THE FOUNDATION DIRECTORY SUPPLEMENT

2014 Edition

THE FOUNDATION DIRECTORY SUPPLEMENT

2014 Edition

William Giles
Coordinator

CONTRIBUTING STAFF

Vice President for Data and Technology Strategy	Jake Garcia
Vice President for Data Architecture	Jeffrey A. Falkenstein
Director, Foundation Information Management	David G. Jacobs
Coordinator, Large Foundations	Cindy B. Martinez
Senior Editorial Associates	Regina Judith Faighes Elia Glenn Joseph W. Guastella Cynthia Y. Manick
Editorial Associate	Lakesha Spiegel-Reneau
Editorial Assistants	Carlos Edwin Estremera Michele Kragalott Casey Robbins
Manager, Corporate Philanthropy	Andrew N. Grabois
Community Foundations Liaison	David Rosado
Publishing Database Administrator	Kathye Giesler
System Administrator	Emmy So
Production Manager	Christine Innamorato
Graphic Designer/Production Coordinator	Betty Saronson

The editors gratefully acknowledge the many other Foundation Center staff who contributed support, encouragement, and information that was indispensable to the preparation of this volume. Special mention should also be made of the staff members of the New York, Washington, DC, Cleveland, San Francisco, and Atlanta libraries who assisted in tracking changes in foundation information. We would like to express our appreciation as well to the many foundations that cooperated fully in updating information prior to the compilation of this volume.

ISBN 978-1-59542-481-5
Printed and bound in the United States of America.

CONTENTS

HOW TO USE THE FOUNDATION DIRECTORY SUPPLEMENT

The Foundation Directory and *The Foundation Directory Part 2* are the standard reference tools for information on the nation's 20,000 largest foundations in terms of total grants paid in the latest fiscal year of record. Six months after the books are published, *The Foundation Directory Supplement* updates this information. The *Supplement* provides complete, revised entries for foundations that have reported substantial changes in personnel, name, address, program interests, limitations, application procedures, or other areas by the midpoint of the yearly *Directory* cycle.

Grantseekers should consult the *Supplement* for the most current information about foundations they have identified as prospects through the *Directory, Directory Part 2,* or other sources. In addition, the *Supplement* may be used to identify foundations that have recently expanded or changed the focus of their giving to incorporate new subjects, types of support, or geographic areas.

The 2014 edition of the *Supplement* contains 3,684 updated entries. To aid in identifying new information quickly, the sections of an entry that have changed are highlighted in bold type. A section called "Other changes" at the end of some entries provides additional information.

In addition, the 2014 *Supplement* contains abbreviated listings for 84 foundations that have ceased operations, merged with another foundation, or have otherwise become ineligible for inclusion during this period. These entries consist only of the foundation's name and city, with a statement explaining the change in its status.

The *Supplement* includes indexes of donors, officers, and trustees; geographic location; international interests; types of support offered; subject areas of interest; and foundation names. Readers of the *Supplement* should bear in mind that the 3,684 foundations listed represent only a portion of the 20,000 foundations appearing in the 2014 editions of *The Foundation Directory* and *The Foundation Directory Part 2*. A complete search for the most appropriate funding prospects should begin with those publications; the Supplement will then be useful in expanding and updating the prospect list with more current information.

Finally, when using the *Directory, Directory Part 2,* and *Supplement* to identify potential funding sources, grantseekers are urged to read each foundation description carefully to determine the nature of the grantmaker's interests and to note any restrictions on giving that would prevent the foundation from considering their proposal. Some foundations limit their giving to a particular subject field or geographic area; others are unable to provide certain types of support, such as funds for buildings and equipment or for general operating budgets.

ARRANGEMENT

The Foundation Directory Supplement is arranged alphabetically by state and, within states, by foundation name. Each descriptive entry is assigned a sequence number, and references in the indexes are to these entry numbers.

WHAT'S IN AN ENTRY?

There are 34 basic data elements that could be included in a *Supplement* entry. The content of entries varies widely due to differences in the size and nature of foundation programs and the availability of information from foundations. Specific data elements that could be included are:

1. The full legal **name of the foundation**.
2. The **former name** of the foundation.
3. The **street address, city,** and **zip code** of the foundation's principal office.
4. The **telephone number** of the foundation.
5. The name and title of the **contact person** of the foundation.
6. Any **additional address** (such as a separate application address) supplied by the foundation. Additional telephone or fax numbers as well as e-mail and/or URL addresses also may be listed here.
7. **Establishment data**, including the legal form (usually a trust or corporation) and the year and state in which the foundation was established.
8. The **donor(s)** or principal contributor(s) to the foundation, including individuals, families, and corporations. If a donor is deceased, the symbol ‡ follows the name.
9. **Foundation type:** community, company-sponsored, independent, or operating.
10. The **year-end date** of the foundation's accounting period for which financial data is supplied.

11. **Assets:** the total value of the foundation's investments at the end of the accounting period. In a few instances, foundations that act as "pass-throughs" for annual corporate or individual gifts report zero assets.
12. **Asset type:** generally, assets are reported at market value (M) or ledger value (L).
13. **Gifts received:** the total amount of new capital received by the foundation in the year of record.
14. **Expenditures:** total disbursements of the foundation, including overhead expenses (salaries; investment, legal, and other professional fees; interest; rent; etc.) and federal excise taxes, as well as the total amount paid for grants, scholarships, and matching gifts.
15. The total amount of **qualifying distributions** made by the foundation in the year of record. This figure includes all grants paid, qualifying administrative expenses, loans and program-related investments, set-asides, and amounts paid to acquire assets used directly in carrying out charitable purposes.
16. The dollar value and number of **grants paid** during the year, with the largest grant paid **(high)** and smallest grant paid **(low)**. When supplied by the foundation, the average range of grant payments is also indicated. Grant figures generally do not include commitments for future payment or amounts spent for grants to individuals, employee matching gifts, loans, or foundation-administered programs.
17. The total dollar value of **set-asides** made by the foundation during the year. Although set-asides count as qualifying distributions toward the foundation's annual payout requirement, they are distinct from any amounts listed as grants paid.
18. The total amount and number of **grants made directly to or on behalf of individuals,** including scholarships, fellowships, awards, and medical payments. When supplied by the foundation, high, low, and average range are also indicated.
19. The dollar amount and number of **employee matching gifts** awarded, generally by company-sponsored foundations.
20. The total dollars expended for **programs administered by the foundation** and the number of foundation-administered programs. These programs can include museums or other institutions supported exclusively by the foundation, research programs administered by the foundation, etc.
21. The dollar amount and number of **loans** made to nonprofit organizations by the foundation. These can include program-related investments, emergency loans to help nonprofits that are waiting for grants or other income payments, etc. When supplied by the foundation, high, low, and average range are also indicated.
22. The number of **loans to individuals** and the total amount loaned. When supplied by the foundation, high, low, and average range are also indicated.
23. The monetary value and number of **in-kind gifts**.
24. The **purpose and activities**, in general terms, of the foundation. This statement reflects funding interests as expressed by the foundation or, if no foundation statement is available, an analysis of the actual grants awarded by the foundation during the most recent two-year period for which public records exist. Many foundations leave statements of purpose intentionally broad, indicating only the major program areas within which they fund. More specific areas of interest can often be found in the "Fields of Interest" section of the entry.
25. The **fields of interest** reflected in the foundation's giving program. The terminology used in this section conforms to the Foundation Center's Grants Classification System (GCS). The terms also provide access to foundation entries through the Subject Index at the back of the volume.
26. The **international giving interests** of the foundation.
27. The **type of support** (such as endowment funds, building/renovation, equipment, fellowships, etc.) offered by the foundation. Definitions of the terms used to describe the forms of support available are provided at the beginning of the Types of Support Index at the back of this volume.
28. Any stated **limitations** on the foundation's giving program, including geographic preferences, restrictions by subject focus or type of recipient, or specific types of support the foundation cannot provide. It is noted here if a foundation does not accept unsolicited applications.
29. **Publications** or other printed materials distributed by the foundation that describe its activities and giving program. These can include annual or multi-year reports, newsletters, corporate giving reports, informational brochures, grant lists, etc.
30. **Application information**, including the preferred form of application, the number of copies of proposals requested, application deadlines, frequency and dates of board meetings, and the general amount of time the foundation requires to notify applicants of the board's decision. Some foundations have indicated that their funds are currently committed to ongoing projects.
31. The names and titles of **officers, principal administrators, trustees,** or **directors,** and members of other governing bodies. An asterisk (*) following the individual's name indicates an officer who is also a trustee or director.
32. The number of professional and support **staff** employed by the foundation, and an indication of part-time or full-time status of these employees, as reported by the foundation.
33. **EIN:** the Employer Identification Number assigned to the foundation by the Internal Revenue Service for tax purposes. This number can be useful when ordering or searching for the foundation's annual information return, Form 990-PF.
34. **Other changes:** any additional information about the foundation, including significant growth in its asset base or grants awarded. Statements here may also highlight specific changes within the entry, as when the foundation relocates to another state.

TERMINATIONS AND MERGERS

Foundations that have recently notified the Center that they have ceased operation, merged with another foundation, or otherwise suspended grantmaking activities are listed in the descriptive directory section along with other updated foundation entries. These entries consist only of the foundation's name, city, and a statement concerning its change of status and the date occurred, if known.

INDEXES

Six indexes to the descriptive entries are provided at the back of the book to assist grantseekers and other users of this volume:

1. The **Index to Donors, Officers, Trustees** is an alphabetical list of individual and corporate donors, officers, and members of governing boards whose names appear in this volume. Many grantseekers find this index helpful in determining whether current or prospective members of their own governing boards, alumni of their schools, or current contributors are affiliated with any foundations.
2. The **Geographic Index** references foundation entries by the state and city in which the foundation maintains its principal offices. The index includes "see also" references at the end of each state section to indicate foundations that have made substantial grants in that state but are located elsewhere. Foundations that award grants on a national, regional, or international basis are indicated in bold type. The remaining foundations generally limit their giving to the state or city in which they are located.
3. The **International Giving Index** provides access to foundations whose funding or giving interests extend beyond the United States. A complete alphabetical list of countries, continents, and regions is provided at the beginning of the index. Under each country, continent, or region, entry numbers are listed by the state location and abbreviated name of the foundation. Organizations whose programs benefit foreign countries should use this index to identify funders with similar geographic interests.
4. The **Type of Support Index** provides access to foundation entries by the specific types of support the foundation awards. A glossary of the forms of support listed appears at the beginning of the index. Under each type of support term, entry numbers are listed by the state location and abbreviated name of the foundation. Foundations that award grants on a national, regional, or international basis are indicated in bold type. When using this index, grantseekers should focus on foundations located in their own state that offer the specific type of support needed, or on foundations listed in bold type if their program has national impact.
5. The **Subject Index** provides access to the giving interests of foundations based on the "Fields of Interest" sections of their entries. The terminology in the index conforms to the Foundation Center's Grants Classification System (GCS). A complete alphabetical list of the subject headings in the current edition is provided at the beginning of the index as well as "see also" references to related subject areas included in this volume. Under each subject term, entry numbers are listed by the state location and abbreviated name of the foundation. As in the Type of Support Index, foundations that award grants on a national, regional, or international basis are indicated in bold type. Again, grantseekers should focus on foundations located in their own state that have shown an interest in their subject area, or on foundations listed in bold type if their program is national in scope.
6. The **Foundation Name Index** is an alphabetical list of all foundations appearing in the *Directory*. Following the foundation name, state, and *Supplement* entry number, the codes (FD) and (FD2) indicate whether the foundation appeared in the previous edition of *The Foundation Directory* or *The Foundation Directory Part 2.* Former names of foundations appear with "see" references to the appropriate entry numbers.

WHAT IS A FOUNDATION?

The Foundation Center defines a foundation as a nongovernmental, nonprofit organization with its own funds (usually from a single source, either an individual, family, or corporation) and program managed by its own trustees and directors that was established to maintain or aid educational, social, charitable, religious, or other activities serving the common welfare, primarily by making grants to other nonprofit organizations. *The Foundation Directory* and *The Foundation Directory Part 2* also include charitable trusts as well as private operating foundations (which administer programs directly and usually make few, if any, grants) and community foundations (which derive their funds from many sources).

The *Directory* and *Directory Part 2* do not include organizations whose giving is restricted by charter to one or more specified organizations; operating foundations that do not maintain active grantmaking programs; organizations that act as associations for industrial or other special groups; and organizations that make general appeals to the public for funds.

RESEARCHING FOUNDATIONS

Foundations receive many thousands of worthy requests each year. Most of these requests are declined simply because there are never enough funds to go around or because the application clearly falls outside the foundation's fields of interest. Sometimes the qualifications of the staff are not well established; the budget or the means of evaluating the project may not be presented convincingly; or the organization may not have asked itself whether it is especially suited to make a contribution to the solution of the problem, whether it can provide the service proposed, or whether others are not already effectively engaged in the same activity.

The first step in researching foundation funding support, then, is to analyze your own program and organization to determine the need you plan to address, the audience you will serve, and the amount and type of support you need. Become familiar with the basic facts about foundations in general and how they operate. Consider other sources of funding, such as individual contributors, government grants, earned income possibilities, and so on. Although foundations are an important source of support for nonprofit organizations, their giving represents a relatively small percentage of the total philanthropic dollars contributed annually, and an even smaller percentage of the total when government grants and earned income are included.

Once you have determined the amount and type of support you need and the reasons why you are seeking foundation support, *The Foundation Directory, The Foundation Directory Part 2,* and *The Foundation Directory Supplement* can help you to develop an initial list of foundations that might be interested in funding your project. In determining whether or not it is appropriate to approach a particular foundation with a grant request, keep in mind the following questions:

1. Has the foundation demonstrated a real commitment to funding in your subject area?
2. Does it seem likely that the foundation will make a grant in your geographic area?
3. Does the amount of money you are requesting fit within the foundation's grant range?
4. Does the foundation have any policy prohibiting grants for the type of support you are requesting?
5. Does the foundation prefer to make grants that cover the full cost of a project or does it favor projects where other foundations or funding sources share the cost?
6. What types of organizations does the foundation tend to support?
7. Does the foundation have specific application deadlines and procedures or does it review proposals continuously?

Some of these questions can be answered from the information provided in the *Directory, Directory Part 2,* and *Supplement,* but grantseekers will almost always want to consult a few additional resources before submitting a request for funding. If the foundation issues an annual report, application guidelines, or other printed materials describing its program or has a Web site, it is advisable to study them carefully before preparing your proposal. The foundation's annual information return (Form 990-PF) includes a list of all grants paid by the foundation, as well as basic data about its finances, officers, and giving policies.

The Center also publishes a number of other reference tools that provide information on private philanthropy, as well as *Foundation Fundamentals,* a guidebook to funding research strategies. Copies of all Foundation Center publications, as well as other relevant state and local foundation directories, are available for free examination at Foundation Center libraries and Cooperating Collections, which are listed at the end of this introduction.

GLOSSARY

The following list includes important terms used by grantmakers and grantseekers. A number of sources have been consulted in compiling this glossary, including *The Handbook on Private Foundations*, 3rd Edition, by David F. Freeman, John A. Edie, Jane C. Nober, and the Council on Foundations (Washington, DC, 2005); *The Law of Tax-Exempt Organizations*, 9th Edition, by Bruce R. Hopkins (Hoboken, NJ: John Wiley & Sons, 2007); and the *AFP Fund-Raising Dictionary*, (2003).

Annual Report: A *voluntary* report issued by a foundation or corporation that provides financial data and descriptions of grantmaking activities. Annual reports vary in format from simple typewritten documents listing the year's grants to detailed publications that provide substantial information about the grantmaking program.

Assets: The amount of capital or principal—money, stocks, bonds, real estate, or other resources—controlled by the foundation or corporate giving program. Generally, assets are invested and the income is used to make grants.

Beneficiary: In philanthropic terms, the donee or grantee receiving funds from a foundation or corporate giving program is the beneficiary, although society benefits as well. Foundations whose legal terms of establishment restrict their giving to one or more named beneficiaries are not included in this publication.

Bricks and Mortar: An informal term for grants for buildings or construction projects.

Capital Support: Funds provided for endowment purposes, buildings, construction, or equipment, and including, for example, grants for "bricks and mortar."

Challenge Grant: A grant awarded that will be paid only if the donee organization is able to raise additional funds from another source(s). Challenge grants are often used to stimulate giving from other donors. (*See also* **Matching Grant**)

Community Foundation: A 501(c)(3) organization that makes grants for charitable purposes in a specific community or region. Funds are usually derived from many donors and held in an endowment independently administered; income earned by the endowment is then used to make grants. Although a few community foundations may be classified by the IRS as private foundations, most are classified as public charities eligible for maximum income tax-deductible contributions from the general public. (*See also* **501(c)(3)**; **Public Charity**)

Community Fund: An organized community program which makes annual appeals to the general public for funds that are usually not retained in an endowment but are used for the ongoing operational support of local social and health service agencies. (*See also* **Federated Giving Program**)

Company-Sponsored Foundation (also referred to as Corporate Foundation): A private foundation whose grant funds are derived primarily from the contributions of a profit-making business organization. The company-sponsored foundation may maintain close ties with the donor company, but it is an independent organization with its own endowment and is subject to the same rules and regulations as other private foundations. (*See also* **Private Foundation**)

Cooperative Venture: A joint effort between or among two or more grantmakers (including foundations, corporations, and government agencies). Partners may share in funding responsibilities or contribute information and technical resources.

Corporate Giving Program: A grantmaking program established and administered within a profit-making company. Corporate giving programs do not have a separate endowment and their annual grant totals are generally more directly related to current profits. They are not subject to the same reporting requirements as private foundations. Some companies make charitable contributions through both a corporate giving program and a company-sponsored foundation.

Distribution Committee: The board responsible for making grant decisions. For community foundations, it is intended to be broadly representative of the community served by the foundation.

Donee: The recipient of a grant. (Also known as the grantee or the beneficiary.)

Donor: The individual or organization that makes a grant or contribution. (Also known as the grantor.)

Employee Matching Gift: A contribution to a charitable organization by a company employee that is matched by a similar contribution from the employer. Many corporations have employee matching gift programs in higher education that stimulate their employees to give to the college or university of their choice.

Endowment: Funds intended to be kept permanently and invested to provide income for continued support of an organization.

Expenditure Responsibility: In general, when a private foundation makes a grant to an organization that is not classified by the IRS as a "public charity," the foundation is required by law to provide some assurance that the funds will be used for the intended charitable purposes. Special reports on such grants must be filed with the IRS. Most grantee organizations are public charities and many foundations do not make "expenditure responsibility" grants.

Family Foundation: An independent private foundation whose funds are derived from members of a single family. Family members often serve as officers or board members of the foundation and have a significant role in grantmaking decisions. (*See also* **Operating Foundation**; **Private Foundation**; **Public Charity**)

Federated Giving Program: A joint fundraising effort usually administered by a nonprofit "umbrella" organization which in turn distributes contributed funds to several nonprofit agencies. United Way and community chests or funds, the United Jewish Appeal and other religious appeals, the United Negro College Fund, and joint arts councils are examples of federated giving programs. (*See also* **Community Fund**)

501(c)(3): The section of the Internal Revenue code that defines nonprofit, charitable (as broadly defined), tax-exempt organizations; 501(c)(3) organizations are further defined as public charities, private operating foundations, and private non-operating foundations. (*See also* **Operating Foundation**; **Private Foundation**; **Public Charity**)

Form 990-PF: The annual information return that all private foundations must submit to the IRS each year and which is also filed with appropriate state officials. The form requires information on the foundation's assets, income, operating expenses, contributions and grants, paid staff and salaries, program funding areas, grantmaking guidelines and restrictions, and grant application procedures.

General Purpose Foundation: An independent private foundation that awards grants in many different fields of interest. (*See also* **Special Purpose Foundation**)

General Purpose Grant: A grant made to further the general purpose or work of an organization, rather than for a specific purpose or project. (*See also* **Operating Support Grant**)

Grantee Financial Report: A report detailing how grant funds were used by an organization. Many corporations require this kind of report from grantees. A financial report generally includes a listing of all expenditures from grant funds as well as an overall organizational financial report covering revenue and expenses, assets and liabilities.

Grassroots Fundraising: Efforts to raise money from individuals or groups from the local community on a broad basis. Usually an organization's own constituents— people who live in the neighborhood served or clients of the agency's services—are the sources of these funds. Grassroots fundraising activities include membership drives, raffles, auctions, benefits, and a range of other activities.

Independent Foundation: A grantmaking organization usually classified by the IRS as a private foundation. Independent foundations may also be known as family foundations, general purpose foundations, special purpose foundations, or private non-operating foundations. The Foundation Center defines independent foundations and company-sponsored foundations separately; however, federal law normally classifies both as private, non-operating foundations subject to the same rules and requirements. (*See also* **Private Foundation**)

In-Kind Contributions: Contributions of equipment, supplies, or other property as distinguished from monetary grants. Some organizations may also donate space or staff time as an in-kind contribution.

Matching Grant: A grant that is made to match funds provided by another donor. (*See also* **Challenge Grant**; **Employee Matching Gift**)

Operating Foundation: A 501(c)(3) organization classified by the IRS as a private foundation whose primary purpose is to conduct research, social welfare, or other programs determined by its governing body or establishment charter. Some grants may be made, but the sum is generally small relative to the funds used for the foundation's own programs. (*See also* **501(c)(3)**)

Operating Support Grant: A grant to cover the regular personnel, administrative, and other expenses of an existing program or project. (*See also* **General Purpose Grant**)

Payout Requirement: The minimum amount that private foundations are required to expend for charitable purposes (includes grants and, within certain limits, the administrative cost of making grants). In general, a private foundation must meet or exceed an annual payout requirement of five percent of the average market value of the foundation's assets.

Private Foundation: A nongovernmental, nonprofit organization with funds (usually from a single source, such as an individual, family, or corporation) and program managed by its own trustees or directors that was established to maintain or aid social, educational, religious or other charitable activities serving the common welfare, primarily through the making of grants. "Private foundation" also means an organization that is tax-exempt under code section 501(c)(3) and is classified by the IRS as a private foundation as defined in the code. The code definition usually, but not always, identifies a foundation with the characteristics first described. (*See also* **501(c)(3)**; **Public Charity**)

Program Amount: Funds that are expended to support a particular program administered internally by the foundation or corporate giving program.

Program Officer: A staff member of a foundation who reviews grant proposals and processes applications for the board of trustees. Only a small percentage of foundations have program officers.

Program-Related Investment (PRI): A loan or other investment (as distinguished from a grant) made by a foundation or corporate giving program to another organization for a project related to the grantmaker's stated charitable purpose and interests. Program-related investments are often made from a revolving fund; the foundation generally expects to receive its money back with interest or some other form of return at less than current market rates, and it then becomes available for further program-related investments.

Proposal: A written application, often with supporting documents, submitted to a foundation or corporate giving program in requesting a grant. Preferred procedures and formats vary. Consult published guidelines.

Public Charity: In general, an organization that is tax-exempt under code section 501(c)(3) and is classified by the IRS as a public charity and not a private foundation. Public charities generally derive their funding or support primarily from the general public in carrying out their social, educational, religious, or other charitable activities serving the common welfare. Some public charities engage in grantmaking activities, although most engage in direct service or other tax-exempt activities. Public charities are eligible for maximum income tax-deductible contributions from the public and are not subject to the same rules and restrictions as private foundations. Some are also referred to as "public foundations" or "publicly supported organizations" and may use the term "foundation" in their names. (*See also* **501(c)(3)**; **Private Foundation**)

Qualifying Distributions: Expenditures of private foundations used to satisfy the annual payout requirement. These can include grants, reasonable administrative expenses, set-asides, loans and program-related investments, and amounts paid to acquire assets used directly in carrying out exempt purposes.

Query Letter: A brief letter outlining an organization's activities and its request for funding sent to a foundation or corporation to determine whether it would be appropriate to submit a full grant proposal. Many grantmakers prefer to be contacted in this way before receiving a full proposal.

RFP: Request For Proposal. When the government issues a new contract or grant program, it sends out RFPs to agencies that might be qualified to participate. The RFP lists project specifications and application procedures. A few foundations occasionally use RFPs in specific fields, but most prefer to consider proposals that are initiated by applicants.

Seed Money: A grant or contribution used to start a new project or organization. Seed grants may cover salaries and other operating expenses of a new project.

Set-Asides: Funds set aside by a foundation for a specific purpose or project that are counted as qualifying distributions toward the foundation's annual payout requirement. Amounts for the project must be paid within five years of the first set-aside.

Special Purpose Foundation: A private foundation that focuses its grantmaking activities in one or a few special areas of interest. For example, a foundation may only award grants in the area of cancer research or child development. (*See also* **General Purpose Foundation**)

Technical Assistance: Operational or management assistance given to nonprofit organizations. It can include fundraising assistance, budgeting and financial planning, program planning, legal advice, marketing, and other aids to management. Assistance may be offered directly by a foundation or corporate staff member, or be offered in the form of a grant to pay for the services of an outside consultant. (*See also* **In-Kind Contributions**)

Trustee: A member of a governing board. A foundation's board of trustees meets to review grant proposals and make decisions. Often also referred to as a "director" or "board member."

ABBREVIATIONS

The following lists contain standard abbreviations frequently used by the Foundation Center's editorial staff. These abbreviations are used most frequently in the addresses of grantmakers and the titles of corporate and grantmaker officers.

STREET ABBREVIATIONS

1st	First*
2nd	Second*
3rd	Third*
Apt.	Apartment
Ave.	Avenue
Bldg.	Building
Blvd.	Boulevard
Cir.	Circle
Ct.	Court
Ctr.	Center
Dept.	Department
Dr.	Drive
E.	East
Expwy.	Expressway
Fl.	Floor
Ft.	Fort
Hwy.	Highway
Ln.	Lane
M.C.	Mail Code
M.S.	Mail Stop
Mt.	Mount
N.	North
N.E.	Northeast
N.W.	Northwest
No.	Number
Pkwy.	Parkway
Pl.	Place
Plz.	Plaza
R.R.	Rural Route
Rd.	Road
Rm.	Room
Rte.	Route
S.	South
S.E.	Southeast
S.W.	Southwest
Sq.	Square
St.	Saint
St.	Street
Sta.	Station
Ste.	Suite
Terr.	Terrace
Tpke.	Turnpike
Univ.	University
W.	West

*Numerics used always

TWO LETTER STATE AND TERRITORY ABBREVIATIONS

AK	Alaska
AL	Alabama
AR	Arkansas
AZ	Arizona
CA	California
CO	Colorado
CT	Connecticut
DC	District of Columbia
DE	Delaware
FL	Florida
GA	Georgia
HI	Hawaii
IA	Iowa
ID	Idaho
IL	Illinois
IN	Indiana
KS	Kansas
KY	Kentucky
LA	Louisiana
MA	Massachusetts
MD	Maryland
ME	Maine
MI	Michigan
MN	Minnesota
MO	Missouri
MS	Mississippi
MT	Montana
NC	North Carolina
ND	North Dakota
NE	Nebraska
NH	New Hampshire
NJ	New Jersey
NM	New Mexico
NV	Nevada
NY	New York
OH	Ohio
OK	Oklahoma
OR	Oregon
PA	Pennsylvania
PR	Puerto Rico
RI	Rhode Island
SC	South Carolina
SD	South Dakota
TN	Tennessee
TX	Texas
UT	Utah
VA	Virginia
VI	Virgin Islands
VT	Vermont
WA	Washington
WI	Wisconsin
WV	West Virginia
WY	Wyoming

ABBREVIATIONS USED FOR OFFICER TITLES

Acctg.	Accounting
ADM.	Admiral
Admin.	Administration
Admin.	Administrative
Admin.	Administrator
Adv.	Advertising
Amb.	Ambassador
Assn.	Association
Assoc(s).	Associate(s)
Asst.	Assistant
Bro.	Brother
C.A.O.	Chief Accounting Officer
C.A.O.	Chief Administration Officer
C.E.O.	Chief Executive Officer
C.F.O.	Chief Financial Officer
C.I.O.	Chief Information Officer
C.I.O.	Chief Investment Officer
C.O.O.	Chief Operating Officer
Capt.	Captain
Chair.	Chairperson
Col.	Colonel
Comm.	Committee
Comms.	Communications
Commo.	Commodore
Compt.	Comptroller
Cont.	Controller
Contrib(s).	Contribution(s)
Coord.	Coordinator
Corp.	Corporate, Corporation
Co(s).	Company(s)
Dep.	Deputy
Devel.	Development
Dir.	Director
Distrib(s).	Distribution(s)
Div.	Division
Exec.	Executive
Ext.	External
Fdn.	Foundation
Fr.	Father
Genl.	General
Gov.	Governor
Govt.	Government
Hon.	Judge
Inf.	Information
Int.	Internal
Intl.	International
Jr.	Junior
Lt.	Lieutenant
Ltd.	Limited
Maj.	Major
Mfg.	Manufacturing
Mgmt.	Management
Mgr.	Manager
Mktg.	Marketing
Msgr.	Monsignor
Mt.	Mount
Natl.	National
Off.	Officer
Opers.	Operations
Org.	Organization
Plan.	Planning
Pres.	President
Prog(s).	Program(s)
RADM.	Rear Admiral
Rels.	Relations
Rep.	Representative
Rev.	Reverend
Rt. Rev.	Right Reverend
Secy.	Secretary
Secy.-Treas.	Secretary-Treasurer
Sen.	Senator
Soc.	Society
Sr.	Senior
Sr.	Sister
Supt.	Superintendent
Supvr.	Supervisor
Svc(s).	Service(s)
Tech.	Technology
Tr.	Trustee
Treas.	Treasurer
Univ.	University
V.P.	Vice President
VADM.	Vice Admiral
Vice-Chair.	Vice Chairperson

ADDITIONAL ABBREVIATIONS

E-mail	Electronic mail
FAX	Facsimile
LOI	Letter of Inquiry
RFP	Request for Proposals
SASE	Self-Addressed Stamped Envelope
TDD, TTY	Telecommunication Device for the Deaf
Tel.	Telephone
URL	Uniform Resource Locator (web site)

Jan.	January
Feb.	February
Mar.	March
Apr.	April
Aug.	August
Sept.	September
Oct.	October
Nov.	November
Dec.	December

FOUNDATION CENTER RESOURCES

Established in 1956 and today supported by close to 550 foundations, Foundation Center is the leading source of information about philanthropy worldwide. Through data, analysis, and training, it connects people who want to change the world to the resources they need to succeed. Foundation Center maintains the most comprehensive database on U.S. and, increasingly, global grantmakers and their grants — a robust, accessible knowledge bank for the sector. It also operates research, education, and training programs designed to advance knowledge of philanthropy at every level. Thousands of people visit Foundation Center's website each day and are served in its five library/learning centers and at more than 470 Funding Information Network locations nationwide and around the world.

ONLINE DATABASES

Foundation Directory Online

Which grantmaker is most likely to fund your organization? *Foundation Directory Online* (FDO) will help you answer this question, making it an essential tool for any grantseeker.

With detailed profiles on 120,000+ grantmakers — including U.S. and international foundations, corporations, and grantmaking public charities — FDO eliminates the guesswork from finding the right funder.

Foundation Directory Online includes:

- **Grantmaker profiles:** Get application information and deadlines, grant limitations, fields of interest, and geographic focus to help narrow your search.
- **Grants information:** Discover grants awarded to organizations similar to yours, with in-depth descriptions.
- **Visualization tools:** Easily map and chart a grantmaker's funding patterns by location and subject area.

Monthly and annual plans are available to fit your research needs.

LEARN MORE: foundationcenter.org/fdo

Foundation Grants to Individuals Online

Need a scholarship, fellowship or award? Visit the new *Foundation Grants to Individuals Online* built specifically for students, artists, researchers, and individuals like you!

$19.95: ONE MONTH
$36.95: THREE MONTHS
$59.95: SIX MONTHS
$99.95: ONE YEAR

TO SUBSCRIBE, VISIT gtionline.foundationcenter.org

TRASI (Tools and Resources for Assessing Social Impact)

Browse or search the TRASI database for proven approaches to social impact assessment, guidelines for creating and conducting an assessment, and ready-to-use tools for measuring social change. TRASI also features a community page where individuals can connect with peers and experts.

FREE

PLEASE VISIT trasi.foundationcenter.org

Foundation Maps

Foundation Maps brings to life data about U.S. and global philanthropy through extensive mapping, charting, and analytic capabilities. This interactive tool for funders is designed to facilitate more transparent, effective, and collaborative philanthropy.

LEARN MORE: maps@foundationcenter.org

Nonprofit Collaboration Database

This database provides hundreds of real-life examples of how nonprofits are working together.

PLEASE VISIT foundationcenter.org/gainknowledge/collaboration

GRANTMAKER DIRECTORIES

The Foundation Directory, 2014 Edition

Key facts include fields of interest, contact information, financials, names of decision makers, and over 51,000 sample grants. Convenient indexes are provided for all *Foundation Directories*.

MARCH 2014 / ISBN 978-1-59542-473-0 / $215 / PUBLISHED ANNUALLY

The Foundation Directory Part 2, 2014 Edition

Thorough coverage for the next 10,000 largest foundations, with nearly 40,000 sample grants.

MARCH 2014 / ISBN 978-1-59542-474-7 / $185 / PUBLISHED ANNUALLY

The Foundation Directory Supplement, 2014 Edition

This single volume provides updates for thousands of foundations in *The Foundation Directory* and the *Directory Part 2*. Changes in foundation status, contact information, and giving interests are highlighted in new entries.

SEPTEMBER 2014 / ISBN 978-1-59542-481-5 / $125 / PUBLISHED ANNUALLY

Guide to Funding for International & Foreign Programs, 11th Edition

Profiles of more than 2,200 grantmakers that provide international relief, disaster assistance, human rights, civil liberties, community development, and education.

MAY 2012 / ISBN 978-1-59542-408-2 / $125

The Celebrity Foundation Directory 5th Digital Edition

This downloadable directory (PDF) includes detailed descriptions of more than 1,880 foundations started by VIPs in the fields of business, entertainment, politics, and sports.

NOVEMBER 2013 / ISBN 978-1-59542-456-3 / $59.95

Foundation Grants to Individuals, 23rd Edition

The only publication devoted entirely to foundation grant opportunities for qualified individual applicants, this directory features more than 10,000 entries with current information including foundation name, address, program description, and application guidelines.

JULY 2014 / ISBN 978-1-59542-489-1 / $75 / PUBLISHED ANNUALLY

The PRI Directory, 3rd Edition Charitable Loans and Other Program-Related Investments by Foundations

This *Directory* lists leading funders, recipients, project descriptions, and includes tips on how to secure and manage PRIs. Foundation listings include funder name and state; recipient name, city, and state (or country); and a description of the project funded.

PUBLISHED IN PARTERNSHIP WITH PRI MAKERS NETWORK.

JULY 2010 / ISBN 978-1-59542-214-9 / $95

Grant Guides

Designed for fundraisers who work within specific areas, 15 digital edition *Grant Guides* list actual foundation grants of $10,000 or more. *Guides* include a keyword search tool and indexes to pinpoint grants of interest to you. As a special bonus, each grantmaker entry contains a link to its *Foundation Directory Online Free* profile for even more details, all in a convenient PDF format.

2014 EDITIONS / $39.95 EACH

TO ORDER, VISIT foundationcenter.org/grantguides

FUNDRAISING GUIDES

After the Grant

The Nonprofit's Guide to Good Stewardship

An invaluable and practical resource for anyone seeking funding from foundations, this *Guide* will help you manage your grant to ensure you get the next one.

MARCH 2010 / ISBN 978-1-59542-301-6 / $39.95

Foundation Fundamentals, 8th Edition

Expert advice on fundraising research and proposal development.

A go-to resource in academic programs on the nonprofit sector. *Foundation Fundamentals* describes foundation funding provides advice on research strategies, including how to best use *Foundation Directory Online*.

MARCH 2008 / ISBN 978-1-59542-156-2 / $39.95

Foundation Center's Guide to Proposal Writing, 6th Edition

Author Jane Geever provides detailed instructions on preparing successful grant proposals, incorporating the results of interviews with 40 U.S. grantmakers.

MAY 2012 / ISBN 978-1-59542-404-4 / $39.95

Guía Para Escribir Propuestas

The Spanish-language translation of *Foundation Center's Guide to Proposal Writing,* 5th edition.

MARCH 2008 / ISBN 978-1-595423-158-6 / $39.95

The Grantseeker's Guide to Winning Proposals

A collection of 35 actual proposals submitted to international, regional, corporate, and local foundations. Each includes remarks by the program officer who approved the grant.

AUGUST 2008 / ISBN 978-1-59542-195-1 / $39.95

Securing Your Organization's Future

A Complete Guide to Fundraising Strategies, Revised Edition

Author Michael Seltzer explains how to strengthen your nonprofit's capacity to raise funds and achieve long-term financial stability.

FEBRUARY 2001 / ISBN 0-87954-900-9 / $39.95

NONPROFIT MANAGEMENT GUIDES

America's Nonprofit Sector

A Primer

The third edition of this publication, by Lester Salamon, is ideal for people who want a thorough, accessible introduction to the nonprofit sector—as well as the nation's social welfare system.

MARCH 2012 / ISBN 978-1-59542-360-3 / $24.95

The 21St Century Nonprofit

Managing in the Age of Governance

This book details the significant improvements in nonprofit management practice that have taken place in recent years.

SEPTEMBER 2009 / ISBN 978-1-59542-249-1 / $39.95

Foundations and Public Policy

This book presents a valuable framework for foundations as they plan or implement their engagement with public policy.

Published in partnership with The Center on Philanthropy & Public Policy.

MARCH 2009 / ISBN 978-1-59542-218-7 / $34.95

Local Mission-Global Vision

Community Foundations in the 21st Century

This book examines the new role of community foundations, exploring the potential impact of transnational evolution on organized philanthropy.

Published in partnership with Transatlantic Community Foundations Network.

AUGUST 2008 / ISBN 978-1-59542-204-0 / $34.95

Wise Decision-Making in Uncertain Times

Using Nonprofit Resources Effectively

This book highlights the critical challenges of fiscal sustainability for nonprofits, and encourages organizations to take a more expansive approach to funding outreach.

AUGUST 2006 / ISBN 1-59542-099-1 / $34.95

Effective Economic Decision-Making by Nonprofit Organizations

Editor Dennis R. Young offers practical guidelines to help nonprofit managers advance their mission while balancing the interests of trustees, funders, government, and staff.

DECEMBER 2003 / ISBN 1-931923-69-8 / $34.95

The Board Member's Book

Making a Difference in Voluntary Organizations, 3rd Edition

Written by former Independent Sector President Brian O'Connell, this is the perfect guide to the issues, challenges, and possibilities facing a nonprofit organization and its board.

MAY 2003 / ISBN 1-931923-17-5 / $29.95

Philanthropy's Challenge

Building Nonprofit Capacity Through Venture Grantmaking

Author Paul Firstenberg explores the roles of grantmaker and grantee within various models of venture grantmaking. He outlines the characteristics that qualify an organization for a venture grant, and outlines the steps a grantmaker can take to build the grantees' organizational capacity.

FEBRUARY 2003 / SOFTBOUND: ISBN 1-931923-15-9 / $29.95
HARDBOUND: ISBN 1-931923-53-1 / $39.95

Investing in Capacity Building

A Guide to High-Impact Approaches

Author Barbara Blumenthal helps grantmakers and consultants design better methods to help nonprofits, while showing nonprofit managers how to get more effective support.

NOVEMBER 2003 / ISBN 1-931923-65-5 / $34.95

ASSOCIATES PROGRAM

For just $995 a year or $695 for six months, the Associates Program experts will answer all of your questions about foundation giving, corporate philanthropy, and individual donors.

You will receive online access to several lists that are updated monthly, including new grantmakers and grantmaker application deadlines. In addition, you will receive most results within the next business day.

JOIN NOW AT foundationcenter.org/associates

ADDITIONAL ONLINE RESOURCES

foundationcenter.org

- *Philanthropy News Digest* is a daily digest of philanthropy-related articles. Read interviews with leaders, look for RFPs, learn from the experts, and share ideas with others in the field.
- Foundation Stats is a web-based tool that provides free and open access to a wealth of data on the U.S. foundation community. The intuitive platform can be used by anyone to generate thousands of custom tables and charts on the size, scope, and giving priorities of the U.S. foundation community.
- Access research studies to track trends in foundation growth and giving in grantmaker policies and practices.
- To stay current on the latest research trends visit foundationcenter.org/gainknowledge.

grantspace.org

GrantSpace, Foundation Center's learning community for the social sector, features resources organized under the 13 most common subject areas of funding research — including health, education, and the arts.

- Dig into the GrantSpace knowledge base for answers to more than 150 questions asked about grantseeking and nonprofits.
- Stay up-to-date on classes and events happening in person and online with the GrantSpace training calendar.
- Add your voice and help build a community-driven knowledge base: share your expertise, rate content, ask questions, and add comments.

glasspockets.org

Glasspockets provides the data, resources, examples, and action steps foundations need to understand the value of transparency, be more open in their own communications, and help shed more light on how private organizations are serving the public good.

- Learn about the online transparency and accountability practices of the largest foundations, and see who has "glass pockets."
- Transparency Talk, the Glasspockets blog and podcast series, highlights strategies, findings, and best practices related to foundation transparency.
- The Giving Pledge is an effort that encourages the world's wealthiest individuals and families to commit the majority of their assets to philanthropic causes. Eye on the Giving Pledge offers an in-depth picture of Giving Pledge participants, their charitable activities, and the potential impact of the Giving Pledge.
- Learn more about the Reporting Commitment, an initiative aimed at developing more timely, accurate, and precise reporting on the flow of philanthropic dollars.

grantcraft.org

GrantCraft combines the practical wisdom of funders worldwide with the expertise of Foundation Center to improve the practice of philanthropy. Since 2001, GrantCraft has delivered the knowledge funders need to be strategic and effective in their work, addressing questions funders face across various strategies and issue areas.

- Search the 13 content types including guides, takeaways, discussions, infographics, and videos to find real-life examples from funders.
- Register for free access to the monthly newsletter, personal dashboard, and to share content and comment.
- All content is free to use and share.

issuelab.org

IssueLab provides free access to resources that analyze the world's most pressing social, economic, and environmental challenges and their potential solutions. The platform contains thousands of case studies, evaluations, white papers, and issue briefs, and represents one the largest collections of social sector knowledge.

- Search and browse the database by social issue area, author, publishing organization, or geography.
- Learn how to add resources to the IssueLab collection.

DESCRIPTIVE DIRECTORY

ALABAMA

1
Andalusia Health Services Inc.
P.O. Box 56
Andalusia, AL 36420-1200 (334) 222-2030
Contact: Gwen Ryland

Established in 1985 in AL; converted from sale of Andalusia Hospital to Hospital Corp. of America.
Foundation type: Independent foundation.
Financial data (yr. ended 06/30/12): Assets, $3,119,055 (M); expenditures, $159,397; qualifying distributions, $149,262; giving activities include $149,262 for grants.
Purpose and activities: Giving primarily for community health services; support also for scholarships, which are limited to residents of Covington County, Alabama, pursuing a health-related field of study, such as nursing, medicine or medical and laboratory technology.
Fields of interest: Medical school/education; Nursing care; Health care; American Red Cross.
Type of support: General/operating support; Equipment; Scholarships—to individuals.
Limitations: Applications accepted. Giving limited to Covington County, AL. No grants to individuals (except for scholarships); no program-related investments.
Publications: Annual report.
Application information: Application form required.
Directors: Cathy Alexander; **Wayne Bennett**; **Carolyn Graham**; John S. Merrill; Harmon Proctor; Charles H. Roland; **Elizabeth Starr.**
Officers: Ivan Bishop, Pres.; Jim Krudop, V.P.; Wilson H. Parker, Secy.-Treas.
Number of staff: 2 part-time support.
EIN: 630793474
Other changes: Ivan Bishop has replaced John S. Merrill as Pres. Jim Krudop has replaced Ivan Bishop as V.P. Wilson H. Parker has replaced Eiland E. Anthony as Secy.-Treas.

2
Atlantis Educational Foundation
c/o Eric Auyang
2101 Dorchester Dr.
Mobile, AL 36695-2920
***E-mail:* contact@aefinc.org**; Main URL: http://aefinc.org/

Donors: Eric Auyang; Sunny Auyang.
Foundation type: Independent foundation.
Financial data (yr. ended 12/31/12): Assets, $109,528 (M); gifts received, $317,000; expenditures, $229,130; qualifying distributions, $229,130; giving activities include $206,000 for 2 grants (high: $150,000; low: $56,000).
Purpose and activities: Provide children from the poorest parts of China with an opportunity to complete a minimum of high school and possibly a college education.
Fields of interest: Education.
Limitations: Applications not accepted. Giving primarily in China.
Application information: Unsolicited requests for funds not accepted.
Directors: Angela Auyang; Eric Auyang; Sunny Auyang.
EIN: 450889464

3
BBVA Compass Foundation
(formerly Compass Bank Foundation)
P.O. Box 10566, M.C. AL/BI/CH/ACT
Birmingham, AL 35296-0002 (205) 297-3464
Contact: Reymundo Ocanas, V.P. and Exec. Dir.
***E-mail:* grants@bbvacompass.com**; Additional contact: Joye Hehn, Mgr., Corp. Responsibility and Reputation; Application address: 2001 Kirby Dr., Ste. C110, Houston, TX 77019, tel.: (713) 831-5705; Main URL: http://www.bbvacompass.com/compass/responsibility/foundations.cfm

Established in 1981 in AL.
Donor: Compass Bank.
Foundation type: Company-sponsored foundation.
Financial data (yr. ended 12/31/12): Assets, $85,929 (M); gifts received, $4,050,000; expenditures, $4,607,990; qualifying distributions, $4,606,800; giving activities include $4,606,800 for 600 grants (high: $150,000; low: $100).
Purpose and activities: The foundation supports organizations involved with arts and culture, education, the environment, health, housing, human services, diversity and inclusion, community development, minorities, and economically disadvantaged people.
Fields of interest: Museums; Arts; Elementary/secondary education; Higher education; Teacher school/education; Education; Environment, natural resources; Environment, energy; Environmental education; Environment; Health care, equal rights; Public health; Health care; Housing/shelter; Children/youth, services; Human services, financial counseling; Human services; Civil rights, race/intergroup relations; Community development, neighborhood development; Business/industry; Community/economic development; United Ways and Federated Giving Programs; Leadership development; Minorities; Economically disadvantaged.
Type of support: General/operating support; Management development/capacity building; Annual campaigns; Program development; Curriculum development; Scholarship funds; Research; Sponsorships; Employee-related scholarships; Matching/challenge support.
Limitations: Applications accepted. **Giving primarily in areas of company operations in AL, AZ, CA, CO, FL, NM, NY, PR, and TX.** No support for political committees or candidates, veterans' or fraternal organizations, alumni organizations, religious organizations not of direct benefit to the entire community, discriminatory organizations, individual pre-college schools including private, parochial, charter, or home schools, or individual schools in public school systems. No grants for sponsorships, golf tournaments, tables at events, fundraising activities that includes tickets, meals, or other benefits, general operating support for organizations supported by the United Way, or political causes.
Publications: Application guidelines; Program policy statement.
Application information: All applicants are encouraged to attend the semi-monthly Charitable Contributions Process conference calls and webinar presentations. Application form required.
Initial approach: Complete online eligibility quiz and application
***Deadline(s):* Jan. 20 to Sept. 30**
Officers and Trustees:* Manolo Sanchez,* Chair.; Tiffany Dunne, Pres.; J. Reymundo Ocanas, V.P. and Exec. Dir.; Joseph B. Cartee, Secy.; Kirk Pressley, Treas.; Rafael Bustillo; William Helms; James G. Heslop; Angel Regiero; **Sandy Salgado**; Jeffery Talpas.
EIN: 630823545
Other changes: B. Shane Clanton is no longer a director.

4
The Black Belt Community Foundation, Inc.
609 Lauderdale St.
P.O. Box 2020
Selma, AL 36702-2020 (334) 874-1126
Contact: Felecia L. Jones, Pres.
FAX: (334) 874-1131;
E-mail: info@blackbeltfound.org; Toll-free tel.: (866) 874-1126; Main URL: http://blackbeltfound.org/
Facebook: http://www.facebook.com/pages/Black-Belt-Community-Foundation/132682343760
Twitter: https://twitter.com/BlackBeltFound

Established in 2003 in AL; status changed to a Community Foundation.
Foundation type: Community foundation.
Financial data (yr. ended 12/31/12): Assets, $2,281,078 (M); gifts received, $654,764; expenditures, $742,825; giving activities include $200,500 for 8+ grants (high: $12,000).
Purpose and activities: The foundation promotes community development in the Black Belt region of Alabama.
Fields of interest: Arts; Education; Environment; Health care; Youth development; Human services; Economic development; Community/economic development; Public affairs; Children/youth; Children; Youth; Adults; Aging; Young adults; Physically disabled; Blind/visually impaired; Mentally disabled; Minorities; African Americans/Blacks; Hispanics/Latinos; Native Americans/American Indians; Indigenous peoples; Women; Girls; Adults, women; Men; Boys; Adults, men; Young adults, male; Military/veterans; Offenders/ex-offenders; Substance abusers; AIDS, people with; Single parents; Crime/abuse victims; Terminal illness, people with; Economically disadvantaged; Homeless; LGBTQ; Lesbians; Gay men; Transgender and gender nonconforming.
Type of support: Annual campaigns; Capital campaigns; Program development; Scholarship funds; Research; Technical assistance; Consulting services; In-kind gifts.
Limitations: Applications accepted. Giving primarily to Bullock, Choctaw, Dallas, Greene, Hale, Lowndes, Macon, Marengo, Perry, Pickens, Sumter, and Wilcox counties, AL. No support for religious organizations for religious purposes, political organizations or candidates for public office, or school systems. No grants to individuals, or for national fundraising drives, tickets for benefits, lobbying activities, or scholarship or endowment funds.
Publications: Application guidelines; Annual report; Informational brochure; Newsletter.
Application information: Attendance at one of the Community Awareness Grant Seekers Workshops is mandatory for all applicant, including new and returning organizations; visit web site for application information. Grants range from $500 to $3,000. Application form required.
Initial approach: Contact foundation
***Deadline(s):* Apr. 15**
Board meeting date(s): Jan., Mar., May, July, Sept. and Nov.
***Final notification:* June**
Officers and Directors:* Felicia L. Jones,* Pres.; RaSheda Workman,* Secy.; Richard Holland,* Treas.; Dr. Royrickers Cook; Calvin Harkness; Dr.

Walter Hill; Thelma L. Hogue; Barbara Howard; Jerria Martin; George McMillan; Cathy McVay; Virginia Norman; Erica Robinson; Sheryl Smedley; Saint Thomas; Kenneth Webb; Lillian Wideman; Dr. Carol Zippert.
EIN: 631270745
Other changes: Imani B. Washington is no longer Prog. Off.

5
Stokes and Sarah Brown Charitable Foundation
c/o Regions Bank Trust Department
P.O. Box 2886
Mobile, AL 36652-2886
Application address: c/o Regions Bank, 315 Deaderick St., 5th Fl., Nashville, TN 37238-3000, tel.: (615) 748-2922

Established in 2005 in TN.
Donor: J. Stokes Brown.
Foundation type: Independent foundation.
Financial data (yr. ended 01/31/13): Assets, $4,628,349 (M); expenditures, $274,871; qualifying distributions, $231,900; giving activities include $231,000 for 8 grants (high: $60,000; low: $5,000).
Fields of interest: Higher education; Libraries (public); Health care; YM/YWCAs & YM/YWHAs; Christian agencies & churches.
Limitations: Applications accepted. Giving primarily in Robertson County, TN, and surrounding communities. No grants to individuals.
Application information: Application form required.
Initial approach: Contact foundation for application form
Deadline(s): Oct. 1
Advisory Commitee Members: Virginia Sory Brown; Joe Gaston; William R. Goodman III; Evelyn A. Smith.
Trustee: Regions Bank.
EIN: 260110679

6
The Caddell Foundation
2700 Lagoon Park Dr.
Montgomery, AL 36109-1110
Contact: Earl Jones

Donor: Caddell Construction Co., Inc.
Foundation type: Company-sponsored foundation.
Financial data (yr. ended 12/31/12): Assets, $6,453,507 (M); expenditures, $308,732; qualifying distributions, $304,002; giving activities include $304,002 for grants.
Purpose and activities: The foundation supports fairs and festivals and organizations involved with performing arts, higher education, and cancer.
Fields of interest: Performing arts; Performing arts, theater; Performing arts, music; Performing arts, orchestras; Higher education; Cancer; Recreation, fairs/festivals; United Ways and Federated Giving Programs.
Type of support: General/operating support.
Limitations: Applications accepted. Giving primarily in Montgomery, AL. No grants to individuals.
Application information: Application form required.
***Initial approach:* Letter**
Deadline(s): None
Officers and Directors:* John A. Caddell,* Pres.; Joyce K. Caddell,* Secy.-Treas.; Cathy L. Caddell; Christopher P. Caddell; Jeffrey P. Caddell; John K. Caddell; Michael A. Caddell.
EIN: 631133304

7
The Caring Foundation
450 Riverchase Pkwy. E.
Birmingham, AL 35244-2858 **(205) 220-9194**
***Contact:* Tim King, Mgr., The Caring Fdn & Corporate Giving**
***E-mail:* TheCaringFoundation@bcbsal.org; Main URL: https://www.bcbsal.org/web/the-caring-foundation-and-corporate-giving.html**

Established in 1990 in AL.
Donor: Blue Cross and Blue Shield of Alabama, Inc.
Foundation type: Company-sponsored foundation.
Financial data (yr. ended 12/31/12): Assets, $43,253,103 (M); gifts received, $972; expenditures, $4,462,393; qualifying distributions, $4,318,044; giving activities include $4,318,044 for 275 grants (high: $1,000,000; low: $250).
Purpose and activities: The foundation supports programs designed to promote health, wellness, and education, with a special interest in assisting children.
Fields of interest: Education; Hospitals (general); Health care; Safety, education; Boy scouts; Salvation Army; Children/youth, services; Human services; United Ways and Federated Giving Programs; Children.
Type of support: General/operating support; Program development.
Limitations: Applications accepted. Giving primarily in AL. **No support for political organizations or provide foundations or charities.** No grants to individuals, or for capital campaigns.
Publications: Application guidelines.
Application information: Application form required.
***Initial approach:* Complete online application**
Copies of proposal: 1
Deadline(s): None
Board meeting date(s): 4th Wed. in Apr.
Final notification: 1 to 2 months
Officers and Directors:* M. Eugene Moor, Jr.,* Chair.; Terry D. Kellogg, Pres.; Timothy L. Kirkpatrick, V.P.; Cynthia M. Vice, Treas.; James M. Aycock; L. Keith Granger; Kenneth E. Hubbard; Fred D. Hunker, M.D.; Donald L. Large, Jr.; William J. Stevens.
EIN: 631035261
Other changes: James L. Priester is no longer Secy. The grantmaker now publishes application guidelines.

8
Central Alabama Community Foundation, Inc.
(formerly Montgomery Area Community Foundation, Inc.)
35 S. Court St.
Montgomery, AL 36104 (334) 264-6223
Contact: Burton Ward, Pres.; For grants: Lynn Broach, V.P., Community Svcs.
FAX: (334) 263-6225;
E-mail: burton.ward@cacfinfo.org; Grant inquiry e-mail: lynne.broach@cacfinfo.org; Main URL: http://www.cacfinfo.org
E-Newsletter: http://www.cacfinfo.org/newsletter.html
Facebook: https://www.facebook.com/cacfinfo?ref=ts
Twitter: https://twitter.com/CACFinfo

Established in 1987 in AL.
Foundation type: Community foundation.
Financial data (yr. ended 12/31/12): Assets, $37,142,203 (M); gifts received, $3,100,192; expenditures, $5,069,018; giving activities include $3,829,153 for 85+ grants (high: $405,000).
Purpose and activities: The foundation was created by and for the people of central Alabama. Individuals and corporate donors make gifts and bequests of any size for the betterment of the community. Through the grants program, the foundation addresses a wide variety of needs and opportunities, supporting programs and projects in education, human services, health, cultural arts, and other civic concerns.
Fields of interest: Arts; Education; Health care; Agriculture/food; Housing/shelter; Children/youth, services; Family services; Family services, domestic violence; Human services; Nonprofit management; Community/economic development; Children/youth.
Type of support: Income development; Management development/capacity building; Program development; Seed money; Scholarship funds; Technical assistance; Scholarships—to individuals; Matching/challenge support.
Limitations: Applications accepted. Giving limited to Autauga, Elmore, Lowndes, Macon, and Montgomery counties, AL. No grants to individuals (except for designated scholarship funds limited to local area residents), or for fundraising events or capital campaigns.
Publications: Application guidelines; Annual report; Financial statement; Grants list; Newsletter.
Application information: Visit foundation web site for online applications and guidelines per grant type. Application form required.
Initial approach: Create online profile
Copies of proposal: 1
Deadline(s): Aug. 29 for CACF grants; varies for geographic affiliates
Final notification: Dec. for CACF grants; varies for geographic affiliates
Officers and Directors:* Kyle Johnson,* Chair.; Burton Ward,* Pres.; **David Allred**; **Rita O. Brown**; Milton C. Davis; Laura Harmon; **Evette Hester**; Louise Jennings; **Jennifer McDonald**; Riley Roby; William J. Scanlan; Shannon G. Speir; K. Roger Teel, Jr.; Daniel Thompson; Clay Torbert.
Number of staff: 4 full-time professional; 1 full-time support.
EIN: 630842355
Other changes: Rita O. Brown is no longer Secy.-Treas. Robert L. Davis, David Jamison and Riley Roby are no longer directors.

9
Community Foundation of Northeast Alabama
(formerly Calhoun County Community Foundation)
1130 Quintard Ave., Ste. 100
P.O. Box 1826
Anniston, AL 36201 (256) 231-5160
Contact: Jennifer S. Maddox, C.E.O.
FAX: (256) 231-5161;
E-mail: info@yourcommunityfirst.org; Additional e-mail: jmaddox@yourcommunityfirst.org; Main URL: http://www.yourcommunityfirst.org/
Facebook: http://www.facebook.com/pages/Community-Foundation-of-Northeast-Alabama/212407278799983

Established in 1997 in AL; reorganized as a community foundation in 1999.
Foundation type: Community foundation.
Financial data (yr. ended 09/30/13): Assets, $34,488,973 (M); gifts received, $2,277,226; expenditures, $1,789,000; giving activities include $1,118,005 for grants, and $409,345 for foundation-administered programs.
Purpose and activities: The foundation is a permanent philanthropic resource dedicated to

enhancing the quality of life in nine counties in Northeast Alabama including Calhoun, Cherokee, Clay, Cleburne, DeKalb, Etowah, Randolph, St. Clair, and Talladega. The foundation's mission is to wisely assess needs and channel donor resources to maximize community well-being, by using donor gifts to grow funds that benefit the community.
Fields of interest: Arts; Child development, education; Education; Health care; Mental health, treatment; Human services.
Type of support: Seed money; Program evaluation; Management development/capacity building; Curriculum development; General/operating support; Building/renovation; Equipment; Emergency funds; Program development; Conferences/seminars; Publication; Scholarship funds; Research; Technical assistance; Matching/ challenge support.
Limitations: Applications accepted. Giving to organizations who provide services to residents of Calhoun County, AL. No support for religious organizations for religious purposes or to influence elections. No grants to individuals (except for scholarships), or for organizations operating less than one year, endowments, special events or fundraising campaigns, or capital campaigns.
Publications: Application guidelines; Annual report; Financial statement; Grants list; Informational brochure; Newsletter; Occasional report; Program policy statement.
Application information: Visit foundation web site for online application forms and guidelines. Application form required.
Initial approach: Varies, see website
Deadline(s): Varies
Board meeting date(s): Quarterly
Officers and Trustees:* Tommie J. Goggans III,* Chair.; Cheryl Potts,* Vice-Chair.; Jennifer Maddox,* C.E.O. and Pres.; Eula Tatman,* V.P., Grants, Scholarships and Initiatives; **Susan Williamson,* V.P., Advancement, Comms.**; Martha G. Lavender,* Secy.; Newman R. Nowlin,* Treas.; Matt Akin; **Gloria K. Bennett**; **Anne S. Carruth**; Terry Graham, Ed.D.; James S. Nolen; Thomas S. Potts, Jr.; Manju Purohit; Albert L. Shumaker; Brenda S. Stedham; Jack Swift.
Number of staff: 4 full-time professional; 1 part-time professional; 1 part-time support.
EIN: 630308398
Other changes: Susan Williamson is now V.P., Advancement, Comms. Martha G. Lavender, Newman R. Nowlin, and Thomas S. Potts are no longer trustees.

10
The Community Foundation of South Alabama
(formerly The Mobile Community Foundation)
212 St. Joseph Rd.
Mobile, AL **36602** (251) 438-5591
***Contact:* Rebecca Byrne, Pres.**
FAX: (251) 438-5592;
E-mail: info@communityendowment.com; **Grant inquiry e-mail: program@communityendowment.com; Mailing address: P.O. Box 990, Mobile, AL 36601-0990**; Main URL: http://www.communityendowment.com
Blog: http://thecommunityfoundationofsouthalabma.blogspot.com/
Twitter: https://twitter.com/CFSouthAlabama
YouTube: http://www.youtube.com/user/CFSouthAlabama?feature=mhee

Incorporated in 1976 in AL.
Foundation type: Community foundation.
Financial data (yr. ended 09/30/12): Assets, $56,148,254 (M); gifts received, $1,697,590; expenditures, $8,861,534; giving activities include $7,267,450 for grants.
Purpose and activities: The foundation works to improve the quality of life in South Alabama by promoting philanthropy. Through wise investments, they help build the financial resources necessary to make effective grants that positively impact our community. They are committed to providing the effective leadership that is necessary to help solve tough problems in their communities. By building strategic partnerships with community leaders, corporations and volunteers we bring the community together to share ideas and identify issues to strengthen South Alabama.
Fields of interest: Arts; Higher education; Adult education—literacy, basic skills & GED; Education; Environment; Animal welfare; Health care, insurance; Health care; Substance abuse, prevention; Crime/violence prevention; Crime/ violence prevention, abuse prevention; Disasters, preparedness/services; Recreation, parks/ playgrounds; Recreation; Youth development, services; Neighborhood centers; Children, day care; Family services; Human services, emergency aid; Aging, centers/services; Human services; Community/economic development; Children/ youth; Youth; Aging; Young adults; Mentally disabled; Minorities; Asians/Pacific Islanders; African Americans/Blacks; Girls; Boys; AIDS, people with; Single parents; Economically disadvantaged; Homeless.
Type of support: Program evaluation; General/ operating support; Management development/ capacity building; Building/renovation; Equipment; Emergency funds; Program development; Publication; Seed money; Curriculum development; Scholarship funds; Program-related investments/ loans; In-kind gifts; Matching/challenge support.
Limitations: Applications accepted. Giving primarily limited to an eight county region in Southwest AL, including Baldwin, Choctaw, Clarke, Conecuh, Escambia, Mobile, Monroe, and Washington counties. No support for religious activities. No grants to individuals, or for national fundraising campaigns, conferences or seminar expenses, tickets for charity benefits, or budget deficits.
Publications: Application guidelines; Annual report; Annual report (including application guidelines); Financial statement; Informational brochure (including application guidelines); Newsletter.
Application information: Visit the foundation's web site for application form and guidelines. Unsolicited applications are not accepted. Application form required.
Initial approach: Submit application form and attachments
Copies of proposal: 1
Deadline(s): Varies
Board meeting date(s): Quarterly
Final notification: Varies
Officers and Directors:* Dr. Bernard H. Eichold, II*, Chair.; Norman D. Pitman, Jr.,* Vice-Chair.; **Rebecca Byrne, C.E.O. and Pres.; Mary Kathleen Miller,* Secy.; Linette Clausman, C.F.O.**; Bob Higgins,* Treas.; Mark Hieronymus; LaShaunda Holly; Jennifer Jenkins; Robert "Bob" Jones; Neil M. Kennedy; Douglas M. Littles, Ph.D.; Champ Meyercord; Samford T. Myers; Mrs. Edna Rivers; A.J. Rudnick; Mary M. Tucker; Raymond R. Wingard; Cynthia H. Zipperly.
Number of staff: 5 full-time professional; 1 part-time professional; 2 full-time support; 1 part-time support.
EIN: 630695166
Other changes: Rebecca Byrne has replaced Alvertha Penny as C.E.O. and Pres. Mary Kathleen Miller has replaced Neil M. Kennedy as Secy. Linette Clausman is now C.F.O. George V. Davis, Mitchell G. Lattof, Michael S. Marshall, and Henry F. O'Connor are no longer directors.

11
Community Foundation of West Alabama
700 Energy Center Blvd., Ste. 406
Northport, AL 35473 (205) 366-0698
Contact: Glenn Taylor, C.E.O.
FAX: (205) 366-0813;
E-mail: CFOWA@bellsouth.net; Mailing address: P.O. Box 3033, Tuscaloosa, AL 35403; Main URL: http://www.thecfwa.org

Established in 1999 in AL as an initiative of the Tuscaloosa Estate Planning Council.
Foundation type: Community foundation.
Financial data (yr. ended 12/31/12): Assets, $8,537,898 (M); gifts received, $2,709,756; expenditures, $1,707,837; giving activities include $1,314,897 for 32+ grants (high: $270,181), and $159,897 for 96 grants to individuals.
Purpose and activities: The foundation seeks to connect people and resources to the real needs of the community. The foundation strives to help build partnerships between donors, nonprofit organizations and the community at large in order to strengthen and enhance the quality of life of the people of western AL.
Fields of interest: Humanities; Arts; Education; Environment; Health care; Disasters, Hurricane Katrina; Recreation; Residential/custodial care, hospices; Aging, centers/services; Human services; Community/economic development; United Ways and Federated Giving Programs; Infants/toddlers; Children/youth; Youth; Disabilities, people with; Physically disabled; Blind/visually impaired; Mentally disabled; Single parents; Crime/abuse victims; Terminal illness, people with; Economically disadvantaged.
Limitations: Applications accepted. Giving limited to western AL, including Bibb, Fayette, Green, Hale, Lamar, Marengo County, Pickens, Sumter, and Tuscaloosa. No support for religious organizations for religious purposes. No grants to individuals (except for scholarships), or for dinners, balls, or other ticketed events, or endowments.
Publications: Application guidelines; Annual report; Annual report (including application guidelines); Financial statement; Grants list; Informational brochure; Newsletter; Program policy statement.
Application information: Visit foundation web site for application form and guidelines. Application form required.
Initial approach: Submit application form and attachments
Copies of proposal: 1
Deadline(s): Apr. 1 and Oct. 1
Board meeting date(s): May and Nov.
Final notification: May and Nov.
Officers and Directors:* Thomas A. Nettles IV,* Chair.; Glenn Taylor,* C.E.O. and Pres.; **Joseph D. Blackburn,* V.P.**; William A. Tate,* V.P.; Anne Moman,* Secy.; Pierce Boyd,* Treas.; Davis S. Burton; Claude D. Edwards; Hon. John England; Sam Faucett; James I. Harrison III; Shelley Jones; Dr. Barry Mason; Gina Miers; Lin Moore; Mary Bess Paluzzi; Pam Parker; Leah Ann Sexton; Dr. Hugh H. Stegall; William W. Walker, Jr.
Number of staff: 2 part-time professional.
EIN: 631225003

12

Day Family Foundation

2001 Park Pl. Twr., Ste. 320
Birmingham, AL 35203-4800

Established in 1979 in NY.
Donor: H. Corbin Day.
Foundation type: Independent foundation.
Financial data (yr. ended 07/31/13): Assets, $305,124 (M); expenditures, $159,249; qualifying distributions, $153,200; giving activities include $150,200 for 40 grants (high: $30,000; low: $100).
Purpose and activities: Giving primarily for the arts, education, and health and human services.
Fields of interest: Arts; Education; Human services.
Limitations: Applications not accepted. Giving primarily in AL, NJ, and NY. No grants to individuals.
Application information: Contributes only to pre-selected organizations.
Trustees: James D. Davis; H. Corbin Day.
EIN: 133025969
Other changes: Stephen Friedman is no longer a trustee.

13

Mike and Gillian Goodrich Foundation

(formerly Mike and Gillian Goodrich Charitable Foundation)
3800 Colonnade Pkwy., Ste. 430
Birmingham, AL 35243-3369 **(205) 443-7809**
Main URL: http://www.mggoodrichfoundation.org/

Established in 2008 in AL.
Donors: T. Michael Goodrich; Gillian W. Goodrich.
Foundation type: Independent foundation.
Financial data (yr. ended 12/31/12): Assets, $72,446,971 (M); gifts received, $1,700,000; expenditures, $4,118,306; qualifying distributions, $3,598,602; giving activities include $3,469,078 for 95 grants (high: $400,000; low: $1,000).
Purpose and activities: Giving primarily for education, neighborhood revitalization, the environment, arts and culture, and positioning strategic community assets. Grant applications must be geared toward achieving specific results in these focus areas.
Fields of interest: Arts; Education; Environment, natural resources; Community development, neighborhood development.
Limitations: Giving primarily in the Birmingham metro, and Woodlawn areas of AL, as well as the Black Belt, AL, area (particularly Greene and Hale Counties). No support for individual school classrooms or programs, private schools, or mission trips or ambassador programs. No grants to individuals, or for scholarships, private awards, health-related research, or fundraising events that are not 100% deductible for charitable purposes.
Publications: Application guidelines.
Application information: Full proposals for Leadership Grants are by invitation only, upon consideration of Letter of Intent. Grants to faith-based organizations may be made to support programs that address the focus areas. See foundation web site for specific application guidelines.
Initial approach: **For Leadership Grants: use Letter of Intent process on foundation web site; use online application process for Community Support Grants**
Deadline(s): **None, for Letters of Intent regarding Leadership Grants; full grant proposals for Leadership Grants and applications for Community Support Grants must be submitted by Feb. 1, May, 1, Aug. 1, and Nov. 1;**
Officers and Directors:* Gillian W. Goodrich,* Chair. and Pres.; T. Michael Goodrich,* V.P.; T. Michael Goodrich II,* Secy.; Carol W. Butler, Exec. Dir.; Alexandra D. Goodrich; Gillian G. Goodrich; Mary B. Goodrich.
EIN: 263587489
Other changes: The grantmaker now publishes application guidelines.

14

Hawkins Educational Foundation

c/o Compass Bank, WMG- Tax Dept.
P. O. Box 10566
Birmingham, AL 35296-0002 **(205) 297-6713**
***Contact:* Patsy Alford, Grants Mgr.**
E-mail: info@HawkinsScholarship.com; Main URL: http://www.hawkinsscholarship.com
Facebook: http://www.facebook.com/pages/Hawkins-Educational-Foundation/112841992133738

Established in 2005 in AL.
Foundation type: Independent foundation.
Financial data (yr. ended 07/31/13): Assets, $4,048,608 (M); expenditures, $236,334; qualifying distributions, $181,204; giving activities include $157,500 for 46 grants to individuals (high: $6,000; low: $1,700).
Purpose and activities: Scholarship awards to residents of Baldwin County, Alabama, who have a minimum of 2.0 GPA from high school and who are pursuing a higher education.
Fields of interest: Higher education.
Type of support: Scholarships—to individuals.
Limitations: Giving primarily to residents of Baldwin County, AL.
Application information: See foundation web site for full application guidelines and requirements, including downloadable application form. Application form required.
Officer: Joyce Woodburn, Chair.
Trustee: Compass Bank.
EIN: 616320623

15

International Retinal Research Foundation, Inc.

1720 University Blvd., Ste. 124
Birmingham, AL 35233-1816 (205) 325-8103
Contact: Sandra Blackwood, Exec. Dir.
FAX: (205) 325-8394;
E-mail: sblackwood@irrfonline.org; Main URL: http://www.IRRFonline.org
E-Newsletter: http://www.irrfonline.org/newsletters.html

Established in 1997 in AL.
Foundation type: Independent foundation.
Financial data (yr. ended 12/31/12): Assets, $29,225,702 (M); gifts received, $55,549; expenditures, $1,809,687; qualifying distributions, $1,515,656; giving activities include $1,515,656 for 17 grants (high: $466,739; low: $1,000).
Purpose and activities: The foundation supports scientific research on the diseases of the human eye, especially its center, the macula, and peripheral retinal research that ultimately will accelerate the outcome of discovery. Specific consideration will be given to those scientists who are actively working toward discovering the causes, preventions, and cures of macular degeneration and diabetic retinopathy. Limited funding is available for postdoctoral training in the area of vision research and for educational and scientific exchange.
Fields of interest: Eye research.
Type of support: Equipment; Conferences/seminars; Fellowships; Research; Matching/challenge support.
Limitations: Applications accepted. Giving on a national and international basis. No support for capital building programs. No grants to individuals, or for building construction, or salary of the Principal Investigator except when matching funds are committed from another funding agency.
Publications: Application guidelines; Grants list; Informational brochure; Newsletter.
Application information: E-mail application are not accepted. Application form required.
Initial approach: Download application form from foundation web site, or telephone requesting it
Copies of proposal: 2
Deadline(s): May 1 (for regular grants); Mar. 1 (for Postdoctoral Scholar nominations)
Board meeting date(s): Mar., May, Aug., and Nov.
Officers and Directors:* Michael A. Callahan, M.D.*, Pres.; John S. Parker, M.D.*, V.P.; Victor Hugo Marx III, M.D.*, Treas.; Sandra Blackwood, Exec. Dir.; Larry A. Donoso, M.D., Ph.D., Scientific Dir.; Paul Sternberg, Jr., M.D., Scientific Advisor.
Number of staff: 2 full-time professional; 1 part-time support.
EIN: 721342841

16

Malone Family Foundation

P.O. Box 531085
Birmingham, AL 35253-1085 (205) 423-0901
Contact: Alyson M. Bagby, Pres.
E-mail: info@themalonefamilyfoundation.org; Main URL: http://www.themalonefamilyfoundation.org
Grants List: http://www.themalonefamilyfoundation.org/initiatives.html

Established in 2007 in AL.
Donor: Wallace D. Malone, Jr.
Foundation type: Independent foundation.
Financial data (yr. ended 02/28/13): Assets, $6,570,801 (M); expenditures, $366,067; qualifying distributions, $353,213; giving activities include $352,008 for 5 grants (high: $179,000; low: $4,533).
Purpose and activities: The foundation primarily, but not solely, focuses on programs and projects that expand the horizons of and opportunities for children and young adults. Those programs and projects with objectives of providing better education, promoting self-esteem and instilling in its beneficiaries a desire to improve oneself are of great interest to the foundation. The foundation concentrates on 501(c)(3), non-profit organizations that provide programs and projects designed to prevent or solve problems and create opportunities, rather than meet basic needs. Preference will be given to creative programs that directly and positively impact the future of children and young adults in the area of education. The foundation feels that a well-educated and motivated population promotes an economically strong community and, thereby, improves everyone's standard of living while simultaneously expanding opportunities for everyone.
Fields of interest: Education; Children; Young adults.
Limitations: Applications accepted. Giving primarily in AL; limited giving in FL and GA.
Application information: Application form required.
Initial approach: Letter

Deadline(s): May 15 for June decisions; Oct. 15 for Dec. decisions
Board meeting date(s): June and Dec.
Officers: Wallace D. Malone, Jr., Chair.; Alyson M. Bagby, Pres. and Treas.; Catherine M. Wilson, V.P. and Secy.
Directors: Ocllo S. Malone; Wallace Davis Malone.
EIN: 204596031

17
McWane Foundation
P.O. Box 43327
Birmingham, AL 35243-0327 **(205) 414-3400**
Contact: C. Phillip McWane, Tr.
***Main URL:* http://www.mcwane.com/community/charitable-giving-guidelines/**

Established in 1961.
Donor: McWane, Inc.
Foundation type: Company-sponsored foundation.
Financial data (yr. ended 12/31/13): Assets, $712,363 (M); gifts received, $1,493,000; expenditures, $1,516,637; qualifying distributions, $1,504,169; giving activities include $1,504,169 for 50 grants (high: $1,000,000; low: $250).
Purpose and activities: The foundation supports programs designed to promote arts and culture; education; environmental stewardship; heath and safety; and children.
Fields of interest: Museums (science/technology); Arts; Higher education; Education; Health care; Safety/disasters; YM/YWCAs & YM/YWHAs; Children, services.
Type of support: Scholarship funds; General/operating support; Capital campaigns; Matching/challenge support.
Limitations: Applications accepted. Giving primarily in areas of company operations, with emphasis on Birmingham, AL. No support for discriminatory organizations, political organizations, or athletic teams, fraternal orders, sectarian religious or veterans' organizations, or labor associations. No grants to individuals, or for telephone or mass mail appeals.
Publications: Application guidelines.
Application information: Application form not required.
Initial approach: Proposal to the nearest company facility
Copies of proposal: 1
Deadline(s): Mar. 15, June 15, Sept. 14, and Dec. 15
Board meeting date(s): Quarterly
Trustees: John McMahon; C. Phillip McWane.
EIN: 636044384

18
Erie Hall Meyer Charitable Fund, Inc.
P.O. Drawer 2527
Mobile, AL **36652-2527** (251) 432-5511
***Application address:* c/o Kenneth E. Niemeyer, Pres., 11 N. Water St., 28th Fl., Mobile, AL 36602; (251) 690-1535,**
e-mail: ken.niemeyer@regions.com

Established in 1991 in AL.
Donor: Erie H. Meyer†.
Foundation type: Independent foundation.
Financial data (yr. ended 09/30/13): Assets, $13,464,161 (M); expenditures, $790,287; qualifying distributions, $699,703; giving activities include $686,750 for 16 grants (high: $457,500; low: $500).
Fields of interest: Education; Environment; Health organizations; Human services; Community/economic development.
Type of support: General/operating support.
Limitations: Giving primarily in the South Baldwin County, AL, area. No grants to individuals.
Application information: Application form not required.
Initial approach: Letter
Deadline(s): None
Officers and Directors:* Herbert J. Malone, Jr.,* Chair.; Kenneth E. Niemeyer,* Pres.; Neil C. Johnston,* V.P.; **Norman D. Pitman III,* Secy.-Treas.**
EIN: 631055074
Other changes: Kenneth E. Niemeyer has replaced Vivian G. Johnston, Jr. as Pres.
Herbert J. Malone, Jr. is now Chair. Norman D. Pitman, III is now Secy.-Treas.

19
Regions Financial Corporation Foundation
(formerly Regions Bancorporation Foundation)
c/o Regions Bank
P.O. Box 11647
Birmingham, AL 35202-1647

Established in 1997 in AL.
Donors: AmSouth Bank; AmSouth Bancorporation; Regions Financial Corp.; Regions Morgan Keegan Trust; Regions Bank.
Foundation type: Company-sponsored foundation.
Financial data (yr. ended 12/31/12): Assets, $517,979 (M); gifts received, $400,000; expenditures, $1,109,380; qualifying distributions, $1,108,480; giving activities include $1,108,480 for 555 grants (high: $2,475; low: $25).
Purpose and activities: The foundation supports organizations involved with health, housing, and human services. Special emphasis is directed toward education and arts and culture.
Fields of interest: Arts; Education; Health care.
Type of support: General/operating support; Continuing support; Employee matching gifts.
Limitations: Applications accepted. Giving primarily in AL and FL; some giving also in GA and TN. No support for religious organizations not of direct benefit to the entire community, political organizations, or alumni groups. No grants to individuals, or for cultural or social events.
Application information: Application form required.
***Initial approach:* Proposal**
***Deadline(s):* None**
Officers and Directors:* Fournier J. Gale III,* Pres.; Douglas J. Jackson,* V.P.; Dale M. Herbert, Secy.; Ann W. Forney, Treas.; David B. Edmonds; William D. Ritter.
Trustee: Regions Bank.
EIN: 631144265
Other changes: The grantmaker no longer lists a phone. The grantmaker no longer lists a primary contact.
The grantmaker now accepts applications. Regions Bank is no longer a member of the governing body.

20
M.A. Rikard Charitable Trust
c/o Synovus Trust Company, N.A.
800 Shades Creek Pkwy., Ste. 225
Birmingham, AL 35209-4526
Application address: c/o Frank A. Rikard, Tr., 9340 Clubhouse Rd., Foley, AL 36535-9322

Established in 2001 in AL.
Donor: M.A. Rikard†.
Foundation type: Independent foundation.
Financial data (yr. ended 09/30/13): Assets, $4,121,524 (M); expenditures, $286,771; qualifying distributions, $248,987; giving activities include $195,500 for 45 grants (high: $65,000; low: $200).
Fields of interest: Education; Health care; Human services.
Limitations: Applications accepted. Giving primarily in GA and HI.
Application information: Application form required.
Initial approach: Letter
Deadline(s): None
Trustees: Frank A. Rikard; Glenn A. Rikard; Elizabeth R. Von Krusenstiern; John Von Krusenstiern; Synovus Trust Company, N.A.
EIN: 636231842

21
The Simpson Foundation
P.O. Box 240548
Montgomery, AL **36124-0548** (334) 386-2516
FAX: (334) 386-2521; Main URL: http://thesimpsonfoundation.org/

Established in 1985 in AL.
Foundation type: Independent foundation.
Financial data (yr. ended 04/30/13): Assets, $6,439,713 (M); expenditures, $356,406; qualifying distributions, $279,435; giving activities include $199,200 for 28 grants (high: $28,800; low: $400).
Purpose and activities: Giving primarily for educational scholarships.
Fields of interest: Education.
Type of support: Scholarship funds.
Limitations: Applications accepted. Giving limited to residents of Wilcox County, AL. No grants to individuals directly.
Application information: Scholarship payments made to the individual's educational institution. Applicants must submit transcripts and letters of recommendation. Application form required.
Initial approach: Proposal
Deadline(s): Jan. 1- Mar. 31
Trustees: Mary Hogen; Chris Stone; AlaTrust, Inc.
EIN: 630925496

22
J. Craig and Page T. Smith Scholarship Foundation, Inc.
400 Caldwell Trace Park
Indian Springs, AL 35242 (205) 202-4076
Contact: Ahrian Tyler Dudley, C.E.O.

Established in 2005 in AL.
Foundation type: Operating foundation.
Financial data (yr. ended 12/31/12): Assets, $30,545,848 (M); gifts received, $23,785,249; expenditures, $1,281,428; qualifying distributions, $986,945; giving activities include $573,587 for grants to individuals.
Purpose and activities: The foundation funds college scholarships for deserving students throughout Alabama, with special consideration given to applicants who would be the first in their mother's and/or father's families to attend college.
Fields of interest: Higher education.
Type of support: Scholarships—to individuals.
Limitations: Applications accepted. Giving limited to AL.
Application information: Application form required.

Initial approach: Letter
Deadline(s): Jan. 15
Officer and Directors:* Ahrian Tyler Dudley,* Exec. Dir.; Lewis G. Burks, Jr.; June Cunniff; C.R. Dudley, Jr.; Stewart R. Dudley; Helen Crow Mills.
Trustees: Barbara J. Belisle; Michael K.K. Choy, Esq.; Deivid Delgado; Richard H. Gill, Esq.; Jason Leger; Fred Phillips; Stephen Powell; Kenneth O. Simon, Esq.; Keith Walker; and 4 additional trustees.
EIN: 202224138
Other changes: At the close of 2012, the fair market value of the grantmaker's assets was $30,545,848, a 302.9% increase over the 2010 value, $7,580,956.
Louis H. Anders, Carolyn B. Featheringill and James W. Gewin are no longer directors. Ahrian Tyler Dudley is now Exec. Dir.

23
Snook Foundation

P.O. Box 725
Summerdale, AL 36580-0725 (251) 952-5810
Contact: Marjorie Y. Snook

Established in AL.
Donor: Marjorie Y. Snook.
Foundation type: Independent foundation.
Financial data (yr. ended 12/31/12): Assets, $34,980,223 (M); expenditures, $1,840,237; qualifying distributions, $1,790,237; giving activities include $1,318,041 for 34 grants (high: $400,000; low: $5,000), and $163,606 for 2 foundation-administered programs.
Fields of interest: Education, single organization support; Education, fund raising/fund distribution; Education; United Ways and Federated Giving Programs.
Limitations: Applications accepted. Giving primarily in AL. No grants to individuals.
Application information: Application form required.
***Initial approach:* Letter requesting application form**
Deadline(s): None
Trustees: Rosemary Johnston; William L. Lambert; Lester Smith; Marjorie Y. Snook; M. Mort Swaim.
EIN: 237250795

24
Stephens Foundation

P.O. Box 1943
Birmingham, AL 35201-1943

Established in 1991.
Donors: Elton B. Stephens†; Dell S. Brooke.
Foundation type: Independent foundation.
Financial data (yr. ended 12/31/12): Assets, $7,740,721 (M); expenditures, $772,072; qualifying distributions, $746,200; giving activities include $746,200 for 83 grants (high: $205,000; low: $250).
Purpose and activities: Giving primarily for the arts, education, health associations, and to a United Methodist church.
Fields of interest: Arts education; Performing arts centers; Performing arts, orchestras; Arts; Education; Health organizations, association; Protestant agencies & churches.
Type of support: General/operating support.
Limitations: Applications not accepted. Giving primarily in AL, with some emphasis on Birmingham and Huntsville. No grants to individuals.
Application information: Contributes only to pre-selected organizations.
Officers: James T. Stephens, Pres.; **Jane S. Comer, V.P.**; Dell S. Brooke, Secy.; Elton B. Stephens, Jr., Treas.
EIN: 631035698
Other changes: Jane S. Comer is now V.P.

25
Wiregrass Foundation

1532 Whatley Dr.
Dothan, AL 36303-1984 (334) 699-1031
Contact: Cindy Bedsole, V.P., Admin. and Grants; Dr. Barbara Alford, Pres.
FAX: (334) 669-2472;
E-mail: Barbara@wiregrassfoundation.org; E-mail address for Cindy White, V.P., Admin. and Grants: cindy@wiregrassfoundation.org; Main URL: http://www.wiregrassfoundation.org
Grants List: http://www.wiregrassfoundation.org/grants-1/

Established in 2003 in AL.
Foundation type: Independent foundation.
Financial data (yr. ended 12/31/13): Assets, $105,065,826 (M); expenditures, $5,559,028; qualifying distributions, $4,600,357; giving activities include $3,951,563 for 83 grants (high: $1,000,000; low: $750).
Purpose and activities: Giving primarily to make grants that have a significant, measurable impact on the health, education and quality of life of the Dothan, Alabama area.
Fields of interest: Education; Health care.
Limitations: Applications accepted. Giving primarily in Houston, Henry, Dale and Geneva counties, AL.
Publications: Application guidelines; Annual report; Financial statement.
Application information: Any application (including micro-grant applications) for projects that will operate in schools, request services from school personnel, or involve students during the school day or in connection with their school-sponsored activities, must include written endorsements by the principal(s) and the superintendent of that school and system. The endorsements will not affect the foundation's funding decision, but are intended to insure that the school and system are aware of the proposed project. All proposals must comply with grant application guidelines which are available on foundation web site. Application form required.
Initial approach: See foundation web site for guidelines and eligibility quiz
Copies of proposal: 2
***Deadline(s):* Applications accepted between Mar. 1, May 1, July 1, and Sept. 1**
Board meeting date(s): Apr. 19, June 21, Aug. 16 and Oct. 18
Officers and Directors:* Steve McCarroll,* Chair.; Mary Julia Lee,* Chair.-Elect; Barbara Alford, Pres.; Cindy Besole, V.P., Admin. and Grant Mgmt.; Steve Shaw,* Secy.; John Dunn; John H. Edge; Bobby Hewes; G. David Johnston; Addie McKinzie; David W. Parsons.
EIN: 200897153

ALASKA

26
Alaska Conservation Foundation
911 W. 8th Ave., Ste. 300
Anchorage, AK 99501 (907) 276-1917
Contact: Ann Rothe, Exec. Dir.
FAX: (907) 274-4145;
E-mail: acfinfo@alaskaconservation.org; Grant inquiry e-mail: grants@alaskaconservation.org; Main URL: http://www.alaskaconservation.org
Facebook: https://www.facebook.com/pages/Alaska-Conservation-Foundation/156006977745168
RSS Feed: http://alaskaconservation.org/feed/

Established in 1980 in AK.
Foundation type: Community foundation.
Financial data (yr. ended 06/30/13): Assets, $9,482,091 (M); gifts received, $5,740,367; expenditures, $6,331,462; giving activities include $3,670,970 for 46 grants (high: $485,147).
Purpose and activities: The foundation protects Alaska's natural environment and the diverse cultures and ways of life it sustains. They do this by promoting conservation philanthropy and by strategically directing resources to conservation leaders, organizations, and initiatives.
Fields of interest: Environment, research; Environment, natural resources; Environmental education; Environment; Animals/wildlife, preservation/protection; Animals/wildlife, sanctuaries; Economic development; Community/economic development; Social sciences, public policy; Public affairs, information services.
Type of support: General/operating support; Continuing support; Equipment; Emergency funds; Program development; Conferences/seminars; Publication; Internship funds; Technical assistance; Consulting services; Program evaluation; Grants to individuals; Scholarships—to individuals; Matching/challenge support.
Limitations: Applications accepted. Giving primarily in AK. No grants for annual campaigns, deficit financing, building funds, land acquisition, renovation projects, general or special endowments, or exchange programs; no student loans.
Publications: Application guidelines; Annual report; Financial statement; Grants list; Informational brochure; Newsletter; Program policy statement.
Application information: Visit foundation web site for letter of inquiry forms and grant guidelines per grant type. Application form required.
Initial approach: Varies
Copies of proposal: 1
Deadline(s): Varies
Board meeting date(s): Feb., May, and Sept.
Final notification: 2 weeks after board meeting
Officers and Directors:* Ruth D. Wood,* Chair.; Jim DeWitt,* Vice-Chair.; Kerry K. Anderson,* Secy.; Ann Rothe,* Exec. Dir.; Rhonda Bennon; Cliff Eames; A.J. Grant; Amy Gulick; Lisa Marie Lang; Dorothy M. Larson; William Leighty; Nancy Lord; Anna Plager; David Robertson; Dorene Schiro; John Schoen; Marilyn Sigman; **Stacy Studebaker**; **Anne M. Wilkas.**
Number of staff: 18 full-time professional; 3 part-time professional; 2 full-time support; 1 part-time support.
EIN: 920061466
Other changes: Sam Snyder is now Prog. Off. David Hardenberg is no longer Treas. Marsha Lamb is no longer National Vice-Chair. Anne M. Wilkas is now At-Large. Bonita Howard is no longer a director.

27
The Aleut Foundation
703 W. Tudor Rd., Ste. 102
Anchorage, AK 99503-6650 (907) 646-1929
***Contact:* Cynthia H. Lind, Exec. Dir.**
***FAX:* (907) 646-1949**;
E-mail: taf@thealeutfoundation.org; Main URL: http://thealeutfoundation.org

Established in 1987.
Donors: The Aleut Corp.; Space Mark Inc.; Aleutian Pribilof Islands Restitution Trust.
Foundation type: Company-sponsored foundation.
Financial data (yr. ended 03/31/13): Assets, $272,954 (M); gifts received, $939,225; expenditures, $895,733; qualifying distributions, $643,374; giving activities include $643,374 for 2 + grants.
Purpose and activities: The foundation awards grants and college scholarships to original enrollees and the descendants of original enrollees of the Aleut Corporation, beneficiaries and the descendants of beneficiaries of the Aleutian Pribilof Islands Restitution Trust, and original enrollees and the descendants of original enrollees of the Isanotski Corporation.
Fields of interest: Arts, cultural/ethnic awareness; Vocational education, post-secondary; Higher education; Education; Native Americans/American Indians.
Type of support: Scholarships—to individuals.
Limitations: Applications not accepted. Giving limited to AK.
Application information: Unsolicited requests for funds not accepted.
Board meeting date(s): Quarterly
Officers: Kathy Griesbaum, Chair.; Cynthia H. Lind, Exec. Dir.
Directors: Jessica Borenin; **Gary Ferguson**; Kathy Greisbaum; Debra Mack; Thomas Mack; Boris Merculief.
Number of staff: 2 full-time professional.
EIN: 920124517
Other changes: Kathy Griesbaum has replaced Debra Mack as Chair.
Debra Mack is no longer Chair. Boris Merculief is no longer a member of the governing body. Millie McKeown is no longer Vice-Chair. Gary Ferguson is no longer Secy.-Treas.

28
Arctic Education Foundation
3900 C. St., Ste. 1002
Anchorage, AK 99503 (907) 852-9456
Contact: Carolyn M. Edwards, Mgr.
***FAX:* (907) 852-2774; E-mail: arcticed@asrc.com**;
Tel. and e-mail for Carolyn M. Edwards: (907) 852-8633, cmedwards@asrc@com; Additional tel.: (800) 770-2772; Main URL: http://www.arcticed.com

Established in 1978 in AK.
Donors: Arctic Slope Regional Corp.; Chevron U.S.A., Inc.; BP Alaska; Shell Oil Co.; Amoco Corp.; Piqunik Management Corp.; UIC Construction LLC.
Foundation type: Company-sponsored foundation.
Financial data (yr. ended 12/31/13): Assets, $38,780,709 (M); gifts received, $947,216; expenditures, $1,606,356; giving activities include $1,474,050 for 420 grants to individuals (high: $23,100).
Purpose and activities: The foundation awards scholarships for training and higher education to Northern Alaska Inupiat Natives currently residing in the Artic Slope Region, original 1971 shareholders of the Artic Slope Regional Corporation, and lineal descendants of original 1971 shareholders of the Arctic Slope Regional Corporation.
Fields of interest: Vocational education; Higher education; Education; Native Americans/American Indians.
Type of support: Scholarships—to individuals.
Limitations: Applications accepted. Giving limited to AK.
Publications: Application guidelines.
Application information: Application form required.
Initial approach: Complete online application or download application form and mail to foundation
Deadline(s): Mar. 1, May 1, Aug. 1, and Dec. 1; Apr. 15 for Anagi Leadership Award
Board meeting date(s): Jan. and Aug.
Officers: George Sielak, Chair. and Pres.; Eddie Ahyakak, V.P.; Sandra Stuermer, Co-Secy.-Treas.; Lucinda Stackhouse, Co-Secy.; Carolyn M. Edwards, Mgr.
Directors: Patsy Aamodt; Paul Bodfish, Sr.; Elizabeth Hollingsworth; Raymond Paneak; Crawford Patkotak.
Number of staff: 1 full-time professional.
EIN: 920068447

29
Atwood Foundation, Inc.
301 W. Northern Lights Blvd., Ste. 440
Anchorage, AK **99503-2648 (907) 274-4900**
Contact: Edward Rasmuson, Chair.
FAX: (907) 274-2415;
E-mail: atwoodfoundation@gci.net; Application address: c/o Natasha Vonimhof, Latash Investments, 301 Northern Lights Blvd., Ste. 412, Anchorage, AK 99503; tel.: (907) 274-4900; Main URL: http://www.atwoodfoundation.org

Established in 1962 in AK.
Donors: Robert B. Atwood; Elaine Atwood‡; Anchorage Times Publishing Co.
Foundation type: Independent foundation.
Financial data (yr. ended 12/31/12): Assets, $27,300,349 (M); gifts received, $33,741; expenditures, $1,504,840; qualifying distributions, $1,028,852; giving activities include $851,200 for 30 grants (high: $250,000; low: $1,500).
Fields of interest: Performing arts; Higher education.
Limitations: Applications accepted. Giving primarily in Anchorage, AK. No grants to individuals.
Publications: Annual report; Grants list.
Application information: Application form available on foundation web site. Application form required.
***Initial approach:* Application via U.S. Mail, e-mail, or hand delivery**
Copies of proposal: 1
***Deadline(s):* See foundation web site for current deadlines**
***Board meeting date(s):* Quarterly in Mar., June, Sept., and Dec.**
Final notification: 90 days
Officers: Edward Rasmuson, Chair.; David J. Tobin, Vice-Chair.; Ira Perlman, Secy.; Nancy Harbour, Treas.
Directors: Gloria Allen; Maria Downey; Carolyn Heyman-Layne.
Number of staff: 1 full-time professional; 1 part-time support.
EIN: 926002571

30
Richard L. and Diane M. Block Foundation
2120 C St., Ste. 100
Anchorage, AK 99503-1916 (907) 563-5121
***Contact:* Richard L. Block, Dir.**
***E-mail:* blockfoundation@arctic.net; Email for Richard L. Block: rlblock@arctic.net**; Main URL: https://online.foundationsource.com/public/home/blockfoundation

Established in 2007 in AK.
Donors: Richard L. Block; Diane M. Block.
Foundation type: Independent foundation.
Financial data (yr. ended 12/31/12): Assets, $9,919,504 (M); gifts received, $3,058,000; expenditures, $259,030; qualifying distributions, $209,572; giving activities include $209,572 for grants.
Purpose and activities: Giving to support those resources in Alaska which can most effectively enhance the quality of life of Alaska's people; the young who will lead and power the state's future, the cultural organizations that inspire the community intellectually and artistically and the social service organizations that lift up the poor so they may permanently and independently share in Alaska's bounty.
Limitations: Applications accepted. Giving primarily in AK and MA. No grants for See part xv, line 2a.
Publications: Application guidelines.
Application information: See foundation web site for complete application guidelines. Application form required.
***Initial approach:* Use online application system on foundation web site**
Directors: Debbie Bellange; Warren Berckmann; David R. Block; Diane M. Block; Patrick Block; Richard L. Block; Jennifer D. Green; Ned McCarty.
EIN: 306136901
Other changes: The grantmaker now publishes application guidelines.

31
Bristol Bay Native Corp., Education Foundation
111 W. 16th Ave., Ste. 400
Anchorage, AK 99501-6299 **(907) 278-3602**
***Contact:* Greta L. Goto, Exec. Dir.**
***FAX:* (907) 276-3924; Toll-free tel.: (800) 426-3602**; Main URL: http://www.bbnc.net/index.php?option=com_content&view=category&layout=blog&id=19&Itemid=40

Established in 1992 in AK.
Donor: Bristol Bay Native Corp.
Foundation type: Company-sponsored foundation.
Financial data (yr. ended 12/31/12): Assets, $6,747,330 (M); gifts received, $1,864,081; expenditures, $389,821; qualifying distributions, $313,375; giving activities include $313,375 for 199 grants to individuals (high: $5,875; low: -$284).
Purpose and activities: The foundation awards college and vocational scholarships to Alaska Native shareholders of Bristol Bay Native Corporation.
Fields of interest: Vocational education; Higher education; Native Americans/American Indians.
Type of support: Scholarships—to individuals.
Limitations: Applications accepted. Giving primarily in AK.
Publications: Application guidelines; Newsletter (including application guidelines).
Application information: Applicants for Short-Term Vocational Education Program Scholarships must also submit a letter of request that includes employment goals, how the training will relate to your employment goals, and employment opportunities after completion of the training. Application form required.
Initial approach: Download application form and mail to foundation
***Deadline(s):* Apr. 4 for Higher Education and Vocational Education Scholarships; None for Short-Term Vocational Education Program Scholarships**
Board meeting date(s): Quarterly
Officers and Directors: Marie Paul, Pres.; Katrina Johnson, V.P.; **Andria Agli, Secy.; Gregory French, Treas.**; Greta L. Goto, Exec. Dir.; Jerry Liboff; Evelyn Mujica-Larson; Patrick Patterson III.
Number of staff: 1 full-time professional.
EIN: 920141709
Other changes: The grantmaker no longer lists an E-mail address. The grantmaker no longer lists a fax. The grantmaker no longer lists a phone.
Andria Agli has replaced April Ferguson as Secy. Gregory French has replaced Cynthia Tisher as Treas.
Richard Y. Lopez is no longer V.P. April Ferguson is no longer Secy. Cynthia Tisher is no longer Treas. Luanne Pelagio is no longer Exec. Dir.

32
Chugach Heritage Foundation
3800 Centerpoint Dr., Ste. 601
Anchorage, AK 99503-4196 (907) 563-8866
***FAX:* (907) 550-4147;**
E-mail: scholarships@chugach-ak.com; Main URL: http://www.chugachheritagefoundation.org/

Established in 1994 in AK.
Donors: Chugach Alaska Regional Corp.; Chugach Alaska Corp.
Foundation type: Company-sponsored foundation.
Financial data (yr. ended 12/31/12): Assets, $243,834 (M); gifts received, $1,113,052; expenditures, $909,184; qualifying distributions, $909,488; giving activities include $821,065 for 227 grants (high: $12,533; low: $132).
Purpose and activities: The foundation awards college scholarships, vocational certificates, and job training to shareholders and the descendants of shareholders of Chugach Alaska Corporation, and works to utilize, preserve, and promote the tradition and cultural heritage of the Chugach region.
Fields of interest: Vocational education; Higher education; Education; Health care; Employment, training; Human services; Native Americans/American Indians.
Type of support: Scholarships—to individuals.
Limitations: Applications accepted. Giving primarily in AK and WA.
Publications: Application guidelines.
Application information: Application form required.
***Initial approach:* Download application form or contact corporate office**
***Deadline(s):* June 30 for Barney Uhart Memorial Scholarship**
Officer: Michael McCanna,* Chair. and Pres.
Trustee: Sheri D. Buretta; **Marchell Espe**; Gabriel Kompkoff.
EIN: 920116128

33
The CIRI Foundation
(also known as The Cook Inlet Region, Inc. Foundation)
3600 San Jeronimo Dr., Ste. 256
Anchorage, AK 99508-2870 (907) 793-3575
FAX: (907) 793-3585;
E-mail: tcf@thecirifoundation.org; Additional tel.: (800) 764-3382; Main URL: http://www.thecirifoundation.org
Education and Heritage Project Grant Recipients: http://www.thecirifoundation.org/project_grants_Awards_2011.html
Facebook: http://www.facebook.com/#!/pages/The-CIRI-Foundation/124737080941125
The Ciri Foundation: Making A Difference Video: http://www.thecirifoundation.org/TCF_Video.html

Established in 1982 in AK.
Donors: CIRI, Inc.; CITC; Salamatof Native Association; AK Village Initiatives; Tyonek Native Corp.; Southcentral Foundation.
Foundation type: Company-sponsored foundation.
Financial data (yr. ended 12/31/12): Assets, $50,389,113 (M); gifts received, $309,360; expenditures, $3,895,457; qualifying distributions, $3,376,290; giving activities include $121,869 for 5 grants (high: $43,869; low: $9,000), and $2,494,575 for 682 grants to individuals (high: $10,000; low: $250).
Purpose and activities: The foundation supports organizations involved with Alaska Native heritage and education, and awards scholarships, grants, and fellowships to Alaska Natives to promote individual self-development and economic self-sufficiency.
Fields of interest: Arts, cultural/ethnic awareness; Visual arts; Performing arts; History/archaeology; Literature; Philosophy/ethics; Historic preservation/historical societies; Arts; Vocational education; Higher education; Graduate/professional education; Business school/education; Engineering school/education; Health sciences school/education; Scholarships/financial aid; Education; Employment, services; Employment, training; Employment; Mathematics; Native Americans/American Indians.
Type of support: General/operating support; Continuing support; Program development; Conferences/seminars; Fellowships; Internship funds; Scholarship funds; Research; Grants to individuals; Scholarships—to individuals.
Limitations: Applications accepted. Giving primarily in the Cook Inlet Region, AK. No grants for endowments, buildings or equipment, completed projects, re-granting, or lobbying or propaganda efforts; no loans.
Publications: Application guidelines; Grants list; Program policy statement.
Application information: Visit website for scholarship endowment funds and named scholarship funds. Additional information may be requested at a later date for project grants. Organizations receiving project grants are asked to submit a final report. Application form required.
Initial approach: Complete online application; download application form and mail proposal and application to foundation for General and Cultural Heritage Fellowships and project grants
Copies of proposal: 1
***Deadline(s):* Mar. 1, June 1, Sept. 1, and Nov. 1 for project grants; Mar. 31, June 30, Sept. 30, and Dec. 1 for Vocational Training, General and Cultural Heritage Fellowships, and internships; June 1 for Achievement, Excellence, and Special Excellence Annual Scholarships; and June 1 and Dec. 1 for General Semester Scholarships**
Board meeting date(s): Quarterly
Final notification: 30 to 60 days for project grants

Officers and Directors:* Jeff Gonnason,* Chair.; Louis Nagy, Jr.,* Vice-Chair.; Susan A. Anderson, C.E.O. and Pres.; Tamara Pickett, MD, Secy.-Treas.; Hallie Bissett; Jessica Greiner; Rayna Hartz; Deanna Sackett; Jaclyn Sallee; **Susan Wells**; David Wright.
Number of staff: 6
EIN: 920087914
Other changes: Patrick Duke is no longer Secy.-Treas. Shirley Holloway is no longer a director.

34
The Doyon Foundation
615 Bidwell, Ste. 101
Fairbanks, AK 99701-7580 (907) 459-2048
Contact: Doris Miller, Exec. Dir.
FAX: (905) 459-2065;
E-mail: foundation@doyon.com; E-mail for Doris Miller: millerd@doyon.com; Additional tel.: (888) 478-4755; Main URL: http://www.doyonfoundation.com/
Doyon Foundation Blog: http://doyonfoundation.wordpress.com/
Facebook: http://www.facebook.com/doyonfoundation
Tel. for Tonya. Garnett; (907) 459-2049, e-mail: garnett@doyon.com

Established in 1988 in AK.
Donor: Doyon Ltd.
Foundation type: Company-sponsored foundation.
Financial data (yr. ended 06/30/13): Assets, $16,359,338 (M); gifts received, $1,492,633; expenditures, $1,066,680; qualifying distributions, $629,392; giving activities include $426,630 for 597 grants to individuals (high: $2,500; low: -$400).
Purpose and activities: The foundation supports programs designed to improve educational, career, and cultural opportunities for Dayan shareholders. Special emphasis is directed toward programs designed to strengthen Native culture and heritage through education.
Fields of interest: Arts, cultural/ethnic awareness; Elementary/secondary education; Vocational education; Higher education; Education; Native Americans/American Indians.
Type of support: General/operating support; Internship funds; Scholarships—to individuals.
Limitations: Applications accepted. Giving primarily in AK.
Publications: Application guidelines; Annual report; Informational brochure; Newsletter.
Application information: Application form required.
Initial approach: Complete online application or download application and mail
Deadline(s): Apr. 15 for Competitive Scholarships; Mar. 15, Apr. 15, and Nov. 15 for Basic Scholarships; Mar. 15, Apr. 15, Sept. 15, and Nov. 15 for Vocational Scholarships
Board meeting date(s): Quarterly
Officers and Directors:* Lanien Livingston, Pres.; Allan Hayton, V.P.; Julie Anderson, Secy.-Treas.; Doris Miller, Exec. Dir.; Paul Mountain; Victor Nicholas; **Joshua Peter**; **Sonta Roach.**
Number of staff: 2 full-time professional.
EIN: 943089624
Other changes: Lanien Livingston has replaced Julie Anderson as Pres. Allan Hayton has replaced Wesley Roberts Dalton as V.P. Julie Anderson has replaced Lorraine B. David as Secy.-Treas.
Mark Holmgren is no longer C.E.O. Julie Anderson is no longer Pres. Wesley Roberts Dalton is no longer V.P. Lorraine B. David is no longer Secy.-Treas. Shane Derendoff and Teisha M. Simmons are no longer members of the governing body.

35
Juneau Community Foundation
350 N. Franklin St., Ste. 2
Juneau, AK 99801 (907) 463-3223
Contact: Amy Skilbred, Exec. Dir.
FAX: (907) 463-4841; E-mail: info@juneaucf.org; E-Mail for Amy Skilbred: amy@juneaucf.org; Main URL: http://www.juneaucf.org/

Established in 2000 in AK.
Foundation type: Community foundation.
Financial data (yr. ended 12/31/12): Assets, $2,298,885 (M); gifts received, $702,233; expenditures, $314,138; giving activities include $262,380 for 12 grants (high: $50,000; low: $65).
Purpose and activities: The foundation promotes philanthropy and effectively responds to the needs of the community to create a healthy, safe, and culturally rich environment.
Fields of interest: Performing arts; Environment, natural resources; Animals/wildlife.
Limitations: Giving primarily in the Juneau, AK, area. No grants to individuals.
Publications: Annual report; Grants list; Informational brochure.
Application information:
***Deadline(s):* Apr. 30 for Scholarships.**
Board meeting date(s): Jan., Apr., June and Oct.
Officers and Directors:* Eric Kueffner,* Pres.; Reed Stoops,* V.P.; Robin Sahnow,* Secy.; Bob Rehfeld,* Treas.; Amy Skilbred, Exec. Dir.; Laraine Derr; Sioux Douglas; Linda Egan; Clark Gruening; Sandro Lane; Geoff Larson; Amanda Mallott; Mike McKrill; Bob Storer.
Number of staff: 1 part-time professional.
EIN: 522395867

36
Koniag Education Foundation
4241 B. St., Ste. 303B
Anchorage, AK 99503-5920 (907) 562-9093
Contact: Tyan Hayes, Exec. Dir.
FAX: (907) 562-9023;
E-mail: kef@koniageducation.org**; Toll-free tel.: (888) 562-9093; e-mail for Tyan Hayes: director@koniageducation.org; e-mail for Christina Fisch: scholarships@koniageducation.org**; Main URL: http://www.koniageducation.org
E-Newsletter: http://www.koniageducation.org/sign-up-for-our-newsletter/
Facebook: http://www.facebook.com/pages/Alaska-Native-Student-Network/59290820727
Grants List: http://www.koniageducation.org/scholarship-awards/
Koniag Education Student Blog: http://www.koniageducation.org/category/student-blog/
Radio Interview with Exective Director Tyan Hayes: http://www.koniageducation.org/wp-content/uploads/2012/03/KEF-on-KMXT-Radio-3-1-2012.mp3
RSS Feed: http://www.koniageducation.org/feed/

Established in 1993 in AK.
Donors: Koniag, Inc.; Exxon Mobile; Alyeska Pipeline Co.; Gary Sampson.
Foundation type: Company-sponsored foundation.
Financial data (yr. ended 03/31/13): Assets, $6,045,140 (M); gifts received, $349,259; expenditures, $589,357; qualifying distributions, $477,459; giving activities include $231,415 for 166 grants to individuals (high: $11,100; low: $132).
Purpose and activities: The foundation awards college scholarships and career development grants to Alaska Native shareholders and descendants of shareholders of Koniag, Inc.
Fields of interest: Vocational education, post-secondary; Higher education; Education; Native Americans/American Indians.
Type of support: Internship funds; Grants to individuals; Scholarships—to individuals.
Limitations: Applications accepted. Giving primarily in AK and the Pacific Northwest, with emphasis on Kodiak Island, AK.
Publications: Application guidelines; Financial statement; Grants list; Informational brochure; Newsletter.
Application information: Multi-year funding is not automatic. Application form required.
Initial approach: Complete online application or download application form and mail to foundation
Deadline(s): Jan. 15 for Angayuk Scholarship & Internship; Mar. 15 for KEF General summer term; June 1 for KEF General fall term; Aug. 10 for Alyeksa, Drabek, ExxonMobil, Godfrey, and Matfay; None for Career Development Grants
Board meeting date(s): Quarterly
Officers and Directors: Edward Ward, Pres.; Jon Panamaroff, V.P.; James Carmichael, Secy.-Treas.; Tyan Hayes, Exec. Dir.; **Loren Anderson**; Peter Boskofsky; Laurie Fagnani; Janissa Johnson; Jacqueline Madsen; Stephen Parsons; Lorena Skonberg; Thomas Swensen.
Number of staff: 1 full-time professional; 1 part-time professional; 1 part-time support.
EIN: 920145017
Other changes: Uwe Gross and William Anderson are no longer members of the governing body.

37
Steve Nash Foundation
9400 Sugar Cir.
Anchorage, AK 99507-6033 (907) 274-0629
Contact: Jenny L. Miller, Exec. Dir.
Main URL: https://stevenash.org/
Twitter: https://twitter.com/SteveNashFdn

Established in 2001 in TX.
Donors: Stephen Nash; Calle; Phebe's Tavern/East Pub; Glaceau; Indochino; Major League Soccer; Neurosurgery and Endovascular Associates; Phoenix Suns Charities; St. Boniface Hospital; Steve Nash Sports Club; United way of Greater Milwaukee; Walton Family Foundation; Namrata Ahuja; Natasha Ahuja; Anne Penn; Icap.
Foundation type: Independent foundation.
Financial data (yr. ended 12/31/12): Assets, $163,275 (M); gifts received, $307,406; expenditures, $445,414; qualifying distributions, $156,240; giving activities include $156,240 for grants.
Purpose and activities: The foundation is dedicated to assisting underserved children in their health, personal development, education and enjoyment of life. The foundation awards grants to youth-focused organizations that foster children's development by addressing underlying conditions of poverty, medical need, and restricted access to those resources that contribute to their well-being. The foundation looks for organizations that work directly with children, or those that work to benefit children through social change and policy reform.
Fields of interest: Health care; Youth development; Children; Economically disadvantaged.
International interests: Canada.
Type of support: General/operating support.
Limitations: Applications accepted. Giving primarily in AZ; some giving also other regions of the U.S. and in British Columbia, Canada, Paraguay, and Uganda. No support for governmental agencies, or for religious programs or programs based within a

religious institution, schools, colleges or university administrations or for sports teams or sporting events. No grants to individuals, or for salaries, general operating expenses or travel.

Application information: Application form required.
Initial approach: See website for application form
Deadline(s): See website for deadline
Board meeting date(s): Mar. and Sept.

Officers: Stephen Nash, Pres.; Joann Nash, Secy.-Treas.; Jenny Miller, Exec. Dir.
EIN: 311753206

ARIZONA

38
Ahearn Family Foundation
2390 E. Camelback Rd., Ste. 203
Phoenix, AZ 85016-3450
Contact: Phil Krevitsky

Established in 2007 in AZ.
Donor: Michael J. Ahearn.
Foundation type: Independent foundation.
Financial data (yr. ended 12/31/11): Assets, $8,108,937 (M); gifts received, $7,891,200; expenditures, $1,265,472; qualifying distributions, $1,265,422; giving activities include $1,265,422 for 19 grants (high: $1,097,500; low: $120).
Purpose and activities: Giving primarily to a college scholarship foundation; some funding also for human services.
Fields of interest: Scholarships/financial aid; Human services.
Limitations: Applications not accepted. Giving primarily in AZ. No grants to individuals.
Application information: Contributes only to pre-selected organizations.
Trustees: Gayle S. Ahearn; Michael J. Ahearn.
EIN: 137582929

39
APS Foundation, Inc.
P.O. Box 53999, M.S. 8657
Phoenix, AZ **85072-3999** 602-250-4736
Contact: Julie Coleman, Exec. Dir.
FAX: 602-250-4492;
E-mail: corporategiving@aps.com; E-mail for Julie Coleman: julie.coleman@aps.com; Main URL: http://www.aps.com/en/communityandenvironment/charitablegiving/ourgivingprograms/Pages/home.aspx

Established in 1981 in AZ.
Donor: Arizona Public Service Co.
Foundation type: Company-sponsored foundation.
Financial data (yr. ended 12/31/13): Assets, $30,349,680 (M); expenditures, $3,220,309; qualifying distributions, $3,121,997; giving activities include $3,023,685 for 25 grants (high: $1,000,000; low: $5,000).
Purpose and activities: The foundation supports education programs designed to promote science, technology, engineering, and math to nurture's tomorrow's leader and create a more educated workforce.
Fields of interest: Elementary/secondary education; Higher education; Education; Environment; Children/youth, services; Foundations (community); Mathematics; Engineering/technology; Science.
Type of support: Building/renovation; General/operating support; Program development.
Limitations: Applications accepted. Giving primarily in APS service territories in AZ. No support for charter or private schools, religious, political, fraternal, legislative, or lobbying organizations, civic service clubs, private or family foundations, start-up organizations, discriminatory organizations, sports teams, scouting troops, or advocacy organizations. No grants to individuals, or for fundraising events, sponsorships, endowments, debt reduction, or capital or building campaigns.
Publications: Application guidelines.
Application information: Support is limited to 1 contribution per organization during any given year. Organizations receiving support are asked to provide a final report. Application form not required.
Initial approach: Complete online application
Deadline(s): Mar. 1 and Sept. 1
Final notification: 30 to 60 days
Officers and Directors:* Donald E. Brandt,* Chair. and Pres.; **David P. Falck,* Secy.**; **Tommy D. McLeod,* Treas.**; Julie Coleman, Exec. Dir.; **Linda R. Fisker**; **John S. Hatfield**; **Donald G. Robinson**; Mark A. Schiavoni.
Number of staff: 2 full-time professional; 1 part-time support.
EIN: 953735903
Other changes: Donald P. Falck is now Secy. Tommy D. McLeod is now Treas.

40
Lon D. and Lucille Barton Charitable Foundation
38093 South Samaniego Dr.
Tucson, AZ 85739-1019

Established in 1984 in IL.
Donor: Florence Lucille Barton.
Foundation type: Independent foundation.
Financial data (yr. ended 12/31/12): Assets, $6,332,153 (M); expenditures, $339,650; qualifying distributions, $328,000; giving activities include $328,000 for grants.
Fields of interest: Higher education; Education; Health organizations, association; Cancer research; Human services; Protestant agencies & churches; Economically disadvantaged.
Limitations: Applications not accepted. Giving primarily in AZ and IL. No grants to individuals.
Application information: Contributes only to pre-selected organizations.
Officers: John F. Schmidt, Pres. and Treas.; Margaret Schmidt, Secy.
Director: Tom Schmidt.
EIN: 371161757
Other changes: The grantmaker has moved from IL to AZ.

41
Christian Scholarship Foundation
(formerly Prescott Christian School Scholarship Foundation)
2126 W. Charteroak Dr.
Prescott, AZ **86305-7711** (928) 771-2018
Contact: William T. Warren, Chair.
***Main URL:* http://www.csf-info.net**

Established in 1999 in AZ.
Foundation type: Independent foundation.
Financial data (yr. ended 12/31/12): Assets, $303,176 (M); gifts received, $271,461; expenditures, $198,999; qualifying distributions, $198,999; giving activities include $181,653 for 145 grants to individuals (high: $2,920; low: $38).
Purpose and activities: Scholarship awards for students at designated Prescott, Arizona, schools.
Fields of interest: Higher education.
Type of support: Scholarships—to individuals.
Limitations: Applications accepted. Giving primarily in AZ.
Application information: Guidelines available on foundation web site. Application form required.
Officers and Directors:* William T. Warren,* Chair.; Charlie Taylor,* Secy.; Bill Patrick,* Treas.; Peter Grey; Lou Higdon; Theresa Higdon.
EIN: 860947958

42
Dorrance Family Foundation
7600 E. Doubletree Ranch Rd., Ste. 300
Scottsdale, AZ 85258-2137 (480) 367-7000

Established in 1991 in AZ.
Donor: Bennett Dorrance.
Foundation type: Independent foundation.
Financial data (yr. ended 12/31/12): Assets, $53,793,078 (M); expenditures, $4,577,504; qualifying distributions, $4,314,106; giving activities include $4,110,100 for 89 grants (high: $1,436,707; low: $500).
Purpose and activities: Giving primarily for education and national resource conservation.
Fields of interest: Museums (science/technology); Arts; Elementary/secondary education; Higher education, college; Environment, natural resources.
Limitations: Applications not accepted. Giving primarily in AZ. No grants to individuals.
Application information: Contributes only to pre-selected organizations.
Officers and Directors:* Bennett Dorrance,* Pres.; Bennett Dorrance, Jr.,* V.P.; Jacquelynn W. Dorrance,* Secy.; Ashley Dorrance Kaplan,* Treas.
Number of staff: 1 full-time professional; 1 part-time professional.
EIN: 860691863
Other changes: Carolyn O'Malley is no longer Exec. Dir. Ashley Dorrance Barker, Treas., is now Ashley Dorrance Kaplan.

43
Every Voice In Action Foundation
1300 S. Belvedere Ave.
Tucson, AZ **85711-5701** (520) 615-2100
Contact: Judith Anderson, C.E.O.; Ruth Marblestone, Oper. Mgr.
FAX: (520) 615-2112
MySpace: http://www.myspace.com/everyvoiceaz
Tumblr: http://everyvoiceaz.tumblr.com/
Twitter: http://twitter.com/everyvoiceaz

Established in 2001 in AZ.
Foundation type: Independent foundation.
Financial data (yr. ended 06/30/13): Assets, $7,048,790 (M); expenditures, $1,172,574; qualifying distributions, $1,071,800; giving activities include $887,668 for 2 grants (high: $785,015; low: $102,653).
Purpose and activities: Every Voice in Action is a small, private foundation supporting Youth Voice-focused nonprofit programs in Tucson and Pima County, Arizona. The mission of the foundation is to ignite and support youth voice, infusing the community with the unique perspectives of young people. The foundation supports Youth Voice programs, including those focused on youth activism, youth media, youth as resources and youth philanthropy.
Fields of interest: Youth development, services; Youth.
Type of support: General/operating support; Equipment; Program development; Film/video/radio; Technical assistance; Matching/challenge support.
Limitations: Giving limited to Tucson and Pima County, AZ. No support for religious programs and any program that practices or promotes discrimination against people. No grants to individuals or for government services, public school services required by law, and projects that jeopardize an organization's tax-exempt status; no loans or deficit funding.
Publications: Grants list.

Application information:
Board meeting date(s): Jan.
Officers and Directors:* Scott Lunn,* Chair.; Judith Anderson, C.E.O. and Pres.; Rofaidah Al Shamir, Secy.; **Daniel Arellano,* Treas.**; David Aquino; Andres Cano; Rosie Garcia; Massie Gebedou; Jose Hoyos; Manny Leon; Trey Spiece.
Number of staff: 3 full-time professional; 1 part-time support.
EIN: 860988206
Other changes: At the close of 2013, the grantmaker paid grants of $887,668, a 311.4% increase over the 2012 disbursements, $215,750. Scott Lunn has replaced Celestino Fernandez as Chair. Daniel Arellano has replaced Scott Lunn as Treas.

44
The Flinn Foundation
1802 N. Central Ave.
Phoenix, AZ 85004-1506 (602) 744-6800
Contact: Jack B. Jewett, C.E.O.
FAX: (602) 744-6815; E-mail: info@flinn.org; Main URL: http://www.flinn.org
Arizona Biosciences Feed: http://www.flinn.org/feed.rss
Bioscience Roadmap: http://www.flinn.org/bio-roadmap/reports-and-multimedia
E-Newsletter: http://www.flinn.org/newsletter-signup
Twitter: http://www.twitter.com/biozonanews
Scholarship tel.: **(602) 744-6802, e-mail: fscholars@flinn.org**

Established in 1965 in AZ.
Donors: Irene Flinn†; Robert S. Flinn, M.D.†.
Foundation type: Independent foundation.
Financial data (yr. ended 12/31/12): Assets, $194,755,468 (M); gifts received, $172,814; expenditures, $10,138,784; qualifying distributions, $8,937,578; giving activities include $5,250,603 for 61 grants (high: $2,500,000; low: $1,620), and $2,470,177 for foundation-administered programs.
Purpose and activities: Giving to improve the quality of life in Arizona to benefit future generations, by improving the competitiveness of Arizona's biomedical/research enterprise; by strengthening universities through an undergraduate scholarship program for outstanding high school students; and by furthering the artistic mission and strengthening the institutional capacity of principal visual and performing arts organizations.
Fields of interest: Arts; Higher education; Medical research, institute; Biology/life sciences.
Type of support: Program development; Seed money; Scholarship funds; Research.
Limitations: Applications accepted. Giving limited to AZ. No grants for building projects, purchase of equipment, endowment projects, annual fundraising campaigns, ongoing operating expenses or deficit needs; requests to support conferences and workshops, publications, or the production of films and video are considered only when these activities are an integral component of a larger foundation initiative.
Publications: Annual report; Financial statement; Newsletter; Occasional report.
Application information: Applications accepted for Flinn Scholarship only. Application form required.
Initial approach: See foundation web site for scholarship information and application form procedures
Deadline(s): Oct. 19 for scholarships
Board meeting date(s): Quarterly
Officers and Directors:* David J. Gullen, M.D.*, Chair.; Steven M. Wheeler,* Vice-Chair.; Jack B. Jewett, C.E.O. and Pres.; Cathy McGonigle, Exec. V.P.; William A. Read, Ph.D., Sr. V.P., Research and Special Programs; Don P. Snider, V.P. and C.F.O.; Bradley W. Halvorsen, V.P., Comms.; Nancy Welch, V.P., Arizona Center for Civic Leadership; Eric M. Reiman, M.D.*, Secy.; Rosellen C. Papp,* Treas.; Robert A. Brooks, M.D., Honorary Dir.; David R. Frazer, Honorary Dir.; Merlin W. Kampfer, M.D., Honorary Dir.; Edward V. O'Malley, Jr., Honorary Dir.; Lisa Wilkinson-Fannin, M.D., Honorary Dir.; Linda J. Blessing, Ph.D.; Drew M. Brown; Richard J. Caselli, M.D.; Shaun A. Kirkpatrick; W. Scott Robertson, M.D.
Number of staff: 10 full-time professional; 7 full-time support.
EIN: 860421476

45
Freedom Wireless Foundation
14850 N. Scottsdale Rd., Ste. 295
Scottsdale, AZ 85254-2882 (480) 584-5354
***Application address:* 18801 N. Thompson Peak Pkwy., Ste. 240, Scottsdale, AZ 85255, email: MTD@freedomwirelessfoundation.org**; Main URL: http://www.freedomwirelessfoundation.org/

Donor: Freedom Wireless Inc.
Foundation type: Independent foundation.
Financial data (yr. ended 12/31/12): Assets, $7,901 (M); gifts received, $230,000; expenditures, $237,729; qualifying distributions, $236,800; giving activities include $236,800 for 3 grants (high: $175,000; low: $1,800).
Fields of interest: Recreation, parks/playgrounds.
Limitations: Applications accepted. Giving primarily in AZ.
Application information: Application form required.
Initial approach: Complted grant application form
Deadline(s): None
Directors: Douglas V. Fougnies; Larry L. Day; Kenneth Widner.
EIN: 262692248

46
William M. & Ann K. Grace Foundation
c/o William Matt Grace Development Co.
7575 N. 16th St., Ste. 1
Phoenix, AZ 85020-4625 (602) 956-8254
Contact: Ron Richards, Dir.
***FAX:* (602) 943-3548**;
E-mail: ronrichards@wmgracefoundation.com; Main URL: http://www.wmgracefoundation.com

Established in 2005 in AZ.
Donor: Ann K. Grace Charitable Lea Ann Trust.
Foundation type: Independent foundation.
Financial data (yr. ended 12/31/12): Assets, $10,727,378 (M); gifts received, $1,875,100; expenditures, $645,827; qualifying distributions, $642,006; giving activities include $642,006 for 54 grants (high: $137,000; low: $500).
Purpose and activities: The foundation provides individual scholarships directly to students (for all levels of school, including private grade schools, high schools, colleges, universities) with scholarships given for merit or need. The foundation also makes grants for existing scholarship funds, as well as grants directly to schools for facilities, scholarships or general support. The foundation strongly encourages and gives preference to matching funds where it concerns grants to organizations.
Fields of interest: Higher education.
Type of support: General/operating support; Scholarship funds; Scholarships—to individuals; Matching/challenge support.
Limitations: Applications accepted. Giving primarily in AZ and northwest MO.
Application information: Application form required.
Initial approach: Submit application form (which can be downloaded from foundation web site) via U.S. mail, fax or e-mail
Deadline(s): Nov. 15
Officers and Board Members: Howard T. Grace,* Pres.; Barb Grace; Matt Grace; Heather G. Kaiser.
Directors: Kate Kaiser; Ron Richards.
EIN: 562529760

47
The George Mason and Lois C. Green Foundation
2440 E. Broadway
Tucson, AZ 85719-6008 (520) 791-3939
Contact: Linda Lohse, Secy.
FAX: (520) 791-3995; Main URL: http://www.tucsonfoundations.org

Established in 1986 in AZ.
Donors: Lois C. Green†; G.M. Green Unitrust; George Mason Green†.
Foundation type: Independent foundation.
Financial data (yr. ended 12/31/12): Assets, $15,168,692 (M); gifts received, $136,412; expenditures, $1,034,193; qualifying distributions, $983,948; giving activities include $897,124 for 8 grants (high: $375,600; low: $1,500).
Fields of interest: Arts; Human services; Children/youth, services.
Type of support: General/operating support; Annual campaigns; Capital campaigns; Building/renovation; Endowments; Emergency funds.
Limitations: Giving primarily in Tucson, AZ. No grants to individuals.
Application information: Unsolicited requests for funds are not currently accepted. Refer to foundation web site for updates.
Officers: Robert Lohse, Pres.; Jennifer Lohse, V.P.; Linda Lohse, Secy.; Patricia Lohse, Treas.
Director: Jason DePizzo.
Number of staff: 3
EIN: 742379340

48
Hill Foundation
c/o Wells Fargo Bank Arizona, N.A.
P.O. Box 53456, MAC S4101-22G
Phoenix, AZ 85072-3456
Application address: c/o Wells Fargo Bank West, N.A., 1740 Broadway, Denver, CO 90274, tel.: (720) 947-6725

Established in 1955 in CO.
Donor: Virginia W. Hill†.
Foundation type: Independent foundation.
Financial data (yr. ended 04/30/13): Assets, $37,096,414 (M); expenditures, $2,594,366; qualifying distributions, $1,982,299; giving activities include $1,887,450 for 172 grants (high: $100,000; low: $3,000).
Purpose and activities: Grants largely for health care for the medically indigent, higher education, services for the elderly, and cultural programs; support also for social service agencies and the disabled, as well as the arts, particularly the opera.
Fields of interest: Performing arts, opera; Arts; Higher education; Education; Hospitals (general);

Health care, financing; Health organizations, association; Human services; Catholic federated giving programs; Catholic agencies & churches; Homeless.
Type of support: Program development; Scholarship funds; Matching/challenge support.
Limitations: Giving primarily in CO and WY. No grants to individuals, or for capital improvements other than equipment acquisition for health care and related purposes.
Publications: Informational brochure; Program policy statement.
Application information:
Initial approach: Letter
Deadline(s): None
Final notification: Within 5 weeks
Trustees: Francis W. Collopy; John R. Moran; **Margaret L. Toal**; Wells Fargo Bank West, N.A.
EIN: 846081879

49
Mabel Y. Hughes Charitable Trust
c/o Wells Fargo Bank, N.A.
P.O. Box 53456, MAC S4101, Ste. 22G
Phoenix, AZ 85072-3456
Application address: c/o Wells Fargo Bank, Attn.: Ian Dreifaldt, Private Client Svcs., Denver, CO 80274, tel.: (720) 947-6630; **Main URL: https://www.wellsfargo.com/privatefoundationgrants/hughes**

Trust established in 1969 in CO.
Donor: Mabel Y. Hughes†.
Foundation type: Independent foundation.
Financial data (yr. ended 08/31/13): Assets, $11,140,630 (M); expenditures, $457,825; qualifying distributions, $366,719; giving activities include $337,513 for 42 grants (high: $22,513; low: $5,000).
Purpose and activities: Support primarily for the arts, health care and education.
Fields of interest: Museums; Museums (art); Museums (children's); Performing arts centers; Performing arts, opera; Higher education; Education; Reproductive health, family planning; Health care; Human services; Children/youth, services; Family services.
Type of support: General/operating support; Continuing support; Annual campaigns; Equipment; Endowments; Emergency funds; Program development; Seed money; Research.
Limitations: Applications accepted. Giving limited to CO, with emphasis on the Denver area. No grants to individuals, or for deficit financing, scholarships, or fellowships; no loans.
Application information: Application form required.
Initial approach: Letter
Copies of proposal: 1
Deadline(s): None
Trustees: W. Robert Alexander; Wells Fargo Bank, N.A.
EIN: 846070398

50
Jasam Foundation Fund B
286 N. Fenceline Dr.
Tucson, AZ **85748-3726**

Established in 2002 in AR.
Foundation type: Independent foundation.
Financial data (yr. ended 12/31/12): Assets, $7,763,700 (M); expenditures, $568,834; qualifying distributions, $506,655; giving activities include $485,000 for 25 grants (high: $75,000; low: $5,000).
Purpose and activities: Giving primarily for education, hospitals and health organizations, Christian organizations, human services and U.S. troop support.
Fields of interest: Education; Hospitals (general); Health organizations, association; Human services; Children/youth, services; Christian agencies & churches.
Limitations: Applications not accepted. Giving limited to western MI, and the greater Tucson, AZ, area. No grants to individuals.
Application information: Contributes only to pre-selected organizations.
Board meeting date(s): Varies
Officer: Joan D. Guylas, Admin.
Number of staff: 1 part-time support.
EIN: 383637370
Other changes: The grantmaker no longer lists a primary contact.

51
John F. Long Foundation, Inc.
5035 W. Camelback Rd.
Phoenix, AZ 85031-1331 (602) 272-0421
***Contact:* Jacob F. Long, Pres. and Dir.**
FAX: (623) 846-7208;
E-mail: foundation@jflong.com; Main URL: http://www.jflong.com/foundation.htm

Established in 1959.
Donor: John F. Long†.
Foundation type: Independent foundation.
Financial data (yr. ended 04/30/13): Assets, $8,754,766 (M); expenditures, $471,347; qualifying distributions, $440,762; giving activities include $430,198 for 142 grants (high: $30,000; low: $162).
Purpose and activities: Giving primarily for groups who are working to help themselves, their own communities, and help others like themselves through self-empowering, community organizing efforts. The foundation's approach to grant requests focuses on fostering local neighborhood vitality and excellence.
Fields of interest: Arts; Elementary/secondary education; Human services; Children/youth, services; Family services; Community/economic development; Christian agencies & churches; Protestant agencies & churches.
Limitations: Applications accepted. Giving primarily in Phoenix, AZ. No grants to individuals.
Application information: Application guidelines and questionnaire available on foundation web site. Grant requests exceeding $1,000 must be accompanied by financial reports for the past and current fiscal year, and a list of past donors going back no more than 2 years. Application form required.
Initial approach: Letter
Deadline(s): None
Officer and Directors:* Jacob F. Long,* Pres.; Shirley Long Lewis; James J. Miller.
EIN: 866052431

52
The Marketplace One Foundation
(formerly The Edson Foundation)
1 N. 1st St., Ste. 700
Phoenix, AZ 85004-2364

Established in 2006 in AZ.
Donors: Brad Edson; Patricia Edson.
Foundation type: Independent foundation.
Financial data (yr. ended 12/31/12): Assets, $1,259,785 (M); expenditures, $856,785; qualifying distributions, $852,500; giving activities include $852,500 for grants.
Fields of interest: Christian agencies & churches.
Limitations: Applications not accepted. Giving primarily in GA; some funding nationally. No grants to individuals.
Application information: Contributes only to pre-selected organizations.
Officers and Directors:* Bret Edson,* Pres.; Brad Edson,* V.P.; Brad Routh,* Secy.-Treas.
EIN: 208066031
Other changes: Paul Palmer is no longer a director.

53
The Kemper and Ethel Marley Foundation
P.O. Box 10392
Phoenix, AZ 85064-0392
Contact: Daniel Corrigan, V.P.

Established in 1990 in AZ.
Donors: Ethel Marley†; Kemper Marley Trust.
Foundation type: Independent foundation.
Financial data (yr. ended 12/31/12): Assets, $221,262,246 (M); gifts received, $147,363; expenditures, $13,879,734; qualifying distributions, $10,641,854; giving activities include $10,317,408 for 77 grants (high: $1,200,000; low: $1,000).
Purpose and activities: Giving primarily for higher education, human service organizations, the arts, and a zoo.
Fields of interest: Museums; Historic preservation/historical societies; Higher education; Zoos/zoological societies; Youth, services.
Type of support: General/operating support.
Limitations: Applications not accepted. Giving limited to AZ. No support for animal welfare organizations. No grants to individuals.
Application information: Contributes only to pre-selected organizations.
Officers and Directors:* Stephen M. Corrigan,* Pres.; **Nancy Elitharp Ball,* V.P. and Treas.**; Daniel Corrigan,* V.P.
EIN: 860653091
Other changes: Nancy Elitharp Ball is now V.P. and Treas.

54
Marshall Foundation
814 E. University Blvd.
P.O. Box 3306
Tucson, AZ 85722-3306 (520) 622-8613
***Contact:* Jane McCollum**
FAX: (520) 622-0124;
E-mail: jane@marshallfoundation.com; Application contact: Jen Dang, Secy., e-mail: jendang@email.arizona.edu; Main URL: http://www.marshallfoundation.com

Incorporated in 1930 in AZ.
Donor: Louise F. Marshall†.
Foundation type: Independent foundation.
Financial data (yr. ended 12/31/12): Assets, $31,144,882 (M); expenditures, $3,794,437; qualifying distributions, $1,069,806; giving activities include $945,394 for 67 grants (high: $197,539; low: $25).
Purpose and activities: Giving primarily for higher education, children and youth programs, cultural organizations and programs, community service organizations, and medical research.

Fields of interest: Arts; Higher education; Scholarships/financial aid; Education; Health organizations, association; Medical research, institute; Human services; Children/youth, services; Foundations (private grantmaking).
Type of support: Capital campaigns; Building/renovation; Scholarship funds.
Limitations: Giving limited to Tucson and Pima County, AZ. No grants to individuals, or for operational support, or annual support.
Publications: Application guidelines; Annual report; Informational brochure.
Application information: Funding to new recipients is limited due to large-scale commitments to the University of Arizona Scholarship Fund and the University Medical Center Artificial Heart Laboratory as well as other long-term commitments. Application form required.

Initial approach: Use online application form via foundation web site
Copies of proposal: 2
Deadline(s): Mar. 15, May 15 and Sept. 15
Board meeting date(s): Monthly

Officers: Charles Jackson, Pres.; **Bruce Shelton, Secy.**; George Steele, V.P.; Anne Nelson, Treas.
Directors: Francisco Aguilar; **Bruce Burke.**
Number of staff: 2 full-time professional; 1 part-time professional; 4 full-time support.
EIN: 860102198
Other changes: Bruce Shelton has replaced Jennifer Dang as Secy.

55
The James H. Napier Foundation

(formerly The Napier Foundation)
c/o Wells Fargo Bank N.A.
P.O. Box 53456, MAC S4101-22G
Phoenix, AZ 85072-3456

Established in 1953 in NY.
Donor: James H. Napier†.
Foundation type: Independent foundation.
Financial data (yr. ended 07/31/13): Assets, $3,381,279 (M); expenditures, $227,162; qualifying distributions, $192,478; giving activities include $185,560 for 25 grants (high: $30,000; low: $250).
Fields of interest: Education; Health care; Human services.
Type of support: Annual campaigns; Capital campaigns; Building/renovation; Endowments; Scholarship funds; Research; Employee matching gifts.
Limitations: Applications not accepted. Giving primarily in the Meriden, CT, area. No grants to individuals, or for loans or program-related investments.
Application information: Contributes only to pre-selected organizations.

Board meeting date(s): Quarterly

Trustee: Wells Fargo Bank.
EIN: 136029883
Other changes: The grantmaker no longer lists a separate application address.
The grantmaker no longer publishes application guidelines.

56
The Ottosen Family Foundation

105 S. 28th St.
Phoenix, AZ 85034-2619

Established in AZ.
Donors: Donald R. Ottosen; Barbara Ottosen.
Foundation type: Independent foundation.
Financial data (yr. ended 12/31/13): Assets, $11,550,693 (M); gifts received, $300,000; expenditures, $447,308; qualifying distributions, $438,654; giving activities include $438,654 for 11 grants (high: $261,850; low: $365).
Fields of interest: Museums (art); Higher education; Botanical gardens; Hospitals (specialty); Human services; Community/economic development.
Limitations: Applications not accepted. Giving primarily in AZ. No grants to individuals.
Application information: Unsolicited requests for funds not accepted.
Officers: Barbara J. Ottosen, Pres.; Diann C. Henderson, Secy.; Donald R. Ottosen, Treas.
EIN: 860778785
Other changes: Pamela L. Perry is no longer V.P.

57
The Virginia G. Piper Charitable Trust

1202 E. Missouri Ave.
Phoenix, AZ 85014-2921 (480) 948-5853
Contact: Judy Jolley Mohraz Ph.D., C.E.O. and Pres.
FAX: (480) 348-1316; E-mail: info@pipertrust.org; Main URL: http://www.pipertrust.org
E-Newsletter: http://visitor.constantcontact.com/manage/optin/ea?v=001IQ4Q15knkjMpZ2OUGVSlcA%3D%3D
Grants Database: http://www.pipertrust.org/our-grants/search-grants/
Knowledge Center: http://www.pipertrust.org/nonprofit-support/piper-academy/
Twitter: https://twitter.com/pipertrust

Established in 1995.
Donor: Virginia G. Piper†.
Foundation type: Independent foundation.
Financial data (yr. ended 03/31/13): Assets, $533,033,849 (M); gifts received, $22; expenditures, $23,682,862; qualifying distributions, $19,891,992; giving activities include $15,016,997 for 399 grants (high: $1,127,364; low: $35), $39,256 for 111 employee matching gifts, and $1,373,729 for 4 foundation-administered programs.
Purpose and activities: The trust seeks to enhance and strengthen the quality of life for the people in Maricopa County through support of healthcare and medical research, children, older adults, arts and culture, education and religious organizations.
Fields of interest: Arts; Youth development, adult & child programs; Aging, centers/services; Youth.
Type of support: Building/renovation; Capital campaigns; Continuing support; Employee matching gifts; Endowments; Equipment; Fellowships; General/operating support; Management development/capacity building; Matching/challenge support; Program development; Technical assistance.
Limitations: Applications accepted. Giving primarily to organizations that serve residents of Maricopa County, AZ, have operated as a Section 501(c)(3) organization or governmental entity for at least three years, and not be a private foundation or ineligible Type III supporting organization. No support for private foundations, or for start-ups. No grants to individuals, or for endowments.
Publications: Biennial report; Financial statement; Grants list; Newsletter; Occasional report.
Application information: The letter of inquiry and Grant Summary Form can be submitted online from the foundation's web site. Applications should be directed to the Grants Manager. An organization must serve residents of Maricopa County, have operated as a Section 501(c)(3) organization or governmental entity for at least three years, and not be a private foundation or ineligible Type III supporting organization. An additional requirement is the adoption of eight best practices listed on the website. Online application form required. Application form required.

***Initial approach:* Online Grant Summary Form and attach a two-page letter of inquiry.**
Copies of proposal: 1
Deadline(s): None
Board meeting date(s): 12 times per year
Final notification: 3 to 6 months

Officers and Trustees:* Susan M. Pepin, C.E.O. and Pres.; Mary Jane Rynd, Exec. V.P. and C.F.O.; Marilee L. Dal Pra, V.P., Programs; James D. Bruner; Jose A. Cardenas; Paul N. Critchfield; Art DeCabooter; Laura R. Grafman; Sharon C. Harper; Judy Jolley Mohraz, Ph.D.; Steven J. Zabilski.
Number of staff: 13 full-time professional; 3 full-time support.
EIN: 866247076
Other changes: Susan M. Pepin has replaced Judy Jolley Mohraz, Ph.D., as C.E.O. and Pres.
The grantmaker now makes its financial statement available online.

58
Prayer Child Foundation

3903 E. Huber St.
Mesa, AZ 85205-3903 **(480) 634-6086**
***Contact:* Laura Washington, Admin.**
E-mail: info@prayerchild.org; Main URL: http://www.prayerchild.org

Established in 2006 in AZ.
Donors: Curt Waisath; Karen Waisath; Melanie Bastian; Nona Persons; Gold Canyon Candle.
Foundation type: Operating foundation.
Financial data (yr. ended 06/30/13): Assets, $58,804 (M); gifts received, $242,752; expenditures, $226,886; qualifying distributions, $226,700; giving activities include $400 for 3 grants (high: $150; low: $100), and $226,300 for 333 grants to individuals (high: $1,000; low: $200).
Purpose and activities: Giving for children (18 years of age and younger) with physical and emotional challenges.
Fields of interest: Children, services.
Limitations: Giving primarily in Mesa, AZ.
Publications: IRS Form 990 or 990-PF printed copy available upon request.
Application information: Application form required.

Initial approach: Use grant request form on foundation web site
Final notification: Within 4-6 weeks

Officers: Karen Waisath, Pres.; Curt Waisath, V.P.; John Makoff, Secy.; Joe Phillips, Treas.
Advisory Board: Brew Crosby; Troy Crosland; Rick Dutriac; Greg Goeser; David Hejl; Brooks Merrill; Nona Persons; Burke Plummer; Bernie Zimmer.
EIN: 030558277

59
Research Corporation for Science Advancement

4703 E. Camp Lowell Dr., Ste. 201
Tucson, AZ 85712-1292 (520) 571-1111
Contact: Daniel Gasch, C.F.O.
FAX: (520) 571-1119; E-mail: awards@rescorp.org; Main URL: http://www.rescorp.org
Facebook: http://www.facebook.com/pages/Research-Corporation-for-Science-Advancement/166231769296?ref=ts
Grants Database: http://www.rescorp.org/grants-and-awards/awards-database

Twitter: http://twitter.com/ResearchCorp

Incorporated in 1912 in NY.
Donors: Rachel Brown‡; Frederick Gardner Cottrell‡; Elizabeth Hazen‡; Donald F. Jones‡; Edward C. Kendall‡; Paul C. Mangelsdorf; Charles H. Townes; Robert E. Waterman‡; Robert R. Williams‡; Robert B. Woodward‡.
Foundation type: Operating foundation.
Financial data (yr. ended 12/31/12): Assets, $146,724,496 (M); gifts received, $664,306; expenditures, $8,752,905; qualifying distributions, $8,554,535; giving activities include $4,169,828 for 206 grants (high: $125,000; low: $75), and $8,554,535 for foundation-administered programs.
Purpose and activities: Giving to advance academic science research and teaching. The awards programs include the Cottrell College Science Awards, Cottrell Scholars Awards, and Scialog Awards and are open to U.S. colleges and universities to support basic research in the physical sciences (physics, chemistry, and astronomy).
Fields of interest: Astronomy; Chemistry; Physics; Science.
Type of support: Program development; Research.
Limitations: Applications accepted. Giving limited to the U.S. No grants to individuals directly, or for building or endowment funds, indirect costs, common supplies and services, tuition, research leave to start new projects, faculty academic year salaries, post-doctoral or graduate student stipends, secretarial assistance, general support, scholarships, fellowships, publications, travel expenses to scientific meetings, or matching gifts; no loans.
Publications: Application guidelines; Annual report; Newsletter; Occasional report.
Application information: Only online applications will be accepted. Application form required.
Initial approach: Fill out application request form on foundation web site
Deadline(s): Deadlines vary from year to year
Board meeting date(s): Feb., Apr., and Nov.
Final notification: Differs by program
Officers and Directors:* Patrick S. Osmer,* Chair.; **Robert Shelton, Ph.D., Pres.**; Robert B. Hallock,* Secy.; Daniel Gasch, C.F.O.; G. Scott Clemons,* Treas.; Patricia C. Barron, Dir. Emeritus; Stuart B. Crampton, Dir. Emeritus; Robert Holland, Jr., Dir. Emeritus; Suzanne D. Jaffe,* Dir. Emeritus; John P. Schaefer, Dir. Emeritus; Peter K. Dorhout; Jonathan Hook; Brent Iverson; Gayle P.W. Jackson; Elizabeth McCormack; David L. Wenner; Joan B. Woodard.
Science Advisory Committee: Bert Chandler; **Mike Dennin**; Jordan Gerton; Martin Gruebele; Peter Iovine; Nicola Pohl; Veronika Szalai.
Number of staff: 9 full-time professional; 5 full-time support.
EIN: 131963407
Other changes: Jairo Sinova is no longer a member of the Science Advisory Committee.

60
Maureen and Paul Rubeli Foundation Inc.
7181 E. Camelback Rd., Unit 1202
Scottsdale, AZ 85251

Established in 2006 in AZ.
Donors: Maureen E. Rubeli; Paul E. Rubeli.
Foundation type: Independent foundation.
Financial data (yr. ended 12/31/13): Assets, $5,781,808 (M); expenditures, $265,121; qualifying distributions, $236,061; giving activities include $235,000 for 32 grants (high: $45,000; low: $2,000).
Fields of interest: Education; Health care; Boys & girls clubs; United Ways and Federated Giving Programs; Catholic agencies & churches.
Limitations: Applications not accepted. Giving primarily in AZ. No grants to individuals.
Application information: Unsolicited requests for funds not accepted.
Officers: Maureen M. Rubeli, Pres.; Paul E. Rubeli, V.P. and Treas.
EIN: 205935203

61
Milton & Harriet Sioles Family Foundation
6021 E. Naumann Dr.
Paradise Valley, AZ 85253

Foundation type: Independent foundation.
Financial data (yr. ended 06/30/13): Assets, $3,753,548 (M); expenditures, $214,341; qualifying distributions, $184,925; giving activities include $184,925 for 5 grants (high: $83,500; low: $500).
Fields of interest: Education; Health care, clinics/centers; Catholic agencies & churches.
Limitations: Applications not accepted. Giving primarily in AZ.
Application information: Unsolicited requests for funds not accepted.
Officers and Directors:* Harriet Z. Sioles,* Pres.; Elyse C. Sioles,* Secy.; Robert M. Sioles,* Treas.
EIN: 272546709

62
The William D. Squires Educational Foundation, Inc.
2338 W. Royal Palm Rd., Rm. J
Phoenix, AZ 85021-9339
***E-mail:* info@wmdsquiresfoundation.org**; Application address: c/o Cynthia Squires Gross, P.O. 2940, Jupiter, FL 33468-2940, tel.: (561) 741-7751; Main URL: http://www.wmdsquiresfoundation.org/index.htm

Established in 1999 in AZ.
Donor: William D. Squires.
Foundation type: Independent foundation.
Financial data (yr. ended 12/31/12): Assets, $2,214,165 (M); expenditures, $261,973; qualifying distributions, $245,292; giving activities include $158,918 for 26 grants to individuals (high: $52,000; low: $1,500).
Purpose and activities: Scholarship awards to financially needy graduating seniors in Ohio, who are graduating from high school in the current year.
Fields of interest: Higher education; Education.
Limitations: Applications accepted. Giving limited to residents of OH.
Application information: Applicants must provide a minimum of 2 letters of recommendation, an official high school transcript, a short essay, and a FAFSA. Application form required.
Initial approach: Letter
Deadline(s): Apr. 5
Officers: Pamela A. Bolen, Pres.; Cynthia Squires Gross, V.P. and Exec. Dir.; Deborah A. Squires, V.P.; Judy K. Perry, Secy.; Lena B. Squires, Treas.
EIN: 860946058

63
Stardust Foundation, Inc.
6730 N. Scottsdale Rd., Ste. 230
Scottsdale, AZ 85253-4416 (480) 607-5800
E-mail: contact@stardustco.com; Main URL: http://www.stardustfoundation.org

Established in 1993 in AZ as successor to the Bisgrove Foundation.
Donors: Gerald Bisgrove; Debra Bisgrove‡; Bisgrove Foundation.
Foundation type: Company-sponsored foundation.
Financial data (yr. ended 12/31/12): Assets, $23,858,952 (M); expenditures, $1,010,471; qualifying distributions, $993,908; giving activities include $985,504 for 22 grants (high: $403,069; low: $100).
Purpose and activities: The foundation supports community foundations and organizations involved with arts and culture, health, human services, and community development. Special emphasis is directed toward programs designed to link concepts of family and neighborhood stability.
Fields of interest: Museums; Performing arts, theater; Performing arts, orchestras; Arts; Higher education; Health care; Children/youth, services; Family services; Homeless, human services; Human services; Community/economic development; Foundations (community); United Ways and Federated Giving Programs.
Type of support: General/operating support; Endowments; Program development; Scholarship funds.
Limitations: Applications not accepted. Giving primarily in Phoenix and Scottsdale, AZ.
Application information: Contributes only to pre-selected organizations.
Officers: Gerald Bisgrove,* Pres.; Jon Munson, Secy.-Treas.
EIN: 860735230

64
Del E. Webb Foundation
P.O. Box 2427
Prescott, AZ 86302-2427 (928) 445-9699
Contact: Lawrence A. Johnson, Pres.
FAX: (928) 445-1584; E-mail: Larry@DEWF.org; Main URL: http://www.DEWF.org
Grants List: http://www.dewf.org/TFM/$WebStatus/AppsApprDateSort.asp

Incorporated in 1960 in AZ.
Donor: Del E. Webb‡.
Foundation type: Independent foundation.
Financial data (yr. ended 12/31/12): Assets, $45,851,203 (M); expenditures, $2,132,870; qualifying distributions, $1,820,177; giving activities include $1,471,500 for 20 grants (high: $500,000; low: $5,000).
Purpose and activities: Giving to support organizations that are primarily involved in providing formal medical services, medical research, or medical education and are located in the states of Arizona, California or Nevada.
Fields of interest: Education; Health care; Infants/toddlers; Children/youth; Children; Youth; Adults; Aging; Young adults; Disabilities, people with; Physically disabled; Blind/visually impaired; Deaf/hearing impaired; Mentally disabled; Minorities; Asians/Pacific Islanders; African Americans/Blacks; Hispanics/Latinos; Native Americans/American Indians; Indigenous peoples; Women; Infants/toddlers, female; Girls; Adults, women; Young adults, female; Men; Infants/toddlers, male; Boys; Adults, men; Young adults, male; Military/veterans; Offenders/ex-offenders; Substance

abusers; AIDS, people with; Single parents; Crime/abuse victims; Terminal illness, people with; Immigrants/refugees; Economically disadvantaged; Homeless; Migrant workers; LGBTQ.
Type of support: General/operating support; Continuing support; Capital campaigns; Building/renovation; Equipment; Land acquisition; Emergency funds; Program development; Seed money; Curriculum development; Scholarship funds; Research; Matching/challenge support.
Limitations: Applications accepted. Giving limited to AZ, CA, and NV. No support for government agencies, sectarian or religious organizations, or pass-through organizations. No grants to individuals, or for deficit financing or indirect costs.
Publications: Application guidelines.
Application information: Application guidelines and form available on foundation web site. Formal proposals are by invitation only, after review of letter of intent. Application form required.
Initial approach: 1-page letter of intent with foundation Contact Information Form which can be downloaded from foundation web site
Deadline(s): None, for letters of intent. Formal grant applications are due 1-month prior to the foundation's next board meeting. (Refer to meeting calendar on foundation web site)
Board meeting date(s): Jan., Apr., July and Oct.
Final notification: Within 1-week for letters of intent
Officers and Directors:* Lawrence A. Johnson,* Pres.; John B. Lees, V.P.; Shielia Johnson, Treas.; Nicole Aubin; Jean Canoose; John W. Smith.
Number of staff: 2 full-time professional; 2 part-time support.
EIN: 866052737

65
The Weil Foundation
(formerly Polaris Foundation)
P.O. Box 13006
Tucson, AZ 85732-3006
Contact: Nancy Olmstead, Recording Secy.
***E-mail:* info@weilfoundation.org; Proposal e-mails: James Dalen: jdalenmd@gmail.com, and Nancy Olmstead: nancy@x9ranch.com; Express package address: c/o Nancy Olmstead, The Weil Foundation, 1670 N. Kolb Rd., Ste. 240, Tucson, AZ 85715**; Main URL: http://www.weilfoundation.org/
Facebook: http://www.facebook.com/WeilFoundation
Twitter: https://twitter.com/WeilFoundation
Vimeo: http://vimeo.com/weilfoundation

Established in 2002 in AZ.
Donors: Andrew Weil; Custom Nutrition Services, LLC; drugstore.com, inc.
Foundation type: Independent foundation.
Financial data (yr. ended 12/31/12): Assets, $654,418 (M); gifts received, $582,849; expenditures, $506,858; qualifying distributions, $435,000; giving activities include $435,000 for grants.
Purpose and activities: Support for the advancement of integrative medicine. The foundation's current strategic focus is the training and education of medical students, physicians and other health care professionals in integrative medicine.
Fields of interest: Higher education; Medical school/education; Holistic medicine.
Limitations: Applications accepted. Giving primarily in AZ; some giving also in ME and NM.
Publications: Application guidelines.
Application information: Grants are funded from July 1 until June 30. If any material that is to be submitted does not exist in electronic form, indicate in e-mail that such material is being sent by regular mail. Specific instructions available on foundation web site. Application form required.
Initial approach: **Proposal (5-10 pages, to be e-mailed to both James Dalen and Nancy Olmstead), along with cover page which is located on foundation web site**
***Deadline(s):* Jan. 31**
***Final notification:* Mar.**
Officers: Andrew Weil, Chair.; Lura M. Lovell, Vice-Chair.; Richard Baxter, Secy.-Treas.; Nancy Olmstead, Recording Secy.; James Dalen, M.D., Exec. Dir.
Directors: Donald Abrams, M.D.; **Janet Lang**; Humberto S. Lopez; Daria Myers; Robert G. Sarver; Adele Simmons.
EIN: 861049023
Other changes: The grantmaker now publishes application guidelines.

ARKANSAS

66
The Buck Foundation
15249 Dutchman's Dr.
Rogers, AR 72756-7868 (479) 925-2597
Contact: Jan Buck, Exec. Dir.
***E-mail:* info@buckforscholarships.com**; Email address for Jan Buck: jan@buckforscholarships.com; Main URL: http://buckforscholarships.com
Facebook: http://www.facebook.com/pages/Buck-Foundation/105830369465112

Established in 1999 in AR.
Foundation type: Independent foundation.
Financial data (yr. ended 04/30/13): Assets, $6,160,358 (M); expenditures, $242,538; qualifying distributions, $235,717; giving activities include $38,000 for 7 grants (high: $10,000; low: $500), and $190,500 for grants to individuals.
Purpose and activities: Giving primarily to help meet financial needs of college students by awarding scholarships to students from Rogers Heritage High School and Rogers High School in Rogers, Arkansas.
Fields of interest: Education; Human services.
Type of support: General/operating support; Scholarships—to individuals.
Limitations: Applications accepted. **Giving limited to residents of Rogers, AR who are students from Rogers Heritage High School or Rogers High School.**
Application information: Complete application guidelines available on foundation web site. Application form required.
Officers and Directors:* Richard E. Buck,* Pres.; Jan G. Buck, Exec. Dir.; John Garner Buck.
EIN: 710824287

67
Horace C. Cabe Foundation
108 N. Front St.
Gurdon, AR 71743-1010 **(903) 794-2223**
Contact: Paul Harris
TX tel.: (903) 794-2223; Main URL: http://horaceccabefoundation.org/

Established in 1991 in TX.
Donor: Horace C. Cabe†.
Foundation type: Independent foundation.
Financial data (yr. ended 06/30/13): Assets, $34,280,761 (M); expenditures, $2,041,313; qualifying distributions, $1,787,462; giving activities include $1,697,347 for 100 grants (high: $113,750; low: $100).
Purpose and activities: Giving primarily for education, health care and hospitals, including children's hospitals, and children and youth services.
Fields of interest: Arts; Higher education; Education; Hospitals (general); Hospitals (specialty); Health care; Youth development; Human services; Children/youth, services; Protestant agencies & churches; Children; Youth; Aging; Young adults; Physically disabled; Terminal illness, people with; Economically disadvantaged; Homeless.
Type of support: Annual campaigns; Building/renovation; Capital campaigns; Conferences/seminars; Continuing support; Curriculum development; Debt reduction; Emergency funds; Endowments; Equipment; General/operating support; Land acquisition; Management development/capacity building; Matching/challenge support; Program development; Program-related investments/loans; Research; Scholarship funds; Seed money.
Limitations: Applications accepted. **Giving primarily in southwest AR and northeast TX.** No grants to individuals.
Publications: Biennial report (including application guidelines); Newsletter.
Application information: Applications should be sent unbound and without folders or binders. Application form required.
Initial approach: Use application form on foundation web site
Copies of proposal: 1
***Deadline(s):* Jan. 1, Apr. 1, and Sept. 1**
Board meeting date(s): Sept. 30, Jan. 31, and May 31
Final notification: 1 week
Officers: Charles Lee "Sandy" Cabe, Pres.; **JJ Barto, V.P.**; Lucille T. Cook, Secy.
Directors: Charles L. Cabe, Jr.; Thomas H. Cabe; John K. Slicker.
Number of staff: 1 part-time professional; 1 part-time support.
EIN: 752402852
Other changes: JJ Barto has replaced Marianne C. Long as V.P.

68
Delta Dental of Arkansas Foundation, Inc.
c/o Edie Arey
1513 Country Club Rd.
Sherwood, AR 72120-5076 (501) 992-1602
E-mail: earey@ddpar.com; **Application contact: Kelly Caldwell, Mgr., tel.: (501) 992-1698, toll-free tel.: (800) 462-5410, e-mail: kcaldwell@deltadentalar.com**; Main URL: http://www.ddarfoundation.com

Established in AR.
Donor: Delta Dental Plan of Arkansas, Inc.
Foundation type: Independent foundation.
Financial data (yr. ended 12/31/12): Assets, $2,574,749 (M); gifts received, $1,765,956; expenditures, $1,391,282; qualifying distributions, $1,380,370; giving activities include $1,380,370 for 24 grants (high: $400,000; low: $3,389).
Fields of interest: Hospitals (specialty); Health care, clinics/centers; Dental care.
Type of support: Equipment.
Limitations: Applications accepted. Giving primarily in AR.
Publications: Application guidelines.
Application information: See foundation web site for specific application form and instructions. Application form required.
***Initial approach:* E-mail grant request to Kelly Caldwell, Mgr.**
***Deadline(s):* See foundation web site for current deadline**
Officers: James Johnston, Chair.; **Weldon Johnson, Vice-Chair.**; Ed Choate, Pres.; Dr. Paul Fitzgerald, Secy.; **Billy Tarpley, Treas.**
Directors: Joyce Dees; **Dr. Bob Mason**; Ron Ownbey; **Dr. Jim Phillips**; Dr. Michael Zweifler.
EIN: 261569324
Other changes: At the close of 2012, the grantmaker paid grants of $1,380,370, a 133.8% increase over the 2010 disbursements, $590,317. Weldon Johnson has replaced Ron Ownbey as Vice-Chair. Billy Tarpley has replaced Dr. Robert Matlock as Treas.
Lynn Mouden is no longer a director.

69
Endeavor Foundation
800 Founders Park Dr. E.
Springdale, AR 72762 (479) 361-4624
Contact: Anita Scism, C.E.O.
FAX: (479) 361-5094;
E-mail: anita@endeavorfoundation.net; Main URL: http://www.endeavorfoundation.net
Blog: http://endeavorfoundation.net/blog/
Facebook: https://www.facebook.com/EndeavorFoundation

Established in 1999 in AR.
Foundation type: Community foundation.
Financial data (yr. ended 12/31/12): Assets, $19,896,547 (M); gifts received, $4,991,071; expenditures, $2,073,759; giving activities include $1,254,481 for 21+ grants (high: $670,000), and $3,000 for grants to individuals.
Purpose and activities: The foundation seeks to impact Northwest Arkansas by identifying community issues, engaging key stakeholders, making grants and leveraging resources to address the issues.
Fields of interest: Education; Human services; Civil/human rights, immigrants; Community/economic development.
Type of support: General/operating support; Annual campaigns; Capital campaigns; Building/renovation; Equipment; Endowments; Program development; Conferences/seminars; Seed money; Curriculum development; Scholarship funds; Program evaluation; Scholarships—to individuals.
Limitations: Applications not accepted. Giving limited to Benton, Carroll, Madison and Washington counties in northwest AR. No support for religious organizations. No grants to individuals (except for scholarships).
Publications: Annual report; Biennial report; Informational brochure; Occasional report.
Application information:
Board meeting date(s): Bimonthly
Officers and Directors:* Lisa Ray,* Chair.; Debi Havner,* Vice-Chair.; Anita Scism,* C.E.O. and Pres.; Lisa McCullough,* C.F.O. and C.O.O.; Rick Parsons,* Treas.; **Victoria Bossler**; Roger Collins; Alan Dranow; Steven Lane; Katie Papasan; Charles Rateliff; Guillermo Rosales; Brad Sikorski; Terry Smith; **Michael Stewart**; Celia Swanson; Warren Wheat; Walter Turnbow.
Number of staff: 5 full-time professional; 2 full-time support.
EIN: 311682365
Other changes: Lisa Ray has replaced Dennis Smiley as Chair. Debi Havner has replaced Lisa Ray as Vice-Chair.
Susan Duke, Debi Havner, Mauricio Herrera, and Michael Schmidt are no longer directors.

70
Charles A. Frueauff Foundation, Inc.
200 River Market Ave., Ste. 100
Little Rock, AR 72201-1762 (501) 324-2233
Contact: Alma Willett, Office Mgr.; Anna Kay F. Frueauff, V.P., Comms. and Prog.
FAX: (501) 324-2236; Main URL: http://www.frueauff.org
Grants Database: http://www.frueauff.org/index.php?fuseaction=p0004.&mod=25

Incorporated in 1950 in NY.
Donor: Charles A. Frueauff†.
Foundation type: Independent foundation.
Financial data (yr. ended 12/31/12): Assets, $104,059,125 (M); expenditures, $5,995,545; qualifying distributions, $5,169,449; giving

activities include $4,475,560 for 157 grants (high: $100,000; low: $5,000).
Purpose and activities: The mission of the foundation is to improve the lives of those in need by awarding grants to nonprofits in the areas of social services, health and hospitals, and higher education.
Fields of interest: Higher education; Hospitals (general); Health care; Human services; Children/youth, services.
Type of support: Annual campaigns; Building/renovation; Capital campaigns; Continuing support; Emergency funds; Endowments; Equipment; General/operating support; Matching/challenge support; Program development; Scholarship funds; Technical assistance.
Limitations: Applications accepted. Giving limited to the U.S. with emphasis on east of the Rockies, the South, and Northeast. **No support for international projects, state supported colleges of universities, primary and secondary schools, or churches.** No grants to individuals, or for multi-year grants, fundraising drives, or special events.
Publications: Grants list.
Application information: The foundation is not considering proposals from first time grant seekers. Grantseekers are encouraged to visit the foundation's web site for additional information prior to calling or submitting a letter of inquiry. Please re-visit the foundation's website periodically for an update on the funding status. Application form not required.

Copies of proposal: 1
Board meeting date(s): May and Nov.
Final notification: After May and Nov. meetings

Officers and Trustees:* David A. Frueauff,* C.E.O. and Pres.; Anna Kay Frueauff-Williams,* V.P., Comms. and Progs.; James P. Fallon,* C.F.O.; Sue M. Frueauff,* C.A.O.; A.C. McCully, M.D.*, Pres. Emeritus.
Number of staff: 3 full-time professional; 1 part-time professional; 1 full-time support.
EIN: 135605371

71
Ottenheimer Brothers Foundation

425 W. Capitol Ave., Ste. 1516
Little Rock, AR 72201-3486
Contact: Gus Blass III, Dir.

Established in 1965 in AR.
Donors: Gus Ottenheimer†; Leonard J. Ottenheimer†; Gladys Ottenheimer Hirsch†; Joseph B. Hirsch†.
Foundation type: Independent foundation.
Financial data (yr. ended 04/30/13): Assets, $6,289,235 (M); expenditures, $343,179; qualifying distributions, $305,939; giving activities include $287,200 for 16 grants (high: $100,000; low: $500).
Purpose and activities: Giving primarily in the health and higher education fields in Little Rock, Arkansas, and surrounding areas.
Fields of interest: Higher education; Aging, centers/services; Community/economic development; Jewish agencies & synagogues; Aging.
Limitations: Applications accepted. Giving primarily in the Little Rock, AR, area. No grants to individuals or for scholarships.
Application information: Application form required.

Initial approach: Letter
Copies of proposal: 1
Deadline(s): None

Officers: Julianne D. Grundfest, Chair.; Steve Bauman, Secy.; Gus Blass III, Project Chair.; Larry Alman, C.F.O.
Board Members: Edward M. Penick, Sr.; Joe Selz; E. Grainger Williams.
Number of staff: 1 part-time support.
EIN: 716059988
Other changes: Julianne D. Grundfest has replaced Edward M. Penick, Sr. as Chair.
Gus Blass, III is now Project Chair. Steve Bauman is now Secy. Larry Alman is now C.F.O. Sam B. Strauss is no longer a board member.

72
The Ross Foundation

P.O. Box 335
Arkadelphia, AR 71923-0335 (870) 246-9881
Contact: Mary Elizabeth Eldridge, Dir. of Progs.
FAX: (870) 246-9674;
E-mail: info@rossfoundation.us; Main URL: http://rossfoundation.us

Established in 1966 in Arkadelphia, AR.
Donors: Esther C. Ross†; Jane Ross†.
Foundation type: Independent foundation.
Financial data (yr. ended 12/31/12): Assets, $91,891,580 (M); expenditures, $2,005,755; qualifying distributions, $1,378,422; giving activities include $610,617 for 24 grants (high: $351,684; low: $200).
Purpose and activities: Giving primarily for education, arts and cultural enrichment, community beautification and improvement, historical preservation, mental health and people who are developmentally disabled, and forestry research and conservation management.
Fields of interest: Arts; Higher education; Education; Environment, natural resources; Environment, forests; Children/youth, services; Community/economic development; Foundations (community); United Ways and Federated Giving Programs; Children/youth; Adults; Disabilities, people with.
Type of support: Scholarship funds; Capital campaigns; General/operating support; Building/renovation; Equipment; Endowments; Emergency funds; Program development; Publication; Seed money; Research; Consulting services; Matching/challenge support.
Limitations: Applications accepted. Giving limited to Arkadelphia and Clark County, AR. No support for political organizations. No grants to individuals, or for scholarships or fellowships; no loans.
Publications: Application guidelines; Informational brochure (including application guidelines).
Application information: Full proposals are by invitation only, upon review of pre-proposal. Application form required.

Initial approach: Pre-proposal
Copies of proposal: 6
Deadline(s): None for pre-proposals; Jan. 1, May 1, and Sept. 1 for full proposals
Board meeting date(s): Monthly
Final notification: Within 1 month for pre-proposals; Mar. 31, July 31, and Nov. 30 for full proposals

Officers and Trustees:* Ross M. Wipple,* Chair.; Mary Whipple,* Secy.; Peggy Clark; Mary Elizabeth Eldridge; Mark Karnes; Clark Tennyson.
Number of staff: 4 full-time professional; 4 full-time support; 1 part-time support.
EIN: 716060574
Other changes: The grantmaker now makes its application guidelines available online.

73
Union County Community Foundation, Inc.

P.O. Box 148
El Dorado, AR 71731-0148 **(870) 862-8223**
***Contact:* Rodney Landes, Chair.**

Established in 1996 in AR.
Foundation type: Community foundation.
Financial data (yr. ended 09/30/12): Assets, $13,617,576 (M); gifts received, $420,850; expenditures, $520,001; giving activities include $320,351 for 39 grants (high: $83,546; low: $500), and $78,513 for 53 grants to individuals.
Purpose and activities: The foundation provides a charitable vehicle that accepts, invests and distributes resources according to the donors' wishes. Giving also to individuals for scholarships.
Fields of interest: Historic preservation/historical societies; Scholarships/financial aid; Education; Human services; Community/economic development; Protestant agencies & churches.
Type of support: Scholarships—to individuals; Employee matching gifts; In-kind gifts.
Limitations: Applications not accepted. Giving limited to the El Dorado, AR, area.
Publications: Financial statement; Grants list; Newsletter.
Officers and Board Members:* Rodney Landes,* Chair.; John McFarland,* Vice-Chair.; Ginger Bullard,* Secy.; Mike Murphy,* Treas.; Gill Colvin; Lynn Landers; Lois Meekins; Tandy Menefee; Lenora Newsome; Bob Risor; Mary Jo Scott; Stacy Scroggins; Matthew Shepherd; Scott Simpson; Kenna Williams.
Number of staff: 1 full-time professional; 1 full-time support.
EIN: 311500805

74
The Wal-Mart Foundation, Inc.

(also known as The Walmart Foundation)(formerly Wal-Mart Foundation)
702 S.W. 8th St., Dept. 8687, No. 0555
Bentonville, AR 72716-0555 (800) 530-9925
Contact: Julie Gehrki, Sr. Dir., Business Integration
FAX: (479) 273-6850; Main URL: http://foundation.walmart.com
RSS Feed: http://walmartstores.com/RSS/FeaturedTopics/rss.ashx?id=11
Twitter: https://twitter.com/WalmartGiving
Walmart Blog: http://blog.walmart.com/giving

Established in 1979 in AR.
Donor: Wal-Mart Stores, Inc.
Foundation type: Company-sponsored foundation.
Financial data (yr. ended 01/31/13): Assets, $21,162,257 (M); gifts received, $182,566,130; expenditures, $182,860,304; qualifying distributions, $182,859,236; giving activities include $182,859,236 for 13,225 grants (high: $7,721,220; low: $30).
Purpose and activities: The foundation supports programs designed to promote hunger relief and healthy eating; sustainability; women's economic empowerment; and career opportunity. The foundation also funds disaster relief, women, military and veterans, and economically disadvantaged people.
Fields of interest: Middle schools/education; Elementary school/education; Secondary school/education; Higher education; Teacher school/education; Adult education—literacy, basic skills & GED; Education, ESL programs; Education, services; Education, drop-out prevention; Education, reading; Education; Health care, equal rights; Hospitals (general); Health care, clinics/centers; Public

health; Health care; Employment, services; Employment, training; Employment, retraining; Goodwill Industries; Employment; Agriculture, sustainable programs; Agriculture, farmlands; Food services; Food banks; Food distribution, meals on wheels; Nutrition; Housing/shelter; Disasters, preparedness/services; Boys & girls clubs; Youth development, business; American Red Cross; Salvation Army; Children, services; Human services, financial counseling; Human services, mind/body enrichment; Developmentally disabled, centers & services; Community development, business promotion; Community development, small businesses; Community/economic development; United Ways and Federated Giving Programs; Military/veterans' organizations; Minorities; Women; Military/veterans; Economically disadvantaged.
Type of support: Management development/ capacity building; Emergency funds; Program development; Scholarship funds; Employee volunteer services; Sponsorships; Employee matching gifts; Employee-related scholarships; Grants to individuals; Matching/challenge support.
Limitations: Applications accepted. Giving on a national basis in areas of company operations, with emphasis on AR, Washington, DC, DE, GA, MA. MD, NY, TN, TX, UT, and VA. No support for faith-based organizations not of direct benefit to the entire community, political candidates or organizations, athletic teams, or discriminatory organizations. No grants to individuals (except for scholarships), or for multi-year funding, annual meetings, contests or pageants, political causes or campaigns, advertising, film, or video projects, research, athletic sponsorships or events, tickets for contests, raffles, or any other activities with prizes, travel, capital campaigns, endowments, association or chamber memberships, or registration fees, research, salaries, stipends, trips, rewards, construction costs, or projects that send products or people to a foreign country.
Publications: Application guidelines; Program policy statement.
Application information: Applications for State Giving Program are accepted designated periods or cycles only and all states have two cycles a year. Visit website for State Giving Program for deadlines. A full proposal may be requested at a later date for National Giving Program. Organizations receiving support are asked to submit an impact report detailing what outcomes were achieved.
Initial approach: **Complete online application for State Giving Program, Walmart U.S. Manufacturing Innovation Fund, Northwest Arkansas Giving Program, and Community Grant Program; complete online letter of inquiry for National Giving Program**
Deadline(s): **Varies per cycle and per state for State Giving Program; April 22 for Walmart U.S. Manufacturing Innovation Fund; Nov. 30 for Northeast Arkansas Giving Program; Dec. 31 for Community Grant Program; None for National Giving Program**
Board meeting date(s): Mar., May, Aug., and Nov.
Final notification: **90 days for Local Giving Program; 8 weeks for Northwest Arkansas Giving Program; 6 to 8 weeks for National Giving Program**
Officers and Directors:* Michael T. Duke, Chair.; Sylvia Mathews Burwell, Pres.; Michelle Gilliard, V.P.; Michael Spencer, Secy.; Tim Culp, Treas.; M. Susan Chambers; Leslie A. Dach; Cindy Davis; Tom Mars; Gisel Ruiz; Cathy Smith.
Number of staff: 31 full-time professional.
EIN: 205639919

75
Windgate Charitable Foundation, Inc.

P.O. Box 826
Siloam Springs, AR 72761-0826
Contact: John E. Brown, III, Exec. Dir.
FAX: (479) 524-3550;
E-mail: windgate@cox-internet.com

Established in 1993 in AR.
Donor: Dorothea W. Hutcheson‡.
Foundation type: Independent foundation.
Financial data (yr. ended 12/31/13): Assets, $174,284,603 (M); gifts received, $79,520,000; expenditures, $42,742,711; qualifying distributions, $90,241,127; giving activities include $41,741,431 for 342 grants (high: $3,000,000; low: $1,500).
Purpose and activities: Giving primarily to promote art and craft education, and projects that strengthen marriage and family relationships. Limited giving also to programs that serve children and Christian higher education.
Fields of interest: Arts education; Children/youth, services; Family services.
Type of support: Program development; Matching/ challenge support.
Limitations: Applications accepted. Giving on a national basis with emphasis on the Midwest and Southwest. No support for private religious schools or churches. No grants to individuals, or for undesignated annual funds, debt retirement, completed projects, or group travel for performance or competition.
Publications: Application guidelines; Program policy statement.
Application information: Application form not required.
Initial approach: 2-page letter
Copies of proposal: 1
Deadline(s): Mar. 1, July 1 and Oct. 1
Board meeting date(s): Varies
Final notification: 3 to 4 months
Officer: John E. Brown III, Exec. Dir.
Directors: Robyn Horn; Karen Hutcheson; Mary E. Hutcheson; Richard Hutcheson; William L. Hutcheson.
Number of staff: 2
EIN: 710723781
Other changes: At the close of 2013, the grantmaker paid grants of $41,741,431, a 57.6% increase over the 2012 disbursements, $26,485,421.

CALIFORNIA

76
Adams Legacy Foundation
P.O. Box 1957
Los Alamitos, CA 90720-1957 (562) 431-0011
Contact: Blair Carty, Exec. Dir.
E-mail for Blair Carty: bcarty@adamslegacyfoundation.org; Main URL: http://www.adamslegacyfoundation.org
Grants List: http://www.adamslegacyfoundation.org/untitled.html

Donor: Peter D. Adams.
Foundation type: Independent foundation.
Financial data (yr. ended 12/31/12): Assets, $4,562,764 (M); expenditures, $241,454; qualifying distributions, $204,817; giving activities include $154,600 for 20 grants (high: $20,500; low: $500).
Purpose and activities: Giving primarily for education and land conservation.
Fields of interest: Education; Environment, land resources.
Limitations: Applications accepted. Giving primarily in CA, OH and Washington, DC.
Application information: See foundation web site for complete application guidelines. Application form required.
Officers: Peter D. Adams, Pres.; Rebecca B. Adams, V.P.; Blair Carty, Exec. Dir.
EIN: 263373791

77
The Ahmanson Foundation
9215 Wilshire Blvd.
Beverly Hills, CA 90210-5501 (310) 278-0770
Contact: Yvonne deBeixedon, Grants Admin.
E-mail: info@theahmansonfoundation.org; Main URL: http://www.theahmansonfoundation.org

Incorporated in 1952 in CA.
Donors: Howard F. Ahmanson‡; Dorothy G. Sullivan‡; William Hayden Ahmanson‡; Robert H. Ahmanson‡.
Foundation type: Independent foundation.
Financial data (yr. ended 10/31/13): Assets, $1,108,002,312 (M); expenditures, $52,416,048; qualifying distributions, $52,530,907; giving activities include $50,359,404 for 525 grants (high: $3,000,000; low: $1,000).
Purpose and activities: Emphasis on education at all levels, the arts and humanities, health and medicine, and a broad range of human service programs.
Fields of interest: Visual arts; Museums; Performing arts; Humanities; Arts; Elementary school/education; Secondary school/education; Higher education; Adult education—literacy, basic skills & GED; Libraries/library science; Education, reading; Education; Health care; Crime/violence prevention, domestic violence; Recreation, public policy; Human services; Youth, services; Homeless, human services; Children/youth; Adults; Aging; Young adults; Disabilities, people with; Physically disabled; Minorities; Substance abusers; Economically disadvantaged; Homeless.
Type of support: Building/renovation; Capital campaigns; Debt reduction; Equipment; General/operating support; Land acquisition; Matching/challenge support; Program-related investments/loans; Scholarship funds; Technical assistance.
Limitations: Applications accepted. Giving primarily in southern CA, with emphasis on the Los Angeles area. No support for religious organizations for sectarian purposes, or advocacy or political organizations. No grants to individuals, or generally for continuing support, endowed chairs, annual campaigns, deficit financing, professorships, internships, film production, media projects, general research and development, workshops, studies, surveys, operational support of regional and national charities, underwriting, or exchange programs.
Publications: Application guidelines.
Application information: Fax or e-mail requests will not be accepted. Application form not required.
Initial approach: Letter of inquiry (following review of guidelines)
Copies of proposal: 1
Deadline(s): None
Board meeting date(s): 4 times annually
Final notification: 60 to 90 days
Officers and Trustees:* William Howard Ahmanson,* Pres.; Karen A. Hoffman,* Secy. and Managing Dir.; Kristen K. O'Connor, C.F.O. and Treas.; Lloyd E. Cotsen, Trustee Emeritus; Leonard E. Walcott, Jr., Managing Dir., Emeritus; Howard F. Ahmanson, Jr.; Mark A. Brooks; Robert M. DeKruif; Stephen D. Rountree; John Wagner; Stephen D. Yslas.
Number of staff: 11 full-time professional; 1 full-time support; 1 part-time support.
EIN: 956089998
Other changes: Robert F. Erburu is no longer Trustee Emeritus.

78
Alalusi Foundation
1975 National Ave.
Hayward, CA 94545-1709 **(510) 887-2374**
E-mail: info@alalusifoundation.org; Main URL: http://www.alalusifoundation.org/
Facebook: https://www.facebook.com/pages/Alalusi-Foundation/497928536916586?ref=br_tf

Established in 2001 in CA.
Donors: Hesham Al-Alusi; Ayam Alshar; Mirza Baig; Patricia Baig; Mohammed Raheemuddin Ahmed; Husam Shuayb; Ahd Shuayb; Syed K. Raza; Nabeela Sajjad.
Foundation type: Independent foundation.
Financial data (yr. ended 03/31/13): Assets, $0 (M); gifts received, $576,325; expenditures, $753,871; qualifying distributions, $752,727; giving activities include $659,530 for 8 grants (high: $253,200; low: $3,200), and $65,734 for grants to individuals.
Purpose and activities: Giving primarily for Muslim and Islamic relief and affairs, as well as for humanitarian assistance in other regions.
Fields of interest: International relief; International human rights; Islam; Religion.
International interests: Middle East; Asia; Africa; China.
Type of support: General/operating support; Grants to individuals.
Limitations: Applications accepted. Giving on an international basis with emphasis on China; some giving also in CA.
Application information:
Initial approach: Letter
Deadline(s): None
Director: Hesham Al-Alusi.
EIN: 912158518

79
The Isabel Allende Foundation
116 Caledonia St.
Sausalito, CA 94965-1925 (415) 289-0992
Contact: Lori Barra, Exec. Dir.
FAX: (415) 289-1154;
E-mail: lori@isabelallendefoundation.org; Main URL: http://www.isabelallendefoundation.org

Established in 1996 in CA.
Donors: Isabel Allende; William C. Gordon.
Foundation type: Independent foundation.
Financial data (yr. ended 11/30/12): Assets, $9,618,102 (M); gifts received, $796,508; expenditures, $925,546; qualifying distributions, $840,732; giving activities include $580,100 for 84 grants (high: $42,500; low: $385).
Purpose and activities: Giving primarily to organizations whose missions are to provide women and girls with reproductive self-determination, healthcare, education, and protection from violence, exploitation and/or discrimination.
Fields of interest: Education; Crime/violence prevention, domestic violence; Youth development; Women, centers/services; Women; Girls.
Type of support: General/operating support; Program development.
Limitations: Applications accepted. Giving limited to the San Francisco Bay Area, CA, and Chile. No support for political, religious and/or military organizations. No grants to individuals, or for capital campaigns, trips, tours, conferences or events.
Publications: Application guidelines.
Application information: New organization proposals for Esperanza Grants are not being accepted at this time. Unsolicited requests for Espiritu Awards and Paula Scholarships are not accepted. Information sent to the foundation by e-mail or U.S. mail is not considered unless the foundation requests such information from an applicant. Complete application policies and guidelines available on foundation web site. Application form required.
Board meeting date(s): Jan.
Officers: Isabel Allende, Pres.; William C. Gordon, Secy.; Lori Barra, Exec. Dir.
Number of staff: 1 full-time professional.
EIN: 911748486

80
The Allergan Foundation
2525 Dupont Dr., T1-4D
P.O. Box 19534
Irvine, CA 92623-9534 (714) 246-2077
Contact: Vanessa Ryan, Dir., Community Rels.
E-mail: AllerganFoundation@Allergan.com**; E-mail for Vanessa Ryan: ryan_vanessa@allergan.com**; Main URL: http://www.allerganfoundation.org

Established in 1998 in GA.
Donor: Allergan, Inc.
Foundation type: Company-sponsored foundation.
Financial data (yr. ended 12/31/12): Assets, $45,991,841 (M); expenditures, $6,456,144; qualifying distributions, $6,298,482; giving activities include $5,954,809 for 308 grants (high: $1,000,000; low: $150).
Purpose and activities: The foundation supports programs designed to enhance and strengthen the communities where Allergan employees live or work, focusing on the areas of health and human services, education, civic and community, and the arts. Special emphasis is directed toward programs designed to serve vulnerable and at-risk populations including children, the elderly, and the infirm.

Fields of interest: Arts; Education; Hospitals (general); Public health; Health care, patient services; Health care; Housing/shelter; Disasters, preparedness/services; Human services; Community/economic development; United Ways and Federated Giving Programs; Public affairs; Children; Aging; Women; Economically disadvantaged.
Type of support: Equipment; Program development; Scholarship funds; Employee volunteer services; Sponsorships.
Limitations: Applications accepted. Giving primarily in areas of company operations in Orange and Santa Barbara counties, CA, and McLennan County, TX, area; giving also to regional and national organizations. No support for religious groups not of direct benefit to the entire community, fraternal, labor, political, or veterans' organizations, discriminatory organizations, athletic leagues, school-affiliated orchestras, bands, or choirs, private K-12 schools, pass-through organizations, consumer interest groups, or agencies normally financed by government sources. No grants to individuals, or for family requests for scholarships, fellowship assistance, or other types of support, matching gifts, university administrative, management, or indirect fees, golf tournaments, athletic events, or team sponsorships, student trips or tours, fundraising activities or advertising sponsorships, conferences, workshops, exhibits, surveys, films, or publishing activities, endowments, capital, or building campaigns, general operating support, debt reduction, or contributions in the name of a memorial tribute; no in-kind gifts.
Publications: Application guidelines; Annual report (including application guidelines).
Application information: Community Grants range from $5,000 to $10,000. Support is limited to 1 contribution per organization during any given year. Videos, faxed, or e-mailed applications are not accepted. Application form required.
Initial approach: Complete online application
Deadline(s): May 1 through July 1
Final notification: Sept.
Officers and Directors:* David E.I. Pyott,* Chair. and C.E.O.; James M. Hindman,* Pres.; Terilea J. Wielenga,* C.F.O.; Matthew J Maletta, Secy. and Genl. Counsel; Daryn A. Martin, Treas.; Gwyn L. Grenrock, Exec. Dir.; Julian S. Gangolli; Gavin S. Herbert; Lynn D. Salo; Scott D. Sherman; Scott M. Whitcup, M.D.
EIN: 330794475

81
Maurice Amado Foundation
3940 Laurel Canyon Blvd., No. 809
Studio City, CA 91604-3709 (818) 980-9190
Contact: Pam Kaizer, Exec. Dir.
FAX: (818) 980-9190;
E-mail: pkaizer@mauriceamadofdn.org; Main URL: http://www.mauriceamadofdn.org
Grants List: http://mauriceamadofdn.org/recent-grants/

Incorporated in 1961 in CA.
Donor: Maurice Amado†.
Foundation type: Independent foundation.
Financial data (yr. ended 11/30/13): Assets, $29,376,220 (M); expenditures, $1,366,394; qualifying distributions, $1,172,919; giving activities include $1,050,000 for 48 grants (high: $346,817; low: $250).
Purpose and activities: Support primarily for activities that promote Sephardic Jewish culture and heritage.
Fields of interest: Arts; Education.
Type of support: Continuing support; Curriculum development; General/operating support; Program development.
Limitations: Applications accepted. Giving in geographical areas of interest to the board. No grants to individuals directly.
Publications: Application guidelines.
Application information: Check foundation web site for guidelines. Letter should be on organizational letterhead. Application form not required.
Initial approach: E-mail
Copies of proposal: 1
***Deadline(s):* Aug. 15 and Feb. 15**
Board meeting date(s): Biannually
Final notification: Late Nov. and late May
Officers and Directors:* Mark E. Tarica,* Pres.; Ellen Amado,* V.P. and Secy.; Samuel Tarica, V.P. and C.F.O.; Richard Amado; Ted Amado; Victor Lavis; Susan Malcom.
Number of staff: 1 part-time professional.
EIN: 956041700

82
American Institute of Mathematics
360 Portage Ave.
Palo Alto, CA 94306-2244 (650) 845-2071
***Contact:* Brian Conrey, Exec. Dir.**
FAX: (650) 845-2074**; Email for Brian Conrey: conrey@aimath.org**; Main URL: http://www.aimath.org

Established in 1994 in CA.
Donors: National Science Foundation; Fry's Electronics; The Fry Foundation; Redwood Neuroscience Institute.
Foundation type: Operating foundation.
Financial data (yr. ended 12/31/12): Assets, $1,635,719 (M); gifts received, $3,193,693; expenditures, $3,840,315; qualifying distributions, $3,838,681; giving activities include $272,000 for 17 grants (high: $50,000; low: $5,000).
Purpose and activities: The institutes goal is to expand frontiers of mathematical knowledge through focused research projects, sponsored conferences, and through the development of an on-line mathematics library.
Fields of interest: Mathematics.
Type of support: Conferences/seminars; Fellowships; Research.
Limitations: Giving in the U.S., with emphasis on AZ.
Publications: Biennial report.
Application information: Application form not required.
Initial approach: Letter
Deadline(s): Nov. 1
Officers: Gerald L. Alexanderson, Chair.; Stephen Sorenson, Pres.; John Fry, Secy.; John Brian Conrey, Exec. Dir.
Directors: Gunnar Carlsson; Harry Saal.
Number of staff: 8 full-time professional.
EIN: 943205114

83
Anaheim Community Foundation
200 S. Anaheim Blvd., Ste. 433
Anaheim, CA 92805-3820 (714) 765-4419
Contact: Terry D. Lowe, C.E.O.
FAX: (714) 765-4454;
E-mail: AnaheimCommunityFoundation@gmail.com; Grant inquiry e-mail: jbranich@anaheim.net; Grant inquiry tel.: (714) 765-5250; Main URL: http://www.anaheimcommfound.org
Facebook: https://www.facebook.com/AnaheimCF
Twitter: https://twitter.com/anaheimcf

Established in 1984 in CA.
Foundation type: Community foundation.
Financial data (yr. ended 06/30/12): Assets, $722,682 (M); gifts received, $385,918; expenditures, $407,650; giving activities include $392,781 for grants to individuals.
Purpose and activities: The foundation seeks to: 1) encourage community participation, partnerships, and collaboration that result in successful responses to community challenges and opportunities; 2) strengthen community-based organizations that effectively address community needs, promote volunteerism, and provide community leadership; 3) promote community-building programs and events that inspire community pride and unity; and 4) provide individuals and business opportunities to make charitable investments that directly benefit the Anaheim community.
Fields of interest: Arts; Libraries/library science; Environment; Medical care, rehabilitation; Public health, obesity; Substance abuse, services; Crime/violence prevention, youth; Athletics/sports, Special Olympics; Youth development, services; Youth development; Human services, emergency aid; Aging, centers/services; Human services; Youth; Aging.
Type of support: General/operating support; Emergency funds; Program development; Scholarships—to individuals.
Limitations: Applications accepted. Giving limited to the Anaheim, CA, area. No support for religious or proselytizing activities. No grants for non program-related salaries or to pay for capital improvements.
Publications: Application guidelines; Annual report; Informational brochure.
Application information: Visit foundation web site for application form and guidelines. Grants will not normally exceed $5,000 but larger amounts may be awarded at the discretion of the foundation's Board. Application form required.
Initial approach: Submit application
Copies of proposal: 6
***Deadline(s):* Mar. 14**
Board meeting date(s): 1st Mon. of each month
Officers and Directors:* Bruce Solari,* Chair., Prog. and Grant Distribution Comm.; Steve Sain,* Pres.; Terry D. Lowe,* C.E.O.; Ed Munson,* Secy.; William Taormina, Chair., Emeritus; Orin Abrams; Sarah Alevizon; Suzi Brown; Steve Faessel; John Guastaferro; Irv Pickler; Michael Rubin; Jim Ruth; Greg Smith; Frances Wiseman-Lewis.
EIN: 330033023

84
Irene W. & Guy L. Anderson Children's Foundation
1111 E. Tahquitz Canyon Way, Ste. 109
Palm Springs, CA 92262-0113 **(760) 778-1777**
***FAX:* (760) 778-1777**; Tel./fax: (760) 778-1777; Grant Program contacts: Jane: tel.: (760) 902-7685, e-mail: jmills@andersonchildrensfoundation.org; Bob: tel.: (760) 861-1513, e-mail: bworswick@andersonchildrensfoundation.org; Main URL: http://www.andersonchildrensfoundation.org/
E-Newsletter: http://www.andersongrants.org/sign-up.htm
Facebook: https://www.facebook.com/andersonchildrensfoundation
Grants List: http://www.andersonchildrensfoundation.org/grant-history
Twitter: https://twitter.com/ACFforkids

Established in 1970 in CA.
Foundation type: Independent foundation.
Financial data (yr. ended 11/30/12): Assets, $20,323,387 (M); expenditures, $2,091,073; qualifying distributions, $895,844; giving activities include $734,570 for 68 grants (high: $37,365; low: $675).
Purpose and activities: The foundation makes grant money available to any non-profit group or organization in the Coachella Valley whose purpose is to meet the unmet needs of the youth of the Coachella Valley.
Fields of interest: Education; Youth development; Youth, services; Family services.
Type of support: General/operating support; Continuing support; Program development; Program evaluation.
Limitations: Applications accepted. Giving limited to the Coachella Valley, CA. No grants to individuals.
Publications: Application guidelines; Grants list; Newsletter.
Application information: Application form required.
Initial approach: Use application format on foundation web site, then submit via U.S. mail
Copies of proposal: 8
Deadline(s): June
Final notification: See online application form final notification
Trustee: R. Diane Schlesinger, M.D.
Number of staff: 2 full-time professional; 7 part-time professional.
EIN: 237089096
Other changes: William A. Schlesinger is no longer trustee.

85
Marion & John E. Anderson Foundation
1800 Ave. of the Stars, Ste. 1400
Los Angeles, CA 90067-4216

Established in 1986 in CA.
Donors: John E. Anderson†; Marion Anderson; Topa Insurance Group; Industrial Tools Inc.; Paradise Beverages Inc.; Ace Beverage Co.
Foundation type: Independent foundation.
Financial data (yr. ended 12/31/12): Assets, $50,119,169 (M); gifts received, $14,250,000; expenditures, $12,484,109; qualifying distributions, $12,277,238; giving activities include $12,277,000 for 6 grants (high: $7,000,000; low: $1,000).
Fields of interest: Education; Human services; YM/YWCAs & YM/YWHAs; United Ways and Federated Giving Programs.
Type of support: Scholarship funds.
Limitations: Applications not accepted. Giving primarily in Los Angeles, CA. No grants to individuals.
Application information: Contributes only to pre-selected organizations.
Officers: Marion Anderson, Pres.; Brenda Seuthe, C.F.O.
Directors: John E. Anderson, Jr.; William S. Anderson; Judith Munzig.
EIN: 954074837
Other changes: Therese D. Curtis is no longer Secy.

86
Annenberg Foundation
2000 Ave. of the Stars, Ste. 1000
Los Angeles, CA 90067-4704 (310) 209-4560
Contact: Leonard Aube, Exec. Dir.
FAX: (310) 209-1631;
E-mail: info@annenbergfoundation.org; **Pennsylvania Address: 101 W. Elm St., Ste. 640, Conshohocken, PA 19428; Washington, DC Address: 1301 Pennsylvania Ave., N.W., No. 302, Washington, DC 20004, tel.: (202) 783-0500, fax: (202) 783-0333**; Main URL: http://www.annenbergfoundation.org
E-Newsletter: http://www.annenbergfoundation.org/enewsletter-sign-up
Facebook: http://www.facebook.com/pages/The-Annenberg-Foundation/257553628444
GiveSmart: http://www.givesmart.org/Stories/Donors/Wallis-Annenberg-and-Leonard-Aube
Grants Database: http://www.annenbergfoundation.org/grants/grants-database
Twitter: http://twitter.com/Annenberg_FDN

Established in 1989 in PA.
Donor: Hon. Walter H. Annenberg†.
Foundation type: Independent foundation.
Financial data (yr. ended 12/31/12): Assets, $1,623,162,045 (M); gifts received, $62,217; expenditures, $168,350,177; qualifying distributions, $136,271,869; giving activities include $104,790,232 for 523 grants (high: $28,333,333; low: $100), and $24,866,730 for 4 foundation-administered programs.
Purpose and activities: The mission of the foundation is to provide funding and support to nonprofit organizations in the United States and globally. The foundation and its Board of Directors are also directly involved in the community with innovative projects that further its mission to advance the public well-being through improved communication. The foundation encourages the development of effective ways to share ideas and knowledge and it is committed to core values of responsiveness, accessibility, fairness and involvement. Also, the foundation believes in funding organizations that have a deep level of community involvement, are led by effective leaders and tackle challenging and timely problems. Specific organizational attributes valued by the foundation are: visionary leadership, impact, sustainability, innovation, organizational strength, network of partnerships plus the population being served (thus, creating the acronym VISION+).
Fields of interest: Arts; Education; Environment; Animal welfare; Public health; Military/veterans.
Limitations: Applications accepted. **Giving on a national and international basis. United States giving has an emphasis on the five-county region of Greater Los Angeles; international giving has an emphasis on countries in Africa, Europe and Asia.** No support for political activities. No grants to individuals. Requests for capital campaigns and multi-year commitments are discouraged.
Publications: Application guidelines; Financial statement; Grants list; Newsletter.
Application information: Review the reference copy of the application and the foundation's vision/grantmaking guidelines prior to starting the online application process. Application form required.
Initial approach: Online grant application
Deadline(s): No later than 45 days after the creation of an online grant application account
Board meeting date(s): Varies
Final notification: 90-120 days
Officers and Directors:* Wallis Annenberg,* Chair., C.E.O. and Pres.; Lauren Bon,* V.P.; Charles Annenberg Weingarten,* V.P.; Gregory Annenberg Weingarten,* V.P.
Number of staff: 39 full-time professional.
EIN: 236257083

87
The Annenberg Foundation Trust at Sunnylands
70-177 Hwy. 111, Ste. 202
Rancho Mirage, CA 92270-5902
E-mail: contact@sunnylands.org; Main URL: http://www.sunnylands.org
Facebook: http://www.facebook.com/pages/Sunnylands/145550105480088
Flickr: https://www.flickr.com/photos/annenbergretreatatsunnylands/
GiveSmart: http://www.givesmart.org/Stories/Donors/Wallis-Annenberg-and-Leonard-Aube
Pinterest: http://www.pinterest.com/sunnylands/
Twitter: https://twitter.com/SunnylandsNews
Vimeo: http://vimeo.com/sunnylands
YouTube: http://www.youtube.com/user/AnnenbergRetreat

Established in 2001 in PA; reclassified as an operating foundation in 2004.
Donor: The Annenberg Foundation.
Foundation type: Operating foundation.
Financial data (yr. ended 06/30/12): Assets, $470,846,227 (M); expenditures, $14,032,838; qualifying distributions, $20,583,289.
Purpose and activities: Giving primarily to mental health services, human services, and higher education.
Fields of interest: Higher education; Mental health/crisis services; Children/youth, services.
Type of support: Conferences/seminars; Research.
Limitations: Applications not accepted. Giving primarily in Philadelphia, PA. No grants to individuals.
Application information: Unsolicited requests for funds not accepted.
Officers: Geoffrey Cowan, Pres.; Edward Doran, Dir., Fin.
Directors: Kathleen Hall Jamieson; Janice Lyle.
Trustees: Wallis Annenberg; Lauren A. Bon; Diane Deshong; Howard Deshong III; Leonore Deshong; **Elizabeth K. Kabler**; Elizabeth R. Kabler; Charles Annenberg Weingarten; Gregory Annenberg Weingarten.
Number of staff: 2 part-time professional.
EIN: 256774871
Other changes: Deborah Hinton Money is no longer C.F.O. L. Dianne Lomonaco is no longer a director. Elizabeth Sorensen is no longer a trustee.

88
The Applied Materials Foundation
3050 Bowers Ave., MS 0106
Santa Clara, CA 95054-3201
Contact: Claudia Schwiefert, Grant Mgr.; Siobhan Kenney, Exec. Dir.
E-mail: applied_materials_foundation@amat.com; E-mail contact for organizations located outside of the U.S.: community_affairs@amat.com; **Main URL: http://www.appliedmaterials.com/company/corporate-responsibility**
Corporate Responsibility: http://blog.appliedmaterials.com/corporate-responsibility

Established in 1994.
Donor: Applied Materials, Inc.
Foundation type: Company-sponsored foundation.
Financial data (yr. ended 10/31/12): Assets, $28,940,963 (M); gifts received, $5,432,293; expenditures, $6,919,674; qualifying distributions, $6,822,343; giving activities include $6,749,103 for 213 grants (high: $215,556; low: $40).

Purpose and activities: The foundation supports programs designed to promote arts and culture; education; environmental awareness and sustainability; and civic engagement.
Fields of interest: Performing arts, theater; Arts; Elementary/secondary education; Higher education; Adult/continuing education; Education, reading; Education; Environmental education; Environment; Food services; Food banks; Housing/shelter; Disasters, preparedness/services; Youth development, adult & child programs; Youth, services; Homeless, human services; Human services; International relief; Mathematics; Science; Leadership development; Economically disadvantaged.
Type of support: Annual campaigns; Continuing support; Curriculum development; Program development; Sponsorships.
Limitations: Applications accepted. Giving primarily in areas of company operations, with emphasis on San Jose, CA, Gloucester, MA, Kalispell, MT and Austin, TX; giving also to organizations outside of the United States (China, Europe, India, Japan, Korea, Singapore, Taiwan). No support for missing children organizations, fraternities, religious or political organizations, commencements, PTAs, or alumni groups. No grants to individuals, or for general operating support, capital campaigns, research, sporting events for schools or civic teams, health-related programs or sponsorships, fundraisers such as walk-a-thons, runs, team in training, etc., or bricks/mortar, equipment, home building, or physical structures.
Publications: Application guidelines; Corporate giving report.
Application information:
Initial approach: Complete online application at http://www.appliedmaterials.com/about/cr/community/grants; e-mail community affairs for organizations located outside of the United States
Deadline(s): Jan. 15 and June 15
Board meeting date(s): Semi-annually
Final notification: Mar. 15 to 31 and Aug. 15 to 31
Officers and Directors:* Michael R. Splinter,* Pres.; **Yvonne Leyba, Secy.**; Robert M. Friess, C.F.O.; Siobhan Kenney, Exec. Dir.; Mary E. Humiston; Joseph M. Pon.
EIN: 770386898
Other changes: Yvonne Leyba has replaced Charmaine F. Mesina as Secy.
George S. Davis and James C. Morgan are no longer members of the governing body. Charmaine F. Mesina is no longer Secy.

89
Aratani Foundation
23505 Crenshaw Blvd., No. 230
Torrance, CA 90505-5223 **(310) 530-9900**
Contact: George T. Aratani, Pres.

Established in 1992 in CA.
Donors: George T. Aratani; Sakaye I. Aratani.
Foundation type: Independent foundation.
Financial data (yr. ended 12/31/12): Assets, $21,679,353 (M); expenditures, $1,698,120; qualifying distributions, $1,089,652; giving activities include $1,089,652 for 54 grants (high: $125,000; low: $125).
Purpose and activities: Giving primarily to Japanese-American cultural organizations.
Fields of interest: Museums; Education; Health care; Recreation; Religion.
Type of support: General/operating support; Continuing support; Income development; Management development/capacity building; Annual campaigns; Capital campaigns; Building/renovation; Endowments; Program development; Conferences/seminars; Seed money; Curriculum development; Fellowships; Scholarship funds; Exchange programs.
Limitations: Giving primarily in Los Angeles, CA. No grants to individuals.
Application information: Application outline is available. Application form not required.
Initial approach: Letter
Copies of proposal: 1
Deadline(s): None
Board meeting date(s): As needed
Officers: George T. Aratani, Pres.; Tetsuo Murata, V.P.; Sakaye I. Aratani, Secy.; Linda Y. Aratani, Treas.
Number of staff: 1 full-time professional; 3 full-time support.
EIN: 954377347

90
Archstone Foundation
401 E. Ocean Blvd., Ste. 1000
Long Beach, CA 90802-4933 (562) 590-8655
Contact: Tanisha David MAG, Grants Mgr.
FAX: (562) 495-0317;
E-mail: archstone@archstone.org; Main URL: http://www.archstone.org
Grants Database: http://www.archstone.org/grants_info2340/grants_info.htm

Established in 1985 in CA; created as a result of the conversion of the nonprofit FHP health maintenance organization; status changed to a private foundation in 1998.
Foundation type: Independent foundation.
Financial data (yr. ended 06/30/12): Assets, $105,723,365 (M); expenditures, $6,137,710; qualifying distributions, $5,687,998; giving activities include $3,667,855 for 99 grants (high: $410,250; low: $500).
Purpose and activities: Giving toward the preparation of society in meeting the needs of an aging population. The majority of the foundation's resources are allocated to programs that address elder abuse prevention, fall prevention among the elderly, end-of-life issues, and emerging needs within the field of aging.
Fields of interest: Palliative care; Geriatrics; Gerontology; Aging.
Type of support: Program development; Conferences/seminars; Curriculum development; Technical assistance; Program evaluation.
Limitations: Applications accepted. Giving primarily in southern CA. No support for biomedical research. No grants to individuals, or for capital expenditures, or bricks and mortar, or building campaigns, endowments or for fundraising.
Publications: Application guidelines; Annual report (including application guidelines); Occasional report.
Application information: Full proposals are by invitation only, upon review of Letter of Inquiry. See foundation web site for specific guidelines and forms. Faxed proposals not accepted. Application form required.
Initial approach: Letter of Inquiry (no more than three pages) for Responsive Grantmaking
Copies of proposal: 1
Deadline(s): None for Responsive Grantmaking
Board meeting date(s): Quarterly
Final notification: Proposals submitted before the 15th of a given month will be reviewed during the following month; Quarterly, the foundation makes funding determinations
Officers and Directors:* Robert C. Maxson, Ed.D.*, Chair.; Joseph F. Prevratil,* C.E.O. and Pres.; Mary Ellen Kullman, V.P.; Diana Bonta; Lynn Daucher; Amye L. Leong; Hon. Renee B. Simon; Mark Douglas Smith, M.D.; Rahamin "Rocky" Suares; Peter C. Szutu.
Number of staff: 5 full-time professional; 2 full-time support.
EIN: 330133359

91
Arkay Foundation
127 University Ave.
Berkeley, CA 94710-1616 (510) 841-4025
Contact: Benita Kline, Fdn. Mgr.
FAX: (510) 841-4093;
E-mail: info@arkayfoundation.org; Main URL: http://www.arkayfoundation.org

Established in 1995 in CA.
Donor: Stephen B. Kahn‡.
Foundation type: Independent foundation.
Financial data (yr. ended 12/31/12): Assets, $24,732,897 (M); gifts received, $886,091; expenditures, $1,421,662; qualifying distributions, $1,303,386; giving activities include $1,085,000 for 112 grants (high: $100,000; low: $500).
Purpose and activities: Giving primarily to enhance democracy and to reduce the human impact on the environment.
Fields of interest: Environment, alliance/advocacy; Human services; Civil rights, voter education; Civil/human rights; Public affairs, citizen participation.
Type of support: General/operating support; Program development; Seed money; Research; Technical assistance.
Limitations: Applications not accepted. Giving on a national basis. No grants to individuals.
Application information: Contributes only to pre-selected organizations.
Board meeting date(s): Mar., Aug., and Dec.
Officers and Directors:* Marian Penn,* Pres.; Laura Flanagan,* Secy.; Susan Reed Clark,* Treas.; David M. Goldschmidt; Cecelia Hurwich, Ph.D.; Karen M. Kahn; **Michael Kieschnick**; William H. Soskin, Esq.
EIN: 770404924

92
The Roland and Dawn Arnall Foundation
c/o Holthouse Carlin and Van Trigt LLP
11444 W. Olympic Blvd., 11th Fl.
Los Angeles, CA **90064-1500**

Established in 2005 in CA.
Donors: Roland Arnall‡; Dawn Arnall.
Foundation type: Independent foundation.
Financial data (yr. ended 01/31/13): Assets, $30,182 (M); expenditures, $19,710,994; qualifying distributions, $19,673,672; giving activities include $19,659,381 for 34 grants (high: $10,141,949; low: $200).
Purpose and activities: Giving primarily to Jewish organizations, as well as for human services.
Fields of interest: Education; Medical research, institute; Jewish federated giving programs; Jewish agencies & synagogues.
Limitations: Applications not accepted. Giving primarily in Los Angeles, CA and New York, NY. No grants to individuals.
Application information: Contributes only to pre-selected organizations.
Officers and Director:* Dawn Arnall,* Pres.; Lewis Greenblatt, Treas.
EIN: 202144658

Other changes: For the fiscal year ended Jan. 31, 2013, the grantmaker paid grants of $19,659,381, a 686.9% increase over the fiscal 2012 disbursements, $2,498,480.

93
Arntz Family Foundation

(formerly Eugene S. Arntz Foundation)
P.O. Box 66488
Scotts Valley, CA **95067-6488**
E-mail: nancy@arntzfamilyfoundation.org; Main URL: http://www.arntzfamilyfoundation.org

Established in 1994 in CA.
Donors: Eugene S. Arntz‡; K. Allan Arntz; Thomas E. Arntz; Donald M. Arntz; Arntz Builders Inc.
Foundation type: Independent foundation.
Financial data (yr. ended 09/30/12): Assets, $13,143,668 (M); expenditures, $776,472; qualifying distributions, $688,601; giving activities include $516,335 for grants.
Purpose and activities: The purpose of the foundation is to support environmental organizations, with an emphasis on those organizations that work toward systematic change and sustainability, particularly where the areas of environment and economic development come together.
Fields of interest: Environment.
International interests: Central America; Mexico.
Type of support: General/operating support; Program development.
Limitations: Applications not accepted. Giving primarily in CA. No grants to individuals.
Publications: Grants list.
Application information: Contributes only to pre-selected organizations. Unsolicited requests for funds not accepted. Proposal submissions are by invitation only.
Board meeting date(s): Feb. and July
Trustees: Donald M. Arntz; K. Allan Arntz; Thomas E. Arntz; Katherine J. Jones.
Number of staff: 1 part-time professional.
EIN: 686109096

94
Aroha Philanthropies

(formerly The Michelson Foundation)
1660 Bush St., Ste. 300
San Francisco, CA 94109-5308 (415) 561-6540
Contact: Hector Melendez, Exec. Dir.
***FAX:* (415) 561-5477;**
E-mail: hmelendez@pfs-llc.net; **Main URL: http://www.arohaphilanthropies.org/**

Established in 1991 in CA.
Foundation type: Independent foundation.
Financial data (yr. ended 12/31/13): Assets, $3,564,699 (M); expenditures, $1,543,727; qualifying distributions, $1,542,717; giving activities include $1,355,082 for 42 grants (high: $220,000; low: $300).
Purpose and activities: Giving primarily to performing arts education programs, particularly ones which expose children and youth to performing arts and link arts-based education with academic achievement; as well as to adult residential mental health programs that provide services to help clients regain independent living.
Fields of interest: Arts, formal/general education; Education, early childhood education; Education; Mental health/crisis services; Children/youth, services; Infants/toddlers; Children/youth; Adults; Economically disadvantaged.
Limitations: Applications not accepted. Giving limited to San Mateo, Santa Clara, and San Francisco counties, CA, and to the Twin Cities metropolitan area, MN. No support for sectarian religious purposes. No grants to individuals, or for annual appeals, deficit reduction, or conferences and events.
Publications: Grants list.
Application information: Unsolicited requests for funds currently not accepted; however would-be applicants should refer to the foundation web site for updates.
Board meeting date(s): Three times annually; see foundation web site for details
Officers: Ellen A. Michelson, Pres.; Susan P. Schoenthaler, Treas. and C.F.O.
Director: Michael W. Michelson.
EIN: 943131676
Other changes: At the close of 2013, the grantmaker paid grants of $1,355,082, a 127.0% increase over the 2012 disbursements, $596,870.

95
AS&F Foundation

(formerly Forest Lawn Foundation)
625 Fair Oaks Ave., Ste. 360
South Pasadena, CA 91030-5813 (626) 403-3283
***Contact:* Julie Lytle Nesbit, V.P. and Exec. Dir., Phil. Svcs., Whitter Trust Co.; Pegine Grayson, V.P., Phil. Svcs., Whitter Trust Co.**
FAX: (626) 441-3672;
E-mail: JLytlenesbit@whittiertrust.com; Contact for Pegine Grayson, tel.: (626) 403-3282, fax: (626) 441-3672, e-mail: PGrayson@whittiertrust.com; Main URL: http://www.forestlawnfoundation.org

Incorporated in 1951 in CA.
Donors: Forest Lawn Co.; Hubert Eaton Estate Trust.
Foundation type: Independent foundation.
Financial data (yr. ended 12/31/12): Assets, $56,270,561 (M); expenditures, $3,549,436; qualifying distributions, $3,344,420; giving activities include $3,220,350 for 39 grants (high: $550,000; low: $5,000).
Purpose and activities: The foundation is primarily interested in providing grants to programs dedicated to youth and camping in Los Angeles and Orange Counties in CA. The foundation favors well-established, volunteer-driven organizations that are primarily supported by private donations.
Fields of interest: Recreation, camps; Boys & girls clubs; Boy scouts; Human services; YM/YWCAs & YM/YWHAs; Children/youth, services.
Type of support: General/operating support; Continuing support; Emergency funds; Program development; Matching/challenge support.
Limitations: Applications not accepted. Giving primarily in Los Angeles and Orange counties, CA. No support for federated appeals, political purposes, or projects or programs normally funded by the government, or arts and culture. No grants to individuals, or for endowment funds, or fundraising events.
Application information: Contributes only to pre-selected organizations.
Board meeting date(s): Quarterly
Officers: John Llewellyn, Chair.; Carol Llewellyn, Pres.; Susan Rule Sandler, Secy.; Russell T. Whittenberg, C.F.O.
Director: Darin B. Drabing.
EIN: 956030792
Other changes: At the close of 2012, the grantmaker paid grants of $3,220,350, a 140.8% increase over the 2011 disbursements, $1,337,500.

96
The Atlas Family Foundation

(formerly Richard & Lezlie Atlas Foundation)
P.O. Box 25338
Los Angeles, CA 90025-0338
Contact: Janis Minton, Exec. Dir.; Casey Rogers, Assoc.
E-mail: Thejmint@janisminton.com; Main URL: http://www.atlasfamilyfoundation.org
GiveSmart: http://www.givesmart.org/Stories/Donors/Richard-Atlas

Established in 1985 in CA.
Donors: Richard S. Atlas; Lezlie Atlas.
Foundation type: Independent foundation.
Financial data (yr. ended 02/28/13): Assets, $1,127,331 (M); expenditures, $1,329,719; qualifying distributions, $1,314,051; giving activities include $1,122,731 for 64 grants (high: $100,000; low: $250).
Purpose and activities: Giving primarily for early childhood education, parenting education, and early child development, pre-natal to age 3, and vulnerable children and families in Los Angeles County, CA.
Fields of interest: Education, early childhood education; Child development, education; Mental health/crisis services; Child development, services.
Type of support: General/operating support; Continuing support; Management development/capacity building; Annual campaigns; Program development; Conferences/seminars; Curriculum development; Technical assistance; Consulting services; Program evaluation; Matching/challenge support.
Limitations: Applications not accepted. Giving primarily in Los Angeles County, CA. No grants to individuals, or for basic research, capital campaigns or legislation.
Application information: Contributes only to pre-selected organizations. Unsolicited requests for funds not considered. Letters of inquiry are by invitation only.
Board meeting date(s): Varies
Officer: Janis Milton, Exec. Dir.
Trustees: Lezlie Atlas; Richard S. Atlas; Michael G. O'Brien; Michelle Atlas O'Brien; Allison Atlas Tannenbaum; David Tannenbaum.
Number of staff: 3 part-time professional.
EIN: 942988629

97
The Ayrshire Foundation

301 E. Colorado Blvd., No. 802
Pasadena, CA 91101-1917
Contact: Margaret G. Boyer, Pres.
FAX: (626) 795-7689;
E-mail: info@AyrshireFoundation.org; Main URL: http://www.ayrshirefoundation.org

Established in 1998 in CA.
Donor: James N. Gamble‡.
Foundation type: Independent foundation.
Financial data (yr. ended 05/31/13): Assets, $19,625,984 (M); expenditures, $1,256,027; qualifying distributions, $1,158,517; giving activities include $1,076,000 for 16 grants (high: $200,000; low: $26,000).
Purpose and activities: Giving primarily for health care, including a hospital, and a cancer center;

some giving also for education, the arts, and youth and social services.
Fields of interest: Arts; Education; Environment; Health care; Children/youth, services; Community/economic development; Children/youth; Youth; Aging; Young adults; Disabilities, people with; Mentally disabled; Women.
Type of support: Capital campaigns; Building/renovation; Equipment; Land acquisition; Endowments; Program development; Conferences/seminars; Professorships; Film/video/radio; Seed money; Scholarship funds; Matching/challenge support.
Limitations: Applications accepted. Giving primarily in Pasadena, San Francisco, and Sonoma, CA; giving also in the Petoskey/Harbor Springs, MI, area. **No grants to individuals, or for continuing support.**
Publications: Annual report; Grants list.
Application information: Following inquiry, an organization may receive a request for proposal from the foundation. Unsolicited requests or proposals are not accepted. Organizations with which Ayrshire board members have some personal involvement are given priority. Application form required.
Initial approach: Inquire through foundation web site before sending an application
Copies of proposal: 1
Deadline(s): Mar. 15 and Sept. 15
Board meeting date(s): May and Oct.
Final notification: One month or less
Officers and Directors:* Margaret G. Boyer,* Pres.; Tracy G. Hirrel,* V.P.; Peter S. Boyer, Secy.; Richard J. Hirrel,* Treas.
Number of staff: 1 full-time professional.
EIN: 954690418

98
The Edward and Rosemary Baker Family Foundation
395 Hampton Rd.
Piedmont, CA 94611-3525 **(510) 428-0955**
Contact: Edward D. Baker III, C.F.O.

Established in 2004 in CA.
Donor: Edward D. Baker III.
Foundation type: Independent foundation.
Financial data (yr. ended 12/31/12): Assets, $1,240,555 (M); expenditures, $238,669; qualifying distributions, $223,240; giving activities include $223,240 for 11 grants (high: $100,000; low: $2,000).
Purpose and activities: Giving to organizations that enhance the education and welfare of children, support or perform research in the mathematical sciences, provide medical care, support or perform medical research, promote the fine and performing arts, promote the welfare of animals, or fund other projects that are consistent with the foundation's general charitable purposes.
Fields of interest: Performing arts, ballet; Performing arts, opera; Child development, education; Animal welfare; Medical research; Mathematics; Children.
Limitations: Applications accepted. Giving primarily in San Francisco Bay Area, CA.
Application information:
Initial approach: Letter
Deadline(s): None
Officers: Rosemary Boccio Baker, Pres.; Edward D. Baker III, Secy. and C.F.O.
EIN: 201175382

99
Bank of the West Charitable Foundation
(formerly Commercial Federal Charitable Foundation)
P.O. Box 5155
San Ramon, CA 94583-5155
Contact: Rebeca Rangel, Tr.
Application address: Community Affairs Dept., 180 Montgomery St., 14th Fl., San Francisco, CA 94104; **Main URL: https://www.bankofthewest.com/**

Established in 2001 in NE.
Donor: Commercial Federal Bank, FSB.
Foundation type: Company-sponsored foundation.
Financial data (yr. ended 12/31/12): Assets, $2,895,682 (M); expenditures, $221,158; qualifying distributions, $200,000; giving activities include $155,000 for 3 grants (high: $75,000; low: $30,000).
Purpose and activities: The foundation supports programs designed to promote education and job training; and community and economic development. Special emphasis is directed toward programs designed to serve low-to-moderate income individuals.
Fields of interest: Higher education; Education, reading; Education; Employment, training; Employment; Housing/shelter, home owners; Housing/shelter; Human services, financial counseling; Homeless, human services; Human services; Business/industry; Community development, business promotion; Community development, small businesses; Microfinance/microlending; Community/economic development; Economically disadvantaged.
Type of support: General/operating support; Annual campaigns; Capital campaigns; Building/renovation; Program development; Scholarship funds.
Limitations: Applications accepted. Giving in areas of company operations in AZ, CA, CO, IA, ID, KS, MN, MO, ND, NE, NM, NV, OK, OR, SD, UT, WA, WI and WY. No support for fraternal or alumni organizations, political action committees, political candidates, or lobbying organizations. No grants to individuals, or for capital campaigns, trips or tours, or talent or beauty contests.
Publications: Application guidelines.
Application information: A full on-line application may be requested at a later date. Support is limited to 1 contribution per organization during any given year. Application form required.
Initial approach: Complete online letter of inquiry
Deadline(s): None
Trustees: Michael Bracco; Rebeca Rangel; Vanessa L. Washington.
EIN: 396765096
Other changes: The grantmaker no longer lists an E-mail address. The grantmaker no longer lists a phone.

100
The William C. Bannerman Foundation
9255 Sunset Blvd., Ste. 400
West Hollywood, CA 90069-3302 (310) 273-9933
Contact: Elliot Ponchick, Pres.

Established in 1958 in CA.
Foundation type: Independent foundation.
Financial data (yr. ended 04/30/13): Assets, $7,208,122 (M); expenditures, $523,914; qualifying distributions, $341,245; giving activities include $242,888 for 33 grants (high: $50,000; low: $500).
Purpose and activities: Giving for education, women and children, and the environment.
Fields of interest: Secondary school/education; Education; Environment; Children, services; Women.
Type of support: General/operating support; Annual campaigns; Capital campaigns; Building/renovation; Equipment; Program development; Seed money; Matching/challenge support.
Limitations: Applications accepted. Giving limited to the Los Angeles, CA, area. No support for political organizations, religious or medical/health organizations, or universities. No grants to individuals.
Publications: Application guidelines.
Application information: Application form required.
Initial approach: Letter no more than 2 pages
Deadline(s): Oct. 31
Board meeting date(s): July and Mar.
Final notification: Mar. 15
Officers: Elliot Ponchick, Pres.; Elizabeth T. Ponchick, V.P.; Gail Matthews, Treas.
Directors: Katie Bibbs; **Will Frost**; William D. Frost.
Number of staff: 1 part-time professional.
EIN: 956061353
Other changes: Mark Eiduson is no longer a director.

101
The Barth Foundation
5 Dos Pasos
Orinda, CA **94563-1849**

Established in 1986 in CA.
Donors: Worldwide Educational Svcs. of California; Eugene F. Barth; Aneila Barth.
Foundation type: Independent foundation.
Financial data (yr. ended 09/30/13): Assets, $3,700,620 (M); expenditures, $254,950; qualifying distributions, $213,143; giving activities include $213,143 for 52 grants (high: $27,000; low: $250).
Fields of interest: Arts, multipurpose centers/programs; Performing arts, theater; Higher education; Environment, natural resources; Environment, land resources.
Type of support: Annual campaigns; Scholarship funds.
Limitations: Applications not accepted. Giving primarily in CA. No grants to individuals.
Application information: Unsolicited requests for funds not accepted.
Trustee: Eugene F. Barth.
EIN: 943025710

102
Beavers Charitable Trust
2053 Grant Rd.
PMB 370
Los Altos, CA 94024-6913 (650) 694-4834
FAX: (650) 694-4836; E-mail: info@thebeavers.org; Main URL: http://www.thebeavers.org/trust.php

Established in 1977 in CA.
Donors: Homer Olsen; Willis North America, Inc.; Tutor-Saliba; Traylor Brothers, Inc.; S & W Scott Foundation; Livorna Investments; Lamberson Consulting, LLC; Kellogg LLC; Jacob Associates; Granite Construction Co.; FMI - Management Consulting; The Fluor Foundation; The Dutra Group; Diablo Contractors, Inc.; Corey Delta Constructors; Chubb & Son; The Beavers, Inc.; Amoroso Construction; CC Myers, Inc.
Foundation type: Independent foundation.

Financial data (yr. ended 04/30/13): Assets, $11,714,370 (M); gifts received, $840,885; expenditures, $776,168; qualifying distributions, $734,000; giving activities include $734,000 for 8 grants (high: $170,000; low: $6,000).
Purpose and activities: Giving primarily for grants to higher education institutions offering engineering degrees.
Fields of interest: Higher education; Engineering school/education.
Type of support: Endowments; Scholarship funds; Matching/challenge support.
Limitations: Applications not accepted. Giving on a national basis. No grants to individuals.
Application information: Contributes only to pre-selected organizations.
Board meeting date(s): Jan., Apr., Aug., and Oct.
Officer and Trustees:* Lynn E. Barr,* Chair.; Ronald M. Fedrick,* Vice-Chair.; **Robert E. Alger,* Pres.; Wilfred W. Clyde,* Sr. V.P.; Paul A. Cocotis,* V.P.; Michael T. Traylor,* Secy.-Treas.; David W. Woods, Exec. Dir.; Michael W. Anderson; John E. Bollier; J.C. Brummond**; and 19 additional directors.
Number of staff: 1 full-time professional; 1 part-time support.
EIN: 953605104
Other changes: Sam E. Baker, Thomas R. Draeger, John R. Lamberson, and Ralph G. Larison are no longer directors.

103
Stephen Bechtel Fund
P.O. Box 193809
San Francisco, CA 94119-3809 (415) 284-8675
FAX: (415) 284-8571;
E-mail: information@sdbjrfoundation.org; Main URL: http://www.sdbjrfoundation.org

Established in 2007 in CA and DE.
Donor: Stephen D. Bechtel, Jr.
Foundation type: Independent foundation.
Financial data (yr. ended 12/31/12): Assets, $659,314 (M); gifts received, $40,000,000; expenditures, $39,998,281; qualifying distributions, $40,137,264; giving activities include $37,627,195 for 275 grants (high: $3,000,000; low: $5,000).
Purpose and activities: The foundation invests in preparing California's children and youth to contribute to the state's economy and communities, and in advancing management of California's water and land resources.
Fields of interest: Education; Environment; Health care; Human services; Children.
Type of support: General/operating support; Management development/capacity building; Annual campaigns; Capital campaigns; Building/ renovation; Program development; Curriculum development; Scholarship funds; Employee matching gifts.
Limitations: Applications not accepted. Giving primarily in CA. No grants to individuals.
Publications: Financial statement.
Application information: Applications are by invitation only. Do not send letters of inquiry or proposals by mail or e-mail unless requested to do so by foundation staff.
Board meeting date(s): Quarterly
Officers and Directors:* Stephen D. Bechtel, Jr.,* Chair.; Lauren B. Dachs,* Vice-Chair., Pres. and Exec. Dir.; Patricia Leicher, Secy. and C.F.O.; Barbara Cartier, Cont.; Elizabeth H. Bechtel; Alan B. Dachs; Deborah L. Duncan; Jude P. Laspa; Bob Peck; Nonie B. Ramsay; John W. Weiser.
EIN: 208680679
Other changes: The grantmaker no longer publishes application guidelines.

104
S.D. Bechtel, Jr. Foundation
(formerly Stephen D. Bechtel, Jr. Charitable Foundation)
P.O. Box 193809
San Francisco, CA 94119-3809 (415) 284-8675
***Contact:* Kelly Hayashi, Sr. Grants Mgr.**
FAX: (415) 284-8571;
E-mail: information@sdbjrfoundation.org; Main URL: http://www.sdbjrfoundation.org

Established in 2005 in CA.
Donors: S.D. Bechtel, Jr.; Elizabeth Hogan Bechtel.
Foundation type: Independent foundation.
Financial data (yr. ended 12/31/12): Assets, $339,549,608 (M); gifts received, $63,317,809; expenditures, $65,137,368; qualifying distributions, $61,878,155; giving activities include $59,422,815 for 326 grants (high: $5,000,000; low: $200).
Purpose and activities: The foundation invests in preparing California's children and youth to contribute to the state's economy and communities, and in advancing management of California's water and land resources.
Fields of interest: Engineering school/education; Education; Environment, natural resources; Environment, beautification programs; Environment; Youth development, scouting agencies (general); Girl scouts; Youth development, services; Youth development; Science; Leadership development; Children/youth.
Type of support: General/operating support; Continuing support; Management development/ capacity building; Annual campaigns; Capital campaigns; Building/renovation; Program development; Curriculum development; Scholarship funds; Research; Program evaluation; Employee matching gifts; Matching/challenge support.
Limitations: Applications not accepted. Giving primarily in the San Francisco Bay, CA, area. No grants to individuals or for endowment activities and no international grants.
Publications: Financial statement.
Application information: Applications are by invitation only. Do not send letters of inquiry or proposals by mail or email unless requested to do so by foundation staff.
Officers and Director:* S.D. Bechtel, Jr.,* Chair.; Lauren B. Dachs,* Vice-Chair., Pres. and Exec. Dir.; Patricia W. Leicher, Secy. and C.F.O.; Barbara Cartier, Cont.; Elizabeth Hogan Bechtel; Alan M. Dachs; Deborah L. Duncan; Jude P. Laspa; Bob Peck; Nonie B. Ramsay; John Weiser.
Number of staff: 1 full-time professional; 4 part-time professional; 1 full-time support.
EIN: 203759208
Other changes: The grantmaker no longer publishes application guidelines.

105
Arnold and Mabel Beckman Foundation
100 Academy
Irvine, CA 92617-3002 (949) 721-2222
Contact: Jacqueline Dorrance, Exec. Dir.
FAX: (949) 721-2225;
E-mail: administration@beckman-foundation.com; Mailing address: P.O. Box 13219, Newport Beach, CA 92658; e-mail (for Kathlene Williams, Exec. Asst.): k.williams@beckman-foundation.com; Main URL: http://www.beckman-foundation.com

Incorporated in 1977 in CA.
Donors: Arnold O. Beckman‡; Mabel M. Beckman‡; Conexant.
Foundation type: Independent foundation.
Financial data (yr. ended 08/31/13): Assets, $548,425,390 (M); expenditures, $26,561,276; qualifying distributions, $24,034,850; giving activities include $22,625,440 for 97 grants (high: $4,000,000; low: $20).
Purpose and activities: The foundation makes grants to program-related, nonprofit research institutions to promote research in chemistry and life sciences, broadly interpreted, to foster the invention of methods, instruments, and materials that will open new avenues of research in science.
Fields of interest: Cancer; Eye diseases; Heart & circulatory diseases; Biomedicine; Medical research, institute; Cancer research; Eye research; Heart & circulatory research; AIDS research; Science; Marine science; Physical/earth sciences; Chemistry; Physics; Engineering/technology; Biology/life sciences.
Type of support: Research; Employee matching gifts.
Limitations: Applications accepted. Giving primarily in the U.S. No support for political or religious purposes, or for research that does not fall within the foundation's areas of interest. No grants to individuals (except for Beckman Young Investigator's Program), or for dinners, mass mailings, or fundraising campaigns; no loans.
Publications: Application guidelines; Program policy statement.
Application information: Grant policy and procedure information is available from the foundation. Application form required.
Initial approach: Pre-proposal letter not to exceed 3 pages
Copies of proposal: 1
Deadline(s): Oct. 1
Board meeting date(s): Quarterly
Final notification: Apr. or May
Officers and Directors:* Stephen Ryan,* Co-Chair.; **Harry B. Gray, Ph.D.*, Co-Chair.**; William H. May,* Secy.; Gary T. Wescombe, Ph.D.*, Treas.; Jacqueline Dorrance, Exec. Dir.; **Theodore Shi, Finance Dir.**; Gerald E. Gallwas; Jon Fosheim; Peter Simon.
Number of staff: 1 full-time professional; 3 full-time support.
EIN: 953169713
Other changes: For the fiscal year ended Aug. 31, 2013, the grantmaker paid grants of $22,625,440, a 115.2% increase over the fiscal 2012 disbursements, $10,514,347.
Harry B. Gray, Ph.D. has replaced Gavin Herbert Sr. as Vice-Chair.

106
Beckman Laser Institute & Medical Clinic
1002 Health Sciences Rd. E.
Irvine, CA 92617-3010

Established in 1982 in CA.
Donor: Kratz Foundation.
Foundation type: Independent foundation.
Financial data (yr. ended 06/30/13): Assets, $12,643,451 (M); expenditures, $1,517,017; qualifying distributions, $1,229,110; giving activities include $1,100,000 for 2 grants (high: $835,000; low: $265,000).
Purpose and activities: Giving to universities for research in laser advancement.
Fields of interest: Higher education; Engineering/ technology.
Type of support: Research.

Limitations: Applications not accepted. Giving limited to Irvine and La Jolla, CA. No grants to individuals.
Application information: Contributes only to pre-selected organizations.
Officers and Directors:* Michael W. Berns,* Chair. and C.E.O.; Art Fine,* Vice-Chair.; **Kenneth Strahs, Secy.**; Richard P. Kratz, C.F.O.; **Shu Chien**; **Robert Hanisee**; **Halina Rubinsztein-Dunlop.**
EIN: 953800459
Other changes: Kenneth Strahs has replaced Jacqueline Dorrance as Secy.
Olav Bergheim and D. Robinson Cluck are no longer directors.

107
Bell Charitable Foundation
P.O. Box 642
Rancho Santa Fe, CA 92067-0642

Established in 1994 in CA.
Donor: Bell Family Trust.
Foundation type: Independent foundation.
Financial data (yr. ended 10/31/13): Assets, $8,153,446 (M); expenditures, $447,708; qualifying distributions, $408,473; giving activities include $402,600 for 44 grants (high: $80,000; low: $500).
Fields of interest: Education; Medical research, institute; Medical research; Boy scouts; Human services; Children/youth, services.
Limitations: Applications not accepted. Giving primarily in CA and Washington, DC; some funding also in VA. No grants to individuals.
Application information: Contributes only to pre-selected organizations.
Officers and Directors:* Kathleen Bell-Flynn,* Pres.; Martha A. Bell,* V.P.; Steve Flynn,* Secy.
EIN: 330640946
Other changes: Kathleen Bell-Flynn has replaced Martha A. Bell as Pres. Martha A. Bell has replaced Kathleen Bell-Flynn as V.P.

108
The Bellwether Foundation, Inc.
(formerly The Shalan Foundation, Inc.)
Encino, CA

The foundation terminated in 2011.

109
The Bengier Foundation
c/o Seiler & Co., LLP
3 Lagoon Dr., Ste. 400
Redwood City, CA 94065-5157
Contact: Gary F. Bengier, Chair.
***E-mail:* ideas@bengierfoundation.org**, Application address: P.O. Box 590308, San Francisco, CA 94159-0308; Main URL: http://www.bengierfoundation.org/

Established in 2004 in CA.
Donors: Gary F. Bengier; Cynthia S. Bengier.
Foundation type: Independent foundation.
Financial data (yr. ended 12/31/12): Assets, $6,429,862 (M); gifts received, $1,501,113; expenditures, $1,058,081; qualifying distributions, $1,019,611; giving activities include $1,015,000 for 9 grants (high: $550,000; low: $5,000).
Fields of interest: Museums (science/technology); Education; Children/youth, services.
Type of support: General/operating support; Annual campaigns; Research.
Limitations: Applications accepted. Giving primarily in CA. No support for political organizations.
Application information: Application form not required.
Initial approach: Proposal
Copies of proposal: 1
Deadline(s): None
Officers: Gary F. Bengier, Chair.; Cynthia S. Bengier, C.F.O.; Brooke N. Bengier, Secy.
Number of staff: 1 part-time professional; 1 part-time support.
EIN: 113729246

110
C.J. Berry Foundation
1484 Pollard Rd., Ste. 406
Los Gatos, CA 95032-1031
***FAX:* (408) 374-9258**; Main URL: http://www.cjberry.org/

Established in CA.
Donors: Nella F. Berry; William F. Berry.
Foundation type: Independent foundation.
Financial data (yr. ended 12/31/12): Assets, $5,096,816 (M); gifts received, $1,250,000; expenditures, $320,805; qualifying distributions, $285,000; giving activities include $285,000 for 8 grants (high: $50,000; low: $10,000).
Fields of interest: Youth development; Human services; Philanthropy/voluntarism.
Limitations: Applications not accepted. Giving primarily in CA.
Application information: Unsolicited requests for funds not accepted.
Officers and Directors:* Derek W. Berry,* Pres. and C.E.O.; Koryne Smith,* V.P.; Joanne Berry,* Secy.; Taylor Smith,* Treas.; Bill Berry; Nella F. Berry.
EIN: 273496864

111
The Lowell Berry Foundation
3685 Mt. Diablo Blvd., Ste. 351
Lafayette, CA **94549-6803** (925) 284-4427
Contact: Katherine Sanders, Office Mgr.; For religious grants: Patricia Berry Conklin; For social service grants: Barbara Berry Corneille
FAX: (925) 284-4332;
E-mail: info@lowellberryfoundation.org; Main URL: http://www.lowellberryfoundation.org

Incorporated in 1950 in CA.
Donors: Lowell W. Berry†; Farm Service Co.; The Best Fertilizer Co. of Texas.
Foundation type: Independent foundation.
Financial data (yr. ended 12/31/12): Assets, $24,289,267 (M); expenditures, $1,373,500; qualifying distributions, $1,366,830; giving activities include $1,234,167 for grants.
Purpose and activities: The purpose of the foundation is to support organizations which are dedicated to strengthening the leadership of the local Christian church ministry. The foundation also serves the local community by providing a safety net for those in need while focusing on organizations that shape lives and build leaders.
Fields of interest: Arts; Education; Human services; Children/youth, services; Christian agencies & churches.
Type of support: General/operating support; Continuing support; Program development; Scholarship funds.
Limitations: Applications accepted. Giving limited to Contra Costa and Alameda counties, CA. No support for newly established organizations. No grants to individuals, or for building or capital funds, equipment, seed money, or land acquisition.
Publications: Grants list.
Application information: See foundation web site for updates regarding grant proposal submissions. Application form not required.
Initial approach: Letter, telephone, or visit the foundation web site for application guidelines
Copies of proposal: 1
Deadline(s): None
Board meeting date(s): Quarterly
Final notification: 3 to 4 months for religious grants; 3 to 4 months for social service grants
Officers and Directors:* Larry R. Langdon,* Pres.; Patricia Berry Conklin,* V.P.; Barbara Berry Corneille,* Secy.; Gary L. Depolo,* Treas.; John D. Asher; Jami S. Kane; Jayne S. Mordell; Annette S. Robison.
Number of staff: 1 part-time support.
EIN: 946108391

112
Better U
11812 San Vicente Blvd., 4th Fl.
Los Angeles, CA 90049-5022
E-mail: comments@betterufoundation.org; Main URL: http://betterufoundation.org/
Facebook: https://www.facebook.com/pages/Better-U-Foundation/127947693921261
Twitter: https://twitter.com/BetterUFound

Established in 2005 in CA.
Donors: James Carrey; Carrey Family Trust.
Foundation type: Independent foundation.
Financial data (yr. ended 12/31/12): Assets, $159,907 (M); gifts received, $409,100; expenditures, $579,967; qualifying distributions, $342,615; giving activities include $342,615 for 13 grants (high: $300,000; low: $229).
Purpose and activities: Giving to provide global assistance that transforms the daily lives of people through imaginative and self-improving methods.
Fields of interest: Higher education; Education, reading; Independent living, disability; International human rights; Physically disabled.
Limitations: Applications not accepted. Giving in the U.S. (particularly in N.Y. and Washington, DC) and internationally. No grants to individuals.
Application information: Contributes only to pre-selected organizations.
Officers: James Carrey, C.E.O. and Pres.; John Rigney, Secy.-Treas. and C.F.O.
EIN: 203752045

113
The Kathryne Beynon Foundation
P.O. Box 90815
Pasadena, CA 91109-0815 (626) 731-1185
***Contact:* Alexandra Laboutin Bannon, Tr.**
***E-mail:* beynonfoundation@gmail.com**

Established in 1967 in CA.
Donor: Kathryne Beynon†.
Foundation type: Independent foundation.
Financial data (yr. ended 10/31/13): Assets, $9,530,528 (M); expenditures, $596,873; qualifying distributions, $472,223; giving activities include $368,510 for 23 grants (high: $50,000; low: $5,000).

Purpose and activities: Giving primarily for hospitals, youth agencies, child welfare, Roman Catholic church support, and higher education.
Fields of interest: Higher education; Hospitals (general); Asthma; Boys & girls clubs; Children/youth, services; Catholic agencies & churches.
Type of support: General/operating support; Building/renovation; Endowments; Scholarship funds.
Limitations: Applications accepted. Giving primarily in southern CA, with emphasis on Pasadena. No grants to individuals.
Application information: Application form not required.
Initial approach: **Proposal**
Deadline(s): **None**
Trustees: Alexandra Laboutin Bannon; Mel B. Bannon; Robert D. Bannon; Mary Ellen Stambaugh.
EIN: 956197328

114
Blue Shield of California Foundation

50 Beale St., 14th Fl.
San Francisco, CA 94105-1819
Contact: Gwyneth Tripp, Grants and Contracts Mgr.
FAX: (415) 229-6268;
E-mail: bscf@blueshieldcafoundation.org; **E-mail for Gwyneth Tripp: gwyneth.tripp@blueshieldcafoundation.org; Additional contact: Jessica Gau, Grants and Contracts Admin, jessica.gau@blueshieldcafoundation.org;** Main URL: http://www.blueshieldcafoundation.org/
Ally for Change - Blue Shield of California Foundation: http://www.blueshieldcafoundation.org/video-and-photo-gallery/ally-change-blue-shield-california-foundation
Blog: http://www.blueshieldcafoundation.org/news/blog
Clinic Leadership Institute on YouTube: http://www.youtube.com/watch?v=D8U77ryTcHM
E-Newsletter: http://www.blueshieldcafoundation.org/news/focus-newsletter-archive
Facebook: http://www.facebook.com/pages/Blue-Shield-of-California-Foundation/222943311073741
Grants Database: http://www.blueshieldcafoundation.org/grants/grantees
Peter Long, Pres. and C.E.O., BSCF: http://twitter.com/PeterLongBSCF
Philanthropy's Promise: http://www.ncrp.org/philanthropys-promise/who
Twitter: http://twitter.com/BSCF
YouTube: http://www.youtube.com/user/BlueShieldCAFdn

Established in 1981 as a grantmaking public charity; status changed to company-sponsored foundation in 2004.
Donor: California Physicians' Service Agency Inc.
Foundation type: Company-sponsored foundation.
Financial data (yr. ended 12/31/12): Assets, $66,284,469 (M); gifts received, $40,114,912; expenditures, $37,220,389; qualifying distributions, $36,980,497; giving activities include $31,167,629 for 449 grants (high: $2,000,000; low: $7,500), and $3,519,033 for foundation-administered programs.
Purpose and activities: The foundation supports programs designed to improve the lives of Californians, particularly underserved populations, by making health care accessible, effective, and affordable for all Californians, and by ending domestic violence.
Fields of interest: Health care, public policy; Health care, reform; Health care, clinics/centers; Health care, insurance; Health care, cost containment; Health care, financing; Health care; Health organizations, reform; Crime/violence prevention, domestic violence; Family services, domestic violence; Leadership development; Economically disadvantaged.
Type of support: General/operating support; Continuing support; Management development/capacity building; Program development; Conferences/seminars; Scholarship funds; Research; Technical assistance; Program evaluation; Employee-related scholarships.
Limitations: Applications accepted. Giving limited to CA. No support for religious organizations not of direct benefit to the entire community or political candidates or organizations. No grants to individuals (except for employee-related scholarships), or for stand-alone sponsorships, award dinners, athletic events, competitions, special events, or tournaments, conferences or seminars, capital construction, television, film, or media production, political causes or campaigns, direct medical, specialty, or social services, subsidies to individuals for insurance coverage, outreach and enrollment activities for public health insurance programs, or case management.
Publications: Application guidelines; Annual report; Financial statement; Grants list; Newsletter; Occasional report; IRS Form 990 or 990-PF printed copy available upon request; Program policy statement (including application guidelines).
Application information: Most BSCF funding is by invitation only, but unsolicited requests for support are welcome for a limited number of funding opportunities. Organizations may be asked to submit a full proposal. Additional information may be requested at a later date. Organizations receiving support are asked to submit final reports, and, potentially, interim reports. Application form required.
Initial approach: Complete online eligibility quiz and letter of inquiry form
Deadline(s): **Feb. 7, May 9, July 18, and Oct. 10 for online letter of inquiry form**
Board meeting date(s): Quarterly
Final notification: **Up to 6 months**
Officers and Trustees:* David J. Kears,* Chair.; Peter Long, Ph.D.*, Pres. and C.E.O.; Aden Bliss, C.F.O.; **Eliza Daniely-Woolfolk**; Thomas W. Epstein; Franklin D. Gilliam, Jr., Ph.D.; William Hauck; Antonia Hernandez; Sandra R. Hernandez, M.D.; **N. Marcus Thygeson.**
Number of staff: 13 full-time professional; 4 full-time support; 1 part-time support.
EIN: 942822302
Other changes: Marianne Jackson and Vivian Clecak are no longer directors. Richard Thomason is now Dir., Health Care and Coverage. Brenda Solorzano is now Chief Prog. Dir. Julie Apana is now Prog. Asst. Bryan Tolentino is now Prog. Asst. Gwyneth Tripp is now Grants and Contracts Mgr. Scott Travasos is no longer C.F.O. and Dir., Finance & Opers. Christine Maulhardt is now Comms. Mgr. Ingrid Madden is now Comms. Assoc. Bryan Tolentino is now Prog. Asst. Lucia Corral Pena is now Sr. Prog. Off., Blue Shield Against Violence.

115
Blum Family Foundation

909 Montgomery St., Ste. 400
San Francisco, CA 94133-4652 (415) 434-1111

Established in 2002 in CA.
Donor: Richard C. Blum.
Foundation type: Independent foundation.
Financial data (yr. ended 12/31/12): Assets, $2,899,560 (M); gifts received, $3,375,000; expenditures, $9,091,144; qualifying distributions, $7,667,843; giving activities include $7,371,960 for 73 grants (high: $2,405,642; low: $500).
Purpose and activities: Giving primarily for the arts, education, health, human services, and for public policy research.
Fields of interest: Arts; Higher education; Education; Health organizations, association; Human services; Foundations (private grantmaking); Public policy, research; Public affairs; Jewish agencies & synagogues.
Limitations: Applications not accepted. Giving primarily in CA. No grants to individuals.
Application information: Contributes only to pre-selected organizations.
Officers and Directors:* Richard C. Blum, Chair. and Pres.; Erica Stone,* V.P.; Michael Klein; Jim Murray; Marc Scholvinck; Jane Jin Wen Su.
EIN: 954894347
Other changes: Richard C. Blum is now Chair. and Pres. Erica Stone is now V.P.

116
Boeckmann Charitable Foundation

15505 Roscoe Blvd.
North Hills, CA 91343-6503 **(818) 787-3800**
Contact: Herbert Boeckmann II, Pres.; Jane F. Boeckmann, C.F.O.

Established in 1982 in CA.
Donors: Herbert F. Boeckmann II; Jane Boeckmann; Todd Rothweiler; Biastre Trust; 8101 Sepulveda LLC; S.M.K.I. PTY LTD.
Foundation type: Independent foundation.
Financial data (yr. ended 11/30/13): Assets, $626,539 (M); gifts received, $326,505; expenditures, $581,829; qualifying distributions, $574,561; giving activities include $574,561 for 107 grants (high: $100,000; low: $500).
Fields of interest: Higher education, university; Children/youth, services; Protestant agencies & churches.
Limitations: Applications accepted. Giving primarily in CA.
Application information: Application form required.
Initial approach: Letter
Deadline(s): None
Officers: Herbert F. Boeckmann II, Pres.; Jane F. Boeckmann, C.F.O.
EIN: 953806976
Other changes: Herbert F. Boeckmann, II is now Pres. Jane Boeckmann is now C.F.O.

117
David Bohnett Foundation

245 S. Beverly Dr.
Beverly Hills, CA 90212-3807
Contact: Michael Fleming, Exec. Dir.
FAX: (310) 276-0007;
E-mail: michael@bohnett.com; **E-mail for David Bohnett, Chair.: david.bohnett@yahoo.com;** Main URL: http://www.bohnettfoundation.org/
Facebook: http://www.facebook.com/pages/David-Bohnett-Foundation/103547889686291

Established in 1999 in CA and DE.
Donor: David C. Bohnett.
Foundation type: Independent foundation.

Financial data (yr. ended 12/31/12): Assets, $17,509,498 (M); expenditures, $4,173,201; qualifying distributions, $4,003,887; giving activities include $3,535,607 for 201 grants (high: $800,000; low: $170).
Purpose and activities: The purpose of the foundation is to improve society through social activism. The foundation supports: 1) Positive portrayals of gays and lesbians in the media; 2) The reduction and elimination of the manufacture and sale of handguns; 3) Eliminating the rare animal trade; 4) Los Angeles organizations that are working to better the civic and cultural life of all who call L.A. home; and 5) Voter registration activities.
Fields of interest: Media/communications; Human services; Civil/human rights, LGBTQ; Civil rights, voter education; LGBTQ.
Type of support: General/operating support; Program development.
Limitations: Giving on a national basis, with emphasis on southern CA. No grants to individuals, or for videos or other film productions.
Publications: Grants list.
Application information: Application information available on web site. Application form required.
Initial approach: New applicants should submit a letter of inquiry (2 pages maximum), through online grant application on foundation web site; Existing applicants may update and submit letters of inquiry in-progress by logging back into their online account from the link on foundation web site
Copies of proposal: 1
Deadline(s): Current deadlines available on foundation web site
Board meeting date(s): Twice a year
Final notification: 4 months
Officers: David C. Bohnett, Chair.; Liz Atherton, Cont.; Michael Fleming, Exec. Dir.
Board of Advisors: Gwendolyn Baba; Christopher Caldwell; Rich Llewellyn; Rob Saltzman.
Number of staff: 1 full-time professional; 1 part-time support.
EIN: 954735846
Other changes: Ed Pierce is no longer a member of the Board of Advisors.

118
Clark and Nancy Bonner Foundation
(formerly Pinetops Foundation)
18552 MacArthur Blvd., Ste. 495
Irvine, CA 92612-1271
Contact: Marlys Pianin

Established in 2002 in CA.
Donor: Clark J. Bonner.
Foundation type: Independent foundation.
Financial data (yr. ended 01/31/13): Assets, $5,085,783 (M); expenditures, $270,099; qualifying distributions, $235,965; giving activities include $235,965 for 24 grants (high: $107,155; low: $40).
Fields of interest: Hospitals (general); United Ways and Federated Giving Programs; Christian agencies & churches.
Limitations: Applications accepted. Giving primarily in CA and OR. No grants to individuals.
Application information: Application form required.
***Initial approach:* Completed application form**
Deadline(s): None
Officers and Director:* Clark J. Bonner,* Pres.; Nancy S. Bonner, C.F.O.
EIN: 460477322

119
Borgman Family Foundation
(formerly Education Support Council)
Monterey, CA

The foundation terminated in 2011 and transferred its assets to Community Hospital Foundation, Cottage Health Systems and Next Door Solutions to Domestic Violence.

120
Bothin Foundation
1660 Bush St., Ste. 300
San Francisco, CA 94109-5308
Contact: Sunnie Kaufmann-Paulman, Prog. Off.
FAX: (415) 561-6477;
E-mail: skaufmann@pfs-llc.net; E-mail for proposal submissions: submissions@bothinfoundation.org;
Main URL: http://www.pfs-llc.net/foundations/bothin-foundation
Grants List: http://www.pfs-llc.net/userfiles/kcfinder/files/bothin_grants_2013.pdf

Incorporated in 1917 in CA.
Donors: Henry E. Bothin†; Ellen Chabot Bothin†; Genevieve Bothin de Limur†.
Foundation type: Independent foundation.
Financial data (yr. ended 12/31/12): Assets, $34,213,506 (M); expenditures, $1,985,065; qualifying distributions, $1,701,658; giving activities include $1,392,689 for 64 grants (high: $50,000; low: $1,200).
Purpose and activities: Support for organizations providing direct services to low-income, at-risk children, youth and families, the elderly, and disabled. To a limited extent, grants may also be made to environmental agencies and arts organizations that serve youth predominately. The foundation prefers to make grants for capital, building, and equipment needs.
Fields of interest: Environment; Human services; Children/youth, services; Child development, services; Family services; Aging, centers/services; Homeless, human services; Disabilities, people with.
Type of support: Capital campaigns; Building/renovation; Equipment.
Limitations: Applications accepted. Giving primarily in CA, with emphasis on San Francisco, Marin, Sonoma and San Mateo counties. No support for religious organizations, or educational institutions (except those directly aiding the developmentally or learning disabled). No grants to individuals, or for general operating expenses, endowment drives, annual appeals, scholarships, medical research, or videos.
Publications: Application guidelines; Annual report; Grants list.
Application information: The Board prefers that three full years elapse between grants. The foundation has ceased its grant making in Santa Barbara. See foundation web site for application guidelines, procedures, and forms. Do not send audio-visual materials, binders or pamphlets, unless requested to do so. Application form not required.
***Initial approach:* Use online grants system on foundation web site**
Copies of proposal: 1
Deadline(s): See web site for current deadline
Board meeting date(s): Feb., May, and Oct.
Final notification: 2 to 3 months
Officers and Directors:* **Lyman H. Casey,* Pres.**; A. Michael Casey,* V.P. and Treas.; **Devon Laycox, V.P.**; **Theodore Griffinger**; **Katherine Joiner**; **Pamela McCosker**; **Christian Miller**; Laura King Pfaff; Paul Sussman.
EIN: 941196182
Other changes: Lyman H. Casey has replaced Genevieve di San Faustino as Pres.
Lyman H. Casey is now Pres. Devon Laycox is now V.P. Lyman R. Casey, Jay Jacobs, and Herb Tully are no longer directors.

121
Bowes Family Foundation
1 Maritime Plz., Ste. 1925
San Francisco, CA 94111-3530

Established in CA.
Donors: John G. Bowes; Frances F. Bowes.
Foundation type: Independent foundation.
Financial data (yr. ended 06/30/13): Assets, $1,292,708 (M); gifts received, $2,500,000; expenditures, $1,282,264; qualifying distributions, $1,277,773; giving activities include $1,277,773 for 16 grants (high: $1,148,023; low: $100).
Purpose and activities: Giving primarily for the arts and health care.
Fields of interest: Arts; Education; Health care.
Limitations: Applications not accepted. Giving primarily in San Francisco, CA and NY. No grants to individuals.
Application information: Unsolicited requests for funds not accepted.
Officers and Directors:* Frances F. Bowes,* Chair. and V.P.; Diana Bowes, Secy.; Elena Bowes; Alexandra Bowes Williamson.
EIN: 200489340
Other changes: At the close of 2013, the grantmaker paid grants of $1,277,773, a 660.3% increase over the 2012 disbursements, $168,070.

122
Boys and Girls Aid Society of San Diego Ltd.
(also known as Boys and Girls Foundation)
2730 Historic Decatur Rd., Ste. 201
San Diego, CA 92106-6013 (619) 683-2192
Contact: Meredith Watwood, Exec. Dir.
FAX: (619) 615-2026;
E-mail: info@boysandgirlsfoundation.org; Main URL: http://www.boysandgirlsfoundation.org
Grants List: http://www.boysandgirlsfoundation.org/grants.php

Foundation type: Independent foundation.
Financial data (yr. ended 06/30/13): Assets, $4,679,203 (M); gifts received, $10,932; expenditures, $276,308; qualifying distributions, $156,794; giving activities include $123,100 for 27 grants (high: $25,850; low: $250).
Purpose and activities: The organization's mission is to identify, support, or create programs that provide preventive services or direct care to abused, neglected, and at-risk youth in San Diego County.
Fields of interest: Crime/violence prevention, abuse prevention; Crime/violence prevention, child abuse; Youth, services; Youth.
Limitations: Applications accepted. Giving primarily in San Diego County, CA. No support for for-profit organizations. No grants for salaries, multi-year grants, adult programs, employee benefits, general operating expenses, field trips, capital improvements, or building funds.
Application information: See foundation web site for complete application guidelines. Application form required.

Officers: Robert A. Goff, Pres.; Doris Alvarez,* V.P.; **Edward S. Fletcher, Secy.**; Susan Thorning, Secy.; Brent Hardy, Treas.; Meredith Watwood, Exec. Dir.
Directors: Kathleen Baldwin; Thomas Braden; Darlene Davies; James Eggert; David M. Gill; Margaret Herring; Gladys Jones-Morrison; James F. Kelly, Jr.; Daniel Larsen; George Saadeh; Dennis Smith; Pam Willmoth-Carlson; **Mitch Williams**; John W. Witt.
EIN: 951643979
Other changes: Edward S. Fletcher is now Secy.

123
Robert C. & Lois C. Braddock Charitable Foundation
c/o Robert C. Braddock
1221 Broadway, 21st Fl.
Oakland, CA 94612-1867
Main URL: http://www.braddockfoundation.org/
Grants List: http://www.braddockfoundation.org/grants.html

Established in 1990; classified as a private operating foundation in 1992.
Donors: Robert C. Braddock; Lois C. Braddock.
Foundation type: Operating foundation.
Financial data (yr. ended 06/30/12): Assets, $5,291,966 (M); expenditures, $374,141; qualifying distributions, $330,712; giving activities include $287,500 for 25 grants (high: $50,000; low: $1,500).
Purpose and activities: The foundation directs funding efforts toward projects that enhance the well being of children, youth, the elderly, the disabled and veterans. The foundation is dedicated to assisting these groups in the areas of basic life necessities, education, job training, rehabilitation, and environmental issues that have an impact upon people's lives.
Fields of interest: Higher education; Business school/education; Libraries (public); Environment, natural resources; Environment; Health organizations, association; Cancer; Arthritis; Food services; Human services; YM/YWCAs & YM/YWHAs; Family services, domestic violence; Space/aviation; Christian agencies & churches.
Limitations: Applications accepted. Giving primarily in San Leandro and Oakland, CA, and in central FL.
Publications: Grants list.
Application information: Complete application information available on foundation web site.
Initial approach: Letter
Deadline(s): Mar. 14
Trustees: Lois C. Braddock; Robert C. Braddock, Jr.; Cheryl Lee Keemar.
EIN: 680234966

124
Linda Brandes Foundation
P.O. Box 535
Rancho Santa Fe, CA 92067-0535 **(858) 756-9850**
***FAX:* (858) 756-9865;**
E-mail: info@lindabrandes.org; Main URL: http://www.lindabrandesfoundation.com

Established in 2005 in CA.
Donors: Brandes Family Foundation; Linda Brandes.
Foundation type: Independent foundation.
Financial data (yr. ended 12/31/12): Assets, $9,341,336 (M); expenditures, $712,077; qualifying distributions, $585,416; giving activities include $585,416 for grants.
Fields of interest: Human services; Family services.
Limitations: Applications not accepted. Giving primarily in CA.
Application information: Unsolicited requests for funds not accepted.
Officer: Linda Brandes, Pres.
Director: Karen Nielson.
EIN: 562511857

125
Saul Brandman Foundation
9595 Wilshire Blvd., No. 511
Beverly Hills, CA 90212-2505

Established in 1993 in CA.
Donor: Saul Brandman.
Foundation type: Independent foundation.
Financial data (yr. ended 12/31/12): Assets, $20,217,012 (M); expenditures, $5,071,170; qualifying distributions, $5,068,962; giving activities include $1,037,427 for grants.
Purpose and activities: Giving primarily for education and human services.
Fields of interest: Higher education; Education; Medical research, institute; Human services; Jewish federated giving programs; Children; Aging.
Limitations: Applications not accepted. Giving primarily in CA.
Application information: Unsolicited requests for funds not accepted.
Officer: Joyce Christian O'Donnell, Pres.
EIN: 954456430
Other changes: At the close of 2012, the fair market value of the grantmaker's assets was $20,217,012, a 483.5% increase over the 2011 value, $3,464,912.

126
The Bravo Foundation
(formerly Everhealth Foundation)
1042 N. El Camino Real, B409
Encinitas, CA 92024-1322 **(619) 889-1244**
Main URL: http://www.bravofdn.org
Grants List: http://www.bravofdn.org/grants_prior.html
Established in 1997 in CA.
Foundation type: Independent foundation.
Financial data (yr. ended 12/31/12): Assets, $11,146,032 (M); expenditures, $751,951; qualifying distributions, $449,166; giving activities include $327,922 for 31 grants (high: $20,000; low: $787).
Purpose and activities: The foundation awards grants only to human service organizations which serve the poor and disadvantaged, with special focus on the Hispanic community.
Fields of interest: Elementary/secondary education; Education; Health organizations, association; Human services; Children/youth, services; Catholic agencies & churches.
Limitations: Applications not accepted. Giving limited to San Diego, Imperial, and Riverside counties, CA, and CO. No support for religious or political purposes. No grants to individuals, or for capital campaigns, endowment funds, research, deficit budgets, conferences, transportation and lodging, testimonial dinners, ceremonies, or for publications or media projects.
Publications: Grants list.
Application information: Unsolicited requests for funds not accepted. See foundation web site for letter of inquiry guidelines.
Officers and Directors:* E. Zeke Lopez, Chair.; Michael J. Lopez,* C.E.O. and Pres.; Beatriz Ramirez, Secy.; Wind W. Ralston, Treas.; Jesus Varela.
Number of staff: 1 full-time professional; 1 full-time support.
EIN: 952160081

127
Leo A. and Minta L. Brisco Foundation
1005 El Camino Real
Arroyo Grande, CA 93420-2518 (805) 489-5536
Established in 1994 in CA.
Foundation type: Independent foundation.
Financial data (yr. ended 02/28/13): Assets, $2,921,712 (M); expenditures, $138,889; qualifying distributions, $131,006; giving activities include $131,006 for 10 grants (high: $66,006; low: $1,000).
Fields of interest: Historic preservation/historical societies; Higher education.
Type of support: Building/renovation; Scholarship funds.
Limitations: Applications accepted. Giving limited to San Luis Obispo County, CA. No grants to individuals (directly).
Application information: Application form required.
Initial approach: Letter
Deadline(s): None
Trustee: Blair Mankins.
EIN: 776110290
Other changes: The grantmaker no longer lists a primary contact.
Howard D. Mankins is no longer a trustee.

128
Brittingham Family Foundation
1482 E. Valley Rd., Ste. 703
Santa Barbara, CA 93108-1200
E-mail: info@brittinghamfoundation.org; Main URL: http://www.brittinghamfamilyfoundation.org

Established in 1997 in CA.
Foundation type: Independent foundation.
Financial data (yr. ended 12/31/12): Assets, $45,675,016 (M); gifts received, $77,355; expenditures, $3,691,814; qualifying distributions, $3,299,906; giving activities include $3,023,528 for 74 grants (high: $660,000; low: $500).
Purpose and activities: Giving primarily for education and health.
Fields of interest: Arts; Education; Environment; Human services; Children/youth, services.
Limitations: Applications accepted. Giving primarily in CA, with emphasis on Santa Barbara and WI; No giving for institutions outside of the U.S. No grants to individuals.
Application information:
Initial approach: Online application
Deadline(s): None; however applications received by Nov. 1 will most likely be considered for funding in the following calendar year.
Officers and Directors:* Scott Brittingham,* Chair. and Pres.; Ella Brittingham,* Exec. V.P.
EIN: 262992045
Other changes: Scott Brittingham is now Chair. and Pres. Ella Brittingham is now Exec. V.P.

129
Eli & Edythe Broad Foundation
(also known as The Broad Foundation)

2121 Ave. of the Stars, Ste. 3000
Los Angeles, CA **90067-5058** **(310) 954-5000**
FAX: (310) 954-5051;
E-mail: info@broadfoundation.org; Main URL: http://www.broadfoundation.org/
Eli and Edythe Broad's Giving Pledge Profile: http://glasspockets.org/philanthropy-in-focus/eye-on-the-giving-pledge/profiles/broad
E-Newsletter: http://broadeducation.org/news/press_releases/index.html
Facebook: http://www.facebook.com/pages/Los-Angeles-CA/The-Broad-Foundation/60623123387
GiveSmart: http://www.givesmart.org/Stories/Donors/Eli-Broad
Twitter: http://www.twitter.com/BroadFoundation

Established in 1999 in CA; As of Jan 1, 2007, the Eli & Edythe L. Broad Foundation merged into the Broad Foundation.
Donors: Eli Broad; U.S. Department of Education.
Foundation type: Independent foundation.
Financial data (yr. ended 12/31/12): Assets, $1,658,457,965 (M); gifts received, $85,740,581; expenditures, $177,994,962; qualifying distributions, $160,444,924; giving activities include $153,400,126 for 247 grants (high: $85,000,000; low: $500), and $250,000 for loans/program-related investments.
Purpose and activities: The foundation's mission is to dramatically improve K-12 urban public education through better governance, management, labor relations and competition; make significant contributions to advance major scientific and medical research; foster public appreciation of contemporary art by increasing access for audiences world wide and contributing to major civic projects in Los Angeles.
Fields of interest: Arts; Elementary/secondary school reform; Biomedicine; Medical research; Science.
Type of support: Program-related investments/loans.
Limitations: Applications accepted. Giving on a national basis. No grants to individuals.
Publications: Annual report.
Application information: See foundation web site for each program area's policies and guidelines. Application form not required.
Copies of proposal: 1
Deadline(s): Rolling basis
Officers and Directors: Eli Broad,* Chair.; Bruce Reed, Pres.; **Gerun Riley, V.P. and Chief of Staff**; Cindy Quane, C.F.O.; Marc A. Schwartz, C.I.O.; Edythe L. Broad.
Number of staff: 29 full-time professional; 4 full-time support.
EIN: 954686318

130
Albert & Rina Brocchini Family Foundation
27011 S. Austin Rd.
Ripon, CA 95366-9625 (209) 599-4229
Contact: Robert Brocchini, Pres.

Established in 2004 in CA.
Donors: Brocchini Farms, Inc.; A&R Enterprises.
Foundation type: Company-sponsored foundation.
Financial data (yr. ended 08/31/13): Assets, $1,747,744 (M); expenditures, $115,023; qualifying distributions, $102,150; giving activities include $102,150 for 31 grants (high: $30,500; low: $100).
Purpose and activities: The foundation supports organizations involved with arts and culture, education, nerve disorders, athletics, and human services.
Fields of interest: Arts; Secondary school/education; Education; Nerve, muscle & bone diseases; Athletics/sports, amateur leagues; Children, services; Aging, centers/services; Human services.
Type of support: Scholarship funds; General/operating support.
Limitations: Applications accepted. Giving primarily in CA. No grants to individuals.
Application information: Application form required.
Initial approach: **Letter**
Deadline(s): None
Officers: Robert Brocchini, Pres.; Stephen Brocchini, V.P.; Kristine Brocchini, Secy.-Treas.
EIN: 270106523

131
Sunshine Brooks Foundation
P.O. Box 34627
San Diego, CA **92163-4627**
Contact: Michael Kearney, Dir.
E-mail: mkearney@costco.com; Main URL: http://www.sunshinebrooks.com

Established in 1985 in CA.
Donors: Hattie H. Brooks; Sol Price; Sunshine Brooks†; Costco Wholesale Corp.
Foundation type: Independent foundation.
Financial data (yr. ended 06/30/13): Assets, $1,576,571 (M); gifts received, $78,000; expenditures, $166,081; qualifying distributions, $156,000; giving activities include $156,000 for 104 grants to individuals.
Purpose and activities: Scholarship awards to employees and children of employees of Costco Wholesale.
Fields of interest: Education.
Type of support: Employee-related scholarships; Scholarships—to individuals.
Limitations: Applications accepted. Giving primarily in CA.
Application information: See foundation web site for application information. Application form required.
Deadline(s): May 1
Officer: John Matthews, Secy.-Treas.
Directors: Michael Kearney; Julius Pearl; Henry Wolff, Jr.
EIN: 330190411

132
Patricia Crail Brown Foundation
6405 River Grove St.
Bakersfield, CA **93308-9694**

Established in 1998 in CA.
Donor: Patricia A. Brown Trust.
Foundation type: Independent foundation.
Financial data (yr. ended 12/31/12): Assets, $3,131,182 (M); gifts received, $73,333; expenditures, $228,497; qualifying distributions, $218,646; giving activities include $201,350 for 22 grants (high: $50,000; low: $2,500).
Fields of interest: Museums; Education; Animal welfare; Cancer; Alzheimer's disease; Children/youth, services.
Limitations: Applications not accepted. Giving primarily to organizations located in Kern County, CA. No grants to individuals.
Application information: Unsolicited requests for funds not accepted.
Officers and Director:* Lynn A. Brown,* Pres.; Patricia M. Soldano, C.F.O. and Secy.
EIN: 330379373

133
Lewis Brunswick and Rebecca Matoff Foundation, Inc.
1015 Calle Amanecer
San Clemente, CA 92673-6260

Established in 2000 in CA.
Donor: Lewis Brunswick†.
Foundation type: Operating foundation.
Financial data (yr. ended 12/31/11): Assets, $6,221,474 (M); gifts received, $562,292; expenditures, $337,846; qualifying distributions, $260,290; giving activities include $260,290 for 15 grants (high: $50,000; low: $3,000).
Fields of interest: Theological school/education; Cystic fibrosis research; Jewish federated giving programs; Jewish agencies & synagogues.
Type of support: General/operating support.
Limitations: Applications not accepted. Giving primarily in CA. No grants to individuals.
Application information: Contributes only to pre-selected organizations.
Officer: Brad Shapiro, V.P.
Trustee: Rebecca Matoff.
EIN: 954748693

134
Susie Tompkins Buell Foundation
(formerly Esprit Foundation)
P.O. Box 29921
San Francisco, CA 94129-9921 (415) 248-7825
Contact: Belinda Viray-Munoz, Exec. Dir.
FAX: (415) 441-6381;
E-mail: belindavm@buellofficesf.com; Additional e-mail: belindavm@earthlink.net; Main URL: http://www.susietompkinsbuell.org
Grants List: http://susietompkinsbuell.org/grantees/

Established in 1990 in CA.
Donor: Susie R. Tompkins Buell.
Foundation type: Independent foundation.
Financial data (yr. ended 11/30/13): Assets, $7,251,305 (M); expenditures, $384,370; qualifying distributions, $283,082; giving activities include $278,250 for 9 grants (high: $100,000; low: $5,000), and $2,740 for 16 employee matching gifts.
Purpose and activities: Primarily funds programs that improve the lives of women and girls, with emphasis on programs aimed at 1) creating an awareness of social responsibility, 2) promoting civic participation, 3) leadership development, and 4) activism training.
Fields of interest: Youth development, equal rights; Women, centers/services; Community development, women's clubs; Science; Women.
Type of support: General/operating support; Continuing support; Program development; Technical assistance; Consulting services; Matching/challenge support.
Limitations: Applications not accepted. Giving limited to San Francisco, CA. No support for international programs, drug and alcohol rehabilitation programs, or for health service organizations. No grants to individuals or for capital campaigns or film and video projects.
Publications: Grants list.
Application information: Unsolicited requests for funds not accepted. However, a 2-page letter of inquiry describing the program's objectives and funding needs is accepted. Formal proposals are to be submitted upon invitation only.
Board meeting date(s): Jan.

Officers and Directors:* Susie R. Tompkins Buell,* Pres.; Mark Buell, V.P.; Joan Steckler, Secy.; Belinda Viray-Munoz,* Exec. Dir.
EIN: 770266801

135
Burns Family Foundation
2055 Woodside Rd., Ste. 250
Redwood City, CA 94061-3379

Established in CA.
Donor: Susan T. Burns†.
Foundation type: Independent foundation.
Financial data (yr. ended 12/31/12): Assets, $27,432,607 (M); expenditures, $1,206,395; qualifying distributions, $1,170,600; giving activities include $1,170,600 for grants.
Fields of interest: Human services; Foundations (public); Catholic agencies & churches.
Officers: Trina R. Dean, Co-Pres.; Tori A. Burns, Co-Pres.; Kelli Kellerman, Secy.-Treas.
EIN: 261120529
Other changes: Trina R. Dean is now Co-Pres. Tori A. Burns is now Co-Pres.

136
Fritz B. Burns Foundation
21800 Oxnard St., No. 490
Woodland Hills, CA **91367-7532** (818) 840-8802
Contact: Rex J. Rawlinson, Pres.

Incorporated in 1955 in CA.
Donor: Fritz B. Burns†.
Foundation type: Independent foundation.
Financial data (yr. ended 09/30/13): Assets, $165,688,610 (M); expenditures, $9,447,277; qualifying distributions, $7,645,182; giving activities include $7,227,293 for 25 grants (high: $3,207,293; low: $25,000).
Purpose and activities: Grants primarily for education, hospitals and medical research organizations; support also for Roman Catholic religious associations and, social welfare agencies, and church support.
Fields of interest: Higher education; Education; Hospitals (general); Medical research, institute; Human services; Catholic federated giving programs; Catholic agencies & churches.
Type of support: Program-related investments/loans.
Limitations: Applications accepted. Giving primarily in the Los Angeles, CA, area; some giving also in Provo, UT. No support for private foundations. No grants to individuals.
Application information:
Initial approach: Letter
Deadline(s): Sept. 30
Board meeting date(s): Feb., May, Aug., and Nov.
Final notification: Approvals in Nov., payments made in Feb.
Officers and Directors:* Rex J. Rawlinson,* Pres.; Maureen E. Rawlinson,* V.P.; Cheryl R. Robinson,* V.P.; Lorraine F. Perry, Secy.-Treas.
EIN: 943218106

137
California Community Foundation
221 S. Figueroa St., Ste. 400
Los Angeles, CA 90012 (213) 413-4130
FAX: (213) 383-2046; E-mail: info@calfund.org;
Grants information e-mail: grantsmanager@calfund.org; Main URL: http://www.calfund.org/
Blog: http://givinginla.org/
California Community Foundation's Philanthropy Promise: http://www.ncrp.org/philanthropys-promise/who
CCF Fellowship for Visual Artists: https://www.facebook.com/CCFArtists
E-Newsletter: https://www.calfund.org/page.aspx?pid=736
Facebook: http://www.facebook.com/pages/California-Community-Foundation/62143496512
Flickr: http://www.flickr.com/photos/calfund/
LinkedIn: http://www.linkedin.com/companies/california-community-foundation
YouTube: http://www.youtube.com/calfundtv

Established in 1915 in CA by bank resolution.
Foundation type: Community foundation.
Financial data (yr. ended 06/30/13): Assets, $1,315,930,000 (M); gifts received, $184,700,000; expenditures, $184,177,000; giving activities include $164,428,000 for grants.
Purpose and activities: The mission of the foundation is to strengthen Los Angeles communities through effective philanthropy and civic engagement. The foundation makes multi-year grants (usually two years) in these main areas: arts, education, health care, housing and neighborhoods, transition aged youth and civic engagement.
Fields of interest: Arts; Education, early childhood education; Elementary school/education; Education; Animal welfare; Health care; Housing/shelter, development; Children/youth, services; Aging, centers/services; Human services; Civil rights, race/intergroup relations; Community/economic development; Aging; Disabilities, people with; Asians/Pacific Islanders; African Americans/Blacks; Hispanics/Latinos; Native Americans/American Indians; Women; Immigrants/refugees; Economically disadvantaged; Homeless; LGBTQ.
Type of support: General/operating support; Continuing support; Management development/capacity building; Capital campaigns; Program development; Scholarship funds; Research; Technical assistance; Consulting services; Program evaluation; Program-related investments/loans; Employee matching gifts; Matching/challenge support; Mission-related investments/loans.
Limitations: Applications accepted. Giving limited to Los Angeles County, CA. No support for sectarian purposes. No grants to individuals (except fellowships for artists or scholarships), or for annual campaigns, equipment, endowment funds, debt reduction, operating budgets, re-granting, fellowships, films, conferences, dinners, or special events.
Publications: Application guidelines; Annual report; Financial statement; Informational brochure; Newsletter.
Application information: Based on initial letter of intent submitted, applicants will receive written notification that either invites or discourages the submission of a full grant application. Application form required.
Initial approach: Visit calfund.org for information on general eligibility and specific requirements for each priority area. Interested applicants must submit a letter of intent.
Deadline(s): Varies
Board meeting date(s): Mar., June, Oct., and Dec.
Final notification: Four months
Officers and Board of Governors:* Cynthia Telles, Ph.D.*, Chair.; Antonia Hernandez,* C.E.O. and Pres.; John E. Kobara, Exec. V.P. and C.O.O.; Nichole D. Baker, V.P., Devel. and Donor Rels.; Steve Cobb, V.P. and C.F.O.; Nike Irvin, V.P., Progs.; Carolyn Steffen, Cont.; Sheldon M. Stone,* Chair. Emeritus; Louis Henry Bryson; Patrick Dowling, M.D.; David W. Fleming; Dennis Gertmenian; Meloni M. Hallock; Preston L.C. Johnson; Joanne Corday Kozberg; Hon. Carlos R. Moreno; Quan Phung; Todd Quinn; Paul Schulz; Jean Bixby Smith; Melanie Staggs; Catherine L. Unger; Tom Unterman; Ronald T. Vera; Marie Brooks Washington.
Number of staff: 54 full-time professional.
EIN: 953510055

138
The California Endowment
1000 N. Alameda St.
Los Angeles, CA 90012-1804 **(800) 449-4149**
FAX: (213) 928-8800;
E-mail: questions@calendow.org; Main URL: http://www.calendow.org
Bob's BLOG: http://tcenews.calendow.org/pr/tce/blog.aspx
CalConnect: http://www.calendow.org/HealthyCommunities/
E-Newsletter: http://calendow.us2.list-manage.com/subscribe?u=afe755296f10c4ca4f725bb4b&id=3d6712e9bb
Facebook: http://www.facebook.com/Calendow
GiveSmart: http://www.givesmart.org/Stories/Donors/Richard-Atlas
Google Plus: https://plus.google.com/100143257574109327234/videos
Grants Database: http://grantfinder.calendow.org/grantfinder_inter/index.cfm
Health Happens Here: http://twitter.com/calendow_here
New Health Law Guide for Buiness: http://www.healthlawguideforbusiness.org/
Pinterest: http://pinterest.com/calendow/
Publications and Reports: http://tcenews.calendow.org/releases
The California Endowment's Philanthropy Promise: http://www.ncrp.org/philanthropys-promise/who
Twitter: http://twitter.com/calendow
Youth-focused Californian Health Care Law Education: http://www.getcoveredca.org/
YouTube: https://www.youtube.com/user/HealthHappensHere

Established in 1996 in CA; converted from Blue Cross of California.
Foundation type: Independent foundation.
Financial data (yr. ended 03/31/13): Assets, $3,562,148,280 (M); expenditures, $196,646,151; qualifying distributions, $182,817,448; giving activities include $115,378,626 for 1,494 grants (high: $1,528,759; low: $260), $390,148 for 121 employee matching gifts, $11,997,782 for 4 foundation-administered programs and $18,016,917 for 7 loans/program-related investments (high: $10,516,917; low: $116,500).
Purpose and activities: To expand access to affordable, quality health care for underserved individuals and communities and to promote fundamental improvements in the health status of all Californians.
Fields of interest: Public health; Youth development; Minorities; African Americans/Blacks; Economically disadvantaged.
Type of support: General/operating support; Management development/capacity building; Conferences/seminars; Technical assistance; Program evaluation; Program-related investments/loans; Employee matching gifts; Mission-related investments/loans.

Limitations: Applications accepted. Giving primarily in CA. No support for lobbying, medical or scientific research, or uncompensated care for direct clinical services. No grants to individuals for scholarships, fellowships or grants, or for endowments, operating deficits or retirement of debt, media projects not part of a broader project or strategy, medical supplies, laboratory fees, X-ray services, medications, vaccines or prescriptions; capital funding for purchase, construction or renovation of facilities or other physical infrastructure; indirect costs that exceed 15 percent of the total of requested personnel and operating cost.
Publications: Application guidelines; Annual report; Occasional report.
Application information: See foundation's web site for Innovative Ideas Challenge grant submission requirements. The foundation currently has very limited resources available for proposed grants outside of its Health Happens Here programs and Building Healthy Communities (BHC) 10-year plan. It is highly unlikely a request will be funded unless there is significant alignment with the BHC's 10 Outcomes or 4 Big Results. Thus, an applicant must be able to state clearly how their work aligns with one or more of the 10 BHC Outcomes or 4 Big Results. Application form required.
Initial approach: Complete online application if proposal meets any of the required objectives. See foundation web site: http://www.calendow.org/grants
Deadline(s): Dec, 1, May 1 and Sept. 1
Board meeting date(s): May 16-17, Aug. 20-21, Nov. 19-20, and Feb. 19-20
Final notification: Up to 120 days
Officers and Directors:* C. Dean Germano,* Chair.; Jane Garcia, Vice-Chair.; Robert K. Ross, M.D.*, C.E.O. and Pres.; B. Kathlyn Mead, Exec. V.P. and C.O.O.; Anthony B. Iton, M.D., Sr. V.P., Healthy Communities; Daniel Zingale, Sr. V.P., Healthy California; Dan C. DeLeon, V.P. and C.F.O.; Brytain Ashford, V.P., Human Resources; Jim Keddy, V.P. and Chief Learning Off.; Ruth Wernig, C.I.O.; Stephen Bennett; Susan V. Berresford; Walter L. Buster, Ed.D.; Shan Cretin, Ph.D.; Adrienne Crowe; Hector Flores, M.D.; Shawn A. Ginwright, Ph.D.; Russ Gould; Zac Guevara; Christina Kazhe, Esq.; Kate Kendell, Esq.; Maurice Lim Miller; Steve PonTell; Winston F. Wong, M.D.
Number of staff: 74 full-time professional; 1 part-time professional; 62 full-time support.
EIN: 954523232

139
California HealthCare Foundation
1438 Webster St., Ste. 400
Oakland, CA 94612-3206 (510) 238-1040
Contact: Lisa Kang, Dir., Grants Admin.
FAX: (510) 238-1388; E-mail: info@chcf.org; **E-mail for questions regarding Letters of Inquiry: grants@chcf.org; Additional address: 1415 L St., No. 820, Sacramento, CA 95814; tel.: (916) 329-4540; fax: (916) 329-4545**; Main URL: http://www.chcf.org
Blog: http://www.chcf.org/innovation-fund/notes-from-the-team
California Healthline: http://www.californiahealthline.org/rss
E-Newsletter: http://www.chcf.org/media
Facebook: http://www.facebook.com/chcfnews
Grants Database: http://www.chcf.org/grants/awarded
iHealthBeat: http://www.ihealthbeat.org/rss
Knowledge Center: http://www.chcf.org/about/assessing-our-impact
Knowledge Center: http://www.chcf.org/almanac
Knowledge Center: http://www.chcf.org/search?type=chcf&se=1&contenttype=publications&sdate=all
Pinterest: http://www.pinterest.com/chcfoundation/the-picture-of-health/
Twitter: https://twitter.com/chcfnews
YouTube: http://www.youtube.com/user/CHCFoundation

Established in 1996 in CA; converted from Blue Cross of California.
Foundation type: Public charity.
Financial data (yr. ended 02/28/13): Assets, $716,354,350 (M); expenditures, $52,443,464; giving activities include $31,775,896 for grants.
Purpose and activities: The foundation's mission is to expand access to affordable, quality health care for underserved individuals and communities, and to promote fundamental improvements in the health status of the people of California. The foundation commissions research and analysis, publishes and disseminates information, convenes stakeholders, and funds the development of programs and models aimed at improving the healthcare delivery and financing systems.
Fields of interest: Health care, HMOs; Health care, insurance; Health care; Health organizations, public policy; Health organizations, public education.
Type of support: Program development; Research; Program evaluation.
Limitations: Applications accepted. Giving primarily in CA. No grants for general operating expenses, capital campaigns, annual campaigns, building, purchases or renovations, direct clinical care costs, or equipment.
Publications: Application guidelines; Informational brochure (including application guidelines); Occasional report; IRS Form 990 or 990-PF printed copy available upon request.
Application information: Projects must have potential to inform or impact healthcare access and health policy issues in California; Application form required only for RFPs; See web site for latest information including available publications. Application form not required.
Initial approach: Letter of inquiry (1-3 pages)
Copies of proposal: 2
Deadline(s): None
Board meeting date(s): Quarterly
Final notification: 6-8 weeks from receipt
Officers and Directors:* Micheline Chau,* Chair.; Barbara N. Lubash,* Vice-Chair.; Sandra R. Hernandez, M.D.*, C.E.O and Pres.; Craig C. Ziegler, M.B.A., V.P., Fin., Admin. and Investments; Collette Clark, Cont.; Michael V. Drake, M.D.; Maria Echaveste; **Daniel L. Gross**; Elizabeth G. Hill; Pamela Joyner; Ian Morrison, Ph.D., M.A.; Walter W. "Bill" Noce, Jr.; John D. Welty, Ph.D.
Number of staff: 43 full-time professional; 10 full-time support; 2 part-time support.
EIN: 954523231
Other changes: Micheline Chau has replaced Ian Morrison, Ph.D., M.A., as Chair. Barbara N. Lubash has replaced Micheline Chau as Vice-Chair. Sandra R. Hernandez, M.D. has replaced Mark Douglas Smith, M.D., M.B.A. as C.E.O. and Pres.
Geoffrey Cowan is no longer a director.
The grantmaker now publishes application guidelines.

140
The California Wellness Foundation
6320 Canoga Ave., Ste. 1700
Woodland Hills, CA 91367-2565 (818) 702-1900
Contact: Amy Scop, Dir., Grants Mgmt.
FAX: (818) 702-1999; E-mail: tcwf@tcwf.org; Branch Office address: 575 Market St., Ste. 1850, San Francisco, CA 94105, tel.: (415) 908-3000, fax: (415) 908-3001; Main URL: http://www.calwellness.org/
Grants Database: http://www.calwellness.org/grants_program/search.php
Job Resource Center: http://www.healthjobsstarthere.com/resources/welcome
Knowledge Center: http://www.calwellness.org/publications/evaluations.htm
Twitter: https://twitter.com/calwellness

Established in 1992 in CA; converted from Health Net HMO.
Foundation type: Independent foundation.
Financial data (yr. ended 12/31/12): Assets, $847,982,323 (M); expenditures, $51,454,654; qualifying distributions, $48,153,295; giving activities include $39,271,251 for 712 grants (high: $500,000; low: $1,000), $150,000 for 6 grants to individuals (high: $25,000; low: $25,000), and $128,854 for 96 employee matching gifts.
Purpose and activities: The foundation's mission is to improve the health of the people of California by making grants for health promotion, wellness education and disease prevention. The foundation pursues the following goals through grantmaking: 1) to address the particular health needs of traditionally underserved populations, including low-income individuals, people of color, youth and residents of rural areas; 2) to support and strengthen nonprofit organizations that seek to improve the health of underserved populations; 3) to recognize and encourage leaders who are working to increase health and wellness within their communities; and 4) to inform policy makers and opinion leaders about important wellness and health care issues.
Fields of interest: Vocational school, secondary; Higher education; Higher education, college (community/junior); Higher education, college; Dental school/education; Medical school/education; Nursing school/education; Public health school/education; Education; Environment, air pollution; Environment, water pollution; Environment, toxics; Environment, waste management; Health care, equal rights; Health care, formal/general education; Medical care, community health systems; Hospitals (general); Health care, clinics/centers; Dental care; Health care, rural areas; Reproductive health; Reproductive health, family planning; Reproductive health, prenatal care; Reproductive health, sexuality education; Public health; Public health, STDs; Public health, communicable diseases; Public health, occupational health; Public health, environmental health; Health care, home services; Health care; Mental health/crisis services, hot-lines; Obstetrics/gynecology; Crime/violence prevention; Offenders/ex-offenders, transitional care; Offenders/ex-offenders, rehabilitation; Offenders/ex-offenders, probation/parole; Offenders/ex-offenders, services; Offenders/ex-offenders, prison alternatives; Food banks; Food distribution, meals on wheels; Nutrition; Housing/shelter, temporary shelter; Housing/shelter, homeless; Youth development, centers/clubs; Boys & girls clubs; Youth development; YM/YWCAs & YM/YWHAs; Youth, pregnancy prevention; Youth, services; Family services; Pregnancy centers; Residential/custodial care, senior continuing care; Aging, centers/services; Women, centers/services; Minorities/immigrants, centers/services; Homeless, human services; Community development, citizen coalitions; Nonprofit management; Military/veterans' organizations; Leadership development; Youth; Aging; Young adults; Minorities; Asians/Pacific Islanders; African

Americans/Blacks; Hispanics/Latinos; Native Americans/American Indians; Indigenous peoples; Women; Girls; Adults, women; Men; Boys; Adults, men; Military/veterans; Offenders/ex-offenders; Immigrants/refugees; Economically disadvantaged; Homeless; Migrant workers; LGBTQ.
Type of support: General/operating support; Continuing support; Program development; Conferences/seminars; Publication; Seed money; Scholarship funds; Research; Technical assistance; Program evaluation; Grants to individuals.
Limitations: Applications accepted. Giving limited to CA; national organizations providing programs in CA are also considered. No support for activities that exclusively benefit the members of religious or sectarian organizations. No grants to individuals (except for TCWF awards), or for annual fund drives, building campaigns, major equipment, or for biomedical research.
Publications: Application guidelines; Annual report; Annual report (including application guidelines); Grants list; Informational brochure; Informational brochure (including application guidelines); Newsletter (including application guidelines); Occasional report.
Application information: Unsolicited letters of interest to the foundation's Responsive Grantmaking Program are suspended until further notice. For updates see foundation homepage. Review the guidelines and eligibility criteria on the "How To Apply" portal on the foundation's web site, which includes answers to frequently asked questions. All requested information should be included in the letter and not sent as separate attachments. Application form not required.
Initial approach: No more than a 1- to 2-page letter of interest
Deadline(s): None
Board meeting date(s): Quarterly
Final notification: 3 months
Officers and Directors:* Barbara C. Staggers, M.D., M.P.H.*, Chair.; Eugene Washington, M.D., M.Sc.*, Vice-Chair.; **Judy Belk, C.E.O. and Pres.**; Margaret W. Minnich, V.P., Finance and Admin.; **Fatima Angeles, V.P., Programs**; Magdalena Beltran-del Olmo, V.P., Comms.; Amy B. Scop, Dir., Grants Mgmt.; David S. Barlow, M.B.A., C.P.A.; M. Isabel Becerra, B.A.; Elizabeth M. Gomez, M.S.W.; Elisabeth Hallman, M.B.A., R.N.
Number of staff: 19 full-time professional; 1 part-time professional; 18 full-time support; 2 part-time support.
EIN: 954292101
Other changes: Judy Belk has replaced Diana M. Bonta as C.E.O. and Pres.
Fatima Angeles is now V.P., Programs. Colburn S. Wilbur is no longer Interim Pres.

141
Camp Foundation
(formerly Doris & Donald Fisher Foundation)
1 Maritime Plz., Ste. 1400
San Francisco, CA 94111-3504

Established in 1986; the foundation's name changed from the D & DF Foundation to the Doris & Donald Fisher Foundation and is now the Camp Foundation.
Donors: Donald G. Fisher‡; Doris F. Fisher; John J. Fisher; DDF 2005 Charitable Remainder Annuity Trust.
Foundation type: Operating foundation.
Financial data (yr. ended 06/30/13): Assets, $140,335,032 (M); expenditures, $136,253,033; qualifying distributions, $135,642,909; giving activities include $135,600,000 for 1 grant.
Fields of interest: Museums (art).
Limitations: Applications not accepted. Giving primarily in Broomfield, CO; some giving also in San Francisco, CA, Atlanta, GA, and New York, NY. No grants to individuals.
Application information: Contributes only to pre-selected organizations.
Officer: Jane Spray, Treas.
Trustee: Doris F. Fisher.
EIN: 943022002
Other changes: At the close of 2013, the grantmaker paid grants of $135,600,000, a 427.6% increase over the 2012 disbursements, $25,700,000.

142
The Keith Campbell Foundation for the Environment, Inc.
1450 Sutter St., Ste. 510
San Francisco, CA 94109-5418 (415) 722-4739
Contact: Pacific Region Proposals: Anna Lindgren, Asst. to the Pres.; Chesapeake and Atlantic Proposals: Rebecca Bednarek, Grants Asst.
E-mail: pacificadmin@campbellfoundation.org;
Chesapeake Office: 410 Severn Ave., Ste. 210, Annapolis MD 21403, tel: (410) 990-0900, fax: (410) 990-0988; E-mail for Chesapeake and Atlantic Coastal Bay proposals: Rebecca Bednarek (rebednarek@campbellfoundation.org); E-mail for Pacific Region proposals: Anna Lindgren (pacificadmin@campbellfoundation.org); Main URL: http://www.campbellfoundation.org/
Grants Database: http://www.campbellfoundation.org/grantee_search

Established in 1998 in MD.
Donor: Keith Campbell.
Foundation type: Independent foundation.
Financial data (yr. ended 12/31/12): Assets, $143,527,562 (M); gifts received, $9,077,769; expenditures, $12,823,381; qualifying distributions, $12,429,189; giving activities include $9,926,527 for 229 grants (high: $500,000; low: $25), $3,715 for 31 employee matching gifts, and $448,650 for foundation-administered programs.
Purpose and activities: The foundation promotes policy, advocacy, and enforcement to improve water quality, restore ecological balance, and foster an engaged citizenry within the watersheds of the Chesapeake Bay, Atlantic Coastal Bays and the Pacific Coast region.
Fields of interest: Environment, alliance/advocacy; Environment, administration/regulation; Environment, research; Environment, public policy; Environment, single organization support; Environment, public education; Environment, formal/general education; Environment, pollution control; Environment, water pollution; Environment, toxics; Environment, water resources; Environmental education; Environment; Animals/wildlife, fisheries; Animals/wildlife, sanctuaries.
Type of support: General/operating support; Continuing support; Management development/capacity building; Emergency funds; Program development; Employee matching gifts; Matching/challenge support.
Limitations: Applications not accepted. Giving primarily in the Chesapeake Bay area, (MD and VA), the San Francisco Bay Area, CA, OR, and HI. No support for No support generally for on-the-ground restoration or classroom environmental education. No grants to individuals.
Publications: Grants list.
Application information: Unsolicited requests for funds are not currently being accepted. See foundation web site for updates.
Officers: D. Keith Campbell, Chair.; Samantha Campbell, Pres.; Verna Harrison, Exec. Dir.
EIN: 522136842

143
Carlston Family Foundation
(formerly Broderbund Foundation)
2933 Quedada
Newport Beach, CA 92660 (415) 388-4763
Contact: Timothy J. Allen, Exec. Dir.
FAX: (949) 640-7841;
E-mail: tima@carlstonfamilyfoundation.com;
Additional telephone: (949) 640-7840; Main URL: http://www.carlstonfamilyfoundation.org
Facebook: https://www.facebook.com/pages/Carlston-Family-Foundation/104985366209091

Established in 1987 in CA.
Donor: Alice Carlston.
Foundation type: Independent foundation.
Financial data (yr. ended 12/31/12): Assets, $3,361,903 (M); expenditures, $313,120; qualifying distributions, $313,120; giving activities include $67,969 for grants, $82,761 for grants to individuals, and $61,219 for 2 foundation-administered programs.
Purpose and activities: The mission of the foundation is to recognize and reward outstanding teachers in California public schools. To be considered for the award, a teacher must be nominated by former students who are either currently enrolled in or who have graduated from four year colleges or universities.
Fields of interest: Secondary school/education.
Type of support: Program development; Grants to individuals.
Limitations: Applications accepted. Giving primarily in CA.
Publications: Annual report; Grants list; Program policy statement.
Application information: Nomination guidelines and nominating form available on foundation web site. Application form required.
Officers and Directors:* Douglas G. Carlston,* Chair.; Alice Carlston,* Secy.-Treas.; Timothy J. Allen, Exec. Dir.; Charles Carlston; Donal Carlston; Erin Carlston; Gary Carlston; Tom Marcus; Diane Rapley; Carisa Showden.
Number of staff: 1 full-time professional; 1 part-time professional.
EIN: 680154752

144
The Lloyd and Carole Carney Foundation
303 Twin Dolphin Dr., Ste. 600
Redwood City, CA 94065-1422

Established in 1999 in CA.
Donors: Lloyd Carney; Carole Carney.
Foundation type: Independent foundation.
Financial data (yr. ended 12/31/12): Assets, $1,342,256 (M); gifts received, $248,556; expenditures, $188,761; qualifying distributions, $183,760; giving activities include $183,760 for grants.
Fields of interest: Higher education, university; Boys & girls clubs; Children, services; Residential/custodial care; Community development, service clubs.
Limitations: Applications not accepted. No grants to individuals.
Application information: Contributes only to pre-selected organizations.

Directors: Carole Carney; Lloyd Carney.
EIN: 770528830

145

Carpenter Family Foundation

(formerly Karen A. Carpenter Memorial Foundation)
16255 Ventura Blvd., Ste. 1250
Encino, CA 91436-2315

Established in 1997 in CA.
Donors: Agnes Carpenter Revocable Trust; Richard Carpenter; Evalyn M. Bauer Foundation.
Foundation type: Independent foundation.
Financial data (yr. ended 01/31/13): Assets, $2,142,363 (M); gifts received, $1,014,450; expenditures, $70,215; qualifying distributions, $32,000; giving activities include $32,000 for 6 grants (high: $20,000; low: $250).
Fields of interest: Performing arts centers; Elementary/secondary education; Higher education, university; Medical research, institute.
Limitations: Applications not accepted. Giving primarily in CA. No grants to individuals.
Application information: Contributes only to pre-selected organizations.
Officers: Richard Carpenter, Pres.; Werner Wolfen, Secy.; **Susan Frazin, Treas.**
EIN: 953854103

146

The CEC Foundation

c/o John R. Fuqua
P.O. Box 1324
Los Alamitos, CA 90720-2420

Established in 1999 in CA.
Donor: Carol Electric Company, Inc.
Foundation type: Operating foundation.
Financial data (yr. ended 12/31/12): Assets, $3,715,646 (M); gifts received, $428,000; expenditures, $325,876; qualifying distributions, $303,605; giving activities include $288,605 for 12 grants (high: $100,000; low: $5,000), and $15,000 for 2 grants to individuals (high: $10,000; low: $5,000).
Fields of interest: Human services; Homeless, human services; Christian agencies & churches.
Type of support: Grants to individuals; General/operating support.
Limitations: Applications not accepted. Giving primarily in CA.
Application information: Unsolicited requests for funds not accepted.
Officers: John R. Fuqua, C.E.O.; **Allen W. Moffitt, C.F.O. and Secy.**
EIN: 330859870
Other changes: Ronald J. Hathaway is no longer Secy.

147

The Champions Volunteer Foundation

78-200 Miles Ave.
Indian Wells, CA **92210-6803**

Donors: Desert Champions, LLC; War Caualty Family Assistance Fund.
Foundation type: Independent foundation.
Financial data (yr. ended 12/31/12): Assets, $10,475 (M); gifts received, $162,670; expenditures, $177,813; qualifying distributions, $177,813; giving activities include $159,100 for 45 grants (high: $10,000; low: $100), and $13,507 for 2 foundation-administered programs.
Fields of interest: Education; Recreation; Human services.
Limitations: Applications not accepted. Giving primarily in CA.
Application information: Unsolicited requests for funds not accepted.
Officers: Georgia D. Felich, Pres.; Mary Kalluski, Secy.; Gudrun Bauer-Farr, Treas.
Directors: Celia M. Pauls; Steven R. Simon.
EIN: 330952475

148

Chan Soon-Shiong Family Foundation

c/o Steve Hassan
10182 Culver Blvd.
Culver City, CA 90232
Dr. Patrick Soon-Shiong's Twitter Feed: https://twitter.com/solvehealthcare
Michele Chan and Dr. Patrick Soon-Shiong's Giving Pledge Profile: http://glasspockets.org/philanthropy-in-focus/eye-on-the-giving-pledge/profiles/soon-shiong

Established in 2008 in CA.
Donors: Michele Chan; Dr. Patrick Soon-Shiong.
Foundation type: Independent foundation.
Financial data (yr. ended 09/30/13): Assets, $132,546,910 (M); expenditures, $5,104,962; qualifying distributions, $4,969,532; giving activities include $4,944,927 for 21 grants (high: $2,000,000; low: $1,000).
Purpose and activities: The mission of the foundation is to fund research and erase disparities in access to health care and education.
Fields of interest: Education; Health care; Medical research, institute.
Limitations: Applications not accepted. Giving primarily in CA, with emphasis on Los Angeles and San Francisco.
Application information: Unsolicited requests for funds not accepted.
Officers and Directors:* Patrick Soon-Shiong,* Pres.; Michele Soon-Shiong,* Secy. and C.F.O.; Charles Kenworthy, Exec. V.P.
EIN: 264384360
Other changes: For the fiscal year ended Sept. 30, 2013, the grantmaker paid grants of $4,944,927, a 283.6% increase over the fiscal 2011 disbursements, $1,289,002.

149

Ping and Amy Chao Family Foundation

445 S. San Antonio Rd., Ste. 204
Los Altos, CA 94022-3638 (650) 924-1104
***Contact:* Ping Chao, Chair.**
FAX: (650) 434-3770;
E-mail: info@chaofoundation.org; China address: No. 1 Shanyuan St., Rm. 1-307, Haidian District, Beijing, China; Main URL: http://www.chaofoundation.org
Facebook: https://www.facebook.com/chaofoundation
Twitter: https://twitter.com/eastvillagers

Established in 2006 in CA.
Donor: Chao Family Trust.
Foundation type: Independent foundation.
Financial data (yr. ended 11/30/12): Assets, $9,906,161 (M); expenditures, $945,948; qualifying distributions, $920,383; giving activities include $646,150 for 15 grants (high: $200,000; low: $150), and $113,270 for 1 foundation-administered program.
Purpose and activities: Giving primarily to fund and nurture initiatives improving the health and well-being of children and youth in economically disadvantaged regions throughout the world, as well as to promote the spirit of philanthropy and developing awareness of non-profit practices and opportunities for service for the younger generation of China and the greater Chinese Diaspora. Because of these focuses, the foundation seeks to fund grants that either are run by a member of the Asian American community, or that focus on work in Asia or the Asian American community.
Fields of interest: Education; Human services; International affairs, goodwill promotion; Christian agencies & churches.
Limitations: Giving primarily in CA; some giving also NY. No grants to individuals.
Application information:
Initial approach: Use online application on foundation web site
Deadline(s): See foundation web site for current deadlines
Officers and Trustees:* Ping Chao,* Chair.; Amy Chao,* V.P.; Nancy Nguyen, Exec. Dir.
EIN: 206750125

150

Chartwell Charitable Foundation

1999 Ave. of the Stars, Ste. 3050
Los Angeles, CA 90067-4613 (310) 556-7600

Established in 1998 in CA.
Donor: A. Jerrold Perenchio.
Foundation type: Independent foundation.
Financial data (yr. ended 12/31/13): Assets, $830 (M); gifts received, $6,661,013; expenditures, $6,659,851; qualifying distributions, $6,637,812; giving activities include $6,615,000 for 89 grants (high: $500,000; low: $2,500).
Fields of interest: Arts; Higher education; Education; Environment; Hospitals (general); Human services; Children/youth, services.
Limitations: Applications accepted. Giving primarily in CA and NY.
Application information:
Initial approach: Letter
Deadline(s): None
Officers and Trustee:* A. Jerrold Perenchio,* Chair. and Exec. V.P.; Margaret A. Perenchio, Pres.; Robert V. Cahill, V.P.; Michael A. Enright, Secy.; Kathleen Antion, C.F.O. and Treas.
EIN: 954679659
Other changes: At the close of 2013, the grantmaker paid grants of $6,615,000, a 66.5% increase over the 2012 disbursements, $3,974,060.

151

The Christensen Fund

260 Townsend St., Ste. 600
San Francisco, CA 94107-1719 (415) 644-1600
Contact: Lourdes Inga, Grants Admin.
FAX: (415) 644-1601;
E-mail: info@christensenfund.org; Main URL: http://www.christensenfund.org
Facebook: http://www.facebook.com/pages/The-Christensen-Fund/170421729636697
Grants Database: http://www.christensenfund.org/funding/grants-search/
Philanthropy's Promise: http://www.ncrp.org/philanthropys-promise/who

The Christensen Fund's Philanthropy Promise: http://www.ncrp.org/philanthropys-promise/who
Twitter: http://twitter.com/christensenfund
YouTube: https://www.youtube.com/user/ChristensenFund?feature=mhee

Incorporated in 1957 in CA.
Donors: Allen D. Christensen‡; Carmen M. Christensen‡.
Foundation type: Independent foundation.
Financial data (yr. ended 12/31/12): Assets, $233,568,073 (M); gifts received, $145,528,544; expenditures, $18,951,176; qualifying distributions, $18,203,202; giving activities include $13,420,603 for grants, and $13,670 for employee matching gifts.
Purpose and activities: The fund believes in the power of biological and cultural diversity to sustain and enrich a world faced with great change and uncertainty. Focus is on "bio-cultural" - the rich but neglected adaptive interweave of people and place, culture and ecology. The fund's mission is to buttress the efforts of people and institutions who believe in a biodiverse world infused with artistic expression and work to secure ways of life and landscapes that are beautiful, bountiful and resilient. The fund pursues this mission through place-based work in the region chosen for their potential to withstand and recover from the global erosion of diversity. Focus is on backing the efforts of locally-recognized community custodians of this heritage, and their alliances with scholars, artists, advocates and others. International efforts are also funded to help build global understanding of these issues. The fund works primarily through capacity and network building, knowledge generation, collaboration and mission-related investments.
Fields of interest: Arts, cultural/ethnic awareness; Visual arts; Museums; Environment, research; Environment, natural resources; Environment; Biology/life sciences; Native Americans/American Indians; Indigenous peoples.
International interests: Papua New Guinea; Kyrgyz Republic; Australia; Vanuatu; Tajikistan; Mexico.
Type of support: Continuing support; Equipment; Program development; Conferences/seminars; Seed money; Fellowships; Research; Program evaluation; Matching/challenge support.
Limitations: Applications accepted. Giving primarily in the Southwest (Four Corners region), northern Mexico (including the Colorado Plateau and Delta, the Pueblo and Hispanic communities of the Rio Arriba/Rio Grande, the Sonoran Desert on both sides of the Mexican-U.S. border and east of the Colorado River, and the Sierra Tarahumara Montane West), Central Asia (the mountains and associated valleys of northeastern Turkey, the Kyrgyz Republic, and Tajikistan), the Rift Valley (especially southwest Ethiopia and adjacent areas of northern Kenya) Northern Australia (especially Arhem Land, Far Northern Queensland, and the Kimberley and Torres Strait Islands), and Melanesia, (Papua New Guinea and Vanuatu). No grants to individuals, or for capital funds, or building or renovation funding; no loans.
Publications: Financial statement; Grants list; Program policy statement (including application guidelines).
Application information: Please refer to the fund's web site for guidelines and program areas. For events such as conferences and workshops, apply at least six months in advance of their starting date to enable timely review and grant processing. Application form required.
Initial approach: Pre-proposal as outlined on fund's web site
Copies of proposal: 1
Deadline(s): Submit pre-proposal between July 15 and Sept. 15 (for next calendar year)
Board meeting date(s): Quarterly
Final notification: 8 weeks
Officers and Directors:* Atossa Soltani,* Chair.; E. Walter Coward, Jr., Ph.D.*, Vice-Chair.; C. Diane Christensen,* Pres.; Albert Fong, C.F.O. and Dir., Finance and Investment; **Peter Liu,* Treas.**; Kenneth Wilson, Ph.D., Exec. Dir.; **Theresa Fay-Bustillos**; Winona LaDuke; Thomas K. Seligman; Richard Williams; Michael Nicoll Yahgulanaas.
Number of staff: 4 full-time professional; 5 full-time support; 1 part-time support.
EIN: 946055879
Other changes: At the close of 2012, the fair market value of the grantmaker's assets was $233,568,073, a 152.3% increase over the 2011 value, $92,581,188.
Peter Liu has replaced Kenneth Kirshenbaum as Treas. Peter Liu has replaced Kenneth Kirshenbaum as Treas.
Albert Fong is now C.F.O. and Dir., Finance and Investment. E. Walter Coward, Jr. is now Vice-Chair. C. Diane Christensen is now Pres. Atossa Soltani is now Chair. John G. Robinson is no longer a trustee. Tara Diann Stein is no longer Secy. Rodolfo Dirzo is no longer a trustee.

152
Clif Bar Family Foundation
1451 66th St.
Emeryville, CA 94608-1004 (510) 596-6383
E-mail: familyfoundation@clifbar.com; E-mail for Seed Matters Program: seedmatters@clifbarfamilyfoundation.org; Main URL: http://www.clifbarfamilyfoundation.org
Grants List: http://clifbarfamilyfoundation.org/Grantees/Grantees-Map
Seed Matters Blog: http://www.seedmatters.org/the-seed-commons/
Seed Matters on Facebook: http://www.facebook.com/seedmatters
Seed Matters on Twitter: http://twitter.com/Seed_Matters/

Established in 2006 in CA.
Donor: Clif Bar & Co.
Foundation type: Company-sponsored foundation.
Financial data (yr. ended 12/31/12): Assets, $607,545 (M); gifts received, $3,278,609; expenditures, $2,775,695; qualifying distributions, $2,875,694; giving activities include $2,410,535 for 308 grants (high: $95,000; low: $550), and $100,000 for loans/program-related investments.
Purpose and activities: The foundation supports programs designed to strengthen the food system and community; enhance public health; and safeguard the environment and natural resources. Special emphasis is directed toward grassroots organizations that have the ability to engage local groups.
Fields of interest: Arts; Education; Environment, pollution control; Environment, air pollution; Environment, waste management; Environment, climate change/global warming; Environment, natural resources; Environment, land resources; Environment, energy; Environment; Employment; Agriculture, community food systems; Agriculture, sustainable programs; Agriculture, farmlands; Food services; Agriculture/food; Housing/shelter; Youth, services; Human services; Community development, small businesses.
Type of support: Donated products; General/operating support; Management development/capacity building; Annual campaigns; Program development; Fellowships; Consulting services.
Limitations: Applications accepted. Giving primarily in CA. No support for religious groups or state agencies. No grants to individuals, or for seminar, media, or fundraising events that are not an integral part of a broader program, capital construction, endowments, or debt reduction.
Publications: Application guidelines; Grants list.
Application information: The average award for Small Grants is $8,000. Capacity-Building Grants, Long-Term Partnerships, and Consulting Grants are by invitation only. Application form required.
Initial approach: Complete online questionnaire and application for Small Grants
***Deadline(s):* Feb. 15, May 15, Aug. 15, and Nov. 1 for Small Grants**
Board meeting date(s): Quarterly
Officers: Kathleen F. Crawford, Pres.; Gary J. Erickson, Secy.-Treas.
EIN: 204345935

153
The Clorox Company Foundation
1221 Broadway
Oakland, CA 94612-1888 (510) 836-3223
E-mail: cloroxfndt@eastbaycf.org; Mailing address: c/o East Bay Community Foundation, De Domenico Bldg., 200 Frank Ogawa Plz., Oakland, CA 94612; Main URL: http://www.thecloroxcompany.com/corporate-responsibility/purpose/clorox-company-foundation/

Incorporated in 1980 in CA.
Donor: The Clorox Co.
Foundation type: Company-sponsored foundation.
Financial data (yr. ended 06/30/13): Assets, $2,147,290 (M); gifts received, $5,705,183; expenditures, $5,996,718; qualifying distributions, $5,793,125; giving activities include $5,793,125 for grants.
Purpose and activities: The foundation supports organizations involved with arts and culture, K-12 education, disaster relief, and youth development. Grants are administered by the East Bay Community Foundation.
Fields of interest: Visual arts; Performing arts; Arts; Elementary/secondary education; Disasters, preparedness/services; Youth development; Voluntarism promotion; Children/youth; Children; Youth; Girls; Boys; Economically disadvantaged.
Type of support: General/operating support; Program development; Scholarship funds; Employee volunteer services; Employee matching gifts; Employee-related scholarships; Donated products.
Limitations: Applications accepted. Giving primarily in areas of company operations, with emphasis on the Oakland, CA, area; giving on a national and international basis for disaster relief. No support for national organizations, religious organizations not of direct benefit to the entire community, political parties, candidates, or organizations, or exclusive membership organizations. No grants for fundraising, athletic events or league sponsorships, travel, advertising or promotional sponsorships, tickets, conferences, conventions, meetings, or similar events, media production, political activities, dues, debt reduction, capital campaigns, or individual school projects.
Publications: Application guidelines; Annual report (including application guidelines).
Application information: Unsolicited requests for scholarship funds are not accepted. East Bay Community Foundation staff receives all applications and reviews them on behalf of The Clorox Company Foundation. Application form required.
Initial approach: Complete online application form

Deadline(s): Jan. 1, Apr. 1, July 1, and Oct. 1
Board meeting date(s): Mar. and Sept.
Final notification: 2 months following deadlines
Officers and Trustees:* Donald R. Knauss,* Chair.; Jacqueline P. Kane,* Pres.; Victoria Jones, V.P. and Secy.; Charles R. Conradi, V.P. and Treas.; Jeffrey R. Brubaker; Benno Dorer; Paola Gonzalez.
EIN: 942674980
Other changes: Nichelle Rachal is now Sr. Community Rels. Specialist.

154
The James and Paula Coburn Foundation
3550 Wilshire Blvd., Ste. 840
Los Angeles, CA 90010-2433
***E-mail:* lynda@jamesandpaulacoburnfoundation.org**; Main URL: http://jamesandpaulacoburnfoundation.org/
Facebook: https://www.facebook.com/JamesandPaulaCoburnFoundation
Grants List: http://jamesandpaulacoburnfoundation.org/beneficiaries/
Twitter: https://twitter.com/jpcoburnfdtn

Donors: Coburn Survivor's Trust; Soleyman John Nobatian; Julius Gianninni.
Foundation type: Independent foundation.
Financial data (yr. ended 06/30/13): Assets, $3,348,455 (M); expenditures, $594,295; qualifying distributions, $530,345; giving activities include $206,000 for 8 grants (high: $100,000; low: $1,000).
Purpose and activities: Giving to support the arts and sciences, and to charities involved in the treatments or cures for cancer and the care of indigent cancer patients.
Fields of interest: Media/communications; Arts; Health care; Cancer; Human services.
Limitations: Applications not accepted. Giving primarily in CA and VA. No grants to individuals.
Application information: Contributes only to pre-selected organizations.
Trustees: Lynda Erkiletian; Robert Harabedian; Cynthia Webb.
EIN: 201512237

155
Teddy Cole Foundation for Horses Inc
4976 Sunline Ave.
San Diego, CA 92117-1613

Established in 2002 in CA.
Donor: Theora Ruth Cole.
Foundation type: Independent foundation.
Financial data (yr. ended 12/31/12): Assets, $0 (M); gifts received, $8,849; expenditures, $238,108; qualifying distributions, $169,298; giving activities include $166,600 for 7 grants (high: $48,000; low: $2,000).
Fields of interest: Animal welfare; Athletics/sports, equestrianism.
Limitations: Applications not accepted. Giving primarily in CA. No grants to individuals.
Application information: Contributes only to pre-selected organizations.
Officers: Jill Eshenbaugh, Pres.; **Kris Kudas, Secy.-Treas.**
Director: Brian Maryott.
EIN: 431957535
Other changes: Jill Eshenbaugh is now Pres. Kris Kudas is now Secy.-Treas.

156
The College Access Foundation of California
(formerly The Education Financing Foundation of California)
1 Front St., Ste. 1325
San Francisco, CA 94111-5325 (415) 287-1800
Contact: Stefanie Charren, Office Admin.; Jessica Eting, Grants. Admin.
FAX: (415) 287-1801;
E-mail: info@collegeaccessfoundation.org; Main URL: http://www.collegeaccessfoundation.org
Facebook: https://www.facebook.com/CollegeAccessCA
LinkedIn: http://www.linkedin.com/company/college-access-foundation-of-california
Twitter: https://twitter.com/CollegeAccessCA

Established in 1979 in CA; status changed to a independent foundation in 2010; created from the sale of Chela Education Financing.
Foundation type: Independent foundation.
Financial data (yr. ended 12/31/12): Assets, $427,137,138 (M); expenditures, $26,063,631; qualifying distributions, $22,882,243; giving activities include $19,773,196 for 407 grants (high: $850,000; low: $730), $24,126 for 55 employee matching gifts, and $533,912 for 4 foundation-administered programs.
Purpose and activities: The foundation helps qualified students in California who have financial need attend and graduate from college, by providing grants to community-based programs that use their funds to award college scholarships to the students they serve. Their grantees also support students by connecting them to on-campus mentoring and other services to help them stay in school and graduate. Current strategies include: 1. Supporting programs that offer college advice and academic support to young adults with significant need, including first generation college-goers and groups that have historically low enrollment or completion rates. 2. Supporting and testing new and innovative approaches to scholarship giving that have the potential to increase college enrollment and persistence in school. 3. Fostering greater networking and sharing of best practices among scholarship programs in the state, and offering evidence that will increase scholarship giving and promote a more effective public financial aid system.
Fields of interest: Higher education; Scholarships/financial aid.
Type of support: Program development; General/operating support; Scholarship funds; Employee matching gifts.
Limitations: Giving primarily in CA. No grants to individuals directly.
Publications: Application guidelines.
Application information: The majority of grants are identified by the proactive work of the foundation's program staff.
Initial approach: Online inquiry form and by invitation
Copies of proposal: 1
Deadline(s): Check web site for inquiry deadlines.
Final notification: 60 days after submission of application
Officers and Directors:* Toby Rosenblatt,* Chair.; Russell S. Gould,* Vice-Chair.; Julia I. Lopez,* C.E.O. and Pres.; Jacqueline Khor, V.P., Progs.; Phillipe Wallace, C.F.O. and Treas.; Krysten Curtis, Cont.; Carlene M. Ellis; Donna Lucas; N. Ross Matthews; Gretchen Hartnack Milligan; Eloy Ortiz Oakley; Linda Davis Taylor; Joseph W. Watson, Ph.D.; Richard Whitmore.
EIN: 942618667
Other changes: James E. Canales is no longer a director.

157
Community Foundation for Monterey County
2354 Garden Rd.
Monterey, CA 93940-5326 (831) 375-9712
***Contact:* Dan Baldwin, C.E.O.**; **For grants: Janet Shing, Sr. Prog. Off.**
FAX: (831) 375-4731; E-mail: info@cfmco.org;
Additional Address: 945 S. Main St., Ste. 207, Salinas, CA 93901; Additional e-mail: danb@cfmco.org; Grant inquiry e-mail: julied@cfmco.org; Main URL: http://www.cfmco.org
Facebook: http://www.facebook.com/cfmco
Grants List: http://www.cfmco.org/index.cfm/id/258/Recent-Grants/
RSS Feed: http://www.cfmco.org/modules/news/rss.cfm?type=3&featured=&limit=6
RSS Feed: http://www.cfmco.org/modules/news/rss.cfm?type=2&featured=1&limit=6
YouTube: http://www.youtube.com/user/cfmcmonterey

Incorporated in 1945 in CA.
Foundation type: Community foundation.
Financial data (yr. ended 12/31/12): Assets, $155,790,404 (M); gifts received, $14,051,003; expenditures, $10,888,180; giving activities include $8,752,128 for grants.
Purpose and activities: The foundation seeks to improve the quality of life in Monterey County by raising, managing, and distributing charitable funds to worthy organizations and by creating positive connections between donors and their interests. Primarily supports arts and cultural organizations, libraries, schools and other educational institutions, and human services organizations.
Fields of interest: Historic preservation/historical societies; Arts; Education; Environment; Animal welfare; Health care; Substance abuse, prevention; Employment; Housing/shelter; Human services; Community/economic development; Infants/toddlers; Children/youth; Children; Youth; Adults; Aging; Young adults; Disabilities, people with; Physically disabled; Blind/visually impaired; Asians/Pacific Islanders; African Americans/Blacks; Hispanics/Latinos; Native Americans/American Indians; Indigenous peoples; Offenders/ex-offenders; Substance abusers; AIDS, people with; Single parents; Crime/abuse victims; Terminal illness, people with; Immigrants/refugees; Economically disadvantaged; Homeless; Migrant workers; LGBTQ.
Type of support: General/operating support; Continuing support; Management development/capacity building; Annual campaigns; Capital campaigns; Building/renovation; Equipment; Emergency funds; Program development; Conferences/seminars; Seed money; Technical assistance; Consulting services; Matching/challenge support.
Limitations: Applications accepted. Giving primarily in Monterey County, CA. No support for sectarian religious programs. No grants to individuals (except for scholarships), or for annual campaigns, deficit financing, general endowments, fellowships, travel, fundraising campaigns or events, academic research, or publications.
Publications: Application guidelines; Annual report (including application guidelines); Informational brochure; Newsletter.
Application information: Visit foundation web site for application forms and specific guidelines per grant type. Application form required.

Initial approach: Attend an Information Session
Copies of proposal: 1
Deadline(s): Varies
Board meeting date(s): 4th Tues. of selected months
Final notification: Generally no longer than 2 months

Officers and Directors:* Gail Delorey,* Chair.; Rick Kennifer,* Vice-Chair.; Dan Baldwin,* C.E.O. and Pres.; Julie Kenny Drezner, V.P., Grants and Progs.; Catherine Kobrinsky Evans,* Secy.; Tina Starkey Lopez,* Treas.; Tonya Antle; Ann Brown; Ida Lopez Chan; Greg Chilton; Jim Claypool; Stephen Dart; Alred Diaz-Infante; Patti Hiramoto; Stephen McGowan; Kelly McMillin; Ken Petersen; John M. Phillips; Ana Marie Ponce; Raul C. Rodriguez; Kenneth R. Wright.
Number of staff: 20 full-time professional.
EIN: 941615897

158
Community Foundation for Oak Park

P.O. Box 291
Agoura Hills, CA 91376-0291 **(818) 390-0060**
Contact: Alon Glickstein, Pres.
E-mail: info@OakParkFoundation.org; Main URL: http://www.OakParkFoundation.org

Established in 1979 in CA.
Foundation type: Community foundation.
Financial data (yr. ended 06/30/13): Assets, $373,748 (M); gifts received, $48,859; expenditures, $249,586; giving activities include $86,915 for 10+ grants (high: $56,619).
Purpose and activities: The purpose of the foundation is to improve and protect the social welfare of the residents of Oak Park, CA, with special emphasis on the cultural, educational and recreational needs of the youth of the community.
Fields of interest: Arts; Elementary/secondary education; Libraries (public); Education; Environment; Recreation; Children/youth, services; Human services.
Type of support: General/operating support; Continuing support; Program development; Scholarship funds; Matching/challenge support.
Limitations: Applications accepted. Giving limited to Oak Park, CA (except Donor-Defined funds). No support for religious purposes. No grants to individuals (except for scholarships), or for endowments or building campaigns.
Publications: Application guidelines; Financial statement; Grants list; Informational brochure; Occasional report.
Application information: Visit foundation web site for application form and guidelines. Application form required.
Initial approach: Submit application form
Copies of proposal: 1
Deadline(s): None
Board meeting date(s): 2nd Tues. of Feb., May, Aug., and Nov.
Final notification: 1-4 months

Officers and Trustees:* Alon Glickstein,* Pres.; Jerry Clebanoff,* V.P.; **Barbara Schwartz,* Secy.**; Jay Kapitz,* Treas.; Eva Larson; Risa Littman; Diane Milavetz; Karen Onifer; Sherwin Samuels; **Mike Paule.**
EIN: 953416510
Other changes: Barbara Schwartz has replaced Mary Pallant as Secy.
Barbara Schwartz is no longer a trustee.

159
Community Foundation for San Benito County

829 San Benito St., Ste. 200
Hollister, CA 95023 (831) 630-1924
Contact: Gary Byrne, C.E.O.
FAX: (831) 630-1934; E-mail: info@cffsbc.org; Mailing address: P.O. Box 2062 Hollister, CA 95024-2062; Additional e-mail: gbyrne@cffsbc.org; Grant application e-mail: grants@cffsbc.org; Main URL: http://www.cffsbc.org/
Facebook: http://www.facebook.com/pages/Community-Foundation-for-San-Benito-County/106418471856

Established in 1992 in CA.
Foundation type: Community foundation.
Financial data (yr. ended 12/31/12): Assets, $5,788,631 (M); gifts received, $1,526,982; expenditures, $1,370,761; giving activities include $839,915 for 47+ grants (high: $165,000), and $25,851 for 13 grants to individuals.
Purpose and activities: The Community Foundation for San Benito County is dedicated to building a stronger community and enhancing the quality of life in San Benito County through support of philanthropic activities.
Fields of interest: Arts; Education; Environment; Medical care, outpatient care; Health care; Human services; Youth.
Limitations: Applications accepted. Giving primarily in San Benito County, CA. No support for private foundations or fundraising organizations, fraternal of service organizations, unless in support of specific programs open to or benefiting the entire community or nonprofit organizations that spend more than 25% of their revenue on management, overhead and/or fundraising costs. No grants to individuals (except for scholarships), or for annual campaigns, walk-a-thons, tournaments, fashion shows, dinners or auctions, or salaries or operating expenses of schools, government departments and agencies or related organizations.
Publications: Application guidelines.
Application information: Visit foundation web site for application forms and guidelines. Grant awards generally will range up to $25,000. Application form required.
Initial approach: E-mail application (if project will be ready to start within three months) or preliminary Intent to Submit Application (if project is expected to start later in the year)
Deadline(s): Oct. 15
Final notification: Applications will be reviewed and approved monthly, with the goal to respond to all applications within 6 to 8 weeks of their acceptance

Officers and Board Members:* Fernando Gonzalez,* Chair.; Phil Fortino,* Vice-Chair.; Gary Byrne,* C.E.O. and Pres.; Kathy Flores,* Secy.; Mike Grace,* C.F.O. and Treas.; Enrique Arreola; Marilyn Ferreira; Kay Filice; Steve Hudner; Susan Schwabacher Modic; Anne Morris; Diane Ortiz; Jim Paxton; Allison Rohnert; **Sandy Rose**; Ed Stephenson; Bob Tiffany; Rebecca Medeiros Wolf.
EIN: 770312582

160
The Community Foundation of Mendocino County, Inc.

(formerly Mendocino County Community Foundation, Inc.)
204 South Oak St.
Ukiah, CA 95482 (707) 468-9882
Contact: Susanne Norgard, Exec. Dir.
FAX: (707) 468-5529;
E-mail: info@communityfound.org; Main URL: http://www.communityfound.org
Facebook: https://www.facebook.com/pages/The-Community-Foundation-of-Mendocino-County/210963148919337

Established in 1993 in CA.
Foundation type: Community foundation.
Financial data (yr. ended 06/30/12): Assets, $15,232,357 (M); gifts received, $1,554,758; expenditures, $1,275,318; giving activities include $757,821 for grants.
Purpose and activities: The foundation helps people give back in ways that matter to them and in ways that strengthen local communities.
Fields of interest: Historic preservation/historical societies; Arts; Libraries/library science; Education; Environment; Health care; Recreation, parks/playgrounds; Recreation; Youth development, centers/clubs; Youth development, adult & child programs; Children/youth, services; Economic development; Community/economic development; Economically disadvantaged.
Type of support: Management development/capacity building; General/operating support; Equipment; Endowments; Emergency funds; Program development; Seed money; Scholarship funds; Technical assistance; Matching/challenge support.
Limitations: Applications accepted. Giving limited to Mendocino County, CA, and its service areas. No support for for-profit organizations. No grants to individuals (except for scholarships).
Publications: Annual report; Informational brochure; Newsletter.
Application information: Visit foundation web site for application form and guidelines. Faxed, e-mailed, or late submissions are not accepted. Application form required.
Initial approach: Letter of inquiry on grant programs and opportunities
Copies of proposal: 1
Deadline(s): Varies by program
Board meeting date(s): 1st Tues. monthly (except for July and Dec.)
Final notification: Varies by program

Officers and Directors:* Jim Mayfield,* Pres.; Judith Bailey,* 1st V.P.; Katie Gibbs,* 2nd V.P.; Francine Selim,* Secy.; Greg Nelson,* Treas.; Susanne Norgard, Exec. Dir.; Guilford Dye; **Claire Ellis**; Gayle Greene; James King; John Knapp; Rudy Light; Jim Moorehead; Santiago Simental.
Number of staff: 1 full-time professional; 3 part-time professional.
EIN: 680330462
Other changes: Claire Ellis and Jim Mayfield are no longer directors.

161
Community Foundation of San Joaquin

217 N. San Joaquin St., Ste. B
Stockton, CA 95202 (209) 943-2375
***Contact:* Linda J. Philipp, Pres. and C.E.O.**
FAX: (209) 593-2333; E-mail: lphilipp@cfosj.org; Main URL: http://www.cfosj.org

Established in 2007 in CA.
Donors: Assistance League of Stockton; Scott Beattie; Scott Beattie; Lorna Boothroyd; Calone Law Group; Child Abuse Prevention Council; Bridget Childs; C. Joseph Crane; Helen Crane; Credit Bureau of San Janquin County Charitable Foundation; Michael P. Duffy; Hospice of San Joaquin; IMPACT; Stefanie Leland; Ted Leland; Sandra Mazzoula; Charles G. Patmon; Dorothy N. Patmon; Irene Perkins; Paul Perkins; Larry Philipp; Linda Philipp;

San Joaquin County Office of Education Educational Foundation; United Cerebral Palsy; Francesca Vera; John R. Vera; Women's Center of San Joaquin County; Nishka M. Yudnich.
Foundation type: Community foundation.
Financial data (yr. ended 12/31/12): Assets, $3,787,204 (M); gifts received, $566,022; expenditures, $761,769; giving activities include $463,008 for 28+ grants (high: $16,616).
Purpose and activities: The foundation facilitates and develops philanthropy by providing services to donors and their advisors and by making grants to benefit the local community.
Fields of interest: Children/youth; Children; Youth; Disabilities, people with; Women; Girls; Adults, women; Young adults, female; Boys; Crime/abuse victims; Economically disadvantaged; Homeless.
Type of support: Management development/ capacity building; Endowments; Consulting services; Annual campaigns; General/operating support; Continuing support; Capital campaigns; Building/renovation; Equipment; Program development; Conferences/seminars; Scholarship funds.
Limitations: Applications accepted. Giving primarily in San Joaquin County, CA.
Publications: Grants list; Informational brochure; Newsletter; Occasional report.
Application information: Application form not required.
Initial approach: Telephone or e-mail
Copies of proposal: 1
Deadline(s): None
Board meeting date(s): Bi-monthly
Officers and Board Members:* Scott Beattie,* Chair.; Teresa Mandella,* Vice-Chair.; Linda Philipp,* Pres. and C.E.O.; Linda A. Guinn,* V.P.; Duane Isetti,* Secy.; David Vaughn,* C.F.O.; Robert Kavanaugh; Ted Leland; Ray McCray; Charles G. Patmon, III; Diana Slawson; Cynthia Souza; **David Vaccarezza**; John Vera.
Number of staff: 1 full-time professional; 2 part-time professional.
EIN: 261476916

162
Community Foundation of the Verdugos

(formerly Glendale Community Foundation)
111 E. Bdwy., Ste. 200
Glendale, CA 91205 (818) 241-8040
Contact: Edna Karinski, C.E.O.
FAX: (818) 241-8045; E-mail: info@cfverdugos.org; Main URL: http://www.cfverdugos.org/
Facebook: https://www.facebook.com/pages/Community-Foundation-of-the-Verdugos/132731506768493?sk=wall
YouTube: https://www.youtube.com/user/cfverdugos

Incorporated in 1956 in CA.
Donors: Albert Dunford‡; Pearl Gray‡; Maryon Greaves‡; Don Packer‡; Juanita Duncan‡; Bernie Larson‡; Dorothy Larson‡.
Foundation type: Community foundation.
Financial data (yr. ended 12/31/12): Assets, $9,238,660 (M); gifts received, $247,344; expenditures, $697,756; giving activities include $218,535 for 12+ grants (high: $42,883), and $89,750 for 62 grants to individuals.
Purpose and activities: The mission of the foundation is to provide financial support to a broad range of charitable and educational endeavors within the geographic area served by the foundation.
Fields of interest: Performing arts; Arts; Higher education; Adult education—literacy, basic skills & GED; Libraries (public); Education; Environment; Hospitals (general); Health care, clinics/centers; Health care; Disasters, preparedness/services; Recreation; Youth development; Children/youth, services; Family services; Residential/custodial care, hospices; Aging, centers/services; Human services; Children; Aging; Disabilities, people with; Economically disadvantaged; Homeless.
Type of support: General/operating support; Equipment; Program development; Seed money; Scholarship funds; Technical assistance; Matching/ challenge support; Student loans—to individuals.
Limitations: Applications accepted. Giving limited to the Glendale, CA, area, including La Canada-Flintridge, La Crescenta, Montrose, and Verdugo City. No support for religious purposes, or athletic groups. **No grants to individuals (except for scholarships and student loans), budget deficits, salaries, maintenance, or repairs, annual campaigns, building campaigns, conferences, multi-year funding for new programs, or endowments.**
Publications: Application guidelines; Annual report; Financial statement; Grants list; Informational brochure; Newsletter; Program policy statement (including application guidelines).
Application information: Visit foundation web site for application form and guidelines. Application form must be mailed and e-mailed to the foundation (attachments accepted via mail only). Application form required.
Initial approach: Letter, telephone, or e-mail
Copies of proposal: 1
Deadline(s): Feb. 1, May 15 and Aug. 1
Board meeting date(s): 6 times a year
Final notification: Within 8 weeks
Officers and Directors:* Robert Knauf,* Pres.; Ernest P. Burger, Esq.*, V.P.; Edna Karinski,* C.E.O.; Mary Ann Plumley,* Secy.; Michael W. Deaktor,* C.F.O.; Charles Alleman, Jr.; Eric A. Ashton, Jr.; Michael Cusumano; Toni Beck Espinoza; Norman H. Green; Arye Gross; Charles L. LeCroy, III; David S. Levy; Lawrence F. Meyer; Sunder Ramani; Jose L. Sierra; Lee Wochner.
Number of staff: 2 full-time professional.
EIN: 956068137
Other changes: Kelsea Mauerhan is now Prog. Coord. Kelsea Mauerhan is now Prog. and Scholarships Coord. Zainul Abedin and Armen Baghdasarian are no longer directors.

163
Community Foundation Santa Cruz County

(formerly The Community Foundation of Santa Cruz County)
7807 Soquel Dr.
Aptos, CA 95003 (831) 662-2000
***Contact:* Lance Linares, C.E.O.; For grants: Christina Cuevas, Prog. Dir.**
FAX: (831) 662-2001; E-mail: cfhelp@cfscc.org; Additional e-mails: lance@cfscc.org and christina@cfscc.org; Grant application e-mail: grants@cfscc.org; Main URL: http://www.cfscc.org
Blog: http://www.cfscc.org/Philanthropy831Blog.aspx
E-Newsletter: http://www.cfscc.org/Home.aspx
E-Newsletter: http://www.cfscc.org/emailnews
Facebook: http://www.facebook.com/CFSantaCruzCounty
Grants List: http://www.cfscc.org/Nonprofits/Grants/RecentGrants.aspx
LinkedIn: http://www.linkedin.com/company/community-foundation-santa-cruz-county
RSS Feed: http://feeds.feedburner.com/AboutNonprofits
Twitter: https://twitter.com/#!/CFSantaCruzCo
YouTube: http://www.youtube.com/user/CFSantaCruzCounty
Scholarship inquiry tel.: (832) 662-2072

Incorporated in 1982 in CA.
Foundation type: Community foundation.
Financial data (yr. ended 12/31/12): Assets, $56,863,547 (M); gifts received, $10,344,010; expenditures, $5,664,793; giving activities include $3,704,920 for 185+ grants (high: $150,000).
Purpose and activities: The foundation promotes local philanthropy in Santa Cruz County, CA, through grants and resources for nonprofits, donors and their professional advisors.
Fields of interest: Historic preservation/historical societies; Arts; Education; Environment; Health care; Youth development; Human services; Community/economic development.
Type of support: General/operating support; Continuing support; Management development/ capacity building; Program development; Technical assistance; Program evaluation; Scholarships—to individuals.
Limitations: Applications accepted. Giving limited to Santa Cruz County, CA. No support for religious organizations or individual (public or private) schools, as distinct from a school district. No grants to individuals (except for scholarships from designated funds), or for annual fund appeals, deficit financing, building campaigns, land acquisition, fellowships, research, endowments, fundraising events, or celebrations; no student loans.
Publications: Application guidelines; Annual report; Financial statement; Grants list; Informational brochure.
Application information: Application form required.
Initial approach: Attend a Grant Information Session
Deadline(s): Apr. 5 and July 31 for online Letter of Intent, May 20 and Sept. 10 for completed application
Board meeting date(s): Quarterly
Final notification: June 28 and Oct. 17
Officers and Directors:* Lance Linares, C.E.O.; Michael K. O'Farrell,* Pres.; Dina Hoffman,* V.P.; Linda Fawcett,* Secy.; Susan J. Farrar, C.F.O.; Michael Meara,* Treas.; Alexandra Urbick, Cont.; Caleb Baskin; Marilyn Calciano; Martin M. Chemers; Ceil Cirillo; Freny Cooper; Cynthia Druley; Janet Heien; Leola Lapides; Jerry Lopez; Rachel Mayo; Ginny Solari Mazry; Terry Medina; Carlos Palacios; Robert Ridino.
Number of staff: 5 full-time professional; 2 part-time professional; 1 full-time support; 2 part-time support.
EIN: 942808039
Other changes: Susan J. Farrar is now C.F.O. Mario Maldonado is no longer a director.

164
Congregation Joseph Jacob Abraham

344 S. Almont Dr.
Beverly Hills, CA 90211-3548

Foundation type: Independent foundation.
Financial data (yr. ended 12/31/12): Assets, $3,924,454 (M); expenditures, $380,451; qualifying distributions, $294,273; giving activities include $196,000 for 6 grants (high: $72,000; low: $6,000).
Fields of interest: Jewish agencies & synagogues.
Limitations: Applications not accepted. Giving primarily in CA and NJ.
Application information: Contributes only to pre-selected organizations.
Officer: Daniel M. Arnall, Pres.

Trustee: Tzepah Freedland.
EIN: 954746504
Other changes: The grantmaker has moved from DE to CA.

165
The Conservation Land Trust
1606 Union St.
San Francisco, CA **94123-4507**
E-mail: info@theconservationlandtrust.org; Main URL: http://www.theconservationlandtrust.org
Facebook: http://www.facebook.com/pages/The-Conservation-Land-Trust/188936124452696

Established in 1999 in CA.
Donors: Douglas R. Tompkins; Kristine M. Tompkins; Addison M. Fischer; Charities Aid Foundation.
Foundation type: Operating foundation.
Financial data (yr. ended 03/31/13): Assets, $108,439,607 (M); gifts received, $269,493; expenditures, $3,190,298; qualifying distributions, $6,753,119; giving activities include $2,141,400 for 2+ grants (high: $2,089,000), $632,911 for foundation-administered programs and $3,982,684 for loans/program-related investments (high: $2,803,684; low: $1,179,000).
Purpose and activities: Giving to the conservation of biodiversity and strategically important biota. Important but secondary considerations are good public access, public educational and interpretive programs, appropriate and ecologically sustainable economic activities, and tourist possibilities.
Fields of interest: Environment, natural resources; Environment, water resources; Environment, forests.
International interests: Argentina; Chile.
Type of support: Program-related investments/loans.
Limitations: Applications not accepted. Giving primarily in Argentina and Chile; funding also in Sausalito, CA for a Chile-based cause. No grants to individuals.
Application information: Contributes only to pre-selected organizations.
Officers and Directors:* Douglas R. Tompkins,* Pres.; Quincey T. Imhoff,* V.P.; **Esther Li, V.P.**; Debra B. Ryker,* Secy.-Treas.; Peter Buckley; Thomas Butler; Kristine M. Tompkins; George Wuerthner.
EIN: 680245471
Other changes: .

166
Helen K. and James S. Copley Foundation
(formerly James S. Copley Foundation)
2251 San Diego Ave., Ste. A-238
San Diego, CA **92110 (619) 269-8220**
***Contact:* Kimberly Koch, Secy.**

Incorporated in 1953 in CA.
Donors: The Copley Press Inc.; San Diego Union Shoe Fund; Helen K. Copley†.
Foundation type: Company-sponsored foundation.
Financial data (yr. ended 12/31/12): Assets, $4,444,966 (M); expenditures, $1,352,036; qualifying distributions, $1,340,641; giving activities include $1,340,641 for 13 grants (high: $666,666; low: $100).
Purpose and activities: The foundation supports organizations involved with arts and culture, education, animals and wildlife, health, recreation, and human services.
Fields of interest: Arts; Education; Health care.
Type of support: Capital campaigns; Building/renovation; Equipment; Endowments; Scholarship funds; Employee matching gifts.
Limitations: Applications accepted. Giving primarily in areas of company operations in CA, IL, and OH. No support for religious, fraternal, or athletic organizations, government agencies, local chapters of national organizations, public elementary or secondary schools, or public broadcasting systems. No grants to individuals, or for research, publications, conferences, general operating support, or large campaigns; no loans.
Publications: Informational brochure (including application guidelines).
Application information: Application form required.
***Initial approach:* Letter**
Copies of proposal: 1
Deadline(s): Jan. 2
Board meeting date(s): Feb.
Final notification: Following board meeting
Officers: Charles F. Patrick, Chair.; **Dean P. Dwyer, Pres.**; Robert F. Crouch, V.P.; Kimberly Koch, Secy.
EIN: 956051770
Other changes: Dean P. Dwyer has replaced David C. Copley as Pres.
Charles F. Patrick is no longer V.P. Dean P. Dwyer is no longer Treas.

167
Cotsen Family Foundation
12100 Wilshire Blvd., Ste. 920
Los Angeles, CA 90025-7100 (310) 826-0504
FAX: (310) 826-2667; E-mail: info@cotsen.org; Main URL: http://www.cotsen.org/index.html
E-Newsletter: http://cotsen.org/topic/news/
Knowledge Center: http://cotsen.org/thoughts-on-teaching-excellence/

Established in 1984 in CA.
Donor: Lloyd E. Cotsen.
Foundation type: Independent foundation.
Financial data (yr. ended 06/30/13): Assets, $70,867,396 (M); expenditures, $5,183,350; qualifying distributions, $5,037,345; giving activities include $3,074,960 for 13 grants (high: $608,541; low: $3,972).
Purpose and activities: The foundation provides grants to schools and districts to support the Art of Teaching mentoring program.
Fields of interest: Elementary/secondary education; Higher education; Education.
Limitations: Applications not accepted. Giving limited to CA. No grants to individuals.
Application information: Contributes only to pre-selected organizations.
Officers and Directors:* Lloyd Cotsen,* Chair.; Dr. Barry Munitz,* Pres.; David Hardacre, V.P. and Secy.; **Marilyn Payne, C.F.O.**; **Jerry Harris, Exec. Dir.**; Margit Cotsen; Peggy Funkhauser; Gary K. Hart; Dr. Steven Koblik; **Lucia Laguarda**; Dr. Steven Lavine.
EIN: 953953038
Other changes: Marilyn Payne has replaced Lyn Tansey as C.F.O. Jerry Harris has replaced Judy Johnson, Ed.D. as Exec. Dir.

168
S. H. Cowell Foundation
595 Market St., Ste. 950
San Francisco, CA 94105-2816 (415) 397-0285
Contact: Lise Maisano, V.P., Grant Progs.
FAX: (415) 986-6786; Main URL: http://www.shcowell.org
Grantee Perception Report: http://www.shcowell.org/docs/Granteeperceptionstudy.pdf
Grants Database: http://www.shcowell.org/sections/grantsinaction/gra_database.php
Grants In Action: http://www.shcowell.org/sections/grantsinaction/gra_results.php
Strategic Plan 2009-2019: http://www.shcowell.org/docs/Strategic%20Plan.pdf

Established in 1956 in CA.
Donor: S.H. Cowell†.
Foundation type: Independent foundation.
Financial data (yr. ended 12/31/12): Assets, $125,826,180 (M); expenditures, $6,348,536; qualifying distributions, $5,265,338; giving activities include $3,699,935 for 86 grants (high: $266,000; low: $1,000).
Purpose and activities: The goal of the foundation is to improve the quality of life of children and families living in Northern and Central California by making grants that directly support and strengthen children, families, and the neighborhoods where they live. Priority is given to communities where Cowell has made, or could make, place-based complementary grants in Northern and Central California towns and neighborhoods where there is widespread and acute poverty and there are strong working relationships among residents and institutional leaders. The foundation funds efforts to increase a town or neighborhood's capacity to engage and serve its low-income families. These guidelines apply across all program areas: Family Resources Centers, K-12 Public Education, Responsive, Youth Development and affordable Housing.
Fields of interest: Education; Housing/shelter; Youth development; Human services; Infants/toddlers; Children/youth; Children; Youth; Minorities; Asians/Pacific Islanders; African Americans/Blacks; Hispanics/Latinos; Native Americans/American Indians; Girls; Boys; Economically disadvantaged.
Type of support: Mission-related investments/loans; General/operating support; Management development/capacity building; Capital campaigns; Building/renovation; Equipment; Land acquisition; Emergency funds; Program development; Seed money; Curriculum development; Technical assistance; Consulting services; Program-related investments/loans; Matching/challenge support.
Limitations: Applications accepted. Giving limited to Northern and Central California. No support for projects restricted to people with specific medical, physical, or health conditions, daycare centers, drug or alcohol abuse programs, environmental or conservation programs, medical service projects, political lobbying, population programs, post-secondary education, projects that are the responsibility of government agencies (except for school districts), or sectarian, politically partisan, or religious projects. No grants to individuals, or for special events conferences, books, films, videos, academic or medical research.
Publications: Application guidelines; Financial statement; Grants list; Occasional report; Program policy statement; Program policy statement (including application guidelines).
Application information: Applicants should submit the following:1. Brief history of organization and description of its mission2. Geographic area and population to be served3. Detailed description of project and amount of funding requested4. Timetable for implementation and evaluation of project5. Results expected from proposed grant6. Copy of most recent annual report/audited financial statement7. Board of Directors Roster8. Budget for

proposed workflow9. Copy of IRS 501 (c) (3) Determination Letter. Application form not required.
Initial approach: Visit foundation web site, then telephone inquiry
Copies of proposal: 1
Deadline(s): None
Board meeting date(s): Five times a year
Final notification: 3 to 6 months
Officers and Directors:* Ann Alpers,* Pres.; **Don Roberts, Secy. and Genl. Counsel**; Dr. Lisa Backus; Charles E. Ellwein; Dr. Mikiko Huang; Scott Mosher; Lydia Tan; **Kim Thompson.**
Number of staff: 7 full-time professional; 4 part-time professional.
EIN: 941392803
Other changes: Don Roberts is now Secy. and Genl. Counsel.

169
Craigslist Charitable Fund
222 Sutter St., 9th Fl.
San Francisco, CA 94108-4460
E-mail: charitable@craigslist.org; Main URL: http://www.craigslist.org/about/charitable

Donor: Craigslist, Inc.
Foundation type: Company-sponsored foundation.
Financial data (yr. ended 12/31/12): Assets, $12,512,514 (M); gifts received, $7,000,000; expenditures, $2,626,341; qualifying distributions, $2,626,341; giving activities include $2,618,669 for 171 grants (high: $206,297).
Purpose and activities: The fund supports programs designed to promote human rights, justice, and education; the environment and transportation; non-violence, world peace, and veteran's issues; and journalism, software, and internet.
Fields of interest: Media, film/video; Media, journalism; Higher education; Education; Environment, energy; Environment; Children/youth, services; Human services; International peace/security; Civil/human rights; Economic development; Computer science; Military/veterans' organizations; Transportation.
Type of support: General/operating support.
Limitations: Applications accepted. Giving primarily in CA and NY.
Publications: Application guidelines.
Application information: Special consideration is given to organizations with annual budgets less than $1 million. Application form required.
Initial approach: E-mail foundation for application inquires
***Deadline(s):* None**
Officers and Directors:* James Buckmaster,* Pres.; Craig Alexander Newmark,* Secy. and C.F.O.
EIN: 263823367

170
Crail-Johnson Foundation
461 W. 6th St., Ste. 300
San Pedro, CA **90731-2678** (310) 519-7413
***Contact:* Alan C. Johnson, Pres.**
FAX: (310) 519-7221;
E-mail: grantrequest@crail-johnson.org; Additional e-mail: carolyn-johnson@crail-johnson.org; Main URL: http://www.crail-johnson.org

Established in 1987 in CA.
Donors: Jerry L. Johnson†; Robert Johnson†; Robert Johnson Charitable Lead Trust.
Foundation type: Independent foundation.
Financial data (yr. ended 12/31/12): Assets, $22,237,269 (M); expenditures, $1,856,693; qualifying distributions, $1,195,228; giving activities include $1,077,415 for 52+ grants (high: $50,000; low: $100), and $19,000 for 30 employee matching gifts.
Purpose and activities: The foundation promotes the well-being of children in need through the effective application of human and financial resources.
Fields of interest: Education, early childhood education; Child development, education; Elementary school/education; Education, reading; Health care; Children/youth, services; Child development, services; Family services; Science; Mathematics; Economically disadvantaged.
Type of support: General/operating support; Capital campaigns; Equipment; Emergency funds; Program development; Seed money; Curriculum development; Employee matching gifts; Matching/challenge support.
Limitations: Giving primarily in Los Angeles County and the greater Los Angeles, CA, area. Generally no support for athletic events, religious programs and causes, political causes, or for university level education. No grants to individuals, or for research.
Publications: Application guidelines; Annual report (including application guidelines); Financial statement; Grants list.
Application information: Please do not send unsolicited proposals with extensive attachments and/or videotapes. Proposals are by invitation only, after review of letter of inquiry. See foundation web site for guidelines. Application form required.
Initial approach: Letter of inquiry (no more than 3 pages)
Copies of proposal: 1
Deadline(s): Oct. through Dec. for letters of inquiry; proposals deadline dates vary
Board meeting date(s): Quarterly
Officers and Directors:* Eric C. Johnson,* Chair.; Alan C. Johnson,* Pres.; Ann L. Johnson,* V.P.; Carolyn E. Johnson,* V.P.; Craig C. Johnson,* V.P.; Jack S. Peterson,* Secy.; Byung Kim,* C.F.O.; Dorothy Courtney; Elizabeth Schindler-Johnson; and 7 additional directors.
Number of staff: 1 full-time professional.
EIN: 330247161

171
James G. Cummings Foundation
c/o Robert Petersen & Randy Decaminada
519 S. School St.
Ukiah, CA 95482-5437 (707) 462-5860
Contact: Robert Petersen, Tr.; Randy Decaminada, Tr.

Established in 1998 in CA.
Donor: James G. Cummings Trust.
Foundation type: Independent foundation.
Financial data (yr. ended 12/31/12): Assets, $3,639,837 (M); expenditures, $210,066; qualifying distributions, $148,804; giving activities include $85,667 for 18 grants (high: $12,000; low: $500).
Purpose and activities: Giving for the health and well-being of children, youth, and families, with priority to early intervention and academic enrichment programs.
Fields of interest: Education; Health care; Human services; Children/youth, services; Family services.
Type of support: General/operating support; Scholarship funds.
Limitations: Applications accepted. Giving limited to Mendocino County, CA.
Application information: Application form required.
Initial approach: Telephone
Deadline(s): None
Trustees: Randy Decaminada; Robert C. Petersen.
Number of staff: 1 full-time professional.
EIN: 686170773

172
Cuore Foundation
859 Corporate Way
Fremont, CA 94539-6115 **(510) 657-2467**
***Main URL:* http://www.cuorefoundation.org/index.html**

Established in 2007 in CA.
Foundation type: Independent foundation.
Financial data (yr. ended 03/31/13): Assets, $697,577 (M); gifts received, $6,822; expenditures, $106,847; qualifying distributions, $102,618; giving activities include $102,618 for 8 grants (high: $60,118; low: $500).
Purpose and activities: Giving for the encouragement of children and teenagers facing social vulnerability.
Fields of interest: Children/youth, services; International affairs.
International interests: Brazil.
Limitations: Applications not accepted. Giving primarily in Brazil.
Application information: Unsolicited requests for funds not accepted.
Officer: Daniel Dalarossa, Pres.; Elza Harumi Dalarossa, Secy.
EIN: 205106120

173
John Curci Family Foundation
P.O. Box 1549
Newport Beach, CA **92663-1549**
***Application address:* c/o Patricia Soldano, 151 Kalmus Dr., Ste. J-1, Costa Mesa, CA 92626, tel.: (714) 641-1402**

Established in 2004 in CA.
Donor: John Curci Trust.
Foundation type: Independent foundation.
Financial data (yr. ended 12/31/12): Assets, $41,603,963 (M); gifts received, $4,768,482; expenditures, $1,733,494; qualifying distributions, $1,518,606; giving activities include $1,482,500 for 22 grants (high: $815,000; low: $1,000).
Purpose and activities: Giving primarily for health care, including a medical center; support also for education.
Fields of interest: Education; Hospitals (general); Health care; Human services; Children/youth, services; Catholic agencies & churches.
Limitations: Applications accepted. Giving primarily in southern CA.
Application information:
Initial approach: Letter
***Deadline(s):* None**
Directors: John Curci; Robert Curci; Janet Curci Walsh.
EIN: 201477014

174
The Shurl & Kay Curci Foundation
(formerly The TDC Foundation)
2377 Crenshaw Blvd., No. 300
Torrance, CA 90501-3330

Established in 2007 in CA.

Donor: Shurl Curci.
Foundation type: Independent foundation.
Financial data (yr. ended 02/28/13): Assets, $28,568,716 (M); gifts received, $7,000,000; expenditures, $970,150; qualifying distributions, $825,000; giving activities include $825,000 for 6 grants (high: $200,000; low: $75,000).
Fields of interest: Cancer; Health organizations; Medical research.
Limitations: Applications not accepted. Giving primarily in CA and NY. No grants to individuals.
Application information: Unsolicited requests for funds not accepted.
Officers: Ronald V. Rosequist,* Pres.; Amy E. Fuermann, Secy.; Roberta P. Irish, Treas. and C.F.O.
Directors: Kay Curci; Shurl Curci; Thomas G. Irish; Bruce Levine.
EIN: 205242604

175
The Cush Family Foundation
(formerly Cush Automotive Charitable Foundation)
10620 Treena St., Ste. 110
San Diego, CA 92131-1140 **(858) 549-2874**
Contact: Johnna Ridenour, Admin.
***FAX:* (866) 707-5843;**
E-mail: jridenour@cushnet.net; Main URL: http://www.cushenterprises.com

Established in 1994 in CA.
Donors: Stephen P. Cushman; Noyce Foundation.
Foundation type: Independent foundation.
Financial data (yr. ended 06/30/13): Assets, $9,037,459 (M); gifts received, $8,700; expenditures, $395,119; qualifying distributions, $395,119; giving activities include $301,810 for 61 grants (high: $180,000; low: $85).
Fields of interest: Education; Health organizations, association; Human services; Children, services; Foundations (community).
Limitations: Applications accepted. Giving primarily in San Diego, CA. No grants to individuals.
Application information: Application form available on foundation web site. Application form required.
Deadline(s): None
Officers: Marjorie L. Cushman, Pres.; Lori A. Moore, V.P.; Debra L. Parrish, Secy.; Johnna Ridenour, Admin.
Director: Stephen P. Cushman.
EIN: 330643458

176
CW Film Foundation, Inc.
(doing business as The Global Film Initiative)
145 9th St., Ste. 105
San Francisco, CA 94103-2637 (415) 934-9500
Contact: Santhosh Daniel, Dir., Progs.
FAX: (415) 934-9501;
E-mail: gfi-info@globalfilm.org; Main URL: http://www.globalfilm.org
Grants List: http://globalfilm.org/granting_past.htm

Foundation type: Independent foundation.
Financial data (yr. ended 06/30/11): Assets, $636,547 (M); gifts received, $511,320; expenditures, $960,048; qualifying distributions, $945,383; giving activities include $157,500 for grants, and $686,921 for 3 foundation-administered programs.
Purpose and activities: The initiative promotes cross-cultural understanding through the medium of cinema by supporting the production of authentic and accessible stories created in the developing world, and their distribution through the schools and leading cultural institutions of the U.S.
Fields of interest: Media, film/video; Education; International affairs.
Type of support: Film/video/radio; Grants to individuals.
Limitations: Applications accepted. Giving limited to Africa, Asia, the Caribbean, Central and Eastern Europe, Latin America, the Middle East, and Oceana. No support for projects from Australia, Cuba, the European Union, Iran, Japan, New Zealand, Singapore, South Korea, and Taiwan. No grants for documentaries or short films.
Publications: Application guidelines.
Application information: Application form required.
Initial approach: Submit application
Copies of proposal: 2
Deadline(s): July 15 for Feature-Film Production Grants
Officer: Susan Weeks Coulter, Chair.
Board Members: Pedro Almodovar; Lucy Barreto; Jean-Pierre Bekolo; Noah Cowan; Sandra den Hamer; Christopher Doyle; Adoor Gopalakrishnan; Rashid Masharawi; Mira Nair; Carlos Reygadas; Pierre Rissient; Lita Stantic; Bela Tarr; Djamshed Usmonov; Lars von Trier; Apichatpong Weerasethakul.
EIN: 010738276

177
Dart-L Foundation
4001 Wilshire Blvd., No. F-165
Los Angeles, CA **90010-3435** (213) 480-3372

Established in 1998 in CA.
Donors: Aaron Friedman; Ira David Friedman; Jacob Friedman; Lea Friedman; Ruchel Friedman Klavan; Libby Friedman Lehmann; Tzippy Friedman Notis.
Foundation type: Independent foundation.
Financial data (yr. ended 12/31/12): Assets, $190,408,323 (M); gifts received, $5,000,000; expenditures, $9,953,688; qualifying distributions, $9,158,813; giving activities include $9,097,580 for 117 grants (high: $6,500,000; low: $180).
Purpose and activities: Giving primarily to Jewish agencies, temples, and schools.
Fields of interest: Education; Human services; Jewish agencies & synagogues.
Limitations: Applications not accepted. Giving primarily in Los Angeles, CA; some funding also in NY, with emphasis on Brooklyn. No grants to individuals.
Application information: Contributes only to pre-selected organizations.
Officers and Directors:* Jacob Friedman, Pres.; Lea Friedman, V.P.; Ira David Friedman,* C.F.O; Aaron Friedman; Ruchel Friedman Klavan; Libby Friedman Lehmann; Tzippy Friedman Notis.
EIN: 954701699

178
The Ruth and Leo David Foundation
2222 E. 17th St.
Santa Ana, CA 92705-8608

Established in 2004 in CA.
Donors: Leo David; JPIII Inc.; PGB Properties.
Foundation type: Independent foundation.
Financial data (yr. ended 12/31/12): Assets, $308,643 (M); gifts received, $109,000; expenditures, $0; qualifying distributions, $0.
Fields of interest: Jewish agencies & synagogues.
International interests: Israel.
Limitations: Applications not accepted. No grants to individuals.
Application information: Unsolicited requests for funds not accepted.
Directors: Leo David; Ruth David; **Dan Wojkowski**.
EIN: 201199793
Other changes: Boros David is no longer a director.

179
De Miranda Foundation, Inc.
P.O. Box 2127
Palos Verdes Peninsula, CA **90274-8127**

Established in 2001.
Donors: Jay R. De Miranda; Shirley Y. De Miranda.
Foundation type: Operating foundation.
Financial data (yr. ended 03/31/13): Assets, $4,445,214 (M); gifts received, $231,700; expenditures, $191,382; qualifying distributions, $191,382; giving activities include $182,054 for 12 grants (high: $72,000; low: $250).
Fields of interest: AIDS; Christian agencies & churches.
Limitations: Applications not accepted. Giving primarily in CA.
Application information: Unsolicited requests for funds not accepted.
Officers: Jay R. De Miranda, Pres.; Mary Harris, Secy.
EIN: 954855401

180
Donald C. & Elizabeth M. Dickinson Foundation
P.O. Box 7078
Rancho Santa Fe, CA 92067-7078
Contact: Martin C. Dickinson, Pres.

Established in 1995 in CA.
Donor: Elizabeth M. Dickinson.
Foundation type: Independent foundation.
Financial data (yr. ended 12/31/12): Assets, $36,018,089 (M); expenditures, $2,019,164; qualifying distributions, $1,944,745; giving activities include $1,903,950 for 26 grants (high: $400,000; low: $2,000).
Purpose and activities: Giving primarily for education, health and human services; some giving also for museums.
Fields of interest: Museums (specialized); Arts; Nursing school/education; Education; Animals/wildlife, special services; Hospitals (specialty); Human services; Children/youth, services.
Limitations: Giving primarily in San Diego, CA, funding also in Oklahoma City, OK and Portland, OR.
Application information: Application form not required.
Initial approach: Letter
Deadline(s): Oct. 31
Officers: Martin C. Dickinson, Pres.; **Donald Smoyer, V.P.**; Barry C. Fitzpatrick, Secy.; **Rebecca Welch, Treas.**
Directors: Kristopher Dickinson; **John Seiber**.
EIN: 330653203
Other changes: Donald Smoyer has replaced Elizabeth D. Smoyer as V.P. Rebecca Welch has replaced Don Smoyer as Treas.

181
The Walt Disney Company Foundation
500 S. Buena Vista St.
Burbank, CA 91521-6444
Main URL: http://corporate.disney.go.com/responsibility/index.html

Incorporated in 1951 in CA.
Donor: The Walt Disney Co.
Foundation type: Company-sponsored foundation.
Financial data (yr. ended 09/29/12): Assets, $2,683,614 (M); expenditures, $4,856,807; qualifying distributions, $4,622,475; giving activities include $1,928,500 for 6 grants (high: $985,000; low: $1,098), and $2,693,975 for 1,132 employee matching gifts.
Purpose and activities: The foundation supports organizations involved with arts and culture, education, the environment, and programs involved with the health and well-being of children and youth.
Fields of interest: Media/communications; Media, film/video; Media, television; Arts; Scholarships/financial aid; Education; Environment, land resources; Environment; Health care, clinics/centers; Health care; Children/youth, services.
Type of support: General/operating support; Continuing support; Annual campaigns; Capital campaigns; Program development; Scholarship funds; Employee matching gifts; Employee-related scholarships.
Limitations: Applications not accepted. Giving primarily in CA, DC, FL, NJ, and NY. No support for public agencies or tax-supported organizations.
Application information: Contributes only to pre-selected organizations.
Officers: Robert A. Iger, Pres.; Jay Rasulo, Sr. Exec. V.P.; Leslie Goodman, Sr. V.P.; Kevin Callahan, V.P.; Marsha L. Reed, Secy.; Christine M. McCarthy, Treas.
EIN: 956037079
Other changes: At the close of 2012, the grantmaker paid grants of $4,622,475, a 77.8% increase over the 2011 disbursements, $2,599,687.
The grantmaker has changed its fiscal year-end from Oct. 1 to Sept. 29.

182
Roy Disney Family Foundation
c/o Shamrock Holdings, Inc.
4444 Lakeside Dr.
P.O. Box 7774
Burbank, CA 91510-7774

Incorporated in 1969 in CA.
Donors: Roy E. Disney; Roy O. Disney†; Edna F. Disney; Patricia Disney†; Redna Inc.; Susan D. Loughman 1997 Charitable Remainder Annuity Trust.
Foundation type: Independent foundation.
Financial data (yr. ended 05/31/13): Assets, $9,814,941 (M); expenditures, $26,772; qualifying distributions, $4,385.
Fields of interest: Environment; Human services.
Limitations: Applications not accepted. Giving primarily in Boise, ID and Washington, DC. No grants to individuals, or for building or endowment funds.
Application information: Contributes only to pre-selected organizations.
Officers: Susan Disney Lord, Pres.; Pierre Hauser, V.P.; **Caitlin Disney, Secy.**; Kathleen Galli, Treas.
Directors: Tom R. Camp; Timothy J. Disney.
EIN: 237028399
Other changes: Caitlin Disney has replaced Roy P. Disney as Secy.

183
The Walt and Lilly Disney Foundation
(formerly The Lillian B. Disney Foundation)
P.O. Box 2566
San Anselmo, CA 94979-2566

Established in 1974 in CA.
Donor: Lillian B. Disney†.
Foundation type: Independent foundation.
Financial data (yr. ended 12/31/12): Assets, $160,439,733 (M); gifts received, $9; expenditures, $12,003,865; qualifying distributions, $11,040,385; giving activities include $11,030,871 for 9 grants (high: $8,809,871; low: $10,000).
Purpose and activities: Giving primarily for the arts, education and human services.
Fields of interest: Arts; Education; Human services.
Type of support: General/operating support.
Limitations: Applications not accepted. Giving primarily in CA. No grants to individuals.
Application information: Contributes only to pre-selected organizations.
Board meeting date(s): Annually
Officers: Ronald W. Miller, Sr., V.P.; Walter E.D. Miller, Secy.
EIN: 237425637
Other changes: Diane Disney Miller, Pres., is deceased. Christopher D. Miller is no longer V.P.

184
DJ & T Foundation
200 N. Larchmont Blvd., No. 3
Los Angeles, CA **90004-3707** (323) 465-9955
Contact: William Prappas
***FAX:* (323) 446-7187**; Main URL: http://www.djtfoundation.org

Established in 1995 in CA.
Donors: Robert W. "Bob" Barker; Nanci's Animal Rights Foundation, Inc.
Foundation type: Independent foundation.
Financial data (yr. ended 05/31/13): Assets, $2,678,019 (M); gifts received, $5,275,265; expenditures, $6,606,340; qualifying distributions, $6,606,090; giving activities include $6,469,617 for 1,438 grants (high: $1,000,000; low: $14).
Purpose and activities: Giving only to free or low cost spay/neuter clinics or spay/neuter voucher programs for companion dogs.
Fields of interest: Animal population control.
Type of support: General/operating support; Continuing support; Capital campaigns; Building/renovation; Equipment.
Limitations: Applications not accepted. Giving on a national basis. No grants to individuals.
Application information: Unsolicited requests for funds not accepted.
Board meeting date(s): As needed
Officers: Robert W. "Bob" Barker, Pres.; Kent T. Valandra, Secy.; Robert Louis Valandra, C.F.O.
Number of staff: 1 full-time support; 1 part-time support.
EIN: 954499239

185
Ray and Dagmar Dolby Family Fund
(formerly Dolby Family Foundation)
3340 Jackson St.
San Francisco, CA 94118-2019 (415) 563-7403
Contact: Dagmar Dolby, Secy.-Treas.

Established in 2002 in CA.
Donors: Ray M. Dolby†; Dagmar Dolby.
Foundation type: Independent foundation.
Financial data (yr. ended 12/31/12): Assets, $110,287,697 (M); expenditures, $1,450,849; qualifying distributions, $1,058,440; giving activities include $1,041,250 for 76 grants (high: $135,000; low: $250).
Fields of interest: Museums; Performing arts, orchestras; Performing arts, opera; Higher education; Health organizations; Human services; Civil liberties, reproductive rights.
Type of support: Annual campaigns; Capital campaigns; Building/renovation.
Limitations: Applications not accepted. Giving primarily in San Francisco, CA. No support for religious organizations.
Application information: Unsolicited requests for funds not accepted.
Board meeting date(s): Oct.
Officers: Ray M. Dolby, Pres.; Dagmar Dolby, Secy.-Treas.
EIN: 912159332
Other changes: At the close of 2012, the fair market value of the grantmaker's assets was $110,287,697, a 92.7% increase over the 2011 value, $57,243,997.

186
Douglas Foundation
(formerly Douglas Charitable Foundation)
141 El Camino Dr., Ste. 209
Beverly Hills, CA **90212-2718** **(310) 274-5294**
***FAX:* (310) 274-2537**;
E-mail: info@douglasfoundation.org; Main URL: http://douglasfoundation.org/

Established in 1964 in CA.
Donors: Kirk Douglas; Anne Douglas; Pepsico, Inc.; Pacific Vascular Research Foundation; AARP.
Foundation type: Independent foundation.
Financial data (yr. ended 12/31/12): Assets, $21,382,030 (M); expenditures, $2,539,740; qualifying distributions, $2,421,222; giving activities include $2,238,025 for 74 grants (high: $400,000; low: $75).
Purpose and activities: Giving primarily for improving the education and health, fostering the well-being, and developing new opportunities for children. Support also to medical research, equipment, and programs within the health system that strive to enhance the quality of care in local communities.
Fields of interest: Performing arts; Performing arts, theater; Arts; Higher education; Education; Hospitals (general); Health care; Medical research, institute; Human services; Jewish agencies & synagogues; Children.
Type of support: General/operating support.
Limitations: Giving primarily in CA, with emphasis on the Southern CA counties of: Los Angeles, Santa Barbara and Ventura. No support for political organizations. No grants to individuals, or for emergency funding, conferences, workshops, exhibits, travel, surveys, films or publishing.
Application information: Formal applications are by invitation only, after review of letter of inquiry. Faxed or e-mailed material is not accepted. See foundation web site for application procedure.
Initial approach: Letter of inquiry via U.S. mail only
Deadline(s): None
Trustees: Peter Douglas,* Pres.; Anne Douglas; Kirk Douglas; Anita May Rosenstein; Fayez Sarofim.
EIN: 956096827

187
Joseph Drown Foundation
1999 Ave. of the Stars, Ste. 2330
Los Angeles, CA 90067-6043 (310) 277-4488
Contact: Wendy Wachtell, Pres.
FAX: (310) 277-4573; E-mail: staff@jdrown.org;
Main URL: http://www.jdrown.org

Established in 1953 in CA.
Donor: Joseph W. Drown‡.
Foundation type: Independent foundation.
Financial data (yr. ended 03/31/13): Assets, $82,126,910 (M); expenditures, $5,473,044; qualifying distributions, $4,474,153; giving activities include $3,988,260 for 124 grants (high: $200,000; low: $5,000).
Purpose and activities: Education is the primary focus of the foundation, and it supports education programs in K-12, at both public and private schools, that seek to solve the existing problems in Los Angeles, CA, area schools. Grants for education reform can be made directly to the schools or to independent organizations which are closely involved with this issue. In addition, the foundation provides funds to private secondary schools, colleges and universities for student financial assistance, in the form of both scholarships and loan programs. Favor is given to programs directed at talented middle income students who are unable to obtain assistance from sources specifically available to low income students. Committed to improving the quality of life in the local community, the foundation supports programs that encourage all individuals to reach their fullest potential. The foundation believes that the best chance a young person has to reach that goal is to stay in school, inside a functioning family, and outside the juvenile justice system. To that end, the foundation supports programs that deal with issues such as the high drop-out rate, lack of sufficient health care, substance abuse and violence. In addition, the foundation will consider programs that address poverty issues and assist the economically disadvantaged. Programs aimed at solutions to or the prevention of these problems are favored. Although it is not the emphasis of the foundation, grants are made for the arts and humanities and are made primarily for outreach and education programs. The foundation also makes grants for medical and scientific research, but these are initiated by the foundation.
Fields of interest: Humanities; Arts; Education, early childhood education; Elementary school/education; Education; Health care; Substance abuse, services; Medical research, institute; Crime/violence prevention, abuse prevention; Human services; Economically disadvantaged.
Type of support: General/operating support; Program development; Seed money; Scholarship funds; Matching/challenge support.
Limitations: Applications accepted. Giving primarily in Los Angeles County, CA. No support for religious purposes. No grants to individuals, or for endowments, multi-year grants, capital campaigns, building funds, tickets for fundraising events, seminars or conferences.
Publications: Application guidelines; Grants list; Informational brochure (including application guidelines).
Application information: Unsolicited applications are not accepted for medical and scientific research. Please do not send videos or materials that need to be returned. Application form not required.
Initial approach: Proposal and letter
Copies of proposal: 1
Deadline(s): Jan. 15, Apr. 15, July 15, and Oct. 15
Board meeting date(s): Mar., June, Sept., and Dec.
Final notification: Immediately after board meeting
Officers and Directors:* Norman C. Obrow,* Chair.; Wendy Wachtell,* Pres.; Elaine Mahoney,* V.P.; Thomas C. Marshall,* V.P.; Philip S. Magaram,* Secy.-Treas.; Ann T. Miller, C.F.O.
Number of staff: 3 full-time professional; 1 full-time support.
EIN: 956093178

188
The Eichenberg-Larson Charitable Foundation
(formerly Robert & LaDorna Eichenberg Charitable Foundation)
1 Collins Island
Newport Beach, CA 92662-1003

Established in 1990 in CA.
Donors: Robert Eichenberg; LaDorna Eichenberg.
Foundation type: Independent foundation.
Financial data (yr. ended 09/30/13): Assets, $6,547,004 (M); gifts received, $1,068,782; expenditures, $321,713; qualifying distributions, $300,000; giving activities include $300,000 for 23 grants (high: $20,000; low: $10,000).
Fields of interest: Performing arts, orchestras; Arts; Higher education; Higher education, university; Health care, patient services; Health organizations, association; Cancer; Alzheimer's disease; Human services; American Red Cross; Salvation Army; Mormon agencies & churches.
Limitations: Applications not accepted. Giving primarily in CA. No grants to individuals.
Application information: Contributes only to pre-selected organizations.
Directors: Ladorna Eichenberg; **Robert Eichenberg;** Jorli Perine.
EIN: 330431855

189
The Eisner Foundation, Inc.
9401 Wilshire Blvd., Ste. 735
Beverly Hills, CA 90212-2947 (310) 228-6808
Contact: Trent Stamp, Exec. Dir.
E-mail: info@eisnerfoundation.org; Main URL: http://www.eisnerfoundation.org
Grants List: http://www.eisnerfoundation.org/what_we_do/grantees.htm

Established in 1996 in CA.
Donors: Michael D. Eisner; Jane B. Eisner.
Foundation type: Independent foundation.
Financial data (yr. ended 12/31/12): Assets, $126,869,201 (M); expenditures, $9,476,428; qualifying distributions, $7,994,591; giving activities include $7,369,232 for 174 grants (high: $500,000; low: $150).
Purpose and activities: The foundation exists to provide access and opportunity for disadvantaged children and the aging of Los Angeles County, CA.
Fields of interest: Arts education; Elementary/secondary education; Health care; Crime/violence prevention, abuse prevention; Athletics/sports, school programs; Children/youth; Children; Aging; Young adults; Economically disadvantaged.
Type of support: General/operating support; Continuing support; Management development/capacity building; Capital campaigns; Building/renovation; Equipment; Program development; Seed money; Matching/challenge support.
Limitations: Applications accepted. Giving limited to Los Angeles County CA. No support for sectarian purposes. Generally, no grants to individuals, annual campaigns, existing obligations, re-granting programs, sponsoring conferences or special events.
Application information: Full applications will be accepted by request only following LOI. See foundation's web site for LOI instructions. Applications sent via fax or E-mail not accepted. Application form required.
Initial approach: Letter of inquiry (LOI) not to exceed 2 pages
Copies of proposal: 2
Board meeting date(s): Mar., June, Sept., and Dec.
Final notification: 2 to 4 weeks
Officers and Directors:* Jane B. Eisner,* Pres.; Michael B. Eisner,* V.P.; Anders D. Eisner,* Secy.; Eric D. Eisner,* C.F.O.; Trent Stamp, Exec. Dir.; **Breck Eisner**; Michael D. Eisner.
Number of staff: 3 full-time professional.
EIN: 954607191

190
The Elfenworks Foundation
20 Park Rd., Ste. D
Burlingame, CA 94011-0431 (650) 347-9700
FAX: (650) 347-9702;
E-mail: admin@elfenworks.org; Main URL: http://www.elfenworksfoundation.org
Blog: http://wp.elfenworksfoundation.org/category/blog/
Facebook: https://www.facebook.com/inharmonywithhope
Twitter: http://twitter.com/elfenworks
YouTube: http://www.youtube.com/elfenworks

Established in 2006 in CA.
Donor: Maples Burlingame, LLC.
Foundation type: Operating foundation.
Financial data (yr. ended 12/31/12): Assets, $2,799,223 (M); gifts received, $416,009; expenditures, $1,195,860; qualifying distributions, $1,164,368; giving activities include $396,020 for 25 grants (high: $200,000; low: $50), and $768,348 for foundation-administered programs.
Purpose and activities: The mission of the foundation is to foster a world in harmony with hope. The foundation seeks to use expertise in communications, computers, film music, the law, finance and business administration to advance their goals of measurable and sustainable transformative change, with emphasis on fighting domestic poverty.
Fields of interest: Human services; Economically disadvantaged.
Limitations: Applications not accepted. Giving in the U.S., with some emphasis on CA.
Application information: Unsolicited requests for funds not accepted. See foundation web site for list of current initiatives.
Officer: Kenneth C. Tam, Exec. Dir.
Trustees: Kim Schoknecht; Lauren Speeth; Mark Vorsatz; Elizabeth Wied.
EIN: 205522254

191
The Lawrence Ellison Foundation
(formerly The Ellison Medical Foundation)
101 Ygnacio Valley Rd., Ste. 310
Walnut Creek, CA 94596-7018 (301) 829-6410
Contact: Kevin Lee Ph.D., Exec. Dir.

E-mail: klee@ellisonfoundation.org; Address for post-award financial reporting: 104 E. Ridgeville Blvd., Mount Airy, MD 21771-5260, tel.: (301) 829-6410, fax: (301) 829-6413; Main URL: http://www.ellisonfoundation.org
Lawrence J. Ellison's Giving Pledge Profile: http://glasspockets.org/philanthropy-in-focus/eye-on-the-giving-pledge/profiles/ellison

Established in 1997 in CA.
Donor: Lawrence J. Ellison.
Foundation type: Operating foundation.
Financial data (yr. ended 12/31/12): Assets, $0 (M); gifts received, $45,632,000; expenditures, $48,903,099; qualifying distributions, $48,747,230; giving activities include $10,295,971 for 31 grants (high: $4,000,000; low: $5,000), $36,122,869 for 209 grants to individuals (high: $291,000; low: $2,000), and $287,599 for 1 foundation-administered program.
Purpose and activities: The foundation supports basic biomedical research on aging relevant to understanding lifespan development processes and age-related diseases and disabilities. The foundation particularly wishes to stimulate new, creative research that might not be funded by traditional sources or that is often under-funded in the U.S.
Fields of interest: Biomedicine; Biomedicine research; Science, research; Biology/life sciences; Gerontology.
Type of support: Conferences/seminars; Research; Grants to individuals.
Limitations: Applications accepted. Giving limited to U.S. institutions only. No support for commercial or for-profit organizations.
Publications: Informational brochure.
Application information: Applications for the Senior Scholar and New Scholar in Aging Awards are currently not being accepted. Any inquiries regarding support for research topics other than aging should be directed to the Exec. Dir. Application form required.
Copies of proposal: 1
Deadline(s): Feb. or early Mar.
Final notification: Late May for letter of intent decision, Aug. for awardees
Officers and Directors:* Lawrence J. Ellison,* Chair. and Pres.; Andrew L. Dudnick, Corp. Secy.; Philip B. Simon, C.F.O.; Kevin Lee, Ph.D., Exec. Dir.; Melanie Craft Ellison.
Scientific Advisory Board: George M. Martin, Chair.; Helen M. Blau, Ph.D.; Eric R. Kandel; Arnold J. Levine; Martin Raff, M.D.; Gary Ruvkun, Ph.D.; Gerald Weissmann.
Number of staff: 2 full-time professional; 3 full-time support; 1 part-time support.
EIN: 943269827
Other changes: The grantmaker has moved from NY to CA.

192
The Jim Hicks Family Foundation
565 Mercury Ln.
Brea, CA 92821

Established in CA.
Donors: Jim Hicks; Jim Hicks & Company, Inc.; Neta Hicks.
Foundation type: Independent foundation.
Financial data (yr. ended 10/31/13): Assets, $6,991,445 (M); expenditures, $235,490; qualifying distributions, $235,316; giving activities include $231,800 for 30 grants (high: $41,800; low: $500).
Fields of interest: Education; Youth development; Philanthropy/voluntarism.
Limitations: Applications not accepted. Giving primarily in CA.
Application information: Unsolicited requests for funds not accepted.
Officers: Jim Hicks, Pres.; Gary H. Edelstone, Secy.
Board Members: Jennifer E. Hicks; Wayland R. Hicks; Gary Milhous.
EIN: 271357705

193
Fansler Foundation
5713 N. West Ave., Ste. 102
Fresno, CA 93711-2366 (559) 432-0544
Contact: Lisa Prudek, Admin. Dir.
FAX: (559) 432-0543; Main URL: http://www.fanslerfoundation.com

Established in 1984 in CA.
Donors: D. Paul Fansler†; Fansler Living Trust.
Foundation type: Independent foundation.
Financial data (yr. ended 10/31/12): Assets, $30,048,646 (M); gifts received, $1,117; expenditures, $2,045,838; qualifying distributions, $1,490,338; giving activities include $1,316,565 for 21 grants (high: $175,000; low: $125).
Purpose and activities: Giving primarily for education and health care, and social services, with emphasis on children and youth; some giving also for a family development center, and handicap accessibility facilities; scholarships to middle school student parishioners are also available.
Fields of interest: Education, early childhood education; Health organizations, association; Cerebral palsy; Crime/violence prevention, child abuse; Children/youth, services; Youth; Disabilities, people with.
Type of support: Scholarships—to individuals.
Limitations: Applications accepted. **Giving primarily in the Fresno, Kings, Tulare, Merced, Madera, or Mariposa counties in CA.**
Publications: Application guidelines.
Application information: Contact the foundation for specifics to be covered, and required attachments. Application form required.
***Initial approach:* Letter of intent, no more than 3 typewritten pages, which needs to address the 9 points indicated in the Grant Guidelines on the foundation's web site**
***Copies of proposal:* 7**
Deadline(s): Mar. 31 for funding by Oct. 31; Mar. 15 for scholarships
Board meeting date(s): As needed
Final notification: July 31 for letters of intent
Officer: Marlene Fansler, C.E.O. and Pres.; Richard Spencer.
Trustees: Margie Cooper; Keith Kompsi; Jim Pardini; William B. Saleh.
Number of staff: 2 full-time professional.
EIN: 770095125

194
The Farese Family Foundation
1660 Bush St., Ste. 300
San Francisco, CA 94109-5308 **(415) 561-6540**
FAX: (415) 561-5477; Main URL: http://www.faresefamilyfoundation.org

Established in 2000 in CA.
Donors: Nancy R. Farese; Robert Farese.
Foundation type: Independent foundation.
Financial data (yr. ended 12/31/12): Assets, $17,630,147 (M); gifts received, $1,007,306; expenditures, $399,548; qualifying distributions, $288,519; giving activities include $209,475 for 43 grants (high: $30,000; low: $325).
Fields of interest: Libraries (public); Education; Human services; Children/youth; Economically disadvantaged.
Type of support: General/operating support.
Limitations: Applications not accepted. Giving primarily in the San Francisco Bay Area, CA. No grants to individuals.
Publications: Grants list; Program policy statement.
Application information: Unsolicited requests for funds not accepted. Proposals are by invitation only.
Board meeting date(s): May and Dec.
Officers: Nancy R. Farese, Pres.; Robert V. Farese, Jr., Secy.-Treas.
Board Members: Conor Farese; Julie Shafer.
Number of staff: 2 part-time professional; 3 part-time support.
EIN: 943376857

195
The Farrah Fawcett Foundation
P.O. Box 6478
Beverly Hills, CA 90212-1478
E-mail: info@thefarrahfawcettfoundation.org; Main URL: http://www.thefarrahfawcettfoundation.org
E-Newsletter: http://www.thefarrahfawcettfoundation.org/documents/FFFNewsletter2013.pdf
Facebook: https://www.facebook.com/pages/The-Farrah-Fawcett-Foundation/175709109105967?ref=hl

Established in 2010.
Donor: Farrah Fawcett†.
Foundation type: Independent foundation.
Financial data (yr. ended 12/31/11): Assets, $5,465,341 (M); gifts received, $562,835; expenditures, $496,121; qualifying distributions, $262,000; giving activities include $262,000 for 9 grants (high: $104,500; low: $2,500).
Purpose and activities: The organization aims to provide funding for alternative methods of cancer research, clinical trials, prevention, and awareness with an emphasis on anal and pediatric cancers.
Fields of interest: Cancer; Cancer research.
Officers and Board Members: Alana Stewart,* Pres. and C.E.O.; Shira Nachshon,* Secy.-Treas.; Dr. Brad Allen; David Kessler; Kim Swartz.
EIN: 208076177

196
Irving Feintech Family Foundation
321 S. Beverly Dr., Ste. K
Beverly Hills, CA 90212-4303

Established in 1990 in CA.
Donors: Irving Feintech; The Feintech Family Foundation; Liberty Building Co.; Shapell Industries.
Foundation type: Independent foundation.
Financial data (yr. ended 12/31/12): Assets, $3,885,960 (M); expenditures, $371,817; qualifying distributions, $355,717; giving activities include $352,174 for 26 grants (high: $87,500; low: $60).
Fields of interest: Education; Human services; Foundations (private grantmaking).
Limitations: Applications not accepted. Giving primarily in CA. No grants to individuals.
Application information: Contributes only to pre-selected organizations.

Officers: Lisa A. Feintech, Pres.; Wendy Feintech, V.P.
EIN: 954268946
Other changes: Lisa A. Feintech has replaced Wendy Feintech as Pres. Wendy Feintech has replaced Lisa A. Feintech as V.P.

197
Ernest L. and Ruth W. Finley Foundation
1400 N. Dutton Ave., No. 12
Santa Rosa, CA 95401-4644 (707) 545-3136
***Contact:* Norma J. Person, Tr.**

Established in 1985 in CA.
Donors: Ernest L. Finley‡; Ruth W. Finley‡; R. Finley Charitable Remainder Unitrust.
Foundation type: Independent foundation.
Financial data (yr. ended 08/31/13): Assets, $32,979,369 (M); expenditures, $6,593,576; qualifying distributions, $6,251,630; giving activities include $6,158,989 for 18 grants (high: $1,500,000; low: $10,000).
Purpose and activities: Giving primarily for the preservation of visual arts, social services, youth activities and support, religious endeavors.
Fields of interest: Arts; Health care; Human services; Children/youth, services.
Type of support: General/operating support; Building/renovation; Endowments; Scholarship funds.
Limitations: Applications accepted. Giving generally limited to Santa Rosa and Sonoma County, CA. No grants to individuals.
Application information: Application form required.
Initial approach: Letter
Copies of proposal: 3
Deadline(s): None
Board meeting date(s): As required
Trustees: Brad Bollinger; William W. Godward; Norma J. Person.
EIN: 941694310
Other changes: For the fiscal year ended Aug. 31, 2013, the grantmaker paid grants of $6,158,989, a 63.7% increase over the fiscal 2012 disbursements, $3,761,829.

198
Firedoll Foundation
1460 Maria Ln., Ste. 400
Walnut Creek, CA 94596-8802
Contact: Neil Sims, Sr.Prog. Off.
FAX: (925) 937-4530; E-mail: info@firedoll.org; **LOI e-mail: LOI@firedoll.org**; Main URL: http://www.firedoll.org

Established in 1998 in CA.
Donor: Straus Family Trust.
Foundation type: Independent foundation.
Financial data (yr. ended 05/31/13): Assets, $9,231,624 (M); gifts received, $1,573,514; expenditures, $2,091,476; qualifying distributions, $2,079,502; giving activities include $1,899,825 for 98 grants (high: $40,000; low: $2,500).
Purpose and activities: The foundation offers grants to nonprofits in the areas of environmental conservation, immigrant/human rights, community development, Mid-East peace, and offers support for Bay Area non-profits servicing victims of traumatic brain injury.
Fields of interest: Environment, natural resources; Environment, water resources; Environment, forests; Animals/wildlife, fisheries; Housing/shelter, homeless; International peace/security; Civil/human rights, immigrants; Community development, small businesses.
International interests: Middle East.
Type of support: General/operating support; Continuing support; Capital campaigns; Building/renovation; Equipment; Land acquisition; Emergency funds; Program development; Seed money; Technical assistance; Program evaluation; Matching/challenge support.
Limitations: Applications accepted. Giving limited to Alameda and Contra Costa Counties in CA, for community development. Giving primarily in Alameda and Contra Costa Counties for land acquisition and conservation, HI for Monk seal conservation, and the Eastern Pacific for fish stock preservation. Giving in Alameda and Contra Costa Counties for immigration and human rights, as well as some giving nationally for civil rights work. Giving in Alameda, Contra Costa, Marin, San Mateo, San Francisco and Solano Counties for traumatic brain injury. Giving to U.S.-based or U.S. fiscally sponsored organizations providing relief in Gaza and the West Bank. **No support for organizations with budgets less than $150,000, wild animal or pet rescue and rehab, or international support (except for Middle East Peace and an occasional grant in Environmental Conservation). No grants to individuals or for the arts, youth (grades K-12), education, LGBT, general support for first time applicants, climate change, community leadership development, youth development (other than aid for emancipated foster youth), films, videos, documentaries, books, web sites and other media, start-up or seed funding for organizations or projects new to the foundation, or for large-scope, long-term initiatives (the foundation prefers discrete projects with concrete end-of-year deliverables).**
Publications: Application guidelines; Grants list; Program policy statement.
Application information: Consult application guidelines on web site before sending proposals. Proposals not following guidelines will be returned. Application form required.
Initial approach: E-mail or written letter of inquiry or proposal after consulting web site
Copies of proposal: 1
Deadline(s): See foundation web site for current deadlines
***Final notification:* Within 3 months**
Officers: Sandor Straus, Pres. and Treas.; Faye Straus, V.P. and Secy.
Number of staff: 1 full-time professional; 1 part-time professional.
EIN: 943301999

199
Fleishhacker Foundation
P.O. Box 29918
San Francisco, CA 94129-0918 (415) 561-5350
Contact: Christine Elbel, Exec. Dir.
FAX: (415) 561-5345;
E-mail: info@fleishhackerfoundation.org; Main URL: http://www.fleishhackerfoundation.org

Incorporated in 1947 in CA.
Donors: Mortimer Fleishhacker, Sr.‡; Mortimer Fleishhacker, Jr.‡; Janet Fleishhacker Bates‡.
Foundation type: Independent foundation.
Financial data (yr. ended 12/31/13): Assets, $18,206,095 (M); expenditures, $935,770; qualifying distributions, $873,072; giving activities include $530,460 for 110 grants (high: $20,000; low: $1,000), and $150,500 for 9 grants to individuals (high: $25,000; low: $500).
Purpose and activities: Grants to visual and performing arts organizations; support also for precollegiate education.
Fields of interest: Media, film/video; Visual arts; Museums; Performing arts; Performing arts, dance; Performing arts, theater; Performing arts, music; Arts; Elementary school/education; Education; Children/youth; Children; Minorities; Asians/Pacific Islanders; African Americans/Blacks; Hispanics/Latinos; Native Americans/American Indians; Girls; Adults, women; Adults, men; Economically disadvantaged; LGBTQ.
Type of support: General/operating support; Equipment; Program development; Film/video/radio; Curriculum development; Fellowships; Technical assistance; Grants to individuals.
Limitations: Applications accepted. Giving limited to the greater San Francisco Bay Area, CA. No support for religious or political organizations. No grants for annual campaigns, endowments, large capital campaigns, deficit financing, fund raising events, matching gifts or scholarships; no loans.
Publications: Application guidelines; Grants list.
Application information: Fellowships not open to individual application. Application form required.
Initial approach: Full proposal
Copies of proposal: 1
Deadline(s): Usually Jan. 15 and July 15
Board meeting date(s): Biannually
Final notification: 3 to 4 months
Officers and Directors:* David Fleishhacker,* Pres.; John Ehrlich, Jr.,* V.P.; Deborah Sloss,* Secy.; William Fleishhacker,* Treas.; Christine Elbel, Exec. Dir.; Delia Fleishhacker Ehrlich; Jodi Ehrlich; Jeffrey Fleishhacker; Marc Fleishhacker; Edie Fleishhacker Rindal; Laura Sloss; Robin Strawbridge.
Number of staff: 1 full-time professional; 1 part-time support.
EIN: 946051048
Other changes: Lois Gordon is no longer a director.

200
Floyd Family Foundation
620 Sand Hill Rd., Apt. 127D
Palo Alto, CA 94304-2096

Established in 1989 in CA.
Donors: William S. Floyd; Mary Bell Floyd‡.
Foundation type: Independent foundation.
Financial data (yr. ended 06/30/13): Assets, $8,379,162 (M); gifts received, $187,576; expenditures, $357,536; qualifying distributions, $312,000; giving activities include $312,000 for 49 grants (high: $128,500; low: $250).
Purpose and activities: Giving primarily for education and human services.
Fields of interest: Education; Human services; Philanthropy/voluntarism.
Limitations: Applications not accepted. Giving on a national basis. No grants to individuals.
Application information: Contributes only to pre-selected organizations. Unsolicited requests for funds not considered.
Officers: William S. Floyd, Pres.; Jeanne Floyd Downs, V.P. and Secy.-Treas.
EIN: 943106119

201
Found Animals Foundation, Inc.
P.O. Box 66370
Los Angeles, CA 90066-0370
E-mail: Info@foundanimals.org; Main URL: http://www.foundanimals.org/
Blog: http://www.foundanimals.org/blog/

E-Newsletter: http://www.foundanimals.org/get-involved/newsletter-signup
Facebook: http://www.facebook.com/foundanimals
Instagram.com: http://instagram.com/foundanimals#
Pinterest: http://www.pinterest.com/foundanimals/
Twitter: http://twitter.com/FoundAnimalsOrg
YouTube: http://www.youtube.com/foundanimals
Application e-mail: michelsonprize@foundanimals.org

Established in 2005 in CA.
Donor: Gary Karlin Michelson, M.D.
Foundation type: Operating foundation.
Financial data (yr. ended 11/30/12): Assets, $796,277 (M); gifts received, $4,306,000; expenditures, $8,971,559; qualifying distributions, $8,516,876; giving activities include $873,447 for 19 grants (high: $200,000; low: $2,500), and $7,234,582 for foundation-administered programs.
Purpose and activities: The foundation is focused on creating innovative, largely self-sustaining programs dedicated to 3 initiatives; spary/neuter; resources for pet owners; and adoption.
Fields of interest: Animal welfare; Hospitals (specialty).
Limitations: Applications not accepted. Giving primarily in CA. No grants to individuals.
Application information: Contributes only to pre-selected organizations.
Officers: Gary Karlin Michelson, M.D., Pres.; Aimee Gilbreath, V.P.; David Cohen, Secy. and C.F.O.; Dennis Phillips, C.O.O.
EIN: 203944602

202
Foundation for Deep Ecology
1606 Union St.
San Francisco, CA **94123-4507** (415) 229-9339
Contact: Lizzie Udwin, Prog. Admin.
FAX: (415) 229-9340;
E-mail: info@deepecology.org; Main URL: http://www.deepecology.org

Established in 1989 in CA.
Donors: Douglas R. Tompkins; Clark Family Foundation.
Foundation type: Independent foundation.
Financial data (yr. ended 06/30/13): Assets, $42,091,210 (M); expenditures, $2,407,003; qualifying distributions, $2,136,937; giving activities include $1,111,353 for 24+ grants (high: $121,000), and $179,780 for foundation-administered programs.
Purpose and activities: Focus on fundamental ecological issues: 1) protection of forests, aquatic ecosystems and other habitats, including wildlands philanthropy (buying land to save it), wilderness recovery (supporting the design and implementation of large-scale wilderness recovery networks), funding for activists fighting for full protection of species and ecosystems and funding for efforts to eliminate resource extraction on public lands; 2) support for alternative models of agriculture that support biodiversity, local self-reliance and healthy agrarian communities, support for efforts in the fight against industrial agriculture, and support for efforts to link conservationists with farmers and activists in order to integrate habitat preservation and restoration with diverse farming practices; 3) campaigns for effective analysis, organizing and action in response to the rapid acceleration in macroeconomic trends toward global economic integration and free trade that has shifted real political power away from citizen democracies to global corporate bureaucracies, and the further centralization of global corporate power caused by new technological innovation. Supported projects include educational programs exposing the full consequences of the global economy and new free trade agreements, technological critiques and campaigns, and groups fighting large road-building, infrastructure, and dam projects.
Fields of interest: Environment, natural resources; Environment, land resources; Environment; Animals/wildlife, preservation/protection; Agriculture; International affairs.
International interests: South America; Argentina; Chile.
Type of support: General/operating support; Continuing support; Land acquisition; Program development; Conferences/seminars; Publication; Seed money; Grants to individuals.
Limitations: Applications not accepted. Giving primarily in CA and South America, with emphasis on Chile and Argentina. No support for curriculum development or K-12 educational projects, or for businesses or debt. No grants for television, video, photography (visual arts) or film productions, research, or individual academic pursuits (including graduate work or scholarships).
Publications: Multi-year report.
Application information: Contributes only to pre-selected organizations. Unsolicited requests for funds will not be accepted.
Board meeting date(s): Annually
Officers and Directors:* Douglas R. Tompkins,* Pres.; Quincey Imhoff,* V.P.; Kristine McDivitt Tompkins,* V.P.; Debra B. Ryker,* Secy.-Treas.; Esther Li, Cont.
Number of staff: 3 full-time professional; 2 part-time professional; 3 full-time support.
EIN: 943106115

203
Foundation for Enterprise Development
1241 Cave St.
La Jolla, CA 92037-3602 (866) 936-4333
Contact: Grants Admin.
E-mail: inquire@fed.org; Main URL: http://www.fed.org
Facebook: https://www.facebook.com/Foundation.for.Enterprise.Development?ref=mf
RSS Feed: http://www.fed.org/feed
Twitter: https://twitter.com/fedfellows
YouTube: http://www.youtube.com/user/fedvideos

Established in 1986 in CA.
Donors: John Robert Beyster; Jim Russel; Barbara Schmidt; Mary Ann Beyster; Employee Ownership Foundation.
Foundation type: Operating foundation.
Financial data (yr. ended 06/30/13): Assets, $3,142,519 (M); gifts received, $761,706; expenditures, $1,403,087; qualifying distributions, $891,049; giving activities include $163,261 for 9 grants (high: $81,434; low: $2,500), and $995,824 for foundation-administered programs.
Purpose and activities: Giving primarily for the development of entrepreneurialism and employee ownership.
Fields of interest: Higher education, university; Business/industry.
Type of support: Grants to individuals.
Limitations: Giving primarily in CA and NJ. No support for political, social or fraternal organizations, or for medical research or international programs. No grants for endowments, the arts, start-up expenses, seed capital, or scholarships; no loans.
Application information: Formal proposals are by invitation only, upon review of the letter of inquiry. Large volumes of material are not accepted. If the foundation deems it fit, it will contact the applicant with a request for more information. Application form not required.
Initial approach: Letter of inquiry (no more than 3 pages)
Deadline(s): None
Final notification: Within 2 weeks if the foundation is willing to consider a formal proposal.
Officers and Trustees:* Dr. John Robert Beyster, Chair.; Mary Ann Beyster, Pres.; David Binns, Secy.; Thomas E. Darcy; Steven P. Fischer.
EIN: 330207662

204
The Foundation for Global Sports Development
(formerly Justice for Athletes)
333 S. Hope St., 48th Fl.
Los Angeles, CA 90071-1406
Main URL: http://www.globalsportsdevelopment.org/
Blog: http://blog.globalsportsdevelopment.org/
Facebook: http://www.facebook.com/GlobalSportsDevelopment
Flickr: http://www.flickr.com/photos/106498917@N08/
LinkedIn: http://www.linkedin.com/company/the-foundation-for-global-sports-development
Twitter: http://twitter.com/GlobalSportsD
YouTube: http://www.youtube.com/user/GlobalSportsD

Donor: Dorot Foundation.
Foundation type: Independent foundation.
Financial data (yr. ended 12/31/12): Assets, $31,363,651 (M); gifts received, $38,600; expenditures, $2,373,770; qualifying distributions, $1,764,013; giving activities include $1,035,500 for 67 grants (high: $400,000; low: $2,000), and $1,764,013 for 4 foundation-administered programs.
Purpose and activities: Giving for programs that promote sportsmanship, education, fair play, and ethics among youth.
Fields of interest: Recreation, centers; Athletics/sports, school programs; Athletics/sports, amateur leagues.
Limitations: Applications accepted. Giving primarily in CA; giving internationally in Switzerland. No grants to individuals.
Application information:
Initial approach: Letter (2-3 pages)
Copies of proposal: 1
Board meeting date(s): Biannually
Officers: David C. Ulich, Esq., Pres.; Steven Ungerleider, Ph.D., V.P.; Steven C. Baum, Secy.-Treas.
EIN: 954560243

205
Frieda C. Fox Family Foundation
12411 Ventura Blvd.
Studio City, CA 91604-2407 (818) 308-4369
Contact: Dana Marcus, Exec. Dir.
E-mail: info@fcfox.org; Tel./fax for Dana Marcus: (408) 358-6966; toll-free tel.: (888) 358-6966; Main URL: http://www.fcfox.org
LinkedIn: http://www.linkedin.com/company/the-frieda-c-fox-family-foundation

Twitter: http://twitter.com/fcfoxfamfound
YouTube: http://www.youtube.com/user/fcfoxorg#p/u/6/nwqRVYS-BMQ

Established in 1999 in CA.
Foundation type: Independent foundation.
Financial data (yr. ended 12/31/12): Assets, $6,404,202 (M); gifts received, $5,285; expenditures, $744,642; qualifying distributions, $683,199; giving activities include $367,032 for 38 grants (high: $65,057; low: $500).
Purpose and activities: The foundation seeks inquiries from programs that improve and expand learning environments of children, especially for those from economically- and socially-disadvantaged families; provides needed financial support for existing, highly-successful, results-oriented programs; and actively promotes positive interactions between children, youth, and adults, through programs that actively involve parents and/or staff and embrace professional development and training for those that deal directly with children or create their learning environments.
Fields of interest: Youth development, formal/general education; Youth development, adult & child programs; Youth development, citizenship; Children/youth, services; Economically disadvantaged.
Type of support: Management development/capacity building; Program development; Technical assistance; Consulting services; In-kind gifts; Matching/challenge support.
Limitations: Giving limited to Los Angeles and Santa Clara counties, CA. No support for schools; religious institutions; organizations that unfairly discriminate against people because of age, race, creed, gender, national origin, handicap, sexual orientation, or ethnicity; or organizations that do not have at least one full year's operational and financial history to share with the foundation. No grants to individuals, or for capital improvement projects, support for past operating deficits, or fundraising events; no loans.
Publications: Application guidelines; Grants list; Program policy statement (including application guidelines).
Application information: See foundation web site for complete application guidelines.
Initial approach: **Online Letter of Introduction through foundation web site**
Board meeting date(s): Summer and winter
Officer: Dana Marcus, Exec. Dir.
Directors: Alan C. Fox, Pres.; Daveen Fox, V.P. and Secy.; Cathy Reynolds, Treas.; Ingrid Fox; Kevin Fox; Sara Fox; Scott Semel.
Number of staff: 1 full-time professional; 1 part-time professional.
EIN: 954775770
Other changes: Jill E. Fox and Carolyn L. Fox are no longer directors.
The grantmaker now makes its grants list available online.

206
The Sidney E. Frank Foundation
575 Market St., Ste. 3165
San Francisco, CA 94105-2854
Contact: Rae Richman, Philanthropic Advisor
FAX: (415) 543-0753; E-mail for Rae Richman: rrichman@rockpa.org

Established in 2004 in NY.
Donor: Sidney E. Frank†.
Foundation type: Independent foundation.
Financial data (yr. ended 12/31/12): Assets, $293,277,041 (M); gifts received, $1,500,000; expenditures, $9,528,570; qualifying distributions, $9,225,278; giving activities include $6,373,341 for 120 grants (high: $550,000; low: $1,000).
Fields of interest: Arts, multipurpose centers/programs; Elementary/secondary education; Education; Environment, beautification programs; Environment; Cancer; Medical research.
Limitations: Applications not accepted. Giving primarily in the San Francisco Bay Area and San Diego, CA, HI, and New York City. No grants to individuals.
Application information: Contributes only to pre-selected organizations.
Officer: Amy C. Fisch, C.I.O.
Trustees: Cathy Halstead; Peter Halstead; **Anne M. Logan; Harold R. Logan, Jr.**
Number of staff: 1 full-time professional.
EIN: 206383779

207
Fremont Bank Foundation
39150 Fremont Blvd.
Fremont, CA 94538-1316
Main URL: **https://www.fremontbank.com/about/community-relations/fremont-bank-foundation**
Recent Grants: https://www.fremontbank.com/about/community-relations/fremont-bank-foundation/recent-grants

Established as a company-sponsored operating foundation in 1996 in CA.
Donor: Fremont Bank.
Foundation type: Company-sponsored foundation.
Financial data (yr. ended 12/31/12): Assets, $8,310,927 (M); gifts received, $3,721,659; expenditures, $633,577; qualifying distributions, $633,577; giving activities include $627,802 for 78 grants (high: $100,000; low: $250).
Purpose and activities: The Fremont Bank Foundation provides financial assistance to nonprofit organizations for the implementation of series and programs that enhance the quality of life for all people in the communities served by Fremont Bank.
Fields of interest: Performing arts; Arts; Education; Environment; Public health; Health care; Mental health/crisis services; Health organizations; Crime/violence prevention, abuse prevention; Crime/violence prevention, domestic violence; Crime/violence prevention, child abuse; Nutrition; Children/youth, services; Human services, financial counseling; Homeless, human services; Human services.
Type of support: Building/renovation; Capital campaigns; Endowments; Equipment; General/operating support; Program development; Research; Scholarship funds.
Limitations: Applications not accepted. Giving primarily in San Francisco Bay Area, CA in areas of company operations. **No support for private foundations, pass-through organizations, or national or international organizations (except for local chapters addressing the needs of the community). No grants to individuals, or for political or labor activities, debt reduction, or membership fees or dues.**
Publications: Grants list.
Application information: Contributes only to pre-selected organizations.
Board meeting date(s): Annually
Officers: Hattie Hyman Hughes, Pres.; Bradford L. Anderson, C.F.O; Howard L. Hyman, V.P.; Chris Chenoweth, Secy.
Directors: Sharon Belshaw-Jones; Brian Hughes; Alan L. Hyman; Michael J. Wallace.
EIN: 943170075

208
Friedman Family Foundation
353 Folsom St., 2nd Fl.
San Francisco, CA 94105-2300 (650) 342-8750
FAX: (866) 223-1078;
E-mail: info@friedmanfamilyfoundation.org; Main URL: http://www.friedmanfamilyfoundation.org
Grants List: http://www.friedmanfamilyfoundation.org/grants/

Established in 1964 in CA.
Donors: Phyllis K. Friedman; Howard Friedman†.
Foundation type: Independent foundation.
Financial data (yr. ended 02/28/13): Assets, $9,810,226 (M); expenditures, $662,937; qualifying distributions, $662,790; giving activities include $530,000 for 88 grants (high: $10,000; low: $100).
Purpose and activities: Support for programs which attempt to end the cycle of poverty, especially programs that provide tools, support, asset building, and opportunity to people in need in order to overcome the root causes of their poverty, and in which the people to be helped are part of the design and decision making of the organization or project. Preference is given to new and creative programs, and programs working for systemic change.
Fields of interest: Economic development; Community/economic development; Economically disadvantaged.
Type of support: General/operating support; Program development; Program-related investments/loans.
Limitations: Applications accepted. Giving primarily in the nine counties of the San Francisco Bay Area, CA. No grants to individuals, or for films, videos, conferences, seminars, capital campaigns, scholarships, research, or special or fundraising events.
Publications: Application guidelines; Grants list; Occasional report (including application guidelines).
Application information: Applications are by invitation only, upon review of letter of inquiry. Fax submissions are not accepted. E-mail is preferred. Application form required.
Initial approach: Letter
Copies of proposal: 1
Deadline(s): None, for letters of inquiry; see foundation web site for current application deadlines
Board meeting date(s): Varies, meets 3 times a year
Final notification: Up to 3 months for letters of inquiry
Officers: Phyllis K. Friedman, Pres.; Eleanor Friedman, V.P.; Robert E. Friedman, Secy.; David A. Friedman, Treas.
Number of staff: 1 part-time professional.
EIN: 946109692

209
The Friend Family Foundation
(formerly The Eugene Friend Family Foundation)
355 Hayes St.
San Francisco, CA **94102-4420**
Contact: Robert B. Friend, Pres.; Additional contact: Donald A. Friend, Secy.
E-mail: bob@friendsf.com

Established in 1967 in CA.
Donors: Donald A. Friend; Eugene L. Friend†; Robert B. Friend.
Foundation type: Independent foundation.
Financial data (yr. ended 06/30/13): Assets, $4,962,747 (M); expenditures, $832,185; qualifying distributions, $812,660; giving activities

include $812,500 for 28 grants (high: $250,000; low: $1,000).
Purpose and activities: Grants primarily for Jewish giving, including Jewish welfare funds; support also for cultural programs.
Fields of interest: Arts; Human services; Jewish federated giving programs; Jewish agencies & synagogues.
Limitations: Applications not accepted. Giving primarily in CA, with emphasis on San Rafael and San Francisco. No grants to individuals.
Application information: Contributes only to pre-selected organizations.
Officers and Directors:* Robert Friend,* Pres.; Donald A. Friend,* Secy.
EIN: 946163916

210
Fund for Nonviolence
303 Potrero, No. 54
Santa Cruz, CA 95060-2760 (831) 460-9321
Contact: Monica Larenas, Prog. Off.
FAX: (831) 460-9137;
E-mail: mail@fundfornonviolence.org; **Toll-free tel.: (866) 454-8006**; Main URL: http://www.fundfornonviolence.org
Grants List: http://www.fundfornonviolence.org/grants/grants.html

Established in 1997 in CA.
Foundation type: Independent foundation.
Financial data (yr. ended 12/31/12): Assets, $3,101,996 (M); expenditures, $1,088,550; qualifying distributions, $902,800; giving activities include $585,287 for 29 grants (high: $70,000; low: $500) and $251,750 for set-asides.
Purpose and activities: The fund cultivates and supports efforts to bring about social change that moves humanity towards a more just and compassionate coexistence. Primary interest is placed on proposals from organizations that: 1) pursue structural changes to root causes of race, class, and gender injustice; 2) value the active involvement of members of the communities most impacted by the violence and social injustice being addressed; 3) understand and articulate the impact of their work on women and promote the leadership of women within the organization; 4) work through networks, coalitions and alliances; 5) reflect the spirit of nonviolence in their organizational relations, structure, and process; and 6) demonstrate the capacity to reflect on their experience and adapt to lessons and insights.
Fields of interest: Offenders/ex-offenders, prison alternatives; Civil/human rights, alliance/advocacy; Civil/human rights, advocacy; Civil liberties, death penalty issues; Offenders/ex-offenders; Crime/abuse victims.
International interests: Colombia; Ecuador; Latin America; Mexico; Peru.
Type of support: Consulting services; General/operating support; Continuing support; Management development/capacity building; Program development; Conferences/seminars; Seed money; Technical assistance; Program evaluation.
Limitations: Giving primarily in CA through the Justice with Dignity Program; giving nationally through the Lifting Voices of Resistance Program. No grants to individuals; no support for one-time events or experiences that are not connected to broader campaigns or movement building or without effective follow up; no support for media production costs.
Publications: Application guidelines; Grants list.
Application information: Unsolicited requests for funding are currently not accepted. Check foundation web site for updates in this area. Application form not required.
Board meeting date(s): Full board: Jan., Apr., and Oct.; grantmaking committees separately
Officers and Directors:* Betsy Fairbanks,* C.E.O. and Pres.; Carolina Martinez, Secy.; Lynda Marin,* Treas.; Kelli Evans; **Rebecca Rittgers**.
Number of staff: 2 full-time professional; 1 part-time professional.
EIN: 770457185

211
Georges and Germaine Fusenot Charity Foundation, Inc.
12711 Ventura Blvd., Ste. 390
Studio City, CA 91604-2491

Trust established in 1967 in CA.
Donors: Germaine Fusenot†; Andre Blanchard†; Marcelle Blanchard†; Virginia W. Markel†.
Foundation type: Independent foundation.
Financial data (yr. ended 07/31/13): Assets, $5,512,950 (M); expenditures, $374,075; qualifying distributions, $325,067; giving activities include $295,000 for 52 grants (high: $36,500; low: $1,000).
Purpose and activities: Giving primarily for education, youth services and the arts.
Fields of interest: Arts; Education; Environment; Hospitals (general); Health care; Health organizations, association; Food distribution, meals on wheels; Youth development, centers/clubs; Human services; YM/YWCAs & YM/YWHAs; Children/youth, services; Child development, services; Religion; Blind/visually impaired.
Type of support: General/operating support; Continuing support; Capital campaigns; Building/renovation; Equipment; Matching/challenge support.
Limitations: Applications not accepted. Giving limited to CA. No support for religious organizations for religious purposes, or for political organizations. No grants to individuals, or for emergency or endowment funds, deficit financing, demonstration projects, publications, conferences, scholarships, or fellowships; no loans.
Application information: Unsolicited requests for funds not accepted.
Officers: Guy Arnold Stone, Chair.; Richard G. Herlihy, Mgr.
Trustees: Viveca Ann S. Berry; Charles F. Gorder; Janet W. Kernon; Patricia H. Stone; Richard H. Stone; Norman C. Walker; Scott L. Whitman.
Number of staff: 1 full-time professional.
EIN: 956207831
Other changes: Michael J. Herlihy is no longer a trustee.

212
Fuserna Foundation
(formerly The Getty Family Foundation)
100 N. Crescent Dr., Ste. 324
Beverly Hills, CA 90210-5411 (775) 412-4322
Contact: Leah Langsdorf
***FAX:* (775) 786-5414;**
E-mail: leah.langsdorf@suttonpl.com; Main URL: http://fusernafoundation.org/

Donors: John Paul Getty III; Ariadne Getty.
Foundation type: Independent foundation.
Financial data (yr. ended 12/31/12): Assets, $2,683 (M); gifts received, $604,244; expenditures, $640,403; qualifying distributions, $613,480; giving activities include $613,480 for 13 grants (high: $200,000; low: $11,000).
Fields of interest: Youth development; Community/economic development.
Limitations: Applications accepted. Giving primarily in CA and NY.
Application information: Application form required.
Initial approach: Email
Deadline(s): Every Quaterly
Officers and Directors:* Ariadne Getty,* Pres. and Exec. Dir.; Erin Otolski,* V.P.; John Ladner,* Secy.; Howard D. Reynolds,* Treas.
Trustees: Louise Creasey; Patrick Maxwell.
EIN: 200461573
Other changes: The grantmaker has moved from NV to CA.
Ariadne Getty is now Pres. and Exec. Dir. D'Andra Walker is no longer V.P.

213
The Gamble Foundation
1660 Bush St., Ste. 300
San Francisco, CA 94109-5308
***Contact:* Emily Schroeder, Grants Mgr.**
E-mail for Emily Schroeder, Grants Mgr.:
eschroeder@pfs-llc.net; tel.: (415) 561-6540, ext. 222; Main URL: http://www.pfs-llc.net/gamble/gamble.html

Established in 1968 in CA.
Donors: Launce E. Gamble; Mary S. Gamble†; George F. Gamble; MSG Charitable Trust; Launce L. Gamble; Mark D. Gamble; Aimee Gamble Price; George T. Gamble; Jim Gamble; Joan L. Gamble.
Foundation type: Independent foundation.
Financial data (yr. ended 12/31/12): Assets, $16,785,747 (M); gifts received, $443,128; expenditures, $435,664; qualifying distributions, $399,979; giving activities include $348,500 for 45 grants (high: $53,500; low: $500).
Purpose and activities: The foundation's primary interest is to support organizations that serve disadvantaged children and youth in San Francisco, Marin and Napa counties. Within the field of youth development, the foundation focuses on educational and personal enrichment programs designed to open doors of opportunity for at risk youth in order to help them succeed in school and become productive, self-sufficient members of society. The foundation is particularly interested in agricultural/environmental education, vocational training, and programs that prevent substance abuse and teen violence. To a lesser degree, the foundation supports environmental organizations that focus on land preservation and sustainability, animal welfare and management, and pollution control. The foundation is interested in promoting green concepts that increase awareness of science-based solutions that help reduce consumption of finite resources.
Fields of interest: Environment, beautification programs; Environment; Youth development.
Type of support: General/operating support; Program development.
Limitations: Applications accepted. Giving primarily in San Francisco, Marin and Napa counties, CA. No support for religious organizations. No grants to individuals, or for medical research, endowment funds, capital improvements, or annual appeals.
Publications: Application guidelines; Annual report; Grants list.
Application information: The foundation accepts proposals for one round of grants each year. Grants range from $10,000 - $25,000 annually over one to four years. The foundation typically funds for no

more than four consecutive years. Application guidelines available on foundation web site. Application form required.

Initial approach: Letter
Deadline(s): None
Board meeting date(s): 2nd quarter of each year

Officers: Launce E. Gamble, Pres.; Aimee Gamble Price, V.P. and Secy.; Mark D. Gamble, V.P. and Treas.; George F. Gamble, V.P.
EIN: 941680503

214
The Fred Gellert Family Foundation

1038 Redwood Hwy., Bldg. B, Ste. 2
Mill Valley, CA 94941-1620 **(415) 381-7575**
***E-mail:* FGFamilyfoundation@gmail.com; Main URL: http://www.fgfamilyfoundation.com**
Grants List: http://www.fgfamilyfoundation.com/grant-awards/

Established in 1958 in CA.
Donor: Fred Gellert, Sr.†.
Foundation type: Independent foundation.
Financial data (yr. ended 12/31/12): Assets, $8,694,848 (M); expenditures, $549,522; qualifying distributions, $372,341; giving activities include $265,252 for 130 grants (high: $20,000; low: $500).
Purpose and activities: Giving primarily in the areas of long-term sustainability planning, community support and social services, advanced and specialized education, and reproductive health.
Fields of interest: Arts; Education; Environment, natural resources; Environment; Hospitals (general); Reproductive health, family planning; Health care; Mental health/crisis services; Human services; Children/youth, services; Youth, pregnancy prevention; Family services; Aging, centers/services; Community/economic development; Children/youth; Youth; Adults; Young adults; Disabilities, people with; Physically disabled; African Americans/Blacks; Women; Crime/abuse victims; Immigrants/refugees; Economically disadvantaged.
Type of support: General/operating support; Continuing support; Capital campaigns; Equipment; Program development; Conferences/seminars; Film/video/radio; Publication; Seed money; Curriculum development; Scholarship funds; Research; Technical assistance; Matching/challenge support.
Limitations: Applications not accepted. **Giving on a national and international basis, but primary focus is San Francisco and Marin counties, CA.** No grants to individuals or for annual campaigns, land acquisition or K-12 school reform; no loans.
Publications: Annual report; Grants list.
Application information: The foundation is currently not accepting any unsolicited letters of inquiry or grant proposals.

Board meeting date(s): Apr. and Nov.

Officers and Trustees:* Annette Gellert,* Co-Chair.; Fred Gellert,* Co-Chair.
Number of staff: 1 full-time professional; 2 part-time professional; 1 part-time support.
EIN: 946062859
Other changes: Annette Gellert is now Co-Chair. Fred Gellert is now Co-Chair.

215
The Carl Gellert and Celia Berta Gellert Foundation

(formerly The Carl Gellert Foundation)
2171 Junipero Serra Blvd., Ste. 310
Daly City, CA 94014-1995 (650) 985-2080
***Contact:* Jack Fitzpatrick, Exec. Dir.; Rosa King, Grants Mgr.**
E-mail: info@gellertfoundation.org; Main URL: http://www.gellertfoundation.org/

Incorporated in 1958 in CA.
Donors: Carl Gellert†; Gertrude E. Gellert†; Celia Berta Gellert†; Atlas Realty Co.; Pacific Coast Construction Co.
Foundation type: Independent foundation.
Financial data (yr. ended 12/31/12): Assets, $40,316,647 (M); expenditures, $2,538,173; qualifying distributions, $2,168,762; giving activities include $1,941,000 for 180 grants (high: $125,000; low: $1,000).
Fields of interest: Literature; Elementary school/education; Secondary school/education; Higher education; Engineering school/education; Education; Hospitals (general); Substance abuse, services; Human services; Youth, services; Aging, centers/services; Engineering.
Type of support: General/operating support; Continuing support; Annual campaigns; Capital campaigns; Building/renovation; Equipment; Endowments; Program development; Publication; Scholarship funds; Research; Technical assistance.
Limitations: Applications accepted. Giving limited to the nine counties of the greater San Francisco Bay Area, CA, (Alameda, Contra Costa, Marin, Napa, San Francisco, San Mateo, Santa Clara, Solano and Sonoma). No support for private foundations or for organizations outside the 9 counties of the San Francisco Bay Area. No grants to individuals or fiscal sponsors, or for seed money, emergency funds, land acquisition, matching gifts, conferences, sponsorships, fundraising events sponsorships, dinners, walk-a-thons, tournaments, or fashion shows; no loans.
Publications: Application guidelines; Grants list; Program policy statement.
Application information: Application form available on web site. Application form required.

Initial approach: Proposal with application form and supporting documentation outlined in posted guidelines
Copies of proposal: 1
Deadline(s): Annually, on Aug. 15
Board meeting date(s): Nov.
Final notification: In writing, for all decisions, annually on Dec. 31

Officers and Directors:* Robert J. Grassilli,* Chair.; Andrew A. Cresci,* Vice-Chair.; Jack Fitzpatrick,* Secy. and Exec. Dir.; Lorraine D'Elia; Michael J. King; J. Malcolm Visbal.
Number of staff: 1 full-time professional; 1 full-time support.
EIN: 946062858
Other changes: Marie C. Bentley is no longer Treas. and Admin. Dir.

216
Genentech Foundation

1 DNA Way, M.S. 24
South San Francisco, CA 94080-4918 (877) 313-5778
E-mail: foundation@gene.com; Main URL: http://www.genentechfoundation.com/index.html

Established in 2002.
Donor: Genentech, Inc.
Foundation type: Company-sponsored foundation.
Financial data (yr. ended 12/31/12): Assets, $28,870,009 (M); expenditures, $2,035,279; qualifying distributions, $2,025,260; giving activities include $1,980,100 for 28 grants (high: $200,000; low: $40,000).
Purpose and activities: The foundation supports programs designed to promote health science education; community-wide civic initiatives; and national patient education and advocacy efforts.
Fields of interest: Higher education; Graduate/professional education; Medical school/education; Libraries (public); Education; Health care, patient services; Health care; Cancer; Pediatrics; Employment, services; Employment, training; Food services; Food banks; Housing/shelter; Community/economic development; Science, formal/general education; Public affairs.
Type of support: General/operating support; Continuing support; Program development; Curriculum development; Fellowships; Research.
Limitations: Applications accepted. Giving primarily in areas of company operations in North San Diego County, Oceanside, South San Francisco, San Francisco County, San Mateo County, Solano County, and Vacaville, CA, Jefferson County, KY, and Washington County, OR; giving also to national organizations. No support for discriminatory organizations, professional sports athletes, religious organizations not of direct benefit to the entire community, or political organizations. No grants to individuals, or for alumni drives, capital campaigns or building funds, infrastructural requests including salary or equipment, memorial funds, professional sports events, sponsorships, or yearbooks.
Publications: Application guidelines; Informational brochure; Program policy statement.
Application information: A site visit may be requested. Application form required.

Initial approach: Complete online application
Copies of proposal: 1
***Deadline(s):* Jan. 30, Apr. 5, July 5, and Sept. 27**
Board meeting date(s): Mar., June, Sept., and Dec.

Officers and Directors:* Richard H. Scheller, Ph.D.*, Chair.; Ashraf Hanna, C.F.O.; Colleen Wilson, Exec. Dir.; Sunil Agarwal, M.D.; Vishva Dixit, M.D.; Markus Gemuend; Nancy Oaks; Michelle Rohrer, Ph.D.; Mary B. Silwkowski, Ph.D.; Denise Smith-Hams; Geoff Teeter.
EIN: 460500264
Other changes: Cynthia Brown-Dunn is now Grants Mgr.

217
Wallace Alexander Gerbode Foundation

77 Van Ness Ave., Ste. 200
San Francisco, CA 94102-6042 (415) 391-0911
Contact: Molly Barrons, Admin. Mgr.
FAX: (415) 992-4723; E-mail: info@gerbode.org; Main URL: http://www.foundationcenter.org/grantmaker/gerbode/
Grants List: http://foundationcenter.org/grantmaker/gerbode/grcomm.html

Incorporated in 1953 in CA.
Donor: Members of the Gerbode family.
Foundation type: Independent foundation.
Financial data (yr. ended 12/31/12): Assets, $59,511,941 (M); expenditures, $3,812,936; qualifying distributions, $3,349,382; giving activities include $2,602,966 for 117 grants (high: $100,000; low: $845).
Purpose and activities: Support for programs and projects offering the potential for significant impact in the areas of arts and culture, the environment, population, reproductive rights, citizen participation/building communities/inclusiveness, strength of the philanthropic process and the

nonprofit sector, and foundation-initiated special projects. Grants also to California artists through its Special Awards in the Arts program, to support fresh, dynamic new work in dance, theater and music.
Fields of interest: Arts; Environment; Civil liberties, reproductive rights; Civil/human rights; Community/economic development; Philanthropy/voluntarism; Public affairs; Adults; Aging; Young adults; Minorities; Asians/Pacific Islanders; African Americans/Blacks; Hispanics/Latinos; Indigenous peoples; Women; Girls; Adults, women; Young adults, female; Men; Adults, men; Young adults, male; Immigrants/refugees; LGBTQ.
Type of support: Management development/capacity building; Program development; Technical assistance; Consulting services; Matching/challenge support.
Limitations: Applications accepted. Giving primarily to programs directly affecting residents of Alameda, Contra Costa, Marin, San Francisco, and San Mateo counties in CA, and HI. No support for religious purposes or private schools. No grants to individuals (except for individual artist sections of the foundation's Special Awards in the Arts program), or for direct services, deficit budgets, general operating funds, building or equipment funds, general fundraising campaigns, publications, or scholarships.
Publications: Application guidelines; Annual report; Financial statement; Grants list.
Application information: Application form not required.
Initial approach: Letter; initial contact should not include materials (including DVDs) requiring a return.
Copies of proposal: 1
Board meeting date(s): 4 times per year
Final notification: Generally 2 to 3 months; the foundation's Special Awards in the Arts grants are announced in Jan.
Officers and Trustees:* Maryanna G. Stockholm,* Chair.; Frank A. Gerbode, M.D.*, Vice-Chair. and Secy.; Charles M. Stockholm,* Vice-Chair. and Treas.; **Stacie Ma'a, Pres.**; Sharon Gerbode, Member; Sarah Shaw, Member.
Number of staff: 2 full-time professional; 2 full-time support; 1 part-time support.
EIN: 946065226
Other changes: Stacie Ma'a has replaced Thomas C. Layton as Pres.

218
The Ann and Gordon Getty Foundation
1 Embarcadero Ctr., Ste. 1350
San Francisco, CA **94111-3700**

Established in 1986 in CA.
Donors: Gordon P. Getty; G.P.G. Foundation.
Foundation type: Independent foundation.
Financial data (yr. ended 12/31/12): Assets, $63,919 (M); gifts received, $9,608,000; expenditures, $9,550,742; qualifying distributions, $9,541,850; giving activities include $9,305,000 for 477 grants (high: $2,000,000; low: $500).
Purpose and activities: Support primarily for symphonies, opera companies, and educational institutions.
Fields of interest: Museums; Performing arts; Performing arts, music; Education; Anthropology/sociology.
Type of support: General/operating support; Continuing support; Annual campaigns; Matching/challenge support.
Limitations: Applications not accepted. Giving primarily in CA, with emphasis on the San Francisco Bay Area. No grants to individuals.
Application information: Contributes only to pre-selected organizations.
Board meeting date(s): Annually
Officer and Directors:* Gordon P. Getty,* Chair. and Pres.; Lisa DeLan; Matthew A. Hall; William A. Newsom.
EIN: 954078340

219
GGS Foundation
(formerly Georgina G. Stevens Foundation)
1660 Bush St., Ste. 300
San Francisco, CA **94109-5308** (415) 561-6540
***Contact:* Shawna Hamilton, Grants Mgr.**
***FAX:* (415) 561-5477;**
E-mail: shamilton@pfs-llc.net; Main URL: http://www.pfs-llc.net/ggs/ggs.html

Established in 1992 in CA.
Donors: Georgiana G. Stevens; The Georgiana G. Stevens 1997 Trust.
Foundation type: Independent foundation.
Financial data (yr. ended 12/31/12): Assets, $19,254,850 (M); expenditures, $1,035,510; qualifying distributions, $922,616; giving activities include $807,010 for 33 grants (high: $50,000; low: $1,510).
Purpose and activities: Giving primarily for: 1) Promoting literacy for children from pre-K through third grade, including access to books, acquisition of reading, writing, and comprehension skills, and application of literacy skills to critical thinking and self-expression; 2) Preventing substance abuse and promoting healthy living for children and youth, with emphasis on programs that enable youth to make healthy decisions and form healthy relationships; and 3) Building vocational and workplace skills for middle and high school-aged youth.
Fields of interest: Substance abuse, prevention; Youth development; Children/youth.
Type of support: Continuing support; Annual campaigns.
Limitations: Applications accepted. Giving primarily in San Francisco, CA. No support for religious organizations, or for medical research. No grants to individuals, or for endowments, events, annual appeals, videos, capital campaigns or conferences.
Publications: Application guidelines; Annual report; Grants list.
Application information: Application form required.
***Initial approach:* Use online application system on foundation web site**
Copies of proposal: 1
***Deadline(s):* See foundation web site for current deadlines**
Board meeting date(s): Spring and Fall
Officers: John H. Kirkwood, Pres.; Amanda H. Kirkwood, V.P.; Jean K. Casey, Secy.-Treas.
Director: A. Michael Casey.
EIN: 943155521

220
The Gibson, Dunn & Crutcher Foundation
333 S. Grand Ave.
Los Angeles, CA 90071-1504 (213) 229-7252
Contact: Charles E. Woodhouse, C.F.O.

Established in 1990 in CA.
Donor: Gibson, Dunn & Crutcher LLP.
Foundation type: Independent foundation.
Financial data (yr. ended 12/31/13): Assets, $965,776 (M); expenditures, $2,123,470; qualifying distributions, $2,111,483; giving activities include $2,111,483 for 133 grants (high: $160,000; low: $3,500).
Fields of interest: Health organizations, association; Medical research, institute; Legal services; Civil/human rights; United Ways and Federated Giving Programs; Jewish federated giving programs; Public policy, research.
Limitations: Applications accepted. Giving primarily in Los Angeles, CA, Washington, DC, and NY.
Application information: Application form not required.
Initial approach: Letter
Deadline(s): None
Officers: Kenneth M. Doran, Pres.; Dean J. Kitchens, Secy.; Charles E. Woodhouse, C.F.O.
Directors: Theodore J. Boutrous, Jr.; **Thomas H. Dupree, Jr.**; Randy M. Mastro.
EIN: 954301635
Other changes: Mary G. Murphy is no longer a director.

221
The William G. Gilmore Foundation
1660 Bush St., Ste. 300
San Francisco, CA 94109-5308
Contact: Eric L. Sloan, Admin.; Maereg Haile, Prog. Coord.
E-mail: esloan@pfs-llc.net; Tel. extension for Maereg Haile: 201; e-mail address for Maereg Haile: mhaile@pfs-llc.org; Main URL: http://www.williamggilmorefoundation.org

Incorporated in 1953 in CA.
Donors: William G. Gilmore†; Mrs. William G. Gilmore†.
Foundation type: Independent foundation.
Financial data (yr. ended 12/31/12): Assets, $22,127,793 (M); expenditures, $1,810,533; qualifying distributions, $1,657,378; giving activities include $1,581,500 for 106 grants (high: $100,000; low: $1,500).
Purpose and activities: The foundation's mission is to support: the educational opportunities for young people; provide for the health and welfare of the ill and disabled; assist those in need of food, shelter, and counseling; and encourage the arts and other activities generally related to the foregoing.
Fields of interest: Human services; Children/youth, services; Children/youth; Youth; Aging; Disabilities, people with; Terminal illness, people with; Economically disadvantaged; Homeless.
Type of support: General/operating support; Continuing support; Building/renovation; Equipment.
Limitations: Applications accepted. Giving primarily in the Alameda, Contra Costa, Marin, San Francisco, and San Mateo counties in CA, and in OR. No grants to individuals.
Publications: Application guidelines.
Application information: Oregon organizations should not send letters of inquiry or any other materials to the foundation. Board trustees will personally invite eligible organizations from Oregon to apply. Application guidelines available on foundation web site. Audio-visual materials, binders, folders or pamphlets should not be submitted unless requested. Application form not required.
***Initial approach:* Bay Area organizations may use online application process on foundation web site**
Copies of proposal: 1

Deadline(s): See foundation web site for current deadlines
Board meeting date(s): June and Dec.
Final notification: Within 2-3 business days for e-mails
Officers and Trustees:* Mary Lee Boklund,* Pres.; Bob Baton,* V.P.; David Jubb,* Secy.; William Mackay, C.F.O. and Treas.; **Emily Schroeder, Mgr., Grants.**
EIN: 946079493

222
GirlSMART Literacy Program
(formerly National Literacy Program Fund)
21 Orinda Way, Ste. C, #358
Orinda, CA **94563-2534 (925) 254-6358**
Contact: Barclay Simpson, Pres.

Established in CA.
Donor: Barclay Simpson.
Foundation type: Independent foundation.
Financial data (yr. ended 12/31/12): Assets, $59,212 (M); gifts received, $410,200; expenditures, $426,016; qualifying distributions, $299,834; giving activities include $299,834 for grants.
Purpose and activities: Giving for the improvement of children's literacy.
Fields of interest: Education, early childhood education.
Limitations: Applications accepted. Giving primarily in Omaha, NE, NH, Buffalo, NY, Rapid City, SD.
Application information:
Initial approach: Letter
Deadline(s): None
Officers: Barclay Simpson, Pres.; Sharon Simpson, Secy.
EIN: 263542627

223
GLA Foundation
Costa Mesa, CA

The foundation terminated on May 31, 2013.

224
Gleason Family Foundation
(formerly Gleason Foundation)
1112 Sir Francis Drake Blvd.
Kentfield, CA 94904-1419
Contact: Marcia Smith, C.O.O.

Established in 2006 in DE a as successor to Gleason Family Foundation located in NY.
Foundation type: Independent foundation.
Financial data (yr. ended 12/31/12): Assets, $167,948,066 (M); expenditures, $11,177,933; qualifying distributions, $10,486,837; giving activities include $6,822,471 for 95 grants (high: $1,717,000; low: $50), $1,717,402 for foundation-administered programs and $37,500 for 1 loan/program-related investment.
Fields of interest: Elementary school/education; Secondary school/education.
Limitations: Applications not accepted. Giving primarily in U.S. No grants to individuals.
Application information: Contributes only to pre-selected organizations.
Officers and Directors:* James S. Gleason,* Chair.; Tracy R. Gleason,* C.E.O. and Pres.; Janis F. Gleason,* Secy.-Treas.; Ralph E. Harper; Gary J. Kimmet; Albert W. Moore; Jeffery P. Robinson.
EIN: 205804684
Other changes: Tracy Gleason is now C.E.O. and Pres.

225
Glenn Foundation for Medical Research, Inc.
(formerly Paul F. Glenn Foundation for Medical Research, Inc.)
1270 Coast Village Cir., St. 200
Santa Barbara, CA 93108-3724
Contact: Mark R. Collins, Pres.
E-mail: mrc@glennfoundation.org; Main URL: http://www.glennfoundation.org

Established in 1965 in NY; reincorporated in 1992 in AZ.
Donor: Paul F. Glenn.
Foundation type: Independent foundation.
Financial data (yr. ended 09/30/13): Assets, $245,703,267 (M); gifts received, $16,479,609; expenditures, $10,346,058; qualifying distributions, $6,478,696; giving activities include $6,448,409 for 18+ grants (high: $1,455,000).
Purpose and activities: The purpose of the foundation is to extend the healthy, productive years of life, through research into the mechanisms of biological aging.
Fields of interest: Medical research, institute; Geriatrics research; Biology/life sciences; Aging.
Type of support: Conferences/seminars; Fellowships; Research.
Limitations: Applications not accepted. Giving on a national basis. No support for sociological, as opposed to biological, aging projects.
Publications: Grants list; Informational brochure; Program policy statement.
Application information: Unsolicited requests for funds not accepted.
Board meeting date(s): Annually
Officers and Directors:* Paul F. Glenn,* Chair. and Treas.; Mark R. Collins,* Pres.; K. Leonard Judson,* Exec. V.P. and Secy.; **A. Ray Copeland**; **Jack N. Rudel**.
Number of staff: None.
EIN: 860710305
Other changes: Paul F. Glenn is now Chair. and Treas. .

226
Thornton S., Jr. and Katrina D. Glide Foundation
28120 Pierce Ranch Rd.
Davis, CA 95616-9447 (530) 753-3803
FAX: (530) 753-3849;
E-mail: glidefoundation@sprynet.com; Main URL: http://www.glidefoundation.org/

Established in 1997 in CA.
Donors: Katrina D. Glide†; The George and Lena Valente Foundation.
Foundation type: Independent foundation.
Financial data (yr. ended 12/31/12): Assets, $36,243,161 (M); expenditures, $1,997,154; qualifying distributions, $1,562,130; giving activities include $632,061 for 121 grants (high: $50,000; low: $500), and $930,069 for foundation-administered programs.
Purpose and activities: Giving to organizations committed to the preservation of lands in their natural state, including wetlands; organizations committed to agricultural purposes; land and wildlife conservancy groups, and animal protection organizations.
Fields of interest: Arts; Environment, land resources; Animal welfare; Animals/wildlife, preservation/protection; Housing/shelter; Human services; United Ways and Federated Giving Programs.
Limitations: Applications accepted. **Giving primarily in CA. Out of state applicants will be considered.** No support for programs focused primarily on a sport, general educational institutions, or religious organizations (except for community social service activities). No grants to individuals; no scholarships.
Application information: See foundation web site for downloadable application form. Application form required.
Deadline(s): May 15 to Aug. 15
Trustees: Richard D. Bruga; Yvonne LeMaitre; Russell E. White.
EIN: 943276694

227
Maxwell H. Gluck Foundation, Inc.
P.O. Box 55516
Sherman Oaks, CA 91413-0516
Contact: Camilla Townsend, Exec. Dir.
Main URL: http://www.gluckfoundation.org

Established in 1955 in NY.
Donor: Maxwell H. Gluck†.
Foundation type: Independent foundation.
Financial data (yr. ended 06/30/13): Assets, $104,239,647 (M); expenditures, $5,646,545; qualifying distributions, $4,806,893; giving activities include $4,679,803 for 20 grants (high: $833,291; low: $24,505).
Purpose and activities: Support for higher and other education, and the arts.
Fields of interest: Arts education; Arts; Higher education; Education; Human services.
Limitations: Applications not accepted. Giving limited to southern CA. No grants to individuals.
Application information: Contributes only to pre-selected organizations. Unsolicited requests for funds not accepted.
Officers and Directors:* Jon A. Kaswick, M.D.*, Pres.; Julie Kaswick, Secy.; Camilla Townsend, Exec. Dir.; Jennifer Kaswick; Richard G. Reinis; Betty S. Shelhamer.
Number of staff: 1 part-time support.
EIN: 953979100

228
The David B. Gold Foundation
44 Montgomery St., Ste. 3750
San Francisco, CA 94104-4826 (415) 288-9530
Contact: Elaine Gold, Exec. Dir.
FAX: (415) 288-9549;
E-mail: rose@goldfoundation.org; Main URL: http://www.goldfoundation.org/
Grants List: http://www.goldfoundation.org/grants_awarded/grants_awarded.htm
Knowledge Center: http://www.goldfoundation.org/information_links/information_links.htm

Established in 1992 in CA.
Donor: David B. Gold†.
Foundation type: Independent foundation.
Financial data (yr. ended 12/31/12): Assets, $95,576,376 (M); expenditures, $5,037,232; qualifying distributions, $4,148,267; giving activities include $3,442,500 for 116 grants (high: $150,000; low: $500).

Purpose and activities: Giving primarily for: 1) children, youth and families, particularly to support early childhood development programs, promote enrichment programs for school age youth, reduce domestic violence, improve the welfare of children, and to help prevent teen parenthood; 2) the environment, particularly to reduce toxic emissions, preserve open space, and promote sustainable energy policy; 3) democratic values, 4) and Jewish culture.
Fields of interest: Environment, natural resources; Reproductive health, family planning; Crime/ violence prevention, child abuse; Youth development; Jewish agencies & synagogues.
Type of support: General/operating support; Continuing support; Capital campaigns; Building/ renovation; Land acquisition; Program development.
Limitations: Applications accepted. Giving primarily to organizations that have an impact on the San Francisco Bay Area, CA, with emphasis on Alameda and San Francisco counties and in the Twin Cities of Minneapolis/St. Paul, MN; some funding to national projects that are particularly relevant to the foundation's mission. No support for sectarian organizations, except for those organizations that fall within the foundation's Jewish Culture program area. **No grants to individuals, which includes projects for research, attending conferences, scholarships, musical works, or film.**
Publications: Application guidelines.
Application information: See foundation web site for complete application guidelines. Application form required.
Initial approach: **On-line proposal via foundation web site**
Copies of proposal: 1
Deadline(s): None
Board meeting date(s): Quarterly
Final notification: Within 4 months after the proposal is received
Officers and Directors:* Barbara Gold-Lurie,* Pres.; Diane Gold-Bubier,* Secy.; Steven A. Gold,* Treas. and C.F.O.; Elaine Gold,* Exec. Dir.; Emily Gold.
EIN: 943169439

229
Sheila Gold Foundation
3940 Laurel Canyon Blvd., Ste. 139
Studio City, CA **91604-3709**
***Contact:* Jeff Gold**

Established in 1997 in CA.
Donors: Dave Gold; Sherry Gold; Jeff Gold; Howard Gold; Karen Schiffer.
Foundation type: Independent foundation.
Financial data (yr. ended 12/31/12): Assets, $43,834,897 (M); gifts received, $32,676,701; expenditures, $1,904,776; qualifying distributions, $1,897,177; giving activities include $1,897,177 for grants.
Purpose and activities: Giving primarily for health organizations and medical research, as well as for Jewish organizations, education, and children, youth, and social services.
Fields of interest: Higher education; Education; Health organizations, association; Medical research, institute; Human services; Children/ youth, services; Jewish agencies & synagogues.
Limitations: Applications not accepted. Giving primarily in Los Angeles, CA. No grants to individuals.
Application information: Contributes only to pre-selected organizations.
Trustees: David Gold; Howard Gold; Jeff Gold; Sherry Gold; Karen Schiffer.
EIN: 954636060

230
The Good Works Foundation
2101 Wilshire Blvd., Ste. 225
Santa Monica, CA 90403-5746 (310) 828-1288
FAX: (310) 829-6090; E-mail: info@goodworks.org;
Main URL: http://www.goodworks.org

Established in 1993 in CA.
Donor: Laura Donnelley Family Trust.
Foundation type: Independent foundation.
Financial data (yr. ended 12/31/12): Assets, $2,195,922 (M); gifts received, $992,322; expenditures, $1,048,571; qualifying distributions, $1,009,330; giving activities include $1,009,330 for 81 grants (high: $301,880; low: $500).
Purpose and activities: Giving primarily for the arts, the environment, social action and education, with an emphasis on grassroots organizations and innovative ideas in the Los Angeles, CA, area.
Fields of interest: Museums (art); Performing arts, opera; Arts; Education; Environment.
Type of support: General/operating support; Seed money; Matching/challenge support.
Limitations: Giving primarily in the Los Angeles, CA, area and NY. No support for political causes. No grants to individuals, for fellowships, capital expenditures, construction or endowments.
Publications: Application guidelines.
Application information: Applications are by invitation only, upon review of initial e-mail. Application form not required.
Initial approach: E-mail via contact page on foundation web site
Deadline(s): None
Board meeting date(s): Quarterly
Officer and Trustees:* Laura Donnelley,* Pres.; Philip Yenawine.
Number of staff: 1 part-time support.
EIN: 954471685

231
Google Foundation
1600 Amphitheatre Pkwy.
Mountain View, CA 94043-1351
Main URL: http://www.google.org/foundation.html
RSS Feed: http://feeds.feedburner.com/OfficialGoogleorgBlog
The Official Google.org Blog: http://blog.google.org/
Twitter: https://twitter.com/#!/googlenonprofit
YouTube: http://www.youtube.com/user/Googleorg

Established in 2004 in CA.
Donor: Google Inc.
Foundation type: Company-sponsored foundation.
Financial data (yr. ended 12/31/12): Assets, $72,412,693 (M); gifts received, $39,560,000; expenditures, $39,984,747; qualifying distributions, $39,647,902; giving activities include $39,606,000 for 14 grants (high: $5,000,000; low: $1,200,000).
Purpose and activities: The foundation supports organizations involved with arts and culture, education and computer science, the environment, international development, women and girls, and poverty.
Fields of interest: Media/communications; Museums; Arts; Higher education; Education; Environment, climate change/global warming; Environment, water resources; Animals/wildlife; Disasters, preparedness/services; Children, services; Human services; International development; International human rights; Anti-slavery/human trafficking; Microfinance/microlending; Computer science; Women; Girls; Economically disadvantaged.
Type of support: General/operating support; Program development.
Limitations: Applications not accepted. **Giving primarily in CA, Washington, DC, and NY; giving also to international organizations in the United Kingdom.**
Publications: Financial statement; IRS Form 990 or 990-PF printed copy available upon request.
Application information: Contributes only to pre-selected organizations. Grants are administered in part by Google.org.
Officers and Directors:* Mathew Stepka,* Pres.; Chris Busselle, Secy.; Kristin Reinke, Treas.; Sergey Brin; Shona Brown; Lawrence Page; Alfred Spector.
EIN: 201548253
Other changes: At the close of 2012, the grantmaker paid grants of $39,606,000, a 247.4% increase over the 2011 disbursements, $11,402,000.
Mathew Stepka has replaced Shona Brown as Pres.
Jay Boren is no longer Secy.

232
The Grass Foundation
P.O. Box 241458
Los Angeles, CA 90024-9258 (424) 832-4188
FAX: (310) 986-2252;
E-mail: info@grassfoundation.org; Main URL: http://www.grassfoundation.org
Blog: http://grasslab11.blogspot.com/
Twitter: https://twitter.com/#!/grassfoundation

Incorporated in 1957 in MA.
Donors: Albert M. Grass†; Ellen R. Grass†; Grass Instrument Co.; Cannon Manufacturing Co.; The Ellen R. Grass Trust.
Foundation type: Independent foundation.
Financial data (yr. ended 12/31/12): Assets, $19,834,897 (M); expenditures, $948,089; qualifying distributions, $766,999; giving activities include $181,500 for 6 grants (high: $55,000; low: $4,500).
Purpose and activities: Giving to encourage research in neurophysiology and the neurosciences; grants primarily for fellowships for summer study at a marine biological laboratory, lectureships, and for higher education.
Fields of interest: Biomedicine; Neuroscience; Medical research; Marine science; Biology/life sciences.
International interests: Africa; Latin America.
Type of support: Fellowships; Research.
Limitations: Applications accepted. Giving primarily in Washington, DC and Woods Hole, MA; with some giving internationally.
Publications: Application guidelines; Informational brochure (including application guidelines); Program policy statement.
Application information: Application formats and deadlines depend upon type of grant; specific information will be sent upon request. Application guidelines and form are available on foundation web site. Application form required.
Initial approach: Refer to foundation web site
Board meeting date(s): Jan. and July
Officers and Trustees:* Felix E. Schweizer, Ph.D.*, Pres.; Bernice Grafstein, Ph.D.*, V.P.; Catherine E. Carr, Ph.D.*, Secy.; Richard Larkin, C.P.A.*, Treas.; Graeme W. Davis, Ph.D; Henry J. Grass, M.D.; **Gregory Holmes, M.D.**; Ronald R. Hoy, Ph.D.; Kamran Khodakhah, Ph.D.; **George Langford, Ph.D.**; **Jeff Lichtman, M.D.**; **Edwin McCleskey,**

Ph.D.; Amy R. Segal, Esq.; Janis C. Weeks, Ph.D.; Steven J. Zottoli, Ph.D.
Number of staff: 2 part-time support.
EIN: 046049529
Other changes: Shelley Adamo and Jeffrey Noebels are no longer directors. Catherine E. Carr is now Secy. Bernice Grafstein is now V.P. Felix E. Schweizer is now Pres.

233
Green Earth Charitable Organization
2906 Belmont Terr.
Fremont, CA **94539-8340**

Donors: Charles Liang; Chiu-Chu Liu; Sara Liang.
Foundation type: Independent foundation.
Financial data (yr. ended 12/31/12): Assets, $3,438,910 (M); expenditures, $272,988; qualifying distributions, $257,903; giving activities include $257,903 for grants.
Fields of interest: Education; Animals/wildlife; Human services.
Limitations: Applications not accepted.
Application information: Unsolicited requests for funds not accepted.
Officer: Carly Kao, Treas.
Director: Sara Liu.
EIN: 261701023

234
Grousbeck Family Foundation
Stanford, CA

The foundation terminated in 2012.

235
GSF Foundation
18301 Von Karman Ave., Ste. 1100
Irvine, CA 92612-0133 (949) 252-2000
E-mail: **helpkids@gsffoundation.org**; Additional tel.: (877) 473-5437; Main URL: http://www.gsffoundation.org
E-Newsletter: http://www.gsffoundation.org/newsletter/
Facebook: https://www.facebook.com/goldenstatefoodsfoundation
GSF Foundation Video: http://www.goldenstatefoods.com/foundationvideo.asp

Established in 2002 in CA and OR.
Donors: Mark S. Wetterau; Golden State Foods Corp.; Mike Echolds; Leslie Echolds; Orange Wood Children's Fdn.
Foundation type: Company-sponsored foundation.
Financial data (yr. ended 12/31/12): Assets, $1,015,384 (M); gifts received, $2,987,586; expenditures, $3,267,939; qualifying distributions, $3,323,984; giving activities include $1,772,125 for 118 grants (high: $418,305; low: $85).
Purpose and activities: The foundation supports programs designed to improve the lives of children and families. Special emphasis is directed toward programs designed to serve children with various needs, including food, shelter, clothes, medical treatment, and social activities.
Fields of interest: Arts; Education; Health care, patient services; Health care; Food services; Food banks; Housing/shelter; Big Brothers/Big Sisters; Boy scouts; Children, services; Family services; Developmentally disabled, centers & services.
Type of support: General/operating support; Capital campaigns; Building/renovation; Equipment; Program development; Employee volunteer services; Sponsorships.
Limitations: Applications accepted. Giving primarily in areas of company operations in AR, CA, GA, IL, MO, NC, NY, OR, SC, VA, WA, and WI. No support for political organizations or candidates, religious, veterans', or fraternal organizations, or sports teams. No grants for individuals, or for sponsorships of fundraising events, tickets or tables, academic or medical research, political causes, sporting events, trips or travel, festivals or parades, or advertising.
Publications: Application guidelines; Newsletter.
Application information: Support is limited to 1 contribution per organization during any given year. Faxed, e-mailed, or videotaped applications are not accepted. Application form not required.
Initial approach: **E-mail letter of inquiry**
Deadline(s): **None**
Officers and Directors:* Mark S. Wetterau,* Chair. and C.E.O.; **Michael Waitukaitis,* Vice-Chair.**; Catherine Duffy, Secy.; Lisa Gottlieb, C.F.O.; Chuck Browne,* Exec. Dir.; Steve Becker; Jim Brooks; Neil Cracknell; Shellie Frey; Jim Fusting; **Mickey Hamer; Daniel Van Hoozer; Frank Listi**; Larry McGill; John Murphy; John Page; Bill Pocilujko; Bill Sanderson; Jeff Steiner; Gregg Tarlton; Scott Thomas.
EIN: 460501728
Other changes: Bob Jorge and Glenn Parish are no longer directors. Michael Waitukaitis is now Vice-Chair. Lisa Gottlieb is now C.F.O.
The grantmaker no longer publishes an annual report.

236
The Josephine S. Gumbiner Foundation
333 W. Broadway, Ste. 312
Long Beach, CA 90802-4438 (562) 437-2882
Contact: Julie Meenan, Secy. and Exec. Dir.
FAX: (562) 437-4212; E-mail: julie@jsgf.org; Main URL: http://www.jsgf.org
Grants List: http://www.jsgf.org/grants-awarded-by-jsgf/

Established in 1989 in CA.
Donor: Josephine S. Gumbiner‡.
Foundation type: Independent foundation.
Financial data (yr. ended 12/31/12): Assets, $13,506,296 (M); expenditures, $880,934; qualifying distributions, $797,065; giving activities include $639,620 for 52 grants (high: $40,000; low: $1,000).
Purpose and activities: The foundation is dedicated to supporting programs that enrich the women and children in the Long Beach area of southern California. It includes programs focusing on day care, job training, housing, after school tutoring, and health care, with a special emphasis on intervention, prevention, and direct service. Previously funded projects by the foundation range from prenatal care to women's shelters to programs for at-risk youth, and participatory cultural programs for children and teens. The foundation's goal is to fund projects that protect and enrich the lives of women and children in Long Beach, California.
Fields of interest: Crime/violence prevention, domestic violence; Crime/violence prevention, child abuse; Human services; Children/youth, services; Family services; Women, centers/services; Minorities/immigrants, centers/services; Civil liberties, reproductive rights; Infants/toddlers; Children/youth; Children; Youth; Aging; Young adults; Disabilities, people with; Physically disabled; Deaf/hearing impaired; Mentally disabled; Minorities; African Americans/Blacks; Hispanics/Latinos; Native Americans/American Indians; Women; Infants/toddlers, female; Girls; Adults, women; Young adults, female; Infants/toddlers, male; Boys; Young adults, male; Substance abusers; Single parents; Crime/abuse victims; Economically disadvantaged; Homeless; LGBTQ.
Type of support: General/operating support; Continuing support; Equipment; Emergency funds; Program development; Technical assistance; Matching/challenge support.
Limitations: Applications accepted. Giving limited to Long Beach, CA. No support for political campaigns, pass through organizations, organizations with endowments greater than $5 million, or organizations with Long Beach, CA client bases of less than 75%. No grants to individuals, or for lobbying efforts, or programs that supplant traditional school funding.
Publications: Application guidelines; Grants list; Informational brochure (including application guidelines).
Application information: Grant application packages are by invitation only, upon review of initial Letter of Intent. Application form required.
Initial approach: E-mail to request Letter of Intent Questionnaire
Copies of proposal: 7
Deadline(s): None
Board meeting date(s): Generally in Mar., June, Sept., and Nov.
Final notification: Within 90 days for Letter of Intent
Officers: Lee Gumbiner,* Pres.; Alis Gumbiner,* C.F.O.; Burke Gumbiner,* V.P.; Julie Meenan,* Secy. and Exec. Dir.
Directors: Art Gottlieb; Alex Norman; Dennis Rockway.
Number of staff: 1 full-time professional; 1 part-time professional.
EIN: 330345249

237
The Guthy-Jackson Charitable Foundation
1018 Pamela Dr.
Beverly Hills, CA **90210-2823**

Established in 2008 in CA.
Donors: William R. Guthy; Victoria Jackson; Mark Madden; David Fett; Kitchelle Custom Homes.
Foundation type: Independent foundation.
Financial data (yr. ended 12/31/13): Assets, $47,725 (M); gifts received, $5,545,273; expenditures, $5,876,506; qualifying distributions, $5,876,346; giving activities include $5,835,966 for 19 grants (high: $2,502,000; low: $39,960).
Fields of interest: Medical research, institute.
Limitations: Applications not accepted. Giving primarily in CA; some giving also in CO, MA, and London, England.
Application information: Contributes only to pre-selected organizations.
Trustees: William R. Guthy; Victoria Jackson.
EIN: 266461545

238
The Guzik Foundation
2443 Wyandotte St.
Mountain View, CA 94043-2350

Established in 1993 in CA.
Donor: Nahum Guzik.
Foundation type: Independent foundation.
Financial data (yr. ended 12/31/12): Assets, $38,904,934 (M); expenditures, $2,188,290; qualifying distributions, $2,031,042; giving

activities include $2,008,000 for 19 grants (high: $1,000,000; low: $2,000).
Purpose and activities: Giving primarily to Jewish organizations, the arts, and for children, youth, and social services; some funding to individuals for their projects.
Fields of interest: Museums; Performing arts; Arts; Higher education; Human services; Children/youth, services; Jewish agencies & synagogues.
Type of support: Grants to individuals.
Limitations: Applications not accepted. Giving primarily in CA.
Application information: Contributes only to pre-selected organizations.
Trustees: Nahum Guzik; **Kira Makagon.**
EIN: 770360079
Other changes: Svetlana Gorzhevskaya is no longer a trustee.

239
Mimi and Peter Haas Fund
(formerly Miriam and Peter Haas Fund)
201 Filbert St., 5th Fl.
San Francisco, CA 94133-3238 (415) 296-9249
Contact: Lynn Merz, Exec. Dir.
FAX: (415) 296-8842

Incorporated in 1982 in CA.
Donors: Peter E. Haas‡; Miriam L. Haas; Elise S. Haas‡.
Foundation type: Independent foundation.
Financial data (yr. ended 12/31/12): Assets, $192,843,330 (M); expenditures, $10,461,454; qualifying distributions, $7,913,522; giving activities include $6,767,270 for 255 grants (high: $250,000; low: $61), and $2,230 for 1 foundation-administered program.
Purpose and activities: The fund's primary focus is early childhood development. Support is for activities that provide San Francisco's young (ages 2-5), low-income children and their families with access to high-quality early childhood programs that are part of a comprehensive, coordinated system. The fund recognizes the importance of connecting the work of its direct service grants to the ongoing discussions of public policy and will seek specific opportunities to share and collaborate with organizations to improve early childhood settings. The fund will also continue trustee-initiated grantmaking to arts, education, public affairs, and health and human services organizations.
Fields of interest: Education, early childhood education.
Type of support: General/operating support; Continuing support; Annual campaigns; Capital campaigns; Building/renovation; Equipment; Endowments; Program development; Curriculum development; Matching/challenge support.
Limitations: Giving primarily in San Francisco, CA; early childhood, direct service component is limited to San Francisco. No grants to individuals.
Publications: Annual report; Financial statement; Grants list.
Application information: Contributes only to pre-selected organizations.
Board meeting date(s): Approximately 4 times per year
Officers and Trustees:* Miriam L. Haas,* Pres.; Lynn Merz, Exec. Dir.; Ari A. Lurie; Daniel L. Lurie.
Number of staff: 5 full-time professional.
EIN: 946064551
Other changes: The grantmaker no longer lists an E-mail address.

240
Robert and Ruth Halperin Foundation
1 Lombard St., Ste. 305
San Francisco, CA **94111-1130**

Established in 1999 in CA.
Donors: Robert Halperin; Ruth Halperin; Philip W. Halperin.
Foundation type: Independent foundation.
Financial data (yr. ended 12/31/12): Assets, $92,325,397 (M); expenditures, $5,287,590; qualifying distributions, $3,960,000; giving activities include $3,960,000 for grants.
Fields of interest: Higher education; Business school/education; Human services.
Limitations: Applications not accepted. Giving primarily in Chicago, IL, Boston, MA and San Francisco and Stanford, CA. No grants to individuals.
Application information: Contributes only to pre-selected organizations.
Officers: Robert Halperin, Pres.; Philip W. Halperin, V.P. and Treas.
Directors: Peggy Dow; Mark Halperin.
EIN: 943334424

241
The Hand Foundation
P.O. Box 5655
Redwood City, CA 94063-0655
Contact: Radha Blackman, Exec. Dir.
FAX: (650) 599-9025;
E-mail: info@thehandfoundation.org; Main URL: http://www.thehandfoundation.org
E-Newsletter: http://thehandfoundation.org/newsletter
Facebook: https://www.facebook.com/pages/The-HAND-Foundation/397390166996630
LinkedIn: http://www.linkedin.com/company/3286976?trk=prof-exp-company-name
Twitter: https://twitter.com/HandFound

Established in 2003 in CA.
Donors: Noosheen Hashemi; Farzad Nazem.
Foundation type: Independent foundation.
Financial data (yr. ended 06/30/13): Assets, $12,812,622 (M); gifts received, $721,799; expenditures, $452,490; qualifying distributions, $354,609; giving activities include $202,191 for 49 grants (high: $50,000; low: $250).
Purpose and activities: The foundation's mission is to advance the philanthropic sector, prevent child sexual abuse, build a global middle class, and prepare and engage the Next Generation.
Fields of interest: Education; Crime/violence prevention, sexual abuse; Community/economic development; Philanthropy/voluntarism.
Type of support: Annual campaigns; Fellowships; Research; Scholarships—to individuals.
Limitations: Applications accepted. Giving primarily in CA and Washington, DC. No support for political and religious organizations. **No grants for travel expenses.**
Publications: Grants list.
Application information: The foundation will accept unsolicited proposals, but for the most part will only fund organizations it knows well. See web site for application and for guidelines. Application form required.
Initial approach: Letter of inquiry
Copies of proposal: 1
***Deadline(s):* Mar. 1, June 1, Sept. 1, and Dec. 1 (for letters of inquiry)**
Board meeting date(s): Varies
Officers and Board Members:* Noosheen Hashemi,* Pres.; Farzad Nazem,* Secy.; Nasrin Hashemi,* Treas.; Radha Blackman, Exec. Dir.
Number of staff: 1 full-time professional; 2 part-time professional.
EIN: 562403164
Other changes: The grantmaker now makes its grants list available online.

242
William H. Hannon Foundation
729 Montana Ave., Ste. 5
Santa Monica, CA 90403-1369
Contact: Kathleen Hannon Aikenhead, Pres.
FAX: (310) 260-9740; Main URL: http://www.hannonfoundation.org

Established in 1983 in CA.
Donor: William Herbert Hannon‡.
Foundation type: Independent foundation.
Financial data (yr. ended 09/30/13): Assets, $31,493,100 (M); expenditures, $3,543,186; qualifying distributions, $3,199,436; giving activities include $3,003,829 for 321 grants (high: $625,000; low: $35).
Purpose and activities: Giving primarily to enhance the welfare and education of students in both public and private elementary schools, high schools, and universities, primarily within the greater Los Angeles, California area; to aid in the advancement of health care and human services, especially for those who are least able to afford quality care; to address the needs of the disadvantaged, aged, sick, and homeless; and to support and promote the values of the founder's faith through the support of the good works of the Roman Catholic Church.
Fields of interest: Elementary/secondary education; Higher education; Education; Health care; Catholic agencies & churches.
Type of support: General/operating support; Continuing support; Capital campaigns; Building/renovation; Program development; Scholarship funds.
Limitations: Giving primarily in Los Angeles and the southern CA area. No support for private foundations, or for political organizations. No grants to individuals, or for underwriting parties, travel funds, advertisements, or radio or television programming.
Publications: Application guidelines.
Application information: Application information and procedures available on foundation web site. Application form not required.
Initial approach: Letter only
Copies of proposal: 1
Deadline(s): Aug. 1, Nov.1, Feb. 1, and May 1
Board meeting date(s): Sept., Dec., Mar., and June
Final notification: 1 month from receipt
Officers and Directors:* Kathleen Hannon Aikenhead,* Pres.; Nancy B. Cunningham,* V.P. and Secy.; James A. Hannon,* V.P. and C.F.O.; David W. Burcham; David A. Herbst; Robert B. Lawton, S.J.; Rev. Msgr. Royale M. Vadakin.
Number of staff: 1 full-time professional; 1 part-time support.
EIN: 953847664
Other changes: For the fiscal year ended Sept. 30, 2013, the grantmaker paid grants of $3,003,829, a 94.5% increase over the fiscal 2012 disbursements, $1,544,647.

243
The John Randolph Haynes and Dora Haynes Foundation
888 W. 6th St., Ste. 1150
Los Angeles, CA 90017-2737 (213) 623-9151
Contact: William J. Burke, Admin. Dir.
FAX: (213) 623-3951;
E-mail: info@haynesfoundation.org; Main URL: http://www.haynesfoundation.org
Grants Database: http://www.haynesfoundation.org/searcharchive/index.asp

Trust established in 1926 in CA.
Donors: John Randolph Haynes‡; Mrs. Dora Fellows Haynes‡.
Foundation type: Independent foundation.
Financial data (yr. ended 08/31/13): Assets, $48,435,186 (M); expenditures, $2,476,013; qualifying distributions, $1,942,746; giving activities include $1,499,500 for grants.
Purpose and activities: The foundation promotes the well-being of mankind by making grants for study and research in the social sciences (economics, history, government, and sociology) with emphasis on education, the environment, immigration and public policy. It also provides doctoral dissertation fellowships, and fellowships for faculty members in the social sciences at colleges and universities in the greater Los Angeles region. Grants made only through local colleges and universities or other nonprofit institutions.
Fields of interest: Social sciences; Public policy, research.
Type of support: Fellowships; Research.
Limitations: Applications accepted. Giving limited to the greater Los Angeles, CA, area. No support for political or religious organizations. No grants to individuals, or for building or endowment funds, operating budgets, or capital improvements.
Publications: Application guidelines; Annual report; Biennial report; Financial statement; Grants list; Informational brochure; Informational brochure (including application guidelines); Newsletter; Program policy statement.
Application information: Application for a faculty fellowship, doctoral dissertation fellowship, or research study grant is made directly to the foundation. See foundation web site for detailed submission guidelines. Application form not required.
Initial approach: Letter or telephone
***Copies of proposal:* 5**
Deadline(s): See foundation web site for deadlines
Board meeting date(s): Quarterly
Final notification: 2 months from receipt
Officer and Trustees:* Jane G. Pisano,* Pres. and Secy.-Treas.; Philip M. Hawley,* V.P.; Gilbert T. Ray,* V.P.; Robert A. Eckert; Gil Garcetti; Enrique Hernandez, Jr.; Daniel A. Mazmanian; Robert Suro; Willis B. Wood, Jr.
Number of staff: 1 full-time professional; 1 full-time support.
EIN: 951644020
Other changes: Jane G. Pisano is now Pres. and Secy.-Treas. Philip M. Hawley and Gilbert T. Ray are now V.P.s. Kent Kresa is no longer a trustee.

244
The HealthCare Foundation for Orange County
(formerly Westmed Health Foundation)
1450 N. Tustin Ave., Ste. 209
Santa Ana, CA 92705-8667 (714) 245-1650
FAX: (714) 245-1653; Main URL: http://www.hfoc.org

Established in 1994 in CA; converted from the sale of United Western Medical Centers and its affiliates.
Donors: United Western Medical Centers; The California Wellness Foundation; Russell Guy and Ruth Louise Morgan Trust.
Foundation type: Independent foundation.
Financial data (yr. ended 03/31/13): Assets, $16,100,156 (M); expenditures, $725,533; qualifying distributions, $513,407; giving activities include $436,623 for 10 grants (high: $133,356; low: $695).
Purpose and activities: Giving to improve the health of the neediest and most underserved residents of Orange County, CA, by advancing access to health promotion, prevention, and basic health care.
Fields of interest: Hospitals (general); Hospitals (specialty); Health care; Mental health/crisis services; Breast cancer; Asthma; Pediatrics; Obstetrics/gynecology; Human services; Children/youth, services; Family services.
Limitations: Giving primarily in Orange County, CA. No support for biomedical research organizations, disease-specific organizations seeking support for their national programs, or for religious or fraternal organizations. No grants to individuals, or for annual campaigns, social events, telethons, building projects or equipment.
Publications: Annual report; Informational brochure (including application guidelines).
Application information: Application guidelines and procedures available on foundation web site. No faxed proposals. Application form required.
Initial approach: Follow proposal guidelines on web site for Gold Fund for Health and Partners for Health program.
Deadline(s): See web site for current deadlines
Board meeting date(s): Quarterly
Officers and Directors:* Lilia M. Tanakeyowma,* Chair.; J. Fernando Niebla,* Vice-Chair.; Marven E. Howard,* C.F.O.; Zee Mabel Allred; **David Dobos**; Donald P. Kennedy; Quynh Kieu, M.D.; Anthony M. Magno; Timothy P. Mullins; William B. Stannard; John O. Strong, M.D.
EIN: 330644620

245
The Heising-Simons Foundation
300 2nd St.
Los Altos, CA 94022-3694

Established in 2007 in CA.
Donors: Elizabeth D. Simons; James H. Simons; The Elizabeth Simons DE TR I; The Elizabeth II Trust-Bermuda; The Elizabeth Simons DE Trust II.
Foundation type: Independent foundation.
Financial data (yr. ended 12/31/12): Assets, $234,508,426 (M); gifts received, $56,959,457; expenditures, $20,834,214; qualifying distributions, $18,762,531; giving activities include $17,701,135 for 57 grants (high: $3,575,000; low: $9,000).
Fields of interest: Education; Environment, natural resources; Environment; Social sciences, public policy.
Limitations: Applications not accepted. Giving primarily in CA; funding also in Washington, DC. No grants to individuals.
Application information: Contributes only to pre-selected organizations.
Officers: Elizabeth D. Simons, Pres.; **Joanne Reed, V.P., Opers.**; Mark W. Heising, Secy.; **Deanna Gomby, Exec. Dir.**
EIN: 260799587

246
Clarence E. Heller Charitable Foundation
44 Montgomery St., Ste. 1970
San Francisco, CA 94104-4718 (415) 989-9839
FAX: (415) 989-1909; E-mail: info@cehcf.org; Contact for Environment and Health Program: Bruce A. Hirsch, Exec. Dir. Contact for Education and Music Program: Stan Hutton, Sr. Prog. Off.; Main URL: http://cehcf.org

Established in 1982 in CA.
Donor: Clarence E. Heller‡.
Foundation type: Independent foundation.
Financial data (yr. ended 12/31/12): Assets, $63,818,931 (M); expenditures, $3,075,305; qualifying distributions, $2,697,311; giving activities include $2,102,550 for 82 grants (high: $150,000; low: $500).
Purpose and activities: The mission of the foundation is to protect and improve the quality of life through support of programs in the environment, human health, education and the arts. Giving to support research, public education, and policy development to reduce health risks from environmental degradation and environmental hazards, innovative educational programs for elementary and secondary students, sustainable natural resource management, and programs that promote the accessibility of symphonic and chamber music.
Fields of interest: Performing arts, music; Performing arts, orchestras; Arts; Higher education; Education; Environment, research; Environment, public policy; Environment, public education; Environment, natural resources; Agriculture.
Type of support: General/operating support; Continuing support; Equipment; Program development; Publication; Seed money; Curriculum development; Scholarship funds; Research; Technical assistance; Consulting services; Program evaluation.
Limitations: Giving primarily in CA. No grants to individuals.
Publications: Application guidelines; Annual report (including application guidelines); Grants list; Program policy statement.
Application information: Applicant should limit the length of the LOI to two pages of narrative and a one-page projected project budget. Full applications are by invitation only, after review of initial letter of inquiry. Application information available on foundation web site. Application form not required.
Initial approach: Letter of inquiry via U.S. mail or e-mail
Copies of proposal: 1
Deadline(s): See foundation web site for current deadline
Board meeting date(s): 3 times a year, usually Mar., June, and Oct.
Officers and Directors:* Anne Heller Andersen,* Pres.; **Rolf Lygren, V.P.**; Sarah Coade Mandell,* Secy.-Treas.; Bruce A. Hirsch, Exec. Dir.; Janet Harckham; Alfred Heller; Katherine Heller; Ruth Heller.
Number of staff: 1 full-time professional; 1 full-time support.
EIN: 942814266
Other changes: Rolf Lygren has replaced Alfred Heller as V.P.

247
Helms Foundation, Inc.
c/o Saddington Shusko LLP
18201 Von Karman Ave., Ste. 150
Irvine, CA 92612-1014

Incorporated in 1946 in CA.
Donors: The Helms family; Helms Bakeries.
Foundation type: Independent foundation.
Financial data (yr. ended 06/30/13): Assets, $3,977,981 (M); expenditures, $246,766; qualifying distributions, $237,645; giving activities include $214,003 for 39 grants (high: $30,000; low: $3).
Purpose and activities: Giving primarily for education and to Christian agencies and churches.
Fields of interest: Arts; Higher education; Education; Health organizations, association; Human services; Children/youth, services; Christian agencies & churches.
Limitations: Applications not accepted. Giving primarily in CA. No support for private foundations. No grants to individuals.
Application information: Unsolicited requests for funds not accepted.
Officers: Stephen Helms Bell, Pres.; Fonza Bell Lawther, Treas.
Trustees: Elizabeth Helms Adams; **Elizabeth Bennett**; Michael F. Kane.
EIN: 956091335

248
The William and Flora Hewlett Foundation
2121 Sand Hill Rd.
Menlo Park, CA 94025-6909 (650) 234-4500
***Contact:* Heath Wickline, Comm. Off.**
FAX: (650) 234-4501; **E-mail for Heath Wickline: hwickline@hewlett.org**; Main URL: http://www.hewlett.org
E-Newsletter: http://www.hewlett.org/newsroom/subscribe
Facebook: http://www.facebook.com/pages/William-and-Flora-Hewlett-Foundation/132972610943?ref=mf
Financials: http://www.hewlett.org/about-us/financials
Grantee Perception Report: http://www.hewlett.org/what-were-learning/grantee-perception-reports
Grants Database: http://www.hewlett.org/grants/search?order=field_date_of_award_value&sort=desc
Library Database: http://www.hewlett.org/library/search
Library Feed: http://www.hewlett.org/rss/library
News Feed: http://www.hewlett.org/rss/newsroom
RSS Grants Feed: http://grantsfeed.hewlett.org/
Twitter: http://www.twitter.com/hewlett_found
Work in Progress: http://www.hewlett.org/blog
YouTube: http://www.youtube.com/hewlettfoundation

Incorporated in 1966 in CA.
Donors: Flora Lamson Hewlett‡; William R. Hewlett‡.
Foundation type: Independent foundation.
Financial data (yr. ended 12/31/13): Assets, $8,607,073,000 (M); expenditures, $298,400,000; qualifying distributions, $271,100,000; giving activities include $238,700,000 for 634 grants, $1,400,000 for employee matching gifts, and $5,200,000 for foundation-administered programs.
Purpose and activities: The foundation makes grants to help people build measurably better lives. It concentrates its resources on activities in education, the environment, global development, performing arts, philanthropy, and population, and makes grants to support disadvantaged communities in the San Francisco Bay Area. A full list of all the Hewlett Foundation's grants can be found on its website.
Fields of interest: Performing arts; Performing arts, dance; Performing arts, theater; Performing arts, music; Arts; Elementary/secondary education; Higher education; Higher education, college (community/junior); Environment, natural resources; Environment; Reproductive health, family planning; International economic development; Urban/community development; Community/economic development; Philanthropy/voluntarism; Population studies; International studies; Public policy, research; Minorities.
International interests: China; India; Latin America; Southern Asia; Sub-Saharan Africa.
Type of support: General/operating support; Continuing support; Program development; Employee matching gifts; Matching/challenge support.
Limitations: Applications accepted. Giving limited to the San Francisco Bay Area and Central Valley, CA, for family and community development programs; performing arts primarily limited to the Bay Area. No funds for individuals and generally the foundation does not fund scholarships, endowments, capital campaigns, building construction, for-profit organizations, or unincorporated associations or groups. In addition, the foundation's funds can be used only for purposes that are consistent with its status as a charitable organization.
Publications: Application guidelines; Annual report; Grants list; Informational brochure; Newsletter; Program policy statement.
Application information: The Hewlett Foundation prefers to receive letters of inquiry via its online submission form on its web site. The foundation is not currently accepting letters of inquiry for the following programs: Global Development and Population, Philanthropy, and Special Projects. The foundation accepts unsolicited letters of inquiry for various areas of work within its Environment and Performing Arts programs. For detailed application information, visit the foundation's web site page For Grantseekers. Application form not required.

Initial approach: **Online letter of inquiry preferred**
Copies of proposal: 1
Deadline(s): None
Board meeting date(s): Mar., July, and Nov.
Final notification: 2 to 3 months

Officers and Directors:* Harvey V. Fineberg, M.D.*, Chair.; Larry Kramer, Pres.; Ana Weichers-Marshall, V.P. and C.I.O.; Elizabeth Peters, Corp. Secy. and Genl. Counsel; Susan Ketcham, C.F.O. and Treas.; Mariano-Florentino Cuellar; Eric Gimon; Walter B. Hewlett; Patricia House; Koh Boon Hwee; Mary H. Jaffe; Richard C. Levin; Stephen C. Neal; Rakesh Ranjani; Jean Gleason Stromberg.
Number of staff: 69 full-time professional; 7 part-time professional; 23 full-time support; 2 part-time support.
EIN: 941655673
Other changes: Harvey V. Fineberg, M.D. has replaced Walter B. Hewlett as Chair.
Eleanor H. Gimon, Byron Auguste and Sarah Singh are no longer directors.

249
Hewlett-Packard Company Foundation
3000 Hanover St.
Palo Alto, CA 94304-1112 (650) 857-4954
E-mail: philanthropy_ed@hp.com; Main URL: http://www8.hp.com/us/en/hp-information/social-innovation/hp-foundation.html
RSS Feed: http://www8.hp.com/us/en/hp-news/newsroom-rss.jsp
Twitter: https://twitter.com/hpglobalcitizen

Established in 1979 in CA.
Donors: Hewlett-Packard Co.; EDS Foundation.
Foundation type: Company-sponsored foundation.
Financial data (yr. ended 10/13/12): Assets, $100,788,169 (M); gifts received, $40,734,000; expenditures, $4,918,537; qualifying distributions, $4,802,550; giving activities include $1,147,750 for 6 grants (high: $681,291; low: $25,000), and $3,654,800 for employee matching gifts.
Purpose and activities: The foundation supports projects designed to improve education; match employee giving; and provide humanitarian relief to communities hit by disaster.
Fields of interest: Education; Health care; Disasters, preparedness/services; Disasters, floods; Disasters, search/rescue; American Red Cross; Human services; United Ways and Federated Giving Programs; Mathematics; Engineering/technology; Science.
Type of support: General/operating support; Building/renovation; Equipment; Employee matching gifts.
Limitations: Applications not accepted. Giving on a national basis in areas of company operations, with emphasis on Washington, DC; giving also to national organizations. No support for sectarian or denominational groups or discriminatory or political organizations. No grants to individuals or for research.
Application information: Contributes only to pre-selected organizations.
Officers and Directors:* Marcela Perez de Alonso,* Chair.; Martin J. Holston,* Secy.; Catherine A. Lesjak,* C.F.O.; Ashley B. Watson, Exec. Dir.
EIN: 942618409
Other changes: At the close of 2012, the fair market value of the grantmaker's assets was $100,788,169, a 57.0% increase over the 2011 value, $64,197,524.

250
The Larry L. Hillblom Foundation, Inc.
755 Baywood Dr., Ste. 180
Petaluma, CA 94954-5509
FAX: (707) 762-6694; E-mail: petaluma@llhf.org; Additional address: 1458 Draper St., Kingsburg, CA 93631, tel.: (559) 897-7050, fax: (559) 897-7590, e-mail: kingsburg@llhf.org; Main URL: http://www.llhf.org
Grants List: http://www.llhf.org/funded-research
RSS Feed: http://www.llhf.org/news-events/all-news-events/RSS

Established in 1996 in CA.
Donor: Larry L. Hillblom‡.
Foundation type: Independent foundation.
Financial data (yr. ended 12/31/12): Assets, $122,342,002 (M); expenditures, $6,124,806; qualifying distributions, $4,942,096; giving activities include $4,123,704 for 54 grants (high: $1,151,347; low: $2,000).
Purpose and activities: Giving for research in Diabetes Mellitus and its complications including studies of normal glucose metabolism; and age-related chronic or degenerative disorders of

the brain or vision including such studies of the healthy aging processes. Studies should target the prevention, diagnosis, treatment and/or cure of diseases described above. Proposals should employ genetic, molecular, cellular and/or metabolic approaches to one of two categories which are the areas of concern to the foundation.
Fields of interest: Diabetes; Geriatrics; Medical research, institute; Eye research; Brain research.
Type of support: Fellowships; Research.
Limitations: Applications accepted. Giving primarily in CA. **No support for cancer, cardiovascular or joint/bone degenerative disease research.** No grants to individuals.
Publications: Grants list; Informational brochure; Occasional report; Program policy statement.
Application information: Grant applications need to be formatted as a single Adobe PDF file. See foundation web site for forms and instructions. Hard copies not accepted.
Initial approach: All applications must be submitted via electronic file using the foundation's online grant management system
***Deadline(s):* See foundation web site for current deadlines**
Board meeting date(s): Feb., May, Aug., and Nov.
Officers and Directors:* Peter J. Donnici,* Chair., C.E.O., and Pres.; Terry C. Hillblom,* Vice-Chair., C.O.O., and Exec. V.P.; Grant A. Anderson,* V.P.; Walter Hillblom,* V.P.; Stephen J. Schwartz,* V.P.; David R. Jones, Secy. and C.F.O.; Paul Kimoto; Ida O'Brien; Janice E. Quistad; E. Lewis Reid; William A. Robinson; Joseph W. Waechter.
Number of staff: 6 full-time professional; 3 full-time support.
EIN: 943241600

251
Conrad N. Hilton Foundation

30440 Agoura Rd.
Agoura Hills, CA 91301-2145 (818) 851-3700
Contact: Jordan Faires, Sr. Grants Mgr.; Rose M. Arnold, Grants Mgr.
FAX: (818) 851-3791;
E-mail: communications@hiltonfoundation.org;
Main URL: http://www.hiltonfoundation.org
Barron Hilton's Giving Pledge Profile: http://glasspockets.org/philanthropy-in-focus/eye-on-the-giving-pledge/profiles/hilton
Blog: http://www.hiltonfoundation.org/horizons
Conrad N. Hilton Fondation Staff: https://twitter.com/hiltonfound/foundation-staff/members
Conrad N. Hilton Foundation's Philanthropy Promise: http://www.ncrp.org/philanthropys-promise/who
Conrad N. Hilton Humanitarian Prize: http://www.hiltonfoundation.org/prize
Facebook: https://www.facebook.com/hiltonfoundation
Flickr: http://www.flickr.com/photos/hiltonfoundation
GiveSmart: http://www.givesmart.org/Stories/Donors/Steve-Hilton
Knowledge Center: http://www.hiltonfoundation.org/impact-learning
RSS Feed: http://hiltonfoundation.org/index.php?option=com_obrss&task=feed&id=1
Twitter: https://twitter.com/@hiltonfound
Vimeo: http://vimeo.com/hiltonfoundation

Established in 1944 in NV.
Donors: Conrad N. Hilton†; Barron Hilton.
Foundation type: Independent foundation.
Financial data (yr. ended 12/31/12): Assets, $2,230,883,024 (M); gifts received, $14,654,129; expenditures, $122,978,532; qualifying distributions, $112,173,713; giving activities include $83,243,022 for 445 grants (high: $5,000,000; low: $100), and $156,079 for 1 foundation-administered program.
Purpose and activities: The Conrad N. Hilton Foundation supports efforts to improve the lives of disadvantaged and vulnerable people throughout the world by focusing on six strategic initiatives and five major program areas. Potential applicants should see Current Programs for more information.
Fields of interest: Education; Environment, water resources; Public health, clean water supply; Public health, hygiene; Public health, sanitation; Mental health/crisis services; Health organizations, association; Multiple sclerosis research; Medical research; Housing/shelter; Safety/disasters; Youth development; Homeless, human services; Human services; Public utilities, water; Public utilities, sewage; Religion; Infants/toddlers; Children/youth; Children; Youth; Young adults; Disabilities, people with; Blind/visually impaired; Substance abusers; AIDS, people with; Economically disadvantaged; Homeless.
International interests: Africa; Asia; Global Programs.
Type of support: General/operating support; Continuing support; Management development/capacity building; Capital campaigns; Building/renovation; Equipment; Endowments; Emergency funds; Program development; Publication; Curriculum development; Fellowships; Scholarship funds; Research; Technical assistance; Program evaluation; Program-related investments/loans; Employee matching gifts; Matching/challenge support.
Limitations: Applications accepted. Giving on a balanced national and international basis. No support for political organizations. No grants to individuals, or for fundraising events.
Publications: Annual report; Financial statement; Grants list; Newsletter; Occasional report.
Application information: The foundation accepts requests for proposals only for the Marilyn Hilton Award for Innovation in MS Research. Full proposals are by invitation only. The foundation accepts applications primarily from its specified beneficiaries; unsolicited proposals generally not considered. If application is invited, information will be requested. Application form required.
***Initial approach:* Electronic submission for RFP**
***Deadline(s):* Pre-proposal: July 28, 2014**
Board meeting date(s): Quarterly
***Final notification:* Nov. 2014**
Officers and Directors:* Steven M. Hilton,* Chair., C.E.O. and Pres.; Randy Kim, V.P. and C.I.O.; Edmund J. Cain, V.P., Grant Progs.; Judy M. Miller, V.P. and Dir., Humanitarian Prize; Patrick J. Modugno, V.P., Admin. and C.F.O.; **Monica Emerson, Cont.**; Barron Hilton, Chair. Emeritus; Donald H. Hubbs, Dir. Emeritus; William H. Foege, M.D., M.P.H.; James R. Galbraith; Conrad N. Hilton III; Eric M. Hilton; William B. Hilton, Jr.; Hawley Hilton McAuliffe; Joyce Meyer; John L. Notter; William G. Ouchi.
Number of staff: 39 full-time professional; 1 part-time professional; 6 full-time support; 1 part-time support.
EIN: 943100217
Other changes: The grantmaker now accepts requests for proposals.

252
William H. Hinkle Charitable Foundation, Inc.

P.O. Box 10
Geyserville, CA 95441-0010
E-mail: gwhhinkle@theHCF.org; Main URL: http://www.thehcf.org
Grants List: http://www.thehcf.org/projects.html

Established in NJ.
Donor: William H. Hinkle.
Foundation type: Independent foundation.
Financial data (yr. ended 10/31/12): Assets, $3,261,170 (M); expenditures, $157,715; qualifying distributions, $137,535; giving activities include $137,535 for 3+ grants (high: $69,523).
Fields of interest: Arts; Education; Human services.
Limitations: Applications not accepted. Giving primarily in Washington, DC and NY. No grants to individuals.
Application information: Unsolicited request for funds not accepted.
Officer: William H. Hinkle, Pres.
Trustees: Howard Leonard; Sherry Jennings.
EIN: 202045526

253
George Hoag Family Foundation

(formerly Hoag Foundation)
2665 Main St., Ste. 220
Santa Monica, CA 90405-4054 **(310) 664-1358**
Contact: Charles W. Smith, Secy. and Exec. Dir.
FAX: (310) 664-1368;
E-mail: csmith@hoagfoundation.org; **E-mail for Sarah Bicknell, Grants Coord.: sbicknell@hoagfoundation.org**; Main URL: http://www.hoagfoundation.org/

Incorporated in 1940 in CA.
Donors: George Grant Hoag†; Grace E. Hoag†; George Grant Hoag II†.
Foundation type: Independent foundation.
Financial data (yr. ended 12/31/12): Assets, $68,564,998 (M); expenditures, $3,772,312; qualifying distributions, $3,351,394; giving activities include $3,045,000 for 93 grants (high: $1,000,000; low: $2,000).
Purpose and activities: Giving to improve social conditions, promote human welfare, and alleviate pain and suffering. Also, giving to improve and expand medical services, and opportunities for youth in CA.
Fields of interest: Arts; Hospitals (general); Medical research, institute; Youth development, services; Children/youth, services; Human services.
Type of support: General/operating support; Capital campaigns; Building/renovation; Equipment; Program development; Scholarship funds; Research.
Limitations: Applications accepted. **Giving limited to CA, primarily to southern CA, with emphasis on Los Angeles, and Orange County, as well as parts of the Central Coast of CA.** No support for government agencies, tax-supported projects, or sectarian or religious organizations for the benefit of their own members. No grants to individuals, or for deficit financing or normal operating expenses.
Publications: Application guidelines; Program policy statement; Program policy statement (including application guidelines).
Application information: Application form required.
Initial approach: Letter (not exceeding 2 pages)
Copies of proposal: 9
Deadline(s): Mar. 31 and Sept. 30

Board meeting date(s): May and Nov.
Final notification: Following meeting at which proposal is reviewed
Officers and Directors:* Melinda Hoag Smith,* C.E.O. and Pres.; George Grant Hoag III,* V.P. and C.F.O.; Charles W. Smith,* Secy. and Exec. Dir.; Michael B. Sedgwick, Treas.; John L. Curci, Jr.; John G. Ebey; Gwyn P. Parry; Michael D. Stephens.
Number of staff: 1 full-time professional; 1 part-time support.
EIN: 956006885

254
The Horne Family Foundation, Inc.
38 Miller Ave., PMB 257
Mill Valley, CA 94941-1927 (415) 388-1831
Contact: Tara Horne, Prog. Off.
FAX: (415) 388-1851;
E-mail: info@hornefamilyfoundation.org; Main URL: http://www.hornefamilyfoundation.org
Grants List: http://www.hornefamilyfoundation.org/pages/grants-awarded.htm

Established in 1990 in MA.
Donor: George B. Horne†.
Foundation type: Independent foundation.
Financial data (yr. ended 11/30/11): Assets, $8,424,498 (M); expenditures, $515,877; qualifying distributions, $418,000; giving activities include $418,000 for 39 grants (high: $20,000; low: $2,500).
Purpose and activities: Giving for community development, conservation, education, health, economic stability, and environmental sustainability initiatives.
Fields of interest: Environment; Animals/wildlife; Health care.
Limitations: Applications accepted. Giving primarily in MA. No grants for capital campaigns.
Application information: Accepts Common Grant Application. See grantmaker web site for application policies, guidelines, and application form. Application form required.
Initial approach: Letter
Copies of proposal: 1
Deadline(s): Mar. 31 and Sept. 30
Board meeting date(s): Oct. 1
***Final notification:* May 31 for proposals received after Sept. 30 and before Mar. 31; Nov. 30 for proposals received after Mar. 31 and before Sept. 30**
Officers and Director:* Timothy P. Horne,* Pres. and Treas.; Walter J. Flowers, Clerk.
Number of staff: 1 part-time support.
EIN: 043104008

255
The Khaled Hosseini Foundation
4848 San Felipe Rd., Ste. 150-221
San Jose, CA 95135-1276 (408) 904-7175
Contact: Omid Grant
***FAX:* (408) 904-7175;**
E-mail: info@khaledhosseinifoundation.org; Main URL: http://www.khaledhosseinifoundation.org/

Donors: Khaled Hosseini; Roya Hosseini; Michael Bealmear; Elaine Koster; Mid Shore Community Foundation; Brandenburg Family Foundation; Pearson Foundation; Texas IB Schools; Notre Dame High School.
Foundation type: Independent foundation.
Financial data (yr. ended 12/31/12): Assets, $151,096 (M); gifts received, $70,266; expenditures, $154,365; qualifying distributions, $141,325; giving activities include $141,325 for 5 grants (high: $111,325; low: $5,000).
Fields of interest: Education; Community/economic development.
Application information: Application form required.
Initial approach: See Website.
Deadline(s): Jan. 1st, Apr. 1st, July 1st, Oct. 1st
Officers: Roya Hosseini, Chair.; Khaled Hosseini, Pres.; Sandra Hosseini, Exec. Dir.
EIN: 264199874
Other changes: Roya Hosseini is now Chair.

256
Humanist Foundation
San Francisco, CA

The foundation terminated in 2013.

257
The Humboldt Area Foundation
373 Indianola Rd.
Bayside, CA **95524-9350** (707) 442-2993
Contact: Patrick Cleary, Exec. Dir.; Kathy VanVleet, Admin. Asst.
FAX: (707) 442-9072;
E-mail: kathyv@hafoundation.org; Additional e-mail: patrickc@hafoundation.org; Main URL: http://www.hafoundation.org
Grants List: http://www.hafoundation.org/haf/grants/grantmaking-summary.html
Philanthropy's Promise: http://www.ncrp.org/philanthropys-promise/who

Established in 1972 in CA by declaration of trust.
Donors: Vera P. Vietor†; Lynn A. Vietor†.
Foundation type: Community foundation.
Financial data (yr. ended 06/30/13): Assets, $90,470,144 (M); gifts received, $8,056,138; expenditures, $6,482,013; giving activities include $2,717,169 for grants.
Purpose and activities: The foundation seeks to serve as an independent staging ground for residents, individually and in concert, to build social, economic and environmental prosperity in the Redwood, Trinity and Wild Rivers Region. Primary areas of interest include youth, health, community development, human services, arts and culture and public safety. The foundation also operates a resource center that hosts public workshops covering a range of nonprofit issues.
Fields of interest: Arts; Health care; Crime/violence prevention; Food services; Housing/shelter; Safety/disasters; Recreation; Children/youth, services; Family services; Human services; Civil rights, race/intergroup relations; Community/economic development; Economically disadvantaged.
Type of support: General/operating support; Management development/capacity building; Capital campaigns; Building/renovation; Equipment; Emergency funds; Program development; Seed money; Scholarship funds; Technical assistance; Consulting services; Grants to individuals; Scholarships—to individuals; Matching/challenge support.
Limitations: Applications accepted. Giving limited to Del Norte, Humboldt, and Trinity counties, CA. No grants to individuals (except from donor-designated funds); generally no grants for endowment funds, unspecified emergency purposes, deficit financing, or operating budgets.
Publications: Application guidelines; Annual report; Financial statement; Grants list.
Application information: Visit foundation web site for application forms and additional guidelines per grant type. Application form required.
Initial approach: Application, telephone, or e-mail
Copies of proposal: 1
Deadline(s): Oct. 1, Jan. 12, Apr. 1, and July 1 for Community Grant Program grants; varies for others
Board meeting date(s): 2nd Wed. of each month
Final notification: Within 10 weeks for Community Grant Program notification; varies for others
Officers and Directors:* Paula Allen,* Chair.; Jon Sapper,* Vice-Chair.; Jim Anderson,* Secy.; Patrick Cleary, Exec. Dir.; Gary Blatnick; Kevin Caldwell; **Neal Ewald**; Julie Fulkerson; Kathryn Lobato; Greg Nesbitt; Steve O'Meara; Terry Supahan.
Number of staff: 9 full-time professional; 1 part-time professional; 5 full-time support; 2 part-time support.
EIN: 237310660
Other changes: Susan Elliot is now Finance Asst. Elysia Frink is now Prog. Asst. Beth Johnson is now Prog. Asst. Claire Reynolds is now Comm. Coord. Cassandra Wagner is now Prog. Coord., Donor Srvs. and Planned Giving. Chris Witt is now Dir., Donor Srvs. and Planned Giving. Mary Wilson is now Depa. Asst. Sara Dronkers is now Dir., Grantmaking. Kate Russell is now Fund Devel. Coord. Helen L'Annunziata is no longer a member of the governing body.

258
Hutto Patterson Charitable Foundation
P.O. Box 80880
San Marino, CA 91118-8880

Established in 1988 in CA.
Donor: Clare P. Hutto†.
Foundation type: Independent foundation.
Financial data (yr. ended 09/30/12): Assets, $9,346,285 (M); expenditures, $1,285,059; qualifying distributions, $1,187,796; giving activities include $1,123,500 for 12 grants (high: $800,000; low: $3,000).
Purpose and activities: Giving primarily for education and children's services.
Fields of interest: Education, early childhood education; Higher education; Education; Human services; Children/youth, services; Family services.
Limitations: Applications not accepted.
Application information: Unsolicited requests for funds not accepted.
Officers and Trustees:* Catherine Hutto Gordon,* Pres.; Eileen C. Hutto,* V.P.; Harry L. Hathaway; Douglas Johnson.
EIN: 954181302
Other changes: For the fiscal year ended Sept. 30, 2012, the grantmaker paid grants of $1,123,500, a 153.3% increase over the fiscal 2011 disbursements, $443,500.

259
i.am.angel Foundation
450 Roxbury Dr.
Beverly Hills, CA 90210-4209
Toll-free tel.: (800) 839-1754; Main URL: http://iamangelfoundation.org/
Causes.com URL: http://www.causes.com/causes/434950-i-am-angel
Facebook: http://www.facebook.com/iamangelfoundation
Foundation Blog: http://iamangelfoundation.org/blog/

Google Plus: https://plus.google.com/118314738112858440523/posts
RSS Feed: http://xml.dipdive.com/community/rss/iamhome
Twitter: https://twitter.com/iamangelfdn
Vimeo: http://vimeo.com/34679422
YouTube: http://www.youtube.com/user/iamangelfnd

Established in 2010.
Donors: William James "will.i.am" Adams, Jr.; Sean Parker; Jennifer M. Van Natta; Misael Vasquez; Michael Murphy; Entertainment Industry Foundation; Jeanne and Sanford Roberston Fund; Quantum Realtors Inc.; Silicon Valley Community Foundation; Wells Fargo bank.
Foundation type: Independent foundation.
Financial data (yr. ended 12/31/12): Assets, $116,264 (M); gifts received, $640,460; expenditures, $2,100,055; qualifying distributions, $2,100,050; giving activities include $1,170,000 for 7 grants (high: $785,000; low: $5,000), and $610,827 for 2 foundation-administered programs.
Purpose and activities: The foundation works to make a difference in the lives of individuals and families through education, opportunity, and inspiration.
Fields of interest: Education; Housing/shelter; Economically disadvantaged.
Limitations: Applications not accepted. Giving primarily in CA.
Application information: Unsolicited requests for funds not accepted.
Officers: William James "will.i.am" Adams, Jr., Pres. and Secy.; Justin Paschal, Exec. Dir.
Directors: Ron Conway; Polo Molina.
EIN: 273419857
Other changes: At the close of 2012, the grantmaker paid grants of $1,170,000, a 532.4% increase over the 2011 disbursements, $185,000.

260
Institute for Healthcare Advancement
501 S. Idaho St., Ste. 300
La Habra, CA 90631-6047 (562) 690-4001
FAX: (562) 690-8988; E-mail: info@iha4health.org; Toll-Free tel.: (800) 434-4633; **Main URL: http://iha4health.org**
Facebook: http://www.facebook.com/IHAhealthliteracy
Twitter: http://twitter.com/IHAhealthlit

Established in 1999 in CA; converted from Friendly Hills Health Care.
Donors: Bambi Holzer; Jason Buck.
Foundation type: Operating foundation.
Financial data (yr. ended 12/31/12): Assets, $29,093,860 (M); gifts received, $389,891; expenditures, $4,080,853; qualifying distributions, $2,588,464; giving activities include $444,041 for grants (high: $438,291), and $3,348,667 for 4 foundation-administered programs.
Purpose and activities: Giving for the advancement of healthcare. Committed to developing, through a variety of means, programs and projects that will demonstrate innovative healthcare delivery. The Institute will be a conduit for leveraging knowledge, resources and relationships to identify specific needs, understand the constantly changing needs and design educational formats that stimulate and facilitate solutions to the challenges that healthcare will face in the future.
Fields of interest: Health care.
Limitations: Applications not accepted. Giving primarily in CA.
Application information: Contributes only to pre-selected organizations.
Officers: Albert E. Barnett, M.D., Chair.; **Michael Villaire, MSLM, C.E.O.; Ronald G. Chow, C.F.O.**
Directors: S. Eric Anderson, Ph.D., MBA; **Kambiz Arman, M.D.**; Juan M. Garcia; George S. Goldstein, Ph.D.; Nancy J. Monk, MPH, MBA; Barbara Price; Duane Saikami, PharmD, MBA.
EIN: 330483197
Other changes: John Applen is no longer a director. Gloria G. Mayer is no longer C.E.O. and Pres. Michael Villaire is now C.E.O.

261
International Humanity Foundation
4311 Pavlov Ave.
San Diego, CA 92122-3709 **(858) 597-0232**
***E-mail:* ihf@ihfonline.org**; Main URL: http://www.ihfonline.org/

Established in 2000 in CA.
Donors: Glen Sasaki; Carol Sasaki; Joseph Didomenico; Suzanne Vazanna; Nancy Santoro; Edmond Sahn; John Formicola; Technical Marine Service.
Foundation type: Operating foundation.
Financial data (yr. ended 12/31/11): Assets, $0 (M); gifts received, $139,577; expenditures, $152,399; qualifying distributions, $136,752; giving activities include $135,094 for 1 grant.
Fields of interest: International affairs.
International interests: Guatemala; India; Kenya; Sri Lanka; Thailand.
Limitations: Applications not accepted. Giving primarily in Asia. No grants to individuals.
Application information: Unsolicited requests for funds not accepted.
Officers: Carol Sasaki, C.E.O.; Catherine Tain, Pres.; Patty Robbins, Secy.; Andi Connor, Treas.
EIN: 330933239

262
Intrepid Philanthropy Foundation
575 Market St., No. 3625
San Francisco, CA **94105-5845** (415) 543-0733
Contact: Karen Leshner, Pres.
Main URL: http://www.intrepid-philanthropy.org/

Donors: Karen Leshner; Brian Leshner; Payne Family Foundation.
Foundation type: Independent foundation.
Financial data (yr. ended 12/31/12): Assets, $6,285,718 (M); gifts received, $619,802; expenditures, $501,390; qualifying distributions, $458,214; giving activities include $279,156 for 17 grants (high: $50,000; low: $4,000).
Purpose and activities: The foundation seeks to improve the U.S. educational system in order to provide opportunity for all students, particularly the poor and disadvantaged, to be productive members of their communities. The overall mission is to support and promote programs that work to close the achievement gap by honoring and supporting teachers, enhancing the environment in which they work and enriching the physical, cultural, academic and social well-being of students.
Fields of interest: Education; Economically disadvantaged.
Limitations: Applications accepted. Giving primarily in CA.
Application information: Application form required.
Initial approach: Letter
Deadline(s): None
Officers and Directors:* Karen Leshner,* Pres.; Rae Richman, Secy.; Rebecca K. Payne.
Trustee: Brian Leshner.
EIN: 300527867

263
The Intuit Foundation
P.O. Box 7850, MS MTV-07-02
Mountain View, CA 94039-7850
Main URL: http://www.intuit.com/about_intuit/philanthropy/how.jsp#Foundation

Established in 2002 in CA.
Donor: Intuit Inc.
Foundation type: Company-sponsored foundation.
Financial data (yr. ended 03/31/13): Assets, $1,067,191 (M); gifts received, $1,050,000; expenditures, $1,418,366; qualifying distributions, $1,385,200; giving activities include $1,313,481 for 1,192+ grants.
Purpose and activities: The foundation supports organizations involved with education, health, human services, community development, and economically disadvantaged people. Special emphasis is directed toward programs designed to foster economic empowerment.
Fields of interest: Education; Health care; Children/youth, services; Human services, financial counseling; Human services; Economic development; Community development, small businesses; Community/economic development; Economically disadvantaged.
Type of support: General/operating support; Program development; Employee volunteer services; Employee matching gifts.
Limitations: Applications not accepted. Giving primarily in AZ, CA, Washington, DC, GA, MA, NV, NY, TX, and VA. No support for religious organizations, political or labor organizations, private foundations, or discriminatory organizations. No grants to individuals, or for fundraising events or sponsorships, advertising, souvenir journals, or dinner programs, or conferences, exhibits, or academic research.
Application information: Contributes only to pre-selected organizations.
Officers and Directors:* Sherry Whiteley,* C.E.O. and Pres.; **Kerry McLean, Secy.**; Scott D. Cook; **Tayloe Stansbury.**
EIN: 470860921
Other changes: Kerry McLean has replaced Tyler Cozzens as Secy.
David Merenbach is no longer Treas. Ken Wach is no longer V.P. Tyler Cozzens is no longer Secy.

264
The James Irvine Foundation
One Bush St., Ste. 800
San Francisco, CA 94104-4425 (415) 777-2244
Contact: Kelly Martin, Dir., Grants Admin.
FAX: (415) 777-0869;
E-mail: grantsadmin@irvine.org; Southern CA office: 865 S. Figueroa St., Ste. 2308, Los Angeles, CA 90017-5430, tel.: (213) 236-0552, fax: (213) 236-0537; Main URL: http://www.irvine.org
E-Newsletter: http://www.irvine.org/index.php?option=com_content&view=article&id=748&Itemid=635
Facebook: http://www.facebook.com/pages/The-James-Irvine-Foundation/107030182653162?ref=ts
Grantee Perception Reports: http://www.irvine.org/evaluation/foundation-assessment/2010-grantee-perception-report
Grants Database: http://www.irvine.org/grantmaking/grants_database

James E. Canales on Twitter: http://www.twitter.com/jcanales
Knowledge Center: http://www.irvine.org/evaluation
News & Insights Blog: http://www.irvine.org/news-insights/latest
RSS Feed: http://www.irvine.org/index.php?option=com_content&view=category&id=129&layout=blog&format=feed&type=rss
Twitter: http://twitter.com/IrvineFdn
YouTube: http://www.youtube.com/user/IrvineFoundation

Incorporated in 1937 in CA.
Donor: James Irvine†.
Foundation type: Independent foundation.
Financial data (yr. ended 12/31/12): Assets, $1,675,267,930 (M); expenditures, $91,806,877; qualifying distributions, $83,167,510; giving activities include $72,272,563 for 618 grants (high: $4,725,000; low: $500), $446,325 for employee matching gifts, and $1,289,927 for 4 foundation-administered programs.
Purpose and activities: The mission of the foundation is to expand opportunity for the people of CA to participate in a vibrant, successful, and inclusive society.
Fields of interest: Arts, multipurpose centers/programs; Arts, cultural/ethnic awareness; Arts, folk arts; Arts councils; Performing arts; Performing arts centers; Performing arts, dance; Performing arts, ballet; Performing arts, theater; Performing arts, orchestras; Performing arts, opera; Employment, training; Youth development, services; Civil rights, race/intergroup relations; Community/economic development, management/technical assistance; Community development, neighborhood development; Economic development; Nonprofit management; Philanthropy/voluntarism, association; Philanthropy/voluntarism, administration/regulation; Philanthropy/voluntarism, information services; Foundations (public); Foundations (community); Voluntarism promotion; Philanthropy/voluntarism; Public policy, research; Economically disadvantaged.
Type of support: Research; General/operating support; Program development; Seed money; Technical assistance; Program evaluation; Employee matching gifts; Matching/challenge support.
Limitations: Applications accepted. Giving limited to CA. No support for agencies receiving substantial government support. No grants to individuals.
Publications: Annual report; Informational brochure; Newsletter.
Application information: See foundation web site for additional application information. Application form required.

Initial approach: Online application form
Copies of proposal: 1
Deadline(s): Online letter of inquiry accepted on a rolling basis
Board meeting date(s): Mar., June, Oct., and Dec.
Final notification: 8 to 10 weeks

Officers and Directors:* Greg Avis,* Chair.; **Frank H. Cruz,* Vice-Chair.**; Don Howard, Interim Pres. and C.E.O., and Exec. V.P.; John R. Jenks, C.I.O. and Treas.; Jane Carney; Paula A. Cordeiro; Robert E. Denham; Samuel Hoi; David Mas Masumoto; Regina L. Muehlhauser; Tim Rios; Virgil Roberts; Steven A. Schroeder; Isaac Stein; Lydia M. Villarreal.
Number of staff: 29 full-time professional; 1 part-time professional; 9 full-time support; 2 part-time support.
EIN: 941236937
Other changes: Frank H. Cruz is now Vice-Chair. Molly Munger is no longer a director. Joseph M. Pon is no longer V.P., Progs. James E. Canales is no longer C.E.O. and Pres. Don Howard is now Interim Pres. and C.E.O., and Exec. V.P.

265
The Isaacs Brothers Foundation
Del Mar, CA

The foundation terminated in 2011.

266
The Jackson Family Foundation, Inc.
(formerly The Kendall-Jackson Foundation, Inc.)
1045 Alexander Mountain Rd.
Geyserville, CA 95441-9315
Contact: Lauren Renken

Established in 1994 in CA.
Donor: Jess S. Jackson†.
Foundation type: Independent foundation.
Financial data (yr. ended 12/31/12): Assets, $4,852,788 (M); expenditures, $333,546; qualifying distributions, $300,655; giving activities include $295,000 for 2 grants (high: $240,000; low: $10,000).
Fields of interest: Education.
Type of support: General/operating support; Annual campaigns; Building/renovation; Program development.
Limitations: Applications not accepted. Giving primarily in Santa Rosa, CA. No grants to individuals.
Application information: Contributes only to pre-selected organizations.
Officer: Barbara R. Banke, Chair. and Pres.
EIN: 680345179
Other changes: Barbara R. Banke is now Chair. and Pres.

267
Jacobs Family Foundation, Inc.
c/o Joe & Vi Jacobs Ctr.
404 Euclid Ave.
San Diego, CA 92114-2221 (619) 527-6161
Contact: Jennifer Vanica, C.E.O. and Pres.
FAX: (619) 527-6162;
E-mail: info@jacobscenter.org; Toll free tel.: (800) 550-6856; Main URL: http://www.jacobsfamilyfoundation.org/
Multimedia: http://www.jacobsfamilyfoundation.org/news/news_video_frame.htm?newsvar=/jacobs/jacobscenter/jacobsnetwork/news/news_video_content.htm

Established in 1988 in CA.
Donors: Joseph J. Jacobs, Ph.D.†; Violet J. Jacobs; Norman Hapke; Valerie Jacobs Hapke.
Foundation type: Independent foundation.
Financial data (yr. ended 06/30/13): Assets, $22,198,311 (M); expenditures, $2,569,519; qualifying distributions, $2,341,096; giving activities include $2,316,588 for 29 grants (high: $2,145,224; low: $20).
Purpose and activities: The foundation invests in and with communities to seed or strengthen projects and programs that build the capacity of under-invested neighborhoods, through neighborhood-based programs, resident-led initiatives, projects that test new ideas, and activities that build community spirit. This is done through five funds: the Partnership Fund, Community-Building Strategies Fund, Spirit of the Diamond Fund, and the Jabara Scholarship Fund.
Fields of interest: Education; Human services; Children/youth, services; Family services; Community/economic development; Economically disadvantaged.
Type of support: Mission-related investments/loans; General/operating support; Endowments; Program development; Conferences/seminars; Seed money; Scholarship funds; Technical assistance; Consulting services; Program-related investments/loans; Employee matching gifts; Matching/challenge support.
Limitations: Applications accepted. Giving in CA, with primary emphasis in the southeastern San Diego communities of Valencia Park, Lincoln Park, Webster, Emerald Hills, Chollas View, Mountain View, Mount Hope, North Encanto, Oak Park, and South Encanto. No support for medical services, religious purposes, athletics, or the arts. No grants to individuals, or for medical research.
Publications: Annual report (including application guidelines); Financial statement; Grants list; Informational brochure; Newsletter.
Application information: Applicants are encouraged to contact the foundation before applying. See foundation web site for full application guidelines and requirements for each grant fund. Application form not required.

Initial approach: Telephone call
Copies of proposal: 1
Deadline(s): None
Board meeting date(s): Quarterly
Final notification: 30 days

Officer and Directors:* Susan Halliday, C.F.O. and Secy.; Andrew Hapke; Claire Hapke; Norman F. Hapke, Jr.; Valerie Jacobs Hapke; Margaret E. Jacobs; Violet Jabara Jacobs.
Advisors: William Hanna; **Kurt Kicklighter**; **John Landis**; **Peter Tanous**; **Christopher Weil**.
Number of staff: 4 full-time professional.
EIN: 954187111
Other changes: For the fiscal year ended June 30, 2013, the grantmaker paid grants of $2,316,588, an 81.8% increase over the fiscal 2012 disbursements, $1,274,288.

268
JAMS Foundation
2 Embarcadero Ctr., Ste. 1500
San Francisco, CA **94111-3906**
Main URL: http://www.jamsadr.com/jamsfoundation/xpqGC.aspx?xpST=JAMSFoundation

Established in 2001 in CA.
Donors: Daniel Weinstein; Alex Polsky; Charles Legge; Charles Vogel; Chris Poole; Dickran Tevrizian; Edward Wallin; Ellen James; Fern Smith; Gary Taylor; Gerald Kurland; James Smith; Jay Folberg; Jay Welsh; Jerry Spolter; John Kennedy, Jr.; John Trotter; Linda Singer; Michael McAllister; Michael Young; Read Ambler; Richard Chernick; Richard Neal; Richard Neville; Richard Silver; Robert Davidson; Robert Sabraw; Ross Feinberg; Stephen Crane; Steven Stone; W. Scott Snowden; William Cahill; William Bettinelli; Viggo Boserup; Bruce Edwards; Michael Loeb; James Melinson; Jerry Roscoe; James Warren; Catherine Yanni; Peter Woodin; Carol Wittenberg; Stephen Sundvold; Kathleen Roberts; Brian Parmelee; John Hinchey; William Bettinelli.
Foundation type: Independent foundation.
Financial data (yr. ended 12/31/12): Assets, $863,225 (M); gifts received, $685,933; expenditures, $997,099; qualifying distributions, $981,459; giving activities include $775,794 for 46 grants (high: $167,500; low: $1,300).

Purpose and activities: Giving primarily for financial assistance for conflict resolution initiatives with national or international impact; also shares its dispute resolution experience and judicial expertise for the benefit of the public interest.
Fields of interest: Courts/judicial administration; Dispute resolution; Community/economic development, public policy; Community/economic development, public education; Law/international law.
Limitations: Applications not accepted. Giving primarily in CA, IL, and MA; some giving in Washington, DC. No grants to individuals.
Application information: Unsolicited requests for funds not accepted.
Officers: Bruce Edwards, Co-Chair.; Warren Knight, Co-Chair.; John J. Welsh, Secy.; Julie Sager, Treas.; Jay Folberg, Exec. Dir.
Board Members: Viggo Boserup; Candace Cooper; Bill Hartgering; Michael Lewis; Chris Poole; Daniel Weinstein; Peter Woodin.
EIN: 912147141

269

Walter S. Johnson Foundation

505 Montgomery St., Ste. 620
San Francisco, CA 94111-6529 (415) 283-1854
Contact: Grant Inquiries: Yali Lincroft, Prog. Off.; General Inquiries: Christina Thompson, Grants Mgr.; Operational/administrative inquiries: Pegine Grayson, Exec. Dir.
FAX: (415) 283-1840; E-mail: info@wsjf.org; Main URL: http://www.wsjf.org
Grants Database: http://wsjf.org/our-funding-priorities/previous-grant-recipients/

Established in 1968 in CA.
Donor: Walter S. Johnson†.
Foundation type: Independent foundation.
Financial data (yr. ended 12/31/12): Assets, $93,122,341 (M); expenditures, $4,771,002; qualifying distributions, $4,643,344; giving activities include $3,360,695 for 60 grants (high: $400,000; low: $10,000).
Purpose and activities: The foundation provides grants to assist youth to become successful adults by promoting positive change in the policies and systems that serve them and by supporting high impact and promising practices. Grantmaking is limited to organizations providing services in Northern California and Washoe County, Nevada, and policy advocacy organizations effecting change that will impact those areas.
Fields of interest: Education, reform; Elementary/secondary education; Graduate/professional education; Youth development, services; Children/youth, services; Family services; Leadership development; Youth; Young adults; Economically disadvantaged.
Type of support: Research; Program evaluation; General/operating support; Program development; Seed money; Technical assistance.
Limitations: Giving primarily in northern CA and the counties of Alameda, Alpine, Amador, Butte, Calaveras, Colusa, Contra Costa, Del Norte, El Dorado, Fresno, Glenn, Humboldt, Inyo, Kings, Lake, Lassen, Madera, Marin, Mariposa, Mendocino, Merced, Modoc, Mono, Monterey, Napa, Nevada, Placer, Plumas, Sacramento, San Benito, San Francisco, San Joaquin, San Mateo, Santa Clara, Santa Cruz, Shasta, Sierra, Siskiyou, Solano, Sonoma, Stanislaus, Sutter, Tehama, Trinity, Tulare, Tuolumne, Yolo, Yuba; funding also in Washoe County, NV. No support for religious organizations for sectarian purposes or for medical purposes, or for private schools. No grants to individuals, or for annual campaigns, deficit financing, memorial funds, capital or endowment funds, conservation or renovation projects, equipment purchases, awards, prizes, one time events, plays or films, camps or school bands, emergency funding, or scholarships.
Publications: Application guidelines; Financial statement.
Application information: Unsolicited proposals not accepted. Interested applicants should contact foundation Program Officer, Yali Lincroft, at yalilncroft@wsjf.org to discuss their needs and the foundation's current funding priorities. If a proposal is invited, an application form will be required, and it is to be submitted electronically. See foundation web site for further information.
Deadline(s): Varies. Check with Prog. Off.
Board meeting date(s): Feb., May, Aug. and Nov.
Final notification: Shortly after each quarterly Board meeting at which funding decisions are made
Officers and Trustees:* Sandra Bruckner,* Pres.; Samuel Lamont Johnson,* Secy.; Hathily Johnson Winston,* Treas.; Pegine Grayson, Exec. Dir.; Gloria Eddie; Gloria Jeneal Eddie; Peter Lillevand; Scott Shackelton.
Number of staff: 2 part-time professional; 1 full-time support; 1 part-time support.
EIN: 237003595

270

The Fletcher Jones Foundation

(formerly The Jones Foundation)
117 E. Colorado Blvd., Ste. 403
Pasadena, CA 91105-3725 (626) 535-9506
Contact: Christine Sisley, Treas. and Exec. Dir.
FAX: (626) 535-9508; Main URL: http://www.fletcherjonesfdn.org

Established in 1969 in CA.
Donor: Fletcher Jones†.
Foundation type: Independent foundation.
Financial data (yr. ended 12/31/12): Assets, $143,372,732 (M); expenditures, $8,235,766; qualifying distributions, $6,911,563; giving activities include $6,605,875 for 81 grants (high: $1,015,000; low: $250).
Purpose and activities: Support primarily for private colleges and universities, particularly those in CA (over 96 percent of available funds).
Fields of interest: Higher education.
Type of support: Capital campaigns; Building/renovation; Equipment; Endowments; Professorships; Fellowships; Scholarship funds; Matching/challenge support.
Limitations: Applications accepted. Giving primarily in CA. No support for K-12 schools; political campaigns or organizations. No grants to individuals, or for operating funds, deficit financing, conferences, seminars, workshops, travel exhibits, surveys, or projects supported by government agencies; no loans.
Publications: Annual report (including application guidelines); Financial statement; Grants list.
Application information: Effective Jan. 1, 2012, the foundation has implemented an online application process for regular grants. Submission in any other form will not be accepted. Please visit the foundation's web site for more detailed application procedures. Application form not required.
Initial approach: Prior to any written submission, it is advisable to consult with the foundation's Exec. Dir. in order to discuss a tentative proposal and to determine suitability of the intended request
Copies of proposal: 1
Deadline(s): 6 weeks prior to board meetings
Board meeting date(s): Mar., June, Sept. and Dec.
Final notification: 3 to 6 months
Officers and Trustees:* Peter K. Barker,* Pres.; **John D. Pettker, V.P. and Secy.**; Samuel P. Bell,* V.P.; Patrick C. Haden,* V.P.; Parker S. Kennedy,* V.P.; Robert W. Kummer, Jr.,* V.P.; Daniel E. Lungren,* V.P.; Donald E. Nickelson,* V.P.; Hon. Rockwell Schnabel,* V.P.; Stewart R. Smith,* V.P.; **Christine Sisley, Treas. and Exec. Dir.**
Number of staff: 1 part-time professional; 1 part-time support.
EIN: 237030155
Other changes: John P. Pollock is no longer V.P. John D. Pettker is now V.P. and Secy. Dickinson C. Ross is no longer V.P. Christine Sisley is now Treas. and Exec. Dir.

271

The Joyard Foundation

La Canada Flintridge, CA

The foundation terminated on June 15, 2013.

272

Just Keep Livin Foundation

9777 Wilshire Blvd., Ste. 805
Beverly Hills, CA 90212 (310) 857-1555
FAX: (310) 388-1084;
E-mail: jklfoundation@jklivin.net; Main URL: http://www.jklivinfoundation.org/
E-Newsletter: http://www.jklivinfoundation.org/contact/join-our-email-list/
Facebook: https://www.facebook.com/jklivin?ref=ts
RSS Feed: http://jklivinfoundation.org/rss/
Twitter: https://twitter.com/jklivinFNDN
YouTube: http://www.youtube.com/user/justkeeplivin

Established in 2006 in CA.
Donors: Matthew McConaughey; Chime on Inc.; Competitor Group Inc.; Entertainment Industry Foundation; Active Network; JK Living Foundation; Texas Rangers Baseball Foundation; JP Morgan Chase; Best Buy.
Foundation type: Independent foundation.
Financial data (yr. ended 12/31/12): Assets, $1,734,744 (M); gifts received, $701,615; expenditures, $813,301; qualifying distributions, $726,898; giving activities include $388,599 for 16 grants (high: $137,426; low: $150).
Purpose and activities: The foundation is dedicated to helping teenage kids lead active lives and make healthy choices to become great men and women. The foundation is partnered with Communities in Schools (CIS), the nation's largest, non-profit, dropout prevention organization in the nation, to implement fitness and wellness programs in large inner-city high schools in the community. Through after school programs, students are encouraged to improve their physical and mental health through exercise, teamwork, gratitude, and positive life choices.
Fields of interest: Education, drop-out prevention; Public health, physical fitness; Nutrition; Youth development; Children/youth.
Limitations: Applications not accepted. Giving primarily in CA. No grants to individuals.
Application information: Contributes only to pre-selected organizations.
Officers and Directors:* Matthew McConaughey,* C.E.O. and Pres.; Todd Gustawes, C.F.O.; P. Kevin Morris, Secy.; Shannon Mabrey Rotenberg, Exec.

Dir.; Rick George; George King; Blaine Lourd; Camila McConaughey; P. Kevin Morris; Jim Toth.
EIN: 203921057

273
Kapor Center for Social Impact
(formerly Mitchell Kapor Foundation)
2201 Broadway, Ste. 727
Oakland, CA 94612-3024 (510) 255-4650
Contact: Cedric Brown, C.E.O.
E-mail: info@kaporcenter.org; Tel./Fax: (510) 488-6600; **Main URL: http://www.kaporcenter.org**
Blog: http://www.kaporcenter.org/blog
Facebook: https://www.facebook.com/KaporCenter
Kapor Center for Social Impact's Philanthropy Promise: http://www.ncrp.org/philanthropys-promise/who
RSS Feed: http://feeds2.feedburner.com/MitchellKaporFoundationWeblog
Twitter: https://twitter.com/KaporCenter
YouTube: https://www.youtube.com/user/KaporCenter

Established in 1997 in MA.
Donor: Mitchell Kapor.
Foundation type: Independent foundation.
Financial data (yr. ended 12/31/12): Assets, $35,589,212 (M); gifts received, $1,175,382; expenditures, $5,545,036; qualifying distributions, $5,013,208; giving activities include $4,201,000 for 95 grants (high: $2,020,000; low: $250).
Purpose and activities: The foundation is based in the San Francisco Bay Area, California, and supports organizations that provoke social change in communities of color en route to equality. It employs three strategies in pursuit of their mission: grantmaking and community partnerships, collaboration with other funders, and technical assistance to organizations. It is particularly interested in working with organizations that have a racial justice analysis and an integrated use of information technology.
Fields of interest: Secondary school/education; Higher education; Education; Environment, administration/regulation; Environment, public policy; Environment, information services; Environment, recycling; Environment, climate change/global warming; Environment; Community/economic development; Public affairs, citizen participation.
Type of support: General/operating support; Continuing support; Management development/capacity building; Program development; Conferences/seminars; Seed money; Curriculum development; Technical assistance; Consulting services; Program evaluation; In-kind gifts; Matching/challenge support; Mission-related investments/loans.
Limitations: Applications accepted. Giving primarily in the San Francisco Bay Area, CA; limited giving in southern CA and nationally. The foundation does not award grants to organizations based or primarily working outside of the U.S. No grants to individuals.
Publications: Application guidelines; Annual report; Financial statement; Grants list; Occasional report.
Application information: Application guidelines available on foundation web site. Application form required.
Initial approach: Apply online only after reviewing guidelines on web site and discussion with staff
Deadline(s): Generally quarterly
Board meeting date(s): Quarterly (some flexibility)
Final notification: Generally within six weeks
Officers and Trustees:* Mitchell Kapor,* Co-Chair.; Freada Kapor Klein, Ph.D.*, Co-Chair.; Cedric Brown, C.E.O.; Stephen DeBerry, Treas.
Number of staff: 3 full-time professional; 1 part-time professional; 1 full-time support.
EIN: 943330604
Other changes: Mitchell Kapor is now Co-Chair.

274
Glorya Kaufman Dance Foundation
Los Angeles, CA

Pursuant to a reorganization, the foundation transferred its assets to the Glorya Kaufman Dance Foundation, EIN: 806167949.

275
The Kavli Foundation
1801 Solar Drive, Ste. 250
Oxnard, CA 93030-8297 (805) 683-6000
Contact: Dr. Robert W. Conn, Pres.
FAX: (805) 988-4800; Main URL: http://www.kavlifoundation.org/
E-Newsletter: http://visitor.constantcontact.com/manage/optin/ea?v=001nQUq2GTjwCh2XVyu9nQt_g%3D%3D
E-Newsletter: http://www.kavlifoundation.org/kavli-newsletter
RSS Feed: http://www.kavlifoundation.org/rss.xml
Twitter: http://twitter.com/KavliFoundation
YouTube: http://www.youtube.com/KavliFoundation

Established in 2000 in CA.
Donor: Fred Kavli†.
Foundation type: Independent foundation.
Financial data (yr. ended 12/31/12): Assets, $176,204,117 (M); gifts received, $10,500,000; expenditures, $12,962,806; qualifying distributions, $9,511,150; giving activities include $4,393,555 for 13 grants (high: $1,250,000; low: $30,000).
Purpose and activities: The foundation is dedicated to the goals of advancing science for the benefit of humanity and promoting increased public understanding of and support for scientists and their work. The foundation has selected three areas in which to focus its activities: astrophysics, neuroscience, and nanoscience. An international program of research institutes, prizes, symposia, and endowed professorships is being established to further these goals.
Fields of interest: Education; Science.
Type of support: Professorships; Research.
Limitations: Applications not accepted. Giving primarily on a national basis; some giving internationally. No grants to individuals.
Publications: Informational brochure.
Application information: Participation in the foundation's programs of fellowships, professorships, symposia and prizes is by invitation only; the foundation does not respond to unsolicited proposals.
Officers and Directors:* Rockell N. Hankin,* Chair.; Dr. Robert W. Conn,* C.E.O. and Pres.; Miyoung Chun, Ph.D., Exec. V.P., Science Progs.; **Mary Sue Coleman**; Thomas E. Everhart; Douglas K. Freeman; **Richard A. Meserve**; **Gunnar K. Nilsen**; Henry T. Yang.
Number of staff: 2 full-time professional; 1 part-time professional; 3 full-time support.
EIN: 770560142
Other changes: Rockell N. Hankin is now Chair. Dr. Robert W. Conn is now C.E.O. and Pres.

276
W. M. Keck Foundation
550 S. Hope St., Ste. 2500
Los Angeles, CA 90071-2617 (213) 680-3833
Contact: Maria Pellegrini, Exec. Dir., Progs.; Matesha Varma, Sr. Prog. Dir.
FAX: (213) 614-0934; E-mail: info@wmkeck.org; E-mail for Maria Pellegrini: mpellegrini@wmkeck.org; Main URL: http://www.wmkeck.org
Grants List: http://www.wmkeck.org/grant-programs/science-engineering/science-and-engineering-grant-abstracts.html
Knowledge Center: http://www.wmkeck.org/impact.html

Established in 1954 and incorporated in 1959 in DE.
Donor: William M. Keck†.
Foundation type: Independent foundation.
Financial data (yr. ended 12/31/13): Assets, $1,254,540,000 (M); expenditures, $68,999,000; qualifying distributions, $54,992,000; giving activities include $54,992,000 for grants.
Purpose and activities: The foundation continues to adhere to the directions and guidelines established by its founder, using an interdisciplinary/cross-program or thematic funding approach. The foundation has designated the following specific areas of funding: Early Learning Program, Science and Engineering Program, Liberal Arts Program, Medical Research Program, and the Southern CA Program. Concentration is placed on strengthening studies and programs in accredited colleges and universities, medical schools, and major independent medical research institutions in the areas of earth science, engineering, medical research, and to some extent, other sciences, and the liberal arts. Some consideration, limited to southern CA, is given to organizations in the categories of arts and culture, civic and community affairs, health care, precollegiate education, and early learning.
Fields of interest: Arts; Elementary school/education; Secondary school/education; Higher education; Engineering school/education; Health care; Medical research, institute; Children/youth, services; Residential/custodial care, hospices; Marine science; Physical/earth sciences; Chemistry; Mathematics; Engineering/technology; Computer science; Engineering; Biology/life sciences; Science.
Type of support: Capital campaigns; Building/renovation; Equipment; Program development; Curriculum development; Research; Employee matching gifts; Matching/challenge support.
Limitations: Applications accepted. Giving nationally to universities, colleges, and major independent medical research institutions. Arts and culture, civic and community, health care, and precollegiate education and early learning are restricted to southern CA, mainly the greater Los Angeles area. No support for conduit organizations or to organizations that have not received permanent tax-exempt ruling determination from the federal government and state of CA (if state exemption is applicable). No grants to individuals, or for routine expenses, general endowments, deficit reduction, fundraising events, dinners, mass mailings, conferences, seminars, publications, films, theatrical productions, or public policy research.
Publications: Annual report (including application guidelines); Grants list; Informational brochure

Application information: Contributes only to pre-selected organizations.
Directors: Maria Hon; **Brent Jeon**; Dong Koo Kim.
EIN: 331059702
Other changes: Pil Jae Lee is no longer a director.

281
The Kimbo Foundation
72 Santa Ana Ave.
San Francisco, CA 94127-1508
E-mail: info@kimbofoundation.org; Main URL: http://www.kimbofoundation.org
Grants List: http://www.kimbofoundation.org/history.html
Application addresses: Northern CA: c/o The SF Korea Daily, Attn.: Business Planning Dept., 33288 Central Ave., Union City, CA 94587-2010, tel.: (510) 429-3230, fax: (510) 429-3260, e-mail: kwang@koreadaily.com; Southern CA and other states: c/o The LA Korean Central Daily, Attn.: Business Planning Dept., 690 Wilshire Pl., Los Angeles, CA 90005-3930, tel.: (213) 368-2607, fax: (213) 389-6196, e-mail: info@jkoreadaily.com

Established in 1987 in CA.
Donors: Sunny S. Hwang; Geon Y. Kim†; Sunrise Foundation.
Foundation type: Independent foundation.
Financial data (yr. ended 12/31/12): Assets, $0 (M); gifts received, $200,000; expenditures, $339,823; qualifying distributions, $329,200; giving activities include $56,200 for 6 grants (high: $33,000; low: $1,000), and $273,000 for grants to individuals.
Purpose and activities: Scholarship awards to Korean-American students; some giving for missions assistance.
Fields of interest: Christian agencies & churches; Protestant agencies & churches; Asians/Pacific Islanders.
Type of support: Scholarships—to individuals.
Limitations: Applications accepted. Giving in the U.S., with an emphasis on CA.
Application information: See web site for complete application policies, guidelines and forms. Application form required.
Initial approach: Complete application form
Deadline(s): May 20 to July 15
Board meeting date(s): July through Aug.
Final notification: Aug. 27
Officer: Jeanne M. Kim, Pres.
EIN: 943047547

282
The Karl Kirchgessner Foundation
c/o Grants Coord.
1525 Aviation Blvd., No. 168
Redondo Beach, CA 90278-2805
Contact: Christine Tuthill, Grants Coord.
FAX: (310) 374-2545;
E-mail: grantscoordinator@kirchgessnerfoundation.org; Main URL: http://www.kirchgessnerfoundation.org

Established in 1979 in CA and reincorporated in NV due to a merger with The Karl Kirchgessner Foundation (CA) in 2003.
Foundation type: Independent foundation.
Financial data (yr. ended 06/30/13): Assets, $17,831,377 (M); expenditures, $1,111,052; qualifying distributions, $837,050; giving activities include $743,720 for 26+ grants (high: $161,530).
Purpose and activities: The foundation's mission is to assist economically disadvantaged persons, especially those among the young, the elderly, and the disabled. While the foundation supports a limited amount of eye research, its emphasis is to support activities in the area of eye care, and in helping those with sight problems to be self-sufficient.
Fields of interest: Health care; Eye diseases; Eye research; Blind/visually impaired.
Type of support: General/operating support; Continuing support; Equipment; Endowments; Program development; Professorships; Seed money; Scholarship funds; Research; Technical assistance; Matching/challenge support.
Limitations: Applications accepted. Giving primarily in CA, with emphasis on southern CA. No support for private foundations, private operating foundations, supporting organizations, or for lobbying organizations or campaigns. No grants to individuals, or for fundraising campaigns, or for dinners.
Publications: Application guidelines; Grants list.
Application information: Letter of intent should not contain any supporting materials. Formal applications will be solicited by the foundation. The foundation strongly encourages applications which incorporate funding through matching grants. Application form required.
Initial approach: Send a brief letter of intent
Copies of proposal: 1
Deadline(s): Nov. 1
Board meeting date(s): May and as required
Officers and Directors:* Robert A. Huber,* Pres.; **Karl F. Kramer,* Sr. V.P.**; **Kathleen McGrath Kramer,* V.P. and Treas.**; Darryl W. Cluster, Secy.; Diana Kramer; Michael Kramer; David M. Todd.
Number of staff: None.
EIN: 680530356
Other changes: Kathleen McGrath Kramer is now V.P. and Treas. Kenneth Rudnick is no longer a director. Karl F. Kramer is now Sr. V.P.

283
The Lloyd E. & Elisabeth H. Klein Family Foundation
c/o First Foundation Advisors
18101 Von Karman Ave., Ste. 700
Irvine, CA 92612-0145 (877) 968-6328
***FAX:* (949) 833-9584**; Main URL: http://www.kleinfamilyfoundation.org

Established in 2002 in CA.
Donors: Elisabeth Klein†; Lloyd E. Klein†.
Foundation type: Independent foundation.
Financial data (yr. ended 12/31/12): Assets, $14,619,413 (M); expenditures, $799,778; qualifying distributions, $680,153; giving activities include $632,000 for 29 grants (high: $125,000; low: $5,000).
Purpose and activities: The mission of the foundation is to empower disadvantaged youth toward improved life achievement through encouragement, education, and emotional support.
Fields of interest: Libraries (public); Education; YM/YWCAs & YM/YWHAs; Children/youth; Youth; Economically disadvantaged.
Limitations: Applications accepted. Giving primarily in CA. No grants to individuals or for endowments.
Application information: Application form required.
Initial approach: Eligibility quiz (available on foundation web site)
Deadline(s): May 15 (Letter of Enquiry); July 25 (Grant Application)
Board meeting date(s): May 1
Officers and Directors:* Catherine H. Sorensen,* Pres.; Kenneth Klein,* V.P.; Christine E. Cross,* Secy.; James L. Klein,* Treas.; Kristi Barens; Kay Carpenter; Paul Kott; Russell Leatherby.
EIN: 300105588

284
Gerald M. Kline Family Foundation
c/o John Brychel, C.P.A.
12657 Alcosta Blvd., Ste. 500
San Ramon, CA 94583-4427

Established in 1999 in CA.
Donor: Gerald M. Kline.
Foundation type: Independent foundation.
Financial data (yr. ended 06/30/13): Assets, $15,511,192 (M); gifts received, $6,000,000; expenditures, $315,860; qualifying distributions, $273,168; giving activities include $267,500 for 21 grants (high: $60,000; low: $2,500).
Fields of interest: Libraries/library science.
Limitations: Applications not accepted. No grants to individuals.
Application information: Unsolicited requests for funds not accepted.
Officer: Gerald M. Kline, C.E.O., C.F.O. and Secy.
EIN: 943316362

285
The Bradford & Lauren Koenig Foundation
c/o Seiler, LLP
3 Lagoon Dr., Ste. 400
Redwood City, CA 94065-1565

Established in 1997 in CA.
Donors: Bradford Koenig; Lauren Koenig.
Foundation type: Independent foundation.
Financial data (yr. ended 12/31/12): Assets, $1,998,833 (M); gifts received, $518,565; expenditures, $200,000; qualifying distributions, $200,000; giving activities include $200,000 for grants.
Fields of interest: Elementary/secondary education; Higher education.
Limitations: Applications not accepted. Giving primarily in CA. No grants to individuals; no loans or scholarships.
Application information: Contributes only to pre-selected organizations.
Trustees: Bradford Koenig; Lauren Koenig; Mark R. Tercek.
EIN: 133993307
Other changes: The grantmaker has moved from NY to CA.

286
The Jean & E. Floyd Kvamme Foundation
P.O. Box 2494
Saratoga, CA 95070-0494
Contact: Jean Kvamme, Tr.
FAX: (408) 354-0804

Established in 1993 in CA.
Donors: E. Floyd Kvamme; Jean Kvamme.
Foundation type: Independent foundation.
Financial data (yr. ended 06/30/13): Assets, $10,481,408 (M); gifts received, $55,000; expenditures, $4,465,918; qualifying distributions, $4,346,017; giving activities include $4,334,000 for 18 grants (high: $3,500,000; low: $1,000).
Purpose and activities: Giving primarily to Christian religious organizations, medical grants for Alzheimer's, leukemia, arthritis, and spondylitis

research and to the community of northern California for education and the arts.
Fields of interest: Arts; Engineering school/education; Education; Health organizations, association; Medical research, institute; Christian agencies & churches.
Type of support: General/operating support; Continuing support; Building/renovation; Equipment; Research; Matching/challenge support.
Limitations: Applications not accepted. Giving primarily in northern CA. No grants to individuals.
Application information: Contributes only to pre-selected organizations.
Trustees: Damon Kvamme; E. Floyd Kvamme; Jean Kvamme; Todd Kvamme.
Number of staff: 3 part-time support.
EIN: 770359484
Other changes: For the fiscal year ended June 30, 2013, the grantmaker paid grants of $4,334,000, a 252.9% increase over the fiscal 2012 disbursements, $1,228,100.

287
LA84 Foundation
(formerly Amateur Athletic Foundation of Los Angeles)
2141 W. Adams Blvd.
Los Angeles, CA 90018-2040 (323) 730-4600
Contact: F. Patrick Escobar, V.P., Grants and Progs.
FAX: (323) 730-9637;
E-mail: info@LA84Foundation.org; Main URL: http://www.la84foundation.org
Facebook: http://www.facebook.com/pages/LA84-Foundation/135796917696
Grants List: http://www.la84foundation.org/1gm/grantees_frmst.htm
Sportsletter Blog: http://www.sportsletter.org/
Twitter: http://twitter.com/LA84Foundation
weplay: http://www.weplay.com/groups/25069-LA84-Foundation/public
YouTube: http://www.youtube.com/user/LA84Foundation/videos

Established in 1982 in CA.
Donor: Los Angeles Olympic Organizing Comm.
Foundation type: Independent foundation.
Financial data (yr. ended 12/31/12): Assets, $139,555,111 (M); gifts received, $6,902; expenditures, $7,549,701; qualifying distributions, $6,797,305; giving activities include $2,811,935 for 67 grants (high: $500,000; low: $5,000), $2,165 for 5 employee matching gifts, and $1,277,421 for foundation-administered programs.
Purpose and activities: Support for youth sports programs (youth ages 6-17), especially in areas where the risk of delinquency is high. Special attention to sectors of the population underserved by current sports programs: girls, minorities, and the disabled.
Fields of interest: Athletics/sports, training; Athletics/sports, amateur leagues; Youth development; Youth, services; Children/youth; Girls.
Type of support: Capital campaigns; Building/renovation; Equipment; Program development; Matching/challenge support.
Limitations: Applications accepted. Giving limited to eight southern CA counties (Imperial, Los Angeles, Orange, Riverside, San Bernardino, San Diego, Santa Barbara, and Ventura). No support for single, public, or private school facilities or programs not including sports schools. No grants to individuals, endowments, travel outside of southern CA, routine operating expenses, purchase of land, debt recovery (or incurring debt liability), or one or two-day annual events.
Publications: Application guidelines; Biennial report; Biennial report (including application guidelines); Grants list; Occasional report.
Application information: Application form available on foundation web site. Application form required.
Initial approach: Use of online application is the method which the foundation strongly recommends; if submitting an online request is not an option, applicants may contact foundation and request a paper copy of the application
Deadline(s): See foundation web site for current deadlines
Board meeting date(s): 3 times per year
Final notification: 4 weeks
Officers and Directors:* Frank M. Sanchez,* Chair.; Anita L. DeFrantz,* Pres.; F. Patrick Escobar, V.P., Grants and Progs.; Wayne Wilson, V.P., Comm. and Education; Marcia Suzuki, Treas.; Yvonne B. Burke; Jae Min Chang; John F. Chavez; Debra Kay Duncan; James L. Easton; Priscilla Florence; Jonathan Glaser; Robert V. Graziano; Mariann Harris; Rafer Johnson; **Stan Kasten**; Maureen Kindel; Patrick McClenahan; Peter V. Ueberroth; Walter F. Ulloa; Gilbert R. Vasquez; John Ziffren.
Number of staff: 11 full-time professional; 1 part-time professional.
EIN: 953792725
Other changes: Frank M. Sanchez has replaced Robert V. Graziano as Chair.

288
Laguna Beach Community Foundation
303 Broadway Ave., Ste. 212
Laguna Beach, CA 92651 (949) 715-8223
***Contact:* Dan Pingaro, Exec. Dir.**
FAX: (949) 661-1475;
E-mail: info@lagunabeachcf.org; Mailing address: P. O. Box 1628, Laguna Beach, CA 92652; Main URL: http://www.lagunabeachcf.org
Facebook: http://www.facebook.com/lagunabeachcf

Established in 2004 in CA.
Foundation type: Community foundation.
Financial data (yr. ended 12/31/12): Assets, $2,209,903 (M); gifts received, $1,184,563; expenditures, $1,204,844; giving activities include $965,540 for 23+ grants (high: $552,000).
Purpose and activities: The foundation strengthens the community by encouraging philanthropy. The foundation provides expertise and resources to assist local charities, connect donor passions with nonprofit needs, and work with local professional advisors in assisting their clients in giving now and beyond their lifetimes with a legacy gift.
Fields of interest: Arts; Education; Environment; Animals/wildlife; Human services.
Type of support: General/operating support; Management development/capacity building; Program development.
Limitations: Applications accepted. Giving primarily in Laguna Beach, CA. No support for labor organizations, fraternal organizations, athletic clubs or social clubs. No grants for annual fund drives, endowments, or for underwriting or sponsoring special events.
Application information: Visit foundation web site for application, guidelines and specific deadline. Application form required.
Initial approach: Contact foundation
Deadline(s): Sept.
Officers and Trustees:* Rick Balzar,* Chair.; Robert J. Harryman,* Treas.; Laura Tarbox,* Treas.; **Dan Pingaro,* Exec. Dir.**; Nicole Anderson; Jerry Bieser; **Dennis Boyer**; Donnie Crevier; Thomas P. Davis; Jane Egly; Mary Ferguson; James P. Fletcher; Lynee M. Kniss; John G. Mansour; Lisa Mansour; Angie Miller.
EIN: 206390272

289
The Stanley S. Langendorf Foundation
P.O. Box 2509
San Francisco, CA 94126-2509 (415) 217-4919
Contact: Jude P. Damasco
FAX: (415) 217-4914;
E-mail: sslfoundation@damasco.com; Main URL: http://www.sslfoundation.org

Established in 1982 in CA.
Donor: Stanley S. Langendorf†.
Foundation type: Independent foundation.
Financial data (yr. ended 12/31/12): Assets, $11,657,926 (M); expenditures, $973,216; qualifying distributions, $867,850; giving activities include $867,850 for 83 grants (high: $200,000; low: $250).
Purpose and activities: The foundation funds organizations that benefit community services/social services, youth, primary and secondary education, and the arts.
Fields of interest: Arts; Elementary/secondary education; Youth development; Human services; Children/youth, services.
Type of support: General/operating support; Program development; Scholarship funds.
Limitations: Applications accepted. Giving limited to San Francisco, CA. No grants to individuals.
Publications: Application guidelines.
Application information: The foundation strongly prefers electronic submissions. Full proposals via invitation only. See foundation web site for application guidelines and forms. Application form required.
Initial approach: See foundation web site for letter of intent instructions and guidelines
Copies of proposal: 1
***Deadline(s):* See foundation web site for current deadlines**
Board meeting date(s): Spring and fall
Officers and Trustees:* Richard J. Guggenhime,* Pres. and Treas.; Lisa Guggenhime Hauswirth,* Secy.; Patricia Capbarat; Charles H. Clifford, Jr.; Andrew Guggenhime.
EIN: 942861512

290
Sherry Lansing Foundation
2121 Ave. of the Stars, Ste. 2020
Los Angeles, CA 90067-5075 (310) 788-0057
FAX: (310) 788-0631;
E-mail: slfasst@sherrylansingfoundation.org; Main URL: http://www.sherrylansingfoundation.org/
Multimedia: https://www.facebook.com/pages/The-Sherry-Lansing-Foundation/362443257112837

Established in 1995 in CA.
Donors: Sherry Lansing; Michael Gordon.
Foundation type: Independent foundation.
Financial data (yr. ended 12/31/12): Assets, $615,808 (M); gifts received, $405,637; expenditures, $565,696; qualifying distributions, $182,206; giving activities include $182,206 for 36 grants (high: $25,550; low: $45).
Purpose and activities: The foundation is committed to making the world a better place by funding and raising awareness for cancer research and by supporting education, art, and culture.

Fields of interest: Performing arts, theater; Arts; Higher education; Hospitals (general); Cancer research; Children/youth, services; Jewish agencies & synagogues.
Limitations: Applications not accepted. Giving primarily in CA. No grants to individuals.
Application information: Unsolicited requests for funds not accepted.
Officers: Sherry Lansing, C.E.O.; **Doug Collins, Pres.**; John C. Stiefel, Secy.-Treas.
EIN: 954533113
Other changes: Doug Collins is now Pres.

291
Las Cumbres Observatory, Inc.
6740 Cortona Dr., Ste. 102
Goleta, CA 93117-5575 (805) 880-1600
FAX: (805) 961-1792; UK address: Unit 2, Hamilton Plz., Duncan St., Birkenhead CH41 5EY UK, tel.: +44 (0) 151 647 8654; Main URL: http://www.lcogt.net
Facebook: https://www.facebook.com/lcogt
RSS Feed: http://lcogt.net/blog/feed
Twitter: http://twitter.com/lcogt

Established in 1995 in CA.
Donors: Wayne E. Rosing; The Tabasgo Foundation.
Foundation type: Operating foundation.
Financial data (yr. ended 12/31/12): Assets, $46,820,975 (M); gifts received, $12,737,540; expenditures, $8,244,244; qualifying distributions, $4,696,922; giving activities include $841,075 for 9 grants (high: $485,031; low: $702), and $3,855,847 for foundation-administered programs.
Fields of interest: Science, public education; Astronomy.
Limitations: Applications not accepted. **Giving primarily in CA, HI and TX; some funding internationally, particularly Australia.** No grants to individuals.
Application information: Contributes only to pre-selected organizations.
Officers: Wayne E. Rosing, Pres.; **Dorothy F. Largay, Secy.-Treas.**
Directors: Lars Bildstein; **Mike Skrutskie, Ph.D.**
EIN: 770361278
Other changes: Dorothy F. Largay is now Secy.-Treas. John Farrell is no longer Treas.

292
Cherese Mari Laulhere Foundation
5800 Spinnaker Bay Dr.
Long Beach, CA 90803-6818
E-mail: info@cherese.org; Main URL: http://www.cherese.org
Twitter: https://twitter.com/cheresemari/

Established in 1996 in CA.
Donors: Larry Laulhere; Mrs. Larry Laulhere; Gwen Laulhere; Wakeman Holdings LP.
Foundation type: Independent foundation.
Financial data (yr. ended 06/30/13): Assets, $14,214,990 (M); gifts received, $4,200,025; expenditures, $819,459; qualifying distributions, $817,011; giving activities include $817,000 for 9 grants (high: $600,000; low: $2,000).
Purpose and activities: Giving to organizations that enrich and better the lives of children, adults and/or families through education, cultural or performing arts, or through medical and health-care related causes.
Fields of interest: Arts; Education; Animals/wildlife; Hospitals (general); Health care; Medical research, institute; Boys & girls clubs; Children/youth, services; Family services.
Limitations: Applications not accepted. Giving primarily in CA.
Application information: Contributes only to pre-selected organizations.
Officers and Directors:* Christine Laulhere,* Pres.; Larry Laulhere,* Secy.-Treas.; **Teresa Laulhere**; Todd Laulhere.
Advisors: Lisa Lungren; Anne-Mare Pedersen; **Sophia Pen**; **Judy Valadez**.
EIN: 330735639

293
The Lawrence Foundation
530 Wilshire Blvd., Ste. 207
Santa Monica, CA 90401-1461
Contact: Lori Mitchell, Exec. Dir.
FAX: (310) 451-7580;
E-mail: info@thelawrencefoundation.org; Direct tel.: (970) 870-9456; Main URL: http://www.thelawrencefoundation.org
Grants Database: http://www.commongrantapplication.com/grantmaker_statistics.php?orgId=20

Established in 2000 in CA.
Donors: Jeff Lawrence; Diane Troth.
Foundation type: Independent foundation.
Financial data (yr. ended 12/31/12): Assets, $3,898,550 (M); expenditures, $279,038; qualifying distributions, $254,409; giving activities include $185,000 for 35 grants (high: $30,000; low: $1,000).
Purpose and activities: The mission of the foundation is to make a difference in the world by providing contributions and grants to organizations that are working to solve pressing educational, environmental, health and other issues.
Fields of interest: Education; Environment, pollution control; Environment; Human services.
Type of support: General/operating support; Emergency funds; Program development; Conferences/seminars; Program evaluation; In-kind gifts.
Limitations: Applications accepted. Giving limited to the U.S., including international organizations that have a U.S.-based office. No support for voter registration, music, gardening, recreational, religious programs, or theater or performance arts programs, hospices or home programs for the elderly, or for international organizations that do not have a qualified domestic 501(c)(3) representative. No grants to individuals or for program related investments, computers or software, audio or video equipment or designing and producing videos, kiosks or promotional material, or dinners, balls or other ticketed events.
Publications: Application guidelines; Grants list.
Application information: Applicants must use Common Grant Application at www.commongrantapplication.com. Full proposal upon invitation, per review of letter. The most efficient way to currently contact the foundation is via e-mail. Application form required.
Deadline(s): Apr. 30 and Oct. 31
Board meeting date(s): May and Nov.
Final notification: June and Nov.
Officer: Lori Read Mitchell, Exec. Dir.
Trustees: Jeff Lawrence; Diane Troth.
Number of staff: 1 part-time professional.
EIN: 954804431

294
Thomas & Dorothy Leavey Foundation
10100 Santa Monica Blvd., Ste. 610
Los Angeles, CA 90067-4110 (310) 551-9936
Contact: Kathleen L. McCarthy, Chair.

Established in 1952 in CA.
Donors: Thomas E. Leavey†; Dorothy E. Leavey†.
Foundation type: Independent foundation.
Financial data (yr. ended 12/31/12): Assets, $249,171,900 (M); expenditures, $14,408,495; qualifying distributions, $11,308,967; giving activities include $10,725,188 for 92 grants (high: $2,000,000; low: $1,200), and $324,000 for grants to individuals.
Purpose and activities: Giving primarily for hospitals, medical research, higher and secondary education, and Catholic church groups; provides scholarships to children of employees of Farmers Group, Inc.
Fields of interest: Education; Health care; Youth, services; Human services; Community/economic development.
Type of support: Scholarships—to individuals.
Limitations: Applications accepted. Giving primarily in southern CA.
Application information:
Initial approach: Letter
Copies of proposal: 1
Deadline(s): None
Board meeting date(s): As required
Officer and Trustees:* Kathleen L. McCarthy,* Chair.; Louis M. Castruccio; Leo E. Denlea, Jr.; Jacqueline Powers Doud; Michael Enright; Karen Hollins; **Tom Lemons**; **John McCarthy**; Colleen Pennell.
EIN: 956060162
Other changes: Kathleen Duncan, James Leavey, and Mark C. Lemons are no longer trustees.

295
The Iara Lee & George Gund III Foundation
c/o T. Suniville
39 Mesa St., Ste. 300
The Presidio
San Francisco, CA **94129-1019**

Established in 2004 in CA, funded in 2005.
Donors: George Gund III; Iara Lee.
Foundation type: Independent foundation.
Financial data (yr. ended 12/31/13): Assets, $6,838 (M); expenditures, $141,165; qualifying distributions, $135,784; giving activities include $135,500 for 4 grants (high: $100,000; low: $500).
Fields of interest: Education; Environment; Health care.
International interests: Africa.
Type of support: General/operating support.
Limitations: Applications not accepted. Giving primarily in CA, CT, Washington, DC, and NY.
Application information: Unsolicited requests for funds not accepted.
Officers: Iara Lee, Pres.; **Thomas Suniville, Secy.-Treas.**
Director: George Gund IV.
EIN: 912146075
Other changes: The grantmaker no longer lists a primary contact.

296
Michael Lee Environmental Foundation
(formerly The Terrassist Foundation)

1922 The Alameda, Ste. 209
San Jose, CA 95126-1458 (408) 244-2949
Contact: Ralph Schardt
Main URL: http://www.mlefoundation.org
Grants List: http://www.mlefoundation.org/page.php?page_id=2276

Established in 1999 in CA.
Foundation type: Independent foundation.
Financial data (yr. ended 12/31/12): Assets, $696,588 (M); expenditures, $221,636; qualifying distributions, $80,813; giving activities include $80,813 for grants.
Purpose and activities: Giving primarily for environmental causes and projects.
Fields of interest: Higher education, university; Environmental education.
Limitations: Applications accepted. Giving primarily in CA.
Application information: Application form required.
Initial approach: Outline of project
Deadline(s): None
Officers: Monique Lee, Pres.; Karen Metz, V.P.; Karen Beck, Secy.; Monique Lee, Treas.; Ralph Schardt, Exec. Dir.
Director: Jennifer Seguin.
EIN: 770519788

297
The Leichtag Foundation
441 Saxony Rd.
Encinitas, CA **92024-2725** (760) 929-1090
E-mail: info@leichtag.org; Main URL: http://jcfsandiego.org/funds-foundations/leichtag-foundation/
Facebook: https://www.facebook.com/LeichtagFoundation?fref=ts

Established in 1991 in CA.
Donors: Max Leichtag; Andre Leichtag; Leichtag Family Trust; Lee and Toni Leichtag Family Trust.
Foundation type: Independent foundation.
Financial data (yr. ended 12/31/12): Assets, $142,042,835 (M); gifts received, $37,617; expenditures, $12,644,312; qualifying distributions, $10,790,478; giving activities include $9,607,787 for 98 grants (high: $1,110,000; low: $162), and $10,790,478 for foundation-administered programs.
Purpose and activities: The foundation strives to alleviate human hardship, advance self-sufficiency, and promote tolerance and understanding, reflecting the Leichtags' pride in their Jewish heritage.
Fields of interest: Human services; Foundations (private independent); Jewish federated giving programs.
International interests: Israel.
Limitations: Giving primarily in the North County Coastal Region of San Diego, CA, and in Jerusalem, Israel. No support for political campaigns or lobbying activities. No grants to individuals, or for fundraising events, endowments, medical or scientific research, individual synagogues or churches, and no funding for capital campaigns.
Publications: Financial statement; Grants list; Program policy statement.
Application information: Unsolicited requests for funds not accepted. However, the foundation is interested in hearing about organizations and programs that may fit within its strategic framework and focus areas. Carefully review the strategic framework on the foundation's website. If you feel your organization is a fit, use the letter of introduction form on the foundation's web site.
Board meeting date(s): May and Nov.
Officers and Trustees:* Bernard Reiter,* Chair.; **Emily Einhorn,* Vice-Chair.**; James S. Farley, C.E.O. and Pres.; Charlene Seidle, V.P. and Exec. Dir.; **Robert Brunst, M.D.*, C.F.O. and Treas.**
Number of staff: None.
EIN: 330466189
Other changes: The grantmaker no longer lists a fax.
Emily Einhorn has replaced Murray Galinson as Vice-Chair.
Murray Galinson, Vice-Chair. and Sheldon Scharlin, Chair., Audit Comm., are deceased. Lenore Bohm is no longer V.P. Dianne Tatum is no longer Secy. Robert Brunst is now C.F.O. and Treas.

298
Lauren B. Leichtman and Arthur E. Levine Family Foundation
c/o Teri McClure
335 N. Maple Dr., Ste. 240
Beverly Hills, CA 90210-3859
Main URL: http://foundationcenter.org/grantmaker/leichtmanlevine/

Established in CA.
Donors: Arthur E. Levine; Lauren B. Leichtman.
Foundation type: Independent foundation.
Financial data (yr. ended 05/31/13): Assets, $313,951 (M); gifts received, $732,500; expenditures, $703,928; qualifying distributions, $701,900; giving activities include $701,900 for 21 grants (high: $300,000; low: $500).
Purpose and activities: Giving primarily for higher and other education; funding also for the arts, children services, and Jewish organizations and temples.
Fields of interest: Performing arts, opera; Elementary/secondary education; Higher education; Law school/education; Education; Human services; Children, services; Family services; Jewish agencies & synagogues.
Type of support: General/operating support.
Limitations: Applications not accepted. Giving primarily in Los Angeles, CA.
Application information: Unsolicited requests for funds not accepted.
Trustees: Lauren B. Leichtman; Arthur E. Levine.
EIN: 954051968

299
Dean & Margaret Lesher Foundation
1333 N. California Blvd., Ste. 330
Walnut Creek, CA 94596-4587 (925) 935-9988
Contact: Kathleen L. Odne, Exec. Dir.
FAX: (925) 935-7459;
E-mail: kodne@lesherfoundation.org; **Contact for LOI and grant application questions: Susan Haley, Grants Mgr., e-mail: shaley@lesherfoundation.org;** Main URL: http://www.lesherfoundation.org
Application Video Tutorial: http://www.foundant.com/applicant-tutorial.php
Grants Database: http://www.lesherfoundation.org/grants_awarded_arts.html

Established in 1989 in CA.
Donors: Lesher Communications, Inc.; Dean S. Lesher†; Margaret L. Lesher†.
Foundation type: Independent foundation.
Financial data (yr. ended 12/31/12): Assets, $71,036,556 (M); gifts received, $143,211; expenditures, $5,010,600; qualifying distributions, $4,478,781; giving activities include $3,820,425 for 162 grants (high: $282,000; low: $400).
Purpose and activities: The foundation is dedicated to improving the quality of life in Contra Costa County, CA, through educational and cultural endeavors and to support children and strengthen families.
Fields of interest: Arts; Education; Children/youth, services; Family services; Children/youth; Children; Youth; Adults; Aging; Young adults; Disabilities, people with; Physically disabled; Blind/visually impaired; Deaf/hearing impaired; Mentally disabled; Minorities; Asians/Pacific Islanders; African Americans/Blacks; Hispanics/Latinos; Women; Girls; Adults, women; Men; Boys; Adults, men; Military/veterans; Substance abusers; Single parents; Crime/abuse victims; Economically disadvantaged; Homeless; LGBTQ.
Type of support: General/operating support; Continuing support; Management development/capacity building; Capital campaigns; Building/renovation; Equipment; Program development; Scholarship funds; Technical assistance; Matching/challenge support.
Limitations: Applications accepted. Giving limited to Contra Costa County, CA. No support for environmental or open space organizations, health care or for other foundations. No grants to individuals, or for conferences, travel costs, fund drives, annual appeals, endowments or debt retirement; no loans.
Publications: Application guidelines; Annual report; Grants list.
Application information: Applications are by invitation only, upon review of initial Letter of Inquiry. The foundation has transitioned to a web-based grant application system, accessible from the web site on the "How to Apply" page. Applicants should submit 1-copy of their proposal online. Application form required.
Initial approach: Letter of Inquiry required for new organizations (see "How to Apply" page on foundation web site for LOI instructions)
Copies of proposal: 1
Deadline(s): None
Board meeting date(s): Monthly
Final notification: Within 90 days
Officers and Directors:* Cynthia A. Lesher,* Pres.; Steve Lesher,* V.P.; Linda L. Tatum,* Secy.-Treas.; Kathleen L. Odne, Exec. Dir.; David Lesher; Joseph Lesher; Tim Lesher; Jill O'Brien.
Number of staff: 1 full-time professional; 1 full-time support.
EIN: 680208980
Other changes: Kris Lesher-Aring is no longer a director.

300
Howard and Irene Levine Family Foundation
1660 Bush St., Ste. 300
San Francisco, CA 94109

Established in 1997 in CA.
Donor: Howard Levine.
Foundation type: Independent foundation.
Financial data (yr. ended 12/31/13): Assets, $15,372,427 (M); gifts received, $1,941,472; expenditures, $1,485,255; qualifying distributions, $1,480,006; giving activities include $1,306,563 for 32 grants (high: $562,500; low: $1,000), and $20,000 for 1 employee matching gift.
Fields of interest: Education.
Type of support: General/operating support.
Limitations: Applications not accepted. Giving primarily in Los Angeles, CA. No grants to individuals.

Application information: Contributes only to pre-selected organizations.
Officers: Howard Levine, Pres.; Irene Levine, V.P.; **Jay Levine, Treas.; David Levine, Exec. Dir.**
Director: Marci Dollinger.
EIN: 954663360
Other changes: At the close of 2013, the grantmaker paid grants of $1,326,563, a 102.2% increase over the 2011 disbursements, $656,149.

301
Lingnan Foundation
(formerly Trustees of Lingnan University)
600 Anton Blvd., Ste. 1100
Costa Mesa, CA 92626-7100 (714) 371-4118
Contact: Leslie Stone, Exec. Dir.
***E-mail:* info@lingnanfoundation.org**; Toll free tel.: (866) 438-4999; Main URL: http://www.lingnanfoundation.org

Established in 1893 in NY.
Donors: Anna Luk Liu; Huey Wong; Pausang Wong; Sinclair Louie; May Louie; Jennie Lee Mui Yi-Ching; I.U. Lai.
Foundation type: Independent foundation.
Financial data (yr. ended 06/30/13): Assets, $21,524,386 (M); gifts received, $28,992; expenditures, $980,336; qualifying distributions, $924,784; giving activities include $757,195 for 8 grants (high: $260,000; low: $902).
Purpose and activities: To contribute to the advancement of higher education in South China, and through that process, to promote understanding between Chinese and Americans. The foundation supports scholarly exchange, educational innovation, and service to society.
Fields of interest: Higher education; Social sciences; International studies.
International interests: China; Hong Kong.
Type of support: General/operating support; Continuing support; Management development/capacity building; Building/renovation; Program development; Conferences/seminars; Professorships; Publication; Seed money; Curriculum development; Fellowships; Internship funds; Scholarship funds; Research; Exchange programs.
Limitations: Applications accepted. Giving primarily in Hong Kong and in the People's Republic of China; some funding in the U.S. No grants to individuals, or for annual campaigns or emergency, capital or endowment funds; no loans.
Publications: Application guidelines; Biennial report; Program policy statement.
Application information: See foundation web site for application guidelines and procedures. Application form not required.
Initial approach: Proposal or letter
Copies of proposal: 1
Deadline(s): Inquire with foundation
Board meeting date(s): May and Nov.
Final notification: 1 month after meetings
Officers and Trustees:* Edward Chow,* Chair.; Jane S. Permaul,* Pres.; Bobby Fong,* Secy.; Alex Banker,* Treas.; Jo H. Currie, Exec. Dir.; Shenyu Belsky; Chi-Chao Chan; Kenyon Chan; Albert Chen; Larry Hudspeth; Helena Kolenda; Ralph Lerner; Roy C. Sheldon; Chui L. Tsang; Michael Woo; Yu "Gary" Zeng.
Number of staff: 2 part-time professional.
EIN: 136400470
Other changes: The grantmaker has moved from CT to CA. The grantmaker no longer lists a fax.

302
The RM Liu Foundation
500 W. 190th St., 6th Fl.
Gardena, CA 90248-4265

Established in 2007 in CA.
Donors: Justin Liu; Emily Liu; Tireco, Inc.
Foundation type: Company-sponsored foundation.
Financial data (yr. ended 12/31/12): Assets, $3,894,304 (M); gifts received, $1,775,000; expenditures, $240,411; qualifying distributions, $221,747; giving activities include $220,372 for 5 grants (high: $202,000; low: $60).
Purpose and activities: The foundation supports organizations involved with arts and culture, education, public policy, and Asian culture.
Fields of interest: Arts, cultural/ethnic awareness; Performing arts centers; Arts; Higher education; Education; Public policy, research; Asians/Pacific Islanders.
Type of support: General/operating support.
Limitations: Applications not accepted. Giving primarily in CA. No grants to individuals.
Application information: Contributes only to pre-selected organizations.
Officers: Justin R. Liu, Pres.; Mimi W. Liu, C.F.O.; Robert W. Liu, V.P.; Emily F. Liu, Secy.
EIN: 208643551
Other changes: The grantmaker no longer lists a phone.

303
Livingston Memorial Foundation
c/o Musick, Peeler & Garrett, LLP
2801 Townsgate Rd., No. 200
Westlake Village, CA 91361-5842 (805) 418-3115
Contact: Laura K. McAvoy, Asst. Secy. and C.F.O.
FAX: (805) 418-3101;
E-mail: l.mcavoy@mpglaw.com; Main URL: http://livingstonmemorialfoundation.org/

Incorporated May, 1974 in CA.
Donor: Ruth Daily Livingston†.
Foundation type: Independent foundation.
Financial data (yr. ended 04/30/13): Assets, $9,750,770 (M); expenditures, $610,079; qualifying distributions, $457,653; giving activities include $352,000 for 26 grants (high: $151,000; low: $1,000).
Purpose and activities: Support for health and health-related agencies serving citizens of Ventura County, California.
Fields of interest: Medicine/medical care, public education; Medical care, community health systems; Hospitals (general); Health care, clinics/centers; Health care, infants; Dental care; Optometry/vision screening; Medical care, rehabilitation; End of life care; Health care, home services; Mental health/crisis services, rape victim services; Mental health, grief/bereavement counseling; Mental health/crisis services.
Type of support: General/operating support; Continuing support; Equipment; Matching/challenge support.
Limitations: Giving limited to organizations benefiting the health of residents of Ventura County, CA. No grants to individuals.
Publications: Application guidelines; Informational brochure (including application guidelines); Program policy statement.
Application information: Application form required.
Initial approach: Letter not exceeding 3 pages
Copies of proposal: 9
Deadline(s): Varies; contact foundation for information
Board meeting date(s): As required
Officers and Directors:* Charles M. Hair, M.D.*, Chair. and Pres.; W.C. Huff, M.D.*, Vice-Chair. and V.P.; Richard Loft, M.D.*, Vice-Chair. and V.P.; Marcia Donlon,* Secy.; Laura K. McAvoy,* C.F.O.; Thomas F. McGrath III; John R. Walters, M.D.
Number of staff: None.
EIN: 237364623
Other changes: The grantmaker now makes its application guidelines available online.

304
Thomas J. Long Foundation
2950 Buskirk Ave., Ste. 160
Walnut Creek, CA 94597-7770 (925) 944-3800
***Contact:* Marcia A. Sander, Cont.; Aimee S. Eng, Sr. Prog. Off.; Pam Matthews, Admin. Asst.; Nancy J. Shills, Prog. Off.**
FAX: (925) 944-3573;
E-mail: info@thomasjlongfdn.org; Main URL: http://www.thomasjlongfdn.org

Established in 1972.
Donor: Thomas J. Long†.
Foundation type: Independent foundation.
Financial data (yr. ended 12/31/13): Assets, $91,036,725 (M); expenditures, $7,417,485; qualifying distributions, $6,692,779; giving activities include $6,076,850 for 225 grants (high: $1,280,000; low: $5,000).
Purpose and activities: Giving primarily for education, the arts, health and human services.
Fields of interest: Arts; Education; Health care; Human services.
Limitations: Applications accepted. Giving primarily in HI and northern CA with preference given to Alameda, Contra Costa, Napa, Solano, and Sonoma counties. No support for supporting organizations. No grants to individuals, or for endowments, loan repayments, research or international grants.
Application information: The foundation does not accept either a Letter of Inquiry or Grant Application in hard copy. Application form required.
Initial approach: Complete online application following instructions posted on foundation website
***Deadline(s):* None. Applications are accepted throughout the year**
Board meeting date(s): Quarterly
Officers and Trustees:* Sidne J. Long,* Chair.; Hank Delevati,* Vice-Chair.; Mark Friedman, C.E.O.; Marcia Sander, Cont.; Catherine M. Fisher,* Secy.; Milton Long,* Treas.; Moira Walsh.
Number of staff: 4 full-time professional; 1 full-time support.
EIN: 237180712
Other changes: Mark Friedman has replaced Bob Coakley as C.E.O.
Robert M. Coakley is no longer Exec. Dir. Hank Delevati is now Vice-Chair. Sidne J. Long is now Chair. Catherine M. Fisher is now Secy. Jill M. Rapier is no longer Secy.-Treas. Milton Long is now Treas. Marcia Sander is now Cont.

305
Los Altos Community Foundation
183 Hillview Ave.
Los Altos, CA 94022-3742 (650) 949-5908
FAX: (650) 949-0807; E-mail: lacf@losaltoscf.org; Grant inquiry e-mail: CGP@losaltoscf.org; Main URL: http://www.losaltoscf.org
Facebook: https://www.facebook.com/pages/Los-Altos-Community-Foundation/138638339553146
Flickr: http://www.flickr.com/photos/losaltoscf/
Google Plus: https://plus.google.com/+LosaltoscfOrg/posts
RSS Feed: http://feeds.feedburner.com/LosAltosCommunityFoundation
Twitter: https://twitter.com/lacforg
YouTube: http://www.youtube.com/user/LosAltosCF

Established in 1991 in CA.
Foundation type: Community foundation.
Financial data (yr. ended 06/30/12): Assets, $5,585,801 (M); gifts received, $876,052; expenditures, $1,112,804; giving activities include $540,579 for 60+ grants (high: $42,000).
Purpose and activities: The foundation supports the community by making grants for local programs, building an endowment for the future, and managing philanthropic funding for other organizations. Giving primarily for the arts, conflict resolution, community building, and leadership development.
Fields of interest: Arts; Higher education; Education; Dispute resolution; Disasters, Hurricane Katrina; Community/economic development; Philanthropy/voluntarism, association; Leadership development; Children/youth.
Type of support: Scholarships—to individuals; General/operating support; Capital campaigns; Building/renovation; Program development; Conferences/seminars; Seed money; Technical assistance; Program evaluation; Program-related investments/loans; Matching/challenge support.
Limitations: Applications accepted. Giving primarily in Los Altos and Los Altos Hills, CA, and surrounding unincorporated areas. No support for governmental, religious, or profit-making organizations. No grants to individuals (except for scholarships).
Publications: Application guidelines; Annual report; Financial statement; Grants list; Informational brochure; Newsletter; Occasional report; Program policy statement.
Application information: Visit foundation web site for grant application, guidelines and specific deadlines. Application form required.
Initial approach: Submit application and attachments
Copies of proposal: 1
***Deadline(s):* 4th Tuesday of June, Sept., and Feb.**
Board meeting date(s): 3rd Wed. of each month
Final notification: 4 weeks
Officers and Directors:* Claudia Coleman,* Co-Chair.; Sherie Dodsworth,* Co-Chair.; Henry Roux,* Corp. Secy.; Joe Eyre,* Exec. Dir.; Roy Lave,* Exec. Dir. Emeritus; Cam Chan; Christina Chu; Judy Hanneman; Mike Kasperzak; Crysta Krames; Bob Kresek; George Limbach; Marilyn Manning; Nancy Manning; Scott Riches; Kevin Schick; George Stafford; **Brenda Taussig**; Emy Thurber; Jim Thurber; Dennis Young.
Number of staff: 1 full-time support.
EIN: 770273721

306
George Lucas Family Foundation
(formerly Lucasfilm Foundation)
101 Ygnacio Valley Rd., Rm. 310
Walnut Creek, CA **94596-7018**
Application address: Kristine Kolton, P.O. Box 2009, San Rafael, CA 94912; Main URL: http://www.lucasfilm.com/inside/faq/
George Lucas's Giving Pledge Profile: http://glasspockets.org/philanthropy-in-focus/eye-on-the-giving-pledge/profiles/lucas

Established in 2005 in CA.
Donors: George W. Lucas, Jr.; Lucasfilm Ltd.
Foundation type: Company-sponsored foundation.
Financial data (yr. ended 12/31/12): Assets, $1,141,488,469 (M); gifts received, $1,076,191,669; expenditures, $7,715,355; qualifying distributions, $7,584,792; giving activities include $7,527,500 for 147 grants (high: $3,900,000; low: $500).
Purpose and activities: The foundation supports organizations involved with arts and culture, education, and human services. Special emphasis is directed toward programs designed to benefit children.
Fields of interest: Media, film/video; Museums; Arts; Higher education; Education; Environment, land resources; American Red Cross; Children, services; Human services; Children.
Type of support: General/operating support; Continuing support; Annual campaigns; Building/renovation; Endowments; Program development; Scholarship funds.
Limitations: Applications accepted. Giving primarily in the San Francisco Bay Area, CA. No grants to individuals.
Publications: Application guidelines.
Application information: Letters of inquiry should be submitted on organization letterhead. Support is limited to 1 contribution per organization during any given year. Application form not required.
Initial approach: Letter of inquiry
Deadline(s): None
Officers and Directors:* George W. Lucas, Jr.,* C.E.O.; Micheline Chau, V.P. and Secy.; Robert Bradley,* V.P.; Angelo Garcia, V.P.; Natalie Talbott, Secy.; Steve Condioti, Treas. and C.F.O.; Mike Rider, Treas.; **Mellody Hobson**; **Kate Nyegaard**.
EIN: 203940983
Other changes: At the close of 2012, the fair market value of the grantmaker's assets was $1,141,488,469, a 1161.3% increase over the 2011 value, $90,498,167.
Micheline Chau is now V.P. and Secy. Steve Condioti is now Treas. and C.F.O.

307
Miranda Lux Foundation
57 Post St., Ste. 510
San Francisco, CA 94104-5020 (415) 981-2966
Contact: Kenneth J. Blum, Exec. Dir.
E-mail: admin@mirandalux.org; Main URL: http://www.mirandalux.org
Grants List: http://www.mirandalux.org/grant-recipients.php

Incorporated in 1908 in CA.
Donor: Miranda W. Lux†.
Foundation type: Independent foundation.
Financial data (yr. ended 06/30/13): Assets, $9,574,586 (M); expenditures, $488,255; qualifying distributions, $474,970; giving activities include $380,452 for 36 grants (high: $25,000; low: $2,500).
Purpose and activities: Support to promising proposals for preschool through junior college programs in the fields of pre-vocational and vocational education. Also supports innovative academic enrichment, technology training, and performing and visual arts programs to help participants develop core job skills. The foundation limits its grantmaking to organizations and programs within the San Francisco Bay area that serve people under the age of 18.
Fields of interest: Vocational education; Adult education—literacy, basic skills & GED; Education, reading; Employment, services; Employment, training; Children/youth, services.
Type of support: General/operating support; Continuing support; Equipment; Program development; Seed money; Fellowships; Internship funds; Scholarship funds; Matching/challenge support.
Limitations: Applications accepted. Giving limited to San Francisco, CA. No support for sectarian religious facilities. No grants to individuals, or for annual campaigns, emergency funds, deficit financing, building or endowment funds, land acquisition, renovations, research, publications, or conferences; no loans.
Publications: Application guidelines; Annual report; Grants list; Informational brochure; Program policy statement.
Application information: Application form required.
Initial approach: Letter
Copies of proposal: 1
Deadline(s): None
Board meeting date(s): Quarterly
Officers: Philip F. Spalding,* Pres.; Robert J. Cappelloni, V.P.; Beatrice Bowles,* Secy.-Treas.; Kenneth J. Blum, Exec. Dir.
Trustees: Bert Damner; Nina Gladish; Betsy Keller; Roland E. Tognazzini, Jr.
EIN: 941170404

308
The Marcled Foundation
235 Montgomery St., Ste. 1270
San Francisco, CA **94104-2912** (415) 346-5757
FAX: (415) 391-7274; E-mail: marcled@marcled.org; Main URL: http://www.marcled.org
Grants List: http://www.marcled.org/grants.html

Established in 2004 in CA and DE.
Donor: The Virginia and Leonard Marx Foundation.
Foundation type: Independent foundation.
Financial data (yr. ended 12/31/12): Assets, $52,656,899 (M); expenditures, $3,486,886; qualifying distributions, $2,917,500; giving activities include $2,917,500 for 33 grants (high: $360,000; low: $25,000; average: $25,000–$50,000).
Purpose and activities: The foundation seeks to build the careers and assets of low-income youth, young adults, and families. The foundation provides financial support to organizations, programs, and policies that effectively reduce barriers to economic success for low-income youth and young adults (especially current and former foster youth). The foundation also supports organizations working to assist low-income individuals who are caring for their child or children while struggling to get ahead.
Fields of interest: Higher education; Adult/continuing education; Employment, services; Employment, job counseling; Employment, training; Employment, vocational rehabilitation; Family services; Financial services; Financial services, credit unions; Youth; Adults; Young adults; Single

parents; Immigrants/refugees; Economically disadvantaged.
Type of support: General/operating support; Program development; Research; Program evaluation; Matching/challenge support.
Limitations: Applications not accepted. Giving in coastal CA, primarily the San Francisco Bay Area, Los Angeles, and the California Central Coast Region. No support for lobbying efforts. No grants to individuals.
Publications: Grants list.
Application information: Contributes only to pre-selected organizations.
Officers and Trustees:* Edwin Solot,* Chair.; Derek Aspacher, Exec. Dir.; Mary Bianco; Claire Solot.
EIN: 200595609

309
Marin Community Foundation
5 Hamilton Landing, Ste. 200
Novato, CA 94949-8263 (415) 464-2500
Contact: Vikki Garrod, V.P., Mktg. and Comms.
FAX: (415) 464-2555; E-mail: info@marincf.org; Main URL: http://www.marincf.org
LinkedIn: http://www.linkedin.com/companies/marin-community-foundation
Making an Impact: http://www.marincf.org/impact
Philanthropy's Promise: http://www.ncrp.org/philanthropys-promise/who
Twitter: http://twitter.com/MarinCmtyFdn

Incorporated in 1986 in CA.
Foundation type: Community foundation.
Financial data (yr. ended 06/30/12): Assets, $1,333,725,159 (M); gifts received, $193,722,307; expenditures, $59,136,825; giving activities include $59,136,825 for grants.
Purpose and activities: The Marin Community Foundation was founded with one simple aspiration: to make a difference in the lives of others through thoughtful, effective philanthropy. The foundation's mission is to encourage and apply philanthropic contributions to help improve the human condition, embrace diversity, promote a humane and democratic society, and enhance the community's quality of life, now and for future generations.
Fields of interest: Arts; Adult education—literacy, basic skills & GED; Education; Environment; AIDS; Legal services; Employment; Housing/shelter, development; Human services; Community/economic development; Religion; Aging; Disabilities, people with; Homeless.
Type of support: General/operating support; Continuing support; Capital campaigns; Building/renovation; Equipment; Land acquisition; Debt reduction; Emergency funds; Program development; Conferences/seminars; Seed money; Curriculum development; Scholarship funds; Research; Technical assistance; Consulting services; Program evaluation; Program-related investments/loans; Employee matching gifts; Scholarships—to individuals; Matching/challenge support.
Limitations: Applications accepted. Giving from Buck Trust limited to Marin County, CA; other giving on a national and international basis with emphasis on the San Francisco Bay Area. No grants to individuals (except for scholarships), or for planning initiatives, or capital projects (except those meeting criteria specified in the funding guidelines). Other limitations specific to each program area are outlined in the funding guidelines.
Publications: Application guidelines; Annual report; Informational brochure (including application guidelines); Newsletter.
Application information: Visit foundation web site for grant applications, deadlines and guidelines. Letters of Intent may be completed online or downloaded and submitted by mail; faxed proposals are not accepted. Application form required.
Initial approach: Register with MCF's online Grant Application Center
Deadline(s): Varies
Board meeting date(s): Monthly
Final notification: 3 months minimum
Officers and Trustees:* Thomas Peters, Ph.D.*, C.E.O. and Pres.; Julie Absey, Ph.D., V.P., Research and Evaluation; Alexandra Derby, V.P., Philanthropic Svcs.; Laura Goff, V.P. and C.I.O.; Sandra Nathan, V.P., Progs.; Fred Silverman, V.P., Mktg. and Comms.; Aileen Sweeney, V.P., Finance; Sid Hartman, C.F.O. and C.O.O.; Deb Terrill, Cont.; George Bull III; Cleveland Justis; Ann Mathieson; Jay L. Paxton; Maria Ramos-Chertok; Robert J. Reynolds; Curtis Robinson; Fu Schroeder; Barbara Clifton Zarate.
Number of staff: 26 full-time professional; 6 part-time professional; 6 full-time support; 1 part-time support.
EIN: 943007979

310
The Marisla Foundation
668 N. Coast Hwy., PMB 1400
Laguna Beach, CA 92651-1513
Contact: Glenda Menges, Admin.
E-mail: glenda@marisla.org; Main URL: http://www.fsrequests.com/marisla

Established in 1986 in CA.
Foundation type: Independent foundation.
Financial data (yr. ended 12/31/12): Assets, $51,482,397 (M); gifts received, $40,000,000; expenditures, $48,391,846; qualifying distributions, $48,295,859; giving activities include $47,404,200 for 345 grants (high: $3,000,000; low: $500).
Purpose and activities: Giving primarily through two programs: an Environmental Program, and a Human Services Program.
Fields of interest: Environment, toxics; Women, centers/services; Marine science; Women.
International interests: Chile; Mexico.
Type of support: General/operating support; Program development.
Limitations: Applications accepted. Giving primarily on the West Coast of the U.S. (including Baja, CA), and in HI, Chile, and the Western Pacific for the environment; funding for women limited to Los Angeles and Orange County, CA. No support for political campaigns. No grants to individuals, or for scholarships, fellowships, or film or video projects.
Publications: Application guidelines.
Application information: Applications accepted via foundation web site. All applicants must complete the online application form which can be found on the foundation's web site. The foundation does not accept applications by mail, fax or e-mail. Application form required.
***Initial approach:* Online**
Copies of proposal: 1
Deadline(s): Jan. 15, Apr. 15, Jul. 15, and Oct. 15
***Board meeting date(s):* Mar., June., Sept., and Dec.**
Final notification: Immediate confirmation of receipt; 2-3 months for a decision
Officers and Directors:* Anne G. Earhart, Pres.; Glenda Menges,* Secy. and Prog. Dir., Admin.; Oliver N. Crary, Treas.; Herbert M. Bedolfe,* Exec. Dir.; Sara M. Lowell.
Number of staff: 2 full-time professional.
EIN: 330200133

311
Matsui Foundation
c/o Teresa Matsui Sanders
1645 Old Stage Rd.
Salinas, CA 93908-9737 **(831) 422-6433, Ext. 206**
E-mail: **teresa@matsuinursery.com**; Main URL: http://andymatsuifoundation.org/

Established in 2003 in CA.
Donors: Toshikiyo Andy Matsui; Yasuko Matsui; Matsui Nursery, Inc.
Foundation type: Operating foundation.
Financial data (yr. ended 12/31/12): Assets, $1,037,375 (M); gifts received, $752,000; expenditures, $632,765; qualifying distributions, $566,885; giving activities include $16,000 for 2 grants (high: $10,000; low: $5,000), $545,000 for 64 grants to individuals, and $619,943 for foundation-administered programs.
Purpose and activities: Giving primarily to improve the quality of life and economic conditions in Monterey County, California; also giving scholarship awards to graduating seniors residing in Monterey County, California.
Fields of interest: Higher education; Community/economic development.
Type of support: General/operating support; Scholarships—to individuals.
Limitations: Applications not accepted. Giving limited to Monterey County, CA.
Application information: Unsolicited requests for funds not accepted.
Officers: Toshikiyo Andy Matsui, Pres.; Yasuko Matsui, Secy. and C.F.O.
EIN: 200483500

312
Mattel Children's Foundation
(formerly Mattel Foundation)
333 Continental Blvd., M.S. M1-0807
El Segundo, CA 90245-5032 (310) 252-6552
Contact: Deidre Lind, Exec. Dir.
E-mail: foundation@mattel.com; Additional e-mail for Deidre Lind: deidre.lind@mattel.com; Additional tel.: (310) 252-3630; Main URL: http://corporate.mattel.com/about-us/philanthropy/
Grants List: http://philanthropy.mattel.com/reports#grants

Established in 1978 in CA.
Donor: Mattel, Inc.
Foundation type: Company-sponsored foundation.
Financial data (yr. ended 12/31/12): Assets, $555,310 (M); gifts received, $5,109,386; expenditures, $4,480,930; qualifying distributions, $4,480,930; giving activities include $4,415,330 for 257 grants (high: $580,910; low: $25).
Purpose and activities: The foundation supports programs designed to enrich the lives of children. Special emphasis is directed toward programs designed to support or enhance the opportunity for children to play.
Fields of interest: Arts; Education, services; Education, reading; Education; Hospitals (general); Health care, clinics/centers; Health care; Disasters, preparedness/services; Athletics/sports, amateur leagues; Athletics/sports, Special Olympics; Youth development; Human services; Children; Girls.

Type of support: General/operating support; Equipment; Program development; Scholarship funds; Technical assistance; Employee volunteer services; Sponsorships; Employee matching gifts; Employee-related scholarships; In-kind gifts.
Limitations: Applications not accepted. Giving primarily in CA, CT, Washington, DC, and NY, and in Argentina, Australia, Brazil, Canada, Chile, China, France, Germany, Hong Kong, Hungary, India, Indonesia, Italy, Japan, Malaysia, Mexico, Poland, Spain, Thailand, and the United Kingdom. No support for political parties, candidates or partisan political organizations, labor or fraternal organizations, athletic or social clubs, sectarian or denominational religious organizations not of direct benefit to the entire community, or schools or school districts. No grants to individuals (except for employee-related scholarships), or for capital campaigns for physical property purchases, renovations, or developments, fundraising events, advertising, sponsorships, or research.
Publications: Annual report; Grants list; IRS Form 990 or 990-PF printed copy available upon request; Program policy statement.
Application information: Unsolicited applications for funding are currently not accepted.
Officers and Directors:* Kevin Farr,* Chair.; Alan Kaye,* Vice-Chair. and Pres.; **Lisa Marie Bongiovanni, V.P. and Secy.; Dianne Douglas, V.P. and Treas.**; **Robert Normile, V.P.**; **Cary Dickson, C.F.O.**; Deidre Lind, Exec. Dir.; **David Allmark**; **Stephanie Cota**; **Tom Debrowski**; **Tony Dimichele**; **Ray Greger**; **Ricardo Ibarra**; **Jean Christophe Pean**; **Tim Kilpin.**
Number of staff: 2 full-time professional; 1 full-time support.
EIN: 953263647

313
The Mazda Foundation (USA), Inc.
7755 Irvine Ctr. Dr.
Irvine, CA 92618-2906 (202) 467-5097
Contact: Tamara Mlynasczyk, Prog. Dir.
FAX: (202) 223-6490;
E-mail: MazdaFoundationApplications@gmail.com;
Application address: Grant Applications, Mazda Foundation, 1025 Connecticut Ave. N.W., Ste. 910, Washington, DC20036; Main URL: http://www.mazdafoundation.org

Established in 1990 in MI.
Donors: Mazda North American Opers.; Mazda Motor of America; Mazda Research & Development of North America.
Foundation type: Company-sponsored foundation.
Financial data (yr. ended 09/30/12): Assets, $8,090,125 (M); expenditures, $331,461; qualifying distributions, $280,971; giving activities include $277,068 for 14 grants (high: $64,568; low: $5,000).
Purpose and activities: The foundation supports programs designed to promote education and literacy; environmental conservation; cross-cultural understanding; social welfare; and scientific research.
Fields of interest: Arts, cultural/ethnic awareness; Historic preservation/historical societies; Education, reading; Education; Environment, natural resources; Hospitals (general); Medical research; Food banks; Human services; Civil rights, race/intergroup relations; Science, research; Youth; Minorities.
Type of support: Exchange programs; Fellowships; General/operating support; Program development; Curriculum development; Scholarship funds; Research.
Limitations: Applications accepted. Giving to national organizations located in CA, Washington, DC, LA, NH, NC, and TX. No support for political or religious organizations. No grants to individuals, or for fundraising dinners or events, capital campaigns, endowments, or debt reduction.
Publications: Application guidelines; Annual report.
Application information: A full proposal may be requested at a later date. Organizations receiving support are asked to submit progress reports. Application form required.
Initial approach: Download application form and mail or fax to foundation
Copies of proposal: 1
Deadline(s): Between May 1 and July 1
Board meeting date(s): Oct.
Final notification: Early Nov.
Officers and Trustees:* James J. O'Sullivan,* Chair.; Jay Amestoy,* Pres.; Renee Lewis, Secy.; Robert T. Davis,* Treas.
EIN: 382952236

314
The Sam Mazza Foundation
P.O. Box 14700
San Francisco, CA 94114-0700 (650) 355-0272
Contact: Jeanette Cool, Pres.
Main URL: http://www.sammazzafoundation.org/

Established in 2005 in CA.
Foundation type: Independent foundation.
Financial data (yr. ended 12/31/12): Assets, $20,475,109 (M); gifts received, $2,590; expenditures, $1,178,759; qualifying distributions, $681,074; giving activities include $529,624 for 28 grants (high: $125,000; low: $3,160).
Fields of interest: Arts; Education; Human services; Children/youth, services.
Limitations: Applications accepted. Giving primarily in the San Francisco Bay Area, CA.
Application information: Application form required.
Initial approach: Proposal
Deadline(s): None
Officers: Robert C. Hood, Treas.; Jeanette Cool, Exec. Dir.
Directors: Dede Estey; David Mazza.
EIN: 203644356
Other changes: Jeanette Cool is now Exec. Dir.

315
McBeth Foundation
c/o DeKarver and Agle
23101 Lake Center Dr., No. 170
Lake Forest, CA 92630-2801
E-mail: info@mcbethfoundation.com; **Application address: c/o Amy Holmes, Wells Fargo Advisors, 19800 MacArthur Blvd., Ste. 1400, Irvine, CA 92612-2442**; Main URL: http://www.mcbethfoundation.com

Established in 1989 in CA.
Donor: Barbara McBeth Woodruff†.
Foundation type: Operating foundation.
Financial data (yr. ended 09/30/12): Assets, $27,984,629 (M); expenditures, $1,752,715; qualifying distributions, $1,418,027; giving activities include $1,347,500 for 33 grants (high: $90,000; low: $5,000).
Fields of interest: Museums; Arts; Higher education; Education; Animal welfare; Veterinary medicine; Zoos/zoological societies; Health organizations, association; Children, services; Blind/visually impaired.
Limitations: Giving primarily in southern CA. No grants to individuals.
Application information: Application form required.
***Initial approach:* Use application form on foundation web site**
Deadline(s): June 1
Final notification: Sept.
Board Members: Martin DeKarver; Amy Holmes; Tim Metcalf; Norm Timmins; Skye Woods; Wells Fargo Bank, N.A.
EIN: 330399736

316
Wendy P. McCaw Foundation
P.O. Box 939
Santa Barbara, CA 93102-0939 (805) 965-8080
Contact: Norman J. Colavincenzo, C.F.O.

Established in 1997 in CA.
Donor: Craig O. McCaw.
Foundation type: Independent foundation.
Financial data (yr. ended 12/31/12): Assets, $30,480,698 (M); expenditures, $1,876,575; qualifying distributions, $1,517,100; giving activities include $1,517,100 for grants.
Purpose and activities: Giving primarily for wildlife conservation and protection as well as for the environment.
Fields of interest: Environment, natural resources; Animals/wildlife, preservation/protection.
Limitations: Applications accepted. Giving primarily in CA and Washington, DC. No grants to individuals.
Application information:
Deadline(s): Oct. 31
Officers: Wendy P. McCaw, Pres.; Norman J. Colavincenzo,* Secy.-Treas. and C.F.O.
EIN: 770469217
Other changes: Jon Clark is no longer Exec. Dir.

317
McClatchy Company Foundation
(formerly Star Tribune Foundation)
2100 Q St.
Sacramento, CA 95816-6816
Contact: Karole Morgan-Prager, Dir.

Incorporated in 1945 in MN.
Donors: Cowles Media Co.; The Star Tribune Co.; The McClatchy Co.
Foundation type: Company-sponsored foundation.
Financial data (yr. ended 12/31/12): Assets, $7,203,540 (M); expenditures, $345,767; qualifying distributions, $342,425; giving activities include $342,425 for 39 grants (high: $25,000; low: $1,000).
Purpose and activities: The foundation supports hospitals and organizations involved with arts and culture, education, mental health, children's services, the first amendment, and Judaism.
Fields of interest: Arts; Agriculture/food; Human services.
Type of support: General/operating support; Continuing support; Annual campaigns; Capital campaigns; Endowments; Program development; Conferences/seminars; Scholarship funds; Employee volunteer services; Employee matching gifts; Matching/challenge support.
Limitations: Applications accepted. Giving primarily in CA; giving also to national organizations.
Application information: Application form required.
***Initial approach:* Requets application form**
Deadline(s): None
Board meeting date(s): Quarterly

Officer: Patrick J. Talamantes, Treas.
Directors: Heather L. Fagundes; **Anders Gyllenhaal**; Elaine Lintecum; Karole Morgan-Prager; **Mark Zieman**.
Number of staff: 1 full-time professional; 1 part-time support.
EIN: 416031373
Other changes: The grantmaker no longer lists a phone.

318
The McConnell Foundation

800 Shasta View Dr.
Redding, CA 96003-8208 (530) 226-6200
Contact: Lee W. Salter, C.E.O. and Pres.
FAX: (530) 226-6230;
E-mail: info@mcconnellfoundation.org; Main URL: http://www.mcconnellfoundation.org
E-Newsletter: http://www.mcconnellfoundation.org/contact/
Facebook: https://www.facebook.com/themcconnellfoundation
Knowledge Center: http://www.mcconnellfoundation.org/about/publications

Established in 1964 in CA.
Donors: Carl R. McConnell‡; Leah F. McConnell‡; National Park Service.
Foundation type: Independent foundation.
Financial data (yr. ended 12/31/12): Assets, $342,881,858 (M); expenditures, $19,489,519; qualifying distributions, $13,316,637; giving activities include $6,077,775 for grants, $706,564 for grants to individuals, $199,335 for 232 employee matching gifts, and $4,467,599 for 4 foundation-administered programs.
Purpose and activities: Primary interests include the children, youth and education, sustainable livable communities, international grantmaking, environment, environmental education, recreation; projects that demonstrate broad based community support, and the promotion of voluntarism and philanthropy.
Fields of interest: Museums; Performing arts; Arts; Secondary school/education; Environment; Health care; Recreation; Aging, centers/services; Community/economic development; Voluntarism promotion.
International interests: Laos; Nepal.
Type of support: Building/renovation; Capital campaigns; Employee matching gifts; Endowments; Equipment; General/operating support; In-kind gifts; Matching/challenge support; Scholarship funds; Technical assistance.
Limitations: Giving limited to Shasta, Trinity, Modoc, Tehama and Siskiyou counties, CA; and Nepal and Laos. No support for sectarian religious purposes or for businesses or non 501(c) (3) organizations. No grants for annual fund drives or budget deficits.
Publications: Annual report; Newsletter.
Application information: Check foundation web site for current active programs.
Board meeting date(s): Feb., Mar., June, Sept., and Dec.
Officers and Directors:* Doreeta J. Domke,* Chair.; Lee W. Salter,* C.E.O. and Pres.; John A. Mancasola,* Exec. V.P. and Secy.; Shannon E. Phillips, V.P., Opers.; William Lox,* Treas.; William B. Nystrom, Dir. Emeritus; Richard J. Stimpel, Dir. Emeritus.
Number of staff: 9 full-time professional; 27 full-time support.
EIN: 946102700

319
Bowen H. and Janice Arthur McCoy Charitable Foundation

3239 N. Verdugo Rd.
Glendale, CA 91208-1633 (818) 249-2085
Contact: Bowen H. McCoy, Tr.

Established in 1989 in CA.
Donor: Bowen H. McCoy.
Foundation type: Independent foundation.
Financial data (yr. ended 12/31/13): Assets, $9,394,330 (M); expenditures, $464,595; qualifying distributions, $400,000; giving activities include $400,000 for 24 grants (high: $100,000; low: $5,000).
Purpose and activities: Giving primarily for higher and other education, the arts, and social services; some funding also for churches.
Fields of interest: Arts; Higher education; Education; Human services; Protestant agencies & churches.
Type of support: General/operating support.
Limitations: Applications accepted. Giving primarily in CA. No grants to individuals.
Application information: Application form not required.
Initial approach: **Letter**
Deadline(s): None
Board meeting date(s): Dec.
Trustees: Elizabeth McCoy Chen; Anne McCoy; Bowen H. McCoy; Janice McCoy Miller.
EIN: 954247192

320
The McCune Foundation

P.O. Box 24340
Ventura, CA 93002-4340 (805) 223-8373
Contact: Claudia Armann, Exec. Dir.
E-mail: claudia@mccunefoundation.org; Main URL: http://www.mccunefoundation.org
McCune Foundation's Philanthropy Promise: http://www.ncrp.org/philanthropys-promise/who

Established in 1990 in CA.
Donors: Sara Miller McCune; Sage Publications, Inc.
Foundation type: Independent foundation.
Financial data (yr. ended 02/28/13): Assets, $1,537,821 (M); gifts received, $1,000,000; expenditures, $979,368; qualifying distributions, $892,668; giving activities include $832,743 for 74 grants (high: $79,000; low: $250).
Purpose and activities: The foundation supports grassroots programs which focus on community capacity building and social justice in Santa Barbara and Ventura Counties, California. The foundation also funds efforts that create a social or societal change, rather than individual empowerment or development of leadership skills in individuals, except where such training is directly linked to community action and participants are committed to remaining in the community.
Fields of interest: Civil liberties, advocacy; Civil/human rights; Community/economic development; Economically disadvantaged.
Type of support: Mission-related investments/loans; General/operating support; Management development/capacity building; Program development; Technical assistance.
Limitations: Applications accepted. Giving primarily in Santa Barbara and Ventura counties, CA. No support for religious organizations. No grants to individuals or for budget deficits, construction or renovation of buildings, general funding drives, or events.
Publications: Application guidelines; Grants list.
Application information: Full proposals are by invitation only, upon review of Letter of Inquiry. Additional material must not accompany the initial letter. See foundation web site for specific application procedures which must be followed. Application form required.
Initial approach: **Letter of Inquiry (no more than 2-pages, in 12-point font on organization letterhead); New applicants should telephone Exec. Dir. to discuss project prior to submitting a Letter of Inquiry**
Copies of proposal: 1
Deadline(s): **See foundation web site for current deadlines**
Board meeting date(s): May and Nov.
Final notification: May and Nov.
Officers and Directors:* Sara Miller McCune,* Chair. and Pres.; Sandra Ball-Rokeach,* V.P.; Vicki Fisher Magasinn, Secy.; Hilda Zacarias,* Treas.; Claudia Armann, Exec. Dir.; David F. McCune; Melvin Oliver; Susan Rose; Margaret Sirot; Susan McCune Trumble; Marcos Vargas.
EIN: 770242953

321
McKesson Foundation, Inc.

(formerly McKesson HBOC Foundation, Inc.)
1 Post St.
San Francisco, CA 94104-5201 (415) 983-9325
FAX: (415) 983-7590;
E-mail: mckessonfoundation@mckesson.com; Contact for Mobilizing Health: tel.: (415) 983-9478, e-mail: mhealth@mckesson.com; Main URL: http://www.mckesson.com/about-mckesson/corporate-citizenship/mckesson-foundation/
Giving Comfort on Facebook: https://www.facebook.com/GivingComfort
Giving Comfort on Pinterest: http://pinterest.com/givingcomfort/
Giving Comfort on Twitter: https://twitter.com/GivingComfort
Mobilizing for Health Recipients: http://www.mckesson.com/about-mckesson/corporate-citizenship/mckesson-foundation/mobilizing-for-health/research-grant-program/grant-winners/

Incorporated in 1943 in FL.
Donors: McKesson Corp.; McKesson HBOC, Inc.
Foundation type: Company-sponsored foundation.
Financial data (yr. ended 03/31/13): Assets, $13,665,988 (M); gifts received, $903,224; expenditures, $5,507,053; qualifying distributions, $5,389,407; giving activities include $3,995,149 for 2,164 grants (high: $225,000; low: $10), and $526,666 for foundation-administered programs.
Purpose and activities: The foundation supports programs designed to improve the health of patients through access to quality healthcare; personal health management; and lower healthcare costs. Special emphasis is directed toward non-medical direct services to low-income cancer patients.
Fields of interest: Higher education; Medical school/education; Nursing school/education; Education; Health care, equal rights; Health care, clinics/centers; Public health; Health care, patient services; Cancer; Diabetes; United Ways and Federated Giving Programs; Children; Youth; Economically disadvantaged.
Type of support: General/operating support; Continuing support; Equipment; Program development; Scholarship funds; Research; Employee volunteer services; Employee matching gifts; Employee-related scholarships.
Limitations: Applications accepted. Giving on a national basis in areas of company operations. No

support for religious organizations not of direct benefit to the entire community or disease-specific organizations. No grants to individuals (except for scholarships), or for endowments, political causes or campaigns, advertising, or research.
Publications: Application guidelines; Corporate giving report.
Application information: Letters of inquiry should be no longer than 1 page. However, unsolicited grant proposals are generally not accepted. Applicants may be invited to submit a full proposal at a later date. Support is limited to 1 contribution per organization during any given year.
Initial approach: **E-mail letter of inquiry**
Deadline(s): **None**
Board meeting date(s): Dec.
Officers and Directors:* John H. Hammergren,* Chair.; Carrie J. Varoquiers,* Pres.; Michele Lau, Secy.; Nicholas A. Loiacono,* Treas.; Patrick Blake; Jorge L. Figueredo; Paul C. Julian; Nigel A. Rees.
Number of staff: 1 full-time professional; 1 part-time professional; 1 full-time support.
EIN: 943140036
Other changes: Jeffrey C. Campbell is no longer V.P.

322
The Joseph R. McMicking Foundation
(formerly McMicking Foundation)
1004B O'Reilly Ave.
San Francisco, CA 94129-2602 (415) 474-1784
Contact: Miriam deQuadros White, Exec. Dir.
FAX: (415) 474-1754;
E-mail: miriam@mcmickingfoundation.org; Main URL: http://www.mcmickingfoundation.org

Established in 1958.
Donor: Joseph R. McMicking†.
Foundation type: Independent foundation.
Financial data (yr. ended 12/31/12): Assets, $13,559,254 (M); expenditures, $1,006,382; qualifying distributions, $984,814; giving activities include $761,000 for 77 grants (high: $30,000; low: $1,000).
Purpose and activities: Giving primarily for the education of children in the areas of the arts, computer science, education, and science.
Fields of interest: Higher education; Education; Science; Children/youth; Children.
Type of support: Scholarship funds.
Limitations: Applications accepted. Giving primarily in the San Francisco Bay Area, CA. No grants to individuals; no loans.
Publications: Application guidelines; Annual report; Grants list.
Application information: Application forms available on foundation web site. Applications sent by fax are not accepted. Telephone calls of inquiry are strongly encouraged. Application form required.
Initial approach: Letter of inquiry and application form
Copies of proposal: 1
Deadline(s): None
Board meeting date(s): Feb., July, and Oct.
Officers and Trustees:* Roderick C.M. Hall,* Chair.; Joseph C.M. Hall,* Pres.; Henry C. McMicking,* Secy.-Treas.; Miriam deQuadros White, Exec. Dir.; **H. Andrew McMicking Hall**; Alaistair C.H. McHugh; Consuelo Hall McHugh; **Kate Trevelyan-Hall.**
Number of staff: 1 part-time professional.
EIN: 946058305

323
McMinn Foundation
P.O. Box 93
St. Helena, CA 94574-0093
E-mail: info@mcminnfoundation.org; Main URL: http://www.mcminnfoundation.org

Established in 2000 in CA.
Donors: Anne McMinn; Charles McMinn.
Foundation type: Independent foundation.
Financial data (yr. ended 10/31/13): Assets, $1,303,770 (M); expenditures, $619,416; qualifying distributions, $607,837; giving activities include $606,159 for 42 grants (high: $100,000; low: $25).
Fields of interest: Education; Health care; Medical research, institute; Housing/shelter; Human services; Community/economic development.
Limitations: Applications not accepted. Giving primarily in northern CA. No grants to individuals.
Publications: Grants list.
Application information: Unsolicited requests for funds not accepted.
Officers: Charles J. McMinn, Pres.; Anne W. McMinn, V.P.
EIN: 770529427

324
Giles W. and Elise G. Mead Foundation
P.O. Box 2218
Napa, CA 94558-0221
Contact: Directors
E-mail: meadfoundation@aol.com; **Tel./fax: (707) 226-2164**; Main URL: http://www.gileswmeadfoundation.org
Grants Database: http://www.mfi.org/display.asp?link=GSRCH1

Incorporated in 1961 in CA.
Donor: Elise G. Mead†.
Foundation type: Independent foundation.
Financial data (yr. ended 10/31/13): Assets, $22,796,028 (M); expenditures, $1,443,546; qualifying distributions, $1,246,660; giving activities include $1,246,660 for 42 grants (high: $155,000; low: $500).
Purpose and activities: The Mead Foundation supports organizations dedicated to preserving and improving the environment, the advancement of medical science, and other important social needs. Environmental organizations supported by the Mead Foundation generally have as their primary emphasis forestry, fisheries, and the sustainable use of natural resources in western North America. Scientific and medical organizations supported by the Mead Foundation generally have as their primary emphasis the endocrine system, and in particular diabetes and its complications.
Fields of interest: Environment, natural resources; Environment, forests; Environment; Animals/wildlife, fisheries; Health care, research; Diabetes.
Type of support: Equipment; Land acquisition; Program development; Seed money; Research; Matching/challenge support.
Limitations: Applications accepted. Giving primarily in the western U.S., with emphasis on AK, northern CA, OR, and WA. No support for local or regional environmental organizations outside the western U.S. No grants to individuals, or for general operating expenses.
Publications: Application guidelines; Annual report (including application guidelines); Biennial report; Grants list.
Application information: Application information available on foundation web site. Proposals are accepted only after a review of letter of inquiry first. If a proposal is requested, submit the proposal and supporting materials in an environmentally sensitive manner. Please use two-sided copying when possible, and do not use binders or plastic packaging. Funding in other program areas except for the environment, medical science, and social needs, are limited to grant proposals initiated by individual board members. A copy of most recent IRS Determination Letter, a copy of most recent annual report/audited financial statement/990, and a listing of board of directors, trustees, officers and other key people and their affiliations, are to be submitted upon request from the foundation only. Additional copies of the proposal will be upon the request of the foundation. Application form not required.
Initial approach: Inquiry by letter
Copies of proposal: 1
Deadline(s): None
***Board meeting date(s):* Jan., June, and Oct.**
Final notification: 2 months
Officers and Directors:* Calder M. Mackay,* C.E.O. and Pres.; Jane W. Mead, V.P.; Parry W. Mead,* V.P.; Richard N. Mackay, Secy.-Treas.; Katherine Cone Keck; Giles W. Mead.
Number of staff: 1 part-time professional.
EIN: 956040921

325
Mediathe Foundation, Inc.
14 Monarch Bay Plz., PMB 485
Dana Point, CA 92629-3424
E-mail: mediathe@yahoo.com; Main URL: http://www.mediathe.org
Grants List: http://www.mediathe.org/html/archive.html

Established in 2001 in NY.
Donors: Nancy Meli Walker; Joseph A. Walker.
Foundation type: Independent foundation.
Financial data (yr. ended 11/30/12): Assets, $935,321 (M); expenditures, $161,645; qualifying distributions, $158,595; giving activities include $157,000 for 13 grants (high: $53,000; low: $2,000).
Purpose and activities: Support for new media performance arts, humanitarian causes, environment, alternative energy and nature preservation.
Fields of interest: Media/communications; Environment.
Limitations: Applications accepted. Giving primarily in NY. No support for scholarship funds.
Application information: See foundation web site for complete application guidelines. Application form required.
***Deadline(s):* Dec. 7**
Officers and Directors:* Joseph A. Walker, Pres. and Treas.; Nancy Meli Walker,* Secy.; Gilbert Hsiao.
EIN: 113641353

326
Mellam Family Foundation
P.O. Box 610091
Redwood City, CA 94061-0091
E-mail: info@mellam.org; Main URL: http://www.mellam.org

Established in 1987 in NY.
Donor: Laural D. Mellam†.
Foundation type: Independent foundation.
Financial data (yr. ended 12/31/13): Assets, $15,609,392 (M); expenditures, $923,628;

qualifying distributions, $761,150; giving activities include $630,510 for 58 grants (high: $20,000; low: $1,000).
Purpose and activities: Giving for programs in the areas of medical and scientific research, education, the environment and social services.
Fields of interest: Education; Health organizations; Medical research.
Limitations: Applications not accepted. Giving primarily in the San Francisco Bay Area, CA, CO, HI, and NY. No grants to individuals.
Publications: Annual report; Financial statement; Grants list.
Application information: Contributes only to pre-selected organizations. All solicited grant proposals must be submitted in electronic format (Word, Excel, or PDF). Hardcopies are not accepted. See foundation web site for complete information.
Board meeting date(s): Quarterly
Officers and Trustees:* Marilyn Rogers,* Pres.; Tracy Rogers, Exec. Dir.; Clay Rogers; Holly Rogers; Timothy Rogers.
Advisory Board: Barry Waldorf.
Number of staff: 1 full-time professional.
EIN: 136894208

327
Menard Family Foundation

c/o Lindsay & Brownell, LLP
4225 Executive Sq., Ste. 1150
La Jolla, CA 92037-9153
E-mail: info@menardfoundation.org; Main URL: http://www.menardfoundation.org
Grants List: http://www.menardfoundation.org/grant-organizations

Established in 1998 in CA.
Donors: Bernard Menard†; Mary Menard†; Menard 1979 Family Trust.
Foundation type: Independent foundation.
Financial data (yr. ended 12/31/12): Assets, $15,262,401 (M); expenditures, $841,304; qualifying distributions, $692,012; giving activities include $619,600 for 55 grants (high: $100,000; low: $1,000).
Purpose and activities: The foundation supports organizations which seek to enhance lives through medicine and medical research, education, music and the arts, direct service to the poor and underserved, and by animal conservation and therapeutic programs. The foundation also provides financial assistance to Roman Catholic and other faith-based organizations, including social service organizations, parishes, schools, retreat centers and retired religious.
Fields of interest: Arts; Education; Animals/wildlife, preservation/protection; Hospitals (general); Health care; Human services; Catholic agencies & churches.
Limitations: Applications not accepted. Giving primarily in CA, with emphasis on San Diego. No support for profit-making enterprises of nonprofit groups, private operating foundations, service clubs, fraternal, labor, military, or similar organizations whose principle activity is for the benefit of their own membership. No grants to individuals, or for fundraising, dinners, advertising, or lobbying.
Application information: Contributes only to pre-selected organizations.
Officer: Barbara Menard, Exec. Dir.
Directors: Don Harrington; Marcel Menard; Marlene Miller.
EIN: 330834790
Other changes: Barbara Menard is now Exec. Dir.

328
The Johnny Mercer Foundation

c/o Prager & Fenton, LLP
2381 Rosecrans Ave., No. 350
El Segundo, CA 90245-7907
Main URL: http://www.johnnymercerfoundation.org/
Facebook: https://www.facebook.com/pages/The-Johnny-Mercer-Foundation/199566596755138?fref=ts
Twitter: https://twitter.com/johnnymercerorg

Established in 1982 in CA.
Donors: Elizabeth M. Mercer†; Alan Oppenheimer.
Foundation type: Operating foundation.
Financial data (yr. ended 07/31/12): Assets, $3,028,078 (M); gifts received, $9,000; expenditures, $621,824; qualifying distributions, $360,993; giving activities include $328,500 for 9 grants (high: $75,000; low: $2,500).
Purpose and activities: The mission of the foundation is to distribute funds to preserve and enhance the legacy of Johnny Mercer, to assist children with illness or disability, to provide educational programs for music appreciation, to assist in the development of songwriters, and to enhance the general appreciation of American popular music.
Fields of interest: Performing arts, music; Arts; Education; Health care; Human services.
Type of support: General/operating support.
Limitations: Applications not accepted. Giving on a national basis.
Application information: Unsolicited requests for funds not accepted.
Board meeting date(s): Feb., June, and Oct.
Officers and Directors:* John Marshall,* Chair. and Pres.; Jonathan Brielle,* V.P.; **Jeanne Roccon Rohm,* V.P.**; Charles S. Tigerman,* Secy.; Neil J. Gillis,* Treas.; Frank P. Scardino, Exec. Dir.; Alan Bergman; Alvin Deutsch; Erin Drake; Bob Fead; Michael A. Kerker; Robert Kimball; Al Kohn; Amanda McBroom; Michael R. Price; Nancy Rishagen; Dianne S. Thurman.
Advisory Board: Tony Bennett; Leslie E. Binder; Michael Feinstein; David Friedman; Barry Manilow; Andre Previn.
Number of staff: 1 full-time professional.
EIN: 953728115
Other changes: The grantmaker has moved from NY to CA.
Jeanne Roccon Rohm is now V.P. Eva Franchi and Patrick Lattore are no longer directors.

329
Metta Fund

(formerly The M Health Foundation)
770 Tamalpais Dr., Ste. 309
Corte Madera, CA 94925-1737 (415) 945-0243
E-mail: info@mettafund.org; Main URL: http://www.mettafund.org

Established around 1986; converted in 1992 from Davies Medical Center.
Donor: Franklin Holding Corp.
Foundation type: Independent foundation.
Financial data (yr. ended 12/31/12): Assets, $75,154,742 (M); expenditures, $7,861,513; qualifying distributions, $6,601,631; giving activities include $4,995,828 for 86 grants (high: $300,000; low: $1,000).
Purpose and activities: Giving primarily for hospitals, health organizations and human services.
Fields of interest: Hospitals (general); Health organizations; Human services; Foundations (private grantmaking).
Limitations: Applications not accepted. Giving primarily in San Francisco, CA. No grants to individuals.
Publications: Annual report; Grants list.
Application information: Contributes only to pre-selected organizations. Grant applications are by invitation only.
Officers and Directors:* Robert Reed,* Chair.; Gregory G. Monardo,* Pres.; **Brigitte Garcia, V.P., Admin.**; Delia Reid, V.P.; Cherie Mohrfeld, M.D.*, Secy.; Beverly Hayon; James E. Loyce, Jr.; Sandy Ouye Mori; H. Marcia Smolens; J. Edward Tippetts.
EIN: 942992640

330
Military Women In Need Foundation

(formerly California Soldiers' Widows Home Association)
10767 National Place, Unit B
Los Angeles, CA 90034 (310) 684-3854
FAX: (310) 380-5277;
E-mail: info@militarywomeninneed.org; Mailing address: c/o Mariana Sosa, Opers. Mgr., 2355 Westwood Blvd., #350, Los Angeles, CA 90064; Main URL: http://www.militarywomeninneed.org
Facebook: https://www.facebook.com/MWINCA
Twitter: https://twitter.com/MWIN_CA

Established in 1921 in CA.
Foundation type: Independent foundation.
Financial data (yr. ended 06/30/12): Assets, $1,979,650 (M); expenditures, $327,463; qualifying distributions, $304,840; giving activities include $253,800 for 1 grant.
Purpose and activities: Giving to provide emergency subsidies, housing subsidies, advocacy and referral services, and home visits to female veterans and widows of veterans, who have an annual income of less than $24,000 per year, assets of $20,000 or less (not including 1 automobile), who are able to live independently, and who are living alone.
Fields of interest: Housing/shelter, expense aid; Aging; Women; Military/veterans.
Type of support: Emergency funds.
Limitations: Applications not accepted. Giving limited to southern CA.
Application information: Unsolicited requests for funds not accepted.
Board meeting date(s): Quarterly
Officers: Meredith Brenalvirez, Pres.; Ranlyn Tiley Hill, Exec. Dir.
Number of staff: 1 full-time professional; 1 part-time professional.
EIN: 953533990

331
The Milken Family Foundation

1250 4th St.
Santa Monica, CA **90401-1353**
Contact: Richard Sandler, Exec. V.P.
FAX: (310) 570-4801; E-mail: admin@mff.org; Main URL: http://www.mff.org
E-Newsletter: http://www.mff.org/connections/connections.taf
Facebook: http://www.facebook.com/pages/Milken-Family-Foundation/22925979701?ref=ts
GiveSmart: http://www.givesmart.org/Stories/Donors/Mike-Milken
Knowledge Center: http://www.mff.org/publications/
Michael and Lori Milken's Giving Pledge Profile: http://glasspockets.org/philanthropy-in-focus/eye-on-the-giving-pledge/profiles/milken

Multimedia: http://www.mff.org/newsroom/news.taf?page=videos
Twitter: http://www.twitter.com/milken
YouTube: http://www.youtube.com/milkenaward

Established in 1982 in CA.
Donors: Lowell Milken; Michael Milken; Lori A. Milken; Sandra Milken; Department of Education.
Foundation type: Independent foundation.
Financial data (yr. ended 11/30/12): Assets, $378,108,280 (M); expenditures, $11,456,371; qualifying distributions, $9,777,930; giving activities include $7,514,862 for 207 grants (high: $2,081,628; low: $272), and $4,372,464 for 6 foundation-administered programs.
Purpose and activities: The purpose of the foundation is to discover and advance inventive and effective ways of helping people help themselves and those around them lead productive and satisfying lives. The foundation advances this mission primarily through its work in education and medical research. In education, the foundation is committed to strengthening the profession by recognizing and rewarding outstanding educators, and by expanding their professional leadership and policy influence; attracting, retaining and motivating the best talent to the teaching profession; stimulating creativity and productivity among educators and students of all ages; fostering the involvement of both family and the community in schools; and helping build vibrant communities, especially by involving young people who have special needs or who live in neighborhoods considered disadvantaged, in school-based programs that contribute to the revitalization of their community and to the well-being of its residents. In medical research, the foundation is committed to advancing and supporting basic and applied medical research, especially in the areas of prostate cancer and epilepsy, and recognizing and rewarding outstanding scientists in these areas; and supporting basic health care programs to assure the well-being of community members of all ages.
Fields of interest: Health care; Medical research, institute; Human services; Jewish federated giving programs; Jewish agencies & synagogues; Children/youth; Economically disadvantaged.
Type of support: General/operating support; Continuing support; Scholarship funds; Research.
Limitations: Applications accepted. Giving primarily in the Los Angeles, CA, area. No loans to individuals.
Application information:
Initial approach: Letter or proposal
Copies of proposal: 1
Deadline(s): None
Officers and Directors:* Lowell Milken,* Chair. and Pres.; Richard Sandler,* Exec. V.P.; Susan M. Fox, Sr. V.P. and C.F.O.; Ralph Finerman,* Sr. V.P. and Treas.; Dr. Jane Foley, Sr. V.P., Educator Awards; Lawrence Lesser, Sr. V.P., Creative Services; Bonnie Somers, Sr. V.P., Comms.; Joni Milken-Noah,* V.P., Mike's Math Club; Gary Panas, V.P., Design; Rosey Grier,* Prog. Dir., Community Affairs; Dr. Thomas C. Boysen,* Ed. Consultant; Mariano Guzman; Katherine Nouri Hughes; Dr. Julius Lesner; Ferne Milken; Gregory A. Milken; Lori A. Milken; Michael Milken; Lynda Resnick; Ellen Sandler.
Number of staff: 41 full-time professional; 1 part-time professional; 5 full-time support; 3 part-time support.
EIN: 954073646
Other changes: Ian Noah is no longer V.P., Mike's Math Club. Dr. Thomas C. Boysen is now Ed. Consultant.

332
Monterey Bay Aquarium Research Institute
7700 Sandholdt Rd.
Moss Landing, CA 95039-9644 (831) 775-1700
Main URL: http://www.mbari.org/
Facebook: https://www.facebook.com/MBARInews
Google Plus: https://plus.google.com/117815878133202293951
RSS Feed: http://www.mbari.org/rssfeed.xml
Tumblr: http://mbari-blog.tumblr.com/
Twitter: http://twitter.com/MBARI_news
YouTube: http://www.youtube.com/user/MBARIvideo

Established in 1987 in CA.
Donors: The David and Lucile Packard Foundation; David Packard.
Foundation type: Operating foundation.
Financial data (yr. ended 12/31/12): Assets, $117,338,627 (M); gifts received, $45,523,145; expenditures, $52,499,812; qualifying distributions, $40,312,058; giving activities include $247,500 for 5 grants (high: $240,000; low: $1,500), and $20,352,618 for foundation-administered programs.
Purpose and activities: Giving primarily for oceanography projects and research.
Fields of interest: Marine science.
Limitations: Applications not accepted. Giving primarily in CA. No grants to individuals.
Application information: Contributes only to pre-selected organizations.
Officers and Directors:* Julie E. Packard,* Chair.; Dr. Franklin M. Orr, Jr., Vice-Chair.; Dr. Christopher A. Scholin, C.E.O. and Pres.; Keith Raybould, C.O.O.; Barbara P. Wright,* Secy.; C. Michael Pinto, C.F.O.; Dr. G. Ross Heath; Nancy Burnett; and 11 additional directors.
EIN: 770150580

333
Gordon and Betty Moore Foundation
1661 Page Mill Rd.
Palo Alto, CA 94304-1209 (650) 213-3000
Contact: Genny Biggs, Comm. Manager
FAX: (650) 213-3003; E-mail for Genny Biggs: genny.biggs@moore.org. Additional e-mail: grantprocessing@moore.org; Main URL: http://www.moore.org/
GiveSmart: http://www.givesmart.org/Stories/Donors/Steve-McCormick
Gordon and Betty Moore's Giving Pledge Profile: http://glasspockets.org/philanthropy-in-focus/eye-on-the-giving-pledge/profiles/moore
Grants Database: http://www.moore.org/grants/list
Grants List: http://www.moore.org/about/financials
Twitter: https://twitter.com/MooreFound

Established in 2000 in CA.
Donors: Gordon E. Moore; Betty I. Moore.
Foundation type: Independent foundation.
Financial data (yr. ended 12/31/12): Assets, $5,697,258,026 (M); expenditures, $286,605,357; qualifying distributions, $259,717,649; giving activities include $233,047,309 for 1,146 grants (high: $7,500,000; low: $50), and $1,935,000 for foundation-administered programs.
Purpose and activities: As responsible stewards of the resources entrusted to them, the foundation forms and invests in partnerships to achieve significant, lasting and measurable results in environmental conservation, science and the San Francisco Bay Area. The majority of funding is directed to organizations whose work supports the foundation's initiatives in its three major program areas.
Fields of interest: Environment; Science.
Type of support: Conferences/seminars; Land acquisition; Program development; Research; Program-related investments/loans.
Limitations: Applications not accepted. Giving on a worldwide basis (North Pacific Rim and Andes-Amazon), with some focus on the San Francisco Bay Area, CA, for selected projects. No grants to individuals, or for arts, building/renovation, endowments, capital campaigns, labor issues, or for sports programs.
Publications: Financial statement; Grants list.
Application information: The foundation does not accept unsolicited proposals.
Officers and Trustees:* Gordon E. Moore,* Chair.; Paul Gray, Ph.D., Vice-Chair. and Interim Pres.; Nancy J. Koch, Genl. Counsel and Secy.; Denise Strack, C.I.O.; Kenneth G. Moore,* Dir., San Francisco Bay Area Prog.; Bruce Alberts, Ph.D.; Rosina Bierbaum, Ph.D.; James C. Gaither; John Hennessy, Ph.D.; Kathleen Justice-Moore; Kristen L. Moore; Steven E. Moore; Kenneth F. Siebel.
Number of staff: 72 full-time professional; 4 part-time professional.
EIN: 943397785
Other changes: Steven J. McCormick is no longer Pres.

334
Jay Morris Foundation, Inc.
(formerly Graff Family Foundation)
c/o Squar Milner
11111 Santa Monica Blvd., Ste. 800
Los Angeles, CA 90025-6395

Established in 1999 in IL.
Donors: Jacob Graff; Pnina Graff.
Foundation type: Independent foundation.
Financial data (yr. ended 12/31/12): Assets, $635,073 (M); expenditures, $1,433,304; qualifying distributions, $1,400,338; giving activities include $1,400,338 for 126+ grants (high: $376,692).
Purpose and activities: Giving primarily to Jewish agencies, temples, and schools.
Fields of interest: Education; Jewish agencies & synagogues.
Limitations: Applications not accepted. Giving primarily in CA and NY. No grants to individuals.
Application information: Contributes only to pre-selected organizations.
Officers and Directors:* Jacob Graff,* Pres.; Pnina Graff, Secy.-Treas.
EIN: 364300685

335
Samuel B. and Margaret C. Mosher Foundation
(also known as The Mosher Foundation)(formerly Samuel B. Mosher Foundation)
1114 State St., No. 248
Santa Barbara, CA 93101-2717 (805) 962-1700
Contact: Edward E. Birch, C.E.O. and Pres.
FAX: (805) 962-1792;
E-mail: info@mosher-foundation.org; Application address: 1114 State St., Ste. 252, Santa Barbara,

CA 93101; Main URL: http://
www.mosher-foundation.org

Incorporated in 1951 in CA.
Donors: Samuel B. Mosher†; Goodwin J. Pelissero†; Deborah S. Pelissero†; Margaret C. Mosher†.
Foundation type: Independent foundation.
Financial data (yr. ended 08/31/13): Assets, $36,024,433 (M); gifts received, $8,907; expenditures, $2,371,602; qualifying distributions, $2,116,170; giving activities include $1,755,864 for 80 grants (high: $882,450; low: $100).
Purpose and activities: Grants mainly for education, health care and the performing arts.
Fields of interest: Arts; Secondary school/ education; Higher education; Health care.
Type of support: General/operating support; Equipment; Endowments; Program development; Scholarship funds; Consulting services; Program evaluation; Program-related investments/loans; Employee-related scholarships.
Limitations: Applications accepted. Giving limited to Santa Barbara County, CA. **No support for international grants, or for requests from organizations outside of Southern Santa Barbara County, CA. No grants to individuals, or for capital campaigns, endowments, fundraising or gala events, annual funds, or multi-year commitments.**
Application information: Full applications by invitation only. Summaries will be kept on file and reviewed when funding is available. See foundation web site for additional information.
Initial approach: **1-page (or less) summary of organization and program**
Board meeting date(s): Quarterly
Officer and Trustees:* Edward E. Birch,* C.E.O. and Pres.; **Yvette Birch Giller,* V.P., Admin.**; **Suzanne Birch**; Robert J. Emmons, Ph.D.; **Jennifer Engmyr**; Bruce McFadden, M.D.; David K. Winter, Ph.D.
Number of staff: 1 full-time professional; 1 part-time professional; 1 full-time support.
EIN: 956037266

336
John and Linda Muckel Foundation
6024 Ocean Terr. Dr.
Rancho Palos Verdes, CA 90275-5755

Established in 1999 in CA.
Donors: Indiana Plumbing Supply Co., Inc.; John Muckel.
Foundation type: Company-sponsored foundation.
Financial data (yr. ended 12/31/12): Assets, $190,774 (M); expenditures, $166,631; qualifying distributions, $166,473; giving activities include $166,473 for grants.
Purpose and activities: The foundation supports organizations involved with historical activities, higher education, animal welfare, human services, and Christianity.
Fields of interest: Historical activities; Higher education; Animal welfare; Homeless, human services; Human services; Christian agencies & churches.
Type of support: General/operating support.
Limitations: Applications not accepted. Giving primarily in CA, Washington, DC, and VA. No grants to individuals.
Application information: Contributes only to pre-selected organizations.
Officers: John Muckel, Pres.; Linda Muckel, Secy. and C.F.O.
EIN: 330882395

337
Mulago Foundation
2435 Polk St., Ste. 21
San Francisco, CA 94109-1600
E-mail: info@mulagofoundation.org; Main URL: http://www.mulagofoundation.org

Established around 1968 in CA.
Donors: Rainer Arnhold Trust; Ruth Steiner†.
Foundation type: Independent foundation.
Financial data (yr. ended 12/31/12): Assets, $212,317,909 (M); expenditures, $8,307,950; qualifying distributions, $7,356,582; giving activities include $6,855,638 for 52 grants (high: $600,526).
Purpose and activities: Giving primarily for education, conservation, and health.
Fields of interest: Higher education; Education; Environment; Hospitals (general); Health care; Human services; Children/youth, services.
Limitations: Applications not accepted. Giving primarily in CA, NY and VA. No grants to individuals.
Application information: Contributes only to pre-selected organizations.
Officers: Henry H. Arnhold, Pres.; Christa Dorrego, Secy.; John P. Arnhold, Treas.
EIN: 946182697
Other changes: The grantmaker has moved from NY to CA.

338
David H. Murdock Institute for Business & Culture
(formerly Castle & Cooke Institute for Business and Culture)
10900 Wilshire Blvd., Ste. 1600
Los Angeles, CA 90024-6500

Established in 1988 in HI.
Donors: David H. Murdock; Dole Food Co., Inc.; Castle & Cooke, Inc.
Foundation type: Company-sponsored foundation.
Financial data (yr. ended 12/31/12): Assets, $1,741 (M); expenditures, $161; qualifying distributions, $0.
Purpose and activities: The foundation supports Duke University and organizations involved with civic affairs.
Fields of interest: Higher education; Public affairs.
Type of support: General/operating support; Research.
Limitations: Applications not accepted. Giving limited to CA and NC. No support for religious organizations. No grants to individuals.
Application information: Contributes only to pre-selected organizations.
Officers and Directors:* David H. Murdock,* C.E.O.; **Roberta Wieman,* Exec. V.P., Admin.**; Scott A. Griswold, Exec. V.P., Finance; Phil Young, V.P., Human Resources.
EIN: 954195213
Other changes: The grantmaker no longer lists a primary contact.
Roberta Wieman is now Exec. V.P., Admin.

339
Muskin Family Foundation
16530 Ventura Blvd., Ste. 305
Encino, CA 91436-4594

Foundation type: Independent foundation.
Financial data (yr. ended 06/30/13): Assets, $2,872,034 (M); expenditures, $238,600; qualifying distributions, $186,500; giving activities include $186,500 for 27 grants (high: $30,000; low: $1,000).
Fields of interest: Education; Human services.
Limitations: Applications not accepted. Giving primarily in Los Angeles, CA.
Application information: Unsolicited requests for funds not accepted.
Officers and Directors:* John E. Saunders,* Pres., V.P. and Secy.; Richard Corleto.
EIN: 261139075
Other changes: Judith Fishman Kolbe is no longer a director.

340
Napa Valley Community Foundation
3299 Claremont Way, Ste. 2
Napa, CA 94558-3382 (707) 254-9565
Contact: Marla B. Tofle, V.P., Philanthropic Svcs.; Julia DeNatale, Mgr., Philanthropic Svcs.
FAX: (707) 254-7955;
E-mail: julia@napavalleycf.org; Main URL: http://
www.napavalleycf.org
Facebook: http://www.facebook.com/
napavalleycommunityfoundation?filter=2
Twitter: http://twitter.com/NapaValleyGives
YouTube: http://www.youtube.com/TerenceCFNV

Established in 1994 in CA.
Foundation type: Community foundation.
Financial data (yr. ended 06/30/14): Assets, $18,547,283 (M); gifts received, $2,665,428; expenditures, $3,607,195; giving activities include $2,689,857 for 367 grants (high: $500,000; low: $250; average: $500–$100,000), and $531,938 for 1 foundation-administered program.
Purpose and activities: The foundation mobilizes resources, inspires giving, builds knowledge and provides leadership on vital community issues to improve the quality of life for all in Napa County.
Fields of interest: Education; Health organizations; Legal services; Safety/disasters; Youth development; Family services; Children/youth; Youth; Adults; Young adults; Immigrants/refugees.
Type of support: General/operating support; Management development/capacity building; Program development; Seed money; Scholarship funds; Technical assistance; Program-related investments/loans.
Limitations: Applications accepted. Giving primarily in the Napa County, CA. No grants to individuals (except for scholarships), or for events or fundraisers, re-granting programs, fundraising by one agency on behalf of another, travel for conferences, workshops or performing arts events outside of Napa County, or for groups or projects that confer goods and services, or other benefits, to the donor advisor in exchange for a grant.
Publications: Application guidelines; Annual report; Financial statement; Grants list; Newsletter; Program policy statement.
Application information: Visit foundation Web site for application guidelines and due dates of competitive grant programs. Application form not required.
Initial approach: Letter submitted via web site
Copies of proposal: 1
Deadline(s): Varies
Board meeting date(s): Alternate months throughout the year
Final notification: Varies
Officers and Directors:* **Patrick Gleeson,* Chair.**; **Blair Lambert,* Co Vice-Chair.**; **Carry Thacher,* Co Vice-Chair.**; Terence P. Mulligan,* Pres.; **Kent Imrie,* Secy.**; **Iain Silverthorne,* Treas.**; Sandra J. Fasold, CPA*, C.F.O.; **Jennifer Byram**; Mary Ann Cleary; Dell Coats; Elba Gonzalez-Mares; Rick

Jones; Richard Meese; Manbin Khaira Monteverdi; Brad Nichinson, M.D.; Melissa Patrino; Loraine Stuart; Marla B. Tofle; Jamie Watson.
Number of staff: 3 full-time professional; 2 part-time professional.
EIN: 680349777
Other changes: Patrick Gleeson has replaced David B. Gaw as Chair. Kent Imrie has replaced Maria L. Cisneros as Secy. Iain Silverthorne has replaced Richard Meese as Treas.
Blair Lambert is now Co Vice-Chair. Carry Thacher is now Co Vice-Chair. Joseph Carillo and Kris Jaeger are no longer directors.

341
Y. & S. Nazarian Family Foundation
1801 Century Park W., 5th Fl.
Los Angeles, CA 90067-6408

Established in 1999 in CA.
Donors: Younes Nazarian; Soraya J. Nazarian.
Foundation type: Independent foundation.
Financial data (yr. ended 12/31/12): Assets, $39,653,878 (M); gifts received, $11,987,508; expenditures, $1,943,501; qualifying distributions, $1,521,505; giving activities include $1,521,505 for 51 grants (high: $699,400; low: $9).
Purpose and activities: Giving primarily for Jewish organizations, temples, and federated giving programs; funding also for the arts, and health organizations.
Fields of interest: Arts; Education; Health organizations, association; Human services; Jewish federated giving programs; Jewish agencies & synagogues.
Limitations: Applications not accepted. Giving primarily in CA, with some emphasis on Los Angeles; some funding also in Tel Aviv, Israel. No grants to individuals.
Application information: Contributes only to pre-selected organizations.
Officers: Sharon Baradaran, Pres.; David Nazarian, C.F.O.
Trustees: Shulamit Nazarian; Soraya J. Nazarian; Younes Nazarian.
EIN: 954774321

342
The Henry Mayo Newhall Foundation
57 Post St., Ste. 510
San Francisco, CA 94104-5020 (415) 981-2966
Contact: Kenneth Blum, Admin. Dir.; John S. Blum, Admin. Dir.
FAX: (415) 981-5218;
E-mail: info@newhallfoundation.org; **Additional e-mail: administrator@newhallfoundation.org**;
Main URL: http://www.newhallfoundation.org

Incorporated in 1963 in CA.
Donors: Alice O'Meara†; Leila G. Newhall†; The Newhall Land and Farming Co.
Foundation type: Independent foundation.
Financial data (yr. ended 12/31/13): Assets, $40,807,034 (M); gifts received, $911; expenditures, $2,385,973; qualifying distributions, $2,140,303; giving activities include $1,964,500 for 76 grants (high: $149,000; low: $1,000).
Purpose and activities: Giving limited to agriculture and conservation, human services and education in San Francisco, Santa Clarita Valley and Santa Maria Valley, CA.
Fields of interest: Arts; Education; Environment; Agriculture; Human services; Children/youth, services; Family services; Children/youth; Adults; Disabilities, people with.
Type of support: Program development; General/operating support; Capital campaigns; Seed money; Scholarship funds; Matching/challenge support.
Limitations: Applications accepted. Giving limited to San Francisco, and the Santa Clarita and Santa Maria Valleys, CA. No grants to individuals, or for scholarships; no loans.
Publications: Application guidelines; Grants list.
Application information: See foundation web site for application guidelines and procedures. The foundation encourages telephone calls to inquire as to whether or not a proposed program is eligible. If so, a full proposal can be submitted. Application form not required.
Initial approach: Letter or telephone
Copies of proposal: 1
Deadline(s): Mar. 15 and Sept. 15
Board meeting date(s): Spring and fall
Final notification: 1 week after board meeting
Officers and Directors:* David Newhall,* Pres.; Angelica C. Simmons, V.P.; Scott Dunham, Secy.; Roger Newhall,* Treas.; Donna Chesebrough; **Robert N. Chesebrough III**; Caroline Conroy; Marion Hill; Natasha Hunt; Anthony Newhall; George A. Newhall; Prudence J. Noon; Francine Woods.
Consultants: John S. Blum, Admin. Dir.; Kenneth Blum, Admin. Dir.
EIN: 946073084
Other changes: Robert C. Chesebrough is no longer a director.

343
Nicholas Endowment
1505 E. 17th St., Ste.101
Santa Ana, CA 92705-3831 (714) 647-0900
FAX: (714) 647-0901;
E-mail: info@nicholas-endowment.org; Main URL: http://www.nicholas-endowment.org/

Established in 2002 in CA; supporting organization of The Bowers Museum in Santa Ana, CHOC Foundation, Harris myCFO Foundation, Justice for Homicide Victims, Mission San Juan Capistrano, The Ocean Institute, Orange County Community Foundation, Pacific Symphony Association, South Coast Repertory, St. Margaret's of Scotland Episcopal School, UCI Foundation, UCLA Foundation, and University of California.
Foundation type: Independent foundation.
Financial data (yr. ended 12/31/12): Assets, $34,923,016 (M); expenditures, $1,905,423; qualifying distributions, $1,680,260; giving activities include $1,680,260 for 21 grants (high: $150,000; low: $3,760).
Purpose and activities: The organization aims to enrich the community of Santa Ana and the world by supporting the performing and visual arts, assisting the advancement of science and education, and engaging other charities to make a difference in people lives.
Fields of interest: Arts; Education; Community/economic development; Science.
Limitations: Applications accepted. **Giving primarily in CA.** No support for salaries or for capacity building. No grants to individuals.
Publications: Financial statement.
Application information: See foundation web site for latest application procedures.
Officers and Trustees:* Claudia Sangster,* Chair.; Daniel T. Stetson,* Treas.; Robert Feller; Paula Tomei.
EIN: 466117991
Other changes: At the close of 2012, the grantmaker paid grants of $1,680,260, a 109.4% increase over the 2011 disbursements, $802,500.

344
Henry T. Nicholas, III Foundation
15 Enterprise, Ste. 550
Aliso Viejo, CA 92656-2656 (949) 448-4480
E-mail: info@htnfoundation.org; Main URL: http://www.htnfoundation.org
Articles of Interest: http://feeds.feedburner.com/htnfoundation/articlesofinterest
News and Events: http://feeds.feedburner.com/htnfoundation/newsandevents

Established in 2006 in CA.
Donor: Henry T. Nicholas III.
Foundation type: Independent foundation.
Financial data (yr. ended 12/31/12): Assets, $4,714,143 (M); expenditures, $1,558,715; qualifying distributions, $1,537,276; giving activities include $1,533,266 for 2 grants (high: $1,483,266; low: $50,000).
Purpose and activities: Giving primarily for improving communities and individual lives through education, youth sports, technology, science, medical research, victim's rights and national defense.
Fields of interest: Education; Employment, services; Human services.
Limitations: Applications accepted. Giving primarily in CA, with emphasis on Santa Ana. No grants to individuals.
Publications: Application guidelines.
Application information: See foundation web site for application procedure and form. Application form required.
Deadline(s): None
Director: Jay Noonan.
Trustee: Henry T. Nicholas III.
EIN: 207201390
Other changes: Robert G. Magnuson is no longer a trustee.

345
Noll Foundation, Inc.
100 Bayview Cir., Ste. 3500
Newport Beach, CA 92660 (949) 725-6504
***Contact:* Frederick McIntosh**
***E-mail:* fmcintosh86@gmail.com**

Established in CA.
Donor: Patricia R. Noll.
Foundation type: Independent foundation.
Financial data (yr. ended 12/31/13): Assets, $13,311,445 (M); expenditures, $936,766; qualifying distributions, $669,919; giving activities include $592,800 for 18 grants (high: $235,000; low: $5,000).
Purpose and activities: Giving primarily for children's organizations, as well as for human services and health. Although the existence of faith-based programs is not a criterion, the existence of faith-based programs by a grantee organization will be a favorable factor.
Fields of interest: Education; Health care; Down syndrome; Human services; Children/youth, services; Christian agencies & churches; Children.
Limitations: Applications accepted. Giving primarily in CA and IL. No grants to individuals.
Application information: Applicants who receive a favorable response to their initial letter of inquiry will be invited to submit a formal proposal with supporting materials. Application form required.

Initial approach: Letter of inquiry
Deadline(s): None
Officers: Thomas J. McIntosh, Pres.; Bruce A. McIntosh, Secy.; Frederick J. McIntosh, C.F.O.
Directors: Jon McIntosh; Katie McIntosh; Calvin Sodestrom; Julie Sodestrom.
EIN: 990209620
Other changes: The grantmaker no longer lists a separate application address.

346
North Valley Community Foundation

(formerly Chico Community Foundation)
3120 Cohasset Rd., Ste. 8
Chico, CA 95973-0978 (530) 891-1150
Contact: Alexa Benson-Valavanis, C.E.O.
FAX: (530) 891-1502; E-mail: nvcf@nvcf.org; Mailing address: P.O. Box 6581, Chico, CA 95927; Additional e-mail: avalavanis@nvcf.org; Main URL: http://www.nvcf.org
Facebook: http://www.facebook.com/northvalleycf
LinkedIn: http://www.linkedin.com/companies/north-valley-community-foundation
Twitter: http://twitter.com/NVCF
YouTube: http://www.youtube.com/user/northvalleycf

Established in 1989 in CA.
Foundation type: Community foundation.
Financial data (yr. ended 06/30/12): Assets, $9,889,012 (M); gifts received, $2,355,204; expenditures, $1,946,459; giving activities include $1,226,526 for 168 grants (high: $49,442; low: $21), and $51,135 for 56 grants to individuals.
Purpose and activities: The mission of the foundation is to facilitate philanthropy in Butte, Colusa, Glenn, and Tehama counties and support community efforts to improve the quality of life in the North Valley.
Fields of interest: Elementary/secondary education; Children/youth, services; Human services; Community development, neighborhood development; Economic development; Christian agencies & churches.
Type of support: General/operating support; Management development/capacity building; Endowments; Program development; Conferences/seminars; Scholarship funds; Research; Technical assistance; Consulting services; In-kind gifts; Matching/challenge support.
Limitations: Applications not accepted. Giving limited to the North Valley area, Butte, Colusa, Glenn, and Tehama counties, CA.
Publications: Annual report; Financial statement; Grants list; Informational brochure; Occasional report.
Application information:
Board meeting date(s): 4th Thurs. monthly
Officers and Directors:* **Joan Stoner,* Co-Chair.**; Carolyn Nava,* Co-Chair.; Alexa Benson-Valavanis,* Pres. and C.E.O.; Vanessa Sundin,* Secy.; Lori Parris,* Treas.; Karen White,* C.F.O.; Lisa Furr; Sherry Holbrook; Marc Nemanic; Diane Ruby; Deborah Rossi.
Number of staff: 1 full-time professional; 1 part-time support.
EIN: 680161455
Other changes: Joan Stoner is now Co-Chair.

347
The Northern California Scholarship Foundation

(formerly The Northern California Scholarship Foundation and the Scaife Scholarship Foundation)
1547 Lakeside Dr.
Oakland, CA 94612-4520
Contact: Clyde Minar, Secy.-Treas.
E-mail: ncsf@pacbell.net; Main URL: http://www.ncsfscholarships.org

Incorporated in 1927 in CA.
Donors: Irene Jones†; Walter B. Scaife†; S. Sidney Morton; Lois Irene Sweeney†; Mrs. John Gifford; Eleanor Monroe DiPietro†; E. & J. West Trusts; Alumni Association Foundation.
Foundation type: Independent foundation.
Financial data (yr. ended 05/31/13): Assets, $19,166,941 (M); gifts received, $1,173,326; expenditures, $915,498; qualifying distributions, $896,681; giving activities include $776,000 for grants to individuals.
Purpose and activities: Scholarships for high school seniors who are attending a Northern or Central California public school.
Fields of interest: Education.
Type of support: Scholarships—to individuals.
Limitations: Giving limited to Kern, San Luis Obispo and Inyo counties, CA, to the Oregon border. Refer to county map on foundation web site for geographic areas served.
Publications: Application guidelines; Informational brochure; Program policy statement.
Application information: Applications sent only to those students recommended by northern and central CA public high school administrations. Only one nomination per high school is accepted. Students are required to maintain a 3.0 accumulative GPA. Applications must be submitted with transcripts of high school records, college entrance exam scores, and statement of financial need. Application form required.
Initial approach: Letter
Copies of proposal: 1
Deadline(s): Mar. 15
Board meeting date(s): Jan., Feb., May, and Aug.
Final notification: Final selections made by May 10
Officers: Bryon Flanders, Pres.; Dave Arp, Vice-Pres.; Cal Gilbert, Secy.-Treas.
Trustees: Wade Bingham; Hans Bissinger; Dallas G. Cason; Robert Crow; Don Emig; Thomas D. Eychner; **Bill K'Burg**; Julius "Sandy" Kahn III; George Klopping; James F. McClung, Jr.; Dan Miller; Clyde D. Minar; Norman Owen; James Sloneker; Hon. Zook Sutton; George Vukasin.
Number of staff: 1 part-time professional; 1 part-time support.
EIN: 941540333
Other changes: Bryon Flanders has replaced Julius "Sandy" Kahn, III as Pres. Dave Arp has replaced Bryon Flanders as Vice-Pres. Cal Gilbert has replaced Clyde Minar as Secy.-Treas.
Charles DiBari is no longer a trustee.

348
The Noyce Foundation

419 S. San Antonio Rd., Ste. 213
Los Altos, CA **94022-3640** (650) 856-2600
Contact: Ann S. Bowers, Chair.
FAX: (650) 856-2601; E-mail: info@noycefdn.org; Main URL: http://www.noycefdn.org
Grants Database: http://www.noycefdn.org/annualReport.php

Established in 1990 in CA.
Donor: Robert N. Noyce Residual Trust.
Foundation type: Independent foundation.
Financial data (yr. ended 12/31/12): Assets, $126,369,989 (M); expenditures, $15,319,290; qualifying distributions, $13,853,845; giving activities include $12,903,294 for 61 grants, and $832,190 for foundation-administered programs.
Purpose and activities: The foundation is dedicated to stimulating ideas and supporting initiatives designed to produce significant improvement in teaching and learning in mathematics and science in grades K-12.
Fields of interest: Education, public education; Elementary/secondary education; Mathematics; Science.
Type of support: General/operating support; Continuing support; Management development/capacity building; Program development; Film/video/radio; Publication; Curriculum development; Research; Technical assistance; Program evaluation; Program-related investments/loans; Matching/challenge support.
Limitations: Applications not accepted. Giving primarily in Silicon Valley, CA and MA. No grants to individuals.
Publications: Annual report; Financial statement; Grants list.
Application information: Contributes only to pre-selected organizations.
Board meeting date(s): Monthly
Officers and Trustees:* Ann S. Bowers,* Chair.; Ronald Ottinger, Exec. Dir.; Phil Daro; Alan J. Friedman; **Paul Goren**; Pendred Noyce, M.D.; Robert Schwartz; Lester Strong.
Number of staff: 2 full-time professional; 1 full-time support.
EIN: 770257009

349
Open Doors International, Inc.

2953 S. Pullman St.
Santa Ana, CA 92705-5840
E-mail for United States Office: opendoorsusa.org; Main URL: http://www.od.org

Established in 1993 in CA.
Foundation type: Operating foundation.
Financial data (yr. ended 12/31/12): Assets, $21,092,571 (M); gifts received, $29,968,993; expenditures, $29,176,650; qualifying distributions, $28,997,913; giving activities include $24,093,767 for 14 grants (high: $8,221,206; low: $1,000), and $25,242,590 for foundation-administered programs.
Purpose and activities: The purpose of the foundation is to "strengthen and equip the Body of Christ living under or facing restriction and persecution because of their faith in Jesus Christ, and to encourage their involvement in world evangelism" by providing bibles and literature, media, leadership training, socio-economic development, as well as mobilizing the free world to identify with threatened and persecuted Christians and be actively involved in assisting them.
Fields of interest: Christian agencies & churches.
International interests: Africa; Asia; Latin America; Middle East; Southeastern Asia.
Limitations: Applications not accepted. Giving on an international basis. No grants to individuals.
Application information: Contributes only to pre-selected organizations.
Officers and Directors:* Brian McFarlane,* Chair.; **Gunnhild Oftedal, Vice-Chair.**; Jeff Taylor, C.E.O.; **Jill Garrett, Secy.**; Kelley Valdez, C.F.O.; Evert Schut, C.O.O.; Robert Dalton; Maarton Dees; Ken Pridmore; Roger Spoelman; Zaldeus Steenkamp; David Stone.
Number of staff: 21 full-time professional; 6 full-time support.
EIN: 330523832

Other changes: Gunnhild Oftedal is now Vice-Chair. Robert Martin, Gabrielle Searle, and Deryck Stone are no longer directors.

350
The Dwight D. Opperman Foundation
c/o Maginnis Knechtel & McIntyre LLP
300 W. Colorado Blvd.
Pasadena, CA 91105-1824

Established in 1996 in MN.
Donor: Dwight D. Opperman.
Foundation type: Independent foundation.
Financial data (yr. ended 12/31/11): Assets, $14,536,812 (M); expenditures, $729,516; qualifying distributions, $724,739; giving activities include $711,614 for 22 grants (high: $134,000; low: $1,000).
Fields of interest: Performing arts; Higher education; Education; Medical research, institute; Courts/judicial administration; Human services; Foundations (private grantmaking).
Limitations: Applications not accepted. Giving primarily in MN, with emphasis on Minneapolis and St. Paul. No grants to individuals.
Application information: Contributes only to pre-selected organizations.
Officer: Dwight D. Opperman, Pres.
Directors: Julie Chrystyn-Opperman; Cathy Farrell; Fane W. Opperman; Vance K. Opperman.
EIN: 411856258
Other changes: The grantmaker has moved from MN to CA.

351
Optivest Foundation
(formerly The Mark Van Mourick Foundation)
24901 Dana Point Harbor Dr., Ste. 230
Dana Point, CA 92629-2930 (949) 363-8686
Contact: Mark Van Mourick, C.E.O.
E-mail: mark@optivestinc.com; **Additional email: reports@optivestinc.com**; Main URL: http://www.optivestinc.com/company/optivestfound

Established in 2002.
Donors: Mark Van Mourick; Tricia Van Mourick; Optivest Properties, LLC; Optivest Inc; Charles Fry; Charles Rosenberge; Dennis Sweeney; Judith Sweeney; Greg Buckingham; Optivest Properties Protection; Stan Gaede; Judy Gaede; Lyn Gossett; John Gossett; Brain Hunsaker; Nancy Hunsaker; Kristen Verdieck; Donna Wertz; Russell Wertz; Frank Childers; John Harzan; Annette Harzan; Patrick Jones; Lisa Jones; David Nix; Virginia Nix; Joanne Sanders; Gregory Skjonsby; Mary Skjonsby; The John L. Cashion Family Foundation; Jodie Lynn Wollman; Monica Younger; John Burke; Christine Burke; Bryan Flynn; Nancy Flynn; Laura Staph; Sandy Grant; Doug Grant; Kirk Wahlberg; Lisa Wahlberg; Gerald Wilkinson; Brenda Wilkinson.
Foundation type: Independent foundation.
Financial data (yr. ended 12/31/12): Assets, $9,721; gifts received, $264,342; expenditures, $276,944; qualifying distributions, $276,944; giving activities include $266,103 for 43 grants (high: $38,904; low: $250).
Purpose and activities: Giving primarily for Christian causes.
Fields of interest: Education; Christian agencies & churches.
Type of support: General/operating support; Grants to individuals; Scholarships—to individuals.
Limitations: Applications accepted. Giving primarily in CA.
Application information: Application form required.
Initial approach: E-mail
Deadline(s): None
Officers: Mark Van Mourick, C.E.O.; Tricia Van Mourick, Secy.
EIN: 260011296

352
The O'Shea Foundation
P.O. Box 31321
San Francisco, CA 94131-0321
E-mail: info@osheafoundation.org; Main URL: http://www.osheafoundation.org
Grants List: http://www.osheafoundation.org/grants

Established in 1958.
Donors: Carole O'Shea†; John P. O'Shea†.
Foundation type: Independent foundation.
Financial data (yr. ended 10/31/12): Assets, $5,865,372 (M); expenditures, $351,848; qualifying distributions, $295,731; giving activities include $290,500 for 27 grants (high: $30,000; low: $2,500).
Fields of interest: Education; Human services.
Limitations: Applications not accepted. Giving primarily in CA. No grants to individuals.
Application information: Contributes only to pre-selected organizations.
Officers and Directors:* Dolores Donahue,* Pres.; Alicia Donahue Silva,* V.P.; Shealagh Meehan,* Secy.; Eddie Niiya,* Treas.; Jay Hurley.
EIN: 946084555

353
June G. Outhwaite Charitable Trust
26 W. Anapamu St., Ste. 103
Santa Barbara, CA **93101-3144** (805) 560-0841
Contact: Jean Volmar
FAX: (805) 560-0811;
E-mail: jean@outhwaitefoundation.org; Main URL: http://www.outhwaitefoundation.org/

Established in 1998 in CA.
Donor: The 1994 June G. Outhwaite Revocable Trust.
Foundation type: Independent foundation.
Financial data (yr. ended 12/31/12): Assets, $19,526,406 (M); expenditures, $1,407,280; qualifying distributions, $1,015,247; giving activities include $946,000 for 71 grants (high: $50,000; low: $500).
Purpose and activities: Giving primarily for medical care support and research, general assistance to the disabled, elderly and children, support for abused women and children, the prevention of cruelty to animals, for the preservation of wildlife and natural resources, historic preservation, and for educational institutions.
Fields of interest: Museums (marine/maritime); Education; Zoos/zoological societies; Cancer; Medical research; Family services; Children; Youth; Aging; Physically disabled.
Type of support: General/operating support; Annual campaigns; Capital campaigns; Building/renovation; Equipment; Program development; Matching/challenge support.
Limitations: Applications accepted. Giving primarily in South Santa Barbara County, CA.
Publications: Application guidelines.
Application information: Santa Barbara Foundation Roundtable's Common Grant Application Form accepted or Outhwaite Foundation Application form accepted; application guidelines and forms available on foundation web site. Application form required.
***Initial approach:* Submit application preferably by e-mail**
Copies of proposal: 1
Deadline(s): July 31
Trustees: C. Michael Cooney; Kent L. Englert; John S. Poucher.
Number of staff: 1 part-time support.
EIN: 776154307
Other changes: The grantmaker now publishes application guidelines.

354
Pacific Forest & Watershed Lands Stewardship Council
155 Bovet Road, Suite 405
San Mateo, CA **94402 (650) 372-9047**
FAX: (650) 372-9303;
E-mail: info@stewardshipcouncil.org; **Contact for Foundation for Youth Investment: 710 Van Ness Avenue,San Francisco, CA 94102, tel.: (415) 654-5460; E-mail for Allene Zanger, Exec. Dir.: azanger@stewardshipcouncil.org**; Main URL: http://www.stewardshipcouncil.org
Foundation for Youth Investment on Facebook: http://www.facebook.com/FYIorg?ref=ts
Foundation for Youth Investment on Twitter: http://twitter.com/FYIorg
Foundation for Youth Investment Website: http://www.fyifoundation.org/home/index2
Youth Investment Grants: http://www.fyifoundation.org/grantmaking/awards/C61/2013-catalyst-fund

Established in 2004 in CA.
Donor: Pacific Gas and Electric Co.
Foundation type: Company-sponsored foundation.
Financial data (yr. ended 12/31/12): Assets, $72,675,908 (M); gifts received, $474,940; expenditures, $4,621,298; qualifying distributions, $4,472,794; giving activities include $1,636,773 for 34 grants (high: $670,000; low: $28), and $4,384,375 for 2 foundation-administered programs.
Purpose and activities: The foundation supports watershed land conservation and invests in programs designed to improve the lives of Californian youth through connections with the outdoors.
Fields of interest: Environment, public education; Environment, land resources; Environmental education; Environment; Recreation, parks/playgrounds; Recreation; Boys & girls clubs; Youth development; Children/youth, services; Youth; Economically disadvantaged.
Type of support: General/operating support; Continuing support; Management development/capacity building; Capital campaigns; Program development.
Limitations: Applications not accepted. Giving primarily in CA, with emphasis on the metropolitan Bay Area, urban areas of the Central Valley, and rural areas with high rates of poverty. No grants to individuals; no multi-year grants.
Application information: The Youth Investment Program is administered by the Foundation for Youth Investment and is currently by invitation only.
Officers and Directors:* Art Baggett,* Pres.; Truman Burns,* V.P.; David Muraki,* V.P.; Soapy Mulholland,* V.P.; Randy Livingston,* Secy.; Mike Schonherr, Treas.; Allene Zanger, Exec. Dir.; **Art Bagget, Jr.**; Truman Burns; Nina Kapoor; John Laird;

Karen Mills; Sandra Morey; Larry Myers; Chris Nota; Tim Quinn; Richard Roos-Collins; David Sutton.
EIN: 201358125
Other changes: Randy Livingston is now Secy. Lee Adams is no longer Treas. Nancy Ryan, David A. Bischel, Cherie Chan, Paul Clanon, Noelle Cremers, Todd Ferrara, Kathy Hardy, and Mark Rentz are no longer directors. Joel Wagner is now Dir. of Special Projects. Robin Flynn is now Exec. Asst. Lauren Kelly is now Dir. of Opers. Ann Coulson is now Public Info. Specialist. Toby Perry, Chantz Joyc, and Vanessa Parker-Geisman are now Sr. Project Mgrs.
The grantmaker no longer publishes application guidelines.

355
Pacific Life Foundation

(formerly Pacific Mutual Charitable Foundation)
700 Newport Center Dr.
Newport Beach, CA 92660-6397 (949) 219-3214
***Contact:* Tennyson S. Oyler, Pres.**
FAX: (949) 719-7614;
E-mail: PLFoundation@PacificLife.com; **Main URL: http://www.pacificlife.com/content/content_corp/crp/foundation/overview.html**
Grants List: http://www.pacificlife.com/content/dam/paclife_corp/crp/public/about_pacific_life/foundation_community/grant_recipients/PLFFundingasof03312014.pdf

Established in 1984 in CA.
Donors: Pacific Life Insurance Co.; Pacific Mutual Holding Co.
Foundation type: Company-sponsored foundation.
Financial data (yr. ended 12/31/12): Assets, $77,116,278 (M); gifts received, $5,214,270; expenditures, $5,713,258; qualifying distributions, $5,548,637; giving activities include $5,542,000 for 747 grants (high: $1,000,000; low: $50).
Purpose and activities: The foundation supports programs designed to address health and human services; education; arts and culture; and civic, community, and the environment.
Fields of interest: Museums; Performing arts centers; Arts; Elementary/secondary education; Adult education—literacy, basic skills & GED; Education; Environment, natural resources; Environment, water resources; Environmental education; Environment; Dental care; Health care; Mental health/crisis services; Food services; Youth development, adult & child programs; American Red Cross; Children, services; Family services; Homeless, human services; Human services; Civil/human rights, equal rights; Biology/life sciences; Science; Leadership development; Public affairs; Youth; Aging; Economically disadvantaged.
Type of support: General/operating support; Continuing support; Management development/capacity building; Capital campaigns; Equipment; Program development; Conferences/seminars; Research; Employee matching gifts.
Limitations: Applications accepted. Giving primarily in areas of company operations in the greater Orange County, CA, area and Omaha, NE; giving also to statewide and national organizations. No support for political parties or candidates or partisan political organizations, labor or fraternal organizations, athletic or social clubs, K-12 schools, school districts, or school foundations (except for 3T's of Education), sectarian or denominational religious organizations not of direct benefit to the entire community, or sports leagues or teams. No grants to individuals, or for fundraising events or advertising sponsorships; no in-kind donations.
Publications: Application guidelines; Annual report (including application guidelines); Grants list.
Application information: Capital grants range from $10,0000 to $100,000 and are given to an agency with an organized campaign already under way. Support is limited to 1 contribution per organization during any given year for three years. Organizations must reapply each year. Multi-year funding is not automatic. Audio and video submissions are not accepted. Unsolicited applications for Focus Program Funding and 3T's of Education Program are not accepted. Application form required.
Initial approach: Download application form and mail proposal and application form to foundation
Copies of proposal: 1
Deadline(s): July 15 to Aug. 15
Board meeting date(s): Oct. or Nov.
Final notification: Nov.
Officers and Directors:* James T. Morris,* Chair.; Carol R. Sudbeck,* Vice-Chair.; Tennyson S. Oyler,* Pres.; Michele A. Townsend,* V.P.; Jane M. Guon, Secy.; Joseph L. Tortorelli, Genl. Counsel; Edward R. Byrd, C.F.O.; **Thomas D. Billard**; **David R. Finear**; Luther N. Martin, Sr.; Chris van Mierlo; Dawn M. Trautman; Madhu Vijay; Rebecca Warwar.
Number of staff: 2 full-time professional; 1 part-time professional; 1 full-time support.
EIN: 953433806
Other changes: Robert G. Haskell is no longer Pres. Carol R. Sudbeck is now Vice-Chair. David L. Garrick, Jenniger L. Portnoff, and Cathy L. Schwartz are no longer directors.

356
Pacific Youth Foundation

1224 Lincoln Blvd., Ste. 5
Santa Monica, CA 90401-1714 (310) 774-0057
Contact: Allan C. Young, Dir.
E-mail: allan@pyfoundation.org; Main URL: http://www.pyfoundation.org

Established in 2008 in CA.
Donor: Wells Fargo Bank.
Foundation type: Independent foundation.
Financial data (yr. ended 12/31/12): Assets, $44,817,916 (M); expenditures, $3,679,564; qualifying distributions, $3,584,301; giving activities include $2,811,030 for 35 grants (high: $700,280; low: $500).
Fields of interest: Boys & girls clubs.
Limitations: Applications accepted. Giving in the U.S., with emphasis on CA and GA. No support for programs that do not directly involve youth, staff or board members of a Boys & Girls' Club; Boys & Girls' Clubs that offer fee based programming (any club that charges more than a nominal membership fee), or Boys & Girls' Clubs that receive more than 50 percent of their funding from government support. No grants for multi-year funds.
Publications: Application guidelines.
Application information: Unsolicited grant applications are not accepted. It is requested that only Executive Directors/CPOs contact the foundation. The amount requested from the foundation should appear in the first paragraph of the concept paper in bold and underlined font. The first page of the concept paper should be on organization's letterhead, and proceeding pages should be footnoted with the page number, organization's name, address and the date of submission. Ensure all addendums are labeled with the organization's name. Follow specific concept paper guidelines on foundation web site.
Initial approach: Concept paper (2 pages maximum)
***Deadline(s):* See foundation web site for current deadline**
Directors: Evan McElroy; James D. Shepard; Allan C. Young.
Advising Trustees: Michelle Arellano; Corey Dantzler; Aaron Young.
EIN: 800162835

357
The David and Lucile Packard Foundation

343 Second St.
Los Altos, CA 94022-3632 (650) 948-7658
Contact: Communications Dept.
E-mail: communications@packard.org; Main URL: http://www.packard.org
Grantee Perception Report: http://www.packard.org/about-the-foundation/how-we-operate-2/grantee-experience/about-grantee-perception-report-content/
Grants Database: http://www.packard.org/grants/grants-database/
Knowledge Center: http://www.packard.org/about-the-foundation/news/

Incorporated in 1964 in CA.
Donors: David Packard†; Lucile Packard†.
Foundation type: Independent foundation.
Financial data (yr. ended 12/31/12): Assets, $6,299,952,716 (M); expenditures, $311,653,368; qualifying distributions, $340,586,438; giving activities include $254,497,853 for 927 grants (high: $66,100,000; low: $2,500), $1,632,609 for employee matching gifts, $6,525,622 for foundation-administered programs and $36,055,512 for 14 loans/program-related investments (high: $10,000,000; low: $217,948).
Purpose and activities: The David and Lucile Packard Foundation is a family foundation. The foundation works on the issues its founders cared about most: improving the lives of children, enabling the creative pursuit of science, advancing reproductive health, and conserving and restoring the earth's natural systems. The foundation invests in effective organizations and leaders, collaborates with them to identify strategic solutions, and supports them over time to reach its common goals.
Fields of interest: Arts, cultural/ethnic awareness; Museums; Performing arts; Arts; Education, early childhood education; Education; Environment, public education; Environment, natural resources; Environment, energy; Environment, beautification programs; Environment; Animals/wildlife, fisheries; Reproductive health; Reproductive health, family planning; Health care, insurance; Food services; Agriculture/food; Housing/shelter; Youth development; Child development, services; Family services; Civil liberties, reproductive rights; Philanthropy/voluntarism, management/technical assistance; Foundations (private operating); Philanthropy/voluntarism; Marine science; Engineering; Science; Population studies.
International interests: Global Programs; Oceania; Southern Asia; Sub-Saharan Africa.
Type of support: General/operating support; Continuing support; Management development/capacity building; Land acquisition; Program development; Fellowships; Research; Consulting services; Program evaluation; Program-related investments/loans; Employee matching gifts; Matching/challenge support.

Limitations: Applications accepted. Giving for national and international grants, with a special focus on the Northern CA counties of San Mateo, Santa Clara, Santa Cruz, Monterey, and San Benito; giving also in Pueblo, Colorado. No support for religious or political organizations. No grants to individuals.
Publications: Application guidelines; Annual report; Financial statement; Grants list; Newsletter; Occasional report; Program policy statement; Program policy statement (including application guidelines).
Application information: Review program guidelines online; foundation does not accept proposals for all of their areas of interest. Application form not required.
Initial approach: Proposal or 2- to 3-page letter of inquiry
Copies of proposal: 1
Deadline(s): None
Board meeting date(s): Mar., June, Sept., and Dec.
Final notification: Varies
Officers and Trustees:* Susan Packard Orr,* Chair.; Nancy Packard Burnett,* Vice-Chair.; Julie E. Packard,* Vice-Chair.; Carol S. Larson,* C.E.O. and Pres.; Chris DeCardy, V.P. and Dir., Progs.; Craig Neyman, V.P. and C.F.O.; John H. Moehling, C.I.O.; Mary Anne Rodgers, Secy. and Genl. Counsel; Edward W. Barnholt; **Ipek S. Burnett**; Jason K. Burnett; Linda Griego; Jane Lubchenco; Linda A. Mason; David Orr; Louise Stephens; Ward W. Woods.
Number of staff: 56 full-time professional; 3 part-time professional; 36 full-time support; 5 part-time support.
EIN: 942278431
Other changes: Sierra Clark, Donald Kennedy, Katy Orr, William K. Reilly and Colburn S. Wilbur are no longer trustees.

358
Parsemus Foundation

P.O. Box 2246
Berkeley, CA 94702-0246
Main URL: http://www.parsemusfoundation.org
Facebook: https://www.facebook.com/ParsemusFoundation
Vimeo: http://vimeo.com/parsemus

Established in 2005 in CA and NV.
Donor: Elaine Lissner.
Foundation type: Independent foundation.
Financial data (yr. ended 12/31/12): Assets, $663,780 (M); gifts received, $591,485; expenditures, $783,950; qualifying distributions, $782,009; giving activities include $408,495 for 6 grants (high: $156,125; low: $14,755).
Purpose and activities: Giving primarily for pharmaceutical and contraceptive development and research, treating breast cancer, and perimenopausal and menopausal rosacea.
Fields of interest: Breast cancer research; Medical research; Pharmacology research.
Limitations: Applications not accepted. Giving primarily in NC and TX; some giving in Italy. No grants to individuals.
Application information: Applications for support are by invitation only.
Officer: Elaine Lissner, Pres. and Secy.
EIN: 203968895

359
The Ralph M. Parsons Foundation

888 W. 6th St., Ste. 700
Los Angeles, CA **90017-2733** (213) 362-7600
Contact: Wendy Garen, C.E.O. and Pres.
Main URL: http://www.parsonsfoundation.org
Grants Database: http://www.rmpf.org/GrantDatabase.html

Incorporated in 1961 in CA.
Donor: Ralph M. Parsons†.
Foundation type: Independent foundation.
Financial data (yr. ended 12/31/12): Assets, $375,283,325 (M); expenditures, $24,957,754; qualifying distributions, $19,610,196; giving activities include $17,706,681 for 300 grants (high: $500,000; low: $1,000).
Purpose and activities: Since 1978, the foundation's grantmaking has helped Southern California nonprofit organizations improve the broad fabric of the entire community. This approach recognizes that museums and arts programs are as important to our collective well-being as after school services, community clinics and food banks. Accordingly, the foundation invests in excellence in social services, health care, the arts and higher education in Los Angeles County. The foundation is a responsive grantmaker. It has always invited local organizations to come to it for what they need to do their best work. This includes core operating support, which is a powerful way to help nonprofits struggling to fulfill their missions in hard economic times.It's not that the foundation does not fund capital campaigns, equipment purchases, and staff positions, because it does. It simply encourage carefully considered requests for top organizational priorities.
Fields of interest: Arts, alliance/advocacy; Arts education; Museums; Performing arts; Arts, services; Education, early childhood education; Secondary school/education; Higher education; Education; Health care; Legal services; Housing/shelter, development; Youth development, centers/clubs; Human services; Children/youth, services; Family services; Aging, centers/services; Homeless, human services; Community/economic development; Science; Children/youth; Youth; Economically disadvantaged; Homeless.
Type of support: General/operating support; Capital campaigns; Building/renovation; Equipment; Program development; Seed money; Fellowships; Internship funds; Scholarship funds; Research; Technical assistance; Matching/challenge support.
Limitations: Applications accepted. Giving limited to Los Angeles County, CA. No support for sectarian, religious, or fraternal purposes, or for political organizations. No grants to individuals, or for annual campaigns, fundraising events, dinners, mass mailings, workshops, federated fundraising appeals, seminars, conferences; no loans.
Publications: Biennial report; Grants list; Informational brochure.
Application information: Unless initiated by a foundation director, personal communication with individual directors by representatives of applicant organizations is not encouraged. The foundation does not accept inquiries or requests submitted via fax or E-mail. An invitation to submit a full proposal will be sent to the most competitive applications. Application form not required.
Initial approach: Brief letter of intent
Copies of proposal: 1
Deadline(s): None. Applications considered in order of receipt
Board meeting date(s): Five times a year
Final notification: 6 months for full proposal and 2 months for letter of intent
Officers and Directors:* Franklin E. Ulf,* Chair.; Walter B. Rose,* Vice-Chair.; Wendy Garen, C.E.O. and Pres.; Astra Anderson Galang, C.F.O.; Angelica K. Clark, C.I.O.; William Bamattre; **Linda M. Griego**; Karen Hill-Scott; Elizabeth Lowe; James A. Thomas; Robert E. Tranquada, M.D.; Gayle Wilson.
Number of staff: 5 full-time professional; 3 full-time support.
EIN: 956085895

360
Partners for Developing Futures, Inc.

850 Colorado Blvd., Ste. 203
Los Angeles, CA 90041-1733 (877) 516-8076
FAX: (323) 739-3697;
E-mail: partners@partnersdevelopingfutures.org; Main URL: http://www.partnersdevelopingfutures.org/

Established in 2008 in DE.
Foundation type: Operating foundation.
Financial data (yr. ended 12/31/12): Assets, $2,166,474 (M); gifts received, $1,497,500; expenditures, $1,973,849; qualifying distributions, $1,919,986; giving activities include $1,300,000 for 13 grants (high: $200,000; low: $5,000).
Fields of interest: Charter schools.
Limitations: Giving in the U.S., with some emphasis on CA.
Application information: The foundation is not accepting investment applications at this time. Please check foundation web site for news regarding the application process.
Initial approach: Letter of interest
Deadline(s): Varies
Officer and Directors:* Ref Rodriguez, Ed.D.*, C.E.O. and Pres.; **Angela Bass, Ed.D., V.P.**; Howard Fuller, Ph.D.; Peter Groff; Delia Pompa.
Advisory Board: Mashea Ashton; Michelle Bullock; Mike Feinberg; Diane Robinson; Johnathan Williams; **Ursula Wright**; **Andrea Zayas**.
EIN: 262045125
Other changes: John Lock is no longer a director.

361
Pasadena Community Foundation

(formerly Pasadena Foundation)
301 E. Colorado Blvd., Ste. 810
Pasadena, CA 91101 (626) 796-2097
Contact: Jennifer Fleming DeVoll, Exec. Dir.
FAX: (626) 583-4738;
E-mail: pcfstaff@pasadenacf.org; Additional E-mail: jdevoll@pasadenacf.org; Main URL: http://www.pasadenacf.org
Facebook: https://www.facebook.com/pages/Pasadena-Community-Foundation/349231191832761

Established in 1953 in CA by resolution and declaration of trust; in 2003, reorganized as a nonprofit public benefit corporation.
Donors: Louis A. Webb†; Marion L. Webb†; Helen B. Lockett†; Dorothy I. Stewart†; Rebecca R. Anthony†; Lucille Crumb†; Cornelia Eaton†; Ralph Norrington†; Margaret Norrington†; Ella C. Price†; Orrin K. Earl†; Jean Hubbard†.
Foundation type: Community foundation.
Financial data (yr. ended 12/31/12): Assets, $36,868,916 (M); gifts received, $7,849,177; expenditures, $3,523,059; giving activities include $2,784,741 for 118+ grants (high: $100,000).
Purpose and activities: The foundation serves as a leader, catalyst, and resource for philanthropy in order to improve the lives of people in the greater

Pasadena area, now and for future generations. To fulfill this mission, the foundation: 1) fosters, builds and preserves permanently endowed charitable funds; 2) provides grants and assistance to nurture and strengthen community organizations; 3) promotes and participates in community partnerships; 4) serves donors to meet their philanthropic goals.
Fields of interest: Humanities; Arts; Education; Environment; Health care; Children/youth, services; Family services; Human services; Community/economic development; Youth; Aging; Disabilities, people with.
Type of support: Capital campaigns; Building/renovation; Equipment.
Limitations: Applications accepted. Giving limited to the Altadena, Pasadena, and Sierra Madre, CA, areas. No support for private foundations, or for educational institutions or sectarian organizations (except for social service programs sponsored by educational institutions or sectarian organizations). No grants to individuals (except for scholarships), or for continuing support, general or operating support, expenses incurred in performance of program services, or elections.
Publications: Application guidelines; Annual report; Financial statement; Informational brochure; Newsletter.
Application information: Visit foundation web site for application forms and guidelines. Eligible organizations must be at least 2 years old. Application form required.
Initial approach: Submit grant application and attachments
Copies of proposal: 14
Deadline(s): Feb. 6
Board meeting date(s): Quarterly
Final notification: Late Apr.
Officers and Directors:* David Davis,* Chair.; Judy Gain,* Vice-Chair.; Jennifer Fleming DeVoll, Exec. Dir.; Ann Dobson Barrett; Rita Diaz; Lois Matthews; Peter McAniff; Margaret Mgrublian; Wendy Munger; Eddie Newman; Corene L. Pindroh; Michael D. Schneickert; Fran Scoble; Les Stocker; Philip V. Swan; Michelle Tyson, M.D.
Number of staff: 2 full-time professional; 1 full-time support.
EIN: 200253310
Other changes: Raymond Ealy, Judy Gain, and Sidney F. Tyler are no longer directors.

362

Patagonia.org

c/o Moss Adams LLP
P.O. Box 24950
Los Angeles, CA **90024-0950**
***Contact for World Trout Initiative:* Bill Klyn, bill_klyn@patagonia.com; Main URL: http://www.patagonia.com/us/patagonia.go?assetid=2927**
Grants List: http://www.patagonia.com/us/patagonia.go?assetid=80551

Established in 2008 in CA.
Donor: Patagonia, Inc.
Foundation type: Company-sponsored foundation.
Financial data (yr. ended 04/30/13): Assets, $6,023,191 (M); gifts received, $6,000,000; expenditures, $5,987,569; qualifying distributions, $5,974,666; giving activities include $5,969,904 for 570 grants (high: $1,170,000; low: $150).
Purpose and activities: The foundation supports programs designed to preserve and promote the environment. Special emphasis is directed toward protecting and restoring native fish populations and the habitat on which they depend.
Fields of interest: Environment, natural resources; Environment, water resources; Environment; Animals/wildlife, fisheries; Public affairs, citizen participation.
Type of support: General/operating support.
Limitations: Applications accepted. Giving primarily in CA, CO, MT, NY, and WY. **No grants for general environmental education efforts, land acquisition, land trusts, or conservation easements, research (unless it's in direct support of a developed pan to alleviate an environmental problem), environmental conferences, endowments, political campaigns, or green building projects.**
Publications: Application guidelines.
Application information: Applications are reviewed by local store employees or the Grants Council at Patagonia headquarters. Grants of up to $12,000 are awarded. Support is limited to 1 contribution per organization during any given year.
***Initial approach:* Complete online application**
***Deadline(s):* Apr. 30 and Aug. 31**
***Final notification:* Aug. and Jan.**
Officers and Directors: Casey Sheahan, Pres.; Rose Marcario, C.F.O.; **Hilary Dessouky, Secy.; Malinda P. Chouinard; Yvon Chouinard.**
EIN: 142004175
Other changes: The grantmaker now accepts applications.
The grantmaker now publishes application guidelines.

363

The Patron Saints Foundation

260 S. Los Robles Ave., Ste. 201
Pasadena, CA 91101-3614
Contact: Kathleen T. Shannon, Exec. Dir.
E-mail: patronsaintsfdn@sbcglobal.net; Tel./fax: (626) 564-0444; Main URL: http://www.patronsaintsfoundation.org

Established in 1986 in CA.
Donors: Rose Trust; St. Luke Medical Staff; Friends of St. Luke.
Foundation type: Independent foundation.
Financial data (yr. ended 06/30/13): Assets, $10,985,461 (M); expenditures, $659,255; qualifying distributions, $584,786; giving activities include $450,856 for 29 grants (high: $36,356; low: $5,000).
Purpose and activities: The foundation provides grants to public charities that improve the health of individuals residing in the West San Gabriel Valley through healthcare programs that are consistent with the moral and religious teachings of the Roman Catholic Church.
Fields of interest: Medicine/medical care, public education; Health care, government agencies; Health care, formal/general education; Medical care, community health systems; Hospitals (general); Hospitals (specialty); Medical care, outpatient care; Health care, clinics/centers; Health care, infants; Dental care; Medical care, rehabilitation; Speech/hearing centers; Health care, support services; Pharmacy/prescriptions; Public health; Health care; Health care, patient services; Nursing care; Health care; Substance abuse, services; Mental health/crisis services; Medical research; Infants/toddlers; Children/youth; Children; Youth; Adults; Aging; Young adults; Disabilities, people with; Physically disabled; Blind/visually impaired; Deaf/hearing impaired; Mentally disabled; Minorities; Women; Infants/toddlers, female; Girls; Adults, women; Young adults, female; Men; Infants/toddlers, male; Boys; Adults, men; Young adults, male; Substance abusers; AIDS, people with; Single parents; Economically disadvantaged; Homeless.
Type of support: General/operating support; Continuing support; Capital campaigns; Building/renovation; Equipment; Research.
Limitations: Applications accepted. Giving limited to Alhambra, Arcadia, Duarte, El Monte, La Canada Flintridge, Monrovia, Monterey Park, Pasadena, Rosemead, San Gabriel, San Marino, Sierra Madre, South El Monte, South Pasadena, Temple City, and unincorporated areas of Los Angeles, known as Altadena and South San Gabriel, CA, along with the unincorporated portions of Los Angeles County bounded by these areas. No support for political or fundraising activities, or for programs unrelated to health care. No grants to individuals, or for endowment funds, travel, or surveys.
Publications: Application guidelines; Grants list; Informational brochure.
Application information: Application forms and guidelines available on foundation web site. A completed H.R. 4 Self-Certification form and a signed accountability statement are required with proposal submission. Application form required.
Initial approach: 3-page proposal
Copies of proposal: 2
Deadline(s): 1st Fri. in Mar. and 1st Fri. in Oct.
Board meeting date(s): Mid-May and early Dec.
Final notification: May and mid-Dec.
Officers and Directors:* Margaret Landry,* Pres.; Britt McConnell, Pres.-Elect.; Kathryn Meagher,* Secy.; Charles Carroll,* Treas.; Kathleen T. Shannon, Exec. Dir.; Thomas Collins; James Gamb; James Graunke; Bryan Herrmann; Susan Kane, Ph.D.; **Margaret Landry**; Nathan Lewis, M.D.; Nan Okum; Sarah Orth; **Comm. John Perez**; Joseph W. Skeehan; Debra Spiegel.
Number of staff: 1 part-time professional.
EIN: 953484257
Other changes: Jack Gurley and Sally Sims are no longer directors.

364

Mario Pedrozzi Scholarship Foundation

1040 Florence Rd., No. 21
Livermore, CA **94550-5543** (925) 456-3700
FAX: (925) 456-3701;
E-mail: info@pedrozzifoundation.org; Main URL: http://www.pedrozzifoundation.org
Facebook: https://www.facebook.com/pages/Pedrozzi-Scholarship-Foundation/123721531934
YouTube: http://www.youtube.com/user/PedrozziFoundation

Established in 2007 in CA.
Donor: Mario Pedrozzi†.
Foundation type: Operating foundation.
Financial data (yr. ended 09/30/13): Assets, $8,578,083 (M); gifts received, $5,200; expenditures, $507,635; qualifying distributions, $461,443; giving activities include $286,000 for grants.
Purpose and activities: Scholarship awards to graduates of Livermore high schools in pursuit of higher education and to graduates of Alameda County high schools who will be attending St. Patrick's Seminary and University in Menlo Park, California.
Fields of interest: Higher education.
Type of support: Scholarship funds; Scholarships—to individuals.
Limitations: Applications accepted. Giving primarily to residents of CA.
Application information: Contact by e-mail preferred. Complete application guidelines available on foundation web site. Application form required.

Initial approach: E-mail
Deadline(s): Mar. 1
Officers and Directors:* **Paula Orrell,* Pres.; Elizabeth Trutner,* Secy.; Steve Bell,* Treas.; Tim Daniels, Exec. Dir.; Carolyn Siegried, Exec. Dir.;** Kathleen Banke; **Lisa Lagorio**; Bob Mendonca; Julie Schnitter; Mark Shawver; Howard Storms.
EIN: 201025764
Other changes: Paula Orrell is now Pres. Elizabeth Trutner is now Secy. Steve Bell is now Treas. Steve Faith is no longer a director.

365
Thomas and Gerd Perkins Foundation
301 Mission St. GPHA
San Francisco, CA **94105**

Established in 1997.
Donor: Genentech, Inc.
Foundation type: Company-sponsored foundation.
Financial data (yr. ended 12/31/12): Assets, $389,691 (M); gifts received, $350,000; expenditures, $373,208; qualifying distributions, $344,391; giving activities include $344,391 for grants.
Purpose and activities: The foundation supports organizations involved with health, leukemia, and other areas.
Fields of interest: Health care; Cancer, leukemia; General charitable giving.
Type of support: Equipment; General/operating support.
Limitations: Applications not accepted. Giving primarily in San Francisco, CA, Centennial, CO, and White Plains, NY. No grants to individuals.
Application information: Contributes only to pre-selected organizations.
Officer: Thomas J. Perkins, Pres.
EIN: 680134693

366
The Peszynski Foundation
1069 Wilhaggin Park Ln.
Sacramento, CA **95864**

Established in 2007 in CA.
Donors: Andrew F. Peszynski; Davison Iron Works, Inc.; Loretto High School.
Foundation type: Company-sponsored foundation.
Financial data (yr. ended 12/31/12): Assets, $3,365,044 (M); expenditures, $193,385; qualifying distributions, $192,000; giving activities include $187,000 for 12 grants (high: $50,000; low: $2,000), and $5,000 for 1 grant to an individual.
Purpose and activities: The foundation supports organizations involved with K-12 and higher education, human services, and Catholicism.
Fields of interest: Education; Health care; Human services.
Type of support: General/operating support; Building/renovation.
Limitations: Applications not accepted. Giving primarily in CA; limited giving in Poland and the United Kingdom. No grants to individuals.
Application information: Contributes only to pre-selected organizations.
Officers and Directors:* Andrew F. Peszynski,* Pres.; Helena Szmit,* V.P.; I.G. Peszynski,* C.F.O.; Elizabeth Perschevitch,* Secy.
EIN: 261349949

367
The PG&E Corporation Foundation
77 Beale St.
San Francisco, CA 94105-1814
E-mail: communityrelations@exchange.pge.com; **Additional e-mail: CharitableContributions@pge.com**; Main URL: http://pgecorporationfoundation.org/
Grants List: http://pgecorporationfoundation.org/resources/docs/2012%20Charitable%20Contributions_Foundation_Website.pdf

Established in 2000 in CA.
Donors: PG&E Corporation; Pacific Gas and Electric Company; PG&E Gas Transmission, Texas Corp.
Foundation type: Company-sponsored foundation.
Financial data (yr. ended 12/31/12): Assets, $42,864,166 (M); gifts received, $39,565,368; expenditures, $17,551,303; qualifying distributions, $16,941,936; giving activities include $16,941,936 for 930 grants (high: $1,017,000; low: $165).
Purpose and activities: The foundation supports programs designed to promote education, environmental stewardship, and economic and community vitality. Special emphasis is directed toward underserved communities and populations.
Fields of interest: Secondary school/education; Education; Environment, natural resources; Environment, land resources; Environment, energy; Environment, plant conservation; Environmental education; Environment; Employment, services; Disasters, preparedness/services; Recreation, parks/playgrounds; American Red Cross; Family services; Human services; Utilities; Disabilities, people with; Minorities; Women; Girls; Economically disadvantaged; LGBTQ.
Type of support: General/operating support; Continuing support; Building/renovation; Program development; Scholarship funds; Employee matching gifts.
Limitations: Applications accepted. Giving primarily in areas of company operations in CA. No support for religious organizations not of direct benefit to the entire community, political or partisan organizations, or discriminatory organizations. No grants to individuals, or for tickets for contests, raffles, or other activities with prizes; endowments, filmmaking, debt-reduction campaigns, or political or partisan events.
Publications: Application guidelines; Grants list; Program policy statement.
Application information: Applications from organizations that do not make preliminary contact with PG&E Public Affairs staff are rarely funded. Grants range from $1,000 to $25,000. Multi-year funding is not automatic. Application form required.
Initial approach: Contact local PG&E Public Affairs representative to discuss grant proposal; complete online application
Deadline(s): **Feb. to Sept.**
Final notification: 3 months
Officers and Directors:* Greg S. Pruett,* Chair.; Linda Y.H. Cheng, Secy.; Christopher P. Johns,* C.F.O.; Ezra Garrett, Exec. Dir.; **Tim Fitzpatrick**; Hyun Park; Dinyar B. Mistry.
EIN: 943358729
Other changes: At the close of 2012, the fair market value of the grantmaker's assets was $42,864,166, a 114.5% increase over the 2011 value, $19,979,401.

368
Philanthropy International
333 N. Indian Hill Blvd.
Claremont, CA 91711-4612 **(909) 625-4511**
Contact: **Duke Draeger**
E-mail: info@picharity.org; Main URL: http://www.picharity.org/

Donors: David Marvin; Tim Triplett; Deborah Triplett; Patrick Leicester; Anna Visser; Doug Faber; Marilyn Faber; Rick Todd; Mary Todd; Kurtwood Smith; Joan Smith; Mitch Allen; Michael Connor; Merlene Connor; Joyce Davis Guine; Mickey McKenzie; Barbara Mckenzie; Conrad Stout; Bruncati Charitable Lead Remainder Trust; Lewis Family Trust; Meisinger Trust; Aidikoff, Uhl & Bakhtiari; David Davis; Tammy Davis; Crystal Heft; Apex Settlement; Langham; Robert & Pamela Smith Investment LP; James Yee; Mckenzie 2008.
Foundation type: Independent foundation.
Financial data (yr. ended 12/31/12): Assets, $11,295,800 (M); gifts received, $1,280,989; expenditures, $1,638,510; qualifying distributions, $1,442,870; giving activities include $1,442,870 for 168 grants (high: $200,000; low: $50).
Purpose and activities: The foundation's mission is to build stronger communities and secure lasting family legacies.
Fields of interest: Education; Animal welfare; Hospitals (general); Health organizations, association; Medical research, institute; Human services; Christian agencies & churches; Protestant agencies & churches; Catholic agencies & churches.
Limitations: Applications accepted. Giving primarily in CA.
Application information:
Initial approach: **Letter**
Deadline(s): **None**
Trustee: Tracy Haraksin.
EIN: 870643877

369
Kenneth A. Picerne Foundation
30950 Rancho Viejo Rd., No. 200
San Juan Capistrano, CA 92675-1766 (949) 267-1517
FAX: (949) 487-6263; Main URL: http://www.picernefoundation.org/
Facebook: https://www.facebook.com/KAPFoundation
Google Plus: https://plus.google.com/106549244621362618329
LinkedIn: http://www.linkedin.com/company/2968469
YouTube: http://www.youtube.com/user/KAPFoundation

Established in 2004 in CA.
Donor: Kenneth A. Picerne.
Foundation type: Operating foundation.
Financial data (yr. ended 11/30/12): Assets, $16,709,860 (M); expenditures, $760,551; qualifying distributions, $764,531; giving activities include $50,000 for 1 grant, $168,459 for 28 grants to individuals (high: $11,000; low: $1,800), and $764,531 for 1 foundation-administered program.
Purpose and activities: Giving to support healthy and adaptive human development throughout the life cycle by creating, developing and evaluating innovative and creative programs that are sustainable and provide significant value to the lives of individuals and a healthy society.
Fields of interest: Arts, artist's services; Youth development.

Type of support: General/operating support; Grants to individuals.
Limitations: Giving primarily in CA.
Officers: Kenneth A. Picerne, Chair. and Pres.; Jon D. Demorest, Secy.; Victor D. Nelson, Exec. Dir.
Directors: Kenneth M. Golden; Michael Whalen.
Number of staff: 1
EIN: 432070561

370
Pisces Foundation
1 Maritime Plz., Ste. 1545
San Francisco, CA 94111-3504
E-mail: admin@piscesfoundation.org; Main URL: http://dev.studionudge.com/pisces/
Blog: http://dev.studionudge.com/pisces/blog/
Twitter: https://twitter.com/PiscesFnd

Established in 2006 in CA.
Donors: Robert J. Fisher; Elizabeth S. Fischer.
Foundation type: Independent foundation.
Financial data (yr. ended 06/30/13): Assets, $49,674,385 (M); gifts received, $43,796,500; expenditures, $9,644,842; qualifying distributions, $9,090,440; giving activities include $8,557,247 for 48 grants (high: $3,500,000; low: $1,000).
Purpose and activities: The foundation works to advance strategic solutions to natural resource challenges and prepare the next generation by supporting environmental education.
Fields of interest: Environment, formal/general education; Environment, climate change/global warming; Environment, water resources; Environment.
Limitations: Applications not accepted. Giving primarily in CA, NY, and VA.
Application information: Contributes only to pre-selected organizations.
Officer: David Beckman, Exec. Dir.
Trustees: Elizabeth S. Fisher; Robert J. Fisher; David Beckman.
EIN: 207415160
Other changes: For the fiscal year ended June 30, 2013, the fair market value of the grantmaker's assets was $49,674,385, a 277.6% increase over the fiscal 2012 value, $13,153,648.

371
Placer Community Foundation
219 Maple St.
Auburn, CA 95603 (530) 885-4920
Contact: Veronica Blake, C.E.O.; Jessica Hubbard, Philanthropic Svcs. Mgr.
FAX: (530) 885-4989; E-mail: info@placercf.org; Mailing address: P.O. 9207, Auburn, CA 95604-9207; Main URL: http://www.placercf.org
Facebook: https://www.facebook.com/placercommunityfoundation
LinkedIn: http://www.linkedin.com/in/placercommunityfoundation
Twitter: https://twitter.com/placercf
YouTube: http://www.youtube.com/user/PlacerCommunityFound

Established in 2004 in CA.
Foundation type: Community foundation.
Financial data (yr. ended 12/31/12): Assets, $10,182,139 (M); gifts received, $1,763,848; expenditures, $1,081,015; giving activities include $598,430 for 31+ grants (high: $33,558).
Purpose and activities: The foundation distributes grants to nonprofit organizations who, through direct services, build sustainable communities and enhance the quality of life for residents of Placer County, CA. The foundation's values are to: 1) be open to learning and listening; 2) act with integrity; 3) value the community and respond to its needs; and 4) lead by example.
Fields of interest: Visual arts; Performing arts; Historic preservation/historical societies; Animals/wildlife; Health care; Youth development; Human services; Children/youth, services; Aging, centers/services; Nonprofit management; Community/economic development; Leadership development.
Type of support: Continuing support; Income development; Management development/capacity building; Conferences/seminars; Scholarship funds; Technical assistance; Consulting services; Program evaluation; Matching/challenge support.
Limitations: Applications accepted. Giving primarily in the western slope of Placer County, CA. No support for for-profit entities. No grants to individuals, or for debt reduction or fundraisers.
Publications: Application guidelines; Annual report; Financial statement; Grants list; Informational brochure; Newsletter.
Application information: Visit foundation web site for application forms and guidelines per grant type.
Initial approach: Submit application
Deadline(s): Varies
Board meeting date(s): Jan., Mar., May, July, Sept. and Nov.
Final notification: Varies
Officers and Directors:* Pamela Constantino,* Chair.; Janice L. Forbes,* Founding Chair.; Hon. Justice Keith F. Sparks,* 1st Vice-Chair.; **Todd Jensen,* 2nd Vice-Chair.**; Veronica Blake,* C.E.O.; **Elizabeth Jansen,* Secy.**; Larry Welch,* Treas.; **Jeff Birkholz**; Ruth Burgess; Guy R. Gibson; Ken Larson; Nadder Mirsepassi; Kelly C. Richardson; Tim Sands; Curt Sproul; Jim Williams.
Number of staff: 1 full-time professional; 3 full-time support.
EIN: 201485011
Other changes: Pamela Constantino has replaced Jeff Birkholz as Chair. Todd Jensen has replaced Pam Constantino as 2nd Vice-Chair.
Janice L. Forbes, Elizabeth Jansen, and Todd Jensen are no longer directors.

372
Plum Foundation
4182 Beck Ave.
Studio City, CA **91604**
***Application address:* c/o Pamela Phillips Kaizer, P.O. Box 1613, Studio City, CA 91604**

Established in 1991 in CA.
Donors: Dorothy Gail Secrest; Debbie Montford; John Montford.
Foundation type: Independent foundation.
Financial data (yr. ended 08/31/13): Assets, $2,900,553 (M); expenditures, $427,734; qualifying distributions, $383,172; giving activities include $332,600 for 17 grants (high: $50,000; low: $2,500).
Fields of interest: Performing arts; Performing arts, dance; Performing arts, theater; Performing arts, music; Arts; Elementary/secondary education; Education; Environment; Animals/wildlife, preservation/protection.
Type of support: Research; General/operating support; Continuing support; Program development; Scholarship funds.
Limitations: Applications accepted. Giving primarily in southern CA and TX for the arts; giving on a national basis for the environment and wildlife preservation and protection. No support for religious organizations for religious purposes, or for local animal shelters. No grants to individuals, or for land acquisition, building or endowment funds, annual fund drives of unified campaigns or capital campaigns, deficit financing, brochures, or public relations campaigns.
Publications: Informational brochure.
Application information: Application form required.
Initial approach: Letter
Deadline(s): Apr. 1 - Aug. 31
Board meeting date(s): Mar.
Officers: John Montford, Pres.; Emily Maupin, V.P.; Bill Baldridge, Secy.-Treas.
Number of staff: 1 part-time professional.
EIN: 752406666

373
The Price Family Charitable Fund
(formerly The Sol & Helen Price Foundation)
7979 Ivanhoe Ave., Ste. 520
La Jolla, CA 92037-4513 (858) 551-2321
Contact: Terry Malavenda
***E-mail:* tmalavenda@pricefamilyfund.org; Main URL: http://www.pricefamilyfund.org**

Established in 1983 in CA.
Donors: Pollyanna Keating; Sol Price; Helen Price.
Foundation type: Independent foundation.
Financial data (yr. ended 12/31/12): Assets, $517,568,212 (M); gifts received, $269,138,289; expenditures, $27,098,099; qualifying distributions, $25,675,658; giving activities include $21,674,976 for 543 grants (high: $3,927,250; low: $25), and $841,178 for foundation-administered programs.
Purpose and activities: Giving primarily for education and philanthropy.
Fields of interest: Elementary/secondary education; Urban/community development; Economically disadvantaged.
Type of support: Scholarships—to individuals; Annual campaigns; Fellowships; Scholarship funds; Program evaluation.
Limitations: Applications accepted. Giving limited to San Diego, CA.
Application information:
***Initial approach:* Online**
Deadline(s): None
Officers and Directors:* Robert Price,* Chair. and Pres.; Sherry Barhrambeygui, Vice-Chair., V.P., and Secy.; Allison Price,* Vice-Chair and V.P.; Ted Parzen, Exec. V.P.; Jeff Fisher, C.F.O.; William Gorham; Don Levi; Maggie Meyer; M. Edward Spring.
Number of staff: 2 full-time professional; 1 part-time professional; 1 full-time support; 1 part-time support.
EIN: 953842468

374
The Arthur & Patricia Price Foundation
(formerly Arthur L. Price Foundation)
c/o Gettleson, Witzer & O'Connor
16000 Ventura Blvd., Ste. 900
Encino, CA 91436-2760

Established in 1990 in CA.
Donors: Arthur L. Price; Patricia A. Price; Arthur Patricia Price Family Trust.
Foundation type: Independent foundation.
Financial data (yr. ended 02/28/13): Assets, $3,013,298 (M); expenditures, $182,842; qualifying distributions, $153,955; giving activities include $148,525 for 60 grants (high: $67,500; low: $50).
Fields of interest: Media/communications; Performing arts, music; Arts; Health care; Health

organizations, association; Human services; Children/youth, services.
Type of support: General/operating support.
Limitations: Applications not accepted. Giving primarily in Santa Monica, CA. No grants to individuals.
Application information: Contributes only to pre-selected organizations.
Officers: Arthur L. Price, Pres. and C.E.O.; **Patricia A. Price, V.P., Secy., and C.F.O.**
Director: David A. Weinstein.
EIN: 954303203

375
The John and Lisa Pritzker Family Fund
c/o Seiler LLP
3 Lagoon Dr., Ste. 400
Redwood City, CA 94065-5157 (650) 365-4646

Established in 2002 in CA and IL.
Donor: John A. Pritzker.
Foundation type: Independent foundation.
Financial data (yr. ended 12/31/12): Assets, $57,799,886 (M); gifts received, $15,882,892; expenditures, $17,766,024; qualifying distributions, $17,199,036; giving activities include $16,683,946 for 212 grants (high: $3,000,000; low: $200).
Purpose and activities: Giving primarily for education, health associations, children, youth, and social services, and Jewish organizations; some funding also for the arts.
Fields of interest: Museums (art); Performing arts, theater; Arts; Elementary/secondary education; Higher education; Education; Hospitals (general); Hospitals (specialty); Health care; Health organizations, association; Human services; Children/youth, services; Jewish federated giving programs; Jewish agencies & synagogues.
Limitations: Applications not accepted. Giving primarily in San Francisco, CA. No grants to individuals.
Application information: Contributes only to pre-selected organizations.
Officers and Directors:* John A. Pritzker,* Chair. and Co-Pres.; Lisa Pritzker,* Co-Pres.; Beverly Symonik, Secy.; Michael Mayer, C.F.O. and Treas.; **Cheryl Polk, Exec. Dir.**; Adam Nicholas Pritzker; Noah Stone Pritzker.
EIN: 300039815
Other changes: At the close of 2012, the grantmaker paid grants of $16,683,946, a 57.5% increase over the 2011 disbursements, $10,594,520.
John A. Pritzker is now Chair. and Co-Pres. Lisa Pritzker is now Co-Pres.

376
Qualcomm Charitable Foundation
5775 Morehouse Dr.
San Diego, CA 92121-1714
***Main URL:* http://www.qualcomm.com/about/citizenship/community/philanthropy**

Established in CA.
Donor: Qualcomm Incorporated.
Foundation type: Independent foundation.
Financial data (yr. ended 09/30/13): Assets, $19,682,507 (M); gifts received, $10,000,000; expenditures, $12,173,914; qualifying distributions, $12,170,226; giving activities include $11,213,787 for 2,628 grants (high: $1,000,000; low: $50).
Purpose and activities: The mission of the foundation is to create educated, healthy, sustainable and culturally vibrant communities.
Fields of interest: Arts; Education; Health care; Medical research, institute; Human services; Children/youth, services.
Limitations: Giving on a national basis and in regions of business operation. No support for sporting events without a charitable beneficiary, sectarian or denominational religious groups, strict faith-based schools, primary and secondary schools. No grants to individuals and no political contributions.
Application information: Grant proposals are by invitation only. Unsolicited proposals will not be considered.
***Initial approach:* Online letter of inquiry**
***Deadline(s):* June 1 to June 30**
***Final notification:* Oct. 1**
Officers and Directors: Paul E. Jacobs, Chair.; Daniel L. Sullivan,* Pres.; William Sailer,* Secy.; Akash Palkhiwala,* Treas.; William Bold; Warren Kneeshaw; Susan Laun; Michelle Sterling.
EIN: 274621444

377
Quest Foundation
P.O. Box 339
Danville, CA 94526-0339 (925) 743-1925

Established in 2005 in CA.
Donors: Herrick-Pacific Corporation; Dorothy Jernstedt Trust.
Foundation type: Company-sponsored foundation.
Financial data (yr. ended 12/31/12): Assets, $87,514,485 (M); expenditures, $4,791,895; qualifying distributions, $4,524,014; giving activities include $4,200,820 for 90 grants (high: $1,504,000; low: $4,620).
Purpose and activities: The foundation supports youth development clubs and community foundations and organizations involved with education and human services.
Fields of interest: Secondary school/education; Charter schools; Higher education; Education, services; Education, reading; Education; Youth development, centers/clubs; Boys & girls clubs; Children/youth, services; Family services; Human services; Foundations (community).
Type of support: General/operating support; Continuing support.
Limitations: Applications not accepted. Giving primarily in CA.
Application information: Contributes only to pre-selected organizations.
Officers and Directors:* Dorothy Jernstedt,* Pres.; **Derek Jernstedt, Exec. Dir.**; Richard Becher,* C.F.O.; **Jennifer Jernstedt, Secy.**; Jaci Jernstedt.
EIN: 201844715
Other changes: Derek Jernstedt is now Exec. Dir. Jennifer Jernsted is now Secy.

378
Rancho Santa Fe Foundation
(formerly Rancho Santa Fe Community Foundation)
162 S. Rancho Santa Fe Rd., Ste. B-30
Encinitas, CA 92024 (858) 756-6557
Contact: Christina Wilson, Exec. Dir.; For grants: Debbie Anderson, Progs. Mgr.
FAX: (858) 756-6561;
E-mail: info@rsffoundation.org; Mailing address: P.O. Box 811, Rancho Santa Fe, CA 92067; Main URL: http://www.rsffoundation.org
Facebook: https://www.facebook.com/RSFFoundation
Twitter: https://twitter.com/rsffoundation
Application e-mail: christy@rsffoundation.org

Established in 1981 in CA.
Foundation type: Community foundation.
Financial data (yr. ended 12/31/12): Assets, $59,385,300 (M); gifts received, $14,753,100; expenditures, $2,670,500; giving activities include $2,143,200 for grants.
Purpose and activities: The foundation seeks to connect donors with regional and global needs through visionary community leadership, personalized service and effective grantmaking.
Fields of interest: Arts; Education; Health care; Human services; Community/economic development.
Type of support: General/operating support; Continuing support; Management development/capacity building; Building/renovation; Equipment; Land acquisition; Emergency funds; Program development; Publication; Seed money; Curriculum development; Scholarship funds; Technical assistance; Grants to individuals.
Limitations: Applications accepted. Giving primarily in San Diego County, CA. No support for religious organizations (from discretionary funds). No grants for capital campaigns, annual campaigns, or endowments (from discretionary funds).
Publications: Annual report; Financial statement; Informational brochure; Newsletter.
Application information: Visit foundation website for application timeline and information. Application form required.
Initial approach: Contact foundation
Board meeting date(s): Bimonthly
Officers and Directors:* Neil C. Hokanson,* Chair.; Gigi Fenley,* Secy.; William J. Ruh,* Treas.; Christina P. Wilson, Exec. Dir.; Alyce Ashcraft; **Terry Atkinson**; Richard Collato; Craig Dado; William Davidson; David Down; Franci Free; Hugh Greenway, M.D.; **Victoria Hanlon**; Mark Holmlund; Candace A. Humber; **Kimberly Davis King**; Constance Levi; Dr. Michael Lobatz; John Major; Ronald D. McMahon; Glenn Oratz; Daniel Platt; Paula Powers; Richard Sapp; **Steve Simpson**; Gordon Swanson; paul Thiel; Robert Vanosky; Donna Walker; Philip White; Betty Williams; Kate Williams.
Number of staff: 1 full-time professional; 3 part-time professional.
EIN: 953709639
Other changes: Sue Pyke is now Donor Srvs. Dir.

379
Nancy Buck Ransom Foundation
P.O. Box 749
Monterey, CA 93942-0749
***Main URL:* http://www.nbrfoundation.org**

Established in 1979 in CA.
Foundation type: Independent foundation.
Financial data (yr. ended 12/31/12): Assets, $40,786,124 (M); expenditures, $4,297,146; qualifying distributions, $3,962,902; giving activities include $3,855,265 for 60 grants (high: $2,725,000; low: $1,000).
Purpose and activities: Support for projects that provide positive enrichment opportunities for mainstream youths.
Fields of interest: Arts; Youth development, centers/clubs; Human services.
Type of support: General/operating support.
Limitations: Applications accepted. Giving primarily in Monterey County, CA; some funding also in WI. No

support for governmental or religious programs. **No grants to individuals or for endowments, regranting, capital projects or campaigns or capacity building; no multi-year grants.**
Application information: Application guidelines and form available on foundation web site.
Initial approach: Proposal
Deadline(s): Feb. 15
Board meeting date(s): Apr.
Officers and Directors:* Lucinda B. Ewing, Pres.; C. Lee Cox, V.P.; **Katherine M. Coopman,* Secy. and Exec. Dir.**; Sandra Stutzman,* Treas.; Richard Arentz.
EIN: 942601172
Other changes: At the close of 2012, the grantmaker paid grants of $3,855,265, a 144.8% increase over the 2011 disbursements, $1,574,814.
Georgiana F. Shepherd is no longer Secy. Katherine M. Coopman is now Secy. and Exec. Dir.

380
Rappaport Family Foundation
1748 Union St.
San Francisco, CA 94123-4407 (415) 593-7111
Contact: Catalina Ruiz-Healy, V.P.
***E-mail:* info@rappaportfamilyfoundation.org**; Main URL: http://www.rappaportfamilyfoundation.org
Facebook: https://www.facebook.com/pages/RFF-Spark/463115230384712
Grants List: http://rappaportfamilyfoundation.org/grants/
Rappaport Family Foundation's Philanthropy Promise: http://www.ncrp.org/philanthropys-promise/who
Twitter: https://twitter.com/RffSpark

Established in 2003 in CA.
Donors: Andrew Rappaport; Deborah Rappaport.
Foundation type: Independent foundation.
Financial data (yr. ended 10/31/12): Assets, $6,858,180 (M); gifts received, $11,760; expenditures, $578,154; qualifying distributions, $554,022; giving activities include $383,500 for 12 grants (high: $41,500; low: $9,000).
Purpose and activities: The foundation's interests are: 1) Finding innovative and promising ideas for engaging community college students in California, especially those focused on pocketbook issues; 2) Identifying and supporting promising institutional or third-party programs, or faculty members who have unique solutions to ignite and maintain civic participation and community engagement among community college students; 3) Solutions that address specific challenges to successful program implementation faced by students, faculty, and administration; 4) Using new tools, technologies and organizing methods to support distributed models of engagement and activism on a community college or among community college students; and 5) Taking a risk on unconventional or untried approaches.
Fields of interest: Education; Philanthropy/voluntarism; Public affairs, research; Public policy, research.
Limitations: Giving in the U.S., with some emphasis on CA and Washington, DC. No support for religious organizations, international or foreign-based programs, or social service programs. No grants to individuals, or for scholarships, or capital campaigns.
Application information: The foundation is currently not accepting unsolicited proposals. Check foundation web site for updates.
Officers: Deborah Rappaport, C.E.O.; Catalina Ruiz-Healy, V.P.; Andrew Rappaport, Treas.
EIN: 200433083
Other changes: Deborah Rappaport is now C.E.O. Andrew Rappaport is now Treas.

381
Rest Haven Preventorium for Children, Inc.
(also known as Children's Health Fund)
P.O. Box 420369
San Diego, CA 92142-0369 (858) 576-0590
Contact: Peggy McNamara, Exec. Secy.
FAX: (858) 576-0029;
E-mail: resthavenchfund@sbcglobal.net; Main URL: http://resthavenchf.org/contact.html

Established in 1963 in CA.
Donors: Anna M. Spring Trust; Jessie Castle Roberts Trust.
Foundation type: Operating foundation.
Financial data (yr. ended 12/31/12): Assets, $10,660,693 (M); expenditures, $341,912; qualifying distributions, $253,307; giving activities include $210,414 for 11 grants (high: $161,683; low: $216), and $48,821 for 1 foundation-administered program.
Purpose and activities: Provides monetary assistance for the benefit of needy children in the San Diego, CA, area for medical, dental, therapy, hearing, child care, and nutrition expenses. No giving to those outside the target area.
Fields of interest: Health care; Youth development, services; Human services; Economically disadvantaged.
Type of support: General/operating support; Grants to individuals.
Limitations: Applications not accepted. Giving exclusively for the benefit of residents of San Diego and Imperial County, CA.
Application information: Unsolicited requests for funds will not be accepted from families outside San Diego or Imperial County, CA.
Officers: Raymond M. Peterson, M.D., Pres.; David N. Allsbrook III, V.P.; Alison F. Gildred, Secy.; **Christine Bryant, Treas.**; **Peggy McNamara, Exec. Dir.**
Directors: Paul S. Condon; Richard B. Hancock, D.D.S.; Beatrice W. Kemp; Patricia Tisdale; W. Harold Tuck; Paul Wozniak, M.D.; and 7 additional directors.
EIN: 952128344
Other changes: Christine Bryant has replaced Paul S. Condon as Treas.
Patricia Carter, Robert C. Hallock and Virginia Hammond are no longer directors.

382
The Mabel Wilson Richards Scholarship Fund
4712 Admiralty Way, Ste. 227
Marina del Rey, CA 90292 **(310) 577-7984**
***Contact:* Joanie C. Freckman, Tr.**

Trust established in 1951 in CA.
Donor: Mabel Wilson Richards†.
Foundation type: Independent foundation.
Financial data (yr. ended 06/30/13): Assets, $8,977,232 (M); expenditures, $792,542; qualifying distributions, $644,260; giving activities include $570,000 for 25 grants (high: $100,000; low: $5,000).
Fields of interest: Education.
Type of support: Scholarship funds.
Publications: Application guidelines; Program policy statement.
Application information: Application form required.
***Initial approach:* Proposal**
Copies of proposal: 1
***Deadline(s):* None**
Board meeting date(s): Jan., Apr., July, and Oct.
Trustees: Joanie C. Freckman; Barbara Sandler.
EIN: 956021322

383
Robert Gore Rifkind Foundation
P.O. Box 662147
Los Angeles, CA 90066-8547 (818) 990-1125
Contact: Max Rifkind-Barron, Dir.

Established in 1979 in CA.
Donors: Robert Gore Rifkind; Max Rifkind-Barron.
Foundation type: Operating foundation.
Financial data (yr. ended 03/31/13): Assets, $8,051,608 (M); expenditures, $532,966; qualifying distributions, $435,186; giving activities include $413,285 for 38 grants (high: $135,000; low: $250).
Purpose and activities: Giving primarily for the arts, especially art museums; in addition, grant awards enable scholars to come to Los Angeles to study at the Rifkind Center for German Expressionist Studies.
Fields of interest: Arts education; Museums; Performing arts, orchestras; Arts; Libraries/library science; Animals/wildlife; Medical research; Jewish agencies & synagogues.
International interests: Israel.
Type of support: General/operating support; Continuing support; Research.
Limitations: Applications accepted. Giving primarily in southern CA.
Application information: Application form required.
Initial approach: Letter
Deadline(s): None
Officers: Max Rifkind-Barron, Pres.; Jane Levikow, Secy.; Jonathan Davidson, Treas.
EIN: 953397350
Other changes: Max Rifkind-Barron is now Pres. Jonathan Davidson is now Treas. Jane Levikow is now Secy.

384
Rivendell Stewards' Trust
P.O. Box 6009
Santa Barbara, CA 93160-6009 (805) 964-9999
Contact: Amity Wicks, Admin.
FAX: (805) 823-4594; E-mail: info@rstrust.org; Main URL: http://www.rstrust.org

Established in 1985 in CA.
Donors: K.N. Hansen, Sr.; K.N. Hansen, Jr.; G.W. Hansen; Vince Nelson; Walter Hansen.
Foundation type: Independent foundation.
Financial data (yr. ended 12/31/13): Assets, $15,385,435 (M); expenditures, $7,345,727; qualifying distributions, $7,199,435; giving activities include $7,111,927 for grants.
Purpose and activities: Giving for Christian institutions and missionary efforts in the two-thirds world.
Fields of interest: Theological school/education; Religion.
International interests: Developing Countries.
Type of support: General/operating support; Management development/capacity building; Program development; Seed money; Curriculum

development; Scholarship funds; Matching/challenge support.
Limitations: Giving limited to developing countries. No support for Western ministries. No grants to individuals (except for program for retired missionaries).
Application information: The foundation does not accept unsolicited proposals for support, but it offers organizations new to the foundation the opportunity to introduce their programs through a Letter of Inquiry, using the foundation's easy online submission process. Application form not required.
Initial approach: **Online letter of inquiry**
Copies of proposal: 1
Deadline(s): See foundation web site for current deadlines
Officers: Walter Hansen, Pres.; Darlene Hansen, Secy.; Vince Nelson, Treas.
Trustees: Steve Hoke; Jean Johnson; Cathy Nelson; Doug Spurlock; Joyce Spurlock.
Number of staff: 1 part-time support.
EIN: 776016389

385
Rosenberg Foundation
131 Steuart St., Ste. 650
San Francisco, CA 94105-1244
Contact: Linda Moll, Business and Grants Mgr.; Tammy Tanner, Exec. Asst. and Office Mgr.
FAX: (415) 357-5016;
E-mail: linda@rosenfound.org; Main URL: http://www.rosenbergfound.org
Facebook: https://www.facebook.com/Rosenbergfound
Rosenberg Foundation's Philanthropy Promise: http://www.ncrp.org/philanthropys-promise/who
Twitter: https://twitter.com/Rosenbergfound

Incorporated in 1935 in CA.
Donors: Max L. Rosenberg†; Charlotte S. Mack†.
Foundation type: Independent foundation.
Financial data (yr. ended 12/31/12): Assets, $56,214,745 (M); expenditures, $3,051,143; qualifying distributions, $3,051,143; giving activities include $2,080,930 for grants.
Purpose and activities: In the more than seven decades since making its first grant, the Rosenberg Foundation has distinguished itself as an ally of the state's most vulnerable residents. From its early work supporting efforts on behalf of Japanese American families returning from internment camps to more recent work to reduce the incarceration rates for women in California, the foundation's aim has remained consistent: to achieve significant and lasting improvements in the life of Californians.
Fields of interest: Legal services; Employment, labor unions/organizations; Human services, reform; Civil/human rights, immigrants; Economics; Poverty studies; Public policy, research; Public affairs, reform; Minorities; Offenders/ex-offenders; Immigrants/refugees; Economically disadvantaged.
Type of support: General/operating support; Continuing support; Management development/capacity building; Program development.
Limitations: Applications accepted. Giving limited to CA, except for national grants. No grants to individuals, or for endowment, building, or capital funds, scholarships, fellowships, continuing support, annual campaigns, emergency funds, deficit financing, matching funds, land acquisition, renovation projects, or conferences and seminars; generally no grants for equipment, films, or publications (except when a necessary part of larger project).
Publications: Application guidelines; Grants list; Multi-year report; Occasional report.
Application information: See foundation web site for application guidelines. The foundation will request additional and specific information if desired after receipt of letter of inquiry. Application form not required.
Initial approach: Letter of Inquiry (1-2 pages)
Deadline(s): None, for letter of inquiry
Final notification: Varies
Officers and Directors:* Hon. Bill Lann Lee,* Chair.; Clara J. Shin,* Vice-Chair. and Secy.; Sarah Stein, 2nd Vice-Chair.; Timothy P. Silard,* Pres.; Robert E. Friedman,* Treas.; Phyllis Cook; Daniel Grossman; Mick Hellman; **Benjamin Todd Jealous**; Herma Hill Kay; **Kate Kendell**; Shauna I. Marshall; Hugo Morales; Albert F. Moreno; Hon. Henry Ramsey, Jr.
Number of staff: 3 full-time professional; 1 full-time support.
EIN: 941186182

386
Dorothy Sargent Rosenberg Memorial Fund
(formerly Anna Davidson Rosenberg Fund)
P.O. Box 431
The Sea Ranch, CA 95497-0431
Main URL: http://www.dorothyprizes.org
Application address: c/o Dorothy Sargent Rosenberg Poetry Prizes, P.O. Box 2306, Orinda, CA 94563

Established in 2003 in CA.
Donors: Marvin Rosenberg†; Violet Ginsburg.
Foundation type: Independent foundation.
Financial data (yr. ended 03/31/13): Assets, $1,471,146 (M); gifts received, $637; expenditures, $105,829; qualifying distributions, $105,829; giving activities include $96,893 for 38 grants to individuals (high: $7,500; low: $250).
Purpose and activities: Literary awards to promising young poets of exceptional talent to pursue their craft and advance their careers.
Fields of interest: Literature.
Type of support: General/operating support; Grants to individuals.
Limitations: Applications accepted. Giving primarily in CA, CT, NE, and NY. No grants for Awards limited to submissions not previously published.
Application information: Complete guidelines available on Fund web site.
Initial approach: Contact Fund for application guidelines
Officers: Barr Rosenberg, Pres. and Secy.; Annette Anderson, Treas.; **Scott Farmer, Treas.**
Trustee: Mary Rosenberg.
EIN: 300041654

387
Rossi Family Foundation
c/o Janeen Tuitupou
1100 Sharon Park Dr., No. 2
Menlo Park, CA 94025-7001

Established in 1989 in CA.
Donors: L. Jay Rossi; Mrs. L. Jay Rossi; Marjorie Rossi.
Foundation type: Independent foundation.
Financial data (yr. ended 06/30/13): Assets, $2,419,640 (M); expenditures, $171,247; qualifying distributions, $146,450; giving activities include $146,450 for 15 grants (high: $51,200; low: $250).
Fields of interest: Higher education; Health care; Health organizations, association; Human services; Human services.
Type of support: Building/renovation; Equipment; Seed money; Research.
Limitations: Applications not accepted. Giving primarily in CA. No support for religious or political organizations. No grants to individuals.
Application information: Unsolicited requests for funds not accepted.
Officers: Marjorie Rossi, Pres.; Safford J. Rossi, Secy.; **Craig Hall Rossi, Treas.; Janeen Rossi Tuitupou, Exec. Dir.**
Directors: Merilee Rossi; Lizabeth Rossi Schuetz.
EIN: 943106122
Other changes: Janeen Rossi Tuitupou is now Exec.Dir. Craig Hall Rossi is no longer a director.

388
Roth Family Foundation
12021 Wilshire Blvd., Ste. 505
Los Angeles, CA **90025-1206** (213) 383-9207
Contact: Sandy Chiang, Grants Mgr.
FAX: (213) 383-9222; E-mail: sandy@roth-la.org; Main URL: http://www.rothfamilyfoundation.org

Established in 1966 in CA.
Donors: Louis Roth and Co.; Louis Roth†; Fannie Roth†; Harry Roth†.
Foundation type: Independent foundation.
Financial data (yr. ended 12/31/13): Assets, $13,054,709 (M); expenditures, $644,299; qualifying distributions, $631,210; giving activities include $569,420 for 86 grants (high: $25,000; low: $500).
Purpose and activities: The foundation seeks to improve lives through a variety of focus areas, primarily in the Los Angeles area. Specifically, it provides general operating support and new and/or on-going program/project support to organizations that fall into the following focus areas: 1) Arts and Culture; 2) Youth; 3) Environment; 4) Economic Development; 5) International Development; 6) Reproductive Health and Rights/Sex Education.
Fields of interest: Media/communications; Media, radio; Performing arts, music; Performing arts, education; Environment, formal/general education; Environment, beautification programs; Environment; Reproductive health; Youth development; International development; Economic development; Children/youth; Youth; Women; Girls; Economically disadvantaged.
International interests: Africa.
Type of support: General/operating support; Program development; Matching/challenge support.
Limitations: Giving primarily in Los Angeles County, CA. No support for fraternal organizations, or for religious or political organizations. No grants to individuals; generally no grants to fund dinners, special events or fundraising events.
Publications: Application guidelines; Annual report; Grants list.
Application information:
Initial approach: **Use Grant Request form on foundation web site for all program areas except for Global Programs**
Copies of proposal: 1
Board meeting date(s): Semiannually
Final notification: **3-6 months for grant request**
Officers and Directors:* Michael P. Roth,* Pres.; Gil Garcetti,* V.P.; Sukey Garcetti,* Secy.-Treas.; Rachel Roth,* Exec. Dir.; Dana Boldt; Eric Garcetti; Sarah Roth; Andrea Roth-Fedida.
Number of staff: 1 full-time professional.
EIN: 880352682

389

Arthur N. Rupe Foundation

(formerly Rupe Foundation)
c/o Susan C. Van Aacken
3887 State St., Ste. 22
Santa Barbara, CA 93105-6111 (805) 687-8586
Contact: Jeffrey J. Cain, Pres. and Exec. Dir.
FAX: (805) 682-5955; E-mail: christine@anrf.net; Main URL: http://www.rupefoundation.org

Established in 1991 in CA.
Donors: Arthur N. Rupe; Arloma Corp.
Foundation type: Independent foundation.
Financial data (yr. ended 06/30/13): Assets, $53,455,405 (M); expenditures, $3,289,180; qualifying distributions, $2,817,064; giving activities include $2,501,528 for 15 grants (high: $1,894,118; low: $12,500).
Purpose and activities: Giving to organizations that promote and/or provide aid, research, and services in the furtherance of select educational, medical, and social studies programs. Areas of focus include the support of qualified organizations that: 1) conduct public debates; 2) provide training to vocational nursing students; and 3) perform research affecting public policy and achieving widespread dissemination.
Fields of interest: Philosophy/ethics; Education, public policy; Education, reform; Education, ethics; Employment, labor unions/organizations; Foundations (public); Social sciences, ethics; Public policy, research.
Type of support: Program development; Professorships; Seed money; Curriculum development; Fellowships; Internship funds; Scholarship funds; Research.
Limitations: Giving on a national basis. No support for organizations lacking 501(c)(3) status. **No grants to individuals, or for fundraising events, conferences, endowments, or capital campaigns.**
Application information: Unsolicited proposals are not accepted. Full proposals are by invitation only, upon review of initial Letter of Inquiry.
Initial approach: **Letter of Inquiry through foundation web site**
Board meeting date(s): Spring and Fall
Officers and Directors:* Arthur N. Rupe,* Chair.; **Jeffrey J. Cain, Ph.D.*, Pres. and Exec. Dir.**; Susan C. Van Aacken, Secy.; Richard L. Hunt, C.P.A.*, Treas.; **Kimberly O. Dennis**; **Lanny Eberstein, Ph.D.**; **Richard L. Hunt, C.P.A.**; **Evan Coyne Maloney**; Beverly Rupe Schwarz, J.D.
EIN: 770278838
Other changes: Alan O. Ebenstein is no longer a director. Jeffrey J. Cain is now Pres. and Exec. Dir.

390

Ryzman Foundation, Inc.

c/o Barak
5967 W. 3rd St., Ste. 102
Los Angeles, CA 90036-2835

Established in 1980 in CA.
Donors: Betty Ryzman; Zvi Ryzman; Mickey Fenig; Elie Ryzman; Sol Majer; Rafael Ryzman; Abraham Ryzman; David Wolf; Mila Kornwasser Life Insurance; SRYZ Corp.; ARYZ Corp.
Foundation type: Independent foundation.
Financial data (yr. ended 11/30/11): Assets, $25,732,345 (M); gifts received, $8,032,000; expenditures, $2,553,400; qualifying distributions, $2,526,800; giving activities include $2,526,800 for 29 grants (high: $1,180,000; low: $1,800).
Purpose and activities: Giving primarily to Jewish agencies, temples, and schools.
Fields of interest: Education; Jewish agencies & synagogues.
Limitations: Applications not accepted. Giving primarily in New York, NY. No grants to individuals.
Application information: Contributes only to pre-selected organizations.
Officers: Zvi Ryzman, Pres.; Betty Ryzman, Secy.
EIN: 953653055
Other changes: For the fiscal year ended Nov. 30, 2011, the grantmaker paid grants of $2,526,800, a 124.0% increase over the fiscal 2010 disbursements, $1,128,000.

391

Sacramento Region Community Foundation

(formerly Sacramento Regional Foundation)
955 University Ave., Ste. A
Sacramento, CA 95825 (916) 921-7723
***Contact:* Linda Beech Cutler, C.E.O.**
FAX: (916) 921-7725; E-mail: info@sacregcf.org; Application e-mail: applications@sacregcf.org; Main URL: http://www.sacregcf.org
Blog: http://www.sacregcf.org/index.cfm/learn/foundation-blog/
Facebook: http://www.facebook.com/sacregcf
Google Plus: https://plus.google.com/105391282457155881466/posts
LinkedIn: http://www.linkedin.com/company/sacramento-region-community-foundation
RSS Feed: http://sacregcf.org/tasks/feed/?feedID=BADCE22E-155D-0204-75B83AD94C7622CC
Twitter: http://twitter.com/sacregcf
YouTube: http://youtube.com/sacregcf
Scholarship contact e-mail: scholarships@sacregcf.org

Incorporated in 1983 in CA.
Foundation type: Community foundation.
Financial data (yr. ended 12/31/12): Assets, $106,540,710 (M); gifts received, $7,758,742; expenditures, $6,357,805; giving activities include $3,354,218 for 117+ grants (high: $218,000; low: $1,000), and $819,894 for 259 grants to individuals.
Purpose and activities: The mission of the foundation is to serve as a leader and trusted partner in expanding philanthropic activity and enhancing its impact for the betterment of the Sacramento region community.
Fields of interest: Visual arts; Museums; Performing arts; Performing arts, theater; Humanities; Historic preservation/historical societies; Arts; Child development, education; Elementary school/education; Vocational education; Higher education; Adult education—literacy, basic skills & GED; Education, reading; Education; Environment, natural resources; Environmental education; Environment; Health care; Mental health/crisis services; Health organizations, association; AIDS; Alcoholism; Legal services; Food services; Housing/shelter, development; Youth development, services; Children/youth, services; Child development, services; Family services; Residential/custodial care, hospices; Aging, centers/services; Minorities/immigrants, centers/services; Homeless, human services; Human services; Urban/community development; Community/economic development; Voluntarism promotion; Social sciences; Public policy, research; Government/public administration; Leadership development; Aging; Disabilities, people with; Minorities; Economically disadvantaged; Homeless.
Type of support: General/operating support; Management development/capacity building; Building/renovation; Emergency funds; Program development; Publication; Seed money; Scholarship funds; Technical assistance; Program evaluation; Employee-related scholarships; Scholarships—to individuals; Matching/challenge support.
Limitations: Applications accepted. Giving primarily focused on organizations within or those offering services to El Dorado, Placer, Sacramento, and Yolo counties, CA. No support for sectarian purposes or private foundations. No grants to individuals (except designated fund scholarships and through the Artists in Crisis Fund), or for annual campaigns, operating funds, capital campaigns, endowments, building funds, continuing support, deficit financing, foundation-managed projects, research, or land acquisition; no loans.
Publications: Annual report; Financial statement; Informational brochure; Newsletter.
Application information: Visit foundation web site for application forms and guidelines. Applications may be submitted via U.S. mail, e-mail, or fax. Application form required.
Initial approach: Submit application form and attachments
Copies of proposal: 10
Deadline(s): Varies
Board meeting date(s): Jan., Mar., May, July, Sept., and Nov.
Officers and Directors:* Henry Wirz,* Chair.; Dennis Mangers,* Vice-Chair.; Linda Beech Cutler, C.E.O.; Jim McCallum, C.F.O.; Carlin Naify, Secy.; Donna L. Courville,* Treas.; Winston Hom, Cont.; Margie Campbell; Jane Einhorn; Cassandra Jennings; Linda Merksamer; Diane Mizell; Darren Morris; William Niemi; Meg Stallard; Martin Steiner; Gary Strong; Stephen Tse; Clarence Williams.
Number of staff: 7 full-time professional; 2 full-time support.
EIN: 942891517
Other changes: Jeannie Howell is now Community Impact Mgr. Dan Cole, Michael Dunlavey, Robert M. Earl, Mario Guiterrez, Robert L. Lorber, Daniel I. Parrish, and Jeanne Reaves are no longer directors.

392

Harriet H. Samuelsson Foundation

P.O. Box 5244
Oxnard, CA 93031-5244 (877) 968-6328
FAX: (949) 833-9584;
E-mail: grants@samuelssonfoundation.org; Additional tel.: (805) 487-5350; Main URL: http://www.samuelssonfoundation.org

Established in 2005 in CA.
Foundation type: Independent foundation.
Financial data (yr. ended 09/30/13): Assets, $27,125,638 (M); expenditures, $1,434,382; qualifying distributions, $1,207,309; giving activities include $1,009,600 for 46 grants (high: $100,000; low: $500).
Purpose and activities: Giving to support organizations that further the health, education, guidance or welfare of youth who reside in Ventura County, CA; organizations that are engaged in cancer research and for the St. John's Regional Medical Center in Oxnard, CA, exclusively for the purchase and maintenance of fetal monitors.
Fields of interest: Cancer research; Boys clubs; Girls clubs; Boys & girls clubs; Human services; Children/youth, services; Children/youth.
Type of support: General/operating support; Capital campaigns; Building/renovation; Equipment; Program development; Conferences/seminars; Research.

Limitations: Giving primarily in Ventura County, CA. No support for non 501(c)(3) organizations. No grants to individuals.
Publications: Application guidelines.
Application information: Letters of inquiry are by invitation only, upon results of eligibility quiz. See foundation web site for information.
Initial approach: Take eligibility quiz on foundation web site
Deadline(s): Mar. 31 and Sept. 30
Board meeting date(s): First Wed. of the month
Trustees: Robert Compton; Thomas Petrovich; **Rick B. Smith**; Irene Yabu.
Number of staff: None.
EIN: 201687782

393
San Luis Obispo County Community Foundation
550 Dana St.
San Luis Obispo, CA 93401 (805) 543-2323
Contact: For grants: Janice Fong Wolf, Dir., Grants & Progs.
FAX: (805) 543-2346; E-mail: info@sloccf.org;
Additional e-mail: jwolf@sloccf.org; Main URL: http://www.sloccf.org
Facebook: http://www.facebook.com/pages/San-Luis-Obispo-County-Community-Foundation/359118103540

Established in 1998 in CA.
Foundation type: Community foundation.
Financial data (yr. ended 12/31/12): Assets, $36,353,519 (M); gifts received, $6,306,230; expenditures, $6,731,821; giving activities include $5,744,157 for 421 grants.
Purpose and activities: The foundation is a public trust established to assist donors in building an enduring source of charitable funds to meet the changing needs and interests of the community. The foundation offers grants for area nonprofits aimed at helping them increase their organizational capacity.
Fields of interest: Historic preservation/historical societies; Arts; Education; Environment; Health care; Recreation; Human services; Nonprofit management; Community/economic development; Children/youth; Youth; Aging; Young adults; Disabilities, people with; Physically disabled; Hispanics/Latinos; Women; Girls; Economically disadvantaged; Homeless; Migrant workers; LGBTQ.
Type of support: General/operating support; Continuing support; Management development/capacity building; Building/renovation; Equipment; Program development; Technical assistance; Consulting services; Scholarships—to individuals; Matching/challenge support.
Limitations: Applications accepted. Giving primarily in San Luis Obispo County, CA. No support for religious programs (unless open to the public regardless of religious affiliation), governmental organizations, or fraternal organizations (unless in support of a specific program open to or benefiting the entire community). No grants to individuals (except for scholarships), or for endowments, debt reduction, fundraising events, fellowships, travel, or technical or specialized research.
Publications: Application guidelines; Annual report; Grants list; Informational brochure; Newsletter; Occasional report.
Application information: Visit foundation web site for application cover sheet and guidelines. Faxed or e-mailed applications are not accepted. Application form required.
Initial approach: Submit application cover sheet, narrative, and attachments
Copies of proposal: 6
Deadline(s): Varies
Board meeting date(s): Monthly
Final notification: Within 3 months
Officers and Directors:* Claire Clark, Interim C.E.O.; Ann Robinson,* Pres.; Steve McCarty,* V.P.; Nick Thille, Secy.; Bill Raver,* C.F.O. and Treas.; Jim Brabeck; Jim Glinn; Lee Hollister; Steven B. Jobst, M.D.; Mike Miner; Barbara Leigh Partridge; Mike Patrick; Johnnie Talley; Mary Verdin.
Number of staff: 1 full-time professional; 5 part-time professional.
EIN: 770496500
Other changes: Barry VanderKelen is no longer Exec. Dir. Claire Clark is now Interim C.E.O. Bill Raver is now C.F.O. and Treas. Pat Holley is now Donor Svcs. and Comms. Assoc. Norman Mendel is no longer a director.

394
Santa Barbara Foundation
1111 Chapala St., Ste. 200
Santa Barbara, CA 93101 (805) 963-1873
Contact: Ronald V. Gallo, C.E.O.
FAX: (805) 966-2345;
E-mail: info@sbfoundation.org; Grant application e-mail: grants@sbfoundation.org; Main URL: http://www.sbfoundation.org
Blog: http://www.sbfoundation.org/feed.rss?id=3
E-Newsletter: http://www.sbfoundation.org/Page.aspx?pid=452
Facebook: https://www.facebook.com/sbfoundation
Flickr: http://www.flickr.com/photos/68044616@N08/sets/
Grants Database: https://www.sbfoundation.org/page.aspx?pid=435
Twitter: http://twitter.com/sbfoundation
YouTube: http://www.youtube.com/user/SBFoundationImpact

Incorporated Oct. 16, 1928 in CA.
Foundation type: Community foundation.
Financial data (yr. ended 12/31/12): Assets, $299,473,778 (M); gifts received, $14,696,210; expenditures, $35,014,687; giving activities include $24,466,934 for grants.
Purpose and activities: The foundation's mission is to enrich the lives of the people of Santa Barbara County through philanthropy. To achieve this mission, the foundation will: 1) serve as a leader, catalyst, and resource for philanthropy; 2) strive for measurable community improvement through strategic funding in such fields as community enhancement, culture, education, environment, health, human services, personal development, and recreation; 3) promote partnerships to address important community issues and leverage resources to meet community needs; 4) build and prudently manage a growing endowment for the community's present and future needs; and 5) provide secure, flexible, and effective opportunities for donors to improve their community.
Fields of interest: Arts; Education; Environment; Animal welfare; Public health; Health care; Substance abuse, services; Housing/shelter; Recreation; Children/youth, services; Children, day care; Human services, personal services; Residential/custodial care, hospices; Aging, centers/services; Human services; Community/economic development; Public affairs, citizen participation.
Type of support: Capital campaigns; Building/renovation; Equipment; Land acquisition; Emergency funds; Program development; Scholarship funds; Scholarships—to individuals; Matching/challenge support; Student loans—to individuals.
Limitations: Applications accepted. Giving limited to Santa Barbara County, CA. No support for religious organizations for religious purposes. **No grants to individuals (except for scholarships), or for deficit financing, endowment funds, capital needs, fundraising drives, fellowships, or for research.**
Publications: Application guidelines; Annual report; Financial statement; Informational brochure; Newsletter; Occasional report.
Application information: Visit foundation web site for application forms and guidelines. Application form required.
Initial approach: Application
***Deadline(s):* Varies**
Board meeting date(s): Jan., Mar., May, June, Sept., Oct., and Dec.
***Final notification:* Varies**
Officers and Trustees:* Eileen F. Sheridan,* Chair.; James Morouse,* Vice-Chair.; Ronald V. Gallo, C.E.O. and Pres.; Jan Campbell, Sr. V.P., Philanthropic Svcs.; Dee Jennings, Sr. V.P., Finance and Admin./C.F.O.; Al Rodriguez, V.P., Community Investments; **Robert Skinner,* Secy.**; Gretchen Milligan,* Treas.; Cheri Savage, Asst. Treas.; Peter MacDougall,* Chair. Emeritus; Diane Adam; Laurie Ashton; Hugh M. Boss; Jon Clark; Frederick W. Gluck; Michael G. Mayfield; Jennifer Murray; Cathy Pepe; Michelle Lee Pickett; Niki Sandoval; Chris Slaughter; Luis Villegas; Polly Firestone Walker; Michael D. Young.
Fund Managers: Alternative Investment Manager; Capital Research & Management Co.; Hammond and Associates; Luther King Capital Management; Straleu and Co.; Wells Fargo Bank, N.A.
Number of staff: 17 full-time professional; 4 full-time support.
EIN: 951866094
Other changes: Robert Skinner has replaced James Morouse as Secy.
Karin Svensson is no longer Cont. Ashley Butler-Soberano is now Special Projects Off. Jessica Sanchez is now Donor Svcs. Off. Kathy Simas is now Community Investment Off. Jessica Tade is now Dir., Comms. and Mktg. Jane Haberman and Cliff Lambert are no longer trustees.

395
Vidal Sassoon Foundation
c/o CBIZ
10474 Santa Monica Blvd., No. 200
Los Angeles, CA 90025-1759

Established in 1979.
Donor: Vidal Sassoon†.
Foundation type: Independent foundation.
Financial data (yr. ended 12/31/12): Assets, $280 (M); gifts received, $206,860; expenditures, $206,881; qualifying distributions, $206,881; giving activities include $202,300 for 7 grants (high: $50,000; low: $2,000).
Purpose and activities: Giving primarily for education and human services.
Fields of interest: Arts; Higher education; Education; Health organizations, association; Human services; Children/youth, services; International affairs; Jewish federated giving programs; Jewish agencies & synagogues.
International interests: Israel.
Limitations: Applications not accepted. Giving primarily in CA, NY and VA. No grants to individuals.
Application information: Contributes only to pre-selected organizations.

Officers: Vidal Sassoon, Pres.; Rhonda Sassoon, Secy.; Cheryl A. Calhoun, C.F.O.; Marilyn B. Esquivel, Exec. Dir.
EIN: 953401086

396
Savage Charitable Foundation
c/o Bruno Skorheim, LLP
9665 Chesapeake Dr., Ste. 470
San Diego, CA 92123-1378
Application address: c/o Ronald J. Savage, 632 Regency Hills Dr., Collegeville, PA 19426, tel.: (703) 987-5407

Established in 2006 in CA.
Donors: Savage Administrative Trust; Visual Communications Co., Inc.
Foundation type: Independent foundation.
Financial data (yr. ended 12/31/12): Assets, $623,689 (M); expenditures, $902,549; qualifying distributions, $865,271; giving activities include $827,995 for 8 grants (high: $500,000; low: $500).
Fields of interest: Catholic agencies & churches.
Limitations: Applications accepted. Giving primarily in CA, IL, PA and VA.
Application information:
***Initial approach:* Letter**
Deadline(s): None
Officers and Trustee:* Ronald J. Savage,* Chair. and Pres.; Samuel Roberts, Secy.-Treas.
EIN: 204589164

397
Scaife Scholarship Foundation
1547 Lakeside Dr.
Oakland, CA 94612-4520 (510) 451-1906
***Contact:* Cal Gilbert, Secy.-Treas.**

Established in fiscal 1992 pursuant to an IRS ruling ending the combined filing of the foundation and the Northern California Scholarship Foundation.
Donors: Clarence Benjamin‡; Rogert Ervin Schulze‡; RBC Dain Rauscher Inc.
Foundation type: Independent foundation.
Financial data (yr. ended 05/31/13): Assets, $12,761,843 (M); expenditures, $601,427; qualifying distributions, $585,006; giving activities include $500,500 for grants to individuals.
Purpose and activities: Scholarship awards to graduates of northern California public high schools whose parents were born in the United States.
Fields of interest: Higher education.
Type of support: Scholarships—to individuals.
Limitations: Giving limited to northern CA residents.
Application information: Written application on pre-printed forms, including transcripts of high school records, college entrance exam scores, and statement of financial need. Application form required.
Initial approach: Letter requesting application form
Deadline(s): Mar. 15
Officers: Byron Flanders, Pres.; Dave Arp, V.P.; Cal Gilbert, Secy.-Treas.
Trustees: Wade Bingham; Hans Bissinger; Dallas G. Cason; Robert Crow; Don Emig; Thomas D. Eychner; **Bill K'Burg**; Julius "Sandy" Khan III; George Klopping; James F. McClung, Jr.; Dan Miller; Clyde Minar; Norman Owen; James Sloenaker; Zook Sutton; George Vukasin.
EIN: 943161402
Other changes: Byron Flanders has replaced Julius "Sandy" Kahn, III, as Pres. Dave Arp has replaced Byron Flanders as V.P. Cal Gilbert has replaced Clyde D. Minar as Secy.-Treas.
Charles DiBari is no longer a trustee.

398
The Schmidt Family Foundation
555 Bryant St., No. 370
Palo Alto, CA 94301-1704
Contact: Sarah Bell, Prog. Mgr., 11th Hour Project
FAX: (650) 454-8993;
E-mail: staff@theschmidt.org; **Main URL: http://www.11thhourproject.org**

Established in 2006 in CA.
Donors: Eric Schmidt; Wendy Schmidt.
Foundation type: Independent foundation.
Financial data (yr. ended 12/31/12): Assets, $312,189,881 (M); gifts received, $143,260,276; expenditures, $22,518,322; qualifying distributions, $21,840,872; giving activities include $17,502,100 for 115 grants (high: $1,500,000; low: $500), $3,746,395 for 3 foundation-administered programs and $608,609 for 3 loans/program-related investments.
Purpose and activities: The foundation supports efforts, using best expert information, to help transform the world's environmental and energy practices in the 21st century. The foundation's mission, at its broadest, is to advance the creation of an increasingly intelligent relationship between human activity and the use of the world's natural resources. The foundation works strategically, and often in collaboration, to create successful models of their vision. This includes the restoration and protection of vulnerable historic places while improving their environmental profile, using new technologies, and the growing knowledge about the impact of the built environment on the Earth's climate system. The foundation supports efforts around the world to improve health, education, transportation and communications through investing in a pattern of economic development that includes green, sustainable environmental practices and design. In addition, the foundation supports public education around issues of energy and the environment and promote public understanding of the science of climate change.
Fields of interest: Environment.
Limitations: Applications not accepted. Giving primarily in CA.
Publications: Annual report; Financial statement; Grants list; IRS Form 990 or 990-PF printed copy available upon request.
Application information: Unsolicited requests for funds not accepted. Grantmaking is by invitation only.
Officers and Directors:* Wendy Schmidt,* Pres., Schmidt Family Foundation; Eric Schmidt,* V.P.; Sophie Schmidt,* V.P.; **William J. Arthur, Secy.**; Jeanne W. Huey, C.F.O.; **Joe Sciortino, Exec. Dir., Schmidt Family Foundation; Amy Rao, Pres., 11th Hour Project.**
EIN: 204170342
Other changes: At the close of 2012, the fair market value of the grantmaker's assets was $312,189,881, a 75.4% increase over the 2011 value, $178,017,994.
Wendy Schmidt is now Pres., Schmidt Family Foundation. Amy Rao is now Pres., 11th Hour Project. Joe Sciortino is now Exec. Dir., Schmidt Family Foundation.

399
Drs. Janene and Tom Scovel Foundation, Inc.
391 S. Rosemead
Pasadena, CA 91107-4955

Established in 2001 in CA.
Donors: Out of the Shell, LLC; Bing Yang.
Foundation type: Independent foundation.
Financial data (yr. ended 12/31/12): Assets, $7,670,183 (M); gifts received, $7,343; expenditures, $161,121; qualifying distributions, $45,700; giving activities include $45,700 for grants.
Fields of interest: Community/economic development.
Limitations: Applications not accepted. Giving primarily in CA and China. No grants to individuals.
Application information: Contributes only to pre-selected organizations.
Officer: Bing Yang, Pres.
Director: Katherine B. Purgason.
EIN: 100002893

400
The Seaver Institute
12400 Wilshire Blvd, Ste. 1240
Los Angeles, CA 90025-1058 (310) 979-0298
Contact: Victoria Seaver Dean, Pres.
FAX: (310) 979-0297;
E-mail: vsd@theseaverinstitute.org

Incorporated in 1955 in CA.
Foundation type: Independent foundation.
Financial data (yr. ended 06/30/13): Assets, $33,413,880 (M); expenditures, $2,799,296; qualifying distributions, $2,424,809; giving activities include $2,058,750 for 88 grants (high: $346,000; low: $100).
Purpose and activities: The Seaver Institute provides seed money to highly regarded organizations for particular projects which offer the potential for significant advancement in their fields.
Fields of interest: Arts; Education, research; Science, research.
Type of support: Seed money; Research.
Limitations: Applications accepted. Giving on a national basis. No grants to individuals, or for operating budgets, continuing support, annual campaigns, emergency or endowment funds, scholarships, fellowships, deficit financing, capital or building funds, equipment, land acquisition, publications, disease-specific research or conferences; no loans.
Publications: Application guidelines; Informational brochure (including application guidelines).
Application information: Application form not required.
Initial approach: Letter addressed to the president, requesting guidelines
Copies of proposal: 1
Deadline(s): Early Apr. and early Nov.
Board meeting date(s): May
Officers and Directors:* Victoria Seaver Dean,* Pres.; Martha Seaver,* Vice-Chair.; Robert Flick,* Secy.; Christopher Seaver,* Treas.; Nancy Bekavac; Margaret Keene; Marie Knowles; Thomas Pfister; Carlton Seaver; Patrick Seaver; Roxanne Wilson.
Number of staff: 2 part-time professional.
EIN: 956054764
Other changes: For the fiscal year ended June 30, 2013, the grantmaker paid grants of $2,058,750, a 62.9% increase over the fiscal 2012 disbursements, $1,263,950.

401

Shasta Regional Community Foundation
1335 Arboretum Dr., Ste. B
Redding, CA 96003-3627 (530) 244-1219
Contact: **Kerri Caranci, C.E.O.; For grants: Amanda Hutchings, Prog. Off.**
FAX: (530) 244-0905; E-mail: info@shastarcf.org; **Grant inquiry e-mail: amanda@shastarcf.org**; Main URL: http://www.shastarcf.org
E-Newsletter: http://visitor.constantcontact.com/manage/optin/ea?v=001Qo1SzxA2oRTl6dK0BelH4w%3D%3D
Facebook: http://www.facebook.com/pages/Shasta-Regional-Community-Foundation/138119199544511

Established in 2000 in CA.
Foundation type: Community foundation.
Financial data (yr. ended 06/30/13): Assets, $21,285,013 (M); gifts received, $3,466,522; expenditures, $3,129,928; giving activities include $1,250,520 for 156+ grants (high: $60,620; low: $100), and $135,308 for 62 grants to individuals (high: $58,508; low: $500).
Purpose and activities: The mission of the foundation is to build resources to meet needs in Shasta and Siskiyou communities through philanthropy, education, and information.
Fields of interest: Arts; Higher education; Education; Environment; Animals/wildlife; Health care; Safety/disasters; Recreation; Youth development; Human services; Nonprofit management; Community/economic development; Leadership development.
Type of support: Student loans—to individuals; General/operating support; Building/renovation; Equipment; Scholarship funds; Scholarships—to individuals.
Limitations: Applications accepted. Giving primarily to Shasta and Siskiyou counties, CA, with limited grantmaking in Modoc, Tehama and Trinity counties, CA.
Publications: Application guidelines; Annual report; Grants list; Informational brochure.
Application information: The foundation currently makes grants from individual Scholarship funds and Donor-Advised funds; visit foundation web site for application forms and guidelines. Application form required.
Initial approach: Telephone
Deadline(s): Varies
Board meeting date(s): Monthly
Final notification: 2-3 months
Officers and Directors:* Joe Tallerico,* Chair.; DeAnne Parker,* Vice-Chair.; Kerry Caranci,* C.E.O.; Mary Rickert,* Secy.; Raiann Wilson,* C.F.O.; Dorian Aiello; Barbara Cross; Joan Favero; Dan Ghidinelli; Leo Graham; Bill Haedrich; Jon Halfhide; Evelyn Jacobs; Bill Kohn; Brian Meek; Jim Zauher.
Number of staff: 2 full-time professional; 2 part-time professional; 1 part-time support.
EIN: 680242276

402

J. F. Shea Company Foundation
655 Brea Canyon Rd.
Walnut, CA 91789-3078

Established in 1967 in CA.
Donor: J.F. Shea Co., Inc.
Foundation type: Company-sponsored foundation.
Financial data (yr. ended 12/31/12): Assets, $5,317,471 (M); expenditures, $259,699; qualifying distributions, $257,060; giving activities include $257,060 for grants.
Purpose and activities: The foundation supports health centers and organizations involved with education, human services, and Catholicism.
Fields of interest: Secondary school/education; Education; Health care, clinics/centers; Children/youth, services; Family services, domestic violence; Human services; United Ways and Federated Giving Programs; Catholic agencies & churches.
Type of support: Program development; General/operating support.
Limitations: Applications not accepted. Giving primarily in CA. No grants to individuals.
Application information: Contributes only to pre-selected organizations.
Officers: John F. Shea, Pres.; Ronald L. Lakey, V.P.; Peter O. Shea, Treas.
EIN: 952554052
Other changes: Edmund H. Shea, Jr. is no longer Secy.

403

Shepherd, Sower, Sentinel and Scholar Foundation
35 Woodcrest
Irvine, CA **92603**

Donors: Nan Lowell; Wayne Lowell.
Foundation type: Independent foundation.
Financial data (yr. ended 12/31/13): Assets, $2,292,983 (M); gifts received, $840,000; expenditures, $122,176; qualifying distributions, $121,074; giving activities include $120,000 for 2 grants (high: $90,000; low: $30,000).
Fields of interest: Education; Human services.
Limitations: Applications not accepted.
Application information: Unsolicited requests for funds not accepted.
Officers: Wayne Lowell, C.E.O. and Pres.; Nan Lowell, Secy.-Treas. and C.F.O.
EIN: 453725115
Other changes: Wayne Lowell is now C.E.O. and Pres.

404

The Thomas and Stacey Siebel Foundation
1300 Seaport Blvd., Ste. 400
Redwood City, CA 94063-5591 (650) 299-5200
Contact: Thomas M. Siebel, Pres.
***FAX:* (650) 299-5250; E-mail: info@fvgroup.com**; Main URL: http://www.fvgroup.com/philanthropy.htm

Established in 1996 in CA.
Donors: Stacey Siebel; Thomas M. Siebel.
Foundation type: Independent foundation.
Financial data (yr. ended 12/31/12): Assets, $223,325,978 (M); expenditures, $8,976,432; qualifying distributions, $7,177,922; giving activities include $6,801,500 for 39 grants (high: $1,000,000; low: $500).
Purpose and activities: Giving primarily to the Salvation Arm as well as for land conservation and children's scholarships and services.
Fields of interest: Education, single organization support; Elementary/secondary education; Higher education, university; Environment, land resources; Salvation Army; Children, services; Homeless, human services.
Limitations: Applications not accepted. Giving primarily in CA, with some giving in MA, MD and NY.
Application information: Contributes only to pre-selected organizations.
Officers: Thomas M. Siebel, Pres.; Stacey Siebel, Secy.; **Bill Dougherty, C.F.O.**; Nitsa Zuppas, Exec. Dir.
EIN: 943256331

405

Sierra Health Foundation
1321 Garden Hwy.
Sacramento, CA 95833-9754
Contact: Chet P. Hewitt, C.E.O. and Pres.
E-mail: info@sierrahealth.org; Additional e-mail: grants@sierrahealth.org; Main URL: http://www.sierrahealth.org
Health Leadership Program: http://www.facebook.com/shfhlp
Knowledge Center: http://www.sierrahealth.org/doc.aspx?9

Established in 1984 in CA; converted from Foundation Health Plan of Sacramento.
Donor: Foundation Health Plan of Sacramento.
Foundation type: Independent foundation.
Financial data (yr. ended 12/31/12): Assets, $107,163,350 (M); gifts received, $1,499,436; expenditures, $10,945,517; qualifying distributions, $8,457,271; giving activities include $3,533,207 for 119 grants (high: $300,000; low: $3,500), $331,739 for 234 employee matching gifts, and $5,907,617 for 4 foundation-administered programs.
Purpose and activities: To invest in and serve as a catalyst for ideas, partnerships and programs to improve health and quality of life in Northern California through convening educating and strategic grantmaking.
Fields of interest: Child development, education; Medical care, rehabilitation; Health care; Substance abuse, services; Mental health/crisis services; Health organizations, association; AIDS; Alcoholism; Biomedicine; Crime/violence prevention, youth; Nutrition; Youth development; Human services; Children/youth, services; Child development, services; Family services; Community/economic development; Leadership development; Youth.
Type of support: Program development; Technical assistance; Program evaluation; Employee matching gifts; In-kind gifts.
Limitations: Applications not accepted. Giving limited to all or a portion of 26 Northern California counties depending on grant program: Alpine, Amador, Butte, Calaveras, Colusa, El Dorado, Glenn, Lassen, Modoc, Mono, Nevada, Placer, Plumas, Sacramento, San Joaquin, Shasta, Sierra, Siskiyou, Solano (eastern), Stanislaus, Sutter, Tehama, Trinity, Tuolumne, Yolo and Yuba. No support for programs, activities, or organizations that are not health-related, No support for activities that exclusively benefit members of sectarian or religious organizations or for support organizations. No grants to individuals or for endowments.
Publications: Biennial report; Informational brochure; Occasional report.
Application information: Newsletter and funding opportunities are available on foundation web site. Application instructions vary by program. See foundation web site for instructions.
Board meeting date(s): Quarterly
Officers and Directors:* Jose Hermocillo,* Chair.; David W. Gordon,* Vice-Chair.; Chet P. Hewitt,* C.E.O and Pres.; Gilbert Alvarado, V.P., Admin. and C.F.O.; Nancy Lee; Robert Petersen, C.P.A.; Dr. Claire Pomeroy; **Dr. Earl Washburn**; **Carol Whiteside.**

Number of staff: 8 full-time professional; 11 full-time support.
EIN: 680050036

406
Sierra Pacific Foundation
c/o Jon D. Gartman
P.O. Box 496028
Redding, CA 96049-6028 **(530) 378-8000**
***E-mail:* foundation@spi-ind.com; Main URL: http://www.spi-ind.com/spf_home.aspx**
Grants List: http://www.spi-ind.com/html/pdf_foundation/spf_contribution11.pdf

Established in 1979 in CA.
Donor: Sierra Pacific Industries.
Foundation type: Company-sponsored foundation.
Financial data (yr. ended 06/30/13): Assets, $22,599 (M); gifts received, $800,500; expenditures, $801,780; qualifying distributions, $776,662; giving activities include $433,690 for 240 grants (high: $100,000; low: -$1,000), and $342,972 for 311 grants to individuals (high: $2,500; low: $375).
Purpose and activities: The foundation supports organizations involved with arts and culture, education, forest conservation, animals and wildlife, health, agriculture, recreation, human services, and youth.
Fields of interest: Performing arts, theater; Arts; Secondary school/education; Education; Environment, forests; Animals/wildlife; Health care, clinics/centers; Health care; Agriculture; Athletics/sports, school programs; Recreation, fairs/festivals; Recreation; Human services; Youth.
Type of support: Sponsorships; General/operating support; Program development; Employee-related scholarships.
Limitations: Applications accepted. Giving primarily in areas of company operations in CA and WA. No support for religious organizations or foundations. No grants to individuals (except for employee-related scholarships), or for salaries, general operating support for schools or public agencies, or religious activities.
Publications: Grants list.
Application information: Application form required.
Initial approach: **Request application form**
Copies of proposal: 1
Deadline(s): Feb. 28
Officers: Carolyn Emmerson Dietz, Pres.; George Emmerson, V.P.; M.D. Emmerson, Secy.
EIN: 942574178

407
The Silicon Valley Bank Foundation
3003 Tasman Dr.
Santa Clara, CA 95054-1191 (405) 987-9147
E-mail: svbfoundation@svb.com.; Main URL: http://www.svb.com/Company/Corporate-Social-Responsibility/Social-Responsibility/

Established in 1995 in CA.
Donor: Silicon Valley Bank.
Foundation type: Company-sponsored foundation.
Financial data (yr. ended 12/31/12): Assets, $1,583,030 (M); expenditures, $161,705; qualifying distributions, $159,750; giving activities include $159,750 for grants.
Purpose and activities: The foundation supports organizations with which employees of Silicon Valley Bank volunteer or serve in leadership positions; and programs designed to serve low-and-moderate income communities.
Fields of interest: Arts; Education; Health care; Employment; Housing/shelter; Homeless, human services; Human services; Community/economic development; United Ways and Federated Giving Programs; Economically disadvantaged.
Type of support: General/operating support; Capital campaigns; Equipment; Program development; Employee volunteer services.
Limitations: Applications accepted. Giving primarily in areas of company operations in northern CA. No support for religious organizations, discriminatory organizations, or parent teacher associations. No grants to individuals, or for memorial campaigns, fundraising, political activities, research, sponsorship of athletic events or programs, endowments, or advertising.
Publications: Application guidelines.
Application information: Preference is given to organizations sponsored by a Silicon Valley Bank employee. Grants range from $500 to $2,500.
Application form required.
***Initial approach:* Email**
Deadline(s): None
Board meeting date(s): Quarterly
Officers: Jim Hori, Chair. and Pres.; Scott Bergquist, V.P.; Michelle Churchill, Treas.
Directors: Pamela Aldsworth; Dan Allred; Anne Bongi; Greg Becker; Don Chandler; Susan Garcia; Katie Knepley; Carrie Merritt; Craig Robinson; Brenda Santoro; Jeff Strawn; Mary Toomey.
EIN: 770414630

408
Silicon Valley Community Foundation
2440 West El Camino Real, Ste. 300
Mountain View, CA 94040-1498 (650) 450-5400
Contact: Vera Bennett, C.O.O. and C.F.O.; Katarina Koster, Exec. Asst. to C.O.O./C.F.O.
FAX: (650) 450-5401;
E-mail: info@siliconvalleycf.org; Additional e-mail: vlbennett@siliconvalleycf.org; Grant inquiry e-mail: grants@siliconvalleycf.org; Grant application e-mail: grantproposals@siliconvalleycf.org; Main URL: http://www.siliconvalleycf.org/
E-Newsletter: http://www.siliconvalleycf.org/content/enewsletters
Facebook: http://www.facebook.com/siliconvalleycf
GiveSmart: http://www.givesmart.org/Stories/Donors/Emmett-Carson
LinkedIn: http://www.linkedin.com/companies/silicon-valley-community-foundation
Silicon Valley Community Foundation's Philanthropy Promise: http://www.ncrp.org/philanthropys-promise/who
Twitter: http://twitter.com/siliconvalleycf
Vimeo: http://vimeo.com/9174091
YouTube: http://www.youtube.com/TheSVCF
Scholarship e-mail: scholarships@siliconvalleycf.org.

Established in 2007 in CA.
Foundation type: Community foundation.
Financial data (yr. ended 12/31/13): Assets, $4,723,897,000 (M); gifts received, $1,388,154,000; expenditures, $398,485,000; giving activities include $362,390,000 for grants.
Purpose and activities: The mission of the foundation is to strengthen the common good, improve quality of life and address the most challenging problems of the community. The foundation's endowment grantmaking strategies are focused on five key areas: Economic Security, Education, Immigrant Integration, Regional Planning, and Community Opportunity Fund.
Fields of interest: Education; Human services; Economic development; Community/economic development; Public affairs; Children/youth; Youth; Adults; Immigrants/refugees; Economically disadvantaged; Homeless.
Type of support: Mission-related investments/loans; General/operating support; Continuing support; Management development/capacity building; Program development; Conferences/seminars; Seed money; Scholarship funds; Scholarships—to individuals.
Limitations: Applications accepted. Giving of endowment grants are restricted to programs, services, and efforts that benefit the San Mateo and Santa Clara counties in CA. No support for religious purposes or private non-operating foundations.
Publications: Application guidelines; Annual report; Financial statement; Grants list; Informational brochure; Newsletter; Occasional report.
Application information: Visit foundation web site for request for proposal forms (which includes application), guidelines, and deadlines per grant type. Application form required.
Initial approach: Attend an information session, request for proposal
Deadline(s): Varies, see web site for requests for proposals specific deadline dates
Board meeting date(s): Mar., June, Oct., and Dec.
Final notification: Within 6 to 12 weeks
Officers and Directors:* Thomas J. Friel,* Chair.; C.S. Park,* Vice-Chair.; Emmett D. Carson, Ph.D., C.E.O. and Pres.; John Stuckey, Sr. V.P., Finance; Don Aguilar, V.P., Human Resources; Bert Feuss, V.P., Investments; Oris Miller, V.P., Information Technology; Samantha Owen, V.P., Business Svcs.; Rebecca Salner, V.P., Mktg. and Comms.; Erica Wood, V.P., Community Leadership and Grantmaking; Vera Bennett, C.O.O. and C.F.O.; Ivonne Montes de Oca,* Secy.-Treas.; Sarah Valencia, Cont.; Mari Ellen Reynolds Loijens, Chief Business, Devel and Brand Off.; Leigh Stilwell, Chief Donor Experience and Engagement Off.; Jane Battey; Gloria Brown; Gregory M. Gallo; Nancy H. Handel; John Hopkins; Samuel Johnson, Jr.; Robert A. Keller; Dan'l Lewin; David P. Lopez; Anne F. Macdonald; Catherine Molnar; Eduardo Rallo; Sanjay Vaswani; Gordon Yamate.
Number of staff: 80 full-time professional; 6 part-time professional; 10 full-time support.
EIN: 205205488
Other changes: At the close of 2013, the fair market value of the grantmaker's assets was $4,723,897,000, a 62.7% increase over the 2012 value, $2,903,166,000.

409
The Silver Giving Foundation
(formerly The Silver Lining Foundation)
1 Lombard St., Ste. 305
San Francisco, CA 94111-1130 (415) 834-9934
FAX: (415) 834-9935; E-mail: info@silvergiving.org; Main URL: http://www.silvergiving.org

Established in 1997 in CA.
Foundation type: Independent foundation.
Financial data (yr. ended 12/31/12): Assets, $35,108,709 (M); expenditures, $2,013,578; qualifying distributions, $1,819,489; giving activities include $1,612,490 for 20 grants (high: $570,500; low: $4,970).
Purpose and activities: The foundation hopes to improve the lives and prospects of low-income children in the San Francisco Bay Area, CA, by affording them increased and more accessible

educational opportunities. To that end, it aims to identify and contribute to organizations whose work promotes success in school or other academically-oriented enrichment activities, with a special focus on literacy.
Fields of interest: Elementary/secondary education; Education; Children/youth, services; Community development, neighborhood development.
Limitations: Giving primarily in the San Francisco Bay Area, CA. No grants to individuals, or for scholarships or multi-year grants.
Application information:
Initial approach: **See foundation web site for proposal guidelines**
Board meeting date(s): Twice yearly
Officers and Directors:* Philip W. Halperin,* Pres.; Peggy Ann Dow,* Secy. and C.F.O.; Natasha Hoehn, Exec. Dir.
EIN: 943285094

410
Simon Foundation for Education and Housing
(formerly Ronald M. Simon Family Foundation)
620 Newport Center Dr., 12th Fl.
Newport Beach, CA 92660-8012 (949) 270-3644
FAX: (949) 729-8072; E-mail: info@sfeh.org; Main URL: http://www.sfeh.org
Facebook: http://www.facebook.com/pages/Simon-Family-Foundation/128337287226682?v=wall

Established in 2003.
Donors: Gilbert E. Levasseur, Jr.; Ronald M. Simon.
Foundation type: Independent foundation.
Financial data (yr. ended 06/30/13): Assets, $857,920 (M); gifts received, $800,000; expenditures, $1,429,816; qualifying distributions, $1,423,153; giving activities include $316,500 for 14 grants (high: $100,000; low: $1,000), and $236,336 for 117 grants to individuals (high: $6,000; low: $168).
Purpose and activities: Giving primarily for enabling deserving individuals to achieve the American dream of higher education and home ownership.
Fields of interest: Education; Health care; Human services.
Type of support: General/operating support; Scholarships—to individuals.
Limitations: Giving primarily to organizations in CA, Washington, DC, and Santa Fe, NM; scholarship giving primarily in CA, GA and NM.
Application information: Unsolicited requests for funds not accepted. See foundation web site for scholarship guidelines and procedures.
Officer and Directors:* Ronald M. Simon,* Chair.; Kathy Simon Abels; Byron Allumbaugh; Alex Calabrese; **James L. Doti, Ph.D.**; David R. Dukes; James B. Freedman; Gilbert E. LeVasseur, Jr.; **Ronald M. Simon**; Steven H. Simon; Gary Singer, Esq.
EIN: 680524905
Other changes: Marguerite W. Kondracke and Sandy Simon are no longer directors.

411
Simpson PSB Fund
(formerly Simpson Foundation)
21 Orinda Way, Ste. C, #358
Orinda, CA 94563-2534
Contact: Barclay Simpson, Chair.; Sharon Simpson

Established in 1988 in CA.
Donors: Simpson Manufacturing Co., Inc.; Barclay Simpson.
Foundation type: Company-sponsored foundation.
Financial data (yr. ended 12/31/12): Assets, $34,616,409 (M); gifts received, $506,789; expenditures, $16,299,225; qualifying distributions, $15,579,090; giving activities include $15,570,090 for 35 grants (high: $7,015,000; low: $1,000).
Purpose and activities: The foundation supports organizations involved with arts and culture, education, rainforests, and domestic violence.
Fields of interest: Museums (art); Performing arts; Performing arts, orchestras; Arts; Elementary school/education; Libraries (public); Education; Environment, forests; Girls clubs; Family services, domestic violence; Children; Youth; Minorities; Hispanics/Latinos; Girls; Young adults, female; Boys; Crime/abuse victims.
Type of support: Annual campaigns; General/operating support; Scholarship funds.
Limitations: Applications accepted. Giving primarily in CA. No grants to individuals.
Application information: Proposal should be submitted on organization letterhead. Application form not required.
Initial approach: Proposal
Copies of proposal: 1
Deadline(s): None
Officer: Barclay Simpson,* Chair.
EIN: 680168017
Other changes: The grantmaker no longer lists a separate application address.

412
The Skoll Foundation
250 University Ave., Ste. 200
Palo Alto, CA 94301-1738 (650) 331-1031
FAX: (650) 331-1033;
E-mail: info@skollfoundation.org; Main URL: http://www.skollfoundation.org/
Flickr: http://www.flickr.com/photos/44608864@N08/with/5576999744/
Foundation News: http://www.skollfoundation.org/latest-news/
iTunes: http://itunes.apple.com/us/podcast/skoll-world-forum-on-social/id348258086
Jeff Skoll's Giving Pledge Profile: http://glasspockets.org/philanthropy-in-focus/eye-on-the-giving-pledge/profiles/skoll
Twitter: http://www.twitter.com/skollfoundation
YouTube: http://www.youtube.com/user/skollfoundation

Established in 2002 in CA. In 2004, the foundation incorporated the Skoll Community Fund, a supporting organization associated with the Silicon Valley Community Foundation of San Jose, CA, into its operations.
Donor: Jeffrey S. Skoll.
Foundation type: Independent foundation.
Financial data (yr. ended 12/31/12): Assets, $521,009,795 (M); gifts received, $42,139,184; expenditures, $32,767,782; qualifying distributions, $29,346,349; giving activities include $18,473,267 for 23 grants (high: $11,000,000; low: $5,000), $4,927,826 for foundation-administered programs and $673,905 for 3 loans/program-related investments (high: $343,510; low: $75,000).
Purpose and activities: The Skoll Foundation drives large-scale change by investing in, connecting, and celebrating social entrepreneurs and other innovators dedicated to solving the world's most pressing problems.
Fields of interest: Social entrepreneurship.
Type of support: Mission-related investments/loans; General/operating support; Program-related investments/loans.
Limitations: Applications accepted. No support for organizations new or early-stage business plans or ideas, schools and school districts, or programs promoting religious doctrine. No grants to individuals, or for scholarships, endowments, deficit reduction or land acquisition.
Publications: Application guidelines; Annual report; Financial statement; Newsletter.
Application information: New SASE award winners celebrated once each year at the annual Skoll World Forum on Social Entrepreneurship. Application form required.
Initial approach: Online eligibility quiz and application
Deadline(s): Online applications are accepted between Jan. 4 and the deadline of Mar. 1
Board meeting date(s): Annually
Final notification: Application status: July. Award decisions: Nov.
Officers and Directors:* Jeffrey S. Skoll,* Chair.; Sally Osberg, C.E.O. and Pres.; Ben Binswanger, C.A.O.; Richard Fahey, C.O.O.; **Renee Kaplan, Chief Strategy Off.**; Larry Brilliant; James G.B. DeMartini III; Debra L. Dunn; Kirk O. Hanson; Peter Hero; Roger L. Martin.
Number of staff: 33
EIN: 113659133

413
Skoll Global Threats Fund
250 University Ave., Ste. 200
Palo Alto, CA 94301-1738
Main URL: http://www.skollglobalthreats.org/
Blog: http://www.skollglobalthreats.org/blog/
Facebook: http://www.facebook.com/pages/Skoll-Global-Threats-Fund/225493127502399
Twitter: http://twitter.com/SkollGlobal

Established in 2010 in CA.
Foundation type: Independent foundation.
Financial data (yr. ended 12/31/12): Assets, $4,435,867 (M); gifts received, $15,000,000; expenditures, $16,952,099; qualifying distributions, $16,510,478; giving activities include $12,291,110 for 49 grants (high: $5,000,000; low: $3,840).
Purpose and activities: The fund's mission is to confront global threats imperiling humanity by seeking solutions, strengthening alliances, and spurring actions needed to safeguard the future.
Fields of interest: Human services; International affairs; Civil/human rights.
Limitations: Applications not accepted. Giving primarily in CA and Washington, DC.
Application information: Unsolicited requests for funds not accepted.
Officers and Directors:* Jeffrey S. Skoll,* Chair.; Larry Brilliant, M.D., MPH*, Pres.; Annie Maxwell, C.O.O.; James G.B. Demartini III; Sally Osberg.
EIN: 270198398
Other changes: Richard Fahey is no longer Treas.

414
Skywords Family Foundation
c/o Cynthia Rowland
235 Montgomery St., 17th Fl.
San Francisco, CA **94104-2902**

Established in 2005 in CA.
Donor: M. Davis Charitable Lead Trust.

Foundation type: Independent foundation.
Financial data (yr. ended 12/31/12): Assets, $71,380,475 (M); gifts received, $6,248,083; expenditures, $1,509,974; qualifying distributions, $1,123,373; giving activities include $1,123,373 for grants.
Fields of interest: Media, film/video; Education, fund raising/fund distribution; Human services; Foundations (private grantmaking).
Limitations: Applications not accepted. Giving primarily in San Francisco, CA.
Application information: Contributes only to pre-selected organizations.
Officers: Michael Davis, Pres.; Janet Jyll Johnstone, Secy.-Treas.
EIN: 201247525

415
Lon V. Smith Foundation
9440 Santa Monica Blvd., Ste. 300
Beverly Hills, CA 90210-4614

Established in 1952 in CA.
Foundation type: Independent foundation.
Financial data (yr. ended 12/31/12): Assets, $27,552,844 (M); expenditures, $1,955,196; qualifying distributions, $1,773,396; giving activities include $1,620,500 for 30 grants (high: $25,000; low: $2,500).
Purpose and activities: Giving primarily for health organizations and medical research, children, youth and social services, and for family services.
Fields of interest: Health care; Health organizations, association; Medical research, institute; Human services; Children/youth, services; Family services; United Ways and Federated Giving Programs; Blind/visually impaired.
Type of support: General/operating support.
Limitations: Applications not accepted. Giving primarily in southern CA. No grants to individuals.
Application information: Contributes only to pre-selected organizations.
Officers: Stefan A. Kantardjieff, Pres.; Lawrence S. Clark, V.P.; John L. Lahn, V.P.; Alexander Rados, V.P.; Matthew Whelan, V.P.; Millicent Anderson, Secy.-Treas.; **Stephan A. Rados, Secy.**
EIN: 956045384

416
The Stanley Smith Horticultural Trust
2320 Marinship Way, Ste. 150
Sausalito, CA 94965-2830 **(415) 379-5350**
E-mail: tdaniel@calacademy.org; **Main URL: http://www.admintrustllc.com/stanley-smith-horticultural-trust/**

Established in 1970 in CA.
Donor: May Smith†.
Foundation type: Independent foundation.
Financial data (yr. ended 12/31/12): Assets, $15,306,176 (M); expenditures, $926,042; qualifying distributions, $786,961; giving activities include $690,630 for 43 grants (high: $47,600; low: $630).
Purpose and activities: Grants to organizations for education and research in ornamental horticulture, particularly in North and South America. Specific interest is in funding organizations that pursue the following activities: 1) the advancement of research in ornamental horticulture and the publication of the results of such research; 2) assisting in the creation, development, preservation, and maintenance of gardens accessible to the public for educational purposes; 3) promotion of the environmentally responsible introduction, cultivation, and distribution of plants which have ornamental horticultural value; 4) assisting in the publication of books or other works relating to the science of horticulture; and 5) informal and/or formal educational activities which further ornamental horticulture.
Fields of interest: Environment, research; Botanical gardens.
Type of support: General/operating support; Equipment; Program development; Publication; Research.
Limitations: Applications accepted. Giving primarily in North and South America. **No grants to individuals, or for endowment funds or for indirect costs.**
Publications: Application guidelines.
Application information: Application form not required.
Initial approach: **Take eligibility quiz on foundation web site, then proceed with Project Description Form (which can be downloaded from foundation web site) if eligible**
Deadline(s): Jan. 1 to Aug. 15
Board meeting date(s): As required
Final notification: Early Dec.
Trustees: John P. Collins, Jr.; Ruth M. Collins; Thomas F. Daniel; James R. Gibbs; Bruce J. Raabe.
EIN: 946209165
Other changes: The grantmaker now makes its application guidelines available online.

417
Smith-Walker Foundation
1260 Coast Village Cir.
Santa Barbara, CA 93108-2790

Established in 1989 in CA.
Foundation type: Independent foundation.
Financial data (yr. ended 09/30/13): Assets, $3,538,576 (M); expenditures, $236,415; qualifying distributions, $210,420; giving activities include $210,000 for 29 grants (high: $30,000; low: $1,500).
Purpose and activities: Giving primarily to Protestant organizations, for youth services, and for health care.
Fields of interest: Historic preservation/historical societies; Arts; Education; Hospitals (general); Health care; Health organizations, association; Recreation, camps; Children/youth, services; Protestant agencies & churches.
Type of support: General/operating support.
Limitations: Applications not accepted. Giving limited to CA. No grants to individuals.
Application information: Contributes only to pre-selected organizations.
Board meeting date(s): Dec.
Officers: Clarke A. Smith, Pres.; Janet G. Gates, Secy.; Kim S. Smith, Treas.
Trustees: Nathan C. Gates; **Matthew McCall**; Shelly S. Royalty; **Walker Smith III.**
EIN: 330327308
Other changes: Clarke A. Smith has replaced Walker Smith, Jr. as Pres. Janet G. Gates has replaced Jean S. Goodrich as Secy.
Joan C. Smith is no longer V.P. and Treas. Kim Smith is now Treas.

418
Y & H Soda Foundation
1635 School St.
Moraga, CA 94556-1150 (925) 631-1133
Contact: Kappy Dye, C.F.O. and Grants Mgr.
FAX: (925) 631-0248; Information for grant inquiries: Program-Assistant@yhsodafoundation.org; Main URL: http://www.yhsodafoundation.org

Established in 1964.
Donors: Y. Charles Soda Trust; Y. Charles Soda†; Helen C. Soda†.
Foundation type: Independent foundation.
Financial data (yr. ended 12/31/12): Assets, $133,287,725 (M); expenditures, $8,322,274; qualifying distributions, $5,878,533; giving activities include $4,812,125 for 180 grants (high: $200,000; low: $250).
Purpose and activities: The foundation focuses grantmaking on four program areas: 1) Family Economic Success; 2) Community Organizing; 3) Immigration Legal Services; and 4) Urban Catholic Education.
Fields of interest: Employment, training; Community/economic development, public policy; Economic development; Community/economic development; Financial services; Catholic agencies & churches; Immigrants/refugees; Economically disadvantaged.
Type of support: Management development/capacity building; General/operating support; Continuing support; Program development; Technical assistance; Program evaluation.
Limitations: Giving limited to Alameda and Contra Costa Counties, CA. No support for private foundations, or for partisan political activities. No grants to individuals, or for annual fundraising campaigns, production of film/video or other media, faculty chairs, or for general fundraisers, benefits or events.
Application information: Program Asst. will steer potential applicants to appropriate Program Officer for application guidance.
Initial approach: After ascertaining that program/organization is a geographic and programmatic fit, contact Prog. Asst. by e-mail or telephone to initiate a discussion regarding potential funding.
Board meeting date(s): 2nd Weds. of each month
Officers and Directors:* Rosemary Soda,* Chair.; Robert Uyeki, C.E.O.; Alfred Dossa,* V.P. and Secy.; Alan Holloway,* V.P.; Judith Murphy,* V.P.; Kappy Dye, C.F.O. and Grants Mgr.; James Dye,* Treas.; **Bob Uyeki, Exec. Dir.**
Number of staff: 4 full-time professional; 1 part-time support.
EIN: 941611668

419
Solano Community Foundation
470 Chadbourne Rd., Ste. D
Fairfield, CA 94534 (707) 399-3846
***Contact:* Constance Harris, Acting C.E.O.**
FAX: (707) 399-3849; E-mail: ceo@solanocf.org; Main URL: http://www.solanocf.org
Facebook: https://www.facebook.com/pages/Solano-Community-Foundation/170743039679397

Established in 2000 in CA.
Foundation type: Community foundation.
Financial data (yr. ended 12/31/12): Assets, $7,959,393 (M); gifts received, $384,119; expenditures, $576,201; giving activities include $264,698 for 24+ grants (high: $20,085).

Purpose and activities: The Solano Community Foundation is dedicated to strengthening the local community both now and for future generations. The foundation is a vehicle for private donors to make a lasting contribution to the community. The Solano Community Foundation fulfills its mission by: 1) encouraging private giving for public good; 2) building and maintaining permanent endowments to respond to changing community needs; 3) providing flexible tax-exempt vehicles for donors with varied charitable interests and abilities to give; 4) serving as a catalyst and resource to effectively respond to community problems; and 5) strengthening the nonprofit sector through capacity-building trainings, workshops, and research tools for donor identification.
Fields of interest: Arts; Elementary/secondary education; Higher education; Environment; Animals/wildlife; Health care, support services; Housing/shelter, temporary shelter; Youth development, adult & child programs; Youth development, intergenerational programs; Human services; Children/youth, services; Children, foster care; Human services; Community/economic development; Children/youth; Youth; Aging; Military/veterans; Economically disadvantaged.
Type of support: General/operating support; Continuing support; Management development/capacity building; Program development; Scholarship funds.
Limitations: Applications accepted. Giving primarily in Solano County, CA. No grants to individuals (except for scholarships), or for capital campaigns, seed money or start up money for organizations applying for tax exempt status.
Publications: Application guidelines; Financial statement; Grants list; Informational brochure.
Application information: The foundation is not currently accepting unsolicited grant proposals. However, grant funds are available from certain program funds held on a recurring basis. For more information about programs and grant schedules, visit website. Application form required.
Initial approach: Letters of Inquiry (LOI) no longer than one page
Copies of proposal: 1
Deadline(s): No deadlines for general requests. Deadlines for RFP's from SCF Programs are listed on foundation website
Board meeting date(s): Each month, except July and Dec.
Officers and Directors:* Teresa Fitzgerald,* Chair.; Sandra Smith,* Vice-Chair.; **Constance Harris,* Acting C.E.O.**; **Tim Kubli,* Secy.-Treas.**; Becky Gardiner; Matt Lucas; Marilyn Manfredi; Gary Passama; **Mark Sievers**; Thomas Snyder, M.D.
Number of staff: 1 full-time professional; 2 part-time support.
EIN: 680354961
Other changes: Teresa Fitzgerald has replaced Mark Sievers as Chair. Tim Kubli has replaced Teresa Fitzgerald as Secy.-Treas.
Tim Kubli and Margaret Payne are no longer directors.

420
Sonora Area Foundation
362 S. Stewart St.
Sonora, CA 95370 (209) 533-2596
Contact: Lin Freer, Prog. Mgr.; Ed Wyllie, Exec. Dir.
FAX: (209) 533-2412;
E-mail: edwyllie@sonora-area.org; Grant application e-mail: leaf@sonara-area.org; Main URL: http://www.sonora-area.org
E-Newsletter: http://www.sonora-area.org/newsletters.html
Established in 1989 in CA.
Foundation type: Community foundation.
Financial data (yr. ended 12/31/12): Assets, $44,076,675 (M); gifts received, $1,872,152; expenditures, $2,640,275; giving activities include $1,829,528 for 51+ grants (high: $487,797), and $178,603 for 162 grants to individuals.
Purpose and activities: The foundation assists donors, makes grants, and provides community leadership. Primary areas of interest include human services, education, arts, culture and humanities, health, public and society benefit, and environment and animals.
Fields of interest: Visual arts; Performing arts; Performing arts, music; Humanities; Arts; Education, early childhood education; Child development, education; Elementary school/education; Libraries/library science; Education; Environment; Animal welfare; Hospitals (general); Health care; Substance abuse, services; Mental health/crisis services; Health organizations, association; Alcoholism; Food services; Recreation; Children/youth, services; Child development, services; Family services; Residential/custodial care, hospices; Aging, centers/services; Women, centers/services; Human services; Community/economic development; Voluntarism promotion; Children/youth; Aging; Disabilities, people with; Women; Economically disadvantaged; Homeless.
Type of support: General/operating support; Continuing support; Management development/capacity building; Capital campaigns; Building/renovation; Equipment; Emergency funds; Program development; Conferences/seminars; Publication; Seed money; Curriculum development; Scholarship funds; Technical assistance; Consulting services; Program evaluation; Grants to individuals; Scholarships—to individuals; Matching/challenge support.
Limitations: Applications accepted. Giving limited to Tuolumne County, CA. No support for sectarian purposes or private foundations. No grants for annual campaigns, endowment funds, or debt retirement.
Publications: Application guidelines; Annual report; Biennial report; Financial statement; Grants list; Informational brochure; Informational brochure (including application guidelines); Newsletter; Occasional report.
Application information: Visit foundation web site for application guidelines. Application form not required.
Initial approach: Mail, e-mail, or fax letter of inquiry (2-page maximum)
Copies of proposal: 1
Deadline(s): Late Jan., Mar., May, July, Sept. and Nov.
Board meeting date(s): 4th Tues. of Feb., Apr., June, Aug., Oct. and Dec.
Final notification: 2 months
Officers and Directors:* Jim Johnson,* Pres.; Roger Francis,* V.P.; Clark Segerstrom,* Secy.; Bob Ozbirn,* Treas.; Ed Wyllie, Exec. Dir.; Gary Dambacher; Carey Haughy; Pete Kerns; William Polley; Tracy A. Russell.
Number of staff: 3 full-time professional.
EIN: 931023051
Other changes: At the close of 2012, the grantmaker paid grants of $2,008,131, a 133.8% increase over the 2011 disbursements, $858,808.

421
William Soroka Charitable Trust
La Jolla, CA

The trust terminated in 2013.

422
The Special Hope Foundation
2225 E. Bayshore Rd., Ste. 200
Palo Alto, CA 94303-3220 (650) 320-1715
Contact: E. Lynne O'Hara, Pres.
FAX: (650) 320-1716;
E-mail: proposals@specialhope.org; **Additional e-mail: info@specialhope.org**; Main URL: http://www.specialhope.org
Facebook: https://www.facebook.com/pages/The-Special-Hope-Foundation/146990365339829?v=wall
Twitter: https://twitter.com/specialhope
Established in 2002 in CA.
Donor: Elena Lynne O'Hara.
Foundation type: Independent foundation.
Financial data (yr. ended 06/30/13): Assets, $14,152,435 (M); expenditures, $780,663; qualifying distributions, $737,688; giving activities include $643,290 for 14 grants (high: $100,000; low: $350).
Purpose and activities: The foundation supports the causes of the physically, emotionally, and developmentally disabled. It welcomes the opportunity to fund innovative projects that challenge the prevailing attitudes towards these special people.
Fields of interest: Health care; Developmentally disabled, centers & services; Adults; Disabilities, people with.
Type of support: General/operating support; Continuing support; Income development; Management development/capacity building; Equipment; Program development; Conferences/seminars; Film/video/radio; Seed money; Curriculum development; Scholarship funds; Research; Program evaluation; Matching/challenge support.
Limitations: Applications accepted. Giving on a national basis. **No support for political campaigns, specific therapies that are provided outside of a formal healthcare setting, i.e. physical fitness and/or nutritional programs ("healthy lifestyle programs"), projects that do not address healthcare delivery, or for organizations or programs that are based and/or provide services to populations outside the U.S. No grants to individuals and/or equipment for individuals, or for endowments, debt reduction, administrative expenses exceeding 20% of the total funding request, or for occupational, physical, and speech therapies, or equestrian therapy.**
Publications: Application guidelines; Program policy statement (including application guidelines).
Application information: Formal grant proposals are by invitation only. The foundation considers international interests only if there is a U.S.-based 501(c)(3) affiliation. Application form required.
Initial approach: Complete pre-application questionnaire on foundation web site
Deadline(s): 4 months prior to quarterly board meeting
Final notification: Per invitation
Officers and Directors:* E. Lynne O'Hara,* Pres.; John W. O'Hara,* V.P.; Margaret Motamed,* Secy.; Jackie Donaho,* Treas.; Lucy Crain; Carrie Jones.
Number of staff: 1 part-time professional.
EIN: 731644863

423

Specialty Foundation
501 Santa Monica Blvd., Ste. 703
Santa Monica, CA **90401-2443 (310) 899-9700**
E-mail: info@specialtyfamilyfoundation.org; Main URL: http://www.specialtyfamilyfoundation.org

Established in 2006 in CA.
Foundation type: Independent foundation.
Financial data (yr. ended 12/31/11): Assets, $54,391,008 (M); gifts received, $99; expenditures, $4,926,458; qualifying distributions, $4,278,631; giving activities include $3,471,491 for 78 grants (high: $1,575,000; low: $180).
Purpose and activities: The foundation seeks to alleviate the conditions that lead to persistent poverty. Primary program areas include expanding educational opportunities in low-income communities, and supporting long-term residential treatment for people struggling with substance abuse and alcoholism. More specifically, the foundation supports inner-city Catholic education, and long-term residential treatment for women with children.
Fields of interest: Elementary/secondary education; Higher education; Education; Catholic agencies & churches.
Type of support: Program-related investments/loans.
Limitations: Applications not accepted. Giving primarily in the Los Angeles metro area, CA. No grants to individuals.
Application information: Contributes only to pre-selected organizations.
Officers and Directors:* Deborah Ann Estes,* Chair.; Joan C. Peter,* V.P.; James B. Peter, Jr.,* Secy.; Arthur L. Peter,* Treas.; Joe Womac, Exec. Dir.; Karen Marie Cane; Christine Mary Gard; Joan Carol Noneman.
EIN: 204896662

424

The W. L. S. Spencer Foundation
1660 Bush St., Ste. 300
San Francisco, CA 94109-5308 **(415) 561-6540**
Contact: **Emily Schroeder, Grants Mgr.**
FAX: (415) 561-5477;
E-mail: eschroeder@pfs-llc.net; Main URL: http://www.pfs-llc.net/spencer/spencer.html

Established in 1994 in DE.
Foundation type: Independent foundation.
Financial data (yr. ended 12/31/12): Assets, $7,941,438 (M); gifts received, $317,065; expenditures, $908,984; qualifying distributions, $878,940; giving activities include $787,400 for 35 grants (high: $100,000; low: $500).
Purpose and activities: The foundation funds educational activities, publications, and outreach associated with innovative art and/or contemporary art exhibitions, especially those focusing on contemporary Asian Art. The foundation has a particular interest in projects that encourage knowledge about art and culture, foster international understanding, and are supported by academic scholarship. Funding also for programs that are innovative and that motivate children to stay in school, do well academically, and continue their education beyond high school (to college or other higher education opportunities). In this area, the foundation may continue to fund programs that it believes in, and may fund replication of a successful program in a new site. The foundation tends to fund programs that are national or regional in nature, but which have a chapter in San Francisco, CA. The foundation prefers specific initiatives that conform with this mission, and enjoys the leverage that arises from seed grants, challenge grants, and matching grants.
Fields of interest: Arts; Education.
International interests: Asia.
Type of support: Program development; Seed money; Matching/challenge support.
Limitations: Applications accepted. Giving on a worldwide basis through intermediaries based in the United States. **No support for individual schools. No grants to individuals, or for films, events, endowments or ongoing operational expenses.**
Publications: Application guidelines; Annual report (including application guidelines); Grants list; Program policy statement.
Application information: The foundation will ONLY consider grant requests for compelling needs within previously funded organizations. Unsolicited full proposals are accepted by invitation only. Application form not required.
Initial approach: **Letter of Intent via foundation web site (for new applicants); renewing applicants should visit the Renewal Procedures page on the foundation's web site**
Copies of proposal: 2
Deadline(s): None
Board meeting date(s): Varies
Final notification: Up to 1 month from receipt of application
Directors: Paul Peppis; Lela Wadsworth; Libby Wadsworth.
EIN: 133799186

425

Stanislaus Community Foundation
1029 16th St.
Modesto, CA 95354 (209) 576-1608
Contact: **Marion Kaanon, C.E.O.**; **For grants: Amanda Hughes, Prog. Off.**
FAX: (209) 576-1609;
E-mail: mkaanon@stanislauscf.org; **Grant inquiry e-mail: ahughes@stanislauscf.org**; Main URL: http://www.StanislausCF.org

Established in 2001 in CA.
Foundation type: Community foundation.
Financial data (yr. ended 12/31/12): Assets, $12,947,136 (M); gifts received, $1,555,742; expenditures, $1,187,818; giving activities include $900,599 for 22+ grants (high: $129,506), and $12,000 for 17 grants to individuals.
Purpose and activities: The foundation seeks to mobilize resources and guide their use to promote a vibrant and sustainable community. In service to the people of the local community, the foundation partners with organizations and donors to create new opportunities while acting as a catalyst for improvement and involvement.
Fields of interest: Arts; Education; Environment; Health care; Human services; Children/youth; Children; Youth.
Type of support: Endowments; Program development; Seed money; Scholarships—to individuals.
Limitations: Applications accepted. Giving primarily in Stanislaus County, CA. No support for religious activities. No grants for individuals (except for scholarships), debt reduction, fundraising events.
Publications: Annual report; Informational brochure; Newsletter.
Application information: Visit foundation web site for application form. Application form required.
Initial approach: Contact foundation
Deadline(s): Aug. 2
Officers and Board Members:* Marian Kaanon,* C.E.O.; Mike Gianelli,* Pres.; Jeff Grover,* V.P.; Craig C. Lewis,* Secy.; John Bellizzi, C.F.O.; Randy Clark, C.F.O.; **Doris Daniel-Brima, Cont.**; Melanie Chiesa; Jeff Coleman; Lynn Dickerson; Joe Duran; John Evans; Bill Jackson; Daryn Kumar; Janine McClanahan.
Number of staff: 3 full-time professional.
EIN: 680483054
Other changes: Connie Bird, Jeff Burda, Denise Costa, J.D. Grothe, Eric Johnston, and Bette Belle Smith are no longer board members.

426

The Donald T. Sterling Charitable Foundation
9441 Wilshire Blvd.
Beverly Hills, CA 90212-2808 (310) 278-8010

Established in 2007 in CA.
Donor: Donald T. Sterling.
Foundation type: Independent foundation.
Financial data (yr. ended 12/31/12): Assets, $49,506 (M); gifts received, $330,000; expenditures, $380,585; qualifying distributions, $370,585; giving activities include $370,500 for 41 grants (high: $10,000; low: $500).
Purpose and activities: The foundation supports nonprofit organizations and events involved with issues of poverty, homelessness, education and literacy. Special emphasis is directed to programs benefiting at-risk children and families located in greater Los Angeles and southern California.
Fields of interest: Education; Health care; Homeless, human services.
Type of support: General/operating support.
Limitations: Applications accepted. Giving primarily in Los Angeles, CA.
Application information: Organizations are limited to one request per calendar year. Application form required.
Initial approach: Letter
Deadline(s): Varies
Officers: Donald T. Sterling, Pres.; Rochelle H. Sterling, V.P.; Douglas L. Walton, Secy.; Darren Schield, C.F.O.
EIN: 208731101

427

The Biz & Livia Stone Foundation
1000 4th St., Ste. 375
San Rafael, CA 94901-3148

Established in 2011 in CA.
Donors: Laura Beck; Biz Stone; Christopher Stone; Livia Stone; Ron Conway; Owlbear Industries Inc.
Foundation type: Independent foundation.
Financial data (yr. ended 12/31/12): Assets, $124,418 (M); gifts received, $275,000; expenditures, $209,097; qualifying distributions, $195,727; giving activities include $172,603 for 7 grants (high: $115,000; low: $1,870).
Purpose and activities: To support education and conservation efforts in CA through scholarships, grants and original programs.
Fields of interest: Education; Animals/wildlife; Philanthropy/voluntarism.
Limitations: Applications not accepted. Giving primarily in CA.
Application information: Unsolicited requests for funds not accepted.
Officers: Christopher Stone, Pres.; Livia Stone, Secy.
EIN: 273744595

Other changes: The grantmaker no longer lists a URL address.

428
The Streisand Foundation

1327 Ocean Ave., Ste. H
Santa Monica, CA **90401-1008**
Contact: Margery Tabankin, Exec. Dir.
FAX: (310) 314-8396; Main URL: http://www.barbrastreisand.com/us/streisand-foundation

Established in 1986 in NY.
Donors: Barbra Streisand; The Lincy Foundation.
Foundation type: Independent foundation.
Financial data (yr. ended 12/31/12): Assets, $7,525,059 (M); gifts received, $258,525; expenditures, $888,576; qualifying distributions, $676,606; giving activities include $666,400 for 88 grants (high: $62,500; low: $500).
Purpose and activities: Giving primarily for environmental issues, women's issues, including reproductive choice and health-related concerns, civil liberties and democratic values, civil rights and race relations, AIDS research, advocacy, service and litigation, and in Los Angeles, CA only: children and youth-related issues with a focus on the economically disadvantaged.
Fields of interest: Arts; Education; Environment; Medical research; Children/youth, services; Civil rights, voter education; Civil liberties, advocacy; Civil/human rights; Women.
Type of support: General/operating support; Continuing support; Program development.
Limitations: Applications not accepted. Giving to nationally-based groups; some local giving in Los Angeles, CA for disadvantaged children and youth. No support for start-up organizations or international organizations. No grants to individuals, or for capital campaigns, endowments, documentaries or audio-visual programming, or publication of books or magazines.
Application information: Unsolicited requests for funds not accepted.
Board meeting date(s): Varies
Officer and Trustees:* Margery Tabankin,* Exec. Dir.; Richard Baskin; Marilyn Bergman; Jason Gould; Barry Hirsh; Lester Knispel; Barbra Streisand.
Number of staff: 1 part-time professional; 1 full-time support.
EIN: 132620702
Other changes: The grantmaker no longer publishes application guidelines.

429
Stuart Foundation

(also known as Elbridge Stuart Foundation)
500 Washington St., 8th Fl.
San Francisco, CA 94111-4735 (415) 393-1551
***Contact:* Carol Ting, C.O.O.; Brad Sink, Cont.**
FAX: (415) 393-1552;
E-mail: rsotelo@stuartfoundation.org; Main URL: http://www.stuartfoundation.org
Grantee Perception Report: http://www.stuartfoundation.org/Files/Stuart%20Foundation%20GPR%20-%20Spring%202006%20-%20For%20Web.pdf
Grants Database: http://www.stuartfoundation.org/GrantSearch
Knowledge Center: http://www.stuartfoundation.org/NewsAndReports
Report on Stuart Foundation Child Welfare Program: http://www.stuartfoundation.org/Files/CEP_Stuart_CaseStudy.pdf

Elbridge Stuart Foundation created in 1937 in CA, Elbridge and Mary Stuart Foundation in 1941 in CA, and Mary Horner Stuart Foundation in 1941 in WA; in 1995 and 1996, the two smaller foundations were merged into the Elbridge Stuart Foundation, DBA Stuart Foundation.
Donors: Elbridge A. Stuart†; Elbridge H. Stuart†; Mary H. Stuart†.
Foundation type: Independent foundation.
Financial data (yr. ended 12/31/12): Assets, $461,733,374 (M); gifts received, $149,713; expenditures, $32,070,974; qualifying distributions, $25,127,370; giving activities include $20,096,321 for 442 grants (high: $425,000; low: $100), and $360,200 for 4 foundation-administered programs.
Purpose and activities: The foundation is dedicated to supporting the education and development of children and youth in California and Washington with a goal of them becoming become self-sustaining, responsible, and contributing members of their communities. The foundation serves as a partner and convener that helps gather the resources, thought, and energy needed to create and sustain change. It is committed to creating powerful partnerships with those who work toward sustainable, scalable, and system-wide change for all young people, especially those who are most in need The foundation looks for partners who share the same mission and values. Many of the foundation's relationships are long-term, with some spanning over a decade of successful collaboration. Its partners share the following characteristics: They support and engage in continuous learning and improvement. Demonstrate, succeed, spread, and engage in practice that informs policy. Recognize the needs of vulnerable youth, and a possess commitment to bolster their education and development. Find, work with, and support the expert implementers and change agents. Build a culture of collaboration; work with others to create a movement. Invest in irresistible information to drive evidence-based decision making. Work on public policy with an incisive role in contributing to statewide system improvement.
Fields of interest: Education, research; Education, public policy; Education, reform; Education, public education; Elementary/secondary school reform; Education; Children/youth, services; Public policy, research; Children/youth.
Type of support: Conferences/seminars; Continuing support; Employee matching gifts; General/operating support; Management development/capacity building; Program development; Program evaluation; Publication; Research; Technical assistance.
Limitations: Applications accepted. Giving primarily in CA and WA. No support for political activities. No grants to individuals, for capital campaigns, or generally for endowments, building funds, or annual campaigns, capital or operating support to sustain existing service capacity.
Application information: Following review of letter of inquiry, program staff will contact you if your request aligns with the foundation's strategy and additional information and/or a full proposal will be invited. At this point, staff will share specific proposal guidelines, provide a list of required documents, and assign a due date for submittal. Please note that it can take an additional four to eight months to conduct the necessary due diligence (which may include but is not limited to a site visit, follow-up meetings, reference checks and program and financial assessment) to bring funding recommendations to the board of directors. During the review process, staff will be in touch to keep you informed of the status of your submittal. Application form required.
Initial approach: Letter of inquiry (can be downloaded from web site and e-mailed)
Copies of proposal: 1
Deadline(s): None
Board meeting date(s): Spring, Summer and Fall
Final notification: Within 60 days for letters of inquiry
Officers and Directors:* Dwight L. Stuart, Jr.,* Chair.; Elbridge H. Stuart III,* Vice.-Chair. and Treas.; Stuart E. Lucas,* Vice-Chair.; **Carol Ting, C.O.O.; Jonathan Raymond, Pres.**; David S. Barlow, C.F.O.; Brad S. Sink, Cont.; Davis Campbell.
Number of staff: 21 full-time professional.
EIN: 200882784
Other changes: Jonathan Raymond has replaced Christy Pichel as Pres. Carol Ting has replaced Rhonnel Sotelo as C.O.O.

430
The Morris Stulsaft Foundation

1660 Bush St., Ste. 300
San Francisco, CA 94109-5308 (415) 561-6540
***Contact:* Emily Schroeder, Grants Mgr.**
FAX: (415) 561-6477;
E-mail: eschroeder@pfs-llc.net; Main URL: http://www.stulsaft.org
Grants List: http://stulsaft.org/grants2011-2012.php

Incorporated in 1953 in CA; sole beneficiary of feeder trust created in 1965.
Donor: The Morris Stulsaft Testamentary Trust.
Foundation type: Independent foundation.
Financial data (yr. ended 06/30/13): Assets, $633,599 (M); gifts received, $1,502,500; expenditures, $1,361,321; qualifying distributions, $1,306,989; giving activities include $1,133,369 for 66 grants (high: $100,000; low: $1,000).
Purpose and activities: The foundation is dedicated to the well-being of children and youth (ages 0-22) through financial support of nonprofit organizations serving foster and homeless youth, and youth with disabilities; providing child care to low-income families and training to childcare providers; and educational enrichment and mentoring to disadvantaged youth. More strategically, the foundation makes grants in four particular areas: 1) Support Services for Vulnerable Children and Youth - funds for services that are provided to children and youth in shelters or transitional housing, or in foster care, that will help them to obtain a good education and to develop healthy relationships with others. The foundation looks for programs that provide safe, supportive and tolerant physical and emotional environments; 2) Preparing Youth for Independent Futures - funds to programs that seek to develop the individual potential in young people ages 13-22, by exposing them to meaningful experiences in the workplace, whether as an intern, a volunteer, or by shadowing someone in a particular job. The foundation funds programs that help participants to determine what work they enjoy doing, are best suited for, and how to pursue it. Programs should also seek to teach soft skills behaviors that help youth to get and keep a job, thereby helping them to ensure independent futures; 3) Setting the Stage for Education - support for pre-schools that predominately service children from low-income backgrounds and that demonstrate their commitment to quality early childhood development through thoughtful curriculum, excellent facilities, and qualified staff who are supported with professional development opportunities. Grants may be made for general support, scholarships, professional development, and occasionally for upgrading facilities; and 4)

Inspiring Youth through Participation in the Arts - support for programs that go beyond the normal classroom curriculum and that offer opportunities for young people to actively participate in the arts (drawing, painting, sculpting, acting, singing, dancing), and that may also expose students to art at museums, theaters, etc. The foundation is most interested in programs that cooperate closely with public schools and are aligned with the California State Board of Education Standards for Visual and Performing Arts.
Fields of interest: Arts; Education; Employment; Human services; Children/youth, services; Children, foster care; Children, day care; Children/youth; Children.
Type of support: General/operating support; Continuing support; Program development; Matching/challenge support.
Limitations: Applications accepted. **Giving limited to the San Francisco Bay Area, CA: Alameda, west Contra Costa, Marin, San Francisco, and northern San Mateo (extending south to Redwood City).** No support for sectarian religious projects or ongoing support for private schools. No grants to individuals, or for emergency funding, endowments, annual campaigns, workshops, conferences, or deficit funding.
Publications: Application guidelines; Financial statement; Grants list; Occasional report.
Application information: Application form not required.
Initial approach: **Use online application process on foundation web site**
Board meeting date(s): Jan., Mar., May, July, and Sept.
Officers and Directors:* Adele K. Corvin,* Pres.; Isadore Pivnick,* V.P.; Dana A. Corvin, Secy.; Mary Gregory, Exec. Dir.; Stuart Corvin; William D. Glenn; Pat Loomes.
Number of staff: None.
EIN: 946064379

431
The Keith and Judy Swayne Family Foundation
668 N. Coast Hwy., PMB #251
Laguna Beach, CA 92651-1513
Grants List: http://swaynefoundation.org/?page_id=70
Keith and Judy Swayne Family Foundation's Philanthropy Promise: http://www.ncrp.org/philanthropys-promise/who

Established in 2005 in CA.
Donors: Keith D. Swayne; Judy K. Swayne.
Foundation type: Independent foundation.
Financial data (yr. ended 12/31/12): Assets, $4,779,634 (M); gifts received, $1,000,000; expenditures, $314,893; qualifying distributions, $268,972; giving activities include $236,000 for 29 grants (high: $18,000; low: $500).
Purpose and activities: Giving primarily for social justice, youth development, education, environmental practices, and also support the health and well-being of women in need.
Fields of interest: Arts; Education; Environmental education; Youth, services; Women.
Limitations: Applications accepted. Giving primarily in CA and HI. No grants to individuals.
Application information:
Initial approach: **Letter of inquiry**
Deadline(s): **Deadline for letter of inquiry is May 25**
Officers and Directors:* Anne Swayne Keir,* Pres.; **Keith D. Swayne,* Secy.-Treas.; Gretchen Weisenburger Carillo**; Robert W. Wright.
EIN: 201577885
Other changes: The grantmaker no longer lists a URL address.
Keith D. Swayne is now Secy.-Treas.

432
The Haeyoung and Kevin Tang Foundation, Inc.
4747 Executive Dr., Ste. 510
San Diego, CA **92121-3100**

Established in 2006 in CA.
Donors: Haeyoung K. Tang; Kevin C. Tang.
Foundation type: Independent foundation.
Financial data (yr. ended 12/31/12): Assets, $25,283,285 (M); gifts received, $3,045,759; expenditures, $1,313,118; qualifying distributions, $1,236,250; giving activities include $1,236,250 for grants.
Fields of interest: Higher education; Environment; Hospitals (specialty); AIDS research.
Limitations: Applications not accepted. Giving primarily in CA and NY. No grants to individuals.
Application information: Unsolicited requests for funds not accepted.
Officers: Haeyoung K. Tang, Chair. and Secy.; Kevin C. Tang, Pres. and Treas.
EIN: 205932781

433
S. Mark Taper Foundation
Comerica Bank Bldg.
12011 San Vicente Blvd., Ste. 400
Los Angeles, CA 90049-4946 (310) 476-5413
Contact: Adrienne Wittenberg, Grants Dir.
FAX: (310) 471-4993;
E-mail: questions@smtfoundation.org; Main URL: http://www.smtfoundation.org/

Incorporated in 1989 in CA.
Donor: S. Mark Taper†.
Foundation type: Independent foundation.
Financial data (yr. ended 12/31/12): Assets, $106,172,433 (M); expenditures, $6,046,903; qualifying distributions, $5,170,762; giving activities include $4,494,550 for 81 grants (high: $250,000; low: $10,000).
Purpose and activities: Giving primarily to children and youth, health care, social services, employment, education, and the environment.
Fields of interest: Arts; Education; Environment; Health care; Crime/violence prevention; Employment; Housing/shelter, development; Human services; Children/youth, services; Family services; Civil liberties, reproductive rights; Government/public administration; Children/youth; Youth; Adults; Aging; Young adults; Disabilities, people with; Blind/visually impaired; Deaf/hearing impaired; Mentally disabled; Asians/Pacific Islanders; Women; Offenders/ex-offenders; AIDS, people with; Economically disadvantaged; Homeless.
Type of support: General/operating support; Annual campaigns; Capital campaigns; Building/renovation; Equipment; Emergency funds; Program development; Conferences/seminars; Publication; Seed money; Curriculum development; Scholarship funds; Research; Program-related investments/loans; Matching/challenge support.
Limitations: Applications accepted. Giving primarily in Los Angeles County, CA. No support for religious organizations or specific diseases. No grants to individuals.
Publications: Application guidelines.
Application information: See foundation web site for specific LOI instructions for general operating support and program/project support. Do not include brochures, annual reports, audited financial statements, Forms 990, and DVDs with LOIs. Application form required.
Initial approach: Letter of inquiry (3 pages maximum, not including attachments)
Copies of proposal: 1
Deadline(s): Dec. 1 through the end of Feb.
Board meeting date(s): As required
***Final notification:* 6-9 months**
Officers and Director:* Janice Taper Lazarof,* Pres.; Cynthia Taper Bolker, V.P.; Amelia Taper Stabler, Secy.; Deborah Taper Ringel, Treas.; Roy Weitz, C.F.O.
Number of staff: 3 full-time professional; 2 full-time support.
EIN: 954245076

434
The Thiel Foundation
(formerly Shire Philanthropic Foundation)
1 Letterman Dr., Bldg. C, Ste. 400
San Francisco, CA 94129-1495
Main URL: http://www.thielfoundation.org

Established in 2005 in CA.
Donor: Peter Thiel.
Foundation type: Independent foundation.
Financial data (yr. ended 12/31/12): Assets, $24,783,613 (M); gifts received, $35,106,000; expenditures, $12,316,484; qualifying distributions, $11,012,416; giving activities include $7,012,549 for 41 grants (high: $760,000; low: $400), and $1,890,861 for 51 grants to individuals (high: $200,000; low: $4,167).
Purpose and activities: The foundation defends and promotes freedom in all its dimensions by supporting innovative scientific research and new technologies that empower people to improve their lives, by championing organizations and individuals who expose human rights abuses and authoritarianism, and by encouraging the exploration of new ideas and new spaces where freedom can flourish.
Fields of interest: Education; Medical research; Human services.
Limitations: Applications not accepted. Giving primarily in the U.S., with some emphasis on CA; some giving internationally, with some emphasis on France. No grants to individuals, except for fellowships.
Application information: Unsolicited requests for funds not accepted. Refer to foundation web site for fellowship application information.
Officers: Robert Hamerton-Kelly, Chair.; Jonathan Cain, Pres.; Amber Fowler, Secy.; James O'Neill, Treas.
Directors: Lynne Fishburne, Exec. Dir.; Peter Thiel.
EIN: 203846597
Other changes: At the close of 2012, the fair market value of the grantmaker's assets was $24,783,613, a 1013.6% increase over the 2011 value, $2,225,531. For the same period, the grantmaker paid grants of $8,903,410, a 111.6% increase over the 2011 disbursements, $4,207,390.

435

The Thomson Family Foundation
P.O. Box 26150
San Francisco, CA **94126-6150 (415) 684-1903**
E-mail: **megan@tffhome.org**; Main URL: http://www.tffhome.org/
Facebook: https://www.facebook.com/pages/Thomson-Family-Foundation/113479115335566

Established in 2007 in CA and TX.
Donors: Clifford L. Thomson; Bonnie M. Thomson.
Foundation type: Independent foundation.
Financial data (yr. ended 12/31/12): Assets, $2,895,939 (M); expenditures, $678,589; qualifying distributions, $673,113; giving activities include $536,904 for 27 grants (high: $200,000; low: $904).
Purpose and activities: Giving to foster opportunities for families to increase their economic success and security by supporting community-based initiatives that improve access to education and asset-building resources and services.
Fields of interest: YM/YWCAs & YM/YWHAs; Family services; Community/economic development.
Type of support: General/operating support.
Limitations: Applications not accepted. Giving primarily in CA and TX. No grants to individuals.
Application information: Unsolicited requests for funds not accepted.
Officers: Clifford L. Thomson, Pres.; C. Jay Thomson, V.P.; Megan McTiernan, Exec. Dir.
Directors: Bonnie M. Thomson; Shannon M. Thomson.
EIN: 208132099

436

The William Hall and Ruth Rathell Tippett Foundation
2604 B El Camino Real, Ste. 356
Carlsbad, CA **92008 (760) 310-3105**
Contact: **Robbin C. Powell, Chief Administrative Officer**
Email for Robbin C. Powell: **powell.robbin@att.net**

Established in 2000 in CA.
Foundation type: Independent foundation.
Financial data (yr. ended 12/31/12): Assets, $4,379,188 (M); expenditures, $247,268; qualifying distributions, $220,000; giving activities include $220,000 for 15 grants (high: $100,000; low: $5,000).
Purpose and activities: Giving primarily for health care and research into the cause and cure of illnesses affecting older people; education, particularly musical arts, for younger people; and animal welfare.
Fields of interest: Performing arts, theater; Arts; Education; Animal welfare; Human services; Youth, services.
Limitations: Applications accepted. Giving primarily in San Diego, CA. No support for athletic organizations, political organizations or to national organizations and/or their local chapters. No grants to individuals, directly; no loans.
Application information: Application form required.
Initial approach: Proposal
Deadline(s): Mar. 15 and Oct. 15
Board meeting date(s): Twice per year
Officers and Trustees:* Barbara Zobell,* Pres.; **Karen Zobell,* V.P.**; Mildred V. Basden,* Secy. and C.F.O.; **Robbin C. Powell, Chief Administrative Officer**.
EIN: 330903811
Other changes: Karen Zobell is now V.P.

437

Tomkat Charitable Trust
1 Maritime Plz., 11th Fl.
San Francisco, CA 94111-3519 (415) 956-9588
GiveSmart: http://www.givesmart.org/Stories/Donors/Tom-Steyer
Tom Steyer and Kathryn Taylor's Giving Pledge Profile: http://www.glasspockets.org/philanthropy-in-focus/eye-on-the-giving-pledge/profiles/steyer

Established in 2008 in CA.
Donors: Thomas Steyer; Kathryn Taylor.
Foundation type: Independent foundation.
Financial data (yr. ended 12/31/12): Assets, $177,849,515 (M); expenditures, $28,130,054; qualifying distributions, $27,986,020; giving activities include $27,225,520 for 85 grants (high: $10,000,000; low: $2,000).
Purpose and activities: Giving primary for education, energy and environmental issues.
Fields of interest: Education; Environment, climate change/global warming; Environment, energy; Environment; Agriculture, sustainable programs.
Limitations: Applications not accepted.
Application information: Contributes only to pre-selected organizations.
Officer: Brooks Shumway, Exec. Dir.
Trustee: Kathryn Hall.
EIN: 386866542

438

The Nick Traina Foundation
P.O. Box 470427
San Francisco, CA 94147-0427
E-mail: **info@nicktrainafoundation.com**; Main URL: http://nicktrainafoundation.com/

Established in 1998 in CA.
Donors: William M. Haber; Alexander Mehran; Danielle Steel; The San Francisco Foundation.
Foundation type: Independent foundation.
Financial data (yr. ended 12/31/12): Assets, $3,039,863 (M); gifts received, $66,048; expenditures, $224,195; qualifying distributions, $201,250; giving activities include $201,250 for grants.
Purpose and activities: Support to organizations involved in the diagnosis, research, treatment, and/or family support of manic-depression, suicide prevention, child abuse and children in jeopardy, and provides assistance to struggling musicians in the areas of health and mental illness.
Fields of interest: Mental health, disorders; Mental health, depression; AIDS; Human services; Children/youth, services; Psychology/behavioral science.
Limitations: Applications accepted. Giving primarily in San Francisco, CA. No support for organizations lacking 501(c)(3) status. No grants to individuals.
Application information: Non-profit organizations can apply for one grant each calendar year. Application form not required.
Initial approach: Proposal, not more than 3 pages
Copies of proposal: 2
Deadline(s): None
Board meeting date(s): Quarterly
Officers and Directors:* Danielle Steel,* Pres.; Beatrix Seidenberg,* Secy.; Cecily Waterman,* C.F.O.
EIN: 943296757

439

The Nora Eccles Treadwell Foundation
1004 B. O'Reilly Ave
San Francisco, CA 94129-2602

Established in 1962 in UT.
Donors: Nora Eccles Treadwell Harrison†; Nora Eccles Treadwell Charitable Trust.
Foundation type: Independent foundation.
Financial data (yr. ended 12/31/12): Assets, $5,457,827 (M); gifts received, $3,746,378; expenditures, $3,645,621; qualifying distributions, $3,605,369; giving activities include $3,269,575 for 44 grants (high: $391,800; low: $500).
Purpose and activities: Grants primarily for health and cardiovascular, diabetes, and arthritis research.
Fields of interest: Health care; Health organizations, association; Heart & circulatory diseases; Medical research, institute; Heart & circulatory research; Arthritis research; Diabetes research.
Type of support: General/operating support; Equipment; Professorships; Research.
Limitations: Applications not accepted. Giving primarily in CA. No grants to individuals, or for research in areas not related to the cardiovascular system, diabetes, or arthritis.
Application information: Contributes only to pre-selected organizations.
Officers and Directors:* Patricia Canepa,* Chair.; Lawrence M. Harrison,* Secy.; Katie A. Eccles; Spencer F. Eccles; Kathryn C. Econome, M.D.; Robert M. Graham.
Number of staff: 3
EIN: 237425351
Other changes: Nicholas T. Prepouses is no longer Treas.

440

The Trio Foundation
1563 Solano Ave.
P.O. Box 174
Berkeley, CA 94707-2116 (510) 527-4605
Contact: Lyda Beardsley, Exec. Dir.
E-mail: lyda@triofoundation.org; Main URL: http://foundationcenter.org/grantmaker/trio
Grants List: http://foundationcenter.org/grantmaker/trio/grantslist.html

Established in 1991 in KS and CA.
Foundation type: Independent foundation.
Financial data (yr. ended 09/30/12): Assets, $2,465,790 (M); expenditures, $561,798; qualifying distributions, $531,162; giving activities include $462,000 for 27 grants (high: $175,000; low: $1,000).
Purpose and activities: The primary focus of the foundation is to provide opportunities for young children of all cultures, who are growing up in poverty, to achieve their fullest and brightest potential. It is especially interested in projects that strengthen low-income families with young children and enhance the ability of caregivers to foster young children's innate gifts and talents. Support also for projects sponsored by Jewish organizations serving Jewish children in need or serving a multi-cultural clientele.
Fields of interest: Education, early childhood education; Child development, education; Mental health, counseling/support groups; Crime/violence prevention, domestic violence; Children/youth, services; Children, day care; Child development, services; Family services; Family services, domestic violence; Family services, adolescent parents; Children/youth.

Type of support: Program development; Seed money; Technical assistance.
Limitations: Giving limited to Alameda and Contra Costa counties, CA and NY. No grants to individuals, or for general operating funds or capital expenditures, including development and purchase of land or buildings; no loans.
Publications: Application guidelines; Grants list; Informational brochure (including application guidelines).
Application information: Initial letter should address the following questions: 1) What is the significance of the issue you seek to address and how does it affect young children and their families; 2) What are the changes you seek to bring about; 3) What project are you proposing to Trio and approximately how much funding are you requesting for it; and 4) How will this project bring about the changes you seek. Applicants whose projects best match the foundation's funding priorities will be asked to submit a longer proposal. Application form not required.
Initial approach: 1-page letter that includes a one-sentence summary of the proposed project
Deadline(s): July 1
Board meeting date(s): June and Dec.
Final notification: Nov.
Officer: Lyda Beardsley, Exec. Dir.
Trustees: Chela Blitt; Irwin Blitt; Rita Blitt.
Number of staff: 2 part-time professional.
EIN: 481104136

441
Truckee Tahoe Community Foundation

11071 Donner Pass Rd.
Truckee, CA 96161 (530) 587-1776
Contact: Phebe Bell, Prog. Off.
FAX: (530) 550-7985; E-mail: phebe@ttcf.net; Mailing address: P.O. Box 366, Truckee, CA 96160; Main URL: http://www.ttcf.net
Facebook: https://www.facebook.com/pages/Tahoe-Truckee-Community-Foundation/188729387821765
Twitter: http://twitter.com/ttcfoundation

Established in 1998 in CA.
Foundation type: Community foundation.
Financial data (yr. ended 06/30/12): Assets, $20,393,202 (M); gifts received, $3,921,023; expenditures, $2,658,235; giving activities include $1,747,830 for 65+ grants (high: $300,000).
Purpose and activities: The foundation seeks to enhance the quality of life in the Truckee/Tahoe, CA area by seeking, accepting, managing, and disbursing funds for the benefit of the community.
Fields of interest: Arts; Education; Environment; Animals/wildlife, preservation/protection; Health care; Mental health/crisis services; Recreation; Youth development; Human services; Children/youth, services; Human services; Community/economic development.
Type of support: General/operating support; Continuing support; Income development; Management development/capacity building; Equipment; Program development; Publication; Seed money; Technical assistance; Consulting services.
Limitations: Applications accepted. Giving limited to the Truckee/North Tahoe, CA, area. No support for direct religious activities. No grants for field trips and participation in activities by parental choice, capital campaigns, activities that have already occurred, or school-based activities (unless they impact students district wide or impact the broader community).

Publications: Application guidelines; Grants list; Newsletter.
Application information: Visit foundation web site for application forms and guidelines per grant type. Application form required.
Initial approach: Telephone
Deadline(s): Varies
Board meeting date(s): 2nd Thurs. of every month
Final notification: 90 days
Officers and Directors:* Steve Gross,* Chair.; **Craig Lundin,* Chair.-Elect. and Treas.**; Stacy Caldwell,* C.E.O.; Wally Auerbach,* Secy.; Paquita Bath; Patti Boxeth; Douglas Dale; **Geoff Edelstein**; David Hansen; **Brad Koch**; Bob Richards; Kathryn Rohlf; Michael Sabarese; Andy Wirth.
Number of staff: 1 full-time support; 3 part-time support.
EIN: 680416404
Other changes: Craig Lundin is now Chair.-Elect. and Treas. Wally Auerbach, Theresa May Duggan, Richard George, and Gail Stephens are no longer directors.

442
True North Foundation

P.O. Box 1177
Grass Valley, CA **95945-1177** (530) 274-1620
Contact: Ms. Kerry Anderson, Pres.
E-mail: kka1119@aol.com

Established in 1986 in CO.
Foundation type: Independent foundation.
Financial data (yr. ended 12/31/12): Assets, $9,760,611 (M); expenditures, $3,454,426; qualifying distributions, $3,360,570; giving activities include $3,130,945 for 70 grants (high: $500,000; low: $5,000).
Purpose and activities: Giving primarily for environmental programs such as environmental work in AK, mining reform in the West, and sustainable agriculture in northern CA; also giving to independent living programs for the frail elderly/disabled in the northern CA region.
Fields of interest: Environment, natural resources; Environment; Aging; Disabilities, people with.
Type of support: General/operating support; Equipment; Program development; Conferences/seminars; Seed money; Technical assistance; Consulting services; Matching/challenge support.
Limitations: Applications accepted. Giving primarily in AK, and northern CA, with emphasis on the San Francisco Bay Area. No support for religious purposes. No grants to individuals.
Publications: Informational brochure (including application guidelines).
Application information: Application form required.
Initial approach: Letter
Copies of proposal: 1
Deadline(s): None
Board meeting date(s): Generally bimonthly
Final notification: 6-8 weeks
Officer and Directors:* Kerry Anderson,* Pres.; Susan O'Hara; Kathy Fong Stephens.
Number of staff: 1 full-time professional; 1 part-time professional.
EIN: 742421528

443
John and Mary Tu Foundation

P. O. Box 8505
Fountain Valley, CA 92728-8505
***Application address:* c/o Albert Kong, 17600 Newhope St., Fountain Valley, CA 92708**

Donors: John Tu; Mary Tu.
Foundation type: Independent foundation.
Financial data (yr. ended 12/31/12): Assets, $3,163,669 (M); gifts received, $2,075,824; expenditures, $2,317,450; qualifying distributions, $2,298,774; giving activities include $2,287,146 for 11 grants (high: $500,000; low: $2,000).
Fields of interest: Museums; Performing arts; Arts; Higher education; Education; Human services.
Limitations: Applications accepted. Giving primarily in CA.
Application information: Application form required.
Initial approach: Letter
Deadline(s): None
Officers: John Tu, Pres.; Mary Tu, Secy.; Albert Kong, C.F.O.
EIN: 271598417
Other changes: At the close of 2012, the grantmaker paid grants of $2,287,146, a 1533.7% increase over the 2011 disbursements, $140,000.

444
UniHealth Foundation

800 Wilshire Blvd., Ste. 1300
Los Angeles, CA 90017-2665 (213) 630-6500
Contact: Mary Odell, Pres.
FAX: (213) 630-6509;
E-mail: webadmin@unihealthfoundation.org; Main URL: http://www.unihealthfoundation.org/
E-Newsletter: http://visitor.constantcontact.com/manage/optin/ea?v=001VGGvr8xQIKg86pN3Wzq9Uw%3D%3D
Grants List: http://www.unihealthfoundation.org/gpf_grants_0910.html

Established in 1998 in CA.
Foundation type: Independent foundation.
Financial data (yr. ended 09/30/13): Assets, $289,569,228 (M); gifts received, $63,107; expenditures, $18,791,660; qualifying distributions, $14,625,316; giving activities include $13,870,985 for 114 grants (high: $500,000; low: $25).
Purpose and activities: To support and facilitate activities that significantly improve the health and well being of individuals and communities within its service area. The majority of funding will be to hospitals in Los Angeles and northern Orange Counties, CA.
Fields of interest: Hospitals (general); Hospitals (specialty); Public health; Palliative care; Health care.
Type of support: Program-related investments/loans; Management development/capacity building; Program development; Curriculum development; Scholarship funds; Technical assistance; Program evaluation; Employee matching gifts.
Limitations: Giving primarily in CA in the following areas: San Fernando and Santa Clarita Valley, Westside and Downtown Los Angeles, San Gabriel Valley, and Long Beach and Orange County. No support for propagandizing and/or influencing legislation, political campaigns, programs that promote religious doctrine, or biomedical/non-applied research. No grants to individuals, or for endowments, annual drives, or retirement of debt.
Publications: Application guidelines; Financial statement; Grants list; Informational brochure (including application guidelines); Newsletter; Occasional report; Program policy statement; Program policy statement (including application guidelines).
Application information: The foundation does not accept unsolicited applications. Grantseekers must send a preliminary letter and those qualified to submit a proposal will be contacted by foundation

program staff. One hard copy and electronic copy of the proposal is required.

Initial approach: Letter of inquiry. If invited, a grant proposal outline will be provided.
Deadline(s): Determined annually
Board meeting date(s): 4 times per year
Final notification: Within 3 months

Officers and Directors:* David R. Carpenter,* Chair. and C.E.O.; Bradley C. Call,* Vice-Chair.; Mary Odell, Pres.; Lydia H. Kennard,* Secy.; Kathleen H. Salazar, C.F.O. and Treas.; David M. Cannom, M.D.; **Patrick C. Haden**; Charles C. Reed; Keith W. Renken; Frank M. Sanchez, Ph.D.; Robert Splawn, M.D.
Number of staff: 7 full-time professional; 1 full-time support; 1 part-time support.
EIN: 955004033

445
Wayne & Gladys Valley Foundation

1939 Harrison St., Ste. 510
Oakland, CA 94612-3532 (510) 466-6060
Contact: Michael D. Desler, Exec. Dir.
FAX: (510) 466-6067; E-mail: info@wgvalley.org;
Main URL: http://fdnweb.org/wgvalley

Established in 1977 in CA.
Donors: F. Wayne Valley†; Gladys Valley†.
Foundation type: Independent foundation.
Financial data (yr. ended 09/30/13): Assets, $454,116,970 (M); expenditures, $29,988,413; qualifying distributions, $27,936,670; giving activities include $27,143,695 for 59 grants (high: $10,000,000; low: $7,500).
Purpose and activities: Primary areas of interest include higher, secondary, and other education, medical research, health care, youth, local parks and recreational facilities and local Catholic organizations. The foundation seeks to make grants to organizations having broad based funding support; specifically defined goals and purposes; demonstrated effectiveness in its programs; expectations for continued success in its activities without future dependence on support from the foundation; and committed, enthusiastic and diligent leadership.
Fields of interest: Elementary/secondary education; Higher education; Health care; Medical research; Recreation, parks/playgrounds; Human services; Children/youth, services; Catholic agencies & churches.
Type of support: General/operating support; Capital campaigns; Building/renovation; Program development; Scholarship funds; Research; Matching/challenge support.
Limitations: Applications accepted. Giving primarily in Alameda and Contra Costa counties, CA. No support for veterans, fraternal, labor, service club, military, or similar organizations. No grants to individuals, or for fundraising events, dinners, advertising, private operating foundations, or generally for endowments.
Publications: Application guidelines; Annual report.
Application information: More detailed application guidelines may be obtained by contacting the foundation. Application form not required.

Initial approach: Letter
Copies of proposal: 1
Deadline(s): None
Board meeting date(s): Mar., June, Sept., and Dec.
Final notification: 3-6 months

Officers and Directors:* Tamara A. Valley,* Pres.; Richard M. Kingsland,* V.P. and C.F.O.; Carolyn A. Worth, Corp. Secy.; Michael D. Desler, Exec. Dir.; Stephen M. Chandler; Barbara B. LaSalle; John P. Stock.
Number of staff: 4 full-time professional; 1 full-time support.
EIN: 953203014

446
van Loben Sels/RembeRock Foundation

(formerly van Loben Sels Foundation)
131 Steuart St., Ste. 301
San Francisco, CA 94105-1241 (415) 512-0500
***Contact:* Gail Shuster, Grants Mgr.; Dan Corsello, Interim Exec. Dir.**
FAX: (415) 371-0227; E-mail: gshuster@vlsrr.org;
Tel. for application information: Gail Shuster, Grants Mgr. Mail applications to Ms. Toni Rembe. Additional tel. for Dan Corsello, Interim Exec. Dir.: (415) 512-0572, e-mail: dcorsello@vlsrr.org; Main URL: http://www.vlsrr.org

Incorporated in 1964 in CA.
Donors: Ernst D. van Loben Sels†; Arthur Rock.
Foundation type: Independent foundation.
Financial data (yr. ended 12/31/12): Assets, $26,923,315 (M); expenditures, $2,455,705; qualifying distributions, $2,342,734; giving activities include $2,024,775 for 168 grants (high: $50,000; low: $275).
Purpose and activities: The van Loben Sels/ RembeRock Foundation's mission is to promote social justice in Northern California by means of legal services and advocacy.
Fields of interest: Legal services; Legal services, public interest law; Civil/human rights, immigrants; Civil/human rights, minorities; Civil/human rights, women; Civil/human rights, LGBTQ; Civil liberties, due process; Civil/human rights.
Type of support: General/operating support; Continuing support.
Limitations: Applications accepted. Giving limited to Northern CA. The foundation defines northern CA as including Santa Cruz, Santa Clara, Stanislaus, Tuolumne, and Mono Counties and all counties north of these five counties. No support for national organizations unless for a specific local project, or to projects requiring medical, scientific, or other technical knowledge for evaluation. No grants to individuals, or for deficit financing, capital or endowment funds, scholarships, stipends, or fellowships or for capital campaigns, fund raisers, annual dinners, galas or award banquets.
Publications: Grants list; Program policy statement.
Application information: See foundation web site for application requirements, guidelines, and application and year-end report templates. Application form and year-end reports are downloaded as a Word documents from the web site, www.vlsrr.org. Videotapes, audiotapes, CDs, etc., are not accepted unless requested. Certified or signature-required mail is not accepted. Application form required.

Initial approach: Proposal
Copies of proposal: 1
Deadline(s): Rolling
Board meeting date(s): Every 8-10 weeks
Final notification: In writing

Officers: Toni Rembe, Pres.; Richard Odgers, Secy.; **Dan Corsello, Treas.**
Trustees: Julie Divola; Tom Layton.
Number of staff: 1 full-time professional.
EIN: 946109309
Other changes: Dan Corsello has replaced Joyce Taylor as Treas.
Katherine Armstrong is no longer Exec. Dir.

447
I. N. & Susanna H. Van Nuys Foundation

400 N. Roxbury Dr., Ste. 600
Beverly Hills, CA **90210-5021**

Established in 1950 in CA.
Foundation type: Independent foundation.
Financial data (yr. ended 05/31/13): Assets, $21,279,989 (M); expenditures, $1,003,638; qualifying distributions, $914,462; giving activities include $914,462 for grants.
Purpose and activities: Support primarily in those fields favored by the original grantor, including a private hospital, secondary schools and colleges, and generally related activities.
Fields of interest: Arts; Elementary/secondary education; Higher education; Education; Hospitals (general); Human services.
Limitations: Applications not accepted. Giving primarily in CA, with emphasis on Los Angeles; some funding also in MA. No grants to individuals.
Application information: Contributes only to pre-selected organizations.
Trustees: George A. Bender; Maribeth A. Borthwick; Stuart M. Ketchum.
EIN: 956006019

448
Versacare, Inc.

c/o The Versafund
4097 Trail Creek Rd., Ste. B
Riverside, CA 92505-5869
FAX: (951) 343-5855; E-mail: versacare@aol.com; Main URL: http://www.versacare.org

Established in 1996 in CA and FL.
Foundation type: Independent foundation.
Financial data (yr. ended 09/30/12): Assets, $28,396,161 (M); expenditures, $1,682,535; qualifying distributions, $1,554,788; giving activities include $1,337,583 for 52 grants (high: $100,000; low: $500; average: $15,000–$100,000).
Purpose and activities: Giving to projects consistent with the principles and mission of the Seventh-day Adventist Church. Priority is given to proposals which advance education and science, promote healthcare activities, assist the distressed and under privileged, and provide general community benefit. Applying organizations should be in operation for two or more years, and provide matching or supporting funds.
Fields of interest: Higher education, university; Health care, association; Hospitals (general); Protestant agencies & churches.
Type of support: Equipment; Program development; Curriculum development; Scholarship funds; Matching/challenge support.
Limitations: Applications accepted. **Giving in the U.S., with some emphasis on CA and WA; Versacare provides a limited number of Non-SDA-related grants that are consistent with its mission, with preference given to organizations located within the Inland Empire of Southern California, or in proximity to a facility or entity that Versacare either operates or is closely affiliated with.** No grants for debt reduction, or for salaries or general operations; no grants to individuals.
Publications: Application guidelines; Grants list; Informational brochure.
Application information: Application guidelines and form available on foundation web site. Application form required.

Initial approach: Submit application online via foundation web site
Copies of proposal: 1

Deadline(s): Dec. 31
Final notification: Mar. 31
Officers: Charles C. Sandefur, Chair.; Robert E. Coy, J.D., Vice-Chair. and Pres.; Ron Wisbey, V.P.; Calvin J. Hanson, C.P.C.U., Secy.; Ellen H. Brodersen, C.P.A., Treas.
Trustees: George W. Brown; Debra Brill; Myrna Costa; Roscoe Howard; Tom Macomber; Richard Pershing.
EIN: 330052434
Other changes: Robert D. Macomber is no longer a trustee.

449
Vera P. Vietor Trust
San Francisco, CA

The trust terminated on Dec. 30, 2010 and transferred its assets to Humboldt Area Foundation.

450
Wadhwani Foundation
(formerly Tekchand Foundation)
2475 Hanover St.
Palo Alto, CA 94304-1114
***U.S. contacts:* Gayatri Agnew, Prog. Dir., and Rishi Chopra, Prog. Coord.**
e-mail: rishi@chopra@wadhwani-foundation.org; India contact: Atul Raja, Exec. V.P., Marketing, e-mail: marketing@wadhwani-foundation.org; Bangalore address: 113/1B, Benaka Tech Park, Block II, 3rd Fl., ITPL Main Rd., Kundalahalli, Bangalore - 560037; New Delhi address: B-315, Basement, Chittaranjan Park, New Delhi - 110 019; Main URL: http://wadhwani-foundation.org/
Dr. Romesh and Kathleen Wadhwani's Giving Pledge Profile: http://glasspockets.org/philanthropy-in-focus/eye-on-the-giving-pledge/profiles/wadhwani

Established in 1997 in CA.
Donors: Kathleen E. Wadhwani; Romesh T. Wadhwani.
Foundation type: Independent foundation.
Financial data (yr. ended 12/31/12): Assets, $62,412,877 (M); gifts received, $54,000,000; expenditures, $4,948,697; qualifying distributions, $2,721,389; giving activities include $1,662,552 for 30 grants (high: $414,882; low: $767).
Purpose and activities: Giving primarily for international affairs, particularly concerning India; funding also for the arts, education, and social services.
Fields of interest: Arts education; Performing arts, music; Arts; Secondary school/education; Disasters, floods; Safety/disasters; Human services; International affairs; Philanthropy/voluntarism.
International interests: India.
Limitations: Giving primarily in CA and India. No grants to individuals.
Application information: Applicants must be a legally registered (under 80G and FCRA) NGO in India. Application information available on foundation web site.
Officers: Dr. Romesh T. Wadhwani, Chair.; Dr. Ajay Kela, C.E.O. and Pres.; **Atul Raja, Exec. V.P., Marketing.**
EIN: 770450893

451
Wallis Foundation
1880 Century Park E., Ste. 950
Los Angeles, CA 90067-1612 (310) 286-9777

Established in 1957 in CA.
Donor: Hal B. Wallis†.
Foundation type: Independent foundation.
Financial data (yr. ended 06/30/13): Assets, $17,769,480 (M); expenditures, $4,310,321; qualifying distributions, $4,025,878; giving activities include $3,894,000 for 164 grants (high: $300,000; low: $1,000).
Purpose and activities: Giving primarily for the arts, education, the environment, health care and human services.
Fields of interest: Performing arts; Arts; Higher education; Education; Environment, natural resources; Health care; Health organizations; Human services; Foundations (community).
Limitations: Applications not accepted. Giving primarily in CA, with emphasis on Los Angeles, San Francisco, and Santa Barbara. No grants to individuals.
Application information: Contributes only to pre-selected organizations.
Officers and Directors:* Beth Wallis,* Pres.; Jeffrey Glassman,* Secy.; Michael Sack,* C.F.O.
EIN: 956027469
Other changes: Jack Baker is no longer a director.

452
Warsh-Mott Legacy
469 Bohemian Hwy.
Freestone, CA 95472-9579 (707) 874-2942
Contact: Roxanne Turnage, Exec. Dir.
FAX: (707) 874-1734; E-mail: inquiries@csfund.org; Main URL: http://www.csfund.org
Grants List: http://www.csfund.org/grants2013-1rg.html

Established in 1985 in CA.
Donors: Maryanne Mott; Herman E. Warsh†.
Foundation type: Independent foundation.
Financial data (yr. ended 09/30/12): Assets, $25,637,525 (M); gifts received, $125,000; expenditures, $2,275,841; qualifying distributions, $2,146,269; giving activities include $1,757,389 for 36 grants (high: $220,000; low: $1,200).
Purpose and activities: Funding in the areas of economic globalization, food sovereignty (seed saving, soil building, and protecting pollinators), civil liberties, and emerging technology.
Fields of interest: Agriculture/food, research; Agriculture/food; Civil liberties, advocacy.
Type of support: General/operating support; Continuing support; Conferences/seminars; Publication; Research; Technical assistance; Matching/challenge support.
Limitations: Applications accepted. Giving on a national basis. **No grants to individuals, or for endowments, capital funds, video or film production, or emergency requests.**
Publications: Application guidelines; Grants list; IRS Form 990 or 990-PF printed copy available upon request.
Application information: Please do not include brochures, reports, news clippings, CDs, DVDs, or other materials with letters of inquiry. Plastic folders, binders or other presentation materials are not necessary. Application form not required.
***Initial approach:* Letter of inquiry (no more than 3 pages) preferred over fax or e-mail**
Copies of proposal: 1
Deadline(s): None
Board meeting date(s): Apr. and Dec.

Officers and Board Members:* Michael Warsh,* Pres.; Marise Meynet Stewart,* V.P.; Maryanne Mott,* C.F.O.; Corinne Meadows-Efram, Secy.; Roxanne Turnage, Exec. Dir.; Kau'i Keliipio; Teresa Robinson.
EIN: 680049658
Other changes: The grantmaker now makes its irs form 990 or 990-pf printed copy available online.

453
Wasserman Foundation
10960 Wilshire Blvd., 5th Fl.
Los Angeles, CA 90024-3708 (310) 407-0200
FAX: (310) 882-4601;
E-mail: feedback@wassermanfoundation.org; Main URL: http://www.wassermanfoundation.org
Facebook: http://www.facebook.com/pages/Wasserman-Foundation/182428898469669?sk=info
Flickr: http://www.flickr.com/photos/wassermanfdn/
Tumblr: http://wassermanfdn.tumblr.com/
Twitter: http://twitter.com/wassermanfdn

Incorporated in 1952 in CA.
Donors: Lew R. Wasserman†; Edith B. Wasserman†.
Foundation type: Independent foundation.
Financial data (yr. ended 12/31/12): Assets, $188,476,343 (M); expenditures, $13,748,666; qualifying distributions, $12,552,798; giving activities include $12,272,298 for 135 grants (high: $1,500,000; low: $1,000).
Purpose and activities: Giving primarily to organizations focused on advancing and promoting education, environmental responsibility, health and welfare, and the arts. With a diversified list of recipients, the foundation continually strives to partner with groups that are committed to assisting those less fortunate, and bettering the community at large.
Fields of interest: Performing arts; Higher education; Environment; Hospitals (general); Medical research, institute; Human services; Jewish federated giving programs; Public policy, research.
Type of support: Capital campaigns; Endowments; Scholarship funds; Research.
Limitations: Applications not accepted. Giving primarily in CA. No grants to individuals or to fund independent film projects.
Application information: Unsolicited requests for funds not accepted.
Officers and Directors:* Casey Wasserman,* C.E.O. and Pres.; Carol A. Leif, V.P.; Lynne Wasserman, V.P.; **Rica Rodman, Exec. Dir.**
EIN: 956038762

454
Paul L. Wattis Foundation
c/o Carlie Wilmans
720 York St., Ste. 103
San Francisco, CA **94110-2148 (415) 986-1571**
FAX: (415) 986-1547;
E-mail: info@wattisfoundation.org; Main URL: http://www.wattisfoundation.org
Grants List: http://www.wattisfoundation.org/grantees.php
Grants List: http://www.wattisfoundation.org/grantees_2011.php

Established in 2003 in CA.
Donor: Phyllis C. Wattis Trust.
Foundation type: Independent foundation.

Financial data (yr. ended 12/31/12): Assets, $6,529,893 (M); expenditures, $351,759; qualifying distributions, $259,697; giving activities include $225,000 for 10 grants (high: $50,000; low: $5,000).
Purpose and activities: In an effort to carry on Mrs. Wattis' legacy and her vision for the arts in the Bay Area, the foundation intends to help the Bay Area arts community become - in her words - "four stars, worth the detour." The foundation will support both the fine arts, including the exhibition of painting and sculpture, and the performing arts, including opera, symphony and dance, in the cities of San Francisco, Berkeley and Oakland, as well as in Marin County, California. The foundation is most interested in supporting smaller, independent arts organizations that are presenting challenging and cutting-edge works.
Fields of interest: Arts.
Limitations: Applications accepted. Giving primarily in the Bay Area, including Alameda, Marin and San Francisco counties, CA. No grants to individuals, or for capital campaigns, or general operating support, operating expenses, capital expansion, endowment funds, seed grants, scholarships, awards, or research and planning.
Application information: Application guidelines and form available on foundation web site. Please do not send any materials that must be returned. The foundation will not be responsible for returning photos, slides, videos, CDs, DVDs, original art work, original documents, and the like. Application form required.
Initial approach: Letter of inquiry
Deadline(s): See foundation web site for current deadlines
Board meeting date(s): Spring and fall
Directors: Carlie Wilmans; Carol W. Casey.
Number of staff: 1 part-time professional.
EIN: 841624183

455
Phyllis C. Wattis Foundation
720 York St., Ste. 103
San Francisco, CA **94110** (415) 986-1571
FAX: (415) 986-1547;
E-mail: info@wattisfoundation.org; Main URL: http://www.wattisfoundation.org
Grants List: http://www.wattisfoundation.org/grantees.php

Donors: Carol Casey; Paul L. Wattis Foundation.
Foundation type: Independent foundation.
Financial data (yr. ended 12/31/12): Assets, $9,510,762 (M); gifts received, $75,000; expenditures, $677,617; qualifying distributions, $470,000; giving activities include $470,000 for grants.
Purpose and activities: Giving for the support of the fine arts, including the exhibition of painting and sculpture, and the performing arts, including opera, symphony, and dance.
Fields of interest: Visual arts; Performing arts; Arts.
Limitations: Giving primarily in San Francisco, Berkeley, and Oakland, as well as in Marin County, California. No grants for general support, operating expenses, capital expansion, endowment funds, seed grants, scholarships, awards, or research and planning.
Publications: Application guidelines.
Application information:
Initial approach: Letter of inquiry of no more than 2 pages
***Deadline(s):* See foundation web site for current deadlines**
Board meeting date(s): Spring and fall
Directors: Carol Casey; Carlie Wilmans.
EIN: 900653262

456
Weingart Foundation
1055 W. 7th St., Ste. 3200
Los Angeles, CA 90017-2305 (213) 688-7799
Contact: Fred J. Ali, C.E.O. and Pres.
FAX: (213) 688-1515; E-mail: info@weingartfnd.org;
Main URL: http://www.weingartfnd.org
Grants Database: http://www.weingartfnd.org/grants-database
Knowledge Center: http://www.weingartfnd.org/Leading-with-Core-Support

Incorporated in 1951 in CA.
Donors: Ben Weingart†; Stella Weingart†.
Foundation type: Independent foundation.
Financial data (yr. ended 06/30/13): Assets, $717,208,865 (M); expenditures, $43,698,402; qualifying distributions, $36,073,321; giving activities include $32,834,578 for 588 grants (high: $500,000; low: $100), $249,735 for 89 employee matching gifts, and $750,000 for 1 loan/program-related investment.
Purpose and activities: The foundation seeks to build a better America by offering constructive assistance to people in need, thereby helping them to lead more rewarding, responsible lives.
Fields of interest: Education, early childhood education; Child development, education; Elementary school/education; Secondary school/education; Higher education; Adult education—literacy, basic skills & GED; Education, reading; Education; Hospitals (general); Medical care, rehabilitation; Nursing care; Health care; Substance abuse, services; AIDS; Crime/violence prevention, youth; Legal services; Employment, services; Food services; Housing/shelter; Recreation; Youth development, services; Human services; Children/youth, services; Child development, services; Family services; Residential/custodial care, hospices; Minorities/immigrants, centers/services; Homeless, human services; Community/economic development, formal/general education; Community/economic development; Leadership development; Infants/toddlers; Children/youth; Children; Youth; Adults; Aging; Young adults; Disabilities, people with; Physically disabled; Blind/visually impaired; Deaf/hearing impaired; Mentally disabled; Minorities; Asians/Pacific Islanders; African Americans/Blacks; Hispanics/Latinos; Native Americans/American Indians; Indigenous peoples; Women; Infants/toddlers, female; Girls; Adults, women; Young adults, female; Men; Infants/toddlers, male; Boys; Adults, men; Young adults, male; Military/veterans; Offenders/ex-offenders; Substance abusers; AIDS, people with; Single parents; Crime/abuse victims; Terminal illness, people with; Sex workers; Immigrants/refugees; Economically disadvantaged; Homeless; Migrant workers; LGBTQ; Lesbians; Gay men; Bisexual; Transgender and gender nonconforming; Intersex.
Type of support: General/operating support; Management development/capacity building; Capital campaigns; Building/renovation; Equipment; Program development; Program-related investments/loans; Employee matching gifts; Matching/challenge support.
Limitations: Applications accepted. Giving for the regular grant program limited to 7 southern CA counties: Los Angeles, Orange, Santa Barbara, Riverside, San Bernardino, Ventura counties, and for the small grant program all the aforementioned and limited grantmaking in San Diego County. No support for religious programs, consumer interest or environmental advocacy, projects or programs exclusively or predominately financed by government sources, social or political issues outside the United States of America, or national organizations that do not have chapters operating in Southern California, or for propagandizing, influencing legislation and/or elections, promoting voter registration; for political candidates, political campaigns; or for litigation. No grants to individuals, or for endowment funds, annual campaigns, emergency funds, deficit financing, fellowships, seminars, conferences, publications, workshops, travel, surveys, films, medical research, or publishing activities.
Publications: Application guidelines; Annual report (including application guidelines); Grants list; Newsletter.
Application information: Applications for the "Small Grant Program" are now being accepted. See foundation web site for application criteria. Application form required.
***Initial approach:* Regular Grant Program (requests over $25,000): Online letter of inquiry; Small Grant Program (requests $25,000 and under): Online application**
Deadline(s): See foundation web site for current deadlines
Board meeting date(s): Sept., Dec., Feb., Apr. and June
Final notification: 3 to 4 months
Officers and Directors:* Steven L. Soboroff,* Chair.; Fred J. Ali, C.E.O. and Pres.; Deborah M. Ives, V.P. and Treas.; Belen Vargas, V.P., Grant Operations; Aileen Adams; William C. Allen; Andrew E. Bogen; Steven D. Broidy; Monica Lozano; John W. Mack; Miriam Muscarolas.
Number of staff: 10 full-time professional; 1 part-time professional; 5 full-time support.
EIN: 956054814
Other changes: Laurence A. Wolfe is no longer V.P., Admin. and Real Estate.

457
Wesley Family Foundation
4201 Via Pinzon
Palos Verdes Estates, CA **90274-1553**

Foundation type: Independent foundation.
Financial data (yr. ended 12/31/12): Assets, $680,762 (M); expenditures, $62,556; qualifying distributions, $62,245; giving activities include $4,110 for 2 grants (high: $3,750; low: $360).
Fields of interest: Higher education; Cystic fibrosis.
Limitations: Applications not accepted. Giving primarily in Los Angeles, CA; some giving also in Bethesda, MD.
Application information: Contributes only to pre-selected organizations.
Trustees: Lisa Bonbright; David Scott Wesley; Jonnie Lynn Wesley; Timothy Andrew Wesley.
EIN: 264106878

458
Gary and Mary West Foundation
(formerly Sunset Foundation)
5796 Armada Dr., Ste. 300
Carlsbad, CA **92008-4693**
E-mail: info@gmwf.org; Main URL: http://www.gmwf.org/

Donors: Gary L. West; Mary L. West.
Foundation type: Independent foundation.
Financial data (yr. ended 12/31/12): Assets, $166,140,959 (M); gifts received, $48;

expenditures, $25,678,492; qualifying distributions, $24,444,523; giving activities include $23,271,905 for 33 grants (high: $17,184,682; low: $500).
Fields of interest: Health care; Health organizations, association; Medical research, institute; Human services; Military/veterans' organizations.
Limitations: Applications not accepted. **Giving primarily in San Diego County CA, and Omaha, NE. No grants to individuals.**
Application information: Unsolicited requests for funds not accepted.
Officers: Gary L. West, Co-Chair.; Mary E. West, Co-Chair.; Shelley M. Lyford, Pres.; **Ginny Merrifield, Exec. Dir.**; Roland J. Santoni, Mgr. Dir.
EIN: 470793015

459
Western Digital Foundation
3355 Michelson Dr., Ste. 100
Irvine, CA 92612-5964
Contact: Rosemary Krupp, Dir.; Milissa Bedell, Mgr., Community Rels.
FAX: (949) 672-9676;
E-mail: Rosemary.Krupp@wdc.com; E-mail for Milissa Bedell: Milissa.bedell@wdc.com; Main URL: http://www.wdc.com/en/company/communityrelations/
Grants List: http://www.wdc.com/en/company/charitablegrantawards.asp

Established in 1997 in CA.
Donors: Western Digital Corp.; Texas Instruments Inc.; Western Digital Technologies, Inc.
Foundation type: Company-sponsored foundation.
Financial data (yr. ended 06/28/13): Assets, $264,927 (M); gifts received, $2,639,310; expenditures, $2,575,795; qualifying distributions, $2,575,795; giving activities include $2,568,905 for 151 grants (high: $300,000; low: $100).
Purpose and activities: The foundation supports organizations involved with education, the environment, disaster relief, human services, community development, science, civic affairs, economically disadvantaged people and veterans.
Fields of interest: Education, computer literacy/technology training; Education; Environment, natural resources; Environment; Disasters, preparedness/services; Family services; Community/economic development; United Ways and Federated Giving Programs; Mathematics; Engineering/technology; Computer science; Science; Military/veterans' organizations; Military/veterans; Economically disadvantaged.
Type of support: Employee volunteer services; Employee matching gifts; Donated products; In-kind gifts.
Limitations: Applications accepted. **Giving limited to areas of company operations, with emphasis on Alameda, Orange, and Santa Clara, CA, Boulder County, CO, and Olmsted County, MN.** No support for religious organization not of direct benefit to the entire community, sports teams, discriminatory organizations, grantmaking foundations, political organizations, hospitals, or museums. No grants to individuals, or for capital campaigns, athletic events, fundraising, conferences or seminars, research, scholarships or stipends, or start-up funds; no multi-year grants.
Publications: Application guidelines; Program policy statement.
Application information: Proposals should be submitted using organization letterhead. Requests for multi-year funding are not accepted. Support is limited to 1 contribution per organization during any given year. Video and audio submissions are not accepted. Application form required.
Initial approach: **Complete online application**
Copies of proposal: 1
Deadline(s): Jan. 15 and July 15
Board meeting date(s): Semi-annual
Final notification: 3 months
Officers: Michael D. Cordano; Jacqueline M. DeMana; Timothy M. Leyden; Stephen D. Miligan; Wolfgang Nickl.
Number of staff: 1 full-time professional; 1 part-time professional.
EIN: 330769372
Other changes: The grantmaker has changed its fiscal year-end from July 31 to June 29.

460
The Westreich Foundation
c/o Stanley I. Westreich
P.O. Box 3601
Rancho Santa Fe, CA 92067-3601 **(858) 735-0811**
E-mail: ruthwestreich@cox.net; Main URL: http://www.thewestreichfoundation.org

Established in 2005 in DE.
Donor: Stanley I. Westreich.
Foundation type: Independent foundation.
Financial data (yr. ended 12/31/12): Assets, $10,551,186 (M); expenditures, $470,461; qualifying distributions, $469,940; giving activities include $469,940 for grants.
Purpose and activities: The focus of the foundation is education and literacy, women and children at risk, and optimum health wellness.
Fields of interest: Higher education; Health organizations; Human services.
Limitations: Applications not accepted. Giving primarily in La Jolla and San Diego, CA. No grants to individuals.
Application information: Contributes only to pre-selected organizations.
Officers: Ruth Westreich, Pres.; Lauren Westriech, 1st V.P.; Dana Westreich Hirt, 2nd V.P.; Anthony Westreich, Secy.; Stanley I. Westreich, Treas.
EIN: 203598096

461
WHH Foundation
333 S. Hope St., 54th Fl.
Los Angeles, CA 90071-1406
Main URL: http://www.whh-foundation.org

Established in 2004 in CA.
Donors: William H. Hurt; Sarah S. Hurt.
Foundation type: Independent foundation.
Financial data (yr. ended 12/31/12): Assets, $14,882,345 (M); gifts received, $1,035,718; expenditures, $831,888; qualifying distributions, $743,299; giving activities include $638,497 for 110 grants (high: $67,731; low: $50).
Purpose and activities: Giving primarily for education, health, the arts, and community-building.
Fields of interest: Museums; Performing arts; Arts; Libraries (public); Education; Medical research; Human services; Children/youth, services.
Type of support: Matching/challenge support.
Limitations: Applications not accepted. Giving in the U.S., with emphasis on CA. No support for religious organizations. No grants to individuals.
Application information: Unsolicited requests for funds not accepted.
Officers and Directors:* Mark L. Purnell,* Chair.; Bernadette Glenn,* Pres.; William H. Hurt,* V.P.; **Molly Purnell, Secy.**; Kelley H. Purnell,* Treas.; Andrew F. Barth; J. Dale Harvey; Otis M. Healey; Kathleen C. Hurt; Sarah S. Hurt; Michael T. Kerr; Courtney D. MacMillan; Terrence A. MacMillan; Douglas S. Murray; Elizabeth Murray; Eve-Lynne G. Murray; James R. Murray; Katharine J. Purnell; Mary L. Purnell.
EIN: 200775264
Other changes: Molly Purnell has replaced Elizabeth Murray as Secy.

462
The Whitman Institute
405 Davis Ct., Ste. 301
San Francisco, CA 94111-2405
The Whitman Institute's Philanthropy Promise: http://www.ncrp.org/philanthropys-promise/who

Established in CA; Classified as a private operating foundation in 1985.
Donor: Frederick C. Whitman.
Foundation type: Operating foundation.
Financial data (yr. ended 06/30/13): Assets, $12,546,314 (M); expenditures, $1,716,986; qualifying distributions, $1,605,590; giving activities include $1,279,000 for grants.
Fields of interest: Education; Human services; Leadership development.
Limitations: Applications not accepted. Giving primarily in CA. No grants to individuals.
Application information: Contributes only to pre-selected organizations.
Officers: John Esterle, Secy. and Exec. Dir.; C.J. Callen, Treas.
Directors: Dr. Les K. Adler; Jill Blair; Sue Ellen McCann.
EIN: 942984079

463
Wilkinson Foundation
3435 Pacific Ave.
San Francisco, CA 94118-2029 (415) 567-5673

Established in 1986 in MI.
Donor: Warren S. Wilkinson.
Foundation type: Independent foundation.
Financial data (yr. ended 01/31/13): Assets, $5,695,958 (M); expenditures, $296,646; qualifying distributions, $277,894; giving activities include $271,951 for 100 grants (high: $21,000; low: $200).
Fields of interest: Historical activities; Arts; Higher education; Education; Environment; Health care; Human services.
Type of support: Continuing support; Annual campaigns; Capital campaigns; Endowments; Program development; Seed money.
Limitations: Applications not accepted. Giving on a national basis, with an emphasis on MI.
Application information: Contributes only to pre-selected organizations.
Trustees: Bary Wilkinson; Bruce Wilkinson; Guerin S. Wilkinson; Dr. Stephen Wilkinson; Tom S. Wilkinson; Warren S. Wilkinson.
EIN: 386497639

464
Wilsey Foundation
2352 Pine St.
San Francisco, CA 94115-2715

Established in 1964 in CA.
Donor: Alfred S. Wilsey, Sr.‡.
Foundation type: Independent foundation.
Financial data (yr. ended 03/31/13): Assets, $352,059 (M); expenditures, $45,362; qualifying distributions, $44,452; giving activities include $44,452 for 18 grants (high: $10,031; low: $503).
Purpose and activities: Giving primarily for the arts, education and social services.
Fields of interest: Arts; Elementary/secondary education; Education; Health organizations; Human services; Children/youth, services.
Type of support: Continuing support; Building/renovation; Program development; Curriculum development.
Limitations: Applications not accepted. Giving primarily in northern CA. No grants to individuals.
Application information: Unsolicited requests for funds not accepted.
Officers: Diane B. Wilsey, Pres.; Michael W. Wilsey, V.P.
Number of staff: 1 part-time support.
EIN: 946098720
Other changes: Diane B. Wilsey is now Pres.

465
Windsong Trust
838 Manhattan Beach Blvd.
Manhattan Beach, CA 90266-4933

Established in 2004 in CA.
Donor: Martin Crowley‡.
Foundation type: Independent foundation.
Financial data (yr. ended 12/31/12): Assets, $514,287,015 (M); expenditures, $27,401,704; qualifying distributions, $25,127,401; giving activities include $23,625,990 for 66 grants (high: $2,000,000; low: $10,710).
Purpose and activities: Giving to support education of underprivileged children across the globe.
Fields of interest: Education; Children/youth.
Limitations: Applications not accepted. Giving in CA and NV.
Application information: Unsolicited requests for funds not accepted.
Trustees: Gigi Osco-Bingeman; Vadim Fridman.
EIN: 562461733
Other changes: At the close of 2012, the grantmaker paid grants of $23,625,990, a 783.7% increase over the 2010 disbursements, $2,673,500.

466
Winiarski Family Foundation
P.O. Box 3327
Yountville, CA 94599-3327

Established in 2007 in CA.
Donors: Warren Winiarski; Barbara Winiarski.
Foundation type: Independent foundation.
Financial data (yr. ended 12/31/12): Assets, $18,224,922 (M); expenditures, $2,727,734; qualifying distributions, $2,571,900; giving activities include $2,571,900 for grants.
Fields of interest: Environment, land resources.
Limitations: Applications not accepted. Giving primarily in CA. No grants to individuals.
Application information: Contributes only to pre-selected organizations.
Officers: Warren Winiarski, Pres.; **Barbara Winiarski, Secy. and Treas.**
EIN: 260474242
Other changes: Barbara Winiarski is now Secy. and Treas.

467
Dean Witter Foundation
57 Post St., Ste. 510
San Francisco, CA 94104-5020 (415) 981-2966
Contact: Kenneth J. Blum, Administrative Dir.
FAX: (415) 981-5218;
E-mail: admin@deanwitterfoundation.org; Main URL: http://www.deanwitterfoundation.org

Incorporated in 1952 in CA.
Donors: Dean Witter‡; Mrs. Dean Witter; Dean Witter & Co.
Foundation type: Independent foundation.
Financial data (yr. ended 06/30/13): Assets, $19,117,353 (M); expenditures, $1,110,496; qualifying distributions, $947,696; giving activities include $822,000 for 40 grants (high: $50,000; low: $5,000).
Purpose and activities: Giving primarily to support specific wildlife conservation projects in Northern California, and seminal opportunities to improve and extend environmental education and to stimulate learning. Funding also to launch and expand innovative K-12 public education initiatives.
Fields of interest: Elementary/secondary education; Environment, natural resources; Animals/wildlife.
Type of support: Equipment; Program development; Publication; Seed money; Research.
Limitations: Applications accepted. Giving for conservation projects limited to northern CA. No support for religious organizations. **No grants to individuals, or for endowment funds, scholarships, capital campaigns, opportunity deficits, and fundraising events; no loans.**
Publications: Application guidelines; Grants list.
Application information: Application guidelines available on foundation web site. Application form not required.
Initial approach: **Applicants are encouraged to telephone or write to the foundation's consultant to determine whether their proposed program falls within the foundation's areas of interest and grantmaking priorities**
Copies of proposal: 1
Deadline(s): None
Board meeting date(s): Jan., Apr., July, and Oct.
Officers and Trustees:* Dean Witter III,* Pres.; Stephen Nessier,* V.P. and C.F.O.; Roland Tognazzini, Jr., Secy.; Deanne Gillette Violich; Malcolm G. Witter; William P. Witter.
EIN: 946065150
Other changes: The grantmaker now makes its grants list available online.

468
World Children's Fund
5442 Thornwood Dr., Ste. 250
San Jose, CA 95123-1207 (408) 363-8100
Contact: Ruth Kendrick
FAX: (408) 629-4846; E-mail: info@wcf-intl.org; Main URL: http://www.worldchildrensfund.org

Established in 1984 in CA.
Donors: Universal Aide Society; World Childrens Fund-Europe (CH); World Harvest Church; Window to Asia.
Foundation type: Operating foundation.
Financial data (yr. ended 03/31/13): Assets, $511,365 (M); gifts received, $4,821,224; expenditures, $4,769,616; qualifying distributions, $3,662,163; giving activities include $3,208,030 for 23 grants (high: $3,000,042; low: $50), and $3,735,052 for foundation-administered programs.
Purpose and activities: Giving for aid to needy, suffering children in crisis situations worldwide.
Fields of interest: Children/youth, services; International relief.
Type of support: In-kind gifts.
Limitations: Applications accepted. Giving on an international basis. No grants to individuals.
Publications: Annual report; Financial statement.
Application information:
Initial approach: Proposal
Deadline(s): None
Officers and Directors:* Joseph Lam,* C.E.O. and Pres.; Ruth Kendrick,* V.P.; Paul Chiar, Secy.; Stanley Chen,* Treas.; Douglas Kendrick, C.F.O.; Anne Chiang, Cont.; Bruce Barnes.
EIN: 770210616
Other changes: For the fiscal year ended Mar. 31, 2013, the grantmaker paid grants of $3,208,030, a 113.9% increase over the fiscal 2012 disbursements, $1,499,917.

469
Wrather Family Foundation
(formerly J. D. & Mazie Wrather Foundation)
c/o Ellis, Bristol, Harmon & Marsh
14310 Ventura Blvd., 2nd Fl.
Sherman Oaks, CA 91423-2738
***Main URL:* http://wrather.org/**

Established in 1962 as the J. D. & Mazie Wrather Foundation, Inc.
Foundation type: Independent foundation.
Financial data (yr. ended 12/31/12): Assets, $4,205,237 (M); expenditures, $181,768; qualifying distributions, $151,750; giving activities include $148,500 for 16 grants (high: $30,000; low: $500).
Purpose and activities: Giving primarily for health care, including a substance abuse treatment center, as well as for education, medical research, and human services.
Fields of interest: Arts; Higher education; Education; Hospitals (general); Health care; Substance abuse, treatment; Cancer; Human services; Children/youth, services; Family services; United Ways and Federated Giving Programs.
Limitations: Applications not accepted. Giving primarily in CA and PA. No grants to individuals.
Application information: Unsolicited requests for funds not accepted.
Officers and Directors:* Christopher C. Wrather, Pres.; Linda W. Finocchiaro,* V.P.; Gerald L. Weisberger, Secy.; Molly W. Dolle,* Treas.
EIN: 956100110
Other changes: The grantmaker no longer lists a URL address.

470
Zafiropoulo Family Foundation
c/o Blanding, Boyer & Rockwell
1340 Treat Blvd., Ste. 525
Walnut Creek, CA 94597-7984
***Contact:* Arthur Zafiropoulo**

Established in 1994 in CA.
Donors: Arthur Zafiropoulo; Lisa Cooper.
Foundation type: Independent foundation.
Financial data (yr. ended 12/31/12): Assets, $4,483,347 (M); expenditures, $190,090; qualifying distributions, $190,000; giving activities include $190,000 for 3 grants (high: $170,000; low: $10,000).

Fields of interest: Performing arts, orchestras; Higher education, college; Cancer; Pediatrics; YM/YWCAs & YM/YWHAs; Children/youth, services.
Type of support: General/operating support.
Limitations: Applications not accepted. Giving primarily in CA. No grants to individuals.
Application information: Unsolicited requests for funds not accepted.
Officers: Arthur Zafiropoulo, Pres.; Lisa Cooper, Secy.-Treas.
EIN: 680344787

471
The Zellerbach Family Foundation

(formerly The Zellerbach Family Fund)
575 Market St., Ste. 2950
San Francisco, CA 94105-2854 (415) 421-2629
***Contact:* Allison Magee, Exec. Dir.**
FAX: (415) 421-6713;
E-mail: info@zellerbachfamilyfoundation.org; Main URL: http://www.zellerbachfamilyfoundation.org
Knowledge Center: http://www.zellerbachfamilyfoundation.org/publications.html

Incorporated in 1956 in CA.
Donor: Jennie B. Zellerbach†.
Foundation type: Independent foundation.
Financial data (yr. ended 12/31/12): Assets, $125,232,175 (M); expenditures, $7,138,386; qualifying distributions, $4,884,760; giving activities include $4,884,760 for 316 grants (high: $140,000; low: $1,000).
Purpose and activities: The foundation focuses its giving in the San Francisco Bay Area, CA and concentrates on the following program areas: Strengthening communities; Improving the management, practice and accountability of public systems with a focus on child welfare, mental health and education; Improving the quality of life for refugees and immigrants and supporting their participation in society; Youth development through the arts; Major community institutions; and Community Arts.
Fields of interest: Arts, single organization support; Performing arts; Youth development; Human services; Minorities/immigrants, centers/services; Immigrants/refugees; Economically disadvantaged.
Type of support: General/operating support; Continuing support; Program development; Technical assistance; Program evaluation.
Limitations: Giving primarily in the San Francisco Bay Area, CA. No grants to individuals, or for capital or endowment funds, research, scholarships, or fellowships; no loans.
Publications: Annual report.
Application information: The foundation accepts proposals only for its Community Arts program. All other program grants are initiated by the foundation. See foundation's web site for Community Arts application information. Application form required.
Initial approach: Community Arts application with application on foundation web site
Deadline(s): See foundation web site for current deadlines
Board meeting date(s): Quarterly
Final notification: Quarterly
Officers and Trustees:* William J. Zellerbach,* Chair.; Thomas H. Zellerbach,* Pres.; Nancy Zellerbach Boschwitz,* V.P. and Secy.; Charles R. Zellerbach,* V.P. and Treas.; Raymond H. Williams,* V.P.; **Allison Magee, Exec. Dir.**; Jeanette M. Dunckel; Philip S. Ehrlich, Jr.; Mary Ann Milias; Stephen R. Shapiro; Suchi Somasekar; Mildred Thompson.
Number of staff: 5 full-time professional; 1 part-time professional; 1 full-time support; 1 part-time support.
EIN: 946069482
Other changes: Allison Magee has replaced Cindy Rambo as Exec. Dir.

COLORADO

472
Animal Assistance Foundation
405 Urban St., Ste. 340
Lakewood, CO 80228-1236 (303) 744-8396
Contact: David L. Gies
FAX: (303) 744-7065; E-mail: info@aaf-fd.org;
Contact for questions: Katie Parker, Prog. Dir., tel.: (303) 744-8396, ext. 302, e-mail: KParker@aaf-fd.org; Main URL: http://www.aaf-fd.org

Established in 1975 in CO.
Donor: Louise C. Harrison†.
Foundation type: Independent foundation.
Financial data (yr. ended 07/31/13): Assets, $27,668,355 (M); gifts received, $11,750; expenditures, $1,289,254; qualifying distributions, $1,197,239; giving activities include $770,278 for 58 grants (high: $234,950; low: $500).
Purpose and activities: The foundation's mission is to provide leadership for the enhancement of animal welfare through charitable, scientific, and educational means. Its vision is to transform the relationship between human beings and all animals, for the betterment of both. Giving for animal welfare, especially to prevent cruelty to cats and dogs; also to promote pet population control, provide for humane treatment education, and expand scientific inquiry.
Fields of interest: Animal welfare; Animal population control.
Type of support: General/operating support; Building/renovation; Emergency funds; Program development; Conferences/seminars; Seed money; Curriculum development; Technical assistance.
Limitations: Applications accepted. Giving limited to CO. No grants to individuals, or for endowment funds, debt retirement, or long-term funding.
Publications: Application guidelines; Annual report; Financial statement; Multi-year report.
Application information: Application form required.
Initial approach: **Use online application system on foundation web site**
Copies of proposal: 8
Deadline(s): Generally, last Fri. in Mar. and Sept.
Board meeting date(s): Bimonthly
Final notification: Within two weeks
Officers and Directors:* Mark Lacy,* Pres.; Todd Towell, V.P.; **Dan Figliola, Secy.**; **Ted J. Cohn, DVM*, Treas.**; **Roger Haston, Exec. Dir.**; Tory Bond; and 8 additional directors.
Number of staff: 4 full-time professional; 1 part-time professional; 1 part-time support.
EIN: 840715412
Other changes: Dan Figliola has replaced Gina Guy as Secy. Mark Lacy has replaced Apryl Steele as Pres. Ted J. Cohn, DVM has replaced Jeff Blomgren as Treas.
David Gies, George Casey, Lauren Immel, and Jon Sands are no longer directors.
The grantmaker now publishes application guidelines.

473
Avenir Foundation, Inc.
215 Union Blvd., Ste. 300
Lakewood, CO 80228-1841 (303) 232-2262

Established in 1993 in CO.
Donors: Alice Dodge Wallace; William Dodge Wallace; Margaret Boynton Wallace; Berkshire Hathaway Inc.; Varki Investments, Inc.; Beaumont Investments, Ltd.
Foundation type: Independent foundation.
Financial data (yr. ended 06/30/13): Assets, $228,479 (M); gifts received, $12,684,500; expenditures, $12,803,578; qualifying distributions, $12,684,500; giving activities include $12,684,500 for 21 grants.
Purpose and activities: Giving primarily for education, and the arts, particularly museums; funding also for a public research center for music theory in Vienna, Austria, which focuses on the methods of Arnold Schoenberg.
Fields of interest: Museums (specialized); Performing arts, opera; Arts; Education; Reproductive health, family planning.
International interests: Austria.
Limitations: Applications not accepted. Giving primarily in CO, MD, NM, NY, as well as in Vienna, Austria. No grants to individuals.
Application information: Contributes only to pre-selected organizations.
Officers and Directors:* Alice Dodge Wallace,* Pres.; William Dodge Wallace,* V.P.; Margaret Boynton Wallace,* Secy.; Norman L. Wilson,* Treas.
EIN: 841245939
Other changes: For the fiscal year ended June 30, 2013, the grantmaker paid grants of $12,684,500, a 99.3% increase over the fiscal 2012 disbursements, $6,365,000.

474
Ballantine Family Fund
(formerly Ballantine Family Charitable Fund)
162 Stewart St.
Durango, CO **81303-7999 (970) 385-2440**
Contact: Nancy Whitson, Exec. Dir.
FAX: (970) 797-6376; Main URL: http://www.ballantinefamilyfund.com/

Established in 1957 in CO.
Donor: Morley C. Ballantine.
Foundation type: Independent foundation.
Financial data (yr. ended 12/31/13): Assets, $4,541,333 (M); expenditures, $281,183; qualifying distributions, $276,507; giving activities include $242,510 for 103 grants (high: $10,000; low: $500).
Fields of interest: Arts; Education; Human services; Foundations (public).
Type of support: General/operating support; Continuing support; Building/renovation; Land acquisition; Research.
Limitations: Applications accepted. Giving primarily in CO. No grants to individuals.
Publications: Application guidelines; Annual report.
Application information: Application guidelines available on Fund web site. Application form required.
Copies of proposal: 1
***Deadline(s):* July 1**
Board meeting date(s): Feb., May, Aug., and Nov.
Officers: Richard G. Ballantine, Pres.; Elizabeth Ballantine, V.P.; Mary Jane Clark, Secy.; Helen B. Healy, Treas.; Nancy Whitson, Exec. Dir.
Directors: Christopher Ballantine; David Ballantine; Morley Healy; Joe Keck; Sarah Leavitt; William Leavitt.
EIN: 846026270

475
Bonfils-Stanton Foundation
Daniels and Fisher Twr.
1601 Arapahoe St., Ste. 500
Denver, CO 80202-2015 (303) 825-3774
Contact: Gary P. Steuer, C.E.O. and Pres.
FAX: (303) 825-0802;
E-mail: webinfo@bonfils-stanton.org; **Main URL: http://www.bonfils-stantonfoundation.org**

Established in 1962 in CO.
Donors: Charles E. Stanton†; Robert E. Stanton†.
Foundation type: Independent foundation.
Financial data (yr. ended 06/30/13): Assets, $77,475,043 (M); expenditures, $4,382,372; qualifying distributions, $4,116,927; giving activities include $3,293,560 for 65 grants (high: $500,000; low: $500), and $35,000 for 1 grant to an individual.
Purpose and activities: The foundation was created to enhance the quality of life for residents of Colorado. Its mission is to advance excellence in the areas of arts and culture, community service, and science and medicine through strategic investments resulting in significant and unique contributions in these fields. In addition to grantmaking, the foundation annually provides 3 awards to Coloradans who have made significant contributions in the fields of arts and humanities, community service, and science and medicine.
Fields of interest: Museums (art); Humanities; Arts; Human services; Economically disadvantaged.
Type of support: Management development/capacity building; Building/renovation; Equipment; Program development; Research; Technical assistance.
Limitations: Applications accepted. Giving limited to CO. No support for activities or initiatives that have a religious purpose or objective, or for organizations that are not for the benefit of CO citizens. Generally no grants to individuals (except for award programs), or for scholarships, loans, fellowships, endowments, seminars, conferences, media productions, fundraising, travel expenses, or to retire debt.
Publications: Application guidelines; Annual report (including application guidelines); Grants list.
Application information: Colorado Common Grant Application form accepted. Application information available on foundation web site. Application form not required.
Initial approach: Telephone call
Copies of proposal: 1
Deadline(s): Last business day of Jan., Apr., Jul., Oct.
Board meeting date(s): Jan., Apr., July, and Oct.
Final notification: Generally 4 months following application deadline
Officers and Trustees:* J. Landis Martin,* Chair.; **Gary P. Steuer, C.E.O and Pres.**; Ann M. Hovland, C.F.O. and Treas.; Louis J. Duman, M.D., Tr. Emeritus; W. Eileen Greenawalt, Tr. Emeritus; Mark G. Falcone; Julanna V. Gilbert, Ph.D.; Harold R. Logan, Jr.; Denise M. O'Leary; John E. Repine, M.D.
Number of staff: 2 full-time professional; 1 part-time professional; 1 full-time support.
EIN: 846029014
Other changes: For the fiscal year ended June 30, 2013, the grantmaker paid grants of $3,328,560, a 55.8% increase over the fiscal 2012 disbursements, $2,136,600.
Gary P. Steuer has replaced Dorothy A. Horrell as C.E.O. and Pres.
Susan H. France is no longer V.P., Progs.
The grantmaker now makes its application guidelines available online.

476
Brett Family Foundation
1123 Spruce St.
Boulder, CO 80302-4001 (303) 442-1200
Contact: Michael Brewer, Exec. Dir.; Claire Hamilton, Grants Admin.
FAX: (303) 442-1221;
E-mail: claire@brettfoundation.org; Main URL: http://www.brettfoundation.org
Grants List: http://www.brettfoundation.org/2009

Established in 1999 in CO.
Donors: Stephen M. Brett; Linda J. Shoemaker.
Foundation type: Independent foundation.
Financial data (yr. ended 12/31/12): Assets, $8,248,055 (M); expenditures, $595,033; qualifying distributions, $527,337; giving activities include $437,550 for 73 grants (high: $65,000; low: $250).
Purpose and activities: Giving primarily for organizations throughout Colorado which work for social justice, and by giving to Boulder County, Colorado, nonprofits which address the needs of underserved communities, primarily disadvantaged youth and their families.
Fields of interest: Education; Health care; Youth, services; Community/economic development; Public policy, research.
Type of support: General/operating support; Continuing support; Program development; Seed money; Technical assistance.
Limitations: Applications accepted. Giving primarily in CO. No support for religious organizations, or for individual public or private schools (K-12, graduate or post graduate), or for large public charities. No grants to individuals.
Publications: Application guidelines; Annual report; Financial statement; Grants list; IRS Form 990 or 990-PF printed copy available upon request.
Application information: Application guidelines and forms available on foundation web site. Application form required.
Copies of proposal: 1
***Deadline(s):* See foundation web site for current deadlines**
Final notification: 2-3 months
Officers and Trustees:* Stephen M. Brett,* Chair.; Linda J. Shoemaker,* Pres.; Michael Brewer, Exec. Dir.; Emily P. Shoemaker Brett; Matthew S. Brett; **Claudia Brett Goldin.**
Number of staff: 1 part-time professional.
EIN: 841525821
Other changes: The grantmaker now makes its application guidelines available online.

477
Bright Mountain Foundation
(formerly The Wessell Family Foundation)
1800 Broadway, Ste. 100
Boulder, CO **80302-5234 (303) 381-2255**
Contact: Irene Lopez-Wessell, Exec. Dir

Established in 1999 in CO.
Donors: Leonard P. Wessell III; Lee Sands; TINA.
Foundation type: Independent foundation.
Financial data (yr. ended 06/30/13): Assets, $1,673,567 (M); expenditures, $380,065; qualifying distributions, $343,855; giving activities include $161,700 for 22 grants (high: $25,000; low: $200).
Purpose and activities: The foundation is committed to programs that assist children and youth, seniors, and persons living with HIV/AIDS.
Fields of interest: Children/youth, services; Aging; AIDS, people with.
Type of support: Program development; Matching/challenge support.
Limitations: Giving limited to CO. No support for religious organizations or their affiliates. No grants to individuals, or for existing scholarships, general endowments, fundraising events, annual fund drives, debt reduction, or administrative costs.
Officers: Cathy Lopez-Wessell, Exec. Dir.; Irene Lopez-Wessell, Exec. Dir.
Directors: Amy P. Wessell; Leonard P. Wessell.
Trustees: Deborah Foy; Gabriel Guillaume; Tony Tapia.
Number of staff: 2 full-time professional.
EIN: 841524099

478
Tim & Libby Brown Family Foundation
(formerly Brown Family Foundation)
1727 Tremont Pl.
Denver, CO 80202-4006

Established in 2002 in CO.
Donor: The Anschutz Foundation.
Foundation type: Independent foundation.
Financial data (yr. ended 11/30/13): Assets, $10,594 (M); gifts received, $340,000; expenditures, $367,333; qualifying distributions, $367,333; giving activities include $367,333 for 30 grants (high: $63,333; low: $1,500).
Fields of interest: Libraries (special); Education; Zoos/zoological societies; Crime/violence prevention, child abuse; Recreation, community.
Limitations: Applications not accepted. Giving primarily in CO. No grants to individuals.
Application information: Contributes only to pre-selected organizations.
Officers: Elizabeth A. Brown, Chair. and Pres.; M. Lavoy Robison, Exec. Dir.
EIN: 460732753
Other changes: Timothy T. Brown is no longer Vice-Chair. or V.P.

479
Nathan B. & Florence R. Burt Foundation, Inc.
1660 Lincoln St., Ste. 3150
Denver, CO 80264-3100 (303) 863-8980
Contact: Harry L. Arkin, Pres.
Main URL: http://www.burtfoundation.org

Established in 1984.
Donors: N.B. Burt†; F.R. Burt†.
Foundation type: Independent foundation.
Financial data (yr. ended 09/30/12): Assets, $4,084,763 (M); expenditures, $224,534; qualifying distributions, $157,350; giving activities include $157,350 for grants.
Purpose and activities: Supports organizations dealing with and affecting the needs of children and senior citizens.
Fields of interest: Health care; Geriatrics; Children/youth, services; Aging.
Type of support: General/operating support; Continuing support; Equipment; Emergency funds; Matching/challenge support.
Limitations: Applications accepted. Giving primarily in the Denver, CO metropolitan area. No support for political organizations or for religious organizations, except those that provide non-denominational assistance within the foundation's fields of interest. No grants for overhead or capital campaigns, or for construction.
Publications: Application guidelines.
Application information: See foundation web site for complete application guidelines. Application form required.
***Initial approach:* Use online application system on foundation web site**
***Deadline(s):* See foundation web site for current deadlines**
Board meeting date(s): Spring and Fall
Officers and Directors:* Harry L. Arkin,* Chair. and Pres.; John C. Baker,* V.P.; Natalie Meyer,* Secy.; Greg Dickson,* Treas.; Margaret Fomer, M.D.; Harrison F. Hayes, M.D.; Bruce W. Jafek, M.D.
Number of staff: 1 part-time professional; 2 part-time support.
EIN: 840972203
Other changes: The grantmaker now makes its application guidelines available online.

480
Catto Charitable Foundation
c/o Woody Creek Mgmt. Grp.
250 Steele St., Ste. 375
Denver, CO **80206-5200**

Established in 1967.
Donors: Jessica Cato; Henry Catto; Hobby Family Foundation.
Foundation type: Independent foundation.
Financial data (yr. ended 12/31/12): Assets, $47,176,277 (M); expenditures, $1,581,784; qualifying distributions, $782,500; giving activities include $782,500 for 102 grants (high: $100,000; low: $125).
Purpose and activities: Giving primarily for the arts, the environment, and human services.
Fields of interest: Media, radio; Arts; Environment, research; Environment, natural resources; Human services; Social sciences, public policy.
Limitations: Applications not accepted. Giving primarily in CO, Washington, DC, and TX. No grants to individuals.
Application information: Contributes only to pre-selected organizations.
Officers and Directors:* Heather Catto Kohout,* Pres.; Elizabeth Pettus Catto,* V.P.; William Halsell Catto,* V.P.; Jennifer A. Crossett, Secy.-Treas.
EIN: 742773632
Other changes: Heather Catto Kohout has replaced Henry E. Catto, Jr. as Pres.

481
Change Happens Foundation
P.O. Box 600
Erie, CO 80516-0600
Contact: Michael D. Troxel, C.F.O.
E-mail: Admin@ChangeHappens.us; Main URL: http://www.changehappens.us/

Established in 2006 in DE and HI.
Foundation type: Independent foundation.
Financial data (yr. ended 12/31/12): Assets, $15,738,885 (M); expenditures, $1,681,005; qualifying distributions, $1,579,036; giving activities include $1,439,735 for 22 grants (high: $1,191,903; low: $3,000).
Purpose and activities: Giving for the development and implementation of innovative technology and progressive ideas to generate a positive force for change in the world.
Fields of interest: Arts; Higher education; Human services; Children/youth, services; Science.
Limitations: Giving primarily in IA; funding also in CA and HI. **No support for faith-based organizations or**

religious activities. No grants to individuals, or for scholarships, land purchases, third-party sponsorships, or special events.
Application information: Formal grant proposals are by invitation only, after review of initial letter of inquiry. Unsolicited grant proposals will not be considered. Application form required.
Initial approach: Use online letter of inquiry on foundation web site
Deadline(s): None
Officers: Douglas D. Troxel, C.E.O. and Pres.; Michael Douglas Troxel, V.P., Admin. and C.F.O.; Sergei George Troxel, Secy.
Directors: Kristin D. Nong; Kenneth D. Troxel.
EIN: 205222620
Other changes: The grantmaker has moved from HI to CO.

482
Colorado Masons Benevolent Fund Association
2400 Consistory Ct.
Grand Junction, CO 81501-2009
E-mail: **tomcox@cmbfa.org**; Main URL: http://www.cmbfa.org/
Scholarship address: c/o Scholarship Admin.: 1130 Panorama Dr., Colorado Springs, CO 80904, tel.: (800) 482-4441

Established in 1899; incorporated in 1912 in CO.
Donors: Irene Houle; Ella Rose†; William D. Hewitt; William Blackwell; A.F. and A.M Grand Lodge of Colorado; Tenet Healtcare Foundation.
Foundation type: Operating foundation.
Financial data (yr. ended 10/31/12): Assets, $9,296,588 (M); gifts received, $53,500; expenditures, $932,535; qualifying distributions, $926,035; giving activities include $730,121 for 88 grants (high: $81,797; low: $250).
Purpose and activities: A private operating foundation; awards assistance grants to needy, distressed CO Masons and their families through local lodges, and scholarships to CO public high school seniors who are planning to attend college in CO. Masonic affiliation not required for scholarships.
Fields of interest: Higher education; Economically disadvantaged.
Type of support: Grants to individuals; Scholarships—to individuals; Matching/challenge support; Student loans—to individuals.
Limitations: Applications accepted. Giving limited to CO.
Application information: Scholarship application forms available on foundation web site. Application form required.
Initial approach: Letter
Deadline(s): Mar. 7
Officers: Richard W. Schmidt, Pres.; Ben H. Bell, Jr., V.P.; Thomas J. Cox, Exec. Secy.; Charles G. Johnson, Secy.; Robert W. Gregory, Jr., Treas.
Trustee: Roy Snyder.
Number of staff: 1 full-time professional; 1 part-time support.
EIN: 840406813

483
The Colorado Trust
1600 Sherman St.
Denver, CO 80203-1604 (303) 837-1200
FAX: (303) 839-9034;
E-mail: questions@coloradotrust.org; Toll free tel.: (888) 847-9140; Additional e-mail: (for Christie McElhinney): christie@coloradotrust.org; e-mail: (for Maggie Frasure): maggie@coloradotrust.org; Main URL: http://www.coloradotrust.org
Blog: http://www.coloradotrust.org/news/blog
Colorado Trust's Instagram: http://instagram.com/thecoloradotrust
Facebook: http://www.facebook.com/pages/The-Colorado-Trust/89447823595
Grants Database: http://www.coloradotrust.org/grants/search-grants
LinkedIn: http://www.linkedin.com/companies/the-colorado-trust
Twitter: http://twitter.com/coloradotrust

Established in 1985 in CO; with the proceeds from the sale of the PSL Health Care corporation.
Donor: PSL Health Care Corporation.
Foundation type: Independent foundation.
Financial data (yr. ended 12/31/12): Assets, $413,795,482 (M); expenditures, $18,161,195; qualifying distributions, $16,462,307; giving activities include $7,243,313 for 222 grants (high: $373,562; low: $20), and $111,084 for 129 employee matching gifts.
Purpose and activities: The Colorado Trust is dedicated to achieving access to health for all Coloradans, with an emphasis on advancing health equity, working together with communities to provide opportunities for the most vulnerable individuals and families to make healthy choices.
Fields of interest: Health care; Mental health/crisis services; Health organizations, association; Family services; Community development, citizen coalitions; Urban/community development; Children/youth; Children; Youth; Adults; Aging; Young adults; Minorities; African Americans/Blacks; Hispanics/Latinos; Immigrants/refugees; Economically disadvantaged; Homeless.
Type of support: Technical assistance; Seed money; Research; Publication; Program evaluation; Program development; Matching/challenge support; General/operating support; Employee matching gifts; Continuing support.
Limitations: Giving limited to CO. No support for religious organizations for religious purposes, political organizations, or private foundations. No grants to individuals, or for endowments, deficit financing or debt retirement, building funds, or real estate acquisition.
Publications: Annual report; Occasional report.
Application information: Unsolicited requests for funds not accepted. Application form not required.
Initial approach: Applications are invited or accepted following the release of requests for proposals (RFP) issued by the foundation; you can print the RFP directly from the foundation web site
Deadline(s): Governed by individual requests for proposals invitations
Board meeting date(s): Quarterly
Final notification: Varies
Officers and Trustees:* R. J. Ross,* Chair.; Gail S. Schoettler, Vice-Chair.; Reginald L. Washington, M.D.*, Vice-Chair.; Ned Calonge, M.D.,* C.E.O. and Pres.; Deb DeMuth, V.P. and C.F.O.; Gay Cook, V.P., Strategy and Philanthropic Relations; Christie McElhinney, V.P., Comm. and Public Affairs; Jennifer Paquette,* Secy.; Colleen Schwarz, Treas.; **Deborah McCluiston, Cont.**; Cara B. Lawrence, Genl. Counsel; John P. Hopkins; Warren T. Johnson; Donald J. Mares; Alan Synn, M.D.; William Wright, M.D.
Number of staff: 15 full-time professional; 8 full-time support.
EIN: 840994055

484
Community Foundation Serving Greeley and Weld County
2425 35th Ave., Ste.201
Greeley, CO 80634 (970) 304-9970
Contact: Judy Knapp, Pres.
FAX: (970) 352-1271; E-mail: judy@cfsgwc.org; Main URL: http://www.cfsgwc.org
Facebook: http://www.facebook.com/pages/The-Community-Foundation-Serving-Greeley-and-Weld-County/135338119125

Established in 1972; merged in 1997 in CO.
Donors: Cameron DeCamp; Annette Fulton; Lucile J. Gray†; Alpine Gardens; H + H Excavation; BMC West; Siegrist Construction; Monfort Family Foundation; Platte Valley Medical Center; Lawrence Hertzke; Rick Jenkins; Barbara Jenkins; Betty Whitson; Bill McDonald; Richard Bond; Reva Bond; Martin Lind; Richard Boettcher; Irene Boettcher; Gerald Shadwick; Jeannine Shadwick; Philip Hood; Robert Kron; Judy Kron; Robert Oshsner†; Lena Ochsner; Poudre Valley Healthcare Inc.; Greeley Rotary Club; Gay and Lesbian Fund for Colorado; Bond Family Foundation; El Pomar; Banner Health and NCMC.
Foundation type: Community foundation.
Financial data (yr. ended 12/31/12): Assets, $13,394,340 (M); gifts received, $1,799,473; expenditures, $1,225,895; giving activities include $883,585 for grants.
Purpose and activities: The Community Foundation Serving Greeley and Weld County promotes philanthropy to build resources, develops partnerships, and provides leadership that will be of lasting benefit to the local communities.
Fields of interest: Arts; Education; Health care; Housing/shelter; Recreation; Youth development; Youth, services; Human services; Community/economic development; General charitable giving; Children/youth; Women; Girls.
Type of support: Equipment; Curriculum development; Emergency funds; General/operating support; Matching/challenge support; Program development; Scholarship funds; Seed money.
Limitations: Applications accepted. Giving primarily to residents of Greeley and Weld County, CO. No support for sectarian religious purposes or for-profit organizations. No grants for capital fund drives, endowments, debt reduction or event sponsorships.
Publications: Application guidelines; Annual report; Financial statement; Informational brochure; Newsletter.
Application information: Visit foundation web site for application forms and guidelines. Application form required.
Initial approach: Submit application form and attachments
Deadline(s): Varies
Board meeting date(s): Feb., May, Aug., and Nov.
Final notification: Within 6 weeks
Officers and Directors:* Tim Ulrich,* Chair.; Rob Waldo,* Vice-Chair.; Judy Knapp,* Pres.; Rochelle Mitchell-Miller,* V.P., Devel.; **Christine Richardson,* Secy.**; Heidi Klepper,* Treas.; John Adams; Matt Anderson; Beth Bashor; **Karen Burd**; Nora Garza; Christine Larsen; Bill Meier; Stephanie McCune.
Number of staff: 4 full-time professional.
EIN: 841315296
Other changes: Christine Richardson has replaced Heidi Klepper as Secy. and Asst. Treas.
Lee Korins is no longer a member of the governing body. Bill Meier is no longer a member of the governing body. Christine Richardson is no longer a member of the governing body. Rob Waldo is no longer a member of the governing body.

485
Comprecare Foundation
P.O. Box 740610
Arvada, CO 80006 (303) 432-2808
Contact: James R. Gilsdorf, Exec. Dir.
Main URL: http://www.comprecarefoundation.org

Established in 1986 in CO.
Foundation type: Independent foundation.
Financial data (yr. ended 12/31/12): Assets, $4,153,877 (M); gifts received, $124,110; expenditures, $362,497; qualifying distributions, $284,861; giving activities include $228,702 for 12 grants (high: $35,000; low: $15,080).
Purpose and activities: To encourage, aid or assist specific health related programs and to support the activities of organizations and individuals who advance and promote healthcare education, the delivery of healthcare services, and the improvement of community health and welfare.
Fields of interest: Health care; Mental health/crisis services; Health organizations, association; Alcoholism; Children/youth, services; Aging, centers/services; Aging.
Type of support: General/operating support; Continuing support; Equipment; Program development; Seed money; Research.
Limitations: Giving limited to CO. No grants to individuals, or for fellowships, scholarships, operating expenses, debt reduction, land acquisition, fundraising events, or testimonial dinners or promotions.
Application information: The foundation is not considering unsolicited requests for funding until further notice. See foundation web site for current information.
Board meeting date(s): Monthly
Officers and Directors:* Dennis E. Baldwin,* Chair.; Milford H. Schulhof II,* Vice-Chair.; Frederick G. Ihrig,* Secy.-Treas.; James R. Gilsdorf, Exec. Dir.; Milton W. Bollman; Bradford L. Darling; Raymond C. Delisle; Ellen J. Mangione, M.D.; M. Eugene Sherman, M.D.
Number of staff: 1 part-time professional; 1 part-time support.
EIN: 840641406

486
Craig-Scheckman Family Foundation
P.O. Box 776429
Steamboat Springs, CO 80477-6429 (970) 879-0148
Contact: Sara Craig-Scheckman, Pres.
Main URL: http://yap4rc.org/
Grants List: http://yap4rc.org/wp-content/uploads/2014/07/CurrentGrantRecipientsMay14Nov13.pdf
Established in 2005 in CO.
Donors: Michael Craig-Scheckman; Sara Craig-Scheckman; Deer Park Road Corp.; STSM.
Foundation type: Independent foundation.
Financial data (yr. ended 12/31/12): Assets, $4,691,557 (M); gifts received, $383,665; expenditures, $356,117; qualifying distributions, $181,000; giving activities include $181,000 for 29 grants (high: $25,000; low: $200).
Fields of interest: Education; Youth development.
Limitations: Applications accepted. Giving limited to Routt County, CO. No grants to individuals.
Application information: Application form required.
Initial approach: Letter
Deadline(s): May 1 and Nov. 1
Officers: Sara Craig-Scheckman, Pres.; Michael Craig-Scheckman, Treas.
EIN: 202835678

487
The Crowell Trust
(also known as Henry P. and Susan C. Crowell Trust)
102 N. Cascade Ave., Ste. 300
Colorado Springs, CO 80903-1418 (719) 645-8119
Contact: Candace "Candy" Sparks, Exec. Dir.
FAX: (719) 418-2695; E-mail: info@crowelltrust.org; Main URL: http://www.crowelltrust.org

Trust established in 1927 in IL.
Donors: Henry P. Crowell†; Henry P. Crowell Benevolence and Education Trust; Henry P. and Susan C. Crowell Trust.
Foundation type: Independent foundation.
Financial data (yr. ended 12/31/12): Assets, $99,963,779 (M); expenditures, $5,466,454; qualifying distributions, $4,766,054; giving activities include $4,225,000 for 113 grants (high: $215,000; low: $500).
Purpose and activities: Created to aid evangelical Christianity by support to organizations having for their purposes its teaching, advancement, and active extension at home and abroad.
Fields of interest: Theological school/education; Christian agencies & churches; Religion.
Type of support: General/operating support; Management development/capacity building; Equipment; Program development; Publication; Curriculum development; Scholarship funds; Technical assistance.
Limitations: Applications accepted. Giving on a national basis. No support for churches or schooling from kindergarten through 12th grade. No grants to individuals, or for endowment funds; no loans.
Application information: Applications accepted online. Application form required.
Initial approach: Preliminary proposal, see foundation web site for full details
Copies of proposal: 1
Deadline(s): See web site for current deadlines
Board meeting date(s): Spring and fall
Final notification: 1 to 2 months
Officers and Trustees:* John T. Lewis,* Chair.; John T. Bass,* Vice-Chair. and Treas.; Dr. Jane Overstreet,* Secy.; Candace "Candy" Sparks, Exec. Dir.; **Paul Borthwick**; Jack Robinson.
Corporate Trustee: The Northern Trust Company.
Number of staff: 1 full-time professional; 2 part-time support.
EIN: 366038028
Other changes: Edwin L. Frizen and Lowell L. Kline is no longer a trustees.

488
Daniels Fund
101 Monroe St.
Denver, CO 80206-4467 (303) 393-7220
Contact: Peter Droege, V.P., Comms.; Barb Danbom, Sr. V.P., Grants Prog.
FAX: (720) 941-4110; E-mail: info@danielsfund.org; Toll free tel.: (877) 791- 4726; Additional e-mails for general contact: grantsinfo@danielsfund.org; For B. Danbom: bdanbom@danielsfund.org; For P. Droege: pdroege@danielsfund.org; Main URL: http://www.danielsfund.org
E-Newsletter: http://www.danielsfund.org/contact/newsletter.asp
Twitter: https://twitter.com/Daniels_Fund

Established in 1997 in CO.
Donor: Bill Daniels†.
Foundation type: Independent foundation.
Financial data (yr. ended 12/31/13): Assets, $1,388,360,517 (M); expenditures, $55,677,151; qualifying distributions, $52,881,939; giving activities include $32,994,514 for 531 grants (high: $1,000,000; low: $750), $13,400,844 for 1,157 grants to individuals, and $10,933 for 22 employee matching gifts.
Purpose and activities: Giving primarily for child care education reform and early childhood education, higher education, youth development, the elderly, homelessness and self-sufficiency, alcoholism, and substance abuse, amateur athletics, and for people with physical disabilities.
Fields of interest: Education, reform; Education, ethics; Education, early childhood education; Education; Substance abuse, services; Alcoholism; Geriatrics; Housing/shelter, homeless; Athletics/sports, amateur leagues; Youth development; Developmentally disabled, centers & services; Homeless, human services; Aging; Disabilities, people with; Economically disadvantaged; Homeless.
Type of support: General/operating support; Annual campaigns; Capital campaigns; Building/renovation; Equipment; Program development; Program evaluation; Scholarships—to individuals; Matching/challenge support.
Limitations: Applications accepted. Giving primarily in CO, with emphasis on Denver; funding also in NM, WY and UT with a limited basis nationally. No support for arts and cultural programs. No grants to individuals (except for Daniels Fund Scholarship Program) or for academic, medical, or scientific research or symposia, or for endowments or debt elimination.
Publications: Annual report; Financial statement; Grants list; Informational brochure; Newsletter; IRS Form 990 or 990-PF printed copy available upon request.
Application information: National Grants applicants should phone the foundation before submitting an application. Generally only one active grant is allowed per organization. Please contact the fund prior to submitting an application if you are applying for a program or project that is part of a larger institution such as a university. Apply for additional funding once all reporting requirements from a previous grant have been fulfilled. Application form required.
Initial approach: Letter, telephone, or submit full proposal
Copies of proposal: 1
Deadline(s): None
Board meeting date(s): Quarterly
Final notification: Within 120 days
Officers and Directors:* Hank Brown,* Chair.; Linda Childears,* C.E.O. and Pres.; Jeb Dickey, Exec. V.P., Finance and Investment; Barb Danborn, Sr. V.P., Grants; Kristin Todd, Sr. V.P., Scholarships Prog.; Saurabh Gupta, V.P., Inf. Tech.; Gretchen Lenamond, V.P., Finance; Vivian Mount, V.P., Human Resources; Bo Peretto, V.P., Admin. and Operations; Janet Friesen, Secy.; Tony Acone; Brian Deevy; Francisco Garcia; Gayle Greer; Jim Griesmer; Tom Marinkovich; Jim Nicholson; Daniel L. Ritchie; June Travis.
Number of staff: 38 full-time professional; 1 full-time support; 2 part-time support.
EIN: 841393308
Other changes: Peter Droege is no longer V.P., Comms.

489
Denver Public Schools Retired Employees Association Foundation
2408 S. Utica St.
Denver, CO 80219-6402 (303) 279-0590
***Contact:* Bernadette Seick**

***E-mail:* brseick@yahoo.com**; Main URL: http://www.dpsrea.org/

Foundation type: Independent foundation.
Financial data (yr. ended 12/31/12): Assets, $8,709,502 (M); gifts received, $30,337; expenditures, $398,572; qualifying distributions, $368,999; giving activities include $368,999 for 39 grants to individuals (high: $10,000; low: $3,333).
Fields of interest: Higher education, college.
Type of support: Scholarships—to individuals.
Limitations: Applications accepted. Giving primarily in CO.
Application information: Application form required.
Initial approach: Letter
Deadline(s): None
Officers: Lynne Williams, Pres.; Leslie Moore, 1st V.P.; Marge Tepper, 2nd V.P.; Jane Rodish, Secy.; Pam Woods, Treas.
EIN: 841331121

490
Donahue Foundation
P.O. Box 2554
Littleton, CO **80161-2254**
Contact: Lisa A. Donahue-Goodwin, Exec. Dir.
E-mail: info@donahuefoundation.org; Main URL: http://www.donahuefoundation.org
Grants List: http://www.donahuefoundation.org/grants.html

Established in 1990 in CO.
Donors: William L. Donahue†; Leonice M. Donahue†.
Foundation type: Independent foundation.
Financial data (yr. ended 12/31/12): Assets, $4,161,435 (M); gifts received, $1,000; expenditures, $308,840; qualifying distributions, $283,511; giving activities include $249,890 for 13 grants (high: $99,274; low: $3,000).
Purpose and activities: Giving primarily for non-public and parochial school education for low-income families.
Fields of interest: Education.
Type of support: General/operating support; Continuing support; Emergency funds; Curriculum development; Scholarship funds.
Limitations: Applications accepted. Giving limited to CO. No grants for capital funding, financial aid for college-level education, or for other foundations.
Publications: Application guidelines; Informational brochure.
Application information: CGA Colorado Common Grant Application accepted. See web site for application policies and guidelines. Application form required.
Initial approach: Preliminary letter
Copies of proposal: 1
Deadline(s): Mar. 1
Board meeting date(s): June
Final notification: 10 days after meeting
Officers: Mark Donahue, Pres. and Treas.; Lisa Donahue-Goodwin, Secy. and Exec. Dir.
Directors: Greg Donahue; William P. Donahue; Teri Goddard; Rita Ochs.
Number of staff: 1 part-time professional.
EIN: 841151637

491
Donnell-Kay Foundation, Inc.
730 17th St., No. 950
Denver, CO 80202-3599 (720) 932-1544
Contact: Carmelita Galicia-Munoz, Dir., Admin.
FAX: (303) 534-5785;
E-mail: cgaliciamunoz@dkfoundation.org; Main URL: http://www.dkfoundation.org
Facebook: https://www.facebook.com/pages/Donnell-Kay-Foundation/134013736616454?ref=search
LinkedIn: http://www.linkedin.com/company/2234127
Twitter: http://twitter.com/donnellkay

Established in 1965 in FL. Incorporated in CO in 2009.
Donor: Elizabeth D. Kay†.
Foundation type: Independent foundation.
Financial data (yr. ended 01/31/13): Assets, $27,040,533 (M); expenditures, $1,793,404; qualifying distributions, $1,622,610; giving activities include $415,000 for 30 grants (high: $35,000; low: $1,000), and $48,142 for 4 foundation-administered programs.
Purpose and activities: The foundation improves public education and drives systemic school reform in Colorado through solid research, creative dialogue, and critical thinking. Giving primarily for public school reform, higher education, and early childhood education.
Fields of interest: Elementary/secondary education; Secondary school/education; Higher education; Education, services; Education; Children/youth, services; Children/youth; Children; Youth.
Type of support: Technical assistance; Fellowships; General/operating support; Continuing support; Annual campaigns; Capital campaigns; Program development; Conferences/seminars; Publication; Research; Consulting services; Matching/challenge support.
Limitations: Applications not accepted. Giving primarily in CO. No support for religious or political organizations. No grants to individuals.
Publications: Newsletter; Occasional report.
Application information: Contributes only to pre-selected organizations; unsolicited applications not considered; however the foundation does accept but does accept one-page concept papers that address statewide educational policy issues.
Board meeting date(s): Varies
Officers and Directors:* Sidney A. Dines,* Pres. and Treas.; Allen Dines,* V.P.; Connie Dines,* Secy.; Tony Lewis, Exec. Dir.
Number of staff: 5 full-time professional; 3 part-time professional.
EIN: 596169704

492
El Pomar Foundation
10 Lake Cir.
Colorado Springs, CO 80906-4201 (719) 633-7733
Contact: William J. Hybl, Chair.
FAX: (719) 577-5702; Additional tel.: (800) 554-7711; Main URL: http://www.elpomar.org
Blog: http://blog.elpomar.org/
Facebook: https://www.facebook.com/elpomarfoundation?v=wall&ref=ts
Grants Database: http://www.elpomar.org/grants
Twitter: http://twitter.com/elpomarfdtn

Incorporated in 1937 in CO.
Donors: Spencer Penrose†; Mrs. Spencer Penrose†.
Foundation type: Independent foundation.
Financial data (yr. ended 12/31/13): Assets, $552,170,661 (M); gifts received, $1,981,050; expenditures, $20,713,894; qualifying distributions, $22,018,826; giving activities include $11,788,502 for 917 grants (high: $1,500,000; low: $272), $169,417 for 49 employee matching gifts, and $256,751 for 56 in-kind gifts.
Purpose and activities: Grants only to nonprofit organizations for public, educational, arts and humanities, health, and welfare purposes, including child welfare, the disadvantaged, and housing; municipalities may request funds for specific projects.
Fields of interest: Visual arts; Museums; Performing arts; Performing arts, theater; Performing arts, music; Humanities; Historic preservation/historical societies; Arts; Child development, education; Vocational education; Higher education; Adult/continuing education; Adult education—literacy, basic skills & GED; Libraries/library science; Education, reading; Education; Environment, natural resources; Environment; Hospitals (general); Pharmacy/prescriptions; Health care; Substance abuse, services; Health organizations, association; Employment; Food services; Nutrition; Housing/shelter, development; Recreation; Human services; Children/youth, services; Child development, services; Family services; Residential/custodial care, hospices; Aging, centers/services; Homeless, human services; Community/economic development; Voluntarism promotion; Transportation; Aging; Disabilities, people with; Minorities; Economically disadvantaged; Homeless.
Type of support: General/operating support; Continuing support; Capital campaigns; Building/renovation; Equipment; Land acquisition; Emergency funds; Program development; Scholarship funds; Employee matching gifts; In-kind gifts.
Limitations: Applications accepted. Giving limited to CO. No support for organizations that distribute funds to other grantees, religious or political organizations, primary or secondary education, or for camps or seasonal facilities. No grants to individuals, or for travel, film or other media projects, conferences, seminars, deficit financing, endowment funds, research.
Publications: Application guidelines; Annual report (including application guidelines); Financial statement; Grants list; Informational brochure.
Application information: Colorado Common Grant Application form accepted. Application form not required.
Initial approach: Proposal
Copies of proposal: 1
Deadline(s): One month before board meeting
Board meeting date(s): 6 to 8 times a year
Final notification: 90 days
Officers and Trustees:* William J. Hybl,* Chair. and C.E.O.; William R. Ward,* Vice-Chair.; **Kyle Hybl,* C.O.O. and Gen. Counsel**; R. Thayer Tutt, Jr.,* Pres. and C.I.O.; **Gary Butterworth, Sr. V.P. ,Dir., El Pomar Fellowship and Dir., Penrose House; Matt Carpenter, Sr. V.P., Grants; George Guerrero, Sr. V.P., Facilities; Theophilus Gregory, Sr. V.P.; Cathy Robbins, Sr. V.P. and Dir., Regional Partnerships**; **Terrence McWilliams, V.P., Military and Veteran Affairs**; **Peter Maiurro, V.P.**; Robert J. Hilbert, C.F.O. and Trustee Emeritus; **Brenda J. Smith, Trustee Emeritus; Andrea Aragon**; Judith M. Bell; **Hon. Dennis Maes**; Bob Manning; **Christina McGrath**; David J. Palenchar; **Genl. Victor Eugene Renuart, Jr.**
Number of staff: 33 full-time professional; 20 full-time support; 7 part-time support.
EIN: 846002373
Other changes: Robert J. Hilbert is now C.F.O. Brenda J. Smith is now Trustee Emeritus. Tim Travis is no longer a trustee.

493

EnCana Cares (USA) Foundation

370 17th St., Ste. 1700
Denver, CO 80202-5632
***Main URL:* http://www.encana.com/**

Established in 2006 in CO.
Donors: Galen Archer; Clark L. Vickers; Julia Gwaltney; Lisa Mallin; David Smith II; John Holmberg; Encana Oil & Gas (USA), Inc.
Foundation type: Company-sponsored foundation.
Financial data (yr. ended 12/31/13): Assets, $0 (M); gifts received, $1,925,138; expenditures, $1,925,138; qualifying distributions, $1,925,138; giving activities include $1,925,138 for 771 grants (high: $46,350; low: $50).
Purpose and activities: The foundation matches contributions made by employees of EnCana to nonprofit organizations.
Fields of interest: Education; Health care; Human services.
Type of support: Employee matching gifts.
Limitations: Applications not accepted. Giving primarily in CO and TX.
Application information: Contributes only through employee matching gifts.
Officers and Directors:* Renee E. Zemljak,* Pres.; Don McClure,* V.P. and Treas.; Doug Hock,* Secy.
EIN: 205064193

494

Erion Foundation

P.O. Box 732
Loveland, CO 80539-0732 (970) 667-4549
Contact: Kristin M. Harmon, Admin., Comm.
FAX: (970) 663-6187;
E-mail: contact@erionfoundation.org; **General inquiries should be directed to Summer Scott, Admin., Comms. at the foundation's main e-mail address; E-mail for applications: GrantRequest@erionfoundation.org; Applications sent via U.S. mail should be to the attention of the Board of Directors**; Main URL: http://www.erionfoundation.org

Established in 1997 in CO.
Donors: Ken Erion†; Helen Erion†.
Foundation type: Independent foundation.
Financial data (yr. ended 12/31/12): Assets, $9,789,647 (M); gifts received, $105,785; expenditures, $701,432; qualifying distributions, $1,222,760; giving activities include $565,449 for 37 grants (high: $311,249; low: $116), and $641,895 for 1 foundation-administered program.
Purpose and activities: The foundation balances its grantmaking between 5 general areas of interest: 1) Major Project Advocacy; 2) Health and Welfare; 3) Basic Needs; 4) Education; and 5) Culture and Community. The foundation prefers grants for capital projects, specific programs, and joint ventures with other funder.
Fields of interest: Arts; Education; Health care; Human services.
Limitations: Applications accepted. Giving primarily in Northern CO, particularly in the Loveland Planning Area, the Thomson and Poudre School Districts, and in Larimer County. No support for private foundations, organizations that don't have fiscal responsibility for the proposed project, private schools, or religious or political programs. No grants to individuals, or for debt reduction.
Application information: The foundation prefers that grant requests be sent via e-mail. Application form required.
Initial approach: Letter requesting application form or download form from foundation web site
Copies of proposal: 1
Deadline(s): Last day of Jan., Apr., July, and Oct.
Board meeting date(s): Quarterly
Final notification: Last day of Mar., June, Sept., and Dec.
Officers and Directors:* Douglas J. Erion,* Pres.; Roger E. Clark,* V.P.; Eli Scott,* Treas.; Janice Pierce Atnip; Justin Erion; Travis Erion; Christine Erion Klein.
Trustee: First National Bank.
EIN: 841358074

495

The Esther Foundation

7979 E. Tufts Ave., Ste. 400
Denver, CO **80237-2521**

Established in 1999 in CO.
Donor: R. Scot Sellers.
Foundation type: Independent foundation.
Financial data (yr. ended 12/31/12): Assets, $4,730,560 (M); gifts received, $900,000; expenditures, $189,780; qualifying distributions, $151,500; giving activities include $151,500 for 2 grants (high: $76,500; low: $75,000).
Purpose and activities: Giving for the support of Christian ministries that strengthen or preserve the family.
Fields of interest: Education; Human services; Foundations (private grantmaking); Christian agencies & churches.
Limitations: Applications not accepted. Giving in the U.S., with emphasis on CO. No grants to individuals.
Application information: Contributes only to pre-selected organizations.
Officer and Director:* R. Scot Sellers,* Pres.
EIN: 841523209
Other changes: Alanna G. Sellers is no longer Secy.-Treas.

496

First Data Foundation

6200 S. Quebec St., Ste. 330
Greenwood Village, CO 80111-4729
***E-mail:* communityrelations@firstdata.com**

Established in 2006 in CO.
Donor: First Data Corp.
Foundation type: Company-sponsored foundation.
Financial data (yr. ended 12/31/13): Assets, $0; gifts received, $1,067,219; expenditures, $1,104,477; qualifying distributions, $1,102,849; giving activities include $1,102,849 for 2,078 grants.
Purpose and activities: The foundation supports food banks and organizations involved with education, health, housing, disaster relief, human services, economically disadvantaged people and other areas. Special emphasis is directed toward programs designed to promote financial literacy and employee engagement.
Fields of interest: Education; Health care; Food banks; Housing/shelter; Disasters, preparedness/services; American Red Cross; Children/youth, services; Human services, financial counseling; Homeless, human services; Human services; United Ways and Federated Giving Programs; General charitable giving; Economically disadvantaged.
International interests: Argentina; Australia; Germany; Greece; United Kingdom.
Type of support: General/operating support; Employee volunteer services; Employee matching gifts.
Limitations: Applications not accepted. Giving primarily in CA, Denver, CO, GA, Omaha, NE, and Long Island, NY, giving also in Australia, Argentina, Germany, Greece, and the United Kingdom. No support for religious or political organizations. No grants for films.
Publications: Corporate report.
Application information: Contributes only to pre-selected organizations.
Board meeting date(s): Jan., Apr., July, and Oct.
Officers: Ed Labry, Chair.; Joe Samuel, Vice-Chair.; Chip Swearngan, Pres.; Alan Bethscheider, Secy.; Barry Cooper, Treas.
Member: Amrish Rau; Javier Mier Y Teran; Karen Whalen; Siobhan Winiberg.
Number of staff: 2 full-time professional.
EIN: 205626313
Other changes: The grantmaker no longer lists a primary contact. The grantmaker no longer lists a URL address.
Ellen Sanderg is no longer Pres.

497

Sheila Fortune Foundation, Inc.

2135 4th St.
Boulder, CO 80302-4901 (303) 443-5348
Contact: Sheila Fortune, Pres.
FAX: (303) 443-5365;
E-mail: sheilafortunefnd@gmail.com; Main URL: http://www.sheilafortunefoundation.com
Grants List: http://www.sheilafortunefoundation.com/glsf.htm

Established in 1998 in CO, IN, and PA.
Donors: Sheila M. Fortune; Martha Murray Fortune Foundation.
Foundation type: Independent foundation.
Financial data (yr. ended 12/31/12): Assets, $6,370,941 (M); gifts received, $63,277; expenditures, $413,410; qualifying distributions, $349,038; giving activities include $328,733 for 66 grants (high: $10,000; low: $2,500).
Purpose and activities: The foundation is dedicated to helping at-risk youth gain access to, and expression through, the performing arts.
Fields of interest: Performing arts; Children/youth, services.
Type of support: Program development.
Limitations: Applications accepted. Giving primarily in CO, IN, NM and PA.
Publications: Newsletter.
Application information: Complete application guidelines available on foundation web site. Application form not required.
Initial approach: Concise request by letter preferred
Deadline(s): See foundation web site
Officers and Directors:* Sheila M. Fortune, Pres.; Sophia Gold,* V.P.; Michelle Winebrenner-Nizam, Secy.-Treas.; Michelle Guyton, Exec. Dir.; Douglas M. Cain; Marc A. Hetzner; William C. Metzger.
EIN: 841467131

498

Foundation for Educational Excellence

4908 Tower Rd., Ste. 108
Denver, CO 80249-6684 (303) 486-8500
Contact: Eric Montoya, Secy.-Treas.
***FAX:* (303) 843-0745**

Established in 1997 in CO.

Donors: Oakwood Homes, LLC; Richmond Homes; The Boeing Co.; Orchard Crossing III; Alpert Companies; Aurora Chamber of Conference.
Foundation type: Independent foundation.
Financial data (yr. ended 12/31/12): Assets, $533,656 (M); gifts received, $5,141,987; expenditures, $4,948,689; qualifying distributions, $4,780,512; giving activities include $4,780,512 for 10 grants (high: $3,530,157; low: $636).
Purpose and activities: The foundation is focused on new school development, school reform, and community engagement on educational issues.
Fields of interest: Education, public policy; Education, reform; Education.
Type of support: Seed money; Program development; Equipment; Consulting services; Conferences/seminars; Building/renovation; General/operating support.
Limitations: Applications accepted. Giving primarily in northeastern Denver, CO. No support for religious or political organizations.
Publications: Informational brochure; Occasional report.
Application information: Application form not required.
Initial approach: Letter
Copies of proposal: 1
Deadline(s): Quarterly
Board meeting date(s): Quarterly (usually the final week of the quarter)
Final notification: 30 days
Officers: Hap Legg, Chair.; Kelly Leid, Vice-Chair.; Eric Montoya, Secy.-Treas.; Amy Schwartz, Exec. Dir.
Directors: Gail Busby; Jeff Carlson; Scott Gilmore; Stacie Gilmore; William T. Golson; Patrick Hamill; Tim Sheahan.
Number of staff: 1 full-time professional.
EIN: 841396597
Other changes: At the close of 2012, the grantmaker paid grants of $4,780,512, an 822.7% increase over the 2011 disbursements, $518,090.

499
Fox Family Foundation
3003 E. 1st Ave., Ste. 400
Denver, CO 80206-5611

Established in 2007 in CO.
Donors: John M. Fox; Marcella F. Fox; John F. Fox, Jr.; Anne E. Fox Mounsey; Kelley P. Fox; Peter Mounsey; Becca Selvidge Fox.
Foundation type: Independent foundation.
Financial data (yr. ended 06/30/13): Assets, $21,497,763 (M); gifts received, $3,351,769; expenditures, $670,022; qualifying distributions, $655,568; giving activities include $621,000 for 42 grants (high: $50,000; low: $2,000).
Fields of interest: Education; Hospitals (specialty); Housing/shelter; Youth, services; Human services; Catholic agencies & churches.
Limitations: Applications not accepted. Giving primarily in CO and LA. No grants to individuals.
Application information: Contributes only to pre-selected organizations.
Officers: John M. Fox, Pres. and Treas.; Marcella F. Fox, V.P.; John M. Fox, Jr., Secy.
Directors: Kelley P. Fox; Anne Mounsey; Rick Simms.
EIN: 205854615
Other changes: Becca Selvidge Fox is no longer a director.

500
The Galena Foundation
4725 S. Monaco St., Ste. 215
Denver, CO **80237-3445 (303) 761-5213**
Contact: Abigail S. Mooney, Pres.; F. Steven Mooney, Secy.

Established in 1996 in CO.
Donors: Abigail S. Mooney; F. Steven Mooney.
Foundation type: Independent foundation.
Financial data (yr. ended 12/31/12): Assets, $39,435,318 (M); gifts received, $1,000,000; expenditures, $3,314,368; qualifying distributions, $3,164,675; giving activities include $3,161,900 for 31 grants (high: $2,000,000; low: $1,000).
Fields of interest: Education; Children/youth, services; Christian agencies & churches.
Limitations: Giving primarily in CO.
Application information:
Initial approach: Proposal
Deadline(s): None
Officers and Trustees:* Abigail S. Mooney, Pres.; F. Steven Mooney,* Secy.; Alice G. Harwood.
EIN: 841326379
Other changes: At the close of 2012, the grantmaker paid grants of $3,161,900, a 99.2% increase over the 2011 disbursements, $1,587,370.

501
General Service Foundation
557 N. Mill St., Ste. 201
Aspen, CO 81611-1513 (970) 920-6834
FAX: (970) 920-4578;
E-mail: info@generalservice.org; E-mail for Letters of Inquiry (if applicant cannot apply online): grantmanager@generalservice.org; Additional tel. (for William M. Repplinger, Cont.): (970) 920-6834, ext. 5; Main URL: http://www.generalservice.org
General Service Foundation's Philanthropy Promise: http://www.ncrp.org/philanthropys-promise/who

Incorporated in 1946 in IL.
Donors: Clifton R. Musser‡; Margaret K. Musser‡.
Foundation type: Independent foundation.
Financial data (yr. ended 12/31/12): Assets, $59,037,431 (M); expenditures, $3,639,462; qualifying distributions, $2,886,840; giving activities include $2,117,180 for 91 grants (high: $80,900; low: $500).
Purpose and activities: The foundation believes it can make its best contribution at this point in time by addressing some of the world's basic long-term problems in three areas: Human Rights and Economic Justice, Reproductive Justice and the Colorado Program.
Fields of interest: Environment, natural resources; Reproductive health; Reproductive health, family planning; Youth, pregnancy prevention; International peace/security; International human rights; Civil liberties, reproductive rights.
International interests: Caribbean; Central America; Mexico.
Type of support: Mission-related investments/loans; General/operating support; Emergency funds; Program development; Conferences/seminars; Seed money; Technical assistance.
Limitations: Applications accepted. Giving limited to the U.S., Mexico, Central America, and the Caribbean.
Publications: Application guidelines; Financial statement; Grants list; Informational brochure (including application guidelines).
Application information: Applicants are strongly encouraged to submit letters of inquiry via e-mail or using the online submission form on the foundation web site. Applicants who are unable to apply online may submit their letters of inquiry via e-mail or U.S. mail, but this only if applying online is not an option. The foundation encourages applicants to who apply via U.S. mail to use non-chlorine bleached recycled paper, and not to use plastic binders. Application form required.
Initial approach: Online letter of inquiry (4 pages)
Copies of proposal: 1
Deadline(s): Feb. 1 and Sept. 1 for letter of inquiry; Mar. 1 and Oct. 1 for invited proposals
Board meeting date(s): Apr. and Nov.
Final notification: 6 months
Officers and Directors:* Robin Snidow,* Chair.; Zoe Estrin,* Vice-Chair.; Marcie J. Musser,* Secy.; Will Halby,* Treas.; William M. Repplinger, CPA, C.F.O.; Lani A. Shaw, Exec. Dir.; Mary Lloyd Estrin; Robert L. Estrin; Zoe L. Foxley; Peter C. Halby; Cleo Hill; Marcie J. Musser; Robert W. Musser; Crystal Plati; Arturo Sandoval; Bill Vandenberg.
Number of staff: 4 full-time professional; 1 full-time support.
EIN: 366018535

502
The Gill Foundation
2215 Market St.
Denver, CO 80205-2026 (303) 292-4455
Contact: Tim Sweeney, C.E.O. and Pres.
FAX: (303) 292-2155;
E-mail: info@gillfoundation.org; Toll free tel.: (888) 530-4455; Main URL: http://www.gillfoundation.org
A program of the Gill Foundation: http://www.facebook.com/gayandlesbianfund
A program of the Gill Foundation: http://www.gayandlesbianfund.org
A program of the Gill Foundation: http://twitter.com/gaylesbianfund
Facebook: http://www.facebook.com/pages/Gill-Foundation/132968166459
Grants Database: http://www.gillfoundation.org/annual-reports/year-2010/grants
Twitter: http://twitter.com/gillfoundation#

Established in 1994 in CO.
Donors: Tim Gill; The Ford Foundation.
Foundation type: Independent foundation.
Financial data (yr. ended 12/31/12): Assets, $222,817,729 (M); gifts received, $1,073,100; expenditures, $21,880,823; qualifying distributions, $19,998,905; giving activities include $14,168,560 for 608 grants (high: $500,000; low: $10), and $1,988,683 for 2 foundation-administered programs.
Purpose and activities: The mission of the foundation is to secure equal opportunity for all people, regardless of sexual orientation or gender expression. The mission is accomplished by: providing grants to nonprofit organizations, strengthening the leadership and managerial skills of nonprofit leaders, increasing financial resources to nonprofit organizations, strengthening democratic institutions, and building awareness of the contributions people of diverse sexual orientations and gender expressions make to American society.
Fields of interest: AIDS; Civil/human rights, LGBTQ; Philanthropy/voluntarism; LGBTQ.
Type of support: General/operating support; Continuing support; Annual campaigns; Emergency funds; Program development; Conferences/seminars; Consulting services; Employee matching gifts; Matching/challenge support.
Limitations: Applications not accepted. Giving on a national basis to national and state-wide

organizations. No support for clinical HIV/AIDS research, prevention or direct client services to community based HIV/AIDS organizations outside CO, or art programs for or about HIV. No support to individuals, endowments, scholarships, capital projects, direct care services, pride events, film or media production.
Publications: Annual report; Grants list.
Application information: Unsolicited requests for funds not accepted at this time. Grants to organizations are by invitation only.
Board meeting date(s): Quarterly
Officers and Board Members:* Tim Gill,* Chair.; Courtney Cuff, C.E.O. and Pres.; Robin Hubbard, C.O.O.; Katherine Peck, Sr. V.P., National Progs.; Lance King, V.P., Donor Resources; Bobby Clark, V.P., Marketing and Comms.; Lauren Arnold, Chief of Staff; **Urvashi Vaid,* Secy.**; **Laurie Meili, C.F.O.**; **John Barabino,* Treas.**
Number of staff: 19 full-time professional; 7 full-time support; 2 part-time support.
EIN: 841264186
Other changes: John Barabino has replaced David Dechman as Treas.
Laurie Meili is now C.F.O.

503
Grand Foundation
(formerly Columbine Foundation for the Grand Foundation)
P.O. Box 1342
Winter Park, CO 80482-1342 (970) 887-3111
Contact: **Megan Ledin, Exec. Dir.; For grants: Stacy Starr, Grants and Mktg. Coord.**
FAX: (970) 887-3176;
E-mail: info@grandfoundation.com; **Grant inquiry e-mail: stacy@grandfoundation.com**; Main URL: http://www.grandfoundation.com
Facebook: http://www.facebook.com/pages/Grand-Foundation/128508847201033
Twitter: http://twitter.com/GrandFoundation
YouTube: http://www.youtube.com/TheGrandFoundation

Established in 1996 in CO.
Foundation type: Community foundation.
Financial data (yr. ended 12/31/11): Assets, $1,697,836 (M); gifts received, $436,408; expenditures, $1,012,603; giving activities include $778,719 for grants.
Purpose and activities: The Grand Foundation is a philanthropic organization serving all of Grand County, Colorado. The foundation seeks to improve the quality of life in Grand County by proactively addressing current and future needs in the areas of Health & Human Services, Arts & Culture, Education, Amateur Sports and Environment.
Fields of interest: Arts; Education; Environment; Health care; Recreation; Human services; Community/economic development.
Limitations: Applications accepted. Giving primarily in Grant County, CO.
Application information: Visit foundation web site for application cover page and guidelines. The standard application is recommended for grant requests of $2,501 or more. Application form required.
Initial approach: Submit cover page and proposal
***Copies of proposal:* 11**
Deadline(s): May 1
Final notification: June
Officers and Board Members:* Ben Watson,* Chair.; Megan Ledin, Exec. Dir.; Barbara Ahrens; Jennifer Colley; Sean Damery; Jerry Groswold; Kyle Harris; Jancie Hughes; David Kafer; **Dr. Jim Kennedy**; C.A. Lane; Dick Lacouture; Sheri Lock; Greg Norwick; Jynnifer Pierro; Mike Ray; Mike Ritschard; Catherine Ross; Dennis Saffell; Julie Watkins; Rob Young.
EIN: 841374928
Other changes: Ben Watson is no longer a board member. Ron Nelson, Judy Schiff, and Ben Watson are no longer board members.

504
The Griffin Foundation, Inc.
303 W. Prospect Rd.
Fort Collins, CO 80526-2003 (970) 482-3030
Contact: David L. Wood, Chair. and Treas.
FAX: (970) 484-6648;
E-mail: carol.wood@thegriffinfoundation.org; Main URL: http://www.thegriffinfoundation.org
Grants List: http://www.thegriffinfoundation.org/about.shtml

Established in 1991 in CO.
Donor: Pat Griffin.
Foundation type: Independent foundation.
Financial data (yr. ended 12/31/12): Assets, $3,082,057 (M); expenditures, $977,585; qualifying distributions, $700,643; giving activities include $700,643 for grants.
Purpose and activities: Giving primarily for health care, higher education and performing arts organizations. Scholarships also to students who have an associate degree or at least sixty academic hours from a junior or community college and are seeking to complete a baccalaureate degree and are attending Colorado State University (Fort Collins campus), the University of Northern Colorado or the University of Wyoming (Laramie campus).
Fields of interest: Performing arts, orchestras; Arts; Higher education; Health care.
Type of support: Building/renovation; Scholarships—to individuals.
Limitations: Applications accepted. Giving primarily in Fort Collins, CO; some giving in Laramie, WY.
Publications: Application guidelines.
Application information: Complete scholarship application guidelines available on foundation web site. Application form required.
***Initial approach:* E-mail; Scholarship application available to download on foundation web site**
Deadline(s): None
Officers and Directors:* David L. Wood,* Chair. and Pres.; Beatrice C. Griffin,* V.P. and Secy.; Jerry W. Rizley,* V.P.
EIN: 841171483
Other changes: The grantmaker now publishes application guidelines online.

505
Helmar Skating Fund
1228 15th St., Ste. 309
Denver, CO 80202-1642

Established in 1986 in CO.
Donors: Helen M. McLoraine; The Pioneer Fund.
Foundation type: Independent foundation.
Financial data (yr. ended 06/30/13): Assets, $891,051 (M); gifts received, $100,000; expenditures, $162,692; qualifying distributions, $161,898; giving activities include $161,898 for 11 grants to individuals (high: $35,954; low: $4,906).
Purpose and activities: Awards grants to amateur U.S.F.S.A. recognized figure-skating participants at novice, junior, and senior levels.
Fields of interest: Recreation.
Type of support: Grants to individuals.
Limitations: Applications not accepted. Giving primarily in CA, MI and PA.
Application information: Unsolicited requests for funds not accepted.
Officers: Scott Hamilton, Pres.; Kathy Casey, V.P.; Robert Anderson, Secy.-Treas.
EIN: 841032757

506
Hewit Family Foundation
191 University Blvd., Ste. 832
Denver, CO **80206-4613** **(303) 955-4983**
Contact: Richard J. Andrews, Pres.
***E-mail:* hewitfamilyfoundation@gmail.com**

Established in 1985 in CO.
Donor: members of the Hewit family.
Foundation type: Independent foundation.
Financial data (yr. ended 11/30/13): Assets, $17,642,655 (M); expenditures, $253,444; qualifying distributions, $215,000; giving activities include $215,000 for 5 grants (high: $125,000; low: $20,000).
Fields of interest: Elementary/secondary education; Higher education; Health care; Human services.
Limitations: Applications accepted. Giving primarily in CO. No support for private foundations or religious organizations. No grants to individuals.
Application information: Application form required.
Initial approach: Letter
Deadline(s): None
Officers: Richard J. Andrews, Pres.; Christie F. Andrews, V.P.; Renee Elise Andrews, Secy.; Candace J. Johnson, Treas.
EIN: 742397040

507
Robert E. Hogsett Foundation, Inc
Fort Morgan, CO

The foundation terminated on June 30, 2013.

508
A. V. Hunter Trust, Inc.
650 S. Cherry St., Ste. 535
Glendale, CO 80246-1897 (303) 399-5450
Contact: Barbara Howie, Exec. Dir
FAX: (303) 399-5499;
E-mail: barbarahowie@avhuntertrust.org; Main URL: http://www.avhuntertrust.org

Trust established in 1924 in CO.
Donor: A.V. Hunter‡.
Foundation type: Independent foundation.
Financial data (yr. ended 12/31/12): Assets, $56,710,136 (M); expenditures, $3,412,278; qualifying distributions, $2,988,330; giving activities include $1,998,240 for 189 grants (high: $30,000; low: $5,000), and $486,200 for 503 grants to individuals.
Purpose and activities: Distributions to organizations giving aid, comfort, support, or assistance to children, aged persons, indigent adults or the disabled.
Fields of interest: Human services; Children/youth, services; Children/youth; Children; Youth; Aging; Disabilities, people with; Physically disabled; Blind/visually impaired; Deaf/hearing impaired; Mentally disabled; Crime/abuse victims; Economically disadvantaged; Homeless.
Type of support: General/operating support.

Limitations: Applications accepted. Giving limited to CO. **No support for tax-supported institutions, political organizations, disease-specific programs, or organizations using a fiscal agent or fiscal sponsor.** No grants to individuals (directly), or for scholarships, capital improvements, acquisitions, staff recruitment and training, endowments, publications, films, media projects, tickets, fundraising benefits, special events, sponsorships, pass-through or start-up funds, research or debt reduction; no loans.
Publications: Application guidelines; Grants list.
Application information: Colorado Common Grant Application form accepted. Organizations applying for funding must have been operating as a 501(c)(3) for at least 3 years. Faxed or e-mailed applications are not accepted. Application form required.
Initial approach: Telephone or 1-page letter
Copies of proposal: 1
Deadline(s): Varies, telephone office before submitting application
Board meeting date(s): Mar., May, Aug., and Nov.
Final notification: Within 20 days after Board meeting
Officers and Trustees:* Allan B. Adams,* Pres.; Mary K. Anstine,* V.P.; Barbara L. Howie, Secy. and Exec. Dir.; George C. Gibson, Treas.; Janet Willson, Cont.; W. Robert Alexander; Bruce K. Alexander.
Number of staff: 3 full-time professional; 1 part-time professional; 1 part-time support.
EIN: 840461332

509
Marion Esser Kaufmann Foundation
1740 Copper Ln.
Evergreen, CO 80439-9406 (303) 674-3472
***Contact:* Julia Keough Esser, Tr.**

Established in 1986 in NY.
Donor: Marion Esser Kaufmann†.
Foundation type: Independent foundation.
Financial data (yr. ended 12/31/12): Assets, $10,619,715 (M); expenditures, $732,177; qualifying distributions, $586,000; giving activities include $586,000 for 16 grants (high: $200,000; low: $5,000).
Purpose and activities: Giving for higher education, health care, including research in cancer, the fields of sudden infant death syndrome (SIDS) and Alzheimer's disease.
Fields of interest: Child development, education; Elementary school/education; Higher education; Hospitals (general); Health care, infants; Health care; Medical research, institute; Cancer research; Alzheimer's disease research; SIDS (Sudden Infant Death Syndrome) research; Pediatrics research; Child development, services; Aging.
Type of support: Program development; Scholarship funds; Research.
Limitations: Applications accepted. Giving primarily in CO, Washington, DC, and NY. No grants to individuals.
Application information: Application form required.
Initial approach: Letter
Deadline(s): None
Final notification: Within 3 months
Trustees: Julia Keough Esser; Richard B. Esser.
EIN: 133339941
Other changes: The grantmaker has moved from FL to CO.

510
Kinder Morgan Foundation
370 Van Gordon St.
Lakewood, CO 80228-1519 **(303) 914-7655**
Contact: Maureen Bulkley, Mgr.
FAX: (303) 984-3306;
E-mail: km_foundation@kindermorgan.com; Main URL: http://www.kindermorgan.com/community/km_foundation.cfm

Established in 1990 in CO.
Donors: Knight Inc.; K N Energy, Inc.; Kinder Morgan, Inc.
Foundation type: Company-sponsored foundation.
Financial data (yr. ended 12/31/13): Assets, $13,836,614 (M); expenditures, $2,074,864; qualifying distributions, $2,064,075; giving activities include $2,064,075 for 708 grants (high: $100,000; low: -$5,000).
Purpose and activities: The foundation supports programs designed to promote the academic and artistic interests of youth. Special emphasis is directed toward academic programs including tutoring; arts education; and environmental education initiatives designed to work with local schools and meet curriculum standards.
Fields of interest: Arts education; Arts; Elementary/secondary education; Higher education; Libraries (public); Education, services; Education; Environmental education; Youth.
Type of support: Continuing support; Program development; Curriculum development; Employee matching gifts.
Limitations: Applications accepted. Giving primarily in areas of company operations in the U.S. and in Canada. No support for political candidates or lobbying organizations, service clubs, fraternal organizations, or organizations located outside the U.S. and Canada. No grants to individuals, or for scholarships, political causes, general operating support, capital projects (excluding libraries), religious projects, advertising, sponsorships, travel, conventions, conferences, or seminars, mentoring, leadership, or social development initiatives.
Publications: Application guidelines; Informational brochure (including application guidelines).
Application information: Grants range between $1,000 and $5,000. Proposals should be no longer than 3 pages. CDs, DVDs, annual reports, and brochures are not accepted. Support is limited to 1 contribution per organization during any given year. Application form not required.
Initial approach: E-mail or mail cover letter and proposal
Copies of proposal: 1
Deadline(s): Jan. 10, Mar. 10, May 10, July 10, Sept. 10, and Nov. 10
Final notification: 60 to 90 days
Directors: Jeffrey R. Armstrong; Larry S. Pierce; C. Park Shaper; James E. Street.
Number of staff: None.
EIN: 841148161

511
Leeoma Charitable Trust
Boulder, CO

The foundation terminated in 2011.

512
The Leighty Foundation
c/o Jane Leighty Justis
P.O. Box 37
Cascade, CO 80809-0037
E-mail: jane@leightyfoundation.org; Main URL: http://www.leightyfoundation.org
Grants List: http://leightyfoundation.org/grantees/

Established in 1985.
Donors: H.D. Leighty; William C. Leighty.
Foundation type: Independent foundation.
Financial data (yr. ended 08/31/13): Assets, $6,050,737 (M); gifts received, $30,000; expenditures, $490,925; qualifying distributions, $455,702; giving activities include $320,150 for 117 grants (high: $18,000; low: $200), and $54,107 for 2 foundation-administered programs.
Purpose and activities: Support for organizations which seek to deal with today's problems and opportunities in ways that meet current needs without compromising the ability of future generations to meet their needs. The foundation concentrates its efforts in areas of special concern to its board members. Priorities include: earth protection, education, promotion of philanthropy and volunteerism.
Fields of interest: Education; Environment; Voluntarism promotion; Philanthropy/voluntarism.
Type of support: General/operating support; Management development/capacity building; Program development; Conferences/seminars; Curriculum development; Internship funds; Technical assistance; Consulting services; Matching/challenge support.
Limitations: Applications not accepted. Giving primarily in AK, CO, and IA. No grants to individuals.
Publications: Annual report.
Application information: Unsolicited requests for funds not accepted.
Board meeting date(s): Mar., May, Aug., Sept., and Dec.
Officers and Directors:* H.D. Leighty,* Pres.; Robert F. Justis, V.P.; William Clyde Leighty, V.P.; Nancy J. Waterman, Secy.-Treas.; Jane Leighty Justis,* Exec. Dir.
Number of staff: 1 full-time professional; 1 part-time support.
EIN: 421264476

513
Maki Foundation
421D Aspen Airport Business Ctr.
Aspen, CO 81611-3551 (970) 925-3272
Contact: Patricia A. Humphry
***E-mail:* makifoundation@gmail.com**; Main URL: http://www.makifoundation.org

Established in 1981 in CO.
Foundation type: Independent foundation.
Financial data (yr. ended 12/31/12): Assets, $2,545,601 (M); expenditures, $218,058; qualifying distributions, $215,131; giving activities include $145,500 for 48 grants (high: $4,000; low: $1,000).
Purpose and activities: Giving primarily for wilderness and wildlands protection, river and wetlands conservation, biological diversity conservation, and public lands management.
Fields of interest: Environment, natural resources; Environment.
Type of support: General/operating support; Program development.
Limitations: Applications accepted. Giving primarily in the western U.S., including NM, CO, UT, ID, WY,

and MT. No support for recycling programs, tree planting projects, toxic waste cleanup, or wildlife rehabilitation centers. No grants for acquisition or construction of community recreation facilities, buildings, municipal parks, reservoirs, film production, fellowships or private land trusts.
Publications: Application guidelines.
Application information: Complete application guidelines available on foundation web site. Application form required.
Initial approach: Letter or telephone
Deadline(s): May 1
Final notification: Sept. 15
Directors: Ann Harvey; Constance Harvey; Mark Harvey; Nelson Harvey; Kim Springer.
Number of staff: 1 full-time professional.
EIN: 840836242

514
The Malone Family Foundation
12300 Liberty Blvd.
Englewood, CO 80112-7009 (720) 875-5201
Contact: Cathie Wlaschin, Admin.; Tracy Amonette, Prog. Dir.
***E-mail:* fdtn@malonefamilyfoundation.org**; E-mail: cathie@malonefamilyfoundation.org. E-mail for Tracy Amonette: tracy.malonefdn@gmail.com; Main URL: http://www.malonefamilyfoundation.org

Established in 1997 in CO.
Donor: John C. Malone.
Foundation type: Independent foundation.
Financial data (yr. ended 12/31/12): Assets, $129,330,118 (M); gifts received, $30,388,068; expenditures, $21,822,516; qualifying distributions, $20,599,667; giving activities include $20,595,652 for 13 grants (high: $2,000,000; low: $58,000).
Purpose and activities: The foundation primarily funds endowments to independent secondary schools for scholarships for underfunded, highly capable students. Also, a small discretionary fund supports gifted research.
Fields of interest: Education, gifted students.
Type of support: Endowments; Research.
Limitations: Applications not accepted. Giving on a national basis. No grants to individuals.
Publications: IRS Form 990 or 990-PF printed copy available upon request.
Application information: Contributes only to pre-selected organizations.
Board meeting date(s): May
Officers and Directors:* John C. Malone,* Pres. and Treas.; Leslie A. Malone,* Secy.; Evan D. Malone; Tracy L. Amonette.
Number of staff: 1 part-time professional.
EIN: 841408520

515
Timothy & Bernadette Marquez Foundation
(formerly Marquez Foundation)
P.O. Box 44354
Denver, CO 80201-4354 (303) 583-1609
Contact: Lisa Roy, Exec. Dir.
E-mail: lisa@tbmfoundation.org; Main URL: http://www.tbmfoundation.org

Established in 2005 in CO.
Foundation type: Independent foundation.
Financial data (yr. ended 12/31/12): Assets, $20,568,653; expenditures, $4,625,939; qualifying distributions, $4,428,599; giving activities include $4,428,599 for 54 grants (high: $2,000,000; low: $10).
Purpose and activities: The foundation currently awards Innovative Planning and Implementation grants in the areas of education, health and human services. Both Planning and Implementation grants will support organizations that are creative in offering innovative solutions to complex problems that promote systems change in one of the foundation's funding areas. The foundation's objective in education is to support student achievement and success within public schools as well as in higher education. The foundation's objective in health is to expand access to and options for quality health care resources to low-income, high-risk individuals and families. The objective in human services is to assist low-income, high-risk individuals and families to improve their life circumstances by promoting self-sufficiency.
Fields of interest: Higher education; Education; Health care; Human services; Family services; Economically disadvantaged.
Type of support: General/operating support; Continuing support; Capital campaigns; Building/renovation; Program development; Matching/challenge support.
Limitations: Applications accepted. Giving primarily in the metropolitan Denver, CO area.
Publications: Application guidelines.
Application information: Application form and guidelines which must be used are available on foundation web site. Application form not required.
Initial approach: E-mail, letter or telephone
Copies of proposal: 1
Board meeting date(s): Monthly
Final notification: 30-60 days
Officer and Directors: Lisa Roy, Exec. Dir.; Bernadette Marquez; Timothy Marquez; David Mokros.
EIN: 203507025

516
McDonnell Family Foundation
609 Cliffgate Ln.
Castle Rock, CO 80108-8395 **(303) 881-9747**
***E-mail:* mcdonnellfamilyfoundation@gmail.com**; Main URL: http://www.mcdonnellfoundation.org/

Established in 1999 in CO.
Donors: John F. McDonnell; Patricia L. McDonnell; Matthew J. McDonnell.
Foundation type: Independent foundation.
Financial data (yr. ended 12/31/12): Assets, $9,715,953 (M); expenditures, $712,441; qualifying distributions, $614,489; giving activities include $566,336 for 16 grants (high: $156,448; low: $1,000).
Fields of interest: Education; Health organizations; Human services; Children/youth, services; Christian agencies & churches.
Limitations: Applications not accepted. Giving primarily in CA and CO. No grants to individuals.
Application information: Contributes only to pre-selected organizations, which the foundation's individual board members seek out.
Officers: John F. McDonnell, Pres.; Patricia L. McDonnell, V.P.; Matthew J. McDonnell, Secy.-Treas.
EIN: 841498562

517
Meadowlark Foundation
Denver, CO

The foundation terminated in 2011.

518
Andre & Katherine Merage Foundation
18 Inverness Pl. E.
Englewood, CO 80112-5622 (303) 789-2664
FAX: (303) 789-2696; **E-mail: info@merage.org**; Main URL: http://www.merage.org
Facebook: https://www.facebook.com/pages/Early-Learning-Ventures/147565111396
Google Plus: https://plus.google.com/103345660533511436759/posts
LinkedIn: http://www.linkedin.com/company/merage-foundation?trk=top_nav_home
YouTube: http://www.youtube.com/user/MerageFoundation

Established in 2002 in CO.
Donor: Katherine Merage.
Foundation type: Independent foundation.
Financial data (yr. ended 11/30/12): Assets, $33,184,610 (M); expenditures, $1,826,981; qualifying distributions, $1,638,055; giving activities include $990,900 for 4 grants (high: $620,000; low: $500).
Purpose and activities: Giving primarily to a donor-advised fund.
Fields of interest: Jewish federated giving programs; Philanthropy/voluntarism.
Limitations: Applications not accepted. **Giving primarily in CO, DE and NY.** No grants to individuals.
Application information: Contributes only to pre-selected organizations.
Officer: Sue Renner, Exec. Dir.
Directors: David Merage; Katherine Merage.
EIN: 450493929

519
David and Laura Merage Foundation
18 Inverness Pl. E.
Englewood, CO 80112-5622 (303) 789-2664
FAX: (303) 789-2696; Main URL: http://www.merage.org
Facebook: https://www.facebook.com/pages/Early-Learning-Ventures/147565111396
Google Plus: https://plus.google.com/103345660533511436759/posts
LinkedIn: http://www.linkedin.com/company/merage-foundation?trk=top_nav_home
YouTube: http://www.youtube.com/user/MerageFoundation

Established in 2002 in CO.
Donors: David Merage; Laura Merage; Katherine Merage.
Foundation type: Independent foundation.
Financial data (yr. ended 11/30/12): Assets, $40,938,247 (M); expenditures, $2,278,733; qualifying distributions, $2,045,980; giving activities include $1,691,900 for 25 grants (high: $940,000; low: $250).
Fields of interest: Arts; Education, early childhood education; Education; Foundations (private grantmaking); Jewish federated giving programs; Philanthropy/voluntarism; Jewish agencies & synagogues.
Limitations: Applications not accepted. **Giving primarily in CO; funding also in CA, DE and Israel.** No grants to individuals.
Application information: Contributes only to pre-selected organizations.
Officer and Directors:* Sue Renner, Exec. Dir.; David Merage; Laura Merage.
EIN: 450493925

520
Monfort Family Foundation
(formerly Monfort Charitable Foundation)
134 Oak Ave.
Eaton, CO 80615-3491 (970) 454-2192
Contact: Patty Penfold
FAX: (970) 454-2535

Established in 1970 in CO.
Donor: Kenneth W. Monfort‡.
Foundation type: Independent foundation.
Financial data (yr. ended 12/31/12): Assets, $22,606,737 (M); gifts received, $200; expenditures, $2,732,829; qualifying distributions, $2,490,967; giving activities include $2,276,108 for 30 grants (high: $745,000; low: $2,000).
Purpose and activities: Giving primarily for education, developing the arts and humanities, conducting scientific research into the causes, treatment and prevention of life-threatening diseases, and providing aid to the disadvantaged.
Fields of interest: Arts; Education, fund raising/fund distribution; Education; Health care, fund raising/fund distribution; Health organizations, association; United Ways and Federated Giving Programs.
Type of support: General/operating support.
Limitations: Giving primarily in Weld County, CO. No support for political or religious organizations, or for environmental organizations, charter schools or lobbying. No grants to individuals.
Application information: Funding for single-year grants will need to be approved each year for continued support; funding for multi-year grants will be limited to a 3-year time frame. Application form required.
Initial approach: 1-page proposal
Copies of proposal: 1
Deadline(s): None
Board meeting date(s): Varies as necessary
Officers: Kaye C. Montford, Pres.; Kyle Monfort Futo, V.P.; Charlie Monfort, V.P.; Myra Monfort, Secy.; Dick Monfort, Treas.
EIN: 237068253
Other changes: Kaye C. Ward, Pres., is now Kaye C. Montford.

521
Pete Morgan Foundation
(formerly McVaney-Fernalld Family Foundation Trust)
1520 W. Canal Ct., Ste. 220
Littleton, CO 80120-5651
Contact: Scott Sprinkle

Established in 2000 in CO.
Donors: Kylee McVaney Fernalld Trust; McVaney Investment Partnership.
Foundation type: Independent foundation.
Financial data (yr. ended 12/31/12): Assets, $4,573,463 (M); gifts received, $1,939,597; expenditures, $0; qualifying distributions, $7,200.
Purpose and activities: Giving primarily for Christian organizations and human services.
Fields of interest: Education; Human services; Christian agencies & churches.
Limitations: Applications not accepted. Giving primarily in CO; some funding nationally.
Application information: Contributes only to pre-selected organizations.
Trustee: C.Edward McVaney.
EIN: 470833529
Other changes: Kylee M. Lourie is no longer a trustee.

522
J. K. Mullen Foundation
5310 DTC Pkwy., Ste. C
Greenwood Village, CO **80111-3010** (303) 722-3557

Incorporated in 1924 in CO.
Donors: John K. Mullen‡; Catherine S. Mullen‡; The J.K. Mullen Foundation.
Foundation type: Independent foundation.
Financial data (yr. ended 07/31/13): Assets, $5,638,173 (M); expenditures, $367,480; qualifying distributions, $298,699; giving activities include $279,020 for 65 grants (high: $47,450; low: $500).
Purpose and activities: Focus is on the poor and disadvantaged members of our society, victims of family and substance abuse, the mentally challenged, physically impaired, and others whose lives are outside the mainstream. Education is also of interest.
Fields of interest: Elementary/secondary education; Secondary school/education; Health organizations, association; Human services; Youth, services; Disabilities, people with.
Type of support: General/operating support; Annual campaigns; Building/renovation; Equipment.
Limitations: Applications accepted. Giving limited to the Denver, CO, metropolitan area. No support for taxpayer-supported organizations. No grants to individuals.
Publications: Application guidelines; Financial statement.
Application information: Application form required.
Initial approach: Letter
Copies of proposal: 1
Deadline(s): June 1
Officers and Trustees:* Timothy M. O'Connor,* Pres.; John K. Weckbaugh,* V.P.; Sheila Sevier,* Secy.; Walter S. Weckbaugh,* Treas.; J. Kenneth Malo, Jr.; **John F. Malo**; Kathleen M. Malo; Marcus Sevier; Heather Weckbaugh.
Number of staff: 1 part-time support.
EIN: 846002475
Other changes: The grantmaker no longer lists a primary contact.
Timothy M. O'Connor has replaced John F. Malo as Pres.

523
National Endowment for Financial Education
(also known as NEFE)
1331 17th St., Ste. 1200
Denver, CO 80202-1595
Contact: Londell Jackson, Asst. Dir., Grants & Research
FAX: (303) 220-0838; E-mail: ldj@nefe.org; Main URL: http://www.nefe.org
E-Newsletter: http://www.nefe.org/NEFENews/PressRoom/Subscribe/tabid/230/Default.aspx
Twitter: http://twitter.com/NEFE_ORG
YouTube: http://www.youtube.com/user/NonprofitNEFE

Established in 1972 in CO.
Foundation type: Operating foundation.
Financial data (yr. ended 12/31/12): Assets, $149,091,736; gifts received, $701,600; expenditures, $7,029,737; qualifying distributions, $5,449,134; giving activities include $169,365 for 3 grants (high: $71,671; low: $40,000), and $5,003,883 for 4 foundation-administered programs.
Purpose and activities: The National Endowment for Financial Education (NEFE) is the only private, nonprofit, national foundation wholly dedicated to improving the financial well-being of all Americans. The mission of the National Endowment for Financial Education is to help individual Americans acquire the knowledge and skills necessary to take control of their financial destiny. NEFE's mission is grounded in the belief that regardless of background or income level, financially informed individuals are better able to 1) take control of their circumstances, 2) improve their quality of life, and 3) ensure a stable future for themselves and their families. NEFE's guiding principles are stated in eight initiatives. These initiatives describe how NEFE achieves its mission, and outlines the goals and standards that guide the foundation's activities. Every project or program undertaken by NEFE must fit within the scope of at least one initiative. NEFE accomplishes its mission primarily by partnering with other organizations to: 1) provide practical, reliable, and unbiased financial education to members of the public, 2) accomplish research in the field of financial literacy education, and 3) create demand for financial education. NEFE's activities place special emphasis on those who face financial challenges that are not being addressed by others. Among the target audiences are: youth, low-income individuals and families, and people in difficult or unusual life circumstances. NEFE's partnerships and the foundation's own efforts result in a wide range of free and low-cost activities and materials, including: resources for consumers, materials for educators and facilitators, the NEFE High School Financial Planning Program, which includes joint efforts with numerous nonprofit, for-profit, and government entities to develop financial literacy resources for specific audiences, research, conferences, and think tanks on a variety of financial literacy topics, and grant awards to organizations and academic institutions whose work can contribute to the field of financial literacy.
Fields of interest: Education, research; Education, public education; Education; Foundations (private grantmaking).
Type of support: Program development; Research; Program evaluation.
Limitations: Applications accepted. Giving on a national basis. No support for organizations lacking 501(c)(3) IRS status, or foreign organizations. No grants to individuals, or for general operating support, deficits, salaries, capital costs, computer equipment, pass-through funding, conferences, seminars, fundraisers, sponsorships, endowments, challenge grants, matching funds, scholarships, or for registration fees.
Publications: Application guidelines; Informational brochure; Newsletter.
Application information: Full proposals will be accepted by invitation only following submission of inquiry. See foundation web site for application information. Application form required.
Initial approach: Complete the Concept Inquiry form after checking guidelines and eligibility
Copies of proposal: 1
Deadline(s): June and Dec.
Board meeting date(s): Apr. and Nov.
Final notification: 5 business days following board meetings
Officers and Directors:* Alexander Gonzalez, Ph.D*, Chair.; Karen Vahouny,* Vice-Chair.; Ted Beck,* C.E.O. and Pres.; **Patrick Bannigan**; **Michael A. Bedke**; Dorothy J. Bridges; Pip Coburn; **Denise V. Crawford**; John R. Woerner; and 5 additional directors.
Number of staff: 10 full-time professional; 5 full-time support; 2 part-time support.
EIN: 840632115
Other changes: Alexander Gonzalez, Ph.D has replaced Richard C. Woltmann as Chair.

Karen Vahouny is now Vice-Chair. William C. Alsover, Sara M. Bentley, Martin Jaffe, Cheryl D. Jennings, Hugh H. Makens, Andrew M. Mecca, Maureen Reeder and Debra L. Wetherby are no longer directors.

524
The Norwood Foundation
P.O. Box 792
Manitou Springs, CO 80829-0792 (719) 593-2600
Contact: Christopher S. Jenkins, Secy.-Treas.

Established in 2002 in CO.
Donors: Carolyn S. Jenkins; David D. Jenkins; Development Mgmt., Inc.; First and Main, LLC.
Foundation type: Independent foundation.
Financial data (yr. ended 02/28/13): Assets, $20,346 (M); gifts received, $1,425,000; expenditures, $1,412,597; qualifying distributions, $1,412,221; giving activities include $1,412,221 for 49+ grants (high: $560,100).
Purpose and activities: Giving primarily for education, Christian organizations, and to a Presbyterian church.
Fields of interest: Health organizations, association; Human services; Child development, services; Christian agencies & churches; Protestant agencies & churches.
Type of support: General/operating support; Scholarships—to individuals.
Limitations: Giving primarily in CO; with some emphasis on Colorado Springs.
Application information: Application form required.
Initial approach: **Letter**
Deadline(s): None
Officers: David D. Jenkins, Pres.; Carolyn S. Jenkins, V.P.; Christopher S. Jenkins, Secy.-Treas.
EIN: 010705471

525
Pikes Peak Community Foundation
730 N. Nevada Ave.
Colorado Springs, CO 80903-5014 (719) 389-1251
Contact: For grants: Michael R. Hannigan, Exec. Dir.; Jamie Brown, Dir., Community Svcs.
FAX: (719) 389-1252; E-mail: info@ppcf.org; Additional E-mails: jbrown@ppcf.org and mhannigan@ppcf.org; Main URL: http://www.ppcf.org
E-Newsletter: http://www.ppcf.org/connect/enews
Facebook: https://www.facebook.com/pikespeakcommunityfoundation
Twitter: https://twitter.com/PPCommFdn

Established in 1996 in CO.
Foundation type: Community foundation.
Financial data (yr. ended 12/31/10): Assets, $46,491,626 (M); gifts received, $6,263,616; expenditures, $6,186,687; giving activities include $3,340,364 for grants.
Purpose and activities: PPCF will boldly commit to dramatically improve the quality of life in the Pikes Peak region. Through education and actions, the foundation will improve the understanding of, appreciation for, and the practice of philanthropy.
Fields of interest: Arts; Education; Environment; Health care; Housing/shelter; Children/youth, services; Human services; Community development, neighborhood development; Economic development; Community/economic development; Public affairs.
Type of support: General/operating support; Continuing support; Income development; Management development/capacity building; Seed money; Matching/challenge support.
Limitations: Applications accepted. Giving primarily in El Paso and Teller counties in CO. No support for religious purposes. No grants to individuals (except for scholarships), or for debt retirement, endowment funds, medical, scientific, or academic research, sponsorships or camperships, travel, publications, fees for conferences, symposiums, or workshops, creation or installation of art objects, or annual memberships of affiliation campaigns, dinners, or special events; no loans.
Publications: Annual report (including application guidelines).
Application information: Visit foundation web site for application guidelines. Application form not required.
Initial approach: E-mail letter of intent (1 page)
Copies of proposal: 1
Deadline(s): None
Board meeting date(s): Varies
Final notification: None
Officers and Directors:* Paula D. Pollet,* Chair.; Michael R. Hannigan, Exec. Dir.; Deborah Adams; Michael Berniger; Suzanne Connaughton; Cari Davis; Susan Foerster; Larry R. Gaddis; Greg Gandy; Alicia McConnell; Kae Rader; Jannie Richardson; Pam Shipp; Wendel P. Torres; Rob Wrubel.
EIN: 841339670
Other changes: Jamie Brown is now Dir., Community Srvs. Eric Cefus is now Dir., Philanthropic Srvs.

526
The Piton Foundation
1705 17th St., Ste. 200
Denver, CO **80202-1293** (303) 825-6246
Contact: Carol Bush, Cont.
FAX: (303) 628-3839; E-mail: info@piton.org; Main URL: http://www.piton.org

Incorporated in 1976 in CO.
Donors: Samuel Gary; Gary Williams Energy Corp.; The Gary Williams Co.
Foundation type: Operating foundation.
Financial data (yr. ended 11/30/12): Assets, $5,971,171 (M); gifts received, $15,186,803; expenditures, $10,730,645; qualifying distributions, $11,750,507; giving activities include $7,630,491 for 172 grants (high: $1,535,182; low: $250), $57,212 for 116 employee matching gifts, $35,100 for 7 in-kind gifts, $968,607 for foundation-administered programs and $1,076,866 for 1 loan/program-related investment.
Purpose and activities: Highly limited funds to support activities of the foundation in 4 areas: Improving Public Education; Revitalizing Neighborhoods; Promoting Economic Opportunities; and Strengthening Families.
Fields of interest: Education; Employment; Youth development; Family services; Community/economic development; Leadership development; Children.
Type of support: General/operating support; Capital campaigns; Program development; Conferences/seminars; Seed money; Curriculum development; Technical assistance; Program evaluation; Employee matching gifts.
Limitations: Applications not accepted. Giving limited to Denver, CO.
Publications: Biennial report; Informational brochure; Occasional report; Program policy statement.
Application information: Unsolicited requests for funds not considered.
Board meeting date(s): As required
Officers and Directors:* Samuel Gary,* Chair.; Dave Younggren,* Pres.; Carol Bush, C.F.O.; Nancy Gary; **Rob Gary**; Tim Howard.
Number of staff: 14 full-time professional; 5 full-time support.
EIN: 840719486
Other changes: For the fiscal year ended Nov. 30, 2012, the grantmaker paid grants of $7,722,803, a 183.2% increase over the fiscal 2011 disbursements, $2,726,741.
Dave Younggren has replaced Mary Gittings Cronin as Pres.
Samuel Gary is now Chair.
The grantmaker now makes its informational brochure available online.

527
Harry L. and Eva J. Puksta Foundation
2221 W. 30th Ave.
Denver, CO 80211-3808 (303) 595-2031
Contact: John Mulstay, Pres.
Main URL: http://www.pukstafoundation.org
Facebook: https://www.facebook.com/pages/The-Puksta-Foundation/54697291984
Tumblr: http://pukstafoundation.tumblr.com/
Twitter: https://twitter.com/PukstaFdn

Established in 2001 in CO.
Foundation type: Independent foundation.
Financial data (yr. ended 12/31/12): Assets, $4,275,630 (M); expenditures, $261,875; qualifying distributions, $195,351; giving activities include $164,320 for 4 grants (high: $80,000; low: $4,500).
Purpose and activities: The mission of the foundation is to provide the opportunity for underprivileged Colorado students to pursue a college education and to develop a commitment to citizenship, leadership and community engagement.
Fields of interest: Higher education; Scholarships/financial aid; Education.
Limitations: Applications accepted. Giving primarily in CO. No grants to individuals.
Application information: See grantmaker web site for application policies, contacts and guidelines. Application form not required.
Initial approach: Letter
Deadline(s): None
Officer: John Mulstay, Pres.
EIN: 841555566

528
Rose Community Foundation
600 S. Cherry St., Ste. 1200
Denver, CO 80246-1712 (303) 398-7400
Contact: For grants: Cheryl McDonald, Grants Mgr.
FAX: (303) 398-7430; E-mail: info@rcfdenver.org; Grant inquiry e-mail: cmcdonald@RCFdenver.org; Grant inquiry tel.: 303-398-7446; Main URL: http://www.rcfdenver.org

Established in 1995 in CO.
Donors: Rose Foundation; DPS Foundation.
Foundation type: Community foundation.
Financial data (yr. ended 12/31/12): Assets, $271,775,000 (M); gifts received, $9,133,000; expenditures, $15,932,000; giving activities include $11,957,000 for grants.
Purpose and activities: The foundation seeks to enhance the quality of life in the greater Denver

community through its leadership, resources, tradition, and values.
Fields of interest: Education; Health care; Children, services; Child development, services; Family services; Human services; Jewish agencies & synagogues; Children/youth; Adults; Aging; Minorities; Hispanics/Latinos; Economically disadvantaged; Homeless.
Type of support: Technical assistance; Research; Publication; Program evaluation; Program development; Matching/challenge support; Management development/capacity building; General/operating support; Equipment; Curriculum development; Consulting services; Capital campaigns; Building/renovation.
Limitations: Applications accepted. Giving limited to the greater Denver, CO, area. No support for political candidates or pass-through organizations. Generally, no grants to individuals, or for endowments, annual appeals, membership drives, or fundraising events.
Publications: Application guidelines; Annual report; Financial statement; Newsletter.
Application information: Visit foundation web site for application guidelines. The foundation encourages prospective applicants to contact the foundation's program staff before submitting a grant request. Application form required.
Initial approach: Telephone
Deadline(s): None
Board meeting date(s): Feb. 5, May 6, July 1, Sept. 2, and Dec. 2
Final notification: Within 4 months
Officers and Trustees:* Jennifer Atler Fischer,* Chair.; Sheila Budganowitz, C.E.O. and Pres.; Anne Garcia, C.F.O. and C.O.O.; Mark Huckenberg, Cont.; Milroy A. Alexander; **Judy Altenberg**; **Steven A. Cohen**; Lisa Reckler Cohn; Jerrold L. Glick; Katherine Gold; Douglas L. Jones; Helayne B. Jones; Rob Klugman; William N. Lindsay III; Evan Makovsky; Ronald E. Montoya; Monte Moses, Ph.D.; Neil Oberfeld; Dean Prina, M.D.; Irit Waldbaum.
Number of staff: 15 full-time professional; 1 part-time professional; 5 full-time support; 1 part-time support.
EIN: 840920862
Other changes: Stephanie Foote is no longer a trustee.

529
Sachs Foundation
90 S. Cascade Ave., Ste. 1410
Colorado Springs, CO 80903-1680 (719) 633-2353
Contact: Morris A. Esmiol, Jr., Pres.
FAX: (719) 633-3663; Main URL: http://www.sachsfoundation.org
Facebook: https://www.facebook.com/SachsFoundation?fref=ts
Twitter: https://twitter.com/SachsScholars

Incorporated in 1931 in CO.
Donors: Henry Sachs†; Henry Sachs Trust.
Foundation type: Independent foundation.
Financial data (yr. ended 12/31/12): Assets, $35,910,854 (M); gifts received, $1,397,000; expenditures, $1,592,703; qualifying distributions, $1,304,031; giving activities include $1,122,789 for grants to individuals.
Purpose and activities: Provides undergraduate scholarships to African-American high school seniors who have a 3.5 GPA or better, and who have been CO residents for five or more years; also, limited graduate scholarships only to African-Americans who have participated in the undergraduate scholarship program and who have been residents of CO five or more years.
Fields of interest: African Americans/Blacks.
Type of support: Grants to individuals; Scholarships—to individuals.
Limitations: Giving limited to residents of CO.
Publications: Application guidelines; Financial statement.
Application information: Applications are accepted only from Jan. 1-Mar. 1. Application form, complete application guidelines, and required financial statement are available on foundation web site. Application form required.
***Initial approach:* Use online application process on foundation web site**
Copies of proposal: 2
***Deadline(s):* Applications accepted from Jan. 1 to Mar. 17 annually**
Board meeting date(s): May
Final notification: 45 days
Officer: Craig Ralston, Pres.; Lisa Harris, Secy.-Treas.; Stewart P. Dodge, 1st V.P.; Wilton W. Cogswell III, 2nd V.P.
Directors: Morris A. Esmiol, Jr.; Thomas M. James.
Number of staff: 2 full-time professional.
EIN: 840500835

530
Schlessman Family Foundation, Inc.
(formerly Schlessman Foundation, Inc.)
c/o Patricia Middendorf
1555 Blake St., Ste. 400
Denver, CO 80202-1866 (303) 831-5683
Contact: Lee E. Schlessman, Pres.
FAX: (303) 831-5676;
E-mail: contact@schlessmanfoundation.org; Main URL: http://www.schlessmanfoundation.org

Incorporated in 1957 in CO.
Donors: Florence M. Schlessman†; Gerald L. Schlessman†; Lee E. Schlessman.
Foundation type: Independent foundation.
Financial data (yr. ended 03/31/13): Assets, $27,630,361 (M); expenditures, $463,941; qualifying distributions, $200,416; giving activities include $200,316 for 17 grants (high: $119,370; low: $100).
Purpose and activities: Giving primarily for: 1) education, 2) disadvantaged youth programs and services, particularly those that foster initiative and a positive work ethic, 3) elderly/senior programs that assist in providing the necessities of life, 4) special needs groups, such as people who are handicapped, homeless families and people who are mentally ill, and 5) established cultural institutions such as museums, libraries and zoos.
Fields of interest: Education; Human services; Children/youth, services; Disabilities, people with.
Type of support: General/operating support; Continuing support; Annual campaigns; Equipment; Endowments; Program development; Curriculum development; Scholarship funds; Matching/challenge support.
Limitations: Applications accepted. Giving limited to CO, primarily the greater Denver area. No support for charter, private or public school programs. No grants to individuals, or for benefits, conferences or start-up grants.
Publications: Application guidelines.
Application information: Colorado Common Grant Application form accepted, but not required. Application form not required.
Initial approach: Proposal
Copies of proposal: 1
Deadline(s): Dec. 31
Board meeting date(s): Mar.
Final notification: Mar. 31
Officers and Board Members:* Lee E. Schlessman,* Pres.; Susan M. Duncan,* V.P.; Dolores J. Schlessman,* V.P.; Gary L. Schlessman,* Secy.; Patricia A. Middendorf, Treas. and Exec. Dir.; Sandra Garnett.
EIN: 846030309
Other changes: At the close of 2013, the fair market value of the grantmaker's assets was $27,630,361, a 2265.9% increase over the 2012 value, $1,167,842.

531
SEAKR Foundation
6221 S. Racine Cir.
Centennial, CO 80111-6427 **(303) 708-5210**
Contact: Raymond E. Anderson, Chair.
***E-mail:* info@seakrfoundation.com**; Additional contact: Melissa Coen, Foundation Rep., tel.: (303) 858-4559; **Main URL: http://www.seakrfoundation.com/**
Facebook: https://www.facebook.com/seakrfoundation
YouTube: https://www.youtube.com/watch?v=mrYQVKPYYOA

Established in 2004 in CO.
Donors: SEAKR Engineering, Inc.; Raymond E. Anderson.
Foundation type: Company-sponsored foundation.
Financial data (yr. ended 12/31/12): Assets, $187,808 (M); gifts received, $262,793; expenditures, $299,722; qualifying distributions, $250,000; giving activities include $250,000 for 13 grants to individuals (high: $24,000; low: $3,000).
Purpose and activities: The foundation awards grants to the families of soldiers killed or wounded in the line of duty.
Fields of interest: Family services; Military/veterans.
Type of support: Grants to individuals.
Limitations: Applications not accepted. Giving primarily in CO.
Application information: Contributes only to pre-selected individuals.
Officer and Director: Raymond E. Anderson,* Chair.; Lorraine W. Anderson.
EIN: 200979291

532
Seay Foundation
c/o American National Bank & Trust Co., Trust Div.
P.O. Box 9250
Colorado Springs, CO 80932-0250 **(719) 381-5623**
Application address: c/o American National Bank, 102 N. Cascade Ave., Colorado Springs, CO 80903-1455
Foundation type: Independent foundation.
Financial data (yr. ended 12/31/12): Assets, $18,130,526 (M); expenditures, $1,610,755; qualifying distributions, $1,369,757; giving activities include $1,088,600 for grants, and $276,056 for grants to individuals.
Fields of interest: Higher education; Youth development; Human services; Christian agencies & churches.
Type of support: General/operating support; Building/renovation; Scholarships—to individuals.
Limitations: Applications accepted. Giving primarily in CO.

Application information: Candidates must be nominated by a member of the foundation's Advisory Committee; application forms available upon request by the nominator. Application form required.
Deadline(s): May 1
Director: Carolyn S. Kopper.
Trustee: American National Bank & Trust Co.
EIN: 436055549

533
Serimus Foundation
148 Remington St.
Fort Collins, CO 80524-2834

Established in 1999 in WY and CO.
Donors: Jill M. Schatz; Douglas S. Schatz.
Foundation type: Independent foundation.
Financial data (yr. ended 12/31/12): Assets, $2,321,305 (M); expenditures, $977,938; qualifying distributions, $961,063; giving activities include $835,444 for 13 grants (high: $686,859; low: $500).
Fields of interest: Education, early childhood education.
Type of support: General/operating support; Program development; Program evaluation; Matching/challenge support.
Limitations: Applications not accepted. Giving primarily in CO. No grants to individuals.
Application information: Contributes only to pre-selected organizations.
Board meeting date(s): Twice per year
Officers: Jill E. Schatz, Pres.; Douglas S. Schatz, V.P. and Treas.; Kirsten Bump, Secy.
Directors: Adrienne Schatz; David Schatz.
EIN: 830328155

534
Society of Economic Geologists Foundation, Inc.
7811 Shaffer Pkwy.
Littleton, CO 80127-3732 (720) 981-7882
FAX: (720) 981-7874; E-mail: seg@segweb.org;
Main URL: http://www.segweb.org/SEG/Foundation/SEG/Foundation.aspx?hkey=18dc5157-3cbd-4cc3-b8bc-7dca63166e04
Facebook: https://www.facebook.com/segweb
LinkedIn: http://www.linkedin.com/company/society-of-economic-geologists-inc-
Twitter: https://twitter.com/societyecongeol
Application e-mail: studentprograms@segweb.org

Established in 1966.
Foundation type: Operating foundation.
Financial data (yr. ended 12/31/12): Assets, $4,553,607 (M); gifts received, $184,729; expenditures, $632,506; qualifying distributions, $1,141,383; giving activities include $519,820 for 9+ grants (high: $192,975).
Purpose and activities: Giving to fund education, research, publications, student support, public outreach and other geoscientific programs endorsed by the Society of Economic Geologists, Inc. (SEG), or other programs considered for funding by the trustees of the corporation. Support is limited to programs, projects, and research in economic geology as they relate to metallic mineral deposits.
Fields of interest: Geology.
International interests: Global Programs.
Type of support: Publication; Seed money; Grants to individuals.
Limitations: Applications not accepted.
Publications: Informational brochure; Newsletter.
Application information: Unsolicited requests for funds not accepted.
Officers and Trustees:* Andrew T. Swarthout,* Pres.; John E. Black, V.P.; Ruth A. Carraher,* Secy.
Number of staff: 1 part-time support.
EIN: 516020487
Other changes: Andrew T. Swarthout has replaced Peter K.M. Megaw as Pres. John E. Black has replaced William X. Chavez, Jr. as Vice-Pres. Ruth A. Carraher has replaced David W. Broughton as Secy.

535
Southern Colorado Community Foundation
121 W. First St., Ste. 240
P.O. Box 1432
Pueblo, CO 81002 (719) 546-6677
Contact: Doris Kester, Exec.Dir.
FAX: (719) 566-7842; E-mail: kester@ddmktg.com;
Main URL: http://www.southerncoloradocommunityfoundation.org

Established in 1998 in CO.
Foundation type: Community foundation.
Financial data (yr. ended 12/31/12): Assets, $9,677,397 (M); gifts received, $156,190; expenditures, $804,823; giving activities include $681,000 for 24+ grants (high: $313,209).
Purpose and activities: The foundation accepts donations and makes grants in accordance with the donor's wishes covering all of southern Colorado.
Fields of interest: Health care; Human services; Community/economic development.
Type of support: Program development.
Limitations: Applications accepted. Giving limited to southern CO.
Application information: Application form required.
***Initial approach:* Submit application**
***Deadline(s):* Mar. 1 and Sept. 1**
Officers and Directors:* Dan Derose,* Pres.; Jane L. Rawlings,* V.P.; Mark Swanson,* Secy.; **Dan Lere,* Treas.;** Doris Kester, Exec. Dir.; Joe Bower; Midori Clark; Barbara Duff; Barbara Fortino; **Priscilla Lucero**; Donna Maes; Kevin McCarthy; Rosemary Reilly; Jeff Shaw; Paulette Stuart; Ken West.
Number of staff: 1 full-time professional.
EIN: 841449305
Other changes: The grantmaker now accepts applications.
Dan Lere has replaced Priscilla Lucero as Treas.
Dan Lere and Dawn M. Mann are no longer directors.

536
The Myron Stratton Home
555 Gold Pass Hts.
Colorado Springs, CO 80906-3894 (719) 579-0930
Contact: Mark Turk, Exec. Dir.
FAX: (719) 579-0447;
E-mail: myronstratton@myron.org; Main URL: http://www.myronstratton.org

Classified as a private operating foundation in 1973.
Foundation type: Operating foundation.
Financial data (yr. ended 12/31/11): Assets, $135,713,781 (M); gifts received, $225; expenditures, $5,283,901; qualifying distributions, $4,416,874; giving activities include $293,000 for 35 grants (high: $20,000; low: $4,000).
Purpose and activities: Giving primarily to maintain and operate residential facilities and services for the elderly poor of El Paso County, Colorado.
Fields of interest: Children/youth, services; Family services; Aging, centers/services; Community/economic development; Economically disadvantaged.
Type of support: General/operating support; Continuing support; Capital campaigns; Building/renovation; Equipment; Emergency funds; Program development; Seed money; Curriculum development.
Limitations: Applications accepted. Giving primarily in Colorado Springs and El Paso County, CO. No grants to individuals, or for fundraising or conferences.
Publications: Informational brochure (including application guidelines); Multi-year report.
Application information: See foundation web site for grants program information. Application form required.
Initial approach: Letter of intent
Copies of proposal: 2
Deadline(s): For letter of intent: May 1 for Sept. cycle and Nov. 1 for Mar. cycle
Final notification: Apr. and Oct.
Officers: Robert G. Baker, Jr., Pres.; **Jon J. Medved, V.P.;** Nechie Hall, Secy.-Treas.; Mark Turk, Exec. Dir.
Trustees: Leonard Farr; C. David McDermott.
Number of staff: 50
EIN: 840404260
Other changes: Jon J. Medved has replaced Joseph C. Woodford as V.P.

537
The Summit Foundation
111 Lincoln Ave.
P.O. Box 4000
Breckenridge, CO 80424-4000 (970) 453-5970
Contact: Lee Zimmerman, Exec. Dir.
FAX: (970) 453-1423;
E-mail: sumfound@summitfoundation.org;
Additional e-mail: TSFADmin@summitfoundation.org; Main URL: http://www.summitfoundation.org

Established in 1984 in CO.
Foundation type: Community foundation.
Financial data (yr. ended 09/30/12): Assets, $7,530,121 (M); gifts received, $2,507,113; expenditures, $2,114,226; giving activities include $1,392,220 for 166 grants (high: $82,000; low: $500), and $181,370 for 109 grants to individuals.
Purpose and activities: The foundation seeks to improve the quality of life for residents and guests of Summit County and neighboring communities. Giving primarily for arts and culture, health and human services, education, environment, sports and recreation, scholarships, and all projects with measurable results.
Fields of interest: Media, film/video; Visual arts; Museums; Performing arts; Performing arts, theater; Performing arts, music; Historic preservation/historical societies; Arts; Elementary/secondary education; Education, early childhood education; Elementary school/education; Secondary school/education; Education; Environment, natural resources; Environment; Health care; Mental health/crisis services; Health organizations, association; Recreation; Children/youth, services; Family services; Residential/custodial care, hospices; Aging, centers/services; Human services; Infants/toddlers; Children/youth; Youth; Adults; Aging; Young adults; Disabilities, people with; Physically disabled; Mentally disabled; Hispanics/Latinos; Women; Girls; Adults, women; Adults, men; Substance abusers; Single parents; Terminal illness, people with; Immigrants/refugees; Economically disadvantaged; Homeless.

Type of support: General/operating support; Continuing support; Management development/capacity building; Annual campaigns; Capital campaigns; Building/renovation; Equipment; Land acquisition; Endowments; Program development; Conferences/seminars; Seed money; Curriculum development; Scholarship funds; Technical assistance; Program evaluation; Exchange programs; In-kind gifts; Matching/challenge support.
Limitations: Applications accepted. Giving limited to Summit County, and the communities of Alma, Fairplay, Kremmling, and Leadville, CO. No support for religious organizations. No grants to individuals (except for designated scholarship programs).
Publications: Application guidelines; Annual report; Grants list; Informational brochure; Newsletter; Program policy statement.
Application information: Visit the foundation's web site for online application and additional guidelines. Application form required.
Initial approach: Telephone
Copies of proposal: 2
Deadline(s): Apr. 11 and Oct. 4
Board meeting date(s): 3rd Wed. of Mar., May, July, Aug., Sept., Oct., and Nov.; 2nd Wed. of Feb., June, and Dec.
Final notification: June and Dec.
Officers and Trustees:* Kevin McDonald,* Pres.; Mike Schilling,* V.P.; Lucy Kay,* Secy.; Lee E. Zimmerman, Exec. Dir.; **Gini Bradley**; John Buhler; Pat Campbell; Ed Casias; **Cary Cooper**; Deb Crook; Thomas Davidson; Nicky DeFord; Wally Ducayet; Greg Finch; Tim Gagen; Kathy Grotemeyer; Millie Hamner; Alan Henceroth; Katha Jenkins; Tom Keltner; Jeff Leigh; Andy Lewis; Phyllis Martinez; Rob Millisor; Rick Oshlo; Susan Propper; Kelly Renoux; Gary Rodgers; Steven Smith; Mark Spiers; Carre Warner; Maureen Westerland; Wendy Wolfe; Hans Wurster.
Number of staff: 3 full-time professional; 2 part-time support.
EIN: 742341399
Other changes: Dick Masica and Michael Schilling are no longer trustees.

538
Telluride Foundation
220 E. Colorado Ave., Ste. 106
P.O. Box 4222
Telluride, CO 81435 (970) 728-8717
Contact: For grants: April Montgomery, Progs. Dir.
FAX: (970) 728-9007;
E-mail: info@telluridefoundation.org; Additional e-mail: april@telluridefoundation.org; Main URL: http://www.telluridefoundation.org
Facebook: http://www.facebook.com/pages/Telluride-Foundation/110163245072
RSS Feed: http://www.telluridefoundation.org/index.php?mact=News,cntnt01,rss,0&cntnt01makerssbutton=true&cntnt01showtemplate=false&cntnt01returnid=15

Established in 2000 in Telluride, CO.
Foundation type: Community foundation.
Financial data (yr. ended 12/31/12): Assets, $9,514,293 (M); gifts received, $3,476,844; expenditures, $3,145,017; giving activities include $2,526,793 for grants.
Purpose and activities: The foundation is committed to preserving and enriching the quality of life of the residents, visitors and workforce of the Telluride, CO, region. It provides year-round support for donors and local community-based organizations by facilitating the charitable intent of donors and grantmaking, technical assistance and education for community groups.
Fields of interest: Arts; Higher education; Education; Environment; Children/youth, services; Children, day care; Child development, services; Human services.
Type of support: Capital campaigns; General/operating support; Annual campaigns; Equipment; Program development; Seed money; Scholarship funds; Technical assistance; Consulting services; Scholarships—to individuals; Matching/challenge support.
Limitations: Applications accepted. **Giving primarily in Ouray, San Miguel, and West Montrose counties, CO, as well as some portions of Dolores County.** No support for religious organizations for religious purposes. **No grants to individuals (except for designated scholarships), debt reduction, non-educational publications, graduate or post-graduate research, economic development, or endowments; no loans.**
Publications: Application guidelines; Annual report (including application guidelines); Financial statement; Grants list; Newsletter; Program policy statement.
Application information: Visit foundation web site for application form and guidelines per grant type. The foundation holds a pre-applications Q&A session; visit web site for details. Application form required.
Initial approach: Submit application form and attachments
***Deadline(s):* Oct. 28 for community grants; varies for others**
Board meeting date(s): Dec. and July
Final notification: Dec. 31 for community grants; varies for others
Officers and Directors:* Bridgitt Evans,* Chair.; Davis Fansler,* Vice-Chair.; Paul Major,* C.E.O. and Pres.; Ron Allred; Anne Andrew; Carol Armstrong; Mike Armstrong; Ed Barlow; Lynne Beck; Richard Betts; Harmon Brown; Joanne Brown; Mark Dalton; Stu Fraser; Tully Friedman; Bunny Freidus; Allan Gerstle; J. Tomilson Hill; Kevin Holbrook; Chuck Horning; Dan Jansen; Jesse Johnson; Andrew Karow; Joan May; Megan McManemin; Melanie Montoya; Brian O'Neill; Michael Plank; Susan Saint James; Kyle Schumacher; Edward Sheridan; Dan Tishman.
Number of staff: 2 full-time professional; 3 part-time professional.
EIN: 841530768
Other changes: Elaine Fischer, Scott Leigh, Tricia Maxon, and George Parker are no longer directors.

539
The Tointon Family Foundation
P.O. Box 9
Greeley, CO 80632-0009 (970) 353-7000
Contact: Travis W. Gillmore

Established in 1989 in CO.
Donors: Robert G. Tointon; Phelps-Tointon, Inc.
Foundation type: Independent foundation.
Financial data (yr. ended 12/31/13): Assets, $46,894 (M); gifts received, $750,000; expenditures, $723,150; qualifying distributions, $723,150; giving activities include $723,150 for 21 grants (high: $511,000; low: $500).
Fields of interest: Higher education; Human services.
Limitations: Applications accepted. Giving primarily in Greeley, CO and Manhattan, KS. No grants to individuals.
Application information: CGA Colorado Common Grant Application accepted. Application form not required.
Initial approach: Letter
Copies of proposal: 1
Deadline(s): None
Final notification: 1-3 weeks
Directors: Travis W. Gillmore; Betty L. Tointon; Bryan E. Tointon; Robert G. Tointon; William I. Tointon.
EIN: 841113542
Other changes: At the close of 2013, the grantmaker paid grants of $723,150, a 449.3% increase over the 2012 disbursements, $131,650.

540
Tomkins Gates Foundation
(formerly Philips Industries Foundation)
1551 Wewatta St., MS 9N A4
Denver, CO 80202

Established in 1986 in OH.
Donors: Tomkins Industries, Inc.; David Newlands.
Foundation type: Company-sponsored foundation.
Financial data (yr. ended 04/30/13): Assets, $6,787,826 (M); expenditures, $370,435; qualifying distributions, $366,446; giving activities include $61,140 for 5 grants, and $305,306 for 162 employee matching gifts.
Purpose and activities: The foundation supports organizations involved with education, cancer, human services, and Christianity.
Fields of interest: Higher education; Scholarships/financial aid; Education; Cancer; Human services; Christian agencies & churches.
Type of support: General/operating support; Scholarship funds; Employee matching gifts.
Limitations: Applications not accepted. Giving primarily in Denver, CO, Chicago, IL, KS, MI, and OH; giving also to national organizations. No grants to individuals.
Application information: Contributes only to pre-selected organizations.
Officers and Trustees:* James Nicol, Pres.; **John W. Zimmerman,* C.F.O. and Treas.**; Sylvia Church,* V.P.; Daniel J. Disser,* V.P.; Thomas C. Reeve,* V.P.; John Barker,* Secy.; **Stephen Meyer**.
EIN: 311207183

541
The Morris & Sylvia Trachten Family Foundation, Inc.
4950 S. Yosemite St., F2-184
Greenwood Village, CO 80111-1349 (303) 488-2057
Contact: Vicki Trachten Schwartz

Established in 1984 in CT.
Donor: Morris Trachten.
Foundation type: Independent foundation.
Financial data (yr. ended 06/30/12): Assets, $682,101 (M); gifts received, $643,024; expenditures, $261,825; qualifying distributions, $240,994; giving activities include $240,994 for grants.
Fields of interest: Higher education; Higher education, university; Jewish federated giving programs; Jewish agencies & synagogues.
Type of support: General/operating support.
Limitations: Applications accepted. Giving primarily in CO, CT, FL, and NY.
Application information: Application form not required.
Initial approach: Letter
Deadline(s): None

Officers and Directors:* David Trachten,* Chair.; Vicki Trachten Schwartz,* Pres. and Treas.; Roberta Zeve, V.P.; Gary Trachten, Secy.; Sylvia Trachten.
EIN: 222518063
Other changes: Gary Trachten has replaced Sylvia Trachten as Secy.
Morris Trachten is no longer C.E.O. and Pres. David Trachten is now Chair. Vicki Trachten Schwartz is now Pres. and Treas.

542
TYL Foundation
(formerly McVaney Family Foundation)
1520 W. Canal Ct., No. 220
Littleton, CO 80120-5651 (303) 297-2142
Contact: Scott Sprinkle

Established in 1993 in CO.
Donors: Charles McVaney; Carole McVaney; Kylee McVaney Fernalld Trust; Kevin Edward McVaney Trust.
Foundation type: Independent foundation.
Financial data (yr. ended 11/30/12): Assets, $18,292,778 (M); expenditures, $1,869,900; qualifying distributions, $1,780,987; giving activities include $1,770,215 for 48 grants (high: $543,125; low: $250).
Purpose and activities: Funding primarily for Christian agencies and churches, human services, and education.
Fields of interest: Education; Health care; Human services; Christian agencies & churches; Protestant agencies & churches.
Limitations: Applications not accepted. Giving primarily in CO. No grants to individuals.
Application information: Unsolicited requests for funds not accepted.
Officers and Directors:* Carole McVaney,* Pres. and Mgr.; Kevin E. McVaney,* V.P.; Kylee Lourie,* Secy.-Treas.
EIN: 841256356
Other changes: For the fiscal year ended Nov. 30, 2012, the grantmaker paid grants of $1,770,215, a 142.7% increase over the fiscal 2010 disbursements, $729,333.

543
Vail Valley Foundation, Inc.
90 Benchmark Rd., Ste. 300
Avon, CO 81620 (970) 777-2015
FAX: (970) 949-9265; E-mail: info@vvf.org; Mailing Address: P.O. Box 309, Vail, CO 81658; Main URL: http://www.vvf.org
Blog: http://www.vailvalleyfoundation.blogspot.com/
Facebook: http://www.facebook.com/pages/Vail-Valley-Foundation/169530086401875
Flickr: http://www.flickr.com/photos/vailvalleyfoundation/
Twitter: http://twitter.com/VVFoundation
YouTube: http://www.youtube.com/vailvalleyfoundation
Tel. for scholarships: (970) 949-1999; Karri Casner Scholarship: c/o Cheryl Lindstrom, P.O. Box 2088, Edwards, CO 81632, tel.: (970) 926-5290, fax: (970) 926-5293

Established in 1981 in CO.
Foundation type: Community foundation.
Financial data (yr. ended 09/30/12): Assets, $24,056,201 (M); gifts received, $11,624,680; expenditures, $20,125,758; giving activities include $463,770 for 6+ grants (high: $257,775), and $38,101 for 17 grants to individuals.
Purpose and activities: The foundation seeks to provide leadership in athletic, cultural, and educational endeavors to enhance the quality of life in the Vail Valley, CO, area.
Fields of interest: Performing arts, dance; Performing arts, music; Arts; Education; Environment; Athletics/sports, winter sports; Human services.
Limitations: Applications accepted. Giving primarily in Eagle County, CO. No grants to individuals (except for scholarships).
Publications: Annual report; Grants list; Newsletter.
Application information: Application form required.
Initial approach: Proposal
Copies of proposal: 1
Deadline(s): Ongoing
Board meeting date(s): Aug. and Dec.
Final notification: Within 12 months
Officers and Directors:* Harry Frampton III,* Chair.; Cecilia Folz,* C.E.O. and Pres.; Katrina Ammer,* V.P., Opers.; John Dakin,* V.P., Comms.; Duncan Horner,* V.P., Mktg.; Mike Imhof,* Sr. V.P., Opers. and Sales; Rob Gaffney,* C.F.O.; Dillon DeMore, Cont.; Andy Arnold; Judy Berkowitz; Marlene Boll; Bjorn Erik Borgen; Steve Coyer; Jack Crosby; Andrew Daly; Ron Davis; Jack Eck; William Esrey; Tim Finchem; Peter Frechette; Steve Friedman; John Garnsey; Margie Gart; Bob Gary; George Gillett, Jr.; Donna Giordano; Sheika Gramshammer; Martha Head; Mike Herman; Robert Hernreich; Al Hubbard; William Hybl; Yvonne Jacobs; Chris Jarnot; Robert Katz; Kent Logan; Peter May; Brian Nolan; Michael Price; Don Remey; Eric Resnick; Doug Rippeto; Dick Rothkopf; Ken Schanzer; Michael Shannon; Stanley Shuman; Rodney Slifer; Ann Smead; Oscar Tang; Stewart Turley; Steve Virostek; Betsy Wiegers.
EIN: 742215035
Other changes: Melisa Rewold-Thuon is now Dir., Edu. Katie Peters is now Sr. Mktg. Mgr. Kathy Brendza is no longer Early Childhood Prog. Consultant.

544
Bee Vradenburg Foundation
730 N. Nevada Ave.
Colorado Springs, CO 80903-1008 (719) 477-0185
***Contact:* David Siegel, Exec. Dir.**
FAX: (719) 389-1252;
E-mail: david@beevradenburgfoundation.org; Main URL: http://www.beevradenburgfoundation.org
Facebook: https://www.facebook.com/BeeVradenburgFoundation
Grants List: http://www.beevradenburgfoundation.org/grantees/grant-recipients/2012-2/

Established in 2001 in CO.
Donors: George A. Vrandenburg, Jr.‡; George A. Vrandenburg III; Beatrice W. Vradenburg; Philip A. Kendall.
Foundation type: Independent foundation.
Financial data (yr. ended 12/31/12): Assets, $4,222,472 (M); gifts received, $20,025; expenditures, $350,758; qualifying distributions, $318,890; giving activities include $192,741 for 24 grants (high: $85,371; low: $1,000).
Purpose and activities: The foundation supports a thriving and diverse cultural community by investing in the excellence, innovation, and sustainability of the arts.
Fields of interest: Arts.
Type of support: General/operating support; Continuing support; Management development/capacity building; Capital campaigns; Building/renovation; Equipment; Emergency funds; Program development; Conferences/seminars; Scholarship funds; Technical assistance; Consulting services; Program evaluation; Matching/challenge support.
Limitations: Applications accepted. Giving limited to organizations based in and serving the Pikes Peak region, defined as El Paso County and the Ute Pass corridor of Teller County, CO, to include Woodland Park but not beyond. No support for religious or political organizations. No grants to individuals or for fund-raisers for non-arts organizations or to advance causes unrelated to the arts.
Publications: Application guidelines; Annual report; Grants list.
Application information: See web site for complete application policies, guidelines and forms. Application form required.
Initial approach: First time applicants should call or e-mail in advance of applying
Copies of proposal: 1
Deadline(s): Quarterly
Board meeting date(s): Jan., Apr., July, Oct.
Final notification: 45 days after submission
Officers: George A. Vradenburg, Chair.; Philip A. Kendall, Pres.; Kathleen Fox Collins, Secy.; Libby Rittenberg, Treas.; **David Siegel, Exec. Dir.**
Trustees: Noel Black; Susan J. Edmondson; Susan Pattee; Alissa Vradenburg; Tyler Vradenburg.
Number of staff: 1
EIN: 841579108

545
Yampa Valley Community Foundation
385 Anglers Dr., Ste. B
Sundance Office Plaza
Steamboat Springs, CO 80487 (970) 879-8632
Contact: Mark Andersen, Exec. Dir.
FAX: (970) 871-0431; E-mail: info@yvcf.org; Mailing address: P.O. Box 881869, Steamboat Springs, CO 80488; Main URL: http://www.yvcf.org
E-Newsletter: http://www.yvcf.org/newsletter.php
Facebook: https://www.facebook.com/yvcf.org
LinkedIn: http://www.linkedin.com/company/yampa-valley-community-foundation?trk=cp_followed_name_yampa-valley-community-foundation
Pinterest: http://www.pinterest.com/yvcf/
Twitter: https://twitter.com/yvcf

Established in 1979 in CO.
Foundation type: Community foundation.
Financial data (yr. ended 12/31/12): Assets, $9,052,088 (M); gifts received, $2,001,004; expenditures, $1,564,236; giving activities include $808,417 for 36+ grants (high: $65,000), and $108,508 for 98 grants to individuals.
Purpose and activities: The foundation provides leadership in raising funds, in partnership with community members, to support innovative programs benefiting the Yampa Valley community. Giving primarily to arts and culture, education, environment, health organizations, recreation and human services.
Fields of interest: Arts; Education; Environment; Health care; Health organizations, association; Recreation; Human services.
Type of support: General/operating support; Continuing support; Annual campaigns; Capital campaigns; Building/renovation; Equipment; Endowments; Emergency funds; Program development; Conferences/seminars; Seed money; Curriculum development; Scholarships—to individuals; Exchange programs.

Limitations: Applications accepted. Giving primarily in Yampa Valley, specifically Moffat and Routt counties, CO. No support for religious purposes. No grants for debt reduction or endowments; generally no grants for team or travel expenses.
Publications: Application guidelines; Annual report; Financial statement; Grants list; Informational brochure; Newsletter.
Application information: Visit foundation web site for the Colorado Common Grant Form and application guidelines. Application form required.
Initial approach: Submit Letter of Intent
Copies of proposal: 1
***Deadline(s):* Aug. 1**
Board meeting date(s): Semi-monthly
***Final notification:* Late Sept.**
Officers and Trustees:* Adonna Allen,* Chair.; Jim Bronner,* Vice-Chair.; Laura Cusenbary,* Vice-Chair.; Dana Tredway,* Secy.-Treas.; Mark Andersen, Exec. Dir.; Paula Cooper Black,* Emeritus; Tammy Delaney; Chris Diamond; **Jay Fetcher; Rod Hanna**; Ron Krall; Gary Neale; Kathryn Pedersen; Tom Sharp; Pam Vanatta.
Number of staff: 2 full-time professional; 2 part-time professional.
EIN: 840794536
Other changes: Ann Barbier is now Finance Dir. Adonna Allen, Elyse Craig, Laura Cusenbary, and Dave Wierman are no longer trustees.

546
Gary & Teresa Yourtz Foundation
825 S. Adams St.
Denver, CO **80209-4946**

Established in 1998 in CO.
Donor: Gary L. Yourtz.
Foundation type: Independent foundation.
Financial data (yr. ended 06/30/13): Assets, $45,735 (M); gifts received, $1,625; expenditures, $51,047; qualifying distributions, $49,422; giving activities include $49,422 for grants.
Limitations: Applications not accepted. Giving primarily in Denver, CO. No grants to individuals.
Application information: Unsolicited requests for funds not accepted.
Officers: Gary L. Yourtz, Pres.; Teresa A. Yourtz, Secy.
Directors: Erin M. Yourtz; Jeffrey M. Yourtz.
EIN: 141482259

CONNECTICUT

547

1772 Foundation, Inc.

P.O. Box 112
Pomfret Center, CT 06259-0112 (860) 928-1772
Contact: Mary Anthony
E-mail: maryanthony@1772foundation.org; Main URL: http://www.1772foundation.org

Established in 1985 in NJ.
Donors: Stewart B. Kean†; Stewart B. Kean Residuary Trust.
Foundation type: Independent foundation.
Financial data (yr. ended 12/31/12): Assets, $75,861,121 (M); gifts received, $2,000,000; expenditures, $3,901,351; qualifying distributions, $3,553,620; giving activities include $3,221,857 for 140 grants (high: $190,000; low: $500).
Purpose and activities: Giving for the preservation and enhancement of American historical entities and projects. Key areas of interest are: 1) Revolving funds for endangered properties, 2) New Jersey inner-city revitalization, 3) Preservation trades and crafts schools and programs, 4) Agricultural endeavors, 5) Historic site sustainability training and conferences, and 6) African American historic site development.
Fields of interest: Historic preservation/historical societies.
Type of support: Building/renovation.
Limitations: Applications accepted. Giving primarily on the East Coast, with emphasis on CT, MA, ME, NJ, NY, and RI. No support for schools and universities, or for non-501(c)(3) organizations, privately owned structures, relocation or purchase of historic structures, hospitals, or religious organizations. No grants to individuals, or for general operating support, scholarships, professional fees, studies and reports, books, strategic planning, endowments, or sabbaticals.
Publications: Annual report.
Application information: Application form required.
Initial approach: **Use application on foundation web site**
Officers and Trustees:* G. Stanton Geary,* Pres.; B. Danforth Ely,* V.P.; Mary Anthony,* Exec. Dir.; Nancy E. Davis; Dr. Robert Raynolds; Dr. Gretchen Sullivan Sorin.
EIN: 222578377
Other changes: J. David Schardien is no longer a trustee.

548

Kenneth and Nira Abramowitz Foundation

(formerly Abramowitz Family Foundation)
P.O. Box 958
Southport, CT 06890-0958

Established in 2002 in NY.
Donors: Kenneth Abramowitz; Nira Abramowitz.
Foundation type: Independent foundation.
Financial data (yr. ended 12/31/12): Assets, $325,079 (M); gifts received, $325,000; expenditures, $340,026; qualifying distributions, $337,140; giving activities include $337,140 for grants.
Purpose and activities: Giving primarily to Jewish organizations.
Fields of interest: Education; Hospitals (general); Human services; Jewish federated giving programs; Jewish agencies & synagogues.
Limitations: Applications not accepted. Giving primarily in NY. No grants to individuals.
Application information: Contributes only to pre-selected organizations.
Trustees: Kenneth Abramowitz; Nira Abramowitz.
EIN: 331017742

549

Ellen H. Adams Foundation, Inc.

16 Old Mill Rd.
Greenwich, CT 06830-3345 (203) 629-0645
***Contact:* Ellen H. Adams, Pres.**

Donor: Ellen H. Adams.
Foundation type: Independent foundation.
Financial data (yr. ended 12/31/12): Assets, $537,785 (M); gifts received, $233; expenditures, $268,063; qualifying distributions, $250,000; giving activities include $250,000 for grants.
Fields of interest: Education; Religion.
Limitations: Applications accepted. Giving primarily in CT, IL and PA.
Application information: Application form required.
Initial approach: Letter
Deadline(s): None
Officers: Ellen H. Adams, Pres.; James W. Adams, V.P.; **Karen Adams, Secy.-Treas.**
EIN: 271495276
Other changes: The grantmaker has moved from NY to CT.
Maria Lamari-Burden is no longer Secy.

550

Aetna Foundation, Inc.

(formerly Aetna Life & Casualty Foundation, Inc.)
151 Farmington Ave., RE2R
Hartford, CT 06156-3180
FAX: (860) 273-7764;
E-mail: aetnafoundation@aetna.com; Main URL: http://www.aetna.com/foundation
AcademyHealth/Aetna Foundation Minority Scholars Recipients: http://www.aetnafoundationscholars.org/2010-scholars.php
Grants List: http://www.aetna.com/about-aetna-insurance/aetna-foundation/aetna-grants/annual-reports-grant-listings.html
Minority Scholars Program Video: http://www.aetnafoundationscholars.org/includes/video_overview
National Medical Fellowships Healthcare Leadership Recipients: http://www.aetna-foundation.org/foundation/aetna-foundation-programs/scholars/nmf-healthcare-leadership-program.html
RSS Feed: http://news.aetnafoundation.org/feeds/press_release/all/rss.xml
The Aetna Foundation: http://news.aetnafoundation.org/multimedia

Incorporated in 1972 in CT.
Donors: Aetna Inc.; Aetna Life Insurance Company; Aetna Health Inc.
Foundation type: Company-sponsored foundation.
Financial data (yr. ended 12/31/12): Assets, $54,426,641 (M); expenditures, $9,580,326; qualifying distributions, $7,864,411; giving activities include $7,864,411 for 205 grants (high: $595,156; low: $92).
Purpose and activities: The foundation supports programs designed to promote wellness, health, and access to high-quality care. Special emphasis is directed toward obesity; racial and ethnic health care equity; and integrated health care.
Fields of interest: Medical school/education; Health care, public policy; Health care, equal rights; Hospitals (general); Health care, clinics/centers; Health care, infants; Public health; Public health, obesity; Public health, physical fitness; Health care, cost containment; Health care, patient services; Health care; Food services; Food banks; Nutrition; Engineering/technology; Children; Minorities; Women; Economically disadvantaged.
Type of support: Program development; Conferences/seminars; Scholarship funds; Research; Employee volunteer services; Sponsorships; Employee matching gifts; Matching/challenge support.
Limitations: Applications not accepted. Giving primarily in areas of company operations in Phoenix, AZ, Los Angeles, Fresno, San Diego, and San Francisco, CA, CT, Washington, DC, Miami and Tampa, FL, Atlanta, GA, Chicago, IL, Baltimore, MD, ME, Charlotte, NC, NJ, New York, NY, Cleveland and Columbus, OH, Philadelphia and Pittsburgh, PA, Austin, Dallas, Houston, and San Antonio, TX, and WA; giving also to national and regional organizations. No support for religious organizations not of direct benefit to the entire community. No grants to individuals, or for scholarships, endowments, capital campaigns, construction, renovation, or equipment, direct delivery of reimbursable healthcare services, biomedical research, advertising, golf tournaments, advocacy, political causes, or events, or general operating support or deficits.
Publications: Annual report; Grants list; Newsletter; Program policy statement.
Application information: Unsolicited requests for national grants are currently not accepted. Sponsorship applications are by invitation only. Visit website for periodic Request for Proposals.
Board meeting date(s): Apr. and Dec.
Officers and Directors:* Mark T. Bertolini,* Chair.; Garth Graham, M.D., M.P.H., Pres.; Gilian R. Barclay, D.D.S., DrPH, V.P.; Sharon C. Dalton,* V.P.; Judith Jones, Secy.; Elaine R. Confranceso, Treas.; Sheryl A. Burke; Molly J. Coye, M.D.; Jeffrey E. Garten; Jerald B. Gooden; Steven B. Kelmar; Susan M. Krosman, RN; Andrew J. Lee; Kristi A. Matus; Margaret M. McCarthy; Kay D. Mooney; Joseph P. Newhouse; Sandip Patel; Lonny Reisman, M.D.
Number of staff: 14 full-time professional.
EIN: 237241940
Other changes: The grantmaker no longer publishes application guidelines.

551

The Josef and Anni Albers Foundation, Inc.

(formerly Josef Albers Foundation, Inc.)
88 Beacon Rd.
Bethany, CT 06524-3074 (203) 393-4089
Contact: Nicholas Fox Weber, Exec. Dir.
FAX: (203) 393-4094;
E-mail: info@albersfoundation.org; Main URL: http://www.albersfoundation.org

Incorporated in 1971 in NY.
Donors: Josef Albers†; Anni Albers†; John Richardson; Margot Wilkie.
Foundation type: Operating foundation.
Financial data (yr. ended 12/31/12): Assets, $14,997,222 (M); gifts received, $197,344; expenditures, $3,241,504; qualifying distributions, $3,565,726; giving activities include $600,839 for

23 grants (high: $249,798), and $1,545,163 for foundation-administered programs.
Purpose and activities: Giving primarily for the preparation and organization of various exhibitions of art by Josef Albers and Anni Albers.
Fields of interest: Arts, management/technical assistance; Arts, administration/regulation; Arts, research; Arts, single organization support; Arts, information services; Arts, public education; Visual arts; Visual arts, painting; Museums; Performing arts; Arts, services; Arts, artist's services; Arts; Higher education; Children/youth, services.
Type of support: Program development; Publication; Seed money.
Limitations: Applications not accepted. Giving primarily in the U.S., with emphasis on CT and NY; funding also in France.
Application information: Unsolicited requests for funds not accepted.
Officer and Directors:* Nicholas Fox Weber,* Exec. Dir.; John Eastman; Charles Kingsley; **Emma Lewis.**
Number of staff: 4 full-time professional; 2 full-time support.
EIN: 237104223

552
The Aronson Family Foundation
15 Westfair Dr.
Westport, CT 06880-4161
***Contact:* Dennis B. Poster, Tr.**

Established in 1992 in NY.
Donor: Independent foundation.
Financial data (yr. ended 12/31/12): Assets, $7,020,175 (M); gifts received, $250; expenditures, $655,977; qualifying distributions, $615,626; giving activities include $610,641 for 16 grants (high: $274,714; low: $1,000).
Fields of interest: Education; Hospitals (general); Hospitals (specialty); Health organizations, association; Human services; Jewish agencies & synagogues.
Limitations: Applications not accepted. Giving primarily in NY. No grants to individuals.
Application information: Contributes only to pre-selected organizations.
Trustees: Henry W. Berinstein; Roger A. Goldman, Esq.; Dennis B. Poster.
EIN: 133693381

553
The Bauer Foundation
206 Dudley Rd.
Wilton, CT 06897-3513

Established in 1989 in CT and GA.
Donor: George P. Bauer.
Foundation type: Independent foundation.
Financial data (yr. ended 12/31/12): Assets, $18,627,121 (M); gifts received, $2,010,841; expenditures, $4,252,832; qualifying distributions, $4,235,737; giving activities include $4,235,000 for 19 grants (high: $2,500,000; low: $5,000).
Fields of interest: Higher education; Education; Health care; Cancer; Children/youth, services; Foundations (private grantmaking).
Limitations: Applications not accepted. Giving primarily in Norwalk, CT and St. Louis, MO. No grants to individuals.
Application information: Contributes only to pre-selected organizations.
Officers: George P. Bauer, Pres.; Carol Bauer, Secy.
Board Members: Brad Bauer; Jocelyn Bauer; Jennifer Bauer Toll.
EIN: 581861919
Other changes: At the close of 2012, the grantmaker paid grants of $4,235,000, a 71.8% increase over the 2011 disbursements, $2,465,000.

554
The Morris S. & Florence H. Bender Foundation, Inc.
c/o J. D. Port
170 Mason St.
Greenwich, CT 06830-6644

Established in 1978 in NY.
Donors: Florence H. Bender†; Morris Bender†
Foundation type: Independent foundation.
Financial data (yr. ended 06/30/13): Assets, $3,395,660 (M); expenditures, $228,124; qualifying distributions, $194,924; giving activities include $174,100 for 36 grants (high: $15,000; low: $100).
Purpose and activities: Giving primarily for the arts, hospitals, and medical research, particularly to an institute for otolaryngology, as well as to organizations for terminally ill children.
Fields of interest: Performing arts; Performing arts, ballet; Arts; Hospitals (general); Medical research, institute; Children, services.
Type of support: General/operating support; Program development; Research.
Limitations: Applications not accepted. Giving primarily in CT, NJ and New York, NY. No grants to individuals.
Application information: Unsolicited requests for funds not accepted.
Officers: Jane Laffend, Pres.; Jennifer D. Port, Secy.; Ralph M. Engel, Treas.
EIN: 132951469

555
The Bok Family Foundation
P.O. Box 966
Canaan, CT 06018-0966

Established in 2005 in CT.
Donors: Scott L. Bok; Roxanne Bok.
Foundation type: Independent foundation.
Financial data (yr. ended 12/31/12): Assets, $51,173,417 (M); gifts received, $467; expenditures, $2,387,387; qualifying distributions, $2,323,060; giving activities include $2,315,000 for 14 grants (high: $1,000,000; low: $20,000).
Fields of interest: Elementary/secondary education; Higher education, university; Education; Environment, natural resources.
Limitations: Applications not accepted. Giving in the U.S., with emphasis on NY and PA. No grants to individuals.
Application information: Contributes only to pre-selected organizations.
Trustees: Elliot P. Bok; Roxanne Bok; Scott L. Bok.
EIN: 256872863

556
Bridgemill Foundation
c/o Foundation Source
55 Walls Dr., 3rd Fl.
Fairfield, CT 06824-5173

Established in 1992 in DE and CT.
Donor: John H.T. Wilson†.
Foundation type: Independent foundation.
Financial data (yr. ended 12/31/12): Assets, $18,361,391 (M); expenditures, $572,207; qualifying distributions, $351,597; giving activities include $337,375 for 17 grants (high: $50,122; low: $5,000).
Purpose and activities: Giving primarily for higher education, health associations, and children and social services.
Fields of interest: Higher education; Health organizations, association; Cancer research; Human services; Children/youth, services.
Limitations: Applications not accepted. Giving primarily in CT and NY. No grants to individuals.
Application information: Contributes only to pre-selected organizations.
Officers: Sandra W. Wilson, V.P.; Emily Wilson Burns, Secy.
Members: David Wilson; William Wilson.
EIN: 133671059

557
The Brightwater Fund
c/o Vogel & Co.
685 Post Rd.
Darien, CT 06820-4718

Established in 2009 in NY.
Donor: The Brightwater Trust.
Foundation type: Independent foundation.
Financial data (yr. ended 06/30/13): Assets, $15,234,881 (M); expenditures, $6,010,332; qualifying distributions, $5,900,787; giving activities include $5,900,787 for 83 grants (high: $500,000; low: $1,000).
Fields of interest: Human services.
Limitations: Applications not accepted. Giving primarily in NY.
Application information: Contributes only to pre-selected organizations.
Officers and Directors:* Gloria Jarecki,* Pres.; **AnnChristine Gormley, Secy.-Treas. and Admin.**; Ellen B. Chandler; Donna M. C. Jarecki; Nancy Jarecki.
EIN: 271041109
Other changes: For the fiscal year ended June 30, 2013, the grantmaker paid grants of $5,900,787, a 197.3% increase over the fiscal 2012 disbursements, $1,985,000.
AnnChristine Gormley is now Secy.-Treas. and Admin.

558
The Louis Calder Foundation
125 Elm St., Ste. 1
New Canaan, CT 06840-5420 (203) 966-8925
Contact: Holly Nuechterlein, Grant Prog. Dir.; Kathryn DiCerto, Prog. Asst.
FAX: (203) 966-5785;
E-mail: proposals@calderfdn.org; Main URL: http://www.louiscalderfdn.org

Trust established in 1951 in NY.
Donor: Louis Calder†.
Foundation type: Independent foundation.
Financial data (yr. ended 10/31/13): Assets, $166,483,274 (M); expenditures, $9,302,449; qualifying distributions, $8,049,011; giving activities include $7,126,367 for 65 grants (high: $375,000; low: $2,000).
Purpose and activities: To promote the scholastic development of children and youth by improving

elementary and secondary education through its support of charter and parochial schools.
Fields of interest: Elementary/secondary education.
Type of support: Capital campaigns; Building/renovation; Program development; Curriculum development; Matching/challenge support.
Limitations: Giving on a national basis. No support for political organizations, private foundations, or governmental organizations. **No grants to individuals; generally no support for annual funds or special events.**
Publications: Application guidelines; Financial statement; Grants list; IRS Form 990 or 990-PF printed copy available upon request.
Application information: Full proposals may only be submitted if requested by the foundation. The foundation accepts the New York/ New Jersey Area Common Application Form and the New York/ New Jersey Common Report Form. The foundation has issued a RFP seeking background letters from charter and parochial schools, charter management organizations and community based organizations for initiatives to develop comprehensive content based core curriculum education programs. Please see the foundation's web site for additional information. Application form required.
Initial approach: E-mail letter of inquiry: proposals@calderfdn.org
Copies of proposal: 1
Deadline(s): None
Board meeting date(s): Monthly
Final notification: Process can take several months
Trustees: Peter D. Calder; Frank E. Shanley; JPMorgan Chase Bank, N.A.
Number of staff: 2 full-time professional; 2 full-time support.
EIN: 136015562

559
The Jane Coffin Childs Memorial Fund for Medical Research
333 Cedar St., SHM L300 MC 0191
P.O. Box 20800
New Haven, CT 06520-8000 (203) 785-4612
Contact: Kim Roberts, Admin. Dir.
FAX: (203) 785-3301; E-mail: jccfund@yale.edu;
E-mail for referees and sponsors with regard to the Fellowship Program: letters@jccfund.org; Main URL: http://www.jccfund.org
Established in 1937 in CT.
Donors: Alice S. Coffin†; Starling W. Childs†; John W. Childs; Merck & Co., Inc.; Agouron Institution; Torrington Area Foundation; Heiman/Fidelity Foundation; Genentech; Howard Hughes Medical Institute; Anna Fuller Fund.
Foundation type: Independent foundation.
Financial data (yr. ended 06/30/12): Assets, $48,706,742 (M); gifts received, $1,615,193; expenditures, $3,893,948; qualifying distributions, $3,661,397; giving activities include $3,281,036 for grants to individuals.
Purpose and activities: Giving primarily for medical research into the causes, origins and treatment of cancer. Grants to institutions only for support of cancer research fellowships.
Fields of interest: Medical research, institute; Cancer research.
Type of support: Fellowships; Research.
Limitations: Giving primarily in CA, CT, and MA; foreign nationals are funded provided they are working in a U.S. lab. No grants to individuals (except for fellowships), or for building or endowment funds, matching gifts, or general purposes; no loans.
Publications: Application guidelines; Annual report; Newsletter; Program policy statement.
Application information: Application form and requirements available on foundation web site. Application form required.
Copies of proposal: 5
Deadline(s): See foundation web site for current deadline
Board meeting date(s): Oct. or Nov. and Apr. or May
Final notification: May
Officers and Managers:* Dr. James E. Childs,* Chair.; William G. Gridley, Jr.,* Vice-Chair.; John W. Childs, Secy.; Hendon C. Pingeon,* Treas.; Alice Childs Anderson; Elizabeth Bordern; John D. Childs; Richard S. Childs, Jr., M.D.; Elisabeth Childs Gill; Brett D. Hellerman; Dr. Richard C. Levin; Gardner Mundy.
Number of staff: 1 full-time professional; 1 full-time support.
EIN: 066034840

560
Colburn-Keenan Foundation, Inc.
P.O. Box 811
Enfield, CT 06083-0811 (860) 749-7522
FAX: (860) 763-6494; E-mail: admin@colkeen.org; Toll free tel.: (800) 966-2431; Main URL: http://www.colkeen.org

Established in 2006 in CT.
Donors: Donald Colburn; Donald Colburn Trust; Kathy Ann Keenan Trust; American Homecare Federation, Inc.; Real State Company.
Foundation type: Independent foundation.
Financial data (yr. ended 12/31/12): Assets, $10,801,497 (M); gifts received, $3,329,299; expenditures, $400,872; qualifying distributions, $289,995; giving activities include $45,000 for 51 grants (high: $25,000; low: $5,000), and $207,397 for 105 grants to individuals (high: $7,745; low: $100).
Purpose and activities: Giving primarily to provide assistance and support to individuals and families impacted by chronic inherited bleeding disorders or other chronic illnesses. The foundation also supports students with bleeding disorders through a designated scholarship program to ten undergraduate students per year for higher education.
Fields of interest: Higher education; Hemophilia; Family services.
Type of support: Research; Grants to individuals.
Limitations: Applications accepted. Giving in the U.S., with emphasis on Enfield, CT.
Publications: Application guidelines.
Application information: Application form and guidelines for all programs available on foundation web site. Application form required.
Initial approach: Letter or telephone
Deadline(s): Oct. 1 (for organizations); none for emergency grants
Officers and Directors:* Sasha Zatyrka,* Chair.; Christine Pineo,* Secy.; Dawn Bryant,* Treas.; Jane Cavanaugh Smith,* Exec. Dir.; Hilary Keenan; Richard Steingart, M.D.
EIN: 204634920
Other changes: Cathy Cornell is no longer Chair. and Secy. Sasha Zatyrka is now Chair. Jane Cavanaugh Smith is now Exec. Dir. Christine Pineo is now Secy.

561
The Common Sense Fund Inc.
c/o Eric Schwartz
10 Glenville St., 1st Fl.
Greenwich, CT 06831-3680
***E-mail:* info@commonsensefund.org**; Main URL: http://www.commonsensefund.org
Grants List: http://www.commonsensefund.org/current-grants

Established in 1983.
Donor: Seymour Schwartz.
Foundation type: Independent foundation.
Financial data (yr. ended 12/31/12): Assets, $4,565,640 (M); gifts received, $2,944,022; expenditures, $900,897; qualifying distributions, $813,000; giving activities include $813,000 for grants.
Purpose and activities: Giving primarily for the environment and for the arts.
Fields of interest: Arts; Elementary/secondary education; Environment, climate change/global warming; Environment, water resources; Environment, energy; Environment; Human services; United Ways and Federated Giving Programs; Jewish agencies & synagogues.
Limitations: Applications not accepted. No grants to individuals.
Application information: Unsolicited requests for funds not accepted.
Officers: Adlyn S. Loewenthal, Pres.; Eric Schwartz, V.P. and Treas.; Ted Loewenthal, Secy.
Trustees: Carolyn Schwartz; David Schwartz; Debra Fram.
EIN: 133157570

562
Community Foundation of Eastern Connecticut
(formerly The Community Foundation of Southeastern Connecticut, Inc.)
68 Federal St.
P.O. Box 769
New London, CT 06320-6302 (860) 442-3572
FAX: (860) 442-0584; E-mail: bmorgan@cfect.org; Main URL: http://www.cfect.org
Scholarship inquiry e-mail: jennob@cfect.org

Established in 1982 in CT.
Donors: J. Martin Leatherman†; Beatrice G. McEwen†; Dorothy Morgan†; Jim Smith; Linda Korolkiewicz†; Priscilla Hodges†; Marjorie Stanton†; Smith Memorial Fund; Edmund O'Brien†; Eleanor Norman; members of the White Family.
Foundation type: Community foundation.
Financial data (yr. ended 12/31/12): Assets, $44,814,192 (M); gifts received, $3,151,066; expenditures, $4,067,300; giving activities include $2,772,986 for 109+ grants, and $315,192 for 202 grants to individuals.
Purpose and activities: The foundation seeks to transform our region into a more vital, caring community, through a number of strategies in pursuit of this goal. Among them are those that focus on grants, scholarships and other resources that serve our partners, the nonprofit agencies and organizations that enrich the local community.
Fields of interest: Arts; Libraries/library science; Education; Environment, natural resources; Environment; Animal welfare; Health care; Substance abuse, services; Mental health/crisis services; Children/youth, services; Family services; Aging, centers/services; Women, centers/services; Human services; Community/economic development; Voluntarism promotion; Children/youth; Children; Youth; Adults; Aging; Disabilities,

people with; Mentally disabled; Minorities; Women; Substance abusers; AIDS, people with; Economically disadvantaged; Homeless.
Type of support: General/operating support; Management development/capacity building; Building/renovation; Equipment; Emergency funds; Program development; Scholarship funds; Technical assistance; Consulting services; Scholarships—to individuals.
Limitations: Applications accepted. Giving limited to Eastern CT: Ashford, Bozrah, Brooklyn, Canterbury, Chaplin, Colchester, Columbia, Coventry, Eastford, East Lyme, Franklin, Griswold, Groton, Hampton, Killingly, Lebanon, Ledyard, Lisbon, Lyme, Mansfield, Montville, New London, North Stonington, Norwich, Old Lyme, Plainfield, Pomfret, Preston, Putnam, Salem, Scotland, Sprague, Stafford, Sterling, Stonington, Thompson, Union, Voluntown, Waterford, Willington, Windham, and Woodstock. No support for sectarian or religious programs. No grants to individuals (except for scholarships), or for fundraising events, or endowment, memorial, or building funds, deficit financing, annual campaigns, or debt retirement; no loans.
Publications: Application guidelines; Annual report; Annual report (including application guidelines); Financial statement; Grants list; Informational brochure; Newsletter; Occasional report; IRS Form 990 or 990-PF printed copy available upon request.
Application information: Visit foundation web site for application form and guidelines. The Connecticut Common Grant Application Form may be submitted in lieu of the foundation's application form. Application form required.
Initial approach: Telephone or e-mail
Copies of proposal: 2
Deadline(s): Nov. 15 for general grants; Apr. 1 for scholarship applications
Board meeting date(s): Jan., Mar., Apr., May, June, Sept., and Nov.
Final notification: General grants are distributed in Mar.; scholarships awarded in June
Officers and Trustees:* Paul Nunes,* Chair.; Susan Pochal,* Vice-Chair.; Maryam Elahi,* C.E.O. and Pres.; **Alison Woods,* V.P. and C.O.O.**; Valerie Grimm,* Secy.; Ruth Crocker,* Treas.; Frederic Anderson; **Thomas Borner**; Theresa Broach; Brian Carey; Sam Childs; John Duggan; Elizabeth Kuszaj; John LaMattina; Stephen Larcen; Marcia Marien; Dyanne Rafal; Mary Seidner; Lee Ellen Terry; Claire Warren, M.D.; Dianne E. Williams.
Number of staff: 6 full-time professional; 2 part-time support.
EIN: 061080097
Other changes: Rebekah Kepple is now Admin. Asst. Alice F. Fitzpatrick is no longer Pres.

563
Community Foundation of Greater New Britain

(formerly New Britain Foundation for Public Giving)
74A Vine St.
New Britain, CT 06052-1431 (860) 229-6018
Contact: James G. Williamson, Pres.; For grants: Joeline Wruck, Dir., Progs.
FAX: (860) 225-2666; E-mail: cfgnb@cfgnb.org; Grant inquiry e-mail: jwruck@cfgnb.org; Main URL: http://www.cfgnb.org
E-Newsletter: http://www.cfgnb.org/EmailSignup/tabid/77/Default.aspx

Established in 1941 in CT.
Foundation type: Community foundation.
Financial data (yr. ended 12/31/12): Assets, $38,034,923 (M); gifts received, $1,883,931; expenditures, $1,960,641; giving activities include $693,327 for grants, and $161,751 for grants to individuals.
Purpose and activities: The foundation seeks to meet the needs of the greater New Britain, CT, community through support of programs dedicated to health and human services, education, community and economic development, the environment, arts and humanities, and civic affairs.
Fields of interest: Humanities; Arts; Child development, education; Secondary school/education; Libraries/library science; Education; Environment; Hospitals (general); Reproductive health, family planning; Health care; Substance abuse, services; Mental health/crisis services; Health organizations, association; Crime/violence prevention, domestic violence; Youth development, services; Children/youth, services; Child development, services; Family services; Aging, centers/services; Homeless, human services; Human services; Economic development; Community/economic development; Leadership development; General charitable giving; Infants/toddlers; Children/youth; Youth; Adults; Aging; Disabilities, people with; Economically disadvantaged.
Type of support: General/operating support; Continuing support; Capital campaigns; Building/renovation; Equipment; Emergency funds; Program development; Seed money; Curriculum development; Research; Technical assistance; Consulting services; Program evaluation; Scholarships—to individuals; Matching/challenge support.
Limitations: Applications accepted. Giving limited to Berlin, New Britain, Plainville, and Southington, CT. No support for sectarian or religious activities. No grants to individuals (except for scholarships), or for annual or endowment campaigns, previously incurred expenses, sponsorships or fundraisers, performances or one-time events, conferences, advertising, or school-sponsored field trips or student trips for cultural, academic, enrichment or competitive purposes.
Publications: Application guidelines; Annual report; Financial statement; Grants list; Informational brochure; Newsletter.
Application information: Visit foundation web site for application guidelines per grant type. Submitted Letters of Intent will be reviewed by staff and selected applicants will be contacted directly to submit a complete, formal application. Application form not required.
Initial approach: Letter of Intent
Copies of proposal: 15
Deadline(s): Feb. 15, June 15, and Oct. 15
Board meeting date(s): Feb., Mar., June, Sept., and Dec.
Officers and Directors:* J. Leo Gagne,* Chair.; **Laurence A. Tanner,* Vice-Chair. and Chair.-Elect**; James G. Williamson,* Pres.; Robert S. Trojanowski,* V.P. Opers.; James G. Williamson,* Secy.; Mark Bernacki; Cori Humes; Rebecca Karabim-Ahern; Dr. John Miller; Marc S. Pelletier; Paul G. Salina; The Rev. Victoria Triano; Patricia M. Walden; Paul Zagorsky, Esq.; and 6 additional directors.
Number of staff: 4 full-time professional; 1 part-time professional; 2 part-time support.
EIN: 066036461
Other changes: Laurence A. Tanner has replaced J. Leo Gagne as Vice-Chair. and Chair. Elect. and Charles W. Bauer Esq. as Vice-Chair.
Manon-Lu Christ. Ken Julian, Charles N. Leach, Steven Maugay, Gail E. Millerick, and Laurence A. Tanner are no longer directors.

564
The Connecticut Community Foundation

(formerly The Waterbury Foundation)
43 Field St.
Waterbury, CT 06702-1906 (203) 753-1315
Contact: For grants and scholarships: Josh Carey, Dir., Grants Mgmt.
FAX: (203) 756-3054; E-mail: info@conncf.org; Grant inquiry e-mail: grants@conncf.org; Main URL: http://conncf.org
LinkedIn: http://www.linkedin.com/companies/ct-community-foundation
Scholarship inquiry e-mail: scholarships@conncf.org

Incorporated in 1923 by special Act of the CT Legislature.
Donors: Katherine Pomeroy†; Edith Chase†.
Foundation type: Community foundation.
Financial data (yr. ended 12/31/12): Assets, $81,761,965 (M); gifts received, $4,485,401; expenditures, $4,390,099; giving activities include $2,285,150 for 81 grants (high: $609,995), and $716,245 for 341 grants to individuals.
Purpose and activities: The foundation serves the people of Central Naugatuck Valley and Litchfield Hills to improve the quality of life by: 1) giving grants, scholarships, and organizational support to address the changing needs of the community; 2) helping donors create a legacy for the future through a permanent endowment fund; 3) promoting informed philanthropy and volunteerism to increase charitable resources for the region; and 4) providing leadership and building partnerships to identify and solve community concerns.
Fields of interest: Humanities; Historic preservation/historical societies; Arts; Education, early childhood education; Child development, education; Secondary school/education; Vocational education; Higher education; Adult/continuing education; Education; Health care; Substance abuse, services; Mental health/crisis services; Health organizations, association; Heart & circulatory diseases; AIDS; Employment; Housing/shelter, development; Recreation; Children/youth, services; Child development, services; Family services; Residential/custodial care, hospices; Aging, centers/services; Homeless, human services; Human services; Economic development; Community/economic development; Children/youth; Youth; Aging; Young adults; Disabilities, people with; Mentally disabled; Minorities; Hispanics/Latinos; Women; Economically disadvantaged; Homeless.
Type of support: Program evaluation; Management development/capacity building; Capital campaigns; Building/renovation; Equipment; Program development; Conferences/seminars; Publication; Seed money; Curriculum development; Scholarship funds; Research; Technical assistance; Consulting services; Scholarships—to individuals; Matching/challenge support.
Limitations: Applications accepted. Giving limited to Beacon Falls, Bethlehem, Bridgewater, Cheshire, Goshen, Litchfield, Middlebury, Morris, Naugatuck, New Milford, Oxford, Prospect, Roxbury, Southbury, Thomaston, Warren, Washington, Waterbury, Watertown, Wolcott, or Woodbury, CT. No support for sectarian or religious purposes. No grants to individuals (except for college scholarships), or for general operating support, capital campaigns for endowments, previously incurred expenses, capital/equipment for public agencies, schools or churches, or fundraising by one agency on behalf of another; no loans.
Publications: Application guidelines; Annual report; Informational brochure; Newsletter; Occasional report.

Application information: Visit foundation web site for application guidelines. Application form required.
Initial approach: E-mail application
Copies of proposal: 1
Deadline(s): Feb. 1 and Oct. 1 for General Grant Program; varies for others
Board meeting date(s): Mar. and Nov.; grants committee meets prior to each board meeting
Final notification: Within 10 weeks for full grant application
Officers and Trustees:* Jack Baker,* Chair.; Margaret W. Field,* Vice-Chair.; Paula Van Ness,* C.E.O. and Pres.; Ann Merriam Feiberg,* V.P.; Wayne P. McCormack,* Secy.; Charles J. Boulier, III*, Treas.; **Robert Bailey; Daniel L. Bedard, C.P.A.**; Martha Bernstein; Daniel Caron; Craig Carragan; Anne Delo; **Michelle Fica**; Brian Henebry; Richard E. Lau; John T. McCarthy; John Michaels; Elner Morrell; David Pelletier, C.P.A.; Antonio Paulo Pinto; Edith Reynolds; Carolyn E. Setlow; Anne Slattery.
Number of staff: 9 full-time professional; 2 part-time professional; 9 full-time support.
EIN: 066038074
Other changes: John Long is now Prog. Off., Nonprofit Assistance Initiative.

565
Carle C. Conway Scholarship Foundation, Inc.
c/o Marsha L. Colten
95 Alexandra Dr.
Stamford, CT 06903-1731
Application address: Carle C. Conway Scholarship Program, P.O. Box 6731, Princeton, NJ 08541

Established in 1950.
Donors: Continental Can Co., Inc.; Franklin Holdings, Inc.
Foundation type: Company-sponsored foundation.
Financial data (yr. ended 06/30/13): Assets, $4,191,616 (M); expenditures, $314,859; qualifying distributions, $285,889; giving activities include $50,000 for 1 grant, and $216,938 for 26 grants to individuals (high: $10,000; low: -$3,938).
Purpose and activities: The foundation supports organizations involved with higher education.
Fields of interest: Higher education.
Type of support: Scholarship funds; General/operating support; Employee-related scholarships.
Limitations: Applications not accepted. Giving primarily in areas of company operations in FL, IL, NY, KS, and PA.
Application information: Contributes only through employee-related scholarships and to pre-selected organizations.
Board meeting date(s): Usually May
Officers: Marsha L. Colten, Pres. and Treas.; Patricia DelTorro Heck, V.P. and Secy.
Trustees: Stephen Bermas; Robert S. Cohen.
EIN: 136088936
Other changes: The grantmaker no longer lists a primary contact.
Marsha L. Colten has replaced Stephen Bermas as Pres.
Patricia DelTorro Heck is now V.P. and Secy.

566
C. S. Craig Family Foundation, Inc.
c/o Craig Capital Corp.
127 Pecksland Rd.
Greenwich, CT 06831-3651 (203) 869-7700
Contact: Charles S. Craig, Dir.

Established in 1997 in DE.
Donor: Charles S. Craig.
Foundation type: Independent foundation.
Financial data (yr. ended 04/30/13): Assets, $2,802,517 (M); expenditures, $279,240; qualifying distributions, $277,450; giving activities include $277,450 for 14 grants (high: $200,500; low: $100).
Fields of interest: Higher education; Education; Health organizations, association.
Type of support: General/operating support.
Limitations: Applications accepted. Giving primarily in New York, NY and RI.
Application information: Application form not required.
***Initial approach:* Proposal**
Deadline(s): None
Directors: Charles S. Craig; Amy W. Harwood; Paul L. Maddock, Jr.
EIN: 061502485

567
Dalio Foundation, Inc.
(formerly Dalio Family Foundation, Inc.)
1 Glendinning Pl.
Westport, CT 06880-1242 (203) 291-5130
Raymond and Barbara Dalio's Giving Pledge Profile: http://glasspockets.org/philanthropy-in-focus/eye-on-the-giving-pledge/profiles/dalio

Established in 2003 in CT.
Donor: Raymond T. Dalio.
Foundation type: Independent foundation.
Financial data (yr. ended 12/31/12): Assets, $590,509,728 (M); gifts received, $223,059,351; expenditures, $30,725,270; qualifying distributions, $30,133,495; giving activities include $29,029,942 for 346 grants (high: $2,832,500; low: $470), $106,544 for foundation-administered programs and $80,723 for 1 loan/program-related investment.
Fields of interest: Elementary/secondary education; Higher education; Health organizations, association; Human services.
Type of support: Program-related investments/ loans.
Limitations: Applications not accepted. Giving primarily in CT, MA, NY, and Washington DC, with some giving in FL and NC. No grants to individuals.
Application information: Contributes only to pre-selected organizations.
Officers and Directors:* Raymond T. Dalio,* Pres.; Devon Dalio,* V.P.; Matthew Dalio,* V.P.; Barbara Dalio.
EIN: 431965846
Other changes: At the close of 2012, the fair market value of the grantmaker's assets was $590,509,728, an 82.9% increase over the 2011 value, $322,846,770.

568
The Daycroft School Foundation, Inc.
1177 High Ridge Rd.
Stamford, CT 06905-1221 **(203) 321-2118**
***FAX:* (203) 321-2119**;
E-mail: info@daycroftschool.org; Main URL: http://www.daycroftschool.org/
Knowledge Center: http://www.daycroftschool.org/online-learning

Established in 1998 in CT.
Foundation type: Independent foundation.
Financial data (yr. ended 12/31/12): Assets, $5,411,653 (M); gifts received, $21,660; expenditures, $356,096; qualifying distributions, $353,919; giving activities include $117,000 for 11 grants (high: $25,500; low: $2,000).
Purpose and activities: Giving for the education of young people in accordance with the teachings of Christian Science.
Fields of interest: Elementary/secondary education; Recreation, camps; Children, services; Christian agencies & churches.
Limitations: Applications not accepted. Giving primarily in MO and PA. No grants to individuals.
Application information: Unsolicited requests for funds not accepted.
Officers and Directors:* Toni Kyriakakis, Chair.; **Erik Olsen, Vice-Chair.**; Al McCready, Pres.; Joy Rendahl, Secy.; David Johnson, Treas.; Barbara Brown, Exec. Dir.; Trude Harper; Jeff Read.
EIN: 237127046
Other changes: Erik Olsen has replaced Fred Haines as Vice-Chair.

569
Deloitte Foundation
(formerly Deloitte & Touche Foundation)
10 Westport Rd.
P.O. Box 820
Wilton, CT 06897-0820
Contact for Doctoral Fellowship Program: Peg Levine, tel.: (203) 761-3413, e-mail: plevine@deloitte.com; Main URL: http://www.deloitte.com/us/df
AAA/Deloitte Wildman Medal Recipients: http://aaahq.org/awards/wildmanhistory.htm#Winners
Doctoral Fellowships Recipients: http://www.deloitte.com/view/en_US/us/press/Press-Releases/bb5b649227024410VgnVCM2000003356f70aRCRD.htm

Incorporated in 1928 in NY.
Donors: Deloitte LLP; Deloitte Haskins & Sells; Deloitte & Touche LLP; Charles Stewart Ludlam†; Charles C. Croggon†; Weldon Powell†; Deloitte & Touche USA LLP; Wayne Williamson.
Foundation type: Company-sponsored foundation.
Financial data (yr. ended 06/01/13): Assets, $15,245,101 (M); gifts received, $7,388,553; expenditures, $7,604,007; qualifying distributions, $7,597,770; giving activities include $2,486,948 for 24 grants (high: $400,000; low: $1,037), and $5,037,373 for 391 employee matching gifts.
Purpose and activities: The foundation supports educational programs designed to promote excellence in teaching, research, and curriculum innovation; and awards fellowships to doctoral accounting students.
Fields of interest: Higher education; Business school/education; Education.
Type of support: Conferences/seminars; Professorships; Curriculum development; Fellowships; Scholarship funds; Research; Sponsorships; Employee matching gifts.
Limitations: Applications accepted. Giving primarily in Washington, DC, FL, IL, KS, TX, and VA; giving on a national basis for fellowships. No grants for general operating support, capital campaigns, special programs, or publications; no loans; no matching support.
Publications: Application guidelines; Grants list; Informational brochure.
Application information: An application form is required for Doctoral Fellowships.
Initial approach: Contact foundation or accounting department head at educational institution for application form for Doctoral Fellowships

Copies of proposal: 1
Deadline(s): Oct. 15 for Doctoral Fellowships
Board meeting date(s): 3 times per year
Final notification: Jan. for Doctoral Fellowships
Officers and Directors:* Punit Renjen, Chair.; Shaun L. Budnik, Pres.; Jennifer Steinmann, Secy.-Treas.; Nathan Andrews; Philip Brunson; Amy Chronis; **Leslie Knowlton**; Adi Padha; **Sandra Shirai**; John Sizer; Sylvia Smyth.
EIN: 136400341
Other changes: Tonie Leatherberry and Lissa Perez are no longer directors.

570
Marie G. Dennett Foundation
c/o Fogarty Cohen Selby & Nemiroff LLC
1700 E. Putnam Ave., No. 406
Old Greenwich, CT **06870-1366**

Incorporated in 1956 in IL.
Donors: Marie G. Dennett†; Priscilla D. Ramsey†.
Foundation type: Independent foundation.
Financial data (yr. ended 08/31/13): Assets, $6,202,711 (M); expenditures, $307,930; qualifying distributions, $297,000; giving activities include $295,000 for 78 grants (high: $25,000; low: $500).
Fields of interest: Arts; Education; Hospitals (general); Health organizations, association; Boys & girls clubs; Human services; Children/youth, services; Christian agencies & churches; Blind/visually impaired.
Limitations: Applications not accepted. No grants to individuals.
Application information: Contributes only to pre-selected organizations.
Officers and Trustees:* Dennett W. Goodrich,* Pres.; John A. Goodrich,* V.P.; Everett Fisher,* Secy.-Treas.; Langdon P. Cook; **Ramsey W. Goodrich**; Anne M. Piedade; **Richard H. Ramsey**; **Richard L. Ramsey.**
EIN: 061060970

571
Deupree Family Foundation
587 Main St.
P.O. Box 126
New Hartford, CT 06057-0126
E-mail: info@deupreefamilyfoundation.org; Main URL: http://www.deupreefamilyfoundation.org

Established in 2000 in OH.
Donor: Ann T. Deupree†.
Foundation type: Independent foundation.
Financial data (yr. ended 06/30/12): Assets, $5,738,518 (M); expenditures, $324,661; qualifying distributions, $285,000; giving activities include $285,000 for 79 grants (high: $27,750; low: $250).
Purpose and activities: Giving preference for local non-profits in the fields of education, the arts, the environment, human services, and animal welfare.
Fields of interest: Arts; Scholarships/financial aid; Environment; Animal welfare; Employment; Recreation, parks/playgrounds; Children/youth; Adults; Young adults; Disabilities, people with; Physically disabled; Crime/abuse victims; Economically disadvantaged.
Type of support: General/operating support; Building/renovation; Equipment; Program development; Seed money; Internship funds; Scholarship funds; Research.
Limitations: Applications accepted. Giving on a national basis. No support for political organizations. No grants to individuals.
Application information: See foundation website for complete application guidelines. Application form required.
***Deadline(s):* June 1**
***Board meeting date(s):* Aug.**
***Final notification:* Sept.**
Officers: Susan D. Jones, Pres.; Richard R. Deupree III, V.P.; Kristine Cramer, Secy.-Treas.
Directors: Martha Chong; Karolen Deupree; Kato Deupree; Taylor Deupree; Thomas R. Deupree; Andi Jones.
Number of staff: None.
EIN: 311746946
Other changes: The grantmaker now accepts applications.

572
Draper Foundation
Winsted, CT

The foundation terminated and transferred its assets to the Community Foundation of Northwest Connecticut, Inc. in 2014.

573
Eder Family Foundation Inc.
(formerly The Andrew J. Eder Family Foundation, Inc.)
11 Eder Rd.
West Haven, CT 06516-4128

Established in 1998 in CT.
Donors: Andrew J. Eder; Eileen F. Eder; Eder Brothers, Inc.; Andrew Eder Annuity Trust.
Foundation type: Independent foundation.
Financial data (yr. ended 09/30/13): Assets, $5,924,594 (M); gifts received, $483,700; expenditures, $306,779; qualifying distributions, $289,980; giving activities include $254,480 for 47 grants (high: $100,000; low: $250), and $35,500 for 17 grants to individuals (high: $7,500; low: $1,000).
Fields of interest: Higher education; Education; Recreation, camps; Human services; United Ways and Federated Giving Programs; Jewish agencies & synagogues.
Type of support: Scholarships—to individuals.
Limitations: Applications not accepted. Giving primarily in PA.
Application information: Unsolicited requests for funds not accepted.
Officers and Director:* Andrew J. Eder,* Pres.; Eileen F. Eder, Secy.
EIN: 061465369

574
The Educational Foundation of America
c/o Foundation Source
55 Walls Dr.
Fairfield, CT 06824-5163
***E-mail:* info@theefa.org**; Main URL: http://www.efaw.org

Trust established in 1959 in NY.
Donors: Richard P. Ettinger†; Elsie Ettinger†; Richard P. Ettinger, Jr.†; Elaine P. Hapgood; Paul R. Andrews†; Virgil P. Ettinger†.
Foundation type: Independent foundation.
Financial data (yr. ended 12/31/12): Assets, $147,060,900 (M); expenditures, $13,042,483; qualifying distributions, $11,105,989; giving activities include $9,950,548 for 184 grants (high: $318,000; low: $5,000).
Purpose and activities: Giving primarily for arts and education, the environment and for sustainable population.
Fields of interest: Arts; Education; Environment; Reproductive health, family planning; Civil liberties, reproductive rights.
Limitations: Applications not accepted. Giving limited to the U.S. No support for political and religious organizations. No grants to individuals, annual fundraising campaigns, or for capital or endowment funds; no loans.
Publications: Annual report.
Application information: Unsolicited requests for funds not accepted at this time.
Board meeting date(s): Varies
Officers and Directors:* Sven Huseby,* Pres.; **Barbara Hapgood,* V.P.**; Christian P. Ettinger,* Secy.; Jerry Babicka,* Treas.; **Melissa Beck, Exec. Dir.**; Lynn P. Babicka; James Bohart, Jr.; Barbara P. Ettinger; Heidi P. Ettinger; Wendy W.P. Ettinger; Matthew Hapgood; John Powers; Trevor Renner.
Adjunct Committee Members: Morey Zuskin, Chair.; **Britton Rollins, Vice-Chair.**; **Jonathan Babicka, Secy.**; **Clarice Annegers**; Missy Babicka; Holly Bohart; **Mackenzie Dawson**; Matthew P. Ettinger; **Dodge Landesman**; North Landesman; Christopher Renner; Jill Renner; Todd Renner; Jonathan Reynolds; Andrew Schumacher; Austin J. Schumacher; Lauren Zuskin.
Number of staff: 3 full-time professional; 2 part-time professional; 1 full-time support.
EIN: 133424750
Other changes: Sven Huseby has replaced Lynn P. Babicka as Pres. Barbara Hapgood has replaced Trevor Renner as V.P.
Jerry Babicka is now Treas. Derek McLane is no longer a director. Morey Zuskin is now Chair., Adjunct Committe. Britton Rollins is now Vice-Chair., Adjunct Committee. Jonathan Babicka is now Secy., Adjunct Committee. James Bohart, Nash Landesman, and Amy Renner are no longer members of the Adjunct Committee.

575
Ensworth Charitable Foundation
c/o US Trust, Philanthropic Solutions
200 Glastonbury Blvd., Ste. 200
Glastonbury, CT 06033-4458 (860) 657-7015
Contact: Amy Lynch, Market Philanthropy Dir., U.S. Trust
E-mail: amy.r.lynch@ustrust.com; **Main URL: https://www.bankofamerica.com/philanthropic/grantmaking.go**

Trust established in 1948 in CT.
Donor: Antoinette L. Ensworth†.
Foundation type: Independent foundation.
Financial data (yr. ended 05/31/13): Assets, $21,787,410 (M); expenditures, $1,111,597; qualifying distributions, $1,020,291; giving activities include $912,800 for 90 grants (high: $25,000; low: $1,000).
Purpose and activities: Primary areas of interest include health and welfare programs, youth activities, enjoyment of the natural environment, relief of human suffering, education, religion, and the arts, particularly music.
Fields of interest: Arts; Education; Environment; Health care; Health organizations, association; AIDS research; Housing/shelter, development; Human services; Youth, services; Family services; Homeless, human services; Community/economic development.

Type of support: Program development; Seed money; Technical assistance; Matching/challenge support.
Limitations: Applications accepted. Giving limited to Hartford, CT, and its surrounding communities. No grants to individuals, or for operating budgets, annual campaigns, deficit financing, building or endowment funds, equipment and materials, land acquisition, scholarships, fellowships, research, or publications; no loans.
Publications: Program policy statement.
Application information: Online proposal available on foundation web site.
Initial approach: Letter
Copies of proposal: 4
Deadline(s): Jan. 15
Board meeting date(s): Mar.
Final notification: Within 3-4 months
Trustee: Bank of America, N.A.
Number of staff: 1 full-time professional.
EIN: 066026018

576
Flavia P. Finucane Charitable Trust
59 Merrimac Dr.
Trumbull, CT 06611-1725 (203) 261-6781
Contact: Christopher J. Koehm, Tr.

Established in CT.
Donor: Flavia P. Finucance†.
Foundation type: Independent foundation.
Financial data (yr. ended 06/30/13): Assets, $500,013 (M); expenditures, $66,521; qualifying distributions, $55,000; giving activities include $55,000 for 2 grants (high: $30,000; low: $25,000).
Fields of interest: Education.
Limitations: Applications accepted. Giving primarily in CT. No grants to individuals.
Application information: Application form not required.
***Initial approach:* Letter**
Deadline(s): Apr. 30
Trustee: Christopher J. Koehm.
EIN: 656403003

577
Fisher Foundation, Inc.
36 Brookside Blvd.
West Hartford, CT 06107-1107 (860) 570-0221
Contact: Hinda Fisher, Pres.
FAX: (860) 570-0225; E-mail: bboyle@fisherfdn.org; Contact for information regarding application form or the foundation's requirements: Beverly Boyle, Exec. Dir.; Main URL: http://www.fisherfdn.org
Grants List: http://www.fisherfdn.org/grants/2011/2011-grants.pdf

Established in 1959.
Donors: Stanley D. Fisher Trust; FIP Corp.
Foundation type: Independent foundation.
Financial data (yr. ended 12/31/12): Assets, $10,143,955 (M); gifts received, $40,947; expenditures, $493,694; qualifying distributions, $369,453; giving activities include $363,710 for 72 grants (high: $60,000; low: $100).
Purpose and activities: Giving primarily for education, arts and culture, health, human services, housing and community needs.
Fields of interest: Performing arts; Arts; Higher education; Education; Health care; Housing/shelter; Human services.
Type of support: General/operating support; Program development.
Limitations: Giving primarily in the greater Hartford, CT, area, (Andover, Avon, Bloomfield, Bolton, Canton, East Hartford, East Granby, East Windsor, Ellington, Enfield, Farmington, Glastonbury, Granby, Hartford, Hebron, Manchester, Marlborough, Newington, Rocky Hill, Simsbury, Somers, South Windsor, Suffield, Tolland, Vernon, West Hartford, Wethersfield, Windsor, and Windsor Locks). No grants to individuals, or for conferences, retreats, performances or events, or for capital campaigns.
Publications: Application guidelines; Annual report (including application guidelines); Grants list; Informational brochure.
Application information: Application information and form available on foundation web site. Audio or videotapes are not accepted, nor are applications submitted via fax or e-mail. Application form required.
Initial approach: Letter or telephone
Copies of proposal: 2
Deadline(s): Jan. 15, Apr. 15, and Sept. 15
Board meeting date(s): Mar., June, and Nov.
Officers and Directors:* Hinda N. Fisher,* Pres. and Treas.; Diane Fisher Bell,* V.P.; Lois Fisher Dietzel,* V.P.; Beverly Boyle, Secy. and Exec. Dir.; Michael Finklestein.
Number of staff: 1 part-time professional.
EIN: 066039415

578
The Floren Family Foundation
210 Round Hill Rd.
Greenwich, CT 06831-3357 (203) 622-5850
Contact: Douglas C. Floren, Pres.

Established in 2000 in CT.
Donor: Douglas C. Floren.
Foundation type: Independent foundation.
Financial data (yr. ended 10/31/13): Assets, $5,716,224 (M); expenditures, $424,078; qualifying distributions, $358,800; giving activities include $358,800 for 18 grants (high: $75,000; low: $2,000).
Fields of interest: Higher education; Higher education, university; Education; Hospitals (general); Health care; Human services; United Ways and Federated Giving Programs; Christian agencies & churches.
Limitations: Applications accepted. Giving primarily in CA, CO, and NH.
Application information: Application form required.
***Initial approach:* Proposal**
Deadline(s): None
Officer: Douglas C. Floren, Pres.
EIN: 066503521

579
Lily Palmer Fry Memorial Trust
(formerly L. P. Fry Memorial Trust)
c/o U.S. Trust
200 Glastonbury Blvd., Ste. 200, CT2-545-02-05
Glastonbury, CT 06033-4056
Contact: Kate Kerchaert
E-mail: kate.kerchaert@ustrust.com; **Main URL: https://www.bankofamerica.com/philanthropic/grantmaking.go**

Trust established in 1954 in CT.
Donor: William Henry Fry†.
Foundation type: Independent foundation.
Financial data (yr. ended 12/31/12): Assets, $5,302,386 (M); expenditures, $299,710; qualifying distributions, $237,009; giving activities include $200,000 for 49 grants (high: $8,000; low: $1,200).
Purpose and activities: The Lily Palmer Fry Memorial Trust was established in 1954 to support and promote summer camp opportunities for underserved children. Special consideration is given to traditional camp programs that take urban children out of the city to experience the natural environment.
Fields of interest: Recreation; Children/youth, services; Children/youth; Youth; Disabilities, people with; Minorities; Economically disadvantaged.
Type of support: General/operating support; Continuing support; Program development.
Limitations: Giving primarily in Fairfield and Hartford counties, CT, and New York City and Westchester County, NY. No grants to individuals.
Publications: Application guidelines.
Application information: Complete application guidelines available on Trust web site.
Initial approach: Online through Trust web site
Deadline(s): Feb. 1
Final notification: 2 to 3 months following deadline
Trustees: Virginia Fry Odell; William Fry Peterson; Bank of America, N.A.
Number of staff: None.
EIN: 066033612

580
E. Clayton and Edith P. Gengras, Jr. Foundation, Inc.
300 Connecticut Blvd.
East Hartford, CT 06108-3065 (860) 289-3461

Established in 1986 in CT.
Donors: Edith P. Gengras; E. Clayton Gengras, Jr.; Gengras Motor Cars, Inc.
Foundation type: Independent foundation.
Financial data (yr. ended 09/30/13): Assets, $427,484 (M); gifts received, $127,405; expenditures, $209,512; qualifying distributions, $204,350; giving activities include $204,350 for 23 grants (high: $150,000; low: $100).
Fields of interest: Arts; Education; Catholic federated giving programs; Christian agencies & churches.
Type of support: General/operating support.
Application information: Application form required.
***Initial approach:* Completed application form**
Deadline(s): None
Officers and Directors:* Edith P. Gengras,* Pres.; E. Clayton Gengras, Jr.,* Secy.; Merrily Moynihan.
EIN: 061188156

581
The Goldstone Family Foundation
445 Main St.
Ridgefield, CT 06877-4513

Established in 2000.
Donors: Steven F. Goldstone; Elizabeth Goldstone.
Foundation type: Independent foundation.
Financial data (yr. ended 12/31/12): Assets, $24,298,481 (M); expenditures, $1,524,932; qualifying distributions, $1,152,821; giving activities include $952,425 for 63 grants (high: $360,000; low: $100).
Purpose and activities: Giving primarily for the arts, education, and human services.
Fields of interest: Museums; Arts; Education; Health organizations, association; Housing/shelter, development; Human services.

Limitations: Applications not accepted. Giving primarily in CT and NY. No grants to individuals.
Application information: Contributes only to pre-selected organizations.
Officers and Directors:* Steven F. Goldstone,* Pres. and Treas.; Elizabeth Goldstone,* V.P. and Secy.; **Kerri Glass, Mgr.**
EIN: 061596255
Other changes: Kerri Glass is now Mgr.

582
Grampy's Charities
(formerly Callahan Foundation, Inc.)
c/o Apache Oil Co.
261 Ledyard St.
New London, CT 06320-5337
***Contact:* Jim Castle; Fran Walenta**
Main URL: http://grampys.com/

Established in 2003 in CT.
Donor: James H. Castle.
Foundation type: Independent foundation.
Financial data (yr. ended 10/31/12): Assets, $1,005,648 (M); gifts received, $28,234; expenditures, $257,753; qualifying distributions, $164,331; giving activities include $164,331 for 23 grants (high: $39,600; low: $1,000).
Fields of interest: Arts; Education; Human services.
Type of support: Scholarships—to individuals.
Limitations: Applications not accepted.
Application information: Unsolicited requests for funds not accepted.
Trustees: Courtney A. Castle; James H. Castle; Jennie Y. Castle; Jonatha Y. Castle; William H. Castle.
EIN: 200523402

583
Harold & Rebecca H. Gross Foundation
c/o U.S. Trust, Philanthropic Solutions
200 Glastonbury Blvd., Ste. 200, CT2-545-02-05
Glastonbury, CT 06033 (860) 657-7016
Contact: Kate Kerchaert, V.P.
E-mail: kate.kerchaert@ustrust.com; **Main URL: https://www.bankofamerica.com/philanthropic/grantmaking.go**

Established in 2006 in CT.
Donors: Rosalind Gross Trust; Rosalind Gross Unitrust.
Foundation type: Independent foundation.
Financial data (yr. ended 05/31/13): Assets, $8,513,909 (M); expenditures, $426,578; qualifying distributions, $359,008; giving activities include $307,870 for 6 grants (high: $70,000; low: $15,000).
Purpose and activities: To support and promote charitable organizations that assist persons with physical disabilities to become better adjusted to their environments.
Fields of interest: Health care; Human services; Physically disabled.
Limitations: Applications accepted. Giving primarily in CT. No grants to individuals.
Application information: Full applications will be accepted by invitation only following submission of a concept paper. Application form required.
Initial approach: Submit 1-page concept paper
Deadline(s): Apr. 1 for concept papers
Final notification: 4-6 weeks following concept paper deadline
Trustee: Bank of America, N.A.
EIN: 597266000

584
Charles H. Hall Foundation
c/o U.S. Trust, Bank of America, N.A.
200 Glastonbury Blvd., Ste. 200, CT2-545-02-03
Glastonbury, CT 06033-4056 (860) 657-7015
Contact: Amy Lynch, Market Director
E-mail: amy.r.lynch@ustrust.com; **Main URL: https://www.bankofamerica.com/philanthropic/grantmaking.go**

Established in 2007 in RI.
Foundation type: Independent foundation.
Financial data (yr. ended 04/30/13): Assets, $4,881,480 (M); expenditures, $246,434; qualifying distributions, $217,404; giving activities include $195,319 for 29 grants (high: $15,000; low: $2,500).
Purpose and activities: The foundation supports and promotes educational, health & human services, religious, and arts & cultural programming for underserved populations. Special consideration is given to programs whose purpose is the prevention of cruelty to children or animals.
Fields of interest: Performing arts, theater; Education; Health care; Boys & girls clubs.
Limitations: Giving to organizations based in Berkshire, Hampden, Hampshire, and Franklin counties, Massachusetts.
Application information:
Initial approach: Online via foundation web site
Deadline(s): Dec. 1
Trustee: Bank of America, N.A.
EIN: 261227617

585
The Maximilian E. & Marion O. Hoffman Foundation, Inc.
970 Farmington Ave., Ste. 203
West Hartford, CT 06107-2134 (860) 521-2949
Contact: Marion L. Barrak, Pres.

Established in 1986 in CT as a successor foundation of the Maximilian E. & Marion O. Hoffman Foundation.
Foundation type: Independent foundation.
Financial data (yr. ended 06/30/13): Assets, $62,472,604 (M); expenditures, $3,917,643; qualifying distributions, $3,157,742; giving activities include $2,942,191 for 65 grants (high: $500,000; low: $2,250).
Fields of interest: Arts; Higher education; Education; Hospitals (general); Human services; Catholic agencies & churches.
Type of support: General/operating support; Program development.
Limitations: Giving primarily in CT. No grants to individuals.
Application information: Application form required.
Initial approach: Letter of inquiry
Copies of proposal: 1
Deadline(s): 2 months prior to board meeting
Board meeting date(s): Mid-Oct., Jan., Apr., and June
Final notification: Few weeks after board meeting
Officers and Directors:* Marion L. Barrak,* Pres.; Joseph B. Chaho, V.P. and Secy.; Michael B. Chaho, M.D., Treas.; **Anne Marie Fauliso**; Marie Gustin, Ph.D.; Robert M. Jeresaty, M.D.
Number of staff: 3 full-time professional.
EIN: 222648036
Other changes: Joseph J. Fauliso is no longer a director.

586
J. S. Howe Family Foundation
c/o Old Hill Partners, Inc.
1120 Post Rd., 2nd Fl.
Darien, CT 06820

Established in 2007 in CT.
Donor: John Howe.
Foundation type: Independent foundation.
Financial data (yr. ended 06/30/13): Assets, $1,649,663 (M); gifts received, $400,000; expenditures, $117,750; qualifying distributions, $115,406; giving activities include $104,000 for 12 grants (high: $50,000; low: $1,000).
Fields of interest: Higher education; Education; Community/economic development; Religion.
Limitations: Applications not accepted. Giving primarily in MA and VA. No grants to individuals.
Application information: Contributes only to pre-selected organizations.
Trustees: Eliza Howe; Jacquelyn Howe; John Howe.
EIN: 223942135
Other changes: The grantmaker no longer lists a phone.

587
Gordon F. and Jocelyn B. Linke Foundation
116 Eleven Levels Rd.
Ridgefield, CT 06877-3009

Established in 1997 in MD.
Foundation type: Independent foundation.
Financial data (yr. ended 12/31/12): Assets, $2,562,561 (M); expenditures, $175,554; qualifying distributions, $157,800; giving activities include $157,800 for grants.
Purpose and activities: Giving primarily for animals, education, health and human services, and to Catholic churches.
Fields of interest: Museums; Arts; Elementary/secondary education; Higher education; Environment; Animals/wildlife; Human services; Catholic agencies & churches.
Limitations: Applications not accepted. Giving primarily in CA, CT, Washington, DC, MD, and NY. No grants to individuals.
Application information: Contributes only to pre-selected organizations.
Officers and Directors:* Gordon F. Linke,* Pres. and Mgr.; Jocelyn B. Linke,* V.P. and Mgr.; Jocelyn S. Witt,* Treas. and Mgr.
EIN: 521985801
Other changes: The grantmaker has moved from MD to CT.

588
George A. & Grace L. Long Foundation
c/o US Trust, Philanthropic Solutions
200 Glastonbury Blvd, Ste. 200
Glastonbury, CT 06033-4056 (860) 657-7019
Contact: Carmen Britt
E-mail: carmen.britt@ustrust.com; **Main URL: https://www.bankofamerica.com/philanthropic/grantmaking.go**

Trust established in 1960 in CT.
Donors: George A. Long†; Grace L. Long†.
Foundation type: Independent foundation.
Financial data (yr. ended 12/31/12): Assets, $10,038,258 (M); expenditures, $482,817; qualifying distributions, $419,759; giving activities include $348,804 for 122 grants (high: $10,000; low: $1,000).

Purpose and activities: The foundation was established in 1960 to support and promote quality educational, cultural, human services, and health care programming for underserved populations in Connecticut.
Fields of interest: Arts; Education, early childhood education; Child development, education; Adult/continuing education; Education; Environment; Hospitals (general); Health care; Health organizations, association; AIDS; AIDS research; Human services; Children/youth, services; Child development, services; Family services; Aging, centers/services; Community/economic development; Aging; Disabilities, people with; Minorities.
Type of support: Program development.
Limitations: Giving limited to CT. No grants to individuals, or for operating budgets or endowment funds; no loans.
Application information: Application guidelines available on foundation's website.
Initial approach: Online
Copies of proposal: 2
Deadline(s): Jan. 15 and June 15
Trustees: Alan S. Parker; Bank of America, N.A.
EIN: 066030953

589
The Macauley Foundation, Inc.
131 Hazel Plain Rd.
Woodbury, CT 06798-1919
E-mail: info@themacauleyfoundation.org; Main URL: http://www.themacauleyfoundation.com

Established in 1995 in CT.
Donors: Alma Jane Macauley; Robert C. Macauley.
Foundation type: Independent foundation.
Financial data (yr. ended 06/30/13): Assets, $1,784,989 (M); gifts received, $713,250; expenditures, $365,141; qualifying distributions, $286,650; giving activities include $286,650 for 16 grants (high: $150,000; low: $3,000).
Fields of interest: Human services; Children, services; International relief; Foundations (public).
Limitations: Applications not accepted. **Giving primarily in CT; some funding also in NY.** No grants to individuals.
Application information: Unsolicted requests for funds not accepted.
Officers and Directors:* Annie Yates, Exec. Dir.; Alma Jane Macauley,* Exec. V.P.; Anne Marie Weirether, Secy.; Melinda Rice Macauley; Robert C. Macauley, Jr., M.D.
Number of staff: 1 part-time professional.
EIN: 061439255

590
Katharine Matthies Foundation
c/o US Trust
200 Glastonbury Blvd., Ste. 200
Glastonbury, CT 06033-4056
Contact: Amy R. Lynch,
E-mail: amy.r.lynch@ustrust.com; **E-mail to discuss application process or for questions about the foundation: ct.grantmaking@ustrust.com (Foundation name should appear in subject line)**; Main URL: http://www.bankofamerica.com/grantmaking

Established in 1987 in CT.
Donor: Katharine Matthies†.
Foundation type: Independent foundation.
Financial data (yr. ended 12/31/12): Assets, $18,290,653 (M); expenditures, $698,843; qualifying distributions, $568,308; giving activities include $512,520 for 42 grants (high: $44,825; low: $1,500).
Purpose and activities: Giving primarily to support and promote quality educational, human services, and health care programming for underserved populations. Special consideration is given to organizations that work to prevent cruelty to children and animals.
Fields of interest: Arts; Animals/wildlife; Recreation; Human services; Youth, services; Family services; Community/economic development.
Type of support: General/operating support; Capital campaigns; Building/renovation; Equipment; Program development; Publication; Seed money; Matching/challenge support.
Limitations: Giving limited to the Lower Naugatuck Valley of CT, particularly the towns of Ansonia, Derby, Oxford, Shelton and Beacon Falls, with special consideration to organizations that serve the people of Seymour.
Publications: Application guidelines; Grants list.
Application information:
Initial approach: Online
Copies of proposal: 6
Deadline(s): May 1
Trustee: Bank of America, N.A.
EIN: 066261860

591
The Meriden Foundation
c/o Webster Bank, N.A.
123 Bank St.
Waterbury, CT 06702-2205 **(860) 692-1751**
***Contact:* Paul M. McAfee**

Established in 1983.
Donors: A. Leo Ricci†; I. Margaret Mesite; Rose Mesite; Jessie Wilcox Clark†; Warren Gardner†; Charles Hasburg†; F. Marino D'Amato†; Shirley Samaris†.
Foundation type: Independent foundation.
Financial data (yr. ended 12/31/12): Assets, $20,927,788 (M); gifts received, $19,159; expenditures, $1,434,124; qualifying distributions, $1,229,757; giving activities include $1,043,594 for 89+ grants (high: $57,200), and $146,185 for 62 grants to individuals (high: $5,000; low: $500).
Purpose and activities: Giving primarily for education, health organizations and hospitals, children and youth services, including children's hospitals, social services, YMCAs, and Protestant and Roman Catholic churches.
Fields of interest: Law school/education; Education; Hospitals (general); Hospitals (specialty); Health organizations, association; Boys & girls clubs; Human services; Salvation Army; YM/YWCAs & YM/YWHAs; Children/youth, services; United Ways and Federated Giving Programs; Protestant agencies & churches; Catholic agencies & churches.
Type of support: General/operating support; Annual campaigns; Scholarships—to individuals.
Limitations: Giving limited to the greater Meriden, CT, area.
Application information: Application form required.
Initial approach: Letter, on organizational letterhead, for grants; application form for scholarship requests
Deadline(s): None
Trustee: Webster Bank, N.A.
Ditribution Committee: Thomas Griglun, Chair.; Walter G. Alwang, Vice-Chair.; Elsa Bradford; Maureen Kane; Peter Vouras, Jr.
EIN: 066037849
Other changes: The grantmaker no longer lists a separate application address.
Thomas Griglun is now Chair. Walter G. Alwang is now Vice-Chair. Jeffery Otis is no longer Director.

592
Middlesex County Community Foundation, Inc.
211 S. Main St.
Middletown, CT 06457 (860) 347-0025
Contact: Cynthia H. Clegg, Pres. and C.E.O.; Ms. Thayer Talbott, Dir., Progs. and Opers.
FAX: (860) 347-0029;
E-mail: info@middlesexcountycf.org; Additional e-mail: cynthia@middlesexcountycf.org and thayer@middlesexcountycf.org; Main URL: http://www.middlesexcountycf.org
E-Newsletter: http://middlesexcountycf.org/news-events/newsletters-annual-reports/
Facebook: https://www.facebook.com/CommunityFoundationMC?rf=126312434089559

Established in 1997 in CT.
Foundation type: Community foundation.
Financial data (yr. ended 12/31/12): Assets, $9,679,802 (M); gifts received, $2,728,772; expenditures, $1,057,579; giving activities include $535,867 for 16+ grants (high: $113,665).
Purpose and activities: The foundation is dedicated to improving the quality of life in Middlesex County, CT. The foundation's grantmaking areas of interest include the arts, the environment, women and girls issues, heritage enhancement, education, neighborhood enhancement, safer communities, and services to help the less fortunate.
Fields of interest: Historic preservation/historical societies; Arts; Education; Environment; Animals/wildlife; Human services; Community development, neighborhood development; Community/economic development.
Type of support: General/operating support; Management development/capacity building; Equipment; Program development; Conferences/seminars; Technical assistance; Program evaluation; Matching/challenge support.
Limitations: Applications accepted. Giving primarily in Middlesex County, CT. No grants to individuals, or for endowment, capital campaigns, building programs, or debt reduction.
Publications: Application guidelines; Annual report; Financial statement; Grants list; Newsletter.
Application information: Visit foundation web site for application forms and guidelines. The foundation's Grants Committee requests full grant proposals from most viable Letters of Intent. Application form required.
Initial approach: Letter of Intent (no more than 2 pages)
***Copies of proposal:* 16**
Deadline(s): Sept. 17
Board meeting date(s): Quarterly
***Final notification:* Dec. 31**
Officers and Directors:* John S. Biddiscombe,* Chair.; Moira B. Martin,* Vice-Chair.; Cynthia H. Clegg,* Pres. and C.E.O.; Nancy Fischbach,* Secy.; Richard W. Tomc,* Asst. Secy.; David Director,* Treas.; John L. Boccalatte; Vincent G. Capece, Jr.; Sharon Griffin; Wallace C. Jones; Jean C. LaTorre; Marc V. Levin; Deborah L. Moore; Gregory P. Rainey; Gary P. Salva; Judith D. Schoonmaker; Eric W. Thornburg; Anna M. Wasescha; Frantz Williams, Jr.
Number of staff: 2 full-time professional; 1 part-time professional; 1 part-time support.
EIN: 061477711

593
Roy R. and Marie S. Neuberger Foundation, Inc.
55 Walls Dr., 3rd Fl.
Fairfield, CT 06824-5163
Contact: Gloria Silverman

Incorporated in 1954 in NY.
Donors: Roy R. Neuberger; Marie S. Neuberger†; Ann N. Aceves; James A. Neuberger; Roy S. Neuberger.
Foundation type: Independent foundation.
Financial data (yr. ended 12/31/12): Assets, $4,501,027 (M); expenditures, $4,923,833; qualifying distributions, $4,868,388; giving activities include $4,810,212 for 57 grants (high: $4,500,737; low: $60).
Purpose and activities: Giving primarily for education, as well as to arts and culture organizations, and Jewish agencies and temples.
Fields of interest: Visual arts; Performing arts; Arts; Higher education; Jewish agencies & synagogues.
Type of support: General/operating support; Continuing support; Annual campaigns.
Limitations: Applications not accepted. Giving primarily in NY. No support for political organizations. No grants to individuals.
Application information: Contributes only to pre-selected organizations.
Board meeting date(s): Varies
Officers and Directors:* Roy R. Neuberger,* Pres.; Roy S. Neuberger,* V.P. and Treas.; Ann N. Aceves,* V.P.; James A. Neuberger,* V.P.
Number of staff: None.
EIN: 136066102
Other changes: The grantmaker has moved from NY to CT.
At the close of 2012, the grantmaker paid grants of $4,810,212, a 434.2% increase over the 2010 disbursements, $900,507.

594
Leo Nevas Family Foundation, Inc.
(formerly Leo & Libby Nevas Family Foundation, Inc.)
P.O. Box 299
Chester, CT 06412-0299
***Contact:* Jo-Ann Price, Pres.**

Established in 1961 in CT.
Donor: Leo Nevas†.
Foundation type: Independent foundation.
Financial data (yr. ended 11/30/12): Assets, $5,714,577 (M); expenditures, $295,861; qualifying distributions, $245,000; giving activities include $245,000 for 6 grants (high: $100,000; low: $10,000).
Fields of interest: Student services/organizations; Education; Jewish agencies & synagogues.
Type of support: General/operating support.
Limitations: Applications accepted. Giving primarily in CT and NY. No grants to individuals.
Application information: Application form not required.
Deadline(s): None
Officers: Jo-Ann Price, Pres.; Bernard Nevas, Treas.
EIN: 066068842
Other changes: Jo-Ann Price is now Pres.

595
NewAlliance Foundation, Inc.
195 Church St., 7th Fl.
New Haven, CT 06510-2009
Contact: Kim A. Healey, Exec. Dir.
E-mail: khealey@newalliancefoundation.org; Additional contacts: Maryann Ott, Assoc. Dir., tel.: (203) 859-6555, e-mail: mott@newalliancefoundation.org; Bobbi Griffith, Admin. Asst., tel.: (203) 859-6543, e-mail: bgriffith@newalliancefoundation.org; Main URL: http://newalliancefoundation.org/

Established in 2004 in CT.
Donor: NewAlliance Bancshares, Inc.
Foundation type: Independent foundation.
Financial data (yr. ended 12/31/12): Assets, $29,062,037 (M); expenditures, $1,807,211; qualifying distributions, $1,650,793; giving activities include $1,212,650 for 185+ grants (high: $35,000).
Purpose and activities: The foundation supports nonprofit and charitable organizations that promote the arts; community development; health and human services; and youth and education.
Fields of interest: Museums; Performing arts; Arts; Elementary/secondary education; Education, services; Education, reading; Education; Environment; Health care; Employment, services; Employment, training; Food services; Food banks; Housing/shelter; Youth development; Children/youth, services; Developmentally disabled, centers & services; Homeless, human services; Human services; Economic development; Community/economic development; Mathematics; Engineering/technology; Science; Children/youth; Aging; Economically disadvantaged.
Type of support: General/operating support; Continuing support; Management development/capacity building; Capital campaigns; Building/renovation; Equipment; Endowments; Program development; Seed money; Sponsorships; Employee matching gifts; Matching/challenge support.
Limitations: Applications accepted. Giving limited to Branford, Centerbrook, Cheshire, Chester, Clinton, Columbia, Coventry, Danielson, Dayville, East Hartford, East Haven, Ellington, Enfield, Essex, Glastonbury, Guilford, Hamden, Hartford, Hebron, Madison, Manchester, Milford, New Haven, North Branford, North Haven, Old Saybrook, Orange, Putnam, Seymour, South Windsor, Stafford Springs, Storrs, Tolland, Vernon, Wallingford, West Hartford, West Haven, Westbrook, Wethersfield, Willington, Willimantic, Windsor, Woodbridge, and Woodstock, CT. No support for religious organizations not of direct benefit to the entire community, service clubs, fraternal organizations, or third party fundraising organizations, Parent Teacher Organizations, state agencies, departments, or organizations raising money for specific diseases. No grants to individuals, or for political or lobbying activities, interest expenses on loans or debt reduction, feasibility studies, trips, tours, transportation, or conference attendance, golf tournaments, animal causes, team sponsorships, "a-thon" fundraising events, pageants, or start-up needs for programs initiated by organizations not located in areas of company operations.
Publications: Application guidelines; Annual report.
Application information: Support is limited to 1 contribution per organization during any given year. Organizations receiving support are asked to provide a final report. Proposal narratives should be no longer than 2 pages. Application form required.
Initial approach: Complete the on-line Application Coversheet on foundation web site
Copies of proposal: 1
Deadline(s): See foundation web site for current deadline
Board meeting date(s): Mar. and Sept.
Final notification: Within a week of board meeting
Officers and Directors:* Robert Lyons, Jr.,* Chair.; Paul A. McCraven,* Secy.-Treas.; Kim A. Healey, Exec. Dir.; **William W. Bouton III**; Shiela B. Flanagan; Marjorie Bussmann Gillis, Ed.D.; D. Anthony Guglielmo; Dr. Dorsey L. Kendrick; Dr. Julia M. McNamara; Joseph H. Rossi; Donald E. Waggaman, Jr.; Diane Wishnafski.
Number of staff: 2 full-time professional; 1 full-time support.
EIN: 562453619

596
Henry E. Niles Foundation
c/o Fogarty, Cohen, Selby, & Nemiroff LLC
1700 E. Putnam Ave., Ste. 406
Old Greenwich, CT **06870-1370**
Contact: Ashley C. Lantz, Admin.
***FAX:* (203) 629-7300; E-mail: agaran@fcsn.com**; Main URL: http://www.heniles.org

Established in 1990 in CT.
Foundation type: Independent foundation.
Financial data (yr. ended 12/31/12): Assets, $27,946,031 (M); expenditures, $1,688,597; qualifying distributions, $1,507,965; giving activities include $1,336,000 for 98 grants (high: $100,000; low: $2,000).
Purpose and activities: The foundation strives to support humanitarian efforts, including faith-based endeavors, that: 1) strengthen education, including special education, literacy, and others; 2) fight economic hardships through self-help opportunities; and 3) enhance public health and sanitation on a global basis. The foundation also has particular interest in organizations that promote partnerships and collaborative efforts among multiple groups and organizations, and it encourages pilot initiatives that test new program models.
Fields of interest: Higher education; Education; Health care; Human services.
Limitations: Applications accepted. Giving primarily in the Northeast, with emphasis on CT and NY. **No support for government agencies or for organizations that subsist mainly on third-party funding, and that have demonstrated no ability or have exerted little effort to attract public funding, or for organizations based outside the U.S.** No grants to individuals or for general fundraising drives.
Publications: Application guidelines.
Application information: Application form required.
***Initial approach:* Use application form on foundation web site**
Copies of proposal: 1
Deadline(s): Rolling
***Board meeting date(s):* 10 times per year**
***Final notification:* 1 week after board meeting**
Officers and Directors:* Geoffrey M. Parkinson,* Pres.; Leland C. Selby,* V.P. and Secy.; James R. Lamb,* Treas.
EIN: 061252486

597
Laura J. Niles Foundation
c/o Fogerty, Cohen, Selby, & Nemiroff LLC
1700 E. Putnam Ave., Ste. 406
Old Greenwich, CT **06870-1370** (203) 629-7314
Contact: Ashley C. Garan, Admin.
***FAX:* (203) 629-7300**; E-mail: agaran@fcsn.com; Main URL: http://www.ljniles.org

Established in 1997 in CT.
Donors: Laura Janet Niles†; Laura J. Niles Revocable Trust.
Foundation type: Independent foundation.

Financial data (yr. ended 12/31/12): Assets, $22,177,129 (M); expenditures, $1,404,081; qualifying distributions, $1,259,846; giving activities include $1,095,000 for 104 grants (high: $90,000; low: $2,500).
Purpose and activities: The foundation encourages and supports efforts to improve the lives of both people and animals. The foundation seeks to benefit animals, primarily dogs, through research, training, and adoption, especially where people and animals benefit simultaneously. Additionally, the foundation strives to nurture and assist individuals in leading responsible and productive lives by enabling them to help themselves.
Fields of interest: Education; Animals/wildlife; Employment; Children/youth, services; Economically disadvantaged.
Limitations: Applications accepted. **Giving in the U.S., but priority is given to organizations in the Northeast. No support for any non-U.S. 501 (c) (3) s, or for spay or neuter projects.** No grants to individuals.
Publications: Application guidelines.
Application information: Application form required.
***Initial approach:* Use application form on foundation web site**
Copies of proposal: 1
Deadline(s): Rolling
***Board meeting date(s):* 10 times per year**
***Final notification:* 1 week after board meeting**
Officers and Directors:* Geoffrey M. Parkinson,* Pres.; **Leland C. Selby,* V.P. and Secy.**; James R. Lamb,* Treas.
EIN: 223188304
Other changes: Leland C. Selby is now V.P. and Secy.

598
Northeast Utilities Foundation, Inc.
P.O. Box 270
Hartford, CT 06141-0270 **(860) 665-3306**
***Contact:* Lindsay Parke, Community Rels.**
FAX: (860) 728-4594;
E-mail: lindsay.parke@nu.com; Additional tel.: (888) 682-4639; Contact in Western MA: Edgar Alejandro, Economic and Community Devel., Western Massachusetts Electric Co., P.O. Box 2010, West Springfield, MA 01090-2010, tel.: (413) 785-5871, fax: (413) 787-9289, ext. 2289, e-mail: alejae@nu.com; Contact in NH: Paulette Faggiano, Comms. and Public Affairs, Public Service Co. of New Hampshire, P.O. Box 330, Manchester, NH 03105, tel.: (603) 634-3386, fax: (603) 634-2367, e-mail: faggips@nu.com; Main URL: http://www.northeastutilitiesfoundation.org
Additional URL: http://www.cl-p.com/community/partners/grants/nufoundation.asp
Grants List: http://www.northeastutilitiesfoundation.org/what/partners.html

Established in 1998 in CT.
Donors: The Connecticut Light and Power Co.; Northeast Nuclear Energy Co.; Northeast Utilities; Public Service Co. of New Hampshire; Western Massachusetts Electric Co.; Select Energy, Inc.; Yankee Gas Services Company.
Foundation type: Company-sponsored foundation.
Financial data (yr. ended 12/31/12): Assets, $22,964,884 (M); expenditures, $1,020,711; qualifying distributions, $983,641; giving activities include $983,641 for 24 grants (high: $125,000; low: $7,217).
Purpose and activities: The foundation supports programs designed to promote economic and community development, workforce development, and environmental stewardship.
Fields of interest: Museums (science/technology); Education; Environment, water resources; Environment, land resources; Environment, energy; Environment; Employment, training; Employment; Salvation Army; Economic development; Community development, small businesses; Community/economic development.
Type of support: General/operating support; Continuing support; Program development; Sponsorships; Employee matching gifts; Employee-related scholarships.
Limitations: Applications accepted. Giving primarily in areas of company operations, with emphasis on CT, western MA, and NH. No support for private foundations, religious, political, or fraternal organizations, or organizations not of direct benefit to the entire community. No grants to individuals (except for employee-related scholarships), or for endowments, debt reduction, or athletic trips.
Publications: Application guidelines; Grants list.
Application information: The foundation supports large regional projects through select partners and through requests for proposals that address a specific issue or focus areas. Inquiries and proposals for small grant requests should be directed toward local state representatives. Application form not required.
Initial approach: Proposal to local state representative in Connecticut, Massachusetts, and New Hampshire
Deadline(s): None
Board meeting date(s): Feb., May, Aug., and Nov.
Officers and Directors:* Thomas J. May,* Chair. and Pres.; Richard J. Morrison, Secy.; James J. Judge,* Treas.; Joseph R. Nolan, Jr.,* Exec. Dir.; Gregory B. Butler; **Christine M. Carmody; David R. McHale**; Leon J. Oliver.
EIN: 061527290
Other changes: Thomas J. May has replaced Charles W. Shivery as Chair.
Charles W. Shivery is no longer Chair. Shirley M. Payne is no longer Pres., Secy., and Exec. Dir. David R. McHale is no longer Treas. Jeffrey D. Butler, Peter J. Clarke, Jean M. LaVecchia, Rodney O. Powell, Marie T. Van Luling, and Gary A. Long are no longer directors.

599
The Old Stones Foundation, Inc.
62 Southfield Ave., No. 101
Stamford, CT **06902-7229**

Established in 1996 in CT.
Donors: Dorothy M. Morris; Anthony P. Morris; Robert E. Morris, Jr.
Foundation type: Independent foundation.
Financial data (yr. ended 06/30/13): Assets, $1,593,508 (M); expenditures, $83,368; qualifying distributions, $82,415; giving activities include $82,000 for 43 grants (high: $15,000; low: $500).
Fields of interest: Arts; Education; Protestant agencies & churches.
Limitations: Applications not accepted. Giving primarily in CT and NY. No grants to individuals.
Application information: Contributes only to pre-selected organizations.
Officers and Directors:* Robert E. Morris, Jr.,* Pres.; Anthony P. Morris,* Secy.; Susan T. Morris; Susan W. Morris.
EIN: 061463304

600
Frank Loomis Palmer Fund
c/o Bank of America, N.A.
200 Glastonbury Blvd., Ste. 200
Glastonbury, CT 06033-4458 (860) 657-7015
E-mail: ct.grantmaking@ustrust.com; **Main URL: https://www.bankofamerica.com/philanthropic/grantmaking.go**

Trust established in 1936 in CT.
Donor: Virginia Palmer†.
Foundation type: Independent foundation.
Financial data (yr. ended 07/31/13): Assets, $33,463,416 (M); expenditures, $1,711,955; qualifying distributions, $1,562,930; giving activities include $1,418,046 for 83 grants (high: $100,000; low: $1,250).
Purpose and activities: Grants to encourage new projects and to provide seed money, with emphasis on child welfare and family services and youth agencies; support also for civic groups, cultural programs, social services, and educational programs.
Fields of interest: Performing arts; Arts; Elementary school/education; Secondary school/education; Higher education; Adult/continuing education; Libraries/library science; Education; Environment, natural resources; Environment; Hospitals (general); Reproductive health, family planning; Health care; Health organizations, association; AIDS; Alcoholism; AIDS research; Legal services; Safety/disasters; Children/youth, services; Family services; Residential/custodial care, hospices; Aging, centers/services; Minorities/immigrants, centers/services; Community/economic development; Engineering/technology; Science; Government/public administration; Transportation; Religion; Aging; Minorities.
Type of support: Equipment; Program development; Conferences/seminars; Publication; Seed money; Scholarship funds; Research; Consulting services; Matching/challenge support.
Limitations: Applications accepted. Giving limited to New London, CT. No grants to individuals, or for endowment funds.
Publications: Informational brochure (including application guidelines).
Application information: Application information available at http://www.bankofamerica.com/grantmaking. Application form required.
Initial approach: Telephone
Copies of proposal: 1
Deadline(s): Nov. 15
Board meeting date(s): Jan. and July
Final notification: Feb. 1 and Aug. 1
Trustee: Bank of America, N.A.
EIN: 066026043

601
Robert E. Leet & Clara Guthrie Patterson Trust
c/o U.S. Trust, Bank of America, N.A.
200 Glastonbury Blvd., Ste. 200
Glastonbury, CT 06033-4458
Contact: Carmen Britt, V.P.
E-mail: carmen.britt@ustrust.com; **Main URL: https://www.bankofamerica.com/philanthropic/grantmaking.go**

Established in 1981 in CT.
Donors: Robert Leet Patterson†; Clara Guthrie Patterson†; Robert Patterson Trust No. 2.
Foundation type: Independent foundation.
Financial data (yr. ended 01/31/13): Assets, $19,576,465 (M); expenditures, $1,024,772; qualifying distributions, $831,120; giving activities

include $775,000 for 6 grants (high: $225,000; low: $50,000).
Fields of interest: Health care.
Type of support: Research.
Limitations: Applications not accepted. Giving limited to CT, NJ, and NY. No grants to individuals, or for operating budgets, continuing support, annual campaigns, emergency funds, deficit financing, endowment funds, consulting services, technical assistance, demonstration projects, publications, conferences and seminars, or for medical equipment; no loans.
Application information: Unsolicited requests for funds are currently not accepted.
Board meeting date(s): Dec.
Trustee: Bank of America Merrill Lynch.
EIN: 066236358

602
The Perna Foundation for Hope, Inc.
50 Knobloch Ln.
Stamford, CT 06902-1702
***Main URL:* http://www.pernafoundationforhope.org/**

Donor: Janet Perna.
Foundation type: Independent foundation.
Financial data (yr. ended 06/30/13): Assets, $3,150,393 (M); gifts received, $100,000; expenditures, $167,584; qualifying distributions, $152,561; giving activities include $148,728 for 13 grants (high: $60,000; low: $1,728).
Fields of interest: Higher education, college; Education; Animals/wildlife; Human services.
Limitations: Applications not accepted. Giving primarily in CT and NY.
Application information: Unsolicited requests for funds not accepted.
Officers: Melanie Rose, Pres. and Secy.; Tina Woodward, V.P.; Janet Perna, Treas.
EIN: 352357099

603
The Perrin Family Foundation
4 Prospect St.
Ridgefield, CT 06877-4510 (203) 438-7349
Contact: Kelly Weldon, Grants Mgr.
E-mail: info@perrinfamilyfoundation.org; **Additional address: The Grove, 760 Chapel St., New Haven, CT 06533, tel.: (203) 438-7349; Laura McCargar e-mail: lmccargar@perrinfamilyfoundation.org.;** Main URL: http://www.perrinfamilyfoundation.org
Blog: http://perrinfamilyfoundation.blogspot.com/
Facebook: https://www.facebook.com/pages/Perrin-Family-Foundation/407486896010548
Pinterest: http://www.pinterest.com/perrinfamilyfdn/
Twitter: http://twitter.com/Perrinfamilyfdn

Established in 1994 in CT.
Donors: Charles Perrin; Sheila Perrin.
Foundation type: Independent foundation.
Financial data (yr. ended 12/31/12): Assets, $15,293,841 (M); gifts received, $1,019,166; expenditures, $948,245; qualifying distributions, $834,623; giving activities include $695,500 for 43 grants (high: $30,000; low: $2,000).
Purpose and activities: The foundation's mission is to provide equal opportunities for children and young adults to lead safe, productive, and creative lives. Giving for education, health and cultural services for children, including after-school programs.
Fields of interest: Arts; Education; Health care; Children, services; Youth, services; Children/youth; Youth; Economically disadvantaged.
Type of support: General/operating support; Continuing support; Program development.
Limitations: Giving in Fairfield County, CT for social services, and in CT for youth engagement. No support for public or private schools. No grants to individuals.
Publications: Application guidelines; Grants list.
Application information: Applications are by invitation only, upon review of letter of inquiry. Complete application guidelines available on foundation web site.
***Initial approach:* Letter of inquiry via e-mail to Laura McCarger, or U.S. mail**
***Deadline(s):* See foundation web site for current deadlines**
Board meeting date(s): Three times a year
Officer and Trustees:* Sheila A. Perrin,* Pres.; Anne Kenan; Charles R. Perrin; David B. Perrin; Jeffrey L. Perrin.
Number of staff: 2 part-time professional.
EIN: 223309886
Other changes: The grantmaker now publishes application guidelines.

604
The Pitney Bowes Foundation
(formerly The Pitney Bowes Employees Involvement Fund, Inc.)
1 Elmcroft Rd., MSC 6101
Stamford, CT 06926-0700
Contact: Kathleen Ryan Mufson, Pres.
FAX: (203) 460-5336;
E-mail: Kathleen.RyanMufson@pb.com; **Main URL: http://www.pitneybowes.com/us/our-company/corporate-responsibility/community.html**
Pitney Bowes Corporate Social Responsibility Video: http://embed.vidyard.com/share/naBRrxwYAcL—x69Pponvw

Donor: Pitney Bowes Inc.
Foundation type: Company-sponsored foundation.
Financial data (yr. ended 12/31/12): Assets, $8,801,042 (M); expenditures, $3,598,240; qualifying distributions, $3,584,089; giving activities include $3,545,994 for 148 grants (high: $1,586,200; low: $300).
Purpose and activities: The foundation supports programs designed to promote literacy and education.
Fields of interest: Education, early childhood education; Higher education; Adult/continuing education; Adult education—literacy, basic skills & GED; Education, continuing education; Education, services; Education, reading; Education; Employment, services; Employment, training; Employment; Youth development, adult & child programs; Engineering; Disabilities, people with; Minorities; Women.
Type of support: Sponsorships; General/operating support; Program development; Curriculum development; Employee volunteer services; Employee matching gifts.
Limitations: Applications accepted. Giving primarily in areas of company operations in Bridgeport, Danbury, Hartford, Shelton, and Stamford, CT, Washington, DC, Atlanta, GA, Waltham, MA, Detroit and Grand Rapids, MI, Troy, NY, Chesapeake, VA, Dallas, TX, Spokane, WA, and Appleton, WI; giving also to national organizations. No support for religious organizations not of direct benefit to the entire community, political candidates or lobbying organizations, organizations with limited constituency including fraternal, labor, veterans' groups, or business associations, anti-business groups, discriminatory organizations, or single disease health organizations. No grants to individuals, or for conferences, sporting events, auctions, trade shows, or other one-time short term events, sponsorships, advertising or television programming, team sponsorships or athletic scholarships, fundraising, or indirect costs that exceeds 20% of program budget.
Publications: Application guidelines.
Application information: Support is limited to 1 contribution per organization during any given year. Application form required.
Initial approach: Complete online application
Deadline(s): Jan. 15 and June 1 for Literacy and Education; Feb. 15 and Aug. 31 for Local Community Grants
Board meeting date(s): Quarterly
Final notification: 4 to 6 months for Literacy and Education
Officers and Directors:* Johnna G. Torsone,* Chair.; Kathleen Ryan Mufson,* Pres.; Polly O'Brien Morrow, V.P.; Juanita James; Murray D. Martin; Michael Monahan; Helen Shan.
Number of staff: 1 full-time professional; 1 part-time professional.
EIN: 200523317

605
Post College Foundation, Inc.
43 Field St.
Waterbury, CT 06702-1906

Established in 2005 in CT.
Foundation type: Independent foundation.
Financial data (yr. ended 06/30/13): Assets, $5,973,394 (M); gifts received, $500; expenditures, $392,241; qualifying distributions, $339,481; giving activities include $325,000 for 122 grants to individuals (high: $8,000; low: $1,500).
Fields of interest: Education.
Limitations: Applications not accepted. Giving primarily in CT.
Application information: Unsolicited requests for funds not accepted.
Officers: Edmund White, Chair.; **Gary Post, Pres.; Peter Meriman, Secy.-Treas.**
EIN: 061298333
Other changes: Gary Post has replaced Benjamin M. DeAngelis as Pres.

606
Praxair Foundation, Inc.
39 Old Ridgebury Rd.-K2
Danbury, CT 06810-5113
Contact: Susan M. Neuman, Pres.
FAX: (203) 837-2454;
E-mail: Praxair_GlobalGiving@praxair.com; Main URL: http://www.praxair.com/our-company/our-people/praxair-foundation

Established in 1994.
Donor: Praxair, Inc.
Foundation type: Company-sponsored foundation.
Financial data (yr. ended 11/30/12): Assets, $760,543 (M); gifts received, $4,099,993; expenditures, $3,842,325; qualifying distributions, $3,842,325; giving activities include $3,842,325 for 221 grants (high: $519,063; low: $250).
Purpose and activities: The foundation supports public libraries and organizations involved with

higher education, the environment, health, disaster relief, diversity, and community development.
Fields of interest: Higher education; Libraries (public); Environment; Hospitals (general); Health care; Disasters, preparedness/services; Civil rights, race/intergroup relations; Community/economic development; United Ways and Federated Giving Programs.
Type of support: General/operating support; Building/renovation; Equipment; Program development; Scholarship funds; Employee volunteer services; Employee matching gifts.
Limitations: Applications accepted. Giving on a national and international basis in areas of company operations, with emphasis on CT, Asia, Brazil, India, and South America. No support for religious organizations, fraternal or labor organizations, or discriminatory organizations. No grants to individuals or for sports programs.
Publications: Application guidelines.
Application information: Organizations receiving support of $25,000 or more are required to submit a final report. Application form required.
Initial approach: Complete online application form
Deadline(s): None
Officers: Susan M. Neumann, Pres.; Anthony M. Pepper, Secy.; Timothy S. Heenan, Treas.
EIN: 061413665

607
The Robbins Family Foundation
(formerly Robbins Foundation, Inc.)
32 Calhoun Dr.
Greenwich, CT 06831-4437
***Contact:* Clifton S. Robbins**

Established in 1993 in NY.
Donors: Clifton S. Robbins; Edwin Robbins; Beverly Robbins; Edward Milstein; Gabe Kaplan; Tobey Maguire; General Atlantic Service Corp.; Larry Robbins.
Foundation type: Independent foundation.
Financial data (yr. ended 12/31/12): Assets, $402,037 (M); gifts received, $755,000; expenditures, $1,025,956; qualifying distributions, $1,020,085; giving activities include $1,020,085 for grants.
Purpose and activities: Giving primarily for Jewish organizations, as well as for health organizations and hospitals, particularly a cancer center; funding also for higher education.
Fields of interest: Higher education; Education; Hospitals (specialty); Health care; Health organizations, association; Cancer; Human services; Children/youth, services; Jewish federated giving programs; Jewish agencies & synagogues.
Limitations: Applications not accepted. Giving primarily in CT and NY; some funding also in MA. No grants to individuals
Application information: Contributes only to pre-selected organizations.
Officers: Clifton S. Robbins, Pres.; Edwin Robbins, V.P.
EIN: 133745914
Other changes: At the close of 2011, the grantmaker paid grants of $1,504,639, a 366.6% increase over the 2010 disbursements, $322,440.

608
Edward C. & Ann T. Roberts Foundation, Inc.
P.O. Box 271588
West Hartford, CT 06127-1588 (860) 233-0228
Contact: Lisa M. Curran, Exec. Dir.
FAX: (860) 233-0228;
E-mail: edwannroberts@att.net; Main URL: http://www.foundationcenter.org/grantmaker/e&aroberts
Grants List: http://foundationcenter.org/grantmaker/e&aroberts/grants.html

Established in 1964 in CT.
Donors: Edward C. Roberts†; Ann T. Roberts†.
Foundation type: Independent foundation.
Financial data (yr. ended 12/31/12): Assets, $6,762,104 (M); expenditures, $383,374; qualifying distributions, $338,385; giving activities include $297,000 for 32 grants (high: $50,000; low: $1,500).
Purpose and activities: Funding for Excellence in the Arts grants to support and encourage excellence in the arts in the Hartford, Connecticut, area.
Fields of interest: Visual arts; Performing arts; Performing arts, dance; Arts.
Type of support: Capital campaigns; Building/renovation; Equipment; Program development.
Limitations: Applications accepted. Giving limited to Hartford, CT, and the immediately surrounding area. No grants to individuals or for scholarship aid, endowment funds, projects that have already occurred or are underway at the time the Board considers the application, proposals that use a fiscal agent or a pass-through organization, or for general operating expenses.
Publications: Application guidelines; Annual report; Grants list.
Application information: 8 copies of the proposal are required for Excellence in Arts grant, 4 copies for Creation of New Work Initiative. When mailing an application, use P.O. Box only. There is no mail delivery to the street address, however proposals may be hand-delivered to the street address. The Connecticut Council for Philanthropy Common Grant Application Form will be accepted. Application guidelines are available on foundation web site. Application form not required.
Initial approach: Proposal
Copies of proposal: 8
Deadline(s): Feb. 1, May 1, Aug. 1, and Nov. 1
Board meeting date(s): Mar., June, Sept., and Dec.
Final notification: Mar. 31, June 30, Sept. 30, and Dec. 31
Officers and Trustees:* Kelley R. Bonn, Chair.; Magrieta L. Willard, Pres.; Jack Kennedy, Secy.; Pierre Guertin, Treas.; Lisa M. Curran, Exec. Dir.; John Alves; Carol Terry; Joyce Willis; Alex H. Vance, Jr.
Number of staff: 1 part-time professional.
EIN: 066067995
Other changes: The grantmaker now makes its annual report available online.

609
Charles Nelson Robinson Fund
(formerly Carse Robinson Foundation)
c/o US Trust, Philanthropic Solutions
200 Glastonbury Blvd., Ste. 200, CT2-545-02-05
Glastonbury, CT 06033 (860) 657-7019
Contact: Carmen Britt, V.P.
E-mail: carmen.britt@ustrust.com; **Main URL: https://www.bankofamerica.com/philanthropic/grantmaking.go**

Established in 1970 in CT.
Donors: Charles Nelson Robinson†; Elizabeth Carse†; Joseph Stackpole†; Mabel Hoffman†; Henry Hall†.
Foundation type: Independent foundation.
Financial data (yr. ended 06/30/13): Assets, $4,338,250 (M); expenditures, $229,229; qualifying distributions, $197,660; giving activities include $170,500 for 46 grants (high: $8,000; low: $1,500).
Purpose and activities: To support and promote quality educational, human services, and health care programming for underserved populations in Hartford, CT.
Fields of interest: Arts, administration/regulation; Education; Health care; Human services; Economically disadvantaged.
Type of support: Program development.
Limitations: Applications accepted. Giving primarily in the Hartford, CT, area. No grants to individuals, or for capital campaigns.
Application information: Forms and guidelines available on foundation web site. Preference is given to organizations that provide human services programming to underserved adults. Application form required.
Initial approach: Letter
Copies of proposal: 5
Deadline(s): Feb. 15 and Aug. 15
Board meeting date(s): Apr. and Oct.
Final notification: Within 2-3 months following deadlines
Trustee: Bank of America, N.A.
EIN: 066029468

610
Saybrook Charitable Trust
P.O. Box 330265
West Hartford, CT **06133-0265** (860) 232-6853
Contact: Caren Foisie Gaudet, Managing Tr.

Established in 1983.
Donor: Robert A. Foisie.
Foundation type: Independent foundation.
Financial data (yr. ended 12/31/12): Assets, $9,833 (M); expenditures, $3,792,248; qualifying distributions, $3,650,743; giving activities include $3,339,500 for 2 grants (high: $2,839,500; low: $500,000), and $311,243 for 106 grants to individuals (high: $7,000; low: $333).
Purpose and activities: The trust is dedicated to assisting high school seniors and college undergraduate students who exhibit strong ethical and moral character, in furthering their education to accredited colleges and universities through the award of annual scholarships for study towards a degree in engineering, technology, science, or education.
Fields of interest: Elementary/secondary education; Higher education; Youth
Type of support: Scholarship funds; Scholarships—to individuals.
Limitations: Applications accepted. Giving primarily to residents of Hartford and Middlesex counties, CT, Windham County, VT and Cheshire County, NH.
Application information: Application form required.
Deadline(s): Mar. 31
Final notification: May 15
Officer: Thomas E. Cross, Mgr.
Trustees: Caren Foisie Gaudet, Managing Tr.; Michael R. Foisie; Robert A. Foisie; Gregory H. Gaudet; Lauren Foisie Glennon.
Number of staff: 2 part-time professional.
EIN: 222501925

611

SBM Charitable Foundation, Inc.
935 Main St., Level C, Unit B-101
Manchester, CT 06040-6050 (860) 533-0355
***Contact:* Doreen Downham, Exec. Dir.**
FAX: (860) 533-0241; Main URL: http://www.sbmfoundation.org
Scholarship contact/inquiry: **Kelley Gunther, Foundation and Scholarship Dir., tel.: (860) 533-1067, e-mail: kgunther@sbmfoundation.org**

Established as a company-sponsored foundation in 2000 in CT; status changed to independent foundation in 2004.
Donor: Savings Bank of Manchester Foundation, Inc.
Foundation type: Independent foundation.
Financial data (yr. ended 12/31/12): Assets, $37,843,533 (M); expenditures, $2,486,078; qualifying distributions, $2,318,858; giving activities include $2,051,987 for 139 grants (high: $175,000; low: $100).
Purpose and activities: The foundation supports organizations involved with arts and culture, education, health, housing, human services, and children and youth. College scholarships of up to $5,000 each are awarded annually to students who are permanent residents of the CT counties which the foundation serves, are in the top 40 percent of their high school class or maintain a 2.5 GPA or higher in college, and who plan on attending an accredited institution of higher learning in CT.
Fields of interest: Arts; Education; Hospitals (general); Health care; Housing/shelter; Children/youth, services; Human services; United Ways and Federated Giving Programs.
Type of support: Scholarships—to individuals; In-kind gifts.
Limitations: Applications accepted. Giving primarily in Hartford, Tolland and Windham counties in CT. No support for public or private schools (both primary and secondary), or for religious institutions, unless the program benefits the community at large. No grants to individuals, (except for scholarships).
Application information: Application forms available on foundation web site. Application form required.
Initial approach: First-time applicants use Pre-Application form; past recipients may use the Request for Grant form; scholarship applicants use scholarship application form
Copies of proposal: 1
Deadline(s): See foundation web site for current deadlines
Officers and Directors:* Laurence P. Rubinow,* Chair.; Richard P. Meduski,* Pres.; Douglas K. Anderson,* V.P.; Charles L. Pike,* V.P.; Brian A. Orenstein,* Treas.; Doreen Downham, Exec. Dir.; Timothy J. Devanney; Sheila B. Flanagan; **Harry S. Gaucher**; Michael J. Hartl; Linda S. Klein; John D. LaBelle, Jr.; Eric A. Marziali; Timothy J. Moynihan; Jon L. Norris; William D. O'Neill; Richard Suski; Gregory S. Wolff.
Number of staff: 2 full-time support; 1 part-time support.
EIN: 061574365
Other changes: A. Paul Berte and John G. Sommers, directors, are deceased. Thomas E. Toomey is no longer a director.

612

SCA Charitable Foundation
326 Round Hill Rd.
Greenwich, CT 06831-3343
E-mail: info@scacharitablefoundation.org; Main URL: http://www.scacharitablefoundation.org

Donor: Michael Pollack.
Foundation type: Independent foundation.
Financial data (yr. ended 12/31/12): Assets, $1,858,250 (M); expenditures, $151,706; qualifying distributions, $150,206; giving activities include $137,350 for 4 grants (high: $82,350; low: $5,000).
Purpose and activities: Giving primarily to organizations with highly scalable business models serving large social needs for education and the reduction of poverty.
Fields of interest: Education; Health care; Economically disadvantaged.
International interests: India.
Limitations: Applications not accepted. Giving primarily in Torrance, CA, New York, NY, and Sugar Land, TX. No grants to individuals.
Application information: Unsolicited requests for funds not accepted.
Officers and Directors:* Michael Pollack,* Pres.; Heleina Bernstein, Secy.-Treas.; Jason Karp; Nadine Mirchandani; Anjali Pollack.
EIN: 900484624

613

Senior Services of Stamford, Inc.
2009 Summer St., Ste. 301
Stamford, CT **06905-5023** (203) 324-6584
Contact: Michael G. Mezzapelle, Treas.

Established in 1908 in CT.
Donors: Katherine D. Uehling†; Katharine J. Adamson; The Advocate and Greenwich Times Holiday Fund; First County Bank; Interfaith Council; Saugatuck Capital; Wachovia Bank, N.A.; St. John's Community Foundation; Friendship House, Inc.; Barry Coutant; Stamford Hospital.
Foundation type: Independent foundation.
Financial data (yr. ended 02/28/13): Assets, $13,354,203 (M); gifts received, $97,492; expenditures, $928,284; qualifying distributions, $840,166; giving activities include $319,334 for 545 grants to individuals.
Purpose and activities: Support for: 1) social service organizations serving the elderly; 2) organizations that provide information, referral, counseling, advocacy, and emergency financial assistance to needy elderly; and 3) operation of a senior center. Focus on programs offering innovative solutions to problems of older persons, particularly in access to health care, housing, transportation, and isolation.
Fields of interest: Health care, home services; Aging, centers/services; Aging.
Type of support: Annual campaigns; Endowments; Grants to individuals.
Limitations: Applications accepted. Giving limited to Stamford, CT.
Publications: Annual report; Informational brochure.
Application information: Application form required.
Initial approach: Letter requesting application form
Copies of proposal: 1
Deadline(s): None
Officers: Carmen Domonkos, Chair.; **Barry Coutant, Vice-Chair.; Jevera Hennessey, Vice-Chair.;** Kate Mulvany, Secy.; Michael G. Mezzapelle, Treas.; Marie Johnson, Exec. Dir.
Trustees: Donald Case; Kathleen Ego; Alejandro Knopoff; Fern Pessin; Karen Kelly; and 4 additional trustees.
Number of staff: 1 full-time professional; 2 part-time professional; 1 full-time support; 1 part-time support.
EIN: 060646916
Other changes: John Louizos is no longer Vice-Chair.

614

Silver Family Foundation
(formerly Barbara Silver Foundation)
c/o Walter, Berlingo and Co.
P.O. Box 4080
Darien, CT 06820-1480

Established in 1998 in CT.
Donors: Barbara Silver; R. Philip Silver.
Foundation type: Independent foundation.
Financial data (yr. ended 06/30/13): Assets, $19,213,061 (M); expenditures, $1,904,596; qualifying distributions, $1,824,602; giving activities include $1,762,696 for 43 grants (high: $400,725; low: $5,000).
Fields of interest: Education; Human services; Children/youth, services.
Limitations: Applications not accepted. Giving primarily in OR and WA. No grants to individuals.
Application information: Contributes only to pre-selected organizations.
Trustees: Barbara Silver; Peter Milo Silver; Philip Silver; Philip Tyler Silver.
EIN: 061532898
Other changes: For the fiscal year ended June 30, 2013, the grantmaker paid grants of $1,762,696, a 64.8% increase over the fiscal 2012 disbursements, $1,069,500.

615

Tauck Family Foundation, Inc.
(formerly The Tauck Foundation, Inc.)
P.O. Box 5020
10 Norden Pl.
Norwalk, CT 06856 (203) 899-6824
Contact: Eden Werring, Exec. Dir.; Mirellise Vazquez, Prog. Off.
FAX: (203) 286-1340; Main URL: http://www.tauckfamilyfoundation.org/
Twitter: https://twitter.com/TauckFamilyFdn

Donors: Elizabeth T. Walters; Arthur C. Tauck III.
Foundation type: Independent foundation.
Financial data (yr. ended 12/31/12): Assets, $18,767,149 (M); gifts received, $60,797; expenditures, $932,030; qualifying distributions, $894,142; giving activities include $292,333 for 50 grants (high: $35,000; low: $100), and $311,667 for foundation-administered programs.
Purpose and activities: The foundation's mission is to invest in the development of essential life skills that lead to better prospects for children from low-income families in Bridgeport, Connecticut. Its vision is that Bridgeport children will cultivate the skills they need to take control of their future, succeed in their education, break the cycle of poverty, and reach their full potential.
Fields of interest: Education; Youth development; Children/youth; Economically disadvantaged.
Limitations: Applications accepted. Giving primarily in Bridgeport, CT.
Application information: Complete application guidelines available on foundation web site. Application form required.
Officers and Directors:* Arthur C. Tauck, Jr.,* Chair. and Secy.-Treas.; Elizabeth T. Walters,* Pres.; Eden Werring, Exec. Dir.; Christopher Duermmeier; Christen Romano Lert; Colleen Ritzau Leth; Arthur C. Tauck III; Chuck Tauck; Peter Tauck; Robin Tauck; Tyler Tauck.
EIN: 270729341

616
The Tow Foundation, Inc.
(formerly The Leonard & Claire Tow Charitable Trust, Inc.)
50 Locust Ave., 2nd Fl.
New Canaan, CT 06840-4737 (203) 761-6604
FAX: (203) 761-6605;
E-mail: info@towfoundation.org; Main URL: http://towfoundation.org/
Claire and Leonard Tow's Giving Pledge Profile: http://glasspockets.org/philanthropy-in-focus/eye-on-the-giving-pledge/profiles/tow

Established in 1988 in CT.
Donors: Claire Tow; Leonard Tow.
Foundation type: Independent foundation.
Financial data (yr. ended 12/31/12): Assets, $196,522,778 (M); gifts received, $3,290,146; expenditures, $19,080,532; qualifying distributions, $17,752,190; giving activities include $16,843,600 for 91 grants (high: $200,000; low: $50).
Purpose and activities: The foundation will fund projects and create collaborative ventures where it see opportunities for reform and benefits for underserved populations. It strives to provide leverage to make possible far greater things than it could achieve alone.
Fields of interest: Performing arts centers; Higher education; Public health; Cancer research; ALS research; Crime/violence prevention, youth.
Type of support: Research; Program development; General/operating support.
Limitations: Applications not accepted. Giving primarily in CT and New York, NY. **No grants to individuals or for capital campaigns.**
Publications: Grants list; Informational brochure.
Application information: Contributes only to pre-selected organizations. Invited applicants will receive a link to an application form.
Officers and Trustees:* Leonard Tow,* Chair.; Emily Tow Jackson,* Pres. and Exec. Dir.; **Claire Tow,* V.P.**; Frank Tow,* V.P.; David Rosensweig,* Secy.; Scott N. Schneider,* Treas.; Pamela Castori, Ph. D.; **Amy Lefkof**; Maureen Strafford, M.D.; David Tobias.
EIN: 066484045
Other changes: At the close of 2012, the fair market value of the grantmaker's assets was $196,522,778, a 77.1% increase over the 2011 value, $110,971,433. For the same period, the grantmaker paid grants of $16,843,600, a 55.6% increase over the 2011 disbursements, $10,827,250.
Claire Tow is now V.P.

617
Emily Hall Tremaine Foundation, Inc.
171 Orange St.
New Haven, CT 06510-3111
Main URL: http://www.tremainefoundation.org

Established in 1987 in CT.
Donors: Emily Hall Tremaine†; Burton G. Tremaine, Sr.†; Burton G. Tremaine, Jr.†.
Foundation type: Independent foundation.
Financial data (yr. ended 12/31/12): Assets, $81,705,175 (M); expenditures, $4,526,556; qualifying distributions, $4,288,275; giving activities include $3,221,309 for 219 grants (high: $100,000; low: $500).
Purpose and activities: The foundation seeks to fund innovative projects that advance practical solutions to basic problems in our society. With an overall emphasis on education principally in the United States, it takes an active role in the arts, the environment, and in learning disabilities.
Fields of interest: Arts; Education; Environment.
Limitations: Applications not accepted. Giving on a national basis. No grants to individuals or for building funds, research projects, or experimental demonstrations.
Application information: Unsolicited requests for funds not accepted; however the foundation does accept 1-page letters of inquiry.
Board meeting date(s): Rolling
Officers and Directors:* Amanda G. Stanley,* Chair.; **Michelle Knapik, Pres.**; Wyndsor DePetro,* Secy.; Atwood Collins III,* Treas.; Lauren Collins; Jordan Nodelman; William O'Brien; Janet T. Stanley; Philip T. Stanley; Burton G. Tremaine III; John M. Tremaine; John M. Tremaine, Jr.; Sarah C. Tremaine; Susan C. Tremaine; Emily R. Wick.
Number of staff: 2 full-time professional; 2 part-time professional; 1 part-time support.
EIN: 222533743
Other changes: Michelle Knapik has replaced Stewart J. Hudson as Pres.

618
The Weatherstone Family Foundation, Inc.
28 Beach Dr.
Darien, CT 06820-5608
Contact: Melissa Moskal, CPA

Established in 1996 in CT.
Donors: Dennis Weatherstone; Marion Weatherstone.
Foundation type: Independent foundation.
Financial data (yr. ended 12/31/12): Assets, $1,696,100 (M); expenditures, $77,212; qualifying distributions, $76,612; giving activities include $76,612 for grants.
Fields of interest: Arts; Libraries (public); Education; Human services; Children/youth, services; Aging, centers/services; United Ways and Federated Giving Programs.
Limitations: Applications not accepted. Giving primarily in CT and NY. No grants to individuals.
Application information: Unsolicited requests for funds not accepted.
Officers: Marion Weatherstone, Pres.; **Peter Hershman, Secy.**
EIN: 061469074
Other changes: Peter Hershman has replaced Brain C. Bandler as Secy.

619
Charles R. Wood Foundation
c/o Foundation Source
55 Walls Dr., Ste. 302
Fairfield, CT 06824-5163 (203) 319-3718
Contact: Georgia Beckos-Wood, Chair.; Shirley Myott
FAX: (800) 839-1764;
E-mail: lfaria@foundationsource.com; Main URL: http://www.charlesrwoodfoundation.com
Facebook: https://www.facebook.com/pages/Charles-R-Wood-Foundation/328326557266429
Grants List: http://charlesrwoodfoundation.com/?page_id=12
Twitter: https://twitter.com/CWFoundationNY

Established in 1978.
Donor: Charles R. Wood†.
Foundation type: Independent foundation.
Financial data (yr. ended 12/31/12): Assets, $32,686,635 (M); gifts received, $815; expenditures, $1,863,526; qualifying distributions, $1,576,551; giving activities include $1,462,914 for 76 grants (high: $250,000; low: $500).
Purpose and activities: Giving primarily to support programs for children, health care, and the arts.
Fields of interest: Arts; Hospitals (general); Health care; Children, services.
Type of support: General/operating support.
Limitations: Applications accepted. Giving primarily in the Lake George, NY, region and its surrounding areas. No support for colleges or universities. No grants to individuals, or for salaries.
Publications: Financial statement; Grants list; Informational brochure.
Application information:
Initial approach: Use application form on foundation web site
Deadline(s): Apr. 1 (for spring meeting), and Sept. 1 (for fall meeting)
Board meeting date(s): May and in the fall
Officers and Trustees:* Georgia Beckos-Wood,* Chair.; Barbara Wages,* Pres.; Barbara J. Beckos,* V.P.; Page Wages,* Secy.; Charlene W. Courtney,* Treas.; Dean J. Beckos; Michael Della Bella; Shirley Myott; Dennis J. Phillips; Chelsea Hoopes Silver; Heather Ward.
Number of staff: None.
EIN: 222237193

620
WorldQuant Foundation Corp.
1700 E. Putnam Ave.
Old Greenwich, CT 06870-1366
***E-mail:* info@worldquant.org**; Main URL: http://worldquant.org/

Donor: Igor Tulchinsky.
Foundation type: Independent foundation.
Financial data (yr. ended 12/31/12): Assets, $3,841,944 (M); gifts received, $100; expenditures, $495,978; qualifying distributions, $432,000; giving activities include $432,000 for grants.
Fields of interest: Education; Human services.
Limitations: Applications not accepted.
Application information: Unsolicited requests for funds not accepted.
Officers: Mina Joy Tulchinsky, Chair. and Secy.; Igor Tulchinsky, Pres.
EIN: 263576736

DELAWARE

621
18 Pomegranates Inc.
c/o Foundation Source
501 Silverside Rd.
Wilmington, DE 19809-1377

Established in 2008 in CO.
Donors: Weaver Family Foundation; Francine Lavin Weaver.
Foundation type: Independent foundation.
Financial data (yr. ended 12/31/12): Assets, $1,799,026 (M); expenditures, $455,143; qualifying distributions, $449,319; giving activities include $261,793 for 57 grants (high: $72,000; low: $18).
Fields of interest: Education; Human services; Jewish agencies & synagogues.
Type of support: General/operating support; Program development.
Limitations: Applications not accepted. Giving primarily in Boulder, CO.
Application information: Unsolicited requests for funds not accepted.
Officer and Director:* Francine Lavin Weaver,* Pres.
EIN: 262000133
Other changes: The grantmaker no longer lists an E-mail address or a URL address. The grantmaker has moved from CO to DE.

622
The AEC Trust
c/o Foundation Source
501 Silverside Rd., Ste. 123
Wilmington, DE 19809-1377
***Contact for technical questions regarding the online submission process:* tel.: (800) 839-1821, e-mail: requests@foundationsource.com**; Main URL: http://www.fsrequests.com/aec

Established in 1980 in IL.
Donor: Members of the Cofrin family.
Foundation type: Independent foundation.
Financial data (yr. ended 12/31/12): Assets, $27,350,956 (M); expenditures, $4,451,316; qualifying distributions, $4,239,584; giving activities include $4,239,584 for 48 grants (high: $2,942,103; low: $5,000).
Purpose and activities: Giving primarily for the arts, educational support for pre-selected schools, the environment, women's issues, and AIDS-related services.
Fields of interest: Museums; Arts; Education; Environment; Women; AIDS, people with.
Type of support: General/operating support; Capital campaigns; Building/renovation; Equipment; Land acquisition; Debt reduction; Conferences/seminars; Professorships; Publication; Research; Technical assistance; Matching/challenge support.
Limitations: Applications accepted. Giving primarily in Boulder, CO, Gainesville, FL, Atlanta or Decatur, GA (within Fulton or Dekalb Counties), and Western MA. No support for religious organizations, government agencies, affiliates of large public charities, or for organizations with budgets over $1 million. No grants to individuals, or for special events, annual campaigns, or sponsorships; endowments generally not funded.
Application information: All proposals must be submitted electronically via foundation web site. Paper documents will not be reviewed or accepted. Grant requests should be made within the $10,000 to $50,000 range and should not exceed 50% of total budget. Application form required.
Initial approach: Take eligibility quiz on foundation web site
Deadline(s): Apr. 1 and Sept. 1
Board meeting date(s): May and Oct.
Final notification: On a rolling basis
Advisory Committee: Edith Dee Cofrin, Chair.; David H. Cofrin; Gladys G. Cofrin; Mary Ann H. Cofrin; Mary Ann P. Cofrin; Paige W. Cofrin.
Corporate Trustee: Atlantic Trust Co., N.A.
EIN: 366725987

623
AstraZeneca HealthCare Foundation
(formerly Zeneca HealthCare Foundation)
1800 Concord Pike
P.O. Box 15437
Wilmington, DE 19850-5437 (302) 886-3000
E-mail: ConnectionsforCardiovascularHealth@astrazeneca.com; Additional tel.: (800) 236-9933; Main URL: http://www.astrazeneca-us.com/foundation/

Established as a company-sponsored operating foundation in 1993 in DE.
Donors: Zeneca Inc.; AstraZeneca Pharmaceuticals LP.
Foundation type: Operating foundation.
Financial data (yr. ended 12/31/13): Assets, $10,380,179 (M); gifts received, $14,783; expenditures, $4,455,652; qualifying distributions, $4,411,574; giving activities include $3,722,921 for 20 grants (high: $250,000; low: $45,000).
Purpose and activities: The foundation promotes public awareness of healthcare issues and provides public education of medical knowledge.
Fields of interest: Education; Health care, clinics/centers; Health care, patient services; Nursing care; Health care; Cancer; Breast cancer; Heart & circulatory diseases; Health organizations; Disasters, preparedness/services.
Type of support: General/operating support; Continuing support; Annual campaigns; Program development; Grants to individuals.
Limitations: Applications accepted. Giving on a national basis. **No support for religious or faith-based programs not of direct benefit to the entire community, for-profit organizations, lobbying, fraternal, or social organizations, or discriminatory organizations. No grants to individuals (except for employee-related disaster relief grants), or for capital investments, unsolicited capital campaigns, media or awareness campaigns, enhancements of existing hospital services or hospital software systems, professional education, training for healthcare professionals, research or clinical trials, healthcare providers or cardiologist salaries, endowments, journals, or advertising.**
Publications: Application guidelines; Annual report; Grants list.
Application information: Grants range from $150,000 to $250,000. Multi-year funding is not automatic. Organizations receiving support are asked to provide a mid-year report and final report. Application form required.
Initial approach: Complete online application for Connections for Cardiovascular Health
***Deadline(s):* Feb. 3 to Feb. 15 for Connections for Cardiovascular Health grants**
Final notification: Nov.
Officers and Directors:* James W. Blasetto,* Chair.; David P. Nicoli, Esq.*, Pres.; Emily Denney,* V.P.; Ann V. Booth-Barbarin,* Secy.; David E. White, Treas.; Joyce Jacobson, Exec. Dir.; Cindy Bertrando; John B. Buse; Timothy J. Gardner; Howard G. Hutchinson; Michael Miller; L. Kristin Newby.
EIN: 510349682

624
Brookwood Foundation
c/o Foundation Source
501 Silverside Rd., Ste. 123
Wilmington, DE 19809-1377

Established in 2000 in WI.
Donors: Charles H. Heide; Charles H. Heide, Jr.; Kathryn H. Thompson.
Foundation type: Independent foundation.
Financial data (yr. ended 12/31/12): Assets, $3,062,963 (M); expenditures, $146,028; qualifying distributions, $118,000; giving activities include $118,000 for grants.
Fields of interest: Secondary school/education; Protestant agencies & churches.
Limitations: Applications not accepted. Giving primarily in WI. No grants to individuals.
Application information: Contributes only to pre-selected organizations.
Trustees: Charles H. Heide; Charles H. Heide, Jr.; Kathryn H. Heide; Paula J. Heide-Waller; Krista J. Reck; Kathryn H. Thompson.
EIN: 392012432
Other changes: The grantmaker has moved from WI to DE.

625
Mary Alice and Bennett Brown Foundation, Inc.
(formerly Bennett A. Brown Family Charitable Fund, Inc.)
c/o Foundation Source
501 Silverside Rd., Ste. 123
Wilmington, DE 19809-1377
E-mail: info@MABBF.org; Main URL: http://www.mabbf.org/

Established in 1998 in GA.
Foundation type: Independent foundation.
Financial data (yr. ended 12/31/12): Assets, $7,883,955 (M); expenditures, $502,514; qualifying distributions, $449,343; giving activities include $399,500 for 23 grants (high: $60,000; low: $5,000).
Purpose and activities: Giving for the support of nonprofits working with underserved children, with an emphasis on education.
Fields of interest: Elementary/secondary education; Boys & girls clubs; Children/youth, services.
Type of support: General/operating support; Equipment; Program development; Scholarship funds; Matching/challenge support.
Limitations: Applications not accepted. Giving primarily in Atlanta, GA. No grants to individuals; no annual funds; no building funds.
Publications: Informational brochure; Program policy statement.
Application information: Proposals are accepted by invitation only.
Board meeting date(s): Fall and spring
Officers: Bennett A. Brown III, Co-Chair.; Charlotte B. Dixon, Co-Chair.
Trustees: Leila B. Armknecht; Katherine B. Ohlhausen.
Number of staff: 1 part-time support.
EIN: 586332776
Other changes: The grantmaker has moved from GA to DE.

626
The Burt's Bees Greater Good Foundation
c/o Foundation Source
501 Sliverside Rd., Ste. 123
Wilmington, DE 19809-1377 (919) 433-4533
Contact: Paula Alexander, Pres. and Exec. Dir.
Application address: C/o. Burts Bees, 210 W. Pettigrew St., Durham, NC 27701, tel.: (919) 433-4533; **Main URL: http://www.burtsbees.com/Community-Partnerships/sustain-community,default,pg.html**

Established in 2007 in DE.
Donor: Burt's Bees.
Foundation type: Company-sponsored foundation.
Financial data (yr. ended 12/31/12): Assets, $43,604 (M); gifts received, $227,452; expenditures, $283,114; qualifying distributions, $283,105; giving activities include $271,080 for 28 grants (high: $50,000; low: $300).
Purpose and activities: The foundation supports programs designed to protect honeybees, support sustainable agriculture, and promote community development in Durham.
Fields of interest: Environment, natural resources; Animals/wildlife; Agriculture; Agriculture, sustainable programs; Human services; Community/economic development.
Type of support: Program development; General/operating support; Employee volunteer services.
Application information: Application form required.
Initial approach: Letter or E-mail.
Deadline(s): None
Officers and Directors:* Paula Alexander, Co-Pres., Co-Secy. and Exec. Dir.; Beth Ritter,* Co-Pres. and Co-Secy.; Matt Kopac,* V.P.; Manah Kulp Eckhardt.
EIN: 260143643

627
CenturyLink-Clarke M. Williams Foundation
(formerly Qwest Foundation)
c/o Foundation Source
501 Silverside Rd., Ste. 123
Wilmington, DE 19809-1377
Main URL: http://www.centurylink.com/Pages/AboutUs/Community/Foundation/
Facebook: http://www.facebook.com/Qwest#!/Qwest?v=app_354459035481

Established in 1985 in CO.
Donors: U S WEST, Inc.; Qwest Communications International Inc.
Foundation type: Company-sponsored foundation.
Financial data (yr. ended 12/31/12): Assets, $16,474,473 (M); gifts received, $2,099,424; expenditures, $4,090,884; qualifying distributions, $3,921,662; giving activities include $3,822,512 for 1,378 grants (high: $261,334; low: -$159,055).
Purpose and activities: The foundation supports programs designed to improve the well-being and overall quality of life for people throughout CenturyLink's communities.
Fields of interest: Elementary/secondary education; Education; Food services; Food banks; Children/youth, services; Homeless, human services; Human services; United Ways and Federated Giving Programs; Engineering/technology; Science.
Type of support: General/operating support; Continuing support; Annual campaigns; Program development; Employee volunteer services; Employee matching gifts; Grants to individuals.
Limitations: Applications accepted. Giving on a national basis in areas of company operations in AR, IA, ID, CO, MN, MO, ND, NE, NM, OR, SD, UT, WA, and WY. No support for political organizations, private foundations, pass-through organizations, or organizations that receive 3 percent or more funding from the United Way. No grants to individuals (except for Qwest Teacher Grants), or for scholarships, sectarian religious activities, capital campaigns, chairs, endowments, general operating support for single-disease health groups, or goodwill advertising.
Publications: Application guidelines.
Application information: Applications for general funding are currently not accepted. Applicants for the Teachers and Technology Program should email local coordinators for more information.
***Initial approach:* Download application form and mail to application address for Teachers and Technology Program**
***Deadline(s):* Oct. 1 to Jan. 10 for Teachers and Technology Program**
***Final notification:* Apr. 1 for Teachers and Technology**
Officers and Directors:* Stacey Goff,* Pres.; Christine Searls, Secy.; Jonathan Robinson, Treas.; Steven Davis; Tony Davis; Odell Riley.
Number of staff: 2 full-time professional.
EIN: 840978668
Other changes: The grantmaker has moved from LA to DE.
At the close of 2012, the grantmaker paid grants of $3,822,512, a 100.9% increase over the 2011 disbursements, $1,902,597.
The grantmaker now makes its application guidelines available online.

628
Chaney Foundation Ltd.
(formerly Eugene Chaney Foundation, Ltd.)
c/o Foundation Source
501 Silverside Rd.
Wilmington, DE 19809-1377
***Main URL:* http://www.chaneyenterprises.com/index.cfm/go/WhoWeAre.Chaney-Foundation**

Established in 1987 in MD.
Donors: Chaney Enterprises, L.P.; B.P.O.E.; Southstar, LP; Renditions Washington DC LLC; Places Inc.
Foundation type: Company-sponsored foundation.
Financial data (yr. ended 12/31/12): Assets, $427,418 (M); gifts received, $5,123; expenditures, $246,786; qualifying distributions, $246,569; giving activities include $235,350 for 53 grants (high: $25,000; low: $100).
Purpose and activities: The foundation supports programs designed to promote children advocacy and services; cultural arts; education; the environment; health care and health education; and historical education and preservation.
Fields of interest: Historical activities; Historic preservation/historical societies; Arts; Education; Environment; Health care; Children, services; Community/economic development.
Type of support: General/operating support; Annual campaigns; Capital campaigns; Building/renovation; Equipment; Program development; Scholarship funds; Scholarships—to individuals; Matching/challenge support.
Limitations: Applications not accepted. **Giving primarily in Waldorf, MD, with emphasis on Anne Arundel, Calvert, Caroline, Charles, Prince George, and St. Mary's County.** No support for religious organizations. No grants for endowments.
Application information: Unsolicited requests for funds not accepted. The grant application process is currently under construction.
Officers and Directors:* Francis H. Chaney II,* Pres.; William F. Childs IV,* V.P.; Carol M. Jackson,* Secy.; **Mike Middleton,* Treas.**; Robert D. Agee; Rebekah Lare; Barbara Lawson.
EIN: 521525001

629
Nancy Sayles Day Foundation
c/o WFO
1100 N. Market St., No. 1010
Wilmington, DE **19801-1289**

Trust established in 1964 in CT.
Donors: Nancy Sayles Day†; Mrs. Lee Day Gillespie.
Foundation type: Independent foundation.
Financial data (yr. ended 09/30/13): Assets, $14,206,830 (M); expenditures, $801,793; qualifying distributions, $682,122; giving activities include $649,000 for 21 grants (high: $250,000; low: $2,500).
Fields of interest: Environment, natural resources; Health organizations; Human services.
Type of support: General/operating support; Continuing support.
Limitations: Applications not accepted. Giving primarily in Nantucket, MA. No grants to individuals, or for building or endowment funds, research, or matching gifts; no loans.
Application information: Contributes only to pre-selected organizations.
Trustees: Mary G. West; Wilmington Trust Co.
EIN: 066071254

630
Delaware Community Foundation
100 W. 10th Street, Ste. 115
P.O. Box 1636
Wilmington, DE 19899 (302) 571-8004
Contact: Elizabeth M. Bouchelle, Dir., Grants
FAX: (302) 571-1553; E-mail: info@delcf.org; Tel. for grant application inquiries: (302) 504-5239; E-mail for grant application inquiries: bbouchelle@delcf.org; Main URL: http://www.delcf.org
Twitter: https://twitter.com/@DelCommunity

Incorporated in 1986 in DE.
Foundation type: Community foundation.
Financial data (yr. ended 06/30/13): Assets, $219,684,923 (M); gifts received, $14,026,726; expenditures, $33,371,595; giving activities include $28,100,711 for grants.
Purpose and activities: The foundation is a nonprofit, philanthropic community organization created by and for the people of Delaware to build community. The DCF is dedicated to inspiring and helping people of all backgrounds and means create lasting legacies to benefit the people of Delaware. It enables people with philanthropic interests to easily and effectively support the issues they care about by establishing a charitable fund at the foundation and recommending grants to nonprofit groups they want to support. The foundation offers personalized service, local expertise and community leadership. The foundation itself awards grants to qualified nonprofit organizations that serve Delawareans for selected programs and capital projects.
Fields of interest: Arts; Education; Environment; Animals/wildlife; Health care; Substance abuse, prevention; Health organizations, association; Crime/violence prevention, child abuse; Nutrition; Housing/shelter, development; Children/youth,

services; Human services; Community/economic development; Aging.
Type of support: Continuing support; Capital campaigns; Building/renovation; Equipment; Program development; Seed money; Technical assistance.
Limitations: Applications accepted. Giving limited to DE. No support for religious organizations for sectarian purposes or educational institutions for capital projects. **No grants to individuals (except for scholarships), or for annual fundraising campaigns, special events, operating costs, endowments, debt reduction, or sports clubs or leagues.**
Publications: Application guidelines; Annual report; Financial statement; Informational brochure; Newsletter.
Application information: Visit foundation web site for application form and guidelines. Handwritten or faxed application forms are not accepted. Application form required.
Initial approach: Submit application form and attachments
Copies of proposal: 1
Deadline(s): Varies
Board meeting date(s): Quarterly
Final notification: Varies
Officers and Directors:* Marilyn Rushworth Hayward,* Chair.; Thomas L. Sager,* Vice-Chair.; Fred C. Sears II, C.E.O. and Pres.; Richard A. Gentsch, Exec. V.P.; David Fleming, Sr. V.P., Devel.; William R. Allan, Sr. V.P., Southern Delaware; Donna D. Stone, Sr. V.P., Central Delaware; Becky Cahill, C.F.O.; Stephen P. Lamb, Secy.; Stephen A. Fowle,* Treas.; Omar Y. McNeill, Asst. Secy.; Doneen Keemer Damon; Bill Dugdale; Martha S. Gilman; Daryl A. Graham; Jennings Hastings; John C. Hawkins; Nancy Karibjanian; Rob MacGovern; Kathleen McDonough; Janice E. Nevin, M.D.; Donald W. Nicholson, Jr.; John W. Noble; Laurisa S. Schutt; Joan L. Sharp; Valerie J. Sill; David Singleton; Gary Stockbridge; Cindy L. Szabo; Michelle A. Taylor; Michelle Whetzel.
Number of staff: 10 full-time professional; 2 part-time professional.
EIN: 222804785
Other changes: Marilyn Rushworth Hayward has replaced Thomas J. Shopa as Chair. Thomas L. Sager has replaced Marilyn Rushworth Hayward as Vice-Chair.
Laura Day, Anne S. Dougherty, Kelly Firment, Mary B. Hickok, and Lynn Adams Kokjohn are no longer directors.

631
Edwards Mother Earth Foundation
c/o Foundation Source
501 Silverside Rd., Ste. 123
Wilmington, DE 19809-1377
E-mail: ruth@tjedwards.com; Main URL: http://www.fsrequests.com/EMEF

Established in 1997 in WA.
Donors: Bob Edwards†; Jane Edwards†.
Foundation type: Independent foundation.
Financial data (yr. ended 12/31/12): Assets, $30,822,403 (M); expenditures, $1,586,515; qualifying distributions, $1,479,799; giving activities include $1,110,400 for 71 grants (high: $105,000; low: $100).
Purpose and activities: The foundation is currently responding to global climate disruption (global warming) by working with utilities to develop energy efficient models and policies within AR, AZ, CO, ID, IL, MO, and OH.
Fields of interest: Environment, climate change/global warming.
Type of support: General/operating support; Continuing support; Management development/capacity building; Equipment; Program development; Technical assistance; Matching/challenge support.
Limitations: Applications not accepted. Giving is currently limited to AR, AZ, CO, ID, IL, MO and OH. See foundation web site for updates on state giving. No support for organizations that are not nationally-based. No grants to individuals.
Application information: Contributes only to pre-selected organizations.
Board meeting date(s): Last Fri/Sat. in April and the 3rd weekend in Oct.
Officers and Directors:* Tara Reinertson, Secy.; Paul Cunningham,* Treas.; Eileen Bell; Garrett Bell; Robbin Finch; Kristina Rayl; Sutter Wehmeier.
Number of staff: 1 part-time professional; 1 part-time support.
EIN: 911789783
Other changes: The grantmaker no longer lists a phone. The grantmaker has moved from WA to DE.

632
The Farmhouse Foundation
Rockland, DE

The foundation terminated in 2011.

633
Freygish Foundation
c/o Foundation Source
501 Silverside Rd.
Wilmington, DE 19809-1377

Established in 2000 in NY.
Donor: Peter Bloom.
Foundation type: Independent foundation.
Financial data (yr. ended 07/31/12): Assets, $3,670,182 (M); gifts received, $864,187; expenditures, $361,288; qualifying distributions, $301,240; giving activities include $301,240 for grants.
Fields of interest: Health care; Health organizations, association; Cancer research; Human services.
Limitations: Applications not accepted. Giving primarily in NY. No grants to individuals.
Application information: Contributes only to pre-selected organizations.
Trustees: Peter Bloom; Janet Greenfield.
EIN: 113578290
Other changes: The grantmaker has moved from CT to DE.

634
Gloria Dei Foundation
c/o Foundation Source
501 Silverside Rd., Ste. 123
Wilmington, DE 19809-1377
E-mail: info@thegloriadeifoundation.org; Main URL: http://www.gloriadeifoundation.org/

Established in 2005 in FL.
Donor: Mary Cade.
Foundation type: Independent foundation.
Financial data (yr. ended 12/31/12): Assets, $3,235,174 (M); expenditures, $499,191; qualifying distributions, $490,591; giving activities include $472,800 for 15 grants (high: $60,000; low: $3,750).
Purpose and activities: Giving primarily for causes dealing with the arts, the community, education, evangelism, discipleship and outreach, justice and public policy, and the sanctity of life.
Fields of interest: Arts; Education; Public health; Civil liberties, right to life; Public affairs; Christian agencies & churches; Economically disadvantaged.
Limitations: Giving on a worldwide basis. No grants to individuals.
Application information: See foundation web site for current application information.
Officers and Directors:* Emily Cade Morrison,* Pres.; Phoebe C. Miles,* V.P.; Robert L. Morrison,* Secy.-Treas.; Martha Cade; Mary Cade.
EIN: 203723933
Other changes: Cecelia Miles is no longer Exec. Dir.

635
The Hasselbeck Family Foundation
c/o Foundation Source
501 Silverside Rd.
Wilmington, DE 19809-1377

Established in 2010 in DE.
Donors: Matthew Hasselbeck; Sarah Hasselbeck.
Foundation type: Independent foundation.
Financial data (yr. ended 12/31/12): Assets, $0 (M); expenditures, $12,626; qualifying distributions, $0.
Fields of interest: Athletics/sports, academies.
Limitations: Applications not accepted.
Application information: Unsolicited requests for funds not accepted.
Directors: Matthew Hasselbeck; Sarah Hasselbeck.
EIN: 273980634

636
The Kendeda Fund
c/o Foundation Source
501 Silverside Rd., Ste. 123
Wilmington, DE 19809-1377 (800) 839-1754

Donor: The March 23, 2006 Trust.
Foundation type: Independent foundation.
Financial data (yr. ended 12/31/12): Assets, $56,413,054 (M); gifts received, $71,579,500; expenditures, $31,249,289; qualifying distributions, $29,619,805; giving activities include $29,188,266 for 101 grants (high: $5,000,000; low: $5,000).
Fields of interest: Higher education; Environment, climate change/global warming; Environment; Animals/wildlife; Housing/shelter, development.
Limitations: Applications not accepted. Giving primarily in CA, Washington, DC, MA, MT, NY and VA.
Application information: Unsolicited requests for funds not accepted.
Trustee: Atlantic Trust Co., N.A.
EIN: 206881642
Other changes: At the close of 2012, the fair market value of the grantmaker's assets was $56,413,054, a 363.6% increase over the 2011 value, $12,168,049.

637
Milton and Hattie Kutz Foundation
101 Garden of Eden Rd.
Wilmington, DE 19803-1511
***Contact:* Leslie Newman, Pres.**

Established in 1955 in DE.
Donors: Milton Kutz†; Hattie Kutz†.
Foundation type: Independent foundation.
Financial data (yr. ended 06/30/13): Assets, $2,462,936 (M); gifts received, $242; expenditures, $184,277; qualifying distributions, $173,533; giving activities include $161,220 for 28 grants (high: $20,000; low: $1,150).
Purpose and activities: Giving largely for social service organizations; grants also for children and youth programs, scholarships to organizations (not individuals), and capital campaigns. Preference for capital rather than program.
Fields of interest: Education; Human services; Children/youth, services; Aging.
Type of support: General/operating support; Capital campaigns; Building/renovation; Program development; Seed money.
Limitations: Applications accepted. Giving limited to DE. No grants to individuals.
Publications: Grants list.
Application information: Application form required.
Initial approach: Proposal
Copies of proposal: 1
Deadline(s): Mar. 31
Board meeting date(s): June and Dec.
Officers: Leslie Newman, Pres.; Suzanne B. Grant, V.P.; Jerome K. Grossman, Secy.; Rolf F. Erikson, Treas.; Seth J. Katzen, Exec. Secy.
Directors: Jack Blumenfeld; Donald F. Parsons; Susan Kirk Ryan, Esq.; Barbara H. Schoenberg; Connie J. Sugarman; Craig Sternberg; Robin Kauffman Saran.
EIN: 510187055
Other changes: The grantmaker no longer lists a separate application address.
Richard Leff is no longer a director.

638
Lennox Foundation
c/o Foundation Source
501 Silverside Rd., Ste 123
Wilmington, DE 19809-1377
Mailing address: c/o David H. Anderson, Treas., 1114 State St., Ste. 200, Santa Barbara, CA 93101-2767, tel.: (805) 963-6503

Incorporated in 1951 in IA.
Donor: Lennox Industries, Inc.
Foundation type: Independent foundation.
Financial data (yr. ended 12/31/12): Assets, $36,425,518 (M); expenditures, $1,827,132; qualifying distributions, $1,729,439; giving activities include $1,619,675 for 26 grants (high: $100,000; low: $7,000).
Purpose and activities: Grants primarily for land conservation, human services, education and health, within geographic areas of the family's involvement.
Fields of interest: Higher education; Education; Environment, land resources; Health care; Human services.
Type of support: General/operating support; Continuing support; Annual campaigns; Capital campaigns; Building/renovation; Equipment; Land acquisition; Program development; Matching/challenge support.
Limitations: Applications not accepted. Giving in the U.S., with some emphasis on MA and ME. No grants to individuals.
Application information: Unsolicited requests for funds not accepted.
Board meeting date(s): Mar. and Sept.
Officers and Trustees:* Jeff Norris,* Co-Chair.; Stefan Norris,* Co-Chair.; Karen Waeschle,* Co-Vice-Chair.; Frank Zink,* Co-Vice-Chair.; Beth A. Booth,* Co-Secy.; **Amy Rattner,* Co-Secy.; Eron Malone,* Co-Treas.**; Andrew Rattner,* Co-Treas.; Lyn Anderson; **Sarah W. Carlan**; Cathy Houlihan; Eileen Murphy.
EIN: 426053380
Other changes: Stefan Norris is now Co-Chair. Beth A. Booth is now Co-Secy. Andrew Rattner is now Co-Treas. Eron Malone is now Co-Treas.

639
Longwood Foundation, Inc.
c/o Eleuthere I. du Pont
100 W. 10th St., Ste. 1109
Wilmington, DE 19801-1653 (302) 654-2477
***Contact:* Eleuthere I. du Pont, Pres.**
E-mail: contactus@longwood.org; Main URL: http://www.longwoodfoundation.org

Incorporated in 1937 in DE.
Donor: Pierre S. du Pont†.
Foundation type: Independent foundation.
Financial data (yr. ended 09/30/13): Assets, $625,762,845 (M); expenditures, $34,801,218; qualifying distributions, $32,780,688; giving activities include $32,386,913 for 94 grants (high: $15,000,000; low: $2,500).
Purpose and activities: The mission is to be thoughtful stewards of Pierre S. dePont's legacy by being creative philanthropic leaders and by providing support to Longwood Gardens.
Fields of interest: Arts; Education; Environment; Health care; Housing/shelter; Human services.
Type of support: Seed money; General/operating support; Management development/capacity building; Capital campaigns; Building/renovation; Equipment; Land acquisition; Program development; Matching/challenge support.
Limitations: Applications accepted. Giving primarily in DE and southern Chester County, PA. No support for religious or political programs. No grants to individuals, or for special projects or events. Generally no grants for endowments and limited operating support.
Application information: The foundation accepts online applications only. Application form required.
***Initial approach:* Online**
Copies of proposal: 1
Deadline(s): Mar. 15 and Sept. 15
Board meeting date(s): May and Nov.
Final notification: The following board meeting (approximately 60 days)
Officers and Trustees:* Charles T.L. Copeland,* Chair.; Eleuthere I. du Pont II,* Pres.; Dr. M. Lynn du Pont,* V.P.; C. Roderick Maroney,* Secy.; Eli R. Sharp,* Treas.; Gerret van S. Copeland; David L. Craven; Edward B. du Pont; Pierre S. du Pont IV.
Number of staff: 4 full-time professional; 1 part-time professional.
EIN: 510066734

640
John B. Lynch Scholarship Foundation
Wilmington, DE

The foundation terminated in 2011 and transferred its assets to The JBL Scholarship Trust, Inc.

641
Frank McHugh-O'Donovan Foundation, Inc.
c/o Foundation Source
501 Silverside Rd., Ste. 123
Wilmington, DE 19809-1377

Established in 2004 in CT.
Donor: Christine O'Donovan Trust A '86.
Foundation type: Independent foundation.
Financial data (yr. ended 12/31/12): Assets, $53,614,553 (M); gifts received, $3,185,449; expenditures, $2,235,302; qualifying distributions, $2,015,709; giving activities include $1,724,456 for 15 grants (high: $1,000,000; low: $10,000).
Fields of interest: Higher education; Education.
Limitations: Applications not accepted. Giving primarily in CA, with emphasis on Los Angeles. No grants to individuals.
Application information: Contributes only to pre-selected organizations.
Officers and Directors:* Frank McHugh,* C.E.O.; **Richard Riordan,* V.P.**; Theresa McHugh,* Secy. and C.F.O.; Katherine Cadiente; Loree A. Vincent; **Oscar Zaldana.**
EIN: 200842449
Other changes: Theresa McHugh is now Secy. and C.F.O. Richard Riordan is now V.P. Joe Reber is no longer a director.

642
Morgridge Family Foundation
501 Silverside Rd., Ste. 123
Wilmington, DE 19809-1377
Contact: Renee Joyce, Prog. Off.
E-mail: reneejoyce@comcast.net
GiveSmart: http://www.givesmart.org/Stories/Donors/Tashia-and-John-Morgridge
John and Tashia Morgridge's Giving Pledge Profile: http://glasspockets.org/philanthropy-in-focus/eye-on-the-giving-pledge/profiles/morgridge

Established in 2008 in CO.
Donors: John P. Morgridge; Tashia Morgridge.
Foundation type: Independent foundation.
Financial data (yr. ended 12/31/12): Assets, $50,985,234 (M); gifts received, $19,502,500; expenditures, $11,642,877; qualifying distributions, $10,191,483; giving activities include $10,000,000 for 135 grants (high: $1,250,000; low: $500), and $13,389 for 1 foundation-administered program.
Purpose and activities: The foundation's mission is to serve the neediest of the needy, with emphasis on support for educational programs. Support also for arts and culture, strengthening the community, health and wellness, and early childhood literacy.
Fields of interest: Arts; Education, reading; Education; Health care; Community/economic development; Economically disadvantaged.
Limitations: Applications not accepted. Giving in the U.S., with emphasis in CO.
Application information: Applications not accepted.
Officers: John D. Morgridge, Pres.; Carrie Morgridge, V.P.
Advisory Directors: John P. Morgridge; Tashia Morgridge.
Number of staff: 1 full-time professional.
EIN: 262336633
Other changes: The grantmaker no longer lists a fax. The grantmaker no longer lists a phone. The grantmaker has moved from CO to DE.
John D. Morgridge is now Pres. . Carrie Morgridge is now V.P. .

643
The Martha Morse Foundation
c/o C.S. Marshall Esq., Wilmington Trust Co.
1100 N. Market St.
Wilmington, DE 19890-0900

Established in NC.
Foundation type: Independent foundation.
Financial data (yr. ended 03/31/13): Assets, $2,568,654 (M); expenditures, $178,848; qualifying distributions, $143,118; giving activities include $138,000 for 26 grants (high: $10,000; low: $1,000).
Purpose and activities: Giving to organizations concerned with animal welfare.
Fields of interest: Animals/wildlife.
Limitations: Applications not accepted. Giving in the New England area, primarily in MA.
Application information: Unsolicited requests for funds not accepted.
Trustee: Colin S. Marshall, Esq.
EIN: 043375373

644
Palmer Home, Inc.
P.O. Box 1751
Dover, DE 19903-1751
Contact: Jean T. Deleo, Pres.

Established in 1930.
Foundation type: Operating foundation.
Financial data (yr. ended 02/28/13): Assets, $4,782,061 (M); gifts received, $18,447; expenditures, $321,082; qualifying distributions, $278,292; giving activities include $275,650 for 15 grants (high: $45,000; low: $3,500).
Purpose and activities: Giving to organizations that benefit the elderly (over 65).
Fields of interest: Hospitals (general); Food services; Human services; Salvation Army; Residential/custodial care, hospices; Aging, centers/services; Catholic agencies & churches; Aging.
Limitations: Applications accepted. Giving primarily in DE. No grants to individuals.
Application information: Application form not required.
Initial approach: Letter
Deadline(s): Sept. 1
Board meeting date(s): Quarterly
Officers: Jean T. DeLeo, Pres.; Carol Braverman, V.P.; Ellen Harbeson, Secy.
EIN: 510066737
Other changes: Jean Hitchens is no longer Treas. Susan Rosello is no longer Treas.

645
Pinkerton Foundation
c/o Foundation Source
501 Silverside Rd., Ste. 123
Wilmington, DE 19809-1377

Established in 1994 in WA.
Donors: Guy C. Pinkerton; Nancy J. Pinkerton.
Foundation type: Independent foundation.
Financial data (yr. ended 04/30/13): Assets, $4,048,640 (M); gifts received, $332,400; expenditures, $258,485; qualifying distributions, $213,710; giving activities include $194,400 for 52 grants (high: $40,000; low: $500).
Purpose and activities: Giving for federated giving programs, Christian churches, youth services, higher education and music organizations.
Fields of interest: Education; Hospitals (general); Youth development; Human services; YM/YWCAs & YM/YWHAs; United Ways and Federated Giving Programs; Christian agencies & churches.
Type of support: General/operating support.
Limitations: Applications not accepted. Giving primarily in WA. No grants to individuals.
Application information: Contributes only to pre-selected organizations.
Officers and Directors: Guy C. Pinkerton,* Pres. and Treas.; Nancy J. Pinkerton,* V.P. and Secy.
EIN: 911665004
Other changes: The grantmaker no longer lists a phone.

646
Prairie Creek Partners Charitable Foundation
c/o Foundation Source
501 Silverside Rd., Ste. 123
Wilmington, DE 19809-1377

Established in 2007 in DE.
Donors: Alan K. Engstrom; Randall Robert Engstrom.
Foundation type: Independent foundation.
Financial data (yr. ended 12/31/12): Assets, $18,923,965 (M); gifts received, $20,834; expenditures, $1,044,939; qualifying distributions, $934,114; giving activities include $854,700 for 32 grants (high: $100,000; low: $1,000).
Fields of interest: Christian agencies & churches.
Limitations: Applications not accepted. Giving primarily in TX. No grants to individuals.
Application information: Unsolicited requests for funds not accepted.
Officers and Directors:* Randall Robert Engstrom,* Pres. and Secy.; Alan K. Engstrom,* V.P.; Alyson T. Engstrom,* V.P.; Randall Robert Engstrom, Jr., V.P.; Ellen Porter,* V.P.; Reid Porter,* V.P.
EIN: 260639084
Other changes: At the close of 2012, the fair market value of the grantmaker's assets was $18,923,965, a 120.6% increase over the 2010 value, $8,579,080. For the same period, the grantmaker paid grants of $854,700, a 247.4% increase over the 2010 disbursements, $246,000.

647
Mariano Rivera Foundation
321 Chattahoochee Dr.
Bear, DE 19701-4809 (847) 291-0603
Contact: Naomi Gandia, Secy.-Treas.
Main URL: **http://www.marianoriverafoundation.org/**

Established in NY.
Donors: Mariano Rivera; Steiner Sports; Charity Buzz; Frozen Ropes of Morris County NJ, LLC; Neuro Rays Imaging; Ridgefield High School Student Activity Account; VF Services; Yes Network; BTIG, LLC; Major League Baseball; Topps Us; Wish You Were Here Productions; OLILVY; Chardan Capital; David R. Tarella; Joseph Nicolla; Racing Rest of America II Inc.; Colorado Rockies Baseball Club Foundation; Mariners Care; Minnesota Twins; Royals Charities Inc.; Michael Weinberger; Arianne Weinberger; KCH Group; Curmark.
Foundation type: Independent foundation.
Financial data (yr. ended 06/30/13): Assets, $4,374,884 (M); gifts received, $402,963; expenditures, $864,975; qualifying distributions, $853,770; giving activities include $773,000 for 2 grants (high: $500,000; low: $273,000).
Fields of interest: Christian agencies & churches.
Limitations: Applications accepted. Giving in the U.S., with some emphasis on NY and TN.
Application information: Application form required.
Initial approach: Letter
Deadline(s): None
Officers: Mariano Rivera, Pres.; Clara Rivera, V.P.; Naomi Gandia, Secy.-Treas.
EIN: 134076067
Other changes: At the close of 2013, the grantmaker paid grants of $773,000, a 271.6% increase over the 2012 disbursements, $208,000.

648
Sylvan/Laureate Foundation, Inc.
(formerly The Sylvan Learning Foundation, Inc.)
c/o Foundation Source
501 Silverside Rd., Ste. 123
Wilmington, DE 19809-1377
Contact: Carol Maivelett, Admin.
E-mail: **Carol.Maivelett@laureate.net**; Main URL: http://www.laureate.net/HereforGood/TheSylvanLaureateFoundation

Established in 1997 in MD.
Donors: Sylvan Learning Systems, Inc.; Laureate Education, Inc.; Leadform Est. LTD.
Foundation type: Company-sponsored foundation.
Financial data (yr. ended 12/31/12): Assets, $11,643,008 (M); gifts received, $4,000,000; expenditures, $2,994,286; qualifying distributions, $2,926,139; giving activities include $2,578,785 for 60 grants (high: $689,812; low: $1,500), and $279,625 for 4 foundation-administered programs.
Purpose and activities: The foundation supports organizations involved with arts and culture, health, children and youth, youth development, international development, public policy research. Special emphasis is directed toward programs designed to promote best practices in education.
Fields of interest: Museums; Performing arts, theater; Performing arts, orchestras; Arts; Elementary/secondary education; Higher education; Teacher school/education; Education; Health care; Youth development, citizenship; Youth development; Children/youth, services; International development; Business/industry; United Ways and Federated Giving Programs; Public policy, research; Leadership development.
Type of support: General/operating support; Annual campaigns; Capital campaigns; Program development; Sponsorships.
Limitations: Applications not accepted. Giving primarily in Baltimore, MD. No support for religious organizations or political or lobbying organizations. No grants to individuals.
Application information: Contributes only to pre-selected organizations.
Board meeting date(s): Apr., July, Oct., and Jan.
Officers and Trustees:* Douglas L. Becker,* Pres.; R. Christopher Hoehn-Saric,* 1st V.P.; Robert W. Zentz, 2nd V.P. and Secy.; Eilif Serck-Hanssen, Treas.; B. Lee McGee.
EIN: 522044008

649
Mark Paul Terk Charitable Trust
c/o Foundation Source
501 Silverside Rd., Ste. 123
Wilmington, DE 19809-1377

Foundation type: Independent foundation.
Financial data (yr. ended 12/31/11): Assets, $127 (M); expenditures, $100,000; qualifying

distributions, $158,261; giving activities include $158,261 for 1 grant.
Fields of interest: Arts.
Limitations: Applications not accepted. Giving primarily in OR.

Application information: Unsolicited requests for funds not accepted.
Trustee: Glenn Staack.
EIN: 806084948

Other changes: The grantmaker has moved from NY to DE.

DISTRICT OF COLUMBIA

650
Bauman Family Foundation, Inc.
c/o Jewett House
2040 S St. N.W.
Washington, DC 20009-1110 (202) 328-2040
Contact: Patricia Bauman, Pres.; John L. Bryant, Jr., Dir.
FAX: (202) 328-2003;
E-mail: baumanfoundation@baumanfoundation.org;
Main URL: http://www.baumanfoundation.org

Established in 1982 in NY.
Donor: Lionel R. Bauman†.
Foundation type: Independent foundation.
Financial data (yr. ended 06/30/13): Assets, $91,997,425 (M); expenditures, $9,192,094; qualifying distributions, $7,954,015; giving activities include $7,124,700 for 89 grants (high: $735,000; low: $1,000).
Purpose and activities: Grants to local, state, or national organizations with a clear strategy for translating their projects into nationally applicable ideas, including support for issues at the intersection of the economy and the environment, e.g., reconciliation of worker and community interests in sustainable economic development, trade and the environment, and jobs and the environment; support also for fostering citizens' access to information, increasing awareness of civic rights and responsibilities, and encouraging a central role for interdisciplinary education in achieving the goals of education reform.
Fields of interest: Arts; Education; Environment; Employment; Economic development; Public policy, research.
Type of support: Conferences/seminars; Continuing support; Curriculum development; General/operating support; Matching/challenge support; Program development; Publication; Research; Seed money; Technical assistance.
Limitations: Applications not accepted. Giving primarily in Washington, DC, and New York, NY. No grants to individuals.
Application information: Only applications solicited by the foundation are accepted.
Board meeting date(s): Quarterly
Officers and Directors:* Patricia Bauman,* Pres.; **John Landrum Bryant, Jr.,* V.P. and Treas.**; Gary D. Bass, Exec. Dir.; Marcia Avner; Anne Bartley; Jessica Bauman; Deepak Bhargava; Anne H. Hess; Rev. Msgr. Kevin W. Irwin; Rev. Walter G. Lewis; Gerald Torres.
Number of staff: 2 full-time professional; 1 full-time support.
EIN: 133119290
Other changes: John Landrum Bryant, Jr. is now V.P. and Treas. .

651
The Berger-Marks Foundation
(formerly Edna Berger-Gerald Marks Foundation)
4301 Connecticut Ave. N.W., Ste. 108
Washington, DC 20008-2304 (202) 243-0133
E-mail: bmarks@bergermarks.org; Main URL: http://www.bergermarks.org
Facebook: https://www.facebook.com/BergerMarks
Google Plus: https://plus.google.com/107060696896718710977/posts
Twitter: https://twitter.com/bergermarks

Established in 1996 in DC; Funded in 2002.
Donor: Gerald Marks†.
Foundation type: Independent foundation.
Financial data (yr. ended 12/31/12): Assets, $3,388,236 (M); gifts received, $242,569; expenditures, $430,016; qualifying distributions, $383,951; giving activities include $265,009 for 55 grants (high: $14,292; low: $120), and $13,000 for 4 grants to individuals.
Purpose and activities: Giving to bring the benefits of unionization to working women and to assist organizations committed to those principles. The goal is to provide financial assistance to women who are engaged in union organizing and to assist working women who want to organize other women into unions through training, research and other resources.
Fields of interest: Employment, labor unions/organizations; Minorities; Women.
Limitations: Applications accepted. Giving primarily in Washington, DC, MA and NY.
Application information: See web site for application policies, guidelines and online application.
Initial approach: Complete online application
Deadline(s): See web site
Officers and Trustees:* Louise Walsh,* Chair.; Linda K. Foley,* Pres.; Carolyn Jacobson,* Secy.-Treas.; Kevin Burton; Yvette Herrera; Kitty Peddicord.
EIN: 522044121

652
Bernstein Family Foundation
(formerly Leo M. Bernstein Family Foundation)
c/o The Bernstein Companies, Attn.: Ami Becker Aronson
3299 K St. N.W., Ste. 700
Washington, DC 20007-4438 (202) 255-4477
FAX: (202) 333-3323;
E-mail: info@bernsteinfamilyfoundationdc.org;
Main URL: http://bernsteinfamilyfoundationdc.org/
Grants List: http://bernsteinfamilyfoundationdc.org/downloads/bff_grants.pdf

Established in 1952 in DC and VA.
Donors: Leo M. Bernstein†; Wayside of Virginia Inc.
Foundation type: Independent foundation.
Financial data (yr. ended 12/31/12): Assets, $10,900,162 (M); expenditures, $1,046,380; qualifying distributions, $528,972; giving activities include $440,700 for 51 grants (high: $50,000; low: $500).
Purpose and activities: Giving primarily for: 1) Jewish causes which strengthen the Jewish community of Washington, DC, through support of spiritual leaders, synagogues and community programs that educate Jewish children and adults, and support the development of Jewish identity. Priority will be given to leaders, institutions and projects that: a) use innovative tools to examine the current state of Jewish identity; b) foster dialogue and bridge cultural divides; and c) expand Jewish culture in a modern way; 2) Programs that advance and promote public understanding and appreciation for the United States of America and American democracy; 3) Arts and Culture programs, including support for museum activities, performing arts, visual arts, film, media and art education programs. Priority will be given to projects that: a) use art as a tool for public dialogue and education; b) use public celebrations of art as a way to bring the community together; c) share community-building models developed by community-based arts institutions; and d) integrate different segments of society and awaken civic engagement; and 4) Special projects as defined by the foundation's Board of Directors.
Fields of interest: Arts education; Arts; Education; Community/economic development; Jewish agencies & synagogues.
Type of support: General/operating support; Capital campaigns; Program development; Conferences/seminars.
Limitations: Applications not accepted. Giving limited to charitable organizations located in or serving areas within a 100-mile radius of Washington, DC, and have a strong interest in focusing on needs within the district itself. No support for private foundations. No grants to individuals, or for general operating support; no loans.
Publications: Grants list.
Application information: Contributes only to pre-selected organizations.
Board meeting date(s): Mar. and Sept.
Officers and Directors:* Amb. Stuart Bernstein,* Pres.; Richard Bernstein,* V.P.; Mauree Jane Perry,* Secy.; Adam K. Bernstein,* Treas.; Ami Becker Aronson, Exec. Dir.; Shawn Becker, M.D.; Baron John Bernstein; Rabbi Boruch Bernstein; Tara Bernstein; Alison Bernstein Shulman.
Number of staff: 1 part-time professional.
EIN: 526041822

653
Herb Block Foundation
1730 M St. N.W., Ste. 901
Washington, DC 20036-4509 (202) 223-8801
***Contact:* Sarah Armstrong Alex, C.O.O. and Exec. Dir.**
FAX: (202) 223-8804; E-mail: info@herbblock.org;
Main URL: http://www.herbblockfoundation.org/
Facebook: https://www.facebook.com/pages/The-Herb-Block-Foundation/194650137248067
Scholarship address: **The Herb Block Scholarship, ISTS, 1321 Murfreesboro Rd., Ste. 800, Nashville, TN 37217, tel.: (855) 670-4787, e-mail: contactus@applyists.com**

Established in 2001 in DC and VA.
Donor: Herbert L. Block†.
Foundation type: Independent foundation.
Financial data (yr. ended 09/30/13): Assets, $53,421,175 (M); expenditures, $2,875,910; qualifying distributions, $3,479,807; giving activities include $1,554,500 for 150 grants (high: $25,000; low: $500).
Purpose and activities: The foundation is committed to defending the basic freedoms guaranteed to all Americans, combating all forms of discrimination and prejudice, and improving the conditions of the poor and underprivileged through the creation or support of charitable and educational programs with the same goals. It is also committed to providing educational opportunity to deserving students through post-secondary education scholarships, and to promoting editorial cartooning through continued research.
Fields of interest: Adult education—literacy, basic skills & GED; Scholarships/financial aid; Education; Employment, services; Youth development; Civil liberties, advocacy; Civil liberties, first amendment; Civil/human rights; Public affairs, citizen participation; Economically disadvantaged.
Type of support: General/operating support; Emergency funds; Program development; Curriculum development; Program evaluation; Matching/challenge support.

Limitations: Applications accepted. Giving limited for the benefit of the greater metropolitan Washington, DC, region, including Montgomery and Prince George's counties, MD, and the counties of Arlington, Fairfax, and the city of Alexandria, VA. Applicants for the Defending Basic Freedoms Program and the Encouraging Citizen Involvement Program may be located in or provide services in areas outside the District of Columbia region. No support for sectarian religious purposes. No grants for capital or endowment programs.
Publications: Application guidelines; Grants list; Informational brochure; Program policy statement; Program policy statement (including application guidelines).
Application information: Washington Regional Association of Grantmakers' Common Grant Application Format accepted. See foundation web site for full application information, including grant program cycles, application timelines, and eligibility requirements. Application form required.
Initial approach: Letter of inquiry; submit full proposals upon foundation invitation only
Copies of proposal: 1
Deadline(s): Check foundation web site for application deadlines
Board meeting date(s): Jan., May, and late Sept.
Final notification: Approximately 4 weeks
Officers and Executive Committee:* Athelia Knight,* Chair.; Marcela Brane,* Pres.; Jean J. Rickard,* V.P. and Exec. Dir. Emerita; **Sarah Armstrong Alex,* C.O.O. and Exec. Dir.**; Robin Meszoly,* Treas.
Directors: Jane Asher; Robert Asher; Raymond Bonieskie; Laura Hutchison; Donna McNulty; Clarence Page; Jill Hammer Stanley; Laurie Strayer; Roger Wilkins.
Number of staff: 3 full-time professional; 1 part-time professional.
EIN: 260008276
Other changes: Lynda Bonieskie is no longer a director. Haynes Johnson, a director, is deceased. Sarah Armstrong Alex is now C.O.O. and Exec. Dir.

654
Bou Family Foundation, Inc.
1629 K St., N.W., No. 700
Washington, DC **20006-1636**
***Contact:* Edward C. Bou; Stephen A. Bou**

Established in 1987 in MD.
Donor: Edward C. Bou.
Foundation type: Independent foundation.
Financial data (yr. ended 09/30/12): Assets, $1,641,174 (M); expenditures, $116,802; qualifying distributions, $94,477; giving activities include $94,477 for grants.
Purpose and activities: Giving primarily for education and Christian organizations.
Fields of interest: Arts; Secondary school/education; Higher education; Human services; Protestant agencies & churches; Catholic agencies & churches.
Type of support: General/operating support; Building/renovation.
Limitations: Applications not accepted. Giving primarily in Stamford, CT, Washington, DC and Bethesda, MD. No grants to individuals.
Application information: Contributes only to pre-selected organizations.
Directors: Edward C. Bou; Stephen A. Bou.
EIN: 521549739

655
The Butler Family Fund
1634 I St. N.W., Ste. 1000
Washington, DC 20006-4015 (202) 463-8288
Contact: Martha A. Toll, Exec. Dir.; Anne H. Morin, Prog. Assoc.
FAX: (202) 783-8499;
E-mail: info@butlerfamilyfund.org; Main URL: http://www.butlerfamilyfund.org
Grants Database: http://www.butlerfamilyfund.org/grantees.php

Established in 1992 in DC.
Donor: J.E. and Z.B. Butler Foundation.
Foundation type: Independent foundation.
Financial data (yr. ended 12/31/12): Assets, $9,673,976 (M); expenditures, $909,263; qualifying distributions, $857,573; giving activities include $653,600 for 26 grants (high: $60,000; low: $2,000).
Purpose and activities: Support for homeless families and criminal justice reform (death penalty and juvenile justice).
Fields of interest: Environment, climate change/global warming; Crime/law enforcement, reform; Housing/shelter; Civil liberties, death penalty issues; Homeless.
International interests: United Kingdom.
Type of support: General/operating support; Program development; Seed money.
Limitations: Applications not accepted. Giving primarily in Los Angeles, San Diego and the San Francisco Bay Area, CA, Washington, DC, Chicago, IL, NY, Philadelphia, PA, WI, and London, England. No grants to individuals.
Publications: Grants list; Multi-year report; Program policy statement.
Application information: Unsolicited proposals or letters of inquiry are not accepted. No grants for more than 3 consecutive years.
Board meeting date(s): Biannually
Officers and Directors:* Eve B. Wildrick,* Pres.; Martha A. Toll, Exec. Dir.; Jennifer Gravin; **Dina Hirsch**; Eleanor Leyden-Dunbar; **Nina Morrison**; Rebecca Morrison; Jody Snider.
Number of staff: 1 part-time professional; 1 part-time support.
EIN: 521786778
Other changes: Alexandra Hirsch is no longer a director.

656
The Morris and Gwendolyn Cafritz Foundation
1825 K St. N.W., Ste. 1400
Washington, DC 20006-1202 (202) 223-3100
Contact: Rose Ann Cleveland, Exec. Dir.
FAX: (202) 296-7567;
E-mail: info@cafritzfoundation.org; Main URL: http://www.cafritzfoundation.org
Grants Database: http://www.cafritzfoundation.org/grantees/recent_grantees.asp

Incorporated in 1948 in DC.
Donors: Morris Cafritz‡; Gwendolyn D. Cafritz‡.
Foundation type: Independent foundation.
Financial data (yr. ended 04/30/13): Assets, $728,428,540 (M); expenditures, $42,614,926; qualifying distributions, $27,185,204; giving activities include $17,124,375 for 604 grants (high: $437,500; low: $5,000), and $40,285 for 46 employee matching gifts.
Purpose and activities: The foundation is committed to building a stronger community for residents of the Washington, D.C. area through support of programs in arts and humanities, community services, education, and health and the environment.
Fields of interest: Museums; Performing arts; Performing arts, dance; Performing arts, theater; Performing arts, music; Arts; Education, early childhood education; Child development, education; Elementary school/education; Secondary school/education; Higher education; Adult/continuing education; Adult education—literacy, basic skills & GED; Environment, formal/general education; Environment, natural resources; Environment; Reproductive health, family planning; Medical care, rehabilitation; Health care; Substance abuse, services; Mental health/crisis services; AIDS; Health organizations; Food services; Housing/shelter, development; Housing/shelter; Human services; Children/youth, services; Child development, services; Family services; Residential/custodial care, hospices; Aging, centers/services; Women, centers/services; Homeless, human services; Civil/human rights, immigrants; Civil/human rights, minorities; Civil/human rights, women; Civil/human rights, aging; Civil liberties, reproductive rights; Civil/human rights; Community/economic development; Voluntarism promotion; Infants/toddlers; Children/youth; Youth; Aging; Young adults; Disabilities, people with; Physically disabled; Blind/visually impaired; Deaf/hearing impaired; Mentally disabled; Minorities; Asians/Pacific Islanders; African Americans/Blacks; Hispanics/Latinos; Women; Infants/toddlers, female; Girls; Military/veterans; Offenders/ex-offenders; Substance abusers; AIDS, people with; Single parents; Crime/abuse victims; Immigrants/refugees; Economically disadvantaged; Homeless; LGBTQ.
Type of support: General/operating support; Management development/capacity building; Program development; Scholarship funds; Technical assistance; Program evaluation; Matching/challenge support.
Limitations: Applications accepted. Giving limited to the Washington, DC, area and the immediate surrounding counties in MD and VA, specifically Prince George's and Montgomery counties, MD, and Arlington and Fairfax counties, and the cities of Alexandria and Falls Church, VA. No grants to individuals, or for emergency funds, deficit financing, endowments, demonstration projects and no loans.
Publications: Application guidelines; Annual report; Grants list.
Application information: Washington Regional Association of Grantmakers' Common Grant Application Format accepted. Proposals may not be submitted via fax or e-mail. Proposals may be submitted online. Application form required.
Initial approach: Telephone e-mail or Full Proposal
Copies of proposal: 1
Deadline(s): Mar. 1, July 1, and Nov. 1
Board meeting date(s): Generally 3 to 9 months after deadline dates
Final notification: 4 to 6 months
Officers and Directors:* Calvin Cafritz,* Chair., C.E.O. and Pres.; **John E. Chapoton,* Vice-Chair.**; Ed McGeogh, V.P., Asset Mgmt.; Rohan Rodrigo, V.P., Finance; **F. Joseph Moravec, Treas.**; Rose Ann Cleveland, Exec. Dir.; Michael F. Brewer; LaSalle D. Leffall, Jr., M.D.; Patricia McGuire; Robert Peck; Earl A. Powell III; Alice M. Rivlin; Norman O. Scribner.
Advisory Board: Anthony W. Cafritz; Elliot S. Cafritz; Jane Lipton Cafritz; Carolyn J. Deaver; Hon. Constance A. Morella; Elizabeth M. Peltekian; Julia Sparkman Shepard.
Number of staff: 12 full-time professional; 2 part-time professional; 5 full-time support.
EIN: 526036989

Other changes: Daniel J. Callahan, III is no longer Vice-Chair. and Treas. John E. Chapoton is now Vice-Chair. F. Joseph Moravec is now Treas.

657
E. Eugene Carter Foundation
3075 Ordway St. N.W.
Washington, DC 20008-3255

Established in 1993 in DC.
Donor: E. Eugene Carter.
Foundation type: Independent foundation.
Financial data (yr. ended 12/31/13): Assets, $6,328,357 (M); expenditures, $249,050; qualifying distributions, $249,050; giving activities include $238,619 for 8 grants (high: $99,793; low: $250).
Fields of interest: Higher education; Engineering; Minorities; Hispanics/Latinos; Women; Immigrants/refugees.
Type of support: Scholarship funds.
Limitations: Applications not accepted. Giving on a national basis. No grants to individuals.
Application information: Contributes only to pre-selected organizations.
Officers: E. Eugene Carter, Chair.; Jane R. O'Neil, Secy.
Trustee: John Aldridge.
Number of staff: None.
EIN: 521829253

658
The Case Foundation
(formerly The Stephen Case Foundation)
1717 Rhode Island Ave. N.W., 7th Fl.
Washington, DC 20036-3023 (202) 467-5788
Contact: Brian Sasscer, Sr. V.P., Strategic Opers.
FAX: (202) 775-8513;
E-mail: contactus@casefoundation.org; Main URL: http://www.casefoundation.org
Case Foundation Blog: http://www.casefoundation.org/blog
Case Foundation Video Library: http://www.casefoundation.org/videos
Case Soup: http://www.casefoundation.org/videos/case-soup
Facebook: http://www.facebook.com/casefoundation
Foundation's Instagram Profile: http://instagram.com/casefoundation
GiveSmart: http://www.givesmart.org/Stories/Donors/Jean-and-Steve-Case
Google Plus: https://plus.google.com/+casefoundation/posts
Jean and Steve Case's Giving Pledge Profile: http://glasspockets.org/philanthropy-in-focus/eye-on-the-giving-pledge/profiles/case
LinkedIn: http://www.linkedin.com/company/the-case-foundation
Pinterest: http://www.pinterest.com/casefoundation/
RSS Feed: http://feed.casefoundation.org/casefoundation
Twitter: http://www.twitter.com/CaseFoundation
YouTube: http://www.youtube.com/casefoundation

Established in 1997 in VA.
Donors: Stephen M. Case; Jean N. Case; Goldhirsh Foundation.
Foundation type: Independent foundation.
Financial data (yr. ended 12/31/12): Assets, $530,289 (M); gifts received, $3,020,000; expenditures, $3,981,190; qualifying distributions, $3,965,784; giving activities include $1,192,211 for 44 grants (high: $300,000; low: $225).
Purpose and activities: Giving to achieve sustainable solutions to complex social problems by investing in collaboration, leadership, and entrepreneurship. Supports individuals and organizations that have the strategy, leadership, and commitment to make positive, widespread social change. The foundation seeks to meet the needs of families and children in poverty; create thriving and sustainable economic development for communities; bridge cultural and religious divides; expand civic engagement and volunteerism; and accelerate innovative approaches to health care.
Fields of interest: Education; Health care; Youth development, services; Community/economic development; Engineering/technology.
International interests: Global Programs.
Type of support: Program-related investments/loans.
Limitations: Giving in the U.S. and abroad. No grants to individuals.
Officers and Directors:* Stephen M. Case,* Chair.; Jean N. Case,* C.E.O. and Pres.; Erich Brokas, Sr. V.P., Innovation and Investment; Brian Sasscer, Sr., V.P., Strategic Operations; Michael Smith, Sr.V.P., Social Innovation; Kari Dunn Saratovsky, V.P., Social Innovation; John Sabin, Secy.-Treas. and C.F.O.
Number of staff: 2 full-time professional; 1 part-time professional; 3 full-time support; 1 part-time support.
EIN: 541848791

659
El-Hibri Charitable Foundation
Ibrahim El-Hibri Bldg.
1420 16th St. N.W.
Washington, DC 20036-2202 (202) 387-9500
FAX: (202) 387-9050;
E-mail: info@elhibrifoundation.org; Application address: c/o Zen Hunter-Ishikawa, 12001 Glen Rd., Potomac, MD 20854, tel.: (301) 983-1133; **Main URL: http://www.elhibrifoundation.org/**
Facebook: https://www.facebook.com/elhibrifoundation
Grants List: http://www.elhibrifoundation.org/granthistory.html
LinkedIn: http://www.linkedin.com/company/el-hibri-charitable-foundation
Twitter: https://twitter.com/ElHibriFdn

Established in 2001 in DC.
Donors: Fuad El-Hibri; Ibrahim Y. El-Hibri†.
Foundation type: Independent foundation.
Financial data (yr. ended 12/31/12): Assets, $38,066,727 (M); gifts received, $520,000; expenditures, $1,678,271; qualifying distributions, $1,468,556; giving activities include $574,500 for 19 grants (high: $110,000; low: $3,000).
Purpose and activities: Giving primarily to: 1) Promote the fields of peace studies and conflict resolution through education, training, media production and related activities; 2) Encourage respect for religious diversity through research, education, interfaith collaboration and dialogue, and related activities; 3) Enable disadvantaged youth, primarily in Lebanon, to become productive members of society by supporting education, training and related activities; and 4) Advance human rights for women in the Middle East by fostering knowledge about Islam and building skills to empower women.
Fields of interest: Education; International relief; International democracy & civil society development; International peace/security; International conflict resolution; International human rights; Islam; Religion, interfaith issues.
International interests: Lebanon; Middle East.
Type of support: General/operating support; Management development/capacity building; Capital campaigns; Seed money.
Limitations: Applications accepted. Giving primarily in the Washington, DC area, and Lebanon.
Publications: Application guidelines.
Application information: Full proposals are by invitation only, upon review of letter of intent. Application form not required.
Initial approach: Letter of intent (1-2 pages)
Deadline(s): Letters of intent are accepted from May 1 until June 30 of the year preceding the grant's proposed start date
Officers and Directors:* Fuad El-Hibri, Chair.; Judy Barsalou, Pres.; Marcia Thayer Nass, V.P., Strategic Planning, Secy. and Genl. Counsel; Greg Siegrist, V.P., Fin. and Admin. and Treas.; Zen Hunter-Ishikawa, V.P., Opers. and Devel.; Karim El-Hibri,* Dir., Grants; Mary Goudie; Lynn Kunkle; Nadia Roumani; Abdo Sabban; Abdul Aziz Said; Allen Shofe.
EIN: 522306995

660
Flamboyan Foundation, Inc.
1730 Massachusetts Ave. N.W.
Washington, DC 20036-1903
E-mail: info@flamboyanfoundation.org; Puerto Rico address: P.O. Box 16699, San Juan, PR 00908-6699, tel.: (787) 977-5522; Main URL: http://www.flamboyanfoundation.org

Established in 2007 in DC.
Donors: Fundacion Flamboyan; Coqui Development Co.
Foundation type: Independent foundation.
Financial data (yr. ended 12/31/12): Assets, $7,699,375 (M); gifts received, $561,062; expenditures, $2,784,479; qualifying distributions, $2,721,688; giving activities include $1,064,643 for 23 grants (high: $340,294; low: $250), and $29,000 for 19 grants to individuals (high: $3,000; low: $1,000).
Purpose and activities: Giving primarily for the improvement of educational outcomes for children in public schools in Washington, DC, and San Juan, PR.
Fields of interest: Education.
Limitations: Applications not accepted. Giving primarily in Washington, DC, and San Juan, PR.
Application information: Contributes only to pre-selected organizations.
Officers and Directors:* Kristin Ehrgood,* Chair. and Pres.; Vadim Nikitine, Treas.; **Rea Carey, Exec. Dir.**; Guiomar Garcia, Exec. Dir.; Susan K. Stevenson, Exec. Dir.
EIN: 208924675
Other changes: Kristin Ehrgood is now Chair. and Pres.

661
Foundation for Middle East Peace
1761 N St. N.W.
Washington, DC 20036-2801 (202) 835-3650
Contact: Philip C. Wilcox, Jr., Pres.
***FAX:* (202) 835-3651; E-mail: info@fmep.org**; Main URL: http://www.fmep.org

Incorporated in 1979 in DC.
Donors: Merle Thorpe, Jr.‡; Stephen Hartwell; Nelson B. Delavan Foundation; W.H. Rosenwald Family Fund.
Foundation type: Independent foundation.
Financial data (yr. ended 09/30/13): Assets, $8,993,360 (M); gifts received, $10,893; expenditures, $872,544; qualifying distributions, $545,197; giving activities include $281,000 for 27 grants (high: $37,500; low: $2,500).
Purpose and activities: To promote an understanding of the Israeli-Palestinian conflict, including the identification of U.S. interests, and to contribute to a just and peaceful resolution of the conflict with security for both peoples. Support directed to elements within the Arab and Jewish communities working for a peaceful resolution of the conflict.
Fields of interest: International peace/security.
International interests: Israel; Middle East.
Type of support: General/operating support; Conferences/seminars; Publication; Research; Matching/challenge support.
Limitations: Applications accepted. Giving primarily in Washington, DC, Israel, and Palestine.
Application information: Application form required.
Initial approach: Request application form
Deadline(s): None
Officers: Amb. Nicholas A. Veliotes, Chair.; Philip C. Wilcox, Jr., Pres.; **Calvin Hayes Cobb, Jr., Co-Secy.**; Richard S.T. Marsh, Co-Secy.; **Jean Newsom, Treas.**
Directors: Landrum R. Bolling; **Edison Dick**; **Joseph Englehardt**; **Arthur H. Hughes**; Richard Murphy; Gail Pressberg; William B. Quandt.
Number of staff: 2 full-time professional; 1 full-time support.
EIN: 526055574
Other changes: Amb. Nicholas A. Veliotes has replaced Calvin Hayes Cobb, Jr. as Chair. Jean Newsom has replaced Stephen Hartwell as Treas. A. Lucius Battle, James J. Cromwell and Peter Gubser are no longer directors.

662
The Freedom Forum, Inc.
555 Pennsylvania Ave., NW
Washington, DC 20001-2114 (202) 292-6100
Contact: James Duff, Pres. and C.E.O.
E-mail: news@freedomforum.org; Main URL: http://www.freedomforum.org

Incorporated in 1991 in VA.
Foundation type: Operating foundation.
Financial data (yr. ended 12/31/12): Assets, $765,567,826 (M); expenditures, $56,052,317; qualifying distributions, $42,201,043; giving activities include $28,463,754 for 83 grants (high: $26,642,008; low: $1,000), and $3,693,085 for 3 foundation-administered programs.
Purpose and activities: The Freedom Forum, based in Washington, D.C., is a nonpartisan foundation that champions the First Amendment as a cornerstone of democracy.
Fields of interest: Civil liberties, first amendment; Civil liberties, freedom of information.
Type of support: Scholarships—to individuals.
Limitations: Applications not accepted. Giving on a national and international basis.
Publications: Annual report; Occasional report.
Application information: Unsolicited requests for funds not accepted.
Board meeting date(s): Quarterly
Officers and Trustees:* Jan Neuharth,* Chair.; **James C. Duff,* Pres. and C.E.O., Freedom Forum and C.E.O., Newseum and Pres. and C.E.O., Newseum Institute**; James W. Abbott,* Chair., Newseum Institute; Peter S. Prichard,* Chair., Newseum; Shelby Coffey III, Vice-Chair., Newseum; Gene Policinski, C.O.O., Newseum Institute; Ken Paulson,* Pres. and C.E.O., First Amendment Center; Jack Marsh, Pres., Al Neuharth Media Ctr.; Pamela Y. Galloway-Tabb, Sr. V.P., Conferences and Special Svcs.; Nicole F. Mandeville, Sr. V.P., Finance, and Treas.; Cathy Trost, Sr. V.P., Exhibits and Prog(s); Paul Sparrow, Sr. V.P., Broadcasting; Courtney L. Surls, Sr. V.P., Devel.; James Thompson, Sr. V.P., Operations; Jim Updike, Sr. V.P., Technology; Scott Williams, Sr. V.P, Marketing; Howard H. Baker, Jr.,* Secy.; Michael Coleman; Malcolm R. Kirschenbaum; H. Wilbert Norton, Jr.; Orage Quarles III; Judy C. Woodruff.
Number of staff: 111 full-time professional; 6 part-time professional; 45 full-time support; 5 part-time support.
EIN: 541604427

663
Philip L. Graham Fund
c/o The Washington Post Co.
1150 15th St. N.W.
Washington, DC 20071-0001 (202) 334-6640
Contact: Eileen F. Daly, Pres.
FAX: (202) 334-4498;
E-mail: plgfund@washpost.com; **Main URL: http://plgrahamfund.org/**
Grants Database: http://plgrahamfund.org/vw_grants_awarded

Trust established in 1963 in DC.
Donors: Katharine Meyer Graham; Frederick S. Beebe‡; The Washington Post Co.; Newsweek, Inc.; Post-Newsweek Stations.
Foundation type: Independent foundation.
Financial data (yr. ended 12/31/12): Assets, $98,338,608 (M); expenditures, $4,785,326; qualifying distributions, $4,600,496; giving activities include $4,232,500 for 132 grants (high: $400,000; low: $2,000).
Purpose and activities: Support for one-time infrastructure investments in health and human services, for children, youth, and families, pre-collegiate education, arts and humanities, and community needs. Grants for journalism, media and communications are extremely limited, and generally awarded only to those who have received media grants in the past.
Fields of interest: Arts; Education, early childhood education; Education; Housing/shelter; Human services; Youth, services; Community development, neighborhood development.
Type of support: Capital campaigns; Building/renovation; Equipment; Program development; Seed money; Matching/challenge support.
Limitations: Applications accepted. Giving primarily in the metropolitan Washington, DC, area. No support for national or international organizations, membership organizations, lobbying or political activities, or for religious purposes. No grants to individuals, or for medical services, research, annual campaigns, fundraising events, endowments, seminars, conferences, publications, tickets, films, travel expenses, courtesy advertising, advocacy, or litigation.
Publications: Application guidelines; Program policy statement.
Application information: Letters of inquiry must be submitted via the foundation's online system. Application form not required.
Initial approach: Review guidelines and qualifications prior to submitting a letter of inquiry
Copies of proposal: 3
Deadline(s): See foundation web site for current deadlines
Board meeting date(s): 120 days from application deadline
Final notification: 6 months
Officers and Trustees:* Eileen F. Daly,* Pres.; Theodore C. Lutz,* Secy.; Martin Cohen,* Treas.; Donald E. Graham; Pinkie D. Mayfield; Carol D. Melamed.
Number of staff: 1 full-time professional; 1 full-time support.
EIN: 526051781

664
Hill-Snowdon Foundation
1201 Connecticut Ave. N.W., 3rd Fl.
Washington, DC 20036-2605
FAX: (202) 833-8606; E-mail: info@hillsnowdon.org; Main URL: http://www.hillsnowdon.org/
Grants Database: http://www.hillsnowdon.org/grantlistings.asp
Hill-Snowden Foundation's Philanthropy Promise: http://www.ncrp.org/philanthropys-promise/who
RSS Feed: http://www.hillsnowdon.org/newsresources.asp

Established in 1959 in NJ.
Donors: Arthur B. Hill‡; Edward Snowdon Charitable Lead Unitrust.
Foundation type: Independent foundation.
Financial data (yr. ended 12/31/12): Assets, $28,138,443 (M); gifts received, $367,358; expenditures, $2,155,413; qualifying distributions, $1,770,369; giving activities include $1,232,540 for 84 grants (high: $35,000; low: $1,000).
Purpose and activities: Giving primarily for organization working with low-income families and communities to create a fair and just society by helping them develop the capacity and leadership skills necessary to influence the decisions that shape their lives. HSF seeks to accomplish this mission by providing grants to organizations that work directly to build the power of low-income families; leveraging our and others' resources; and promoting opportunities for learning and growth.
Fields of interest: Employment, services; Youth development; Human services; Children/youth, services; Family services; Civil/human rights, advocacy; Economic development; Community/economic development; Leadership development; Youth; Minorities; Women; Economically disadvantaged; Homeless.
Type of support: General/operating support.
Limitations: Applications not accepted. **Giving in Washington, DC, for the Fund for DC program; 60-70% of the Youth Organizations and Economic Justice Organizing program areas will be directed toward the U.S. South; and strategic investments made nationally to help promote the goals of Youth Organizing and Economic Organizing program areas.** No grants to individuals.
Publications: Grants list; Program policy statement.
Application information: While unsolicited proposals are not considered, the foundation will accept initial inquiry contacts from nonprofits whose work intersects with its areas of interest. Refer to foundation web site for guidelines.
Board meeting date(s): Nov.
Officers and Trustees:* Elizabeth Snowdon Bonner,* Pres.; Ashley Snowdon Blanchard,* V.P.; Richard Snowdon III,* Secy.-Treas.; Nat Chioke Williams, Ph.D., Exec. Dir.; Andrew L. Snowdon; Ariana Snowdon; Edward W. Snowdon, Jr.; Marguerite Snowdon.

Number of staff: 3 full-time professional; 1 part-time professional.
EIN: 226081122

665
Paul & Annetta Himmelfarb Foundation Inc.
1240-A Upshur St. N.W.
Washington, DC 20011-5626

Incorporated in 1947 in DE.
Donor: Members of the Himmelfarb family.
Foundation type: Independent foundation.
Financial data (yr. ended 12/31/12): Assets, $5,573,111 (M); expenditures, $296,107; qualifying distributions, $223,763; giving activities include $215,000 for 5 grants (high: $140,000; low: $10,000).
Purpose and activities: Support primarily to organizations that combat homelessness and/or addiction in Washington, D.C.; giving also to organizations that provide summer camp services to Washington, D.C. youth.
Fields of interest: Mental health, addictions; Recreation, camps; Children/youth, services; Homeless, human services; Children/youth; Homeless.
Limitations: Applications accepted. Giving primarily in the Washington, DC, area. No support for political organizations. No grants to individuals.
Publications: Annual report.
Application information: Application form required.
Initial approach: Letter
Deadline(s): None
Officers and Directors:* Paul Himmelfarb,* Pres.; Norma Lee Naiman,* V.P.; Lauren K. Hester,* Secy.; Michael E. Preston, Treas. and Exec. Dir.; Lisa Ulanow.
Number of staff: 1 full-time professional; 1 part-time professional.
EIN: 520784206
Other changes: The grantmaker no longer lists a URL.

666
The Hitachi Foundation
1215 17th St., N.W., 3rd Fl.
Washington, DC 20036-3019 (202) 457-0588
Contact: Barbara Dyer, C.E.O. and Pres.; Mark Popovich, Sr. Prog. Off.
FAX: (202) 298-1098;
E-mail: info@hitachifoundation.org; Main URL: http://www.hitachifoundation.org
Facebook: https://www.facebook.com/pages/The-Hitachi-Foundation/542427755792314?ref=br_rs
Flickr: https://www.flickr.com/photos/75775267@N03/
LinkedIn: http://www.linkedin.com/company/the-hitachi-foundation
Twitter: http://twitter.com/HitachiFdn#
YouTube: http://www.youtube.com/user/TheHitachiFoundation

Established in 1985 in DC.
Donor: Hitachi, Ltd.
Foundation type: Independent foundation.
Financial data (yr. ended 12/31/12): Assets, $23,469,501 (M); gifts received, $3,177,122; expenditures, $3,334,689; qualifying distributions, $3,177,489; giving activities include $1,535,572 for 269 grants (high: $281,388; low: $100).
Purpose and activities: The foundation supports organizations involved with education, employment, and economically disadvantaged people and awards grants to high school seniors.
Fields of interest: Employment; Economically disadvantaged.
Type of support: Mission-related investments/loans; Program development; Employee volunteer services; Matching/challenge support.
Limitations: Applications accepted. Giving on a national basis. No grants to individuals (except for Yoshiyama Awards), or for capital campaigns or fundraising.
Publications: Application guidelines; Annual report; Financial statement; Grants list; Informational brochure; Occasional report.
Application information: Application forms are available online. Application form required.
Initial approach: Complete online letter of inquiry form for Business and Communities Grants; complete online narration form for Yoshiyama Awards
Copies of proposal: 1
Deadline(s): Apr. 1 for Yoshiyama Awards
Board meeting date(s): Spring, summer, and fall
Final notification: Aug. or Sept. for Yoshiyama Awards
Officers and Directors:* Patrick W. Gross,* Chair.; Barbara Dyer,* C.E.O. and Pres.; **Takashi Kawamura, Honorary Chair.**; **Jason Baron**; Sherry Salway Black; Albert D. Fuller; **David Langstaff**; Bruce MacLaury, Ph.D.; **Jennifer Pryce**; **Kelly Ryan.**
Number of staff: 4 full-time professional; 3 full-time support.
EIN: 521429292
Other changes: Patrick W. Gross has replaced Bruce MacLaury as Chair.
David Dodson and Frances Garcia are no longer board members.

667
Institute of Current World Affairs, Inc.
(also known as The Crane-Rogers Foundation)
4545 42nd St. N.W., Ste. 311
Washington, DC 20016-4623 (202) 364-4068
Contact: Steven Butler, Exec. Dir.
FAX: (202) 364-0498; E-mail: icwa@icwa.org; Main URL: http://www.icwa.org
Twitter: https://twitter.com/ICWAnews
Application e-mail: apply@icwa.org

Incorporated in 1925 in NY as a private operating foundation.
Donors: Charles R. Crane; Robert McColl; Suzanne McColl; The Beinecke Foundation; Friendship Fund, Inc.
Foundation type: Operating foundation.
Financial data (yr. ended 12/31/12): Assets, $6,058,064 (M); gifts received, $800,159; expenditures, $773,735; qualifying distributions, $705,303; giving activities include $130,616 for 5 grants (high: $36,191; low: $9,469), and $29,387 for 2 grants to individuals (high: $27,632; low: $1,755).
Purpose and activities: Support for a limited number of long-term fellowships to persons 35 years or younger of exceptional ability to enable them to work in and write about foreign areas of significance to the U.S.
Fields of interest: International affairs.
Type of support: Fellowships.
Limitations: Applications accepted. Giving limited to fellowships conducted outside the U.S. No support for formal education. No grants for research projects.
Publications: Application guidelines; Informational brochure.
Application information: Complete application information available on Institute web site. Application form not required.
Initial approach: Letter of interest and resume (by email preferred)
Copies of proposal: 1
Deadline(s): See Institute web site for deadlines for letter of interest and resume. If appropriate, candidates will be invited to submit a more detailed written application
Board meeting date(s): June and Dec.
Officers and Trustees:* Gary Hartshorn,* Chair.; Pramila Jayapal,* Vice-Chair.; Boris Weintraub,* Secy.; Edmund Sutton,* Treas.; Steven Butler,* Exec. Dir.; Bryn Barnard; Carole Beaulieu; Mary Lynne Bird; Virginia Foote; Peter Geithner; Robert Levinson; Cheng Li; David Robinson; John Spencer; Susan Stemer.
Number of staff: 1 full-time professional; 2 full-time support.
EIN: 131621044

668
Jovid Foundation
5335 Wisconsin Ave. N.W., Ste. 440
Washington, DC 20015-2003 (202) 686-2616
Contact: Bob Wittig, Exec. Dir.
FAX: (202) 686-2621;
E-mail: jovidfoundation@gmail.com**; Main URL: http://fdnweb.org/jovid/**
Grants List: http://fdnweb.org/jovid/grants-awarded/

Established in 1990 in DC; funded in 1991.
Donors: David O. Maxwell; Joan P. Maxwell.
Foundation type: Independent foundation.
Financial data (yr. ended 12/31/13): Assets, $3,932,820 (M); gifts received, $250,000; expenditures, $527,576; qualifying distributions, $518,851; giving activities include $371,500 for 34 grants (high: $30,000; low: $1,500).
Purpose and activities: The foundation's primary interest is in supporting nonprofit organizations in the District of Columbia whose work is aimed at helping people in or at risk of long-term poverty to become more self-sufficient. Because the foundation is small and seeks to make a real difference to the projects it funds, it is particularly interested in neighborhood-based efforts that provide programs and services to adults, including its funding for vocational education and job counseling. The foundation also has a modest budget for support of the arts.
Fields of interest: Vocational education; Employment, job counseling; Youth; Adults; Young adults; Minorities; Asians/Pacific Islanders; African Americans/Blacks; Hispanics/Latinos; Native Americans/American Indians; Women; Adults, women; Young adults, female; Men; Adults, men; Young adults, male; Offenders/ex-offenders; Substance abusers; Single parents; Immigrants/refugees; Economically disadvantaged; Homeless.
Type of support: Technical assistance; General/operating support; Continuing support; Management development/capacity building; Program development; Seed money; Research; Program evaluation.
Limitations: Applications accepted. Giving primarily in Washington, DC. No support for sectarian projects. No grants to individuals.
Publications: Annual report (including application guidelines); Grants list.
Application information: Jovid will consider letters of inquiry from organizations which have not received previous funding from the foundation. Please note that the foundation's funding remains

very limited. Therefore the letter of inquiry must clearly address the proposal's anticipated effectiveness and impact in helping DC adults obtain and retain employment. Full proposals are by invitation only, upon consideration of letter of inquiry. See Foundation web site for application guidelines. Application form not required.

Initial approach: Letter of inquiry (not exceeding 3 pages) by fax or e-mail; or telephone Exec. Dir. prior to submission
Copies of proposal: 1
Deadline(s): See foundation web site for current deadlines
Board meeting date(s): Mar., June, and Nov.
Final notification: After board meeting

Officers and Directors:* Joan P. Maxwell,* Pres.; David O. Maxwell,* V.P. and Treas.; Doris D. Blazek-White,* Secy.; Bob Wittig, Exec. Dir.
Number of staff: 1 full-time professional.
EIN: 521694387

669
The Krauthammer Foundation, Inc.
1225 19th St. N.W., Rm. 700
Washington, DC 20036

Established in 1988 in NY.
Donor: Charles Krauthammer.
Foundation type: Independent foundation.
Financial data (yr. ended 09/30/13): Assets, $617,497 (M); expenditures, $242,861; qualifying distributions, $226,435; giving activities include $226,435 for 6 grants (high: $175,000; low: $500).
Fields of interest: Performing arts, music; Elementary/secondary education; Jewish agencies & synagogues.
Type of support: General/operating support.
Limitations: Applications not accepted. Giving primarily in Washington, DC. No grants to individuals.
Application information: Contributes only to pre-selected organizations.
Officer: Charles Krauthammer, Pres.
EIN: 222927289

670
Jacob and Charlotte Lehrman Foundation, Inc.
1836 Columbia Rd. N.W.
Washington, DC 20009-2002 (202) 328-8400
FAX: (202) 328-8405;
E-mail: info@lehrmanfoundation.org; Main URL: http://www.lehrmanfoundation.org
Grants List: http://www.lehrmanfoundation.org/grants.html

Incorporated in 1953 in DC.
Donors: Jacob J. Lehrman†; Charlotte F. Lehrman†.
Foundation type: Independent foundation.
Financial data (yr. ended 10/31/12): Assets, $11,017,885 (M); expenditures, $650,029; qualifying distributions, $566,270; giving activities include $544,000 for grants.
Purpose and activities: The foundation supports and seeks to enrich Jewish life in Washington, DC, Israel, and around the world. It is committed to making Washington a better place for all people and it supports the arts, education and underserved children, the environment, and health care.
Fields of interest: Museums; Arts; Vocational education; Education; Health care; Health organizations, association; Medical research, institute; Human services; Aging, centers/services; Community/economic development; Jewish federated giving programs; Jewish agencies & synagogues; Aging.
Type of support: General/operating support; Scholarship funds; Research.
Limitations: Applications not accepted. Giving primarily in metropolitan Washington, DC. No grants to individuals; no loans.
Publications: Grants list.
Application information: Unsolicited requests for funds not accepted; however an organization may be asked to submit a grant/request for proposal (RFP) by a Trustee of the Board and/or staff member. See foundation web site for details.

Board meeting date(s): Apr. and Oct.

Officers and Trustees:* Robert Lehrman,* Pres.; Mark A. Dubick,* V.P. and Admin.; Elizabeth Berry,* Secy.; Samuel Lehrman,* Treas.
EIN: 526035666

671
Lichtenberg Family Foundation, Inc.
(formerly William R. & Nora Lichtenberg Foundation)
1025 Connecticut Ave. N.W., Ste. 400
Washington, DC 20006-5405 (202) 659-6773
Contact: Glenn Bonard Esq., Dir.

Established in 1980 in DC.
Donors: Nora Lichtenberg†; William Lichtenberg†; Linda Kaplan.
Foundation type: Independent foundation.
Financial data (yr. ended 10/31/13): Assets, $2,462,023 (M); gifts received, $73,350; expenditures, $281,267; qualifying distributions, $252,790; giving activities include $252,790 for 25 grants (high: $225,000; low: $70).
Fields of interest: Visual arts; Performing arts; Arts; Higher education; Health care; Women.
Type of support: Endowments; Emergency funds; Program development; Matching/challenge support.
Limitations: Applications accepted. Giving primarily in Washington, DC. No grants to individuals; no loans.
Application information:

Initial approach: Letter
Deadline(s): None

Officers and Directors:* Linda Kaplan,* Pres.; Louis Kaplan,* Treas.; Glenn R. Bonard.
EIN: 526036659

672
Eugene and Agnes E. Meyer Foundation
1250 Connecticut Ave. N.W., Ste. 800
Washington, DC 20036-2620 (202) 483-8294
FAX: (202) 328-6850; E-mail: info@meyerfdn.org; Main URL: http://www.meyerfoundation.org
E-Newsletter: https://app.e2ma.net/app/view:Join/signupId:1357652/acctId:1356193
Eugene and Agnes E. Meyer Foundation's Philanthropy's Promise: http://www.ncrp.org/philanthropys-promise/who
Facebook: http://www.facebook.com/meyerfoundation
Grants Database: http://www.meyerfoundation.org/grantees/recent/search
Strategic Framework: http://app.e2ma.net/app2/campaigns/archived/1356193/08ec0493039d1dc3264520f4e4f1007f/
Twitter: http://twitter.com/meyerfoundation
Vimeo: http://vimeo.com/meyerfoundation
YouTube: http://www.youtube.com/user/TheMeyerFoundation

Incorporated in 1944 in NY.
Donors: Eugene Meyer†; Agnes E. Meyer†; Marpat Foundation.
Foundation type: Independent foundation.
Financial data (yr. ended 12/31/12): Assets, $199,664,078 (M); gifts received, $3,023; expenditures, $10,909,533; qualifying distributions, $8,733,644; giving activities include $5,992,970 for 241 grants (high: $100,000; low: $1,000), and $29,020 for 4 foundation-administered programs.
Purpose and activities: The mission of the foundation is to identify and invest in visionary leaders and effective community-based nonprofit organizations that are working to create lasting improvements in the lives of low-income people in the Washington, D.C. metropolitan region, and to work to strengthen the region's nonprofit sector as a vital and respected partner in meeting community needs.
Fields of interest: Education, early childhood education; Child development, education; Elementary school/education; Secondary school/education; Vocational education; Adult education—literacy, basic skills & GED; Education, reading; Education; Dental care; Health care; Substance abuse, services; Mental health/crisis services; Health organizations; Legal services; Employment; Youth development, services; Human services; Children/youth, services; Child development, services; Family services; Women, centers/services; Minorities/immigrants, centers/services; Homeless, human services; Civil rights, race/intergroup relations; Civil/human rights; Urban/community development; Community/economic development; Leadership development; Economically disadvantaged.
Type of support: General/operating support; Management development/capacity building; Program development; Technical assistance; Consulting services; Matching/challenge support.
Limitations: Applications accepted. Giving limited to the Washington, DC, metropolitan area, including, Montgomery and Prince George's counties in MD; Arlington County, City of Alexandria, City of Falls Church, City of Manassas Park, City of Manassas, Fairfax County, and Prince William County in VA. No support for sectarian purposes, or for programs that are national or international in scope. No grants to individuals, or for annual campaigns, deficit financing, endowment funds, equipment, scholarships, fellowships, scientific or medical research, publications, special events or conferences.
Publications: Application guidelines; Grants list; Newsletter.
Application information: Applicants should read the foundation's guidelines thoroughly at www.meyerfoundation.org. Letters of inquiry should be submitted online via a link on the foundation's web site. The foundation will acknowledge receipt of all applications within two weeks. If further information is needed, the applicant will be contacted by a foundation staff member. The foundation may or may not invite a full proposal. Application form required.

Initial approach: Online application available on foundation web site
Deadline(s): See foundation web site for current deadline
Board meeting date(s): May and Oct.
Final notification: Within 2 weeks after board meetings

Officers and Directors:* Joshua B. Bernstein,* Chair.; Deborah Ratner Salzberg, Vice-Chair.; **Nicky Goren, Pres.**; Janice A. Thomas, V.P., Finance and Opers.; Richard L. Moyers, V.P. Progs. and Comm.; Barbara Lang, Secy.-Treas; Antoinett "Toni" Cook Bush; William Dunbar; Newman T. Halvorson, Jr.;

Barbara J. Krumsiek; Ginger Lew; Jim Sandman; Lidia Soto-Harmon; Robert G. Templin, Jr., Ph.D.; Kerrie B. Wilson.
Number of staff: 5 full-time professional; 2 part-time professional; 4 full-time support.
EIN: 530241716
Other changes: Nicky Goren is now Pres. Julie L. Rogers is no longer C.E.O. and Pres.

673
Monarch Fund
c/o Alison Olsen
1901 Pennsylvania Ave. N.W., Ste. 701
Washington, DC 20006-3447

Established in 2007 in DC.
Donor: Donald E. Graham.
Foundation type: Independent foundation.
Financial data (yr. ended 12/31/12): Assets, $2,051,459 (M); expenditures, $1,102,232; qualifying distributions, $1,100,724; giving activities include $1,100,724 for 3 grants (high: $500,362; low: $100,000).
Fields of interest: Medical research, institute; Foundations (community).
Limitations: Applications not accepted. Giving primarily in Washington, DC, and MA. No grants to individuals.
Application information: Contributes only to pre-selected organizations.
Director: Mary Graham.
EIN: 266049750

674
The National Academy of Education
500 5th St. N.W., No. 307
Washington, DC 20001-2736 (202) 334-2093
Contact: Gregory White, Exec. Dir.; Philip Perrin, Sr. Prog. Off., Professional Devel. Progs.; Jack Busbee
FAX: (202) 334-2350; E-mail: info@naeducation.org; Main URL: http://www.naeducation.org/

Established in 1965 in NY; classified as a private operating foundation in 1973.
Donors: Carnegie Corporation of New York; Spencer Foundation.
Foundation type: Operating foundation.
Financial data (yr. ended 12/31/12): Assets, $6,769,453 (M); gifts received, $266,447; expenditures, $2,736,370; qualifying distributions, $2,630,550; giving activities include $1,583,750 for 61 grants (high: $55,000; low: $12,500).
Purpose and activities: Awards fellowships to dissertation completion and to recent recipients of Ph.D., Ed.D., or equivalent degrees planning to study matters relevant to the improvement of education.
Fields of interest: Education, research; Education.
Type of support: Fellowships.
Limitations: Applications accepted. Giving on an international basis. No support for organizations.
Publications: Application guidelines; Informational brochure.
Application information: Applications must be in English. Application guidelines are available on The Academy's web site. Application form required.
Initial approach: Letter, telephone, e-mail, or download application from web site
Deadline(s): See web site for details
Board meeting date(s): Spring and fall
Final notification: Mid-May
Officers and Directors:* Michael Feuer,* Pres.; James Pellegrino,* V.P.; Catherine Snow,* Secy.-Treas.; Gregory White, Exec. Dir.; Greg Duncan; Margaret Eisenhart; Susan H. Fuhrman; **Pamela Grossman**; Kenji Hakuta; Margaret Beale Spencer; Claude Steele.
Number of staff: 4 full-time professional; 2 part-time professional.
EIN: 770415802
Other changes: Michael Feuer has replaced Susan H. Fuhrman as Pres. James Pellegrino has replaced Edward Haertel as V.P. Catherine Snow has replaced Susan Moore Johnson as Secy.-Treas. Edward Haertel is no longer V.P. Jacquelynne Eccles is no longer a director.

675
National Public Education Foundation
1825 K St. N.W., Ste. 400
Washington, DC **20006**

Donors: Margaret & Richard Lipmanson Foundation; Liselotte Leeds; Gerard Leeds.
Foundation type: Independent foundation.
Financial data (yr. ended 03/31/13): Assets, $6,465,020 (M); gifts received, $20,000; expenditures, $314,012; qualifying distributions, $302,486; giving activities include $300,000 for 1 grant.
Fields of interest: Education.
Limitations: Applications not accepted. Giving primarily in DC and MA.
Application information: Unsolicited requests for funds not accepted.
Officers and Directors:* Daniel H. Leeds,* Pres.; Sunita Leeds,* Secy.-Treas.; Gerard G. Leeds; Liselotte J. Leeds; **Michelle Leeds.**
EIN: 262818981

676
New Futures
(formerly Allen Gould Youth & Family Learning Association, Inc.)
805 15th St. N.W., Ste. 100
Washington, DC 20005-2232 **(202) 384-5854**
Contact: Michael Gould
***E-mail:* info@newfuturesdc.org**; Main URL: http://www.newfuturesdc.org
Facebook: http://www.facebook.com/pages/NEW-FUTURES-Transforming-lives-through-learning/112970223155?ref=ts

Reclassified as a private foundation in 2001 in DC.
Donors: Citybridge Foundation; Junior League of Washington; Morris and Gwendolyn Cafritz Foundation; Sunrise Foundation; The Arcana Foundation; The Lodestar Foundation; United Way of the NATL Capital Area; Betsy Banks; Greg Banks; Hemingway Foundation; Capital One; The Weissberg Foundation; IMF Civic Program; May and Stanley Smith Charitable Trust; Sonya Memorial Trust Fund; Armeane Choksi; Catalogue for Philanthropy; John Edward Fowler Memorial Foundation; Paul Giordano.
Foundation type: Independent foundation.
Financial data (yr. ended 12/31/12): Assets, $1,518,373 (M); gifts received, $736,933; expenditures, $400,972; qualifying distributions, $218,159; giving activities include $218,159 for 9 grants (high: $94,122; low: $1,486).
Purpose and activities: Scholarship funds provided in partnership with community organizations to help very low income, at risk young people complete their post-secondary education and become financially self-sufficient.
Fields of interest: Education; Youth; Economically disadvantaged.
Type of support: Scholarship funds.
Limitations: Applications not accepted. Giving primarily in Washington, DC.
Publications: Annual report.
Application information: Unsolicited requests for funds not accepted.
Officers and Directors:* Greg Banks,* Chair.; Michael Gould,* Pres.; Barbara Kafka,* Vice-Chair.; Michael Kershow,* Secy.; Christina Dykstra Mead,* Treas.; Martina Bradford; Lauren Cross; Donna Gerstenfeld; **Emily Leveille**; Romana Li; Earl McJett; Mark Popofsky; Ilene Rosenthal; Emily van Agtmael.
EIN: 522180378
Other changes: Michael Kershow has replaced Christina Dykstra Mead as Secy. Christina Dykstra Mead has replaced Steve Ettinger as Treas. Christina Dykstra Mead replaced Steve Ettinger as Treas. Michael Kershow replaced Christina Dykstra Mead as Secy. Kristen Desanti and Laura Hinz are no longer directors.

677
The Palmer Foundation
1201 Connecticut Ave. N.W., Ste. 300
Washington, DC **20036-2656**
FAX: (202) 833-5540;
E-mail: admin@thepalmerfoundation.org; Main URL: http://www.thepalmerfoundation.org

Established in 1990 in IL.
Donors: Rogers Palmer‡; Mary Palmer‡; Mary P. Enroth.
Foundation type: Independent foundation.
Financial data (yr. ended 12/31/12): Assets, $14,380,061 (M); gifts received, $200,000; expenditures, $697,275; qualifying distributions, $652,906; giving activities include $498,000 for 27 grants (high: $60,000; low: $1,000).
Purpose and activities: Giving primarily for youth, the environment and public health.
Fields of interest: Environment; Public health; Human services; Children/youth; Youth.
International interests: Guatemala; Mexico.
Type of support: Program development; Matching/challenge support.
Limitations: Applications not accepted. Giving limited to the Midwest states of: IL and WI, and the Mid Atlantic states of: MD, NC, VA, and in Washington, DC, unless one of the foundation's directors has a personal interest elsewhere. No support for lobbying, sectarian religious purposes, individual medical purposes, or for scientific research. No grants to individuals, or for multi-year grants, endowment drives, operational support, annual campaigns, or salaries.
Publications: Annual report; Grants list; Program policy statement.
Application information: Unsolicited requests for funds not accepted.
Board meeting date(s): Apr. and Oct.
Officers: Mary P. Enroth, Chair.; Karen E. Lischick, Pres.; Susan Le Mieux Enroth, V.P.; Jay L. Owen, Secy.; Peter Lischick, Treas.
Director: Charlly Enroth.
Number of staff: 1 part-time support.
EIN: 363700897
Other changes: Karen E. Lischick has replaced Mary P. Enroth as Pres. Susan Le Mieux Enroth has replaced Karen E. Lischick as V.P.
Mary P. Enroth is now Chair. Jay L. Owen is now Secy. Matthew Lischick is no longer a director.

678

Alicia Patterson Foundation

1090 Vermont Ave. NW, Ste. 1000
Washington, DC 20005-4965 (202) 393-5995
Contact: Margaret Engel, Exec. Dir.
FAX: (301) 951-8512;
E-mail: info@aliciapatterson.org; Main URL: http://aliciapatterson.org/
Blog: http://aliciapatterson.org/blog
Facebook: https://www.facebook.com/pages/Alicia-Patterson-Foundation/38469057147

Incorporated in 1960 in NY.
Donors: Alicia Patterson‡; Cissy Patterson Foundation; Aria Foundation.
Foundation type: Operating foundation.
Financial data (yr. ended 12/31/13): Assets, $5,537,766 (M); gifts received, $60,000; expenditures, $432,635; qualifying distributions, $420,201; giving activities include $40,000 for 1 grant, and $234,775 for 10 grants to individuals (high: $40,000; low: $3,333).
Purpose and activities: Grants one-year fellowships for a small number of print journalists and photojournalists to examine and write about areas or problems of special interest; candidates must be U.S. citizens who have been working professionally as print journalists for five years or longer.
Fields of interest: Media, print publishing; Adults.
Type of support: Fellowships.
Publications: Application guidelines; Annual report; Grants list; Informational brochure; Newsletter.
Application information: Application guidelines available on foundation web site. Application form required.
Initial approach: Typewritten statement not exceeding 3 single-spaced pages. Contact foundation for full submission details
Copies of proposal: 3
Deadline(s): Submit proposal between June and Sept.; deadline Oct. 1
Board meeting date(s): Annually in Dec.
Final notification: Early Dec.
Officers: Joseph M.P. Albright, Chair.; Alice Arlen, Pres.; Adam Albright, Treas.; Margaret Engel, Exec. Dir.
Trustees: Anne K. Albright; Kai Bird; Patrick Hoge; Robert Lee Hotz; Tom Kunkel; Michael Massing; Geneva Overholser.
Number of staff: 1 part-time professional.
EIN: 136092124
Other changes: The grantmaker now makes its application guidelines available online.

679

Rumsfeld Foundation

1718 M St. N.W., No. 366
Washington, DC 20036-4504
***E-mail:* contact@rumsfeldfoundation.org**; Main URL: http://rumsfeldfoundation.org/
Facebook: https://www.facebook.com/rumsfeldfoundation
LinkedIn: http://www.linkedin.com/company/rumsfeld-foundation
Twitter: https://twitter.com/RumsfeldOffice

Established in 2007 in DC.
Donors: Donald H. Rumsfeld; Joyce P. Rumsfeld; Ralph Eberhart; Joyce and Donald Rumsfeld Foundation; DHR Holdings, LLC; Charity Buzz; Infosoft Group, Inc.; Morgan Stanley; Forrest Fenn; Data Tresary Charitable Foundation.
Foundation type: Independent foundation.
Financial data (yr. ended 12/31/12): Assets, $11,482,329 (M); gifts received, $827,560; expenditures, $1,832,727; qualifying distributions, $1,588,931; giving activities include $1,588,931 for 79 grants (high: $281,912; low: $40).
Fields of interest: Higher education; Human services; International affairs, research; Military/veterans' organizations.
Limitations: Applications not accepted. Giving in the U.S., with emphasis on Washington, DC.
Application information: Unsolicited requests for funds not accepted.
Officers and Directors:* Donald H. Rumsfeld,* Pres. and Secy.; Joyce P. Rumsfeld,* V.P. and Treas.; Edward G. Biester, Jr.; **Dr. Steve Cambone**; Lawrence Di Rita.
EIN: 260580915
Other changes: The grantmaker has moved from IL to DC.

680

Sasakawa Peace Foundation U.S.A. Inc

1819 L St., N.W., Ste. 300
Washington, DC 20036-3855 (202) 296-6694
FAX: (202) 296-8272; E-mail: info@spfusa.org; Main URL: http://spfusa.org/

Established in 1990 in DC; funded in 1991.
Donors: Sasakawa Peace Foundation; Christy's Charity; Community Foundation of Nat'l Capit; Japanese American National Museum; Pratima Gupta; George F. Russell; United Biosource Corp Speciality Cli; Sasakawa Peace Foundation Tokyo.
Foundation type: Operating foundation.
Financial data (yr. ended 03/31/13): Assets, $16,055,646 (M); gifts received, $296,877; expenditures, $1,962,540; qualifying distributions, $890,456; giving activities include $81,060 for 6 grants (high: $28,000; low: $340), and $480,574 for 3 foundation-administered programs.
Purpose and activities: The mission of the foundation is to introduce elements of contemporary Japanese society and culture to the people of the U.S. The foundation provides a full-service library and art gallery, both of which are open to the public.
Fields of interest: Education; Safety/disasters; Human services.
Limitations: Applications not accepted. Giving primarily in Tokyo, Japan; some giving also in Los Angeles, CA, Washington, DC, New York, NY, and Bangkok, Thailand.
Application information: Unsolicited requests for funds not accepted.
Officers: Jiro Hanyu, Chair.; Junko Chano, Pres.; Tatsuya Tanami, Secy.; Akinori Sugai, Treas.
Directors: Masahiro Akiyama; Takahiro Nanri.
EIN: 521728688
Other changes: Keiji Iwatake is no longer a director.

681

Searle Freedom Trust

(formerly D & D Foundation)
1055 Thomas Jefferson St. N.W., Ste. L26
Washington, DC 20007-5259 (202) 375-7820
Contact: Kimberly O. Dennis, C.E.O. and Pres.
FAX: (202) 375-7821; Kim Berly O. Dennis, C.E.O. and Pres. Phone: (202) 375-7822, and E-mail: Kdennis@searlefreedomtrust.org; Main URL: http://www.searlefreedomtrust.org

Established in 1998 in IL.
Donor: Daniel C. Searle‡.
Foundation type: Independent foundation.
Financial data (yr. ended 12/31/12): Assets, $111,578,641 (M); gifts received, $13,817; expenditures, $18,747,813; qualifying distributions, $14,912,835; giving activities include $14,001,422 for 102 grants (high: $1,500,000; low: $9,218).
Purpose and activities: The trust aims to foster research and encourage public policies that promote individual freedom and economic liberty while at the same time advancing a commitment to personal responsibility and a respect for traditional American values. One of the foundation's chief objectives is to help develop policies that advance liberty without encouraging license, and that demand personal responsibility without compromising freedom. Issues the foundation supports include: Tax and budget issues, cost-benefit analysis of regulatory practices, welfare policy, K-12 reform, environmental policy, and legal reform.
Fields of interest: Elementary/secondary education; Higher education; Environment, public policy; Social sciences; Welfare policy/reform; Public affairs.
Type of support: Conferences/seminars; Publication; Fellowships; Research.
Limitations: Applications accepted. Giving on a national basis. No support for for-profit organizations. No grants to individuals, or for endowments, operating support capital campaigns, or building projects.
Application information:
Initial approach: Online grant proposal
Board meeting date(s): Apr., July and Nov.
Officer and Trustees:* Kimberly O. Dennis,* C.E.O. and Pres.; D. Gideon Searle; Kinship Trust Co.
EIN: 367244615
Other changes: Kimberly O. Dennis is now C.E.O. and Pres.

682

Alexander and Margaret Stewart Trust

888 17th St. N.W., Ste. 610
Washington, DC 20006-3321 (202) 785-9892
Contact: Lori A. Jackson, Exec. Mgr.
FAX: (202) 785-0918;
E-mail: ljackson@stewart-trust.org; Main URL: http://www.stewart-trust.org
RSS Feed: http://www.stewart-trust.org/?feed=rss2

Trust established in 1947 in DC; in 1997 combined with the Helen S. Devore Trust that was established in 1960.
Donors: Helen S. Devore‡; Mary E. Stewart‡.
Foundation type: Independent foundation.
Financial data (yr. ended 12/31/12): Assets, $96,846,721 (M); expenditures, $4,806,174; qualifying distributions, $4,661,304; giving activities include $4,366,074 for 49+ grants (high: $400,000).
Purpose and activities: Giving for the care, prevention, and treatment of cancer, and for the care of children who are physically or mentally ill or handicapped; and research, education, or prevention of diseases common to childhood, including societal behavioral patterns having a negative impact on the welfare of children.
Fields of interest: Health care, infants; Health care; Cancer; Children/youth, services; Economically disadvantaged.
Type of support: General/operating support; Continuing support; Equipment; Program development; Research.
Limitations: Applications accepted. Giving primarily in the Washington, DC, area. No grants to individuals, or for endowment funds, annual campaigns, building funds, land acquisition, renovation projects, scholarships, or fellowships.

Publications: Application guidelines; Grants list.
Application information: Applications by invitation only, upon review of initial Letter of Inquiry. Applicants who have received a grant from the trust within the past three years already pre-quality, and may submit an application through foundation web site. Application form required.
Initial approach: **Online Letter of Inquiry form on foundation web site**
Copies of proposal: 1
Deadline(s): See foundation web site for current deadline
Board meeting date(s): Monthly
Final notification: Usually by late Dec.
Officer: Lori A. Jackson, Exec. Mgr.
Trustees: William J. Bierbower; George Hamilton; Rockefeller Trust Co., N.A.
Number of staff: 1 full-time professional.
EIN: 526020260

683
Wallace Genetic Foundation, Inc.
4910 Massachusetts Ave., NW, Ste. 221
Washington, DC 20016-4368 (202) 966-2932
Contact: Patricia Lee, Co-Exec. Dir.; Carolyn Sand, Co-Exec. Dir.
FAX: (202) 966-3370;
E-mail: info@wallacegenetic.org; Additional e-mail: president@wallacegenetic.org; Main URL: http://www.wallacegenetic.org

Incorporated in 1959 in NY.
Donors: Henry A. Wallace†; Jean Douglas.
Foundation type: Independent foundation.
Financial data (yr. ended 12/31/12): Assets, $153,434,358 (M); expenditures, $8,498,534; qualifying distributions, $7,656,689; giving activities include $7,328,000 for 146 grants (high: $300,000; low: $10,000).
Purpose and activities: Areas of interest are sustainable agriculture, protection of farmland near cities, plant genetic research, biodiversity protection, and environmental education.
Fields of interest: Environment, natural resources; Environmental education; Public health, clean water supply; Agriculture; Public policy, research.
International interests: Latin America; Soviet Union.
Type of support: General/operating support; Continuing support; Land acquisition; Program development; Seed money; Research; Matching/challenge support.
Limitations: Applications accepted. Giving on a national basis. No grants to individuals, or for scholarships, endowments, multi-year commitments, or university overhead expenses; no loans.
Publications: Grants list.
Application information: Faxed or e-mailed proposals will not be accepted; application guidelines available on foundation web site. Application form not required.
Initial approach: 1- or 2-page letter and proposal
Copies of proposal: 1
Deadline(s): None
Board meeting date(s): Six times a year
Final notification: None
Officers and Directors:* Joan D. Murray,* Pres.; Ann D. Cornell,* V.P. and Secy.; David W. Douglas,* V.P. and Treas.; Patricia Lee, Co-Exec. Dir.; Carolyn H. Sand, Co-Exec. Dir.
Number of staff: 2 part-time professional.
EIN: 136162575

684
Wallace Global Fund II
1990 M. St., NW, Ste. 250
Washington, DC 20036-3430 (202) 452-1530
FAX: (202) 452-0922; E-mail: tkroll@wgf.org; Main URL: http://www.wgf.org
Wallace Global Fund II's Philanthropy's Promise: http://www.ncrp.org/philanthropys-promise/who

Foundation type: Independent foundation.
Financial data (yr. ended 12/31/12): Assets, $155,471,213 (M); expenditures, $10,122,114; qualifying distributions, $8,875,955; giving activities include $7,413,625 for 146 grants (high: $150,000; low: $500).
Purpose and activities: The fund's mission is to promote an informed and engaged citizenry to fight injustice, and to protect the diversity of native and the natural systems upon which all life depends.
Fields of interest: Environment; Public affairs.
Type of support: General/operating support; Management development/capacity building; Program development; Program evaluation; Matching/challenge support.
Publications: Grants list; Occasional report.
Application information: No e-mail or mailed proposals accepted; application guidelines available on foundation web site. Application form required.
Initial approach: Letter of inquiry, no more than 2 pages, submitted via foundation web site.
Deadline(s): Quarterly, in Mar., June, Sept., and Dec.
Board meeting date(s): Quarterly
Officer: Ellen Dorsey, Exec. Dir.
Directors: Scott Fitzmorris; Annie Leonard; Christy Wallace; Scott Wallace.
Number of staff: 3 full-time professional; 2 part-time professional.
EIN: 800424607

685
The Wyss Medical Foundation, Inc.
(formerly The Wyss Peace Foundation, Inc.)
1601 Connecticut Ave., N.W., Ste. 802
Washington, DC 20009-1055 (202) 232-4418
Hansjorg Wyss' Giving Pledge Profile: http://glasspockets.org/philanthropy-in-focus/eye-on-the-giving-pledge/profiles#w

Donor: Hansjoerg Wyss.
Foundation type: Independent foundation.
Financial data (yr. ended 12/31/13): Assets, $86,444,416 (M); expenditures, $3,413,559; qualifying distributions, $3,407,074; giving activities include $3,336,600 for 6 grants (high: $1,000,000; low: $100,000).
Fields of interest: Higher education; Education; Health care; Orthopedics; Spine disorders research; International peace/security; Civil/human rights.
Limitations: Applications not accepted. Giving primarily in Switzerland; some giving also in Washington, DC, Philadelphia, PA, Layton, UT, and Richland, WA.
Application information: Contributes only to pre-selected organizations.
Officers: Patricia Davis, Secy.; Joseph Fisher, Treas.
Directors: David Helfet; Steve Schwartz; Hansjoerg Wyss.
EIN: 263962795
Other changes: Robert Bland is no longer a director.

FLORIDA

686
A. & R. Charitable Foundation, Inc.
c/o Robert D. Falese, Jr.
10661 Copper Lake Dr.
Bonita Springs, FL 34135-8438

Established in 2005 in NJ.
Donors: Robert D. Falese; Robert D. Falese, Jr.
Foundation type: Independent foundation.
Financial data (yr. ended 06/30/13): Assets, $43,719 (M); gifts received, $153,939; expenditures, $175,228; qualifying distributions, $170,000; giving activities include $170,000 for 4 grants (high: $105,000; low: $10,000).
Fields of interest: Higher education, university; Education; Human services; Christian agencies & churches.
Limitations: Applications not accepted. Giving primarily in NJ and PA. No grants to individuals.
Application information: Contributes only to pre-selected organizations.
Officer: Robert D. Falese, Jr., Pres.
EIN: 201647309

687
Alpha Foundation, Inc.
c/o John R. Wynn
P.O. Box 3688
Fort Pierce, FL 34948-3688
E-mail: info@alphafoundationhsv.org; **Application address: c/o John Wynn, 2101 Clinton Ave., Huntsville, AL 35805**; Main URL: http://alphafoundationhsv.org

Donor: Lonnie S. McMillian.
Foundation type: Operating foundation.
Financial data (yr. ended 12/31/12): Assets, $43,853,927 (M); expenditures, $2,899,626; qualifying distributions, $2,485,000; giving activities include $2,485,000 for 18 grants (high: $890,000; low: $5,000).
Purpose and activities: Giving primarily for education, youth development, and human services.
Fields of interest: Education; Medical research; Youth development; Human services; Homeless, human services; Protestant agencies & churches.
Limitations: Applications accepted. **Giving primarily in Huntsville, AL.** No support for churches and religious organizations for projects that primarily benefit their own members or adherence. No grants to individuals, or for event tickets, productions, performances, dinners, conferences or seminars, or for debt.
Publications: Application guidelines.
Application information: Application form not required.
Initial approach: Letter
Copies of proposal: 2
Deadline(s): None
Directors and Officers:* Lonnie M. McMillian,* Pres.; Hellen W. McMillian, V.P.; Glynda Cavalcanti, Treas.; Barbara M. Fisk; **Kelly Fisk; Lonnie Key; Robert Key; Emily M. Robertson**; Andy Whitehead; Susan M. Whitehead; John R. Wynn.
EIN: 631188643
Other changes: Lonnie M. McMillian is now Pres. Hellen W. McMillian is now V.P. Glynda Cavalcanti is now Treas.
The grantmaker now publishes application guidelines.

688
The Anna Fund, Inc.
Lauderdale By The Sea, FL

The foundation terminated on Dec. 7, 2011.

689
Ansin Foundation
P.O. Box 610727
N. Miami, FL 33261-0727

Established in 1957.
Donors: Sunbeam Television Corp.; WHDH-TV, Inc.; Sunbeam Development Corp.; Sunbeam Properties, Inc.; Edmund N. Ansin.
Foundation type: Company-sponsored foundation.
Financial data (yr. ended 12/31/13): Assets, $55,850,601 (M); gifts received, $1,000,000; expenditures, $1,703,567; qualifying distributions, $1,667,432; giving activities include $1,667,432 for 45 grants (high: $530,000; low: $100).
Purpose and activities: The foundation supports hospitals and organizations involved with arts and culture, education, youth development, and community development.
Fields of interest: Museums (art); Performing arts, ballet; Performing arts, theater; Arts; Secondary school/education; Higher education; Education, services; Education; Hospitals (general); Boys & girls clubs; Community/economic development; United Ways and Federated Giving Programs.
Type of support: General/operating support; Scholarship funds.
Limitations: Applications not accepted. Giving primarily in FL and Boston, MA. No grants to individuals.
Application information: Contributes only to pre-selected organizations.
Trustee: Edmund N. Ansin.
EIN: 046046113

690
The Applebaum Foundation, Inc.
11111 Biscayne Blvd., Twr. 3, Apt. 853
North Miami, FL 33181-3404

Incorporated in 1949 in NY.
Donors: Joseph Applebaum‡; Leila Applebaum.
Foundation type: Independent foundation.
Financial data (yr. ended 02/28/13): Assets, $46,420,683 (M); gifts received, $522,900; expenditures, $2,432,255; qualifying distributions, $2,306,500; giving activities include $2,301,000 for 66 grants (high: $600,000; low: $500).
Purpose and activities: Giving primarily for higher education, hospitals and medical research, and to Jewish organizations, including welfare agencies, schools, and temple support; some funding for children, youth, and social services.
Fields of interest: Elementary/secondary education; Higher education; Medical school/education; Hospitals (general); Health organizations, association; Pediatrics; Medical research, institute; Cancer research; Human services; Children/youth, services; Jewish federated giving programs; Jewish agencies & synagogues.
Limitations: Applications not accepted. Giving primarily in Miami, FL and in the metropolitan New York, NY area. No grants to individuals.
Application information: Contributes only to pre-selected organizations.
Officers and Directors:* Leila Applebaum,* C.E.O. and Treas.; Warren Weiss, Esq.*, Pres.; Alan T. Applebaum,* V.P. and Secy.; Judy Borger,* V.P.; Jane Weiss.
EIN: 591002714
Other changes: For the fiscal year ended Feb. 28, 2013, the grantmaker paid grants of $2,301,000, a 71.5% increase over the fiscal 2012 disbursements, $1,341,700.

691
Ted Arison Family Foundation USA, Inc.
(formerly Arison Foundation, Inc.)
c/o Safo, LLC
20900 N. E. 30th Ave., Ste. 1015
Aventura, FL 33180-2166 (305) 891-0017
E-mail: hanna@SAFOUSA.com; **Main URL: http://www.shariarison.com/en/content/ted-arison-family-foundation**

Incorporated in 1981 in FL.
Donors: Carnival Cruise Lines, Inc.; Festivale Maritime, Inc.; Intercon Overseas, Inc.; Ted Arison Charitable Trust.
Foundation type: Independent foundation.
Financial data (yr. ended 12/31/12): Assets, $471,347,559 (M); gifts received, $345,175; expenditures, $22,185,780; qualifying distributions, $21,744,763; giving activities include $15,569,705 for 59 grants (high: $3,638,922; low: $5,000).
Purpose and activities: Emphasis on arts and cultural programs; support also for Jewish welfare funds.
Fields of interest: Arts; Education; Health care; Human services; Children/youth, services; Jewish federated giving programs; Disabilities, people with.
Limitations: Applications accepted. Giving primarily in NY and Israel.
Publications: Grants list.
Application information:
Initial approach: Letter
Deadline(s): None
Officers and Trustees:* Jason Arison,* Chair.; Shlomit de Vries, C.E.O.; Rachel Cohen, Deputy C.E.O. and C.F.O.; Kaynan Rabino, V.P., Vision Ventures; Cassie Arison; David Arison; Marilyn Arison; Shari Arison Glazer.
EIN: 592128429
Other changes: Jason Arison has replaced Shari Arison Glazer as Chair. Shlomit de Vries has replaced Jason Arison as C.E.O.
Arnaldo Perez is no longer V.P.

692
The Around Foundation
748 Windsor Ln.
Key West, FL 33040-6441
***Contact:* J. Gleick**

Established in 1997 in NY.
Donor: James Gleick.
Foundation type: Independent foundation.
Financial data (yr. ended 04/30/13): Assets, $4,890,401 (M); expenditures, $243,182; qualifying distributions, $234,500; giving activities include $234,500 for 32 grants (high: $15,000; low: $500).
Fields of interest: Media, radio; Arts; Education; Human services; International human rights.
Limitations: Applications not accepted. Giving primarily in NY. No grants to individuals.
Application information: Contributes only to pre-selected organizations.
Trustees: Cynthia Crossen; James Gleick.
EIN: 113377271

693
The Atkins Foundation, Inc.
(formerly The PBSJ Foundation, Inc.)
4030 W. Boy Scout Blvd., Ste. 700
Tampa, FL 33607-1757

Foundation type: Operating foundation.
Financial data (yr. ended 12/31/12): Assets, $536,599 (M); gifts received, $129,229; expenditures, $297,049; qualifying distributions, $297,049; giving activities include $295,565 for 54 grants (high: $31,000; low: $500).
Fields of interest: Higher education, university; Scholarships/financial aid; Education.
Limitations: Applications not accepted. Giving in the U.S., with emphasis on FL. No grants to individuals.
Application information: Contributes only to pre-selected organizations.
Officers: C. Ernest Edgar, Secy.; **Judith Aldrovandi, Cont.**; **Carol L. Craft, Admin.**
Directors: John Buckley; **Marvin N. Fisher**; **Richard W. Galloway**; Cecilia Green; Victor P. Poteat.
EIN: 204235058

694
The Azeez Foundation
(formerly The Michael and Kathleen Azeez Foundation)
2187 Marseille Dr.
Palm Beach Gardens, FL 33410-1279

Established in 1998 in NJ.
Donors: Michael Azeez; Kathleen Azeez; Anne Azeez.
Foundation type: Independent foundation.
Financial data (yr. ended 12/31/12): Assets, $12,179,737 (M); expenditures, $952,617; qualifying distributions, $764,339; giving activities include $764,333 for 49 grants (high: $214,990; low: $485).
Purpose and activities: Giving primarily to Jewish organizations, including a Jewish history museum.
Fields of interest: Museums (ethnic/folk arts); Health care; Human services; Jewish federated giving programs; Jewish agencies & synagogues.
Limitations: Applications not accepted. Giving primarily in NJ; funding also in CA, CO, Washington, DC, and FL. No grants to individuals.
Application information: Contributes only to pre-selected organizations.
Directors and Officers:* Michael Azeez,* Chair. and Pres.; Kathleen Azeez, Secy.; Anne Azeez, Treas.
EIN: 232967146
Other changes: Anne Azeez is now Treas. Kathleen Azeez is now Secy. Michael Azeez is now Chair. and Pres.

695
Bank of America Client Foundation
(also known as BOA Client Foundation)
50 Central Ave., Ste. 750, MC FL4-234-07-01
Sarasota, FL 34236-5743 (941) 951-4103
***Contact:* Maryann L. Smith, V.P.**
E-mail: maryann.l.smith@ustrust.com; **Main URL: http://fdnweb.org/boacf**
Grants List: http://fdnweb.org/boacf/grants/category/annual-grants/

Established in 1961 in FL as the Sarasota Bank and Trust Company Community Foundation.
Donors: Eileen Kroeger; Julius Brandenburg†; Leona Hughes†.
Foundation type: Independent foundation.
Financial data (yr. ended 12/31/12): Assets, $16,346,446 (M); expenditures, $772,538; qualifying distributions, $659,210; giving activities include $569,763 for 40 grants (high: $37,500; low: $315), and $117,500 for 4 foundation-administered programs.
Purpose and activities: Giving primarily for the arts, education, human services, natural science, youth and family organizations, and historic preservation.
Fields of interest: Media, film/video; Visual arts; Museums; Performing arts; Performing arts, dance; Performing arts, theater; Humanities; Historic preservation/historical societies; Arts; Education, early childhood education; Child development, education; Elementary school/education; Secondary school/education; Vocational education; Higher education; Adult education—literacy, basic skills & GED; Education, reading; Education; Environment, natural resources; Environment; Reproductive health, family planning; Health care; Mental health/crisis services; Health organizations, association; AIDS; Crime/violence prevention, youth; Recreation; Human services; Children/youth, services; Child development, services; Family services; Residential/custodial care, hospices; Aging, centers/services; Women, centers/services; Minorities/immigrants, centers/services; Homeless, human services; Urban/community development; Community/economic development; Marine science; Protestant agencies & churches; Aging; Disabilities, people with; Minorities; Women; Economically disadvantaged; Homeless.
Type of support: Building/renovation; Equipment; Program development; Matching/challenge support.
Limitations: Applications accepted. Giving limited to organizations operating in or providing services to residents of Sarasota County, FL and DE. No support for individual schools or child care facilities. No grants to individuals, or for general operating expenses, endowment or annual giving campaigns, debt reduction or financing, conferences, seminars, workshops, travel, surveys or advertising.
Publications: Application guidelines.
Application information: Electronic transmittals are not acceptable. Applications must have arrived by deadline. See web site for full application guidelines. Application form required.
Initial approach: Proposal
Copies of proposal: 10
Deadline(s): Apr. 15 and Sept. 15
Board meeting date(s): End of June and Nov.
Final notification: Within 3 to 4 months after the deadline
Trustee: Bank of America, N.A.
EIN: 596142753

696
Bartner Family Foundation Trust
601 Heritage Dr., Ste. 484
Jupiter, FL 33458-2777

Established in 2000 in CT.
Donors: Robert G. Bartner; Beverly D.N. Bartner; Nicole Bartner; Jennifer Indeck; Arabella Higgins.
Foundation type: Independent foundation.
Financial data (yr. ended 12/31/12): Assets, $388,660 (M); gifts received, $283,811; expenditures, $249,422; qualifying distributions, $247,945; giving activities include $246,080 for 7 grants (high: $134,930; low: $750).
Purpose and activities: Giving primarily for the arts; funding also for education and human services.
Fields of interest: Performing arts; Performing arts, orchestras; Performing arts, opera; Arts; Education; Human services.
Limitations: Applications not accepted. Giving primarily in FL and NY; some funding also in CT. No grants to individuals.
Application information: Unsolicited requests for funds not accepted.
Trustees: Beverly D.N. Bartner; Robert G. Bartner; Nicole Bartner Graff; Arabella Bartner Higgins; Jennifer Bartner Indeck.
EIN: 137235081
Other changes: The grantmaker has moved from VI to FL.

697
The Batchelor Foundation, Inc.
1680 Michigan Ave., No. PH 1
Miami Beach, FL 33139-2538 (305) 534-5004
Contact: Anne O. Batchelor-Robjohns, Co-C.E.O.

Established in 1990 in FL.
Donors: International Air Leases, Inc.; Batchelor Enterprises; George E. Batchelor†.
Foundation type: Company-sponsored foundation.
Financial data (yr. ended 06/30/13): Assets, $352,753,085 (M); gifts received, $40,125,144; expenditures, $23,057,999; qualifying distributions, $20,281,144; giving activities include $19,674,515 for 192 grants (high: $3,520,000; low: $800).
Purpose and activities: The foundation supports organizations involved with arts and culture, education, animals and wildlife, health, agriculture and food, housing, recreation, human services, and economically disadvantaged people. Special emphasis is directed toward programs designed to engage in medical research and provide care for childhood diseases; and promote study, preservation, and public awareness of the natural environment.
Fields of interest: Museums; Arts; Higher education; Education; Environment, research; Environment, public education; Environment, natural resources; Botanical gardens; Environment; Animals/wildlife, preservation/protection; Zoos/zoological societies; Animals/wildlife; Hospitals (general); Health care; Diabetes research; Medical research; Food services; Agriculture/food; Housing/shelter, development; Recreation; Boy scouts; YM/YWCAs & YM/YWHAs; Children/youth, services; Homeless, human services; Human services; United Ways and Federated Giving Programs; Economically disadvantaged.
Type of support: General/operating support; Continuing support; Capital campaigns; Endowments; Program development; Matching/challenge support.
Limitations: Applications accepted. Giving primarily in Miami, FL. No grants to individuals.
Application information: Application form not required.
Initial approach: Letter of inquiry
Deadline(s): None
Officers and Trustees:* Anne O. Batchelor-Robjohns,* Co-C.E.O.; Daniel J. Ferraresi,* Co-C.E.O.; Jon Batchelor, Exec. V.P.; Nancy Ansley, C.F.O.; Caridad Velasco, Cont.; Jack Falk.
EIN: 650188171
Other changes: At the close of 2013, the grantmaker paid grants of $19,674,515, a 88.2% increase over the 2012 disbursements, $10,451,744.

698
The James E. and Constance L. Bell Foundation, Inc.
(formerly Bell Foundation, Inc.)
11450 Southeast Dixie Hwy., Ste. 208
Hobe Sound, FL **33455-5235**

Established in 1984 in FL.
Donors: James E. Bell; Constance L. Bell.
Foundation type: Independent foundation.
Financial data (yr. ended 06/30/13): Assets, $0 (M); expenditures, $322,424; qualifying distributions, $272,975; giving activities include $272,975 for 67 grants (high: $95,000; low: $100).
Purpose and activities: Giving primarily for education, social services, federated giving programs, and Episcopal and Presbyterian churches and organizations.
Fields of interest: Higher education; Education; Health care; Boys & girls clubs; Human services; Community/economic development; Foundations (community); United Ways and Federated Giving Programs; Protestant agencies & churches.
Type of support: General/operating support.
Limitations: Applications not accepted. Giving primarily in CT, FL, NC, and PA. No grants to individuals.
Application information: Contributes only to pre-selected organizations.
Officers & Directors:* Constance B. Moser,* Pres.; Constance L. Bell,* V.P.; Stuart M. Bell,* Secy.-Treas.
EIN: 592473417

699
The Bennie & Martha Benjamin Foundation, Inc.
55 S.E. 2nd Ave., Ste. 301
Delray Beach, FL 33444-3615 (561) 243-1477
Contact: David A. Beale, Exec. Dir.
***E-mail:* info@benniebenjaminfoundation.org**; Main URL: http://www.benniebenjaminfoundation.org

Established in 1989 in NY.
Donor: Claude Benjamin†.
Foundation type: Independent foundation.
Financial data (yr. ended 10/31/12): Assets, $1,846,834 (M); expenditures, $258,282; qualifying distributions, $161,931; giving activities include $145,454 for 8 grants (high: $45,429; low: $615), and $3,128 for 4 grants to individuals (high: $1,000; low: $128).
Purpose and activities: Giving to improve health and health care facilities, as well as health-related educational systems in the U.S. Virgin Islands.
Fields of interest: Education; Health care; Human services.
Type of support: Building/renovation; Equipment; Program development; Conferences/seminars; Professorships; Fellowships; Internship funds; Scholarship funds; Scholarships—to individuals; Student loans—to individuals; Loans—to individuals.
Limitations: Applications accepted. Giving limited to the U.S. Virgin Islands.
Application information: See foundation web site for complete application guidelines. Application form required.
Deadline(s): None
Directors: Jack N. Albert; David A. Beale; Seymour Braun, Esq.
EIN: 133555717

700
Bi-Lo/Winn-Dixie Foundation, Inc.
5050 Edgewood Ct.
Jacksonville, FL 32254-3601 (904) 783-5000
Contact: Melissa Adams
Main URL: https://www.winndixie.com/CO/Community%20Events/Default.aspx
Grants List: https://www.winndixie.com/CO/Our%20Sponsorships/GrantRecipients2011.aspx

Incorporated in 1943 in FL.
Donors: PGA Tour Charities, Inc.; Winn-Dixie Stores, Inc.
Foundation type: Company-sponsored foundation.
Financial data (yr. ended 12/31/12): Assets, $1,438,037 (M); gifts received, $1,722,895; expenditures, $1,195,352; qualifying distributions, $1,157,646; giving activities include $1,157,646 for 105 grants (high: $100,000; low: $450).
Purpose and activities: The foundation supports organizations involved with education, health, hunger, and women.
Fields of interest: Elementary school/education; Higher education; Education; Hospitals (general); Health care, clinics/centers; Health care; Cancer; Food services; Food banks; Women.
Type of support: Continuing support; Annual campaigns; Building/renovation; Equipment; Program development; Conferences/seminars; Scholarship funds; Research; Employee matching gifts; Matching/challenge support.
Limitations: Applications accepted. Giving primarily in areas of company operations in AL, FL, GA, LA, and MS. No support for religious or political organizations or schools. No grants to individuals, or for capital campaigns, general operating support, multi-year commitments, capital campaigns, fundraising, or sponsorships.
Publications: Application guidelines; Grants list.
Application information: Application form required.
Initial approach: Download application form and mail proposal and application form to foundation
Copies of proposal: 3
***Deadline(s):* June 30**
Board meeting date(s): As required
Officers: Mary Kellmanson, Pres.; M. Sandlin Grimm, Secy.; D. Michael Byrum, Treas.
Director: Anthea Jones.
EIN: 590995428

701
Goldie & David Blanksteen Foundation
P.O. Box 43250
Jacksonville, FL 32203-3250
***Application address:* c/o David Blanksteen, 866 United Nations Plz., New York, NY 10017**

Established in 1995 in NY.
Donors: David Blanksteen; Goldie Blanksteen.
Foundation type: Independent foundation.
Financial data (yr. ended 06/30/13): Assets, $1,752,696 (M); expenditures, $158,372; qualifying distributions, $155,295; giving activities include $154,795 for 23 grants (high: $75,000; low: $50).
Fields of interest: Museums; Arts; Higher education; Graduate/professional education; Education; Human services; Jewish agencies & synagogues.
Type of support: General/operating support.
Limitations: Applications accepted. Giving primarily in New York, NY. No grants to individuals.
Application information: Application form required.
Initial approach: Letter
Deadline(s): None
Trustees: David Blanksteen; Goldie Blanksteen.
EIN: 137072675
Other changes: The grantmaker has moved from IL to FL.

702
Hilda Sutton & William D. Blanton Charitable Foundation, Inc.
200 Lake Morton Dr.
Lakeland, FL 33801-5318 (863) 688-7611
Contact: E. Snow Martin, Jr., V.P.

Established in 1993 in FL.
Donor: Hilda Sutton Blanton†.
Foundation type: Independent foundation.
Financial data (yr. ended 12/31/13): Assets, $4,859,164 (M); expenditures, $207,128; qualifying distributions, $151,600; giving activities include $151,600 for 17 grants (high: $55,000; low: $1,000).
Purpose and activities: Giving primarily for scholarships for the study of organ and church music, and for humanitarian causes.
Fields of interest: Performing arts, music; Performing arts, orchestras; Higher education; Athletics/sports, golf.
Type of support: General/operating support; Scholarship funds; Scholarships—to individuals.
Limitations: Applications accepted. Giving primarily in FL.
Application information: Contact foundation for application guidelines. Application form required.
***Initial approach:* Contact foundation**
Deadline(s): None
Officers and Directors:* E. Snow Martin, Jr.,* V.P.; Mettie Withers,* Secy.-Treas.; Beth Mason.
EIN: 593162785

703
Bohnert Foundation, Inc.
24 Dockside Ln., Ste. 209
Key Largo, FL 33037-5267

Established in 2002 in NJ.
Donor: Robert Manzo.
Foundation type: Independent foundation.
Financial data (yr. ended 12/31/12): Assets, $4,104,769 (M); expenditures, $210,909; qualifying distributions, $170,150; giving activities include $170,150 for 10 grants (high: $100,000; low: $1,650).
Fields of interest: Higher education; Education.
Limitations: Applications not accepted. Giving primarily in NJ and NY.
Application information: Contributes only to pre-selected organizations.
Officers: Robert Manzo, Pres.; Cynthia Manzo, V.P.
Trustee: Ellen Jacob Wraith.
EIN: 542072845
Other changes: The grantmaker has moved from NJ to FL.

704
Booth Foundation, Inc.
2001 Sailfish Point Blvd., No. 316
Stuart, FL 34996-1971

Established in 2004 in FL.
Donors: Alex E. Booth, Jr.; HTOOB, Inc.
Foundation type: Independent foundation.
Financial data (yr. ended 12/31/12): Assets, $23,368,076 (M); expenditures, $1,530,995;

qualifying distributions, $1,430,924; giving activities include $1,430,000 for 2 grants (high: $1,400,000; low: $30,000).
Purpose and activities: Giving primarily for Presbyterian churches.
Fields of interest: Protestant agencies & churches.
Limitations: Applications not accepted. Giving primarily in TN and WV. No grants to individuals.
Application information: Contributes only to pre-selected organizations.
Officers and Directors:* Alex E. Booth, Jr.,* Pres. and Treas.; Katherine Booth,* V.P.; Beth Terdo Prinz,* Secy.; William Bryant; **Susan Machamer.**
EIN: 200667161

705
Boston Center for Blind Children, Inc.
859 N.W. Sorrento Ln.
Port Saint Lucie, FL 34986-2199 (617) 296-4232
***Contact:* Donald E. Boucher, Grants Coordinator**
E-mail: info@bostoncenterforblindchildren.org; Main URL: http://www.bostoncenterforblindchildren.org

Established in 1901 in MA.
Donor: Evelyn L. Kendall Charitable Remainder.
Foundation type: Independent foundation.
Financial data (yr. ended 06/30/13): Assets, $4,491,362 (M); gifts received, $1,063; expenditures, $232,511; qualifying distributions, $212,780; giving activities include $212,780 for 14 grants (high: $40,000; low: $5,000).
Purpose and activities: Giving primarily to organizations that provide care, treatment, and services to blind, visually impaired, or otherwise disabled children as well as other children and families in need.
Fields of interest: Education; Recreation; Children, services; Blind/visually impaired.
Limitations: Applications accepted. Giving primarily in MA. No grants to individuals.
Publications: Application guidelines; Grants list.
Application information: Application guidelines available on foundation web site.
Deadline(s): **Apr. 15 and Oct. 15**
Board meeting date(s): **May and Nov.**
Officers: William G. McDevitt III, Pres.; Carol C. Cleven, Treas.
Directors: Caroline B. Grady; Anne V. McBride; John T. Bennett, Jr.
EIN: 042103910
Other changes: William G. McDevitt, III is now Pres.
The grantmaker now publishes application guidelines.

706
Harry L. Bradley, Jr. Charitable Fund
777 S. Flagler Dr., 8th Fl., West Tower
West Palm Beach, FL 33401-6161
E-mail: info@hlbjr.org; Main URL: http://www.hlbjrfund.org/

Established in 1981 in MA.
Donor: Mark S. Bradley Trust.
Foundation type: Independent foundation.
Financial data (yr. ended 06/30/13): Assets, $159,063,775 (M); gifts received, $750,000; expenditures, $4,411,704; qualifying distributions, $3,148,230; giving activities include $3,148,230 for 39 grants (high: $2,260,000; low: $500).
Purpose and activities: Giving primarily for education, human services, and Catholic organizations.
Fields of interest: Museums; Higher education; Law school/education; Education; Health organizations; Human services; Catholic agencies & churches.
Type of support: General/operating support.
Limitations: Applications not accepted. Giving primarily in MA, with emphasis on the Boston area. No grants to individuals.
Publications: IRS Form 990 or 990-PF printed copy available upon request.
Application information: Contributes only to pre-selected organizations. Unsolicited requests for funds not accepted.
Officer: Robert F. Morrissey, Exec. Dir.
Trustee: Robert J. Morrissey.
EIN: 042747025
Other changes: The grantmaker has moved from MA to FL.

707
Brown Shoe Co., Charitable Trust
(formerly Brown Group, Inc. Charitable Trust)
P.O. Box 1908
Orlando, FL 32802-1908 **(314) 854-4000**
***E-mail:* charitablegiving@brownshoe.com;**
Additional address: 8400 Maryland Ave., St. Louis, MO 36166; Main URL: http://brownshoe.com/brown-shoe-company/community/charitable-trust/

Trust established in 1951 in MO.
Donors: Brown Group Inc., Charitable Trust, Inc.; Brown Shoe Co., Inc.
Foundation type: Company-sponsored foundation.
Financial data (yr. ended 12/31/13): Assets, $5,468,919 (M); gifts received, $3,000,000; expenditures, $3,069,066; qualifying distributions, $3,057,483; giving activities include $3,043,752 for 113 grants (high: $2,000,000; low: $50).
Purpose and activities: The foundation supports programs designed to develop strong families through opportunity enrichment; encourage individuals to live better lives through health and wellness efforts; and provide occasions for families and individuals to step feet first into the arts and cultural opportunities in the community.
Fields of interest: Arts councils; Media, television; Museums (art); Performing arts, theater; Performing arts, orchestras; Arts; Higher education; Education; Hospitals (general); Health care, clinics/centers; Health care; Boy scouts; Youth development, business; YM/YWCAs & YM/YWHAs; Family services; Human services; Foundations (community); United Ways and Federated Giving Programs; Jewish federated giving programs.
Type of support: General/operating support; Continuing support; Annual campaigns; Capital campaigns; Program development.
Limitations: Applications accepted. Giving limited to areas of major company operations, with emphasis on St. Louis, MO. No support for private foundations, organizations primarily funded by state or federal taxes, fraternal organizations, political or advocacy groups, organizations located outside of the U.S. operating primarily in the U.S., international charities, religious organizations not of direct benefit to the entire community, pass-through organizations, or United Way-supported organizations. No grants to individuals, or for endowments, special projects, research, publications, or conferences; no loans.
Publications: Application guidelines.
Application information: Application form not required.
Initial approach: **Complete online application**
Copies of proposal: 1
Deadline(s): **Mar. 31, June 30, Sept. 30, and Dec. 31**
Board meeting date(s): **Quarterly**
Officer: Ronald A. Fromm, Chair.
Board Members: Bill Berberich; Ann Joos; Michael Oberlander.
Trustee: SunTrust Banks, Inc.
EIN: 237443082
Other changes: At the close of 2013, the grantmaker paid grants of $3,043,752, a 126.2% increase over the 2012 disbursements, $1,345,592.

708
Al and Nancy Burnett Charitable Foundation, Inc.
(formerly Al Burnett Charitable Foundation, Inc.)
2465 Snook Trail
Palm Beach Gardens, FL 33410-1270

Established in 1985 in FL.
Donors: J. Albert Burnett†; Nancy L. Burnett.
Foundation type: Independent foundation.
Financial data (yr. ended 11/30/13): Assets, $7,192,805 (M); gifts received, $2,923,000; expenditures, $316,687; qualifying distributions, $313,462; giving activities include $304,175 for 16 grants (high: $50,000; low: $500).
Fields of interest: Higher education; Health care; Protestant agencies & churches.
Limitations: Applications not accepted. Giving primarily in FL and ME. No grants to individuals.
Application information: Unsolicited requests for funds not accepted.
Officers and Directors:* Amy Gravina,* Pres.; Becky B. Moore,* Treas.; Bruce K. Burnett; Melinda Steele.
EIN: 592620060
Other changes: Amy Gravina is now Pres. Becky B. Moore is now Treas. J. Albert Burnett, donor and director, is deceased.

709
Burnetti Childrens Foundation Inc.
211 S. Florida Ave.
Lakeland, FL 33801-4621

Established in 2002.
Donor: Patricia A. Burnetti.
Foundation type: Independent foundation.
Financial data (yr. ended 12/31/12): Assets, $31,116 (M); gifts received, $135,200; expenditures, $216,814; qualifying distributions, $216,814; giving activities include $204,595 for 30 grants (high: $38,830; low: $50).
Fields of interest: Higher education; Protestant agencies & churches.
Type of support: General/operating support.
Limitations: Applications not accepted. Giving primarily in FL. No grants to individuals.
Application information: Contributes only to pre-selected organizations.
Officers: Douglas K. Burnetti, Pres.; Dean Burnetti, V.P.; Denise L. Burnetti, Secy.; Patricia A. Burnetti, Treas.
EIN: 593760786

710
Donald A. Burns Foundation Inc.
450 Royal Palm Way, Ste. 450
Palm Beach, FL 33480-4100 (561) 655-7855
Contact: Ginger Gibas

Established in 1998 in FL.
Donor: Donald A. Burns.
Foundation type: Independent foundation.
Financial data (yr. ended 12/31/12): Assets, $10,190,885 (M); expenditures, $1,267,582; qualifying distributions, $480,994; giving activities include $461,690 for 18 grants (high: $322,790; low: $100).
Fields of interest: Arts, formal/general education; Museums; Elementary/secondary education; Reproductive health, prenatal care; Human services; Children/youth, services; Family services; Christian agencies & churches; LGBTQ.
Type of support: Annual campaigns; Equipment; Program development; Curriculum development; Technical assistance.
Application information: Application form required.
Initial approach: Contact foundation for the application form
Copies of proposal: 1
Deadline(s): None
Officer: Donald A. Burns, Pres.
Number of staff: 2 full-time professional.
EIN: 650870379
Other changes: The grantmaker no longer lists a URL address.

711
Burton Foundation, Inc.
1899 Sycamore Ln.
Fernandina Beach, FL 32034-7857

Established in 2001 in FL.
Donors: Dr. Barry A. Gray; Mrs. Barry A. Gray; David Gray.
Foundation type: Independent foundation.
Financial data (yr. ended 12/31/12): Assets, $26,418,884 (M); gifts received, $15,039; expenditures, $2,294,774; qualifying distributions, $2,058,483; giving activities include $1,884,500 for 50 grants (high: $1,500,000; low: $500).
Fields of interest: Higher education; Education; Environment, natural resources; Human services; Foundations (community); Catholic agencies & churches.
Limitations: Applications not accepted. Giving in the U.S., with emphasis on OK. No grants to individuals.
Application information: Contributes only to pre-selected organizations.
Officers and Trustees:* David Gray,* Pres.; Gretchen Gray,* Secy.; Sherrie Schroeder, Treas.; Joseph Gray; Robert Gray; **Lisa Wall.**
EIN: 731584983
Other changes: E.D. Wall is no longer a trustee.

712
Edyth Bush Charitable Foundation, Inc.
199 E. Welbourne Ave.
P.O. Box 1967
Winter Park, FL 32790-1967 (407) 647-4322
Contact: David A. Odahowski, C.E.O. and Pres.; Deborah Hessler, Corp. Secy. and Prog.Off.
FAX: (407) 647-7716;
E-mail: dhessler@edythbush.org; Deborah Hessler direct tel.: (407) 647-4322 x17; additional tel.: (888) 647-4322; Main URL: http://www.edythbush.org
Facebook: https://www.facebook.com/EdythBushCharitableFoundation
Google Plus: https://plus.google.com/+EdythbushOrg/about
Grants List: http://www.edythbush.org/awarded.html
YouTube: http://www.youtube.com/channel/UCkToIOhE9pRdpobW8hd7FGw

Originally incorporated in 1966 in MN; reincorporated in 1973 in FL.
Donors: Edyth Bassler Bush†; H. Clifford Lee†; Richard Conlee†.
Foundation type: Independent foundation.
Financial data (yr. ended 08/31/12): Assets, $71,603,069 (M); expenditures, $4,906,454; qualifying distributions, $2,886,130; giving activities include $2,813,065 for 60 grants (high: $333,333; low: $971; average: $5,000–$50,000), and $73,065 for 56 employee matching gifts.
Purpose and activities: Support for charitable, educational, and health service organizations, with emphasis on human services, the elderly, youth services, the handicapped, and nationally recognized quality arts or cultural programs. Provides limited number of program-related investment loans for construction, land purchase, emergency or similar purposes to organizations otherwise qualified to receive grants. Active programs directly managed and/or financed for management/volunteer development of nonprofits.
Fields of interest: Arts education; Arts; Education; Health care; Crime/violence prevention, domestic violence; Employment; Housing/shelter; Human services; Children/youth, services; Nonprofit management; Children/youth; Aging; Young adults; Disabilities, people with; Women; Military/veterans; Crime/abuse victims; Economically disadvantaged; Homeless.
Type of support: Management development/capacity building; Capital campaigns; Building/renovation; Equipment; Land acquisition; Emergency funds; Program development; Technical assistance; Consulting services; Program-related investments/loans; Employee matching gifts; Matching/challenge support.
Limitations: Giving limited to organizations that are headquartered within Orange, Seminole, Lake, and Osceola counties, FL. No support for alcohol or drug abuse prevention/treatment projects or organizations, religious facilities or functions, primarily (50 percent or more) tax-supported institutions, advocacy organizations, foreign organizations, or, generally, for cultural programs. No grants to individuals, or for scholarships or individual research projects, endowments, fellowships, travel, routine operating expenses, annual campaigns, or deficit financing.
Publications: Application guidelines; Financial statement; Grants list; Informational brochure; Program policy statement.
Application information: Application guidelines and form available on foundation web site. The foundation is open to discussing your funding needs. If we determine there is significant interest, the foundation may invite you to submit an online application. With the many needs facing the people of Central Florida in this challenging economic environment, the foundation receives far more requests than it can possibly fund. Due to this increased demand on the foundation's limited resources, we are unable to fund every new request. Check foundation web site periodically for further updates. Application form required.
Initial approach: Telephone, e-mail, personal visit, or stated interest by foundation.
Deadline(s): None
Board meeting date(s): May and Nov.
Final notification: Varies depending on scope of request
Officers and Directors:* Gerald F. Hilbrich,* Chair.; Herbert W. Holm, Vice-Chair.; David A. Odahowski,* C.E.O. and Pres.; Mary Ellen Hutcheson, V.P., Treas. and C.F.O.; Deborah J. Hessler, Corp. Secy. and Prog. Off.; Matthew Certo; Elizabeth Dvorak; Deborah C. German, M.D.; Harvey L. Massey; Richard J. Walsh.
Number of staff: 3 full-time professional; 2 full-time support.
EIN: 237318041

713
Campbell Foundation
5975 N. Federal Hwy., Ste. 126
Fort Lauderdale, FL 33308-2685 (954) 493-8822
Contact: William Venuti, Tr.
FAX: (954) 493-8801; E-mail: campfound@aol.com; Main URL: http://www.campbellfoundation.net/
Facebook: https://www.facebook.com/pages/The-Campbell-Foundation/239925086157653
Google Plus: https://plus.google.com/101791887848110694616#101791887848110694616/posts
Grants List: http://www.campbellfoundation.net/Resources/Campbell%20Foundation%20Funding%201995-Present.pdf

Established in 1986 in FL.
Donors: Richard Campbell Zahn†; Thomas Todd†.
Foundation type: Independent foundation.
Financial data (yr. ended 12/31/12): Assets, $8,026,975 (M); gifts received, $25,529; expenditures, $754,866; qualifying distributions, $639,951; giving activities include $451,856 for 28 grants (high: $100,000; low: $100).
Purpose and activities: The foundation supports other nonprofit organizations conducting clinical research into the prevention and treatment of HIV/AIDS, and related conditions and illnesses. The focus of the Campbell Foundation's funding lies in alternative, nontraditional avenues of research.
Fields of interest: AIDS; AIDS research.
Type of support: Research.
Limitations: Applications accepted. Giving primarily on a national basis; some consideration also for foreign nonprofit entities. No support for educational effects or behavioral research (only for clinical research). No grants to individuals, or for discretionary grants, equipment or travel expenses.
Publications: Application guidelines; Grants list.
Application information: Full proposals are by invitation only, upon review of letter of inquiry.
Initial approach: Letter of Inquiry (no more than 2 pages)
Deadline(s): Jan., Apr., July, and Oct. for letters of inquiry
Trustee: William Venuti.
Directors: David Ferebee, Jr.; Jeanne R. Kos, MSN, RN; Sandy Kristoff; Frederick R. MacLean; Robert H. Samuels; Corkin R. Steinhart, M.D.; Patricia M. Whetstone-Foltz.
Number of staff: 2 full-time professional.
EIN: 586205065

714
Cape Coral Community Foundation
(formerly Philanthropic Foundation of Cape Coral, Inc.)
1405 S.E. 47th St., Unit 2
Cape Coral, FL **33904** (239) 542-5594
Contact: Beth T. Sanger, Exec. Dir.
FAX: (239) 549-8307;
E-mail: cccf@capecoralcf.org; **Main URL: http://www.capecoralcf.planyourlegacy.org/**

Established in 1973 in FL.
Foundation type: Community foundation.

Financial data (yr. ended 06/30/12): Assets, $7,839,692 (M); gifts received, $198,824; expenditures, $533,419; giving activities include $226,726 for 17+ grants (high: $25,000), and $57,000 for 35 grants to individuals.
Purpose and activities: The mission of the foundation is to support the public well being and to improve the quality of life in the greater Cape Coral community through the stewardship of permanently endowed and gifted funds.
Fields of interest: Arts; Education; Environment; Animals/wildlife; Health care; Youth development; Human services; Youth; Aging; Disabilities, people with.
Type of support: Equipment; Program development; Scholarship funds; Matching/challenge support.
Limitations: Applications accepted. Giving primarily in Cape Coral, FL. No grants for general operating expenses, travel, training seminars, or staff salaries.
Publications: Application guidelines; Annual report; Informational brochure; Newsletter.
Application information: Visit foundation web site for application form and guidelines. Applications must be mailed or hand delivered. Application form required.
Initial approach: Letter or telephone
Copies of proposal: 3
Deadline(s): July 10
Board meeting date(s): 3rd Thurs. monthly
Final notification: Oct.
Officers and Directors:* Joe Padgett,* Chair.; Brian D. Gomer,* Vice-Chair.; **ToniRae Hurley,* Secy.**; Karen Mosteller,* Treas.; Beth T. Sanger, Exec. Dir.; John G. Bobb; Donna Caruso; Donna Giannuzzi; Pastor Dennis Gingerich; Alison Hussey; **Wayne R. Kirkwood**; Robert D. Knight; Steve Pohlman; Tyra Read; Steve Riggs; Rebecca Ross; Keith A. Veres; Warchol.
Number of staff: 1 full-time professional; 2 part-time support.
EIN: 237410312
Other changes: ToniRae Hurley is now Secy.

715
Hazel Crosby Carlton Foundation Inc.
3500 Reynolds Rd.
Lakeland, FL 33803-7327
***E-mail:* info@hcc-foundation.org**; Main URL: http://www.hcc-foundation.com

Established in 2005 in FL.
Donors: Cynthia L. Bunch; James D. Bunch; Lief Goodson; Charles Funk; Kathy Sergi; Bunch and Assocs., Inc.
Foundation type: Independent foundation.
Financial data (yr. ended 12/31/12): Assets, $1,624,322 (M); gifts received, $26,393; expenditures, $282,709; qualifying distributions, $266,306; giving activities include $265,309 for 10 grants (high: $108,663; low: $120).
Fields of interest: Education; Health organizations; Human services; Family services; Pregnancy centers; Civil liberties, right to life; Women.
Limitations: Applications not accepted. Giving primarily in FL and OH.
Application information: Unsolicited requests for funds not accepted.
Officers: Cynthia L. Bunch, Pres. and Treas.; James D. Bunch, V.P. and Secy.
Directors: Charles A. Funk; Lief G. Goodson; Kathy J. Sergi; Nila C. Watkins.
EIN: 203163711

716
Catalina Marketing Charitable Foundation
200 Carillon Pkwy.
St. Petersburg, FL 33716-1242
Contact: Bill Protz, Pres.

Established in 1991 in CA.
Donors: Catalina Marketing Corp.; trademark Metals Recycling LLC.
Foundation type: Company-sponsored foundation.
Financial data (yr. ended 07/31/13): Assets, $2,824,070 (M); gifts received, $2,229; expenditures, $263,440; qualifying distributions, $231,511; giving activities include $231,511 for 151 grants (high: $30,000; low: $10).
Purpose and activities: The foundation supports organizations involved with education, water conservation, health, hunger, housing development, athletics, youth business development, and children services.
Fields of interest: Education; Health care; Human services.
Type of support: General/operating support; Continuing support; Annual campaigns; Program development; Scholarship funds.
Limitations: Applications accepted. Giving primarily in FL.
Application information: Application form not required.
Initial approach: Proposal
Deadline(s): None
Officers and Directors:* Debbie Booth, Chair.; Bill Protz, Pres.; Justin Summer,* Secy.; **James Flanigan, Co-Treas.**; **Rick Frier,* Co-Treas.**; **Joni Elmore**; **Chad Keller**; Edward Kuehnle; **John Miles**; Tricia Stelges.
EIN: 330489905
Other changes: James Flanigan is now Co-Treas. Rick Frier is now Co-Treas.

717
Alvah H. & Wyline P. Chapman Foundation, Inc.
P.O. Box 55398
St. Petersburg, FL 33732-5398
E-mail: vsayler@saylerfamily.com; Additional e-mail: cfsecretary@aol.com; **Main URL: http://www.chapmanfoundation.org**

Established in 1967 in FL.
Donors: Wyline Chapman Sayler; Chris Chapman Hilton; Alvah H. Chapman; Betty Bateman Chapman; Dale Chapman Webb; Van C. Sayler; Wyline Page Chapman†.
Foundation type: Independent foundation.
Financial data (yr. ended 12/31/12): Assets, $3,712,201 (M); expenditures, $184,635; qualifying distributions, $151,114; giving activities include $145,000 for 22 grants (high: $10,000; low: $1,000).
Fields of interest: Performing arts, orchestras; Literature; Arts; Education; Medical care, rehabilitation; Substance abuse, prevention; YM/YWCAs & YM/YWHAs; Children/youth, services; Family services; Homeless, human services; Civil rights, race/intergroup relations; Science; Christian agencies & churches.
Type of support: General/operating support; Continuing support; Capital campaigns; Building/renovation; Endowments; Emergency funds.
Limitations: Giving primarily in FL. No grants to individuals, and no endowments or loans to organizations engaged in partisan political activities.
Publications: Application guidelines; Informational brochure (including application guidelines).
Application information: Letter of inquiry should include requested amount and description of project. After letter of inquiry, if endorsed by a foundation director, submit application. Application form not required.
***Initial approach:* Email brief letter of inquiry**
Copies of proposal: 1
Board meeting date(s): Early summer and late fall
Final notification: After board meeting
Officers and Trustees:* Van C. Sayler,* Chair.; Chris Hilton,* Pres.; Bob Hilton,* V.P.; Lee B. Sayler,* Secy.-Treas.; Page Beckwith; Alan P. Sayler; Brey Webb; **Kristy Webb.**
Number of staff: 1 part-time support.
EIN: 586069146
Other changes: Bob Hilton has replaced Van C. Sayler as V.P. Lee B. Sayler has replaced Bob Hilton as Secy.-Treas.
Van C. Sayler is now Chair. Chris Hilton is now Pres.
The grantmaker now publishes application guidelines online.

718
Charlotte Community Foundation, Inc.
(formerly Charlotte County Foundation, Inc.)
227 Sullivan St.
P. O. Box 512047
Punta Gorda, FL 33950-5244 (941) 637-0077
Contact: Connie Kantor, C.E.O.
FAX: (941) 637-6202;
E-mail: ccf@charlottecommunityfoundation.org; Additional e-mail: gbobonich@charlottecommunityfoundation.org; Main URL: http://www.charlottecommunityfoundation.org

Established in 1993 in FL.
Foundation type: Community foundation.
Financial data (yr. ended 12/31/12): Assets, $4,833,742 (M); gifts received, $166,363; expenditures, $1,611,395; giving activities include $1,120,497 for 14+ grants (high: $852,138).
Purpose and activities: The foundation seeks to enhance the quality of life in Charlotte County, FL. The foundation's mission is to advance the common good by nurturing a giving community and connecting people who care with causes that matter.
Fields of interest: Historic preservation/historical societies; Arts; Education; Environment; Animal welfare; Health care; Human services; Nonprofit management; Community/economic development; Aging.
Type of support: Management development/capacity building; Equipment; Program development; Film/video/radio; Publication; Program evaluation; Scholarships—to individuals; Matching/challenge support.
Limitations: Applications accepted. Giving limited to Charlotte County, FL. No support for religious organization for sectarian purposes, or fraternal organizations, societies or orders. **No grants for general operating support, building or capital campaigns, deficit financing or debt reduction, endowment funds, fundraising events, basic scientific research, start-up funding, or travel expenses; no loans.**
Publications: Application guidelines; Annual report; Grants list; Informational brochure; Multi-year report; Occasional report; Occasional report (including application guidelines); Program policy statement.
Application information: Visit foundation web site for letter of intent, application form, and guidelines. The foundation will invite applicants to submit a full

application based on letter of intent. Application form required.

Initial approach: Complete online letter of intent
Copies of proposal: 1
Deadline(s): Apr. 8 for letter of intent; July 1 for full grant application
Board meeting date(s): 2nd Thurs. of each 2nd month
Final notification: Within 3 weeks for letter of intent determination; Sept. 26 for award notification

Officers and Directors:* Brian Presley,* Chair.; David A. Holmes,* Vice-Chair.; Connie Kantor,* C.E.O.; Robin Bayne,* Secy.; Ronald Olsen,* Treas.; Mary Byrski; Jimmy Dean; Hasan A. Hammami; Ronald R. Monck; Vernon Peeples; Douglas L. Young.
Number of staff: 1 full-time professional; 1 part-time professional; 1 full-time support.
EIN: 650455319

719
The Chartrand Foundation, Inc.

2038 Gilmore St.
Jacksonville, FL 32204-3210
E-mail: info@thechartrandfoundation.org; Main URL: http://www.thechartrandfoundation.org/

Established in 2006 in FL.
Donor: Gary R. Chartrand.
Foundation type: Independent foundation.
Financial data (yr. ended 12/31/12): Assets, $7,104,562 (M); expenditures, $983,320; qualifying distributions, $711,356; giving activities include $711,356 for 27 grants (high: $153,255; low: $500).
Fields of interest: Elementary/secondary education; Education.
Limitations: Applications not accepted. Giving primarily in Jacksonville, FL; some giving in New York, NY. No grants to individuals.
Application information: The foundation is currently redesigning its grantmaking strategy, systems and timeline. Check foundation web site for updates in this matter.
Officers: Nancy J. Chartrand, Chair.; Sandy Ramsey, V.P.; Ashley Smith Juarez, Exec. Dir.
Directors: Gary R. Chartrand; Jeffrey Chartrand; Meredith Chartrand.
EIN: 205440166

720
Jack Chester Foundation

333 S.E. 2nd Ave., Ste. 4400
Miami, FL 33131-2184 (305) 579-0503
Contact: Norman H. Lipoff, Chair.
FAX: (305) 961-5503; E-mail: lipoffn@gtlaw.com; Address for applications and grant-related inquiries: c/o SunTrust Bank Foundations & Endowments, 200 S. Orange Ave., S.O.A.B. 10, Orlando, FL 32801-3410; Main URL: http://jackchesterfoundation.org

Established in 2001 in FL.
Donor: Jack Chester†.
Foundation type: Independent foundation.
Financial data (yr. ended 12/31/12): Assets, $9,557,550 (M); expenditures, $694,711; qualifying distributions, $634,803; giving activities include $534,000 for 70 grants (high: $125,000; low: $1,000).
Purpose and activities: giving primarily for: 1) Jewish education (formal and informal) and Jewish identity, in Miami and Israel; 2) Social services for vulnerable segments of the Jewish communities of Miami and Israel (including people with disabilities and children at risk); 3) Israel Experience programs; 4) Higher education in Israel; 5) Holocaust education; 6) Israel education and Zionist initiatives; and 7) Health care in Israel or serving the Jewish community in Miami.
Fields of interest: Education, formal/general education; Higher education; Human services; Jewish federated giving programs; Jewish agencies & synagogues.
International interests: Israel.
Type of support: General/operating support; Annual campaigns; Capital campaigns; Scholarship funds.
Limitations: Applications accepted. Giving on a national and international basis, particularly in Miami, FL and Israel.
Publications: Application guidelines.
Application information: Application form required.

***Initial approach:* The foundation recommends the use of its online application procedure on its web site. Applications sent by U.S. mail are also accepted, and the grant proposal format for mailing is also located on the foundation's web site**
Deadline(s): Dec. 31
Board meeting date(s): Feb.
Final notification: Mar.

Officer and Trustees:* Norman H. Lipoff,* Chair.; Jorge Lerman; Bernardo Pedro Szwarc.
EIN: 316660664

721
John and Golda Cohen Trust

P.O. Box 607772
Orlando, FL 32860-7772

Established in 2002 in FL.
Donor: The John S. Cohen Foundation.
Foundation type: Independent foundation.
Financial data (yr. ended 12/31/12): Assets, $10,601,984 (M); expenditures, $766,398; qualifying distributions, $548,000; giving activities include $548,000 for 74 grants (high: $71,500; low: $250).
Fields of interest: Media/communications; Education; Human services; Homeless, human services; Jewish agencies & synagogues.
Limitations: Applications not accepted. Giving primarily in FL and MA. No grants to individuals.
Application information: Contributes only to pre-selected organizations.
Trustees: Elizabeth Ann Cohen; Jenny Cohen; Richard S. Cohen; Jolyon Ellis Cowan.
EIN: 597222346

722
The Community Foundation, Inc.

(doing business as The Community Foundation of Northeast Florida, Inc.)
(also known as The Community Foundation in Jacksonville)(formerly The Community Foundation in Jacksonville)
245 Riverside Ave., Ste. 310
Jacksonville, FL 32202 (904) 356-4483
FAX: (904) 356-7910; E-mail: info@jaxcf.org; Grant application e-mail: applications@jaxcf.org; Main URL: http://www.jaxcf.org
Facebook: http://www.facebook.com/cfjacksonville
Twitter: http://twitter.com/CFJacksonville
YouTube: http://www.youtube.com/user/TCFJacksonville

Established in 1964 in FL.
Foundation type: Community foundation.
Financial data (yr. ended 12/31/12): Assets, $257,249,260 (M); gifts received, $99,162,430; expenditures, $33,308,777; giving activities include $30,588,464 for 532+ grants (high: $6,092,644), and $58,888 for 47 grants to individuals.
Purpose and activities: The foundation's mission is to stimulate philanthropy to build a better community.
Fields of interest: Performing arts, theater; Arts; Children/youth, services; Aging, centers/services; Infants/toddlers; Children/youth; Aging.
Type of support: Endowments; Emergency funds; Program development; Seed money; Internship funds; Scholarship funds; Technical assistance; Consulting services; Program-related investments/loans; Grants to individuals; Matching/challenge support.
Limitations: Applications accepted. Giving primarily in northeastern FL, including Baker, Clay, Duval, Nassau and St. Johns counties. No support for religious programming. No grants for general operating support of existing programs, construction or renovation, equipment, or tickets for fundraising activities.
Publications: Application guidelines; Annual report; Informational brochure; Newsletter.
Application information: Visit foundation web site for preliminary application form and guidelines. If preliminary application is selected for further consideration, the foundation will provide a full grant application and related information to the organization's contact person (full applications are available only to organizations which are invited to apply based on preliminary applications). Application form required.

Initial approach: Submit preliminary application
Copies of proposal: 1
Deadline(s): Varies
Board meeting date(s): Mar., June, Sept., and Nov.
Final notification: Varies

Officers and Trustees:* Paul Perez,* Chair.; William D. Brinton,* Vice-Chair.; Nina M. Waters, Pres.; **Grace Sacerdote, Exec. V.P. and C.F.O.**; Joanne Cohen, V.P., Philanthropic Svcs.; Susan Datz Edelman, V.P., Strategic Comms.; **Kathleen Shaw, V.P., Progs.**; John Zell, V.P., Devel.; Yan Cumper, Cont.; Martha Baker; Peggy Bryan; Hon. Brian J. Davis; Michael DuBow; Cindy Edelman; Charles D. "Chuck" Hyman; Deborah S. Pass-Durham; Hon. Harvey E. Schlesinger; Ryan Schwartz; James Van Vleck; Dori Walton; Tracey Westbrook; Jim Winston.
Number of staff: 8 full-time professional; 4 full-time support.
EIN: 596150746
Other changes: At the close of 2012, the fair market value of the grantmaker's assets was $257,249,260, a 56.4% increase over the 2011 value, $164,467,941. For the same period, the grantmaker paid grants of $30,647,352, a 112.6% increase over the 2011 disbursements, $14,413,049.
Kathleen Shaw has replaced Cheryl Riddick as V.P., Grantmaking.
C. Daniel Rice is no longer a trustee.

723
Community Foundation of Brevard

(formerly Community Foundation of Brevard County, Inc.)
1361 Bedford Dr., Ste. 102
Melbourne, FL 32940 (321) 752-5505
Contact: Sandi Scannelli, C.E.O.

E-mail: info@cfbrevard.org; Main URL: http://www.cfbrevard.org
Scholarship submission e-mail: foundation@cfbrevard.org

Established as a community foundation in 1981 in FL.
Foundation type: Community foundation.
Financial data (yr. ended 12/31/12): Assets, $12,708,264 (M); gifts received, $1,414,840; expenditures, $1,934,668; giving activities include $1,580,896 for 26+ grants (high: $600,000).
Purpose and activities: The foundation seeks to provide a cost-effective bridge for all donors to the community's changing needs, serve as a leader, catalyst, and resource for philanthropy, produce an expanding pool of permanent endowment funds for now and all time, improve the quality of life with grants and technical assistance to local charities and partner with and be an advocate for the endowment of local charities.
Fields of interest: Arts; Education; Environment; Animal welfare; Health care; Food services; Housing/shelter; Recreation; Family services; Human services; Community/economic development; Youth; Aging.
Type of support: Program development; Management development/capacity building.
Limitations: Applications accepted. Giving limited to Brevard County, FL. No support for sectarian religious activities. No grants to individuals, or for endowment campaigns, event sponsorships or advertising, debt retirement or budget deficits, sustaining operating support, or group trips.
Publications: Application guidelines; Grants list; Informational brochure.
Application information: Visit foundation web site for application Cover Page and guidelines. Application form required.
Initial approach: Create online profile
Copies of proposal: 6
Deadline(s): Feb. 14
Board meeting date(s): Monthly
Final notification: 90 days after deadline
Officers and Directors:* Brian Fisher,* Chair.; Ronald E. Bray,* Vice-Chair.; Sandi Scannelli,* C.E.O. and Pres.; Matthew Kucera,* Secy.; Michael S. Cerow,* Treas.; **Dale Dettmer, Esq., Emeritus**; **William Harris, Emeritus**; I. Wayne Cooper; Bill Fillmore; Juliana Kreul; Linda J. May; Gina H. Rall; Todd Russell; Erik Shuman, Esq.; Lynne Strynchuk; Bob Sukolsky; Kurt C. Weiss, Esq.; Mick Welch; Holly Woolsey.
Number of staff: 1 full-time professional.
EIN: 592114988
Other changes: Matthew Kucera and Lynne Laughna-Strynchuk are no longer directors.

724
Community Foundation of Central Florida, Inc.

1411 Edgewater Dr., Ste. 203
Orlando, FL 32804-6361 (407) 872-3050
Contact: Mark Brewer, C.E.O.
FAX: (407) 425-2990; E-mail: info@cfcflorida.org; Additional Address: P.O. Box 2071, Orlando, FL 32802; Main URL: http://www.cfcflorida.org
RSS Feed: http://mycfcf.wordpress.com/
Twitter: https://twitter.com/cffound

Established in 1993 in FL.
Foundation type: Community foundation.
Financial data (yr. ended 04/30/13): Assets, $58,085,963 (M); gifts received, $2,464,079; expenditures, $5,854,187; giving activities include $4,796,146 for grants.
Purpose and activities: The mission of the foundation is "Building Community by Building Philanthropy." The foundation works to fulfill this mission by managing and investing donor funds, connecting people with charitable causes they feel passionate about and empowering donors to make informed decisions through research and evaluation.
Fields of interest: Arts; Elementary/secondary education; Higher education; Health care; Children/youth, services; Youth, services; Human services; Community/economic development; Aging.
Type of support: Management development/capacity building; Program development; Seed money; Scholarship funds; Scholarships—to individuals.
Limitations: Applications accepted. Giving limited to central FL, with emphasis on Orange, Osceola, and Seminole counties. No grants to individuals (except for scholarships).
Publications: Application guidelines; Annual report; Financial statement; Grants list; Informational brochure; Informational brochure (including application guidelines); Newsletter.
Application information: Visit foundation web site for application guidelines. Application form required.
Copies of proposal: 1
Board meeting date(s): Monthly
Officers and Board Members:* Martin A. Rubin,* Chair.; Robert Panepinto,* Vice-Chair.; Mark Brewer,* C.E.O. and Pres.; Michelle Chapin,* V.P., Community Investment; Meghan Warrick,* Exec. V.P. and C.F.O.; Robert F. Thomson II,* Secy.; Kaki Rawls,* Treas.; Elizabeth Gordon, Cont.; Waymon Armstrong; Eugene Campbell; Thomas V. Durkee; Aaron Gorovitz; Stacey Prince-Troutman; Thomasa Sanchez; James Scrivener.
Number of staff: 4 full-time professional; 2 full-time support.
EIN: 593182886
Other changes: Avanish Aggarwal and Robert F. Thomson are no longer directors.

725
Community Foundation of North Central Florida, Inc.

(formerly Gainesville Community Foundation)
3919 W. Newberry Rd., Ste. 3
Gainesville, FL 32607 (352) 367-0060
FAX: (352) 378-1718; E-mail: office@gnvcf.org; Main URL: http://www.gnvcf.org
Facebook: https://www.facebook.com/pages/Community-Foundation-of-North-Central-Florida/132775353446284
RSS Feed: http://cfncf.org/feed/

Established in 1998 in FL.
Foundation type: Community foundation.
Financial data (yr. ended 12/31/12): Assets, $11,276,761 (M); gifts received, $543,496; expenditures, $1,063,610; giving activities include $714,163 for 22+ grants (high: $200,000).
Purpose and activities: The foundation seeks to promote and sustain philanthropy among the communities of North Central Florida.
Fields of interest: Arts; Higher education; Libraries/library science; Education; Environment; Animal welfare; Hospitals (general); Health care; Substance abuse, prevention; Medical research; Housing/shelter; Athletics/sports, water sports; Recreation; Family services; Human services; Philanthropy/voluntarism; Religion; Children/youth; Aging; Women; Girls; Economically disadvantaged; Homeless.
International interests: Costa Rica.
Type of support: General/operating support; Program development; Scholarship funds.
Limitations: Giving limited to Gainesville and the surrounding areas in north central FL.
Publications: Application guidelines; Annual report; Financial statement.
Application information:
Board meeting date(s): 3rd Thurs of Jan., Mar. May, Sept. and Nov.
Officers and Directors:* Eric Godet,* Chair.; Mitch Gleaser,* Vice-Chair.; Barzella Papa,* C.E.O. and Pres.; Tony Kendzior,* Secy.; WJ Rossi,* Treas.; Mark Avera; Phil Emmer; Stan Given; Dink Henderson; Clark Hodge; Cathy Jenkins; Linda Kallman; Carrie Lee; Peter Maren; Wes Marston; Howard Patrick; Susannah Peddie; Mike Ryals; **Melanie Shore**; Ester Tibbs; Marilyn Tubb; Terry Van Nortwick; Richard White; and 6 additional Directors.
Number of staff: 1 full-time professional; 1 full-time support.
EIN: 593532330
Other changes: Luis Diaz, Perry McGriff, Nancy Perry, and Melanie Shore are no longer directors.

726
The Community Foundation of North Florida, Inc.

1621 Metropolitan Blvd., Ste. A
Tallahassee, FL 32308-3792 (850) 222-2899
Contact: Joy R. Watkins, Pres.
FAX: (850) 222-3624; E-mail: info@cfnf.org; Additional e-mail: jwatkins@cfnf.org; Main URL: http://www.cfnf.org/
: http://www.firstfd.com

Established in 1997 in FL.
Foundation type: Community foundation.
Financial data (yr. ended 12/31/12): Assets, $26,614,076 (M); gifts received, $6,844,549; expenditures, $2,846,205; giving activities include $2,302,992 for 37+ grants (high: $1,100,000), and $4,500 for grants to individuals.
Purpose and activities: The foundation's primary purpose is to receive and raise charitable giving from third parties and to distribute property and extend financial aid and support through grants, gifts, and assistance to qualified charitable organizations.
Fields of interest: Arts; Education; Environment; Housing/shelter; Youth, services; Family services; Human services; Economic development; Community/economic development.
Limitations: Applications accepted. Giving limited to the North Florida counties of Franklin, Gadsden, Gulf, Jackson, Jefferson, Leon, Liberty, Madison, Taylor and Wakulla. No grants to individuals (except for scholarships).
Publications: Application guidelines; Annual report; Financial statement; Grants list; Informational brochure.
Application information: Visit foundation web site for application guidelines. Faxed or e-mailed proposals are not accepted. Application form not required.
Initial approach: Telephone or e-mail
Copies of proposal: 1
Board meeting date(s): 2nd Thurs. of Jan., Mar., May, July, Sept., and Nov.
Officers and Directors:* Everitt Drew,* Chair.; **Joy R. Watkins, J.D.*, Pres. and C.E.O.**; Rick Shapley,* Secy.-Treas.; Todd Abernethy,* C.F.O.; **Carrol Dadisman, Emeritus**; **Louise Humphrey, Emeritus**; **Brooks Pettit, Emeritus**; Mildred Dadisman; Kathy Dahl; Erin Ennis; Alex Hinson, Esq.; Winston Howell; Rob Langford; Julie Moreno; Martin Proctor; Katrina Rolle.

Number of staff: 2 full-time professional; 1 part-time support.
EIN: 593473384
Other changes: Debara Jump is now Dir., Mktg. and COmms. Debara Jump is now Dir., Mktg. and Comms. Joy R. Watkins is now Pres. and C.E.O.

727
The Community Foundation of Sarasota County, Inc.

(formerly The Sarasota County Community Foundation, Inc.)
2635 Fruitville Rd.
Sarasota, FL 34237-5222 (941) 955-3000
Contact: For grants: Patricia Martin, Mgr., Grants and Community Initiatives
FAX: (941) 952-1951; E-mail: info@cfsarasota.org; Email for grant inquiries: patricia@cfsarasota.org; Main URL: http://www.cfsarasota.org
E-Newsletter: https://www.cfsarasota.org/AboutUs/GoodNewsENewsletterSignup/tabid/510/Default.aspx
Facebook: http://www.facebook.com/pages/Sarasota-FL/Community-Foundation-of-Sarasota-County/74962141153
Google Plus: https://plus.google.com/+CfsarasotaOrg
LinkedIn: http://www.linkedin.com/company/community-foundation-of-sarasota-county
Twitter: https://twitter.com/#!/CFSarasota
YouTube: http://www.youtube.com/user/CFSC34237
Scholarship inquiries: tel. (941) 556-7114 or e-mail eyoung@cfsarasota.org

Incorporated in 1979 in FL.
Foundation type: Community foundation.
Financial data (yr. ended 05/31/13): Assets, $239,462,234 (M); gifts received, $36,098,583; expenditures, $20,627,031; giving activities include $15,831,757 for grants.
Purpose and activities: The foundation brings together citizens and organizations who care deeply about their community and who believe that people can act locally to improve quality of life. The foundation supports organizations involved with the arts, education, environment, animal protection, health care, human services, and community development.
Fields of interest: Humanities; Arts; Child development, education; Higher education; Education; Environment; Animals/wildlife; Health care; Mental health/crisis services; Health organizations, association; Youth development, centers/clubs; Children/youth, services; Family services; Residential/custodial care, hospices; Human services; Community/economic development; Youth; Aging; Disabilities, people with; Economically disadvantaged.
Type of support. Equipment; Emergency funds; Program development; Seed money; Scholarship funds; Scholarships—to individuals.
Limitations: Applications accepted. Giving primarily in Sarasota County, FL, and surrounding communities. No support for fraternal organizations, societies or orders, or religious organizations for sectarian purposes. No grants to individuals (except for selected scholarships), or for annual campaigns, building campaigns, endowment funds, deficit financing, debt retirement, publications, operating expenses, travel, fundraising events, scientific research, or conferences.
Publications: Application guidelines; Annual report; Grants list; Informational brochure; Newsletter; Occasional report; Program policy statement.
Application information: The foundation is currently not accepting competitive grant requests for EdExplore Exploration, Immediate Impact, discretionary or unrestricted grants. Visit the foundation's web site donor-advised grant guidelines and scholarship information. Application form required.
Board meeting date(s): Jan., Mar., May, July, Sept., and Nov.
Officers and Directors:* Philip A. Delaney, Jr.,* Chair.; Orion Marx,* Vice-Chair.; Kathleen Roberts, Vice-Chair., Governance Committee; Roxanne Jerde, C.E.O. and Pres.; John Annis, V.P., Community Investment; Janet K. Ginn, Sr. V.P., Devel. and Donor Rels.; Laura Spencer, C.F.O.; Patricia Courtois,* Secy.; Vicente Medina,* Treas.; Erin Jones, Cont.; Audrey Coleman; Dr. Duncan Finlay; C.J. Fishman; Barbara Freeman; Richard Gans, Esq.; Victoria Leopold; Rodney Linford; Michael P. Martella; Jeffrey McCurdy; Vincente Medina; Austin Nadwondny; Michael R. Pender, Jr.; William M. Seider; Richard Smith; Terri Vitale.
Number of staff: 7 full-time professional; 1 part-time professional; 9 full-time support; 2 part-time support.
EIN: 591956886
Other changes: Jocelyn Stevens is no longer V.P., Donor Engagement. Earl Young is now Mgr., Grants and Scholarships. Melody Porter is now Acct. Kathleen Roberts is now Vice-Chair., Governance Committee. L. Thomas Baker, Steve Dahlquist, Patrick Dorsey, and Manuel Pineiro are no longer directors.

728
Conn Memorial Foundation

3410 Henderson Blvd., Ste. 200
Tampa, FL 33609-3975 **(813) 554-1210**
Contact: Beth Doyle, Grant Dir.
***tel./fax:* (813) 554-1210;**
e-mail: Beth@connfoundation.org; Main URL: http://www.connfoundation.org

Incorporated in 1954 in FL.
Donors: Fred K. Conn†; Edith F. Conn†.
Foundation type: Independent foundation.
Financial data (yr. ended 07/31/13): Assets, $22,982,249 (M); expenditures, $1,495,902; qualifying distributions, $1,275,207; giving activities include $1,024,000 for 50 grants (high: $75,000; low: $1,000).
Purpose and activities: Giving primarily for programs that support at-risk children and families in Hillsborough County, Florida; funding also for inner-city youth outreach, college scholarships, and capacity grants.
Fields of interest: Education; Human services; Family services; Children; Economically disadvantaged.
Type of support: General/operating support; Continuing support; Management development/capacity building; Capital campaigns; Building/renovation; Equipment; Emergency funds; Program development; Conferences/seminars; Seed money; Scholarship funds; Technical assistance; Consulting services; Program evaluation; Matching/challenge support.
Limitations: Applications accepted. Giving limited to Hillsborough County, FL. No grants for individual scholarships, no loans.
Publications: Application guidelines; Informational brochure (including application guidelines); Multi-year report.
Application information: Applications are by invitation only upon review of letter of intent. Application form required.
Initial approach: 1-page letter of intent using form on foundation web site
Copies of proposal: 1
Deadline(s): Jan. 1 (for spring cycle), and June 1 (for fall cycle)
Board meeting date(s): Monthly
Final notification: Following board meetings
Officers: Ron Peterson, Chair.; Dr. Mario Hernandez, Vice-Chair.; Sheff Crowder, Pres.; **Sonja Garcia, Secy.; Peter J. Gardner, Treas.**
Directors: Nuri Delacruz Ayres; Dave Kennedy; Scott Pieper.
Number of staff: 2 part-time professional; 1 part-time support.
EIN: 590978713
Other changes: Ron Peterson has replaced Carolyn Bricklemeyer as Chair. Dr. Mario Hernandez has replaced Dave Kennedy as Vice-Chair. Peter J. Gardner has replaced Ken Collier as Treas.

729
Coral Gables Community Foundation

(formerly The Coral Gables Foundation)
3001 Ponce de Leon Blvd., Ste. 203
Coral Gables, FL 33134-6817 (305) 446-9670
***Contact:* Mary Snow, Exec. Dir.**
FAX: (305) 446-3773;
E-mail: info@gablesfoundation.org; **Grant inquiry e-mail: mary@gablesfoundation.org**; Main URL: http://www.gablesfoundation.org
E-Newsletter: http://www.gablesfoundation.org/subscribe.php
Facebook: http://www.facebook.com/GablesHomePage
Twitter: http://twitter.com/CGCF
YouTube: http://www.youtube.com/gableshomepage

Established in 1991 in FL.
Donors: Suzanna P. Tweed; Jose Calvo; Ralph Moore; Kerdyle Liljedahl†; Shelly Roberts.
Foundation type: Community foundation.
Financial data (yr. ended 12/31/11): Assets, $824,804 (M); gifts received, $295,796; expenditures, $768,955; giving activities include $406,474 for 7+ grants (high: $250,000).
Purpose and activities: The foundation seeks to promote programs and initiatives that enhance the quality of life for people living and working in Coral Gables, FL.
Fields of interest: Museums; Historic preservation/historical societies; Arts; Education; Health care; Recreation, parks/playgrounds; Youth development, services; Community/economic development; Children/youth; Aging; Disabilities, people with.
Type of support: General/operating support; Annual campaigns; Building/renovation; Land acquisition; Emergency funds; Conferences/seminars; Scholarship funds; Grants to individuals; In-kind gifts; Matching/challenge support.
Limitations: Applications accepted. Giving limited to Coral Gables, FL. No support for religious or sectarian purposes. No grants to individuals (except for scholarships), or for tickets for charitable functions.
Publications: Annual report; Newsletter.
Application information: Grants are reviewed on a bi-annual basis; visit foundation web site for application information. Application form not required.
Initial approach: Letter
Copies of proposal: 5
***Deadline(s):* Apr. 25 and Sept. 19**

Board meeting date(s): Mar., June, Sept., and Dec.
Final notification: **45 following the bi-annual review period**

Officers and Directors:* Carlos F. Garcia, C.P.A.*, Chair.; Anthony L. Rogers,* Chair.-Elect; F. David Olazabal,* Treas.; **Mary Snow, Exec. Dir.**; **Karelia Martinez Carbonell, Asst. Secy.**; John Allen; Pat Blanco; **William Colas**; **Sissy DeMaria**; **Wayne Cameron Eldred**; Zeke Guilford, Esq.; Andria Hanley; Paul Lowenthal; Matthew Meehan; Lee J. Osiason, Esq.; Aurelia A. Reinhardt; Ari Rollnick; Jose Valdes-Fauli; Marielena Villamil.
Number of staff: 2 full-time professional.
EIN: 650208290
Other changes: Mary Snow has replaced Andria Hanley as Exec. Dir.
Jerry Santeiro is no longer Secy. Marc Berenfeld, Amanda Bonifay, Catherine Grieve, Andy S. Gomez, Michael Harris, Vicente Lago, Jason Neal, and F. David Olazabal are no longer directors.

730
Peter C. Cornell Trust
Amelia Island, FL

The foundation terminated in 2011.

731
Dahl Family Foundation, Inc.
P.O. Box 449
Ponte Vedra Beach, FL **32204-0449**

Donors: James H. Dahl; William L. Dahl.
Foundation type: Independent foundation.
Financial data (yr. ended 12/31/12): Assets, $1,638,931 (M); gifts received, $200,000; expenditures, $130,943; qualifying distributions, $124,000; giving activities include $124,000 for 6 grants (high: $50,000; low: $500).
Fields of interest: Education, research; Higher education; Education; Hospitals (general); Athletics/sports, amateur leagues; Human services.
Limitations: Applications not accepted. Giving primarily in FL, NC, NE, and NY. No grants to individuals.
Application information: Contributes only to pre-selected organizations.
Officers and Directors:* James H. Dahl,* Pres.; William L. Dahl,* V.P. and Secy.-Treas.; Trina Dahl Miller.
EIN: 562360547

732
Darden Restaurants, Inc. Foundation
P.O. Box 695011
Orlando, FL 32869-5011 (407) 245-5366
FAX: (407) 245-4462;
E-mail: communityaffairs@darden.com; **Additional address: 1000 Darden Center Dr., Orlando, FL 32837; e-mail: dardeninthecommunity@darden.com**; Main URL: http://www.dardenfoundation.com/cms/index.php
Darden Digest Blog: http://www.darden.com/sustainability/default.aspx?lang=en&page=sustainability§ion=blog
Facebook: https://www.facebook.com/DardenCitizen
Twitter: https://twitter.com/DardenCitizen
YouTube: http://www.youtube.com/DardenTV

Established in 1995 in FL.
Donor: Darden Restaurants, Inc.
Foundation type: Company-sponsored foundation.
Financial data (yr. ended 06/26/13): Assets, $277,076 (M); gifts received, $5,842,661; expenditures, $6,478,006; qualifying distributions, $6,478,006; giving activities include $6,478,006 for 648 grants (high: $700,000; low: $100).
Purpose and activities: The foundation supports organizations involved with arts and culture, education, the environment, animal welfare, hunger, and human services.
Fields of interest: Arts; Middle schools/education; Secondary school/education; Higher education; Education, services; Education; Environment, natural resources; Environment, water resources; Environment, land resources; Environmental education; Environment; Animal welfare; Food services; Food banks; Recreation, parks/playgrounds; Boys & girls clubs; American Red Cross; Children/youth, services; Human services; United Ways and Federated Giving Programs.
Type of support: General/operating support; Program development; Conferences/seminars; Scholarship funds; Employee volunteer services; Employee matching gifts; In-kind gifts; Matching/challenge support.
Limitations: Applications accepted. Giving primarily in areas of company operations, with some emphasis on central FL; giving also to national organizations. No support for discriminatory organizations, religious organizations not of direct benefit to the entire community, or political, lobbying, anti-business, international, or disease-specific organizations, fraternities, or sororities. No grants to individuals, or for event sponsorships, health-related funding, national conferences, capital campaigns, travel, athletic team sponsorships or scholarships, fundraising, galas, benefits, dinners, or sporting events, goodwill advertising, souvenir journals, or dinner programs.
Publications: Application guidelines; Corporate giving report.
Application information: National or regional grants are by invitation only. Organizations receiving support of $5,000 or more are asked to submit a grant report. Application form required.
Initial approach: Complete online application form
Copies of proposal: 1
Deadline(s): Nov. 15 to Dec. 10
Board meeting date(s): Feb., May, Sept., and Nov.
Final notification: March

Officers and Trustees:* Clarence Otis, Jr.,* Chair. and Pres.; Robert S. McAdam,* V.P.; Teresa Sebastian,* Secy.; Bradford C. Richmond, Treas.; Laurie Burns; Mary Darden; Tom Gathers; Valerie L. Insignares.
Number of staff: 1 full-time professional.
EIN: 593332929
Other changes: The grantmaker has changed its fiscal year-end from May 27 to June 26.

733
John & Norma Darling Foundation
c/o Northern Trust N.A.
755 Beachland Blvd.
Vero Beach, FL 32963-1746 **(772) 231-2400**

Established in IL.
Donors: John S. Darling; Norma W. Darling.
Foundation type: Independent foundation.
Financial data (yr. ended 03/31/13): Assets, $1,529,836 (M); expenditures, $133,111; qualifying distributions, $116,350; giving activities include $112,500 for 11 grants (high: $30,000; low: $1,000).
Purpose and activities: Giving primarily to religious and educational organizations.
Fields of interest: Arts; Education; Health care.
Limitations: Applications accepted. Giving primarily in Chicago, IL. No grants to individuals.
Application information: Application form not required.
Initial approach: Proposal
Deadline(s): None

Officers: Thomas A. Donahue, Pres.; Martha D. Gallo, Secy.; Sara D. Donahue, Treas.
Directors: John J. Donahue; Susan D. Gally.
EIN: 366132977

734
DeBartolo Family Foundation
15436 N. Florida Ave., Ste. 200
Tampa, FL 33613-1226 (813) 964-8302
***Contact:* Melissa Johnson, Exec. Dir.**
FAX: (813) 964-8321;
E-mail: mjohnson@debartoloholdings.com; Main URL: http://www.debartolofamilyfoundation.com
Community Grants List: http://www.debartolofamilyfoundation.com/programs/community-grants/
Facebook: http://www.facebook.com/DeBartoloFamilyFoundation
Scholarship Awards List: http://www.debartolofamilyfoundation.com/programs/scholarship-awards/
Twitter: http://twitter.com/DeBartoloFndtn

Established in 2001 in OH; reincorporated in 2003 in FL.
Donors: Edward J. DeBartolo, Jr.; The DeBartolo Family Foundation; Edward J. DeBartolo Memorial Scholarship Foundation; and 33 additional donors.
Foundation type: Independent foundation.
Financial data (yr. ended 01/31/13): Assets, $3,151,836 (M); gifts received, $929,897; expenditures, $912,291; qualifying distributions, $417,189; giving activities include $329,730 for 68 grants (high: $25,000; low: $200), and $87,459 for 32 grants to individuals (high: $9,959; low: $2,500).
Purpose and activities: The foundation's mission is to provide leadership and financial resources to extraordinary organizations and individuals to improve the community. The foundation annually awards scholarships to deserving students (graduating high school seniors), provides grants to individuals and organizations with exceptional requirements, and presents the Spirit of Humanity Award, honoring those organizations that provide extraordinary assistance to Tampa, FL, residents with special needs.
Fields of interest: Arts; Elementary/secondary education; Higher education; Education; Animal welfare; Health organizations, association; Medical research, institute; Cancer research; Human services; Children/youth, services; Christian agencies & churches.
Type of support: Grants to individuals; General/operating support; Scholarships—to individuals.
Limitations: Applications accepted. Giving primarily in the Tampa, FL, area.
Publications: Grants list; Newsletter.
Application information: See grantmaker web site for application guidelines and procedures and to download scholarship application form. Application form required.
Deadline(s): Apr. 15 for scholarships

Officers: Edward J. DeBartolo, Jr., Pres.; Cynthia R. DeBartolo, V.P.; Lisa DeBartolo, V.P.; Nikki DeBartolo, V.P.; Tiffanie DeBartolo, V.P.; James D.

Palermo, Secy.; David S. Mallitz, Treas.; Melissa Johnson, Exec. Dir.
EIN: 311739677
Other changes: Edward J. DeBartolo, Jr. is now Pres. Cynthia R. DeBartolo, Lisa DeBartolo, Nikki DeBartolo and Tiffanie DeBartolo are now V.P.s.

735
Arthur S. DeMoss Foundation
777 S. Flagler Dr., Ste. 215E
West Palm Beach, FL 33401-6165
***Contact:* Nancy S. DeMoss, Chair.**

Incorporated in PA in 1955 as the National Liberty Foundation of Valley Forge, Inc.
Donor: Arthur S. DeMoss†.
Foundation type: Independent foundation.
Financial data (yr. ended 12/31/12): Assets, $138,066,389 (M); expenditures, $32,839,577; qualifying distributions, $30,711,265; giving activities include $28,326,011 for 32+ grants (high: $10,356,724), and $1,942,799 for 1 foundation-administered program.
Purpose and activities: Support primarily for operating programs initiated and managed by the foundation itself that are evangelistic and disciplined in nature in the U.S. and other countries, primarily the Third World. To a limited extent, a few grants are made to organizations both in the U.S. and overseas that have these same goals.
Fields of interest: Christian agencies & churches.
International interests: Kenya; Tanzania; Uganda.
Type of support: Program development.
Limitations: Applications not accepted. Giving on an international basis. No support for local churches, denominational agencies and/or schools or colleges. No grants to individuals, or for scholarships or endowments; no loans.
Publications: Informational brochure.
Application information: Unsolicited requests for funds not accepted.
Board meeting date(s): Quarterly
Officers and Directors:* Nancy S. DeMoss,* Chair., C.E.O., and Treas.; Robert G. DeMoss,* Pres.; Charlotte DeMoss,* Secy.; Larry R. Nelson, C.F.O.; Elizabeth J. DeMoss.
Number of staff: 9 full-time professional; 8 full-time support.
EIN: 236404136
Other changes: The grantmaker has moved from DC to FL.

736
Diermeier Family Foundation
2113 Canna Way
Naples, FL 34105-3069 **(630) 655-8845**
***Contact:* Julie Diermeier, Tr.**
***FAX:* (630) 789-6249;**
E-mail: diermeier1@comcast.net; Main URL: http://www.diermeierff.org/

Established in 2003 in IL.
Donors: Jeffrey J. Diermeier; Julia M. Diermeier.
Foundation type: Independent foundation.
Financial data (yr. ended 12/31/12): Assets, $8,769,677 (M); expenditures, $476,784; qualifying distributions, $428,410; giving activities include $422,200 for 19 grants (high: $100,000; low: $1,000).
Fields of interest: Elementary/secondary education; Higher education; Health care; Mental health, treatment; Cancer research; Human services.
Type of support: General/operating support.
Limitations: Giving primarily in FL, GA, IL, and WI. No grants to individuals.
Application information: Application form available on foundation web site. Application form required.
Initial approach: Download application form from foundation web site. Applications may be submitted via fax or e-mail.
Trustees: Jeffrey J. Diermeier; Julie M. Diermeier.
EIN: 364545339

737
The Paul J. DiMare Foundation
P.O. Box 900460
Homestead, FL 33090-0460

Established in 1995 in FL.
Donors: Paul J. DiMare; DiMare Management, Inc.
Foundation type: Independent foundation.
Financial data (yr. ended 12/31/12): Assets, $37,244,585 (M); gifts received, $2,100,000; expenditures, $707,901; qualifying distributions, $596,500; giving activities include $596,500 for 39 grants (high: $75,000; low: $100).
Purpose and activities: Giving primarily for education, children and youth services, health organizations and medical research, including a children's hospital, and social services.
Fields of interest: Arts; Higher education; Botanical gardens; Hospitals (specialty); Health organizations, association; Medical research, institute; Human services; Children/youth, services; Christian agencies & churches.
Limitations: Applications not accepted. Giving primarily in FL. No grants to individuals.
Application information: Contributes only to pre-selected organizations.
Officer: Anthony DiMare, V.P.
Trustee: Paul J. DiMare.
EIN: 650537843

738
Dunspaugh-Dalton Foundation Inc.
1500 San Remo Ave., Ste. 103
Coral Gables, FL 33146-3054 (305) 668-4192
***FAX:* (305) 668-4247;**
E-mail: ddf@dunspaughdalton.org; Main URL: http://www.dunspaughdalton.org
Grants List: http://www.dunspaughdalton.org/giving-grantees.html

Incorporated in 1963 in FL.
Donor: Ann V. Dalton†.
Foundation type: Independent foundation.
Financial data (yr. ended 12/31/12): Assets, $34,313,822 (M); expenditures, $2,264,727; qualifying distributions, $1,892,752; giving activities include $1,404,789 for 51 grants (high: $225,000; low: $695).
Purpose and activities: Giving primarily for the arts, education, social services, and for health care.
Fields of interest: Performing arts; Performing arts, theater; Elementary/secondary education; Higher education; Education; Hospitals (general); Health care; Human services.
Type of support: General/operating support; Continuing support; Capital campaigns; Endowments; Program development; Professorships; Matching/challenge support.
Limitations: Applications accepted. Giving primarily in Monterey, CA, and Miami, FL, and NC. No grants to individuals; no loans.
Application information: See foundation website for complete application guidelines. Application form required.
***Deadline(s):* None**
Officers: Sarah L. Bonner, Pres.; Alexina Lane, V.P.; Leslie Buchanan, Secy.-Treas.
Number of staff: 3 full-time professional; 1 full-time support.
EIN: 591055300
Other changes: The grantmaker now accepts applications.

739
Albert E. & Birdie W. Einstein Fund
P.O. Box 310
Melbourne, FL 32902-0310 (864) 241-8562
Contact: Michael S. Lee, Pres.

Established about 1967 in FL.
Donors: Albert E. Einstein†; Birdie W. Einstein†.
Foundation type: Independent foundation.
Financial data (yr. ended 06/30/13): Assets, $10,143,734 (M); expenditures, $636,621; qualifying distributions, $528,000; giving activities include $528,000 for 28 grants (high: $75,000; low: $2,500).
Fields of interest: Human services; Children/youth, services; Jewish federated giving programs; Christian agencies & churches; Jewish agencies & synagogues; Economically disadvantaged.
Limitations: Applications accepted. Giving generally limited to FL. No grants to individuals.
Application information: Application form required.
Initial approach: Letter or telephone
Deadline(s): None
Officers: Michael S. Lee, Pres.; J. Michael Smith, V.P.; Debi Malone, Secy.-Treas.
EIN: 596127412
Other changes: Joyce Boyer is no longer a director.

740
Erdle Foundation
3720 S. Ocean Blvd.
Highland Beach, FL 33487

Established around 1964 in NY.
Donors: Jack A. Erdle; Norma Erdle.
Foundation type: Independent foundation.
Financial data (yr. ended 12/31/12): Assets, $0 (M); gifts received, $160,780; expenditures, $194,502; qualifying distributions, $194,502; giving activities include $192,563 for grants.
Purpose and activities: Giving primarily for education and human services.
Fields of interest: Higher education; Human services; Jewish federated giving programs; Jewish agencies & synagogues.
Type of support: Program development; Grants to individuals; Capital campaigns; General/operating support; Continuing support; Annual campaigns; Emergency funds; Scholarship funds; Employee-related scholarships; Scholarships—to individuals.
Limitations: Applications not accepted. Giving primarily in FL and NY.
Application information: Unsolicited requests for funds not accepted.
Officers: Jack A. Erdle, Pres. and C.E.O.; Harvey B. Erdle, V.P.; Lee C. Moss, V.P.; Norma Erdle, Secy.
Number of staff: None.
EIN: 237002682
Other changes: The grantmaker has moved from NY to FL. The grantmaker no longer lists a primary contact.

741
The Albert E. Feder Family Foundation
c/o Steven Feder
2501 Mercedes Dr.
Fort Lauderdale, FL **33316-2325**

Established in 2000.
Donors: West Interactive Corp.; Steven Feder.
Foundation type: Independent foundation.
Financial data (yr. ended 12/31/12): Assets, $103,698 (M); gifts received, $7,000; expenditures, $85,927; qualifying distributions, $83,742; giving activities include $83,742 for 10 grants (high: $37,867; low: $200).
Fields of interest: Higher education, university; Animals/wildlife; Boys & girls clubs; Civil/human rights, LGBTQ; Jewish agencies & synagogues.
Type of support: Capital campaigns; General/operating support.
Limitations: Applications not accepted. Giving primarily in FL and NY.
Application information: Unsolicited requests for funds not accepted.
Trustee: Steven Feder.
EIN: 656346215

742
The Figg Foundation
Tallahassee, FL

The foundation terminated in 2012.

743
The Doak Finch Foundation
c/o Bank of America, N.A.
P.O. Box 40200, FL9-100-10-19
Jacksonville, FL 32203-0200
***Application address:* c/o David R. Williams, M.D., 705 Salem St., Thomasville, NC 27360-2810, tel.: (336) 475-2348**

Trust established in 1961 in NC.
Donor: Doak Finch†.
Foundation type: Independent foundation.
Financial data (yr. ended 10/31/13): Assets, $3,170,898 (M); expenditures, $234,914; qualifying distributions, $213,746; giving activities include $200,000 for 12 grants (high: $60,000; low: $2,000).
Purpose and activities: Giving primarily for human services.
Fields of interest: Arts; Secondary school/education; Human services; YM/YWCAs & YM/YWHAs; Protestant agencies & churches.
Limitations: Giving limited to the Thomasville, NC, area.
Application information: Application form not required.
Initial approach: Letter
Deadline(s): None
Board meeting date(s): Nov.
Trustee Bank: Bank of America, N.A.
EIN: 566042823

744
Florida Blue Foundation
(formerly Blue Cross and Blue Shield of Florida Foundation)
4800 Deerwood Campus Pkwy., DC 3-4
Jacksonville, FL **32246-6498 (800) 477-3736 ext. 63215**
Contact: Susan B. Towler, V.P.; Susan F. Wildes, Sr. Prog. Mgr.
FAX: (904) 357-8367;
E-mail: thebluefoundationfl@bcbsfl.com; E-mail for Susan B. Towler: susan.towler@bcbsfl.com; E-mail for Sapphire Award: TheSapphireAward@bcbsfl.com; E-mail for Embrace a Healthy Florida: embrace@bcbsfl.com; E-mail for Improve Quality of Life Grants: communityrelations@floridablue.com; Main URL: http://www3.bcbsfl.com/wps/portal/bcbsfl/bluefoundation

Established in 2001 in FL.
Donors: Blue Cross and Blue Shield of Florida, Inc.; Health Options, Inc.; Tracy Leinbach.
Foundation type: Company-sponsored foundation.
Financial data (yr. ended 12/31/13): Assets, $156,519,933 (M); gifts received, $19,163,253; expenditures, $11,779,694; qualifying distributions, $11,655,052; giving activities include $9,864,078 for 472 grants (high: $1,000,000; low: $244), and $496,118 for 4 foundation-administered programs.
Purpose and activities: The foundation supports programs designed to improve the health of Floridians and their communities. Special emphasis is directed toward programs designed to improve access to health care; consumer health; the quality and safety of patient care; quality of life; and the healthcare system.
Fields of interest: Arts; Elementary/secondary education; Higher education; Nursing school/education; Education, reading; Education; Health care, alliance/advocacy; Health care, public policy; Health care, equal rights; Health care, clinics/centers; Dental care; Optometry/vision screening; Public health; Public health, obesity; Public health, physical fitness; Health care, financing; Health care, patient services; Health care; Mental health, counseling/support groups; Mental health/crisis services; Nutrition; Family services; Human services; Civil/human rights, equal rights; Community/economic development; Leadership development; Children; Minorities; Economically disadvantaged.
Type of support: General/operating support; Continuing support; Management development/capacity building; Capital campaigns; Equipment; Program development; Scholarship funds; Technical assistance.
Limitations: Applications accepted. Giving limited to areas of company operations in FL. No support for political or lobbying organizations, fraternal, athletic, or social organizations, or religious organizations not of direct benefit to the entire community, private foundations, or Type III supporting organizations. No grants to individuals (except for the Sapphire Award) or for fundraising.
Publications: Application guidelines; Corporate giving report; Grants list; Newsletter.
Application information: Organizations may apply for support only once during a 12-moth period. Unsolicited applications for Embrace a Healthy Florida are not accepted. An interview may be requested for the Sapphire Award. Organizations receiving support are asked to submit a final report. Application form required.
***Initial approach:* Complete online nomination form for Sapphire Award; complete online application for Build Healthy, Strong Communities**
***Deadline(s):* Varies for Sapphire Award; None for Build Healthy, Strong Communities**
Board meeting date(s): Feb., Apr., June, Aug., Oct., and Dec.
***Final notification:* Varies for Sapphire Award**
Officers and Directors:* Charles S. Joseph,* Chair.; **Jason Altmire, Vice-Chair.**; Susan B. Towler, V.P.; Mark S. McGowan,* Secy.; Gary M. Healy, Treas.; **Chuck Divita**; Renee Finley; Camille Harrison; Joyce A. Kramzer; **Robert Lufrano**; Maria Moutinho; Penelope S. Shaffer; Darnell Smith.
Number of staff: 4 full-time professional.
EIN: 593707820
Other changes: Jason Altmire has replaced Charles S. Joseph as Vice-Chair.
Cyrus M. "Russ" Jollivette is no longer Chair.
Cheryl O. Mose is no longer Treas. Michael Cascone and V. Sheffield Kenyon are no longer directors. Sharon Hackney is now Sr. Prog. Mgr.

745
Flournoy-Theadcraft Trust
c/o SunTrust Bank
P.O. Box 1908
Orlando, FL 32802-1908

Established in VA.
Donor: Georgia T. Flournoy Unitrust No. 2.
Foundation type: Independent foundation.
Financial data (yr. ended 11/30/13): Assets, $2,386,481 (M); gifts received, $61,059; expenditures, $6,027,598; qualifying distributions, $5,918,108; giving activities include $5,760,951 for 12 grants (high: $1,146,878; low: $8,798).
Fields of interest: Children/youth, services; Foundations (community); United Ways and Federated Giving Programs.
Limitations: Applications not accepted. Giving primarily in VA. No grants to individuals.
Application information: Contributes only to pre-selected organizations.
Trustee: SunTrust Bank.
EIN: 546191989
Other changes: For the fiscal year ended Nov. 30, 2013, the grantmaker paid grants of $5,760,951, a 1,844.8% increase over the fiscal 2011 disbursements, $296,227.

746
Focus on Excellence, Inc.
7035 Philips Hwy. 36
Jacksonville, FL 32216
Main URL: http://www.focusonexcellenceofflorida.com/

Donor: Chartered Foundation.
Foundation type: Independent foundation.
Financial data (yr. ended 12/31/12): Assets, $58,417 (M); gifts received, $542,789; expenditures, $506,329; qualifying distributions, $500,826; giving activities include $310,008 for 5 grants (high: $183,104; low: $9,199).
Fields of interest: Education.
Limitations: Applications not accepted. Giving primarily in FL.
Application information: Unsolicited requests for funds not accepted.
Officers: James R. Swanson, Chair. and Pres.; **Mike Baxter, Secy.**
Directors: Marcus Broadnax; Joel Settembrini.
EIN: 262483759
Other changes: The grantmaker has moved from IL to FL.
Mike Baxter has replaced Cheryl L. Highland as Secy.

747
The Mary Alice Fortin Foundation
201 Chilean Ave.
Palm Beach, FL 33480-6118

Established in 1993 in FL.
Donors: Mary Alice Fortin†; Fortin Foundation of Florida; Mary Alice Fortine Irrevocable Trust.
Foundation type: Independent foundation.
Financial data (yr. ended 12/31/12): Assets, $136,355,236 (M); gifts received, $57,900,425; expenditures, $4,972,513; qualifying distributions, $3,019,601; giving activities include $2,335,618 for 114 grants (high: $500,000; low: $1).
Fields of interest: Education; Health care; Boys & girls clubs; Human services; Children/youth, services; Community/economic development; Foundations (private grantmaking).
Limitations: Applications not accepted. Giving primarily in FL. No grants to individuals.
Application information: Contributes only to pre-selected organizations.
Officers: Danielle Hickox Moore, Pres. and Treas.; **Carol McCracken, Secy.**
Directors: Larry Alexander; Susan Stockard Channing; Nick R. Cladis; Mary Alice Plisco; Lesly S. Smith.
EIN: 592469696
Other changes: At the close of 2012, the fair market value of the grantmaker's assets was $136,355,236, a 250.1% increase over the 2010 value, $38,951,119. For the same period, the grantmaker paid grants of $2,335,618, a 234.2% increase over the 2010 disbursements, $698,825. Carol McCracken has replaced John McCracken as Secy.

748
Wilson P. & Anne W. Franklin Foundation
7395 Acorn Way
Naples, FL **34119-9611** (404) 312-8951
Contact: W. Stevens Franklin, Tr.

Established in 1996 in GA.
Donors: Wilson P. Franklin†; Richard R. Franklin†.
Foundation type: Independent foundation.
Financial data (yr. ended 09/30/13): Assets, $2,972,589 (M); gifts received, $48,196; expenditures, $270,049; qualifying distributions, $250,000; giving activities include $250,000 for 2 grants (high: $150,000; low: $100,000).
Fields of interest: Education; Health care.
Limitations: Applications accepted. Giving primarily in GA. No grants to individuals.
Application information: Application form required.
Initial approach: Proposal
Deadline(s): None
Trustees: James D. Bryce; Tammy G. Franklin; W. Stevens Franklin.
EIN: 586329924

749
The Gate Foundation, Inc.
9540 San Jose Blvd.
P.O. Box 23627
Jacksonville, FL 32241-3627 (904) 448-2979
***Contact:* Kathy J. Brady**
Main URL: http://www.gatepetro.com

Established in FL.
Donor: Gate Petroleum Company.
Foundation type: Company-sponsored foundation.
Financial data (yr. ended 06/30/13): Assets, $8,637 (M); gifts received, $376,419; expenditures, $363,143; qualifying distributions, $279,606; giving activities include $279,606 for 33 grants (high: $114,000; low: $50).
Purpose and activities: The foundation supports programs designed to create affordable housing for low-to-moderate income families; provide shelter for those in crisis; provide youth activity initiatives to reduce crime in communities; offer food, nourishment, and clothing to those in need; protect the communities; provide assisted or independent living for the disabled or elderly; and promote access to quality health care and health education.
Fields of interest: Health care; Cancer; Crime/violence prevention, youth; Food services; Nutrition; Housing/shelter, temporary shelter; Housing/shelter, homeless; Housing/shelter; Big Brothers/Big Sisters; Youth, services; Family services; Independent living, disability; Human services; Aging; Disabilities, people with; Economically disadvantaged.
Type of support: General/operating support.
Limitations: Applications accepted. **Giving primarily in Jacksonville, FL. No support for discriminatory organizations, international organizations, political committees or candidates, fraternal or alumni organizations, religious-based organizations, private foundations, individual pre-college schools or individual public school systems, or athletic teams. No grants to individuals, or for travel or conferences for employees of nonprofit organizations, political causes, books, research papers, or articles in professional journals, general operating expenses for organizations supported by the United Way, sponsorships, events, or projects for which the GATE Petroleum Company receive tangible benefits.**
Publications: Application guidelines.
Application information: Application form required.
***Initial approach:* Download application form and mail to foundation**
Deadline(s): None
Officers and Directors:* Hill Peyton,* Chair. and Pres.; Frank Gwaltney,* V.P. and Secy.-Treas.; David Dill; Drew Frick; Dean Gwin; Dale Haney; Sammy Patten.
EIN: 262990671
Other changes: The grantmaker now publishes application guidelines online.

750
Glazer Family Foundation, Inc.
c/o Coord.
1 Buccaneer Pl.
Tampa, FL 33607-5701 (813) 870-2700
E-mail: GlazerFamilyFoundation@buccaneers.nfl.com; Main URL: http://www.glazerfamilyfoundation.com/
Facebook: http://www.facebook.com/glazerfamilyfoundation
Grants List: http://www.glazerfamilyfoundation.org/our-programs/grant-program/who-has-received-grants

Established in 1999 in FL.
Donors: Buccaneer L.P.; Florida Sports Foundation.
Foundation type: Company-sponsored foundation.
Financial data (yr. ended 12/31/12): Assets, $1,014,825 (M); gifts received, $3,591,204; expenditures, $2,588,441; qualifying distributions, $2,561,236; giving activities include $2,561,236 for 55 grants (high: $1,010,000; low: $875).
Purpose and activities: The foundation supports programs designed to serve disadvantaged youth and families.
Fields of interest: Museums; Libraries (public); Education, reading; Education; Hospitals (general); Health care, clinics/centers; Optometry/vision screening; Health care, patient services; Health care; Food services; Safety/disasters; Athletics/sports, amateur leagues; Athletics/sports, football; Recreation; Children/youth, services; Human services; Community/economic development; Youth; Economically disadvantaged.
Type of support: Equipment; Program development; Donated products; In-kind gifts.
Limitations: Applications not accepted. Giving primarily in Tampa Bay and central FL, with emphasis on Charlotte, Citrus, De Soto, Hardee, Hernando, Highlands, Hillsborough, Lake, Manatee, Marion, Orange, Osceola, Pasco, Pinellas, Polk, Sarasota, Seminole, Sumter counties. No support for political organizations. No grants to individuals, or for fundraising, celebrations, administrative/training costs, capital campaigns, sponsorships, scholarships, basic research/conferences, or political campaigns.
Publications: Program policy statement.
Application information: The foundation currently practices an invitation only process for giving.
Officers and Directors: Darcie Glazer Kassewitz, Co-Pres.; Edward Glazer, Co-Pres.; **Avie Glazer**; Bryan Glazer; Joel Glazer; **Kevin Glazer**.
EIN: 593578188
Other changes: The grantmaker no longer publishes application guidelines.

751
Green Family Foundation, Inc.
2601 S. Bayshore Dr., 9th Fl.
Coconut Grove, FL 33133-5417 (305) 858-4225
E-mail: info@greenff.org; **Miami Beach address: 1820 Bay Rd., Miami Beach, FL 33139, tel.: (305) 538-4848, ext. 14; fax: (305) 538-4890; e-mail for information about current grant opportunities or to be added to the foundation's RFP contact list: grants@greenff.org**; Main URL: http://www.greenff.org
Facebook: http://www.facebook.com/greenff
Twitter: https://twitter.com/GreenFamilyFdn
YouTube: http://www.youtube.com/greenfamilymiami

Established in 1991 in FL.
Donor: Steven J. Green.
Foundation type: Independent foundation.
Financial data (yr. ended 12/31/12): Assets, $25,098,656 (M); gifts received, $12,511,316; expenditures, $1,999,265; qualifying distributions, $1,523,749; giving activities include $1,512,186 for 37 grants (high: $1,200,000; low: $100), and $11,563 for foundation-administered programs.
Purpose and activities: The foundation provides seed grants to support holistic programs that empower entire communities. The end goal is to enable underserved communities to achieve sustainability and self-reliance by alleviating the cycle of poverty and disease. The foundation lends resources to programs that focus on, 1) global health and development, 2) community empowerment, 3) youth arts, and 4) education.
Fields of interest: Arts; Education; Human services; Children/youth, services; International development; Foundations (private grantmaking); Immigrants/refugees; Economically disadvantaged.
Limitations: Applications not accepted. Giving primarily in Miami, FL. No grants to individuals, or for emergency funding to cover ongoing program or operational deficits.
Publications: Grants list.

Application information: Contributes only to pre-selected organizations. See foundation web site for current RFP information.
Officers: Kimberly Green, Pres.; Kevin Coster, V.P.
EIN: 650284913

752
Greenburg May Foundation, Inc.
9999 Collins Ave., Apt. 15A
Bal Harbour, FL 33154-1834

Incorporated in 1947 in DE.
Donors: Harry Greenburg†; Samuel D. May†.
Foundation type: Independent foundation.
Financial data (yr. ended 12/31/12): Assets, $10,668,182 (M); expenditures, $831,909; qualifying distributions, $685,969; giving activities include $685,969 for 24 grants (high: $500,000; low: $9).
Purpose and activities: Grants almost entirely for medical research, primarily cancer, heart, diabetes, Parkinson's, and neurological research; support also for the aged, hospitals, Jewish welfare funds, and temples.
Fields of interest: Hospitals (general); Cancer; Heart & circulatory diseases; Neuroscience; Medical research, institute; Cancer research; Human services; Aging, centers/services; Jewish federated giving programs; Jewish agencies & synagogues; Children; Aging; Blind/visually impaired.
International interests: Israel.
Type of support: General/operating support; Continuing support; Annual campaigns; Endowments; Emergency funds; Program development; Internship funds; Scholarship funds; Research; Consulting services.
Limitations: Applications accepted. Giving primarily in southern FL and Long Island, NY. No grants to individuals, or for conferences; generally no grants for scholarships or fellowships; no loans.
Application information: Application form required.
Initial approach: Letter
Copies of proposal: 1
Deadline(s): None
Board meeting date(s): Jan., Apr., July, and Oct.
Final notification: 1 to 2 mos.
Officer: Isabel May, Pres.
Directors: Peter May; Linda Sklar.
Number of staff: 2 part-time support.
EIN: 136162935

753
Audrey and Martin Gruss Foundation
c/o Gruss & Co., Inc.
777 S. Flagler Dr., Ste. 801-E
West Palm Beach, FL 33401-6134

Established in 2009 in FL.
Donors: Martin D. Gruss; Joseph S. Gruss Settlor Trust; Joseph S. Gruss Trust.
Foundation type: Independent foundation.
Financial data (yr. ended 08/31/13): Assets, $102,220,548 (M); gifts received, $2,593,661; expenditures, $8,484,291; qualifying distributions, $6,573,074; giving activities include $6,560,982 for grants.
Fields of interest: Medical research; Human services.
Limitations: Applications not accepted. Giving primarily in San Francisco, CA and New York, NY.
Application information: Unsolicited requests for funds not accepted.
Officers: Audrey B. Gruss, Co-Pres.; Martin D. Gruss, Co-Pres.; Brash Lalta, V.P.
EIN: 900445575
Other changes: Howard R. Guberman is no longer V.P. and Secy.-Treas.

754
Gulf Coast Community Foundation, Inc.
(doing business as Gulf Coast Community Foundation)
(formerly Gulf Coast Community Foundation of Venice)
601 Tamiami Trail South
Venice, FL 34285-3237 (941) 486-4600
***Contact:* Teri A. Hansen, C.E.O./Pres.; Wendy Deming, Chief of Staff and Corp. Secy.**
FAX: (941) 486-4699; E-mail: info@gulfcoastcf.org; Additional e-mail: thansen@gulfcoastcf.org; Main URL: http://www.gulfcoastcf.org/
Facebook: https://www.facebook.com/GulfCoastCommFnd
LinkedIn: http://www.linkedin.com/companies/gulf-coast-community-foundation-of-venice
Twitter: http://www.twitter.com/gulfcoastcf
YouTube: http://www.youtube.com/user/GulfCoastCF

Established in 1995 in FL.
Foundation type: Community foundation.
Financial data (yr. ended 06/30/13): Assets, $232,647,057 (M); gifts received, $19,904,665; expenditures, $22,670,492; giving activities include $16,432,516 for grants.
Purpose and activities: Together with donors, the Gulf Coast Community Foundation transforms the local region through bold and proactive philanthropy. Gulf Coast is a public charity that was created in 1995 through the sale of the Venice Hospital. Since then, the foundation has welcomed more than 500 charitable funds established by generous donors and invested $148 million in grants in the areas of health and human services, civic and economic development, education, arts and culture, and the environment.
Fields of interest: Media, film/video; Arts; Higher education; Education; Environmental education; Environment; Health care; Mental health/crisis services; Disasters, preparedness/services; Youth development; Youth, services; Aging, centers/services; Human services; Community development, neighborhood development; Community development, citizen coalitions; Public affairs, citizen participation; Public affairs.
Type of support: Emergency funds; Program development; Scholarship funds; Consulting services.
Limitations: Applications accepted. Giving limited to Charlotte, DeSoto, Lee, Manatee, Sarasota counties in FL. No support for religious purposes. No grants to individuals (except for scholarships), or for endowments, debt reduction, basic scientific research, events, or travel.
Publications: Application guidelines; Annual report; Grants list; Informational brochure (including application guidelines); Occasional report.
Application information: Each year, the foundation's grantmaking evolves to stay ahead of emerging issues and to make the greatest positive impact throughout the region. The foundation invites nonprofit organizations to partner with them as they transform the region through bold ideas, creative projects, and proactive philanthropy. This year, Gulf Coast will fund Leveraged grants and Transformative grants greater than $10,000, and Community grants of $10,000 and under. Application form required.
Initial approach: Visit grant page on website: http://www.gulfcoastcf.org/resources.php
Deadline(s): Varies
Board meeting date(s): Bimonthly
Final notification: Varies
Officers and Directors:* Tommy Taylor,* Chair.; Jay McHarque,* Vice-Chair.; Teri A. Hansen,* C.E.O. and Pres.; Veronica Brady, Sr. V.P., Philanthropy; Mark Pritchett, Sr. V.P., Community Investment; Rich Jones, V.P., Finance; Wendy Deming, Chief of Staff and Corp. Secy.; Judy Cahn; Lisa Carlton; Scott Collins; Norbert Donelly; Janis Fawn; Jim Gallogly; Benjamin Hanan; Phil Humann; Michael Saunders; Bayne Stevenson; R. Elton White.
Number of staff: 15 full-time professional.
EIN: 591052433

755
The Hand Foundation, Inc.
1499 Forest Hill Blvd., Ste. 116
West Palm Beach, FL 33406-6050 (561) 439-0171
Contact: Ruben Ledesma, Jr., Dir.

Established in 1989 in FL.
Donors: Homer J. Hand; Frances R. Hand.
Foundation type: Independent foundation.
Financial data (yr. ended 12/31/12): Assets, $26,784 (M); gifts received, $190,000; expenditures, $191,306; qualifying distributions, $191,306; giving activities include $191,245 for 48 grants to individuals (high: $16,300; low: $1,000).
Fields of interest: Higher education; Scholarships/financial aid.
Type of support: Scholarships—to individuals.
Limitations: Applications accepted. Giving primarily in FL.
Application information: Application form required.
Initial approach: Letter
Deadline(s): None
Directors: Thomas L. Altman; Homer J. Hand; Ruben Ledesma, Jr.; Paul R. Orsemigo.
EIN: 650118848
Other changes: Frances R. Hand is no longer a director.

756
Hard Rock Cafe Foundation, Inc.
6100 Old Park Ln.
Orlando, FL 32835-2466
Established in 2000 in FL.
Donors: Hard Rock Cafe International (USA) Inc.; WDI Corporation.
Foundation type: Company-sponsored foundation.
Financial data (yr. ended 12/31/12): Assets, $962 (M); gifts received, $2,268,478; expenditures, $2,267,758; qualifying distributions, $2,267,184; giving activities include $2,211,389 for 15 grants (high: $630,976; low: $14), and $55,795 for 91 grants to individuals (high: $3,000; low: $200).
Purpose and activities: The foundation supports organizations involved with music, substance abuse services, cancer research, hunger, agriculture, human services, civil and human rights, and economically disadvantaged people.
Fields of interest: Health organizations; Agriculture/food; Recreation.
Type of support: General/operating support; Program development; Research; Grants to individuals.
Limitations: Applications not accepted. Giving limited to Washington, DC and New York, NY.

Application information: Contributes only to pre-selected organizations.
Officers and Directors:* Hamish Dodds,* Pres.; Jay Wolszczak,* Secy.; Thomas Gispanski,* Treas.
EIN: 593686985
Other changes: At the close of 2012, the grantmaker paid grants of $2,267,184, a 56.8% increase over the 2011 disbursements, $1,446,153.

757
Heartbeat International Worldwide, Inc.
(formerly Heartbeat International of West Central Florida)
4302 Henderson Blvd., Ste. 102
Tampa, FL 33629-5693 (813) 259-1213
FAX: (813) 259-1215;
E-mail: connect@HeartbeatSavesLives.org; Main URL: http://www.heartbeatsaveslives.org
E-Newsletter: https://www.heartbeatsaveslives.org/?nav=6&pos=0&sub=0
Facebook: https://www.facebook.com/pages/Heartbeat-Saves-Lives-Heartbeat-International-Foundation/281723716762
Flickr: http://www.flickr.com/photos/65420182@N06
Google Plus: https://plus.google.com/114014326670221637661/posts
Twitter: https://twitter.com/HeartbeatSaves
YouTube: http://www.youtube.com/user/HeartbeatSavesLives

Established in 1984.
Donors: Medtronic, Inc.; Pacesetter Systems, Inc.; Intermedics, Inc.; St. Joseph's Hospital; Watson Clinic Foundation; St. Jude Medical, CRM Div.; George Lorton; Biotronik SE & Co. KG; Boston Scientific.
Foundation type: Independent foundation.
Financial data (yr. ended 12/31/12): Assets, $7,818,506 (M); gifts received, $4,015,066; expenditures, $3,100,527; qualifying distributions, $3,100,527; giving activities include $3,032,722 for 12 grants (high: $1,252,722; low: $8,000).
Purpose and activities: Heartbeat International provides free cardiac pacemakers, implantable defibrillators and medical care to needy patients around the world.
Fields of interest: Health care.
Limitations: Applications not accepted. Giving worldwide.
Application information: Unsolicited requests for funds not accepted.
Officers and Directors:* Benedict Maniscalco, M.D.*, Chair. and C.E.O.; Albert Salem, Jr.,* Chair.; Laura DeLise, Exec. V.P.; Jorge Bahena, M.D.; **Sandra Kreul**; Basha G. Mohammed; **Arthur Noriega IV**.
Number of staff: 1 full-time professional; 2 full-time support; 1 part-time support.
EIN: 593236060
Other changes: Andres A. Baffico Fuentes, Gerald F. Fletcher, Hary G. Mond are no longer directors.

758
The A. D. Henderson Foundation, Inc.
P.O. Box 14096
Fort Lauderdale, FL 33302-4096 (954) 764-2819
Contact: Karen Pfeiffer, Sr. Admin.
E-mail: karen@hendersonfdn.org; **Additional FL office contact: Monica Menahem, Admin, Asst. and Prog. Assoc., tel.: (954) 764-2819, ext. 2, e-mail: monica@hendersonfdn.org; VT. office contact: Eddie Gale, Prog. Dir., tel.: (902) 888-1188, e-mail: egale@hendersonfdn.org**; Main URL: http://www.hendersonfdn.org

Established in 1969.
Foundation type: Independent foundation.
Financial data (yr. ended 09/30/13): Assets, $56,763,509 (M); expenditures, $2,788,448; qualifying distributions, $2,378,377; giving activities include $1,806,017 for 36 grants (high: $400,000; low: $2,500).
Purpose and activities: In FL, the foundation supports high quality early care and education for children ages 0-5. In VT, the foundation supports high quality early care and education for children ages 0-5, and capacity building for the non-profit sector, with a focus on mentoring and early learning.
Fields of interest: Education, early childhood education; Child development, education; Education; Children/youth, services.
Type of support: Continuing support; Management development/capacity building; Program development; Seed money; Curriculum development; Technical assistance; Matching/challenge support.
Limitations: Applications accepted. Giving primarily in Broward and Marion counties, FL, and VT. No support for private foundations or organizations lacking 501(c)(3) status, or for sectarian purposes. **No grants to individuals, or for scholarships, annual campaigns or fundraising events, operating budgets, endowments, building or renovation, equipment (unless it is an integral part of an eligible project), capital campaigns, debt reduction, general operating support, or medical or clinical research; no loans.**
Publications: Application guidelines; Grants list; Program policy statement; Program policy statement (including application guidelines).
Application information: Applications are by invitation, based on initial telephone call. Application guidelines available on foundation web site.
Initial approach: Telephone a foundation Program Dir. prior to formal submission to discuss project idea
Deadline(s): Quarterly
Board meeting date(s): Quarterly
Officers and Trustees:* Allen Douglas Henderson,* Pres.; Lucia Henderson,* 1st V.P.; Anne Rider, 2nd V.P.; Barbara K. Henderson,* 3rd V.P.; Karen M. Pfeiffer,* Secy. and Sr. Admin.; Maureen C. Tompkins,* Treas.; **A. Holly Fouladi**; James Hasson, Jr.; Robert S. Hinrichs.
Number of staff: 1 full-time professional; 1 part-time professional; 1 full-time support; 1 part-time support.
EIN: 237047045

759
Jack Holloway Foundation
390 N. Orange Ave., MC FL0-800-07-08
Orlando, FL 32801-1640
Application address: John W. Holloway, P.O. Box 593688, Orlando, FL 32859-3688

Established in 1960.
Donor: John D. Holloway Revocable Trust.
Foundation type: Independent foundation.
Financial data (yr. ended 05/31/13): Assets, $4,941,417 (M); expenditures, $269,539; qualifying distributions, $234,991; giving activities include $233,500 for 15 grants (high: $80,000; low: $3,500).
Fields of interest: Hospitals (specialty); Cerebral palsy; Health organizations; Human services; Children/youth, services; Protestant agencies & churches; Catholic agencies & churches.
Limitations: Applications accepted. Giving limited to FL. No grants to individuals.
Application information: Application form required.
Initial approach: Letter
Deadline(s): None
Trustees: Jacqueline H. Bailes; John W. Holloway.
EIN: 596076468

760
The Ann & Joel Horowitz Family Foundation, Inc.
800 S. Pointe Dr., Ste. 2003
Miami Beach, FL 33139-7190
***Contact:* Ann Horowitz**

Established in 1997 in NJ and DE.
Donor: Joel J. Horowitz.
Foundation type: Independent foundation.
Financial data (yr. ended 11/30/11): Assets, $612,649 (M); expenditures, $230,866; qualifying distributions, $216,532; giving activities include $216,000 for 9 grants (high: $100,000; low: $1,000).
Fields of interest: Arts, research; Public affairs, equal rights; Jewish agencies & synagogues.
Limitations: Applications not accepted. No grants to individuals.
Application information: Unsolicited requests for funds not accepted.
Officers: Ann P. Horowitz, Pres.; Joel J. Horowitz, V.P.
Director: Dustin Horowitz.
EIN: 223554513
Other changes: The grantmaker has moved from NV to FL.

761
Jacksonville Jaguars Foundation
1 EverBank Field Dr.
Jacksonville, FL 32202-1920 (904) 633-5437
Contact: Peter M. Racine, Pres.
FAX: (904) 633-5683;
E-mail: sahil@nfl.jaguars.com; **E-mail for Peter Racine: racinep@jaguars.nfl.com; Contact for Honor Rows: T-Neisha Tate, tel.: (904) 633-6516, e-mail: tatet@nfl.jaguars.com; Community Scholars: Heather Burk, University of North Florida, Service Learning Coord., tel.: (904) 620-3922, E-mail: hburk@unf.edu**; Main URL: http://www.jaguars.com/foundation-community/index.html
Facebook: https://www.facebook.com/JaguarsFoundation

Established in 1994 in FL.
Donor: Jacksonville Jaguars, Ltd.
Foundation type: Company-sponsored foundation.
Financial data (yr. ended 12/31/12): Assets, $4,976,349 (M); gifts received, $1,943,596; expenditures, $2,296,353; qualifying distributions, $2,233,072; giving activities include $1,244,316 for 99 grants (high: $78,500; low: $500).
Purpose and activities: The foundation supports programs designed to serve economically and socially disadvantaged youth and families.
Fields of interest: Media/communications; Arts; Education, reading; Education; Public health, physical fitness; Nutrition; Recreation; YM/YWCAs & YM/YWHAs; Family services; Human services; Youth; Economically disadvantaged.

Type of support: General/operating support; Continuing support; Capital campaigns; Program development; Scholarship funds; In-kind gifts; Matching/challenge support.
Limitations: Applications accepted. Giving limited to the greater Jacksonville, FL, area, including Baker, Clay, Duval, Nassau, and St. Johns counties. No support for schools, religious organizations not of direct benefit to the entire community, or disease-specific organizations. No grants to individuals or for fundraising or sponsorships.
Publications: Application guidelines.
Application information: A full proposal may be requested at a later date for new applicants. Multi-year funding is limited to a maximum of 2 to 3 consecutive years. Requests for general operating support and capital campaigns must include a long-term (3-5 year) strategic plan. Organizations receiving support are asked to submit a progress report and a final report.
Initial approach: **Complete online eligibility quiz and letter of inquiry for new applicants; complete online application for returning grantees and for Honor Rows**
Deadline(s): **None for new applicants; Feb. 15 for Cycle 1 and July 15 for Cycle 2 for returning grantees; Mar. 24 for Honor Rows deadline**
Board meeting date(s): Generally, summer and winter
Final notification: 30 days; June 1 for Honor Rows
Officer: Peter M. Racine, Pres.
Number of staff: 3 full-time professional; 1 full-time support; 1 part-time support.
EIN: 593249687

762
Hans & Cay Jacobsen Charitable Foundation Inc.

P.O. Box 2149
Winter Park, FL 32790-2149 (407) 810-6672
Contact: Teresa W. Borcheck, Pres.
E-mail: **info@hansandcayjacobsenfoundation.org**; Main URL: http://www.hansandcayjacobsenfoundation.org
Grants List: http://www.hansandcayjacobsenfoundation.org/index.php?p=updates

Established in 1990 in FL.
Foundation type: Independent foundation.
Financial data (yr. ended 05/31/13): Assets, $5,558,900 (M); expenditures, $343,683; qualifying distributions, $282,427; giving activities include $240,000 for 15 grants (high: $45,000; low: $1,000).
Purpose and activities: Giving primarily for services for children.
Fields of interest: Elementary/secondary education; Scholarships/financial aid; Education; Health organizations, equal rights; Boys & girls clubs; Human services; Children, services; Children/youth; Disabilities, people with; Physically disabled; Economically disadvantaged.
Type of support: General/operating support; Program development; Scholarship funds; Matching/challenge support.
Limitations: Applications accepted. **Giving primarily in the Lake and Sumpter County, FL, area.** No grants to individuals.
Publications: Application guidelines.
Application information: Application guidelines and form available on foundation web site. Application form required.
Copies of proposal: 1
Deadline(s): May 1 and Nov. 1
Board meeting date(s): Feb., May, Aug. and Nov.
Officers: Teresa W. Borcheck, Pres.; Tom Brooks, V.P.; Shannon McLin Carlyle, Secy.; Brian Brooks, Treas.
EIN: 593010451

763
Mohsin & Fauzia Jaffer Foundation

3410 Stallion Ln.
Weston, FL 33331-3035

Established in 2005 in FL.
Donors: Mohsin Jaffer; Fauzia Jaffer; Family Doctors of Broward; Medina Properties, Inc.; Sam Weston Properties, Inc.; Mayfair Medical Mgmt.
Foundation type: Independent foundation.
Financial data (yr. ended 12/31/12): Assets, $5,031,903 (M); gifts received, $5,684,000; expenditures, $1,044,800; qualifying distributions, $1,044,800; giving activities include $1,044,800 for 35 grants (high: $101,000; low: $200).
Fields of interest: Education; Human services; Islam; Religion.
Type of support: General/operating support.
Limitations: Applications not accepted. Giving primarily in FL, and on an international basis. No grants to individuals.
Application information: Contributes only to pre-selected organizations.
Directors: Fauzia Jaffer; Mohsin Jaffer.
EIN: 202965144

764
Kantner Foundation, Inc.

3801 PGA Blvd., Ste. 902
Palm Beach Gardens, FL **33410-2757 (561) 296-2682**
Contact: Thomas N. Silverman, Chair., Pres., and Secy.
E-mail: **info@kantnerfoundation.org**; Main URL: http://kantnerfoundation.org/
Facebook: https://www.facebook.com/pages/Kantner-Foundation/234417809954572?fref=ts
Google Plus: https://plus.google.com/105692082967518438128/about
LinkedIn: http://www.linkedin.com/company/kantner-foundation

Established in 1987 in FL.
Donors: Woodrow A. Kantner; Karen Kantner; Byron C. Wiswell; Woodrow A. Kantner Charitable Trust.
Foundation type: Independent foundation.
Financial data (yr. ended 12/31/12): Assets, $4,957,379 (M); expenditures, $290,111; qualifying distributions, $231,677; giving activities include $171,000 for 16 grants (high: $50,000; low: $3,000).
Purpose and activities: Giving primarily for scholarships to high school students from the local community to obtain a degree from a four-year college or university and to community-based philanthropic organizations.
Fields of interest: Education; Hospitals (general); Legal services; Human services; Residential/custodial care, hospices; Foundations (private grantmaking).
Type of support: General/operating support; Scholarships—to individuals.
Application information: For scholarships, use online application on foundation web site. Application form required.
Initial approach: Request application form
Deadline(s): **See foundation web site for deadlines**
Officers and Trustees:* Thomas N. Silverman, Chair., Pres., and Secy.; Connie P. Santini, V.P. and Treas.; Richard C. Jarchow, Sr.,* V.P.; Richard C. Geisinger; Michael Moehle; Samuel B. Silverman; Tim B. Wright.
EIN: 650011831

765
The Katcher Family Foundation, Inc.

4197 S. Douglas Rd.
Miami, FL **33133-6832**
Contact: Gerald Katcher, Dir.

Established in 1996 in DE and FL.
Donors: Gerald Katcher; Dorothy Katcher†.
Foundation type: Independent foundation.
Financial data (yr. ended 11/30/12): Assets, $3,246,366 (M); gifts received, $1,200,000; expenditures, $1,088,689; qualifying distributions, $1,084,475; giving activities include $1,082,372 for 30 grants (high: $357,932; low: $40).
Purpose and activities: Giving primarily for the arts, particularly to museums, as well as for higher education, and Jewish organizations.
Fields of interest: Museums (art); Museums (ethnic/folk arts); Performing arts, music; Arts; Higher education; Education; Environment, research; Children/youth, services; United Ways and Federated Giving Programs; Jewish federated giving programs; Jewish agencies & synagogues.
Limitations: Applications not accepted. Giving primarily in CO, FL and NY.
Application information: Unsolicited requests for funds not accepted.
Directors: Lesley Heller; Gerald Katcher; Jane Katcher.
EIN: 650715498

766
Kazma Family Foundation

1 N. Federal Hwy., Ste. 400
Boca Raton, FL 33432-3930
Contact: Leigh-Anne Kazma, Pres.

Established in 1997 in IL.
Donors: Gerald Kazma; Amzak Corp.
Foundation type: Independent foundation.
Financial data (yr. ended 04/30/13): Assets, $276,748 (M); gifts received, $793,408; expenditures, $1,635,866; qualifying distributions, $1,525,854; giving activities include $1,525,854 for grants.
Purpose and activities: Giving primarily to Roman Catholic schools and organizations, and for social services.
Fields of interest: Elementary/secondary education; Higher education; Education; Human services; Children, services; Catholic federated giving programs; Catholic agencies & churches.
Limitations: Giving primarily in Chicago, IL; some funding also in El Salvador.
Officers: Leigh-Anne Kazma, Pres.; Gerald Kazma, Treas.
Directors: Margaret Kazma; Michael Kazma.
EIN: 364206371
Other changes: The grantmaker has moved from IL to FL.

767
The Ethel & W. George Kennedy Family Foundation, Inc.
1550 Madruga Ave., Ste. 225
Coral Gables, FL 33146-3051 (305) 666-6226
Contact: Kathleen Kennedy-Olsen, Managing Dir.
FAX: (305) 666-2441;
E-mail: admin@kennedyfamilyfdn.org; Main URL: http://www.kennedyfamilyfdn.org

Established in 1968 in FL.
Donor: W. George Kennedy†.
Foundation type: Independent foundation.
Financial data (yr. ended 12/31/12): Assets, $26,155,045 (M); expenditures, $1,480,915; qualifying distributions, $1,215,761; giving activities include $1,038,150 for 97 grants (high: $80,000; low: $250).
Purpose and activities: Giving primarily to organizations that directly support children and families by means of education, health care, technological assistance, rehabilitation and welfare.
Fields of interest: Education; Human services; Children/youth, services; Child development, services; Family services; Infants/toddlers; Children/youth; Children; Youth; Economically disadvantaged.
Type of support: General/operating support; Capital campaigns; Building/renovation; Equipment; Endowments; Program development; Seed money; Scholarship funds; Technical assistance; Matching/challenge support.
Limitations: Applications not accepted. Giving limited to Miami-Dade County, FL. No grants to individuals.
Application information: Unsolicited requests for funds not accepted. The foundation now receives and reviews all grant proposals by Board invitation only.
Board meeting date(s): Mar. and Oct.
Officers and Directors:* Karyn Kennedy Herterich,* Pres.; Kendel Kennedy,* V.P.; Kimberly Kennedy,* V.P.; Kathleen Kennedy-Olsen,* Secy.-Treas. and Managing Dir.; Morgan Herterich; Forrest Mulcahy; Martin Nash; Guy Rizzo.
Number of staff: 2 full-time professional.
EIN: 596204880
Other changes: The grantmaker no longer publishes application guidelines.

768
Basil L. King Scholarship Foundation, Inc.
(formerly Fort Pierce Memorial Hospital Scholarship Foundation, Inc.)
c/o Indian River State College Foundation, Inc.
3209 Virginia Ave.
Fort Pierce, FL 34981-5596 (772) 462-7246
E-mail: lthomas@irsc.edu; Main URL: http://www.blksf.org/

Established in 1973 in FL.
Donor: Yearsley Memorial Fund.
Foundation type: Independent foundation.
Financial data (yr. ended 09/30/13): Assets, $6,032,419 (M); gifts received, $21,035; expenditures, $312,490; qualifying distributions, $267,698; giving activities include $247,035 for 2 grants (high: $226,000; low: $21,035).
Purpose and activities: Scholarships to St. Lucie County, Florida, residents, who are pursuing study in health sciences, medicine, dentistry and pharmacy; payments also made for the medical care of indigent children under 14 years of age.
Fields of interest: Medical school/education; Dental care; Nursing care; Health care; Health organizations, association; Economically disadvantaged.
Type of support: Scholarship funds; Grants to individuals; Scholarships—to individuals.
Limitations: Applications accepted. Giving limited to residents of St. Lucie County, FL.
Application information: Complete guidelines and application available on foundation web site. Application form required.
***Deadline(s):* See foundation web site for current deadline**
Officers and Directors:* Frank H. Fee III,* Chair.; Frederick T. Johnston,* Secy.-Treas.; **Jimmie Anne Haisley, Exec. Dir.**; Bruce Abernethy, Jr.; Barbara Allen; Margaret Benton; Ann Decker; Jimmie Anne Haisley; Betty King.
EIN: 590651084
Other changes: Jimmie Anne Haisley has replaced Craig Harris as Exec. Dir.

769
The Kislak Family Fund, Inc.
7900 Miami Lakes Dr. W.
Miami Lakes, FL 33016-5897
Contact: Stephanie Chace
FAX: (305) 821-1267; E-mail: schace@kislak.com

Established in 1992 in FL.
Donors: Jay I. Kislak; J.I. Kislak, Inc.
Foundation type: Independent foundation.
Financial data (yr. ended 12/31/12): Assets, $20,236,741 (M); gifts received, $1,612,639; expenditures, $894,992; qualifying distributions, $825,018; giving activities include $805,297 for 65 grants (high: $100,000; low: $25).
Purpose and activities: Giving primarily for human services, animal welfare, and to Jewish agencies.
Fields of interest: Museums; Museums (art); Museums (marine/maritime); Museums (specialized); Higher education; Animal welfare; United Ways and Federated Giving Programs; Jewish agencies & synagogues.
Limitations: Applications not accepted. Giving primarily in FL. No grants to individuals.
Application information: Contributes only to pre-selected organizations.
Officers and Directors:* Jay I. Kislak,* Pres.; Jean Kislak,* Secy.; **Thomas Bartelmo, Treas.**; Philip Thomas Kislak; Paula Mangravite.
EIN: 650350930

770
Kiwanis Club of Bradenton Foundation, Inc.
P.O. Box 1032
Bradenton, FL 34206-1032
***Contact:* Teri Roberts, Club Admin.**
***E-mail for Teri Roberts:* palmroberts@gmail.com**;
Main URL: http://www.bradentonkiwanis.org

Established in 1990 in FL.
Donors: Dozier Hilliard; Kiwanis Club of Bradenton, Inc.; Stanley Nieby Revocable Trust; Revocable Living Trust of Elmer J. Trulaske.
Foundation type: Independent foundation.
Financial data (yr. ended 09/30/12): Assets, $9,923,874 (M); gifts received, $2,080; expenditures, $568,427; qualifying distributions, $449,332; giving activities include $449,332 for 27 grants (high: $158,000; low: $100).
Fields of interest: Higher education; Education; Youth development, business; YM/YWCAs & YM/YWHAs; Children/youth, services; United Ways and Federated Giving Programs.
Type of support: Scholarship funds; General/operating support.
Limitations: Applications accepted. Giving primarily in FL.
Publications: Application guidelines.
Application information: Complete application guidelines available on foundation web site. Application form required.
***Initial approach:* For grants e-mail the Club Admin. to request application; for scholarships download the scholarship application on the foundation web site**
Officers: Jack Hawkins, Pres.; Gary Bogart, V.P.; Mark Nelson, Secy.; Bob Sweat, Treas.
Directors: David Bassett; Jim Farr; Hon. Robert Farrance; Hon. Thomas A. Gallen; Mike McCoy; John Tucker.
EIN: 650221660
Other changes: The grantmaker now publishes application guidelines.

771
John S. and James L. Knight Foundation
(formerly Knight Foundation)
200 S. Biscayne Blvd., Ste. 3300
Miami, FL 33131-2349 (305) 908-2600
Contact: Grant Admin.
FAX: (305) 908-2698;
E-mail: web@knightfoundation.org; Additional tel. for publication requests: (305) 908-2630; Main URL: http://www.knightfoundation.org
Community foundations guide for developing a Giving Day: http://www.givingdayplaybook.org/
Facebook: http://www.facebook.com/knightfdn
Grant Assessments: http://knightfoundation.org/publications/browse/?q=%22%22&page=1&selected_facets=pubtype_exact:%22Grant%20Assessments%22
John S. and James L. Knight Foundation Staff: https://twitter.com/knightfdn/knightstaff/members
KnightBlog: http://www.knightblog.org/
Pinterest: http://pinterest.com/knightfnd/pins/
RSS Feed: http://www.knightfoundation.org/rss/
Twitter: http://www.twitter.com/knightfdn
Vimeo: http://www.vimeo.com/knightfdn/videos

Incorporated in 1950 in OH.
Donors: John S. Knight†; James L. Knight†; and their families.
Foundation type: Independent foundation.
Financial data (yr. ended 12/31/13): Assets, $2,395,608,862 (M); expenditures, $135,987,628; qualifying distributions, $120,694,865; giving activities include $107,825,135 for grants, $10,928,230 for foundation-administered programs and $1,941,500 for loans/program-related investments.
Purpose and activities: The foundation advances journalism in the digital age and invests in the vitality of communities where the Knight brothers owned newspapers. The foundation focuses on projects that promote informed, engaged communities and that lead to transformational change. The foundation promotes these goals through its journalism, communities and national programs.
Fields of interest: Media, print publishing; Media, journalism; Arts; Education; Children, services; Family services; Civil rights, race/intergroup relations; Community development, neighborhood development; Economic development; Public affairs, citizen participation; African Americans/Blacks.
Type of support: General/operating support; Management development/capacity building; Capital campaigns; Building/renovation;

Endowments; Emergency funds; Program development; Seed money; Curriculum development; Fellowships; Technical assistance; Program evaluation; Program-related investments/ loans; Employee matching gifts; Matching/ challenge support; Mission-related investments/ loans.
Limitations: Applications accepted. Giving limited to projects serving the 26 communities where the Knight brothers published newspapers for communities and local grants: Long Beach and San Jose, CA, Boulder, CO, Bradenton, Miami, Palm Beach County, and Tallahassee, FL, Columbus, Macon, and Milledgeville, GA, Fort Wayne and Gary, IN, Wichita, KS, Lexington, KY, Detroit, MI, Duluth and St. Paul, MN, Biloxi, MS, Charlotte, NC, Grand Forks, ND, Akron, OH, Philadelphia and State College, PA, Columbia and Myrtle Beach, SC, and Aberdeen, SD; international for Journalism. No support for organizations whose mission is to prevent, eradicate and/or alleviate the effects of a specific disease; hospitals, unless for community-wide capital campaigns; activities to propagate a religious faith or restricted to one religion or denomination; political candidates; international programs, except U.S.-based organizations supporting free press around the world; charities operated by service clubs; or activities that are the responsibility of government (the foundation will in selective cases, join with units of government in supporting special projects). No grants to individuals, or for fundraising events; second requests for previously funded capital campaigns; operating deficits; general operating support; films, videos, or television programs; honoraria for distinguished guests-except in initiatives of the foundation in all three cases; group travel; memorials; medical research; or conferences.
Publications: Newsletter.
Application information: Please do not submit a proposal until you have been invited to do so by the Grants Admin. or a Prog. Off. Journalism and media grantees are required to disclose the identities of major donors and amounts contributed. The requirement applies to gifts of at least $5,000. Application form required.
Initial approach: Online inquiry
Copies of proposal: 1
Deadline(s): None, except for special initiatives (approximately 6-month grant cycle)
Board meeting date(s): Mar., June, Sept., and Dec.
***Final notification:* Full proposal: 1 month**
Officers and Trustees:* John Palfrey,* Chair.; Alberto Ibarguen,* C.E.O. and Pres.; Carol Coletta, V.P., Community and National Initiatives; **Terese Coudreaut Curiel, V.P., HR and Admin.**; Michael Maness, V.P., Journalism Prog. and Media Innovation; Juan J. Martinez, V.P., C.F.O. and Treas.; Dennis Scholl, V.P., Arts and Prog. Dir., Miami; Jorge Martinez, V.P., Inf. Systems; Andrew Sherry, V.P., Comm.; **Elena Stetsenko, Cont.; Christopher M. Austen**; Stephanie Bell-Rose; Francisco L. Borges; William Considine; James N. Crutchfield; Chris Hughes; Joi Ito; Susan D. Kronick; Anna Spangler Nelson; Beverly Knight Olson; Ray Rodriguez; E. Roe Stamps IV; Paul Steiger.
Number of staff: 61 full-time professional; 1 part-time professional.
EIN: 650464177
Other changes: John Palfrey has replaced Robert W. Briggs as Chair.
Marjorie Knight Crane, Mariam C. Noland, Earl W. Powell are no longer trustees. Mayur Patel is no longer V.P., Strategy and Assessment.

772
The Korf Family Foundation, Inc.
200 S. Biscayne Blvd., Ste. 5500
Miami, FL 33131-2333

Established in 2006 in FL.
Donor: Mordechai Korf.
Foundation type: Independent foundation.
Financial data (yr. ended 11/30/13): Assets, $204,959 (M); gifts received, $2,368,000; expenditures, $2,354,718; qualifying distributions, $2,351,155; giving activities include $2,351,155 for 25 grants (high: $1,208,265; low: $350).
Purpose and activities: Giving primarily to Jewish agencies, temples, and schools.
Fields of interest: Education; Jewish federated giving programs; Jewish agencies & synagogues.
Limitations: Applications not accepted. Giving primarily in FL and NY.
Application information: Contributes only to pre-selected organizations.
Officers: Mordechai Y. Korf, C.E.O. and Pres.; Nechama A. Korf, V.P.
EIN: 203942766

773
C. L. C. Kramer Foundation, Inc.
3840 Prairie Dunes Dr.
Sarasota, FL 34238-2816
E-mail: rzabelle@verizon.net; **Tel./fax: (941) 924-2533**; Main URL: http://www.clckramerfoundation.org

Established in 1966.
Donor: Catherine Kramer†.
Foundation type: Independent foundation.
Financial data (yr. ended 09/30/12): Assets, $7,871,934 (M); expenditures, $576,600; qualifying distributions, $479,058; giving activities include $445,000 for 31 grants (high: $60,000; low: $500).
Purpose and activities: Giving primarily for hospitals, as well as to an organization for people who are blind; funding also for the performing arts and Jewish organizations.
Fields of interest: Performing arts; Hospitals (general); Medical research, institute; Human services; Jewish federated giving programs.
Type of support: General/operating support; Continuing support.
Limitations: Applications not accepted. Giving primarily in New York, NY. No grants to individuals.
Publications: IRS Form 990 or 990-PF printed copy available upon request.
Application information: Contributes only to pre-selected organizations.
Officers: Robert Zabelle, Pres.; Lawrence Rothenberg, Secy.; Erica Harold, Treas.
EIN: 136226513

774
Krouse Family Foundation, Inc.
c/o Sun Capital Partners, Inc.
5200 Town Center Cir., Ste. 650
Boca Raton, FL 33486-1045
***Contact:* Donna Wohlfarth**

Donors: Rodger Krouse; Hillary Krouse.
Foundation type: Independent foundation.
Financial data (yr. ended 09/30/13): Assets, $8,562,954 (M); gifts received, $10,000,000; expenditures, $2,345,762; qualifying distributions, $2,323,888; giving activities include $2,322,333 for 10 grants (high: $1,100,000; low: $1,000).
Fields of interest: Education; Human services; Foundations (private grantmaking).
Limitations: Applications not accepted. Giving primarily in Boca Raton, FL; some funding also in New York, NY, and Philadelphia, PA.
Application information: Contributes only to pre-selected organizations.
Officers and Directors:* Rodger R. Krouse,* Pres.; Hillary Krouse,* Secy.; Marc J. Leder,* Treas.
EIN: 261514117
Other changes: For the fiscal year ended Sept. 30, 2013, the grantmaker paid grants of $2,322,333, a 227.1% increase over the fiscal 2011 disbursements, $710,000.

775
Fanny Landwirth Foundation, Inc.
830-13 US AIA N., No. 103
Ponte Vedra Beach, FL 32082 (904) 860-4409
E-mail: info@fannylandwirthfoundation.org; Main URL: http://fannylandwirthfoundation.org/
Grants List: http://fannylandwirthfoundation.org/Recent_Grants.html

Established in 1980 in FL.
Donor: Henri Landwirth.
Foundation type: Independent foundation.
Financial data (yr. ended 12/31/12): Assets, $4,982,558 (M); expenditures, $312,537; qualifying distributions, $237,101; giving activities include $196,650 for 30 grants (high: $20,000; low: $200).
Purpose and activities: Giving primarily for human services, education and Jewish affiliations.
Fields of interest: Arts; Education; Human services; Youth, services; Family services; Jewish agencies & synagogues; Religion; Children/youth; Children; Adults; Young adults; Indigenous peoples; Crime/abuse victims; Terminal illness, people with; Economically disadvantaged; Homeless.
Type of support: General/operating support; Continuing support; Program development; Seed money; Matching/challenge support.
Limitations: Applications not accepted. Giving primarily in FL and Asheville, NC. No grants to individuals or for capital campaigns; no loans.
Publications: Financial statement; Program policy statement.
Application information: Unsolicited requests for funds not accepted.
Board meeting date(s): Oct. and Nov.
Officers and Trustees:* Henri Landwirth,* Chair.; **Gregory D. Landwirth,* Pres.**; Gary M. Landwirth,* V.P.; **Glenn Ullmann,* Secy.**; Linda Landwirth, Treas.; Margot Glazer; Theresa Landwirth; Lisa Landwirth Ullmann.
Number of staff: 2 part-time support.
EIN: 592080560
Other changes: Gregory D. Landwirth has replaced Lisa Landwirth Ullmann as Pres. Glenn Ullmann has replaced Gregory D. Landwirth as Secy.

776
Lattner Family Foundation, Inc.
777 E. Atlantic Ave., Ste. 317
Delray Beach, FL 33483-5352 (561) 278-3781
Contact: Patty Gerhart, Fund Mgr.
E-mail: lattner@bellsouth.net; Main URL: http://www.lattnerfoundation.org

Established in 2006 in FL with assets from the Forrest C. Lattner Foundation.
Foundation type: Independent foundation.

Financial data (yr. ended 12/31/12): Assets, $78,032,683 (M); expenditures, $4,850,441; qualifying distributions, $4,205,500; giving activities include $4,205,500 for grants.
Purpose and activities: Giving primarily in the areas of education, environment, health and social services, arts and humanities, and religion, including Christian organizations that provide health and social services. Special emphasis on the following geographical areas related to where the trustees live: Palm Beach County, Florida, Kansas, Rhode Island, Texas, and Georgia.
Fields of interest: Humanities; Arts; Education; Environment; Health care; Community/economic development; Christian agencies & churches; Religion.
Type of support: General/operating support.
Limitations: Applications accepted. Giving primarily in Palm Beach County, FL, GA, KS, RI, and TX.
Publications: Application guidelines.
Application information: The foundation is not accepting any unsolicited grants from organizations unless they have received a grant in the past. See foundation web site for specific application guidelines which must be followed. The foundation does not accept grant requests via e-mail, fax or phone. Please mail in all grant requests for review. Upon receipt, each request will be reviewed on a preliminary basis. Application form not required.
Initial approach: Letter
Copies of proposal: 1
Deadline(s): Mar. 1 and Sept. 1
Board meeting date(s): Late spring and fall
Final notification: Notification letters are sent out approximately twelve weeks after board meetings
Officer and Trustees:* Martha L. Walker,* Chair.; Janet Barnes; Forrest C. Brown, M.D.; Andrew L. Harris; Richard M. Harris; Thomas Shoof; Susan B. Funke Walker.
EIN: 203100839

777
Josephine S. Leiser Foundation, Inc.
2438 E. Las Olas Blvd.
Fort Lauderdale, FL **33301**
***Contact:* Robert Judd, Pres. and Treas.**

Established in 1992 in FL.
Donor: Josephine S. Leiser†.
Foundation type: Independent foundation.
Financial data (yr. ended 05/31/13): Assets, $7,485,595 (M); expenditures, $638,066; qualifying distributions, $388,682; giving activities include $269,150 for 13 grants (high: $100,000; low: $5,000).
Purpose and activities: Giving primarily for the arts, and children, youth and social services.
Fields of interest: Media, television; Performing arts; Performing arts, opera; Arts; Human services; Children/youth, services; United Ways and Federated Giving Programs.
Type of support: General/operating support.
Limitations: Applications not accepted. Giving primarily in FL. No grants to individuals.
Application information: Contributes only to pre-selected organizations.
Officers: Robert Judd, Pres. and Treas.; Theodore Friedt, V.P.; Ruth Turner Camp, Secy.
EIN: 650347903

778
Lennar Foundation
700 N.W. 107th Ave., Ste. 400
Miami, FL 33172-3139 (305) 229-6400
***Contact:* Marshall Ames, Pres.**
FAX: (305) 228-8383;
E-mail: marshall.ames@lennar.com; Main URL: http://www.lennar.com/about/community/foundation.aspx

Established in 1989 in FL.
Donor: Lennar Corp.
Foundation type: Company-sponsored foundation.
Financial data (yr. ended 11/30/12): Assets, $40,949,556 (M); expenditures, $2,579,760; qualifying distributions, $1,773,338; giving activities include $1,369,523 for 33 grants (high: $425,500; low: $4,023).
Purpose and activities: The foundation supports organizations involved with education, water resources, cancer, multiple sclerosis, disaster relief, and human services. Special emphasis is directed toward programs designed to assist people who are less fortunate.
Fields of interest: Middle schools/education; Higher education; Education, services; Education; Environment, water resources; Health care, patient services; Health care; Cancer; Multiple sclerosis; Disasters, preparedness/services; Children/youth, services; Children, foster care; Homeless, human services; Human services; United Ways and Federated Giving Programs; Economically disadvantaged.
Type of support: General/operating support; Seed money.
Limitations: Applications accepted. Giving primarily in CA, Miami, FL, Las Vegas, NV, SC, and TX. No grants to individuals.
Application information: Application form not required.
***Initial approach:* Letter**
Deadline(s): None
Officers and Directors:* Marshall Ames,* Pres.; Samantha Fels,* Secy.; Jim Carr; Ezra Katz; Waynewright Malcolm; Stuart A. Miller; Allan J. Pekor; Shelley Rubin.
EIN: 650171539

779
Lois Pope Life Foundation Inc.
6274 Linton Blvd., Ste. 103
Delray Beach, FL 33484-6508 (561) 865-0955
FAX: (561) 865-0938; E-mail: life@life-edu.org; Main URL: http://www.life-edu.org/

Established in FL.
Donor: The Lois Pope Life Foundation.
Foundation type: Independent foundation.
Financial data (yr. ended 12/31/12): Assets, $4,032,904 (M); expenditures, $993,611; qualifying distributions, $945,821; giving activities include $650,250 for 19 grants (high: $250,000; low: $500).
Purpose and activities: Giving primarily for animal welfare, medical research, education, summer camp programs, humanitarian relief, and the performing arts.
Fields of interest: Performing arts; Education; Animals/wildlife; Medical research, institute; Recreation, camps; Human services; Military/veterans' organizations.
Type of support: Scholarships—to individuals.
Limitations: Applications not accepted. **Giving primarily in FL.**
Publications: Newsletter.
Application information: Unsolicited requests for funds not accepted.
Officers: Lois B. Pope, Chair.; Paul D. Pope, Pres.; Robert C. Miller, Secy.; Elsa Johnson, Treas.
EIN: 273158367

780
Lindemann Charitable Foundation II
505 S. Flagler Dr., No. 900
West Miami Beach, FL **33401-5923**

Established in FL.
Donor: George L. Lindemann.
Foundation type: Independent foundation.
Financial data (yr. ended 06/30/12): Assets, $5,211,515 (M); gifts received, $320,000; expenditures, $2,353,581; qualifying distributions, $2,351,710; giving activities include $2,350,310 for 24 grants (high: $1,503,060; low: $250).
Fields of interest: Performing arts; Performing arts, opera; Arts; Education; Human services; United Ways and Federated Giving Programs; Jewish federated giving programs.
Limitations: Applications not accepted. Giving primarily in FL and NY.
Application information: Contributes only to pre-selected organizations.
Officers: George L. Lidemann, Pres.; Frayda B. Lindemann, V.P.; Sloan N. Lindemann, Secy.; George L. Lindemann, Jr., Treas.
EIN: 582119083

781
Lipton Foundation
655 Ocean Blvd.
Golden Beach, FL 33160-2217 **(305) 935-3338**
***FAX:* (305) 935-3440**; Main URL: http://liptonfoundation.com/

Established in 1988 in CA and FL.
Donors: Alan Lipton; Janice Lipton.
Foundation type: Independent foundation.
Financial data (yr. ended 12/31/12): Assets, $5,944,848 (M); expenditures, $360,474; qualifying distributions, $308,639; giving activities include $257,511 for 16 grants (high: $101,800; low: $180).
Fields of interest: Human services; Foundations (private grantmaking); Jewish federated giving programs; Jewish agencies & synagogues.
Limitations: Applications not accepted. Giving primarily in FL.
Application information: Unsolicited requests for funds not accepted.
Trustees: Alan Lipton; Janice Lipton.
EIN: 650098730

782
Daniel M. Lyons & Bente S. Lyons Foundation
13685 Rivoli Dr.
Palm Beach Gardens, FL 33410-1239 **(561) 627-1573**
Contact: Bente S. Lyons, Tr.

Established in 1984 in FL.
Donors: Bente S. Lyons; Daniel M. Lyons†.
Foundation type: Independent foundation.
Financial data (yr. ended 12/31/13): Assets, $3,216,474 (M); gifts received, $336; expenditures, $932,761; qualifying distributions,

$826,164; giving activities include $784,600 for 5 grants (high: $335,000; low: $5,000).
Fields of interest: Jewish federated giving programs; Jewish agencies & synagogues.
Limitations: Applications accepted. Giving primarily in FL and NY. No grants to individuals.
Application information:
Initial approach: Letter
Deadline(s): Aug. 1
Board meeting date(s): As needed
Trustee: Bente S. Lyons.
EIN: 592315047
Other changes: Joe B. Cox is no longer a trustee.

783
Dr. John T. Macdonald Foundation, Inc.
1550 Madruga Ave., Ste. 215
Coral Gables, FL 33146-3017 (305) 667-6017
FAX: (305) 667-9135;
E-mail: info@jtmacdonaldfdn.org; **Contact for application procedures: Kim Greene, Exec. Dir., e-mail: kgreene@tjmacdonaldfdn.org;** Main URL: http://www.jtmacdonaldfdn.org
Facebook: https://www.facebook.com/DrJohnTMacDonaldFoundation
Twitter: http://www.twitter.com/drjtmacdonaldfn

Established in 1992 in FL; converted from sale of Doctors' Hospital to HEALTHSOUTH Rehabilitation Corporation; became a private foundation in 1992.
Donor: Adele H. Goddard Trust.
Foundation type: Independent foundation.
Financial data (yr. ended 12/31/12): Assets, $26,306,275 (M); gifts received, $26,233; expenditures, $5,181,843; qualifying distributions, $4,799,753; giving activities include $4,799,753 for 17 grants (high: $7,500; low: $5,000).
Purpose and activities: To provide funding for programs and projects designed to improve, preserve or restore the health and health care of the people in Miami-Dade County, FL.
Fields of interest: Medical school/education; Health care; Mental health/crisis services; Human services.
Type of support: General/operating support; Continuing support; Equipment; Program development; Seed money; Scholarship funds; Technical assistance; Program evaluation.
Limitations: Applications accepted. Giving limited to Miami-Dade County, FL. No support for projects that promote religious faith, political candidates or campaigns, national projects which would result in funding leaving Miami-Dade County, for-profit organizations, or other grantmaking foundations. No grants to individuals directly, or for fundraising campaigns.
Publications: Application guidelines; Annual report; Grants list.
Application information: Application form and deadlines are available on foundation web site. Application form required.
Initial approach: Letters of inquiry submitted online, through foundation web site. Selected applicants are then invited to fill out application
Copies of proposal: 1
Deadline(s): Feb. 1 to Apr. 15
Board meeting date(s): Quarterly
Final notification: June
Officers and Directors:* Steven S. Pabalan, M.D.*, Chair.; Thomas M. Mark, M.D., Vice-Chair.; Karl Smiley, Secy.; Kim Greene, Exec. Dir.; Robert G. Breier; Aldo C. Busot, M.D.; Gary W. Dix; Charles A. Dunn, M.D.; R. Rodney Howell, M.D.; George D. Mekras, M.D.; John C. Nordt III, M.D.; Latanae R. Parker, Jr., M.D.; Dean H. Roller, M.D.; Stuart H. Savedoff, D.D.S.; Dazelle D. Simpson, M.D.; Margaret C. Starner; David A. Wolfberg.
Number of staff: 1 full-time professional; 1 part-time professional.
EIN: 590818918

784
MAH Foundation, Inc.
7121 Fairway Dr., Ste. 400
Palm Beach Gardens, FL 33418-3776 (561) 656-0609
Contact: Mark Albers, C.F.O.
Main URL: http://www.mahfoundation.org/
Grants List: http://www.mahfoundation.org/recipients.html

Established in 2002 in FL.
Donor: Allan E. Hadhazy.
Foundation type: Independent foundation.
Financial data (yr. ended 11/30/12): Assets, $3,695,252 (M); expenditures, $160,500; qualifying distributions, $155,500; giving activities include $155,500 for 35 grants (high: $30,000; low: $1,500).
Fields of interest: Safety/disasters; Human services; Religion.
Type of support: General/operating support.
Limitations: Applications accepted. Giving primarily in CA and FL.
Application information: Application form required.
Initial approach: Letter
Deadline(s): None
Officer: Mark N. Albers, C.F.O.
Directors: Helen J. Barrionnuevo; Allan E. Hadhazy; Andrew H. Kayton.
EIN: 651165800

785
Martin Z. Margulies Foundation, Inc.
445 Grand Bay Dr.
Key Biscayne, FL 33149-1905

Established in FL.
Donor: Martin Z. Margulies.
Foundation type: Operating foundation.
Financial data (yr. ended 07/31/13): Assets, $56,434,204 (M); expenditures, $799,888; qualifying distributions, $4,425,912; giving activities include $130,260 for 6 grants (high: $125,500; low: $360).
Fields of interest: Human services; United Ways and Federated Giving Programs.
Limitations: Applications not accepted. Giving primarily in FL. No grants to individuals.
Application information: Contributes only to pre-selected organizations.
Officers and Director:* Martin Z. Margulies,* Pres.; Katherine Hinds, Secy.
EIN: 592130476
Other changes: At the close of 2013, the fair market value of the grantmaker's assets was $56,434,204, a 53.8% increase over the 2012 value, $36,700,153.

786
G. Roxy & Elizabeth C. Martin Charitable Trust
c/o SunTrust Bank, Charitable Services Group
300 S. Orange Ave., Ste. 1600
Orlando, FL 32801-3382
E-mail: fdnsvcs.fl@suntrust.com; Application address: c/o SunTrust Bank, 200 S. Orange Ave., SOAB-10, Orlando, FL 32801; **Main URL: http://fdnweb.org/martin**

Established in 1988 in FL.
Donors: Alfred S. Martin; Elizabeth C. Martin; G. Roxy Martin.
Foundation type: Independent foundation.
Financial data (yr. ended 11/30/13): Assets, $4,071,044 (M); expenditures, $249,126; qualifying distributions, $225,905; giving activities include $90,500 for 9 grants (high: $20,000; low: $3,000), and $112,250 for 87 grants to individuals (high: $2,500; low: $750).
Purpose and activities: Giving primarily for education, health and human services, arts and culture, religion, children and youth services, and environment.
Fields of interest: Arts; Secondary school/education; Higher education; Environment; Human services; Children/youth, services; Christian agencies & churches.
Type of support: General/operating support; Capital campaigns; Scholarships—to individuals.
Limitations: Applications accepted. Giving primarily in Lake County, FL.
Application information: Application guidelines available on trust web site. Application form required.
Initial approach: Telephone for application
Copies of proposal: 1
Deadline(s): Mar. 31 for scholarships. Oct. 1 for grants
Board meeting date(s): Nov.
Final notification: May for scholarships
Directors: Alfred C. Haliday, Jr.; J. Stephen Pullum; David Weiss.
Trustee: SunTrust Bank.
EIN: 596920693

787
The Patrick J. Martin Family Foundation
5286 Kensingston High St.
Naples, FL 34105 (303) 931-3723
Contact: Patrick J. Martin, Tr.
FAX: (239) 643-3263; E-mail: patmartin@qwest.net; Main URL: http://thepatrickjmartinfoundation.com/
Blog: http://thepatrickjmartinfoundation.com/blog/

Established in 2005 in CO.
Donor: Patrick J. Martin.
Foundation type: Independent foundation.
Financial data (yr. ended 12/31/12): Assets, $4,396,087 (M); expenditures, $300,832; qualifying distributions, $273,844; giving activities include $58,844 for 6 grants (high: $26,400; low: $250), and $215,000 for 43 grants to individuals (high: $5,000; low: $5,000).
Purpose and activities: Giving primarily to encourage the study of math, science, and engineering at the college or undergraduate level. Preference is given to students who wish to study at Iona College in New Rochelle, NY, or The George Washington University in Washington, DC. Applicants must 1) demonstrate financial need, 2) be in the top 10 percent of their graduating class and have a desire to study math, science, or engineering, 3) take a challenging course of study in math and science and have successfully completed available AP Science and Math courses, 4) score in the top ten percentile in the Math, Reading and Writing SATs or equivalent, and 5) have strong character demonstrated in school and/or community. The foundation also supports efforts in the arts, the environment and humanitarian needs.
Fields of interest: Higher education.

Type of support: General/operating support; Scholarships—to individuals.
Limitations: Applications accepted. Giving primarily in NY.
Publications: Application guidelines; Annual report.
Application information: Complete guidelines and scholarship eligibility criteria available on foundation web site. Application form required.
Initial approach: Proposal; Scholarship applicants use form on foundation web site
Deadline(s): None
Trustee: Patrick J. Martin.
EIN: 206758585
Other changes: The grantmaker now publishes an annual report online.

788
Esther M. Mertz Charitable Trust
c/o Nancy Close
4951 Windsor Park
Sarasota, FL 34235-2610

Established in 1999 in FL.
Donor: Esther M. Mertz.
Foundation type: Independent foundation.
Financial data (yr. ended 10/31/13): Assets, $1,852,233 (M); expenditures, $4,000; qualifying distributions, $3,200.
Fields of interest: Performing arts, theater; Performing arts, education; Arts; Education; Health organizations, association; Human services.
Type of support: General/operating support.
Limitations: Applications not accepted. Giving primarily in FL. No grants to individuals.
Application information: Contributes only to pre-selected organizations.
Trustee: Nancy L. Close.
EIN: 137231616
Other changes: Esther M. Mertz is no longer trustee.

789
Minto Foundation, Inc.
4400 W. Sample Rd.
Coconut Creek, FL 33073-3473 (954) 973-4490
Contact: Lilliam Costello

Established in 1996 in FL.
Donors: Minto Communities, Inc.; Kenneth Greenberg; Michael Greenberg.
Foundation type: Company-sponsored foundation.
Financial data (yr. ended 04/30/13): Assets, $4,409,150 (M); expenditures, $206,113; qualifying distributions, $181,392; giving activities include $180,500 for 21 grants (high: $50,000; low: $1,000).
Purpose and activities: The foundation supports public charities and community foundations and organizations involved with education, heath care, human services, and the arts.
Fields of interest: Elementary/secondary education; Education; Cancer; Multiple sclerosis; Health organizations; Children, services; Aging, centers/services; Developmentally disabled, centers & services; Human services; Foundations (public); Foundations (community); Jewish agencies & synagogues.
Type of support: Employee volunteer services; General/operating support.
Limitations: Applications accepted. Giving primarily in FL, MA, and NC. No grants to individuals.
Application information: Application form not required.
Initial approach: Proposal
Deadline(s): None
Directors: Michael Greenberg; Roger Greenberg.
EIN: 650655805
Other changes: The grantmaker no longer lists an E-mail address. The grantmaker no longer lists a URL address.

790
Paul Moos Foundation
c/o Edward I. Speer, C.P.A.
5550 Glades Rd., Ste. 500
Boca Raton, FL **33431-7277**
Application address: c/o Pearl Lamberg, 880 5th Ave., New York, NY 10021

Established in 1964 in NY.
Foundation type: Independent foundation.
Financial data (yr. ended 01/31/13): Assets, $885,235 (M); expenditures, $140,119; qualifying distributions, $136,581; giving activities include $133,250 for 9 grants (high: $75,000; low: $350).
Purpose and activities: Giving to Jewish organizations and to medical organizations.
Fields of interest: Hospitals (general); Health organizations, association; United Ways and Federated Giving Programs; Jewish agencies & synagogues.
Limitations: Applications accepted. Giving primarily in New York, NY. No grants to individuals.
Application information:
Initial approach: Letter
Deadline(s): None
Trustees: Carol Lamberg; Pearl Lamberg; Anne L. Zeff.
EIN: 237275464

791
The Morningstar Foundation
c/o Bank of America, N.A.
P.O. Box 40200, FL9-100-10-19
Jacksonville, FL 32203-0200
***Application address:* c/o Bank of America, N.A., Attn.: Sarah D. Kay, P.O. Box 26688 (VA2-300-12-92), Richmond, VA 23261-6688, tel.: (804) 887-8773**

Established in 2007 in VA.
Donor: Mary Ann Elliott.
Foundation type: Independent foundation.
Financial data (yr. ended 06/30/13): Assets, $4,013,915 (M); expenditures, $245,237; qualifying distributions, $204,476; giving activities include $192,550 for 42 grants (high: $21,500; low: $1,000).
Purpose and activities: The mission of the foundation is twofold: to provide support for the environment and to nurture, serve and minister in the areas of health research, education, children's initiatives and animal welfare.
Fields of interest: Education; Animal welfare; Health care, research.
Type of support: General/operating support.
Limitations: Applications accepted. Giving primarily in NC and VA. No grants to individuals.
Application information: Application form required.
Trustees: Daniel Keith Elliott; James Ray Elliott, Jr.; Mary Ann Elliott; Sharon Elliott Hensely.
EIN: 261557579

792
Glenn W. & Hazelle Paxson Morrison Foundation, Inc.
P.O. Box 7518
Lakeland, FL 33807-7518 (863) 602-2968
Contact: R. Lynn Noris

Established in 1982 in FL.
Donor: Hazelle Paxson Morrison Eduction Fund.
Foundation type: Independent foundation.
Financial data (yr. ended 06/30/13): Assets, $4,074,639 (M); expenditures, $266,457; qualifying distributions, $241,391; giving activities include $126,300 for 29 grants (high: $10,000; low: $1,000), and $83,250 for 29 grants to individuals (high: $3,500; low: $1,000).
Purpose and activities: Giving primarily for scholarships for students from Polk County, FL who are interested in religion and music, and to help small churches in Polk County, FL.
Fields of interest: Higher education; Scholarships/financial aid; Boys & girls clubs; Foundations (community); Christian agencies & churches.
Type of support: General/operating support; Continuing support; Scholarship funds; Scholarships—to individuals.
Limitations: Applications accepted. Giving primarily in FL, with emphasis on the Polk County area.
Application information: Applications should be typed or written and should include a copy of the applicant's (if self supporting) or parents' tax return. Application form not required.
Initial approach: Letter
Copies of proposal: 1
Deadline(s): 2 months
Board meeting date(s): May and Dec.
Officers: Ralph C. Allen, Pres.; John Attaway, Secy.
Trustees: Hunt Berryman; Mary E. Jenko; Patricia Ricker.
EIN: 592220612

793
Richard C. Munroe Foundation
466 Champion Oaks Cir.
Havana, FL 32333-4804 (404) 351-6976
***Contact:* Bobbie D. Munroe**
FAX: (404) 355-0157

Established in 1990 in GA; funded in 1991.
Donor: Richard C. Munroe†.
Foundation type: Independent foundation.
Financial data (yr. ended 12/31/12): Assets, $3,654,536 (M); expenditures, $202,449; qualifying distributions, $179,245; giving activities include $161,545 for 46 grants (high: $8,000; low: $1,000).
Purpose and activities: Giving primarily for technology education for underprivileged and at-risk youth in the metropolitan Atlanta, GA area.
Fields of interest: Education; Housing/shelter; Human services; YM/YWCAs & YM/YWHAs; Children/youth, services.
Type of support: General/operating support; Capital campaigns; Building/renovation; Equipment; Program development.
Limitations: Applications accepted. Giving primarily in the Atlanta, GA area. No grants to individuals.
Publications: Application guidelines.
Application information: Application form required.
Initial approach: Request application form
Copies of proposal: 3
Deadline(s): Aug. 15
Board meeting date(s): Annually, usually between Aug. and Nov.

Officers: Richard G. Munroe, Pres.; Bobbie D. Munroe, Secy.; Jan H. Munroe, Treas.
EIN: 581925844
Other changes: The grantmaker has moved from GA to FL.

794
C. Olsen 1990 Private Foundation

11891 U.S. Highway 1, Ste. 100
North Palm Beach, FL 33408-2864
***Contact:* Joshua M. Fleming**

Established in 2002 in FL.
Donor: Christian Olsen Charitable Trust.
Foundation type: Independent foundation.
Financial data (yr. ended 09/30/13): Assets, $9,179,790 (M); expenditures, $683,674; qualifying distributions, $471,629; giving activities include $392,913 for 71 grants (high: $13,000; low: $1,000).
Fields of interest: Education; Cancer; Health organizations; Food banks; Human services; Children/youth, services; Developmentally disabled, centers & services.
Limitations: Applications accepted. Giving primarily in FL; some emphasis on West Palm Beach. No grants to individuals.
Application information:
Initial approach: Proposal
Deadline(s): Feb. 15, May 15, Aug. 15, and Nov. 15
Trustee: Joseph M. Fleming.
EIN: 656400515

795
Paul Palank Memorial Foundation, Inc.

70 Bay Colony Ln.
Fort Lauderdale, FL 33308-2004
E-mail: palankfoundation@bellsouth.net; Main URL: http://www.palankfoundation.org

Established in 2000 in FL.
Donor: Angelica Palank.
Foundation type: Independent foundation.
Financial data (yr. ended 10/31/13): Assets, $13,018,114 (M); gifts received, $1,360; expenditures, $659,028; qualifying distributions, $600,050; giving activities include $595,708 for 18 grants (high: $115,000; low: $5,000).
Purpose and activities: The foundation will strive to facilitate creative, effective programming that addresses the immediate needs of children in crisis while seeking long term solutions to the abuse, neglect, and abandonment problems facing the children of our economy.
Fields of interest: Human services; Children/youth, services.
Limitations: Applications accepted. Giving primarily in Dade and Broward counties, FL.
Publications: Application guidelines.
Application information: Application form required.
Initial approach: Use pre-application form on foundation web site
***Deadline(s):* See foundation web site for deadlines**
Directors: Angelica Palank-Sharlet; **Anne Richards Rothe; Lisa Collins Stamp.**
EIN: 651050806

796
The Richard Laurence Parish Foundation
(formerly Psychists, Inc.)

100 Lakeshore Dr., No. L-7
North Palm Beach, FL 33408-3660

Incorporated in 1943 in NY.
Donors: Richard L. Parish†; American Flange & Manufacturing Co., Inc.
Foundation type: Independent foundation.
Financial data (yr. ended 08/31/13): Assets, $6,975,251 (M); expenditures, $317,922; qualifying distributions, $312,189; giving activities include $304,000 for 62 grants (high: $62,000; low: $250).
Purpose and activities: Support primarily for secondary education; giving also for hospitals, higher education, and health care services.
Fields of interest: Secondary school/education; Medical school/education; Education; Health care; Human services.
Limitations: Applications not accepted. Giving primarily in CT, FL, NJ, and NY. No grants to individuals.
Application information: Contributes only to pre-selected organizations.
Directors: Richard C. Bondy; David L. McKissock; Richard L. Parish, Jr.; Richard L. Parish III.
EIN: 131869530

797
Drs. Kiran & Pallavi Patel Family Foundation, Inc.

5600 Mariner St., Ste. 227
Tampa, FL 33609-3471
Contact: Kiran C. Patel M.D., Secy.-Treas.

Established in 2006 in FL.
Donors: Kiran C. Patel, M.D.; Pallavi C. Patel, M.D.; Ace Endowment Fund; Bay Area Primary Care; The Aids Institute, Inc.; Glance HR LLC.
Foundation type: Independent foundation.
Financial data (yr. ended 06/30/13): Assets, $7,058,381 (M); gifts received, $1,369,610; expenditures, $1,478,454; qualifying distributions, $1,424,430; giving activities include $1,386,894 for 15 grants (high: $1,000,000; low: $1,008).
Fields of interest: Performing arts centers; Education; Health care; Human services; International development; International relief; International human rights.
International interests: India.
Type of support: General/operating support; Program development; Scholarships—to individuals.
Limitations: Applications accepted. Giving primarily in FL; some funding also in India.
Application information:
Initial approach: Proposal
Deadline(s): None
Officers: Pallavi C. Patel, M.D., Pres.; Shilen Patel, V.P.; Kiran C. Patel, M.D., Secy.-Treas.
Trustees: Sonali Judd; Sheetal Patel.
EIN: 203916634
Other changes: For the fiscal year ended June 30, 2013, the grantmaker paid grants of $1,386,894, a 242.9% increase over the fiscal 2012 disbursements, $404,455.

798
The Patterson Foundation

2 N. Tamiami Trail, Ste. 206
Sarasota, FL 34236-5574 (941) 952-1413
Contact: Carol Lipp
FAX: (941) 952-1435;
E-mail: clipp@thepattersonfoundation.org; Main URL: http://www.thepattersonfoundation.org
Blog: http://www.thepattersonfoundation.org/blog/
Facebook: http://www.facebook.com/pages/The-Patterson-Foundation/233909564806
Google Plus: https://plus.google.com/u/0/+ThepattersonfoundationOrg/posts
Twitter: http://twitter.com/ThePattersonFdn
YouTube: http://www.youtube.com/user/ThePattersonFdn

Established in 1997 in FL.
Donors: Dorothy Clarke Patterson†; James J. Patterson†; Dorothy C. Patterson Trust.
Foundation type: Independent foundation.
Financial data (yr. ended 06/30/13): Assets, $222,423,695 (M); expenditures, $12,557,541; qualifying distributions, $10,498,134; giving activities include $4,961,681 for 23 grants (high: $1,500,000; low: $1,250).
Purpose and activities: The foundation believes that through communications, technology, and financial innovations, improvements may be achieved that transcend any single issue, entity, or geographic area. The foundation provides resources to facilitate, expedite, and share methods, techniques, and tools, joining with others in creating New Realities. Current initiatives focus on aging, diabetes, arthritis, and educational opportunities in the community.
Fields of interest: Higher education; Arthritis; Diabetes; Human services; Aging, centers/services; Aging.
Limitations: Applications not accepted. Giving primarily FL, with emphasis on Sarasota. No grants to individuals.
Application information: Contributes only to pre-selected organizations.
Officer: Debra M. Jacobs, C.E.O. and Pres.
Designation Committee: John T. Berteau, Chair.; Charles D. Bailey, Jr.; Ric Gregoria.
Trustee: Northern Trust Bank.
EIN: 656230256

799
Folke H. Peterson Charitable Foundation
c/o SunTrust Bank Foundations Endowment

200 S. Orange Ave., SOAB-10
Orlando, FL 32801-3410 **(407) 237-4354**
FAX: (407) 237-5604; **Main URL: http://fdnweb.org/peterson**

Established in 1988 in FL.
Donor: Folke H. Peterson†.
Foundation type: Independent foundation.
Financial data (yr. ended 11/30/13): Assets, $10,019,182 (M); expenditures, $307,011; qualifying distributions, $286,286; giving activities include $256,500 for 22 grants (high: $80,000; low: $2,000).
Purpose and activities: Giving primarily for nonprofit organizations involved in the health and well-being of animals, including no-kill animal shelters.
Fields of interest: Animal welfare.
Type of support: Program development; Emergency funds; General/operating support; In-kind gifts.
Limitations: Applications accepted. Giving primarily in FL. No grants to individuals.
Application information: See foundation website for complete application guidelines. Application form required.
Initial approach: Letter
Copies of proposal: 1
Deadline(s): None

Trustees: SunTrust Bank; University of Florida; University of Miami; Wildlife Care Center.
EIN: 656040055

800
The Dr. P. Phillips Foundation

P.O. Box 692709
Orlando, FL 32869-2709 (407) 422-6105
Contact: Robert L. Mellen III, Pres.
FAX: (407) 422-4952; E-mail: info@drphillips.org; Main URL: http://www.drphillips.org

Incorporated in 1953 in FL.
Donors: Della Phillips†; Howard Phillips†; Dr. Phillips, Inc.
Foundation type: Independent foundation.
Financial data (yr. ended 05/31/13): Assets, $39,351,518 (M); expenditures, $534,711; qualifying distributions, $483,545; giving activities include $382,816 for 23 grants (high: $124,404; low: $750), and $73,954 for 2 foundation-administered programs.
Fields of interest: Arts; Health care; Employment; Children/youth, services; Human services; Community/economic development; Public affairs.
Type of support: Capital campaigns; Building/renovation; Equipment; Program development; Program-related investments/loans; Matching/challenge support.
Limitations: Applications accepted. Giving generally limited to Orange and Osceola counties, FL. No support for social, religious, fraternal or veterans' groups that primarily benefit their own members or adherents, or for legislative lobbying. No support to Type III support organizations. No grants to individuals, or for endowment funds, or to retire accumulated debt.
Publications: Application guidelines; Grants list; Newsletter.
Application information: Application guidelines available on foundation web site. Application form required.
Copies of proposal: 1
Officers and Directors:* J.A. Hinson,* Chair.; **Kenneth D. Robinson,* Pres. and C.E.O.; H.L. Burnett,* Secy.; Eva M. Tukdarian,* Treas.**; Don Ammerman; James W. Ferber; Margaret G. Miller.
Number of staff: None.
EIN: 596135403
Other changes: Kenneth D. Robinson has replaced Robert L. Mellen, III as Pres. and C.E.O.
Eva M. Tukdarian is now Treas. H.L. Burnett is now Secy.

801
Pinellas County Community Foundation

5200 East Bay Dr., Ste. 202
Clearwater, FL 33764 (727) 531-0058
Contact: Julio Scalco, Exec. Dir.
FAX: (727) 531-0053; E-mail: info@pinellasccf.org; Main URL: http://www.pinellasccf.org

Established in 1969 in FL by trust agreement.
Foundation type: Community foundation.
Financial data (yr. ended 12/31/12): Assets, $78,287,771 (M); gifts received, $825,884; expenditures, $12,494,140; giving activities include $11,727,266 for 100+ grants (high: $695,327).
Purpose and activities: The purpose of the foundation is to receive donations from people and organizations interested in helping their community and to oversee the investment of those funds by monitoring the work of the trustees and then to distribute the income to sound charitable organizations that meet community needs. Primary areas of interest include family services, the disadvantaged, low income, handicapped, and other social services.
Fields of interest: Arts; Education; Environment; Animal welfare; Health care; Substance abuse, services; Mental health/crisis services; Crime/violence prevention, abuse prevention; Housing/shelter; Children/youth, services; Family services; Aging, centers/services; Developmentally disabled, centers & services; Women, centers/services; Human services; Religion; Children/youth; Adults; Aging; Disabilities, people with; Blind/visually impaired; Deaf/hearing impaired; Mentally disabled; Economically disadvantaged; Homeless.
Type of support: General/operating support; Continuing support; Building/renovation; Equipment; Scholarship funds; Scholarships—to individuals.
Limitations: Applications accepted. Giving limited to Pinellas County, FL area. No grants for endowment funds, or for research, fellowships, or matching gifts; no loans.
Publications: Application guidelines; Annual report (including application guidelines); Informational brochure; Newsletter; Occasional report.
Application information: Only agencies receiving Operating Grants from the foundation are eligible to apply for Competitive Grants; visit foundation web site for application information. Application form required.
Initial approach: Telephone
Copies of proposal: 1
Deadline(s): Oct. 1 for Operating Grants; June 15 and Oct. 1 for Competitive Grants
Board meeting date(s): Feb., Sept., and Dec.
Final notification: 2 months
Officers and Governors:* Sallie Parks,* Chair.; Byron Smith,* Vice-Chair.; Julie Scales, Exec. Dir.; Louis N. Adcock, Jr.; Sandra F. Diamond; **Maria N. Edmonds**; Robert Entel, M.D.; Joseph W. Fleece III; **Peggy O'Shea**; Judith Powers; Virginia Rowell; David Sietsma; Irene Sullivan; Sarah Williams, Esq.
Trustee Banks: Bank of America, N.A.; Fifth Third Bank; Merrill Lynch Trust Co.; Northern Trust Bank of Florida, N.A.; Raymond James Trust Co.; Regions Morgan Keegan Trust; Sabal Co.; SunTrust Bank; Synovus Trust Co.; Wachovia Bank, N.A.
Number of staff: 1 full-time professional; 1 part-time support.
EIN: 237113194
Other changes: Sallie Parks has replaced Maria N. Edmonds as Chair. Byron Smith has replaced Sallie Parks as Vice-Chair.
Marty Klemperer and Bryon C. Smith are no longer directors.

802
Plangere Foundation, Inc.

c/o Quail Ridge
3829 Partridge Pl.
Boynton Beach, FL 33436-5413

Established in 1997 in FL.
Donors: Jules L. Plangere, Jr.; Alfred Colantoni; The Plangere KCA Charitable Trust; The Plangere KRDJ Charitable Trust.
Foundation type: Independent foundation.
Financial data (yr. ended 04/30/13): Assets, $7,383,391 (M); gifts received, $628,460; expenditures, $1,638,768; qualifying distributions, $1,609,415; giving activities include $1,565,500 for 24 grants (high: $1,025,000; low: $1,000).
Fields of interest: Higher education; Human services; Community/economic development.
Limitations: Applications not accepted. Giving primarily in NJ. No grants to individuals.
Application information: Contributes only to pre-selected organizations.
Officers and Directors:* Jules Plangere, Jr.,* Chair.; **E. Donald Lass, Secy.**; Jules L. Plangere III, Treas.; Wendy Bickart; Alfred Colantoni; John C. Conover III.
EIN: 650747053

803
The Lois Pope Life Foundation

1720 S. Ocean Blvd.
Manalapan, FL 33462-6222 (561) 582-8083
***FAX:* (561) 582-8086**; E-mail: life@life-edu.org; Main URL: http://www.life-edu.org

Established in 1996 in FL.
Donors: Lois B. Pope; The Cessna Aircraft Co.
Foundation type: Independent foundation.
Financial data (yr. ended 12/31/11): Assets, $0 (M); expenditures, $545,058; qualifying distributions, $510,735; giving activities include $439,015 for 18 grants (high: $175,000; low: $365).
Purpose and activities: Giving primarily for education, health associations, social services, and to disabled veterans' organizations.
Fields of interest: Education; Animal welfare; Health organizations, association; Human services; Children/youth, services; Military/veterans' organizations.
Limitations: Applications not accepted. Giving primarily in FL; funding also in CA and NY.
Publications: Newsletter.
Application information: Unsolicited requests for funds not accepted.
Trustees: Elsa G. Johnson; Lois B. Pope; Michele Ritter.
EIN: 137086087

804
Publix Super Markets Charities

(formerly George W. Jenkins Foundation, Inc.)
3300 Publix Corporate Pkwy.
Lakeland, FL 33811-3311 (863) 686-8754
Contact: Sharon Miller, Exec. Dir.
Application address: P.O. Box 407, Lakeland, FL 33802-0407

Incorporated in 1967 in FL.
Donor: George W. Jenkins†.
Foundation type: Independent foundation.
Financial data (yr. ended 12/31/12): Assets, $599,221,858 (M); expenditures, $32,084,394; qualifying distributions, $30,044,452; giving activities include $30,006,085 for 3,173 grants (high: $2,100,000; low: $100).
Purpose and activities: Giving primarily for education, children and youth, and the United Way and its agencies.
Fields of interest: Education; Children/youth, services; Children, services; Youth, services; United Ways and Federated Giving Programs.
Type of support: General/operating support; Capital campaigns; Building/renovation; Equipment; Program development; Employee matching gifts.
Limitations: Applications accepted. Giving primarily in AL, FL, GA, SC, and TN. No grants to individuals.
Application information:
Initial approach: Letter of request
Copies of proposal: 1
Deadline(s): None

Board meeting date(s): Monthly
Final notification: 6 to 8 weeks
Officers and Directors:* Carol Barnett,* Chair. and C.E.O.; Hoyt Barnett,* V.P.; John Attaway, Secy.; Tina Johnson, Treas.; **Kelly Williams-Puccio,* Exec. Dir.**; Barbara Hart.
Number of staff: 3 full-time professional.
EIN: 596194119
Other changes: Kelly Williams-Puccio has replaced Sharon Miller as Exec. Dir.

805
Quantum Foundation
2701 N. Australian Ave. Ste. 200
West Palm Beach, FL 33407-4526 (561) 832-7497
Contact: Eric Kelly, Pres.
FAX: (561) 832-5794;
E-mail: tmay@quantumfnd.org; Main URL: http://www.quantumfnd.org
Facebook: http://www.facebook.com/pages/West-Palm-Beach-FL/Quantum-Foundation/131113414501
Foundation News Feed: http://www.quantumfnd.org/index.cfm?fuseaction=news.main&rss=true&x=9836582
Grants Database: http://www.cybergrants.com/cybergrants/plsql/quantum.grant_search.search_page
LinkedIn: http://www.linkedin.com/groups?home=&gid=2342204&trk=anet_ug_hm
President's Blog: http://www.quantumfnd.org/index.cfm?fuseaction=blog.main&x=5431130
Twitter: http://twitter.com/quantumfnd

Established in 1995 in FL; converted from sale of John F. Kennedy Hospital to Columbia/HCA.
Foundation type: Independent foundation.
Financial data (yr. ended 12/31/12): Assets, $139,453,453 (M); expenditures, $8,569,297; qualifying distributions, $7,446,051; giving activities include $6,268,578 for 197 grants (high: $650,000; low: $400).
Purpose and activities: The foundation works in Palm Beach County to increase health care access, improve science and health education, and enhance the health care workforce.
Fields of interest: Education; Health care; Community/economic development; Children; Adults; Economically disadvantaged.
Type of support: General/operating support; Management development/capacity building; Capital campaigns; Building/renovation; Equipment; Emergency funds; Program development; Seed money; Technical assistance; Consulting services; Program evaluation; Employee matching gifts; Matching/challenge support.
Limitations: Applications accepted. Giving limited to Palm Beach County, FL. No support for religious organizations for religious purposes, health research, or for political organizations or causes. No grants to individuals, or individual requests for scholarships, or for endowments, operating deficits or retirement of debt.
Publications: Application guidelines; Annual report; Grants list; Newsletter; Occasional report.
Application information: Letters of Inquiry are received and reviewed on an on-going basis. If your LOI is approved to move forward in the review process, you will be invited to submit a full proposal. If you are invited to submit a full proposal, you will be directed to the foundation's online proposal form. All areas to address in your full proposal will be clearly identified. The foundation invites submission of full proposals at least three times per year. Full proposals must be submitted online and must be received by close of business on the full proposal due date. Application form required.
Initial approach: Submit a letter of inquiry online at foundation's web site
Deadline(s): See foundation web site for current full proposal due dates
Board meeting date(s): Year-round
Final notification: 3-4 weeks
Officers and Trustees:* Donna A. Mulholland, 2nd Vice-Chair.; William A. Meyer,* Chair.; Denis P. Coleman, Jr.,* 1st Vice-Chair.; Eric M. Kelly, Pres.; Joe Paskoski, C.F.O.; Jeannette M. Corbett; Kerry A. Diaz; James P. Kintz; Anthony J. McNicholas III; Stephen C. Moore; Richard Sussman; Ethel Isaacs Williams.
Number of staff: 6 full-time professional; 2 full-time support.
EIN: 590812783

806
The Querrey Simpson Charitable Foundation
700 Kings Town Dr.
Naples, FL 34102-7831
Contact: Kimberly Querry, Tr.

Established in 2007 in IL.
Donors: Louis A. Simpson; Kimberly Querrey.
Foundation type: Independent foundation.
Financial data (yr. ended 12/31/12): Assets, $1,860,814 (M); gifts received, $4,968,430; expenditures, $7,190,081; qualifying distributions, $7,136,102; giving activities include $7,136,102 for 23 grants (high: $6,000,000; low: $2,000).
Fields of interest: Museums; Education.
Limitations: Giving primarily in Chicago, IL; some giving also in CA and NY.
Application information: Application form not required.
Initial approach: Letter
Deadline(s): None
Trustee: Kimberly Querrey.
EIN: 261346418
Other changes: At the close of 2012, the grantmaker paid grants of $7,136,102, a 325.0% increase over the 2011 disbursements, $1,678,950.

807
Carmen Rebozo Foundation, Inc.
6274 S.W. 35th St.
Miami, FL 33155-4934
Contact: Olga Guilarte, V.P.

Established in 1985 in FL.
Donors: Charles G. Rebozo†; Mary Bouterse†.
Foundation type: Independent foundation.
Financial data (yr. ended 06/30/13): Assets, $18,314,578 (M); expenditures, $967,527; qualifying distributions, $867,125; giving activities include $867,125 for grants.
Purpose and activities: Giving primarily for a boys and girls club, as well as for education and children, youth and social services.
Fields of interest: Education; Boys & girls clubs; Human services; Children/youth, services.
Limitations: Applications not accepted. Giving primarily in FL.
Application information: Contributes only to pre-selected organizations.
Officers: Charles F. Rebozo, Pres.; James Bernhardt, V.P.; **E. Andres Guilarte, V.P.**; Olga Guilarte, V.P.; Teresa Rebozo Hood, V.P.; Michael Rebozo, V.P.; **Thomas Rebozo, Jr., V.P.; William Rebozo, Jr., V.P.**
EIN: 592667397
Other changes: Patricia Nixon Cox is no longer a V.P.

808
Paul E. & Klare N. Reinhold Foundation, Inc.
(formerly Paul E. & Ida Klare Reinhold Foundation, Inc.)
1845 Town Ctr. Blvd., Ste. 105
Fleming Island, FL 32003-3358 **(904) 269-5857, ext. 404**
Contact: Amy Parker, Exec. Dir.
FAX: (904) 269-8382; E-mail: aparker@reinhold.net; Main URL: http://www.reinhold.net/
Blog: http://www.reinhold.net/blog/
RSS Feed: http://reinhold.net/blog/?feed=rss2

Established in 1954.
Donor: Paul E. Reinhold†.
Foundation type: Independent foundation.
Financial data (yr. ended 12/31/12): Assets, $7,458,986 (M); expenditures, $352,720; qualifying distributions, $321,411; giving activities include $165,602 for 77 grants (high: $62,000; low: $500), and $86,544 for 1 employee matching gift.
Purpose and activities: The mission of the foundation is to perpetuate the ethos of cathedral building in doing good in the community, within the context of Christian values and family continuity (unity), and to share in the celebration of family heritage. The foundation also operates a program dedicated to enhancing the leadership skills of senior staff members and volunteers that manage non-profit organizations. This grant program is restricted to organizations that provide meaningful services to the citizens of Clay County, Florida.
Fields of interest: Education; Hospitals (general); Health care; Health organizations, association; Youth development; Human services; YM/YWCAs & YM/YWHAs; Foundations (community); Christian agencies & churches; Religion.
Type of support: Capital campaigns; Building/renovation; Equipment; Land acquisition; Emergency funds; Seed money; Matching/challenge support.
Limitations: Applications accepted. Giving limited to Clay County, FL. No support for private operating foundations. No grants to individuals.
Publications: Application guidelines; Program policy statement.
Application information: See web site for complete application policies and guidelines. Application form required.
Initial approach: 2-3 page proposal
Copies of proposal: 1
Deadline(s): See web site
Board meeting date(s): Oct.
Final notification: See web site
Officers: J.F. Bryan IV, Chair.; Leah B. Burnette, Secy.-Treas.
Trustees: Megan Baptist; Jeff Bryan; George Egan; Jack Myers; John C. Myers IV; June R. Myers; Paul Myers; Neely D. Towe.
EIN: 596140495

809

The Rendina Family Foundation

661 University Blvd., Ste. 200
Jupiter, FL 33458-2795
Main URL: http://www.rendinafamilyfoundation.com/
Facebook: https://www.facebook.com/RendinaFamilyFoundation
Google Plus: https://plus.google.com/+RendinafamilyfoundationOrg/about
RSS Feed: http://rendinafamilyfoundation.org/feed/
Twitter: https://twitter.com/RendinaFF
YouTube: http://www.youtube.com/user/RendinaFF

Established in 1997 in FL.
Donors: Bruce A. Rendina; Marjorie Rendina; Edward M. Feigeles; Andy Malik; Dr. Peter Slavin; Fred Jaeckle; Marc Roberts; S.M. Wilson & Co.; Health Care Reit, Inc.; BDI Capital Mgmt.; Harcone 4 LLC; Rendina Companies.
Foundation type: Independent foundation.
Financial data (yr. ended 06/30/13): Assets, $78,697 (M); gifts received, $16,250; expenditures, $124,546; qualifying distributions, $124,476; giving activities include $121,842 for 4 grants (high: $100,000; low: $3,000).
Purpose and activities: Giving primarily to enhance the quality of life for families and individuals who have been affected by cancer, by supporting organizations, hospitals and biotechnology companies that excel in researching and developing cures for cancer. In addition, the foundation supports efforts to increase the general welfare of the communities in which the foundation is actively involved.
Fields of interest: Secondary school/education; Health care; Health organizations, association; Cancer; Human services; Children/youth, services; Foundations (private grantmaking).
Type of support: General/operating support.
Limitations: Applications accepted. **Giving primarily in FL and MA.** No grants to individuals.
Application information:
Initial approach: Letter
Deadline(s): None
Officers and Directors:* Michael D. Rendina,* Pres. and Treas.; Richard M. Rendina,* V.P. and Secy.; Marji Rendina,* V.P.; Richard B. Comiter; Frank Coniglio; David B. Rendina; **Lainie Rendina**; Tricia Rendina.
EIN: 650800240

810

Marshall E. Rinker, Sr. Foundation, Inc.

310 Okeechobee Blvd., No. 100
West Palm Beach, FL 33401-6419
Contact: Fdn. Admin.

Established in 1998 in FL.
Donor: M.E. Rinker, Sr.
Foundation type: Independent foundation.
Financial data (yr. ended 12/31/12): Assets, $28,545,829 (M); expenditures, $1,551,411; qualifying distributions, $1,340,425; giving activities include $1,228,898 for 31 grants (high: $250,000; low: $400).
Purpose and activities: Giving primarily for higher education.
Fields of interest: Higher education; Education; Health care; Community/economic development; Religion.
Type of support: Capital campaigns; Endowments.
Limitations: Applications not accepted. Giving primarily in FL. No grants to individuals.
Application information: Unsolicited requests for funds not accepted.
Board meeting date(s): Quarterly
Officers and Directors:* David B. Rinker,* Pres.; Leighan R. Rinker,* 1st V.P.; Paul C. Bremer,* Secy.-Treas.; Marshall M. Criser; Richard S. Johnson; **Richard A. Krause**; **Christopher R. Rinker**; **David S. Rinker**.
EIN: 650871532

811

River Branch Foundation

177 4th Ave. N., 2nd Fl.
Jacksonville, FL 32250-7016 (904) 396-5831
***E-mail:* JLeroux@RiverBranchFoundation.org**; Main URL: http://riverbranchfoundation.org/

Trust established in 1963 in NJ.
Donors: J. Seward Johnson 1951 and 1961 Charitable Trusts; The Atlantic Foundation; Jennifer Johnson Duke.
Foundation type: Independent foundation.
Financial data (yr. ended 12/31/12): Assets, $17,813,732 (M); gifts received, $8,105; expenditures, $1,270,573; qualifying distributions, $1,135,848; giving activities include $1,135,848 for grants.
Purpose and activities: Giving primarily for human services, children's services, education, the arts and the environment.
Fields of interest: Higher education; Environment; Children/youth, services.
Limitations: Applications accepted. Giving primarily in the Jacksonville, FL, area. No grants to individuals.
Publications: Application guidelines.
Application information: Application form not required.
Initial approach: Letter
Copies of proposal: 1
Deadline(s): None
Director: Jennifer Johnson Duke.
Trustees: Jason Gregg; Simon Gregg; Judith Leroux.
EIN: 226054887

812

The Sage & Dice Foundation

c/o William C. Stone
425 Gulf Shore Blvd. N.
Naples, FL 34102-5548

Established in 2005 in CT.
Donor: William C. Stone.
Foundation type: Independent foundation.
Financial data (yr. ended 12/31/12): Assets, $1,563,921 (M); expenditures, $1,253,398; qualifying distributions, $1,251,242; giving activities include $1,250,523 for 8 grants (high: $1,000,000; low: $300).
Fields of interest: Education; United Ways and Federated Giving Programs.
Type of support: General/operating support.
Limitations: Applications not accepted. Giving primarily in CT and IN. No grants to individuals.
Application information: Contributes only to pre-selected organizations.
Trustees: Mary R. Stone; William C. Stone.
EIN: 206771152
Other changes: The grantmaker has moved from CT to FL.

813

Gordon Samstag Fine Arts Trust

c/o Bank of America, N.A.
P.O. Box 40200, FL9-100-10-19
Jacksonville, FL 32203-0200
E-mail: samstag@unisa.edu.au
Application address: c/o Ross Wolfe, Dir., Samstag Scholarship Program, University of South Australia, GPO Box 2471, Adelaide, South Australia 5001, tel.: (08) 8302-0865; fax: (08) 8302-0866; International Code for Australia is 618

Established in 1991 in FL.
Donor: Gordon Samstag‡.
Foundation type: Independent foundation.
Financial data (yr. ended 12/31/12): Assets, $8,493,486 (M); expenditures, $511,957; qualifying distributions, $457,270; giving activities include $233,506 for 8 grants to individuals (high: $63,382; low: $206).
Purpose and activities: Scholarships are awarded for the furtherance of overseas studies in the visual arts. The scholarships cover the reasonable costs for a period of twelve months overseas, and include a tax-exempt stipend, plus return airfares and institutional fees for one academic year. Eligible individuals are graduates of not more than six years standing of a studio-based course at an Australian institution of higher education, and must be either Australian citizens or have permanent residency status, and be at least 18 years of age. Persons currently overseas may apply provided they are otherwise eligible in accordance with the above. Samstag application forms and detailed guidelines can be requested through the Trust web site by filling out the electronic form.
Fields of interest: Visual arts; Performing arts.
International interests: Australia.
Type of support: Scholarship funds; Scholarships—to individuals.
Limitations: Giving limited to residents of Australia.
Publications: Application guidelines.
Application information: Application form required.
Initial approach: Letter, e-mail, telephone
Deadline(s): June 30
Final notification: Sept.
Trustee: Bank of America, N.A.
EIN: 656064217
Other changes: The grantmaker no longer lists a URL address.

814

Sandelman Foundation

185 N.W. Spanish River Blvd., Ste. 100
Boca Raton, FL 33431-4230

Established in 1977 in NY.
Donors: Sanford Sandelman‡; Susan Sandelman.
Foundation type: Independent foundation.
Financial data (yr. ended 06/30/13): Assets, $3,851,606 (M); expenditures, $77,693; qualifying distributions, $73,700; giving activities include $73,700 for 15 grants (high: $24,600; low: $500).
Purpose and activities: Giving primarily to Jewish agencies.
Fields of interest: Higher education; Health care; Human services; Jewish federated giving programs; Jewish agencies & synagogues.
Limitations: Applications not accepted. Giving primarily in CO, FL, and NY. No grants to individuals.
Application information: Contributes only to pre-selected organizations.
Officers: Jeffrey Sandelman, Pres.; Andrew Schreier, V.P.; Susan Sandelman, Secy.; **Alison Schreier, Treas.**
EIN: 132910436

815

Seacor Foundation
Ft. Lauderdale, FL

The foundation has terminated in 2012.

816

William G. Selby and Marie Selby Foundation
1800 2nd St., Ste. 954
Sarasota, FL **34236-5930** (941) 957-0442
Contact: Evan Jones, Grants Mgr,
FAX: (941) 957-3135; E-mail: ejones@selbyfdn.org;
Main URL: http://www.selbyfdn.org/

Trust established in 1955 in FL.
Donors: William G. Selby†; Marie Selby†.
Foundation type: Independent foundation.
Financial data (yr. ended 05/31/13): Assets, $69,415,321 (M); expenditures, $3,593,894; qualifying distributions, $3,222,201; giving activities include $2,002,187 for grants, and $811,820 for grants to individuals.
Purpose and activities: The foundation seeks to make capital grants that will improve the quality of life in Sarasota County, FL, and its bordering counties. Scholarships are also given to students who can demonstrate financial need, who maintain a 3.0 (unweighted) GPA, who are residents of Sarasota, Manatee, Charlotte or DeSoto counties in FL, and who are pursuing a bachelors degree from a four-year college or university. Scholarships will be awarded up to $7,000 per year.
Fields of interest: Visual arts; Performing arts; Historic preservation/historical societies; Arts; Child development, education; Elementary school/education; Secondary school/education; Higher education; Education; Housing/shelter, development; Recreation, parks/playgrounds; Human services; Youth, services; Child development, services; Aging, centers/services; Community/economic development; Physical/earth sciences; Aging.
Type of support: Capital campaigns; Building/renovation; Equipment; Land acquisition; Scholarships—to individuals.
Limitations: Applications accepted. Giving limited to Charlotte, DeSoto, Manatee, and Sarasota counties, FL. No support for private K-12 schools, public schools, childcare facilities, or churches and their individual ministries. No grants to individuals (except through Selby Scholars Program), or for debt reduction, annual campaigns, deficit financing, operating budgets, endowment funds, surveys, program advertising, research, seminars, workshops, travel, fundraising, or conferences; no loans.
Publications: Application guidelines; Grants list; Informational brochure (including application guidelines).
Application information: Application must be submitted using the foundation's guidelines and online system. No applications for amounts under $10,000. Application guidelines and form for Selby Scholars available on foundation web site. Application form required.
Initial approach: Letter
Copies of proposal: 1
Deadline(s): Feb. 1 and Aug. 1 for grants; Apr. 1 for scholarships
Board meeting date(s): Apr. and Nov.
Final notification: May 15 and Dec. 15
Officer: Sarah Pappas, Pres.
Trustee: Wells Fargo, N.A.
Number of staff: 1 full-time professional; 2 full-time support.
EIN: 596121242

817

Sender Charitable Trust
1000 5th St., Ste. 303
Miami Beach, FL 33139-6510

Established in 1999 in NY.
Donor: Adam Sender.
Foundation type: Independent foundation.
Financial data (yr. ended 12/31/12): Assets, $581 (M); gifts received, $375,353; expenditures, $375,207; qualifying distributions, $371,619; giving activities include $371,619 for 19,000 grants (high: $130,000; low: $1,000).
Fields of interest: Museums (art); Animal welfare; Human services; Foundations (private grantmaking); Jewish federated giving programs; Jewish agencies & synagogues.
Limitations: Applications not accepted. Giving primarily in Washington, DC, FL and NY. No grants to individuals.
Application information: Unsolicited requests for funds not accepted.
Trustees: Adam Sender; Lenore Sender.
EIN: 137187854
Other changes: The grantmaker has moved from NY to FL.

818

Setzer Family Foundation Inc.
8650-12 Old Kings Rd. S.
Jacksonville, FL 32217

Established in 1986 in FL.
Donor: Sidney Setzer.
Foundation type: Independent foundation.
Financial data (yr. ended 06/30/13): Assets, $1,990,314 (M); gifts received, $1,150; expenditures, $187,125; qualifying distributions, $155,500; giving activities include $155,500 for 3 grants (high: $100,000; low: $13,500).
Purpose and activities: Giving primarily for Jewish organizations and hospitals.
Fields of interest: Hospitals (general); Human services; Jewish federated giving programs; Jewish agencies & synagogues.
Limitations: Applications not accepted. Giving primarily in Jacksonville, FL. No grants to individuals.
Application information: Contributes only to pre-selected organizations.
Trustees: Debra Setzer; Leonard R. Setzer.
EIN: 592685979
Other changes: The grantmaker no longer lists a phone.

819

Sierra Foundation, Inc.
509 Guisando de Avila, Ste. 200
Tampa, FL 33613-5235 (813) 549-7707
Contact: Thomas H. Gray, Secy.-Treas.; John Robert Sierra, Pres.

Established in 1987 in FL.
Donors: J. Robert Sierra; Mary Sierra.
Foundation type: Independent foundation.
Financial data (yr. ended 06/30/13): Assets, $9,407,614 (M); expenditures, $448,216; qualifying distributions, $447,492; giving activities include $397,361 for 66 grants (high: $200,000; low: $100).
Fields of interest: Education; Health organizations, association; Cancer research; Human services; YM/YWCAs & YM/YWHAs; Children/youth, services; Foundations (community); Religion.
Limitations: Applications accepted. Giving primarily in FL. No grants to individuals.
Application information: Application form not required.
Initial approach: Proposal
Deadline(s): None
Officers: John Robert Sierra, Pres.; Mary Sierra, V.P.; Thomas H. Gray, Secy.-Treas.; **James Kilbride, Secy.**
EIN: 592846736

820

The Gertrude E. Skelly Charitable Foundation
4600 N. Ocean Blvd., Ste. 206
Boynton Beach, FL 33435-7365 (561) 276-1008
Contact: Erik Edward Joh, Tr.
E-mail: skelly@erikjoh.com

Established in 1991 in FL.
Donor: Gertrude E. Skelly†.
Foundation type: Independent foundation.
Financial data (yr. ended 12/31/12): Assets, $15,124,697 (M); expenditures, $1,052,705; qualifying distributions, $906,372; giving activities include $765,000 for 47 grants (high: $30,000; low: $5,000).
Purpose and activities: The foundation's primary mission is to provide educational opportunities, mainly at colleges and universities, and needed medical care for those who are unable to afford them. All grants must affect multiple individuals and meet some educational, medical or emergency need.
Fields of interest: Scholarships/financial aid; Education; Hospitals (general).
Type of support: Emergency funds; Fellowships; Internship funds; Scholarship funds; Research; Matching/challenge support.
Limitations: Applications accepted. Giving on a national basis. No support for political or advocacy groups, or for organizations similar to the United Way which called funds for distribution to other charities. No grants to individuals.
Publications: Application guidelines.
Application information: Application form not required.
***Initial approach:* Contact foundation for complete guidelines**
Copies of proposal: 7
***Deadline(s):* June 30**
Board meeting date(s): Oct.
Trustees: Erik Edward Joh; SunTrust Bank.
Number of staff: 1 full-time professional; 1 part-time support.
EIN: 656085406

821

Randolph Snell Family Foundation
175 1st St. S., Ste. 3303
St. Petersburg, FL **33701**

Donors: Jake Randolph; Marvis Snell.
Foundation type: Independent foundation.
Financial data (yr. ended 08/31/13): Assets, $118,119 (M); expenditures, $67,616; qualifying

distributions, $65,833; giving activities include $65,833 for 5 grants (high: $33,333; low: $5,000).
Fields of interest: Performing arts, orchestras; Arts; Education; Human services; Christian agencies & churches.
Limitations: Applications not accepted. Giving primarily in AL and FL.
Application information: Unsolicited request for funds not accepted.
Trustee: Randolph R. Snell.
EIN: 274115291

822
Sontag Foundation, Inc.

c/o Frederick Sontag
816 A1A North, Ste. 201
Ponte Vedra Beach, FL 32082-8213
E-mail: kverble@sontagfoundation.com; Main URL: http://www.sontagfoundation.com
E-Newsletter: http://www.sontagfoundation.com/display.aspx?page=newsletter

Established in 2000 in FL.
Donor: Frederick B. Sontag.
Foundation type: Independent foundation.
Financial data (yr. ended 12/31/12): Assets, $53,483,785 (M); expenditures, $3,569,986; qualifying distributions, $3,236,660; giving activities include $2,910,812 for 41 grants (high: $784,286; low: $250).
Purpose and activities: Giving primarily for brain cancer and brain tumor research, rheumatoid arthritis research, and grants to programs that help individuals in northeast FL to become more self-sufficient.
Fields of interest: Brain research; Arthritis research; Human services.
Type of support: General/operating support.
Limitations: Applications not accepted. **Giving primarily in northeast FL, with emphasis on Baker, Clay, Duval, Flagler, Nassau, Putnam, and St. John's counties. No grants to individuals or for building funds, capital campaigns, sponsorship of fundraising events, long range program support.**
Application information: See foundation web site for the application guidelines and procedures which must be followed.
Officers and Directors:* Frederick B. Sontag,* Pres.; Frederick T. Sontag,* V.P.; **Daniel M. Ryan,* Secy.-Treas.**; Kay W. Verble, Exec. Dir.; Jeffrey Hudgins; Bradley D. Mottier; Susan T. Sontag; John D. Strom.
EIN: 593634325
Other changes: Daniel M. Ryan has replaced Matthew Miller as Secy.-Treas.

823
The Southwest Florida Community Foundation, Inc.

8771 College Pkwy., Bldg. 2, Ste. 201
Fort Myers, FL 33919 (239) 274-5900
Contact: For grants: Anne Douglas, Dir., Progs.
FAX: (239) 274-5930;
E-mail: info@floridacommunity.com; Main URL: http://www.floridacommunity.com
Facebook: https://www.facebook.com/SWFLCF
Twitter: https://twitter.com/SWFLCFnd

Incorporated in 1976 in FL.
Donors: Dorothy M. Beall‡; Beryl Berry‡; Marguerite Covington‡; Herbert E. Hussey‡; Isabel Kirkpatrick‡; Leonard Santini‡; Earl Riggs‡; Mrs. Earl Riggs‡; Daniel J. Berktold; Jane H. Berktold; Betty Houkom; Lillia Hodges; Richard T. Thompson.
Foundation type: Community foundation.
Financial data (yr. ended 06/30/12): Assets, $63,957,237 (M); gifts received, $5,166,046; expenditures, $3,989,627; giving activities include $2,454,892 for 143+ grants (high: $123,515).
Purpose and activities: The goals of the foundation are: 1) to significantly strengthen the ability of existing institutions to reach a broader segment of the community; 2) to provide innovative responses to community needs which do not unnecessarily duplicate other efforts; and 3) to create a sense of community through neighborhood involvement and outreach. Emphasis also on organizational capacity-building for area nonprofit organizations.
Fields of interest: Historic preservation/historical societies; Arts; Higher education; Education; Environment; Animal welfare; Health care; Mental health/crisis services; Safety/disasters; Children/youth, services; Human services; Community/economic development; Infants/toddlers; Children/youth; Children; Youth; Young adults; Disabilities, people with; Physically disabled; Blind/visually impaired; Deaf/hearing impaired; Mentally disabled; Minorities; Substance abusers; AIDS, people with; Single parents; Crime/abuse victims; Immigrants/refugees; Economically disadvantaged; Homeless.
Type of support: Technical assistance; Management development/capacity building; Capital campaigns; Building/renovation; Equipment; Endowments; Emergency funds; Program development; Scholarship funds; Consulting services; Scholarships—to individuals; Matching/challenge support.
Limitations: Applications accepted. Giving limited to Charlotte, Collier, Glades, Hendry and Lee counties, FL. No support for fraternal organizations, societies, or orders, or religious organizations for sectarian purposes (except where designated by a fund donor). No grants to individuals (except for scholarships), or for operating budgets, research, annual funds, debt retirement, feasibility studies, sports team travel, class trips, or fundraising events; no loans.
Publications: Application guidelines; Annual report (including application guidelines); Financial statement; Grants list; Informational brochure; Newsletter; Occasional report; Program policy statement; Program policy statement (including application guidelines); Quarterly report.
Application information: Visit foundation website for the online application portal and application guidelines. Application form required.
Initial approach: Complete online application
Deadline(s): Varies
Board meeting date(s): Quarterly
Final notification: Several days after board meetings
Officers and Trustees:* Joe Mazurkiewicz, Jr., Ph. D*, Chair.; Guy E. Whitesman,* Vice-Chair.; Sarah Owen,* C.E.O. and Pres.; Gay Thompson,* Secy.-Treas.; Deborah M. Braendle; **Carolyn E. Conant**; Patricia K. Dobbins; Dawn-Marie Driscoll; Kevin L. Erwin; Craig Folk; John Gamba; Charles Green; Archie B. Hayward, Jr.; Christopher Hill, CFA; Larry A. Hobbs, M.D.; Howard Leland; Sarah Owen; Darren Robertshaw; Sandy Robinson; **Robbie B. Roepstorff**; Myra Hale Walters; A. Scott White; Steven R. Whitley.
Number of staff: 6 full-time professional; 3 full-time support; 1 part-time support.
EIN: 596580974
Other changes: Gay Rebel Thompson is no longer a trustee. Andrea McKiddie is now Donor Srvs. Coord. Steven Mills is now Data Integrity Coord. and Admin. Asst. Robert Raymond is now Acct. Asst. Anne Douglas is now Regional Initiatives Dir. Janet Remmel is now Opers. Asso. Janet Remmel is now Opers. Asso. Carolyn Rogers is no longer V.P. of Devel. and Comm. Gay Rebel Thompson is no longer a trustee. Marie M. Ackord, Gary Aubuchon, M. Jaqueline McCurdy, David F. Shellenbarger, Robbie Roepstorff, and Guy E. Whitesman are no longer trustees.

824
Roy M. Speer Foundation

2535 Success Dr.
Odessa, FL 33556-3401
***Contact:* Lynnda L. Speer, Tr.**

Established in 1986 in FL.
Donors: Richard W. Baker; Roy M. Speer‡.
Foundation type: Independent foundation.
Financial data (yr. ended 06/30/13): Assets, $32,414,151 (M); gifts received, $20,089,627; expenditures, $1,089,385; qualifying distributions, $1,001,383; giving activities include $669,500 for 15 grants (high: $297,000; low: $2,500).
Fields of interest: Medical school/education; Hospitals (general); Hospitals (specialty); Heart & circulatory diseases; Health organizations; Religious federated giving programs; Protestant agencies & churches.
Limitations: Applications accepted. Giving primarily in FL. No grants to individuals.
Application information: Application form not required.
Initial approach: Letter
Deadline(s): None
Trustees: Lynnda L. Speer; Richard M. Speer.
EIN: 592785945
Other changes: For the fiscal year ended June 30, 2013, the fair market value of the grantmaker's assets was $32,414,151, a 166.6% increase over the fiscal 2012 value, $12,159,492.
Roy Speer, a trustee, is deceased.

825
The John R. and Inge P. Stafford Foundation

16682 Captiva Dr.
P.O. Box 355
Captiva, FL 33924-0355
Contact: John R. Stafford, Tr.

Established in 1996 in NJ.
Donors: John R. Stafford; Inge P. Stafford.
Foundation type: Independent foundation.
Financial data (yr. ended 06/30/13): Assets, $1,979,724 (M); expenditures, $201,198; qualifying distributions, $201,129; giving activities include $201,031 for 40 grants (high: $50,000; low: $35).
Purpose and activities: Giving primarily for education, health, particularly a cancer hospital, human services, and to a Presbyterian church.
Fields of interest: Education; Hospitals (specialty); Health care; Cancer; Boys & girls clubs; Human services; Protestant agencies & churches.
Limitations: Applications accepted. Giving primarily in NJ and NY. No grants to individuals.
Application information: Application form not required.
Initial approach: Letter
Deadline(s): None
Trustees: Christina Stafford Chaplin; Jennifer Stafford Farrow; Charlotte Stafford; John R. Stafford; Carolyn Stafford Stein.
EIN: 226710521
Other changes: Inge P. Stafford is no longer a trustee.

826
The Stellar Foundation
2900 Hartley Rd.
Jacksonville, FL 32257-8221 (904) 260-2900
***FAX:* (904) 260-2959;**
E-mail: info@thestellarfoundation.org; Main URL: http://www.thestellarfoundation.org/

Established in 2006 in FL.
Donors: The Stellar Group; Dilling Mechanical; Hansen; McGladrey LLP; Rogers Towers, P.A.; Structural Components; Amex Evapco.; Dryco LLC.; Assurance Dimensions; Cooper Steel.
Foundation type: Independent foundation.
Financial data (yr. ended 12/31/12): Assets, $3,122 (M); gifts received, $162,752; expenditures, $201,129; qualifying distributions, $180,993; giving activities include $180,993 for 59 grants (high: $19,500; low: $300).
Fields of interest: Secondary school/education; Higher education, university; Health care; Residential/custodial care, hospices; United Ways and Federated Giving Programs.
Limitations: Applications accepted. Giving primarily in FL. No grants to individuals.
Application information: See foundation website for complete application guidelines. Application form required.
Directors: Richard M. Lovelace; Clint E. Pyle; Michael S. Santarone; **Allison Korman Shelton**; Scott V. Witt.
EIN: 203808875
Other changes: Ronald H. Foster and Michael A. Wodrich are no longer directors.

827
The Robert J. Stransky Foundation
c/o Michael C. Trimboli
3308 Purple Martin Dr., No. 126
Punta Gorda, FL 33950-6747

Established in 1987 in NY.
Donors: Robert J. Stransky†; Stransky, Inc.
Foundation type: Independent foundation.
Financial data (yr. ended 06/30/12): Assets, $5,869,651 (M); expenditures, $349,104; qualifying distributions, $284,299; giving activities include $284,299 for 5 grants (high: $157,534; low: $1,000).
Purpose and activities: Giving primarily for education, human services, and Roman Catholic organizations and churches.
Fields of interest: Elementary/secondary education; Higher education; Education; Human services; Catholic agencies & churches.
Type of support: General/operating support.
Limitations: Applications not accepted. Giving in the U.S., with some emphasis on Buffalo, NY. No grants to individuals.
Application information: Contributes only to pre-selected organizations.
Trustees: Norman E. Benz; Rosemary Burgio; Michael C. Trimboli.
EIN: 222849600
Other changes: The grantmaker has moved from AZ to FL.

828
Harry Sudakoff Foundation Inc.
c/o U.S. Trust
50 Central Ave., Ste. 750
Sarasota, FL **34236-5743**
***Contact:* Janet Lynn Dickens, A.V.P.**
E-mail: janet.dickens@ustrust.com; **Main URL: http://fdnweb.org/sudakoff**
Grants List: http://fdnweb.org/sudakoff/grants/year/grants-for-2012/

Incorporated in 1956 in NY.
Donors: The Harry and Ruth Sudakoff Trust; Ruth Sudakoff†; Harry Sudakoff.
Foundation type: Independent foundation.
Financial data (yr. ended 12/31/12): Assets, $6,025,004 (M); expenditures, $409,209; qualifying distributions, $409,209; giving activities include $310,368 for 8 grants (high: $85,302; low: $10,000).
Fields of interest: Arts; Education; Environment; Health care; Boys & girls clubs; YM/YWCAs & YM/YWHAs; Family services; Aging, centers/services; Science; Children/youth; Disabilities, people with.
Limitations: Applications accepted. Giving primarily in Sarasota County, FL. No grants to individuals, or for endowments, deficit financing, debt reduction, operating expenses, conferences, seminars, workshops, travel, surveys, advertising, fund raising, research, or for annual campaigns.
Application information: Complete application guidelines available on foundation web site.
Initial approach: Letter
Deadline(s): Aug. 14
Officers: Gary A. Bucholtz, Pres.; Bertram Axelrad, V.P. and Treas.; William T. Harrison, Jr., Secy.
EIN: 650439722

829
Sunburst Foundation, Inc.
2285 Potomac Rd.
Boca Raton, FL 33431-5518 (561) 995-7755
Contact: James M. Hankins, Pres.
***E-mail:* sunfound@bellsouth.net**; Main URL: http://www.sunburst-foundation.org/

Established in 1986 in FL.
Foundation type: Independent foundation.
Financial data (yr. ended 06/30/13): Assets, $5,488,714 (M); expenditures, $265,952; qualifying distributions, $254,589; giving activities include $125,000 for 1 grant, and $102,250 for 31 grants to individuals (high: $6,000; low: $1,500).
Purpose and activities: Scholarship awards to minority seniors graduating from participating Florida high schools who are planning to study the physical sciences at a four year college or university; also some community giving.
Fields of interest: Higher education; Foundations (community); Physical/earth sciences.
Type of support: General/operating support; Scholarships—to individuals.
Application information: Application guidelines available on foundation web site. Application form required.
Officers and Trustees:* James M. Hankins,* Pres.; John M. Wargo,* V.P. and Treas.; Kenneth A. Wenzel,* Secy.
Number of staff: 1 part-time professional.
EIN: 592637289

830
TECO Energy Foundation Inc.
P.O. Box 11
Tampa, FL **33601 (813) 228-4111**
Contact: Jack Amor, Exec. Dir.
***Application address:* 702 N. Franklin St., Tampa, FL 33602**

Established as a company-sponsored operating foundation.
Donor: TECO Energy, Inc.
Foundation type: Operating foundation.
Financial data (yr. ended 12/31/12): Assets, $318,523 (M); gifts received, $445,036; expenditures, $481,131; qualifying distributions, $479,700; giving activities include $479,700 for 5 grants (high: $180,000; low: $50,000).
Purpose and activities: The foundation supports museums and performing art centers and organizations involved with higher education.
Fields of interest: Arts; Education.
Type of support: Capital campaigns; Matching/challenge support.
Limitations: Applications accepted. Giving primarily in Tampa, FL.
Application information: Application form required.
Initial approach: Proposal
Deadline(s): None
Officers and Directors: Sandra W. Callahan,* V.P.; David E. Schwartz, Secy.; Kim M. Caruso, Treas.; Jack Amor, Exec. Dir.; **Charles A. Attal; Phil Barringer; Deirdre A. Brown; Gordon L. Gillete; Bruce Narzissenfeld.**
EIN: 010598444
Other changes: The grantmaker no longer lists a URL address.

831
William and Helen Thomas Charitable Trust
c/o U.S. Trust, Bank of America, N.A.
900 S.E. Federal Hwy., 2nd Fl., M/C: FL5-359-02-6
Stuart, FL 34994-3733 (772) 403-1623
Contact: Bonney A. Johnson, V.P., Bank of America, N.A.
FAX: (772) 403-1617;
E-mail: bonney.johnson@ustrust.com; **Main URL: http://fdnweb.org/thomas**

Established in 1990 in FL.
Donors: William A. Thomas†; Helen S. Thomas; Emily Thomas†.
Foundation type: Independent foundation.
Financial data (yr. ended 12/31/12): Assets, $22,031,356 (M); gifts received, $1,222; expenditures, $1,445,468; qualifying distributions, $1,236,825; giving activities include $1,135,000 for 37 grants (high: $165,000; low: $5,000).
Purpose and activities: Giving primarily for: 1) Educational opportunities for deserving and needy students; 2) Preservation and protection of the natural environment; 3) Medical research and care for the treatment, prevention and cure of arthritis, blindness and diabetes; 4) Assistance for the poor, especially those of Appalachia and those of American Indian ancestry; and 5) Assistance and care for orphaned children who are unlikely to be adopted because of age, handicap, or for other reasons.
Fields of interest: Education; Environment; Health organizations, association; Human services; Children/youth, services; Disabilities, people with; Blind/visually impaired; Native Americans/American Indians.
Type of support: General/operating support; Continuing support; Annual campaigns; Capital campaigns; Building/renovation; Equipment; Endowments; Program development; Curriculum development; Scholarship funds; Matching/challenge support.
Limitations: Applications accepted. Giving primarily in FL and Appalachia. No grants to individuals.
Application information: Applicants are encouraged to submit applications in advance of the deadline. Application form required.

Initial approach: **Use online application on foundation web site**
Deadline(s): Sept. 15
Board meeting date(s): Nov.
Final notification: Within 3 months
Trustees: Dennis Blanz; James H. Elam; James Keffler; Marilyn Moore; U.S. Trust Co., N.A.
Number of staff: 1
EIN: 366917007

832
Thomsen Foundation, Inc.
701 E. Commercial Blvd., Ste. 300
Fort Lauderdale, FL 33334-3391

Established in FL.
Donors: Pipp, Inc.; Carl J. Thomsen; Frances D. Thomsen; Robert J. Thomsen.
Foundation type: Independent foundation.
Financial data (yr. ended 10/31/13): Assets, $6,587,349 (M); expenditures, $353,867; qualifying distributions, $332,972; giving activities include $320,000 for 1 grant.
Fields of interest: Higher education; Health care.
Limitations: Applications not accepted. Giving primarily in MI and MN. No grants to individuals.
Application information: Contributes only to pre-selected organizations.
Officers and Directors:* Carl J. Thomsen,* Secy.; Susan Davis,* Treas.; **Valerie S. Armagno**; Kathleen M. McMillan.
EIN: 592070983

833
Liz Whitney Tippett Foundation, Inc.
3325 Griffin Rd., Ste. E-186
Fort Lauderdale, FL 33312-5500

Established in 1998 in FL.
Foundation type: Operating foundation.
Financial data (yr. ended 12/31/12): Assets, $5,345,056 (M); expenditures, $285,966; qualifying distributions, $268,416; giving activities include $198,000 for 28 grants (high: $20,000; low: $2,500).
Fields of interest: Arts; Higher education; Hospitals (general); Cancer research; Food distribution, meals on wheels; Human services; Christian agencies & churches.
Limitations: Applications not accepted. Giving primarily in FL, MO, and NC.
Application information: Contributes only to pre-selected organizations.
Officer: Janet Lindsley, Mgr.
Director: William Lindsley.
EIN: 650083442

834
Tsunami Foundation
c/o Anson M. Beard, Jr.
421 Peruvian Ave.
Palm Beach, FL 33480-4518

Established in 1993 in CT.
Donor: Anson McCook Beard, Jr.
Foundation type: Independent foundation.
Financial data (yr. ended 12/31/12): Assets, $20,256,595 (M); gifts received, $10,000; expenditures, $1,191,400; qualifying distributions, $937,485; giving activities include $914,400 for 22 grants (high: $70,000; low: $2,500).
Purpose and activities: Giving primarily for education, conservation, health, and human services.
Fields of interest: Arts; Education; Environment, natural resources; Health care; Human services.
Limitations: Applications not accepted. Giving primarily in NY and PA. No grants to individuals.
Application information: Contributes only to pre-selected organizations.
Trustees: Anson H. Beard; Anson McCook Beard, Jr.; Debra Beard; James M. Beard; Veronica M. Beard; Veronica S. Beard.
EIN: 137019761

835
The Turock Family Foundation
2929 E. Commercial Blvd., Ste. 501
Fort Lauderdale, FL 33308-4221
***Contact:* Stuart Wardlaw, CPA**

Established in 1998 in NJ.
Foundation type: Independent foundation.
Financial data (yr. ended 12/31/12): Assets, $3,851,190 (M); expenditures, $328,300; qualifying distributions, $294,925; giving activities include $294,925 for grants.
Purpose and activities: Giving primarily for education and for children, youth, and social services, including a children's hospital.
Fields of interest: Elementary/secondary education; Higher education; Hospitals (specialty); Human services; Children/youth, services.
Limitations: Applications not accepted. Giving primarily in MD; with some giving in New York, NY.
Application information: Unsolicited requests for funds not accepted.
Trustees: David L. Turock; Nancy G. Turock.
EIN: 223758083
Other changes: The grantmaker has moved from NJ to FL.

836
The TWS Foundation
c/o Thomas W. Smith
2200 Butts Rd., No. 320
Boca Raton, FL 33431-7453 (561) 314-0800
Contact: Thomas W. Smith, Tr.

Established in 1984 in NY.
Donor: Thomas W. Smith.
Foundation type: Independent foundation.
Financial data (yr. ended 12/31/12): Assets, $6,845,959 (M); gifts received, $6,327,750; expenditures, $5,884,565; qualifying distributions, $5,826,514; giving activities include $5,619,287 for grants.
Fields of interest: Arts; Education; Health care; Health organizations, association; Human services; Community/economic development; Public policy, research.
Type of support: General/operating support; Scholarship funds.
Limitations: Giving primarily in CT, ID, NY, RI, and VA. No grants to individuals.
Application information:
Initial approach: Letter
Deadline(s): None
Trustee: Thomas W. Smith.
EIN: 133258067
Other changes: The grantmaker has moved from CT to FL.

837
The Walter Foundation
(formerly Jim Walter Corporation Foundation)
13623 N. Florida Ave.
Tampa, FL 33613-3216 (813) 961-0530
Contact: W.K. Baker, Tr.

Established in 1966 in FL.
Donor: Walter Industries, Inc.
Foundation type: Company-sponsored foundation.
Financial data (yr. ended 08/31/13): Assets, $16,284,707 (M); expenditures, $1,008,147; qualifying distributions, $831,000; giving activities include $831,000 for 51 grants (high: $100,000; low: $2,000).
Purpose and activities: The foundation supports hospitals and organizations involved with orchestras, historical activities, secondary and higher education, mental health and crisis services, hunger, human services, and Christianity.
Fields of interest: Performing arts, orchestras; Historical activities; Secondary school/education; Higher education; Hospitals (general); Mental health/crisis services; Food distribution, meals on wheels; Boys & girls clubs; Salvation Army; Children, services; Residential/custodial care; Developmentally disabled, centers & services; Human services; Christian agencies & churches.
Type of support: General/operating support.
Limitations: Applications accepted. Giving primarily in FL. No grants to individuals.
Application information: Application form not required.
Initial approach: Proposal
Deadline(s): None
Trustees: W. K. Baker; S. L. Myers; **A.J. Walter**; R. A. Walter.
EIN: 596205802

838
The Ware Foundation
5825 Sunset Dr., Ste. 306
South Miami, FL 33143-5222
E-mail: info@warefoundation.org; Application address: 6609 S.W. 65th St., Miami, FL 33143, tel.: (305) 662-5002; Main URL: http://www.warefoundation.org

Trust established in 1950 in PA.
Donor: John H. Ware, Jr.‡.
Foundation type: Independent foundation.
Financial data (yr. ended 12/31/12): Assets, $19,432,030 (M); expenditures, $1,062,615; qualifying distributions, $841,923; giving activities include $678,508 for 31 grants (high: $75,000; low: $1,000).
Purpose and activities: The foundation's mission is to promote social responsibility by providing grants that improve the quality of people's lives, particularly the lives of children.
Fields of interest: Higher education; Education; Environment, water resources; Environment; Medical research; Crime/violence prevention, child abuse; Human services.
Limitations: Giving primarily in CO and FL. No support for private foundations. No grants to individuals.
Publications: Application guidelines.
Application information: When forwarding an application or correspondence electronically please put a copy in the mail. Telephone inquiries are not accepted. Application form not required.
Initial approach: Letter or proposal, no more than 2 pages
Final notification: Positive responses only; up to 6 months from receipt of letter

Officer: Mark Edwards, Secy.-Treas.
Trustees: Elizabeth Eason; John Edwards; James Odom; Morgan Ware-Soumah.
EIN: 237286585

839
Wells Family Foundation, Inc.
680 Via Lugano
Winter Park, FL 32789-1534

Established in 2005 in FL.
Donors: Stephen L. Wells; Stephanie Shackelford; John Shackelford.
Foundation type: Independent foundation.
Financial data (yr. ended 06/30/13): Assets, $4,653,592 (M); gifts received, $102,415; expenditures, $210,939; qualifying distributions, $191,430; giving activities include $180,580 for 9 grants (high: $83,000; low: $100).
Fields of interest: Children/youth, services; Christian agencies & churches; Children.
Limitations: Applications not accepted. Giving primarily in FL. No grants to individuals.
Application information: Contributes only to pre-selected organizations.
Directors: Stephanie W. Shackelford; Kristi Wells; Stephen L. Wells.
EIN: 204003386
Other changes: Stephanie Wells, a director, is now Stephanie W. Shackelford.

840
Whitehall Foundation, Inc.
P.O. Box 3423
Palm Beach, FL 33480-1623 (561) 655-4474
Contact: George M. Moffett II, Pres.; Catherine M. Thomas, Asst. Treas.
E-mail: email@whitehall.org; Express mail address: 125 Worth Ave., Ste. 220, Palm Beach, FL 33480; Main URL: http://www.whitehall.org
Grants List: http://www.whitehall.org/recipients/

Incorporated in 1937 in NJ.
Donor: George M. Moffett†.
Foundation type: Independent foundation.
Financial data (yr. ended 09/30/12): Assets, $107,121,135 (M); expenditures, $5,117,606; qualifying distributions, $4,839,791; giving activities include $4,566,558 for 125 grants (high: $300,000; low: $500).
Purpose and activities: Support for scholarly research in the life sciences, with emphasis on behavioral neuroscience and invertebrate neurophysiology; innovative and imaginative projects preferred. Research grants are paid to sponsoring institutions, rather than directly to individuals.
Fields of interest: Biology/life sciences.
Type of support: Equipment; Program development; Research.
Limitations: Applications accepted. Giving limited to the U.S. No support for investigators who already have, or expect to receive, substantial support from other quarters. No grants for salary support for principal investigator, travel to conferences or for consultation, secretarial or office expenses, construction projects or laboratory renovations, or tuition or fellowships.
Publications: Application guidelines; Grants list.
Application information: See foundation web site for specific application guidelines. Though the foundation encourages use of electronic mail, the letter of intent must be submitted in hard copy, via U.S. mail, on institutional letterhead. Foundation telephone available 9:00am-12:00pm, weekdays.
Initial approach: 2-page letter of intent
Deadline(s): Letter of intent: Jan. 15, Apr. 15, and Oct. 1; Application: Feb. 15, June 1, and Sept. 1
Board meeting date(s): 3 grant review sessions per year
Final notification: May 1, Aug. 15, and Dec. 1
Officers and Trustees:* George M. Moffett II,* Pres. and Treas.; J. Wright Rumbough, Jr.,* V.P.; Peter Gibbons Neff,* Assoc. V.P.; Catherine M. Thomas, Corp. Secy.; Kenneth S. Beall, Jr.; E. Anthony Newton.
Number of staff: 1 full-time professional; 1 part-time professional.
EIN: 135637595

841
Wiegand Morning Star Foundation, Inc.
3010 Grand Bay Blvd., Ste. 474
Longboat Key, FL 34228-4419
***Contact:* Phillips Wiegand**

Established in 2004 in PA.
Donors: Phillips Wiegand; PW Financial Partners.
Foundation type: Independent foundation.
Financial data (yr. ended 12/31/12): Assets, $5,925,318 (M); gifts received, $908,278; expenditures, $925,666; qualifying distributions, $915,700; giving activities include $915,700 for grants.
Fields of interest: Human services; Family services; Christian agencies & churches.
Limitations: Applications not accepted. Giving primarily in CO, LA, PA and TN. No grants to individuals.
Application information: Contributes only to pre-selected organizations.
Directors: Sara Valentine; Ben Wiegand; Phillips Wiegand; Phillips Wiegand, Jr.; Ruth Wiegand.
EIN: 562449126
Other changes: The grantmaker has moved from PA to FL.
At the close of 2011, the grantmaker paid grants of $868,700, a 170.1% increase over the 2010 disbursements, $321,630.

842
Winter Park Health Foundation
(formerly Winter Park Memorial Hospital Association, Inc.)
220 Edinburgh Dr.
Winter Park, FL 32792-4160 (407) 644-2300
FAX: (407) 644-0174; Main URL: http://www.wphf.org
E-Newsletter: http://feedburner.google.com/fb/a/mailverify?uri=WinterParkHealthFoundation
Facebook: https://www.facebook.com/WinterParkHealthFoundation
Flickr: https://www.flickr.com/photos/109856427@N08/
LinkedIn: http://www.linkedin.com/company/winter-park-health-foundation?trk=tyah&trkInfo=tas%3Awinter+park+health+foundation%2Cidx%3A1-1-1
Pinterest: http://www.pinterest.com/WPHealthFdn/
Twitter: https://twitter.com/WPHealthFdn
Vimeo: http://vimeo.com/user4160462/videos
YouTube: http://www.youtube.com/user/WPHealthFdn

Established in 1951 as Winter Park Memorial Hospital Association; name changed in 1994.
Donors: Lola E. Nowers Fund; Carl J. Brunoehler Scholarship Fund.
Foundation type: Independent foundation.
Financial data (yr. ended 12/31/12): Assets, $113,474,123 (M); gifts received, $140,211; expenditures, $6,164,466; qualifying distributions, $5,141,882; giving activities include $2,751,630 for 180 grants (high: $447,469; low: $250), and $1,095,520 for foundation-administered programs.
Purpose and activities: Giving primarily for children and youth, community health, and older adults.
Fields of interest: Education; Health care; Human services; Children/youth; Youth; Adults; Aging.
Type of support: Management development/capacity building; Emergency funds; Program development; Conferences/seminars; Scholarship funds; Research; Consulting services; Program evaluation; Matching/challenge support.
Limitations: Applications not accepted. Giving primarily in the greater Winter Park, FL, area. No support for political purposes, lobbying, electioneering, or for-profit organizations. No grants to individuals.
Publications: Grants list; Informational brochure; Newsletter; Occasional report.
Application information: Unsolicited applications not accepted.
Board meeting date(s): Quarterly
Officers and Trustees:* George H. Herbst,* Chair.; Toni Jennings, Vice Chair., Children and Youth; Eddie Needham, M.D., FAAFP, Vice-Chair., Community Health; Joyce Swain,* Vice-Chair., Older Adults; Patricia Maddox,* C.E.O. and Pres.; Debbie Watson, V.P.; **Harold W. Barley,* Secy.; Marisa Carnevale-Henderson,* Treas.**; Ron Lambert, C.F.O.; **Rita Bornstein, Ph.D.**; Debbie Chang; Matthew M. Davies; **W. Marvin Hardy IV, M.D.**; Christine Jablonski, M.D.; **Christopher Jacobs; Barbara Jenkins, Ed.D.**; Jean D. Leuner; Charles F. Pierce; Joseph D. Portoghese, M.D.; David Stanley; **J. Kurt Wood.**
Number of staff: 6 full-time professional; 1 part-time professional; 3 full-time support.
EIN: 590669460
Other changes: George H. Herbst has replaced Sandra G. Hostetter as Chair. Toni Jennings has replaced David Stanley as Vice-Chair., Children and Youth. Eddie Needham, M.D., FAAFP has replaced Joseph D. Portoghese, M.D. as Vice-Chair., Community Health. Joyce Swain has replaced Gerald Sutton, C.P.A. as Vice-Chair., Older Adults. Harold W. Barley has replaced Marisa Carnevale-Henderson as Secy. Marisa Carnevale-Henderson has replaced George Herbst as Treas.
Lewis M. Duncan, Brenda Holson, Mary B. Rumberger, Debra A. St. Louis, and Judith G. Thames are no longer trustees.

843
Wollowick Family Foundation
(formerly Rubin and Gladys Wollowick Foundation, Inc.)
c/o Golomb, Schwartz & Cove, P.A.
2000 N.W. 150th Ave., Ste. 2106
Pembroke Pines, FL **33028-2870 (954) 889-0075**

Established in 1984 in FL.
Donor: Gladys Wollowick†.
Foundation type: Independent foundation.
Financial data (yr. ended 01/31/13): Assets, $4,104,242 (M); expenditures, $676,452; qualifying distributions, $601,193; giving activities

include $589,550 for 96 grants (high: $150,000; low: $800).
Purpose and activities: Giving primarily for education, hospitals and health organizations, social services, and Jewish organizations.
Fields of interest: Higher education; Hospitals (general); Health organizations, association; Medical research, institute; Human services; American Red Cross; Jewish federated giving programs; Jewish agencies & synagogues.
International interests: Israel.
Type of support: General/operating support; Annual campaigns; Equipment; Emergency funds; Research; Matching/challenge support.
Limitations: Applications accepted. Giving primarily in Boca Raton and Miami, FL. No grants to individuals.
Application information: Application form not required.
Initial approach: Letter
***Deadline(s):* Sept. 30**
Board meeting date(s): Varies
Directors: Megan Lowe; Richard Lowe; Sandra Lois Lowe; Jason Stein; Rhoda Stein; Ronnit Stein; Dr. Robert Tesher; Janet Amy Wollowick.
Trustee: BNY Mellon, N.A.
EIN: 592469452

844
Woodbery Carlton Foundation
222 S. 6th Ave.
Wauchula, FL 33873-2921
***Application address:* c/o Doyle E. Carlton III, Rt. 1, P.O. Box 412, Cloverhill, Wauchula, FL 33873-0412**

Established in 1988 in FL.
Donor: Doyle E. Carlton, Jr.
Foundation type: Independent foundation.
Financial data (yr. ended 08/31/13): Assets, $2,307,761 (M); expenditures, $203,503; qualifying distributions, $190,602; giving activities include $177,500 for 12 grants (high: $95,000; low: $500), and $11,820 for 4 grants to individuals (high: $6,820; low: $1,000).
Fields of interest: Education; Recreation, community; Christian agencies & churches.
Type of support: General/operating support; Scholarship funds.
Limitations: Applications accepted. Giving primarily in FL.
Application information: Application form not required.
Initial approach: Letter
Deadline(s): July 1
Directors: Doyle E. Carlton III; Jane Carlton Durando; Walter S. Farr; Susan C. Smith.
EIN: 650068703

845
Charles G. Wright Endowment for Humanity Inc.
91750 Overseas Hwy.
Tavernier, FL 33070-2642

Established in 2006 in FL.
Donors: Jeanette S. Wright; JSW & JCW, LP; Jeffrey C. Wright.
Foundation type: Independent foundation.
Financial data (yr. ended 12/31/12): Assets, $0 (M); expenditures, $248,328; qualifying distributions, $209,500; giving activities include $209,500 for grants.
Fields of interest: Horticulture/garden clubs; Christian agencies & churches.
Limitations: Applications not accepted. Giving primarily in ME and NJ; some funding also in FL. No grants to individuals.
Application information: Contributes only to pre-selected organizations.
Directors: Matthew M. Jeans; Kate Wright; **Laura Wright.**
EIN: 203514304
Other changes: Michael R. Danatos and Jeffrey C. Wright are no longer directors.

GEORGIA

846
May P. & Francis L. Abreu Charitable Trust
(formerly M & F Abreu Charitable Trust)
c/o SunTrust Bank
P.O. Box 502407
Atlanta, GA 31150-2407 (404) 549-6743
Contact: Peter M. Abreu, Chair.; Katherine M. Abreu, Prog. Dir.
FAX: (404) 549-6752;
E-mail: info@abreufoundation.org; Main URL: http://www.abreufoundation.org

Established in 2003 in GA.
Donor: Francis Abreu Trust.
Foundation type: Independent foundation.
Financial data (yr. ended 12/31/13): Assets, $9,036,640 (M); expenditures, $376,205; qualifying distributions, $355,218; giving activities include $245,500 for 21 grants (high: $142,500; low: $1,000).
Purpose and activities: The trust benefits others by providing grants to arts and cultural programs, education, health associations, human services, and children and youth services.
Fields of interest: Arts, cultural/ethnic awareness; Human services; Infants/toddlers; Children/youth; Children; Adults; Young adults; Disabilities, people with; Physically disabled; Blind/visually impaired; Deaf/hearing impaired; Mentally disabled; Minorities; Women; Infants/toddlers, female; Girls; Adults, women; Young adults, female; Infants/toddlers, male; Boys; Adults, men; Young adults, male; Substance abusers; AIDS, people with; Single parents; Crime/abuse victims; Terminal illness, people with; Economically disadvantaged; Homeless.
Type of support: Capital campaigns; Building/renovation; Equipment; Program development; Seed money; Curriculum development; Fellowships; Matching/challenge support.
Limitations: Applications accepted. Giving primarily in the Atlanta, GA, area. No grants for operating support.
Publications: Application guidelines.
Application information: Applications must be submitted through the online application system. Complete application form and guidelines available on Trust web site. No international proposals accepted. Application form required.
Copies of proposal: 1
Deadline(s): Mar. 31 for Apr. consideration or Sept. 30 for Oct. consideration
Officer: Peter M. Abreu, Chair.
Committee Members: Claire Abreu; Katherine M. Abreu; Michael Abreu; Charles D. Menser, Jr.; John A. Wallace.
Trustee: SunTrust Bank.
Number of staff: 3
EIN: 586455665

847
AIM Foundation
1555 Peachtree St. N.E., Ste. 1800
Atlanta, GA 30309-2499

Established in 1997 in TX.
Donors: Robert H. Graham; AIM Management Group Inc.; AMVESCAP.
Foundation type: Company-sponsored foundation.
Financial data (yr. ended 12/31/12): Assets, $1,280,553 (M); expenditures, $14,355; qualifying distributions, $5,023.
Purpose and activities: The foundation supports organizations involved with education.
Fields of interest: Elementary/secondary education; Education, early childhood education; Higher education; Education.
Type of support: Scholarship funds; General/operating support.
Limitations: Applications not accepted. Giving primarily in TX, with emphasis on Houston. No support for religious organizations or grantmaking foundations. No grants to individuals, or for benefits, dinners, galas, or special fundraising events, mass appeal solicitations, scientific or medical research projects, feasibility studies, costs for trips, meetings, attendance, conferences, or group competitions or performances, or political candidates; no loans.
Application information: Contributes only to pre-selected organizations.
Trustees: Washington C. Dender; Loren M. Starr; Kevin M. Carome.
EIN: 760522586
Other changes: Robert H. Graham is no longer Pres. Gary T. Crum is no longer V.P. and Secy.-Treas.

848
Daniel P. Amos Family Foundation
(formerly Daniel P. and Shannon L. Amos Foundation, Inc.)
c/o Selection Comm.
P.O. Box 5346
Columbus, GA 31906-0346
E-mail: CCBradshaw@AmosFamilyFoundation.org; Main URL: http://amosfamilyfoundation.org/index.htm

Established in 1992 in GA.
Donors: Daniel P. Amos; Paul Amos Trust; Jean Amos Trust; Paul S. and Jean R. Amos Trust.
Foundation type: Independent foundation.
Financial data (yr. ended 12/31/12): Assets, $140,670,140 (M); gifts received, $7,147,917; expenditures, $8,105,347; qualifying distributions, $6,772,000; giving activities include $6,772,000 for 58 grants (high: $1,500,000; low: $500).
Purpose and activities: Giving primarily to Christian organizations whose goals, activities, and operating principles are consistent with the foundation's Statement of Faith.
Fields of interest: Higher education; Human services; Christian agencies & churches; Protestant agencies & churches.
Type of support: Building/renovation.
Limitations: Applications accepted. Giving primarily in Columbus, GA. No grants to individuals.
Application information: Application forms available on foundation web site. Application form required.
Initial approach: Complete appropriate application form
Trustee:* Daniel P. Amos, Pres.
EIN: 582005391
Other changes: Lauren A. Amos is no longer Vice-Chair. David B. Plyler is no longer Secy.

849
Amos-Cheves Foundation, Inc.
(formerly His Trust Foundation, Inc.)
6867 Mountainbrook Dr., Ste. 107
Columbus, GA **31904-3379**

Established in 2002 in GA.
Donors: Olivia D. Amos; Bettye A. Cheves; Cecil Chevez; Elizabeth Cheves Meeks; Olivia D. Amos Charitable Lead Trust.
Foundation type: Independent foundation.
Financial data (yr. ended 12/31/12): Assets, $18,313,390 (M); gifts received, $941,277; expenditures, $2,311,082; qualifying distributions, $2,289,535; giving activities include $2,257,702 for 78 grants, and $18,500 for 23 grants to individuals.
Purpose and activities: Giving primarily for Christian-based education, youth programs, and human services.
Fields of interest: Higher education; Youth development; Human services; YM/YWCAs & YM/YWHAs; Children/youth, services; International relief; Christian agencies & churches; Economically disadvantaged.
Type of support: Building/renovation; Equipment; Program development; Scholarship funds; Grants to individuals; Scholarships—to individuals.
Limitations: Applications not accepted. Giving primarily in GA; some giving also in AL, SC, and TN.
Application information: Unsolicited requests for funds not accepted.
Officers and Board Members:* Cecil M. Cheves,* Chair.; Bettye A. Cheves,* Pres. and Secy.-Treas.; William R. Blanchard; Elizabeth C. Meeks; **Ryan L. Meeks**; Blanchard C. Olivia; Avery C. Wolf; Luther H. Wolf III.
EIN: 582634947
Other changes: At the close of 2012, the grantmaker paid grants of $2,276,202, a 129.1% increase over the 2011 disbursements, $993,517.

850
The Peyton Anderson Foundation, Inc.
577 Mulberry St., Ste. 830
Macon, GA 31201-8223 (478) 743-5359
Contact: Karen J. Lambert, Pres.
FAX: (478) 742-5201; E-mail: grants@pafdn.org; Main URL: http://www.peytonanderson.org/
Peyton Anderson Scholarship tel. (Scholarship Mgr.): (478) 314-0948, e-mail: scholarships@pafdn.org

Incorporated in 1988 in GA; funded in 1989.
Donor: Peyton Tooke Anderson, Jr.†.
Foundation type: Independent foundation.
Financial data (yr. ended 12/31/12): Assets, $83,950,135 (M); gifts received, $21,000; expenditures, $5,394,956; qualifying distributions, $4,626,601; giving activities include $3,219,000 for 49 grants (high: $717,500; low: $500), and $267,750 for grants to individuals.
Purpose and activities: Giving primarily for community development and human services; funding also for the arts. Scholarships have also been established to help fund the college education of highly promising high school students in Bibb County, GA, who have been residents for the past 2 years and who are graduating high school seniors with a 2.0 GPA, who are graduating from a Bibb County public high school or private high school accredited by the Southern Association of Colleges and Schools (SACS), and demonstrate academic promise, strong character, community involvement, and financial need. All scholarship recipients must register as full-time students in an undergraduate degree program at one of the following Georgia schools: Central Georgia Technical College, Fort Valley State University, Georgia College and State University, Georgia Institute of Technology, Georgia Southern University, Georgia State University, Kennesaw State University, Macon State College, Mercer University, Middle Georgia Technical

College, University of Georgia, or Wesleyan College. Scholarships are paid directly to the school and not the individual.
Fields of interest: Performing arts, theater; Arts; Higher education; Scholarships/financial aid; Education; Human services; Children/youth, services; Community/economic development.
Type of support: Program development; Seed money; Matching/challenge support.
Limitations: Applications accepted. Giving limited to Bibb County and Macon, GA. No support for private foundations, private schools, sports related events, or churches. No grants to individuals directly, or for endowments, festivals, trips or special events.
Publications: Application guidelines; Grants list; Informational brochure (including application guidelines).
Application information: Specific application guidelines and form available on foundation web site. Information and application guidelines and form for Peyton Anderson Scholars maybe be found on http://www.peytonandersonscholars.org. Application forms may also be obtained at high school guidance counselor's office. Peyton Anderson Scholarship may be combined with the HOPE scholarship and other financial aid awards. Application form required.
Initial approach: Use online application form, or letter or telephone requesting guidelines and form
Deadline(s): Apr. 1 and Aug. 1 for grants; see foundation web site for current scholarship deadline
Board meeting date(s): 2 times per year
Final notification: Grants awarded twice a year
Officers and Trustees:* Ed S. Sell III,* Chair.; Tom Johnson,* V.P.; Karen J. Lambert, Pres.; **R. Kirby Godsey, Secy.**; R. Reid Hanson,* Treas.; John D. Comer,* Chair. Emeritus.
Number of staff: 1 full-time professional; 2 full-time support.
EIN: 581803562
Other changes: R. Kirby Godsey is now Secy.

851
The Barbara Cox Anthony Foundation
Atlanta, GA

The foundation merged with the Trailsend Foundation on Dec. 7, 2012.

852
Atlanta Foundation
c/o Wachovia Bank, N.A.
100 Terminus Building, Ste. 400
3280 Peachtree Rd., N.W., Ste. 400, MC GA8023
Atlanta, GA 30305-2422 **(888) 234-1999**
E-mail: grantadministration@wellsfargo.com; Main URL: https://www.wellsfargo.com/privatefoundationgrants/atlanta

Established in 1921 in GA by bank resolution and declaration of trust.
Foundation type: Independent foundation.
Financial data (yr. ended 12/31/12): Assets, $18,532,321 (M); expenditures, $1,232,345; qualifying distributions, $1,041,394; giving activities include $995,500 for 114 grants (high: $30,000; low: $1,000).
Purpose and activities: The foundation provides assistance to charitable and educational institutions to promote education and improve local living conditions. Primary areas of interest include education, cultural programs, housing, and other general charitable activities in Fulton and DeKalb counties, Georgia.
Fields of interest: Arts; Adult education—literacy, basic skills & GED; Education, reading; Education; Hospitals (general); Health care; Housing/shelter, development; Recreation; Human services; Youth, services; Community/economic development; United Ways and Federated Giving Programs.
Type of support: General/operating support; Capital campaigns; Building/renovation; Equipment; Program development.
Limitations: Applications accepted. Giving limited to Fulton and DeKalb counties, GA. No grants to individuals, or for scholarships or fellowships; no loans.
Publications: Application guidelines; Grants list.
Application information: Guidelines available on foundation web site. Application form required.
Initial approach: Use online application via foundation web site
Copies of proposal: 1
Deadline(s): Mar. 1 or Sept. 1
Board meeting date(s): Apr. and Oct.
Final notification: Sept. 1
Committee Members: Elaine B. Alexander; Linda Selig; **Ty Smith**; Dom H. Wyant.
Trustee: Wells Fargo Bank, N.A.
EIN: 586026879

853
Clark and Ruby Baker Foundation
c/o US Trust, Bank of America, N.A.
3414 Peachtree Rd. NE GA7-813-14-04
Atlanta, GA 30326-1113 (404) 264-1377
Contact: Quanda Allen, V.P.
E-mail: quanda.allen@ustrust.com; **Main URL: https://www.bankofamerica.com/philanthropic/grantmaking.go**

Established in 1974 in GA.
Donor: Clark A. Baker‡.
Foundation type: Independent foundation.
Financial data (yr. ended 12/31/12): Assets, $3,252,901 (M); expenditures, $176,175; qualifying distributions, $161,882; giving activities include $156,000 for 21 grants (high: $18,000; low: $2,000).
Purpose and activities: Emphasis on higher education at a college or university operated by or affiliated with the Methodist Church. Support also for Protestant welfare funds and pensions for Methodist ministers.
Fields of interest: Higher education; Protestant agencies & churches.
Type of support: General/operating support; Endowments; Conferences/seminars; Scholarship funds.
Application information: Application form not required.
Initial approach: Check online
Deadline(s): June 1
Trustee: Bank of America, N.A.
Number of staff: None.
EIN: 581429097

854
The Bancker-Williams Foundation Inc.
130 Riverwood Pl.
Atlanta, GA 30327-4280
Contact: Thomas Oastler

Established in 1989 in GA.
Foundation type: Independent foundation.
Financial data (yr. ended 06/30/13): Assets, $2,776,326 (M); expenditures, $226,591; qualifying distributions, $226,591; giving activities include $181,000 for 19 grants (high: $26,000; low: $1,000).
Fields of interest: Environment, natural resources; Environment; Animals/wildlife, preservation/protection; Human services; Women, centers/services; Women.
International interests: Africa; Latin America.
Type of support: Continuing support; Program development; Seed money; Scholarship funds.
Limitations: Applications not accepted. Giving in the U.S., with emphasis on GA. No grants to individuals.
Application information: Contributes only to pre-selected organizations.
Officers and Trustees:* Elaine O. Blackmon,* Chair.; Beverly Kelly, Secy.-Treas.; Belitje B. Bull; Elizabeth O. Jackson; Katharine B. Johnson; **Sunni Johnson**; Dorothy B. Robertson; Charlotte H. Versfeld.
EIN: 581868577

855
Lewis H. Beck Educational Foundation
Atlanta, GA
The foundation terminated in 2013.

856
The Arthur M. Blank Family Foundation
3223 Howell Mill Rd. N.W.
Atlanta, GA 30327-4105 (404) 367-2100
***Contact:* Penelope "Penny" McPhee, Pres.**
FAX: (404) 367-2059; Main URL: http://www.blankfoundation.org
Annual reports: http://www.blankfoundation.org/annual-reports
Arthur Blank's Giving Pledge Profile: http://glasspockets.org/philanthropy-in-focus/eye-on-the-giving-pledge/profiles/blank
Facebook: http://www.facebook.com/ArthurBlankFamilyFoundation
Grants List: http://www.blankfoundation.org/2011-grants
RSS Feed: http://blankfoundation.org/feed.xml
Twitter: http://twitter.com/blankfoundation
YouTube: http://www.youtube.com/user/BlankFoundation

Established in 1995 in GA.
Donor: Arthur M. Blank.
Foundation type: Independent foundation.
Financial data (yr. ended 12/31/12): Assets, $39,718,177 (M); gifts received, $4,762,418; expenditures, $5,766,036; qualifying distributions, $5,873,997; giving activities include $4,761,024 for 221 grants (high: $275,000; low: $25), and $201,814 for 4 foundation-administered programs.
Purpose and activities: The mission going forward is to promote positive change in people's lives and to build and enhance the communities in which they live. The foundation has an especially strong interest in supporting innovative endeavors leading to better circumstances for low-income youth and their families. The foundation seeks to learn from their investments, share what they have learned, and inspire others in the public and private sectors to make similar commitments. The foundation has established two primary initiatives: 1) Fostering Opportunity - to support efforts that help create access to opportunity and improve life chances for low-income young people and their families; and 2)

Enhancing Quality of Life - to preserve green space and parks, and sustain a vibrant arts community.
Fields of interest: Performing arts, theater; Education; Environment; Youth development, services.
Type of support: Research; Employee matching gifts.
Limitations: Applications not accepted. Giving primarily in Maricopa County, AZ, Atlanta, GA, and Beaufort County, SC. No support for government agencies, municipalities, parochial or private schools, houses of worship, or therapeutic programs. No grants to individuals, or for events.
Publications: Annual report.
Application information: Within the scope of its strategic plan, the Blank Family Foundation will identify and invite potential partners to apply for grants around its specific initiatives. The foundation will seek partners from all sectors - public, private and nonprofit. The foundation will no longer accept unsolicited grant requests.
Board meeting date(s): Aug. and Dec.
Officers and Trustees:* Arthur M. Blank,* Chair.; Penelope "Penny" McPhee,* Pres.; **John Bare, V.P.**; Frank Fernandez, V.P., Community Development; Dena Kimball; Kenny Blank; Michael Blank; Nancy Blank; Josh Kimball; Danielle Thomsen.
Number of staff: 8 full-time professional; 1 part-time professional; 3 full-time support.
EIN: 586292769

857
The R. A. Bowen Trust
P.O. Box 4611
Macon, GA **31208-4611 (478) 345-0317**
Contact: R.A. Bowen, Jr., Tr.
FAX: **(866) 823-9410**; E-mail: rabtrust@juno.com; Main URL: http://www.rabowentrust.org

Established in 1943 in GA.
Donor: R. A. Bowen, Jr.
Foundation type: Independent foundation.
Financial data (yr. ended 12/31/12): Assets, $4,210,747 (M); gifts received, $100,000; expenditures, $186,817; qualifying distributions, $184,097; giving activities include $181,377 for 40 grants (high: $51,000; low: $250).
Purpose and activities: The trust awards scholarships to undergraduate students for the purpose of attending an accredited college or university full time.
Fields of interest: Higher education; Education.
Type of support: Scholarship funds.
Limitations: Applications accepted. Giving through scholarships are limited to residents of GA, particularly Bibb County and its surrounding counties of Crawford, Houston, Jones, Monroe, Peach and Twiggs, and to undergraduate students who plan to attend college in Macon, GA, at Wesleyan College or Mercer University.
Publications: Informational brochure (including application guidelines).
Application information: See foundation web site for complete application guidelines. Application form required.
Initial approach: Proposal
Copies of proposal: 1
Deadline(s): Jun. 1
Trustees: R.A. Bowen, Jr.; Robert A. Bowen III; Charles H. Yates.
Number of staff: 1 part-time support.
EIN: 586032145

858
Bradley-Turner Foundation, Inc.
P.O. Box 140
Columbus, GA 31902-0140 (706) 571-6040
Contact: Phyllis Wagner, Exec. Secy.

Incorporated in 1943 in GA as W.C. and Sarah H. Bradley Foundation; in 1982 absorbed the D.A. and Elizabeth Turner Foundation, Inc., also of GA.
Donors: W.C. Bradley†; D.A. Turner†; Elizabeth B. Turner†; Elizabeth T. Corn.
Foundation type: Independent foundation.
Financial data (yr. ended 12/31/12): Assets, $113,100,709 (M); gifts received, $3,885,753; expenditures, $6,029,035; qualifying distributions, $5,648,836; giving activities include $5,648,836 for 118 grants (high: $313,497; low: $1,800).
Purpose and activities: Giving primarily for higher education, religious associations, community funds, and youth and social service agencies; support also for cultural and health-related programs.
Fields of interest: Arts; Higher education; Education; Health care; Health organizations, association; Human services; Youth, services; Religion.
Type of support: General/operating support.
Limitations: Applications accepted. Giving primarily in GA, with emphasis on Columbus. No grants to individuals.
Application information: Application form not required.
Initial approach: Letter
Copies of proposal: 2
Deadline(s): None
Board meeting date(s): Quarterly
Final notification: None
Officers: D. Abbott Turner II,* Chair.; **Katherine C. Wilson,* Vice-Chair.**; William B. Turner, Treas.
EIN: 586032142
Other changes: Katherine C. Wilson has replaced Lovick P. Corn as Vice-Chair.

859
The Thomas C. Burke Foundation
c/o Bank of America, N.A.
3414 Peachtree Rd. NE, Ste. 1475, GA7-813-14-04
Atlanta, GA 30326-1113
E-mail: ga.grantmaking@ustrust.com; **Main URL: https://www.bankofamerica.com/philanthropic/grantmaking.go**

Established in 1965 in GA.
Donor: Thomas C. Burke†.
Foundation type: Independent foundation.
Financial data (yr. ended 09/30/13): Assets, $6,342,378 (M); expenditures, $315,099; qualifying distributions, $283,706; giving activities include $259,748 for 8 grants (high: $80,000; low: $7,800).
Purpose and activities: The foundation has a strong interest in programs focused on cancer prevention and treatment. The foundation specifically serves Bibb County, Georgia and its surrounding communities.
Fields of interest: Health care, patient services; Cancer; Cancer research.
Limitations: Applications accepted. Giving in Bibb County, GA and its surrounding communities.
Application information:
Initial approach: Consult online guidelines on foundation web site
Deadline(s): July 1
Advisory Board Members: Mrs. John D. Comer; Cheryl Jones, M.D.; Donald Rhame, M.D.
Trustee: Bank of America, N.A.
EIN: 586047627

860
J. Bulow Campbell Foundation
3050 Peachtree Rd., N.W., Ste. 270
Atlanta, GA 30305-2212 (404) 658-9066
Contact: Betsy Hamilton Verner, Assoc. Dir.
FAX: (404) 659-4802; Main URL: http://www.jbcf.org

Trust established in 1940 in GA.
Donors: J. Bulow Campbell†; Virginia Campbell Courts†.
Foundation type: Independent foundation.
Financial data (yr. ended 12/31/12): Assets, $504,096,661 (M); expenditures, $32,248,358; qualifying distributions, $26,716,571; giving activities include $25,577,361 for 39 grants (high: $3,000,000; low: $25,000).
Purpose and activities: Broad purposes include, but are not limited to, privately-supported education, human welfare, youth development, the arts, Christian church-related agencies and agencies of the Presbyterian Church (not congregations) operating within the foundation's giving area. Concern for improving quality of spiritual and intellectual life, preferably projects of permanent nature or for capital funds. Gives anonymously and requests no publicity.
Fields of interest: Arts; Secondary school/education; Higher education; Education; Youth development; Human services; Children/youth, services; Family services; Christian agencies & churches; Protestant agencies & churches.
Type of support: Capital campaigns; Building/renovation; Land acquisition; Endowments; Matching/challenge support.
Limitations: Applications accepted. Giving primarily in GA; very limited giving in AL, FL, NC, SC, and TN. No support for local church congregations. No grants to individuals, or for current scholarships, fellowships, operating budgets, or recurring items; no loans.
Publications: Application guidelines; Informational brochure (including application guidelines).
Application information: Submit 1-page proposal, 1 copy of tax information. Application form not required.
Initial approach: One page letter or telephone
Copies of proposal: 1
Deadline(s): 1st of Jan., Apr., July, and Oct.
Board meeting date(s): Jan., Apr., July, and Oct.
Final notification: Within 1 week of board meetings
Officers and Trustees:* Bickerton W. Cardwell, Jr., Chair.; Richard C. Parker, Vice-Chair.; John W. Stephenson, Exec. Dir.; Malon W. Courts; George H. Lane III; James B. Patton; William C. Warren IV, M.D.; S. Zachary Young.
Number of staff: 2 full-time professional; 3 full-time support.
EIN: 580566149
Other changes: At the close of 2012, the grantmaker paid grants of $25,577,361, a 70.0% increase over the 2011 disbursements, $15,045,151.

861
Camp-Younts Foundation
c/o SunTrust Bank
P.O. Box 4655, MC 221
Atlanta, GA 30302-4655 (404) 813-2021
Contact: Emily Butler, Grants Mgr., SunTrust Banks
E-mail: fdnsvsc.ga@suntrust.com; Application address for applicants outside of Metro Atlanta: P.O. Box 813, Franklin, VA 23851; **Main URL: http://fdnweb.org/campyounts**

Established in 1955 in GA.
Donors: Charles Younts†; Willie Camp Younts†.
Foundation type: Independent foundation.
Financial data (yr. ended 12/31/12): Assets, $39,395,029 (M); expenditures, $2,029,189; qualifying distributions, $1,940,077; giving activities include $1,875,355 for 317 grants (high: $177,025; low: $500).
Purpose and activities: Giving primarily for education, with emphasis on higher and secondary educational institutions (including colleges and universities), and social services; support also for youth, Protestant giving, and health associations and hospitals with focus on helping poor and needy people.
Fields of interest: Arts, alliance/advocacy; Secondary school/education; Higher education; Education; Hospitals (general); Health organizations, association; Human services; Youth, services; Protestant agencies & churches; Children/youth; Children; Young adults.
Type of support: Management development/capacity building; General/operating support; Emergency funds; Capital campaigns; Annual campaigns.
Limitations: Applications accepted. Giving primarily in GA (only for operating and program grants) and VA. No grants to individuals.
Application information: In Georgia, only operating and non-capital grants will be considered. Application form not required.
Initial approach: Use application form on foundation web site; organizations outside of Metro Atlanta that wish to be considered should submit requests via U.S. mail to Franklin, VA, address
Copies of proposal: 1
Deadline(s): Aug. 31
Board meeting date(s): Dec.
Final notification: 3 months
Trustees: Harold S. Atkinson; John M. Camp, Jr.; Paul Camp Marks; Gilford Walker; SunTrust Bank.
EIN: 586026001

862
The Raymond M. Cash Foundation, Inc.
Smyrna, GA

The foundation terminated in Sept. 2013.

863
Ty Cobb Educational Fund
P.O. Box 937
Sharpsburg, GA 30277-0937
Contact: Cathy Scott, Schol. Coord.
E-mail: tycobb@mindspring.com; Main URL: http://www.tycobbfoundation.com

Trust established in 1953 in GA.
Donor: Tyrus R. Cobb†.
Foundation type: Independent foundation.
Financial data (yr. ended 12/31/12): Assets, $12,954,021 (M); expenditures, $641,488; qualifying distributions, $604,762; giving activities include $509,000 for grants to individuals.
Purpose and activities: The foundation was established by the late Tyrus R. Cobb for the purpose of assisting capable and deserving residents of GA (who have resided in GA for at least 2 years prior to attending college, or have graduated from high school in GA), who need financial assistance in completing their college education. Foundation scholarships are granted to qualified students who have completed at least 30 semester hours or 45 quarter hours, with a 3.0 GPA or better, for the purpose of attending an accredited college or university full time. Professional students pursuing their dentistry or MD degrees, who are residents of GA, and have demonstrated financial need are eligible to apply.
Fields of interest: Higher education; Medical school/education; Dental care.
Type of support: Scholarships—to individuals.
Limitations: Giving limited to GA residents. No grants for building or endowment funds, operating budgets, special projects, or matching gifts; no loans.
Publications: Application guidelines; Informational brochure.
Application information: Application must include a letter of recommendation from student's academic dean or advisor and transcripts of all college studies; transcripts must be received by June 15th. Application form maybe downloaded from a PDF file on the foundation web site. Funds are paid directly to the applicant's institution. Application form required.
Initial approach: Letter or e-mail for guidelines between Mar. 15 and June 10 (postmark date), or see foundation web site
Copies of proposal: 1
Deadline(s): June 15
Board meeting date(s): Jan. and July
Final notification: Within 5 business days
Officers and Scholarship Board:* Francis J. Tedesco, M.D.,* Chair.; Cathy Cox*; Sherm Day; Dr. Harry S. Downs; Bill Gerspacher; **Dr. Valerie Hepburn**; Hank Huckaby.
Trustee: SunTrust Bank.
Number of staff: 1 part-time support.
EIN: 586026003

864
The Coca-Cola Foundation, Inc.
1 Coca-Cola Plaza, N.W.
Atlanta, GA 30313-2420 (404) 676-2568
Contact: Helen Smith Price, Exec. Dir.
FAX: (404) 676-8804;
E-mail: cocacolacommunityrequest@coca-cola.com; Additional tel.: (404) 676-3525; Main URL: http://www.thecoca-colacompany.com/citizenship/foundation_coke.html
Grants List: http://assets.coca-colacompany.com/c0/91/5c8a678246dd96470f4e306938ed/2011_grants_contributions_paid.pdf

Incorporated in 1984 in GA.
Donor: The Coca-Cola Co.
Foundation type: Company-sponsored foundation.
Financial data (yr. ended 12/31/12): Assets, $191,508,505 (M); expenditures, $70,331,780; qualifying distributions, $69,658,157; giving activities include $64,103,179 for 3,644 grants (high: $5,250,000; low: $10,000), and $5,554,978 for employee matching gifts.
Purpose and activities: The foundation supports programs designed to promote water stewardship; healthy and active lifestyles; community recycling, and education.
Fields of interest: Higher education; Scholarships/financial aid; Education, services; Education, drop-out prevention; Education; Environment, water pollution; Environment, recycling; Environment, water resources; Hospitals (general); Public health, obesity; Public health, physical fitness; Public health, clean water supply; Public health, sanitation; AIDS; Nutrition; Disasters, preparedness/services; Big Brothers/Big Sisters; Girl scouts; Youth development; Economic development; Community/economic development; Women.
International interests: Africa; Europe; Latin America.
Type of support: General/operating support; Continuing support; Emergency funds; Program development; Fellowships; Scholarship funds; Sponsorships; Employee matching gifts.
Limitations: Applications accepted. Giving on a national and international basis in areas of company operations, with emphasis on CA, Washington, DC, Atlanta, GA, New York, NY, TX, VA, Africa, Australia, Chile, China, Colombia, Europe, Italy, Japan, Latin America, Philippines, and Russia. No support for discriminatory organizations, political, legislative, or lobbying organizations, fraternal organizations, athletic teams, or U.S. based local schools, including charter schools, pre-schools, elementary schools, middle schools, or high schools. No grants to individuals (except for the Coca-Cola First Generation Scholarship), or for movie, film, or television documentaries, website development, concerts or other entertainment events, beauty contests, fashion shows, or hair shows, local sports, travel or organized field trips, family reunions, marketing sponsorships, cause marketing, or advertising projects, land, building, or equipment, or construction or renovation projects.
Publications: Application guidelines; Grants list; Program policy statement.
Application information: Faxed or e-mailed applications are not accepted. Application form required.
Initial approach: Complete online application form; contact participating universities for Coca-Cola First Generation Scholarship
Copies of proposal: 1
Deadline(s): None
Board meeting date(s): Quarterly
Final notification: 60 days
Officers and Directors:* Lisa M. Borders, Chair.; Alexander B. Cummings, Secy.; Gary P. Fayard,* Treas.; Lawton Hawkins, Genl. Legal Counsel; William Hawkins,* Genl. Tax Counsel; Helen Smith Price,* Exec. Dir.; Ahmet C. Bozer; Beatriz Perez; Sonya Soutus; Dominique Reiniche; Clyde C. Tuggle.
Number of staff: 6 full-time professional; 5 full-time support.
EIN: 581574705
Other changes: Ingrid Saunders Jones is no longer Chair.

865
The Edward Colston Foundation, Inc.
299 Glencastle Dr.
Atlanta, GA 30327-4823

Established in 1988 in GA.
Donors: Edward C. Mitchell, Jr.; Virginia C. Mitchell.
Foundation type: Independent foundation.
Financial data (yr. ended 12/31/12): Assets, $5,717,850 (M); expenditures, $246,929; qualifying distributions, $236,000; giving activities include $236,000 for 29 grants (high: $30,000; low: $2,500).
Fields of interest: Elementary/secondary education; Higher education; Hospitals (specialty); Health care; Children/youth, services; Homeless, human services; United Ways and Federated Giving Programs; Protestant agencies & churches; Catholic agencies & churches.
Limitations: Applications not accepted. Giving primarily in Atlanta, GA. No grants to individuals.
Application information: Contributes only to pre-selected organizations.

Officers and Directors:* Edward C. Mitchell, Jr.,* Pres.; Jennifer B. Mitchell, Secy.; **Dustin Martin**; **Amanda K. Mitchell**; **Edward C. Mitchell III**; Virginia C. Mitchell.
EIN: 581818739
Other changes: Jennifer B. Mitchell is now Secy.

866
Communities of Coastal Georgia Foundation, Inc.

1626 Frederica Rd., Ste. 201
Saint Simons Island, GA 31522 (912) 268-4442
***Contact:* For grant inquiries: Ellen E. Post, Grants and Opers. Mgr.; Valerie A. Hepburn, C.E.O.**
FAX: (912) 268-2316;
E-mail: vhepburn@coastalgeorgiafoundation.org; Grant inquiry tel.: (912) 268-2561, and e-mail: epost@coastalgeorgiafoundation.org; Main URL: http://www.coastalgeorgiafoundation.org
Facebook: https://www.facebook.com/pages/Communities-of-Coastal-Georgia-Foundation-Inc/503084426417621

Established in 2005 in GA.
Foundation type: Community foundation.
Financial data (yr. ended 12/31/12): Assets, $8,514,944 (M); gifts received, $1,641,040; expenditures, $903,270; giving activities include $559,680 for 20 grants (high: $100,000).
Purpose and activities: The mission of the foundation is to improve the quality of life in Coastal Georgia by promoting and increasing responsible, effective philanthropy now and for future generations.
Fields of interest: Arts; Education, early childhood education; Education; Environment; Animals/wildlife; Health care; Youth development; Human services; Community development, neighborhood development; Community/economic development.
Type of support: Management development/capacity building; Equipment; Program development; Conferences/seminars; Curriculum development; Technical assistance; Consulting services; Program evaluation.
Limitations: Applications accepted. Giving limited to Glynn, McIntosh, and Camden counties, GA. No support for medical or academic research, religious purposes, or international NGOs. No grants to individuals, or for annual fundraising campaigns, debt or deficit reduction, capital building campaigns, general operating support, endowments, grants for re-granting or retroactive funding.
Publications: Application guidelines; Annual report; Financial statement; Grants list; Informational brochure; Newsletter.
Application information: Visit foundation web site for application deadlines and guidelines. Full proposals accepted through invitation only, following letter of intent. Application form required.
Initial approach: Letter of intent
Copies of proposal: 1
***Deadline(s):* Dec. 13 for letter of intent; Mar. 4 for full proposals**
Board meeting date(s): First Wed. of June
Final notification: Approx. 4 weeks for RFP invitation; Early June for grant determination
Officers and Directors:* Rees Sumerford,* Chair.; Arthur M. Lucas,* Vice-Chair. and Secy.; Jeff Barker,* Treas.; Frank DeLoach, Jr., Dir. Emeritus; Jack Dinos, Dir. Emeritus; Bill Jones III, Dir. Emeritus; Edward Andrews, Jr.; **Mark Bedner**; **Claude Booker**; Martha Brumley Ellis; Ellen Fleming; S. Michael Hardy; Diane Laws; Michael Maloy; **Jeanne Manning**; William Bernard McCloud; Diana M. Murphy; **S. Lloyd Newberry**; Mary T. Root; Alfred Sams III; Bonney Stamper Shuman; Bill Stembler.
Number of staff: 2 full-time professional.
EIN: 202454729
Other changes: Lee Hiers Owen is no longer Exec. Dir. Mark Bedner is no longer a director. Jeff Barker and Dennie McCrary are no longer directors.

867
Community Foundation for Northeast Georgia

6500 Sugarloaf Pkwy., Ste. 220
Duluth, GA 30097 (770) 813-3380
Contact: Margaret Bugbee, Dir., Finance
FAX: (770) 813-3375; E-mail: info@cfneg.org; Main URL: http://www.cfneg.org
Facebook: https://www.facebook.com/pages/Community-Foundation-for-Northeast-Georgia/190357550996590
Twitter: https://twitter.com/CFNEG

Incorporated in 1985 in GA.
Foundation type: Community foundation.
Financial data (yr. ended 12/31/12): Assets, $26,680,210 (M); gifts received, $3,409,949; expenditures, $4,218,983; giving activities include $3,701,318 for 51+ grants.
Purpose and activities: The foundation seeks to: 1) provide a cost-effective bridge for all donors to our community's changing needs; 2) serve as a leader, catalyst, and resource for philanthropy; 3) produce an expanding pool of permanent endowment funds for now and all time; 4) Improve the quality of life with grants and technical assistance to local charities; and 5) partner with and be an advocate for the endowment of local charities.
Fields of interest: Performing arts; Arts; Education; Health care; Human services; Community/economic development; Children/youth; Youth; Aging.
Type of support: Capital campaigns; Building/renovation; Equipment; Emergency funds; Program development; Seed money.
Limitations: Applications accepted. Giving limited to organizations or services directly benefiting citizens of northeast GA. No support for religious purposes, or commonly accepted community services. No grants for individuals, or for endowment support, debt reduction, fundraising or annual campaigns, membership contributions, research, travel, or ongoing operating support.
Publications: Annual report (including application guidelines); Grants list; Newsletter.
Application information: Visit foundation web site for application cover sheet and guidelines. Faxed applications are not accepted. Application form required.
Initial approach: Submit grant proposal cover sheet and attachments
Copies of proposal: 15
Deadline(s): Mar. 1
Board meeting date(s): 5 times annually
Final notification: June
Officers and Directors:* Robert D. Fowler,* Chair.; William R. Short,* Pres.; Greg Shumate,* V.P.; Richard B. Chandler, Jr.,* Secy.; William E. McLendon,* Treas.; Judy Waters, Exec. Dir.; **Tom Abernathy**; Ethel D. Anderson; Julie Keeton Arnold; Doug Bridges; Stephen K. Hill; Barbara Howard; Dan Kaufman; James Pack; Scott Phelan; Maxie Price, Jr.; Karen Fine Saltiel; Ruth Strickland; Sandra Strickland; Perry Tindol; **T. Michael Tennant**; Kathryn Willis; **A. Ray Weeks, Jr.**
Number of staff: 2 full-time professional; 2 part-time support.
EIN: 581557995
Other changes: Paige Havens is now Mktg. Consultant. Karyl Kaye Miller is now Exec. Asst. to Judy Waters. Fran Forehand is no longer a director. Joe McCart and T. Michael Tennant are no longer directors.

868
Community Foundation of Northwest Georgia, Inc.

714 S. Thorton Ave., Ste. 5
P.O. Box 942
Dalton, GA 30722-0942 (706) 275-9117
Contact: David Aft, Pres.
FAX: (706) 275-9118;
E-mail: thefoundation@communityfoundationnwga.org; Additional e-mail: david.aft@communityfoundationnwga.org; Main URL: http://www.communityfoundationnwga.org
Facebook: https://www.facebook.com/CommunityFoundationNWGA

Established in 1998 in GA.
Foundation type: Community foundation.
Financial data (yr. ended 12/31/12): Assets, $23,452,320 (M); gifts received, $3,180,293; expenditures, $3,597,369; giving activities include $2,875,777 for 61+ grants (high: $100,000; low: $200).
Purpose and activities: The foundation seeks to enhance the quality of life in the northwest GA region for both present and future generations by: 1) promoting philanthropy; 2) building and maintaining permanent endowment funds to be used for the broad charitable needs of the region; 3) serving as a leader in identifying and prioritizing needs in the community; 4) serving as a catalyst in developing effective responses to community issues; 5) encouraging collaboration between organizations and agencies to shape solutions; and 6) serving as a steward of the funds in the endowment.
Fields of interest: Historic preservation/historical societies; Arts; Education; Environment; Animal welfare; Health care; Youth development; Children/youth, services; Human services; Community/economic development; Religion.
Type of support: Program development; Seed money; Matching/challenge support.
Limitations: Applications accepted. Giving limited to Bartow, Catoosa, Chattooga, Dade, Fannin, Floyd, Gilmer, Gordon, Murray, Pickens, Walker, and Whitfield, GA.
Publications: Application guidelines; Annual report; Informational brochure.
Application information: Visit foundation web site for online application and guidelines. Application form required.
Initial approach: Submit online application or call foundation
Deadline(s): Mar. 31 and Oct. 1
Board meeting date(s): Jan., Mar., May, July, Sept., and Nov.
Final notification: 30 to 60 days
Officers and Directors:* Harris R. Thompson,* Chair.; David Aft, Pres.; Vance D. Bell; Jim Bethel; Linda Blackman; Ed Brush; George Crowley*; Bill Davies; Bryan McAllister*.
Number of staff: 1 full-time professional; 1 full-time support; 1 part-time support.
EIN: 582360356
Other changes: Randy Thompson is no longer a director.

869
Community Foundation of South Georgia, Inc.
(formerly Community Foundation of Southwest Georgia, Inc.)
135 N. Broad St., Ste. 202
Thomasville, GA 31792-8103 (229) 228-5088
Contact: David M. Carlton, Pres.; Randae Davis, Dir., Donor Svcs.
FAX: (229) 228-0848; E-mail: cfsga@rose.net; Additional tel.: (888) 544-2317; Main URL: http://www.cfsga.net/

Established in 1995 in GA.
Foundation type: Community foundation.
Financial data (yr. ended 12/31/11): Assets, $52,719,564 (M); gifts received, $4,746,024; expenditures, $5,079,236; giving activities include $4,003,727 for grants, and $89,487 for 112 grants to individuals.
Purpose and activities: The foundation seeks to: 1) be a catalyst for the establishment of charitable funds which benefit the community for generations to come; 2) serve the varied interests and needs of donors; 3) promote local philanthropy; 4) serve as a steward of funds; and 5) provide leadership and resources in identifying and meeting local needs.
Fields of interest: Arts; Education; Health care; Human services.
Type of support: Scholarships—to individuals.
Limitations: Applications not accepted. Giving primarily in southwest GA.
Publications: Annual report; Grants list; Informational brochure.
Application information: Unsolicited requests for funds are currently not accepted.
Board meeting date(s): Mar., June, Sept., and Dec.
Officers and Trustees:* Alston Watt,* Chair.; Vann K. Parrott,* Vice-Chair.; **David Carlton,* Pres.**; George Lilly II,* Secy.; W. Ralph Rodgers, Jr.,* Treas.; Lisa Hitt, Cont.; Jimmy Allen; Bill Burke; John M. Carlton, Jr.; David Cone; Russ Henry; Ann Hopkins; James M. Jeter; Bruce W. Kirbo, Jr.; John McTier; John Prince III; E.J. Vann IV; Randy Wages; Jo Stott Wingate.
Number of staff: 3 full-time professional; 1 part-time professional.
EIN: 582210876
Other changes: David Carlton is now Pres. Meghan Warrick is no longer Exec. V.P. and C.F.O. Vann K. Parrott is no longer a trustee.

870
Frederick E. Cooper and Helen Dykes Cooper Charitable Foundation, Inc.
170 W. Paces Ferry Rd. N.E.
Atlanta, GA 30305-1352 (404) 467-0905

Established in 1998 in FL.
Donors: Frederick E. Cooper; Helen D. Cooper.
Foundation type: Independent foundation.
Financial data (yr. ended 09/30/13): Assets, $6,950,557 (M); expenditures, $302,076; qualifying distributions, $290,285; giving activities include $288,975 for 17 grants (high: $119,900; low: $500).
Fields of interest: Museums (art); Historic preservation/historical societies; Higher education; Health care; Cancer; Human services; Christian agencies & churches.
Type of support: General/operating support.
Limitations: Applications accepted. Giving primarily in GA, NC and VA.
Application information: Application form required.
Initial approach: Proposal
Deadline(s): None
Directors: Beckwith Archer Cooper; Frederick E. Cooper; Frederick E. Cooper, Jr.; Johnson Joseph Cooper; Bernard Lanigan, Jr.
EIN: 582433546

871
The Correll Family Foundation, Inc.
191 Peachtree St., Ste. 4050
Atlanta, GA 30303-1786 **(404) 478-6779**

Established in 2006 in GA.
Donor: Alston D. Correll.
Foundation type: Independent foundation.
Financial data (yr. ended 06/30/13): Assets, $39,146,425 (M); expenditures, $6,212,051; qualifying distributions, $5,892,500; giving activities include $5,892,500 for 29 grants (high: $2,000,000; low: $2,500).
Purpose and activities: Giving primarily for higher education, and children, youth and social services.
Fields of interest: Higher education; Environment, natural resources; Health care; Boys & girls clubs; Human services; Children/youth, services; United Ways and Federated Giving Programs.
Limitations: Applications not accepted. Giving primarily in Atlanta, GA; some funding also in ME. No grants to individuals.
Application information: Contributes only to pre-selected organizations.
Officers and Directors:* Ada F. Correll,* Secy.; Alston D. Correll,* Treas.; Alston D. Correll III; Elizabeth Richards.
EIN: 134311179
Other changes: For the fiscal year ended June 30, 2013, the fair market value of the grantmaker's assets was $39,146,425, a 525.1% increase over the fiscal 2012 value, $6,262,024. For the same period, the grantmaker paid grants of $5,892,500, a 165.5% increase over the fiscal 2012 disbursements, $2,219,500.

872
R. Howard Dobbs, Jr. Foundation, Inc.
(formerly Helen and Howard Dobbs Foundation, Inc.)
133 Peachtree St. N.E., Ste. 4950
Atlanta, GA 30303-1861 (404) 574-2970
FAX: (404) 574-2971; E-mail: dgray@rhdobbs.net; Main URL: http://www.dobbsfoundation.org

Established in 1959.
Donor: R. Howard Dobbs, Jr.†.
Foundation type: Independent foundation.
Financial data (yr. ended 12/31/12): Assets, $66,076,520 (M); expenditures, $2,726,435; qualifying distributions, $2,419,558; giving activities include $1,871,285 for 51 grants (high: $250,000; low: $100).
Purpose and activities: The mission of the foundation is to improve the quality of life for individuals, families and communities by supporting educational opportunities, improving access to health services, promoting environmental stewardship, and enriching the arts. The foundation is committed to honoring the life and impact of R. Howard Dobbs, Jr. through its grant-making activities. In the field of education, the foundation seeks to improve teacher quality and classroom outcomes by investing in the development of new and veteran educators with an emphasis on innovative teaching practices and the delivery of a 21st century education. The foundation will place priority on projects with potential for scaling and replication. In its environmental giving, the foundation focuses on land conservation and watershed protection with particular interest in the coastal Georgia and longleaf pine ecosystems. Health priorities include age related macular degeneration (ARMD) research, access to basic health services including low vision services. The foundation does not support medical research outside of ARMD. Arts funding is limited to mid-size organizations with an operating budget less than $2,000,000. Maximum award amount is $40,000. The foundation will support requests for discrete capital purchases that improve content delivery or increase organizational capacity; or requests that support cultural opportunities for school groups.
Fields of interest: Arts; Education; Environment; Health care.
Limitations: Giving primarily in the metropolitan Atlanta, GA area. Consideration will also be given to proposals that serve other parts of the state of GA as well as states in which the Life Insurance Company of Georgia operated. Giving outside of GA is by invitation only and must be strongly aligned with stated interests. No support for churches or religious organizations. No grants or loans to individuals, or for endowments, special events, performances, dinners, booster clubs, or for reduction of debts/deficits.
Publications: Application guidelines; Grants list.
Application information: Unsolicited full proposals will not be reviewed. See foundation web site for application guidelines and application form. Although the foundation prefers the use of its application form, it is not required. However when not using the foundation's form, please ensure all questions on the form are addressed in your proposal. Application form not required.
Initial approach: Letter of inquiry
Copies of proposal: 1
Deadline(s): Dec. 1, Mar. 1, June 1 and Sept. 1
Board meeting date(s): Jan., Apr., July, and Oct.
Final notification: The board will vote on the grant generally two months after the receipt of an invited proposal and following a site visit.
Officers and Trustees:* E. Cody Laird, Jr.,* Chair.; David Weitnauer, Pres.; Nancy L. Crosswell,* Secy.; C. Mark Crosswell,* Treas.; William Clarkson IV; Ciannat M. Howett; Nancy Clair Laird McInaney; Dorothy L. Williams; Laird M. Williams.
Number of staff: 2 full-time professional.
EIN: 586033186

873
The Exposition Foundation
P.O. Box 421099
Atlanta, GA 30342-8099

Incorporated in 1950 in GA.
Donor: Frances F. Cocke.
Foundation type: Independent foundation.
Financial data (yr. ended 08/31/13): Assets, $2,095,854 (M); expenditures, $200,841; qualifying distributions, $182,500; giving activities include $182,500 for 9 grants (high: $80,500; low: $1,000).
Purpose and activities: Giving primarily for historical preservation, higher education, particularly a university for agricultural sciences, and natural resources.
Fields of interest: Historic preservation/historical societies; Higher education; Environment, formal/general education; Botanical gardens; Human services; United Ways and Federated Giving Programs.

Type of support: General/operating support; Annual campaigns; Capital campaigns; Building/renovation; Equipment; Endowments; Program development; Scholarship funds.
Limitations: Applications not accepted. Giving primarily in Atlanta, GA.
Publications: Annual report.
Application information: Contributes only to pre-selected organizations.
Board meeting date(s): Varies
Officers: Jane Cocke Black, Pres.; James Floyd Black, V.P.; Dameron Black III, V.P.; Dameron Black IV, V.P.
EIN: 586043273
Other changes: Jane Cocke Black is now Pres. James Floyd Black, Dameron Black, III, and Dameron Black, IV are now V.P.s.

874
The EZ Agape Foundation
12850 Highway 9, Ste. 600, PMB 328
Alpharetta, GA **30004-4248** (404) 633-9360
Contact: Nancy Walker, Fdn. Mgr.
E-mail: grantrequest@ezagapefoundation.org

Established in 1994 in GA.
Donors: Mary Louise Brown Jwell; Nancy Louise Brown Markham; Elizabeth Irene Brown Dixon.
Foundation type: Independent foundation.
Financial data (yr. ended 12/31/12): Assets, $8,813,504 (M); expenditures, $892,490; qualifying distributions, $776,702; giving activities include $776,702 for 76 grants (high: $25,000; low: $1,500).
Purpose and activities: Giving primarily for those who are poor, disabled and needy; funding also for smaller charities, and helping handicapped children and adults.
Fields of interest: Housing/shelter, development; Human services; Children, services; Children; Women; Homeless.
Type of support: General/operating support; Building/renovation; Program development; Scholarship funds.
Limitations: Applications accepted. Giving primarily in Atlanta, GA. No grants to individuals.
Application information: Application form not required.
Initial approach: E-mail
Copies of proposal: 1
Deadline(s): None
Board meeting date(s): Generally in the 1st quarter, summer, and fall; however no set schedule.
Officer: Nancy Walker, Mgr.
Trustees: Elizabeth Irene Brown Dixon; Nancy Louise Brown Markham.
EIN: 586289241

875
Allan C. and Leila J. Garden Foundation
c/o U.S. Trust, Bank of America, N.A.
3414 Peachtree Rd. NE, Ste. 1475, GA7-813-14-04
Atlanta, GA 30326-1113 (404) 264-1377
Contact: Quanda Allen, V.P.
E-mail: quanda.allen@ustrust.com; **Main URL: https://www.bankofamerica.com/philanthropic/grantmaking.go**

Established in 1972 in GA.
Foundation type: Independent foundation.
Financial data (yr. ended 05/31/13): Assets, $5,046,569 (M); expenditures, $205,589; qualifying distributions, $174,006; giving activities include $69,500 for 5 grants (high: $50,000; low: $3,000), and $83,875 for 43 grants to individuals (high: $2,250; low: $1,000).
Purpose and activities: The mission of the foundation is to support charitable organizations that maintain, care, and educate orphan or underprivileged children. It is also the foundation's intent to support organizations that provide medical, dental, hospital care, nursing, and treatment of physically handicapped children.
Limitations: Applications accepted. Giving primarily in Ben Hill, Irwin, and Wilcox counties in Georgia.
Application information:
Initial approach: Online via foundation web site
Deadline(s): June 1
Trustee: Bank of America, N.A.
EIN: 586103546

876
Georgia Health Foundation, Inc.
3050 Peachtree Rd., Ste. 270
Atlanta, GA 30305-2283 (404) 658-9066
Contact: John Borek, Treas.
***E-mail:* info@gahealthfdn.org**; Main URL: http://www.gahealthfdn.org
Grants List: http://gahealthfdn.org/grants-awarded-in-2013

Established in 1985 in GA; converted from Georgia Medical Plan, Inc.
Donor: Georgia Medical Plan, Inc.
Foundation type: Independent foundation.
Financial data (yr. ended 12/31/13): Assets, $10,087,648 (M); expenditures, $466,160; qualifying distributions, $402,360; giving activities include $326,250 for 47 grants (high: $25,000).
Purpose and activities: Giving for public health education, as well as for health-related projects and programs in GA. Consideration is given to proposals that are of local importance, and to opportunities that may address regional and national issues.
Fields of interest: Medical school/education; Public health school/education; Public health; Health care; Health organizations, association; Medical research, institute.
Type of support: General/operating support; Equipment; Program development; Conferences/seminars; Publication; Seed money; Research; Matching/challenge support.
Limitations: Applications accepted. Giving limited to GA.
Publications: Application guidelines; Grants list; Informational brochure (including application guidelines).
Application information: Between Jan. 1 and May 1, submit a thorough request outlining the project or proposal. Complete application guidelines and procedures are available on foundation web site. Application form not required.
***Initial approach:* Outline of the project or proposal (3 page limit)**
Copies of proposal: 1
***Deadline(s):* Aug. 1 final deadline**
Board meeting date(s): Feb., May, Aug., and Nov.
Officers and Directors:* Martha Katz,* Chair.; Nancy M. Paris,* Vice-Chair.; S. Jarvin Levison, J.D.*, Secy.; John M. Borek, Jr., Ph.D.*, Treas.; Jaquelin Gottieb, M.D.; Robert L. Zwald.
Number of staff: 3 part-time support.
EIN: 581352076
Other changes: John M. Borek, Jr. is now Treas. Martha Katz is now Chair. S. Jarvin Levison is now Secy. Nancy M. Paris is now Vice-Chair.

877
Georgia Power Foundation, Inc.
241 Ralph McGill Blvd., N.E., Bin 10131
Atlanta, GA 30308-3374 (404) 506-6784
Contact: Susan M. Carter, Secy. and Exec. Dir.
FAX: (404) 506-1485;
E-mail: gpfoundation@southernco.com; Main URL: http://www.georgiapower.com/in-your-community/charitable-giving/overview-and-focus.cshtml

Established in 1986 in GA.
Donors: Georgia Power Co.; Savannah Electric Foundation, Inc.
Foundation type: Company-sponsored foundation.
Financial data (yr. ended 12/31/12): Assets, $128,972,580 (M); gifts received, $10,000,000; expenditures, $8,621,772; qualifying distributions, $8,016,375; giving activities include $8,016,375 for 547 grants (high: $1,330,000; low: $250).
Purpose and activities: The foundation supports organizations involved with arts and culture, education, the environment, cancer, diversity, and workforce planning.
Fields of interest: Arts; Higher education; Education; Environment, air pollution; Environment, water pollution; Environment, natural resources; Environment; Health care; Cancer; Salvation Army; Human services; Community development, neighborhood development.
Type of support: General/operating support; Continuing support; Annual campaigns; Capital campaigns; Equipment; Emergency funds; Program development; Conferences/seminars; Scholarship funds; Sponsorships; Employee matching gifts.
Limitations: Applications accepted. Giving primarily in GA. No support for private foundations, political or religious organizations, private elementary or secondary schools, or non-public charities. No grants to individuals, or for political campaigns or causes.
Publications: Application guidelines; Informational brochure (including application guidelines).
Application information: Support is limited to 1 contribution per organization during any given year. Multi-year funding is not automatic. Video submissions are not encouraged. Application form not required.
***Initial approach:* Complete online application form or mail proposal to foundation**
Copies of proposal: 1
Deadline(s): Feb. 15, May 15, Aug. 15, and Nov. 15 for requests over $25,000
Board meeting date(s): Mar., June, Sept., and Dec.
Final notification: 1 month following board meetings for requests over $25,000
Officers and Directors:* Michael K. Anderson,* Pres. and C.E.O.; Susan M. Carter, Secy. and Exec. Dir.; Roger S. Steffens, Treas.; W. Ron Hinson, C.F.O.; W. Craig Barrs; Brad J. Gates; Valerie D. Searcy; Anthony L. Wilson.
EIN: 581709417
Other changes: Ronnie R. Labrato is no longer C.F.O.

878
Georgia-Pacific Foundation, Inc.
133 Peachtree St. N.E., 39th FL
Atlanta, GA 30303-1808 **(404) 652-4000**
***Contact:* Curley M. Dossman, Jr., Pres.**
FAX: (404) 749-2754;
E-mail: GPFoundation@gapac.com; Additional contact: Charmaine Ward, Dir., Community Affairs, tel.: (404) 652-5302; e-mail for Bucket Brigade:

gpbucketbrigade@gapac.com; Main URL: http://www.gp.com/gpfoundation/index.html

Incorporated in 1958 in OR.
Donor: Georgia-Pacific Corp.
Foundation type: Company-sponsored foundation.
Financial data (yr. ended 12/31/12): Assets, $249,025 (M); gifts received, $3,303,617; expenditures, $4,161,881; qualifying distributions, $4,161,881; giving activities include $4,134,739 for 405 grants (high: $398,145; low: $100).
Purpose and activities: The foundation supports programs designed to promote education; environment; community enrichment; and entrepreneurship.
Fields of interest: Arts; Elementary/secondary education; Higher education; Education, reading; Education; Environment, air pollution; Environment, recycling; Environment, natural resources; Environment, land resources; Environmental education; Environment; Employment, training; Employment; Housing/shelter, development; Housing/shelter; Disasters, preparedness/services; Disasters, fire prevention/control; Safety/disasters; Youth development, business; Youth development; Family services, domestic violence; Social entrepreneurship; Community development, small businesses; Community/economic development; United Ways and Federated Giving Programs; Youth; Minorities; Women.
Type of support: General/operating support; Continuing support; Management development/capacity building; Annual campaigns; Capital campaigns; Building/renovation; Equipment; Program development; Conferences/seminars; Scholarship funds; Employee volunteer services; Sponsorships; Employee-related scholarships; In-kind gifts.
Limitations: Applications accepted. Giving limited to areas of company operations in AL, AR, AZ, CA, Washington, DC, DE, FL, GA, IA, IL, IN, KS, KY, LA, MA, MI, MN, MO, MS, NH, NJ, NM, NV, NY, NC, OH, OK, OR, PA, SC, TN, VA, WA, WI, WV, WY, and Africa, Asia, Europe, and South America. No support for discriminatory organizations, political candidates, churches or religious denominations, religious or theological schools, social, labor, veterans', alumni, or fraternal organizations not of direct benefit to the entire community, athletic associations, national organizations with local chapters already receiving support, medical or nursing schools, or pass-through organizations. No grants to individuals (except for employee-related scholarships), or for emergency needs for general operating support, political causes, legislative lobbying, or advocacy efforts, goodwill advertising, sporting events, general operating support for United Way member agencies, tickets or tables for testimonials or similar benefit events, named academic chairs, social sciences or health science programs, fundraising events, or trips or tours.
Publications: Application guidelines; Program policy statement.
Application information: Extraneous proposal materials are not encouraged. Photos, videos, CD's, and DVD's are not encouraged. Firefighting units must process applications through their local GP facility contact. Application form not required.
Initial approach: **Complete online eligibility quiz and mail application or proposal to foundation; download application form for Bucket Brigade**
Copies of proposal: 1
Deadline(s): **Between Jan. 1 and Oct. 31; Apr. 1 to July 11 for Bucket Brigade**
Board meeting date(s): As required
Final notification: **Within 60 days; Sept. for Bucket Brigade**

Officers and Directors:* Curley M. Dossman, Jr.,* Pres.; Gerald Shirk, V.P. and Treas.; Mark Berry,* Secy.; Philip Ellender; Shiela Weidman.
Number of staff: 5 full-time professional; 1 full-time support.
EIN: 936023726
Other changes: Tye Darland is no longer V.P. and Secy. Tyler Woolson is no longer C.F.O. Marty Agard is no longer Treas.

879
J. Knox Gholston Foundation

c/o US Trust, Bank of America, N.A.
3414 Peachtree Rd., NE GA7-813-14-04
Atlanta, GA 30326-1113 (404) 264-1377
Contact: **Mark Drake**
E-mail: **ga.grantmaking@ustrust.com**; Main URL: http://www.bankofamerica.com/grantmaking

Established in 1967 in GA.
Donor: J. Knox Gholston†.
Foundation type: Independent foundation.
Financial data (yr. ended 02/28/13): Assets, $6,820,927 (M); expenditures, $339,065; qualifying distributions, $312,400; giving activities include $298,135 for 60 grants (high: $281,035; low: $100).
Purpose and activities: The mission of the foundation is to support charitable organizations that provide for the education of children within the City of Comer in Madison County, GA.
Fields of interest: Education; Human services.
Limitations: Giving in GA, with emphasis on City of Comer. No grants to individuals directly.
Application information:
Initial approach: **See foundation information on web site**
Deadline(s): **June 1**
Trustee: Bank of America, N.A.
EIN: 586056879

880
J. William Gholston Foundation

(formerly J. William Gholston Trust)
c/o U.S. Trust, Bank of America, N.A.
3414 Peachtree Rd. N.E., Ste. 1475, GA7-813-14-04
Atlanta, GA 30326-1113 (404) 264-1377
Contact: Quanda Allen, V.P.
E-mail: quanda.allen@ustrust.com; **Main URL: https://www.bankofamerica.com/philanthropic/grantmaking.go**

Foundation type: Independent foundation.
Financial data (yr. ended 12/31/12): Assets, $4,248,229 (M); expenditures, $214,791; qualifying distributions, $200,191; giving activities include $191,683 for 4 grants (high: $190,483; low: $200).
Purpose and activities: Support for charitable organizations that provide for the education of children within the city of Comer in Madison County, Georgia.
Fields of interest: Elementary/secondary education; Protestant agencies & churches.
Limitations: Giving primarily in the city of Comer in Madison County, GA. No grants to individuals.
Application information:
Initial approach: Consult guidelines online on foundation web site
Deadline(s): Feb. 1
Trustee: Bank of America, N.A.
EIN: 586027903

881
Price Gilbert, Jr. Charitable Fund

c/o Wells Fargo Philanthropic Svcs.
3280 Peachtree Rd. N.E., Ste. 400
Atlanta, GA 30305-2449 (888) 234-1999
Contact: Joyce Yamaato
FAX: (877) 746-5889;
E-mail: grantadministration@wellsfargo.com; Information telephone number for technical assistance regarding the online grant application: 1-888-235-4351; Main URL: https://www.wellsfargo.com/privatefoundationgrants/gilbert

Established in 1973 in GA.
Foundation type: Independent foundation.
Financial data (yr. ended 05/31/13): Assets, $8,733,866 (M); expenditures, $471,194; qualifying distributions, $378,834; giving activities include $351,500 for 41 grants (high: $100,000; low: $2,500).
Purpose and activities: Giving primarily for arts and culture, education, human services, and federated giving programs.
Fields of interest: Arts; Education; Environment; Human services; United Ways and Federated Giving Programs.
Limitations: Giving limited to the Atlanta, GA, area. No grants to individuals.
Publications: Application guidelines; Grants list.
Application information: Application guidelines and form available on fund web site. Application form required.
Initial approach: 1-page letter
Deadline(s): Aug. 1
Board meeting date(s): Sept.
Trustee: Wells Fargo Bank, N.A.
Number of staff: 4
EIN: 582064640

882
Jack and Anne Glenn Charitable Foundation

c/o SunTrust Bank
P.O. Box 4655, MC221
Atlanta, GA 30302-4655 (404) 813-2021
Contact: Emily Butler, Grants Mgr., SunTrust Bank
E-mail: fdnsvcs.ga@suntrust.com; **Main URL: http://fdnweb.org/glenn**

Established in 2004 in FL.
Donors: Anne Glenn; Jack Glenn; John Fitten Glen†.
Foundation type: Independent foundation.
Financial data (yr. ended 12/31/12): Assets, $9,952,168 (M); expenditures, $521,261; qualifying distributions, $498,454; giving activities include $477,000 for 26 grants (high: $75,000; low: $2,000).
Fields of interest: Elementary/secondary education; Environment; Health care; Human services; Community/economic development.
Type of support: Scholarship funds; Endowments; Program development.
Limitations: Applications accepted. Giving primarily in Atlanta, GA. No grants to individuals.
Application information:
Initial approach: Proposal
Copies of proposal: 1
Deadline(s): Feb. 15 and July 15
Board meeting date(s): Spring and Fall
Directors: Alston Glenn; Jack Glenn; Lewis Glenn; Robert Glenn.
Trustee: SunTrust Bank.
EIN: 200545315

883
The Goizueta Foundation
4401 Northside Pkwy., Ste. 400
Atlanta, GA 30327-3057 (404) 239-0390
Contact: Amanda Smith, Prog. Dir.
FAX: (404) 239-0018;
E-mail: info@goizuetafoundation.org; Main URL: http://www.goizuetafoundation.org

Established in 1992 in GA.
Donor: Roberto C. Goizueta†.
Foundation type: Independent foundation.
Financial data (yr. ended 12/31/12): Assets, $565,374,356 (M); gifts received, $2,000,000; expenditures, $36,694,175; qualifying distributions, $35,741,288; giving activities include $34,741,977 for 26 grants (high: $9,750,000; low: $5,000), and $17,000 for 2 employee matching gifts.
Purpose and activities: The primary focus of the foundation is to assist organizations that empower individuals and families through educational opportunities to improve the quality of their lives.
Fields of interest: Education, early childhood education; Elementary school/education; Secondary school/education; Higher education; Education; Legal services; Employment, services; Youth development; Youth, services; Family services, parent education; Residential/custodial care; Developmentally disabled, centers & services; Minorities/immigrants, centers/services; Disabilities, people with; Immigrants/refugees.
Type of support: Program development; Scholarship funds; Employee matching gifts.
Limitations: Applications accepted. Giving primarily in GA. No support for political organizations, government agencies, or public schools. No grants to individuals, or for general operating expenses, capital investment, construction/renovation, equipment purchase, retirement of debt, annual appeals, special events, conferences, or awards, prizes, or competitions; no loans.
Publications: Informational brochure (including application guidelines).
Application information: Review the Types of Funding and Eligibility sections of the web site to ensure that your organization matches the foundation's geographic parameters and strategic priorities. Application form not required.
Initial approach: **Online application process**
Copies of proposal: 1
Deadline(s): None
Board meeting date(s): May and Nov.
Final notification: **Following each board meeting**
Officers and Distribution Committee:* Olga Goizueta Rawls,* Chair. and C.E.O.; Olga C. de Goizueta,* Chair. Emeritus; Javier C. Goizueta; Roberto S. Goizueta.
Number of staff: 6 full-time professional.
EIN: 586269421
Other changes: Olga C. de Goizueta is now Chair. Emeritus. Olga Goizueta Rawls is now Chair. and C.E.O. Eduardo M. Carreras and Katherine R. Stearns are no longer directors. Maria Elena Retter is no longer Exec. Dir.

884
Guanacaste Ventures U.S., Inc.
P.O. Box 1047
Decatur, GA 30031-1047

Established in 2005 in GA.
Donors: H.G. Pattillo; John J. McMahon, Jr.
Foundation type: Independent foundation.
Financial data (yr. ended 12/31/12): Assets, $1,257,722 (M); gifts received, $50,700; expenditures, $508,360; qualifying distributions, $508,300; giving activities include $507,000 for 5 grants (high: $250,000; low: $18,000).
Fields of interest: Higher education; United Ways and Federated Giving Programs.
Limitations: Applications not accepted. Giving primarily in GA; funding also in Santa Cruz, Costa Rica.
Application information: Contributes only to pre-selected organizations.
Officers and Trustees:* H.G. Pattillo,* Pres.; **Carolyn Wagnon, Secy.-Treas.**; Jack Guynn; **Bree Patillo**; Christine W. Pierce.
EIN: 203885468

885
John H. and Wilhelmina D. Harland Charitable Foundation, Inc.
2 Piedmont Ctr., Ste. 710
Atlanta, GA 30305-1567 (404) 264-9912
Contact: Jane G. Hardesty, Exec. Dir.
***Main URL:* http://harlandfoundation.org**

Incorporated in 1972 in GA.
Donors: John H. Harland†; Miriam H. Conant†; John A. Conant†.
Foundation type: Independent foundation.
Financial data (yr. ended 12/31/12): Assets, $26,654,275 (M); expenditures, $1,992,259; qualifying distributions, $1,725,673; giving activities include $1,432,500 for 39 grants (high: $500,000; low: $10,000).
Purpose and activities: Support for youth services, arts and culture, and community services. The focus is local rather than regional or national, and priority is given to institutions in metropolitan Atlanta, Georgia.
Fields of interest: Arts; Education, early childhood education; Adult education—literacy, basic skills & GED; Children/youth, services; Child development, services; Children/youth; Disabilities, people with.
Type of support: General/operating support; Capital campaigns; Building/renovation; Equipment; Program development; Matching/challenge support.
Limitations: Applications accepted. Giving limited to GA, with emphasis on DeKalb and Fulton counties in metropolitan Atlanta. No support for private, primary, or secondary schools, except for those serving the handicapped. No grants to individuals, or for annual campaigns or special events; no loans.
Publications: Annual report (including application guidelines).
Application information: 21-month waiting period for new grant proposals from previously considered applicants. Application form required.
Initial approach: Telephone call preferred
Copies of proposal: 1
Deadline(s): Mar. 15 and Oct. 1
Board meeting date(s): June 1 and Dec. 1
Final notification: 3 to 4 weeks after board meeting
Officers: Margaret C. Reiser, Pres.; Winifred S. Davis, V.P. and Treas.; Robert E. Reiser, Jr., Secy.; Jane G. Hardesty, Exec. Dir.
Trustees: Kathleen B. Patillo; Joseph E. Patrick, Jr.; Sam Pettway.
Number of staff: 1 full-time professional; 1 full-time support; 2 part-time support.
EIN: 237225012

886
Healthcare Georgia Foundation, Inc.
191 Peachtree St. N.E., Ste. 2650
Atlanta, GA **30303** (404) 653-0990
Contact: Javier Sanchez, Grants Mgr.
FAX: (404) 577-8386;
E-mail: info@healthcaregeorgia.org; Main URL: http://www.healthcaregeorgia.org/
E-Newsletter: http://www.healthcaregeorgia.org/publications-and-research/issues-category.cfm/type/Catalyst#signup
Grant Applicants Survey: http://www.healthcaregeorgia.org/grantmaking/grant-applicants-survey.cfm
Grants Database: http://www.healthcaregeorgia.org/grantees/grants-search.cfm
Podcasts: http://www.healthcaregeorgia.org/news-and-information/news-details.cfm/news_id/D2CDF3B7-3048-7C59-19EA37D285C896B0

Established in 1999 in GA; converted from the merger of Blue Cross Blue Shield of Georgia with Wellpoint Health Networks.
Donor: Blue Cross and Blue Shield of Georgia, Inc.
Foundation type: Independent foundation.
Financial data (yr. ended 12/31/12): Assets, $111,633,150 (M); expenditures, $7,029,474; qualifying distributions, $5,476,391; giving activities include $3,893,525 for 75 grants (high: $128,000; low: $2,050), and $65,000 for 21 employee matching gifts.
Purpose and activities: The foundation's mission is to advance the health of all Georgians and to expand access to affordable, quality health care for underserved individuals and communities. Specific goals include protecting and promoting the health of individuals, families and communities; improving the availability, quality, appropriateness and financing of health care services; and integrating and coordinating efforts to improve health and health care services. The foundation has also established the following grantmaking priorities: 1) addressing health disparities; 2) strengthening nonprofit health organizations; and 3) expanding access to primary health care.
Fields of interest: Public health; Health care.
Type of support: Publication; General/operating support; Income development; Management development/capacity building; Program development; Conferences/seminars; Research; Technical assistance; Program evaluation.
Limitations: Applications accepted. Giving limited to GA. No support for sectarian programs (benefiting only one religious organization). No grants to individuals (except for award program), or for capital campaigns, or major equipment.
Publications: Application guidelines; Annual report; Grants list; Informational brochure (including application guidelines); Occasional report; Program policy statement.
Application information: The foundation is currently reviewing its Grantmaking Priorities and Guidelines. Please visit its web site for more information. The foundation engages in both proactive (solicited) and responsive (unsolicited) grantmaking. Proactive grantmaking will be carried out through an RFP process that addresses specific areas within the foundation's funding priorities. Responsive grantmaking will allow the foundation to support unsolicited proposals that fit its mission and fall within its funding priorities. See foundation web site for full application requirements and guidelines. Application form required.
Initial approach: Potential applicants should view pre-application webinar on foundation web site. All applications should be submitted online via web site

Copies of proposal: 2
Deadline(s): See foundation web site for current deadline
Board meeting date(s): Quarterly
Final notification: Within 3 months for letters of inquiry; within 8 to 9 months for proposals; declinations are announced quarterly

Officers and Directors:* Diane Zabak Weems, M.D.*, Chair.; Francis Tedesco, M.D.*, Vice-Chair.; Gary D. Nelson, Ph.D., Pres.; Lynn Thogerson,* Secy.; Teri Hartman,* Treas.; Michael J. Sweeney III, C.F.O. and Dir., Finance; Cheryl Christian; Gene Godfrey; Anne Griffith Hennessy; Scott Kroell; Pierluigi Mancini, Ph.D.; Steven P. Merz; Robert Nesbitt, M.D.; Charles T. Stafford, M.D.
Number of staff: 8 full-time professional; 1 full-time support.
EIN: 582418091

887
The Holder Construction Foundation

3333 Riverwood Pkwy., Ste. 400
Atlanta, GA 30339-3304 (770) 988-3280
Contact: J.C. Pendrey, Jr., Tr.

Donor: Holder Construction Co.
Foundation type: Company-sponsored foundation.
Financial data (yr. ended 12/31/12): Assets, $4,936,655 (M); gifts received, $1,250,000; expenditures, $955,794; qualifying distributions, $953,294; giving activities include $953,294 for grants.
Purpose and activities: The foundation supports zoos and organizations involved with arts and culture, education, health, human services, and business.
Fields of interest: Museums (art); Performing arts, ballet; Arts; Elementary/secondary education; Higher education; Education; Zoos/zoological societies; Health care; Children/youth, services; Human services; Business/industry; United Ways and Federated Giving Programs.
Type of support: General/operating support.
Limitations: Applications accepted. Giving in the greater metropolitan Atlanta, GA, area.
Application information: Application form required.
***Initial approach:* Letter or telephone**
Deadline(s): None
Trustee: J.C. Pendrey, Jr.
EIN: 586412965

888
The Imlay Foundation, Inc.

945 E. Paces Ferry Rd., Ste. 2450
Atlanta, GA 30326-1125 (404) 239-1777
Contact: Mary Ellen Imlay, V.P. and Exec. Dir.
FAX: (404) 239-1779; Main URL: http://theimlayfoundation.org
Grants List: http://theimlayfoundation.org/pdf/imlay-recipients.pdf

Established in 1989 in GA.
Donor: John P. Imlay, Jr.
Foundation type: Independent foundation.
Financial data (yr. ended 12/31/12): Assets, $21,523,481 (M); expenditures, $1,642,844; qualifying distributions, $1,497,268; giving activities include $1,490,812 for 91 grants (high: $100,000; low: $5,000).
Purpose and activities: Giving primarily for health care, and children, youth and social services.
Fields of interest: Botanical gardens; Hospitals (general); Health care; Human services; Children/youth, services; Foundations (community).
Type of support: General/operating support; Annual campaigns; Capital campaigns; Building/renovation; Program development; Curriculum development; Scholarship funds; Research.
Limitations: Giving primarily in Atlanta, GA and Hilton Head, SC; some funding also in Scotland. No grants to individuals.
Application information: Applications may be hand delivered or mailed. The foundation does not accept e-mailed applications because of the required attachments. Application form not required.
Initial approach: Letter of intent
Deadline(s): Feb. 1, June 1, and Oct. 1
Board meeting date(s): Apr., Sept., and Dec.
Officers: John P. Imlay, Jr., Chair.; Mary Ellen Imlay, Pres.; I. Sigmund Mosley, Jr., V.P. and Secy.
Directors: John Dayton; Wimberly Charlotte Dayton; William Evans; Donald Hardie; Cindy Imlay; John P. "Scott" Imlay III; Cori Zubay.
Number of staff: 1 part-time professional; 1 part-time support.
EIN: 581868936

889
Abraham J. & Phyllis Katz Foundation

c/o Alexander S. Katz
1579F Monroe Dr., Ste. 933
Atlanta, GA 30324-5016
Contact: Peter A. Katz, Tr.
E-mail: contact@katzfoundation.org; Main URL: http://katzfoundation.org/
Grants List: http://katzfoundation.org/recent_grants.html

Established in 1994 in NY.
Donors: Abraham J. Katz†; Phyllis Katz†; Peter A. Katz; Kason Industries, Inc.; World Trade Ventures, Ltd.
Foundation type: Operating foundation.
Financial data (yr. ended 12/31/12): Assets, $67,944,440 (M); gifts received, $28,863; expenditures, $3,799,545; qualifying distributions, $3,696,674; giving activities include $3,376,647 for 33 grants.
Purpose and activities: Giving to support young musicians both in performance and composition, and for scientific and medical research. Medical research projects must be related to the use of cord blood to promote wellness, prevent disease or save lives. Of particular interest to the foundation are programs that benefit low-income and under-resourced populations.
Fields of interest: Performing arts, music; Higher education; Medical school/education; Hospitals (general).
Limitations: Applications accepted. Giving primarily in NY and OH. The Small Grants Program is limited to organizations located in the City of Atlanta, GA and the counties of Coweta, DeKalb, Fayette, and Fulton, GA. No grants to individuals or government agencies; no funding for events.
Application information: To be considered, organizations must have at least one paid staff member. The foundation is not accepting applications for the Traditional and Small Grants programs in 2014. See foundation web site for updates about this. Application form required.
***Initial approach:* For medical research requests: 1-page Letter of Intent outlining proposed research**
Deadline(s): Varies; application deadlines available on foundation web site
Board meeting date(s): Jan. and Apr.
Trustees: Ellen B. Doft; Alexander S. Katz; David Katz; Esther Katz.
Number of staff: 1 part-time professional.
EIN: 116442077

890
The Knox Foundation

3133 Washington Rd. N.W.
Thomson, GA 30824-5451 **(706) 595-1907**
Contact: Boone A. Knox, Tr.

Established in 1981 in GA.
Donors: Boone A. Knox†; Julia P.R. Knox; The George Ann Knox Charitable Lead Annuity Trust; The Pat Knox Charitable Lead Annuity Trust; Knox, Ltd.; Folkstone Ltd.; The Pat Knox Charitable Lead Annuity Trust.
Foundation type: Independent foundation.
Financial data (yr. ended 12/31/12): Assets, $64,880,599 (M); gifts received, $337,292; expenditures, $3,436,654; qualifying distributions, $2,891,130; giving activities include $2,719,387 for 121 grants (high: $360,000; low: $600).
Fields of interest: Arts; Higher education; Human services.
Type of support: General/operating support; Continuing support; Annual campaigns; Capital campaigns; Building/renovation; Endowments; Program development; Matching/challenge support.
Limitations: Applications accepted. Giving generally primarily in Augusta and Thomson, GA. No grants to individuals.
Application information: Application form not required.
Initial approach: Letter
Copies of proposal: 2
Deadline(s): None
Board meeting date(s): Apr. and Oct.
Final notification: Feb. 15 and Aug. 15
Director: Jefferson B.A. Knox.
EIN: 586163728

891
The Sartain Lanier Family Foundation, Inc.

950 Lowery Blvd. N.W.
25 Puritan Mill
Atlanta, GA 30318-5279 (404) 564-1259
Contact: Mark B. Riley, Dir.; Patricia E. Lummus, Assoc. Dir.
FAX: (404) 564-1251;
E-mail: plummus@lanierfamilyfoundation.org; Main URL: http://www.lanierfamilyfoundation.org

Established in 1963 in GA.
Donor: Sartain Lanier†.
Foundation type: Independent foundation.
Financial data (yr. ended 12/31/12): Assets, $50,816,050 (M); expenditures, $4,826,864; qualifying distributions, $4,042,562; giving activities include $3,940,450 for 92 grants (high: $1,230,000; low: $950).
Purpose and activities: The foundation will focus the majority of new grantmaking on education, which has traditionally been primary to the foundation's mission. Specifically the foundation will focus on educational organizations which have broad, systemic impact with the aim of enhancing available options for K-12 education in the metro Atlanta area. The foundation will not be establishing new relationships with private schools at this time, but may continue to make grants to private schools which have received grants from the foundation in the past. In the areas of health and human services, arts, environment and community development, special consideration will continue to be given to institutions that were supported by Mr. Lanier during

his lifetime and that his family has supported since his death.
Fields of interest: Arts; Elementary/secondary education; Education; Environment; Human services; Community/economic development.
Type of support: General/operating support; Capital campaigns; Building/renovation; Endowments; Program development; Program-related investments/loans.
Limitations: Giving primarily in New grants will be limited to organizations in the metro Atlanta, GA area. There will be a few grants each year to organizations outside Atlanta, but those will be based on commitments to organizations with which the foundation has had a lengthy history. No support for churches or religious organizations (for projects that primarily benefit their own members), or for partisan political purposes. No grants to individuals, or for tickets to charitable events or dinners, or to sponsor special events or fundraisers.
Publications: Application guidelines.
Application information: Applications are by invitation only. See foundation web site for further information. Application form not required.
Initial approach: E-mail or telephone
Copies of proposal: 1
Deadline(s): No deadlines, but those invited to submit are encouraged to apply by Apr. 1 for the May meeting and Oct. 1 for the Nov. meeting
Board meeting date(s): May and Nov.
Final notification: Within 1 week of Board of Trustee meeting in May and Nov.
Officers and Trustees:* J. Hicks Lanier,* Chair.; Cecil D. Conlee,* Vice-Chair.; Julie W. Lanier Balloun; John B. Ellis; Claudia M. Livingston; E. Jenner Wood III.
Director: Mark B. Riley.
Number of staff: 2 part-time professional; 1 part-time support.
EIN: 586045056

892
The Ligon Foundation
512 Reston Mill Ln.
Marietta, GA 30067-4982
***E-mail:* ligonfoundation@comcast.net**; Main URL: http://ligonfoundation.com/

Foundation type: Independent foundation.
Financial data (yr. ended 12/31/12): Assets, $3,655,235 (M); expenditures, $250,923; qualifying distributions, $218,949; giving activities include $140,180 for 14 grants (high: $40,000; low: $300).
Fields of interest: Education; Health care; Agriculture/food.
Limitations: Applications not accepted. Giving primarily in GA.
Application information: Unsolicited requests for funds not accepted.
Trustees: Glenn H. Shaw; Nancy Peterson Shaw; William H. Shaw III.
EIN: 207307605

893
Livingston Foundation, Inc.
171 17th St. N.W., Ste. 2100
Atlanta, GA 30363-1031 (404) 873-8500
Contact: Milton W. Brannon, Pres.

Incorporated in 1964 in GA.
Donors: Roy N. Livingston†; Leslie Livingston Kellar†; Bess B. Livingston†.
Foundation type: Independent foundation.
Financial data (yr. ended 09/30/13): Assets, $8,862,246 (M); expenditures, $514,459; qualifying distributions, $414,916; giving activities include $400,097 for 23+ grants (high: $37,250).
Purpose and activities: Giving primarily for education, the fine arts, and health care.
Fields of interest: Arts, cultural/ethnic awareness; Visual arts; Museums; Performing arts; Historic preservation/historical societies; Arts; Education; Environment; Animal welfare; Hospitals (general); Health care; Medical research, institute; Human services; Community/economic development; International studies; Public affairs.
Type of support: General/operating support; Continuing support; Annual campaigns; Capital campaigns; Building/renovation; Endowments; Seed money; Curriculum development; Matching/challenge support.
Limitations: Applications accepted. Giving primarily in the metropolitan Atlanta, GA, area. No support for religious or political organizations. No grants to individuals, or for scholarships or fellowships; no loans.
Application information: Application form required.
***Deadline(s):* None**
Board meeting date(s): Quarterly
Officers and Trustees:* Jonathan Golden,* Chair.; Milton W. Brannon,* Pres. and Treas.; C.E. Gregory III,* Secy.; Greer Brannon; Michael Golden; Charles Gregory; Bill Jacobs.
Number of staff: 1 part-time support.
EIN: 586044858
Other changes: The grantmaker now accepts applications.

894
The Thomas H. and Jarman F. Lowder Foundation
c/o Pathstone Family Office
P.O. Box 52047
Atlanta, GA 30355-0047

Established in 1995 in AL.
Donors: Thomas H. Lowder; Jarman F. Lowder; Catherine Lowder†; Charlotte Lowder.
Foundation type: Independent foundation.
Financial data (yr. ended 12/31/12): Assets, $21,370,005 (M); expenditures, $1,508,695; qualifying distributions, $1,310,225; giving activities include $1,310,225 for 16 grants (high: $500,000; low: $100).
Purpose and activities: Giving primarily for education, health organizations, social services, federated giving programs, and Roman Catholic organizations and churches.
Fields of interest: Education; Health organizations; Human services; United Ways and Federated Giving Programs; Catholic agencies & churches.
Limitations: Applications not accepted. Giving primarily in Birmingham, AL. No grants to individuals.
Application information: Contributes only to pre-selected organizations.
Officers: Thomas H. Lowder, Pres. and Treas.; **Susan A. Carrington, V.P. and Secy.; Heather Anne Lowder, V.P.; James K. Lowder, V.P.**
EIN: 631139498

895
Mattie H. Marshall Foundation
c/o SunTrust Bank
P.O. Box 4655, MC221
Atlanta, GA 30302-4655 (404) 813-2021
Contact: Emily Butler, Grants Mgr., SunTrust Bank
E-mail: fdnsvcs.ga@suntrust.com; **Main URL: http://fdnweb.org/marshall**

Established in 1963 in GA.
Donors: Thomas O. Marshall; Mrs. Thomas O. Marshall.
Foundation type: Independent foundation.
Financial data (yr. ended 12/31/12): Assets, $7,956,182 (M); expenditures, $395,714; qualifying distributions, $368,074; giving activities include $347,000 for 24 grants (high: $35,000; low: $7,000).
Purpose and activities: Giving to organizations that provide support to orphans, hospitals, nursing for the aged, and Methodist churches that assist retired ministers.
Fields of interest: Higher education; Animal welfare; Hospitals (general); Human services; Aging, centers/services; Protestant agencies & churches; Aging.
Type of support: General/operating support; Annual campaigns; Capital campaigns; Building/renovation; Endowments; Program development.
Limitations: Applications accepted. Giving limited to GA, with emphasis on Americus and southern GA. No grants to individuals.
Publications: Application guidelines.
Application information: Application form not required.
Initial approach: Letter
Copies of proposal: 1
Deadline(s): Feb. 15 and Aug. 15
Board meeting date(s): Spring and fall
Final notification: Dec. 31
Director: Martha Marshall Dykes.
Trustee: SunTrust Bank.
EIN: 586042019

896
The Carlos and Marguerite Mason Fund
c/o Wells Fargo Bank, N.A.
3280 Peachtree Rd. N.E., MAC G0141-041
Atlanta, GA 30305-2430
Contact: Joyce Yamaato, V.P. and Sr. Trust and Fiduciary Specialist in Philanthropic Svcs.; Lydia Whitman
Main URL: https://www.wellsfargo.com/privatefoundationgrants/mason

Established in 1991 in GA.
Donor: Marguerite F. Mason†.
Foundation type: Independent foundation.
Financial data (yr. ended 12/31/12): Assets, $92,551,805 (M); expenditures, $4,885,894; qualifying distributions, $4,257,830; giving activities include $4,056,963 for 8 grants (high: $2,068,000; low: $25,000).
Purpose and activities: Support only for Georgia organizations involved with organ transplantation and related research.
Fields of interest: Health care, organ/tissue banks; Organ research.
Type of support: Equipment; Program development; Professorships; Research.
Limitations: Applications accepted. Giving limited to GA. **No support for indirect or overhead expenses for projects at colleges, universities, governmental units, or other established organizations. No grants to individuals, or for general goodwill advertising,**

or grants that would replace existing sources of funding.
Publications: Application guidelines.
Application information: Application form not required.
Initial approach: Proposal
Copies of proposal: 3
Deadline(s): June 1
Board meeting date(s): Sept.
Final notification: Sept. 30
Officer and Advisory Committee:* George W.P. Atkins,* Chair.; Carol Hoffman; John Libby; Alice Sheets; Joyce Yamaato.
Trustee: Wells Fargo Bank, N.A.
EIN: 581996431

897
The Sara Giles Moore Foundation
1355 Peachtree St., Ste. 1560
Atlanta, GA 30309-3275 (404) 249-2800
Contact: Lisa B. Williams, Exec. Dir.
E-mail: lwilliams@thesaragilesmoorefoundation.org; Main URL: http://www.thesaragilesmoorefoundation.org
Grants List: http://thesaragilesmoorefoundation.org/recent-grants/

Established in 1997 in GA.
Donor: Sara Giles Moore†.
Foundation type: Independent foundation.
Financial data (yr. ended 12/31/12): Assets, $36,831,014 (M); expenditures, $1,840,325; qualifying distributions, $1,779,595; giving activities include $1,651,000 for 51 grants (high: $150,000; low: $5,000).
Purpose and activities: Giving to art and cultural institutes.
Fields of interest: Visual arts; Museums; Education, early childhood education.
Type of support: General/operating support; Management development/capacity building; Annual campaigns; Capital campaigns; Building/renovation; Emergency funds; Scholarship funds; Matching/challenge support.
Limitations: Applications accepted. Giving primarily in Atlanta, GA.
Application information: Application form required.
Initial approach: E-mail
Copies of proposal: 1
Board meeting date(s): Oct. and May
Final notification: 3 to 6 months
Officers and Trustees:* Sara A. Hehir,* Chair.; Elizabeth Pritchard, Secy.; Frank Butterfield,* Treas.; Lisa B. Williams, Exec. Dir.; Frank McGaughey; Kathleen Riley.
Number of staff: 1 part-time professional.
EIN: 586343477

898
Katherine John Murphy Foundation
c/o SunTrust Bank
P.O. Box 4655, MC GA-ATL-0221
Atlanta, GA 30302-4655
Contact: Emily Butler, Grants Mgr., SunTrust Bank
E-mail: info@murphyfoundation.org; **E-mail for questions regarding grantmaking: fdnsvcs.ga@suntrust.com**; Main URL: http://www.murphyfoundation.org/

Trust established in 1954 in GA.
Donor: Katherine Murphy Riley†.
Foundation type: Independent foundation.
Financial data (yr. ended 12/31/13): Assets, $17,023,482 (M); expenditures, $948,545; qualifying distributions, $848,923; giving activities include $820,000 for 32 grants (high: $170,000; low: $5,000).
Fields of interest: Arts; Higher education; Environment; Health care; Children/youth, services.
International interests: Latin America.
Limitations: Applications not accepted. Giving primarily in Atlanta, GA. No grants to individuals, or for research, or matching gifts; no loans.
Application information: The foundation has suspended grantmaking for the foreseeable future. Please check foundation web site for updates.
Board meeting date(s): Annually, and as necessary
Officer and Trustees:* Martin Gatins,* Chair.; Dameron Black III; Phillip Gatins.
Number of staff: None.
EIN: 586026045

899
Stuart & Eulene Murray Foundation
c/o Joel Reed
2800 Century Pkwy., Ste. 900
Atlanta, GA **30345-3140**

Established in 1991 in GA.
Donor: Eulene H. Murray†.
Foundation type: Independent foundation.
Financial data (yr. ended 06/30/13): Assets, $47,331,568 (M); expenditures, $2,651,489; qualifying distributions, $2,212,963; giving activities include $2,210,834 for 12 grants (high: $1,000,000; low: $2,000).
Fields of interest: Arts; Education; Human services.
Limitations: Applications not accepted. Giving primarily in GA, with some emphasis on Atlanta. No grants to individuals.
Application information: Contributes only to pre-selected organizations.
Trustees: Joe McDonald, Jr.; Joel Reed; Marilyn Rowland.
EIN: 581936483

900
North Georgia Community Foundation
615F Oak St., Ste. 1300
Gainesville, GA 30501-8562 (770) 535-7880
FAX: (770) 503-0439; E-mail: info@ngcf.org; **Additional tel.: (866) 535-7880; Grant application e-mail: grants@ngcf.org**; Main URL: http://www.ngcf.org
Facebook: http://www.facebook.com/pages/Gainesville-GA/North-Georgia-Community-Foundation/128405248648

Established in 1985 in GA.
Foundation type: Community foundation.
Financial data (yr. ended 12/31/12): Assets, $39,520,415 (M); gifts received, $3,089,197; expenditures, $5,136,855; giving activities include $4,214,631 for 67+ grants (high: $728,724), and $187,300 for 150 grants to individuals.
Purpose and activities: The foundation supports nonprofit organizations and donors by building, distributing and preserving philanthropic assets to enhance the spirit of community and the quality of life of the region.
Fields of interest: Arts; Education; Environment; Health care; Human services; Economic development; Community/economic development; Philanthropy/voluntarism; Religion.
Type of support: General/operating support; Management development/capacity building; Equipment; Program development; Seed money; Technical assistance; Program evaluation; Matching/challenge support.
Limitations: Applications accepted. Giving limited to the 15-county area of northeast GA for discretionary funding. No grants to individuals (except for scholarships), or for annual fund campaigns.
Publications: Application guidelines; Annual report; Financial statement; Informational brochure; Occasional report.
Application information: Visit foundation Web site for RFP announcements and application guidelines. Application form not required.
Initial approach: Submit application letter (not to exceed two type-written pages)
Copies of proposal: 1
Deadline(s): June 16 for Community Impact grants
Board meeting date(s): 2nd Wed. monthly
Final notification: Late July for Community Impact grants
Trustees: James McCoy,* Chair.
Trustees: Strother Randolph,* Vice-Chair.; James E. Mathis, Jr.,* C.E.O.
Trustees: Julie Ferguson,* Secy.; Henry Ridgon,* Treas.; Loveanne Addison; **Richard M. Asbill**; Jeff Ash; Kathleen Carter; Jim Coyle; Tim Darrah; Rob Fowler; Chip Frierson; Haines Hill; Ronnie Hopkins; Rusty Hopkins; Mary Helen McGruder; Cara Mitchell; Virgilio Perez Pascoe; Lona Pope; Helen Ray; Lydia Starke; Kevin Tallant; Daren Wayne.
Number of staff: 4 full-time professional.
EIN: 581610318
Other changes: Blair Diaz, Shane Gaddy, Kirk Knous, Kris Nordholz, Strother Randolph, and Moss Robertson are no longer directors. Donald S. Pirkle, Russell M. Roush, and Kathy L. Tillman are no longer directors.

901
The Orianne Society
579 Highway 441 S.
Clayton, GA 30525-5482 (706) 212-0112
FAX: (706) 212-0113;
E-mail: info@oriannesociety.org; Main URL: http://www.oriannesociety.org/
Blog: http://www.oriannesociety.org/blog
Facebook: https://www.facebook.com/OrianneSociety

Donors: Rudolf G. Amdt; Andrew Sabin Family Foundation; National Fish and Wildlife Foundation; Thomas Kaplan and Family; Fidelity Charitable Gift Fund; The Recanati-Kaplan Foundation; Daphne Recanati Kaplan.
Foundation type: Operating foundation.
Financial data (yr. ended 06/30/13): Assets, $8,149,955 (M); gifts received, $6,367,089; expenditures, $1,782,551; qualifying distributions, $1,626,398; giving activities include $39,784 for 1 grant, and $1,782,551 for 5 foundation-administered programs.
Purpose and activities: Giving primarily for the conservation of imperiled snakes around the world.
Fields of interest: Education; Environment; Animal welfare; Recreation.
Limitations: Applications not accepted.
Application information: Unsolicited requests for funds not accepted.
Officers and Directors:* Christopher Jenkins,* C.E.O.; Gary Baldaeus,* C.F.O.; **Thomas Kaplan**; **William Nabony.**
EIN: 262444068

902
Patrick Family Foundation, Inc.
P.O. Box 1048
Decatur, GA 30031-1048
Contact: Hilda B. Patrick, Secy.-Treas.

Established in 1988 in GA.
Donors: Joseph E. Patrick, Sr.†; Geraldine A. Patrick.
Foundation type: Independent foundation.
Financial data (yr. ended 09/30/13): Assets, $5,435,776 (M); expenditures, $303,475; qualifying distributions, $262,094; giving activities include $255,000 for 40 grants (high: $22,000; low: $1,000).
Purpose and activities: The primary emphasis of the foundation is support of institutions of the Presbyterian Church (USA), and a secondary focus is on the capital expenditures of local charities in the communities of the directors.
Fields of interest: Higher education; Human services; Protestant agencies & churches.
Type of support: Capital campaigns.
Limitations: Applications accepted. Giving primarily in GA and OH, and nationally for institutions of the Presbyterian Church. No support for private, primary, or secondary schools or national organizations. No grants to individuals.
Application information: Application form required.
Initial approach: Proposal
Deadline(s): Nov. 1 for Winter meeting and May 1 for Summer meeting
Board meeting date(s): Summer
Officers: Dorothea P. Smith, Pres.; Joseph E. Patrick, Jr., 1st V.P.; William L. Smith IV, 2nd V.P.; Hilda B. Patrick, Secy.-Treas.
EIN: 581820403
Other changes: The grantmaker no longer lists a phone.

903
Pickett & Hatcher Educational Fund, Inc.
6001 River Rd., Ste. 408
Columbus, GA 31904-4558 **(800) 864-8308, ext. 100**
FAX: (706) 324-6788; E-mail: info@phef.org; **Mailing address: P.O. Box 8169, Columbus, GA 31908-8169; tel.: (706) 327-6586; e-mail for Scholarships: info@phef.org**; Main URL: http://www.phef.org
Facebook: https://www.facebook.com/phefinc

Incorporated in 1938 in GA.
Donor: Claud A. Hatcher†.
Foundation type: Independent foundation.
Financial data (yr. ended 09/30/13): Assets, $47,057,882 (M); gifts received, $1,000; expenditures, $4,087,428; qualifying distributions, $3,929,669; giving activities include $3,376,752 for 520 loans to individuals.
Purpose and activities: The fund makes student loans to U.S. citizens who are full-time students (12 hours per term), who are enrolled in classroom instructional credit hours on the campus of a 4-year college or university in the U.S., who are enrolled in a bachelor's degree program with a broad liberal education component, who possess a good credit history (or have no credit), and who have a GPA no less than 2.0 on a 4.0 scale (per term and overall). Entering freshmen must have a minimum composite ACT score of 20 or combined verbal/critical reading and math score of 950 on the SAT. Loans are available to medical health care students studying nursing, physical therapy, etc.
Fields of interest: Economically disadvantaged.
Type of support: Student loans—to individuals.
Limitations: Applications accepted. Giving limited to the U.S. No support for students planning to enter career fields of medicine, law, or the ministry. No grants for any purpose other than educational loans.
Publications: Application guidelines; Informational brochure (including application guidelines).
Application information: Loans cannot be made if applicant will be enrolled in a vocational or technical school/college, a 2-year college, at a branch campus, or an online-program. See foundation web site for current application guidelines, procedures and deadlines. Application form required.
Initial approach: Use online application on foundation web site
Copies of proposal: 1
Deadline(s): Varies based on availability of funds
Board meeting date(s): Feb., May, Aug. and Nov.
Final notification: Usually 1-2 weeks
Officers and Directors:* William B. Hardegree, Jr.,* Chair.; Kenneth R. Owens, Pres.; Margaret G. Zollo,* Secy.; Frank D. Brown, Ph.D.; Frank S. Etheridge III; Donna S. Hand; Anne H. Matthews; Jerry M. Smith.
Number of staff: 1 full-time professional; 3 full-time support; 2 part-time support.
EIN: 580566216
Other changes: William B. Hardegree, Jr. has replaced William K. Hatcher as Chair.

904
William I. H. and Lula E. Pitts Foundation
c/o SunTrust Bank, Atlanta
P.O. Box 4655, MC221
Atlanta, GA 30302-4655 (404) 813-2021
Contact: Emily Butler, Grants Mgr., SunTrust Bank
E-mail: fdnsvcs.ga@suntrust.com; Main URL: http://www.pittsfoundation.org

Trust established in 1941 in GA.
Donors: William I.H. Pitts†; Margaret A. Pitts.
Foundation type: Independent foundation.
Financial data (yr. ended 12/31/12): Assets, $76,559,269 (M); expenditures, $3,607,061; qualifying distributions, $3,440,391; giving activities include $3,319,872 for 13 grants (high: $1,102,936; low: $5,000).
Purpose and activities: Giving exclusively to organizations affiliated with the United Methodist Church; specific areas of interest include education, children's homes, charitable hospitals, and.
Fields of interest: Higher education; Human services; Aging, centers/services; Protestant agencies & churches; Aging.
Type of support: General/operating support; Continuing support; Building/renovation; Equipment; Conferences/seminars; Professorships; Scholarship funds.
Limitations: Applications accepted. Giving limited to GA. No grants to individuals, or for endowment funds, research, scholarships, fellowships, or matching gifts; no loans.
Publications: Application guidelines.
Application information: Application form required.
Initial approach: Use online grant application form on foundation web site
Copies of proposal: 1
Deadline(s): Mar. 1
Board meeting date(s): Apr.
Officers and Directors:* Bishop L. Bevel Jones III,* Chair.; Allen Mast, Secy.; Columbus Gilmore; Dan McAlexander; Philip Millians; Ralph R. Morrison; Elizabeth C. Ogie; David Seyle; E. Jenner Wood III.
Trustee: SunTrust Bank.
EIN: 586026047

905
The Pittulloch Foundation, Inc.
5830 E. Ponce de Leon Ave.
Stone Mountain, GA 30083-1504

Established in 1985 in GA.
Donors: Stone Mountain Industrial Park, Inc.; Pattillo Split Interest Trust; Rockdale Industries, Inc.; Genuine Parts Co.; Peter Winters.
Foundation type: Independent foundation.
Financial data (yr. ended 12/31/12): Assets, $32,394,258 (M); gifts received, $526,000; expenditures, $1,595,266; qualifying distributions, $1,552,002; giving activities include $1,544,500 for 34 grants (high: $350,000; low: $500).
Purpose and activities: Support primarily for mental health services for children and for education.
Fields of interest: Education, early childhood education; Higher education; Education, reading; Mental health, treatment; Human services; Leadership development; Children/youth.
Limitations: Applications not accepted. Giving primarily in GA. No grants to individuals.
Application information: Contributes only to pre-selected organizations.
Officers and Directors:* Lynn L. Pattillo-Cohen, Chair.; Michael G. Kerman, Secy.; Robert C. Goddard; Anita Kern.
EIN: 581651352
Other changes: Peter Winter is no longer a director.

906
Carolyn King Ragan Charitable Foundation
(formerly Ragan and King Charitable Foundation)
c/o Wells Fargo Bank, N.A.
3280 Peachtree Rd. N.W., Ste. 300
Atlanta, GA 30305-2449 (404) 238-0444
Contact: Joyce Yamaato
E-mail: grantinquiries8@wachovia.com; **Main URL: https://www.wellsfargo.com/privatefoundationgrants/ragan-king**

Established in 1972 in GA.
Donor: Carolyn King Ragan†.
Foundation type: Independent foundation.
Financial data (yr. ended 09/30/12): Assets, $4,736,880 (M); expenditures, $303,675; qualifying distributions, $244,596; giving activities include $225,500 for 8 grants (high: $56,375; low: $8,000).
Purpose and activities: Giving primarily for Baptist organizations and churches; funding also for higher education and human services.
Fields of interest: Higher education; Human services; Protestant agencies & churches.
Limitations: Applications accepted. Giving limited to GA (except for two specific out-of-state beneficiaries). No grants to individuals.
Application information: Application form not required.
Initial approach: Letter
Copies of proposal: 1
Deadline(s): None
Board meeting date(s): Fall
Trustee: Wells Fargo Bank, N.A.
EIN: 586138950

907
W. G. Raoul Foundation
c/o SunTrust Bank
P.O. Box 4655, MC GA-ATL-0221
Atlanta, GA 30302-4655 (404) 813-2021
Contact: Emily Butler, Grants Mgr., SunTrust Bank

E-mail: fdnsvcs.ga@suntrust.com; **Main URL: http://fdnweb.org/raoul**

Established in 1913 in GA; supporting organization of the American Lung Association and Children's Healthcare of Atlanta.
Foundation type: Independent foundation.
Financial data (yr. ended 12/31/12): Assets, $4,094,659 (M); expenditures, $204,122; qualifying distributions, $196,317; giving activities include $187,700 for 3 grants (high: $89,700; low: $27,500).
Purpose and activities: The foundation was established to address lung-related diseases in the State of Georgia. The foundation is particularly interested in pediatric asthma programs.
Fields of interest: Lung diseases; Lung research; Asthma research.
Type of support: General/operating support; Capital campaigns; Program development.
Limitations: Applications accepted. Giving limited to GA. No grants to individuals.
Application information: Online application on foundation web site. Application form required.
Board meeting date(s): Spring and fall
Officers: Frederick VanWinkle, Chair.; Brenda Rambeau, Pres.; Charles Stokes, V.P.; Greg Gerhard, Secy.-Treas.
Trustee: Linda Laird.
EIN: 586026051

908
The Richards Foundation, Inc.
(also known as Judy Windom)(formerly Roy Richards, Jr. Foundation for Charitable Giving)
P.O. Box 800
Carrollton, GA 30112-0015 (770) 832-4097
***Contact:* Roy Richards, Dir.**
FAX: (770) 832-5265;
E-mail: Judy_Windom@southwire.com

Established in 1990 in GA.
Donor: Roy Richards, Jr.
Foundation type: Independent foundation.
Financial data (yr. ended 12/31/12): Assets, $7,263,365 (M); gifts received, $1,997,420; expenditures, $1,183,424; qualifying distributions, $1,180,562; giving activities include $1,143,000 for 12 grants (high: $500,000; low: $1,000).
Fields of interest: Education; Environment, natural resources; Environment, land resources; Foundations (community).
Limitations: Applications accepted. Giving primarily in Charleston, SC; funding also in Carroll County, GA, and surrounding counties.
Application information:
Initial approach: Letter
Copies of proposal: 1
Deadline(s): Ongoing
Director: Roy Richards.
EIN: 581933598
Other changes: At the close of 2012, the grantmaker paid grants of $1,143,000, a 471.5% increase over the 2011 disbursements, $200,000. Robin R. Donohoe is no longer a director.

909
The Rockdale Foundation Inc.
(formerly Rockdale Fund for Social Investment, Inc.)
916 Joseph E. Lowery Blvd. N.W., Ste. 4
Atlanta, GA **30318-5280**

Established in GA.
Donor: Kathleen M. Barksdale.
Foundation type: Independent foundation.
Financial data (yr. ended 12/31/12): Assets, $5,166,015 (M); expenditures, $603,411; qualifying distributions, $501,208; giving activities include $446,217 for 58 grants (high: $105,875; low: $100).
Fields of interest: Education; Human services; Children, services; International migration/refugee issues; Foundations (community); Economically disadvantaged.
Limitations: Applications not accepted. Giving primarily in Atlanta, GA. **No grants to individuals.**
Application information: Contributes only to pre-selected organizations.
Officers: Kathleen M. Barksdale, Pres.; Winsome Hawkins, Secy.; **Jody Stephenson, C.F.O.**
Board Members: Jonna Adams; Beverly Hall.
EIN: 582668065
Other changes: Lisa Morris is no longer Treas.

910
Murray & Sydell Rosenberg Foundation, Inc.
(formerly Murray M. Rosenberg Foundation)
3330 Cumberland Blvd., Ste. 900
Atlanta, GA 30339-5998

Established in 1991 in GA.
Donor: Greystone Funding Corp.
Foundation type: Company-sponsored foundation.
Financial data (yr. ended 06/30/13): Assets, $39,860 (M); gifts received, $4,308,010; expenditures, $4,218,900; qualifying distributions, $4,215,084; giving activities include $4,215,084 for 65 grants (high: $429,632; low: $500).
Purpose and activities: The foundation supports programs designed to help impoverished Jewish families.
Fields of interest: Education; Jewish agencies & synagogues; Economically disadvantaged.
International interests: Israel.
Type of support: General/operating support; Grants to individuals.
Limitations: Applications not accepted. Giving primarily in NJ and NY, and in Israel.
Application information: Contributes only to pre-selected organizations and individuals.
Directors: Lisa Lifshitz; Cheryl Rosenberg; Stephen Rosenberg.
Number of staff: 3 full-time professional.
EIN: 581947342
Other changes: At the close of 2013, the grantmaker paid grants of $4,215,084, a 152.8% increase over the 2012 disbursements, $1,667,342.

911
The Sapelo Foundation, Inc.
(formerly Sapelo Island Research Foundation, Inc.)
4503 New Jesup Hwy.
Brunswick, GA **31520-1798** (912) 265-0520
Contact: Phyllis Bowen, Exec. Dir.
FAX: (912) 265-1888;
E-mail: sapelofoundation@mindspring.com; Main URL: http://www.sapelofoundation.org
Grants List: http://sapelofoundation.org/resources

Incorporated in 1949 in GA.
Donor: Richard J. Reynolds, Jr.‡.
Foundation type: Independent foundation.
Financial data (yr. ended 06/30/12): Assets, $32,492,613 (M); expenditures, $1,653,655; qualifying distributions, $1,376,725; giving activities include $895,294 for 62 grants (high: $65,000; low: $308), and $142,750 for grants to individuals.
Purpose and activities: The foundation promotes progressive social change affecting, in particular, vulnerable populations, rural communities and the natural environment. Scholarships also to financially needy residents of McIntosh County, GA, who are graduates of McIntosh County Academy, and who have a 2.0 GPA or better, for attendance at accredited colleges, universities, or technical colleges.
Fields of interest: Higher education; Environment, public policy; Environment, air pollution; Environment, toxics; Environment, water resources; Environment, forests; Animals/wildlife, preservation/protection; Crime/violence prevention, youth; Legal services, public interest law; Civil liberties, due process; Civil/human rights.
Type of support: General/operating support; Continuing support; Annual campaigns; Program development; Matching/challenge support.
Limitations: Applications accepted. Giving limited to rural and statewide GA (with the exception of the Metro Atlanta area). No support for projects focusing on and/or implemented in the Metro Atlanta, GA, area, or for indirect or overhead expenses for projects at colleges, universities, public schools or governmental units. No grants or scholarships to individuals directly, or for capital, emergency, or endowment funds, deficit financing, or publications; no loans.
Publications: Application guidelines; Annual report; Grants list.
Application information: The foundation will not fund 100 percent of any organization or project. Applicants may include only 1-3 pages of news articles, letters of support, or other information. Such information must be formatted on an easy-to-copy 8.5" x 11" page. Attachments in color must be mailed to the Sapelo Foundation (15 copies). See foundation web site for complete and specific application guidelines and procedures, as incomplete proposals are not accepted. Application form required.
***Initial approach:* For grants use online application system on foundation web site; For scholarships use application form on foundation web site and send via U.S. mail**
***Deadline(s):* See foundation web site for specific deadlines**
Board meeting date(s): May and Nov.
Final notification: Within two weeks following board meeting
Officers and Trustees:* Irene Reynolds Schier,* Pres.; Nicole Bagley,* V.P.; Hon. Nan Grogan Orrock,* Secy.; Bettieanne Hart,* Treas.; Phyllis Bowen, Exec. Dir.; William K. Broker; Henry H. Carey; Philip N. Carey; Jerry Gonzalez; Katharine R. Grant; Michael Grant; Midge Sweet.
Number of staff: 2 full-time professional.
EIN: 580827472
Other changes: Irene Reynolds Schier has replaced Henry H. Carey as Pres. Nicole Bagley has replaced Irene Reynolds Schier as V.P. Hon. Nan Grogan Orrock has replaced Katharine R. Grant as Secy.

912
The Savannah Community Foundation
(formerly The Savannah Foundation)
7393 Hodgson Memorial Dr., Ste. 204
Savannah, GA 31406-1507 (912) 921-7700
Contact: K. Russell Simpson, Pres.
E-mail: Russ@SavFoundation.org; Additional e-mails: russ@savfoundation.org and

grants@savfoundation.org; Main URL: http://www.savfoundation.org

Established in 1953 in GA; re-incorporated as a community foundation in 1986.
Foundation type: Community foundation.
Financial data (yr. ended 06/30/12): Assets, $16,415,432 (M); gifts received, $1,395,973; expenditures, $2,343,992; giving activities include $1,958,511 for grants, and $87,700 for grants to individuals.
Purpose and activities: The foundation supports organizations involved with arts, education, health, human services, and religion.
Fields of interest: Arts; Education; Health care; Health organizations, association; Medical research, institute; Human services; Religion.
Type of support: Scholarships—to individuals; Endowments; Equipment; Emergency funds; Conferences/seminars; Scholarship funds; In-kind gifts.
Limitations: Applications accepted. Giving limited primarily to southeastern GA, but Donor-Advised Funds may support any qualified U.S. charity. No grants to individuals (except for scholarships).
Publications: Application guidelines; Financial statement; Grants list; Informational brochure (including application guidelines).
Application information: Visit foundation web site for application information. Application form required.
Initial approach: E-mail
Deadline(s): None
Board meeting date(s): Feb., May, Aug., and Nov.
Final notification: Varies
Officers and Directors:* Linda J. Evans,* Chair.; K. Russell Simpson,* Pres.; Michael Traynor,* V.P.; Stephen W. Schwarz,* Secy.; Christopher Cay,* Treas.; **Michael F. Kemp,* Asst. Treas.**; Jennifer Abshire; Dale C. Critz, Jr.; Justin A. Godchaux; John C. Helmken II; James R. Hungerpiller; Russell C. Jacobs III; Al Kennickell, Jr.; Frank S. Macgill; Melanie L. Marks; Michael Traynor.
Number of staff: 1 part-time professional; 1 part-time support.
EIN: 586033468
Other changes: Melanie L. Marks is no longer a director. Christopher Cay, Linda J. Evans, Dolly Chisholm, Stephen W. Schwarz, and Michael F. Kemp are no longer directors.

913
Raymond F. Schinazi and Family Foundation, Inc.
1860 Montreal Rd.
Tucker, GA 30084

Established in 2005 in GA.
Donors: Raymond F. Schinazi; William H. Prusoff.
Foundation type: Independent foundation.
Financial data (yr. ended 03/31/13): Assets, $14,005,295 (M); gifts received, $4,908,193; expenditures, $688,918; qualifying distributions, $420,172; giving activities include $416,960 for 21 grants (high: $120,339; low: $105).
Fields of interest: Education; Medical research; Christian agencies & churches; Jewish agencies & synagogues.
Limitations: Applications not accepted. Giving primarily in Atlanta, GA. No grants to individuals.
Application information: Unsolicited requests for funds not accepted.
Officers: Raymond F. Schinazi, Pres.; **Nicholas Guttridge, V.P**; Charlene Mcnabb, Secy.-Treas.
EIN: 203693012
Other changes: Nicholas Guttridge has replaced Rebecca E. Williams as V.P.

914
Warren P. & Ava F. Sewell Foundation, Inc.
217 Davis Blvd.
Bremen, GA **30110-2569**
***Application address:* c/o The Meigs Group, PC, Attn.: Richard Meigs, 411 Alabama Ave., Bremen, GA, tel.: (770) 537-2326**

Established in 1989 in GA as successor to Warren P. and Ava F. Sewell Foundation.
Foundation type: Independent foundation.
Financial data (yr. ended 06/30/13): Assets, $4,865,328 (M); expenditures, $297,112; qualifying distributions, $237,243; giving activities include $215,002 for 47 grants (high: $30,000; low: $50).
Purpose and activities: Giving primarily to Baptist churches and for education.
Fields of interest: Elementary school/education; Secondary school/education; Recreation; Human services; Protestant agencies & churches.
Type of support: Capital campaigns; Building/renovation.
Limitations: Applications accepted. Giving primarily in eastern AL and Haralson and Carroll counties, GA. No grants to individuals.
Publications: Annual report.
Application information: Application form not required.
Initial approach: Letter
Copies of proposal: 1
Deadline(s): None
Board meeting date(s): Every 60 days
Trustees: L. Richard Plunkett; Warren P. Sewell, Jr.; Robin S. Worley.
EIN: 581791240

915
Southern Company Charitable Foundation, Inc.
241 Ralph McGill Blvd., N.E., BIN 10131
Atlanta, GA 30308-3374 (404) 506-6784
Contact: Susan M. Carter, Secy.
FAX: (404) 506-1485; Main URL: http://www.southerncompany.com/corporate-responsibility/social-responsibility/communityInvolvement.aspx

Established in 1999 in GA.
Donor: The Southern Co.
Foundation type: Company-sponsored foundation.
Financial data (yr. ended 12/31/11): Assets, $29,338,399 (M); gifts received, $25,000,000; expenditures, $1,012,525; qualifying distributions, $863,511; giving activities include $861,111 for 10 grants (high: $260,000; low: $10,000).
Purpose and activities: The foundation supports organizations involved with education, the environment, and disaster relief.
Fields of interest: Education; Environment; Disasters, preparedness/services.
Type of support: Annual campaigns; Capital campaigns; Continuing support; Emergency funds; General/operating support; Grants to individuals; Program development.
Limitations: Applications accepted. Giving primarily in AL, FL, GA, and MS. No support for religious organizations or private or secondary schools or non-public foundations. No grants to individuals (except for employee-related emergency assistance grants).
Application information: Multi-year funding is not automatic. Application form not required.
Initial approach: Proposal
Copies of proposal: 1
Deadline(s): None
Board meeting date(s): May
Final notification: 1 month
Officers and Directors:* Michael K. Anderson,* Pres.; Susan M. Carter, Secy.; Roger S. Steffens, Treas.; Arthur P. Beattie; **Mark S. Lantrip**; Christopher C. Womack.
EIN: 582514027
Other changes: Michael K. Anderson has replaced Edison G. Holland as Pres.
G. Edison Holland is no longer Pres.

916
Trailsend Foundation
(formerly James M. Cox, Jr. Foundation, Inc.)
c/o Cox Enterprises, Inc.
6205 Peachtree Dunwoody Rd., N.E.
Atlanta, GA 30328-4524
Contact: Nancy K. Rigby, Treas.

Established in 1969 in OH.
Donors: James M. Cox, Jr.†; Cox Enterprises, Inc.
Foundation type: Independent foundation.
Financial data (yr. ended 12/31/12): Assets, $102,228,740 (M); gifts received, $8,187,768; expenditures, $2,767,342; qualifying distributions, $2,262,500; giving activities include $2,262,500 for 35 grants (high: $1,000,000; low: $2,500).
Purpose and activities: Giving primarily for conservation, environment and education.
Fields of interest: Higher education; Education; Environment, natural resources; Environment, beautification programs.
Type of support: Capital campaigns; Building/renovation; Program development.
Limitations: Applications not accepted.
Application information: Unsolicited requests for funds not accepted.
Officers and Trustees:* James C. Kennedy,* Chair.; Blair Parry-Okeden,* Pres.; Jimmy W. Hayes,* V.P.; Shauna Sullivan Muhl, Secy.; Nancy K. Rigby, Treas.
EIN: 237256190

917
The Tull Charitable Foundation
191 Peachtree St. N.E., Ste. 3950
Atlanta, GA **30303-1740** (404) 659-7079
Contact: Barbara Cleveland, Secy.-Treas and Exec. Dir.
E-mail: bobbi@tullfoundation.org; Main URL: http://www.tullfoundation.org

Trust established in 1952 in GA as The J.M. Tull Foundation; reorganized under current name in 1984 with the Tull Charitable Foundation.
Donors: J.M. Tull†; J.M. Tull Metal and Supply Co., Inc.
Foundation type: Independent foundation.
Financial data (yr. ended 12/31/12): Assets, $78,147,846 (M); expenditures, $3,651,365; qualifying distributions, $3,150,398; giving activities include $2,410,000 for 59 grants (high: $200,000; low: $1,000; average: $10,000–$100,000).
Purpose and activities: Giving to assist Georgia nonprofit organizations with one-time capital costs associated with the implementation of strategic growth initiatives.
Fields of interest: Museums; Performing arts; Arts; Secondary school/education; Higher education;

Education; Environment; Health care; Housing/shelter, development; Youth development; Human services; Children/youth, services; Residential/custodial care; Homeless, human services; Children/youth; Youth; Economically disadvantaged; Homeless.
Type of support: Capital campaigns; Building/renovation.
Limitations: Applications accepted. Giving limited to organizations based in and serving GA. No support for government agencies, churches, projects of religious organizations that primarily benefit their own adherents, PTAs or Booster Clubs. No grants to individuals or for conferences or seminars; scientific research, purchase of tickets to benefit events; sponsorship of performances; program or project support; operating support; to retire accumulated debt; or for scholarships (except for scholarship endowments); no loans.
Publications: Informational brochure (including application guidelines).
Application information: The foundation does not accept grant proposals via e-mail. Application form not required.
Initial approach: Letter of intent
Copies of proposal: 1
***Deadline(s):* None for letters of intent; see foundation web site for current proposal deadlines**
Board meeting date(s): Jan., Apr., July, and Oct.
Final notification: 1 week after board meeting, in writing
Officers and Trustees:* Larry L. Prince,* Chair.; Warren Y. Jobe,* Vice-Chair.; Barbara Cleveland, Secy.-Treas. and Exec. Dir.; Clair (Yum) Arnold; Sylvia Dick; Lillian C. Giornelli; Jack Guynn; B. Harvey Hill, Jr.
Agent: SunTrust Bank.
Number of staff: 1 full-time professional; 1 full-time support.
EIN: 581687028

918
The University Financing Foundation, Inc.
(formerly Georgia Scientific and Technical Research Foundation)
3333 Busbee Dr., Ste. 150
Kennesaw, GA 30144-3089 (404) 214-9440
Contact: Thomas H. Hall III, Pres.
FAX: (404) 214-9441; E-mail: tuff@tuff.org; Main URL: http://www.tuff.org
Blog: http://www.tuff.org/news/
E-Newsletter: http://www.tuff.org/newsletter

Classified as a private operating foundation in 1989.
Donor: Florida Institute of Technology.
Foundation type: Operating foundation.
Financial data (yr. ended 12/31/12): Assets, $444,185,932 (M); expenditures, $38,310,054; qualifying distributions, $12,982,601; giving activities include $199,650 for 17 grants (high: $92,500; low: $1,000), $19,750 for 21 employee matching gifts, $12,515,085 for foundation-administered programs and $467,516 for loans/program-related investments.
Purpose and activities: Giving primarily to institutions of education and research, and assists such institutions in the planning, development, and financing of facilities and equipment.
Fields of interest: Higher education; Public policy, research.
Type of support: Building/renovation; Equipment; Program-related investments/loans.
Limitations: Giving primarily in Atlanta, GA.
Application information: Very limited outright grants or gifts awarded. Application form not required.
Initial approach: Letter, telephone or fax
Deadline(s): None
Officers and Directors:* Thomas Ventulett,* Chair.; Thomas H. Hall III,* C.E.O. and Pres.; Kevin Byrne, C.O.O. and V.P.; John E. Aderhold, Dir. Emeritus; James M. Sibley, Dir. Emeritus; Lisa A. Beall, Cont.; David M. McKenney; A.J. Robinson.
EIN: 581505902

919
Shirley and Billy Weir Scholarship Foundation Trust
7804 Eagles Landing Ct.
Columbus, GA 31909-2028 (706) 573-2255
Contact: Mike McCollum, Tr.
E-mail: mmccollum@weir-foundation.org; **Additional e-mail: mcgolf@knology.net**; Main URL: http://www.weir-foundation.org/
Grants List: http://www.weir-foundation.org/recipients.html

Established in 2006 in GA.
Donors: Billy Weir‡; Shirley Weir.
Foundation type: Independent foundation.
Financial data (yr. ended 12/31/12): Assets, $1,553,855 (M); expenditures, $170,456; qualifying distributions, $170,456; giving activities include $145,275 for 10 grants to individuals (high: $43,856; low: $268).
Purpose and activities: Scholarship awards to employees or children of employees of golf course facilities located within the state of Georgia served by golf professionals who are members of the Georgia section of the PGA America.
Fields of interest: Higher education.
Type of support: Employee-related scholarships.
Limitations: Applications accepted. Giving limited to residents of GA.
Publications: Application guidelines.
Application information: See foundation web site for complete application guidelines. Application must include golf course affiliation, general education and college admission information, financial need, recommendations, and a personal essay that describes career objectives. Application form required.
Initial approach: Use application on foundation web site
Deadline(s): See foundation web site for current deadlines
Trustees: Michael McCollum; Stephen Sims; Synovus Trust Company, N.A.
EIN: 597257621

920
James M. & Ruth E. Wilder Foundation
171 17th St. N.W., Ste. 2100
Atlanta, GA 30363-1031

Established in 1982 in GA.
Donor: Ruth E. Wilder.
Foundation type: Independent foundation.
Financial data (yr. ended 12/31/12): Assets, $1,332,760 (M); expenditures, $186,985; qualifying distributions, $110,500; giving activities include $110,500 for 37 grants (high: $7,000; low: $500).
Fields of interest: Human services; Children/youth, services; Christian agencies & churches.
Limitations: Applications not accepted. Giving primarily in GA, with some emphasis on Atlanta. No grants to individuals.
Application information: Contributes only to pre-selected organizations.
Board Members: Marc Peterzell; William Wilder.
EIN: 581486417
Other changes: The grantmaker has changed its fiscal year-end from May 31 to Dec. 31.

921
WinShape Foundation, Inc.
(formerly WinShape Centre, Inc.)
5200 Buffington Rd.
Atlanta, GA 30349-2998
FAX: (706) 238-7742;
E-mail: rskelton@winshape.org; Additional address: P.O. Box 490009, Mt. Berry, GA 30149-0009, tel.: (877) 977-3873, e-mail: info@winshape.org; Main URL: http://www.winshape.org
Scholarship application address: c/o Berry College, P.O. Box 490159, Mt. Berry, GA 30149-0009, tel.: (706) 236-2215, e-mail: admissions@berry.edu, collegeprogram@winshape.org

Established as a company-sponsored operating foundation in 1984 in GA.
Donors: Chick-fil-A, Inc.; S. Truett Cathy; CFA Properties, Inc.
Foundation type: Operating foundation.
Financial data (yr. ended 12/31/12): Assets, $71,523,969 (M); gifts received, $20,973,966; expenditures, $26,372,699; qualifying distributions, $17,165,351; giving activities include $569,547 for 2 grants (high: $507,547; low: $62,000), and $20,519,733 for 4 foundation-administered programs.
Purpose and activities: The foundation supports programs involved with education, children and youth, families, marriage enrichment, and religion; also awards college scholarships to undergraduate students attending Berry College.
Fields of interest: Child development, education; Secondary school/education; Education; Youth development; Children/youth, services; Child development, services; Family services; Christian agencies & churches; Religion; Children/youth; Children.
Type of support: Continuing support; Scholarships—to individuals.
Limitations: Applications accepted. Giving primarily in GA.
Publications: Application guidelines; Informational brochure (including application guidelines).
Application information: Unsolicited requests accepted only for scholarship program. An interview may be required for scholarships. Scholarship applicants must apply to the WinShape College Program and to Berry College. Application form required.
Initial approach: Complete online application form or contact foundation for application form for scholarships
Deadline(s): Feb. 1 for scholarships
Board meeting date(s): Varies
Final notification: Apr. 15 for scholarships
Officers and Directors: S. Truett Cathy, Pres.; Donald M. Cathy, V.P.; **John W. White, III, V.P.**; James B. McCabe, Secy.-Treas.; Robert M. Skelton, Exec. Dir.; **Brett Whorton**.
Number of staff: 62 full-time professional.
EIN: 581595471

922
J. W. & Ethel I. Woodruff Foundation, Inc.
c/o J. Barnett Woodruff
P.O. Box 750
Columbus, GA 31902-0750

Established in 1960 in GA.
Donors: Ethel I. Woodruff; James W. Woodruff; J. Barnett Woodruff; members of the Woodruff family.
Foundation type: Independent foundation.
Financial data (yr. ended 07/31/13): Assets, $31,660,411 (M); expenditures, $1,538,535; qualifying distributions, $1,434,006; giving activities include $1,430,000 for 58 grants (high: $350,000; low: $2,000).
Fields of interest: Performing arts, opera; Arts; Higher education; Education; Health care; Health organizations, association; Boys & girls clubs; Human services; Children/youth, services.
Limitations: Applications not accepted. Giving primarily in GA, with emphasis on Columbus. No grants to individuals; no loans.
Application information: Contributes only to pre-selected organizations.
Officers and Directors:* Katherine F. Woodruff,* Chair. and C.E.O.; Christopher S. Woodruff, Secy.-Treas.; Timothy L. Decamp; Stephen E. Draper; Dina Woodruff; James W. Woodruff III.
EIN: 586049589
Other changes: Katherine F. Woodruff has replaced J. Barnett Woodruff as Chair. and C.E.O.

923
David, Helen, and Marian Woodward Fund
(also known as Marian W. Ottley Trust-Atlanta)
c/o Wells Fargo Bank, N.A.
3280 Peachtree Rd., N.E., Ste. 400, MAC G0141-041
Atlanta, GA 30305-2422 **(888) 234-1999**
Contact: Joyce Yamaato
FAX: (877) 746-5889;
E-mail: grantadministration@wellsfargo.com; Main URL: https://www.wellsfargo.com/privatefoundationgrants/woodward

Established in 1975 in GA.
Donor: Marian W. Ottley‡.
Foundation type: Independent foundation.
Financial data (yr. ended 05/31/13): Assets, $48,680,409 (M); expenditures, $2,501,914; qualifying distributions, $2,164,739; giving activities include $2,080,500 for 46 grants (high: $150,000; low: $7,500).
Fields of interest: Arts; Education; Health organizations; Human services.
Type of support: Capital campaigns; Building/renovation; Equipment.
Limitations: Giving primarily in the metropolitan Atlanta, GA, area. No grants to individuals, or for scholarships or student loans.
Publications: Application guidelines.
Application information: Application form required.
Initial approach: **Use online application form on foundation web site**
Deadline(s): **Apr. 1 and Sept. 1**
Board meeting date(s): **May and Nov.**
Officers and Distribution Committee:* Benjamin T. White,* Chair.; Crawford F. Barnett, Jr., M.D.; **Mike Donnelly**; Florida Huff; Horace Sibley.
Trustee: Wells Fargo Bank, N.A.
Number of staff: 1 full-time professional; 1 full-time support.
EIN: 586222004
Other changes: Joyce Yaamato is no longer a trustee.

HAWAII

924
Alexander & Baldwin Foundation
Honolulu, HI

The foundation terminated.

925
Atherton Family Foundation
c/o Hawaii Community Foundation
827 Fort Street Mall
Honolulu, HI 96813-4317 (808) 537-6333
Contact: Amy Luersen, Dir., Philanthropic Svcs., HCF
FAX: (808) 521-6286;
E-mail: foundations@hcf-hawaii.org; **Toll free tel.: (888) 731-3863 (Hawaii and neighbor islands only); Contact if applicant is not able to submit proposal online: Pam Funai, tel.: (808) 566-5537, e-mail: pfunai@hcf-hawaii.org**; Main URL: http://www.athertonfamilyfoundation.org

Incorporated in 1975 in HI as successor to Juliette M. Atherton Trust established in 1915; F. C. Atherton Trust merged into the foundation in 1976.
Donors: Juliette M. Atherton‡; Frank C. Atherton‡.
Foundation type: Independent foundation.
Financial data (yr. ended 12/31/12): Assets, $92,259,292 (M); expenditures, $5,061,604; qualifying distributions, $4,339,624; giving activities include $3,939,746 for 190 grants (high: $200,000; low: $1,814), and $129,300 for 27 grants to individuals (high: $6,500; low: $500).
Purpose and activities: The foundation is concerned with education, human services, culture and the arts, health, religion, and the environment. Focus also on programs that benefit the people of Hawaii. Scholarships for the postgraduate education of Protestant ministers, Protestant ministers' children for undergraduate study, and for graduate theological education at a Protestant seminary. Foundation staff and grants administration is provided by the Hawaii Community Foundation.
Fields of interest: Humanities; Arts; Theological school/education; Education; Environment; Health care; Health organizations, association; Youth development; Human services; Community/economic development; Protestant agencies & churches.
Type of support: Management development/capacity building; Annual campaigns; Capital campaigns; Building/renovation; Equipment; Program development; Seed money; Curriculum development; Research; Technical assistance; Program evaluation; Scholarships—to individuals; Matching/challenge support.
Limitations: Applications accepted. Giving limited to HI; student aid for HI residents only. **Generally, no support for private foundations, or for lobbying, individual Department of Education schools, or for organizations engaged in fundraising for the purpose of distributing grants to recipients of their own choosing, or to the University of Hawai`i other than an annual grant to the University of Hawai`i Foundation. No grants to individuals (except for scholarships), generally no giving for endowment funds, or for annual operating support or funds for re-granting; no conferences, festivals or one-time events; no loans.**
Publications: Annual report; Financial statement; Grants list.
Application information: Application form required for scholarships and automation grants. See foundation web site for application details. If an organization applies through a fiscal sponsor, the fiscal sponsor must agree that the purpose of the grant is charitable, to monitor the grant project, control the expenditure of grant funds, and ensure compliance with the terms and conditions of the grant. Application form required.
Initial approach: **Applicant must first establish an online account with the Hawaii Community Foundation in order to access the online application at: https://nexus.hawaiicommunityfoundation.org/SSLPage.aspx?pid=330**
Copies of proposal: 1
Deadline(s): Jan. 2, Apr. 1, July 1, and Oct. 1
Board meeting date(s): Mar., June, Sept., and Dec.
Final notification: 2 to 3 months
Officers and Directors:* Judith M. Dawson,* Pres.; Joan H. Rohlfing,* V.P. and Secy.; Frank C. Atherton,* V.P. and Treas.; Patricia R. Giles,* V.P.; Robin S. Midkiff,* V.P.; Paul F. Morgan,* V.P.
Agent: Bank of Hawaii.
EIN: 510175971

926
Fred Baldwin Memorial Foundation
827 Fort Street Mall
Honolulu, HI **96813-4317 (808) 242-6184**
Contact: Amy Luersen
***E-mail:* foundations@hcf-hawaii.org**; Application address: c/o The Hawaii Community Foundation, 1164 Bishop St., Ste. 800, Honolulu, HI 96813, tel.: (808) 537-6333 or toll-free (888) 731-3863 from neighbor islands; e-mail: foundations@hcf-hawaii.org; e-mail for Amy Luersen: aluersen@hcf-hawaii.org; URL: http://www.hawaiicommunityfoundation.org; Main URL: http://www.fredbaldwinfoundation.org
Grants List: http://www.hawaiicommunityfoundation.org/index.php?id=338

Established in 1910 in HI as the Fred Baldwin Memorial Foundation.
Donors: Fred Baldwin‡; and other members of the Baldwin family.
Foundation type: Independent foundation.
Financial data (yr. ended 12/31/13): Assets, $5,638,595 (M); expenditures, $256,504; qualifying distributions, $197,082; giving activities include $159,735 for 28 grants (high: $12,000; low: $2,000).
Purpose and activities: The foundation is interested in supporting projects that will benefit the people of Maui County, HI. The foundation is most interested in health and human services projects. However, the foundation also supports arts and cultural organizations, as well as education and the environment.
Fields of interest: Arts; Education; Environment; Health care; Health organizations, association; Human services; Children/youth, services.
Type of support: Building/renovation; Program development; Seed money.
Limitations: Applications accepted. Giving limited to Maui County, HI. No grants to individuals; no loans or debt service, endowments, funds for re-granting, scholarships, grants to units of government, or activities that have already occurred.
Publications: Application guidelines.
Application information: See Hawaii Community Foundation web site (http://www.hawaiicommunityfoundation.org/privatefoundations) for complete application policies, guidelines and forms. Completed coversheet required with proposal. Application form not required.
Initial approach: Complete 2-page cover sheet. No cover letters, executive summaries, business cards, videos or CDs accepted
Copies of proposal: 1
Deadline(s): Jan. 2 for Apr. meeting and July 2 for Oct. meeting
Board meeting date(s): Apr. and Oct.
Final notification: One month following board meetings
Officers and Trustees:* Kristina E. Lyons,* Pres.; Shaun B. Lyons,* V.P.; **Mary Sanford,* Secy.**; Elizabeth Norcross,* Treas.; **Edward Baldwin**; Jeremy C. Baldwin; **Frances Ort**; Wendy Rice Peterson; Henry F. Rice; Claire C. Sanford.
EIN: 990075264
Other changes: Mary Sanford has replaced John C. Baldwin as Secy.

927
Paul & Irene Buehner - Joan B. Merrill Family Foundation
(formerly Paul & Irene Buehner Foundation)
50 Pu'U Anoano St., No. 11201
Lahaina, HI 96761-1954 (808) 667-6608
***Contact:* Joan B. Merrill, Dir.**

Established in 2007 in UT.
Foundation type: Independent foundation.
Financial data (yr. ended 05/31/13): Assets, $595,876 (M); expenditures, $2,258,456; qualifying distributions, $2,239,212; giving activities include $2,239,212 for 13 grants (high: $585,056; low: $1,000).
Fields of interest: Cancer; Family services; United Ways and Federated Giving Programs.
Limitations: Applications accepted. Giving primarily in CA, ID and UT. No grants to individuals.
Application information: Application form not required.
Initial approach: Letter
Deadline(s): None
Directors: Joan B. Merrill; **Mark B. Merrill**; **Scott B. Merrill.**
EIN: 260272154
Other changes: The grantmaker has moved from UT to HI.
For the fiscal year ended May 31, 2013, the grantmaker paid grants of $2,239,212, a 1290.8% increase over the fiscal 2012 disbursements, $161,000.
Carolyn Buehner, Paul W. Buehner and Kenneth Marsh are no longer directors.

928
James & Abigail Campbell Family Foundation
(formerly James & Abigail Campbell Foundation)
1001 Kamokila Blvd., Ste. 200
Kapolei, HI 96707-2030 (808) 674-3167
Contact: D. Keola Lloyd, Grants Mgr.
FAX: (808) 674-3349;
E-mail: keolal@jamescampbell.com; Main URL: http://www.campbellfamilyfoundation.org

Established in 1980 in HI.
Donor: Members of the Campbell family.
Foundation type: Independent foundation.
Financial data (yr. ended 12/31/12): Assets, $20,183,041 (M); gifts received, $676,432; expenditures, $1,186,519; qualifying distributions,

$912,009; giving activities include $772,426 for 27 grants (high: $150,000; low: $5,000).
Purpose and activities: Giving primarily for: 1) programs that address the challenges of young people; 2) public schools, early childhood education and environmental stewardship; and 3) programs that promote values and the health and welfare of Hawaiians.
Fields of interest: Education; Human services; Children/youth, services.
Type of support: Continuing support; Building/renovation; Equipment; Program development; Seed money; Curriculum development; Scholarship funds.
Limitations: Applications accepted. Giving limited to HI, with emphasis on West Oahu: Ewa/Ewa Beach, Kapolei, Makakilo and the Wai'anae Coast. No support for sectarian or religious programs. No grants to individuals, or for endowments, or highly technical research projects; no loans.
Publications: Annual report; Grants list.
Application information: The foundation considers 1 request per organization per calendar year. Application guidelines available on foundation web site. Application form not required.
Initial approach: Proposal (2-3 pages)
Copies of proposal: 1
Deadline(s): Feb. 1 and Aug. 1
Board meeting date(s): Last working day of Apr. and Oct.
Final notification: 2 weeks after board meeting
Officers and Directors:* Wendy B. Crabb,* Pres.; Alice K. Shingle,* V.P.; Alice F. Guild,* Secy.; Jonathan E. Staub,* Treas.; Richard J. Dahl; Kapi 'Olani K. Marignoli; Dorna M. Robinson; **Juliette K. Sheehan; Cynthia K. Sorenson.**
Number of staff: 2 part-time professional; 1 part-time support.
EIN: 990203078
Other changes: Wendy B. Crabb has replaced Kapi'olani K. Marignoli as Pres. Alice K. Shingle has replaced Wendy B. Crabb as V.P. Alice F. Guild has replaced Jonathan E. Staub as Secy. Jonathan E. Staub has replaced Alice F. Guild as Treas. James K. Campbell is no longer a director.

929
Harold K. L. Castle Foundation

1197 Auloa Rd.
Kailua, HI 96734-4658 (808) 263-7073
Contact: Ann Matsukado, Cont.
FAX: (808) 261-6918;
E-mail: jguerrero@castlefoundation.org; E-mail for Ann Matsukado: amatsukado@castlefoundation.org; Main URL: http://www.castlefoundation.org
Facebook: http://www.facebook.com/pages/Kailua-HI/Harold-KL-Castle-Foundation/56297956988?ref=ts
Foundation Investment Trends: http://www.castlefoundation.org/overall-investment-trends.htm
Grants List: http://www.mcgregorfund.org/html/5_1_grants.htm
Twitter: http://twitter.com/HaroldKLCastle
YouTube: https://www.youtube.com/user/hklcastle

Incorporated in 1962 in HI.
Donors: Harold K.L. Castle†; Mrs. Harold K.L. Castle†.
Foundation type: Independent foundation.
Financial data (yr. ended 12/31/12): Assets, $165,470,137 (M); expenditures, $11,980,744; qualifying distributions, $8,032,561; giving activities include $5,948,273 for 105 grants (high: $750,000; low: $190).
Purpose and activities: As the largest private foundation in the state of Hawaii, the foundation grants approximately $7,000,000 per year to organizations that serve Hawaii. The foundation is currently focusing on three strategic program areas: 1) Public Education Redesign and Enhancement; 2) Near-Shore Marine Resource Conservation; and 3) Windward Oahu.
Fields of interest: Education, management/technical assistance; Education, public policy; Education, reform; Education, public education; Elementary school/education; Elementary/secondary school reform; Education; Environment, public policy; Environment, water resources; Environment; Youth development; Community/economic development.
Type of support: Management development/capacity building; Program development; Seed money; Technical assistance; Program evaluation.
Limitations: Applications accepted. Giving limited to HI with priority given to Windward Oahu. No grants to individuals, or for ongoing operating expenses, endowments, annual fund drives, vehicles, or sponsorships or special events.
Application information: Within one month of receipt of inquiry, the foundation will contact applicant either to invite a full proposal or to inform applicant that the foundation will be unable to consider the request due to a mismatch with current foundation priorities. If applicant does not receive notification within a month after submitting online application, please contact Elizabeth Murph, Grants Mgr., at tel.: (808) 263-7073 or e-mail: bmurph@castlefoundation.org. Additionally, all prospective applicants must submit information explaining the extent to which the proposed project will help the foundation achieve its strategic goals. Application form required.
Initial approach: Submit online inquiry on foundation's web site
Copies of proposal: 1
Deadline(s): None
Board meeting date(s): Bimonthly
Final notification: Within 1 month of scheduled meeting
Officers and Directors:* H. Mitchell D'Olier,* Chair.; Terrence R. George, C.E.O. and Pres.; Carlton K.C. Au, C.F.O., V.P., and Treas.; Ann Matsukado, Cont.; **Dr. Claire L. Asam; Dr. Kittredge A. Baldwin**; Corbett A.K. Kalama; James C. McIntosh; Eric K. Yeaman.
Number of staff: 2 full-time professional; 2 part-time professional; 2 full-time support.
EIN: 996005445
**Other changes: H. Mitchell D'Olier has replaced James C. McIntosh as Chair.
Terrence R. George is now C.E.O. and Pres. .
Carlton K.C. Au is now C.F.O., V.P., and Treas.**

930
Samuel N. and Mary Castle Foundation

Pacific Guardian Ctr., Makai Twr.
733 Bishop St., Ste. 1275
Honolulu, HI 96813-4019 (808) 522-1101
Contact: Alfred L. Castle, Exec. Dir.
FAX: (802) 522-1103;
E-mail: snandmarycastle@hawaii.rr.com; Main URL: http://foundationcenter.org/grantmaker/castle/

Founded as S.N. Castle Memorial Trust in 1894; incorporated as a foundation in 1925 in HI.
Donors: Mary Castle†; Samuel N. Castle†.
Foundation type: Independent foundation.
Financial data (yr. ended 12/31/12): Assets, $42,622,956 (M); expenditures, $2,355,284; qualifying distributions, $2,046,189; giving activities include $1,765,446 for 75 grants.
Purpose and activities: The foundation is committed to providing resources to improve the life of Hawaii's children and families by improving the quality and quantity of early education, K-12, independent schools, and arts and cultural institutions. Preference is given to pre-schools, K-12 independent schools and other organizations which improve the lives of low income children and families.
Fields of interest: Historical activities; Arts; Education, early childhood education; Elementary school/education; Teacher school/education; Child development, services; Children/youth; Children; Economically disadvantaged.
Type of support: Capital campaigns; Building/renovation; Equipment; Program development; Seed money; Curriculum development; Scholarship funds; Technical assistance; Program evaluation; Matching/challenge support.
Limitations: Applications accepted. Giving generally limited to HI. Generally, no support for publicly funded organizations, public and government funded charter schools, or for lobbying organizations. No grants to individuals, or for continuing support; generally, no support for general operating budgets, endowment funds, more than 30 percent of total project cost, projects in which parents and community have not been properly involved in planning and funding, annual campaigns, scholarships, or research; no loans.
Publications: Application guidelines; Annual report; Annual report (including application guidelines); Financial statement; Grants list; Occasional report; Program policy statement.
Application information: Major capital requests of $25,000 or more considered at Dec. meeting only, with preferences given to organizations with which trustees are involved or that trustees have invited to apply. Application form not required.
***Initial approach:* Contact Exec. Dir. by mail, e-mail, telephone or in-person visit prior to submitting a proposal**
Copies of proposal: 2
Deadline(s): Feb. 1, June 1, and Oct. 1
Board meeting date(s): Apr., Aug., and Dec.
Final notification: 2 months
Officers and Trustees:* Dr. Robert G. Peters,* Pres.; Kitt Baldwin,* V.P.; James C. McIntosh,* V.P.; Cynthia Quisenberry,* Secy.; Alfred L. Castle,* Treas. and Exec. Dir.
Number of staff: 1 full-time professional; 1 part-time support.
EIN: 996003321
**Other changes: Dr. Robert G. Peters has replaced Randolph Moore as Pres.
The grantmaker now makes its application guidelines available online.**

931
Hung Wo & Elizabeth Lau Ching Foundation

841 Bishop St., Ste. 940
Honolulu, HI 96813-3910 (808) 521-4961
***Contact:* Han Hsin Ching, V.P.; Han P. Ching, V.P.**

Established around 1963.
Donors: Hung Wo Ching; Elizabeth Lau Ching; Chui Ying Soo Rev Trust Dtd.
Foundation type: Independent foundation.
Financial data (yr. ended 01/31/13): Assets, $5,642,679 (M); gifts received, $1,500; expenditures, $462,545; qualifying distributions, $379,900; giving activities include $364,900 for 40 grants (high: $125,000; low: $200), and $15,000

for 12 grants to individuals (high: $2,500; low: $625).
Fields of interest: Education; Health organizations; Human services.
Type of support: Grants to individuals.
Limitations: Giving primarily in HI.
Application information:
Initial approach: Proposal
Deadline(s): None
Officers and Directors:* Han Hsin Ching,* V.P.; Han Ping Ching,* V.P.; Edric M. Ching,* Secy.; Marie Sakamoto, Treas.; Shelli Mei Li Ching.
EIN: 996008990

932
Cooke Foundation, Ltd.
827 Fort St. Mall
Honolulu, HI 96813-4317 (808) 566-5524
Contact: Amy Luersen
FAX: (808) 521-6286;
E-mail: foundations@hcf-hawaii.org**; Contact if applicant cannot submit proposal online: Terry Savage, tel.: (808) 566-5508, e-mail: tsavage@hcf-hawaii.org; toll-free tel. from neighboring islands: (888) 731-3863, ext. 508**; Main URL: http://www.cookefdn.org

Trust established in 1920 in HI; incorporated in 1971.
Donor: Anna C. Cooke†.
Foundation type: Independent foundation.
Financial data (yr. ended 06/30/13): Assets, $22,040,871 (M); expenditures, $1,415,237; qualifying distributions, $1,228,727; giving activities include $1,070,885 for 65 grants (high: $100,000; low: $4,000).
Purpose and activities: Giving to assure the continuance of, and also to expand and extend all worthy endeavors for the betterment and welfare of the people of Hawaii.
Fields of interest: Humanities; Education; Environment; Health care; Health organizations, association; Human services.
Type of support: Management development/capacity building; Capital campaigns; Building/renovation; Equipment; Program development; Seed money; Technical assistance; Consulting services; Program evaluation; Matching/challenge support.
Limitations: Applications accepted. Giving limited to HI and to organizations serving the people of HI. No support for religious organizations, unless the forebears were involved with them, or to supporting organizations classified under section 509(a)(3). No grants to individuals, or for scholarships, fellowships, general operations, or endowment funds; no loans.
Publications: Application guidelines; Annual report (including application guidelines); Financial statement; Grants list.
Application information: Applicants must first establish an online account with the Hawaii Community Foundation to access the online application. If the applicant is requesting an account for the first time, it may take two to three days to receive the account information. It is recommended to request an account early enough in order to allow adequate time to complete the application by the submission deadline. Applicants must be in existence for 5 years and be in stable financial condition. Applications from a unit of the University of Hawai'i must be submitted through the University of Hawai'i Foundation. Requests for more than $20,000 must be sponsored by a trustee. Requests for more than $5,000 should demonstrate that the Cooke Foundation portion of the budget does not exceed 30 percent of the total project budget. Application form required.
***Initial approach:* Use online application process on foundation web site**
Copies of proposal: 1
***Deadline(s):* See foundation web site for current deadlines**
Board meeting date(s): May and Nov.
Final notification: Early June for Mar. submissions, and early Dec. for Sept. submissions
Officers and Trustees:* Dale S. Bachman,* Pres.; Caroline Bond Davis,* V.P. and Secy.; Charles C. Spalding, Jr.,* V.P. and Treas.; Catherine Cooke,* V.P.; Lissa Dunford,* V.P.; Lynne Johnson,* V.P.
EIN: 237120804
Other changes: The grantmaker now publishes application guidelines.

933
Hawaii Community Foundation
(formerly The Hawaiian Foundation)
827 Fort St. Mall
Honolulu, HI 96813 (808) 537-6333
Contact: Kelvin H. Taketa, C.E.O.
FAX: (808) 521-6286; E-mail: info@hcf-hawaii.org; Additional tel.: (888) 731-3863; Main URL: http://www.hawaiicommunityfoundation.org
Facebook: http://www.facebook.com/pages/Hawaii-Community-Foundation/31768973510
Flickr: http://www.flickr.com/photos/hcfhawaii
GiveSmart: http://www.givesmart.org/Stories/Donors/Kelvin-Taketa
LinkedIn: http://www.linkedin.com/in/hcfhawaii
Twitter: http://twitter.com/hcfhawaii
YouTube: http://www.youtube.com/hcfhawaii
Scholarship inquiry e-mail: scholarships@hcf-hawaii.org

Established in 1916 in HI by trust resolution; incorporated in 1987; reorganized in 1988.
Foundation type: Community foundation.
Financial data (yr. ended 12/31/12): Assets, $426,636,217 (M); gifts received, $23,901,041; expenditures, $37,161,178; giving activities include $25,843,999 for 462+ grants (high: $1,477,422), and $1,517,980 for 1,431 grants to individuals.
Purpose and activities: The foundation helps people make a difference by inspiring the spirit of giving and by investing in people and solutions to benefit every island community.
Fields of interest: Historic preservation/historical societies; Arts; Adult/continuing education; Education, reading; Education; Environment, natural resources; Environmental education; Environment; Health care; Mental health, treatment; Medical research, institute; Residential/custodial care; Aging, centers/services; Human services; Nonprofit management; Community/economic development; Leadership development; Aging; Economically disadvantaged.
Type of support: Travel awards; Management development/capacity building; Program development; Scholarship funds; Research; Technical assistance; Consulting services; Scholarships—to individuals.
Limitations: Applications accepted. Giving limited to HI. No grants to individuals (except for scholarships), or for annual campaigns, emergency support, endowments, major capital projects, ongoing operating support, tuition aid programs, or deficit financing; no loans.
Publications: Application guidelines; Annual report; Financial statement; Informational brochure; Newsletter; Program policy statement.
Application information: Application procedures vary with the foundation's different grantmaking programs. Visit foundation web site for application instructions, application forms, and specific deadlines. Application form required.
Initial approach: Contact foundation
Copies of proposal: 1
Deadline(s): Varies
Board meeting date(s): Varies
Final notification: Within 3 months of proposal deadline
Officers and Board Members:* Paul Kosasa,* Chair.; Deborah Berger,* Vice-Chair.; Kelvin H. Taketa, C.E.O. and Pres.; Wally Chin, V.P. and C.F.O.; Tom Kelly, V.P., Knowledge, Evaluation and Learning; Joseph Martyak, V.P., Comms.; **Tammi Chun, V.P., Progs.**; Curtis Saiki, V.P., Philanthropy and Genl. Counsel; Myles Shibata, V.P., Mktg. Initiatives; Chris van Bergeijk, V.P. and C.O.O.; Gary Caulfield,* Secy.; Cathy Luke,* Treas.; Robert R. Bean; Mary G.F. Bitterman; Michael Broderick; Kimberly W. Dey; Elizabeth Rice Grossman; Richard W. Gushman II; Robert S. Harrison; Dorothy "Honey Bun" Haynes; Peter Ho; Tyrie Lee Jenkins; Micah A. Kane; Katherine G. Richardson; Jennifer Goto Sabas; Barry K. Taniguchi; James Wei; Eric K. Yeaman.
Number of staff: 39 full-time professional; 3 part-time professional; 12 full-time support; 1 part-time support.
EIN: 990261283
Other changes: Myles Shibata is now V.P., Mktg. Initiatives. Jessica Calilao is no longer Cont. Forest Frizzell is no longer C.I.O. Micah A. Kane and Colbert Matsumoto is no longer board members.

934
Hawaiian Electric Industries Charitable Foundation
(also known as H.E.I. Charitable Foundation)
P.O. Box 730
Honolulu, HI 96808-0730 **(808) 543-7960**
Contact: Denise Tanaka
FAX: (808) 203-1390; E-mail: heicf@hei.com**; Main URL: http://www.hei.com/phoenix.zhtml?c=101675&p=charitable-foundation**

Established in 1984 in HI.
Donor: Hawaiian Electric Industries, Inc.
Foundation type: Company-sponsored foundation.
Financial data (yr. ended 12/31/12): Assets, $2,573,271 (M); expenditures, $1,653,393; qualifying distributions, $1,575,958; giving activities include $1,539,164 for 68 grants (high: $440,000; low: -$10,000), and $36,794 for 1 employee matching gift.
Purpose and activities: The foundation supports programs designed to promote educational excellence, economic growth, and environmental sustainability.
Fields of interest: Education; Environment; Family services; Community/economic development.
Type of support: Employee volunteer services; General/operating support; Continuing support; Capital campaigns; Program development; Employee matching gifts.
Limitations: Applications accepted. Giving limited to HI. No support for political, religious, veterans', fraternal, or labor organizations. No grants to individuals or for advertising, dinners, or tournaments.
Publications: Application guidelines; Annual report.
Application information: Support is limited to 1 contribution per organization during any given year. Organizations receiving support are asked to submit a final report. Application form required.

Initial approach: Download application form and mail proposal and application form to foundation
Copies of proposal: 1
Deadline(s): Jan. 1, Apr. 1, July 1, and Oct. 1
Board meeting date(s): Quarterly
Officers and Directors:* Alan Oshima,* Chair.; Constance H. Lau,* Pres.; James A. Ajello, V.P., Finance and Treas.; Chester A. Richardson,* Secy.; Richard M. Rosenblum; Richard F. Wacker; Jeffrey N. Watanabe.
Number of staff: 1 full-time professional; 1 full-time support.
EIN: 990230697

935
The Kahiau Foundation
2969 Kalakaua Ave., Ste. 1101
Honolulu, HI 96815-4626

Established in 2005 in CA.
Donors: David Eckles; Allene Wong.
Foundation type: Independent foundation.
Financial data (yr. ended 12/31/12): Assets, $3,291,542 (M); expenditures, $372,082; qualifying distributions, $321,446; giving activities include $319,748 for 7 grants (high: $104,748; low: $5,000).
Fields of interest: Arts, cultural/ethnic awareness; Elementary school/education; Foundations (community); Science, formal/general education.
Limitations: Applications not accepted. Giving primarily in HI.
Application information: Contributes only to pre-selected organizations.
Officers: Allene Wong, Chair. and Pres.; Colleen Wong, Secy.
Directors: Morgan Eckles; Zachary Kau.
EIN: 050629872
Other changes: The grantmaker has moved from CA to HI.
Allene Wong has replaced David Eckles as Chair. and Pres.

936
Kaneta Foundation
(formerly Kaneta Charitable Foundation)
827 Fort Street Mall
Honolulu, HI 96813-4317 **(808) 566-5550**
Contact: Lester Kaneta, Pres.; Amy Luersen, Dir. Phil. Svcs.
FAX: (808) 521-6286;
E-mail: info@kanetafoundation.org; Main URL: http://kanetafoundation.org
Grants List: http://www.kanetafoundation.org/grants/

Established in 1999 in HI.
Donors: Lester Kaneta; Marian Kaneta; JII Capital, Inc.
Foundation type: Independent foundation.
Financial data (yr. ended 12/31/12): Assets, $3,772,109 (M); expenditures, $387,715; qualifying distributions, $310,127; giving activities include $128,627 for 4 grants (high: $103,627; low: $10,000), and $181,500 for grants to individuals.
Purpose and activities: Giving primarily for human services, community development, religion and spiritual development, and youth development; funding also for scholarships to graduating Christian high school seniors who are residents of HI.
Fields of interest: Education; Youth development; Human services; Christian agencies & churches.
Type of support: General/operating support; Income development; Annual campaigns; Program development; Scholarships—to individuals.
Limitations: Applications not accepted. Giving primarily in HI and NV. No support for political organizations.
Application information: Unsolicited requests for funds not accepted.
Board meeting date(s): Apr. 15
Officers: Lester Kaneta, Pres. and V.P.; Marian Kaneta, Secy.-Treas.
EIN: 311655882

937
The Makana Aloha Foundation
P.O. Box 342190
Kailua, HI 96734-8998 (808) 683-8363
Contact: Jami Lynn Burks, Pres.
E-mail: makanaalohafoundation@gmail.com; Main URL: http://makanaalohafoundation.org

Established in 2008 in CA.
Donors: Gunars E. Valkirs; Jorene Valkirs.
Foundation type: Independent foundation.
Financial data (yr. ended 03/31/12): Assets, $6,561,017 (M); expenditures, $374,524; qualifying distributions, $321,475; giving activities include $277,195 for 16 grants (high: $52,000; low: $3,000).
Purpose and activities: Giving primarily for education, health, and human services.
Fields of interest: Higher education; Education; Health care; Human services.
Limitations: Giving primarily in CA and HI.
Application information: Application form required.
Initial approach: Letter requesting application form
Deadline(s): None
Officers: Jami Lynn Burks, Pres. and Secy.; Gunars E. Valkirs, V.P.
Director: JoRene Valkirs.
EIN: 208877756
Other changes: The grantmaker has moved from CA to HI.

938
McInerny Foundation
c/o Bank of Hawaii, Fdn. Admin.
P.O. Box 3170
Honolulu, HI 96802-3170
Contact: Paula Boyce, Asst. V.P.
FAX: (808) 694-4006;
E-mail: paula.boyce@boh.com; Additional contact: Elaine Moniz, Trust Specialist, tel.: (808) 694-4944, fax: (808) 694-4006, e-mail: elaine.moniz@boh.com; Toll-free tel. from neighbor islands: 1 (800) 272-7262; Main URL: https://www.boh.com/apps/foundations/FoundationDetails.aspx?foundation=7&show=0

Trust established in 1937 in HI.
Donors: William H. McInerny‡; James D. McInerny‡; Ella McInerny‡.
Foundation type: Independent foundation.
Financial data (yr. ended 09/30/12): Assets, $69,880,787 (M); expenditures, $4,720,478; qualifying distributions, $3,556,318; giving activities include $3,353,550 for 89 grants (high: $275,000; low: $2,500).
Purpose and activities: Giving primarily for arts and culture, community, education, the environment, health, and human services.
Fields of interest: Arts; Education; Environment; Health care; Health organizations, association; AIDS; Human services; Youth, services.
Type of support: General/operating support; Continuing support; Capital campaigns; Building/renovation; Equipment; Program development; Seed money; Scholarship funds; Matching/challenge support.
Limitations: Applications accepted. Giving limited to HI. No support for religious institutions. **No grants to individuals, or for endowment funds, deficit financing, the purchase of real estate, or research; no loans.**
Publications: Application guidelines; Grants list; Occasional report (including application guidelines).
Application information: Application guidelines with specific instructions and cover sheet available on foundation web site. Application form required.
Initial approach: Proposal (3 pages maximum) with cover sheet
Copies of proposal: 7
Deadline(s): None
Board meeting date(s): Distribution Committee generally meets monthly
Final notification: 3-4 months
Officers and Distribution Committee:* Peter Ho,* Chair.; Thurston Twigg-Smith, Vice-Chair.; Paula Boyce, Grants Admin. Off.; Mrs. Gerry Ching.
Trustee: Bank of Hawaii.
EIN: 996002356

939
Watumull Foundation
c/o Business Advisory Svcs.
7192 Kalanianaole Hwy., Ste. A143A-190
Honolulu, HI 96825

Established in 1942 in MI.
Donors: G.J. Watumull; E. Watumull.
Foundation type: Independent foundation.
Financial data (yr. ended 06/30/12): Assets, $25,688 (M); expenditures, $1,318; qualifying distributions, $0.
Purpose and activities: Giving primarily for rural development in India; some support also for education and culture in Hawaii.
Fields of interest: Arts; Education; Human services; International development; Rural development.
International interests: India.
Type of support: Endowments; Emergency funds.
Limitations: Applications not accepted. Giving on an international basis, with emphasis in India; giving also in HI. No grants to individuals, or for scholarships or travel grants.
Application information: Unsolicited requests for funds not accepted.
Officers: Rann J. Watumull, Pres. and Treas.; Gina Watumull, Secy.
Director: Bluebell Standal.
EIN: 990080681
Other changes: Rann J. Watumull has replaced Lila Watumull Sahney as Pres. and Treas. Gina Watumull has replaced Rann Watumull as Secy.

940
Hans and Clara Davis Zimmerman Foundation
c/o Bank of Hawaii, No. 758
P.O. Box 3170
Honolulu, HI 96802-3170
For scholarship information contact Hawai'i Community Foundation at scholarships@hcf-hawaii.org or tel.: 1-(808)

566-5570 (or toll-free from neighbor islands 1-(888) 731-3863)

Established in 1963 in HI.
Donors: Hans Zimmerman†; Clara Zimmerman†.
Foundation type: Independent foundation.
Financial data (yr. ended 12/31/12): Assets, $13,613,978 (M); expenditures, $799,948; qualifying distributions, $661,753; giving activities include $568,650 for 199 grants to individuals (high: $10,000; low: $1,000).
Purpose and activities: Giving for scholarships thereby assisting Hawaiian residents to obtain a college education. The foundation allows the Hawai'i Community Foundation's scholarship program to administer its scholarship funds.
Fields of interest: Higher education; Scholarships/financial aid.
Type of support: Scholarships—to individuals.
Limitations: Giving limited to residents of HI.
Application information: Application form required.
Board meeting date(s): May
Trustee: Bank of Hawaii.
EIN: 996006669

IDAHO

941

The Hop & Mae Adams Foundation

P.O. Box 9500
Boise, ID 83707-9500

Foundation type: Independent foundation.
Financial data (yr. ended 03/31/13): Assets, $32,188,910 (M); gifts received, $14,242,850; expenditures, $523,582; qualifying distributions, $3,339,332; giving activities include $127,311 for 7 grants (high: $50,000; low: $3,500), and $3,109,133 for 6 loans/program-related investments (high: $904,684; low: $88,302).
Fields of interest: Education; Youth development; Community/economic development.
Limitations: Applications not accepted. Giving primarily in NV.
Application information: Unsolicited requests for funds not accepted.
Trustees: Edward D. Ahrens; Andrew MacKenzie; Steven G. Neighbors.
EIN: 271393341
Other changes: For fiscal year ended Mar. 31, 2013, the fair market value of the grantmaker's assets was $32,188,910, an 18285.9% increase over the fiscal 2012 value, $175,074.

942

J. A. & Kathryn Albertson Foundation, Inc.

501 Baybrook Ct.
P.O. Box 70002
Boise, ID 83707-0102 (208) 424-2600
Contact: Jamie MacMillian, Exec. Dir.
Main URL: http://www.jkaf.org
Go On Idaho Initiative Facebook: http://www.facebook.com/GoOnIdaho?sk=wall
Go On Idaho Initiative Twitter: http://twitter.com/go_on_idaho
Go On Idaho Initiative YouTube: http://www.youtube.com/user/IdahoGoOn

Established in 1966 in ID.
Donors: J.A. Albertson‡; Kathryn Albertson‡.
Foundation type: Independent foundation.
Financial data (yr. ended 12/31/12): Assets, $650,068,822 (M); gifts received, $53,874,675; expenditures, $34,875,619; qualifying distributions, $29,881,276; giving activities include $28,862,561 for 90 grants (high: $11,173,178; low: $1,000).
Purpose and activities: The vision and mission of the foundation is to discover, develop and expand environments of limitless learning for all Idahoans.
Fields of interest: Elementary/secondary education; Education, early childhood education; Higher education, college (community/junior).
Type of support: Program development; Conferences/seminars; Curriculum development.
Limitations: Applications not accepted. **Giving primarily in ID.** No grants to individuals.
Publications: Annual report; Informational brochure; Newsletter.
Application information: Unsolicited requests for funds not accepted. All giving done through RFPs or invitations to apply. Check web site for current initiatives and programs.
Board meeting date(s): Quarterly
Officers and Directors:* Joseph B. Scott,* Chair.; **Brady Panatopoulos,* C.E.O.; Jamie MacMillian,* Pres.; Brian Naeve,* V.P. and Secy.-Treas.**; Rex Butler, Cont.; **Roger Quarles, Exec. Dir.**; Gary Michael; **Toby Prehn**; Brian Scott; J.L. Scott.
Number of staff: 6 full-time professional; 1 part-time support.
EIN: 826012000
Other changes: Roger Quarles has replaced Jamie MacMillan as Exec. Dir. Brady Panatopoulos has replaced Thomas J. Wilford as C.E.O.
Jamie MacMillian is now Pres. Brian Naeve is now V.P. and Secy.-Treas. Barbara J. Newman is no longer Dir. Emeritus. Tony Scott is no longer Secy.-Treas. and Prog. Developer.

943

Angels Among Us, Inc.

10151 W. River Rock Ln.
Garden City, ID 83714-8088
Contact: Angie Harrison, Pres.
Main URL: http://www.aauinc.org/

Donor: Angie Harrison.
Foundation type: Independent foundation.
Financial data (yr. ended 12/31/12): Assets, $10,752 (M); gifts received, $200,000; expenditures, $200,853; qualifying distributions, $200,853; giving activities include $199,915 for 29 grants (high: $64,571; low: $100), and $381 for 1 grant to an individual.
Fields of interest: Education; Health care; Housing/shelter; Homeless, human services; Human services.
Type of support: Building/renovation.
Publications: Application guidelines.
Application information: Complete application guidelines available on grantmaker web site. Application form required.
Initial approach: See grantmaker web site for application form
Deadline(s): None
Officers and Directors:* Angie Harrison,* Pres.; Kirsten Heffner,* V.P.; Amber Mallett,* Secy.; Sharon Burke,* Treas.; **Teresa Tavelli.**
EIN: 264682140

944

The Caven Foundation

911 E. Winding Creek Way, Ste. 100
Eagle, ID 83616-7053

Established in ID.
Foundation type: Independent foundation.
Financial data (yr. ended 07/31/13): Assets, $145,217 (M); gifts received, $101,605; expenditures, $136,801; qualifying distributions, $135,592; giving activities include $134,671 for 4 grants (high: $114,477; low: $3,000).
Fields of interest: Christian agencies & churches.
Limitations: Applications not accepted. Giving primarily in ID and TN.
Application information: Unsolicited requests for funds not accepted.
Trustees: Jay Caven; Jerry Caven; Mike Caven; Muriel Caven.
EIN: 916475449

945

CHC Foundation

245 N. Placer Ave.
P.O. Box 1644
Idaho Falls, ID 83402-4020 (208) 522-2368
E-mail: info@chcfoundation.net; Main URL: http://www.chcfoundation.net

Established in 1985 in ID.
Foundation type: Independent foundation.
Financial data (yr. ended 12/31/12): Assets, $10,886,052 (M); expenditures, $497,344; qualifying distributions, $399,423; giving activities include $337,161 for 43 grants (high: $38,000; low: $394).
Purpose and activities: The foundation gives priority to innovative and enriching projects which serve the public interest and well-being, and significantly improve the quality of life for the people of the ID region which it serves.
Fields of interest: Arts; Elementary/secondary education; Education; Environment, natural resources; Human services; Children/youth, services; Aging, centers/services; Community/economic development.
Type of support: Capital campaigns; Building/renovation; Equipment; Matching/challenge support.
Limitations: Giving limited to the following 10 counties in eastern ID: Bonneville, Bingham, Butte, Clark, Custer, Fremont, Jefferson, Madison, Lemhi, and Teton. No support for religious organizations, or for lobbying groups, interstate organizations or other charitable foundations, or for projects that deliver basic educational services. No grants to individuals or for operating expenses, trips, workshops, competitions, scholarships, advertising, specialized training, real estate, equipment, machinery, or for annual fund drives.
Publications: Application guidelines; Informational brochure (including application guidelines).
Application information: Application coversheet available on foundation web site. Applications by fax, internet or e-mail, or that include staples, binding, or cover folders are not accepted. Application form required.
Initial approach: Telephone, letter or e-mail to request application forms and information, or refer to foundation web site
Copies of proposal: 6
Deadline(s): See grantmaker web site for proposal deadlines
Board meeting date(s): 1st Wed. of the month
Final notification: 10 weeks
Officers and Directors:* Peggy Sharp,* Pres.; Ron Lechelt, M.D.*, V.P.; Milton F. Adam,* Secy.; Carole Lentz,* Treas.; **Dick Fowler**; Ralph Isom; Scott Lee; Margaret A. Leverett; Leslee Martin; **Alice Pike**; John G. St. Clair.
Number of staff: 1 part-time support.
EIN: 820211282
Other changes: Keith Ormond and Anne S. Voilleque are no longer directors.

946

Laura Moore Cunningham Foundation, Inc.

P.O. Box 1157
Boise, ID 83701-1157
Contact: Harry Bettis, Pres.
E-mail: lmcf_idaho@msn.com; Main URL: http://www.lauramoorecunningham.org

Incorporated in 1964 in ID.
Donors: Harry Bettis; Laura Moore Cunningham‡; Doreen Moore‡; Anna Parsons‡.
Foundation type: Independent foundation.
Financial data (yr. ended 08/31/13): Assets, $103,685,169 (M); gifts received, $110,000; expenditures, $4,188,646; qualifying distributions, $4,113,828; giving activities include $4,102,985 for 63 grants (high: $500,004; low: $1,000).
Purpose and activities: Emphasis on higher and other education, particularly for scholarship funds;

support also for hospitals, child welfare, and educational programs.
Fields of interest: Arts; Higher education; Health care; Human services; Children/youth, services; Children/youth; Economically disadvantaged.
Type of support: General/operating support; Building/renovation; Equipment; Endowments; Program development; Seed money; Scholarship funds.
Limitations: Applications accepted. Giving limited to ID. No grants to individuals.
Publications: Informational brochure (including application guidelines).
Application information: The foundation only accepts unsolicited grant applications from tax-exempt organizations within the State of ID. Unsolicited applications from outside ID, from individuals, or from organizations not providing proof of current tax exempt status will not be reviewed or acknowledged. Application form required.
Initial approach: Request application via e-mail
Copies of proposal: 2
Deadline(s): May 15
Board meeting date(s): Summer
Final notification: By Aug. 31
Officers: Harry L. Bettis, Pres. and Treas.; Janelle A. Wise, V.P.; Laura MacGregor Bettis, Secy.
Number of staff: None.
EIN: 826008294

947
Equinox Foundation, Inc.

(formerly Fenton Family Foundation, Inc.)
P.O. Box 2021
Sandpoint, ID 83864-2021
***E-mail:* info@theequinoxfoundation.org; Main URL: http://theequinoxfoundation.org/**

Established in 2006 in ID as Fenton Family Foundation, Inc.; 2008 name changed to Equinox Foundation, Inc.
Donors: Joyce R. Fenton; Steven Fenton.
Foundation type: Independent foundation.
Financial data (yr. ended 12/31/13): Assets, $6,349,774 (M); expenditures, $304,407; qualifying distributions, $273,590; giving activities include $271,500 for 4 grants (high: $220,000; low: $1,500).
Purpose and activities: The foundation partners with the Inland Northwest Community Foundation to provide a grant program for the benefit of the communities in Bonner and Boundary counties of North Idaho.
Fields of interest: Environment; Youth development.
Limitations: Applications accepted. Giving primarily in Boundary and Bonner counties, ID. No grants to individuals.
Application information: To learn more about applying for a grant, visit the web site of the Inland Northwest Community Foundation: http://www.inwcf.org.
Officers: Julie R. Kubiak, Pres.; Susan L. Kubiak, V.P. and Treas.; J. Ted Diehl, Secy.
Directors: Mark S. Kubiak; Steve Meyer.
EIN: 203751438

948
Idaho Community Foundation

210 W. State St.
Boise, ID 83702-6052 (208) 342-3535
Contact: Holly Motes, Cont.
FAX: (208) 342-3577; E-mail: info@idcomfdn.org; Additional tel.: (800) 657-5357; Additional E-mail: hmotes@idcomfdn.org; Grant inquiry E-mail: grants@idcomfdn.org; Main URL: http://www.idcomfdn.org
Facebook: http://www.facebook.com/pages/Idaho-Community-Foundation/261769331685?ref=ts
Twitter: http://twitter.com/idahocf
YouTube: http://www.youtube.com/user/IDCommFoundation

Incorporated in 1988 in ID.
Foundation type: Community foundation.
Financial data (yr. ended 12/31/12): Assets, $94,957,136 (M); gifts received, $6,138,115; expenditures, $7,628,377; giving activities include $5,652,871 for grants, and $1,016,932 for 371 grants to individuals (high: $6,895; low: $250).
Purpose and activities: The mission of the foundation is to enrich the quality of life throughout ID.
Fields of interest: Humanities; Arts; Libraries/library science; Education; Environment; Animals/wildlife; Health care; Recreation; Human services, emergency aid; Human services; Community development, neighborhood development.
Type of support: General/operating support; Continuing support; Management development/capacity building; Building/renovation; Equipment; Emergency funds; Program development; Seed money; Curriculum development; Scholarship funds; Matching/challenge support.
Limitations: Applications accepted. Giving primarily in ID. No support for religious purposes, or organizations typically funded by the government, or national organizations, unless monies expended are for sole benefit of ID citizens. No grants to individuals (except for scholarships), or for debt reduction, fundraising projects, travel, conferences or seminars, or endowments.
Publications: Application guidelines; Annual report; Financial statement; Grants list; Informational brochure (including application guidelines); Newsletter; Program policy statement.
Application information: Visit foundation web site for application and guidelines. Application form required.
Initial approach: Complete online grant application
Copies of proposal: 1
Deadline(s): Jan. 15 for northern region, Apr. 1 for eastern region, and July 1 for southwestern region
Board meeting date(s): Feb., May, Aug., and Nov.
Final notification: May for northern region; Aug. for eastern region; Nov. for southwestern region
Officers and Directors:* Mike McBride,* Chair.; Mary Lynn Hartwell,* Vice-Chair.; Bob Hoover,* C.E.O. and Pres.; Bill Berg,* Secy.; Greg Braun,* Treas.; Holly Motes, Cont.; Bill Allen; Steve Carr; Trent Clark; Gerard Connelly; Frances Ellsworth; Jean Elsaesser; Shannon E.H. Erstad; Sandra L. S. Fery; C. K. Haun; C. Timothy Hopkins; Dr. Ellen Jaeger; Dan Klocko; Tena Lokken; Mike Martin; Joe Marshall; Debbie McDonald; Mark Nye; Art Rammell; Brenda Sanford; Denise Smith; Tricia Swartling; Sue Thilo; Alan Van Orden; Marc Wallace; Linda Watkins; Ray Wolfe; Robert J. Yuditsky.
Number of staff: 5 full-time professional; 2 part-time professional; 2 full-time support; 1 part-time support.
EIN: 820425063
Other changes: Debbie McDonald is no longer a director.

949
Jeker Family Trust

199 N. Capitol Blvd., Ste. 502
Boise, ID 83701-5964

Established in 2006 in ID.
Foundation type: Independent foundation.
Financial data (yr. ended 12/31/12): Assets, $15,210,314 (M); expenditures, $1,057,266; qualifying distributions, $794,037; giving activities include $574,805 for 56 grants (high: $85,463; low: $500).
Purpose and activities: Giving primarily for scholarships and higher education, as well as for health, and children, youth and social services.
Fields of interest: Higher education; Health organizations, association; Human services; Children/youth, services.
Type of support: Scholarships—to individuals.
Limitations: Applications not accepted. Giving primarily to residents of ID, with emphasis on Boise, Eagle and Moscow.
Application information: Unsolicited requests for funds not accepted.
Directors: Diane M. Bagley; Catherine Parkinson; Charles Winder.
Trustees: E. Don Copple; Terry Copple.
EIN: 204120889

950
Micron Technology Foundation, Inc.

8000 S. Federal Way, MS 1-407
P.O. Box 6
Boise, ID 83707-0006
***Contact:* Kami Faylor, Community Rels. Mgr.**
E-mail: mtf@micron.com; **E-mail for Micron's K-12 Programs: k-12programs@micron.com**; Main URL: http://www.micron.com/foundation
Micron Students site: http://students.micron.com/
The Micron Bulletin: http://bulletin.micron.com/
Twitter: http://twitter.com/Micron_Giving

Established in 1999 in ID.
Donors: Micron Technology, Inc.; Micron Semiconductor Products, Inc.; Blue Cross of Idaho Health Service, Inc.
Foundation type: Company-sponsored foundation.
Financial data (yr. ended 12/31/12): Assets, $86,805,324 (M); expenditures, $5,756,844; qualifying distributions, $5,192,051; giving activities include $4,340,124 for 328 grants (high: $1,500,000; low: $25).
Purpose and activities: The foundation supports organizations involved with K-12 and higher education. Special emphasis is directed toward programs designed to promote education in the areas of engineering, science, chemistry, mathematics, and computer science.
Fields of interest: Education, research; Elementary/secondary education; Secondary school/education; Higher education; Teacher school/education; Engineering school/education; Education; Science, formal/general education; Chemistry; Mathematics; Engineering/technology; Computer science.
International interests: Italy; Singapore.
Type of support: Continuing support; Program development; Professorships; Curriculum development; Fellowships; Scholarship funds; Research; Employee volunteer services; Sponsorships; Employee matching gifts; Scholarships—to individuals.
Limitations: Applications accepted. Giving limited to areas of company operations in Boise, ID, Manassas, VA, Avezzano, Italy, and Singapore. No support for religious, fraternal, veterans', or political

organizations, discriminatory organizations, pass-through organizations, or private foundations. No grants to individuals (except for scholarships), or for general operating support, luncheons, dinners, auctions, or events, travel or related expenses, courtesy advertisements, endowments, annual campaigns, or lobbying activities.
Publications: Application guidelines.
Application information: University participation in the University Partnerships program is by invitation only. Applications for Chip Camp require a teacher recommendation. Application form required.
Initial approach: Download application form and mail proposal and application form to foundation for Community and K-12 Grants; visit website for Chip Camp
Deadline(s): None for Community and K-12 Grants; Apr. 15 for Chip Camp
Final notification: Monthly
Officers and Directors:* Mark D. Duncan,* Chair.; Kipp A. Bedard,* Pres.; Roderick W. Lewis,* Secy.; Tom L. Laws, Treas.; Dee K. Mooney, Exec. Dir.; Jay L. Hawkins.
Number of staff: 8 full-time professional; 2 part-time professional.
EIN: 820516178

951
Schneidmiller Family Foundation, Inc

1511 N. Chase Rd.
Post Falls, ID 83854-9225 (208) 773-5466
***Contact:* Gladys V. Schneidmiller, Secy.-Treas.**

Established in 2001 in ID.
Donors: Gary T. Schneidmiller; Gladys V. Schneidmiller.
Foundation type: Independent foundation.
Financial data (yr. ended 06/30/13): Assets, $959,740 (M); gifts received, $77,550; expenditures, $122,525; qualifying distributions, $122,067; giving activities include $122,067 for 7 grants (high: $80,367; low: $250).
Fields of interest: Education; Human services; Foundations (community).
Limitations: Applications accepted. Giving primarily in ID, with emphasis on Boise and Pullman and WA. No grants to individuals.
Application information: Application form required.
Initial approach: Letter
Deadline(s): None
Officers: Gary T. Schneidmiller, Pres.; Kevin E. Schneidmiller, V.P.; Gladys V. Schneidmiller, Secy.-Treas.
Director: Raymond R. Bradley, C.P.A.
EIN: 820527600

952
Supervalu Eastern Region Community First Foundation

(formerly The Richfood Foundation)
c/o Corp. Tax Dept. 70428
P.O. Box 20
Boise, ID 83726-0020
***Application address:* Foundation Manager, P.O. Box 26967, Richmond, VA 23261**

Established in 1995 in VA.
Donors: Bunzl Mid Atlantic Region; Creps United Publications; Flowers Foods Bakeries Group; Furr & Associates Sales & Marketing; Hess Brothers Fruit Co, Inc.; Irving Consumer Products; Kraft Foods Global; Masters Gallery Foods, Inc.; Progressive Logistics Services, LLC; Sara Lee; General Mills; Acosta Sales & Marketing; Procter & Gamble Distributing; Kimberly-Clark Corporation; Del Monte.
Foundation type: Independent foundation.
Financial data (yr. ended 04/27/13): Assets, $65,488 (M); expenditures, $54,335; qualifying distributions, $54,335; giving activities include $54,150 for 6 grants (high: $25,000; low: $2,000).
Fields of interest: Arts; Agriculture/food; Human services.
Limitations: Applications accepted. Giving primarily in Richmond, VA. No grants to individuals.
Application information: Application form not required.
Initial approach: Proposal
Deadline(s): None
Officers and Directors:* Kevin L. Kemp,* Pres.; Doyle J. Troyer, V.P.; John F. Boyd, V.P. and Treas.; Tammy R. Moore, Secy.
EIN: 541813921
Other changes: Sherry M. Smith is no longer Exec. V.P.

953
Claude R. and Ethel B. Whittenberger Foundation

P.O. Box 1073
Caldwell, ID 83606-1073 **(208) 459-4649**
Contact: Coralie Weston, Chair.
FAX: (208) 454-0136
Grants List: http://www.whittenberger.org/awardedgrants.html

Established in 1970 in ID; commenced grantmaking activities in 1973.
Donor: Ethel B. Whittenberger†.
Foundation type: Independent foundation.
Financial data (yr. ended 12/31/13): Assets, $5,657,086 (M); expenditures, $216,604; qualifying distributions, $176,918; giving activities include $172,324 for 43 grants (high: $34,475; low: $1,000).
Purpose and activities: The Whittenberger Foundation currently gives priority to innovative and enriching projects which significantly improve the quality of life for children and young people. The foundation's areas of interest relating to children and young people are education, arts and culture, health, social welfare, recreation and the environment.
Fields of interest: Arts; Libraries/library science; Education; Environment; Health care; Recreation; Human services; Children/youth, services; Children/youth; Children; Youth; Young adults.
Type of support: Equipment; Program development; Publication; Seed money; Curriculum development; Scholarship funds.
Limitations: Applications accepted. Giving limited to ID, with emphasis on the southwestern area. No support for political involvement of any kind. No grants to individuals, or for endowment funds, general operating funds, research, individual scholarships, fundraisers, capital campaigns, construction or advertising.
Publications: Application guidelines; Grants list; Multi-year report; Program policy statement.
Application information: No audio or videotapes accepted. Application form required.
Initial approach: Letter requesting application form
Copies of proposal: 8
***Deadline(s):* None**
Board meeting date(s): Apr., July, Oct., and Jan.
Final notification: Second week in Nov.
Officer: Coralie Weston, Chair.
Directors: Elaine Carpenter; Scott Gipson; Michael Groff; **Joe Miller**; **Laura Moylan**; Estella Zamora.
Number of staff: 2 part-time support.
EIN: 237092604
Other changes: The grantmaker no longer lists a URL address or an E-mail address.
Coralie Weston has replaced Dean J. Miller as Chair.
Donald D. Price is no longer director.

ILLINOIS

954
The Clara Abbott Foundation
1175 Tri-State Pkwy., Ste. 200
Gurnee, IL **60031-9141** (800) 972-3859
Contact: Christy Wistar, V.P. and Exec. Dir.
FAX: (847) 938-6511;
E-mail: claraabbottfoundation@abbott.com; **Additional tel.: (847) 937-1090**; Main URL: http://clara.abbott.com

Established in 1940 in IL.
Donors: Clara Abbott‡; Louis B. Kyle; Joseph Miller, Jr.; Mrs. Joseph Miller, Jr.; Marie Wilkinson; Jack Moss Trust for Euluos Moss; Rieker Charitable Remainder Trust; Charles S. Brown; Mrs. Charles S. Brown; Marcia Thomas; John C. Kane; Bernard Semler; Gary P. Coughlan; W. Thomas Brady; Lucilee Heine.
Foundation type: Independent foundation.
Financial data (yr. ended 12/31/12): Assets, $220,498,413 (M); gifts received, $103,560; expenditures, $7,049,286; qualifying distributions, $6,575,135; giving activities include $3,218,096 for grants to individuals.
Purpose and activities: The mission of the foundation is to efficiently and responsibly provide needed assistance to Abbott families worldwide. Grants, loans, financial education and counseling services are made to Abbott Laboratories employees and retirees for financial aid due to financial hardships. Educational grants are made only to dependents of Abbott Laboratories employees (of at least one year) and retirees based on a financial need criteria.
Fields of interest: Education; Human services; Aging; Economically disadvantaged.
Type of support: Continuing support; Emergency funds; Consulting services; Program-related investments/loans; Employee-related scholarships; Grants to individuals; Scholarships—to individuals.
Limitations: Applications accepted. Giving primarily to Abbott Laboratories employees (of at least one year) and retirees worldwide.
Publications: Annual report (including application guidelines); Financial statement; Informational brochure.
Application information: Application and guidelines available on foundation's web site. Application form required.
Deadline(s): Varies
Board meeting date(s): Apr. and Oct.
Final notification: 5 business days of receiving application.
Officers and Directors:* **Stephen R. Fussell,* Pres.**; Christy Wistar, V.P. and Exec. Dir.; **John Tebbets, Treas.**; **Hubert Allen**; Charles M. Brock; William J. Chase; Jaime Contreras; Charles D. Foltz; **Robert Funck**; Jose M. Ibanez; Laurence Kraus; Elaine R. Leavenworth; John F. Lussen; Corlis Murray; D. Stafford O'Kelly; William H. Preece; Robert E. Tweed; Grice E. Williams; Diane Winnard; Valentine Yien; Brian Yoor.
Number of staff: 25 full-time professional; 4 part-time professional; 12 full-time support; 1 part-time support.
EIN: 366069632
Other changes: Stephen R. Fussell has replaced Michael J. Warmuth as Pres. John Tebbets has replaced Rebecca Kinnavy as Treas.
Catherine V. Babington, Stanley R. Flood, Greg W. Linder, Laura J. Schumacher, and Guy R. Wiebking are no longer directors.

955
G.A. Ackermann Memorial Fund
c/o US Trust, Bank of America, N.A.
231 S. LaSalle St., IL1-231-13-32
Chicago, IL 60604-1426 (312) 828-4154
Contact: George Thorn, Market Dir.
E-mail: ilgrantmaking@ustrust.com; **Main URL: https://www.bankofamerica.com/philanthropic/grantmaking.go**

Established in 1937.
Foundation type: Independent foundation.
Financial data (yr. ended 12/31/12): Assets, $23,103,403 (M); expenditures, $533,151; qualifying distributions, $433,920; giving activities include $400,000 for 5 grants (high: $100,000; low: $50,000).
Purpose and activities: Giving to Catholic and Protestant church-affiliated organizations.
Fields of interest: Secondary school/education; Theological school/education; Human services; Salvation Army; Catholic federated giving programs; Protestant federated giving programs; Catholic agencies & churches.
Limitations: Giving limited to organizations that are geographically located within the city limits of New York City, NY or Chicago, IL.
Application information: Application form not required.
Initial approach: Online
Deadline(s): Jan. 15 and June 1
Trustee: Bank of America, N.A.
EIN: 366039158

956
Marjorie C. Adams Charitable Trust
c/o JPMorgan Chase Bank, N.A.
10 S. Dearborn St., 21st Fl.
Chicago, IL 60603-2300
***Application address:* c/o JPMorgan Chase Bank, N.A., Attn.: Frank Lemma, 270 Park Ave., 16th Fl., New York, NY 10017, tel.: (212) 648-1477**

Established in 1987 in NY.
Donor: Marjorie Carr Adams†.
Foundation type: Independent foundation.
Financial data (yr. ended 08/31/12): Assets, $3,617,222 (M); expenditures, $245,829; qualifying distributions, $197,279; giving activities include $184,000 for 1 grant.
Purpose and activities: Giving primarily for care and treatment of deaf and blind people, research into the causes and the treatment of deafness and blindness, and K-12 education.
Fields of interest: Education; Blind/visually impaired; Deaf/hearing impaired.
Type of support: Capital campaigns; Building/renovation; Endowments.
Limitations: Applications accepted. Giving primarily in NY. No grants to individuals; no loans or program-related investments.
Publications: Grants list.
Application information: Application form not required.
Deadline(s): None
Trustee: JPMorgan Chase Bank, N.A.
EIN: 136897539
Other changes: The grantmaker has moved from WI to IL.

957
J.R. Albert Charitable Foundation
55 S. Main St.
Naperville, IL 60540-5372 (630) 335-7098
Contact: Patricia Belly Robb, Pres. and C.E.O.
E-mail: staff@jralbertfoundation.org; Main URL: http://www.jralbertfoundation.org/
Grants List: http://www.jralbertfoundation.org/recent.htm

Foundation type: Independent foundation.
Financial data (yr. ended 12/31/12): Assets, $35,271,218 (M); expenditures, $1,790,194; qualifying distributions, $1,626,092; giving activities include $1,355,600 for 78 grants (high: $100,000; low: $1,000).
Fields of interest: Arts; Education; Health care.
Limitations: Giving primarily in IL, KS, MI, MO, and WI. No support for programs outside of the foundation's geographic area, or for those with political affiliations or for religious organizations' operating expenses. Generally, no grants for conferences, seminars, forums, summits, or think-tanks; no support for museum or art exhibits or for private school tuition.
Application information: As of June 2013, the Board is not accepting unsolicited applications, but has decided to focus on multi-year commitments to several of the foundation's existing grantees. See foundation web site for updates and application guidelines.
Officers and Directors:* B. Joanne Sante,* Chair.; Trish Robb, C.E.O. and Pres.; Carol Deese; Harry Robb; Patty Robb; Sandy Robb; Sue Robb; Mike Sante.
EIN: 260147405

958
Fred & Jean Allegretti Foundation, Inc.
830 W. Rte. 22, Ste. 119
Lake Zurich, IL 60047-2389 (224) 655-6405
Contact: Carol Allegretti, Pres.; Lynn Larson, Fdn. Admin.
FAX: (224) 677-4992;
E-mail: fjallegrettifoundation@gmail.com; **Toll-free tel.: (866) 819-3301**; Main URL: http://allegrettifoundation.org

Established in 1997 in IL.
Donors: Jean Allegretti†; Carol Allegretti; Joseph Zielinski†.
Foundation type: Operating foundation.
Financial data (yr. ended 10/31/12): Assets, $17,743,126 (M); gifts received, $5,398,541; expenditures, $785,523; qualifying distributions, $640,250; giving activities include $640,250 for 61 grants (high: $60,000; low: $3,050).
Purpose and activities: The foundation provides financial support to various domestic charitable organizations that work to improve the lives, minds, health and well being of children, adults, the elderly, animals, those who are physically challenged, and veterans. It is our goal to provide a quality of life and dignity through humanitarian support, medical treatment, housing, education, and the arts.
Fields of interest: Arts; Education; Animals/wildlife, preservation/protection; Health care; Housing/shelter; Human services; Children/youth, services; Residential/custodial care; Military/veterans' organizations; Aging; Military/veterans; Economically disadvantaged.
Type of support: Program development; Advocacy.
Limitations: Applications accepted. Giving primarily in CO, FL, and IL; some funding nationally. **No grants to individuals, or for endowments or international grants.**

Application information: Online application process accessed from foundation web site. Application guidelines available on foundation web site.
Initial approach: Letter of Inquiry—through online application system on foundation web site
***Deadline(s):* For new organizations: May 31 for Letter of Inquiry, July 31 for application. For renewal applications: June 30**
Board meeting date(s): Aug.
Final notification: Varies
Officers: Carol Allegretti, Pres.; Thomas Bucaro, Secy.; James Allegretti, Treas.
Directors: Karen Allegretti; Kim Allegretti.
EIN: 364110761

959
Alphawood Foundation

(formerly WPWR-TV Channel 50 Foundation)
P.O. Box 146340
Chicago, IL 60614-8544 (773) 477-8984
Contact: Agnes Meneses, Prog. Off. and Grants Mgr.
FAX: (773) 477-9019;
E-mail: info@alphawoodfoundation.org; Main URL: http://www.alphawoodfoundation.org/

Established in 1991 in IL.
Donors: Fred Eychaner; Newsweb Corp.
Foundation type: Independent foundation.
Financial data (yr. ended 02/28/13): Assets, $169,408,379 (M); gifts received, $6,883,616; expenditures, $12,356,541; qualifying distributions, $11,788,820; giving activities include $11,349,545 for 208 grants (high: $1,000,000; low: $5,000).
Purpose and activities: The foundation provides general operating support to nonprofit organizations whose primary mission involves the arts, arts education for children, institutional advocacy for social change, domestic violence intervention/prevention, and architecture and historical preservation. Arts education funding is specifically for children only.
Fields of interest: Arts education; Visual arts; Performing arts, dance; Performing arts, theater; Performing arts, music; Performing arts (multimedia); Literature; Historic preservation/historical societies; Arts; Family services, domestic violence.
Type of support: General/operating support.
Limitations: Giving primarily in the metropolitan Chicago, IL, area and northwestern IN. No support for religious or fraternal purposes, political campaigns or for public schools. No grants to individuals, or for scholarships, underwriting or tables for events, capital campaigns, or special projects.
Publications: Program policy statement (including application guidelines).
Application information: New proposals from organizations not currently being funded are by invitation only. Prospective new applications for funding must demonstrate a very strong match between their work and the foundation's priorities and guidelines; in order to be invited to apply contact foundation for more information.
Board meeting date(s): Varies
Officers and Directors:* Fred Eychaner,* Pres. and Treas.; Don Hilliker,* Secy.; Barbara Richardson; **Tom Yoder.**
Number of staff: 2 full-time professional.
EIN: 363805338

960
American Friends of the National Institute for Psychobiology in Israel

5825 S. Dorchester Ave., Ste. 9W
Chicago, IL 60637-1701 **(773) 546-8037**
***FAX:* (773) 834-3562**; Application address: c/o Nipi Scientific Advisory Committee, 5841 S. Maryland Ave., MC 3077, Chicago, IL 60637; Main URL: http://www.afnipi.org/
Grants List: http://www.afnipi.org/grants/byyear/2012

Donors: Charles E. Smith Family Foundation; Morton B. & Blance S. Prince Philanthropic Fund.
Foundation type: Independent foundation.
Financial data (yr. ended 12/31/12): Assets, $9,919 (M); gifts received, $219,360; expenditures, $209,441; qualifying distributions, $209,441; giving activities include $209,426 for 1 grant.
Fields of interest: Education; Jewish agencies & synagogues.
Limitations: Applications accepted. Giving limited to Jerusalem, Israel.
Application information: Application form required.
Initial approach: Letter or E-mail
Deadline(s): 1st year funding Dec. 31, 2nd & 3rd year funding Apr. 30
Officers and Directors:* Elliot S. Gershon,* Pres.; Shaul Hochstein,* Secy.-Treas.; **Lisa Adler Covitz; Orley M. Desser; Vance Liebman; Anita Roe; Leona Z. Rosenberg; David Bruce Smith; Joseph Walder;** and 2 additional directors.
EIN: 900794238

961
Amicus Foundation

98 E. Chicago Ave., Ste. 201
Westmont, IL 60559-1559

Established in 1985 in IL.
Donors: Joan C. Erickson; Peter E. Erickson; Hubbard H. Erickson, Jr.; Peggy Bigelow; Peter H. Erickson; Michael G. Beemer; John Erickson.
Foundation type: Independent foundation.
Financial data (yr. ended 12/31/12): Assets, $16,743,877 (M); expenditures, $1,019,756; qualifying distributions, $900,000; giving activities include $900,000 for grants.
Fields of interest: Human services; Philanthropy/voluntarism.
Limitations: Applications not accepted. Giving primarily in OH, some giving in IL. No grants to individuals.
Application information: Contributes only to pre-selected organizations.
Officers and Directors:* Hubbard H. Erickson, Jr.,* Pres.; Karen E. Cronin, V.P.; Joanne E. Smith, V.P.; Zachary Erickson,* Secy.; Peter H. Erickson,* Treas.; John H. Erickson*; Joan C. Erickson.
EIN: 363378462
Other changes: Hubbard H. Erickson, Jr. has replaced John H. Erickson as Pres. Karen E. Cronin has replaced Joan C. Erickson as V.P. Joanne E. Smith has replaced Peter H. Erickson as V.P. Zachary Erickson has replaced Mary Christine Flannery as Secy. Peter H. Erickson has replaced Hubbard H. Erickson, Jr. as Treas.
Michael G. Beemer and Ernest A. Janus are no longer directors.

962
Paul M. Angell Family Foundation

4140 W. Fullerton Ave.
Chicago, IL 60639-2106 **(773) 628-6980**
***Contact:* Kim Van Horn, Chief Admin. Off.**
***E-mail:* kim@pmangellfamfound.org**; Main URL: http://pmangellfamfound.org
Grants List: http://pmangellfamfound.org/Fall_2013_Grants.html

Donor: Charles T. Angell.
Foundation type: Independent foundation.
Financial data (yr. ended 12/31/13): Assets, $418,155 (M); gifts received, $2,596,149; expenditures, $2,515,532; qualifying distributions, $2,498,884; giving activities include $2,411,500 for 103 grants (high: $150,000; low: $5,000).
Purpose and activities: Giving primarily for: 1) Conservation, particularly the protection of the world's oceans and species. The foundation is interested in site-specific projects designed to improve the health of ocean habitats and to enhance their ability to withstand the challenges of climate change. The foundation also supports efforts to fund species protection, particularly regarding the seas' apex predators. Eligible projects include research, conservation and/or restoration. Grants for other types of water-related conservation efforts may be considered on a limited basis; 2) Performing Arts, primarily classical music and theater; and 3) Social Causes, particularly to support efforts that address the root causes of poverty and inequality, particularly in urban areas. Priority will be given to programs that emphasize evidence-based early intervention and prevention approaches. The foundation seeks to support efforts designed to help alter the life trajectories of socioeconomically disadvantaged individuals and families. Specific areas of interest include early childhood education, teenage pregnancy prevention, school completion for at-risk youth, workforce preparedness, and African-American male achievement. Although not limited exclusively to Chicago, grant making in Social Causes will focus on the Chicago area.
Fields of interest: Museums (natural history); Arts; Environment; Youth development; Community/economic development.
Limitations: Applications accepted. Giving primarily in CA, Washington, DC and IL. **No support for religious institutions. No grants for debt reeducation, fundraising events, or endowments.**
Application information: Applications are by invitation only, upon review of Letter of Inquiry. Application form required.
***Initial approach:* Create an account on the foundation's web site, then use the online Letter of Inquiry process**
***Deadline(s):* See foundation web site for current deadlines**
Officers: Charles T. Angell, Pres.; James S . Angell, Secy.; Michael T. Angell, Treas.
EIN: 274818015

963
Aon Foundation

(formerly Combined International Foundation)
200 East Randolph
Chicago, IL 60601-6419 (312) 381-3555
Contact: Carolyn Barry Frost, Pres. and Treas.
FAX: (312) 381-6166;
E-mail: aon_foundation@aon.com; **Main URL: http://www.aon.com/about-aon/global-citizenship/giving.jsp**

Established in 1984 in IL.

Donor: Aon Corp.
Foundation type: Company-sponsored foundation.
Financial data (yr. ended 12/31/12): Assets, $50,035 (M); gifts received, $10,024,731; expenditures, $9,431,769; qualifying distributions, $9,431,769; giving activities include $9,431,769 for 3,082 grants (high: $500,000; low: $25).
Purpose and activities: The Aon Foundation is the principal vehicle for Aon's philanthropic programs in the U.S. and focuses on empowering people and working with communities at risk. Aon invests in educational programs that make a marked difference in the academic achievement of young people, as well as in organizations that help develop the future workforce.
Fields of interest: Arts; Education; Environment; Disasters, preparedness/services; Youth development; American Red Cross; Human services; Community/economic development; Youth; Disabilities, people with; Minorities; Economically disadvantaged.
Type of support: General/operating support; Program development; Employee volunteer services; Employee matching gifts.
Limitations: Applications not accepted. Giving on a national basis in areas of company operations, with emphasis on Chicago, IL. No support for fraternal, labor, political, religious, or discriminatory organizations. No grants to individuals.
Publications: Corporate giving report.
Application information: Contributes only to pre-selected organizations. The foundation utilizes an invitation only process for giving.
Board meeting date(s): 3 times per year
Officers and Directors: Carolyn Barry Frost, Pres. and Treas.; Ram Padmanabhan, Secy.; Gregory J. Besio; Gregory C. Case; Christa Davies.
Number of staff: 4
EIN: 363337340

964
ArcelorMittal USA Foundation, Inc.
(formerly Mittal Steel USA Foundation, Inc.)
1 S. Dearborn St., 19th Fl.
Chicago, IL **60603-2307**
Contact: William C. Steers, Pres.

Established in 2000 in IN.
Donors: Mittal Steel USA Inc.; ArcelorMittal USA, Inc.
Foundation type: Company-sponsored foundation.
Financial data (yr. ended 12/31/12): Assets, $342,400 (M); gifts received, $1,225,000; expenditures, $1,506,015; qualifying distributions, $1,505,500; giving activities include $1,505,500 for 15 grants (high: $700,000; low: $1,500).
Purpose and activities: The foundation supports organizations involved with education, animal welfare, disaster relief, and to the United Way.
Fields of interest: Education; Animal welfare; Disasters, preparedness/services; United Ways and Federated Giving Programs.
Type of support: Scholarship funds; General/operating support; Program development.
Limitations: Applications accepted. Giving in the U.S., with emphasis on IN and MN.
Application information: Application form required.
***Initial approach:* Proposal**
Deadline(s): None
Officers: William C. Steers, Pres.; Paul Liebenson, Secy.; Martha Gonzalez, Treas.
Directors: Josephine Heil; Gary Lefko; Heather Loebner; Cordell Petz.
EIN: 352121803

965
Bergstrom Inc. Charitable Foundation
10 S. Dearborn, IL1-0117
Chicago, IL 60603 **(815) 394-4655**

Established in 1979.
Donors: Bergstrom Manufacturing Co., Inc.; Bergstrom Climate Systems, Inc.; Bergstrom Inc.
Foundation type: Company-sponsored foundation.
Financial data (yr. ended 04/30/13): Assets, $1,446,442 (M); gifts received, $180,868; expenditures, $360,425; qualifying distributions, $355,988; giving activities include $354,560 for 48 grants (high: $37,500; low: $1,000).
Purpose and activities: The foundation supports history museums, parks, and community foundations and organizations involved with education, health, golf, and human services.
Fields of interest: Education; Health care; Human services.
Type of support: Program development.
Limitations: Applications accepted. Giving primarily in Rockford, IL. No grants to individuals.
Application information: Application form required.
***Initial approach:* Letter**
Deadline(s): None
Trustees: David R. Rydell; JPMorgan Chase Bank, N.A.
EIN: 366692339
Other changes: The grantmaker no longer lists a separate application address. The grantmaker no longer lists a primary contact.

966
Alfred Bersted Foundation
c/o US Trust
231 S. LaSalle St., IL1-231-13-32
Chicago, IL 60697-0001 (312) 828-4154
Contact: Debra Grand, Sr. V.P.
E-mail to discuss application process or for questions: ilgrantmaking@ustrust.com (the name of the foundation must be indicated in subject line); Main URL: http://www.bankofamerica.com/grantmaking

Established in 1972 in IL.
Donor: Alfred Bersted†.
Foundation type: Independent foundation.
Financial data (yr. ended 12/31/13): Assets, $21,945,266 (M); expenditures, $1,110,226; qualifying distributions, $967,258; giving activities include $822,200 for 59 grants (high: $25,000; low: $5,000).
Purpose and activities: The foundation was established in 1972 to support and promote quality educational, human services, and health care programming for underserved populations. It specifically serves the people of DeKalb, DuPage, Kane, and McHenry counties in Illinois.
Fields of interest: Health organizations; Human services; Children/youth, services.
Type of support: General/operating support; Continuing support; Building/renovation; Technical assistance.
Limitations: Applications accepted. Giving limited to DeKalb, DuPage, Kane, and McHenry counties, in IL. No support for religious houses of worship, degree-conferring institutions of higher learning or for organizations that are testing for public safety. No grants to individuals; or for endowment funds exclusively, deficit financing or political campaigns.
Application information: Application form and guidelines available online. Application form required.
Initial approach: Online application
Deadline(s): Apr. 15 and Sept. 15
***Final notification:* June 30 (for the Apr. deadline), and Dec. 15 (for the Sept. deadline)**
Trustee: Bank of America, N.A.
EIN: 366493609

967
Grace Bersted Foundation
c/o U.S. Trust
231 S. LaSalle St., IL1-231-13-32
Chicago, IL 60604
Contact: Debra Grand, Senior V.P.
E-mail: ilgrantmaking@ustrust.com; **Main URL: https://www.bankofamerica.com/philanthropic/grantmaking.go**

Established in 1986 in IL.
Donor: Grace A. Bersted†.
Foundation type: Independent foundation.
Financial data (yr. ended 12/31/12): Assets, $8,574,331 (M); expenditures, $481,998; qualifying distributions, $418,941; giving activities include $372,500 for 28 grants (high: $25,000; low: $5,000).
Purpose and activities: Giving primarily for health care programming for underserved populations. Special consideration is given to charitable organizations that serve the needs of children or the disabled.
Fields of interest: Secondary school/education; Higher education; Environment, natural resources; Health care; Human services; YM/YWCAs & YM/YWHAs; Family services; Foundations (private independent); Children.
Limitations: Applications accepted. Giving limited to DuPage, Kane, Lake, and McHenry counties, IL. No grants to individuals.
Application information: Application form required.
Initial approach: Online through foundation web site
Deadline(s): Aug. 1
Trustee: Bank of America, N.A.
EIN: 366841348

968
The Blowitz-Ridgeway Foundation
1701 E. Woodfield Rd., Ste. 201
Schaumburg, IL 60173-5127 (847) 330-1020
Contact: Serena L. Moy, Admin.; Laura Romero, Prog. Assoc.
FAX: (847) 330-1028;
E-mail: laura@blowitzridgeway.org; Main URL: http://www.blowitzridgeway.org/

Status changed from public charity to private foundation in 1984; converted from Ridgeway Hospital.
Foundation type: Independent foundation.
Financial data (yr. ended 09/30/13): Assets, $23,437,664 (M); expenditures, $1,706,033; qualifying distributions, $1,582,591; giving activities include $1,137,679 for 56 grants (high: $50,000; low: $2,000), and $100,000 for 1 loan/program-related investment.
Purpose and activities: Giving through program, general operating capital, and research grants primarily in the areas of health, mental and physical disability, and social services, with emphasis on children and youth.
Fields of interest: Health care; Mental health/crisis services; Medical research, institute; Human services; Children/youth, services; Children/youth; Youth; Adults; Aging; Young adults; Disabilities,

people with; Physically disabled; Mentally disabled; Women; Adults, women; Young adults, female; Adults, men; Young adults, male; Terminal illness, people with; Economically disadvantaged.
Type of support: General/operating support; Continuing support; Capital campaigns; Program development; Research; Program-related investments/loans.
Limitations: Applications accepted. Giving generally limited to IL, except for medical research grants. No support for government agencies, religious purposes, or organizations that subsist mainly on third-party funding. No grants to individuals, or for production or writing of audio-visual materials.
Publications: Annual report; Annual report (including application guidelines); Grants list; Informational brochure (including application guidelines).
Application information: See foundation web site for application guidelines and forms. Return applicants are required to submit their final report for the previous grant, before the new grant request can be reviewed. In addition, the foundation is requiring all grant applicants to include, with their grant application, a copy of the Schedule A form from the IRS form 990. Application form required.
Initial approach: Letter or telephone requesting guidelines
Copies of proposal: 5
Deadline(s): Ongoing
Board meeting date(s): Monthly
Final notification: 3-6 months
Officers and Trustees:* Daniel L. Kline,* Pres.; Pierre R. LeBreton, Ph.D., V.P.; Sandra Swantek, M.D.*, Secy.; Thomas P. FitzGibbon, Jr.,* Treas.; Rev. Barbara Bolsen; Anthony M. Dean; Marvin J. Pitluk, Ph.D.; Marva E. Williams, Ph.D.
Number of staff: 1 full-time professional; 1 full-time support.
EIN: 362488355
Other changes: Deborah J. DiLeonard and Samuel G. Winston are no longer trustees.

969
The Blue Knight Foundation
(formerly The Kenneth and Anne Griffin Foundation)
Chicago, IL

The foundation terminated in 2013.

970
The Bobolink Foundation
(formerly Henry M. & Wendy J. Paulson, Jr. Foundation)
c/o Robbins and Assocs. LLC
333 W. Wacker Dr., Ste. 830
Chicago, IL 60606-1225

Established in 1985 in IL.
Donors: Henry M. Paulson, Jr.; Goldman Sachs & Co.
Foundation type: Independent foundation.
Financial data (yr. ended 03/31/13): Assets, $76,534,456 (M); expenditures, $19,327,856; qualifying distributions, $19,039,146; giving activities include $18,869,486 for 49 grants (high: $12,641,986; low: $5,000).
Purpose and activities: Support primarily for environmental conservation and wildlife preservation.
Fields of interest: Environment, natural resources; Animals/wildlife, preservation/protection; Animals/wildlife, bird preserves.
Limitations: Applications not accepted. Giving primarily in New York, NY, Washington, DC, Chicago, IL, Arlington, VA, and Boston, MA. No grants to individuals; no loans.
Application information: Contributes only to pre-selected organizations.
Trustees: Amanda Clark Paulson; Henry M. Paulson, Jr.; Henry Merritt Paulson III; Wendy J. Paulson.
EIN: 942988627
Other changes: For the fiscal year ended Mar. 31, 2013, the grantmaker paid grants of $18,869,486, a 460.4% increase over the fiscal 2012 disbursements, $3,367,000.

971
Charles H. and Bertha L. Boothroyd Foundation
175 W. Jackson Blvd., Ste. 1600
Chicago, IL 60604-2827
Contact: **Thomas C. Kaufmann, Pres.**

Incorporated in 1958 in IL.
Donors: Mary T. Palzkill†; Agnes K. McAvoy Trust; Gudrun Alcock.
Foundation type: Independent foundation.
Financial data (yr. ended 06/30/13): Assets, $4,826,237 (M); expenditures, $393,914; qualifying distributions, $332,975; giving activities include $287,000 for 17 grants (high: $40,000; low: $3,000).
Purpose and activities: Giving primarily for the arts and education.
Fields of interest: Arts; Education; Health organizations, association; Human services.
Type of support: General/operating support; Continuing support; Program development; Scholarship funds; Research.
Limitations: Applications accepted. Giving primarily in IL.
Application information: Application form required.
Initial approach: Proposal
Deadline(s): None
Officers: Thomas C. Kaufmann, Pres. and Treas.; Owen Beacon, V.P.; Dennis A Marks, Secy.
Number of staff: 1 part-time support.
EIN: 366047045
Other changes: Thomas C. Kaufmann has replaced Donald C. Gancer as Pres.
Owen Beacon is now V.P.

972
Boulder Historical Society Trust
Chicago, IL

Status changed to Public Charity.

973
Helen V. Brach Foundation
104 S. Michigan Ave., Ste. 1301
Chicago, IL **60603-6114** (312) 372-4417
Contact: John P. Hagnell, Assoc. Dir.
FAX: (312) 372-0290

Established in 1974 in IL.
Donor: Helen Brach†.
Foundation type: Independent foundation.
Financial data (yr. ended 03/31/14): Assets, $122,603,508 (M); expenditures, $7,454,801; qualifying distributions, $6,826,566; giving activities include $5,448,900 for 408 grants (high: $75,000; low: $500), and $637,550 for 153 employee matching gifts.
Purpose and activities: The foundation's charter provides that it should operate for the following purposes: charitable, educational, literary, prevention of cruelty to animals, prevention of cruelty to children, promotion of music, arts and theater, religious and scientific.
Fields of interest: Arts; Secondary school/education; Higher education; Education; Environment; Animal welfare; Housing/shelter; Youth development, services; Human services; Children/youth, services; Homeless, human services; Disabilities, people with; Economically disadvantaged.
Type of support: General/operating support; Annual campaigns; Building/renovation; Equipment; Program development; Conferences/seminars; Publication; Scholarship funds.
Limitations: Applications accepted. Giving primarily in the Chicago, IL, metropolitan area. No grants outside continental U.S. No support for political organizations. No grants to individuals, or to organizations with less than one year of budget history.
Publications: Application guidelines; Biennial report (including application guidelines).
Application information: No grants under $5,000. Prior year's minimum expenses must have been $50,000. Application form required.
Initial approach: Letter. Faxed applications or inquiries not accepted
Copies of proposal: 6
Deadline(s): Dec. 31 (earlier preferred)
Board meeting date(s): Quarterly; grants considered at Mar. meeting
Final notification: Mar. and Apr.
Officers and Directors:* Raymond F. Simon,* Chair.; R. Matthew Simon,* Pres.; Richard Curry; James J. O'Connor; John J. Sheridan; Charles A. Vorhees.
Number of staff: 3 full-time professional.
EIN: 237376427

974
The Brennan Family Charitable Trust
11950 South Harlem Ave., Ste. 201-8
Palos Heights, IL **60463-1998**
E-mail: dbz3864@ameritech.net

Established in 2000 in IL.
Donors: Daniel G. Brennan; Victoria A. Brennan.
Foundation type: Independent foundation.
Financial data (yr. ended 12/31/12): Assets, $865,387 (M); expenditures, $168,155; qualifying distributions, $154,592; giving activities include $154,592 for 22 grants (high: $45,525; low: $50).
Fields of interest: Education; Protestant agencies & churches.
Type of support: General/operating support.
Limitations: Applications not accepted. Giving primarily in IL and WI. No grants to individuals.
Application information: Contributes only to pre-selected organizations.
Trustees: Daniel G. Brennan; Victoria A. Brennan.
EIN: 364371135
Other changes: The grantmaker no longer lists a fax. The grantmaker no longer lists a phone.

975

Howard G. Buffett Foundation
145 N. Merchant St.
Decatur, IL 62523-1442 (217) 423-9286
Main URL: http://www.thehowardgbuffettfoundation.org/
Multimedia: http://www.thehowardgbuffettfoundation.org/media/

Established in 1999 in IL and NE.
Donors: Warren E. Buffett; Susan T. Buffett†.
Foundation type: Independent foundation.
Financial data (yr. ended 12/31/12): Assets, $255,867,080 (M); gifts received, $53,089,976; expenditures, $52,469,651; qualifying distributions, $67,861,354; giving activities include $41,563,348 for 96 grants (high: $3,637,320; low: $500), and $22,365,464 for 3 foundation-administered programs.
Purpose and activities: The foundation's mission is to improve the standard of living and quality of life for the world's most impoverished and marginalized populations. It works to achieve its mission by focusing its funding in three core areas: 1) food security; 2) water security; and 3) conflict resolution, management and post-conflict development.
Fields of interest: Education; Environment; Public health, clean water supply; Agriculture; Agriculture, farmlands; Human services; International conflict resolution.
Limitations: Applications not accepted. Giving primarily in GA, IL and MD, and in England and Italy. No grants to individuals.
Application information: Contributes only to pre-selected organizations.
Officers and Directors:* Howard G. Buffett,* Chair. and C.E.O.; Ann M. Kelly, Pres.; Trisha A. Cook, V.P., Opers. and Treas.; Devon G. Buffett,* Exec. V.P. and Secy.; Howard W. Buffett, Exec. Dir.; Nicolette DeBruyn; Erin M. Morgan; Michael D. Walter; Chelsea M. Zillmer.
EIN: 470824756
Other changes: Ann M. Kelly has replaced Howard G. Buffett as Pres.
Trisha A. Cook is now V.P., Opers. and Treas. Howard G. Buffett is now Chair. and C.E.O. Susan S. Bell is no longer a director.

976

Buonacorsi Foundation
330 S. Naperville Rd., Ste. 300
Wheaton, IL 60187-5442

Donors: Marguerite Doyle; Michael Doyle.
Foundation type: Independent foundation.
Financial data (yr. ended 12/31/12): Assets, $45,022 (M); gifts received, $201,135; expenditures, $184,006; qualifying distributions, $184,006; giving activities include $152,913 for 2 grants (high: $120,000; low: $32,913).
Purpose and activities: Giving primarily for use and development of medical imaging software.
Fields of interest: Human services.
Limitations: Applications not accepted. Giving primarily in IL.
Application information: Unsolicited requests for funds not accepted.
Officers and Directors:* Michael Doyle,* Pres.; Marguerite Doyle,* Secy.; Geoffrey Doyle.
EIN: 264147697
Other changes: The grantmaker no longer lists a URL address.

977

Henrietta Lange Burk Fund
c/o U.S. Trust, Philanthropic Solutions
231 S. LaSalle St., IL-1-231-13-32
Chicago, IL 60604 (312) 828-4154
Contact: George Thorn, Market Director
E-mail: ilgrantmaking@ustrust.com; Main URL: http://www.bankofamerica.com/grantmaking

Established in 1995 in IL.
Donor: Henrietta Lange Burk Trust.
Foundation type: Independent foundation.
Financial data (yr. ended 09/30/13): Assets, $8,921,788 (M); expenditures, $461,011; qualifying distributions, $393,605; giving activities include $326,000 for 19 grants (high: $30,000; low: $5,000).
Purpose and activities: Giving primarily for the arts and human services.
Fields of interest: Arts; Education; Health care; Human services; Children/youth, services; Religion.
Limitations: Applications accepted. Giving primarily in Chicago, IL.
Application information: Application guidelines available at Fund web site. Application form required.
Initial approach: **E-mail**
Copies of proposal: 1
Deadline(s): June 1 and Nov. 1
Final notification: Varies
Trustee: Bank of America, N.A.
EIN: 367092200

978

C.W.B. Foundation
1252 Bell Valley Rd., Ste. 300
Rockford, IL 61108-4439

Established in 1986 in IL.
Donor: Cedric Blazer.
Foundation type: Independent foundation.
Financial data (yr. ended 12/31/12): Assets, $4,432,065 (M); gifts received, $1,000; expenditures, $279,703; qualifying distributions, $269,036; giving activities include $267,900 for 20 grants (high: $75,000; low: $650).
Fields of interest: Arts; Education; Hospitals (general); Human services; Independent living, disability.
Limitations: Applications not accepted. Giving primarily in Rockford, IL. No grants to individuals.
Application information: Contributes only to pre-selected organizations.
Directors: Mark Blazer; James W. Keeling; Jay Maddox; Patrick Shaw; Jim Vitale; Bob Yocum.
EIN: 363480054

979

John P. Cadle Foundation
11 E. North St.
Danville, IL 61832-5803 **(217) 442-0350**
Contact: Phillip Stephen Miller

Established in 2000 in IL.
Donor: John P. Cadle†.
Foundation type: Independent foundation.
Financial data (yr. ended 08/31/13): Assets, $14,224,426 (M); expenditures, $971,097; qualifying distributions, $313,406; giving activities include $275,553 for 49 grants (high: $22,900; low: $500).
Fields of interest: Arts; Elementary/secondary education; Education; Human services; Religion.
Type of support: General/operating support.
Limitations: Applications accepted. Giving primarily in IL. No grants to individuals.
Application information: Application form required.
Deadline(s): Oct. 31
Trustees: John C. Alexander; Thomas Beckner; Steve Miller; Stan Seaman.
EIN: 371389249

980

The Chartered Foundation
5430 W. Roosevelt Rd., Ste. 232
Chicago, IL 60644-1493

Established in 1998 in IL.
Donor: James R. Swanson.
Foundation type: Independent foundation.
Financial data (yr. ended 06/30/13): Assets, $2,829,108 (M); expenditures, $1,319,498; qualifying distributions, $1,116,855; giving activities include $1,095,922 for 3 grants (high: $960,922; low: $10,000).
Purpose and activities: Giving to provide students, children, and adults with opportunities and incentives to improve their competitive positions in society; to provide food, clothing, housing, transportation, health care, nutrition, child care, job placement, and counseling for students and their families; and to provide scholarships to certain students who might benefit from them.
Fields of interest: Health care; Boys & girls clubs; Youth development, services; Human services; Family services; Community/economic development.
Limitations: Applications not accepted. Giving primarily in FL and IL. No grants to individuals.
Application information: Contributes only to pre-selected organizations.
Officer: James R. Swanson, Pres.
Director: Mark T. Swanson.
EIN: 364239391
Other changes: At the close of 2013, the grantmaker paid grants of $1,095,922, a 191.7% increase over the 2012 disbursements, $375,684.

981

Elizabeth F. Cheney Foundation
120 S. LaSalle St., Ste. 1740
Chicago, IL 60603-3568 **(312) 782-1234**
Contact: Elisabeth Geraghty, Exec. Dir.
***FAX:* (312) 782-1242;**
E-mail: egeraghty@cheneyfoundation.org; Main URL: http://www.cheneyfoundation.org
Grants List: http://www.cheneyfoundation.org/grants2012-2013.pdf

Established in 1985 in IL.
Donor: Elizabeth F. Cheney Trust.
Foundation type: Independent foundation.
Financial data (yr. ended 05/31/13): Assets, $10,814,662 (M); expenditures, $1,180,832; qualifying distributions, $1,002,706; giving activities include $1,002,706 for grants.
Purpose and activities: The Elizabeth F. Cheney Foundation is a private independent foundation. Its principal focus is to support the arts and cultural organizations. Organizations supported include, but are not limited to, musical performance organizations, theater and dance companies, historical societies and museums. The overall grant making focus of the foundation is on artistic achievement in presentation or performance rather than education enrichment or outreach.

Fields of interest: Visual arts; Museums; Performing arts, dance; Performing arts, theater; Performing arts, music; Literature.
Type of support: Program development.
Limitations: Applications accepted. Giving primarily in the metropolitan Chicago, IL, area. No grants to individuals.
Publications: Application guidelines; Annual report; Grants list.
Application information: See foundation web site for complete application guidelines. Application form required.
Initial approach: See website for application form
Copies of proposal: 1
Deadline(s): 30 days prior to meeting based on programmatic schedule
Board meeting date(s): Mar., May, July, Sept., and Nov.
Officers: Lawrence L. Belles, Pres.; Howard M. McCue III, Secy.; Allan R. Drebin, Treas.; Elisabeth Geraghty, Exec. Dir.
Number of staff: 1 part-time professional.
EIN: 363375377

982
The Chicago Community Trust
225 N. Michigan Ave.
Chicago, IL 60601 (312) 616-8000
Contact: For grants: Ms. Sandy Phelps, Dir., Grants Mgmt.
FAX: (312) 616-7955; E-mail: info@cct.org; TDD: (312) 856-1703; Grant inquiries e-mail: grants@cct.org; Main URL: http://www.cct.org
Facebook: http://www.facebook.com/thechicagocommunitytrust
Grants Database: http://www.cct.org/grants/grant-list
RSS Feed: http://www.cct.org/news/updates
Twitter: http://twitter.com/ChiTrust

Established in 1915 in IL by bank resolution and declaration of trust.
Donors: Albert W. Harris; and members of the Harris family.
Foundation type: Community foundation.
Financial data (yr. ended 09/30/12): Assets, $1,804,362,755 (M); gifts received, $156,178,784; expenditures, $196,010,249; giving activities include $169,744,869 for grants.
Purpose and activities: The trust's mission is to lead and inspire philanthropic efforts that measurably improve the quality of life and the prosperity of the region. With new strategic focus, the trust seeks to advance four overarching goals in the community: 1) advancing opportunities for human and economic development; 2) securing conditions for healthy, safe, just and caring communities; 3) promoting civic and cultural vitality; and 4) transforming the region through sustainable development.
Fields of interest: Visual arts; Performing arts; Humanities; Arts; Child development, education; Elementary school/education; Secondary school/education; Education; Health care; Employment, training; Housing/shelter, development; Youth development, services; Children/youth, services; Child development, services; Aging, centers/services; Women, centers/services; Minorities/immigrants, centers/services; Homeless, human services; Human services; Economic development; Community/economic development; Public policy, research; Government/public administration; Leadership development; Children/youth; Children; Adults; Aging; Young adults; Disabilities, people with; Blind/visually impaired; Minorities; Asians/Pacific Islanders; African Americans/Blacks; Hispanics/Latinos; Native Americans/American Indians; Indigenous peoples; Women; Girls; Adults, women; Young adults, female; Men; Boys; Adults, men; Young adults, male; Offenders/ex-offenders; Immigrants/refugees; Economically disadvantaged; Homeless; Migrant workers; LGBTQ.
Type of support: General/operating support; Continuing support; Income development; Management development/capacity building; Capital campaigns; Building/renovation; Equipment; Land acquisition; Program development; Curriculum development; Research; Technical assistance; Consulting services; Program evaluation; Employee matching gifts; Matching/challenge support.
Limitations: Applications accepted. Giving primarily in Cook County and the adjacent 5 counties of northeastern, IL. No support for sectarian purposes or support of single-disease oriented research, treatment or care. No grants to individuals (except for limited fellowship programs), or for reducing operating deficits or liquidating existing debt, or for the sole purpose of writing, publishing, producing or distributing audio, visual or printing material, or for conducting conferences, festivals, exhibitions or meetings.
Publications: Application guidelines; Annual report; Financial statement; Grants list.
Application information: Visit foundation web site for strategic grant opportunities, guidelines, RFPs and to access online application system. Application form required.
Initial approach: Create online account to submit application
Copies of proposal: 1
Deadline(s): Varies
Board meeting date(s): Jan., May, and Sept.
Officers and Executive Committee:* Frank M. Clark,* Chair.; Terry Mazany, C.E.O. and Pres.; Carol Y. Crenshaw, V.P., Finance; Jamie Phillippe, V.P., Devel. and Donor Svcs.; Frank Soo Hoo, Cont.; Tom Irvine, C.I.O.; Leslie Bluhm; Carol L. Brown; Martin R. Castro; John "Jack" Catlin; William M. Daley; Shawn M. Donnelley; Michael W. Ferro, Jr.; Denise Gardner; King W. Harris; Christopher G. Kennedy; Audrey R. Peeples; Mary B. Richardson-Lowry; John W. Rowe; Jesse H. Ruiz; Michael Tang; Linda S. Wolf.
Trustees: Bank of America, N.A.; BMO Harris Bank, N.A.; JPMorgan Chase Bank, N.A.; The Northern Trust Company; U.S. Bank, N.A.
Number of staff: 32 full-time professional; 11 full-time support.
EIN: 362167000
Other changes: Chae Dawning is now Sr. Dir., Human Resources and Admin. Maria C. Bechily is no longer a member of the Executive Committee.

983
The Children's Care Foundation
333 N. Michigan Ave., Ste. 2131
Chicago, IL 60601-4110 (312) 201-0540
Contact: Robert L. Campbell, Exec. Dir.
Main URL: http://www.childrenscarefoundation.org

Established in 1990 in IL.
Donors: Mary L. Medlock Trust; William J. Watson Trust; C. Lydia Frederick Trust; Hobart W. Williams Trust; Ava W. Farwell Trust; Robert & Janet McMurdy Fund; George J. Williams Charitable Trust; The Chicago Community Trust; Caroline Williams Charitable Trust.
Foundation type: Independent foundation.
Financial data (yr. ended 06/30/13): Assets, $48,356,310 (M); gifts received, $363,427; expenditures, $2,543,910; qualifying distributions, $2,308,459; giving activities include $1,977,000 for 24 grants (high: $530,000; low: $5,000).
Purpose and activities: Support limited to organizations that benefit children in the state of Illinois. Funding interests include programmatic services that give accountable results addressing such issues as: access to primary pediatric and related child health care, child abuse, educational and youth development, social services and delinquency prevention. Priority is given to community-based health care and health services for medically underserved poor children living in metropolitan Chicago, Illinois.
Fields of interest: Hospitals (general); Human services; Children/youth, services.
Type of support: Program-related investments/loans; Matching/challenge support.
Limitations: Applications accepted. Giving limited to metropolitan Chicago, IL. No support for political organizations or governmental entities. No grants to individuals, or for endowments, capital campaigns, general operating support, advocacy, start-up projects, research, lobbying groups, fundraising benefits, or courtesy advertisements.
Publications: Application guidelines; Informational brochure (including application guidelines).
Application information: Full proposals are by invitation only, upon review of letter of inquiry. Electronic submissions, including faxes and e-mails, are not accepted. Organizations that expend more than fifteen percent of their annual revenue for administration, overhead and fundraising will usually not be considered for funding. Application guidelines available on foundation web site. Application form not required.
Initial approach: Letter of inquiry
Copies of proposal: 1
Deadline(s): None
Board meeting date(s): Twice a year
Final notification: 30 days
Officers and Directors:* Anthony Pertile,* Chair.; Joseph S. Johnson,* Pres.; Edward X. Clinton, V.P.; Bruce E. Huey,* V.P.; George S. Trees, Jr.,* V.P.; Roxanne M. Warble,* V.P.; Justin A. Stanley, Jr., Secy.-Treas.; Robert L. Campbell,* Exec. Dir.; Marvin Kamensky; Michael E. Reed; Samuel H. Young.
Number of staff: 1 full-time professional.
EIN: 366088708
Other changes: Anthony Pertile is now Chair.

984
CME Group Foundation
20 S. Wacker Dr.
Chicago, IL 60606-7431 (312) 930-3292
Contact: Kassie Davis, Exec. Dir.
E-mail: kassie.davis@cmegroupfoundation.org; Main URL: http://www.cmegroupfoundation.org

Established in 2008 in IL.
Donor: Chicago Mercantile Exchange Trust.
Foundation type: Company-sponsored foundation.
Financial data (yr. ended 12/31/12): Assets, $17,238,849 (M); gifts received, $3,897,660; expenditures, $3,285,475; qualifying distributions, $3,099,716; giving activities include $3,099,716 for grants.
Purpose and activities: Giving primarily in the Chicago, Illinois region to promote research, teaching and learning specific to financial markets; to promote the education of children and youth; and to promote the health and education of young children.
Fields of interest: Elementary/secondary education; Higher education; Education; Youth development; Human services.

Limitations: Applications not accepted. Giving primarily in the Chicago, IL region. No support for political campaigns or for organizations not in compliance with all applicable anti-terrorist financing and asset control laws. **No grants to individuals, or for deficit reduction, debt, benefit events or advertising.**
Application information: Contributes only to pre-selected organizations.
Officers and Directors:* Howard J. Siegel,* Chair.; Charles P. Carey,* Vice-Chair.; Terrance A. Duffy,* Vice-Chair.; Phupinder Gill,* Vice-Chair.; Leo Melamed,* Vice-Chair.; John F. Sandner,* Vice-Chair.; James E. Oliff,* Secy.-Treas.; Kassie Davis,* Exec. Dir.
EIN: 450575574

985
Lizanell and Colbert Coldwell Foundation

c/o JPMorgan Chase Bank, N.A.
10 S. Dearborn, ILI-0117
Chicago, IL 60603
***Application address:* c/o JPMorgan Chase Bank, Attn.: Larry Bothe, 420 Throckmorton, Fl. 3, Fort Worth, TX 76102, tel.: (817) 884-4022**

Established in 1990 in TX.
Donor: Lizanell Coldwell†.
Foundation type: Independent foundation.
Financial data (yr. ended 03/31/13): Assets, $4,886,648 (M); expenditures, $289,428; qualifying distributions, $245,852; giving activities include $233,238 for 5 grants (high: $100,232; low: $10,000).
Purpose and activities: Giving limited to TX organizations furthering the advancement of medical sciences, and research institutions dedicated to medical research, especially for the cure and prevention of heart disease and cancer.
Fields of interest: Higher education; Medical research, institute.
Type of support: General/operating support; Equipment; Research.
Limitations: Giving limited to TX, with emphasis on El Paso. No support for political organizations. No grants to individuals, or for endowment funds.
Trustees: Colbert Coldwell; Annette Hoy, M.D.; JPMorgan Chase Bank, N.A.
EIN: 742576133
Other changes: The grantmaker has moved from TX to IL.

986
The Coleman Foundation, Inc.

651 W. Washington Blvd., Ste. 306
Chicago, IL 60661-2134 (312) 902-7120
***Contact:* Michael W. Hennessy, C.E.O. and Pres.**
FAX: (313) 902-7124;
E-mail: info@colemanfoundation.org; Main URL: http://www.colemanfoundation.org
Blog: http://colemanfoundation.typepad.com/cfi_blog/

Trust established in 1951 in IL.
Donors: J.D. Stetson Coleman†; Dorothy W. Coleman†.
Foundation type: Independent foundation.
Financial data (yr. ended 12/31/12): Assets, $142,934,063 (M); expenditures, $7,818,772; qualifying distributions, $7,048,895; giving activities include $5,893,359 for 125 grants (high: $250,000; low: $2,000).
Purpose and activities: Giving for postsecondary, community, secondary and elementary education programs which focus on developing awareness of self-employment, and other selected postsecondary, secondary, and elementary education projects. Support also for cancer care and research well as for programs to aid the developmentally disabled in the metropolitan Chicago area.
Fields of interest: Elementary school/education; Secondary school/education; Higher education; Business school/education; Adult/continuing education; Education; Medical care, rehabilitation; Cancer; Cancer research; Human services; Community development, small businesses; Community/economic development; Disabilities, people with; Economically disadvantaged.
Type of support: General/operating support; Income development; Capital campaigns; Building/renovation; Equipment; Program development; Conferences/seminars; Professorships; Curriculum development; Scholarship funds; Research; Program-related investments/loans; Matching/challenge support.
Limitations: Applications accepted. Giving primarily in the Midwest, with emphasis on the metropolitan Chicago, IL, area; support outside the Midwest is only for selected programs. No support for religious or political organizations. No grants to individuals, or for deficit financing, ticket purchases, or student loans to individuals.
Publications: Application guidelines; Financial statement; Grants list; Occasional report.
Application information: Brochures, videotapes, CDs and other attachments should not be sent with the letter of inquiry. Full grant proposals should only be submitted upon invitation by the foundation. Refer to website for application requirements. Application form available on website. Application form required.
Initial approach: Concise letter of inquiry. The foundation may then contact the applicant for a full application
Copies of proposal: 1
Deadline(s): Rolling deadline schedule with quarterly consideration
Board meeting date(s): Usually in Feb., May, Aug., and Nov.
Final notification: 3 months
Officers and Directors:* Michael W. Hennessy,* C.E.O. and Pres.; James H. Jones,* Secy.; Trevor C. Davies,* C.F.O. and Treas.; John E. Hughes,* Chair. Emeritus; R. Michael Furlong; Daniel Wanzenberg.
Number of staff: 4 full-time professional; 1 full-time support.
EIN: 363025967

987
Comer Science & Education Foundation

c/o Lawrence Richman
2 N. LaSalle St.
Chicago, IL 60602-3963

Established in 1998 in IL.
Donors: The Comer Foundation; Gary C. Comer†.
Foundation type: Independent foundation.
Financial data (yr. ended 12/31/12): Assets, $129,049,033 (M); gifts received, $1,285,257; expenditures, $10,135,781; qualifying distributions, $8,263,820; giving activities include $1,374,595 for 20 grants (high: $393,600; low: $1,000).
Purpose and activities: Giving primarily for climate change and the redevelopment of a Chicago neighborhood.
Fields of interest: Museums (natural history); Higher education; Education; Hospitals (general); Urban/community development.
Type of support: General/operating support; Program development.
Limitations: Applications not accepted. Giving primarily in Chicago, IL. No grants to individuals.
Application information: Contributes only to pre-selected organizations.
Officers and Directors:* Guy Comer,* Pres.; Stephanie Comer,* V.P.; William T. Schleicher, Jr.,* Secy.; Vicki Kalnins, Treas.; Gregory Mooney, Exec. Dir.
Number of staff: 20
EIN: 364244783
Other changes: Lee Reid is no longer Exec. Dir.

988
Community Foundation of Central Illinois

(formerly Peoria Area Community Foundation)
331 Fulton St., Ste. 310
Peoria, IL 61602-1449 (309) 674-8730
Contact: Mark Roberts, C.E.O.
FAX: (309) 674-8754;
E-mail: mark@communityfoundationci.org; Main URL: http://www.communityfoundationci.org
Facebook: http://www.facebook.com/pages/Community-Foundation-of-Central-Illinois/322998507749395
Twitter: https://twitter.com/CFCIllinois

Incorporated in 1987 in IL.
Foundation type: Community foundation.
Financial data (yr. ended 06/30/13): Assets, $22,776,804 (M); gifts received, $567,607; expenditures, $1,233,327; giving activities include $802,973 for 81+ grants (high: $38,500).
Purpose and activities: The foundation seeks to serve the Central Illinois area by providing an intelligent bridge between needs and resources through a growing endowment, entrepreneurial grantmaking service to the nonprofit sector, and promotion of philanthropy. Primary areas of interest include community development, the arts and humanities, education, health, and human services.
Fields of interest: Arts education; Visual arts; Museums; Performing arts; Performing arts, dance; Performing arts, music; Humanities; Historic preservation/historical societies; Arts; Education, early childhood education; Child development, education; Elementary school/education; Secondary school/education; Higher education; Adult/continuing education; Adult education—literacy, basic skills & GED; Education, reading; Education; Environment, natural resources; Environment; Animal welfare; Animals/wildlife, preservation/protection; Reproductive health, family planning; Medical care, rehabilitation; Health care; Substance abuse, services; Mental health/crisis services; Health organizations, association; Cancer; Heart & circulatory diseases; AIDS; Alcoholism; Cancer research; Heart & circulatory research; AIDS research; Crime/violence prevention, youth; Food services; Nutrition; Recreation; Youth development, services; Children/youth, services; Child development, services; Family services; Aging, centers/services; Homeless, human services; Human services; Civil/human rights; Urban/community development; Community/economic development; Voluntarism promotion; United Ways and Federated Giving Programs; Social sciences; Government/public administration; Leadership development; Aging; Disabilities, people with; Minorities; Women; Economically disadvantaged; Homeless.
Type of support: General/operating support; Capital campaigns; Equipment; Program development; Conferences/seminars; Seed money; Scholarship

funds; Employee matching gifts; In-kind gifts; Matching/challenge support.
Limitations: Applications accepted. Giving limited to the central IL area. No support for sectarian religious purposes. No grants to individuals (except for scholarships), or for annual campaigns or endowments; no loans.
Publications: Application guidelines; Annual report (including application guidelines); Financial statement; Informational brochure; Newsletter.
Application information: Visit foundation web site for application form and application guidelines. Application form required.
Initial approach: Submit application and attachments
Copies of proposal: 17
***Deadline(s):* Mar. 1 for Community Arts Grants and Jean M. Ligon Animal Welfare Grant; Sept. 1 for Community Needs Grants**
Board meeting date(s): Monthly
Final notification: Within 1 month
Officers and Directors:* Bashir Ali,* Chair.; Cathy Butler,* Vice-Chair. and Treas.; Mark Roberts,* C.E.O.; Donna Marcacci,* Secy.; Nathan Bach; Alma Brown; Ray Busam; Christopher Glynn; Dawn Harris Jeffries; Ron Miller; Debbie Ritschel; **Sarah Stabler-Cordis**; Karen Stumpe; Dr. Maxine Wortham; David Wynn.
Number of staff: 2 full-time professional; 1 part-time professional.
EIN: 371185713

989
Community Foundation of Kankakee River Valley

(formerly Kankakee River Valley Foundation)
701 S. Harrison Ave.
Kankakee, IL 60901 (815) 939-1611
***Contact:* Rick Manuel, Exec. Dir.**
FAX: (815) 936-9633;
E-mail: info@endowthefuture.org; Main URL: http://www.endowthefuture.org
Facebook: https://www.facebook.com/CommunityFoundationKankakeeRiverValley
Parent's Page -Success by 6, an early childhood initiative: http://www.parentspage.org/

Established in 1982 in IL.
Foundation type: Community foundation.
Financial data (yr. ended 12/31/12): Assets, $6,703,442 (M); gifts received, $74,145; expenditures, $963,325; giving activities include $198,543 for 4+ grants (high: $12,500).
Purpose and activities: The foundation: 1) promotes visionary philanthropy to create and support vital and caring communities; 2) builds and preserves funds of many individuals and institutions; 3) distributes to nonprofit organizations that serve members of the community; and 4) convenes concerned individuals to shape flexible responses to changing needs of the community.
Fields of interest: Arts; Education; Environment, land resources; Health care; Employment, services; Children, day care; Human services.
Type of support: Equipment; Program development; Seed money; Consulting services; Matching/challenge support.
Limitations: Applications accepted. Giving for the benefit of residents of the area, including Aroma Park, Bourbonnais, Bradley, and Kankakee in Kankakee County, IL.
Publications: Application guidelines; Informational brochure; Newsletter.
Application information: Visit foundation web site for application form and guidelines. Application form required.
***Initial approach:* Submit online application**
***Deadline(s):* Mar. 7**
Board meeting date(s): 3rd Thurs. of each month
Officers and Directors:* Paul Snellenberger,* Chair.; **Kari Sargeant,* Chair.-Elect.**; Roger Benson,* Secy.; Mary Elise Burnett,* Treas.; Rick Manuel, Exec. Dir.; Ann Brezinski; Hollice Clark; Dale Gerretse; Joy Hansen-Irps; Karl Kruse; Elizabeth Kubal; Dr. Stonewall McCuiston; Mike O'Brien; **Cindi Reddish**; **Camille Rose**; Kari Sargeant; Mike Van Mill.
Number of staff: 1 full-time professional; 1 part-time professional; 1 full-time support.
EIN: 363235540
Other changes: Kari Sargeant is now Chair.-Elect.

990
Community Foundation of Northern Illinois

(formerly Rockford Community Foundation)
946 N. 2nd St.
Rockford, IL 61107-3005 (815) 962-2110
FAX: (815) 962-2116; E-mail: info@cfnil.org; Grant application tel.: (815) 962-2110, ext. 15 and e-mail: bnelson@cfnil.org; Main URL: http://www.cfnil.org
Facebook: http://www.facebook.com/cfnil
Twitter: http://twitter.com/resources4ever

Established in 1953 in IL.
Foundation type: Community foundation.
Financial data (yr. ended 06/30/12): Assets, $49,636,480 (M); gifts received, $927,870; expenditures, $2,822,552; giving activities include $1,819,784 for 50+ grants (high: $144,525), and $140,027 for 129 grants to individuals.
Purpose and activities: The foundation seeks to serve the four-county area through philanthropy, to provide leadership in meeting charitable needs, and to be a responsible steward to donors of the endowment. Giving primarily for social services; support also for arts and culture, education, health services, and housing, neighborhoods, economic and community development, youth, children, and families. The "In Youth We Trust" group of the foundation supports programs initiated by and operated for people under 21.
Fields of interest: Humanities; Historic preservation/historical societies; Arts; Education; Health care; Housing/shelter; Youth, services; Child development, services; Family services; Human services; Economic development; Community/economic development; Children; Youth; Disabilities, people with; Economically disadvantaged.
Type of support: Management development/capacity building; Equipment; Emergency funds; Program development; Seed money; Scholarship funds; Research; Technical assistance; Program evaluation; Program-related investments/loans; Scholarships—to individuals; Matching/challenge support.
Limitations: Applications accepted. Giving primarily in the metropolitan Rockford, IL, area, including Boone, Ogle, Stephenson, and Winnebago counties. No grants to individuals (except for scholarships), or for ongoing project support or operating support, annual or capital campaigns, budget deficit, endowments, or regranting of funds.
Publications: Application guidelines; Annual report; Grants list; Informational brochure (including application guidelines); Newsletter; Program policy statement.
Application information: Visit foundation web site for online application and additional guidelines per grant type. Applicant may attend a Grant Seekers meeting held on the 1st Tues. of every May and Nov.; call for reservations. Application form required.
Initial approach: Complete online application
Copies of proposal: 1
Deadline(s): Sept. 1 and May 1
Board meeting date(s): Feb., Apr., May, Aug., Sept., Oct., and Nov.
Final notification: 2 1/2 months
Officers and Trustees:* Patrick T. Derry,* Chair.; Gloria Lundin,* Pres. and Secy.; Jon Bates,* Exec. V.P.; Roger Reithmeier,* Asst. Treas.; Richard Leighton, Tr. Emeritus; Thomas S. Johnson, Legal Counsel; Cheryl Balsam; Judith A. Barnard; Williard C. Brenner; Larry Bridgeland; Russ Dennis; Robert M. Hammes; Nancy Hyzer; Chris Janke; Jeffrey Layng; James E. Lee; Erin Maggio-Calkins; William Reilly II; Thomas R. Walsh; Janice Westlund; Michael White, Jr.; Jonathan Whitlock; Brenten Witherby.
Trustee Bank: JPMorgan Chase Bank, N.A.
Number of staff: 8 full-time professional.
EIN: 364402089
Other changes: LuAnn Groh is now Exec. Asst. and Off. Mgr. Thomas S. Johnson and Nancy Hyzer are no longer trustees.

991
Community Foundation of the Fox River Valley

(formerly The Aurora Foundation)
111 W. Downer Pl., Ste. 312
Aurora, IL 60506-5136 (630) 896-7800
Contact: Sharon Stredde, C.E.O.
FAX: (630) 896-7811;
E-mail: info@CommunityFoundationFRV.org;
Additional e-mails:
sstredde@communityfoundationfrv.org and grant@communityfoundationfrv.org; Main URL: http://www.communityfoundationfrv.org
E-mail for scholarship: Sch@CommunityFoundationFRV.org

Incorporated in 1948 in IL.
Foundation type: Community foundation.
Financial data (yr. ended 12/31/12): Assets, $63,649,777 (M); gifts received, $5,707,727; expenditures, $6,263,631; giving activities include $4,668,516 for 70+ grants, and $823,400 for 426 grants to individuals.
Purpose and activities: The foundation is a non-profit philanthropic organization that administers individual charitable funds from which grants and scholarships are distributed to benefit the citizens of the Greater Aurora Area, the TriCities and Kendall County, Illinois.
Fields of interest: Humanities; Arts; Higher education; Education; Hospitals (general); Health care; Health organizations, association; Children/youth, services; Human services.
Type of support: Capital campaigns; Building/renovation; Equipment; Seed money; Scholarship funds; Scholarships—to individuals; Matching/challenge support.
Limitations: Applications accepted. Giving limited to City of Aurora, Southern Kane County, and Kendall County, IL. No support for private foundations, sectarian or religious purposes, or for organizations operated primarily for the benefit of their own membership. No grants to individuals (except for scholarships), or for operating budgets, research, annual campaigns, continuing support, endowments, contingency funds, reserves, deficits, benefit tickets, or national fundraising efforts.
Publications: Application guidelines; Annual report; Newsletter.
Application information: Visit foundation web site for application guidelines.

Initial approach: Telephone or e-mail
Copies of proposal: 8
Deadline(s): May 1 and Nov. 3
Board meeting date(s): Mar. and Sept.; Exec. Comm. meets as required
Officers and Directors:* Mark E. Truemper,* Chair.; Hedy K. Lindgren,* Vice-Chair.; **Sharon Stredde,* Pres. and C.E.O.**; William B. Skoglund,* Treas.; Duncan Alexander; Christina S.T. Anderson; **Austin M. Dempsey**; John Diederich; Patricia Fabian; Rick Guzman; Jane W. Harris; Frank R. Miller; Katherine Navota; Robert J. O'Connor; Timothy J. Reuland; Edward H. Schmitt, Jr.; Scott Voris; Donna J. Williams; Kyle D. Witt.
Number of staff: 1 full-time professional; 1 full-time support.
EIN: 366086742
Other changes: Sharon Stredde is now Pres. and C.E.O. Roger O. Anderson and Kyle D. Witt are no longer directors.

992
Community Foundation of the Quincy Area
(formerly Quincy Area Community Foundation)
4531 Maine, Ste. A.
Quincy, IL 62305 (217) 222-1237
Contact: Jill Arnold Blickhan, Exec. Dir.; For grants: Amy Meyer Lehenbauer, Outreach Coord.
FAX: (217) 222-2260;
E-mail: info@mycommunityfoundation.org; Mailing address: P.O. Box 741, Quincy, IL 62306-0741; Additional e-mail: execdir@mycommunityfoundation.org; Grant inquiry e-mail: grants@mycommunityfoundation.org; Main URL: http://www.mycommunityfoundation.org
Facebook: http://www.facebook.com/mycommunityfoundation
YouTube: http://www.youtube.com/user/qacf2010?feature=watch

Established in 1997 in IL.
Foundation type: Community foundation.
Financial data (yr. ended 12/31/12): Assets, $14,836,803 (M); gifts received, $1,084,089; expenditures, $510,497; giving activities include $270,012 for 12+ grants (high: $30,000), and $6,525 for 9 grants to individuals.
Purpose and activities: The foundation seeks to enrich the quality of life in the tri-state area by offering a way for people from all walks of life to easily and effectively support the groups and issues they care about most.
Fields of interest: Arts; Education; Health care; Human services; Community/economic development.
Type of support: Management development/capacity building; General/operating support; Building/renovation; Equipment; Program development; Publication; Seed money; Curriculum development; Scholarship funds; Matching/challenge support.
Limitations: Applications accepted. Giving limited to Adams, Brown, Hancock, and Pike counties, IL, Lee County, IA, and Clark, Knox, Lewis, Marion, Monroe, Pike, Ralls, and Shelby counties, MO. No support for religious purposes. No grants to individuals (except for scholarships), or for annual campaigns, endowments, debt reductions, national fundraising efforts, sponsorships for fundraising or for-profit events or recurring events.
Publications: Application guidelines; Annual report; Grants list; Informational brochure; Newsletter.
Application information: Visit foundation web site for guidelines and to access online application. Grants from the foundation's competitive fund are generally limited to $1,000 or less. Application form required.
Initial approach: Online, telephone or e-mail
Deadline(s): June 1
Board meeting date(s): 4th Tues. of each month
Final notification: Sept.-Nov.
Officers and Directors:* Andy Sprague,* Chair.; William McCleery, Jr.,* Vice-Chair.; Virgil Welker,* Secy.; Gary L. Blickhan,* Treas.; Jill Arnold Blickhan, Exec. Dir.; Lydia Ahrens; Leah Berry; Julie Bowen; Tony Crane; Tom Dale; Larry Fischer; Tanya Harvey; Chris Kirn; Philip Krupps; Blake Roderick; Steve Siebers; Sharon Tenhouse; Catherine Tracy; Byron Webb III; Dennis R. Williams.
Number of staff: 1 full-time professional; 1 part-time professional; 1 part-time support.
EIN: 371366611
Other changes: Andy Sprague has replaced Brian A. Ippensen as Chair. William McCleery, Jr. has replaced Andy Sprague as Vice-Chair.
Jim Schlepphorst is no longer a director.

993
Community Memorial Foundation
15 Spinning Wheel Rd., Ste. 326
Hinsdale, IL 60521-2986 (630) 654-4729
Contact: Deb Kustra, Grants Mgr.
FAX: (630) 654-3402; E-mail: info@cmfdn.org; Main URL: http://cmfdn.org/
Facebook: https://www.facebook.com/CommunityMemorialFoundation

Established in 1995 in IL; converted from sale of La Grange Memorial Hospital to Columbia/HCA.
Donors: Helen Prempas Trust; LaGrange Memorial Health System; Marion O. Crion Trust; Harris Associates.
Foundation type: Independent foundation.
Financial data (yr. ended 12/31/12): Assets, $83,876,342 (M); gifts received, $305,734; expenditures, $4,960,616; qualifying distributions, $4,449,005; giving activities include $3,333,240 for 87 grants (high: $1,004,150; low: $250), and $624,164 for 2 foundation-administered programs.
Purpose and activities: The foundation is dedicated to measurably improving the health of people who live and work in the western suburbs of Chicago, Illinois.
Fields of interest: Health care, clinics/centers; Dental care; Health care; Substance abuse, services; Mental health, clinics; Mental health, counseling/support groups; Housing/shelter, temporary shelter; Housing/shelter, homeless; Housing/shelter, services.
Type of support: Management development/capacity building; General/operating support; Continuing support; Program development; Technical assistance; Consulting services; Program evaluation; Matching/challenge support.
Limitations: Applications accepted. Giving limited to the 27 communities of Bridgeview, Broadview, Brookfield, Burr Ridge, Clarendon Hills, Countryside, Darien, Downers Grove, Hickory Hills, Hinsdale, Hodgkins, Indian Head Park, Justice, La Grange, LaGrange Park, Lyons, McCook, North Riverside, Oak Brook, Riverside, Stickney, Summit, Westchester, Western Springs, Westmont, Willow Springs and Willowbrook in the western suburbs of Chicago, IL. No support for organizations which limit services to any one religious group or members of a specific sectarian perspective. No grants to individuals, or for endowments, in-patient care, capital projects, sponsoring dinners, or advertising space.
Publications: Application guidelines; Financial statement; Grants list; Informational brochure; Newsletter; Program policy statement.
Application information: See foundation web site for downloadable General Grant Application Packet. Application form required.
Copies of proposal: 1
Deadline(s): See foundation web site for current deadlines
Board meeting date(s): Varies
Final notification: June and Dec.
Officers and Directors:* Jeffrey Simmons,* Chair.; **Beth Prohaska,* Vice-Chair. and Treas.**; Gregory DiDomenico,* C.E.O and Pres.; **Neil James,* Secy.**; Michael Bruni; Deborah Daro, Ph.D.; **Gustavo Espinosa**; Grace B. Hou; Anthony Perry, M.D.; Hon. Patrick Rogers; Ruby Roy, M.D.; **Richard Shanley.**
Number of staff: 5 full-time professional.
EIN: 364012380
Other changes: Beth Prohaska has replaced John J. Madden as Vice-Chair. and Treas. Neil James has replaced Beth Prohaska as Secy.
Maria del Socorro Pesqueira is no longer a director.

994
The Conduit Foundation
c/o Strategic Philanthropy
1700 W. Irving Park Rd., No. 203
Chicago, IL 60613-2599 (773) 360-5998
Main URL: http://www.theconduitfoundation.org

Established in 2002.
Donor: Oak Tree Trust.
Foundation type: Independent foundation.
Financial data (yr. ended 12/31/12): Assets, $21,003,442 (M); expenditures, $1,617,796; qualifying distributions, $2,561,374; giving activities include $1,548,000 for 3 grants.
Purpose and activities: Giving primarily for Jewish education.
Fields of interest: Elementary/secondary education.
Limitations: Applications not accepted. **Giving primarily in CT, MA and NY.** No grants to individuals.
Application information: Contributes only to pre-selected organizations.
Officers: William M. Doyle, Jr., Pres. and Secy.; Dennis J. Kelly, Treas.; Betsy Brill, Exec. Dir.
EIN: 043684566

995
Leslie & Loretta Copeland Foundation
c/o JPMorgan Chase Bank, N.A.
10 S. Dearborn St., IL1-0117
Chicago, IL 60603-2300

Established in 1999 in IL.
Donor: Loretta M. Copeland†.
Foundation type: Independent foundation.
Financial data (yr. ended 12/31/12): Assets, $8,551,114 (M); expenditures, $494,055; qualifying distributions, $430,873; giving activities include $412,802 for 13 grants (high: $31,754; low: $31,754).
Fields of interest: Higher education; Protestant agencies & churches.
Limitations: Applications not accepted. Giving primarily in IL. No grants to individuals.
Application information: Contributes only to pre-selected organizations.
Trustee: JPMorgan Chase Bank, N.A.
EIN: 367278445
Other changes: The grantmaker has moved from WI to IL.

996

Cord Vanderpool Foundation

10470 W. 163rd Pl.
Orland Park, IL 60467-5445 **(708) 590-6253**
***FAX:* (708) 873-5509**; Main URL: http://www.cordvanderpool.com/
Facebook: https://www.facebook.com/Cord.Vanderpool

Established in 2009 in IL.
Donors: Floridamae Vanderpool 2005 Trust; Parkview Christian Church.
Foundation type: Independent foundation.
Financial data (yr. ended 12/31/12): Assets, $3,725,871 (M); gifts received, $25,110; expenditures, $776,493; qualifying distributions, $353,499; giving activities include $177,599 for 25 grants (high: $50,000; low: $150).
Fields of interest: Education; Human services.
Limitations: Applications not accepted. Giving primarily in IL.
Application information: Unsolicited requests for funds not accepted.
Officers: Gary Bertacchi, Pres.; Thomas Lavin, V.P.
Director: Therese Foster.
EIN: 204817193

997

Arie and Ida Crown Memorial

(doing business as Crown Family Philanthropies)
222 N. LaSalle St., Ste. 1000
Chicago, IL 60601-1109 (312) 750-6671
Contact: Caren Yanis, Exec. Dir.
FAX: (312) 984-1499;
E-mail: aicm@crown-chicago.com; Main URL: http://www.crownmemorial.org/

Incorporated in 1947 in IL.
Donor: members of the Crown family.
Foundation type: Independent foundation.
Financial data (yr. ended 12/31/12): Assets, $670,711,031 (M); gifts received, $15,979,096; expenditures, $28,155,593; qualifying distributions, $23,627,848; giving activities include $22,915,737 for 444 grants (high: $1,125,000; low: $15).
Purpose and activities: Giving primarily for arts and culture, civic affairs, education, the environment, health, human services, and Jewish causes.
Fields of interest: Arts; Education; Environment; Health care; Human services; Public affairs; Jewish agencies & synagogues.
International interests: Israel.
Type of support: General/operating support; Continuing support; Annual campaigns; Capital campaigns; Building/renovation; Equipment; Endowments; Program development; Professorships; Fellowships; Scholarship funds; Employee matching gifts; Matching/challenge support.
Limitations: Applications accepted. Giving primarily in metropolitan Chicago, IL, with some giving in NY. No support for government-sponsored programs, or to organizations with budgets under $200,000. No grants to individuals, or for film, video, exhibitions, conference, associations or coalitions.
Publications: Application guidelines.
Application information: Application guidelines available on foundation web site. Application form not required.
Initial approach: E-mail letter of intent (2 pages maximum)
Copies of proposal: 1
Deadline(s): See web site deadlines for specific program areas
Board meeting date(s): Spring and fall
Officers and Directors:* Susan Crown, Pres.; A. Steven Crown,* V.P.; James S. Crown,* V.P.; Rebecca Crown,* V.P.; William Crown,* V.P.; Charles Goodman, V.P.; Barbara Goodman Manilow,* V.P.; Sara Crown Star,* V.P.; Arnold Weber,* V.P.; Lester Crown, Treas.; Caren Yanis, Exec. Dir.
Number of staff: 6 full-time professional.
EIN: 366076088

998

The de Kay Foundation

10 S. Dearborn St., IL1-0117
Chicago, IL 60603
Contact: Yvette Boisnier MSW, Prog. Dir.
Application address: c/o JPMorgan Chase Bank, N.A., Attn.: Daniel Ordan, V.P., 270 Park Ave., New York, NY 10017; tel.: (212) 648-1489

Established in 1967 in CT.
Donor: Helen M. de Kay‡.
Foundation type: Independent foundation.
Financial data (yr. ended 02/28/13): Assets, $32,797,098 (M); expenditures, $1,307,556; qualifying distributions, $1,107,961; giving activities include $700,000 for 3 grants (high: $350,000; low: $175,000), and $351,794 for grants to individuals.
Purpose and activities: The foundation traditionally awards monthly stipends directly to elderly individuals and couples to help them remain in their home in safety and comfort, to protect their dignity and individuality, and to encourage them to continue contributing to their community. Stipendiary program applicants must be 65 years of age or older and must be referred by social service agencies and have an assigned social worker. Applicants must demonstrate a history of self-sufficiency and minimal dependence on private charitable or government assistance. Individuals should also demonstrate a history of volunteering or engaging in civic or cultural activities. Applicants may have assets up to $25,000, excluding their primary residence.
Fields of interest: Hospitals (specialty); Aging.
Type of support: Grants to individuals.
Limitations: Applications accepted. Giving limited to the New York, NY metropolitan area, including the five boroughs of New York City, Westchester, Rockland, and Nassau counties, NY, Fairfield County, CT, and Essex, Bergen, Hudson, and Passaic counties, NJ. No grants for building or endowment funds, scholarships, fellowships, or matching gifts; no loans.
Publications: Application guidelines.
Application information: Monthly stipends range from $150-$1,000. Application form required.
Initial approach: Application form
Copies of proposal: 1
Deadline(s): None
Board meeting date(s): Quarterly
Final notification: 3 months
Trustee: JPMorgan Chase Bank, N.A.
EIN: 136203234
Other changes: The grantmaker has moved from DE to IL.

999

DeKalb County Community Foundation (IL)

475 DeKalb Ave.
Sycamore, IL 60178 (815) 748-5383
Contact: Daniel P. Templin, Executive Director; Anita Zurbrugg, Prog. Dir.
FAX: (815) 748-5873; E-mail: dan@dekalbccf.org; Main URL: http://www.dekalbccf.org
Facebook: http://www.facebook.com/pages/DeKalb-County-Community-Foundation/IL/92913581842

Established in 1991 in IL; re-incorporated in 1993 under current name.
Foundation type: Community foundation.
Financial data (yr. ended 12/31/12): Assets, $38,592,381 (M); gifts received, $7,210,004; expenditures, $1,184,352; giving activities include $793,151 for 31+ grants (high: $85,729).
Purpose and activities: The foundation seeks to enhance the quality of life for the citizens of DeKalb County, IL, by: 1) serving donors in achieving their philanthropic objectives; 2) creating and building a lasting source of revenue to benefit the residents of the local community; and 3) providing leadership and resources in addressing community needs.
Fields of interest: Arts; Education; Health care; Human services; Community/economic development.
Type of support: Building/renovation; Equipment; Seed money; Matching/challenge support.
Limitations: Applications accepted. Giving primarily in DeKalb County, IL. No support for religious purposes, political campaigns, or direct support to individuals. Generally no grants for operational phases of established programs, debt reduction, or advertising.
Publications: Application guidelines; Annual report; Financial statement; Grants list; Informational brochure; Newsletter; Occasional report.
Application information: Visit foundation Web site for application forms and guidelines. Application form required.
Initial approach: Contact foundation
Copies of proposal: 7
Deadline(s): Mar. 1 and Sept. 3 for Community Needs Grant
Board meeting date(s): Jan., Apr., July, and Oct.
Final notification: Approx. 60 days for Community Needs Grant
Officers and Directors:* Tim Suter,* Pres.; Donna Larson,* V.P.; Daniel P. Templin,* Secy. and Exec. Dir.; Frank Roberts,* Treas.; Marcy Billington; Larry D. Bolles; Kevin Buick; **Amie Carey**; Tim Dunlop; Patricia A. Foster; Kevin Fuss; Kristina Garcia; Marcia Goodrich; Lana Haines; Alethia Hummel; Dean Lundeen; Kevin McArtor; Charles McCormick; Penny Rosenow; Donna Turner; Beth White.
Number of staff: 2 full-time professional; 2 part-time professional.
EIN: 363788167
Other changes: Daniel P. Templin is now Secy. and Exec. Dir. Donna Larson is now V.P. Tim Suter is now Pres. Frank Roberts is now Treas. Thomas J. Matya and Mary E. Pritchard are no longer directors.

1000

Frank C. Diener Foundation

1711 Mayfair Rd.
Champaign, IL 61821-5522

Established in 1967 in CA.
Donor: Shining D Farms.
Foundation type: Independent foundation.
Financial data (yr. ended 06/30/13): Assets, $3,547,194 (M); expenditures, $441,402; qualifying distributions, $410,000; giving activities include $410,000 for 3 grants (high: $300,000; low: $10,000).
Purpose and activities: Giving primarily to Roman Catholic agencies and churches, including a high school and a hospital.

Fields of interest: Elementary/secondary education; Hospitals (general); Catholic federated giving programs; Catholic agencies & churches; Aging.
Type of support: General/operating support.
Limitations: Applications not accepted. Giving primarily in Fresno County, CA. No grants to individuals.
Application information: Contributes only to pre-selected organizations.
Officers: Edward F. Diener, Pres.; Marie C. DeMera, V.P.; Marissa Diener, Secy.; M. Dolores Brown, Treas.
EIN: 946165307
Other changes: The grantmaker has moved from CA to IL.

1001
Gaylord and Dorothy Donnelley Foundation
35 E. Wacker Dr., Ste. 2600
Chicago, IL 60601-2102 (312) 977-2700
Contact: Susan Clark, Grants Mgr.
FAX: (312) 977-1686; E-mail: info@gddf.org; **Address for Lowcountry Charleston office: 4 N. Atlantic Wharf, Charleston, SC 29401, tel. and fax: (843) 651-3793; mailing address: 5465 Huntington Marsh Rd., Murrells Inlet, SC 29576**; Main URL: http://www.gddf.org
Blog: http://gddf.org/blog
E-Newsletter: http://gddf.org/signup/

Incorporated in 1952 in IL.
Donors: Gaylord Donnelley†; Dorothy Ranney Donnelley†.
Foundation type: Independent foundation.
Financial data (yr. ended 12/31/12): Assets, $167,911,567 (M); expenditures, $8,665,514; qualifying distributions, $8,126,341; giving activities include $6,061,021 for 363 grants (high: $250,000; low: $2,500), and $61,736 for 49 employee matching gifts.
Purpose and activities: Primary areas of interest include conservation and environment, and arts and culture.
Fields of interest: Arts; Environment, natural resources; Environment.
Type of support: General/operating support; Program development; Program-related investments/loans; Employee matching gifts; Mission-related investments/loans.
Limitations: Applications accepted. Giving primarily in the Chicago, IL, area and in the Lowcountry area of SC. No support for religious purposes. No grants to individuals, or for pledges, endowments, capital campaigns, benefits, conferences, meetings, eradication of deficits, research, or studies, publications, films, videos or fundraising events; no loans (except for program-related investments).
Publications: Application guidelines; Grants list; Occasional report; Occasional report (including application guidelines).
Application information: Complete guidelines for each program are available on the foundation web site. Application form required.
Initial approach: Telephone or e-mail prior to applying online
Copies of proposal: 1
Deadline(s): Generally, Apr., July and Dec. See web site for exact dates
Board meeting date(s): Mar., July, and Nov.
Final notification: 1 month
Officers and Directors:* Laura Donnelley,* Chair.; Shawn M. Donnelley,* Secy.-Treas.; J. David Farren, Exec. Dir.; Julia Antonatos; Timothy H. Brown; Peter R. Crane; Ceara Donnelley; Vivian Donnelley; Charles Lane; Cheryl Mayberry McKissack; Dr. John Rashford; Alex Shuford; Max E. Wheeler; Mimi Wheeler.
Number of staff: 4 full-time professional; 3 full-time support.
EIN: 366108460

1002
The Richard H. Driehaus Foundation
737 N. Michigan Ave., Ste. 2000
Chicago, IL **60611-6745** (312) 641-5772
FAX: (312) 641-5736; Contact for arts and culture groups with budgets under $500,000: Richard Cahan, Prog. Off., e-mail: RichardCahan@aol.com, tel.: (847) 722-9244; Contact for small theater and dance companies with budgets under $150,000, Peter Handler, Prog. Dir., e-mail: peterhandler@driehausfoundation.org; E-mail for general inquiries, Kim Romero, Admin.: kimromero@driehausfoundation.org; Main URL: http://www.driehausfoundation.org
RSS Feed: http://www.driehausfoundation.org/rss.xml
YouTube: http://www.youtube.com/user/DriehausFoundation

Established in 1983 in IL.
Donors: Richard H. Driehaus; John D. and Catherine T. MacArthur Foundation; Reva and David Logan Foundation; Leveraging Investment in Creativity.
Foundation type: Independent foundation.
Financial data (yr. ended 12/31/12): Assets, $68,459,646 (M); gifts received, $10,007,879; expenditures, $5,185,749; qualifying distributions, $4,806,223; giving activities include $3,966,529 for 442 grants (high: $100,000; low: $87).
Purpose and activities: The foundation benefits individuals and communities primarily by supporting the preservation and enhancement of the built and natural environments through historic preservation, encouragement of quality architectural and landscape design, and conserving open space. The foundation also supports the performing and visual arts, investigative reporting and government accountability, and makes grants to organizations that provide opportunities for working families who remain poor.
Fields of interest: Visual arts, design; Historic preservation/historical societies; Arts; Housing/shelter, development; Human services; Economic development.
International interests: Scotland.
Type of support: General/operating support; Capital campaigns; Emergency funds; Program development; Publication; Seed money; Grants to individuals; Matching/challenge support.
Limitations: Giving primarily in the metropolitan Chicago, IL, area which includes Cook, DuPage, Lake, McHenry, Kane and Will counties. Generally, no support for arts education or arts outreach, community theater or community dance, public, private or parochial education, or health care.
Publications: Application guidelines; Biennial report; Multi-year report.
Application information: Applications accepted only for MacArthur grants. Application guidelines and form are available on foundation web site. Faxed proposals are not accepted. Application form required.
Initial approach: Letter of inquiry or telephone for Built Environment, Economic Opportunity for the Working Poor, Government Accountability/Investigative Reporting, Small Museums and Cultural Centers funding areas; Arts and culture groups with budgets under $500,000, and small theater and dance companies with budgets under $150,000 may apply online through foundation web site
Copies of proposal: 2
Deadline(s): See foundation web site for current deadlines in each funding area
Final notification: 4 - 5 months
Officers and Directors:* Richard H. Driehaus,* Pres.; Elizabeth Driehaus,* Secy.; Dorothy Mellin,* Treas.; **Kim Coventry, Exec. Dir.**
Number of staff: 2 full-time professional; 1 full-time support.
EIN: 363261347
Other changes: Kim Coventry has replaced Sonia Fischer as Exec. Dir.

1003
Walter S. and Lucienne Driskill Charitable Foundation
311 W. Superior St., Ste. 207
Chicago, IL 60654-2619
***Contact:* June Barnard, Exec. Dir.**
FAX: (312) 266-1797;
E-mail: rlb@driskillfoundation.com; Main URL: http://www.driskillfoundation.com

Established in 1986 in FL.
Donors: Walter S. Driskill†; Lucienne Driskill†.
Foundation type: Independent foundation.
Financial data (yr. ended 12/31/12): Assets, $29,886,799 (M); expenditures, $9,291,927; qualifying distributions, $8,673,810; giving activities include $8,598,946 for 13 grants (high: $3,412,500; low: $15,000).
Purpose and activities: The objectives of the foundation are to benefit research, development and use of medical treatments and medicines used in such treatments. Also, the foundation will seek to provide assistance to relieve and eliminate child abuse and provide assistance to infants and children who are without proper homes.
Fields of interest: Health care; Medical research; Crime/violence prevention, child abuse; Children/youth, services.
Limitations: Applications accepted. Giving on a national basis. No support for religious institutions, or for sports organizations, political organizations or performing arts organizations. No grants to individuals, or for endowments, or capital improvements.
Application information: Summary proposal form available on foundation web site. Formal proposals accepted by invitation only. Application form required.
Deadline(s): Nov. 1 for Summary proposals
Final notification: Foundation will request formal applications by Jan. 1
Officer and Directors:* June Barnard,* Exec. Dir.; Laura F. Gutierrez; Edward A. Kennedy III.
EIN: 061190296
Other changes: June Barnard has replaced Ronald L. Barnard as Exec. Dir.
Edward A. Kennedy and Carmine Figlilio are no longer directors.

1004
Edward T. & Ellen K. Dryer Charitable Foundation
P.O. Box 803878
Chicago, IL 60680-3878

Donor: Ellen Dryer†.
Foundation type: Independent foundation.
Financial data (yr. ended 11/30/13): Assets, $2,621,770 (M); expenditures, $1,180,076;

qualifying distributions, $1,155,000; giving activities include $1,140,000 for 6 grants (high: $1,000,000; low: $15,000).
Fields of interest: Education, public education; Education; Health care; Human services; Blind/ visually impaired.
Type of support: General/operating support.
Limitations: Applications not accepted. Giving primarily in MI. No grants to individuals.
Application information: Contributes only to pre-selected organizations.
Trustees: Joseph Drobot; Judy Drobot; Elizabeth Mower Gandelot; Jon B. Gandelot.
EIN: 371451429
Other changes: At the close of 2013, the grantmaker paid grants of $1,140,000, a 647.5% increase over the 2012 disbursements, $152,500.

1005
The Duchossois Family Foundation
(formerly The Duchossois Foundation)
1515 W. 22nd St., Ste. 650
Oak Brook, IL 60523 (312) 641-5765

Established in 1984 in IL.
Donors: Duchossois Industries, Inc.; Thrall Car Manufacturing Co.; Duchossois Technology Partners, LLC; Chamberlain Group, Inc.
Foundation type: Company-sponsored foundation.
Financial data (yr. ended 12/31/12): Assets, $185,385 (M); gifts received, $527; expenditures, $910,854; qualifying distributions, $907,646; giving activities include $762,580 for 64 grants (high: $100,000; low: $500).
Purpose and activities: The foundation supports organizations involved with mental health, cancer, and human services.
Fields of interest: Education; Health organizations; Human services.
Type of support: General/operating support; Annual campaigns; Capital campaigns; Research; Employee matching gifts.
Limitations: Applications not accepted. Giving primarily in the metropolitan Chicago, IL, area.
Application information: Contributes only to pre-selected organizations.
Board meeting date(s): 4 times per year
Officers and Directors:* Kimberly T. Duchossois,* Pres.; Craig J. Duchossois,* V.P. and Treas.; Richard L. Duchossois,* Secy.
Number of staff: 1 part-time professional; 1 part-time support.
EIN: 363327987
Other changes: The grantmaker no longer lists an E-mail address. The grantmaker no longer lists a primary contact.

1006
Dunard Fund USA, Ltd.
555 Skokie Blvd., Ste. 555
Northbrook, IL 60062-2845

Established around 1993 in IL.
Donors: Consolidated Electrical Distributors, Inc.; LCR-M Corp.; Carol C. Hogel.
Foundation type: Company-sponsored foundation.
Financial data (yr. ended 12/31/12): Assets, $34,331,373 (M); gifts received, $15,005,000; expenditures, $3,464,471; qualifying distributions, $3,186,803; giving activities include $3,171,445 for 23 grants (high: $1,332,950; low: $8,930).
Purpose and activities: The foundation supports organizations involved with arts and culture and education.
Fields of interest: Museums; Performing arts, music; Performing arts, orchestras; Performing arts, opera; Performing arts, education; Arts; Higher education.
Type of support: Matching/challenge support; General/operating support; Continuing support; Annual campaigns; Endowments; Program development; Scholarship funds.
Limitations: Applications not accepted. Giving primarily in CA, New York, NY, and Philadelphia, PA. No grants to individuals.
Application information: Contributes only to organizations referred by known and highly respected figures.
Board meeting date(s): Weekly
Officers and Directors:* Carol C. Hogel,* Pres. and Treas.; David T. Bradford, Secy.; Catherine C. Hogel; Elisabeth Hogel.
EIN: 980087034
Other changes: At the close of 2012, the fair market value of the grantmaker's assets was $34,331,373, a 71.8% increase over the 2011 value, $19,977,846.

1007
The Dunham Fund
8 E. Galena Blvd., Ste. 202
Aurora, IL 60506-4161 (630) 844-2774
FAX: (630) 844-4405;
E-mail: info@dunhamfund.org; Main URL: http://www.dunhamfund.org
Facebook: https://www.facebook.com/DunhamFund
Twitter: https://twitter.com/DunhamFund
Wordpress: http://dunhamfund.wordpress.com/
YouTube: https://www.youtube.com/user/DunhamFund?feature=mhee

Established in 2007 in IL.
Donor: John C. Dunham Trust.
Foundation type: Independent foundation.
Financial data (yr. ended 12/31/12): Assets, $76,764,979 (M); expenditures, $3,282,530; qualifying distributions, $2,858,603; giving activities include $2,358,603 for 30 grants (high: $535,000; low: $2,250).
Purpose and activities: The mission of the fund is to honor the legacy of John C. Dunham. In that spirit, the fund supports organizations that work to make the world a safer and more comfortable place for mankind to live and prosper, giving special consideration to Aurora, Illinois-area organizations engaged in providing education and to organizations engaged in assisting individuals to attain heights they may not have attained without the benefit of such assistance. Areas of interest include: education within formal academic settings such as licensed early childhood education, K-12, college, and graduate school, including STEM (Science, Technology, Mathematics and Science) education, workforce development, and other accredited professional certifications; and community development, which the fund describes as the expansion of infrastructure, capital, resources, human capital or aggregate capability available to the community on a long term basis that provides support for stronger social or economic interaction and performance.
Fields of interest: Vocational education; Education; Housing/shelter.
Type of support: Scholarship funds; Program-related investments/loans.
Limitations: Giving primarily in the Aurora, IL area; the fund gives preference to applicants located within Kane, DuPage and Kendall Counties, more specifically, the geography bounded on the north by Illinois State Route 38 and on the south by U.S. Route 34; on the east by Illinois State Route 59 and on the west by Illinois State Route 47.
Publications: Application guidelines.
Application information: Full grant applications by invitation only, upon review of letter of inquiry. The fund prefers to provide one-time, startup funding for new or uniquely enhanced educational or community development programs and capital projects. See foundation web site for detailed application information.
***Initial approach:* Use online grant application on foundation web site**
Deadline(s): Feb. 1 and June 1
Officers and Directors:* Mark Treumper, Chair.; Robert W. Vaughn, Exec. Dir.; Stewart Beach; Wendy Hirsch; Ryan Maley; Michael J. Morcos; Christine Tunney.
EIN: 376416138

1008
The DuPage Community Foundation
104 E. Roosevelt Rd., Ste. 204
Wheaton, IL 60187-5200 (630) 665-5556
Contact: David M. McGowan, Pres.; For grants: Barb Szczepaniak, Dir., Progs.
FAX: (630) 665-9571; E-mail: dmm@dcfdn.org; Grant application e-mail: barbs@dcfdn.org; Main URL: http://www.dcfdn.org
Facebook: http://www.facebook.com/pages/The-DuPage-Community-Foundation/101853007709
LinkedIn: http://www.linkedin.com/company/the-dupage-community-foundation
Twitter: https://twitter.com/DCFDN

Established in 1986 in IL as fund of Chicago Community Trust; became a separate entity in 1994.
Foundation type: Community foundation.
Financial data (yr. ended 06/30/13): Assets, $47,016,028 (M); gifts received, $4,412,199; expenditures, $3,351,925; giving activities include $2,360,061 for 97+ grants (high: $250,000).
Purpose and activities: The foundation was created to benefit the residents of DuPage County, IL. It receives contributions and bequests into a permanent endowment that continues to grow and help meet the needs of its community. Priorities in grantmaking are arts and culture, environment, education, health, and human services.
Fields of interest: Arts; Education; Environment, pollution control; Environmental education; Environment; Animals/wildlife, preservation/ protection; Health care; Mental health/crisis services; Children/youth, services; Human services.
Type of support: General/operating support; Building/renovation; Equipment; Program development; Seed money; Scholarship funds; Matching/challenge support.
Limitations: Applications accepted. Giving primarily in DuPage County, IL. No support for religious purposes, disease-specific organizations, historic societies and foundations, food pantries for the purchase of food, hospitals, private foundations or private operating foundations. **No grants to individuals, or for endowments.**
Publications: Application guidelines; Annual report; Grants list; Informational brochure; Newsletter; Occasional report.
Application information: Visit foundation web site for application form and guidelines. The foundation accepts requests for up to $2,500 for Community Needs mini-grants, and $20,000 for Community Needs general grants. Application form required.

Initial approach: Telephone
Copies of proposal: 2
Deadline(s): 1st Fri. in Mar. for Health and Human Services and 1st Fri. in Sept. for Arts and Culture, Education, and Environment
Board meeting date(s): Bimonthly
Final notification: 10 weeks

Officers and Trustees:* Stephen M. Burt,* Chair.; Joan S. Morrissey,* Vice-Chair.; David M. McGowan,* Pres.; Denice A. Gierach,* Secy.; Ernest J. Mrozek,* Treas.; **Betsy K. Brosnan**; Phillip R. Cabrera; Brett M. Dale; Marilyn K. Gaston; Janet A. Hodge; Frank C. Hudetz; Christopher M. Janc; William J. Kennedy; **Mary Kay Kluge**; Richard W. Kuhn; **Bruce K. Lee**; **Daniel Maguire**; Charles B. McKenna; Charles G. Mueller; Nathaniel P. Wasson; Joyce A. Webb; Joseph L. Weidenbach.
Number of staff: 5 full-time professional; 1 part-time support.
EIN: 363978733
Other changes: Dalip Bammi, Josephine Beavers, James C. Bridgman, and Denice A. Gierach are no longer trustees.

1009
Edlis-Neeson Foundation
175 E. Delaware Pl., No. 5116
Chicago, IL **60611-1756**

Established in 2007 in IL.
Donor: Stefan Edlis.
Foundation type: Independent foundation.
Financial data (yr. ended 12/31/13): Assets, $19,062,247 (M); expenditures, $2,316,547; qualifying distributions, $2,237,038; giving activities include $2,227,150 for 46 grants (high: $446,000; low: $1,000).
Fields of interest: Arts education; Museums (art); Human services; Social sciences.
Limitations: Applications not accepted. Giving primarily in CO, Washington, DC, IL, and NY.
Application information: Contributes only to pre-selected organizations.
Directors: Stefan Edlis; Jack Guthman; Heather Gael Neeson.
EIN: 208986573

1010
Greater Edwardsville Area Community Foundation
(also known as Your Community Foundation)
P.O. Box 102
Edwardsville, IL 62025-1911 (855) 464-3223
Contact: Mary Westerhold, Chair.
E-mail: contact@edwardsvillefoundation.org; Main URL: http://www.geacf.org/
Blog: http://www.geacf.org/category/news/
E-Newsletter: http://edwardsvillefoundation.us2.list-manage.com/subscribe?u=9401e8e863419e971bb8aad42&id=356341c88c
Facebook: http://www.facebook.com/edwardsvillecommunityfoundation
Twitter: http://twitter.com/TheGEACF

Established in 1997 in IL.
Foundation type: Community foundation.
Financial data (yr. ended 12/31/12): Assets, $1,697,395 (M); gifts received, $463,984; expenditures, $547,196; giving activities include $445,315 for 14+ grants (high: $170,000), and $68,950 for 58 grants to individuals.
Purpose and activities: The foundation's mission is to enhance the quality of life in the Greater Edwardsville area by: 1) leading the development of collaboration and understanding among all members of the community; 2) ascertaining community needs and opportunities; 3) providing a flexible permanent vehicle for donors with diverse interests; 4) protecting the community's endowment through prudent investment and effective stewardship; 5) expanding the community's endowment through appropriate solicitations; and 6) acting as an informed grant maker.
Fields of interest: Arts; Education; Environment; Health care; Human services; Community/economic development.
Type of support: Building/renovation; Equipment; Land acquisition; Emergency funds; Program development; Conferences/seminars; Curriculum development; Consulting services; Scholarships—to individuals.
Limitations: Applications accepted. **Giving primarily in Edwardsville, Glen Carbon, Hamel, Worden, Dorsey, and Moro, IL.** No support for sectarian religious programs. No grants for operating budgets, basic municipal services, basic educational functions, or endowment campaigns.
Publications: Informational brochure; Newsletter.
Application information: Visit foundation web site for application form and guidelines. Application form required.
Initial approach: Submit application form and attachments
Copies of proposal: 1
Deadline(s): Oct. 1
Board meeting date(s): Jan., Mar., May, July, Sept., and Nov.
Final notification: Nov.

Officers and Directors:* Mary Westerhold,* Chair.; Patty Thiede,* Vice-Chair., Chair, Gifts and Funds Comm., and Treas.; Chad Abernathy,* Chair., Community Awareness Comm.; Suzanne Weiss,* Chair., Education Comm.; Scott Weber,* Chair., Grants Review Comm.; Steve Mudge,* Secy.; Calvin Brown; Greg Coffey; Faye Coffman; Jill Dorsey; Pete Fornof; David Gerber; Phil Lading; Linda Lynch; Joseph Malench; Carol Mestemacher; John Motley; Will Shashack.
EIN: 367146151

1011
Eisenberg Family Charitable Trust
c/o JPMorgan Chase Bank, N.A.
10 S. Dearborn St., IL1-0117
Chicago, IL 60603-2300
***Application address:* c/o Carolyn O'Brien, Program Officer, 270 Park Ave., NY1-K348, New York, NY 10017, tel.: (212) 464-2350**

Established in 1996 in NY.
Donor: Estelle Eisenberg†.
Foundation type: Independent foundation.
Financial data (yr. ended 04/30/13): Assets, $7,200,784 (M); expenditures, $404,909; qualifying distributions, $344,644; giving activities include $325,000 for 1 grant.
Fields of interest: Health care; Alzheimer's disease.
Limitations: Applications accepted. Giving primarily in FL; some funding also in IL. No grants to individuals.
Publications: Grants list.
Application information:
***Deadline(s):* None**
Board meeting date(s): Apr.

Trustee: JPMorgan Chase Bank, N.A.
EIN: 527091392

1012
Evanston Community Foundation
1560 Sherman Ave., Ste. 535
Evanston, IL **60201** (847) 492-0990
Contact: Sara L. Schastok Ph.D., C.E.O.; For grants: Marybeth Schroeder, V.P., Progs.
FAX: (847) 492-0904;
E-mail: info@evanstonforever.org; Additional e-mail: schastok@evanstonforever.org; Grant inquiry e-mail: schroeder@evanstonforever.org; Grant inquiry tel.: (847) 492-0990; Main URL: http://www.evanstonforever.org
Facebook: https://www.facebook.com/evanstonforever
Twitter: http://www.twitter.com/evanstonforever

Established in 1986 in IL.
Foundation type: Community foundation.
Financial data (yr. ended 12/31/12): Assets, $17,138,221 (M); gifts received, $2,050,801; expenditures, $2,333,103; giving activities include $1,404,948 for 45+ grants (high: $108,250).
Purpose and activities: The foundation was established as a publicly supported philanthropic organization. Helping Evanston thrive now and forever as a vibrant, inclusive, and just community, the Evanston Community Foundation builds, connects, and distributes resources and knowledge through local organizations for the common good.
Fields of interest: Arts; Education, early childhood education; Education; Environment; Health care; Health organizations, association; AIDS; Employment, services; Housing/shelter, development; Youth development, services; Children/youth, services; Family services; Aging, centers/services; Minorities/immigrants, centers/services; Homeless, human services; Human services; Community development, neighborhood development; Community/economic development; Public affairs, citizen participation; Leadership development; Infants/toddlers; Children/youth; Youth; Aging; Disabilities, people with; Minorities; Women; Girls; Boys; Economically disadvantaged; Homeless.
Type of support: Income development; Management development/capacity building; Program development; Seed money; Curriculum development; Program evaluation.
Limitations: Applications accepted. Giving limited to organizations serving the Evanston, IL community. No grants to individuals.
Publications: Annual report; Grants list; Informational brochure; Newsletter; Occasional report.
Application information: Visit foundation web site for applications and guidelines per grant type. Application form required.
Initial approach: Create an online eGrant account
Copies of proposal: 15
***Deadline(s):* Jan. 28 for Responsive Grants program; varies for others**
Board meeting date(s): Jan., Mar., May, June, Sept., Nov., and Dec.
Final notification: Varies

Officers and Directors:* Joan Gunzberg,* Chair.; Mike Brody,* 1st Vice-Chair.; Judith Aiello-Fantus,* 2nd Vice-Chair.; **Sara L. Schastok, Ph.D.*, Pres. and C.E.O.**; **Gwen Jessen,* V.P., Philanthropy**; Marybeth Schroeder,* V.P., Progs.; Anne Murdoch,* Secy.; Bill Blanchard,* Treas.; Jan Fischer,* C.F.O.; Lisa Altenbernd; Lun Ye Crim Barefield; Julie Chernoff; Diana Cohen; **Pete Henderson**; Burgie Howard; Bill Logan; **John McCarthy**; Kevin Mott; Richard Peach; **Patty Reece**; Eric Robison; **Penelope Sachs**; Keith Sarpolis, M.D.; **Gene Servillo**; Sandra Waller Shelton, C.P.A.; Larry Singer; Keith Terry; Judy Witt.

Number of staff: 4 full-time professional; 3 part-time professional.
EIN: 363466802
Other changes: Amy Monday is now Devel. Off. Sara L. Schastok is now Pres. and C.E.O. Judith Aiello-Fantus, Bill Blanchard, Julie Captain, Mary Finnegan, Naomi Lovinger, Anne Murdoch, and Shabnum Sanghvi are no longer directors.

1013
FDC Foundation
1415 W. 55th St., Ste. 202
Countryside, IL 60525-6543 (847) 235-2170
Contact: John C. Doyle, Pres.
E-mail: fcluck@fdcfoundation.org**; Additional e-mail: jdoyle@fdcfoundation.org**; Main URL: http://www.fdcfoundation.org/

Foundation type: Independent foundation.
Financial data (yr. ended 12/31/12): Assets, $10,270,805 (M); expenditures, $614,462; qualifying distributions, $479,500; giving activities include $479,500 for 27 grants (high: $30,000; low: $4,500).
Purpose and activities: Giving primarily for: 1) Health, particularly to organizations that support a) improved nutrition for Americans, including organizations supplying food and food supplements to people in need as well as those providing education regarding proper nutrition; b) the treatment of persons with diabetes, including education, nutrition, medication and supplies for persons who either now have or who are at high risk of developing diabetes; and c) the expanded use of alternative medicines, including all forms of non-traditional therapies and medications that offer promise of improving the lives of people, whether healthy or ill; 2) Education, particularly to organizations that support a) early childhood development programs, including but not limited to educational institutions currently doing outstanding work in the field; b) programs for returning scholars, supporting organizations that provide financial support (such as reimbursement of tuition, fees, cost of books and additional living expenses) incurred by persons who return to school to continue their education later in life; and c) literary achievement, specifically organizations (such as colleges and universities) offering financial support or programs to gifted individuals pursuing the creation of meritorious literary works (poetry, fiction, drama, non-fiction prose, or translation) over a specific time period (such as one year); and 3) Housing, particularly to organizations that provide opportunities to those who have difficulty finding housing or achieving home ownership. The organizations may support construction of new housing, rehabilitation of existing housing, or financing of housing for people having unusual needs or facing extraordinary challenges. The foundation may also offer grants to organizations supporting education for careers within the real estate industry, such as the endowment of a chair with the business department of a university.
Fields of interest: Education, early childhood education; Education; Health care; Diabetes; Nutrition; Housing/shelter; Human services.
Limitations: Applications accepted. Giving primarily in IL. **No support for international organizations, or for-profit businesses.**
Application information: Application form required.
Initial approach: Letter
***Deadline(s):* See foundation web site for current deadlines**
Final notification: Within 3 months
Officers: Frank D. Cluck, Jr., Chair. and Treas.; John C. Doyle, Pres.; Bruce W. Cluck, V.P.; Cynthia Heynen, V.P.; Susan Patke, V.P.; Maria Begona Pulido, Secy.
EIN: 263349582

1014
The Field Foundation of Illinois, Inc.
200 S. Wacker Dr., Ste. 3860
Chicago, IL 60606-5848 (312) 831-0910
Contact: Aurie A. Pennick, Exec. Dir.; Beatrice Young, Opers./Grants Mgr.
FAX: (312) 831-0961;
E-mail: byoung@fieldfoundation.org; Main URL: http://www.fieldfoundation.org

Incorporated in 1960 in IL.
Donor: Marshall Field IV†.
Foundation type: Independent foundation.
Financial data (yr. ended 04/30/13): Assets, $60,814,807 (M); expenditures, $2,087,156; qualifying distributions, $3,361,186; giving activities include $2,462,250 for 143 grants (high: $25,000), and $106,875 for 87 employee matching gifts.
Purpose and activities: The foundation seeks to provide support for community, civic, and cultural organizations in the Chicago, Illinois area, enabling both new and established programs to test innovations, to expand proven strengths or to address specific, time-limited operational needs. The foundation supports giving in the fields of health, community welfare, primary and secondary education, cultural activities, conservation, and urban and community affairs.
Fields of interest: Museums; Arts; Education, early childhood education; Elementary school/education; Secondary school/education; Adult education—literacy, basic skills & GED; Education; Environment; Health care; Substance abuse, services; Mental health/crisis services; AIDS; Employment; Food services; Human services; Children/youth, services; Aging, centers/services; Homeless, human services; Civil rights, race/intergroup relations; Community/economic development; Public policy, research; Public affairs; Children/youth; Youth; Aging; Disabilities, people with; Minorities; Women; Girls; Offenders/ex-offenders; AIDS, people with; Crime/abuse victims; Immigrants/refugees; Economically disadvantaged; Homeless; LGBTQ.
Type of support: General/operating support; Capital campaigns; Building/renovation; Equipment; Land acquisition; Emergency funds; Program development; Seed money; Curriculum development; Technical assistance; Employee matching gifts; Matching/challenge support.
Limitations: Applications accepted. Giving primarily in the Chicago, IL, metropolitan area. No support for member agencies of community funds, medical research, national health agencies, neighborhood health clinics, small cultural groups, or religious purposes. No grants to individuals, or for endowment funds, continuing operating support, conferences, operating support of day care centers, fundraising events, advertising, scholarships, printed materials or video equipment, or fellowships; no loans.
Publications: Biennial report; Informational brochure (including application guidelines); Occasional report.
Application information: Application guidelines available on foundation web site. Application form not required.
***Initial approach:* Proposal, including Self-Certification Checklist**
Copies of proposal: 1
***Deadline(s):* Jan. 15, May 15, and Sept. 15 (if these dates fall on a weekend, the deadline is the following Monday)**
Board meeting date(s): 3 times per year
Final notification: Within 4 months
Officers and Directors:* Lyle Logan, Chair.; Sarah Linsley,* Secy.; Aurie A. Pennick, Treas. and Exec. Dir.; Judith S. Block; Gloria Castillo; Marshall Field V; Rita A. Fry; Philip Wayne Hummer; F. Oliver Nicklin; George A. Ranney, Jr.
Number of staff: 4 full-time professional; 1 full-time support; 1 part-time support.
EIN: 366059408
Other changes: Lyle Logan has replaced Judith S. Block as Chair.
Lyle Logan is now Chair.

1015
Foglia Family Foundation
190 S. LaSalle St., Ste. 1700
Chicago, IL 60603-3411

Established in 1993 in IL.
Donor: Vincent W. Foglia.
Foundation type: Independent foundation.
Financial data (yr. ended 09/30/13): Assets, $73,911,868 (M); gifts received, $75,020,000; expenditures, $7,226,910; qualifying distributions, $7,017,080; giving activities include $7,017,080 for 94 grants (high: $750,000; low: $300).
Fields of interest: Higher education; Education; Hospitals (general); Health care; Human services; YM/YWCAs & YM/YWHAs; Children/youth, services; Residential/custodial care, hospices.
Limitations: Applications not accepted. Giving primarily in Chicago, IL. No grants to individuals.
Application information: Contributes only to pre-selected organizations.
Officers and Directors:* Patricia A. Foglia,* Pres.; Vincent W. Foglia,* Secy.-Treas.; Kymberly A. Foglia; Vincent J. Foglia.
EIN: 363925857
Other changes: For the fiscal year ended Sept. 30, 2013, the fair market value of the grantmaker's assets was $73,911,868, a 1,655.2% increase over the fiscal 2012 value, $4,210,926.

1016
Herman Forbes Charitable Trust
c/o JPMorgan Chase Bank, N.A.
10 S. Dearborn St., IL1-0117
Chicago, IL 60603-2300
Application address: c/o JPMorgan Chase Bank, N.A., 270 Park Ave., 16th Fl., New York, NY 10017-2014, tel.: (212) 464-1020

Incorporated in 1982 in NY.
Donor: Herman Forbes†.
Foundation type: Independent foundation.
Financial data (yr. ended 03/31/13): Assets, $7,188,033 (M); expenditures, $476,039; qualifying distributions, $387,779; giving activities include $360,000 for 31 grants (high: $43,000; low: $2,000).
Fields of interest: Education; Jewish agencies & synagogues.
Limitations: Applications accepted. Giving primarily in FL and New York, NY; some giving in NH. No grants to individuals or for matching gifts or loans.
Publications: Grants list.
Application information: Application form not required.
Deadline(s): None
Board meeting date(s): Mar. and Dec.

Trustees: William H. Fleece, Esq.; Benjamin Ari Herring; Gerald Moss; JPMorgan Chase Bank, N.A.
EIN: 136814404
Other changes: The grantmaker has moved from WI to IL.

1017
Frankel Family Foundation

c/o Peter Frankel
1700 W. Irving Park Rd., Ste. 203
Chicago, IL 60613-2599 (773) 360-5412
FAX: (773) 224-5187;
E-mail: info@frankelfamilyfoundation.org; Main URL: http://www.frankelfamilyfoundation.org/index.aspx
Grants Database: http://www.frankelfamilyfoundation.org/grantlist.aspx

Established in 2000 in IL.
Donors: Bernard Frankel; Peter Frankel; Miriam Frankel; Frankel Family LP; Matthew Frankel Living Trust.
Foundation type: Independent foundation.
Financial data (yr. ended 10/31/12): Assets, $10,196,517 (M); gifts received, $3,269,657; expenditures, $760,831; qualifying distributions, $732,548; giving activities include $630,000 for 54 grants (high: $100,000; low: $1,000).
Purpose and activities: Giving primarily for the environment, a democratic and peaceful Israel as a homeland for Jews, fighting anti-Semitism wherever it exists, and for providing education for refugees and displaced persons.
Fields of interest: Arts; Education; Environment; Human services; Children/youth, services; Jewish federated giving programs.
Type of support: General/operating support; Continuing support; Annual campaigns; Capital campaigns; Building/renovation; Equipment; Land acquisition; Endowments; Debt reduction; Emergency funds; Program development; Conferences/seminars; Professorships; Publication; Seed money; Curriculum development; Fellowships; Internship funds; Scholarship funds; Research; Technical assistance; Consulting services; Matching/challenge support.
Limitations: Giving primarily in Chicago and Evanston, IL; some funding nationally, particularly in NY. No grants to individuals.
Publications: Application guidelines.
Application information: Full proposals by invitation only; application guidelines available on foundation web site.
Initial approach: Letter of inquiry via foundation web site
Deadline(s): None
Final notification: Within 6 weeks
Officers and Directors:* Peter Frankel,* Pres.; Miriam Frankel,* V.P.; Bernard Frankel,* Treas.; **Marya Frankel**; Matthew Frankel.
EIN: 367337220
Other changes: The grantmaker now publishes application guidelines.

1018
Lloyd A. Fry Foundation

120 S. LaSalle St., Ste. 1950
Chicago, IL 60603-3419 (312) 580-0310
***Contact:* Unmi Song, Pres. and Secy.**
FAX: (312) 580-0980;
E-mail: usong@fryfoundation.org; Main URL: http://www.fryfoundation.org

Established in 1959 in IL.
Donor: Lloyd A. Fry†.
Foundation type: Independent foundation.
Financial data (yr. ended 06/30/13): Assets, $164,492,986 (M); expenditures, $10,109,550; qualifying distributions, $9,181,748; giving activities include $7,389,379 for 276 grants (high: $150,000; low: $200).
Purpose and activities: The foundation supports organizations with the strength and commitment to address persistent problems of urban Chicago resulting from poverty, violence, ignorance and despair. The foundation seeks to build the capacity of individuals and the systems that serve them. The vision is of a Chicago that offers education, prosperity and hope for all.
Fields of interest: Arts; Elementary school/education; Secondary school/education; Education; Health care; AIDS; Employment; Minorities/immigrants, centers/services; Children/youth; Children; Adults; Young adults; Minorities; Asians/Pacific Islanders; African Americans/Blacks; Hispanics/Latinos; Women; Girls; Adults, women; Young adults, female; Men; Boys; Adults, men; Young adults, male; AIDS, people with; Immigrants/refugees; Economically disadvantaged.
Type of support: General/operating support; Continuing support; Program development; Curriculum development; Technical assistance; Program evaluation.
Limitations: Applications accepted. Giving generally limited to Chicago, IL. No support for medical research, religious purposes, governmental bodies, or tax-supported educational institutions for services that fall within their responsibilities. No grants to individuals, or for general operating support for new grantees, annual campaigns, emergency funds, deficit financing, building funds, fundraising benefits, land acquisition, renovation projects, or endowment funds; no loans.
Publications: Application guidelines; Annual report (including application guidelines); Financial statement; Grants list.
Application information: Organizations outside of Chicago, IL are rarely funded. The foundation now requires demographic information from applicant organizations. Chicago Area Grant Application Form accepted. Application form not required.
Initial approach: Letter of inquiry
Copies of proposal: 1
Deadline(s): Mar. 1, June 1, Sept. 1, and Dec. 1
Board meeting date(s): Feb., May, Aug., and Nov.
Final notification: 3 months
Officers and Directors:* Howard M. McCue III,* Chair.; Lloyd A. Fry III,* Vice-Chair.; **Unmi Song, Pres. and Secy.**; Stephanie Pace Marshall,* V.P.; Graham C. Grady, Treas.; **Diane Sotiros, Cont.**; **Amina J. Dickerson**; David A. Donovan.
Number of staff: 5 full-time professional; 2 full-time support; 1 part-time support.
EIN: 366108775
Other changes: Unmi Song is now Pres. and Secy.

1019
Charles F. & Esther M. Frye Foundation

P.O. Box 803878
Chicago, IL 60680-3878

Established in 1999 in FL.
Donors: Esther M. Frye; Esther Frye Interim Trust.
Foundation type: Independent foundation.
Financial data (yr. ended 05/31/13): Assets, $2,386,122 (M); expenditures, $165,142; qualifying distributions, $141,904; giving activities include $138,849 for 19 grants (high: $25,000; low: $2,500).
Fields of interest: Hospitals (specialty); Cancer; Salvation Army; Residential/custodial care, hospices; Protestant agencies & churches; Children.
Limitations: Applications not accepted. Giving primarily in FL. No grants to individuals.
Application information: Unsolicited requests for funds not accepted.
Trustee: The Northern Trust Co.
EIN: 656303071
Other changes: The grantmaker no longer lists a phone.

1020
Fulk Family Foundation, Inc.

10 S. Wacker Dr., Ste. 2675
Chicago, IL 60606-7475 (312) 236-2233

Established in 1989 in NE.
Donors: Wilma B. Fulk†; Robert W. Fulk; Fulk Farms, Inc.
Foundation type: Independent foundation.
Financial data (yr. ended 07/31/13): Assets, $26,636,952 (M); gifts received, $1,538,774; expenditures, $1,080,843; qualifying distributions, $913,185; giving activities include $910,000 for 32 grants (high: $100,000; low: $1,000).
Fields of interest: Arts; Education; Health care; Medical research; Human services.
Limitations: Giving in the U.S., with emphasis on IL.
Application information:
***Initial approach:* Letter to the Board**
Deadline(s): Dec. 1
Final notification: Dec. 31
Officer and Directors:* Robert W. Fulk,* Pres. and Treas.; Alice Brunner; Marcia Coffman; N. Jane Morrison.
EIN: 470732237

1021
Paul A. Funk Foundation

115 W. Jefferson St., Ste. 200
Bloomington, IL 61702-3217

Established in 1967 in IL.
Foundation type: Independent foundation.
Financial data (yr. ended 06/30/13): Assets, $10,531,927 (M); gifts received, $100; expenditures, $414,719; qualifying distributions, $465,313; giving activities include $213,400 for 40 grants (high: $50,000; low: $500), and $251,913 for foundation-administered programs.
Purpose and activities: Giving primarily for education, health, human services, and to a nature center foundation.
Fields of interest: Higher education; Health organizations; Human services; Children/youth, services; Community/economic development; Foundations (private grantmaking).
Limitations: Applications not accepted. Giving primarily in McLean County, IL. No grants to individuals.
Application information: Unsolicited requests for funds not accepted.
Trustees: Duncan Funk; Rey Jannusch; Justin McLaughlin; Clint Rehtmeyer; Leigh Ann Sharp.
EIN: 376075515
Other changes: Carla A. Hickey is no longer a trustee.

1022
Geneseo Foundation
P.O. Box 89
Geneseo, IL 61254-0089
***Application address:* c/o Central Bank Illinois, Attn.: Michael Kelly, Trust Off., 101 N. State St., Geneseo, IL 61254, tel.: (309) 944-5601**
Grants List: http://www.geneseofoundation.org/GiftsAwarded.html

Established in 1961 in IL.
Donors: George B. Dedrick; Catherine Cambell†; Walter & Carol Keppy Memorial Trust; Geneseo Lions Club; Hayden Dedecker; Faith Dedecker.
Foundation type: Independent foundation.
Financial data (yr. ended 03/31/13): Assets, $7,689,821 (M); gifts received, $1,650; expenditures, $326,373; qualifying distributions, $309,672; giving activities include $237,212 for 37 grants (high: $50,000; low: $742), and $53,542 for 80 grants to individuals.
Purpose and activities: Giving for civic organizations, social services, youth, recreation, and education, including for scholarships for graduates of Geneseo High School.
Fields of interest: Arts; Education; Recreation; Human services; Children/youth, services; Community/economic development; Government/public administration.
Type of support: General/operating support; Scholarships—to individuals.
Limitations: Applications accepted. Giving primarily in Geneseo, IL.
Application information: Application form required.
Initial approach: Letter or telephone to request application form
Copies of proposal: 1
Board meeting date(s): Monthly
Managers: Bryce B. Chamberlain; John J. DuBois; Michael L. Gernant; John T. Greenwood; Eric Johnson; **Brett Lohman**; Roger Pray; **Todd W. Sieben**; Central Bank Illinois.
EIN: 366079604
Other changes: Bruce R. Fehlman is no longer a manager.

1023
Good Heart Work Smart Foundation
830 North Blvd.
Oak Park, IL 60301-1354

Established in 2006 in IL.
Donors: Stephen G. Schuler; Mary Jo Schuler; Shu Trading, Inc.
Foundation type: Independent foundation.
Financial data (yr. ended 12/31/12): Assets, $1,211,211 (M); gifts received, $635,000; expenditures, $529,086; qualifying distributions, $509,364; giving activities include $509,364 for 370 grants (high: $40,000; low: $11).
Fields of interest: Education; Human services; YM/YWCAs & YM/YWHAs; Foundations (community); Catholic agencies & churches.
Limitations: Applications not accepted. Giving primarily in IL.
Application information: Unsolicited requests for funds not accepted.
Trustees: Susan Mika; Melvin P. Phillips, Jr.; Mary Jo Schuler; Stephen G. Schuler; Stacy Wettstein.
EIN: 205836042
Other changes: The grantmaker no longer lists a URL address.

1024
The Grainger Foundation Inc.
100 Grainger Pkwy.
Lake Forest, IL 60045-5201 (847) 535-1000
Contact: Gloria J. Sinclair, V.P. and Secy.

Incorporated in 1967 in IL as successor to the Grainger Charitable Trust established in 1949.
Donors: William W. Grainger†; Hally W. Grainger†; David W. Grainger.
Foundation type: Independent foundation.
Financial data (yr. ended 12/31/13): Assets, $445,096,516 (M); gifts received, $230,860,000; expenditures, $58,019,938; qualifying distributions, $54,710,239; giving activities include $54,710,239 for 809 grants (high: $24,938,241; low: $1,000).
Purpose and activities: Emphasis on capital funds, and special program funds for education, cultural institutions (museums, the arts, and symphony orchestras), hospitals, and human service organizations.
Fields of interest: Museums; Arts; Education; Health care; Medical research; Human services; Engineering; Science.
Type of support: General/operating support; Continuing support; Capital campaigns; Building/renovation; Equipment; Endowments; Program development; Professorships; Fellowships; Scholarship funds; Research.
Limitations: Applications not accepted. Giving on a national basis. No grants to individuals, or for seed money, emergency funds, deficit financing, publications, conferences, or matching gifts; no loans.
Application information: The foundation contributes only to pre-selected charitable organizations as determined by its directors and officers. For this reason, and due to staffing constraints, grant requests received from organizations other than those first contacted by The Grainger Foundation cannot be acknowledged.
Board meeting date(s): Periodically
Officers and Directors:* David W. Grainger,* Pres.; Gloria J. Sinclair, V.P. and Secy.; William B. Hayden, V.P.; Chris J. Bellmore, Treas.; John S. Chapman; John L. Howard; David L. Kendall.
Number of staff: 4 part-time professional; 1 part-time support.
EIN: 366192971
Other changes: At the close of 2013, the fair market value of the grantmaker's assets was $445,096,516, a 137.0% increase over the 2012 value, $187,799,835. For the same period, the grantmaker paid grants of $54,710,239, a 63.3% increase over the 2012 disbursements, $33,504,661.

1025
Grant Healthcare Foundation
500 N. Western Ave., Ste. 204
Lake Forest, IL 60045-1955 (847) 735-1590
Contact: Joan Eldridge Ridell, Exec. Dir.
FAX: (847) 735-8770;
E-mail: koconnor@granthealthcare.org; Main URL: http://www.granthealthcare.org
Grants List: http://www.granthealthcare.org/awards.html

Established in 1996 in IL.
Foundation type: Independent foundation.
Financial data (yr. ended 12/31/12): Assets, $16,351,367 (M); expenditures, $1,574,339; qualifying distributions, $1,228,063; giving activities include $1,228,063 for 39 grants (high: $100,000; low: $5,000).
Purpose and activities: Giving primarily for healthcare organizations in the greater Chicago, IL, area.
Fields of interest: Reproductive health; Health care; Substance abuse, services; Economically disadvantaged.
Type of support: Matching/challenge support; General/operating support; Seed money.
Limitations: Applications accepted. Giving only in Chicago, IL, and the surrounding metropolitan area. No support for religious and political organizations. No grants to individuals.
Publications: Application guidelines; Grants list.
Application information: Grant applications are not to be submitted without prior approval of preliminary grant inquiry. Application form required.
Initial approach: Preliminary grant inquiry—must be submitted electronically
Copies of proposal: 1
***Deadline(s):* See foundation web site for current deadlines**
Board meeting date(s): May, June, Aug., Oct., Nov. and Dec.
Final notification: Dec. 15
Officers and Directors:* Robert Friedlander,* Chair.; Richard M. Norton,* Secy.-Treas.; Kate Grubbs O'Connor, Exec. Dir.; Joseph S. Carr; George M. Covington; Richard Ross, Jr.
Number of staff: 1 full-time professional.
EIN: 362167090
Other changes: Robert Friedlander has replaced Richard Ross as Chair. Kate Grubbs O'Connor has replaced Joan Eldridge Ridell as Exec. Dir. Richard M. Norton is now Secy.-Treas.

1026
Grant Thornton Foundation
175 W. Jackson Blvd.
Chicago, IL 60604

Established in 2007 in IL.
Donor: Grant Thornton LLP.
Foundation type: Company-sponsored foundation.
Financial data (yr. ended 07/31/12): Assets, $1,120 (M); gifts received, $691,687; expenditures, $691,687; qualifying distributions, $682,015; giving activities include $682,015 for grants.
Fields of interest: Higher education.
Type of support: General/operating support.
Limitations: Applications not accepted. Giving primarily in areas of company operations in AK, AL, AR, AZ, CA, CO, CT, DC, FL, GA, HI, IL, KS, KY, MA, MD, ME, MI, MN, MO, MS, NC, ND, NH, NJ, NM, NY, OH, OK, OR, PA, RI, SC, TN, UT, VA, WA, WI, and WV.
Application information: Contributes only to pre-selected organizations.
Officers and Directors:* Stan I. Levy,* Pres.; Margaret M. Zagel,* Secy.; Fred K. Walz,* Treas.; Anne Lang; **Michael McGuire**; **Russell G. Wieman**.
EIN: 300438415

1027
The Leo S. Guthman Fund
c/o Iris Krieg Assocs.
333 N. Michigan Ave., No. 510
Chicago, IL 60601-3901 (312) 641-6330
***FAX:* (312) 641-5736**; E-mail: iriskrieg1@aol.com;
Additional e-mail: Lauren Krieg, Prog. Off., EQUIP Dir.: lauren@ikriegassoc.com; Main URL: http://www.lsgfchicago.org
Grants List: http://www.lsgfchicago.org/our_grantees0.aspx

1038

Marion Gardner Jackson Charitable Trust

c/o U.S. Trust, Philanthropic Solutions
231 S. LaSalle St., IL1-231-13-32
Chicago, IL 60604 (312) 828-4154
Contact: Debra Grand, Sr. V.P.
E-mail: ilgrantmaking@ustrust.com; Main URL: http://www.bankofamerica.com/grantmaking

Foundation type: Independent foundation.
Financial data (yr. ended 12/31/12): Assets, $10,874,100 (M); expenditures, $550,261; qualifying distributions, $494,210; giving activities include $443,230 for 23 grants (high: $35,000; low: $5,000).
Purpose and activities: Giving primarily to aid religious, charitable, scientific, literary, and educational organizations in the Quincy, Illinois area and surrounding communities in Adams County, Illinois.
Fields of interest: Higher education; Education; Big Brothers/Big Sisters; Youth development; Human services; Community/economic development.
Type of support: Building/renovation.
Limitations: Giving primarily in Quincy, IL, and surrounding communities in Adams County. No grants to individuals.
Application information: Application guidelines available on Trust web site.
Initial approach: Online through Trust web site
Deadline(s): July 31
***Final notification:* Jan. 15**
Trustee: Bank of America, N.A.
EIN: 046010559

1039

Mead Johnson Nutrition Foundation

2701 Patriot Blvd.
Glenview, IL 60026
***Main URL:* http://www.meadjohnson.com/corporate-citizenship/nurturing-communities**

Donor: Mead Johnson Nutrition Company.
Foundation type: Company-sponsored foundation.
Financial data (yr. ended 12/31/12): Assets, $3,316,573 (M); expenditures, $600,000; qualifying distributions, $600,000; giving activities include $600,000 for 5 grants (high: $170,000; low: $50,000).
Purpose and activities: Giving primarily to support infants and children in fragile circumstances.
Fields of interest: Children, services; Human services; Infants/toddlers.
Application information: Application form not required.
Initial approach: Proposal
Deadline(s): None
Officers and Directors:* Stephen W. Golsby,* Chair.; Charles M. Urbain, Vice-Chair.; William C. P'Pool,* Secy.; Kevin Wilson, Treas.; Christopher Perille, Exec. Dir.
EIN: 274243966

1040

The Joyce Foundation

c/o Dir. Communication
321 North Clark Street, Ste. 1500
Chicago, IL 60654-4714 (312) 782-2464
Contact: Dir. Comms.
FAX: (312) 595-1350; E-mail: info@joycefdn.org; Main URL: http://www.joycefdn.org
LinkedIn: http://www.linkedin.com/company/122729
Twitter: https://twitter.com/joyceawards

Incorporated in 1948 in IL.
Donor: Beatrice Joyce Kean‡.
Foundation type: Independent foundation.
Financial data (yr. ended 12/31/12): Assets, $832,164,870 (M); gifts received, $4,000,000; expenditures, $46,560,518; qualifying distributions, $42,450,667; giving activities include $36,040,503 for 303 grants (high: $530,000; low: $1,000), and $38,420 for employee matching gifts.
Purpose and activities: The foundation supports the development of policies that both improve the quality of life for people in the Great Lakes region and serve as models for the rest of the country. The foundation focuses on today's most pressing problems while also informing the public policy decisions critical to creating opportunity and achieving long-term solutions. The work is based on sound research and is focused on where the foundation can add the most value. The foundation encourages innovative and collaborative approaches with a regional focus and the potential for a national reach.
Fields of interest: Arts; Education; Environment; Crime/violence prevention; Crime/violence prevention, gun control; Employment; Public affairs, finance; Public affairs, political organizations.
Type of support: General/operating support; Continuing support; Program development; Conferences/seminars; Research; Program evaluation; Employee matching gifts.
Limitations: Applications accepted. Giving primarily in the Great Lakes region, specifically the states of Illinois, Indiana, Michigan, Minnesota, Ohio, and Wisconsin. A limited number of environment grants are made to organizations in Canada. Education grant making in K-12 focuses on Chicago, Indianapolis, and Minneapolis. The Employment Program primarily focuses on federal and state policy grants, but will make some grants to support targeted metro-level progress in Chicago, Indianapolis, and Minneapolis/St. Paul. Culture grants are primarily focused on the Chicago metropolitan area, except for the Joyce Awards, which extend to other Midwest cities. No support for religious activities, or for political organizations. No grants to individuals or for endowment campaigns, scholarships, direct service programs, commercial ventures, or capital proposals.
Publications: Annual report (including application guidelines); Financial statement; Newsletter; Occasional report.
Application information: Program policy and grant proposal guidelines reviewed annually in Dec. Proposals in all program areas will be considered at each board meeting. Applicants are encouraged to submit their proposals for the Apr. or July meeting, since most grant funds will be distributed at those times. Proposal cover sheet available on foundation web site. Online proposals will not be considered. Application form required.
Initial approach: Contact foundation for application guidelines prior to submitting 2- to 3-page letter of inquiry
Copies of proposal: 1
***Deadline(s):* Letter of inquiry required at least 6 to 8 weeks before proposal deadlines. For formal proposals: Apr. 8 (for July meeting); Aug. 13 (for Dec. meeting). For Joyce Awards: Apr. 4 for letter of inquiry and June 16 for proposal (if requested by foundation)**
Board meeting date(s): Apr., July, and Dec.
Final notification: 2 weeks after meeting
Officers and Directors:* Roger R. Fross,* Chair.; Charles U. Daly, Vice-Chair.; Ellen S. Alberding,* Pres.; Deborah Gillespie, V.P., Finance and Admin. and Treas.; Gretchen Crosby Sims, V.P., Progs.; **Gil M. Sarmiento, Cont.**; Jane R. Paterson, C.I.O.; Jose B. Alvarez; John T. Anderson; Roger G. Bottoms; Michael F. Brewer; Anthony S. Earl; Carlton L. Guthrie; Daniel P. Kearney; Tracey L. Meares; Margot M. Rogers; Paula Wolff.
Number of staff: 17 full-time professional; 2 part-time professional; 8 full-time support.
EIN: 366079185

1041

Mayer and Morris Kaplan Family Foundation

1780 Green Bay Rd., Ste. 205
Highland Park, IL 60035-3276 (847) 926-8350
Contact: Dinaz Mansuri, Exec. Dir.
FAX: (847) 681-1363;
E-mail: dmansuri@kapfam.com; Main URL: http://www.kapfam.com/

Incorporated in 1957 in IL.
Donors: Burton B. Kaplan‡; Morris Kaplan‡.
Foundation type: Independent foundation.
Financial data (yr. ended 12/31/12): Assets, $35,704,893 (M); gifts received, $797,397; expenditures, $4,008,660; qualifying distributions, $3,493,394; giving activities include $3,108,485 for 173 grants (high: $500,000; low: $500).
Purpose and activities: Giving primarily for education and the environment.
Fields of interest: Education; Environment.
Type of support: General/operating support; Management development/capacity building; Program development.
Limitations: Applications not accepted. Giving in Los Angeles, CA, and Chicago, IL, for Education Grants; and CO and WY for Environment Grants. No support for religious organizations, organizations that accept abstinence-only educational funding; employment, housing and emergency services organizations, national organizations, health care institutions, or medical, scientific, or academic research. **No grants to individuals, or for capital campaigns, building funds, equipment or materials, research, publications, meetings, ticket purchases, films or recordings.**
Publications: Annual report; Financial statement; Grants list.
Application information: The foundation is currently not accepting proposals or Letters of Inquiry. Refer to foundation web site for updates in the RFP process.
Board meeting date(s): 2 times per year
Officers and Directors:* Curt Kaplan,* Chair.; Beth Kaplan Karmin,* Pres.; **Anne Kaplan,* V.P.**; Jessica Kaplan Lundevall,* Secy.; Michael Kaplan,* Treas.; Dinaz Mansuri, Exec. Dir.; Aura de la Fuente; Charles Kaplan; David Kaplan; Jean Kaplan; Robert Kaplan; Hannah Karmin; Hilary Kaplan Loretta; Kaja Lundevall; Sarah Kaplan Moore.
Number of staff: 3 full-time professional.
EIN: 366099675
Other changes: Anne Kaplan is now V.P. Dolores Kohl Kaplan is no longer a director.

1042

Katten Muchin Rosenman Foundation, Inc.

(formerly Katten Muchin Zavis Rosenman Foundation, Inc.)
525 W. Monroe St., Ste. 1900
Chicago, IL 60661-3693 **(312) 902-5200**
***FAX:* (312) 902-1061; Main URL: http://www.kattenlaw.com/katten-cares**

Established in 1982 in IL.

Donors: Katten Muchin Zavis; Katten Muchin Zavis Rosenman; Katten Muchin Rosenman LLP; Wander Revocable Trust.
Foundation type: Company-sponsored foundation.
Financial data (yr. ended 12/31/12): Assets, $312,391 (M); gifts received, $1,856,812; expenditures, $1,946,787; qualifying distributions, $1,946,787; giving activities include $1,945,990 for 338 grants (high: $66,162; low: $25).
Purpose and activities: The foundation supports organizations involved with arts and culture, education, health, cancer, heart disease, legal aid, human services, international relief, civil rights, Judaism, and women.
Fields of interest: Museums; Performing arts; Performing arts, theater; Arts; Higher education; Law school/education; Education; Health care, volunteer services; Hospitals (general); Health care; Cancer; Cancer, leukemia; Heart & circulatory diseases; Legal services; Boys & girls clubs; Children/youth, services; Human services; International relief; Civil/human rights; United Ways and Federated Giving Programs; Jewish agencies & synagogues; Women.
Type of support: General/operating support.
Limitations: Applications not accepted. Giving primarily in the Chicago, IL, area. No grants to individuals.
Application information: Contributes only to pre-selected organizations.
Officers: Vincent A.F. Sergi, Pres.; Herbert S. Wander, Secy.; Howard S. Lanznar, Treas.
Directors: David J. Bryant; **Henry Bregstein**; **Roger P. Furey**; Daniel S. Huffenus; David H. Kistenbroker; **Laura Keidan Martin**; **Kenneth E. Noble**; Joshua S. Rubenstein; Stuart P. Shulruff; Ross O. Silverman; Steven P. Solow; Joshua D. Wayser.
EIN: 363165216
Other changes: The grantmaker no longer lists a primary contact.
Karen Artz Ash is no longer a member of the governing body.

1043
The Chaim, Fanny, Louis, Benjamin and Anne Florence Kaufman Memorial Trust

c/o JPMorgan Chase Bank, N.A.
10 S. Dearborn St., IL1-0117
Chicago, IL 60603-2300
***Application address:* c/o JPMorgan Chase Bank, N.A., Trust Dept., Attn.: Kimberly Kalmar, 1116 W. Long Lake, 2nd Fl., Bloomfield Hills, MI 48302, tel.: (248) 645-8419**

Established in 1986 in MI.
Donor: Anne F. Kaufman‡.
Foundation type: Independent foundation.
Financial data (yr. ended 05/31/13): Assets, $2,468,321 (M); expenditures, $163,109; qualifying distributions, $143,674; giving activities include $137,333 for 13 grants (high: $25,000; low: $2,500).
Fields of interest: Museums; Performing arts; Education; Reproductive health, family planning; Health care; Human services; Jewish federated giving programs.
Type of support: General/operating support; Building/renovation; Program development; Seed money; Research.
Limitations: Applications accepted. Giving primarily in southeastern MI, with emphasis on Detroit. No grants to individuals.
Application information: Application form not required.
Copies of proposal: 1
Deadline(s): None

Trustee: JPMorgan Chase Bank, N.A.
EIN: 386504432
Other changes: The grantmaker has moved from WI to IL.

1044
Kenny's Kids

(formerly Comdisco Foundation)
c/o John D. Marshall
520 N. Hicks Rd., Ste. 120
Palatine, IL 60067-2694
***Application address:* c/o Nicholas K. Pontikes, 1230 W. Altgeld, Chicago, IL 60614, tel.: (773) 871-7597**

Established in 1994 in IL.
Donor: Comdisco, Inc.
Foundation type: Independent foundation.
Financial data (yr. ended 09/30/13): Assets, $13,346,910 (M); expenditures, $486,362; qualifying distributions, $354,702; giving activities include $247,178 for 11 grants (high: $100,000; low: $1,000).
Purpose and activities: The primary target of grants is giving support to organizations which seek to give youth greater opportunities outside of the classroom to learn and grow, to teach them skills that will enable them to thrive in a technology-oriented society, and to offer them the guidance and attention necessary to develop such skills. Also consideration for youth-oriented organizations and other organizations that promote the welfare of youth, such as those that offer hope and encouragement to the sick and terminally ill, protect those who have suffered from abuse, and offer after-school programs for the underprivileged.
Fields of interest: Elementary/secondary education; Education; Hospitals (general); Sickle cell disease; Youth development, services; Children/youth, services; Children, services.
Type of support: General/operating support; Annual campaigns; Program development.
Limitations: Applications accepted. Giving primarily in the Chicago, IL, area. No support for private foundations, schools (public or private), or corporations, political campaigns. No grants to individuals, film, video, or audio productions.
Publications: Annual report.
Application information: Grant requests are processed monthly. Application form required.
Initial approach: Letter
Deadline(s): None
Board meeting date(s): Quarterly
Officers and Directors:* Nicholas K. Pontikes,* Pres.; Melissa Pontikes,* Secy.; Victoria L. Gallegos,* Treas.
EIN: 363977234

1045
Kobe College Corporation

540 W. Frontage Rd., Ste. 3335
Northfield, IL 60093-1233
Main URL: http://www.kccjee.org/

Donor: Mary Longbrake Trust.
Foundation type: Independent foundation.
Financial data (yr. ended 03/31/13): Assets, $4,144,991 (M); gifts received, $91,915; expenditures, $267,623; qualifying distributions, $199,141; giving activities include $194,500 for 3 grants (high: $119,500; low: $12,000).
Fields of interest: Higher education.
International interests: Japan.
Type of support: Scholarships—to individuals.
Limitations: Applications not accepted. Giving primarily in Nishinomiya, Hyogo, Japan.
Application information: Unsolicited requests for funds not accepted.
Officers: Go Sugiura, Pres.; Angie Gaspar, V.P., Admin. and Secy.; Ken Tornheim, Treas.
Directors: Lynn Cohee; **Robert Head**; Takuzo Ishida; Bradley Knotts; Robert Mason; Reiko Mrozik; **Jeanne Sokolowski**; **Cindi Sturtz-Sreetharan**; Roberta Wollons; Fumiyo Young.
EIN: 362110366
Other changes: The grantmaker no longer lists an E-mail address, fax, or phone.
Angie Gaspar has replaced Fumivo Young as V.P., Admin. and Secy. Ken Tornheim has replaced Robert Head as Treas.
Robert Mason is no longer Co-Pres. Marjorie Kinsey is no longer V.P., Programs. Yasuko Sanborn is no longer a member of the governing body.

1046
Blanche M. Koffler Charitable Trust

Chicago, IL

The foundation terminated on Sept. 24, 2013.

1047
Lars Foundation

10 S. Dearborn, IL1-0117
Chicago, IL 60603
***Application address:* c/o Andrew Schulert and Joy Lucas, 23 Lee St., Cambridge, MA 02139**

Established in 1999 in WA.
Donors: Andrew Schulert; Joy Lucas.
Foundation type: Independent foundation.
Financial data (yr. ended 06/30/13): Assets, $3,318,877 (M); expenditures, $158,883; qualifying distributions, $150,738; giving activities include $148,344 for 18 grants (high: $30,000; low: $1,000).
Fields of interest: Arts; Higher education; YM/YWCAs & YM/YWHAs; Science; Christian agencies & churches.
Type of support: General/operating support.
Limitations: Applications accepted. Giving primarily in MA. No grants to individuals.
Application information: Application form not required.
Initial approach: Proposal
Deadline(s): None
Directors: Joy Lucas; Andrew Schulert.
EIN: 912003530
Other changes: The foundation no longer lists a telephone number.

1048
Michael Lascaris Scholarship Trust

c/o Schiff Hardi
233 S. Wacker Dr.
Chicago, IL 60606-5096
Contact: Sarah K. Severson
E-mail: info@lascaristrust.gr; Main URL: http://lascaristrust.gr/
Facebook: http://www.facebook.com/Lascaris.Trust
Grants List: http://lascaristrust.gr/?cmd=receipients

Established in 1997 in IL.
Foundation type: Independent foundation.

Financial data (yr. ended 12/31/12): Assets, $4,935,868 (M); expenditures, $530,145; qualifying distributions, $475,468; giving activities include $206,400 for 177 grants to individuals.
Purpose and activities: Scholarship awards to individuals of Greek ancestry from Greece, Cyprus and Istanbul for the purpose of learning the English language. The scholarships are only for English language instruction at all levels from beginner up to and including the Certificate of Proficiency (Universities of Cambridge and Michigan) and are applicable to candidates of all ages, provided they have had their 12th birthday. Candidates must also be Greek Orthodox. The scholarships cover all tuition and educational materials for one year, with the possibility of renewal for further years for those recipients who are conscientious in their study and attendance.
Fields of interest: Education; Human services.
Type of support: Scholarships—to individuals.
Limitations: Applications accepted. Giving primarily in Cyprus, Greece and Istanbul.
Application information: See web site for scholarship application information and guidelines. Application form required.
Initial approach: Telephone or e-mail
Deadline(s): May 4
Officers: Sherry Cossyphas, Mgr.; **Evangelia Laiou, Mgr.**; Maria Rallis, Mgr.
Trustee: Koula Pagonis.
EIN: 367144785

1049
The Lefkofsky Family Foundation

600 W. Chicago Ave., Ste. 775
Chicago, IL 60654-2526
E-mail: info@lffoundation.com; Main URL: http://www.lefkofskyfoundation.com
Liz and Eric Lefkofsky's Giving Pledge Profile: http://glasspockets.org/philanthropy-in-focus/eye-on-the-giving-pledge/profiles#l
Twitter: https://twitter.com/Lfforg

Established in 2006 in IL.
Donors: Elizabeth Lefkofsky; Eric Lefkofsky.
Foundation type: Independent foundation.
Financial data (yr. ended 12/31/12): Assets, $14,674,024 (M); gifts received, $15,944,220; expenditures, $4,800,429; qualifying distributions, $4,612,235; giving activities include $4,612,235 for 121 grants (high: $847,300; low: $100).
Fields of interest: Arts; Education; Medical research; Civil/human rights.
Limitations: Applications not accepted. Giving primarily in IL.
Application information: Unsolicited requests for funds not accepted.
Trustees: Dawn Denberg; Bradley Keywell; Kim Keywell; Manuel Kramer; Susan Kramer; Elizabeth K. Lefkofsky; Eric P. Lefkofsky; Sandra Lefkofsky; Steven Lefkofsky; William Lefkofsky; Jodi Neff.
EIN: 207066362

1050
The Libra Foundation

1700 W. Irving Park Rd., Ste. 203
Chicago, IL 60613-2599 (773) 325-1235
Contact: Hilda Vega, Sr. Prog. Off.; Betsy Brill, Exec. Dir.; Leah Zamora, Grant Admin.
E-mail: info@thelibrafoundation.org; Main URL: http://www.thelibrafoundation.org
The Libra Foundation's Philanthropy Promise: http://www.ncrp.org/philanthropys-promise/who

Established in 2002 in IL.
Donors: Rhoda Pritzker‡; Nicholas J. Pritzker; Pritzker Foundation.
Foundation type: Independent foundation.
Financial data (yr. ended 12/31/12): Assets, $149,434,186 (M); gifts received, $76,209,306; expenditures, $5,873,296; qualifying distributions, $5,021,027; giving activities include $4,760,286 for 82 grants (high: $1,599,000; low: $1,000).
Purpose and activities: The foundation funds organizations that integrate human rights into their work in and across the following priority areas: women's rights, with an emphasis on reproductive rights and the elevation of women's rights as human rights; environmental sustainability, with an emphasis on promoting social justice within climate change mitigation and adaptation strategies; social justice, with an emphasis on fair application of the law, government accountability and human rights field-building; and drug policy reform, focusing on protecting rights and advancing reforms that lessen the social and economic impacts of the "war on drugs".
Fields of interest: International human rights; Civil/human rights, alliance/advocacy; Civil/human rights, public policy; Civil/human rights, reform; Civil/human rights, advocacy; Civil liberties, advocacy; Civil liberties, reproductive rights; Civil liberties, due process; Environmental and resource rights; Civil/human rights; Economically disadvantaged.
International interests: Africa; Asia; Europe; Latin America.
Type of support: General/operating support; Management development/capacity building; Emergency funds; Seed money; Program evaluation; Matching/challenge support.
Limitations: Giving is limited to state-specific work in CA and IL, for projects with national level impact and for work covering multiple regions outside of the U.S. (but funded through a U.S. home office). The foundation does not fund international work directly, nor does it fund international work focused on a single country. No support for international organizations not registered in the U.S., or for organizations that are heavily supported by the government (except for specific advocacy or public policy projects of interest). No grants to individuals, or for fundraising events, capital fund drives or campaigns, debt reduction, international work that focuses on a single country or on a small set of countries, or for religious activities.
Publications: Application guidelines; Grants list.
Application information: The foundation does not accept unsolicited proposals. Brief letters of inquiry are accepted however, on a rolling basis. Letters must be submitted via our website. Paper inquiries will not be accepted. Refer to foundation web site for complete application information and guidelines. Application form required.
Initial approach: Letter of Inquiry, with a preference for brief phone discussion first to determine alignment.
Deadline(s): None
Board meeting date(s): June and Dec.
Final notification: Letters of inquiry are reviewed on a monthly basis.
Officers and Directors:* Nicholas J. Pritzker,* C.E.O.; Susan S. Pritzker,* Pres. and Treas.; Regan Pritzker,* V.P. and Secy.; Thomas Dykstra, V.P.; Betsy Brill, Exec. Dir.; Isaac Pritzker; Jacob Pritzker; Joseph Pritzker.
Number of staff: 1 full-time professional; 1 part-time professional; 1 part-time support.
EIN: 300031117

1051
Reva and David Logan Foundation

c/o Jonathan Logan
980 N. Michigan Ave., Ste. 1122
Chicago, IL 60611-4522 (312) 664-3350
***Contact:* Peter Handler, Exec. Dir.**
FAX: (312) 664-9103; E-mail: jon@loganfdn.org; **Peter Handler, Exec. Dir., contact for Letters of Inquiry, tel.: (312) 664-3350, e-mail: peter@loganfdn.org**; Main URL: http://www.loganfdn.org
Grants List: http://www.loganfdn.org/grants.html

Established in 1965 in IL.
Donors: David Logan; Daniel Logan; Richard Logan; Jonathan Logan.
Foundation type: Independent foundation.
Financial data (yr. ended 12/31/12): Assets, $2,614,017 (M); gifts received, $2,042,000; expenditures, $590,334; qualifying distributions, $548,538; giving activities include $418,499 for 19 grants (high: $125,000; low: $2,000), and $100,018 for 1 employee matching gift.
Purpose and activities: Giving primarily for education, community and social welfare, Jewish life and concerns, public service and civil society, the upkeep and support of a library of modern illustrated and photographic books, and investigative reporting.
Fields of interest: Media/communications; Literature; Arts; Journalism school/education; Education; Aging, centers/services; Philanthropy/voluntarism; Leadership development; Jewish agencies & synagogues; Children; Aging; LGBTQ.
Type of support: General/operating support; Annual campaigns; Building/renovation; Endowments; Publication; Curriculum development; Research; Matching/challenge support.
Limitations: Giving primarily in the metropolitan areas of San Francisco, CA, and Chicago, IL. No grants to individuals.
Application information: Unsolicited proposals are not accepted.
***Initial approach:* Letter of Inquiry or telephone call**
Officers and Directors:* Jonathan Logan,* Pres.; Richard Logan,* Secy.; Cecelia Simmons,* Treas.; **Peter Handler, Exec. Dir.**; Daniel Logan; Ben Rothblatt.
Number of staff: None.
EIN: 366139439

1052
Wesley Luehring Foundation

807 Cherry St.
Wheaton, IL 60187-4303 (630) 668-7663
***Contact:* Gary Crocus, Pres.**
Established in 1989 in IL.
Donors: Marian D. Luehring Trust; Ruth E. Luehring Irrevocable Trust.
Foundation type: Independent foundation.
Financial data (yr. ended 12/31/12): Assets, $7,274,360 (M); expenditures, $477,840; qualifying distributions, $419,494; giving activities include $400,000 for 18 grants (high: $35,000; low: $10,000).
Fields of interest: Historic preservation/historical societies; Hospitals (specialty); Health organizations, association; Cancer; Youth

development, centers/clubs; Boy scouts; Human services; Salvation Army; Christian agencies & churches; Protestant agencies & churches; Blind/ visually impaired.
Limitations: Applications accepted. Giving primarily in IL. No grants to individuals.
Application information: Application form required.
Initial approach: Letter
Deadline(s): None
Officers: Gary E. Crocus, Pres.; R. Terrence Kalina, Secy.; Michael Celer, Treas.
Directors: Lisa Patterson; Corinne Schaefer; **Joseph M. Schaefer, Sr.**
EIN: 363616086
Other changes: The grantmaker no longer lists a separate application address. The grantmaker has moved from WI to IL.

1053
The Lumpkin Family Foundation
121 S. 17th St.
Mattoon, IL 61938-3915 (217) 235-3361
Contact: Bruce Karmazin, Exec. Dir.
FAX: (217) 258-8444;
E-mail: info@lumpkinfoundation.org; Main URL: http://www.lumpkinfoundation.org/

Incorporated in 1953 in IL.
Donors: Besse Adamson Lumpkin†; Mary G. Lumpkin†; Richard Adamson Lumpkin†; Illinois Consolidated Telephone Co.; Richard Anthony Lumpkin; Mary Lee Sparks; Margaret L. Keon; Elizabeth Lumpkin Celio; Benjamin I. Lumpkin.
Foundation type: Independent foundation.
Financial data (yr. ended 12/31/12): Assets, $41,608,936 (M); gifts received, $201,620; expenditures, $2,763,723; qualifying distributions, $2,503,413; giving activities include $1,984,134 for 186 grants (high: $347,500; low: $25), and $112,219 for foundation-administered programs.
Purpose and activities: The foundation supports people pursuing innovation and long-lasting improvements in the environment, health, education, and community access to the arts.
Fields of interest: Arts; Libraries (public); Education; Environment, natural resources; Health care; Human services; Children, services.
Type of support: General/operating support; Management development/capacity building; Annual campaigns; Program development; Seed money; Internship funds; Technical assistance; Program evaluation; Employee matching gifts; Matching/challenge support.
Limitations: Applications accepted. Giving primarily in central IL; giving also in the San Francisco Bay Area, CA, Albuquerque, NM, Chicago, IL, Philadelphia, PA, the Jamestown area in western NY, and Wilton, CT. No support for religious organizations, political causes, or organizations who influence legislation. No grants to individuals.
Publications: Application guidelines; Annual report; Grants list.
Application information: Online application process. See complete application guidelines on foundation web site. Application form required.
Initial approach: Online letter of inquiry
Deadline(s): **For Regional Grants Program, Apr. 4 for Letter of Inquiry and May 30 for invited applications; for Lumpkin Family Foundation, see calendar on foundation web site for deadlines**
Board meeting date(s): Feb., Apr., June, Sept. and Nov.
Final notification: May, July and Nov.
Officers and Directors:* Christina Duncan,* Pres.; Benjamin Lumpkin,* V.P.; Richard Anthony Lumpkin,* Treas.; Bruce Karmazin, Exec. Dir.; Elizabeth Celio; Richard DeWyngaert; Susan DeWyngaert; Joseph Dively; Barbara Federico; S.L. Grissom.
Number of staff: 2 full-time professional; 1 full-time support.
EIN: 237423640

1054
The Robert Lyon Leukemia Foundation
1406 N. Astor St.
Chicago, IL 60610-1615
Main URL: http://rhlfoundation.com/

Donor: Donna Lyon.
Foundation type: Independent foundation.
Financial data (yr. ended 12/31/12): Assets, $3,445,204 (M); gifts received, $138,758; expenditures, $267,208; qualifying distributions, $208,500; giving activities include $208,500 for 9 grants (high: $120,000; low: $2,500).
Purpose and activities: Giving primarily for research programs delivering treatment improvements for patients struggling with leukemia.
Fields of interest: Cancer, leukemia; Health organizations; Housing/shelter.
Limitations: Applications not accepted. Giving primarily in IL.
Application information: Unsolicited requests for funds not accepted.
Officer: Donna Lyon, Exec. Dir.
Director: David Lyon.
EIN: 261500324

1055
MacArthur Family Charitable Foundation
c/o Pasquesi Sheppard LLC
585 Bank Ln.
Lake Forest, IL 60045-5307

Donors: C.J. MacArthur; Gina G. MacArthur.
Foundation type: Independent foundation.
Financial data (yr. ended 06/30/13): Assets, $4,858,999 (M); gifts received, $300,000; expenditures, $268,271; qualifying distributions, $257,000; giving activities include $257,000 for 7 grants (high: $200,000; low: $1,000).
Fields of interest: Theological school/education; Education.
Type of support: General/operating support.
Limitations: Applications not accepted. Giving primarily in CA and New York, NY.
Application information: Unsolicited requests for funds not accepted.
Officers: Gina G. MacArthur, Chair.; Alan Halperin, Secy.-Treas.
EIN: 273141382

1056
The John D. and Catherine T. MacArthur Foundation
140 S. Dearborn St., Ste. 1200
Chicago, IL 60603-5285 (312) 726-8000
Contact: Richard J. Kaplan, Assoc. V.P., Institutional Research and Grants Mgmt.
FAX: (312) 920-6258;
E-mail: 4answers@macfound.org; TDD: (312) 920-6285; Main URL: http://www.macfound.org
E-Newsletter: http://www.macfound.org/site/c.lkLXJ8MQKrH/b.4357343/k.7FF4/Subscribe_to_eNews__Custom/apps/ka/ct/contactcustom.asp
Grants Database: http://www.macfound.org/site/c.lkLXJ8MQKrH/b.4979973/k.8E29/Recent_Grants.htm
Knowledge Center: http://www.macfound.org/site/c.lkLXJ8MQKrH/b.2722017/k.62D0/What_We_Have_Learned.htm
RSS Feed: http://feeds.feedburner.com/macfound
Spotlight on Digital Media and Learning: http://spotlight.macfound.org/blog
Twitter: http://www.twitter.com/macfound
YouTube: http://www.youtube.com/macfound

Incorporated in 1970 in IL.
Donors: John D. MacArthur†; Catherine T. MacArthur†.
Foundation type: Independent foundation.
Financial data (yr. ended 12/31/12): Assets, $5,987,438,524 (M); expenditures, $271,209,395; qualifying distributions, $252,641,628; giving activities include $197,759,152 for 1,579 grants (high: $3,500,000; low: $150), and $12,100,000 for 121 grants to individuals (high: $100,000; low: $100,000).
Purpose and activities: The John D. and Catherine T. MacArthur Foundation supports creative people and effective institutions committed to building a more just, verdant, and peaceful world. In addition to selecting the MacArthur Fellows, the foundation works to defend human rights, advance global conservation and security, make cities better places, and understand how technology is affecting children and society.
Fields of interest: Media/communications; Media, film/video; Education, public education; Higher education; Environment, natural resources; Reproductive health; Mental health/crisis services, public policy; Crime/violence prevention, youth; International peace/security; International human rights; Community development, neighborhood development; Public policy, research.
International interests: India; Mexico; Nigeria; Russia.
Type of support: General/operating support; Program development; Fellowships; Research; Program-related investments/loans; Employee matching gifts; Matching/challenge support.
Limitations: Applications accepted. Giving on a national and international basis. No support for religious programs, political activities or campaigns. No grants for fundraising appeals, institutional benefits, honorary functions or similar projects, tuition expenses, scholarships, or fellowships (other than those sponsored by the foundation).
Publications: Annual report; Newsletter.
Application information: Please do not send the letter of inquiry by fax. Send it by mail to the office of Grants Management or by e-mail. Direct applications for MacArthur Fellows programs not accepted. Grants increasingly initiated by the board. Application form not required.
Initial approach: Letter of inquiry (2 to 3 pages) and one-page summary
Copies of proposal: 1
Deadline(s): None
Board meeting date(s): Mar., June, Sept., and Dec.
Final notification: 8 to 10 weeks
Officers and Directors:* Marjorie M. Scardino,* Chair.; **Julia Stasch, Pres.**; Marc P. Yanchura, V.P., and C.F.O.; Susan E. Manske, V.P. and C.I.O.; Joshua J. Mintz, V.P. and Genl. Counsel; Cecilia Conrad, V.P., MacArthur Fellows Prog.; Elspeth A. Revere, V.P., Media, Culture and Special Initiatives; Andrew Solomon, V.P., Public Affairs; Elizabeth Kane, Secy.; Kevin Doherty, Cont.; John Seely Brown; Jack Fuller; Jamie S. Gorelick; Mary Graham; Donald R. Hopkins, M.D.; Daniel Huttenlocher; Joi

Ito; Julie T. Katzman; Paul Klingenstein; Martha Minow; Mario J. Molina; Sendhil Mullainathan; Claude M. Steele.
Number of staff: 92 full-time professional; 85 full-time support.
EIN: 237093598
Other changes: Julia Stasch has replaced Robert L. Gallucci.
Barry Lowenkron is no longer V.P., Intl. Progs.
Karen S. Menke is no longer Cont.

1057
Web Maddox Trust
c/o JP Morgan Chase Bank N.A.
10 S. Dearborn St., IL1-0117
Chicago, IL 60603-2300
Application address: P.O. Box 2050, Fort Worth, TX 76113-2050, tel.: (817) 884-4159

Established in 1986 in TX.
Foundation type: Independent foundation.
Financial data (yr. ended 03/31/13): Assets, $4,384,016 (M); expenditures, $280,478; qualifying distributions, $208,791; giving activities include $196,000 for 10 grants (high: $50,000; low: $3,000).
Fields of interest: Museums; Performing arts; Performing arts, orchestras; Performing arts, opera; Arts; Higher education; Human services.
Type of support: General/operating support.
Limitations: Applications accepted. Giving primarily in Tarrant County, TX. No support for organizations supported by the United Way. No grants to individuals.
Application information: Application form required.
Initial approach: Letter
Deadline(s): None
Trustee: JPMorgan Chase Bank, N.A.
EIN: 756347669
Other changes: The grantmaker has moved from WI to IL.

1058
Magnus Charitable Trust
600 W. Rand Rd., Ste. A-104
Arlington Heights, IL 60004-2355 (847) 255-1100
***Contact:* Delores Dorothy**
FAX: (847) 632-0616;
E-mail: info@magnuscharitable.org; Toll free tel.: (888) 259-5044; Main URL: http://www.magnuscharitable.org

Established in 1995 in IL.
Donors: Alexander B. Magnus, Jr.†; The Magnus Asset Management Trust.
Foundation type: Independent foundation.
Financial data (yr. ended 12/31/12): Assets, $9,865,836 (M); expenditures, $1,444,082; qualifying distributions, $498,266; giving activities include $479,388 for 10 grants (high: $180,000; low: $1,997).
Purpose and activities: The mission of the Trust is to make a positive impact on the world by helping to educate those that are greatly in need. Since its inception, the trust has partnered with many organizations to help eliminate hunger and obstacles to obtaining education. Giving primarily for education scholarships to needy individuals; some funding for higher education, health and human services.
Fields of interest: Higher education; Education; Health organizations, association; Human services; International human rights.
Limitations: Applications accepted. Giving in the U.S., with emphasis on IL.
Application information: Application form required.
Deadline(s): Apr. 18
Director: Victoria Magnus.
EIN: 364049284

1059
Luther T. McCauley Charitable Trust
c/o JPMorgan Chase Bank, N.A.
10 S. Dearborn St., IL1-0117
Chicago, IL 60603-2300
Application address: c/o JPMorgan Chase Bank, N.A., 370 17th St., Denver, CO 80202-1370, tel.: (303) 607-7710

Established in 1978 in CO.
Foundation type: Independent foundation.
Financial data (yr. ended 04/30/13): Assets, $5,528,710 (M); expenditures, $303,820; qualifying distributions, $263,518; giving activities include $251,000 for 21 grants (high: $35,000; low: $3,500).
Purpose and activities: Support primarily for programs benefiting economically deprived, socially disadvantaged, and mentally or physically handicapped citizens of El Paso County, Colorado.
Fields of interest: Zoos/zoological societies; Health organizations, association; Human services; Family services; Government/public administration.
Type of support: General/operating support; Equipment; Matching/challenge support.
Limitations: Applications accepted. Giving primarily in El Paso County, CO. No grants to individuals.
Publications: Application guidelines.
Application information: Application form required.
Initial approach: Letter
Copies of proposal: 1
Deadline(s): None
Board meeting date(s): Quarterly
Trustee: JPMorgan Chase Bank, N.A.
EIN: 846152258
Other changes: The grantmaker has moved from WI to IL.

1060
Max McGraw Wildlife Foundation
P.O. Box 9, Rte. 25
Dundee, IL 60118-0009 (847) 741-8000
Contact: Charles S. Potter, Exec. Dir.
Main URL: http://www.mcgrawwildlife.org

Established in 1962 in IL. Classified as an operating foundation in 1987.
Donor: McGraw Foundation.
Foundation type: Operating foundation.
Financial data (yr. ended 04/30/13): Assets, $24,024,822 (M); gifts received, $2,933,414; expenditures, $5,780,733; qualifying distributions, $2,251,111; giving activities include $65,830 for 2 grants (high: $65,800; low: $30), $96,146 for 9 grants to individuals (high: $20,350; low: $3,200), and $1,480,912 for 2 foundation-administered programs.
Purpose and activities: Giving primarily to organizations that sponsor wildlife research projects, especially those related to upland game birds, song birds, waterfowl, fisheries, and endangered species.
Fields of interest: Higher education; Environment, natural resources; Animals/wildlife, preservation/protection.
Type of support: Donated land; Internship funds; Technical assistance.
Limitations: Applications accepted. Giving primarily in the midwestern U.S. No grants to individuals directly.
Publications: Informational brochure.
Application information:
Initial approach: Letter
Deadline(s): None
Board meeting date(s): Mid-June
Officers: Scott M. Elrod, Chair.; J. Stanley Pepper, Vice-Chair.; Charles S. Potter, Jr., C.E.O. and Pres.; **Wendy Romero, C.O.O. and V.P.**; Clark E. Ganshirt, V.P.; Joseph J. Slawek, Secy.; Bruce Crowther, Treas.
Directors: Thomas Anderson; Robert G. Donnelley; Thomas G. Fitzgerald; Terence M. Graunke; Michael C. Hillstrom; Eugene M. Lerner; Lawrence R. Lucas; Carol E. Moorman; Timothy N. Thoelecke; Allen M. Turner.
EIN: 362519612
Other changes: Wendy Romero is now C.O.O. and V.P.

1061
Edward Arthur Mellinger Educational Foundation, Inc.
1025 E. Broadway
Monmouth, IL 61462-1983 (309) 734-2419
FAX: (309) 734-4435; E-mail: info@mellinger.org; Main URL: http://www.mellinger.org/

Incorporated in 1959 in DE.
Donor: Inez M. Hensleigh†.
Foundation type: Independent foundation.
Financial data (yr. ended 12/31/12): Assets, $19,973,976 (M); gifts received, $1,130; expenditures, $1,602,457; qualifying distributions, $1,414,211; giving activities include $406,160 for 5 grants (high: $400,000; low: $160), $895,660 for 730 grants to individuals, and $7,500 for loans to individuals.
Purpose and activities: The Mellinger foundation is committed to the support of education. Accordingly, the foundation devotes a major portion of its resources to providing scholarship and loan assistance to young men and women from western Illinois who attend colleges and universities throughout the nation. In addition, the foundation offers support to a variety of educational organizations and programs in its local area.
Fields of interest: Higher education; Education; Young adults.
Type of support: Seed money; Scholarships—to individuals; Student loans—to individuals.
Limitations: Applications accepted. Giving limited to students residing in any of the 6 western IL counties of Fulton, Henderson, Knox, McDonough, Mercer and Warren.
Publications: Application guidelines; Program policy statement.
Application information: Application information available on foundation web site. Application form required.
Initial approach: Request application form
Copies of proposal: 1
Deadline(s): Applications are accepted from Feb. 1 to May 1 only
Board meeting date(s): Scholarship committee meets in June
Final notification: Early July
Officers and Trustees:* Tom Johnson,* Pres.; Gary D. Willhardt, Ph.D.*, V.P.; Daniel G. Kistler,* Secy.; Debra L. Grand; Gary Martin.
Number of staff: 1 part-time professional; 4 part-time support.
EIN: 362428421

Other changes: Mary Frances Miller is no longer a V.P.

1062
Nathan & Isabel Miller Family Foundation
Chicago, IL

The foundation terminated on Dec. 2011.

1063
The Moline Foundation
817 11th Ave.
Moline, IL 61265-1222 (309) 736-3800
Contact: Joy Boruff, Exec. Dir.
FAX: (309) 736-3721;
E-mail: molinefoundation@qconline.com; Main URL: http://www.molinefoundation.org
Facebook: https://www.facebook.com/pages/Moline-Foundation/104847132915358
Scholarship e-mail: ldaily@qconline.com

Established in 1953 in Illinois.
Foundation type: Community foundation.
Financial data (yr. ended 09/30/12): Assets, $16,717,428 (M); gifts received, $775,994; expenditures, $1,425,007; giving activities include $1,043,595 for 17+ grants (high: $459,800), and $34,614 for grants to individuals.
Purpose and activities: The foundation is a community-based, nonprofit organization which provides grants to health, human services, education, community development, the arts, and other charitable organizations which benefit the citizens of Moline and the Quad Cities, IL, region.
Fields of interest: Arts; Education; Health care; Employment; Human services; Community development, neighborhood development; Economic development.
Type of support: Scholarship funds.
Limitations: Applications accepted. Giving limited to the Quad Cities area of eastern IA and western IL.
Publications: Annual report; Grants list; Newsletter.
Application information: Visit foundation web site for grant application guidelines. Application form not required.
Initial approach: Letter
Copies of proposal: 11
Deadline(s): Apr. 15, and Sept. 30
Board meeting date(s): Scheduled as needed
Final notification: Within 2 weeks of interview
Officers and Trustees:* Sandra Kramer,* Chair.; Darcy Callas,* Vice-Chair.; Ann Millman,* Secy.; **Stephen Krause,* Treas.**; Joy Boruff, Exec. Dir.; Gene Blanc; Dennis Fox; Dr. Kerry Humes; Mary Lagerblade; Dr. David Markward; Larry Meeske.
EIN: 366036867
Other changes: Ann Millman, Peter Benson, and Dennis Schwartz are no longer trustees.

1064
The Mondelez International Foundation
(formerly The Kraft Foods Foundation)
3 Pkwy. North Blvd.
Deerfield, IL **60015-2504**
***Main URL:* http://www.mondelezinternational.com/well-being**

Established in 2005 in IL.
Donor: Kraft Foods Global, Inc.
Foundation type: Company-sponsored foundation.
Financial data (yr. ended 12/31/12): Assets, $35,740,779 (M); gifts received, $12,000,219; expenditures, $3,309,359; qualifying distributions, $3,309,071; giving activities include $1,552,689 for grants, and $1,756,382 for employee matching gifts.
Purpose and activities: The foundation supports programs designed to combat obesity; nutrition education; promote active play; and provide access to fresh foods.
Fields of interest: Public health, obesity; Public health, physical fitness; Health care; Agriculture; Food services; Food banks; Nutrition; Disasters, preparedness/services; American Red Cross; Salvation Army; YM/YWCAs & YM/YWHAs; Human services; Community/economic development; Children; African Americans/Blacks; Hispanics/Latinos.
Type of support: General/operating support; Continuing support; Program development; Employee volunteer services; Sponsorships; Employee matching gifts; Donated products; In-kind gifts.
Limitations: Applications not accepted. Giving on a national and international basis in areas of company operations, with emphasis on CA, CO, Washington, DC, FL, GA, IA, IL, MN, MO, NJ, NY, PA, TX, VA, WI, Argentina, Australia, Brazil, Canada, France, Germany, Indonesia, Italy, Mexico, Philippines, Spain, Russia, and the United Kingdom.
Application information: Contributes only to pre-selected organizations.
Officers and Directors:* Nicole R. Robinson,* Pres.; Carol J. Ward, V.P. and Secy.; **Kim Harris Jones, V.P., Treas., and Cont.; Ernest L. Duplessis, V.P.**; Marc S. Firestone,* V.P.; **Julia Gin, V.P.**; Joseph Klauke, Counsel; James Portnoy, Counsel.
EIN: 203881590
Other changes: Nicole R. Robinson has replaced Cynthia P. Yeatman as Pres.
Nancy Daigle is no longer V.P. and Secy.

1065
The Monticello College Foundation
c/o The Evergreens
5800 Godfrey Rd.
Godfrey, IL 62035-2426 (618) 468-2370
Contact: Linda K. Nevlin, Exec. Dir.
E-mail: lnevlin@lc.edu; Main URL: http://monticellofound.org/
Grants List: http://monticellofound.org/awards.cfm

Incorporated in 1843 in IL as Monticello College; reorganized as a foundation in 1971.
Donors: Lucile Porter Charitable Trust; Patricia Adams Elliott Trust.
Foundation type: Independent foundation.
Financial data (yr. ended 06/30/13): Assets, $14,088,729 (M); gifts received, $12,388; expenditures, $717,122; qualifying distributions, $647,810; giving activities include $647,810 for grants.
Purpose and activities: Support for programs that assist in advancing education for women.
Fields of interest: Higher education; Education; Women; Young adults, female.
Type of support: Endowments; Fellowships; Internship funds; Scholarship funds.
Limitations: Applications accepted. No support for foreign schools or foreign-based American schools, or for social service agencies. No grants to individuals, or for capital, bricks and mortar, operating expenses, or for endowed chairs and exchange students.
Publications: Application guidelines; Annual report (including application guidelines); Financial statement; Grants list.
Application information: Proposals may be stapled. Please do not place proposals in folders or other binders. Application form required.
Initial approach: Letter (2-pages maximum)
Copies of proposal: 18
Deadline(s): Feb. 28 (for spring meeting), and Aug. 31 (for fall meeting)
Board meeting date(s): Oct. and Apr.
Officers and Board Members: Janet Biermann,* Chair.; Alice Norton,* Vice-Chair.; Dianne P. Saul,* Secy.; Karl K. Hoagland, Jr.,* Treas.; Linda K. Nevlin, Exec. Dir.; Mary Dell Pritzlaff, Tr. Emeritus; Sara Anschuetz; Sarah Hoagland; Christopher Kreid; Cathy Maude; Barbara P. Pierce; Enola Proctor; Jenny Levis Sadow; Janet A. Schweppe; Mary Anschuetz Vogt; Julie Jones Williams.
Number of staff: 1 part-time professional.
EIN: 370681538

1066
Motorola Solutions Foundation
(formerly Motorola Foundation)
1303 East Algonquin Rd.
Schaumburg, IL 60196-4041 (847) 538-7639
Contact: Matt Blakely, Dir.
FAX: (847) 538-1456;
E-mail: foundation@motorolasolutions.com; **Main URL: http://responsibility.motorolasolutions.com/index.php/solutions-for-community/com02-foundation/**
Facebook: http://www.facebook.com/MSIFoundation
Innovation Generation Grant Recipients: http://responsibility.motorolasolutions.com/images/downloads_page/2013_Innovation_Generation_Grant_Descriptions.pdf
International Grant Recipients: http://responsibility.motorolasolutions.com/images/downloads_page/2013_Motorola_Solutions_Foundation_International_Grants.pdf
Motorola Responsibility Blog: http://communities.motorolasolutions.com/blogs/corporate_responsibility/
Public Safey Grant Recipients: http://responsibility.motorolasolutions.com/images/downloads_page/2013_Motorola_Solutions_Foundation_Public_Safety_Grants.pdf
Twitter: http://twitter.com/msifoundation

Established in 1953 in IL.
Donors: Motorola, Inc.; Motorola Solutions, Inc.
Foundation type: Company-sponsored foundation.
Financial data (yr. ended 12/31/12): Assets, $61,362,029 (M); gifts received, $61,362,029; expenditures, $17,037,678; qualifying distributions, $16,904,625; giving activities include $16,672,432 for 353 grants (high: $2,000,000; low: $143).
Purpose and activities: The Motorola Solutions Foundation focuses its funding on education, especially science, technology, engineering, and math programming; public safety; disaster relief and preparedness; and employee involvement.
Fields of interest: Museums (science/technology); Education, formal/general education; Elementary/secondary education; Education; Disasters, preparedness/services; Disasters, fire prevention/control; Safety/disasters; American Red Cross; Human services; Mathematics; Engineering/technology; Science; Youth; Minorities; Girls.

Type of support: General/operating support; Equipment; Program development; Curriculum development; Employee volunteer services.
Limitations: Applications accepted. **Giving primarily on a national and international basis in areas of company operations, with emphasis on CA, Washington, DC, FL, GA, IL, MA, MD, NJ, NY, Argentina, Belgium, Brazil, Canada, China, England, France, Mexico, Poland, and Singapore.** No support for political or lobbying organizations, political candidates, religious organizations, or private foundations described under the U.S. IRS Code Section 509(a). No grants to individuals, or for endowments, sports sponsorships, or capital campaigns; no Motorola Solutions product or equipment donations.
Publications: Application guidelines; Grants list; Program policy statement.
Application information: Support is limited to 1 contribution per organization during any given year. Organizations receiving support are asked to submit a program evaluation. Application form required.
Initial approach: Complete online eligibility quiz and application
***Deadline(s):* None for general grants; Jan. to Apr. 11 for Innovation Generation Grants; Mar. to June for International Grants for International Countries; May to July for Public Safety Grans**
Board meeting date(s): Monthly and as required
***Final notification:* June for Innovation Generation Grants**
Director: Matt Blakely, Dir.
Number of staff: 1 full-time professional; 3 part-time professional; 1 full-time support.
EIN: 366109323

1067
James & Aune Nelson Foundation
P.O. Box 5146
Godfrey, IL 62035-5146

Established in IL.
Donor: Aune Nelson‡.
Foundation type: Independent foundation.
Financial data (yr. ended 12/31/12): Assets, $19,069,516 (M); expenditures, $869,841; qualifying distributions, $672,670; giving activities include $660,000 for 4 grants (high: $380,000; low: $80,000).
Purpose and activities: Giving primarily for conservation and the environment.
Fields of interest: Environment, natural resources; Environment, land resources.
Type of support: General/operating support; Land acquisition; Program development.
Limitations: Applications not accepted. Giving primarily in IL and CA. No grants to individuals.
Application information: Contributes only to pre-selected organizations.
Officers: Judy Hoffman, Pres.; Richard Keating, V.P.; **Laura Asher, Secy.; Robert McClellan, Treas.**
Directors: Anita Cooper; Karen Eckert; Mark Maggos; **Jeff Weber**; John Williams.
EIN: 371371840
Other changes: Laura Asher has replaced Chestnut Booth as Secy.
James Hoefert is no longer Co-Treas. Richard Snyder is no longer Co-Treas. Julie Blase, Timothy Campbell, and Wayne Politsch are no longer directors.

1068
Oak Park/River Forest Community Foundation
1049 Lake St., No. 204
Oak Park, IL 60301-6708 (708) 848-1560
Contact: Sophia Lloyd, Exec. Dir.
FAX: (708) 848-1531; E-mail: slloyd@oprfcf.org;
Main URL: http://www.oprfcf.org
Facebook: https://www.facebook.com/OPRFCF

Established in 1958 in IL.
Foundation type: Community foundation.
Financial data (yr. ended 12/31/12): Assets, $22,989,653 (M); gifts received, $2,110,394; expenditures, $2,857,097; giving activities include $2,178,511 for 52+ grants (high: $555,673).
Purpose and activities: The foundation serves the community by: 1) stimulating and facilitating individual philanthropy; 2) being accountable and prudent managers of donor funds; 3) making responsive and informed grants; and 4) convening resources to address community priorities and interests.
Fields of interest: Arts; Education; Environment; Health care; Crime/violence prevention; Housing/shelter; Recreation; Family services; Human services; Community development, neighborhood development; Community/economic development; Children/youth; Aging; Disabilities, people with; Minorities.
Type of support: General/operating support; Income development; Management development/capacity building; Program development; Seed money; Consulting services; Scholarships—to individuals; Matching/challenge support.
Limitations: Applications accepted. Giving limited to Oak Park and River Forest, IL, for discretionary grantmaking. No grants to individuals (except for specific funds designated for scholarships), or for endowments, capital campaigns or for debt retirement.
Publications: Application guidelines; Annual report (including application guidelines); Grants list; Informational brochure; Newsletter; Occasional report.
Application information: Visit foundation web site for application form and guidelines. Applications are sent to an extensive mailing list of Oak Park and River Forest organizations; to be placed on the list, organizations can call the foundation or e-mail staff. E-mailed or faxed applications are not accepted. Application form required.
Initial approach: Telephone or e-mail
Copies of proposal: 3
Deadline(s): Apr. 1 for CommunityWorks grants; Aug. 1 for others
Board meeting date(s): 2nd Tues. in Jan., Mar., May, Sept., and Nov.
Officers and Directors:* Sheila Price,* Pres.; Clare Golla,* V.P.; Donna Myers,* Secy.; Matthew Grote,* Treas.; Sophia Lloyd, Exec. Dir.; Case Hoogendoorn, Counsel; Cuyler Brown; **Susan Conti; Michele Donley**; Sonny Ginsberg; Janet Hanley; John Hedges; John Houseal; Phillip Jimenez; Annese Piazza; Brian Plain; Pravin Rao; Mary Jo Schuler; Michelle Vanderlaan; Barbara Watkins; Eric Weinheimer; Stacey Williams.
Number of staff: 3 full-time professional; 1 part-time professional; 1 full-time support.
EIN: 364150724
Other changes: Clarmarie I. Keenan, Virginia Martinez, and Donna Myers are no longer directors.

1069
Oberweiler Foundation
1250 S. Grove St., Ste. 200
Barrington, IL 60010-5011
FAX: (847) 277-7446;
E-mail: oberw1@ameritech.net
Google Plus: https://plus.google.com/110987600611257280915/about?gl=us&hl=en

Established in 2000 in IL.
Donor: Siegfried Weiler.
Foundation type: Independent foundation.
Financial data (yr. ended 12/31/12): Assets, $10,115,544 (M); expenditures, $687,237; qualifying distributions, $509,760; giving activities include $409,771 for 30 grants (high: $35,000; low: $178).
Purpose and activities: Giving primarily to 1) help individuals achieve higher levels of wellness through the application of alternative medicine procedures, 2) prevent the demise of America's wilderness/wetlands as a result of private exploitation and/or public encroachment, and 3) assist disadvantaged, sick, and/or abused children.
Fields of interest: Environment; Health care; Health organizations, association; Children/youth, services; Children/youth; Children.
Type of support: Equipment; Land acquisition; Emergency funds; Internship funds; Research; Matching/challenge support.
Limitations: Applications not accepted. Giving primarily in northern IL. No grants for operational support.
Application information: Contributes only to pre-selected organizations.
Board meeting date(s): Feb.
Officers: Siegfried Weiler, Pres.; James R. Bartell, V.P.; **Anna Weiler, Secy.-Treas.**
Directors: Ruth S. Flynn; Ronald Ohlsen; Martha Heylin.
Number of staff: 1 full-time professional.
EIN: 364376705
Other changes: Anna Weiler is now Secy.-Treas.

1070
Omron Foundation, Inc.
c/o Omron Managment Center of America
55 Commerce Dr.
Schaumburg, IL 60173-5302 (224) 520-7654
Contact: James P. Eberhart, Treas.
Main URL: http://www.components.omron.com/components/web/webfiles.nsf/philanthropy.html

Established in 1989 in IL.
Donors: Omron Electronics Inc.; Omron Electronics LLC; Omron Healthcare, Inc.; Omron Electronics Components, LLC; Omron Automotive Electronics, Inc.
Foundation type: Company-sponsored foundation.
Financial data (yr. ended 03/31/13): Assets, $1,044,704 (M); gifts received, $914,658; expenditures, $621,292; qualifying distributions, $621,292; giving activities include $617,977 for 219 grants (high: $90,000; low: $10).
Purpose and activities: The foundation supports food banks and organizations involved with arts and culture, education, health, breast cancer, heart disease, housing development, disaster relief, human services, the disabled, and the elderly.
Fields of interest: Arts, cultural/ethnic awareness; Arts; Secondary school/education; Higher education; Engineering school/education; Education; Health care; Breast cancer; Heart & circulatory diseases; Food banks; Housing/shelter, development; Disasters, preparedness/services; American Red Cross; Aging, centers/services;

Developmentally disabled, centers & services; Human services; United Ways and Federated Giving Programs; Disabilities, people with.
Type of support: General/operating support; Continuing support; Building/renovation; Endowments; Program development; Scholarship funds; Employee matching gifts; Employee-related scholarships.
Limitations: Applications accepted. Giving primarily in CA, IL, NY, and TX. No support for political, fraternal, veterans', athletic, or lobbying organizations, or religious organizations not of direct benefit to the entire community. No grants to individuals (except for employee-related scholarships).
Application information: Application form required.
Initial approach: Letter
Deadline(s): None
Board meeting date(s): Quarterly
Officers and Directors: Nigel Blakeway,* Pres. and V.P.; K. Blake Thatcher,* Secy.; James P. Eberhart, Treas.; **Yutaka Miyanaga.**
EIN: 363644055
Other changes: Nigel Blakeway has replaced Takuji Yamamoto as Pres.

1071
The Pangburn Foundation
c/o JPMorgan Chase Bank, N.A.
10 S. Dearborn St., IL1-0117
Chicago, IL 60603-2300
***Application address:* c/o JPMorgan Chase Bank, N.A., Attn.: Larry Bothe, P.O. Box 2050, Fort Worth, TX 76113, tel.: (817) 884-4022**

Established in 1962 in TX.
Foundation type: Independent foundation.
Financial data (yr. ended 03/31/13): Assets, $7,036,502 (M); expenditures, $387,810; qualifying distributions, $340,309; giving activities include $325,000 for 6 grants (high: $100,000; low: $30,000).
Purpose and activities: Emphasis on cultural programs, especially music and the performing arts; funding also for education and human services.
Fields of interest: Museums; Performing arts; Performing arts, ballet; Performing arts, theater; Performing arts, orchestras; Performing arts, opera; Education; Human services.
Limitations: Applications accepted. Giving primarily in the Fort Worth, TX, area. No grants to individuals.
Application information:
Initial approach: Letter
Copies of proposal: 1
Deadline(s): Sept. 30
Board meeting date(s): Oct. or Nov.
Trustee: JPMorgan Chase Bank, N.A.
EIN: 756042630
Other changes: The grantmaker has moved from WI to IL.

1072
Martha Sue Parr Trust
c/o JPMorgan Chase Bank, N.A.
10 S. Dearborn St., IL1-0117
Chicago, IL 60603-2300
***Application address:* c/o JPMorgan Chase Bank, N.A.; Attn.: Larry Bothe, 420 Throckmorton St., Fort Worth, TX 76102-3700, tel.: (817) 884-4022**

Established in TX.
Donor: Martha Sue Parr†.
Foundation type: Independent foundation.
Financial data (yr. ended 03/31/13): Assets, $26,713,084 (M); expenditures, $1,298,224; qualifying distributions, $1,134,238; giving activities include $1,085,000 for 9 grants (high: $200,000; low: $5,000).
Purpose and activities: Giving primarily for children and youth services.
Fields of interest: Health care, association; Hospitals (general); Hospitals (specialty); Children, services; Residential/custodial care.
Limitations: Applications accepted. Giving primarily in Fort Worth, TX.
Application information:
Initial approach: Letter
Deadline(s): None
Trustee: JPMorgan Chase Bank, N.A.
EIN: 416519559
Other changes: The grantmaker has moved from WI to IL.

1073
The Pattis Family Foundation
600 Central Ave., Ste. 205
Highland Park, IL 60035-3256

Established in 1985 in IL.
Donors: S. William Pattis; Rose Q. Corp; Bette L. Pattis; Mark Pattis; Next Chapter Holdings; Pattis Family Investments.
Foundation type: Independent foundation.
Financial data (yr. ended 06/30/13): Assets, $5,135,947 (M); gifts received, $154,562; expenditures, $208,265; qualifying distributions, $113,820; giving activities include $113,820 for 46 grants (high: $50,000; low: $15).
Fields of interest: Arts; Higher education; Education; Hospitals (general); Health organizations, association; Human services; Jewish federated giving programs; Jewish agencies & synagogues.
Limitations: Applications not accepted. Giving primarily in Chicago, IL; some funding in CA, FL, and PA. No grants to individuals.
Application information: Unsolicited requests for funds not accepted.
Officers: Mark R. Pattis, Pres.; Robin Q. Pattis Himovitz, V.P.; **S. William Pattis, V.P.**; Bette L. Pattis, Secy.
EIN: 363433310

1074
The Pierce Family Charitable Foundation
(doing business as Pierce Family Foundation)
c/o Pierce and Assocs.
1 N. Dearborn St., Ste. 1300
Chicago, IL 60602-4321
***Contact:* Heather D. Parish, Prog. Dir.; Marianne Philbin, Exec. Dir.**
Main URL: http://www.piercefamilyfoundation.org
Facebook: https://www.facebook.com/thepiercefamilyfoundation

Established in 2007 in DE and IL.
Donors: Denis Pierce; Martha V. Pierce.
Foundation type: Independent foundation.
Financial data (yr. ended 12/31/12): Assets, $10,607,961 (M); gifts received, $2,249,780; expenditures, $1,893,321; qualifying distributions, $1,779,943; giving activities include $1,095,171 for 149 grants (high: $55,741; low: $200), and $564,564 for foundation-administered programs.
Purpose and activities: The foundation supports nonprofit organizations providing essential social services in the areas of housing and opportunities for homeless people.
Fields of interest: Environment, natural resources; Housing/shelter; Human services; Family services; Homeless, human services; Protestant agencies & churches; Homeless.
Type of support: Management development/ capacity building; General/operating support.
Limitations: Applications not accepted. Giving primarily in Chicago, IL, as well as to select programs in MI. No grants to individuals.
Application information: Contributes only to pre-selected organizations.
Officers and Director:* Denis Pierce,* Pres.; Martha V. Pierce, Secy.; Marianne Philbin, Exec. Dir.
EIN: 261459612

1075
Polk Bros. Foundation, Inc.
20 W. Kinzie St., Ste. 1110
Chicago, IL 60654-5815 (312) 527-4684
Contact: Sheila A. Robinson, Grant Admin.
FAX: (312) 527-4681; E-mail: info@polkbrosfdn.org; E-mail for Sheila A. Robinson:srobinson@polkbrosFdn.org; Main URL: http://www.polkbrosfdn.org/
Grants Database: http://www.polkbrosfdn.org/grants.asp

Incorporated in 1957 in IL.
Donors: David D. Polk†; Harry Polk†; Morris G. Polk†; Samuel H. Polk†; Sol Polk†; Rand Realty and Development Co.; Polk Bros., Inc.; and members of the Polk family.
Foundation type: Independent foundation.
Financial data (yr. ended 08/31/13): Assets, $434,206,007 (M); expenditures, $23,353,181; qualifying distributions, $22,998,209; giving activities include $19,464,480 for 455 grants (high: $350,000; low: $100), and $1,357,985 for 453 employee matching gifts.
Purpose and activities: The mission is to improve the quality of life for the people of Chicago. The foundation partners with local nonprofit organizations that work to reduce the impact of poverty and provide area residents with better access to quality education, preventive health care and basic human services. Through its grantmaking, the foundation strives to make Chicago a place where all people have the opportunity to reach their full potential.
Fields of interest: Museums; Performing arts; Performing arts, theater; Arts; Education, early childhood education; Child development, education; Vocational education; Higher education; Adult/continuing education; Adult education—literacy, basic skills & GED; Education, reading; Education; Health care; Mental health/crisis services; Health organizations, association; AIDS; Crime/violence prevention, domestic violence; Legal services; Employment; Youth development, services; Human services; Children/youth, services; Child development, services; Family services; Women, centers/services; Minorities/immigrants, centers/services; Homeless, human services; Civil rights, race/intergroup relations; Urban/community development; Community/economic development; Jewish federated giving programs; Leadership development; Jewish agencies & synagogues; Disabilities, people with; Minorities; Women; Economically disadvantaged; Homeless.
Type of support: Pro bono services - legal; Management development/capacity building; General/operating support; Continuing support; Equipment; Program development; Curriculum development; Scholarship funds; Technical

assistance; Program evaluation; Employee matching gifts.
Limitations: Applications accepted. Giving primarily in Chicago, IL. No support for political organizations or religious institutions seeking support for programs whose participants are restricted by religious affiliation, or for tax-generating entities (municipalities and school districts) for services within their normal responsibilities. No grants to individuals, or for medical, scientific or academic research, or purchase of dinner or raffle tickets.
Publications: Annual report (including application guidelines).
Application information: An organization that is new to the foundation or has not received a grant from the foundation in the last five years should review the foundation's program area guide before submitting a pre-application form. Current grantees or those that have received a grant from the foundation within the last five years may call or e-mail the foundation for an application packet. Proposals for health-related services are not reviewed at the Feb., May and Nov. board meeting. Application form required.
Initial approach: Letter of inquiry and online pre-application request
Copies of proposal: 1
Deadline(s): None
Board meeting date(s): Feb., May, Aug., and Nov.
Final notification: 3 - 4 weeks
Officers and Directors:* Sandra P. Guthman,* Chair.; Gillian Darlow, C.E.O.; Evette M. Cardona, V.P., Progs.; Raymond F. Simon,* V.P.; Gordon S. Prussian,* Secy.; Theodore S. Weymouth, C.F.O.; Sidney Epstein,* Treas.; Bruce R. Bachmann; Howard J. Polk; Cherryl T. Thomas.
Number of staff: 9 full-time professional; 2 part-time professional; 2 full-time support.
EIN: 366108293

1076
Prince Charitable Trusts
140 S. Dearborn St., Ste. 1410
Chicago, IL 60603-5208 (312) 419-8700
Contact: Benna Wilde, Prog. Dir.; For Chicago and RI Proposals: Sharon Robison, Grants Mgr.
FAX: (312) 419-8558;
E-mail: tfron@prince-trusts.org; Additional address: 816 Connecticut Ave. N.W., Washington, DC 2006, tel.: (202) 728-0636, fax: (202) 466-4726. Proposals should be addressed to: Charles C. Twichell, Mgr. Dir. (Chicago office); Main URL: http://princetrusts.org

Frederick Henry Prince Trust dated July 9, 1947 established in 1947 in IL. Frederick Henry Prince Testamentary Trust established in 1947 in RI. Abbie Norman Prince Trust established in 1949 in IL.
Donor: Frederick Henry Prince†.
Foundation type: Independent foundation.
Financial data (yr. ended 12/31/12): Assets, $137,035,968 (M); expenditures, $6,634,705; qualifying distributions, $6,380,922; giving activities include $4,965,327 for 333 grants (high: $250,000; low: $100).
Purpose and activities: Support for cultural programs, youth organizations, social services, hospitals, hospital morale, rehabilitation, and environment.
Fields of interest: Arts; Education, early childhood education; Environment, natural resources; Environment; Hospitals (general); Reproductive health, family planning; Medical care, rehabilitation; Health care; Human services; Children/youth, services; Children/youth; Children; Minorities; Economically disadvantaged; Homeless.
Type of support: General/operating support; Continuing support; Capital campaigns; Program development; Seed money; Technical assistance; Program-related investments/loans; Employee matching gifts.
Limitations: Applications accepted. Giving limited to local groups in Washington, DC, Chicago, IL, and RI, with emphasis on Aquidneck Island. No support for national organizations, or for religious or political organizations. No grants to individuals.
Publications: Application guidelines.
Application information: The DC office will not be accepting unsolicited proposals - applications by invitation only. Some funding areas for the Chicago office are via invitation only- applicants should check web site prior to applying. Application form not required.
***Initial approach:* On-line proposal (4 to 6 pages for proposal) to be submitted via http://www.egrant.net. Check foundation web site for application guidelines**
Copies of proposal: 1
***Deadline(s):* Chicago: Jan. 13 for Social Svcs., May 1 for Health, June 2 for Arts/Culture, Environment and Capital; Rhode Island: May 1**
***Board meeting date(s):* Chicago: spring and fall; Rhode Island: fall; Washington, DC: late spring and late fall**
Final notification: Within 5 months of proposal deadline
Trustees: Frederick Henry Prince IV; Patrick B. Wood-Prince.
Number of staff: 4 full-time professional; 1 part-time professional; 2 full-time support.

1077
Prince Foundation
140 S. Dearborn St., Ste. 1410
Chicago, IL 60603 (312) 419-8700
***Main URL:* http://www.princetrusts.org/chicago.html**

Incorporated in 1955 in IL.
Donors: F.H. Prince & Co., Inc.; John D. MacArthur Foundation; Catherine T. MacArthur Foundation.
Foundation type: Company-sponsored foundation.
Financial data (yr. ended 12/31/12): Assets, $2,563,313 (M); gifts received, $1,658,000; expenditures, $1,696,325; qualifying distributions, $1,694,175; giving activities include $1,537,500 for 51 grants (high: $37,000; low: $6,000).
Purpose and activities: The foundation supports organizations involved with arts and culture and children and youth.
Fields of interest: Museums; Performing arts, dance; Performing arts, theater; Performing arts, orchestras; Performing arts, opera; Performing arts, music (choral); Arts; Elementary/secondary education; Children/youth, services.
Type of support: General/operating support; Employee matching gifts.
Limitations: Applications accepted. Giving primarily in IL. No grants to individuals.
Application information: Application form required.
Initial approach: Letter
Deadline(s): None
Officers and Trustees:* Patrick Wood-Prince,* Pres.; Randall M. Highley,* V.P.; Frederick Henry Prince,* V.P.
EIN: 366116507

1078
Colonel (IL) James N. Pritzker Charitable Distribution Fund
(doing business as The Tawani Foundation)
104 S. Michigan Ave., Ste. 525
Chicago, IL 60603-5950 (312) 374-9390
Contact: Lisa M. Lanz, Exec. Dir.
E-mail: www.info@tawanifoundation.net; Main URL: http://www.tawanifoundation.org/

Established in 2002 in IL.
Donors: James Pritzker; Pritzker Foundation; Pritzker Cousins Foundation.
Foundation type: Independent foundation.
Financial data (yr. ended 12/31/12): Assets, $47,501,281 (M); gifts received, $18,358,574; expenditures, $3,795,499; qualifying distributions, $3,541,058; giving activities include $3,021,187 for 242+ grants.
Purpose and activities: Giving primarily for historical preservation of military heritage, projects that provide access to public spaces and services that enhance and improve quality of life, conservation and preservation of historic sites, as well as the foundation provides cadet awards for JROTC and ROTC units, and supports programs that reward, study and document the promotion of the citizen soldier ideal and military service.
Fields of interest: Museums; Historical activities; Education.
Type of support: Capital campaigns; Building/renovation; Program development; Publication; Research; Matching/challenge support.
Limitations: Applications not accepted. Giving primarily in Chicago, IL. No support for political campaigns. No grants to individuals, or for building endowments or scholarships.
Application information: Letters of inquiry and applications are by invitation only.
Board meeting date(s): Fall and spring
Officer and Directors: Lisa M. Lanz, Exec. Dir.; Lew Collens; Charles E. Dobrusin; Mary Parthe; Col. David Pelizzon; Guy Sellars.
Number of staff: 5 full-time professional.
EIN: 300040386

1079
Pritzker Foundation
300 N. LaSalle St., Ste. 1500
Chicago, IL **60654-3413** (312) 873-4884
FAX: (312) 577-0847

Incorporated in 1944 in IL.
Donors: Members of the Pritzker family; H. Group Holding, Inc. and Subsidiaries; Marmon Holdings, Inc. and Subsidiaries.
Foundation type: Independent foundation.
Financial data (yr. ended 12/31/12): Assets, $384,212,520 (M); expenditures, $14,243,023; qualifying distributions, $8,876,744; giving activities include $8,848,000 for 41 grants (high: $2,500,000; low: $500).
Purpose and activities: Grants largely for higher education, including medical education, and religious welfare funds; giving also for hospitals, temple support, and cultural programs.
Fields of interest: Arts; Higher education; Higher education, university; Medical school/education; Hospitals (general); Human services; Foundations (private grantmaking); Philanthropy/voluntarism; Religious federated giving programs; Jewish agencies & synagogues.
Limitations: Applications not accepted. Giving primarily in Chicago, IL. No grants to individuals.

Application information: Contributes only to pre-selected organizations.

Board meeting date(s): Dec. and as required

Officers and Directors:* **Gigi Pritzker Pucker,* Pres.**; **Ronald D. Wray, V.P. and Secy.**; Nicholas J. Pritzker,* V.P.; Thomas J. Pritzker,* V.P.; **Brian S. Traubert,* V.P.**

EIN: 366058062

Other changes: Ronald D. Wray is now V.P. and Secy. Mark Hoplamazian is no longer V.P. Penny S. Pritzker is no longer V.P. Brian S. Traubert is now V.P.

1080
The Pritzker Traubert Family Foundation

(formerly The Bryan Traubert and Penny Pritzker Charitable Foundation)

300 N. La Salle St., Ste. 1500
Chicago, IL **60654-3413**
Contact: **Jody Boutell, Grants Mgr.**
E-mail: **jboutell@ptffoundation.org**; Main URL: http://www.ptffoundation.org/

Established in 2000 in IL.

Donors: Bryan Traubert; Penny Pritzker.

Foundation type: Independent foundation.

Financial data (yr. ended 12/31/12): Assets, $172,339,177 (M); gifts received, $54,192,710; expenditures, $4,644,567; qualifying distributions, $3,387,826; giving activities include $3,231,844 for 78 grants (high: $495,000; low: $250).

Purpose and activities: Giving primarily for education, health and fitness, and art and culture programs.

Fields of interest: Arts; Education; Public health.

Limitations: Applications not accepted. Giving primarily in Chicago, IL. No grants to individuals.

Application information: Contributes only to pre-selected organizations.

Board meeting date(s): Annually

Officers and Directors:* Bryan S. Traubert, M.D.*, Pres.; Ronald D. Wray, V.P. and Secy.; Penny Pritzker,* V.P.; Kevin Poorman,* Treas.

EIN: 364347781

Other changes: At the close of 2012, the fair market value of the grantmaker's assets was $172,339,177, a 63.9% increase over the 2011 value, $105,138,372.

1081
George M. Pullman Educational Foundation

55 W. Monroe St., Ste. 3460
Chicago, IL 60603-5086 (312) 422-0444
Contact: Robin Redman, Exec. Dir.
FAX: (312) 422-0448;
E-mail: info@pullmanfoundation.org; Main URL: http://www.pullmanfoundation.org
Facebook: https://www.facebook.com/pages/George-M-Pullman-Educational-Foundation/141896812511358
LinkedIn: http://www.linkedin.com/groups?gid=4239215&trk=hb_side_g
Twitter: https://twitter.com/pullmanfdn

Incorporated in 1949 in IL.

Donors: George Mortimer Pullman†; Harriet Sanger Pullman†.

Foundation type: Independent foundation.

Financial data (yr. ended 07/31/13): Assets, $27,740,913 (M); gifts received, $76,590; expenditures, $1,539,850; qualifying distributions, $1,201,842; giving activities include $559,683 for 161 grants to individuals (high: $6,000; low: $300).

Purpose and activities: The foundation was established in 1949 to support qualified individuals primarily for post-secondary education. Graduating high school seniors who are residents of Cook County, IL are eligible for consideration for scholarships for college.

Fields of interest: Education.

Type of support: Program development; Scholarship funds.

Limitations: Giving primarily to residents of Cook County, IL. No grants to individuals directly.

Publications: Informational brochure.

Application information: Scholarship applicants must be residents of Cook County, IL. Awards are paid directly to the scholar's chosen college or university. Application information available on the foundation's website. Application form required.

Initial approach: Online application available at foundation's website

Deadline(s): Mar. 31

Board meeting date(s): Quarterly

Officers and Directors:* Barbara H. Miller,* Pres.; John P. Hergert, V.P.; Rev. Sam A. Portaro, Jr.,* Secy.; Marc Christman,* Treas.; Robin Redmond, Exec. Dir.; Robert W. Bennett; Edward McCormick Blair, Jr.; Peter Braxton; Robert W. Fioretti; **Kimberley Freedman**; Alejandra Garza; Richard J. Hoskins; Warren Pullman Miller; Harry M. Oliver, Jr.

Number of staff: 4 full-time professional; 2 full-time support.

EIN: 362216171

1082
Redhill Foundation - Sam and Jean Rothberg Family Charitable Trust

(also known as Redhill Foundation - Rothberg Family Charitable Trust)

c/o Kavanagh, Scully, Sudow, White & Frederick, P.C.
301 S.W. Adams St., Ste. 700
Peoria, IL 61602-1570 (309) 676-1381

Established in 1987 in IL.

Donors: Samuel Rothberg; Lee Patrick Rothberg; Kathleen M. Barnett; Heidi B. Munday; Jean Rothberg; Samuel Rothberg Trust.

Foundation type: Independent foundation.

Financial data (yr. ended 12/31/12): Assets, $122,278,261 (M); expenditures, $8,333,385; qualifying distributions, $5,899,735; giving activities include $5,899,735 for 6+ grants (high: $5,860,000).

Purpose and activities: Giving primarily for Jewish organizations and for human services.

Fields of interest: Human services; United Ways and Federated Giving Programs; Jewish federated giving programs; Jewish agencies & synagogues.

Type of support: General/operating support; Scholarship funds; Research.

Limitations: Giving primarily in Peoria, IL and New York, NY. No grants to individuals.

Application information:

Initial approach: Letter

Deadline(s): None

Trustees: Kathleen M. Barnett; Heidi B. Rothberg; Jean C. Rothberg; Lee Patrick Rothberg; Michael Rothberg.

EIN: 371217165

1083
Michael Reese Health Trust

(formerly Michael Reese Hospital Foundation)

150 N. Wacker Dr., Ste. 2320
Chicago, IL 60606-1608 (312) 726-1008
Contact: Gregory S. Gross Ed.D., Pres.; Jennifer M. Rosenkranz, Sr. Prog. Off., Responsive Grants
FAX: (312) 726-2797;
E-mail: wpalmer@healthtrust.net; E-mail for Responsive Grant Program: jrosenkranz@healthtrust.net (Jennifer Rosenkranz); Main URL: http://www.healthtrust.net
Knowledge Center: http://www.healthtrust.net/index.php?option=com_content&task=view&id=14&Itemid=43

Established in 1995 in IL; converted from sale of Michael Reese Hospital to Humana (now Columbia/HCA).

Donors: Foreman Trust; Lazarus Charitable Fund; Kirchheimer Trust; Blum Trust; Alice Schimberg.

Foundation type: Independent foundation.

Financial data (yr. ended 06/30/13): Assets, $135,030,710 (M); gifts received, $443,143; expenditures, $7,844,624; qualifying distributions, $6,804,140; giving activities include $5,927,374 for 150 grants (high: $417,000; low: $700), and $199,260 for foundation-administered programs.

Purpose and activities: The trust is committed to improving the health of the Chicago area's most vulnerable residents: the poor, children and youth, people with disabilities, the elderly, immigrants and refugees, and the uninsured. Its grants and initiatives support the work of organizations serving these populations, as well as efforts to achieve lasting change in the region's healthcare delivery system.

Fields of interest: Education, public education; Public health; Health care; Medical research, institute; Children/youth, services; Civil/human rights, disabled; Jewish agencies & synagogues; Aging; Disabilities, people with; Military/veterans; Immigrants/refugees.

Type of support: General/operating support; Program development; Research; Technical assistance; Program evaluation.

Limitations: Applications accepted. Giving limited to the metropolitan Chicago, IL, area with emphasis on the city of Chicago. No support for private foundations, secular purposes or for durable medical equipment. **No grants to individuals, or for capital campaigns, endowment funds, fundraising events, debt reduction, or scholarships.**

Publications: Financial statement; Grants list; Multi-year report.

Application information: If an organization's letter of inquiry is accepted, a full proposal will be invited. Online application process. Application form not required.

Initial approach: Use online Letter of Inquiry found on foundation web site

Deadline(s): Dec. 15 and June 15 for receipt of letter of inquiry

Board meeting date(s): Twice per year

Final notification: Approx. 5-6 weeks after deadlines for letters of inquiry; approx. 3 months for proposals

Officers and Trustees:* Herbert S. Wander,* Chair.; Hon. Howard W. Carroll,* Vice-Chair.; Gregory S. Gross, Ed.D.*, Pres.; Walter R. Nathan,* Secy.; Ellard Pfaelzer, Jr.,* Treas.; Harvey J. Barnett; John F. Benjamin; Andrew K. Block; **Bechara Choucair, M.D.**; **Nancy Glick**; Ann-Louise Kleper; **Gregory C. Mayer**; Mally Z. Rutkoff; **Michelle R. B. Saddler**; **Max R. Schrayer II**; **Michael B. Tarnoff**; **Joseph F. West, ScD**; Andrea Rozran Yablon.

Number of staff: 4 full-time professional.

EIN: 362170910

Other changes: Frederick J. Manning, Enrique Martinez, Steven B. Nasatir, Ph.D, Angela R. Perry, M.D., Midge Perlman Shafton, Marc H. Slutsky,

M.D., and John L. Wilhelm, M.D. are no longer trustees.

1084
Jeffrey J. Rhodes Family Foundation
c/o Kevin Hodges, CPA, Miller Cooper and Co. Ltd.
1751 Lake Cook Rd., Ste. 400
Deerfield, IL 60015-5286

Established in 1988 in IL.
Donor: Jeffrey J. Rhodes.
Foundation type: Independent foundation.
Financial data (yr. ended 11/30/11): Assets, $112,969 (M); expenditures, $24,550; qualifying distributions, $24,550; giving activities include $24,550 for 6 grants (high: $20,000; low: $50).
Fields of interest: Higher education, university; Education; Cancer; Human services.
Limitations: Applications not accepted. Giving primarily in PA. No grants to individuals.
Application information: Contributes only to pre-selected organizations.
Officers: Jeffrey J. Rhodes, Pres.; Arthur Rhodes, V.P.; Nina B. Matis, Secy.
EIN: 363624203

1085
Richard Benevolent Foundation
720 Hampton Course
West Chicago, IL 60185-5807

Established in 2002 in IL.
Donors: Betty J. Richard; Elwood Richard.
Foundation type: Independent foundation.
Financial data (yr. ended 06/30/13): Assets, $398,008 (M); gifts received, $300,000; expenditures, $309,869; qualifying distributions, $307,600; giving activities include $301,500 for 8 grants (high: $125,000; low: $5,000).
Purpose and activities: Giving primarily for missionary work, health research, and for the disabled.
Fields of interest: Health care, research; Human services; Religious federated giving programs; Christian agencies & churches; Disabilities, people with.
Limitations: Applications not accepted. Giving primarily in IL and VA. No grants to individuals.
Application information: Contributes only to pre-selected organizations.
Officers and Directors:* Elwood Richard,* Pres.; Beth Richard,* V.P.; Betty J. Richard,* V.P.; Sharon Wong,* Secy.
EIN: 753089935
Other changes: The grantmaker no longer lists a phone.

1086
Michael Alan Rosen Foundation
10 S. Dearborn, ILI-0117
Chicago, IL 60603

Established in 1986 in CA. Classified as a private operating foundation in 1991.
Donors: Tobi Haleen; Conrad Hilton Foundation; The AGR Trust.
Foundation type: Operating foundation.
Financial data (yr. ended 12/31/12): Assets, $4,773,148 (M); gifts received, $350,104; expenditures, $316,206; qualifying distributions, $275,320; giving activities include $266,350 for 14 grants (high: $136,200; low: $150).
Fields of interest: Higher education, university; Hospitals (general); Substance abuse, services; Substance abuse, treatment.
Type of support: General/operating support; Program-related investments/loans.
Limitations: Applications not accepted. Giving primarily in CA. No grants to individuals.
Application information: Contributes only to pre-selected organizations.
Officers: Arlene Rosen, Pres. and Treas.; William Kroger, V.P.; Tobi Haleen, Secy.
Number of staff: 2 full-time professional; 7 full-time support; 6 part-time support.
EIN: 943024736
Other changes: The grantmaker has moved from DE to IL.

1087
Patrick G. & Shirley W. Ryan Foundation
150 N. Michigan Ave., Ste. 2100
Chicago, IL 60601-7559

Established in 1984 in IL.
Donors: Patrick G. Ryan; Shirley W. Ryan; Ryan Holding Corp. of Illinois; Ryan Enterprises Corp. of Illinois.
Foundation type: Independent foundation.
Financial data (yr. ended 11/30/13): Assets, $31,239,805 (M); gifts received, $9,808,507; expenditures, $6,428,833; qualifying distributions, $6,385,549; giving activities include $6,361,962 for 110 grants (high: $1,500,000; low: $100).
Purpose and activities: Giving primarily for education, the arts, Roman Catholic churches and schools, and children and youth services.
Fields of interest: Performing arts; Arts; Elementary/secondary education; Higher education; Education; Youth development, services; Human services; Children/youth, services; Residential/custodial care, hospices; United Ways and Federated Giving Programs; Catholic agencies & churches.
Limitations: Applications not accepted. Giving primarily in IL, with emphasis on Chicago. No grants to individuals.
Application information: Contributes only to pre-selected organizations.
Officers and Directors:* Patrick G. Ryan,* Chair. and V.P.; Shirley W. Ryan, Pres. and Treas.; Dawn Moore, Secy.; **Corbett M.W. Ryan**; Patrick G. Ryan, Jr.; Robert J.W. Ryan.
EIN: 363305162
Other changes: For the fiscal year ended Nov. 30, 2012, the fair market value of the grantmaker's assets was $23,749,598, a 594.7% increase over the fiscal 2011 value, $3,418,698.

1088
Arthur J. Schmitt Foundation
P.O. Box 340
LaGrange, IL 60525-0340 **(708) 522-9361**
***Contact:* Patricia A. Shevlin, Exec. Dir.**
E-mail: schmittfoundation@gmail.com; Main URL: http://www.schmittfoundation.org

Incorporated in 1941 in IL.
Donor: Arthur J. Schmitt†.
Foundation type: Independent foundation.
Financial data (yr. ended 06/30/13): Assets, $15,965,294 (M); expenditures, $1,115,375; qualifying distributions, $980,616; giving activities include $891,000 for 14 grants (high: $100,000; low: $15,000).
Purpose and activities: Giving for institutional scholarship support to universities for undergraduate and graduate studies, and to organizations that sponsor and mentor under-privileged students attending Catholic high schools. Funding also for organizations that develop and support learning and leadership in students of various learning levels.
Fields of interest: Education; Human services.
Type of support: General/operating support; Continuing support; Fellowships; Scholarship funds.
Limitations: Giving primarily in the metropolitan Chicago, IL, area. No grants to individuals, or for capital or building funds, research, or matching gifts; no loans.
Publications: Informational brochure.
Application information: The foundation does not encourage new grant applications at this time.
Board meeting date(s): Sept., Dec., Mar., and June
Officers and Directors:* John J. Gearen,* Pres.; Mary M. Dwyer,* Treas.; Daniel E. Mayworm,* V.P.; Peter J. Wrenn,* V.P.; Patricia A. Shevlin, Exec. Dir.; Richard C. Becker, Pres. and Board Member Emeritus; **Patrick C. Eilers**; **Carol H. Sullivan**.
Number of staff: 1 part-time professional.
EIN: 362217999

1089
The Schnadig-Belgrad Foundation
P.O. Box 90
Glencoe, IL 60022-0090

Established in 1999 in IL.
Donor: Dorothy D. Schnadig.
Foundation type: Independent foundation.
Financial data (yr. ended 12/31/13): Assets, $193,571 (M); gifts received, $175,000; expenditures, $112,643; qualifying distributions, $112,643; giving activities include $111,825 for 46 grants (high: $30,000; low: $75).
Fields of interest: Family services; Jewish federated giving programs.
Limitations: Applications not accepted. Giving primarily in Chicago, IL. No grants to individuals.
Application information: Contributes only to pre-selected organizations.
Trustees: Donald A. Belgard; Dorothy D. Schnadig; Richard H. Schnadig.
EIN: 367293195
Other changes: The grantmaker no longer lists a phone.

1090
Schuler Family Foundation
28161 N. Keith Dr.
Lake Forest, IL 60045-4528
E-mail: info@schulerprogram.org; Main URL: http://www.schulerfoundation.org/
Blog: http://www.schulerscholar.blogspot.com
Facebook: https://www.facebook.com/schulerprogram
Google Plus: https://plus.google.com/107506573411218462200/posts
LinkedIn: http://www.linkedin.com/company/schuler-scholar-program
Twitter: https://www.twitter.com/SchulerScholar
YouTube: http://www.youtube.com/channel/UCVxXfByTFbtCjW5JqCuNc5A

Established in 1997 in IL.
Donors: Jack W. Schuler; AmeriCorps.
Foundation type: Independent foundation.

Financial data (yr. ended 12/31/12): Assets, $109,900,452 (M); gifts received, $972,634; expenditures, $4,437,951; qualifying distributions, $4,383,230; giving activities include $1,152,826 for grants to individuals, and $593,120 for foundation-administered programs.
Purpose and activities: The foundation sponsors a scholarship program to motivate and change behavior of high potential students to strive towards a goal of graduating from college, recognizing that even high potential students are vulnerable to outside influences during high school and college years. Schuler Scholars are Illinois students selected at the end of the freshman year in high school. They are offered a 4 year college scholarship of $5,000 per year provided they maintain the requirements of the Scholar program for their remaining 3 years of high school and 4 years of college. Each student will have a team of advisors, including her/his parents to help him or her navigate through high school and college. At Highland Park and Maine East high schools, applications will be accepted from 8th grade students only; at Waukegan High School, applications will be accepted from Freshman only; at Round Lake and Warren Township high schools, applications will be accepted from both 8th grade and Freshman students.
Fields of interest: Arts; Higher education; Health care; Human services; Children/youth, services; Women, centers/services.
Type of support: Scholarships—to individuals.
Limitations: Giving primarily in IL.
Application information: Contributes only to pre-selected organizations for general grants. See foundation web site for Schuler Scholar guidelines and application. Application form required.
Deadline(s): Varies
Officers: Jack W. Schuler, Pres. and Secy.; Therese H. Hoffman, V.P.; Tino H. Schuler, V.P.; Tanya E. Sharman, V.P.; Renate R. Schuler, Treas.; Candace A. Browdy, Exec. Dir.
EIN: 364154510

1091
W. L. & Louise E. Seymour Foundation
c/o JPMorgan Chase Bank, N.A.
10 S. Dearborn St., IL1-0117
Chicago, IL 60603-2300
Application address: 420 Throckmorton St., 3rd Fl., Fort Worth, TX 76102, tel.: (817) 884-4022

Established in 1983 in TX.
Donor: Louise E. Seymour†.
Foundation type: Independent foundation.
Financial data (yr. ended 03/31/13): Assets, $4,468,435 (M); expenditures, $239,693; qualifying distributions, $204,468; giving activities include $193,946 for 7 grants (high: $75,000; low: $500).
Purpose and activities: Grants only for crippled children, mentally retarded children, handicapped and homeless children, and the elderly.
Fields of interest: Human services; Children, services; Family services; Residential/custodial care; Developmentally disabled, centers & services; Homeless, human services; Aging.
Type of support: General/operating support; Equipment; Program development; Research.
Limitations: Applications accepted. Giving limited to TX, with emphasis on El Paso. No support for political organizations. No grants to individuals or for endowments.
Application information: Application form required.
Initial approach: Letter
Deadline(s): None
Trustee: JPMorgan Chase Bank, N.A.
EIN: 746315820
Other changes: The grantmaker has moved from WI to IL.

1092
Shamrock Foundation
747 Sheridan Rd.
Wilmette, IL 60091-1959
Main URL: http://www.shamrockfound.org/
Blog: http://www.shamrockfound.org/?page_id=7

Established in 2004 in IL.
Donors: Edwardson Family Foundation; Catharine O. Edwardson; Catherine O. Edwardson Charitable Lead Annuity Trust; Catherine O. Edwardson Charitable Lead Annuity Trust 2.
Foundation type: Independent foundation.
Financial data (yr. ended 12/31/12): Assets, $4,066,106 (M); gifts received, $250,000; expenditures, $199,272; qualifying distributions, $183,000; giving activities include $183,000 for 8 grants (high: $100,000; low: $5,000).
Fields of interest: International economic development; Christian agencies & churches.
Limitations: Applications not accepted. Giving primarily in DC, IL and TX. No grants to individuals.
Application information: Contributes only to pre-selected organizations.
Officer: Catharine O. Edwardson, Pres.
Trustees: Laura K. Barrett; Anne L. Edwardson; Shelly M. Edwardson.
EIN: 061720127

1093
Charles and M. R. Shapiro Foundation, Inc.
(formerly Fern G. Shapiro, Morris R. Shapiro, and Charles Shapiro Foundation, Inc.)
191 N. Wacker Dr., Ste. 1800
Chicago, IL 60606-1615

Incorporated in 1958 in IL.
Donors: Charles Shapiro†; Mary Shapiro†; Molly Shapiro†; Morris R. Shapiro†.
Foundation type: Independent foundation.
Financial data (yr. ended 07/31/12): Assets, $37,261,515 (M); expenditures, $2,041,593; qualifying distributions, $1,903,299; giving activities include $1,729,429 for 87 grants (high: $155,039; low: $2,500).
Purpose and activities: Giving primarily to Jewish organizations and for human services; funding also for higher education.
Fields of interest: Arts; Higher education; Health organizations, association; Medical research, institute; Human services; Youth, services; Jewish federated giving programs; Jewish agencies & synagogues.
Limitations: Applications not accepted. Giving primarily in Chicago, IL; funding also in New York, NY. No grants to individuals.
Application information: Contributes only to pre-selected organizations.
Officers and Directors:* Norman A. Shubert,* Pres.; Joan Pines,* V.P. and Secy.; Linda Godlewski,* Treas.
EIN: 366109757
Other changes: Michael D. Vick is no longer Treas.

1094
Arnold Simonsen Family Charitable Foundation, Inc.
P.O. Box 5139
Buffalo Grove, IL 60089-5139
Application address: c/o Sharon Brennan, 1N599 Augusta Ct., Winfield, IL 60190-2361, tel.: (847) 941-0100

Established in 2007 in FL.
Donor: Arnold J. Simonsen.
Foundation type: Independent foundation.
Financial data (yr. ended 06/30/13): Assets, $2,256,424 (M); gifts received, $10,000; expenditures, $152,586; qualifying distributions, $122,900; giving activities include $122,900 for 17 grants (high: $25,000; low: $1,000).
Fields of interest: Performing arts; Human services.
Limitations: Applications accepted. Giving primarily in FL and IL.
Application information: Application form required.
Initial approach: Letter
Deadline(s): None
Officers and Directors:* Arnold J. Simonsen,* Pres.; Sharon Brennan,* V.P. and Secy.; Benjamin A. Hurwitz,* V.P. and Treas.
EIN: 261624741

1095
The Alexandrine and Alexander L. Sinsheimer Fund
10 S. Dearborn St., IL1-0117
Chicago, IL 60603-2300
***Application address:* c/o Wing Wilson, V.P., 270 Park Ave., 16th Fl., New York, NY 10017-2014; tel.: (212) 464-1497**

Established in 1959 in NY.
Donors: Alexander L. Sinsheimer†; Alexandrine Sinsheimer†.
Foundation type: Independent foundation.
Financial data (yr. ended 04/30/13): Assets, $10,222,378 (M); expenditures, $534,287; qualifying distributions, $453,890; giving activities include $430,000 for 7 grants (high: $100,000; low: $50,000).
Purpose and activities: Grants to medical schools to support scientific research relating to the prevention and cure of human diseases.
Fields of interest: Medical school/education; Medical research, institute.
Type of support: Research.
Limitations: Giving primarily in the metropolitan New York, NY, area; some funding also in Rochester, and Syracuse, NY.
Application information: Application form required.
Deadline(s): Feb. 15
Final notification: Apr. 30
Trustee: JPMorgan Chase Bank, N.A.
EIN: 136047421
Other changes: The grantmaker has moved from DE to IL.

1096
The Siragusa Foundation
1 E. Wacker Dr., Ste 2910
Chicago, IL 60601-1474 (312) 755-0064
Contact: Irene S. Phelps, Pres.
FAX: (312) 755-0069; E-mail: info@siragusa.org;
Main URL: http://www.siragusa.org
Grants List: http://www.siragusa.org/pages/recent_grants_2013/176.php

Trust established in 1950 in IL; incorporated in 1980.
Donor: Ross D. Siragusa†.
Foundation type: Independent foundation.
Financial data (yr. ended 12/31/12): Assets, $23,766,211 (M); gifts received, $1,000; expenditures, $1,936,537; qualifying distributions, $1,610,250; giving activities include $1,164,321 for 132 grants (high: $200,000; low: $46), and $19,176 for employee matching gifts.
Purpose and activities: The foundation strives to improve the quality of life for people living in the metropolitan Chicago, IL, area, by funding projects and programs that help care for those in need, as well as nurture the environments in which they live, work and play. Building on the foundation's founder Ross D. Siragusa's compassion and generosity, the foundation believes in working with organizations, communities and other philanthropic entities to connect people with people, engage people in issues and bridge people to services, all with the purpose of fulfilling their basic needs, enhancing their lives, and fostering a sense of community. The foundation supports charitable organizations that reflect the founder's special interests in arts and culture, education, the environment, health services and medical research, and human services.
Fields of interest: Humanities; Arts; Higher education; Education; Environment; Hospitals (general); Health care; Medical specialties; Youth, services; Child development, services; Aging, centers/services; Homeless, human services; Human services; Infants/toddlers; Children/youth; Children; Youth; Adults; Aging; Young adults; Disabilities, people with; Physically disabled; Blind/visually impaired; Mentally disabled; Minorities; African Americans/Blacks; Hispanics/Latinos; Native Americans/American Indians; Women; Girls; Military/veterans; Offenders/ex-offenders; AIDS, people with; Immigrants/refugees; Economically disadvantaged; Homeless.
Type of support: General/operating support; Continuing support; Emergency funds; Program development; Fellowships; Scholarship funds; Technical assistance; Employee matching gifts.
Limitations: Applications not accepted. Giving primarily in the metropolitan Chicago, IL, area. No support for political advocacy programs. No grants to individuals, or for endowment funds or medical research; no loans.
Publications: Annual report; Financial statement; Grants list.
Application information: Unsolicited requests for funds not accepted. Refer to foundation web site for future giving deadlines.
Board meeting date(s): Apr. and Nov.
Officers and Directors:* John E. Hicks, Jr., Chair.; Ross D. Siragusa III,* Vice-Chair.; Irene S. Phelps, C.E.O. and Pres.; Sinclair C. Siragusa,* Secy.; John R. Siragusa III,* Treas.; James Durkan; Caitlyn Hicks; Alisa Perrotte; Andrew Perrotte; Melvyn H. Schneider; Alexander C. Siragusa; Isabel Siragusa.
Number of staff: 2 full-time professional; 1 full-time support.
EIN: 363100492

1097
Albert J. & Claire R. Speh Foundation
10700 W. Higgins Rd., Ste. 250
Rosemont, IL 60018-3711 (847) 299-7011
Contact: Kevin Malinger, Exec. Dir.
FAX: (847) 299-7044; E-mail: Alanna@speh.org;
Main URL: http://www.speh.org
Grants List: http://www.speh.org/grantees.php

Established in 1996 in IL.
Donors: Albert J. Speh, Jr.†; Claire R. Speh.
Foundation type: Independent foundation.
Financial data (yr. ended 12/31/12): Assets, $9,540,873 (M); expenditures, $818,937; qualifying distributions, $666,681; giving activities include $470,374 for 35 grants (high: $100,000; low: $500).
Purpose and activities: Giving for programs that directly impact youth between the ages of 13 and 19.
Fields of interest: Education; Youth development; Children/youth, services; Family services.
Type of support: General/operating support; Continuing support; Management development/capacity building; Annual campaigns; Capital campaigns; Building/renovation; Equipment; Emergency funds; Program development; Seed money; Curriculum development; Internship funds; Scholarship funds; Technical assistance; Consulting services; Employee-related scholarships; Matching/challenge support.
Limitations: Applications accepted. Giving primarily in the metropolitan Chicago, IL, area. Generally, no grants to individuals, government agencies, medical/healthcare agencies and programs, or for research or political activity.
Publications: Grants list; Informational brochure (including application guidelines).
Application information: Letter of intent must be submitted 60 days prior to grant application deadline. Full proposals are by invitation only, upon review of letter of interest. Chicago Area Grant Application Form accepted, and can be downloaded from foundation web site (if full proposal is requested). Organizations that are not approved for grants are welcome to submit a new letter of interest the subsequent year. Application form required.
Initial approach: Letter of interest (no longer than 2 typewritten pages, via e-mail. Attachments, brochures, reports, articles, etc., will not be accepted)
Copies of proposal: 1
Deadline(s): Mar. 15 and July 15 for applications
Board meeting date(s): Feb., June, and Oct.
Final notification: June 30 and Oct. 30
Officers and Members:* Kevin Malinger,* Exec. Dir.; Alanna Golden,* Prog. Off.; Justin Bennett; Lorene Caravello; Erik Jorgenson; Megan Jorgenson; Lynette Malinger; Shannon Neal; Matthew Sharko; Michelle Sharko; Albert J. Speh IV; **Michael Speh.**
Executive Committee: Jonathan Speh; Kathleen M. Malinger.
Number of staff: 2 full-time professional; 1 part-time support.
EIN: 364118596
Other changes: Lawrence J. Speh is no longer a member of the Executive Committee.

1098
The Spencer Foundation
625 N. Michigan Ave., Ste. 1600
Chicago, IL 60611-3109 (312) 337-7000
Contact: Michael S. McPherson, Pres.
FAX: (312) 337-0282; E-mail: pres@spencer.org;
Main URL: http://www.spencer.org
Grants List: http://www.spencer.org/content.cfm/foundation-reports

Incorporated in 1962 in IL.
Donor: Lyle M. Spencer†.
Foundation type: Independent foundation.
Financial data (yr. ended 03/31/13): Assets, $472,399,062 (M); expenditures, $18,322,570; qualifying distributions, $16,599,251; giving activities include $11,221,187 for 144 grants (high: $1,577,216; low: $2,000), $224,188 for employee matching gifts, and $445,298 for foundation-administered programs.
Purpose and activities: The foundation is committed to supporting high-quality investigation of education through its research programs and to strengthening and renewing the educational research community through its fellowship and by strengthening the connections among education research, policy and practice through its communication and networking.
Fields of interest: Education, research.
Type of support: Fellowships; Research; Employee matching gifts.
Limitations: Applications accepted. Giving on a national and international basis. No grants to individuals, or for capital funds, general purposes, operating or continuing support, sabbatical supplements, work in instructional or curriculum development, any kind of training or service program, scholarships, travel fellowships, endowment funds, or pre-doctoral research; no loans.
Publications: Annual report; Financial statement; Grants list; Informational brochure; Newsletter.
Application information: Application information for specific foundation programs available on foundation website. Submit full proposal only upon request. Information on program and application forms required for NAEd/Spencer Postdoctoral Fellowships or NAEd/Spencer Dissertation Fellowships should be requested from the National Academy of Education, 500 5th St. N.W., Washington, DC 20001. Application form not required.
Initial approach: See foundation web site for program-specific guidelines
Deadline(s): See program-specific deadlines on foundation website
Board meeting date(s): Jan., June, and Oct.
Final notification: Program-specific dates available on foundation website
Officers and Directors:* Deborah Lowenberg Ball,* Chair.; Pamela Grossman,* Vice-Chair.; Michael S. McPherson,* Pres.; Diana Hess, Sr. V.P.; **Elizabeth Carrick, V.P., Admin. and Chief of Staff**; Julie Hubbard, C.F.O.; **Mary J. Cahillane, C.I.O.**; Carol R. Johnson; Richard Murnane; Stephen Raudenbush; C. Cybele Raver; Mario Small; T. Dennis Sullivan; Mark Vander Ploeg.
Number of staff: 11 full-time professional; 10 full-time support; 2 part-time support.
EIN: 366078558
Other changes: Deborah Lowenberg Ball has replaced Derek C. Bok as Chair. Pamela Grossman has replaced Deborah Lowenberg Ball as Vice-Chair.
Elizabeth Carrick is now V.P., Admin. and Chief of Staff. Judy Klippenstein is no longer Secy. Mary J. Cahillane is now C.I.O. Maria H. Carlos is no longer Cont. Christopher Jencks, Lyle Logan, and Richard J. Shavelson are no longer directors.

1099
Square D Foundation
1415 S. Roselle Rd.
Palatine, IL 60067-7399
Contact: Aurelie Richard, Treas.
Main URL: http://www.schneider-electric.us/sites/us/en/company/community/community.page

Established in 1956 in MI.
Donors: Schneider Electric USA, Inc.; Square D Co.
Foundation type: Company-sponsored foundation.
Financial data (yr. ended 12/31/13): Assets, $0; gifts received, $52,815; expenditures, $139,961;

qualifying distributions, $138,433; giving activities include $61,006 for grants.
Purpose and activities: The foundation supports organizations involved with arts and culture, education, health, human services, community development, civic affairs, senior citizens, disabled people, and economically disadvantaged people.
Fields of interest: Arts; Education; Hospitals (general); Health care; Housing/shelter, development; Youth, services; Human services; Community/economic development; Public affairs; Aging; Disabilities, people with; Economically disadvantaged.
Type of support: General/operating support; Continuing support; Annual campaigns; Capital campaigns; Building/renovation; Emergency funds; Professorships; Scholarship funds; Sponsorships; Employee matching gifts; Employee-related scholarships; Matching/challenge support.
Limitations: Applications not accepted. Giving primarily in areas of company operations, with emphasis on IA, IL, IN, KY, MO, NC, NE, OH, SC, TN, and TX; giving also national organizations. No support for religious organizations, labor unions, or political organizations. No grants to individuals (except for employee-related scholarships).
Application information: Telephone calls are not encouraged.
Board meeting date(s): As necessary
Officers and Directors:* **Mary Ann Maclean, Pres.**; Ted Klee, V.P.; Aurelie Richard,* Treas.; **Gladys Juarez**; John Mcpherson; **Karen Miranda**; Jean Pelletier.
Number of staff: None.
EIN: 366054195
Other changes: Mary Ann Maclean has replaced George Powers as Pres.
George Powers is no longer Pres. Allen Breeze, Jeff Dress, Robert Fiorani, and Gwen Magner are no longer directors. Geraldo Oliuares is no longer a director.

1100
Irvin Stern Foundation
4 E. Ohio St., Studio 22
Chicago, IL 60611-2783
Contact: Christine Flood, Grants Admin.
E-mail: christine@irvinstern.org; Main URL: http://www.irvinstern.org

Established in 1957 in IL.
Donor: Irvin Stern†.
Foundation type: Independent foundation.
Financial data (yr. ended 09/30/13): Assets, $13,476,782 (M); expenditures, $1,008,111; qualifying distributions, $880,962; giving activities include $798,000 for 56 grants (high: $120,000; low: $1,000).
Purpose and activities: Grants for human services, particularly aid to the underserved, the poor and disadvantaged, via innovative social service programs, physical and mental health outreach, literacy and vocational training; civic affairs aimed at improving the quality of life in urban communities through grass roots and neighborhood organizations; and for the enhancement of the Jewish community through education and spirituality.
Fields of interest: Education; Mental health/crisis services; Health organizations; Food services; Human services; Homeless, human services; Jewish federated giving programs; Public affairs; Jewish agencies & synagogues.
International interests: Israel.
Type of support: General/operating support; Continuing support; Equipment; Program development; Seed money.
Limitations: Applications accepted. Giving primarily in Chicago, IL. Some giving in New York by invitation only. No support for organizations outside of Chicago, IL without an invitation from the foundation. No grants to individuals, or for endowment funds, deficit financing, building funds, capital campaigns, construction projects, medical research, or advertising or program books.
Publications: Application guidelines.
Application information: Letter of inquiry form and application guidelines available on foundation web site. All requests for funding from outside the City of Chicago are by invitation only. Unsolicited requests for funds accepted only from applicants in Chicago. Application form required.
Initial approach: Brief letter of inquiry form available on foundation web site
Copies of proposal: 1
Deadline(s): Submit proposal preferably by Mar. 1 or Sept. 1
Board meeting date(s): Apr./May and Oct./Nov.
Final notification: Up to 90 days
Trustees: Heidi Boncher; Kristen Boncher; **Ian Epstein**; Jeffrey R. Epstein; Nicholas Epstein; Samantha Epstein; Stuart A. Epstein; Arthur Winter; Dorothy Winter; **Emma Winter**.
Number of staff: 1 part-time professional.
EIN: 366047947

1101
Stewart Foundation
c/o The Northern Trust Co.
P.O. Box 803878
Chicago, IL 60680-3878

Established in 1984 in IL.
Donors: John Alexander; Thomas S. Alexander; Alexander S. Rudolph; Geoffrey E. Rudolph; Emily H. Alexander; Martha J. Alexander; Brett W. Barnes; Kenneth W. Barnes; Eliza A. Cummings; Walter Alexander; Chris Barnes; Barbara A. Harty; American Livestock Insurance Co.; Alexander-Stewart Lumber Co.; Alexander Building Co.
Foundation type: Independent foundation.
Financial data (yr. ended 08/31/13): Assets, $965,838 (M); expenditures, $1,584,842; qualifying distributions, $1,566,015; giving activities include $1,565,000 for 5 grants (high: $1,275,000; low: $20,000).
Fields of interest: Arts education; Higher education, college; Higher education, university; Environment; Zoos/zoological societies; Aquariums; Animals/wildlife; Catholic agencies & churches.
Limitations: Applications not accepted. Giving primarily in CT, FL, IL, MA, MN, and NY. No grants to individuals.
Application information: Contributes only to pre-selected organizations.
Officers and Directors:* John Alexander,* Pres.; Duncan M. Alexander,* V.P.; Emily H. Alexander,* Secy.-Treas.; Eliza A. Cummings; Margaret A. Pemberton; Martha A. Porter; Emily A. Strong.
EIN: 363339135
Other changes: For the fiscal year ended Aug. 31, 2013, the grantmaker paid grants of $1,565,000, a 434.1% increase over the 2012 disbursements, $293,000.

1102
W. Clement & Jessie V. Stone Foundation
1100 Lake St., Ste. 202
Oak Park, IL 60301-1015 (800) 288-4859
FAX: (415) 561-0927;
E-mail: Brian@wcstonefnd.org; Main URL: http://www.wcstonefnd.org
Grants List: http://www.wcstonefnd.org/grantees/index.html
Knowledge Center: http://www.wcstonefnd.org/reports.html

Incorporated in 1958 in IL.
Donors: W. Clement Stone†; Jessie V. Stone†.
Foundation type: Independent foundation.
Financial data (yr. ended 12/31/12): Assets, $110,161,070 (M); gifts received, $100; expenditures, $5,691,134; qualifying distributions, $5,203,051; giving activities include $4,392,583 for 111 grants (high: $165,000; low: $500).
Purpose and activities: The foundation is committed to providing the educational and developmental opportunities to disadvantaged children and young people that enable them to fulfill their potential. Its grantmaking programs in education, youth development and early childhood development are designed to tackle the problems children and youth face in obtaining an excellent education, accessing the skills that will serve them as they transition into adulthood, and experiencing quality developmental experiences in their earliest years. It seeks to work with great leaders doing promising work that has the potential for advancing the knowledge and practice in its grantmaking fields.
Fields of interest: Education; Youth development.
Type of support: General/operating support; Management development/capacity building; Program development; Curriculum development; Scholarship funds; Program evaluation.
Limitations: Applications not accepted. Giving limited to Chicago, IL, the San Francisco Bay Area, CA, New York, NY, and Boston, MA. No grants to individuals.
Publications: Annual report; Grants list.
Application information: Contributes only to pre-selected organizations. See foundation web site for further information.
Board meeting date(s): May and Oct.
Officers and Directors:* Norman C. Stone, Ph.D.*, Pres.; Steven Stone, J.D.*, 1st V.P. and Treas.; Michael A. Stone,* V.P. and Secy.; Barbara Samuels, V.P.; Tony Smith, Exec. Dir.; **Jeff Donoghue, C.O.O.**; Alexander Knecht; Amy M. Stone; Barbara West Stone; David Stone; Deborah Stone; Jennifer Stone; Norah Sharpe Stone, J.D.; Sandra Stone; Sara Stone; Chad Tingley.
Number of staff: 3 full-time professional.
EIN: 362498125

1103
The Sumac Foundation
c/o JPMorgan Services Inc.
10 S. Dearborn, IL1-0117
Chicago, IL 60603

Established in NY.
Donor: Freebairn Char Lead Annuity Trust.
Foundation type: Independent foundation.
Financial data (yr. ended 03/31/13): Assets, $4,507,824 (M); gifts received, $353,306; expenditures, $199,115; qualifying distributions, $188,968; giving activities include $188,000 for 8 grants (high: $50,000; low: $5,000).
Fields of interest: Legal services; Civil/human rights, immigrants; Minorities; Hispanics/Latinos.

Limitations: Applications not accepted. Giving primarily in AR, CA and IL. No grants to individuals.
Application information: Contributes only to pre-selected organizations.
Trustees: Elizabeth A. Freebairn; Kenneth T. Freebairn; William A. Freebairn.
EIN: 137115395
Other changes: The grantmaker has moved from DE to IL.

1104
Tracy Family Foundation
P.O. Box 25, Highway 99 South
Mount Sterling, IL 62353-0025
Contact: Kim Bielik, Grants Mgr.
E-mail: kbielik@tracyfoundation.org; Additional contact: Jean Buckley, Pres., e-mail: jbuckley@tracyfoundation.org; Main URL: http://www.tracyfoundation.org

Established in 1997 in IL.
Donor: Dot Foods, Inc.
Foundation type: Company-sponsored foundation.
Financial data (yr. ended 12/31/12): Assets, $8,638,642 (M); gifts received, $3,060,000; expenditures, $2,545,918; qualifying distributions, $2,485,198; giving activities include $2,137,560 for 278 grants (high: $321,747; low: $300).
Purpose and activities: The foundation supports programs designed to promote education; youth and families; leadership; and economic development. Additional support is given to address pre-k to grade 12 academics; youth development; and the unmet needs of at-risk families.
Fields of interest: Elementary/secondary education; Education, early childhood education; Education, services; Education; Youth development; YM/YWCAs & YM/YWHAs; Children/youth, services; Family services; Human services; Community/economic development; Leadership development; Catholic agencies & churches.
Type of support: General/operating support; Management development/capacity building; Annual campaigns; Capital campaigns; Program development; Curriculum development; Scholarship funds; Employee matching gifts.
Limitations: Applications accepted. Giving primarily in Adams, Brown, Cass, Greene, Hancock, McDonough, Morgan, Pike, Schuyler, and Scott County, IL. No grants to individuals.
Publications: Application guidelines; IRS Form 990 or 990-PF printed copy available upon request; Program policy statement.
Application information: Organizations receiving Formal Funding, Capacity Building, Brown County T.E.A.C.H.E.R. Fund, or Catholic School grants are asked to submit a final report. Final Reports are due within 1 year of receipt of the grant. Application form required.
Initial approach: Complete online pre-application for Formal Funding Grant Program, Brown County T.E.A.C.H.E.R. Fund, and Catholic School Grants; complete online application for Capacity Building Grant
Deadline(s): Jan 1, May 1, and Sept. 1 for Formal Funding Grant Program and Brown County T.E.A.C.H.E.R. Fund; Sept. 1 for Catholic Schools Grants; None for Capacity Building Grant
Board meeting date(s): Feb., June, and Oct.
Final notification: Apr., Aug., and Dec. for Formal Funding Grant Program and Brown County T.E.A.C.H.E.R. Fund; Dec. for Catholic School Grants
Officers: Jean C. Buckley, Pres. and C.E.O.; Pat Smith, V.P.; John Oliver, Secy.; Rob Tracy, Treas.
Directors: Mary Sullivan; Alex Tracy; Don Tracy; Jane Tracy; Linda Tracy; Liz Tracy.
EIN: 364163760

1105
Tyndale House Foundation
351 Executive Dr.
Carol Stream, IL 60188-2420 (630) 790-9532
Contact: Mary Kleine Yehling, Exec. Dir.
FAX: (630) 790-2446;
E-mail: foundation@tyndalehousefdn.org; Main URL: http://www.TyndaleHouseFdn.org

Established in 1964 in IL.
Donors: Howard A. Elkind‡; Kenneth N. Taylor‡; ENB Charitable Trust; Elizabeth Taylor Char. Trust.
Foundation type: Independent foundation.
Financial data (yr. ended 12/31/12): Assets, $68,038,274 (M); expenditures, $4,433,816; qualifying distributions, $4,374,384; giving activities include $3,958,000 for 254 grants (high: $200,000; low: $2,000).
Purpose and activities: Giving to promote the Gospel through Christian literature projects, Bible translations, and Christian services and activities in the U.S. and abroad. The main area of interest is Christian literature and media.
Fields of interest: Language/linguistics; Literature; Human services; Religious federated giving programs; Christian agencies & churches; Protestant agencies & churches.
Type of support: General/operating support; Program development; Conferences/seminars; Publication; Matching/challenge support.
Limitations: Applications accepted. Giving in the U.S.; international projects are funded through U.S.-based organizations. No grants to individuals, or for building or endowment funds, scholarships, fellowships, or personnel support.
Publications: Financial statement; Informational brochure (including application guidelines).
Application information: The foundation only accepts online applications. Organizations that apply need to have a faith-based component. See foundation web site for instructions. Application form required.
Initial approach: Letter or telephone
Deadline(s): Dec. 1
Board meeting date(s): Apr. for grantmaking; as required for administrative business
Final notification: May of the subsequent year
Officers and Directors:* C. Douglas McConnell,* Chair.; Edward A. Elliott,* Vice-Chair.; Mark D. Taylor, C.E.O. and Pres.; Mary Kleine Yehling, V.P. and Exec. Dir.; Edwin L. Frizen, Jr.; David M. Howard; Ted Noble; Jeremy P. Taylor; Peter W. Taylor; Rebecca Wilson.
Number of staff: 1 full-time professional; 1 full-time support; 5 part-time support.
EIN: 362555516

1106
John Ullrich Foundation Trust
c/o Busey Trust Co.
130 N. Water St.
Decatur, IL 62523-1310

Foundation type: Independent foundation.
Financial data (yr. ended 12/31/12): Assets, $26,919,250 (M); expenditures, $1,478,627; qualifying distributions, $957,040; giving activities include $957,040 for 21 grants (high: $275,000; low: $1,000).
Purpose and activities: Giving primarily for higher education, and federated giving programs.
Fields of interest: Higher education; Youth development; Human services; United Ways and Federated Giving Programs.
Type of support: General/operating support.
Limitations: Applications not accepted. Giving primarily in IL. No grants to individuals.
Application information: Contributes only to pre-selected organizations.
Trustee: Busey Trust Co.
EIN: 376279232

1107
VNA Foundation
(doing business as Visiting Nurse Association of Chicago)
20 N. Wacker Dr., Ste. 3118
Chicago, IL 60606-3101 (312) 214-1521
Contact: Robert N. DiLeonardi, Exec. Dir.; Claudia Baier, Sr. Prog. Off.; Ann C. Schaefer, Prog. Assoc.
FAX: (312) 214-1529;
E-mail: info@vnafoundation.net; Main URL: http://www.vnafoundation.net
LinkedIn: http://www.linkedin.com/company/vna-foundation
Twitter: https://twitter.com/vnafoundation
YouTube: http://www.youtube.com/user/VNAFoundation

Established in 1995 in IL; converted from the transfer of VNA-C operations to CareMed Chicago; status changed to a private foundation in July 1998.
Foundation type: Independent foundation.
Financial data (yr. ended 06/30/13): Assets, $48,808,866 (M); gifts received, $32,816; expenditures, $3,174,890; qualifying distributions, $2,800,722; giving activities include $2,361,172 for 67 grants (high: $150,000; low: $305).
Purpose and activities: The grantmaking goal of the foundation is to support home- and community-based health care and health services for the medically underserved in Cook and the collar counties, IL, with a focus on Chicago. Capital, program and general operating grants to support home, health, community and school-based services, prevention and health promotion, and early intervention are available to nonprofits. Priority is given to programs in which care is provided by nurses. The population targeted by the program must be medically underserved.
Fields of interest: Dental care; Health care, support services; Nursing care; Health care, home services; Health care; Economically disadvantaged; Homeless.
Type of support: General/operating support; Capital campaigns; Equipment; Program development; Seed money; Program evaluation; Matching/challenge support.
Limitations: Applications accepted. Giving primarily in Cook, DuPage, Kane, Lake, Will, and McHenry counties, IL. No support for profit organizations. No grants for research or inpatient services.
Publications: Application guidelines; Financial statement; Grants list.
Application information: Both unsolicited and solicited applicants are invited to submit grant ideas via a Letter of Intent. Full proposals must be invited, with invitations offered following foundation's review of letter of inquiry. The foundation uses an online grants management system that can be accessed through its website. Letters of Intent and proposals submitted to the foundation through means other than the online grants management system will not be considered. Application form required.

Initial approach: Telephone calls, (encouraged) and letter of intent submitted through the foundation's online system.
Copies of proposal: 1
Deadline(s): Call for deadlines or see foundation web site.
Board meeting date(s): Quarterly
Final notification: 7 weeks

Officers and Directors:* M. Catherine Ryan, Chair.; Sandra Wilks, MS, RN, Vice-Chair.; Brigid E. Kenney,* Secy.; Dian Langenhorst, Treas.; Robert N. DiLeonardi, Exec. Dir.; Marie W. Harris; Arlene Michaels Miller, Ph.D., RN, FAAN; Katherine H. Miller; Denise Palmer; David R. Rutter; Nancy Scinto.
Number of staff: 2 full-time professional; 1 part-time professional.
EIN: 362167943

1108
The Von Blon Family Charitable Foundation

Chicago, IL

The foundation terminated in 2011.

1109
Walgreens Assistance, Inc.

300 Wilmot Rd., M.S. 3301
Deerfield, IL **60015**
Main URL: http://www.walgreens.com/topic/sr/sr_giving_back_flu_shot.jsp

Donor: Walgreen Co. and Subsidiaries.
Foundation type: Operating foundation.
Financial data (yr. ended 08/31/13): Assets, $0; gifts received, $7,587,000; expenditures, $7,587,000; qualifying distributions, $7,587,000; giving activities include $7,587,000 for grants to individuals.
Purpose and activities: The foundation provides flu shot vouchers to the uninsured or underinsured ill, needy, and infants to prevent influenza and improve health.
Fields of interest: Health care; Infants/toddlers; Economically disadvantaged.
Type of support: Grants to individuals; Donated products; In-kind gifts.
Limitations: Applications not accepted. Giving on a national basis and in Laos.
Application information: The foundation partners with the U.S. Department of Health and Human Services to distribute flu vaccine vouchers to local health agencies and community partners.
Officers and Directors:* John Gremer,* Pres.; John Mann,* V.P.; Robert Silverman,* Secy.; Rick Hans,* Treas.
EIN: 274521750
Other changes: At the close of 2012, the grantmaker paid grants of $17,197,200, a 720.4% increase over the 2011 disbursements, $2,096,100.

1110
Byron L. Walter Family Trust

c/o JPMorgan Chase Bank, N.A.
10 S. Dearborn St., IL1-0117
Chicago, IL 60603-2300 (312) 732-7553
***Contact:* Mackenzie Currans, Trust Off., JPMorgan Chase Bank, N.A.**

Established in 1981 in WI.

Donor: Arlene B. Walter†.
Foundation type: Independent foundation.
Financial data (yr. ended 04/30/13): Assets, $13,241,388 (M); expenditures, $702,300; qualifying distributions, $595,165; giving activities include $562,552 for 14 grants (high: $77,552; low: $5,000).
Fields of interest: Arts; Higher education; Nursing school/education; Education; Health care; Human services; YM/YWCAs & YM/YWHAs; Children/youth, services; Foundations (private grantmaking).
Type of support: Capital campaigns; Building/renovation; Equipment; Program development.
Limitations: Applications accepted. Giving limited to Brown County, WI. No grants to individuals, or for matching gifts; no loans.
Publications: Application guidelines.
Application information: Application form not required.
Initial approach: Letter
Copies of proposal: 2
Deadline(s): None
Board meeting date(s): Jan., Apr., June, Sept., and Dec.
Final notification: 6 months

Trustees: Richard J. Blahnik; JPMorgan Chase Bank, N.A.
EIN: 396346563
Other changes: The grantmaker no longer lists a separate application address. The grantmaker has moved from WI to IL.

1111
A. Montgomery Ward Foundation

c/o Bank of America, N.A.
231 S. LaSalle St. IL1-231-13-32
Chicago, IL 60604-1206
E-mail: ilgrantmaking@ustrust.com; **Main URL: https://www.bankofamerica.com/philanthropic/grantmaking.go**

Trust established in 1959 in IL.
Donor: Marjorie Montgomery Ward Baker†.
Foundation type: Independent foundation.
Financial data (yr. ended 06/30/13): Assets, $15,155,469 (M); expenditures, $853,693; qualifying distributions, $693,461; giving activities include $562,627 for 40 grants (high: $66,000; low: $1,848).
Purpose and activities: The foundation's grantmaking emphasizes those institutions in the Chicago, IL, area which provide its many citizens with high-quality, well established educational and cultural activities, with emphasis on museums; funding also for children, youth, families, women, and social services including recordings for the blind and dyslexic, and treatment for families where child abuse and neglect have occurred, focusing on children from birth to 5 years.
Fields of interest: Museums; Museums (natural history); Planetarium; Arts; Education; Hospitals (general); Health care; Human services; Children/youth, services; Community/economic development.
Type of support: General/operating support; Capital campaigns; Scholarship funds.
Limitations: Giving primarily in Chicago, IL, and surrounding metropolitan areas. No grants to individuals.
Publications: Application guidelines.
Application information: Application guidelines and form available on foundation web site. Application form required.
Initial approach: Proposal
Copies of proposal: 2
Deadline(s): Apr. 15, and Oct. 15
Board meeting date(s): May and Nov.
Final notification: June 30 and Dec. 31

Trustees: Jack Hutchings; Richard Oloffson; Bank of America, N.A.
EIN: 362417437

1112
Washington Square Health Foundation, Inc.

875 N. Michigan Ave., Ste. 3516
Chicago, IL 60611-1957 (312) 664-6488
***Contact:* Howard Nochumson, Exec. Dir.; Catherine Baginski, Prog. Dir.**
***FAX:* (312) 664-7787**;
E-mail: washington@wshf.org; Main URL: http://www.wshf.org
Facebook: https://www.facebook.com/WashingtonSquareHealthFoundation

Established in 1985 in IL; converted from Henrotin Hospital.
Donors: Henrotin Hospital; George Zendt Charitable Trust.
Foundation type: Independent foundation.
Financial data (yr. ended 09/30/13): Assets, $20,702,949 (M); gifts received, $11,353; expenditures, $1,200,472; qualifying distributions, $1,448,977; giving activities include $426,344 for 72 grants (high: $30,000; low: $200), and $350,000 for 1 loan/program-related investment.
Purpose and activities: Giving to promote and maintain access to adequate primary health care, through grants for medical and nursing education scholarships, medical research, and direct healthcare services.
Fields of interest: Medical school/education; Nursing school/education; Nursing care; Nursing home/convalescent facility; Health care; AIDS; Medical research, institute; AIDS research; Crime/violence prevention, domestic violence; Aging; Disabilities, people with; Minorities; Women; AIDS, people with; Immigrants/refugees; Homeless; LGBTQ.
Type of support: Equipment; Program development; Seed money; Fellowships; Scholarship funds; Research; Program-related investments/loans; Matching/challenge support.
Limitations: Applications accepted. Giving primarily in the Chicago, IL, area for direct healthcare services; giving nationally for medical research and education grants. No grants to individuals, or for general operating or administrative expenses, land acquisition, or construction.
Publications: Application guidelines; Annual report; Grants list.
Application information: Application form required.
***Initial approach:* Use online grant form on foundation web site**
Board meeting date(s): Feb., May, and July

Officers and Directors:* William N. Werner, M.D., Pres.; Richard B. Patterson, DPM, MSPH*, V.P.; William B. Friedeman,* Secy.; James M. Snyder,* Treas.; Howard Nochumson,* Exec. Dir.; **Barbara Berendt**; Catherine M. Creticos Poulos, M.D.
Number of staff: 2 full-time professional; 1 part-time support.
EIN: 361210140

1113
Webb Foundation

P.O. Box 432
Winthrop Harbor, IL 60096-0432
***Application address:* P.O. Box 423, Winthrop Harbor, IL 60096, tel.: (262) 948-1033**

Established in 1969 in MO.
Donors: Francis M. Webb†; Pearl M. Webb†.
Foundation type: Independent foundation.
Financial data (yr. ended 12/31/12): Assets, $5,451,818 (M); expenditures, $380,899; qualifying distributions, $330,832; giving activities include $289,500 for grants.
Fields of interest: Secondary school/education; Higher education; Hospitals (general); Health care; Health organizations, association; Human services; Children/youth, services; Christian agencies & churches; Aging; Economically disadvantaged.
Type of support: General/operating support; Continuing support; Annual campaigns; Building/renovation; Equipment; Seed money; Scholarship funds; Research.
Limitations: Applications accepted. Giving limited to the metropolitan area of Chicago, IL, and St. Louis, MO; Chicago grants limited to pre-selected organizations. No grants to individuals, or for emergency funds, deficit financing, land acquisition, endowment funds, matching gifts, special projects, publications, conferences, or fundraising or special events; no loans.
Publications: Informational brochure (including application guidelines).
Application information: Awardees must submit final report before next application. Application form not required.
Initial approach: Proposal
Copies of proposal: 1
Deadline(s): Feb. 28 and Aug. 31
Board meeting date(s): June and Nov.
Final notification: After board meetings
Officer: Greg Preves, Secy.; Linda Barry, Admin.
Advisors: John Barry; Donald D. McDonald; Evelyn M. McDonald; Donna Sue Preves; Robert Preves.
Number of staff: 1 part-time professional.
EIN: 237028768
Other changes: The grantmaker no longer lists a primary contact.

1114
Westlake Health Foundation
1 Lincoln Ctr.
18 W. 140 Butterfield Rd., Ste. 1660
Oakbrook Terrace, IL 60181-4257 (630) 495-3800
Contact: Leonard J. Muller, Chair.
E-mail: info@westlakehf.com**; Additional e-mail: rosewesolek@aol.com**; Main URL: http://www.westlakehf.com

Established in 1998 in IL; converted from Westlake Hospital.
Donor: Westlake Hospital.
Foundation type: Independent foundation.
Financial data (yr. ended 12/31/12): Assets, $103,730,914 (M); expenditures, $5,616,503; qualifying distributions, $4,922,563; giving activities include $4,303,044 for 49 grants (high: $500,000; low: $3,000).
Purpose and activities: The foundation supports and encourages the development of healthcare services by making grants to nonprofit community organizations.
Fields of interest: Health care.
Limitations: Applications accepted. Giving primarily in west suburban Cook County, IL. No support for political organizations, direct religious activities or for fraternal societies. No grants to individuals; or for endowment campaigns, campaigns or lobbying activities, fundraising or for telephone solicitations.
Publications: Application guidelines.
Application information: See web site for application guidelines.
Deadline(s): May 1 and Nov. 1
Board meeting date(s): June and Dec.
Officers and Trustees:* Leonard J. Muller,* Chair. and C.E.O.; David R. Hey,* Pres. and C.O.O.; J. Melvin Smith, M.D.*, Secy.; Fred M. Tomera, M.D.*, Treas.; Richard M. Montalbano, Sr.; Saundra L. Spilotro; Raul Villasuso, M.D.
EIN: 363104071

1115
Wieboldt Foundation
53 W. Jackson Blvd., Ste. 1252
Chicago, IL 60604-3611 (312) 786-9377
Contact: Carmen Prieto
***E-mail for letter of inquiry:* awards@wieboldt.org.; Main URL: http://www.wieboldt.org**
Wieboldt Foundation's Philanthropy Promise: http://www.ncrp.org/philanthropys-promise/who

Incorporated in 1921 in IL.
Donors: William A. Wieboldt†; Anna Krueger Wieboldt†.
Foundation type: Independent foundation.
Financial data (yr. ended 12/31/12): Assets, $18,292,850 (M); expenditures, $1,031,990; qualifying distributions, $1,032,778; giving activities include $653,600 for 37 grants (high: $35,000; low: $2,600).
Purpose and activities: The foundation's highest priority is the support of multi-issue community organizations that work in low-income neighborhoods, that are accountable to neighborhood residents, and through which people are empowered to have a major voice in shaping decisions that affect their lives. A second priority is given to organizations that support community organizations through training, technical assistance, legal strategies, coalition building, advocacy, and policy development. The foundation's recognition of community organizing or community action as its prime concern is promoted by its conviction that a sense of powerlessness and the apathy and alienation bred of this sense are at the root of many of the ills of our time. It believes that funding those efforts that give people hope that they can exercise a degree of control over their lives and that involve them working together toward jointly defined ends is an important contribution to the resolution of social ills.
Fields of interest: Urban/community development.
Type of support: General/operating support; Continuing support; Program-related investments/loans.
Limitations: Applications accepted. Giving limited to the metropolitan Chicago, IL, area. No grants to individuals, or for endowment funds, studies and research, capital campaigns, scholarships, fellowships, conferences, direct service projects, or economic development.
Publications: Application guidelines; Annual report (including application guidelines); Grants list.
Application information: Complete application guidelines available on foundation web site. Application form required.
Initial approach: Letter of inquiry via e-mail for general grant requests; telephone regarding Program Related Investments
Copies of proposal: 1
***Deadline(s):* See foundation web site for current deadlines**
Board meeting date(s): Monthly, except Apr., Aug., and Dec.
Officers and Directors:* Jennifer Corrigan,* Pres.; Ben Darrow,* V.P.; John S. Darrow,* Treas.; Regina McGraw, Exec. Dir.; Jessica Darrow; Bill Davis; T. Lawrence Doyle; Carol Larson; Maureen Loughnane; Janet Smith; Nancy Wieboldt.
Number of staff: 2 full-time professional.
EIN: 362167955
Other changes: Anne W. Burghard, Philip Darrow, Heather D. Parish, Sonia Silva and John W. Straub are no longer directors.
The grantmaker now publishes application guidelines.

1116
Abbey Woods Foundation
Frankfort, IL

The foundation terminated in 2011.

1117
John R. Woods Foundation
111 W. Monroe St., Tax Div. 10C
Chicago, IL 60603
***Application address:* c/o BMO Harris Bank, N.A., P.O. Box 5000, Janesville, WI 53547, tel.: (608) 755-4265**

Foundation type: Independent foundation.
Financial data (yr. ended 11/30/12): Assets, $3,815,196 (M); expenditures, $239,008; qualifying distributions, $194,799; giving activities include $186,000 for 33 grants (high: $30,000; low: $250).
Fields of interest: Arts; Education; Human services.
Limitations: Applications accepted. Giving primarily in CO.
Application information: Application form required.
Initial approach: Letter
Deadline(s): None
Trustees: Catherine W. Hill; BMO Harris Bank, N.A.
EIN: 276155799
Other changes: The grantmaker has moved from WI to IL.

1118
The Martha Hursh Yowell Charitable Trust
c/o W. Peithmann & J. Sandburg
403 E. Main St.
P.O. Box 80
Mahomet, IL **61853 (217) 586-6102**

Established in 2005 in IL.
Foundation type: Public charity.
Financial data (yr. ended 12/31/12): Revenue, $458,043; assets, $6,266,802 (M); expenditures, $426,149; program services expenses, $401,149; giving activities include $346,149 for 2 grants (high: $242,304; low: $103,845).
Fields of interest: Aging, centers/services; Protestant agencies & churches.
Limitations: Applications not accepted. Giving primarily in IL.
Application information: Contributes only to pre-selected organizations.
Trustees: William A. Peithmann; JoEllen Sandburg.
EIN: 206799151

1119
Zell Family Foundation
(formerly Samuel Zell Family)
2 N. Riverside Plz., Ste. 600
Chicago, IL 60606-2639 (312) 466-3852

Established in 1986 in IL.
Donor: Samuel Zell.
Foundation type: Independent foundation.
Financial data (yr. ended 12/31/13): Assets, $58,225,154 (M); gifts received, $33,427,508; expenditures, $14,801,072; qualifying distributions, $14,744,201; giving activities include $14,739,900 for 88 grants (high: $2,000,000; low: $1,000).
Purpose and activities: Giving primarily for the arts, education, medicine, cancer research, recreation, youth development, and human service organizations.
Fields of interest: Museums (art); Arts; Education; Health care; Cancer research; Recreation; Youth development; Human services.
Limitations: Applications not accepted. Giving primarily in Chicago, IL, with some giving in MI. No grants to individuals.
Application information: Contributes only to pre-selected organizations.
Officers and Directors:* Samuel Zell,* Pres.; Philip Tinkler, V.P.; Helen H. Zell,* V.P.; Joann L. Zell,* V.P.; Kellie Zell,* V.P.; Matthew M. Zell,* V.P.; Carleen Schreder, Secy.; James Bunegar, Treas.
EIN: 363487811
Other changes: At the close of 2013, the fair market value of the grantmaker's assets was $58,225,154, an 85.0% increase over the 2012 value, $31,465,486.

INDIANA

1120
Edward D. & Ione Auer Foundation
c/o Monarch Capital, Attn.: David Meyer
127 W. Berry St., Ste. 402
Fort Wayne, IN 46802-2310 (260) 415-5743
E-mail: AuerFoundation@MonarchCapitalMgmt.com; Main URL: http://www.auerfoundation.org/

Established in IN.
Donor: Ione Breeden Auer Irrevocable Trust.
Foundation type: Independent foundation.
Financial data (yr. ended 12/31/12): Assets, $33,200,571 (M); expenditures, $5,102,305; qualifying distributions, $4,873,758; giving activities include $4,779,000 for 59 grants (high: $1,000,000; low: $4,000).
Purpose and activities: Some emphasis in the foundation's giving includes literature, music, art, education, and parks.
Fields of interest: Performing arts; Performing arts, orchestras; Arts; Higher education; Libraries (public); Zoos/zoological societies; Human services; Children/youth, services.
Type of support: Equipment; Land acquisition.
Limitations: Giving limited to Fort Wayne, IN. No support for individual public schools or school districts. No grants to individuals, or for scholarships (unless through an endowment), travel, conferences, deficits, sponsorships, special events, advertising, or annual appeals.
Publications: Application guidelines.
Application information: Full proposals are by invitation only, upon review of initial concept letter. Refer to foundation web site for Application Packet.
Initial approach: 1-page concept letter (with print no smaller than an 11 point font)
Deadline(s): Jan. 15, Apr. 15, July 15, and Oct. 15 for concept letters
Board meeting date(s): Feb. 1, May 1, Aug. 1, and Nov. 1
Trustees: David Meyer; Lake City Bank.
EIN: 311097946

1121
Ball Brothers Foundation
P.O. Box 1408
Muncie, IN 47308-1408 (765) 741-5500
Contact: Jud Fisher, C.O.O. and Pres.
FAX: (765) 741-5518; E-mail: info@ballfdn.org; Additional address: 222 S. Mulberry St., Muncie, IN 47305. Additional e-mail: donna.munchel@ballfdn.org; Main URL: http://www.ballfdn.org
Grants List: http://www.ballfdn.org/index/grantees.asp
News Feed: http://www.ballfdn.org/news/rss/sitenews.xml

Incorporated in 1926 in IN.
Donors: Edmund B. Ball†; Edmund F. Ball†; Frank C. Ball†; George A. Ball†; Lucius L. Ball, M.D.†; Janice B. Fisher†; John W. Fisher†; Virginia B. Ball†; William A. Ball†.
Foundation type: Independent foundation.
Financial data (yr. ended 12/31/12): Assets, $145,711,100 (M); expenditures, $7,681,594; qualifying distributions, $6,812,155; giving activities include $6,252,541 for 120 grants (high: $2,599,500; low: $1,000; average: $1,000–$250,000).
Purpose and activities: Support for the environment, humanities and cultural programs, higher and other education, health and medical education, youth, and family and social services.
Fields of interest: Museums; Humanities; Arts; Elementary school/education; Secondary school/education; Higher education; Medical school/education; Adult education—literacy, basic skills & GED; Education, reading; Education; Environment; Hospitals (general); Health care; Health organizations, association; Human services; Children/youth, services; Family services; Community/economic development; Public affairs.
Type of support: Program evaluation; Annual campaigns; Building/renovation; Capital campaigns; Conferences/seminars; Consulting services; Curriculum development; Endowments; Equipment; General/operating support; In-kind gifts; Management development/capacity building; Matching/challenge support; Professorships; Program development; Publication; Research; Technical assistance.
Limitations: Applications accepted. Giving limited to IN. No support for non-secular religious programs or booster organizations. No grants to individuals.
Publications: Application guidelines; Annual report; Grants list.
Application information: Applications now accepted via foundation web site. Application form required.
Initial approach: Submit letter of inquiry via web site
Copies of proposal: 1
Deadline(s): Letters of inquiry: Feb. 15 and July 15
Board meeting date(s): Quarterly and as necessary
Final notification: Varies
Officers and Directors:* James A. Fisher,* Vice-Chair.; Jud Fisher,* C.O.O. and Pres.; Terry L. Walker,* Secy.; Tammy Phillips, Treas.; William M. Bracken; Stephanie Duckmann; Douglas J. Foy; Nancy B. Keilty; Terri E. Matchett; Judith F. Oetinger; Scott Shockley.
Number of staff: 2 full-time professional; 1 part-time professional; 1 full-time support.
EIN: 350882856
Other changes: Frank E. Ball, Chair. and C.E.O., is deceased.

1122
Blackford County Community Foundation, Inc.
121 N. High St.
P.O. Box 327
Hartford City, IN 47348-0327 (765) 348-3411
Contact: Patricia D. Poulson, Exec. Dir.
FAX: (765) 348-4945;
E-mail: foundation@blackfordcounty.org; Additional e-mail: ppoulson@blackfordcounty.org; Main URL: http://www.blackfordcofoundation.org
Facebook: http://www.facebook.com/BlackfordCoFoundation

Established in 1989 in IN.
Foundation type: Community foundation.
Financial data (yr. ended 12/31/12): Assets, $5,402,025 (M); gifts received, $210,369; expenditures, $547,018; giving activities include $171,622 for 5+ grants (high: $37,170), and $87,743 for grants to individuals.
Purpose and activities: The foundation's mission is to enhance and improve the quality of life in Blackford County, Indiana. The foundation accomplishes this by continually increasing their endowed assets so that they can better meet to the needs of the community.
Fields of interest: Arts; Scholarships/financial aid; Education; Environment, beautification programs; Health care; Mental health/crisis services; Recreation, parks/playgrounds; Children/youth, services; Family services; Aging, centers/services; Human services; Community development, neighborhood associations; Community/economic development.
Type of support: General/operating support; Scholarships—to individuals.
Limitations: Applications accepted. Giving primarily in Blackford County, IN. No support for sectarian or religious purposes. **No grants for building campaigns, endowments or operating budgets.**
Publications: Application guidelines; Annual report; Financial statement; Grants list; Informational brochure; Newsletter; IRS Form 990 or 990-PF printed copy available upon request.
Application information: Visit foundation web site for application guidelines. Application form required.
Initial approach: Contact foundation
Copies of proposal: 6
Deadline(s): Jan. 30, Mar. 27, June 26, and Sept. 25
Board meeting date(s): Monthly
Officers and Directors:* Maxie A. Malott,* Pres.; Diana L. Holsten,* V.P.; Julie A. Forcum,* Secy.; Peggy L. Fisher,* Treas.; Patricia D. Poulson, Exec. Dir.; Robert Benbow; Gary D. Cheesman; Jon Creek; David K. Neff; Lisa C. Weeks; J. Nolan Willman.
EIN: 351772356

1123
Brotherhood Mutual Foundation Inc.
6400 Brotherhood Way
Fort Wayne, IN 46825-4235

Established in 2005 in IN.
Donor: Brotherhood Mutual Insurance Co.
Foundation type: Company-sponsored foundation.
Financial data (yr. ended 12/31/12): Assets, $202,272 (M); gifts received, $570,612; expenditures, $458,696; qualifying distributions, $458,537; giving activities include $458,537 for 85 grants (high: $60,857; low: $200).
Purpose and activities: The foundation supports organizations involved with higher education, housing development, human services, international relief, and Christianity.
Fields of interest: Higher education; Housing/shelter, development; Human services; International relief; United Ways and Federated Giving Programs; Christian agencies & churches; Religion.
Type of support: General/operating support; Annual campaigns; Capital campaigns; Building/renovation; Program development; Sponsorships.
Limitations: Applications not accepted. Giving primarily in IN. No grants to individuals.
Application information: Contributes only to pre-selected organizations.
Officers: James A. Blum, Chair.; Mark A. Robison, Pres.; Hugh W. White, V.P.; Matthew G. Hirschy, Treas.
EIN: 203618117
Other changes: Michael J. Allison is no longer Secy.

1124
Brown County Community Foundation, Inc.

91 W. Mound St. Unit 4
P.O. Box 191
Nashville, IN 47448 (812) 988-4882
Contact: Judy Bowling, Office and Financial Mgr.
FAX: (812) 988-0299; E-mail: jenise@bccfin.org;
Main URL: http://www.bccfin.org/
Facebook: https://www.facebook.com/bccfin

Established in 1993 in IN.
Foundation type: Community foundation.
Financial data (yr. ended 12/31/12): Assets, $8,455,132 (M); gifts received, $1,040,849; expenditures, $769,143; giving activities include $536,536 for grants, $28,720 for 250 grants to individuals, and $63,480 for foundation-administered programs.
Purpose and activities: The foundation seeks to receive, hold, and distribute funds for charity. Primary areas of focus include arts and humanities, education, the environment, health care, human services, and community development.
Fields of interest: Humanities; Arts; Higher education; Education; Environment; Health care; Human services; Community/economic development; Children/youth; Youth; Adults; Disabilities, people with; Physically disabled; Women; Adults, women; Substance abusers.
Type of support: Continuing support; Capital campaigns; Building/renovation; Equipment; Land acquisition; Emergency funds; Program development; Conferences/seminars; Film/video/radio; Publication; Seed money; Scholarship funds; Technical assistance; Scholarships—to individuals; Matching/challenge support.
Limitations: Applications accepted. Giving primarily in Brown County, IN. No support for religious organizations. No grants for operating expenses (generally).
Publications: Application guidelines; Annual report; Financial statement; Informational brochure (including application guidelines); Newsletter.
Application information: Visit foundation web site for application information. Application form required.
Initial approach: Attend a mandatory grants workshop meeting
Copies of proposal: 1
***Deadline(s):* Late May for grants; Jan. for scholarships**
Board meeting date(s): 4th Monday of every month
***Final notification:* Late June or July.**
Officers and Trustees:* Michael Laros,* Chair.; Robert Andrew,* Vice-Chair.; Larry Pejeau,* C.E.O.; Shirley Boardman,* Secy.; **Karen Avery**; **Timothy Burke**; Mark LindenLaub; Terry Norman; Jack Winn; Joan Wright.
Number of staff: 2 full-time professional; 1 part-time professional.
EIN: 351960379
Other changes: Robert Andrew, Michael Laros, and Richard Rhyant are no longer trustees.

1125
Cass County Community Foundation, Inc.

417 N. St., Ste. 102
P.O. Box 441
Logansport, IN 46947-3172 (574) 722-2200
Contact: Deanna Crispen, Pres.
FAX: (574) 753-7501;
E-mail: cccf@casscountycf.org; Additional e-mail: dcrispen@casscountycf.org; Main URL: http://www.casscountycf.org

Established in 1993 in IN.
Foundation type: Community foundation.
Financial data (yr. ended 12/31/12): Assets, $14,283,051 (M); gifts received, $1,296,140; expenditures, $823,219; giving activities include $390,307 for 14 grants (high: $49,781), and $146,673 for 91 grants to individuals.
Purpose and activities: The foundation honors the spirit of giving and assists donors in building enduring sources of charitable assets to promote education, enhance humanity and advance community development throughout Cass County, IN.
Fields of interest: Education; Human services; Community/economic development.
Type of support: Seed money; Matching/challenge support; Equipment; Program development; Scholarships—to individuals.
Limitations: Applications accepted. Giving primarily in Cass County, IN. No support for public schools. **No grants to individuals (except for scholarships), travel expenses, ongoing operating expenses, advocacy, or endowments; no loans.**
Publications: Application guidelines; Annual report; Informational brochure; Newsletter.
Application information: Visit foundation web site for application form and information. Scholarship Orientation Session mandatory for scholarships. Application form required.
Initial approach: Contact foundation
***Copies of proposal:* 7**
***Deadline(s):* July 30**
Board meeting date(s): Monthly
Officers and Board Members:* Susan Platt,* Chair.; Dr. Herb Price,* Vice-Chair.; Deanna Crispen,* Pres.; Deb Shanks,* Secy.; Keith Cole,* Treas.; Lucy Burns; Brad Duerr; Randy Head; Tom Heckard; Paul Kroeger; Dan Layman; Burton Reed; Dr. Sue Ridlen; Jesse Robinson; Adam Strasser.
Number of staff: 1 full-time professional; 1 part-time professional; 1 full-time support.
EIN: 352125727

1126
Central Indiana Community Foundation, Inc.

615 N. Alabama St., Ste. 119
Indianapolis, IN 46204-1498 (317) 634-2423
Contact: Brian Payne, C.E.O.
FAX: (317) 684-0943; E-mail: info@cicf.org; Additional tel.: (317) 634-7497; Grant application e-mail: applications@cicf.org; Main URL: http://www.cicf.org
E-Newsletter: http://www.cicf.org/page26606.cfm
LinkedIn: http://www.linkedin.com/companies/central-indiana-community-foundation
Twitter: https://twitter.com/cicfoundation

Established in 1997 in IN through a partnership between the Indianapolis Foundation and the Legacy Fund of Hamilton County.
Foundation type: Community foundation.
Financial data (yr. ended 12/31/11): Assets, $566,257,151 (M); gifts received, $27,110,505; expenditures, $49,367,963; giving activities include $41,155,380 for grants.
Purpose and activities: The foundation is committed to improving and strengthening the metropolitan region community, with grantmaking focused on helping where the needs are greatest and the benefits to the region are most extensive.
Fields of interest: Arts, cultural/ethnic awareness; Arts; Education; Health care; Mental health/crisis services; Health organizations, association; Housing/shelter; Children/youth, services; Family services; Human services, emergency aid; Aging, centers/services; Human services; Community development, neighborhood development; Economic development; Economic development, visitors/convention bureau/tourism promotion; Community development, business promotion; Community/economic development; Philanthropy/voluntarism; Government/public administration; Disabilities, people with.
Type of support: Mission-related investments/loans; General/operating support; Annual campaigns; Capital campaigns; Building/renovation; Equipment; Land acquisition; Emergency funds; Program development; Conferences/seminars; Publication; Seed money; Curriculum development; Scholarship funds; Technical assistance; Consulting services; Program evaluation; Scholarships—to individuals; Matching/challenge support.
Limitations: Applications accepted. Giving limited to the central IN region. No support for religious or sectarian purposes, or for post-event or after-the-fact situations. No grants to individuals (except for scholarships), or for long-term operating support, endowment funds, medical, scientific or academic research, publications, travel, fundraising events, annual appeals, or membership contributions.
Publications: Application guidelines; Annual report; Financial statement; Grants list; Informational brochure; Newsletter.
Application information: Visit foundation web site for online grants management system and application guidelines. Application form required.
Initial approach: Complete online application
Copies of proposal: 1
Deadline(s): Feb. 28 and July 31
Board meeting date(s): Feb., May., Sept., and Nov.
Final notification: By year-end for both cycles
Officers and Directors:* **Charles P. Sutphin,* Chair.**; Cynthia Simon Skjodt,* Vice-Chair.; Brian Payne,* C.E.O. and Pres.; Rob MacPherson, V.P., Devel.; **Liz Tate, V.P., Community Investment**; Alan A. Levin,* Secy.; **Jennifer K. Bartenbach, C.F.O.**; Gregory F. Hahn,* Treas.; Brenda Delaney, Cont.; Elaine Bedel; Michael Daugherty; Kathy Davis; Traci M. Dolan; Henry L. Fernandez; Marianne Glick; Mark E. Hill; Myrta Pulliam; Marisol Sanchez; Jerry D. Semler; Michael Simmons; Joseph L. Smith, Jr.; Corby D. Thompson; Milton O. Thompson; Lee White.
EIN: 351793680
Other changes: Charles P. Sutphin has replaced Mark Hill as Chair.
Liz Tate is now V.P., Community Investment. Jan Edmondson is now Dir., Charitable Gift Planning. Angie Carr Klitzsch is now Community Impact Dir., Family Success. Roderick Wheeler is now Community Impact Dir., Education. Mary Stanley is now Dir. Gift Planning and Legal Affairs. Peggy O. Monson, Larry J. Sablosky, Sarah Wilson Otte, Frank Esposito, and Brian Myers are no longer directors.

1127
Olive B. Cole Foundation, Inc.

6207 Constitution Dr.
Fort Wayne, IN 46804-1517
Contact: Maclyn T. Parker, Pres.
E-mail: gwentip@ligtel.com

Incorporated in 1954 in IN.
Donors: Richard R. Cole†; Olive B. Cole†.

Foundation type: Independent foundation.
Financial data (yr. ended 03/31/13): Assets, $30,527,314 (M); expenditures, $1,535,774; qualifying distributions, $1,378,634; giving activities include $977,393 for grants, and $229,706 for 194 grants to individuals (high: $1,200; low: $500).
Purpose and activities: Grants largely for education, including student aid for graduates of Noble County, IN, high schools, hospitals, civic affairs, youth agencies, and cultural programs.
Fields of interest: Arts; Higher education; Hospitals (general); Youth, services; Government/public administration.
Type of support: General/operating support; Continuing support; Building/renovation; Equipment; Land acquisition; Seed money; Scholarships—to individuals; Matching/challenge support.
Limitations: Giving limited to Noble County, IN, and immediate adjacent areas in northern IN. No grants for endowment funds or research.
Publications: Application guidelines; Program policy statement.
Application information: Scholarship applications available through foundation and at all Noble and LaGrange County, IN, secondary schools. Application form required.

Initial approach: Letter
Copies of proposal: 7
Deadline(s): None
Board meeting date(s): Feb., May, Aug., and Nov.
Final notification: 4 months

Officers and Directors:* John N. Pichon, Jr.,* Chair.; Maclyn T. Parker,* Pres.; Emily E. Pichon, Secy.; **Michael Barranda**; Kristi P. Celico; Jack Hunter; John Riemke; **Tracy Tipton.**
Scholarship Administrator: Gwen I. Tipton.
Number of staff: 1 full-time professional; 1 full-time support.
EIN: 356040491

1128
Community Foundation Alliance, Inc.

5000 E. Virginia St., Ste. 4
Evansville, IN **47715** (812) 429-1191
Contact: Jill Tullar, Exec. Dir.
FAX: (812) 429-0840; E-mail: info@alliance9.org; Toll free tel.: (877) 429-1191; Main URL: http://www.alliance9.org

Established in 1991 in IN.
Foundation type: Community foundation.
Financial data (yr. ended 06/30/12): Assets, $63,918,571 (M); gifts received, $1,607,673; expenditures, $3,877,053; giving activities include $2,093,127 for 110+ grants (high: $99,283), and $196,532 for 45 grants to individuals.
Purpose and activities: The alliance seeks to provide leadership and support for member community foundations as they promote philanthropy and build endowments to serve their communities.
Fields of interest: Humanities; Arts; Education; Environment, beautification programs; Environment; Health care; Recreation; Youth development; Human services; Community/economic development.
Type of support: Management development/capacity building; Program development; Program evaluation; Scholarships—to individuals.
Limitations: Applications accepted. Giving limited to Daviess, Gibson, Knox, Perry, Pike, Posey, Spencer, Vanderburgh, and Warrick counties, IN. No support for religious organizations for religious purposes. No grants for endowment creation or debt reduction, operating costs, capital campaigns, annual appeals or membership contributions, or travel requests for groups or individuals such as bands, sports teams, or classes.
Publications: Application guidelines; Annual report; Financial statement; Grants list; Informational brochure; Newsletter.
Application information: Visit foundation web site or contact foundation for application forms, deadlines, and guidelines. Application form required.

Initial approach: Telephone
Deadline(s): Varies according to county
Board meeting date(s): 2nd Tues. of each month, except for July and Dec.

Officers and Directors:* Chris Harmon,* Chair.; Jody Giles,* Vice-Chair.; Jill Tullar,* Secy. and Exec. Dir.; Dave Osmon,* Treas.; Jean Blanton; Shane Bonaparte; John Dudenhoeffer; Bill Gillenwater; Jim Gislason; Bill Goedde; Randall Haaff; Tim Hayden; Kim Keene; Carla Kidwell; Pam Lock; Jim Pearson; Mason Seay; Paul Singleton; Grant Taylor; Wil Teague; Carolyn Veale; Tom Virgin.
Number of staff: 2 full-time professional; 13 full-time support; 4 part-time support.
EIN: 351830262

1129
Community Foundation of Grant County

505 W. 3rd St.
Marion, IN 46952-3748 (765) 662-0065
Contact: Dawn Brown, Exec. Dir.; For grants and scholarships: Ashley McKnight, Prog. Mgr.
FAX: (765) 662-1438;
E-mail: foundationoffice@comfdn.org; Main URL: http://www.comfdn.org
Facebook: http://www.facebook.com/comfdn
Twitter: http://twitter.com/comfdn

Incorporated in 1984 in IN.
Foundation type: Community foundation.
Financial data (yr. ended 03/31/13): Assets, $19,465,148 (M); gifts received, $970,260; expenditures, $2,105,587; giving activities include $562,155 for 150 grants (high: $110,792; low: $100), and $350,412 for 266 grants to individuals (high: $29,941; low: $500).
Purpose and activities: The foundation offers creative and imaginative grantmaking, coupled with strict volunteer review that assures responsible funding.
Fields of interest: Arts; Education; Environment, beautification programs; Health care; Mental health/crisis services; Recreation, parks/playgrounds; Youth development, services; Youth development; Children/youth, services; Family services; Aging, centers/services; Human services; Community development, neighborhood associations; Economic development; Community/economic development; Philanthropy/voluntarism.
Type of support: Technical assistance; Seed money; Program development; Matching/challenge support; Equipment; Emergency funds; Conferences/seminars; Building/renovation.
Limitations: Applications accepted. Giving limited to Grant County, IN. No support for sectarian or religious purposes. No grants for endowments or salaries.
Publications: Application guidelines; Annual report; Financial statement; Newsletter.
Application information: Visit foundation web site for proposal summary form and guidelines. Application form required.

Initial approach: Letter of intent
Copies of proposal: 12
Deadline(s): Prior to noon on the last Friday in Jan, Apr, July, and Oct.
Board meeting date(s): Feb., May, Aug., and Nov.
Final notification: Feb., May, Aug., and Nov. - approximately one month after deadline date

Officers and Directors:* Martin Harker,* Pres.; **Chad Leighty,* V.P.**; Mary Eckerle,* Secy.; Karen Behnke,* Treas.; Dawn Brown, Exec. Dir.; Sherri Rush,* C.F.O.; Dennis Banks; Janet Barnett; Jackie Certain; Mike Cline; Trent Dailey; Mike Falder; Judy Fitzgerald; John Jones; Dru McCoy; Jane Merchant; Georgette Miller; Reggie Nevels; Chris Oliver; Kyle Persinger; Dave Raabe; Nedra Sutter; Steven A. Wampner.
Number of staff: 7 full-time professional; 3 full-time support; 2 part-time support.
EIN: 311117791
Other changes: Chad Leighty has replaced Wilbur Webb as V.P.
Chad Leighty and Royce Mitchell are no longer directors.

1130
The Community Foundation of Greater Lafayette

1114 State St.
Lafayette, IN 47905-1219 (765) 742-9078
Contact: Greg Kapp, C.E.O.
FAX: (765) 742-2428; E-mail: info@cfglaf.org; Main URL: http://www.cfglaf.org
Facebook: http://www.facebook.com/pages/Lafayette-IN/The-Community-Foundation-of-Greater-Lafayette/109336922422126

Established in 1970 in IN.
Foundation type: Community foundation.
Financial data (yr. ended 12/31/12): Assets, $36,716,354 (M); gifts received, $1,861,502; expenditures, $1,606,472; giving activities include $728,908 for 32+ grants (high: $69,522), and $110,361 for 68 grants to individuals.
Purpose and activities: The mission of the foundation is to inspire, nurture, and practice philanthropy, stewardship, and leadership in local community.
Fields of interest: Performing arts, music; Performing arts, education; Humanities; Arts; Higher education; Education; Environment, beautification programs; Environment; Health care; Substance abuse, services; Mental health/crisis services; Food services; Housing/shelter, homeless; Housing/shelter; Children, day care; Human services; Community development, neighborhood development; Youth.
Type of support: Capital campaigns; Equipment; Emergency funds; Seed money; Scholarship funds; Program-related investments/loans; Scholarships—to individuals.
Limitations: Applications accepted. Giving primarily in Tippecanoe County and the greater Lafayette, IN, area, including the surrounding counties. No support for government agencies or public institutions, or sectarian or religious purposes. No grants to individuals (except for scholarships), or for ongoing expenses, endowments, special events, multi-year grants, debt or deficit reduction, or operating support.
Publications: Application guidelines; Annual report; Grants list; Informational brochure; Newsletter.
Application information: Visit foundation web site for application form and guidelines. Application form required.

Initial approach: Mail grant proposal form and attachments
Deadline(s): Discretionary Grants: Apr. 1 for grants over $15,000; Sept. 3 for grants over $7,500; none for grants under $7,500

Board meeting date(s): Last Thurs. of each month except June and Dec.
Final notification: Discretionary Grants: May 31 for grants over $15,000; Oct. 31 for grants over $7,500; within 4 weeks for grants under $7,500

Officers and Directors:* Dave Luhman,* Chair.; Jim Bodenmiller,* Vice-Chair.; Marianne Curtis Rose,* C.E.O. and Pres.; George Ramsey,* Secy.; Charlie Shook,* Treas.; **Maryann Santos de Barona**; **Carolyn Gery**; Scott Hanback; Sue Holder-Price; Steve Horne; Jeff Love; John Martin; Sonya Margerum; Amy Moulton; Rick Olson.
Number of staff: 3 full-time professional; 1 full-time support.
EIN: 237147996
Other changes: Angela Strader is now Opers. Coord. Sue Holder-Price, George Ramsey, and Charlie Shook are no longer directors.

1131
The Community Foundation of Howard County, Inc.

215 W. Sycamore
Kokomo, IN 46901 (765) 454-7298
Contact: For grants: Kim Abney, V.P., Progs.
FAX: (765) 868-4123; E-mail: info@cfhoward.org; Additional tel.: (800) 964-0508; Grant application e-mail: kim@cfhoward.org; Main URL: http://www.cfhoward.org
E-Newsletter: http://www.cfhoward.org/enews_signup.html
Facebook: https://www.facebook.com/pages/Community-Foundation-Serving-Howard-Clinton-Carroll-Counties/112393758833133

Established in 1991 in IN.
Foundation type: Community foundation.
Financial data (yr. ended 12/31/11): Assets, $41,479,056 (M); gifts received, $720,309; expenditures, $1,751,172; giving activities include $807,286 for 33+ grants (high: $82,572), and $350,280 for 167 grants to individuals.
Purpose and activities: The foundation seeks to improve the quality of life in the community through the accumulation and stewardship of enduring the charitable gifts. Primary areas of interest include health and medical, social services, education, cultural affairs, civic affairs and community beautification.
Fields of interest: Historic preservation/historical societies; Arts; Elementary/secondary education; Education, early childhood education; Education, special; Higher education; Education; Environment, beautification programs; Hospitals (general); Health care; Employment; Youth, services; Human services; Community/economic development; Leadership development.
Type of support: Capital campaigns; Building/renovation; Equipment; Program development; Seed money; Scholarship funds; Scholarships—to individuals; Matching/challenge support.
Limitations: Applications accepted. Giving limited to Carroll, Clinton, and Howard counties, IN. No support for sectarian religious purposes. No grants to individuals (except for scholarships), or for seminars, equipment, normal operating expenses or salaries, or endowments.
Publications: Application guidelines; Annual report (including application guidelines); Informational brochure; Newsletter.
Application information: Visit foundation web site for application form and guidelines. First-time applicants must contact the foundation to discuss grant proposals prior to submission. Application form required.
Initial approach: Mail, e-mail, or fax letter of Inquiry
Copies of proposal: 21
Deadline(s): Jan. 25, May 10, Aug. 2 and Oct. 4 for letter of inquiry; Feb. 22, May 31, Sept. 6 and Nov. 1 for full application
Board meeting date(s): Monthly
Final notification: Letters of inquiry will receive a prompt response. Grant determination within 1 month of full application deadline

Officers and Directors:* Scott McClelland,* Chair.; Rick Smith,* Vice-Chair.; Hilda Burns,* Pres.; Kim Abney,* V.P., Progs.; Bob Hingst,* Secy.-Treas.; Nanette Bowling; Joe Dunbar; Melissa Ellis; Brian Hayes; Betsy Hoshaw; Brad Howell; Beth MacDonald; Paul Manning; James B. McIntyre; Dr. Greg Norman; Stan Rebber; Steve Rothenberger; Laura Sheets; John Shoup; Mike Ullery; Doug Vaughn; J.D. Young; and 6 additional directors.
Number of staff: 1 full-time professional.
EIN: 351844891
Other changes: Tiana Maclin, Kent Ryan, Marilyn Skinner, Mike Stegall are no longer directors.

1132
The Community Foundation of Jackson County, Inc.

107 Community Dr.
P.O. Box 1231
Seymour, IN 47274 (812) 523-4483
***Contact:* Bud Walther, Pres. and C.E.O.**
FAX: (812) 523-1433;
E-mail: info@cfjacksoncounty.org; Additional e-mails: president@cfjacksoncounty.org, vicepresident@cfjacksoncounty.org, accounting@cfjacksoncounty.org and development@cfjacksoncounty.org; Main URL: http://www.cfjacksoncounty.org
Facebook: https://www.facebook.com/CFJacksonCounty

Established in 1992 in IN.
Foundation type: Community foundation.
Financial data (yr. ended 12/31/11): Assets, $10,770,679 (M); gifts received, $707,646; expenditures, $785,138; giving activities include $275,902 for 10+ grants, and $52,901 for grants to individuals.
Purpose and activities: The foundation seeks to promote philanthropy in Jackson County. It is a community-focused organization dedicated to: 1) building visionary partnerships with donors and local service organizations; 2) trustworthy stewardship of gifts; 3) providing funds to enhance the quality of life across Jackson County; 4) and being a catalyst for change in the community.
Fields of interest: Arts; Education; Environment; Youth development; Human services; Community/economic development; Children/youth; Adults; Deaf/hearing impaired; Homeless.
Type of support: Income development; Management development/capacity building; Building/renovation; Emergency funds; Seed money; Curriculum development; Scholarship funds; Technical assistance; Consulting services; Program evaluation; Employee-related scholarships; Scholarships—to individuals; Matching/challenge support.
Limitations: Applications accepted. Giving limited to Jackson County, IN. No support for sectarian programs. No grants for seminars, trips, endowments, or state or national fundraising efforts.
Publications: Application guidelines; Annual report; Financial statement; Informational brochure (including application guidelines); Newsletter.
Application information: Visit foundation web site application form and guidelines. Application form required.
Initial approach: Submit application form
Copies of proposal: 1
Deadline(s): July 31
Board meeting date(s): 3rd Wed. of Jan., Apr., July and Oct.
Final notification: 30 days

Officers and Directors:* **Denise Connell,* Chair.**; **Gary Meyer,* Vice-Chair.**; **Priscilla Wischmeier,* Secy.**; Ray Eakins,* Treas.; Dan Davis,* C.E.O. and Pres.; **Sue Smith,* V.P., Prog. and Admin.**; John Beatty; Susan Bevers; **Patricia Butt**; **Kevin Gabbard**; Ron Harrison; Jim Johnson; Tom Lantz; **Sue Nehrt**; Darrell Persinger; Jim Plump; Andy Royalty; Ron Sibert.
Number of staff: 2 full-time professional; 1 full-time support; 1 part-time support.
EIN: 311119856
Other changes: Denise Connell has replaced Kevin Gabbard as Chair. Gary Meyer has replaced Denise Connell as Vice-Chair. Priscilla Wischmeier has replaced Gary Meyer as Secy. Bud Walther has replaced C.W. Walther as Pres. and C.E.O. Bill Bailey is no longer a director.

1133
Community Foundation of Madison and Jefferson County, Inc.

416 W. St., Ste. B
P.O. Box 306
Madison, IN 47250-0306 (812) 265-3327
***Contact:* Bill Barnes, Pres. and C.E.O.**
FAX: (812) 273-0181; E-mail: info@cfmjc.org; Main URL: http://www.cfmjc.org
Facebook: http://www.facebook.com/cfmjc
Scholarship e-mail: **kelly@cfmjc.org**

Established in 1992 in IN.
Foundation type: Community foundation.
Financial data (yr. ended 12/31/12): Assets, $18,126,846 (M); gifts received, $273,207; expenditures, $731,134; giving activities include $369,584 for 19+ grants (high: $42,615), and $71,845 for 51 grants to individuals.
Purpose and activities: The mission of the foundation is to build a strong, vibrant community by helping donors provide perpetual funding for the people, projects and passions of Jefferson County, IN.
Fields of interest: Arts; Education; Environment; Animal welfare; Health organizations, association; Human services; Community/economic development; Youth; Aging.
Type of support: Management development/capacity building; Capital campaigns; Building/renovation; Equipment; Endowments; Emergency funds; Program development; Conferences/seminars; Seed money; Scholarship funds; Technical assistance; Consulting services; Scholarships—to individuals; Matching/challenge support.
Limitations: Applications accepted. Giving limited to Jefferson County, IN. No support for religious purposes or programs requiring religious participation, public or private educational institutions, or government agencies. **No grants to individuals (except for scholarships), or for debt reduction, annual appeals or membership contribution, ongoing operating expenses or regular programming of well-established agencies, or travel expenses.**
Publications: Application guidelines; Annual report; Financial statement; Grants list; Informational brochure; Newsletter; Program policy statement.

Application information: Visit foundation web site for the Initial Proposal form and application information. Application form required.
Initial approach: Contact foundation
***Deadline(s):* Aug. 1 for Initial Proposal, Sept. 5 for full application**
Board meeting date(s): 1st Wed. of each month
Final notification: Mar. 19
Officers and Directors:* Bonnie Hare,* Chair.; Carri Dirksen,* Vice-Chair.; Bill Barnes,* C.E.O. and Pres.; Donn Vecchie-Campbell,* Secy.; Charles McKay,* Treas.; Mark Wynn, Counsel; Anthony D. Brandon; Dr. Ben Canida; Clifford Carnes; Darleen Connolly; Al Huntington; Eric Phagan; Michael Robinson; Margaret Seifert-Russell; Steve Telfer.
Number of staff: 2 full-time professional; 1 full-time support; 1 part-time support.
EIN: 351847297

1134
The Community Foundation of Muncie and Delaware County, Inc.

P.O. Box 807
Muncie, IN 47308-0807 (765) 747-7181
Contact: Roni Johnson, Pres.
FAX: (765) 289-7770;
E-mail: commfound@cfmdin.org; Main URL: http://www.cfmdin.org
Facebook: http://www.facebook.com/pages/The-Community-Foundation-of-Muncie-and-Delaware-County-Inc/98358219043
Twitter: http://twitter.com/CFofMuncieDelCo

Incorporated in 1985 in IN.
Foundation type: Community foundation.
Financial data (yr. ended 12/31/12): Assets, $45,648,869 (M); gifts received, $1,608,584; expenditures, $2,542,788; giving activities include $1,777,631 for grants.
Purpose and activities: The foundation seeks to encourage philanthropy, assist donors in building and enduring source of charitable assets, and exercise leadership in directing resources to enhance the quality of life of the residents of Muncie and Delaware County, Indiana.
Fields of interest: Arts; Education; Human services; Community development, neighborhood development; Economic development; Children/youth; Children; Adults; Aging; Young adults; Disabilities, people with; Women; Men; Economically disadvantaged; Homeless.
Type of support: General/operating support; Capital campaigns; Building/renovation; Equipment; Emergency funds; Program development; Conferences/seminars; Seed money; Curriculum development; Scholarship funds; Technical assistance; Consulting services; Scholarships—to individuals; In-kind gifts; Matching/challenge support.
Limitations: Applications accepted. Giving limited to Muncie and Delaware County, IN. No support for religious purposes or public agency projects. No grants to individuals (except for scholarships), or for endowment support, travel, fundraising events, or budget deficits.
Publications: Application guidelines; Annual report; Financial statement; Grants list; Informational brochure; Newsletter; Occasional report.
Application information: Visit foundation web site for application form and specific guidelines per grant type. Application form required.
Initial approach: Telephone
Copies of proposal: 2
Deadline(s): Jan. 10, Apr. 11, July 11, and Oct. 10 for the quarterly competitive grants; varies for others
Board meeting date(s): 3rd Mon. of each month
Final notification: 3rd Mon. of Feb., May, Aug., and Nov. for the quarterly competitive grants; varies for others
Officers and Board Members:* Mark A. Ervin,* Chair.; Marianne Vorhees,* Vice-Chair.; **Kelly Shrock,* Pres.; Suzanne Kadinger,* V.P.;** Catharine P. Stewart,* Treas.; Mary L. Dollison; Jud Fisher; Michael B. Galliher; **Mark K. Hardwick;** Jeffrey R. Lang; Michael O. Lunsford.
Number of staff: 3 full-time professional; 1 part-time professional; 2 full-time support.
EIN: 351640051
Other changes: Kelly Shrock has replaced Roni Johnson as Pres.
Jon H. Moll is no longer Secy. Steven M. Smith is no longer a board member.

1135
Community Foundation of Randolph County, Inc.

213 S. Main St.
Winchester, IN 47394-1824 (765) 584-9077
Contact: Ruth B. Mills, Exec. Dir.
FAX: (765) 584-7710;
E-mail: info@cfrandolphcounty.org; Additional e-mail: rmills@cfrandolphcounty.org; Main URL: http://www.randolphcountyfoundation.org/
Facebook: https://www.facebook.com/#!/pages/Community-Foundation-of-Randolph-County/205746446129959
Twitter: http://www.twitter.com/CFofRC

Established in 1992 in IN.
Foundation type: Community foundation.
Financial data (yr. ended 12/31/12): Assets, $7,009,628 (M); gifts received, $364,371; expenditures, $521,415; giving activities include $249,795 for 16 grants (high: $21,629), and $95,331 for 70 grants to individuals.
Purpose and activities: The Community Foundation of Randolph County, Inc. seeks to bring people and resources together to enrich the lives of Randolph County residents.
Fields of interest: Historic preservation/historical societies; Arts; Higher education; Scholarships/financial aid; Education; Environment; Health care; Human services; Economic development; Community/economic development; Youth; Aging.
Type of support: Program development; Curriculum development; Scholarship funds.
Limitations: Applications accepted. Giving limited to Randolph County, IN. No support for religious or sectarian purposes. No grants to individuals (except for scholarships), or for make-up of operating deficits, post-event or after-the-fact situations, or endowments campaigns.
Publications: Application guidelines; Annual report; Newsletter; Occasional report (including application guidelines).
Application information: Visit foundation web site for application cover sheet and guidelines. Completed typewritten application forms should be sent or delivered to the foundation's office. Applications cannot be submitted online. Application form required.
Initial approach: Submit application
Copies of proposal: 11
Deadline(s): Mar. 31 and Sept. 30
Board meeting date(s): 3rd Thursday of each month
Final notification: 4 to 6 weeks
Officers and Directors:* Chip Loney,* Pres.; Cheryl Jones,* V.P.; Sheryl Thurston,* Secy.; Lisa Jennings,* Treas.; Ruth B. Mills, Exec. Dir.; Kathy Beumer; Christen Commers; Dick Gause; Richard Gough; Jane Grove; Joyce Husmann; Rev. Cherie Isakson; James Meinerding; Ronn Shumaker; Kent Thornburg.
Number of staff: 2 full-time professional.
EIN: 351903148

1136
Community Foundation of Southern Indiana

4104 Charlestown Rd.
New Albany, IN 47150-9538 (812) 948-4662
Contact: For grants: Crystal Gunther, Grants and Prog. Off.
FAX: (812) 948-4678;
E-mail: lspeed@cfsouthernindiana.com; Grant inquiry e-mail: cgunther@cfsouthernindiana.com; Main URL: http://www.cfsouthernindiana.com
Facebook: https://www.facebook.com/cfsouthernindiana
Twitter: https://twitter.com/CFofSI
YouTube: http://www.youtube.com/user/cfsouthernindiana

Established in 1991 in IN.
Foundation type: Community foundation.
Financial data (yr. ended 06/30/12): Assets, $28,263,609 (M); gifts received, $1,981,480; expenditures, $2,840,592; giving activities include $1,467,039 for grants.
Purpose and activities: The foundation builds enduring charitable resources used to positively impact the community by: 1) serving as a partner and resource for donors, their advisors, and area nonprofits; 2) making it simple for donors to fulfill their individual goals in giving back; 3) providing stewardship of donor gifts and charitable intent for generations to come; and 4) fulfilling a leadership role on important community issues.
Fields of interest: Arts; Education; Environment; Health care; Recreation; Youth development; Human services; Community/economic development.
Type of support: Management development/capacity building; Capital campaigns; Building/renovation; Emergency funds; Program development; Conferences/seminars; Seed money; Scholarship funds; Scholarships—to individuals; Matching/challenge support.
Limitations: Applications accepted. Giving limited to Clark and Floyd counties, IN. No support for medical, scientific or academic research, or for religious or sectarian purposes. No grants to individuals (except for designated scholarship funds), or for annual appeals, endowment funds, membership contributions, fundraising events, existing obligations, travel expenses, long-term operating support, or multi-year grants or repeat funding; no loans.
Publications: Annual report (including application guidelines); Financial statement; Informational brochure; Newsletter.
Application information: Visit foundation web site for application forms and guidelines. Application form required.
Initial approach: Submit online application and attachments
Copies of proposal: 2
Deadline(s): Sept. 1 for competitive grant cycle
Board meeting date(s): Bimonthly
Final notification: Late Oct.
Officers and Directors:* **Julie Larner,* Chair.;** Susie Stewart,* Vice-Chair.; Linda S. Speed,* C.E.O. and Pres.; **Gary Banet,* Secy.;** Phillip Beaman,* Treas.; Jessica Bergman; Helen Bryant; Bill Hanson; Tom Hardy; Jorge Lanz; Leslie Lewis-Sheets; Pat More;

Greg Neely; Kyle Ridout; Sue Sanders; Andrew Takami; Bill White.
Number of staff: 4 full-time professional; 2 part-time professional; 1 full-time support; 1 part-time support.
EIN: 351827813
Other changes: Julie Larner has replaced Kevin Cecil as Chair. Gary Banet has replaced Susie Stewart as Secy.
Kenton M. Wooden is now Comm. and Outreach Off. Margaret Brinkworth is now Grants and Scholarships Asso.

1137
Community Foundation of Switzerland County, Inc.
303 Ferry St.
P.O. Box 46
Vevay, IN 47043-1103 (812) 427-9160
Contact: Pam W. Acton, Exec. Dir.
E-mail: info@cfsci.org; Main URL: http://www.cfsci.org
Facebook: http://www.facebook.com/cfsci

Established in 1999 in IN.
Foundation type: Community foundation.
Financial data (yr. ended 12/31/12): Assets, $10,629,567 (M); gifts received, $457,645; expenditures, $648,810; giving activities include $430,821 for 8 grants (high: $173,271), and $33,065 for 59 grants to individuals.
Purpose and activities: The mission of the foundation is to connect people who care with causes that matter for good, for ever, for Switzerland County.
Fields of interest: Arts; Education; Environment; Health care; Human services; Community/economic development.
Limitations: Applications accepted. Giving limited to Switzerland County, IN. No support for religious organizations for direct religious activities. **No grants to individuals (except for scholarships), operating expenses, debt reduction, endowments, annual appeals or memberships, travel expenses, or endowment building.**
Publications: Application guidelines; Annual report; Grants list; Informational brochure; Program policy statement; Program policy statement (including application guidelines).
Application information: Visit foundation web site for grant application and guidelines. Application form required.
Initial approach: Complete online application through web site
Deadline(s): Mar. 10, The maximum amount that may be requested is $5,000.
Board meeting date(s): 3rd Tues. of month
Officers and Directors:* Steve Lyons,* Pres.; Wilma Swango,* V.P.; Ruth Lohide,* Secy.; Phyllis Collier,* Treas.; Pam W. Acton, Exec. Dir.; Jessica Archer; Adam Cole; Nancy Craig; Roy Leap; Rick Lewis.
Number of staff: 2 full-time professional.
EIN: 352087649

1138
Compassionate Spirit Foundation, Inc.
Lafayette, IN

The foundation terminated on Dec. 5, 2011.

1139
Crosser Family Foundation, Inc.
14701 Cumberland Rd., Ste. 190
Noblesville, IN 46060-3098
Twitter: http://twitter.com/crosserfamily

Established in 2001 in IN.
Donors: Richard H. Crosser†; Janet R. Crosser.
Foundation type: Independent foundation.
Financial data (yr. ended 12/31/12): Assets, $0 (M); gifts received, $1,100; expenditures, $312,590; qualifying distributions, $248,804; giving activities include $248,804 for 17 grants (high: $110,634; low: $270).
Purpose and activities: Giving to improve the lives of our youth and their families by providing them with everyday needs and opportunities to help them achieve a bright future.
Fields of interest: Performing arts, music; Hospitals (general); Food banks; Boys & girls clubs; Human services; Children, services; International relief.
Type of support: General/operating support.
Limitations: Applications not accepted. Giving primarily in IN. No grants to individuals.
Application information: Unsolicited requests for funds not accepted.
Officers: Janet R. Crosser, Pres. and Treas.; Craig Crosser, V.P.; Clark Crosser, Secy.
Director: Carrie Crosser-Renner.
EIN: 352145332
Other changes: The grantmaker no longer lists an E-mail or a URL address.

1140
Darling Family Foundation, Inc.
P.O. Box 11648
Fort Wayne, IN 46859-1648
***Application address:* c/o Benjamin S. J. Williams, 229 W. Berry St., Ste. 400, Fort Wayne, IN 46802, tel.: (260) 423-1430**

Established in 2002 in IN.
Donors: William A. Darling; William A. Darling 2002 Charitable Lead Annuity Trust.
Foundation type: Independent foundation.
Financial data (yr. ended 05/31/13): Assets, $1,897,780 (M); gifts received, $140,000; expenditures, $155,081; qualifying distributions, $140,752; giving activities include $140,002 for 8 grants (high: $67,500; low: $2,500).
Fields of interest: Performing arts; Animal welfare; Human services; Protestant agencies & churches.
Type of support: General/operating support.
Limitations: Applications accepted. Giving primarily in IL and IN. No grants to individuals.
Application information: Application form required.
Initial approach: Letter
Deadline(s): None
Officers: Philip W. Darling, Pres.; Benjamin S.J. Williams, Secy.
Director: Nancy A. Darling.
EIN: 300106082

1141
Dearborn Community Foundation
(formerly Dearborn County Community Foundation)
322 Walnut St.
Lawrenceburg, IN 47025 (812) 539-4115
Contact: Fred McCarter, Exec. Dir.; For grants: Denise Sedler, Dir., Progs.
FAX: (812) 539-4119;
E-mail: fmccarter@dearborncf.org; Grant information e-mail: dsedler@comcast.net; Main URL: http://www.dearborncf.org
Facebook: http://www.facebook.com/DearbornCommunityFoundation
Established in 1997 in IN.
Donors: The Greater Cincinnati Foundation; Lilly Endowment; Rising Sun Regional Foundation.
Foundation type: Community foundation.
Financial data (yr. ended 12/31/12): Assets, $14,623,632 (M); gifts received, $3,920,298; expenditures, $3,886,508; giving activities include $3,054,388 for 56+ grants (high: $359,524), and $318,000 for 206 grants to individuals.
Purpose and activities: The foundation is a catalyst to connect people who care with causes that improve the quality of life in the community by advancing cultural, educational and social opportunities, while preserving its heritage and helping donors to create a permanent legacy in Dearborn County.
Fields of interest: Arts; Elementary/secondary education; Education; Environment, natural resources; Environment; Hospitals (general); Health care; Crime/law enforcement, government agencies; Human services; Community/economic development; Children/youth.
Type of support: Building/renovation; Equipment; Program development; Seed money; Scholarships—to individuals; Matching/challenge support.
Limitations: Applications accepted. Giving limited to Dearborn County, IN. No support for sectarian or religious purposes. No grants to individuals (except for scholarships), or exclusively for endowment creation or debt reduction, or for travel expenses or after-the-fact funding.
Publications: Application guidelines; Annual report; Newsletter.
Application information: Visit foundation web site for application cover form, guidelines, and specific deadline per grant type. Application form required.
Initial approach: Submit grant application cover form and attachments
Copies of proposal: 8
Deadline(s): Varies
Board meeting date(s): Last Thurs. of every month except Apr., July, and Dec.
Final notification: Varies
Officers and Directors:* Jim Stock,* Chair.; Perry Taylor,* Pres.; David Wismann,* V.P.; Mary Ewbank,* Secy.; John Rumsey,* Treas.; Fred McCarter, Exec. Dir.; Lisa DeHart Lehner, Counsel; Tami Bovard; Paula Bruner; Dave Deddens; Mark Graver; Deanna Hacker; Mike Hornbach; Becky Lyons; Barry Nanz; Jon Strautman; Judy Ullrich.
Number of staff: 4 full-time professional; 1 full-time support.
EIN: 352036110
Other changes: Andrea Nappier is now Admin. Asst.

1142
Decatur County Community Foundation, Inc.
101 E. Main St., Ste. 1
P.O. Box 72
Greensburg, IN 47240-2031 (812) 662-6364
Contact: Deb Locke, Exec. Dir.
FAX: (812) 662-8704;
E-mail: contact@dccfound.org; Main URL: http://www.dccfound.org
Facebook: https://www.facebook.com/dccfound

Established in 1992 in IN.
Foundation type: Community foundation.

Financial data (yr. ended 12/31/11): Assets, $14,873,816 (M); gifts received, $499,187; expenditures, $709,933; giving activities include $279,256 for 18+ grants (high: $81,438), and $186,210 for 94 grants to individuals.
Purpose and activities: The foundation seeks to provide a general depository for charitable contributions that will service Decatur County. The foundation supports the following areas of interest: civic and community, education, health and human services, arts and literacy, historic preservation, safety, and youth and recreation.
Fields of interest: Historic preservation/historical societies; Arts; Education, reading; Education; Public health; Health care; Safety, education; Recreation; Youth development, services; Youth development; Human services; Community/economic development.
Type of support: Building/renovation; Equipment; Emergency funds; Program development; Seed money; Scholarship funds; Technical assistance; Program-related investments/loans; Scholarships—to individuals; Matching/challenge support.
Limitations: Applications accepted. Giving primarily in Decatur County, IN. No support for religious purposes. No grants for debt reduction, post-event or after the fact funding, make-up operating deficits, or ongoing operating expenses.
Publications: Application guidelines; Annual report (including application guidelines); Financial statement; Informational brochure; Informational brochure (including application guidelines); Newsletter; Occasional report.
Application information: Visit foundation web site for Letter of Intent form and additional guidelines per grant type. Upon approval of Letter of Intent, grant applications will be sent to eligible applicants. Organizations may not receive foundation grants more than once in a 12-month period; maximum grant amount is $15,000. Application form required.
Initial approach: Submit Letter of Intent form
Copies of proposal: 10
***Deadline(s):* Feb. 15, May 15, and Sept. 15 for large grants; 10th of each month for grants under $1,500; Oct. 1 and Feb. 1 for Teacher Grants.**
Board meeting date(s): 3rd Fri. monthly
Final notification: Normally within 2 months
Officers and Directors:* Gail Rueff,* Pres.; Dennis Wilson,* V.P.; Bob Cupp,* Secy.-Treas.; Deb Locke, Exec. Dir.; Steve Doerflinger; **Sharon Hollowell**; Roland Shirk; Lynda Smith; Carrie Stapp; Dave Stults; Mark Vice.
Number of staff: 1 full-time professional; 1 part-time support.
EIN: 351870979

1143
Christel DeHaan Family Foundation

(formerly RCI Foundation)
c/o Joe Schneider
10 W. Market St., Ste. 1990
Indianapolis, IN 46204-2973 (317) 464-2038
***Contact:* Melynne Klaus, Exec. Dir.**
E-mail: mklaus@cde-ltd.com; **Main URL: http://www.christeldehaanfamilyfoundation.org/**

Established in 1992 in IN.
Donor: Christel DeHaan.
Foundation type: Independent foundation.
Financial data (yr. ended 12/31/12): Assets, $43,358,672 (M); expenditures, $1,160,899; qualifying distributions, $776,694; giving activities include $662,650 for 64 grants (high: $80,000; low: $100).
Purpose and activities: Giving to meaningfully preserve and enhance for future generations the rich artistic and cultural fabric of the Indianapolis, Indiana community.
Fields of interest: Arts.
Type of support: General/operating support; Continuing support; Annual campaigns; Program development; Matching/challenge support.
Limitations: Giving primarily in central IN. No support for religious organizations, political candidates, parties or lobbyists, federal/state/local governmental bodies, or for other private foundations. No grants for individual artistic endeavors, media advertising, or public awareness campaigns.
Publications: IRS Form 990 or 990-PF printed copy available upon request.
Application information: Full applications are accepted by invitation only, upon consideration of initial tel., e-mail or letter. See foundation web site for additional information. Application form required.
***Initial approach:* Tel., e-mail or letter to request additional information and funding guidelines**
Copies of proposal: 1
Board meeting date(s): June and Dec.
Officers and Directors:* Christel DeHaan,* Pres.; Cheryl J. Wendling,* Sr. V.P. and Secy.; Keith A. DeHaan,* V.P.; Kirsten A. DeHaan,* V.P.; Timothy E. DeHaan,* V.P.; **Joe Schneider, Treas.**; **Melynne Klaus, Exec. Dir.**; Mark Willis, C.I.O.; **Nelson Hitchcock**; **Jim Reed.**
Number of staff: 1 part-time professional.
EIN: 351939960
Other changes: Joe Schneider is now Treas.

1144
DeKalb County Community Foundation, Inc.

650 W. N. St.
P.O. Box 111
Auburn, IN 46706-0111 (260) 925-0311
Contact: Wendy Oberlin, Exec. Dir.; For grants: Diane Wilson, Grant and Scholarship Mgr.
FAX: (260) 925-0383;
E-mail: woberlin@dekalbfoundation.org; Additional tel.: (888) 727-3834; Grant application e-mail: dwilson@dekalbfoundation.org; Main URL: http://www.dekalbfoundation.org
Scholarship application e-mail: scholarships@dekalbfoundation.org

Established in 1996 in IN.
Foundation type: Community foundation.
Financial data (yr. ended 12/31/13): Assets, $14,041,958 (M); gifts received, $794,433; expenditures, $1,112,341; giving activities include $486,546 for grants.
Purpose and activities: The foundation promotes community philanthropy by offering local citizens the opportunity to leave a charitable legacy that will sustain and improve life in DeKalb County.
Fields of interest: Arts; Education; Environment; Health care; Youth development; Human services; Community/economic development.
Type of support: General/operating support; Capital campaigns; Building/renovation; Equipment; Program development; Technical assistance; Scholarships—to individuals; Matching/challenge support.
Limitations: Applications accepted. Giving limited to projects/programs that benefit residents of DeKalb County, IN.
Publications: Application guidelines; Annual report; Financial statement; Grants list; Newsletter.
Application information: Visit foundation web site for application form and guidelines. Handwritten proposals are not accepted. The foundation offers free 60-minute workshops to help grantseekers understand the application process and how to submit a request; contact Prog. Mgr. to register. Application form required.
Initial approach: Contact foundation to schedule meeting
Copies of proposal: 1
***Deadline(s):* July 1**
Board meeting date(s): Varies
Officers and Directors:* Marcia K. Weller,* Pres.; W. Erik Weber,* V.P.; Holly Albright,* Secy.; Todd W. Custer,* Treas.; Wendy Oberlin, Exec. Dir.; Matthew A. Bechdol; Randall J. Deetz; Michael W. Hasselman; Don B. Hollman; Ken McCrory; Ian Mercer; Terry Rayle; Michael L. Slentz; Vanessa Sterling; Trenton Stuckey; Peg Yoder.
Number of staff: 2 full-time professional; 4 part-time support.
EIN: 351992897

1145
Richard M. Fairbanks Foundation, Inc.

(formerly Fairbanks Foundation, Inc.)
9292 N. Meridian St., Ste. 304
Indianapolis, IN 46260-1828 (317) 846-7111
Contact: Betsy Bikoff, V.P. and Chief Grantmaking Off.
FAX: (317) 844-0167; E-mail (for Betsy Bikoff): bikoff@rmff.org; Main URL: http://www.rmff.org
CEP Study: http://www.rmff.org/page.aspx?PageID=f82d510d-d596-41e7-8848-704060f2d6dd&ParentPageID=814be4f6-2d1d-46f5-acef-8235b323be12

Established in 1986 in IN.
Donor: Richard M. Fairbanks†.
Foundation type: Independent foundation.
Financial data (yr. ended 12/31/12): Assets, $281,793,008 (M); gifts received, $116,984; expenditures, $13,917,206; qualifying distributions, $10,387,445; giving activities include $9,635,755 for grants.
Purpose and activities: Support primarily for health care, the vitality of Indianapolis, sustainable employment as well as organizations historically supported by the foundation.
Fields of interest: Health care; Employment, services; Human services; Community/economic development.
Type of support: General/operating support; Continuing support; Management development/capacity building; Annual campaigns; Capital campaigns; Building/renovation; Equipment; Endowments; Program development; Seed money; Fellowships; Research; Technical assistance; Program evaluation; Matching/challenge support.
Limitations: Applications accepted. **Giving primarily in greater Indianapolis, IN, with an emphasis on Marion County.** No support for political organizations. **No grants to individuals, or for conference, seminars, media events, or workshops unless they are an integral part of a broader program, and no grants to for-profit organizations.**
Publications: Application guidelines; Financial statement; Grants list.
Application information: Proposals should be submitted to the foundation only upon request. Unsolicited full proposals will not be accepted. Application form not required.
Initial approach: Telephone or letter of inquiry (2-3 pages)
Copies of proposal: 1
***Deadline(s):* No**

Board meeting date(s): Spring, summer, and fall
Final notification: Day after board meetings
Officers and Directors:* Leonard J. Betley,* Chair., C.E.O. and Pres.; Mary E. "Betsy" Bikoff, V.P. and Chief Grantmaking Off.; Ellen White Quigley, Secy. and Grants Off.; Roger S. Snowdon,* Treas.; Steffanie Rhinesmith, C.I.O.; Daniel C. Appel; Christopher M. Callahan, M.D.; Jonathan B. Fairbanks; Elizabeth N. Mann; Bryan A. Mills; **Thomas H. Ristine**.
Number of staff: 4 full-time professional; 1 part-time professional; 2 part-time support.
EIN: 311189885

1146
Fayette County Foundation

521 N. Central Ave., Ste. A
P.O. Box 844
Connersville, IN 47331 (765) 827-9966
***Contact:* Anna Dungan, Exec. Dir.; For grants: Katherine Good, Prog. Off.**
FAX: (765) 827-5836;
E-mail: info@fayettefoundation.com**; Grant application e-mail: kgood@fayettefoundation.com**;
Main URL: http://www.fayettefoundation.com
Facebook: http://www.facebook.com/pages/Connersville-IN/Fayette-County-Foundation/369719452177

Established in 1985 in IN.
Foundation type: Community foundation.
Financial data (yr. ended 12/31/12): Assets, $9,585,063 (M); gifts received, $146,830; expenditures, $544,052; giving activities include $307,644 for grants.
Purpose and activities: The foundation seeks to inspire a spirit of philanthropy in Fayette County, IN, by enhancing the quality of life through impacting grantmaking, strategic endowment building, and community leadership.
Fields of interest: Arts; Higher education; Education; Environment; Animal welfare; Health care; Health organizations, association; Youth development, adult & child programs; Human services; Economic development; Community/economic development; Religion; Youth.
Type of support: Building/renovation; Endowments; Emergency funds; Conferences/seminars; Scholarship funds; Scholarships—to individuals; In-kind gifts.
Limitations: Applications accepted. Giving limited to Fayette County, IN. No support for religious organizations. No grants for deficit funding, or for salaries, annual campaigns, repeat funding, or for travel expenses.
Publications: Annual report; Grants list; Informational brochure; Newsletter.
Application information: Visit foundation web site for application information. Application form required.
Initial approach: Letter of intent
Copies of proposal: 9
Deadline(s): Jan. 31, June 1, and Oct. 1 for letter of intent
Board meeting date(s): Once a month
Final notification: 4 weeks
Officers and Directors:* Andy Yaryan,* Pres.; Jane Oakley,* Treas.; Anna Dungan, Exec. Dir.; Brett Adams; Jon Eakins; Mahershall Gardner; Becky Gibson; Doug Hornsby; Duane Keaffaber; Cyndi Nesbitt; Donna Stern; Nick Thomas.
Number of staff: 2 full-time professional.
EIN: 311185980

1147
Foellinger Foundation, Inc.

520 E. Berry St.
Fort Wayne, IN 46802-2002 (260) 422-2900
Contact: Cheryl K. Taylor, C.E.O. and Pres.; Terry Stevens, Exec. and Prog. Specialist
FAX: (260) 422-9436; E-mail: info@foellinger.org; E-mail for Cheryl K. Taylor: cheryl@foellinger.org; E-mail for Terry Stevens: terry@foellinger.org; Main URL: http://www.foellinger.org

Incorporated in 1958 in IN.
Donors: Esther A. Foellinger†; Helene R. Foellinger†.
Foundation type: Independent foundation.
Financial data (yr. ended 08/31/13): Assets, $172,748,697 (M); expenditures, $9,294,455; qualifying distributions, $7,920,656; giving activities include $6,939,909 for 126 grants (high: $893,000; low: $3,000), and $139,846 for 4 foundation-administered programs.
Purpose and activities: Giving in Allen County, IN, for early childhood development, youth development and family development, especially the most in need with the least opportunity, and organizational effectiveness.
Fields of interest: Children/youth, services; Family services; Children/youth; Youth; Economically disadvantaged.
Type of support: General/operating support; Continuing support; Management development/capacity building; Program development; Research; Technical assistance; Consulting services; Program evaluation.
Limitations: Applications accepted. Giving in Allen County, IN, area. Generally, no grants for religious groups for religious purposes, elementary or secondary schools independent of their school systems, or purposes taxpayers are expected to support. No grants to individuals, or for endowments, deficit financing, sponsorships, camperships, special events, conferences, commercial advertising, capital projects, annual campaigns or appeals, or for capital projects.
Publications: Application guidelines; Annual report; Grants list; Occasional report.
Application information: See foundation's web site for downloadable grant guideline packet. Not currently accepting applications for capital support. Only 1 application for operation or program support per organization per year. Application form required.
Initial approach: Grant application
Copies of proposal: 1
Deadline(s): No deadline for grants for Inspire, Renew or Transform grant applications. First Mon. in Feb. for Community Interests; First Mon. in Aug. for Early Childhood Development and Family Development; First Mon. in Nov. for Youth Development; and as invited for all other foundation-invited initiatives
Board meeting date(s): Quarterly in Feb., May, Aug., and Nov.
Final notification: One week after board meeting
Officers and Directors:* David A. Bobilya,* Chair.; **Robert N. Taylor,* Vice-Chair. and Secy.**; Cheryl K. Taylor,* C.E.O. and Pres.; Helen J. Murray, Treas.; **Darryl R. Olson, C.F.O.; Hon. Thomas J. Felts**; Carolyn R. Hughes; Richard B. Pierce; Todd C. Rumsey, M.D.; Sarah Strimmenos, CPA.
Number of staff: 3 full-time professional; 3 full-time support.
EIN: 356027059

1148
The Froderman Foundation, Inc.

4325 U.S. Highway 41
P.O. Box 10039
Terre Haute, IN 47802-4406
Contact: Mark Fuson, Pres.
FAX: (812) 232-8414;
E-mail: markfuson@drivefuson.com; Main URL: http://www.frodermanfoundation.com

Established in 1962 in IN.
Donors: Harvey Froderman†; Mrs. Harvey Froderman.
Foundation type: Independent foundation.
Financial data (yr. ended 06/30/13): Assets, $10,989,878 (M); expenditures, $561,847; qualifying distributions, $463,373; giving activities include $463,373 for 20 grants (high: $90,000; low: $925).
Purpose and activities: The foundation's mission is to provide funds to qualified applicants whose emphasis is to promote religious, educational, medical, and/or charitable causes.
Fields of interest: Higher education; Health organizations, association; Human services; Christian agencies & churches.
Type of support: Building/renovation; Equipment; Publication; Scholarship funds.
Limitations: Applications accepted. Giving primarily in Indianapolis and Terre Haute, IN. No grants to individuals, or for operating budgets.
Application information: Application form required.
Initial approach: Request application
Copies of proposal: 1
Deadline(s): None
Board meeting date(s): Apr., June, Sept., and Dec.
Officers: Mark Fuson, Pres.; Carl Froderman, V.P.; Chris Froderman, Secy.; Brad Fuson, Treas.
EIN: 356025283

1149
FSJ Foundation, Inc.

6900 S. Gray Rd.
Indianapolis, IN 46237-3209

Established in 1994 in IN.
Donor: Franklin L. Jackson.
Foundation type: Independent foundation.
Financial data (yr. ended 12/31/12): Assets, $0 (M); gifts received, $2,000,000; expenditures, $325,946; qualifying distributions, $325,941; giving activities include $325,941 for grants.
Purpose and activities: Giving primarily for evangelical Christian programs.
Fields of interest: Christian agencies & churches.
Limitations: Applications not accepted. Giving primarily in IN. No grants to individuals.
Application information: Contributes only to pre-selected organizations.
Directors: Jody A. Gregg; Franklin L. Jackson; Jonathon F. Jackson; Mark A. Jackson; Michael L. Jackson; Sharon M. Jackson; **Lisa Mauceri**; Shelly I. Todd.
EIN: 351888190

1150
Eugene and Marilyn Glick Foundation Corporation

P.O. Box 40177
Indianapolis, IN 46240-0177 (317) 469-5877
Contact: David O. Barrett, C.E.O. and Pres.

Established in 1982 in IN.
Donors: Eugene B. Glick†; Marilyn K. Glick†.

Foundation type: Independent foundation.
Financial data (yr. ended 11/30/13): Assets, $167,733,905 (M); gifts received, $2,543,167; expenditures, $2,994,089; qualifying distributions, $1,571,407; giving activities include $1,518,661 for 134 grants (high: $347,000; low: $750).
Fields of interest: Arts; Higher education; Education; Eye research; Human services; Children/youth, services; Foundations (community).
Type of support: General/operating support; Capital campaigns; Program development; Matching/challenge support.
Limitations: Applications accepted. Giving primarily in Indianapolis, IN. No grants to individuals.
Application information:
Initial approach: Letter
Deadline(s): None
Officers and Directors:* **David O. Barrett,* Vice-Chair., C.E.O. and Pres.**; Marianne Glick,* Vice-Chair.; James T. Bisesi,* Secy.; Anita S. Smith,* C.F.O. and Treas.; Sharon Kibbe, Exec. Dir.; Thomas J. Grande,* C.I.O.; Jacqueline Barrett; Arlene Grande; Alice Meshbane; Lynda Schwartz.
Number of staff: 1 full-time professional.
EIN: 351549707
Other changes: Eugene B. Glick, Donor, is deceased. Marilyn K. Glick, Donor and Chair., is deceased. David O. Barrett is now Vice-Chair., C.E.O. and Pres.

1151
Globe Foundation Limited
3392 Eden Hollow Pl.
Carmel, IN 46033-3033
E-mail: info@globefoundation.org; Main URL: http://www.globefoundation.org
Flickr: https://www.flickr.com/photos/77184629@N08
Twitter: http://twitter.com/GlobeFoundation

Established in 2008 in IN.
Donors: Suzanne Fehsenfeld; Fred M. Fehsenfeld, Jr.
Foundation type: Independent foundation.
Financial data (yr. ended 12/31/12): Assets, $171,042 (M); gifts received, $579,500; expenditures, $457,608; qualifying distributions, $402,342; giving activities include $375,475 for 6 grants (high: $106,350; low: $2,200).
Purpose and activities: Giving primarily to organizations and individuals addressing humanitarian, animal and environmental conservation needs worldwide.
Fields of interest: Environment; Animals/wildlife; Human services.
Limitations: Applications not accepted.
Application information: Unsolicited requests for funds not accepted.
Officers: Suzanne Fehsenfeld, Chair.; Fred M. Fehsenfeld, Jr., Vice-Chair.; Karen A. Kennelly, Secy.-Treas.
EIN: 263282195

1152
Greene County Foundation, Inc.
(formerly Greene County Community Foundation, Inc.)
4513 W St., Hwy. 54
Bloomfield, IN 47424 (812) 659-3142
Contact: Cam Trampke, Exec. Dir.
FAX: (812) 659-3142;
E-mail: gcf@greenecountyfoundation.org; Additional e-mail: ctrampke@greenecountyfoundation.org; Main URL: http://www.greenecountyfoundation.org

Established in 1990 in IN.
Foundation type: Community foundation.
Financial data (yr. ended 12/31/12): Assets, $5,064,399 (M); gifts received, $151,075; expenditures, $299,206; giving activities include $150,702 for 3+ grants (high: $44,251), and $49,041 for 29 grants to individuals.
Purpose and activities: The foundation seeks to work with charitably minded individuals and organizations to strengthen Greene County now and for future generations to come.
Fields of interest: Arts; Environment, beautification programs; Health care; Recreation; Human services; Community/economic development; Philanthropy/voluntarism.
Type of support: Program development.
Limitations: Applications accepted. Giving limited to Greene County, IN. **No support for religious purposes. No grants for annual appeals or membership contributions.**
Publications: Application guidelines; Annual report; Occasional report.
Application information: Visit foundation web site for more information.
Initial approach: Contact foundation
***Copies of proposal:* 6**
***Deadline(s):* July 22**
Board meeting date(s): 2nd Mon. of every month
***Final notification:* Aug.**
Officers and Directors:* Linda Thomas,* Pres.; Kevin Kramer,* V.P.; Patti Jones,* Secy.; Kim Hughes,* Treas.; Cam Trampke,* Exec. Dir.; beth Clark; Daryn Lewellyn; Scott Powers; Tom Roberts; Dan Sichting; Todd Walton; Bob Weeks; John Wells.
Number of staff: 1 part-time professional; 1 part-time support.
EIN: 351815060
Other changes: The grantmaker now publishes application guidelines online.

1153
Robert and Helen Haddad Foundation, Inc.
3460 Commerce Dr.
Columbus, IN 47201-2204
E-mail: tlhaddad@me.com; Main URL: http://www.thehaddadfoundation.org
Grants List: http://haddadfoundation.org/projects/

Established in 2002 in IN.
Donor: Robert W. and Helen Haddad Trust.
Foundation type: Independent foundation.
Financial data (yr. ended 12/31/12): Assets, $4,429,111 (M); gifts received, $461,574; expenditures, $187,091; qualifying distributions, $166,711; giving activities include $141,450 for 19 grants (high: $17,000; low: $1,950).
Fields of interest: Arts; Education; Health care; Health organizations; Medical research; Christian agencies & churches; Mutual aid societies.
Limitations: Applications accepted. Giving primarily in IN. No grants to individuals.
Application information: Proposals must be submitted via foundation web site. Application form required.
Officers: Robert W. Haddad, Jr., Pres.; Hayden L.H. Bishop, Secy.; Tamara L. Burton, Treas.
Directors: Kevin Alerding; Tracy L. Haddad.
EIN: 300127786

1154
Hancock County Community Foundation, Inc.
312 E. Main St.
Greenfield, IN 46140-2348 (317) 462-8870
Contact: Mary Gibble, Pres.; For grants: Alyse Vail, Prog. Off.
FAX: (317) 467-3330;
E-mail: info@givehcgrowhc.org; Grant inquiries e-mail: avail@giveHCgrowHC.org; Main URL: http://givehcgrowhc.org/
Facebook: https://www.facebook.com/HancockCountyCommunityFoundation
RSS Feed: http://www.givehcgrowhc.org/feed
Twitter: https://twitter.com/HancockCountyCF
YouTube: http://www.youtube.com/user/HCCFGreenfield

Established in 1992 in IN.
Foundation type: Community foundation.
Financial data (yr. ended 12/31/12): Assets, $21,396,827 (M); gifts received, $1,665,169; expenditures, $1,591,648; giving activities include $659,583 for 29+ grants (high: $45,543), and $157,350 for 96 grants to individuals.
Purpose and activities: The foundation provides philanthropic leadership to effectively manage and direct the resources of community donors in ways which enrich and enhance the quality of life in Hancock County, IN.
Fields of interest: Arts; Education; Health care; Human services; Community/economic development; Youth.
Type of support: Program development; Equipment; Conferences/seminars; Seed money; Curriculum development; Scholarship funds; Technical assistance; Consulting services; Matching/challenge support.
Limitations: Applications accepted. Giving limited to Hancock County, IN. No support for sectarian religious purposes. **No grants to individuals, or for endowments, deficit financing, or fundraising.**
Publications: Application guidelines; Annual report; Informational brochure; Newsletter.
Application information: Visit foundation web site for application guidelines per grant type. Application form required.
Initial approach: Attend Grant Workshop
***Deadline(s):* Aug. 23 for Fall Grants; Feb. 28 for Scholarships**
Board meeting date(s): 3rd Thurs. of each month
Officers and Directors:* Tom Seng,* Chair.; Teri Dunlavy,* Vice-Chair.; Mary Gibble,* Pres.; Fred Powers,* Secy.; P. Jon Miller,* Treas.; Wayne Beck; Bob Bogigian; **Barbara Campbell**; Tim Clark; Josh Daugherty; David Dellacca; Lorraine Ewing; Jim Greig; Debi Hill; Leah Janes; Chris McQueeney; Florence May; Sandy Miller; **Linda Muegge**; Susan Nichter; **Adam Schultz**; Bill Weldon; Stephenie White-Longworth.
Number of staff: 4 full-time professional.
EIN: 351837729
Other changes: Pam Hayes, Ann Vail, and Mike Burrow are no longer directors.

1155
Harrison County Community Foundation, Inc.
1523 Foundation Way
P.O. Box 279
Corydon, IN 47112-1552 (812) 738-6668
Contact: Steven A. Gilliland, C.E.O.; For grants: Anna Curts, Grants Mgr.
FAX: (812) 738-6864;
E-mail: steveg@hccfindiana.org; Additional e-mail:

staff@hccfindiana.org; Grant inquiry e-mail: annac@hccfindiana.org; Main URL: http://www.hccfindiana.org
E-Newsletter: http://www.hccfindiana.org/category/httpwww-icontact-archive-comcmi0k5-gqgmskpcbq5hwlgjr-dvfqxmj03i6m_6sjlywrk8bp-d0ojwww3/
Facebook: http://www.facebook.com/pages/Harrison-County-Community-Foundation/155052747849474
Scholarship inquiry e-mail: heathers@hccfindiana.org

Established in 1996 in IN.
Foundation type: Community foundation.
Financial data (yr. ended 12/31/13): Assets, $146,536,171 (M); gifts received, $11,189,787; expenditures, $5,298,850; giving activities include $4,660,063 for grants.
Purpose and activities: The foundation was established for the receipt of donations and distribution of income from permanent endowments for the philanthropic purposes of Harrison County, IN. Giving primarily for arts and culture, human services, recreation, government, health and safety, historical preservation, community projects, education and environment.
Fields of interest: Historic preservation/historical societies; Arts; Secondary school/education; Higher education; Adult education—literacy, basic skills & GED; Scholarships/financial aid; Education; Environment; Health care; Recreation; Youth development; Human services; Community/economic development; Government/public administration; Aging.
Type of support: General/operating support; Continuing support; Management development/capacity building; Capital campaigns; Building/renovation; Equipment; Land acquisition; Emergency funds; Program development; Conferences/seminars; Publication; Seed money; Curriculum development; Research; Consulting services; Program evaluation; Employee-related scholarships; Scholarships—to individuals; Matching/challenge support.
Limitations: Applications accepted. Giving limited to Harrison County, IN. No support for religious organizations for the purpose of furthering their religion. **No grants to individuals (except for scholarships), or for reimbursement for previously purchased items or previously incurred expenses, or to purchase souvenirs or other personal items or real estate that has not been identified and appraised.**
Publications: Application guidelines; Annual report; Financial statement; Grants list; Informational brochure; Multi-year report; Newsletter; Program policy statement (including application guidelines).
Application information: Visit foundation web site for application forms and guidelines. All applicants are strongly encouraged to attend formal training sessions as announced, typically in May and Nov. Application form required.
Initial approach: See web site
Deadline(s): Jan. 15 and July 15
Board meeting date(s): Monthly, first Mon.
Final notification: Mar. 15 and Sept. 15
Officers and Directors:* Jason Copperwaite,* Chair.; Heather Clunie,* Vice-Chair.; Steve A. Gilliland, C.E.O. and Pres.; Scott Berkley,* Secy.-Treas.; Paul Beckort; Kevin Burch; Chad Coffman; Scott Estes; Cheryl Fisher; Jim Isbell; Phyllis J. Krush; Barbara Middleton; Shirley Raymond; joe Shireman; Glenn Walker; Carolyn Wallace.
Number of staff: 5 full-time professional; 1 full-time support.
EIN: 351986569
Other changes: At the close of 2013, the grantmaker paid grants of $4,660,063, a 75.3% increase over the 2012 disbursements, $2,658,641.

1156
The Health Foundation of Greater Indianapolis, Inc.
429 E. Vermont St., Ste. 400
Indianapolis, IN **46202-3732** (317) 630-1805
Contact: Betty H. Wilson, C.E.O. and Pres.
FAX: (317) 630-1806; E-mail: betty@thfgi.org; **Additional e-mail: info@thfgi.org**; Main URL: http://www.thfgi.org

Established as a private foundation in 1985 in IN; converted from an HMO, Metro Health.
Donors: Deborah Simon; James Spain; Wm. Kingston; David Suess; Betty H. Wilson; Mary D. Richardson; Steven Reeves; AIDSERVE Indiana; Anthem, Inc.; Broadway Cares; Cooke Investment Group; Community Hospitals of Indiana; Indiana Thrift for AIDS; Endagered Species Chocolate; The National Bank of Indianapolis; National City Bank; Efromyson Fund; Central Indiana Community Foundation; Christel DeHaan Family Foundation; Joseph F. Miller Foundation; Indiana State Dept. of Health; Marion County Health Department; Indy Pride; St. Francis Hospital; The Indianapolis Foundation; Wishard Hospital; Health and Hospital Corp.; Samerian Foundation; Baker and Daniels, LLP; Bose McKinney, Attorneys; Bingham McHale, LLP; Back Home Again Foundation; Financial Partners.
Foundation type: Independent foundation.
Financial data (yr. ended 12/31/12): Assets, $21,035,160 (M); gifts received, $656,982; expenditures, $2,717,294; qualifying distributions, $2,314,457; giving activities include $1,401,868 for 52 grants (high: $300,000; low: $1,000).
Purpose and activities: Primary areas of focus are adolescent health, including childhood obesity and school-based health clinics, and HIV/AIDS education and services. Grants will be made to neighborhood-based service centers such as neighborhood health centers, multi-service centers, churches, and other nonprofit agencies and organizations.
Fields of interest: Health care; AIDS; Nutrition; Human services; Children/youth, services; Minorities; African Americans/Blacks; Hispanics/Latinos; Women; AIDS, people with; Economically disadvantaged.
Type of support: Program evaluation; Management development/capacity building; Consulting services; General/operating support; Continuing support; Equipment; Program development; Conferences/seminars; Seed money; Technical assistance.
Limitations: Applications not accepted. Giving limited to Marion County, IN and the seven contiguous counties. No support for sectarian or religious purposes. No grants to individuals, or for advertising, event tickets, research, payment of financial deficit, production and design of educational materials that are currently available for purchase, endowments, or short- or long- term loans.
Publications: Grants list; Informational brochure; Occasional report.
Application information: Unsolicited requests for funds not accepted.
Board meeting date(s): 2nd Wed. of Jan., Mar., May, July, Sept. and Nov.
Officers and Directors:* David Suess,* Chair.; Anne Belcher,* Vice-Chair.; Betty H. Wilson, C.E.O. and Pres.; **Teresa Craig, C.P.A.*, Secy.; David Kelleher,* Treas.; Michael Carter**; John Hall; Kenneth Hull; Monica Medina; Robert D. Robinson, M.D.; James Trulock.
Number of staff: 3 full-time professional; 2 full-time support.
EIN: 356203550
Other changes: David Suess has replaced Dwayne Isaacs as Chair. Anne Belcher has replaced Moncia Medina as Vice-Chair. Teresa Craig, C.P.A. has replaced David Suess as Secy. David Kelleher has replaced Kenneth Hill as Treas.
Lawrence M. Ryan and Beverly Swinney are no longer directors.
The grantmaker no longer publishes application guidelines.

1157
Hendricks County Community Foundation
(formerly The White Lick Heritage Community Foundation, Inc.)
6319 E. U.S. Hwy. 36, Ste. 211
Avon, IN 46123 (317) 268-6240
***Contact:* William A. Rhodehamel, Exec. Dir.**
FAX: (317) 268-6164;
E-mail: info@hendrickscountycf.org; Additional e-mail: william@hendrickscountycf.org; Main URL: http://www.hendrickscountycf.org/
Alternate URL: http://www.HCGives.orgs
E-Newsletter: http://www.hendrickscountycf.org/signup/
Facebook: http://facebook.com/pages/Hendricks-County-Community-Foundation/103732686862
Scholarship inquiry e-mail:
eric@hendrickscountycf.org

Established in 1996 in IN.
Foundation type: Community foundation.
Financial data (yr. ended 12/31/12): Assets, $8,463,511 (M); gifts received, $589,555; expenditures, $1,136,373; giving activities include $501,114 for 12+ grants (high: $50,000), and $149,235 for 337 grants to individuals.
Purpose and activities: The foundation is a vehicle for people of all means to make a difference in the Hendricks County, IN, community. The foundation seeks to: 1) professionally manage and distribute revenues from charitable contributions and bequests in a manner consistent with the donor's specific or general interests; 2) maintain and enhance the educational, social, cultural, health and civic resources of the community through support of appropriate community organizations; and 3) provide philanthropic leadership and promote efforts to improve the quality of life in the community.
Fields of interest: Arts; Education; Environment; Health care; Youth development; Human services; Community/economic development.
Type of support: Continuing support; Building/renovation; Equipment; Land acquisition; Emergency funds; Program development; Seed money; Curriculum development; Research; Grants to individuals; Scholarships—to individuals; Matching/challenge support.
Limitations: Applications accepted. Giving limited to Hendricks County, IN. **No support for projects aimed at promoting a particular religion or construction projects for religious institutions. No grants to individuals (except for scholarships), bands, sports teams or other groups without a philanthropic project, annual appeals, galas, or membership contributions, fundraising events, post-event, after-the-fact situations or debt retirement, or medical, scientific or academic research.**

Publications: Annual report; Financial statement; Informational brochure; Newsletter.
Application information: Visit foundation web site for application guidelines. Application form not required.
Initial approach: E-mail grant application
Copies of proposal: 1
Deadline(s): Mar. 4 for Opportunity Fund grants
Board meeting date(s): Monthly
Officers and Board Members:* Judy Wyeth,* Pres.; Rhonda Wiles,* V.P.; Jim Hall,* Secy.; Carrie Hanni,* Treas.; William A. Rhodehamel, Exec. Dir.; David Durell; Steve Eichenberger; Janie Hardin; Matt Howrey; Terri McCoy; Alice McColgin; Larry Paynter; Teresa Ray; Melaney Sargent; Marland Villanueva; Dan Whipple; Dan Young.
Number of staff: 1 part-time professional; 2 part-time support.
EIN: 351878973

1158
Henry County Community Foundation, Inc.
700 S. Memorial Dr.
P.O. Box 6006
New Castle, IN 47362-6006 (765) 529-2235
Contact: Beverly Matthews, Pres.
FAX: (765) 529-2284;
E-mail: info@henrycountycf.org; Additional e-mail: beverly@henrycountycf.org; Main URL: http://www.henrycountycf.org
E-Newsletter: http://www.henrycountycf.org/index.php?src=forms&ref=enews
Facebook: http://www.facebook.com/pages/Henry-Community-Foundation/32495688002

Established in 1985 in IN.
Foundation type: Community foundation.
Financial data (yr. ended 12/31/12): Assets, $30,177,807 (M); gifts received, $725,156; expenditures, $2,094,134; giving activities include $1,081,793 for 21+ grants (high: $600,000), and $181,229 for 197 grants to individuals.
Purpose and activities: The mission of the foundation is to help where the needs are greatest, and the benefits to the community and its citizens are most substantial. The foundation seeks to provide public-spirited donors a vehicle for using their gifts in the best possible way now and in the future, and to provide stewardship for those gifts.
Fields of interest: Arts; Education; Health care; Mental health/crisis services; Recreation; Children/youth, services; Developmentally disabled, centers & services; Human services; Community/economic development; Government/public administration; Infants/toddlers; Children/youth; Disabilities, people with; Physically disabled; Women; Men; Economically disadvantaged; Homeless.
Type of support: Technical assistance; Continuing support; Capital campaigns; Building/renovation; Equipment; Endowments; Emergency funds; Program development; Conferences/seminars; Publication; Seed money; Scholarship funds; Research; Consulting services; Exchange programs; Matching/challenge support.
Limitations: Applications accepted. Giving limited to Henry County, IN. No support for sectarian religious purposes. No grants to individuals (except for scholarships), or for endowments or operating costs including salaries.
Publications: Application guidelines; Annual report; Financial statement; Grants list; Informational brochure (including application guidelines); Newsletter.
Application information: Visit foundation web site for grant application workshop dates, application forms and additional guidelines. Application form not required.
Initial approach: Attend Spring or Fall Grant Workshop
Copies of proposal: 15
Deadline(s): Feb. 28 and Aug. 29
Board meeting date(s): Monthly
Final notification: Within 30 days
Officers and Directors:* Susan Falck Neal,* Chair.; Dick Armstrong,* 1st Vice-Chair.; **Duke Hamm,* 2nd Vice-Chair.; Beverly Matthews, Pres. and Exec. Dir.; Debi Ware,* Treas.**; Herb Bunch, Dir., Emeritus; Danny Danielson, Dir., Emeritus; Patty Danielson, Dir., Emeritus; Morris Edwards, Dir., Emeritus; **Judy Melton, Dir., Emeritus**; Dick Myers, Dir., Emeritus; Rex Slick, Dir., Emeritus; Mike Broyles; Jeff Galyen; Soni Jones; Steve Pfenninger; Jim Ray; Steve Weidert; and 5 additional Directors.
Number of staff: 3 full-time professional; 1 full-time support; 1 part-time support.
EIN: 311170412
Other changes: Susan Falck Neal has replaced Jeff Smiley as Chair. Duke Hamm has replaced Susan Falck Neal as 2nd Vice-Chair. Beverly Matthews has replaced Jerry Schaeffer as Exec. Dir. Debi Ware has replaced David McCord as Treas. Nicole Broyles, Greg L. Crider, Roger Dickinson, Duke Hamm, and Debi Ware are no longer directors.

1159
Hoover Family Foundation
860 E. 86th St., Ste. 5
Indianapolis, IN 46240-6860 (317) 815-9553
***Contact:* David C. Hoover, Pres., Indianapolis, IN; Glen H. Friedman, Exec. Dir, Portland, OR**
FAX: (317) 815-9663; **OR address: P.O. Box 551, West Linn, OR 97068, Attn: Glen Friedman, Exec. Dir., Oregon, tel.: (503) 699-1363**; Main URL: http://www.gosw.org/hff/

Established in 1992 in IN.
Donors: James E. Hoover; Katherine C. Hoover†; Mildred M. Hoover†.
Foundation type: Independent foundation.
Financial data (yr. ended 06/30/13): Assets, $13,714,303 (M); expenditures, $1,214,943; qualifying distributions, $1,163,829; giving activities include $895,172 for 84 grants (high: $350,000; low: $2,000).
Purpose and activities: Giving primarily for human services and promoting self-sufficiency.
Fields of interest: Education; Human services; Economically disadvantaged.
Limitations: Applications accepted. Giving primarily in Indianapolis, IN, and Portland, OR. No support for religious or sectarian organizations. No grants to individuals, or for operating budgets, continuous support, capital campaigns, event (or post event) funding, multi-year funding, college scholarships, medical research, private foundations or endowment funds, or for long term funding.
Publications: Application guidelines.
Application information: Only grantseekers in IN should contact the foundation's IN office, and grantseekers in the metropolitan Portland, OR, area should contact the OR office. Applications for the Indianapolis, North Webster and Syracuse, IN, area are accepted by invitation only. Unsolicited applications from these areas will not be considered. See foundation web site for specific guidelines which must be followed. Application form required.
***Initial approach:* Use format and cover sheet which is available on foundation web site**
Copies of proposal: 3
Board meeting date(s): Jan., May, and Sept.
Final notification: 3-4 months
Officers and Directors:* David C. Hoover,* Pres.; Cynthia K. Hoover,* V.P.; Glen H. Friedman, Exec. Dir., Oregon; **Anne Hoover**.
Number of staff: 2 full-time professional; 1 part-time professional.
EIN: 351873953
Other changes: David C. Hoover has replaced James E. Hoover as Pres.

1160
Jasper Foundation, Inc.
301 N. Van Rensselaer St.
P.O. Box 295
Rensselaer, IN 47978-2630 (219) 866-5899
Contact: Kristen Ziese, Exec. Dir.
FAX: (219) 866-0555; E-mail: jasper@liljasper.com; Additional e-mail: kziese@jasperfdn.org; Main URL: http://www.jasperfdn.org

Established in 1992 in IN.
Foundation type: Community foundation.
Financial data (yr. ended 12/31/12): Assets, $13,957,576 (M); gifts received, $1,528,430; expenditures, $449,059; giving activities include $248,193 for 1+ grant (high: $18,209).
Purpose and activities: The foundation seeks to assist donors in creating a source of assets to meet the ongoing and changing charitable needs and interests of the people living in all of the Jasper County communities. The foundation seeks to make philanthropic grants in response to community needs for education, arts and culture, health, social concerns, and historic preservation.
Fields of interest: Historic preservation/historical societies; Arts; Higher education; Scholarships/financial aid; Education; Environment; Hospitals (general); Health care; Recreation; Human services; Community/economic development.
Type of support: Seed money; Scholarship funds; Matching/challenge support.
Limitations: Applications accepted. Giving limited to Jasper County, IN. No support for religious purposes or for national organizations (unless the monies are to. No grants for budget deficits, endowments, annual giving campaigns, or for projects normally the responsibility of a government agency; generally no grants for travel.
Publications: Application guidelines; Annual report.
Application information: Visit foundation web site for application form and guidelines. Application form required.
Initial approach: Contact Exec. Dir. before submitting application
***Copies of proposal:* 6**
***Deadline(s):* Apr. 1 and Oct. 1**
Officers and Directors:* Dr. Kathy Parkison,* Pres.; Stephen J. Kinsell,* V.P.; Dawn Kearney,* Secy.; David F. Schrum,* Treas.; Kristen Ziese, Exec. Dir.; Norman P. Chappell; Russell Collins; Hubert Doughty; Dr. Jack Drone; Brian Egan; Ashley Hayworth-Hopp; Craig Hooker; Calvin Ilingworth; Ron Jordan; Gene Lehman; Todd Sammons; Patty Stringfellow; John Tillema; Gina Van Baren.
EIN: 351842404

1161
Jasteka Foundation
266 America Pl.
Jeffersonville, IN 47130-4286 (502) 454-9013
Contact: Debbie Smith

Established in 1999 in KY.

Donor: James S. Karp.
Foundation type: Independent foundation.
Financial data (yr. ended 10/31/13): Assets, $6,765,096 (M); gifts received, $1,000,000; expenditures, $419,617; qualifying distributions, $399,000; giving activities include $399,000 for 13 grants (high: $100,000; low: $500).
Fields of interest: Arts; Education; Jewish federated giving programs.
Type of support: General/operating support.
Limitations: Applications accepted. Giving primarily in FL and KY.
Application information: Application form not required.
Initial approach: **Proposal**
Deadline(s): None
Officers: James S. Karp, Chair.; Irene J. Karp, Secy.-Treas.
EIN: 611356020

1162
Jennings County Community Foundation, Inc.
111 N. State St.
North Vernon, IN 47265 (812) 346-5553
***Contact:* Barbara Shaw, Exec. Dir.**
FAX: (812) 352-4061;
E-mail: jccf@jenningsfoundation.net; Main URL: http://www.jenningsfoundation.net
Facebook: https://www.facebook.com/pages/Jennings-County-Community-Foundation/144210068953807?ref=ts

Established in 1994 in IN.
Foundation type: Community foundation.
Financial data (yr. ended 12/31/12): Assets, $4,252,446 (M); gifts received, $210,019; expenditures, $373,768; giving activities include $139,810 for 3+ grants (high: $32,094), and $84,157 for 49 grants to individuals.
Purpose and activities: The foundation seeks to serve philanthropic and charitable needs in Jennings County, IN, by offering endowment services, grantmaking, scholarships, donor estate and planned gift services to individuals and qualified organizations serving the community.
Fields of interest: Arts; Education; Environment; Health care; Human services; Community/economic development.
Type of support: Building/renovation; Equipment; Endowments; Program development; Curriculum development; Scholarship funds; Consulting services; Program-related investments/loans; Employee-related scholarships; In-kind gifts; Matching/challenge support.
Limitations: Applications accepted. Giving primarily in Jennings County, IN. No grants to individuals (except for scholarships).
Publications: Application guidelines; Annual report; Financial statement; Informational brochure; Newsletter.
Application information: Visit the foundation's web site for application form, guidelines and specific deadline dates. Application form required.
Initial approach: Submit application and attachments
Copies of proposal: 10
Deadline(s): Mar. and Sept.
Board meeting date(s): Monthly
Officers and Board Members:* Darlene Bradshaw,* Pres.; Linda Erler,* V.P.; Brenda Habenicht,* Secy.; Carolyn Frey,* Treas.; Barb Shaw, Exec. Dir.; **Bill Black**; Dr. Bill Burnett; Bill Dillon; Teri Doran; Jennifer Franklin; Greg Hicks; Kathryn Johnson; Brian Sawyer; Dixie Tempest; Sandy Vance; Bob Weeks.
Number of staff: 1 full-time professional; 2 part-time support.
EIN: 351922885
Other changes: Carolyn Frey is no longer a board member.

1163
Johnson County Community Foundation, Inc.
(formerly Greater Johnson County Community Foundation)
398 S. Main St.
P.O. Box 217
Franklin, IN 46131 (317) 738-2213
Contact: Gail Richards, C.E.O.; For grants and scholarships: Stephanie Walls, Prog. Assoc., Grants and Scholarships
FAX: (317) 738-9113; E-mail: frontdesk@jccf.org; Grant and scholarship inquiries e-mail: stephaniew@jccf.org; Main URL: http://www.jccf.org
Facebook: http://www.facebook.com/jccfindiana
Twitter: https://twitter.com/JCCFIndiana
YouTube: http://www.youtube.com/jccfindiana

Established in 1991 in IN.
Foundation type: Community foundation.
Financial data (yr. ended 12/31/12): Assets, $17,410,671 (M); gifts received, $891,372; expenditures, $1,094,601; giving activities include $383,551 for 8+ grants (high: $32,350), and $164,493 for 130 grants to individuals.
Purpose and activities: The foundation exists to encourage local philanthropy and to improve the quality of life in the Johnson County community through leadership and grant support to local nonprofit organizations. Scholarships are awarded to high school seniors from specific high schools primarily in Johnson County, IN, and/or students enrolled at specific IN colleges or universities.
Fields of interest: Arts; Higher education; Education; Environment; Health care; Agriculture; Disasters, preparedness/services; Human services; Community/economic development.
Type of support: General/operating support; Management development/capacity building; Building/renovation; Equipment; Emergency funds; Program development; Seed money; Scholarship funds; Technical assistance; Consulting services; Program evaluation; Scholarships—to individuals; Matching/challenge support.
Limitations: Applications accepted. Giving limited to Johnson County, IN, and vicinity. No support for sectarian or religious programs, or for medical research. No grants to individuals (except for scholarships), or for endowments, conferences, travel, publications or media projects, annual campaigns, capital campaigns, ongoing operating budgets, fundraising events, deficit funding, equipment, construction and renovation, land acquisition, public school services required by state law, repeat funding supported through prior grants, or athletic leagues or teams.
Publications: Application guidelines; Annual report (including application guidelines); Grants list; Informational brochure (including application guidelines); Newsletter.
Application information: Visit foundation web site for application guidelines. If the grant request meets funding guidelines, the foundation will invite the organization to submit a full application. Application form required.
Initial approach: E-mail letter of inquiry
Copies of proposal: 1
***Deadline(s):* Apr. 4 and Aug. 1 for letter of inquiry; Apr. 26 and Aug. 30 for full grant application**
Board meeting date(s): 6 times per year
Final notification: Within 30-60 days
Officers and Directors:* Andy Walker,* Chair.; Gail Richards, C.E.O. and Pres.; Kim Minton, V.P., Devel.; Erin Smith,* Secy.; Steve Sonntag,* Treas.; John Shell,* Chair.-Elect; Dean Abplanalp; Benji Betts; Brian V. Biehn; Susie Bixler; Chris Cosner; Don Cummings; Virginia Davis; Ed Deiwert; Bill Kiesel; Amy Kelsay; Courtney Krudy; Seth Perigo; Bob Romack; Loren Snyder; Joe Waltermann; Richard Wertz; Brooke Worland.
Number of staff: 3 full-time professional.
EIN: 351797437
Other changes: Keith Jewell, Steve Spencer, and Pat Van Valer are no longer directors.

1164
Ove W. Jorgensen Foundation Inc.
c/o Wells Fargo Bank Indiana, N.A.
300 N. Meridian St., Ste. 1600
Indianapolis, IN 46204-1751

Established in 1998 in IN.
Donor: Ove W. Jorgensen.
Foundation type: Independent foundation.
Financial data (yr. ended 01/31/13): Assets, $3,967,794 (M); expenditures, $134,618; qualifying distributions, $98,634; giving activities include $97,500 for 9 grants (high: $25,000; low: $2,500).
Fields of interest: Arts; Higher education; Education; Environment; Youth development, business; YM/YWCAs & YM/YWHAs; United Ways and Federated Giving Programs.
Type of support: General/operating support.
Limitations: Applications not accepted. Giving primarily in Fort Wayne, IN. No grants to individuals.
Application information: Contributes only to pre-selected organizations.
Officer: Diane Oberlin, Mgr.
Directors: Jay O. Jorgensen; Winifred M. Jorgensen.
Trustee: Wells Fargo Bank Indiana, N.A.
EIN: 352050475

1165
The Georgina Joshi Foundation Inc
215 S. Hawthorne Dr.
South Bend, IN 46617-3440
Contact: Yatish J. Joshi, Chair.
Main URL: http://www.thegeorginajoshifoundation.org/
E-Newsletter: http://www.thegeorginajoshifoundation.org/guestbook/

Established in 2007 in IN.
Donors: Yatish J. Joshi; USB Financial Services; GTA Containers Inc.
Foundation type: Independent foundation.
Financial data (yr. ended 12/31/12): Assets, $0 (M); gifts received, $2,341,683; expenditures, $2,358,630; qualifying distributions, $2,306,194; giving activities include $2,249,349 for 9 grants (high: $1,200,000; low: $700).
Purpose and activities: Giving primarily for educational and career development opportunities for young musicians and singers, and to encourage and support the public performance of music.
Fields of interest: Performing arts, music; Arts; Education.
Type of support: Scholarships—to individuals.

Limitations: Applications accepted. Giving primarily in IN.
Application information: Application form not required.
Initial approach: Proposal
Deadline(s): None
Officers and Directors:* Yatish J. Joshi,* Chair.; Glenda G. Lamont,* Treas.; Avatar A. Joshi; Tenzing H. Joshi.
EIN: 208791238
Other changes: At the close of 2012, the grantmaker paid grants of $2,249,349, a 120.4% increase over the 2011 disbursements, $1,020,500.

1166
Kendrick Foundation, Inc.

(formerly Kendrick Memorial Hospital, Inc.)
c/o The Academy Bldg.
250 N. Monroe St.
Mooresville, IN 46158-1551 (317) 831-1232
FAX: (317) 831-2854;
E-mail: info@kendrickfoundation.org; **Toll free tel.: (855) 280-3095 (tel. is in c/o the Community Foundation of Morgan County, Inc.)**; Main URL: http://www.kendrickfoundation.org

Established in 2001 in IN from proceeds of the sale of Kendrick Memorial Hospital.
Foundation type: Independent foundation.
Financial data (yr. ended 06/30/13): Assets, $29,315,922 (M); expenditures, $1,852,868; qualifying distributions, $1,708,119; giving activities include $1,212,270 for 36 grants (high: $200,000; low: $1,500), and $378,113 for 43 grants to individuals (high: $15,000; low: $1,144).
Purpose and activities: The foundation supports healthcare programs in Morgan County, IN.
Fields of interest: Medical school/education; Health care.
Type of support: Land acquisition; Equipment; Scholarships—to individuals.
Limitations: Applications accepted. Giving limited to Morgan County, IN.
Publications: Application guidelines; Annual report; Financial statement.
Application information: Full proposals for grants will not be accepted. Only those who have their Letters of Intent approved may submit a full proposal. Scholarship application form available on foundation web site. Letters of Intent are accessible on foundation web site for a limited amount of time during the opening of the grant cycle. Paper applications are not accepted. Application form required.
Initial approach: **Letter of intent for grants via foundation web site; fill out application form for scholarships**
Copies of proposal: 6
Deadline(s): See foundation web site for current deadlines
Board meeting date(s): Quarterly
Final notification: 60 days
Officer: Shelley D. Voelz, Chair. and Pres.; **Mae Cooper, Secy.-Treas.**
Directors: Alicia Boyd; **Lynn Gordon**; **Greg McKelfresh**; R. Barry Melbert, M.D.
EIN: 351124905
Other changes: Mae Cooper is now Secy.-Treas. John D. Ehrhart is no longer a director.

1167
Koch Foundation, Inc.

(formerly George Koch Sons Foundation, Inc.)
10 S. 11th Ave.
Evansville, IN 47744-0001
Contact: Jennifer K. Slade, Secy.
***Main URL:* http://www.kochenterprises.com/foundation**

Incorporated in 1945 in IN.
Donors: George Koch Sons, Inc.; George Koch Sons, LLC; Gibbs Die Casting Corp.; Koch Enterprises, Inc.
Foundation type: Company-sponsored foundation.
Financial data (yr. ended 12/31/13): Assets, $29,722,060 (M); gifts received, $902,000; expenditures, $1,085,457; qualifying distributions, $1,000,699; giving activities include $1,000,546 for 112 grants (high: $202,500; low: $50).
Purpose and activities: The foundation supports organizations involved with arts and culture, education, health, human services, civic affairs, and religion. Special emphasis is directed toward organizations with which employees of Koch Enterprises are involved.
Fields of interest: Arts; Education; Health care; Human services; Public affairs; Religion.
Type of support: Annual campaigns; Capital campaigns; Building/renovation; Program development; Research; Employee volunteer services; Sponsorships; Employee matching gifts; Employee-related scholarships; Matching/challenge support.
Limitations: Applications accepted. Giving limited to IN, KY, MO, Elko, NV, Schertz, TX, Beckley, WV, and Casper, WY, with emphasis on the Evansville and the Vanderburgh County, IN, area. No grants to individuals (except for employee-related scholarships).
Publications: Application guidelines.
Application information: Application form not required.
Initial approach: Proposal
Copies of proposal: 1
Deadline(s): None
Final notification: 3 months
Officers and Directors:* Robert L. Koch II,* Pres.; Kevin R. Koch, V.P.; James H. Muehlbauer,* V.P.; Jennifer K. Slade, Secy.; Susan E. Parsons, Treas.; Steve A. Church; Josh Gilberg; David M. Koch; Glen J. Muehlbauer; Brad J. Muehlbauer; Christopher L. Slade.
Number of staff: 2 part-time support.
EIN: 356023372

1168
Kosciusko 21st Century Foundation, Inc.

(also known as K21 Health Foundation)
2170 N. Pointe Dr.
Warsaw, IN 46581-1810 (574) 269-5188
FAX: (574) 269-5193;
E-mail: rhaddad@k21foundation.org; Mailing address: c/o Richard Haddad, C.E.O. and Pres., P.O. Box 1810, Warsaw, IN 46581-1810; Main URL: http://www.k21foundation.org
Facebook: http://www.facebook.com/pages/K21-Health-Foundation/107302855974304
Grants List: http://www.k21foundation.org/what-weve-done/index.cfm

Established in 1999 in IN from the proceeds of the sale of Kosciusko Community Hospital to Quorum Health Group, Inc.
Foundation type: Independent foundation.
Financial data (yr. ended 12/31/12): Assets, $64,068,199 (M); gifts received, $164,918; expenditures, $5,049,765; qualifying distributions, $4,620,004; giving activities include $4,620,004 for 40 grants (high: $2,000,000; low: $920), and $4,457,467 for 2 loans/program-related investments (high: $4,348,792; low: $108,675).
Purpose and activities: The foundation exists for the benefit of Kosciusko County, Indiana citizens to ensure healthcare services are provided, and to advance prevention and healthy lifestyles. This will be accomplished by identifying health needs in our community and maintaining an endowment so funding is available, through investments and grants, for those needs.
Fields of interest: Medical care, community health systems; Medical care, rehabilitation; Physical therapy; Health care, EMS; Pharmacy/prescriptions; Health care; Mental health/crisis services; Cancer; Crime/violence prevention, domestic violence; Disasters, preparedness/services; Residential/custodial care, hospices.
Type of support: Capital campaigns; Building/renovation; Equipment; Program development; Scholarship funds; Matching/challenge support.
Limitations: Applications accepted. Giving primarily in Kosciusko County, IN.
Publications: Application guidelines; Annual report; Grants list; Newsletter.
Application information: Refer to: http://www.kcfoundation.org/seekingfunds/documents/K21FoundationMedicalTraditional.pdf for scholarship guidelines. Application form required.
***Initial approach:* Use online application form and/or online program to see if the applicant qualifies. See foundation web site for details**
Copies of proposal: 1
Deadline(s): Feb. 1, May 1, Aug. 1, and Nov. 1 for grants
Board meeting date(s): Quarterly
Final notification: 2 months
Officers and Directors:* Dr. Jennifer Lucht, Chair.; Jim Tinkey, Vice-Chair.; Richard A. Haddad,* C.E.O. and Pres.; Shari Boyle, Secy.; Lee Heyde,* Treas.; Karen Boling; David C. Cates; Dr. David Dick; Becky Doll; Dr. Michael E. Grill; Dr. David Haines; Officer Joe Hawn; Rosy Jansma; Mr. Dana L. Krull; Max Mock; Jon Sroufe; Scott Tucker; Valerie Warner.
Number of staff: 2 full-time professional; 1 full-time support; 1 part-time support.
EIN: 351187105

1169
Charles W. Kuhne Foundation Trust

c/o Wells Fargo Bank N.A., MAC 8622-031
P.O. Box 960
Fort Wayne, IN 46801-6632
***Application address:* c/o Wells Fargo Bank, Attn.: Jennifer King, 111 E. Wayne St., Fort Wayne, IN 46802, tel.: (260) 461-6458, email: jennifer.i.king@wellsfargo.com**

Established in IN during the 1950's.
Foundation type: Independent foundation.
Financial data (yr. ended 07/31/13): Assets, $6,512,226 (M); expenditures, $387,906; qualifying distributions, $359,434; giving activities include $306,984 for 39 grants (high: $25,000; low: $2,009).
Purpose and activities: Giving primarily for education, the arts, particularly theater and public television, community development, and social services.
Fields of interest: Museums (history); Arts; Higher education; Education; Food banks; Human services; YM/YWCAs & YM/YWHAs; Children/youth, services; Community/economic development.
Type of support: General/operating support; Annual campaigns; Capital campaigns; Building/renovation; Equipment; Program development; Matching/challenge support.

Limitations: Applications accepted. Giving limited to Allen County, IN. No grants to individuals, or for scholarships, exhibitions or seminars.
Application information: Application form not required.
Initial approach: Letter
Copies of proposal: 4
Deadline(s): None
Board meeting date(s): Quarterly
Trustee: Wells Fargo Bank, N.A.
EIN: 356011137

1170
LaGrange County Community Foundation, Inc.

109 E. Central Ave., Ste. 3
LaGrange, IN 46761-2301 (260) 463-4363
***Contact:* Laura Lemings, Exec. Dir.; For grants: Laney Kratz, Prog. Off.**
FAX: (260) 463-4856; E-mail: lccf@lccf.net; Additional e-mail: llemings@lccf.net; Main URL: http://www.lccf.net

Established in 1991 in IN.
Foundation type: Community foundation.
Financial data (yr. ended 12/31/12): Assets, $10,877,533 (M); gifts received, $698,656; expenditures, $507,725; giving activities include $223,995 for grants.
Purpose and activities: The foundation seeks to encourage philanthropy and charitable giving throughout LaGrange County, IN.
Fields of interest: Arts; Higher education; Education; Environment; Youth development; Children/youth, services; Human services; Community/economic development.
Type of support: General/operating support; Management development/capacity building; Building/renovation; Equipment; Land acquisition; Endowments; Emergency funds; Program development; Conferences/seminars; Seed money; Scholarship funds; Technical assistance; Consulting services; Program evaluation; Scholarships—to individuals; In-kind gifts; Matching/challenge support.
Limitations: Applications accepted. Giving limited to LaGrange County, IN.
Publications: Annual report; Financial statement; Grants list; Informational brochure; Newsletter; Occasional report.
Application information: Visit foundation web site for updates.
Initial approach: Mail or hand-deliver grant proposal
Copies of proposal: 8
Deadline(s): Varies
Board meeting date(s): 4th Tues. of each month
Final notification: 30 - 45 days
Officers and Directors:* Paul Johnston,* Pres.; Steven Scott Welty,* V.P.; Jeff Wible,* Secy.; Dr. Rhonda Sharp,* Treas.; Laura Lemings, Exec. Dir.; Mahlon Bontrager; Dr. John Egli; Vickie Guyas; Jama Keaffaber; Sue Keenan; Crystal Leu; **Gene Mory**; Jayne Perkins; Dalonda Young.
Number of staff: 2 full-time professional; 2 part-time professional; 1 full-time support.
EIN: 351834679

1171
Legacy Foundation, Inc.

1000 E. 80th Pl.
Merrillville, IN 46410 (219) 736-1880
FAX: (219) 736-1940; E-mail: legacy@legacyfdn.org; Main URL: http://www.legacyfdn.org
E-Newsletter: http://
www.legacyfoundationlakeco.org/emailsignup.html
Facebook: http://www.facebook.com/pages/
Merrillville-IN/Legacy-Foundation/314525729630
Flickr: http://www.flickr.com/photos/legacyfdn/
sets/
Twitter: http://twitter.com/legacyfdn

Established in 1992 in IN.
Foundation type: Community foundation.
Financial data (yr. ended 06/30/13): Assets, $46,819,671 (M); gifts received, $2,116,606; expenditures, $2,791,918; giving activities include $1,796,037 for 87+ grants (high: $40,000), and $157,023 for 152 grants to individuals.
Purpose and activities: The mission of the foundation is to enhance the quality of life for all citizens of Lake County, IN, now and for generations to come. The mission is achieved by building a community endowment, addressing needs through grantmaking, and by providing leadership on key community issues.
Fields of interest: Arts; Education; Environment; Public health; Health care; Youth, services; Human services; Community development, neighborhood development; Community/economic development; Philanthropy/voluntarism; Public affairs.
Type of support: Building/renovation; Equipment; Program development; Seed money; Scholarship funds; Technical assistance; Scholarships—to individuals; Matching/challenge support.
Limitations: Applications accepted. Giving primarily in Lake County, IN. No support for sectarian religious programs or basic municipal or educational functions and services. No grants to individuals (except through designated scholarship funds), or for operating budgets, endowment funds, debt reduction, continuing support, general operating expenses (except for start up), annual campaigns, fundraising events, or travel; no multi-year grants or scholarly research grants.
Publications: Application guidelines; Annual report; Grants list; Informational brochure; Newsletter.
Application information: Visit foundation Web site for application forms and guidelines. If application deadline falls on a non-business day, proposals must be received on the last business day prior to the deadline. Application form required.
Initial approach: Contact foundation
Copies of proposal: 1
Deadline(s): Mar. 1, May 1, Sept. 1, and Nov. 1
Board meeting date(s): 1st Tues. of Feb., Apr., June, Aug., Oct., and Dec.
Final notification: Approx. 6 weeks
Officers and Directors:* Nancy L. Clifford,* Chair.; Robert Johnson,* Vice-Chair.; Carolyn Saxton,* Pres.; Sandra Snearly-Vosberg,* Treas.; Dave Austgen; Benjamin Bochnowski; Margot Clark; Danette Garza; Matthew Glaros; Gregory Gordon; Amy Han, Ph.D.; J. Brian Hittinger; Debara Howe; Jill Jones; Tom Keilman; Shar Miller; Janet Moran; Dana Rifai; Marti Rivas-Ramos; Dave Ryan; Michael Suggs; Alexis Vazquez-Dedelow; Chris White.
Number of staff: 4 full-time professional; 1 part-time professional; 1 full-time support.
EIN: 351872803
Other changes: Nancy L. Clifford has replaced Robert Nickovich as Chair. Leigh Morris has replaced Harry J. Vande as C.E.O. and Pres. Tina Rongers has replaced Lara Lawinski as V.P.
Howard Cohen is no longer Secy. Amy Han, J. Brian Hittinger, and Robert Nickovich are no longer directors.

1172
Judd Leighton Foundation, Inc.

211 W. Washington Ave., Ste. 2400
South Bend, IN 46601-1708 (574) 232-5970
Contact: Charles F. Nelson, Exec. Dir.
E-mail: CNelson@juddleightonfoundation.org; Main URL: http://www.juddleightonfoundation.org/

Established in 2000 in IN.
Donor: Judd Leighton.
Foundation type: Independent foundation.
Financial data (yr. ended 12/31/12): Assets, $97,051,165 (M); gifts received, $1,525,500; expenditures, $5,802,021; qualifying distributions, $4,767,533; giving activities include $4,501,209 for 34 grants (high: $1,671,109; low: $350).
Purpose and activities: Giving primarily to enhance the quality of life in St. Joseph County, IN, by providing funds for health, education, and economic development.
Fields of interest: Higher education; Medical research, institute; Heart & circulatory research; Human services.
Limitations: Giving primarily in St. Joseph County, IN. No support for programs that are sectarian or religious in nature, political organizations or candidates or organizations without 501 (c) (3) designation. No grants to individuals.
Publications: Application guidelines.
Application information: Application guidelines available on foundation web site. Application form required.
Initial approach: Use online application on foundation web site
Deadline(s): By the end of the month preceding a Board Meeting month
Board meeting date(s): Mar., June, Sept., and Dec.
Officers: James F. Keenan, Pres. and Treas.; John M. Pycik, V.P. and Secy.; Charles F. Nelson, Exec. Dir.
Directors: Mary Stanfield; Donald F. Walter.
EIN: 352120550
Other changes: The grantmaker now publishes application guidelines.

1173
Ruth Lilly Philanthropic Foundation

c/o PNC Bank, N.A.
101 W. Washington St., No. 600E
Indianapolis, IN 46255-5000 (317) 267-3731
Contact: Regina Smith
FAX: (317) 267-3959; E-mail for Regina Smith: regina.smith@pnc.com

Established in 2006 in OH.
Donor: Ruth Lilly†.
Foundation type: Independent foundation.
Financial data (yr. ended 12/31/12): Assets, $154,094,161 (M); gifts received, $54,878,842; expenditures, $17,114,238; qualifying distributions, $16,611,836; giving activities include $16,311,285 for 130 grants (high: $2,876,876; low: $1,000).
Purpose and activities: Giving primarily for the arts, higher education and youth development.
Fields of interest: Arts; Higher education; Boys & girls clubs; Youth development.

Limitations: Applications not accepted. Giving fifty percent to IN charities, and fifty percent is unrestricted.
Application information: Unsolicited requests for funds not accepted.
Trustee: PNC Bank, N.A.
EIN: 347206415
Other changes: At the close of 2012, the fair market value of the grantmaker's assets was $154,094,161, a 55.9% increase over the 2011 value, $98,862,283.

1174
Lumina Foundation

P.O. Box 1806
Indianapolis, IN 46206-1806 (317) 951-5300
Contact: Juan Suarez, Sr. V.P., External Affairs; Lucia Anderson, Comms. Dir.
FAX: (317) 951-5063;
E-mail: jsuarez@luminafoundation.org; E-mail for Lucia Anderson: landerson@luminafoundation.org. Toll free: (800) 834-5756; Main URL: http://www.luminafoundation.org
E-Newsletter: http://www.luminafoundation.org/newsroom/newsletter/subscription.html
Foundation News: http://www.luminafoundation.org/category/newsroom
Grants Database: http://www.luminafoundation.org/grants/database/
iTunes: http://itunes.apple.com/podcast/lumina-foundation-for-education/id311515249
Jamie Merisotis on Twitter: http://twitter.com/jamieindy/
Knowledge Center: http://www.luminafoundation.org/publications.html
Mobile Device Downloads: http://www.luminafoundation.org/newsroom/mobile.html
Multimedia: http://www.luminafoundation.org/newsroom/multimedia.html
Podcast Feed: http://luminafoundation.libsyn.com/rss
Podcasts: http://www.luminafoundation.org/podcasts
Twitter: http://twitter.com/LuminaFound

Established in 2000.
Donors: USA Group, Inc.; SLM Holding Corp.
Foundation type: Independent foundation.
Financial data (yr. ended 12/31/12): Assets, $1,137,783,686 (M); expenditures, $75,250,651; qualifying distributions, $68,931,737; giving activities include $47,035,267 for 275 grants (high: $1,700,000; low: $150), $1,352,882 for 492 employee matching gifts, and $8,760,391 for 4 foundation-administered programs.
Purpose and activities: The foundation's primary goal is to raise the proportion of the U.S. adult population who earn college degrees to 60 percent by 2025. The foundation is dedicated to expanding access and success in education beyond high school.
Fields of interest: Higher education; Youth; Adults; Young adults; Minorities; Asians/Pacific Islanders; African Americans/Blacks; Hispanics/Latinos; Native Americans/American Indians; Immigrants/refugees.
Type of support: General/operating support; Continuing support; Management development/capacity building; Program development; Conferences/seminars; Film/video/radio; Publication; Seed money; Research; Technical assistance; Consulting services; Program evaluation; Employee matching gifts; Matching/challenge support.
Limitations: Applications accepted. Giving on a national basis. No support for P-12 education reform, discipline-specific schools of study and training or religious activities (except for activities that promote educational access and success and that serve diverse recipients without regard to their religious background); no grants that support single institutions; and no support for electioneering or lobbying activities. No grants to individuals (except for employee matching gifts), or for scholarships, fundraisers, corporate sponsorships, meetings and conferences (except for those related to a strategic initiative of the foundation), capital campaigns, or endowment funds.
Publications: Application guidelines; Financial statement; Grants list; Informational brochure (including application guidelines); Newsletter; Occasional report.
Application information: See foundation web site for LOI instructions. Only selected LOIs will receive a response. Application form required.
Initial approach: **Online letter of inquiry**
Copies of proposal: 1
Deadline(s): None
Board meeting date(s): Mar., Jun., Sept., and Nov.
Final notification: 3 to 6 months
Officers and Directors:* James C. Lintzenich,* Chair.; Jamie P. Merisotis, C.E.O. and Pres.; **J. David Maas, V.P., Finance and Investments and C.F.O.; Danette Howard, V.P., Policy and Mobilization;** Dewayne Matthews, V.P., Policy and Strategy; Samuel D. Cargile, V.P., Sr. Advisor to C.E.O.; **Kiko Suarez, V.P., Comm. and Innovation;** David A. Brown, Cont.; Holiday Hart McKiernan, Chief of Staff and Genl. Counsel; Frank D. Alvarez; Kathy Davis; Allan Hubbard; F. Joseph Loughrey; Marie V. McDemmond; J. Bonnie Newman; Laura Palmer Noone; Michael L. Smith; Belle S. Wheelan; Mark G. Yudof.
Number of staff: 27 full-time professional; 9 full-time support.
EIN: 351813228
Other changes: Gerald L. Bepko and Randolph H. Waterfield are no longer a directors. J. David Maas is now V.P., Finance and Investments and C.F.O. Holiday Hart McKiernan is now Chief of Staff and Genl. Counsel. James Applegate is no longer Sr. V.P., Prog. Devel. Juan Suarez is no longer Sr. V.P., External Affairs.

1175
Madison County Community Foundation

33 W. 10th St., Ste. 600
P.O. Box 1056
Anderson, IN 46015-1056 (765) 644-0002
Contact: Sally A. DeVoe, Exec. Dir.
FAX: (765) 644-3392; E-mail: info@madisonccf.org; Additional e-mail: sdevoe@madisonccf.org; Main URL: http://www.madisonccf.org
Facebook: https://www.facebook.com/madisonccf

Established in 1992 in IN.
Foundation type: Community foundation.
Financial data (yr. ended 12/31/11): Assets, $13,874,636 (M); gifts received, $913,484; expenditures, $1,189,387; giving activities include $663,199 for 31+ grants (high: $49,515).
Purpose and activities: The foundation seeks to enhance the quality of life of the citizens of Madison County, IN, by attracting charitable gifts, making philanthropic grants, providing responsible financial stewardship and community leadership.
Fields of interest: Arts; Education; Health care; Human services; Economic development; Public affairs.
Type of support: General/operating support; Capital campaigns; Building/renovation; Equipment; Emergency funds; Program development; Curriculum development; Scholarship funds; Scholarships—to individuals; Matching/challenge support.
Limitations: Applications accepted. Giving limited to Madison County, IN. No support for religious or sectarian activities. No grants to individuals (except for scholarships), for budget deficits, annual fund campaigns, capital debt reduction, endowments, medical, scientific, or health research, or travel; no student loans.
Publications: Annual report (including application guidelines); Informational brochure; Newsletter.
Application information: Visit foundation web site for application form and guidelines. Application form required.
Initial approach: Submit application
Copies of proposal: 8
***Deadline(s):* May 9 and Nov. 5 for General Grants; varies for others**
Board meeting date(s): 6 times a year
Final notification: Within 6 weeks
Officers and Directors:* Tom Cassidy,* Pres.; Craig Dunkin,* V.P.; Lynn Rowley,* Secy.; Tom Beeman,* Treas.; Sally A. DeVoe,* Exec. Dir.; James F. Ault; Sherri Contos; Gary Erskine; Gloria Gaither; Joe Kilmer; Rob Loose; Bob Pensec; Marcia Simmermon; Chuck Staley.
Number of staff: 1 full-time professional; 1 part-time professional; 1 full-time support.
EIN: 351859959

1176
Marshall County Community Foundation, Inc.

2701 N. Michigan St.
P.O. Box 716
Plymouth, IN 46563 (574) 935-5159
FAX: (574) 936-8040;
E-mail: info@marshallcountycf.org; Main URL: http://www.marshallcountycf.org
Facebook: https://www.facebook.com/pages/Marshall-County-Community-Foundation/218830374800800
RSS Feed: http://marshallcountycf.org/feed/

Established in 1991 in IN.
Foundation type: Community foundation.
Financial data (yr. ended 06/30/12): Assets, $25,831,909 (M); gifts received, $1,364,178; expenditures, $1,257,847; giving activities include $840,352 for 29+ grants (high: $59,102).
Purpose and activities: The foundation seeks to enhance the quality of life in Marshall County by providing funds through a grant making process for humanitarian, cultural, educational, recreational and environmental activities. The general policy of the foundation is to make grants for innovative and creative projects serving Marshall County, and to programs which are responsive to changing community needs.
Fields of interest: Arts; Secondary school/education; Higher education; Libraries (public); Scholarships/financial aid; Education; Environment; Animals/wildlife, preservation/protection; Hospitals (general); Health care; Recreation, parks/playgrounds; Recreation; Family services; Human services; Community/economic development; Government/public administration; Children/youth.
Type of support: Building/renovation; Equipment; Emergency funds; Program development; Publication; Seed money; Research; Technical assistance; Consulting services; Scholarships—to individuals; Matching/challenge support.
Limitations: Applications accepted. Giving limited to Marshall County, IN. No support for sectarian or religious purposes. No grants to individuals (except

for scholarships), or for operating expenses, long-term funding or for endowments.
Publications: Application guidelines; Annual report (including application guidelines); Financial statement; Grants list; Informational brochure (including application guidelines); Newsletter; Program policy statement.
Application information: Visit foundation web site for application form and guidelines. Application form required.
Initial approach: Submit application form and attachments
Copies of proposal: 3
Deadline(s): Feb. 3 and Aug. 1
Board meeting date(s): Jan., Mar., May, July, Sept., and Nov.
Final notification: Within 90 days
Officers and Directors:* Jerry Gates,* Chair.; Patti Kitch,* Vice-Chair.; Jayne Gibson,* V.P., Opers.; Carolyn Kline,* Secy.; Jared Weidner,* Treas.; Richard Parker,* Co-Treas.; Linda K. Yoder, Exec. Dir.; Derek Jones, Legal Counsel; Brian Baker; Don Balka; Kevin Boyer; Tim Harman; Joan Hunt; Connie Lemler; Louise Mason; Amy Middaugh; Ginny Munroe; Don Newton; Paul Nye; Michael Overmyer; John Small, Jr.; Beth Styers; Don Thompson; Barbara Winters; John Zeglis; Ron Zeltwanger; and 4 additional Directors.
Number of staff: 2 part-time professional; 1 full-time support; 2 part-time support.
EIN: 351826870
Other changes: Bruce Emerick, Verna Kay Finlay, Kurt Garner, Kevin Hickman, Jenny Beck Sheedy, Jerry Gates, Patti Kitch, Jared Weidner, Richard Parker, Carolyn Kline, and Derek Jones are no longer directors.

1177
Master Works Foundation, Inc.

2879 E. Dupont Rd.
Fort Wayne, IN 46825-1668 **(260) 487-4005**
***Contact:* Zach Lesser**

Established in 1988 in IN.
Donors: Daryle L. Doden; Matt Lesser.
Foundation type: Independent foundation.
Financial data (yr. ended 12/31/12): Assets, $314,119 (M); expenditures, $15,932; qualifying distributions, $14,506; giving activities include $1,500 for 1 grant.
Purpose and activities: Giving primarily to select Christian ministries that demonstrate a primary desire to engage in long-term Christian fellowship and relationship with the foundation apart from any financial consideration.
Fields of interest: Higher education; Theological school/education; Education; Christian agencies & churches; Protestant agencies & churches.
Type of support: Scholarship funds; Program development; Building/renovation; Capital campaigns.
Limitations: Giving primarily in Auburn, Fort Wayne, and Indianapolis, IN; some giving nationally.
Application information: Application form not required.
Deadline(s): None
Officers: Daryle L. Doden, Pres.; Brenda J. Doden, Secy.
EIN: 351752152

1178
MIBOR Foundation, Inc.

1912 N. Meridian St.
Indianapolis, IN 46202-1304 (317) 956-5255
***Contact:* Gabie Benson, Fdn. Mgr.**
E-mail: Gabiebenson@realtorfoundation.com; **Email for Gabie Benson: Gabiebenson@realtorfoundation.com**; Main URL: http://www.realtorfoundation.org
Blog: http://blog.realtorfoundation.org
Facebook: https://www.facebook.com/realtorfoundation
Flickr: https://www.flickr.com/photos/realtorfoundation
Twitter: https://twitter.com/REALTORFnd
YouTube: http://www.youtube.com/user/REALTORFoundation

Established in 1984 in IN.
Donors: Janne Steadman; MIBOR Service Corp.; Chicago Title Insurance Company; Wertern Division Of Mibor; Mick Scheetz; Kristie Smith; Williams Keller; National Bank Of Indianapolis; Steve Sullivan; United Consulting; Indiana Association Of Realtors; Sentrilock,LLC.
Foundation type: Public charity.
Financial data (yr. ended 12/31/11): Assets, $684,091 (M); gifts received, $334,163; expenditures, $478,324; giving activities include $297,000 for 20 grants (high: $167,000; low: $1,500).
Purpose and activities: Giving to organizations in central Indiana who serve and house the homeless.
Fields of interest: Housing/shelter, homeless.
Type of support: General/operating support.
Limitations: Applications accepted. Giving primarily in Indianapolis, IN. No grants to individuals.
Application information: Application guidelines available on foundation web site. Application form required.
Officers: Joyce Scotten, Pres.; Gail Watts, Secy.
Directors: Jeri Ballantine; Diane Bussell; Bill Hacker; Kaye Hirt-Eggleston; Don Hunter; Katherine Griffin; Tom Johnson; Kevin Kirkpatrick; Jodi O'Neill; Jeffrey Risley; Cindy Sylvester; Nick Tillema; Lynette Wuethrich.
Board Member: Dan Bowden.
EIN: 351158610

1179
Noble County Community Foundation

1599 Lincolnway S.
Ligonier, IN 46767-9731 (260) 894-3335
Contact: Linda Speakman-Yerick, Exec. Dir.; For grants: Margarita White, Prog. Off.
FAX: (260) 894-9020;
E-mail: info@noblecountycf.org; Grant inquiry e-mail: margarita@noblecountycf.org; Grant inquiry tel.: (260) 894-3335; Main URL: http://www.noblecountycf.org/
Facebook: https://www.facebook.com/pages/Noble-County-Community-Foundation/486692855042
RSS Feed: http://noblecountycf.org/feed/

Established in 1991 in IN.
Foundation type: Community foundation.
Financial data (yr. ended 12/31/12): Assets, $20,563,794 (M); gifts received, $525,781; expenditures, $1,248,996; giving activities include $358,533 for grants, $155,547 for 67 grants to individuals, and $134,758 for foundation-administered programs.
Purpose and activities: The foundation seeks to improve the quality of life in Noble County by serving as a catalyst for positive change, enabling donors to carry out charitable intent, and making grants. Primary areas of interest include health, human services, education, arts and culture, and civic affairs.
Fields of interest: Arts, cultural/ethnic awareness; Arts; Education; Health care; Safety/disasters; Youth development, services; Family services, parent education; Human services; Community/economic development; Public affairs; Girls.
Type of support: Management development/capacity building; In-kind gifts; Building/renovation; Capital campaigns; Conferences/seminars; Consulting services; Emergency funds; Equipment; General/operating support; Land acquisition; Matching/challenge support; Program development; Scholarship funds; Scholarships—to individuals; Seed money; Technical assistance.
Limitations: Applications accepted. Giving primarily limited to Noble County, IN. No support for sectarian religious purposes, or for conduit organizations. No grants for annual fund campaigns, routine operating support for ongoing programs, multi-year funding, travel, augmenting endowments, deficit spending, underwriting for fundraising events, or research; no loans.
Publications: Application guidelines; Annual report; Grants list; Informational brochure (including application guidelines); Newsletter.
Application information: Visit foundation Web site for application guidelines. Faxed proposals are not accepted. The foundation offers a free grant writing workshop from time to time; e-mail or call Prog. Off. to register. Application form not required.
Initial approach: Telephone or letter of intent
Copies of proposal: 1
Deadline(s): Mar. 2, May 2, July 2, and Nov. 2
Board meeting date(s): 4th Wed. in Feb., Apr., June, Aug., Oct., and 3rd Wed. in Dec.
Final notification: 60 days after deadline
Officers and Directors:* Valerie Hague,* Pres.; Dr. Doug Jansen,* V.P.; Jolene Durham,* Secy.; Monte Egolf,* Treas.; Linda Speakman-Yerick, Exec. Dir.; **Jim Abbs**; **Arthur Grawcock**; Gary Leatherman; Jonthan Leman; Craig Lichlyter; Josh Munson; Leigh Pranger; Jarrod Ramer; Rodney Schoon; Janet Sweeney.
Number of staff: 3 full-time professional; 1 full-time support; 1 part-time support.
EIN: 351827247
Other changes: Larry Baker, David Blackman, Jolene Durham, Valerie Hague, Doug Jansen, Robert Probst, and Roger Schermerhorn are no longer directors.

1180
Northern Indiana Community Foundation, Inc.

715 Main St.
P.O. Box 807
Rochester, IN 46975-1543 (574) 223-2227
***Contact:* Jay Albright, Exec. Dir.**
FAX: (574) 224-3709; **E-mail: jay@nicf.org; Additional tel.: (877) 432-6423; additional e-mail: jay@nicf.org**; Main URL: http://www.nicf.org
Facebook: http://www.facebook.com/pages/Northern-Indiana-Community-Foundation/207271679290731

Established in 1993 in IN.
Foundation type: Community foundation.
Financial data (yr. ended 12/31/12): Assets, $23,704,972 (M); gifts received, $1,664,358; expenditures, $2,608,434; giving activities include $1,163,556 for 28+ grants (high: $150,000), and $230,563 for 293 grants to individuals.

Purpose and activities: The foundation seeks to improve the quality of life in the community by assisting donors in fulfilling their charitable wishes.
Fields of interest: Arts; Education; Environment; Health organizations, association; Recreation; Youth development; Human services; Community/economic development; Youth.
Type of support: General/operating support; Building/renovation; Equipment; Endowments; Emergency funds; Program development; Seed money; Scholarship funds; Consulting services; Matching/challenge support.
Limitations: Applications accepted. Giving limited to Fulton, Miami, and Starke counties, IN. No support for sectarian or religious organizations operated primarily for the benefit of their own members. No grants to individuals (except for scholarships), or for annual fundraisers or campaigns, ongoing operating expenses, deficits, direct or grass-roots lobbying, sponsorships, special events, commercial advertising, films or videos, television, conferences, or group uniforms or trips.
Publications: Application guidelines; Annual report; Informational brochure; Newsletter.
Application information: Visit foundation web site for specific county application forms, guidelines, and deadlines. Application form required.
Initial approach: Telephone or fax
Copies of proposal: 1
Deadline(s): Varies
Board meeting date(s): 3rd Wed. of each month
Final notification: Approx. 6 weeks
Officers and Directors:* Ron Douglas,* Pres.; Jennifer Gappa,* V.P.; Judy Climie,* Secy.; Gene Miles,* Treas.; Jay Albright, Exec. Dir.; Suzy Bishop; **Larry Cunningham**; **Jeff Finke**; **Evan Gottschalk**; **Jerry Gurrado**; Max Hattery; Leon Huskey; Gene Ladd; Tom McKaig; Marcia Minard; Pat Mitchell; Susie Perkins; Kirk Robinson; Marilyn Wickert; Jim Yates.
Number of staff: 1 full-time professional; 4 full-time support.
EIN: 351912317
Other changes: Ron Douglas has replaced Larry Cunningham as Pres. Jennifer Gappa has replaced Ron Douglas as V.P. Judy Climie has replaced Nancy Day as Secy.

1181
Ohio County Community Foundation, Inc.

330 Industrial Access Dr.
P.O. Box 170
Rising Sun, IN 47040 (812) 438-9401
Contact: Peggy Dickson, Exec. Dir.; For grants: Stephanie Scott, Prog. Coord.
FAX: (812) 438-9488;
E-mail: pdickson@occfrisingsun.com; Grant inquiry e-mail: sscott@occfrisingsun.com; Main URL: http://www.occfrisingsun.com

Established in 1998 in IN.
Foundation type: Community foundation.
Financial data (yr. ended 12/31/12): Assets, $24,719,808 (M); gifts received, $1,317,140; expenditures, $718,822; giving activities include $140,005 for 9+ grants (high: $15,000), and $108,808 for 138 grants to individuals.
Purpose and activities: The foundation seeks to assist donors with building, managing and distributing a lasting source of charitable resources for Ohio County, IN. The foundation makes grants in the fields of community development, education, human services, cultural affairs and health.
Fields of interest: Arts; Education; Environment; Health care; Human services; Community/economic development.
Limitations: Applications accepted. Giving limited to Ohio County, IN. No support for sectarian religious purposes. No grants to individuals (except for scholarships).
Publications: Application guidelines; Annual report; Grants list; Informational brochure; Newsletter.
Application information: Visit foundation web site for application form and guidelines. Application form required.
Initial approach: Submit application form
Copies of proposal: 10
***Deadline(s):* Apr. 15 and Oct. 15**
Board meeting date(s): 10 times per year
Final notification: May and Dec.
Officers and Board Members:* Monte Denbo,* Pres.; Ken McIntosh,* V.P.; Nancy Gililland,* Secy.; April Hautman,* Treas.; Peggy Dickson,* Exec. Dir.; **Douglas Baker**; **Wayne Chipman**; **Rosie Hewitt**; **Barb Scranton**; **John Spina**.
Number of staff: 1 full-time professional; 1 part-time support.
EIN: 352038531
Other changes: Sue Alwin is no longer a member of the governing body. April Hautman is no longer a member of the governing body. Steven Timms is no longer a member of the governing body. Yvotte Walton is no longer a member of the governing body.

1182
Old National Bank Foundation, Inc.

c/o Janet H. Baas, Fdn. Pres.
1 Main St.
Evansville, IN 47708 **(812) 464-1515**
***Contact:* Janet Heldt Baas, Pres.; Linda Ford, Fdn. Prog. Admin.**
E-mail: grants&sponsorships@oldnational.com; Main URL: https://www.oldnational.com/about-us/community-partnership/foundation-grants/index.asp

Established in 2006.
Donor: Old National Bank.
Foundation type: Company-sponsored foundation.
Financial data (yr. ended 12/31/13): Assets, $0 (M); expenditures, $883,107; qualifying distributions, $883,107; giving activities include $874,872 for 160 grants, and $8,235 for employee matching gifts.
Purpose and activities: The foundation supports organizations involved with arts and culture, health, and human services. Special emphasis is directed toward programs designed to promote community and economic development and education.
Fields of interest: Arts, cultural/ethnic awareness; Education, early childhood education; Higher education; Education, reading; Housing/shelter, rehabilitation; Housing/shelter, home owners; Youth development; Human services, financial counseling; Human services; Economic development; Urban/community development; Community development, small businesses; Microfinance/microlending; Community/economic development; Mathematics; Leadership development; Economically disadvantaged.
Type of support: Building/renovation; Capital campaigns; Continuing support; Curriculum development; In-kind gifts; Program development.
Limitations: Applications accepted. Giving limited to areas of company operations in IL, IN, KY, and MI. **No support for school clubs/organizations, including bands, athletic or academic teams, booster clubs, or PTO/PTA, summer camps, political, labor, military, veterans', international, or fraternal organizations, discriminatory organizations, or religious organizations, not of direct benefit to the entire community.** No grants to individuals, or for endowments, salaries or general operating support, meals, tickets, dues, memberships, fees, travel, tuition, subscriptions, or other tangible benefits, childcare fees/subsidies or K-12 tuition, meetings, conferences, or workshops, debt retirement, contests, competitions, athletic events, beauty pageants, or talent contests, operating costs or capital campaigns for faith-based organizations, sponsorships, fundraisers, races, telethons, marathons, benefits, banquets, galas, golf tournaments, festivals or other events, or scholarly or medical research, feasibility studies, project research or development phases, including the cost of hiring consultants or planners.
Publications: Application guidelines; Corporate giving report; Program policy statement.
Application information: A full proposal may be required at a later date. Support is limited to 1 contribution per organization during any given year. **Application form required.**
Initial approach: Complete online application
Copies of proposal: 1
***Deadline(s):* Mar. 16 and July 11**
Board meeting date(s): Spring and Fall
***Final notification:* 2-3 weeks following deadlines**
Officers: Janet Heldt Baas, Pres.; Doug Gregurich, V.P.; **Linda Ford, Secy.**; Jackie Russell, Treas.
EIN: 260130059
Other changes: Linda Ford has replaced Danyelle Granger as Secy.
Danyelle Granger is no longer Secy. Danyelle Granger is no longer Secy.

1183
The OneAmerica Foundation, Inc.

(formerly AUL Foundation, Inc.)
1 American Sq.
P.O. Box 368
Indianapolis, IN **46206-0368 (317) 285-1877**
***Contact:* Jim Freeman, V.P.**
FAX: (317) 285-1979

Established in 1985 in IN.
Donor: American United Life Insurance Co.
Foundation type: Company-sponsored foundation.
Financial data (yr. ended 12/31/12): Assets, $9,268,106 (M); expenditures, $630,272; qualifying distributions, $622,141; giving activities include $622,141 for 49 grants (high: $321,366; low: $100).
Purpose and activities: The foundation supports museums and zoological societies and organizations involved with orchestras, education, human services, and leadership development.
Fields of interest: Museums; Performing arts, orchestras; Higher education; Education; Zoos/zoological societies; American Red Cross; Children, services; Human services; Leadership development.
Type of support: General/operating support.
Limitations: Applications accepted. Giving limited to the Indianapolis, IN, area. No grants to individuals.
Application information: Application form required.
***Initial approach:* Letter**
Deadline(s): Sept. 30
Officers and Directors:* Dayton H. Molendorp,* Chair. and Pres.; James W. Freeman, V.P.; **Thomas M. Zurek,* Secy.**; **Douglas W. Collins, Treas.**; **J. Scott Davison**; Jeffrey D. Holley; **John C. Mason**; Mark C. Roller.
EIN: 311146437
Other changes: Thomas M. Zurek has replaced Kaye A. Palmer as Secy. Douglas W. Collins has replaced Daniel Schluge as Treas.

1184
Orange County Community Foundation, Inc.
112 W. Water St.
Paoli, IN 47454-1347 (812) 723-4150
Contact: Imojean Dedrick, Exec. Dir.
FAX: (812) 723-7304;
E-mail: contact@orangecountycommunityfoundation.org; Main URL: http://www.orangecountycommunityfoundation.org
Facebook: https://www.facebook.com/orangecountycf
Twitter: http://twitter.com/OrangeCountyCF

The foundation was incorporated in 2000 in IN.
Foundation type: Community foundation.
Financial data (yr. ended 09/30/12): Assets, $8,265,461 (M); gifts received, $1,921,784; expenditures, $1,420,355; giving activities include $813,997 for grants.
Purpose and activities: The goal of the foundation is to provide a pool of funds to help meet the needs of Orange County, IN, citizens and, in so doing, to help donors carry out their philanthropic purposes as effectively as possible.
Fields of interest: Humanities; Historical activities; Arts; Education; Environment; Animals/wildlife; Health care; Recreation; Human services; Children/youth; Terminal illness, people with.
Type of support: Building/renovation; Equipment; Program development; Conferences/seminars; Film/video/radio; Publication; Curriculum development; Research; Technical assistance; Consulting services; Program evaluation; Scholarships—to individuals.
Limitations: Applications accepted. Giving limited to Orange County, IN. No support for religious purposes. No grants to individuals (except for scholarships), or for operating revenue, endowment creation, debt reduction, or travel expenses; no loans.
Publications: Application guidelines; Annual report; Financial statement; Grants list; Informational brochure; Newsletter.
Application information: Visit foundation web site for application form and additional information. Application form required.
Initial approach: Contact foundation
Copies of proposal: 7
Deadline(s): Varies
Board meeting date(s): 4th Thurs. of every month
Final notification: Varies
Officers and Directors:* Carolyn Clements,* Pres.; Peter Grigsby,* V.P.; Larry Hollan,* Secy.; Mary Jane Harrison,* Treas.; Imojean Dedrick, Exec. Dir.; Hon. Larry Blanton; Brett Busick; Pete Conrad; Donnie Crockett; Linda Gerkin; Barbara Gilliatt; Todd Hitchcock; Kay Lynn Kaiser; Glenda Lamb; Louanne Lashbrook; Timothy Leehe.
Number of staff: 3 full-time professional; 1 part-time support.
EIN: 352117084
Other changes: Cathy Hardin is now Mgr., Finance and Admin.

1185
Owen County Community Foundation
201 W. Morgan St., Ste. 202
P.O. Box 503
Spencer, IN 47460-0503 (812) 829-1725
***Contact:* Mark E. Rogers, Exec. Dir.; For grants: Marilyn Hart, Admin. Dir.**
FAX: (812) 829-9958;
E-mail: mark@owencountycf.org; **Grant inquiry e-mail: marilyn@owencountycf.org**; Main URL: http://www.owencountycf.org
Facebook: https://www.facebook.com/pages/Owen-County-Community-Foundation/401226016658416
Twitter: https://twitter.com/OwenCounty_CF
YouTube: http://www.youtube.com/user/OwenCountyCF

Established in 1994 in IN.
Foundation type: Community foundation.
Financial data (yr. ended 12/31/12): Assets, $4,391,156 (M); gifts received, $171,366; expenditures, $306,528; giving activities include $101,390 for 3+ grants (high: $25,360), and $19,090 for 37 grants to individuals.
Purpose and activities: The foundation is committed to help make the local communities become better places to grow, work and live.
Fields of interest: Arts; Education; Environment, natural resources; Animal welfare; Health care; Recreation, camps; Human services; Community/economic development.
Type of support: General/operating support; Continuing support; Capital campaigns; Endowments; Curriculum development; Employee matching gifts; Scholarships—to individuals.
Limitations: Applications accepted. Giving limited to Owen County, IN. No support for religious purposes. No grants for endowments, deficit funding, conferences, publications, films, television, or radio programs, travel, annual appeals, or membership contributions.
Publications: Annual report; Grants list; Informational brochure.
Application information: Visit foundation web site for application form and guidelines. Application form required.
Initial approach: Letter of intent (1 page)
Copies of proposal: 1
Deadline(s): Jan. 15 for Scholarships; June 1 for letter of intent; Sept. 15 for full proposal
Board meeting date(s): Monthly
Final notification: Mid-Nov.
Officers and Directors:* Phyllis Tucker,* Pres.; Bob Livingston,* V.P.; Doris Scully,* Secy.; Tad Wilson,* Treas.; Mark E. Rogers, Exec. Dir.; Gary Armstrong; Barbara Bonness; Josh Clark; John Hackworthy; Nancy Lorenz; Steve Mader; Connie Neihart; Marge Neumeyer; Brad Thurston, M.D.; Sally Vance; Dale Walker.
Number of staff: 2 full-time professional; 1 part-time support.
EIN: 351934464

1186
Parke County Community Foundation, Inc.
115 N. Market St.
P.O. Box 276
Rockville, IN 47872-1719 (765) 569-7223
Contact: Brad C. Bumgardner, Exec. Dir.
FAX: (765) 569-5383; E-mail: parkeccf@yahoo.com; Main URL: http://www.parkeccf.org
Facebook: https://www.facebook.com/pages/Parke-County-Community-Foundation/188650397850473
RSS Feed: http://www.parkeccf.org/newsreleases.html?rss

Established in 1993 in IN.
Foundation type: Community foundation.
Financial data (yr. ended 12/31/12): Assets, $11,249,782 (M); gifts received, $300,882; expenditures, $776,703; giving activities include $286,178 for 4+ grants (high: $63,388), and $202,261 for 166 grants to individuals.
Purpose and activities: The foundation's mission is to assist donors in meeting charitable need in Parke County and to build community capacity, thereby, enhancing the quality of life in Parke County.
Fields of interest: Performing arts, theater; Historic preservation/historical societies; Elementary/secondary education; Higher education; Education; Animal welfare; Health organizations, association; Disasters, fire prevention/control; Human services; Community/economic development; Protestant agencies & churches; Cemeteries/burial services.
Type of support: General/operating support; Program development; Scholarship funds; Scholarships—to individuals.
Limitations: Applications accepted. Giving primarily in Parke County, IN.
Publications: Financial statement; Newsletter.
Application information: Visit foundation web site for application form and guidelines. For requests $1,000 or undera one-page letter or email will suffice. Application form required.
Initial approach: Submit application
Deadline(s): None
Final notification: Within 90 days
Officers and Directors:* Nathan Adams,* Chair.; Wilma Wooten,* Vice-Chair.; Donna McVay,* Secy.; Tom Rohr,* Treas.; Brad C. Bumgardner, Exec. Dir.; Andrew Allen; Jana Crites; **Mark Davis**; Renee Hartman; Jenn Kersey; **Cliff Kunze**; Barbara Livezey; Nellie Myers; Gary Staadt.
EIN: 351881810
Other changes: John Hartman and Wilma Wooten are no longer directors.

1187
Porter County Community Foundation, Inc.
57 S. Franklin St., Ste. 207
P.O. Box 302
Valparaiso, IN 46384 (219) 465-0294
Contact: For grants: Brenda Sheetz, V.P.
FAX: (219) 464-2733;
E-mail: info@portercountyfoundation.org; Grant inquiry e-mail: bsheetz@portercountyfoundation.org; Main URL: http://www.portercountyfoundation.org
Facebook: http://www.facebook.com/pages/Porter-County-Community-Foundation/133136959185
LinkedIn: http://www.linkedin.com/company/porter-county-community-foundation
Twitter: https://twitter.com/pccfoundation

Established in 1996 in IN.
Foundation type: Community foundation.
Financial data (yr. ended 12/31/12): Assets, $31,456,644 (M); gifts received, $1,256,708; expenditures, $2,665,117; giving activities include $1,914,407 for 83+ grants (high: $85,105), and $14,000 for 14 grants to individuals.
Purpose and activities: The foundation provides resources and ideas by which donors can make lasting contributions to humanitarian, cultural, educational, recreational and environmental causes in Porter County, IN, and provides asset management which maximizes the effectiveness of these gifts.
Fields of interest: Arts; Education; Environment; Human services.
Type of support: Capital campaigns; Emergency funds; Management development/capacity building; Program development; Equipment.
Limitations: Applications accepted. Giving primarily in Porter County, IN. No support for programs that are sectarian or religious in nature. No grants to individuals (except scholarships from scholarship funds), operational funding, annual appeals or

membership contributions, event sponsorship, endowment campaigns (except for endowment building grants), debt reduction, camp scholarships or fees related to camp programs, or travel for bands, sports teams, or similar groups.
Publications: Application guidelines; Annual report; Grants list; Newsletter.
Application information: Visit foundation web site for application cover sheet and specific guidelines. Application form required.
Initial approach: Proposal
Copies of proposal: 1
Deadline(s): Feb. 17 and Aug. 15
Final notification: 60 days after deadline
Officers and Directors:* Barbara A. Young,* Pres.; Brenda A. Sheetz,* V.P.; Jan Barsophy; Rick Calinski; Laura Campbell; Dr. John Felton; Stephanie Gerdes; Minaski Ghuman; Carol Hall; John Hannon; Heather Harrigan-Hitz; Susan Kelly-Johnson; Geoff Laciak; Judy Leetz; William P. Maar; Kent Mishler; Ralph Neff; Douglas Olson; Gregory Sobkowski; Jacki Stutzman; Spero Valavanis; John Walsh; Katharine Wehling; and 7 additional directors.
EIN: 352000788
Other changes: Debora Butterfield, David Kelly, Sharon Kish, Mark Maassel, Jane Maxwell, Jonathan Nalli, and Paul Reisen are no longer directors.

1188
The Portland Foundation
112 E. Main St.
Portland, IN 47371-2105 (260) 726-4260
Contact: Douglas L. Inman, Exec. Dir.; For grant applications: Jessica L. Cook, Prog. Off.
FAX: (260) 726-4273;
E-mail: tpf@portlandfoundation.org; Main URL: http://www.portlandfoundation.org
Facebook: https://www.facebook.com/pages/The-Portland-Foundation/138673816247793

Established in 1951 in IN.
Foundation type: Community foundation.
Financial data (yr. ended 12/31/13): Assets, $28,720,250 (M); gifts received, $2,131,715; expenditures, $994,196; giving activities include $442,316 for grants, and $191,487 for grants to individuals.
Purpose and activities: The foundation provides support for all aspects of the quality of life in the Jay County, IN, community.
Fields of interest: Arts; Child development, education; Higher education; Libraries/library science; Education; Animal welfare; Health care; Children/youth, services; Family services; Human services, emergency aid; Human services; Community/economic development; Youth; Disabilities, people with.
Type of support: Capital campaigns; Building/renovation; Equipment; Program development; Seed money; Scholarship funds; Scholarships—to individuals; Matching/challenge support.
Limitations: Applications accepted. Giving limited to Jay County, IN. No support for religious or sectarian purposes. No grants to individuals (except through designated scholarship funds); generally no grants for regular operating budgets, operating costs, operating deficits, after-the-fact funds, endowments, or long-term funding; no loans.
Publications: Application guidelines; Annual report; Newsletter; IRS Form 990 or 990-PF printed copy available upon request.
Application information: Visit foundation web site for application form and guidelines. Applications must be typed; handwritten copies will not be accepted. Application form required.
Initial approach: Submit application form and attachments
Copies of proposal: 1
Deadline(s): Jan. and July
Board meeting date(s): Bimonthly
Final notification: Feb. and Aug.
Officers and Trustees:* Mary Davis,* Pres.; Dean Jetter,* V.P.; Emily Goodrich Roberts,* Secy.-Treas.; Douglas L. Inman, Exec. Dir.; Pat Bennett; David Fullenkamp; Rex Journay; Ronald Laux; **John Moore**; **Stephanie Robinson**.
Number of staff: 1 full-time professional; 1 part-time support.
EIN: 356028362
Other changes: Rosalie Clamme and Eric Reynolds are no longer trustees.

1189
The Putnam County Community Foundation
2 S. Jackson St.
P.O. Box 514
Greencastle, IN 46135-0514 (765) 653-4978
Contact: M. Elaine Peck, Exec. Dir.
FAX: (765) 653-6385;
E-mail: info@pcfoundation.org; Additional e-mail: epeck@pcfoundation.org; Main URL: http://www.pcfoundation.org
E-Newsletter: http://www.pcfoundation.org/about_newsletter.html
Facebook: https://www.facebook.com/pages/Putnam-County-Community-Foundation/128261640565285?ref=ts
Scholarship e-mail: dgambill@pcfoundation.org

Established in 1985 in IN.
Foundation type: Community foundation.
Financial data (yr. ended 12/31/12): Assets, $21,533,458 (M); gifts received, $632,866; expenditures, $950,577; giving activities include $448,602 for 18+ grants (high: $66,308), and $135,413 for 145 grants to individuals.
Purpose and activities: The foundation partners with those who give to enrich life and strengthen community for current and future generations.
Fields of interest: Arts; Education; Environment; Animals/wildlife; Public health, obesity; Health care; Recreation; Human services; Economic development; Community/economic development; Public affairs, citizen participation; Transportation; Youth; Aging.
Type of support: Income development; Building/renovation; Program development; Seed money; Scholarship funds; Technical assistance; Consulting services; Program-related investments/loans; Matching/challenge support.
Limitations: Applications accepted. Giving limited to Putnam County, IN. No support for sectarian religious purposes, or national or state-wide fundraising projects. No grants to individuals (except for scholarships), or for salaries, utilities or rent, projects normally fully funded by units of government, endowment funds, fundraising projects, or retroactive funding.
Publications: Application guidelines; Annual report; Financial statement; Grants list; Informational brochure; Newsletter.
Application information: Visit foundation web site for application forms and guidelines. To be considered for funding, organizations must first submit a Preliminary Grant Application form; eligible organizations will then be mailed application materials and an invitation in writing to submit a full application. Application form required.
Initial approach: Submit 1-page Preliminary Grant Application form
Copies of proposal: 1
Deadline(s): Feb. 1 and Aug. 1 for preliminary application; Mar. 1 and Sept. 1 for full application
Board meeting date(s): Monthly
Final notification: Feb. 15 and Aug. 15 for full application invitation; 3 months for funding decisions
Officer and Directors:* M. Elaine Peck, Exec. Dir.; David Archer; Keith Archer; Keith Brackney; **Debbi Christy**; Ellen Dittmer; **Ken Eitel**; Brad Hayes; Karen Nelson Heavin; **Scott Herrick**; Susan Lemon; M. Todd Lewis; Vickie Parker; Susan Price; Nancy Wells; Vivian Whitaker; Rodger Winger; Ellie Ypma.
Number of staff: 4 full-time professional.
EIN: 311159916
Other changes: Jeff Rich, Phyllis Rokicki, and Vicki Timm are no longer directors.

1190
Regenstrief Foundation, Inc.
9292 N. Meridian, Ste. 202
Indianapolis, IN 46260-1828
Contact: Susan Luse, Secy.
FAX: (317) 848-9586

Established in IN in 1969.
Foundation type: Independent foundation.
Financial data (yr. ended 06/30/13): Assets, $165,175,602 (M); expenditures, $10,666,192; qualifying distributions, $8,951,025; giving activities include $8,735,573 for 2 grants (high: $5,780,361; low: $2,955,212).
Purpose and activities: Giving for innovative research directed toward improving the efficiency, quality, and accessibility of health care.
Fields of interest: Higher education; Medical research, institute; Medical research, information services; Medical research, formal/general education.
Type of support: Research.
Limitations: Applications not accepted. Giving primarily in Indianapolis, IN.
Application information: Unsolicited requests for funds not considered.
Board meeting date(s): Jan. and June
Officers and Directors:* **Jack Snyder,* Chair.**; **Jack R. Shaw, C.E.O., Pres., and Treas.**; Susan M. Luse, Secy.; Daniel Appel; Leonard J. Betley; **D. Craig Brater**; **Richard Buckius**; Allan L. Cohn; Ronald W. Dollens; Harvey Feigenbaum, M.D.; Stephen L. Ferguson; David W. Knall; Sally F. Mason, Ph.D.; Lesley B. Olswang, Ph.D.; Bart Peterson.
Number of staff: 4 part-time professional; 2 part-time support.
EIN: 356066023
Other changes: Jack R. Shaw is now C.E.O., Pres., and Treas. Jack Snyder is now Chair. .

1191
Ripley County Community Foundation, Inc.
4 S. Park, Ste. 210
Batesville, IN 47006 (812) 933-1098
Contact: Sally Morris, Exec. Dir.
FAX: (812) 933-0096;
E-mail: office@rccfonline.org; Additional tel.: (887) 234-5220; Additional e-mail: smorris@rccfonline.org and office@rccfonline.org; Main URL: http://rccfonline.org/
Facebook: https://www.facebook.com/RipleyCountyCommunityFoundation?fref=ts

Established in 1997 in IN.
Foundation type: Community foundation.
Financial data (yr. ended 12/31/12): Assets, $8,714,956 (M); gifts received, $1,712,806; expenditures, $1,500,344; giving activities include $293,552 for 14+ grants (high: $44,290), and $796,131 for 26,040 grants to individuals.
Purpose and activities: The foundation seeks to: 1) assist donors to build an enduring source of charitable assets to benefit Ripley County; 2) provide responsible stewardship of the gifts donated; 3) promote leadership in addressing Ripley County's issues; and 4) to make grants in the fields of community service, social service, education, health, environment, and the arts.
Fields of interest: Arts; Education; Environment; Health care; Human services; Community/economic development.
Type of support: General/operating support; Seed money; Matching/challenge support.
Limitations: Applications accepted. Giving limited to Ripley County, IN. No support for sectarian religious purposes. No grants to individuals (except for scholarships), or for seminars, trips, or endowments.
Publications: Application guidelines; Annual report.
Application information: Visit foundation web site for application form and guidelines. Application form required.
Initial approach: Submit application
Deadline(s): First Friday of Apr., June, Sept. and Nov. for small projects grants for amounts up to $500; Aug. 2 for larger projects grants for amounts of $500 to $5,000.
Officers and Board Members:* Amy Kellerman Streator,* Pres.; Mark Collier,* V.P.; Linda Chandler,* Secy.; Eric Benz,* Treas.; Marie Dausch; Tim Dietz; **John Kellerman II**; Jenny Miles; **Chris Nichols**; Alesha Neal; Herman Struewing.
EIN: 352048001
Other changes: At the close of 2012, the grantmaker paid grants of $1,089,683, a 199.7% increase over the 2011 disbursements, $363,564. Cheryll Obendorf is now Prog. Coord. Jane Deiwert is now Prog. Off. Brenda Wetzler is no longer Pres. The grantmaker now publishes an annual report.

1192
Rush County Community Foundation, Inc.
c/o Alisa Henderson
117 N. Main St.
Rushville, IN 46173-1927 (765) 938-1177
***Contact:* Alisa Henderson, Exec. Dir.**
FAX: (765) 938-1719;
E-mail: info@rushcountyfoundation.org; Main URL: http://www.rushcountyfoundation.org

Established in 1991 in IN.
Foundation type: Community foundation.
Financial data (yr. ended 12/31/12): Assets, $10,449,544 (M); gifts received, $271,881; expenditures, $391,885; giving activities include $163,066 for 7+ grants (high: $26,569), and $86,966 for 115 grants to individuals.
Purpose and activities: The foundation seeks to enrich and enhance the quality of life in Rush County, Indiana.
Fields of interest: Arts; Education; Hospitals (general); Recreation, parks/playgrounds; Athletics/sports, training; Athletics/sports, soccer; Human services; United Ways and Federated Giving Programs; Public affairs.
Type of support: Building/renovation; Equipment; Program development; Seed money; Scholarship funds; Technical assistance; Matching/challenge support.
Limitations: Applications accepted. Giving limited to Rush County, IN. No support for religious purposes. No grants to individuals (except for scholarships), or for operating expenses, annual drives, building campaigns, debt reduction, endowments, multi-year grants, or travel expenses; no loans.
Publications: Application guidelines; Annual report; Financial statement; Grants list; Informational brochure; Newsletter.
Application information: Contact the foundation's Grants Prog. Dir. or Exec. Dir. for a current set of grant guidelines and application form. Application form required.
Initial approach: Telephone or e-mail
Copies of proposal: 14
***Deadline(s):* Jan. 31, Feb. 18, Mar. 3, Apr. 1, Apr. 15 for Grants**
Board meeting date(s): 4th Tues. of the month
Officers and Directors:* Terry VanNatta, C.F.O. and Asst. Exec. Dir.; Garry E. Cooley, Exec. Dir.; Robert Bridges; David Burkhardt; J.B. Gardner; Mary Hill; Greg Krodel; Michele King; Tony Laird; Dr. Amy Meyer-Ploeger; Dahl Petry; Keith Perin; Anna Jo Richards; Cindy Taff.
Number of staff: 1 full-time professional; 1 full-time support.
EIN: 351835950
Other changes: Terry VanNatta is now C.F.O. and Asst. Exec. Dir.

1193
Olin B. and Desta Schwab Foundation, Inc.
c/o Michael Earls, C.P.A.
200 E. Main St.
Fort Wayne, IN 46802-2316
***Application address:* 110 W. Berry St., Ste. 2401, Fort Wayne, IN 46802, tel.: (260) 461-6128**

Established in 2008 in IN following a merger with the Olin B. & Desta Schwab Foundation.
Foundation type: Independent foundation.
Financial data (yr. ended 06/30/13): Assets, $7,197,965 (M); expenditures, $360,587; qualifying distributions, $276,973; giving activities include $221,418 for 7 grants (high: $63,000; low: $10,000).
Purpose and activities: Grants are made for the following purposes: 1) To assist people, especially youth, in the process of career development decision-making; 2) To provide career services; and 3) To provide funding to services as a common community good that impacts the greatest number of clients.
Fields of interest: Employment, services; Employment.
Limitations: Applications accepted. Giving primarily in IN. No grants for salaries, or for curriculum development.
Application information: Application form required.
***Initial approach:* Contact foundation for application guidelines**
***Deadline(s):* Mar. 31 and Aug. 31**
Officers: M. James Johnston,* Pres.; **Jerrilee K. Mosier, Secy.; Michael Earls, Treas.**
Directors: Holly Brady; John Ferguson; Courtney Tritch; Bill Zielke.
EIN: 352284008
Other changes: Jerrilee K. Mosier has replaced Matt Bell as Secy. Michael Earls has replaced Kerry Burda as Treas.

1194
Steven M. Seger Memorial Foundation, Inc.
1365 W. 15th St.
Jasper, IN 47546-9107 (812) 678-2891
Contact: Thomas W. Seger, Secy.

Established in 1993 in IN.
Donors: Thomas W. Seger; Cynthia J. Seger; Andy Seger; Audrey Seger; Kelly Seger.
Foundation type: Independent foundation.
Financial data (yr. ended 12/31/12): Assets, $1,210,121 (M); gifts received, $48,843; expenditures, $160,808; qualifying distributions, $160,045; giving activities include $160,045 for 6 grants (high: $100,000; low: $1,000).
Fields of interest: Education; Health care; Cancer research; Human services; Christian agencies & churches.
Type of support: Building/renovation.
Limitations: Applications accepted. Giving primarily in IN, PA, and TX.
Application information: Application form required.
Initial approach: Letter
Deadline(s): None
Officers and Directors:* Cynthia J. Seger,* Pres.; Thomas W. Seger,* Secy.; Randolph L. Seger.
EIN: 351906210

1195
Shoop Sports and Youth Foundation Inc.
(formerly International Palace of Sports, Inc.)
P.O. Box 332
North Webster, IN 46555-0332 (574) 834-4422
Contact: Joan Rhodes, Treas.

Foundation type: Independent foundation.
Financial data (yr. ended 03/31/13): Assets, $4,225,076 (M); expenditures, $154,624; qualifying distributions, $124,784; giving activities include $21,060 for 15 grants (high: $5,500; low: $100), and $97,457 for 45 grants to individuals (high: $6,000; low: $500).
Purpose and activities: Scholarships only to graduates of school districts within Warsaw, Wawasee or Whitko, Indiana. Support also for community projects and programs.
Fields of interest: Libraries/library science; Scholarships/financial aid; Education; Recreation, community; Youth, services.
Type of support: General/operating support; Scholarship funds; Scholarships—to individuals.
Limitations: Applications accepted. Giving limited to the Warsaw, Wawasee and Whitko, IN, school districts.
Application information: Application form required.
Deadline(s): Apr. 1
Officers: Sandra Kissene, Pres.; David Whalen, Secy.; Joan Rhodes, Treas.
EIN: 351331032
Other changes: Sandra Kissene has replaced Robert Merchant as Pres. David Whalen has replaced Tammy O'Dell as Secy.

1196
The Steel Dynamics Foundation, Inc.
7575 W. Jefferson Blvd.
Fort Wayne, IN 46804-4131
Contact: Beth Burke
***Main URL:* http://www.steeldynamicsfoundation.org/**

Donor: Steel Dynamics, Inc.
Foundation type: Company-sponsored foundation.

Financial data (yr. ended 12/31/12): Assets, $6,552,263 (M); expenditures, $2,092,312; qualifying distributions, $2,074,750; giving activities include $2,074,750 for 35 grants (high: $300,000; low: $10,000).
Purpose and activities: The foundation supports organizations involved with children and family services. Special emphasis is directed toward programs designed to promote economic development, including education in business and technology fields.
Fields of interest: Business school/education; Children/youth, services; Family services; Economic development.
Type of support: Equipment; Building/renovation; Capital campaigns; Sponsorships; General/operating support.
Limitations: Applications accepted. Giving primarily in areas of company operations in Wayne, IN.
Publications: Application guidelines.
Application information: General grant requests should be submitted to the division general manager who will determine if the request is suited for the foundation.
Initial approach: **Contact local general management for general grants; complete online eligibility form for major impact grants**
Deadline(s): **None**
Officer and Directors: Theresa E. Wagler, Pres. and Secy.; Keith E. Busse; **Mark Millet.**
Number of staff: None.
EIN: 263012038
Other changes: The grantmaker now accepts applications.
Theresa E. Wagler is now Pres. and Secy. Joseph D. Ruffolo is deceased.
The grantmaker now publishes application guidelines.

1197
TCU Foundation Inc.
110 S. Main St.
P.O. Box 1395
South Bend, IN **46624 (800) 333-3828**
Contact: **Karol Griffin**

Established in 1995 in IN.
Donors: Teacher's Credit Union; Community Foundation of St. Joseph County.
Foundation type: Company-sponsored foundation.
Financial data (yr. ended 12/31/12): Assets, $595,753 (M); gifts received, $146,155; expenditures, $225,321; qualifying distributions, $220,377; giving activities include $220,377 for grants.
Purpose and activities: The foundation supports organizations involved with education and other member-driven initiatives. Special emphasis is directed toward programs that promote life-long learning and financial literacy.
Fields of interest: Museums (art); Arts; Education, reading; Education; Health care; Children/youth, services; Voluntarism promotion.
Type of support: Endowments; Program development; Curriculum development; Scholarship funds; Research; Employee matching gifts; Scholarships—to individuals; Donated equipment; Matching/challenge support.
Limitations: Applications accepted. Giving limited to areas of company operations in IN.
Application information: Application form not required.
Initial approach: **Proposal**
Copies of proposal: 1
Deadline(s): **None**

Officers: David Sage, Chair.; William Hojnacki, Vice-Chair.; **Roger Thornton, Secy.; Paul March, Treas.**
Directors: Alfred Bias; Shirley Golichowski; Vincent Henderson; Thea Kelly; John Myers.
Number of staff: None.
EIN: 351939838
Other changes: The grantmaker no longer lists a URL address. The grantmaker no longer lists a separate application address.

1198
Tipton County Foundation, Inc.
1020 W. Jefferson St.
P.O. Box 412
Tipton, IN 46072-0412 (765) 675-8480
Contact: **Frank M. Giammarino, Pres. and C.E.O.; For scholarships: Megan Zanto, Educ. Prog. Off.**
FAX: (765) 675-8488; E-mail: tcf@tiptoncf.org; Grant e-mail: grants@tiptoncf.org; Main URL: http://www.tiptoncf.org
Blog: http://tiptoncountyfoundation.blogspot.in/
Facebook: https://www.facebook.com/tiptoncountyfoundation
YouTube: http://www.youtube.com/intiptoncounty
Scholarship e-mail: megan@tiptoncf.org

Established in 1986 in IN.
Foundation type: Community foundation.
Financial data (yr. ended 12/31/12): Assets, $24,913,580 (M); gifts received, $304,592; expenditures, $1,140,509; giving activities include $639,859 for 13 grants (high: $313,370), and $142,836 for 87 grants to individuals.
Purpose and activities: The foundation is a nonprofit public charity established to serve donors, award grants, and provide leadership to improve the quality of life in Tipton County.
Fields of interest: Arts; Education; Recreation; Youth development; Human services; Community/economic development; Public affairs.
Type of support: Income development; Management development/capacity building; Annual campaigns; Capital campaigns; Building/renovation; Equipment; Emergency funds; Program development; Conferences/seminars; Seed money; Curriculum development; Scholarship funds; Consulting services; Scholarships—to individuals; Matching/challenge support.
Limitations: Applications accepted. Giving limited to Tipton County, IN. No support for religious purposes. **No grants for individuals (except for scholarships), or for ongoing operating expenses, debt reduction, annual appeals or membership contributions, travel, or endowment building.**
Publications: Application guidelines; Annual report; Financial statement; Grants list; Informational brochure; Newsletter; Occasional report; IRS Form 990 or 990-PF printed copy available upon request.
Application information: Visit foundation web site for application form and guidelines. Application form required.
Initial approach: Mail or e-mail letter of intent
Copies of proposal: 1
Deadline(s): **Apr. 1, Aug. 1 and Sept. 15 for full proposals, letters of intent should be submitted a few weeks beforehand**
Board meeting date(s): Mar., May, Sept., and Dec.
Officers and Directors:* Mark Raver,* Chair.; Jan Henderson,* Vice-Chair.; Frank M. Giammarino,* C.E.O. and Pres.; Nancy A. Nicholson,* Secy.; Mark Baird,* Treas.; Dr. Kevin Condict; Joe Cottingham; Lary Graves; Ben B. Hobbs; Janice Legg; Tom McKinney; JoAnn McQuinn; Brad Nichols; Sharon Smith.

Number of staff: 1 full-time professional; 1 part-time support.
EIN: 311175045
Other changes: Vernon Schmaltz is no longer a director.

1199
The Randall L. and Deborah F. Tobias Foundation, Inc.
(formerly Randall L. Tobias Foundation, Inc.)
10330 Laurel Ridge Ln.
Carmel, IN 46032-8818

Established in 1994 in IN.
Donor: Randall L. Tobias.
Foundation type: Independent foundation.
Financial data (yr. ended 12/31/12): Assets, $490,437 (M); expenditures, $61,599; qualifying distributions, $57,000; giving activities include $57,000 for grants.
Purpose and activities: Giving to support learning for children and youth through opportunity and experience.
Fields of interest: Arts; Elementary/secondary education; Education, early childhood education; Higher education; Children/youth, services.
Type of support: Program development; Curriculum development.
Limitations: Applications not accepted. Giving primarily in Indianapolis, IN.
Application information: Unsolicited requests for funds not accepted.
Officers: Randall L. Tobias, Chair.; Paige N. Tobias-Button, Pres.; **Eric Tobias, Secy.; Deborah Flanagan Tobias, Treas.**
EIN: 351938355
Other changes: Eric Tobias has replaced Meg Linden as Secy.
Randall L. Tobias is now Chair.

1200
Union County Foundation, Inc.
404 Eaton St.
Liberty, IN 47353-1407 (765) 458-7664
Contact: Danka Klein, Exec. Dir.
FAX: (765) 458-0522; E-mail: ucf@frontier.com; Additional e-mail: dklein@ucfoundationinc.org; Main URL: http://www.ucfoundationinc.org

Established in 1989 in IN.
Foundation type: Community foundation.
Financial data (yr. ended 12/31/12): Assets, $5,378,463 (M); gifts received, $128,437; expenditures, $315,423; giving activities include $84,065 for 3 grants (high: $12,374), and $73,867 for 74 grants to individuals.
Purpose and activities: The foundation seeks to assist donors to build and preserve a perpetual fund; to meet the changing needs of the community and to enrich the quality of life for the residents of Union County.
Fields of interest: Higher education; Human services; Community/economic development.
Type of support: Scholarships—to individuals.
Limitations: Applications accepted. Giving limited to Union County, IN. No support for sectarian religious purposes. No grants to individuals (except for scholarships), or for previously incurred debt, or seminars or trips.
Publications: Application guidelines.
Application information: Visit foundation web site for application packet.
Initial approach: Submit application
Copies of proposal: 8

Deadline(s): Mar. 31, June 30, Sept. 30, and Dec. 31
Final notification: May 1, Aug. 1, Sept. 30 and Feb. 1
Officers and Directors:* **Richard Worcester,*** **Pres.**; **David Bertch,*** **V.P.**; Gena Hartman,* Secy.; Gene Sanford,* Treas.; Danka Klein, Exec. Dir.; **Wendell Bias,*** **Dir. Emeritius**; **Mike Blackwell,*** **Dir. Emeritius**; Julie Abbott; Nancy Blank; Karen Briggs; Landon Coyle; Marsha Chambers Eldridge; Arthur Redinger.
EIN: 351769294
Other changes: Richard Worcester has replaced Landon Coyle as Pres. David Bertch has replaced Dic Worcester as V.P.
Wendell Bias is now Dir. Emeritius. Mike Blackwell is now Dir. Emeritius. David Bertch is no longer a director.

1201
Unity Foundation of La Porte County, Inc.
115 E. 4th St.
Michigan City, IN 46360 (219) 879-0327
Contact: Margaret A. Spartz, Pres.
FAX: (219) 210-3881; E-mail: info@uflc.net; Mailing address: P.O. Box 527 Michigan City, IN 46361; Additional tel.: (888) 89-UNITY; Main URL: http://www.uflc.net
Facebook: https://www.facebook.com/pages/The-Unity-Foundation/241204849231027
LinkedIn: http://www.linkedin.com/company/unity-foundation-of-la-porte-county
Twitter: http://twitter.com/unityfndtn
YouTube: http://www.youtube.com/user/UnityFound

Established in 1992 in IN.
Foundation type: Community foundation.
Financial data (yr. ended 12/31/12): Assets, $23,797,446 (M); gifts received, $3,143,116; expenditures, $1,741,174; giving activities include $744,995 for 369+ grants, and $142,629 for grants to individuals.
Purpose and activities: The foundation seeks to accept and pool charitable contributions from a variety of resources, and use the proceeds to support other charitable activities and organizations to benefit the residents of La Porte County, IN. The foundation makes discretionary and field of interest grants to charitable organizations in the area of the arts, education, health and human services, the environment, and the community.
Fields of interest: Historic preservation/historical societies; Arts; Libraries/library science; Education, reading; Education; Environment; Animals/wildlife; Health care; Mental health/crisis services; Housing/shelter, homeless; Housing/shelter; Recreation; Youth development; Children/youth, services; Human services; Community/economic development.
Type of support: Building/renovation; Equipment; Land acquisition; Endowments; Program development; Conferences/seminars; Seed money; Scholarship funds; Technical assistance; Employee matching gifts.
Limitations: Applications accepted. Giving limited to residents of La Porte County, IN. No support for sectarian religious programs. No grants to individuals (except for scholarship funds), or for operating budgets, basic municipal or educational functions and services, debt reduction, long-term funding, or after-the-fact funding.
Publications: Application guidelines; Annual report; Annual report (including application guidelines); Financial statement; Grants list; Newsletter.
Application information: Community fund grant requests should be no more than $3000. Visit foundation web site for application forms and guidelines. Application form required.
Initial approach: Submit letter and attachments
Copies of proposal: 1
***Deadline(s):* July 20**
Board meeting date(s): 1st Mon. of month
Final notification: Mid-Sept.
Officers and Directors:* Michael Brennan,* Co-Chair.; Edward Volk,* Co-Chair.; Margaret A. Spartz,* Pres.; Sandy Gleim,* V.P.; Elizabeth Bernel; Daryl Crockett; Jon Gilmore; Jim Jessup; Jack L. Jones; Jerry Kabelin; Vidya Kora, M.D.; Daniel E. Lewis; Mary Lou Linnen; Ronald J. Ragains; Burton B. Ruby; Kim Sauers; Marti Swanson; Michele Thompson.
Number of staff: 2 full-time professional; 1 part-time professional; 3 part-time support.
EIN: 351658674
Other changes: Gabby Dziadkowiec is no longer Devel. Asst.

1202
Vectren Foundation, Inc.
(formerly Indiana Energy Foundation, Inc.)
1 Vectren Sq.
Evansville, IN 47708-1251 (812) 491-4176
Contact: Mark Miller, Mgr., Community Affairs
E-mail: mmiller@vectren.com; Additional application address and contact: Lynda Hoffman, Community Affairs, Mgr., Vectren Corp., 120 W. 2nd St., Ste. 1212, Dayton, OH 45402-1685, tel.: (937) 222-2936, e-mail:lkhoffman@vectren.com; Main URL: http://www.vectrenfoundation.org/

Established in 2000 in IN.
Donors: Indiana Energy, Inc.; Vectren Corp.
Foundation type: Company-sponsored foundation.
Financial data (yr. ended 12/31/12): Assets, $4,679,283 (M); gifts received, $6,000,000; expenditures, $2,184,665; qualifying distributions, $2,184,665; giving activities include $2,181,368 for 458 grants (high: $100,000; low: -$5,000).
Purpose and activities: The foundation supports programs designed to promote community development; energy conservation and environmental stewardship; and education. Special emphasis is directed toward programs designed to contribute to sustainable future.
Fields of interest: Elementary/secondary education; Higher education; Education, services; Education, reading; Education; Environment, natural resources; Environment, energy; Environmental education; Environment; Health care, clinics/centers; Health care; Employment, training; Employment; Housing/shelter, development; Housing/shelter; Youth development, adult & child programs; American Red Cross; YM/YWCAs & YM/YWHAs; Children/youth, services; Economic development; Community/economic development; Foundations (community); United Ways and Federated Giving Programs; Leadership development; Public affairs.
Type of support: General/operating support; Capital campaigns; Equipment; Program development; Employee volunteer services; Sponsorships; Employee matching gifts.
Limitations: Applications accepted. **Giving limited to areas of company operations in IN and west central OH.** No support for political, religious, fraternal, labor, or veterans' organizations or issue-oriented organizations. No grants to individuals or for scholarships.
Publications: Application guidelines; Annual report.
Application information: Application form required.
***Initial approach:* Complete online application**
Deadline(s): None
Final notification: 90 days
Officers and Directors:* Jeffrey W. Whiteside,* Pres.; **Ronald E. Christian,*** **V.P.**; **Joshua Claybourn, Secy.**; Jerome A. Benkert, Jr.; Carl L. Chapman; **J. Bradley Ellsworth**; Colleen Ryan.
EIN: 351950691
Other changes: Ronald E. Christian is now V.P.

1203
Wabash Valley Community Foundation, Inc.
2901 Ohio Blvd., Ste. 153
Terre Haute, IN 47803-2239 (812) 232-2234
Contact: Beth A.A. Tevlin, Exec. Dir.; Kate Kollinger, Financial Mgr.
FAX: (812) 234-4853; E-mail: info@wvcf.com; Additional tel.: (877) 232-2230; Additional e-mails: beth@wvcf.com, kate@wvcf.com; Main URL: http://www.wvcf.com
Facebook: http://www.facebook.com/pages/Wabash-Valley-Community-Foundation/134088539978330
RSS Feed: http://161.58.109.117/wvcf-news/rss.php?category=1,8&number=10

Established in 1991 in IN.
Foundation type: Community foundation.
Financial data (yr. ended 09/30/12): Assets, $37,761,328 (M); gifts received, $1,275,302; expenditures, $1,958,665; giving activities include $864,401 for 163+ grants (high: $84,658), and $434,475 for 36 grants to individuals.
Purpose and activities: The foundation's mission is to promote community investment for a better tomorrow. Giving primarily for arts and culture, education, human services, community development, and religion in west central IN, specifically in Clay, Sullivan and Vigo counties.
Fields of interest: Arts; Education; Health care; Youth, services; Human services; Community/economic development; Religion.
Type of support: General/operating support; Capital campaigns; Building/renovation; Equipment; Endowments; Emergency funds; Seed money; Scholarship funds; Scholarships—to individuals; Matching/challenge support.
Limitations: Applications accepted. Giving primarily in Clay, Sullivan, and Vigo counties, IN; requests from other counties occasionally considered. No support for religious purposes. No grants for endowments, deficit funding, annual appeals and membership contributions, travel for groups such as bands, sports teams and classes, conferences, publications, films, television, or radio programs (unless integral to the project for which the grant is sought).
Publications: Application guidelines; Annual report; Financial statement; Grants list; Informational brochure; Newsletter.
Application information: Visit foundation web site for application guidelines, varying per grant type. 17 to 22 copies depending on grant cycle. Application form required.
Initial approach: Letter of Intent (1 page)
Copies of proposal: 1
Deadline(s): June 1 for Clay, Sullivan, and Vigo counties' letters of intent, Nov. 1 for Vigo County letter of intent; Feb. 1 for Vigo County full proposal, Aug. 1 for Clay, Sullivan, and Vigo counties' full proposals

Board meeting date(s): Jan., Mar., May, July, Sept., and Nov.
Final notification: Approx. 1 month for letter of intent determination; Approx. 4 months for full grant proposals
Officers and Directors:* Fred Nation,* Pres.; Michael Lawson,* V.P.; Jeff Perry,* Secy.; David Doti,* Treas.; Beth A.A. Tevlin, Exec. Dir.; **Daryl Andrews**; Cynthia Cox; Lant Davis; Jo Einstandig; Jon Ford; Judy Harris; Jackie Lower; Malinda Medsker; Dave Piker; Lakshmi Reddy; Nancy Rogers; Dr. Randall Stevens; Renee Stewart; Dick Vining.
Number of staff: 2 full-time professional; 1 part-time professional; 1 part-time support.
EIN: 351848649
Other changes: Joyce Emmert is no longer a director.

1204
Walther Cancer Foundation, Inc.

(formerly Walther Cancer Institute Foundation, Inc.)
9292 N. Meridian St., Ste. 300
Indianapolis, IN 46260-1828 (317) 708-6101
Contact: James E. Ruckle Ph.D., C.E.O. and Pres.
FAX: (317) 708-6102; E-mail: info@walther.org;
Main URL: http://www.walther.org
Grants List: http://www.walther.org/grants-and-programs/active-grant-list.aspx

Established in 1985 in IN; The grantmaker changed its status from Public Charity to Private Foundation in 2007.
Foundation type: Independent foundation.
Financial data (yr. ended 06/30/13): Assets, $146,183,284 (M); gifts received, $10,407; expenditures, $5,979,879; qualifying distributions, $5,185,036; giving activities include $4,755,643 for 147 grants (high: $333,334; low: $32).
Purpose and activities: The mission of the foundation is to eliminate cancer as a cause of suffering and death through interdisciplinary and inter-institutional basic laboratory, clinical, and behavioral cancer research initiatives.
Fields of interest: Cancer research.
Type of support: Research.
Limitations: Applications not accepted. Giving limited to the U.S., with emphasis on IN. No grants for building/renovation, debt reduction, emergency funds, land acquisition, equipment, or technical assistance; no loans.
Publications: Grants list; IRS Form 990 or 990-PF printed copy available upon request.
Application information: Unsolicited requests for funds not accepted.
Board meeting date(s): Second Tues. of each month
Officers and Directors:* Leonard J. Betley,* Chair.; Gregory L. Pemberton,* Vice-Chair.; James E. Ruckle, Ph.D., C.E.O. and Pres.; D. Craig Brater, M.D., V.P., Progs.; Donald C. Danielson,* Secy.; Sue Peebles, C.F.O.; Stephen C. Gaerte,* Treas.; Steffanie Rhinesmith, C.I.O.; Daniel Appel; Mary Beth Gadus; Richard Gaynor, M.D.; Thomas W. Grein; **Bryan A. Mills**; Sharon Pierce; Nancy Yaw.
Number of staff: 2 full-time professional; 2 part-time professional; 1 full-time support.
EIN: 351650570

1205
Welborn Baptist Foundation, Inc.

(formerly Welborn Foundation, Inc.)
21 S.E. 3rd St., Ste. 610
Evansville, IN 47708-1418
Contact: Gary W. Bauer, C.F.O.
FAX: (812) 437-8269; E-mail: info@welbornfdn.org;
Main URL: http://www.welbornfdn.org
Grants List: http://www.welbornfdn.org/news/funded-projects
Knowledge Center: http://www.welbornfdn.org/community-resources/publications

Established in 1999 in IN; converted from Welborn Hospital.
Donor: WBH Evansville, Inc.
Foundation type: Independent foundation.
Financial data (yr. ended 12/31/12): Assets, $110,263,986 (M); gifts received, $1,156,100; expenditures, $6,885,324; qualifying distributions, $6,570,847; giving activities include $3,657,791 for 117 grants (high: $425,000; low: $24).
Purpose and activities: Giving primarily in support of improved community health, well being and quality of life for all members of the Tri-State Community, particularly in the areas of 1) Promotion of Early Childhood Education, 2) Faith Based Initiatives, 3) Promotion of Healthy Adolescent Development, 4) Improvements in Community Health Status, and 5) School Based Health Programs. The foundation will apply Christian principles when evaluating and selecting applications for granting.
Fields of interest: Health care; Substance abuse, services; Crime/violence prevention; Nutrition; Youth development; Community/economic development; Religion.
Type of support: Building/renovation; Capital campaigns; Conferences/seminars; Curriculum development; Equipment; Matching/challenge support; Program development.
Limitations: Giving limited to Gallatin, Saline, Wabash, Wayne and White counties, IL; Dubois, Gibson, Perry, Pike, Posey, Spencer, Vanderburgh, and Warrick counties, IN; and Henderson County, KY. No support for basic scientific research. No grants to individuals, or for endowments, annual fund drives, debt service, deficit spending, scholarships, fellowships, general operating costs, venture capital or fund-raising; no loans.
Publications: Application guidelines; Annual report; Financial statement; Multi-year report; Program policy statement.
Application information: Applications are not accepted via U.S. Mail, e-mail or any other method apart from the foundation's online process.
***Initial approach:* Use application process on foundation web site**
***Deadline(s):* See foundation web site for current deadline**
Board meeting date(s): Varies
Officers: Daniel Schenk, Ph.D., Chair.; Ellis S. Redd, 1st Vice-Chair.; John C. Schroeder, 2nd Vice-Chair.; Kevin Bain, C.E.O. and Exec. Dir.; Connie K. Nass, Secy.; Lisa N. Collins, Treas.; Gary W. Bauer, C.F.O.
Directors: Norm Bafunno; Linda Bennett, Ph.D.; W. Harold Calloway; **Don Chaudoin**; John M. Dunn; Carrie Ellspermann; C. Mark Hubbard; E. Lynn Johnson; Thomas A. Kazee, Ph.D; Marilyn Klenck; David L. Knapp; **James Muehlbauer**; John Pulcini, M.D.; Ronald Romain; Jaleigh J. White.
Number of staff: 8 full-time professional; 3 part-time professional; 1 full-time support.
EIN: 352056722
Other changes: Daniel Schenk, Ph.D. has replaced Ronald Romain as Chair. Ellis S. Redd has replaced Daniel Schenk, Ph.D. as 1st Vice-Chair. John C. Schroeder has replaced David L. Knapp as 2nd Vice-Chair.
Rita Eykamp is no longer a director.
The grantmaker now publishes application guidelines.

1206
WellPoint Foundation, Inc.

(formerly Anthem Foundation, Inc.)
120 Monument Cir.
Indianapolis, IN 46204-4906
Contact: Lance Chrisman, Exec. Dir.
E-mail: wellpoint.foundation@wellpoint.com; Additional e-mail: communityrelations@wellpoint.com; **Main URL: http://wellpointcorporateresponsibility.com/cr/wellPoint_foundation.html**
Tumblr: http://wellpointfoundation.tumblr.com/
Twitter: https://twitter.com/@wellpointfdn_Pr

Established in 2000 in IN.
Donors: Anthem Insurance Cos., Inc.; Anthem Health Plans of New Hampshire, Inc.; Anthem, Inc.; WellPoint, Inc.; Howard Cashion Living Trust.
Foundation type: Company-sponsored foundation.
Financial data (yr. ended 12/31/12): Assets, $123,585,891 (M); expenditures, $11,590,892; qualifying distributions, $10,983,238; giving activities include $7,699,508 for 45 grants (high: $1,643,481; low: $3,000), and $1,939,562 for employee matching gifts.
Purpose and activities: The foundation supports programs designed to enhance the health and well-being of individuals and families. Special emphasis is directed toward programs designed to promote healthy generations.
Fields of interest: Hospitals (general); Health care, infants; Reproductive health, prenatal care; Public health; Public health, communicable diseases; Public health, obesity; Public health, physical fitness; Health care, insurance; Health care; Mental health, smoking; Cancer; Heart & circulatory diseases; Diabetes; Disasters, preparedness/services; Boys & girls clubs; American Red Cross; YM/YWCAs & YM/YWHAs; Public policy, research.
Type of support: General/operating support; Continuing support; Emergency funds; Program development; Scholarship funds; Research; Employee volunteer services; Sponsorships; Employee matching gifts.
Limitations: Applications accepted. **Giving primarily in areas of company operations in AZ, CA, CO, CT, FL, GA, IN, KS, KY, LA, MD, ME, MO, NV, NH, NJ, NM, NY, OH, TN, TX, UT, VA, WA, and WI.** No support for private charities or foundations, religious organizations not of direct benefit to the entire community, political candidates or organizations, discriminatory organizations, or association memberships. No grants to individuals, or for political causes or campaigns, lobbying activities, endowments, film, music, TV, video, or media production projects or broadcast program underwriting, fundraising events, sports sponsorships, performing arts tours, or requests that provide benefit to WellPoint, Inc. or WellPoint employees.
Publications: Application guidelines.
Application information: Organizations receiving support are asked to submit an interim and a final report. Unsolicited applications for capital projects, initiatives, or campaigns are not accepted. Research and policy grants are by invitation only and must align with the Healthy Generations signature initiative. Organizations with research or policy projects should e-mail the foundation with a brief summary. Application form required.

Initial approach: Complete online eligibility quiz and application
***Deadline(s):* May 9 and Sept. 12**
Board meeting date(s): Quarterly
Final notification: 4 to 6 months

Officers and Directors:* Kathleen S. Kiefer, Secy.; Wayne S. DeVeydt,* C.F.O.; R. David Kretschmer, Treas.; Lance Chrisman, Exec. Dir.; Angela F. Braly; Randal L. Brown; Lisa Moriyama; Samuel R. Nussbaum, M.D.
EIN: 352122763
Other changes: Brian A. Sassi is no longer a director.

1207
The Wells County Foundation, Inc.

360 N. Main St., Ste. C
Bluffton, IN 46714 (260) 824-8620
***Contact:* Tammy Slater, C.E.O.**
FAX: (260) 824-3981;
E-mail: wellscountyfound@wellscountyfound.org;
Additional e-mail: tslater@wellscountyfound.org;
Additional E-mail: light@wellscountyfound.org;
Main URL: http://www.wellscountyfound.org

Established in 1957 in IN.
Foundation type: Community foundation.
Financial data (yr. ended 12/31/12): Assets, $15,899,163 (M); gifts received, $174,822; expenditures, $684,174; giving activities include $178,972 for 12+ grants (high: $16,830), and $246,770 for 97 grants to individuals.
Purpose and activities: The foundation seeks to enhance the quality of life of the Wells County, IN, community through the generation and prudent administration of entrusted donor funds to meet present and future changing community needs. Grantmaking fields of interest include arts and culture, education, economic and community development, health and human services, and other charitable purposes.
Fields of interest: Arts; Scholarships/financial aid; Education; Environment; Animals/wildlife; Health care; Recreation; Children/youth, services; Human services; Economic development; Community/economic development; Public affairs.
Type of support: Building/renovation; Equipment; Emergency funds; Program development; Seed money; Technical assistance; Scholarships—to individuals; Matching/challenge support.
Limitations: Applications accepted. Giving primarily in Wells County, IN. No support for religious organizations for religious purposes, or private or parochial schools. No grants to individuals (except for scholarships), or for operating support, financial deficits, or travel; no multi-year funding.
Publications: Application guidelines; Annual report; Informational brochure; IRS Form 990 or 990-PF printed copy available upon request.
Application information: Visit foundation web site for grant application format and guidelines. Scholarships only to residents of Wells County, IN; application guidelines available upon request. Application form not required.
Initial approach: Telephone
Copies of proposal: 1
***Deadline(s):* Feb. 14, June 16, and Oct. 15**

Officers and Directors:* Laura Gentis,* Pres.; Tammy Slater,* C.E.O.; **Alan Gunkel,* V.P. and Chair., Finance Committee**; Chuck King,* Secy.; Trent Bucher,* Treas.; Amy Greiner,* Chair., Mktg. Comm.; Jeremy Todd,* Chair., Grants Comm.; Tim Babcock; Barbara Barbieri; **Ginny Fenstermaker**; Adam Harder; **Mitch Harnish**; **Mike Kracium**; Olivia Reeves; Greg Roembke; Pat Trant.
Number of staff: 1 full-time professional.
EIN: 356042815
Other changes: Alan Gunkel has replaced Laura Gentis as V.P.
Ted Ellis, Kim Gentis, Rick Singer, Laura Gentis, Alan Gunkel, Chuck King, Trent Bucher, Amy Greiner, and Jeremy Todd are no longer directors.

1208
Western Indiana Community Foundation, Inc.

(formerly Covington Community Foundation, Inc.)
135 S. Stringtown Rd.
P.O. Box 175
Covington, IN 47932-0175 (765) 793-0702
Contact: Dale A. White, Exec. Dir.
FAX: (765) 793-0703; E-mail: info@wicf-inc.org;
Main URL: http://www.wicf-inc.org
Scholarship tel.: (765) 793-0702 ext. 3,
e-mail: keaton@wicf-inc.org

Established in 1990 in IN.
Foundation type: Community foundation.
Financial data (yr. ended 12/31/12): Assets, $10,457,381 (M); gifts received, $447,636; expenditures, $484,766; giving activities include $203,098 for grants, and $72,053 for grants to individuals.
Purpose and activities: The foundation seeks to support, encourage, and maintain core Christian values leading to a community which recognizes the benefits of individual commitment to honesty, integrity, reliability, marriage, respect for others, church and traditional family, and to provide public-spirited donors a vehicle for using their gifts in the best possible way now and in the future as conditions inevitably change.
Fields of interest: Arts; Education; Health care; Recreation; Community development, neighborhood development; Economic development.
Type of support: Capital campaigns; Building/renovation; Equipment; Emergency funds; Program development; Seed money; Curriculum development; Scholarship funds; Scholarships—to individuals; Matching/challenge support.
Limitations: Applications accepted. Giving limited to the Attica, Covington, and Southeast Fountain school districts, IN. No grants for individuals (except for scholarships), or for operating budgets, endowments, apparel such as school/sport uniform, or long-term funding.
Publications: Application guidelines; Annual report; Financial statement; Informational brochure; Newsletter; Occasional report (including application guidelines).
Application information: Visit foundation web site for application form and guidelines. Application form required.
Initial approach: Submit application form and attachments
Copies of proposal: 1
Deadline(s): None
Board meeting date(s): Monthly
Final notification: 2 to 4 weeks

Officers and Directors:* Dick Minnette,* Pres.; Kevin Martin,* V.P.; Kim Eaton,* Secy.; Raquel Stultz,* Treas.; Dale A. White, Exec. Dir.; Beth Mason; Thomas A. McGurk, Jr.; Susan Reynolds; John L. Shambach; Robert C. Wright.
Number of staff: 2 full-time professional; 1 part-time support.
EIN: 351814927

1209
Whitley County Community Foundation

400 N. Whitley St.
P.O. Box 527
Columbia City, IN 46725 (260) 244-5224
Contact: September McConnell, Exec. Dir.; For grant applications: John Slavich, Prog. Off.
FAX: (260) 244-5724; E-mail: sepwccf@gmail.com;
Main URL: http://whitleycountycommunityfoundation.org
Facebook: https://www.facebook.com/WhitleyCountyCommunityFoundation
Twitter: https://twitter.com/#!/WhitleyCountyCF

Established in 1992 in IN.
Foundation type: Community foundation.
Financial data (yr. ended 12/31/11): Assets, $16,044,604 (M); gifts received, $1,049,606; expenditures, $1,819,461; giving activities include $1,157,029 for 29 grants (high: $142,514), and $124,325 for 109 grants to individuals.
Purpose and activities: The mission of the foundation is to champion the spirit of philanthropy and grow permanent endowments. Utilizing collaborative leadership, it will assess and address local needs and direct funding to best meet community aspirations. Funding categories include: arts and culture, health, civic affairs, recreation, community development, welfare, and education.
Fields of interest: Arts; Education; Health care; Recreation; Human services; Community development, neighborhood development; Community/economic development; Voluntarism promotion; Public affairs; Youth; Women.
Type of support: Capital campaigns; Endowments; Emergency funds; Seed money; Scholarships—to individuals; Matching/challenge support; Student loans—to individuals.
Limitations: Applications accepted. Giving limited to Whitley County, IN. No support for private schools, or religious or sectarian causes. No grants for operating budgets, budget deficits, annual campaigns, advertising, or debt retirement.
Publications: Application guidelines; Biennial report; Grants list; Informational brochure (including application guidelines); Newsletter.
Application information: Visit foundation web site for application form and guidelines. Application form required.
Initial approach: Submit application form and attachments
Copies of proposal: 1
Deadline(s): May 1 and Dec. 1
Board meeting date(s): 2nd Thurs. of each month

Officers and Directors:* Laurie Steill,* Pres.; Sharlene Berkshire,* Secy.; September McConnell, Exec. Dir.; Dale Duncan; Greg Fahl; Rhonda Jones; John Lefever; Rob Marr; Aileen Meier; Harold Norman; Bill Overdeer; **David Smith**; John Whiteleather.
Number of staff: 2 full-time professional; 1 part-time professional; 1 full-time support.
EIN: 351860518

IOWA

1210
The Claude W. & Dolly Ahrens Foundation
1510 Penrose St.
P.O. Box 284
Grinnell, IA 50112-1203
FAX: (641) 236-5590;
E-mail: info@ahrensfamilyfoundation.org; Main URL: http://www.ahrensfamilyfoundation.org/
Facebook: http://www.facebook.com/pages/Claude-W-Dolly-Ahrens-Foundation-Ahrens-Park-Foundation/122607224452384
Twitter: https://twitter.com/CDAFoundation

Established in 1993 in IA.
Donor: Claude W. Ahrens†.
Foundation type: Independent foundation.
Financial data (yr. ended 10/31/12): Assets, $11,309,515 (M); gifts received, $12,500; expenditures, $1,036,350; qualifying distributions, $878,243; giving activities include $386,436 for 21 grants (high: $270,392; low: $1,000), and $312,975 for 1 foundation-administered program.
Purpose and activities: Giving primarily for education, health, and parks and recreation.
Fields of interest: Arts; Education; Health care; Recreation, parks/playgrounds; Human services; Youth, services.
Type of support: Capital campaigns; Building/renovation; Equipment; Program development; Conferences/seminars; Seed money; Technical assistance; Matching/challenge support.
Limitations: Applications not accepted. Giving limited to central IA. No support for religious and political organizations. No grants to individuals, or for scholarships, general operating support, or international.
Publications: Annual report; Grants list; Informational brochure.
Application information: Unsolicited requests for funds not accepted.
Board meeting date(s): Jan., Mar., May, July, Sept., and Nov.
Officers and Trustees:* Julie Gosselink,* C.E.O. and Pres.; Susan E. Ahrens Witt,* V.P.; Shannon Fitzgerald-Schultz, Secy.-Treas.; Chad W. Ahrens; David Clay.
Number of staff: 3 full-time professional.
EIN: 391906775

1211
Aviva Charitable Foundation
(formerly AmerUs Group Charitable Foundation)
7700 Mills Civic Pkwy.
West Des Moines, IA 50266-3862 (515) 342-3910
Contact: Karen Lynn, V.P.
***E-mail:* AvivaFoundation@avivausa.com**; E-mail for Karen Lynn: karen.lynn@avivausa.com; Main URL: http://www.avivausa.com

Established in 1994 in IA.
Donors: American Mutual Life Insurance Co.; AmerUs Group Co.; Aviva Life and Annuity Co.
Foundation type: Company-sponsored foundation.
Financial data (yr. ended 12/31/12): Assets, $3,869,486 (M); gifts received, $4,000,000; expenditures, $1,949,381; qualifying distributions, $1,949,381; giving activities include $1,949,381 for 64 grants (high: $696,191; low: $25).
Purpose and activities: The foundation supports organizations involved with arts and culture, education, community development, and civic affairs.
Fields of interest: Media, television; Visual arts; Museums; Performing arts; Arts; Higher education; Education; Health care, association; Health care; Human services; Community/economic development; United Ways and Federated Giving Programs; Economics; Public affairs.
Type of support: General/operating support; Continuing support; Scholarship funds; Employee volunteer services; Employee matching gifts.
Limitations: Applications accepted. Giving primarily in areas of company operations in Des Moines, IA, Indianapolis, IN, Topeka, KS, Quincy, MA, and Woodbury, NY. No support for athletes or athletic organizations, fraternal organizations, hospitals or health care facilities, K-8 schools, military or veterans' groups, pass-through organizations, political parties, candidates, or organizations, private foundations, sectarian, religious or denominational organizations, social organizations, trade, industry, or professional associations, or United Way organizations seeking funds for operating expenses of United Way-funded programs. No grants to individuals, or for conference or seminar attendance, courtesy or goodwill advertising, endowments, fellowships, festival participation, or political campaigns.
Publications: Application guidelines.
Application information: Support is limited to 1 contribution per organization during any given year. Multi-year funding is not automatic. Organizations receiving support are asked to provide a final report. Application form required.
Initial approach: Contact foundation for application form
Copies of proposal: 1
Deadline(s): None
Board meeting date(s): Three times per year
Final notification: 8 weeks
Officers and Director:* Christopher J. Littlefield, Pres.; Karen Lynn, V.P.; Michael H. Miller, Secy.; Brenda J. Cushing, Treas.
Number of staff: 2 part-time professional.
EIN: 421431745

1212
Harold R. Bechtel Charitable Trust
201 W. 2nd St., Ste. 1000
Davenport, IA 52801-1817 **(563) 328-3353**
Contact: R. Richard Bittner, Tr.

Foundation type: Independent foundation.
Financial data (yr. ended 04/30/13): Assets, $38,057,443 (M); expenditures, $1,768,157; qualifying distributions, $1,603,658; giving activities include $1,535,558 for 29 grants (high: $366,000; low: $2,000).
Fields of interest: Museums; Arts; Education; YM/YWCAs & YM/YWHAs; United Ways and Federated Giving Programs.
Limitations: Applications accepted. Giving primarily in Scott County, IA.
Application information: Application form required.
Initial approach: Letter or telephone requesting application form
Deadline(s): None
Officers and Trustee:* R. Richard Bittner,* Pres.; Lucille Oseland, Secy.
EIN: 261284636
Other changes: R. Richard Bittner is now Pres.

1213
F. William Beckwith Charitable Foundation
(formerly F. William Beckwith & Leola I. Beckwith Charitable Foundation)
1502 220th St.
Boone, IA **50036-7523**
***Application address:* c/o F. William Beckwith, P.O. Box 70, Boone, IA 50036, tel.: (515) 432-9164**

Established in 1995 in IA.
Donors: F. William Beckwith; Leola I. Beckwith†.
Foundation type: Operating foundation.
Financial data (yr. ended 12/31/12): Assets, $3,561,530 (M); gifts received, $3,028; expenditures, $231,243; qualifying distributions, $200,000; giving activities include $200,000 for 2 grants (high: $100,000; low: $100,000).
Fields of interest: Libraries (public); Education; Botanical gardens; Recreation, camps; Youth development, agriculture; Family services; Christian agencies & churches.
Limitations: Giving primarily in IA and TN. No grants to individuals.
Application information:
Initial approach: Letter
Deadline(s): None
Officer: F. William Beckwith, Pres. and Treas.
EIN: 421448419

1214
The Clarinda Foundation
114 E. Washington St.
P.O. Box 273
Clarinda, IA 51632 (712) 542-4412
Contact: Pam Herzberg, Exec. Dir.
FAX: (712) 542-4412;
E-mail: clarindafound@iowatelecom.net; Main URL: http://www.clarindafoundation.com

Established in 1986 in IA.
Foundation type: Community foundation.
Financial data (yr. ended 12/31/12): Assets, $3,865,321 (M); gifts received, $658,091; expenditures, $589,995; giving activities include $382,791 for 12+ grants (high: $113,328), and $29,328 for 22 grants to individuals.
Purpose and activities: The foundation seeks to provide prospective donors an effective way to invest in the future of Clarinda, IA, and to maximize tax savings to the donors and their estates.
Fields of interest: Education; Health care; Human services; Community/economic development; Public affairs.
Type of support: Building/renovation; Equipment; Program development; Scholarship funds; Scholarships—to individuals; Exchange programs.
Limitations: Applications accepted. Giving limited to within 15 miles of Clarinda, IA.
Publications: Application guidelines; Annual report; Newsletter.
Application information: Visit foundation web site for grant application form. Application form required.
Initial approach: Mail application form
Copies of proposal: 1
***Deadline(s):* June 2**
Board meeting date(s): 3rd Thursday of every month
Final notification: Within 90 days
Officers and Directors:* Dale McAllister,* Pres.; Jennifer McCall,* 1st V.P.; Martin Mattes,* 2nd V.P.; Sandy Geer,* 3rd V.P.; Connie Richardson,* Secy.; Jon Baier,* Treas.; Pam Herzberg,* Exec. Dir.; Elaine Armstrong; Scott Brown; Paul Honnold; Scott Keys; Katie Lowrie; Tom McAndrews; Scott Sump; Laura Swanson; Lynn Whitmore.

Number of staff: 1 part-time professional; 1 part-time support.
EIN: 421285187

1215
Community Foundation of Fort Dodge and United Way
822 Central Ave., Ste. 405
Fort Dodge, IA 50501 (515) 573-3179
Contact: For grants: Randy Kuhlman, C.E.O.
FAX: (515) 955-5421;
E-mail: mail.fdfoundation@frontier.com; Main URL: http://www.fd-foundation.org/
Facebook: http://www.facebook.com/pages/Fort-Dodge-Community-Foundation-and-United-Way/163888696985010

Established in IA in 1995.
Foundation type: Community foundation.
Financial data (yr. ended 12/31/11): Assets, $1,985,738 (M); gifts received, $1,219,160; expenditures, $1,281,885; giving activities include $1,037,858 for 18+ grants (high: $100,000).
Purpose and activities: The foundation's mission is to serve as a catalyst for charitable giving - developing charitable resources to support important community programs, services and projects that will benefit the public good and improve the quality of life of all citizens, families and youth in Fort Dodge, Webster County and North Central Iowa.
Fields of interest: Arts; Education; Environment; Health care; Crime/violence prevention; Recreation; Youth development; Human services, emergency aid; Human services; Community/economic development.
Limitations: Applications accepted. Giving primarily in Fort Dodge, Webster County, and North Central Iowa.
Publications: Annual report.
Application information: All applications are to submitted in hard-copy form and electronically. Visit foundation web site for application form and additional information. Application form required.
Initial approach: Submit application
Deadline(s): Nov. 15 for the Endow Iowa grant
Officers and Board Members:* Randy Kuhlman,* C.E.O.; Timothy J. Carmody,* Pres.; John Bruner,* V.P.; Deb Johnson,* Secy.; Scott Johnson,* Treas.; Tim Burns; Nick Cochrane; Jim Humes; Susan Ahlers Leman; Troy Martens; **Scott McQueen**; Don Schnurr; Troy K. Shaner; Lin Simpson; Bill Thatcher; Lisa Wilson; Karen Wood.
EIN: 421439853
Other changes: Chris Hayek is no longer Opers. Mgr. John Bruner is no longer a board member.

1216
Community Foundation of Greater Dubuque
700 Locust St., Ste. 195
Dubuque, IA 52001-6824 (563) 588-2700
Contact: Nancy Van Milligen, C.E.O.; For grants: Eric Dregne, V.P., Strategic Inititiatives
FAX: (563) 583-6619;
E-mail: office@dbqfoundation.org; Grant inquiry and information e-mail: eric@dbqdoundation.org; Main URL: http://www.dbqfoundation.org
Facebook: http://www.facebook.com/pages/Community-Foundation-of-Greater-Dubuque/119274054070?ref=mf
Google Plus: https://plus.google.com/111491904102395018243
LinkedIn: http://www.linkedin.com/companies/community-foundation-of-greater-dubuque
RSS Feed: http://www.dbqfoundation.org/news-events/news/feed
Twitter: http://twitter.com/CFGD
YouTube: http://www.youtube.com/user/yapperscfgd

Established in 2001 in IA.
Foundation type: Community foundation.
Financial data (yr. ended 06/30/12): Assets, $31,179,245 (M); gifts received, $6,534,658; expenditures, $4,384,297; giving activities include $3,080,190 for 85+ grants (high: $633,147).
Purpose and activities: The foundation works to improve the quality of life in the Dubuque region by: serving donors, making grants and providing community leadership through convening and collaboration.
Fields of interest: Community/economic development; Children/youth; Youth; Aging; Physically disabled; Economically disadvantaged.
Type of support: General/operating support; Management development/capacity building; Seed money; Scholarship funds; Technical assistance; Consulting services.
Limitations: Applications accepted. Giving limited to northeast IA. No support for religious purposes. No grants for operating support, annual and capital campaigns, budget deficit, endowments, or equipment (unless it is essential for the program).
Publications: Application guidelines; Annual report; Grants list; Informational brochure; Newsletter.
Application information: Visit foundation web site for applications and guidelines per grant type. Application form required.
Initial approach: Complete online application for Community Impact Grants
Deadline(s): Dec. 31 for Community Impact Grants; varies for others
Board meeting date(s): 4 times a year
Final notification: Early Oct. for Community Impact Grants; varies for others
Officers and Directors:* Tim Conlon,* Chair.; John O'Connor,* Vice-Chair.; Nancy Van Milligen,* C.E.O. and Pres.; Eric Dregne,* V.P., Strategic Initiatives; **Amy Manternach,* V.P., Philanthropic Srvs.**; Ken Furst,* Secy.; Brian Kane,* Treas.; Dr. Ed Alt; Jesus Aviles; Chad Chandlee; Charlie Glab; Sarah Harris; Jane Hasek; Bob Hoefer; William R. Klauer, Jr.; Keith Kramer; Jeanne Lauritsen; Phillip Ruppel; Jim Theisen; Teri Zuccaro.
Number of staff: 5 full-time professional; 8 part-time professional; 1 full-time support; 1 part-time support.
EIN: 421526614
Other changes: Hillary Baker is now Dir., Comms. Dick Friedman and Stephen J. Juergens are no longer directors.

1217
Community Foundation of Greater Muscatine
208 W. 2nd St., Ste. 13
Muscatine, IA 52761 (563) 264-3863
Contact: Judi Holdorf, Exec. Dir.; For grants: Betsy Baker, Finance and Office Mgr.
FAX: (563) 264-3383; E-mail: cfgm@machlink.com; Grant application e-mail: bbaker.cfgm@machlink.com; Main URL: http://www.muscatinecommunityfoundation.org
Twitter: http://twitter.com/MuscatineComFnd

Established in 1999 in IA.
Foundation type: Community foundation.
Financial data (yr. ended 12/31/12): Assets, $7,376,113 (M); gifts received, $1,174,114; expenditures, $587,690; giving activities include $309,533 for 4 grants.
Purpose and activities: The foundation actively works to improve the quality of life in Muscatine County through philanthropy. The foundation seeks to accomplish this mission by: 1) building a substantial endowment to provide for community needs for generations to come; 2) serving donors' needs by providing flexible, convenient and cost-effective means to achieve charitable giving goals; 3) educating the public about charitable giving strategies and encourage inclusion of charitable giving in will; 4) promoting philanthropy in the service area; and 5) providing a neutral place for collaboration of community improvement initiatives.
Fields of interest: Arts; Education; Environment; Health care; Youth, services; Family services; Human services; Community/economic development.
Type of support: General/operating support; Continuing support; Income development; Management development/capacity building; Capital campaigns; Building/renovation; Equipment; Land acquisition; Endowments; Debt reduction; Emergency funds; Program development; Conferences/seminars; Seed money; Scholarship funds; Technical assistance; Consulting services; Employee matching gifts; In-kind gifts; Matching/challenge support.
Limitations: Applications accepted. Giving limited to the greater Muscatine, IA, area.
Publications: Annual report; Financial statement; Grants list; Informational brochure.
Application information: Visit foundation web site for grant information and application form. Application form required.
Initial approach: Submit application form
Copies of proposal: 2
***Deadline(s):* Mar. 28**
Board meeting date(s): 3rd Tues. of each month
Officers and Directors:* Bob Jensen,* Pres.; Sarah Lande,* V.P.; Keith Porter,* Secy.; Diana Gradert,* Treas.; Judi Holdorf, Exec. Dir.; Joan U. Axel; Rich Dwyer; Timothy M. Heth; Jonathon Holthe; Shelly Maharry; Cindy Mays; Brett Nelson; Michael Wilson.
Number of staff: 1 full-time professional; 2 part-time professional.
EIN: 421495980
Other changes: Tim Nelson is no longer a director.

1218
Community Foundation of Johnson County
325 E. Washington St.
Iowa City, IA 52240-3968 (319) 337-0483
Contact: Michael L. Stoffregen, Exec. Dir.
FAX: (319) 338-9958;
E-mail: info@communityfoundationofjohnsoncounty.com; Main URL: http://www.communityfoundationofjohnsoncounty.org/

Established in 2000 in IA.
Foundation type: Community foundation.
Financial data (yr. ended 06/30/12): Assets, $8,870,600 (M); gifts received, $1,935,168; expenditures, $1,626,519; giving activities include $1,312,376 for 20+ grants (high: $746,592).
Purpose and activities: The organization provides a means for citizens to make gifts to specific organizations, general areas of concern or the common good, to pool and manage endowment funds for local nonprofit organizations, and to distribute funds to benefit the community.

Fields of interest: Arts; Education; Environment; Animals/wildlife; Youth development; Human services.
Limitations: Applications accepted. Giving limited to the Johnson County, IA, area.
Publications: Annual report; Grants list; Newsletter.
Application information: Visit web site for application form and guidelines. Application form required.
Initial approach: Create online profile
Deadline(s): July 15
Officers and Directors:* Tim Krumm,* Pres.; **John Schneider,* V.P.**; Steve Atkins,* Secy.; Dean Price,* Treas.; Michael L. Stoffregen, Exec. Dir.; Betsy Boyd; Chuck Coulter; Maggie Elliott; **Bart Floyd**; Pat Harney; Michael Heinrich; Sarah Maiers; Sharon Oglesby; Nancy Richardson; Chuck Skaugstad, Jr.; Greg Turner; Anne Vandenberg; Steve Weeber; Joe Wegman; Mary Westbrook; Nancy Williams.
EIN: 421508117
Other changes: John Schneider is now V.P. Ross DeValois, Bill Furlong, Tim Krumm, and Christine Scheetz are no longer directors.

1219
Greater Delaware County Community Foundation
200 E. Main St.
Manchester, IA **52057 (563) 927-4141**
E-mail: **macc@manchesteriowa.org; Main URL: http://www.manchesteriowa.org/GDCCF/index.html**

Established in 1976 in IA.
Foundation type: Community foundation.
Financial data (yr. ended 10/31/12): Assets, $2,306,147 (M); gifts received, $309,672; expenditures, $233,114; giving activities include $106,353 for 4+ grants (high: $27,796), and $67,575 for 172 grants to individuals.
Purpose and activities: Giving for scholarships and community development.
Fields of interest: Higher education; Education; Community/economic development.
Type of support: Scholarships—to individuals.
Limitations: Giving primarily in IA.
Officers and Trustees:* John E. Tyrrell,* Chair.; Cheryl Stufflebeaum,* Vice-Chair.; Jack Klaus,* Secy.; Tom Allyn; Kay Harris; Fred Phelps; Ed Poynor; Doug Tuetken.
EIN: 421045184

1220
deStwolinski Family Foundation
2911 Hamilton Blvd.
P.O. Box 270
Sioux City, IA 51104-2405

Established in 1998 in NE.
Donor: Lance W. deStwolinski.
Foundation type: Independent foundation.
Financial data (yr. ended 05/31/13): Assets, $1,931,617 (M); expenditures, $203,517; qualifying distributions, $203,517; giving activities include $174,566 for grants.
Fields of interest: Education; Military/veterans' organizations.
Type of support: Capital campaigns; Endowments; Scholarship funds.
Limitations: Applications not accepted. Giving primarily in AZ, IA, NE and NM.
Application information: Unsolicited requests for funds not accepted.
Board meeting date(s): Nov. and May
Officers: Lance W. deStwolinski, Pres.; Elizabeth H. deStwolinski, V.P. and Secy.-Treas.
Directors: Matthew deStwolinski; Kim Sealey; Pat Sealey.
EIN: 470812539
Other changes: Lori deStwolinski is no longer a director.

1221
Max and Helen Guernsey Charitable Foundation
P.O. Box 1172
Waterloo, IA 50704-1172 (319) 226-3434
Contact: Soo Greiman, Exec. Dir.
E-mail: **GuernseyFoundatn@aol.com; Physical address to apply in person for a grant: Regions Bank Building, 100 E. Park Ave., Ste. 230, Waterloo, IA**; Main URL: http://www.guernseyfoundation.com

Established in 1996 in IA.
Donors: Helen Guernsey; Max E. Guernsey†; Waverly Plastics, Inc.
Foundation type: Independent foundation.
Financial data (yr. ended 06/30/13): Assets, $18,825,315 (M); gifts received, $5,000; expenditures, $1,322,757; qualifying distributions, $1,098,794; giving activities include $1,098,794 for 92 grants (high: $50,000; low: $500).
Purpose and activities: The foundation's mission is to work in partnership with others to improve the vitality of the community, addressing issues important now and in the future. The foundation focuses its support on a broad spectrum of needs including education that builds character, programs that enhance family life, key social issues, science, programs that aim for community betterment, health and life skills, sports, fitness, and activities that recognize the value of people.
Fields of interest: Museums; Education; Botanical gardens; Crime/law enforcement, police agencies; YM/YWCAs & YM/YWHAs; Children/youth, services; Children, services; Family services.
Type of support: General/operating support; Continuing support; Annual campaigns; Capital campaigns; Building/renovation; Endowments; Emergency funds; Conferences/seminars.
Limitations: Applications accepted. Giving primarily in the Cedar Valley, IA, area. No support for national health organizations and their local affiliates, veteran, labor and political organizations or campaigns, or fraternal, athletic, and social clubs; no operating expenses of organizations supported by United Way. No grants to individuals, or for business ventures, endowments, advertising, loans or debt retirements, conferences, seminars, trips or similar events; no grants for religious purposes or to sectarian programs for religious purposes.
Publications: Application guidelines; Informational brochure.
Application information: Brochures and application forms are available at the foundation office. Application form required.
Initial approach: Telephone Exec. Dir. to determine appropriateness of request
Copies of proposal: 1
Deadline(s): Mar. 15 and Aug. 15
Board meeting date(s): Spring and Fall
Final notification: June 1 and Nov. 1
Officers and Directors:* Thomas R. Paulsen,* Pres.; Helen Guernsey,* V.P.; Shirley Kreger,* Secy.; Gary Nelson,* Treas.; **Soo Greiman, Exec. Dir.**; Harold B. Strever, Jr.
EIN: 421460664

1222
The Hall-Perrine Foundation
(formerly The Hall Foundation, Inc.)
115 3rd St., S.E., Ste. 803
Cedar Rapids, IA 52401-1222 (319) 362-9079
Contact: **Kristin Novak, Prog. Off.; Jack Evans, Pres.**
FAX: (319) 362-7220;
E-mail: kristin@Hallperrine.org; Main URL: http://www.hallperrine.org/

Incorporated in 1953 in IA.
Donor: Members of the Hall family.
Foundation type: Independent foundation.
Financial data (yr. ended 12/31/12): Assets, $109,995,615 (M); expenditures, $6,194,121; qualifying distributions, $5,595,424; giving activities include $5,422,878 for 17+ grants (high: $1,000,000), and $100,000 for 1 loan/program-related investment.
Purpose and activities: The foundation is dedicated to improving the quality of life for people in Linn County, IA by responding to changing social, economic, and cultural needs. Primary areas of interest include the arts, higher education, social services, community funds, and health care. Support also for cultural programs, including fine and performing art groups, youth agencies, and health services.
Fields of interest: Arts; Higher education; Health care; Youth, services; Human services.
Type of support: Capital campaigns; Building/renovation; Matching/challenge support.
Limitations: Applications accepted. Giving limited to Linn County, IA. No support for churches or their programs, or elementary or secondary schools. No grants to individuals, or for deficit financing, endowment funds, continuing operating support, benefits, special events, conferences, or fellowships; no loans.
Publications: Application guidelines; Informational brochure.
Application information: Application form required.
Initial approach: Letter or in-person conversation
Copies of proposal: 1
Deadline(s): Varies according to meeting dates
Board meeting date(s): Quarterly
Final notification: After board meetings
Officers and Directors:* Jack B. Evans,* Pres.; Darrel A. Morf,* V.P.; Iris E. Muchmore,* Secy.; Charles M. Peters,* Treas.; Dee Baird; Todd M. Bergen; Dennis L. Boatman, M.D.; Ernie Buresh; Kathy E. Eno; Carleen Grandon; Alex A. Meyer.
Number of staff: 2 full-time professional.
EIN: 426057097

1223
HNI Charitable Foundation
(formerly HON INDUSTRIES Charitable Foundation)
P.O. Box 1109
Muscatine, IA 52761-0071 (563) 252-7503
Contact: Dianna Stelzner, Secy.-Treas.
FAX: (563) 264-7217;
E-mail: stelznerd@hnicorp.com; Application address: 408 W. Second St., Muscatine, IA 52761

Established in 1985 in IA.
Donors: HON Industries Inc.; HNI Corp.
Foundation type: Company-sponsored foundation.

Financial data (yr. ended 12/31/12): Assets, $2,836,611 (M); gifts received, $443,396; expenditures, $796,256; qualifying distributions, $766,431; giving activities include $766,431 for grants.
Purpose and activities: The foundation supports organizations involved with arts and culture, education, health, disaster preparedness, and human services.
Fields of interest: Historic preservation/historical societies; Arts; Higher education; Libraries (public); Education, services; Education; Hospitals (general); Health care, clinics/centers; Health care; Disasters, preparedness/services; Disasters, fire prevention/control; Boy scouts; YM/YWCAs & YM/YWHAs; Human services; United Ways and Federated Giving Programs.
Type of support: General/operating support; Capital campaigns; Building/renovation.
Limitations: Applications accepted. Giving limited to areas of company operations, with emphasis on IA, IL, KY, MN, NC and WA. No support for national, statewide, or religious organizations. No grants to individuals.
Application information: Application form not required.
Initial approach: Proposal
Copies of proposal: 1
Deadline(s): None
Officers: Stan A. Askren,* Pres.; Gary L. Carlson,* V.P.; Dianna Stelzner, Secy.-Treas.; **Tim Heth**; **Jack Michaels**; **Karen Olderog.**
Number of staff: 1 full-time professional.
EIN: 421246787

1224
Holthues Trust
209 Iowa Ave.
Muscatine, IA 52761-3730

Established in 1997 in IA.
Donor: The Stanley Foundation.
Foundation type: Independent foundation.
Financial data (yr. ended 12/31/12): Assets, $23,275,606 (M); expenditures, $1,139,133; qualifying distributions, $1,044,000; giving activities include $1,044,000 for grants.
Purpose and activities: Giving primarily for projects that will advance the goals of peace, security, freedom and justice globally, as well as community services locally in Iowa.
Fields of interest: Education; Human services; International peace/security; International human rights; International affairs; Civil/human rights; Community/economic development.
Limitations: Applications not accepted. Giving in the U.S., with emphasis on Washington, DC, IA, MA, MN, and NY. No support for private foundations. No grants to individuals.
Application information: Contributes only to pre-selected organizations.
Officers and Directors:* Richard H. Stanley, Pres.; Joseph H. Stanley,* V.P.; Betty Anders, Secy.; Dana W. Pittman, Treas.; Donna J. Buckles; **Brian Hanson**; Elizabeth Shriver; Lincoln Stanley; Lynne E. Stanley.
EIN: 421466786

1225
Iowa Foundation for Agricultural Advancement
131 240th St.
Durant, IA 52747-9616
Contact: Taci Lilienthal
Application address: c/o Winner's Circle Scholarship, Attn: Dr. Hodson, 30805 595th Ave., Cambridge, IA 50046, tel.: (515) 383-4386
Facebook: https://www.facebook.com/IowaFoundationforAgAdvancement

Established in IA.
Donor: Robert Schlutz.
Foundation type: Independent foundation.
Financial data (yr. ended 12/31/12): Assets, $0 (M); gifts received, $144,534; expenditures, $249,112; qualifying distributions, $257,558; giving activities include $144,000 for 118 grants to individuals (high: $5,500; low: $100).
Purpose and activities: Scholarship awards to students pursuing a degree relating to the animal industry at any 2-year or 4-year post secondary educational institution in Iowa.
Fields of interest: Education; Agriculture.
Type of support: Scholarships—to individuals.
Limitations: Applications accepted. Giving primarily in IA.
Application information: Application form required.
Deadline(s): June 1
Officers: Jack Bair, Pres.; Stephen Weldon, V.P.; Scott Wiley, Treas.; Shelley Wing, Secy.
Directors: Rob Bohnsack; Dick Danielson; Dustin Ford; Lindsay Greiner; Harold Hodson; Cat Penton; Taylor Sweeney; Gary Vanaernam; Linda Weldon.
EIN: 421183067
Other changes: The grantmaker no longer lists a URL address.

1226
Iowa West Foundation
25 Main Pl., Ste. 550
Council Bluffs, IA 51503-0700 (712) 309-3000
***Contact:* Deb Debbaut, Grants. Mgr.**
E-mail: grantinfo@iowawest.com; Main URL: http://www.iowawestfoundation.org
Facebook: https://www.facebook.com/IowaWestFoundation
Grants List: http://www.iowawestfoundation.org/grantmaking/grant-archive/
Twitter: https://twitter.com/IowaWestFdn

Established in 1992 in IA, began grant operations in 1994.
Donor: Iowa West Racing Assn.
Foundation type: Independent foundation.
Financial data (yr. ended 12/31/12): Assets, $336,793,463 (M); gifts received, $6,942,922; expenditures, $29,768,744; qualifying distributions, $27,102,738; giving activities include $21,648,633 for 235 grants (high: $3,406,684; low: $1,000), and $3,785,808 for 7 foundation-administered programs.
Purpose and activities: The mission of the foundation is to improve lives and strengthen communities for present and future generations. The foundation strives to provide leadership, create partnerships, leverage resources and serve as a catalyst in identifying and supporting community needs. The foundation has a special interest in the areas of community development and beautification, economic development, education, and human and social needs. Current focus includes assisting local schools to reduce the dropout rate, and to improve neighborhoods in Pottawattamie County, IA.
Fields of interest: Education; Human services; Community/economic development.
Type of support: General/operating support; Management development/capacity building; Capital campaigns; Building/renovation; Equipment; Program development; Seed money; Curriculum development; Consulting services; Scholarships—to individuals; Matching/challenge support.
Limitations: Applications accepted. **Giving primarily in southwest IA and eastern NE.** No support for medical research or church-affiliated organizations for religious purposes. No grants for fundraising, benefit, and social events, capital requests (for improvements to school property or for hospitals, medical facilities, assisted living projects, nursing homes, independent care, and extended care facilities), operating deficits or long-term operating support, publications, films, books, seminars, symposia or for conferences.
Publications: Application guidelines; Annual report; Quarterly report.
Application information: After foundation staff review letter of inquiry, they notify each prospective applicant usually within one business day and only by foundation invitation are applicants requested to complete an on-line proposal. Application form required.
Initial approach: Complete on-line eligibility quiz and, if eligible, submit an on-line letter of inquiry via foundation's web site
Copies of proposal: 1
Deadline(s): For letter of inquiry: Jan. 1, Apr. 1, July 1, and Oct. 1; For full proposal: Jan. 15, Apr. 15, July 15, and Oct. 15
Final notification: 3 months from full proposal deadline
Officers and Directors:* Sue M. Miller,* Chair.; Rick Crowl, Vice-Chair.; Peter Tulipana, C.E.O. and Pres.; Jerry Mathiasen, Sr. V.P; Tim Miller, V.P., Finance; **Kathleen Rapp, V.P., Grants and Initiatives; Rick Killion, Secy.-Treas.; Amy Crawford; Mark Genereux; John P. Nelson**; Suellen Overton; Robert Schlott; **Warren Weber.**
Number of staff: 9 full-time professional.
EIN: 421391990
Other changes: At the close of 2012, the grantmaker paid grants of $25,434,441, a 63.6% increase over the 2011 disbursements, $15,550,169.

1227
Greater Jefferson County Community Foundation
P.O. Box 1325
Fairfield, IA 52556-1325 (641) 472-0758
***Contact:* Barbara Kistler, Admin.**
FAX: (641) 472-0758;
E-mail: gjcf0758@iowatelecom.net; Main URL: http://greaterjeffersoncountyfoundation.org/

Established in 1975 in IA.
Foundation type: Community foundation.
Financial data (yr. ended 03/31/12): Assets, $2,148,928 (M); gifts received, $344,021; expenditures, $262,662; giving activities include $156,372 for 12 grants (high: $22,000), and $74,692 for 38 grants to individuals.
Purpose and activities: The Greater Jefferson County Foundation receives, accepts and distributes funds for educational, cultural, civic and charitable purposes for the benefit of the greater community of Jefferson County, Iowa.
Fields of interest: Humanities; Arts; Scholarships/financial aid; Education; Safety/disasters; Athletics/sports, baseball; Recreation; Youth development; Children/youth, services.
Type of support: Building/renovation; Equipment; Endowments; Scholarships—to individuals.
Limitations: Applications accepted. Giving limited to Jefferson County, IA. No support for churches. No grants for operating expenses.

Publications: Application guidelines; Annual report; Financial statement; Grants list; Informational brochure.
Application information: Visit foundation's web site for additional guidelines and online application. Application form required.
Initial approach: Complete online grant application
Copies of proposal: 1
Deadline(s): June 1
Board meeting date(s): May and Nov.
Final notification: 30 days
Officers and Directors:* Bob Wiegert,* Pres.; Ken Malloy,* V.P.; Peggy Small,* Secy.; Dave Eastburn,* Treas.; Joe Carr; Dave Dickey; **David Eastburn**; Sarah Flattery; **Marty Gleason**; Nancy Horras; Tim Kuiken; Greg Lowenbery; Ken Malloy; Pat McMahon; Pam Mitchell; Linda Pettit; Renee Rebling; Peggy Small; Bob Wiegert.
Number of staff: 1 part-time support.
EIN: 510172078
Other changes: Amanda Beasley and Sharyn Workman are no longer directors.

1228
Zach Johnson Foundation
P.O. Box 2336
Cedar Rapids, IA 52406-2336 **(319) 730-3734**
***E-mail:* tmyers@zachjohnsongolf.com; Main URL: http://www.zachjohnsongolf.com/foundation.page**
Facebook: https://www.facebook.com/pages/Zach-Johnson-Foundation/122406031136754
Twitter: https://twitter.com/ZJFClassic

Donors: Gary Rozek; David Ekland; William Mowery; Patrick Cobb; SFX Escrow - Blood PSA; TrueNorth Companies; DSD Realty, Inc.; Cedar Rapids Bank & Trust; Infinity Contact; AEGON Transamerica Foundation; PGA of America; Zach Johnson; Kimala Johnson; Pat Baird.
Foundation type: Independent foundation.
Financial data (yr. ended 12/31/12): Assets, $1,714,789 (M); gifts received, $1,249,218; expenditures, $659,125; qualifying distributions, $331,875; giving activities include $331,814 for 8 grants (high: $241,015; low: $1,000).
Fields of interest: Children/youth, services; Human services; United Ways and Federated Giving Programs; Children.
Limitations: Applications not accepted. Giving primarily in IA.
Publications: Annual report; IRS Form 990 or 990-PF printed copy available upon request.
Application information: Unsolicited requests for funds not accepted.
Officers and Directors:* Patrick Cobb,* Chair.; Zach Johnson,* Pres.; Kimala Johnson,* V.P.; Craig Vermie, Secy.; Patrick Baird,* Treas.; Brad Buffoni; Larry Gladson; Craig Hotchkiss; Beth Malicki; Lon Olejniczak.
EIN: 272683100
Other changes: The grantmaker now publishes an annual report online.

1229
The F. Maytag Family Foundation
(formerly The F. Maytag Family Foundation)
P.O. Box 366
Newton, IA 50208
Contact: Edna Parrish, Secy.

Trust established in 1945 in IA.
Donors: Fred Maytag II†; and members of the Maytag family.
Foundation type: Independent foundation.
Financial data (yr. ended 12/31/12): Assets, $56,066,191 (M); expenditures, $6,302,524; qualifying distributions, $6,044,084; giving activities include $6,028,696 for 81 grants (high: $1,100,000; low: $500).
Purpose and activities: Giving primarily for higher and other education, arts and culture, public affairs, social services, health, and aid for the handicapped.
Fields of interest: Arts; Higher education; Education; Environment, natural resources; Health care; Health organizations, association; Human services; Community/economic development; Public affairs; Disabilities, people with.
Type of support: General/operating support; Continuing support; Annual campaigns; Capital campaigns; Building/renovation; Equipment; Land acquisition; Endowments; Emergency funds; Program development; Conferences/seminars; Professorships; Publication; Seed money; Curriculum development; Fellowships; Internship funds; Scholarship funds; Research; Technical assistance; Matching/challenge support.
Limitations: Applications accepted. Giving primarily in Des Moines and Newton, IA. No grants to individuals, or for emergency funds, deficit financing, scholarships, fellowships, demonstration projects, or conferences; no loans.
Publications: Application guidelines.
Application information: Application form not required.
Initial approach: Telephone or write for guidelines
Copies of proposal: 3
Deadline(s): None
Officer and Directors:* Kenneth P. Maytag,* Pres.; Frederick L. Maytag III,* Vice-Pres.; Edna Parrish, Secy.; William C. Weinsheimer.
Number of staff: 1 full-time support.
EIN: 421444870
Other changes: At the close of 2012, the grantmaker paid grants of $6,028,696, a 72.2% increase over the 2011 disbursements, $3,501,824.

1230
R. J. McElroy Trust
425 Cedar St., Ste. 312
Waterloo, IA 50701-1351 (319) 287-9102
Contact: Stacy Van Gorp, Exec. Dir.
FAX: (319) 287-9105;
E-mail: vangorp@mcelroytrust.org; Additional e-mail: office@mcelroytrust.org; Main URL: http://www.mcelroytrust.org
Blog: http://mcelroytrust.org/news/
Grants List: http://mcelroytrust.org/grants/previous-grants/

Established in 1965 in IA; private foundation status attained in 1984.
Donor: R.J. McElroy†.
Foundation type: Independent foundation.
Financial data (yr. ended 12/31/12): Assets, $39,977,113 (M); gifts received, $6,455; expenditures, $2,190,439; qualifying distributions, $1,702,820; giving activities include $1,338,291 for 69 grants (high: $500,000; low: $300), and $74,300 for 24 grants to individuals (high: $10,000; low: $100).
Purpose and activities: Primary emphasis on education, especially scholarship and loan programs; public secondary education, particularly for the disadvantaged; early childhood and elementary education and programs for minorities; and youth, including internships. The trust awards scholarships to 1-3 high school seniors in each of the school districts in the trust's 19-county area. Scholarship selection is made locally, not by the trust. Giving also for the arts, recreation, and the environment; some support through matching funds and fellowships for graduate study.
Fields of interest: Visual arts; Performing arts; Arts; Education, early childhood education; Child development, education; Elementary school/education; Secondary school/education; Higher education; Education; Environment; Recreation; Youth development, services; Human services; Children/youth, services; Child development, services; Leadership development; Infants/toddlers; Children/youth; Children; Youth; Young adults.
Type of support: General/operating support; Capital campaigns; Building/renovation; Equipment; Emergency funds; Program development; Professorships; Seed money; Fellowships; Internship funds; Scholarship funds; Research; Matching/challenge support.
Limitations: Applications accepted. Giving primarily in 15 counties in northeast IA, (Allamakee, Black Hawk, Bremer, Buchanan, Butler, Chickasaw, Clayton, Delaware, Dubuque, Fayette, Floyd, Grundy, Howard, Tama, and Winneshiek). No support for religious organizations for religious education. No grants to individuals (except for fellowship and scholarship programs that are already established).
Publications: Application guidelines; Grants list; Informational brochure; Informational brochure (including application guidelines); Program policy statement; Program policy statement (including application guidelines).
Application information: Application guidelines and form available on foundation web site. Application form required.
Initial approach: E-mail or telephone to Exec. Dir.
Copies of proposal: 1
Deadline(s): Mar. 1, June 1, Sept. 1, and Dec. 1
Board meeting date(s): Monthly
Final notification: May 1, Aug. 1, Nov. 1, and Feb. 1
Officers and Trustees:* James B. Waterbury,* Chair.; Stacy Van Gorp, Exec. Dir.; Raleigh D. Buckmaster; Rick Young.
Number of staff: 1 full-time professional; 1 full-time support.
EIN: 426173496

1231
Mount Saint Clare Education Foundation
Clinton, IA

The foundation terminated on June 14, 2013 and transferred its assets to Mount Saint Clare Education Charitable Trust.

1232
NCMIC Foundation, Inc.
14001 University Ave., Ste. A3E
Clive, IA 50325-8258
Contact: Matt Gustafson
***E-mail:* info@ncmicfoundation.org**; Main URL: http://www.ncmicfoundation.com

Established in IA.
Donors: NCMIC Insurance Company; National University of Health Sciences; Logan College of Chiropractic; NCMIC Group, Inc.
Foundation type: Independent foundation.
Financial data (yr. ended 12/31/12): Assets, $10,511,210 (M); gifts received, $80,956;

expenditures, $577,732; qualifying distributions, $508,068; giving activities include $474,625 for 16 grants (high: $232,437; low: $1,000).
Purpose and activities: Giving for research and educational projects relating to chiropractic care and/or alternative approaches to healthcare.
Fields of interest: Education; Chiropractic research.
Limitations: Applications accepted. Giving primarily in CA and IA.
Publications: Application guidelines.
Application information: See grantmaker web site for application policies and guidelines. Application form required.
Initial approach: **Submit plan**
Deadline(s): None
Officers and Directors:* Gerald Strubinger, Jr., Esq.*, Pres.; Thomas Schmidt, Sr.,* Secy.; Stanley Bushner, C.P.A.,* Treas.; Ronald Segel; Gerald Strubinger, Esq., Jr.
EIN: 680570762
Other changes: Gerald Strubinger, Jr., Esq. has replaced Gary Tarola as Pres.
The grantmaker now publishes application guidelines.

1233
On His Path
604 N. Parkway St.
Wayland, IA 52654-7638 **(319) 256-5656**
***E-mail:* info@onhispath.com**; Main URL: http://www.onhispath.com/
Blog: http://blog.onhispath.com/
Facebook: https://www.facebook.com/pages/On-His-Path/203691329662316

Established in IA.
Donor: M.D. Orthopaedics Inc.
Foundation type: Independent foundation.
Financial data (yr. ended 12/31/12): Assets, $48,409 (M); gifts received, $840,121; expenditures, $817,527; qualifying distributions, $766,604; giving activities include $638,228 for 36 grants (high: $157,581; low: $70), $23,535 for 8 grants to individuals (high: $13,308; low: $227), and $92,651 for 4 foundation-administered programs.
Purpose and activities: Giving primarily for children and social services, particularly for the manufacturing and distribution of a superior low-cost clubfoot brace to developing countries. Support also for research on devices and techniques to more effectively treat and care for a variety of pediatric and adult conditions and deformities. The foundation is also focused on bringing potable water and adequate nutrition to the developing world.
Fields of interest: Health care; Human services; Children/youth, services; International relief.
Limitations: Applications accepted. Giving in the U.S., with some emphasis on IA.
Application information: Application form available on foundation web site. Application form required.
Officers: John Mitchell, Pres.; Jean Mitchell, V.P.; Emily Ferguson, Secy.-Treas.
EIN: 271354039

1234
The Peregrine Charities
1 Peregrine Way
Cedar Falls, IA 50613-4707 (319) 553-2118
Facebook: http://www.facebook.com/pctri

Established in 2005 in IL.
Donors: Russell R. Wasendorf, Sr.; Ken Wood; Minneola Co-op; Riverbend Industries, LLC; PFC Best; City of Waterloo.
Foundation type: Independent foundation.
Financial data (yr. ended 12/31/11): Assets, $27,441 (M); gifts received, $233,244; expenditures, $243,430; qualifying distributions, $211,125; giving activities include $187,060 for 2 grants (high: $142,210; low: $44,850).
Fields of interest: Health care; Pediatrics; Children, services.
Limitations: Giving primarily in IA. No grants to individuals.
Application information: Accepts applications by invitation only through a formal request for proposals.
Officers: Russell R. Wasendorf, Sr., Chair. and Pres.; Russell R. Wasendorf, Jr., V.P.; Connie Wasendorf, Treas.; Amber Wasendorf, Exec. Dir.
EIN: 412152771
Other changes: The grantmaker no longer lists an E-mail or a URL address.

1235
Pottawattamie County Community Foundation
536 E. Broadway
Council Bluffs, IA 51503 **(712) 256-7007**
***Contact:* Dawn Hovey, Pres. and C.E.O.**
E-mail: info@ourpccf.org; Main URL: http://www.ourpccf.org/
Facebook: http://www.facebook.com/pages/Pottawattamie-County-Community-Foundation/120183394687048

Foundation type: Community foundation.
Financial data (yr. ended 12/31/12): Assets, $9,278,178 (M); gifts received, $1,661,971; expenditures, $426,436; giving activities include $124,093 for 3+ grants (high: $34,821), and $87,037 for 142 grants to individuals.
Purpose and activities: The Pottawattamie County Community Foundation is a partnership of rural and urban citizens dedicated to improving the lives of all residents of the county's communities by: 1) serving as an effective catalyst for responses to community issues; 2) supporting continuous efforts to meet changing needs stimulating donor-driven philanthropy; 3) raising the capacity of nonprofit organizations in the county; and 4) providing careful stewardship of the foundation's resources.
Limitations: Applications accepted. Giving primarily in Pottawattamie County, IA. No grants for clinical or medical research, capital campaigns, operating deficits or retirement of debt, construction projects or real estate acquisitions, gift cards or prizes, or .
Publications: Application guidelines; Annual report; IRS Form 990 or 990-PF printed copy available upon request.
Application information: Visit foundation web site for application forms and guidelines per grant type. Application form required.
Initial approach: Submit application and attachments
Deadline(s): Mar. 15 and Sept. 15 for the Community Grants Program
Final notification: 45 days for Community Grants Program
Officers and Directors:* Kelly Summy,* Chair.; Marie Knedler,* Vice-Chair.; Dawn Hovey,* Pres. and C.E.O.; Jerry Banks,* Secy.; Robert McCarthy,* Treas.; Bobbette Behrens; Dean R. Fischer; Walter Keast; Frank Pechacek.
EIN: 261382215
Other changes: Dawn Hovey is no longer C.E.O. and Pres. Rex Hardie is now Acct. Jerry Banks, Marie Knedler, Robert McCarthy, and Kelly Summy are no longer directors.

1236
R & R Realty Group Foundation
1225 Jordan Creek Pkwy., Ste. 200
West Des Moines, IA 50266-2346

Established in 1999 in IA.
Donors: R&R Investors Inc.; Daniel P. Rupprecht.
Foundation type: Company-sponsored foundation.
Financial data (yr. ended 06/30/13): Assets, $58,853 (M); gifts received, $247,360; expenditures, $257,632; qualifying distributions, $256,360; giving activities include $255,540 for 42 grants (high: $43,158; low: $100).
Purpose and activities: The foundation supports organizations involved with education, health, athletics, human services, and Catholicism.
Fields of interest: Secondary school/education; Higher education; Education; Health care; Athletics/sports, amateur leagues; Athletics/sports, golf; United Ways and Federated Giving Programs; Catholic agencies & churches.
Type of support: General/operating support.
Limitations: Applications not accepted. Giving primarily in Ames, Des Moines, Urbandale, and West Des Moines, IA. No grants to individuals.
Application information: Contributes only to pre-selected organizations.
Directors: Susan M. Bosworth; Daniel P. Rupprecht; **Paul S. Rupprecht**; Phyllis M. Rupprecht; Thomas P. Rupprecht.
Officers: Judy A. Price, Pres.; Mark A. Rupprecht, Secy.; Anthony J. Rogers, Treas.
EIN: 421494641

1237
Rockwell Collins Charitable Corporation
400 Collins Rd., N.E., M.S. 124-302
Cedar Rapids, IA 52498-0001 (319) 295-8122
Contact: Jennifer Becker, Exec. Dir.
FAX: (319) 295-9374;
E-mail: jlbecker@rockwellcollins.com**; Additional e-mail: communityrelations@rockwellcollins.com; Contact for Green Communities Prog.: Joan Schaffer, Community Rels., tel.: (319) 295-5131, e-mail: jmschaff@rockwellcollins.com**; Main URL: http://www.rockwellcollins.com/Our_Company/Corporate_Responsibility/Community_Overview/Charitable_Giving.aspx

Established in 2001 in IA.
Donor: Rockwell Collins, Inc.
Foundation type: Company-sponsored foundation.
Financial data (yr. ended 09/30/13): Assets, $385,095 (M); gifts received, $4,450,000; expenditures, $4,596,751; qualifying distributions, $4,531,828; giving activities include $4,107,750 for 151 grants, and $424,078 for employee matching gifts.
Purpose and activities: The foundation supports organizations involved with the environment, health, human services, and civic affairs. Special emphasis is directed toward programs designed to promote math, science, engineering, and technology education; and arts and culture with a focus on youth educational initiatives.
Fields of interest: Arts education; Arts; Engineering school/education; Education; Environment, natural resources; Environment, water resources; Environment, land resources; Environment; Youth development; Science, formal/general education;

Mathematics; Engineering/technology; Science; Youth.
Type of support: Capital campaigns; Continuing support; Employee matching gifts; General/operating support; Program development; Scholarship funds.
Limitations: Applications accepted. Giving in the U.S. in areas of company operations, with emphasis on Tustin, CA, Melbourne, FL, IA, Portland, OR, and Richardson, TX; giving also to international organizations in Australia, Canada, France, and the United Kingdom for the Green Communities Program. No support for private foundations, political candidates or organizations, religious organizations not of direct benefit to the entire community, fraternal or social organizations, or discriminatory organizations. No grants to individuals, or for memorials, endowments, annual campaigns, debt reduction, federated campaigns, political campaigns, sports events or scholarships for designated athletes, gifts, door prizes, or raffles, equipment or playground funding, classroom donations, or school fundraisers.
Publications: Application guidelines.
Application information: All grant applications should be preceded by an e-mail or telephone inquiry. Applicants for Green Communities Program must be teamed with a Rockwell Collins employee or retiree. Organizations receiving Green Communities grants may be asked to provide interim reports and a final report. Application form required.
Initial approach: Telephone or e-mail foundation; download application form and mail to foundation for organizations located in IA or mail to nearest company facility for organizations located outside IA; download application form and e-mail form to contact for Green Communities Program
Copies of proposal: 1
***Deadline(s):* Apr. 1 to Apr. 30 and Aug. 1 to Aug. 30; Feb. 14 for Green Communities Program**
Board meeting date(s): Oct. and July
Final notification: 3 months; Apr. for Green Communities Program
Officers and Directors:* Martha May,* Pres.; Gary R. Chadick,* V.P. and Secy.; Patrick E. Allen, V.P. and Treas.; Jennifer Becker, Exec. Dir.; **Robert K. Ortberg.**
Number of staff: None.
EIN: 421526774
Other changes: Ronald W. Kirchenbauer is no longer Pres. Clayton M. Jones is no longer a director.

1238
Schildberg Foundation
P.O. Box 358
Greenfield, IA 50849

Established in 1986 in IA.
Donors: S.K. Schildberg; Sylvia K. Schildberg Irrev. Trust.
Foundation type: Independent foundation.
Financial data (yr. ended 04/30/13): Assets, $4,104,999 (M); expenditures, $234,745; qualifying distributions, $197,021; giving activities include $185,500 for 36 grants (high: $25,000; low: -$1,000).
Fields of interest: Nursing school/education; Libraries (public); Education; Disasters, fire prevention/control; YM/YWCAs & YM/YWHAs; Community/economic development, volunteer services; Christian agencies & churches.
Type of support: General/operating support.
Limitations: Applications not accepted. Giving primarily in IA. No grants to individuals.
Application information: Unsolicited requests for funds not accepted.
Officers: Bernadette M. Youngblood, Pres.; Mark Schildberg, V.P.; Marlene Schildberg, Secy.
Director: Kathy Hellebuyck.
EIN: 421282794
Other changes: The grantmaker has moved from MO to IA.

1239
Dale D. Schroeder Trust
12086 120th St.
Rippey, IA 50235-4703 **(866) 228-8142**
E-mail: daleschroeder@act.org; Main URL: http://www.act.org/daleschroeder/

Established in 2004 in IA.
Foundation type: Independent foundation.
Financial data (yr. ended 12/31/12): Assets, $1,285,525 (M); expenditures, $276,665; qualifying distributions, $209,105; giving activities include $209,105 for 21 grants to individuals (high: $22,749; low: $2,916).
Purpose and activities: Scholarship awards to qualifying graduating high school seniors in Iowa with a G.P.A. of at least 2.5, who plan to attend Iowa State University, University of Iowa, or University of Northern Iowa. Applicants must be legal residents of Iowa and must live in an Iowa community with a population between 1 and 10,000.
Fields of interest: Higher education.
Type of support: Scholarships—to individuals.
Limitations: Applications accepted. Giving limited to residents of IA.
Application information: Complete application guidelines available on Trust web site.
***Deadline(s):* Mar. 26**
Trustee: Walt Tomenga.
EIN: 206519954

1240
Siouxland Community Foundation
(formerly Siouxland Foundation)
505 5th St., Ste. 412
Sioux City, IA 51101-1507
Contact: Debbie Hubbard, Exec. Dir.
FAX: (712) 293-3303;
E-mail: office@siouxlandcommunityfoundation.org; Main URL: http://www.siouxlandcommunityfoundation.org

Established in 1988 in IA.
Foundation type: Community foundation.
Financial data (yr. ended 12/31/12): Assets, $16,086,227 (M); gifts received, $1,848,004; expenditures, $2,062,415; giving activities include $1,839,660 for grants, and $222,755 for grants to individuals.
Purpose and activities: The foundation awards grants to social service agencies that offer assistance with addiction, domestic violence and other issues. Giving also for arts and culture, education, civic affairs, and health.
Fields of interest: Arts education; Museums; Performing arts, dance; Performing arts, theater; Performing arts, music; Arts; Education, early childhood education; Child development, education; Medical school/education; Adult education—literacy, basic skills & GED; Education, reading; Education; Nursing care; Health care; Substance abuse, services; Mental health/crisis services; Health organizations, association; Alcoholism; Crime/violence prevention, domestic violence; Safety/disasters; Recreation, parks/playgrounds; Recreation; Children/youth, services; Child development, services; Family services; Aging, centers/services; Minorities/immigrants, centers/services; Human services; Community/economic development; Government/public administration; Youth; Aging; Disabilities, people with; Minorities; Asians/Pacific Islanders; African Americans/Blacks; Hispanics/Latinos; Native Americans/American Indians; Economically disadvantaged; Homeless.
Type of support: Building/renovation; Equipment; Program development; Conferences/seminars; Seed money; Scholarship funds; Research; Employee-related scholarships; Scholarships—to individuals.
Limitations: Applications accepted. Giving limited to the greater Sioux City, IA, tri-state area (within a 50-mile radius of Sioux City, including NE and SD). No support for religious purposes. No grants to individuals (except for scholarships), or for endowment funds, deficit financing, fundraising campaigns, capital campaigns, general operating support, or school playground equipment or uniforms.
Publications: Application guidelines; Annual report; Annual report (including application guidelines); Grants list; Informational brochure; Newsletter.
Application information: Visit foundation web site for application cover sheet and guidelines. Foundation grants do not generally exceed $5,000. Application form required.
Initial approach: Letter or telephone
Copies of proposal: 2
Deadline(s): Jan. 16 and May 15
Board meeting date(s): Mar., June, Sept., and Dec.
Final notification: Late Mar. and late June
Officers and Directors:* Matthew J. Basye,* Chair., Grant Review Committee and V.P.; Richard J. Dehner,* Chair., Investment/Finance Comm.; Laura A. Schiltz,* Chair., Mktg. and Devel. Comm.; Lesley M. Bartholomew,* Pres.; Barbara F. Orzechowski,* Secy.; Paul A. Bergmann,* Treas.; **Rebecca Krohn, Exec. Dir.**; Marie L. Buckley; Todd DeMoss; Lance D. Ehmcke; Marilyn J. Hagberg; Robert W. Houlihan; Charles A. Knoepfler; Matthew J. Lawler; Robert F. Meis; Pam Miller; Michael H. Prosser; Leon D. Rozeboom; Garrett K. Smith; Richard G. Wagner; Charese E. Yanney.
Number of staff: 1 full-time professional; 1 part-time professional; 1 part-time support.
EIN: 421323904
Other changes: Rebecca Krohn has replaced Debbie Hubbard as Exec. Dir.
Matthew J. Basye is now Chair., Grant Review Committee and V.P.

1241
South Central Iowa Community Foundation
108 North Card
Chariton, IA 50049 (641) 217-9105
Contact: Diane Bear, Exec. Dir.
E-mail: scicf.diane@mediacombb.net; Main URL: http://www.scicf.org
Facebook: https://www.facebook.com/pages/South-Central-Iowa-Community-Foundation/167804839939700
Twitter: https://twitter.com/SCICF1

Established in 1993 in IA.
Foundation type: Community foundation.
Financial data (yr. ended 06/30/12): Assets, $9,305,740 (M); gifts received, $1,612,348;

expenditures, $1,289,030; giving activities include $1,095,123 for 34+ grants (high: $47,805).
Purpose and activities: The foundation's mission is to contribute to a better life for people of South Central Iowa by helping donors to carry out their charitable intent and by providing responsible stewardship of gifts for community purposes.
Fields of interest: Arts; Education; Human services; Community/economic development.
Limitations: Applications accepted. Giving primarily in Clarke, Decatur, Lucas, Ringgold, and Union counties, IA. No grants for existing debts, operating expenses or salaries, or consumable items.
Application information: Visit foundation web site for application form and guidelines. Application form required.
Initial approach: Submit application form and attachments
Copies of proposal: 6
Deadline(s): Varies
Officers and Directors:* Betty Hansen,* Chair.; Lori Borcherding,* Vice-Chair.; Diane Bear,* Pres. and C.E.O.; Michell Ricker,* Secy.; Kay Herring,* Treas.; Peg Anderson; Adam Bahr; Sue Beck; Pennie Gonseth Cheers; Kevin Creveling; Mike Frost; Jason Gibbs; Dennis Jeter; Mellony Klemesrud; Jan Knock; Gloria Salsman; Mary Seales; Don Sheridan; Melissa Snell; Clinton Spurrier; Barb Stephens; Mary Stierwalt; Ray Thurlby; Jim Wright; and 2 additional directors.
Number of staff: 1 full-time professional; 1 full-time support.
EIN: 421411234
Other changes: Betty Hansen has replaced Don Sheridan as Pres.
Lori Borcherding is now Vice-Chair. Diane Bear is now Pres. and C.E.O. Ginny Galigiuri and Sharon South are no longer directors.

1242
Bertha Stebens Charitable Foundation
119 2nd St. N.W.
Mason City, IA 50401-3105 (641) 423-1913
Contact: Harold R. Winston, Secy.

Established in 1986 in IA.
Foundation type: Independent foundation.
Financial data (yr. ended 07/31/13): Assets, $3,477,506 (M); expenditures, $194,367; qualifying distributions, $149,668; giving activities include $136,940 for 49 grants (high: $15,000; low: $500).
Fields of interest: Performing arts, theater; Education; YM/YWCAs & YM/YWHAs; Children/youth, services; Government/public administration; Christian agencies & churches; Protestant agencies & churches; Infants/toddlers; Children/youth; Children; Adults; Aging; Young adults; Disabilities, people with; Mentally disabled; Women; Girls; Adults, women; Men; Boys; Adults, men; Military/veterans; Crime/abuse victims; Economically disadvantaged; Homeless.
Type of support: Capital campaigns; Building/renovation; Equipment; Land acquisition; Endowments; Scholarship funds; Consulting services.
Limitations: Applications accepted. Giving limited to Mason City and Cerro Gordo County, IA. No grants to individuals.
Publications: Application guidelines.
Application information: Application form required.
Initial approach: Letter
Copies of proposal: 3
Deadline(s): May 31
Board meeting date(s): As needed
Officers and Directors:* Gary Blodgett,* Pres.; Harold R. Winston,* Secy.; **Gregory C. Nicholas,* Treas.**
Number of staff: 1 part-time professional.
EIN: 421280907
Other changes: Gregory C. Nicholas has replaced Terry E. Nettleton as Treas.

1243
United Fire Group Foundation
118 2nd Ave. S.E.
Cedar Rapids, IA 52401-1212

Established in 2001 in IA.
Donors: United Fire & Casualty Co.; United Life Insurance Co.
Foundation type: Company-sponsored foundation.
Financial data (yr. ended 12/31/12): Assets, $182,239 (M); gifts received, $46,858; expenditures, $579,725; qualifying distributions, $565,725; giving activities include $565,725 for grants.
Purpose and activities: The foundation supports museums and organizations involved with theater, education, employment, and human services and awards grants to individuals for higher education and disaster relief.
Fields of interest: Museums; Performing arts, theater; Higher education; Business school/education; Libraries (public); Education; Goodwill Industries; YM/YWCAs & YM/YWHAs; Children, services; Residential/custodial care; Residential/custodial care, hospices; Developmentally disabled, centers & services; Human services; United Ways and Federated Giving Programs.
Type of support: Emergency funds; General/operating support; Program development; Grants to individuals.
Limitations: Applications not accepted. Giving primarily in IA.
Application information: Contributes only to pre-selected organizations and individuals.
Officers: Randy A. Ramlo, Pres.; Michael T. Wilkens, Secy.; Dianne M. Lyons, Treas.
Director: Jack Evans.
EIN: 421492320

1244
Wahlert Foundation
P.O. Box 736
Dubuque, IA 52004-0736
Contact: Amy Principi, Pres.; R.H. Wahlert, V.P. and Treas.
E-mail: info@wahlertfoundation.org; Summer address: P.O. Box 736, Dubuque, IA 52004-0736. E-mail: Bob16307@aol.com; Main URL: http://www.wahlertfoundation.org

Incorporated in 1948 in IA.
Donors: H.W. Wahlert†; and officers of the foundation.
Foundation type: Independent foundation.
Financial data (yr. ended 08/31/13): Assets, $6,401,270 (M); gifts received, $6,692; expenditures, $413,645; qualifying distributions, $334,544; giving activities include $334,544 for 43 grants (high: $60,000; low: $500).
Purpose and activities: Support primarily for higher, secondary, and medical education; grants also for health services and hospitals, including medical and cancer research, social service agencies, including drug abuse prevention programs and services for families, the homeless and the handicapped, child welfare programs for minorities, cultural activities, including the arts and museums, and Catholic welfare organizations and schools.
Fields of interest: Secondary school/education; Higher education; Health care; Human services; Aging, centers/services; Catholic agencies & churches; Children; Aging; Hispanics/Latinos; Native Americans/American Indians; Women; Terminal illness, people with; Economically disadvantaged; Homeless; Migrant workers.
International interests: Honduras.
Type of support: General/operating support; Annual campaigns; Capital campaigns; Building/renovation; Equipment; Emergency funds; Program development; Scholarship funds.
Limitations: Applications accepted. Giving primarily in IA, IL and WI. No grants to individuals, or for publications, conferences, or matching gifts; no loans.
Publications: Application guidelines.
Application information: Complete application procedures and guidelines available on foundation web site. Application form required.
***Initial approach:* Application form on foundation web site**
Copies of proposal: 1
Board meeting date(s): 2nd Sat. of Sept.
Officers: Amy Wahlert Principi,* Pres.; Robert H. Wahlert,* Exec. V.P. and Treas.; David Wahlert,* V.P.; Mark Wahlert, V.P.; Brian J. Kane,* Secy.
Directors: Kathleen C. Chameli; Marni L. Peck; Alan Wahlert; Donna Wahlert; Nancy Wahlert; James R. Wahlert; Robert C. Wahlert; Susan Wahlert.
Number of staff: 1 part-time professional.
EIN: 426051124

1245
Wallace Research Foundation
c/o RSM McGladrey, Inc., Attn.: Kay Hegarty
221 3rd Ave. S.E., Ste. 300
Cedar Rapids, IA 52401-1525

Established in 1996 in IA.
Donors: H.B. Wallace†; Jocelyn M. Wallace; Henry D. Wallace; Linda Wallace-Gray; H.A. Wallace†; Eric Gilchrist Charitable Trust.
Foundation type: Independent foundation.
Financial data (yr. ended 12/31/12): Assets, $75,424,265 (M); gifts received, $7,587; expenditures, $4,657,117; qualifying distributions, $4,189,985; giving activities include $4,140,921 for 52 grants (high: $350,000; low: $5,000).
Purpose and activities: Giving primarily for education, the environment, and medical research.
Fields of interest: Higher education; Environment, natural resources; Animal welfare; Medical research, institute.
Type of support: General/operating support; Endowments; Research.
Limitations: Applications not accepted. Giving primarily in the U.S., with some emphasis on AZ. No support for religious or political purposes. No grants to individuals.
Publications: Annual report.
Application information: Contributes only to pre-selected organizations.
Officers and Director:* Henry D. Wallace, Pres.; Linda Wallace-Gray, V.P. and Secy.-Treas.; Alex Gilchrist; Angus Gilchrist.
EIN: 426540579

1246
The Wellmark Foundation
(formerly The IASD Health Care Foundation)

1331 Grand Ave., Station 3W739
Des Moines, IA 50309-2551 (515) 376-4819
***Contact:* Stephanie Perry, Interim Dir.**
FAX: (515) 376-9082;
E-mail: wmfoundation@wellmark.com**; Contact for Stephanie Perry: (605) 373-7429, e-mail: perryss@wellmark.commcgarveym@wellmark.com; Additional contact: Mike Gerrish, Corporate & Mktg. Comms, (515) 376-4611, e-mail gerrishm@wellmark.com**; Main URL: http://www.wellmark.com/foundation/index.asp
Grants List: http://www.wellmark.com/foundation/grants/grant_awards.htm

Established in 1991 in IA.
Donors: Blue Cross and Blue Shield of Iowa; Blue Cross and Blue Shield of South Dakota; Wellmark, Inc.
Foundation type: Company-sponsored foundation.
Financial data (yr. ended 12/31/12): Assets, $48,259,255 (M); gifts received, $11,378,598; expenditures, $2,904,984; qualifying distributions, $2,476,724; giving activities include $2,476,724 for 24+ grants (high: $59,993).
Purpose and activities: The foundation supports programs designed to improve the health of Iowans, South Dakotans, and their communities. Special emphasis is directed toward childhood obesity prevention; and community-based wellness and prevention.
Fields of interest: Elementary/secondary education; Dental care; Reproductive health; Reproductive health, prenatal care; Public health; Public health, obesity; Public health, physical fitness; Health care; Food services; Nutrition; Family services, parent education; United Ways and Federated Giving Programs; Children.
Type of support: Employee volunteer services; Continuing support; Management development/capacity building; Program development; Publication; Seed money; Curriculum development.
Limitations: Applications accepted. Giving limited to IA and SD. **No support for for-profit organizations.** No grants to individuals, or for biomedical research not of direct benefit to local residents, uncompensated care for direct clinical services, or services that are billable for third-party reimbursement, capital campaigns, equipment, organizations indirect/overhear costs, debt reduction, annual campaigns, fundraising events, or endowments.
Publications: Application guidelines; Annual report; Grants list; Newsletter.
Application information: Proposals for Healthy Communities Small Grants should be no longer than 4 pages. A full proposal may be requested at a later date for MATCH grants. Application form required.
***Initial approach:* Proposal for Healthy Communities Small Grants; letter of interest for MATCH grants**
Copies of proposal: 4
***Deadline(s):* Mar. 3 for Healthy Communities Small Grants; May 6 for MATCH grants**
Board meeting date(s): Mar. 30, May 24, Aug. 11, and Nov. 1
***Final notification:* Late Apr. for Healthy Communities Small Grants; early Aug. for MATCH grants**
Officers and Directors: John D. Forsyth, Chair.; Janet Griffin, Secy.; Christa Kuennen, Treas.; Theodore J. Boesen, Jr.; Ruth Litchfield; Edward R. Lynn; Robert E. O'Connell; Robert J. Richard; Sheila Riggs; Roberta Wattlesworth.
Number of staff: 2 full-time professional; 1 part-time professional.
EIN: 421368650
Other changes: Mary Ann Abrams and Eldon E. Huston are no longer directors.

1247
Woodward Foundation, Inc.

801 Bluff St.
Dubuque, IA 52001-4661
Contact: Thomas Woodward, Pres.

Established in 1956 in IA.
Donor: Woodward Communications, Inc.
Foundation type: Independent foundation.
Financial data (yr. ended 12/31/12): Assets, $96,551 (M); gifts received, $77,496; expenditures, $187,900; qualifying distributions, $186,850; giving activities include $186,850 for 16 grants (high: $30,000; low: $1,000).
Fields of interest: Museums (art); Performing arts, opera; Higher education; Higher education, college; Libraries (public); Recreation, centers; Human services; United Ways and Federated Giving Programs.
Limitations: Applications accepted. Giving primarily in Dubuque, IA; some giving in WI. No grants to individuals or for scholarships or endowments; no loans or program-related investments.
Application information: Application form required.
Initial approach: Letter
Deadline(s): Apr. 1 and Nov. 1
Board meeting date(s): Annually
Officers: Thomas Woodward, Pres.; Cheri Phipps, Secy.; Steve Larson, Treas.
Directors: Mary anne Drewek; Jim Normandin; Barbara Sullivan Woodward; Kristin Woodward.
EIN: 426070224
Other changes: The grantmaker no longer lists a URL address.

1248
World Food Prize Foundation

666 Grand Ave., Ste. 1700
Des Moines, IA 50309-2500 (515) 245-3783
Contact: Judith Pim, Dir., Secretariat Operations
FAX: (515) 245-3785;
E-mail: wfp@worldfoodprize.org; Main URL: http://www.worldfoodprize.org
Facebook: http://www.facebook.com/pages/The-World-Food-Prize/51072466793
RSS Feed: http://www.worldfoodprize.org/RSS/newsfeed.xml
Twitter: http://twitter.com/worldfoodprize
YouTube: http://www.youtube.com/user/WorldFoodPrize
E-mail for Judith Pim: jpim@worldfoodprize.org

Established in 1990 in IA.
Foundation type: Independent foundation.
Financial data (yr. ended 12/31/12): Assets, $48,839,505 (M); gifts received, $3,099,159; expenditures, $4,107,841; qualifying distributions, $2,905,170; giving activities include $250,000 for 1 grant to an individual.
Purpose and activities: Awards prizes to individuals for achievement in improving the world food supply.
Fields of interest: Agriculture.
Type of support: Grants to individuals; General/operating support; Capital campaigns; Endowments; Internship funds; In-kind gifts.
Publications: Informational brochure; Informational brochure (including application guidelines).
Application information: See foundation web site for application and nomination information. Application form not required.
Copies of proposal: 1
Deadline(s): Apr. 1
Officers: John Ruan III, Chair.; **Kenneth Quinn, Pres.**
Number of staff: 7 full-time professional.
EIN: 421356715
Other changes: Kenneth Quinn is now Pres.

1249
The William J. Zimmerman Foundation

1603 Pleasant Plain Rd.
Fairfield, IA 52556

Established in 1983 in IL.
Donor: Zimmerman Family Trust, No. 1.
Foundation type: Independent foundation.
Financial data (yr. ended 12/31/12): Assets, $13,621,432 (M); expenditures, $862,690; qualifying distributions, $600,000; giving activities include $600,000 for grants.
Fields of interest: Education; Human services.
Limitations: Applications not accepted. Giving primarily in CA. No grants to individuals.
Application information: Contributes only to pre-selected organizations.
Officers and Directors:* David J. Johnson, Pres.; John E. Mallard, V.P.; William M. Doyle, Jr.,* Secy.; **Susan E. Chroman**; Christopher J. Podoll.
EIN: 421223262
Other changes: David J. Johnson has replaced Christopher J. Podoll as Pres.
Marc S. Zimmerman is no longer a director.

KANSAS

1250
The Ross and Marianna Beach Foundation, Inc.
P.O. Box 1752
Lawrence, KS 66044-8752
Contact: Carrie Edwards
E-mail: beachfoundation@gmail.com

Established in 2001 in KS.
Donors: Marianna Beach; Ross Beach.
Foundation type: Independent foundation.
Financial data (yr. ended 09/30/13): Assets, $12,037,359 (M); expenditures, $604,619; qualifying distributions, $558,643; giving activities include $527,853 for 25 grants (high: $100,000; low: $500).
Purpose and activities: The foundation is dedicated to the enrichment of Kansans, specifically through the support of education, the arts, and the environment, and to the enhancement of the lives of children and adults with special needs.
Fields of interest: Arts; Education, early childhood education; Child development, education; Education, special; Human services; Civil/human rights, disabled; Disabilities, people with; Mentally disabled.
Type of support: General/operating support; Building/renovation; Endowments.
Limitations: Applications accepted. Giving limited to KS. No grants to individuals.
Publications: Annual report.
Application information: The foundation prefers email contact.
Officers and Directors:* Marianna Beach,* Pres.; Terry Edwards,* Secy.-Treas.; Elizabeth Jane Hipp.
Number of staff: 1 part-time support.
EIN: 431947099
Other changes: The grantmaker no longer lists a phone.
The grantmaker now accepts applications.

1251
Capitol Federal Foundation
700 S. Kansas Ave., Ste. 517
Topeka, KS 66603-3809 **(785) 270-6041**
***Contact:* Tammy Dishman, Pres. and Exec. Dir.**
***Additional tel.:* (785) 270-6040**; Main URL: http://www.capfed.com/site/en/home/community.html

Established in 1999 in KS.
Donor: Capitol Federal Financial.
Foundation type: Company-sponsored foundation.
Financial data (yr. ended 12/31/12): Assets, $94,589,305 (M); expenditures, $3,689,163; qualifying distributions, $3,277,708; giving activities include $3,162,245 for 394 grants (high: $300,000; low: $37).
Purpose and activities: The foundation supports performing art centers and organizations involved with education, health, affordable housing, human services, and community development.
Fields of interest: Performing arts centers; Higher education; Education; Health care; Housing/shelter; Boys & girls clubs; Big Brothers/Big Sisters; Youth, services; Human services; Community/economic development; Foundations (community); United Ways and Federated Giving Programs.
Type of support: General/operating support; Continuing support; Income development; Management development/capacity building; Annual campaigns; Capital campaigns; Building/renovation; Equipment; Emergency funds; Program development; Conferences/seminars; Professorships; Seed money; Fellowships; Internship funds; Scholarship funds; Technical assistance; Employee volunteer services; Employee matching gifts; Matching/challenge support.
Limitations: Applications accepted. Giving limited to areas of company operations in central and northeastern KS. No support for religious or political organizations.
Application information: Application form not required.
Initial approach: Letter or telephone
Copies of proposal: 1
Deadline(s): None
Board meeting date(s): Quarterly
Final notification: 90 to 120 days
Officers: John C. Dicus, Chair.; **Tammy Dishman, Pres. and Exec. Dir.**; John B. Dicus, Secy.-Treas.
Number of staff: 1 full-time professional.
EIN: 481214952
Other changes: The grantmaker no longer lists a fax.
Tammy Dishman is now Pres. and Exec. Dir.

1252
Barton P. and Mary Davidson Cohen Charitable Fund Part One
5901 College Blvd., Ste. 100
Overland Park, KS 66211-1834 (913) 319-0391
***Contact:* Mary Davidson Cohen**
E-mail: MCohen@midwesttrust.com; Main URL: http://cohentrust.org/

Established in KS.
Donor: Barton P. Cohen†.
Foundation type: Independent foundation.
Financial data (yr. ended 12/31/12): Assets, $10,452,397 (M); gifts received, $215; expenditures, $680,574; qualifying distributions, $575,413; giving activities include $510,514 for 16 grants (high: $204,350; low: $1,000).
Fields of interest: Arts; Education; Jewish agencies & synagogues.
Limitations: Applications accepted. Giving primarily in Kansas City, Overland Park, and Johnson and Wyandotte counties, KS.
Publications: Grants list.
Application information: Applicants are encouraged to contact the foundation prior to submitting an application to determine if their program fits the foundation's guidelines. Application form required.
***Initial approach:* Use application form on foundation web site**
Deadline(s): None
Trustees: Mary Cohen; Midwest Trust Co.
EIN: 266205947

1253
Collective Brands Foundation
(formerly Payless ShoeSource Foundation)
3231 S.E. 6th Ave.
Topeka, KS 66607-2207 (785) 233-5171
Main URL: http://www.collectivebrands.com/foundation

Established in 1998 in KS and MO.
Donors: Payless ShoeSource, Inc.; Collective Brands, Inc.
Foundation type: Company-sponsored foundation.
Financial data (yr. ended 02/02/13): Assets, $699,725 (M); gifts received, $748,500; expenditures, $493,815; qualifying distributions, $493,815; giving activities include $463,180 for 108 grants (high: $78,000; low: $850).
Purpose and activities: The foundation supports programs designed to address women's preventative health; promote children's physical activity and fitness; improve the lives of children and youth in need; preserve the environment; and support the footwear industry.
Fields of interest: Arts; Education; Environment; Public health, physical fitness; Health care; Children/youth, services; Human services; Business/industry; United Ways and Federated Giving Programs; Children; Women.
Type of support: Continuing support; Annual campaigns; Capital campaigns; Building/renovation; Program development; Scholarship funds; Sponsorships; In-kind gifts.
Limitations: Applications accepted. Giving primarily in areas of company operations, with emphasis on Redlands, CA, Denver, CO, Topeka, the Kansas City metropolitan area, and Lawrence, KS, greater Boston and Lexington, MA, New York, NY, and Brookville, OH. No support for private charities or foundations, private schools, or religious or political organizations. No grants to individuals, or for capital campaigns, debt reduction, travel, or conferences.
Publications: Application guidelines.
Application information: Application form required.
Initial approach: Complete online application for grants and sponsorship requests
Deadline(s): Aug. 15
Board meeting date(s): Quarterly
Officers and Directors:* Betty J. Click,* Pres.; Curtis Sneden,* V.P. and Secy.; Gary C. Madsen,* V.P. and Treas.; Rob Hallam, V.P.
EIN: 481196508
Other changes: The grantmaker has changed its fiscal year-end from Jan. 28 to Feb. 2.

1254
Damon Family Foundation
5601 S.W. Barrington Ct. S.
Topeka, KS 66614 (785) 273-7722
Contact: Karen L. Damon, Pres.
Main URL: http://www.damonfamilyfoundation.org/
Facebook: https://www.facebook.com/damonfamilyfoundation

Established in KS.
Donors: Donald H. Damon; Kathleen J. Damon.
Foundation type: Independent foundation.
Financial data (yr. ended 12/31/12): Assets, $4,176,411 (M); expenditures, $319,684; qualifying distributions, $222,400; giving activities include $131,000 for 7 grants (high: $100,000; low: $2,500), and $91,400 for 11 grants to individuals (high: $25,000; low: $500).
Fields of interest: Safety/disasters; Human services; Economically disadvantaged.
Type of support: Grants to individuals; General/operating support.
Limitations: Applications accepted. Giving primarily in KA.
Application information: Application form required.
Initial approach: Completed application form
Deadline(s): None
Officers and Directors:* Karen L. Damon,* Pres.; Alan E. Streit,* V.P.; Kelly Strayer, Secy.; Donald H. Damon, Treas.; Carla Damm; Brenden A. Damon; Kathleen J. Damon.
EIN: 271568326

1255
Delta Dental of Kansas Foundation, Inc.
(formerly Delta Dental Plan of Kansas Foundation)
1619 N. Waterfront Pkwy.
Wichita, KS **67278 (316) 264-1099 ext. 114**
***Contact:* Nancy Wiebe, Exec. Dir.**
***FAX:* (316) 462-3393;**
E-mail: nwiebe@deltadentalks.com; Additional contact: Tammy Penrow, Fdn. Asst., tel.: (913) 327-3728, e-mail: tpenrow@deltadentalks.com; Main URL: http://www.deltadentalksfoundation.org
Facebook: http://www.facebook.com/DeltaDentalKSFoundation

Established in 2004 in KS.
Donor: Delta Dental Plan of Kansas, Inc.
Foundation type: Company-sponsored foundation.
Financial data (yr. ended 12/31/12): Assets, $2,680,515 (M); gifts received, $1,244,692; expenditures, $754,845; qualifying distributions, $743,868; giving activities include $618,288 for 98 grants (high: $83,004; low: $21).
Purpose and activities: The foundation supports programs designed to increase access to dental care by underserved populations; build the capacity to provide dental care; increase public awareness of oral health; and promote the prevention of oral disease. Special emphasis is directed toward programs that emphasize prevention; have significant and/or large impact; and are sustainable solutions.
Fields of interest: Dental school/education; Health care, clinics/centers; Dental care; Employment, training; Children; Aging; Economically disadvantaged.
Type of support: Building/renovation; Equipment; Program development; Seed money; Scholarship funds; Program evaluation; Employee matching gifts; Donated products.
Limitations: Applications accepted. Giving limited to areas of company operations in KS. No support for political, lobbying, or religious organizations. No grants or dental treatment funds for individuals, or for administrative costs, salaries, fundraising events, ongoing programs, general operating expenses, or existing deficits.
Publications: Application guidelines; Annual report; Annual report (including application guidelines); Grants list.
Application information: Faxed or e-mailed applications are not accepted. Additional information may be requested at a later date. Organizations receiving support are asked to provide periodic reports. Application form required.
Initial approach: Download application form and mail proposal and application form to foundation for Community Dental Health Grants and Toothbrush Kit Program
Copies of proposal: 10
Deadline(s): May 1 for Community Dental Health Grants; Aug. 27 for Toothbrush Kit Program
Board meeting date(s): Apr. to Dec.
Final notification: June for Community Dental Health Grants
Officers and Directors:* **Lucynda Raben, Chair.; Jill Quigley, Vice-Chair.; Greg Peppes, Secy.**; Nancy Wiebe, Exec. Dir.; **Barbara Bollier**; Michael Herbert*; Brick Scheer; **R. Wayne Thompson; Bruce Witt.**
Number of staff: 1 full-time professional; 1 part-time professional.
EIN: 680554527
Other changes: Lucynda Raben has replaced Brad Clothier as Chair. Jill Quigley has replaced Stanley Wint as Vice-Chair. Greg Peppes has replaced Darlene Harrell as Secy.
Brad Clothier is no longer Chair. Stanley Wint is no longer Vice-Chair. Darlene Harrell is no longer Secy. Karen Finstad is no longer Exec. Dir. Linda Branter, Hugh Brunner, and Elizabeth Kinch are no longer members of the governing body.

1256
Douglas County Community Foundation
900 Massachusetts St., Ste. 406
Lawrence, KS 66044-2868 (785) 843-8727
Contact: Chip Blaser, Exec. Dir.; For grants: Marilyn Hull, Prog. Off.
FAX: (785) 843-8735;
E-mail: dccfoundation@sbcglobal.net; Additional tel.: (785) 843-8735; Grant proposal e-mail: marilynhull@dccfoundation.org; Main URL: http://www.dccfoundation.org
Facebook: https://www.facebook.com/pages/Douglas-County-Community-Foundation/236784366389403
Twitter: http://twitter.com/DCCFoundation

Established in 2000 in KS.
Foundation type: Community foundation.
Financial data (yr. ended 12/31/12): Assets, $21,132,010 (M); gifts received, $1,696,028; expenditures, $2,060,787; giving activities include $1,742,665 for 33+ grants (high: $450,507), and $5,500 for 8 grants to individuals.
Purpose and activities: The foundation connects the diverse citizens and communities of Douglas County, KS through charitable action. Their mission is to enrich the quality of life by: 1) building philanthropic resources and relationships; 2) providing attractive options for donors to make philanthropist contributions; and 3) being a catalyst for the betterment of the lives of the citizens of Douglas County.
Fields of interest: Arts; Education; Environment; Health care; Housing/shelter; Children/youth, services; Youth, services; Human services; Community/economic development; United Ways and Federated Giving Programs; Children/youth.
Type of support: Management development/capacity building; Building/renovation; Equipment; Emergency funds; Program development; Publication; Curriculum development; Program evaluation; Scholarships—to individuals; Matching/challenge support.
Limitations: Applications accepted. Giving primarily in Douglas County, KS. No support for religious purposes. No grants to individuals (except for scholarships), or for administrative or general operating expenses, tickets, marketing plans or projects, annual campaigns, endowment funds, or debt retirement.
Publications: Application guidelines; Annual report; Annual report (including application guidelines); Grants list.
Application information: Visit foundation web site for application form and guidelines. Faxed applications are not considered. Application form required.
Initial approach: Submit application form and attachments
Copies of proposal: 12
Deadline(s): Feb. 10
Board meeting date(s): 9 to 12 times per year
Final notification: Apr.
Officers and Directors:* Web Golden,* Chair.; John Elmore,* Vice-Chair.; Chip Blaser, Exec. Dir.; **Harry Gibson**; Pat Long; Mike McGrew; Vickie Randel; Reggie Robinson; Dan Sabatini; Dolph Simons, Jr.; Evan Williams.
Number of staff: 2 part-time professional.
EIN: 481209687
Other changes: Hortense Oldfather is no longer a director.

1257
Emporia Community Foundation
527 Commercial St., Ste. 501
Emporia, KS 66801 (620) 342-9304
E-mail: emporiacf@emporiacf.org; Main URL: http://emporiacf.org/
Facebook: https://www.facebook.com/emporiacommunityfoundation?fref=ts

Established in 1996 in KS.
Foundation type: Community foundation.
Financial data (yr. ended 12/31/12): Assets, $11,981,273 (M); gifts received, $1,879,459; expenditures, $2,642,851; giving activities include $2,328,825 for grants to individuals.
Purpose and activities: The mission of the foundation is to improve the quality of life in the Emporia area, consisting of Lyon County and those six counties that are contiguous to Lyon County: Chase, Morris, Coffey, Greenwood, Osage and Wabaunsee counties.
Fields of interest: Arts; Education; Health care; Recreation; Human services; Children/youth; Blind/visually impaired; Deaf/hearing impaired.
Limitations: Applications accepted. Giving primarily in Chase, Morris, Coffey, Greenwood, Lyon, Osage and Wabaunsee counties. No grants for operational expenses.
Publications: Application guidelines; Annual report.
Application information: Application form required.
Copies of proposal: 9
Deadline(s): Feb. 15
Final notification: Approx. 45 days
Officers and Trustees:* Mark Schreiber,* Chair.; Cynthia Kraft,* Vice-Chair.; Shirley M. Antes,* Exec. Dir. and C.O.O.; Bill Barnes; Tom Bell; **Ken Buchele; Jeff DeBauge**; Skip Evans; Eddie Gilpin; D.J. Glaser; Jim Kessler; Mary Kretsinger; Dr. Thomas Kriss; Kay Lauer; Janis Meyer; Larry Putnam; Sally Sanchez; Bob Symmonds; Jennell Tebbetts; Nancy Thomas; Bobby Thompson.
Officers and Directors:* Ken Buchele, Pres.; Mark Schreiber,* V.P.; Jeff DeBauge,* Treas.; Ken Calhoun, Emeritus; Elvin Perkins, Emeritus; Cynthia Kraft; Kay Lauer; Bob Symmonds.
EIN: 481169158
Other changes: Mark Schreiber has replaced Jackie Scott as Chair. Mark Schreiber has replaced Jackie Scott as Chair.
Loni Heinen is now Prog. Off. Ken Calhoun, Brian Schmidt, and Mark Schreiber are no longer trustees. Mark Schreiber is now V.P. Chuck Hanna, Jackie Scott, and Chris Walker are no longer trustees.

1258
Virginia H. Farah Foundation
P.O. Box 457
Wichita, KS 67201-0457 **(316) 682-1939**
Contact: Eric S. Namee, Pres.
E-mail: contact@farahfoundation.org; Main URL: http://www.farahfoundation.org
Grants List: http://www.farahfoundation.org/pastrecipients.html

Established in 1983.
Foundation type: Independent foundation.
Financial data (yr. ended 12/31/12): Assets, $240,441 (M); gifts received, $27,392; expenditures, $202,645; qualifying distributions, $152,950; giving activities include $152,950 for 13 grants (high: $36,200; low: $1,500).
Purpose and activities: Giving primarily for the maintenance and growth of the Orthodox Christian Church in the U.S. and the world.
Fields of interest: Orthodox agencies & churches.

Type of support: Management development/capacity building; Capital campaigns; Building/renovation; Program development; Publication; Seed money.
Application information: See foundation web site for current information. Application form required.
Initial approach: Letter
Copies of proposal: 4
Deadline(s): July 1
Board meeting date(s): Fall
Officers and Trustees:* Eric S. Namee,* Pres.; Valerie DeBolt,* V.P.; **Bruce Ferris, Secy.-Treas.**
EIN: 760067300
Other changes: Bruce Ferris is now Secy.-Treas.

1259
Dane G. Hansen Foundation
P.O. Box 187
Logan, KS 67646-0187 (785) 689-4832
Contact: Don Stahr, Tr.
***FAX:* (785) 689-4833; Main URL: http://www.danehansenfoundation.org**

Incorporated in 1965 in KS.
Donors: Dane G. Hansen†; Dane G. Hansen Trust.
Foundation type: Independent foundation.
Financial data (yr. ended 09/30/13): Assets, $161,755,823 (M); gifts received, $380,857; expenditures, $7,067,413; qualifying distributions, $6,211,097; giving activities include $5,527,436 for 132 grants (high: $500,398; low: $333).
Purpose and activities: Grants largely for higher education, including undergraduate, graduate, theological, and vocational scholarships to individuals, civic affairs and public interest groups, youth agencies, services for the handicapped, and hospitals.
Fields of interest: Vocational education; Higher education; Hospitals (general); Youth, services; Public policy, research; Government/public administration; Disabilities, people with.
Type of support: General/operating support; Continuing support; Building/renovation; Equipment; Publication; Scholarship funds; Scholarships—to individuals.
Limitations: Giving primarily in Logan, Phillips County, and northwestern KS; scholarships limited to residents of 26 northwestern KS counties, which include: Cheyenne, Cloud, Decatur, Ellis, Ellsworth, Gove, Graham, Jewell, Lincoln, Logan, Mitchell, Norton, Osborne, Ottawa, Phillips, Rawlins, Republic, Rooks, Russell, Saline, Sheridan, Sherman, Smith, Thomas, Trego and Wallace.
Application information: Scholarship application information and form available on foundation web site. Application form required.
Deadline(s): See web site for latest deadlines
Board meeting date(s): Monthly
Final notification: Within 2 weeks for grants to organizations; 30 days after graduation for scholarships
Officers and Trustees:* Doyle D. Rahjes,* Pres.; F. Doyle Fair,* V.P.; Robert Hartman,* Secy.-Treas.; Douglas M. Albin; Carol Bales; Charles I. Moyer; Gary Poore; Don Stahr.
Number of staff: 7 full-time support.
EIN: 486121156
Other changes: Doyle D. Rahjes has replaced Carol Bales as Pres.
F. Doyle Fair is now V.P. Robert Hartman is now Secy.-Treas.

1260
Hutchinson Community Foundation
1 N. Main St., Ste. 501
P.O. Box 298
Hutchinson, KS 67504-0298 (620) 663-5293
Contact: Aubrey Abbott Patterson, Pres.; For grants: Eileen Yamauchi, Donor Svcs. Assoc.
FAX: (620) 663-9277; E-mail: info@hutchcf.org; Grant inquiry e-mail: eileen@hutchcf.org; Main URL: http://www.hutchcf.org
Facebook: https://www.facebook.com/Hutchcf
Twitter: http://twitter.com/hutchcf

Established in 1989 in KS.
Foundation type: Community foundation.
Financial data (yr. ended 12/31/11): Assets, $32,148,448 (M); gifts received, $6,205,427; expenditures, $4,686,070; giving activities include $3,498,887 for 57+ grants (high: $169,247).
Purpose and activities: The foundation connects donors to community needs and opportunities, increases philanthropy and provides community leadership. Giving primarily for arts, education, health care, mental health/crisis services, health associations, housing/shelter development, human services, children and youth services, hospices, aging centers and services, civil rights, community development, voluntarism promotion, federated giving programs, disabled, aging, economically disadvantaged, and general charitable giving.
Fields of interest: Visual arts; Performing arts; Performing arts, theater; Arts; Education, early childhood education; Higher education; Education; Health care; Substance abuse, services; Mental health/crisis services; Health organizations, association; Housing/shelter, development; Youth development; Children/youth, services; Child development, services; Residential/custodial care, hospices; Aging, centers/services; Human services; Civil/human rights; Economic development; Community/economic development; Voluntarism promotion; United Ways and Federated Giving Programs; Aging; Disabilities, people with; Men; Economically disadvantaged.
Type of support: Scholarships—to individuals; General/operating support; Continuing support; Annual campaigns; Capital campaigns; Equipment; Endowments; Debt reduction; Program development; Conferences/seminars; Seed money; Curriculum development; Scholarship funds; Technical assistance; Matching/challenge support.
Limitations: Applications accepted. Giving primarily in Reno County, KS. No grants to individuals (except for scholarships).
Publications: Application guidelines; Annual report; Financial statement; Grants list; Informational brochure; Newsletter; Occasional report; Program policy statement.
Application information: Visit foundation web site for application form and guidelines. Application form required.
Initial approach: Submit application
Copies of proposal: 13
Deadline(s): Sept. 4
Board meeting date(s): Quarterly
Final notification: Nov. 14
Officers and Directors:* Marilyn Bolton,* Chair.; Aubrey Abbott Patterson,* Pres. and Exec. Dir.; Terri L. Eisiminger,* V.P., Admin. and Secy.; Paul W. Dillon,* Co-Treas.; Kenneth E. Vogel,* Co-Treas.; **Chelsea Barker**; Susan Buttram; **Ryan Diehl**; David Dick; Dan Garber; Wendy C. Hobart; Kory Jackson; John D. Montgomery; Richard Russell; Bill Southern; Dell Marie Shanahan Swearer; Mark Trotman.
Number of staff: 4 full-time professional; 1 part-time support.
EIN: 481076910
Other changes: Ann Bush is no longer a member of the governing body.

1261
Insurance Management Associates Foundation
(also known as IMA Foundation)
8200 E. 32nd St. North
Wichita, KS 67226 (316) 267-9221
Contact: Ruth Rohs, Exec. Dir.
***FAX:* (316) 266-6254;**
E-mail: foundation@imacorp.com; **Main URL: http://www.imafg.com/Community.html**
Donors: The IMA Financial Group Inc.; Insurance Management Associates, Inc.
Foundation type: Company-sponsored foundation.
Financial data (yr. ended 12/31/12): Assets, $1,953,535 (M); gifts received, $319,515; expenditures, $239,267; qualifying distributions, $238,850; giving activities include $238,850 for 46 grants (high: $25,000; low: $500).
Purpose and activities: The foundation supports programs designed to advance youth; promote arts and culture; enhance economic vitality; and promote health and wellness.
Fields of interest: Museums (art); Performing arts; Arts; Elementary/secondary education; Education, early childhood education; Higher education; Education; Hospitals (general); Health care; Employment; Boy scouts; Children/youth, services; Aging, centers/services; Human services; Business/industry; Community/economic development; United Ways and Federated Giving Programs; Leadership development; Youth.
Type of support: General/operating support; Capital campaigns; Program development; Scholarship funds.
Limitations: Applications accepted. Giving primarily in areas of company operations in Denver, CO, Kansas City, Topeka, and Wichita, KS, and Dallas TX. No support for fiscal agents or sponsors. No grants to individuals.
Publications: Application guidelines; Corporate giving report; Program policy statement.
Application information: Applicants are encouraged to email the foundation in advance of submitting a letter of inquiry to ensure that the organization's request is a fit for the IMA Foundation. Letters of inquiry should not exceed 4 pages. Average grant awards range from $5,000 to $10,000.
***Initial approach:* E-mail letter of inquiry**
***Deadline(s):* Apr. 1 and Oct. 1**
Trustees: Anita Bourke; Robert L. Cohen; William C. Cohen, Jr.; Robert Reiter; Kurt D. Watson.
EIN: 237432160
Other changes: The grantmaker has moved from KS to CO.
The grantmaker now accepts applications.
The grantmaker now publishes application guidelines. The grantmaker no longer publishes application guidelines.

1262
Walter S. and Evan C. Jones Foundation
(also known as Jones Foundation, Inc.)
2501 W. 18th Ave., Ste. D
Emporia, KS 66801-6195 (620) 342-1714
Contact: Sharon L. Tidwell, Exec. Dir.
FAX: (620) 342-4701; E-mail: dir@jonesfdn.org; Main URL: http://www.jonesfdn.org

Established in 1974 in KS.
Donor: Walter S. and Evan C. Jones Trust.
Foundation type: Independent foundation.
Financial data (yr. ended 06/30/13): Assets, $30,191 (M); gifts received, $2,282,500; expenditures, $2,253,951; qualifying distributions, $2,089,761; giving activities include $2,076,361 for grants.
Purpose and activities: Grants awarded are limited to educational and medical expenses of children of 3 specified counties who have resided there continuously for a minimum of 1 year.
Fields of interest: Education; Health care; Children/youth, services; Economically disadvantaged.
Type of support: Grants to individuals; Scholarships—to individuals.
Limitations: Applications accepted. Giving limited to children who have resided continuously for a minimum of one year in Osage, Coffey, or Lyon counties, KS. No support for non U.S. citizens.
Publications: Informational brochure; Program policy statement.
Application information: Applicants must contact office prior to submitting an application. Must be under 21 for medical grants. Medical services must be pre-approved generally, except in emergency cases. Individuals who move to Coffey, Lyon or Osage County and attend a post-secondary institution prior to fulfilling the residency requirement are not eligible for medical or educational assistance. Copy of current federal income tax return (both personal and business, if applicable), a minimum of 1 month's pay stubs, proof of all other income, and a copy of insurance card (if applicable) are required with application. Application form required.
Initial approach: Telephone
Deadline(s): None
Board meeting date(s): Monthly
Final notification: 1-2 months
Officers: Tom Thomas, Pres.; Jeff Larson, V.P.; Max Stewart, Jr., Secy.; **Megan A. Evans, Treas.**; Sharon L. Tidwell, Exec. Dir.
Trustees: Greg Bachman; Jeff Longbine; Cheryl Mussato.
Number of staff: 1 full-time professional; 1 full-time support; 1 part-time support.
EIN: 237384087
Other changes: Megan A. Evans is now Treas.

1263
Kansas Health Foundation

(formerly Kansas Health Foundation/Kansas Health Trust)
309 E. Douglas
Wichita, KS 67202-3405
***Contact:* Chris Power, V.P., Comms.; Valerie Black, Information Technoloy Specialist**
FAX: (316) 262-2044; E-mail: info@khf.org; Additional tel.: (800) 373-7681; E-mail for Valerie Black: vblack@khf.org; Main URL: http://www.kansashealth.org
Blog: http://www.kansashealth.org/blog
E-Newsletter: http://www.kansashealth.org/publications/happenings
Facebook: http://www.facebook.com/pages/Kansas-Health-Foundation/131838311319
Grants Database: http://www.kansashealth.org/grantmaking/grants
Twitter: https://twitter.com/kansashealthorg

Established in 1978 in KS as the Wesley Medical Endowment Foundation; converted from funds resulting from the sale of Wesley Medical Center to HCA in 1985; current name adopted in 1991.
Foundation type: Independent foundation.
Financial data (yr. ended 12/31/12): Assets, $474,033,125 (M); expenditures, $19,852,622; qualifying distributions, $20,824,322; giving activities include $12,927,232 for 215 grants (high: $1,500,000; low: $500), and $1,195,165 for 4 foundation-administered programs.
Purpose and activities: The foundation is driven by a mission to improve the health of all Kansans. The foundation joins with the World Health Organization in defining health, believing that health is a state of complete physical, mental and social well-being and not merely the absence of disease or infirmity.
Fields of interest: Public health; Children/youth, services; Leadership development; Children/youth; Adults.
Type of support: General/operating support; Continuing support; Management development/capacity building; Program development; Technical assistance; Program evaluation; Matching/challenge support.
Limitations: Applications accepted. Giving limited to KS. No support for political campaigns or political advocacy. No grants to individuals, or for medical research, deficit or debt retirement, endowments not initiated by the foundation, vehicles, construction projects, mental health or for direct medical services.
Publications: Application guidelines; Annual report (including application guidelines); Grants list; Informational brochure; Newsletter; Occasional report.
Application information: Application forms required for Recognition Grants. Forms are available on foundation web site. Application form required.
Initial approach: Application through Recognition Grant program form on web site
Deadline(s): Mar. 15 and Sept. 15 for Recognition Grants
Board meeting date(s): Quarterly
Final notification: 60 days for Recognition Grants
Officers and Directors:* Shelly Buhler,* Chair.; Steve Coen,* C.E.O. and Pres.; Evan Meyers, V.P. and C.F.O.; Christopher Power, V.P., Admin.; Blythe Thomas, V.P., Comms.; Jeffrey Willett, V.P., Progs.; Matt Allen; **Claudia Bakely**; Mollie H. Carter; **Junetta Everett**; Jeffrey L. Jack; Michael Lennen; Donna Shank; Andy Tompkins.
Number of staff: 12 full-time professional; 8 full-time support; 2 part-time support.
EIN: 480873431
Other changes: Gary Brooks is no longer Vice-Chair. Ronald W. Holt is no longer a director.

1264
David H. Koch Charitable Foundation

c/o Kara Washington
4111 E. 37th St., N.
Wichita, KS 67220-3203
Contact: Vonda Holliman, Treas.
E-mail: inquiries@kochfamilyfoundations.org; Additional address: P.O. Box 2256, Wichita, KS 67201-2256; Main URL: http://www.kochfamilyfoundations.org/FoundationsDHK.asp

Established in 1982 in KS.
Donors: David H. Koch; Fred C. Koch Trusts for Charity.
Foundation type: Independent foundation.
Financial data (yr. ended 12/31/12): Assets, $60,567,797 (M); expenditures, $10,504,239; qualifying distributions, $10,502,790; giving activities include $10,500,000 for 2 grants (high: $10,000,000; low: $500,000).
Fields of interest: Arts; Higher education; Hospitals (specialty); Prostate cancer research; Science, formal/general education; Science; Public affairs.
Type of support: Research.
Limitations: Applications not accepted. Giving primarily in Washington, DC and New York, NY. No grants to individuals, for deficit financing, exchange programs, land acquisition, seed money or professorships; no loans.
Application information: Contributes only to pre-selected organizations.
Officers and Director:* David H. Koch,* Pres.; Ruth E. Williams, Secy.; Vonda Holliman, Treas.
EIN: 480926946

1265
The Fred C. and Mary R. Koch Foundation, Inc.

(formerly The Fred C. Koch Foundation)
4111 E. 37th St. N.
Wichita, KS 67220-3203
Contact: Grant Admin.
E-mail: email@fmkfoundation.org; Main URL: http://www.fmkfoundation.org/
Scholarship e-mail: scholarships@fmkfoundation.org

Incorporated in 1953 in KS.
Donors: Fred C. Koch‡; Mary R. Koch‡; Koch Industries, Inc.
Foundation type: Independent foundation.
Financial data (yr. ended 12/31/12): Assets, $31,775,151 (M); gifts received, $408,000; expenditures, $2,127,153; qualifying distributions, $2,043,000; giving activities include $1,638,000 for 22 grants (high: $626,000; low: $2,500), and $405,000 for 204 grants to individuals (high: $2,000; low: $2,000).
Purpose and activities: Grants for the arts and art education, environmental stewardship, human services, the enablement of at-risk youth, and education in KS. Scholarships are limited to dependents of full-time employees of Koch Industries, Inc. and its subsidiaries.
Fields of interest: Arts; Higher education; Environment; Children/youth, services.
Type of support: General/operating support; Continuing support; Program development; Scholarship funds; Research; Employee-related scholarships.
Limitations: Giving primarily in KS. No support for athletic associations or sports teams, or for political or fraternal organizations. No grants to individuals (except for dependents of Koch Industries employees); or for venture capital grants, fundraising events, trips, tours, endowment funds, or for capital campaigns (unless the organization has received previous grants from the foundation).
Publications: Application guidelines.
Application information: Application required for scholarships. Application form not required.
Initial approach: Letter for grants (3 pages maximum); scholarship applicants should send for guidelines or refer to foundation web site
Copies of proposal: 1
Deadline(s): Submit proposal preferably Oct. 1; Mar. 1 deadline for scholarship
Board meeting date(s): Mar.
Officers and Directors:* Elizabeth B. Koch,* Pres.; Susan Addington, Secy.; Heather Love, Treas.; Richard Fink; Charles G. Koch; David H. Koch.
EIN: 486113560

1266
Claude R. Lambe Charitable Foundation
Wichita, KS

The foundation terminated in 2013, and transferred its assets to the Fidelity Investments Charitable Gift Fund.

1267
Harry J. Lloyd Charitable Trust
(formerly Share Foundation)
7200 W. 132nd St., Ste. 190
Overland Park, KS 66213-1136 (913) 851-2174
FAX: (913) 851-4892; E-mail: ltrust@ltrust.org; Main URL: http://www.hjltrust.org/

Established in 1965 in MO.
Donors: House of Lloyd, Inc.; Harry J. Lloyd†.
Foundation type: Independent foundation.
Financial data (yr. ended 12/31/12): Assets, $92,101,581 (M); expenditures, $10,924,121; qualifying distributions, $10,545,415; giving activities include $9,486,685 for 158 grants (high: $200,000; low: $500).
Purpose and activities: The foundation concentrates its support on projects that have a spiritual dimension, with special attention given to evangelical work, especially in the foreign mission field. Interest also in human services and educational organizations that are Christian-based.
Fields of interest: Education; Health care; Cancer; Cancer research; Food services; Christian agencies & churches.
International interests: Africa; China; India; Middle East.
Type of support: Capital campaigns; Equipment; Program development; Seed money; Scholarship funds.
Limitations: Applications accepted. Giving worldwide. No support for the arts, organizations that support or prohibit abortion or abortion rights, or for political organizations.
Publications: Application guidelines.
Application information: The foundation's web site is restricted to information on and applications for melanoma research related grants. Not more than one application per institution in each of the three melanoma grant type categories will be funded. See foundation's web site for complete melanoma research grant application policies, guidelines and forms. Application form required.
Initial approach: Proposal
Deadline(s): Feb. 1 for melanoma research grants
Board meeting date(s): Quarterly
Final notification: May for melanoma research grants
Officer: Russell Brown, Pres.
Trustees: Don Carson; Dan Doty; **G. Richard Hastings**; Jami Kay; Demi Lloyd; Jeanette Lloyd; Jane Overstreet.
Number of staff: 6 full-time support.
EIN: 436689416
Other changes: Jim Plueddemann is no longer a trustee.

1268
Greater Manhattan Community Foundation
555 Poyntz Avenue, Ste. 269
P.O. Box 1127
Manhattan, KS 66505-1127
E-mail: foundation@mcfks.org; Main URL: http://www.mcfks.org/
Facebook: https://www.facebook.com/GreaterManhattanCommunityFoundation?ref=ts&fref=ts

Established in 1999 in KS.
Foundation type: Community foundation.
Financial data (yr. ended 12/31/12): Assets, $16,027,111 (M); gifts received, $1,498,123; expenditures, $1,201,742; giving activities include $993,840 for 80+ grants (high: $250,000).
Purpose and activities: The mission of the foundation is to enhance quality of life in the Greater Manhattan area, both today and in the future, by: 1) enabling donors to fulfill their charitable desires; 2) building a permanent endowment; 3) facilitating prudent management and care of funds; and 4) meeting needs through grants, awards, and scholarships.
Fields of interest: Humanities; Arts; Education; Environment; Health care; Mental health/crisis services; Safety/disasters; Human services; Community/economic development; Youth; Aging.
Type of support: Capital campaigns; Equipment; Program development.
Limitations: Applications accepted. Giving primarily in greater Manhattan, KS. No support for religious organizations for religious purposes. No grants for annual appeals in membership drives.
Publications: Annual report; Informational brochure.
Application information: Visit foundation web site for application guidelines. Application form required.
Initial approach: Contact foundation
Copies of proposal: 3
Deadline(s): Varies
Officers and Trustees:* James Gordon,* Pres.; Neil Horton,* V.P.; Jodi Kaus,* Secy.; Tom Fryer,* Treas.; Jerry Banaka; Matt Crocker; Cheryl Grice; Neal Helmick; Vern Henricks; Jo Lyle; Dennis Mullin; Bill Richter; Karen Roberts; Jim Armendariz; Bahr Bahr.
EIN: 481215574
Other changes: Vernon J. Henricks is now Pres. and C.E.O. Jim Armendariz, Jon Bechtel, Charlie Busch, Connie Casper, Mike Daniels, Mary DeLucci, Mavis Fletcher, Rick Fulton, John Graham, Terry Harts, Vern Henricks, Doug Hinkinm Mike Holtman, Evan Howe, Kevin Ingram, C. Clyde Jones, and Mark Knackendoffel are no longer board members.

1269
Miller-Mellor Association
5301 W. 67th St.
Prairie Village, KS 66208-1409 (913) 432-5301
***Contact:* Craig W. Patterson, Dir.**

Established in 1950 in MO.
Foundation type: Independent foundation.
Financial data (yr. ended 06/30/13): Assets, $6,248,980 (M); expenditures, $332,691; qualifying distributions, $317,300; giving activities include $317,300 for 52 grants (high: $50,000; low: $100).
Purpose and activities: Grants primarily for higher education and cultural programs; support also for Roman Catholic churches and health services.
Fields of interest: Arts; Higher education; Hospitals (general); Hospitals (specialty); Human services; Catholic agencies & churches.
Limitations: Applications accepted. Giving primarily in Kansas City, MO.
Application information: Application form not required.
Initial approach: Proposal
Deadline(s): None
Officers and Directors:* Anne Patterson,* Pres.; JoZach James Miller,* V.P.; James Ludlow Miller,* Secy.-Treas.; **Marika Ivanko**; **Craig W. Patterson**; **Mark Elliot Patterson**.
EIN: 446011906

1270
Albert Morgan and Leona A. Morgan Charitable Foundation
711 3rd St.
P.O. Box 266
Phillipsburg, KS 67661-1915 (785) 543-6561
Contact: Denis Miller, Dir.

Established in 1992 in KS.
Donors: Albert Morgan†; Leona Morgan†.
Foundation type: Independent foundation.
Financial data (yr. ended 09/30/13): Assets, $10,643,839 (M); expenditures, $623,479; qualifying distributions, $448,642; giving activities include $386,045 for 25+ grants (high: $90,901).
Purpose and activities: Giving primarily to benefit the residents of Phillips County, KS.
Fields of interest: Historic preservation/historical societies; Hospitals (specialty); Boy scouts; American Red Cross; Human services.
Limitations: Applications accepted. Giving limited to Phillipsburg, KS. No grants to individuals.
Application information: Application form required.
Initial approach: Request application
Copies of proposal: 6
Deadline(s): 2 weeks prior to board meeting
Board meeting date(s): Semi-monthly
Final notification: 1 week following board meeting
Officers: Denis Miller, Chair.; Lowell Hahn, Secy.; Lori Ferguson, Treas.
Directors: John Beim; Daniels Heinze.
EIN: 481126706
Other changes: Denis Miller is now Chair. Lowell Hahn is now Secy. Lori Ferguson is now Treas.

1271
Muchnic Foundation
704 N. 4th St.
P.O. Box 329
Atchison, KS 66002-1924 **(913) 367-4164**
***Contact:* Sharon Meier**

Trust established in 1946 in KS.
Donors: Valley Co., Inc.; Helen Q. Muchnic†; H.E. Muchnic†.
Foundation type: Independent foundation.
Financial data (yr. ended 11/30/13): Assets, $9,675,237 (M); expenditures, $532,865; qualifying distributions, $500,139; giving activities include $397,704 for 64 grants (high: $45,000; low: $1,000).
Purpose and activities: Giving primarily for higher education and cultural programs, including museums, and civic affairs; support also for health associations and medical research.
Fields of interest: Museums; Arts; Higher education; Health organizations, association; Medical research, institute.
Limitations: Applications accepted. Giving on a national basis. No grants to individuals.
Application information: Large brochures are not helpful. Application form not required.

Initial approach: Letter
Deadline(s): Oct. 31
Board meeting date(s): As required
Officer: David C. Mize, Pres.; Sharon Meier, Secy.-Treas.
Directors: Ann Mize; Daphne Nan Muchnic.
Number of staff: 1
EIN: 486102818
Other changes: David C. Mize is now Pres. Elizabeth M. Elicker is no longer trustee.

1272
George H. Nettleton Foundation
(formerly George H. Nettleton Home)
P.O. Box 8707
Prairie Village, KS 66208-0707
Contact: Susann Riffe, Pres.
***E-mail:* susannriffe@aol.com**; Application address: 13820 W. 77th Terr., Lenexa, KS 66216; Main URL: http://www.gnettleton.org/

Re-classified as a private foundation in 2001.
Donors: Nettleton Trust; Aduh Hudson-Jaccard Charitable Trust Fund; Susie M. Root Charitable Trust; TUW Minerva Gundelfinger; A.H. Jaccard Memorial Trust; L.A. Jaccard Memorial Trust.
Foundation type: Independent foundation.
Financial data (yr. ended 12/31/12): Assets, $4,061,256 (M); gifts received, $55,293; expenditures, $316,901; qualifying distributions, $281,754; giving activities include $275,892 for 8 grants (high: $70,550; low: $15,000), and $5,000 for 1 grant to an individual.
Purpose and activities: Giving limited to organizations providing services for the elderly.
Fields of interest: Aging.
Type of support: General/operating support.
Limitations: Applications accepted. Giving limited to the greater Kansas City, MO area. No support for faith-based organizations. No grants to individuals.
Application information: Application form required.
Initial approach: Letter
Copies of proposal: 10
Deadline(s): Oct. 1
Board meeting date(s): 6 times per year
Officers: Susann Riffe, Pres.; Teresa L. Clark, V.P.; Jody Carroll, Secy.; Ken Lawrence, Treas.
Board Members: Paul Becker; Don Davis; Bob Frazier; David Ross; Lucina Noches Talbert.
EIN: 440369625

1273
David and Mary P. Rush Educational Trust
c/o Dennis Bieker
P.O. Box 579
Hays, KS 67601-0579 (785) 625-3537

Established in 1993 in KS.
Foundation type: Independent foundation.
Financial data (yr. ended 01/31/13): Assets, $5,577,727 (M); expenditures, $319,062; qualifying distributions, $223,818; giving activities include $202,500 for 21 grants (high: $74,500; low: $1,750).
Purpose and activities: Scholarships only available to graduates of Graham County High School in Kansas, who are full-time students, have involvement in high school and community activities, maintain a 2.0 GPA or better, and are in financial need.
Fields of interest: Higher education.
Type of support: Scholarship funds.
Limitations: Applications accepted. Giving limited to residents of Graham County, KS.
Application information: Application form required.
***Initial approach:* Request application form**
Deadline(s): May 1
Trustees: Dennis L. Bieker; Keith Riley; Brad Trexler.
EIN: 486243254

1274
Greater Salina Community Foundation
113 N. 7th St., Ste. 201
P.O. Box 2876
Salina, KS 67402-2876 (785) 823-1800
Contact: Betsy Wearing, Pres.
FAX: (785) 823-9370;
E-mail: communityfoundation@gscf.org; Main URL: http://www.gscf.org

Established in 1999 in KS.
Foundation type: Community foundation.
Financial data (yr. ended 06/30/12): Assets, $77,404,131 (M); gifts received, $6,486,991; expenditures, $3,732,513; giving activities include $3,130,146 for 646 grants (high: $254,104; low: $120), and $122,263 for 306 grants to individuals (high: $2,500; low: $15).
Purpose and activities: The foundation seeks to enhance quality of life, both today and in the future, by enabling donors to fulfill their charitable desires, building a permanent endowment, facilitating prudent management and care of funds, and meeting needs through grants, awards, and scholarships.
Fields of interest: Visual arts; Performing arts; Arts; Scholarships/financial aid; Education; Environment; Health care; Employment, training; Human services.
Type of support: General/operating support; Management development/capacity building; Capital campaigns; Equipment; Endowments; Emergency funds; Program development; Conferences/seminars; Publication; Seed money; Scholarship funds; Grants to individuals; Scholarships—to individuals.
Limitations: Applications accepted. Giving primarily in Saline County, KS, and the surrounding area. No grants for operating deficits or retirement of debt.
Publications: Annual report; Financial statement; Newsletter.
Application information: Visit foundation web site for application forms and additional guidelines per grant type. Contact the foundation for specific deadlines for the Fund for Greater Salina grants. Application form required.
Initial approach: Submit application form
Copies of proposal: 14
Deadline(s): Dec./Jan. and July/Aug. for the Fund for Greater Salina grants; none for others
Board meeting date(s): Bi-monthly
Final notification: Spring and fall for Fund for Greater Salina grants
Officers and Directors:* Dan Mendicina,* Chair.; Betsy Wearing,* Pres. and Exec. Dir.; Ray Perez,* Secy.-Treas.; Mark Berkley; Stephanie Klingzell Carlin; Ruth Cathcart-Rake; Olaf Frandsen; Frieda Mai-Weis; Rex Matlack; Dusty Moshier; Peter L. Peterson; Susy Reitz; Martha Rhea; Mark Speer; Glenn Stroer; Galen Swenson; Paula Tomlins; Susan Young.
Number of staff: 1 full-time professional; 4 part-time professional; 1 part-time support.
EIN: 481215503
Other changes: Lisa Peters is no longer a director.

1275
Sarver Charitable Trust
c/o The Peoples Bank
P.O. Box 307
Smith Center, KS 66967-0307 (785) 346-5445
***Application address:* c/o Paul Gregory, P.O. Box 12, Osborne, KS 67473**

Established in 1990 in KS.
Donors: Gail Sarver†; Sarver, Inc.
Foundation type: Independent foundation.
Financial data (yr. ended 12/31/12): Assets, $11,540,941 (M); expenditures, $383,440; qualifying distributions, $308,806; giving activities include $163,486 for 46 grants (high: $28,866; low: $250), and $117,950 for 136 grants to individuals (high: $1,800; low: $300).
Purpose and activities: Awards scholarships to high school graduates in Osborne County, KS; support also for leukemia research, human services, education, and to a Roman Catholic church.
Fields of interest: Education; Hospitals (general); Cancer, leukemia; Human services; Salvation Army; Catholic agencies & churches.
Type of support: General/operating support; Curriculum development; Scholarship funds; Scholarships—to individuals.
Limitations: Applications accepted. Giving limited to Osborne County, KS.
Application information: Application form required.
Initial approach: Letter
***Deadline(s):* Dec. 31 for charitable organizations; Apr. 1 for scholarships**
Board meeting date(s): Varies
Board Members: Pete Bohm; George Eakin; Paul S. Gregory; Frances Leadabrand; Melvin Wilcoxson.
Trustee: The Peoples Bank.
EIN: 486298990

1276
The Shumaker Family Foundation
1948 E. Santa Fe St., Ste. G
Olathe, KS 66062-1894
Contact: Judy Wright, Exec. Dir.
E-mail: request@shumakerfamilyfoundation.net; Tel./fax: (913) 764-1772; Main URL: http://www.shumakerfamilyfoundation.org

Established in 2005 in KS.
Donors: Paul K. Shumaker†; Dianne C. Shumaker.
Foundation type: Independent foundation.
Financial data (yr. ended 12/31/13): Assets, $19,030,203 (M); expenditures, $955,502; qualifying distributions, $811,475; giving activities include $710,500 for 72 grants (high: $55,000; low: $100).
Purpose and activities: The foundation exists to promote social justice, environmental justice, spirituality and education. Within social justice, the foundation emphasizes domestic violence prevention and the development of leadership among inner-city youth. Within environmental justice, the foundation supports projects that promote animal rights, animal welfare, and that address global warming. Within education, the foundation favors projects that show the fascination and potentiality of math, physical science, engineering, and the arts to children who otherwise might not receive such exposure. The foundation also funds projects that address the education of children 0-3 years of age. The foundation prefers innovative projects led by people and organizations with a history of successful innovation; projects that connect 2 or more of foundation funding areas; and projects that

can demonstrate significant outcomes within 3 years.
Fields of interest: Arts, public education; Education, early childhood education; Engineering school/education; Education; Environment; Animal welfare; Animals/wildlife, preservation/protection; Crime/violence prevention, domestic violence; International peace/security; Civil/human rights; Science; Religion, interfaith issues; Spirituality.
Type of support: Management development/capacity building; Capital campaigns; Curriculum development; Program evaluation.
Limitations: Applications accepted. Giving primarily in the greater bi-state Kansas City area; national and international giving for environmental and animal rights. No support for non 501(c)3 organizations, or for churches, or organizations that discriminate or promote violence (including to the environment). In general, no support for schools, except for select organizations. No grants to individuals, or for bricks and mortar, annual campaigns, capital campaigns or for special events.
Publications: Application guidelines; Grants list.
Application information: Application form available on foundation web site. Requests for $10,000 or less need only a letter description plus the required documentation. Application form required.
Initial approach: Letter, telephone or e-mail inquiry to ensure applicant's request fits the foundation's criteria
Copies of proposal: 1
***Deadline(s):* Mar. 15 for Spirituality and Environmental Justice; July 15 for Social Justice and Education**
Board meeting date(s): Feb., Apr., July and Nov.
Final notification: Within 6 weeks of decision
Trustees: Dianne C. Shumaker; Eric A. Shumaker; Megan I. Shumaker.
Number of staff: 1 full-time professional.
EIN: 656406193

1277
Skillbuilders Fund

4701 College Blvd., Ste. 214
Leawood, KS 66211-1689 (913) 608-7545
Main URL: http://www.skillbuildersfund.org

Established in 1984; Incorporated in 1983 in KS.
Donor: Marjorie P. Allen†.
Foundation type: Independent foundation.
Financial data (yr. ended 12/31/11): Assets, $4,414,511 (M); expenditures, $224,928; qualifying distributions, $195,108; giving activities include $138,250 for 23 grants (high: $61,000; low: $100).
Purpose and activities: Giving to organizations that enhance the capabilities of women of all ages to realize their full potential, with emphasis on women in the Kansas City region. Interested in programs that help women gain economic independence, build their capacity to function effectively in our society, and become full-participatory citizens.
Fields of interest: Employment, services; Human services; Family services; Women.
Type of support: General/operating support; Continuing support; Emergency funds; Program development; Seed money; Internship funds.
Limitations: Applications accepted. Giving primarily in the Greater Kansas City area. No support for political activities, or religious purposes. No grants to individuals, or for endowments, building programs, or annual giving campaigns.
Publications: Informational brochure (including application guidelines).
Application information: Application guidelines available on Fund web site. Application form required.
***Initial approach:* Email a letter via the fund web site, no longer than 2 pages**
***Deadline(s):* April 15**
Board meeting date(s): Spring and fall
Officers and Directors:* Barbara P. Allen,* Chair.; Betsy Vander Velde,* Vice-Chair.; Debbie Sosland-Edelman,* Secy.-Treas.; Debbie Allen; **Hon. Brenda Cameron**; **Margo Quiriconi**; Beth K. Smith.
EIN: 480984713
Other changes: Wendy J. Powell is no longer a director.

1278
Sunderland Foundation

(formerly Lester T. Sunderland Foundation)
P.O. Box 25900
Overland Park, KS 66225-5900 (913) 451-8900
Contact: Kent Sunderland, Pres.
E-mail: sunderlandfoundation@ashgrove.com; Main URL: http://www.sunderlandfoundation.org
Grants List: http://www.sunderlandfoundation.org/2009Contributions.asp

Incorporated in 1945 in MO.
Donors: Lester T. Sunderland†; Paul Sunderland†.
Foundation type: Independent foundation.
Financial data (yr. ended 12/31/12): Assets, $92,581,628 (M); expenditures, $4,915,805; qualifying distributions, $4,644,683; giving activities include $4,624,000 for 92 grants (high: $250,000; low: $5,000).
Purpose and activities: Giving primarily for higher education, youth services, arts and culture, health care and hospitals.
Fields of interest: Arts; Higher education; Hospitals (general); Health care; Children/youth, services.
Type of support: General/operating support; Continuing support; Annual campaigns; Capital campaigns; Building/renovation; Equipment; Land acquisition; Endowments; Emergency funds.
Limitations: Applications accepted. **Giving primarily in geographic areas that have connections to the Ash Grove Cement Co., particularly AR, Western IA, KS, Western MO and NE, and, to a lesser extent, ID, MT, OR, UT, and WA.** No grants to individuals, or for programs, endowments, special events, scholarships or operating expenses; no loans.
Publications: Application guidelines; Financial statement; Grants list; Program policy statement.
Application information: Application guidelines available on foundation web site. Application form not required.
Initial approach: Proposal via U.S. mail or e-mail as a PDF file
Copies of proposal: 1
Deadline(s): None
Board meeting date(s): As required
Officers and Trustees:* Kent Sunderland,* Pres.; James P. Sunderland,* Secy.; Charles Sunderland,* Treas.; William Sunderland, Ph.D.
Number of staff: 1 part-time support.
EIN: 446011082
Other changes: Lori D. Sunderland is no longer a trustee.

1279
Topeka Community Foundation

5431 S.W. 29th St., Ste. 300
Topeka, KS 66614-4483 (785) 272-4804
Contact: Roger K. Viola, Pres.; For grants: Marsha Pope, V.P.
FAX: (785) 273-4644;
E-mail: info@topekacommunityfoundation.org; Grant inquiry e-mail: pope@topekacommunityfoundation.org; Main URL: http://www.topekacommunityfoundation.org
Facebook: https://www.facebook.com/pages/Topeka-Community-Foundation/124452534291100

Incorporated in 1983 in KS.
Foundation type: Community foundation.
Financial data (yr. ended 12/31/12): Assets, $43,295,040 (M); gifts received, $3,571,443; expenditures, $3,622,108; giving activities include $2,484,310 for 46 grants (high: $250,000), and $147,052 for 150 grants to individuals.
Purpose and activities: The foundation seeks to connect donors with their interests and community needs, increasing charitable giving in our community, providing leadership on key community issues and ensuring stewardship and accountability for effective community investment of donor dollars.
Fields of interest: Performing arts; Arts; Education, early childhood education; Education; Environment, natural resources; Environment; Public health; Substance abuse, services; Children/youth, services; Family services; Homeless, human services; Human services; Community/economic development; Government/public administration; Children/youth; Youth; Adults; Disabilities, people with; Mentally disabled; Women; Adults, women; Homeless.
Type of support: General/operating support; Continuing support; Annual campaigns; Capital campaigns; Building/renovation; Emergency funds; Program development; Seed money; Scholarship funds; Employee matching gifts; Employee-related scholarships; Scholarships—to individuals; In-kind gifts; Matching/challenge support.
Limitations: Applications accepted. Giving limited to Topeka and Shawnee County, KS. No support for religious organizations for religious purposes. No grants to individuals (directly), or for ongoing general operating expenses or existing deficits, endowments, or fundraising events.
Publications: Application guidelines; Annual report; Financial statement; Informational brochure; Informational brochure (including application guidelines); Newsletter; Quarterly report.
Application information: Visit foundation web site for application forms and attachments. Faxed or e-mailed applications are not accepted. Application form required.
Initial approach: Submit application and attachments
Copies of proposal: 17
Deadline(s): Varies
Board meeting date(s): Quarterly, 3rd Thurs. of Feb., May, Aug. and Nov.
Final notification: Varies
Officers and Directors:* Grace A. Morrison, M.D.*, Chair.; Nancy Lewis,* Vice-Chair.; Roger K. Viola,* Pres.; Marsha Pope,* V.P.; James Schmank,* Secy.; Brad Owen,* Treas.; Steve Briman; Mary Brownback; Shelly Buhler; Dan Crow; John B. Dicus; Tim Etzel; Cathy McCoy; Chris McGee; Maynard Oliverius; Larry Robbins; Ford Ross; **Stephen Tempero, M.D.**; Susan Krenbiel William; C. Patrick Woods; **Lambert Wu.**
Number of staff: 2 full-time professional; 2 full-time support.
EIN: 480972106

1280

Western Kansas Community Foundation

402 No. Main
Garden City, KS 67846
Contact: For grants: Melissa Gallegos, Opers. Mgr.
E-mail: wkcf@wkcf.org; Grant inquiry e-mail: melissa@wkcf.org; Main URL: http://www.wkcf.org/
E-Newsletter: http://wkcf.org/news/newsletters
Facebook: https://www.facebook.com/pages/Western-Kansas-Community-Foundation/115598408500639

Established in 1996 in KS.
Foundation type: Community foundation.
Financial data (yr. ended 12/31/11): Assets, $18,650,062 (M); gifts received, $2,891,419; expenditures, $1,710,665; giving activities include $1,454,240 for 30+ grants (high: $500,000).
Purpose and activities: The foundation enriches western Kansas life through philanthropy, collaboration and leadership.
Fields of interest: General charitable giving.
Type of support: Program development.
Limitations: Applications accepted. Giving primarily in the 15-county service area of Western Kansas: Greeley, Wichita, Scott, Lane, Hamilton, Kearny, Finney, Stanton, Grant, Haskell, Gray, Morton, Stevens, Seward, and Meade counties, KS. No support for religious organizations for religious purposes. No grants to individuals (except for scholarship funds), or operating or maintenance expenses, medical or scholarly research, membership fees, banquet or luncheon expenses, ticket sales or fundraising efforts, travel expenses, capital debt reduction, endowments, or marketing tools.
Publications: Application guidelines; Newsletter.
Application information: Visit foundation web site for additional information. Application form required.
Initial approach: Submit application
Copies of proposal: 1
Deadline(s): Feb. 1, May 1, Aug. 1, Nov. 1
Officer and Directors:* Shea Sinclair, Exec. Dir.; Michael Cearley; Troy Dirks; Neil Hawley; Sharla Krenzel; Bob Kreutzer; Pat LeClerc; Marlene Lee; Don Linville; Emily Miller; Martin Nusser; Brenda Reeve; Liz Sosa; Bill Stewart.
EIN: 481184667
Other changes: Alice Banning, Dennis Jones, and Janie Welsh are no longer directors.

1281

Western Professional Associates, Inc.

5020 Bob Billings Pkwy., Ste. C
Lawrence, KS 66049-3873

Established in 1994 in CO, FL, IN, KS, MO, OK, and SD.
Donor: Kansas Legal Services, Inc.
Foundation type: Operating foundation.
Financial data (yr. ended 12/31/12): Assets, $614,654 (M); expenditures, $1,769,815; qualifying distributions, $187,129; giving activities include $187,129 for 3 grants (high: $150,000; low: $15), and $1,582,687 for 1 foundation-administered program.
Fields of interest: Human services; Civil/human rights; Philanthropy/voluntarism.
Limitations: Applications not accepted. Giving limited to Topeka, KS.
Application information: Unsolicited requests for funds not accepted.
Officers: Dr. Robert C. Harder, Pres.; Chuck Briscoe, Secy.-Treas.
Directors: Anne Fehrenbacher Haught; Roger L. McCollister; Charles E. Worden.
EIN: 431655154
Other changes: The grantmaker no longer lists a URL address.

KENTUCKY

1282
Blue Grass Community Foundation, Inc.
(formerly Blue Grass Foundation, Inc.)
499 E. High St., Ste. 112
Lexington, KY 40507 (859) 225-3343
Contact: For grants: Kassie L. Branham, Dir., Grants and Scholarships
FAX: (859) 243-0770; E-mail: info@bgcf.org; Grant inquiry e-mail: kbranham@bgcf.org; Main URL: http://www.bgcf.org
Blog: http://bgcf.org/engage/news-events/
Facebook: http://www.facebook.com/bgcf.org
Flickr: http://www.flickr.com/photos/bgcf/
LinkedIn: http://www.linkedin.com/companies/blue-grass-community-foundation
RSS Feed: http://bgcf.org/feed/
Twitter: http://twitter.com/BGCF
YouTube: http://www.youtube.com/bluegrasscf

Incorporated in 1967 in KY.
Foundation type: Community foundation.
Financial data (yr. ended 06/30/13): Assets, $65,790,534 (M); gifts received, $13,605,326; expenditures, $9,936,019; giving activities include $7,799,413 for 147 grants (high: $2,500,000), and $113,686 for 56 grants to individuals.
Purpose and activities: The foundation receives gifts and gives grants to people and causes in central and eastern Kentucky.
Fields of interest: Arts; Education, early childhood education; Education, reading; Education; Environment; Animal welfare; Health care; Health organizations, association; Housing/shelter, homeless; Housing/shelter; Disasters, Hurricane Katrina; Children/youth, services; Human services; Economic development; Community/economic development; Public affairs; Religion; Infants/toddlers.
Type of support: General/operating support; Management development/capacity building; Building/renovation; Equipment; Endowments; Program development; Seed money; Scholarship funds; Technical assistance; Consulting services; Employee-related scholarships; Scholarships—to individuals; Matching/challenge support.
Limitations: Applications accepted. Giving limited to central and eastern KY.
Publications: Application guidelines; Annual report; Financial statement; Grants list; Quarterly report.
Application information: The foundation's grant committee will review all letters of inquiry and decide which agencies will be asked to complete a full application for Community Grants. Visit foundation web site for application forms and guidelines per grant type. Application form required.
Initial approach: E-mail Letter of inquiry (1 to 2 pages) for Community Grants
Copies of proposal: 1
Deadline(s): Aug. 15 for Community Grants; varies for others
Board meeting date(s): Quarterly
Final notification: Varies
Officers and Directors:* Buckner Woodford IV,* Chair.; Arthur R. Salomon,* Vice-Chair.; **Lisa Adkins,* Pres. and C.E.O.**; Madonna Turner,* Secy.; James Rouse,* Treas.; Jonathan Barker; Eunice Beatty; **Garland H. Barr III**; Bruce Florence; Rufus Friday; Phil Holoubek; Logan Marskbury; John Milward; Travis Musgrave; P.G. Peeples, Sr.; Ashley Robbins; Joe Rosenberg; Dr. Ronald Saykaly; Brandi Skirvin; Fran Taylor; Nancy Allen Turner; Griffin VanMeter; Bud Watson; Tracee Whitley.
Number of staff: 4 full-time professional.
EIN: 616053466
Other changes: Lisa Adkins is now Pres. and C.E.O. Jill Springate is now Dir., Donor & Board Relations.

1283
James Graham Brown Foundation, Inc.
4350 Brownsboro Rd., Ste. 200
Louisville, KY 40207-1681 (502) 896-2440
Contact: Mason B. Rummel, Pres. and Treas.
FAX: (502) 896-1774; E-mail: grants@jgbf.org; Additional tel.: (866) 896-5423. E-mail for Mason B. Rummel : mason@jgbf.org; Main URL: http://www.jgbf.org
Grants List: http://www.jgbf.org/Home/GrantsAwarded/tabid/69/Default.aspx

Trust established in 1943 in KY; incorporated in 1954.
Donors: J. Graham Brown†; Agnes B. Duggan†.
Foundation type: Independent foundation.
Financial data (yr. ended 12/31/12): Assets, $336,587,494 (M); expenditures, $23,146,729; qualifying distributions, $19,492,826; giving activities include $18,725,108 for 35 grants (high: $2,666,666; low: $500).
Purpose and activities: Giving for higher education, civic organizations, community and economic development, human service organizations, culture and humanities, and health.
Fields of interest: Museums; Historic preservation/historical societies; Higher education; Education; Health care; Human services; Youth, services; Urban/community development.
Type of support: Building/renovation; Capital campaigns; Equipment; Land acquisition; Matching/challenge support; Research.
Limitations: Applications accepted. Giving limited to KY, with emphasis on the Jefferson County and Louisville metropolitan areas. No support for private foundations or the performing arts, primary or secondary schooling, religious institutions for religious purposes, including theological seminaries, or political or national organizations. No grants to individuals.
Publications: Application guidelines; Grants list; Informational brochure (including application guidelines).
Application information: Application form required if board approves request for permission to apply. Application form required.
Initial approach: Online Pre-Grant Request
Copies of proposal: 1
***Deadline(s):* Social Services: July 7; Culture and Civic: May 5; Education: Mar. 3**
Board meeting date(s): Six annually
Final notification: Grants paid Dec. 31
Officers and Trustees:* R. Alex Rankin,* Chair. and C.E.O.; **Mason B. Rummel, Pres.**; W. Barrett Nichols,* V.P.; **Kathy Kotcamp, Treas.**; Alice Houston; Fr. Ron Knott; J.A. Paradis, III; Robert W. Rounsavall III; R. Ted Steinbock, M.D.
Number of staff: 4 full-time professional; 1 part-time professional.
EIN: 610724060
Other changes: Mason B. Rummel is now Pres. Dodie L. McKenzie is no longer Secy. and Grants Dir.

1284
The C.E. and S. Foundation, Inc.
101 S. 5th St., Ste. 1650
Louisville, KY 40202-3122 (502) 583-0546
Contact: Bruce A. Maza, Exec. Dir.
FAX: (502) 583-7648;
E-mail: Bruce@cesfoundation.com; Main URL: http://www.cesfoundation.com

Established in 1984 in FL.
Donors: David A. Jones; and family.
Foundation type: Independent foundation.
Financial data (yr. ended 12/31/12): Assets, $65,532,418 (M); expenditures, $3,316,957; qualifying distributions, $3,402,136; giving activities include $2,949,505 for 121 grants (high: $300,000; low: $600).
Purpose and activities: Giving primarily for higher education, (with a focus on undergraduate liberal arts programs in Louisville, KY), as well as for colleges and universities, and for disaster relief and prevention, international cooperation, Louisville's urban environment, and special projects initiated by the grants committee. The foundation will give priority to organizations and programs that: 1) have demonstrated effectiveness, proven management, clear plans and a high level of competence; 2) are committed to measuring outcomes and examining the lasting impact of their efforts; 3) have strong levels of funding from other donors; and 4) offer unique, highly innovative solutions to recognized social problems.
Fields of interest: Education; Safety/disasters; International affairs, goodwill promotion; Urban/community development.
Type of support: General/operating support; Income development; Management development/capacity building; Capital campaigns; Land acquisition; Endowments; Emergency funds; Program development; Seed money; Internship funds; Scholarship funds; Research; Technical assistance; Consulting services; Program-related investments/loans.
Limitations: Applications accepted. Giving primarily in Louisville, KY. No support for medical research organizations, or for political organizations. No grants to individuals, or for scholarships.
Publications: Application guidelines; Annual report; Grants list; Program policy statement.
Application information: Letters sent to the foundation that propose projects outside of the guidelines are immediately declined. Application form not required.
Initial approach: Letter, telephone, or web site for guidelines
Copies of proposal: 1
Deadline(s): None
Board meeting date(s): Jan., May, Sept. and Nov.
Final notification: Up to two months
Officers and Trustee:* David A. Jones,* Pres.; Bruce A. Maza, Exec. Dir.
Number of staff: 3 full-time professional.
EIN: 592466943

1285
Alex G. Campbell, Jr. Foundation, Inc.
831 E. Main St.
Lexington, KY 40502-1603 (859) 268-2701
Contact: Rebecca L. Reinhold, Secy.

Established in 1997 in KY.
Donor: Alex G. Campbell, Jr.
Foundation type: Independent foundation.
Financial data (yr. ended 04/30/13): Assets, $1,268,454 (M); expenditures, $127,911; qualifying distributions, $106,275; giving activities include $100,000 for 2 grants (high: $50,000; low: $50,000).
Fields of interest: Media, television; Performing arts, education; Historic preservation/historical societies; Arts; Higher education; Education;

Environment, natural resources; Animal welfare; Cancer; Human services; Salvation Army; YM/YWCAs & YM/YWHAs; Children/youth, services; Community/economic development.
Limitations: Applications accepted. Giving primarily in KY. No grants to individuals.
Application information: Application form not required.
Initial approach: Letter
Deadline(s): None
Officers and Directors:* Alex G. Campbell, Jr.,* Pres.; Rebecca L. Reinhold,* Secy.; Edward S. Barr,* Treas.
EIN: 311532423

1286
Community Foundation of West Kentucky
(formerly Paducah Area Community Foundation)
333 Broadway, Ste. 615
P.O. Box 7
Paducah, KY 42002-0007 (270) 442-8622
Contact: Tony Watkins, C.E.O.
FAX: (270) 442-8623; E-mail: info@cfwestky.org; Main URL: http://www.cfwestky.org

Established in 1995 in KY.
Foundation type: Community foundation.
Financial data (yr. ended 12/31/12): Assets, $16,972,502 (M); gifts received, $1,639,229; expenditures, $1,249,485; giving activities include $670,350 for 30+ grants (high: $25,000), and $42,000 for 35 grants to individuals (high: $2,000; low: $500).
Purpose and activities: The foundation supports areas of art and culture, community development, education, environment, health and social needs.
Fields of interest: Arts, cultural/ethnic awareness; Arts; Education; Environment; Public health; Health care; Human services; Community/economic development.
Type of support: Equipment; General/operating support; Annual campaigns; Capital campaigns; Endowments; Debt reduction; Emergency funds; Program development; Scholarship funds.
Limitations: Applications not accepted. Giving primarily in western KY and Massac County, IL.
Publications: Annual report; Informational brochure; Newsletter.
Application information:
Board meeting date(s): Quarterly in Feb., May, Aug., and Nov.
Officers and Directors:* Tony Watkins,* C.E.O.; Scott Powell,* Pres.; Vicki Brantley,* Secy.-Treas.; Carney Allen; Chris Black; Terry Bunnell; Eugenia Drossos; Joseph H. Framptom; B.A. Hamilton; Mark Hequembourg; Chris Hutson; Ronald Jackson; Eugene Katterjohn, Jr.; Robin Kelly; C. Thomas Miller; **Gerry Montgomery**; Bonnie Schrock; Jerr Severns; George Shaw; Chris Smith; Tim Thomas; Ken Wheeler.
Number of staff: 1 full-time professional; 1 full-time support; 1 part-time support.
EIN: 611304905
Other changes: Gerry Montgomery and Jennifer Revell are no longer directors.

1287
Irvin F. & Alice S. Etscorn Charitable Foundation
c/o Hilliard Lyons Trust Company
P.O. Box 32760
Louisville, KY 40232-2760 (502) 588-8623

Established in 1996 in KY.
Donor: Alice S. Etscorn†.
Foundation type: Independent foundation.
Financial data (yr. ended 06/30/13): Assets, $7,656,673 (M); gifts received, $200,000; expenditures, $458,062; qualifying distributions, $418,000; giving activities include $418,000 for 42 grants (high: $35,000; low: $1,500).
Purpose and activities: Giving to YMCAs, and for pediatrics, eye diseases, and Christian organizations.
Fields of interest: Higher education; Health care, organ/tissue banks; Eye diseases; Pediatrics; Human services; YM/YWCAs & YM/YWHAs; Christian agencies & churches.
Type of support: Capital campaigns; Building/renovation; Equipment; Professorships; Fellowships; Scholarship funds; Matching/challenge support.
Limitations: Applications accepted. Giving primarily in Louisville and Jefferson County, KY. No grants to individuals.
Application information: Application form required.
Initial approach: Letter
Copies of proposal: 1
Deadline(s): 2nd Thurs. in Nov.
Board meeting date(s): Nov.
Final notification: 4 weeks
Trustee: Hilliard Lyons Trust Co.
Number of staff: None.
EIN: 611314419

1288
The Gheens Foundation, Inc.
401 W. Main St., Ste. 705
Louisville, KY 40202-2937 (502) 584-4650
Contact: Carl M. Thomas, Pres.
FAX: (502) 584-4652;
E-mail: carl@gheensfoundation.org; Main URL: http://www.gheensfoundation.org

Incorporated in 1957 in KY.
Donors: C. Edwin Gheens†; Mary Jo Gheens Hill†.
Foundation type: Independent foundation.
Financial data (yr. ended 10/31/13): Assets, $123,333,385 (M); expenditures, $6,800,277; qualifying distributions, $5,886,160; giving activities include $5,607,021 for 138 grants (high: $250,000; low: $2,500).
Purpose and activities: Emphasis on higher and secondary education, ongoing teacher education, social service agencies, health associations, programs for the physically and mentally handicapped, and cultural programs.
Fields of interest: Arts; Secondary school/education; Higher education; Education; Mental health/crisis services; Health organizations, association; Human services; Children/youth; Disabilities, people with; Economically disadvantaged.
Type of support: General/operating support; Capital campaigns; Building/renovation; Equipment; Program development; Scholarship funds; Research.
Limitations: Applications accepted. Giving primarily in Louisville, KY, and LaFourche and Terrebone parishes, LA. No support for private high schools. No grants to individuals.
Publications: Application guidelines; Grants list.
Application information: Application form, guidelines and information is available on foundation web site. Application form required.
Initial approach: Ask for application by letter, phone, fax, or e-mail
Copies of proposal: 7
Deadline(s): One week before the last business day of the month prior to board meeting
Board meeting date(s): Quarterly
Final notification: Within 30 days after board meeting
Officers and Trustees:* Michael B. Mountjoy,* Chair. and C.E.O.; Carl M. Thomas, Pres. and Treas.; William G. Duncan, Jr., Secy.; **Morton Boyd**; John R. Crockett III; Dr. Laman A. Gray, Jr.; Phoebe A. Wood.
Number of staff: 2 full-time professional; 2 full-time support.
EIN: 616031406

1289
Good Samaritan Foundation, Inc.
c/o Grant Review Comm.
7400 Floydsburg Rd.
Crestwood, KY 40014-8202 (800) 530-7236
***E-mail:* gsf@kyumc.org**; Main URL: http://kyumc.org/gsf
Facebook: https://www.facebook.com/KentuckyAnnualConference

Established in 1888 in KY, Incorporated as Good Samaritan Hospital of KY in 1929; Good Samaritan Foundation is a hospital conversion foundation.
Donors: Thomas Clark†; F.W. Rickard†; Elisabeth Spanton†.
Foundation type: Independent foundation.
Financial data (yr. ended 06/30/13): Assets, $19,076,591 (M); gifts received, $31,437; expenditures, $1,175,170; qualifying distributions, $860,000; giving activities include $860,000 for 28 grants (high: $180,456; low: $2,500).
Purpose and activities: The foundation initiates, participates in, and supports activities which focus on improving the health status of Kentuckians. Primary/preventive health care proposals serving low income and uninsured individuals in underserved areas of KY are a priority for funding.
Fields of interest: Health care.
Type of support: General/operating support; Equipment; Seed money; Curriculum development; Fellowships; Scholarship funds; Research.
Limitations: Applications accepted. Giving limited to KY. No support for indirect costs, or for fraternal or veterans' organizations. No grants to individuals, or capital improvements, endowment funds. charitable tournaments, meal functions, team sponsorships, ticket purchases, or athletic activities.
Publications: Application guidelines; Informational brochure (including application guidelines); Newsletter; Occasional report.
Application information: In addition to the online applications, applicants must mail both a paper copy of all attachments and a CD containing a pdf file which contains all attachments. All attachments should be placed in one pdf file and not in multiple files. See foundation web site for complete application requirements. Application form required.
Initial approach: Use online application on foundation web site
Copies of proposal: 2
Deadline(s): See web site for current deadline
Final notification: May 31
Officers: Jackson Brewer, Chair.; **William Martin Moore, Vice-Chair.**; Marian Bensema, Secy.; **Joni B. Way, Treas.**
Directors: Carlyle Ackley; **Randy Capps**; Leanne Diakov; **Frank Fitzpatrick**; Paul Fryman; Terry L. Reffett; Marian R. Smith; Tukea Talbert.
Number of staff: 1 full-time support.
EIN: 311087598
Other changes: The grantmaker no longer lists a fax.
William Martin Moore has replaced James Tennill as Vice-Chair. Joni B. Way has replaced Michael B. Watts as Treas.

Mike Johnson and Mike Mullins are no longer directors.

1290
Hayswood Foundation, Inc.
1 W. McDonald Pkwy., Ste. 3A
Maysville, KY 41056-1138 (606) 563-9333
Contact: Lloyd Schlitz, Exec. Dir.
FAX: (606) 563-9444;
E-mail: hfound@maysvilleky.net; Main URL: http://www.hayswood.org
Grants List: http://www.hayswood.org/Recent%20Grant%20Recipients.html

Established in 1985.
Foundation type: Independent foundation.
Financial data (yr. ended 12/31/12): Assets, $7,961,583 (M); gifts received, $14,706; expenditures, $424,412; qualifying distributions, $318,723; giving activities include $318,723 for grants.
Purpose and activities: Giving to support mental and physical health, and education.
Fields of interest: Education; Health care; Mental health/crisis services.
Type of support: General/operating support; Capital campaigns; Building/renovation; Equipment; Program development; Scholarship funds; Scholarships—to individuals; Matching/challenge support.
Limitations: Applications accepted. Giving limited to Bracken, Fleming, Lewis, Mason, and Robertson Counties in KY, and Adams and Brown Counties in OH. No support for religious or political organizations. No grants to individuals (except for scholarships) or for endowments.
Publications: Application guidelines.
Application information: Application forms are available starting June 1 of each year, and are available on foundation web site. Application form required.
Initial approach: See web site
Copies of proposal: 1
Deadline(s): Aug. 1
Board meeting date(s): Jan., May, Aug. and Oct.
Final notification: Oct.
Officers and Directors:* Dave Wallingford,* Pres.; Ronald Rice,* V.P.; Dr. Robert Ross,* Secy.; Douglas Hendrickson,* Treas.; Lloyd Schlitz, Exec. Dir.; Michael Clarice; Dave Clarke; Romey Griffey; Dr. John McDowell; William McNeill; John Parker; Dr. Robert Ross; Kirk Tolle; Ann Tomlin; Debra Wallingford; Sally Walton.
Number of staff: 1 part-time professional.
EIN: 237345996

1291
The J & L Foundation
(formerly The Joan and Lee Thomas Foundation, Inc.)
2602 Grassland Dr.
Louisville, KY 40299-2524 (502) 495-1958
Contact: Lee B. Thomas, Dir.

Established in 1989 in KY.
Donors: Lee B. Thomas; Joan Thomas.
Foundation type: Independent foundation.
Financial data (yr. ended 06/30/13): Assets, $20,492,143 (M); expenditures, $1,270,539; qualifying distributions, $1,230,167; giving activities include $1,208,000 for 28 grants (high: $125,000; low: $5,000).
Purpose and activities: Giving primarily for human services and education.
Fields of interest: Higher education; Education; Human services; Children/youth, services; Family services; Religion, interfaith issues.
Limitations: Applications accepted. Giving primarily in Louisville, KY; some funding also in Washington, DC. No grants to individuals.
Application information: Application form not required.
Deadline(s): None
Officers and Directors:* Lee B. Thomas,* Chair. and Treas.; Glenn E. Thomas, Pres. and Secy.
EIN: 611166955
Other changes: Glenn E. Thomas is now Pres. and Secy. Lee B. Thomas is now Chair. and Treas.

1292
Kentucky Foundation for Women, Inc.
1215 Heyburn Bldg.
332 W. Broadway
Louisville, KY 40202-2184 (502) 562-0045
FAX: (502) 561-0420; **E-mail: team@kfw.org**; Toll free tel.: (866) 654-7564; Main URL: http://www.kfw.org
Grants List: http://www.kfw.org/grrec.html

Established in 1985 in KY.
Donor: Sallie Bingham.
Foundation type: Independent foundation.
Financial data (yr. ended 06/30/13): Assets, $12,934,418 (M); gifts received, $10,522; expenditures, $637,884; qualifying distributions, $597,040; giving activities include $60,225 for 16 grants (high: $7,500; low: $500), $144,775 for 54 grants to individuals (high: $7,444; low: $1,000), and $74,434 for 1 foundation-administered program.
Purpose and activities: Support for feminist artists and arts-related organizations, with the goal of bringing about social change through the arts. Giving to 1) feminist visual art: painting, sculpture, puppetry, crafts, photography exhibits, multi-media, etc.; 2) feminist performing arts: dance, theater, music, including performers, directors, producers, composers, lyricists, choreographers, and conductors; 3) feminist writers and playwrights; and 4) feminist video/filmmakers.
Fields of interest: Media, film/video; Visual arts; Visual arts, photography; Visual arts, painting; Performing arts; Performing arts, choreography; Performing arts, theater; Performing arts, music composition; Literature; Arts; Civil/human rights, women; Social sciences; Women.
Type of support: Grants to individuals.
Limitations: Giving limited to persons who live or work in KY, or to persons and organizations whose projects directly affect the lives of women in KY. No grants for scholarships or for any expenses associated with work towards a college degree; or for endowments, capital campaigns or facilities renovation.
Publications: Application guidelines; Annual report; Grants list; Newsletter.
Application information: Applicants are requested to write a 4-page proposal addressing the relationship between their art activities and social change, and/or the direct impact of their art-making upon KY women and girls. Application form required.
Initial approach: Request application form by letter or telephone; also available on foundation web site
Copies of proposal: 4
Deadline(s): For the Artist Enrichment Program, typically the first Friday of September; for the Art Meets Activism Program, typically the first Friday of March
Final notification: Nov. 30 for Artist Enrichment program; May 30 for Art Meets Activism program
Officers and Board Members:* Gail Martin,* Chair; Katie Ward,* Treas.; Judith Jennings, Dir.; Gabriela Alcalde; Sallie Bingham; Leah Ottersbach; Cynthia Resor; Mae Suramek.
Number of staff: 2 full-time professional; 1 part-time professional; 1 full-time support; 1 part-time support.
EIN: 611070429

1293
Lift A Life Foundation, Inc.
(formerly The David C. and Wendy L. Novak Foundation, Inc.)
4350 Brownsboro Rd., Ste. 110
Louisville, KY 40207-1681 (502) 893-4540
E-mail: info@listalifefoundation.org; Main URL: http://www.liftalifefoundation.org
Facebook: https://www.facebook.com/LiftALifeFoundation
LinkedIn: http://www.linkedin.com/company/lift-a-life-foundation?trk=top_nav_home
Twitter: https://twitter.com/LiftALifeFdtn

Established in 1999 in KY.
Donors: David C. Novak; Wendy L. Novak.
Foundation type: Independent foundation.
Financial data (yr. ended 12/31/12): Assets, $34,938,198 (M); gifts received, $9,535,542; expenditures, $4,511,363; qualifying distributions, $4,239,950; giving activities include $4,239,950 for 27 grants (high: $500,000; low: $5,000).
Purpose and activities: Giving primarily to organizations that impact individuals and families in need in the areas of hunger, education, leadership, juvenile diabetes research and family support programs, and youth and family issues.
Fields of interest: Diabetes research; Food services; Human services; Family services; Christian agencies & churches; Youth.
Limitations: Giving primarily in KY; some funding also in Washington, DC. **No support for political activities. No grants to individuals, or for travel, surveys or fundraising activities (unless exception is made by the foundation's Board of Directors).**
Application information: Full proposals are by invitation only, upon review of Partnership Interest Form. Proposals submitted without a request from the foundation will not be considered.
***Initial approach:* Submit Partnership Interest Form through foundation web site**
***Deadline(s):* See foundation web site for current deadlines**
Officers and Directors:* David C. Novak,* Pres.; Wendy L. Novak,* V.P. and Secy.-Treas.; Ashley Novak Butler; Susan B. Novak.
EIN: 611359337

1294
The Steel Foundation, Inc.
15415 Shelbyville Rd.
Louisville, KY 40245-4137

Established in 2004 in KY.
Donors: Steel Technologies, Inc.; Bradford T. Ray; Michael Carroll.
Foundation type: Company-sponsored foundation.
Financial data (yr. ended 12/31/11): Assets, $869,036 (M); gifts received, $142,101; expenditures, $205,933; qualifying distributions,

$174,741; giving activities include $170,071 for 56 grants (high: $60,000; low: $160).
Purpose and activities: The foundation supports organizations involved with health, cancer, recreation, youth development, and human services.
Fields of interest: Recreation; Human services; Religion.
Type of support: General/operating support; Scholarship funds.
Limitations: Applications not accepted. Giving primarily in areas of company operations in Louisville, KY. No grants to individuals.
Application information: Unsolicited applications are not accepted.
Officers and Directors:* Stuart Ray,* Pres.; Patrick M. Flanagan,* Secy.; Bradford Ray,* Treas.
EIN: 562468607
Other changes: The grantmaker no longer lists a URL address.

1295
Trim Masters Charitable Foundation, Inc.
401 Enterprise Dr.
Nicholasville, KY 40356-2294

Donor: Trim Masters Inc.
Foundation type: Company-sponsored foundation.
Financial data (yr. ended 06/30/13): Assets, $1,675,838 (M); expenditures, $238,672; qualifying distributions, $236,989; giving activities include $236,989 for 48 grants (high: $25,000; low: $325).
Purpose and activities: The foundation supports festivals and parks and organizations involved with arts and culture, education, health, cancer, child welfare, agriculture, athletics, and human services.
Fields of interest: Arts, cultural/ethnic awareness; Arts; Elementary/secondary education; Higher education; Libraries (public); Education; Health care; Cancer; Crime/violence prevention, child abuse; Agriculture; Recreation, parks/playgrounds; Recreation, fairs/festivals; Athletics/sports, amateur leagues; Boy scouts; YM/YWCAs & YM/YWHAs; Children, services; Human services; United Ways and Federated Giving Programs.
Type of support: Capital campaigns; General/operating support; Building/renovation; Equipment; Program development; Scholarship funds; Sponsorships; Matching/challenge support.
Limitations: Applications not accepted. Giving primarily in KY. No grants to individuals.
Application information: Contributes only to pre-selected organizations.
Officers: Dale Kihlman, Pres.; Steve Hesselbrock, V.P.; **Scarlett Ingram, Secy.-Treas.**
Directors: Larry Carter; Anji Flint; Mike French.
EIN: 611225606
Other changes: Scarlett Ingram has replaced Beth Rohrback as Secy.-Treas.
Julie Frank is no longer a member of the governing body. Scarlett Ingram is no longer a member of the governing body. Mark Jennings is no longer a member of the governing body.

1296
USA Equestrian Trust Inc.
P.O. Box 13321
Lexington, KY 40583-3321
***E-mail:* grants@trusthorses.org**; Main URL: http://trusthorses.org/

Foundation type: Independent foundation.
Financial data (yr. ended 11/30/12): Assets, $4,347,209 (M); expenditures, $441,999; qualifying distributions, $326,357; giving activities include $213,204 for 13 grants (high: $50,000; low: $8,000).
Fields of interest: Education; Employment.
Application information: Inquiries about grant applications or the grant process are handles only by email. See Trust web site for complete application guidelines. Application form required.
Deadline(s): Before May and Oct.
Officers: Alan F. Balch, Pres.; Lisa Blackstone, V.P.; Georgie F. Green, Secy.; Guy R. Warner, Treas.
Directors: Linda A. Allen; Karl V. Hart; Kate Jackson; Marianne Ludwig; Fred K. Sarver.
EIN: 131764840
Other changes: The grantmaker no longer lists a phone.

1297
The Zantker Charitable Foundation Inc
Lexington, KY

The foundation terminated in 2011 and transferred its funds to Blue Grass Community Foundation.

LOUISIANA

1298
Albemarle Foundation
451 Florida St.
Baton Rouge, LA 70801-1700 (225) 388-7552
Contact: Sandra M. Holub, Mgr.
E-mail: AlbemarleFoundation@albemarle.com; E-mail for Sandra Holub: sandra_holub@albemarle.com; Main URL: http://www.albemarle.com/Sustainability/Albemarle-Foundation-42.html
Grants List: http://www.albemarle.com/Sustainability/2013-Giving-by-Agency-838C42.html
YouTube: https://www.youtube.com/watch?feature=player_embedded&v=BJnANeuLUD8

Established in 2006 in VA.
Donors: M. Rohr; J. Steitz; L. Kissam; Albemarle Corp.
Foundation type: Company-sponsored foundation.
Financial data (yr. ended 12/31/12): Assets, $10,121,573 (M); gifts received, $11,070,282; expenditures, $3,883,642; qualifying distributions, $3,591,091; giving activities include $3,591,091 for 675 grants (high: $281,487; low: $50).
Purpose and activities: The foundation supports programs designed to promote future workforce and education; social and health services; and cultural resources and advocacy.
Fields of interest: Arts education; Arts; Charter schools; Adult/continuing education; Education; Hospitals (general); Health care; Employment, services; Food banks; Housing/shelter, development; Disasters, preparedness/services; Children/youth, services; Family services; Human services; Community/economic development; Engineering/technology.
Type of support: General/operating support; Annual campaigns; Building/renovation; Program development; Curriculum development; Employee volunteer services; Employee matching gifts; Employee-related scholarships.
Limitations: Applications accepted. **Giving limited to communities in which Albemarle Corporation operates in Magnolia, AR, Baton Rouge, LA, South Haven, MI, Twinsburg, OH, Tyrone, PA, Orangeburg, SC, and Bayport, Clearlake, and Pasadena, TX.** No support for discriminatory organizations or legislative organizations. No grants for telephone solicitations.
Publications: Application guidelines; Grants list; Informational brochure.
Application information: Grant requests of $5,000 and less are forwarded to site councils for review. Grant requests of $5,001 must be approved by the Board of Directors at the January meeting. Organizations receiving support are asked to submit a final report. Application form required.
Initial approach: Complete online application
***Deadline(s):* Feb. to Nov.**
Board meeting date(s): First week of May and Nov.
***Final notification:* 4 to 12 weeks**
Officers and Directors:* Luke Kissam,* Pres.; Nicole C. Daniel, Secy.; Richard G. Fishman, Treas.; Mark C. Rohr, Pres.; John M. Steitz; **Ron Zumstein.**
EIN: 204798471
Other changes: Luke Kissam has replaced Mark C. Rohr as Pres.

1299
Baptist Community Ministries
(formerly Christian Health Ministries)
400 Poydras St., Ste. 2950
New Orleans, LA 70130-3245 (504) 593-2323
***Contact:* Charles Beasley, Interim C.E.O. and Pres.**
FAX: (504) 593-2301; E-mail: info@bcm.org; Main URL: http://www.bcm.org

Established in 1996 in LA; converted from the sale of the assets of Mercy + Baptist Medical Center. In 2009, the organization changed their name following a merger with the original Baptist Community Ministries.
Donors: C.E. McFarland Trust; D.A. McFarland Trust; Baptist Community Ministries; Christian Health Ministries Foundation.
Foundation type: Independent foundation.
Financial data (yr. ended 09/30/12): Assets, $234,671,410 (M); gifts received, $1,379,400; expenditures, $13,247,337; qualifying distributions, $12,290,022; giving activities include $7,182,379 for 112 grants (high: $638,850; low: $2,000), and $1,454,333 for foundation-administered programs.
Purpose and activities: Baptist Community Ministries is committed to the development of a healthy community offering a wholesome quality of life to its residents and to improving the physical, mental, and spiritual health of the individuals it serves.
Fields of interest: Education; Health care; Crime/violence prevention; Public affairs, citizen participation.
Type of support: General/operating support; Continuing support; Program development; Seed money; Curriculum development; Research; Technical assistance; Program evaluation; Matching/challenge support.
Limitations: Applications accepted. Giving primarily in Jefferson, Orleans, Plaquemines, St. Bernard and St. Tammany parishes, LA. No support for operating budgets of individual churches. No grants to individuals, or for capital grants.
Publications: Application guidelines; Annual report (including application guidelines); Informational brochure.
Application information: Provide material on standard 8-1/2 by 11 inch paper with 2 filing holes punched at top and secured with binder clips. Do not use staples, binders or folders. Application form required.
Initial approach: Check foundation web site for updated application information before applying. Application form available on foundation web site
Copies of proposal: 3
Deadline(s): Spring: Feb. 15 - Feb. 28. Fall: Aug. 15 - Aug. 31
Board meeting date(s): May and Nov.
Final notification: May and Nov.
Officers and Trustees:* H. Merritt Lane III,* Chair.; **David Guidry,* Vice-Chair.**; **Charles E. Beasley, Interim C.E.O. and Pres.**; Laurie G. DeCuir, Sr. V.P. and C.F.O.; Frances L. Hawkins, R.N., V.P., Congregational Wellness; James E. Hightower, Jr., Ed. D., V.P., Chaplaincy; Luceia LeDoux, V.P., Public Safety and Gov. Oversight; Jennifer P. Roberts, V.P., Education; Elizabeth L. Scheer, V.P., Health; **Patricia M. Prechter, Ed.D., M.S.N*, Secy.-Treas.**; **Herschel L. Abbott, Jr.**; **Dianne C. Boazman**; Tina S. Clark; Richard Estrada; John J. Graham; Robert A. "Drew" Jardine, Jr.; Hans B. Jonassen; Frank Kelly; Kenneth E. Pickering; Jerry St. Pierre, M.D.; Rep. James Tucker.
Number of staff: 11 full-time professional; 3 full-time support; 1 part-time support.
EIN: 720423887
Other changes: Patricia M. Prechter, Ed.D., M.S.N has replaced David Guidry as Secy.-Treas. Charles E. Beasley is now Interim C.E.O. and Pres. Lauri Ashton is no longer V.P., Eval. Research and Strategy. David Guidry is now Vice-Chair. Thomas L. Callicutt is no longer a trustee.

1300
Baton Rouge State Fair Foundation
(formerly Baton Rouge Jaycee Foundation)
P.O. Box 15010
Baton Rouge, LA **70895-5010 (225) 755-3247**
***E-mail:* gbrsf@eatel.net**; Main URL: http://www.gbrsf.com/

Established in 2000 in LA.
Foundation type: Independent foundation.
Financial data (yr. ended 12/31/12): Assets, $1,776,025 (M); expenditures, $988,045; qualifying distributions, $184,563; giving activities include $171,063 for 18 grants (high: $50,000; low: $1,000), and $13,500 for 27 grants to individuals (high: $500; low: $500).
Fields of interest: Higher education; Children/youth, services; Community/economic development.
Type of support: Scholarships—to individuals.
Limitations: Applications accepted. Giving primarily in Baton Rouge, LA.
Application information: See foundations web site for grant outline and application. Application form required.
Initial approach: Proposal
Deadline(s): None
Officers: J.H. Martin, Pres.; Douglas M. Gonzales, Secy.; David M. Broussard, Treas.
Board Members: Cliff Barton; Greg Edwards; Stan Prutz; Warren Wilson.
EIN: 721036440
Other changes: The grantmaker no longer lists a separate application address.

1301
Carolyn W. and Charles T. Beaird Family Foundation
(formerly Charles T. Beaird Foundation)
330 Marshall St., Ste. 1112
Shreveport, LA 71101-3015 (318) 221-2823
Contact: Susan Beaird, Pres.
FAX: (318) 221-5993**;**
E-mail: brandy@beairdfoundation.org; Main URL: http://www.beairdfoundation.org/

Established in 1960 in LA.
Donors: Dr. Charles T. Beaird‡; Carolyn W. Beaird‡; John B. Beaird; Marjorie Beaird Seawell; Susan Beaird.
Foundation type: Independent foundation.
Financial data (yr. ended 12/31/12): Assets, $21,571,390 (M); expenditures, $1,263,231; qualifying distributions, $1,183,446; giving activities include $1,031,483 for 108 grants (high: $60,000; low: $20).
Purpose and activities: Giving to enable organizations or entities to add opportunity, freedom of action and choice, self-betterment and a climate for change to the lives of residents of the Shreveport, LA, area.
Fields of interest: Humanities; Arts; Employment; Housing/shelter; Human services; Children/youth, services; Women, centers/services; Children; Minorities; Women; Economically disadvantaged.
Type of support: General/operating support; Continuing support; Management development/

capacity building; Capital campaigns; Building/renovation; Equipment; Program development; Seed money; Technical assistance; Program evaluation; Mission-related investments/loans.
Limitations: Applications accepted. **Giving primarily in the Shreveport-Bosssier City, LA, area.** No support for national programs and organizations. No grants to individuals.
Publications: Application guidelines; Financial statement; Grants list.
Application information: Application guidelines available on foundation web site. Application form and proposal must be submitted via the foundation's web site. Application form required.
Initial approach: Not required, but the foundation strongly suggests e-mail, telephone or letter, especially from first-time applicants, prior to filing an application.
Copies of proposal: 1
Deadline(s): Mar. 1 and Sept. 1
Board meeting date(s): Spring, summer, and fall
Final notification: May 15 and Nov. 15
Officers and Directors:* Susan Beaird, Pres.; Leslie M. Darr,* V.P.; Susie Seawell,* Secy.; John B. Beaird, Treas.; **Brandy Stroud, Exec. Dir.**; Ben McCormick; Jennifer McCormick; David Seawell; Katie Seawell; Marjorie B. Seawell.
Number of staff: 1 full-time professional.
EIN: 726027212
Other changes: Brandy Stroud has replaced Jim Montgomery as Exec. Dir.

1302
Blue Cross and Blue Shield of Louisiana Foundation

(formerly Louisiana Child Caring Foundation, Inc.)
P.O. Box 98029
Baton Rouge, LA 70898-9022 **(225) 298-7979**
Contact: Christy Oliver Reeves, Exec. Dir.
FAX: (225) 298-3175;
E-mail: foundation@bcbsla.com; Tel. and e-mail for Christy Oliver Reeves: (225) 298-7051, Christy.Reeves@bcbsla.com; tel. and e-mail for The Angel Award: (888) 219-2583, e-mail: angel.award@bcbsla.com; Contact for Challenge for a Healthier Louisiana: Elizabeth Gollub, tel.: (225) 763-0945, e-mail: BCBSChallenge@pbrc.edu; Main URL: http://www.bcbsla.com/web/reddotcm/html/64_205.asp
Angel Award Database: http://ourhomelouisiana.org/signature-programs/angel-award/angel-award-database/
Angel Award Winners video: http://ourhomelouisiana.org/programs/the-angel-award/2011-angel-award-winners/
Challenge for a Healthier Louisiana Video: http://www.youtube.com/watch?feature=player_embedded&v=wwo3aLXJfac
Our Home, Louisiana on Facebook: http://www.facebook.com/ourhomela
Our Home, Louisiana on Twitter: https://twitter.com/#!/ourhomela
Our Home, Lousiana Coalition: A Resource Website for BCBSL and the BCBSL Foundation: http://ourhomelouisiana.org/
RSS Feed: http://ourhomelouisiana.org/feed/

Donor: Blue Cross Blue Shield of Louisiana.
Foundation type: Company-sponsored foundation.
Financial data (yr. ended 12/31/12): Assets, $29,278,325 (M); gifts received, $295,813; expenditures, $7,315,947; qualifying distributions, $7,146,207; giving activities include $6,850,894 for 100 grants (high: $877,500; low: $1,000).
Purpose and activities: The foundation supports programs designed to improve health and education in Louisiana.
Fields of interest: Elementary/secondary education; Education, early childhood education; Education; Medicine/medical care, public education; Hospitals (general); Health care, clinics/centers; Public health; Public health, obesity; Public health, physical fitness; Health care; Nutrition; Children/youth; Aging; Economically disadvantaged.
Type of support: General/operating support; Management development/capacity building; Program development; Faculty/staff development; Research; Employee volunteer services; Sponsorships; Program evaluation; Matching/challenge support.
Limitations: Applications accepted. Giving primarily in areas of company operations in LA. No support for political candidates or organizations, athletes or athletic teams, labor, fraternal, or veterans' organizations, parent-teacher organizations, or religious organizations. No grants to individuals, or for beauty pageants, students raising funds for travel, capital projects or campaigns, or memorials.
Publications: Application guidelines; Informational brochure.
Application information: The foundation generally practices an invitation only process for giving; however letter of inquiries are accepted from organizations aligned with the foundation's priorities. Grants range from $5,000 to $20,000. Organizations receiving support are asked to submit a final report. Application form required.
***Initial approach:* E-mail letter of inquiry; complete online nomination form for The Angel Award**
***Deadline(s):* None; Apr. 4 for The Angel Award**
Officers and Directors:* C. Richard Atkins, D.D.S.*, Chair.; Peggy B. Scott,* Pres.; **Kevin McCotter, Secy.-Treas.**; Christy Oliver Reeves, Exec. Dir.; Dan Borne; **David Carmouche**; **Jerome "Jerry" Greig**; Frances Turner Henry; Sybil H. Morial.
EIN: 721232379
Other changes: At the close of 2012, the grantmaker paid grants of $6,850,894, a 241.8% increase over the 2011 disbursements, $2,004,076.
Kevin McCotter is now Secy.-Treas. Todd Schexnayder is no longer a director.

1303
The William T. and Ethel Lewis Burton Foundation

641 W. Prien Lake Rd.
Lake Charles, LA 70601-8315
Contact: William T. Drost, Dir.

Incorporated in 1963 in LA.
Donors: William T. Burton; Wm. T. Burton Industries, Inc.; William B. Lawton Company, L.L.C.; William B. Lawton‡; Tower Land Co, LLC.
Foundation type: Independent foundation.
Financial data (yr. ended 05/31/13): Assets, $5,096,508 (M); gifts received, $1,000,000; expenditures, $1,082,817; qualifying distributions, $1,077,311; giving activities include $1,059,033 for 5 grants (high: $1,000,000; low: $164), and $10,000 for 8 grants to individuals (high: $1,250; low: $1,250).
Purpose and activities: Giving primarily for higher education and Protestant churches; giving also in the form of scholarships to Southwest Louisiana High School seniors and members of the McNeese State University, Louisiana football team.
Fields of interest: Higher education; Protestant agencies & churches.
Type of support: General/operating support; Scholarships—to individuals.
Limitations: Applications accepted. Giving primarily in LA. No grants for endowment funds or matching gifts; no loans.
Application information: Application form not required.
Initial approach: Proposal
Deadline(s): None
Directors: Ernest Gerald Conner; Charles Mitchell Drost; William T. Drost; Jack E. Lawton, Jr.; Gus W. Schram III; Roderick Smith.
EIN: 726027957
Other changes: For the fiscal year ended May 31, 2013, the grantmaker paid grants of $1,069,033, a 327.2% increase over the fiscal 2012 disbursements, $250,240.

1304
Chambers Charitable Foundation

P.O. Box 61540, Trust Tax Compliance
New Orleans, LA 70161-1540

Established in 2006 in TX.
Donor: Florence Chambers‡.
Foundation type: Independent foundation.
Financial data (yr. ended 01/31/14): Assets, $13,804,574 (M); expenditures, $640,855; qualifying distributions, $518,474; giving activities include $460,361 for 5 grants (high: $276,217; low: $46,036).
Purpose and activities: Giving primarily for historical property preservation.
Fields of interest: Museums (art); Historic preservation/historical societies; American Red Cross; Protestant agencies & churches.
Limitations: Applications not accepted. Giving primarily in New Orleans, LA. No grants to individuals.
Application information: Contributes only to pre-selected organizations.
Trustee: Capital One Bank, N.A.
EIN: 202123840
Other changes: The grantmaker has moved from TX to LA.

1305
Christen Elizabeth Clement Foundation, Inc.

5959 S. Sherwood Forest Blvd.
Baton Rouge, LA 70816-6038 (225) 299-3508
Contact: Michael Pitts
FAX: (225) 295-9624

Established in 2003 in LA.
Donor: Amdisys, Inc.
Foundation type: Independent foundation.
Financial data (yr. ended 12/31/13): Assets, $535,796 (M); gifts received, $718,284; expenditures, $869,619; qualifying distributions, $876,890; giving activities include $868,095 for grants.
Fields of interest: Human services.
Application information: Application form required.
Initial approach: Letter
Deadline(s): Monthly
Officers: Scott Ginn, Pres.; **Michael D. Lutgring, V.P.; Mark R. Phillips, Treas.**
EIN: 200122620
Other changes: Mark R. Phillips has replaced Michael D. Lutgring as Treas.
Michael D. Lutgring is now V.P.

1306
The Community Foundation of North Louisiana

(also known as The Community Foundation)(formerly Community Foundation of Shreveport-Bossier)
401 Edwards St., Ste. 105
Shreveport, LA 71101-5508 (318) 221-0582
Contact: Paula H. Hickman, Exec. Dir.; Finance: Paige Carlisle, Dir., Finance; Marketing, PR, Communications: Jennifer Steadman, Dir., External Rels.
FAX: (318) 221-7463; E-mail: hickman@cfnla.org; Grant application e-mail: laborde@cfnla.org; Main URL: http://www.cfnla.org
Blog: http://www.nlacf.org/?Blog_home
E-Newsletter: http://www.nlacf.org/news/newsletter
Facebook: https://www.facebook.com/TheCommunityFoundation
Twitter: https://twitter.com/commfoundnla
YouTube: http://www.youtube.com/cfnla

Incorporated in 1961 in Louisiana.
Foundation type: Community foundation.
Financial data (yr. ended 12/31/12): Assets, $86,561,057 (M); gifts received, $2,820,936; expenditures, $4,144,998; giving activities include $2,709,238 for 313 grants (high: $175,000; low: $55).
Purpose and activities: The foundation seeks to promote philanthropy and improve the quality of life in North Louisiana by serving as a permanent and growing resource of expertise and funds. The mission of The Community Foundation is to strengthen the community through philanthropy.
Fields of interest: Arts, single organization support; Arts, formal/general education; Performing arts; Performing arts, dance; Performing arts, theater; Performing arts, theater (musical); Performing arts, orchestras; Performing arts, opera; Arts; Education, research; Education, public education; Education, formal/general education; Elementary/secondary education; Child development, education; Middle schools/education; Elementary school/education; Secondary school/education; Elementary/secondary school reform; Higher education; Higher education, college (community/junior); Higher education, college; Higher education, university; Higher education reform; Adult education—literacy, basic skills & GED; Education, reading; Education, community/cooperative; Education; Environment, natural resources; Environment; Animals/wildlife; Public health; Public health, obesity; Public health, physical fitness; Health care; Mental health/crisis services; Employment, services; Employment, training; Goodwill Industries; Agriculture, community food systems; Nutrition; Housing/shelter; Disasters, Hurricane Katrina; Recreation, community; Youth development, centers/clubs; Boys & girls clubs; Youth development, adult & child programs; American Red Cross; Salvation Army; Volunteers of America; YM/YWCAs & YM/YWHAs; Youth, services; Family services; Aging, centers/services; Homeless, human services; Human services; Economic development; Urban/community development; Nonprofit management; Community/economic development; Foundations (community); Science; Public affairs, citizen participation; Children/youth; Children; Aging; Disabilities, people with; Women; Economically disadvantaged; Homeless.
Type of support: Continuing support; Management development/capacity building; Capital campaigns; Building/renovation; Equipment; Land acquisition; Endowments; Emergency funds; Program development; Conferences/seminars; Seed money; Curriculum development; Scholarship funds; Research; Technical assistance; Employee matching gifts; Matching/challenge support; Mission-related investments/loans.
Limitations: Applications accepted. Giving strictly limited to 501(c)3 organizations in Caddo and Bossier Parishes for the competitive grant process. No support for religious purposes. No grants to individuals, or for debt retirement, general operating expenses, or annual sustaining fund drives.
Publications: Application guidelines; Annual report; Annual report (including application guidelines); Grants list; Informational brochure; Newsletter.
Application information: Visit foundation web site for online application forms and guidelines. All organizations interested in submitting a proposal must send a representative to attend one of the scheduled Grant Overview Sessions prior to submission; reservations are required by calling or e-mailing the foundation. Application form required.
Initial approach: Attend a Grant Overview Session
Deadline(s): After Labor Day
Board meeting date(s): Feb., Apr., Aug. and Dec.
Final notification: Late Apr. for final grant notifications
Officers and Directors:* Edward Crawford III,* Chair.; Paula H. Hickman, J.D., Exec. Dir.; **Dr. Terry C. Davis,* Secy.**; Thomas Murphy,* Treas.; Janie D. Richardson,* Vice-Chair.; Rand Falbaum; Bobby Jelks; Margaret Thompson.
Trustee Banks: JPMorgan Chase Bank, N.A.; Regions Bank.
Number of staff: 3 full-time professional; 2 full-time support; 1 part-time support.
EIN: 726022365
Other changes: Mike Alost is no longer a director.

1307
Community Foundation of Southwest Louisiana

(formerly Southwest Louisiana Community Foundation)
1625 Ryan St., Ste. C
P.O. Box 3125
Lake Charles, LA 70602 (337) 491-6688
***Contact:* Sara Judson, Pres. and C.E.O.**
FAX: (337) 491-6710;
E-mail: sjudson@foundationswla.org; Main URL: http://www.foundationswla.org

Established in 2001 in LA.
Foundation type: Community foundation.
Financial data (yr. ended 12/31/12): Assets, $7,456,740 (M); gifts received, $1,135,526; expenditures, $1,982,067; giving activities include $1,530,495 for 26 grants (high: $611,635).
Purpose and activities: The foundation seeks to enhance the quality of life in Southwest Louisiana by becoming a strong and effective catalyst for building philanthropy for present and future generations.
Publications: IRS Form 990 or 990-PF printed copy available upon request.
Application information:
***Deadline(s):* Varies**
Officers and Directors:* Greg Webb,* Chair.; Tom Sherman,* Vice-Chair.; Sara Judson,* C.E.O. and Pres.; Dan Donald, M.D.*, Secy.; Jonald Walker,* Treas.; Susan Blake; Edwin F. Hunter III; Mary Shaddock Jones; Brent Lumpkin; Jon Manns; **Dr. Lehrue Stevens**; Mary Leach Werner.
EIN: 721508036
Other changes: Mark Boniol, Reed Mendelson, Rick Richard, Lehrue Stevens, and Ulysses Thibodeaux are no longer directors.

1308
Entergy Charitable Foundation

639 Loyola Ave.
New Orleans, LA 70113-3125 (504) 576-6980
Additional address: P.O. Box 61000, New Orleans, LA 70161, tel.: (504) 576-2674; Main URL: http://www.entergy.com/our_community/ECF_grant_guidelines.aspx

Established in 2000 in AR and LA.
Donor: Entergy Corp.
Foundation type: Company-sponsored foundation.
Financial data (yr. ended 12/31/12): Assets, $1,285,757 (M); gifts received, $2,904,679; expenditures, $3,116,063; qualifying distributions, $3,116,063; giving activities include $3,111,563 for 147+ grants (high: $460,000).
Purpose and activities: The foundation supports programs designed to create and sustain thriving communities. Special emphasis is directed toward programs designed to promote low-income initiatives and solutions; and education and literacy.
Fields of interest: Museums; Education, reading; Education; Environment, energy; Housing/shelter, development; Housing/shelter; Disasters, fire prevention/control; Family services; Human services, financial counseling; Community/economic development, management/technical assistance; United Ways and Federated Giving Programs; Children; Aging; Economically disadvantaged.
Type of support: Scholarship funds; Building/renovation; Program development.
Limitations: Applications accepted. Giving primarily in areas of company operations in AR, LA, MA, MS, NH, NY, TX, and VT, with emphasis on New Orleans. No support for political organizations, religious organizations not of direct benefit to the entire community, or organizations owned or operated by an employee of Entergy. No grants to individuals, or for utility bills, administrative expenses or recurring expenses exceeding 15 percent of the requested amount, capital campaigns, gala events, testimonials, or fundraising meals, advertisements, or uniforms, equipment, or trips for school-related organizations or amateur sports teams; no loans.
Publications: Application guidelines.
Application information: Visit website for contact information for contributions coordinators in each state. Application form required.
Initial approach: Complete online application form
***Deadline(s):* Feb. 1 and Aug. 1**
Board meeting date(s): 3 times per year
Final notification: 3 months
Officers and Directors:* Kim Despeaux, Pres.; Kay Kelley Arnold, V.P.; Leo P. Denault,* Treas.; Renea Conley; Haley R. Fisackerly; John Herron; William Mohl; Gary J. Taylor; Rod K. West.
EIN: 710845366

1309
The Ella West Freeman Foundation

6028 Magazine St.
New Orleans, LA 70118-5824 (504) 895-1984
Contact: Louis M. Freeman, Chair.; Catherine Freeman, Exec. Admin.
FAX: (504) 895-1988; E-mail: info@ellawest.org; Main URL: http://www.ellawest.org
Grants List: http://www.ellawest.org/grants.html

Established in 1941 in LA.
Donors: Richard W. Freeman†; Alfred B. Freeman†.
Foundation type: Independent foundation.
Financial data (yr. ended 12/31/12): Assets, $29,937,008 (M); gifts received, $42,000; expenditures, $1,726,167; qualifying distributions,

$1,449,060; giving activities include $1,432,060 for 36+ grants (high: $279,000).
Purpose and activities: Giving primarily for education with an emphasis on private education, arts, both performing and applied, community improvement and governmental oversight, and human service organizations with an emphasis on capital projects for established agencies.
Fields of interest: Arts; Higher education; Human services; Government/public administration.
Type of support: Annual campaigns; Capital campaigns; Building/renovation; Endowments; Program development; Seed money.
Limitations: Applications accepted. Giving primarily in the greater New Orleans, LA, area. No support for organizations supported by community giving campaigns such as the United Way and the Archbishop's Community Appeal. No grants to individuals.
Publications: Application guidelines; Grants list.
Application information: Application form and guidelines available on foundation web site. Application form required.

Initial approach: Proposal summary sheet, which may be sent either via e-mail, fax or surface mail
Copies of proposal: 2
Deadline(s): Jan. 20 or Sept. 1 for proposal summary sheet; Mar. 1 or Oct. 15 for full proposal
Board meeting date(s): Spring and fall
Final notification: Feb. 1 or Sept. 15, via e-mail for proposal summary; after board meetings for full proposal

Officer and Trustees:* Louis M. Freeman,* Chair.; Richard W. Freeman, Jr.; R. West Freeman III; Virginia Rowan; Philip Woollam; Tina Freeman Woollam.
EIN: 726018322
Other changes: The grantmaker now makes its grants list available online.

1310
German Protestant Orphan Asylum Association Foundation
(also known as GPOA Foundation)
1441 Canal St., Ste. 211
New Orleans, LA **70112-2714 (504) 895-2361**
Contact: Lisa M. Kaichen, Fdn. Mgr.
***E-mail:* lisa@gpoafoundation.org**; Main URL: http://www.gpoafoundation.org/

Parent organization founded in 1855; foundation established in 1979 in LA.
Foundation type: Independent foundation.
Financial data (yr. ended 11/30/13): Assets, $14,448,269 (M); gifts received, $90; expenditures, $666,493; qualifying distributions, $573,321; giving activities include $468,133 for 44 grants (high: $40,000; low: $2,500).
Purpose and activities: Grants only for the benefit and welfare of children and youth in Metro New Orleans, LA.
Fields of interest: Children/youth, services.
Type of support: General/operating support; Program development; Seed money; Matching/challenge support.
Limitations: Giving limited to LA, with emphasis on the New Orleans metropolitan area. No support for programs not focused on children, or for out-of-state organizations (unless request is to serve LA children). No grants to individuals, or for capital campaigns, building or renovation expenses, computers, special events, or traditional scholarships.
Publications: Application guidelines; Annual report; Grants list.
Application information: Full proposals are by invitation only, upon review of concept paper. Applications accepted by mail only. Hand delivery or deliveries which require a signature are not accepted. The foundation will also accept the Southern Grantmakers Common Application Form. Application form required.

Initial approach: Use 1-page concept paper application on foundation web site
Copies of proposal: 12
Deadline(s): Feb. 1, May 1, Aug. 1, and Nov. 1
Board meeting date(s): Jan., Apr., July, and Oct.
Final notification: May 15 (for Feb. 1 deadline), Aug. 15 (for May 1 deadline), Nov. 15 (for Aug. 1 deadline), and Feb. 15 (for Nov. 1 deadline)

Officers and Trustees:* Charles B. Mayer,* Pres.; Camille Jones Strachan,* V.P.; Walter C. Flower III,* Secy.; G. Price Crane,* Treas.; Lisa M. Kaichen, Mgr.; **Henry Bodenheimer**; Ralph C. Cox, Jr.; Paul Haygood III; Barbara C. MacPhee; Gordon R. Wadge.
Number of staff: 2 part-time professional.
EIN: 720423621
Other changes: The grantmaker no longer lists a fax.
Charles B. Mayer has replaced Gary J. Haller as Pres.
Camille Jones Strachan is now V.P.

1311
Jerome S. Glazer Foundation Inc.
2100 St. Charles Ave., Ste. 5
New Orleans, LA **70130-7603**
Contact: Kim Glazer Goldberg, Pres.

Established in 1961 in LA.
Donors: Jerome S. Glazer†; Bradford A. Glazer; Kim Glazer Goldberg.
Foundation type: Independent foundation.
Financial data (yr. ended 12/31/12): Assets, $3,205,889 (M); expenditures, $233,592; qualifying distributions, $114,760; giving activities include $79,534 for 46 grants (high: $10,000; low: $50).
Fields of interest: Arts; Education; Human services; Religion.
Limitations: Applications not accepted. Giving primarily in CA, LA, and NY. No grants to individuals.
Application information: Contribute only to pre-selected organizations.
Officers and Director:* Kim Glazer Goldberg,* Pres.; Brooke Goldberg, V.P.; Evan Goldberg, Secy.
Board Member: Debra Fallis.
Number of staff: 2 part-time professional; 1 part-time support.
EIN: 726020850

1312
The Merice "Boo" Johnson Grigsby Foundation
15635 Airline Hwy.
Baton Rouge, LA 70817-7318 (225) 753-5857
FAX: (225) 751-9777;
E-mail: grants@boogrigsbyfoundation.com;
Additional address: P.O. Box 104, Baton Rouge, LA 70821, tel.: (225) 938-7584; Main URL: http://www.boogrigsbyfoundation.com
Grants List: http://www.boogrigsbyfoundation.com/pastgiving.html

Established in 2006 in LA.
Donor: Cajun Constructors, Inc.
Foundation type: Company-sponsored foundation.
Financial data (yr. ended 12/31/12): Assets, $5,145,231 (M); gifts received, $2,132,650; expenditures, $2,547,370; qualifying distributions, $2,506,200; giving activities include $2,506,200 for 40 grants (high: $1,730,000; low: $1,000).
Purpose and activities: The foundation supports organizations involved with arts and humanities, education, conservation and science, medical and health services, human services, and community initiatives.
Fields of interest: Visual arts; Performing arts; Humanities; Arts; Higher education; Education; Environment, natural resources; Environmental education; Environment; Health care; Family services; Human services; Community/economic development; Science.
Type of support: General/operating support; Continuing support; Program development; Scholarship funds; Research.
Limitations: Applications accepted. Giving primarily in Baton Rouge, LA; giving also to national organizations.
Publications: Application guidelines.
Application information: Grants range from $1,000 to $5,000. Application form required.

Initial approach: Complete online application
***Deadline(s):* Mar. 15, June 15, Sept. 15, and Dec. 15**
Board meeting date(s): Quarterly

Directors: L. Lane Grigsby; Todd William Grigsby; Tami Grigsby Moran; Tricia Grigsby Sanchez.
EIN: 208091007

1313
Heymann Foundation
P.O. Box 51529
Lafayette, LA 70505-1529 (337) 232-4343
***Contact:* Board of Dirs.**

Established in 1974 in LA.
Donors: Maurice Heymann†; Jacqueline Cohn†; Herbert Heymann†; Southern Comm Buildings, LLC.
Foundation type: Independent foundation.
Financial data (yr. ended 05/31/13): Assets, $4,815,692 (M); expenditures, $259,663; qualifying distributions, $231,597; giving activities include $114,378 for 39 grants (high: $33,724; low: $100).
Purpose and activities: Giving for higher education, the arts, human services, and health care associations in the Lafayette, Louisiana, area.
Fields of interest: Arts; Higher education; Environment; Alzheimer's disease; Health organizations; Human services; Community/economic development.
Type of support: General/operating support.
Limitations: Applications accepted. Giving primarily in Lafayette, LA. No grants to individuals.
Application information: Application form not required.

Initial approach: Contact foundation
Copies of proposal: 1
Deadline(s): None

Officers: Joan Heymann Bergmann, Co-Pres.; Claire Lynn Heymann, Co-Pres.; Lila R. Heymann, Co-Pres.; Rick Dickerson, Treas.
EIN: 237397293

1314
The Emeril Lagasse Foundation
829 St. Charles Ave.
New Orleans, LA 70130-3715
Main URL: http://www.emeril.org/
E-Newsletter: http://www.emeril.org/news/

Facebook: https://www.facebook.com/EmerilLagasseFoundation
Foundation's Instagram Profile: http://instagram.com/emerilorg
Grants List: http://emeril.org/beneficiaries/
Twitter: http://twitter.com/emerilorg

Established in 2002 in LA.
Donors: Emeril J. Lagasse III; Charles Merinoff; Judy Girard; H. Coleman Davis III; Keep Memory Alive; Whirlpool; LRA; M. Hammer/Pontchartrain Capital, LLC; New Orleans Wine and Food Experience; Shows, Cali, Berthelot, Morris, LLP.
Foundation type: Independent foundation.
Financial data (yr. ended 03/31/13): Assets, $5,752,947 (M); gifts received, $2,062,516; expenditures, $1,958,217; qualifying distributions, $406,048; giving activities include $406,048 for 38 grants (high: $175,000; low: $22).
Purpose and activities: The foundation supports programs creating developmental opportunities for children within the following areas: public education, culinary arts, the arts and humanities, and life skills development. The foundation seeks to inspire, mentor and enable all young people, especially those from disadvantaged circumstances, to realize their full potential as productive and creative individuals. It supports and encourages programs creating developmental and educational opportunities for children within communities where Emeril's restaurants operate.
Fields of interest: Arts education; Child development, education; Children, services.
Type of support: General/operating support.
Limitations: Applications accepted. Giving limited to Orlando, FL, New Orleans, LA, and Las Vegas, NV. No grants to individuals.
Application information: Requests for grants sent via e-mail are not accepted.
Initial approach: Concept letter no longer than 3 pages
Officers and Directors:* Emeril J. Lagasse III,* Chair.; Tony Cruz, Pres.; Mark S. Stein, Secy.-Treas.; Kristin Shannon, Exec. Dir.; Mario Batali; Paul Frank; Robert Goldstein; Eric Linquest; Mark Romig; Gary N. Solomon; Michael C. Thompson.
EIN: 421536915

1315
Lincoln Health Foundation
1809 Northpointe Ln., Ste. 203
Ruston, LA **71270-3852** (381) 251-3226
Contact: Norman Hanes, Exec. Dir.
E-mail: nhanes@lincolnhealth.com; Main URL: http://www.lincolnhealth.com/

Established in LA.
Foundation type: Independent foundation.
Financial data (yr. ended 09/30/12): Assets, $26,735,102 (M); gifts received, $157,711; expenditures, $1,643,319; qualifying distributions, $1,415,457; giving activities include $1,340,150 for 12 grants (high: $413,482; low: $5,000).
Purpose and activities: Giving to improve health care and outcomes for residents of Lincoln Parish, LA.
Fields of interest: Health care, research; Health care, formal/general education; Health care.
Limitations: Giving primarily in Lincoln Parish, LA. **No support for disease-specific organizations seeking support for national projects and programs, for-profit organizations, hospitals, religious, fraternal, athletic or veterans groups when primary beneficiaries of such undertakings would be their own members, or for social or political actions programs that advocate a specific point of view. No grants to individuals, or for trips, tours, travel to professional meetings, social events or similar fundraising activities, telethons, or grants awarded for an indeterminate period of time.**
Publications: Application guidelines.
Application information: Refer to application guidelines on foundation web site for specific instructions and budget form.
***Initial approach:* Letter on letterhead**
Officers and Board Members:* Ben P. Haley, M.D.*, Chair.; Wilbert Ellis,* Vice-Chair.; **Norman Hanes, C.E.O.**; James Davison, Secy.-Treas.; John Belton; Benjamin L. Denny; Allen Herbert, M.D.; Fredric Hoogland; Shirley P. Reagan, Ph.D.; Jo Tatum.
EIN: 721335146
Other changes: Ben P. Haley, M.D. has replaced Shirley P. Reagan, Ph.D., as Chair.
Norman Hanes is now C.E.O.
The grantmaker now publishes application guidelines.

1316
The Greater New Orleans Foundation
1055 St. Charles Ave., Ste. 100
New Orleans, LA 70130-3981 (504) 598-4663
Contact: Dr. G. Albert Ruesga, C.E.O.
FAX: (504) 598-4676; E-mail: albert@gnof.org; Main URL: http://www.gnof.org
Blog: http://www.gnof.org/our-community/
Facebook: http://www.facebook.com/pages/Greater-New-Orleans-Foundation/200124173059?ref=ts
Philanthropy's Promise: http://www.ncrp.org/philanthropys-promise/who
RSS Feed: http://feeds2.feedburner.com/gnof
Twitter: http://twitter.com/GNOFoundation

Established in 1924 in LA as the Community Chest; became a community foundation in 1983.
Foundation type: Community foundation.
Financial data (yr. ended 12/31/12): Assets, $276,454,560 (M); gifts received, $822,578; expenditures, $23,277,015; giving activities include $19,006,768 for grants.
Purpose and activities: The ultimate goal of the Greater New Orleans Foundation is to create a resilient, sustainable, vibrant community in which individuals and families flourish and in which the special character of the New Orleans region and its people is preserved, celebrated, and given the means to develop. The foundation has a critical role to play in attaining this goal, as community leader and convener; as champion of civil society; and as supporter of effective nonprofit leaders and organizations. By serving as a philanthropic partner to members of the donor community, the foundation helps add meaning and value to the giving of individuals, families and institutions, increasing the effectiveness of their philanthropy and connecting them with the very best nonprofit work in Greater New Orleans and surrounding regions.
Fields of interest: Arts; Education; Environment; Health care; Crime/law enforcement; Housing/shelter; Safety/disasters; Youth development; Human services; Economic development; Community/economic development; Public affairs; Children/youth; Adults, women.
Type of support: General/operating support; Management development/capacity building; Endowments; Emergency funds; Program development; Seed money; Research; Technical assistance; Program evaluation; Matching/challenge support.
Limitations: Applications accepted. Giving limited to southeastern LA, including the greater New Orleans area. No support for religious activities. No grants to individuals, or for annual fund campaigns, capital expenditures, sponsorship of special events, trips, continuing support, endowment funds, equipment, building funds, or deficit financing.
Publications: Annual report; Informational brochure; Newsletter; Program policy statement.
Application information: Each competitive grantmaking fund is governed by different grantmaking priorities, criteria and guidelines. Visit foundation web site for application information per grant type.
Deadline(s): Varies
Board meeting date(s): Quarterly
Final notification: Varies
Officers and Trustees:* Ludovico Feoli, Ph.D.*, Chair.; Cheryl R. Teamer,* Vice-Chair.; Dr. G. Albert Ruesga, C.E.O. and Pres.; Ryan Crespino, V.P., Finance and Admin.; Martha McDermott Landrum, V.P., Mktg. and Comms.; Alice B. Parkerson, V.P., Devel.; Joann Ricci, V.P., Organizational Effectiveness; Leann O. Moses,* Secy.; Robert Bories,* Treas.; Cherie F. Thompson, Cont.; David Barksdale; Mark Blanchard; Robert S. Boh; Christian T. Brown; Robert W. Brown; James J. Buquet III; Daryl G. Byrd; Arnold W. Donald; David Edwards; Monica Edwards; Conrad N. Hilton, III; Pat LeBlanc; Dr. Silas H. Lee III; Walter J. Leger, Jr.; Nancy M. Marsiglia; Monika McKay; R. King Milling; Andree K. Moss; Elizabeth S. Nalty; Anthony Recasner, Ph.D.; Charles L. Rice, Jr.; Edwin "Rod" Rodriguez, Jr.; Ileana Suquet; Dr. Vera Triplett; Madeline D. West; George V. Young; Luis Zervigon.
Number of staff: 13 full-time professional; 1 part-time professional; 3 full-time support.
EIN: 720408921

1317
Irene W. & C. B. Pennington Foundation
2237 S. Acadian Thruway, Ste. 705
Baton Rouge, LA 70808-2380 (225) 928-8346
Contact: To Discuss Current or Proposed Projects: Vonnie L. Hawkins, Prog. Off.
FAX: (225) 928-8375;
E-mail: rec@penningtonfamilyfoundation.org; Main URL: http://www.penningtonfamilyfoundation.org

Established in 1982 in LA.
Donors: C.B. Pennington†; Irene W. Pennington†.
Foundation type: Independent foundation.
Financial data (yr. ended 12/31/12): Assets, $7,036,919 (M); expenditures, $9,318,797; qualifying distributions, $6,629,675; giving activities include $6,629,675 for 139 grants (high: $300,000; low: $400).
Purpose and activities: Giving primarily to provide philanthropic support to promote the overall well-being of families and communities.
Fields of interest: Secondary school/education; Medical specialties research; Youth development, centers/clubs; Human services; Youth, services.
Type of support: General/operating support; Capital campaigns; Building/renovation; Program development.
Limitations: Giving limited to communities within or near Baton Rouge, LA. No grants to individuals.
Publications: Application guidelines.
Application information: Paper proposals which have not been invited will not be accepted, considered or returned. Fax or e-mail proposals, or proposals in spiral or ring binders are not accepted. Unsolicited applications are reviewed once per year in a single step process. Proposal guidelines available on foundation web site. Application form required.
Initial approach: Online proposal submission

Copies of proposal: 1
Deadline(s): Aug. 15
***Final notification:* Dec.**
Officers and Trustees:* William E. Hodgkins,* Chair.; Lori Bertman, C.E.O. and Pres.; Richard Blackstone; Paula P. Delabretonne; Claude B. Pennington III; Daryl B. Pennington, Sr.; Daryl B. Pennington, Jr.; Sharon Palmer Pennington.
Number of staff: 2
EIN: 720938097

1318
Pugh Family Foundation
P.O. Box 51366
Lafayette, LA 70505-1366
***E-mail:* nanpugh@pughfamilyfoundation.org**; Main URL: http://www.pughfamilyfoundation.org/

Established in 2000 in LA.
Donors: Francis Tillou Nicholls Pugh III; Jo Ann Lewis Pugh; Francis Nicholls Pugh IV; Michael Lewis Pugh; Nancy Lewis Marie Pugh.
Foundation type: Independent foundation.
Financial data (yr. ended 12/31/12): Assets, $5,016,804 (M); expenditures, $285,539; qualifying distributions, $276,357; giving activities include $250,215 for 4 grants (high: $245,000; low: $50).
Fields of interest: Higher education; Education; Housing/shelter, development; Human services; Foundations (community); United Ways and Federated Giving Programs.
Limitations: Applications not accepted. Giving primarily in LA. No grants to individuals.
Application information: Unsolicited request for funds not accepted.
Officer: Nancy Pugh, Exec. Dir.
Directors: Francis T.N. Pugh III; Francis T.N. Pugh IV; JoAnn Pugh; Michael L. Pugh.
EIN: 721491038

1319
Edward G. Schlieder Educational Foundation
201 St. Charles Ave., Ste. 2508
New Orleans, LA 70170-1000 **(504) 533-5535**
Contact: Pierre F. Lapeyre, Consultant

Incorporated in 1945 in LA.
Donor: Edward G. Schlieder†.
Foundation type: Independent foundation.
Financial data (yr. ended 12/31/12): Assets, $63,794,587 (M); expenditures, $3,957,508; qualifying distributions, $3,021,386; giving activities include $2,925,333 for 19 grants (high: $375,000; low: $25,000).
Purpose and activities: Giving limited to educational institutions in Louisiana, particularly to institutions involved in biomedical research.
Fields of interest: Higher education; Education; Biomedicine research.
Type of support: Capital campaigns; Equipment; Research.
Limitations: Giving limited to LA. No grants to individuals, or for general purposes, endowment funds, scholarships, fellowships, or operating budgets; no loans.
Publications: Annual report.
Application information: Application form not required.
Initial approach: Letter
Copies of proposal: 3
Deadline(s): None
Board meeting date(s): As required
Final notification: 30 to 45 days
Officers and Directors:* Elizabeth S. Nalty,* Pres.; Thomas D. Westfeldt,* V.P.; John M. Waid,* Secy.; Jill K. Nalty, Treas.; Laura S. Shields.
Number of staff: 1 part-time professional; 1 part-time support.
EIN: 720408974

1320
B. A. and Elinor Steinhagen Benevolent Trust
c/o Trust Tax Compliance
P.O. Box 61540
New Orleans, LA 70161-1540 (409) 880-1415

Established in 1939 in TX.
Donors: B.A. Steinhagen†; Elinor Steinhagen†.
Foundation type: Independent foundation.
Financial data (yr. ended 12/31/12): Assets, $6,467,511 (M); expenditures, $345,951; qualifying distributions, $290,875; giving activities include $255,850 for 12 grants (high: $50,000; low: $1,000).
Purpose and activities: Giving for the housing and general assistance of the elderly and the helpless and afflicted of any age.
Fields of interest: Arts; Education; Health care; Housing/shelter, development; Human services; Aging, centers/services; Aging; Disabilities, people with; Economically disadvantaged.
Type of support: Building/renovation; Equipment; Program development; Publication; Seed money; Research; Matching/challenge support.
Limitations: Applications accepted. Giving limited to southeast TX. No grants to individuals, or for operating budgets, continuing support, annual campaigns, emergency funds, deficit financing, conferences, scholarships, or fellowships; no loans.
Publications: Application guidelines.
Application information: Application form required.
Initial approach: Letter
Copies of proposal: 1
Deadline(s): May 31
Board meeting date(s): June and July
Final notification: Aug.
Trustee: Capital One Bank, N.A.
EIN: 746039544
Other changes: The grantmaker has moved from TX to LA.

1321
The Whitman Family Foundation
423 Ridgeway Dr.
Metairie, LA 70001-3046

Established in 2006 in LA.
Donor: Wayne Whitman.
Foundation type: Independent foundation.
Financial data (yr. ended 12/31/12): Assets, $6,605,377 (M); expenditures, $286,654; qualifying distributions, $249,240; giving activities include $249,240 for 34 grants (high: $50,740; low: $100).
Fields of interest: Education; Youth development, volunteer services; Children, services; Urban/community development; Catholic agencies & churches.
Type of support: General/operating support.
Limitations: Applications not accepted. Giving primarily in LA. No grants to individuals.
Application information: Contributes only to pre-selected organizations.
Officer: Leigh Whitman, Pres.
EIN: 205666003
Other changes: Leigh Whitman has replaced Wayne Whitman as Pres.

1322
William B. Wiener, Jr. Foundation
333 Texas St., Ste. 2290
Shreveport, LA 71101-3681

Established in LA.
Donor: William B. Wiener, Jr.
Foundation type: Independent foundation.
Financial data (yr. ended 02/28/13): Assets, $30,762,807 (M); expenditures, $2,104,172; qualifying distributions, $1,445,399; giving activities include $1,439,000 for 71 grants (high: $405,000; low: $1,000).
Fields of interest: Environment, reform; Environment, government agencies; Animals/wildlife; Health organizations; Human services.
International interests: Israel.
Limitations: Applications not accepted. Giving primarily in LA; some giving also in Washington, DC and New York, NY. No grants to individuals.
Application information: Contributes only to pre-selected organizations.
Officers and Directors:* William B. Wiener, Jr., Pres.; Donald B. Wiener,* V.P. and Secy.; Jeffrey W. Weiss,* Treas.; Peter G. Case; David Rockefeller, Jr.
EIN: 726024398
Other changes: Theodore Smith is no longer a director.

MAINE

1323
Aicher Family Foundation, Inc.
1303 Naples Rd.
Harrison, ME **04040**
***Contact:* Peter Aicher, Pres.**
Application address: c/o Kathryn Slawson, 19 Sawmill Rd., Lebanon, NJ 08833-4620, tel.: (908) 832-8994

Established in 1997 in CT.
Donors: Paul J. Aicher‡; The Paul J. Aicher Trust.
Foundation type: Independent foundation.
Financial data (yr. ended 12/31/12): Assets, $7,724,390 (M); expenditures, $1,168,715; qualifying distributions, $1,125,000; giving activities include $1,125,000 for grants.
Fields of interest: Foundations (private operating).
Limitations: Giving primarily in East Hartford, CT; some giving also in New York, NY.
Application information:
Initial approach: Letter
Deadline(s): None
Officers: Peter Aicher, Pres.; Diana Johnson, V.P.; Kathryn Aicher Slawson, Secy.; Bradford Sparrow, Treas.
EIN: 061398331

1324
Harold Alfond Foundation
c/o Dexter Enterprises
2 Monument Sq.
Portland, ME 04101-4093 (207) 828-7999
Contact: Gregory Powell, Chair.
E-mail: info@haroldalfondfoundation.org; Main URL: http://www.haroldalfondfoundation.org/

Established in 1993 in ME as successor to Harold Alfond Trust.
Donors: Harold Alfond‡; Dorothy Alfond‡.
Foundation type: Independent foundation.
Financial data (yr. ended 12/31/12): Assets, $611,923,275 (M); expenditures, $31,747,490; qualifying distributions, $28,469,669; giving activities include $27,917,452 for 39 grants (high: $10,335,333; low: $150).
Purpose and activities: Support primarily for higher education, the arts, and health care.
Fields of interest: Arts; Higher education; Hospitals (general); Health care; Health organizations, association; Youth development; Human services; Children/youth, services.
Type of support: Annual campaigns; Capital campaigns; Building/renovation; Endowments; Scholarship funds; Research; Matching/challenge support.
Limitations: Applications accepted. Giving primarily in ME, with emphasis on central ME. No support for religious organizations for religious purposes, for political campaigns or causes, or for legislative lobbying efforts. No grants to individuals, start-up organizations, or for organizations or programs that provide benefits outside the U.S., and no support for private foundations.
Application information: Application form not required.
Initial approach: Online
Copies of proposal: 1
Deadline(s): None
Final notification: 3-6 months
Officer and Trustees:* Gregory Powell,* Chair.; Steven P. Akin; Peter Alfond; Theodore B. Alfond; William Alfond; Peter Lunder; Larry Pugh; Theresa M. Stone.
EIN: 223281672
Other changes: Robert Marden is no longer a trustee.

1325
The Borman Family Foundation
166 Old Waterville Rd., Ste. 3
Oakland, ME 04963-5358

Established in 2000 in ME.
Donor: Cornelius H. Borman.
Foundation type: Independent foundation.
Financial data (yr. ended 07/31/13): Assets, $6,735,256 (M); gifts received, $41,953; expenditures, $369,368; qualifying distributions, $328,823; giving activities include $301,549 for 38 grants (high: $34,000; low: $1,000).
Fields of interest: Performing arts, opera; Arts; Higher education; Environment, natural resources; Alzheimer's disease; Health organizations; Human services; Disabilities, people with.
Type of support: Annual campaigns; Capital campaigns; Equipment; Building/renovation; Scholarship funds; Program development; General/operating support.
Limitations: Applications not accepted. Giving primarily in IL, IN, ME and NJ. No grants to individuals.
Application information: Unsolicited requests for funds not accepted.
Officers: Cornelius H. Borman, Pres.; Robert Borman, V.P.; Donald Borman, Secy.-Treas.
Directors: Adam Borman; Kate Borman; Matthew Borman; **Robert Borman, Jr.**; Megan Frowery.
EIN: 010522171

1326
Catalyst for Peace
(formerly The Catalyst Fund)
50 Exchange St., 3rd Fl.
Portland, ME 04101-3308 **(207) 775-2616**
E-mail: info@catalystforpeace.org; Main URL: http://www.catalystforpeace.org/

Established in ME.
Donors: Elisabeth Hoffman; Alan Lukas; Tides Foundation.
Foundation type: Independent foundation.
Financial data (yr. ended 12/31/11): Assets, $12,709,093 (M); gifts received, $55,715; expenditures, $1,463,149; qualifying distributions, $1,202,702; giving activities include $1,047,791 for 2 grants (high: $1,047,291; low: $500).
Purpose and activities: The foundation identifies and supports community based peacebuilding work around the world.
Fields of interest: Higher education; International peace/security; International human rights; Religion, interfaith issues.
International interests: Africa.
Limitations: Applications not accepted. Giving primarily in ME and VA; some funding also in Sierra Leone.
Application information: Unsolicited requests for funds not accepted.
Officers: Elisabeth Hoffman, Pres.; Seth Johnson, Secy.-Treas.
Directors: Alfred Hoffman, Jr.; Cynthia Sampson.
EIN: 352202654

1327
Sam L. Cohen Foundation
50 Foden Rd., Ste. 5
Portland, ME 04106-1718 (207) 871-5600
Contact: Nancy Brain, Exec. Dir.; Stephanie Eglinton, Prog. Off.
FAX: (207) 871-9043;
E-mail: nbrain@samlcohenfoundation.org; Mailing address: P.O. Box 1123, Portland, ME 04104; Main URL: http://www.samlcohenfoundation.org

Re-established in 2005 in ME. Successor to Sam L. Cohen Foundation established in 1983.
Donors: Sam L. Cohen‡; Sam L. Cohen Foundation.
Foundation type: Independent foundation.
Financial data (yr. ended 12/31/12): Assets, $38,422,120 (M); expenditures, $2,343,300; qualifying distributions, $1,941,360; giving activities include $1,568,923 for 80 grants (high: $400,000; low: $1,000).
Purpose and activities: The foundation strives to ensure that people have the opportunity to develop their potential and to provide healthy, productive futures for themselves, their families and their communities. It supports nonprofit organizations that benefit individuals living in southern Maine, York and Cumberland counties.
Fields of interest: Arts; Education; Health care; Jewish agencies & synagogues.
Type of support: General/operating support; Management development/capacity building; Program development; Research; Matching/challenge support; Pro bono services - legal; Pro bono services - medical.
Limitations: Applications accepted. Giving primarily in York and Cumberland counties in southern ME. No grants to individuals, or for annual appeals, endowments or for multi-year grants.
Publications: Application guidelines; Grants list.
Application information: Maine Philanthropy Center Common Grant Application Form accepted. See foundation web site for application information and current guidelines.
Deadline(s): See foundation website for current deadlines
Board meeting date(s): May and Nov.
Officers and Directors:* Jerome Goldberg,* Pres.; Jeffrey Nathanson,* Secy.; Edward Simensky,* Treas.; **John Shoos, Exec. Dir.**; Sherry Broder; Elinor Miller; Kenneth Spirer.
Number of staff: 2 full-time professional; 1 part-time professional.
EIN: 202262822
Other changes: John Shoos has replaced Nancy Brain as Exec. Dir.

1328
Sadie and Harry Davis Foundation, Inc.
135 Sheridan St., No. 303
Portland, ME **04101-2678 (207) 253-1865**
Contact: Sharon L. Rosen, Exec. Dir.
E-mail: slrosen@sadieandharrydavis.org; Main URL: http://www.sadieandharrydavis.org

Established in 2007 in NY.
Donor: Sadie Davis‡.
Foundation type: Independent foundation.
Financial data (yr. ended 12/31/11): Assets, $12,144,723 (M); expenditures, $359,946; qualifying distributions, $304,799; giving activities include $270,899 for 9 grants (high: $229,899).
Purpose and activities: Giving primarily for the advancement of children's health in Maine.
Fields of interest: Health care; Health organizations.

Limitations: Applications accepted. Giving primarily in ME.
Application information: See foundation web site for complete application guidelines.
Officers and Directors:* Andrew Davis Klingenstein,* Pres.; Sally Martell,* Secy.-Treas.; John Klingenstein; Julie Klingenstein; Patricia Davis Klingenstein; Thomas Davis Klingenstein; C. Michael Martell; Nancy Perlman; Nancy Simpkins.
EIN: 203515375

1329
The Golden Rule Foundation, Inc.

P.O. Box 658
Camden, ME 04843-0658
E-mail: **laurel@goldrule.org**; Main URL: http://www.goldrule.org

Established in 1981 in DC.
Donor: Jack Evans†.
Foundation type: Independent foundation.
Financial data (yr. ended 10/31/13): Assets, $3,814,558 (M); expenditures, $334,452; qualifying distributions, $286,159; giving activities include $235,080 for 39 grants (high: $30,000; low: $500).
Purpose and activities: Giving primarily for the arts, environmental programs, and social services.
Fields of interest: Arts; Education; Environment, alliance/advocacy; Environment, toxics; Environment, natural resources; Human services; Children, services; Community/economic development.
International interests: Mexico.
Type of support: General/operating support; Program development; Seed money.
Limitations: Applications not accepted. **Giving on a national basis.** No grants to individuals.
Publications: Informational brochure.
Application information: Unsolicited requests for funds not considered.
Board meeting date(s): Late Aug.
Officers: Jean Evans, Pres.; Tegan Stephens, Secy.; Salvadore Messina, Treas.
Directors: Gareth Evans; Trevor Evans.
Advisory Board: Sian Evans.
Number of staff: 1 part-time support.
EIN: 599207701

1330
Hannaford Charitable Foundation

P.O. Box 1000
Portland, ME 04104-5005
Main URL: **http://www.hannaford.com/content.jsp?pageName=charitableFoundation&leftNavArea=AboutLeftNav**

Established in 1993 in ME.
Donor: Hannaford Bros. Co.
Foundation type: Company-sponsored foundation.
Financial data (yr. ended 12/31/12): Assets, $1,365,743 (M); gifts received, $1,182,000; expenditures, $782,446; qualifying distributions, $1,412,446; giving activities include $1,372,850 for 93 grants (high: $200,000; low: $1,000).
Purpose and activities: The foundation supports organizations involved with arts and culture, education, fisheries, health, human services, marine science, and civic affairs.
Fields of interest: Arts; Higher education; Education; Animals/wildlife, fisheries; Hospitals (general); Health care, clinics/centers; Health care; YM/YWCAs & YM/YWHAs; Children/youth, services; Human services; United Ways and Federated Giving Programs; Marine science; Public affairs.
Type of support: Program development; Capital campaigns; Building/renovation; Employee-related scholarships.
Limitations: Applications accepted. Giving primarily in areas of company operations in MA, ME, NH, NY, and VT. No support for tax-supported organizations or veterans', fraternal, or religious organizations not of direct benefit to the entire community. No grants to individuals (except for employee-related scholarships), or for advertising or general operating support.
Publications: Application guidelines.
Application information: Application form required.
Initial approach: Proposal
Copies of proposal: 10
Deadline(s): 6 to 8 weeks prior to need
Officers: Bob Schools, Pres.; Donna J. Boyce, Secy.; Jim Kacer, Treas.
Directors: Rudy DiPietro; Rick Meyerkopf; Heather Paquette; Mary Wright.
EIN: 010483892

1331
Horizon Foundation, Inc.

1 Monument Way, 2nd Fl.
Portland, ME 04101-4078 (207) 773-5101
E-mail: **info@horizonfoundation.org**; Main URL: http://www.horizonfoundation.org

Established in 1997 in MA and PA.
Donors: Alexander K. Buck, Sr.; Alexander K. Buck, Jr.; N. Harrison Buck; Alexander K. Buck, 1997 Trust No. 1, Jr.; Alexander K. Buck, 1997 Trust No. 2, Jr.
Foundation type: Independent foundation.
Financial data (yr. ended 06/30/13): Assets, $17,604,234 (M); gifts received, $160,000; expenditures, $857,924; qualifying distributions, $695,499; giving activities include $695,499 for grants.
Purpose and activities: The foundation supports organizations that effect positive change among children, the adults who work with them, and the communities in which they live. The foundation will support programs and organizations that aspire to create and maintain sustainable and livable communities by protecting and conserving land and water resources, educating children and adults about being good stewards of the environment, promoting vibrant, child-oriented arts, teaching respect for and preservation of historic assets, enabling children and adults to lead their communities in thoughtful, creative, and healthy ways, and encouraging service to others. Giving primarily for education in the arts, history, the environment, and leadership training for children; funding also for community services and mentoring.
Fields of interest: Arts education; Historic preservation/historical societies; Education; Environmental education; Leadership development; Children/youth; Adults.
Type of support: Equipment; Program development; Conferences/seminars; Seed money; Curriculum development; Internship funds; Program evaluation; Matching/challenge support.
Limitations: Applications accepted. Giving limited to Fairfield County, CT, Barnstable County, MA, Cumberland, Franklin, Lincoln, and York counties, ME, and Mercer County, NJ. No support for religion, state agencies, mental health agencies, colleges and universities, or public and private schools. No grants to individuals, or for international or foreign affairs, emergency requests, building, capital or endowment funds, or health/mental health.
Publications: Application guidelines; Annual report; Grants list; Informational brochure (including application guidelines).
Application information: Complete application guidelines available on foundation web site. Application form required.
Initial approach: 1-page letter of inquiry; no faxed or e-mailed letters of inquiry or proposals
Copies of proposal: 1
Deadline(s): See foundation web site for latest deadlines; proposals arriving after deadlines will be considered in next awards cycle.
Board meeting date(s): May, July, and Nov.
Officers: Sara L. Buck, Chair. and V.P.; Alexander K. Buck, Jr., Pres.; Nancy B. Buck, V.P.; Anne E. Buck, Secy.; N. Harrison Buck, Treas.
Number of staff: 1 part-time professional.
EIN: 232867116

1332
Kennebec Foundation

(formerly Kennebec Savings Bank Foundation)
P.O. Box 50
Augusta, ME 04332-0050
Contact: Andrew Silsby

Established in 1985 in ME.
Donor: Kennebec Savings Bank.
Foundation type: Independent foundation.
Financial data (yr. ended 12/31/12): Assets, $2,239,307 (M); gifts received, $285,355; expenditures, $319,987; qualifying distributions, $306,875; giving activities include $306,875 for grants.
Fields of interest: Arts; Boys & girls clubs; Human services; YM/YWCAs & YM/YWHAs; Youth, services; Community/economic development; United Ways and Federated Giving Programs.
Limitations: Applications not accepted. Giving primarily in the Kennebec County, ME, area. No grants to individuals.
Application information: Contributes only to pre-selected organizations.
Officers: Mark L. Johnston, Pres., Secy. and Clerk; Andrew Silsby, V.P.; Debra A. Getchell, Treas.
Directors: Mary A. Denison; Norman S. Elvin; Diane F. Hastings; Charles W. Hays, Jr.; Laura J. Hudson; **William E. Mitchell**; Richard D. O'Connor; Douglas E. Reinhardt; William W. Sprague, Jr.
EIN: 222624600
Other changes: Mark L. Johnston is now Pres., Secy. and Clerk., Peter T. Dawson is no longer Secy. and Clerk. Andrew Silsby is now V.P. .

1333
Stephen and Tabitha King Foundation, Inc.

P.O. Box 855
Bangor, ME 04402-0855 (207) 990-2910
Contact: Stephanie Leonard
FAX: (207) 990-2975; Main URL: http://www.stkfoundation.org

Established in 1986 in ME.
Donor: Stephen E. King.
Foundation type: Independent foundation.
Financial data (yr. ended 12/31/12): Assets, $150,586 (M); gifts received, $1,526,738; expenditures, $2,863,505; qualifying distributions, $2,858,380; giving activities include $2,838,844 for 150 grants (high: $150,000; low: $500).
Purpose and activities: Giving primarily for the arts, education (including libraries), and human services.

Fields of interest: Arts; Higher education; Libraries (public); Education; Health organizations, association; Human services; United Ways and Federated Giving Programs.
Type of support: General/operating support; Capital campaigns; Building/renovation; Equipment; Land acquisition; Endowments; Program development; Seed money; Research; Matching/challenge support.
Limitations: Applications accepted. Giving limited to ME. No support for hospice programs or facilities, animal shelters, hospitals or rehabilitation centers. No grants to individuals, or for fellowships, scholarships, or for travel or sponsorships, student or athletic groups, graduation parties or events, renovations to churches or other religious properties or institutions, or renovations to historical society property unless connected to a library, or for film or video productions, transportation, book or publishing projects, conferences, meetings, exhibits, or workshops, construction of playgrounds; no wheelchair vans; no organizations whose policies encourage discrimination; no academic research, fellowships or publication; no loans.
Publications: Application guidelines.
Application information: Application guideline and form available on foundation web site. Application form required.
Initial approach: Use online application process on foundation web site
Deadline(s): Dec. 31 and June 30. If the deadline falls on the weekend, the foundation will accept applications until the end of the following Monday.
Board meeting date(s): Spring and fall
Final notification: Within 8 weeks of application deadlines
Officers and Directors:* Stephen E. King,* Pres.; **Tabitha King,* Secy.; Arthur B. Greene, Treas.; Mark Levenfus.**
Number of staff: 1 full-time professional.
EIN: 133364647
Other changes: Tabitha King has replaced Arthur B. Greene as Secy.
Arthur B. Greene is now Treas.

1334
Libra Foundation
3 Canal Plz.
P.O. Box 17516
Portland, ME 04112-8516 (207) 879-6280
Contact: Elizabeth C. Flaherty, Exec. Asst.
FAX: (207) 879-6281; Main URL: http://www.librafoundation.org
Grants List: http://librafoundation.org/grant-lists

Established in 1989 in ME.
Donor: Elizabeth B. Noyce†.
Foundation type: Independent foundation.
Financial data (yr. ended 12/31/12): Assets, $93,721,509 (M); expenditures, $9,732,579; qualifying distributions, $10,540,451; giving activities include $7,755,769 for 45 grants (high: $4,390,000; low: $1,000), and $1,805,000 for 3 loans/program-related investments.
Purpose and activities: Areas of giving include arts, culture & humanities, education, environment, health, human services, justice, public/society benefit and religion.
Fields of interest: Arts; Education; Animals/wildlife; Health care; Athletics/sports, winter sports; Human services.
Type of support: Building/renovation; Capital campaigns; Continuing support; Curriculum development; Emergency funds; Endowments; Equipment; General/operating support; Land acquisition; Program development; Program-related investments/loans; Research; Seed money; Technical assistance.
Limitations: Applications accepted. Giving limited to ME. No grants to individuals.
Publications: Application guidelines; Annual report; Financial statement; Grants list; Informational brochure (including application guidelines).
Application information: Application form required.
Initial approach: Letter or telephone
Copies of proposal: 1
Deadline(s): Feb. 15, May 15, Aug. 15, and Nov. 15
Board meeting date(s): Mar., June, Sept., and Dec.
Final notification: Within 1 week of board meeting
Officers and Trustees:* Pendred E. Noyce, M.D.*, Chair.; **Owen W. Wells,* Vice-Chair.**; Craig N. Denekas,* C.E.O. and Pres.; **Jere G. Michelson, Exec. V.P. and C.F.O.; Erik K. Hayward, V.P.**; William J. Ryan.
Number of staff: 4 full-time professional; 3 full-time support.
EIN: 046626994
Other changes: Owen W. Wells is now Vice-Chair. Jere G. Michelson is now Exec. V.P. and C.F.O. Erik K. Hayward is now V.P.

1335
Hattie A. and Fred C. Lynam Trust
P.O. Box 1100
Ellsworth, ME 04605-1100 **(877) 475-5399**
Grant application address: c/o Julie Zimmerman, Trust Officer, Bar Harbor Trust Services, P.O. Box 1100, Ellsworth, ME 04605; email for Julie Zimmerman: jzimmerman@bhbt.com; Main URL: http://www.lynamtrust.com
Grants List: http://www.lynamtrust.com/grant_recipients.html
Scholarship application address: c/o Maine Community Foundation, 245 Main St., Ellsworth, ME 04605-1613, tel.: (207) 667-9735, toll free: (877) 700-6800, fax: (207) 667-0447

Established in 2007 in ME.
Donor: Fred C. Lynam†.
Foundation type: Independent foundation.
Financial data (yr. ended 12/31/12): Assets, $5,109,317 (M); expenditures, $321,853; qualifying distributions, $290,873; giving activities include $273,738 for 32 grants (high: $135,000; low: $1,000).
Purpose and activities: Giving primarily for charitable, religious, and educational organizations which are particularly beneficial to and advantageous for the people of Mount Desert Island, Maine; giving also for scholarships to graduates of Mount Desert Island High School.
Fields of interest: Education; Human services; Foundations (community); Religion.
Type of support: General/operating support; Capital campaigns; Equipment.
Limitations: Applications accepted. Giving primarily in Mount Desert Island, ME. No grants to individuals (only scholarships).
Application information: Application guidelines available on Trust web site.
Trustee: Bar Harbor Trust Svcs.
EIN: 010222218

1336
Maine Health Access Foundation
150 Capitol St., Ste. 4
Augusta, ME 04330-6858 (207) 620-8266
Contact: Wendy J. Wolf M.D., M.P.H., C.E.O. and Pres.; Barbara A. Leonard M.P.H., V.P., Progs.; Catherine L. Luce MBA, Grants Mgr.
FAX: (207) 620-8269; E-mail: Cluce@mehaf.org; Toll-free tel.: (866) 848-9210; Main URL: http://www.mehaf.org
CEP Study: http://www.mehaf.org/cep-survey-results/
Knowledge Center: http://mehaf.org/resources/
RSS Feed: http://mehaf.org/feeds/news/

Established in 2000 in ME.
Foundation type: Independent foundation.
Financial data (yr. ended 12/31/12): Assets, $113,216,690 (M); gifts received, $41,700; expenditures, $6,420,935; qualifying distributions, $5,527,310; giving activities include $3,846,053 for 94 grants (high: $160,000; low: $500), and $1,687,257 for foundation-administered programs.
Purpose and activities: The foundation's mission is to promote access to quality health care, especially for those who are uninsured and underserved, and to improve the health of everyone in Maine. The foundation uses its human and financial resources to ensure that all people have access to high quality, affordable health care to achieve or preserve better health. The foundation directs its program, grantmaking, and staff resources to advance four strategic priorities in pursuit of its mission. The foundation's priorities are: advancing health system reform, promoting patient-centered care, improving access to quality care, and achieving better health in communities.
Fields of interest: Health care, public policy; Health care.
Type of support: Program-related investments/loans; Management development/capacity building; Equipment; Program development; Conferences/seminars; Research; Technical assistance; Program evaluation.
Limitations: Applications accepted. Giving primarily in ME. No grants to individuals, or for endowments, debt retirement, annual appeals or membership campaigns, fundraising or social events, or public relations campaigns.
Publications: Application guidelines; Annual report; Grants list; Newsletter; Occasional report.
Application information: Online application form required. See foundation web site for application guidelines and procedures, as well as new funding priorities. Application form required.
Initial approach: Phone discussion with program staff
Deadline(s): Varies
Board meeting date(s): 2nd Thurs. Bimonthly
Final notification: Variable depending on type of grant
Officers and Trustees:* Sara Gagne-Holmes, Esq., Chair.; Constance Sandstrom, M.P.A., Vice-Chair.; Nancy Fritz,* Secy.; Anthony Marple,* Treas.; Constance Adler, M.D., FAAFP; **John Benoit; Deborah Deatrick, MPH**; Roy Hitchings, Jr., FACHE; Frank Johnson; Bruce G. Nickerson, CPA; **Catherine Ryder**; Lisa Sockabasin, BSN; Ted Sussman; Jeff Wahlstrom*; Shirley Weaver, Ph.D.
Number of staff: 7 full-time professional; 3 full-time support.
EIN: 010535144
Other changes: Karen O'Rourke, Cheryl Lee Rust, and Lee Webb are no longer trustees.

1337
Narragansett Number One Foundation

P.O. Box 779
Bar Mills, ME 04004-0779
Contact: Patricia M. Wales, Pres.
Main URL: http://www.nnof.org/

Established in 2001 in ME.
Donors: Patricia M. Wales; R. Erwin Wales†.
Foundation type: Independent foundation.
Financial data (yr. ended 06/30/13): Assets, $5,965,296 (M); expenditures, $347,098; qualifying distributions, $306,099; giving activities include $306,099 for 46 grants (high: $20,000; low: $600).
Fields of interest: Museums; Historic preservation/historical societies; Education; Animal welfare; Veterinary medicine; Recreation; Human services; Community/economic development; Foundations (public); Religion.
Type of support: General/operating support.
Limitations: Applications accepted. Giving primarily in Buxton, ME, and surrounding areas. No grants to individuals or to political campaigns.
Publications: Application guidelines.
Application information: See web site for application policies, guidelines and forms. Application forms may also be obtained by stopping by the Buxton, Hollis, Limington or Standish Town Halls during normal business hours. Application form required.
Initial approach: Letter
Copies of proposal: 2
Deadline(s): Nov. 1 - Mar. 1
Final notification: June 30
Officers and Directors:* Patricia M. Wales,* Pres.; Angela H. DesRuisseaux,* Secy.-Treas.; David DesRuisseaux; **Libby DesRuisseaux**; Reid DesRuisseaux; Pamela H. Haines; Thomas Charles Holding; Eric P. Wales; Wendy York Wales.
EIN: 010546133

1338
Quimby Family Foundation

P.O. Box 148
Portland, ME 04112-0148
E-mail: info@quimbyfamilyfoundation.org; Main URL: http://www.quimbyfamilyfoundation.org

Established in 2004 in ME.
Donor: Roxanne Quimby.
Foundation type: Independent foundation.
Financial data (yr. ended 12/31/12): Assets, $22,011,252 (M); gifts received, $4,977,292; expenditures, $1,735,268; qualifying distributions, $1,561,915; giving activities include $1,330,382 for 69 grants (high: $50,000; low: $500).
Purpose and activities: The mission of the foundation is to advance wilderness values and to increase access to the arts throughout Maine. The foundation accomplishes this mission by supporting and encouraging non-profit organizations that: 1) Address critical environmental issues such as the protection of wildlife, preservation of wildlands and promotion of non-consumptive, non-motorized recreation; and 2) Foster an active, vibrant, and successful art community, including non- profit galleries, exhibit space, art schools, and community outreach programs.
Fields of interest: Arts, multipurpose centers/programs; Arts; Education; Environment, natural resources; Environmental education; Animals/wildlife, preservation/protection; Animals/wildlife.
Type of support: General/operating support.
Limitations: Applications accepted. Giving primarily in ME. **No grants to individuals; no multi-year grants.**
Publications: Application guidelines; Grants list.
Application information: Full applications will be accepted by invitation only. Application information for invited applicants available on foundation web site. The foundation prefers e-mail correspondence.
Initial approach: One-page concept letter submitted through foundation web site
***Deadline(s):* Feb. 1 - Feb. 28 (for concept letter)**
Final notification: Aug. 1
Directors: Hannah Quimby; **Rachelle Quimby**; Roxanne Quimby; **Rebecca Rowe**; Rebecca Rundquist; Lucas St. Clair.; **Yemana St. Clair**; Liliane Willens.
EIN: 200041017
Other changes: Walter A. Anderson, Liane Judd, Jed Rathband and Andres Verzosa are no longer directors.

1339
Elmina B. Sewall Foundation

15 Maine St., Ste. 230
Freeport, ME 04032-1100 (207) 865-3810
Contact: Jay Espy, Exec. Dir.
FAX: (207) 865-3811;
E-mail: info@sewallfoundation.org; Main URL: http://www.Sewallfoundation.org

Established in 1982 in ME.
Donor: Elmina B. Sewall†.
Foundation type: Independent foundation.
Financial data (yr. ended 09/30/13): Assets, $183,240,921 (M); expenditures, $10,647,921; qualifying distributions, $9,496,940; giving activities include $8,951,352 for 164 grants (high: $1,085,515; low: $246).
Purpose and activities: The mission of the foundation is to support conservation of the natural environment and the well-being of animals and human beings, primarily in Maine. Through its giving, the foundation seeks to make a significant impact, inspire the generosity of others and empower those who share its vision.
Fields of interest: Environment, plant conservation; Environment; Animal welfare; Animals/wildlife, preservation/protection; Human services; Children/youth, services.
Type of support: General/operating support; Management development/capacity building; Capital campaigns; Program development; Matching/challenge support.
Limitations: Giving primarily in ME, with the exception of a moderate amount of routine annual giving which may take place in other regions. No grants to individuals, or for operating endowments. In general, multi-year projects will not be supported.
Publications: IRS Form 990 or 990-PF printed copy available upon request.
Application information: The foundation now follows a one-step grant application process. To start a new application, visit foundation web site, select the "New Application" tab. Returning applicants will be prompted to enter the appropriate e-mail address and password for their organization. New applicants will be prompted to establish an account and password. Refer to the foundation web site for more detailed information and instructions.
Initial approach: Submit online application
***Deadline(s):* Jan. 15 for environment and human well-being; June 15 for animal welfare and legacy**
Board meeting date(s): Apr., Jul. and Sept.
***Final notification:* Early June for environment and human well-being; early Oct. for animal welfare and legacy**
Officers and Directors:* Margaret Sewall Barbour,* Pres.; Kent W. Wommack,* V.P.; **David E. Norris,* Treas.**; Jay Espy, Exec. Dir.; **Betsy Biemann**; William E. Curran; Robert E. McAfee, M.D.; H. Roy Partridge, Jr., Ph.D.; Lisa J. Sockabasin; Carol Wishcamper.
Number of staff: 3 full-time professional.
EIN: 010387404
Other changes: David E. Norris has replaced William E. Curran as Treas.
Elaine D. Rosen is no longer a director. John S. Kaminski, Jr. is no longer Secy.

1340
The Margaret Chase Smith Foundation

10 Free St.
P.O. Box 4510
Portland, ME 04112-4510
Contact: Merton G. Henry, Pres.
E-mail: mhenry@jbgh.com

Established in 1983 in ME.
Donors: Margaret Chase Smith†; Alden B. Dow Charitable Trust; Dexter Shoe Co.; Evelyn Shaw Trust; Muriel & Robert List Trusts.
Foundation type: Independent foundation.
Financial data (yr. ended 12/31/12): Assets, $10,402,117 (M); gifts received, $58,316; expenditures, $665,536; qualifying distributions, $555,881; giving activities include $68,244 for 7 grants (high: $30,500; low: $1,000), $25,000 for 1 grant to an individual, and $462,637 for 1 foundation-administered program.
Purpose and activities: Giving primarily to support the Margaret Chase Smith Library in Skowhegan, ME, and the Margaret Chase Smith Center for Public Policy at the University of Maine in Orono, ME.
Fields of interest: Libraries (public); Education; Social sciences, public policy.
Type of support: General/operating support; Conferences/seminars; Publication; Fellowships.
Limitations: Applications not accepted. Giving primarily in ME. No grants to individuals.
Application information: Contributes only to pre-selected organizations.
Board meeting date(s): June and Dec.
Officers: Charles L. Cragin, Esq., Pres.; Michael J. Quinlan, Secy.-Treas.; **Merton G. Henry, Esq., V.P.**
Directors: Davida D. Barter; John Bernier; Paul H. Mills; **Paula D. Silsby**.
EIN: 010388680

1341
Virginia Hodgkins Somers Foundation, Inc.

P.O. Box 367
Kennebunk, ME **04043-0367**
E-mail: admin@vhsfoundation.org; **Application address: c/o Gordon C. Ayer, Pres., 16 Locke St., Kennenbunkport, ME 04046, tel.: (207) 289-4109; Main URL: http://www.vhsfoundation.org**

Established in 1991 in ME.
Foundation type: Independent foundation.
Financial data (yr. ended 09/30/12): Assets, $6,080,412 (M); expenditures, $373,297; qualifying distributions, $290,840; giving activities include $278,882 for 27 grants (high: $50,000; low: $1,000).
Purpose and activities: Giving primarily for children and education.

Fields of interest: Education; Human services; Children/youth, services; Family services.
Type of support: Conferences/seminars; Capital campaigns; General/operating support; Continuing support; Annual campaigns; Equipment; Land acquisition; Program development; Seed money; Curriculum development; Research; Matching/challenge support.
Limitations: Applications accepted. Giving primarily in New England, with a focus on southern ME and York County. No support for political, religious or governmental organizations.
Publications: Informational brochure (including application guidelines).
Application information: See foundation web site for application guidelines. Application form required.
Initial approach: Letter or e-mail
Copies of proposal: 1
***Deadline(s):* Varies**
Board meeting date(s): Jan. 15 and June 15
***Final notification:* Varies**
Officers: Gordon C. Ayer, Pres.; Susan Ayer, V.P.; Carolyn B. May, Treas.
Number of staff: 1 full-time professional; 2 part-time professional.
EIN: 010537127

1342
Robert and Patricia Switzer Foundation
(formerly Switzer Foundation)
P.O. Box 293
Belfast, ME 04915-0293 (207) 338-5654
***Contact:* Erin Lloyd, Prog. Off.**
***E-mail:* info@switzernetwork.org; Application e-mail: erin@switzernetwork.org**; Main URL: http://www.switzernetwork.org/
Blog: http://www.switzernetwork.org/blogs/opentopics/
Facebook: http://www.facebook.com/SwitzerFoundation
Twitter: http://twitter.com/switzernetwork

Established in 1985 in OH.
Donors: Robert Switzer‡; Patricia Switzer.
Foundation type: Independent foundation.
Financial data (yr. ended 06/30/13): Assets, $18,088,083 (M); expenditures, $969,600; qualifying distributions, $895,225; giving activities include $502,097 for grants.
Purpose and activities: Graduate fellowships awarded for one year to individuals most apt to be leaders in environmental fields. Only awarded to students in CA, and in New England. Grants also to environmental non-profits to hire Switzer Fellow(s) in leadership positions.
Fields of interest: Environment.
Type of support: Mission-related investments/loans; Fellowships.
Limitations: Applications accepted. Giving limited to CA, CT, MA, ME, NH, RI, and VT for fellowship program, leadership grants available on a national basis.
Publications: Application guidelines; Annual report.
Application information: See foundation web site for specific application instructions and requirements. Application form required.
Deadline(s): See foundation web site for deadlines
Board meeting date(s): Varies
Final notification: Varies
Officer and Trustees:* Lissa Widoff,* Exec. Dir.; **Adrienne Alvord**; **Bruce Kahn**; Margaret Rubega; Jennifer Sokolove; **Elise Switzer**; Jessica Switzer; Patricia D. Switzer; Carol Tucker.
Number of staff: 3 full-time professional.
EIN: 341504501
Other changes: Steve Parry, Deborah Spalding, and Mark Switzer are no longer trustees.
The grantmaker now publishes application guidelines.

1343
Otto and Fran Walter Foundation, Inc.
(formerly Walter & Lorenz Foundation, Inc.)
c/o The Brick House
7 Oak St.
Boothbay Harbor, ME 04538-1972 (207) 633-7300
Contact: Martha H. Peak, V.P. and Grants Dir.
E-mail: grants@walterfoundation.org; Main URL: http://www.walterfoundation.org/

Established in 1952 in NY.
Donors: Anton Lorenz‡; Otto L. Walter‡; Fran D. Walter‡.
Foundation type: Independent foundation.
Financial data (yr. ended 12/31/12): Assets, $13,226,443 (M); expenditures, $921,303; qualifying distributions, $765,863; giving activities include $546,710 for 9 grants (high: $312,500; low: $324).
Purpose and activities: Primary areas of interest include education, the arts, the disadvantaged, Holocaust survivorship and international amity.
Fields of interest: Arts; Education; Human services; International affairs, goodwill promotion; Aging; Economically disadvantaged.
Type of support: Seed money; Matching/challenge support.
Limitations: Applications accepted. Giving on a national and international basis. No support for purely religious or ethnic programs, or for programs with political agendas or programs that discriminate; no support for projects with only local impact. No grants or scholarships to individuals, or for annual or capital campaigns.
Application information: Application form not required.
***Initial approach:* E-mail**
Copies of proposal: 1
Deadline(s): None
Board meeting date(s): As necessary
Officers and Directors:* Frank G. Helman,* Pres.; Martha H. Peak,* V.P.; Carl R. Griffin III,* Secy.; Fritz Weinschenk,* Treas.
Number of staff: 3 part-time professional; 1 part-time support.
EIN: 131625529

MARYLAND

1344

ABMRF/The Foundation for Alcohol Research

(formerly Alcoholic Beverage Medical Research Foundation)
1200-C Agora Dr., No. 310
Bel Air, MD **21014-6849** (410) 821-7066
Contact: Mack C. Mitchell, Jr. M.D., Pres.
FAX: (410) 821-7065; E-mail: info@abmrf.org; Grant Program e-mail: grantinfo@abmrf.org; Main URL: http://www.abmrf.org/
Facebook: http://www.facebook.com/AlcoholResearch?ref=ts
Grants List: http://www.abmrf.org/grants_awarded
LinkedIn: http://www.linkedin.com/company/1137768?trk=NUS_CMPE-updater
Twitter: http://twitter.com/AlcoholResearch

Established in 1982 in MD.
Donors: Beer Institute; Brewers Association of Canada; National Beer Wholesalers Association.
Foundation type: Independent foundation.
Financial data (yr. ended 12/31/12): Assets, $3,703,616 (M); gifts received, $2,576,056; expenditures, $2,198,822; qualifying distributions, $2,174,925; giving activities include $1,608,835 for grants, and $2,198,822 for foundation-administered programs.
Purpose and activities: The mission of the foundation is to achieve a better understanding of the effects of alcohol on the health and behavior of individuals; to provide the scientific basis for prevention and treatment of alcohol misuse and alcoholism; to fund innovative, high-quality research; to support promising new investigations; to communicate effectively with the research community and with other interested parties.
Fields of interest: Alcoholism; Medical research.
International interests: Canada.
Type of support: Research.
Limitations: Applications accepted. Giving primarily in the U.S. and Canada. No grants to individuals, or for education projects, public awareness efforts, treatment or referral services, training of pre- and post-doctoral fellows, undergraduates, graduate students, medical students, interns or residents, or for thesis or dissertation research.
Publications: Annual report; Financial statement; Grants list; Informational brochure.
Application information: See foundation web site for application form and guidelines. Application form required.
Initial approach: Use grant application available on foundation web site
Copies of proposal: 1
Deadline(s): See foundation web site for current deadline
Board meeting date(s): Apr. and Nov.
Final notification: Within 2 weeks of board meeting
Officers and Trustees:* Bruce Ambler, M.B.A.*, Chair.; Raymond Anton, Jr., M.D.*, Vice-Chair.; Mack C. Mitchell, Jr., M.D.*, Pres.; Janet L. Hanratty, Cont.; David A. Brenner, M.D.; Thomas A. Collier, M.D.; Ivan Diamond, M.D., Ph.D.; R. Stuart Dickson; Luke Harford; Stephen Hindy; Arthur L. Klatsky; Louis G. Lange, M.D., Ph.D.; Steven W. Leslie, Ph.D.; James G. Martin, Ph.D.; Joseph S. McClain; Craig Purser; Timothy Scully, Jr.; John Sleeman; James Villenueve.
Number of staff: 1 full-time professional; 2 part-time professional; 1 part-time support.
EIN: 521234277

1345

The William L. and Victorine Q. Adams Foundation, Inc.

1040 Park Ave., Ste. 300
Baltimore, MD 21201-5635 **(410) 783-3203**
Contact: Blanche Rodgers, Prog. Off.

Established in 1984.
Donor: William L. Adams.
Foundation type: Operating foundation.
Financial data (yr. ended 09/30/13): Assets, $3,140,514 (M); gifts received, $284,415; expenditures, $426,373; qualifying distributions, $405,067; giving activities include $280,710 for 50 grants (high: $25,000; low: $300), and $42,777 for 8 grants to individuals (high: $12,519; low: $814).
Purpose and activities: Awards scholarships only to African-American residents of Baltimore City, Maryland, for undergraduate study in a business-related field. Giving also for schools, human services, and community support.
Fields of interest: Business school/education; Education; Human services; Community/economic development.
Type of support: General/operating support; Scholarships—to individuals.
Limitations: Applications accepted. Giving primarily in Baltimore, MD.
Application information: The foundation is no longer accepting applications for the Adams Future Business Leadership Scholarship Program, but is honoring previous awards. Application form not required.
Initial approach: Letter
***Deadline(s):* None**
***Board meeting date(s):* June**
Final notification: July
Officers and Trustees:* Theo C. Rodgers,* Pres. and Treas.; Marjorie J. Rodgers Cheshire,* V.P. and Secy.; Blanche D. Rodgers.
EIN: 521369556
Other changes: The grantmaker no longer lists a URL address.
Theo C. Rodgers is now Pres. and Treas.

1346

The Kathryn Ames Foundation, Inc.

c/o Pierson & Pierson
305 W. Chesapeake Ave., Ste. 308
Towson, MD 21204-4440 (410) 821-3006
Contact: Ms. Lu Pierson, Grant Admin.
FAX: (410) 821-3007;
E-mail: info@kathrynames.org; Main URL: http://www.kathrynames.org/

Established in 1993 in MD.
Donor: Kathryn Ames‡.
Foundation type: Independent foundation.
Financial data (yr. ended 12/31/12): Assets, $7,588,046 (M); expenditures, $625,784; qualifying distributions, $591,560; giving activities include $527,000 for 39 grants (high: $175,000; low: $1,000).
Purpose and activities: Giving primarily to organizations benefiting Israel in social and economic welfare, religious and ethnic pluralism, social justice, and education.
Fields of interest: Education; Economic development; Social sciences; Religion, interfaith issues; Religion.
International interests: Israel.
Type of support: General/operating support; Building/renovation; Equipment; Program development.
Limitations: Applications accepted. Giving primarily in Washington, DC, and New York, NY. **No grants to individuals, or for special events, benefit dinners, advertising, or publications.**
Publications: Application guidelines.
Application information: See grantmaker web site for complete application guidelines and form. Application form should only be submitted upon an invitation from the foundation (following receipt and consideration of Letter of Inquiry). Application form required.
***Initial approach:* Letter of Inquiry (not more than 2 pages, and sent via e-mail or U.S. mail)**
***Deadline(s):* None, for Letters of Inquiry**
Board meeting date(s): Quarterly
Officers: W. Michel Pierson, Pres.; Esther E. Saltzman, V.P.; Robert L. Pierson, Secy.-Treas.
EIN: 521828472
Other changes: The grantmaker now publishes application guidelines online.

1347

The William G. Baker, Jr. Memorial Fund

2 E. Read St., 9th Fl.
Baltimore, MD 21202-6903 (410) 332-4171
Contact: Melissa Warlow, Exec. Dir.; Aaron Meyers, Philanthropic Svcs. Coord.
FAX: (410) 837-4701; E-mail: mwarlow@bcf.org; Tel. for Melissa Warlow: (410) 332-4172, ext. 150; e-mail for Aaron Meyers: ameyers@bcf.org; Main URL: http://www.bcf.org/BaltimoreCFGrants/GrantProgramDetails/tabid/166/Default.aspx?grid=1

Established in 1964 in MD.
Foundation type: Independent foundation.
Financial data (yr. ended 12/31/12): Assets, $22,113,921 (M); expenditures, $1,175,247; qualifying distributions, $1,086,243; giving activities include $919,000 for 38 grants (high: $215,800; low: $3,000).
Purpose and activities: Giving to support cultural and artistic organizations and programs that enhance Baltimore, MD's, civic participation and economic health. The fund's objectives are to celebrate metropolitan life, spur economic development, improve the quality of life, provide access to cultural opportunities for all, support civic engagement through the arts, and create opportunities for self-expression and reflection.
Fields of interest: Arts, alliance/advocacy; Museums (art); Performing arts; Performing arts centers; Historic preservation/historical societies; Arts.
Type of support: Income development; Management development/capacity building; Equipment; Program development; Seed money; Technical assistance; Consulting services.
Limitations: Applications accepted. Giving limited to 501(c)(3) organizations in the metropolitan Baltimore, MD, area. No support for religious or sectarian purposes. No grants to individuals, or for annual campaigns, event sponsorships, or deficit financing; no loans.
Application information: Specific application guidelines available on foundation web site. Association of Baltimore Area Grantmakers Common Grant Application Form accepted. Grant applicants must complete a Maryland Cultural Data Project data profile and receive a "review complete" status.
Deadline(s): See web site for current deadlines

Board meeting date(s): Mar., May, Sept., and Nov.
Final notification: 2 months
Officer and Governors:* Connie E. Imboden,* Pres.; Louis R. Cestello; Gwen Davidson; Steven G. Ziger.
Trustee: P.N.C. Bank, N.A.
Number of staff: None.
EIN: 526057178

1348
The Kenneth S. Battye Charitable Trust
2330 W. Joppa Rd., Ste. 107-A
Lutherville, MD 21093-4605

Established in 1992 in MD.
Donors: Kenneth S. Battye†; Susan A. Battye.
Foundation type: Independent foundation.
Financial data (yr. ended 06/30/13): Assets, $49,728,869 (M); gifts received, $3,954,496; expenditures, $2,294,212; qualifying distributions, $1,865,600; giving activities include $1,737,295 for 31 grants (high: $250,000; low: $50).
Fields of interest: Health organizations, association; Food banks; Human services; American Red Cross; Salvation Army; United Ways and Federated Giving Programs; Catholic agencies & churches; Blind/visually impaired.
Type of support: General/operating support.
Limitations: Applications not accepted. Giving primarily in Baltimore, MD. No grants to individuals.
Application information: Contributes only to pre-selected organizations.
Trustees: Audrey B. Drossner; Charlotte B. Floyd; **Raymond A. Mason.**
EIN: 521748587
Other changes: Kenneth S. Battye, Donor and a trustee, is deceased. Susan A. Battye is no longer a trustee.

1349
The Jacob and Hilda Blaustein Foundation, Inc.
1 South St., Ste. 2900
Baltimore, MD **21202-3334** (410) 347-7201
Contact: Betsy F. Ringel, Exec. Dir.
FAX: (410) 347-7210; E-mail: info@blaufund.org; Main URL: http://www.blaufund.org/foundations/jacobandhilda_f.html

Incorporated in 1957 in MD.
Donors: Jacob Blaustein†; American Trading and Production Corp.; Barbara B. Hirschhorn; Elizabeth B. Roswell.
Foundation type: Independent foundation.
Financial data (yr. ended 12/31/12): Assets, $113,603,431 (M); gifts received, $1,595,466; expenditures, $8,123,300; qualifying distributions, $7,822,759; giving activities include $7,200,085 for 186 grants (high: $1,200,000; low: $100).
Purpose and activities: The foundation promotes social justice and human rights through its five program areas: Jewish life, strengthening Israeli democracy, health and mental health, educational opportunity, and human rights. The foundation supports organizations that promote systematic change; involve constituents in planning and decision making; encourage volunteer and professional development; and engage in ongoing program evaluation.
Fields of interest: Arts education; Arts; Education, reform; Education, public education; Health care; Mental health, treatment; International human rights; Jewish federated giving programs; Jewish agencies & synagogues.
International interests: Israel.
Type of support: General/operating support; Capital campaigns; Building/renovation; Endowments; Program development; Technical assistance; Program evaluation; Program-related investments/loans; Employee matching gifts; Matching/challenge support.
Limitations: Applications accepted. Giving primarily in MD (no local projects outside Baltimore, MD); giving also in Israel. No support for unaffiliated schools or synagogues. No grants to individuals, or for fundraising events, or direct mail solicitations; no loans (except for program-related investments).
Publications: Application guidelines; Grants list.
Application information: The foundation accepts applications that conform to the Association of Baltimore Area Grantmakers Common Grant Application. Application form not required.
Initial approach: Letter
Copies of proposal: 1
Deadline(s): None
Board meeting date(s): Quarterly
Final notification: 4 to 6 months
Officers and Trustees:* Michael J. Hirschhorn,* Pres.; Barbara B. Hirschhorn, V.P.; Arthur E. Roswell,* V.P.; Elizabeth B. Roswell,* V.P.; Jill R. Robinson, Secy.; Anne Patterson, Treas.; Betsy F. Ringel, Exec. Dir.
Number of staff: 1 part-time professional.
EIN: 526038382

1350
The Morton K. and Jane Blaustein Foundation, Inc.
1 South St., Ste. 2900
Baltimore, MD **21202-3334** (410) 347-7201
Contact: Mary Jane Blaustein, Pres.
FAX: (410) 347-7210; E-mail: info@bloufund.org; Main URL: http://www.blaufund.org/foundations/mortonandjane_f.html

Established in 1988 in MD.
Donors: Morton K. Blaustein†; Mary Jane Blaustein; Lord Baltimore Capital Corp.
Foundation type: Independent foundation.
Financial data (yr. ended 12/31/12): Assets, $52,795,115 (M); gifts received, $350,000; expenditures, $3,181,385; qualifying distributions, $2,816,357; giving activities include $2,816,357 for grants.
Purpose and activities: Giving primarily for education, health, human rights, and social justice.
Fields of interest: Education; Health care; Mental health/crisis services; International human rights.
Type of support: General/operating support; Continuing support; Emergency funds; Program development.
Limitations: Applications accepted. Giving primarily in Washington, DC, Baltimore, MD, and New York, NY. No support for fundraising events, direct mail solicitations, or unsolicited proposals for academic, scientific or medical research. No grants or scholarships to individuals, or for fundraising, capital campaigns, annual campaigns, membership campaigns; no loans.
Application information: See foundation web site for program guidelines. Association of Baltimore Area Grantmakers Common Grant Application Form accepted. Application form not required.
Initial approach: Letter
Copies of proposal: 1
Deadline(s): None
Final notification: 4 to 6 months
Officers and Trustees:* Mary Jane Blaustein,* Pres.; Alan Berlow,* V.P.; Jeanne P. Blaustein,* V.P.; Susan B. Blaustein,* V.P.; Peter Bokor,* V.P.; Jill R. Robinson, Secy.; Anne Patterson, Treas.; Betsy Ringel, Exec. Dir.
Number of staff: 1 full-time professional.
EIN: 521607300

1351
The Braitmayer Foundation
6470 Freetown Rd., Ste. 20087
Columbia, MD 21044-4016 (410) 480-2799
Contact: Sabina Taj, Advisor
E-mail: sabina@braitmayerfoundation.org; Main URL: http://www.braitmayerfoundation.org
Grants List: http://www.braitmayerfoundation.org/grant-recipients/
Grants List: http://www.braitmayerfoundation.org/2014/2013-grant-recipients/
Grants List: http://www.braitmayerfoundation.org/2013/2012-grant-recipients/
Grants List: http://www.braitmayerfoundation.org/2012/2011-grant-recipients/

Trust established in 1964 in MA.
Donor: Marian S. Braitmayer†.
Foundation type: Independent foundation.
Financial data (yr. ended 12/31/12): Assets, $3,991,777 (M); gifts received, $3,525; expenditures, $265,182; qualifying distributions, $209,055; giving activities include $160,800 for 14 grants (high: $35,000; low: $1,000).
Purpose and activities: Support primarily for K-12 education. Of particular interest are curricular and school reform initiatives and preparation of, and professional development opportunities for, K-12 teachers. In addition, the foundation provides modest support of activities in Marion, MA, and surrounding communities which will improve the quality of life for residents in the area.
Fields of interest: Elementary school/education; Secondary school/education; Elementary/secondary school reform; Education, community/cooperative; Education.
Type of support: Program development; Seed money; Curriculum development; Matching/challenge support.
Limitations: Applications accepted. Giving on a national basis; interest also in Marion, MA, and surrounding communities. No grants to individuals, or for building, general operating purposes, endowment funds, multi-year grants, child care or pre-kindergarten programs or equipment.
Publications: Application guidelines; Grants list; Program policy statement.
Application information: Faxed or e-mailed applications are not accepted. See foundation web site for additional details. Application form not required.
Initial approach: For grants up to $10,000, 3-page proposal; for grants up to $35,000, 2-page letter of inquiry
Copies of proposal: 8
Deadline(s): Mar. 15
Board meeting date(s): Biannually
Final notification: Aug. 1 for grants up to $10,000; Mar. 15 of following year for grants up to $35,000
Officer and Trustees:* R. Davis Webb, Jr.,* Chair.; Eric A. Braitmayer; John W. Braitmayer; Karen L. Braitmayer; Nancy W. Corkery; Kristina B. Hewey; Anne B. Webb.
Number of staff: 1 part-time professional.
EIN: 046112131

1352
The Mary Catherine Bunting Foundation, Inc.
c/o Bunting Mgmt. Group
217 International Cir.
Hunt Valley, MD 21030-1332

Established in 1998 in MD.
Donor: Mary Catherine Bunting.
Foundation type: Independent foundation.
Financial data (yr. ended 12/31/12): Assets, $8,627,994 (M); gifts received, $48,076; expenditures, $450,000; qualifying distributions, $450,000; giving activities include $450,000 for grants.
Fields of interest: Higher education; Human services; Catholic agencies & churches.
Limitations: Applications not accepted. Giving primarily in Washington, DC, and Baltimore, MD. No grants to individuals.
Application information: Contributes only to pre-selected organizations.
Officers and Directors:* Mary Catherine Bunting,* Chair.; **Eleanor Smith,* Secy.-Treas.**; Christopher L. Bunting; Geraldine Fiakowski.
Trustee: Kevin D. Irwin.
EIN: 522106057
Other changes: Eleanor Smith has replaced Judith Needham as Secy.-Treas.
Judith Claire Boyce is no longer a director.

1353
The Annie E. Casey Foundation
701 St. Paul St.
Baltimore, MD 21202-2311 (410) 547-6600
***Contact:* Satonya C. Fair, Dir., Grants Mgmt.**
FAX: (410) 547-6624; E-mail: webmail@aecf.org; E-mail for S.C. Fair: sfair@aecf.org; Main URL: http://www.aecf.org
Casey Places: http://www.aecf.org/CaseyPlaces.aspx
E-Newsletter: http://www.aecf.org/Newsroom/NewsletterSubscribe.aspx
Knowledge Center: http://www.aecf.org/KnowledgeCenter.aspx
The Annie E. Casey Foundation Staff: https://twitter.com/AECFNews/casey-foundation-staff/members
Twitter: http://twitter.com/aecfnews

Incorporated in 1948 in CA.
Donors: Annie E. Casey†; James E. "Jim" Casey†; and members of the Casey family.
Foundation type: Independent foundation.
Financial data (yr. ended 12/31/12): Assets, $2,666,068,266 (M); gifts received, $2,063,157; expenditures, $225,437,214; qualifying distributions, $241,888,903; giving activities include $98,475,361 for 996 grants (high: $6,127,523; low: $550), $205,655 for 346 employee matching gifts, $67,544,428 for 135 foundation-administered programs and $28,400,000 for 7 loans/program-related investments (high: $19,000,000; low: $500,000).
Purpose and activities: The primary mission of the foundation is to foster public policies, human service reforms, and community supports that more effectively meet the needs of today's vulnerable children and families. In pursuit of this goal, the foundation makes grants that help states, cities, and communities fashion more innovative, cost-effective responses to these needs.
Fields of interest: Education; Youth development, services; Human services; Children/youth, services; Urban/community development; Public affairs; Children/youth; Children; Adults; African Americans/Blacks; Economically disadvantaged.
Type of support: General/operating support; Management development/capacity building; Program development; Conferences/seminars; Publication; Fellowships; Research; Technical assistance; Consulting services; Program evaluation; Program-related investments/loans; Grants to individuals; Mission-related investments/loans.
Limitations: Applications accepted. Giving on a national basis, with emphasis on the ten sites that consist of the Making Connections initiative, as well as the foundation civic sites in Baltimore, MD, New Haven, CT, and Atlanta, GA. No support for political committees-529s (PACs). No grants to individuals (except for Casey Children and Family Fellowship Program), or for capital projects or medical research.
Publications: Financial statement; Informational brochure; Newsletter; Occasional report.
Application information: The foundation does not often fund unsolicited grant applications. The foundation's approach to grant making focuses on making multi-year, multi-site commitments that enable them to invest in long-term strategies and partnerships that strengthen families and communities. Most grantees are by invitation. Application form not required.
Initial approach: Letter (no more than 3 pages)
Deadline(s): None
Board meeting date(s): 5 times annually
Final notification: Approximately 30 days after receiving letter
Officers and Trustees:* Michael L. Eskew,* Chair.; Patrick McCarthy, C.E.O. and Pres.; Ralph Smith, Sr. V.P.; **Kenneth M. Jones II, V.P. and C.F.O.**; Stefan Strein, V.P. and C.I.O.; **Ryan Chao, V.P., Civic Sites and Community Change**; Bob Giloth, V.P., Ctr. for Community and Economic Opportunity; Donna Stark, V.P., Talent Mgmt. and Leadership Devel.; Lisa M. Hamilton, V.P., External Affairs; **Teresa Markowitz, V.P., Center for Systems Innovation**; **Debra Joy Perez, V.P., Research, Evaluation and Learning**; Maurice Agresta; Diana M. Bonta; Robert J. Clannin; D. Scott Davis; John Engler; Joseph Moderow; Gabriella E. Morris; **Teri Plummer McClure**; Lea N. Soupata; Arnold Wellman; Jim Winestock; Sam Zamarripa.
Number of staff: 141 full-time professional; 2 part-time professional; 49 full-time support; 1 part-time support.
EIN: 521951681
Other changes: Kenneth M. Jones, II is now V.P. and C.F.O. Raymond Torres is no longer V.P. and Exec. Dir., Casey Family Svcs. Steve Cohen is no longer V.P. and Chief Prog. Off.

1354
Ceres Foundation
18606 Reliant Dr.
Gaithersburg, MD 20879-5422
***E-mail:* ceresmd1@gmail.com; Main URL: http://fdnweb.org/ceres**
Grants List: http://fdnweb.org/ceres/foundation-grantees/

Established in 2000 in MD.
Donor: Donald B. Milder.
Foundation type: Independent foundation.
Financial data (yr. ended 12/31/12): Assets, $26,185,976 (M); expenditures, $1,179,158; qualifying distributions, $1,087,485; giving activities include $898,500 for 19 grants (high: $165,000; low: $3,000).
Purpose and activities: The foundation's mission is to provide the catalyst needed to mobilize human energies and talents that lie dormant. The foundation will focus on programs that aim to produce permanent improvements in peoples' lives by means of short-term interventions. The foundation will favor applicants who can best demonstrate a tangible, direct connection between the services their programs provide and the positive shifts that take place in individuals' lives.
Fields of interest: Education; Youth development; Human services; Children/youth, services; Family services; Women, centers/services; Young adults; Crime/abuse victims; Economically disadvantaged; Homeless.
Type of support: General/operating support; Program-related investments/loans.
Limitations: Applications accepted. Giving restricted to the West Coast or the Eastern Seaboard, from Raleigh northward. No support for foreign organizations, programs that serve those with disabilities, injuries, addictions or HIV, programs focused only on particular immigrant, ethnic or religious groups, programs that primarily serve pre-school kids or adults over 30 without children, and youth development programs that are after-school or considered learning centers. No grants to individuals.
Publications: Application guidelines; Program policy statement.
Application information: Full proposals are only accepted via invitation following submission of an application. Application form required.
Initial approach: Send short summary application of 3 - 6 pages following review of application criteria
Copies of proposal: 1
Deadline(s): None
Board meeting date(s): Nov.
Final notification: By Dec.
Officers: Daniel C. Milder, Pres.; Terri L. Milder, Secy.; Donald B. Milder, C.F.O.
EIN: 912170962

1355
Naomi and Nehemiah Cohen Foundation
P.O. Box 30100
Bethesda, MD 20824-0639 (301) 652-2230
Contact: Alison McWilliams, Exec. Dir.
FAX: (301) 652-2260; E-mail: info@nncf.net; Main URL: http://www.nncf.net

Incorporated in 1959 in DC.
Donors: Emanuel Cohen†; N.M. Cohen†; Naomi Cohen†; Israel Cohen†; Daniel Solomon; Lillian Cohen Solomon†; David Solomon; Stuart Brown; Dr. Diane Solomon Brown.
Foundation type: Independent foundation.
Financial data (yr. ended 12/31/12): Assets, $76,507,135 (M); gifts received, $2,500; expenditures, $4,205,999; qualifying distributions, $3,821,244; giving activities include $3,431,100 for 97 grants (high: $510,100; low: $600).
Purpose and activities: The focus of the foundation is on human services, reproductive health care, and civic affairs in Washington, DC, and Jewish-Arab shared society in Israel.
Fields of interest: Environment; Human services; International human rights; Civil liberties, reproductive rights; Civil/human rights; Minorities; Women; Young adults, female; Economically disadvantaged; Homeless.
International interests: Israel.
Type of support: General/operating support; Annual campaigns; Capital campaigns; Building/renovation; Program evaluation.
Limitations: Giving primarily in Washington, DC, and Israel. No support for private or parochial schools,

universities, or for medical research. No grants to individuals.
Publications: Grants list.
Application information: Unsolicited requests for funds not accepted. Current grantees should refer to application guidelines on foundation web site, and may use the Washington Regional Association of Grantmakers' Common Grant Application Format. Proposals sent by e-mail, fax, FedEX or messenger are not accepted.
Deadline(s): **Current grantees should refer to foundation web site for deadlines**
Board meeting date(s): Quarterly
Officers and Directors:* Dr. Diane Solomon Brown,* Pres.; Daniel Solomon,* V.P.; Jane Solomon,* Secy.; Stuart Brown,* Treas.; Alison McWilliams, Exec. Dir.
Number of staff: 1 full-time professional.
EIN: 201135004

1356
Commonweal Foundation, Inc.

10770 Columbia Pike, Ste. 150
Silver Spring, MD 20901-4451 (240) 450-0000
Contact: Rozita Green, V.P., Programs
FAX: (240) 450-4115; E-mail: grants@cweal.org; Main URL: http://www.cweal.org

Established in 1968 in Washington, DC.
Donors: Stewart Bainum, Sr.; Roberta Bainum; Jane Bainum; Realty Investment Company, Inc.; Rose-Marie and Jack R. Anderson Foundation.
Foundation type: Operating foundation.
Financial data (yr. ended 06/30/13): Assets, $220,581,715 (M); gifts received, $13,996,769; expenditures, $15,684,057; qualifying distributions, $15,853,223; giving activities include $5,480,108 for 204 grants (high: $1,625,000; low: $20), and $8,656,650 for 2 foundation-administered programs.
Purpose and activities: The foundation's vision is that children living in poverty have the opportunity to break the bonds of their circumstance by gaining access to quality educational opportunities and services, and graduate from high school prepared to enter and succeed in higher education or pursue gainful employment to become contributing members of society.The foundation operates and supports educational programs and projects assisting underserved children and youth. The foundation focuses on primary and secondary education.
Fields of interest: Child development, education; Elementary school/education; Secondary school/education; Human services; Children/youth, services; Child development, services; Minorities.
Type of support: General/operating support; Continuing support; Program development; Seed money; Scholarship funds; Matching/challenge support.
Limitations: Applications accepted. Giving limited to Washington, DC, MD, and northern VA for Community Assistance Grants. **No support for political organizations. No grants to individuals, or for endowments or building funds, capital campaigns, special events, lobbying activities, local organizations that raise funds to send to other countries and .**
Publications: Application guidelines; Grants list; Program policy statement.
Application information: Organizations with operating budget above 1 million will not be considered for funding. Application form required.
Initial approach: Apply online via foundation web site
Deadline(s): Feb. 1 and Aug. 1 for Community Assistance Grants
Board meeting date(s): June and Dec.
Final notification: 4 to 6 weeks after deadline
Officers and Directors:* Barbara Bainum,* Chair., C.E.O., and Pres.; Stewart Bainum, Sr.,* Vice-Chair.; Christopher Sharkey, V.P. and C.F.O.; Bruce Bainum, Ph.D.; Roberta Bainum; Alexander Froom; Charles A. Ledsinger, Jr.; James MacCutcheon; Scott Renschler.
Number of staff: 11 full-time professional; 4 full-time support.
EIN: 237000192
Other changes: For the fiscal year ended June 30, 2013, the grantmaker paid grants of $5,480,108, a 143.4% increase over the fiscal 2012 disbursements, $2,251,169.

1357
Community Foundation of Carroll County, Inc.

255 Clifton Blvd. St. 313
Westminster, MD 21157-4690 (410) 876-5505
***Contact:* Audrey S. Cimino, Exec. Dir.**
FAX: (410) 871-9031;
E-mail: cfccinfo@carrollcommunityfoundation.org; Main URL: http://
www.carrollcommunityfoundation.org

Established in 1994 in MD.
Foundation type: Community foundation.
Financial data (yr. ended 12/31/11): Assets, $4,659,369 (M); gifts received, $795,705; expenditures, $1,054,694; giving activities include $261,587 for 3+ grants (high: $11,745), and $320,212 for 206 grants to individuals.
Purpose and activities: The foundation seeks to maintain and enhance the quality of life in the community of Carroll County through philanthropic means. The foundation will receive, invest, and distribute funds for charitable, cultural, and educational purposes for the benefit of the citizens of Carroll County.
Fields of interest: Historic preservation/historical societies; Arts; Education; Health care; Recreation; Human services.
Limitations: Applications accepted. Giving limited to Carroll County, MD. No support for sectarian religious programs. No grants for to individuals (except for scholarships), or for operational deficits, fundraisers, or debt retirement.
Application information: Visit foundation web site for application form and guidelines. Application form required.
Initial approach: Contact foundation
Officers and Trustees:* Caroline Babylon,* Chair.; Audrey S. Cimino, Exec. Dir.; **Gregg Blair**; **Mel Blizzard**; Dean Camlin; **Stanley Dill**; William Gering; **Emily Johnston**; Bernie Jones; **Donna Lewis**; Phil Mullikin; Sue Myers; Tom Rasmussen; Carolyn Scott; Seth Shipley; Jason Stambaugh; Sue Yingling; Pam Zappardino.
EIN: 521865244
Other changes: Neil J. Borrelli is no longer Secy. Gary Davis is no longer Treas. Eileen Gist is no longer a member of the governing body. Robin L. Weisse is no longer a member of the governing body. Missie Wilcox is no longer a member of the governing body.

1358
The Community Foundation of Frederick County, MD, Inc.

312 E. Church St.
Frederick, MD 21701-5611 (301) 695-7660
Contact: Elizabeth Y. Day, Pres.
FAX: (301) 695-7775;
E-mail: info@frederickcountygives.org; Additional e-mail: donor.services@cffredco.org; Main URL: http://www.frederickcountygives.org/
Blog: http://www.frederickcountygives.org/about/blog
Facebook: https://www.facebook.com/CommunityFoundationFredCo

Established in 1986 in MD.
Foundation type: Community foundation.
Financial data (yr. ended 06/30/13): Assets, $88,402,511 (M); gifts received, $3,392,290; expenditures, $4,174,419; giving activities include $2,314,108 for 74+ grants (high: $320,856), and $561,588 for 281 grants to individuals.
Purpose and activities: The Community Foundation is dedicated to connecting people who care with causes that matter to enrich the quality of life in Frederick County now and for future generations.
Fields of interest: Historic preservation/historical societies; Arts; Higher education; Education; Environment, pollution control; Health care; Housing/shelter; Youth, services; Aging, centers/services; Human services; Community/economic development; Public affairs; Religion.
Type of support: Capital campaigns; Building/renovation; Emergency funds; Program development; Publication; Seed money; Scholarship funds; Scholarships—to individuals.
Limitations: Applications accepted. Giving limited to Frederick County, MD. No grants for operating costs, annual campaigns, endowments, or multi-year funding.
Publications: Application guidelines; Annual report; Grants list; Informational brochure; Newsletter.
Application information: Visit foundation web site for application guidelines. Application form required.
Initial approach: Contact foundation
Copies of proposal: 1
***Deadline(s):* Aug. 15 for affordable healthcare, housing/homelessness, and school readiness grants, Sept. 15 for arts, agriculture, civic causes, animal welfare, education, youth programs, elder care, and other grants**
Board meeting date(s): 4th Fri. of each month
Final notification: Mid-Dec.
Officers and Trustees:* James R. Shoemaker, Esq.,* Chair.; Cynthia S. Palmer,* 1st Vice-Chair.; Debra S. Borden, Esq.,* 2nd Vice-Chair.; Elizabeth Y. Day,* Pres.; Gail M. Fitzgerald,* C.F.O.; Joanne R. McCoy,* Secy.; Dale T. Summers,* Treas.; **Bill Blakeslee**; Robert E. Broadrup, D.D.S.; Colleen Chidester; Lisa Y. Coblentz; Cornelius Ryan Fay III; **Harry George III**; Kevin Hessler, C.P.A.; David L. Hoffman; Ted Luck; Brenda M. Main; Mark Mayer; Janet I. McCurdy, Esq.; Shabri Moore; Joy Hall Onley; J. Ray Ramsburg III; Tod P. Salisbury, Esq.; Shirley A. Shores; Daniel K. Tregoning; Barbara K. Walker.
Number of staff: 4 full-time professional; 5 full-time support; 1 part-time support.
EIN: 521488711
Other changes: Dezirae Farrell is now Acct. Asst. Tonyia Miller is now Exec. Asst. Valerie Proudfoot is now Mktg. and Comm. Asst. Nancy Williford is now Acct. and Technology Asst. Neil Fay is no longer a trustee.

1359
Community Foundation of the Eastern Shore, Inc.
1324 Belmont Ave., Ste. 401
Salisbury, MD 21804 (410) 742-9911
***Contact:* For grants: Heather Towers, Prog. Off.**
FAX: (410) 742-6638; E-mail: cfes@cfes.org; **Grant inquiry e-mail: htowers@cfes.org**; Main URL: http://www.cfes.org
Facebook: http://www.facebook.com/pages/Community-Foundation-of-the-Eastern-Shore/178920515477
LinkedIn: http://www.linkedin.com/company/2292766
Twitter: http://twitter.com/cfesnonprofit
Vimeo: http://vimeo.com/cfes
YouTube: http://www.youtube.com/user/CFEasternShore
Scholarship inquiry e-mail: **bjsummers@cfes.org**

Established in 1984 in MD.
Foundation type: Community foundation.
Financial data (yr. ended 06/30/13): Assets, $88,723,926 (M); gifts received, $4,742,431; expenditures, $6,238,774; giving activities include $5,166,559 for 87+ grants (high: $1,090,000), and $256,551 for 69 grants to individuals.
Purpose and activities: The foundation serves the Lower Eastern Shore of Maryland, specifically Somerset County, Wicomico County, and Worcester County. Established in 1984, the foundation is a local philanthropic expert committed to connecting donors with community needs. Gifts to the foundation create permanent endowment funds that steadily grow in value over time and produce income for grants to local charitable nonprofit organizations. The foundation seeks to encourage philanthropy and strengthen our communities.
Fields of interest: Historic preservation/historical societies; Arts; Higher education; Education; Environment; Health care; Human services; Community/economic development; Children/youth; Youth; Women; Girls.
Type of support: Management development/capacity building; Equipment; Emergency funds; Program development; Conferences/seminars; Seed money; Technical assistance; Consulting services; Scholarships—to individuals.
Limitations: Applications accepted. Giving limited to the Lower Eastern Shore of MD, area, encompassing Somerset, Wicomico, and Worcester counties. No support for sectarian religious programs. No grants to individuals (except for scholarships), or for annual campaigns, building campaigns, fundraising campaigns, major capital campaigns, building or endowment funds, continuing support, land acquisition, general operating support, playground equipment, or debt retirement or budget deficits; no program-related investments.
Publications: Application guidelines; Annual report; Financial statement; Informational brochure; Newsletter.
Application information: Visit foundation web site for application form and guidelines per grant type. Application form required.
Initial approach: Letter or telephone
Copies of proposal: 1
Deadline(s): Feb. 1 and Aug. 1 for Community Needs Grant Program; varies for others
Board meeting date(s): Feb., Apr., June, Aug., Oct., and Dec.
Final notification: Apr. and Oct. for Community Needs Grant Program; varies for others
Officers and Directors:* Melody S. Nelson,* Chair.; John J. Allen,* Vice-Chair.; Dr. Doug Wilson,* C.E.O. and Pres.; Erica N. Joseph,* V.P., Community Investment; **James R. Thomas, Jr.,* Secy.; David A. Vorhis,* Treas.**; David Plotts, Cont.; **James W. Almand**; John P. Barrett; Todd E. Burbage; Thomas K. Coates; Jane R. Corcoran; Charles G. Goslee; Dr. Carolyn Johnston; Andy Kim; Dwight W. Marshall, Jr.; Kathleen G. McLain; James F. Morris; Susan K. Purnell; Ernest R. Satchell; John M. Stern, Jr.; Greg Tawes; Donald K. Taylor; Lauren C. Taylor; Louis H. Taylor; Michael P. Truitt; Stephanie T. Willey; Julius D. Zant, M.D.
Number of staff: 8 full-time professional.
EIN: 521326014
Other changes: Melody S. Nelson has replaced Donald K. Taylor as Chair. John J. Allen has replaced Melody S. Nelson as Vice-Chair. James R. Thomas, Jr. has replaced James W. Almand as Secy. David A. Vorhis has replaced James R. Thomas Jr. as Treas.
Dr. Doug Wilson is now C.E.O. and Pres. Jacqueline R. Cassidy and Annemarie Dickerson are no longer directors.

1360
Community Foundation of Washington County Maryland, Inc.
33 W. Franklin St., Ste. 203
Hagerstown, MD 21740-4863 (301) 745-5210
Contact: Bradley N. Sell, Exec. Dir.
FAX: (301) 791-5752; E-mail: cfwc@cfwcmd.org; Additional e-mail: brads@cfwcmd.org; Main URL: http://www.cfwcmd.org
Facebook: http://www.facebook.com/cfwashingtoncountymd

Established in 1996 in MD.
Foundation type: Community foundation.
Financial data (yr. ended 06/30/13): Assets, $25,213,114 (M); gifts received, $439,329; expenditures, $1,742,840; giving activities include $1,085,240 for 31+ grants (high: $100,000).
Purpose and activities: The foundation's mission includes: 1) serving as a leader, resource, and catalyst to enrich the quality of life in the community; 2) providing a variety of flexible and cost-effective ways for donors to create permanent endowments; 3) providing donor services that allow the foundation to respond to changing community needs and opportunities; 4) making financial gifts to qualified organizations and other community needs; and 5) encouraging philanthropy at all levels.
Fields of interest: Arts; Education; Health care; Boys & girls clubs; YM/YWCAs & YM/YWHAs; Children, services; Family services; Human services; Economic development, visitors/convention bureau/tourism promotion; United Ways and Federated Giving Programs; Infants/toddlers; Children/youth; Youth; Adults; Aging; Young adults; Disabilities, people with; Physically disabled; Mentally disabled; Minorities; Substance abusers; Single parents; Crime/abuse victims; Economically disadvantaged; Homeless.
Type of support: Program development; Seed money; Scholarship funds.
Limitations: Applications accepted. Giving primarily in Washington County, MD. No support for projects that would ordinarily receive public tax support, sectarian religious programs, or K-12 educational institutions. No grants for annual operating expenses, or for capital campaigns, endowment campaigns, deficit retirement, special fundraising events, or celebration functions.
Publications: Application guidelines; Annual report; Newsletter.
Application information: Visit foundation web site for application and additional information. Application form required.
Initial approach: Complete online application
Deadline(s): Nov. 15
Board meeting date(s): 3rd Thurs. of each month
Final notification: Awards will be made by Mar. 1
Officers and Trustees:* John P. Itell,* Chair.; Mike Day,* Vice-Chair.; Rev. D. Suart Dunnan,* Vice-Chair.; Ted Reeder,* Secy.; Cindy Moore,* Treas.; Bradley N. Sell, Exec. Dir.; John F. Barr; Dr. Carol R. Becker; Howard Bowen; Andy Bruns; Jason Divelbiss; Bob Ernst; Douglas A. Fiery; Mark Fulton; Lou Giustini; John R. Hershey III; Stuart L. Mullendore; Brad Pingrey; Melissa Reabold; Ann Marie Rotz; Elizabeth Schulze; Todd Snook; Mary Helen Strauch; Robin Twigg.
Number of staff: 1 full-time professional; 1 part-time professional; 1 full-time support; 2 part-time support.
EIN: 522001455
Other changes: Ruth Ann Callaham is no longer a member of the governing body.

1361
Cornell Douglas Foundation, Inc.
4701 Sangamore Rd., Ste. 133
Bethesda, MD 20816-2524 (301) 229-3008
FAX: (301) 229-3342; **E-mail for Ann Cornell: ann@cornelldouglas.org; e-mail for Holly Cornell: cdf@cornelldouglas.org**; Main URL: http://www.cornelldouglas.org/

Established in 2006 in MD.
Donors: Jean Douglas; Ann Cornell; W. Leslie Douglas‡; Wallace Genetic Foundation.
Foundation type: Independent foundation.
Financial data (yr. ended 12/31/12): Assets, $10,772,524 (M); gifts received, $1,996,820; expenditures, $361,475; qualifying distributions, $359,991; giving activities include $328,000 for 32 grants (high: $15,000; low: $5,000).
Purpose and activities: The foundation provides small grants to organizations which promote the foundation's vision: advocating for environmental health and justice, encouraging stewardship of the environment, and furthering respect for sustainability of resources.
Fields of interest: Education; Environment, plant conservation.
Application information: Application guidelines available on foundation web site.
Officers and Directors:* Ann Cornell,* Pres.; Elizabeth Sword,* Secy.; George L. Cornell, Jr.,* Treas.; Gillian C. Shinkman, Exec. Dir.; Alex Cornell; Holly Cornell.
EIN: 651287707

1362
L. Gordon Gordon Croft Foundation Inc.
(formerly Leominster-Croft Foundation, Inc.)
Canton House, 300 Water St.
Baltimore, MD 21202-3330 **(410) 576-8231**
Contact: L. Gordon Croft, V.P.

Established in 1990 in MD.
Donors: Leominster, Inc.; L. Gordon Croft; Jane Aurell Croft.
Foundation type: Company-sponsored foundation.
Financial data (yr. ended 12/31/12): Assets, $5,536,595 (M); expenditures, $220,082; qualifying distributions, $202,970; giving activities include $199,883 for 71+ grants (high: $125,500).
Purpose and activities: The foundation supports organizations involved with education, the environment, health, human services, economically disadvantaged people, and homeless people.

Fields of interest: Education; Agriculture/food; Community/economic development.
Type of support: General/operating support; Building/renovation.
Limitations: Applications accepted. Giving primarily in MD.
Application information: Application form required.
Initial approach: **Letter**
Deadline(s): None
Officers: Kent Gordon Croft, Pres.; L. Gordon Croft, V.P.; Jane Aurell Croft, Secy.
EIN: 521682796

1363
The Cupid Foundation, Inc.
(formerly The KDP Foundation, Inc.)
1010 Hull St., No. 220
Baltimore, MD **21230-5330** (410) 454-6472
Contact: Amy S. Larkin, Exec. Dir.

Established in 2007 in MD.
Donor: Kevin A. Plank.
Foundation type: Independent foundation.
Financial data (yr. ended 12/31/12): Assets, $18,175,405 (M); expenditures, $4,462,638; qualifying distributions, $3,993,376; giving activities include $3,993,376 for grants.
Fields of interest: Education; Medical research, institute; Athletics/sports, school programs; Family services.
Limitations: Applications accepted. Giving primarily in Baltimore and College Park, MD, and Washington, DC.
Application information:
Initial approach: Letter of request
Deadline(s): None
Officer: Amy S. Larkin, Exec. Dir.
Directors: Desiree Jacqueline Plank; Kevin A. Plank; Thomas J. Sippel.
EIN: 261300940

1364
The Haron Dahan Foundation, Inc.
6225 Smith Ave.
Baltimore, MD **21209-3626**
Contact: Haron Dahan, Pres.

Established in 1986 in MD.
Donors: Haron Dahan; Caddie Homes, Inc.; Dahan Homes, Inc.
Foundation type: Independent foundation.
Financial data (yr. ended 12/31/12): Assets, $42,521,041 (M); expenditures, $2,303,293; qualifying distributions, $2,181,977; giving activities include $2,170,280 for 12 grants (high: $1,902,780; low: $500).
Purpose and activities: Giving primarily for Jewish agencies, temples, and education.
Fields of interest: Higher education; Human services; Jewish federated giving programs; Jewish agencies & synagogues.
International interests: Israel.
Limitations: Applications not accepted. Giving in the U.S., primarily in Brooklyn and New York, NY, and MD, with emphasis on Baltimore.
Application information: Contributes only to pre-selected organizations.
Officer: Haron Dahan, Pres.
Number of staff: 1 part-time support.
EIN: 521473704
Other changes: The grantmaker no longer lists a telephone.

1365
The Davis Family Foundation, Inc.
c/o Mr. & Mrs. James C. Davis
P.O. Box 468
Hanover, MD 21076-0468 (877) 388-3823

Established in 2002 in MD.
Donors: James C. Davis; Kimberly J. Davis; William Davis; Deborah Davis.
Foundation type: Independent foundation.
Financial data (yr. ended 12/31/12): Assets, $291,542,383 (M); gifts received, $100,000,000; expenditures, $10,214,634; qualifying distributions, $9,831,020; giving activities include $9,821,900 for 48 grants (high: $4,300,000; low: $900).
Purpose and activities: Giving primarily for education, including Roman Catholic education.
Fields of interest: Elementary/secondary education; Higher education; Catholic agencies & churches.
Limitations: Applications not accepted. Giving primarily in Baltimore, MD and PA. No grants to individuals.
Application information: Contributes only to pre-selected organizations.
Officers and Directors:* James C. Davis,* Pres.; Kimberly J. Davis,* V.P. and Secy.-Treas.
EIN: 010751429
Other changes: At the close of 2012, the fair market value of the grantmaker's assets was $291,542,383, a 62.4% increase over the 2011 value, $179,501,821.

1366
de Beaumont Foundation, Inc.
7501 Wisconsin Ave., Ste. 1310E
Bethesda, MD **20814-6597** (301) 961-5800
Contact: James B. Sprague M.D., Chair.
FAX: (301) 961-5802;
E-mail: info@deBeaumont.org; Main URL: http://www.deBeaumont.org

Established in 1999 in MA.
Donor: Pierre de Beaumont.
Foundation type: Independent foundation.
Financial data (yr. ended 12/31/12): Assets, $116,433,394 (M); gifts received, $103,304,000; expenditures, $5,230,767; qualifying distributions, $4,755,832; giving activities include $4,124,444 for 23 grants (high: $1,267,194; low: $750).
Purpose and activities: Giving primarily for developing the public health workforce, encouraging health departments to collaborate and implement best practices, and improving information and data management through effective campaigns and innovative technology.
Fields of interest: Public health; Public health, communicable diseases; Public health, epidemiology; Public health, bioterrorism; Health care; Immunology; Disasters, preparedness/services.
Type of support: Conferences/seminars; Curriculum development; Fellowships; General/operating support; Management development/capacity building; Professorships; Program development; Program evaluation; Publication; Research; Scholarship funds; Seed money.
Limitations: Applications not accepted. Giving limited to the U.S. No support for religious or political organizations, or for international programs. No grants to individuals, or for scholarships, endowment funds, cash reserves, capital campaigns, debt, or lobbying.
Publications: Financial statement; Grants list.
Application information: Proposals by invitation only.
Board meeting date(s): Feb., May, Aug., and Oct.
Officers and Directors:* James B. Sprague, M.D.*, Chair. and C.E.O.; Murray Brennan, M.D.*, Vice-Chair.; Leroy Parker, M.D.*, Secy.-Treas.; Ariel C. Moyer, C.O.O.; John M. Auerbach, MBA; Richard M. Burnes, Jr.; Carol H. Massoni; John M. Stevens; Gregory R. Wagner, M.D.
Number of staff: 1 full-time professional.
EIN: 043467074
Other changes: Murray Brennan is now Vice-Chair.

1367
Delaplaine Foundation, Inc.
c/o Great Southern Enterprises, Inc.
244 W. Patrick St.
P.O. Box 3829
Frederick, MD 21701-6945 (301) 662-2753
Contact: Marlene B. Young, Pres.
FAX: (301) 620-1689;
E-mail: info@delaplainefoundation.org; Main URL: http://www.delaplainefoundation.org/

Established in 2001 in MD.
Donors: Edward S. Delaplaine; Elizabeth B. Delaplaine; George B. Delaplaine, Jr.; George B. Delaplaine III; James W. Delaplaine; John F. Delaplaine.
Foundation type: Independent foundation.
Financial data (yr. ended 12/31/13): Assets, $17,462,252 (M); gifts received, $5,000; expenditures, $954,204; qualifying distributions, $763,500; giving activities include $763,500 for 89 grants (high: $127,000; low: $500).
Purpose and activities: Giving primarily for the enrichment of communities and families within Maryland, nearby states, and the District of Columbia, by supporting programs that strengthen the arts and sciences, historical preservation, educational advancement, spiritual enlightenment and physical well-being.
Fields of interest: Historic preservation/historical societies; Arts; Higher education; Health care; Community/economic development; Spirituality.
Type of support: General/operating support; Continuing support; Annual campaigns; Capital campaigns; Endowments; Program development.
Limitations: Applications accepted. Giving primarily in Frederick County, MD, and its surrounding area, including Washington, DC. No grants to individuals.
Publications: Application guidelines; Informational brochure (including application guidelines).
Application information: See foundation web site for complete guidelines and application. Application form required.
Initial approach: Use application form on foundation web site
Copies of proposal: 1
Deadline(s): Nov. 1
Board meeting date(s): 1st Wed. in Nov.
Final notification: 4-6 weeks
Officers and Trustees:* George B. Delaplaine, Jr.,* Chair.; Marlene B. Young,* Pres.; **Edward S. Delaplaine II,* V.P.**; George B. Delaplaine III,* Secy.; Philip W. Hammond,* Treas.; Bettie Delaplaine*; James W. Delaplaine; **John P. Delaplaine.**
Number of staff: 2 part-time professional.
EIN: 522278038
Other changes: Edward S. Delaplaine II has replaced Bettie Delaplaine as V.P.
John F. Delaplaine is no longer a trustee.

1368
The Carl DelSignore Foundation, Inc.
927 Braddock Rd.
Cumberland, MD **21502-2624** (301) 777-2772
Contact: G. Douglas Reinhard, Secy.

Established in 1986 in MD.
Donor: Carl DelSignore†.
Foundation type: Independent foundation.
Financial data (yr. ended 04/30/13): Assets, $4,185,680 (M); expenditures, $270,501; qualifying distributions, $171,347; giving activities include $171,347 for 38 grants (high: $52,000; low: $719).
Fields of interest: Higher education; Hospitals (general); Children/youth, services; Community/economic development; Protestant agencies & churches; Catholic agencies & churches.
Limitations: Applications accepted. Giving primarily in western MD and WV. No grants to individuals.
Application information:
Initial approach: Proposal
Deadline(s): None
Officers: R. Donald Cussins, Pres.; Carmen P. DelSignore, V.P.; G. Douglas Reinhard, Secy.; James L. Crickard, Treas.
EIN: 521489402

1369
Robert W. Deutsch Foundation
1122 Kennilworth Dr., Ste. 201
Towson, MD 21204-2143 (443) 275-1144
Contact: Jane Brown, Exec. Dir.
FAX: (410) 321-4882;
E-mail: info@rwdfoundation.org; Main URL: http://www.rwdfoundation.org

Established in 1991 in MD.
Donors: Robert W. Deutsch; RWD Technologies.
Foundation type: Independent foundation.
Financial data (yr. ended 12/31/12): Assets, $96,575,541 (M); gifts received, $13,000,000; expenditures, $4,741,915; qualifying distributions, $4,274,467; giving activities include $3,709,965 for 23 grants (high: $520,000; low: $2,000).
Purpose and activities: The foundation is in the process of reconsidering its mission and goals. It supports innovation broadly.
Fields of interest: General charitable giving.
Type of support: General/operating support; Continuing support; Program development; Seed money; Curriculum development; Fellowships; Internship funds; Research.
Limitations: Applications not accepted. Giving primarily in MD. No support for religious or political organizations.
Application information: Unsolicited requests for funds not accepted.
Officers: Jane Brown, Pres. and Exec. Dir.; Neil Didriksen, C.O.O.
Directors: David Deutsch; Mac Maclure.
Number of staff: 2 full-time professional; 1 full-time support.
EIN: 521758252
Other changes: At the close of 2012, the fair market value of the grantmaker's assets was $96,575,541, a 483.2% increase over the 2010 value, $16,559,013. For the same period, the grantmaker paid grants of $3,709,965, an 882.8% increase over the 2010 disbursements, $377,500.

1370
The Dresher Foundation, Inc.
4940 Campbell Blvd., Ste. 110
Baltimore, MD 21236-5910 (410) 933-0384
Contact: Robin Platts, Exec. Dir.
FAX: (410) 931-9052;
E-mail: info@dresherfoundation.org; E-mail for Robin Platts: robin@dresherfoundation.org; Main URL: http://www.dresherfoundation.org

Established in 1989 in MD.
Donor: James T. Dresher, Sr.†.
Foundation type: Independent foundation.
Financial data (yr. ended 12/31/12): Assets, $50,438,383 (M); expenditures, $2,577,261; qualifying distributions, $2,132,622; giving activities include $1,913,260 for 100 grants (high: $205,000; low: $500).
Purpose and activities: Giving primarily for education, including after school programs, and human services, in specific geographic areas.
Fields of interest: Health care; Recreation, camps; Human services; Youth, services; Children/youth; Youth; Disabilities, people with; Mentally disabled; Women; Economically disadvantaged; Homeless.
Type of support: General/operating support; Capital campaigns; Building/renovation; Equipment; Scholarship funds; Technical assistance; Matching/challenge support.
Limitations: Giving primarily in Baltimore City, eastern Baltimore County, and Harford county in MD. **No support for adult literacy, charter or public schools and political organizations, or for national/local chapters for specific diseases, legal service organizations, or environmental programs.** No grants to individuals, or for annual campaigns, legal services, events or conferences, galas or golf tournaments, one-time only events, seminars or workshops.
Publications: Application guidelines; Grants list; Occasional report.
Application information: Funding for educational institutions is pre-selected.
***Initial approach:* Use online application process via foundation web site**
***Deadline(s):* See foundation web site for current deadlines**
Board meeting date(s): See foundation web site for current meeting dates
Officers: Jeffrey M. Dresher, Pres.; Michael Meoli, V.P.; Virginia M. Dresher, Secy.; Joshua Dresher, Treas.; Robin Platts, Exec. Dir.
Trustees: James R. Butcher; Jeanne D. Butcher; Patricia K. Dresher; Anthony J. Meoli; **Virginia Meoli**; Marcie Michael; James T. Dresher, Jr.; Susan Roarty; Melanie Robinson.
Number of staff: 1 full-time professional.
EIN: 521610465
Other changes: Patti Dresher is no longer a trustee.

1371
Dupkin Educational and Charitable Foundation, Inc.
10045 Red Run Blvd., No. 330
Owings Mills, MD 21117-5903

Established in 2000 in MD.
Donors: Manuel Dupkin II; Carol N. Dupkin.
Foundation type: Independent foundation.
Financial data (yr. ended 12/31/12): Assets, $30,328,809 (M); expenditures, $1,561,315; qualifying distributions, $1,500,000; giving activities include $1,500,000 for 21 grants (high: $1,457,150; low: $500).
Purpose and activities: Giving primarily to a Jewish federated giving program, as well as for education.
Fields of interest: Elementary/secondary education; Higher education; Education; Human services; Jewish federated giving programs.
Limitations: Applications not accepted. Giving primarily in Baltimore, MD. No grants to individuals.
Application information: Contributes only to pre-selected organizations.
Officers and Trustees:* Manuel Dupkin II,* Pres.; Carol N. Dupkin,* V.P.; Dr. Sally P. Thanhouser,* Secy.-Treas.
EIN: 522277075
Other changes: Stanford Z. Rothschild is no longer a trustee.

1372
John Edward Fowler Memorial Foundation
4340 East-West Hwy., Ste. 206
Bethesda, MD 20814-4467 (301) 654-2700
Contact: Richard H. Lee, Pres.
FAX: (301) 654-6700; **Main URL: http://fdnweb.org/fowler**
Grants List: http://fdnweb.org/fowler/recent-grants/

Incorporated in 1964 in DE.
Donor: Pearl Gunn Fowler†.
Foundation type: Independent foundation.
Financial data (yr. ended 12/31/12): Assets, $33,461,466 (M); expenditures, $1,762,599; qualifying distributions, $1,596,677; giving activities include $1,342,000 for 83 grants (high: $118,000; low: $5,000).
Purpose and activities: Primary areas of interest include the disadvantaged, with emphasis on the homeless, housing, food programs and youth education. Giving primarily to small community service organizations with little public funding, especially for programs that benefit children and youth; support also for social service agencies, literacy programs, and programs that help the elderly maintain their independence.
Fields of interest: Child development, education; Adult education—literacy, basic skills & GED; Education, reading; Food services; Housing/shelter, development; Human services; Children/youth, services; Child development, services; Aging, centers/services; Homeless, human services; Infants/toddlers; Children/youth; Youth; Adults; Aging; Physically disabled; Mentally disabled; Minorities; Economically disadvantaged; Homeless.
Type of support: Continuing support; General/operating support; Building/renovation; Equipment; Consulting services; Matching/challenge support.
Limitations: Applications accepted. Giving limited to the Washington, DC, Beltway area, including suburbs in MD and VA that abut the District of Columbia. No support for agencies principally funded by local, state or federal government sources, national health organizations, or for medical research programs or national organizations. No grants to individuals, or for capital grants (with the exception of long-time grantees); no loans.
Publications: Application guidelines; Grants list; IRS Form 990 or 990-PF printed copy available upon request.
Application information: Washington Grantmakers' Common Grant Application Form accepted, but not required. Application form and application guidelines available on foundation web site.
Initial approach: Telephone call requesting application form and guidelines. Do not send letters of inquiry
Copies of proposal: 1

Deadline(s): None
Board meeting date(s): Periodically
Final notification: Approximately 6 months

Officers and Trustees:* Richard H. Lee,* Pres.; Michael P. Bentzen,* Secy.; Jeffery P. Capron,* Treas.
Number of staff: 1 part-time professional.
EIN: 516019469

1373
The Carl M. Freeman Foundation, Inc.
111 Rockville Pike
Rockville, MD **20850**
Contact: Patti A. Grimes, Exec. Dir.
E-mail: patti@freemafoundation.org; **Telephone for Patti Grimes: (302) 436-3003**; Main URL: http://www.carlfreemanfoundation.org/

Established in 1960.
Donors: Joshua M. Freeman‡; Carl M. Freeman Charitable Lead Trust; The Freeman Foundation Charitable Lead Annuity Trust.
Foundation type: Independent foundation.
Financial data (yr. ended 12/31/12): Assets, $26,302,934 (M); gifts received, $3,316,161; expenditures, $2,323,882; qualifying distributions, $2,019,723; giving activities include $1,550,013 for 88 grants (high: $870,000; low: $100).
Purpose and activities: The foundation commits its time, talent and treasure to facilitate, support, and promote innovative community-based leadership and giving. The foundation seeks to honor our founders' legacies and passions by endorsing excellence and leveraging resources. Generally, the foundation limits donations to communities where the customers, employees, and vendors of the Carl M. Freeman Companies live and work.
Fields of interest: Performing arts; Performing arts centers; Arts; Education; Human services; Child development, services; Jewish federated giving programs; Jewish agencies & synagogues.
Type of support: General/operating support; Continuing support; Annual campaigns; Equipment; Program development; Technical assistance; Employee matching gifts; Matching/challenge support.
Limitations: Giving in the greater Washington, DC, area, (Delmarva communities), as well as the Eastern Panhandle of WV. No support for religious organizations for religious work. No grants to individuals.
Publications: Application guidelines; Annual report; Grants list.
Application information: Application information and guidelines available on foundation web site. Application form required.
Deadline(s): See foundation web site for current deadlines
Board meeting date(s): Generally on a quarterly basis

Officers and Trustees:* Michelle D. Freeman,* Chair. and Pres.; Stephen B. Huttler,* Secy.; Christine A. Shreve,* Treas.; Patti Grimes, Exec. Dir.
EIN: 526047536

1374
Morris Goldseker Foundation of Maryland, Inc.
(also known as Goldseker Foundation)
c/o Symphony Center
1040 Park Ave., Ste. 310
Baltimore, MD 21201-5635 (410) 837-5100
***Contact:* Laurie Latuda Kinkel, Prog. Off.**
FAX: (410) 837-7927;
E-mail: laurie@goldsekerfoundation.org; Laurie Latuda Kinkel tel.: (410) 837-6115; Main URL: http://www.goldsekerfoundation.org
Facebook: http://www.facebook.com/pages/Goldseker-Foundation/141220962603871?v=wall
Grants Database: http://www.goldsekerfoundation.org/search_the_grants_database
Twitter: http://twitter.com/GoldsekerFdn

Incorporated in 1973 in MD.
Donor: Morris Goldseker‡.
Foundation type: Independent foundation.
Financial data (yr. ended 12/31/12): Assets, $89,855,843 (M); expenditures, $4,657,475; qualifying distributions, $4,175,778; giving activities include $2,941,528 for 92+ grants (high: $261,550).
Purpose and activities: In 2000, the Goldseker Foundation's Board of Trustees and its Selection Committee adopted a two-track approach to grantmaking. This approach designates priority areas that build on existing experience and investments, but it also retains the ability to respond to new ideas and opportunities within the established program areas. The foundation's grantmaking funds will focus on the first-track priority areas. In these areas - community development, regionalism, and the nonprofit sector - the foundation will be a more directly engaged and active partner. The existing grantmaking policies apply to the priority areas. Grants will include a mix of foundation initiatives and projects submitted independently by potential grantees. The second track focuses on the foundation's established program areas: neighborhood development, community affairs, human services, and education.
Fields of interest: Education; Housing/shelter, search services; Human services; Community development, neighborhood development; Public affairs, association.
Type of support: Program development; Seed money; Technical assistance; Consulting services; Program-related investments/loans; Matching/challenge support.
Limitations: Applications accepted. Giving limited to the Baltimore, MD, area. No support for advocacy or political action groups, religious purposes, arts or cultural affairs, specific diseases or disabilities, or for projects normally financed with public funds. No grants to individuals, or for building or endowment funds, deficit financing, annual campaigns, or publications.
Publications: Annual report; Financial statement; Informational brochure (including application guidelines).
Application information: Submit preliminary letter as early as possible before deadlines. See foundation web site for application information, and information on applying for Management Assistance Grants. Association of Baltimore Area Grantmakers Common Grant Application Form accepted. Application form not required.
Initial approach: Letter or telephone inquiry
Copies of proposal: 1
Deadline(s): Feb. 1, May 1, and Sept. 1
Board meeting date(s): Distribution committee meets 3 times a year (Mar., June, and Oct.)
Final notification: Following committee meetings

Officers and Directors:* Sheldon Goldseker,* Chair.; Simon Goldseker,* Vice-Chair.; Matthew D. Gallagher, C.E.O. and Pres; Sheila L. Purkey, V.P., Secy.-Treas. and Cont.; Ana Goldseker; Deby Goldseker; Sharna Goldseker; Susan B. Katzenberg; Howard M. Weiss.
Advisory Selection Committee: Ronald J. Daniels; Marc B. Terrill; David Wilson.
Number of staff: 2 full-time professional; 2 part-time professional; 1 full-time support.
EIN: 520983502

1375
Monica and Hermen Greenberg Foundation
Bethesda, MD

The foundation terminated in 2011.

1376
The Homer and Martha Gudelsky Family Foundation, Inc.
11900 Tech Rd.
Silver Spring, MD 20904-1910
Contact: Medda Gudelsky, V.P.

Incorporated in 1968 in MD.
Donors: Percontee, Inc.; Jonathan Genn; Members of the Gudelsky family.
Foundation type: Independent foundation.
Financial data (yr. ended 12/31/12): Assets, $55,186,123 (M); gifts received, $29,347,372; expenditures, $2,802,744; qualifying distributions, $2,797,500; giving activities include $2,797,500 for 35 grants (high: $250,000; low: $2,500).
Fields of interest: Higher education; Health care; Jewish agencies & synagogues.
Type of support: Annual campaigns; Capital campaigns; Building/renovation; Equipment; Scholarship funds; Research.
Limitations: Applications accepted. Giving primarily in FL and MD. No grants to individuals.
Application information:
Initial approach: Letter
Deadline(s): None

Officers and Directors:* John Gudelsky,* Pres.; Medda Gudelsky,* V.P.; Rita Regino,* V.P.; Holly Stone,* V.P.; Jonathan Genn,* Secy.; Samuel Yedlin, Treas.
EIN: 520885969
Other changes: At the close of 2012, the fair market value of the grantmaker's assets was $55,186,123, a 108.0% increase over the 2011 value, $26,532,509. For the same period, the grantmaker paid grants of $2,797,500, a 97.6% increase over the 2011 disbursements, $1,416,000.

1377
John and Maureen Hendricks Charitable Foundation
8484 Georgia Ave., Ste. 700
Silver Spring, MD 20910-5619

Established in 2001 in MD.
Donors: John S. Hendricks; Maureen D. Hendricks.
Foundation type: Operating foundation.
Financial data (yr. ended 03/31/13): Assets, $13,416 (M); gifts received, $1,934,240; expenditures, $1,934,400; qualifying distributions, $1,934,304; giving activities include $1,931,454 for 19 grants (high: $451,489; low: $4,550).
Fields of interest: Higher education; Education; Environment; Athletics/sports, soccer; Foundations (community).
Type of support: General/operating support.
Limitations: Applications not accepted. Giving in the U.S., with emphasis on MD and Washington DC;

funding also in CO, MT, NJ, NY and VA. No grants to individuals.
Application information: Contributes only to pre-selected organizations.
Trustees: John S. Hendricks; Maureen D. Hendricks; Elizabeth Hendricks North; Eric W. Shaw.
EIN: 137180307
Other changes: For the fiscal year ended Mar. 31, 2013 the foundation paid grants of $1,931,454, a 1169.1% increase over fiscal 2012 disbursements of $152,196.

1378
The Richard A. Henson Foundation, Inc.

P.O. Box 151
Salisbury, MD 21803-0151 (410) 742-7057
Contact: Donna S. Altvater, Exec. Dir.
FAX: (410) 742-4036;
E-mail: dsaltvater@ymail.com; Main URL: http://www.richardhensonfoundation.org

Established in 1989 in MD; funded in 1990.
Donor: Richard A. Henson†.
Foundation type: Independent foundation.
Financial data (yr. ended 12/31/12): Assets, $31,634,284 (M); expenditures, $1,422,197; qualifying distributions, $1,231,269; giving activities include $1,180,930 for 15 grants (high: $300,000; low: $1,000).
Purpose and activities: Giving primarily to enrich the quality of life primarily in (but not exclusively to), the greater Salisbury, MD, area.
Fields of interest: Arts; Higher education; Hospitals (general); Children/youth, services; Foundations (community).
Type of support: Continuing support; Annual campaigns; Capital campaigns; Building/renovation; Equipment; Endowments; Scholarship funds; In-kind gifts; Matching/challenge support.
Limitations: Giving limited to the Salisbury, MD, area. No support for denominational religious organizations. No grants to individuals.
Publications: Application guidelines; Financial statement; Informational brochure.
Application information: Letters of Inquiry are by invitation only, upon consideration during initial telephone call, or of the e-mail. Application information and guidelines available on foundation web site.
***Initial approach:* Telephone or e-mail**
Copies of proposal: 1
***Deadline(s):* 2nd Mon. of every month (except Aug. and Dec.) for Letters of Inquiry**
***Board meeting date(s):* 4th Tues. of every month (except Aug. and Dec.)**
Final notification: Within 30 days
Officer: Donna S. Altvater, Exec. Dir.
Trustees: Thomas H. Evans; Stephen R. Farrow; Gordon D. Gladden; Gregory J. Olinde; Jon P. Sherwell; Thomas L. Trice IV.
Number of staff: 1 full-time professional.
EIN: 521642558

1379
The David and Barbara B. Hirschhorn Foundation, Inc.

c/o AFS
1 South St., Ste. 2900
Baltimore, MD **21202-3334** (410) 347-7201
Contact: Daniel B. Hirschhorn, Pres.
***FAX:* (410) 347-7210**; E-mail: info@blafund.org;
Main URL: http://www.blaufund.org/foundations/davidandbarbara_f.html

Established in 1986 in MD.
Donors: Barbara B. Hirschhorn; David Hirschhorn†; Daniel B. Hirschhorn; 3510 LLC.
Foundation type: Independent foundation.
Financial data (yr. ended 12/31/12): Assets, $38,970,237 (M); expenditures, $2,550,903; qualifying distributions, $2,437,811; giving activities include $2,264,446 for 146 grants (high: $116,666; low: $1,000).
Purpose and activities: Giving primarily for Jewish and secular initiatives in the program areas of: education and literacy, summer camping, human services, and intergroup understanding.
Fields of interest: Human services; International relief; Civil rights, race/intergroup relations; Jewish federated giving programs; Jewish agencies & synagogues; Religion, interfaith issues.
Type of support: General/operating support; Annual campaigns; Capital campaigns; Endowments.
Limitations: Applications accepted. Giving primarily in the metropolitan Baltimore, MD, area. No grants to individuals or for fundraisers; no loans.
Publications: Grants list.
Application information: Association of Baltimore Area Grantmakers Common Grant Application Form accepted. Application form not required.
Initial approach: Letter
Copies of proposal: 1
Deadline(s): None
Final notification: 4 to 6 months
Officers and Trustees:* Barbara B. Hirschhorn,* Chair.; Daniel B. Hirschhorn,* Pres.; Michael J. Hirschhorn,* V.P.; Sarah H. Shapiro,* V.P.; Deborah H. Vogelstein,* V.P.; Jill R. Robinson, Secy.; Betsy F. Ringel, Exec. Dir.
EIN: 521489400
Other changes: The grantmaker no longer lists a separate application address.

1380
Israelson Family Foundation, Inc.

409 Washington Ave., Ste. 900
Towson, MD 21204-4905

Established in 2000 in MD.
Donors: Bernice F. Israelson; Max R. Israelson†.
Foundation type: Independent foundation.
Financial data (yr. ended 06/30/13): Assets, $4,760,279 (M); expenditures, $221,543; qualifying distributions, $191,800; giving activities include $191,800 for 7 grants (high: $60,000; low: $1,800).
Fields of interest: Hospitals (general); Philanthropy/voluntarism; Jewish agencies & synagogues; Children.
Type of support: Capital campaigns.
Limitations: Applications not accepted. Giving primarily in FL, MD and NJ. No grants to individuals.
Application information: Unsolicited requests for funds not accepted.
Officers and Directors:* Stuart G. Israelson,* Pres. and Treas.; Wendy I. Carroll,* V.P.; Louis F. Friedman,* Secy.; Cynthia Israelson.
EIN: 522256896
Other changes: Thomas Carroll is no longer a director.

1381
Izzo Family Foundation

4853 Cordell Ave., Ste. P-6
Bethesda, MD 20814-7015

Established in 2008 in MD.
Donors: Anthony J. Izzo, Jr.; Genco Masonry, Inc.
Foundation type: Independent foundation.
Financial data (yr. ended 06/30/13): Assets, $1,825,972 (M); gifts received, $550,000; expenditures, $220,156; qualifying distributions, $216,500; giving activities include $216,500 for 11 grants (high: $150,000; low: $500).
Fields of interest: Education; Hospitals (general); Health care.
Limitations: Applications not accepted. Giving primarily in MD. No grants to individuals.
Application information: Contributes only to pre-selected organizations.
Directors: Anthony J. Izzo, Jr.; Anthony J. Izzo III; Mary Ann Richardson.
EIN: 260844190
Other changes: The grantmaker no longer lists a primary contact.

1382
Jehovah-Jireh Foundation, Inc.

c/o James F. Bosse
2605 Chapel Lake Dr., Unit 412
Gambrills, MD 21054-1689 (410) 960-2390
E-mail: jjirfdn@aol.com; Main URL: http://www.jehovahjirehministries.org
Grants List: http://www.jehovahjirehministries.org/projects.html

Established in 2001 in FL.
Donor: James F. Bosse.
Foundation type: Operating foundation.
Financial data (yr. ended 12/31/12): Assets, $1,653,804 (M); gifts received, $63,851; expenditures, $483,306; qualifying distributions, $483,306; giving activities include $295,000 for 5 grants (high: $75,000; low: $45,000).
Purpose and activities: Provides financial assistance to new Baptist churches world-wide.
Fields of interest: Protestant agencies & churches.
Limitations: Giving on a national and international basis. No grants to individuals.
Application information: Application form required.
Initial approach: Contact foundation for application form
Deadline(s): Dec. 15
Officers and Board Members:* James F. Bosse,* Pres.; **Robert Vallier, V.P.**; Rev. Robert Warnick,* Secy.; Rev. Craig Bennett; Rev. Chris Chadwick; Dr. Pat Creed; Dr. Daniel K. Hicks; Rev. Curtis King; Dr. Kevin E. Schaal; Rev. Jeff Sizemore; Rev. Rick Wilder.
EIN: 651104291
Other changes: Robert Vallier has replaced Rev. Daniel S. MacAvoy as V.P.

1383
The Kahlert Foundation, Inc.

5848 Pinebrook Farm Rd.
Sykesville, MD **21784-8679**
Contact: Greg W. Kahlert, Pres.

Established in 1996 in MD.
Donor: William E. Kahlert.
Foundation type: Independent foundation.
Financial data (yr. ended 06/30/13): Assets, $21,201,972 (M); gifts received, $16,496,636; expenditures, $1,294,372; qualifying distributions, $1,254,000; giving activities include $1,254,000 for 19 grants (high: $1,000,000; low: $1,000).
Fields of interest: Hospitals (general); Human services.
Limitations: Applications not accepted. Giving primarily in MD and VA. No grants to individuals.

Application information: Contributes only to pre-selected organizations.
Officers: Greg W. Kahlert, Pres.; Harold W. Walsh, V.P.; James D. Stone, Secy.; Robert F. Wilson, Treas.
Directors: Roberta Kahlert; Ronald F. Tutrone, Jr.
EIN: 521798711
Other changes: At the close of 2013, the fair market value of the grantmaker's assets was $21,201,972, a 393.3% increase over the 2012 value, $4,298,138. For the same period, the grantmaker paid grants of $1,254,000, a 523.9% increase over the 2012 disbursements, $201,000.

1384
The Kay Family Foundation, Inc.
(formerly L & S Foundation)
8720 Georgia Ave., Ste. 410
Silver Spring, MD 20910-3638 **(301) 589-8045**
Contact: Jack Kay

Established in 1976 in MD.
Donors: Jack Kay; Ina Kay†; Lauren Hawkins; Shelley Joan Kay.
Foundation type: Independent foundation.
Financial data (yr. ended 12/31/12): Assets, $7,811,731 (M); expenditures, $322,368; qualifying distributions, $307,740; giving activities include $307,740 for grants.
Fields of interest: Hospitals (general); Human services; Foundations (private grantmaking); Jewish federated giving programs; Jewish agencies & synagogues.
Limitations: Giving primarily in MD; some funding in New York, NY, and Washington, DC. No grants to individuals.
Application information:
Initial approach: Letter
Deadline(s): None
Officer: Lauren K. Pollin, V.P. and Secy.
EIN: 521045650

1385
Kentfields Foundation Inc.
c/o Philip J. Rauch
P.O. Box 437
Brooklandville, MD 21022-0437

Established in 1992 in MD.
Donors: Philip J. Rauch; Lynn H. Rauch.
Foundation type: Independent foundation.
Financial data (yr. ended 12/31/12): Assets, $1,386,514 (M); expenditures, $171,529; qualifying distributions, $171,050; giving activities include $171,050 for 7 grants (high: $100,000; low: $200).
Fields of interest: Arts; Education; Philanthropy/voluntarism.
Limitations: Applications not accepted. Giving primarily in MD. No grants to individuals.
Application information: Unsolicited requests for funds not accepted.
Officers: Lynn H. Rauch, Pres.; Philip J. Rauch, V.P.
EIN: 521841472

1386
The Kirk Family Foundation
P.O. Box 477
Ellicott City, MD **21041-0477**

Established in 2001 in MD.
Donor: Donald H. Kirk, Jr.
Foundation type: Independent foundation.
Financial data (yr. ended 12/31/12): Assets, $1,140,351 (M); gifts received, $200,000; expenditures, $182,068; qualifying distributions, $169,160; giving activities include $165,100 for 9 grants (high: $102,500; low: $250).
Fields of interest: Education; Human services.
Limitations: Applications not accepted. Giving primarily in MD. No grants to individuals.
Application information: Contributes only to pre-selected organizations.
Officers: Donald H. Kirk, Jr., Pres. and Treas.; Patricia M. Kirk, V.P. and Secy.
EIN: 522358200

1387
Lutheran Home and Hospital Foundation, Inc.
2571 Hanover Pike
Hampstead, MD 21074-1145 (410) 258-0398
***Contact:* Rev. Michael Dubsky, Exec. Dir.**
***E-mail:* dubsky@aol.com**

Donor: Catherine Stehman†.
Foundation type: Independent foundation.
Financial data (yr. ended 06/30/13): Assets, $2,086,755 (M); gifts received, $3,563; expenditures, $386,087; qualifying distributions, $366,360; giving activities include $364,177 for 18 grants (high: $150,000; low: $800).
Purpose and activities: Giving primarily for Lutheran and health organizations.
Fields of interest: Higher education, college (community/junior); Higher education, university; Health care, home services; Substance abuse, treatment; Youth, services; Protestant agencies & churches.
Limitations: Applications accepted. Giving limited to Baltimore, MD. No grants to individuals.
Application information:
Initial approach: Proposal
Deadline(s): None
Officers and Directors:* Pastor Robert Kretzschmar, Pres.; Claire Workneh, V.P.; Sue Fitzsimmons, Secy.; Gertrude Hinson,* Treas.; Rev. Michael Dubsky,* Exec. Dir.
EIN: 521081449
Other changes: The grantmaker no longer lists a separate application address.

1388
Morton and Sophia Macht Foundation, Inc.
15 E. Fayette St.
Baltimore, MD 21202-1606 (410) 539-2370
Contact: Amy Macht, Pres.

Established in 1956 in MD.
Donors: Philip Macht; Sophia Macht†; Westland Gardens Co.; Mallview; Queensgate Co.; Windsor; Automatic Service Corp.; Baltoland Inc.; Conwill Co.; Dahley Co.; Builders; Compression; Developers; Halldane; Macwell; Patience; Realsearch; Tracery; Transmaryland Co.; Huron Co.; Outpost; Raintree; Scholar; Stranden; Lodestone; Masterplan, Inc.; Northrail; Tensiltech Corp.; Walden Co.; Talltimber; Thunderwood Co.; Wolfwind; College Gardens; Elmcroft Co.; Welsh Construction; Gradient; Folcroft Co.; Cosmo Co.; Lawford Co.; Cedlair Corp.; Park Grove Realty Co.
Foundation type: Independent foundation.
Financial data (yr. ended 04/30/13): Assets, $1,303,647 (M); gifts received, $360,800; expenditures, $460,115; qualifying distributions, $451,898; giving activities include $411,389 for 63 grants (high: $268,652; low: $50).
Fields of interest: Arts; Higher education; Education; Environment; Human services; YM/YWCAs & YM/YWHAs; Children/youth, services.
Type of support: General/operating support; Continuing support; Annual campaigns; Capital campaigns; Equipment; Program development; Conferences/seminars; Publication; Seed money; Scholarship funds; Research.
Limitations: Applications accepted. Giving primarily in the metropolitan Baltimore, MD, area. No grants to individuals.
Application information: Application form required.
Initial approach: Proposal
Copies of proposal: 1
Deadline(s): None
Final notification: Letter
Officers and Trustees:* Amy Macht,* Pres.; Katherine Kelly Howard,* V.P. and Secy.; Jill Gansler,* V.P. and Treas.; Bette D. Cohen,* V.P.; William A. Goodhardt,* V.P.; George R. Grose,* V.P.; Peter Grose,* V.P.; Robert W. Mastropieri,* V.P.
EIN: 526035753
Other changes: Philip Macht is no longer a V.P.

1389
Mann-Paller Foundation, Inc.
5404 Falmouth Rd.
Bethesda, MD 20816-1841

Donors: Alan T. Paller; Marsha Paller.
Foundation type: Independent foundation.
Financial data (yr. ended 09/30/13): Assets, $4,611,941 (M); gifts received, $3,000,000; expenditures, $2,130,687; qualifying distributions, $2,130,000; giving activities include $2,130,000 for 3 grants (high: $2,000,000; low: $10,000).
Fields of interest: Performing arts, dance; Education; Foundations (community).
Limitations: Applications not accepted. Giving in Washington, DC. No grants to individuals.
Application information: Contributes only to pre-selected organizations.
Officers: Marsha Paller, Pres. and Treas.; Channing Paller, V.P.; Alan T. Paller, Secy.
EIN: 521316829
Other changes: At the close of 2013, the grantmaker paid grants of $2,130,000, a 868.2% increase over the 2012 disbursements, $220,000.

1390
The J. Willard and Alice S. Marriott Foundation
(formerly The J. Willard Marriott Foundation)
10400 Fernwood Rd., Dept. 52/925
Bethesda, MD 20817-1102
Contact: Anne Gunsteens, Exec. Dir.

Established in 1966 in DC.
Donors: J. Willard Marriott†; Alice S. Marriott†; J. Willard Marriott Charitable Annuity Trust.
Foundation type: Independent foundation.
Financial data (yr. ended 12/31/13): Assets, $630,758,193 (M); gifts received, $6,847,789; expenditures, $33,408,199; qualifying distributions, $30,724,962; giving activities include $29,827,002 for 246 grants (high: $5,203,099; low: $1,000).
Purpose and activities: Grants primarily to local, previously supported charities, and a few general scholarship funds.
Fields of interest: Arts; Education; Health care; Human services.

Limitations: Applications not accepted. Giving primarily in Washington, DC. No grants to individuals.
Application information: Contributes only to pre-selected organizations.
Board meeting date(s): Spring and Fall
Officers: Anne Gunsteens, Exec. Dir.; Amanda Farnum, Grants Mgr.; Angela Williams, Finance and Prog. Mgr.
Trustees: J. Willard Marriott, Jr.; Richard E. Marriott; Stephen Marriott.
Number of staff: 3 full-time professional; 3 part-time professional; 1 full-time support.
EIN: 526068678
Other changes: At the close of 2013, the grantmaker paid grants of $29,827,002, a 55.8% increase over the 2012 disbursements, $19,149,403.

1391
Maryland Home & Community Care Foundation
c/o Cavagna
3902 Dance Mill Rd.
Phoenix, MD 21131-2116
Contact: Linda J. Safran, Exec. Dir.

Established in MD.
Foundation type: Independent foundation.
Financial data (yr. ended 06/30/13): Assets, $1,193,182 (M); expenditures, $572,853; qualifying distributions, $550,079; giving activities include $530,000 for 2 grants (high: $265,000; low: $265,000).
Purpose and activities: The foundation is dedicated to improving the quality of life for those in need of health and supportive services at home and in the community, regardless of age, by providing grants to organizations in Maryland.
Fields of interest: Health care, support services; Health care, patient services; Health care, home services; Health care; Residential/custodial care.
Limitations: Applications not accepted. Giving primarily in MD. No grants for general operating costs.
Application information: Contributes only to pre-selected organizations.
Officers: Joseph F. Cavagna, Pres. and Secy.; Jeffrey L. Friedman, Esq., Treas.
Trustees: Esther Bonnet; Lynda Burton, Sc.D.; Neetu Dhawan-Gray; Stanley A. Levi; Kantahyanee Murray; Edyth H. Schoenrich, M.D.
EIN: 521574346
Other changes: Joseph F. Cavagna is now Pres. and Secy.

1392
The Lyn P. Meyerhoff Foundation, Inc.
1 South St., Ste. 1000
Baltimore, MD 21202-7301 (410) 727-3200
Contact: Misty Gibson
FAX: (410) 625-1075; E-mail: info@magnajm.com; **Additional email: misty@magnajm.com**; Main URL: http://www.meyerhoffcharitablefunds.org

Established in 1989 in MD.
Donor: Lenore P. Meyerhoff†.
Foundation type: Independent foundation.
Financial data (yr. ended 12/31/12): Assets, $5,208,034 (M); expenditures, $293,070; qualifying distributions, $209,664; giving activities include $196,237 for 12 grants (high: $100,000; low: $500).
Fields of interest: Education; Human services; Jewish agencies & synagogues.
Type of support: General/operating support.
Limitations: Applications accepted. Giving primarily in MD and New York, NY. No grants to individuals.
Application information: See foundation web site for application guidelines. Application form required.
Initial approach: Letter
Deadline(s): None
Officers: Joseph Meyerhoff II, Pres.; Lee M. Hendler, V.P.; Jill M. Hieronimus, Secy.; Terry M. Rubenstein, Treas.
EIN: 521624876

1393
The Joseph Meyerhoff Fund, Inc.
1 South St., Ste. 1000
Baltimore, MD 21202-7301
***Contact:* Terry Rubenstein, V.P. and Secy.**
E-mail: info@magnajm.com; **Additional contact: Misty Gibson, Grants Admin.**; Main URL: http://www.meyerhoffcharitablefunds.org/

Incorporated in 1953 in MD.
Donors: Joseph Meyerhoff†; Mrs. Joseph Meyerhoff†; Meyerhoff Charitable Income Trust; Katz Charitable Income Trust; Meyerhoff Charitable Income Trust II; Katz Charitable Income Trust II; Rebecca Meyerhoff Memorial Trusts; The Rebecca Meyerhoff Philanthropic Fund.
Foundation type: Independent foundation.
Financial data (yr. ended 12/31/12): Assets, $70,215,246 (M); expenditures, $3,772,350; qualifying distributions, $3,016,395; giving activities include $2,902,609 for 97 grants (high: $350,000; low: $1,000).
Purpose and activities: Giving primarily to support and encourage cultural and higher educational programs and institutions and to facilitate immigration and absorption of new immigrants into Israel.
Fields of interest: Arts; Higher education; Human services; Jewish federated giving programs; Jewish agencies & synagogues; Immigrants/refugees.
International interests: Israel.
Type of support: General/operating support; Continuing support; Annual campaigns; Capital campaigns; Building/renovation; Equipment; Land acquisition; Endowments; Debt reduction; Emergency funds; Program development; Professorships; Publication; Seed money; Fellowships; Scholarship funds; Research; Matching/challenge support.
Limitations: Applications not accepted. Giving primarily in Baltimore, MD, and New York, NY; some funding also to organizations in Israel. No grants to individuals.
Application information: Contributes only to pre-selected organizations.
Board meeting date(s): May and Oct.
Officer: Jill M. Hieronimus, Pres.; Terry M. Rubenstein, V.P. and Secy.; Joseph Meyerhoff II, V.P. and Treas.; Eleanor Katz, V.P.
Number of staff: 1 part-time professional; 1 part-time support.
EIN: 526035997

1394
Middendorf Foundation, Inc.
2 E. Read St., 5th Fl.
Baltimore, MD 21202-2470
Contact: Laura A. Holter, Grants Admin.

Incorporated in 1953 in MD.
Donors: J. William Middendorf, Jr.†; Alice C. Middendorf†.
Foundation type: Independent foundation.
Financial data (yr. ended 03/31/13): Assets, $33,339,838 (M); expenditures, $1,554,255; qualifying distributions, $1,280,490; giving activities include $1,182,300 for 26 grants (high: $200,000; low: $1,000).
Purpose and activities: Giving primarily for higher education, particularly to scholarship funds, and for community and social services.
Fields of interest: Museums (art); Higher education; Education; Environmental education; Human services.
Type of support: General/operating support; Capital campaigns; Building/renovation; Endowments; Professorships; Matching/challenge support.
Limitations: Applications accepted. Giving primarily in MD, with emphasis on Baltimore; some giving also in Charlottesville, VA. No support for political organizations, or for programs. No grants to individuals, or for annual funds.
Application information: Application form not required.
Initial approach: Letter
Copies of proposal: 1
Deadline(s): None
Board meeting date(s): Quarterly (Apr., July, Sept. and Dec.)
Final notification: 2 weeks for acknowledgement, 1 week after trustee meetings for determination
Officers and Trustees:* Craig Lewis,* Pres.; Forrest F. Bramble, Jr., Esq.*, V.P.; **Sealy H. Hopkinson,* Secy.**; Benjamin F. Lucas II, Esq.*, Treas.; Phillips Hathaway; Linda W. McCleary; Theresa N. Knell.
Number of staff: 2 part-time professional.
EIN: 526048944
Other changes: Sealy H. Hopkinson has replaced Theresa N. Knell as Secy.

1395
Mid-Shore Community Foundation, Inc.
102 E. Dover St.
Easton, MD 21601-3002 (410) 820-8175
Contact: W. W. "Buck" Duncan, Pres.
FAX: (410) 820-8729; E-mail: info@mscf.org; Additional e-mail: wduncan@mscf.org; Main URL: http://www.mscf.org
Facebook: http://www.facebook.com/pages/Mid-Shore-Community-Foundation/175044307692

Established in 1992 in MD.
Foundation type: Community foundation.
Financial data (yr. ended 06/30/12): Assets, $41,109,757 (M); gifts received, $4,252,576; expenditures, $2,141,791; giving activities include $1,072,286 for 70+ grants (high: $115,734), and $9,164 for 17 grants to individuals.
Purpose and activities: The foundation connects private resources with public needs to enhance the quality of life for the citizens of Caroline, Dorchester, Kent, Queen Anne's and Talbot counties, MD.
Fields of interest: Arts; Education; Environment; Animals/wildlife; Health care; Youth development; Human services; Community/economic development.
Type of support: General/operating support; Management development/capacity building; Capital campaigns; Building/renovation; Equipment; Land acquisition; Emergency funds; Program development; Seed money; Curriculum development; Scholarship funds; Employee matching gifts; In-kind gifts; Matching/challenge support.

Limitations: Applications accepted. Giving limited to the mid-shore and eastern-shore areas of MD (Caroline, Dorchester, Kent, Queen Anne, and Talbot counties). No support for veterans groups or fraternal organizations. No grants to individuals (except for scholarships), or for fundraisers, conferences, public relations, publications, or for multi-year commitments.
Publications: Application guidelines; Annual report; Financial statement; Informational brochure; Newsletter.
Application information: Visit foundation web site for application form and guidelines. Application form required.
Initial approach: Submit application form and attachments
Copies of proposal: 1
Deadline(s): Apr. 1 and Oct. 1
Board meeting date(s): Mar., June, Sept., and Dec.
Final notification: June 30 and Dec. 30
Officers and Directors:* W. Moorhead Vermilye,* Chair.; **John Dillon,* Vice-Chair.**; W.W. Duncan,* Pres.; **Brett Summers,* Secy.**; **David Nagel,* Treas.**; Heather D. Moore,* C.F.O.; E. Jean Anthony; Joseph M. Anthony; Dick Barker; Scott Beatty; William B. Boyd; Elizabeth Brice; Art Cecil; Mickey Elsberg; Mark Freestate; Wayne Howard; Lynn Knight; Neil Lecompte; John Lewis; Sandy McAllister; John McGinnis; Alice Ryan; Win Trice; Barbara A. Viniar; Hubert Wright.
Number of staff: 2 full-time professional; 1 full-time support.
EIN: 521782373
Other changes: John Dillon is now Vice-Chair. Brett Summers is now Secy. David Nagel is now Treas. Derick Daly, Keith A. McMahan, R. Michael S. Menzies, and Margaret K. Riehl are no longer directors.

1396
The Clement C. Moore II and Elizabeth W. Y. Moore Charitable Trust
P.O. Box 1058
Chestertown, MD 21620-5058 (410) 788-5225

Established in 2001 in DE.
Donor: Clement C. Moore II.
Foundation type: Independent foundation.
Financial data (yr. ended 06/30/13): Assets, $2,620,569 (M); expenditures, $227,187; qualifying distributions, $179,241; giving activities include $175,451 for 12 grants (high: $53,951; low: $3,000).
Fields of interest: Arts; Libraries (public); Education; Botanical/horticulture/landscape services; Veterinary medicine, hospital; Reproductive health, family planning; Food banks; Human services.
Limitations: Applications accepted. Giving primarily in NY.
Application information: Application form required.
***Initial approach:* Completed application form**
Deadline(s): None
Trustees: Clement C. Moore II; Elizabeth W. Moore.
EIN: 527059395

1397
The Morningstar Foundation
c/o Gelman, Rosenberg & Freedman
4550 Montgomery Ave., Ste. 650 N.
Bethesda, MD 20814-3250
Contact: Michael C. Gelman, V.P.
FAX: (301) 913-9042

Established in 1982 in DC and MD.
Donors: Michael C. Gelman; Susan R. Gelman; Richard Goldman 1997 Charitable Lead Annuity Trust; Susan R. Gelman Charitable Lead Trust; SSR Charitable Lead Annuity Trust 2004; Susan R. Gelman 2001 Trust; Richard and Rhoda Goldman Fund.
Foundation type: Independent foundation.
Financial data (yr. ended 12/31/12): Assets, $235,898,287 (M); gifts received, $136,704,812; expenditures, $9,208,026; qualifying distributions, $8,144,217; giving activities include $7,306,374 for 134 grants (high: $1,090,040; low: $300).
Fields of interest: Arts; Education; Environment; Human services; International peace/security; Jewish federated giving programs; Jewish agencies & synagogues.
International interests: Israel.
Type of support: General/operating support; Annual campaigns; Capital campaigns.
Limitations: Applications not accepted. Giving primarily in the greater Washington, DC, area and in Israel. No grants to individuals.
Application information: Contributes only to pre-selected organizations. Unsolicited requests for funds not accepted.
Board meeting date(s): Quarterly
Officers: Susan R. Gelman, Pres.; Michael C. Gelman, V.P.; George P. Levendis, Esq., Secy.-Treas.
Number of staff: 1 part-time support.
EIN: 521270464
Other changes: At the close of 2012, the fair market value of the grantmaker's assets was $235,898,287, a 142.1% increase over the 2010 value, $97,419,707. For the same period, the grantmaker paid grants of $7,306,374, a 56.5% increase over the 2010 disbursements, $4,667,418.

1398
Mpala Wildlife Foundation, Inc.
P.O. Box 137
Riderwood, MD 21139-0137 **(410) 244-7507**
***Contact:* Kay Berney**
***E-mail for Kay Berney:* kberney@mpala.org;**
Tel.: (410) 889-0194; Main URL: http://www.mpala.org
E-Newsletter: http://www.mpala.org/Get_our_Newsletter.php

Established in 1989 in MD; funded in 1990.
Donors: George L. Small‡; Princeton University; Smithsonian Institute.
Foundation type: Operating foundation.
Financial data (yr. ended 12/31/12): Assets, $10,862,190 (M); gifts received, $300,609; expenditures, $326,625; qualifying distributions, $617,361; giving activities include $222,546 for 2 grants (high: $202,546; low: $20,000).
Purpose and activities: Giving primarily to a wildlife sanctuary and preserve, and operation of a scientific research center, as well as for the operation of a mobile clinic.
Fields of interest: Animals/wildlife, preservation/protection.
International interests: Kenya.
Limitations: Applications not accepted. Giving primarily in Nanyuki, Kenya. No grants to individuals.
Application information: Contributes only to pre-selected organizations.
Trustees: William S. Eisenhart, Jr., Tr. Emeritus; Giles Davies; Howard Ende; Jeffrey K. Gonya; Laurel Harvey; Dennis Keller; Dr. Ira Rubinoff; **Paul Rudy**; John Wreford-Smith.
EIN: 521656147

Other changes: Robert King is no longer a trustee.

1399
The Murthynayak Foundation, Inc.
(formerly The Murthy Foundation, Inc.)
11 Cool Spring Ct.
Lutherville, MD 21093-3529
***E-mail:* info@murthynayak.org**; Main URL: http://www.murthynayak.org/
Blog: http://www.murthynayak.org/?cat=81

Established in 2001 in MD.
Donors: Sheela Murthy; Murthy Law Firm.
Foundation type: Independent foundation.
Financial data (yr. ended 12/31/12): Assets, $5,936,777 (M); gifts received, $100,000; expenditures, $250,000; qualifying distributions, $250,000; giving activities include $250,000 for 9 grants (high: $175,000; low: $5,000).
Fields of interest: Human services; United Ways and Federated Giving Programs.
Limitations: Applications not accepted. Giving primarily in Washington, DC, and Baltimore, MD. No grants to individuals.
Application information: Unsolicited requests for funds not accepted.
Officers: Sheela Murthy, Pres.; Vasant Nayak, V.P.
Trustees: Kenneth B. Coehlo; Srinivas Murthy; Joseph E. Pollak.
EIN: 800016494

1400
Mustard Seed Foundation
7101 Wisconsin Ave., Ste. 1011
Bethesda, MD 20814-4805

Established in 1986 in DC and MD.
Donor: Sandra P. Spedden.
Foundation type: Independent foundation.
Financial data (yr. ended 11/30/13): Assets, $850,205 (M); gifts received, $75,224; expenditures, $208,390; qualifying distributions, $186,400; giving activities include $172,150 for 32 grants (high: $25,000; low: $150).
Purpose and activities: Giving primarily for Christian organizations.
Fields of interest: Education; Human services; Religion, formal/general education; Christian agencies & churches.
Limitations: Applications not accepted. Giving primarily in MD. No grants to individuals.
Application information: Unsolicited requests for funds not accepted.
Officers: Sandra P. Spedden, Pres.; Yvonne Alexander Matthews, V.P.; John C. Hendricks, Secy.; Joann Knauer, Treas.
Directors: Ralph Scott; Blake Wise.
EIN: 521492276
Other changes: Elva Eareckson is no longer a member of the governing body.

1401
NASDAQ OMX Group Educational Foundation, Inc.
(formerly The Nasdaq Stock Marked Educational Foundation, Inc.)
805 King Farm Blvd.
Rockville, MD **20850** (800) 842-0356
E-mail: foundation@nasdaqomx.com; Main URL: http://www.nasdaqomx.com/services/initiatives/educationalfoundation

Established in 1993 in MD and DE.
Donor: The Nasdaq Stock Market, Inc.
Foundation type: Company-sponsored foundation.
Financial data (yr. ended 12/31/12): Assets, $27,463,287 (M); expenditures, $4,679,411; qualifying distributions, $4,309,768; giving activities include $4,309,768 for 41 grants (high: $500,000; low: $7,900).
Purpose and activities: The foundation supports programs designed to promote capital formation, financial markets, and entrepreneurship through education and awards fellowships to individuals for the purpose of conducting independent academic study or research on financial markets.
Fields of interest: Elementary/secondary education; Higher education; Education; Disasters, preparedness/services; Human services, financial counseling; Community/economic development; Economics.
Type of support: Continuing support; Program development; Curriculum development; Fellowships; Research.
Limitations: Applications accepted. Giving primarily in CA, CT, Washington, DC, IN, MD, MN, NY, NC, and TX. No support for discriminatory organizations.
Publications: Application guidelines; Grants list.
Application information: Letters of inquiry should be no longer than one page. Grant seekers may be invited to submit a full proposal at a later date. Ph.D. dissertation fellowships are granted in a set amount of $15,000. Application form not required.
Initial approach: E-mail or mail letter of inquiry
***Deadline(s):* Feb. 3 and Aug. 1**
***Final notification:* Mar. 1 and Oct. 1**
Officers and Directors:* Robert Greifeld,* Chair.; **Joan C. Conley, Secy. and Managing Dir.**; Peter Strandell, Treas.; **Bruce E. Aust**; H. Furlong Baldwin; Marc Baum; John J. Lucchese.
EIN: 521864429
Other changes: Bruce E. Aust is now Exec. V.P. Eric W. Noll is no longer a director. Joan C. Conley is now Secy. and Managing Dir.

1402
Northern Kenya Fund
c/o Bunting Mgmt. Group
217 International Cir.
Hunt Valley, MD 21030-1332
***E-mail:* chris@northernkenyafund.org**; Main URL: http://www.northernkenyafund.org
Facebook: https://www.facebook.com/pages/Northern-Kenya-Fund/204405872933612

Donors: Christopher L. Bunting; Mary Catherine Bunting; George L. Bunting, Jr.; Anne R. Bunting; Arthur B. Schultz Foundation; Judith Needham; Marc Bunting; Mary Ellen Kranzlin; Samuel P. Pardoe Foundation; The Bunting Family Foundation; Travis Jordan; Karen Jordan; Dorothy B. Duffy; Joseph J. Duffy, Jr.
Foundation type: Independent foundation.
Financial data (yr. ended 12/31/12): Assets, $67,581 (M); gifts received, $107,532; expenditures, $156,044; qualifying distributions, $156,044; giving activities include $154,500 for 6 grants (high: $80,000; low: $5,000).
Purpose and activities: Scholarship awards paid directly to the college for deserving and high-achieving students of Marsabit, Kenya, who have completed primary school but do not have the financial means to attend secondary school.
Fields of interest: Higher education.
Limitations: Applications not accepted. Giving primarily in Nairobi, Kenya. No grants to individuals.
Application information: Unsolicited requests for funds not accepted.
Officers and Directors:* Christopher L. Bunting,* Pres.; Rebekah S. Bunting,* Secy.-Treas.; Deb Kmon Davidson.
EIN: 743196803
Other changes: Rebekah S. Bunting has replaced Judith Needham as Secy.-Treas.
Christopher L. Bunting is now Pres.

1403
The Osprey Foundation
1 Olympic Pl., 8th Fl.
Towson, MD 21204-4104

Established in 2002 in MD.
Donors: William C. Clark III; Mrs. William C. Clarke III.
Foundation type: Independent foundation.
Financial data (yr. ended 12/31/12): Assets, $46,629,854 (M); gifts received, $845,000; expenditures, $3,833,993; qualifying distributions, $3,527,464; giving activities include $3,527,464 for 43 grants (high: $307,500; low: $5,000).
Purpose and activities: Giving primarily for health organizations, children, youth and social services, and to Presbyterian organizations.
Fields of interest: Health organizations; Disasters, Hurricane Katrina; Human services; Children/youth, services; Protestant agencies & churches.
Type of support: General/operating support; Scholarship funds.
Limitations: Applications not accepted. Giving in the U.S., with some emphasis on MD, particularly Baltimore. No grants to individuals.
Application information: Contributes only to pre-selected organizations.
Officers: William C. Clarke III, Pres.; Bonnie A. Clarke, Secy.-Treas.
Directors: Jesse Clarke; Steven W. Clarke; Christopher Powell; Meredith Powell; Christopher Wells; Lindsey B. Wells.
EIN: 141862154
Other changes: The grantmaker has changed its fiscal year-end from June 30 to Dec. 31.

1404
Clarence Manger & Audrey Cordero Plitt Trust
c/o Natalie Stengel
25 S. Charles St., MD2-CS51
Baltimore, MD 21203-1596
Application address: c/o Mary Anne Kirgan, 968 Bellview Rd., McLean, VA 22102, tel.: (410) 244-4630

Established in 1979 in MD.
Donor: Clarence M. Plitt†.
Foundation type: Independent foundation.
Financial data (yr. ended 08/31/13): Assets, $13,229,577 (M); expenditures, $662,390; qualifying distributions, $576,500; giving activities include $451,000 for 1 grant.
Fields of interest: Education.
Type of support: Program-related investments/loans; Matching/challenge support; Student loans—to individuals.
Limitations: Applications accepted. Giving primarily in MA.
Publications: Annual report.
Application information: Application form required.
Initial approach: Letter
Copies of proposal: 2
Deadline(s): May 31
Managers: Mary Anne Kirgan; Robert S. Kirgan.
Trustee: M&T Bank, N.A.
Number of staff: 1 full-time professional.
EIN: 526195778

1405
Howard and Geraldine Polinger Family Foundation
(formerly Howard and Geraldine Polinger Foundation)
5530 Wisconsin Ave., Ste. 1000
Chevy Chase, MD 20815-4330
Contact: Lorre Polinger, Pres.
E-mail: info@polingerfoundation.org; Tel./fax: (617) 964-6199; Main URL: http://foundationcenter.org/grantmaker/polinger/

Incorporated in 1968 in MD.
Donors: Howard Polinger†; Geraldine Polinger; Geraldine Polinger Family Trust.
Foundation type: Independent foundation.
Financial data (yr. ended 06/30/13): Assets, $41,414,540 (M); expenditures, $2,105,405; qualifying distributions, $1,919,875; giving activities include $1,626,000 for 58 grants (high: $150,000; low: $1,000).
Purpose and activities: Giving primarily to foster Jewish identity, showcase Jewish arts and culture, build and strengthen Jewish life in emerging communities, specifically the in spurring Jewish identity in Central and Eastern Europe and the Former Soviet Union, combat anti-Semitism, and help people in need. Funding also for the cultivation of the performing arts, and enhancing the well-being of families.
Fields of interest: Performing arts; Youth development; Family services; Jewish federated giving programs; Jewish agencies & synagogues.
International interests: Israel.
Type of support: General/operating support; Continuing support; Program development; Curriculum development; Matching/challenge support.
Limitations: Giving primarily in the Washington, DC, and Montgomery County, MD, area. No grants to individuals. Requests for capital and endowment grants are not normally accepted.
Publications: Grants list; Newsletter.
Application information: Unsolicited applications are not accepted. The foundation prefers to take the initiative to develop projects in conjunction with organizations that are in accord with its mission and funding priorities. Only brief e-mails are accepted if applicant feels their program or project would be a good fit with the foundation's funding priorities.
***Initial approach:* Brief e-mail**
Board meeting date(s): Spring and fall
Officers and Directors:* Lorre Beth Polinger,* Pres.; Arnold Lee Polinger,* V.P., Fin.; Jan Polinger,* V.P., Grants; **Erica Pressman, Secy.**; David Marc Polinger,* Treas.; Geraldine H. Polinger.
Number of staff: 3 part-time professional.
EIN: 526078041
Other changes: Erica Pressman has replaced Margaret Siegel as Secy.

1406
The RCM & D Foundation
555 Fairmount Ave.
Towson, MD 21286-5417 (410) 339-7263
Contact: Albert R. Counselman

Established in 1999 in MD.

Donors: Riggs Conselman Michaels & Downes, Inc.; L. Patrick Deering; Charles C. Counselman; Catherine R. Counselman.
Foundation type: Independent foundation.
Financial data (yr. ended 03/31/13): Assets, $3,373,998 (M); gifts received, $50,000; expenditures, $183,805; qualifying distributions, $155,460; giving activities include $155,460 for 41 grants (high: $13,610; low: $50).
Fields of interest: Performing arts, orchestras; Arts; Higher education; Education; Aquariums; Hospitals (general); Cancer; United Ways and Federated Giving Programs; Catholic agencies & churches.
Limitations: Applications accepted. Giving primarily in Baltimore, MD.
Application information: Application form required.
Initial approach: Letter
Deadline(s): None
Officers and Directors:* Albert R. Counselman,* Chair. and Pres.; Thomas P. Healy,* V.P.; J. Kevin Carnell, Secy.; Price Poore, Treas.; Margaret K. Counselman.
EIN: 522204935
Other changes: Francis G. Riggs is no longer a director.

1407
Rembrandt Foundation, Inc.
(formerly Constellation Energy Group Foundation, Inc.)
c/o Community Partnerships
100 Constellation Way, Ste. 1800
Baltimore, MD 21202-6302
Contact: Ashley Freeman
FAX: (410) 470-4098;
E-mail: exeloncorporatecontributions@exeloncorp.com
E2 Energy to Educate Grants List: http://www.constellation.com/documents/2013_grant_winners.pdf
EcoStar Grants List: http://www.constellation.com/Documents/2012%20Final%20EcoStar%20Awardee%20List.pdf

Established in 1986 in MD.
Donors: Baltimore Gas and Electric Co.; Constellation Energy Group, Inc.
Foundation type: Company-sponsored foundation.
Financial data (yr. ended 12/13/12): Assets, $24,331,164 (M); expenditures, $4,430,747; qualifying distributions, $4,400,438; giving activities include $4,400,438 for grants.
Purpose and activities: The foundation supports organizations involved with education, energy assistance, the environment, and economic growth.
Fields of interest: Higher education; Education; Environment, pollution control; Environment, natural resources; Environment, land resources; Environmental education; Environment; Housing/shelter, development; Recreation, parks/playgrounds; Athletics/sports, golf; Youth development, business; Children/youth, services; Economic development; United Ways and Federated Giving Programs; Mathematics; Engineering/technology; Youth; Economically disadvantaged.
Type of support: Employee volunteer services; General/operating support; Continuing support; Capital campaigns; Building/renovation; Program development; Conferences/seminars; Scholarship funds; Employee matching gifts; Matching/challenge support.
Limitations: Applications not accepted. Giving primarily in areas of company operations, with emphasis on DE, KY, central MD, NJ, NY, PA, TX,. No support for churches not of direct benefit to the entire community, organizations actively opposing Constellation's position on issues, individual schools, or sports teams. No grants to individuals, or for general operating or program development support for United Way agencies, start-up needs, or hospital capital campaigns.
Application information: The foundation is in the process of transitioning into new giving guidelines.
Board meeting date(s): June and Oct.
Officers and Directors:* Mayo A. Shattuck II,* Chair. and Pres.; C. A. Berardesco,* V.P. and Secy.; S. M Ulrich, V.P.; James L. Connaughton.
Number of staff: None.
EIN: 521452037
Other changes: The grantmaker no longer lists a URL address.
The grantmaker no longer publishes application guidelines.

1408
Frederick W. Richmond Foundation, Inc.
31 S. Harrison St.
Easton, MD 21601-3020 (410) 820-7676

Incorporated in 1962 in NY.
Donor: Frederick W. Richmond.
Foundation type: Independent foundation.
Financial data (yr. ended 06/30/13): Assets, $4,961,321 (M); expenditures, $216,367; qualifying distributions, $206,569; giving activities include $200,065 for 57 grants (high: $25,000; low: $250).
Purpose and activities: The foundation is interested in funding pilot projects, primarily in the arts, education, health, and the environment.
Fields of interest: Arts; Education; Environment.
Type of support: Annual campaigns; Capital campaigns; Building/renovation; Program development; Professorships; Seed money; Fellowships; Scholarship funds.
Limitations: Applications accepted. Giving primarily in Talbot County, MD; some giving also in NY. No support for non-exempt organizations. No grants to individuals.
Publications: Program policy statement.
Application information: Application form not required.
Initial approach: Proposal
Deadline(s): None
Board meeting date(s): Aug.
Officers: Timothy E. Wyman, Chair. and Treas.; Elizabeth Wyman, V.P.; James L. Myers, Secy.; Erin Geyelin, Exec. Dir.
Director: Karin W. Morgan.
Number of staff: 1 part-time professional.
EIN: 136124582
Other changes: The grantmaker no longer lists a primary contact.

1409
The Henry and Ruth Blaustein Rosenberg Foundation, Inc.
1 South St., Ste. 2900
Baltimore, MD **21202-3334** (410) 347-7201
Contact: Henry A. Rosenberg, Jr., Pres.
FAX: (410) 347-7210; E-mail: info@blaufund.org; Main URL: http://www.blaufund.org/foundations/henryandruth_f.html

Incorporated in 1959 in MD.
Donors: Ruth Blaustein Rosenberg†; Henry A. Rosenberg, Jr.; Ruth R. Marder; Judith R. Hoffberger; American Trading and Production Corp.; Rosemore, Inc.
Foundation type: Independent foundation.
Financial data (yr. ended 12/31/12): Assets, $26,285,041 (M); gifts received, $100,000; expenditures, $1,654,128; qualifying distributions, $1,508,529; giving activities include $1,354,750 for 80 grants (high: $85,000; low: $1,500).
Purpose and activities: The mission of the foundation is to improve the human condition through promoting life-long educational opportunities, research advances and a spectrum of cultural programming.
Fields of interest: Arts; Higher education; Adult education—literacy, basic skills & GED; Education; Health care; Employment, services; Youth development, adult & child programs; Jewish federated giving programs.
Type of support: General/operating support; Annual campaigns; Capital campaigns; Building/renovation; Matching/challenge support.
Limitations: Giving primarily in the greater Baltimore, MD, area. No support for unaffiliated schools. No grants to individuals, or for fundraising events, direct mail solicitations; no loans.
Publications: Application guidelines; Grants list.
Application information: The foundation does not accept unsolicited proposals for health research. Complete application guidelines available on foundation web site; Association of Baltimore Area Grantmakers Common Grant Application Form accepted. Application form not required.
Initial approach: Letter
Copies of proposal: 1
Deadline(s): None
Board meeting date(s): Semiannually
Final notification: 4 to 6 months
Officers and Trustees:* Henry A. Rosenberg, Jr.,* Pres.; Judith R. Hoffberger,* V.P.; Ruth R. Marder,* V.P.; Robert A. Delp, Treas.; Betsy F. Ringel, Exec. Dir.
EIN: 526038384

1410
The Aaron Straus & Lillie Straus Foundation, Inc.
2 E. Read St., Ste. 100
Baltimore, MD 21202-6912 (410) 539-8308
Contact: Jan Rivitz, Exec. Dir.
FAX: (410) 837-7711;
E-mail: info@strausfoundation.org; Main URL: http://www.strausfoundation.org

Established in 1926 in MD.
Foundation type: Independent foundation.
Financial data (yr. ended 12/31/12): Assets, $63,409,106 (M); expenditures, $3,972,585; qualifying distributions, $3,217,012; giving activities include $2,791,230 for 80 grants (high: $600,000; low: $36).
Purpose and activities: Giving primarily for Jewish community services; families, children, and youth; building infrastructure in the non-profit sector; and alternative grantmaking.
Fields of interest: Arts; Education, public policy; Human services; Children, services; Family services; United Ways and Federated Giving Programs; Public policy, research; Jewish agencies & synagogues.
Type of support: General/operating support; Income development; Annual campaigns; Capital campaigns; Building/renovation; Program development; Seed money; Scholarship funds; Technical assistance; Consulting services; Program evaluation.
Limitations: Applications accepted. Giving primarily in Baltimore, MD. No grants to individuals, or for endowments.

Publications: Application guidelines; Informational brochure; Program policy statement (including application guidelines).
Application information: Association of Baltimore Area Grantmakers Common Grant Application Format required. This form is available on the foundation's web site. Unsolicited applications not accepted for Arts and Culture. Application form required.
Initial approach: Proposal
Copies of proposal: 1
Deadline(s): Feb. 1, July 1, and Oct. 1
Final notification: 8-10 weeks
Officers: Jan Rivitz, Pres. and Treas.; Lee E. Coplan, V.P. and Secy.; Terry Underberg, Secy.
Directors: Jane Abraham; Stephen H. Abraham; **Charles Baum**; Samuel Himmelrich; Susan Leviton.
Number of staff: 1 full-time professional.
EIN: 522040073

1411
Leonard and Helen R. Stulman Charitable Foundation, Inc.
2 E. Read St., 9th Fl.
Baltimore, MD **21202-6903**
Contact: Shale D. Stiller, Pres.; Laurie Baker Crosley, Dir., Philanthropic Svcs.; Cathy Brill, Exec. Dir.
E-mail: lcrosley@bcf.org; E-mail for Cathy Brill: cbrill@bcf.org

Established in 1986 in MD.
Donor: Leonard Stulman‡.
Foundation type: Independent foundation.
Financial data (yr. ended 12/31/12): Assets, $70,557,014 (M); expenditures, $2,521,870; qualifying distributions, $2,163,112; giving activities include $1,976,158 for 27 grants (high: $547,318; low: $5,500).
Purpose and activities: Supports programs in research and treatment for mental illness, aging and health care in MD.
Fields of interest: Mental health, treatment; Mental health, schizophrenia; Mental health, association; Civil/human rights, aging; Gerontology; Children; Adults; Aging; Mentally disabled; Economically disadvantaged.
Type of support: Matching/challenge support; General/operating support.
Limitations: Applications accepted. Giving primarily in Baltimore, MD. No support for organizations that further religious doctrine. No grants to individuals, or for debt retirement, membership campaigns, public primary and secondary education, or conferences/seminars.
Application information: See Web site of Baltimore Community Foundation for application guidelines, procedures, and application deadlines. Association of Baltimore Area Grantmakers Common Grant Application Format accepted. Application form not required.
Initial approach: Letter of inquiry
Copies of proposal: 1
Deadline(s): Rolling
Board meeting date(s): Varies
Final notification: 3 to 6 months
Officers: Shale D. Stiller, Pres.; Frank T. Gray, V.P. and Secy.; Walter D. Pinkard, Jr., Treas.
Number of staff: None.
EIN: 521491609

1412
The Laszlo N. Tauber Family Foundation
6000 Exec. Blvd., Ste. 600
North Bethesda, MD 20852-3818
E-mail: info@tauberfoundation.com; **Additional address: 12 Moshe Hess St., Jerusalem, Israel Email: office@tauberfoundation.org.il**; Main URL: http://www.tauberfoundation.org/page1/about.html
Grants List: http://www.tauberfoundation.org/page3/grants.html

Established in 2004 in MD.
Donor: Laszlo N. Tauber‡.
Foundation type: Independent foundation.
Financial data (yr. ended 12/31/12): Assets, $150,310,339 (M); gifts received, $1,928,435; expenditures, $9,867,971; qualifying distributions, $8,126,884; giving activities include $7,215,780 for 65 grants (high: $67,000; low: $1,000).
Purpose and activities: The foundation is committed to philanthropy in four major areas: education, biomedical research, services to persons with psychosocial and psychiatric disabilities, and social welfare. 1) Educational grants support scholarships and innovative academic programs; 2) biomedical research projects focus on the regulation and organization of complex biological systems; 3) services for persons with psychosocial disabilities include innovative rehabilitation programs and clinical research; 4) social welfare programs encompass a wide array of support for the economically under-privileged. Grants in each area are awarded to institutions of the United States and Israeli affiliates.
Fields of interest: Elementary/secondary education; Mental health/crisis services, research; Mental health, disorders; Medical research; Human services; Jewish agencies & synagogues; Mentally disabled; Economically disadvantaged.
Limitations: Applications not accepted. Giving primarily in Baltimore, MD. No grants to individuals.
Application information: Contributes only to pre-selected organizations.
Officers and Directors:* Ingrid D. Tauber,* Pres.; Alfred I. Tauber,* Secy.-Treas.; **Jay Grossman, Cont.**
Number of staff: 2 full-time professional.
EIN: 300208793

1413
Town Creek Foundation, Inc.
121 N. West St.
Easton, MD 21601-2709 (410) 763-8171
Contact: Stuart A. Clarke, Exec. Dir.
FAX: (410) 763-8172;
E-mail: info@towncreekfdn.org; Main URL: http://www.towncreekfdn.org

Established in 1981 in MD.
Donor: Edmund A. Stanley, Jr.‡.
Foundation type: Independent foundation.
Financial data (yr. ended 12/31/13): Assets, $46,350,512 (M); expenditures, $7,102,104; qualifying distributions, $6,828,328; giving activities include $6,373,500 for 81 grants (high: $300,000; low: $10,000).
Purpose and activities: The foundation supports programs that engage citizens in challenging and reversing the unsustainable use of natural resources and in protecting biological diversity. Strategies supported are grassroots activism, monitoring the enforcement of environmental laws, public policy advocacy, collaborative opportunities, media outreach, and model or demonstration projects fostering sustainable policies and practices. The foundation has restructured its focus to have a more in depth and targeted approach to restoring the Chesapeake Bay and transitioning Maryland to a low carbon economy. In order to attain this mission, the foundation has three programmatic focuses: Chesapeake Bay, Climate Change, and Sustainability.
Fields of interest: Environment, climate change/global warming; Environment, natural resources; Environment.
Type of support: General/operating support; Continuing support; Program development; Seed money; Matching/challenge support.
Limitations: Applications accepted. Giving primarily in the Mid Atlantic region. No support for primary or secondary schools, hospitals, healthcare institutions, or religious organizations. No support for colleges or universities except when some aspect of their work is an integral part of a program supported by the foundation, or for government organizations. No grants to individuals, or for endowment, capital, or building fund campaigns, purchase of land or buildings, research, scholarship programs, conferences, the publication of books or periodicals, or visual or performing arts projects.
Publications: Application guidelines; Grants list.
Application information: All applications must be submitted online, via foundation web site. Full proposals accepted by invitation only. Application guidelines available on foundation web site. Application form required.
Initial approach: Letter of inquiry
Deadline(s): See foundation web site for current deadlines
***Board meeting date(s):* Spring and summer**
Officers and Directors:* Jennifer Stanley,* Pres.; Lisa A. Stanley,* V.P.; Philip E.L. Dietz, Jr.,* Treas.; Stuart A. Clarke, Exec. Dir.; Donald Boesch, Ph.D.; Betsy Taylor.
Number of staff: 3 full-time professional; 1 part-time support.
EIN: 521227030

1414
The Jim and Carol Trawick Foundation
7979 Old Georgetown Rd., 10th Fl.
Bethesda, MD 20814-2429 (301) 654-7030
FAX: (301) 654-7032; Main URL: http://www.trawick.org/
Grants Database: http://www.trawick.org/grants-search

Established in 2005 in MD.
Donors: Carol Trawick; James Trawick; Class Act Arts; Teamup Team of Stars; Howard & Geraldine Polinger Family Foundation; Montgomery County Dept. of Recreation; HSC Health Care Foundation; Casey Family Programs.
Foundation type: Independent foundation.
Financial data (yr. ended 12/31/12): Assets, $7,525,745 (M); gifts received, $378,318; expenditures, $1,284,069; qualifying distributions, $1,094,608; giving activities include $820,379 for 79 grants (high: $50,000; low: $10).
Purpose and activities: The foundation assists local health and human service and arts nonprofit organizations in Montgomery County, Maryland. Giving also for specific projects that will make a demonstrable impact on the local community by reaching people in need and encouraging and sustaining creative activities.
Fields of interest: Arts; Health care; Human services.
Limitations: Giving limited to Montgomery County, MD. No grants to individuals, or for debt reduction, fundraising, general operating support, capital campaigns, endowment funds, or special events.

Publications: Grants list.
Application information: See foundation web site for full application guidelines and requirements. Applications submitted by fax, e-mail or hand delivery are not accepted.
Officers and Directors:* Carol Trawick,* Pres.; Robby Brewer; Gail Nachman.
EIN: 203932082

1415
Marcia Brady Tucker Foundation, Inc.

P.O. Box 1149
Easton, MD 21601-8922

Incorporated in 1941 in NY.
Donor: Marcia Brady Tucker†.
Foundation type: Independent foundation.
Financial data (yr. ended 12/31/12): Assets, $9,827,909 (M); expenditures, $658,286; qualifying distributions, $522,839; giving activities include $391,518 for 160 grants (high: $20,000; low: $100).
Purpose and activities: Giving primarily for the arts, education, the environment, social services, and religious institutions.
Fields of interest: Museums; Arts; Higher education; Environment; Human services; Residential/custodial care, hospices; Christian agencies & churches; Jewish agencies & synagogues; Religion.
Type of support: General/operating support; Annual campaigns; Capital campaigns; Building/renovation; Endowments; Program development; Seed money; Matching/challenge support.
Limitations: Applications not accepted. Giving primarily in CA, CO, MD, NY, and OH. No grants to individuals.
Application information: Unsolicited requests for funds not accepted.
Officers: Marcia B. Loughran, Pres.; Barbara Bartlett, V.P.; Emily Tucker, Secy.; David Randell, Jr., Treas.
Directors: Marcia Boogaard; Thomas Boogaard; Naomi Gerwin; Cam Sanders; Elizabeth Sanders; Elizabeth Stoehr; Ben Tucker; Noah Tucker; Toinette Tucker.
Number of staff: 1 part-time support.
EIN: 136161561
Other changes: The grantmaker no longer lists a URL address.

1416
The Harry and Jeanette Weinberg Foundation, Inc.

7 Park Center Ct.
Owings Mills, MD 21117-4200 (410) 654-8500
***Contact:* Craig Demchak, Dir., Marketing and Communications**
***For Hawaii operations correspondence:* 3660 Waialae Ave., Ste. 400, Honolulu, HI 96816-3260, tel.: (808) 924-1000, fax: (808) 922-3975**; Main URL: http://www.hjweinbergfoundation.org
Annual Reports and Grants Summaries: http://hjweinbergfoundation.org/publications/annual-reports/
E-Newsletter: http://hjweinbergfoundation.org/publications/e-newsletters/e-newsletter-sign-up/
Facebook: http://www.facebook.com/pages/The-Harry-and-Jeanette-Weinberg-Foundation-Inc/169299436473114
Get to Know: http://hjweinbergfoundation.org/wp-content/uploads/downloads/2013/12/Get-to-Know.pdf
Grantee Perception Report: http://hjweinbergfoundation.org/publications/what-we-have-learned/
Twitter: https://twitter.com/hjweinbergfdn
YouTube: http://www.youtube.com/user/HJWeinbergFoundation

Incorporated in 1959 in MD.
Donors: Harry Weinberg†; and various companies.
Foundation type: Independent foundation.
Financial data (yr. ended 02/28/13): Assets, $2,046,251,873 (M); expenditures, $116,914,158; qualifying distributions, $99,430,204; giving activities include $95,928,547 for 756 grants (high: $3,000,000; low: $100), and $504,512 for 1 foundation-administered program.
Purpose and activities: Support for programs and direct services (including general operating grants) and capital projects that assist low-income and vulnerable individuals and families primarily located in Maryland, Hawaii, Northeastern Pennsylvania, Israel and the Former Soviet Union.
Fields of interest: Education; Health care; Food services; Housing/shelter; Human services; Aging, centers/services; Aging; Disabilities, people with; Economically disadvantaged.
International interests: Israel; Soviet Union.
Type of support: Program development; Building/renovation; Capital campaigns; Equipment; General/operating support; Matching/challenge support.
Limitations: Applications accepted. **Giving nationally, primarily in MD, HI, Northeastern PA, NY, and internationally within Israel and the Former Soviet Union.** No support for political organizations, colleges, universities, think tanks, or for arts organizations. No grants to individuals, or for deficit financing, annual giving, publications or for scholarships.
Application information: Unsolicited full proposals will not be accepted. The foundation will invite appropriate proposals following submission of Letter of Inquiry. Guidelines for LOI and invited proposals available on foundation website.
Application form not required. Application form not required.
Initial approach: Complete Letter of Inquiry after reviewing funding guidelines
Copies of proposal: 1
Deadline(s): Rolling basis
***Board meeting date(s):* Weekly**
***Final notification:* The foundation will confirm receipt of each LOI within 30 days. Within 60 days, the grant application will receive notification either that the LOI was declined or that the applicant is invited to submit a full grant proposal.**
Officers and Trustees:* Ellen M. Heller,* Chair.; **Rachel Garbow Monroe,* C.E.O. and Pres.; Alvin Awaya,* V.P.; Barry I. Schloss,* Treas.; Jonathan D. Hook, C.I.O.**; Robert T. Kelly, Jr.; **Donn Weinberg.**
Number of staff: 26
EIN: 526037034
Other changes: The grantmaker no longer lists an E-mail address.
Alvin Awaya is now V.P. Rachel Garbow Monroe is now C.E.O. and Pres. John F. Lingenfelter is no longer V.P., Finance. Joel Winegarden is no longer Corp. Off. Barry I. Schloss is now Treas.

1417
Wolpoff Family Foundation

9841 Washingtonian Blvd., Ste. 410
Gaithersburg, MD **20878-7339 (301) 917-2350**
***FAX:* (301) 917-2398;**
E-mail: info@wolpoff-familyfoundation.org; Application address: c/o Suzanne Oliwa, 5002 Dalton Rd., Chevy Chase, MD 20815, tel.: (240) 888-3563; Main URL: http://www.wolpoff-familyfoundation.org/

Foundation type: Independent foundation.
Financial data (yr. ended 10/31/12): Assets, $9,257,272 (M); expenditures, $465,177; qualifying distributions, $414,777; giving activities include $310,000 for 14 grants (high: $65,000; low: $2,000).
Fields of interest: Education; Hospitals (general); Cancer; Residential/custodial care, hospices; Jewish federated giving programs.
Limitations: Giving primarily in Washington, DC, MD and MA.
Publications: Application guidelines.
Application information: After letter of inquiry grant applications are extended by invitation only. Complete application guidelines available on foundation web site.
***Initial approach:* Letter of inquiry**
Officers: Harry K. Wolpoff, Pres.; Carol Wolpoff, Secy.; Suzanne Oliwa, EXec. Dir.
EIN: 261419703
Other changes: The grantmaker now publishes application guidelines.

1418
Wright Family Foundation

14626 Thornton Mill Rd.
Sparks, MD 21152-9633 (410) 472-3398
Contact: Mari Beth C. Moulton, Assoc. Exec. Dir. - Baltimore; Secondary Contact: Katherine B. Wright, Exec. Dir.
FAX: (410) 472-3394;
E-mail: mcmoulton@wrightfamilyfdn.org**; Additional e-mail: info@wrightfamilyfdn.org**; Main URL: http://www.wrightfamilyfdn.org

Established in 2000 in MD.
Donors: Vernon H.C. Wright; Lucy B. Wright.
Foundation type: Independent foundation.
Financial data (yr. ended 12/31/12): Assets, $15,928,565 (M); expenditures, $1,114,152; qualifying distributions, $911,792; giving activities include $911,792 for 79 grants (high: $75,000; low: $250).
Purpose and activities: Giving primarily to organizations and programs that will help achieve the foundation's goals for education that fall within the following areas: in Austin, TX: K-12 education, out-of-school time, and teenage pregnancy; in Baltimore City, MD: early childhood education, K-5 education, and out-of-school time.
Fields of interest: Arts; Elementary/secondary education; Higher education; Youth development, services; Children/youth; Children; Youth; Economically disadvantaged.
Type of support: General/operating support; Program development; Curriculum development; Research; Matching/challenge support.
Limitations: Applications accepted. Giving limited to Baltimore City, MD, and Austin, TX. No support for political organizations. No grants to individuals.
Publications: Application guidelines; Financial statement; Grants list.
Application information: See foundation web site for specific application guidelines. Association of

Baltimore Area Grantmakers Common Grant Application Format accepted. Application form required.

Initial approach: Letter of inquiry
Copies of proposal: 1
***Deadline(s):* None, for Baltimore; Jan. 15 for Austin; Mar. 1 for proposals (if invited)**
Board meeting date(s): May, Sept., and Nov.
Final notification: Two weeks after board meeting

Officers: Katherine B. Wright, Exec. Dir., Austin, TX; **Mari Beth C. Moulton, Exec. Dir., Baltimore, MD.**
Number of staff: 1 full-time professional.
EIN: 522278319

1419
Zickler Family Foundation, Inc.
5630 Wisconsin Ave., Ste. 1405
Chevy Chase, MD **20815-4457**

Established in 2000 in MD.
Donors: Leo E. Zickler; Judy Zickler.
Foundation type: Independent foundation.
Financial data (yr. ended 12/31/12): Assets, $5,368,817 (M); expenditures, $383,660; qualifying distributions, $345,594; giving activities include $337,220 for 31 grants (high: $125,000; low: $250).
Fields of interest: Arts; Elementary/secondary education; Higher education; Education; Health care; Human services.
Type of support: General/operating support; Continuing support; Management development/ capacity building; Annual campaigns; Capital campaigns; Building/renovation; Endowments; Seed money; Curriculum development; Research; Matching/challenge support.
Limitations: Applications not accepted. Giving primarily in Washington, DC, MD and VA. No grants to individuals.
Application information: Contributes only to pre-selected organizations.
Officers: Leo E. Zickler, Chair.; Judith Zickler, Pres.
Number of staff: 1 part-time support.
EIN: 522283882

MASSACHUSETTS

1420
A Child Waits Foundation
1136 Barker Rd.
Pittsfield, MA 01201-8043 (413) 499-7859
E-mail: cnelson@achildwaits.org; Main URL: http://www.achildwaits.org

Established in 1998 in NY.
Donors: Cynthia Nelson; Randolph Nelson; Ira and Beth Leventhal Foundation; Dove Givings Foundation.
Foundation type: Operating foundation.
Financial data (yr. ended 12/31/12): Assets, $2,697,884 (M); gifts received, $114,196; expenditures, $441,606; qualifying distributions, $440,307; giving activities include $87,492 for 18 grants (high: $10,000; low: $26), and $228,241 for 63 grants to individuals (high: $9,090; low: $1,388).
Purpose and activities: Giving primarily to provide financial assistance to individuals adopting foreign-born children. Support for adoption, adoption funding, international adoption and child welfare and the child must meet special needs criteria, and adoptive family must meet financial criteria.
Fields of interest: Human services; Religion.
Type of support: Grants to individuals.
Limitations: Applications accepted. Giving on a national basis.
Application information: Application form required.
Initial approach: Letter
Copies of proposal: 1
Deadline(s): None
Board meeting date(s): Weekly
Officers: Cynthia Nelson, Pres.; Randolph Nelson, V.P.; Richard Cayne, Secy.
Number of staff: 2 full-time professional.
EIN: 133978652
Other changes: The grantmaker has moved from NY to MA.

1421
The Aaron Foundation
(formerly The Stop & Shop Charitable Foundation)
10 Possum Rd.
Weston, MA 02493-2318 (781) 899-4445
Contact: Avram J. Goldberg, Tr.

Trust established in 1951 in MA.
Donors: The Stop & Shop Cos., Inc.; The Stop & Shop Supermarket Co.; Avram J. Goldberg.
Foundation type: Independent foundation.
Financial data (yr. ended 12/31/13): Assets, $218,364 (M); expenditures, $2,923,461; qualifying distributions, $2,887,520; giving activities include $2,876,309 for 18 grants (high: $946,451; low: $3,083).
Purpose and activities: Giving primarily for education and to Jewish organizations.
Fields of interest: Higher education; Education; Human services; Youth, services; United Ways and Federated Giving Programs; Jewish federated giving programs; Jewish agencies & synagogues.
Limitations: Applications accepted. Giving primarily in San Francisco, CA, and MA. No grants to individuals.
Application information: Application form required.
Initial approach: Proposal
Copies of proposal: 1
Deadline(s): None
Trustees: Hope R. Edison; Avram J. Goldberg; Carol R. Goldberg; James M. Rabb; Jane M. Rabb; Betty R. Schafer.
Number of staff: 1 full-time professional; 2 full-time support.
EIN: 046039593
Other changes: At the close of 2013, the grantmaker paid grants of $2,876,309, a 404.6% increase over the 2011 disbursements, $570,000.

1422
Access Strategies Fund, Inc.
675 Massachusetts Ave., 8th Fl., Ste. B
Cambridge, MA 02139-3309 (617) 494-0715
Contact: Kelly Bates, Exec. Dir.
FAX: (617) 494-0718;
E-mail: info@accessstrategies.org; Toll-free tel.: (888) 920-1969; Main URL: http://www.accessstrategies.org
Access Strategies Fund's Philanthropy Promise: http://www.ncrp.org/philanthropys-promise/who
Civic Engagement Initiative Grant Awards: http://www.accessstrategies.org/funding/civic-engagement-fund-grant-recipients
Drawing Democracy Project Grant Awards: http://www.accessstrategies.org/funding/drawing-democracy-project-grant-partners
Economic Democracy Fund Grant Awards: http://www.accessstrategies.org/funding/economic-democracy-fund-grant-awards
Facebook: https://www.facebook.com/AccessStrategies
Movement Building Fund Grant Awards: http://www.accessstrategies.org/funding/movement-building-fund-grant-awards

Established in 1999 in DE.
Foundation type: Independent foundation.
Financial data (yr. ended 10/31/12): Assets, $7,785,544 (M); expenditures, $601,495; qualifying distributions, $530,161; giving activities include $159,418 for 16 grants (high: $25,000; low: $100).
Purpose and activities: Helps underserved communities in Massachusetts harness their collective power to access the democratic process to improve their lives.
Fields of interest: Disabilities, people with; Minorities; Asians/Pacific Islanders; African Americans/Blacks; Hispanics/Latinos; Native Americans/American Indians; Indigenous peoples; Women; Offenders/ex-offenders; Immigrants/refugees; Economically disadvantaged.
Type of support: General/operating support; Management development/capacity building; Program development; Seed money; Technical assistance.
Limitations: Applications accepted. Giving primarily in MA. No support for direct service programs or partisan programs, or for municipal, state, or federal agencies. No grants to individuals, or for scholarships or capital campaigns.
Publications: Application guidelines; Grants list; Newsletter.
Application information: After reviewing letters of inquiry, the foundation will seek proposals from only a limited number of organizations. Unsolicited full proposals are not accepted. See grantmaker web site for application policies and guidelines. Associated Grant Makers Common Proposal Form accepted. Application form required.
Initial approach: Call or 1-page letter of inquiry
Final notification: 2 to 3 months
Officers and Directors:* Maria Jobin-Leeds,* Chair.; John Bonifaz; Dayna Cunningham; Jeanette Huezo.
Number of staff: 2 full-time professional.
EIN: 043464581

1423
Frank W. & Carl S. Adams Memorial Fund
(formerly Charles E. & Caroline J. Adams Trust)
c/o US Trust, Bank of America, N.A.
225 Franklin St., 4th Fl., MA1-225-04-02
Boston, MA 02110-2800 (866) 778-6859
Contact: Miki C. Akimoto
***E-mail:* ma.grantmaking@ustrust.com**; Main URL: http://www.bankofamerica.com/grantmaking

Established in 1925 in MA.
Donors: Charles E. Adams‡; Caroline J. Adams‡.
Foundation type: Independent foundation.
Financial data (yr. ended 05/31/13): Assets, $14,174,292 (M); expenditures, $715,339; qualifying distributions, $637,089; giving activities include $590,000 for 19 grants (high: $147,500; low: $10,000).
Purpose and activities: Giving to support and promote quality educational, human services, and health care programming for underserved populations. Annual gifts are also awarded to the Harvard University Medical School and the Massachusetts Institute of Technology for student scholarships.
Type of support: General/operating support.
Limitations: Giving primarily in MA. No support for national organizations. No grants to individuals, or for conferences, film production, travel, research projects, or publications; no loans.
Application information: Complete application guidelines available at http://www.bankofamerica.com/grantmaking.
Initial approach: E-mail (Indicate foundation name in subject line)
Deadline(s): See foundation web site for current deadlines
Trustee: Bank of America, N.A.
EIN: 046011995

1424
Dr. Miriam and Sheldon G. Adelson Medical Research Foundation
300 1st Ave.
Needham, MA 02494-2736 (781) 972-5900
Contact: Marissa White
E-mail: info@adelsonfoundation.org; **Main URL: http://www.adelsonfoundation.org/amrfphil.html**

Established in 2006 in MA.
Donors: Sheldon G. Adelson; Dr. Miriam Adelson.
Foundation type: Independent foundation.
Financial data (yr. ended 12/31/12): Assets, $1,336,346 (M); gifts received, $24,940,727; expenditures, $24,013,584; qualifying distributions, $23,957,691; giving activities include $22,754,124 for 49 grants (high: $3,060,133; low: $145,080).
Purpose and activities: Giving primarily to foster collaboration in biomedical research in order to accelerate medical innovation and to facilitate commercialization of innovative medical products for the public good. The foundation is designed to encourage a model in which scientists from different institutions (referred to as Collaborating Scientists) come together to identify and conduct a synergetic group of research studies to answer a particular question (each individual study is referred to as a Component Project and the grouping is referred to as a Collaboration). The Collaborating Scientists

determine the sequence, timing, scope and direction of the Component Projects, and the foundation provides infrastructure and financial support to foster the Collaborations and to protect and commercialize resulting biomedical innovation. Currently, the foundation is focusing on collaborations in the areas of neurology, oncology, and immunology.
Fields of interest: Cancer research; Brain research; Biomedicine research; Neuroscience research; Medical research.
Limitations: Giving on a national basis.
Application information: Funding for collaborations within program areas only. Application form required.
Initial approach: Letter
Deadline(s): None
Officers: Kenneth H. Fasman, Ph.D., V.P. and C.T.O.; Steven Garfinkel, V.P. and General Counsel.
Trustees: Dr. Miriam Adelson; Sheldon G. Adelson.
EIN: 047023433

1425
John W. Alden Trust
c/o Bank of America, N.A.
225 Franklin St., 4th Fl.
Boston, MA 02110-2800 (866) 778-6859
Contact: Miki Akimoto, V.P.
FAX: (617) 542-7437;
E-mail: miki.akimoto@ustrust.com; **Grants Coordinator: Susan T. Monahan, tel.: (617) 951-1108, email: smonahan@rackemann.com**;
Main URL: http://www.cybergrants.com/alden
Grants List: http://www.cybergrants.com/alden/2009_final_grants.xls

Established in 1986 in MA.
Donor: Priscilla Alden†.
Foundation type: Independent foundation.
Financial data (yr. ended 09/30/13): Assets, $9,962,762 (M); expenditures, $475,400; qualifying distributions, $413,108; giving activities include $349,000 for grants.
Purpose and activities: Grant support directed toward organizations providing care and administering to the needs of children who are blind, retarded, disabled, or who are either mentally or physically ill, or to organizations engaged in medical and scientific research, directed toward the prevention or cure of diseases and disabilities particularly affecting children.
Fields of interest: Arts education; Child development, education; Hospitals (general); Medical research, institute; Children/youth, services; Child development, services; Disabilities, people with.
Type of support: Program development; Seed money; Research.
Limitations: Applications accepted. Giving limited to eastern MA. No grants to individuals.
Publications: Application guidelines.
Application information: Applications must be submitted online through the trust web site; AGM Common Proposal Form accepted. Application form not required.
Initial approach: Email
Deadline(s): Jan. 15, Apr. 15, July 15, and Oct. 15
Board meeting date(s): Feb., May, Aug., and Nov.
Final notification: Within 1 month
Trustees: Susan T. Monahan; William B. Tyler; Bank of America, N.A.
Number of staff: 1 part-time professional; 1 part-time support.
EIN: 222719727
Other changes: The grantmaker now makes its application guidelines available online.

1426
Arbella Insurance Group Charitable Foundation, Inc.
(formerly Arbella Charitable Foundation, Inc.)
101 Arch St., Ste. 1860
Boston, MA 02110-1118 (617) 769-3040
***Contact:* Beverly Tangvik, Dir. of Charitable Giving**
E-mail: charitable.foundation@arbella.com; **E-mail for BSO Bus Program: bsoschoolbus@arbella.com**;
Main URL: https://www.arbella.com/arbella-insurance/why-arbella/arbella-insurance-foundation

Established in 2004 in MA.
Donor: Arbella, Inc.
Foundation type: Company-sponsored foundation.
Financial data (yr. ended 12/31/12): Assets, $25,234,330 (M); expenditures, $2,573,403; qualifying distributions, $2,129,451; giving activities include $1,688,270 for 578 grants (high: $314,145; low: $20), and $441,181 for foundation-administered programs.
Purpose and activities: The foundation supports organizations involved with arts and culture, education, breast cancer, hunger, disaster relief, automotive safety, human services, community development, and veterans.
Fields of interest: Museums; Performing arts, orchestras; Arts; Education; Hospitals (general); Breast cancer; Food services; Food banks; Disasters, preparedness/services; Safety, automotive safety; Children/youth, services; Family services; Homeless, human services; Human services; Community/economic development; United Ways and Federated Giving Programs; Military/veterans' organizations.
Type of support: General/operating support; Continuing support; Program development; Scholarship funds; Employee volunteer services; Employee matching gifts.
Limitations: Applications not accepted. Giving primarily in areas of company operations, with emphasis on CT, NH, and MA. No grants to individuals.
Application information: Unsolicited applications are currently not accepted. The foundation is currently working with established partners. Visit website for BSO Bus Program.
Officers and Directors:* John F. Donohue,* Chair. and Pres.; Frances X. Bellotti,* Vice-Chair.; Gail Eagan, Sr. V.P. and Genl. Counsel; Beverly J. Tangvik, Secy. and Dir. of Charitable Giving; Christoper E. Hall, Treas.; Patricia B. Bailey; Thomas S. Carpenter; Anne DeFrancesco; Edmund J. Doherty; J. Robert Dowling; William H. DuMouchel; Andrea Gargiulo; David W. Hattman; Thomas R. Kiley; Jeannette M. Orsino.
EIN: 050613355

1427
Archibald Family Charitable Foundation
c/o Nutter McClennen & Fish LLP
155 Seaport Blvd.
Boston, MA **02210-2698**
***Application address:* c/o K&L Gates, Attn.: David W. Lewis, Jr., 1 Lincoln St., Boston, MA 02111-2950, tel.: (617) 261-3100**

Established in 1998 in MA.
Donor: Anne G. Archibald.
Foundation type: Independent foundation.
Financial data (yr. ended 03/31/13): Assets, $4,045,550 (M); expenditures, $203,970; qualifying distributions, $181,835; giving activities include $164,000 for 27 grants (high: $27,000; low: $500).
Purpose and activities: Giving primarily for education; some funding for conservation, animal and wildlife protection, and health and human services.
Fields of interest: Historic preservation/historical societies; Higher education; Education; Environment, natural resources; Animal welfare; Health care; Human services.
Type of support: General/operating support.
Limitations: Applications accepted. Giving primarily in MA. No grants to individuals.
Application information: Application form not required.
Initial approach: Proposal
Deadline(s): None
Trustees: John L.G. Archibald; Mary A. Poor; **Nutter McClennen & Fish LLP.**
EIN: 043417222

1428
Association for the Relief of Aged Women of New Bedford
432 County St.
New Bedford, MA 02740-5018

Established in 1866 in MA.
Donor: George D. Barnard Trust.
Foundation type: Operating foundation.
Financial data (yr. ended 03/31/13): Assets, $17,699,049 (M); gifts received, $265,210; expenditures, $1,014,387; qualifying distributions, $974,646; giving activities include $421,816 for 10 grants (high: $85,305; low: $4,500), and $349,693 for grants to individuals.
Purpose and activities: A private operating foundation; furnishes assistance to and promotes the welfare and relief of elderly women in New Bedford, Dartmouth, Fairhaven, and Acushnet, Massachusetts. Applicants for aid must be 60 years of age or older, have liquid assets of under $5,000, and live alone. Only women who have been residents of the above named towns for at least five years are eligible.
Fields of interest: Health care; Children, services; Family services; Aging; Women; Economically disadvantaged.
Type of support: Grants to individuals.
Limitations: Applications not accepted. Giving limited to residents of New Bedford, Dartmouth, Fairhaven, and Acushnet, MA.
Application information: Unsolicited requests for funds not accepted.
Board meeting date(s): 1st Mon. of each month
Officers and Directors:* Nancy Kurtz,* Pres.; **Roseanne O'Connell,* V.P.; Deborah Brooke, Clerk; Jo-Ann Beaulieu, Treas.**; Cheryl Randall-Mach, Exec. Dir.; **Shannon Bachman**; Elizabeth Brinkerhoff; Sandra Fogg; Gillian Harris; Hannah Lloyd; Lorraine Mello; **Emily Pinheiro**; Susan Rothschild; **Rosemary Saber**; Jean Silver; **Barbara Wackowski-Faria**; Gretchen Whipple; Lynn Wylde.
EIN: 046056367
Other changes: Deborah Brooke has replaced Roseanne O'Connell as Clerk. Jo-Ann Beaulieu has replaced Lynn Wylde as Treas.
Roseanne O'Connell is now V.P. Hope Atkinson, Sally Hand, Carol Munger, and Anne Webb are no longer directors.

1429
The Susan A. & Donald P. Babson Charitable Foundation
c/o GMA Foundations
77 Summer St., 8th Fl.
Boston, MA 02110-1006 (617) 391-3087
Contact: Michelle Jenney, Fdn. Admin.
FAX: (617) 523-8949;
E-mail: mjenney@gmafoundations.com; **Main URL: http://www.babsonfoundation.org**
Grants List: http://www.babsonfoundation.org/grants-awarded-2

Established in 1995 in MA.
Donor: Susan Babson†.
Foundation type: Independent foundation.
Financial data (yr. ended 12/31/12): Assets, $4,633,886 (M); expenditures, $265,710; qualifying distributions, $231,242; giving activities include $199,816 for 67 grants (high: $10,000; low: $1,000).
Purpose and activities: Giving primarily for the enrichment and empowerment of people of all ages around the world, so as to prevent exploitation, poverty, and injustice.
Fields of interest: Education; Youth development; Human services; Youth, services.
Type of support: General/operating support; Program development.
Publications: Application guidelines; Grants list.
Application information: Complete application information is available on foundation web site. Application form required.
Initial approach: Letter of Inquiry using online application form
Board meeting date(s): May and Oct.
Trustees: Averill Babson; Deborah E. Babson; James A. Babson; Katherine L. Babson, Jr.; Richard L. Babson; James R. Nichols.
EIN: 046782460

1430
Paul and Edith Babson Foundation
c/o GMA Foundations
77 Summer St., 8th Fl.
Boston, MA **02110 (617) 391-3088**
Contact: Betty Nichols, Prog. Off.; Daniel Roundy, Fdn. Asst.
E-mail: pebabson@gmafoundations.com; **Main URL: http://pebabsonfoundation.org/**
Grants List: http://pebabsonfoundation.org/grants/

Trust established in 1957 in MA.
Donor: Paul T. Babson†.
Foundation type: Independent foundation.
Financial data (yr. ended 12/31/12): Assets, $14,739,598 (M); expenditures, $624,446; qualifying distributions, $602,297; giving activities include $586,716 for 107 grants (high: $25,050; low: $1,000).
Purpose and activities: The competitive grant program focuses on providing opportunities for the people of Greater Boston, Massachusetts, through grants in four program areas: entrepreneurship and economic development, culture, education and leadership development, environment and community building, and health and social services.
Fields of interest: Arts; Education; Environment, beautification programs; Youth, services; Economic development; Community development, small businesses.
Type of support: General/operating support; Program development; Scholarship funds.
Limitations: Applications accepted. Giving limited to the greater Boston, MA, area as generally defined by Route 128. Communities touched by Route 128 will be included. No grants to individuals, or for individual scholarships, conferences, films, fundraising, or donor cultivations.
Publications: Application guidelines; Grants list; Program policy statement.
Application information: Application form required.
***Initial approach:* Use online application process on foundation web site**
***Deadline(s):* See foundation web site for current deadlines**
Board meeting date(s): Late May and early Dec.
Trustees: James A. Babson; Katherine L. Babson; James R. Nichols.
Number of staff: 1 part-time professional; 1 part-time support.
EIN: 046037891

1431
Lloyd G. Balfour Foundation
c/o US Trust, Bank of America, N.A.
225 Franklin St., 4th Fl.
Boston, MA 02110-2801 (866) 778-6859
Contact: Miki C. Akimoto, Market Dir.
***E-mail:* ma.grantmaking@ustrust.com; Main URL: https://www.bankofamerica.com/philanthropic/grantmaking.go**
Scholarship contact: Wendy Holt, Exec. Dir., Attleboro Scholarship Foundation, tel.: 1 (508) 226-4414

Established in 1973 in MA.
Donor: L.G. Balfour†.
Foundation type: Independent foundation.
Financial data (yr. ended 03/31/13): Assets, $106,987,027 (M); expenditures, $5,215,669; qualifying distributions, $4,624,919; giving activities include $4,239,030 for 60 grants (high: $398,000; low: $5,000).
Purpose and activities: Giving primarily for programs that provide access to education, especially those that promote college readiness, access, and success for underserved populations in New England. The foundation's other giving is to favored charities listed in Mr. Balfour's will, and organizations serving the community of Attleboro, Massachusetts, where giving is for general charitable purposes.
Fields of interest: Education.
Type of support: General/operating support; Program development.
Limitations: Giving primarily in New England, with emphasis on Attleboro, MA. No grants to individuals.
Publications: Application guidelines.
Application information: Online application at www.bankofamerica.com/grantmaking.
Initial approach: E-mail
Deadline(s): See foundation web site for current deadlines
Final notification: May/June for Attleboro-based organizations; ongoing for general education requests.
Trustee: Bank of America, N.A.
Number of staff: 5
EIN: 222751372

1432
Barakat, Inc.
552 Massachusetts Ave., Ste. 215
Cambridge, MA 02139-0039 (617) 876-3830
***Contact:* Angha Sirpurkar-Childress, Exec. Dir.**
FAX: (617) 876-3800;
E-mail: info@barakatworld.org; Main URL: http://barakatworld.org
Community Blog: http://barakatblog.blogspot.com/
Facebook: http://www.facebook.com/pages/Barakat-Inc/8728933924?ref=ts
Flickr: https://www.flickr.com/photos/barakatworld/
Twitter: http://twitter.com/barakatinc
YouTube: http://www.youtube.com/barakatinc

Donors: Yayla Tribal Rugs, Inc.; Cultural Survival.
Foundation type: Independent foundation.
Financial data (yr. ended 09/30/13): Assets, $353,753 (M); gifts received, $92,360; expenditures, $333,785; qualifying distributions, $332,839; giving activities include $156,252 for grants.
Purpose and activities: Giving primarily for education in South and Central Asia, with a focus on providing basic education, increasing access to higher education, and advancing literacy, especially for women and children.
Fields of interest: Education; Environment, research; Environment, water resources; Environment, land resources; Health organizations; Human services.
Limitations: Giving primarily in South and Central Asia.
Application information:
Initial approach: Proposal
Deadline(s): None
Officers: Ian Crowley, Pres.; Jennifer Z. Flanagan, V.P.; **Ike Syed, Secy.**; William Mor, Treas.; **Angha Sirpurkar-Childress, Exec. Dir.**
Directors: Thomas J. Barfield; Habibullah Karimi; **Bilal Paracha**; Christopher K. Walter.
EIN: 043493675
Other changes: Ike Syed has replaced Ian Crowley as Secy.
Edward A. Scribner is no longer Chair. Ian Crowley is now Pres. Peggy Simons and Thomas Simons are no longer directors.

1433
Barr Foundation
(formerly The Hostetter Foundation)
The Pilot House
Lewis Wharf
Boston, MA 02110 (617) 854-3500
Contact: Kerri Ann Hurley, Grants Mgr.
FAX: (617) 854-3501;
E-mail: info@barrfoundation.org; Main URL: http://www.barrfoundation.org
Grantee Perception Report: http://www.barrfoundation.org/news/barr-foundation-2007-grantee-perception-report/
Knowledge Center: http://www.barrfoundation.org/news/

Established in 1987 in MA.
Donors: Amos B. Hostetter, Jr.; Barbara W. Hostetter.
Foundation type: Independent foundation.
Financial data (yr. ended 12/31/12): Assets, $1,313,184,018 (M); gifts received, $10,001,820; expenditures, $77,756,048; qualifying distributions, $64,765,522; giving activities include $58,380,364 for 354 grants (high: $3,000,000).
Purpose and activities: The foundation's mission is guided by a vision of a vibrant, just, and sustainable world with hopeful futures for children. Its mission is to support gifted leaders and networked organizations working in Boston and beyond to enhance educational and economic opportunities, to achieve environmental sustainability, and to

create rich cultural experiences - all with particular attention to children and families living in poverty.
Fields of interest: Performing arts; Arts; Elementary/secondary education; Education, early childhood education; Elementary school/education; Education, services; Education; Environment, climate change/global warming; Environment, natural resources; Environment, land resources; Environment; Community/economic development; Children/youth; Children; Youth; Young adults; Minorities; Economically disadvantaged.
International interests: India; Ethiopia; Haiti.
Type of support: General/operating support; Management development/capacity building; Annual campaigns; Capital campaigns; Building/renovation; Land acquisition; Endowments; Emergency funds; Program development; Conferences/seminars; Fellowships; Research; Technical assistance; Consulting services; Program evaluation; Matching/challenge support.
Limitations: Giving primarily in the greater Boston, MA, area, and on an international basis in sub-Saharan Africa, Haiti and India. No grants to individuals, or for scholarships, lobbying or elective activity.
Application information: After completing an online inquiry form, staff review and follow up with only selected submissions. Grant applications are by invitation only.
Initial approach: **Online inquiry**
Board meeting date(s): Quarterly
Officers and Trustee:* Barbara W. Hostetter,* Chair.; James Canales,* Pres.; Amos B. Hostetter, Jr.
Number of staff: 11 full-time professional; 3 full-time support.
EIN: 046579815
Other changes: Patricia H. Brandes is no longer Exec. Dir. Barbara W. Hostetter is now Chair.

1434
The Allen H. and Selma W. Berkman Charitable Trust

c/o GMA Foundations
77 Summer St., 8th Fl.
Boston, MA 02110-1006
Contact: Amy Shorey

Established in 1972 in PA.
Donors: Allen H. Berkman†; Selma W. Berkman†.
Foundation type: Independent foundation.
Financial data (yr. ended 10/31/13): Assets, $17,335,266 (M); expenditures, $887,794; qualifying distributions, $819,373; giving activities include $747,000 for 31 grants (high: $200,000; low: $5,000).
Purpose and activities: Giving primarily to promote education, the arts, health and human services, social justice, and Judaism.
Fields of interest: Performing arts; Higher education; Human services; YM/YWCAs & YM/YWHAs; Children/youth, services; Civil/human rights; Jewish federated giving programs; Jewish agencies & synagogues.
Type of support: General/operating support; Capital campaigns; Building/renovation; Endowments; Emergency funds; Program development; Seed money; Fellowships; Scholarship funds; Research; Program-related investments/loans; Matching/challenge support.
Limitations: Applications not accepted. Giving primarily in NY, OH and PA. No support for private foundations. No grants to individuals.
Application information: Unsolicited requests for funds not accepted.
Board meeting date(s): Quarterly
Trustees: Barbara Berkman Ackerman; James S. Berkman; Richard L. Berkman; Helen Berkman Habbert; Susan Berkman Rahm.
EIN: 256144060

1435
Bilezikian Family Foundation, Inc.

231 Willow St.
Yarmouth Port, MA **02675-1744**

Established in MA.
Donors: Charles G. Bilezikian; Doreen Bilezikian.
Foundation type: Independent foundation.
Financial data (yr. ended 12/31/12): Assets, $19,735,280 (M); expenditures, $1,092,857; qualifying distributions, $929,094; giving activities include $929,094 for 51 grants (high: $100,000; low: $2,100).
Fields of interest: Education; Environment, water resources; Human services; Children/youth, services.
Limitations: Applications not accepted. Giving primarily in Boston and Cape Cod, MA.
Application information: Contributes only to pre-selected organizations.
Officers and Directors:* Doreen Bilezikian,* Pres.; Gregory C. Bilezikian,* V.P.; Jeffrey D. Bilezikian,* V.P.; Henry L. Murphy, Jr.,* Clerk; Charles G. Bilezikian,* Treas.
EIN: 043504021

1436
Blue Hills Bank Charitable Foundation Inc.

1196 River St.
Hyde Park, MA 02136-2906 (617) 360-6542
Contact: Richard L. Thompson, Dir.
***E-mail:* rthompson@bluehillsbank.com; Main URL: https://www.bluehillsbank.com/about/charitable-foundation/**

Donor: Blue Hills Bank.
Foundation type: Independent foundation.
Financial data (yr. ended 12/31/12): Assets, $3,714,297 (M); gifts received, $444,050; expenditures, $389,874; qualifying distributions, $384,837; giving activities include $292,544 for 102 grants (high: $42,750; low: $20).
Fields of interest: Education; Recreation; Youth development; Human services.
Limitations: Applications accepted. Giving primarily in MA.
Application information: See foundation web site for complete application guidelines. Application form required.
Initial approach: Proposal
***Deadline(s):* Feb. 1, May 1, Aug. 1, and Nov. 1**
***Board meeting date(s):* Mar., June, Sept., and Dec.**
***Final notification:* Mar. 31, June 30, Sept. 30 and Dec. 31**
Officers and Directors:* Janice Kenny,* Chair.; William M. Parent,* Pres.; Richard L. Thompson,* Clerk; Stephen McNulty,* Treas.; Karen Marryat; Karen O' Connell; Elain Piselli; Samuel L. Smith, Jr.
EIN: 274283786

1437
John W. Boynton Fund

c/o U.S. Trust, Bank of America, N.A.
225 Franklin St., 4th Fl.
Boston, MA 02110-2800 (866) 778-6859
Contact: Michealle Larkins, V.P.
E-mail: michealle.larkins@ustrust.com; **Main URL: https://www.bankofamerica.com/philanthropic/grantmaking.go**

Trust established in 1952 in MA.
Donor: Dora C. Boynton†.
Foundation type: Independent foundation.
Financial data (yr. ended 12/31/12): Assets, $3,772,545 (M); expenditures, $211,236; qualifying distributions, $182,105; giving activities include $168,350 for 16 grants (high: $21,000; low: $5,000).
Purpose and activities: Grants principally to organizations serving low-income elderly; special consideration also to the town of Athol, MA.
Fields of interest: Housing/shelter; Human services; Youth, services; Aging, centers/services; Aging; Economically disadvantaged.
Type of support: General/operating support; Continuing support; Building/renovation; Equipment; Program development; Seed money.
Limitations: Applications accepted. Giving limited to Athol and eastern MA. No grants to individuals, or for endowment funds, research, scholarships, fellowships, or matching gifts; no loans.
Publications: Application guidelines; Grants list.
Application information: Online application; complete application guidelines available on Fund web site.
Initial approach: Email
Trustee: Bank of America, N.A.
Number of staff: 2 part-time support.
EIN: 046036706

1438
Brabson Library & Educational Foundation

120 Sippewisset Rd.
Falmouth, MA 02540-1819
Contact: John Brabson, Pres.
***E-mail:* gatekeeper@brabsonfamilyfoundation.org**; Application address: c/o Elizabeth Feathers, V.P., 4649 Country Rd. 9, East Nassau, NY 12062, tel.: (812) 332-6507; Main URL: http://www.brabsonfamilyfoundation.org

Established in 1990 in FL.
Donors: George Brabson Trust; Evelyn Brabson Trust.
Foundation type: Independent foundation.
Financial data (yr. ended 06/30/13): Assets, $6,568,320 (M); gifts received, $398,189; expenditures, $376,760; qualifying distributions, $327,762; giving activities include $298,836 for 26 grants (high: $33,000; low: $500).
Fields of interest: Museums (science/technology); Performing arts, orchestras; Performing arts, opera; Education; Animals/wildlife; Children/youth; Children; Economically disadvantaged.
Type of support: General/operating support; Annual campaigns; Endowments; Seed money; Research.
Limitations: Applications accepted. Giving on a national basis. No support for religious or political organizations. No grants to individuals, or for food, housing, clothing, or medical support.
Publications: Application guidelines; Grants list; Occasional report; Program policy statement.
Application information: Application form required.
Copies of proposal: 1
Deadline(s): 2 weeks prior to annual meeting
Board meeting date(s): Apr.
Final notification: Varies
Officers: John Brabson, Pres.; Elizabeth Feathers, V.P.; Andrew Brabson, Treas.
Directors: Margaret Becker; Bennet Brabson; G. Dana Brabson, Jr.; Jessica Brabson; Steve Brabson.

Number of staff: None.
EIN: 593021777

1439
Brooks Family Foundation

(formerly Brooks Family Charitable Foundation)
20 Walnut St., Ste. 318
Wellesley, MA 02481-2104
***Contact:* Andrew P. Prague**

Established in 2001 in MA.
Donors: James E. Brooks; Mary C. Brooks‡.
Foundation type: Independent foundation.
Financial data (yr. ended 06/30/13): Assets, $10,128,044 (M); expenditures, $924,297; qualifying distributions, $825,500; giving activities include $825,500 for 94 grants (high: $255,000; low: $1,000).
Fields of interest: Arts; Higher education; Libraries (public); Community/economic development; United Ways and Federated Giving Programs.
Limitations: Applications not accepted. Giving primarily in ME and NY. No grants to individuals.
Application information: Contributes only to pre-selected organizations.
Trustee: Andrew P. Prague.
Advisory Committee: James E. Brooks; Cherie Wendelken.
EIN: 043582018
Other changes: At the close of 2013, the grantmaker paid grants of $825,500, a 166.7% increase over the 2012 disbursements, $309,500.

1440
Harold Brooks Foundation

c/o Bank of America, N.A.
225 Franklin St.
Boston, MA 02110-2804 (866) 778-6859
E-mail: ma.grantmaking@ustrust.com; **Main URL: https://www.bankofamerica.com/philanthropic/grantmaking.go**

Established in 1984 MA.
Donor: Harold Brooks‡.
Foundation type: Independent foundation.
Financial data (yr. ended 12/31/12): Assets, $9,460,561 (M); expenditures, $540,603; qualifying distributions, $494,817; giving activities include $467,500 for 27 grants (high: $50,000; low: $5,000).
Purpose and activities: The foundation provides assistance to causes and organizations that help the largest possible number of residents of Massachusetts' South Shore communities, especially those that support the basic human needs of South Shore residents. More specifically, the foundation supports: 1) Educational programs for all ages, including but not limited to academic access, educational enrichment, and remedial programming for children, youth, adults, and senior citizens that focus on preparing individuals to achieve while in school and beyond; 2) Health and Mental Health programming that: a) makes possible care or expands care in response to priority community health needs of residents of the South Shore, b) improves access to care (especially basic services) for traditionally underserved individuals, or c) prepares individuals to be independent and to assist themselves; and 3) Food, Agriculture, Nutrition and Housing and Shelter programs.
Fields of interest: Education; Health care; Mental health/crisis services; Agriculture/food; Housing/shelter; Human services.
Type of support: General/operating support; Program development.
Limitations: Giving limited to MA, with emphasis on the South Shore area including Abington, Braintree, Bridgewater, Brockton, Carver, Cohasset, Duxbury, Hanover, Hanson, Hingham, Holbrook, Hull, Marshfield, Norwell, Pembroke, Plymouth, Quincy, Randolph, Rockland, Scituate, Weymouth, and Whitman. No grants to individuals, or for general operating expenses or endowments.
Publications: Application guidelines.
Application information: Complete application guidelines available on foundation web site. Application form not required.
Initial approach: Letter
Copies of proposal: 1
Deadline(s): Apr. 1 and Oct. 1
Board meeting date(s): June and Dec.
Final notification: June 30 and Dec. 31
Trustees: Paul Taylor; Rev. M. James Workman; Bank of America Merrill Lynch.
EIN: 046043983

1441
Bruner Foundation Inc.

130 Prospect St.
Cambridge, MA 02139-1844 (617) 492-8404
Contact: Emily Axelrod, Exec. Dir.
***FAX:* (617) 876-4002**;
E-mail: info@brunerfoundation.org; Main URL: http://www.brunerfoundation.org

Incorporated in 1967 in NY.
Donors: Rudy Bruner‡; Martha Bruner‡.
Foundation type: Independent foundation.
Financial data (yr. ended 12/31/12): Assets, $5,817,153 (M); expenditures, $485,932; qualifying distributions, $288,695; giving activities include $288,695 for grants.
Purpose and activities: Support primarily for the Rudy Bruner Award for Excellence and evaluation of nonprofit service delivery.
Fields of interest: Visual arts, architecture; Arts; Urban/community development; Nonprofit management; Community/economic development.
Type of support: Conferences/seminars; Program development; Research.
Limitations: Applications accepted. Giving on a national basis within the lower 48 states only. No grants to individuals, or for general support, building or endowment funds, scholarships, or fellowships.
Publications: Application guidelines; Informational brochure (including application guidelines); Program policy statement.
Application information: The foundation is not currently making any new grants. See foundation web site for application guidelines, procedures, and publications for the Rudy Bruner Award. Application form required.
Initial approach: Letter
Copies of proposal: 1
Deadline(s): See Website
Board meeting date(s): As required
Officers: Joshua E. Bruner, Pres.; R. Simeon Bruner, Treas.; Emily Axelrod, Exec. Dir.
Number of staff: 1 part-time professional; 1 part-time support.
EIN: 136180803

1442
Cabot Family Charitable Trust

70 Federal St., 7th Fl.
Boston, MA 02110-1906 (617) 226-7505
Contact: Katherine S. McHugh, Exec. Dir.
FAX: (617) 451-1733;
E-mail: kmchugh@cabwel.com; Main URL: http://www.cabwel.com/cabot_family_charitable_trust_v3.htm

Trust established in 1942 in MA.
Donor: Godfrey L. Cabot‡.
Foundation type: Independent foundation.
Financial data (yr. ended 12/31/13): Assets, $44,176,821 (M); expenditures, $2,188,474; qualifying distributions, $2,021,424; giving activities include $1,705,000 for 78 grants (high: $40,000; low: $7,500).
Purpose and activities: Program includes a wide range of organizations and activities important in Boston, MA, as well as nonprofit programs that represent particular family interests.
Fields of interest: Arts; Education; Environment; Health care; Youth development; Human services; Public affairs; Infants/toddlers; Children/youth; Youth.
Type of support: General/operating support; Capital campaigns; Program development.
Limitations: Applications accepted. Giving primarily in Boston, MA. No support for religious institutions for sectarian purposes, or for fraternal organizations. No grants to individuals, or for research, event sponsorship, or matching gifts.
Publications: Application guidelines; Annual report; Annual report (including application guidelines).
Application information: Concept paper format available on foundation web site. Application form required.
Initial approach: Concept letter (3 pages) with Cabot Family Charitable Trust cover sheet
Copies of proposal: 1
Deadline(s): Feb. 1 and Sept. 1
Board meeting date(s): June and Dec.
Final notification: June and Dec.
Officer and Trustees:* John G.L. Cabot,* Chair.; Frank Bradley; Laura Cabot Carrigan; Mary Schneider Enriquez; Greenfield Sluder; Hendrika Sluder.
Number of staff: 1 part-time professional.
EIN: 046036446

1443
The Virginia Wellington Cabot Foundation

c/o Cabot-Wellington, LLC
70 Federal St., 7th Fl.
Boston, MA 02110-1906 **(617) 451-1855, ext. 204**
Contact: Joan M. Whelton, Exec. Dir.
FAX: (857) 239-9724; E-mail: Jowhelton@aol.com; Main URL: http://www.cabwel.com/v_w_cabot_foundation.htm

Established in 1992 in MA.
Donors: Thomas D. Cabot, Jr.; Thomas D. Cabot 1986 Conduit Trust; Thomas D. Cabot 1994 Charitable Lead Unitrust; Virginia W. Cabot Revocable Trust; Virginia W. Cabot 1996 Charitable Lead Unitrust.
Foundation type: Independent foundation.
Financial data (yr. ended 12/31/12): Assets, $34,165,591 (M); expenditures, $1,605,221; qualifying distributions, $1,465,142; giving activities include $1,063,801 for 119 grants (high: $60,000; low: $500).
Purpose and activities: The foundation grants program includes a wide range of organizations and activities that represent particular interests of family members.
Fields of interest: Arts; Higher education; Education; Environment; Youth development; Human services; Public affairs.

Type of support: General/operating support; Annual campaigns; Capital campaigns; Building/renovation; Endowments; Program development; Fellowships; Scholarship funds; Matching/challenge support.
Limitations: Giving in the U.S., primarily in MA and ME. No support for religious or political organizations. No grants for one-time events.
Publications: Application guidelines; Grants list.
Application information: Unsolicited applications are generally not accepted. All grant applications are sponsored by family members who initiate the process. Application form required.
Copies of proposal: 1
Deadline(s): Mar. 1, and Sept. 13
Board meeting date(s): Semiannually
Final notification: 1 week after meeting
Officers: Helen C. McCarthy, Chair.; Laura Cabot Carrigan, Secy.; James W. Cabot, Treas.; Joan M. Whelton, Exec. Dir.
Trustees: Linda C. Black; Sophie C. Black; Alexis Cabot; Amiel Cabot; Bradford W. Cabot; Elizabeth C. Cabot; Timothy Eiserle; Carole Ganz; Alexander McCarthy; Peter Myers.
EIN: 046728351
Other changes: Helen C. McCarthy has replaced Amanda Cabot as Chair. Laura Cabot Carrigan has replaced Louis W. Cabot as Secy. James W. Cabot has replaced Dr. Edmund B. Cabot as Treas. Jeremy Black, Emlen Cabot, Helen Cabot, Virginia Cabot, Kieran Fitzgerald, Michael Fitzgerald, and Diane Scanlon are no longer trustees.

1444
Calderwood Charitable Foundation
c/o Choate Hall & Stewart LLP
P.O. Box 961019
Boston, MA 02196-1019 **(617) 248-4760**

Established in 1968 in MA.
Donors: Stanford M. Calderwood; Stanford Calderwood Trust.
Foundation type: Independent foundation.
Financial data (yr. ended 12/31/12): Assets, $29,884,768 (M); expenditures, $5,911,812; qualifying distributions, $5,682,814; giving activities include $5,618,978 for 13 grants (high: $2,350,000; low: $1,000).
Purpose and activities: Giving for the performing arts, as well as to an artists' colony; funding also for higher education, and to an academic library.
Fields of interest: Museums (art); Performing arts, theater; Performing arts, orchestras; Performing arts, opera; Higher education; Libraries (academic/research); Hospitals (general).
Limitations: Applications not accepted. Giving primarily in MA, with emphasis on Boston, Chestnut Hill, and Wesley Hills; some funding also in NH, with emphasis on Greenfield and Peterborough. No grants to individuals.
Application information: Contributes only to pre-selected organizations.
Trustees: John M. Cornish; William A. Lowell.
EIN: 046186166

1445
The Cape Cod Foundation
(formerly The Community Foundation of Cape Cod)
259 Willow St.
P.O. Box 406
Yarmouthport, MA 02675-1762 (508) 790-3040
***Contact:* For grants: Kristin O'Malley, Exec. Dir.**
FAX: (508) 790-4069;
E-mail: info@capecodfoundation.org; Additional tel.: (800) 947-2322; Grant and scholarship inquiry e-mail: komalley@capecodfoundation.org; Main URL: http://www.capecodfoundation.org
E-Newsletter: http://www.capecodfoundation.org/index.php?module=FormExpress&func=display_form&form_id=3
Scholarship e-mail: **dbryan@capecodfoundation.org**

Established in 1989 in MA.
Foundation type: Community foundation.
Financial data (yr. ended 12/31/12): Assets, $40,793,851 (M); gifts received, $2,199,388; expenditures, $3,268,739; giving activities include $2,489,912 for grants.
Purpose and activities: The foundation seeks to improve community life on Cape Cod through philanthropy and grantmaking. One of the ways this mission is accomplished is by developing permanent and flexible endowment funds to help nonprofit organizations respond to the existing and emerging needs of the Cape. Therefore, the foundation's grantmaking program is broad; grants may be made in the areas of health, human services, the environment, education, the arts, and community development.
Fields of interest: Humanities; Arts; Education; Environment; Health care; Youth development, community service clubs; Youth, services; Human services; Economic development; Nonprofit management; Community/economic development; Economically disadvantaged.
Type of support: General/operating support; Continuing support; Management development/capacity building; Annual campaigns; Equipment; Land acquisition; Emergency funds; Conferences/seminars; Seed money; Scholarship funds; Technical assistance; Consulting services; Grants to individuals; Scholarships—to individuals; In-kind gifts; Matching/challenge support; Student loans—to individuals.
Limitations: Applications accepted. Giving limited to Barnstable County, MA. No grants for capital campaigns or improvements, endowment building, or monuments or memorials.
Publications: Application guidelines; Annual report; Informational brochure; Newsletter.
Application information: Visit foundation web site for application and guidelines per grant type. Faxed or e-mailed applications are not accepted. Associated Grant Makers Common Proposal Form accepted. Application form required.
Initial approach: Complete online application
Deadline(s): General Grant requested on a rolling basis; Oct. 1 for Strategic Focus Grants; varies for others
Board meeting date(s): Bimonthly; Grant Review meetings are held semiannually
Final notification: 6 to 8 weeks for General Grants; 2 to 3 months for Strategic Focus Grants; varies for others
Officers and Directors:* Eileen C. Miskell,* Chair. and Pres.; **Henry R. Holden,* Vice-Chair.**; James T. Hoeck,* Treas.; Kristin O'Malley,* Exec. Dir.; **Matthew J. Bresette,* Clerk**; Jake F. Brown II; Larry Capodilupo; **Elliott Carr**; Thomas Evans; Rev. Thomas M. Nelson; Jennifer S.D. Roberts; Myer R. Singer; Sidney H. Snow; Larry R. Thayer; Sheila Vanderhoef.
Number of staff: 4 full-time professional; 1 full-time support; 1 part-time support.
EIN: 510140462
Other changes: Henry R. Holden has replaced Eileen C. Miskell as Vice-Chair. Matthew J. Bresette has replaced Linda Zammer as Clerk. Maura K. White is now Off. Mgr. John D. OBrien and Christopher D. Wise are no longer directors.

1446
Alfred E. Chase Charity Foundation
c/o Bank of America, N.A.
225 Franklin St.
Boston, MA 02110
E-mail: ma.grantmaking@ustrust.com; Main URL: http://www.bankofamerica.com/grantmaking

Established in 1956 in MA.
Donor: Alfred E. Chase†.
Foundation type: Independent foundation.
Financial data (yr. ended 10/31/13): Assets, $8,785,725 (M); expenditures, $466,660; qualifying distributions, $416,518; giving activities include $370,000 for 18 grants (high: $80,000; low: $10,000).
Purpose and activities: The foundation was established in 1956 to support and promote quality educational, human services, and health care programming for underserved populations. Special consideration is given to charitable organizations that serve the people of the city of Lynn and the North Shore of Massachusetts.
Fields of interest: Education; Boys & girls clubs; Human services; Children/youth, services.
Type of support: General/operating support; Program development.
Limitations: Giving limited to MA, with special consideration for Lynn and North Shore areas. No grants to individuals, or for research, scholarships, or fellowships; no loans.
Publications: Application guidelines.
Application information: Online application; complete guidelines available on foundation web site.
Initial approach: E-mail
***Deadline(s):* Mar. 1**
Trustee: Bank of America, N.A.
EIN: 046026314

1447
Child Relief International Foundation
(formerly The Andrew and Bonnie Weiss Foundation)
58 Commonwealth Ave.
Boston, MA 02116-3003 (617) 262-0071
Contact: Andrew Weiss, Tr.

Established in 2004 in MA.
Donors: Andrew Weiss; Bonnie Weiss.
Foundation type: Independent foundation.
Financial data (yr. ended 12/31/12): Assets, $35,294,384 (M); gifts received, $7,355,723; expenditures, $1,886,999; qualifying distributions, $2,923,801; giving activities include $1,823,801 for 17 grants (high: $1,000,000; low: $500).
Fields of interest: Health care; Children, services; Jewish agencies & synagogues.
Limitations: Applications accepted. Giving primarily in MA and NY.
Application information:
Initial approach: Letter
Deadline(s): None
Trustees: Andrew M. Weiss; Bonnie K. Weiss.
EIN: 206391910
Other changes: At the close of 2012, the grantmaker paid grants of $1,823,801, a 58.1% increase over the 2011 disbursements, $1,153,872.

1448
The John Clarke Trust
c/o US Trust, Bank of America, N.A.
225 Franklin St., MA1-225-04-02
Boston, MA 02110-2804
Contact: Emma Greene, Market Dir.; Charles Tickner
E-mail: ma.ri.grantmaking@ustrust.com; **Main URL: https://www.bankofamerica.com/philanthropic/grantmaking.go**

Established in 1676 in Rhode Island.
Donor: John Clark†.
Foundation type: Independent foundation.
Financial data (yr. ended 12/31/12): Assets, $8,942,404 (M); expenditures, $509,334; qualifying distributions, $490,408; giving activities include $465,785 for 73 grants (high: $20,000; low: $2,000).
Purpose and activities: Giving primarily for education and to provide relief to people who are economically disadvantaged.
Fields of interest: Higher education; Education; Health care, clinics/centers; Human services; Children/youth, services; Community/economic development.
Type of support: General/operating support; Equipment; Program development; Curriculum development; Scholarship funds; Matching/challenge support.
Limitations: Applications accepted. Giving primarily in The trustees have established a policy of giving preference to organizations located on Aquidneck Island, RI, and within the East Bay area. However, applications from any RI 501(c)(3) are acceptable. The trustees will consider capital grant requests ONLY from Aquidneck Island.
Application information:
Initial approach: Online
Deadline(s): Apr. 1 and Nov. 1
Trustees: William W. Corcoran, Esq.; Barbara N. Watterson; Bank of America, N.A.
EIN: 056006062

1449
Clipper Ship Foundation, Inc.
c/o GMA Foundations
77 Summer St., 8th Fl.
Boston, MA 02110-1006 (617) 426-7080
Contact: Katy Fyrberg, Fdn. Asst.
FAX: (617) 426-7087;
E-mail: kfyrberg@gmafoundations.com; Tel. for Katy Fyrberg: (617) 391-3094; **Main URL: http://clippershipfoundation.org/**
Grants List: http://clippershipfoundation.org/previous-grants/

Established in 1979 in MA.
Donor: David Parmely Weatherhead†.
Foundation type: Independent foundation.
Financial data (yr. ended 10/31/12): Assets, $25,024,838 (M); expenditures, $1,649,035; qualifying distributions, $1,574,280; giving activities include $1,460,253 for 136 grants (high: $75,000; low: $2,500).
Purpose and activities: Giving primarily to public charities that serve the sick and poor residents of the Greater Boston, MA, community and the cities of Brockton and Lawrence. Preference is given to organizations devoted to helping: 1) the homeless and under-housed; 2) people in need; 3) children; 4) elders; 5) people with disabilities; 6) new immigrant populations; and 7) low-income communities and neighborhoods. Consideration is also given to emergency disaster situations, worldwide.
Fields of interest: Food services; Food banks; Housing/shelter, development; Disasters, preparedness/services; Human services; Children/youth, services; Aging, centers/services; Minorities/immigrants, centers/services; Homeless, human services; Community/economic development; Public affairs; Aging; Disabilities, people with; Minorities; Homeless.
Type of support: General/operating support; Continuing support; Capital campaigns; Building/renovation; Equipment; Emergency funds; Program development; Technical assistance; Consulting services; Matching/challenge support.
Limitations: Applications accepted. Giving primarily in Brockton, Lawrence, and the greater Boston, MA, area (in cities and towns lying on or within Rte. 128). No support for religion, hospitals, higher education, legal services, or advocacy programs. No grants to individuals, campaigns for endowment funds; for the production of motion pictures, television, video tapes or film strips; for conferences or conventions; for consulting, research, scholarships, fellowships, student loans or travel; for the writing or publishing of books or articles.
Publications: Application guidelines; Annual report (including application guidelines); Grants list; Informational brochure (including application guidelines).
Application information: The foundation prefers that the applying organization's Executive Director register with the foundation as the main contact. Proposals sent by e-mail or U.S. mail will not be accepted. Application form required.
Initial approach: Use online registration and application forms on foundation web site only
Copies of proposal: 1
Deadline(s): See foundation web site for current deadlines
Board meeting date(s): Jan, Apr., July, and Oct.
Final notification: Within 2 months
Officers and Directors:* Benjamin H. Lacy,* Chair.; Kay B. Frishman,* Pres.; Katy Fyrberg,* Clerk; Kathleen O'Connor,* Treas.; Brooks A. Ames; Celia Grant; Donald J. Greene; Brian S. Kelley; Mayra Rodriguez-Howard; Bryan Spence; Christine Swistro.
Number of staff: 1 part-time professional.
EIN: 042687384

1450
Cogan Family Foundation
c/o Choate LLP
P.O. Box 961019
Boston, MA **02196-1019**

Established in 2000 in MA.
Donor: John F. Cogan, Jr.
Foundation type: Independent foundation.
Financial data (yr. ended 08/31/13): Assets, $21,310,225 (M); expenditures, $1,197,830; qualifying distributions, $1,010,700; giving activities include $1,010,000 for 94 grants (high: $50,000; low: $2,500).
Purpose and activities: Giving primarily for education and for human services; funding also for the arts.
Fields of interest: Performing arts, orchestras; Arts; Education; Health care; Human services; Children/youth, services; United Ways and Federated Giving Programs.
Limitations: Applications not accepted. Giving primarily in CA, MA, and NY. No grants to individuals.
Application information: Contributes only to pre-selected organizations.
Trustees: Gregory Cogan; John F. Cogan, Jr.; **Jonathan Cogan**; Peter G. Cogan; Mary Cornille; Pamela Cogan Riddle.
EIN: 046923387

1451
Ben And Rose Cole Charitable Pria Foundation
c/o Joseph Savy
33 Broad St., Ste. 1001
Boston, MA **02109-4237**
***Application address:* c/o Rose Cole, Tr., 85 E. India Row, Apt. 33-C, Boston, MA 02110-3394, tel.: (617) 723-3922**

Donors: Ben Cole; Rose Cole.
Foundation type: Independent foundation.
Financial data (yr. ended 06/30/13): Assets, $4,759,005 (M); expenditures, $285,565; qualifying distributions, $250,000; giving activities include $250,000 for 1 grant.
Fields of interest: Hospitals (specialty); Health care; Cancer research.
Limitations: Applications accepted. Giving primarily in MA.
Application information: Application form not required.
Initial approach: Proposal
Deadline(s): None
Trustees: Rose Cole; Kathleen Curry; Ira Deitsch; Joseph Savy.
EIN: 453513929

1452
Colombe Foundation
15 Research Dr., Ste. B
Amherst, MA 01002-2776
FAX: (413) 256-0349;
E-mail: info@proteusfund.org; Contact for new applicants: Dini Merz, Prog. Dir.: tel.: (203) 439-0076, e-mail: dmerz@proteusfund.org; Contact for current grantees: Beery Adams Jimenez, Grants Mgr., tel.: (413) 256-0349, ext. 12, e-mail: grantsmanager@proteusfund.org; Main URL: http://www.proteusfund.org/programs/colombe-foundation

Established in 1996 in DE.
Donor: Edith W. Allen.
Foundation type: Independent foundation.
Financial data (yr. ended 06/30/13): Assets, $30,293,012 (M); expenditures, $2,482,262; qualifying distributions, $2,052,000; giving activities include $2,052,000 for 26 grants (high: $460,000; low: $7,000).
Purpose and activities: The foundation supports organizations that are: 1) working for the elimination of weapons of mass destruction; 2) advocating for foreign policy that is balanced with diplomacy and prevention rather than dominated by war and aggression; and 3) supporting a shift from wasteful military spending to investments in programs that create real national security, grounded in environmental protection, alternative energy, education and human services. The foundation's current grantmaking priorities are: 1) changing U.S. policy with regards to nuclear weapons disarmament and non-proliferation and complex transformation; 2) shifting the priorities of the military budget; and 3) ending the wars in Afghanistan and Iraq.
Fields of interest: Education, public education; Environment, research; International affairs, information services; International peace/security; Social sciences, public policy; Social sciences, government agencies; Social sciences, formal/general education; Political science.
Limitations: Applications accepted. **Giving primarily in Washington, DC.** No grants to individuals, or for research, conferences, or films/documentaries.
Publications: Application guidelines; Grants list.
Application information:

Initial approach: Telephone or e-mail to Dina Merz to discuss proposal prior to submitting an application; Current grantees should contact Beery Adams Jimenez for current guidelines
Copies of proposal: 2
Deadline(s): See foundation web site for latest deadlines
Final notification: Spring and fall
Officers: Edith W. Allen, Pres.; Frederick Allen, Secy.
EIN: 137103356

1453
Community Foundation of Southeastern Massachusetts
63 Union St.
New Bedford, MA 02740-6361 (508) 996-8253
Contact: Craig J. Dutra, Pres.
FAX: (508) 996-8254; E-mail: info@cfsema.org; Additional e-mail: cdutra@cfsema.org; Main URL: http://www.cfsema.org
Facebook: http://www.facebook.com/pages/Community-Foundation-of-Southeastern-Massachusetts/323838137171

Established in 1995 in MA.
Foundation type: Community foundation.
Financial data (yr. ended 12/31/12): Assets, $27,429,151 (M); gifts received, $3,807,717; expenditures, $3,388,168; giving activities include $1,906,026 for 37+ grants (high: $143,915), and $61,250 for 7 grants to individuals.
Purpose and activities: The foundation seeks to support programs that improve the quality of life for residents of the 41 towns and cities in Southeastern MA.
Fields of interest: Historic preservation/historical societies; Arts; Child development, education; Education; Environment; Health care; Mental health, treatment; Medical research, institute; Housing/shelter; Disasters, preparedness/services; Children/youth, services; Children, services; Child development, services; Family services; Human services; Economic development; Community/economic development; Leadership development.
Type of support: Technical assistance; General/operating support; Management development/capacity building; Building/renovation; Emergency funds; Program development; Seed money; Scholarship funds.
Limitations: Applications accepted. Giving primarily in southeastern MA.
Publications: Financial statement; Informational brochure; Multi-year report.
Application information: Visit the foundation's web site for more information on current requests for proposals.
Deadline(s): Varies
Board meeting date(s): Monthly
Officers and Directors:* Edward G. Siegal, C.P.A.*, Chair.; **Seth Garfield,* Vice-Chair.**; Craig J. Dutra,* Pres.; June A. Smith, Esq.*, Clerk; Mary Louise Nunes,* Treas.; **Linda Bondenmann, Asst. Clerk**; Elizabeth Isherwood, Asst. Treas.; Kim Clark, Dir. Emeritus; **Peter C. Bogle, Esq.**; Terry Boyle; Peter Bullard; Carl J. Cruz; Matthew J. Downey; Paul C. Downey; Sr. Kathleen Harrington; James S. Hughes; Gerry Kavanaugh; Richard L. Lafrance; Thomas F. Lyons; Deborah A. McLaughlin; Joan Menard; George Oliveira; Eric H. Strand; Leonard W. Sullivan; Dr. Paul Vivino; Dean Robert V. Ward.
Number of staff: 3 full-time professional; 1 full-time support; 1 part-time support.
EIN: 043280353
Other changes: Seth Garfield has replaced Edward G. Siegal as Vice-Chair.
Carole A. Fiola is no longer a director.

1454
Conservation, Food and Health Foundation, Inc.
77 Summer St., 8th Fl.
Boston, MA 02110-1006 (617) 391-3092
Contact: Prentice Zinn, Admin.
FAX: (617) 426-7087;
E-mail: pzinn@gmafoundations.com; Main URL: http://cfhfoundation.grantsmanagement08.com/
Grants List: http://cfhfoundation.grantsmanagement08.com/?page_id=8

Established in 1985 in MA.
Foundation type: Independent foundation.
Financial data (yr. ended 12/31/12): Assets, $15,995,635 (M); expenditures, $1,984,147; qualifying distributions, $1,014,616; giving activities include $976,787 for 43 grants (high: $50,000; low: $6,678).
Purpose and activities: The purpose of the foundation is to assist in the conservation of natural resources, the production and distribution of food, and the improvement and promotion of health in the developing world. The foundation is especially interested in supporting projects which lead to the transfer of responsibility to the citizens of developing countries for managing and solving their own problems and for developing the capacity of local organizations. Preference will be given to projects, including research projects, in areas that tend to be under-funded.
Fields of interest: Environment, natural resources; Environment; Animals/wildlife, preservation/protection; Health care; Agriculture; Agriculture/food.
International interests: Developing Countries.
Type of support: Program development; Seed money; Research; Technical assistance.
Limitations: Giving to benefit developing countries. No support for famine, emergency relief, direct delivery of medical care, or for overhead expenses of large institutions. No grants to individuals (except for research efforts sponsored by organizations and institutions), or for building or land purchase, endowments, fundraising activities, scholarships, tuition, and travel grants or general operating support.
Publications: Application guidelines; Grants list.
Application information: Faxed or e-mailed proposals will not be accepted. In order to try to reduce the number of applicants who are turned down for lack of available funds, and to save time loss and expense to the applicants, the foundation has adopted a 2-phase application system, comprised of a short concept application, followed by a limited number of full proposals, at the invitation of the foundation. This system is designed to screen out, at the concept application level, projects which appear unlikely to receive final funding. Application guidelines available on foundation web site. Application form required.
***Initial approach:* Submit concept application through the online application system on foundation web site**
Copies of proposal: 5
***Deadline(s):* See foundation web site for current deadlines**
Board meeting date(s): May and Nov.
Final notification: June 1 and Dec. 1
Officer: Philip M. Fearnside, Pres.
EIN: 222625024
Other changes: The grantmaker now makes its application guidelines available online.

1455
Currents of Change, Inc.
(formerly Common Stream)
P.O. Box 300757
Jamaica Plain, MA 02130 (617) 522-6858
E-mail: peter@commonstream.org; Main URL: http://www.commonstream.org
Grants Database: http://commonstream.org/grants

Established in MA.
Foundation type: Independent foundation.
Financial data (yr. ended 12/31/12): Assets, $23,871,344 (M); expenditures, $1,823,621; qualifying distributions, $1,687,653; giving activities include $1,451,000 for 61 grants (high: $60,000; low: $1,000).
Purpose and activities: Giving primarily for the defense of wild areas, environmental and economic justice, youth organizing, and LGBT rights.
Fields of interest: Environment; Human services; LGBTQ.
Limitations: Applications not accepted. Giving primarily in MA and NY. No grants to individuals.
Application information: Contributes only to pre-selected organizations.
Officers: Julia Satti Cosentino, Pres.; Robert D. Webb, Clerk; Mary Ryan, Treas.
EIN: 721556093

1456
The Gerald & Paul D'Amour Founders Scholarship for Academic Excellence
2145 Roosevelt Ave.
Springfield, MA 01104 (413) 504-4218
2012 Big Y Scholarship Recipients: http://www.bigy.com/Community/Scholarships/Awards#.UNCfpayrDTM

Established in 1994 in MA.
Donor: Big Y Foods, Inc.
Foundation type: Company-sponsored foundation.
Financial data (yr. ended 06/30/13): Assets, $1,829,854 (M); gifts received, $290,404; expenditures, $220,037; qualifying distributions, $219,078; giving activities include $219,078 for 296 grants to individuals (high: $1,026; low: $500).
Purpose and activities: The foundation awards college scholarships to students residing in Big Y Foods, Inc. marketing areas.
Fields of interest: Higher education.
Type of support: Employee-related scholarships; Scholarships—to individuals.
Limitations: Applications accepted. Giving limited to areas of company operations in CT and central and western MA.
Publications: Application guidelines; Grants list.
Application information: Application form required.
Initial approach: Proposal
Deadline(s): Feb. 1
Trustees: Charles L. D'Amour; Donald H. D'Amour.
EIN: 223305742
Other changes: The grantmaker no longer lists a URL address.
The grantmaker has changed its fiscal year-end from July 1 to June 30.

1457
Irene E. and George A. Davis Foundation
1 Monarch Pl., Ste. 1300
Springfield, MA 01144-4011 (413) 734-8336
Contact: Mary E. Walachy, Exec. Dir.

FAX: (413) 734-7845; E-mail: info@davisfdn.org; Additional e-mail (for Mary E. Walachy): mwalachy@davisfdn.org; Main URL: http://www.davisfdn.org
Join E-mail List: http://www.davisfdn.org/matriarch/default.asp

Established in 1970 in MA.
Foundation type: Independent foundation.
Financial data (yr. ended 12/31/12): Assets, $95,224,786 (M); gifts received, $4,440,672; expenditures, $4,423,224; qualifying distributions, $4,173,042; giving activities include $3,670,929 for 176 grants (high: $400,000; low: $250).
Purpose and activities: The mission of the foundation is to support the development of Hampden County, MA, children, youth and families by insuring that they have the opportunities needed to achieve their full potential. The foundation accomplishes this by: 1) investing in a continuum of services with a particular focus on young children, ages birth through 8, while at the same time, sustaining these early investments through a variety of learning supports and experiences for youth ages 9 through 18; and 2) a holistic approach that encompasses the social, emotional, physical and cognitive needs of children and youth, and supports them within the context of their families.
Fields of interest: Arts; Elementary/secondary education; Education, early childhood education; Health care; Human services; Infants/toddlers; Children/youth; Children; Minorities; Economically disadvantaged.
Type of support: General/operating support; Continuing support; Management development/capacity building; Annual campaigns; Capital campaigns; Building/renovation; Equipment; Land acquisition; Emergency funds; Program development; Seed money; Technical assistance; Consulting services; Program evaluation; Matching/challenge support.
Limitations: Applications accepted. Giving generally limited to Hampden County, MA. **No support for other private foundations.** No grants to individuals, or for scholarships, internships, continuing support of current programs, debt reduction or endowments; no program-related investments or loans.
Publications: Application guidelines.
Application information: All submissions must be done on-line at foundation web site. Application form required.
Initial approach: Online application form
Deadline(s): Feb. 1, May 1, Aug. 1, and Nov. 1 for grants
Board meeting date(s): Mar., June, Sept., and Dec.
Final notification: 2 weeks after board meeting
Officer: Mary E. Walachy, Exec. Dir.
Trustees: John H. Davis; Stephen A. Davis; Jane Davis-Kusek.
Number of staff: 3 full-time professional.
EIN: 263713735

1458
Demoulas Foundation
286 Chelmsford St.
Chelmsford, MA 01824-2403 (978) 244-1024
Contact: Arthur T. Demoulas, Tr.

Established in 1964 in MA.
Donors: Demoulas Super Markets, Inc.; Members of the Demoulas family.
Foundation type: Company-sponsored foundation.
Financial data (yr. ended 12/31/13): Assets, $29,687,427 (M); expenditures, $1,583,662; qualifying distributions, $1,551,412; giving activities include $1,504,094 for 131 grants (high: $265,000; low: -$1,000).
Purpose and activities: The foundation supports hospitals and organizations involved with arts and culture, education, cancer, human services, and religion.
Fields of interest: Higher education; Education; Hospitals (general); Medical care, rehabilitation; Health care; Cancer; Boys & girls clubs; Residential/custodial care, hospices; Human services; Religion.
Type of support: General/operating support; Annual campaigns; Endowments; Program development; Scholarship funds.
Limitations: Applications accepted. Giving primarily in MA.
Application information: Application form required.
***Initial approach:* Letter**
Deadline(s): None
Trustee: Arthur T. Demoulas.
EIN: 042723441

1459
DentaQuest Foundation
(formerly Oral Health Services Foundation, Inc.)
465 Medford St.
Boston, MA 02129-1454 **(617) 886-1700**
Contact: Andrea Forscht, Grants and Progs. Assoc.
FAX: (617) 886-1799;
E-mail: andrea.forscht@dentaquestfoundation.org;
Additional contact: Mathew Bond, Mgr., Grants and Progs., e-mail: mathew.bond@dentaquestfoundation.org; Main URL: http://www.dentaquestfoundation.org/
Grants Database: http://dentaquestfoundation.org/impact/search
Oral Health Matters: http://oralhealthmatters.blogspot.com/

Established in 2000 in MA.
Donors: Dental Services of Massachusetts Inc.; Delta Dental Plan of Massachusetts.
Foundation type: Company-sponsored foundation.
Financial data (yr. ended 12/31/12): Assets, $85,651,234 (M); gifts received, $25,625,000; expenditures, $12,989,345; qualifying distributions, $12,810,931; giving activities include $9,518,845 for 85 grants (high: $380,000; low: $500).
Purpose and activities: The foundation supports programs designed to improve oral health. Special emphasis is directed toward public policy that improves oral health; increased public and private funding for oral health initiatives; improved delivery of oral health care and prevention; and community engagement on oral health issues.
Fields of interest: Dental school/education; Health care, management/technical assistance; Health care, public policy; Health care, equal rights; Medicine/medical care, public education; Health care, clinics/centers; Dental care; Health care, insurance; Health care; Children/youth, services; Children; Economically disadvantaged.
Type of support: Continuing support; Management development/capacity building; Building/renovation; Equipment; Program development; Technical assistance; Sponsorships.
Limitations: Applications accepted. Giving primarily in areas of company operations, with emphasis on FL, IL, MA, and MD; giving also to national organizations. No support for lobbying organizations. No grants to individuals, or for scholarships, general overhead or indirect costs, capital campaigns, debt reduction, or endowments.
Publications: Application guidelines; Annual report; Grants list; Program policy statement.
Application information: A full proposal may be requested at a later date for Oral Health 2020 and Innovation Fund for Oral Health.
***Initial approach:* Complete online concept form for Oral Health 2020, Community Response Fund, President Fund, and Innovation Fund for Oral Health**
***Deadline(s):* None**
Officers and Directors:* Caswell A. Evans, Jr., DDS, MPH*, Chair.; Michael McPherson, Vice-Chair.; Ralph Fuccillo, MA*, Pres.; Myra Green, Clerk; Scott Frock, Treas.; Alice Huan-mei Chen, MD, MPH; Jamie Collins; Harold D. Cox, MSSW; Fay Donohue; Shephard Goldstein, DMD; Leslie E. Grant, DDS, MSPA; Donald J. Kenney; Linda C. Niessen, DMD, MPH, MPP; Alonzo L. Plough, Ph.D., MPH; Norman A. Tinanoff, DDS; Mary Vallier-Kaplan, MHSA.
EIN: 043265080
Other changes: Mathew Bond is now Mgr., Grants and Progs. Palmer Corson is no longer Mgr., Progs. and Opers. Andrea Henry is no longer Grants and Prog. Assoc.

1460
East Boston Savings Charitable Foundation Inc.
(formerly Meridian Charitable Foundation, Inc.)
c/o Kenneth Fisher
67 Prospect St.
Peabody, MA 01960-1604 **(617) 567-1500**
Contact: Deborah J. Jackson, Treas.
Additional tel.: (617) 567-1500; **Main URL: http://www.ebsb.com/**
Grants List: http://ebsb.com/about-us/community/charitable-foundation/recipients.aspx

Established in 1998 in MA.
Donors: East Boston Savings Bank; Ralph R. Bagley, Esq.
Foundation type: Company-sponsored foundation.
Financial data (yr. ended 12/31/12): Assets, $5,125,193 (M); expenditures, $189,655; qualifying distributions, $177,755; giving activities include $177,755 for 38 grants (high: $10,000; low: $2,000).
Purpose and activities: The foundation supports camps and organizations involved with education, health, hunger, housing, human services, and community development.
Fields of interest: Secondary school/education; Education; Health care; Food services; Housing/shelter, homeless; Housing/shelter; Recreation, camps; YM/YWCAs & YM/YWHAs; Youth, services; Family services; Residential/custodial care, hospices; Aging, centers/services; Developmentally disabled, centers & services; Homeless, human services; Human services; Community/economic development.
Type of support: Scholarship funds; Equipment; General/operating support; Capital campaigns; Program development.
Limitations: Applications accepted. Giving limited to East Boston, Everett, Lynn, Lynnfield, Melrose, Peabody, Revere, Saugus, Wakefield, and Winthrop, MA, and other North Shore, MA, areas. No support for national organizations or city, town, state, or federal agencies. No grants to individuals or for annual campaigns or salaries.
Publications: Application guidelines; Grants list.
Application information: Grants range from $1,000 to $5,000. Proposal narratives should be no longer than 3 pages. If brochures or pamphlets are included with the application, the applicant must provide 10 copies of each. Support is limited to 1 contribution per organization during any given year. Application form required.

Initial approach: Download application form and mail proposal and form to foundation
Deadline(s): July
Final notification: 60 to 90 days
Officers and Directors: Richard J. Gavegnano, Pres.; Deborah J. Jackson, Treas.; Martha R. Bagley, Esq.; Paula M. Cotter; Grace Previte Magoon; Peter F. Scolaro; Ruth A. Sheets.
EIN: 043406328

1461
Eastern Bank Charitable Foundation
195 Market St., EP5-02
Lynn, MA 01901-1508 (781) 598-7530
Contact: Laura Kurzrok, Exec. Dir.
FAX: (781) 596-4445;
E-mail: Foundation@easternbank.com; TDD/TTY tel.: (781) 596-4408; Main URL: https://www.easternbank.com/foundation

Established in 1994 in MA.
Donor: Eastern Bank.
Foundation type: Company-sponsored foundation.
Financial data (yr. ended 12/31/12): Assets, $64,452,431 (M); gifts received, $7,500,000; expenditures, $3,988,909; qualifying distributions, $3,664,104; giving activities include $3,056,419 for 1,528 grants (high: $100,000; low: $50).
Purpose and activities: The foundation supports organizations involved with education, the environment, community health, workforce development, hunger, affordable housing, children and families, human services, civil liberties, and economic revitalization.
Fields of interest: Higher education; Education, services; Education, computer literacy/technology training; Education; Health care, clinics/centers; Health care; Employment, services; Employment, training; Food banks; Nutrition; Housing/shelter; Boys & girls clubs; Youth development; Children, services; Family services; Family services, domestic violence; Human services, financial counseling; Human services; Civil/human rights; Economic development; United Ways and Federated Giving Programs.
Type of support: General/operating support; Annual campaigns; Capital campaigns; Building/renovation; Endowments; Program development; Scholarship funds; Sponsorships; Employee matching gifts.
Limitations: Applications accepted. Giving primarily in areas of company operations in eastern MA.
Publications: Application guidelines; Annual report (including application guidelines).
Application information: Partnership Grants are limited to 1 contribution per organization during any 3-year period. Application form required.
Initial approach: Complete online application
***Deadline(s):* None for Community Grants and Neighborhood Support; Mar. 1 for Targeted Grants; Mar. 1 and Sept. 1 for Partnership Grants; None for Neighborhood Support**
Board meeting date(s): Monthly for Community Grants and Neighborhood Support; Semi-annually for Partnership Grants
***Final notification:* 60 days for Community Grants and Neighborhood Support; May and Nov. for Partnership Grants**
Trustees: Richard C. Bane; Deborah Hill Bornheimer; Paul M. Connolly; Robert A. Glassman; Daryl A. Hellman; Richard E. Holbrook; Deborah C. Jackson; Wendell J. Knox; Stanley J. Lukowski; Peter K. Markell; George A. Massaro; Henry L. Murphy, Jr., Esq.; E. Joel Peterson; John M. Plukas; Roger D. Scoville; Michael B. Sherman.
Number of staff: 1 full-time professional; 2 part-time support.
EIN: 223317340

1462
Edwards Scholarship Fund
89 South St., Ste. 603
Boston, MA 02111-2651 **(617) 737-3400**

Established in 1939 in MA.
Donor: Grace M. Edwards‡.
Foundation type: Independent foundation.
Financial data (yr. ended 07/31/12): Assets, $7,905,831 (M); gifts received, $1,850; expenditures, $353,373; qualifying distributions, $306,670; giving activities include $196,991 for 108 grants to individuals (high: $5,000; low: $1,000).
Purpose and activities: Giving for scholarships to Boston, Massachusetts residents for higher education.
Fields of interest: Higher education.
Type of support: Scholarships—to individuals.
Limitations: Applications accepted. Giving limited to students residing in Boston, MA since the beginning of their junior year of high school.
Publications: Application guidelines.
Application information: Application form required.
Initial approach: Letter requesting application
Copies of proposal: 1
Deadline(s): Mar. 1
Board meeting date(s): Summer and winter
Trustees: Bernard Bonn III; Margaret Flanagan.
Number of staff: 1 part-time professional.
EIN: 046002496

1463
The Elsevier Foundation
2 Newton Pl., Ste. 350
Newton, MA 02458-1637
Contact: John Regazzi, Chair.
E-mail: foundation@elsevier.com; **Application address: 360 Park Ave. S., New York, NY 10010-1710, tel.: (212) 633-3933**; Main URL: http://www.elsevierfoundation.org
Facebook: https://www.facebook.com/TheElsevierFoundation
Twitter: https://twitter.com/ELsFoundation
YouTube: http://www.youtube.com/user/ElsevierFoundation

Established in NY.
Donor: Elservier, Inc.
Foundation type: Independent foundation.
Financial data (yr. ended 12/31/12): Assets, $559,337 (M); gifts received, $1,340,160; expenditures, $853,894; qualifying distributions, $853,894; giving activities include $853,894 for grants.
Purpose and activities: The foundation provides grants to institutions around the world, with a focus on support for the world's libraries and for scholars in the early stages of their careers.
Fields of interest: Higher education; Libraries/library science; Education; Health organizations; Human services.
Type of support: General/operating support; Employee matching gifts.
Limitations: Applications accepted. Giving on an international basis. No grants for individuals, nor for basic research, sectarian religious activities or to organizations that lack tax exemption.
Publications: Application guidelines.
Application information:
Initial approach: See foundation web site for guidelines
Officer: David A. Ruth, Exec. Dir.
Directors: YoungSuk "YS" Chi; Dr. Rita Colwell; Paula Kaufman; Dr. Emilie Marcus; Kenneth R. Thompson II; Wu Yishan.
EIN: 431976990

1464
Essex County Community Foundation, Inc.
175 Andover St., Ste. 101
Danvers, MA 01923-2833 (978) 777-8876
Contact: David Welbourn, C.E.O. and Pres.; For grants: Julie Bishop, V.P., Grants and Svcs.
FAX: (978) 777-9454; E-mail: info@eccf.org; Grant inquiry e-mail: j.bishop@eccf.org; Grant application e-mail: grantsubmit@eccf.org; Main URL: http://www.eccf.org
Facebook: http://www.facebook.com/ECCFBulletin
Pinterest: http://www.pinterest.com/eccfgives/
Twitter: https://twitter.com/ECCFGives
YouTube: https://www.youtube.com/channel/UCazR-5XlxUdqkvbhaDcjzDg

Established in 1998 in MA.
Foundation type: Community foundation.
Financial data (yr. ended 06/30/13): Assets, $21,342,520 (M); gifts received, $6,016,811; expenditures, $5,662,960; giving activities include $4,283,977 for 62 grants (high: $350,000).
Purpose and activities: The mission of the foundation is to connect people, ideas and resources for the common good. The foundation promotes local philanthropy and strengthens the nonprofit organizations of Essex County by: 1) partnering with donors, helping them meet their philanthropic goals by managing donor funds and organization's assets with efficiency, security, expertise and privacy; 2) supporting nonprofit organizations across the county with grants, strategic planning, board development, fundraising, professional training and sustainability; and 3) building collaboration between individuals and organizations to address current issues through programs and collaborative funds.
Fields of interest: Arts; Education; Environment; Youth development; Human services; Children/youth; Youth; Adults; Aging; Young adults; Disabilities, people with; Minorities; Women; Girls; Young adults, female; Offenders/ex-offenders; Economically disadvantaged; Homeless.
Type of support: General/operating support; Management development/capacity building; Capital campaigns; Equipment; Emergency funds; Program development; Seed money; Curriculum development; Scholarship funds; Technical assistance; Consulting services; Program evaluation; Scholarships—to individuals.
Limitations: Applications accepted. Giving limited to Essex County, MA for competitive grantmaking; Donor-Advised funds may grant outside Essex County. No support for sectarian or religious purposes. No grants to individuals (except for scholarships), or for debt or deficit reduction, academic research, feasibility studies, capital campaigns for buildings, land acquisition, or endowment.
Publications: Application guidelines; Annual report; Financial statement; Grants list; Informational brochure; Newsletter.
Application information: Visit foundation web site for application cover sheet and guidelines. Application form required.
Initial approach: Submit online application

Deadline(s): **Varies**
Board meeting date(s): Usually held monthly, except in Aug.
Final notification: **Varies**
Officers and Directors:* Jonathan Payson,* Chair.; **Robert R. Fanning, Jr., Chair., Finance**; Allan Huntley,* Vice-Chair.; Dave Welbourn,* C.E.O. and Pres.; Jay Caporale,* Exec. V.P. and Dir., Philanthropy; Julie Bishop,* V.P., Grants and Services; Susan Perry, Cont.; Karen Ansara; Mollie Byrnes; **Benjamin Chigier**; Steven Cohen; Matthew P. Doring; Theresa M. Ellis; **Benigno Espaillat; Tracy Abedon Filosa**; Susan Gray; **Joseph Grimaldi; Joe Knowles**; Patricia Maguire Meservey; Michael Prior; Richard Sumberg; Kevin M. Tierney, Sr.
Number of staff: 8 part-time professional; 1 full-time support; 1 part-time support.
EIN: 043407816
Other changes: At the close of 2013, the grantmaker paid grants of $4,328,573, a 90.7% increase over the 2012 disbursements, $2,269,654.
Jo Kadlecek is now Dir., Comms. Pat Kelleher is now Philanthropy and Donor Srvs. Carol Lavoie Schuster is now Asst. Mgr. of Grants and Services. Carol Lavoie Schuster is now Asst. Mgr., Grants and Srvs. Joan Henkels is now Prog. Asst. Robert R. Fanning, Jr. is now Chair., Finance.

1465
Charles H. Farnsworth Trust
c/o US Trust, Bank of America, N.A.
225 Franklin St., 4th Fl., MA1-225-04-02
Boston, MA 02110-2804 (866) 778-6859
Contact: Michealle Larkins, V.P.
E-mail: michealle.larkins@ustrust.com; **E-mail to discuss application process or for questions: ma.grantmaking@ustrust.com (Foundation name should appear in subject line)**; Main URL: http://www.bankofamerica.com/grantmaking

Trust established in 1930; became a charitable trust in 1978.
Donor: Charles H. Farnsworth†.
Foundation type: Independent foundation.
Financial data (yr. ended 09/30/13): Assets, $26,940,381 (M); expenditures, $1,394,724; qualifying distributions, $1,235,251; giving activities include $1,139,000 for 26 grants (high: $333,000; low: $2,000).
Purpose and activities: Giving to assist elderly persons to live with dignity and independence. Special focus on services which help prevent premature institutionalization. Grants fostering the development of housing for the elderly are of special interest.
Fields of interest: Housing/shelter, development; Aging, centers/services; Aging.
Type of support: General/operating support; Capital campaigns; Building/renovation; Equipment; Program development; Seed money; Technical assistance.
Limitations: Giving limited to MA. No grants to individuals.
Publications: Application guidelines; Grants list.
Application information: Submit applications online at www.bankofamerica.com/grantmaking.
Initial approach: Proposal online via foundation web site
Deadline(s): See foundation web site for current deadlines
Final notification: See foundation web site
Trustee: Bank of America, N.A.
Number of staff: 2 part-time support.
EIN: 046096075

1466
F. Felix Foundation
6 University Dr., Ste. 206
P.O. Box 240
Amherst, MA **01002-2265**

Established in 2000 in DE and MA.
Foundation type: Independent foundation.
Financial data (yr. ended 09/30/13): Assets, $4,175,722 (M); expenditures, $298,751; qualifying distributions, $261,529; giving activities include $182,755 for 25 grants (high: $50,000; low: $200).
Fields of interest: Human services; Foundations (community).
Limitations: Applications not accepted. Giving primarily in MA. No grants to individuals.
Application information: Contributes only to pre-selected organizations.
Officers and Directors:* Robert Mazer,* Pres.; Magdalena Mazer,* Secy.-Treas.
EIN: 043464255

1467
Fields Pond Foundation, Inc.
5 Turner St.
P.O. Box 540667
Waltham, MA 02454-0667 (781) 899-9990
FAX: (718) 899-2819; E-mail: info@fieldspond.org; Main URL: http://www.fieldspond.org
Grants List: http://www.fieldspond.org/grants.htm

Established in 1993 in MA.
Foundation type: Independent foundation.
Financial data (yr. ended 12/31/12): Assets, $13,508,507 (M); gifts received, $50; expenditures, $696,687; qualifying distributions, $674,304; giving activities include $525,084 for 50 grants (high: $25,000; low: $1,000), and $25,000 for 1 loan/program-related investment.
Purpose and activities: The foundation provides assistance to nature and land conservation organizations which are community based, and which serve to increase environmental awareness by involving local residents in conservation issues. The foundation makes grants under the following priorities: 1) project grants for trailmaking and other enhancement of public access to conservation lands, rivers, coastlines, and other natural resources; 2) land acquisition for conservation; 3) assistance in the establishment of endowments as a means of funding stewardship of conservation areas; and 4) related education programs and publications. The foundation encourages proposals from municipal government agencies. It may also consider short-term loans to conservation groups for the purpose of acquiring conservation lands. Outside of the primary mission, it will also consider grant requests from other nonprofit organizations that have a demonstrated local impact on precollegiate education.
Fields of interest: Elementary/secondary education; Environment, natural resources; Environment.
Type of support: Capital campaigns; Land acquisition; Endowments; Emergency funds; Seed money; Matching/challenge support.
Limitations: Applications accepted. Giving primarily in New England and New York. No support for sectarian religious activities. No grants to individuals; or for deficit financing, routine operating budgets, or for funding usually supported by public subscription or through national appeals.
Publications: Application guidelines; Grants list.
Application information: AGM Common Proposal Format is accepted. Application form not required.
Initial approach: Telephone or submit a 1-page outline prior to submitting full proposal
Copies of proposal: 1
Deadline(s): None
Board meeting date(s): Bimonthly
Final notification: 3-4 weeks
Officers and Directors:* Rhoda R. Cohen,* Pres.; Brian H. Rehrig,* V.P. and Treas.; Walter Angoff, V.P. and Secy.; Russell A. Cohen.
Number of staff: 1 part-time professional; 1 part-time support.
EIN: 043196041

1468
Lincoln and Therese Filene Foundation, Inc.
c/o Nutter McClennen & Fish LLP
P.O. Box 5140
Boston, MA 02206-5140 (617) 439-2498
E-mail: awallis@nutter.com; Application address: c/o Alane Harrington Wallis, Charitable Foundation Mgr., World Trade Center W., 155 Seaport Blvd., Boston, MA 2210-2604; Main URL: http://www.filenefoundation.org/
Grants List: http://www.filenefoundation.org/current-grant-list-1/

Incorporated in 1937 in MA.
Donor: Lincoln Filene†.
Foundation type: Independent foundation.
Financial data (yr. ended 12/31/12): Assets, $20,083,150 (M); expenditures, $1,133,587; qualifying distributions, $963,504; giving activities include $881,675 for 47 grants (high: $159,500; low: $100).
Purpose and activities: General purposes; grants primarily for civic education, human development and self-sufficiency, music and performing arts education, citizenship, and public education. Funds largely committed to long-term support of existing projects.
Fields of interest: Arts education; Media, television; Arts; Education.
Type of support: Program development.
Limitations: Applications accepted. Giving primarily in the New England area, with emphasis on MA. No support for political groups. No grants to individuals, or for endowment funds, capital campaigns, operating costs, scholarships, fellowships, or religious groups; no loans.
Publications: Application guidelines.
Application information: Funds largely committed. Application guidelines and forms available on foundation web site; AGM Common Proposal Form accepted. Application form required.
Initial approach: Cover letter, Grant Request Cover Sheet and Request for Funding forms via U.S. mail or e-mail
Copies of proposal: 1
Deadline(s): March 1 and Sept. 1
Board meeting date(s): May and Nov.
Final notification: After next semiannual meeting
Officers and Directors:* G. Michael Ladd, Jr.,* Pres.; David A. Robertson,* V.P.; Peter A. Brown, Secy.-Treas.; Kimberly R. Dietel; David J. Ladd; Donna J. Ladd; William L. Ladd; Michael E. Mooney; John J. Robertson; Heather C. Sears.
EIN: 237423946

1469
The Paul and Phyllis Fireman Charitable Foundation
c/o Watermill Ctr.
800 South St., Ste. 610
Waltham, MA **02453-1445** (617) 482-5620
Contact: Ana Jimenez, Grants and Projects Specialist
FAX: (617) 482-5624; E-mail: info@ppffound.org; Main URL: http://www.ppffound.org

Established in 1985 in MA.
Foundation type: Independent foundation.
Financial data (yr. ended 12/31/12): Assets, $138,768,935 (M); expenditures, $5,176,093; qualifying distributions, $3,751,893; giving activities include $2,900,495 for 37 grants (high: $475,000; low: $250).
Purpose and activities: The foundation dedicates a major share of its resources to ending family homelessness in the Commonwealth and beyond.
Fields of interest: Performing arts centers; Hospitals (general); Housing/shelter, homeless; Human services; Homeless, human services; Jewish agencies & synagogues; Children/youth; Women; Economically disadvantaged; Homeless.
Type of support: General/operating support; Continuing support; Capital campaigns; Emergency funds; Seed money; Program-related investments/loans.
Limitations: Applications not accepted. Giving primarily in MA, with limited funding to Jersey City, NJ. No grants to individuals.
Application information: Unsolicited full proposals not accepted. See foundation web site for updates in this area.
Board meeting date(s): May
Officer: Deborah Fung, Exec. Dir.
Trustees: Paul Fireman; Phyllis Fireman.
EIN: 222677986

1470
Fish Family Foundation
(formerly The Lawrence K. Fish Charitable Foundation)
75 State St.
Boston, MA **02109-1827**
E-mail: fishfamfound@aol.com

Established in 1999 in MA.
Donors: Lawrence K. Fish; Citizens Bank; Members of the Lawrence K. Fish Family.
Foundation type: Independent foundation.
Financial data (yr. ended 06/30/12): Assets, $10,047,193 (M); gifts received, $900,000; expenditures, $1,657,297; qualifying distributions, $1,624,613; giving activities include $1,281,080 for 137 grants (high: $125,000; low: $10).
Fields of interest: Museums (art); Performing arts, orchestras; Arts; Education; Boys & girls clubs; Human services; United Ways and Federated Giving Programs; Public policy, research.
Type of support: General/operating support.
Limitations: Applications not accepted. Giving primarily in MA, with emphasis on Boston. No grants to individuals.
Application information: Contributes only to pre-selected organizations.
Officer: Alice Borden, Exec. Dir.
Trustees: Atsuko Toko Fish; Edward Takezo Fish; Emily Fish; Lawrence K. Fish; Leah Okajima Toko Fish; Matias Sacerdote; Thaleia Schlesinger.
Number of staff: 1 part-time support.
EIN: 046905753

1471
Saint Francis Community Health Care, Inc.
c/o Stowe & Degon
95A Turnpike Rd.
Westborough, MA 01581-2878 (508) 755-8605
Contact: Michael D. Stowe, Vice-Chair.
Main URL: http://www.saintfrancischc.com/

Foundation type: Independent foundation.
Financial data (yr. ended 12/31/12): Assets, $3,439,757 (M); expenditures, $187,004; qualifying distributions, $164,021; giving activities include $144,250 for 19 grants (high: $20,000; low: $1,000).
Fields of interest: Health care; Human services; Catholic agencies & churches.
Limitations: Applications accepted. Giving primarily in Worcester, MA.
Application information: See foundation web site for application guidelines. Application form required.
Initial approach: Letter
Deadline(s): Jan. 1 through Sept. 15
Officers: David Grenon, Chair. and Pres.; Michael D. Stowe, Vice-Chair. and V.P.; Lawrence Brodeur, Clerk; **Jill Cosgrove Danksewicz, Treas.**
Directors: Henry Braverman; Roger Dauphinais; Stephen Granger; **Ralph D. Marois**; Ronald Racine; E. Paul Tinsley.
EIN: 222755649
Other changes: Jill Cosgrove Danksewicz has replaced Edward Starkus as Treas.
David Grenon is now Chair. and Pres. Michael D. Stowe is now Vice-Chair. and V.P. Robert Vaudreuil is no longer director.

1472
Franklin Square House Foundation
P.O. Box 78037
Belmont, MA 02478 (617) 312-3400
FAX: (617) 484-9252;
E-mail: robertg@franklinsquarehousefoundation.org ; Main URL: http://www.franklinsquarehousefoundation.org

Established in 1902 in MA.
Foundation type: Independent foundation.
Financial data (yr. ended 12/31/12): Assets, $21,695,191 (M); expenditures, $1,876,541; qualifying distributions, $1,756,087; giving activities include $1,574,869 for 33 grants (high: $100,000; low: $4,320).
Purpose and activities: The foundation works to provide grants for housing and shelter organizations, primarily in the Boston area, that protect women and preserve families.
Fields of interest: Housing/shelter, services; Family services; Family services, domestic violence; Women.
Limitations: Giving limited to the Boston, MA metropolitan area.
Publications: Application guidelines.
Application information: Application forms available on foundation web site. Application form required.
Initial approach: Telephone to Exec. Dir.
Deadline(s): See foundation web site for current deadline
Officers and Directors:* Susan Shelby,* Pres.; George Marsh, Jr.,* V.P.; Vanessa Calderon-Rosado,* Clerk; David Parker,* Treas.; Robert Goldstein, Exec. Dir.; Peter Smith, Board Member Emeritus; Jack Curtin, Board Member Emeritus; Hemmie Chang; Ellen Christie; Cheryl Forte; Janet Frazier; John Hickey; **Anita Huggins**; Suzanne Kenney; Vincent McCarthy; Jeanne Pinado; **Robert Rubin**.
EIN: 042103780

Other changes: Yoon J. Lee and Adam Robinson are no longer board members.

1473
Gardinor-Prunaret Foundation
c/o John R.D. McClintock
P.O. Box 639
North Andover, MA 01845-0639

Donors: Mildred Gardinor Prunaret‡; Henri Prunaret Trust.
Foundation type: Independent foundation.
Financial data (yr. ended 03/31/13): Assets, $7,046,904 (M); expenditures, $14,131; qualifying distributions, $0.
Fields of interest: Medical school/education; Hospitals (general); Health organizations, research; Human services; Children/youth, services.
Type of support: General/operating support.
Limitations: Applications not accepted. Giving primarily in MA. No grants to individuals.
Application information: Unsolicited requests for funds not accepted.
Trustee: John R.D. McClintock.
EIN: 042598211

1474
Germeshausen Foundation, Inc.
c/o Silver Bridge Advisors
255 State St., 6th Fl.
Boston, MA 02109-2167 (617) 526-6610
Contact: Martin S. Kaplan, Tr.
FAX: (617) 526-5000;
E-mail: trustee@germeshausen.org; Main URL: http://www.germeshausen.org

Established in 1999 in MA.
Foundation type: Independent foundation.
Financial data (yr. ended 12/31/12): Assets, $25,612,811 (M); expenditures, $1,657,084; qualifying distributions, $1,441,871; giving activities include $1,293,590 for 49 grants (high: $225,000; low: $150).
Purpose and activities: Giving primarily for innovative approaches to positive change in youth culture, leadership development for young adults, environmental and ecological values, and imaginative media projects on current issues. In all grants, the foundation seeks to advance the idea of interconnectedness among people, and between people and the environment.
Fields of interest: Environment; Human services; Leadership development; Youth.
Type of support: General/operating support.
Limitations: Applications accepted. Giving on a national basis. No grants to individuals.
Publications: Application guidelines.
Application information: Application form not required.
***Initial approach:* Letter of inquiry (no more than 2 pages) via e-mail**
Copies of proposal: 1
Deadline(s): None
Board meeting date(s): As needed
Officers and Trustees:* Nancy G. Klavans,* Pres.; Martin S. Kaplan,* Secy.-Treas.
EIN: 043485516

1475

Gordon Family Foundation

c/o Michael S. Gordon
260 Franklin St., Ste. 1900
Boston, MA 02110-3115

Established in 1997 in MA.
Donor: Michael S. Gordon.
Foundation type: Independent foundation.
Financial data (yr. ended 12/31/12): Assets, $38,587,100 (M); expenditures, $2,878,237; qualifying distributions, $2,763,900; giving activities include $2,763,900 for 27 grants (high: $500,000; low: $100).
Purpose and activities: Giving for education and Jewish organizations; funding also for children, youth, and social services.
Fields of interest: Education; Human services; Children/youth, services; Jewish federated giving programs.
Type of support: General/operating support; Scholarship funds.
Limitations: Applications not accepted. Giving primarily in MA. No grants to individuals.
Application information: Contributes only to pre-selected organizations.
Trustees: Christina M. Gordon; Michael S. Gordon.
EIN: 137130595
Other changes: At the close of 2012, the grantmaker paid grants of $2,763,900, a 67.0% increase over the 2011 disbursements, $1,655,401.

1476

Anna Gould Charitable Foundation, Inc.

38 Robinson Dr.
Bedford, MA 01730-1360 **(781) 538-6767**
Contact: Anna Gould, Dir.

Established in MA.
Donor: Anna Gould.
Foundation type: Independent foundation.
Financial data (yr. ended 12/31/12): Assets, $294,320 (M); expenditures, $141,395; qualifying distributions, $138,800; giving activities include $138,800 for 4 grants (high: $106,800; low: $2,000).
Fields of interest: Recreation, camps.
Type of support: General/operating support.
Limitations: Applications accepted. Giving primarily in ME.
Application information: Application form required.
Initial approach: Proposal
Deadline(s): None
Director: Anna Gould.
EIN: 262219241

1477

The Gould Charitable Foundation

One International Pl., 17th Fl.
Boston, MA 02110-2602
E-mail: info@gouldgiving.org; Main URL: http://www.gouldcharitabletrust.org
Grants List: http://www.gouldcharitabletrust.org/recipients.html

Established in 1988 in MA.
Donor: Donna R. Gould.
Foundation type: Independent foundation.
Financial data (yr. ended 12/31/12): Assets, $3,605,943 (M); expenditures, $302,847; qualifying distributions, $253,045; giving activities include $239,245 for 13 grants (high: $30,000; low: $6,000).
Fields of interest: Human services; Children, services; Family services.
Limitations: Applications accepted. Giving primarily in KS, MA, and MO. No grants to individuals or for general operating support.
Application information: Application guidelines available on foundation web site. Application form required.
Initial approach: Letter of inquiry
Deadline(s): Aug. 1 for letter of inquiry
Board meeting date(s): Oct.
Trustees: Karen Courtney; Linda S. Dalby; Donna R. Gould; Joel Gould; Matthew Gould; Day Pitney LLP.
Number of staff: None.
EIN: 226444275

1478

Grew Family Charitable Foundation

c/o RH&B, Inc.
50 Congress St., Ste. 900
Boston, MA **02109-4023**

Established in 2004 in MA.
Donor: Alma Grew Trust.
Foundation type: Independent foundation.
Financial data (yr. ended 04/30/13): Assets, $3,141,263 (M); expenditures, $165,873; qualifying distributions, $142,053; giving activities include $135,000 for 5 grants (high: $40,000; low: $20,000).
Fields of interest: Performing arts, orchestras; Higher education; Libraries (public).
Limitations: Applications not accepted. Giving primarily in MA. No grants to individuals.
Application information: Contributes only to pre-selected organizations.
Trustees: Adrienne Smith; James Wheeler.
EIN: 206269517

1479

The Harold Grinspoon Charitable Foundation

67 Hunt St., Ste. 100
Agawam, MA 01001-1913 **(413) 276-0700**
Contact: Joanna S. Ballantine, Exec. Dir.
FAX: (413) 276-0804; E-mail: info@hgf.org; Main URL: http://www.hgf.org

Established in 1986 in MA.
Donors: Harold Grinspoon; Diane Troderman; Massmutual Financial Group.
Foundation type: Independent foundation.
Financial data (yr. ended 08/31/12): Assets, $7,676,501 (M); gifts received, $793,746; expenditures, $945,923; qualifying distributions, $898,542; giving activities include $636,421 for grants.
Purpose and activities: Giving primarily to: 1) encourage young people to reach their academic and leadership potential; 2) promote literacy and early childhood education; 3) reward excellence in teaching and education; 4) support entrepreneurship among young people; and 5) promote education and health in Cambodia.
Fields of interest: Arts; Education; Cancer research; Youth development; Human services; Jewish agencies & synagogues; Women.
International interests: Cambodia; Israel.
Type of support: General/operating support; Annual campaigns; Endowments; Program development; Scholarship funds; Program-related investments/loans.
Limitations: Giving primarily in western MA. No grants to individuals (except for research projects), or for scholarships or student aid.
Publications: Financial statement; Multi-year report.
Application information: See foundation web site for specific application instructions.
Trustees: Stuart Anfang; Michael Bohnen; **Andy Eder**; David Galper; Rabbi Irving "Yitz" Greenberg; Harold Grinspoon; Winnie Sandler Grinspoon; Jeremy Pava; Diane Troderman.
Number of staff: 2 full-time professional; 2 part-time support.
EIN: 222738277
Other changes: Dan Backer is no longer a trustee.

1480

Frank B. Hazard General Charity Fund

c/o U.S. Trust, Philanthropic Solutions
225 Franklin St., MA1-225-04-02
Boston, MA 02110-2801
Contact: Emma Greene, Market Director
E-mail: emma.m.greene@ustrust.com; **Main URL: https://www.bankofamerica.com/philanthropic/grantmaking.go**

Foundation type: Independent foundation.
Financial data (yr. ended 12/31/12): Assets, $4,958,344 (M); expenditures, $250,882; qualifying distributions, $217,984; giving activities include $186,500 for 34 grants (high: $12,500; low: $1,500).
Purpose and activities: Giving primarily for human services.
Fields of interest: Education; Human services; Urban League; Neighborhood centers; Children/youth, services; Family services; Women, centers/services; United Ways and Federated Giving Programs; Economically disadvantaged.
Type of support: General/operating support; Endowments.
Limitations: Giving primarily in Providence, RI. No grants to individuals.
Application information: Complete application guidelines available on Fund web site.
Initial approach: Online through Fund web site
Deadline(s): Dec. 1
Trustee: Bank of America, N.A.
EIN: 056004659

1481

The Victor Herbert Foundation, Inc.

11 Doris Cir.
Newton, MA 02458-1929
***Contact:* Carolyn Jacoby Gabbay, Pres.**

Established in 1969 in NY.
Foundation type: Independent foundation.
Financial data (yr. ended 04/30/13): Assets, $2,651,107 (M); expenditures, $176,618; qualifying distributions, $140,386; giving activities include $138,200 for 16 grants (high: $20,000; low: $250).
Purpose and activities: Emphasis on promoting musical performances and cultural programs, also higher education in music and the arts; support also for medical research.
Fields of interest: Museums; Performing arts; Arts; Higher education; Libraries/library science; Hospitals (general); Health care; Cancer; Diabetes; Cancer research; Human services; Jewish agencies & synagogues.
Type of support: General/operating support; Scholarship funds.

Limitations: Applications accepted. Giving primarily in New York, NY. No grants to individuals.
Application information: Application form not required.
Initial approach: Proposal
Deadline(s): None
Officers: Carolyn Jacoby Gabbay, Pres.; Lois C. Schwartz, Secy.; **Jonathan Jacoby, Treas.**
EIN: 237044623
Other changes: The grantmaker no longer lists a separate application address.

1482
High Meadows Foundation
c/o Carl Ferenbach
P.O. Box 171754
Boston, MA 02116
***E-mail:* info@highmeadowsgroup.org**; Main URL: http://www.highmeadowsfoundation.com

Established in 2007 in MA.
Donors: Carl Ferenbach; Judy Ferenbach.
Foundation type: Independent foundation.
Financial data (yr. ended 12/31/12): Assets, $7,534,960 (M); gifts received, $15,462,398; expenditures, $7,967,807; qualifying distributions, $7,912,070; giving activities include $7,912,070 for 29 grants (high: $2,000,000; low: $10,000).
Purpose and activities: Giving primarily to ensure sound environmental stewardship of our planet; for the management and conservation of non-working farm land in northern New England; for the development of a 21st century social contract; and for the preservation and enhancement of the art of the book beyond the content of its pages. Giving also, on a program specific basis, for education and fellowships that are related to the work of the organizations that the foundation supports.
Fields of interest: Higher education; Education; Environment, natural resources.
Limitations: Applications not accepted. Giving primarily in CO and NJ; some funding in MA and NY.
Application information: Contributes only to pre-selected organizations.
Officers and Trustees:* Carl Ferenbach,* Chair.; Lynne Ball, Secy.-Treas.; Jeffrey L. Berenson; Jane Brock-Wilson; Daniel P. Carbonneau; Judy Ferenbach.
EIN: 208521462

1483
The Honey Dew Family Foundation, Inc.
2 Taunton St., Ste. 261
Plainville, MA 02762 **(508) 699-0079**
***E-mail:* info@honeydewfamilyfoundation.org**; Main URL: http://www.honeydewfamilyfoundation.org
Facebook: https://www.facebook.com/pages/Honey-Dew-Family-Foundation-Inc/234823796534101?ref=ts&fref=ts

Established in 2008 in MA.
Donors: Richard Bowen; Golf Tournament.
Foundation type: Independent foundation.
Financial data (yr. ended 06/30/13): Assets, $8,633 (M); gifts received, $210,685; expenditures, $203,756; qualifying distributions, $142,048; giving activities include $119,798 for 28 + grants (high: $31,850; low: $50), and $22,250 for 77 grants to individuals.
Fields of interest: YM/YWCAs & YM/YWHAs.
Type of support: Scholarships—to individuals.
Limitations: Applications not accepted. Giving primarily in MA.
Application information: Unsolicited requests for funds not accepted.
Officers and Directors:* Richard J. Bowen,* Pres.; Kara J. Bowen,* Clerk; Amanda J. Bowen; Stacy L. DeMaria; Jennifer A. Fellman; Tracie L. Pond; Kelly A. Sofronas.
EIN: 261116810

1484
The Mabel A. Horne Fund
c/o U.S. Trust, Bank of America, N.A.
225 Franklin St., 4th Fl., MA1-225-04-02
Boston, MA 02110-2801 (866) 778-6859
Contact: Phung Pham, V.P.
E-mail: phung.pham@ustrust.com; **Main URL: https://www.bankofamerica.com/philanthropic/grantmaking.go**

Trust established in 1957 in MA.
Donor: Mabel A. Horne‡.
Foundation type: Independent foundation.
Financial data (yr. ended 09/30/13): Assets, $6,468,769 (M); expenditures, $314,963; qualifying distributions, $275,091; giving activities include $238,000 for 24 grants (high: $15,000; low: $1,000).
Purpose and activities: The Trust was established in 1957 to support and promote quality educational, human services, and health care programming for underserved populations.
Fields of interest: Education; Health care; Human services.
Type of support: General/operating support.
Limitations: Giving limited to MA. No support for national organizations. No grants to individuals, or for conferences, film production, scholarships, travel, book publication, or research projects not under the aegis of a recognized organization; no loans.
Publications: Application guidelines.
Application information: Online application and complete application guidelines available on Fund web site.
Initial approach: Online via Fund web site
Deadline(s): Please consult Fund web site
Trustee: Bank of America, N.A.
EIN: 046089241

1485
Howard Home for Aged Men in the City of Brockton
71 Legion Pkwy., 3rd Fl.
Brockton, MA 02301-7225 (508) 584-4088
Contact: John F. Creedon, Pres.

Established in 1942 in MA.
Donors: Horace Howard‡; Daniel W. Field Trust.
Foundation type: Operating foundation.
Financial data (yr. ended 03/31/13): Assets, $4,654,119 (M); expenditures, $330,927; qualifying distributions, $330,927; giving activities include $235,000 for 16 grants (high: $25,000; low: $5,000).
Purpose and activities: Giving for elderly situations (60 years or older).
Fields of interest: Human services.
Limitations: Applications accepted. Giving limited to within 35 miles of Boston, MA. No grants to individuals, salaries, or capital building projects.
Application information: Application form required.
Initial approach: Letter
Deadline(s): None
Officers: John F. Creedon, Pres.; Vaughn Boyajian, Clerk; **Eugene Marrow, Treas.**
EIN: 042103796
Other changes: Eugene Marrow has replaced Robert Prince as Treas.

1486
The Hyams Foundation, Inc.
(formerly Sarah A. Hyams Fund)
50 Federal St., 9th Fl.
Boston, MA 02110-2509 (617) 426-5600
Contact: Elizabeth B. Smith, Exec. Dir.
FAX: (617) 426-5696;
E-mail: info@hyamsfoundation.org; Contact for questions regarding application process: Susan Perry: sperry@hyamsfoundation.org; (617) 426-5600 ext. 307; Main URL: http://www.hyamsfoundation.org
Grantee Perception Report Highlights: http://www.hyamsfoundation.org/documents/CEP_-_Letter_to_Grantees_and_Applicants.pdf
The Hyams Foundation, Inc.'s Philanthropy's Promise: http://www.ncrp.org/philanthropys-promise/who

Established in 1929 in MA as the Sarah A. Hyams Fund; in 1991 merged with the Godfrey Hyams Trust and adopted current name.
Donors: Godfrey M. Hyams‡; Sarah A. Hyams‡.
Foundation type: Independent foundation.
Financial data (yr. ended 12/31/12): Assets, $134,908,398 (M); expenditures, $8,046,210; qualifying distributions, $6,871,822; giving activities include $5,519,531 for 122 grants (high: $150,000; low: $300), and $416,387 for 4 foundation-administered programs.
Purpose and activities: The mission of the foundation is to increase economic, social justice and power within low-income communities. The foundation believes that investing in strategies that enable low-income people to increase their communities will have the greatest social return in these times. The foundation will carry out its mission by: supporting civic participation by low-income communities; promoting economic development that benefits low-income neighborhoods and their residents; and developing the talents and skills of low-income youth.
Fields of interest: Adult/continuing education; Housing/shelter, development; Human services; Youth, services; Family services; Civil rights, race/intergroup relations; Urban/community development; Community/economic development; Disabilities, people with; Asians/Pacific Islanders; African Americans/Blacks; Hispanics/Latinos; Immigrants/refugees; Economically disadvantaged; LGBTQ.
Type of support: Mission-related investments/loans; General/operating support; Continuing support; Program development; Technical assistance; Program-related investments/loans; Matching/challenge support.
Limitations: Applications accepted. Giving primarily in Boston and Chelsea, MA. No support for municipal, state, or federal agencies; institutions of higher learning for standard educational programs, hospitals and health centers, religious organizations for sectarian religious purposes; support for medical research is being phased out. No grants to individuals, or for endowment funds, capital campaigns, fellowships, publications, conferences, films or videos or curriculum development.
Publications: Application guidelines; Annual report; Grants list; Informational brochure (including application guidelines).
Application information: Application form required.

Initial approach: Use online application system via foundation web site. Applicants who are unsure about whether their organization meets the foundation's funding priorities may send a 2-page letter of interest via e-mail
Copies of proposal: 1
Deadline(s): Mar. 1, Sept. 2, and Dec. 2
Board meeting date(s): Mar., June, and Dec.
Final notification: 3 to 4 months

Officers and Trustees:* Marti Wilson-Taylor,* Chair.; Adam D. Seitchik,* Treas.; Iris Gomez,* Clerk; Elizabeth B. Smith, Exec. Dir.; **Wilma H. Davis**; **Lucas H. Guerra**; M. Elena Letona; Penn S. Loh; Karen L. Mapp; **Lily Mendez-Morgan**; **Omar Simmons**; **Roslyn M. Watson**.
Number of staff: 6 full-time professional; 2 full-time support; 1 part-time support.
EIN: 046013680
Other changes: John H. Sarvey is no longer a trustee.

1487
The Iacocca Family Foundation
(formerly The Iacocca Foundation)
867 Boylston St., 6th Fl.
Boston, MA 02116-2774 (617) 267-7747
Contact: Margaret A. Laurence, Exec. Dir.
FAX: (617) 267-8544;
E-mail: info@iacoccafoundation.org; Main URL: http://www.iacoccafoundation.org

Established in 1984 in MI.
Donor: Lido A. "Lee" Iacocca.
Foundation type: Independent foundation.
Financial data (yr. ended 12/31/12): Assets, $35,515,140 (M); gifts received, $215,842; expenditures, $2,409,881; qualifying distributions, $1,446,285; giving activities include $1,446,285 for grants.
Purpose and activities: Giving primarily for innovative and promising type 1 diabetes research programs and projects that will lead to a cure for the disease and alleviate complications caused by it.
Fields of interest: Hospitals (general); Diabetes; Diabetes research; Foundations (private grantmaking).
Type of support: Conferences/seminars; Professorships; Fellowships; Research; Matching/challenge support.
Publications: Application guidelines.
Application information: See foundation web site for full application guidelines and requirements, including downloadable application form. Application form submitted by fax not accepted. Application form required.
Initial approach: Call for proposals via web site or announcement on web site
Copies of proposal: 6
Deadline(s): See foundation web site for application deadline
Board meeting date(s): Fall and spring
Final notification: June 30

Officers and Trustees:* **Lido A. "Lee" Iacocca,* Chair.**; Kathryn Iacocca Hentz, Pres.; Louis E. Lataif, Secy.; Margaret Laurence, Exec. Dir.; Ken Anderson; Lia Iacocca Assad; Edward Bousa; John Gerace; Desmond Heathwood.
Number of staff: 3 full-time professional.
EIN: 386071154
Other changes: Lido A. "Lee" Iacocca is now Chair.

1488
Inavale Foundation, Inc.
c/o KLR
800 South St., No. 300
Waltham, MA **02453-1478**

Established in 1998 in MA.
Donors: Katherine Buffett; William N. Buffett; Susan Kennedy.
Foundation type: Independent foundation.
Financial data (yr. ended 12/31/12): Assets, $16,351,507 (M); expenditures, $1,014,799; qualifying distributions, $896,860; giving activities include $891,300 for 66 grants (high: $95,000; low: $150).
Fields of interest: Arts; Higher education; Education; Health organizations; Human services; Foundations (private grantmaking); Protestant agencies & churches.
Type of support: General/operating support.
Limitations: Applications not accepted. Giving in the U.S., with emphasis on MA. No grants to individuals.
Application information: Contributes only to pre-selected organizations.
Officers and Directors:* William N. Buffett,* Pres.; Susan Kennedy,* Treas.; Thomas M. Buffett; Wendy O. Buffett; Noah E. Buffett-Kennedy.
EIN: 043409789

1489
Informed Medical Decisions Foundation, Inc.
(formerly Foundation for Informed Medical Decisions Foundation)
40 Court St., Ste. 300
Boston, MA 02108-2202 (617) 367-2000
Main URL: http://informedmedicaldecisions.org
Facebook: http://www.facebook.com/imdfoundation?v=app_106171216118819
Google Plus: https://plus.google.com/114164346716236100178/posts
LinkedIn: http://www.linkedin.com/company/informed-medical-decisions-foundation
RSS Feed: http://www.informedmedicaldecisions.org/feed/?cat=15
Scoop.it!: http://www.scoop.it/u/imdfoundation
Slideshare: http://www.slideshare.net/fimdm
Twitter: http://twitter.com/fimdm
YouTube: http://www.youtube.com/user/FIMDM?feature=mhum

Established in MA.
Donor: David Wennberg.
Foundation type: Operating foundation.
Financial data (yr. ended 06/30/12): Assets, $23,221,021 (M); expenditures, $11,509,581; qualifying distributions, $11,440,124; giving activities include $3,333,573 for 58 grants (high: $662,574; low: $4,194).
Purpose and activities: The foundation is dedicated to assuring that people understand their choices and have the information they need to make sound decisions affecting their health and well-being.
Fields of interest: Higher education; Hospitals (general); Health care.
Limitations: Giving primarily in the U.S., with some emphasis on NH; some funding internationally, particularly in the UK.
Application information: Application information and updates available on foundation web site.
Initial approach: Proposal not to exceed 10 pages
Deadline(s): Varies

Officers and Directors:* John Billings, J.D.*, Chair.; Michael J. Barry, M.D., Pres.; **Leslie Kelly Hall, Sr. V.P., Policy**; **Benjamin W. Moulton, JD, MPH, Sr. V.P.**; Christine M. Fisler,* C.O.O. and C.F.O.; James R. Bell, Ph.D.; Clarence H. Braddock III, M.D., MPH; Richard A. Deyo, M.D., MPH; Susan Edgman-Levitan; Arthur Levin, MPH; Margaret E. O'Kane; Carmen Hooker Odom; Lee Sechrest, Ph.D.; Harold C. Sox, M.D.
EIN: 020434037

1490
The Jacobson Family Trust Foundation
240 Newbury St., Fl. 2
Boston, MA 02116-2580

Established in 1997 in MA.
Donor: Jonathon Jacobson.
Foundation type: Independent foundation.
Financial data (yr. ended 12/31/12): Assets, $384,311,294 (M); gifts received, $25,000,000; expenditures, $22,299,765; qualifying distributions, $17,490,154; giving activities include $16,499,565 for 117 grants (high: $2,000,000; low: $500).
Fields of interest: Elementary/secondary education; Higher education; Education; Human services; Children/youth, services; Foundations (private grantmaking); Jewish federated giving programs; Jewish agencies & synagogues.
Limitations: Applications not accepted. Giving primarily in MA, with emphasis on the Boston area. No grants to individuals.
Application information: Contributes only to pre-selected organizations.
Officers and Trustees:* **Joanna Jacobson,* Pres.**; William Foster, Exec. Dir.; Jonathon Jacobson.
EIN: 046836735
Other changes: Joanna Jacobson is now Pres.

1491
The Jaffe Foundation
c/o 8 Pine St.
P.O. Box 307
Stockbridge, MA 01262 **(413) 298-0000**
Contact: Holly Seagrave
***FAX:* (413) 298-3199**

Established in 1962 in MA.
Donors: Meyer Jaffe†; Edwin A. Jaffe.
Foundation type: Independent foundation.
Financial data (yr. ended 06/30/13): Assets, $167,961 (M); expenditures, $192,875; qualifying distributions, $148,629; giving activities include $105,963 for 25 grants (high: $25,000; low: -$1,837).
Purpose and activities: The foundation is dedicated to the support of disadvantaged persons in the U.S. and other parts of the world and is committed to the survival of the Jewish people as a cultural unity. In pursuing these goals, the foundation focuses its support mainly in the areas of health, education, and the arts.
Fields of interest: Visual arts; Performing arts; Arts; Higher education; Hospitals (general); Health care; Human services; Jewish federated giving programs; Public affairs, finance; Jewish agencies & synagogues; Economically disadvantaged.
Limitations: Applications accepted. Giving primarily in MA and NY. No grants to individuals.
Application information: Application form required.
Initial approach: Proposal
Deadline(s): None
Board meeting date(s): Summer

Officers: Robert Jaffe, Chair.; Lola Jaffe, Vice-Chair.
EIN: 046049261

1492

Esther B. Kahn Charitable Foundation

c/o Choate Hall & Stewart LLP
Two International Pl.
Boston, MA **02110** **(617) 248-4814**
***Contact:* John M. Cornish, Tr.**
E-mail: estherbkahn@choate.com; Main URL: http://www.estherbkahn.org

Established in 1998 in MA.
Donor: Esther B. Kahn†.
Foundation type: Independent foundation.
Financial data (yr. ended 05/31/13): Assets, $4,499,403 (M); expenditures, $264,020; qualifying distributions, $225,893; giving activities include $190,000 for 24 grants (high: $12,500; low: $5,000).
Purpose and activities: The foundation supports and funds innovative approaches to education, the arts, and medical research.
Fields of interest: Performing arts, theater; Performing arts, opera; Performing arts, education; Education; Hospitals (specialty); Medical research.
Type of support: Annual campaigns; Capital campaigns; Conferences/seminars; Continuing support; Curriculum development; Endowments; Equipment; Fellowships; Internship funds; Program development; Program evaluation; Publication; Research; Scholarship funds; Seed money; Technical assistance.
Limitations: Applications accepted. Giving on a national basis. No support for private foundations. No grants to individuals.
Publications: Application guidelines; Informational brochure (including application guidelines).
Application information: Preliminary application through foundation web site; final application by invitation only. See foundation web site for application policies, guidelines and application form. Application form required.
***Initial approach:* E-mail**
***Copies of proposal:* 4**
Deadline(s): June 30 and Dec. 30
Board meeting date(s): Jan. and July.
Final notification: 3 weeks following board meeting
Trustees: John M. Cornish; Richard J. Eckstein; Robert A. Russo.
Number of staff: 2 part-time professional.
EIN: 046869254

1493

The Kelsey Trust

99 Trapelo Rd.
Lincoln, MA 01773-2107

Established in 1988 in MA.
Donor: Sally Patrick Johnson.
Foundation type: Independent foundation.
Financial data (yr. ended 06/30/13): Assets, $4,148,280 (M); expenditures, $221,545; qualifying distributions, $196,500; giving activities include $196,500 for 20 grants (high: $20,000; low: $2,500).
Purpose and activities: Primary areas of interest include the environment, children and families, education, and health.
Fields of interest: Child development, education; Vocational education; Adult education—literacy, basic skills & GED; Education, reading; Education; Environment, natural resources; Environment; Reproductive health, family planning; Health care; Nutrition; Housing/shelter, public policy; Youth, services; Child development, services; Family services; Infants/toddlers; Children/youth; Children; Youth; Aging; Single parents; Immigrants/refugees; Economically disadvantaged; Homeless.
Type of support: General/operating support; Continuing support; Capital campaigns; Land acquisition; Emergency funds; Publication; Seed money; Scholarship funds; Technical assistance; Program evaluation; Program-related investments/loans; Matching/challenge support.
Limitations: Applications not accepted. Giving limited to the Lake Champlain Drainage Basin. No support for religious or political organizations. No grants to individuals.
Application information: Unsolicited requests for funds not accepted.
Board meeting date(s): June and Dec.
Trustees: Paula D. Johnson; Sally P. Johnson; Stephen P. Johnson.
Number of staff: None.
EIN: 046609917
Other changes: The grantmaker has moved from VT to MA.
The grantmaker no longer publishes application guidelines.

1494

The Henry P. Kendall Foundation

176 Federal St.
Boston, MA 02110-2214 (617) 951-2525
Contact: Theodore M. Smith, Exec. Dir.
FAX: (617) 951-2556; E-mail: info@kendall.org; Main URL: http://www.kendall.org
Grants List: http://www.kendall.org/grantseekers

Trust established in 1957 in MA.
Donors: Henry Kendall†; Henry Way Kendall Trust; and members of the Henry P. Kendall family.
Foundation type: Independent foundation.
Financial data (yr. ended 12/31/12): Assets, $79,815,633 (M); expenditures, $4,699,279; qualifying distributions, $4,571,376; giving activities include $3,659,950 for 34 grants (high: $1,600,000; low: $5,000).
Purpose and activities: Emphasis on strategic environmental policies/ecosystem management.
Fields of interest: Environment, natural resources.
International interests: Canada.
Type of support: Management development/capacity building; Research; General/operating support; Program development; Seed money; Internship funds.
Limitations: Applications not accepted. Giving primarily in New England and the Northeast. No support for waste clean-ups, toxic or air/water pollution prevention or pollution monitoring initiatives, land trusts, or species-specific preservation efforts. No grants to individuals, or for capital or endowment funds, building construction/operation, basic research, scholarships, fellowships, equipment, debt reduction, or conference participation/travel.
Publications: Biennial report.
Application information: Unsolicited proposals and inquiries will not be reviewed.
Board meeting date(s): Mar., June, and Nov.
Officer and Trustees:* Andrew W. Kendall,* Exec. Dir.; John P. Kendall; Ken Meyers; Phoebe Winder.
Number of staff: 6 full-time professional.
EIN: 046029103
Other changes: At the close of 2012, the grantmaker paid grants of $3,659,950, a 76.9% increase over the 2011 disbursements, $2,068,366.
Andrew W. Kendall has replaced Theodore M. Smith as Exec. Dir.

1495

The D. Kim Foundation for The History of Science and Technology In East Asia, Inc.

663 Lowell St.
Lexington, MA 02420-1961
***E-mail:* info@dkimfoundation.org**; Main URL: http://www.dkimfoundation.org

Donor: Don-Won Kim.
Foundation type: Independent foundation.
Financial data (yr. ended 06/30/13): Assets, $3,843,156 (M); expenditures, $219,839; qualifying distributions, $201,374; giving activities include $136,500 for 8 grants to individuals (high: $55,000; low: $2,500).
Purpose and activities: Dedicated to furthering the study of the history of science and technology in East Asia by providing fellowships and grants.
Fields of interest: Education, research.
Type of support: Fellowships; Grants to individuals.
Limitations: Applications not accepted. **Giving primarily in MA; funding also in CA and internationally.**
Application information: Unsolicited requests for funds not accepted.
Officer and Trustees:* Dong-Won Kim,* Pres. and Treas.; **Christopher Cullen**; **Takehiko Hashimoto**; **Shigehisa Kuriyama**; **Stuart W. Leslie**; **Angela K.C. Leung.**
EIN: 800297127

1496

The Kittredge Foundation

P.O. Box 52570
Boston, MA 02205-2570

Established in 2000 in MA.
Donors: Michael J. Kittredge; Lisa R. Kittredge.
Foundation type: Independent foundation.
Financial data (yr. ended 04/30/13): Assets, $2,559,301 (M); gifts received, $2,845; expenditures, $690,071; qualifying distributions, $648,533; giving activities include $648,533 for 9 grants (high: $275,000; low: $1,000).
Fields of interest: Education; Hospitals (general); Cancer; Children/youth, services; Religion; Women.
Type of support: General/operating support.
Limitations: Applications not accepted. Giving primarily in MA. No grants to individuals.
Application information: Unsolicited requests for funds not accepted.
Trustees: Lisa R. Kittredge; Michael J. Kittredge.
EIN: 046911444
Other changes: For the fiscal year ended Apr. 30, 2013, the grantmaker paid grants of $648,533, a 376.7% increase over the fiscal 2012 disbursements, $136,033.

1497

Krieger Charitable Trust

63 Beethoven Ave.
Waban, MA 02468-1732 **(617) 467-5643**
Contact: Roger M. Klein, Tr.
***E-mail:* rogerklein2000@yahoo.com**

Established in 1986 in NJ.
Foundation type: Independent foundation.
Financial data (yr. ended 12/31/11): Assets, $8,383,127 (M); expenditures, $386,001; qualifying distributions, $386,001; giving activities include $351,530 for 90 grants (high: $100,000; low: $100).
Purpose and activities: Giving primarily to Jewish organizations, including Jewish education.

Fields of interest: Higher education; Human services; United Ways and Federated Giving Programs; Jewish agencies & synagogues.
Type of support: General/operating support; Continuing support; Annual campaigns; Capital campaigns; Endowments; Scholarship funds.
Limitations: Applications accepted. Giving primarily in northern NJ. No grants to individuals; no loans.
Application information: Application form not required.
Deadline(s): None
Trustees: Herbert C. Klein; Roger M. Klein.
EIN: 226374448

1498
The Lalor Foundation, Inc.
c/o GMA Foundations
77 Summer St., 8th Fl.
Boston, MA 02110-1006 **(617) 391-3088**
***Contact:* Hannah Blaisdell**
***FAX:* (617) 426-7087;**
E-mail: hblaisdell@gmafoundations.com; Main URL: http://www.lalorfound.org

Incorporated in 1935 in DE.
Donors: Willard A. Lalor†; and members of the Lalor family.
Foundation type: Independent foundation.
Financial data (yr. ended 09/30/12): Assets, $12,786,442 (M); expenditures, $608,368; qualifying distributions, $551,183; giving activities include $438,136 for 28 grants (high: $33,000; low: $500).
Purpose and activities: The foundation awards fellowships to institutions for basic postdoctoral research in mammalian reproductive biology as related to the regulation of fertility.
Fields of interest: Reproductive health, family planning.
Type of support: Program development; Fellowships.
Limitations: Applications accepted. Giving on a national and international basis. No support for private organizations. No grants to individuals directly, or for operating budgets, capital or endowment funds, continuing support, annual campaigns, seed money, emergency funds, deficit financing, or matching gifts; no loans.
Publications: Application guidelines; Grants list.
Application information: Full proposals are by invitation only, upon review of initial concept paper. Only online applications are accepted. Application form required.
***Initial approach:* Submit concept paper through foundation web site**
Copies of proposal: 1
Deadline(s): May 1 and Nov. 1
Board meeting date(s): June and Dec.
***Final notification:* Within 6-8 weeks for concept paper**
Officers: Cynthia B. Patterson, Pres.; Lalor Burdick, Secy.-Treas.
Trustees: Andrew G. Braun; Christopher Burdick; Carol Chandler; Sally H. Zeckhauser.
EIN: 516000153

1499
The Leadership and Learning Foundation, Inc.
Boston, MA

The foundation terminated in 2013 and transferred its assets to Advisors Charitable Gift Fund.

1500
Learning by Giving Foundation Inc.
304 Newbury St.
Boston, MA **02115**
Main URL: http://www.learningbygivingfoundation.org
Facebook: https://www.facebook.com/learningbygivingfoundation?fref=ts
Google Plus: https://plus.google.com/+LearningbygivingfoundationOrg/posts
LinkedIn: http://www.linkedin.com/company/3037922?trk=tyah
Twitter: https://twitter.com/learngive
YouTube: https://www.youtube.com/channel/UC1dcJTrsjzE30Q8LmXamL0g

Donors: Doris Buffett; Kristen E. Williams.
Foundation type: Independent foundation.
Financial data (yr. ended 06/30/13): Assets, $5,001,510 (M); gifts received, $3,718,557; expenditures, $614,061; qualifying distributions, $315,000; giving activities include $315,000 for 33 grants (high: $20,000; low: $500).
Fields of interest: Education.
Limitations: Applications not accepted. **Giving primarily in MA and NY.**
Application information: Unsolicited requests for funds not accepted.
Officer: Louise Sawyer, Mgr.
Directors: Doris Buffett; Howard W. Buffett; Margaret Johnson; Alex Rozek; **Mimi Rozek.**
EIN: 452324555
Other changes: Sarah Krueger is no longer a director.

1501
June Rockwell Levy Foundation, Inc.
20 Oak St.
Beverly Farms, MA 01915-2230
Application address: c/o Jonathan B. Loring, Fiduciary Trust, 175 Federal St., Boston, MA 02110-2289, tel.: (617) 574-3426

Incorporated in 1947 in CT.
Donor: Austin T. Levy†.
Foundation type: Independent foundation.
Financial data (yr. ended 12/31/11): Assets, $23,093,218 (M); expenditures, $1,415,560; qualifying distributions, $1,269,557; giving activities include $1,223,925 for 100 grants (high: $90,000; low: $1,700).
Purpose and activities: Giving primarily for the arts, education, health, and children and social services.
Fields of interest: Arts; Education; Health care; Human services; Children/youth, services; United Ways and Federated Giving Programs.
Type of support: General/operating support; Continuing support; Capital campaigns; Building/renovation; Equipment; Seed money; Scholarship funds; Research.
Limitations: Giving primarily in northern RI. No support for religious purposes. No grants to individuals.
Application information: Application form required.
Initial approach: Letter
Copies of proposal: 1
Deadline(s): None
Board meeting date(s): Starting in Feb., 1st Tues. of every other month
Officers and Trustees:* Jonathan B. Loring,* Pres.; Paul F. Greene,* Secy.; Nancy B. Smith, Treas.; Karen Delponte; Raymond G. Leveille, Jr.; Raymond N. Menard; Robert P. Picard; Thomas H. Quill, Jr.; Dr. H. Denman Scott; **Nancy B. Smith.**
EIN: 046074284
Other changes: James K. Edwards is no longer a trustee.

1502
The Liberty Mutual Foundation, Inc.
175 Berkeley St.
Boston, MA 02116-5066
E-mail: foundation@LibertyMutual.com; Main URL: http://www.libertymutualfoundation.org

Established in 2003 in MA.
Donor: Liberty Mutual Insurance Co.
Foundation type: Company-sponsored foundation.
Financial data (yr. ended 12/31/12): Assets, $43,027,164 (M); gifts received, $28,675,872; expenditures, $10,934,124; qualifying distributions, $10,493,200; giving activities include $10,492,500 for 6,302 grants (high: $250,000; low: $2).
Purpose and activities: The foundation supports organizations involved with arts and culture, education, health, human services, community development, and civic affairs. Special emphasis is directed toward programs designed to serve youth, low-income families and individuals, and people with disabilities.
Fields of interest: Museums; Performing arts, orchestras; Arts; Elementary/secondary education; Elementary school/education; Higher education; Education, services; Education; Health care; Food banks; Safety/disasters; Recreation, camps; Boys & girls clubs; Youth development, adult & child programs; American Red Cross; Salvation Army; Family services; Developmentally disabled, centers & services; Homeless, human services; Human services; Community/economic development; Assistive technology; Leadership development; Public affairs; Youth; Disabilities, people with; Economically disadvantaged; Homeless.
Type of support: General/operating support; Continuing support; Capital campaigns; Program development; Curriculum development; Scholarship funds; Employee volunteer services; Employee matching gifts.
Limitations: Applications accepted. **Giving primarily in areas of company operations in MA, with emphasis on Boston.** No support for grantmaking foundations, religious organizations not of direct benefit to the entire community, or fraternal, social, or political organizations. No grants to individuals, or for trips, tours, or transportation, debt reduction, conferences, forums, or special events.
Publications: Application guidelines.
Application information: Support is limited to 1 contribution or RFP per organization during any given year. Organizations receiving support are asked to submit a final assessment report. Application form required.
Initial approach: Complete online application form
***Deadline(s):* None; preferably Mar. 6 for Accessibility and Inclusion RFP; Mar. 31 for the Basic Services Initiative RFP;**
Board meeting date(s): Monthly
***Final notification:* 6 to 8 weeks; May for Basic Services Initiative RFP**
Officers and Directors:* David H. Long,* Chair. and C.E.O.; Dexter R. Legg,* V.P. and Secy.; Dennis J. Langwell,* V.P., C.F.O., and Treas.; Christopher C. Mansfield,* V.P. and Genl. Counsel; A. Alexander Fontanes,* V.P. and C.I.O; Melissa M. Macdonnell, V.P.; Gary J. Ostrow, V.P.
EIN: 141893520
Other changes: At the close of 2012, the fair market value of the grantmaker's assets was

$43,027,164, a 82.2% increase over the 2011 value, $23,617,914.

1503
Lincoln Institute of Land Policy
(formerly Lincoln Foundation, Inc.)
113 Brattle St.
Cambridge, MA 02138-3400 (617) 661-3016
FAX: (617) 661-7235; **E-mail: help@lincolnist.edu; Phoenix office: c/o Kathryn J. Lincoln, Chair. and C.I.O., and Dione A. Etter, Asst. to the Chair. and Corp. Secy., 11010 N. Tatum Blvd., Ste. D-101, Phoenix, AZ 85028, tel.: (602) 393-4300; Additional tel.: (800) 526-3873, additional fax: (800) 526-3944**; Main URL: http://www.lincolninst.edu
Blog: http://www.lincolninst.edu/news/atlincolnhouse.asp
Facebook: https://www.facebook.com/lincolninstituteoflandpolicy
LinkedIn: http://www.linkedin.com/company/1210434
Twitter: http://twitter.com/landpolicy
YouTube: http://www.youtube.com/user/LincolnLandPolicy

Established in 1946 in AZ and MA; Founded as Lincoln Foundation; merged into the Lincoln Institute of Land Policy and adopted current name in 2006.
Foundation type: Operating foundation.
Financial data (yr. ended 06/30/13): Assets, $471,656,024 (M); expenditures, $17,509,698; qualifying distributions, $14,346,101; giving activities include $205,429 for 12 grants (high: $24,000; low: $12,829), $265,750 for 21 grants to individuals (high: $22,200; low: $10,000), and $9,867,508 for foundation-administered programs.
Purpose and activities: The Institute improves the dialogue about urban development, the built environment, and tax policy in the United States and abroad. Through research, training, conferences, demonstration projects, publications, and multi-media, the organization provides non-partisan analysis and evaluation for today's regulatory, planning, and policy decisions.
Fields of interest: Public affairs, research; Public affairs, information services; Public affairs, public education.
International interests: China; Europe; Latin America.
Type of support: Research; Publication; Fellowships.
Limitations: Applications not accepted. Giving on a national and international basis.
Publications: Informational brochure; Newsletter.
Application information: Unsolicited requests for funds not accepted.
Officers and Directors:* Kathryn Lincoln,* Chair. and C.I.O.; George McCarthy,* C.E.O. and Pres.; Dennis W. Robinson, V.P., Finance and Opers., and Treas.; Dione Etter, Secy.; Roy W. Bahl; and 14 additional directors.
EIN: 866021106
Other changes: Henry Coleman and Gary Cornia are no longer directors.

1504
The Linden Foundation Inc.
c/o GMA Foundations
77 Summer St., 8th Fl.
Boston, MA 02110-1006 **(617) 426-7080, ext. 288**
***Contact:* Ruth Victorin, Fdn. Asst.**
FAX: (617) 426-7087;
E-mail: rvictorin@gmafoundations.com; **Ruth Victorin direct tel. line: (617) 391-3101**; Main URL: http://www.lindenfoundation.org

Established in 1996 in NJ.
Donors: Thomas V.A. Kelsey 1968 Revocable Trust; Elizabeth S. Kelsey 1988 Revocable Trust.
Foundation type: Independent foundation.
Financial data (yr. ended 12/31/12): Assets, $7,344,360 (M); gifts received, $299,737; expenditures, $780,345; qualifying distributions, $702,463; giving activities include $672,500 for 36 grants (high: $40,000; low: $7,000).
Purpose and activities: Giving to organizations that strengthen disadvantaged and homeless families by helping provide them with the skills and support systems they need to become cohesive, internally supportive, and self-sufficient. Preference is given to comprehensive programs that most directly help those in need, involve multiple family members, provide sustained support to the participants, and are administered by community-based organizations.
Fields of interest: Family services; Homeless, human services; Economically disadvantaged; Homeless.
Type of support: General/operating support; Program development; Matching/challenge support.
Limitations: Applications not accepted. Giving in the northern side of the greater Boston, MA, area, with emphasis on communities inside Route 128 and the North Shore to the Gloucester area, as well as in the counties of the Lakes Region and northern NH. No support for public schools, charter schools or universities, or for community organizing or political lobbying efforts. No grants to individuals, or for tickets to artistic performances, computer centers, or operating support for community centers.
Application information: Unsolicited requests for funds not accepted.
Officers: Thomas V.A. Kelsey, Pres. and Treas.; Margen S. Kelsey, Secy.
Directors: Elizabeth S. Kelsey; Suzanne V.A. Kelsey; Lea Dobbs Kelsey; William C. Kelsey; Mark J. Pine; Kenneth V. Siegert.
Number of staff: None.
EIN: 226678640

1505
Greater Lowell Community Foundation
100 Merrimack St., Ste. 202
Lowell, MA 01852-1723 (978) 970-1600
Contact: Raymond E. Riddick, Jr., Exec. Dir.
FAX: (978) 970-2444;
E-mail: ray@glcfoundation.org; Main URL: http://www.glcfoundation.org

Established in 1996 in MA.
Donors: Joe Donahue; Richard K. Donahue, Sr.; Human Svcs. Corp.; Lowell Museum Corp.; The Theodore Edson Parker Foundation.
Foundation type: Community foundation.
Financial data (yr. ended 12/31/12): Assets, $23,739,426 (M); gifts received, $2,230,513; expenditures, $1,755,450; giving activities include $778,911 for 46 grants (high: $57,250), and $203,818 for 150 grants to individuals.
Purpose and activities: The foundation seeks to improve the quality of life in the greater Lowell, MA, area by attracting funds, distributing grants, making loans and striving as a catalyst and leader among funders, agencies and individuals to address identified and emerging community needs.
Fields of interest: Arts; Education; Environment, water pollution; Environment, water resources; Environment; Health care; Human services; Economic development; Community/economic development; Voluntarism promotion.
Type of support: Income development; Management development/capacity building.
Limitations: Applications accepted. Giving limited to the greater Lowell, Nashoba, and Western Merrimack Valley, MA, regions. No support for religious organizations or government agencies. No grants to individuals (except for scholarships), or for continuing support, operating expenses, building funds or endowment funds; no multi-year commitments.
Publications: Application guidelines; Annual report; Financial statement; Grants list.
Application information: Visit foundation web site for application deadlines and guidelines. Full proposals may be submitted by invitation only. Application form required.
Initial approach: E-mail Concept Paper and Cover Sheet
Deadline(s): Varies
Officers and Directors:* Steven Joncas,* Pres.; Kay Doyle, Ph. D.*, V.P.; James C. Shannon III,* Treas.; Brian J. Stafford, C.P.A.*, Asst. Treas.; **Susan Winship, Exec. Dir.**; Janinne Nocco, Cont.; Jeff Bergart,* C.F.O.; Annmarie Roark,* Clerk; **Richard K. Donahue, Sr., Emeritus; George L. Duncan, Emeritus; Luis Pedroso, Emeritus**; Joseph Bartolotta; Brian Chapman; John P. Chemaly; Dorothy Chen-Courtin, Ph.D.; Scott Flagg; Karen Frederick; Jacqueline F. Moloney, Ed.D.; Amsi Y. Morales; James D. Nolan; James H. Reichheld, M.D.; Timothy M. Sweeney.
EIN: 043401997
Other changes: Susan Winship has replaced Raymond E. Riddick Jr. as Exec. Dir.
William Samaras is no longer a director.

1506
George W.P. Magee Trust
c/o U.S. Trust, Bank of America, N.A.
225 Franklin St., MA1-225-04-02
Boston, MA 02110
Contact: Augusta Haydock, Sr. V.P.
E-mail: augusta.k.haydock@ustrust.com; **Main URL: https://www.bankofamerica.com/philanthropic/grantmaking.go**
Foundation type: Independent foundation.
Financial data (yr. ended 09/30/13): Assets, $7,516,854 (M); expenditures, $385,237; qualifying distributions, $341,511; giving activities include $298,700 for 10 grants (high: $40,000; low: $25,000).
Purpose and activities: Supports the councils of the Boy Scouts of America that are located in Massachusetts.
Fields of interest: Boy scouts.
Limitations: Giving primarily in MA.
Application information: Complete application guidelines available on Trust web site.
Deadline(s): Sept. 15
Trustee: Bank of America, N.A.
EIN: 046011097

1507
Makepeace Neighborhood Fund
158 Tihonet Rd.
Wareham, MA 02571-1104 (508) 295-1000
***Contact:* Linda M. Burke**
***Main URL:* http://admakepeace.com/**

Established in 2004 in MA.
Donor: A. D. Makepeace Co.

Foundation type: Company-sponsored foundation.
Financial data (yr. ended 12/31/12): Assets, $166,038 (M); gifts received, $140,000; expenditures, $140,363; qualifying distributions, $135,260; giving activities include $135,260 for grants.
Purpose and activities: The fund supports organizations involved with historic preservation, education, environmental protection, health care, agriculture, and community housing.
Fields of interest: Historic preservation/historical societies; Education; Environment, natural resources; Environment; Animals/wildlife; Health care; Agriculture/food; Housing/shelter.
Type of support: Scholarship funds; General/operating support; Program development.
Limitations: Applications accepted. Giving limited to Carver, Middleborough, Plymouth, Rochester, and Wareham, MA. No grants to individuals.
Publications: Application guidelines; Grants list.
Application information: Grants range from $5,000 to $10,000. Application form required.

Initial approach: Download application form and mail to foundation
Copies of proposal: 1
Deadline(s): Mar. 15
Board meeting date(s): Nov.
Final notification: May

Trustees: Joanna Bennett; Richard Canning; Michael P. Hogan; Christopher Makepeace; Elizabeth Snow.
EIN: 412163159

1508
Massachusetts Maternity & Foundling Hospital Corporation
P.O. Box 600805
Newtonville, MA 02460-0008 (617) 928-1725
Contact: Cheryl Forte, Treas.
E-mail: info@massmaternity.org; Main URL: http://massmaternity.org

Established in 1893 in MA.
Foundation type: Independent foundation.
Financial data (yr. ended 10/31/13): Assets, $2,901,100 (M); expenditures, $149,941; qualifying distributions, $148,296; giving activities include $147,011 for 5 grants (high: $50,000; low: $10,136).
Purpose and activities: Giving to organizations that provide care for young unwed mothers of limited means and their infant children and for the prevention of teenage pregnancies.
Fields of interest: Health organizations; Human services.
Type of support: Annual campaigns; Building/renovation; Emergency funds; Program development; Conferences/seminars.
Limitations: Applications accepted. Giving limited to the greater metropolitan Boston, MA, area. No support for day care programs. No grants to individuals.
Publications: Application guidelines.
Application information: See foundation web site for complete application guidelines. Application form required.

***Initial approach:* Submit via e-mail the Associated Grant Makers Common Proposal Form, available on foundation web site, along with other requested items.**
Deadline(s): Nov. 1
***Final notification:* Late Apr.**

Officers and Directors:* Thomas J. Connolly, M.D.*, Pres.; Douglas A. Morash,* V.P.; Nolly E. Corley,* Secy.; Cheryl Forte,* Treas.; Anne Groves; Lori B. Leeth.
EIN: 042628366
Other changes: The grantmaker now makes its application guidelines available online.

1509
John A. McNeice, Jr. Charitable Foundation
c/o Choate
P.O. Box 96109
Boston, MA **02196**

Established in 1997 in MA.
Donors: John A. McNeice, Jr.; John McNeice.
Foundation type: Independent foundation.
Financial data (yr. ended 04/30/13): Assets, $5,207,898 (M); expenditures, $371,456; qualifying distributions, $336,679; giving activities include $250,000 for 9 grants (high: $202,500; low: $500).
Purpose and activities: Giving primarily for education.
Fields of interest: Elementary/secondary education; Hospitals (general); Health organizations; Housing/shelter, homeless; Salvation Army.
Limitations: Applications not accepted. Giving primarily in MA. No grants to individuals.
Application information: Unsolicited requests for funds not accepted.
Officer and Trustees:* Margarete Anne Portanova,* Exec. Dir.; George Ashur; Edward G. Casey; A. Silvana Giner; John A. McNeice, Jr.; William B. Neenan, S.J.; John Shaughnessy, Jr.
EIN: 043371560
Other changes: The grantmaker no longer lists a phone.

1510
The Meelia Family Foundation
26 Patriot Pl., Ste. 104
Foxboro, MA **02035-3304**

Established in 2006 in MA.
Donors: Richard J. Meelia; Mary J. Meelia.
Foundation type: Independent foundation.
Financial data (yr. ended 12/31/12): Assets, $10,095,649 (M); gifts received, $5,002,016; expenditures, $280,085; qualifying distributions, $279,000; giving activities include $279,000 for grants.
Fields of interest: Education; Health care; Health organizations; Human services; Catholic agencies & churches.
Limitations: Applications not accepted. Giving primarily in MA. No grants to individuals.
Application information: Contributes only to pre-selected organizations.
Trustee: Richard J. Meelia.
EIN: 207198269
Other changes: Mary J. Meelia is no longer trustee.

1511
The Melville Charitable Trust
11 Beacon St., Ste. 914
Boston, MA 02108-3020 (617) 236-2244
Contact: Aimee Hendrigan
FAX: (617) 307-4590;
E-mail: ahendrigan@melvilletrust.org; Main URL: http://www.melvilletrust.org
Grants List: http://www.melvilletrust.org/grantee-partners/
Melville Charitable Trust's Philanthropy Promise: http://www.ncrp.org/philanthropys-promise/who
Twitter: https://twitter.com/MelvilleTrust

Established in 1987 in NY.
Donor: Dorothy Melville†.
Foundation type: Independent foundation.
Financial data (yr. ended 12/31/12): Assets, $148,390,535 (M); gifts received, $12,024,018; expenditures, $8,815,681; qualifying distributions, $5,983,474; giving activities include $4,493,338 for 47 grants (high: $600,000; low: $250), and $2,481,513 for 4 foundation-administered programs.
Purpose and activities: The trust concentrates its efforts on supporting solutions to prevent and end homelessness. The trust supports service and housing programs in Connecticut that can serve as models throughout the country. The trust also funds educational, research and advocacy initiatives in the state and on the national level.
Fields of interest: Housing/shelter, development; Housing/shelter, services; Homeless, human services; Community development, neighborhood development; Economic development; Homeless.
Type of support: General/operating support; Management development/capacity building; Program development; Conferences/seminars; Publication; Seed money; Research; Technical assistance; Consulting services; Program evaluation; Program-related investments/loans; Matching/challenge support.
Limitations: Applications accepted. Giving primarily in CT. No support for religious organizations for religious purposes. No grants to individuals, for scholarships, budget deficits, or general fundraising drives or events.
Publications: Application guidelines; Grants list; Program policy statement; Program policy statement (including application guidelines).
Application information: See foundation web site. Application form not required.

Initial approach: Concept paper
Copies of proposal: 1
Deadline(s): Rolling
Board meeting date(s): Varies
Final notification: Varies

Officer and Board Members:* Stephen Melville,* Chair.; **Arthur Evans**; Shelley Geballe; **David Hadden**; **Robert M. Haggett**; Carla Javits; Ruth Melville.
Trustee: Bank of America, N.A.
Number of staff: 2 full-time professional; 2 part-time professional.
EIN: 133415258

1512
Memorial Foundation for the Blind Inc.
(formerly Memorial Homes for the Blind)
799 W. Boylston St.
Worcester, MA 01606-3071 **(508) 854-9980**
***E-mail:* raymondlma@charter.net**; Main URL: http://www.mfblind.org/

Established in 1951 in MA.
Foundation type: Independent foundation.
Financial data (yr. ended 03/31/13): Assets, $3,986,492 (M); gifts received, $192,175; expenditures, $257,312; qualifying distributions,

$227,537; giving activities include $221,742 for 3 + grants (high: $105,000).
Purpose and activities: Support primarily for the care of the visually handicapped.
Fields of interest: Media, radio; Libraries (public); Eye diseases; Human services.
International interests: Greece.
Type of support: General/operating support.
Limitations: Applications accepted. Giving primarily to residents of the Worcester, MA, area.
Application information: Application form required.
Initial approach: Proposal
Copies of proposal: 1
Deadline(s): None
Officers: Larry Raymond, Pres.; **Elizabeth Myska, V.P.**; Jane Weisman, Secy.; Gary MacConnell, Treas.
Directors: Eleanor Brockway; **T. Ashley Edwards**; Helen D. Fifield; James Gettens; Roger W. Greene; Barbara Higgins; Nancy Jeppson; **Maggie Lawler**; Diane MacConnell; **Nicholas McNamara**; Janice Reidy; Joseph Reidy.
EIN: 041611615
Other changes: Elizabeth Myska has replaced T. Ashley Edwards as V.P.

1513
The MENTOR Network Charitable Foundation, Inc.
313 Congress St., 5th Fl.
Boston, MA 02210-1218
E-mail: foundation@thementornetwork.com; Main URL: http://www.thementornetwork.com/foundation
Facebook: https://www.facebook.com/likementor
Twitter: https://twitter.com/The_MENTOR_Ntwk
YouTube: https://www.youtube.com/user/TheMENTORNetwork

Established in 2006 in MA.
Donors: Hugh R. Jones; Robert Digia; Madison Dearborn Partners; The MENTOR Network.
Foundation type: Independent foundation.
Financial data (yr. ended 09/30/12): Assets, $1,160,239 (M); gifts received, $114,381; expenditures, $257,587; qualifying distributions, $248,651; giving activities include $220,667 for 35 grants (high: $103,183; low: $1,000).
Purpose and activities: The foundation works to build on innovative approaches to human services by seeking new solutions and creative ideas for enhancing the lives of persons with disabilities and youth and families facing emotional, behavioral and other challenges, and by expanding opportunity.
Fields of interest: Education; Human services; Family services; Youth; Disabilities, people with.
Application information: Online application process; paper-based applications no longer accepted. Complete application guidelines available on foundation web site. Application form required.
Officers and Directors:* Gregory Torres,* Chair.; Dwight D. Robson,* Pres.; Linda DeRenzo,* Secy.; Chris M. Kozakis,* Treas.; **Kathleen Federico**; **Denis Holler**; **Sarah Magazine**; **Edward Murphy**; **Bruce Nardella.**
EIN: 204935290

1514
The John Merck Fund
2 Oliver St., 8th Fl.
Boston, MA **02109-4901** (617) 556-4120
Contact: Ruth G. Hennig, Secy. and Exec. Dir.
FAX: (617) 556-4130; E-mail: info@jmfund.org; Main URL: http://www.jmfund.org
Grants List: http://www.jmfund.org/program.list.php

Established in 1970 in NY as a trust.
Donor: Serena S. Merck‡.
Foundation type: Independent foundation.
Financial data (yr. ended 12/31/12): Assets, $73,942,428 (M); expenditures, $9,415,670; qualifying distributions, $8,811,191; giving activities include $7,319,500 for 105 grants (high: $300,000; low: $2,000), and $300,000 for 1 loan/program-related investment.
Purpose and activities: Grants are made in the following areas: for medical research on causes of developmental disabilities in children; to build supply and demand for clear, renewable energy and reduce reliance on coal-fired power plants; to improve the health and vitality of rural communities in Maine, New Hampshire and Vermont by developing a sustainable food systems sector in the region; and to eliminate persistent bio-accumulative toxic chemicals and to encourage comprehensive precaution-based chemicals policy reforms in states to provide both models and upward pressure for eventual reform at the federal level.
Fields of interest: Environment, public policy; Environment, toxics; Environment, climate change/global warming; Environment; Employment, services.
Type of support: Mission-related investments/loans; General/operating support; Program development.
Limitations: Giving on a national basis in the areas of the environment. Generally, no support for large organizations with well-established funding sources. No grants to individuals, or for endowment or capital fund projects, generally no general support grants.
Publications: Grants list; Program policy statement.
Application information: The fund does not encourage the submission of unsolicited applications for grants. The fund prefers to request a grant proposal after receiving preliminary written or verbal information about a project. Application form required.
Initial approach: Letter of inquiry
Deadline(s): Approximately six weeks before quarterly board meetings
Board meeting date(s): Mar., June, Sept., and Dec.
Final notification: Within 2 months
Officers and Trustees:* Ruth G. Hennig, Exec. Dir.; Rick Burnes; Olivia H. Farr; Robert Gardiner; George Hatch; Whitney Hatch; Frederica Perera; Anne Stetson; Serena M. Whitridge.
Number of staff: 3 full-time professional.
EIN: 237082558
Other changes: Ruth G. Hennig is now Exec. Dir.

1515
MetroWest Health Foundation
(formerly MetroWest Community Health Care Foundation, Inc.)
c/o The Meadows Bldg.
161 Worcester Rd., Ste. 202
Framingham, MA 01701-5232 (508) 879-7625
Contact: Martin Cohen, Pres.
FAX: (508) 879-7628; E-mail: info@mwhealth.org; Main URL: http://www.mwhealth.org
Blog: http://www.mwhealth.org/NewsEvents/MWHealthBlog/tabid/248/PostID/15/Default.aspx
E-Newsletter: http://www.mwhealth.org/PublicationsampMedia/Newsletters/tabid/221/Default.aspx
Facebook: http://www.facebook.com/mwhealth
LinkedIn: http://www.linkedin.com/company/2174503?trk=tyah
YouTube: http://www.youtube.com/user/MetroWestCHCF

Established in 1999 in MA; converted from the proceeds of the sale of a non-profit medical center. Serves 25 communities in the MetroWest area of Massachusetts.
Foundation type: Independent foundation.
Financial data (yr. ended 09/30/13): Assets, $99,955,446 (M); gifts received, $352,893; expenditures, $4,690,784; qualifying distributions, $3,725,222; giving activities include $2,418,094 for grants, and $272,944 for foundation-administered programs.
Purpose and activities: The foundation is focused on the health status of the MetroWest area of Massachusetts, its individuals, and its families, through informed and innovative leadership.
Fields of interest: Medicine/medical care, public education; Health care, formal/general education; Medical care, community health systems; Public health; Nursing care; Health care; Children/youth; Adults; Aging; Young adults.
Type of support: Continuing support; Program development; Technical assistance; Scholarships—to individuals.
Limitations: Giving limited to Ashland, Bellingham, Dover, Framingham, Franklin, Holliston, Hopedale, Hopkinton, Hudson, Marlborough, Medfield, Medway, Mendon, Milford, Millis, Natick, Needham, Norfolk, Northborough, Sherborn, Southborough, Sudbury, Wayland, Wellesley, and Westborough, MA.
Publications: Application guidelines; Annual report; Financial statement; Grants list; Newsletter; Occasional report.
Application information: Grant submission guidelines and forms are available on the foundation web site. The foundation usually has 2 grant cycles - fall and spring. Grant guidelines and submission requirements are included with each announcement. Grant proposals must be submitted online. Application form required.
Initial approach: Organizations must submit a 2-page concept letter via e-mail or mail
Deadline(s): For scholarships: Apr. 15 to May 31 for the academic term following Sept.; Oct. 15 to Nov. 30 for academic term beginning the following Jan.
Board meeting date(s): Last Thurs. of each month
Final notification: 4-6 weeks
Officers and Trustees:* Dana Neshe,* Chair.; Joel Barrera,* Vice-Chair.; Martin D. Cohen, C.E.O. and Pres.; **Rosemarie Coelho, Clerk**; Adam Rogers,* Treas.; Cynthia Bechtel, Ph.D.; Maria DaSilva; Alan Geller, Esq.; John Krikorian, M.D.; Meyer Levy; Regina Marshall, Esq.; Julie Reed.
Number of staff: 3 full-time professional.
EIN: 042121342
Other changes: Rosemarie Coelho is now Clerk. Ken Foley is no longer a trustee.

1516
Herman and Frieda L. Miller Foundation
c/o GMA Foundations
77 Summer St., Ste. 800
Boston, MA 02110-1006
Contact: Amy Segal Shorey, Admin.
FAX: (617) 426-7087;
E-mail: ashorey@gmafoundations.com; **Additional contact: Ruth Victorin, Fdn. Asst., tel.: (617) 391-3101, e-mail: rvictorin@gmafoundations.com;**

Main URL: http://
millerfoundation.grantsmanagement08.com/

Established in 1997 in MA.
Donor: Herman Miller†.
Foundation type: Independent foundation.
Financial data (yr. ended 11/30/12): Assets, $46,659,067 (M); expenditures, $2,856,123; qualifying distributions, $2,777,561; giving activities include $2,665,000 for 60 grants (high: $120,000; low: $10,000).
Purpose and activities: The foundation supports civic engagement, advocacy, and community organizing in Greater Boston and Eastern Massachusetts. The foundation is also dedicated to improving the infrastructure that supports vibrant urban community life. Key elements toward achieving this goal include: strong civic culture and community empowerment, neighborhood and citywide; development and maintenance of healthy physical settings that facilitate vigorous communities; and access by individuals of all income-levels and backgrounds to employment, housing, education, health care, transportation, and cultural activities.
Fields of interest: Arts; Environment, natural resources; Environment; Human services; Community/economic development.
Type of support: General/operating support; Annual campaigns; Capital campaigns; Building/renovation; Program development; Program evaluation; Matching/challenge support.
Limitations: Applications not accepted. Giving primarily in Boston, MA. No grants to individuals.
Publications: Grants list.
Application information: Unsolicited requests for funds not accepted. Proposals by invitation only. Phone inquires to staff are welcome.
Board meeting date(s): Varies
Trustee: Myron Miller.
Number of staff: 2 part-time professional; 1 part-time support.
EIN: 137131926

1517
Mount Washington Charitable Foundation, Inc.
430 W. Broadway
South Boston, MA 02127-2216 (617) 269-5738

Established in 2002 in MA.
Donors: Mt. Washington Co-operative Bank; Auburn Construction; Fitzgerald Cleaning; East Boston Savings Bank.
Foundation type: Independent foundation.
Financial data (yr. ended 06/30/13): Assets, $770 (M); gifts received, $104,506; expenditures, $151,830; qualifying distributions, $151,830; giving activities include $151,760 for 214 grants (high: $5,000; low: $50).
Fields of interest: Education; Human services; Community/economic development.
Limitations: Applications accepted. Giving primarily in Boston, MA. No grants to individuals.
Application information: Application form not required.
Initial approach: Proposal
Deadline(s): None
Officers and Directors:* Richard Gavegnano,* Chair.; Edward J. Merritt,* Pres.; James A. Morgan, V.P. and Clerk; Mary E. Hagen, V.P and Treas.; Thomas Henderson, V.P.; **Vincent D. Basile; Marilyn A. Censullo**; Anna R. DiMaria; Thomas J. Gunning; Edward Lynch; Gail Snowden; and 8 additional directors.
EIN: 450488207

1518
New Balance Foundation
20 Guest St.
Boston, MA 02135-2040 (617) 783-4000
Contact: Anne M. Davis, Managing Tr.
E-mail: newbalancefoundation@newbalance.com; Main URL: http://www.newbalancefoundation.org/
New Balance Foundation Video: http://www.newbalancefoundation.org/NewBalance_v8_RT332_FullFrame.wmv

Established in 1981 in MA.
Donor: New Balance Athletic Shoe, Inc.
Foundation type: Company-sponsored foundation.
Financial data (yr. ended 11/20/13): Assets, $124,450,793 (M); gifts received, $1,076,570; expenditures, $6,531,997; qualifying distributions, $6,319,579; giving activities include $6,318,079 for 87 grants (high: $900,000; low: $200).
Purpose and activities: The foundation supports organizations involved with education, the environment, health, nutrition, disaster relief, school athletics, and human services. Special emphasis is directed toward programs designed to promote healthy lifestyles and prevent childhood obesity.
Fields of interest: Education; Environment; Hospitals (general); Public health, obesity; Public health, physical fitness; Health care; Nutrition; Disasters, preparedness/services; Athletics/sports, academies; Family services; Human services; United Ways and Federated Giving Programs; Children; Economically disadvantaged.
Type of support: Research; General/operating support; Continuing support; Scholarship funds; Matching/challenge support.
Limitations: Applications accepted. Giving primarily in Boston and Lawrence, MA and Norridgewock, Norway, and Skowhegan, ME. No support for political parities or discriminatory organizations. No grants to individuals, or for capital campaigns, fundraising dinners or galas, team sponsorships, sporting events, or film or television underwriting.
Publications: Application guidelines; Financial statement; Grants list; Program policy statement.
Application information: Concept papers should be no longer than 1 page. Proposals should be no longer than 3 pages and existing grant partners should submit 4 copies of that proposal.. Support is limited to 1 contribution per organization during any given year. Organizations receiving support are asked to submit interim reports and a final report. Application form not required.
Initial approach: Concept paper for new grant seekers; proposal for existing grant partners
***Deadline(s):* Mar. 3 for new grant seekers; Feb. 3 for existing grant partners**
Final notification: Apr. 1 for new grant seekers
Trustees: Anne M. Davis; James S. Davis; Paul R. Gauron.
EIN: 046470644

1519
Newburyport Society for the Relief of Aged Women, Inc.
P.O. Box 787
Newburyport, MA 01950-0987 (978) 463-8801
Contact: Lori Davis, Chair.
***E-mail:* nsraw1835@gmail.com**; Main URL: http://www.nsraw.org/

Established in MA.
Foundation type: Independent foundation.
Financial data (yr. ended 03/31/13): Assets, $3,347,452 (M); expenditures, $187,018; qualifying distributions, $153,110; giving activities include $147,753 for 7+ grants (high: $40,000).
Fields of interest: Health care; Human services; Community/economic development.
Limitations: Applications accepted. Giving primarily in Newburyport, MA.
Application information: Application form required.
Initial approach: Proposal
Deadline(s): Feb. 15 and Sept. 15
Officers: Melissa Foley, Co-Chair; Lori Davis, Co-Chair.; Ardis Campbell, Pres.; Dorothy Lafrance, V.P.; Lyn Parker, Secy.; Eleanora Paciulan, Treas.
Directors: Jean Coffman; Jocelyne Consentino; Jean Doyle; Linda Lynehan; Alice McLeod; Sally Plourde; Janet Sheenan; Elizabeth Swanson.
EIN: 042121771

1520
Deborah Munroe Noonan Memorial Fund
c/o US Trust, Bank of America, N.A.
225 Franklin St., MA1-225-04-02
Boston, MA 02110-2804 (866) 778-6859
Contact: Phung Pham, Philanthropic Rels. Mgr.
***E-mail regarding application process or for questions:* ma.grantmaking@ustrust.com (indicate foundation name in subject line); Main URL: https://www.bankofamerica.com/philanthropic/grantmaking.go**

Foundation type: Independent foundation.
Financial data (yr. ended 12/31/11): Assets, $8,172,801 (M); expenditures, $488,301; qualifying distributions, $400,000; giving activities include $400,000 for grants.
Purpose and activities: Giving to support and promote quality educational, human services, and health care programming for underserved populations.
Fields of interest: Arts; Education; Health care; Human services.
Type of support: Program development; General/operating support.
Limitations: Giving primarily in greater Boston, MA. No grants to individuals.
Application information: Apply online at www.bankofamerica.com/grantmaking.
Initial approach: E-mail
Deadline(s): Sept. 1
Final notification: Nov. 30
Trustee: Bank of America, N.A.
EIN: 046025983

1521
Deborah Munroe Noonan Memorial Research Fund
(formerly Frank M. Noonan Trust)
c/o US Trust, Bank of America, N.A.
225 Franklin St., MA1-225-04-02
Boston, MA 02110-2801 (866) 778-6859
Contact: Miki Akimoto, Market Dir.
***E-mail regarding application process or for questions:* ma.grantmaking@ustrust.com (indicate foundation name in subject line0; Main URL: https://www.bankofamerica.com/philanthropic/grantmaking.go**

Trust established in 1947 in MA.
Donor: Frank M. Noonan†.
Foundation type: Independent foundation.
Financial data (yr. ended 09/30/13): Assets, $9,945,006 (M); expenditures, $511,404; qualifying distributions, $457,006; giving activities include $405,560 for 6 grants to individuals (high: $80,000; low: $5,960).

Purpose and activities: Grants solely for organizations and hospitals directly serving children with disabilities.
Fields of interest: Education; Health care; Human services.
Type of support: General/operating support; Program development.
Limitations: Giving limited to the greater Boston, MA, area. No grants to individuals, or for scholarships or fellowships; no loans.
Publications: Application guidelines.
Application information: The fund's grant review process is externally administered by The Medical Foundation, a division of Health Resources in Action. Consult fund web site for more information. Application form required.
Initial approach: Proposal with cover sheet
Copies of proposal: 16
***Deadline(s):* Mar. 15**
Board meeting date(s): Distribution committee meets as required
***Final notification:* June 30**
Trustee: Bank of America, N.A.
EIN: 046025957

1522
Samuel P. Pardoe Foundation
c/o Grants Mgmt. Assoc., Inc.
77 Summer St., 8th Fl.
Boston, MA 02110-1006 **(617) 391-3088**
***Contact:* Hannah Blaisdell, Admin.**
FAX: (617) 426-7087;
E-mail: hblaisdell@gmafoundations.com; Main URL: http://www.pardoefoundation.grantsmanagement08.com
Grants List: http://pardoefoundation.grantsmanagement08.com/?page_id=4

Established in 1989 in DC.
Donors: Samuel P. Pardoe‡; Helen P. Pardoe Trust.
Foundation type: Independent foundation.
Financial data (yr. ended 06/30/13): Assets, $11,857,457 (M); expenditures, $550,238; qualifying distributions, $550,238; giving activities include $514,000 for 38 grants (high: $373,500; low: $500).
Purpose and activities: Support primarily for programs that provide educational and economic opportunities for underprivileged persons. Other areas of interest include health and social services, cultural programs, community development activities, education, and land and resource management, with a focus on support for programs related to specific conservation initiatives. The foundation also supports programs that educate New Hampshire residents about conservation and environmental issues. Educational support focuses primarily on programs on a pre-collegiate level, with a special interest in increasing access to educational opportunities, particularly experiential learning. The foundation also supports literacy, tutoring, and arts education programs.
Fields of interest: Education; Environment, land resources; Human services; Children/youth; Economically disadvantaged.
Type of support: Capital campaigns; Building/renovation; Equipment; Program development; Program-related investments/loans.
Limitations: Applications accepted. Giving limited to organizations located within or serving the Lakes Region of NH, with a priority focus on Laconia. No support for religious or sectarian purposes. No grants to individuals, or for operating expenses, endowments, scholarships, deficit financing, advertising, special events, or fundraising activities.
Publications: Application guidelines; Grants list.
Application information: Application form required.
Initial approach: Use online application form on foundation web site
Copies of proposal: 2
Deadline(s): See foundation web site for current deadline
Board meeting date(s): Spring and fall
Officers and Directors:* Charles H. Pardoe II,* Pres.; Prescott Bruce Pardoe,* V.P.; E. Spencer Pardoe Ballou,* Secy.; Charles E. Pardoe,* Treas.; Elizabeth Pardoe Grey.
Number of staff: None.
EIN: 521660757

1523
The Theodore Edson Parker Foundation
c/o GMA Foundations
77 Summer St., 8th Fl.
Boston, MA 02110-1006 (617) 391-3097
Contact: Kirstie David, Prog. Off.; Philip Hall, Admin.
FAX: (617) 426-7087;
E-mail: phall@gmafoundations.com**; Contact for Kristie David, Prog. Off.: tel.: (617) 391-3081, e-mail: kdavid@gmafoundations.com**; Main URL: http://parkerfoundation.gmafoundations.com

Incorporated in 1944 in MA.
Donor: Theodore Edson Parker‡.
Foundation type: Independent foundation.
Financial data (yr. ended 12/31/12): Assets, $23,105,719 (M); expenditures, $1,258,361; qualifying distributions, $1,040,538; giving activities include $875,181 for 36 grants (high: $100,750; low: $500).
Purpose and activities: The foundation's primary goal is to make effective grants that benefit the city of Lowell, MA, and its residents. Giving for a variety of purposes including social services, cultural programs, community development activities, education, community health needs and urban environmental projects.
Fields of interest: Arts; Education; Environment; Health care; Substance abuse, services; Employment; Housing/shelter, development; Human services; Children/youth, services; Minorities/immigrants, centers/services; Community/economic development; Public affairs; Children/youth; Minorities; Immigrants/refugees; Economically disadvantaged.
Type of support: Conferences/seminars; Capital campaigns; Building/renovation; Equipment; Land acquisition; Program development; Seed money; Research; Consulting services; Program-related investments/loans; Matching/challenge support.
Limitations: Applications accepted. Giving primarily in Lowell, MA. No grants to individuals, or for operating budgets, matching gifts, continuing support, annual campaigns, emergency funds, deficit financing, scholarships, or fellowships.
Publications: Application guidelines; Annual report; Grants list.
Application information: Applicants are limited to 1 application per year. See foundation web site for application guidelines and procedures. Application form not required.
***Initial approach:* Use online application system on foundation web site**
Deadline(s): Jan. 15, May 15, and Sept. 15
Board meeting date(s): Apr. or May; Sept., and Dec.
Final notification: 4 months
Officers and Trustees:* Newell Flather,* Pres.; Andrew C. Bailey,* Secy.-Treas.; Karen H. Carpenter; David Donahue, Jr.; Sophie Theam.
Number of staff: 3 part-time professional.
EIN: 046036092

1524
The Patagonia Sur Foundation
P. O. Box 2428
Edgartown, MA 02539-2428 **(917) 300-1076**
***Contact:* Daniela Diaz, Exec. Dir.**
***FAX:* (508) 503-3788;**
E-mail: info@fundacionpatagoniasur.cl; Chilean Address: La Concepcion 141, Office 304, Providencia, Santiago, Chile, tel.: (56) 2-2897-3538; Main URL: http://patagoniasur.com/subpage.php?sid=47&l=e&l=e

Established in 2007.
Donors: Warren Adams; Megan Adams; David Tufaro; Sharon Tufaro; Fred Mouawad; Jim Levitt; Jane Levitt; Brian Hoesterey; Dawn Hoesterey; Elizabeth Daisy Helman; Stephen Reifenberg; Chris Cervenak; Daniel Nowiszewski; Bechler River Partners, LLC; Tufaro Family Ltd. Partnership; Patagonia Resources, LLC; BJP Ventures, LLC; Small Pond Investments, Ltd.; Basant LTDA; Hvalbukta Ans.
Foundation type: Independent foundation.
Financial data (yr. ended 12/31/12): Assets, $22,755 (M); gifts received, $84,050; expenditures, $180,905; qualifying distributions, $176,458; giving activities include $176,458 for grants.
Purpose and activities: Giving primarily to encourage conservation and promote social and economic development in the Patagonia region of Chile.
Fields of interest: Higher education, university; Environment; International development.
Type of support: General/operating support.
Limitations: Applications not accepted. Giving primarily in Chile; some funding also in the U.S., with emphasis on Cambridge, MA and Portland, ME. No grants to individuals.
Application information: Contributes only to pre-selected organizations.
Directors: Steve Reifenberg; Pablo Allard; Francisca Cortes.
EIN: 208875388

1525
Perennial Foundation
10 Rocky Hill Rd.
Plymouth, MA 02360-5501

Established in 1989 in MA.
Donors: T. David Parks; Rosemary T. Parks.
Foundation type: Independent foundation.
Financial data (yr. ended 06/30/13): Assets, $262,357 (M); gifts received, $45,990; expenditures, $43,553; qualifying distributions, $39,903; giving activities include $39,000 for 5 grants (high: $29,500; low: $1,000).
Fields of interest: Christian agencies & churches; Protestant agencies & churches.
Limitations: Applications not accepted. Giving primarily in MA and NC. No grants to individuals.
Application information: Unsolicited requests for funds not accepted.
Trustees: Laura T. Garth; Rosemary T. Parks; T. David Parks; Elizabeth J. Parks-Stamm; Jennifer P. Rinne.
EIN: 043059472
Other changes: The grantmaker no longer lists a phone. The grantmaker no longer lists a primary contact.

1526

Perpetual Trust for Charitable Giving
c/o US Trust, Bank of America, N.A.
225 Franklin St., 4th Fl.
Boston, MA 02110-2801
Contact: Miki Akimoto, Market Dir.
E-mail: miki.akimoto@ustrust.com; **E-mail regarding application or for questions: ma.grantmaking@ustrust.com (include foundation name in subject line)**; Main URL: http://www.bankofamerica.com/grantmaking

Established in 1957 in MA.
Foundation type: Independent foundation.
Financial data (yr. ended 12/31/13): Assets, $23,799,915 (M); expenditures, $1,192,194; qualifying distributions, $1,028,928; giving activities include $934,769 for 50 grants (high: $100,000; low: $267).
Purpose and activities: Giving primarily to organizations that support education, health care, and family services.
Fields of interest: Education; Health care; Human services.
Type of support: General/operating support; Program development.
Limitations: Giving limited to MA. No grants to individuals.
Publications: Application guidelines.
Application information: Complete guidelines available on trust website. Application form required.
Initial approach: Proposal with cover sheet
Copies of proposal: 1
Deadline(s): Sept. 1
Board meeting date(s): Nov.
Final notification: Nov. 30
Trustee: Bank of America, N.A.
EIN: 046026301

1527

Frank Reed & Margaret Jane Peters Memorial Fund I
c/o US Trust, Bank of America, N.A.
225 Franklin St., MA1-225-04-02
Boston, MA 02110-2801 (866) 778-6859
Contact: Phung Pham, V.P.
E-mail: phung.pham@ustrust.com; **Main URL: https://www.bankofamerica.com/philanthropic/grantmaking.go**

Established in 1935 in MA.
Foundation type: Independent foundation.
Financial data (yr. ended 12/31/12): Assets, $9,012,153 (M); expenditures, $420,128; qualifying distributions, $353,697; giving activities include $320,000 for 22 grants (high: $20,000; low: $10,000).
Purpose and activities: Giving primarily to support and promote quality educational, human services, and health care programming for underserved populations. Special consideration is given to charitable organizations that serve youth and children.
Fields of interest: Education; Human services; Children/youth, services; Family services.
Limitations: Giving primarily in Boston, MA. No grants to individuals, for independent research projects, or for publications or national organizations.
Application information: Complete application guidelines available on fund's web site.
Initial approach: E-mail
Trustee: Bank of America, N.A.
EIN: 046012009

1528

Richard J. Phelps Charitable Foundation
599 North Ave., Door 8, 2nd Fl.
Wakefield, MA 01880-1648

Established in 1990 in MA.
Donor: Richard J. Phelps.
Foundation type: Independent foundation.
Financial data (yr. ended 06/30/13): Assets, $43,424 (M); gifts received, $26,829; expenditures, $253,651; qualifying distributions, $251,148; giving activities include $248,685 for 43 grants (high: $62,350; low: $100).
Fields of interest: Arts; Secondary school/education; Higher education; Higher education, university; Housing/shelter, development; Athletics/sports, amateur leagues.
Type of support: General/operating support; Building/renovation; Scholarship funds.
Limitations: Applications not accepted. Giving primarily in CT, FL and MA.
Application information: Unsolicited requests for funds not accepted.
Trustees: Ann Jacobs; Richard J. Phelps.
EIN: 223090828

1529

Stephen Phillips Memorial Charitable Trust
P.O. Box 870
Salem, MA 01970-0970 **(978) 744-2111**
Contact: Karen Emery, Scholarship Coord.
FAX: (978) 744-0456;
E-mail: staff@spscholars.org; Main URL: http://www.phillips-scholarship.org/
Facebook: https://www.facebook.com/phillipsscholarship
Twitter: https://twitter.com/PhillipsScholar

Established in 1973.
Donor: Bessie Wright Phillips†.
Foundation type: Independent foundation.
Financial data (yr. ended 12/31/12): Assets, $6,956,969 (M); gifts received, $7,565; expenditures, $4,094,662; qualifying distributions, $3,650,991; giving activities include $2,924,200 for grants to individuals.
Purpose and activities: Scholarships for permanent residents of New England states who demonstrate academic excellence, seriousness of purpose, good citizenship and character, a strong work ethic and who meet the foundation's financial-need requirements. Applicants must be an entering or returning student at an accredited undergraduate institution in the United States and must be enrolled full-time (at least 12 hours). Applicants must also be pursuing a bachelor's degree (BA, BS, BFA, BSN, for example) for the first time, have a GPA of 3.0 or higher on a 4.0 scale, be enrolled in a demanding course of study, and demonstrate skilled writing. Students in 1-year or 2-year certificate or associate's degree programs do not qualify. Students in 5-plus year programs ending in a master's degree program or beyond may apply for the first four (undergraduate) years of their programs.
Fields of interest: Education; Economically disadvantaged.
Type of support: Scholarships—to individuals.
Limitations: Applications accepted. Giving limited to all permanent residents of the New England states.
Publications: Application guidelines; Informational brochure (including application guidelines); Newsletter.
Application information: Specific application requirements and forms are available on foundation web site. Application form required.
***Initial approach:* Use online application process on foundation web site**
***Deadline(s):* See foundation web site for current deadlines**
Officer: Barbara Welles Iler, Exec. Dir.
Trustees: Lawrence Coolidge; John H. Finley IV; Dr. Richard F. Gross; Robert M. Randolph.
Number of staff: 2 full-time professional; 1 part-time professional.
EIN: 237235347
Other changes: Arthur H. Emery is no longer a trustee.

1530

The Ramsey McCluskey Family Foundation
P.O. Box 275
Lincoln, MA 01773-0275 (781) 259-9948
Contact: Margaret A. Ramsey, Tr.
E-mail: Meg.Ramsey@verizon.net; Main URL: http://www.ramseymccluskeyfndn.org
Grants List: http://www.ramseymccluskeyfndn.org/recentGrants.aspx

Established in 1999 in MA.
Donor: Margaret A. Ramsey.
Foundation type: Independent foundation.
Financial data (yr. ended 03/31/13): Assets, $3,119,953 (M); gifts received, $75,000; expenditures, $189,258; qualifying distributions, $165,014; giving activities include $155,600 for 32 grants (high: $75,000; low: $100).
Purpose and activities: Giving primarily to support projects in education and the arts.
Fields of interest: Arts, multipurpose centers/programs; Arts education; Museums; Arts; Scholarships/financial aid; Education, reading; Education; Animals/wildlife; Food services.
Type of support: Program development; Scholarship funds.
Limitations: Applications accepted. Giving primarily in MA. No grants for capital campaigns, endowments, or general operating expenses.
Publications: Application guidelines.
Application information: Application form required.
***Initial approach:* Letter or email (strongly encouraged over telephone calls)**
Copies of proposal: 1
Deadline(s): Annually
Board meeting date(s): Late Mar.
Trustees: John M. McCluskey; Margaret A. Ramsey.
EIN: 043464899

1531

A.C. Ratshesky Foundation
c/o GMA Foundations
77 Summer St., 8th Fl.
Boston, MA 02110-1006 (617) 391-3092
Contact: Susan Haff, Fdn. Asst.; Prentice Zinn, Prog. Off.
FAX: (617) 426-7087;
E-mail: pzinn@gmafoundations.com; Main URL: http://www.ratsheskyfoundation.org
Grants List: http://www.ratsheskyfoundation.org/grants/past-grants

Incorporated in 1916 in MA.
Donors: A.C. Ratshesky†; and family.
Foundation type: Independent foundation.

Financial data (yr. ended 12/31/12): Assets, $6,855,780 (M); expenditures, $395,454; qualifying distributions, $331,750; giving activities include $276,000 for 27 grants (high: $25,000; low: $2,500).
Purpose and activities: The foundation is committed to fostering economic and social justice for low- and moderate-income families residing in Boston, Massachusetts and surrounding communities. The foundation gives priority consideration to programs from the following fields of interest: education and training, and arts and culture. Support for programs that serve disadvantaged Jewish populations is also of special interest, provided that these programs are aligned with one or more of the foundation's other fields of interest.
Fields of interest: Arts education; Arts; Vocational education; Adult education—literacy, basic skills & GED; Education, services; Education; Employment, services; Children/youth, services; Family services; Jewish agencies & synagogues; Economically disadvantaged.
Type of support: General/operating support; Continuing support; Program development; Seed money.
Limitations: Applications accepted. Giving limited to the metro Boston, MA, area, within Rte. 128. No support for public schools, or for health programs, national organizations, municipal, state or federal agencies, or religious programs. No grants to individuals, or for annual campaigns, general endowments, deficit financing, land acquisition, web sites, scientific or other research, publications, or conferences; no loans.
Publications: Application guidelines; Grants list.
Application information: The foundation uses an online application process. See foundation web site for complete application information. Associated Grant Makers Common Proposal Form accepted. Application form required.
Initial approach: Proposal or telephone
Copies of proposal: 1
Deadline(s): Feb. 1, July 1, and Oct. 1
Board meeting date(s): May, Oct., and Jan.
Final notification: Following board meetings
Officers and Trustees:* Timothy Morse,* Pres.; Laurie Morse Sprague, V.P.; Rebecca Morse Steinfield,* Secy.; Linda G. Ortwein, Treas.; Craig Levy; Roberta Morse Levy; Alan R. Morse, Jr.; Eric Robert Morse; Jennifer Morse.
Number of staff: 2 part-time professional; 1 part-time support.
EIN: 046017426

1532
Raymond Family Foundation
29 Commonweatlh Ave., 4th Fl.
Boston, MA **02116-2349**

Established in 1989 in MA.
Donor: Neil St. John Raymond.
Foundation type: Independent foundation.
Financial data (yr. ended 12/31/12): Assets, $334,000 (M); expenditures, $256; qualifying distributions, $0.
Fields of interest: Environment, natural resources; Environment, land resources.
Limitations: Applications not accepted. Giving in MA. No grants to individuals.
Application information: Contributes only to pre-selected organizations.
Trustee: Neil St. John Raymond.
EIN: 043076151

1533
Albert W. Rice Charitable Foundation
c/o Bank of America, N.A.
225 Franklin St., 4th Fl., MA1-225-04-02
Boston, MA 02110-2801 (866) 778-6859
E-mail: ma.grantmaking@ustrust.com; **Main URL: https://www.bankofamerica.com/philanthropic/grantmaking.go**

Established in 1959 in MA.
Donors: Albert W. Rice†; Mary Gage Rice†.
Foundation type: Independent foundation.
Financial data (yr. ended 12/31/12): Assets, $6,509,903 (M); expenditures, $610,359; qualifying distributions, $561,877; giving activities include $520,000 for 24 grants (high: $45,000; low: $10,000).
Purpose and activities: The foundation supports and promotes quality educational, human services, and health care programming for underserved populations. Special consideration is given to charitable organizations that serve the people of Worcester, Massachusetts, and surrounding communities.
Fields of interest: Education; Health care; Human services.
Type of support: General/operating support; Program development.
Limitations: Giving primarily in Worcester, MA and surrounding communities. No grants to individuals.
Publications: Application guidelines.
Application information: Online application; complete application guidelines available on foundation web site.
Initial approach: Email
Trustee: Bank of America, N.A.
EIN: 046028085

1534
The Mabel Louise Riley Foundation
(also known as The Riley Foundation)
c/o GMA
77 Summer St., 8th Fl.
Boston, MA 02110-1006 (617) 399-1850
Contact: Nancy A. Saunders, Admin.
FAX: (617) 399-1851;
E-mail: nsaunders@rileyfoundation.com; E-mail for Letters of Inquiry: info@rileyfoundatrion.com; Main URL: http://www.rileyfoundation.com

Established in 1971 in MA as the Mabel Louise Riley Charitable Trust.
Donor: Mabel Louise Riley†.
Foundation type: Independent foundation.
Financial data (yr. ended 12/31/12): Assets, $58,538,112 (M); expenditures, $3,465,470; qualifying distributions, $3,117,909; giving activities include $2,800,682 for 48 grants (high: $100,000; low: $1,292).
Purpose and activities: Giving primarily for 1) education and social services for disadvantaged children and adolescents; 2) preschool reading programs; 3) community development that will benefit low-income and minority neighborhoods, including job development and training, and housing; 4) citywide efforts in Boston and vicinity that promote cultural improvements and the arts; 5) grants that, despite some risk, offer a potential of high impact or significant benefits for a community, (the foundation is especially interested in leveraging its grants by funding new programs that can become self-sufficient or which may serve as a model in other geographic areas); and 6) improvements of race relations and neighborhood safety issues.
Fields of interest: Arts; Education; Employment; Housing/shelter, development; Human services; Children/youth, services; Family services; Minorities/immigrants, centers/services; Community/economic development; Minorities.
Type of support: Capital campaigns; Building/renovation; Equipment; Program development; Seed money; Curriculum development; Technical assistance; Matching/challenge support.
Limitations: Applications accepted. Giving limited to MA, with strong emphasis on Boston's Dudley Street neighborhood. No support for political or sectarian religious purposes, or for national organizations. No grants to individuals, or for operating budgets, continuing support, annual campaigns, emergency funds, deficit financing, research, publications, conferences, professorships, scholarships, travel, internships, exchange programs, fellowships, no loans.
Publications: Application guidelines; Annual report; Grants list.
Application information: Proposals will come at the invitation of the foundation only, following review of Letter of Inquiry. Unsolicited proposals will not be accepted. Associated Grant Makers Common Proposal Form accepted. Application form not required.
Initial approach: Letter of Inquiry, not more than 2 pages (without a cover letter)
Copies of proposal: 1
Deadline(s): None for Letters of Inquiry
Board meeting date(s): Mar., June, Sept., and Dec.
Final notification: 30 days for Letters of Inquiry
Officer: Nancy A. Saunders, Admin.
Trustees: Grace Fey; Robert W. Holmes, Jr.; BNY Mellon.
Number of staff: 1 full-time support.
EIN: 046278857
Other changes: Andrew C. Bailey is no longer a trustee.

1535
Rodman Ford Sales, Inc. Charitable Trust
Route 1
Foxboro, MA 02035-1388 **(508) 698-4001**
Contact: Donald E. Rodman, Tr.
FAX: (508) 543-7683;
E-mail: cchaplin@rodmanford.com

Established in 1986 in MA.
Donors: R. & R. Realty Co.; Rodman Five Realty Trust; Rodman Ford Sales, Inc.; Donald E. Rodman.
Foundation type: Company-sponsored foundation.
Financial data (yr. ended 12/31/12): Assets, $60,415 (M); gifts received, $283,522; expenditures, $266,530; qualifying distributions, $253,826; giving activities include $253,826 for grants.
Purpose and activities: The foundation supports organizations involved with arts and culture, education, health, and human services.
Fields of interest: Arts; Education; Health care; Children/youth, services; Human services.
Limitations: Applications accepted. Giving primarily in MA. No grants to individuals.
Application information: Application form not required.
***Initial approach:* Proposal**
***Deadline(s):* None**
Trustees: Donald E. Rodman; Gene D. Rodman.
Number of staff: None.
EIN: 222780804
Other changes: The grantmaker now accepts applications.

1536
Rogers Family Foundation
c/o GMA Foundations, Attn: Susan Haff
77 Summer St., 8th Fl.
Boston, MA 02110-1006 **(617) 426-7080**
Contact: Amy Rogers Dittrich, Managing Tr.
FAX: (617) 426-7087;
E-mail: shaff@gmafoundations.com; Main URL: http://www.rogersfamilyfoundation.com

Established in 1957 in MA.
Donors: Irving E. Rogers†; Martha B. Rogers†; Eagle-Tribune Publishing Co.; Andover Publishing Co.; Rogers Investment Corp.; Consolidated Press, Inc.; Derry Publishing Co.
Foundation type: Independent foundation.
Financial data (yr. ended 12/31/12): Assets, $20,481,770 (M); expenditures, $1,045,360; qualifying distributions, $980,855; giving activities include $939,039 for 58 grants (high: $100,000; low: $1,500).
Purpose and activities: Giving primarily for education, religion, medicine, and the arts.
Fields of interest: Museums; Secondary school/education; Education; Hospitals (general); Human services; Community/economic development; Christian agencies & churches.
Type of support: Scholarship funds; General/operating support.
Limitations: Applications accepted. Giving limited to Merrimack Valley-North Shore, MA, including Andover, Amesbury, Beverly, Boxford, Byfield, Danvers, Dracut, Essex, Gloucester, Georgetown, Groveland, Haverhill, Ipswich, Lynn, Lynnfield, Lawrence, Marblehead, Manchester, Middleton, Methuen, Merrimac, North Reading, North Andover, Newbury, Newburyport, Peabody, Rockport, Rowley, Swampscott, Salem, South Hamilton, Salisbury, Topsfield, Wenham, and West Newbury; and to Southeastern NH, including Auburn, Atkinson, Chester, Derry, Danville, Exeter, East Kingston, Epping, East Hampstead, Fremont, Hudson, Hampstead, Kingston, Litchfield, Londonderry, Newton, Plaistow, Pelham, Raymond, Stratham, Salem, Sandown, and Windham. No grants to individuals, or for fellowships, or matching gifts; no loans.
Publications: Annual report; Grants list; Program policy statement.
Application information: Application form required.
Initial approach: Online application on foundation web site
Deadline(s): Mar. 1 and Sept. 1
Board meeting date(s): June and Nov.
Final notification: 2 months
Trustees: Amy Rogers Dittrich; T. Tyler Dittrich; Kathryn Doherty; Deborah R. Pratt.
Number of staff: 1 full-time professional.
EIN: 046063152

1537
Ruderman Family Foundation
(formerly Ruderman Family Charitable Foundation)
2150 Washington St.
Newton, MA 02462-1498 (617) 599-9919
Contact: Sharon E. Shapiro, Tr.
Main URL: http://www.rudermanfoundation.org/
Facebook: https://www.facebook.com/RudermanFamilyFoundation
Google Plus: https://plus.google.com/106645418281817434488/about
Twitter: https://twitter.com/RudermanFdn

Established in 1996 in MA.
Donors: Marcia Ruderman; Morton E. Ruderman.
Foundation type: Independent foundation.
Financial data (yr. ended 12/31/12): Assets, $112,043,942 (M); gifts received, $89,628,808; expenditures, $4,084,821; qualifying distributions, $4,043,560; giving activities include $3,448,381 for 52 grants (high: $925,000; low: $118).
Purpose and activities: The foundation supports effective programs, innovative partnerships and a dynamic approach to philanthropy in its core areas of interest: advocating for and advancing the inclusion of people with disabilities throughout the Jewish community; fostering a more nuanced understanding of the American Jewish community among Israeli leaders; and modeling the practice of strategic philanthropy worldwide.
Fields of interest: Education; Jewish federated giving programs; Jewish agencies & synagogues; Disabilities, people with.
Limitations: Applications not accepted. Giving primarily in MA and NY. No grants to individuals.
Application information: Unsolicited requests for funds not accepted.
Officers and Trustees:* Jay Seth Ruderman,* Pres.; Michal Bineth-Horowitz, C.O.O.; Steven P. Rosenthal; Marcia Ruderman; Todd Adam Ruderman; Sharon Ellen Shapiro.
EIN: 043334973
Other changes: Jay Seth Ruderman is now Pres.

1538
Rx Foundation
P.O. Box 23
Hadley, MA 01035-0023
Contact: Jennie Riley

Established in 2002 in MA and DE.
Donor: Serena M. Hatch.
Foundation type: Independent foundation.
Financial data (yr. ended 12/31/12): Assets, $37,011,349 (M); expenditures, $1,964,097; qualifying distributions, $1,691,556; giving activities include $1,671,555 for 9 grants (high: $500,000; low: $62,435).
Purpose and activities: The purpose of the foundation is to fund innovative projects to improve the quality of health care in the United States.
Fields of interest: Health care.
Limitations: Applications not accepted. Giving in the U.S., primarily in Boston, MA. No grants to individuals, or for capital campaigns.
Application information: Contributes only to pre-selected organizations.
Officers and Directors:* George Hatch,* Pres.; **Jennie Riley, Secy.-Treas.**; Christopher C. Angell; Donald M. Berwick; Atul Gawande; Serena M. Hatch; Howard Hiatt; Whitney Hatch; Matthew H. Liang.
EIN: 810556499
Other changes: Jennie Riley has replaced Rowan Murphy as Secy.-Treas.

1539
Sailors' Snug Harbor of Boston, Inc.
c/o GMA Foundations
77 Summer St., 8th Fl.
Boston, MA 02110-1006 (617) 426-7080
Contact: Gracelaw Simmons, Fdn. Admin.; Ruth Victorin, Fdn. Asst.
FAX: (617) 426-7087;
E-mail: info@gmafoundations.com**; Tel. and e-mail for Gracelaw Simmons, Admin.: (617) 426-7080, ext. 312; gsimmons@gmafoundations.com**; Main URL: http://www.sailorssnugharbor.org
Grants List: http://www.sailorssnugharbor.org/?page_id=6

Established in 1852 in MA.
Foundation type: Independent foundation.
Financial data (yr. ended 04/30/13): Assets, $7,494,785 (M); expenditures, $460,453; qualifying distributions, $415,171; giving activities include $373,200 for 31 grants (high: $25,000; low: $700).
Purpose and activities: Giving to help current and former fishing families in MA achieve sustainable self-sufficiency, as well as to help Greater Boston's low-income elderly population live independently.
Fields of interest: Health care; Health organizations, association; Human services; Family services; Aging, centers/services; Aging; Economically disadvantaged.
Type of support: General/operating support; Continuing support; Building/renovation; Matching/challenge support.
Limitations: Applications accepted. Giving to agencies that serve seamen, fishermen, and their families is targeted toward MA organizations, with a particular focus on services in New Bedford, Gloucester, and Cape Cod. Grants for services to the elderly are awarded to agencies in greater Boston, with a preference for the City of Boston. No grants to individuals, or for conferences, seminars, debt reduction, cash reserves, multi-year pledges, or for publications, films or videos.
Publications: Application guidelines; Grants list; Occasional report; Program policy statement (including application guidelines).
Application information: All grantmaking guidelines are available on foundation web site. Application form not required.
Initial approach: Online proposal
Deadline(s): For Fishing Communities Initiative: Last Mon. in Aug. for Oct. meeting; for Elder Programs: Dec. 15, or the first Mon. after that date for Feb. meeting
Board meeting date(s): Usually in Feb., June, and Oct.
Officers and Trustees:* William C. Eaton,* Pres.; William B. Perkins,* V.P.; Arthur Page,* Clerk.; Pamela S. Evans,* Treas.; William N. Bancroft; Herbert P. Dane; Charles R. Eddy; **Tristan Eddy**; Edward M. Howland; Amy E. Saltonstall Isaac; E. Amory Loring; Robert W. Loring; Everett Morss, Jr.; George B. Motley; Jonathan Nash; Thomas Rogerson; G. West Saltonstall; **Caroline Gates Slocum**; Jo-Ann Watson; Benjamin J. Williams; David Willis.
EIN: 042104430
Other changes: William C. Eaton has replaced Robert W. Loring as Pres. William B. Perkins has replaced William C. Eaton as V.P.
Courtney Evans is no longer a trustee.

1540
Elizabeth and George L. Sanborn Foundation for the Treatment and Cure of Cancer, Inc.
P.O. Box 417
Arlington, MA 02476-0052 (781) 643-7775
Contact: Evelyn Smith-Demille
Main URL: http://www.sanbornfoundation.org/
Facebook: https://www.facebook.com/pages/Sanborn-Foundation/167060606639954

Established in 1999 in MA.
Foundation type: Independent foundation.
Financial data (yr. ended 12/31/12): Assets, $5,662,668 (M); gifts received, $2,505; expenditures, $233,464; qualifying distributions, $184,587; giving activities include $113,137 for 5 grants (high: $46,422; low: $5,000).

Fields of interest: Education, public education; Hospitals (general); Health care, emergency transport services; Cancer; Aging.
Limitations: Applications accepted. Giving primarily in Arlington, MA.
Application information: Application form required.
Initial approach: Proposal
Deadline(s): 2nd Tues. in Mar.
Officers: Lourie August, Pres.; Victoria Palmer-Erbs, V.P.; Daniel Brosnan, C.P.A., Treas.
Directors: Robert Lafyatis, M.D.; Debra A. Kaden, Ph.D.; Christopher J. Nauman, M.D.; Kevin F. Wall, C.P.A., Esq.
EIN: 043452444

1541
Santander Bank Foundation
(formerly Sovereign Bank Foundation)
c/o Foundation Mgr.
75 State St., MA1-SST-0407
Boston, MA 02109 (617) 757-3410
Contact: Craig Williams, V.P.
Additional application addresses: DE, MD, NJ, and PA organizations: CRA Div. Mgr., Sovereign Bank, 20-536-CD2, 2 Aldwyn Lane, Villanova, PA 19085, e-mail: MIDAFoundation@sovereignbank.com; CT, MA, NH, and RI organizations: CRA Division Mgr., Sovereign Bank, MA1-MB2-03-06, 2 Morrissey Blvd., Dorchester, MA 02125, e-mail: NEFoundation@sovereignbank.com; Metro-New York, NY organizations: CRA Division Mgr., Sovereign Bank, NY1-6528-LG12, 195 Montague St., Brooklyn, NY 11201, e-mail: NYFoundation@sovereignbank.com; **Main URL: https://www.santanderbank.com/us/about/community/grant-application-guidelines**

Established in 1989 in PA.
Donor: Sovereign Bank.
Foundation type: Company-sponsored foundation.
Financial data (yr. ended 12/31/13): Assets, $0 (M); gifts received, $1,737,504; expenditures, $1,737,504; qualifying distributions, $1,737,504; giving activities include $1,737,504 for 1 grant.
Purpose and activities: The foundation supports organizations involved with arts and culture, education, health, employment, housing, human services, and community and economic development. Special emphasis is directed toward programs targeting low-and moderate-income individuals and communities.
Fields of interest: Media/communications; Visual arts; Museums; Performing arts; Arts; Education, early childhood education; Child development, education; Libraries (public); Education; Environment; Health care; Employment, training; Housing/shelter, home owners; Housing/shelter, services; Housing/shelter; Children/youth, services; Human services, financial counseling; Human services; Economic development; Community/economic development; Economically disadvantaged.
Type of support: General/operating support; Continuing support; Annual campaigns; Building/renovation; Emergency funds; Program development; Curriculum development; Employee matching gifts; Employee-related scholarships.
Limitations: Applications accepted. Giving primarily in areas of company operations in CT, New Castle, DE, MA, MD, NH, Central and Southern NJ, NY, Mid-Atlantic, PA, and RI. No support for political organizations, or organizations traditionally supported by parents, including Little League, Parent Teacher Organizations, and Scouting. No grants to individuals (except for employee-related scholarships), or for capital campaigns, sectarian or religious purposes, pageants, team sponsorships or sporting events, advertising in programs, bulletins, schedules, maps, yearbooks, book covers, or brochures, trips or tours, or walk-a-thon races or similar fundraising events.
Publications: Application guidelines; Annual report; Program policy statement.
Application information: Proposal narratives should be no longer than 2 pages. Submissions of videos, folders, and plastic covers are not encouraged. Additional information may be requested at a later date. Application form not required.
Initial approach: Download grant proposal cover sheet and e-mail cover sheet and proposal to foundation
Copies of proposal: 1
***Deadline(s):* Mar. 7, June 6, and Sept. 5**
***Final notification:* Apr. 30, July 31, and Oct. 31**
Officers and Directors:* John V. Killen,* Pres.; Sonia L. Alleyne, V.P.; Patricia Rock, V.P.; Joseph E. Schupp, V.P.; Craig M. Williams, V.P.; Cynthia Kelly, Secy.; Jay Bobb, Treas.; Lawrence F. Delp; Patrick Sullivan.
Number of staff: 1 part-time professional; 1 part-time support.
EIN: 232548113
Other changes: The grantmaker has moved from PA to MA.

1542
The Schelzi Family Foundation
Wakefield, MA

The foundation terminated in 2011 and transferred its assets to Fidelity Investments Charitable Gift Fund.

1543
William E. Schrafft and Bertha E. Schrafft Charitable Trust
77 Summer St., 8th Fl.
Boston, MA 02110-1006
Contact: Karen Faulkner, Exec. Dir.
E-mail: funding@schrafftcharitable.org; Main URL: http://www.schrafftcharitable.org
Grants List: http://www.schrafftcharitable.org/?page_id=91

Trust established in 1946 in MA.
Donors: William E. Schrafft†; Bertha E. Schrafft†.
Foundation type: Independent foundation.
Financial data (yr. ended 12/31/12): Assets, $31,281,798 (M); expenditures, $1,791,862; qualifying distributions, $1,450,000; giving activities include $1,450,000 for 93 grants (high: $83,000; low: $2,000).
Purpose and activities: Grants primarily for educational programs in the Boston, MA, inner-city area, for minorities and higher and secondary education; support also for community funds, cultural programs, and youth agencies.
Fields of interest: Arts; Elementary school/education; Secondary school/education; Higher education; Children/youth, services; Youth, services; Minorities; Economically disadvantaged.
Type of support: Continuing support; Scholarship funds.
Limitations: Applications accepted. Giving limited to the inner-city Boston, MA, area. No grants to individuals, or for matching gifts, seed money, emergency funds, capital campaigns, or deficit financing; no loans.
Publications: Application guidelines; Grants list.
Application information: Associated Grant Makers Common Proposal Form accepted, which is available through the trust's web site. Application form required.
Initial approach: Proposal
Copies of proposal: 1
Deadline(s): None
Board meeting date(s): About 6 times per year
Final notification: 2 months
Officer: Karen Faulkner, Exec. Dir. and Grants Mgr. Admin.
Trustees: Lavinia B. Chase; Kristen J. McCormack; Arthur H. Parker.
EIN: 046065605

1544
The Clinton H. & Wilma T. Shattuck Charitable Trust
c/o K & L Gates
1 Lincoln St.
Boston, MA 02111-2950

Established in 1985 in MA.
Foundation type: Independent foundation.
Financial data (yr. ended 08/31/13): Assets, $6,397,848 (M); expenditures, $444,204; qualifying distributions, $396,345; giving activities include $395,000 for 43 grants (high: $40,000; low: $2,000).
Fields of interest: Museums; Arts; Education; Environment; Animal welfare; Children/youth, services; Residential/custodial care, hospices; Law/international law.
Limitations: Applications not accepted. Giving primarily in MA. No grants to individuals.
Application information: Contributes only to pre-selected organizations.
Trustee: Walter G. Van Dorn.
EIN: 222659654

1545
Sheehan Family Foundation
P.O. Box K
Kingston, MA 02364-0510
E-mail: director@sheehanfoundation.org; Application address: c/o Laura Gang, Exec. Dir., 631 South St., Roslindale, MA 02131; Main URL: http://www.sheehanfoundation.org/

Established in 1993 in MA.
Donors: Gerald V. Sheehan; Elizabeth Sheehan; Margaret Sheehan; L. Knife & Son, Inc.
Foundation type: Operating foundation.
Financial data (yr. ended 12/31/12): Assets, $3,080,216 (M); gifts received, $287,820; expenditures, $946,040; qualifying distributions, $865,000; giving activities include $865,000 for 39 grants (high: $500,000; low: $500).
Purpose and activities: Giving primarily for education, including after school programs, youth development and natural resource protection.
Fields of interest: Education, early childhood education; Education; Environment, natural resources; Youth development.
Type of support: General/operating support; Continuing support; Land acquisition; Conferences/seminars; Curriculum development; Scholarship funds; Technical assistance; Program evaluation; Matching/challenge support.
Limitations: Giving limited to Essex, Middlesex, Plymouth, Barnstable, and Dukes counties, MA; and Brooklyn, Liverpool, and Westmoreland, NY; some funding also in Milwaukee, WI. No grants to individuals.

Publications: Annual report; Multi-year report.
Application information:
Initial approach: Letter
Deadline(s): Rolling basis
Board meeting date(s): Jan., May and Sept.
Officer: Laura Gang, Exec. Dir.
Trustees: Chris Sheehan; John Sheehan; Timothy Sheehan.
EIN: 043197325
Other changes: Matthew Sheehan is no longer trustee.

1546
Richard and Susan Smith Family Foundation

1 Newton Executive Park, Ste. 104
Newton, MA 02462-1435 **(857) 404-0700**
Contact: Lynne J. Doblin, Exec. Dir.
FAX: (857) 404-0719;
E-mail: info@smithfamilyfoundation.net; Main URL: http://www.smithfamilyfoundation.net

Trust established in 1970 in MA.
Donors: Marian Smith‡; Richard A. Smith; Susan F. Smith.
Foundation type: Independent foundation.
Financial data (yr. ended 04/30/13): Assets, $253,764,175 (M); gifts received, $163,946; expenditures, $15,813,365; qualifying distributions, $13,306,565; giving activities include $11,443,260 for 142 grants (high: $500,000; low: $100).
Purpose and activities: Grants for health, education, and for children and youth; the arts are a secondary field of interest. Of particular interest are organizations providing opportunities for economically disadvantaged populations, especially children and youth. Toward this end, the foundation has directed most of its support toward highly successful operators of non-traditional public schools that are playing an important role in Massachusetts's efforts to eliminate the achievement gap.
Fields of interest: Arts; Education, early childhood education; Elementary school/education; Education; Hospitals (general); Medical research; Children/youth, services; Homeless, human services; Children/youth; Youth; Young adults; Minorities; Economically disadvantaged; Homeless.
Type of support: General/operating support; Management development/capacity building; Annual campaigns; Capital campaigns; Building/renovation; Equipment; Program development; Seed money; Curriculum development; Research; Program evaluation; Matching/challenge support.
Limitations: Applications accepted. **Giving primarily in the greater Boston, MA; giving also to agencies that serve the communities of Lawrence, Lowell, Lynn, Brocton, Fall River, and New Bedford, MA. No support for sectarian religious activities, federal, state or municipal agencies or political causes.** No grants to individuals, or for deficit financing, or endowment funds.
Publications: Application guidelines; Grants list.
Application information: Applications for all grants, except Small Capital Grants, are by invitation only. Unsolicited applications will not be accepted. See foundation web site for additional application information for the Small Capital Grants program. Application form not required.
Initial approach: Letter
Copies of proposal: 1
Deadline(s): See foundation web site
Board meeting date(s): As needed, 4 or more times per year
Final notification: After board meeting
Officers and Trustees:* Richard A. Smith,* Co-Chair.; Susan F. Smith,* Co-Chair.; Lynne J. Doblin, Exec. Dir.; Amy Smith Berylson; James Berylson; John G. Berylson; Jennifer Berylson Block; Jonathan Block; Elizabeth Berylson Katz; **Robert Katz**; Andrew Knez; Debra S. Knez; Jessica Knez; Dana W. Smith; Robert A. Smith.
Number of staff: 3 full-time professional; 1 part-time support.
EIN: 237090011
Other changes: Elizabeth Berylson, a trustee, is now Elizabeth Berylson Katz.

1547
The Horace Smith Fund

1441 Main St.
Springfield, MA 01103 (413) 739-4222
***FAX:* (413) 739-1108**; Main URL: http://www.horacesmithfund.org

Established in 1898 in MA.
Donors: Horace Smith‡; Jean M. Smith‡.
Foundation type: Independent foundation.
Financial data (yr. ended 03/31/13): Assets, $6,700,423 (M); gifts received, $50; expenditures, $420,867; qualifying distributions, $219,750; giving activities include $219,750 for grants to individuals.
Purpose and activities: Scholarship grants for high school seniors in Hampden County, Massachusetts, and fellowships for Hampden County residents or qualified former residents.
Fields of interest: Higher education.
Type of support: Fellowships; Scholarships—to individuals.
Limitations: Applications accepted. Giving limited to Hampden County, MA, residents.
Application information: Application form required.
Initial approach: Contact foundation website for application form
Deadline(s): Dec. 20 for scholarship; Feb. 1 for fellowship
Officers: Michael P. Williams, Pres.; Anne Mahoney, V.P. and Admin.; Benjamin Bump, Exec. Secy.; Josephine Sarnelli, Clerk; Adonis E. Miller,* Treas.
Trustees: Katleen Bourque; James W. Brodrick, Jr.; Samalid Hogan; Jerome Linehan; Michael E. Tucker; Wayne L. Webster.
Number of staff: 1 full-time professional; 1 part-time professional; 1 part-time support.
EIN: 042235130

1548
Sociological Initiatives Foundation, Inc.

c/o GMA Foundations
77 Summer St., 8th Fl.
Boston, MA 02110-1006 **(617) 426-7080**
Contact: Prentice Zinn, Admin.
FAX: (617) 426-7087;
E-mail: pzinn@gmafoundations.com; Main URL: http://www.sifoundation.org/

Established in 2001 in NY.
Foundation type: Independent foundation.
Financial data (yr. ended 11/30/12): Assets, $3,775,405 (M); expenditures, $225,338; qualifying distributions, $177,992; giving activities include $139,000 for 7 grants (high: $20,000; low: $19,000).
Purpose and activities: To support research projects that help solve social problems.
Fields of interest: Community/economic development, research; Public affairs, research.
Type of support: Research.
Limitations: Applications accepted. Giving on a national basis. No support for direct service programs. No grants to individuals, or for dissertation research, honoraria, or capital campaigns.
Publications: Application guidelines; Grants list; Program policy statement.
Application information: See web site for complete application guidelines and forms. Eight copies of a brief concept letter summarizing proposal are required. Application form required.
Initial approach: The foundation generally does not accept unsolicited proposals. No fax or e-mail applications accepted.
Deadline(s): Aug. 15 for concept letter; Nov. 15 for proposal
Board meeting date(s): Jan. 5
Final notification: Grants awarded in Jan.
Trustees: Barbara Freed; Ramona Hernandez; Glenn Jacobs; Randy Stoecker; Irene Thomson.
Number of staff: 1 part-time professional; 1 full-time support.
EIN: 112000581

1549
Staples Foundation, Inc.

(formerly Staples Foundation for Learning, Inc.)
500 Staples Dr., 4 W.
Framingham, MA 01702-4478 (508) 253-5000
FAX: (508) 253-9600;
E-mail: foundationinfo@staples.com; Main URL: http://www.staplesfoundation.org/
Grants Database: http://www.staplesfoundation.org/grant-recipients-list.php

Established in 2002 in MA.
Donor: Staples, Inc.
Foundation type: Company-sponsored foundation.
Financial data (yr. ended 01/31/13): Assets, $72,967 (M); gifts received, $3,083,000; expenditures, $3,042,400; qualifying distributions, $3,034,200; giving activities include $3,034,200 for 475 grants (high: $600,000; low: $1,000).
Purpose and activities: The foundation supports programs designed to provide education and job skills. Special emphasis is directed toward programs designed to support disadvantaged youth.
Fields of interest: Vocational education; Education, reading; Education; Employment, training; Boys & girls clubs; Youth; Economically disadvantaged.
Type of support: Program development; Curriculum development.
Limitations: Applications not accepted. Giving primarily in CA, CO, GA, MA, NJ, and VA. No support for public schools without 501(c)(3) status, athletic teams, fiscal sponsors, government agencies, substance abuse agencies, discriminatory organizations, international organizations, political organizations, religious organizations not of direct benefit to the entire community, fraternal or veterans' organizations, professional associations, or similar membership groups. No grants to individuals, or for capital campaigns, athletic events, educational loans, travel, conferences or conventions, books, research papers, or articles in professional journals, medical research, or public or commercial broadcasting.
Publications: Annual report; Corporate giving report; Grants list.
Application information: Unsolicited requests for funding are not accepted.
Board meeting date(s): June, Sept., and Jan.
Officers and Directors: John Burke, Pres.; Steve Fund, Exec. V.P.; Erich Rhynhart, Clerk; Laura Granahan, Treas.; **Alison Corcoran**; **Katy Dobbs**;

Patrick Girard; **Gordon Glover**; Conor Kearny; Regis Mulot; Neil Ringel; Mary Sagat; Melissa Tetreault.
Number of staff: 2
EIN: 470867951
Other changes: The grantmaker no longer lists a primary contact.
John Burke has replaced Mike Miles as Pres.
Mike Miles is no longer Pres. Stephanie Shores Lambert is no longer Clerk. Steve Bussberg, Jay Mutschler, Paul Mullen, Amy Shanler, Mary Tivnan, and Denise Zielecki are no longer directors.

1550
State Street Foundation, Inc.

1 Lincoln St
Boston, MA 02111-2900
Contact: Wayne Young, V.P., Global Grants Mgr.
***E-mail:* wyoung@statestreet.com; E-mail address for international applicants: Europe, Middle East and Africa: statestreet@cafoline.org Asia Pacific: statestreet@give2asia.org**; Main URL: http://www.statestreet.com/wps/portal/internet/corporate/home/aboutstatestreet/corporatecitizenship/globalphilanthropy/statestreetfoundation/

Established in 2006 in MA.
Donor: State Street Bank & Trust Co.
Foundation type: Company-sponsored foundation.
Financial data (yr. ended 12/31/12): Assets, $28,707,695 (M); gifts received, $1,682,000; expenditures, $20,717,350; qualifying distributions, $20,714,350; giving activities include $20,651,795 for 584 grants (high: $1,887,651; low: $400).
Purpose and activities: The mission of State Street Foundation's strategic grantmaking program is to contribute to the sustainability of communities where State Street operates, primarily by investing in education and workforce development programs related to employability for disadvantaged populations.
Fields of interest: Vocational education; Adult/continuing education; Adult education—literacy, basic skills & GED; Employment, services; Employment, training; Employment; Youth development; Adults; Young adults; Economically disadvantaged.
Type of support: Continuing support; Employee matching gifts; Employee volunteer services; General/operating support; Program development; Sponsorships; Use of facilities.
Limitations: Applications accepted. Giving primarily in areas of company operations in CA, GA, IL, Boston and Quincy, MA, MO, NJ, NY, and PA and in Australia, Austria, Belgium, Canada, Cayman Islands, Europe, France, Germany, India, Ireland, Italy, Japan, Luxembourg, the Middle East, Netherlands, Poland, Qatar, Singapore, South Africa, South Korea, Switzerland, Taiwan, and the United Kingdom. No support for political candidates or organizations, lobbying, labor, or fraternal organizations, or religious organizations not of direct benefit to the entire community. No grants to individuals, or for endowments, political causes or campaigns, sectarian activities for religious organizations, travel, team sponsorships, or sporting events, or medical research or disease specific initiatives.
Publications: Application guidelines; Grants list.
Application information: Applicants may be asked to submit a full grant application. Organizations receiving support are asked to provide a final report. Visit website for nearest community contact information.
Initial approach: Complete online preliminary grant application; e-mail preliminary grant applications for organizations located in the Asia Pacific, Canada, the Cayman Islands, Europe, Middle East, and South Africa
Deadline(s): None for preliminary grant applications
Final notification: 8 weeks for preliminary grant applications
Officers and Directors:* Joseph A. McGrail, Jr., C.O.O.; **Michael Scannell, Pres.**; Amanda Northrop, V.P.; Simon Zornoza,* Clerk; James J. Malebra,* Treas.; Paul Selian.
EIN: 562615567
Other changes: Michael Scannell has replaced George A. Russell Jr. as Pres.
George A. Russell, Jr. is no longer Pres.

1551
Sudbury Foundation

326 Concord Rd.
Sudbury, MA 01776-1819 (978) 443-0849
Contact: Marilyn Martino, Exec. Dir.
FAX: (978) 579-9536;
E-mail: contact@sudburyfoundation.org; **Main URL: http://www.sudburyfoundation.org**
Blog: http://www.sudburyfoundation.org/sudbury-foundation-blog/
Twitter: http://twitter.com/SudburyFdn

Trust established in 1952 in MA.
Donors: Esther M. Atkinson†; Herbert J. Atkinson†.
Foundation type: Independent foundation.
Financial data (yr. ended 12/31/12): Assets, $30,420,278 (M); expenditures, $1,599,436; qualifying distributions, $1,442,193; giving activities include $887,310 for 48 grants (high: $175,000; low: $500), and $309,447 for 64 grants to individuals (high: $7,500; low: $1,200).
Purpose and activities: Scholarships to residents of Sudbury, Lincoln or Boston, MA, who are graduating from Lincoln-Sudbury Regional High School or are dependents of employees of the Town of Sudbury; support also for community building and civic issues, the environment, local social services, and arts and culture.
Fields of interest: Arts; Environment; Human services; Youth, services; Community/economic development.
Type of support: Program evaluation; Management development/capacity building; Consulting services; Program development; Scholarships—to individuals; Matching/challenge support.
Limitations: Applications accepted. Giving primarily in Sudbury, MA, and surrounding towns. No support for sectarian religious activities. No grants to individuals (except for the scholarship program), or for ongoing operating support, deficit financing, general appeals, or graduate study.
Publications: Application guidelines; Financial statement; Informational brochure; Program policy statement.
Application information: Unsolicited requests for funds are not accepted for the Environmental Program. Program and application information and forms are available on foundation web site. Application form required.
Initial approach: Telephone inquiries and concept papers are welcome prior to proposal submission
Copies of proposal: 1
Deadline(s): Feb. 1 for Atkinson Scholarships; Jan. 1, Apr. 1, July 1, and Oct. 1 for The Sudbury Program
Board meeting date(s): Dates available on request
Final notification: 2 months
Officer: Marilyn Martino, Exec. Dir.
Trustees: Susan Iuliano, Chair.; Miner Crary; Richard H. Davison; Jill M. Stansky; Bank of America, N.A.
Number of staff: 1 full-time professional; 1 part-time professional.
EIN: 046037026
Other changes: Susan Iuliano is now Chair.
The grantmaker now makes its application guidelines available online.

1552
Swan Society in Boston

(formerly Widows Society in Boston)
581 Boylston St., Ste. 705
Boston, MA 02116-3626 (617) 536-7951
Contact: Jackie Husid, Exec. Dir.
FAX: (617) 536-0725

Established in 1816 in MA. Incorporated in 1828.
Foundation type: Operating foundation.
Financial data (yr. ended 10/31/13): Assets, $5,055,202 (M); gifts received, $6,000; expenditures, $289,609; qualifying distributions, $284,287; giving activities include $229,232 for 10 grants (high: $61,241; low: $5,000).
Purpose and activities: Support for widowed, divorced, or single women who are over 65 years old and in need of financial aid, and live within a 25 mile radius of the State House in Boston, MA.
Fields of interest: Aging, centers/services; Women, centers/services; Aging; Women; Economically disadvantaged.
Type of support: Emergency funds.
Limitations: Applications accepted. Giving limited to applicants living within 25 miles of the State House in Boston, MA.
Publications: Application guidelines; Annual report; Informational brochure.
Application information: Application form required.
Initial approach: Referrals from public and social organizations
Copies of proposal: 1
Deadline(s): None
Board meeting date(s): Jan.
Final notification: 1-2 weeks
Officers and Directors:* Lucy Goreham,* Pres.; Jill Newman,* Secy.; Richard V. Howe, Treas.; Jackie Husid, Exec. Dir.; **Eleanor Marsh**; Ms. Lee Smith.
Number of staff: 1 part-time professional.
EIN: 042306840

1553
Swartz Foundation

c/o Ropes & Gray LLP
800 Boylston St.
Boston, MA 02199-3600 (617) 951-7000
Contact: Janet C. Taylor, Philanthropic Advisor

Established in 1994 in MA.
Donors: Sidney W. Swartz; Judith W. Swartz.
Foundation type: Independent foundation.
Financial data (yr. ended 12/31/12): Assets, $226,162,423 (M); expenditures, $17,349,933; qualifying distributions, $16,595,213; giving activities include $16,490,905 for 31 grants (high: $9,007,000; low: $500), and $104,308 for foundation-administered programs.
Purpose and activities: Giving primarily to Jewish organizations for medical research, as well as to Jewish temples and federated giving programs; funding also for social services, and education.
Fields of interest: Medical research, institute; Human services; Jewish federated giving programs; Jewish agencies & synagogues; Women.

Type of support: General/operating support; Capital campaigns; Program development.
Limitations: Applications not accepted. Giving primarily in eastern MA, and Palm Beach, FL. No grants to individuals.
Application information: Contributes only to pre-selected organizations.
Trustees: Robert N. Shapiro; **Sydney Swartz**.
EIN: 043255974

1554
Sweet Water Trust
1 Short St.
Northampton, MA 01060-2567
Contact: Eve Endicott, Exec Dir.
E-mail: eendicott@sweetwatertrust.org; Main URL: http://www.sweetwatertrust.org

Established in 1991 in MA.
Donor: Walker G. Buckner, Jr.
Foundation type: Independent foundation.
Financial data (yr. ended 12/31/12): Assets, $22,721,919 (M); gifts received, $40,216; expenditures, $2,285,369; qualifying distributions, $1,652,824; giving activities include $1,652,824 for 9 grants (high: $470,000; low: $12,000).
Purpose and activities: Support for environmental preservation through its Land Protection Program: Wildlands, Wildwaters - to help purchase land and conservation easements. The trust seeks partners (land trusts, government agencies, businesses and individuals) to work toward the ecological and biotic health of New England by establishing, enlarging, and connecting reserve areas. Grants range from $1,000-$1,000,000 for land acquisition.
Fields of interest: Environment, natural resources; Environment, water resources; Environment, land resources; Animals/wildlife, preservation/protection; Biology/life sciences.
Type of support: Land acquisition; Technical assistance; Matching/challenge support.
Limitations: Giving generally limited to New England and upstate NY; giving also to Canada. No support for projects for the protection of farmland, timberlands, parks, and trails unless they are a small part of a reserve design of a natural area which exceeds 10,000 acres. No grants to individuals, or for operating support or scientific studies (unless tied to qualifying land project that has received approval).
Publications: Application guidelines; Grants list.
Application information: After preliminary e-mail contact, grant application is by invitation only. Grant guidelines and information are available on foundation web site. Application form not required.
Initial approach: E-mail
Copies of proposal: 1
Deadline(s): None
Board meeting date(s): Bi-monthly
Final notification: Varies
Officer: Eve Endicott, Exec. Dir.
Trustee: Walker G. Buckner, Jr.
Number of staff: 1 full-time professional; 1 part-time professional.
EIN: 043118545
Other changes: At the close of 2012, the grantmaker paid grants of $1,652,824, an 84.2% increase over the 2011 disbursements, $897,500.

1555
Symes Family Charitable Foundation
50 Dodge St.
Beverly, MA 01915-1711

Established in 1999 in MA.
Donors: Albert R. Symes; Barbara Symes.
Foundation type: Independent foundation.
Financial data (yr. ended 06/30/13): Assets, $2,080,404 (M); expenditures, $286,619; qualifying distributions, $200,872; giving activities include $200,872 for 2 grants (high: $190,872; low: $10,000).
Fields of interest: Performing arts, theater.
Limitations: Applications not accepted. Giving primarily in MA. No grants to individuals.
Application information: Unsolicited requests for funds not accepted.
Officers and Directors:* Albert R. Symes,* Pres.; Arica Symes-Elmer,* V.P. and Treas.; Landers Symes, Clerk; Barbara Symes.
EIN: 043494605
Other changes: Landers Symes has replaced Arica Symes-Elmer as Clerk.
Arica Symes-Elmer is now V.P. and Treas.

1556
Thee Mustard Seed Foundation
38 Newbury St., Ste. 6
Boston, MA 02116

Foundation type: Independent foundation.
Financial data (yr. ended 12/31/11): Assets, $2,348,308 (M); expenditures, $141,860; qualifying distributions, $141,860; giving activities include $141,860 for 10 grants (high: $50,000; low: $3,250).
Fields of interest: Health care; Agriculture/food; Religion.
Limitations: Applications not accepted.
Application information: Unsolicited requests for funds not accepted.
Officer: Arthur S. Demoulas.
EIN: 260873247

1557
Two Sisters and a Wife Foundation, Inc.
c/o Sara Whitman
10 Blueberry Cir.
Newton, MA **02462-1437**

Donor: Catherine A. Whitman Charitable Remainder Trust.
Foundation type: Independent foundation.
Financial data (yr. ended 06/30/13): Assets, $11,198,018 (M); gifts received, $333,007; expenditures, $686,978; qualifying distributions, $573,000; giving activities include $573,000 for 14 grants (high: $150,000; low: $1,000).
Fields of interest: Arts; Education; Health organizations; LGBTQ.
Limitations: Applications not accepted.
Application information: Unsolicited requests for funds not accepted.
Directors: Jeanine M. Cowen; Sara G. Whitman.
EIN: 264607134

1558
Ray Tye Medical Aid Foundation
175 Campanelli Dr.
P.O. Box 850376
Braintree, MA 02184-0376
Contact: Terri Carlson, Dir.
FAX: (781) 356-4551;
E-mail: rtmaf@unitedliquors.com; **Additional e-mail: info@rtmaf.org**; Main URL: http://www.rtmaf.org
Facebook: https://www.facebook.com/raytyemedicalaidfoundation
RSS Feed: http://feeds.feedburner.com/TheRayTyeMedicalAidFoundation

Established in 2002 in MA.
Donors: Harvey R. Chaplin; Maurice Halter Foundation; National Distributing Co., Inc.
Foundation type: Independent foundation.
Financial data (yr. ended 12/31/12): Assets, $3,998,269 (M); gifts received, $36,183; expenditures, $813,531; qualifying distributions, $780,347; giving activities include $780,347 for 11 grants (high: $425,946; low: $125).
Purpose and activities: Grants are made for medical care of indigents in U.S. hospitals.
Fields of interest: Hospitals (general); Health care; Economically disadvantaged.
Limitations: Giving primarily in the Boston, MA, area, including Cambridge.
Publications: Newsletter.
Application information:
Initial approach: Use Medical Aid Request form on foundation web site
Copies of proposal: 1
Board meeting date(s): As necessary
Final notification: 30 days
Officers: Eileen Tye, Pres.; Terri Carlson, V.P.
EIN: 046958143
Other changes: Terri Carlson has replaced Eileen Tye as V.P.
Eileen Tye is now Pres.

1559
United Charitable Foundation
95 Elm St.
West Springfield, MA 01089-2704 **(413) 787-1292**
Contact: Dena M. Hall, Pres.
***Main URL:* https://www.bankatunited.com/about-us/united-bank-foundation/**

Established in 2005 in MA.
Donor: United Financial Bancorp, Inc.
Foundation type: Independent foundation.
Financial data (yr. ended 12/31/12): Assets, $5,662,580 (M); expenditures, $307,314; qualifying distributions, $304,389; giving activities include $243,050 for 52 grants (high: $32,000; low: $750).
Fields of interest: Arts; Education; Health care; Youth development; Human services.
Type of support: Technical assistance; Program development; Matching/challenge support; Equipment; Capital campaigns; Building/renovation.
Limitations: Applications accepted. Giving primarily in MA. No grants to individuals.
Application information: See foundation website for complete application guidelines. Application form required.
Initial approach: Letter of intent
***Deadline(s):* Jan. 15, Apr. 15, July 15., and Oct. 15**
Board meeting date(s): Quarterly in Feb., May, Aug., and Nov.
Officers: Dena M. Hall, Pres.; Mark A. Roberts, V.P. and Treas.; Jennifer Shaw, Secy.
Directors: Richard B. Collins; Carol Moore Cutting; Carol A. Leary; Kevin E. Ross; Robert A. Stewart, Jr.; Peter F. Straley; Thomas H. Themistos.
Number of staff: None.
EIN: 203128745

1560
Verrochi Family Charitable Trust
33 Beaver Pl.
Boston, MA **02108-3303**

Established in 1993 in MA.
Donor: Paul M. Verrochi.
Foundation type: Independent foundation.
Financial data (yr. ended 07/31/13): Assets, $2,409,017 (M); gifts received, $1,267,036; expenditures, $217,993; qualifying distributions, $211,539; giving activities include $206,940 for 34 grants (high: $53,625; low: $50).
Fields of interest: Museums; Arts; Education; Youth development, centers/clubs; Catholic agencies & churches; Children.
Limitations: Applications not accepted. Giving primarily in MA. No grants to individuals.
Application information: Contributes only to pre-selected organizations.
Trustee: Paul M. Verrochi.
EIN: 046740855

1561
The Vingo Trust III
c/o LWC
230 Congress St., 12th Fl.
Boston, MA 02110-2409

Established in 1991 in MA.
Donor: Catherine Lastavica.
Foundation type: Independent foundation.
Financial data (yr. ended 12/31/12): Assets, $3,321,256 (M); expenditures, $321,762; qualifying distributions, $265,088; giving activities include $247,500 for 1 grant.
Fields of interest: Historical activities.
Limitations: Applications not accepted. Giving primarily in Boston, MA. No grants to individuals.
Application information: Contributes only to pre-selected organizations.
Trustees: David W. Fitts, Esq.; **Catherine C. Lastavica.**
EIN: 223106692
Other changes: Lawrence Coolidge is no longer a trustee.

1562
George C. Wadleigh Foundation, Inc.
(formerly George C. Wadleigh Home for Aged Men, Inc.)
P.O. Box 226
Groveland, MA 01834-0226 (978) 374-0115

Established in 1981 in MA.
Donor: George C. Wadleigh†.
Foundation type: Independent foundation.
Financial data (yr. ended 12/31/12): Assets, $12,972,227 (M); expenditures, $680,712; qualifying distributions, $585,321; giving activities include $568,323 for 17 grants (high: $85,000; low: $11,000).
Purpose and activities: Grants primarily to organizations benefiting aged and indigent individuals in the greater Haverhill, MA, area.
Fields of interest: Human services; Aging, centers/services; Aging.
Type of support: Seed money; Equipment; Building/renovation.
Limitations: Applications accepted. Giving primarily in the greater Haverhill, MA, area. No grants to individuals, or for general operating expenses, or research.
Publications: Application guidelines; Informational brochure.
Application information: Application form not required.
Initial approach: Letter
Copies of proposal: 1
Deadline(s): Aug. 30
Board meeting date(s): 2nd Tues. of Feb., May, Aug., and Nov.
Final notification: Dec.
Officers and Directors:* Edmund J. Cote, Jr.,* Pres.; A. Bruce McGregor,* Secy.; Richard Cammett,* Treas.; David Hindle; William Kluber; Charles Traver; Zoe Veasey.
Number of staff: None.
EIN: 042720087
Other changes: Donald Ruhl is no longer a director.

1563
Vila B. Webber 1985 Charitable Trust
c/o Choate LLP
P.O. Box 961019
Boston, MA **02196-1019**

Established in 1989 in MA.
Foundation type: Independent foundation.
Financial data (yr. ended 06/30/13): Assets, $4,217,734 (M); expenditures, $261,236; qualifying distributions, $224,978; giving activities include $220,000 for grants.
Purpose and activities: Giving primarily for education and human services.
Fields of interest: Language (classical); Arts; Education; Hospitals (general); Human services.
Limitations: Applications not accepted. Giving primarily in MA. No grants to individuals.
Application information: Unsolicited requests for funds not accepted.
Trustees: A. Silvana Giner; John J. Regan; Jennifer C. Snyder.
EIN: 222824617
Other changes: Cheryl B. Gemborys, a trustee, is deceased.

1564
The Frederick E. Weber Charities Corporation
89 South St.
Boston, MA 02110 (617) 292-6264
Contact: Thanda Brassard, Pres.

Incorporated in 1902 in MA.
Donor: Frederick E. Weber†.
Foundation type: Independent foundation.
Financial data (yr. ended 03/31/13): Assets, $5,936,352 (M); expenditures, $350,630; qualifying distributions, $266,000; giving activities include $266,000 for 51 grants (high: $18,000; low: $1,000).
Purpose and activities: Giving primarily to social service agencies for emergency financial assistance to indigent families or individuals.
Fields of interest: Hospitals (general); Human services; Children/youth, services; Family services; Economically disadvantaged.
Type of support: Emergency funds; Grants to individuals.
Limitations: Applications accepted. Giving limited to MA, with emphasis on Boston. No grants for research, capital projects, or equipment.
Publications: Annual report; Program policy statement.
Application information: Application form not required.
Initial approach: Letter
Copies of proposal: 1
Deadline(s): None
Board meeting date(s): Weekly except in Aug.
Final notification: 30 days
Officers: Thanda Brassard, Pres.; **Lisa Van Vleck, Clerk**; Nathaniel Butler, Treas.
Members: Elizabeth Aguilo; Linda Braun; Jeffrey Katz; **Mitchell Pomerance**; **Kevin Queally**; Jay Scollins; Kate Taylor.
Number of staff: 1 part-time support.
EIN: 042133244
Other changes: Lisa Van Vleck has replaced Janet W. Eustis as Clerk.

1565
Edwin S. Webster Foundation
c/o GMA Foundations
77 Summer St., 8th Fl.
Boston, MA 02110-1006 (617) 391-3087
Contact: Michelle Jenney, Admin.
FAX: (617) 426-7080;
E-mail: mjenney@gmafoundations.com; **Duplicate application contact: Alex Hiam, Tr., The Edwin S. Webster Foundation, 24 Chestnut St., Amherst, MA 01002**; Main URL: http://websterfoundation.grantsmanagement08.com/

Established in 1948 in MA.
Donor: Edwin S. Webster†.
Foundation type: Independent foundation.
Financial data (yr. ended 12/31/12): Assets, $27,802,778 (M); expenditures, $1,824,074; qualifying distributions, $1,684,287; giving activities include $1,610,000 for 71 grants (high: $75,000; low: $5,000).
Purpose and activities: Giving primarily to organizations that are well known to the foundation's trustees, with emphasis on hospitals, medical research, education, youth agencies, cultural activities, and programs addressing the needs of minorities.
Fields of interest: Arts; Education; Hospitals (general); Medical research, institute; Boys & girls clubs; Human services; Children/youth, services; Minorities/immigrants, centers/services; United Ways and Federated Giving Programs; Minorities.
Type of support: General/operating support; Capital campaigns; Building/renovation; Endowments; Program development; Research.
Limitations: Applications accepted. Giving primarily in the U.S., with emphasis on MA, MD, NH, NY, VA and VT. No grants to individuals, or for emergency funds, deficit financing, publications, or conferences; no loans.
Publications: Application guidelines; Grants list.
Application information: Applications sent by mail should conform generally to the AGM Common Proposal Form. A duplicate of application on paper (whether you apply on paper or electronically) is required and should be sent to Alex Hiam, Tr. Application form not required.
***Initial approach:* U.S. Mail or electronically**
Copies of proposal: 1
***Deadline(s):* May 1 and Nov. 1**
Board meeting date(s): June and Dec.
Trustees: Thomas C. Beck; Henry U. Harris III; Alexander W. Hiam; Suzanne Harte Sears.
Number of staff: 1 part-time professional.
EIN: 046000647

1566

George W. Wells Foundation

c/o U.S. Trust, Bank of America, N.A.
225 Franklin St., 4th Fl.
Boston, MA 02110 (866) 778-6859
Contact: Michealle Larkins, V.P.
E-mail: michealle.larkins@ustrust.com; **Main URL: https://www.bankofamerica.com/philanthropic/grantmaking.go**

Established in MA.
Foundation type: Independent foundation.
Financial data (yr. ended 12/31/12): Assets, $4,468,389 (M); expenditures, $265,476; qualifying distributions, $224,886; giving activities include $202,500 for 9 grants (high: $35,000; low: $7,500).
Purpose and activities: The Foundation was established in 1934 to support and promote quality educational, human services, and health care programming for underserved populations. Special consideration is given to charitable organizations that serve the people of Southbridge, Massachusetts and its surrounding communities.
Fields of interest: Education; Health care; Human services.
Type of support: General/operating support; Program development.
Limitations: Giving primarily in Southbridge, MA and surrounding communities. No grants to individuals.
Application information: Online application; complete application guidelines available on foundation web site.
Initial approach: Email
Trustee: Bank of America Merrill Lynch.
EIN: 046038039

1567

Arthur Ashley Williams Foundation

379 Underwood St.
Holliston, MA 01746-1562
FAX: (508) 893-0757; E-mail: ctlambert@rcn.com; **Application address: P.O. Box 6280, Holliston, MA 01746, tel.: (508) 429-6228**

Incorporated in 1951 in MA.
Donor: Arthur A. Williams†.
Foundation type: Independent foundation.
Financial data (yr. ended 12/31/12): Assets, $3,311,913 (M); expenditures, $306,281; qualifying distributions, $168,788; giving activities include $130,000 for 30 grants (high: $22,000; low: $1,000), and $168,788 for 1 foundation-administered program.
Purpose and activities: Giving primarily for historical and natural history societies, as well as to churches; funding also for arts and culture, animals and wildlife, health associations, food services, and women's and social services.
Fields of interest: Historic preservation/historical societies; Arts; Animals/wildlife; Health organizations, association; Food banks; Human services; Women, centers/services; Christian agencies & churches; Aging.
Type of support: Annual campaigns; Capital campaigns; Seed money; Scholarship funds; Research; Scholarships—to individuals.
Limitations: Applications accepted. Giving primarily in CA, CT, MA, and Canaan and Plymouth, NH.
Publications: Application guidelines; Annual report; Grants list; Informational brochure.
Application information: See foundation web site for additional policies and guidelines. Associated Grantmakers (AGM) form accepted. Application form required.
Initial approach: Letter
Copies of proposal: 1
Deadline(s): None
Board meeting date(s): May and Nov.
Officers: Elbert F. Tuttle, Chair.; Martha Anderson, Clerk; Clement T. Lambert, Treas.
Trustees: Melissa W. Laverack; Nancy C. Rose; Polly Williams.
Number of staff: None.
EIN: 046044714
Other changes: The grantmaker no longer lists a URL address.

1568

The Windover Foundation

c/o Nutter McClennen
155 Seaport Blvd.
Boston, MA **02210-2698**
***Application address:* c/o K&L Gates, Attn.: David W. Lewis, Jr., 1 Lincoln St., Boston, MA 02111-2950, tel.: (617) 261-3100**

Established in 1999 in MA.
Donors: Constance B. Fuller; Constance Fuller Marital Trust.
Foundation type: Independent foundation.
Financial data (yr. ended 07/31/13): Assets, $19,152,500 (M); expenditures, $614,539; qualifying distributions, $496,873; giving activities include $456,500 for 8 grants (high: $250,000; low: $1,000).
Fields of interest: Arts; Hospitals (general); Human services.
Limitations: Applications accepted. Giving primarily in MA and ME. No grants to individuals.
Application information: Application form not required.
Initial approach: Proposal
Deadline(s): None
Trustees: Moira H. Fuller; Randolph J. Fuller; Robert G. Fuller, Jr.; Nutter McClennen; K&L Gates.
EIN: 046897800

1569

Winning Home Inc.

c/o CFC Investments
P.O. Box 1308
Concord, MA **01742-1308 (978) 287-1414**
***FAX:* (978) 287-6009**; Main URL: http://www.winninghome.org/

Established in MA.
Foundation type: Independent foundation.
Financial data (yr. ended 12/31/12): Assets, $5,493,232 (M); expenditures, $297,933; qualifying distributions, $235,000; giving activities include $235,000 for grants.
Purpose and activities: Giving primarily for services and support to children who are economically, socially, physically, emotionally, or mentally handicapped.
Fields of interest: Food services; Boys & girls clubs; Children/youth, services; Disabilities, people with; Economically disadvantaged.
Limitations: Applications accepted. Giving primarily in MA. No grants to individuals.
Application information: See foundation's web site for application guidelines. Application form required.
Officers: Thomas Martin,* Pres.; Donald Foley,* V.P.; Ernest Jones,* Secy.; Albert F. Curran, Jr.,* Treas.
Directors: John Brophy; Larry Byron; **Sean Coakley**; **Robert Maguire**; **Steve Palladino**; **Mark Salvati**; Robert Simons; Mark Sullivan.
EIN: 046049776
Other changes: Paul Paris is no longer director.

1570

Xeric Foundation

351 Pleasant St.
PMB 214
Northampton, MA 01060-3900 (413) 585-0671
E-mail: xericgrant@aol.com; Main URL: http://www.xericfoundation.org/
Grants List: http://www.xericfoundation.org/xericchargrants.html

Established in 1991 in MA.
Donor: Peter A. Laird.
Foundation type: Independent foundation.
Financial data (yr. ended 09/30/13): Assets, $3,712,994 (M); expenditures, $192,350; qualifying distributions, $188,561; giving activities include $103,859 for 36 grants (high: $10,000; low: $500), and $47,702 for 13 grants to individuals (high: $6,985; low: $857).
Purpose and activities: Giving to self-publishing comic book creators in the U.S. and Canada; support also for nonprofit organizations in western MA, in the 413 area code, for unique projects or services.
Fields of interest: Arts; Education; Housing/shelter, development; Youth development.
Type of support: Continuing support; Building/renovation; Land acquisition; Program development; Publication; Seed money; Scholarship funds; Technical assistance; Grants to individuals.
Limitations: Applications accepted. Giving limited to western MA for organizations. No grants for operating budgets or capital costs.
Application information: Complete application guidelines available on foundation web site. Application form required.
Initial approach: Letter
Copies of proposal: 6
Officers: Peter A. Laird, Pres.; Christopher B. Milne, V.P.; Kendall Clark Engelman, Secy.-Treas.
Number of staff: 1 part-time professional.
EIN: 223149258

MICHIGAN

1571
James C. Acheson Foundation
405 Water St., Ste. 200
Port Huron, MI 48060-5469

Established in 1999 in MI.
Donor: James C. Acheson.
Foundation type: Independent foundation.
Financial data (yr. ended 12/31/12): Assets, $17,170,694 (M); gifts received, $1,000; expenditures, $413,856; qualifying distributions, $357,929; giving activities include $323,381 for 25 grants (high: $148,400; low: $100).
Fields of interest: Museums; Education; Hospitals (specialty); Human services; YM/YWCAs & YM/YWHAs; Foundations (community).
Limitations: Applications not accepted. Giving primarily in MI. No grants to individuals.
Application information: Contributes only to pre-selected organizations.
Officers: James C. Acheson, Pres.; **Donna M. Niester, Secy.-Treas.**
EIN: 383463509
Other changes: Donna M. Niester has replaced Douglas R. Austin as Secy.-Treas.

1572
The Alix Foundation
(formerly Jay & Maryanne Alix Foundation)
c/o Jay Alix
151 S. Old Woodward Ave., Ste. 400
Birmingham, MI 48009-6103

Established in 1994 in MI.
Donors: Jay Alix; Maryanne Alix†; Jay Alix Living Trust.
Foundation type: Independent foundation.
Financial data (yr. ended 12/31/12): Assets, $6,555,740 (M); gifts received, $6,001,190; expenditures, $524,590; qualifying distributions, $521,805; giving activities include $518,999 for 5 grants (high: $151,499; low: $20,000).
Purpose and activities: Giving primarily for education, health care and medical research, and to religious organizations.
Fields of interest: Elementary/secondary education; Health care; Medical research, institute; Human services; Religion.
Limitations: Applications not accepted. Giving primarily in MI. No grants to individuals.
Application information: Contributes only to pre-selected organizations.
Officers and Director:* Jay Alix,* Chair.; Robert E. Shields, C.E.O. and Pres.; **Arthur J. Kubert, V.P., Secy.-Treas., and C.F.O.**
EIN: 383171122
Other changes: Jean A. Wiley is no longer Secy. and Cont. Arthur J. Kubert is now V.P., Secy.-Treas., and C.F.O.

1573
Allen Foundation, Inc.
P.O. Box 1606
Midland, MI 48641-1606
Contact: Dale Baum, Secy.
FAX: (989) 832-8842;
E-mail: dbaum@allenfoundation.org; Additional e-mail: Lucille@allenfoundation.org; Main URL: http://www.allenfoundation.org/

Established in 1975 in MI.
Foundation type: Independent foundation.
Financial data (yr. ended 12/31/12): Assets, $10,564,734 (M); expenditures, $489,701; qualifying distributions, $475,671; giving activities include $475,671 for 16 grants (high: $70,150; low: $1,500).
Purpose and activities: The foundation focuses on projects that benefit nutritional programs in the areas of education, training and research. A lower priority is given to proposals that help solve immediate or emergency hunger and malnutrition problems.
Fields of interest: Higher education; Hospitals (general); Nutrition.
Limitations: Applications accepted. Giving on a national basis. No grants to individuals.
Publications: Application guidelines; Annual report; Grants list.
Application information: Application forms and latest information available on foundation web site. All applications are to be submitted online. Application form not required.
  ***Initial approach:* Take eligibility quiz on foundation web site**
  Copies of proposal: 1
  Deadline(s): Dec. 31
  Board meeting date(s): Annually
  Final notification: June
Officers and Trustees:* Gail E. Lanphear,* Chair.; Mark Ostahowski, M.D.*, Pres.; **William Lauderbach,* V.P., Finance and Treas.**; Dale Baum, Ph.D.*, Secy.; William James Allen; Laurie Bouwman; Leslie Hildebrandt, Ph.D.; Ann F. Jay; Charles B. Kendall; Mary M. Neely; Pat Oriel, Ph.D.
Number of staff: 1 part-time support.
EIN: 510152562
Other changes: William Lauderbach is now V.P., Finance and Treas.

1574
The Alro Steel Foundation
3100 E. High St.
Jackson, MI 49203-3467

Established in 2004 in MI.
Donors: Li-Cor of Lincoln LLC; Alro Steel Corp.
Foundation type: Company-sponsored foundation.
Financial data (yr. ended 12/31/12): Assets, $9,345,483 (M); gifts received, $4,400,000; expenditures, $2,069,580; qualifying distributions, $2,065,845; giving activities include $2,065,825 for 48 grants (high: $2,000,000; low: $100).
Purpose and activities: The foundation supports orchestras and organizations involved with education, athletics, human services, and community development.
Fields of interest: Performing arts, orchestras; Higher education; Education; Athletics/sports, amateur leagues; Human services; Community/economic development; United Ways and Federated Giving Programs.
Type of support: General/operating support; Building/renovation; Program development; Scholarship funds.
Limitations: Applications not accepted. Giving primarily in MI, with emphasis on Jackson. No grants to individuals.
Application information: Contributes only to pre-selected organizations.
Officers: Carlton L. Glick, Pres.; Alvin L. Glick, V.P. and Secy.; Barry J. Glick, V.P.; Randal L. Glick, Treas.
EIN: 300254220
Other changes: Carlton L. Glick is now Pres. Alvin L. Glick is now V.P. and Secy.

1575
Paul M. Anderson Foundation
c/o Comerica Charitable Svcs. Grp.
101 N. Main St., Ste. 100
Ann Harbor, MI 48104-5515 (734) 930-2413
Contact: Gregory A. Schupra, Trust Off., Comerica Charitable Svcs. Grp.

Established in 1994 in WA.
Donors: John Privat; Priscilla Privat.
Foundation type: Independent foundation.
Financial data (yr. ended 09/30/13): Assets, $3,478,347 (M); expenditures, $167,719; qualifying distributions, $140,000; giving activities include $140,000 for 2 grants (high: $137,000; low: $3,000).
Fields of interest: Philanthropy/voluntarism.
Type of support: Land acquisition; Program development; Curriculum development.
Limitations: Applications accepted. Giving primarily in MI and WA. No grants to individuals.
Application information:
  Initial approach: None
  Deadline(s): None
  Board meeting date(s): Nov.
Officers: Monica Jo Privat, Pres.; Michael Obermeyer, V.P.; Michelle Privat Obermeyer, Secy.; Jim Privat, Treas.
Director: John Privat.
Number of staff: None.
EIN: 911697666

1576
Ann Arbor Area Community Foundation
(formerly Ann Arbor Area Foundation)
301 N. Main St., Ste. 300
Ann Arbor, MI 48104-1296 (734) 663-0401
Contact: For grants: Jillian Rosen, Prog. Off.
FAX: (734) 663-3514; E-mail: info@aaacf.org; Grant inquiry e-mail: jrosen@aaacf.org; Main URL: http://www.aaacf.org
Facebook: http://www.facebook.com/pages/Ann-Arbor-Area-Community-Foundation/112856658825507?sk=wall
Flickr: http://www.flickr.com/photos/aaacf
Twitter: http://twitter.com/AAACF
YouTube: https://www.youtube.com/user/ForGoodForEver

Incorporated in 1963 in MI.
Foundation type: Community foundation.
Financial data (yr. ended 12/31/12): Assets, $65,836,192 (M); gifts received, $5,003,084; expenditures, $3,345,449; giving activities include $1,951,305 for 133+ grants.
Purpose and activities: The Ann Arbor Area Community Foundation enriches the quality of life in the region through its knowledgeable leadership, engaged grantmaking, and creative partnerships with donors to make philanthropic investments and build endowment.
Fields of interest: Visual arts; Performing arts; Performing arts, theater; Arts; Higher education; Education; Environment, natural resources; Environment; Health care; Health organizations, association; Crime/violence prevention, domestic violence; Safety/disasters; Children/youth, services; Family services; Aging, centers/services; Homeless, human services; Human services; Economic development; Community/economic development; Public affairs, citizen

participation; Public affairs; Aging; African Americans/Blacks; Homeless.
Type of support: Income development; Management development/capacity building; Emergency funds; Program development; Conferences/seminars; Publication; Seed money; Scholarship funds; Research; Matching/challenge support.
Limitations: Applications accepted. Giving limited to Washtenaw County, MI. No support for religious or sectarian purposes. No grants to individuals (except for scholarships), or for construction projects (new building or routine maintenance), re-granting, annual giving campaigns, fundraising events, or computer hardware equipment; no loans.
Publications: Application guidelines; Annual report (including application guidelines); Newsletter; Program policy statement.
Application information: Visit foundation web site for application guidelines per grant type. Applicants must log on to http://www.communitygrants.org to create an online agency profile and complete the Short Community Grants Application. Application form required.
Initial approach: **E-mail Program Officer**
Deadline(s): **Apr. 8 for general grantmaking; varies for others**
Board meeting date(s): Jan., Mar., May, June, July, Sept., Oct., and Nov.
Final notification: **Early June**
Officers and Trustees:* Bhushan Kulkarni,* Chair.; Michelle Crumm,* Vice-Chair.; Cheryl W. Elliott, C.E.O. and Pres.; Neel Hajra, C.O.O.; Jennifer Poteat,* Secy.; Brian P. Campbell,* Treas.; Dr. Rose B. Bellanca; George E. Borel, CPA; Cynthia L. Cattran; Martha Darling; Ann S. Davis; Jeff Hauptman; Robert Laverty; Nancy Margolis; Frederick L. McDonald, II; Jackie Qiu; Paul Schutt; Kevin Thompson; Dr. Levi T. Thompson; Chris Vaughan.
Number of staff: 6 full-time professional; 4 part-time professional; 1 full-time support.
EIN: 386087967
Other changes: Cheryl W. Elliott is now Pres. and C.E.O. Stephanie Freeth is no longer V.P., Development and Donor Services.

1577
Baiardi Family Foundation Inc.
2328 Pinecrest St.
Harbor Springs, MI 49740-9261
E-mail: info@baiardifoundation.org; **Additional email: grants@baiardifoundation.org**; Main URL: http://www.baiardifoundation.org

Established in 1999.
Donors: Chris A. Baiardi; Cindy J. Baiardi; Angelo Baiardi†.
Foundation type: Independent foundation.
Financial data (yr. ended 12/31/12): Assets, $7,186,994 (M); expenditures, $371,654; qualifying distributions, $364,206; giving activities include $363,965 for 76 grants (high: $15,000; low: $500).
Purpose and activities: The foundation's mission remains to support and effect positive change within several main categories of giving. Specifically, the foundation has an interest in health care, education, the arts, environmental stewardship, land use and conservation, Catholic and Judeo-Christian traditions and values, and community resources.
Fields of interest: Arts; Education; Environment, natural resources; Environment, land resources; Hospitals (general); Health organizations; Human services; United Ways and Federated Giving Programs.
Limitations: Applications accepted. Giving primarily in MI, with concentrations in the Detroit metropolitan area community and in northwest lower Michigan, specifically Emmet County. No grants to individuals.
Application information: Application guidelines available on foundation web site. Application form required.
Initial approach: Review and complete Initial Contact Form on foundation web site
Officers: Chris A. Baiardi, Pres.; Kristen L. Baiardi, V.P.; Suzanne M. Baiardi, V.P.; Cindy J. Baiardi, Secy.-Treas.
EIN: 383430867

1578
The Bay Harbor Foundation
750 Bay Harbor Dr.
Bay Harbor, MI 49770-8056 (231) 439-2700
Contact: Candace Fitzsimons, Exec. Dir.
FAX: (231) 439-2701;
E-mail: info@bayharborfoundation.org; Main URL: http://www.bayharborfoundation.org

Established in 2004 in MI.
Foundation type: Community foundation.
Financial data (yr. ended 12/31/12): Assets, $325,674 (M); gifts received, $182,968; expenditures, $295,578; giving activities include $76,373 for 3+ grants (high: $15,000), and $61,000 for 30 grants to individuals.
Purpose and activities: The foundation is a charitable, nonprofit organization established to provide a structure for receiving donations and distributing grants in northern, lower Michigan for programs in the arts, education, the environment, and health and human services.
Fields of interest: Arts; Education; Environment; Health care; Human services.
Limitations: Applications accepted. Giving in northern lower MI.
Publications: Application guidelines; Grants list.
Application information: Visit foundation web site for application information. The foundation will invite selected organizations to submit a full grant application based on letters of intent. Application form required.
Initial approach: Submit letter of intent
Deadline(s): June 2 for letter of intent; Aug. 9 for full grant application
Final notification: Dec. 21
Officers and Directors:* Scot A. Morrison,* Chair.; James Ramer,* Vice-Chair.; Catherine Musto,* Secy.; Rodney Phillips,* Treas.; Candace Fitzsimons, Exec. Dir.; Jason Allen; Tracy Bacigalupi; Sally Cannon; Carole Cobb; William Conner; Christine Etienne; **Leonard Frescoln**; Tina Frescoln; Heather Frick; Debra Goodman; Michael Higgins; David V. Johnson; Paul Knapp; Linda Lyon; John McFarland; Julie Munford; Catherine Phillips; Judy Phillips; Robert Roskam; Kimberley Searengen; Clayton Walford; Kathryn Wisne.
EIN: 371491024

1579
Guido A. & Elizabeth H. Binda Foundation
15 Capital Ave. N.E., Ste. 205
Battle Creek, MI 49017-3557 (269) 968-6171
Contact: Nancy Taber, Exec. Dir.
FAX: (269) 968-5126;
E-mail: grants@bindafoundation.org; **E-mail for general information: info@bindafoundation.org**; Main URL: http://www.bindafoundation.org

Established in 1977 in MI.
Donor: Guido A. Binda†.
Foundation type: Independent foundation.
Financial data (yr. ended 06/30/13): Assets, $22,463,191 (M); gifts received, $188; expenditures, $1,186,146; qualifying distributions, $1,062,638; giving activities include $939,132 for 69 grants (high: $465,000; low: $90).
Purpose and activities: Giving primarily for education, including health and environmental education, as well as for arts and culture, and human services. Creative educational projects receive the highest consideration.
Fields of interest: Arts; Higher education; Education; Environment, formal/general education; Environment; Health care, formal/general education; Human services.
Type of support: Program development; Seed money; Curriculum development; Scholarship funds.
Limitations: Giving limited to Calhoun County, MI. No grants to individuals, or for endowments, capital campaigns, trips, conferences or summer camps.
Publications: Application guidelines; Occasional report.
Application information: Following a review of the letter of inquiry, the foundation will forward its grant application if the grant request is within the scope of the foundation's mission. Application form required.
Initial approach: Letter of Inquiry (via e-mail or U.S. mail)
Copies of proposal: 11
Deadline(s): **None, for letters of inquiry**
Board meeting date(s): Jan. and June
Final notification: 10 days
Officers and Trustees:* John H. Hosking,* Pres.; Richard Tsoumas,* V.P.; Nancy Taber, Exec. Dir.; Robert Binda; LaVerne H. Boss; Chris T. Christ; Joel Orosz; Cindy S. Ruble.
Number of staff: 1 part-time support.
EIN: 382184423
Other changes: Norman Brown is no longer a trustee.

1580
Branch County Community Foundation
2 W. Chicago St., Ste. E-1
Coldwater, MI 49036-1602 (517) 278-4517
Contact: Colleen Knight, Exec. Dir.
FAX: (888) 479-8640;
E-mail: info@brcofoundation.org; Additional E-mail: colleen@brcofoundation.org; Grant inquiry E-mail: grants@brcofoundation.org; Main URL: http://www.brcofoundation.org
Facebook: https://www.facebook.com/brcofoundation

Established in 1991 in MI.
Foundation type: Community foundation.
Financial data (yr. ended 09/30/12): Assets, $4,957,523 (M); gifts received, $373,929; expenditures, $602,517; giving activities include $362,139 for 6+ grants (high: $40,443), and $63,550 for 55 grants to individuals.
Purpose and activities: The foundation serves the community by promoting charitable giving, building permanent endowments, and connecting community resource.
Fields of interest: Humanities; Arts; Education, early childhood education; Education; Environment; Health care; Employment; Housing/shelter, homeless; Youth development; Family services; Human services; Economic development; Community/economic development.
Type of support: General/operating support; Equipment; Endowments; Conferences/seminars;

Scholarship funds; Technical assistance; In-kind gifts; Matching/challenge support.
Limitations: Applications accepted. Giving limited to Branch County and Colon, MI. No support for sectarian religious programs. No grants to individuals (except for scholarships); no loans or program-related investments.
Publications: Application guidelines; Annual report; Financial statement; Informational brochure; Newsletter; Occasional report.
Application information: Visit foundation web site for grant application guidelines. Applicants are strongly encouraged to meet with the foundation's staff prior to submitting an application. Application form required.

Initial approach: **Submit a Pre-Application Questionnaire**
Deadline(s): May 31 and Sept. 30 for Forever Fund and other Community Grant Funds; varies for others
Board meeting date(s): Monthly
Final notification: 2 months

Officers and Directors:* Dave Wright,* Pres.; Wayne Reese,* V.P. and Treas.; Curt Proctor,* Secy.; Colleen Knight, Exec. Dir.; Paul Creal, Dir. Emeritus; Hillary Eley, Dir. Emeritus; Bob Mayer, Dir. Emeritus; Remus Rigg, Dir. Emeritus; Patricia Shoemaker, Dir. Emeritus; Bruce Bloom; Jay Carlson; Joe Chase; Roberta Gagnon; Rachel Hard; Mary Jo Kranz; Chuck Lillis; Kim Morgan; Dale Norton; Ron Rose; Connie Winbigler.
Number of staff: 1 full-time professional; 1 full-time support.
EIN: 383021071

1581
Capital Region Community Foundation

330 Marshall St., NO 300
Lansing, MI 48912 (517) 272-2870
Contact: Dennis W. Fliehman, C.E.O.
FAX: (517) 272-2871;
E-mail: dfliehman@crcfoundation.org; Main URL: http://www.crcfoundation.org
Facebook: http://www.facebook.com/givelansing
Flickr: http://www.flickr.com/photos/givelansing
RSS Feed: http://crcfoundation.org/rss/articles/all
Twitter: http://twitter.com/givelansing

Established in 1987 in MI.
Foundation type: Community foundation.
Financial data (yr. ended 12/31/11): Assets, $63,027,230 (M); gifts received, $3,964,430; expenditures, $5,200,638; giving activities include $4,059,241 for 79+ grants (high: $851,120; low: $33), $207,780 for 125 grants to individuals (high: $24,590; low: $175), and $337,829 for 1 foundation-administered program.
Purpose and activities: The purpose of the foundation is to build the number and size of permanent endowment funds, income from which is used for grants that meet the charitable needs of Clinton, Eaton, and Ingham counties, MI. The foundation provides support for humanities, education, environment, health care, human services, and public benefit.
Fields of interest: Humanities; Education; Environment; Health care; Children/youth, services; Human services; Community/economic development; Public affairs.
Type of support: Management development/capacity building; General/operating support; Capital campaigns; Building/renovation; Equipment; Program development; Seed money; Technical assistance; Matching/challenge support.
Limitations: Applications accepted. Giving limited to Clinton, Eaton, and Ingham counties, MI. No support for international organizations, religious programs, or sectarian purposes. No grants to individuals (except for scholarships), or for endowment funds, administrative costs of fundraising campaigns, annual meetings, routine operating expenses, or for existing obligations, debts, or liabilities.
Publications: Application guidelines; Annual report; Financial statement; Grants list; Informational brochure.
Application information: To apply for any CRCF grant applicants must use the foundation's online system; visit foundation web site for online application and guidelines. Application form required.

Initial approach: Telephone
Deadline(s): Mar. 1 for grants; Jan. 31 for Youth Fund
Board meeting date(s): Bimonthly
Final notification: Oct. 1 for grants

Officers and Trustees:* Denise Schroeder,* Chair.; Kira Carter-Robertson,* Chair.-Elect.; Dennis W. Fliehman,* C.E.O. and Pres.; Richard Comstock,* V.P., Finance; Robin Miner-Swartz,* V.P., Comms.; John Abbott,* Secy.; Andy Hopping,* Treas.; Mark E. Alley; April M. Clobes; Tina Ferland; Bo Garcia; Joan Jackson Johnson, Ph.D.; Helen Pratt Mickens; Douglas A. Mielock; Brian Priester; Laurie Robison; John Sirrine; Robert L. Trezise, Jr.; and 11 additional trustees.
Number of staff: 5 full-time professional; 1 part-time professional; 1 full-time support; 1 part-time support.
EIN: 382776652
Other changes: Diana Rodriguez Algra, Kira Carter-Robertson, Sam L. Davis, Nancy A. Elwood, Vincent J. Ferris, Pat Gillespie, Alexandra Hopping, David Kositchek, Dorothy E. Maxwell, Kate Snyder, Carmen Turner, and Steven Webster are no longer trustees.

1582
The Carls Foundation

6001 N. Adams Rd., Ste. 215
Bloomfield Hills, MI 48304-1576 (248) 434-5512
Contact: Elizabeth A. Stieg, Exec. Dir.
Main URL: http://www.carlsfdn.org

Established in 1961 in MI.
Donor: William Carls†.
Foundation type: Independent foundation.
Financial data (yr. ended 12/31/12): Assets, $112,282,382 (M); expenditures, $5,990,405; qualifying distributions, $5,411,955; giving activities include $4,826,811 for 45 grants (high: $500,000; low: $11,618).
Purpose and activities: The principal purpose and mission of the foundation is: 1) Children's Welfare including: health care facilities and programs, with special emphasis on the prevention and treatment of hearing impairment, and recreational, educational, and welfare programs especially for children who are disadvantaged for economic and/or health reasons; and 2) Preservation of natural areas, open space and historic buildings and areas having special natural beauty or significance in maintaining America's heritage and historic ideals, through assistance to land trusts and land conservancies and directly related environmental educational programs.
Fields of interest: Historic preservation/historical societies; Education; Environment, natural resources; Hospitals (general); Speech/hearing centers; Health care; Recreation; Children/youth, services.
Type of support: Capital campaigns; Seed money.
Limitations: Applications accepted. Giving primarily in MI. No grants to individuals, or for publications, film, research, endowments, fellowships, travel, conferences, special event sponsorships, playground or athletic facilities, or seminars; no educational loans.
Publications: Annual report; Grants list.
Application information: Letter of inquiry is not required and phone calls are welcome. Use of the CMF Common Grant Application Form is optional and acceptable. Application form not required.

Initial approach: Proposal
Copies of proposal: 1
Board meeting date(s): Jan., May, and Sept.
Final notification: Notification letter sent to all applicants

Officers and Trustees:* Elizabeth A. Stieg,* Pres. and Exec. Dir.; Henry Fleischer,* V.P.; Teresa R. Krieger; Dr. Homer E. Nye; Robert A. Sajdak; Edward C. Stieg.
Advisory Board: Donald A. Delong, Esq.; Bruce M. Fleischer, Ph.D.; Teresa Krieger-Burke, Ph.D.
Number of staff: 1 full-time professional; 1 part-time professional; 1 full-time support.
EIN: 386099935
Other changes: Elizabeth A. Stieg is now Pres. Henry Fleischer is now V.P.

1583
Charlevoix County Community Foundation

507 Water St.
P.O. Box 718
East Jordan, MI 49727-9476 (231) 536-2440
FAX: (231) 536-2640; E-mail: info@c3f.org; Main URL: http://www.c3f.org

Established in 1992 in MI.
Foundation type: Community foundation.
Financial data (yr. ended 12/31/11): Assets, $21,993,193 (M); gifts received, $1,725,685; expenditures, $1,338,490; giving activities include $963,688 for grants.
Purpose and activities: The foundation seeks to enhance the quality of life in Charlevoix County, MI, now and for generations to come, by building a permanent charitable endowment from a wide range of donors, addressing needs through grantmaking, and providing leadership on matters of community concern.
Fields of interest: Arts; Higher education; Education; Environment; Health care; Recreation; Children/youth, services; Family services; Human services; Economic development; Community/economic development; Government/public administration; Aging.
Type of support: Endowments; Emergency funds; Program development; Seed money; Scholarship funds; Technical assistance; Consulting services; Scholarships—to individuals.
Limitations: Applications accepted. Giving limited to Charlevoix County, MI. No support for sectarian purposes. No grants to individuals (except for scholarships), or for ongoing organizational operating expenses, office equipment, deficit spending, or fundraising projects; no loans.
Publications: Annual report (including application guidelines); Grants list.
Application information: Visit foundation web site for grant application cover sheet and guidelines. Application form required.

Initial approach: Telephone
Deadline(s): Mar. 1 and Oct. 1

Board meeting date(s): 4th Tues. of the month, 5 times per year
Final notification: May and Dec.

Officers and Trustees:* **Valerie Snyder,*** **Chair.**; Chip Hansen, Jr., Pres.; Hugh Conklin; **Michelle Cortright**; Jim Howell; Fay Keane; John Kempton; David Leusink; Barbara Malpass; Linda Mueller; Don Spencer; Rachel Swiss; **Paul Witting**; Connie Wojan.
Number of staff: 3 full-time professional; 1 part-time professional.
EIN: 383033739
Other changes: Valerie Snyder has replaced Bill Aten as Chair.
Mike Hinkle, Pat O'Brien, and Valerie Snyder are no longer trustees.

1584
The Chelsea Health and Wellness Foundation

310 N. Main St., Ste. 203
Chelsea, MI 48118-1291 (734) 433-4599
Contact: Amy Heydlauff, Exec. Dir.
***FAX:* (734) 433-4598;**
E-mail: info@5healthytowns.org; Main URL: http://5healthytowns.org
Facebook: https://www.facebook.com/5healthytowns

Foundation type: Independent foundation.
Financial data (yr. ended 03/31/13): Assets, $40,703,462 (M); gifts received, $13,050; expenditures, $4,516,698; qualifying distributions, $729,945; giving activities include $729,945 for grants.
Fields of interest: Education; Health care; Human services.
Application information: See foundation web site for guidelines. Application form required.
Deadline(s): Varies
Officers: Jeff Hardcastle, Chair.; Larry Cobler, Vice-Chair.; Alison Pollard, Secy.; John R.C. Wheeler, Treas.; Amy Heydlauff, Exec. Dir.
Directors: Patrick J. Conlin, Jr.; Randall T. Forsch; Kenneth Gietzen; Nancy Graebner; Kathleen Griffiths; Diane Howlin; Susan Kheder; James F. Woods.
EIN: 263040367

1585
Christian Missionary Scholarship Foundation

1899 Orchard Lake Rd., Ste. 203
Sylvan Lake, MI 48320-1776
***E-mail:* cmsf01@gmail.com**; Main URL: http://www.christianmissionaryscholarship.org
Scholarship application address: 3230 Lake Dr. S.E., Grand Rapids, MI 49546, tel.: (616) 526-7731, fax: (616) 526-6777

Established in MI.
Donors: Stanley Van Reken; Randall S. Van Reken; Capital Ventures of NV.
Foundation type: Independent foundation.
Financial data (yr. ended 12/31/12): Assets, $5,368,712 (M); gifts received, $13,045; expenditures, $291,651; qualifying distributions, $281,850; giving activities include $281,850 for 6 grants (high: $146,250; low: $1,000).
Purpose and activities: Giving for scholarships to children of missionaries attending one of the following six colleges: Calvin College, Dordt College, Hope College, Kuyper College, Trinity Christian College and Wheaton College.
Fields of interest: Theological school/education; Christian agencies & churches.
Type of support: Scholarship funds.
Limitations: Applications accepted. Giving primarily in IA, IL and MI. No grants to individuals.
Application information: See web site for complete application policies and guidelines and for an online application. Application form required.
Deadline(s): Feb. 15
Final notification: Apr. 1
Officers: Stanley R. Van Reken, Pres.; Randall Van Reken, Treas.
Directors: Brett Holleman; Marge Hoogeboom; Walter Olsson; Thomas Stuit; Calvin P. Van Reken; Robert Weeldreyer.
EIN: 363553749

1586
Community Foundation for Muskegon County

(formerly Muskegon County Community Foundation, Inc.)
425 W. Western Ave., Ste. 200
Muskegon, MI 49440-1101 (231) 722-4538
Contact: Chris Ann McGuigan, C.E.O.
FAX: (231) 722-4616; E-mail: grants@cffmc.org; Main URL: http://www.cffmc.org
E-Newsletter: http://www.cffmc.org/e-newsletter
Facebook: http://www.facebook.com/pages/Community-Foundation-for-Muskegon-County/100319078604

Incorporated in 1961 in MI.
Donors: Alta Daetz†; Harold Frauenthal†; Charles Goodnow†; George Hilt; Jack Hilt; John Hilt; Paul C. Johnson†; Henry Klooster†; Ernest Settle†.
Foundation type: Community foundation.
Financial data (yr. ended 12/31/11): Assets, $113,996,605 (M); gifts received, $5,860,926; expenditures, $7,233,409; giving activities include $3,994,364 for grants.
Purpose and activities: The foundation seeks to build community endowment, effect positive change through grantmaking, and provide leadership on key community issues, all to serve donor's desires to enhance the quality of life for the people of Muskegon County, MI. The foundation presently supports efforts in the areas of arts, education, environment, community development, health and human services as well as youth development issues.
Fields of interest: Arts education; Performing arts, theater; Arts; Scholarships/financial aid; Education; Environment, air pollution; Environment, water pollution; Environment, land resources; Environment; Health organizations, association; Youth development; Human services; Economic development; Urban/community development; Community/economic development; Infants/toddlers; Children.
Type of support: Management development/capacity building; Building/renovation; Emergency funds; Program development; Seed money; Scholarship funds; Research; Consulting services; Program-related investments/loans; Exchange programs; Matching/challenge support.
Limitations: Applications accepted. Giving limited to Muskegon County, MI. No support for sectarian religious programs, or individual schools or districts. No grants to individuals (except for scholarships), or for deficit financing, routine operating expenses, capital equipment, endowment campaigns, special fundraising events, conferences, camps, publications, videos, films, television or radio programs, or for advertising.
Publications: Application guidelines; Annual report (including application guidelines); Financial statement; Grants list; Informational brochure (including application guidelines); Newsletter.
Application information: Visit foundation web site for grant application information.
Initial approach: Register an account with eGrant on the foundation's web site
Deadline(s): Varies
Board meeting date(s): Feb., Apr., June, Aug., Oct., and Dec.
Final notification: 3 months
Officers and Trustees:* John W. Swanson II,* Chair.; Richard W. Peters, M.D.*, Vice-Chair.; Chris Ann McGuigan,* C.E.O. and Pres.; Robert Chapla,* V.P., Devel.; Ann Van Tassel,* V.P., Finance; Susan Meston, Ph.D.*, Treas.; Nancy L. Crandall; **Jan Deur**; Wes Eklund; Amy Heisser; Charles E. Johnson III; Dick Kamps, M.D.; Kathleen Long; Marvin Nash; Dale K. Nesbary, Ph.D.; Kay Olthoff; Asaline Scott; Michael S. Soimar; Roger Spoelman; Alan D. Steinman, Ph.D.; John M. Sytsema; Kathleen Tyler; James L. Waters.
Trustee Banks: Comerica Bank; Fifth Third Bank; The Huntington National Bank; National City Bank.
Number of staff: 7 full-time professional; 5 full-time support.
EIN: 386114135
Other changes: Barbara Jarman is now Finance Asst. Janelle Mair is now Dir., Grantmaking.
Michael D. Gluhanich and Bernice L. Sydnor are no longer trustees.

1587
Community Foundation for Northeast Michigan

(formerly Northeast Michigan Community Foundation)
100 N. Ripley, Suite F
P.O. Box 495
Alpena, MI 49707-2838 (989) 354-6881
Contact: Barbara Frantz, Exec. Dir.
FAX: (989) 356-3319; E-mail: bfrantz@cfnem.org; Main URL: http://www.cfnem.org
Facebook: http://www.facebook.com/pages/Community-Foundation-for-Northeast-Michigan/211282204045
Twitter: http://twitter.com/CFNEM
Scholarship e-mail: wiesenj@cfnem.org

Incorporated in 1974 in Alpena, MI.
Foundation type: Community foundation.
Financial data (yr. ended 09/30/12): Assets, $24,243,748 (M); gifts received, $1,576,476; expenditures, $1,133,535; giving activities include $545,777 for 432 grants (high: $86,574; low: $50), and $282,784 for 242 grants to individuals (high: $8,000; low: $250).
Purpose and activities: The foundation seeks to serve the community and to preserve the charitable goals of a wide range of donors now and for generations to come.
Fields of interest: Humanities; Arts; Libraries/library science; Education; Environment; Health care; Health organizations, association; Children/youth, services; Human services; Government/public administration.
Type of support: Equipment; Program development; Conferences/seminars; Seed money; Scholarship funds; Technical assistance; Scholarships—to individuals.
Limitations: Applications accepted. Giving limited to Alcona, Alpena, Montmorency, and Presque Isle counties, MI and through affiliates: Crawford, Cheboygan, Iosco, Ogemaw, and Oscoda counties, MI. No support for religious purposes. No grants to

individuals (except for scholarships), or for annual giving campaigns or capital campaigns, normal operating expenses, or multi-year or sustained funding; no loans.
Publications: Application guidelines; Annual report; Financial statement; Grants list; Informational brochure; Newsletter; Program policy statement.
Application information: Visit foundation web site for application forms, guidelines, and deadlines. For grants of $300 or less, organizations should use the 2-page mini-grant application and follow its specific guidelines. Application form required.
Initial approach: Submit application forms and attachments
Copies of proposal: 1
Deadline(s): Generally Feb. 1, Aug. 1, and Nov. 1, but applicants should check our web site to be sure of dates
Board meeting date(s): 2nd Tuesday in March, June, September, and December
Final notification: Within 6 weeks
Officers and Trustees:* Chuck Manning,* Pres.; Esther Ableidinger,* V.P.; Tom Sobeck,* Secy.; Sue Fitzpatrick,* Treas.; Barbara Frantz, Exec. Dir.; Christine Baumgardner; Benjamin Bolser; Kate Bruski; Dave Cook; Brendan Fleishans; Jerry Gosnell; Lora Greene; Kara Grulke; Shanna Johnson; Tony Johnson; Sue Keller; Tim Kuehnlein; Jennifer Lee; John MacMaster; Dave Post; Terri Rondeau; Gina Roose; Carl Woloszyk.
Number of staff: 3 full-time support; 2 part-time support.
EIN: 237384822

1588
Community Foundation for Southeast Michigan

(formerly Community Foundation for Southeastern Michigan)
333 W. Fort St., Ste. 2010
Detroit, MI 48226-3134 (313) 961-6675
Contact: Mariam C. Noland, Pres.
FAX: (313) 961-2886; E-mail: cfsem@cfsem.org; Main URL: http://www.cfsem.org
Facebook: https://www.facebook.com/cfsem
Knowledge Center: http://cfsem.org/initiatives-and-programs
RSS Feed: http://cfsem.org/rss
Twitter: http://twitter.com/cfsem
YouTube: http://www.youtube.com/user/TheCFSEM
Scholarship inquiry e-mail: sfoster@cfsem.org

Established in 1984 in MI.
Foundation type: Community foundation.
Financial data (yr. ended 12/31/13): Assets, $734,226,708 (M); gifts received, $21,594,980; expenditures, $58,566,218; giving activities include $52,560,486 for grants.
Purpose and activities: The foundation exists in perpetuity to enhance the quality of life of the citizens in southeast Michigan. The foundation promotes and facilitates community philanthropy in the seven counties of Wayne, Oakland, Macomb, Monroe, Washtenaw, Livingston and St. Clair, and also help donors invest in organizations they care about nationwide. They are building permanent community capital in the form of endowments that create a base of stable financial support for the region. The foundation does this by: 1) making strategic investments in programs and organizations that benefit the region equipping organizations and the public with knowledge and information that will lead to positive change; 2) building endowment - community capital - to meet the region's needs today and tomorrow; and 3) providing expert assistance to donors and their advisers in their charitable planning.
Fields of interest: Arts; Education; Environment; Health care; Health organizations, association; Youth development, services; Youth, services; Human services; Civil rights, race/intergroup relations; Economic development; Community/economic development; Government/public administration; Leadership development; Public affairs; Economically disadvantaged.
Type of support: Program development; Seed money; Scholarship funds; Technical assistance; Scholarships—to individuals.
Limitations: Applications accepted. Giving primarily to Livingston, Macomb, Monroe, Oakland, St. Clair, Washtenaw, and Wayne counties, MI. No support for sectarian religious programs. No grants to individuals (from unrestricted funds), or for capital projects, endowments, annual campaigns, general operating support, conferences, computers and computer systems, fundraising, annual meetings, buildings, or equipment.
Publications: Application guidelines; Annual report (including application guidelines); Grants list; Informational brochure (including application guidelines); Newsletter.
Application information: There may be separate grantmaking guidelines for targeted grantmaking projects. These guidelines and special application forms are available by contacting the foundation or consulting the foundation's Guidelines for Grantmaking. Visit foundation web site for general grant application guidelines. Application form not required.
Initial approach: Complete online pre-application questionnaire
Deadline(s): Recommended dates of Feb. 15, May 15, Aug. 15, and Nov. 15
Board meeting date(s): Mar., June, Sept., and Dec.
Final notification: 3 months after submission of proposal
Officers and Trustees:* Allan D. Gilmour,* Chair.; **Penny B. Blumenstein,* Vice-Chair.**; **W. Frank Fountain,* Vice-Chair.**; **David M. Hempstead,* Vice-Chair.**; Mariam C. Noland, Pres.; Katie G. Brisson, V.P., Prog.; Robin D. Ferriby, V.P., Philanthropic Svcs.; Karen L. Leppanen, V.P., Finance and Admin.; **Mary H. Weiser,* Secy.**; Michael T. Monahan,* Treas.; Diane M. Kresnak, Cont., Finance and Admin.; James B. Nicholson,* Chair.-Elect; Frederick M. Adams, Jr.; Terence E. Adderley; Margaret Acheson Allesee; Gerard M. Anderson; Michael E. Bannister; Albert M. Berriz; Thomas C. Buhl; Andrew L. Camden; Ahmad Chebbani; Matthew P. Cullen; Paul R. Dimond; Deborah I. Dingell; Irma B. Elder; John M. Erb; David T. Fischer; Phillip W. Fisher; Jenice C. Mitchell Ford; Alfred R. Glancy III; Kouhaila G. Hammer; Steven K. Hamp; William M. Hermann; George G. Johnson; Eric B. Larson; David Baker Lewis; John D. Lewis; Henry W. Lim; Dana M. Locniskar; Florine Mark; Jack Martin; Edward J. Miller; Eugene A. Miller; Bruce E. Nyberg; David K. Page; Cynthia J. Pasky; William F. Pickard; Dr. Glenda D. Price; David T. Provost; Jack A. Robinson; Pamela Rodgers; Alan E. Schwartz; William W. Shelden, Jr.; Vivian Day Stroh; Gary Torgow; Reginald M. Turner; Barbara C. Van Dusen; Dale L. Watchowsky; Mary H. Weiser; Sean K. Werdlow; Ken Whipple.
Number of staff: 18 full-time professional; 1 part-time support.
EIN: 382530980
Other changes: Mary H. Weiser has replaced W. Frank Fountain as Vice-Chair.
James B. Nicholson is now Chair.-Elect. Frank Fountain, Penny B. Blumenstein, and David M. Hempstead are now Vice-Chairs. Joseph L. Hudson is no longer a trustee.

1589
Community Foundation of Greater Rochester

(formerly Greater Rochester Area Community Foundation)
127 W. University Dr.
Rochester, MI 48308 (248) 608-2804
Contact: Peggy Hamilton, Exec. Dir.
FAX: (248) 608-2826; E-mail: cfound@cfound.org; Main URL: http://www.cfound.org

Incorporated in 1983 in MI.
Foundation type: Community foundation.
Financial data (yr. ended 12/31/12): Assets, $7,257,570 (M); gifts received, $1,088,328; expenditures, $892,017; giving activities include $137,865 for 3+ grants (high: $65,000), and $97,145 for 75 grants to individuals.
Purpose and activities: To enhance the quality of life, the foundation is committed to act as the center for philanthropy and serve as the community's endowment builder and grant maker by: 1) attracting charitable funds for permanent endowments; 2) encouraging charitable giving from a wide range of donors; 3) serving as a catalyst for change, innovator to resolve problems, a partner with other local groups and a resource to provide solutions for current and emerging community needs.
Fields of interest: Museums; Performing arts; Performing arts, music; Arts; Elementary school/education; Education; Environment, natural resources; Environment; Health care; Recreation; Youth, services; Family services; Human services; Economic development; Community/economic development; Youth; Disabilities, people with.
Type of support: General/operating support; Annual campaigns; Building/renovation; Equipment; Endowments; Emergency funds; Seed money; Scholarship funds; Scholarships—to individuals; Matching/challenge support.
Limitations: Applications accepted. Giving limited to the greater Rochester, MI, area. No grants to individuals (except for designated scholarship funds), or for operating budgets.
Publications: Annual report (including application guidelines); Financial statement; Informational brochure; Newsletter.
Application information: Visit the foundation web site for application forms and specific guidelines per grant type. A foundation staff member will contact applicants who have submitted a letter of intent to discuss their submitted proposal and funding opportunities available. Application form required.
Initial approach: Letter of Intent
Copies of proposal: 7
Deadline(s): Mar. 31 and Sept. 30 for grant application forms; Mar. 4 for scholarships
Board meeting date(s): Quarterly
Officers and Trustees:* Shirley E. Gofrank,* Chair.; David Bray,* Vice-Chair., Investments; Robert Justin,* Vice-Chair., Devel.; Patricia Botkin,* Secy.; Ed Golick,* Treas.; Peggy Hamilton, Exec. Dir.; Mark Aiello; Ken Bilodeau; **Julie A. Byrd, M.D.**; Jack DiFranco; Michael Glass; Sal LaMendola; Tom Mines; John Schultz; Beth Talbert.
Number of staff: 1 full-time professional; 1 part-time support.
EIN: 382476777
Other changes: Linda Bermingham and Vern Pixley are no longer trustees.

1590
Community Foundation of St. Clair County
516 McMorran Blvd.
Port Huron, MI 48060-3826 (810) 984-4761
Contact: Randy D. Maiers, C.E.O.
FAX: (810) 984-3394;
E-mail: info@stclairfoundation.org; Main URL: http://www.stclairfoundation.org
Facebook: https://www.facebook.com/CommunityFoundationSCC
Pinterest: http://www.pinterest.com/GiveLocalMi/
Twitter: https://twitter.com/@GiveLocalMi

Established in 1944 in MI.
Foundation type: Community foundation.
Financial data (yr. ended 12/31/13): Assets, $47,695,286 (M); gifts received, $6,486,260; expenditures, $2,146,211; giving activities include $1,048,696 for grants.
Purpose and activities: The foundation seeks to serve the charitable needs and enhance the quality of life of the community by: 1) providing a flexible and convenient vehicle for donors having a variety of charitable goals and needs; 2) receiving and investing contributions to build permanent endowments; 3) responding to changing and emerging community needs; 4) serving as a steward for individuals, families, foundations, and organizations entrusting assets to its care; and 5) providing grants to philanthropic organizations, social services, civic concerns, education, arts and culture, recreation and youth.
Fields of interest: Arts; Education; Recreation; Family services; Human services; Economic development; Community/economic development; Youth; Aging.
Type of support: Emergency funds; Management development/capacity building; Building/renovation; Equipment; Program development; Publication; Seed money; Scholarship funds; Technical assistance; Program-related investments/loans; Scholarships—to individuals; Matching/challenge support.
Limitations: Applications accepted. Giving limited to St. Clair County, MI. No support for religious activities. No grants to individuals directly, or for endowments, equipment, annual meetings, conferences, travel expenses, venture capital funds, or film, video, or TV projects, deficit reduction, annual fundraising, capital campaigns, marketing or public relations, general operating expenses, or land use.
Publications: Application guidelines; Annual report; Financial statement; Grants list; Informational brochure; Newsletter.
Application information: Visit foundation web site for application form and guidelines. Application form required.
Initial approach: Contact foundation
Copies of proposal: 1
Deadline(s): Jan. 1, Apr. 1, July 1, and Oct. 1
Board meeting date(s): Quarterly
Final notification: Mar., June, Sept., and Dec.
Officers and Trustees:* Donna Niester,* Chair.; Dr. Sushma Reddy,* Vice-Chair.; **Randy D. Maiers,* Pres. and C.E.O.**; Lynn Alexander,* V.P.; Michael J. Cansfield,* Secy.; Roy W. Klecha, Jr.,* Treas.; Beth A. Belanger; Denise M. Brooks; Rasha Demashkieh; William C. Gratopp; Jackie Hanton; Connie Harrison; Steve L. Hill; Thomas A. Hunter; **Mike Hulewicz**; Charles G. Kelly; **Dr. Randa Jundi-Samman**; Jenifer Kusch; Phyllis Ledyard; Dan Lockwood; Michael McCartan; Will G. Oldford, Jr.; **Dr. Bassam Nasr**; Frank Poma; F. William Schwarz III; Douglas S. Touma; Hale Walker; Chuck Wanninger; Cathy Wilkinson.
Number of staff: 6 full-time professional.
EIN: 381872132
Other changes: Randy D. Maiers is now Pres. and C.E.O. Dr. Donna M. Niester is no longer a trustee.

1591
The Community Foundation of the Holland/Zeeland Area
(formerly Holland Community Foundation, Inc.)
85 E. 8th St., Ste. 110
Holland, MI 49423-3528 (616) 396-6590
Contact: Janet DeYoung, C.E.O.; Elizabeth Kidd, Dir., Grantmaking
FAX: (616) 396-3573; E-mail: info@cfhz.org;
Additional E-mail: jdeyoung@cfhz.org; Grant inquiry e-mail: ekidd@cfhz.org; Main URL: http://www.cfhz.org
Facebook: https://www.facebook.com/cfohz
LinkedIn: http://www.linkedin.com/in/janetdeyoung
Twitter: http://twitter.com/cfohz

Incorporated in 1951 in MI.
Foundation type: Community foundation.
Financial data (yr. ended 12/31/12): Assets, $48,409,622 (M); gifts received, $8,524,432; expenditures, $5,342,564; giving activities include $3,639,721 for 71+ grants (high: $860,953), $398,186 for 168 grants to individuals, and $750,000 for 2 loans/program-related investments (high: $500,000; low: $250,000).
Purpose and activities: The mission of the foundation is to create lasting positive change. The foundation works to build a permanent community endowment that supports high impact charitable projects, helps donors achieve their charitable goals, and leads and partners in community level initiatives.
Fields of interest: Visual arts, art conservation; Historic preservation/historical societies; Arts; Education; Environment; Health care; Housing/shelter; Recreation; Children/youth, services; Human services; Community/economic development; Children/youth; Aging.
Type of support: Capital campaigns; Building/renovation; Equipment; Emergency funds; Program development; Seed money; Curriculum development; Scholarship funds; Technical assistance; Program evaluation; Employee-related scholarships; In-kind gifts.
Limitations: Applications accepted. Giving limited to the Holland/Zeeland, MI, area and surrounding townships. No support for sectarian religious programs. No grants for endowment funds, operating budgets, expenses for established programs, fundraising drives, capital equipment, conference speakers, salaries, stipends, sabbatical leaves, debt reduction, research, endowments, fellowships, matching gifts, travel or tours, or computers, video equipment, or vehicles; no loans.
Publications: Application guidelines; Annual report; Financial statement; Grants list; Informational brochure; Newsletter; IRS Form 990 or 990-PF printed copy available upon request.
Application information: Visit foundation web site for current application form, guidelines and copies required. Application form required.
Initial approach: Contact Dir. of Grantmaking before preparing and submitting proposal
Copies of proposal: 11
***Deadline(s):* Jan. 13, May 12, and Sept. 8**
***Board meeting date(s):* Monthly**
Final notification: Within 5 weeks of deadline
Officers and Trustees:* Sue Den Herder,* Chair.; Janet DeYoung,* C.E.O. and Pres.; Mike Goorhouse, V.P., Donor Devel.; Juanita Bocanegra,* Secy.; **Lori Bush**; Eleanor Lopez; Nancy Miller; P. Haans Mulder; Jane Patterson; Judith Smith; Scott Alan Spoelhof.
Number of staff: 6 full-time professional; 1 part-time professional.
EIN: 386095283
Other changes: Randy Thelan is no longer Treas. Daniel Zwier is no longer a trustee. Ann Query is no longer a trustee.

1592
Dorothy U. Dalton Foundation, Inc.
c/o Greenleaf Trust
211 S. Rose St.
Kalamazoo, MI 49007-4713 (269) 388-9800
Contact: Ronald N. Kilgore, Secy.-Treas.

Incorporated in 1978 in MI as successor to Dorothy U. Dalton Foundation Trust.
Donor: Dorothy U. Dalton†.
Foundation type: Independent foundation.
Financial data (yr. ended 12/31/12): Assets, $31,728,594 (M); expenditures, $2,226,137; qualifying distributions, $1,947,252; giving activities include $1,917,266 for 71 grants (high: $400,000; low: $500).
Purpose and activities: Giving primarily for the arts, human services, and to YMCAs.
Fields of interest: Performing arts; Performing arts, music; Arts; Human services; YM/YWCAs & YM/YWHAs; Youth, services; Foundations (private grantmaking).
Type of support: General/operating support; Continuing support; Capital campaigns; Building/renovation; Equipment; Land acquisition; Debt reduction; Emergency funds; Program development; Seed money; Research; Matching/challenge support.
Limitations: Giving primarily in Kalamazoo County, MI. No support for religious organizations. No grants to individuals, or for annual campaigns, scholarships, fellowships, publications, or conferences; no loans.
Application information: Application form required.
Initial approach: Proposal
Copies of proposal: 5
Deadline(s): Submit proposal preferably in Apr. and Oct.
***Board meeting date(s):* June, Sept. and Dec.**
Final notification: 30 days after board meetings
Officers and Directors:* Howard Kalleward,* V.P.; Ronald N. Kilgore,* Secy.-Treas.; **Elizabeth A. Bennett**; **Sarah A. Johansson**; **Judy K. Jolliffe.**
EIN: 382240062
Other changes: Thompson Bennett is no longer a director.

1593
Dana Foundation
1 Village Center Dr.
Van Buren Township, MI 48111 **(419) 887-5141**
Contact: Joe Stancati, Secy.
***Application address:* P.O. Box 1000, Maumee, OH 43537, Tel.: (419) 887-5141**

Incorporated in 1956 in OH.
Donors: Dana Corporation; Dana Holding Corporation.
Foundation type: Company-sponsored foundation.
Financial data (yr. ended 03/31/13): Assets, $72,134 (M); gifts received, $200,000; expenditures, $445,299; qualifying distributions, $439,726; giving activities include $363,327 for 52

grants (high: $100,000; low: $500), and $76,399 for employee matching gifts.
Purpose and activities: The foundation supports organizations involved with arts and culture, education, cancer, food distribution, and human services.
Fields of interest: Museums (art); Performing arts, theater; Performing arts, orchestras; Arts; Education; Cancer; Food distribution, meals on wheels; Boys & girls clubs; Youth development, business; American Red Cross; Children/youth, services; Human services; United Ways and Federated Giving Programs.
Type of support: General/operating support; Continuing support; Annual campaigns; Capital campaigns; Building/renovation; Equipment; Emergency funds; Employee matching gifts; Employee-related scholarships.
Limitations: Applications accepted. Giving primarily in areas of company operations in KY and OH. No grants to individuals (except for the Driveshaft Scholarship Fund), or for fellowships; no loans.
Application information: Application form not required.
Initial approach: Proposal
Copies of proposal: 1
Deadline(s): None
Officers and Directors:* Marc Levin,* Pres.; Dave Benson,* V.P.; Joe Stancati,* Secy.; Rick Dyer,* Treas.; **Jeffrey Cole**; **David Nash**; Maureen Tackett.
Number of staff: 1 part-time professional.
EIN: 346544909
Other changes: Cindy Simon is no longer Treas.

1594
The Dart Foundation
500 Hogsback Rd.
Mason, MI 48854-9547 (517) 244-2190
Contact: Claudia Deschaine, Grants Mgr.
FAX: (517) 244-2631;
E-mail: dartfoundation@dart.biz; Main URL: http://www.dartfoundation.org

Established in 1984 in MI.
Donor: William & Claire Dart Foundation.
Foundation type: Independent foundation.
Financial data (yr. ended 10/31/12): Assets, $559,629 (M); gifts received, $4,169,500; expenditures, $3,847,826; qualifying distributions, $3,847,826; giving activities include $3,765,303 for 222 grants (high: $1,400,000; low: $250), and $65,465 for foundation-administered programs.
Purpose and activities: Giving primarily for: education, with emphasis on Science, Technology, Engineering, and Mathematics (STEM); community services, with emphasis on youth programs and basic needs such as food, shelter, clothing, and health services; disaster relief, and to other programs of interest to trustees.
Fields of interest: Higher education; Education; Hospitals (general); Health organizations, association; Alzheimer's disease research; Boys & girls clubs; Human services; Children/youth, services; Engineering/technology; Public affairs; Children/youth; Economically disadvantaged.
Type of support: General/operating support; Continuing support; Annual campaigns; Capital campaigns; Building/renovation; Equipment; Program development; Publication; Curriculum development; Scholarship funds; Research; Matching/challenge support.
Limitations: Applications accepted. **Giving primarily in Sarasota, FL, mid-Michigan, and in the immediate vicinities of the following communities: Corona and Lodi, CA; Deerfield Beach and Plant City, FL; Augusta, Conyers, Thomaston, and Lithonia, GA; Twin Falls, ID; North Aurora, Urbana, and some parts of Chicago, IL; Horse Cave and Owensboro, KY; Federalsburg, MD; Quitman, MS; Randleman, NC; Ada, OK; Leola and Lancaster, PA; Dallas and Waxahachie, Texas; and Tumwater, Washington.** No grants to individuals.
Publications: Application guidelines; Annual report; Annual report (including application guidelines); Grants list.
Application information: Application guidelines and forms available on foundation web site. Application form required.
Initial approach: Letter, telephone or e-mail
Copies of proposal: 1
Deadline(s): Mar. 15, June 15, Sept. 15, Dec. 15
Final notification: Feb. 1, May 1, Aug. 1, and Nov. 1
Officer: James D. Lammers, V.P. and Secy.
Directors: Ariane L. Dart; Claire T. Dart; Kenneth B. Dart; Robert C. Dart.
Number of staff: 1 full-time professional.
EIN: 382849841

1595
M. E. Davenport Foundation
433 E. Fulton St.
Stewart White Hall
Grand Rapids, MI 49503-5926 (616) 234-6280
Contact: Margaret E. Moceri, Pres.
FAX: (616) 732-1147;
E-mail: info@medavenport.org; Main URL: http://www.medavenport.org

Established in 1986 in MI.
Donors: Robert W. and Margaret D. Sneden Foundation; Margaret Moceri; Gregory Moceri; Kathleen Sneden; Mary Sneden Sullivan; Watson Pierce; Elsie Pierce; Barbara DeMoor.
Foundation type: Independent foundation.
Financial data (yr. ended 09/30/13): Assets, $18,562,008 (M); gifts received, $1,500; expenditures, $997,982; qualifying distributions, $842,963; giving activities include $742,031 for 18 grants (high: $399,643; low: $2,500).
Purpose and activities: Support primarily for private institutions of higher education, and specific social and community needs, usually related to business education, training, employment, and community stability, such as housing.
Fields of interest: Higher education; Employment, training; Youth development, business.
Type of support: Building/renovation; Capital campaigns; Program development; Seed money; Curriculum development.
Limitations: Applications accepted. **Giving primarily in Grand Rapids, MI.** No support for religious or political agendas. No grants to individuals or for debt retirement or budget deficit remediation, and taxable organizations or activities.
Publications: Application guidelines; Annual report; Financial statement; Grants list; Occasional report.
Application information: Full proposals are by invitation, upon review of initial letter. Application form not required.
Initial approach: Letter (via e-mail preferred)
Copies of proposal: 1
Board meeting date(s): Triennially
***Final notification:* 4-5 months**
Officers and Trustees:* Margaret E. Moceri,* Chair. and Pres.; Gregory C. Moceri, V.P. and Treas.; Mary Sneden Sullivan, Secy.; Donald Maine, Exec. Dir.; Marcia A. Sneden; William Sullivan.
Number of staff: 2 full-time professional.
EIN: 382646809
Other changes: The grantmaker now makes its grants list available online.

1596
The Mignon Sherwood Delano Foundation
834 King Hwy., Ste. 110
Kalamazoo, MI 49001-2579 (269) 344-9236
Main URL: http://www.delanofoundation.com/
Grants List: http://www.delanofoundation.com/recipients.html

Incorporated in 1985 in MI.
Donor: Mignon Sherwood Delano†.
Foundation type: Independent foundation.
Financial data (yr. ended 12/31/12): Assets, $4,182,246 (M); expenditures, $222,779; qualifying distributions, $203,957; giving activities include $164,297 for 31 grants (high: $15,000; low: $1,100).
Purpose and activities: Giving for the furtherance of humanitarian, educational, cultural and environmental enrichment in the City of Allegan, Allegan County and southwestern Michigan.
Fields of interest: Arts; Education; Reproductive health, family planning; Health care; Health organizations; Food banks; Housing/shelter; Youth development; Human services; Residential/custodial care; Community/economic development; Catholic agencies & churches.
Type of support: General/operating support; Equipment; Program development.
Limitations: Applications accepted. Giving limited to the City of Allegan, Allegan County and southwestern MI. No grants to individuals.
Application information: See foundation web site for application policies and application form. Application form required.
Deadline(s): 2nd Tues. in Sept.
Officers and Directors:* Bernard Riker,* Pres.; Ellen Altamore,* V.P.; Julie Sosnowski,* Secy.; Thomas Hunter,* Treas.; Thomas Berlin; Rebecca Burnett.
Trustee: PNC Bank, N.A.
EIN: 382557743

1597
The Herbert H. and Grace A. Dow Foundation
1018 W. Main St.
Midland, MI 48640-4292 (989) 631-3699
Contact: Margaret Ann Riecker, Pres.
FAX: (989) 631-0675;
E-mail: info@hhdowfoundation.org; Grant application e-mail: grants@hhdowfoundation.org; Main URL: http://www.hhdowfoundation.org

Established in 1936 in MI.
Donor: Grace A. Dow†.
Foundation type: Independent foundation.
Financial data (yr. ended 12/31/12): Assets, $406,635,798 (M); gifts received, $5,130; expenditures, $22,601,725; qualifying distributions, $19,948,862; giving activities include $17,728,638 for 188 grants (high: $1,000,000; low: $1,000), and $2,689,240 for 1 foundation-administered program.
Purpose and activities: Support for religious, charitable, scientific, literacy, or educational purposes for the public benefaction of the inhabitants of the city of Midland and of the people of the state of Michigan. Grants largely for education, particularly higher education, community and social services, civic improvement, conservation, scientific research, church support (only in Midland County, MI), and cultural programs; maintains Dow Gardens, a public horticultural garden.
Fields of interest: Arts; Higher education; Libraries/library science; Education; Environment, natural

resources; Human services; Community/economic development; Engineering/technology; Science.
Type of support: General/operating support; Building/renovation; Equipment; Endowments; Program development; Seed money; Research; Matching/challenge support.
Limitations: Applications accepted. Giving limited to MI, with emphasis on Midland County. No support for political organizations or sectarian religious organizations or programs, other than churches in Midland County. No grants to individuals, or for travel or conferences; no loans.
Publications: Annual report (including application guidelines); Financial statement; Grants list.
Application information: Application form not required.
Initial approach: Proposal
Copies of proposal: 1
Deadline(s): None
Board meeting date(s): Bimonthly
Final notification: 2 months
Officers and Trustees:* Macauley Whiting, Jr.,* Pres. and Treas.; Michael Lloyd Dow,* V.P.; Margaret E. Thompson,* Secy.; Julie Carol Arbury; Ruth Alden Doan; Alden Lee Hanson; Diane Dow Hullet; Andrew N. Liveris; Bonnie B. Matheson; **Suzanna McCuan**; Willard Mott; **Elias Buchanan Ohrstrom**; David Ramaker.
EIN: 381437485
Other changes: Margaret Ann Riecker, Pres. and trustee, is deceased. Macauley Whiting, Jr. is now Pres. and Treas. Julie Carol Arbury is no longer a trustee.

1598
DTE Energy Foundation

(formerly Detroit Edison Foundation)
1 Energy Plz., 1578 WCB
Detroit, MI 48226-1279 (313) 235-9271
Contact: Jennifer Whitteaker, Mgr., Corp. Contribs. and Community Involvement
E-mail: foundation@dteenergy.com; Main URL: https://www2.dteenergy.com/wps/portal/dte/aboutus/community/

Established in 1986 in MI.
Donors: The Detroit Edison Co.; DTE Energy Ventures, Inc.
Foundation type: Company-sponsored foundation.
Financial data (yr. ended 12/31/12): Assets, $65,636,182 (M); gifts received, $21,300,000; expenditures, $9,912,018; qualifying distributions, $9,857,713; giving activities include $9,606,192 for 538 grants (high: $625,000; low: $25).
Purpose and activities: The foundation supports programs designed to promote LEAD initiatives including, leadership, education, environment, achievement, development, and diversity in DTE Energy service territories.
Fields of interest: Arts, cultural/ethnic awareness; Museums (science/technology); Performing arts; Arts; Elementary/secondary education; Higher education; Business school/education; Engineering school/education; Education, services; Education; Environment, natural resources; Environment, energy; Environment, forests; Environmental education; Environment; Employment; Food distribution, meals on wheels; Youth development; American Red Cross; Human services; Civil/human rights, equal rights; Community development, neighborhood development; Urban/community development; Business/industry; Community/economic development; Mathematics; Engineering/technology; Science; Leadership development; Minorities; Women.
Type of support: General/operating support; Continuing support; Capital campaigns; Program development; Curriculum development; Employee volunteer services; Sponsorships; Employee matching gifts.
Limitations: Applications accepted. Giving primarily in areas of company operations in MI. No support for political parties or organizations, religious organizations not of direct benefit to the entire community, discriminatory organizations, national or international organizations (unless they provide benefits directly to DTE Energy service areas), single purpose health organizations, or hospitals for building or equipment needs. No grants to individuals, or for political activities, student group trips, conferences, or building or equipment needs for hospitals.
Publications: Application guidelines; Program policy statement.
Application information: Telephone calls and video submissions are not encouraged. Organizations receiving support are asked to provide a final report. Application form required.
Initial approach: Download application form and E-mail proposal and application form to foundation
Copies of proposal: 1
***Deadline(s):* Feb. 3 to Feb. 14; Apr. 21 to May 2; July 21 to Aug. 1; and Oct. 13 to Oct. 25**
Board meeting date(s): Quarterly
***Final notification:* Apr. 17, July 11, Oct. 17, and Jan. 9**
Officers and Directors:* Frederick E. Shell, Chair.; Faye Anderson Nelson, Pres.; Karla D. Hall,* V.P. and Secy.; Naif A. Khouri,* Treas.; **Joann Chavez**; Paul C. Hillegonds; **Steven E. Kurmas; Jerry Norcia**; Bruce D. Peterson; David Rudd; Larry E. Steward.
Number of staff: 1 full-time professional; 2 full-time support.
EIN: 382708636
Other changes: Frederick E. Shell has replaced Joyce V. Hayes-Giles as Chair.
Joyce V. Hayes-Giles is no longer Chair. Michael C. Porter and Lynne Ellyn are no longer directors.

1599
Fred A. and Barbara M. Erb Family Foundation

(doing business as Erb Family Foundation)
38710 Woodward Ave., Ste. 210
Bloomfield Hills, MI 48304-5075 (248) 498-2501
Contact: John M. Erb, Pres.; Jodee Fishman Raines, V.P., Progs.
FAX: (248) 644-1517; E-mail: jraines@erbff.org;
Main URL: http://www.erbff.org/
Grants List: http://www.erbff.org/recent-grants

Established in 2008 in MI.
Donors: Barbara M. Erb†; Fred A. Erb†.
Foundation type: Independent foundation.
Financial data (yr. ended 06/30/12): Assets, $106,529,587 (M); gifts received, $8,574,202; expenditures, $5,920,436; qualifying distributions, $5,328,633; giving activities include $5,248,281 for 130+ grants (high: $250,000).
Purpose and activities: The mission of the foundation is to nurture environmentally healthy and culturally vibrant communities in metropolitan Detroit and support initiatives to restore the Great Lakes Basin.
Fields of interest: Arts; Environment, water resources; Alzheimer's disease research.
Type of support: General/operating support; Management development/capacity building; Program development; Seed money; Matching/challenge support.
Limitations: Applications accepted. Giving primarily in the metropolitan Detroit, MI area (Wayne, Oakland and Macomb counties) though water quality programs will be considered in the watersheds impacting Detroit and the Bayfield area of Ontario. Certain Great Lakes basin-wide efforts will also be considered. No support for religious activities. No grants to individuals, for capital projects, research (unless solicited from the foundation) fundraisers or conferences; no loans.
Publications: Application guidelines; Annual report; Program policy statement.
Application information: Letter of inquiry and application instructions and forms available on foundation web site. Unsolicited applications for Alzheimer's Research and Special Opportunities are not accepted. Proposals in these areas are by invitation only. Application form required.
Initial approach: Letter of inquiry (via foundation web site)
Deadline(s): None
Board meeting date(s): Mar., June, Sept. and Dec.
Final notification: Following board meetings
Officers and Directors:* Ira J. Jaffe,* Chair.; John M. Erb,* Pres.; Jodee Fishman Raines, V.P., Progs.; Patricia D. Smotherman, Secy. and Grants Mgr.; Daryl Larsen, C.F.O.; Susan E. Cooper; Debbie D. Erb; John M. Erb; Chacona W. Johnson; Leslie Erb Liedtke.
Number of staff: 2 full-time professional; 2 part-time professional.
EIN: 205966333

1600
Dick & Betsy Family DeVos Foundation

P.O. Box 230257
Grand Rapids, MI 49523-0257 (616) 643-4700
Contact: Ginny Vander Hart, Exec. Dir.; Sue Volkers, Grants Mgr.
E-mail: info@dbdvfoundation.org; FAX (for Ginny Vander Hart): (616) 774-0116; E-mail (for Ginny Vander Hart): virginiav@rdvcorp.com; Main URL: http://www.dbdvfoundation.org/

Established in 1989 in MI.
Donors: Dick DeVos; Betsy DeVos; Prince Foundation.
Foundation type: Independent foundation.
Financial data (yr. ended 12/31/12): Assets, $59,920,363 (M); gifts received, $10,000,500; expenditures, $14,660,823; qualifying distributions, $16,722,163; giving activities include $13,758,058 for 153 grants (high: $3,365,000; low: $250), and $350,000 for 1 loan/program-related investment.
Purpose and activities: The foundation seeks to create a legacy of caring and stewardship through its support of projects that build a strong community. To demonstrate this commitment, the foundation concentrates its funding in support of various initiatives that promote a healthier community, with a focus on the arts, health and children's causes.
Fields of interest: Arts; Education; Children/youth, services; Family services; Public policy, research; Christian agencies & churches.
Type of support: Program-related investments/loans; General/operating support; Continuing support; Annual campaigns; Capital campaigns.
Limitations: Applications accepted. Giving primarily in west MI. No grants to individuals.
Publications: Application guidelines.

Application information: See foundation web site for online application process. Application form not required.
Initial approach: Online application
Copies of proposal: 1
Board meeting date(s): Quarterly
Final notification: 4 to 5 months
Officers and Directors:* Richard M. DeVos, Jr.,* Pres.; Robert H. Schierbeek, Exec. V.P. and Secy-Treas.; Jerry L. Tubergen,* Exec. V.P.; Elisabeth DeVos,* V.P.; Jeffrey K. Lambert, V.P., Finance and Admin.; Ginny Vander Hart, Exec. Dir. and Fdn. Dir.
EIN: 382902412
Other changes: At the close of 2012, the grantmaker paid grants of $13,758,058, a 105.9% increase over the 2011 disbursements, $6,683,500.

1601
The Farver Foundation
626 Depot St.
Blissfield, MI 49228-1399
Contact: Patrick Farver, Tr.
Main URL: http://www.farverfoundation.org/

Established in 1988 in MI.
Donors: Orville W. Farver†; Constance Farver; Herbert Farver.
Foundation type: Independent foundation.
Financial data (yr. ended 12/31/12): Assets, $3,378,101 (M); expenditures, $352,026; qualifying distributions, $321,525; giving activities include $321,525 for 42 grants (high: $60,000; low: $125).
Fields of interest: Arts; Higher education; Education; Health organizations; Youth development; Human services; Community/economic development; Foundations (private grantmaking).
Type of support: General/operating support; Continuing support; Annual campaigns; Capital campaigns; Building/renovation; Equipment; Emergency funds.
Publications: Application guidelines.
Application information: Complete application guidelines are available on the foundation web site. Application form required.
***Initial approach:* Download application from foundation web site**
Deadline(s): None
Trustees: Constance Farver; Michael Farver; Patrick Farver; Cynthia Farver-Galiette.
EIN: 386540398
Other changes: The grantmaker now publishes application guidelines.

1602
Drusilla Farwell Foundation
675 E. Big Beaver, Ste. 111
Troy, MI **48083 (248) 817-2425**
Contact: Leslie Wise, Secy.

Established in 1937 in MI.
Foundation type: Independent foundation.
Financial data (yr. ended 08/31/13): Assets, $2,827,275 (M); expenditures, $186,453; qualifying distributions, $155,132; giving activities include $142,000 for 89 grants (high: $4,900; low: $100).
Fields of interest: Arts; Higher education; Education; Health organizations; Human services; Children/youth, services; Christian agencies & churches.
Type of support: General/operating support; Scholarship funds.
Application information: Application form not required.
Initial approach: Proposal
Deadline(s): None
Officers: Randolph Fields, Pres.; Leslie Wise, Secy.
Trustee: Charles Peltz.
EIN: 386082430

1603
Four County Community Foundation
(formerly Four County Foundation)
231 E. St. Clair
P.O. Box 539
Almont, MI 48003-0539 (810) 798-0909
***Contact:* Janet Bauer, Pres. and C.E.O.; For grants: Ross Moore, Prog. Asso.**
FAX: (810) 798-0908; E-mail: info@4ccf.org; Additional e-mail: janet@4ccf.org; Grant inquiry e-mail: program@4ccf.org; Main URL: http://www.4ccf.org
Facebook: https://www.facebook.com/4CountyCommunityFoundation
Twitter: http://twitter.com/4CCFMI

Established in 1987 in MI; originally converted from Community Hospital Foundation and sold to Saint Joseph Mercy of Macomb North.
Foundation type: Community foundation.
Financial data (yr. ended 12/31/12): Assets, $10,948,995 (M); gifts received, $448,559; expenditures, $520,036; giving activities include $157,287 for 11+ grants (high: $24,482), and $121,395 for 159 grants to individuals.
Purpose and activities: The foundation is committed to serving the current and emerging needs of the local community, continuing the tradition of philanthropy begun generations ago. The foundation is dedicated to bringing together human and financial resources to support progressive ideas in education, health, community, youth and adult programs. The foundation provides a secure, flexible vehicle for individuals, families, foundations and organizations to positively impact the quality of life in communities. The foundation recognizes that in order to meet its commitments to the community it serves it must seek growth through its permanent endowment funds from a wide range of donors.
Fields of interest: Education; Environment; Health care; Health organizations, association; Recreation; Children/youth, services; Community/economic development.
Type of support: General/operating support; Program development; Scholarship funds; Program evaluation; Grants to individuals.
Limitations: Applications accepted. Giving limited to northeast Oakland, northwest Macomb, southeast Lapeer, and southwest St. Clair counties, MI. No support for sectarian religious programs. No grants for operating expenses or basic educational or municipal functions (generally).
Publications: Application guidelines; Annual report; Informational brochure.
Application information: Visit foundation web site for application forms and additional guidelines per grant type. Faxed applications are not accepted. Application form required.
Initial approach: Submit application form
Copies of proposal: 9
***Deadline(s):* Jan. 1, Apr. 1, July 1, and Oct. 1 for Grants. and Apr. 1 for Scholarship.**
Board meeting date(s): 6 meetings per year
Final notification: Within 1 month
Officers and Trustees:* Sean O'Bryan,* Chair.; Jennifer Parker-Moore,* Vice-Chair.; Janet Bauer,* C.E.O. and Pres.; John Brzozowski,* Secy.; **Joe Worden,* Treas.**; **Peggy Domenick-Muscat**; Randy Jorgensen; Denis McCarthy; Sheila McDonald; Dina Miramonti; Nancy Parmenter; Barb Redding; Dr. Gary Richards; Laura Schapman; Janaea Smith; **Jake Sliman**; Greg Tarr; Al Verlinde.
Number of staff: 2 full-time professional; 1 part-time professional.
EIN: 382736601
Other changes: Sean O'Bryan has replaced Gary Richards as Chair. Joe Worden has replaced Sean O'Bryan as Treas.
Andrew Hunter and Joe Worden are no longer trustees.

1604
Samuel & Jean Frankel Foundation
2301 W. Big Beaver Rd., Ste. 900
Troy, MI 48084-3332 (248) 649-2600

Established in 1970.
Donors: Samuel Frankel; Jean Frankel.
Foundation type: Independent foundation.
Financial data (yr. ended 12/31/12): Assets, $87,649,256 (M); gifts received, $7,001,000; expenditures, $8,722,649; qualifying distributions, $8,398,372; giving activities include $8,398,372 for 12 grants (high: $4,000,000; low: $1,000).
Purpose and activities: Giving primarily for Jewish services, the fine and performing arts, higher education, health organizations, and human services.
Fields of interest: Museums; Performing arts; Education; Health organizations; Youth development, services; Human services; United Ways and Federated Giving Programs; Jewish federated giving programs; Jewish agencies & synagogues.
Limitations: Applications not accepted. Giving primarily in MI. No grants to individuals.
Application information: Contributes only to pre-selected organizations.
Officer: Stanley Frankel, Pres. and Treas.
Trustees: Bruce Frankel; Stuart Frankel; Joelyn Nyman; Arthur Weiss.
EIN: 386088399
Other changes: Stanley Frankel is now Pres. and Treas. Samuel Frankel is no longer Pres. Jean Frankel is no longer V.P. and Secy.

1605
The Samuel and Jean Frankel Health and Research Foundation
1004 Brookwood St.
Birmingham, MI 48009-1147

Established in 2004 in MI.
Donors: Bruce Frankel; Jean Frankel.
Foundation type: Independent foundation.
Financial data (yr. ended 12/31/12): Assets, $22,404,596 (M); expenditures, $1,212,184; qualifying distributions, $1,125,000; giving activities include $1,125,000 for 11 grants (high: $250,000; low: $5,000).
Fields of interest: Mental health, depression; Health organizations, association; Children/youth, services; Jewish federated giving programs.
Limitations: Applications not accepted. Giving in MI.
Application information: Contributes only to pre-selected organizations.
Officers and Trustees:* Bruce Frankel,* Pres. and Treas.; **Jo Elyn Nyman,* V.P.,Treas., and Mgr.**; George Nyman,* Secy.
EIN: 300095044

Other changes: Jo Elyn Nyman is now V.P.,Treas., and Mgr. Jean Frankel is no longer a trustee.

1606
Frankenmuth Community Foundation
(formerly Greater Frankenmuth Area Community Foundation)
P.O. Box 386
Frankenmuth, MI 48734-0386 **(989) 284-4674**
Contact: Stephen C. List, Exec. Dir.; For grants: Scott Zimmer, Treas.
E-mail: steve@frankenmuthcommunityfoundation.org; Grant inquiry tel.: 989-652-3476; Main URL: http://www.frankenmuthfoundation.org

Established in 1976 in MI.
Foundation type: Community foundation.
Financial data (yr. ended 12/31/12): Assets, $5,694,325 (M); gifts received, $230,211; expenditures, $422,154; giving activities include $348,956 for 7+ grants (high: $139,591), and $17,300 for grants to individuals.
Purpose and activities: The foundation seeks to support the public, educational, recreational, charitable, and benevolent organizations of the greater Frankenmuth, MI, community.
Fields of interest: Education; Recreation; Youth development, services; Urban/community development; Community/economic development; United Ways and Federated Giving Programs; Leadership development; General charitable giving.
Type of support: Building/renovation; Emergency funds; Program development; Scholarship funds; Scholarships—to individuals.
Limitations: Applications accepted. Giving limited to the Frankenmuth, MI, area. No support for religious organizations for religious purposes. No grants to individuals (except through scholarship funds), annual fund drives, debt liability, or general operating expenses.
Publications: Application guidelines; Informational brochure.
Application information: Visit foundation web site for application form and guidelines. Application form required.
Initial approach: Submit application
***Deadline(s):* Jan. 17, Mar. 21, June 15, and Sept. 21**
Board meeting date(s): Feb., Apr., July and Oct.
Final notification: After Board Meetings
Officers and Board Members:* Jon Webb,* Chair.; Tim Hildner,* Vice-Chair.; Dennis Krafft,* Secy.; Scott Zimmer,* Treas.; Stephen C. List,* Exec. Dir.; **Joe Cramer**; Julie Gafkay; Nancy Haskin; W. Don Zehnder; Bob Zeilinger.
Trustee: Tri-Star Trust Bank.
EIN: 382140032
Other changes: Karen Zehnder is no longer a member of the governing body.

1607
Fremont Area Community Foundation
(formerly The Fremont Area Foundation)
4424 W. 48th St.
P.O. Box B
Fremont, MI 49412-8721 (231) 924-5350
Contact: Carla A. Roberts, Pres. and C.E.O.; For grants: Todd Jacobs, V.P., Community Investment
FAX: (231) 924-5391; E-mail: info@tfacf.org; Additional fax: (231) 924-7637; Additional e-mail: croberts@tfacf.org; Grants inquiry e-mail: grants@tfacf.org or tjacobs@tfacf.org; Main URL: http://www.tfacf.org
Facebook: http://www.facebook.com/pages/Fremont-Area-Community-Foundation/183815588324852
Twitter: https://twitter.com/FremontAreaCF
E-mail for scholarship inquiries: rcowles@tfacf.org

Incorporated in 1951 in MI as private foundation; became a community foundation in 1972.
Foundation type: Community foundation.
Financial data (yr. ended 12/31/12): Assets, $188,094,887 (M); gifts received, $2,720,759; expenditures, $9,572,607; giving activities include $7,609,807 for 653 grants (high: $675,000; low: $125; average: $5,000–$50,000), $720,832 for 529 grants to individuals (high: $5,000; low: $125; average: $500–$1,500), and $3,500 for 1 loan/program-related investment.
Purpose and activities: The foundation has established six broad funding categories: 1) TrueNorth: to sustain operations of this autonomous agency established for the delivery of general social welfare services and educational programs; 2) Community Development: to strengthen the municipal activities of villages, cities, governmental units, and other related organizations; 3) Education: to augment and promote the special projects of schools, libraries, and other organizations for instruction and training, and for scholarships to promote higher education and learning in specialized programs; 4) Arts and Culture: to support activities that promote appreciation of and participation in artistic expression such as music, theater, dance, sculpture, and painting; 5) Human Services: to foster the delivery of services and the operation of programs to help meet basic human needs and to support the provision of rehabilitative services; and 6) Health Care: made to health care providers and other related organizations for activities designed to promote optimal well-being and to provide health-related education. The foundation is also interested in supporting programs that address the particular needs of youth and older (aged) adults.
Fields of interest: Visual arts; Performing arts; Arts; Libraries/library science; Education; Environment; Medical care, rehabilitation; Health care; Substance abuse, services; Health organizations, association; Recreation; Children/youth, services; Family services; Aging, centers/services; Human services; Community/economic development; Government/public administration; Children/youth; Youth; Adults; Aging; Disabilities, people with; Physically disabled; Deaf/hearing impaired; Mentally disabled; Women; Girls; Economically disadvantaged.
Type of support: General/operating support; Continuing support; Management development/capacity building; Capital campaigns; Building/renovation; Equipment; Endowments; Emergency funds; Program development; Conferences/seminars; Seed money; Curriculum development; Scholarship funds; Technical assistance; Consulting services; Program evaluation; Program-related investments/loans; Employee matching gifts; Scholarships—to individuals; Matching/challenge support.
Limitations: Applications accepted. Giving primarily in Newaygo County, MI. No support for religious organizations for religious purposes. No grants to individuals (except for scholarships), or for contingencies, reserves, services which are considered general government or school obligations, or deficit financing.
Publications: Application guidelines; Annual report; Grants list; Informational brochure; Newsletter.
Application information: Visit foundation web site for application, agency profile and grantmaking guidelines. Application form required.
Initial approach: Please call or e-mail
Copies of proposal: 1
Deadline(s): Feb. 1 and Sept. 1 for competitive grants
Board meeting date(s): Bi-monthly
Final notification: Within 3 months
Officers and Trustees:* Robert Zeldenrust,* Chair.; William Johnson,* Vice-Chair.; Carla Roberts, C.E.O. and Pres.; Todd Jacobs, V.P., Community Investment; Robert Jordan, V.P., Philanthropic Svcs.; Kathy Pope, V.P., Finance; Lynne Robinson,* Secy.; Richard Dunning,* Treas.; Robert Clouse; Maria Gonzalez; Lindsay Hager; Carolyn Hummel; Hendrick Jones; Cathy Kissinger; Mary Rangel; Joseph Roberson; Dale Twing; Tom Williams; Kirk Wyers.
Number of staff: 12 full-time professional; 1 part-time professional; 3 full-time support; 3 part-time support.
EIN: 381443367
Other changes: Tammy Cowley is now Exec. Asst. Mary Crisman is now Dir., Admin. Svcs. Robin Cowles is now Philanthropic Svcs. Mgr.

1608
Twink Frey Charitable Trust
(doing business as Nokomis Foundation)
161 Ottawa Ave. N.W., Ste. 409-A
Grand Rapids, MI **49503-2794** (616) 451-0267
Contact: Mary Alice Williams, Pres.
***E-mail:* ahagen@nolomisfoundation.org**; Main URL: http://www.nokomisfoundation.org

Established in MI.
Foundation type: Independent foundation.
Financial data (yr. ended 12/31/12): Assets, $11,037,859 (M); expenditures, $1,226,070; qualifying distributions, $1,067,738; giving activities include $769,300 for grants.
Fields of interest: Education, public policy; Health care; Human services; Women; Girls.
Limitations: Applications not accepted. Giving primarily in western MI. No support for religious organizations for religious purposes. No grants to individuals; no funding for scholarships, fellowships, medical research, capital requests, endowments or conferences.
Application information: Unsolicited requests for funds not accepted. From time to time, the foundation will send out Requests for Proposals specifically related to its focus areas of women's economic self-sufficiency as well as civic engagement. For questions regarding the grantmaking process, e-mail Anne Hagen, Prog. Dir.
Officers and Trustees:* Twink Frey,* Chair.; **Mary Alice Williams, C.E.O. and Pres.**; Carroll Velie,* Secy.
EIN: 261131263
Other changes: Mary Alice Williams is now C.E.O. and Pres.

1609
Frey Foundation
40 Pearl St. N.W., Ste. 1100
Grand Rapids, MI 49503-3028 (616) 451-0303
Contact: Steve Wilson, Pres.
FAX: (616) 451-8481; E-mail: freyfdn@freyfdn.org; Main URL: http://www.freyfdn.org
Grants List: http://www.freyfdn.org/grants

Established in 1974 in MI; endowed in 1988.
Donors: Edward J. Frey, Sr.†; Frances T. Frey†.
Foundation type: Independent foundation.

Financial data (yr. ended 12/31/12): Assets, $136,566,394 (M); expenditures, $9,739,880; qualifying distributions, $8,612,207; giving activities include $7,400,961 for 213 grants (high: $1,000,000; low: $50).
Purpose and activities: Foundation priorities are: 1) nurturing community arts; 2) community capital projects; 3) enhancing the lives of children and their families; 4) encouraging civic progress; 5) protecting the environment; and 6) strengthening philanthropy.
Fields of interest: Arts; Human services; Children/youth, services; Family services; Community/economic development; Philanthropy/voluntarism.
Type of support: Capital campaigns; Land acquisition; Program development; Seed money; Research; Technical assistance; Employee matching gifts.
Limitations: Applications accepted. Giving primarily in the Grand Rapids, MI, area, as well as Charlevois and Emmet counties. No support for sectarian charitable activity. No grants to individuals, or for endowment funds, debt retirement, general operating expenses, scholarships, conferences, speakers, travel, or to cover routine, current, or emergency expenses.
Publications: Application guidelines; Annual report.
Application information: Application form required for all requests; follow detailed application guidelines on foundation web site. Application form required.
Initial approach: The foundation encourages a pre-proposal meeting with applicants, or telephone, e-mail or letter of inquiry before submitting full application
Copies of proposal: 1
Board meeting date(s): Feb., May, Aug., and Nov.
Officers and Trustees:* David G. Frey,* Chair.; John M. Frey,* Vice-Chair.; Steve Wilson, Pres.; Edward J. Frey, Jr.,* Secy.-Treas.; Mary Caroline "Twink" Frey, Tr. Emeritus; Mary E. Frey Bennett; Eleonora H. Frey; **William O. Frey**; Sarah R. Frey Rose.
Number of staff: 5 full-time professional; 1 full-time support.
EIN: 237094777
Other changes: At the close of 2012, the grantmaker paid grants of $7,400,961, a 58.4% increase over the 2011 disbursements, $4,673,607.

1610
G. II Charities
c/o Ken Cregel
55 Campau Ave. NW, Ste. 501
Grand Rapids, MI 49503-2609 **(616) 363-9209**
Contact: Ken Kregel

Established in MI.
Donor: Gordon Food Service Inc.
Foundation type: Independent foundation.
Financial data (yr. ended 12/31/12): Assets, $11,224,208 (M); gifts received, $4,500,000; expenditures, $4,584,751; qualifying distributions, $4,584,385; giving activities include $4,584,385 for 58 grants (high: $1,000,000; low: $6,000).
Purpose and activities: Giving limited to Christian organizations and limited to effective evangelization activities emphasizing proclamation, church planting, discipleship, and leadership development.
Fields of interest: Christian agencies & churches.
Limitations: Giving primarily in MI.
Application information:
Initial approach: Letter
Deadline(s): None
Officers: Ronald K. Williams, Pres.; James D. Gordon, V.P.; John M. Gordon, Jr., Secy.-Treas.
EIN: 900098975

1611
The Gerber Foundation
(formerly The Gerber Companies Foundation and The Gerber Baby Food Fund)
4747 W. 48th St., Ste. 153
Fremont, MI 49412-8119 (231) 924-3175
Contact: Catherine A. Obits, Prog. Mgr.
FAX: (231) 924-7906; E-mail: tgf@ncresa.org; Additional e-mail (Catherine A. Obits): cobits@ncresa.org; Main URL: http://www.gerberfoundation.org

Incorporated in 1952 in MI with funds from Gerber Products Co.
Foundation type: Independent foundation.
Financial data (yr. ended 12/31/13): Assets, $74,314,600 (M); expenditures, $4,116,500; qualifying distributions, $3,733,300; giving activities include $3,076,343 for grants, $302,018 for 70 grants to individuals (high: $9,200; low: $2,300), and $132,939 for 300 employee matching gifts.
Purpose and activities: The foundation seeks to enhance the quality of life for infants and children by focusing on their nutrition, care, and development.
Fields of interest: Health care, infants; Health organizations, research; Pediatrics; Pediatrics research; Nutrition; Science, research; Infants/toddlers; Children.
Type of support: Research; Scholarships—to individuals.
Limitations: Applications accepted. Giving on a national basis. No support for national child welfare or international based programs. No grants or loans to individuals (except for scholarships), or for capital campaigns or operating support.
Publications: Application guidelines; Annual report (including application guidelines); Grants list; Program policy statement.
Application information: The foundation prefers that applications be submitted only after receiving approval of a letter of inquiry. Application guidelines are available on foundation web site. All materials should be submitted on CD along with the 7 hard copies. Application form required.
Initial approach: Proposal, of no more than 15 pages
Copies of proposal: 7
Deadline(s): Feb. 15 and Aug. 15; June 1 and Dec. 1 for letter of inquiry
Board meeting date(s): Feb., May, Aug., Nov.
Final notification: May and Nov.
Officers and Trustees:* Barbara J. Ivens,* Pres.; Fernando Flores-New,* V.P.; Tracy A. Baker,* Secy.; Stan M. VanderRoest,* Treas.; William L. Bush, M.D.; Michael G. Ebert; Raymond J. Hutchinson, M.D.; Jane M. Jeannero; David C. Joslin; Carolyn R. Morby; Nancy Nevin-Folino; Steven W. Poole; Randy Puff; Robert Schumacher, M.D.
Number of staff: 1 full-time professional; 1 part-time support.
EIN: 386068090
Other changes: John J. James is no longer a trustee.

1612
Irving S. Gilmore Foundation
136 E. Michigan Ave., Ste. 900
Kalamazoo, MI 49007-3915 (269) 342-6411
Contact: Richard M. Hughey, Jr., Exec. V.P. and C.E.O.
FAX: (269) 342-6465; Main URL: http://www.isgilmore.org

Established in 1972 in MI.
Donor: Irving S. Gilmore‡.
Foundation type: Independent foundation.
Financial data (yr. ended 12/31/13): Assets, $260,838,595 (M); expenditures, $11,338,100; qualifying distributions, $9,832,481; giving activities include $8,857,132 for 166 grants (high: $1,000,000; low: $850), and $25,802 for employee matching gifts.
Purpose and activities: The mission of the foundation is to support and enrich the cultural, social, and economic life of the greater Kalamazoo, MI, area. The priorities of the foundation are: 1) arts, culture, and humanities; 2) human services; 3) education and youth activities; 4) community development; and 5) health and well-being.
Fields of interest: Performing arts; Arts; Education; Health care; Youth development; Human services; Community/economic development.
Type of support: General/operating support; Continuing support; Annual campaigns; Capital campaigns; Building/renovation; Equipment; Land acquisition; Debt reduction; Emergency funds; Program development; Conferences/seminars; Publication; Seed money; Scholarship funds; Technical assistance; Consulting services; Program evaluation; Employee matching gifts; Matching/challenge support.
Limitations: Applications accepted. Giving primarily in the greater Kalamazoo, MI, area. No support for political organizations. No grants to individuals.
Publications: Application guidelines; Annual report.
Application information: Organizations that are first time foundation applicants or have not received foundation funding since 2007 must contact the foundation at least four weeks prior to an applicable submission deadline. Please refer to foundation web site for further guidelines and deadlines. Application form not required.
***Initial approach:* Single, unbound proposal including cover letter; narrative, limited to 6 numbered pages, at least 12-point font**
Copies of proposal: 1
Deadline(s): Jan. 10, Mar. 1, May 2, July 1, Sept. 1 and Nov. 1
Board meeting date(s): Jan., Mar., May, July, Sept., and Nov.
Final notification: Acknowledgement letter within 2 weeks
Officers and Trustees:* Richard M. Hughey, Jr., C.E.O. and Exec. V.P.; Floyd L. Parks,* Pres.; Judith H. Moore,* 1st V.P.; Janice C. Elliott, V.P., Admin.; **Robert M. Beam,* Secy.**; Charles D. Wattles,* Treas.; **Russell L. Gabier, Tr. Emeritus**; Howard D. Kalleward,* Tr. Emeritus; Ronald N. Kilgore.
Number of staff: 3 full-time professional; 2 full-time support.
EIN: 237236057
Other changes: Robert M. Beam has replaced Russell L. Gabier as Secy.

1613
Donald & Norma Golden Family Foundation
2000 Town Ctr., Ste. 1500
Southfield, MI 48075-1195
Contact: Barry R. Bess, Dir.

Established in 2005 in MI.
Donors: Donald L. Golden; Richard S. Golden; Bradley Golden; Michael Golden; Randal E. Golden.
Foundation type: Independent foundation.
Financial data (yr. ended 12/31/12): Assets, $4,602 (M); gifts received, $76,047; expenditures, $270,098; qualifying distributions, $257,798; giving activities include $257,798 for 3 grants (high: $230,798; low: $10,000).
Fields of interest: Hospitals (specialty); Medical research, institute.

Limitations: Applications not accepted. No grants to individuals.
Application information: Unsolicited requests for funds not accepted.
Directors: Barry R. Bess; Donald L. Golden; Marion Golden.
EIN: 202354028
Other changes: Donald L. Golden is no longer Pres.

1614
Grand Haven Area Community Foundation, Inc.

1 S. Harbor Dr.
Grand Haven, MI 49417-1385 (616) 842-6378
Contact: Holly Johnson, Pres.; For grants: Beth Larson, Dir., Grants and Nonprofit Svcs.
FAX: (616) 842-9518; E-mail: lgrevel@ghacf.org; Grant application E-mail: blarsen@ghacf.org; Main URL: http://www.ghacf.org
Facebook: http://www.facebook.com/pages/Grand-Haven-Area-Community-Foundation/416194020318
Scholarship e-mail: bpost@ghacf.org

Incorporated in 1971 in MI.
Foundation type: Community foundation.
Financial data (yr. ended 12/31/12): Assets, $64,970,989 (M); gifts received, $5,779,717; expenditures, $4,261,336; giving activities include $3,214,028 for 128+ grants (high: $400,107), and $245,565 for 199 grants to individuals.
Purpose and activities: The foundation seeks to improve and enhance the quality of life in the Tri-Cities area by: 1) serving as a leader, catalyst and resource for philanthropy; 2) building and holding a permanent and growing endowment for the community's changing needs and opportunities; 3) striving for community improvement through strategic grantmaking in such fields as the arts, education, health, the environment, youth, social services and other human needs; and 4) providing a flexible and cost-effective way for donors to improve their community now and in the future.
Fields of interest: Arts; Vocational education, post-secondary; Business school/education; Education; Environment; Health care; Crime/law enforcement; Human services; Community/economic development; Mathematics.
Type of support: Capital campaigns; Equipment; Land acquisition; Program development; Seed money; Scholarship funds; Scholarships—to individuals; Matching/challenge support.
Limitations: Applications accepted. Giving primarily in the MI Tri-Cities area. No support for profit-making organizations or religious programs that serve, or appear to serve, specific religious denominations. No grants to individuals (except for scholarships), or for annual campaigns, emergency or deficit financing, operating costs or ongoing operating support, fundraising events, or endowments.
Publications: Application guidelines; Annual report (including application guidelines); Financial statement; Informational brochure (including application guidelines); Newsletter; Program policy statement.
Application information: Visit foundation web site for more information. Application form required.
Initial approach: Contact foundation
Deadline(s): Jan. 10, Apr. 4, June 27, and Oct. 10
Board meeting date(s): Distribution committee meets quarterly: Jan., Apr., July, and Oct.; board meetings are usually 2 weeks following the distribution committee meeting
Final notification: 1 week after board meeting
Officers and Trustees:* Timothy Parker,* Chair.; Lana Jacobson,* Vice-Chair.; Holly Johnson,* Pres.; Sheila Steffel,* Secy.; Steven Moreland,* Treas.; Tammy Bailey; Kennard Creason; Edward Hanenburg; Randy Hansen; Sandy Huber; Mark Kleist; Monica Verplank.
Number of staff: 4 full-time professional.
EIN: 237108776
Other changes: Beth Larsen is now Dir., Grants and Non-Profit Srvs. Lauren Grevel is now Philanthropic Srvs. Asso. Jan Reenders is now Admin. Asst.

1615
Grand Rapids Community Foundation

(formerly The Grand Rapids Foundation)
185 Oakes Street SW
Grand Rapids, MI 49503-4219 (616) 454-1751
***Contact:* Diana R. Sieger, Pres.; For grant inquiries: Shavon Doyle, Grants Admin.**
FAX: (616) 454-6455;
E-mail: grfound@grfoundation.org; Grant inquiry tel.: (616) 454-1751, ext. 111; Main URL: http://www.grfoundation.org
E-Newsletter: http://www.grfoundation.org/enews
Facebook: http://www.facebook.com/GRCommFound
Podcasts: http://feeds.feedburner.com/grfoundation/gigr
President's Page: http://www.grfoundation.org/president
Twitter: http://twitter.com/GRCommFound
Vimeo: http://vimeo.com/channels/grcommfound
Scholarship contact: Ruth Bishop, tel.: (616) 454-1751, ext. 103,
e-mail: rbishop@grfoundation.org

Established in 1922 in MI by resolution and declaration of trust; Incorporated 1989.
Foundation type: Community foundation.
Financial data (yr. ended 06/30/13): Assets, $279,286,131 (M); gifts received, $18,925,770; expenditures, $13,035,367; giving activities include $7,048,466 for 928+ grants (high: $232,155; low: $50), and $871,850 for 552 grants to individuals.
Purpose and activities: The Community Foundation seeks to build and manage the community's permanent endowment and lead the community to strengthen the lives of its people. Grants are awarded to expand impact in Grand Rapids and surrounding communities. Leadership goals areas are academic achievement, economic prosperity, healthy ecosystems, healthy people, social enrichment and vibrant neighborhoods.
Fields of interest: Performing arts; Performing arts, theater; Arts; Higher education; Education, reading; Education; Environment; Health organizations, association; Employment; Housing/shelter, development; Youth development, services; Family services; Minorities/immigrants, centers/services; Human services; Civil/human rights, immigrants; Civil/human rights, minorities; Civil/human rights, disabled; Civil/human rights, women; Civil/human rights, aging; Civil/human rights, LGBTQ; Civil rights, race/intergroup relations; Civil liberties, reproductive rights; Community/economic development; Infants/toddlers; Children/youth; Children; Youth; Adults; Aging; Young adults; Disabilities, people with; Blind/visually impaired; Deaf/hearing impaired; Minorities; Asians/Pacific Islanders; African Americans/Blacks; Hispanics/Latinos; Native Americans/American Indians; Indigenous peoples; Women; Girls; Adults, women; Men; Boys; Adults, men; Single parents; Crime/abuse victims; Immigrants/refugees; Economically disadvantaged; Homeless; LGBTQ; Gay men; Bisexual.
Type of support: Capital campaigns; Building/renovation; Land acquisition; Program development; Seed money; Technical assistance; Program-related investments/loans; Employee matching gifts; Employee-related scholarships; Scholarships—to individuals.
Limitations: Applications accepted. Giving limited to Greater Grand Rapids, MI area. No support for religious programs, hospitals, child care centers, or nursing homes/retirement facilities. No grants to individuals (except for scholarships), or for continued operating support, annual campaigns, travel expenses, medical or scholarly research, deficit financing, endowment funds, computers, vehicles, films, videos, or conferences; no student loans; no venture capital for competitive profit-making activities.
Publications: Annual report; Informational brochure; Newsletter.
Application information: Visit foundation web site for online applications and guidelines per grant type. The foundation will request a full proposal based on the pre-application for the Fund for Community Good. Application form required.
Initial approach: Submit online pre-application (reviewed every 2 weeks) for Fund for Community Good
Deadline(s): Varies
Board meeting date(s): 6 times a year (bimonthly)
Final notification: 30 days
Officers and Trustees:* Wayman P. Britt,* Chair.; Paul Keep,* Vice-Chair.; Diana R. Sieger, Pres.; Lynne Black, V.P., Finance and Admin.; Roberta F. King, V.P., Public Rels. and Mktg.; Marcia Rapp, V.P., Progs.; **Kevin Harmelink, Cont.**; Laurie F. Beard; Eva Aguirre Cooper; Carol J. Karr; Christina Keller; Arend Lubbers; Michael Rosloniec; Robert W. Roth; E. Miles Wilson.
Number of staff: 15 full-time professional; 9 full-time support.
EIN: 382877959
Other changes: Wayman P. Britt has replaced Robert W. Roth as Chair. Paul Keep has replaced Wayman P. Britt as Vice-Chair.
Cecile Cave Fehsenfeld and Alex Tarr are no longer trustees.

1616
Grand Traverse Regional Community Foundation

250 E. Front St., Ste. 310
Traverse City, MI 49684-2552 (231) 935-4066
***Contact:* Phil Ellis, Exec. Dir.; For grants: Gina Limbocker, Grantmaking and Prog. Assoc.**
FAX: (231) 941-0021; E-mail: info@gtrcf.org; Grant application e-mail: glimbocker@gtrcf.org; Main URL: http://www.gtrcf.org
Facebook: https://www.facebook.com/grandtraverseregionalcommunityfoundation

Established in 1992 in MI.
Foundation type: Community foundation.
Financial data (yr. ended 12/31/12): Assets, $51,932,338 (M); gifts received, $5,331,727; expenditures, $2,430,791; giving activities include $1,674,021 for 280+ grants (high: $208,111; low: $50), and $131,349 for 148 grants to individuals.
Purpose and activities: The foundation seeks to enhance the quality of life and facilitate philanthropy in Antrim, Benzie, Grand Traverse, Kalkaska, and Leelanau counties, MI.
Fields of interest: Arts; Education; Environment; Community/economic development; Youth.

Type of support: Building/renovation; Equipment; Endowments; Program development; Seed money; Curriculum development; Scholarship funds; Technical assistance; Scholarships—to individuals; Matching/challenge support.
Limitations: Applications accepted. Giving limited to the counties of Antrim, Benzie, Grand Traverse, Kalkaska, and Leelanau, MI. No grants for routine training or professional conferences, annual events, budget shortfalls, or payroll or other general operating expenses.
Publications: Annual report; Informational brochure; Newsletter.
Application information: Visit foundation Web site for application information. Application form required.
Initial approach: Submit application
Copies of proposal: 1
***Deadline(s):* Mar. 31 for Spring Grant and Oct. 1 for Fall Grant.**
Board meeting date(s): Quarterly
Officers and Directors:* Phil Ellis, Exec. Dir.; Ed Arbut; Truman Bicum; Blake Brooks; Amy Burk; Dale Claudepierre; Bud Cline; Susan Cogswell; Doug Cook; Gail Dall'Olmo; **David DesAutels**; Jack Findlay; Dick Garcia; Penny Hill; Gary Hoensheid; Wesley Jacobs; Sherrie Jones; Dick Kennedy; Larry Miller; Courtney Morris; Virginia Mouch; Rex O'Connor; Roger Perry; Pam Prairie; Steve Rawlings; Bob Robbins; Neal Ronquist; Janet Sieting; Gregg Smith; Bill Stege; Ryan Sterkenburg; Ken Waichunas; Tom Wiltse; Jeff Wonacott.
Number of staff: 3 full-time professional; 2 part-time support.
EIN: 383056434
Other changes: Alison Metiva is now Dir., Comms. Rels. Gina Limbocker is now Grantmaking and Prog. Assoc. Colleen Etue, David DesAutels, and Teresa Mensching are no longer directors.

1617
Granger Foundation

P.O. Box 22187
Lansing, MI 48909-7185 (517) 393-1670
Contact: Eva Lee
E-mail: elee@grangerconstruction.com; Main URL: http://www.grangerfoundation.org/

Established in 1978.
Donors: Granger Associates, Inc.; Granger Construction Co.; and members of the Granger family.
Foundation type: Independent foundation.
Financial data (yr. ended 12/31/12): Assets, $10,213,570 (M); gifts received, $795,600; expenditures, $988,932; qualifying distributions, $948,821; giving activities include $948,821 for 71 grants (high: $67,146; low: $100).
Purpose and activities: The foundation's primary mission is to support Christ-centered activities. It also supports efforts that enhance the lives of youth in the community.
Fields of interest: Health care; Youth development; Human services; YM/YWCAs & YM/YWHAs; Christian agencies & churches; Youth.
Type of support: Annual campaigns; Capital campaigns.
Limitations: Applications accepted. Giving primarily in the greater Lansing and the Tri-County (Ingham, Eaton and Clinton counties), MI, areas. No support for capital funds or improvements for churches or public schools. No grants to individuals, or for endowments, fundraising, social events, conferences, or exhibits.
Publications: Application guidelines; Annual report; Program policy statement.
Application information: Form letters and lengthy proposals are not accepted. Application form required.
Initial approach: Completed Request for Funding form that is available on foundation web site
Copies of proposal: 4
Deadline(s): Apr. 15 and Oct. 15
Board meeting date(s): Semiannually
Trustees: Alton L. Granger; Donna Granger; Janice Granger; Jerry P. Granger; Lynne Granger; Ronald K. Granger.
EIN: 382251879

1618
Great Lakes Capital Fund Nonprofit Housing Corporation

(formerly Michigan Capital Fund for Non-Profit Housing Corporation)
1000 S. Washington Ave., Ste. 200
Lansing, MI 48910-1647
Main URL: http://www.capfund.net/
Facebook: https://www.facebook.com/Greatlakescapfund
Google Plus: https://plus.google.com/116783011127817898294/videos
LinkedIn: http://www.linkedin.com/company/great-lakes-capital-fund
Twitter: https://twitter.com/GLCapFund/
YouTube: https://www.youtube.com/user/GLCapFund

Foundation type: Operating foundation.
Financial data (yr. ended 12/31/12): Assets, $30,076,000 (M); expenditures, $12,675,000; qualifying distributions, $21,836,213; giving activities include $989,510 for 32 grants (high: $500,000; low: $50).
Purpose and activities: Giving primarily for the delivery of quality, affordable housing to the poor and underprivileged, the promotion of efforts to facilitate self-sufficiency and upward mobility of very-low and low-income households, and the preservation of social welfare through efforts to facilitate the construction and development of housing for very low-, low- and moderate-income households in a manner directed to eliminate prejudice and discrimination, lessen neighborhood tensions, and combat the deterioration of communities throughout Michigan.
Fields of interest: Housing/shelter; Economically disadvantaged.
Limitations: Applications not accepted. Giving primarily in MI.
Application information: Unsolicited requests for funds not accepted.
Officers and Directors:* Wendell Johns,* Chair.; Mark McDaniel, Pres. and C.E.O.; **Michael Taylor,* Secy.-Treas.**; James Logue III, C.O.O.; Christopher Cox, C.F.O.; Jennifer Everhart, Exec. V.P.; Ricky Laber, Exec. V.P.; **Catherine A. Cawthon; Derrick C. Collins; Christine Hobbs; William C. Perkins; Rob Rossiter; James Stretz; Donald F. Tucker; Paul J. Weaver.**
EIN: 383126310

1619
Hebert Memorial Scholarship Fund

c/o Kim M. Gardey
100 Harrow Ln.
Saginaw, MI 48638-6095
***E-mail:* info@saginawfoundation.org**
Application address: **c/o Saginaw Community Foundation, 100 S. Jefferson, Ste. 201, Saginaw, MI 48607, tel.: (989) 755-0545**

Foundation type: Independent foundation.
Financial data (yr. ended 12/31/12): Assets, $1,974,149 (M); expenditures, $172,686; qualifying distributions, $172,686; giving activities include $150,000 for 50 grants to individuals (high: $3,000; low: $3,000).
Purpose and activities: The fund pays expenses of deserving individuals that are pursuing their studies at a college or university of their choice in Saginaw County, MI.
Fields of interest: Education.
Type of support: Scholarships—to individuals.
Limitations: Applications accepted. Giving primarily in MI.
Application information: Application forms are available through the Saginaw Community Foundation's web site: http://www.saginawfoundation.org/site/hebert-memorial-scholarship/. Application form required.
***Initial approach:* Letter or telephone**
Deadline(s): Feb. 1
Trustee: Kim M. Gardey.
EIN: 262764191

1620
Hillsdale County Community Foundation

2 S. Howell St.
P.O. Box 276
Hillsdale, MI 49242-0276 (517) 439-5101
Contact: Sharon E. Bisher, Exec. Dir.
FAX: (517) 439-5109; E-mail: info@abouthccf.org; Additional e-mail: s.bisher@abouthccf.org; Main URL: http://www.abouthccf.org
Facebook: https://www.facebook.com/pages/Hillsdale-County-Community-Foundation/105456042855711

Established in 1991 in MI.
Foundation type: Community foundation.
Financial data (yr. ended 09/30/12): Assets, $11,594,701 (M); gifts received, $581,514; expenditures, $858,874; giving activities include $285,947 for 15+ grants (high: $46,930), and $196,830 for grants to individuals.
Purpose and activities: The foundation receives and administers funds for artistic, charitable, educational, and scientific purposes in a manner that both promotes the spirit of philanthropy and meets the needs of the people of Hillsdale County, MI.
Fields of interest: Visual arts; Performing arts; Performing arts, theater; Arts; Education, association; Education, early childhood education; Child development, education; Elementary school/education; Higher education; Libraries/library science; Education; Environment, natural resources; Environment; Animal welfare; Hospitals (general); Health care; Health organizations, association; Crime/violence prevention, youth; Crime/law enforcement; Employment; Food services; Recreation; Youth development, services; Children/youth, services; Child development, services; Family services; Residential/custodial care, hospices; Aging, centers/services; Human services; Community/economic development; Voluntarism promotion; Biology/life sciences; Economics; Leadership development; Public affairs; Aging; Economically disadvantaged.
Type of support: Scholarships—to individuals; Conferences/seminars; Publication; Seed money; Scholarship funds; In-kind gifts; Matching/challenge support.
Limitations: Applications accepted. Giving limited to Hillsdale County, MI. No support for religious or sectarian purposes. No grants to individuals (except

for scholarships), or for administrative costs, new building campaigns, routine maintenance, remodeling, or capital campaigns; no loans.
Publications: Application guidelines; Annual report; Financial statement; Informational brochure (including application guidelines); Newsletter.
Application information: Visit foundation web site for application form and guidelines. Application form required.
Initial approach: Telephone or in person
Copies of proposal: 1
***Deadline(s):* May 1 and Nov. 1 for general grants; Apr. 1 and Nov. 1 for Kellogg YOUTH grants; and Mar. 1 for scholarships**
Board meeting date(s): 1st Tues. of the month
Final notification: Within 2 months
Officers and Trustees:* David Pope,* Pres.; Jeff Lantis,* V.P.; Michelle Bianchi,* Secy.; John Barrett,* Treas.; Sharon E. Bisher, Exec. Dir.; Clint Barrett; Branden Bisher; Pat Dillon; Jeremiah Hodshire; Les Hutchinson; Tim Raker; Don Sanderson; Bambi Somerlott; Shawn Vondra; Jason Wade; Jim Whitehill; Jay Williams.
Number of staff: 1 full-time professional; 2 part-time professional.
EIN: 383001297

1621
The Isabel Foundation
111 E. Court St., Ste. 3D
Flint, MI 48502-1649 (810) 767-0136
Contact: Frederick S. Kirkpatrick
FAX: (810) 767-1207; Main URL: http://www.isabel.org

Established in 1988 in MI.
Foundation type: Independent foundation.
Financial data (yr. ended 06/30/12): Assets, $57,272,443 (M); expenditures, $3,203,412; qualifying distributions, $2,848,093; giving activities include $2,742,200 for 65 grants (high: $250,000; low: $3,000).
Purpose and activities: Funding primarily for organizations dedicated to supporting or contributing to the cause of Christian Science; support also for the arts, education, and convalescent facilities.
Fields of interest: Arts; Higher education; Nursing home/convalescent facility; Recreation, camps.
Type of support: General/operating support; Continuing support; Annual campaigns; Capital campaigns; Building/renovation; Equipment; Program development.
Limitations: Applications accepted. Giving in the U.S., including but not limited to CA, CO, FL, MA, ME, MI, MO, NY, OH, PA, TX, and WA. **No support for Christian Science branch churches.** No grants to individuals.
Publications: Application guidelines.
Application information: Application form not required.
***Initial approach:* Letter of introduction (in triplicate)**
Deadline(s): Mar. 1
Final notification: Grants are primarily made in June
Officers and Trustees:* Claire Mott White,* Pres.; William S. White,* V.P.; Tiffany W. Lovett; Ridgeway H. White.
Number of staff: 2 part-time professional.
EIN: 382853004

1622
Isabella Bank & Trust Foundation
400 N. Main
Mount Pleasant, MI 48858 (989) 772-9471

Established in 1997 in MI.
Donor: Isabella Bank and Trust.
Foundation type: Company-sponsored foundation.
Financial data (yr. ended 12/31/12): Assets, $916,331 (M); gifts received, $250,000; expenditures, $238,709; qualifying distributions, $234,300; giving activities include $234,300 for grants.
Purpose and activities: The foundation supports hospitals and community foundations and organizations involved with arts and culture, higher education, and human services.
Fields of interest: Education; Community/economic development; Religion.
Type of support: General/operating support; Sponsorships.
Limitations: Applications accepted. Giving primarily in Isabella County, MI, with emphasis on the Mt. Pleasant area. No grants to individuals.
Application information: Application form not required.
Initial approach: Proposal
Deadline(s): None
Officers and Directors:* William J. Strickler,* Chair.; Richard J. Barz,* Pres.; Roxanne Schultz,* Secy.; Steven D. Pung,* Treas.; Dennis P. Angner.
EIN: 383348258

1623
Jackson Community Foundation
(formerly The Jackson County Community Foundation)
1 Jackson Sq.
100 East Michigan Ave., Ste. 308
Jackson, MI 49201-1406 (517) 787-1321
FAX: (517) 787-4333; E-mail: jcf@jacksoncf.org; Main URL: http://www.jacksoncf.org/

Incorporated in 1948 in MI.
Foundation type: Community foundation.
Financial data (yr. ended 12/31/12): Assets, $19,724,146 (M); gifts received, $1,522,833; expenditures, $1,471,578; giving activities include $833,884 for 30+ grants (high: $95,000), and $160,000 for 69 grants to individuals.
Purpose and activities: The foundation seeks to improve the quality of life for the residents of Jackson County, MI.
Fields of interest: Humanities; Historic preservation/historical societies; Arts; Adult education—literacy, basic skills & GED; Education, reading; Education; Environment; Health care; Substance abuse, services; Recreation; Children/youth, services; Human services; Economic development; Community/economic development.
Type of support: Building/renovation; Capital campaigns; Consulting services; Equipment; General/operating support; Land acquisition; Matching/challenge support; Program development; Program evaluation; Scholarships—to individuals; Seed money; Technical assistance.
Limitations: Applications accepted. Giving limited to Jackson County, MI. No support for religious activities. No grants to individuals (except for scholarships), or for endowment funds, debt retirement, fellowships, publications, or conferences.
Publications: Application guidelines; Annual report (including application guidelines); Grants list; Newsletter.

Application information: Visit foundation web site for application forms, guidelines, and specific deadlines. Application form required.
Initial approach: Telephone, e-mail, or letter
Deadline(s): Varies
Board meeting date(s): Jan., Mar., May, July, Sept., and Nov.
Officers and Trustees:* Hendrik Schuur,* Chair.; Monica M. Moser,* C.E.O. and Pres.; John Butterfield; Anne E. Campau; Karen A. Chaprnka; Rick Davies; Tom Draper; Travis Fojtasek; **Michael Funkhouser**; H. Ronald Griffith; John Gruel; Jim Miller; Phil Moilanen; Kevin Oxley; Randy Purvis; Sarah Richmond; Cynthia A. Rider, D.M.D.; Jon Robinson; Jim Serino.
Number of staff: 2 full-time professional; 2 full-time support; 2 part-time support.
EIN: 386070739
Other changes: Katherine Patrick is no longer a member of the governing body.

1624
Jubilee Foundation
(formerly Herman Miller Design Foundation)
P.O. Box 75000
Detroit, MI 48275-3462

Established in 1994 in MI.
Donor: Herman Miller Inc.
Foundation type: Company-sponsored foundation.
Financial data (yr. ended 05/31/13): Assets, $4,608,780 (M); gifts received, $1,210,242; expenditures, $1,574,999; qualifying distributions, $1,570,961; giving activities include $1,570,961 for 150 grants (high: $235,554; low: $500).
Purpose and activities: The foundation supports community foundations and organizations involved with arts and culture, education, the environment, hunger, human services, international affairs, Christianity, neighborhood development, and economically disadvantaged people.
Fields of interest: Arts; Elementary/secondary education; Higher education; Theological school/education; Education; Environment, natural resources; Environment, water resources; Environment; Health care; Food services; Developmentally disabled, centers & services; Human services; International relief; International affairs; Community development, neighborhood development; Foundations (community); Christian agencies & churches; Economically disadvantaged.
Type of support: Scholarship funds; General/operating support.
Limitations: Applications not accepted. Giving primarily in CA, GA, and VA, with emphasis on MI. No grants to individuals.
Application information: Contributes only to pre-selected organizations.
Officers: Michael A. Volkema, Pres.; James E. Christenson, Secy.; James R. Kackley, Treas.
Directors: Mary Vermeer Andringa; Douglas D. French; Brian C. Walker.
EIN: 383003821

1625
The D. Dan and Betty Kahn Foundation
(formerly Kahn Family Foundation)
8655 E. Eight Mile Rd.
Warren, MI 48089-3019
Contact: David D. Kahn, Pres.

Established in 1986 in MI.
Donor: David D. Kahn.
Foundation type: Independent foundation.

Financial data (yr. ended 03/31/13): Assets, $121,182,613 (M); gifts received, $119,696,065; expenditures, $2,399,431; qualifying distributions, $2,367,578; giving activities include $2,337,000 for 8 grants (high: $1,430,000; low: $1,000).
Purpose and activities: Giving primarily for higher education as well as for Jewish organizations and Jewish federated giving programs; some funding for children and social services.
Fields of interest: Higher education; Education; Human services; Children/youth, services; Jewish federated giving programs; Jewish agencies & synagogues.
Type of support: General/operating support; Building/renovation; Scholarship funds.
Limitations: Applications not accepted. Giving primarily in MI and NY. No grants to individuals.
Application information: Contributes only to pre-selected organizations.
Officers and Trustees:* Lawrence A. Wolfe,* Pres.; Patrice Aaron,* V.P.; Arthur Weiss, Secy.-Treas.
EIN: 382712361
Other changes: For the fiscal year ended Mar. 31, 2013, the fair market value of the grantmaker's assets was $121,182,613, a 6423.7% increase over the fiscal 2011 value, $1,857,564. For the same period, the grantmaker paid grants of $2,337,000, a 1402.9% increase over the fiscal 2011 disbursements, $155,500.
Lawrence A. Wolfe has replaced David D. Kahn as Pres.
Arthur Weiss is now Secy.-Treas. Patrice Aaron is now V.P.
The grantmaker has changed its fiscal year-end from Nov. 30 to Mar. 31.

1626
Kalamazoo Community Foundation
(formerly Kalamazoo Foundation)
151 S. Rose St., Ste. 332
Kalamazoo, MI 49007-4775 (269) 381-4416
Contact: For grants: Kari Benjamin, Community Investment Asst.
FAX: (269) 381-3146; E-mail: info@kalfound.org; Main URL: http://www.kalfound.org
Facebook: https://www.facebook.com/kalfound
LinkedIn: http://www.linkedin.com/company/kalfound
Twitter: http://twitter.com/kalfound

Established in 1925; incorporated in 1930 in MI.
Foundation type: Community foundation.
Financial data (yr. ended 12/31/12): Assets, $343,972,044 (M); gifts received, $11,118,482; expenditures, $18,905,346; giving activities include $15,722,579 for grants.
Purpose and activities: The foundation is dedicated to enhancing the spirit of the community and quality of life in the greater Kalamazoo area through its stewardship of permanently endowed funds. Primary areas of giving include: 1) economic development; 2) early childhood learning and school readiness; 3) youth development; and 4) individuals and families. Grants largely for capital purposes and innovative programs.
Fields of interest: Education; Environment; Health care; Employment; Housing/shelter, development; Youth development; Family services; Economic development; Community/economic development.
Type of support: General/operating support; Equipment; Emergency funds; Program development; Seed money; Scholarship funds; Technical assistance; Program-related investments/loans; Employee matching gifts; Scholarships—to individuals; Matching/challenge support; Mission-related investments/loans.
Limitations: Applications accepted. Giving generally limited to Kalamazoo County, MI. No support for for-profit business development projects. No grants to individuals (except for scholarships), or for private land purchases, private home purchases, or endowment funds.
Publications: Application guidelines; Annual report; Financial statement; Grants list; Informational brochure; Informational brochure (including application guidelines); Newsletter; Quarterly report.
Application information: Visit foundation web site for more information and online application. Application form required.
Initial approach: **Submit Letter of Inquiry**
Copies of proposal: 1
Deadline(s): **Mar. 10, Sept. 3, and Dec. 4 for Letters of Inquiry for requests over $10,000**
Board meeting date(s): Jan., Mar., May, June, July, Sept., Nov., and Dec.
Final notification: 10 weeks
Officers and Trustees:* Si Johnson,* Chair.; Frank Sardone,* Vice-Chair.; Carrie Pickett-Erway, C.E.O. and Pres.; Joanna Donnelly Dales, V.P., Donor Rels.; Susan Springgate, V.P., Finance and Admin.; Suprotik Stotz-Ghosh, V.P., Community Investment; Karen Racette, Cont.; James Escamilla; Barbara L. James; Ronda E. Stryker; Hon. Carolyn H. Williams; Dr. Eileen B. Wilson-Oyelaran.
Custodian Bank: PNC Bank, N.A.
Number of staff: 17 full-time professional; 3 part-time professional; 3 full-time support; 3 part-time support.
EIN: 383333202

1627
Keller Foundation
5225 33rd St. S.E.
Grand Rapids, MI 49512-2071
***Contact:* Zelene Wilkins, Exec. Dir.**
***E-mail:* zelene@kellerfoundation.org**; Main URL: http://www.kellerfoundation.org

Established around 1980 in MI.
Donors: Paragon Die & Engineering Co.; Bernedine Keller; Keller Charitable Remainder Annuity.
Foundation type: Independent foundation.
Financial data (yr. ended 06/30/13): Assets, $7,114,069 (M); gifts received, $6,198; expenditures, $342,799; qualifying distributions, $335,682; giving activities include $293,350 for 69 grants (high: $50,000; low: $100).
Purpose and activities: Giving to support innovative programs for city youth in Grand Rapids, Michigan, that foster nurturing environments, spark curiosity, enhance opportunities for self-sufficiency, and inspire high aspirations.
Fields of interest: Museums (art); Performing arts; Education; Botanical/horticulture/landscape services; Zoos/zoological societies; Health care; Human services; Children/youth, services.
Type of support: General/operating support; Continuing support; Capital campaigns; Building/renovation; Program development; Seed money; Curriculum development; Scholarship funds; Matching/challenge support.
Limitations: Applications accepted. Giving primarily in the Grand Rapids, MI, area. No support for political organizations. No grants to individuals.
Publications: Application guidelines.
Application information: Application form required.
Initial approach: Cover Letter
Deadline(s): May 15
Board meeting date(s): June
Officers: Kathleen Muir Laidlaw, Chair.; **Andrew J. Keller, Vice-Chair.; David F. Muir, Treas.**; Zelene Wilkins, Exec. Dir.; Lorissa K. MacAllister; Wesley MacAllister; Catherine L. Muir; Elizabeth M. Muir; Lea Ann Muir; William M Muir; Christina L. Keller; Frederick P. Keller; Lars Whitman.
Number of staff: 1 part-time professional.
EIN: 382331693
Other changes: The grantmaker has moved from IL to MI. The grantmaker no longer lists a separate application address.
Andrew J. Keller has replaced Lorissa K. MacAllister as Vice-Chair.
David F. Muir is now Treas. William Laidlaw, Bernedine J. Keller, Linn Maxwell Keller, Susan T.K. Whitman are no longer trustees.

1628
W. K. Kellogg Foundation
1 Michigan Ave. E.
Battle Creek, MI 49017-4005 (269) 968-1611
Main URL: http://www.wkkf.org
America Healing: https://www.facebook.com/americahealing
Blog: http://blog.wkkf.org
Facebook: https://www.facebook.com/WKKelloggFoundation
Food & Community: https://www.facebook.com/foodandcommunity
GR8by8 - For Education and Learning Grantees: http://www.facebook.com/GR8by8
Grants Database: http://www.wkkf.org/grants
Knowledge Center: http://www.racialequityresourceguide.org/index.cfm
Knowledge Center: http://www.wkkf.org/resource-directory
RSS Feed: http://www.wkkf.org/shared/syndication/rss/news-and-media-rss
Twitter: http://www.twitter.com/WK_Kellogg_Fdn
W.K. Kellogg Foundation's Philanthropy Promise: http://www.ncrp.org/philanthropys-promise/who
YouTube: http://www.youtube.com/KelloggFoundation
Fellowship application URL: http://www.wkkf.org/leadership

Incorporated in 1930 in MI.
Donors: W.K. Kellogg†; W.K. Kellogg Foundation Trust; Carrie Staines Kellogg Trust.
Foundation type: Independent foundation.
Financial data (yr. ended 08/31/13): Assets, $8,155,292,105 (M); expenditures, $347,270,256; qualifying distributions, $259,898,647; giving activities include $259,898,647 for grants.
Purpose and activities: The W.K. Kellogg Foundation supports children, families, and communities as they strengthen and create conditions that propel vulnerable children to achieve success as individuals and as contributors to the larger community and society. The foundation's work is carried out by partners and programs that help it achieve its three organizational goals and embody its commitments to community and civic engagement, and to racial equity. The three goals are: 1) Educated kids: Success by third grade. Increase the number of children who are reading-and-math proficient by third grade; 2) Healthy Kids: Healthy birth weight and optimal development. Increase the number of children born at a healthy birth weight and who receive the care and healthy food they need for optimal development; and 3) Secure Families: Children and families at 200 percent above poverty. Increase the number of

children and families living at least 200 percent above the poverty level.
Fields of interest: Education, early childhood education; Elementary school/education; Secondary school/education; Education; Health care, reform; Health care; Health organizations, association; Agriculture; Agriculture/food; Youth development, services; Youth, services; Minorities/immigrants, centers/services; Community development, neighborhood development; Rural development; Community/economic development; Voluntarism promotion; Leadership development; Infants/toddlers; Children/youth; Children; Youth; Minorities; Asians/Pacific Islanders; African Americans/Blacks; Hispanics/Latinos; Native Americans/American Indians; Indigenous peoples; Single parents; Immigrants/refugees; Economically disadvantaged.
International interests: Brazil; Haiti; Mexico; Southern Africa.
Type of support: Fellowships; General/operating support; Program development; Seed money; Technical assistance; Program evaluation; Program-related investments/loans; Employee matching gifts; Matching/challenge support; Mission-related investments/loans.
Limitations: Applications accepted. Giving primarily in the U.S., with emphases on Michigan, Mississippi, New Mexico and New Orleans, LA, funding also for programs in Mexico, Haiti, northeastern Brazil and southern Africa. No support for religious purposes or for capital facilities. No grants to individuals (except for fellowship), or for scholarships, endowment funds, development campaigns, films, equipment, publications, conferences, or radio and television programs unless they are an integral part of a project already being funded; no grants for operating budgets.
Publications: Annual report; Financial statement; Grants list.
Application information: The foundation requires all proposals to be submitted online via its website. No funds directly to individuals. Funding is limited to the United States (with priority funding in Michigan, Mississippi, New Mexico and New Orleans), two micro-regions in southern Mexico and two micro-regions in Haiti. Unsolicited proposals are not currently being accepted for the southern Africa and northeastern Brazil. In general, it does not provide funding for operational phases of established programs, capital requests (which includes the construction, purchase, renovation, and/or furnishing of facilities), equipment, conferences and workshops, scholarships or tuition assistance, films, television and/or radio programs, endowments, development campaigns, or research/studies unless they are an integral part of a larger program budget being considered for funding. Application form required.
Initial approach: Online submission is required. For additional questions, contact the Central Proposal Processing office at (269) 969-2329
Copies of proposal: 1
Deadline(s): None
Board meeting date(s): Monthly
Final notification: 45 days
Officers and Trustees:* Bobby Moser,* Chair.; La June Montgomery-Tabron, C.E.O.and Pres.; **Ross Comstock, V.P., Technology and Information Systems**; Donald G. Williamson, V.P., Finance and Treas.; Joel R. Wittenberg, V.P. and C.I.O.; Gail C. Christopher, V.P., Prog. Strategy; Joanne K. Krell, V.P., Comms.; James E. McHale, V.P., Prog. Strategy; Linh C. Nguen, V.P., Learning and Impact; Carla D. Thompson, V.P., Prog. Strategy; Kathryn A. Kreckle, General Counsel and Corp. Secy.; Celeste A. Clark; Roderick D. Gillum; Fred P. Keller; Hanmin Liu; Cynthia H. Milligan; Ramon Murguia; Joseph M. Stewart; Richard M. Tsoumas.
Number of staff: 126 full-time professional; 60 full-time support.
EIN: 381359264
Other changes: Wenda Weekes Moore and Sterling K. Speirn are no longer trustees.

1629
Edward M. and Henrietta M. Knabusch Charitable Trust No. 1
Monroe, MI

The foundation terminated in 2014.

1630
James A. and Faith Knight Foundation
180 Little Lake Dr., Ste. 6B
Ann Arbor, MI 48103-6219 (734) 769-5653
***Contact:* Carol Knight-Drain, Pres. and Treas.**
FAX: (734) 769-8383;
E-mail: info@knightfoundationmi.org; **E-mail for Carol Knight-Drain: carol@KnightFoundationMI.org**; Main URL: http://www.knightfoundationmi.org

Established in 1999 in MI.
Donor: James A. Knight Trust.
Foundation type: Independent foundation.
Financial data (yr. ended 12/31/12): Assets, $14,517,201 (M); expenditures, $881,054; qualifying distributions, $753,099; giving activities include $702,516 for 36 grants (high: $44,000; low: $7,500).
Purpose and activities: Primarily serving Jackson and Washtenaw counties, Michigan, the foundation is dedicated to improving communities by providing grant support to qualified nonprofit organizations including, but not limited to, those that address the needs of women and girls, animals and the natural world, and internal capacity. Giving primarily for human services, including a neighborhood center, women's organizations, and family services; support also for nonprofit management, the United Way, housing, the arts, education, and environmental conservation.
Fields of interest: Arts; Adult education—literacy, basic skills & GED; Environment, natural resources; Housing/shelter, development; Human services; Family services; Women, centers/services; Nonprofit management; Women; Girls; Young adults, female.
Type of support: Building/renovation; Capital campaigns; Debt reduction; General/operating support; Management development/capacity building; Program development.
Limitations: Applications accepted. Giving limited to MI, with emphasis on Jackson and Washtenaw counties. No support for religious or political organizations. No grants to individuals, or for conferences or special events, or for annual campaigns.
Publications: Application guidelines; Grants list; Occasional report; Program policy statement.
Application information: All applicants are encouraged to submit applications online using the Community Grants online system at http://www.communitygrants.org. If applicant does not have access to a computer, applicant can mail application (three copies plus one copy of attachments). Complete application guidelines available on foundation web site. Application form required.
***Initial approach:* Online application**
Copies of proposal: 3
***Deadline(s):* See foundation web site for current deadlines**
Board meeting date(s): 10 times per year
Officers: Carol Knight-Drain, Pres. and Treas.; Scott Drain, Secy.
Directors: Christopher Ballard.
Number of staff: 1 part-time professional; 1 part-time support.
EIN: 383465904

1631
The Kresge Foundation
3215 W. Big Beaver Rd.
Troy, MI 48084-2818 (248) 643-9630
Contact: Rip Rapson, C.E.O. and Pres.
FAX: (248) 643-0588; E-mail: info@kresge.org; Main URL: http://www.kresge.org
E-Newsletter: http://kresge.org/subscribe?quicktabs_1=0#quicktabs-1
Facebook: http://www.facebook.com/TheKresgeFoundation
Grantee Perception Survey: http://www.kresge.org/sites/default/files/Kresge%202011%20Grantee%20Perception%20Report%20FINAL%2020120305.pdf
Grants Database: http://maps.foundationcenter.org/grantmakers/index.php?gmkey=KRES002
Knowledge Center: http://www.kresge.org/library
Kresge Blog: http://www.kresge.org/kresge-blog
RSS Feed: http://kresge.org/subscribe?quicktabs_1=0#quicktabs-1
Twitter: https://twitter.com/kresgefdn
YouTube: http://www.youtube.com/user/TheKresgeFoundation

Incorporated in 1924 in MI.
Donor: Sebastian S. Kresge†.
Foundation type: Independent foundation.
Financial data (yr. ended 12/31/12): Assets, $3,301,625,267 (M); expenditures, $171,021,660; qualifying distributions, $167,117,780; giving activities include $140,608,387 for 661 grants (high: $2,500,000; low: $5,000), $1,351,193 for 360 employee matching gifts, and $10,000,000 for 3 loans/program-related investments (high: $5,000,000; low: $2,500,000).
Purpose and activities: The foundation seeks to strengthen nonprofit organizations by catalyzing their growth, connecting them to their stake holders, and challenging greater support through grants. The foundation believes that strong, sustainable, high capacity organizations are positioned to achieve their missions and strengthen communities. Grants are awarded to nonprofit organizations operating in the fields of education, health and long-term care, human services, arts and humanities, public affairs, and science, nature, and the environment.
Fields of interest: Arts, artist's services; Arts; Higher education; Environment, public policy; Environment, government agencies; Environment, natural resources; Environment, energy; Environment; Health care; Human services; Community/economic development; Public policy, research; Economically disadvantaged.
Type of support: Employee matching gifts; General/operating support; Program development; Program-related investments/loans; Research; Technical assistance.
Limitations: Applications accepted. Giving on a national basis with emphasis on Detroit, MI, as well as some international funding. No support for religious organizations, (unless applicant is operated by a religious organization and it serves

secular needs and has financial and governing autonomy separate from the parent organization with space formally dedicated to its programs) private foundations, or elementary and secondary schools (unless they predominantly serve individuals with physical and/or developmental disabilities). No grants to individuals, or for debt retirement, projects that are already substantially completed, minor equipment purchases, or for constructing buildings for worship services.
Publications: Annual report; Financial statement; Grants list; Informational brochure.
Application information: See foundation web site for more application information for each program. Application procedures vary for each foundation program area. See foundation web site for information on its Social Investment Practice. Application form required.
Initial approach: Online submission of proposal. Some grant opportunities are by invitation only.
Copies of proposal: 1
Deadline(s): Announced when grant opportunities open
Board meeting date(s): Mar., June, Sept. and Dec.
***Final notification:* Generally within 10 to 12 weeks of the submission date**
Officers and Trustees:* Elaine D. Rosen,* Chair.; Rip Rapson,* C.E.O. and Pres.; **Amy B. Coleman, V.P. and C.F.O.**; Robert J. Manilla, V.P. and C.I.O.; Sheryl Madden, Cont.; James L. Bildner; Lee C. Bollinger; Phillip L. Clay; Steven K. Hamp; Paul C. Hillegonds; Irene Y. Hirano; Cynthia L. Kresge; Maria Otero; Nancy M. Schlichting.
Number of staff: 23 full-time professional.
EIN: 381359217
Other changes: David W. Horvitz is no longer a trustee. Amy B. Coleman is now V.P. and C.F.O. Richard K. Rappleye is no longer V.P., Admin. Susan K. Drewes is no longer a trustee.

1632
Lear Corporation Charitable Foundation
21557 Telegraph Rd.
Southfield, MI 48033-4248

Established in 2003 in MI.
Donor: Lear Corp.
Foundation type: Company-sponsored foundation.
Financial data (yr. ended 12/31/12): Assets, $6,554,846 (M); gifts received, $27,750; expenditures, $1,676,677; qualifying distributions, $1,663,878; giving activities include $1,663,878 for 24 grants (high: $500,000; low: $1,250).
Purpose and activities: The foundation supports organizations involved with arts and culture, education, youth development, and human services.
Fields of interest: Museums (science/technology); Performing arts, orchestras; Arts; Higher education; Education; Boy scouts; Girl scouts; Human services; United Ways and Federated Giving Programs.
Type of support: Scholarship funds; General/operating support; Program development.
Limitations: Applications not accepted. Giving primarily in MI, with emphasis on Detroit.
Application information: Contributes only to pre-selected organizations.
Officers: Mathew J. Smoncini, Pres.; William P. McLaughlin, V.P.; Dave Mullin, V.P.; Mel Stephens, V.P.; Terrence B. Larkin, Secy.; Shari L. Burgess, Treas.
EIN: 200302085

1633
The Legion Foundation
1750 S. Telegraph Rd., Ste. 301
Bloomfield Hills, MI 48302-0179 (248) 253-1100
Contact: James E. Mulvoy Esq., Pres.
FAX: (248) 253-1142;
E-mail: mulvoy@thelegionfoundation.org; Main URL: http://www.thelegionfoundation.org/Pages/default.aspx

Established in 1997 in MI.
Donors: The Thewes Trust; The TT Trust; The Thewes Charitable Annuity Lead Trust.
Foundation type: Independent foundation.
Financial data (yr. ended 12/31/12): Assets, $9,574,084 (M); expenditures, $1,364,119; qualifying distributions, $1,121,124; giving activities include $1,121,124 for grants.
Purpose and activities: Giving for 1) the development and administration of religious, educational, and/or charitable programs to foster and promote public awareness and adoption of the moral and ethical principles of Christian religions, with special emphasis on supporting the Roman Catholic Church and its members; 2) the distribution of financial support to qualified individuals to promote their physical and spiritual development in order to facilitate and encourage the study and maintenance of their Christian faith in the secular world, with preference given to Roman Catholics for such purposes; and 3) the distribution of financial support to other qualifying organizations engaged in similar work.
Fields of interest: Education; Christian agencies & churches; Catholic agencies & churches.
Type of support: General/operating support; Scholarships—to individuals.
Application information: Application forms available on foundation web site. Scholarships will be paid directly to the educational institution. Application form required.
Initial approach: Send application form via U.S. mail or fax
Deadline(s): None, for grants; June 30 for scholarships
Officers: James E. Mulvoy, Pres.; Maree R. Mulvoy, V.P.; William C. Hanson, Secy.
EIN: 383330588

1634
Lenawee Community Foundation
(formerly Tecumseh Community Fund Foundation)
603 N. Evans St.
P.O. Box 142
Tecumseh, MI 49286-1166 (517) 423-1729
Contact: Suann D. Hammersmith, C.E.O.
FAX: (517) 424-6579;
E-mail: shammersmith@ubat.com; Main URL: http://www.lenaweecommunityfoundation.com/
Blog: http://volunteerlenawee.wordpress.com/
Facebook: https://www.facebook.com/LenaweeCommunityFoundation
YouTube: http://www.youtube.com/lenaweefoundation

Established in 1961 in MI.
Foundation type: Community foundation.
Financial data (yr. ended 09/30/12): Assets, $18,965,901 (M); gifts received, $761,567; expenditures, $1,549,432; giving activities include $1,180,068 for 12+ grants (high: $250,000), and $83,255 for 114 grants to individuals.
Purpose and activities: The mission of the foundation is to enhance the quality of life of the citizens of Lenawee County, Michigan by: 1) identifying and addressing current and anticipated community needs; and 2) raising, managing, and distributing funds for charitable purposes in the areas of civic, cultural, health, education, and social services with an emphasis on permanent endowments.
Fields of interest: Arts; Education; Health organizations, association; Human services; Community/economic development; Youth.
Type of support: Program development; General/operating support; Capital campaigns; Building/renovation; Management development/capacity building; Equipment; Endowments; Conferences/seminars; Scholarship funds; Employee-related scholarships.
Limitations: Applications accepted. Giving limited for the benefit of Lenawee County, MI. No support for religious purposes. No grants to individuals (except for scholarships), or for fundraising.
Publications: Application guidelines; Annual report (including application guidelines); Grants list; Informational brochure; Newsletter.
Application information: Visit foundation web site for application guidelines. Application form required.
Initial approach: Inquiry by telephone or e-mail
Copies of proposal: 1
Deadline(s): Varies
Board meeting date(s): Bimonthly, 4th Thurs. of the month
Final notification: Varies
Officers and Directors:* Charles H. Gross,* Co-Chair.; Bob Vogel,* Co-Chair.; David S. Hickman, Chair. Emeritus; Suann D. Hammersmith,* C.E.O. and Pres.; Scott Hill,* Secy.; Jim Kapnick,* Treas.; **Laura Bell**; **Michele Buku**; **Alison Carpenter**; Charlotte Coberley; Carlton Cook; Frank Dick; Jack Patterson; Kris Schmidt; Amy Stamats.
Number of staff: 2 full-time professional; 2 part-time professional.
EIN: 386095474
Other changes: Charles H. Gross has replaced David E. Maxwell as Vice-Chair. Bob Vogel has replaced David S. Hickman as Chair.
Bob Vogel is no longer a director.

1635
Edward & Helen Mardigian Foundation
c/o Comerica Bank
P.O. Box 75000, MC 3318
Detroit, MI 48275-3318
Application address: c/o Edward Mardigian, Jr., 39400 Woodward Ave., Ste. 225, Bloomfield Hills, MI 48304, tel.: (248) 647-0077

Incorporated in 1955 in MI.
Donors: Edward S. Mardigian‡; Helen Mardigian; Arman Mardigian‡.
Foundation type: Independent foundation.
Financial data (yr. ended 12/31/12). Assets, $38,631,591 (M); gifts received, $22,545,047; expenditures, $8,268,386; qualifying distributions, $7,897,276; giving activities include $7,824,900 for 32 grants (high: $3,735,000; low: $400).
Purpose and activities: Giving primarily for Armenian organizations and churches in the U.S.; funding also for children, youth and social services, and health associations.
Fields of interest: Arts; Higher education; Zoos/zoological societies; Health organizations, association; Human services; Children/youth, services; Christian agencies & churches.
Limitations: Applications accepted. Giving primarily in MI; some funding nationally. No grants to individuals.

Application information: Application form not required.
Initial approach: Letter
Deadline(s): None
Officers: Edward S. Mardigian, Pres.; Janet M. Mardigian, V.P.; Grant Mardigian, Secy.; Matthew Mardigian, Treas.
Director: Robert D. Mardigian.
EIN: 386048886
Other changes: At the close of 2012, the fair market value of the grantmaker's assets was $38,631,591, a 76.1% increase over the 2011 value, $21,939,610. For the same period, the grantmaker paid grants of $7,824,900, a 421.5% increase over the 2011 disbursements, $1,500,425.
Helen Mardigian is no longer Pres. and Secy. Edward S. Mardigian is now Pres.

1636
Marquette County Community Foundation
(formerly Marquette Community Foundation)
401 E. Fair Ave.
P.O. Box 37
Marquette, MI 49855-2951 (906) 226-7666
Contact: Gail Anthony, C.O.O.
FAX: (906) 226-2104; E-mail: mcf@chartermi.net; Main URL: http://www.mqt-cf.org
Facebook: https://www.facebook.com/mqtccf?ref=search&sid=219708050.3543819631..1

Established in 1988 in MI.
Foundation type: Community foundation.
Financial data (yr. ended 12/31/12): Assets, $12,116,478 (M); gifts received, $609,162; expenditures, $867,015; giving activities include $641,690 for 7 grants (high: $203,305), and $36,236 for 43 grants to individuals.
Purpose and activities: The foundation supports organizations involved with the arts, education, health, human services, and other projects and programs that enhance life.
Fields of interest: Arts; Education; Health care; Health organizations, association; Recreation; Children/youth, services; Human services.
Type of support: Film/video/radio; Technical assistance; Consulting services; Capital campaigns; Building/renovation; Equipment; Program development; Seed money; Scholarship funds; Scholarships—to individuals.
Limitations: Applications accepted. Giving limited to Marquette County, MI. No support for religious programs that promote their particular religion.
Publications: Application guidelines; Annual report; Financial statement; Informational brochure; Newsletter; Program policy statement; Program policy statement (including application guidelines).
Application information: Visit foundation web site for application form and guidelines. Application form required.
***Initial approach:* Create online profile**
***Deadline(s):* Apr. 1 and Oct. 3**
Board meeting date(s): Six times annually
Final notification: Within one week of board meeting
Officers and Trustees:* Jack Lenten,* Chair.; Tom Baldini,* Vice-Chair.; Maura Davenport,* Secy.; Tom Humphrey,* Treas.; Pam Benton; Stu Bradley; Brad Canale; Mark Canale; Robert Cowell; Anne Giroux; James Hewitt; Don Mourand; Nancy Wiseman Seminoff; Fred Taccolini; Tom Vear; Karl Weber.
Number of staff: 2 full-time professional.
EIN: 382826563

1637
Masco Corporation Foundation
(formerly Masco Corporation Charitable Trust)
c/o Corp. Affairs
21001 Van Born Rd.
Taylor, MI 48180-1340 (313) 274-7400
Contact: Melonie B. Colaianne, Pres.
FAX: (313) 792-6262; **Main URL: http://masco.com/corporate-responsibility/masco-foundation/**

Trust established in 1952 in MI.
Donor: Masco Corp.
Foundation type: Company-sponsored foundation.
Financial data (yr. ended 12/31/12): Assets, $12,182,077 (M); gifts received, $3,000,000; expenditures, $3,087,118; qualifying distributions, $2,994,027; giving activities include $2,817,690 for 71 grants (high: $375,000; low: $300).
Purpose and activities: The foundation supports organizations involved with arts and culture, the environment, affordable housing, human services, civic affairs, economically disadvantaged, and military and veteran's.
Fields of interest: Performing arts; Arts; Environment; Food services; Housing/shelter, development; Housing/shelter; Homeless, human services; Human services; Military/veterans' organizations; Public affairs; Economically disadvantaged.
Type of support: General/operating support; Annual campaigns; Capital campaigns; Building/renovation; Employee matching gifts.
Limitations: Applications accepted. Giving primarily in areas of company operations, with emphasis on the greater Detroit, MI, area. No support for discriminatory organizations, political organizations or candidates, lobbying organizations, athletic clubs, religious organizations not of direct benefit to the entire community, or organizations benefiting few people. No grants to individuals, or for debt reduction, endowments, sports programs or events or school extracurricular activities, or conferences, travel, seminars, or film or video projects; no loans.
Publications: Application guidelines; Occasional report.
Application information: A full proposal may be requested after inquiry. The Council of Michigan Foundations Common Grant Application form is also accepted. Application form not required.
Initial approach: Letter of inquiry or telephone
Copies of proposal: 1
Deadline(s): None
Board meeting date(s): Spring and fall
Final notification: Within 6 weeks following receipt of proposal
Officers and Directors: Sharon Rothwell,* Chair.; Melonie B. Colaianne, Pres.; Eugene A. Gargaro, Jr., Secy.; Richard A. Manoogian; Timothy J. Wadhams.
Trustee: Comerica Bank.
Number of staff: 2 part-time professional; 2 part-time support.
EIN: 386043605

1638
McGregor Fund
333 W. Fort St., Ste. 2090
Detroit, MI 48226-3134 (313) 963-3495
Contact: C. David Campbell, Pres.
FAX: (313) 963-3512;
E-mail: info@mcgregorfund.org; Main URL: http://www.mcgregorfund.org

Incorporated in 1925 in MI.
Donors: Tracy W. McGregor†; Katherine W. McGregor†.
Foundation type: Independent foundation.
Financial data (yr. ended 06/30/13): Assets, $164,329,580 (M); expenditures, $7,251,104; qualifying distributions, $5,822,884; giving activities include $4,638,800 for 63 grants (high: $300,000; low: $300), and $275,323 for 87 employee matching gifts.
Purpose and activities: A private foundation organized to relieve misfortune and improve the well-being of people. The foundation provides grants to support activities in human services, education, health care, arts and culture, and public benefit.
Fields of interest: Arts; Higher education; Education; Medical care, in-patient care; Health organizations, association; Human services; Youth, services; Homeless.
Type of support: General/operating support; Continuing support; Capital campaigns; Building/renovation; Equipment; Program development; Seed money; Employee matching gifts.
Limitations: Applications accepted. Giving primarily in the metropolitan Detroit, MI, area, including Wayne, Oakland, and Macomb counties. No support for disease-specific organizations (or their local affiliates). No grants to individuals, or for scholarships directly, fellowships, travel, workshops, seminars, special events, film or video projects, or conferences; no loans.
Publications: Application guidelines; Annual report (including application guidelines); Grants list.
Application information: Grantmaking guidelines and application procedures are available on the foundation's Web site. Potential applicants are encouraged to contact the foundation to discuss proposed projects before submitting a proposal. Organizations are limited to submitting one grant application per year. Application form not required.
Initial approach: Cover letter and proposal
Copies of proposal: 1
Deadline(s): Applicants are encouraged to submit proposals at least 3 months in advance of board meetings
Board meeting date(s): Mar., June, Sept., and Dec.
Final notification: 90 to 120 days
Officers and Trustees:* James B. Nicholson,* Chair.; **Denise J. Lewis,* Vice-Chair.; Norah M. O'Brien, C.F.O.; Kate Levin Markel, C.O.O.;** William W. Shelden, Jr.,* Treas.; Dave Bing, Tr. Emeritus; Ira J. Jaffe, Tr. Emeritus; Eugene A. Miller, Tr. Emeritus; Bruce W. Steinhauer, M.D.*, Tr. Emeritus; **Peter P. Thurber, Tr. Emeritus;** Gerard M. Anderson; Cynthia N. Ford; Reuben A. Munday; Richard L. Rogers; Susan Schooley, M.D.
Number of staff: 4 full-time professional; 1 full-time support.
EIN: 380808800
Other changes: Denise J. Lewis has replaced Ruth R. Glancy as Vice-Chair.
Ira J. Jaffe is now Tr. Emeritus. Kate Levin Markel is now C.O.O. Norah M. O'Brien is now C.F.O. C. David Campbell, Pres. and Secy., is deceased.

1639
The Meijer Foundation
c/o Michael R. Julien
2929 Walker Ave. NW
Grand Rapids, MI 49544-6402
E-mail for Mike Julien: Mikejulien@meijer.com

Established in 1990 in MI.
Donors: Frederik G.H. Meijer†; Meijer, Inc.; Lena Meijer.
Foundation type: Independent foundation.
Financial data (yr. ended 09/30/12): Assets, $82,630,115 (M); gifts received, $12,033,000;

expenditures, $19,659,914; qualifying distributions, $18,772,489; giving activities include $18,717,521 for 93 grants (high: $2,000,000; low: $326).
Purpose and activities: Giving primarily to a horticultural society, and to a charitable trust; funding also for community foundations and an art museum. The foundation administers a donor-advised fund.
Fields of interest: Museums (art); Botanical gardens; Horticulture/garden clubs; Foundations (community).
Type of support: Program-related investments/loans.
Limitations: Applications not accepted. Giving primarily in Grand Rapids, MI. No grants to individuals.
Application information: Contributes only to pre-selected organizations.
Trustees: Douglas F. Meijer; Hendrik O. Meijer; Mark D. Meijer.
EIN: 386575227
Other changes: Donald F. Meijer is no longer a trustee.

1640
Orville D. & Ruth A. Merillat Foundation
1800 W. U.S. Hwy. 223
Adrian, MI 49221-8479

Established in 1983 in MI.
Donors: Orville D. Merillat†; Ruth A. Merillat.
Foundation type: Independent foundation.
Financial data (yr. ended 02/28/13): Assets, $54,867,982 (M); expenditures, $3,629,535; qualifying distributions, $3,464,490; giving activities include $3,449,550 for 66 grants (high: $200,000; low: $600).
Purpose and activities: Support primarily for churches and religious welfare.
Fields of interest: Elementary/secondary education; Human services; Religious federated giving programs; Christian agencies & churches.
Type of support: General/operating support; Building/renovation; Equipment.
Limitations: Applications not accepted. Giving primarily in MI. No grants to individuals.
Application information: Contributes only to pre-selected organizations.
Officers and Directors:* Ruth A. Merillat,* Pres. and Secy.; Richard D. Merillat,* V.P.; John D. Thurman, Treas.; **Tricia L.M. McGuire**.
EIN: 382476813

1641
Roy G. Michell Charitable Foundation and Trust
c/o Janz & Knight, PLC
300 E. Long Lake Rd., Ste. 360
Bloomfield Hills, MI 48304-2377

Established in 1963 in MI.
Donor: Roy G. Michell†.
Foundation type: Independent foundation.
Financial data (yr. ended 04/30/13): Assets, $5,472,861 (M); expenditures, $290,366; qualifying distributions, $225,000; giving activities include $225,000 for 65 grants (high: $73,500; low: $100).
Fields of interest: Health organizations, association; Human services; Christian agencies & churches.
Limitations: Applications not accepted. Giving primarily in MI. No grants to individuals.
Application information: Contributes only to pre-selected organizations.
Trustees: Roy G. Michell, Jr.; William Michell; Kenneth E. Zink.
EIN: 386071109
Other changes: Lloyd C. Michell is no longer a trustee.

1642
Midland Area Community Foundation
(formerly Midland Foundation)
76 Ashman Cir.
Midland, MI 48640 (989) 839-9661
Contact: For grants: Nancy Money, Prog. Off.
FAX: (989) 839-9907;
E-mail: info@midlandfoundation.org; Additional tel: (800) 906-9661; Grant application e-mail: nmoney@midlandfoundation.org; Main URL: http://www.midlandfoundation.org
Facebook: http://www.facebook.com/pages/Midland-MI/Midland-Area-Community-Foundation/56875302551
Twitter: https://twitter.com/MidlandFDN
YouTube: http://www.youtube.com/user/MidlandAreaCommFound

Established in 1973 in MI.
Foundation type: Community foundation.
Financial data (yr. ended 12/31/12): Assets, $73,391,036 (M); gifts received, $1,914,834; expenditures, $3,481,841; giving activities include $2,012,384 for 184+ grants (high: $245,000), and $334,281 for 151 grants to individuals.
Purpose and activities: The foundation strengthens the community by providing leadership, fostering collaboration on local needs and issues, and encouraging a legacy of giving through grants, scholarships and events.
Fields of interest: Humanities; Arts; Adult/continuing education; Education; Environment, energy; Environment; Health care; Recreation; Youth, services; Human services; Economic development; Community/economic development; Infants/toddlers; Children/youth; Children; Youth; Adults; Aging; Young adults; Disabilities, people with; Physically disabled; Deaf/hearing impaired; Mentally disabled; Minorities; African Americans/Blacks; Women; Infants/toddlers, female; Girls; Adults, women; Young adults, female; Men; Infants/toddlers, male; Adults, men; Young adults, male; Military/veterans; Substance abusers; Single parents; Crime/abuse victims; Terminal illness, people with; Economically disadvantaged; Homeless.
Type of support: Building/renovation; Equipment; Seed money; Scholarship funds; Technical assistance; Consulting services; Matching/challenge support.
Limitations: Applications accepted. Giving primarily in full support services to Midland and Gladwin counties, MI, and also Clare County through affiliate. No support for sectarian religious programs, basic governmental services, or basic educational functions. No grants for operating budgets, continuing support, annual campaigns or fundraising, normal office equipment, deficit financing, or endowment funds.
Publications: Application guidelines; Annual report; Grants list; Informational brochure; Newsletter.
Application information: Visit foundation web site for application guidelines. Application form required.
Initial approach: Telephone Prog. Off. to discuss project
Copies of proposal: 3
Deadline(s): Jan. 15, Apr. 15, July 15, and Oct. 15
Board meeting date(s): 4th Mon. of every month
Final notification: Early in Mar., June, Sept., and Dec.
Officers and Trustees:* Elizabeth Lumbert,* Chair.; Angela Hine,* Vice-Chair.; Sharon Mortensen,* C.E.O. and Pres.; Kevin Gay,* Treas.; Sam Howard; **Cal Ieuter**; Liz Kapla; Kevin Kendrick; **Craig McDonald**; Dave Ramaker; Mike Rush; **Duncan Stuart**; Beth Swift; Kay Wagner; Kim White.
Number of staff: 4 full-time professional; 1 part-time professional; 2 full-time support.
EIN: 382023395
Other changes: Carole Donaghy, Kevin Gay, and Angela Hine are no longer trustees.

1643
Frances Goll Mills Fund
328 S. Saginaw St., M/C 001065
Flint, MI 48502-1923
***Application address:* c/o First Merit Bank, N.A., Attn.: Helen James, 101 N. Washington Ave., M/C 332021, Saginaw, MI 48607, tel.: (989) 776-7368**

Established in 1982 in MI.
Donor: Frances Goll Mills†.
Foundation type: Independent foundation.
Financial data (yr. ended 09/30/13): Assets, $5,786,465 (M); expenditures, $306,104; qualifying distributions, $266,342; giving activities include $230,000 for 11 grants (high: $50,000; low: $5,000).
Fields of interest: Elementary/secondary education; Higher education; Environmental education; Health care, cost containment; Health care; Employment, vocational rehabilitation; Youth development; Human services; YM/YWCAs & YM/YWHAs; Protestant agencies & churches.
Type of support: General/operating support; Scholarship funds.
Limitations: Applications accepted. Giving limited to MI, with emphasis on Bay City, Midland, and Saginaw. No grants to individuals; no loans.
Publications: Application guidelines.
Application information: Application form required.
Initial approach: Letter or proposal requesting application guidelines
Copies of proposal: 1
Deadline(s): None
Board meeting date(s): 3rd Thurs. of Mar., June, Sept., and Dec.
Trustee: FirstMerit Bank, N.A.
EIN: 382434002

1644
Morley Foundation
(formerly Morley Brothers Foundation)
P.O. Box 2485
Saginaw, MI 48605-2485 (989) 753-3438
***Contact:* David H. Morley, Pres.**
Main URL: http://www.morleyfdn.org/

Incorporated in 1948 in MI.
Donors: Ralph Chase Morley, Sr.†; Mrs. Ralph Chase Morley, Sr.†.
Foundation type: Independent foundation.
Financial data (yr. ended 12/31/12): Assets, $4,217,259 (M); gifts received, $6,970; expenditures, $292,035; qualifying distributions, $218,153; giving activities include $208,533 for grants.
Purpose and activities: Giving primarily in the areas of welfare, health, education, civic improvement,

and the humanities in Michigan, with major emphasis on Saginaw County.
Fields of interest: Museums; Performing arts; Arts; Elementary school/education; Secondary school/education; Higher education; Business school/education; Education; Hospitals (general); Health care; Health organizations, association; Human services; Children/youth, services; Community/economic development.
Type of support: General/operating support; Continuing support; Annual campaigns; Capital campaigns; Building/renovation; Equipment; Emergency funds; Program development; Seed money; Research; Employee matching gifts; Matching/challenge support.
Limitations: Applications accepted. Giving primarily in the greater Saginaw County, MI, area. No grants to individuals, or for endowment funds, deficit financing, land acquisition, renovation projects, publications, or conferences; no loans.
Publications: Application guidelines; Informational brochure.
Application information: Application guidelines available on foundation web site. Application form required.
Initial approach: Letter
Copies of proposal: 1
Board meeting date(s): Feb., May, Aug., and Nov.
Final notification: 3 months
Officers and Trustees:* David H. Morley,* Pres.; Carol Morley Beck,* V.P.; **Peter Morley, Jr.,* Treas.**; Chase Brand; Michael Morley Brand; **Jodona Morley Kinney**; Sara Morley LaCroix; Burrows Morley, Jr.; Christopher Morley; George B. Morley, Jr.; Katharyn Morley; Michael Morley; Peter Morley; Lucy Thomson.
Number of staff: 1 part-time professional.
EIN: 386055569
Other changes: Lois K. Guttowsky is no longer Secy. Peter Morley, Jr. is now Treas. Burrows Morley and Richard B. Thomson are no longer trustees.

1645
Charles Stewart Mott Foundation

Mott Foundation Bldg.
503 S. Saginaw St., Ste. 1200
Flint, MI 48502-1851 (810) 238-5651
FAX: (810) 766-1753; E-mail: info@mott.org; Main URL: http://www.mott.org/
E-Newsletter: http://www.mott.org/about/thefoundation/newslettersubscribe.aspx
Facebook: http://www.facebook.com/mottfoundation
Flint Area Program's Facebook page: http://www.facebook.com/mottfoundationflint
Grants Database: http://www.mott.org/about/searchgrants.aspx
Program News Feeds: http://feeds.feedburner.com/mott/news/General
RSS Grants Feed: http://feeds.feedburner.com/mott/grant/General
Twitter: http://www.twitter.com/mottfoundation
YouTube: http://www.youtube.com/csmottfoundation

Incorporated in 1926 in MI.
Donors: Charles Stewart Mott†; and members of the Mott family.
Foundation type: Independent foundation.
Financial data (yr. ended 12/31/12): Assets, $2,304,865,937 (M); expenditures, $115,910,853; qualifying distributions, $105,379,925; giving activities include $86,439,686 for 1,240 grants, and $1,201,615 for 17 foundation-administered programs.
Purpose and activities: To support efforts that promote a just, equitable and sustainable society with the primary focus on civil society, the environment, the area of Flint, MI and poverty. The foundation makes grants for a variety of purposes within these program areas including: philanthropy and voluntarism; assisting emerging civil societies in Central/Eastern Europe, Russia and South Africa; conservation of fresh water ecosystems in North America; reform of international finance and trade; improving the outcomes for children, youth and families at risk of persistent poverty; education and neighborhood and economic development. The foundation also makes grants to strengthen the capacity of local institutions in its home community of Flint, MI.
Fields of interest: Education; Environment, pollution control; Environment, natural resources; Employment, services; Human services; Children, services; Child development, services; Family services, parent education; Civil rights, race/intergroup relations; Economic development; Urban/community development; Rural development; Community/economic development; Voluntarism promotion; Leadership development; Children/youth; Young adults; Minorities; Economically disadvantaged.
International interests: Ukraine; Eastern Europe; Latin America; Russia; South Africa.
Type of support: General/operating support; Continuing support; Management development/capacity building; Program development; Conferences/seminars; Seed money; Technical assistance; Program evaluation; Program-related investments/loans; Employee matching gifts; Matching/challenge support.
Limitations: Applications accepted. Giving nationally and to emerging countries in Central and Eastern Europe, Russia, and South Africa. No support for religious activities or programs serving specific religious groups or denominations. Faith based organizations may submit inquiries if the project falls within the foundation's guidelines and serves a broad segment of the population. No grants to individuals or for capital development (with the exception of the Flint area and legacy institutions). Grants for research, project replication or endowments are rarely funded unless these activities grow out of work the foundation already supports. No support for local projects, except in the Flint area, unless they are part of a Mott-planned national demonstration or network of grants. Film and video projects, books, scholarships, and fellowships are rarely funded; no loans.
Publications: Annual report (including application guidelines); Financial statement; Occasional report.
Application information: Full proposals by invitation only. Application form not required.
***Initial approach:* Online letter of inquiry**
Deadline(s): None; grants are determined by Aug. 31 of any given year
Board meeting date(s): Mar., June, Sept., and Dec.
Final notification: 60-90 days
Officers and Trustees:* William S. White,* Chair., C.E.O. and Pres.; Frederick S. Kirkpatrick,* Vice-Chair.; Jay C. Flaherty, V.P. and C.I.O.; Neal R. Hegarty, V.P., Progs.; Phillip H. Peters, V.P., Admin. Group and Secy.-Treas.; Gavin T. Clabaugh, V.P., Inf. Svcs.; Kathryn A. Thomas, V.P., Comms.; Ridgway H. White, V.P., Special Projects and Prog. Off., Flint Area; Douglas X. Patino, Tr. Emeritus; A. Marshall Acuff, Jr.; Lizabeth Ardisana; Tiffany W. Lovett; Webb F. Martin; Olivia P. Maynard; John Morning; Maryanne Mott; Charlie Nelms; William H. Piper; Marise M.M. Stewart.
Number of staff: 54 full-time professional; 1 part-time professional; 24 full-time support.
EIN: 381211227
Other changes: Claire M. White is no longer a trustee.

1646
Ruth Mott Foundation

111 E. Court St., Ste. 3C
Flint, MI 48502-1649 (810) 233-0170
Contact: Dolores Ennis, Secy.
FAX: (810) 233-7022;
E-mail: ruthmott@ruthmott.org; Main URL: http://www.ruthmottfoundation.org

Established in 1989 in MI.
Donor: Ruth R. Mott†.
Foundation type: Independent foundation.
Financial data (yr. ended 12/31/12): Assets, $208,154,161 (M); gifts received, $61,685; expenditures, $11,528,471; qualifying distributions, $9,894,598; giving activities include $6,148,440 for 131 grants (high: $500,000; low: $112), and $1,965,242 for 4 foundation-administered programs.
Purpose and activities: The foundation's mission is to advocate, stimulate, and support community vitality. Its commitment is to base the foundation in its home community of Flint, Michigan.
Fields of interest: Arts, cultural/ethnic awareness; Arts; Youth development; Children/youth, services; Community/economic development.
Type of support: Technical assistance; Program evaluation; Program development; Matching/challenge support; Management development/capacity building; General/operating support; Continuing support.
Limitations: Applications accepted. Giving primarily in Genesee County and Flint, MI. No grants to individual scholarships or fellowships, or for capital projects, major equipment, land purchases, deficit financing, endowments, or renovations; no loans.
Publications: Annual report; Annual report (including application guidelines); Grants list; Informational brochure (including application guidelines); Multi-year report; Program policy statement.
Application information: See foundation web site for grant guidelines, and more information. Application form not required.
***Initial approach:* Phone call**
***Deadline(s):* See web site for annual deadlines**
Board meeting date(s): Mar., June, and Nov.
Officers and Trustees:* Maryanne Mott,* Chair.; Harriet Kenworthy,* Vice-Chair.; Cris Doby, Interim Pres.; Dolores Ennis, Secy.; Joseph R. Robinson, Treas.; **Maria Jordan, Dir., Finance**; Gloria Coles; Lawrence E. Moon; Melissa Patterson; Robert Pestronk.
Number of staff: None.
EIN: 382876435
Other changes: The grantmaker now makes its annual report, its annual report (including application guidelines), its grants list and its program policy statement available online.

1647
Mount Pleasant Area Community Foundation

(formerly Mount Pleasant Community Foundation)
306 S. Univ.
P.O. Box 1283
Mount Pleasant, MI 48804-1283 (989) 773-7322
Contact: Amanda Schafer, Exec. Dir.

FAX: (989) 773-1517; E-mail: info@mpacf.org; Main URL: http://www.mpacf.org
Facebook: http://www.facebook.com/MPACF
YouTube: http://www.youtube.com/user/mpareacf

Established in 1990 in MI.
Foundation type: Community foundation.
Financial data (yr. ended 12/31/12): Assets, $12,636,443 (M); gifts received, $715,262; expenditures, $705,715; giving activities include $252,919 for grants, and $66,405 for 65 grants to individuals.
Purpose and activities: The foundation seeks to enhance the quality of life for all citizens of Isabella County, both current and future generations, by holding and attracting permanent, endowed funds from a wide range of donors, addressing needs through grant making, and providing leadership on key community issues.
Fields of interest: Arts; Education, research; Education; Environment; Health care; Recreation; Youth development; Human services; Community development, neighborhood development; Children/youth; Children; Aging; Women; Girls; Adults, women.
Type of support: Consulting services; Management development/capacity building; Building/renovation; Equipment; Land acquisition; Endowments; Emergency funds; Program development; Conferences/seminars; Film/video/radio; Publication; Seed money; Curriculum development; Scholarship funds; Research; Technical assistance; Program evaluation; Scholarships—to individuals; Matching/challenge support; Student loans—to individuals.
Limitations: Applications accepted. Giving limited to Isabella County, MI. No support for the promotion of religious organizations. No grants to individuals (except for scholarships), or for annual operating expenses including salaries, ongoing program support, debt reduction, and travel for groups such as school classes, clubs or sports teams.
Publications: Application guidelines; Annual report; Financial statement; Grants list; Informational brochure; Newsletter; IRS Form 990 or 990-PF printed copy available upon request.
Application information: Visit foundation web site for specific deadline dates, application and guidelines. Incomplete, late and/or faxed proposals will not be accepted. Application form required.
Initial approach: Contact foundation staff
Copies of proposal: 1
***Deadline(s):* Jan. 29, May 28, and Sept. 24 for general grants; Mar. for scholarships**
Board meeting date(s): Bimonthly
Final notification: Within 2 weeks of board meeting
Officers and Trustees:* Jan Strickler,* Pres.; Bob Long,* V.P.; Steve Pung,* Secy.; Terrie Zitzelsberger,* Treas.; Amanda Schafer, Exec. Dir.; **Jay Anders**; Jill Bourland; Bill Chilman; Shirley Martin Decker; Dan Eversole; **Cheryl Gaudard**; Joanne Golden; Dyke Heinze; Shelly Hinck; Chuck Hubscher; Al Kaufmann; Dave Keilitz; Lon Morey; Mary Ann O'Neil; Darcy Orlik; Lynn Pohl; Laura Richards; Nancy Ridley; Donald Schuster; Harold Stegman; Thomas Sullivan; Robert L. Wheeler.
Number of staff: 1 full-time professional; 1 full-time support; 1 part-time support.
EIN: 382951873

1648
Nartel Family Foundation
(formerly Werner and Ruth Nartel Foundation)
141 Harrow Ln., Ste. 1
Saginaw, MI 48638-6093

Foundation type: Independent foundation.
Financial data (yr. ended 06/30/13): Assets, $4,734,849 (M); expenditures, $280,879; qualifying distributions, $280,879; giving activities include $227,017 for 20 grants (high: $66,667; low: $250).
Fields of interest: Museums (history); Breast cancer; Heart & circulatory diseases; Alzheimer's disease; Human services; Children/youth, services; Jewish federated giving programs; Jewish agencies & synagogues.
Type of support: General/operating support.
Limitations: Applications not accepted. Giving primarily in IL and MI. No grants to individuals.
Application information: Contributes only to pre-selected organizations.
Officers: Evelyn Nartelski, Pres. and Treas.; **Kathy Rembowski, V.P.**
Trustees: Timothy Allen; Sherwood DeVisser; Sylvia McCown.
EIN: 382477768
Other changes: Kathy Rembowski is now V.P.

1649
Oleson Foundation
P.O. Box 904
Traverse City, MI 49685-0904
Contact: Kathryn L. Huschke, Exec. Dir.
E-mail: kathy@olesonfoundation.org; Main URL: http://www.olesonfoundation.org

Established in 1959 in MI.
Donors: Don Oleson; Gerald Oleson; Gerald W. Oleson†; Frances M. Oleson†.
Foundation type: Independent foundation.
Financial data (yr. ended 12/31/12): Assets, $16,019,172 (M); gifts received, $3,600; expenditures, $1,520,698; qualifying distributions, $1,017,742; giving activities include $967,484 for 112 grants (high: $100,000; low: $500).
Purpose and activities: The foundation's mission is to help people help themselves achieve the greatest good for the greatest number efficiently over a broad range of social and environmental interests.
Fields of interest: Historic preservation/historical societies; Elementary/secondary education; Higher education; Environment; Health care; Youth development, centers/clubs; Human services; United Ways and Federated Giving Programs; Christian agencies & churches.
Type of support: General/operating support; Continuing support; Annual campaigns; Capital campaigns; Building/renovation; Equipment; Land acquisition; Curriculum development; Technical assistance; Matching/challenge support.
Limitations: Applications accepted. **Giving limited to the Lower Peninsula region in northwestern MI, mainly the counties of Benzie, Emmet, Grand Traverse, and Manistee. No grants to individuals, or for endowments or scholarships.**
Application information: Application form required.
***Initial approach:* Use forms on foundation web site**
Copies of proposal: 1
Deadline(s): Apr. 1
Board meeting date(s): June
***Final notification:* Usually in mid-June**
Officers and Directors:* Donald W. Oleson,* Pres.; Gerald E. Oleson,* V.P.; Richard Ford,* Secy.-Treas.; Kathryn Wise Huschke, Exec. Dir.; John Tobin.
Number of staff: 1 part-time professional.
EIN: 386083080

1650
Onequest Foundation
(formerly Jack and Mary DeWitt Family Foundation)
205 Norwood Dr.
Holland, MI 49424-2730

Established in 1992 in MI.
Donors: Jack L. DeWitt; Jacqueline Curtis; Linda E. Berghorst; Laurie S. Wierda; Mary DeWitt; Jim DeWitt; Lyne DeWitt; Kyle Curtis; Jackie Curtis; Steve DeWitt; Melissa DeWitt; Ryan Berghorst.
Foundation type: Independent foundation.
Financial data (yr. ended 12/31/12): Assets, $1,049,693 (M); gifts received, $29,065; expenditures, $510,030; qualifying distributions, $353,691; giving activities include $341,000 for 42 grants (high: $60,500; low: $500).
Purpose and activities: Giving primarily for education, human services, and Christian agencies and churches.
Fields of interest: Higher education; Human services; Family services; Philanthropy/voluntarism; Christian agencies & churches.
Type of support: Annual campaigns.
Limitations: Applications not accepted. Giving primarily in MI. No grants to individuals.
Application information: Unsolicited requests for funds not accepted.
Officers: Jack L. DeWitt, Pres. and Treas.; Mary E. DeWitt, V.P. and Secy.
Directors: Linda Ellen Berghorst; Jacqueline DeWitt Curtiss; James Russell DeWitt; Steven Lee DeWitt; Laurie Sue Wierda.
EIN: 383080740

1651
Rose and Lawrence C. Page, Sr. Family Charitable Foundation
(formerly Lawrence C. Page, Sr. Family Charitable Foundation)
c/o Mr. David C. Stone, Bodman LLP
201 W. Big Beaver, Ste. 500
Troy, MI 48084-4160

Established in 2007 in MI.
Donors: Lawrence C. Page, Sr.; L.C. Page Char Tr f/b/o Page Fam Char.
Foundation type: Independent foundation.
Financial data (yr. ended 12/31/12): Assets, $3,889,936 (M); expenditures, $264,459; qualifying distributions, $186,842; giving activities include $184,000 for 14 grants (high: $50,000; low: $4,000).
Fields of interest: Elementary/secondary education; Human services.
Limitations: Applications not accepted. Giving primarily in MI.
Application information: Unsolicited requests for funds not accepted.
Directors: Marlene Holly Kunick; Michael N. Rice; David Stone.
EIN: 260367507

1652
Pardee Cancer Treatment Fund of Bay County
c/o County Michigan
P.O. Box 541
Bay City, MI 48707-0541 (989) 891-8815
Contact: Carol Wells

Classified as a private operating foundation in 1991.
Donor: Elsa U. Pardee Foundation.
Foundation type: Operating foundation.
Financial data (yr. ended 09/30/13): Assets, $0 (M); gifts received, $164,581; expenditures, $203,082; qualifying distributions, $186,276; giving activities include $186,276 for grants.
Purpose and activities: Financial assistance provided to help pay medical bills of cancer patients who are residents of Bay County, Michigan.
Fields of interest: Health care.
Type of support: Grants to individuals.
Limitations: Applications accepted. Giving limited to residents of Bay County, MI.
Publications: Annual report.
Application information: Application form required.
Initial approach: Letter
Deadline(s): None
Board meeting date(s): Varies
Officers: Pastor Andreas Teich, Pres.; George Heron, V.P.; Dennis R. Geno, Secy.; **Walter G. Szostak, Treas.**
Directors: Kim Bejcek; Aaron Madzior; Cathleen Schell; Richard Steele; Carol VanderHarst.
Number of staff: 1 part-time professional.
EIN: 382877951

1653
Elsa U. Pardee Foundation
P.O. Box 2767
Midland, MI 48641-2767
Contact: James A. Kendall, Secy.
***E-mail:* kmcdonald@pardeefoundation.org**; Main URL: http://www.pardeefoundation.org

Incorporated in 1944 in MI.
Donor: Elsa U. Pardee†.
Foundation type: Independent foundation.
Financial data (yr. ended 12/31/12): Assets, $81,950,984 (M); expenditures, $3,964,022; qualifying distributions, $3,334,277; giving activities include $3,334,277 for 20 grants (high: $419,937; low: $7,200).
Purpose and activities: Giving primarily to support: 1) research programs directed toward discovering new approaches for cancer treatment and cure; and 2) financial support for cancer treatment.
Fields of interest: Cancer; Medical research, institute; Cancer research.
Type of support: Research.
Limitations: Applications accepted. Giving on a national basis. No grants to individuals, or for capital campaigns, building, or endowment funds, equipment (except when used in a specific project), scholarships, fellowships, general purposes, matching gifts, or fundraising campaigns; no loans.
Publications: Application guidelines; Annual report.
Application information: Application form not required.
Initial approach: Use online application on foundation web site
***Deadline(s):* See foundation web site for deadline information**
Board meeting date(s): 3 times per year
Final notification: 4 to 6 months
Officers and Trustees:* Gail E. Lanphear,* Pres.; Lisa J. Gerstacker,* V.P.; Mary M. Neely, Secy.; Alan W. Ott,* Treas.; W. James Allen; Laurie G. Bouwman; William C. Lauderbach; William D. Schuette; Michael Woolhiser.
Number of staff: 1 part-time support.
EIN: 386065799

1654
Suzanne Upjohn Delano Parish Foundation
(formerly Suzanne D. Parish Foundation)
211 S. Rose St.
Kalamazoo, MI 49007-4713
Contact: Ronald N. Kilgore, V.P.

Established in MI.
Donors: Suzanne U.D. Parish; Suzanne U.D. Parish Irrevocable Trust.
Foundation type: Independent foundation.
Financial data (yr. ended 12/31/12): Assets, $3,914,994 (M); gifts received, $36,819,900; expenditures, $37,770,942; qualifying distributions, $37,735,717; giving activities include $37,725,000 for 7 grants (high: $35,000,000; low: $10,000).
Purpose and activities: Support primarily to an aviation history museum.
Fields of interest: Museums (history); Space/aviation.
Type of support: General/operating support.
Limitations: Applications not accepted. Giving primarily in Portage and Kalamazoo, MI. No grants to individuals; no loans.
Application information: Contributes only to pre-selected organizations.
Officers and Directors:* Katharine P. Miller,* Pres.; P. William Parish,* V.P.; Preston L. Parish,* V.P.; Ronald N. Kilgore,* Secy.-Treas.
EIN: 382484268
Other changes: At the close of 2012, the grantmaker paid grants of $37,725,000, a 1,995.8% increase over the 2010 disbursements, $1,800,000.

1655
Perrigo Company Charitable Foundation
515 Eastern Ave.
Allegan, MI 49010-9070
***E-mail:* perrigofoundation@perrigo.com; Main URL: http://www.perrigo.com/**

Established in 2000 in MI.
Donor: Perrigo Co.
Foundation type: Company-sponsored foundation.
Financial data (yr. ended 06/30/13): Assets, $902,408 (M); gifts received, $1,758,550; expenditures, $1,777,004; qualifying distributions, $1,731,620; giving activities include $1,185,597 for 174+ grants (high: $75,000).
Purpose and activities: The foundation supports organizations involved with arts and culture, education, health, substance abuse prevention, cancer, and human services.
Fields of interest: Arts; Higher education; Education; Hospitals (general); Health care; Substance abuse, prevention; Cancer; Boy scouts; Girl scouts; American Red Cross; Developmentally disabled, centers & services; Homeless, human services; Human services; United Ways and Federated Giving Programs.
Type of support: Scholarship funds; General/operating support; Building/renovation; Program development.
Limitations: Applications accepted. Giving primarily in areas of company operations in MI. No grants to individuals.
Application information: Application form required.
***Initial approach:* Online application form**
Deadline(s): None
Officers and Directors:* Joseph C. Papa,* Pres.; **Judy L. Brown,* Exec. V.P.**; John T. Hendrickson,* Exec. V.P.; **Scott R. Rush, V.P.**; Todd W. Kingma,* Secy.; Ronald L. Winowiecki, Treas.; Michael R. Stewart.
EIN: 383553518
Other changes: The grantmaker no longer lists a phone. The grantmaker no longer lists a primary contact.
At the close of 2013, the grantmaker paid grants of $1,731,620, a 104.3% increase over the 2012 disbursements, $847,502.
Judy L. Brown has replaced Douglas R. Schrank as Exec. V.P.

1656
Petoskey-Harbor Springs Area Community Foundation
616 Petoskey St., Ste. 203
Petoskey, MI 49770-2779 (231) 348-5820
Contact: David L. Jones, Exec. Dir.; For grants: Sara Ward, Prog. Off.
FAX: (231) 348-5883; E-mail: info@phsacf.org; Additional e-mails: djones@phsacf.org, lwendland@phsacf.org and sward@phsacf.org; Main URL: http://www.phsacf.org
Facebook: https://www.facebook.com/PetoskeyHarborSpringsAreaCommunityFoundation
Application inquiry e-mail: sward@phsacf.org

Established in 1991 in MI.
Foundation type: Community foundation.
Financial data (yr. ended 03/31/13): Assets, $30,871,261 (M); gifts received, $1,058,283; expenditures, $1,221,070; giving activities include $822,213 for 41+ grants (high: $85,000), and $29,544 for 21 grants to individuals.
Purpose and activities: The foundation's to improve the quality of life for all people in Emmet County, by: 1) connecting donors with community needs; 2) building a permanent source of charitable funds to serve our area; 3) addressing a broad range of community issues through innovative grantmaking; 4) championing philanthropy and active citizenship.
Fields of interest: Historic preservation/historical societies; Arts; Higher education; Education; Environment; Health care; Agriculture/food; Recreation; Youth development; Human services; Economic development; Community/economic development.
Type of support: Building/renovation; Equipment; Program development; Seed money; Scholarship funds; Technical assistance; Scholarships—to individuals; Matching/challenge support.
Limitations: Applications accepted. Giving limited to Emmet County, MI. No support for sectarian religious purposes. No grants to individuals (except for scholarships), or for endowments, debt reduction, annual fundraising drives, operational phases of established programs, conferences, travel, or scholarly research; no loans.
Publications: Application guidelines; Annual report; Financial statement; Grants list; Informational brochure.
Application information: Potential applicants must contact the foundation prior to submitting an application to discuss their project. Visit foundation web site for application information. Application form required.
Initial approach: Telephone
Copies of proposal: 30
Deadline(s): Mar. 1 and Oct. 1
Board meeting date(s): Monthly
Final notification: Approx. 2 months
Officers and Directors:* Charles H. Gano,* Pres.; Lisa G. Blanchard,* V.P.; Mike Eberhart,* Secy.; Todd Winnell,* Treas.; David L. Jones, Exec. Dir.; Robert W. Charlton; J. Wilfred Cwikiel; Jennifer E. Deegan; Kathy Erber; Michael J. FitzSimons; James

W. Ford; Ann K. Irish; Hon. Charles W. Johnson; Kelsey L. Nuorala; Jill O'Neill; B. Thomas Smith.
Number of staff: 3 full-time professional; 1 part-time professional.
EIN: 383032185
Other changes: Laurissa Wendland is now Finance and Opers. Off. Valerie Wilson is now Admin. Off. Ellen Lively and Virginia B. McCoy are no longer directors.

1657
The Pokagon Fund, Inc.

821 E. Buffalo St.
New Buffalo, MI 49117-1522 (269) 469-9322
Contact: Mary L. Dunbar, Exec. Dir.
E-mail: info@pokagonfund.org; E-mail address for applications: grants@pokagonfund.org; Main URL: http://www.pokagonfund.org/
Facebook: http://www.facebook.com/pages/the-pokagon-fund/123810620966970
Grants List: http://www.pokagonfund.org/Grants.asp
E-mail address for scholarships: scholarships@pokagonfund.org

Established in 2007 in MI.
Donor: Four Winds Casino Resort.
Foundation type: Company-sponsored foundation.
Financial data (yr. ended 06/30/13): Assets, $8,859,236 (M); gifts received, $2,376,667; expenditures, $3,774,758; qualifying distributions, $3,726,854; giving activities include $3,455,074 for 190 grants (high: $500,000; low: $450).
Purpose and activities: The fund supports programs designed to enhance the lives of residents in the New Buffalo, Michigan, region and the communities where the Pokagon Band of Potawatomi Indians own land. Special emphasis is directed toward arts and culture, education, the environment, health, recreation, and human services.
Fields of interest: Performing arts; Arts; Libraries (public); Education, reading; Education; Environment, recycling; Environment, land resources; Environment; Health care; Food services; Food banks; Recreation, camps; Recreation, parks/playgrounds; Recreation, fairs/festivals; Recreation; Residential/custodial care, hospices; Human services; Community/economic development; Native Americans/American Indians.
Type of support: General/operating support; Continuing support; Management development/capacity building; Building/renovation; Equipment; Land acquisition; Emergency funds; Program development; Conferences/seminars; Film/video/radio; Curriculum development; Scholarship funds; Research; Consulting services; Program-related investments/loans; Scholarships—to individuals; Matching/challenge support.
Limitations: Applications accepted. Giving in primarily in New Buffalo, MI, region, including the townships of Chikaming, Grand Beach, Michiana, and Three Oaks; some giving also in South Bend, IN, and Dowagia and Hartford MI. No support for political candidates, political advocacy, or religious organizations not of direct benefit to the entire community. No grants to individuals (except for scholarships), or for endowments.
Publications: Application guidelines; Annual report (including application guidelines); Grants list; IRS Form 990 or 990-PF printed copy available upon request.
Application information: The foundation supports municipalities, nonprofit organizations, and charities in areas where the Pokagon Band of Potawatomi Indians are located, and other organizations. An application form is available for each type of organization. Application form required.
Initial approach: Complete online application
***Deadline(s):* 90 days prior to need; Mar. 19 for high school scholarships; Mar. 31 for adult scholarships**
Board meeting date(s): Second Thurs. of each month
Final notification: Within 90 days; May for scholarships
Officers and Directors:* Roger Radar,* Chair.; Robert Carpenter,* Vice-Chair; Viki Gudas,* Secy.; **Robert Gow, Treas.**; Mary L. Dunbar, Exec. Dir.; Ryan Fellows; Marie Manley.
Number of staff: 1 full-time professional; 1 full-time support.
EIN: 300130499
Other changes: Roger Radar has replaced Rose Dudiak as Chair. Robert Gow has replaced Michaelina Magnuson as Treas.
Vickie Wagner and Alice Overly are no longer directors. Rose Dudiak is no longer Chair. Michaelina Magnuson is no longer Treas.
The grantmaker now makes its grants list available online.

1658
Edgar and Elsa Prince Foundation

(formerly Prince Foundation)
190 River Ave., Ste. 300
Holland, MI 49423-2825

Established in 1977.
Donors: Edgar D. Prince‡; Elsa D. Prince; Prince Corp.; Elsa D. Prince Living Trust; Prince Charitable Remainder Unitrust.
Foundation type: Independent foundation.
Financial data (yr. ended 06/30/13): Assets, $34,973,049 (M); gifts received, $18,999,889; expenditures, $4,929,604; qualifying distributions, $4,748,470; giving activities include $4,740,000 for 146 grants (high: $700,000; low: $1,000).
Purpose and activities: Giving to Christian organizations, churches, and schools and community activities.
Fields of interest: Elementary/secondary education; Health organizations, association; Family services; Aging, centers/services; Community development, neighborhood development; Christian agencies & churches; Aging.
Type of support: General/operating support.
Limitations: Applications not accepted. Giving primarily in MI. No grants to individuals.
Application information: Contributes only to pre-selected organizations.
Officers: Elsa D. Prince Brokehuizen, Pres.; Elisabeth DeVos, V.P.; Eileen Ellens, V.P.; Erik D. Prince, V.P.; Emilie Wierda, V.P.; Robert Haveman, Secy.-Treas.
EIN: 382190330
Other changes: For the fiscal year ended June 30, 2013, the fair market value of the grantmaker's assets was $34,973,049, a 149.4% increase over the fiscal 2012 value, $14,022,831.

1659
RNR Foundation, Inc.

2212 Old Falls Dr.
Ann Arbor, MI **48103**

Established in 1994 in FL.
Donor: Rhoda Newberry Reed.
Foundation type: Independent foundation.
Financial data (yr. ended 07/31/13): Assets, $5,973,807 (M); expenditures, $729,852; qualifying distributions, $661,314; giving activities include $574,779 for 9 grants (high: $208,668; low: $290).
Purpose and activities: Giving primarily for education, human services, community foundations, and health care programs, particularly a foundation's clinical nurse program.
Fields of interest: Higher education; Health care; Human services; Foundations (public); Foundations (community); Leadership development.
Limitations: Applications not accepted. Giving primarily in FL and MI. No grants to individuals.
Application information: Contributes only to pre-selected organizations.
Officers: David Lord, Pres.; Charles Lord, V.P.; Edith Lord-Wolff, Secy.; Richard Lord, Treas.
Director: Heather Lord.
EIN: 650539370
Other changes: The grantmaker no longer lists a phone.

1660
Roscommon County Community Foundation

701 Lake St.
P.O. Box 824
Roscommon, MI 48653 (989) 275-3112
Contact: Mary Fry, Pres. and C.E.O.
FAX: (989) 275-3112; E-mail: rococofo@yahoo.com; Main URL: http://www.roscommoncountycommunityfoundation.org
Facebook: https://www.facebook.com/myrccf
RSS Feed: http://myrccf.org/feed/

Established in 1997 as an affiliate of NCMCF; recognized as an independent community foundation in 2001.
Donors: Rex Gillen‡; Arlene Gillen‡.
Foundation type: Community foundation.
Financial data (yr. ended 12/31/12): Assets, $6,189,935 (M); gifts received, $451,511; expenditures, $313,659; giving activities include $19,792 for grants, and $118,419 for 50 grants to individuals.
Purpose and activities: The foundation seeks to improve the quality of life for all present and future residents of Roscommon County by: 1) providing stewardship and leadership; 2) attracting and holding permanent endowment funds from a wide range of donors; and 3) by making grants of the income from its permanent endowment funds. The foundation is committed to protecting the personal investments that all residents have made, demonstrating concern for youth and many issues affecting their future, recognizing the value and importance of the natural environment now and for the future, and improving and building the future for families.
Fields of interest: Arts, public education; Arts education; Education, formal/general education; Child development, education; Adult education—literacy, basic skills & GED; Education, community/cooperative; Education; Animals/wildlife, single organization support; Animals/wildlife, public education; Animals/wildlife, volunteer services; Animals/wildlife, formal/general education; Animal welfare; Animals/wildlife, special services; Animals/wildlife; AIDS; AIDS research; Crime/law enforcement, management/technical assistance; Crime/law enforcement, single organization support; Crime/law enforcement, public education; Crime/law enforcement, government agencies; Crime/law enforcement, formal/general education; Crime/law enforcement, missing persons; Crime/

law enforcement, police agencies; Crime/law enforcement; Agriculture/food, single organization support; Agriculture/food, public education; Agriculture/food, government agencies; Disasters, search/rescue; Athletics/sports, training; Athletics/sports, school programs; Athletics/sports, basketball; Athletics/sports, baseball; Athletics/sports, soccer; Athletics/sports, football; Athletics/sports, golf; Boy scouts; American Red Cross; Children/youth, services; Children, day care; Children, services; Community/economic development, single organization support; Community development, women's clubs; Christian agencies & churches.
Type of support: Endowments; Scholarship funds.
Limitations: Applications accepted. Giving limited to Roscommon County, MI. No support for religious or for-profit organizations. **No grants to individuals (except for scholarships).**
Publications: Application guidelines; Annual report; Annual report (including application guidelines); Financial statement; Grants list; Informational brochure; Newsletter.
Application information: Visit foundation web site for application cover sheet and guidelines. Application form required.
Initial approach: Submit application
***Copies of proposal:* 8**
Deadline(s): Apr. 30 and Oct. 31
Board meeting date(s): Varies
Final notification: 2 months
Officers and Trustees:* Ron Duquette,* Chair.; Tim Scherer,* Vice-Chair.; Mary Fry,* C.E.O. and Pres.; Susan Tyer,* Secy.; John Sinnaeve,* Treas.; Tom Richardson,* C.F.O.; Suzanne Luck, Exec. Dir.; Dave Harned; Matt Jernigan; Sonia Lake; Kathleen Lawrence, Jr.; Tom Moreau; Greg Rogers.
Number of staff: 1 full-time professional; 2 part-time support.
EIN: 383612480

1661
May Mitchell Royal Foundation
P.O. Box 75000, MC 7874
Detroit, MI 48275-7874
Application address: c/o Susan Hartley, 45 W. 74th St., New York, NY 10023-4725, tel.: (917) 612-2756

Established in 1981 in MI.
Donor: May Mitchell Royal Trust.
Foundation type: Independent foundation.
Financial data (yr. ended 09/30/13): Assets, $2,297,486 (M); expenditures, $139,866; qualifying distributions, $107,400; giving activities include $98,000 for 5 grants (high: $25,000; low: $12,500).
Purpose and activities: Giving for the research and treatment of cancer, vision, and heart disease; support also for hospital equipment and nursing training.
Fields of interest: Health care; Health organizations; Medical research.
Type of support: General/operating support; Equipment; Scholarship funds; Research.
Limitations: Applications accepted. Giving limited to FL, HI, and MI. No grants to individuals.
Application information: Application form required.
Initial approach: Letter
Deadline(s): May 30
Officer: Susan J. Hartley, Chair.
Committee Members: Breann Kennerly; Michael Kennerly; **Ross Kennerly**; Jim Lucius.
Trustee: Comerica Bank, N.A.
EIN: 382387140

1662
Saginaw Community Foundation
1 Tuscola, Ste. 100
Saginaw, MI 48607-1282 (989) 755-0545
Contact: Renee S. Johnston, C.E.O.
FAX: (989) 755-6524;
E-mail: info@saginawfoundation.org; Main URL: http://www.saginawfoundation.org
Facebook: http://www.facebook.com/pages/Saginaw-MI/Saginaw-Community-Foundation/59408999148
Twitter: http://twitter.com/SCFoundation

Incorporated in 1984 in MI.
Foundation type: Community foundation.
Financial data (yr. ended 12/31/12): Assets, $41,787,699 (M); gifts received, $1,947,649; expenditures, $3,550,088; giving activities include $712,351 for grants, and $334,592 for grants to individuals.
Purpose and activities: Support for projects not currently being served by existing community resources and for projects providing leverage for generating other funds and community resources.
Fields of interest: Arts; Education; Environment; Health care; Recreation; Family services; Human services; Economic development; Community/economic development; General charitable giving; Youth; Aging.
Type of support: Building/renovation; Equipment; Emergency funds; Program development; Publication; Seed money; Scholarship funds; Technical assistance; Scholarships—to individuals; Matching/challenge support.
Limitations: Applications accepted. Giving limited to Saginaw County, MI. No support for churches or sectarian religious programs. No grants to individuals (except for designated scholarship funds), or for operating budgets, endowment campaigns, debt reduction, travel, or basic municipal or educational services; generally no multi-year grants.
Publications: Application guidelines; Annual report (including application guidelines); Newsletter; Occasional report.
Application information: Visit foundation web site for application cover form and guidelines. Application form required.
Initial approach: Telephone
Copies of proposal: 1
Deadline(s): Feb. 1, May 1, Aug. 1 and Nov. 1
Board meeting date(s): Monthly
Final notification: 2 months after deadline
Officers and Directors:* David J. Abbs,* Chair.; Heidi A. Bolger,* Vice-Chair.; Renee Johnston,* C.E.O. and Pres.; Smallwood Holoman,* Secy.; Frederick C. Gardner,* Treas.; Bridget Smith,* Asst. Treas.; Andre Buckley; Paul Chaffee; Desmon Daniel, Ph.D.; James Fabiano II; Victor Gomez; Todd Gregory; Dr. Carlton Jenkins; Shari Kennett; Dr. John Kosanovich; Trish Luplow; Leslie Orozco; Francine Rifkin; Cheri Sammis; Kari Shaheen; John Shelton; Richard Syrek; Laura Yockey.
Number of staff: 4 full-time professional; 2 full-time support.
EIN: 382474297
Other changes: Brian Jackson is no longer V.P., Donor Rels. and Devel.

1663
Sanilac County Community Foundation
47 Austin St.
P.O. Box 307
Sandusky, MI 48471-0307 (810) 648-3634
Contact: Joan Nagelkirk, Exec. Dir.
FAX: (810) 648-4418;
E-mail: director@sanilaccountycommunityfoundation.org; Additional e-mail: joan@clearideas.biz; Main URL: http://www.sanilaccountycommunityfoundation.org
Facebook: https://www.facebook.com/sanilacgives
Google Plus: https://plus.google.com/107478376549568362154/posts
Instagram: http://instagram.com/sanilacgives
Pinterest: http://www.pinterest.com/sanilacgives/
Twitter: https://twitter.com/sanilacgives

Established in 1994 in MI.
Foundation type: Community foundation.
Financial data (yr. ended 12/31/11): Assets, $3,631,077 (M); gifts received, $82,858; expenditures, $273,209; giving activities include $114,410 for 4+ grants (high: $54,645), and $58,489 for 80 grants to individuals.
Purpose and activities: The foundation holds a collection of endowed funds, contributed by many individuals, corporations, private foundations and government agencies to benefit the Sanilac County, MI, area.
Fields of interest: Arts; Education; Environment; Health care; Recreation; Youth development; Children/youth, services; Human services; Community/economic development; United Ways and Federated Giving Programs; Infants/toddlers; Children/youth; Children; Youth; Adults; Aging; Young adults; Disabilities, people with; Physically disabled; Blind/visually impaired; Deaf/hearing impaired; Mentally disabled; Minorities; African Americans/Blacks; Indigenous peoples; Women; Infants/toddlers, female; Girls; Adults, women; Young adults, female; Men; Infants/toddlers, male; Boys; Adults, men; Young adults, male; Substance abusers; Single parents; Crime/abuse victims; Economically disadvantaged; Homeless.
Type of support: Technical assistance; Seed money; Program development; Film/video/radio; Equipment; Emergency funds; Curriculum development; Continuing support; Building/renovation; Annual campaigns.
Limitations: Applications accepted. Giving limited to Sanilac County, MI. No support for religious or sectarian purposes. No support for loans.
Publications: Annual report; Financial statement; Grants list; Informational brochure; Informational brochure (including application guidelines); Program policy statement.
Application information: Visit foundation web site for application information. An application form for grants of $5,000 or less is available online. Application form required.
Initial approach: Telephone
Copies of proposal: 12
Deadline(s): May 1 and Nov. 1
Board meeting date(s): 3rd Tues. of every month
Final notification: May 30 or Nov. 30
Officers and Board Members:* Linda Kelke,* Co-Chair.; Bill Sarkella,* Co-Chair.; Ed Gamache,* Vice-Chair.; Susan Dreyer,* Secy.; Joe Nartker,* Treas.; Joan Nagelkirk,* Exec. Dir.; Judy Albrecht; Bob Armstrong; Curt Backus; Robert Barnes; Louise Blasius; Henry Buxton; Steve Coffelt; Paul Cowley; Sharon Danek; Roger Dean; Katie Dunn; Judy Ferguson; David Hearsch; Duane Lange; Gary Macklem; Bill Monroe; Paul Muxlow; Tricia Muxlow; Dorothy Ross; Erica Sheridan; Dave Tubbs; Sandy Willis.
EIN: 383204484

1664
The Art and Mary Schmuckal Family Foundation
6004 E. Gallivan Rd.
Cedar, MI **49621 (231) 935-1470**
***Contact:* Evelyn K. Richardson, Secy.**

Established in 1999 in MI.
Donors: Arthur M. Schmuckal; Schmuckal Land Co.
Foundation type: Independent foundation.
Financial data (yr. ended 06/30/13): Assets, $5,191,641 (M); gifts received, $316,749; expenditures, $312,510; qualifying distributions, $254,709; giving activities include $251,700 for 25 grants (high: $50,000; low: $1,000).
Purpose and activities: Giving primarily to enhance the well-being of children, to strengthen the residents economically, and for community development.
Fields of interest: Theological school/education; Medical care, community health systems; Human services; YM/YWCAs & YM/YWHAs; Residential/custodial care, hospices; Community/economic development; Foundations (community); Children; Homeless.
Type of support: Annual campaigns; Capital campaigns; Program development; Scholarship funds.
Limitations: Applications accepted. Giving primarily in Traverse City, MI.
Application information: Application form required.
Initial approach: Letter
Deadline(s): None
Officers: Barbara F. Benson, Pres.; Donald A. Schmuckal, V.P.; Evelyn K. Richardson, Secy.; Paul M. Schmuckal, Treas.
Directors: Andrew Benson; **Jacob Richardson**; Kevin P. Schmuckal.
EIN: 383498264
Other changes: Barbara F. Benson has replaced Arthur M. Schmuckal as Pres.

1665
Bill and Vi Sigmund Foundation
P.O. Box 1128
Jackson, MI 49204-1128 (517) 784-5464
Contact: Carolyn M. Pratt, Secy.
E-mail: sigmundfoundation@sbcglobal.net; Main URL: http://www.sigmundfoundation.org

Established in 2002 in MI.
Foundation type: Independent foundation.
Financial data (yr. ended 12/31/12): Assets, $10,287,234 (M); expenditures, $648,514; qualifying distributions, $591,193; giving activities include $250,300 for grants, and $337,125 for grants to individuals.
Purpose and activities: Scholarships primarily awarded to students majoring in the medical and aviation fields who are residents of Jackson or Lenawee County, Michigan; have been acceptance to an accredited college or university; have proof of financial need; have a cumulative grade point average of 2.5 or higher; and who have completed the Free Application for Federal Student Aid (FAFSA).
Fields of interest: Salvation Army; United Ways and Federated Giving Programs.
Type of support: Scholarships—to individuals.
Limitations: Applications accepted. **Giving limited to Jackson and Lenawee Counties, MI.**
Publications: Application guidelines; Grants list.
Application information: Letter of intent and application form available on foundation web site.
***Initial approach:* For grants submit a letter of intent; for scholarships submit an application**
***Deadline(s):* See foundation web site for current deadlines**
Officers and Directors:* Ralph L. Bodman, Pres.; Carolyn M. Pratt, Secy.; Charles C. McClafferty,* Treas.; Kenneth A. Dillon; John Macchia; Kent Mauer.
EIN: 300002491
Other changes: Ralph L. Bodman is now Pres.
The grantmaker now publishes application guidelines.

1666
The Skillman Foundation
100 Talon Centre Dr., Ste. 100
Detroit, MI 48207-4266 (313) 393-1185
***Contact:* Suzanne Moran, Grants Mgr.**
FAX: (313) 393-1187;
E-mail: mailbox@skillman.org; Main URL: http://www.skillman.org
A Rose for Detroit Blog: http://skillman.org/News-and-Events/A-Rose-for-Detroit-Blog
E-Newsletter: http://www.skillman.org/newsletter/
Facebook: http://www.facebook.com/pages/The-Skillman-Foundation/83980402909
Grants Database: http://www.skillman.org/browse-grants/
Multimedia: http://www.skillman.org/news-events/multimedia/
Skillman News: http://www.skillman.org/rss/news.xml
The Skillman Foundation's Philanthropy Promise: http://www.ncrp.org/philanthropys-promise/who
Twitter: http://twitter.com/skillmanfound
YouTube: http://www.youtube.com/skillmanfoundation

Incorporated in 1960 in MI.
Donor: Rose P. Skillman†.
Foundation type: Independent foundation.
Financial data (yr. ended 12/31/12): Assets, $438,399,476 (M); gifts received, $300,000; expenditures, $24,758,554; qualifying distributions, $21,283,292; giving activities include $16,366,730 for 217 grants (high: $500,000; low: $150), and $546,851 for 215 employee matching gifts.
Purpose and activities: The foundation is a resource for improving the lives of children in metropolitan Detroit, MI. Children in disadvantaged situations are of special concern. The foundation applies its resources to foster positive relationships between children and adults, support high quality learning opportunities and strengthen healthy, safe and supportive homes and communities.
Fields of interest: Visual arts; Performing arts; Arts; Education, early childhood education; Child development, education; Education, reading; Education; Health care; Substance abuse, services; Crime/violence prevention, youth; Food services; Recreation; Human services; Children/youth, services; Child development, services; Family services; Homeless, human services; Children/youth; Children; Youth; Economically disadvantaged; Homeless.
Type of support: Continuing support; General/operating support; Program development; Program-related investments/loans; Employee matching gifts.
Limitations: Applications accepted. Giving primarily in metropolitan Detroit, with emphasis on six neighborhoods in the city of Detroit. No support for long-term projects not being aided by other sources, sectarian religious activities, political lobbying or legislative activities, or new organizations which do not have an operational and financial history. The foundation does not make grants to organizations that had public support and revenues of less than $100,000 for the preceding year. No grants to individuals, or for endowment funds, annual campaigns, purchase, construct or renovate facilities, basic research or deficit financing.
Publications: Application guidelines; Annual report; Informational brochure (including application guidelines); Newsletter; Occasional report; Program policy statement.
Application information: Complete online Grant Inquiry for new applicants. Previous grantees should contact their program officer before starting application process. Application form required.
Initial approach: Online application process
Deadline(s): For new inquiries, 2 months prior to trustee meeting date
Board meeting date(s): March, June, Sept. and Dec.
Final notification: 6 weeks after board meeting
Officers and Trustees:* Lizabeth Ardisana,* Chair.; Herman B. Gray, M.D.*, Vice-Chair.; **Tonya Allen, C.E.O. and Pres.**; Danielle Olekszyk, V.P., Opers. and C.F.O.; Kristen McDonald, V.P., Programs; Chris Uhl, V.P., Social Innovation; David Baker Lewis; Stephen E. Ewing; Denise Ilitch; Mary L. Kramer; Amyre Makupson; Eddie R. Munson; Jerry Norcia.
Number of staff: 20 full-time professional; 5 full-time support.
EIN: 381675780
Other changes: Tonya Allen has replaced Carol A. Gross as C.E.O. and Pres.
Edsel B. Ford is no longer a trustee.

1667
Steelcase Foundation
P.O. Box 1967, GH-4E
Grand Rapids, MI 49501-1967
Contact: Phyllis Gebben, Donations Coord.
FAX: (616) 475-2200;
E-mail: pgebben@steelcase.com; Main URL: http://www.steelcase.com/en/company/who/steelcase-foundation/pages/steelcasefoundation.aspx
Grants List: http://www.steelcase.com/en/Company/Who/Steelcase-Foundation/Documents/2014%20Second%20Quarter%20Grant%20Awards.pdf

Established in 1951 in MI.
Donor: Steelcase Inc.
Foundation type: Company-sponsored foundation.
Financial data (yr. ended 11/30/13): Assets, $97,773,053 (M); gifts received, $516,100; expenditures, $5,509,752; qualifying distributions, $4,037,425; giving activities include $3,531,757 for 59 grants (high: $400,000; low: $176), and $485,668 for 824 employee matching gifts.
Purpose and activities: The foundation supports organizations involved with arts and culture, education, the environment, health, human services, and community development. Special emphasis is directed toward programs designed to assist youth, the elderly, people with disabilities, and economically disadvantaged people.
Fields of interest: Arts; Education, early childhood education; Libraries (public); Education; Environment; Health care; Homeless, human services; Human services; Economic development; Community/economic development; Youth; Aging; Disabilities, people with; Economically disadvantaged.
Type of support: General/operating support; Management development/capacity building;

Capital campaigns; Building/renovation; Equipment; Program development; Seed money; Scholarship funds; Employee matching gifts; Employee-related scholarships.
Limitations: Applications accepted. Giving limited to areas of company operations, with emphasis on Athens, AL and Grand Rapids, MI. No support for churches or religious organizations not of direct benefit to the entire community, or discriminatory organizations. No grants to individuals (except for employee-related scholarships), or for endowments or conferences or seminars.
Publications: Application guidelines; Annual report; Grants list.
Application information: Letters of inquiry should be submitted using organization letterhead. A full proposal may be requested at a later date. Support is limited to 1 contribution per organization during any given year. Application form required.
Initial approach: Letter of inquiry for application form
Copies of proposal: 1
Deadline(s): Quarterly
Board meeting date(s): Quarterly
Final notification: At least 90 days
Officers and Trustees:* Kate Pew Wolters,* Chair.; Julie Ridenour, Pres.; James P. Hackett; Mary Anne Hunting; Elizabeth Welch Lykins; Mary Goodwillie Nelson; Craig Niemann; Robert C. Pew III.
Number of staff: 1 full-time professional; 1 full-time support.
EIN: 386050470

1668
Technical Assistance Mission Inc.
2764 Lorraine St.
Marlette, MI **48453-1070**

Donors: David Hall; Charlotte Hall.
Foundation type: Independent foundation.
Financial data (yr. ended 03/31/13): Assets, $6,548,542 (M); expenditures, $320,186; qualifying distributions, $260,231; giving activities include $235,387 for 25 grants (high: $89,900; low: $500), and $260,231 for 3 foundation-administered programs.
Fields of interest: Human services; Protestant agencies & churches.
Type of support: General/operating support.
Limitations: Applications not accepted. Giving primarily in FL.
Application information: Contributes only to pre-selected organizations.
Officers: David Hall, Pres.; **Christy Hines, Secy.**; **Charlotte Hall, Treas.**
EIN: 237241202
Other changes: Charlotte Hall has replaced Christy Hines as Treas.
Christy Hines is now Secy.

1669
Steve Van Andel Foundation
(formerly Steve & Cindy Van Andel Foundation)
P.O. Box 172
Ada, MI 49301-0172 (616) 787-6554
Contact: Deb Rushlo

Established in 2005 in MI.
Donor: Jay and Betty Van Andel Foundation.
Foundation type: Independent foundation.
Financial data (yr. ended 12/31/12): Assets, $70,977,688 (M); expenditures, $11,185,791; qualifying distributions, $4,606,543; giving activities include $4,606,543 for 61 grants (high: $1,500,000; low: $25).
Fields of interest: Hospitals (general); Youth development; Human services; Children/youth, services; Community/economic development; Public policy, research; Children/youth; Aging; Adults, women; Economically disadvantaged; Homeless.
Type of support: General/operating support; Annual campaigns; Capital campaigns; Program development; Scholarship funds.
Limitations: Applications accepted. Giving primarily in MI, with some emphasis on Grand Rapids.
Application information:
Initial approach: Letter of request
Deadline(s): None
Number of staff: 1 full-time support.
EIN: 202110604
Other changes: At the close of 2012, the grantmaker paid grants of $4,606,543, a 100.4% increase over the 2011 disbursements, $2,298,436.

1670
Van Kampen Boyer Molinari Charitable Foundation
5440 Farr Rd.
Fruitport, MI 49415-9751 (231) 865-6000
***Contact:* Joan M. Mack**

Donor: Kimberly Van Kampen Boyer.
Foundation type: Independent foundation.
Financial data (yr. ended 12/31/12): Assets, $2,682,590 (M); gifts received, $1,000,000; expenditures, $942,770; qualifying distributions, $749,557; giving activities include $749,557 for 21 grants (high: $125,000; low: $1,267).
Fields of interest: Arts; Education; Hospitals (specialty); Cancer; Health organizations; Athletics/sports, equestrianism; Human services; Children/youth, services; Children/youth.
Limitations: Applications accepted. Giving primarily in MI; funding also in FL, KY, NY, and OH.
Application information: Application form required.
Deadline(s): None
Officers and Directors:* Kimberly Van Kampen Boyer,* Pres.; Frederic Jacques Boyer,* Secy.; Michael William Molinari.
EIN: 201190854
Other changes: The grantmaker has moved from FL to MI.

1671
VanderWeide Family Foundation
(formerly Robert & Cheri VanderWeide Foundation)
P.O. Box 230257
Grand Rapids, MI 49523-0257 (616) 643-4700
Contact: Ginny Vander Hart, Exec. Dir.; Sue Volkers, Fdn. Admin.
FAX: (616) 774-0116;
E-mail: info@vw-foundation.org; E-mail: virginiav@rdvcorp.com (for G. Vander Hart) or SueV@rdvcorp.com (for S. Volkers); Main URL: http://www.vw-foundation.org

Established in 1992 in MI.
Donor: Suzanne DeVos Vanderweide.
Foundation type: Independent foundation.
Financial data (yr. ended 12/31/12): Assets, $42,646,642 (M); gifts received, $11,000,000; expenditures, $9,897,851; qualifying distributions, $9,709,665; giving activities include $9,379,650 for 93 grants (high: $3,810,900; low: $250).
Purpose and activities: The foundation seeks to create a legacy of caring and stewardship through their support of projects that build community and improve the quality of people's lives. To carry out this commitment, it focuses on organizations, projects, or programs that demonstrate Christian charity to meet both the spiritual and physical needs of people, which strengthen the bond of families and communities, and bring opportunity to disadvantaged persons. Giving primarily for Christian churches; giving also for education and human services.
Fields of interest: Education; Medical specialties; Human services; Youth, services; Family services; Community/economic development; United Ways and Federated Giving Programs; Christian agencies & churches; Protestant agencies & churches.
Type of support: General/operating support; Continuing support; Annual campaigns; Capital campaigns; Building/renovation; Program development; Matching/challenge support.
Limitations: Applications accepted. Giving primarily in west MI and central FL. No grants to individuals.
Publications: Application guidelines.
Application information: Tapes, DVD's CD's, brochures or bound proposals are not accepted. Application form not required.
Initial approach: On-line application
Copies of proposal: 1
Deadline(s): 3 weeks prior to review
Board meeting date(s): 3 times annually
Final notification: 3 to 5 months
Officers and Trustees:* Suzanne C. Devos Vanderweide,* Pres.; Robert H. Schierbeek,* Exec. V.P. and Secy.-Treas.; Jerry L. Tubergen,* Exec. V.P.; Jeffrey Lambert,* V.P., Finance; **Douglas L. Devos**; **Hannah J. Vanderweide**; **Katelyn S. Vanderweide.**
Number of staff: 3 full-time professional.
EIN: 383035978
Other changes: Jerry L. Tubergen is now Exec. V.P. Jeffrey Lambert is now V.P., Finance. Robert A. Vanderweide is no longer V.P. Robert H. Schierbeek is now Exec. V.P. and Secy.-Treas.

1672
Ted & Jane Von Voigtlander Foundation
109 W. Clinton St.
Howell, MI 48843-1565

Established in 2007 in MI.
Foundation type: Independent foundation.
Financial data (yr. ended 12/31/12): Assets, $36,588,545 (M); expenditures, $3,692,458; qualifying distributions, $3,242,800; giving activities include $3,242,800 for grants.
Fields of interest: Health organizations; Human services; Residential/custodial care, hospices; United Ways and Federated Giving Programs.
Type of support: General/operating support.
Limitations: Applications not accepted. Giving primarily in MI. No grants to individuals.
Application information: Contributes only to pre-selected organizations.
Officers and Directors:* C. Gwen Haggerty-Bearden,* Pres.; Steven W. Bearden,* V.P.; **Mary T. Cole, Secy.**; **Peter Bowen, Treas.**; Jacquelin A. Moody*; Jeffrey P. Von Voigtlander.
EIN: 205003935

1673
The Wayne and Joan Webber Foundation
c/o Richard Gibbs
44710 Morley Dr.
Clinton Township, MI 48036-1357

Established in 1998 in MI.
Donors: Joan Webber; Wayne Webber; Hanson Aggregates West, Inc.; Southern Crushed Concrete, Inc.
Foundation type: Independent foundation.
Financial data (yr. ended 12/31/12): Assets, $43,642,024 (M); expenditures, $2,530,256; qualifying distributions, $2,207,075; giving activities include $2,141,639 for 23 grants (high: $500,000; low: $2,332).
Fields of interest: Arts, formal/general education; Education; Hospitals (general); Human services.
Type of support: Capital campaigns.
Limitations: Applications not accepted. Giving primarily in MI. No grants to individuals.
Application information: Contributes only to pre-selected organizations.
Officers and Directors:* Cynthia Helisek, Pres.; Joan Webber,* Secy.; Wayne Webber,* Treas.; David Stone.
EIN: 383390733
Other changes: Joan Webber is now Secy. Wayne Webber is now Treas.

1674
The Wege Foundation
P.O. Box 6388
Grand Rapids, MI 49516-6388 **(616) 957-0480, Ext. 206**
***Contact:* Jody Price, C.F.O.**
E-mail for Jody Price: jprice@wegefoundation.org; Main URL: http://wegefoundation.org/index.html
YouTube: https://www.youtube.com/user/wegefoundation

Established on July 13, 1967 in MI.
Donor: Peter M. Wege.
Foundation type: Independent foundation.
Financial data (yr. ended 12/31/12): Assets, $84,647,413 (M); gifts received, $84,647,413; expenditures, $12,971,072; qualifying distributions, $12,171,450; giving activities include $11,372,480 for 541 grants (high: $200,000; low: $5,000).
Purpose and activities: Giving primarily to the environment, education, arts and culture, community service and health care.
Fields of interest: Museums; Performing arts; Elementary/secondary education; Higher education; Environment, natural resources; Hospitals (general); Human services; Children/youth, services; Community/economic development.
Type of support: Scholarship funds; General/operating support; Annual campaigns; Capital campaigns; Building/renovation; Equipment; Endowments; Program development; Curriculum development; Matching/challenge support.
Limitations: Applications accepted. Giving primarily in greater Kent County, MI, with emphasis on the Grand Rapids area. No grants to individuals.
Publications: Application guidelines; Annual report.
Application information: See foundation's web site for online grant application and eligibility quiz. Application form required.
Initial approach: Online grant application
Copies of proposal: 1
Deadline(s): Spring and fall. Check web site for dates
Board meeting date(s): Apr. 15
Officers and Directors:* Peter M. Wege,* Chair.; Ellen Satterlee,* C.E.O. and Treas.; Peter M. Wege II,* Pres.; Terri McCarthy, V.P., Progs; Jonathan M. Wege,* V.P.; W. Michael Van Haren,* Secy.; Jody Price, C.F.O.; Mary Goodwillie Nelson; Christopher M. Wege; Diana Wege.
Number of staff: 3 full-time professional.
EIN: 386124363

1675
Ralph C. Wilson Foundation
63 Kercheval Ave., Ste. 200
Grosse Pointe Farms, MI 48236-3652

Established around 1954.
Donor: Ralph C. Wilson, Jr.‡.
Foundation type: Independent foundation.
Financial data (yr. ended 10/31/12): Assets, $2,427,179 (M); expenditures, $1,876,642; qualifying distributions, $1,876,642; giving activities include $1,873,350 for 40 grants (high: $1,000,000; low: $200).
Purpose and activities: Giving primarily for education, health associations, and social services.
Fields of interest: Museums (sports/hobby); Higher education; Education; Hospitals (general); Health organizations; Human services; Children/youth, services; Residential/custodial care, hospices.
Type of support: General/operating support.
Limitations: Applications not accepted. Giving primarily in MI, NY, and OH. No grants to individuals.
Application information: Contributes only to pre-selected organizations.
Officers and Trustees:* Mary M. Owen, Secy.; Jeffrey C. Littmann,* Treas.; Eugene Driker; Mary M. Wilson.
EIN: 386091638
Other changes: Ralph C. Wilson, Jr., Pres. and Donor, is deceased.

MINNESOTA

1676
3M Foundation
(also known as Minnesota Mining and Manufacturing Foundation)
3M Ctr., Bldg., 225-01-S-23
St. Paul, MN 55144-1000 (651) 733-0144
Contact: Cynthia F. Kleven, Secy.
FAX: (651) 737-3061; E-mail: cfkleven@mmm.com; Main URL: http://www.3Mgives.com

Incorporated in 1953 in MN.
Donors: Minnesota Mining and Manufacturing Co.; 3M Co.
Foundation type: Company-sponsored foundation.
Financial data (yr. ended 12/31/12): Assets, $23,877,379 (M); gifts received, $17,500,000; expenditures, $19,251,645; qualifying distributions, $19,242,220; giving activities include $19,143,906 for 2,314 grants (high: $1,150,000; low: $13).
Purpose and activities: The foundation supports organizations involved with arts and culture, education, the environment, disaster relief, youth development, science, and economics. Special emphasis is directed toward initiatives with defined and measurable results that target underserved populations.
Fields of interest: Arts, cultural/ethnic awareness; Museums (science/technology); Performing arts, orchestras; Arts; Elementary/secondary education; Education, early childhood education; Higher education; Business school/education; Engineering school/education; Education, services; Education; Environment, climate change/global warming; Environment, natural resources; Environment; Disasters, preparedness/services; Youth development; United Ways and Federated Giving Programs; Science, formal/general education; Mathematics; Engineering; Science; Economics; Children/youth; Minorities; Economically disadvantaged.
Type of support: General/operating support; Capital campaigns; Program development; Curriculum development; Scholarship funds; Employee volunteer services; Employee matching gifts; In-kind gifts.
Limitations: Applications accepted. **Giving on a national basis in areas of company operations.** No support for religious, fraternal, social, or veterans' organizations, disease-specific organizations, government agencies, hospitals, clinics, or nursing homes, treatment centers or hospices, or individual K-12 schools. No grants to individuals, or for capital endowments, advocacy or lobbying efforts, conferences, seminars, or workshops, publications, film or video production, fundraising, testimonial, athletic or special events, playground or athletic equipment, non-3M equipment, travel, or scholarship funds; no loans or investments.
Publications: Application guidelines; Annual report; Grants list; Program policy statement.
Application information: Unsolicited requests are rarely funded. The foundation utilizes an invitation only Request For Proposal (RFP) process for organizations located in Minneapolis and St. Paul, MN, and Austin, TX and for humanitarian and disaster relief requests. Application form required.
Initial approach: Complete online eligibility quiz
Copies of proposal: 1
Deadline(s): None
Board meeting date(s): June and Dec.
Final notification: 6 weeks

Officers: Ian F. Hardgrove, Pres.; Kimberly F. Price, V.P.; Cynthia F. Kleven, Secy.; S. D. Krohn, Treas.
Number of staff: 6 full-time professional; 3 full-time support.
EIN: 416038262

1677
Marshall H. and Nellie Alworth Memorial Fund
402 Alworth Bldg.
306 W. Superior St., Ste. 402
Duluth, MN 55802-5017 (218) 722-9366
Contact: Patty Salow Downs, Exec. Dir.
FAX: (218) 529-3760;
E-mail: alworth@alworthscholarship.org; Main URL: http://www.alworthscholarship.org/
E-mail for scholarship questions and recent IRS 1040 forms: alworth@cpinternet.com; Additional URL: http://www.futurestakeflight.com

Incorporated in 1949 by Marshall W. Alworth to honor parents who were early pioneers in northeastern MN.
Donor: Marshall W. Alworth†.
Foundation type: Independent foundation.
Financial data (yr. ended 06/30/13): Assets, $6,343,449 (M); gifts received, $749,928; expenditures, $112,974; qualifying distributions, $71,242; giving activities include $18,650 for grants to individuals.
Purpose and activities: Giving scholarships to high school seniors who: 1) are graduating from a high school in one of the following MN counties: Aitkin, Beltrami, Carlton, Cass, Cook, Crow Wing, Lake, Itasca, Koochiching, and St. Louis; 2) have a composite score of 26 or higher on the American College Test (ACT); 3) will be graduating in the top 20 percent of their class (if not in the top 20 percent but has an ACT score of 28 or higher); 4) will commit to majoring in one of the designated fields of study which are detailed on the foundation's web site; 5) have demonstrated qualities of character, perseverance and ambition; 6) have a high scholastic standing among their peers; 7) have shown promise for a career in the sciences; and 8) are from a family whose taxable income is less than $120,000.
Fields of interest: Visual arts, architecture; Medical school/education; Nursing school/education; Engineering school/education; Environment, research; Animals/wildlife, research; Veterinary medicine; Animals/wildlife; Pharmacy/prescriptions; Genetic diseases and disorders; Biomedicine; Neuroscience; Medical research, institute; Agriculture; Physical/earth sciences; Chemistry; Mathematics; Physics; Geology; Engineering/technology; Computer science; Engineering; Biology/life sciences; Botany; Science.
Type of support: Scholarships—to individuals.
Limitations: Applications accepted. Giving limited to graduates of high schools in Aitkin, Beltrami, Carlton, Cass, Cook, Crow Wing, Lake, Itasca, Koochiching, and St. Louis counties in MN. No grants for building or endowment funds or matching gifts; no loans.
Publications: Application guidelines; Informational brochure; Informational brochure (including application guidelines).
Application information: Application form available from high school counselors in northern MN or from foundation web site, along with application guidelines. Electronic submissions only. Application form required.
Initial approach: Via application form on foundation web site
Copies of proposal: 1
Deadline(s): Jan. 15
Board meeting date(s): Apr. and Oct.
Final notification: May 1

Officers and Directors:* Tere Ivanca,* Pres.; James Abelsen, V.P.; Patty Salo Downs, Secy. and Exec. Dir.; Eric Norberg, Treas.; Patricia Altrichter; Gerald S. Dodd; John Hyduke; Linda Niskanen; Tom Renier.
Number of staff: 1 part-time professional; 1 part-time support.
EIN: 410797340
Other changes: The grantmaker has changed its fiscal year-end from Dec. 31 to June 30.

1678
Andersen Corporate Foundation
(formerly The Bayport Foundation of Andersen Corporation)
White Pine Bldg.
342 5th Ave. N., Ste. 200
Bayport, MN 55003-1201 (651) 275-4450
Contact: Chloette Haley, Prog. Off.
FAX: (651) 439-9480;
E-mail: andersencorpfdn@srinc.biz; Additional tel.: (651) 439-1557; **Main URL: http://www.andersencorporation.com/corporate-responsibility/community-involvement/andersen-corporate-foundation/**

Incorporated in 1941 in MN.
Donor: Andersen Corp.
Foundation type: Company-sponsored foundation.
Financial data (yr. ended 11/30/13): Assets, $43,349,719 (M); gifts received, $100; expenditures, $2,252,377; qualifying distributions, $2,085,785; giving activities include $1,914,400 for 151 grants (high: $100,000; low: $1,500).
Purpose and activities: The foundation supports programs designed to provide community, social, and support services to better people's lives and strengthen communities. Special emphasis is directed toward programs designed to promote affordable housing; health and safety; education and youth development; human services; and civic support.
Fields of interest: Media/communications; Visual arts; Museums; Performing arts; Performing arts, music; Arts; Elementary/secondary education; Education, services; Education; Environment, natural resources; Hospitals (general); Public health; Health care; Substance abuse, prevention; Mental health/crisis services; Employment, services; Housing/shelter, temporary shelter; Housing/shelter, owner/renter issues; Housing/shelter; Disasters, preparedness/services; Safety/disasters; Recreation; Aging, centers/services; Minorities/immigrants, centers/services; Independent living, disability; Human services; Mathematics; Engineering/technology; Science; Children/youth; Aging; Disabilities, people with; Economically disadvantaged.
International interests: Canada.
Type of support: General/operating support; Annual campaigns; Capital campaigns; Building/renovation; Emergency funds; Program development.
Limitations: Applications accepted. Giving primarily in areas of company operations in Des Moines and Dubuque, IA, East Metro, MN, North Brunswick, NJ, Luray and Page County, VA, Dunn County, Menomonie, and St. Croix Valley, WI, and to national organizations; some giving also in Huron, London, Middlesex, and Perth, Ontario Province, Canada. No support for national research organizations. No grants to individuals, or for endowments, or the purchase of Andersen products.

Publications: Application guidelines; IRS Form 990 or 990-PF printed copy available upon request.
Application information: Call foundation before sending request. Visit foundation Web site for application address and guidelines. Application form required.
Initial approach: Download application form and mail proposal and application form to nearest application address
Copies of proposal: 1
Deadline(s): Oct. 15, Feb. 15, and June 15
Board meeting date(s): Mar., July, and Nov.
Final notification: 10 working days
Officers and Directors: Keith D. Olson, Pres.; Susan Roeder, V.P., Grants Admin., and Secy.; Phil Donaldson, Treas.; Laurie Bauer; Jay Lund; Jerry Redmond.
Number of staff: 1 full-time professional; 1 full-time support.
EIN: 416020912

1679
L. & N. Andreas Foundation
(formerly Cayman Conand Foundation)
c/o Andreas Office
P.O. Box 3584
Mankato, MN 56002-3584

Established in MN.
Donors: Lowell W. Andreas‡; Andreas Lee.
Foundation type: Independent foundation.
Financial data (yr. ended 11/30/13): Assets, $37,146,442 (M); gifts received, $1,397; expenditures, $2,086,259; qualifying distributions, $2,002,050; giving activities include $2,002,050 for 117 grants (high: $217,500; low: $1,000).
Fields of interest: Higher education; Human services; Foundations (community); Christian agencies & churches; Protestant agencies & churches.
Limitations: Applications not accepted. Giving primarily in MN. No grants to individuals.
Application information: Contributes only to pre-selected organizations.
Officers: Andreas Lee, Pres. and Secy.; David Andreas, V.P. and Treas.
Trustees: Cayman Campbell; Jason Lee.
EIN: 363382956
Other changes: The foundation has changed its fiscal year-end from Dec. 31 to Nov. 30.

1680
Avocet Foundation
1660 S. Hwy. 100, Ste. 426
St. Louis Park, MN 55416-1533
Contact: Joanne Kletscher, Secy., C.E.O., and C.F.O.

Established in 1996 in MN
Donor: Charles H. Bell‡.
Foundation type: Independent foundation.
Financial data (yr. ended 12/31/12): Assets, $3,872,339 (M); gifts received, $190,106; expenditures, $227,894; qualifying distributions, $164,525; giving activities include $164,500 for 15 grants (high: $35,000; low: $5,000).
Fields of interest: Education; Environment; Human services; Youth.
Type of support: General/operating support.
Limitations: Applications not accepted. Giving limited to MN. No grants to individuals.
Application information: Contributes only to pre-selected organizations.
Officer: Joanne Kletscher, C.E.O., Secy. and C.F.O.
EIN: 411859473

1681
The Bahl Foundation
P.O. Box 22094
St. Paul, MN 55122-0094 (952) 895-8654

Established in 2002 in CT.
Donors: Tracy L. Bahl; Felicia V. Bahl.
Foundation type: Independent foundation.
Financial data (yr. ended 12/31/12): Assets, $67,885 (M); gifts received, $10,631; expenditures, $331,006; qualifying distributions, $329,907; giving activities include $317,600 for 15 grants (high: $150,000; low: $1,200).
Purpose and activities: The foundation is dedicated to advancing the well being of children around the world through education, health, faith and the arts.
Fields of interest: Higher education, college; Education; Youth, services; United Ways and Federated Giving Programs.
Limitations: Applications accepted. Giving primarily in MN and NY.
Application information: Application form required.
Initial approach: Letter
Deadline(s): None
Officer: Penny Bailey, Exec. Dir.
Trustee: Tracy L. Bahl.
EIN: 146216533
Other changes: The grantmaker no longer lists a URL address.

1682
Edward R. Bazinet Foundation
Minneapolis, MN

The foundation terminated in 2011.

1683
The Beim Foundation
318 W. 48th St.
Minneapolis, MN 55419-5418 (612) 825-1404
E-mail: beimfoundation@earthlink.net; Main URL: http://www.beimfoundation.org
Grants List: http://www.beimfoundation.org/recent-grants.asp

Incorporated in 1947 in MN.
Donors: N.C. Beim‡; Raymond N. Beim‡.
Foundation type: Independent foundation.
Financial data (yr. ended 12/31/12): Assets, $11,153,303 (M); expenditures, $569,801; qualifying distributions, $541,724; giving activities include $455,000 for 49 grants (high: $20,000; low: $500).
Purpose and activities: Primary areas of interest are arts, education, environment, and human services.
Fields of interest: Arts; Education; Environment, natural resources; Environment; Human services; Children/youth; Youth; Adults; Aging; Disabilities, people with; Mentally disabled.
Type of support: Equipment; Program development.
Limitations: Applications accepted. Giving primarily in MN; some giving also in selected communities outside of MN. No support for private foundations, or for political or religious organizations or international organizations. No grants to individuals, or for deficit financing memberships, endowments, subscriptions, tickets, conferences, fundraisers, or annual campaigns, multi-year support, capital campaigns or for general operating support; no grants for building or equipment, except for equipment qualifying under small arts capital grants; no loans.
Publications: Application guidelines.

Application information: Complete application policies and guidelines available on foundation web site. Application form required.
Initial approach: See foundation web site
Copies of proposal: 1
Deadline(s): See foundation web site for current deadlines
Board meeting date(s): Board meeting dates available on foundation web site
Final notification: See foundation web site
Officers: Carol Nulsen, Pres.; Patricia Arnold, Treas.
Directors: Jim McKim; David Nulsen; Julie Packard; Barbara Peters; Jack Stephenson; Allison Villani.
Number of staff: None.
EIN: 416022529
Other changes: The grantmaker now publishes application guidelines.

1684
Bentson Foundation
315 Lake St. E., No. 302
Wayzata, MN 55391-1700 (952) 923-1040
Contact: Judy Dutcher

Established in 1956 in MN.
Foundation type: Independent foundation.
Financial data (yr. ended 06/30/13): Assets, $97,704,496 (M); gifts received, $1,438,290; expenditures, $8,578,452; qualifying distributions, $7,675,352; giving activities include $7,675,352 for 28 grants (high: $5,000,000; low: $2,000).
Fields of interest: Higher education, university; Hospitals (general); Jewish agencies & synagogues.
Limitations: Applications accepted. Giving primarily in MN. No grants to individuals.
Application information: Application form not required.
Initial approach: Proposal
Deadline(s): None
Officers: Laurie Bentson Kauth, Pres.; George Reilly, Secy.; Mark S. Niblick, Treas.; Judi Dutcher, Exec. Dir.
Board Member: Lowell Stortz.
EIN: 416020204

1685
Best Buy Foundation
(formerly Best Buy Children's Foundation)
7601 Penn Ave. S.
Richfield, MN 55423-3645 **(866) 625-4350**
FAX: (612) 292-4001;
E-mail: bestbuygrants@easymatch.com; **Additional e-mail and tel.: communityrelations@bestbuy.com, (612) 291-6108; Main URL: http://www.bby.com/community-relations/**

Established in 1994 in MN.
Donor: Best Buy Co., Inc.
Foundation type: Company-sponsored foundation.
Financial data (yr. ended 03/02/13): Assets, $52,912 (M); gifts received, $8,804,089; expenditures, $9,936,715; qualifying distributions, $8,067,994; giving activities include $7,742,839 for 602 grants (high: $1,100,000; low: $950).
Purpose and activities: The foundation supports programs designed to provide teens with opportunities to develop technology skills that inspire future education and careers.
Fields of interest: Media/communications; Media, film/video; Interactive games; Mobile media; Elementary/secondary education; Education; Disasters, preparedness/services; Boys & girls clubs; Human services; United Ways and Federated Giving Programs; Engineering/

technology; Leadership development; Youth; Economically disadvantaged.
Type of support: General/operating support; Continuing support; Capital campaigns; Program development; Curriculum development; Scholarship funds.
Limitations: Applications accepted. Giving limited to areas of company operations, with emphasis on the Twin Cities, MN area. No support for fraternal organizations or social clubs, units of government or quasi-governmental agencies, labor or lobbying organizations, for-profit organizations, religious organizations not of direct benefit to the entire community, or athletic teams. No grants to individuals or for political campaigns, general operating support, endowments, travel, national ceremonies, memorials, fundraising dinners, testimonials, conferences, or similar events, health, medical, therapeutic programs, or living subsidies, athletic events, or multi-year requests; no product donations.
Publications: Application guidelines; Grants list; Program policy statement.
Application information: Capital requests are limited to the Twin Cities, MN, area organizations that have previously received funding from the foundation. Support is limited to 1 contribution per organization during any given year. Organizations receiving support are asked to provide a final report. Multi-year funding is not automatic. Application form required.
Initial approach: Complete online eligibility quiz and application form
Copies of proposal: 1
***Deadline(s):* June 2 to June 27 for Community Grants; Feb. 1, May 1, Aug. 1, and Nov. 1 for National Program and Twin Cities Fund; Feb. 1 for Twin Cities capital grants**
Board meeting date(s): Annually
***Final notification:* Sept. 15 for Community Grants**
Officers and Trustees:* Susan S. Hoff,* Chair.; Todd Hartman, Secy.; Lisa Erickson, Treas.; Matt Furman; Hubert Joly; Dean Kimberly; Scott Moore; Susan Bass Roberts; Raymond Slivia.
Number of staff: 1 full-time professional.
EIN: 411784382
Other changes: Marc D. Gordon is no longer Treas. Stephen Gillett, Bill Hoffman, and Patricia Mcphee are no longer trustees. Shawn Score is no longer Pres.

1686
The Boss Foundation
5858 Centerville Rd.
St. Paul, MN 55127-6804 (651) 653-0599
Contact: Daniel W. McKeown, Treas.

Established around 1957.
Donor: The Specialty Manufacturing Co.
Foundation type: Company-sponsored foundation.
Financial data (yr. ended 06/30/13): Assets, $6,480,718 (M); gifts received, $50,000; expenditures, $333,558; qualifying distributions, $283,525; giving activities include $283,500 for 55 grants (high: $10,000; low: $2,000).
Purpose and activities: The foundation supports zoos and organizations involved with arts and culture, higher education, and human services.
Fields of interest: Museums; Performing arts; Performing arts, theater; Performing arts, opera; Historic preservation/historical societies; Arts; Higher education; Zoos/zoological societies; Youth, services; Human services.
Type of support: General/operating support.
Limitations: Applications accepted. Giving primarily in the Minneapolis and St. Paul, MN, metropolitan area. No grants to individuals.
Publications: Application guidelines.
Application information: Proposals should be limited to 5 pages. Application form not required.
Initial approach: Proposal
Deadline(s): June 1
Board meeting date(s): June
Officers: W. Andrew Boss, Pres.; **Desmond McKeown, Secy.**; Daniel W. McKeown, Treas.
Director: Heidi McKeown.
EIN: 416038452
Other changes: Desmond McKeown is now Secy. Heidi Sandberg McKeown is no longer Secy.

1687
Briggs and Morgan Foundation
(formerly Chancery Lane Foundation)
332 Minnesota St., Ste. 2200
St. Paul, MN 55101
***Main URL:* http://www.briggs.com/about-leadership.html**

Established in 1960 in MN.
Donors: Alan Maclin; Brian Wenger; Jack Perry; Charles Rogers; Frank Taylor; Joseph Roach; Lauren Lonergan; Mark Ayotte; Mary Ippel; Michael Grimes; Michael Krikava; Timothy Thorton; Terry Slye; Sam Hanson; Gregory Stemoe; Joseph Kinning; Michael McEllistrem.
Foundation type: Company-sponsored foundation.
Financial data (yr. ended 12/31/13): Assets, $94,019 (M); gifts received, $339,769; expenditures, $371,032; qualifying distributions, $370,318; giving activities include $370,318 for 61 grants (high: $40,000; low: $600).
Purpose and activities: The foundation supports organizations involved with education, legal aid, and civil rights.
Fields of interest: Higher education; Law school/education; Education; Legal services; Crime/law enforcement; Human services; Civil/human rights.
Type of support: Continuing support; Annual campaigns; Capital campaigns; Program development.
Limitations: Applications not accepted. Giving primarily in the Minneapolis and St. Paul, MN, area. No grants to individuals.
Application information: Contributes only to pre-selected organizations.
Officers and Directors:* Alan Maclin,* Pres.; Steve Ryan,* V.P.; Dawn Iacarella, Secy.; Terry Slye,* Treas.; Greg Stemoe.
EIN: 416009924

1688
Patrick and Aimee Butler Family Foundation
2356 University Ave. W., Ste. 420
St. Paul, MN 55114-3801 (651) 222-2565
Contact: Kerrie Blevins, Dir.
E-mail: kerrieb@butlerfamilyfoundation.org; **E-mail for assistance with application problems: bffinfo@visi.com**; Main URL: http://www.butlerfamilyfoundation.org
Grants Database: http://www.butlerfamilyfund.org/grantees.php

Incorporated in 1951 in MN.
Donors: Patrick Butler‡; Aimee Mott Butler‡; Kate Butler Peterson‡.
Foundation type: Independent foundation.
Financial data (yr. ended 12/31/12): Assets, $90,217,318 (M); gifts received, $747,666; expenditures, $3,552,544; qualifying distributions, $3,198,269; giving activities include $3,015,405 for 113 grants (high: $450,000; low: $5,000).
Purpose and activities: Giving primarily for the arts and humanities, the environment, human services and philanthropy and non-profit management.
Fields of interest: Arts; Environment; Substance abuse, services; Housing/shelter, development; Human services; Family services; Women, centers/services; Philanthropy/voluntarism.
Type of support: General/operating support; Continuing support; Annual campaigns; Program development; Consulting services.
Limitations: Applications accepted. Giving primarily in the St. Paul and Minneapolis, MN, area. No support for criminal justice, secondary and elementary education, health or hospitals, employment or vocational programs, theater or dance programs, or economic education. No grants to individuals, or for medical research, films or videos, capital funds, endowment funds or events; no loans.
Publications: Application guidelines; Annual report (including application guidelines); Grants list.
Application information: Application process available on foundation web site. Application form required.
Initial approach: See foundation web site for guidelines
***Deadline(s):* May 15 (for Arts and Environment applications)**
Board meeting date(s): Oct.
***Final notification:* July 15 (status notification for Arts and Environment applications)**
Officers and Trustees:* John K. Butler,* Pres.; Patrick Butler, Jr.,* V.P.; Catherine C. Butler,* Secy.; Peter M. Butler,* Treas.; Brigid M. Butler; Patricia M. Butler; Paul S. Butler; Sandra K. Butler; Suzanne A. LeFevour; Melanie Martinez; Temple Peterson.
Director: Kerrie Blevins.
Number of staff: 2 part-time professional; 1 part-time support.
EIN: 416009902

1689
Margaret A. Cargill Foundation
6889 Rowland Rd.
Eden Prairie, MN 55344-3380
E-mail: info@macfoundation.org; E-mail for restricted grants program: grantinfo@macfoundation.org; Main URL: http://macphilanthropies.org/macfoundation/
GiveSmart: http://www.givesmart.org/Stories/Donors/Christy-Morse

Established in 2006 in MN.
Donor: Margaret A. Cargill‡.
Foundation type: Independent foundation.
Financial data (yr. ended 12/31/12): Assets, $2,954,027,761 (M); expenditures, $69,100,124; qualifying distributions, $53,734,866; giving activities include $38,406,484 for 622 grants (high: $3,000,000; low: $50), and $3,831,374 for loans/program-related investments.
Purpose and activities: The purpose of the foundation is to provide meaningful assistance and support to society, the arts, environment, and all living things.
Fields of interest: Arts; Environment; Animals/wildlife; Health care; Human services; Family services; Native Americans/American Indians.
Limitations: Applications not accepted. **No grants to individuals.**

Application information: Unsolicited requests for funds not accepted.
Officers and Trustees:* Christine M. Morse,* Chair. and C.E.O.; Paul B. Busch,* Pres.; **Terrence R. Meersman, V.P., Prog(s).**; Naomi Horsager, C.F.O. and Treas.; Shawn Wischmeier, C.I.O.
Number of staff: 75
EIN: 205434405

1690
Douglas and Wendy Dayton Foundation
(formerly Meadowood Foundation)
c/o Okabena Co.
1800 IDS Ctr.
80 S. 8th St.
Minneapolis, MN 55402-4523

Established in 1968 in MN.
Donor: Douglas J. Dayton.
Foundation type: Independent foundation.
Financial data (yr. ended 12/31/12): Assets, $10,892,242 (M); expenditures, $539,535; qualifying distributions, $411,651; giving activities include $400,876 for grants.
Purpose and activities: Giving primarily for land and natural resource conservation and a Protestant church; support also for arts and culture and human services.
Fields of interest: Arts; Education; Environment, natural resources; Animals/wildlife, preservation/protection; Hospitals (general); Human services; Community/economic development; Protestant agencies & churches.
Type of support: General/operating support; Building/renovation.
Limitations: Applications not accepted. Giving primarily in Minneapolis, MN. No grants to individuals.
Application information: Unsolicited requests for funds not accepted.
Officers and Directors:* Douglas J. Dayton,* Pres. and Treas.; Wendy W. Dayton,* V.P.; James M. Karges, Secy.
EIN: 410943749

1691
The Depot Foundation
130 W. Superior St.
302 U.S. Bank Pl.
Duluth, MN 55802-2032 (218) 279-9913
FAX: (218) 279-9914;
E-mail: info@depotfoundation.org; Main URL: http://www.depotfoundation.org

Established in 1979 in MN.
Foundation type: Independent foundation.
Financial data (yr. ended 06/30/13): Assets, $5,975,711 (M); gifts received, $201,804; expenditures, $292,603; qualifying distributions, $206,498; giving activities include $195,484 for 13 grants (high: $50,000; low: $53).
Purpose and activities: The foundation raises, manages, and distributes charitable capital to benefit primarily the St. Louis County Heritage and Arts Center and the nine arts and cultural organizations affiliated at the center.
Fields of interest: Arts.
Type of support: General/operating support; Building/renovation; Program development.
Limitations: Giving primarily in northeastern MN and northwestern WI.
Publications: Annual report; Informational brochure; Newsletter.
Application information: Eligible applicants for all grants funding must have 501(c)(3) status and have a mission to preserve or present arts, culture, or history within northeastern Minnesota and/or northwestern Wisconsin. Application form required.
Initial approach: Telephone or letter
Copies of proposal: 6
Deadline(s): Jan. 31 for Prindle/Wood Family Memorial Endowment Fund; Sept 30 for Designated Funds; Oct. 31 for Undesignated Funds
Board meeting date(s): Bimonthly on the 4th Wed.
Final notification: Feb. 28 for Prindle/Wood Family Memorial Endowment Fund; Oct. 31 for Designated Funds; Dec. 31 for Undesignated Fund
Officers and Directors:* Richard Fischer,* Chair.; Jean B. Olsen,* Vice-Chair.; **Thomas Whittaker,* Secy.**; **Melinda Machones,* Treas.**; Linda Boben; **Laura Budd**; **Pat Cutshall**; Ben Fornear; Dexter Larson; and 4 additional directors.
Number of staff: 1 full-time professional; 1 part-time support.
EIN: 411356072
Other changes: Thomas Whittaker has replaced Marilyn Bowes as Secy. Melinda Machones has replaced Jay Stoffel as Treas.
Joe Konradt and Kenneth Schoen are no longer directors.

1692
Donaldson Foundation
P.O. Box 1299, MS 104
Minneapolis, MN 55440-1299 **(952) 887-3043**
***Main URL:* http://www.donaldson.com/**

Established in 1966 in MN.
Donor: Donaldson Co., Inc.
Foundation type: Company-sponsored foundation.
Financial data (yr. ended 07/31/13): Assets, $2,693,806 (M); gifts received, $200,000; expenditures, $1,146,370; qualifying distributions, $1,143,870; giving activities include $1,143,870 for grants.
Purpose and activities: The foundation supports organizations involved with education.
Fields of interest: Education; United Ways and Federated Giving Programs.
Type of support: Continuing support; Annual campaigns; Capital campaigns; Building/renovation; Scholarship funds; Employee matching gifts; Employee-related scholarships.
Limitations: Applications accepted. Giving on a national basis in areas of company operations. No support for religious organizations. No grants to individuals (except for employee-related scholarships).
Application information: Application form required.
***Initial approach:* Letter**
Copies of proposal: 1
Deadline(s): None
Officers: Lillian Perez, Pres.; Shen Weber, Secy.; Mike Dwyer, Treas.
Directors: Peter Lucas; Catherine Luebke; Grace Ngunu; Rod Radosevich; Robert Van Nelson; Paul Way.
EIN: 416052950
Other changes: The grantmaker no longer lists an E-mail address. The grantmaker no longer lists a fax. The grantmaker no longer lists a primary contact.
Laura Russell is no longer Fdn. Mgr. Shen Weber is now Secy. Mike Dwyer is now Treas. Steve Johnson is no longer a member of the governing body. Tamara Keeler is no longer a member of the governing body. Jeff May is no longer a member of the governing body.
The grantmaker no longer publishes application guidelines or an annual report (including application guidelines).

1693
Duluth Superior Area Community Foundation
Zeitgeist Arts Building
222 E. Superior St., Ste. 302
Duluth, MN 55802 (218) 726-0232
Contact: Holly C. Sampson, Pres.
FAX: (218) 726-0257;
E-mail: info@dsacommunityfoundation.com; Grant application e-mail: grantsinfo@dsacommunityfoundation.com; Main URL: http://www.dsacommunityfoundation.com
Facebook: http://www.facebook.com/pages/Duluth-Superior-Area-Community-Foundation/128701853838939
Scholarship application e-mail: dhammer@dsacommunityfoundation.com

Established in 1982 in MN.
Foundation type: Community foundation.
Financial data (yr. ended 12/31/12): Assets, $53,678,765 (M); gifts received, $1,860,658; expenditures, $2,900,014; giving activities include $1,599,646 for 70+ grants (high: $274,554), and $261,012 for 138 grants to individuals.
Purpose and activities: The foundation supports a wide variety of activities in five interest areas: Arts, Community and Economic Development, Education, Environment, and Human Services.
Fields of interest: Visual arts; Performing arts; Performing arts, music; Arts; Child development, education; Higher education; Education; Environment; Animal welfare; Crime/violence prevention; Employment; Food services; Housing/shelter, development; Children/youth, services; Child development, services; Family services; Homeless, human services; Human services; International affairs, goodwill promotion; International peace/security; Civil rights, race/intergroup relations; Economic development; Community/economic development; Government/public administration; Disabilities, people with; Minorities; Native Americans/American Indians; Women; Economically disadvantaged; Homeless.
Type of support: Film/video/radio; General/operating support; Emergency funds; Program development; Publication; Seed money; Curriculum development; Scholarship funds; Research; Technical assistance; Consulting services; Program evaluation; Scholarships—to individuals.
Limitations: Applications accepted. Giving primarily in Ashland, Bayfield and Douglas counties, WI, and Atkin, Carlton, Cook, Itasca, Koochiching, Lake, and St. Louis counties in northeastern MN. No support for religious organizations for religious activities. No grants to individuals (except for scholarships initiated or managed by the foundation), or for capital or annual campaigns, endowments, debt retirement, medical research, fundraising, continuing support, deficit financing, land acquisition, tickets for benefits, telephone solicitations, or for grants beyond single funding cycle; no loans.
Publications: Application guidelines; Annual report; Grants list; Informational brochure (including application guidelines); Newsletter.
Application information: Based on the outcome of the online inquiry, an organization may be encouraged to submit a full proposal. Visit

foundation web site for application forms and guidelines. Application form required.

Initial approach: E-mail
Copies of proposal: 3
Deadline(s): Apr. 1 and Oct. 1 for Community Opportunity Fund grants; varies for others
Board meeting date(s): Monthly
Final notification: 60 to 90 days

Officers and Board Members:* Claudia Scott Welty,* Chair.; Amy Kuronen,* Vice-Chair.; Holly C. Sampson, Pres.; Howard T. Klatzky,* Secy.; **Philip D. Rolle,* Treas.**; Ryan Boman; **Jennifer L. Carey**; Marlene David; Bethany M. Owen; **Branden Robinson**; Arend J. Sandbulte; Mia Thibodeau; Renee Wachter; Tony Yung; Jim Zastrow.
Number of staff: 8 full-time professional; 1 full-time support.
EIN: 411429402
Other changes: Claudia Scott Welty has replaced Jennifer L. Carey as Chair. Amy Kuronen has replaced Claudia Scott Welty as Vice-Chair. Philip D. Rolle has replaced Amy Kuronen as Vice-Chair.

1694
Edina Realty Foundation

6800 France Ave. S., Ste. 600
Minneapolis, MN 55435-2017 (952) 928-5356
Contact: Susan Cowsert, Dir.

Established in 1996 in MN.
Donor: Edina Realty, Inc.
Foundation type: Company-sponsored foundation.
Financial data (yr. ended 09/30/13): Assets, $376,314 (M); gifts received, $355,029; expenditures, $354,247; qualifying distributions, $341,880; giving activities include $341,880 for 136 grants (high: $18,800; low: $125).
Purpose and activities: The foundation supports programs designed to provide housing and related services to homeless individuals and families.
Fields of interest: Health care; Housing/shelter; Human services.
Type of support: General/operating support; Capital campaigns; Building/renovation; Emergency funds; Program development; Curriculum development; Research.
Limitations: Applications accepted. Giving primarily in MN. No grants to individuals.
Publications: Application guidelines; Annual report; Program policy statement.
Application information: Application form required.

***Initial approach:* Letter**
Copies of proposal: 1
Deadline(s): None
Board meeting date(s): Quarterly

Directors: Michelle Cici; Mark Christopherson; Susan Cowsert; Kevin Folkerts; Scott Harris; Amy Kleinschmidt; Marc Kuhnley; Jodi Lucast; Debra Stumne.
Number of staff: 1 full-time support; 1 part-time support.
EIN: 411826980
Other changes: The grantmaker no longer lists a URL address.

1695
Farmers Union Marketing & Processing Foundation

P.O. Box 319
Redwood Falls, MN 56283-0319
Contact: Dwight Bassingthwaite, Pres.

Established in 1998 in MN.
Donor: Farmers Union Marketing & Processing Assoc.
Foundation type: Company-sponsored foundation.
Financial data (yr. ended 06/30/13): Assets, $2,726,717 (M); expenditures, $406,470; qualifying distributions, $375,062; giving activities include $300,172 for 26 grants (high: $90,000; low: $500), and $8,000 for 5 grants to individuals (high: $1,500; low: $1,000).
Purpose and activities: The foundation supports research and education programs designed to promote agriculture production, management, and cooperative ventures.
Fields of interest: Higher education; Education; Agriculture; Agriculture, sustainable programs; Agriculture, farmlands; Agriculture/food.
Type of support: Equipment; Conferences/seminars; Seed money; Research; Program development; Sponsorships; Employee-related scholarships.
Limitations: Applications accepted. Giving primarily in MN, MT, ND, SD, and WI.
Publications: Annual report; Informational brochure.
Application information: Application form required.

***Initial approach:* Request application form**
Copies of proposal: 3
Deadline(s): None

Officers: Dwight Bassingthwaite, Pres.; Dennis Rosen, Secy.-Treas.
Directors: William Day; Doug Peterson; Doug Somke; Paul Symens.
EIN: 311634460
Other changes: The grantmaker no longer lists an E-mail address. The grantmaker no longer lists a phone. The grantmaker no longer lists a separate application address.

1696
Frey Foundation

5000 Wells Fargo Ctr.
90 S. 7th St.
Minneapolis, MN 55402-3903 (612) 359-6215
Contact: Jo Ann Gruesner
FAX: (612) 359-6210;
E-mail: joann@freyfoundationmn.org; Main URL: http://freyfoundationmn.org/

Established in 1988 in MN.
Foundation type: Independent foundation.
Financial data (yr. ended 06/30/13): Assets, $25,641,993 (M); expenditures, $1,427,897; qualifying distributions, $1,235,628; giving activities include $960,229 for 43 grants (high: $150,000; low: $100).
Purpose and activities: The foundation strives to be a catalyst in strengthening its community through effective, direct giving which promotes self-sufficiency and stimulates creative change, resulting in an improved quality of life for all.
Fields of interest: Education, early childhood education; Higher education; Housing/shelter, development; Housing/shelter; Human services; Children/youth; Homeless.
Type of support: General/operating support; Annual campaigns; Program development; Matching/challenge support.
Limitations: Applications accepted. Giving primarily in the Minneapolis-St. Paul, MN, area and in Naples, FL. No support for political organizations. No grants to individuals, including scholarships and tuition assistance, or for endowments.
Publications: Annual report; Grants list; Program policy statement.
Application information: See foundation web site for application information and form. Full applications will be accepted by invitation only. All letters of inquiry, applications and evaluations must be e-mailed. The foundation requests that materials not be sent via USPS. Application form required.

***Initial approach:* Letter of inquiry (no more than 2 pages) via e-mail, and in word format (not in .pdf), to Jo Ann Gruesner, Exec. Asst.**
Copies of proposal: 1
***Deadline(s):* See foundation web site for deadlines**
Board meeting date(s): June, Sept., and Dec.
Final notification: 3 days following board meetings

Officers and Directors:* Eugene U. Frey,* Chair.; Mary F. Frey,* Vice-Chair.; James R. Frey,* C.E.O. and Pres.; Carol F. Wolfe,* V.P. and Prog. Mgr.; **Flor Frey**; John J. Frey; Mary W. Frey; **Peter J. Frey**; Jane E. Letourneau; **Andrew Wilson**; **Sarah F. Wilson**; Andrew Frey Wolfe; Daniel T. Wolfe; **Molly Frey Wolfe**.
Number of staff: 1 full-time professional; 2 part-time professional.
EIN: 363588505
Other changes: The grantmaker now publishes an annual report.

1697
General Mills Foundation

1 General Mills Blvd.
MS CC-01
Minneapolis, MN 55426-1347
***Contact:* Ellen Luger, Exec. Dir.**
FAX: (763) 764-4114;
E-mail: CommunityActionQA@genmills.com; Application address: P.O. Box 1113, Minneapolis, MN 55440; Main URL: http://www.genmills.com/en/Responsibility/Community_Engagement.aspx
Champions for Healthy Kids Recipients: http://www.genmills.com/Home/Responsibility/Community_Engagement/Grants/Champions_for_healthy_kids/2011_recipients.aspx
Communities of Color Recipients: http://content.generalmills.com/Home/Responsibility/community_engagement/Grants/Twin%20Cities_area/Communities_of_color/grant_recipients_2012.aspx
Facebook: http://www.facebook.com/GeneralMillsGives
General Mills Foundation's Philanthropy Promise: http://www.ncrp.org/philanthropys-promise/who
Grants Database: http://content.generalmills.com/Responsibility/Community_Engagement/Grants/Grantees.aspx?cat={4020A4F2-C35C-40DD-9CE4-2374486831E7}
Philanthropy's Promise: http://www.ncrp.org/philanthropys-promise/who

Incorporated in 1954 in MN.
Donor: General Mills, Inc.
Foundation type: Company-sponsored foundation.
Financial data (yr. ended 05/31/13): Assets, $110,841,484 (M); gifts received, $25,100,000; expenditures, $27,259,015; qualifying distributions, $27,259,015; giving activities include $24,789,661 for 706 grants, and $2,108,664 for employee matching gifts.
Purpose and activities: The foundation supports programs designed to support hunger and nutrition wellness; education; and arts and culture.
Fields of interest: Performing arts; Arts; Elementary/secondary education; Education; Public health, physical fitness; Food services; Food banks; Nutrition; Disasters, preparedness/services; YM/YWCAs & YM/YWHAs; Family services; Human services; United Ways and

Federated Giving Programs; Children/youth; Adults; Minorities; Economically disadvantaged.
Type of support: Capital campaigns; Employee matching gifts; Employee volunteer services; Employee-related scholarships; General/operating support; Program development; Scholarship funds.
Limitations: Applications accepted. **Giving primarily in areas of major company operations and headquarters of Twin Cities, MN area; giving also in CA, GA, IA, IL, IN, MA, MD, MI, MO, MT, NJ, NM, NY, OH, TN, WA, and WI for the Community Action Councils Program.** No support for discriminatory organizations, religious, political, social, labor, veterans', alumni, or fraternal organizations, disease-specific organizations, or athletic associations. No grants to individuals (except for employee scholarships), or for endowments, annual appeals, federated campaigns, fund drives, recreational or sporting events, healthcare, research, advertising, political causes, travel, emergency funding, debt reduction or operating deficits, conferences, seminars or workshops, publications, film, or television, sponsorships, special events, or fundraisers; no loans.
Publications: Application guidelines; Corporate report; Corporate giving report; Financial statement; Grants list.
Application information: Applications for Community Action Council grants are available by invitation only. A full proposal may be requested at a later date for Twin Cities grants. E-mail letter of inquiry to foundation for capital requests. Telephone calls and personal visits are not encouraged. Organizations receiving support may be asked to submit an evaluation report. Application form required.
Initial approach: Complete online letter of inquiry for Twin Cities grants; complete online application for Celebrating Communities of Color
Deadline(s): **None for Twin Cities grants; Dec. See website for Celebrating Communities of Color annual information**
Board meeting date(s): Ongoing
Final notification: **Varies depending on program, see website for additional information per program**
Officers and Trustees:* Kendall J. Powell,* Chair.; Kimberly A. Nelson,* Pres.; Ellen Goldberg Luger, V.P., Secy., and Exec. Dir.; Marie Pillai, Treas.; Marc Belton; John R. Church; Michael L. Davis; Peter C. Erickson; Ian R. Friendly; Donal Leo Mulligan; Shawn O'Grady; Christopher O'Leary; Roderick A. Palmore.
Number of staff: 7 full-time professional; 2 full-time support.
EIN: 416018495
Other changes: Allison Olson is now Assoc. Jeff Peterson is no longer Dir., Innovation and Strategy. Cynthia A. Thelen is now Grants Mgr.

1698
George Family Foundation
1818 Oliver Ave. S.
Minneapolis, MN 55405-2208 **(612) 377-3356**
FAX: (612) 233-2194**; Letter of Inquiry contact: Robin Barker, e-mail: robin@georgefamilyfoundation.org**; Main URL: http://www.georgefamilyfoundation.org

Established in 1992 in MN.
Donors: Penny Pilgram George; William W. George.
Foundation type: Independent foundation.
Financial data (yr. ended 12/31/12): Assets, $57,398,847 (M); gifts received, $1,065,230; expenditures, $5,361,936; qualifying distributions, $4,743,319; giving activities include $4,289,840 for 77 grants (high: $250,000; low: $1,000).
Purpose and activities: The foundation's current focus is integrated health and healing (programs and initiatives that advance an integrated, patient-centered approach to health, healing and well being), authentic leadership (programs that are developing future leaders who are authentic, values-based and empowering of the leadership of others), and community.
Fields of interest: Health organizations, association; Leadership development.
Type of support: General/operating support; Continuing support; Program development.
Limitations: Giving primarily in the Twin Cities area of MN. **No support for fraternal or veterans organizations, school athletic programs, or for disease-specific organizations. No grants to individuals, or for endowments, capital campaigns, memberships, debt reduction, fundraisers, special events, courtesy, goodwill or public service advertisements, re-granting, or for operating expenses.**
Publications: Annual report.
Application information:
Initial approach: **E-mail Letter of Inquiry after reviewing application requirements on foundation web site**
Officers: Penny Pilgram George, Pres.; William W. George, V.P.; Gayle M. Ober, Exec. Dir.
Trustees: Jeffrey Pilgram George; Jonathan R. George.
EIN: 411730855

1699
Grand Rapids Area Community Foundation
350 N.W. First Ave., Ste. E
Grand Rapids, MN 55744-2756 (218) 999-9100
Contact: Chris Fulton, Exec. Dir.; For grants: Sarah Copeland, Dir., Grants and Progs.
FAX: (218) 999-7430; E-mail: info@gracf.org; Grant application e-mail: sarah.copeland@gracf.org; Main URL: http://www.gracf.org
Facebook: http://www.facebook.com/pages/Grand-Rapids-Area-Community-Foundation/115442225148512

Established in 1994 in MN.
Donors: Blandin Foundation; Itasca Medical Center Foundation; Larry Latterell.
Foundation type: Community foundation.
Financial data (yr. ended 12/31/11): Assets, $12,330,429 (M); gifts received, $1,643,421; expenditures, $1,301,182; giving activities include $896,090 for 19+ grants.
Purpose and activities: The foundation seeks to provide individuals and organizations opportunities to invest in their community to improve the quality of life.
Fields of interest: Humanities; Arts; Education; Environment; Health care; Recreation; Family services; Community/economic development.
Type of support: Endowments; Emergency funds; Conferences/seminars; Curriculum development; Technical assistance; Scholarships—to individuals.
Limitations: Applications accepted. Giving in the greater Itasca County, MN, area. No support for religious groups for religious purposes. No grants to individuals (except for scholarships), or for fundraising events or activities, communications including video tapes, brochures, and advertising, building campaigns, travel or conferences.
Publications: Application guidelines; Annual report (including application guidelines); Financial statement; Informational brochure; Newsletter; IRS Form 990 or 990-PF printed copy available upon request.
Application information: Visit foundation web site for online grant applications and guidelines. Application form required.
Initial approach: Letter of Inquiry
Copies of proposal: 1
Deadline(s): Sept. 15
Board meeting date(s): 1st Tues. of alternate months
Final notification: 1 month
Officers and Directors:* Mark White,* Chair.; Daryl Erdman,* Chair.-Elect.; Mike Lentz,* Vice-Chair.; Kelly Kirwin,* Secy.; Steve Burggraf,* Treas.; Chris Fulton, Exec. Dir.; **Edwin A. Anderson, M.D.**; Dennis Anderson; **Keith Anderson**; Derek Bostyancic; Megan Christianson; Chris Deadrick; Skip Drake; Mary Jo Gibbons; Mary Ives; Rhett Johnson; Tina Kane; Cynthia Margo; Sonja Merrild; Mike Olson; Cyrus White.
Number of staff: 3 full-time professional; 1 full-time support.
EIN: 411761590
Other changes: Mark White has replaced Keith Anderson as CHair. Daryl Erdman has replaced Mark White as Chiar.-Elect. Mike Lentz has replaced Daryl Erdman as Vice-Chair. Kelly Kirwin has replaced Peggy Schagh as Secy. Steve Burggraf has replaced Mike Lentz as Treas. Steve Burgraff and Kelly Kirwin are no longer directors.

1700
The Greystone Foundation
730 2nd Ave. S., Ste. 1300
Minneapolis, MN 55402-2475 (612) 752-1772

Established in 1948 in MN.
Donor: Members of the Paul A. Brooks family.
Foundation type: Independent foundation.
Financial data (yr. ended 12/31/12): Assets, $10,933,722 (M); gifts received, $371,195; expenditures, $1,319,565; qualifying distributions, $1,120,512; giving activities include $1,089,725 for 300 grants (high: $50,000; low: $250).
Purpose and activities: Giving for health and medical research, community funds, private secondary and higher education, and arts and cultural programs.
Fields of interest: Arts; Secondary school/education; Higher education; Hospitals (general); Health care; Medical research, institute; Human services; United Ways and Federated Giving Programs.
Type of support: General/operating support; Continuing support; Annual campaigns; Building/renovation; Equipment; Land acquisition; Emergency funds; Program development; Conferences/seminars; Publication; Seed money; Research.
Limitations: Applications not accepted. Giving primarily in MN, with emphasis on the Twin Cities. No grants to individuals, or for endowment funds, matching gifts, scholarships, or fellowships; no loans.
Application information: Unsolicited requests for funds not accepted.
Board meeting date(s): As required
Trustees: Julie Hara; Katherine M. Leighton.
EIN: 416027765
Other changes: Michael P. Hollern is no longer a trustee.

1701
Jessie F. Hallett Charitable Trust
(formerly Hallett Charitable Trust)
c/o Trust Tax Services
P.O. Box 64713
St. Paul, MN 55164-0713
***Application address:* c/o U.S. Bank, N.A., Att.: Duane Feragen, 155 1st Ave. S.W., Rochester, MN 55902, tel.: (507) 285-7925**

Established in 1984 in MN.
Donor: Jessie F. Hallett†.
Foundation type: Independent foundation.
Financial data (yr. ended 11/30/12): Assets, $8,926,891 (M); expenditures, $531,091; qualifying distributions, $451,025; giving activities include $390,930 for 17 grants (high: $77,319; low: $250).
Purpose and activities: Giving for higher education and Protestant agencies.
Fields of interest: Education; Youth development; Christian agencies & churches.
Limitations: Applications accepted. Giving primarily in the Midwest, with emphasis on MN. No grants to individuals.
Application information: Application form required.
Initial approach: Completed application form
Deadline(s): None
Trustees: Tom Jensen; Desiree Parker; Paul Schliesman; Kirk Springsted; U.S. Bank, N.A.
EIN: 416211994

1702
HRK Foundation
(formerly The MAHADH Foundation)
345 Saint Peter St., Ste. 1200
St. Paul, MN 55102-1216
Contact: Kathleen Fluegel, Fdn. Dir.
FAX: (651) 298-0551;
E-mail: Info@HRKFoundation.org; Toll-free tel.: (866) 342-5475; Main URL: http://www.hrkfoundation.org

Established in 1962 in MN.
Donors: Mary Andersen Hulings†; Albert D. Hulings†; Fred C. Andersen†; Katherine B. Andersen†; Katherine D. Rice; Katherine D.R. Hayes; Julia L. Hynnek; Frederick C. Kaemmer; Martha H. Kaemmer; Mary E. Rice; Mary H. Rice.
Foundation type: Independent foundation.
Financial data (yr. ended 12/31/12): Assets, $24,886,174 (M); gifts received, $999,146; expenditures, $2,464,679; qualifying distributions, $2,071,199; giving activities include $1,672,166 for 270 grants (high: $100,234; low: $250), and $21,300 for 10 employee matching gifts.
Purpose and activities: HRK Foundation s defined by quiet leadership and philanthropy. The Board seeks to improve the fabric of our society by promoting healthy families and healthy communities. It supports all families, both traditional and non-traditional.
Fields of interest: Arts, single organization support; Arts, formal/general education; Arts, cultural/ethnic awareness; Child development, education; Education; Reproductive health, sexuality education; Health care, patient services; Health care; AIDS; Children/youth, services; Family services; Community/economic development; AIDS, people with.
Type of support: General/operating support; Continuing support; Annual campaigns; Program development; Employee matching gifts; Matching/challenge support.
Limitations: Applications accepted. Giving primarily in MN, with emphasis on the metropolitan Twin Cities and St. Croix Valley areas, and in Ashland and Bayfield counties, WI. No grants to individuals, or for scholarships, fellowships or capital requests.
Publications: Application guidelines.
Application information: Application form required.
***Deadline(s):* See foundation web site for current deadlines**
Board meeting date(s): Generally May., and Nov.
Officer and Directors:* Julia L. Kaemmer,* Chair.; Arthur W. Kaemmer, M.D.*, Vice-Chair.; Kathleen Fluegel, Exec. Dir.; James D. Hayes; Katherine D.R. Hayes; Frederick C. Kaemmer; Martha H. Kaemmer; Daniel Priebe; Mary H. Rice; Molly E. Rice; Katherine R. Tilney.
Number of staff: 1 full-time professional; 2 part-time professional.
EIN: 416020911
Other changes: The grantmaker now publishes application guidelines.

1703
Initiative Foundation
(formerly Central Minnesota Initiative Fund)
405 1st St., S.E.
Little Falls, MN 56345-3007 (320) 632-9255
Contact: Kathy Gaalswyk, Pres.
FAX: (320) 632-9258; E-mail: info@ifound.org; Additional tel: (877) 632-9255; Grant inquiry e-mail: grants@ifound.org; Additional e-mail: kgaalswyk@ifound.org; Main URL: http://www.ifound.org
Facebook: http://www.facebook.com/ifound
KeyNOTES Blog: http://ifoundmn.blogspot.com/
LinkedIn: http://www.linkedin.com/groups?gid=1928428&trk=hb_side_g
Twitter: http://twitter.com/ifoundmn
YouTube: http://www.youtube.com/user/initiativefoundation

Established in 1986 in MN.
Foundation type: Community foundation.
Financial data (yr. ended 12/31/12): Assets, $54,942,906 (M); gifts received, $5,705,748; expenditures, $4,010,100; giving activities include $1,049,931 for 100+ grants (high: $35,000), and $256,580 for 101 grants to individuals.
Purpose and activities: The foundation awards grants and loans, pools resources, and creates partnerships to enhance the quality of life only in the 14-county area of central Minnesota. Focus is on activities that support resilient businesses, thriving communities, effective organizations and local philanthropy.
Fields of interest: Environment, water pollution; Children/youth, services; Family services; Human services; Civil rights, race/intergroup relations; Community development, public/private ventures; Economic development; Nonprofit management; Community/economic development.
Type of support: General/operating support; Program development; Seed money; Technical assistance; Program-related investments/loans; Scholarships—to individuals; Matching/challenge support.
Limitations: Applications accepted. Giving limited to Benton, Cass, Chisago, Crow Wing, Isanti, Kanabec, Mille Lacs, Morrison, Pine, Sherburne, Stearns, Todd, Wadena, and Wright counties, MN. No support for religious programs. No grants to individuals (except for scholarships) or for continuing support, endowments, capital expenses, curriculum development, or video production.
Publications: Application guidelines; Annual report; Grants list; Informational brochure; Program policy statement; Quarterly report.
Application information: Visit foundation website for application information. Contact Don Hickman, VP for Community and Economic Development, for information concerning the foundation's business financing programs. Application form required.
Initial approach: Complete online Letter of Inquiry for general grants
***Deadline(s):* Feb. 28, May 9, Sept. 5, and Nov. 21 for full proposals**
Board meeting date(s): Mar., June, Sept., and Dec.
***Final notification:* Within 45 days**
Officers and Directors:* Linda Eich DesJardins,* Chair.; Larry Korf,* Vice-Chair.; Kathy Gaalswyk,* Pres.; Don Hickman,* V.P., Community and Economic Devel.; Linda Holliday,* V.P., Organization Devel.; Eric Stommes, V.P., External Rels.; **Lynn Bushinger,* Treas. and C.F.O.**; John E. Babcock; **John J. Babcock**; Mayuli Bales; **Rick Bauerly**; Charles Black Lance; Reggie Clow; Pat Gorham; Lee Hanson; Dan Meyer; Dr. Earl Potter; Steve Shurts; Traci Tapani; Wayne Wolden.
Number of staff: 13 full-time professional; 1 part-time professional; 8 full-time support.
EIN: 363451562
Other changes: Kris Kowalzek is now Accounting Assoc. Jolene Howard is now Inf. Systems Coord. Chris Fastner is now Sr. Prog. Mgr., Organizational Devel.

1704
The Lynn Johnson Family Foundation
(formerly The Johnson Brothers Charitable Foundation)
1999 Shepard Rd.
St. Paul, MN 55116-3210
***Contact:* Todd Johnson, V.P.**

Established in 1980 in MN.
Donors: Lynn Johnson; Johnson Brothers Liquor Co.
Foundation type: Independent foundation.
Financial data (yr. ended 09/30/13): Assets, $11,446,319 (M); gifts received, $125,000; expenditures, $331,678; qualifying distributions, $305,092; giving activities include $305,092 for 27 grants (high: $100,000; low: $250).
Fields of interest: Higher education, university; Health organizations, association; Health organizations, fund raising/fund distribution; Cancer; Foundations (public); Jewish agencies & synagogues.
Limitations: Applications not accepted. Giving primarily in HI, MN and WI. No grants to individuals.
Application information: Contributes only to pre-selected organizations.
Officers: Lynn Johnson, Pres. and Treas.; Gloria Johnson, V.P.; Robin Johnson, V.P.; Todd Johnson, V.P.; Michael Johnson, Secy.
EIN: 411407595

1705
Lloyd K. Johnson Foundation
130 W. Superior St., Ste. 710
Duluth, MN 55802-4035 (218) 726-9000
Contact: Joan Gardner-Goodno, Exec. Dir.
FAX: (218) 726-9002;
E-mail: jgardner@lloydkjohnsonfoundation.org; Main URL: http://www.lloydkjohnsonfoundation.org/

Established in 1975 in MN.
Donor: Lloyd K. Johnson.
Foundation type: Independent foundation.
Financial data (yr. ended 12/31/12): Assets, $19,999,830 (M); gifts received, $150;

expenditures, $1,133,046; qualifying distributions, $1,036,960; giving activities include $911,157 for 71 grants (high: $60,000; low: $20).
Purpose and activities: Support for: 1) Arts and Culture, primarily activities that contribute to the creation and development of a healthy and vibrant arts community including new and traditional forms of the visual, performing, and interdisciplinary arts; 2) Community and Economic Development causes that enhance the economic and social well-being of all residents, and to support opportunities for economic self-sufficiency, particularly for low-income individuals and families; 3) Educational activities that contribute to the development and advancement of quality educational and training opportunities, and promote opportunities for life-long learning; 4) Environmental projects that support educational programs that promote respect for the natural environment, and encourage efforts to maintain quality air, water and land resources for future generations; and 5) Social Welfare programs that support the health and well-being of all members of the community, and support activities that promote healthy youth development.
Fields of interest: Arts; Education; Environment; Human services; Economic development; Community/economic development.
Type of support: General/operating support; Building/renovation; Program development.
Limitations: Applications accepted. Giving limited to organizations benefiting residents within Cook, Lake, and southern St. Louis counties, MN, including the communities of Duluth, Hermantown, and Proctor. No support for political organizations. No grants to individuals, or for endowments, debt reduction, loans or research.
Publications: Application guidelines; Annual report; Grants list.
Application information: Letters of Intent and full proposals are by invitation only. Application form required.

Initial approach: **Telephone or e-mail to determine if the project is consistent with the foundation's goals and interests**
Deadline(s): None for letter of intent. For grant application: Jan. 15, Apr. 15, July 15 and Oct. 15
Board meeting date(s): Mar., June, Sept., and Dec.
Final notification: Within 2 months after submittal

Officers and Directors:* Mark Smithson,* C.E.O. and Pres.; **Bill Hansen, V.P.**; Scott Harrison, C.F.O. and Treas.; Joan Gardner-Goodno, Exec. Dir.; Darryl E. Coons; Ruth Ann Eaton; Heidi Johnson; **Susan Michels.**
Number of staff: 1 full-time professional.
EIN: 510180842
Other changes: Bill Hansen has replaced Heidi Johnson as V.P.

1706
The Jostens Foundation, Inc.

3601 Minnesota Dr., Ste. 400
Minneapolis, MN 55435-5281 (952) 830-3235
Contact: Veronica Sanderson, Secy.
E-mail: foundation@jostens.com; **Main URL: http://www.jostens.com/misc/aboutus/about_jostens_cp_involvement.html**

Established in 1976 in MN.
Donor: Jostens, Inc.
Foundation type: Company-sponsored foundation.
Financial data (yr. ended 12/31/12): Assets, $119,451 (M); gifts received, $500,000; expenditures, $580,802; qualifying distributions, $580,802; giving activities include $534,357 for 50 grants (high: $25,000; low: $25), and $33,000 for 15 grants to individuals (high: $5,000; low: $2,000).
Purpose and activities: The foundation supports organizations involved with education and youth development.
Fields of interest: Elementary/secondary education; Higher education; Education, drop-out prevention; Education, reading; Education; Youth development.
Type of support: General/operating support; Program development; Employee matching gifts; Employee-related scholarships.
Limitations: Applications accepted. Giving in areas of company operations, with emphasis on MN. No support for schools, school districts, or school foundations, organizations involved with highly political or controversial issues, churches or religious groups, or fraternal, veterans', or professional organizations. No grants to individuals (except for employee-related scholarships), or for personal needs, political campaigns or political lobbying activities, benefit fundraising events or tickets to fundraisers, recognition or testimonial events, disease-specific fundraising campaigns, athletic scholarships or activities, advertising, endowments, or capital campaigns.
Publications: Application guidelines; Informational brochure (including application guidelines); Program policy statement.
Application information: Requests may be submitted using the Minnesota Common Grant Form. Application form required.

Initial approach: Proposal
Copies of proposal: 1
Deadline(s): Feb. 22, May 24, Aug. 23, and Nov. 22.
Board meeting date(s): Quarterly
Final notification: Within 1 month of board meetings

Officers and Directors:* Charley Nelson, Pres.; Veronica Sanderson, Secy.; Randall Wilson, Treas.; Tricia Bishop; Sheri Hank; Aaron Kjolhaug; Marin Koentopf; Lindsey Robertson; Natalie Stute.
EIN: 411280587

1707
Kaplan Family Foundation

6566 France Ave. S., No. 701
Edina, MN 55435-1714
E-mail: aryeh1@aol.com

Established in 1994 in MN.
Donors: Harvey Kaplan; Helen Kaplan; Leah Kaplan; Marjorie Kaplan; Rachel Kaplan; Ross Kaplan.
Foundation type: Independent foundation.
Financial data (yr. ended 12/31/12): Assets, $4,105,409 (M); expenditures, $193,299; qualifying distributions, $179,218; giving activities include $179,218 for grants.
Purpose and activities: Giving primarily to Jewish agencies to support Jewish cultural arts, education and camping.
Fields of interest: Education; Human services; Family services; Jewish federated giving programs; Jewish agencies & synagogues.
International interests: Israel.
Type of support: Continuing support; Annual campaigns; Endowments.
Limitations: Applications not accepted. Giving primarily in AZ, IL, MN, NY, PA, the Midwest, and Israel. No support for political organizations. No grants to individuals.
Application information: Contributes only to pre-selected organizations.

Board meeting date(s): July-Aug.

Officers and Directors:* Harvey Kaplan,* Pres.; Marjorie Kaplan,* V.P.; **Helen Kaplan, Treas.**; Rachel Kaplan, Secy.; Laura Kaplan; Leah Kaplan; Ross Kaplan; Robert Riesman; Jon Smollen.
Number of staff: None.
EIN: 411794327
Other changes: Helen Kaplan has replaced Ross Kaplan as Treas.

1708
Peter J. King Family Foundation

3001 Broadway St. N.E., Ste. 665
Minneapolis, MN 55413-2297
***E-mail:* info@pjkingfamilyfoundation.org**; Main URL: http://www.pjkingfamilyfoundation.org/

Established in 1985 in MN.
Donor: Peter J. King‡.
Foundation type: Independent foundation.
Financial data (yr. ended 11/30/12): Assets, $79,925,154 (M); gifts received, $13,199,167; expenditures, $2,839,476; qualifying distributions, $2,392,437; giving activities include $2,077,800 for 11 grants (high: $850,000; low: $1,000).
Purpose and activities: The foundation's focus is to provide brick-and-mortar facilities to local communities and organizations whose activities are dedicated to the improvement of children's health, education and welfare and the family environment.
Fields of interest: Elementary/secondary education; Education, early childhood education; Hospitals (general); Medical care, outpatient care; Health care, support services; Health care, EMS; Youth development, centers/clubs; Youth development, adult & child programs; Children/youth, services; Family services.
Type of support: General/operating support; Capital campaigns; Building/renovation; Equipment; Land acquisition; Matching/challenge support.
Limitations: Giving primarily in the Twin Cities, MN metropolitan area; some giving also in Tanzania. No grants for programming needs.
Application information: Submission of application form is by invitation only, upon review of Letter of Inquiry. Application form required.

***Initial approach:* Letter of Inquiry**

Officers and Directors:* Russell S. King,* Pres.; Stephen D. Higgins,* V.P.; James C. Teal; James A. Weichert.
EIN: 261600569

1709
Ida C. Koran Trust

c/o Ecolab Inc.
370 Wabasha St. N
St. Paul, MN 55102-1323 (651) 293-2392
FAX: (651) 452-0485;
E-mail: Sue@idakorantrust.org; Main URL: http://idakoran.com/

Established around 1992.
Donor: Ida Koran‡.
Foundation type: Independent foundation.
Financial data (yr. ended 12/31/12): Assets, $40,961,033 (M); expenditures, $2,180,808; qualifying distributions, $2,284,868; giving activities include $1,638,753 for grants to individuals, and $424,350 for loans to individuals.
Purpose and activities: Academic assistance to dependents of Ecolab employees, and hardship grants and loans to employees of Ecolab, Inc., MN.
Fields of interest: Education; Human services, emergency aid.

Type of support: General/operating support; Scholarship funds; Grants to individuals.
Limitations: Giving primarily in MN.
Publications: Application guidelines.
Application information: Only Ecolab, Inc., employees are eligible for grant awards. See foundation web site for guidelines.
Trustees: Diana D. Lewis; Stanley Osborn; U.S. Bank, N.A.
EIN: 416124022
Other changes: The grantmaker now publishes application guidelines.

1710
Land O'Lakes Foundation
P.O. Box 64150
St. Paul, MN 55164-0150
Contact: Lydia Botham, Exec. Dir.
E-mail: mlatkins-sakry@landolakes.com; **Contact for California Regions Grant Prog., Mid-Atlantic Grants Prog., and John Brandt Scholarship Program: LandOLakesFoundation@LandOLakes.com; Additional contact: Martha Atkins-Sakry, Exec. Asst., tel.: (651) 375-2470; Main URL: http://www.foundation.landolakes.com/**

Established in 1996 in MN.
Donor: Land O'Lakes, Inc.
Foundation type: Company-sponsored foundation.
Financial data (yr. ended 12/31/12): Assets, $10,546,206 (M); gifts received, $2,885,503; expenditures, $3,134,989; qualifying distributions, $3,066,955; giving activities include $2,848,785 for 1,400 grants (high: $25,000; low: $125).
Purpose and activities: The foundation supports organizations involved with arts and culture, education, human services, civic improvements, and youth and awards graduate scholarships to graduate students studying the dairy sciences. Special emphasis is directed toward programs designed to alleviate rural hunger.
Fields of interest: Media, film/video; Media, television; Visual arts; Performing arts; Literature; Arts; Elementary/secondary education; Higher education; Libraries (public); Education; Environment, water resources; Environment, land resources; Environment, plant conservation; Hospitals (general); Agriculture, sustainable programs; Food services; Food banks; Nutrition; Agriculture/food; Disasters, fire prevention/control; Recreation, parks/playgrounds; Youth development, agriculture; Youth development; Human services; Rural development; Community/economic development; United Ways and Federated Giving Programs; Leadership development; Public affairs; Youth; Native Americans/American Indians.
Type of support: Building/renovation; Capital campaigns; Employee matching gifts; Employee volunteer services; Equipment; General/operating support; Matching/challenge support; Scholarships—to individuals; Seed money.
Limitations: Applications accepted. **Giving on a national basis in areas of company operations in AR, CA, IA, ID, IL, IN, KS, MD, MI, MN, MS, MO, ND, NE, OH, OR, PA, SD, TX, WA, and WI; giving also to statewide, regional, and national organizations.** No support for lobbying or political organizations, religious organizations not of direct benefit to the entire community, or veterans', fraternal, or labor organizations. No grants to individuals (except for scholarships), or for fundraising events, dinners, or benefits, advertising, higher education capital campaigns or endowments, travel, racing or sports sponsorships, or disease or medical research or treatment.
Publications: Application guidelines; Annual report; Grants list; Informational brochure (including application guidelines); IRS Form 990 or 990-PF printed copy available upon request.
Application information: Application form required.
Initial approach: Complete online application for Community Grants Program; contact a Land O'Lakes dairy farmer or unit delegate for application form for California Regions Grants and Mid-Atlantic Grants; download application and mail for John Memorial Scholarships
Copies of proposal: 1
***Deadline(s):* May 1 for Education, July 1 for Hunger, and Oct. 2 for all other proposals for the Community Grants Program; None for California Regions Grants and Mid-Atlantic Grants; May 2 for John Brandt Memorial Scholarships**
Board meeting date(s): Feb., June, Aug., and Dec.
Final notification: 2 to 4 weeks for California Regions Grants and Mid-Atlantic Grants
Officers and Directors:* Jim Hager,* Chair.; **Tom Wakefield, Vice-Chair.**; Nancy Breyfogle,* Treas.; Lydia Botham,* Exec. Dir.; Tanya Dowda; John Ellenberger; Pete Janzen; Stephen Mancebo; Ronnie Mohr; Doug Reimer.
Number of staff: 1 full-time professional; 1 full-time support.
EIN: 411864977
Other changes: Tom Wakefield has replaced James Netto as Vice-Chair.
James Netto is no longer Vice-Chair.

1711
John Larsen Foundation
2002 W. Lake of the Isles Pkwy.
Minneapolis, MN **55105-2438 (612) 377-9010**
Main URL: http://johnlarsenfoundation.org

Established in 1991 in MN.
Donors: John A. Larsen; Karen R. Larsen; Lillian Regenberg.
Foundation type: Independent foundation.
Financial data (yr. ended 12/31/12): Assets, $5,962,732 (M); expenditures, $294,814; qualifying distributions, $243,093; giving activities include $238,000 for 21 grants (high: $50,000; low: $1,000).
Purpose and activities: To better the lives of individuals and families, both traditional and non-traditional.
Fields of interest: Arts; Education; Environment; Human services, equal rights; Human services; Community/economic development; Children/youth; Youth; Adults; Offenders/ex-offenders; Substance abusers; Crime/abuse victims; Homeless; LGBTQ.
Type of support: General/operating support; Continuing support; Management development/capacity building; Annual campaigns; Capital campaigns; Building/renovation; Endowments; Film/video/radio; Curriculum development; Program-related investments/loans; Matching/challenge support.
Limitations: Applications not accepted. Giving primarily in MN and WI. No support for religious or political organizations, umbrella organizations, or for fraternal societies. No grants to individuals.
Publications: Grants list; Multi-year report.
Application information: The foundation accepts grant requests by invitation only; unsolicited requests for funds are not accepted.
Board meeting date(s): Varies
Officers: John E. Larsen, Pres.; John A. Larsen, Treas.
Director: Karen R. Larsen.
Board Member: Kristen L. Rose.
Number of staff: 1 part-time support.
EIN: 411715465

1712
Leslie Foundation Irrevocable Trust
Minneapolis, MN

The foundation terminated in 2011.

1713
Marbrook Foundation
730 2nd Ave. S., Ste. 1300
Minneapolis, MN 55402-2475 (612) 752-1783
***Contact:* Julie Hara, Exec. Dir.**
FAX: (612) 752-1780;
E-mail: jhara@marbrookfoundation.org; Main URL: http://marbrookfoundation.org
Grants Database: http://marbrookfoundation.org/2013-grants/

Established in 1948 in MN.
Donors: Edward Brooks†; Markell C. Brooks†.
Foundation type: Independent foundation.
Financial data (yr. ended 12/31/12): Assets, $14,551,370 (M); expenditures, $954,030; qualifying distributions, $700,000; giving activities include $700,000 for grants.
Purpose and activities: Primary areas of interest include organizations that create equal opportunities for immigrants and refugees in the Twin Cities metropolitan area. Focuses include: 1) Equal opportunity and empowerment; 2) Environmental justice and advocacy for immigrants; 3) Expanding access to healthy food; 4) Academic success for children of immigrants; 5) English language instruction; 6) Cultural preservation for new Americans; 7) Integrating a "mind-body-spirit" approach to the well being of immigrants; and 8) Arts projects that highlight cultural awareness or address social issues of immigrants.
Fields of interest: Arts, cultural/ethnic awareness; Visual arts; Museums; Performing arts; Performing arts, theater; Historic preservation/historical societies; Arts; Elementary school/education; Education; Environment, natural resources; Environment; Employment; Housing/shelter; Human services; Children/youth, services; Community/economic development; Spirituality; Immigrants/refugees.
Type of support: Annual campaigns; Building/renovation; Capital campaigns; Continuing support; Endowments; Equipment; General/operating support; Land acquisition; Matching/challenge support; Professorships; Program development; Research; Scholarship funds.
Limitations: Applications accepted. Giving limited to the Minneapolis-St. Paul, MN, area. No support for political purposes, or for start-up organizations, programs for the elderly, domestic abuse programs, disease-related organizations, homeless shelters, food shelves, or programs servicing the mentally or physically disabled. No grants to individuals, or for early-childhood education, legal services, conferences or events.
Publications: Annual report (including application guidelines); Financial statement; Grants list.
Application information: Complete application guidelines available on foundation web site. Application form required.
***Initial approach:* Online application on foundation web site**
Copies of proposal: 1

Deadline(s): **See foundation web site for current deadlines**
Board meeting date(s): June and Dec.
Officer: Julie S. Hara, Exec. Dir.
Trustees: Conley Brooks; Conley Brooks, Jr.; Markell C. Brooks; Stephen B. Brooks; Markell Kiefer; Katherine M. Leighton; Julie B. Zelle.
Number of staff: 1 part-time professional.
EIN: 416019899
Other changes: Julia S. Hara is now Exec. Dir.

1714
The McKnight Endowment Fund for Neuroscience

710 2nd St. S., Ste. 400
Minneapolis, MN 55401-2290 (612) 333-4220
Contact: Kathleen Rysted
FAX: (612) 332-3833; E-mail: emaler@mcknight.org; Main URL: http://www.mcknight.org/neuroscience

Established in 1987 in MN.
Donor: The McKnight Foundation.
Foundation type: Operating foundation.
Financial data (yr. ended 12/31/12): Assets, $8,037 (M); gifts received, $3,490,000; expenditures, $3,492,831; qualifying distributions, $3,492,831; giving activities include $2,966,958 for 35 grants to individuals (high: $100,000; low: $25,000), and $279,889 for foundation-administered programs.
Purpose and activities: Awards grants for neuroscience research, especially as it pertains to memory and to a clearer understanding of diseases affecting memory and its biological substrates.
Fields of interest: Medical research, institute; Neuroscience research.
Type of support: Research.
Limitations: Applications accepted. Giving limited to U.S. citizens or permanent residents.
Publications: Application guidelines.
Application information: Application form required.
Initial approach: Letter or telephone for application forms and guidelines; materials for Scholar Awards available in Sept. annually
Deadline(s): See foundation web site for current deadlines
Board meeting date(s): Apr.
Final notification: See foundation web site
Officers and Directors:* Thomas M. Jessell, Ph.D.*, Pres.; Huda Yahya Zoghbi, V.P.; Patricia S. Binger; Allison J. Doupe, M.D., Ph.D.; Michael Ehlers, M.D., Ph.D.; David Julius, Ph.D.; Anthony Movshon, Ph.D.; Carla J. Shatz, Ph.D.; **Wendy Suzuki, Ph.D.**; David Tank; Kate Wolford.
EIN: 411563321
Other changes: Eric Nestler is no longer a director.

1715
The McKnight Foundation

710 S. 2nd St., Ste. 400
Minneapolis, MN 55401-2290 (612) 333-4220
***Contact:* Kate Wolford, Pres.**
FAX: (612) 332-3833; E-mail: info@mcknight.org; Main URL: http://www.mcknight.org
Blog: http://blog.mcknight.org/
E-Newsletter: http://visitor.constantcontact.com/manage/optin/ea?v=001mBomMP0GdY8UKXJsN5z3Cw%3D%3D
Facebook: http://www.facebook.com/pages/McKnight-Foundation/131199140270392
Grantee Perception Report: http://www.mcknight.org/resource-library/grant-programs/general-information/grantee-perception-report
Grants Database: http://www.mcknight.org/grantsprograms/findagrantee.aspx
Knowledge Center: http://www.mcknight.org/resource-library
McKnight Foundation's Philanthropy Promise: http://www.ncrp.org/philanthropys-promise/who
RSS Feed: http://www.mcknight.org/rss
State of the Artist: http://www.stateoftheartist.org/
The Mcknight Foundation Staff: https://twitter.com/McKnightFdn/mcknight-staff-on-twitter/members
Twitter: https://twitter.com/McKnightFdn

Incorporated in 1953 in MN.
Donors: William L. McKnight†; Maude L. McKnight†; Virginia M. Binger†; James H. Binger†.
Foundation type: Independent foundation.
Financial data (yr. ended 12/31/12): Assets, $2,063,472,860 (M); gifts received, $87,881; expenditures, $112,560,597; qualifying distributions, $96,051,063; giving activities include $85,024,278 for 752 grants (high: $5,200,000; low: $1,000), $90,714 for 204 employee matching gifts, and $488,262 for 4 foundation-administered programs.
Purpose and activities: The grant maker seeks to improve the quality of life for present and future generations. Through grant making, coalition-building, and encouragement of strategic policy reform, it uses its resources to attend, unite, and empower those it serves.
Fields of interest: Arts; Environment, energy; Environment; Neuroscience; Housing/shelter, development; Youth development; Children/youth, services; Child development, services; Community/economic development; Transportation; Children/youth; Economically disadvantaged.
International interests: Cambodia; Laos; Tanzania; Uganda; Vietnam.
Type of support: Program-related investments/loans; General/operating support; Capital campaigns; Building/renovation; Equipment; Program development; Fellowships; Technical assistance; Program evaluation; Employee matching gifts; Matching/challenge support.
Limitations: Applications accepted. Giving limited to organizations in MN, especially the seven-county Twin Cities, MN, area, except for programs in the environment which are made mainly in the 10 states bordering the Mississippi River and in the Twin Cities region, international aid, or research. No support for religious organizations for religious purposes, or for medical health or health-related services, including those for chemical dependency, services for seniors or people with disabilities. No grants to individuals (except for the Virginia McKnight Binger Awards in Human Service and the McKnight Distinguished Artist Award.), or for basic research in academic disciplines (except for defined programs in crop research and neuroscience) endowment funds, scholarships, fellowships, national fundraising campaigns, ticket sales, travel or conferences.
Publications: Application guidelines; Annual report; Financial statement; Grants list; Informational brochure; Newsletter; Occasional report.
Application information: The foundation will e-mail to decline requests or to provide additional instructions for submitting a full proposal online. Application form not required.
Initial approach: Online grant application
***Deadline(s):* Jan. 15, Apr. 15, July 15, and Oct. 15 for arts, and region and communities; Feb. 1, May 1, Aug. 1, Nov. 1 for Mississippi River. See foundation web site for additional program deadlines**
Board meeting date(s): Feb., May, Aug., Nov.
Final notification: 5 months
Officers and Directors:* Ted Staryk,* Chair.; Kate Wolford, Pres.; Richard J. Scott, V.P., Finance and Compliance, and Secy.; Richard D. McFarland,* Treas.; **Anne Binger**; Erika L. Binger; Meghan Binger Brown; Robert Bruininks; David Crasby; **Phyllis Goff**; Bill Gregg; Debby Landesman; Perry Moriearty; Robert J. Struyk.
Number of staff: 21 full-time professional; 1 part-time professional; 15 full-time support; 1 part-time support.
EIN: 410754835
Other changes: Patricia S. Binger and Noa Staryk are no longer directors.

1716
Midcontinent Media Foundation

(formerly Midcontinent Foundation)
3600 Minnesota Dr., Ste. 700
Minneapolis, MN 55435-7979
***Contact:* Steven E. Grosser**

Established in 1987.
Donors: Midcontinent Media, Inc.; Midcontinent Communications.
Foundation type: Company-sponsored foundation.
Financial data (yr. ended 12/31/12): Assets, $80,544 (M); gifts received, $179,996; expenditures, $163,789; qualifying distributions, $154,543; giving activities include $154,543 for grants.
Purpose and activities: The foundation supports zoos and organizations involved with arts and culture, education, health, diabetes, crime and violence prevention, housing development, recreation, human services, and community economic development.
Fields of interest: Arts; Elementary school/education; Higher education; Education; Zoos/zoological societies; Nursing home/convalescent facility; Health care; Diabetes; Crime/violence prevention; Crime/violence prevention, domestic violence; Housing/shelter, development; Disasters, fire prevention/control; Recreation, centers; Recreation; Youth development, business; American Red Cross; YM/YWCAs & YM/YWHAs; Children, services; Human services; Community/economic development; United Ways and Federated Giving Programs.
Type of support: Building/renovation; Equipment; Emergency funds; Program development; Seed money; Employee matching gifts.
Limitations: Applications accepted. Giving primarily in areas of company operations in MN, ND, and SD. No support for organizations not endorsed by a Midcontinent Media employee.
Publications: Application guidelines.
Application information: The foundation gives priority to organizations endorsed by a Midcontinent Communications employee. Application form required.
Initial approach: Letter
Copies of proposal: 1
Deadline(s): None
Board meeting date(s): Mar. and Sept.
Officers: Judy Johnson, Secy.; Tom Simmons, Exec. Dir.
Directors: Steve Mattern; Pat McAdaragh; Brad Schoenfelder; Debbie Stang.
EIN: 363556764

1717
The Minneapolis Foundation
800 IDS Ctr.
80 S. Eighth St.
Minneapolis, MN 55402-2100 (612) 672-3878
Contact: For grants: Andrea Porter, Grants Admin.
FAX: (612) 672-3846;
E-mail: e-mail@mplsfoundation.org; Grants application request e-mail: grants@mplsfoundation.org; Main URL: http://www.MinneapolisFoundation.org
Additional URL: http://www.mplsfoundation.org
At The Table Blog: http://atthetable.minneapolisfoundation.org/
At The Table Blog Feed: http://atthetable.minneapolisfoundation.org/feed/
Facebook: http://www.facebook.com/MinneapolisFoundation
The Minneapolis Foundation's Philanthropy Promise: http://www.ncrp.org/philanthropys-promise/who
Twitter: http://twitter.com/mplsfoundation

Incorporated in 1915 in MN.
Foundation type: Community foundation.
Financial data (yr. ended 03/31/13): Assets, $631,073,506 (M); gifts received, $38,204,009; expenditures, $59,859,761; giving activities include $52,591,314 for grants.
Purpose and activities: The foundation believes that the well-being of each citizen is connected to that of every other and that the vitality of any community is determined by the quality of those relationships. With this principle in mind, the foundation's purpose is to join with others to strengthen the community, in measurable and sustainable ways, for the benefit of all citizens, especially those who are disadvantaged. The foundation is committed to being an effective resource developer and a responsible steward of those resources, an active grantmaker and convener addressing crucial community needs, and a constructive catalyst, changing systems to serve people better.
Fields of interest: Arts; Education, early childhood education; Child development, education; Education; Health care; Crime/violence prevention, domestic violence; Housing/shelter; Disasters, Hurricane Katrina; Children/youth, services; Child development, services; Family services; Women, centers/services; Human services; International development; Civil/human rights, immigrants; Civil/human rights, minorities; Civil/human rights, disabled; Civil/human rights, women; Civil/human rights, aging; Civil rights, race/intergroup relations; Civil/human rights; Economic development; Community/economic development; Public policy, research; Aging; Disabilities, people with; Minorities; Asians/Pacific Islanders; African Americans/Blacks; Hispanics/Latinos; Native Americans/American Indians; Immigrants/refugees; Economically disadvantaged; Homeless.
Type of support: General/operating support; Continuing support; Capital campaigns; Equipment; Program development; Seed money; Technical assistance; Program-related investments/loans.
Limitations: Applications accepted. Giving limited to MN, with emphasis on organizations in the Twin Cities metropolitan region. No support for national campaigns, direct religious activities, veterans' or fraternal organizations, or organizations within umbrella organizations. **No grants to individuals, or for annual campaigns, capital support, deficit financing, building or endowment funds, emergency/safety net services, production of housing units, conferences, purchase or repair of vehicles, direct fundraising efforts, or memberships.**
Publications: Application guidelines; Annual report; Annual report (including application guidelines); Financial statement; Grants list; Informational brochure; Newsletter.
Application information: Visit foundation web site for online application and guidelines. Application form required.
Initial approach: Submit Letter of Inquiry
***Deadline(s):* Aug. 8 for Letter of Inquiry; Sept. 22 for full proposals**
Board meeting date(s): Committee meets 4 times a year
***Final notification:* Dec. 17**
Officers and Trustees:* Lowell Stortz,* Chair.; Norman Rickeman,* Vice-Chair.; Sandy L. Vargas,* C.E.O. and Pres.; Jean Adams,* C.O.O. and C.F.O.; Beth Halloran, Sr. V.P., Advancement; Luz Maria Frias, V.P., Community Impact; Teresa Morrow, V.P., External Rels. and Mktg.; William M. Sternberg, V.P., Philanthropic Svcs.; Archie Givens, Jr.,* Secy.; Jane Wyatt,* Treas.; Tim Baylor; Maureen Bazinet Beck; Ann Burns; Jan Conlin; Terrance R. Dolan; Robert Fullerton; J. Andrew Herring; Suzanne Koepplinger; Nekima Levy-Pounds, Esq.; Todd J. Lifson; David C. Mortenson; Patty Murphy; Gloria Perez; Brian J. Pietsch; Gretchen Piper; Steven Rothschild; Catherine Shreves; Nancy Siska; Phil Smith; David Sternberg; John Sullivan; Ellen Valde; Sven Wehrwein; Ben Whitney.
Trustee Banks: U.S. Bank, N.A.; Wells Fargo Bank Minnesota, N.A.
Number of staff: 26 full-time professional; 2 part-time professional; 13 full-time support; 1 part-time support.
EIN: 416029402
Other changes: Marshall J. Besikof, Lynn Casey, and Sima Griffith are no longer trustees. Eric L. Anderson is now Dir., Stewardship.

1718
Mosaic Company Foundation
3033 Campus Dr., Rm. E490
Plymouth, MN 55441-2655 (763) 577-2700
FAX: (763) 559-2860;
E-mail: community.relations@mosaicco.com; Toll free tel.: (800) 918-8270; **Main URL: http://www.mosaicco.com/sustainability/givingmap/index.htm**
RSS Feed: http://www.mosaicco.com/2650.htm?subcat=ALL

Established in 2009 in MN.
Donor: The Mosaic Company.
Foundation type: Company-sponsored foundation.
Financial data (yr. ended 05/31/13): Assets, $3,065,396 (M); gifts received, $7,001,125; expenditures, $8,331,844; qualifying distributions, $8,326,483; giving activities include $8,326,009 for 74 grants.
Purpose and activities: The foundation supports programs designed to address food; water; and local community investments.
Fields of interest: Education; Environment, natural resources; Environment, water resources; Environment; Agriculture; Agriculture, community food systems; Agriculture, farmlands; Food services; Nutrition; Disasters, preparedness/services; Human services; Community/economic development; Public affairs.
Type of support: General/operating support; Continuing support; Capital campaigns; Program development; Employee volunteer services; Sponsorships; Donated products; In-kind gifts.
Limitations: Applications accepted. Giving primarily in areas of company operations in FL, LA, MN, Argentina, Brazil, Canada, Chile, China, and India; giving also to national organizations. No support for political, private membership, or faith-based organizations not of direct benefit of the entire community. No grants to individuals, or for endowments, public policy, grassroots organizing, advocacy, or electoral campaigns, residential recycling, energy development including dams or renewable energy, or sewage improvement projects in developed countries.
Publications: Application guidelines.
Application information: Minnesota applicants are encouraged to visit website for additional application guidelines.
***Initial approach:* Complete online application; e-mail letter of inquiry for international organizations**
***Deadline(s):* Sept. 30, Dec. 20, Apr. 4, and June 27**
***Final notification:* Jan. 28, Apr. 18. Aug. 1, and Oct. 24**
Officers and Directors: Mark E. Kaplan, Pres.; Richard L. Mack, Secy.; Lawrence Stranghoener, Treas.; Christopher Lambe, Exec. Dir.; **Gary Bo Davis**; Richard Mclellan; Todd Madden; James Joc O'Rourke; Walt Precourt.
EIN: 270304734
Other changes: At the close of 2012, the grantmaker paid grants of $7,732,816, a 96.1% increase over the 2011 disbursements, $3,942,421.
The grantmaker now accepts applications.
Richard L. Mack has replaced Mark E. Kaplan as Secy.
James T. Prokopanko is no longer Chair. Mark E. Kaplan is now Pres.
The grantmaker now publishes application guidelines.

1719
The Laura Jane Musser Fund
(formerly The Musser Fund)
c/o Trust Tax Services
P.O. Box 64713
St. Paul, MN 55164-0713 (612) 303-3208
***Contact:* Mary Karen Lynn-Klimenko, Grants Prog. Mgr.**
FAX: (612) 822-8587;
E-mail: ljmusserfund@earthlink.net; **Application address: c/o U.S. Bank, N.A., Att.: Sally Godfrey, 800 Nicollet Mall, Minneapolis, MN 55402, tel.: (612) 303-3208**; Main URL: http://www.musserfund.org/

Established in 1990 in MN.
Donor: Laura J. Musser‡.
Foundation type: Independent foundation.
Financial data (yr. ended 12/31/12): Assets, $18,088,877 (M); expenditures, $955,089; qualifying distributions, $831,391; giving activities include $597,250 for 90 grants (high: $35,000; low: $500).
Purpose and activities: Primary areas of interest include community-based approaches to solving environmental problems, smaller participatory arts programs, securing intercultural harmony and developing leadership in rural communities.
Fields of interest: Arts; Environment; Civil rights, race/intergroup relations; Rural development.
Type of support: Program development; Seed money.
Publications: Application guidelines; Grants list; Program policy statement.
Application information: See foundation web site for complete application guidelines. Application form required.
Initial approach: Letter

Copies of proposal: 1
Deadline(s): None
Directors: Lisa Walker Duke; Joseph S. Micallef; Ivy Parish; Robert Strasburg; James Kahea Taylor; Jane Taylor; Drew Walker; Timothy Walker.
Trustee: U.S. Bank, N.A.
Number of staff: None.
EIN: 416334475

1720
The Nash Foundation
90 S. 7th St., Ste. 5300
Minneapolis, MN 55402-3903
E-mail: contact@nashfoundation.org; Main URL: http://www.nashfoundation.org
Heritage Grants: http://www.nashfoundation.org/Special-Projects.html
Minnesota Grants: http://www.nashfoundation.org/Grants_Minnesota.html

Established in 1922 in MN.
Foundation type: Independent foundation.
Financial data (yr. ended 06/30/13): Assets, $4,198,136 (M); expenditures, $191,383; qualifying distributions, $162,672; giving activities include $126,755 for 88 grants (high: $3,000; low: $50).
Purpose and activities: Funding primarily for arts and cultural programs, children and youth services, environment and community services.
Fields of interest: Museums; Performing arts, orchestras; Arts; Higher education, university; Environment; Mental health/crisis services; Agriculture; Food services; Human services; Youth, services; Civil liberties, reproductive rights.
Type of support: General/operating support; Continuing support; Annual campaigns; Capital campaigns; Program development.
Limitations: Applications accepted. Giving primarily in the Twin Cities Minneapolis-St. Paul, MN, metropolitan area. No support for religious, health or medical organizations, or for athletic programs and facilities. No grants to individuals, or for endowments or fundraising events.
Publications: Application guidelines.
Application information: Proposals by U.S. mail are not accepted. Application form required.
***Initial approach:* Online application form**
Deadline(s): July 1
Board meeting date(s): May
Officers: Steve Brautigam, Secy.; Rebecca Nash, V.P.; Peter Norton, Treas.
Directors: Henry Atwood; Nicholas Atwood; Tom Atwood; Will Dietz; Jim Norton; Monty Schmitt.
Number of staff: 1 part-time professional.
EIN: 416019142

1721
George W. Neilson Foundation
P.O. Box 692
Bemidji, MN 56619-0692 (218) 444-4963
Contact: Suzanne Liapis, Secy.
E-mail: sueliapis@excite.com; Main URL: http://www.gwnf.org

Trust established in 1962 in MN.
Donors: George W. Neilson†; Catherine Neilson Cram†.
Foundation type: Independent foundation.
Financial data (yr. ended 12/31/12): Assets, $27,884,705 (M); expenditures, $1,079,441; qualifying distributions, $953,846; giving activities include $874,005 for 30 grants (high: $200,000; low: $1,000).
Purpose and activities: Emphasis on matching funds for community needs, leadership, and rural and economic development in the Bemidji, MN, area.
Fields of interest: Arts; Human services; Children/youth, services; Community/economic development.
Type of support: Building/renovation; Equipment; Program development; Matching/challenge support.
Limitations: Applications accepted. Giving primarily in the Bemidji, MN, area. No support for religious activities or governmental services. No grants to individuals, or for endowment funds, scholarships, fellowships, or basic research.
Publications: Application guidelines; Grants list; Informational brochure (including application guidelines).
Application information: Accepts MN Common Grant Application Form; questions answered via telephone Wednesdays 12:30pm-4:30pm. Application form required.
Initial approach: Letter (1-2 pages)
Copies of proposal: 5
Deadline(s): 2nd Wed. of each month
Board meeting date(s): 3rd Tues. of each month
Final notification: 1 week following board meeting
Officers and Trustees:* **Paul Welle,* Chair.**; **Marcus Wiechmann, Vice-Chair.**; Suzanne Liapis,* Secy.; **James Naylor,* Treas.**
Number of staff: 1 part-time support.
EIN: 416022186
Other changes: Paul Welle has replaced Lowell Gillett as Chair. James Naylor has replaced Paul Welle as Treas.
Marcus Wiechmann is now Vice-Chair.

1722
Northwest Area Foundation
60 Plato Blvd. E., Ste. 400
St. Paul, MN 55107-1832 (651) 224-9635
FAX: (651) 225-7701; E-mail: info@nwaf.org; E-mail for grant inquiries: grants@nwaf.org; Main URL: http://www.nwaf.org
Delicious Bookmarks: http://delicious.com/northwestarea
Facebook: http://www.facebook.com/pages/Northwest-Area-Foundation/394883336881
Grants Database: http://www.nwaf.org/Content/Grantsearch
Knowledge Center: http://toolbox.nwaf.org/
Knowledge Center: http://www.grassrootsandgroundwork.org/
Lessons Learned From a Decade of Philanthropy: http://www.nwaf.org/content/Lessons
LinkedIn: http://www.linkedin.com/companies/northwest-area-foundation?trk=fc_badge
Northwest Area Foundation's Philanthropy Promise: http://www.ncrp.org/philanthropys-promise/who
RSS Feed: http://www.nwaf.org/Content/RSS
Twitter: http://twitter.com/NWAFound

Incorporated in 1934 in MN as Lexington Foundation; name changed to Louis W. and Maud Hill Family Foundation in 1950; present name adopted 1975.
Donors: Louis W. Hill, Sr.†; Maud Hill†.
Foundation type: Independent foundation.
Financial data (yr. ended 12/31/12): Assets, $416,977,402 (M); expenditures, $25,612,606; qualifying distributions, $21,867,863; giving activities include $14,671,362 for grants, and $3,945,868 for 3 foundation-administered programs.
Purpose and activities: The mission of the foundation is to support the efforts by the people, organizations and communities in the eight state region, (MN, IA, SD, ND, MT, ID, WA, and OR), to reduce poverty and achieve sustainable prosperity. By funding the work of proven and promising organizations, the foundation will focus on three outcomes: Increased assets and wealth among people with low incomes; Increased capacity and leadership to reduce poverty; and Improved public policy solutions to reduce poverty.
Fields of interest: Community/economic development; African Americans/Blacks; Hispanics/Latinos; Native Americans/American Indians; Indigenous peoples; Immigrants/refugees; Economically disadvantaged.
Type of support: General/operating support; Management development/capacity building; Program development; Conferences/seminars; Technical assistance; Program-related investments/loans; Employee matching gifts.
Limitations: Applications not accepted. Giving limited to IA, ID, MN, MT, ND, OR, SD, and WA. No grants to individuals, or for lobbying activities.
Publications: Annual report; Financial statement; Grants list; Informational brochure; Occasional report; Program policy statement.
Application information: The foundation does not accept unsolicited proposals. The foundation will support the work of proven or promising organizations working towards reducing poverty and increasing prosperity for low income people.
Board meeting date(s): Feb., May, Aug. and Nov.
Officers and Directors:* Rev. Kevin M. McDonough,* Chair.; Sally Pederson,* Vice-Chair.; Kevin F. Walker, C.E.O. and Pres.; Millie Acamovic, V.P., Fin. and Admin., and C.F.O.; Gary Cunningham, V.P., Progs.; Terrence Glarner, Tr.; Rodney W. Jordan, Tr.; Nicholas Slade, Tr.; M. Lorena Gonzalez; Louis Fors Hill; Linda L. Hoeschler; Hyeok Kim; Jim Laducer; Elsie Meeks; Natalie Camacho Mendoza; Lynda Bourque Moss; William Thorndike, Jr.; Sarah Vogel; Nicholas Walrod.
Number of staff: 22 full-time professional; 6 part-time professional; 1 part-time support.
EIN: 410719221
Other changes: Darrell Robes Kipp, a director, is deceased.

1723
Northwest Minnesota Foundation (NWMF)
201 3rd St. N.W.
Bemidji, MN 56601 (218) 759-2057
Contact: For grants: Nate Dorr, Grants Off.
FAX: (218) 759-2328; E-mail: info@nwmf.org; Additional tel. for MN residents: (800) 659-7859; Grant request e-mail: nated@nwmf.org; Main URL: http://www.nwmf.org

Established in 1986 in MN.
Donors: The McKnight Foundation; The Bremer Foundation; Blandin Foundation.
Foundation type: Community foundation.
Financial data (yr. ended 06/30/12): Assets, $48,212,224 (M); gifts received, $3,239,485; expenditures, $4,336,767; giving activities include $1,583,855 for 48+ grants (high: $40,953), $204,650 for 151 grants to individuals (high: $3,000; low: $100), and $1,848,112 for 8 foundation-administered programs.
Purpose and activities: The foundation invests resources, creates opportunities, and promotes philanthropy to make the region a better place to live and work.
Fields of interest: Arts; Education; Environment, natural resources; Environment; Health care;

Housing/shelter; Recreation; Youth development; Economic development; Community development, small businesses; Infants/toddlers; Children/youth; Youth; Aging; Economically disadvantaged.
Type of support: In-kind gifts; Management development/capacity building; Emergency funds; Program development; Conferences/seminars; Seed money; Scholarship funds; Research; Technical assistance; Consulting services; Program evaluation; Program-related investments/loans; Scholarships—to individuals; Matching/challenge support; Loans—to individuals.
Limitations: Applications accepted. Giving limited to Beltrami, Clearwater, Hubbard, Kittson, Lake of the Woods, Mahnomen, Marshall, Norman, Pennington, Polk, Red Lake, and Roseau counties, MN. No support for religious activities. No grants to individuals (except for scholarships), businesses, or for capital campaigns, major equipment purchases, annual campaigns, endowments, building construction, past operating deficits, publicity or advertising, or general/operating expenses.
Publications: Application guidelines; Annual report; Grants list; Informational brochure; Newsletter.
Application information: Online application process beginning July 1. The foundation strongly encourages all potential applicants to contact the foundation's staff before sending a pre-proposal. To be considered for grant funding, a pre-proposal must be submitted on the foundation's pre-proposal application form; if a project is determined to be eligible, a full application is invited. Visit foundation Web site for pre-proposal form and guidelines. Application form required.
Initial approach: Telephone inquiry preferred
Copies of proposal: 2
Deadline(s): None for pre-proposal
Board meeting date(s): 3rd Fri. of each month
Final notification: 3 weeks for full proposal determination
Officers and Directors:* Bob Hager,* Chair.; Pete Haddeland,* Vice-Chair.; Nancy Vyskocil,* Pres.; Marty Sieve,* V.P., Progs.; Faye Auchenpaugh,* Secy.; Judy Roy,* Treas.; Tom Anderson; Kristin Eggerlirg; Cathy Forgit; Jody Horntvedt; Jon Linnell; Leah Pigatti; Jon Quistgaard; Edie Ramstad.
Number of staff: 13 full-time professional; 2 part-time professional; 4 full-time support.
EIN: 411556013
Other changes: Pete Haddeland is no longer a director.

1724
Opus Foundation
10350 Bren Rd. W., Tax Dept.
Minnetonka, MN 55343-9014
Main URL: http://www.opus-group.com/AboutUs/Community

Established in 2000 in MN.
Donors: Opus Corp.; Opus, LLC; North Star Ventures.
Foundation type: Company-sponsored foundation.
Financial data (yr. ended 12/31/12): Assets, $70,001,407 (M); expenditures, $3,385,850; qualifying distributions, $3,280,478; giving activities include $3,041,035 for 104 grants (high: $1,000,000; low: $100).
Purpose and activities: The foundation supports programs designed to enhance school readiness for pre-school aged children through early childhood education; achieve healthy social and academic development of school-aged youth through youth development; position and prepare individuals for better futures through workforce development; increase the vitality of struggling neighborhoods or communities through community revitalization; and respond to emergency needs resulting from economically challenging times.
Fields of interest: Education, early childhood education; Higher education; Education; Employment, training; Employment; Housing/shelter; Boys & girls clubs; Youth development; Human services; Community development, neighborhood development; Community/economic development; United Ways and Federated Giving Programs.
Type of support: General/operating support; Annual campaigns; Capital campaigns; Building/renovation; Endowments; Program development; Scholarship funds; Sponsorships.
Limitations: Applications not accepted. Giving limited to AZ, FL, and MN. No grants to individuals.
Application information: Contributes only to pre-selected organizations.
Officers and Directors:* Mark H. Rauenhorst,* Chair. and Pres.; Kate Seng, V.P.; Becky Finnigan, Secy.-Treas.; Kristen Grubb, Tax Off.; John Albers; Tim Murnane; Mark Murphy; Joe Rauenhorst; Thomas Shaver.
EIN: 411983284

1725
I. A. O'Shaughnessy Foundation, Inc.
2001 Killebrew Dr., No. 120
Bloomington, MN 55425-1865 (952) 698-0959
Contact: Timothy J. O'Shaughnessy, Pres.
FAX: (952) 698-0958;
E-mail: iaoshaughnessyfdn@tds.net; Main URL: http://www.iaoshaughnessyfdn.org

Incorporated in 1941 in MN.
Donors: I.A. O'Shaughnessy†; John F. O'Shaughnessy†; Globe Oil and Refining Companies; Lario Oil and Gas Co.
Foundation type: Independent foundation.
Financial data (yr. ended 12/31/12): Assets, $82,087,832 (M); gifts received, $200,000; expenditures, $4,267,203; qualifying distributions, $3,927,090; giving activities include $3,588,529 for 74 grants (high: $500,000; low: $695).
Purpose and activities: The foundation's current interest is the support of high quality education that prepares students in disadvantaged communities for educational and life success. The foundation funds organizations that: provide support networks, remove impediments to student success, are broadly supported by the community, and have a record of demonstrated success. The foundation is especially interested in funding endeavors that are broad in scope, widespread in influence, high-impact, innovative, and replicable models.
Fields of interest: Elementary/secondary education; Education, early childhood education; Elementary school/education; Children/youth; Children; Youth; Young adults; Minorities; Girls; Young adults, female; Boys; Young adults, male; Economically disadvantaged.
Type of support: General/operating support; Continuing support; Annual campaigns; Capital campaigns; Endowments; Program development; Curriculum development; Scholarship funds; Research; Matching/challenge support.
Limitations: Applications not accepted. Giving limited to the U.S., with emphasis on areas where foundation directors live. No support for religious missions or individual parishes, or for national fundraising organizations, or political organizations. No grants to individuals, or for operational dependence, lobbying, or capital campaign gifts exceeding twenty percent of the campaign goal; no loans.
Publications: Grants list; Program policy statement.
Application information: Letters of inquiry are not being accepted at this time. See foundation web site for updates in this area.
Board meeting date(s): Varies
Officers and Directors:* John F. O'Shaughnessy, Jr.,* Pres.; Eileen A. O'Shaughnessy,* V.P. and Secy.; Teresa O'Shaughnessy Duggan, V.P.; Charles Lyman, V.P.; Chevonne E. O'Shaughnessy,* V.P.; Daniel J. O'Shaughnessy, V.P.; **Karen J. O'Shaughnessy, V.P.; Terence P. O'Shaughnessy, V.P.**; Michele O'Shaughnessy Traeger,* V.P.; Kathryn Lyman Wysong,* V.P.; Michael F. Sullivan, Treas.
Number of staff: 1 part-time support.
EIN: 416011524
Other changes: Dennis M. O'Shaughnessy is no longer a V.P.

1726
Patterson Foundation
(formerly Patterson Dental Foundation)
1031 Mendota Heights Rd.
St. Paul, MN 55120-1419 (651) 686-1929
Contact: Admin.
E-mail: information@pattersonfoundation.net; Main URL: http://www.pattersonfoundation.net

Established in 2003 in MN.
Donor: Several individuals associated with Patterson Cos.
Foundation type: Independent foundation.
Financial data (yr. ended 12/31/12): Assets, $16,890,021 (M); gifts received, $84,261; expenditures, $981,875; qualifying distributions, $846,393; giving activities include $796,755 for 28 grants (high: $210,000; low: $5,000).
Purpose and activities: The foundation provides resources to programs and to nonprofit organizations in the areas of oral health, animal health, and occupational and physical rehabilitation. The foundation also supports educational programs, and programs for youth and for the economically disadvantaged. It also provides educational scholarships for dependents of Patterson Dental Co. employees. Within oral health, animal health, and occupational and physical rehabilitation, the foundation is focuses on services to those most in need. In addition the foundation seeks to increase the number of underrepresented people in these fields. There is very strong preference for one-time projects or start-up costs, or programs involving as volunteers a number of professionals or students in dentistry, veterinary medicine, occupational or physical rehabilitation.
Fields of interest: Museums (specialized); Higher education; Higher education, college (community/junior); Graduate/professional education; Dental school/education; Animals/wildlife, volunteer services; Veterinary medicine; Animals/wildlife, training; Dental care; Medical care, rehabilitation; Physical therapy; Athletics/sports, Special Olympics.
Type of support: Employee-related scholarships; Capital campaigns; Continuing support; Program development; Seed money.
Limitations: Applications accepted. Giving in North America with emphasis on the United States. No support for religious, political or advocacy organizations. No grants for purchase of products sold by Patterson Companies, or for film/video productions, fundraising events, conferences or seminars; no funding of direct costs of treatment or therapies.

Publications: Application guidelines; Grants list; Informational brochure (including application guidelines).
Application information: Scholarships to dependents of Patterson Companies employees paid through Scholarship America. Contact the foundation office for current due dates and decision dates. Application form required.
Initial approach: Letter of inquiry (e-mail accepted)
Copies of proposal: 2
Deadline(s): At least 6 weeks prior to board meetings
Board meeting date(s): 4 times per year
Final notification: Within 30 days of decision
Officers: Gary D. Johnson, Pres.; Robert C. Clifford, V.P.; Matthew L. Levitt, Secy.; R. Stephen Armstrong, Treas.; **Michelle Mennicke, Mgr.**
Directors: Scott P. Anderson; Jeffrey B. Baker; Ronald E. Ezerski; Raymond D. (Tad) Godsil III; Pam Hemmen; George Henriques; David G. Misiak; Todd W. Mueller; James W. Wiltz.
EIN: 743076772

1727
The Pentair Foundation
5500 Wayzata Blvd., Ste. 800
Golden Valley, MN 55416-1261 (763) 545-1730
Contact: Susan Carter, Fdn. Mgr.
FAX: (763) 656-5404; **Main URL: http://www.pentair.com/about-us/corporate-social-responsibility/team-pentair**

Established in 1998 in MN.
Donor: Pentair, Inc.
Foundation type: Company-sponsored foundation.
Financial data (yr. ended 12/31/13): Assets, $3,725,813 (M); gifts received, $5,355,996; expenditures, $5,457,788; qualifying distributions, $5,456,233; giving activities include $4,839,083 for 252 grants (high: $350,000; low: $1,000), and $178,383 for 119 employee matching gifts.
Purpose and activities: The foundation supports programs designed to promote education, sustainability in water and energy, and workforce readiness.
Fields of interest: Arts, cultural/ethnic awareness; Arts education; Elementary/secondary education; Vocational education; Higher education; Education; Environment, water resources; Environment, energy; Public health, clean water supply; Employment, services; Employment, training; Employment; American Red Cross; Youth, services; Family services; Community/economic development; United Ways and Federated Giving Programs; Mathematics; Engineering/technology; Science; Economically disadvantaged.
Type of support: General/operating support; Program development; Scholarship funds; Employee matching gifts.
Limitations: Giving primarily in areas of company operations in Moorpark, CA, Hanover Park and North Aurora, IL, Kansas City, KS, Mt. Sterling, KY, Anoka, Minneapolis/St. Paul, and New Brighton, MN, Sanford, NC, Ashland and Chardon, OH, Warwick, RI, Radford, VA, Brookfield and Delavan, WI and Colon, Honduras. No support for political, lobbying, or fraternal organizations, religious groups for religious purposes, athletic or sports-related organizations, or non 501 (c)(3) organizations or those operating under a fiscal agent. No grants to individuals, or for scholarships, medical research, fundraising events, sponsorships, or advertising, travel or tour expenses, conferences, seminars, workshops, or symposiums.
Publications: Application guidelines.
Application information: The foundation is currently conducting a strategic program and awards grants only to current or past grant recipients. Application form not required.
***Initial approach:* Complete online application**
***Deadline(s):* June 30 for current or past grant recipients**
Board meeting date(s): Feb. and Aug.
Officers and Directors:* Michael G. Meyer, Pres. and Treas.; Michael Conklin,* Secy.; **Amy Skoczlas Cole, Exec. Dir.**; Todd R. Gleason; Randall J. Hogan; Frederick S. Koury; Angela D. Lageson; John L. Stauch.
Number of staff: 1 full-time professional.
EIN: 411890149
Other changes: Eric Dettmer, Pete Dyke, and Michael V. Schrock are no longer directors.

1728
The Jay and Rose Phillips Family Foundation of Minnesota
615 1st Ave. N.E., Ste. 330
Minneapolis, MN 55413-2640 **(612) 623-1654**
E-mail: info@phillipsfamilyfoundationnm.org; Main URL: http://www.phillipsfamilyfoundationmn.org
Twitter: https://twitter.com/JayRosePhillips

Established in 2011 in MN.
Foundation type: Independent foundation.
Financial data (yr. ended 12/31/12): Assets, $63,247,173 (M); expenditures, $4,077,340; qualifying distributions, $3,680,269; giving activities include $3,049,720 for 149 grants (high: $200,000; low: $1,000), and $87,330 for 1 foundation-administered program.
Purpose and activities: Giving to address the unmet human and social needs of individuals, families, and communities that have the least access to resources.
Fields of interest: Education; Crime/violence prevention, domestic violence; Human services; Family services; Civil/human rights, immigrants; Civil/human rights, minorities; Civil/human rights, disabled; Civil/human rights, women; Civil/human rights, LGBTQ; Civil liberties, reproductive rights; Jewish federated giving programs; Jewish agencies & synagogues; Disabilities, people with; Minorities; Asians/Pacific Islanders; African Americans/Blacks; Hispanics/Latinos; Native Americans/American Indians; Women; AIDS, people with; Immigrants/refugees; Economically disadvantaged; Homeless; LGBTQ.
Type of support: General/operating support; Management development/capacity building; Program development; Curriculum development; Consulting services; Program evaluation.
Limitations: Applications not accepted. Giving primarily in the Twin Cities metropolitan, MN, area. No support for political campaigns or lobbying efforts to influence legislation. No grants to individuals.
Publications: Annual report.
Application information: Unsolicited requests for funds not accepted.
Officers: Dean Phillips,* Co-Chair. and Treas.; Jeanne Phillips,* Co-Chair.; Patrick J. Troska, Exec. Dir.
Trustees: Walter Harris; Karin Philips; Tyler Phillips.
EIN: 274196509
Other changes: Eddie Phillips, Chair. and a trustee, is deceased.
The grantmaker now publishes an annual report.

1729
The Irwin Andrew Porter Foundation
7201 Ohms Ln., Ste. 100
Edina, MN 55439-2155
Main URL: http://www.iapfoundation.org
Domestic Grant Awards: http://www.iapfoundation.org/?q=about/granthistory
International Grant Awards: http://www.iapfoundation.org/?q=about/granthistory/international

Established in 1996 in MN.
Donor: Amy L. Hubbard.
Foundation type: Independent foundation.
Financial data (yr. ended 08/31/12): Assets, $3,017,293 (M); expenditures, $156,117; qualifying distributions, $149,286; giving activities include $149,286 for 18 grants (high: $16,000; low: $1,000).
Purpose and activities: The mission of the foundation is to fund innovative projects that foster connections between individuals, communities, the environment and the world at large.
Fields of interest: Museums (art); Arts; Education; Environment, water resources; Environment; Health care; Human services; YM/YWCAs & YM/YWHAs; International economic development.
Type of support: Matching/challenge support.
Limitations: Applications accepted. Giving primarily in the U.S., with a focus on IA, IL, MN, ND, SD, and WI; international giving limited to Central and South America, the Caribbean, and Africa. No support for political organizations or religious programs. No grants to individuals, or for operating expenses, capital campaigns, or endowments.
Application information: Complete application guidelines available on foundation web site.
Copies of proposal: 1
Board meeting date(s): Quarterly
Officer and Directors:* Amy L. Hubbard,* Chair.; Arta Cheney; Scott Elkins; Jay Goldberg; Gloria Perez Jordan; Geoffrey Kehoe; Cari O'Brien.
EIN: 411852392

1730
RBC Foundation USA
(formerly RBC Dain Rauscher Foundation)
60 S. 6th St., M.S. P20
Minneapolis, MN 55402-4422 (612) 371-2936
***Contact:* Julie Allen, Mgr.**
FAX: (612) 371-7933;
E-mail: fndapplications@rbc.com; **Additional tel.: (612) 371-2218; Main URL: http://www.rbcwm-usa.com/community/cid-275952.html**

Incorporated in 1960 in MN.
Donors: Dain Rauscher Inc.; RBC Dain Rauscher Corp.; RBC Capital Markets Corp.
Foundation type: Company-sponsored foundation.
Financial data (yr. ended 10/31/12): Assets, $622,667 (M); gifts received, $1,687,000; expenditures, $2,220,921; qualifying distributions, $2,220,921; giving activities include $2,220,921 for 1,209 grants (high: $125,000; low: $50).
Purpose and activities: The foundation supports organizations involved with arts and culture, human services, and civic affairs. Special emphasis is directed toward programs designed to promote education and health.
Fields of interest: Arts, cultural/ethnic awareness; Visual arts; Performing arts, music; Arts; Elementary/secondary education; Adult education—literacy, basic skills & GED; Education, services; Education, reading; Education; Health care; Mental health/crisis services, public education; Mental

health, treatment; Mental health, disorders; Mental health, depression; Mental health/crisis services; Employment, training; Food services; Youth development, adult & child programs; Youth development; Family services; Human services, financial counseling; Human services; Community/economic development; Public affairs, citizen participation; Public affairs; Children; Youth; Economically disadvantaged.
Type of support: Program development; General/operating support; Continuing support; Annual campaigns; Employee volunteer services; Employee matching gifts.
Limitations: Applications accepted. Giving on a national basis in areas of company operations, with emphasis on the Twin Cities, MN, metropolitan area. **No support for religious, political, fraternal, or veterans' organizations, athletic teams, or hospitals, nursing homes, hospices, or daycare facilities; generally no start-up organizations. No grants to individuals, or for sponsorships, fundraising events, athletic events or scholarships, travel, academic, medical, or scientific research, recreational or athletic programs, audio or video recording projects, literary or media art projects, artist enrichment programs, medical, health, mental health, or disease-specific or disease-related services, senior citizen programs, or developmental disabilities or disorders, including deafness and blindness, non-K-12 educational programs, environmental education programs, programs limited to special needs students, or childcare or day care programs; generally no capital or endowment campaigns or multi-year commitments.**
Publications: Application guidelines; Program policy statement.
Application information: Letters of inquiry for organizations located in the Twin Cities, MN, area should be submitted if the applying organization did not receive funding from the RBC Foundation last year. Support is limited to 1 contribution per organization during any given year. Application form required.
Initial approach: Complete online letter of inquiry for new applicants located in Twin Cities, MN; complete online application form for returning grantees located in Twin Cities, MN; complete online application form for organizations located outside of the Twin Cities, MN metropolitan area
***Deadline(s):* Jan. 17 and June 13 for new applicants located in Twin Cities, MN; Jan. 31 and June 27 for returning grantees located in Twin Cities, MN; Feb. 18 and July 18 for organizations located outside of Twin Cities, MN, metropolitan area**
Board meeting date(s): Feb., Mar., Aug., and Sept.
Final notification: Within 90 days
Directors: Martha Baumbach; John Taft; Mary Zimmer.
Number of staff: 1 full-time professional; 1 full-time support.
EIN: 416030639
Other changes: Mike Kavanagh is no longer a director.

1731
Redwood Area Communities Foundation, Inc.
c/o Pat Dingels
P.O. Box 481
Redwood Falls, MN 56283-0127 (507) 637-4004
FAX: (507) 637-4082;
E-mail: radc@redwoodfalls.org; **Main URL: http://www.radc.org/index.asp?SEC={B2FCB60D-6D2F-4FE4-8E5F-8FD869AAD646}**

Established in 1987 in MN.
Foundation type: Independent foundation.
Financial data (yr. ended 12/31/12): Assets, $2,471,569 (M); gifts received, $542,632; expenditures, $1,165,540; qualifying distributions, $245,026; giving activities include $245,026 for 1 grant.
Fields of interest: Health care; Human services; Community/economic development; Christian agencies & churches.
Type of support: General/operating support; Program development; Scholarships—to individuals; Student loans—to individuals.
Limitations: Applications not accepted. Giving for the benefit of Redwood County, MN, residents and organizations.
Application information: Contributes only to pre-selected organizations.
Board meeting date(s): Monthly
Officers: Don Yrjo, Pres.; Tom Hollatz, V.P.; Duane Heiling,* Secy.
Board Members: Gordon Alexander; Kathy Anderson; Royce Heffelfinger; Tom Hollatz; David Homan; Rhonda Kerkhoff; Kevin Passe; Dorothy Sarrazin.
EIN: 363611923

1732
Regis Foundation
7201 Metro Blvd.
Minneapolis, MN 55439-2103 (952) 947-7777
***Contact:* Eric Bakken, Secy.**
***Main URL:* http://www.regiscorp.com/**

Established in 1981 in MN.
Donors: Regis Corp.; Regis, Inc.
Foundation type: Company-sponsored foundation.
Financial data (yr. ended 06/30/13): Assets, $248,078 (M); gifts received, $16,437; expenditures, $512,768; qualifying distributions, $512,768; giving activities include $511,728 for 6 grants (high: $155,000; low: $10,000).
Purpose and activities: The foundation supports organizations involved with arts and culture, education, human services, and Judaism.
Fields of interest: Arts; Elementary/secondary education; Higher education; Libraries (public); Education; Human services; United Ways and Federated Giving Programs; Jewish federated giving programs; Jewish agencies & synagogues.
Type of support: Annual campaigns; Capital campaigns; General/operating support; Building/renovation; Scholarship funds.
Limitations: Applications accepted. Giving primarily in the Minneapolis, MN, area.
Application information: Application form required.
***Initial approach:* Letter**
Deadline(s): None
Officers: Dan Hanrahan, Pres.; Eric A. Bakken, Secy.; **Steven Spiegel, Treas.**
EIN: 411410790
Other changes: Dan Hanrahan has replaced Paul Finkelstein as Pres. Steven Spiegel has replaced Randy Pearce as Treas.

1733
Riverway Foundation
8400 Normandale Lake Blvd., Ste. 920
Bloomington, MN 55437 (952) 921-3994
***Contact:* H.M. Baskerville, Jr., Tr.; Terry R. Becker, Tr.**

Established in 1995 in MN.
Donors: Riverway Co.; H.M. Baskerville, Jr.; Terry R. Becker.
Foundation type: Company-sponsored foundation.
Financial data (yr. ended 12/31/12): Assets, $3,617,466 (M); expenditures, $216,631; qualifying distributions, $179,274; giving activities include $178,419 for 29 grants (high: $50,000; low: $1,200).
Purpose and activities: The foundation supports organizations involved with Alzheimer's disease, cancer research, domestic violence, housing, children and youth, family counseling, and senior citizens.
Fields of interest: Education; Human services; Community/economic development.
Type of support: General/operating support; Continuing support; Annual campaigns; Capital campaigns; Building/renovation; Equipment; Endowments; Debt reduction; Emergency funds; Program development; Consulting services; Program evaluation; Matching/challenge support.
Application information: Application form required.
Initial approach: Letter
Copies of proposal: 1
Deadline(s): None
Trustees: H.M. Baskerville, Jr.; Laura Lee Baskerville Becker; Terry R. Becker.
Number of staff: 1 part-time support.
EIN: 416406915

1734
Robina Foundation
4900 IDS Ctr.
80 S. 8th St.
Minneapolis, MN 55402-2100
Contact: Penny Hunt, Exec. Dir.
E-mail: info@robinafoundation.org; Main URL: http://www.robinafoundation.org

Established in 2004.
Donor: James H. Binger‡.
Foundation type: Independent foundation.
Financial data (yr. ended 12/31/12): Assets, $76,591,184 (M); gifts received, $18,246,500; expenditures, $27,235,883; qualifying distributions, $26,776,523; giving activities include $26,428,609 for 11 grants (high: $18,000,000; low: $1,000).
Purpose and activities: The foundation seeks to positively impact critical social issues by encouraging innovation and financially supporting transformative projects of its four industrial partners. These partners, selected by the foundation's founder, James H. Binger, are: Abbott Northwestern Hospital, Minneapolis, MN; The Council on Foreign Relations, New York, NY; University of Minnesota Law School, Minneapolis, MN; and Yale University, New Haven, CT.
Fields of interest: Education; Environment, natural resources; Animals/wildlife, preservation/protection; Hospitals (general).
Limitations: Applications not accepted. Giving primarily in MN; some giving nationally. No grants to individuals.
Application information: Contributes only to pre-selected organizations.
Board meeting date(s): 4 times per year
Officers and Directors:* Kathleen Blatz, Chair.; Steven A. Schroeder, M.D.*, Vice-Chair.; **Susan Berresford, Secy.; Stephen R. Lewis, Jr., Treas.**; Penny Hunt, Exec. Dir.; Gordon M. Aamoth, M.D.; H. Peter Karoff; Marianne D. Short.
Number of staff: 2 part-time professional.
EIN: 201163610

Other changes: Steven A. Schroeder is now Vice-Chair. . Susan Berresford is now Secy. Kathleen Blatz is now Chair. .

1735
Rochester Area Foundation
400 S. Broadway, Ste. 300
Rochester, MN 55904 (507) 282-0203
Contact: JoAnn Stomer, Pres.
FAX: (507) 282-4938;
E-mail: raf-info@rochesterarea.org; Main URL: http://www.rochesterarea.org
Facebook: https://www.facebook.com/pages/Rochester-Area-Foundation/132787263554048
LinkedIn: http://www.linkedin.com/groups/Rochester-Area-Foundation-4844420
Twitter: http://twitter.com/rochesterarea
YouTube: http://www.youtube.com/user/RochAreaFoundation

Established in 1944 in MN by resolution of corporation.
Foundation type: Community foundation.
Financial data (yr. ended 12/31/11): Assets, $38,004,741 (M); gifts received, $2,045,247; expenditures, $3,035,858; giving activities include $1,486,568 for grants.
Purpose and activities: The foundation is dedicated to using its resources to improve the quality of life, promote greater equality of opportunities, and to develop effective methods to assist those in need in the greater Rochester area. The foundation makes grants in the fields of arts and culture, community development, education, human services and recreation.
Fields of interest: Arts; Child development, education; Higher education; Education; Environment; Health care; Housing/shelter, development; Recreation; Child development, services; Family services; Aging, centers/services; Minorities/immigrants, centers/services; Human services; Civil/human rights; Community/economic development; Voluntarism promotion; Government/public administration; Public affairs; Children; Youth; Adults; Aging; Disabilities, people with; Mentally disabled; Minorities.
Type of support: Management development/capacity building; Building/renovation; Emergency funds; Seed money; Technical assistance; Consulting services; Matching/challenge support.
Limitations: Applications accepted. Giving limited to the greater Rochester, MN, area. No support for religious organizations for sectarian purposes. No grants to individuals (except for scholarships), or for endowment funds, annual campaigns, operating budgets, continuing support, land acquisition, deficit financing, fellowships, or research.
Publications: Application guidelines; Annual report; Informational brochure (including application guidelines); Newsletter.
Application information: Visit foundation web site for application forms and guidelines. If the foundation's Board of Trustees approves the applicant's pre-application for a grant, they will be notified and asked to submit a full application. Application form required.
Initial approach: Submit pre-application form
Deadline(s): Jan. and June for pre-application form; Feb. 15 and July 15 for full application
Board meeting date(s): Jan., Feb., Apr., May, Aug., Sept., Oct., Nov., and Dec.
Final notification: Mid Jan. and mid June for pre-application determination; mid Mar. and mid Aug. for grants
Officers and Trustees:* Wendy Shannon,* Vice-Chair.; Dr. Hugh Smith,* Co-Pres.; JoAnn Stormer,* Co-Pres.; **Barbara Porter,* Secy.**; Tom Wente,* Treas.; Jane Campion, Emeritus; **John Benike**; Paul Gorman; Leigh Johnson; **Denise Kelly**; **Greg Layton**; **Walt Ling**; **Jean Locke**; Joe Powers; Jose Rivas; Mark Utz; Karel Weigel; Vivien Williams.
Number of staff: 6 full-time professional.
EIN: 416017740
Other changes: Wendy Shannon has replaced Jean Locke as Vice-Chair. Barbara Porter has replaced Hugh Smith as Secy.
Steve Borchardt is now Devel. Off. Ann Fahy-Gust is now Donor and Grant Srvs. Mgr. Paul Harkess is now Devel. Off. John Benike is no longer Chair. Barbara Porter and Wendy Shannon are no longer trustees.

1736
Sauer Children's Renew Foundation
P.O. Box 9088
North St. Paul, MN 55109-0088 (651) 633-6165
Contact: Colleen O'Keefe, Exec. Dir.
Main URL: http://scrfmn.org/index.html
Grants List: http://scrfmn.org/2012grants.html
Grants List: http://scrfmn.org/2011grants.html

Established in 1997 in MN.
Donors: Gary B. Sauer; Patricia A. Sauer; Barriere Construction Company; Spring Lake Park Lions Club.
Foundation type: Independent foundation.
Financial data (yr. ended 12/31/12): Assets, $4,872,855 (M); gifts received, $31,014; expenditures, $346,773; qualifying distributions, $317,859; giving activities include $214,880 for 15 grants (high: $25,000; low: $10,000).
Purpose and activities: Giving to improve the lives of disadvantaged children and their families.
Fields of interest: Children/youth, services; Children, adoption; Children, day care; Residential/custodial care.
Limitations: Applications accepted. Giving primarily in MN, with priority in the Twin Cities metro area. No support for political activities. No grants to individuals or for lobbying activities, endowments, deficit or debt reduction, fundraising activities or advertising.
Application information: See web site for additional policies and guidelines. Application form required.
Initial approach: Cover letter including brief summary of the project or program
Deadline(s): See web site
Final notification: Grant proposals will be reviewed by the Charity Review Committee in Oct. and approved for funding by the Board of Trustees in late Nov.
Officers: Patricia A. Sauer, Pres.; Gary B. Sauer,* Treas.; Colleen O'Keefe,* Exec. Dir.
EIN: 411859711

1737
The Sayer Charitable Foundation
1730 Meadow Woods Trail
Long Lake, MN **55356-9311**
Contact: Michael Scott Sayer, Treas.

Established in 1994 in MN.
Donors: George W. Sayer†; Evelyn W. Sayer†.
Foundation type: Independent foundation.
Financial data (yr. ended 12/31/13): Assets, $1,767,052 (M); gifts received, $185; expenditures, $245,059; qualifying distributions, $215,990; giving activities include $210,885 for 5 grants (high: $210,000; low: $100).
Purpose and activities: Giving for Catholic education and the economically disadvantaged.
Fields of interest: Education; Foundations (community); Catholic agencies & churches; Economically disadvantaged.
Type of support: Continuing support; Endowments; Program development; Employee matching gifts.
Limitations: Applications not accepted. Giving primarily in MN, with emphasis on the Twin Cities area.
Application information: Contributes only to pre-selected organizations.
Board meeting date(s): Aug.
Officers: Patricia Sayer, Pres.; Michael Scott Sayer, Treas.
Directors: George Sayer III; **John Sayer**.
EIN: 411793832
Other changes: George Sayer is no longer Secy.

1738
Richard M. Schulze Family Foundation
3033 Excelsior Blvd., Ste. 525
Minneapolis, MN 55416-3375 (952) 324-8910
FAX: (952) 324-8982; Main URL: http://www.schulzefamilyfoundation.org/

Established in 2004 in MN.
Donor: Richard M. Schulze.
Foundation type: Independent foundation.
Financial data (yr. ended 12/31/12): Assets, $29,547,422 (M); gifts received, $7,172,930; expenditures, $3,572,303; qualifying distributions, $3,221,911; giving activities include $3,221,911 for 14 grants (high: $2,000,000; low: $695).
Purpose and activities: Giving primarily for: 1) education, particularly to organizations that offer Kindergarten through 5th grade programs that focus on reading, writing, math and science, as well as tutoring and after-school support programs; 2) human services, particularly to organizations which provide food, meals, temporary housing/shelter and services to families and children to assist them back to self-sufficiency; 3) agencies that assist adults and their families with initial transitional needs when dealing with a new medical challenge; and 4) organizations that provide educational camps for children ages 5-11.
Fields of interest: Elementary/secondary education; Health organizations; Recreation, camps; Human services; Children/youth, services.
Limitations: Giving primarily in Dakota, Hennepin and Ramsey counties in MN. No support for the arts.
Publications: Application guidelines; Grants list.
Application information: If invited after staff review of LOI, submit full application through online application portal. Complete application guidelines available of foundation web site.
***Initial approach:* Submit Letter of Inquiry via online application portal on foundation web site**
***Deadline(s):* See foundation web site for current deadlines**
Officer: Mark Dienhart, C.E.O. and Pres.
Directors: Kevin Bergman; **Robert Bruininks**; **Maureen Schulze**; Richard M. Schulze; **Allen Lenzmeier**; Nancy JS Tellor; **Ann Winblad**.
EIN: 200752440
Other changes: The grantmaker now makes its application guidelines available online.

1739

Securian Foundation

Minnesota Mutual Bldg.
400 Robert St. N
St. Paul, MN 55101-2098 (651) 665-3501
Contact: Lori J. Koutsky, Mgr.
FAX: (651) 665-3551;
E-mail: lori.koutsky@securian.com; Main URL: http://www.securian.com/Securian/About+Us/Securian+Financial+Group/Community+commitment

Established in 1988 in MN.
Donors: Minnesota Life Insurance Co.; Securian Holding Co.
Foundation type: Company-sponsored foundation.
Financial data (yr. ended 12/31/12): Assets, $40,382,444 (M); gifts received, $2,062,140; expenditures, $2,097,564; qualifying distributions, $2,036,980; giving activities include $1,740,955 for 91+ grants (high: $408,550), and $217,590 for 1 employee matching gift.
Purpose and activities: The foundation supports organizations involved with arts and culture, education, employment, youth development, human services, community economic development, and economically disadvantaged people.
Fields of interest: Arts; Higher education; Education; Health care; Employment, services; Employment, training; Employment; Youth development; Human services; Economic development; Business/industry; Community/economic development; United Ways and Federated Giving Programs; Mathematics; Economics; Public affairs; Economically disadvantaged.
Type of support: General/operating support; Annual campaigns; Capital campaigns; Program development; Technical assistance; Employee volunteer services; Employee matching gifts.
Limitations: Applications accepted. Giving primarily in areas of company operations, with emphasis on MN; giving also to national organizations. No support for political, lobbying, fraternal, or international organizations, athletic, recreation, or sports-related organizations, religious organizations not of direct benefit to the entire community, or public or private K-12 schools. No grants to individuals, or for scholarships, start-up funds for new organizations, endowments, benefits, sponsorships, fundraising events, advertising, conferences, seminars, workshops, symposiums, trips, or tours.
Publications: Application guidelines; Grants list; Informational brochure; IRS Form 990 or 990-PF printed copy available upon request; Program policy statement.
Application information: Proposals should be no longer than 7 pages. Proposals may be submitted using the Minnesota Common Grant Application Form. Application form required.
Initial approach: Proposal
Copies of proposal: 1
Deadline(s): Feb. 1, June 1, and Oct. 1
Final notification: Apr., Aug., and Dec.
Officers and Directors:* Robert L. Senkler,* Pres.; Kathleen Pinkett,* V.P.; Gary Christensen, Secy.; David LePlavy, Treas.
Number of staff: 1 part-time professional; 1 part-time support.
EIN: 363608619
Other changes: Dwayne C. Radel is no longer Secy.

1740

Southwest Initiative Foundation

(formerly Southwest Minnesota Foundation)
15 3rd Ave. N.W.
Hutchinson, MN 55350-1643 (320) 587-4848
Contact: Sherry E. Ristau, C.E.O.
FAX: (320) 587-3838;
E-mail: info@swifoundation.org; Toll-free tel.: (800) 594-9480; Main URL: http://www.swifoundation.org
RSS Feed: http://feeds.feedburner.com/swif

Established in 1986 in MN.
Foundation type: Community foundation.
Financial data (yr. ended 06/30/12): Assets, $64,842,237 (M); gifts received, $4,024,754; expenditures, $4,508,110; giving activities include $1,416,545 for 321 grants (high: $254,000; low: $100), $3,383,524 for 5 foundation-administered programs and $1,323,610 for 77 loans/program-related investments.
Purpose and activities: The mission of the foundation is to be a catalyst, facilitating opportunities for economic and social growth by developing and challenging leaders to build on the assets of southwestern Minnesota.
Fields of interest: Youth development; Economic development; Community/economic development; Philanthropy/voluntarism; Children/youth; Aging.
Type of support: Program development; Conferences/seminars; Technical assistance; Program-related investments/loans; Loans—to individuals.
Limitations: Applications accepted. Giving limited to Big Stone, Chippewa, Cottonwood, Jackson, Kandiyohi, Lac Qui Parle, Lincoln, Lyon, McLeod, Meeker, Murray, Nobles, Pipestone, Redwood, Renville, Rock, Swift, and Yellow Medicine counties, MN. No support for for-profit businesses (except loans), or for arts programs. No grants to individuals, or for capital expenses, video production, fundraising, past operating debts or ongoing, open-ended grants.
Publications: Application guidelines; Annual report; Grants list; Informational brochure (including application guidelines); Newsletter.
Application information: Only those organizations with successful pre-application questionnaires will be invited by the foundation to submit a full proposal. Application form required.
Initial approach: Online pre-application questionnaire
Copies of proposal: 1
Deadline(s): Rolling
Board meeting date(s): Every other month
Officers and Trustees:* Rob Saunders,* Chair.; Robert Thurston,* Vice-Chair.; Sherry Ristau,* Pres. and C.E.O.; Diana Anderson,* V.P. and C.O.O.; Scott Marquardt,* V.P.; Tim Connell,* Secy.; Janice Nelson,* Treas.; Marcy Costello; Jim Keul; Patricia Loehr-Dols; Jan Lundebrek; Mary Maertens; William McCormack; Greg Raymo; Bob Taubert.
Number of staff: 16 full-time professional; 1 part-time professional; 5 full-time support; 1 part-time support.
EIN: 411555592
Other changes: Deb Berggren is now Acct. Specialist. Jodi Gorres is no longer Community Engagement Specialist.

1741

St. Jude Medical Foundation

1 St. Jude Medical Dr.
St. Paul, MN 55117-1761 (651) 756-2157
FAX: (877) 291-7569;
E-mail: info@sjmfoundation.com; Main URL: http://www.sjmfoundation.com/

Established in 1997 in MN.
Donor: St. Jude Medical, Inc.
Foundation type: Company-sponsored foundation.
Financial data (yr. ended 12/31/12): Assets, $492,722 (M); gifts received, $3,225,000; expenditures, $3,137,088; qualifying distributions, $3,135,362; giving activities include $3,133,887 for 74 grants (high: $600,000; low: $2,500).
Purpose and activities: The foundation supports organizations involved with arts and culture, K-12 education, health, disaster relief, human services, community development, science, and civic affairs. Special emphasis is directed toward programs designed to improve awareness and treatment of cardiac and chronic pain conditions.
Fields of interest: Arts; Elementary/secondary education; Health care; Health organizations, public education; Heart & circulatory diseases; Health organizations; Surgery; Disasters, preparedness/services; Human services; Community/economic development; Mathematics; Engineering/technology; Science; Public affairs.
Type of support: General/operating support; Continuing support; Conferences/seminars; Seed money; Fellowships; Research; Sponsorships; Employee matching gifts.
Limitations: Applications accepted. Giving on a national basis, with some emphasis on CA, Washington, DC, MA, and MN. No grants to individuals.
Publications: Application guidelines; Program policy statement.
Application information: Applications for community outreach, research study, and mission trips are also accepted. Organizations receiving general operating support are asked to submit narrative and financial progress reports near the end of each one-year grant period. Application form required.
Initial approach: Complete online application
Copies of proposal: 1
Deadline(s): 60 days prior to need
Officers and Directors:* Rachel Ellingson,* Pres.; John C. Heinmiller,* V.P.; Daniel J. Starks, V.P.; Donald Zurbay,* V.P.; Pamela S. Krop,* Secy.; Robert Frenz,* Treas.
EIN: 411868372
Other changes: Rachel Ellingson has replaced Angela D. Craig as Pres.
John C. Heinmiller is now V.P. Angela D. Craig is no longer Pres.

1742

Sundance Family Foundation

944 Grand Ave.
St. Paul, MN **55105 (612) 822-8580**
***Contact:* Jeneen Hartley Sago**
FAX: (612) 822-8587;
E-mail: sundancefamilyfoundation@earthlink.net; Main URL: http://www.sundancefamilyfoundation.org
Grants List: http://www.sundancefamilyfoundation.org/grantlists.html
YouTube: http://www.youtube.com/user/SundanceFamilyFdn

Established in 2003 in MN.
Donors: Nancy Jacobs; Mark Sandercott.
Foundation type: Independent foundation.
Financial data (yr. ended 12/31/12): Assets, $3,338,179 (M); expenditures, $306,968; qualifying distributions, $295,496; giving activities include $190,401 for 42 grants (high: $15,000; low: $212).
Purpose and activities: Giving to support family stability worldwide.

Fields of interest: Housing/shelter; Human services; Family services; Social entrepreneurship; Youth.
International interests: Africa; Latin America; Russia.
Type of support: Program evaluation; Technical assistance; Program development.
Application information: See foundation web site for current application guidelines. Application form required.
Copies of proposal: 1
Trustees: Yvonne Barrett; Yvonne Cheek; Mark Hamel; Nancy Jacobs; Mark Sandercott; John Savereide; Rob Scarlett; Segundo Velasquez.
EIN: 200685298

1743
SUPERVALU Foundation
P.O. Box 990
Minneapolis, MN 55440-0990
Contact: Sherry Smith, Sr. V.P. and Co-Treas.
***Main URL:* http://www.supervalu.com/responsibility/community.html**

Established in 1993 in MN.
Donors: General Mills; SUPERVALU INC.
Foundation type: Company-sponsored foundation.
Financial data (yr. ended 02/28/13): Assets, $2,676,126 (M); gifts received, $1,825,946; expenditures, $1,169,219; qualifying distributions, $1,169,219; giving activities include $1,160,894 for 160 grants (high: $430,000; low: $25).
Purpose and activities: The foundation supports programs designed to promote hunger relief; dietary health and nutrition; and environmental stewardship.
Fields of interest: Environment, natural resources; Environment; Health care; Diabetes; Food services; Food banks; Nutrition.
Type of support: Sponsorships; General/operating support; Program development; Scholarship funds; Employee matching gifts.
Limitations: Applications accepted. Giving primarily in areas of company operations in MN. **No support for United Way-supported organizations (over 30 percent of budget) or veterans', fraternal, or labor organizations, or religious organizations. No grants to individuals, or for third-party requests, conferences, seminars, or travel, advertising, emergency relief, fundraising, travel or academic research, parties, ceremonies, or memorials, lobbying or political initiatives, school field trips, or workforce readiness programs.**
Publications: Application guidelines.
Application information: Application form required.
***Initial approach:* Complete online application**
***Deadline(s):* None**
Board meeting date(s): Quarterly
Final notification: Within 90 days
Officers and Directors: John F. Boyd, V.P. and Treas.; Liz Pham,* Secy.; **Mary Vander Leest.**
EIN: 411752955
Other changes: John F. Boyd is now V.P. and Treas. Stacey Nelson-Kumar is no longer Pres. Janet Sparkman, Dave Pylipow, Diane Harper, Joel Guth, Shannon Bennett, and Mike Erlandson are no longer directors.

1744
Target Foundation
(formerly Dayton Hudson Foundation)
c/o Community Rels.
1000 Nicollet Mall, TPN1144
Minneapolis, MN 55403-2467 (800) 388-6740
Contact: Jeanne Kavanaugh, Sr. Specialist
FAX: (612) 696-4706;
E-mail: community.relations@target.com; Main URL: https://corporate.target.com/corporate-responsibility/grants

Incorporated in 1918 in MN.
Donors: Dayton Hudson Corp.; Target Corp.
Foundation type: Company-sponsored foundation.
Financial data (yr. ended 02/02/13): Assets, $17,200,751 (M); gifts received, $4,750,000; expenditures, $9,714,803; qualifying distributions, $9,699,006; giving activities include $9,690,000 for 174 grants (high: $1,225,000; low: $5,000).
Purpose and activities: The foundation supports programs designed to promote arts and culture accessibility; and provide for basic needs of individuals and families at risk. Support is limited to the Minneapolis/St. Paul, Minnesota 7-county metropolitan area.
Fields of interest: Museums; Arts; Food services; Housing/shelter; Salvation Army; Family services; Human services; Community/economic development; United Ways and Federated Giving Programs.
Type of support: General/operating support.
Limitations: Applications accepted. Giving limited to the Minneapolis/St. Paul, MN 7-county metropolitan area. No support for religious organizations not of direct benefit to the entire community; generally, no support for health organizations. No grants to individuals, or for endowments, national ceremonies, memorials, conferences, fundraising dinners, testimonials, or similar events, recreation, therapeutic programs, or living subsidies.
Publications: Application guidelines; Annual report; Grants list; Program policy statement.
Application information: Applicants are required to register through the Minnesota Cultural Data Project. Application form required.
Initial approach: Complete online application
***Deadline(s):* Jan 1. to Feb. 1 for Arts; Apr. 1 to May 1 for Social Services**
Board meeting date(s): Varies
***Final notification:* June 30 for Arts; Sept. 30 for Social Services**
Officers and Trustees:* Gregg W. Steinhafel,* Chair.; Laysha Ward,* Pres.; Timothy R. Baer,* Secy.; John J. Mulligan, Treas.; John D. Griffith; Beth M. Jacob; Jodeen A. Kozlak; Terrance J. Scully; Kathee Tesjia.
Number of staff: 1 full-time professional.
EIN: 416017088
Other changes: The grantmaker has changed its fiscal year-end from Jan. 28 to Feb. 2.

1745
James R. Thorpe Foundation
5866 Oakland Ave.
Minneapolis, MN **55417-3114 (763) 250-9304**
Contact: Kerrie Blevins
***E-mail:* info@jamesrthorpefoundation.org; Email for Kerrie Blevins: kerrieblevins@jamesthorpefoundation.org**; Main URL: http://www.jamesrthorpefoundation.org

Incorporated in 1974 in MN.
Donor: James R. Thorpe†.
Foundation type: Independent foundation.
Financial data (yr. ended 11/30/12): Assets, $6,348,605 (M); expenditures, $296,777; qualifying distributions, $263,344; giving activities include $206,465 for 32 grants (high: $10,000; low: $465).
Purpose and activities: Primary areas of interest include the disadvantaged, youth, the elderly, education, and cultural programs. Giving for social service agencies and higher and secondary education; support also for community health care.
Fields of interest: Performing arts; Performing arts, dance; Performing arts, ballet; Performing arts, orchestras; Arts; Education; Environment; Health care; Mental health/crisis services; Housing/shelter, development; Human services; Children/youth, services; Family services; Aging, centers/services; Homeless, human services; Disabilities, people with; Economically disadvantaged.
Type of support: General/operating support; Capital campaigns; Equipment; Program development; Internship funds; Scholarship funds.
Limitations: Applications accepted. Giving limited to Minneapolis, MN; funding to a lesser extent in the western metropolitan suburbs. No support for organizations in the greater MN area, the east metro area, or outside of MN. No grants to individuals, or for continuing support, emergency or endowment funds, deficit financing, land acquisition, matching gifts, publications, seminars, tours, benefits, multi-year commitments, or conferences; no loans.
Publications: Application guidelines; Annual report (including application guidelines).
Application information: See foundation web site for complete application guidelines. Application form not required.
***Initial approach:* Foundation's online application system**
Copies of proposal: 1
***Deadline(s):* Consult foundation web site for current deadlines**
Board meeting date(s): May and Nov.
Officers and Directors:* Timothy Thorpe,* Pres.; Robert C. Cote,* Treas.; Kerrie Blevins, Fdn. Mgr.; S. Ruggles Cote; Samuel A. Cote; **Carolyn Jones**; Margaret T. Richards; **Richard Thorpe.**
Number of staff: 1 part-time professional.
EIN: 416175293
Other changes: Mary C. Boos is no longer a director.
The grantmaker now publishes application guidelines.

1746
Trust for the Meditation Process
2751 Hennepin Ave. S., No. 259
Minneapolis, MN 55408-1002 (612) 825-3116
Contact: Martha Bolinger, Dir.
E-mail: trustmed@bitstream.net; Main URL: http://www.trustformeditation.org/

Established in 1986 in MN.
Donor: Stephen M. Taylor.
Foundation type: Independent foundation.
Financial data (yr. ended 12/31/12): Assets, $4,349,689 (M); expenditures, $243,519; qualifying distributions, $197,841; giving activities include $157,896 for 23 grants (high: $25,000; low: $450).
Purpose and activities: Giving to organizations that reclaim and teach Christian contemplative traditions, that introduce meditation in the Christian community or that further understanding of contemplative practice in all spiritual traditions.
Fields of interest: Offenders/ex-offenders, rehabilitation; Youth development; Human services; Human services, mind/body enrichment; Foundations (private grantmaking); Religion.
Type of support: Continuing support; Building/renovation; Equipment; Program development; Conferences/seminars; Publication; Seed money; Curriculum development; Scholarship funds;

Research; Technical assistance; Consulting services; Employee-related scholarships; Matching/challenge support.
Limitations: Giving on a national and international basis, primarily in the U.S.
Publications: Application guidelines.
Application information: See trust web site for application guidelines and requirements. Two copies are required: one submitted electronically as an email attachment and one submitted via surface mail. Application form required.
Initial approach: Submit online inquiry form
Copies of proposal: 2
Board meeting date(s): Spring, Summer and Fall
Officer and Trustees:* Deborah Chernick,* Chair.; Michael Lilja; Paul Taylor.
Director: Martha Bolinger.
EIN: 416286503
Other changes: Deborah Chernick has replaced Carole Baker as Chair.
Ward Bauman, Robert Taylor, Helen Welter, Mary White and Charles Wright are no longer trustees.

1747
W.M. Foundation
1800 IDS Ctr., Rm. 1800
80 S. 8th St.
Minneapolis, MN 55402-4523

Established in MN.
Donors: Wallace C. Dayton; Mary Lee Dayton.
Foundation type: Independent foundation.
Financial data (yr. ended 12/31/12): Assets, $18,577,137 (M); expenditures, $1,473,925; qualifying distributions, $1,255,430; giving activities include $1,240,500 for grants.
Purpose and activities: Giving primarily for the environment.
Fields of interest: Environment, natural resources; Animals/wildlife, preservation/protection.
Limitations: Applications not accepted. Giving primarily in MA, and the Minneapolis-St. Paul, MN, area; funding also in Arlington, VA. No grants to individuals.
Application information: Contributes only to pre-selected organizations.
Officers: Ellen D. Grace, Co-Chair.; Katherine D. Nielsen, Co-Chair.; James M. Karges, Secy.
Directors: Sally D. Clement; Mary L. Dayton; Elizabeth D. Dovydenas.
EIN: 416080486
Other changes: Katherine D. Nielsen is now Co-Chair.

1748
Wallin Education Partners
(formerly Northstar Partners Scholarship Fund)
5200 Willson Rd., Ste. 209
Minneapolis, MN 55424-1343 (952) 345-1920
FAX: (952) 345-1930;
E-mail: wallin.staff@wallinpartners.org**; Additional e-mail: info@wallinpartners.org**; Main URL: http://www.wallinfoundation.org
Facebook: https://www.facebook.com/wallin.education.partners
Wallin Education Partners Alumni Assoc.: http://www.linkedin.com/groups?gid=4038198

Established in 2007 in MN.
Donors: Winston R. Wallin; Maxine H. Wallin; Ron Cornwell; Joan Cornwell; Marilyn Erickson; James C. Hayes; Carol Pfleiderer; Peter Pierce; Janice Pierce; Ardes Johnson; St. Paul Foundation; Medtronic Foundation; Alpha Kappa Psi Scholarship Foundation; Wallin Foundation; Simpson Family Charitable Foundation; Junior League; Tom and Mary McCary Foundation.
Foundation type: Operating foundation.
Financial data (yr. ended 06/30/13): Assets, $0 (M); gifts received, $2,664,390; expenditures, $2,687,900; qualifying distributions, $2,684,900; giving activities include $1,830,681 for grants to individuals.
Fields of interest: Higher education, university.
Type of support: Scholarships—to individuals.
Limitations: Giving primarily in MN. No grants to.
Application information:
Initial approach: Use online application form for scholarships
Officers and Directors:* Tom Holman,* Chair.; Bradford W. Wallin, Vice-Chair.; Charles M. Denny, Jr., Treas.; Susan Basil King, Exec. Dir.; Joan Cornwell; Stephen R. Lewis, Jr.; Brian C. Rosenberg; Sandra L. Vargas; Maxine H. Wallin.
EIN: 208505156

1749
WCA Foundation
(formerly Woman's Christian Association)
10249 Yellow Circle Dr., Ste. 101
Minnetonka, MN 55343-9111 (952) 932-9032
Contact: Karen Reamer, Exec. Dir.
FAX: (952) 932-9036; Main URL: http://www.wcafoundation.org

Established in 1866 in MN.
Donors: Minneapolis Foundation; John Windhorst, Jr.; Peter Windhorst.
Foundation type: Independent foundation.
Financial data (yr. ended 12/31/12): Assets, $15,909,792 (M); gifts received, $11,383; expenditures, $982,972; qualifying distributions, $786,552; giving activities include $583,329 for 44 grants (high: $50,000; low: $1,000).
Purpose and activities: Primary area of interest is in programs helping women achieve or sustain self-sufficiency and general human services. Grants also may be awarded for (but are not limited to) battered women's programs, subsidized housing programs, programs for homeless persons, recovery programs, day care subsidies, children's and youth programs, scholarships for education or jobs training, and programs for immigrants.
Fields of interest: Education; Employment, training; Employment, retraining; Human services; Children/youth, services; Family services; Aging, centers/services; Women.
Type of support: General/operating support; Capital campaigns; Building/renovation; Emergency funds; Program development; Scholarship funds; Program evaluation.
Limitations: Applications accepted. Giving limited to MN. No support for private foundations, political or veterans' organizations, religious organizations for religious purposes, national medical associations, pro-life/pro-choice programs, organizations which require employees to raise some or all of their own salaries in individual fundraising, or organizations affiliated with the foundation. No grants to individuals, or for annual fund drives, medical research, costs of litigation or previously incurred deficits, or multi-year awards.
Publications: Application guidelines; Grants list.
Application information: Application form required.
Initial approach: Telephone to Karen Reamer, Exec. Dir., between 8:00am and 4:00pm on weekdays to request application form
Copies of proposal: 1
Deadline(s): May 1 and Nov. 1
Board meeting date(s): 1st Fri. of each month
Final notification: 2 to 6 months following deadline dates
Officers: Patricia Scott, Pres.; Lori Waage, 1st V.P.; Carol Freeburg, 2nd V.P.; Barbara Lyons, 3rd V.P.; Dale Crawford, Secy.; Barbara Rose, Treas.; Karen Reamer, Exec. Dir.
Directors: Mary Jo Henning; Joanne Lieske; Barbara Montgomery.
Number of staff: 1 full-time professional; 1 full-time support.
EIN: 410694712

1750
J.A. Wedum Foundation
2615 University Ave. S.E.
Minneapolis, MN 55414-3207
***Contact:* Jay J. Portz, Pres.**
FAX: (612) 789-4044; E-mail: jayportz@wedum.org; Main URL: http://www.wedum.org
Grants List: http://www.wedumfoundation.org/wedum_grant.html

Established in 1959 in MN.
Donors: Maynard C. Wedum†; John A. Wedum†.
Foundation type: Independent foundation.
Financial data (yr. ended 12/31/12): Assets, $158,283,160 (M); gifts received, $311,008; expenditures, $38,923,549; qualifying distributions, $1,204,378; giving activities include $1,204,378 for 60 grants (high: $344,892; low: $400).
Purpose and activities: The mission of the foundation is to develop and utilize the resources of the foundation to help organizations and individuals change and improve people's lives in the spirit of stewardship and generosity exemplified by John A. Wedum, the grandfather, and carried forward by John A. Wedum, the grandson. The vision of the foundation is to provide needed housing for communities, invest its assets to increase the capital available for its mission, expend its income to change and improve the lives of people in a very efficient manner, giving priority to the support of education, and be recognized as an organization that seeks excellence in whatever it chooses to do.
Fields of interest: Higher education, university; Education; Human services.
Type of support: Continuing support; Seed money; Scholarship funds; Matching/challenge support.
Limitations: Applications not accepted. **Giving primarily in MN; funding also in ID, ND, and WI.** No grants to individuals.
Publications: Annual report; Informational brochure.
Application information: Unsolicited requests for funds will not be accepted.
Board meeting date(s): Apr. and Sept.
Officers and Board Members:* Frank Starke,* Chair.; Jay J. Portz, Pres.; Dawn Downs; Dana Wedum Kennelly; David Kjos; Joseph A. Rusche; Gary Slette; Dayton Soby; Dale Vesledahl.
Number of staff: 2 full-time professional.
EIN: 416025661

1751
West Central Initiative
(formerly West Central Minnesota Initiative Fund)
P.O. Box 318
Fergus Falls, MN 56538-0318 (218) 739-2239
Contact: Nancy Straw, Pres.; Sandra King, V.P., Opers.

FAX: (218) 739-5381; E-mail: info@wcif.org; Additional tel.: (800) 735-2239 (MN only).; Main URL: http://www.wcif.org
Facebook: https://www.facebook.com/westcentralinitiative
Twitter: http://twitter.com/WCIMinn

Established in 1986 in MN.
Foundation type: Community foundation.
Financial data (yr. ended 06/30/13): Assets, $57,232,868 (M); gifts received, $3,795,773; expenditures, $5,532,258; giving activities include $3,608,637 for 485 grants (high: $50,000; low: $100).
Purpose and activities: The fund seeks to improve the region's economic and social viability by expanding quality employment opportunities, addressing shortages of skilled labor, strengthening families, addressing critical regional needs, and developing leadership capacity within local communities.
Fields of interest: Education; Employment, training; Employment; Youth development, services; Children/youth, services; Family services; Economic development; Nonprofit management; Community/economic development; Leadership development.
Type of support: Mission-related investments/loans; Income development; Program development; Seed money; Curriculum development; Scholarship funds; Research; Technical assistance; Program-related investments/loans.
Limitations: Applications accepted. Giving limited to Becker, Clay, Douglas, Grant, Otter Tail, Pope, Stevens, Traverse, and Wilkin counties, MN. No support for religious activities, sports or recreational programs, arts, historical or cultural activities, or groups without physical presence in region. No grants to individuals.
Publications: Application guidelines; Annual report; Financial statement; Grants list; Informational brochure; Newsletter.
Application information: Visit foundation web site for application form and guidelines per grant type. Application form required.
Initial approach: Telephone
Copies of proposal: 1
Deadline(s): Generally at least 6 weeks prior to planned commencement of project for grants exceeding $5,000; at least 3 weeks for grants less than $5,000
Board meeting date(s): Monthly
Final notification: 4 to 6 weeks for grants over $5,000; 2 to 3 weeks for less
Officers and Directors:* David Nelson,* Chair.; Nancy Straw,* Pres.; Kim Embretson,* V.P., Fund Devel.; Sandy King,* V.P., Opers.; Dale Umlauf,* V.P., Business Devel.; Warrenn Anderson; Jerry Arneson; Jessica Boyer; Amy Coley; Sue Dieter; **Dan Ellison**; Cheri Johnson; John MacFarlene; Melissa Persing; Dean Simpson; **Merle Wagner**; Rebecca Worner.
Number of staff: 12 full-time professional; 1 part-time professional; 2 full-time support; 3 part-time support.
EIN: 363453471
Other changes: Merle Wagner is now Vice-Chair. Dan Ellison is now Treas.

1752
Weyerhaeuser Family Foundation

(formerly Weyerhaeuser Foundation)
30 7th St. E., Ste. 2000
St. Paul, MN 55101-4930 (303) 993-5385
***Contact:* Peter Konrad Ed.D., C.P.A.**
E-mail: pkonrad@konradconsulting.com; Main URL: http://www.wfamilyfoundation.org

Incorporated in 1950 in MN.
Donors: Bette D. Moorman; Stanley R. Day, Jr.; Dana L. Day; George H. Weyerhaeuser; Mrs. George H. Weyerhauser; Lucy R. Jones; Jane Weyerhaeuser-Johnson; Hayley M. Reiter; Kyle W. Reiter; Leilee Weyerhaeuser; Elizabeth Bentinck-Smith; Cody N. Reiter; Carol R. Caruthers; Cherbec Advancement Foundation; Rosenberry Charitable Term Trust; Wendy Weyerhaeuser; Ian Weyehaeuser; Lucy Rosenberry Jones Charitable Tust; Robert M. Weyerhaeuser; Stan Day; Vivian W. Day; John Stroh III.
Foundation type: Independent foundation.
Financial data (yr. ended 12/31/12): Assets, $23,090,394 (M); gifts received, $207,141; expenditures, $1,160,720; qualifying distributions, $1,106,931; giving activities include $900,014 for 36 grants (high: $75,000; low: $1,000).
Purpose and activities: The foundation supports programs of national and international significance that promote the welfare of human and natural resources.
Fields of interest: Environment, natural resources; Environment; Health care; Mental health, treatment; Children, services; International development; International peace/security.
Type of support: Program development; Seed money.
Limitations: Applications accepted. Giving for international programs only through U.S.-based organizations. No support for elementary or secondary education, or for books or media projects, unless the project is connected to other areas of foundation interest. No grants to individuals, or for building or endowment funds, annual campaigns, operating budgets, equipment, land acquisitions or trades, research, scholarships, fellowships, travel, or matching gifts; no loans.
Publications: Application guidelines; Annual report (including application guidelines); Grants list.
Application information: See foundation web site for specific application guidelines for each program, as well as application cover sheets. Application form required.
Initial approach: Letter
Copies of proposal: 1
***Deadline(s):* See foundation web site for the current deadline for each program**
Board meeting date(s): Program committee meets annually in early summer to review proposals; board usually meets in June and Nov.
Officers and Trustees:* Frederick W. Titcomb,* Pres.; John B. Driscoll,* V.P.; Blaine Gaustad, Secy.; Peter E. Heymann,* Treas.; John L. Davis; Melissa M. Davis; Lucie C. Greer; Anne W. Henderson; Rebecca Martin; Kristin Rasmussen; Kyle W. Reiter; Amy W. Stried; Daniel L. Titcomb; John W. Titcomb, Jr.; W. Drew Weyerhaeuser; Ian Weyerhaeuser.
Number of staff: 1 part-time professional.
EIN: 416012062

1753
Winona Community Foundation

(formerly Greater Winona Area Community Foundation)
51 E. 4th St., Ste. 314
Winona, MN 55987-6203 (507) 454-6511
***Contact:* Jeni Arnold, Exec. Dir.**
FAX: (507) 454-0441; E-mail: adminwcf@hbci.com; Grant inquiry e-mail: jarnold@hbci.com; Grant inquiry tel.: (507) 454-6511; Main URL: http://www.winonacommunityfoundation.com
Facebook: https://www.facebook.com/adminwcf1
Twitter: http://twitter.com/wcfpres

Established in 1987 in MN.
Foundation type: Community foundation.
Financial data (yr. ended 12/31/12): Assets, $11,544,315 (M); gifts received, $1,249,191; expenditures, $1,206,769; giving activities include $804,181 for 35+ grants (high: $58,150).
Purpose and activities: The foundation improves the quality of life in the Winona area by: 1) educating the public about the practice of philanthropy and its benefits both to donors and to the community; 2) connecting people with charitable intent and resources with organizations and causes that can advance the public good; 3) gathering, preserving, and stewarding philanthropic resources; 4) collaborating with other charitable organizations; 5) serving as a catalyst for selected community initiatives; 6) making grants to projects and causes that address both the needs; and the 7) opportunities present in the community.
Fields of interest: Arts, multipurpose centers/programs; Arts; Elementary/secondary education; Education; Environment; Health care; Recreation; Human services; Public affairs.
Type of support: General/operating support; Continuing support; Management development/capacity building; Annual campaigns; Equipment; Emergency funds; Program development; Conferences/seminars; Technical assistance; Program evaluation; Scholarships—to individuals; Matching/challenge support.
Limitations: Applications accepted. Giving primarily in Winona, MN, and its surrounding community. No support for religious programs or fraternal organizations, societies, or order. No grants to individuals (except for scholarships), or for capital campaigns, endowments, debt retirements or debt financing, tickets for benefits, telephone solicitations, fundraising drives or activities, or travel; no loans.
Publications: Application guidelines; Annual report; Grants list; Informational brochure (including application guidelines); Newsletter.
Application information: Visit foundation web site for application guidelines. Applicants must call foundation staff to review projects prior to submission of any materials. Application form required.
Initial approach: Telephone
Copies of proposal: 1
***Deadline(s):* Mar. 1, June 1, and Sept. 1**
Board meeting date(s): 4th Tues. of each month
***Final notification:* 4th Tues. of deadline month**
Officers and Directors:* Judy Davis,* Chair.; Shelley Milek,* Secy.; Gary Watts,* Treas.; **Jeni Arnold, Exec. Dir.**; Diane Amundson; Sandra Burke; Vicki Decker; Susan Eddy; **Fred Fletcher**; Joan Greshik; Andrea Herczeg; Ann Lavine; Tedd Morgan; Kelley Olson; Ryan Ping; Tom Wynn.
Number of staff: 1 full-time professional; 3 part-time professional; 1 part-time support.
EIN: 363500853
Other changes: Judy Davis has replaced Sandra Burke as Chair.
Jeni Arnold is now Exec. Dir. Ted Biesanz, Andy Blomsness, Steve Blue, Dan Florness, Jennifer Knapp, and Dan Trainor are no longer directors.

1754
Xcel Energy Foundation

414 Nicollet Mall
Minneapolis, MN 55401-1927
***Contact:* James R. Garness, Sr. Fdn. Rep., MN**
FAX: (612) 215-4522;
E-mail: foundation@xcelenergy.com; **Additional e-mail contacts: Monique Lovato, Dir., Corporate Giving and Xcel Energy Fdn. CO, monique.l.lovato@xcelenergy.com; Jeanne Fox,**

Grants Contact, MI and WI, jean.fox@xcelenergy.com; Judith Paukert, Community Rels.. Mgr., ND and SD, judith.n.paukert@xcelenergy.com; Kathy Aas, Community Rels. Mgr., Minot, ND, kathleen.a.aas@xcelenergy; Terry Price, Sr. Fdn.. Rep., TX and NM, terry.price@xcelenergy.com; Eric Pauli, Community Rels.. Mgr., SD, eric.pauli@xcelenergy.com; Main URL: http://www.xcelenergy.com/About_Us/Community/Corporate_Giving
Arts and Culture Grantee List: http://www.xcelenergy.com/staticfiles/xe/Corporate/Corporate%20PDFs/2013_Art_and_Culture.pdf
Economic Sustainability Grantee List: http://www.xcelenergy.com/staticfiles/xe/Corporate/Corporate%20PDFs/2013_Economic_Sustainability.pdf
Education Grantee List: http://www.xcelenergy.com/staticfiles/xe/Corporate/Corporate%20PDFs/2013_Education.pdf
Environment Grantee List: http://www.xcelenergy.com/staticfiles/xe/Corporate/Corporate%20PDFs/2013_Environment.pdf

Established in 2001.
Donor: Xcel Energy Inc.
Foundation type: Company-sponsored foundation.
Financial data (yr. ended 12/31/12): Assets, $13,549,039 (M); gifts received, $18,123,702; expenditures, $7,535,935; qualifying distributions, $7,532,606; giving activities include $7,436,826 for 753 grants.
Purpose and activities: The foundation supports programs designed to improve science, technology, engineering, economics and math education; improve and enhance the natural environment; help individuals achieve economic self-sufficiency; and provide access to arts and culture.
Fields of interest: Arts, equal rights; Arts education; Visual arts; Performing arts; Performing arts, music; Arts; Elementary/secondary education; Scholarships/financial aid; Education, services; Education; Environment, alliance/advocacy; Environment, public education; Environment, natural resources; Environment, water resources; Environment, land resources; Environment, energy; Environment, beautification programs; Environmental education; Environment; Animals/wildlife; Employment, training; Employment, retraining; Employment; Disasters, preparedness/services; Boy scouts; Economic development; Business/industry; Community/economic development; United Ways and Federated Giving Programs; Science, formal/general education; Mathematics; Engineering/technology; Science; Economically disadvantaged.
Type of support: General/operating support; Program development; Curriculum development; Employee volunteer services; Employee matching gifts.
Limitations: Applications accepted. Giving limited to areas of company operations in CO, MI, MN, ND, NM, SD, TX, and WI. No support for national organizations, government agencies, religious, political, veterans', or fraternal organizations not of direct benefit to the entire community or disease-specific organizations. **No grants to individuals, or for research programs, endowments, capital campaigns, energy efficiency projects or improvements, athletics or sports, or benefits or fundraising; no multi-year commitments.**
Publications: Application guidelines; Grants list; Informational brochure; Program policy statement.
Application information: The foundation is currently not accepting new partners for organizations located in CO and MN, but check website for periodic announcements. Organizations receiving support are asked to submit a final report. Application form required.
Initial approach: **Complete online eligibility quiz**
Deadline(s): **Mar. 10 and May 9 for organizations in CO and MN; Mar. 3 for organizations in NM and TX; Mar. 3 for Education and Environment focus areas for organizations in ND, SD, and WI; and May 9 for Arts and Culture and Economic Sustainability focus areas for organizations in ND, SD, and WI**
Final notification: **Early June and Aug.**
Officers and Directors:* Benjamin G.S. Fowke III,* Chair. and Pres.; Roy Palmer,* Secy.; George E. Tyson II,* Treas.; David L. Eves; **David T. Hudson; Marvin McDaniel; David Sparby**; Mark E. Stoering.
EIN: 412007734
Other changes: At the close of 2012, the fair market value of the grantmaker's assets was $13,549,039, a 372.7% increase over the 2011 value, $2,866,161.
James R. Garness is now Sr. Fdn. Rep., MN. Cathy J. Hart, C. Riley Hill, and Judy M. Poferl are no longer directors.

MISSISSIPPI

1755
Biloxi Regional Medical Center, Inc.
P.O. Box 128
Biloxi, MS 39533-0128
***Main URL:* http://www.biloxiregional.net/**

Established in 2003 in MS.
Foundation type: Operating foundation.
Financial data (yr. ended 09/30/13): Assets, $15,940,673 (M); expenditures, $867,409; qualifying distributions, $866,880; giving activities include $866,880 for 9 grants (high: $366,900; low: $1,800).
Fields of interest: Nursing school/education; Education; Hospitals (general); Health organizations.
Limitations: Applications not accepted. Giving primarily in MS. No grants to individuals.
Application information: Contributes only to pre-selected organizations.
Officers: Robert B. Briscoe, Chair.; Andy Carpenter, Vice-Chair.
Directors: Erroll Bradley; Larry Drawdy; Ann LaRosa; John McKee, M.D.; Alfred McNair, M.D.; Jeffrey O'Keefe; Edward Shumski, M.D.; Argile Smith.
EIN: 640657989
Other changes: At the close of 2013, the grantmaker paid grants of $866,880, a 142.1% increase over the 2012 disbursements, $358,000.

1756
The Bower Foundation, Inc.
(formerly Kidney Care, Inc.)
578 Highland Colony Pkwy., Ste. 120
Ridgeland, MS 39157-8779 (601) 607-3163
FAX: (601) 607-3164;
E-mail: info@bowerfoundation.org; Additional e-mail (for grant concept submissions): atravis@bowerfoundation.org; Main URL: http://www.bowerfoundation.org

Established in 1972 in MS.
Foundation type: Independent foundation.
Financial data (yr. ended 12/31/13): Assets, $94,620,475 (M); expenditures, $4,512,874; qualifying distributions, $4,059,683; giving activities include $3,601,323 for 15+ grants.
Purpose and activities: The foundation is committed to the promotion of fundamental improvements in the health status of all Mississippians through the creation, expansion, and support of quality healthcare initiatives. The goals of the foundation are: 1) Access to health care: All children and adults should have reasonable access to health care services so that all citizens have the opportunity to live healthy and productive lives. 2) Health Care Services: To promote health, prevent disease, and reduce health risks among children, young adults, and the underserved. 3) Health Policy and Education: To support approaches that match the needs of the underserved with existing public and private providers. 4) End Stage Renal Disease: To improve the quality of life for patients with End Stage Renal Disease.
Fields of interest: Health care; Kidney diseases.
Limitations: Applications accepted. Giving primarily in Jackson, MS. No grants to individuals.
Publications: Grants list.
Application information: Application guidelines and form available on foundation web site. Nearly all the foundation's grantmaking activities are pro-active. A small percentage of grants develop from grant concepts submitted by prospective grantees. The grant concept can be mailed, faxed, or e-mailed to the foundation.
Initial approach: Grant concept proposal (no more than 2 pages)
Deadline(s): None
Final notification: Within 4 to 6 months
Officers and Directors:* Anne Travis,* C.E.O. and V.P.; John Bower, M.D.*, Pres.; James F. Dorris,* Secy.-Treas.; Ralph Didlake, M.D.; Kathy Ellis; Alan Hull, M.D.; Walter Neely, Ph.D.; William S. Painter; Dana Shires, M.D.
Number of staff: 2 full-time professional.
EIN: 640540635

1757
Center for Mississippi Health Policy
120 N. Congress St., Ste. 700
Jackson, MS 39201-2615 **(601) 709-2133**
***FAX:* (601) 709-2134;**
E-mail: info@mshealthpolicy.com; Main URL: http://www.mshealthpolicy.com
Twitter: https://twitter.com/mshealthpolicy

Established in 2005 in MS.
Donors: The Bower Foundation; The Robert Wood Johnson Charitable Trust.
Foundation type: Operating foundation.
Financial data (yr. ended 12/31/12): Assets, $2,083,327 (M); gifts received, $20,021; expenditures, $1,199,534; qualifying distributions, $1,189,095; giving activities include $393,904 for 2 grants (high: $243,681; low: $150,223).
Purpose and activities: The mission of the Center for Mississippi Health Policy is to serve as a catalyst for health policy debate, providing information to policymakers and the general public and communicating research findings that will stimulate dialogue and inform decision-making.
Fields of interest: Medical research.
Limitations: Applications not accepted. Giving primarily in MS. No grants to individuals.
Application information: Unsolicited requests for funds not accepted.
Officers: Anne B. Travis, Pres.; Ralph Didlake, M.D., V.P.; John Sturdivant, Secy.-Treas.; Therese Hanna, Exec. Dir.
EIN: 203471008

1758
Community Foundation of East Mississippi
P.O. Box 865
Meridian, MS 39302-0865 (601) 696-3035
Contact: M'Lea Davis, Exec. Dir.
FAX: (601) 696-3037; E-mail: office@cfem.org; Main URL: http://www.cfem.org
Facebook: https://www.facebook.com/cfeastmississippi
YouTube: http://www.youtube.com/user/cfem304

Established in 1984 in MS.
Foundation type: Community foundation.
Financial data (yr. ended 12/31/11): Assets, $4,534,162 (M); gifts received, $860,253; expenditures, $500,772; giving activities include $229,063 for 8 grants (high: $50,679).
Purpose and activities: The foundation seeks to: 1) establish permanent charitable endowments; 2) promote philanthropy throughout East MS; 3) provide a vehicle for donors' charitable interests; and 4) provide leadership and resources in addressing ever changing challenges and opportunities.
Fields of interest: Crime/violence prevention; Recreation, parks/playgrounds; Children/youth, services; Community development, neighborhood development; Economic development.
Type of support: Curriculum development; Consulting services; Program-related investments/loans; Matching/challenge support.
Limitations: Applications accepted. Giving limited to eastern MS. No support for sectarian religious purposes, state, regional, or national organizations, or veterans' or fraternal organizations. No grants for operating support for existing programs, endowment campaigns, conference attendance expenses, memberships or tickets to events, advertising and telephone solicitations, feasibility studies for capital campaigns, or fundraising expenses.
Publications: Annual report.
Application information: Visit foundation web site for application guidelines. Application form required.
Initial approach: Telephone
Board meeting date(s): Quarterly
Officers and Directors:* Patricia Thomasson,* Pres.; Clay E. Holladay,* V.P.; Michael Dudley,* Secy.; Jack Christopher,* Treas.; M'Lea Davis, Exec. Dir.; John G. Compton; Maurice Hall; John Johnson; Joe Jordan; James L. McRae; Lee R. Meyer, Jr.; Melanie Mitchell; Brenda Nowell; George R. Rea, Jr.; David T. Stephens; Ron Turner, Sr.; Kim Waters.
Number of staff: 1 full-time professional; 1 part-time support.
EIN: 640702225

1759
Community Foundation of Greater Jackson
(formerly Greater Jackson Foundation)
525 E. Capitol St., Ste. 5B
Jackson, MS 39201-2702 (601) 974-6044
Contact: Jane Alexander, C.E.O.
FAX: (601) 974-6045; E-mail: info@cfgj.com; Main URL: http://www.cfgreaterjackson.org
Facebook: https://www.facebook.com/communityfoundationofgreaterjackson

Established in 1994 in MS.
Foundation type: Community foundation.
Financial data (yr. ended 03/31/13): Assets, $33,102,122 (M); gifts received, $4,939,151; expenditures, $2,647,670; giving activities include $1,958,243 for 74 grants (high: $151,436), and $47,300 for 138 grants to individuals.
Purpose and activities: The foundation helps charitable donors establish permanent giving funds that reflect individual philanthropic interests while also making a long term, positive impact on the community. Giving for the arts, education, health, families/children, environment, and community building.
Fields of interest: Museums; Performing arts; Arts; Elementary/secondary education; Higher education; Environment; Health organizations, association; Disasters, Hurricane Katrina; Youth development; Children/youth, services; Family services; Human services; Community development, neighborhood development.
Type of support: General/operating support; Continuing support; Annual campaigns; Capital campaigns; Building/renovation; Endowments; Program development; Conferences/seminars; Professorships; Curriculum development; Scholarship funds; Scholarships—to individuals; Matching/challenge support.

Limitations: Applications accepted. Giving primarily in Hinds, Madison, and Rankin counties, MS. No support for religious activities.
Publications: Application guidelines; Annual report; Financial statement; Informational brochure; Newsletter; Occasional report.
Application information: Visit foundation web site for online application form and guidelines. Application form required.
Initial approach: Submit Project/Concept Outline
Copies of proposal: 1
Deadline(s): Quarterly
Board meeting date(s): Feb., May, Aug., and Nov.
Final notification: 90 days
Officers and Trustees:* Luther Ott,* Chair.; Jane Alexander,* C.E.O. and Pres.; Jackie Bailey,* C.O.O.; **Amanda Alexander**; Hogan Allen; Tommy Darnell; **Janet Harris**; Jane Hiatt; **Jamie Houston**; **Jan Lewis**; Paul McNeill; Mike McRee; Hibbett Neel; **Chuck Nicholson**; Worth Thomas; Lee Unger; Judy Wiener; Dudley Wooley; Wirt Yerger, Jr.
Number of staff: 5 full-time professional; 1 full-time support.
EIN: 640845750
Other changes: Alveno N. Castilla is no longer Treas. Jon Turner and Rita Wray are no longer trustees.

1760
Community Foundation of Northwest Mississippi
315 Losher St.
Hernando, MS 38632-2124 (662) 449-5002
Contact: Tom Pittman, Pres.; For grants: Peggy Linton, Community Devel. Dir.
FAX: (662) 449-5006;
E-mail: tompittman@cfnm.org; Grant application e-mail: plinton@cfnm.org; Main URL: http://www.cfnm.org
Facebook: https://www.facebook.com/CFNM315
RSS Feed: http://cfnm.org/feed/
Twitter: https://twitter.com/CFNM_2002
YouTube: http://www.youtube.com/cfnm2002

Established in 2002 in MS.
Foundation type: Community foundation.
Financial data (yr. ended 12/31/12): Assets, $13,774,906 (M); gifts received, $4,970,594; expenditures, $2,995,354; giving activities include $848,500 for 29 grants (high: $56,000).
Purpose and activities: The mission of the foundation is to impact its communities by connecting people who care with causes that matter; priorities include education, health care and young people. Its current strategies to address these issues are initiatives in pre-kindergarten education, prevention of childhood obesity and place-based education.
Fields of interest: Education, early childhood education; Education; Environment; Public health; Health care; Nutrition; Children/youth; Children; Youth; Adults; Aging; Young adults; Minorities; African Americans/Blacks; Hispanics/Latinos; Native Americans/American Indians; Women; Girls; Adults, women; Young adults, female; Men; Boys; Adults, men; Young adults, male; Military/veterans; Single parents; Economically disadvantaged.
Type of support: Matching/challenge support; Management development/capacity building; Endowments; General/operating support; Continuing support; Program development; Scholarship funds.
Limitations: Applications accepted. Giving limited to the northwest MS: Bolivar, Coahoma, DeSoto, Marshall, Panola, Quitman, Sunflower, Tallahatchie, Tate and Tunica counties. No support for organizations lacking 501(c)(3) status, or for exclusively religious purposes. No grants to individuals (except for scholarships).
Publications: Application guidelines; Annual report; Financial statement; Grants list; Informational brochure; Newsletter.
Application information: Visit foundation web site for application form, guidelines, and requirements. Application form required.
Initial approach: Submit application form and attachments
Copies of proposal: 1
Deadline(s): Nov. 1, Feb. 1, May 1, and Aug. 1
Board meeting date(s): Mar., May, Aug. and Nov.
Final notification: Within 4 months
Officers and Directors:* Steve Beene,* Chair.; Josephine Rhymes,* Vice-Chair.; Tom Pittman,* Pres. and C.E.O.; Scott Burnham Hollis,* Secy.; Mackey Moore,* Treas.; **Joe Azar**; **Bob Bowen**; Charles Burnett III; **Scott Coopwood**; Kevin Doddridge; Betty Jo Dulaney; Dr. Ishmell Edwards; Joan Ferguson; Dr. Eleanor Gill; Tom Gresham; Lucy Janoush; Pete Johnson; Manuel Killebrew; Campbell Melton; Frank Mitchener; Rev. Bartholomew Orr.
Number of staff: 5 full-time professional; 1 part-time professional; 2 full-time support.
EIN: 943421724
Other changes: Scott Burnham Hollis, Kirk Moore, William L. Pride, Vinson Smith, and Greg Taylor are no longer directors.

1761
Ergon Foundation, Inc.
P.O. Drawer 1639
Jackson, MS 39215-1639

Established in 1980.
Donors: Diversified Technology, Inc.; Ergon Exploration, Inc.; Ergon Nonwovens, Inc.; Ergon Refining, Inc.; Ergon, Inc.; Magnolia Marine Transport Co.; Ergon Asphalt & Emulsions, Inc.; Ergon-West Virginia, Inc.
Foundation type: Company-sponsored foundation.
Financial data (yr. ended 06/30/13): Assets, $54,028,957 (M); gifts received, $19,240,000; expenditures, $1,269,956; qualifying distributions, $663,345; giving activities include $656,400 for 38 grants (high: $50,000; low: $5,000).
Purpose and activities: The foundation supports organizations involved with education, health, cancer, human services, and Christianity.
Fields of interest: Elementary/secondary education; Education, special; Higher education; Theological school/education; Health sciences school/education; Education; Hospitals (general); Health care; Cancer; Salvation Army; Children/youth, services; Family services; Residential/custodial care, group home; Homeless, human services; Human services; Christian agencies & churches.
Type of support: General/operating support; Annual campaigns.
Limitations: Applications not accepted. Giving primarily in MS. No grants to individuals.
Application information: Contributes only to pre-selected organizations.
Officers and Directors:* Leslie B. Lampton,* Pres.; Dorothy Lee Lampton,* V.P.; Lee C. Lampton,* V.P.; Leslie B. Lampton III, V.P.; Robert H. Lampton,* V.P.; William W. Lampton,* V.P.; Kathryn W. Stone,* Secy.-Treas.
EIN: 640656341

1762
Feild Co-Operative Association Inc.
4400 Old Canton Rd., Ste. 170
Jackson, MS 39211-5982 (601) 713-2312
Contact: Cindy May, Secy.
FAX: (601) 713-2314; Application address: P.O. Box 5054, Jackson, MS 39296

Incorporated in 1919 in TN.
Donor: Sons of the late Dr. and Mrs. Monfort Jones.
Foundation type: Independent foundation.
Financial data (yr. ended 12/31/12): Assets, $19,180,701 (M); expenditures, $868,467; qualifying distributions, $770,767; giving activities include $220,200 for 46 grants (high: $20,000; low: $500), and $352,000 for loans to individuals.
Purpose and activities: Awards interest-bearing student loans to residents of MS, who are juniors or seniors in college, graduate and professional students, or students in special fields; some grants to local hospitals and social service agencies.
Fields of interest: Museums; Performing arts; Arts; Higher education; Education; Hospitals (specialty); Health organizations; Human services; Children/youth, services; Christian agencies & churches.
Type of support: General/operating support; Student loans—to individuals.
Limitations: Applications accepted. **Giving primarily in MS.** No grants for building or endowment funds, operating budgets, or for special projects.
Publications: Application guidelines; Informational brochure.
Application information: Application guidelines for student loans are available online. Students must be enrolled on a full-time basis in order to qualify for loans. Application form required.
***Initial approach:* Call to schedule an interview prior to receiving an application for student loans**
Copies of proposal: 1
Deadline(s): 6 to 8 weeks before a semester begins for student loans
Board meeting date(s): Annually
Officers: Cindy S. May, Secy.; Suzanne Neely, Treas.
Directors: Amanda Link Greenlee; John Henry Jackson; B. Bryan Jones III; B. Bryan Jones IV; William M. Link, Jr.; Betty R. May; Hobson C. McGehee, Jr.; Hobson C. McGehee III; Cynthia J. Thompson.
Number of staff: 3
EIN: 640155700
Other changes: The grantmaker now makes its application guidelines available online.

1763
Foundation for the Mid South
134 E. Amite St.
Jackson, MS 39201-2101 (601) 355-8167
Contact: For grants: Denise Ellis, Grants and Technology Mgr.
FAX: (601) 355-6499;
E-mail: bdellis@fndmidsouth.org; Grant Inquiry Form e-mail: concept@fndmidsouth.org; Main URL: http://www.fndmidsouth.org
Facebook: http://www.facebook.com/pages/Foundation-for-the-Mid-South/103086276414874
Flickr: http://www.flickr.com/photos/midsouth/
Foundation for the Mid-South's Philanthropy Promise: http://www.ncrp.org/philanthropys-promise/who

Established in 1989 in MS.
Foundation type: Community foundation.
Financial data (yr. ended 12/31/12): Assets, $16,639,255 (M); gifts received, $1,854,707;

expenditures, $2,968,467; giving activities include $1,691,222 for 61+ grants (high: $100,000).
Purpose and activities: The foundation invests in people and strategies that build philanthropy and promote racial, social, and economic equity in Arkansas, Louisiana, and Mississippi. Priority areas include health and wellness, education, wealth building, and community development.
Fields of interest: Education, early childhood education; Education; Health care; Disasters, Hurricane Katrina; Youth development, services; Children/youth, services; Family services; Minorities/immigrants, centers/services; Economic development; Community/economic development; Leadership development; Religion; Children/youth; Aging; Minorities; African Americans/Blacks.
Type of support: Technical assistance; General/operating support; Continuing support; Management development/capacity building; Program development; Conferences/seminars; Curriculum development; Consulting services; Matching/challenge support.
Limitations: Applications accepted. Giving limited to AR, LA, and MS. No grants to individuals, or to make grants for personal needs or business assistance. No grants for ongoing general operating expenses or existing deficits, endowments, capital costs including construction, renovation, or equipment, or international programs.
Publications: Application guidelines; Annual report; Financial statement; Grants list; Informational brochure (including application guidelines); Multi-year report; Newsletter; Occasional report.
Application information: Visit foundation web site for Grant Inquiry Form application guidelines. Application form required.
Initial approach: E-mail Grant Inquiry Form
Copies of proposal: 1
Deadline(s): None
Board meeting date(s): Feb., May, Aug., and Nov.
Final notification: Within 6 weeks for full proposal invitation; Generally within 3 months for grant determination
Officers and Directors:* Paul E. Davis,* Chair.; Kay Kelly Arnold,* Vice-Chair.; Ivye L. Allen,* Pres.; Hon. Robert Jackson,* Secy.; Patrick C. Moore,* Treas.; **Bill Bynum**; C. Chad Causey; Diana Lewis; Ted Kendall III; Ed Lupberger; Carla Martin; Victor McTeer; Sip B. Mouden; James Rutherford; Don Munro; Hon. William Winter.
Number of staff: 7 full-time professional; 3 full-time support.
EIN: 721151070
Other changes: Elizabeth Sandifer is now Devel. and Comms. Asst. Vickie Wells is now Fiscal Asst. William J. Bynum and Sip B. Mouden are no longer directors.

1764
Gulf Coast Community Foundation
11975 Seaway Rd., Ste. B-150
Gulfport, MS 39503 (228) 897-4841
Contact: Ashley Bryan, Cont.
FAX: (228) 897-4843; E-mail: abryan@mgccf.org; Main URL: http://www.mgccf.org
Facebook: http://www.facebook.com/pages/Gulf-Coast-Community-Foundation/252350845777
LinkedIn: http://www.linkedin.com/groups?homeNewMember=&gid=2654681&trk=
Philanthropy's Promise: http://www.ncrp.org/philanthropys-promise/who
Twitter: http://twitter.com/gccf

Established in 1989 in MS.
Foundation type: Community foundation.
Financial data (yr. ended 06/30/13): Assets, $19,624,158 (M); gifts received, $6,168,957; expenditures, $6,693,684; giving activities include $5,578,923 for 37+ grants (high: $2,679,728), and $164,750 for 511 grants to individuals.
Purpose and activities: The foundation is a public charity dedicated to the progressive development of worthy causes, providing donor services, and promoting and providing leadership in response to changing community needs. The foundation is a vehicle for charitable giving through which individuals, families, corporations, nonprofit organizations and private foundations can meet charitable objectives in the fields of education, arts and culture, historic preservation, neighborhood enrichment, and health and human services.
Fields of interest: Historic preservation/historical societies; Arts; Education; Health care; Disasters, Hurricane Katrina; Human services; Community/economic development; Infants/toddlers; Children/youth; Children; Adults; Young adults; Disabilities, people with; Mentally disabled; Minorities; Men; Economically disadvantaged.
Type of support: General/operating support; Continuing support; Scholarship funds; Technical assistance; Matching/challenge support.
Limitations: Applications accepted. Giving limited to George, Hancock, Harrison, Jackson, Pearl River, and Stone counties, MS. No support for religious organizations or for religious purposes. **No grants to individuals (except for scholarships), or for capital or operating endowment drives.**
Publications: Application guidelines; Annual report; Financial statement; Informational brochure; Newsletter; Occasional report.
Application information: Visit foundation web site for application forms, guidelines, and specific deadlines. Application form required.
Initial approach: Complete Letter of Intent
Copies of proposal: 9
Deadline(s): Varies
Board meeting date(s): Monthly
Final notification: Varies
Officers and Directors:* Dorothy Shaw,* Chair.; Dr. Kaizad Tamboli,* Chair.-Elect; Roger Wilder, Pres.; Raymond Brown,* Secy.; Cindy Shaw,* Treas.; Ashley Bryan, Cont.; **Wynn Alexander**; **Ron Barnes**; **John Baxter**; Mike Bruffey; Greg Cronin; George Cullinan; Jane Dennis; Henry Dick; Trent Favre; Angie Juzang; Bill McDonough; H. Gordon Myrick; Robert F. Neal; Virginia Shanteau Newton; Donald Perkins; Joy Phillips; Rufus Smith; Genl. Joe Spraggins; Stan Tiner; David Treutel, Jr.; Susan Walker; John Walton; Linda Watts; Tom Wicks; H. Rodger Wilder.
Number of staff: 2 full-time professional; 1 part-time professional.
EIN: 570908490
Other changes: Dorothy Shaw has replaced Ron Barnes as Chair. Dr. Kaizad Tamboli has replaced Dorothy Shaw as Chair.-Elect.
Paul Guichet, Marc Holman, Kay Kell, Steve Renfroe, Kaitlin Truong, and Tish Williams are no longer directors.

1765
Hall Foundation, Inc.
Meridian, MS

The foundation terminated in 2011.

1766
King's Daughters & Sons Circle No. 2
P.O. Box 932
Greenville, MS 38702-0932
***Application address:* c/o Becky Tindall, 244 Woodlawn, Greenville, MS 38701, tel.: (662) 335-4953**

Established in MS.
Foundation type: Independent foundation.
Financial data (yr. ended 09/30/13): Assets, $3,814,950 (M); expenditures, $225,357; qualifying distributions, $182,000; giving activities include $182,000 for 23 grants (high: $25,000; low: $1,000).
Purpose and activities: Giving primarily to attend the sick, help the poor and needy, and engage in any and all charitable works to benefit the community in the field of general welfare.
Fields of interest: Health care; Human services; Community/economic development.
Limitations: Applications accepted. Giving primarily in MS.
Application information: Application form required.
Initial approach: Request and complete application
Deadline(s): Apr. 1
Officers: Pattye Wilson, Pres.; Brenda Kretchmar, V.P.; Betsy Dyer, Secy.; William F. Baird, Treas.
Directors: Katherine Crump; **Kathy Bowman**; **Jan Engel**; **Lisa Percy**.
EIN: 640303080

1767
The Luckyday Foundation
1020 Highland Colony Parkway, Ste. 804
Ridgeland, MS **39157-2128 (601) 354-5869**
Contact: Holmes S. Adams, Chair.

Established in 1978 in MS.
Donor: Frank R. Day†.
Foundation type: Independent foundation.
Financial data (yr. ended 12/31/12): Assets, $95,810,379 (M); expenditures, $5,674,927; qualifying distributions, $5,297,834; giving activities include $5,159,118 for 10 grants (high: $3,216,500; low: $125).
Purpose and activities: Giving primarily to educational institutions, churches, and organizations to benefit sick and needy people.
Fields of interest: Higher education; Youth development; Protestant agencies & churches.
Limitations: Applications accepted. Giving primarily in MS, with emphasis on Jackson. No grants to individuals.
Application information: Application form required.
Initial approach: Letter
Copies of proposal: 1
Deadline(s): None
Final notification: Usually within 3 months
Officer and Managers:* Holmes S. Adams,* Chair.; Patricia G. Smith, Exec. Dir.; Barbara Arnold Day; Roger P. Friou; **Jerry Host**; Jamie G. Houston III; S. Griffin Norquist, Jr.
Number of staff: 1 full-time professional.
EIN: 640617746

1768
Mississippi Common Fund Trust
c/o Maggie Abernathy, Memory House
P.O. Box 249
University, MS 38677-0249 (662) 915-1581

Established in 1996 in MS.

Donors: James L. Barksdale; Sally M. Barksdale‡; Robert Seymour; R. Faser Triplett; Jane C. Thomas.
Foundation type: Independent foundation.
Financial data (yr. ended 06/30/13): Assets, $453,664 (M); gifts received, $9,224,034; expenditures, $10,745,072; qualifying distributions, $10,742,251; giving activities include $10,742,251 for 10 grants (high: $6,929,267; low: $50,000).
Purpose and activities: Giving primarily for education and human services.
Fields of interest: Higher education; Education; Human services; Protestant agencies & churches.
Limitations: Applications not accepted. Giving primarily in MS. No grants to individuals.
Application information: Contributes only to pre-selected organizations.
Officers: Wendell W. Weakley, Sr., C.E.O. and Pres.; Sandra M. Guest, V.P. and Secy.; Maggie E. Abernathy, Treas.
Trustee: The University of Mississippi Foundation.
Number of staff: 7
EIN: 640875827

1769
Mississippi Power Foundation Inc.

P.O. Box 4079
Gulfport, MS 39502-4079 (228) 865-5925
Contact: Rebecca Montgomery, Pres.
FAX: (228) 865-5616

Established in 1997 in MS.
Donors: Mississippi Power Co.; Mississippi Power Education Fdn.
Foundation type: Company-sponsored foundation.
Financial data (yr. ended 12/31/12): Assets, $17,650,504 (M); expenditures, $2,553,388; qualifying distributions, $2,144,065; giving activities include $2,144,065 for grants.
Purpose and activities: The foundation supports organizations involved with arts and culture, education, the environment, health, cancer, heart disease, housing, youth development, human services, and community development.
Fields of interest: Museums; Museums (art); Arts; Higher education; Education; Environment, natural resources; Environment, water resources; Environment, beautification programs; Environment; Health care; Cancer; Heart & circulatory diseases; Housing/shelter, repairs; Housing/shelter; Youth development, centers/clubs; American Red Cross; Children/youth, services; Human services; Nonprofit management; Community/economic development; United Ways and Federated Giving Programs.
Type of support: General/operating support; Continuing support; Annual campaigns; Capital campaigns; Building/renovation; Program development; Scholarship funds; Employee matching gifts.
Limitations: Applications accepted. Giving primarily in MS. No support for lobbying or legislative organizations. No grants to individuals, or for voter registration drives, electric appliance purchases, athletic field lighting installation, or any activity that provides a tangible economic benefit to Mississippi Power Company.
Application information: Application form required.
Initial approach: Request application form
Deadline(s): None
Officers: John Atherton, Chair.; Rebecca Montgomery, Pres.; Moses Feagin, Secy.; Vicki L. Pierce, Treas.
Board Members: Michael G. Collins; Cindy Webb.
EIN: 721370746

1770
Regions Foundation

(formerly AmSouth Foundation)
P.O. Box 23100
Jackson, MS **39225-3100**

Incorporated in 1962 in MS.
Donors: Deposit Guaranty National Bank; First American National Bank.
Foundation type: Company-sponsored foundation.
Financial data (yr. ended 12/31/12): Assets, $11,059,847 (M); expenditures, $833,923; qualifying distributions, $753,084; giving activities include $740,000 for 21 grants (high: $100,000; low: $5,000).
Purpose and activities: The foundation supports hospitals and organizations involved with arts and culture, education, youth development, human services, and Christianity.
Fields of interest: Arts; Education; Youth development.
Type of support: General/operating support; Annual campaigns; Capital campaigns; Scholarship funds; Program-related investments/loans; Employee matching gifts.
Limitations: Applications not accepted. Giving limited to MS. No grants to individuals.
Application information: Contributes only to pre-selected organizations.
Officers and Directors:* Charles L. Irby, Chair.; James W. Hood, Vice-Chair. and Pres.; Debbie Purvis, Secy.; Richard D. McRae, Jr., Treas.; Sharon S. Greener; William R. James; James L. Moore; W.R. Newman III; E.B. Robinson, Jr.; Ronnie Smith.
EIN: 646026793
Other changes: The grantmaker no longer lists a fax.

1771
The Algernon Sydney Sullivan Foundation

P.O. Box 1113
1109 Van Buren
Oxford, MS 38655-1113 (662) 236-6335
Contact: Allan E. Strand, Pres.
FAX: (662) 281-8353;
E-mail: admin@sullivanfdn.org; Main URL: http://www.sullivanfdn.org
Facebook: https://www.facebook.com/pages/Sullivan-Foundation-Service-Social-Entrepreneurship-Program/155744524468715
Twitter: https://twitter.com/sullivanfdn

Incorporated in 1930 in NY.
Donors: Mrs. Algernon Sydney Sullivan‡; George Hammond Sullivan‡; Zilph P. Devereaux‡; Charles Watson‡.
Foundation type: Independent foundation.
Financial data (yr. ended 06/30/13): Assets, $15,076,648 (M); expenditures, $887,615; qualifying distributions, $765,358; giving activities include $445,859 for 32 grants (high: $30,730; low: $1,500).
Purpose and activities: Grants primarily to colleges and universities for scholarship funds.
Fields of interest: Higher education.
Type of support: General/operating support; Endowments; Scholarship funds.
Limitations: Applications not accepted. Giving primarily in the Appalachian region of the southeastern U.S. No grants to individuals, or for capital construction.
Application information: Contributes only to pre-selected organizations.
Board meeting date(s): May and Nov.
Officers and Directors:* Stephan L. McDavid,* Pres.; Randolph V. Merrick, M.D.*, V.P.; Darla J. Wilkinson, Esq.*, Secy.; John C. Hardy, Treas.
Trustees: John Clayton Crouch; Thomas S. Rankin; Peter Rooney; Elizabeth H. Verner; Perry Wilson.
Number of staff: 1 part-time professional; 1 part-time support.
EIN: 136084596
Other changes: David C. Farrand is no longer a director.

1772
Walker Foundation

(formerly W. E. Walker Foundation)
c/o Belinda Styres
1020 Highland Colony Pkwy., Ste. 802
Ridgeland, MS 39157-8880 (601) 939-3003
Contact: Marcie Skelton, Dir.
FAX: (601) 939-4433;
E-mail: mskelton@walkercos.com

Established in 1972 in MS.
Donors: Gloria Walker; W.E. Walker, Jr.‡; Walker Lands; The Walker Cos.; His Way Homes.
Foundation type: Independent foundation.
Financial data (yr. ended 12/31/12): Assets, $11,397,384 (M); gifts received, $350,000; expenditures, $941,385; qualifying distributions, $608,150; giving activities include $608,150 for 30 grants (high: $115,300; low: $100).
Purpose and activities: Giving primarily for education, conservation, the arts and human services.
Fields of interest: Museums (art); Arts; Education; Environment; Animals/wildlife, bird preserves; Human services; Children/youth, services; Foundations (private independent); Christian agencies & churches.
Type of support: General/operating support; Annual campaigns; Capital campaigns.
Limitations: Applications accepted. Giving primarily in MS, with emphasis on Jackson. Generally no grants for deficit reduction, operating budgets, endowment programs, personnel costs, welfare agencies, physical plant construction, or individual scholarships.
Publications: Annual report; Occasional report.
Application information: Application form required.
Initial approach: Proposal
Copies of proposal: 1
Deadline(s): None
Board meeting date(s): As needed
Officer: Belinda Styres, Secy.
Trustees: Merry Dougherty; Andrew Mallison; Katie McBrayer; Gloria Walker; W.E. Walker III.
Director: Marcie Skelton.
Number of staff: 1 part-time professional.
EIN: 237279902
Other changes: The grantmaker no longer lists a separate application address.

MISSOURI

1773
Albers/Kuhn Family Foundation
555 N. New Ballas Rd., Ste. 130
St. Louis, MO 63141-6884 **(314) 997-4027, Ext. 2**
Contact: James D. Eckhoff, Tr.
E-mail: jdeckhoff@earthlink.net

Established in 1999 in MO.
Donor: Hilda Albers Kuhn†.
Foundation type: Independent foundation.
Financial data (yr. ended 12/31/13): Assets, $5,139,260 (M); expenditures, $219,477; qualifying distributions, $202,500; giving activities include $200,000 for 16 grants (high: $25,000; low: $5,000).
Fields of interest: Human services; Science.
Limitations: Applications accepted. Giving limited to St. Louis and Versailles, MO. No grants to individuals.
Application information: Application form not required.
Initial approach: Letter
Copies of proposal: 1
Deadline(s): None
Trustees: James D. Eckhoff; Lois Shuford; Robert Thieme.
EIN: 436813186

1774
Anheuser-Busch Foundation
c/o Anheuser-Busch Cos., Inc.
1 Busch Pl.
St. Louis, MO 63118-1849 (314) 577-2000
Main URL: http://anheuser-busch.com/index.php/our-responsibility/

Established in 1975 in MO.
Donor: Anheuser-Busch Cos., Inc.
Foundation type: Company-sponsored foundation.
Financial data (yr. ended 12/31/12): Assets, $59,382,993 (M); gifts received, $4,625,400; expenditures, $13,703,246; qualifying distributions, $13,236,298; giving activities include $12,125,722 for 106 grants (high: $2,000,000; low: $1,500), and $908,811 for 950 employee matching gifts.
Purpose and activities: The foundation supports programs designed to promote disaster relief and preparedness; increase access to and completion of higher education; raise consciousness and action for water conservation and recycling; and increase the quality of life through homeownership and entrepreneurship.
Fields of interest: Higher education; Scholarships/financial aid; Education; Environment, recycling; Environment, natural resources; Environment, water resources; Environmental education; Housing/shelter, development; Housing/shelter; Disasters, preparedness/services; American Red Cross; Human services; Economic development; Community/economic development; United Ways and Federated Giving Programs; Military/veterans' organizations; Minorities; African Americans/Blacks; Hispanics/Latinos; Economically disadvantaged.
Type of support: General/operating support; Continuing support; Building/renovation; Program development; Scholarship funds; Employee volunteer services; Employee matching gifts; Matching/challenge support.
Limitations: Applications not accepted. Giving primarily in areas of company operations, with emphasis on Fairfield, Los Angeles, and San Diego, CA, Fort Collins, CO, Jacksonville, Orlando, and Tampa, FL, Cartersville, GA, St. Louis, MO, Merrimack, NH, Newark, NJ, Baldwinsville, NY, Columbus, OH, Houston and San Antonio, TX, and Williamsburg, VA. No support for discriminatory, political, fraternal, social, or religious organizations, legislators, athletic organizations or teams, charter schools, pre-schools, elementary, middle, or high schools, or hospitals or healthcare-related organizations. No grants to individuals, or for political campaigns, annual or capital campaigns, conferences or seminars, travel or organized field trips, family reunions, general operating support for United Way agencies, or endowments; no multi-year commitments.
Application information: The foundation is moving to an invitation-only process for giving.
Board meeting date(s): Approximately every 3 months
Trustees: Gary L. Rutledge; James Villeneuve; U.S. Bank, N.A.
EIN: 510168084
Other changes: The grantmaker no longer publishes application guidelines.

1775
The Bellwether Foundation, Inc.
231 S. Bemiston Ave., Ste. 925
St. Louis, MO 63105-1991
E-mail: info@bellwetherstl.org; Main URL: http://www.bellwetherstl.org

Established in 1985 in MO.
Donors: Robert B. Smith†; Nancy M. Smith†; Wallace H. Smith†; Nancy Morrill Smith Revocable Trust; Robert Brookings Smith Marital Trust; Nancy M. Smith Charitable Remainder Unitrust; Smith Joint Charitable Remainder Unitrust.
Foundation type: Independent foundation.
Financial data (yr. ended 12/31/12): Assets, $69,658,068 (M); expenditures, $4,221,633; qualifying distributions, $3,641,025; giving activities include $3,453,850 for 21 grants.
Purpose and activities: Primarily supports projects which anticipate the future in the areas of the arts, computer science, education, finance, health care, medicine, and the social sciences, including research in any of these areas.
Fields of interest: Arts; Education; Environment, natural resources; Botanical gardens; Medical research, institute.
Type of support: Management development/capacity building; Program development; Research.
Limitations: Applications accepted. Giving primarily in St. Louis, MO. No grants to individuals.
Application information: Application form required.
Initial approach: Use form on foundation web site
***Deadline(s):* Preliminary grant inquires are accepted between Feb. 1 and June 30**
Officers: Robert B. Smith III, Chair.; Virginia V. Smith, Pres. and Secy.
Trustees: Sally Duffield; Robert B. Smith II; John J. Wolfe.
Number of staff: 2 full-time support.
EIN: 222635309

1776
Helen S. Boylan Foundation
P.O. Box 731
Carthage, MO 64836-0731 (417) 359-6558
Contact: Elizabeth S. Simmons, Pres.
***E-mail:* info@boylanfoundation.org**; Main URL: http://www.boylanfoundation.org

Established in 1982.
Donors: Helen S. Boylan Trust; Elbert Elwyn Boylan, Jr.
Foundation type: Independent foundation.
Financial data (yr. ended 09/30/12): Assets, $4,460,976 (M); expenditures, $386,045; qualifying distributions, $314,226; giving activities include $248,314 for 31 grants (high: $61,839; low: $1,000).
Fields of interest: Performing arts, music; Elementary/secondary education; Higher education; Recreation; Human services; Salvation Army; Children/youth, services; Community/economic development.
Type of support: Building/renovation; Equipment; Land acquisition; Program development; Curriculum development.
Limitations: Applications accepted. Giving primarily in MO and TX. No support for political organizations or religious activities. No grants to individuals, or for annual campaigns or endowments.
Publications: Application guidelines; Annual report; Financial statement.
Application information: Application form not required.
Initial approach: Proposal
Copies of proposal: 8
Deadline(s): None
Board meeting date(s): Quarterly: Feb., May, Aug., and Nov.
Officers and Directors:* Elizabeth S. Simmons, Pres.; Jennifer A. Hering,* V.P.; Sally Spradling Stuart, Secy.-Treas.; James A. Deberry; Helen L. Duff; Eugene C. Hall; Ida S. Locarni; J. Shannon Spradling.
Number of staff: 1 part-time professional.
EIN: 431254043

1777
William J. Brace Charitable Trust
c/o Bank of America, N.A.
1200 Main St., 14th Fl.
Kansas City, MO 64121-9119 (816) 292-4301
Contact: Spence Heddens, Market President
E-mail: spence.heddens@ustrust.com; **Main URL: https://www.bankofamerica.com/philanthropic/grantmaking.go**

Established in 2002 in MO.
Donor: W.J. Brace Charitable Trust.
Foundation type: Independent foundation.
Financial data (yr. ended 02/28/13): Assets, $7,196,498 (M); expenditures, $398,611; qualifying distributions, $354,878; giving activities include $323,718 for 13 grants (high: $50,000; low: $10,000).
Purpose and activities: Giving primarily for the education and health of children, the health and care of aged persons and hospitals in Kansas City, MO.
Fields of interest: Arts; Education; Hospitals (general); Health care; Human services; Children/youth, services; United Ways and Federated Giving Programs.
Limitations: Giving limited to MO, with emphasis on Kansas City. No grants for capital support.
Application information: Application form required.
Initial approach: Letter, no more than 3 pages
Copies of proposal: 2
Deadline(s): None
Trustee: Bank of America, N.A.
EIN: 597244050

1778

Marion I. Breen Charitable Foundation
c/o Spencer Fane Britt Browne LLP
1 N. Brentwood Blvd.
St. Louis, MO **63105-3925**

Established in 2007 in MO.
Donor: Marion I. Breen.
Foundation type: Independent foundation.
Financial data (yr. ended 12/31/12): Assets, $11,954,491 (M); expenditures, $1,109,276; qualifying distributions, $1,100,276; giving activities include $1,056,652 for 1 grant.
Purpose and activities: Giving primarily for higher education and Lutheran agencies and churches.
Fields of interest: Higher education; Theological school/education; Protestant agencies & churches.
Limitations: Applications not accepted. Giving primarily in Selma, AL. No grants to individuals.
Application information: Contributes only to pre-selected organizations.
Trustees: Kathleen Helge; Leonard J. Pranschke.
EIN: 260640175

1779

Bunge North America Foundation
(formerly Bunge Corporation Foundation)
11720 Borman Dr.
St. Louis, MO 63146-4129 (314) 292-2300
Contact: Geralyn F. Hayes

Established in 1993 in MO.
Donor: Bunge North America, Inc.
Foundation type: Company-sponsored foundation.
Financial data (yr. ended 12/31/12): Assets, $14,426 (M); gifts received, $750,000; expenditures, $755,707; qualifying distributions, $755,707; giving activities include $145,007 for 165 grants (high: $25,000; low: $20), and $610,700 for 30 employee matching gifts.
Purpose and activities: The foundation supports organizations involved with arts and culture, education, the environment, and community development.
Fields of interest: Arts; Education.
Type of support: General/operating support; Program development; Sponsorships; Employee matching gifts.
Limitations: Applications accepted. Giving primarily in areas of company operations, with emphasis on KS, MA, MO, and NY. No grants to individuals.
Application information: Application form required.
Initial approach: **Letter**
Deadline(s): None
Officers and Directors:* Soren Schroder,* Pres.; Todd A. Bastean,* V.P.; Geralyn F. Hayes,* V.P.; David G. Kabbes, Secy.; **Aaron L. Elliot, Treas.;** John P. Sabourin, Cont.
EIN: 431617648
Other changes: Soren Schroder has replaced Carl L. Hausmann as Pres. Aaron L. Elliot has replaced John P. Gilsinn as Treas.
Todd A. Bastean is now V.P.

1780

Butler Manufacturing Company Foundation
1540 Genessee St.
P.O. Box 419917
Kansas City, MO 64141-0917 **(816) 968-3208**
FAX: (816) 627-8993

Incorporated in 1952 in MO.
Donor: Butler Manufacturing Co.
Foundation type: Company-sponsored foundation.
Financial data (yr. ended 06/30/13): Assets, $6,181,903 (M); expenditures, $433,657; qualifying distributions, $356,375; giving activities include $344,000 for 120 grants (high: $10,000; low: -$9,000), and $8,150 for 40 employee matching gifts.
Purpose and activities: The foundation supports organizations involved with arts and culture, education, health, employment, housing, youth development, community development, disabled people, minorities, women, and economically disadvantaged people.
Fields of interest: Arts; Elementary/secondary education; Higher education; Education; Hospitals (general); Health care; Employment, training; Employment; Housing/shelter; Youth development; Community development, neighborhood development; Community/economic development; United Ways and Federated Giving Programs; Disabilities, people with; Minorities; Women; Economically disadvantaged.
Type of support: General/operating support; Continuing support; Annual campaigns; Capital campaigns; Seed money; Employee volunteer services; Employee matching gifts; Employee-related scholarships; Grants to individuals.
Limitations: Applications accepted. Giving primarily in areas of company operations, with emphasis on the greater Kansas City, MO, area. No support for political organizations, religious organizations not of direct benefit to the entire community, pre-K-12 educational institutions, fraternal or veterans' organizations, national health organizations, local or regional chapters of national health organizations, or grantmaking foundations. No grants to individuals (except for employee-related hardship grants and employee-related scholarships), or for tours, conferences, seminars, workshops, or similar events, fundraising, or endowments.
Publications: Application guidelines; Informational brochure (including application guidelines).
Application information: Application form not required.
Initial approach: **Letter, E-mail or Telephone call**
Copies of proposal: 1
Deadline(s): **None**
Board meeting date(s): **Aug., Nov., Feb., and May**
Final notification: Following board meetings
Officers: Harry Yeatman, Pres.; Dan Kumm, V.P. and Secy.; Natalie Treff, Treas.
Trustees: Barbara Bridger; Barbara Deloach.
Number of staff: 1 part-time support.
EIN: 440663648
Other changes: The grantmaker no longer lists an E-mail address. The grantmaker no longer lists a primary contact.
Harry Yeatman has replaced Patrick Finan as Pres. Dan Kumm has replaced Harry Yeatman as V.P. and Secy. Natalie Treff has replaced Justin Powell as Treas.
Gary Coder is no longer a member of the governing body. Tanya Bennett is no longer a member of the governing body. Alec Hignam is no longer a member of the governing body.

1781

Canfield Family Foundation
c/o Linda Currier Talx Corp.
9034 Sedgwick Pl. Dr.
St. Louis, MO **63124-1891**

Established in 2000 in MO.
Donor: William W. Canfield.
Foundation type: Independent foundation.
Financial data (yr. ended 06/30/13): Assets, $5,340,279 (M); gifts received, $502,780; expenditures, $379,030; qualifying distributions, $364,170; giving activities include $356,750 for 20 grants (high: $80,000; low: $500).
Fields of interest: Education; Christian agencies & churches; Youth.
Type of support: General/operating support.
Limitations: Applications not accepted. Giving primarily in MO. No grants to individuals.
Application information: Unsolicited requests for funds not accepted.
Officer: William W. Canfield, Pres.
EIN: 436854712

1782

The Centene Charitable Foundation
7700 Forsyth Blvd., Ste. 800
St. Louis, MO 63105-1837 (314) 505-6992
E-mail: CCF@centene.com; Main URL: http://www.centene.com/about-us/responsible-enterprise/charitablefoundation/

Established in 2005 in MO.
Donor: Centene Management Company, LLC.
Foundation type: Company-sponsored foundation.
Financial data (yr. ended 05/31/13): Assets, $1,771,957 (M); gifts received, $6,234,500; expenditures, $6,456,343; qualifying distributions, $6,452,999; giving activities include $6,449,753 for 226 grants (high: $500,000; low: $200).
Purpose and activities: The foundation supports programs designed to help individuals in need, with emphasis on families and children.
Fields of interest: Media, radio; Museums; Performing arts; Performing arts centers; Performing arts, ballet; Performing arts, orchestras; Arts; Secondary school/education; Higher education; Libraries (public); Education; Hospitals (general); Health care; Athletics/sports, amateur leagues; Boys & girls clubs; Boy scouts; Children, services; Family services; Developmentally disabled, centers & services; Human services; Community/economic development; United Ways and Federated Giving Programs; Children; Minorities; African Americans/Blacks.
Type of support: General/operating support; Continuing support; Annual campaigns; Capital campaigns; Building/renovation; Endowments; Program development; Scholarship funds; Sponsorships.
Limitations: Applications accepted. Giving primarily in areas of company operations, with emphasis on St. Louis, MO. **No support for political, religious, or similar groups. No grants to individuals.**
Publications: Application guidelines.
Application information: Application form required.
Initial approach: Complete online application
Deadline(s): 6 months prior to need
Final notification: 1 month
Officers: Michael F. Neidorff, Pres.; Keith H. Williamson, Secy.; William N. Scheffel, Treas.
EIN: 201298192

1783

Community Foundation of the Ozarks
(formerly Community Foundation, Inc.)
425 E. Trafficway
Springfield, MO 65806-1121 (417) 864-6199
Contact: Bridget Dierks, Dir., Nonprofit Svcs.
FAX: (417) 864-8344;
E-mail: mlemmon@cfozarks.org; Mailing address:

P.O. Box 8960, Springfield, MO, 65801; Additional tel.: (888) 266-6815; Main URL: http://www.cfozarks.org
Facebook: http://www.facebook.com/pages/Community-Foundation-of-the-Ozarks/131151120248309?ref=ts
RSS Feed: http://www.cfozarks.org/feed/
Twitter: http://twitter.com/cfozarks
Vimeo: http://vimeo.com/cfozarks

Incorporated in 1973 in MO.
Foundation type: Community foundation.
Financial data (yr. ended 06/30/13): Assets, $225,287,783 (M); gifts received, $37,633,336; expenditures, $26,736,890; giving activities include $22,331,261 for grants.
Purpose and activities: The mission of the foundation is to enhance the quality of life in our region through resource development, community grantmaking, collaboration, and public leadership.
Fields of interest: Arts; Education; Environment; Health care; Children, services; Human services; Civil/human rights; Community/economic development; Aging.
Type of support: General/operating support; Continuing support; Management development/capacity building; Annual campaigns; Capital campaigns; Building/renovation; Equipment; Endowments; Emergency funds; Program development; Conferences/seminars; Seed money; Curriculum development; Scholarship funds; Research; Technical assistance; Consulting services; Program evaluation; Program-related investments/loans; Matching/challenge support; Mission-related investments/loans.
Limitations: Applications accepted. Giving limited to southern MO.
Publications: Application guidelines; Annual report (including application guidelines); Financial statement; Informational brochure; Newsletter.
Application information: Visit foundation web site for online application form and guidelines. Application form required.
Initial approach: Submit online grant application
Deadline(s): Varies. See foundation website for deadline information
Board meeting date(s): 6 times per year
Final notification: Within 1 month
Officers and Directors:* Richard Cavender,* Chair.; Stephanie Stenger Montgomery,* Vice-Chair.; Brian Fogle,* C.E.O. and Pres.; Julie Leeth, Exec. V.P.; Michael Chatman, Sr. V.P., Philanthropy; Louise Whall Knauer, Sr. V.P., Comms. and Mktg.; **Jami S. Peebles,* Secy.**; Susanne Gray, C.F.O.; **Roger D. Shaw, Jr.,* Treas.**; **Dr. Gloria Galanes, Chair.-Emeritus**; Margie Berry; Chris Craig; Rob Foster; Judith Gonzales; Brian Hammons; **Mitch Holmes**; Randy Howard; Bill Lee; **Jared Lightle**; **Karen Miller**; Mark Nelson; Ron Penney; Gary Powell; Sandra Thomason; **Jean Twitty**; Robin Walker; Rosalie O'Reilly Wooten.
Number of staff: 16 full-time professional; 3 full-time support.
EIN: 237290968
Other changes: At the close of 2013, the grantmaker paid grants of $22,331,261, a 78.0% increase over the 2012 disbursements, $12,546,539.
Richard Cavender has replaced Dr. Gloria Galanes as Chair. Stephanie Stenger Montgomery has replaced Richard Cavender as Vice-Chair. Jami S. Peebles has replaced Roger D. Shaw Jr. as Secy. Roger D. Shaw, Jr. has replaced Shari Hoffman as Treas. Richard Cavender has replaced Dr. Gloria Galanes as Chair. Roger D. Shaw, Jr. has replaced Shari Hoffman as Treas.
Roger D. Shaw, Jr. is now Secy. Jill Reynolds is now Chair. Emeritus. Evelyn Mangan and William W. Miller are no longer directors.

1784
The Curry Family Foundation
(formerly Mid-America Foundation)
4900 Main St., Ste. 210
Kansas City, MO 64112-1372
Contact: Lee Ellen Curry, Pres.; Steve O'Neill, V.P.
E-mail for Lee Ellen Curry: lee@curryfoundationkc.org, tel.: (816) 931-2528; E-mail for Steve O'Neill: steve@curryfoundationkc.org, tel.: (816) 931-2529, Fax: (816) 931-2531; Main URL: http://www.curryfoundationkc.org
Grants List: http://www.curryfoundationkc.org/index.php?option=com_content&view=category&layout=blog&id=11&Itemid=8

Established in 1986 in MO.
Donors: William H. Curry; Dorothy F. Curry.
Foundation type: Independent foundation.
Financial data (yr. ended 12/31/12): Assets, $11,857,784 (M); gifts received, $15,000; expenditures, $474,325; qualifying distributions, $416,983; giving activities include $262,000 for 34 grants (high: $30,000; low: $250).
Purpose and activities: Giving primarily for the arts and human services.
Fields of interest: Performing arts, orchestras; Performing arts, education; Arts; Elementary school/education; Higher education, college; Education; Health care, clinics/centers; Food distribution, meals on wheels; Housing/shelter, development; Human services.
Type of support: Scholarship funds; General/operating support; Continuing support; Capital campaigns; Building/renovation; Equipment; Endowments; Program development; Matching/challenge support.
Limitations: Applications accepted. Giving primarily in Kansas City, MO. No grants to individuals.
Application information: Complete application guidelines available on foundation web site.
Initial approach: Letter of Intent
Deadline(s): Feb. 28 and Sep. 30
Board meeting date(s): Jan., Apr., July and Oct.
Officers and Directors:* Bill Curry, Chair.; Lee Curry, Pres. and Treas.; Steven O'Neill, V.P. and Secy.; Dorothy F. Curry; Doug Curry; John Crowe.
Number of staff: 2 full-time professional.
EIN: 431428340

1785
Darr Family Foundation
2870-D S. Ingram Mill Rd.
Springfield, MO **65804-4127** (417) 888-1490
Contact: Thomas L. Slaight, Pres.
***FAX:* (417) 887-0283**; Main URL: http://www.darrff.org

Established in 2002 in MO.
Donors: William N. Darr; Marsha D. Slaight; Sheryl D. Hellweg.
Foundation type: Independent foundation.
Financial data (yr. ended 06/30/13): Assets, $5,292,284 (M); gifts received, $500,000; expenditures, $329,625; qualifying distributions, $294,433; giving activities include $243,350 for 7 grants (high: $200,000; low: $5,000).
Fields of interest: Higher education, university; Big Brothers/Big Sisters; Girl scouts.
Limitations: Applications accepted. Giving primarily in Springfield, MO. No grants to individuals.
Application information: Application form required.
Initial approach: Letter
Deadline(s): Feb. 28
Officers and Directors:* Thomas L. Slaight,* Pres.; Marsha D. Slaight,* V.P.; Erin D. Danastasio,* Secy.; Zachary D. Slaight,* Treas.; **Cody Danastasio**; Kurt D. Hellweg; Sheryl D. Hellweg; Tyler D. Hellweg; Tara L. Slaight.
EIN: 371439200

1786
Deer Creek Foundation
720 Olive St., Ste. 1975
St. Louis, MO 63101-2307 (314) 241-3228
Contact: Mary Stake Hawker, Dir.

Established in 1964 in MO.
Donors: Aaron Fischer†; Teresa M. Fischer†.
Foundation type: Independent foundation.
Financial data (yr. ended 12/31/12): Assets, $36,370,686 (M); expenditures, $2,247,433; qualifying distributions, $1,804,144; giving activities include $1,494,678 for 26+ grants (high: $200,000).
Purpose and activities: Support primarily for programs that preserve and advance our democratic system and government accountability, with civil liberties and civil rights protection provided by the Constitution and the Bill of Rights, and to promote education about democracy; grants primarily to 'action programs' with promise of making a significant national or regional impact; some preference to projects in Missouri.
Fields of interest: Visual arts, sculpture; Environment, climate change/global warming; Environment; Civil rights, race/intergroup relations; Civil liberties, advocacy; Civil liberties, reproductive rights; Public affairs, citizen participation.
Type of support: Program development; Seed money.
Limitations: Applications accepted. Giving on a national basis, with some emphasis on MO. No grants to individuals, or for building or endowment funds, equipment, or operating budgets.
Publications: Informational brochure.
Application information: Letter of inquiry should contain items specified in grantmaker's brochure. See programs for additional information for each area. Application form not required.
Initial approach: Letter of inquiry
Deadline(s): None
Board meeting date(s): Apr. and Sept.
Officer and Trustees:* M. Peter Fischer,* Pres.; Martha C. Fischer; Matthew A. Fischer; Michael P. Fischer.
Director: Mary Stake Hawker.
Number of staff: 1 full-time professional; 1 full-time support; 1 part-time support.
EIN: 436052774
Other changes: At the close of 2012, the grantmaker paid grants of $1,494,678, a 60.5% increase over the 2011 disbursements, $931,239.

1787
Dunn Family Foundation
1001 Locust St.
Kansas City, MO 64106-1904
Contact: Robert P. Dunn, Pres.

Established in 1981 in MO.
Donors: William H. Dunn, Sr.; Terrence P. Dunn; J.E. Dunn Construction; Steven D. Dunn; Terry Dunn; Robert P. Dunn.
Foundation type: Independent foundation.
Financial data (yr. ended 06/30/13): Assets, $2,542,649 (M); gifts received, $753,669; expenditures, $478,605; qualifying distributions,

$442,362; giving activities include $442,362 for 152 grants (high: $100,000; low: $75).
Fields of interest: Education; Health care; Human services; Community/economic development; Religion; Youth; Aging; Disabilities, people with; Minorities.
Type of support: Debt reduction; General/operating support; Building/renovation; Equipment.
Limitations: Applications accepted. Giving within a 75-mile radius of the greater metropolitan Kansas City, MO, area. No support for the visual or performing arts. No grants to individuals, or for research, endowments, travel, conferences, or telethons.
Application information: Application form required.
Initial approach: Letter
Deadline(s): None
Board meeting date(s): Quarterly
Officers and Directors:* William H. Dunn, Sr.,* Chair.; Robert P. Dunn,* Pres.; **Kevin A. Dunn,* V.P. and Treas.**; Terrence P. Dunn,* V.P.; William H. Dunn, Jr.,* V.P.; **Stephen D. Dunn.**
EIN: 431244010
Other changes: Kevin A. Dunn has replaced Stephen D. Dunn as V.P. and Treas.

1788
Fabick Charitable Trust Inc.
1 Fabick Dr.
Fenton, MO 63026-2928 (636) 343-5900
Contact: David Kramer

Incorporated in 1969 in MO.
Donor: John Fabick Tractor Co.
Foundation type: Company-sponsored foundation.
Financial data (yr. ended 12/31/12): Assets, $3,400 (M); gifts received, $258,797; expenditures, $268,100; qualifying distributions, $268,100; giving activities include $268,100 for grants.
Purpose and activities: The foundation supports hospitals and organizations involved with education, disaster relief, human services, and Christianity.
Fields of interest: Theological school/education; Education; Hospitals (general); Disasters, preparedness/services; Boy scouts; Salvation Army; Children/youth, services; Homeless, human services; Human services; Christian agencies & churches; Catholic agencies & churches.
Type of support: General/operating support.
Limitations: Applications accepted. Giving primarily in St. Louis, MO. No grants to individuals.
Application information: Application form required.
***Initial approach:* Letter**
Copies of proposal: 1
Deadline(s): Oct. 15
Officers: Harry Fabick, Pres.; Scott R. Borlinghaus, Secy.
EIN: 237013262

1789
Gateway Foundation
720 Olive St., Ste. 1977
St. Louis, MO 63101-2307 (314) 241-3337
Contact: Christy B. Fox, Admin.
FAX: (314) 241-3559;
***E-mail:* info@gateway-foundation.org**; Main URL: http://www.gateway-foundation.org

Established in 1986 in MO under the EIN of 431420333; reincorporated in 2004 under the current EIN.
Donor: Deer Creek Foundation.
Foundation type: Independent foundation.
Financial data (yr. ended 12/31/12): Assets, $58,361,473 (M); expenditures, $1,749,946; qualifying distributions, $1,325,501; giving activities include $916,309 for 7 grants (high: $741,403; low: $1,293), and $55,367 for 1 loan/program-related investment.
Purpose and activities: Support for the arts and cultural projects and, on occasion, related educational activities. Priority given to acquisition, creation, or improvement of items of a physical, durable nature. Focus on enhancing the physical environment in the St. Louis, Missouri, metropolitan area.
Fields of interest: Visual arts; Visual arts, architecture; Museums; Performing arts; Arts; Recreation, parks/playgrounds; Recreation; Urban/community development.
Type of support: Building/renovation; Equipment; Technical assistance; Matching/challenge support.
Limitations: Applications accepted. Giving limited to the metropolitan St. Louis, MO, area. Generally no support for programmatic operating expenses or for endowments.
Publications: Application guidelines; Grants list; Informational brochure.
Application information: The foundation does not consider grant presentations. Written application is required. See foundation Web site for application guidelines, programs and procedures. Application form not required.
Initial approach: Telephone
Copies of proposal: 1
Deadline(s): Feb. 1, May 1, Aug. 1 and Nov. 1
Board meeting date(s): Quarterly
Final notification: Mar., Jun., Sept., Dec.
Officers and Directors:* M. Peter Fischer,* Pres.; James D. Burke,* V.P.; Susan R. Rava,* Secy.-Treas.; Martha Fischer; Matthew G. Fischer; Michael P. Fischer; Christy B. Fox; Paul Ha; David Mesker; Gyo Obata; Susan Philpott.
Number of staff: 1 full-time professional; 1 full-time support; 1 part-time support.
EIN: 206294706

1790
Allen P. & Josephine B. Green Foundation
c/o Greater Kansas City Community Foundation
1055 Broadway, Ste. 130
Kansas City, MO 64105-1595 **(816) 627-3420**
Contact: Matthew Fuller, Mgr., Community Investment, Greater Kansas City Community Foundation
FAX: (816) 268-3420;
E-mail: greenfoundation@gkccf.org; Main URL: http://www.greenfdn.org

Trust established in 1941 in MO.
Donors: Allen P. Green†; Josephine B. Green†.
Foundation type: Independent foundation.
Financial data (yr. ended 12/31/12): Assets, $10,748,762 (M); expenditures, $612,946; qualifying distributions, $518,885; giving activities include $485,000 for 43 grants (high: $25,000; low: $1,000), and $20,000 for 4 grants to individuals (high: $5,000; low: $5,000).
Purpose and activities: Giving primarily for human service programs providing direct services to people in need, youth development programs, innovative developmental and educational programs for children, health and hospitals (with the exception of research projects), and religious institutions with an emphasis on projects that support community churches and the provision of social services. Each year the foundation also offers a $7,500 scholarship, renewable for three years, to a graduating senior of Mexico High School in Missouri.
Fields of interest: Education; Hospitals (general); Health care; Youth development; Human services; Religion; Children.
Type of support: Building/renovation; Equipment; Land acquisition; Endowments; Emergency funds; Program development; Conferences/seminars; Seed money; Curriculum development; Scholarship funds; Matching/challenge support.
Limitations: Applications accepted. Giving limited to central and eastern MO. No support for political organizations, programs located outside of the U.S., or to a charity that is not publicly supported. No grants to individuals, or for operating budgets, social causes or social activism, or lobbying; no loans.
Publications: Application guidelines; Annual report (including application guidelines); Grants list.
Application information: Scholarship application forms are available on Sept. 15 at Mexico High School. Application form required.
Initial approach: Use application form on foundation web site only
Copies of proposal: 1
Deadline(s): See foundation web site for current deadlines for grants; Jan. 15 for scholarships
Officers: Laura White Erdel, Pres.; **Franklin E.W. Staley, V.P.**; Carl D. Fuemmeler, Secy.-Treas.
Directors: A.D. Bond III; Christopher S. Bond; Nancy A. Ekern; Walter G. Staley III; Larry D. Webber; Nancy G. White; John F. Wood; Robert A. Wood.
Number of staff: 1 part-time support.
EIN: 436030135
Other changes: Franklin E.W. Staley is now V.P.

1791
Anna M. Guilander Scholarship Trust
c/o First Bank Wealth Management
135 N. Meramec 3rd Fl.
Clayton, MO 63105-3751

Donor: Robert M. Guilander f/b/o Trust.
Foundation type: Independent foundation.
Financial data (yr. ended 09/30/13): Assets, $5,759,052 (M); expenditures, $327,112; qualifying distributions, $272,112; giving activities include $272,112 for 37 grants to individuals (high: $52,580; low: $2,000).
Purpose and activities: Support for graduating seniors of Jersey Community Unit School District 100 H.S. who will be attending a college, university or trade school.
Fields of interest: Education.
Type of support: Scholarships—to individuals.
Limitations: Applications not accepted. Giving primarily in IL.
Application information: Contributes only to pre-selected organizations.
Trustees: Jill Bastian; Robert Guilander.
EIN: 271847433
Other changes: Darlene Ward is no longer a trustee.

1792
The Hagan Scholarship Foundation
P.O. Box 1225
Columbia, MO 65205-1225 (573) 875-2020
Contact: Dan Hagan, Tr.
***E-mail:* scholarships@hsfmo.org**; Main URL: http://haganscholarships.org
Grants Database: http://haganscholarships.org/recipients.php

Established in MO.
Donors: Dan Hagan; The Hagan Endowment Foundation; The Hagan Trust.

Foundation type: Independent foundation.
Financial data (yr. ended 12/31/12): Assets, $112,403,908 (M); gifts received, $37,186,111; expenditures, $519,784; qualifying distributions, $1,160,210; giving activities include $281,252 for grants.
Fields of interest: Education.
Limitations: Applications accepted. Giving primarily in MO.
Application information:
Initial approach: Use forms on foundation web site
Deadline(s): Nov.15
Trustee: Dan Hagan.
EIN: 686260880

1793
Hall Family Foundation
P.O. Box 419580, Dept. 323
Kansas City, MO 64141-6580 (816) 274-8516
FAX: (816) 274-8547; Main URL: http://www.hallfamilyfoundation.org

Hallmark Educational Foundation incorporated in 1943 in MO; Hallmark Educational Foundation of KS incorporated in 1954 in KS; combined funds formerly known as Hallmark Educational Foundations; current name adopted due to absorption of Hall Family Foundation of Kansas in 1993.
Donors: Hallmark Cards, Inc.; Joyce C. Hall†; E.A. Hall†; R.B. Hall†.
Foundation type: Independent foundation.
Financial data (yr. ended 12/31/13): Assets, $880,600,000 (M); expenditures, $42,152,716; qualifying distributions, $38,152,716; giving activities include $38,152,716 for 117 grants (high: $5,450,000; low: $8,500).
Purpose and activities: The foundation is dedicated to enhancing the quality of human life. Programs that enrich the community, help people and promote excellence are considered to be of prime importance. The foundation views its primary function as that of a catalyst. It seeks to be responsive to programs that are innovative, yet strive to create permanent solutions to community needs in the Greater Kansas City area.
Fields of interest: Performing arts; Arts; Education, early childhood education; Child development, education; Elementary school/education; Secondary school/education; Higher education; Education; Housing/shelter, development; Human services; Youth, services; Child development, services; Family services; Minorities/immigrants, centers/services; Homeless, human services; Urban/community development; Community/economic development.
Type of support: General/operating support; Capital campaigns; Building/renovation; Equipment; Land acquisition; Emergency funds; Program development; Technical assistance; Program evaluation; Program-related investments/loans; Employee-related scholarships.
Limitations: Applications accepted. Giving limited to greater Kansas City, MO. No support for international or religious organizations or for political purposes. **No grants to individuals (except for employee-related scholarships), or for travel, operating deficits, conferences, scholarly research, or fundraising campaigns or event promotion such as telethons, or for endowments.**
Publications: Annual report; Grants list; Informational brochure (including application guidelines).
Application information: Scholarships are for the children and close relatives of Hallmark Cards employees only. Only eligible applicants should apply. Application form not required.
Initial approach: Letter
Copies of proposal: 1
Deadline(s): 6 weeks before board meetings
Board meeting date(s): Mar., June, Sept., and Dec.
Final notification: 6 to 8 weeks
Officers and Directors:* Donald J. Hall,* Chair.; William A. Hall, Pres.; John A. MacDonald, V.P. and Treas.; Jeanne Bates, V.P.; Tracy McFerrin Foster, V.P. and Secy.; Richard C. Green; Robert E. Hemenway; Irvine O. Hockaday, Jr.; Robert A. Kipp; Sandra A.J. Lawrence; Margaret Hall Pence; Morton I. Sosland; David A. Warm.
EIN: 446006291

1794
Hallmark Corporate Foundation
P.O. Box 419580, M.D. 323
Kansas City, MO 64141-6580
Contact: Carol Hallquist, Pres.; Cora Storbeck
E-mail: contributions@hallmark.com; Main URL: http://corporate.hallmark.com/Corporate-Citizenship/Community-Involvement

Established in 1983 in MO.
Donors: Hallmark Cards, Inc.; Crayola, LLC.
Foundation type: Company-sponsored foundation.
Financial data (yr. ended 12/31/12): Assets, $805,619 (M); gifts received, $1,677,000; expenditures, $1,688,883; qualifying distributions, $1,688,534; giving activities include $1,688,524 for 426 grants (high: $294,750; low: $200).
Purpose and activities: The foundation supports programs designed to address the needs of children and families; promote arts and culture; address human service infrastructure and civic assets; and support the military.
Fields of interest: Performing arts; Performing arts, theater; Performing arts, orchestras; Arts; Child development, education; Education; Hospitals (general); Children/youth, services; Family services; Human services; Urban/community development; United Ways and Federated Giving Programs; Military/veterans' organizations; Public affairs.
Type of support: General/operating support; Continuing support; Capital campaigns; Building/renovation; Equipment; Program development; Technical assistance; Employee volunteer services; Program evaluation; Employee matching gifts.
Limitations: Applications accepted. Giving limited to areas of company operations in Columbus, GA, Metamora, IL, Lawrence, Leavenworth, and Topeka, KS, Liberty and the Kansas City, MO, area, and Center, TX. No support for religious, fraternal, political, international, or veterans' organizations, athletic or labor groups, social clubs, or disease-specific organizations. **No grants to individuals, or for scholarships, endowments, debt reduction, travel, conferences, sponsorships, scholarly or health-related research, advertising, mass media campaigns, or fundraising; no furniture, machines, computers, or other equipment donations.**
Publications: Application guidelines; Informational brochure (including application guidelines).
Application information: Support is limited to 1 contribution per organization during any given year. Additional information may be requested at a later date. A personal or telephone interview or site visit may be requested. Application form required.
Initial approach: Complete online application form
Copies of proposal: 1
Deadline(s): None
Board meeting date(s): Periodic
***Final notification:* Up to 6 weeks**
Officers and Directors:* Donald J. Hall, Jr., Chair.; Carol Hallquist, Pres.; Cora Storbeck, V.P.; Albert P. Mauro, Jr., Secy.; Terri R. Maybee, Treas.; Stephen D. Doyal; David E. Hall.
Number of staff: 3 full-time professional; 1 full-time support.
EIN: 431303258

1795
Lewis H. Humphreys Charitable Trust
c/o US Trust, Philanthropic Solutions
1200 Main St., 14th Fl.
P.O. Box 219119
Kansas City, MO 64121-9119
Contact: James Mueth, V.P.
E-mail: james.mueth@ustrust.com; **E-mail to discuss application process or for questions about the foundation: mo.grantmaking@ustrust.com (Foundation name should be indicated in subject line)**; Main URL: http://www.bankofamerica.com/grantmaking

Established in 2004 in KS and MO.
Donor: Lewis H. Humphreys†.
Foundation type: Independent foundation.
Financial data (yr. ended 09/30/13): Assets, $97,630,924 (M); expenditures, $4,511,953; qualifying distributions, $3,906,724; giving activities include $3,822,300 for 35 grants (high: $392,000; low: $5,000).
Purpose and activities: Giving to support and promote quality educational, cultural, human services, and health care programming for underserved and disadvantaged populations.
Fields of interest: Higher education; Human services; Children/youth, services; Foundations (private grantmaking); Protestant agencies & churches; Aging; Economically disadvantaged.
Type of support: Scholarship funds.
Limitations: Applications accepted. Giving primarily in Osage and Coffey counties, KS.
Application information: Application form required.
***Initial approach:* Use application form on the trust's web site**
Copies of proposal: 2
Deadline(s): Between Aug. 1 and Sept. 30
Final notification: Nov. 30
Trustee: Bank of America, N.A.
EIN: 597276551

1796
Innovative Technology Education Fund
(formerly Humanities Instructional Television Educational Center)
7201 Delmar, Ste. 202
St. Louis, MO **63130-4106 (314) 725-4833**
Contact: Lisa Dinga, Exec. Dir.
***E-mail:* itef@innovteched.com; Main URL: http://innovteched.com**
Grants List: http://innovteched.com/grants-we-give

Established in 1986 in MO.
Foundation type: Independent foundation.
Financial data (yr. ended 12/31/12): Assets, $3,385,304 (M); expenditures, $629,349; qualifying distributions, $577,110; giving activities include $328,484 for 26 grants (high: $44,815; low: $600).
Purpose and activities: The Innovative Technology Education Fund (ITEF) offers a competitive grant program for schools located within the Greater St.

Louis area. It invites accredited K-12 educational institutions and their classroom educators to apply for a grant. Successful projects bring innovative learning to life through the integration of technology. ITEF supports leading edge, outside of the box ideas and models that positively impact student learning and support classroom educators by focusing on: (1) Student Achievement: Students reach new levels of educational success with the integration of technology to support a strong technology based curriculum, (2) Mobile / Extended Learning: Using technology to extend and enhance learning outside of the traditional classroom, and (3) Technology Skill Development: Projects that support students and teachers in developing the skills and knowledge needed to function in and contribute to a technology-rich society.
Fields of interest: Education.
Limitations: Applications accepted. Giving limited to the bi-state St. Louis region.
Publications: Application guidelines.
Application information: Online application form required. See Fund web site under Grants tab for full application guidelines. Application form required.
Initial approach: **Use online application system on Fund web site**
Copies of proposal: 1
Deadline(s): See Fund web site for specific dates
Officers and Directors:* **Tracy Toft Downing,*** **Chair.**; **Brenda Watt,*** **Vice-Chair.**; Anne E. Dill,* Secy.; **Joseph P. Komos,*** **Treas.**; Beth Bender, Ph.D.; Kathryn Kiefer.
Number of staff: 2
EIN: 431689900
Other changes: Tracy Toft Downing has replaced Gerald Arbini as Chair. Brenda Watt has replaced Andrew Thorp as Vice-Chair. Joseph P. Komos has replaced Barb Bollefer as Treas.
The grantmaker now publishes application guidelines.

1797
Ewing Marion Kauffman Foundation
4801 Rockhill Rd.
Kansas City, MO 64110-2046 (816) 932-1000
Contact: **Barbara Pruitt, Dir., Comms.**
FAX: (816) 932-1100; E-mail: info@kauffman.org;
Main URL: http://www.kauffman.org
E-Newsletter: http://www.kauffman.org/StayConnected.aspx?T=Y
Entrepreneurship.Org: http://www.entrepreneurship.org
Facebook: http://www.facebook.com/kauffmanfdn
Grants Database: http://www.kauffman.org/KauffmanGrants.aspx
Kauffman Foundation's Small Business America Blog on Huffington Post: http://www.huffingtonpost.com/tag/ewing-kauffman-foundation
Multimedia: http://www.kauffman.org/KauffmanMultimedia.aspx
RSS Directory: http://www.kauffman.org/StayConnected.aspx?id=3832&ekmensel=e4e07dfa_70_0_3832_6
Twitter: http://www.twitter.com/kauffmanfdn

Established in 1966 in MO.
Donor: Ewing M. Kauffman‡.
Foundation type: Independent foundation.
Financial data (yr. ended 12/31/12): Assets, $1,880,334,000 (M); expenditures, $85,487,000; qualifying distributions, $28,443,000; giving activities include $28,443,000 for grants.
Purpose and activities: The foundation's mission is to help individuals attain economic independence by advancing educational achievement and entrepreneurial success, consistent with the aspirations of its founder Ewing Marion Kauffman. To fulfill the mission, the foundation: 1) Identifies opportunities where application of the foundation's people, ideas, and capital can benefit society in significant and measurable ways; 2) Develops innovative, research-based programs leading to practical, sustainable solutions that are widely accepted and implemented; 3) Treats the Kansas City region as a program incubator where feasible, in which new approaches can be tried and tested before being disseminated nationally; and 4) Partners with others to leverage its resources and capabilities while avoiding the creation of dependency.
Fields of interest: Education, public policy; Elementary/secondary education; Education, services; Education; Community development, business promotion; Community development, small businesses; Science; Mathematics.
Type of support: General/operating support; Emergency funds; Program development; Conferences/seminars; Curriculum development; Fellowships; Research; Program evaluation; Program-related investments/loans; Employee matching gifts; Matching/challenge support.
Limitations: Applications accepted. Giving limited to the U.S., with emphasis on the bi-state metropolitan Kansas City area (KS/MO) for K-12 education initiatives focused on math and science. No support for international programs, political, social, fraternal, or arts organizations, and capital campaigns or construction projects. No grants for fund endowments, or for special events.
Publications: Application guidelines; Annual report; Financial statement; Grants list; Newsletter.
Application information: To receive a copy of the foundation's Guidelines for Grantseekers brochure, visit foundation's web site or send a request via e-mail or by mail. Application form not required.
Initial approach: Letter of inquiry, less than 3 pages
Deadline(s): None
Board meeting date(s): Mar., June, Sept., and Dec.
Final notification: As soon as possible
Officers and Trustees:* Janice Kreamer,* Chair.; **Wendy Guillies, Acting Pres. and C.E.O. and V.P., Comm.**; Dane Stangler, V.P., Research and Policy; Thom Ruhe, V.P., Entrepreneurship; Aaron North, V.P., Education; Kristin Bechard, Cont.; Mary McLean, C.I.O.; John E. Tyler III, Genl. Counsel; Julia Irene Kauffman; Barbara Mowry; Benno C. Schmidt, Jr.; Michael Schultz; John Sherman; Michael Stolper; Jeannine Strandjord.
Number of staff: 48 full-time professional; 4 part-time professional; 35 full-time support; 1 part-time support.
EIN: 436064859
Other changes: Wendy Guillies is now Acting Pres. and C.E.O. and V.P. Comm. Thomas A. McDonnell is no longer C.E.O. and Pres. Ramon de Oliveira, Siobhan Nicolau, Frank L. Douglas, Thomas M. Hoenig and Thomas J. Rhone are no longer trustees. Nancy McCullough is no longer V.P. and Treas. Judith Cone is no longer V.P., Emerging Strategies. Lesa Mitchell is no longer V.P., Advancing Innovation. Joy Torchia is no longer Comms. Mgr.

1798
Kuhn Foundation
4568 Meramec Bottom Rd., Ste. 6
St. Louis, MO **63128** **(314) 845-7700**
Contact: Thomas E. Kuhn, Pres.

Established in 2005 in MO.
Foundation type: Independent foundation.
Financial data (yr. ended 05/31/13): Assets, $8,520,270 (M); expenditures, $437,247; qualifying distributions, $379,905; giving activities include $367,357 for 49 grants (high: $178,700; low: $50).
Fields of interest: Education; Zoos/zoological societies; Human services; United Ways and Federated Giving Programs; Jewish federated giving programs; Jewish agencies & synagogues.
Limitations: Applications accepted. Giving primarily in MO.
Application information: Application form required.
Initial approach: Letter
Deadline(s): None
Officer and Directors:* Thomas E. Kuhn,* Pres.; Michael J. Kuhn; Steven L. Kuhn.
EIN: 203067498

1799
The Laclede Group Foundation
(formerly Laclede Gas Charitable Trust)
720 Olive St., Ste. 1306
St. Louis, MO 63101-2338
Main URL: **http://www.thelacledegroup.com/aboutthelacledegroup/foundation/**

Established in 1966 in MO.
Donor: Laclede Gas Co.
Foundation type: Company-sponsored foundation.
Financial data (yr. ended 09/30/13): Assets, $7,188,343 (M); gifts received, $2,000,000; expenditures, $669,793; qualifying distributions, $657,411; giving activities include $635,293 for 21 grants (high: $410,320; low: $325), and $22,118 for 40 employee matching gifts.
Purpose and activities: The foundation supports the United Way; community enrichment programs designed to support educational, diversity, and inclusion efforts and cultural institutions; and sustainability initiatives designed to protect and preserve community's environmental and natural resources.
Fields of interest: Arts; Education; Environment, natural resources; Environment; Health care; Human services; United Ways and Federated Giving Programs.
Type of support: General/operating support; Continuing support; Annual campaigns; Building/renovation; Equipment; Program development; Employee matching gifts.
Limitations: Applications accepted. Giving primarily in areas of company operations in St. Louis, MO. No support for political, labor, fraternal, or religious organizations, civic clubs, K-8 schools, or school-affiliated clubs. No grants to individuals, or for family services, advertising, school-affiliated events, sports, athletic events, or athletic programs, travel related events, student trips or tours, development or production of books, films, videos, or television programs, endowments, or memorial campaigns.
Application information: The Missouri Common Grant Application is also accepted. Support is limited to 1 contribution per organization during any given year. Application form required.
Initial approach: **Complete online eligibility quiz and application**
Copies of proposal: 1
Deadline(s): None
Board meeting date(s): **Quarterly**
Officers and Trustees:* Mary Caola Kullman,* Chair. and Pres.; Micheal R. Spotanski,* V.P.; P.S.

Kramer, Secy.; Lynn D. Rawlings, Treas.; Scott E. Jaskowiak; **Steven L. Lindsey.**
EIN: 436068197
Other changes: D.M. Seevers is no longer a trustee.
The grantmaker no longer publishes application guidelines.

1800
James S. McDonnell Foundation
(also known as JSMF)
1034 S. Brentwood Blvd., Ste. 1850
St. Louis, MO 63117-1229 **(314) 721-1532**
Contact: Susan M. Fitzpatrick, V.P.
FAX: (314) 721-7421; E-mail: info@jsmf.org;
Additional e-mail: help@jsmf.org; Main URL: http://www.jsmf.org
E-Newsletter: http://www.jsmf.org/about/mailinglist.htm
Facebook: http://www.facebook.com/JSMFoundation
Grants Database: http://www.jsmf.org/grants/search.php
Twitter: http://twitter.com/jsmf

Established in MO.
Foundation type: Independent foundation.
Financial data (yr. ended 12/31/12): Assets, $485,863,318 (M); gifts received, $21,121; expenditures, $32,743,661; qualifying distributions, $29,298,233; giving activities include $27,891,969 for 130 grants (high: $4,328,562; low: $25,000).
Purpose and activities: JSMF believes that private philanthropic support for science is most effective when it invests in the acquisition of new knowledge and in the responsible application of knowledge for solving the real world problems. The 21st Century Science Initiative, the foundation's revised program and funding strategy, will award two types of grants in three program areas. The three program areas are Mathematical & Complex Systems Approaches for Brain Cancer Research, Studying Complex Systems, and Understanding Human Cognition. Projects supported through the 21st Century Science Initiative are expected to meet highly selective intellectual standards.
Fields of interest: Cancer research; Brain research; Medical research; Science, research; Science.
Type of support: Research.
Limitations: Applications accepted. Giving on a local, national and international basis. No support for religious, educational or political organizations. No grants to individuals or for ongoing operational support for university-based centers, programs or institutes, no support for tuition, stipends, scholarships, underwriting or sponsoring of charitable functions, or museum exhibitions, expenses tied to projects whose explicit goal is the publication of a work, or expenses tied to the establishment or day-to-day running of a journal or small press.
Publications: Financial statement; Grants list; Program policy statement.
Application information: See foundation's web site for application information, all proposals must be electronically submitted. Institutions sponsoring an application on behalf of a particular principal investigator to JSMF programs (Research Awards, Collaborative Activity Awards) can only submit one application every 3 years on behalf of the named principal investigator. Application form not required.
Initial approach: Letter of inquiry for collaborative activity awards
Copies of proposal: 1
Deadline(s): Early to mid-Mar. for research awards; no deadline for letters of inquiry for collaborative activity awards
Board meeting date(s): Varies
Final notification: Varies depending on submission date
Officers and Directors:* John T. Bruer, Ph.D, Pres.; Susan M. Fitzpatrick, Ph.D., V.P.; James S. McDonnell III,* Secy.; John F. McDonnell,* Treas.; Jeanne M. Champer; Holly M. James; Alicia S. McDonnell; Jeffrey M. McDonnall; Marcella M. Stevens.
Number of staff: 2 full-time professional; 2 full-time support.
EIN: 542074788

1801
Millstone Foundation
7733 Forsyth Blvd., No. 1525
St. Louis, MO **63105-1867**
***Application address:* c/o Robert D. Millstone, 7701 Forsyth Blvd., Ste. 925, St. Louis, MO 63105, tel.: (314) 721-1932**

Incorporated in 1955 in MO.
Donors: I.E. Millstone; Goldie G. Millstone†.
Foundation type: Independent foundation.
Financial data (yr. ended 05/31/13): Assets, $7,750,609 (M); expenditures, $570,896; qualifying distributions, $514,049; giving activities include $498,742 for 62 grants (high: $78,232; low: $250).
Purpose and activities: Giving primarily for higher education and to Jewish organizations.
Fields of interest: Higher education; Education; Hospitals (specialty); Human services; Jewish federated giving programs; Jewish agencies & synagogues.
International interests: Israel.
Type of support: General/operating support; Continuing support; Annual campaigns; Emergency funds; Scholarship funds; Research.
Limitations: Applications accepted. Giving primarily in St. Louis, MO. No grants to individuals; no loans.
Application information: Application form required.
Initial approach: Letter
Copies of proposal: 1
Deadline(s): None
Officer and Directors:* Robert D. Millstone,* Pres.; Colleen Millstone.
Number of staff: 2 part-time professional.
EIN: 436027373

1802
Moneta Group Charitable Foundation
100 S. Brentwood Blvd., Ste. 500
Saint Louis, MO 63105 (314) 726-2300
***Contact:* Janet Bandera**
Main URL: http://www.monetagroup.com
: http://www.monetagroup.com/Foundation.aspx

Established in 2000 in MO.
Donors: Peter G. Schick; Joe Sheehan; Donald T. Kula; Chandler Taylor; Daniel West; Joseph Sheehan; Dave Sadler; Don Kukla; Jim Blair; Linda Pietroburgo; Michael Johnson; Steve Finerty; Tim Halls; Tom O' Meara.
Foundation type: Company-sponsored foundation.
Financial data (yr. ended 12/31/12): Assets, $1,436,298 (M); gifts received, $161,517; expenditures, $168,670; qualifying distributions, $163,861; giving activities include $163,861 for grants.
Purpose and activities: The foundation supports organizations involved with education, housing, human services, community development, senior citizens, economically disadvantaged people, and other areas.
Fields of interest: Education; Housing/shelter; Children/youth, services; Human services; Community/economic development; Aging; Economically disadvantaged.
Limitations: Applications not accepted. Giving limited to St. Louis, MO, including the Metro East area. No support for churches or religious organizations not of direct benefit to the entire community, national organizations (except for local branches), or controversial organizations. No grants to individuals, or for fundraising events, endowments, debt reduction, general operating support for private or parochial schools, or start-up needs.
Application information: Contributes to organizations recommended by Moneta Group employees.
Board meeting date(s): Feb., May, and Oct.
Officers: Chandler Taylor, Chair.; Daniel West, Treas.
Trustees: Katie Kearins; Donald T. Kukla; Doug Weber.
EIN: 431871586

1803
Monsanto Fund
800 N. Lindbergh Blvd.
St. Louis, MO 63167-7843 (314) 694-4391
Contact: Deborah J. Patterson, Pres.
FAX: (314) 694-7658;
E-mail: monsanto.fund@monsanto.com; Additional tel.: (314) 694-1000, fax: (314) 694-1001; Contact for America's Farmers Grow Communities and America's Farmers Grow Rural Education: Eileen Jensen, 914 Spruce St., St. Louis, MO 63102, tel.: (877) 267-3332; Main URL: http://www.monsantofund.org/
America's Farmers Campaign on Facebook: http://www.facebook.com/AmericasFarmers
America's Farmers Campaign on Twitter: https://twitter.com/americasfarmers
America's Farmers: Grow Communities Winners: http://www.americasfarmers.com/recognition-programs/grow-communities-2014-winners/
America's Farmers: Grow Rural Education Winners: http://www.americasfarmers.com/recognition-programs/grow-rural-education-2013-winners/

Incorporated in 1964 in MO as successor to the Monsanto Charitable Trust.
Donor: Monsanto Co.
Foundation type: Company-sponsored foundation.
Financial data (yr. ended 12/31/13): Assets, $14,466,836 (M); gifts received, $14,450,000; expenditures, $22,138,072; qualifying distributions, $22,106,265; giving activities include $20,004,683 for 2,916 grants (high: $900,000; low: $250), and $1,761,596 for 6,803 employee matching gifts.
Purpose and activities: The fund supports programs designed to strengthen farming communities and the communities where Monsanto employees live and work. Special emphasis is directed toward programs designed to improve education in farming communities, including schools, libraries, science centers, farmer training, and academic initiatives that enrich school programming; and meet critical needs in communities through food security,

sanitation, access to clean water, public safety, and various other local needs.
Fields of interest: Arts education; Visual arts; Performing arts; Literature; Arts; Elementary/secondary education; Libraries (public); Education; Environment, pollution control; Environment, water pollution; Botanical/horticulture/landscape services; Environment; Public health, clean water supply; Public health, sanitation; Agriculture/food, research; Agriculture/food, public education; Agriculture; Agriculture, farmlands; Agriculture, farm bureaus/granges; Food services; Nutrition; Disasters, fire prevention/control; Safety, education; Safety/disasters; Youth development, agriculture; Human services; Science, formal/general education; Mathematics; Science; Public affairs; Children; Youth; Economically disadvantaged.
Type of support: General/operating support; Continuing support; Equipment; Program development; Conferences/seminars; Seed money; Curriculum development; Research; Program evaluation; Employee matching gifts; Matching/challenge support.
Limitations: Applications accepted. Giving on a national and international basis primarily in areas of company operations in GA, IA, ID, IL, and LA, with emphasis on the greater St. Louis, MO, area. Giving outside the U.S. in Canada, Mexico, the United Kingdom, and Africa, including Malawi, Burkina Faso, Kenya, South Africa, and Uganda, Asia, including China, India, Indonesia, Philippines, and Thailand, and South America including Argentina, Brazil, Chile, Columbia, Guatemala, Honduras, Paraguay, and Uruguay. No support for start-up organizations, fraternal, labor, or veterans' organizations not of direct benefit to the entire community, religious, politically partisan, or similar organizations, or discriminatory organizations. No grants to individuals, or for debt reduction, benefits, dinners, or advertisements, endowments, marketing, or projects in which Monsanto Company has a financial interest or could derive a financial benefit through cash or rights to intellectual property; no donations of printers, computer software, copiers, scanners, or computers.
Publications: Application guidelines; Annual report; Grants list; Program policy statement.
Application information: Support is limited to 1 contribution per organization during any given year. Organizations receiving support are asked to submit a mid-year report and a final report. A site visit may be requested for Kids Garden Fresh Program. All applicants are welcome to attend a grant information session at Monsanto headquarters. Session dates are available on Monsanto's website.
Initial approach: Complete online application; complete online nomination for America's Farmers: Grow Rural Education
Deadline(s): **Feb. 28 and Aug. 31 for Math & Science Education K-12 and Access to Arts; Feb. 28 for US Site Grants; Feb. 28 and Aug. 31 for international organizations; Apr. 21 for America's Farmers: Grow Rural Education; June 1 for Kids Garden Fresh Program; and Nov. 30 for America's Farmers: Grow Communities**
Board meeting date(s): Twice per year
Final notification: July for Kids Garden Fresh Program
Officers and Directors:* Derek K. Rapp,* Chair.; Deborah J. Patterson,* Pres.; Sonya Meyers Davis, Secy.; Thomas D. Hartley, Treas.; **Michael J. Frank**; Janet M. Holloway; Jesus Madrazo; **Nicole M. Ringenberg**; **Michael K. Stern.**
Number of staff: 1 full-time professional; 1 part-time professional; 2 full-time support.
EIN: 436044736
Other changes: Derek K. Rapp has replaced Brett D. Begemann as Chair.
Brett D. Begemann is no longer Chair. Consuelo E. Madere, Gerald A. Steiner, and Kerry J. Preete are no longer directors.

1804
The David and Barbara Mungenast Foundation, Inc.

(formerly The Mungenast Foundation, Inc.)
5939 S. Lindbergh Blvd.
St. Louis, MO **63123-7039**
Main URL: **http://www.mungenast.com/Mungenast_Foundation.htm**
Facebook: https://www.facebook.com/MungenastAutomotiveFamily
Google Plus: https://plus.google.com/102879762827110904658/posts
Pinterest: http://www.pinterest.com/mungenastauto/
Twitter: https://twitter.com/MungenastAuto
YouTube: https://www.youtube.com/user/MungenastAutomotive

Established in 1996 in MO.
Donors: David F. Mungenast; Barbara J. Mungenast; Capco Sales, Inc.; DAR, Inc.; DDR Invesment Co., Inc.; DRK Investment Co., Inc.; DFM Investment Co., Inc.; Mungenast Group Dealer Services.
Foundation type: Independent foundation.
Financial data (yr. ended 11/30/13): Assets, $4,399,465 (M); gifts received, $255,064; expenditures, $223,581; qualifying distributions, $218,124; giving activities include $216,700 for 10 grants (high: $74,000; low: $500), and $1,424 for 1 foundation-administered program.
Fields of interest: Medical care, in-patient care; Food services; Youth development, centers/clubs; Human services; Residential/custodial care, hospices.
Limitations: Applications not accepted. Giving primarily in St. Louis, MO. No grants to individuals.
Application information: Unsolicited requests for funds not accepted.
Officers: Raymond J. Mungenast, Secy.; David F. Mungenast, Jr., Treas.
Directors: Barbara J. Mungenast; Kurt A. Mungenast.
EIN: 431766152

1805
Musgrave Foundation

1 Corporate Ctr.
1949 E. Sunshine, Ste. 1-130
Springfield, MO **65804-1601** (417) 841-4698
FAX: (417) 882-2529;
E-mail: contact@musgravefoundation.org; Application address: c/o Jerry L. Redfern, Mgr., Musgrave Foundation, P.O. Box 10327, Springfield, MO 65808; Main URL: http://www.musgravefoundation.org

Established in 1983 in MO.
Donor: Jeannette Musgrave.
Foundation type: Independent foundation.
Financial data (yr. ended 06/30/13): Assets, $15,029,153 (M); expenditures, $1,062,719; qualifying distributions, $834,236; giving activities include $677,017 for 54 grants (high: $138,500; low: $500).
Purpose and activities: Giving primarily for arts and community betterment, healthcare and education, and children and senior services.
Fields of interest: Arts; Higher education; Nursing school/education; Nursing care; Boys & girls clubs; Boy scouts; Human services; Salvation Army; Children/youth, services; Community/economic development; Christian agencies & churches; Economically disadvantaged.
Type of support: General/operating support; Continuing support; Annual campaigns; Capital campaigns; Building/renovation; Equipment; Program development; Scholarship funds; Matching/challenge support.
Limitations: Applications accepted. **Giving limited to Green County, MO, and to other counties that share a border with Greene.** No grants to individuals.
Application information: Application form required.
Initial approach: **Use online application form on foundation web site; alternatively, applications may be downloaded from web site and submitted via U.S. Mail**
Deadline(s): **Mar. 1 and Aug. 1**
Officers: Charles Fuller, Chair.; Jerry L. Redfern, Mgr.
Directors: Rob Baird; Junior Cline; **Dr. Peggy Riggs**; Thomas L. Slaight.
Trustee: U.S. Bank, N.A.
Number of staff: 1 part-time professional.
EIN: 431304514
Other changes: Neil Wortley is no longer a director.

1806
Nichols Company Charitable Trust

4706 Broadway Ave., Ste. 260
Kansas City, MO 64112-1910 (816) 561-3456
Contact: Daniel Hollman, Treas.
***Application address:* 310 Ward Pkwy., Kansas City, MO 64112**

Trust established in 1952 in MO.
Donors: J.C. Nichols Co.; Highwoods Realty L.P.
Foundation type: Company-sponsored foundation.
Financial data (yr. ended 12/31/12): Assets, $3,195,015 (M); expenditures, $165,732; qualifying distributions, $149,229; giving activities include $147,600 for 63 grants (high: $10,500; low: $500).
Purpose and activities: The foundation supports art museums and hospitals and organizations involved with education, patient services, human services, and the real estate industry.
Fields of interest: Arts; Human services; Community/economic development.
Type of support: General/operating support.
Limitations: Applications accepted. Giving primarily in Kansas City, MO. No grants to individuals.
Application information: Application form not required.
Initial approach: **Letter**
Deadline(s): None
Officers: Barrett Brady, Pres.; Daniel Hollman, Treas.
EIN: 446015538

1807
Pendergast-Weyer Foundation

9300 E. 155th St.
Kansas City, MO 64149-1161 (816) 322-0491

Established about 1976 in MO.
Donors: Mary Louise Weyer Pendergast‡; Thomas J. Pendergast, Jr.‡.
Foundation type: Independent foundation.
Financial data (yr. ended 06/30/13): Assets, $4,072,548 (M); gifts received, $58,949;

expenditures, $625,447; qualifying distributions, $484,503; giving activities include $357,172 for 91 grants.
Purpose and activities: Giving primarily for Roman Catholic church-related pre-schools, elementary schools, high schools, and religious organizations. A minimum of 80 percent of all grants must go to Catholic institutions.
Fields of interest: Education; Health organizations; Human services.
Type of support: Continuing support; Program development; Consulting services.
Limitations: Applications accepted. Giving limited to MO. No support for clergymen, chanceries, or church foundations. No grants to individuals, or for annual campaigns, seed money, building funds, land acquisition, endowment funds, matching gifts, research, publications, or conferences; no loans.
Publications: Application guidelines.
Application information: Application form required.
Initial approach: **Request application form**
Copies of proposal: 1
Deadline(s): None
Officers: R. Kenneth Burnett, Pres.; Lynn Burnett, V.P.; Beverly J. Brayman, Secy.
Directors: Roger Brayman; Bernadette C. Cleary; Terry Dotson; Michael Heydon; Michael McGlenn; Mary Weir.
EIN: 431070676

1808
Prime Health Foundation

c/o UMB Bank
1010 Grand Blvd., 3rd Fl.
Kansas City, MO 64106-2220 (816) 860-7711
Contact: Kristen Comment
FAX: (816) 860-5080;
E-mail: director@primehealthfoundation.org; Main URL: http://www.primehealthfoundation.org
Grants List: http://www.primehealthfoundation.org/programs.htm

Established in 1978 in MO; converted from Prime Health Plan.
Foundation type: Independent foundation.
Financial data (yr. ended 12/31/12): Assets, $116,922 (M); expenditures, $354,100; qualifying distributions, $296,840; giving activities include $296,840 for 14 grants (high: $50,000; low: $7,000).
Purpose and activities: The foundation enhances the development of healthcare delivery systems designed to provide appropriate health care services suitable for treatment. Areas of special interest include: disease prevention, including early detection of disease; improvement of conditions that contribute to morbidity and/or mortality (clinical, social or otherwise); improvements in quality of care and/or service delivery; promotion of wellness and healthy lifestyles; increased availability and accessibility of health care; consumer health education; health care provider education; appropriate use of health care resources; awareness about social issues affecting health, such as domestic violence, mental health, etc.; and other projects showing potential to improve community health.
Fields of interest: Health care.
Limitations: Applications accepted. Giving primarily in the Kansas City, MO, metropolitan area, but will fund projects with nationwide impact. No grants for capital equipment.
Publications: Application guidelines.
Application information: See foundation web site for application requirements.
Directors: Robert Barrientos; Alvin Brooks; Karin Chang-Rios, Ph.D; Dr. Mary Corcoran; Robert E. Eisler, Jr.; W.T. Hembree; James T. Nunnelly; Dr. Elizabeth S. Peterson; Margo Quiriconi; Edna Rindner; Melissa Robinson; Thomas Ryan; Dr. Thomas Simmons; Dr. Susan Wilson.
EIN: 431057862

1809
Joseph H. & Florence A. Roblee Foundation

P.O. Box 191255
St. Louis, MO 63119-7255 (314) 963-7713
***Contact:* Kathy Doellefeld-Clancy, Exec. Dir.**
***FAX:* (314) 963-7716;**
E-mail: grantapplication@robleefoundation.org; Address for FL organizations to submit their 3 additional application copies: 5003 S.W. 71st Pl., Miami, FL 33155; Main URL: http://www.robleefoundation.org
Grants List: http://www.robleefoundation.org/past.php

Trust established in 1971 in MO.
Donors: Louise Roblee McCarthy‡; Florence Roblee Trust.
Foundation type: Independent foundation.
Financial data (yr. ended 12/31/12): Assets, $16,832,727 (M); expenditures, $943,326; qualifying distributions, $855,127; giving activities include $712,900 for 72 grants (high: $25,000; low: $500).
Purpose and activities: The foundation awards grants to enable organizations to promote change by addressing significant social issues in order to improve the quality of life and help fulfill the potential of individuals. The foundation arises out of a Christian framework, and values ecumenical endeavors. The foundation particularly supports programs which work to break down cultural, racial, and ethnic barriers. Organizations and churches are encouraged to collaborate in achieving positive change through advocacy, prevention, and systemic improvements.
Fields of interest: Education, reform; Teacher school/education; Substance abuse, prevention; Crime/violence prevention; Crime/violence prevention, domestic violence; Housing/shelter; Youth development, citizenship; Children/youth, services; Youth, pregnancy prevention; Family services; Women, centers/services; Civil rights, race/intergroup relations; Civil liberties, reproductive rights; Public affairs, citizen participation; Women; Economically disadvantaged; Homeless.
Type of support: Technical assistance.
Limitations: Applications accepted. Giving limited to the greater bi-state St. Louis region, and Miami/Dade, FL. No grants to individuals, or for annual campaigns; no loans.
Publications: Application guidelines.
Application information: Organizations in FL should submit their 3 additional application copies to the foundation's Miami, FL address. Proposals submitted by fax are not accepted. Application forms and specific submission requirements available on foundation web site. Application form required.
Initial approach: **Cover letter, proposal summary and application form**
Copies of proposal: 3
Deadline(s): Jan. 15 and June 15
Officers: Jeffrey Allen Von Arx, Pres.; **Kathy Doellefeld-Clancy, Exec. Dir.**
Trustees: Carol M. Duhme; Carol Von Arx; Bank of America, N.A.
Board Members: David W. Duhme; Jeremy Duhme; Sally Welker McAdam; Eugenie Ross McCarthy; Juliana Allen McCarthy; Roblee McCarthy, Jr.; Jeanne R. Radley; Robyn Ann Von Arx; Lisa Welker.
Number of staff: 1 full-time professional.
EIN: 436109579
Other changes: The grantmaker has moved from IL to MO.
The grantmaker now makes its application guidelines available online.

1810
John S. Ross Family Foundation

(formerly John S. & Jody J. Ross Foundation)
P.O. Box 11356
Clayton, MO 63105-0156

Established in 1992 in MO.
Donor: John S. Ross.
Foundation type: Independent foundation.
Financial data (yr. ended 12/31/13): Assets, $1,657,222 (M); expenditures, $180,764; qualifying distributions, $171,323; giving activities include $169,000 for 19 grants (high: $50,000; low: $100).
Fields of interest: Museums (art); Arts; Philanthropy/voluntarism; Religion.
Type of support: General/operating support.
Limitations: Applications not accepted. Giving primarily in St. Louis, MO. No grants to individuals.
Application information: Unsolicited requests for funds not accepted.
Officers: John S. Ross, Pres.; Jody J. Ross, V.P.
EIN: 431544557
Other changes: Jeffrey J. Ross and John S. Ross are no longer directors.

1811
The Saigh Foundation

7777 Bonhomme Ave., Ste. 2007
St. Louis, MO 63105-1911 (314) 862-3055
Contact: JoAnn Hejna, Exec. Dir.
FAX: (314) 862-9288;
E-mail: saigh@thesaighfoundation.org; Main URL: http://www.thesaighfoundation.org/

Established in 1998 in NY.
Donor: Fred M. Saigh‡.
Foundation type: Independent foundation.
Financial data (yr. ended 03/31/13): Assets, $65,517,148 (M); expenditures, $3,307,382; qualifying distributions, $2,823,821; giving activities include $2,298,383 for 92 grants (high: $380,000; low: $2,500).
Purpose and activities: Supports funding for St. Louis, Missouri metropolitan, area organizations benefiting children and youth in the areas of education and health care.
Fields of interest: Education; Health care; Children/youth, services; Children/youth; Children; Youth; Physically disabled; Minorities; Girls; Boys.
Type of support: Endowments; Program development; Scholarship funds; Research; Matching/challenge support.
Limitations: Applications accepted. Giving limited to St. Louis, MO. No grants for capital campaigns, annual appeals, dinner functions, fundraising events, or for films and travel; no loans.
Application information: Proposals may be submitted by mail or fax. Missouri Common Grant Application accepted. Application form required.
Initial approach: Letter
Copies of proposal: 1

Deadline(s): Jan, 15, Apr. 15, July 15, and Oct. 15
Board meeting date(s): Jan., Apr., July, and Oct.
Final notification: 2 days after quarterly meeting
Officer and Trustees:* JoAnn Hejna,* Exec. Dir.; Heidi Veron; Franklin F. Wallis; Fiduciary Trust Co. Int'l.
Number of staff: 2 full-time professional.
EIN: 516511117

1812
Schneider Foundation
c/o U.S. Bank, N.A., Trust Dept.
1615 S. Glenstone Ave.
Springfield, MO 65808-3357
***Application address:* c/o Henry Schneider, Schneider Foundation, 2135 E. Edgewood St., Springfield, MO 65804-3843, tel.: (417) 883-1154**

Established around 1990 in MO.
Donors: Henry Schneider; Jane Schneider.
Foundation type: Independent foundation.
Financial data (yr. ended 09/30/13): Assets, $6,965,696 (M); gifts received, $46,035; expenditures, $285,421; qualifying distributions, $253,772; giving activities include $250,000 for 6 grants (high: $125,000; low: $5,000).
Fields of interest: Education, public education; Elementary/secondary education; Higher education; Higher education, university; Boys & girls clubs; YM/YWCAs & YM/YWHAs; Children/youth, services.
Type of support: General/operating support.
Limitations: Applications accepted. Giving limited to Springfield, MO.
Application information: Application form required.
Initial approach: Letter
Deadline(s): None
Officers: Henry Schneider, Pres.; **R. Barnes Whitlock, Secy.**
Directors: Susan Holliday; James Johnson; Douglas R. Nickell; Jane Schneider; Ross M. Schneider.
EIN: 431530098
Other changes: R. Barnes Whitlock has replaced Douglas R. Nickell as Secy.

1813
Victor E. Speas Foundation
c/o U.S. Trust
1200 Main St., 14th Fl.
P.O. Box 219119
Kansas City, MO 64121-9119 (816) 292-4300
Contact: Spence Heddens, Sr. V.P.
E-mail: Spence.heddens@ustrust.com; **E-mail to discuss application process or for questions about the foundation: mo.grantmaking@ustrust.com (Foundation name should be indicated in subject line)**; Main URL: http://www.bankofamerica.com/grantmaking

Trust established in 1947 in MO.
Donors: Effie E. Speas‡; Victor E. Speas‡; Speas Co.; Alice J. Speas Unitrust.
Foundation type: Independent foundation.
Financial data (yr. ended 12/31/12): Assets, $34,686,124 (M); expenditures, $1,261,604; qualifying distributions, $1,002,168; giving activities include $933,107 for 32 grants (high: $100,000; low: $2,500).
Purpose and activities: Giving restricted to improving the quality of health care in the Kansas City, MO, area. Support mainly for medically-related higher education, including loans for medical students at the University of Missouri at Kansas City, and for a school for dentistry; funding also for preventive health care, and medical research; grants also for agencies serving the healthcare needs of the elderly, youth, and the handicapped.
Fields of interest: Medical school/education; Health care; Health organizations; Human services; Children/youth, services; Economically disadvantaged.
Type of support: General/operating support; Capital campaigns; Building/renovation; Equipment; Emergency funds; Program development; Seed money; Research; Matching/challenge support; Student loans—to individuals.
Limitations: Giving limited to Kansas City, MO. No grants for endowment funds, capital support, or scholarships; no loans (except to medical students at the University of Missouri at Kansas City).
Publications: Application guidelines.
Application information: Application form available online. Application form required.
Copies of proposal: 2
Deadline(s): Rolling
Trustee: Bank of America, N.A.
Number of staff: 1 full-time professional.
EIN: 446008340

1814
Greater St. Louis Health Foundation
(formerly Group Health Foundation of Greater St. Louis)
412 S. Clay Ave., Ste. 100
Kirkwood, MO 63122-5860 **(314) 835-9991**
Contact: Robert W. Swanson, Secy.
E-mail: info@gstlhf.com; Main URL: http://gstlhf.com/

Established in 1986 in MO; converted from Group Health Plan.
Foundation type: Independent foundation.
Financial data (yr. ended 12/31/12): Assets, $3,349,530 (M); gifts received, $10; expenditures, $341,178; qualifying distributions, $180,722; giving activities include $180,722 for grants.
Purpose and activities: To promote health and prevent illness in the greater St. Louis, MO, area through support and financial aid to nonprofit organizations.
Fields of interest: Medical school/education; Nursing school/education; Medical care, rehabilitation; Nursing care; Health organizations, association; Biomedicine; Chiropractic; Medical research, institute.
Type of support: Program development; Conferences/seminars; Seed money; Curriculum development; Scholarship funds; Research.
Limitations: Applications accepted. Giving limited to the greater metropolitan St. Louis, MO, area. No grants to individuals, or for overhead costs or continuing support.
Application information: See foundation web site for guidelines.
Initial approach: Letter
Deadline(s): Feb 28, May 31, Aug 31, Nov 30
Board meeting date(s): Feb., May, Aug., and Nov.
Officers and Directors:* Richard Ellerbrake,* Pres.; Ralph L. Biddy,* V.P.; Robert W. Swanson,* Secy.; Taylor C. Scott, Treas.; Kenneth Guethle; Thomas H. Lake; Darwin W. Schlag.
EIN: 431141117

1815
The Tilles Fund
(formerly Rosalie Tilles Nonsectarian Charity Fund)
c/o U.S. Bank, N.A
The Private Client Reserve, Attn.: Carol Eaves, Mail Loc: SL-MO-CTCS
10 N. Hanley Rd.
Clayton, MO **63105-3426 (314) 505-8204**
Contact: Garth Silvey, V.P.
Application information: Carol Eaves, tel.: (314) 418-8391; Main URL: http://www.thetillesfund.org
Trust established in 1926 in MO.
Donor: Cap Andrew Tilles‡.
Foundation type: Independent foundation.
Financial data (yr. ended 06/30/13): Assets, $12,930,390 (M); expenditures, $586,763; qualifying distributions, $504,756; giving activities include $148,400 for 15 grants (high: $15,000; low: $400), and $341,783 for grants to individuals.
Purpose and activities: Giving primarily for scholarship awards for recent high school graduates who are residents of the City or County of St. Louis, Missouri, to attend any Missouri university or college; funding also available for St. Louis area organizations for a one-year period that provide services for the special needs of children with physical and/or mental disabilities.
Fields of interest: Higher education; Scholarships/financial aid; Health organizations; Human services; Children/youth, services.
Type of support: Scholarship funds.
Limitations: Applications accepted. Giving limited to the city of St. Louis and St. Louis County, MO. No support for political causes and candidates, or for-profit entities. No grants to individuals directly, or for operating costs, fundraising dinners, courtesy advertising or other benefits and endowment projects.
Publications: Application guidelines.
Application information: The foundation generally does not accept unsolicited applications, and is not currently accepting new scholar applications. See foundation web site for additional information. Application form not required.
Initial approach: 1-page concept paper
Copies of proposal: 7
Deadline(s): Aug. 15th for grants; May 1 for scholarships
Board meeting date(s): Monthly
Trustees: Rabbi Mark L. Shook; Richard W. Braun; Paul P. Weil; Archdiocese of St. Louis; U.S. Bank, N.A.
Number of staff: 1 part-time professional; 1 part-time support.
EIN: 436020833
Other changes: The grantmaker now makes its application guidelines available online.

1816
The Trudy Foundation
301 Bellefontaine Ave., No. 1N
Kansas City, MO **64124-1860**

Foundation type: Independent foundation.
Financial data (yr. ended 12/31/12): Assets, $1,837,100 (M); expenditures, $134,040; qualifying distributions, $98,500; giving activities include $98,500 for 25 grants (high: $10,000; low: $1,000).
Fields of interest: Medical research; Human services; Protestant agencies & churches.
Limitations: Applications not accepted.
Application information: Unsolicited requests for funds not accepted.
Officers and Trustees:* Roberta Murphy,* Chair.; Catherine Lobash; Susan Meehan; Arthur Murphy III; Julia Murphy.
EIN: 206389901

1817

Truman Heartland Community Foundation

(formerly Independence Community Foundation)
4200 Little Blue Parkway, Ste. 340
Independence, MO 64057-8303 (816) 836-8189
Contact: Elizabeth A. McClure, Dir., Progs. and Rels.
FAX: (816) 836-8898; E-mail: hanson@thcf.org;
Additional e-mail: mcclure@thcf.org; Main URL: http://www.thcf.org

Incorporated in 1982 in MO; received assets converted from merger of Independence Community Foundation with Independence Regional Health Center Foundation in 1994.
Foundation type: Community foundation.
Financial data (yr. ended 12/31/12): Assets, $27,875,910 (M); gifts received, $2,610,153; expenditures, $5,176,573; giving activities include $4,139,059 for 143+ grants (high: $289,694), and $189,441 for 173 grants to individuals.
Purpose and activities: The mission of the Truman Heartland Community Foundation is to improve area communities by promoting and serving private giving for the public good. The foundation primarily provides support for arts, culture, and historic preservation, building stronger neighborhoods, education, fostering a sense of community spirit, health needs for the community, leadership development for youth and adults, programs for seniors, positive youth development, transportation and violence prevention.
Fields of interest: Historic preservation/historical societies; Arts; Adult/continuing education; Education; Health care; Crime/violence prevention; Employment, training; Housing/shelter, development; Youth development; Children/youth, services; Family services, domestic violence; Aging, centers/services; Human services; Community/economic development; Transportation; Leadership development; Aging.
Type of support: General/operating support; Continuing support; Program development; Seed money; Scholarship funds; In-kind gifts; Matching/challenge support.
Limitations: Applications accepted. Giving limited to suburban Jackson County, MO. No grants to individuals (except for scholarships).
Publications: Application guidelines; Annual report; Informational brochure; Newsletter.
Application information: Visit foundation web site for application forms and guidelines. Organizations whose letters of interest show the greatest potential for serving or strengthening the community will be invited to submit full applications. Application form required.
Initial approach: Letter of interest
Deadline(s): First Thurs. in Apr. for letter of interest; fourth Thursday in May for full proposal
Board meeting date(s): Quarterly
Final notification: Mid-May for full proposal invitation; early October for funding decisions
Officers and Directors:* Martha Cockerell,* Chair.; Judy Forrester,* Vice-Chair.; Phillip J. Hanson,* C.E.O. and Pres.; **Joy Hobick,* Secy.**; **Rick Kreher,* Treas.**; Beverly J. Powell,* C.F.O.; Paul Broome; Cindy Cavanah; Brad Constance; William C. Esry; Randall Ferguson; Ron Finke; Eleanor Frasier; **Chuck Foudree**; Helen Hatridge; Darrel Hensely; Robert Hepting; David Jeter; Cliff Jones; Barbara Koirtyohann; Steve Krueger; Dr. Allan Markley; Tracey Mershon; Melanie Moentmann; Jim Pryde; Charlie Shields; Dr. Barbara Thompson; Brenda West; David Williams; Sharon Williams.
Number of staff: 2 full-time professional; 2 full-time support; 1 part-time support.
EIN: 431482136
Other changes: Martha Cockerell has replaced Chuck Foundree as Chair. Judy Forrester has replaced Martha Cockerell as Vice-Chair. Joy Hobick has replaced Doug Hammer as Secy. Rick Kreher has replaced Mike McGraw as Treas. Greg Finke, Judy Forrester, Joy Hobick, Richard N. Kreher, and Sherri Lozano are no longer directors.

1818

The Earl E. Walker and Myrtle E. Walker Foundation

120 W. Adams Ave., Ste. 306
St. Louis, MO 63122-4084

Established in 1987 in MO.
Donors: Earl E. Walker; Myrtle E. Walker; CARR Lane Manufacturing; Walker Family Trust; W & W, Inc.; Home Towne Suites - Bowling Green LLC; Home Towne Suites - Clarksville LLC; All American Products.
Foundation type: Independent foundation.
Financial data (yr. ended 12/31/12): Assets, $10,969,908 (M); expenditures, $272,829; qualifying distributions, $208,564; giving activities include $208,564 for 5 grants (high: $100,000; low: $764).
Fields of interest: Arts; Higher education; Zoos/zoological societies.
Type of support: General/operating support; Building/renovation; Endowments; Scholarships—to individuals.
Limitations: Applications not accepted. Giving primarily in MO.
Application information: Unsolicited requests for funds not accepted.
Trustees: Nancy E. Frost; **Brian K. Humes**; **Peggy E. Swisher**; **Mary E. Walker**; Myrtle E. Walker; **Thomas E. Walker**.
EIN: 431466121
Other changes: Earl E. Walker is no longer a trustee.

1819

James L. & Nellie M. Westlake Scholarship Fund

c/o U.S. Bank, N.A.
P.O. Box 387
St. Louis, MO 63166-0387
***Main URL:* http://sms.scholarshipamerica.org/westlake/**

Established in 1981 in MO.
Donors: James L. Westlake†; Nellie M. Westlake.
Foundation type: Independent foundation.
Financial data (yr. ended 06/30/13): Assets, $20,930,963 (M); gifts received, $5,000; expenditures, $1,069,280; qualifying distributions, $964,319; giving activities include $878,381 for grants to individuals.
Purpose and activities: Awards scholarships to graduates of Missouri high schools, based on need and scholastic achievement, for higher education scholarships. Applicants must be enrolled in full-time undergraduate study for the entire upcoming academic year at an accredited 4-year college or university, or have completed 1 or 2 full years at a Missouri community college with sufficient credits to transfer to an accredited 4-year college or university at the sophomore or junior level. Applicants must also demonstrate limited financial resources with a family adjusted gross income of $50,000 or less, and an expected family contribution toward college of $7,000 or less, and have at least a cumulative GPA of 2.5 on a 4.0 scale, except community college applicants with 1-year transferable credits who must have 2.25 or higher on a 4.0 scale.
Fields of interest: Young adults.
Type of support: Scholarships—to individuals.
Limitations: Giving limited to high school graduates who are residents of MO. No loans or program-related investments.
Publications: Application guidelines.
Application information: Application form available on program web site. Application form required.
***Deadline(s):* See program web site for current deadline**
Trustee: U.S. Bank, N.A.
EIN: 436248269
Other changes: The grantmaker now makes its application guidelines available online.

1820

Whitaker Foundation

(also known as Lyndon C. and Mae M. Whitaker Charitable Foundation)
308 N. 21st St., Ste. 400
St. Louis, MO 63103-1642 (314) 241-4352
Contact: Christy E. Gray, Exec. Dir.
FAX: (314) 241-4381;
E-mail: cgray@thewhitakerfoundation.org;
Additional e-mail: info@thewhitakerfoundation.org; Main URL: http://www.thewhitakerfoundation.org

Trust established in 1975 in MO.
Donor: Mae M. Whitaker†.
Foundation type: Independent foundation.
Financial data (yr. ended 04/30/13): Assets, $26,181,495 (M); expenditures, $1,378,065; qualifying distributions, $1,193,683; giving activities include $948,786 for 21 grants (high: $141,086; low: $6,000).
Purpose and activities: Giving primarily to strengthen arts organizations and local park preservation and use.
Fields of interest: Arts; Recreation, parks/playgrounds.
Type of support: Capital campaigns; Building/renovation; Program development.
Limitations: Applications accepted. Giving in the metropolitan St. Louis, MO, area, particularly within 50 miles of the Arch. No grants to individuals, or for galas, tournaments, or other social events.
Publications: Application guidelines; Annual report; Grants list.
Application information: Paper letters and proposals are no longer accepted. Full proposals are by invitation only, after review of Letter of Inquiry. Application form required.
***Initial approach:* Letter of Inquiry via online application process through foundation web site**
Copies of proposal: 1
***Deadline(s):* For Letters of Inquiry: Feb. 1, Aug. 1, and Nov. 1; For invited proposals: Mar. 1, Sept. 1 and Dec. 1**
Board meeting date(s): Jan., Apr., July and Oct.
Final notification: Jan., Apr., and Oct.
Officer: Christy E. Gray, Exec. Dir.
Trustees: Arnold Donald; Barbara Eagleton; Dr. Gerald Early; Shaun Hayes; Kiku Obata.
Number of staff: 1 full-time professional; 1 part-time support.
EIN: 510173109

1821
Herbert A. & Adrian W. Woods Foundation
c/o Bank of America, N.A.
100 North Broadway, MO2-100-07-15
St. Louis, MO 63102-2728
Contact: Shanise Evans, V.P.
E-mail: shanise.evans@baml.com; **Main URL: https://www.bankofamerica.com/philanthropic/grantmaking.go**

Established in 1999 in MO.
Donor: Adrian W. Woods Trust.
Foundation type: Independent foundation.
Financial data (yr. ended 12/31/12): Assets, $6,989,746 (M); expenditures, $350,435; qualifying distributions, $318,935; giving activities include $297,500 for 27 grants (high: $35,000; low: $5,000).
Purpose and activities: The foundation is dedicated to the founders' interests in charitable organizations that serve abused, neglected, or troubled children; the poor; the Episcopal Church and its affiliates, including outreach programs; art and culture in the metropolitan St. Louis, Missouri area; animal welfare in Missouri; and victims of illness or disability, including research in this area.
Fields of interest: Hospitals (specialty); Youth development; Children, services; Human services; Christian agencies & churches.
Limitations: Applications accepted. Giving primarily in St. Louis, MO. No grants to individuals.
Application information:
Initial approach: Online approach via foundation web site
Deadline(s): Sept. 1
Trustee: Bank of America, N.A.
EIN: 436826365

MONTANA

1822
Cross Charitable Foundation, Inc.
3805 Valley Commons Dr., Ste. 7
Bozeman, MT 59718-6510
***Contact:* John R. Clark**
***Application address:* P.O. Box 1789, West Yellowstone, MT 59758, tel. (406) 585-3393; Main URL: http://crosscharitablefoundation.org/**

Established in WY.
Donors: C. Walker Cross; C. Walker Cross Living Trust.
Foundation type: Independent foundation.
Financial data (yr. ended 12/31/12): Assets, $24,548,374 (M); gifts received, $2,434,500; expenditures, $1,123,384; qualifying distributions, $891,500; giving activities include $891,500 for grants.
Fields of interest: Environment; Animals/wildlife.
Application information:
Deadline(s): Aug. 1
Officers: Charles Folland, Pres.; Terri Anderson, V.P.; Rex Child, Secy.; Carol Gonella, Secy.; John R. Clark, Treas.
EIN: 830331707

1823
The Greater Montana Foundation
1038 Monroe Ave.
Helena, MT 59601-2661 (406) 443-5693
Contact: Sidney Armstrong, Exec. Dir.
E-mail: info@greatermontana.org; Application address: c/o Robert Hoene, 281 Chapman Hill Rd., Ste. 1, Big Fork, MT 59911; Main URL: http://www.greatermontana.org
Grants List: http://greatermontana.org/category/awarded-grants-list/

Established in 1959 in MT.
Foundation type: Independent foundation.
Financial data (yr. ended 12/31/12): Assets, $8,776,186 (M); expenditures, $389,022; qualifying distributions, $316,065; giving activities include $281,561 for 16 grants (high: $65,000; low: $1,500).
Fields of interest: Media/communications; Media, radio; Historic preservation/historical societies; Higher education, university.
Limitations: Applications accepted. Giving primarily in MT.
Application information: Application forms available on foundation web site. Application form required.
Initial approach: Proposal
Deadline(s): Apr. 1
Officers: Randal Morger, Chair.; Sarah Etchart, Co. Vice-Chair.; William Whitsitt, Co. Vice-Chair.; Steve Browning, Secy.; Jerry Black, Treas.; Sidney O'Malley Armstrong, Exec. Dir.
Trustees: Norma Ashby; Brody Craney; Darlene Craney; Ronald Davis; Fred J. Flanders; Vic Miller; Daniel Synder; Monty Wallis.
EIN: 816009847

1824
Groskinsky Foundation
Sidney, MT

The foundation terminated in 2013.

1825
The High Stakes Foundation
(formerly Montana Good Works Foundation)
P.O. Box 96
Arlee, MT 59821-0096 (406) 726-2030
***Contact:* Cherie Garcelon, Prog. Off.**
Main URL: http://www.highstakesfoundation.org
Grants List: http://www.highstakesfoundation.org/2013_Grants.html

Established in 2007 in MT.
Donors: Mary Stranahan; Mary Stranahan Trust.
Foundation type: Independent foundation.
Financial data (yr. ended 12/31/12): Assets, $1,717,339 (M); expenditures, $497,685; qualifying distributions, $478,173; giving activities include $368,700 for 30 grants (high: $25,000; low: $1,000).
Fields of interest: Environment, natural resources; Environmental education; Animals/wildlife, preservation/protection; Human services; Social sciences, public policy.
Limitations: Applications accepted. Giving primarily in MT.
Application information: See foundation web site for complete application guidelines. Application form required.
Initial approach: Completed application form
***Deadline(s):* April 1 and Sept. 1**
Officer: Dawn McGee, Pres. and Secy.; Cherie Garcelon, Mgr.
Directors: Joel Solomon; Mary Stranahan; Molly Stranahan.
EIN: 205815274

1826
The Lair Family Foundation, Inc.
Big Timber, MT

The foundation terminated in 2011.

1827
Elizabeth A. Lynn Foundation
P.O. Box 439
Lakeside, MT 59922-0439
Contact: Diane Titch, Grant Admin.
Main URL: http://www.elizabethalynnfoundation.org

Established in 1981 in WA.
Donor: Elizabeth A. Lynn†.
Foundation type: Independent foundation.
Financial data (yr. ended 11/30/13): Assets, $6,830,223 (M); expenditures, $373,071; qualifying distributions, $300,758; giving activities include $300,758 for 40 grants (high: $39,758; low: $5,000).
Fields of interest: Elementary/secondary education; Health care; Substance abuse, treatment; Mental health, treatment; Employment; Housing/shelter; Youth development; Human services.
Type of support: Building/renovation; Capital campaigns; Equipment; General/operating support; Program development; Scholarship funds.
Limitations: Applications accepted. Giving primarily in WA, with emphasis on the Puget Sound corridor, and in Ada, Blaine, Lincoln, and Jerome counties in southern Idaho. No grants to individuals.
Publications: Application guidelines; Financial statement.
Application information: Visit foundation web site for information on focus of foundation, guidelines, application format, deadlines, and all requirements and attachments. Application form required.
Board meeting date(s): 3 times annually
Trustees: Traci Kennedy; Jeff Lynn; Jody Moss.
EIN: 911156982
Other changes: The grantmaker no longer lists a phone.

1828
Montana Community Foundation
1 N. Last Chance Gulch, Ste. 1
Helena, MT 59624-1145 (406) 443-8313
FAX: (406) 442-0482; E-mail: info@mtcf.org; Mailing address: P.O. box 1145, Helena, MT 59624-1145; Main URL: http://www.mtcf.org
Facebook: http://www.facebook.com/pages/Montana-Community-Foundation/187434094625353

Incorporated in 1988 in MT.
Foundation type: Community foundation.
Financial data (yr. ended 06/30/12): Assets, $59,658,108 (M); gifts received, $2,956,696; expenditures, $4,674,299; giving activities include $2,567,904 for 120+ grants (high: $112,720).
Purpose and activities: The foundation seeks to cultivate a culture of giving so Montana communities can flourish.
Fields of interest: Arts; Education; Environment, natural resources; Human services; Economic development; Minorities; Native Americans/American Indians; Girls; Adults, women; Young adults, female; LGBTQ.
Type of support: Continuing support; Emergency funds; Employee-related scholarships; Scholarships—to individuals.
Limitations: Applications accepted. Giving limited to MT. No support for religious purposes. No grants for annual or capital campaigns, endowment funds, or generally for debt retirement.
Publications: Annual report; Financial statement; Newsletter.
Application information: Visit foundation web site for Application Cover Sheet and application guidelines. Application form required.
Initial approach: Submit Application Cover Sheet with proposal
Board meeting date(s): 3 times per year
Officers and Directors:* Dan Clark,* Chair.; Brian Patrick,* Vice-Chair.; **Mary Rutherford,* C.E.O.**; Mary Craigle,* Secy.; Dale Woolhiser,* Treas.; Emily Kovarik,* C.F.O.; Jeff Bretherton; Mike Gustafson; Stacey Mueller; Cynthia R. Woods.
Number of staff: 5 full-time professional; 2 full-time support; 1 part-time support.
EIN: 810450150

1829
The Sample Foundation, Inc.
P.O. Box 279
Billings, MT 59103 **(406) 245-6342**
***Contact:* Barbara Sample, Pres.**
FAX: (406) 245-8303;
E-mail: applications@samplefoundation.org; Main URL: http://www.samplefoundation.org

Incorporated in 1954 in FL.
Donors: Helen S. Sample†; John Glen Sample†; Joseph S. Sample; Miriam T. Sample; Michael S. Sample; David F. Sample; Patrick G. Sample.
Foundation type: Independent foundation.
Financial data (yr. ended 10/31/12): Assets, $7,427,446 (M); gifts received, $256,498; expenditures, $379,916; qualifying distributions,

$362,555; giving activities include $362,555 for 59 grants (high: $35,000; low: $100).
Purpose and activities: Giving primarily for health, social welfare, and services for the disadvantaged. Grant support primarily for capital outlays or to assist in initiating a particular project.
Fields of interest: Human services.
Type of support: Capital campaigns; Equipment; Land acquisition.
Limitations: Applications accepted. Giving primarily in Collier County, FL, and MT. No support for lobbying, or religious groups. No grants to individuals, or for scholarships, operating budgets, or duplication of services.
Publications: Application guidelines; Annual report; Grants list; Informational brochure (including application guidelines); Program policy statement.
Application information: Application information and form available on foundation web site. Application form required.
Copies of proposal: 1
Deadline(s): Aug. 1
Board meeting date(s): Oct. 6th
Final notification: Oct. 31
Officers and Trustees:* Joseph S. Sample,* Chair.; **Barbara Sample, Pres. & Exec. Dir.**; Michael S. Sample,* V.P.; T.A. Cox,* Treas.; David F. Sample; Patrick G. Sample.
Number of staff: None.
EIN: 596138602
Other changes: Barbara Sample is now Pres. & Exec. Dir.

1830
Morris & Helen Silver Foundation
P.O. Box 3297
Missoula, MT 59806-3297 (406) 240-6353
Contact: Karrie Montgomery
Main URL: http://www.silverfoundation.org
Grants List: http://www.silverfoundation.net/grantees

Established in 2001 in MT.
Donor: F. Morris Silver†.
Foundation type: Independent foundation.
Financial data (yr. ended 12/31/12): Assets, $4,562,895 (M); expenditures, $321,927; qualifying distributions, $148,120; giving activities include $148,120 for grants.
Fields of interest: Performing arts, theater; Arts; Elementary/secondary education; Human services; YM/YWCAs & YM/YWHAs; Foundations (community).
Type of support: Capital campaigns; Building/renovation; Emergency funds; Program development; Curriculum development; Program evaluation; Matching/challenge support.
Limitations: Applications accepted. Giving limited to Missoula, MT. No support for religious or political organizations.
Publications: Application guidelines; Informational brochure (including application guidelines).
Application information: Application form required.
Initial approach: Contact foundation for application form
Copies of proposal: 1
Deadline(s): None
Board meeting date(s): Quarterly
Final notification: 2 months
Officers: Timothy J. Sather, Pres.; Carolyn R. Montgomery, V.P.; Thomas H. Boone, Secy.-Treas.
EIN: 841398903

1831
Wendy's of Montana Foundation Inc.
2906 2nd Ave. N., Ste. 212
Billings, MT 59101-2026 (406) 252-5125
Contact: Gregory C. McDonald, Pres.

Established in 1998 in NV.
Donors: Wendy's of Montana Inc.; Sam E. McDonald, Jr.; Martin Family Foundation; Food Services of America.
Foundation type: Company-sponsored foundation.
Financial data (yr. ended 12/31/12): Assets, $705,553 (M); gifts received, $869,292; expenditures, $246,748; qualifying distributions, $199,435; giving activities include $199,435 for grants.
Purpose and activities: The foundation supports organizations involved with arts and culture, education, athletics, adoption, and community development.
Fields of interest: Museums (art); Performing arts, theater; Performing arts, orchestras; Arts; Higher education; Education; Athletics/sports, amateur leagues; Athletics/sports, baseball; Boys & girls clubs; YM/YWCAs & YM/YWHAs; Children, adoption; Community/economic development.
Type of support: General/operating support; Program development; Sponsorships.
Limitations: Applications accepted. Giving primarily in Billings, MT.
Application information: Application form required.
***Initial approach:* Request application form**
***Deadline(s):* Contact foundation for deadlines**
Officers: Gregory C. McDonald, Pres.; John Wilcox, Secy.-Treas.
Director: John T. Jones.
EIN: 880393923

1832
Whitefish Community Foundation
214 2nd St. W.
P.O. Box 1060
Whitefish, MT 59937 (406) 863-1781
Contact: Linda Engh-Grady, Exec. Dir.
FAX: (406) 863-2628;
E-mail: info@whitefishcommunityfoundation.org;
Main URL: http://www.whitefishcommunityfoundation.org
Facebook: http://www.facebook.com/pages/Whitefish-MT/Whitefish-Community-Foundation/192411305234

Established in 2000 in MT.
Foundation type: Community foundation.
Financial data (yr. ended 12/31/11): Assets, $6,457,974 (M); gifts received, $2,766,021; expenditures, $1,382,731; giving activities include $1,263,893 for grants.
Purpose and activities: The mission of the Whitefish Community Foundation is to enrich the quality of life in the Whitefish area by fostering philanthropy, building endowments, and helping donors and nonprofits benefit the local community.
Type of support: Technical assistance; Scholarship funds; Research; Publication; Program development; Matching/challenge support; Management development/capacity building; General/operating support; Film/video/radio; Equipment; Endowments; Emergency funds; Capital campaigns; Building/renovation.
Limitations: Applications accepted. Giving primarily in Flathead County, MT. No support for organizations or institutions operated primarily by religious organizations, or medical research. No grants to individuals, or for conduit organizations.
Publications: Application guidelines; Annual report; Financial statement; Grants list; Informational brochure; Multi-year report; Newsletter.
Application information: Visit foundation web site for application form and guidelines. Faxed or e-mailed applications are not accepted. Application form required.
Initial approach: Submit application form
Copies of proposal: 10
Deadline(s): June 1
Board meeting date(s): Jan., Apr., July and Oct.
Final notification: Nov.
Officers and Executive Committee: David Dittman,* Pres.; Jay Latimer,* Secy.-Treas.; Linda Engh-Grady, Exec. Dir.; Carol Atkinson; Judah Gersh; Doug Reed; Ardyce Whisler.
Board Members: Lin Akey; Betsy Bayne; Michael Jenson; James Kenyon III; **John Kramer**; Lori Miller; Tom Quinn; **Karen Rosenberg**; **Jamie Shennan**; Kristin Tabor; Kelly Talsma; Kenneth Wessels; John Witt.
Number of staff: 1 full-time professional; 1 part-time support.
EIN: 810533002
Other changes: David Dittman has replaced Carol B. Atkinson as Pres.
Daria Perez is now Cont. Bart Erickson and Virginia V. Weldon are no longer Executive Committee members.

NEBRASKA

1833
The Susan Thompson Buffett Foundation
(formerly The Buffett Foundation)
222 Kiewit Plz.
Omaha, NE 68131-3302
Contact: Allen Greenberg, Pres.
E-mail: scholarships@stbfoundation.org; Main URL: http://www.buffettscholarships.org
Warren Buffett's Giving Pledge Profile: http://glasspockets.org/philanthropy-in-focus/eye-on-the-giving-pledge/profiles/buffett
Tel. for scholarship information: (402) 943-1383

Incorporated in 1964 in NE. In 2006, Warren Buffett pledged almost $3 billion worth of his Berkshire-Hathaway, Inc. stock to the foundation to be paid out over time. As a result, the Susan Thompson Buffett Foundation's assets and annual giving have risen sharply.
Donors: Warren E. Buffett; Susan T. Buffett‡.
Foundation type: Independent foundation.
Financial data (yr. ended 12/31/12): Assets, $2,384,070,265 (M); gifts received, $153,136,793; expenditures, $374,616,566; qualifying distributions, $374,159,456; giving activities include $346,094,516 for 243 grants (high: $39,892,246; low: $2,091), and $21,073,377 for grants to individuals.
Purpose and activities: Grants primarily for family planning programs, and scholarships to residents of Nebraska attending Nebraska public colleges or universities.
Fields of interest: Reproductive health, family planning; Civil liberties, reproductive rights.
Type of support: General/operating support; Scholarships—to individuals.
Limitations: Applications accepted. Giving on a national and international basis; scholarships awarded only to residents in NE. No grant to individuals (except for Teacher Awards and scholarships).
Application information: Unsolicited requests for grants not accepted. The foundation accepts scholarship applications. The foundation only responds to questions about scholarships and awards. Please see the foundation's web site for additional details.
Initial approach: Application form required for scholarship program only
***Deadline(s):* Feb. 1 for scholarships**
Officers and Directors:* Susan A. Buffett,* Chair. and Treas.; Allen Greenberg, Pres.; Melissa How, Secy.; Peter A. Buffett; **Allison Cowan**; Geoffrey Cowan; Carol Loomis; Patti Matson.
Number of staff: 9 full-time professional; 3 full-time support.
EIN: 476032365

1834
Cooper Foundation
870 Wells Fargo Ctr.
1248 O St.
Lincoln, NE 68508-1493 (402) 476-7571
Contact: E. Arthur Thompson, Pres.; Victoria Kovar, Sr. Prog. Off.
FAX: (402) 476-2356;
E-mail: info@cooperfoundation.org; Main URL: http://www.cooperfoundation.org/
Facebook: https://www.facebook.com/CooperFoundation
Grants List: http://cooperfoundation.org/2013-grants-approved

Incorporated in 1934 in NE.
Donor: Joseph H. Cooper‡.
Foundation type: Independent foundation.
Financial data (yr. ended 12/31/13): Assets, $24,458,351 (M); gifts received, $100; expenditures, $1,040,916; qualifying distributions, $959,171; giving activities include $606,491 for 69 grants (high: $40,000; low: $100).
Purpose and activities: The mission of the foundation is to support strong, sustainable organizations, innovative ideas, and ventures of significant promise in Nebraska.
Fields of interest: Humanities; Arts; Education; Environment; Human services.
Type of support: Advocacy; General/operating support; Management development/capacity building; Program development.
Limitations: Giving limited to NE, with emphasis on Lincoln and Lancaster County. No support for religious, health or political purposes, private foundations, or for businesses. No grants to individuals, or for multi-year grants, memberships, travel, or endowment funds.
Publications: Application guidelines; Financial statement; Grants list; Occasional report.
Application information: If the foundation is interested in the proposal, it will request that an inquiry be submitted via its online application website. Unsolicited applications are not accepted. See foundation web site for complete application guidelines and procedures. Application form required.
Initial approach: Contact foundation in person, or via telephone, letter or e-mail to discuss proposal
Copies of proposal: 1
Deadline(s): Jan. 15, Apr. 1, Aug. 1, and Oct. 1
Board meeting date(s): Quarterly
Final notification: 2 months
Officers and Trustees:* Jack D. Campbell,* Chair.; Robert Nefsky,* Vice-Chair.; E. Arthur Thompson,* Pres.; Victoria Kovar,* Corp. Secy.; Brad Korell,* Treas.; Richard Knudsen, Genl. Counsel; Linda Crump; Jane Renner Hood; Kim Robak; Richard J. Vierk; Norton Warner.
Number of staff: 2 full-time professional; 1 part-time professional.
EIN: 470401230

1835
Robert B. Daugherty Foundation
1 Valmont Plz., Ste. 202
Omaha, NE 68154-5301 (402) 933-4663
Contact: Kimberly Yungtum, C.A.O. and Grants Off.
FAX: (402) 933-4248;
E-mail: grants@daughertyfdn.org; Main URL: http://www.daughertyfdn.org

Established in NE.
Donor: Robert B. Daugherty.
Foundation type: Independent foundation.
Financial data (yr. ended 12/31/12): Assets, $716,182,668 (M); expenditures, $30,750,745; qualifying distributions, $26,666,645; giving activities include $25,523,958 for 97 grants (high: $5,000,000; low: $2,000).
Purpose and activities: The foundation provides grants to organizations that conduct religious, charitable, scientific, cultural or education activities exclusively.
Fields of interest: Education; Science; Religion.
Type of support: Matching/challenge support.
Limitations: Applications accepted. Giving primarily in NE, with emphasis on the greater Omaha area. Generally, no support for religious organizations for religious purposes or to international organizations that do not have a qualified domestic representative. Generally, no grants to individuals or for endowments or other discretionary funding pools, dinners, balls, and other events.
Publications: Application guidelines.
Application information: Application guidelines available on foundation web site.
***Initial approach:* Online application**
Deadline(s): None
***Final notification:* Response via e-mail to the submitting organization confirming receipt of the preliminary grant application**
Officers and Trustees:* John K. Wilson, Exec. Dir.; Rebecca J. Nadgwick, Cont. and Grants Mgr.; Mogens Bay; F. Joe Daugherty; J. Timothy Daugherty; Robert Daugherty III; Ken Stinson.
EIN: 363766006
Other changes: John K. Wilson has replaced J. Timothy Daugherty as Exec. Dir.
The grantmaker now publishes application guidelines.

1836
Fremont Area Community Foundation
1005 E. 23rd St., Ste. 2
P.O. Box 182
Fremont, NE 68025-4932 (402) 721-4252
Contact: Jessica Janssen, Exec. Dir.
FAX: (402) 721-9359;
E-mail: info@facfoundation.org; Main URL: http://www.facfoundation.org
Blog: http://www.facfoundation.wordpress.com
Facebook: http://www.facebook.com/FremontAreaCommunityFoundation

Established in 1980 in NE.
Foundation type: Community foundation.
Financial data (yr. ended 06/30/12): Assets, $14,338,572 (M); gifts received, $4,057,466; expenditures, $1,938,057; giving activities include $1,546,904 for 16+ grants (high: $337,500).
Purpose and activities: The foundation seeks to improve the quality of life by connecting donor interests with community needs. Grantmaking primarily for social services, health and recreation, education, arts and culture, and civic purposes.
Fields of interest: Arts; Education; Health care; Recreation; Human services; Government/public administration.
Type of support: Annual campaigns; Management development/capacity building; Capital campaigns; Building/renovation; Equipment; Endowments; Program development; Seed money; Scholarships—to individuals; In-kind gifts; Matching/challenge support.
Limitations: Applications accepted. Giving primarily in the Fremont and Dodge County, NE, area. Some limited grantmaking in Burt, Colfax, Douglas, Cuming, Saunders and Washington counties in NE. No support for religious organizations for religious purposes. No grants to individuals (except for designated scholarship funds).
Publications: Application guidelines; Annual report; Informational brochure (including application guidelines); Newsletter.
Application information: Visit foundation web site for application form and guidelines. Application form required.
Initial approach: Contact foundation
Copies of proposal: 1
Deadline(s): Jan. 3, Apr. 1, July 1, and Oct. 1; May 16 for field-of-interest grants

Board meeting date(s): Monthly; grant committee meets quarterly
Final notification: Within 2 months
Officers and Directors:* Dick Hendriksen,* Pres.; **Russ Peterson,* V.P.; Chris Leech,* Secy.-Treas.**; Melissa Diers,* Exec. Dir.; Dolores Bang; Mary Buller; Barbara Christensen; Cindy Coffman; Larry Flamme; Todd Hansen; Dr. Greg Haskins; Bob Hillis; Cyndy Koerber; Martin Koopman; Ron Kortan; Cheryl Lamme; Sheila Monke; Gaylord Mussman; Steve Navarrette; Dale Olson; Cathy Saeger; Joe Sajevic; Toni Vering; Marvin G. Welstead; and 3 additional directors.
Number of staff: 2 full-time professional; 1 part-time support.
EIN: 470629642
Other changes: Chris Leech is now Secy.-Treas. Russ Peterson, Jr. is now Pres.-Elect. Russ Peterson is now V.P. Bill Ekeler and Joanne Thietje are no longer directors.

1837
Grand Island Community Foundation, Inc.
1811 W. 2nd St., Ste. 480
Grand Island, NE 68803 (308) 381-7767
***Contact:* Tammy Morris M.S., C.E.O.**
FAX: (308) 384-4069; E-mail: info@gicf.org; Main URL: http://www.gicf.org

Established in 1960 in NE.
Foundation type: Community foundation.
Financial data (yr. ended 12/31/12): Assets, $7,077,774 (M); gifts received, $636,374; expenditures, $763,287; giving activities include $499,132 for 66 grants to individuals.
Purpose and activities: The foundation is a community endowment established to accept charitable contributions in order to preserve and enhance the quality of life in Central Nebraska and to assist donors in realizing their charitable goals.
Fields of interest: Arts; Libraries/library science; Education; Health care; Youth development; Human services; Economic development; Community/economic development; United Ways and Federated Giving Programs; Government/public administration; Public affairs; Children/youth; Youth.
Type of support: Scholarships—to individuals; General/operating support; Emergency funds; Program development; Scholarship funds; Matching/challenge support.
Limitations: Applications accepted. Giving limited to Hall County, NE. No support for religious purposes. **No grants to individuals (except for scholarships), or for endowments, capital campaigns, or annual fund drives.**
Publications: Application guidelines; Annual report; Annual report (including application guidelines); Financial statement; Grants list; Informational brochure; Informational brochure (including application guidelines); Newsletter; Occasional report.
Application information: Visit foundation web site for application form and guidelines. Faxed or e-mailed applications are not accepted. Application form required.
Initial approach: Submit application
Copies of proposal: 8
***Deadline(s):* May 1 and Nov. 1**
Board meeting date(s): Every other month
Officers and Directors:* Lynn Cronk,* Chair.; Tim Wojcik,* Chair.-Elect.; Tammy Morris, M.S.*, C.E.O.; Kris Nolan Brown,* Secy.; Tom Gdowski,* Treas.; June Andrews; Meta Armstrong; Derek Apfel; Roger Bullington; Kim Dinsdale; Ken Grandt; Harry Hoch; Ellen Hornady; Ann Martin; Jodi Maruska; Raymond O'Connor; Densel Rasmussen; Judy Smith; Liana Steele.
Number of staff: 1 full-time professional.
EIN: 476032570

1838
Hawkins Charitable Trust
2516 Deer Park Blvd.
Omaha, NE 68105-3771 (402) 342-1607
Contact: Fred Hawkins Sr., Tr.

Established in 1964 in NE.
Donor: Hawkins Construction Co.
Foundation type: Company-sponsored foundation.
Financial data (yr. ended 12/31/12): Assets, $4,555,833 (M); gifts received, $50,000; expenditures, $192,771; qualifying distributions, $191,591; giving activities include $191,591 for grants.
Purpose and activities: The foundation supports organizations involved with education, health, baseball, human services, and business promotion.
Fields of interest: Higher education; Education; Hospitals (specialty); Health care; Athletics/sports, baseball; Boys & girls clubs; Boy scouts; Children/youth, services; Human services; Community development, business promotion; United Ways and Federated Giving Programs.
Type of support: General/operating support; Annual campaigns; Building/renovation; Scholarship funds.
Limitations: Applications accepted. Giving primarily in NE. No grants to individuals.
Application information: Application form required.
Initial approach: Proposal
Deadline(s): None
Trustees: Chris Hawkins; Kim Hawkins; Fred Hawkins, Sr.; Fred Hawkins, Jr.
EIN: 476041927

1839
Hirschfeld Family Foundation, Inc.
3606 4th Ave.
Kearney, NE 68847-2828 **(308) 234-5579**
Contact: Dan Hirschfeld

Established in 1992 in NE.
Donor: Daniel J. Hirschfeld.
Foundation type: Independent foundation.
Financial data (yr. ended 08/31/13): Assets, $167,606,170 (M); expenditures, $7,438,841; qualifying distributions, $6,437,491; giving activities include $6,437,491 for 28 grants (high: $2,000,000; low: $3,000).
Purpose and activities: Giving primarily for education and for human services.
Fields of interest: Museums; Elementary/secondary education; Higher education; Hospitals (general); Human services; YM/YWCAs & YM/YWHAs; Aging, centers/services.
Type of support: General/operating support; Capital campaigns; Building/renovation; Equipment; Land acquisition; Emergency funds; Program development; Professorships; Seed money; Curriculum development; Scholarship funds; Matching/challenge support.
Limitations: Applications accepted. Giving primarily in NE. No grants to individuals.
Application information: Application form required.
Initial approach: Letter requesting application form
Copies of proposal: 1
Deadline(s): None
Board meeting date(s): As needed
Final notification: 1 month
Officers and Director:* Daniel J. Hirschfeld,* Pres. and Treas.; Benjamin G. Hirschfeld, V.P.; David J. Hirschfeld, V.P.; Letitia A. Spencer, V.P.; Monya A. Hirschfeld,* Secy.
EIN: 470762188

1840
The Holland Foundation
1501 S. 80th St.
Omaha, NE 68124-1423
Contact: Richard D. Holland, Pres.

Established in 1996 in NE.
Donors: Marilyn M. Holland; Richard D. Holland.
Foundation type: Independent foundation.
Financial data (yr. ended 12/31/13): Assets, $137,267,832 (M); gifts received, $4,500,000; expenditures, $18,367,608; qualifying distributions, $18,221,128; giving activities include $18,221,128 for 95 grants (high: $4,261,138; low: $500).
Purpose and activities: Giving primarily for the arts, education and human services.
Fields of interest: Performing arts; Performing arts, orchestras; Arts; Education; Human services.
Limitations: Applications accepted. Giving primarily in NE. No grants to individuals.
Application information:
Initial approach: Proposal
Deadline(s): None
Officers: Richard D. Holland, Pres.; Thomas R. Pansing, Secy.
Directors: Gerald Hoberman; Mary A. Holland; Barbara H. Kral; Wallace R. Weitz; Kathryn A. Weitz White.
Number of staff: 1 part-time support.
EIN: 470804949
Other changes: At the close of 2013, the grantmaker paid grants of $18,221,128, a 187.1% increase over the 2012 disbursements, $6,346,296.

1841
Home Instead Senior Care Foundation
13323 California St.
Omaha, NE 68154-5241 (402) 455-0883
Contact: Judith Sexton
E-mail: info@homeinsteadseniorcarefoundation.org; Main URL: http://www.homeinsteadseniorcarefoundation.org
Grants List: http://www.homeinsteadseniorcarefoundation.org/grant-awards/

Established in 2003 in NE.
Donors: Home Instead, Inc.; Paul R. Hogan; Lori L. Hogan.
Foundation type: Independent foundation.
Financial data (yr. ended 12/31/12): Assets, $84,734 (M); gifts received, $182,195; expenditures, $245,017; qualifying distributions, $243,691; giving activities include $232,500 for 23 grants (high: $20,000; low: $5,000).
Purpose and activities: Giving to support activities designed to improve the quality of life for seniors. Such opportunities may include research and development, education, scholarships, and/or advocacy for the health and well being of older adults.
Fields of interest: Human services; Aging, centers/services.
Application information: Letters of Inquiry must be submitted online through the Foundation web site. When all Letters of Inquiry have been reviewed, the

Foundation will request full proposals from selected organizations. See Foundation web site for complete application guidelines. Application form required.

Initial approach: Letter of Inquiry
Deadline(s): May 1 for Fall grants and Nov. 1 for Spring grants

Officers: Paul R. Hogan, Pres. and Treas.; Lori L. Hogan, V.P. and Secy.
Directors: Mary Alexander; April Cavanaugh; Kathy Curry; Joe Sanders; Patricia Wells.
EIN: 510457609

1842
Kearney Area Community Foundation

412 W. 48th St., Ste. 12
Kearney, NE 68845 (308) 237-3114
Contact: Judi Sickler, Exec. Dir.
FAX: (308) 237-9845;
E-mail: kacf@kearneyfoundation.org; Mailing address: P.O. Box 1694, Kearney, NE 68848; Additional e-mail: judi@kearneyfoundation.org; Main URL: http://www.kearneyfoundation.org
Facebook: http://www.facebook.com/pages/Kearney-Area-Community-Foundation/118780074843224

Established in 1995 in NE.
Foundation type: Community foundation.
Financial data (yr. ended 12/31/12): Assets, $9,598,323 (M); gifts received, $4,269,340; expenditures, $7,247,265; giving activities include $4,334,498 for grants (high: $30,000), and $54,139 for grants to individuals.
Purpose and activities: The foundation exists to enhance the quality of life in the Kearney area by promoting the spirit of charitable giving and effectively responding to the community's needs.
Fields of interest: Visual arts; Museums; Performing arts; Arts; Libraries/library science; Education; Horticulture/garden clubs; Hospitals (general); Health care; Mental health/crisis services; Disasters, Hurricane Katrina; Recreation; Human services; Economic development; Community/economic development; Children; Adults; Aging.
Type of support: Building/renovation; Equipment; Emergency funds; Seed money; Scholarships—to individuals; Matching/challenge support.
Limitations: Applications accepted. Giving limited to Kearney and surrounding area. No support for religious activities (unless non-denominational and serving a broad segment of the population) or private or parochial schools (unless serving a broad segment of the population), as well as other private organizations. No grants to individuals (except for scholarships), or for annual fund drives, galas, or other special-event fundraising activities, capital campaigns/renovation projects, debt reduction, dissertations or student/faculty research projects, endowment funds, indirect/administrative costs, fellowships, travel, tours or trips; no loans.
Publications: Application guidelines; Grants list.
Application information: Visit foundation web site for application form and guidelines. Faxed or e-mailed applications are not accepted. Application form required.

Initial approach: Telephone
Copies of proposal: 9
***Deadline(s):* Feb. 1 and Aug. 1**

Officers and Directors:* Susan Bigg,* Chair.; Mike Tye,* Vice-Chair.; Marsha Fairbanks,* Secy.; Roxanne Bascom,* Treas.; Judi Sickler, Exec. Dir.; John Bancroft, M.D.; Dottie Bowman; Rachelle Bryant; Corliss Dixon; Ron Eckloff; Bob Huddleston; Teresa Ibach; Michaela Lewis; Tom McCarty; Sherry Morrow; Dirk Nickel; Bill Ross; Greg Shea; Lori Smith.
EIN: 470786586

1843
Peter Kiewit Foundation

1125 S. 103rd St., Ste. 500
Omaha, NE 68124-6022 (402) 344-7890
Contact: Lyn Wallin Ziegenbein, Exec. Dir.
FAX: (402) 344-8099; Main URL: http://www.peterkiewitfoundation.org/

Established in 1975 in NE.
Donor: Peter Kiewit†.
Foundation type: Independent foundation.
Financial data (yr. ended 06/30/13): Assets, $397,287,545 (M); gifts received, $346,312; expenditures, $14,845,364; qualifying distributions, $13,709,786; giving activities include $9,806,688 for 136 grants (high: $1,000,000; low: $472), $1,088,750 for grants to individuals, $275,762 for 2 foundation-administered programs and $952,259 for 1 loan/program-related investment.
Purpose and activities: Giving primarily for cultural programs, including the arts, civic affairs, community development, higher and other education, health and social service agencies, and youth programs. Contributions almost always made as challenge or matching grants.
Fields of interest: Arts; Higher education; Education; Human services; Youth, services; Community development, neighborhood development; Rural development; Community/economic development.
Type of support: General/operating support; Capital campaigns; Building/renovation; Equipment; Land acquisition; Program development; Seed money; Program-related investments/loans; Matching/challenge support.
Limitations: Applications accepted. Giving limited to Rancho Mirage, CA, western IA (within 100 miles of Omaha), NE, and Sheridan, WY. No support for elementary or secondary schools (public or private), churches, or religious groups. No grants to individuals or for endowment funds or annual campaigns.
Publications: Application guidelines; Annual report; Informational brochure (including application guidelines).
Application information: All applicants are required to submit the standard Peter Kiewit Foundation application form and required attachments. The form and instructions must be requested from the foundation office. Application form required.

Initial approach: Letter or telephone
Copies of proposal: 4
Deadline(s): Jan. 15, Apr. 15, July 15, and Oct. 15 for grants
Board meeting date(s): Mar., June, Sept., and Dec.
Final notification: Within quarter submitted

Officers and Trustees:* John W. Hancock,* Chair.; Jane E. Miller,* Vice-Chair.; **Jeff Ziegenbein, Exec. Dir.**; Mogens C. Bay; Michael L. Gallagher; G. Richard Russell; U.S. Bank, N.A.
Number of staff: 4 full-time professional; 2 full-time support.
EIN: 476098282
Other changes: Jeff Ziegenbein has replaced Lyn Wallin Ziegenbein as Exec. Dir.

1844
Kim Foundation

c/o Larry J. Courtnage
13609 California St., Ste. 500
Omaha, NE 68154-5245
E-mail: info@thekimfoundation.org; Main URL: http://www.thekimfoundation.org/
Blog: http://blog.thekimfoundation.org/
E-Newsletter: http://www.thekimfoundation.org/html/mh_happenings/newsletter.html
Facebook: http://www.facebook.com/pages/The-Kim-Foundation-Advocating-for-Mental-Health-Services/120739160051

Established in 2000 in NE.
Donors: Larry J. Courtnage; C&A Industries, Inc.; United Way of The Midlands.
Foundation type: Independent foundation.
Financial data (yr. ended 12/31/12): Assets, $4,398,343 (M); gifts received, $230,844; expenditures, $556,765; qualifying distributions, $538,039; giving activities include $475,500 for 17 grants (high: $300,000; low: $1,000).
Purpose and activities: Giving primarily to organizations that assist individuals with mental health difficulties.
Fields of interest: Mental health/crisis services; Health organizations; Human services; Children/youth, services.
Limitations: Applications not accepted. Giving primarily in NE.
Application information: Unsolicited requests for funds not accepted.
Officers: Larry J. Courtnage, Pres.; Kathleen A. Courtnage, V.P. and Secy.; Vicki F. Witkovski, Treas.
EIN: 470837377

1845
Lexington Community Foundation

607 N. Washington St.
P.O. Box 422
Lexington, NE 68850-1915 (308) 324-6704
Contact: Jacqueline Berke, Exec. Dir.
E-mail: lexfoundation@windstream.net; Main URL: http://www.lexfoundation.org
Facebook: http://www.facebook.com/pages/Lexington-Community-Foundation/133425550027265
Twitter: https://twitter.com/lexfoundation

Established in 1982 in NE.
Foundation type: Community foundation.
Financial data (yr. ended 12/31/12): Assets, $7,104,616 (M); gifts received, $7,282,424; expenditures, $722,440; giving activities include $333,778 for 46+ grants (high: $191,935), and $38,800 for 61 grants to individuals.
Purpose and activities: The foundation seeks to encourage and strengthen philanthropy in order to provide a permanent source of funding for opportunities to improve the quality of life, strengthen the sense of community, and benefit future generations in Lexington, NE.
Fields of interest: Arts; Education; Health care; Recreation, camps; Recreation; Children/youth, services; Human services; Community development, neighborhood development; Community/economic development.
Type of support: Capital campaigns; Building/renovation; Equipment; Program development; Seed money; Technical assistance; Scholarships—to individuals; Matching/challenge support.
Limitations: Applications accepted. Giving limited to the Lexington, NE, area. No support for religious activities (unless non-denominational and serving a brand segment of the population). No grants to

individuals directly, or for operational expenses, debt servicing, trips, tours, camps, or endowment funds.
Publications: Application guidelines; Annual report; Financial statement; Grants list; Informational brochure; Newsletter; Program policy statement.
Application information: Visit foundation web site for application form and guidelines. Application form required.
Initial approach: Contact foundation
Copies of proposal: 1
Deadline(s): None
Board meeting date(s): 4th Mon. in Jan., Mar., May, July, Sept., and Nov.
Final notification: 1 to 2 months
Officers and Directors:* Amy Biehl-Owens,* Pres.; Tom Fagot,* V.P.; Bill Stewart,* Secy.-Treas.; Jacqueline Berke, Exec. Dir.; Rob Anderson; Bill Barrett; Dean Brand; Stephanie Buell; Dan Clark; Jill Denker; David Fairbanks; Tom Feltes; Wes Lubberstedt; Patty Mandelko; Barry McFarland; Tod McKeone; Linda Miller; Larry Reynolds; Curt Rickertson; Tempie Roberts; Mark Sarratt; Steve Smith; Dave Stenberg; Rusty Sutton; Gail Wightman; John Wightman.
Number of staff: 1 full-time professional; 1 part-time support.
EIN: 470794760
Other changes: Bill Stewart is no longer a director.

1846
Lienemann Charitable Foundation, Inc.
P.O. Box 81407
Lincoln, NE 68501-1407

Established in 1967.
Donors: Del Lienemann, Sr.; Charlotte Lienemann; Douglas Lienemann.
Foundation type: Independent foundation.
Financial data (yr. ended 08/31/13): Assets, $1,164,280 (M); gifts received, $67,250; expenditures, $221,370; qualifying distributions, $221,370; giving activities include $203,458 for 7 grants (high: $107,200; low: $1,000).
Fields of interest: Performing arts, orchestras; Higher education; Hospitals (general); Human services; American Red Cross; Foundations (private grantmaking); Protestant agencies & churches.
Limitations: Applications not accepted. Giving primarily in CO and NE. No grants to individuals.
Application information: Unsolicited requests for funds not accepted.
Officers: Del Lienemann, Sr., C.E.O. and Pres.; Douglas Lienemann, V.P.; Denise Scholz, Secy.; **Del Lienemann, Jr., Treas.**
Trustee: Dorothy Pflug.
EIN: 476044090
Other changes: Del Lienemann, Jr. is now Treas.

1847
Lincoln Community Foundation, Inc.
(formerly Lincoln Foundation, Inc.)
215 Centennial Mall S., Ste. 100
Lincoln, NE 68508-1813 (402) 474-2345
Contact: For grants: Sarah Peetz, V.P., Community Outreach
FAX: (402) 476-8523; E-mail: lcf@lcf.org; Main URL: http://www.lcf.org
Facebook: https://www.facebook.com/LincolnCommunityFoundation

Incorporated in 1955 in NE.
Foundation type: Community foundation.
Financial data (yr. ended 12/31/11): Assets, $63,437,945 (M); gifts received, $5,417,053; expenditures, $6,025,270; giving activities include $4,026,777 for grants.
Purpose and activities: The foundation seeks to enrich the quality of life in the greater Lincoln, NE, area by responding to emerging and changing needs and sustaining existing organizations and institutions through grants for education, arts and culture, health, social services, economic development, and civic affairs in Lincoln/Lancaster County, NE. Primary areas of interest include family issues, children's issues, older adults, environmental enhancement, higher education, and basic needs.
Fields of interest: Arts, cultural/ethnic awareness; Museums (marine/maritime); Arts; Child development, education; Higher education; Environment; Health care; Child development, services; Family services; Aging, centers/services; Human services; Economic development; Public affairs; Aging.
Type of support: General/operating support; Management development/capacity building; Capital campaigns; Building/renovation; Equipment; Land acquisition; Emergency funds; Program development; Seed money; Scholarship funds; Research; Technical assistance; Consulting services; Program evaluation; Employee matching gifts; Matching/challenge support.
Limitations: Applications accepted. Giving limited to the Lincoln-Lancaster County, NE, area. No support for religious purposes. No grants to individuals (except for scholarships), or for endowments, large capital expenditures, budget deficits, or projects with long future commitments.
Publications: Application guidelines; Annual report; Grants list; Informational brochure (including application guidelines); Newsletter; Program policy statement.
Application information: Visit foundation web site for application forms and guidelines. Letters of inquiry will be reviewed and those receiving approval will be notified and asked to submit a full application. Application form required.
Initial approach: Telephone
Deadline(s): May 1, Aug. 1 and Nov. 1 for letter of inquiry; June 1, Sept. 1 and Dec. 1 for full application
Board meeting date(s): 3rd Thurs. of Feb., May, Aug., and Nov.
Final notification: Full application within 3 months of deadline
Officers and Directors:* Rich Vierk,* Chair.; Cathy Lang,* Vice-Chair.; Barbara Bartle,* Pres.; Chip DeBuse,* V.P., Devel.; Pam Hunzeker,* V.P., Mktg.; Scott Lawson,* V.P., Finance; Paula Metcalf,* V.P., Gift Planning and General Counsel; Sarah Peetz,* V.P., Community Outreach; **Bill Mueller,* Secy.; Bill Cintani,* Treas.**; Rich Bailey; Christi Ball; John Bergmeyer; Bob Caldwell; John Dittman; Juan Franco; Randy Haas; Dave Landis; Diane Mendenhall; William Olson; Deb Schorr; Mark Whitehead; Nancy Wiederspan; Sue Wilkinson; Hank Woods; and 9 additional directors.
Number of staff: 5 full-time professional; 5 full-time support; 1 part-time support.
EIN: 470458128
Other changes: Rich Vierk has replaced Carl Sjulin as Chair. Cathy Lang has replaced Angie Muhleisen as Vice-Chair. Bill Mueller has replaced Candy Henning as Secy.
Rhonda Page is now Gift Planning Coord. Bill Cintani is now Treas,. Bill Cintani is now Treas. Rich Vierk, Cathy Lang, Bill Mueller, Todd Duncan, and Mike Young are no longer directors.

1848
Midlands Community Foundation
217 N. Jefferson St.
Papillion, NE 68046-3111 (402) 991-8027
Contact: Tonee Gay, Exec. Dir.; Diane Knicky, Dir., Opers. and Public Rels.
FAX: (402) 991-8047;
E-mail: info@midlandscommunity.org; Main URL: http://www.midlandscommunity.org

Established in 1994 in NE.
Foundation type: Community foundation.
Financial data (yr. ended 06/30/12): Assets, $5,379,892 (M); gifts received, $683,298; expenditures, $612,654; giving activities include $297,411 for grants.
Purpose and activities: Giving primarily for arts and culture, human services, community and economic development, health care and education.
Fields of interest: Performing arts; Arts; Higher education; Education; Hospitals (general); Health care; Mental health/crisis services; Cancer; Disasters, fire prevention/control; Recreation; YM/YWCAs & YM/YWHAs; Children/youth, services; Human services; Economic development; Community/economic development; Infants/toddlers; Young adults; Disabilities, people with; Physically disabled; Blind/visually impaired; Deaf/hearing impaired; Mentally disabled; Minorities; Hispanics/Latinos; Native Americans/American Indians; Indigenous peoples; Infants/toddlers, female; Girls; Adults, women; Infants/toddlers, male; Boys; Adults, men; Military/veterans; Substance abusers; Single parents; Crime/abuse victims; Terminal illness, people with; Economically disadvantaged; Homeless.
Type of support: Continuing support; Capital campaigns; Building/renovation; Equipment; Land acquisition; Conferences/seminars; Seed money; Scholarship funds; Research; Technical assistance.
Limitations: Applications accepted. Giving limited to Sarpy and Cass counties, NE. No support for political organizations or political programs, or projects of religion-based organizations (unless the project is secular and does not give priority or preferential treatment to the religious organization or its members. No grants to individuals, or for routine general operating expenses, deficit reduction or general or administrative overhead expenses, or dinners, tickets, or conferences.
Publications: Application guidelines; Annual report; Informational brochure; Informational brochure (including application guidelines).
Application information: Visit the foundation's web site for application form and guidelines. Application form required.
Initial approach: Telephone
Copies of proposal: 10
Deadline(s): Feb. 1 and Aug. 1
Board meeting date(s): Second Tues. of every other month
Final notification: Within 60 days
Officers and Directors:* Karla Rupiper,* Pres.; Terri Scholting,* V.P.; Randy Sump,* V.P.; Kevin Dasher,* Secy.-Treas.; Tonee Gay, Exec. Dir.; Tom Ackley; Janet Barna; Julie Bear; Brenda Carlson; Jan Davis; Bob Frederick; Mary Beth Harrold; Dr. Jim Langley; Bonnie Miller; Phil Pankonin; Lee Polikov; Jeff Rennter; Barb Slattery; Jim Thompson.
Number of staff: 1 full-time professional; 1 part-time professional.
EIN: 510191738

1849
Mid-Nebraska Community Foundation, Inc.
120 N. Dewey
P.O. Box 1321
North Platte, NE 69101 (308) 534-3315
Contact: Eric Seacrest, Exec. Dir.
FAX: (308) 534-6117; E-mail: mncf@hamilton.net; Main URL: http://www.midnebraskafoundation.org

Established in 1978 in NE.
Foundation type: Community foundation.
Financial data (yr. ended 05/31/12): Assets, $19,520,620 (M); gifts received, $1,000,109; expenditures, $1,015,268; giving activities include $593,192 for 17+ grants (high: $99,515), and $179,781 for 155 grants to individuals.
Purpose and activities: The foundation seeks to enhance the quality of life in the mid-Nebraska area by providing a vehicle for the pooling of financial resources and wisely managing those resources to allow the making of grants for present and future charitable purposes. The foundation is interested in supporting innovative solutions to community problems, including collaborative efforts.
Fields of interest: Arts; Elementary/secondary education; Education; Environment; Health care; Human services; Community/economic development.
Type of support: Scholarships—to individuals; Capital campaigns; Building/renovation; Equipment; Land acquisition; Program development; Conferences/seminars; Seed money; Curriculum development.
Limitations: Applications accepted. Giving primarily limited to Custer, Dawson, Frontier, Hayes, Keith, Lincoln, Logan, McPherson and Perkins counties, NE. No support for religious organizations for religious activities, or for-profit organizations. No grants to individuals (except through designated scholarship funds), or for current operating budgets or deficit financing.
Publications: Application guidelines; Annual report; Financial statement; Informational brochure; Occasional report.
Application information: Visit foundation web site for application information. Scholarship applications generally available only through area school counselors, except for non-traditional students or for college students from the North Platte area. Application form required.
Initial approach: 1-page letter of inquiry or telephone for grants; complete current application form for scholarships
Copies of proposal: 1
Deadline(s): Jan. 15, Apr. 15, July 15, and Oct. 15
Board meeting date(s): Quarterly
Final notification: Approx. 45 days after deadline
Officers and Directors:* Bob Spady,* Pres.; John A. Patterson,* V.P.; J. Patrick Keenan,* Secy.-Treas.; Eric Seacrest, Exec. Dir.; Gary D. Byrne; Olivia Conrad; Alan J. Erickson; Jo Anne Grady; Dr. Todd E. Hlavaty; Mary Lynn Horst; Don Kilgore; Connie Klemm; Jim McClymont; Cynthia D. Norman; Sam Perry, M.D.; Brenda Robinson; Charlene Schneider; Betty Sones; Jean States; Larry Stobbs; Mary Thompson; Glenn Van Velson; Dorothy Wycoff; and 2 additional directors.
Number of staff: 1 full-time professional; 2 full-time support.
EIN: 470604965
Other changes: Francene McKenzie and Ella Ochoa are no longer directors.

1850
Mutual of Omaha Foundation
Mutual of Omaha Plz.
Omaha, NE 68175-0002 (866) 663-5665
Contact: Christine Johnson, Pres. and Secy.
E-mail: mutualofomaha.foundation@mutualofomaha.com; Main URL: http://www.mutualofomahafoundation.org
Facebook: http://www.facebook.com/mutualofomahafoundation?ref=ts
Grants List: http://www.mutualofomahafoundation.org/documents/2014_year_end.pdf
Twitter: https://twitter.com/MutualFdn

Established in 2005.
Donor: Mutual of Omaha Insurance Co.
Foundation type: Company-sponsored foundation.
Financial data (yr. ended 12/31/13): Assets, $65,180,294 (M); gifts received, $16,500,000; expenditures, $3,416,694; qualifying distributions, $3,402,674; giving activities include $3,402,674 for 128 grants (high: $327,329; low: $25).
Purpose and activities: The foundation supports programs designed to break the cycle of poverty. Special emphasis is directed toward programs designed to prevent and end homelessness; increase self-sufficiency; increase educational achievement; and prevent and end violence.
Fields of interest: Education, early childhood education; Secondary school/education; Education, drop-out prevention; Education; Mental health/crisis services; Crime/violence prevention, youth; Food services; Food banks; Children, services; Family services; Family services, domestic violence; Human services, financial counseling; Homeless, human services; Human services; United Ways and Federated Giving Programs.
Type of support: General/operating support; Capital campaigns; Building/renovation; Emergency funds; Program development; Employee volunteer services; Employee matching gifts; In-kind gifts; Matching/challenge support.
Limitations: Applications accepted. Giving primarily in areas of company operations in Council Bluffs, IA and Omaha, NE. No support for religious or sectarian organizations, social clubs, fraternal organizations, or political organizations or candidates. No grants to individuals, or for tickets and tables, endowment funds, travel, team sponsorships or athletic scholarships, civic or commemorative advertising, festivals, monuments or memorials.
Publications: Application guidelines; Grants list; Informational brochure.
Application information: Applicants are encouraged to apply early. Support is limited to 1 contribution per organization during any given year. Organizations receiving support are asked to submit a final report. Application form required.
Initial approach: Complete online application
Deadline(s): See website for deadline
Board meeting date(s): Quarterly
***Final notification:* Up to 90 days**
Officers and Directors:* Christine D. Johnson,* Pres. and Secy.; Richard A. Witt,* V.P.; Laura Fender,* Treas.; Richard C. Anderi; Michelle Lebens; Jeffrey R. Schmid; Dana Washington.
EIN: 202176636
Other changes: Michael J. Jareske is no longer Treas. Daniel P. Martin, Jeffrey R. Schmid, Stacy A. Scholtz, and Michael C. Weekly are no longer directors.

1851
Nebraska Community Foundation
3833 S. 14th St.
P.O. Box 83107
Lincoln, NE 68501-3107 (402) 323-7330
Contact: Jeffrey G. Yost, Pres. and C.E.O.
FAX: (402) 323-7349;
E-mail: info@nebcommfound.org; Main URL: http://www.nebcommfound.org
Facebook: http://www.facebook.com/nebraskacommunityfoundation
YouTube: http://www.youtube.com/user/nebcommfound?feature=mhee

Established in 1993 in NE.
Foundation type: Community foundation.
Financial data (yr. ended 06/30/12): Assets, $78,664,829 (M); gifts received, $32,111,156; expenditures, $24,460,826; giving activities include $172,231 for grants to individuals, and $22,671,629 for foundation-administered programs.
Purpose and activities: The Nebraska Community Foundation uses the tools of philanthropy, community development and economic development to help communities help themselves. NCF creates a path to greater prosperity for all by helping communities: 1) envision a better future; 2) develop local leadership and talent; 3) inspire charitable giving and grow endowments; 4) fund community needs and opportunities; 5) manage financial resources; and 6) build and leverage every local asset.
Fields of interest: Education; Community/economic development.
Type of support: General/operating support; Management development/capacity building; Endowments; Program development; Conferences/seminars; Publication; Consulting services; Employee matching gifts; Scholarships—to individuals; Matching/challenge support.
Limitations: Applications not accepted. Giving primarily limited to Nebraska via Affiliated Fund giving. No grants to individuals (except for scholarships).
Publications: Annual report; Financial statement; Informational brochure; Newsletter; Occasional report; Program policy statement.
Application information: All grantmaking occurs through the foundation's 227 affiliated funds.
Board meeting date(s): Quarterly
Officers and At-Large Members:* Brandon Day,* Chair.; Richard Walter,* Chair., Fundraising; Dennis Stara,* Vice-Chair.; Jeffrey G. Yost,* Pres. and C.E.O.; Judy Brockmeier,* Secy.; Diane M. Wilson,* C.O.O. and C.F.O.; Hon. Douglas Bereuter,* Treas.; K.C. Belitz; Lora Damme; Joe Ferguson; Casey Garrigan; Lori Pankonin; Judy Parks; Sara Coffee Radil; Lynn Roper; Al Steuter; Kurt Tjaden; Greg Vasek; Ray Welsh; Sandi Wendell.
Number of staff: 10 full-time professional; 3 part-time professional; 4 full-time support.
EIN: 470769903
Other changes: Marcia White is no longer Dir., Community Development Philanthropy. Brian Thompson is no longer a member of the governing body.

1852
Oregon Trail Community Foundation, Inc.
115 W. Railway St.
P.O. Box 1344
Scottsbluff, NE 69361-1344 (308) 635-3393
Contact: Bev Overman, Exec. Admin.
FAX: (308) 635-3393; E-mail: info@otcf.org; Main URL: http://www.otcf.org

Established in 1977 in NE.
Foundation type: Community foundation.
Financial data (yr. ended 12/31/12): Assets, $3,408,473 (M); gifts received, $593,588; expenditures, $401,459; giving activities include $225,671 for 7+ grants (high: $49,750), and $47,700 for 33 grants to individuals.
Purpose and activities: The foundation seeks to receive, administer, and disburse funds for such charitable or educational purposes as will, in the discretion of the Board of Directors, promote the mental, moral, intellectual and physical improvement, and well-being of the inhabitants of Goshen and Platte Counties, Wyoming, and primarily of Scotts Bluff County, Nebraska.
Fields of interest: Arts; Higher education; Health care; Substance abuse, services; Recreation; Youth development; Community development, neighborhood development; Economic development; Community/economic development; Aging.
Type of support: Annual campaigns; Capital campaigns; Building/renovation; Endowments; Scholarships—to individuals.
Limitations: Applications accepted. Giving limited to Scotts Bluff County, NE, and Goshen County, WY. No grants for operating support.
Publications: Grants list; Informational brochure (including application guidelines); Newsletter.
Application information: Visit foundation web site for application form and guidelines. Application form required.
Initial approach: Submit application form and attachments
Copies of proposal: 7
Deadline(s): Feb. 1, June 1, and Oct. 1
Board meeting date(s): Bimonthly
Final notification: Within 6 weeks
Officers and Directors:* Barb Schlothauer,* Chair.; Joanne Krieg,* Vice-Chair.; Travis Hiner,* Pres.; Marilyn Rahmig,* V.P.; Lonnie Miller,* Treas.; Bev Overman,* Exec. Admin.; Ann Baker; Judy Chaloupka; Lee Glenn; Marv Hefti; Jim Holland; Tom Holyoke; Bob Kelley; Doug Kent; Hod Kosman; Julie Marshall; John Massey; Howard Olsen; Jim Reinhardt; Dr. Tom Rohrick; Cricket Simmons; Dr. Todd Sorensen; John Stinner.
Number of staff: 1 part-time support.
EIN: 470596705
Other changes: Tom Flaherty, Joanne Krieg, Travis Hiner, Lonnie Miller, and Bev Overman are no longer directors.

1853
Quivey-Bay State Foundation
P.O. Box 2308
Scottsbluff, NE 69363-2757
***Application Address:* c/o Ted Cannon, 1515 E. 20th St., Scottsbluff NE 69361, tel.: (308) 635-1153**

Established in 1948 in NE.
Donors: M.B. Quivey; Mrs. M.B. Quivey.
Foundation type: Independent foundation.
Financial data (yr. ended 01/31/13): Assets, $5,028,410 (M); expenditures, $301,873; qualifying distributions, $292,750; giving activities include $292,750 for 44 grants (high: $50,000; low: $150).
Fields of interest: Historic preservation/historical societies; Higher education; Animal welfare; Youth development, scouting agencies (general); Boy scouts; Human services; YM/YWCAs & YM/YWHAs; Children/youth, services; Christian agencies & churches.
Limitations: Applications accepted. Giving primarily in western NE. No grants to individuals, or for endowment funds.
Application information: Application form required.
Initial approach: Letter
Copies of proposal: 1
Deadline(s): None
Board meeting date(s): Oct. and Nov.
Officers: Gary Kelley, Pres.; Ted Cannon, Secy.; Zac Karpf, Treas.
Directors: John Koenig; Steve Olsen; Charles Richardson; Jerry Williams.
EIN: 476024159
Other changes: Gary Kelley is now Pres.

1854
Robert Herman Storz Foundation
10050 Regency Cir., Ste. 101
Omaha, NE **68114-3721**
Contact: Herbert A. Engdagl, Tr.

Established in 1957.
Donor: Robert Herman Storz†.
Foundation type: Independent foundation.
Financial data (yr. ended 12/31/12): Assets, $5,386,698 (M); expenditures, $431,298; qualifying distributions, $396,588; giving activities include $381,412 for 33 grants (high: $57,012; low: $1,000).
Fields of interest: Arts; Human services.
Type of support: Annual campaigns; Capital campaigns; Building/renovation; Matching/challenge support.
Limitations: Applications accepted. Giving primarily in the Omaha, NE, area. No support for political organizations. No grants to individuals.
Application information: Application form not required.
Initial approach: Letter
Copies of proposal: 1
Deadline(s): May 1, Sept. 1, Dec. 1
Board meeting date(s): 2nd Mon. in May, Sept., and Dec.
Trustees: Susan Storz Butler; Herbert A. Engdahl; Diane Higgins; Robert S. Howard.
Number of staff: 1 full-time professional.
EIN: 476025980

1855
Weitz Family Foundation
110 N. 92nd St.
Omaha, NE 68114-3903
Contact: Wallace R. Weitz, Pres. and Treas.

Established in 1999 in NE.
Donors: Wallace R. Weitz; Barbara V. Weitz; Roger Weitz.
Foundation type: Independent foundation.
Financial data (yr. ended 08/31/13): Assets, $49,116,157 (M); gifts received, $500; expenditures, $6,718,725; qualifying distributions, $6,718,173; giving activities include $6,718,173 for 82 grants (high: $2,011,673; low: $250).
Purpose and activities: Giving primarily for higher education, the arts, federated giving programs, and children, youth, family and social services.
Fields of interest: Media, radio; Performing arts; Arts; Education; Housing/shelter, development; Housing/shelter; Human services; Community/economic development; Children/youth; Girls; Economically disadvantaged.
Type of support: General/operating support; Continuing support; Professorships; Seed money; Research.
Limitations: Applications not accepted. Giving primarily in Chicago, IL, and Omaha, NE. No support for religious organizations or anti-choice organizations.
Application information: Unsolicited requests for funds not accepted.
Board meeting date(s): Apr. and Oct.
Officers: Wallace R. Weitz, Pres. and Treas.; Barbara V. Weitz, V.P. and Secy.
Directors: Andrew S. Weitz; Kate Noble Weitz; Meredith Weitz; Roger T. Weitz; Kathryn W. White.
Number of staff: 1 part-time support.
EIN: 470834133
Other changes: For the fiscal year ended Aug. 31, 2013, the grantmaker paid grants of $6,718,173, a 102.7% increase over the fiscal 2012 disbursements, $3,314,355.
Watie White is no longer a director.

1856
Warren and Velda Wilson Foundation
c/o Landmark Ctr.
2727 W. 2nd St., No. 211
Hastings, NE 68901-4684

Established in 1993 in NE.
Donor: Velda Wilson†.
Foundation type: Independent foundation.
Financial data (yr. ended 06/30/13): Assets, $11,368,855 (M); expenditures, $412,726; qualifying distributions, $327,145; giving activities include $277,629 for 48 grants (high: $24,375; low: $375).
Fields of interest: Higher education.
Limitations: Applications not accepted. Giving limited to NE.
Application information: Unsolicited requests for funds not accepted.
Officers and Directors:* John F. Farrell,* Pres.; **Jennifer Fleischer, V.P.**; Janet A. Hajny, Secy.; Lulabelle Loehr, Treas.; **Willard Essex**; **Randy Gilson.**
Trustee: Wells Fargo Bank, N.A.
EIN: 470741012
Other changes: Jennifer Fleischer is now V.P.
The grantmaker has changed its fiscal year-end from Dec. 31 to June 30.

1857
Woods Charitable Fund, Inc.
1248 O St., Ste. 1130
Lincoln, NE 68508-1409 (402) 436-5971
Contact: Tom Woods, Exec. Dir.; Joan Stolle, Opers. Mgr.
E-mail: info@woodscharitable.org; Additional e-mails: twoods@woodscharitable.org (Tom Woods); azmarly@woodscharitable.org (Angie Zmarly); jstolle@woodscharitable.org (Joan Stolle);ksteinauersmith@woodscharitable.org (Kathy Steinauer Smith); Main URL: http://www.woodscharitable.org
Facebook: https://www.facebook.com/pages/Woods-Charitable-Fund-Inc/168904933137312
Grants List: http://woodscharitable.org/recent-grants/
Philanthropy In/Sight Grants Map: http://woods.insight.foundationcenter.org

Incorporated in 1941 in NE.
Donors: Frank H. Woods†; Nelle C. Woods†; Frank H. Woods, Jr.†; Thomas C. Woods, Jr.†; Henry C. Woods†; Sahara Coal Co., Inc.
Foundation type: Independent foundation.

Financial data (yr. ended 12/31/13): Assets, $33,553,457 (M); expenditures, $2,028,998; qualifying distributions, $1,712,947; giving activities include $1,165,500 for 53 grants (high: $60,000; low: $4,500), and $40,000 for 1 loan/program-related investment.
Purpose and activities: Giving to improve the quality of life in Lincoln, Nebraska, by expanding prosperity and justice, advancing diverse and balanced participation of community residents, and stimulating creativity and ingenuity.
Fields of interest: Visual arts; Performing arts; Humanities; Arts; Elementary school/education; Education; Crime/violence prevention, domestic violence; Housing/shelter, development; Human services; Children/youth, services; Family services; Community/economic development; Children/youth; Children; Aging; Disabilities, people with; Minorities; Asians/Pacific Islanders; African Americans/Blacks; Hispanics/Latinos; Native Americans/American Indians; Women; Adults, women; Adults, men; Crime/abuse victims; Immigrants/refugees; Economically disadvantaged; Homeless.
Type of support: General/operating support; Program development; Seed money; Technical assistance; Consulting services; Program evaluation; Program-related investments/loans; Matching/challenge support.
Limitations: Applications accepted. Giving primarily in Lincoln, NE. No support for religious activities, recreational programs, healthcare programs, and individual school programs, or for college or university programs that do not involve students and/or faculty in projects of benefit to the Lincoln, NE, area, or for environmental programs, recreational programs, individual school programs, or healthcare programs or residential care and medical clinics. No grants to individuals, or for endowments, scholarships, fellowships, fundraising benefits or for program advertising.
Publications: Application guidelines; Annual report; Financial statement; Grants list; Informational brochure; Newsletter.
Application information: Applications submitted only through on-line application. No hard copies required or accepted. If a full proposal is requested, please use the link to the Woods on-line application system. The proposal itself should not exceed 10 pages. Application form required.

Initial approach: Prior to submitting application, grantseekers must contact the fund (phone, e-mail or letter of intent) to determine eligibility
Copies of proposal: 1
Deadline(s): Mar. 15, July. 15 and Nov. 15 for full proposals only
Board meeting date(s): Mar., June, and Nov.
Final notification: 1 week after board meeting

Officers and Directors:* Donna W. Woods,* Chair.; Kathleen Rutledge,* Vice-Chair.; Thomas C. Woods IV, Pres. and Secy.; Hank Woods,* Treas.; Ernesto Castillo; Carl Eskridge; Nelle Woods Jamison; Orville Jones III; Michael J. Tavlin.
Number of staff: 3 full-time professional; 1 part-time professional.
EIN: 476032847
Other changes: The grantmaker now publishes an annual report online.

1858
Zollner Foundation

c/o Wells Fargo Bank, N.A.
1919 Douglas St., 2nd Fl.
Omaha, NE 68102-1310 (877) 214-0762
***E-mail:* grantadministration@wellsfargo.com; Main URL: https://www.wellsfargo.com/privatefoundationgrants/zollner**

Established in 1983 in IN.
Donor: Fred Zollner†.
Foundation type: Independent foundation.
Financial data (yr. ended 12/31/12): Assets, $10,108,314 (M); expenditures, $531,353; qualifying distributions, $403,810; giving activities include $402,560 for 16 grants (high: $200,000; low: $4,000).
Purpose and activities: Giving primarily for education and youth development.
Fields of interest: Higher education; Education; Boy scouts; Youth development; YM/YWCAs & YM/YWHAs; United Ways and Federated Giving Programs.
Type of support: General/operating support; Continuing support; Annual campaigns; Capital campaigns; Building/renovation; Equipment.
Limitations: Applications accepted. **Giving primarily in Golden Beach, FL, and Fort Wayne, IN.** No grants to individuals.
Application information: See foundation website for complete application guidelines. Application form required.

Initial approach: Letter
***Deadline(s):* June 1**
Board meeting date(s): June

Trustee: Wells Fargo Bank Indiana, N.A.
EIN: 356381471

NEVADA

1859
Bendon Family Foundation
7881 W. Charleston Blvd., Ste. 250
Las Vegas, NV 89117-8327

Established in 1995 in FL.
Donors: Dorothy Bendon; Bendon Clut.
Foundation type: Independent foundation.
Financial data (yr. ended 06/30/13): Assets, $9,362,992 (M); gifts received, $187,521; expenditures, $463,457; qualifying distributions, $404,650; giving activities include $285,000 for 46 grants (high: $50,000; low: $1,000).
Fields of interest: Arts; Elementary/secondary education; Human services; Children/youth, services; Family services; United Ways and Federated Giving Programs.
Limitations: Applications not accepted. Giving primarily in Maui, HI. No grants to individuals.
Application information: Unsolicited requests for funds not accepted.
Officers: James A. Bendon, Pres.; Susan Kaylor Bendon, V.P.
Director: John James Bendon.
EIN: 650631534
Other changes: The grantmaker has moved from NJ to NV.

1860
Caesars Foundation
(formerly The Harrah's Foundation)
1 Caesars Palace Dr.
Las Vegas, NV 89109-8969 (702) 880-4728
***Contact:* Torben Cohrs, Treas,**
FAX: (702) 407-6520;
E-mail: caesarsfoundation@caesars.com; Main URL: http://www.caesarsfoundation.com/
Facebook: https://www.facebook.com/CaesarsFoundation
YouTube: https://www.youtube.com/channel/UCCHa6zB7mDMWbTntZw6mIRw

Established in 2002 in NV.
Donors: Caesars Entertainment Operating Company, Inc.; Harrah's Operating Co., Inc.
Foundation type: Company-sponsored foundation.
Financial data (yr. ended 12/31/13): Assets, $1,422,279 (M); gifts received, $4,106,392; expenditures, $4,017,188; qualifying distributions, $3,824,337; giving activities include $3,695,588 for 113 grants (high: $300,000; low: $10).
Purpose and activities: The foundation supports programs designed to help older individuals live longer, healthier, and more fulfilling lives; promote a more sustainable world through environmental and educational initiatives; and improve the quality of life in communities where Caesars operates.
Fields of interest: Higher education; Environment, natural resources; Environment, land resources; Environment; Hospitals (general); Health care, clinics/centers; Health care, patient services; Health care; Mental health/crisis services; Alzheimer's disease; Food services; Food distribution, meals on wheels; Nutrition; Disasters, preparedness/services; American Red Cross; Youth, services; Human services, mind/body enrichment; Aging, centers/services; Developmentally disabled, centers & services; Human services; Public affairs; Aging.
Type of support: General/operating support; Continuing support; Capital campaigns; Building/renovation; Program development; Scholarship funds; Research; Employee volunteer services; Sponsorships.
Limitations: Applications accepted. Giving primarily in areas of company operations in AZ, CA, IA, IL, IN, LA, MO, MS, NC, NJ, Las Vegas and Reno, NV, and PA. No grants to individuals; no in-kind gifts.
Publications: Application guidelines; Informational brochure.
Application information: The foundation generally funds programs and projects of $10,000 or more. Application form required.
Initial approach: Complete online application
Deadline(s): None
Board meeting date(s): Quarterly
Officers and Trustees:* Janet Beronio,* Chair.; Jan Jones Blackhurst,* Vice-Chair.; Scott Weigand,* Secy.; Torben Cohrs, Treas.; Thom Reilly, Exec. Dir.; Thomas M. Jenkin; Fred Keeton; Dan Nita; John Payne; Diane Wilfong.
EIN: 743050638

1861
The Frank M. Doyle Foundation, Inc.
3495 Lakeside Dr., No. 34
Reno, NV 89509-4841 (775) 829-1972
FAX: (775) 829-1974;
E-mail: FMDFoundation@aol.com; Main URL: http://www.frankmdoyle.org

Established in 1996 in CA and NV.
Donors: Gertrude R. Doyle; Shirley Freedland; Steve Inch; Tara Inch; F. Patrick Doyle; Molly K.D. Glen.
Foundation type: Operating foundation.
Financial data (yr. ended 08/31/13): Assets, $69,711,491 (M); expenditures, $4,259,601; qualifying distributions, $3,703,863; giving activities include $2,383,173 for 24 grants (high: $350,000; low: $3,500), and $1,043,757 for 409 grants to individuals (high: $10,000; low: $67).
Purpose and activities: Scholarships to high school graduates of the Huntington Beach Union High School District and Huntington Beach Adult High School in CA; as well as students and graduates of community colleges in Coastline, Cypress, Fullerton, Golden West, Irvine Valley, Orange Coast, Saddleback, Santa Ana, or Santiago Canyon, CA. Scholarships also to students and graduates of the Washoe County School District or Washoe Adult High School in NV. Some funding also for human services.
Fields of interest: Higher education; Human services.
Type of support: Scholarships—to individuals.
Limitations: Giving primarily in CA; funding also in NV.
Publications: Application guidelines.
Application information: Cover letters must be formatted and labeled in the particular order that appears in the "Guidelines for New Grants" section (under "Grants" tab) of the foundation web site. Application form required.
***Initial approach:* Cover letter**
Copies of proposal: 1
***Deadline(s):* May 1 (for grants); Mar. 1 (for scholarships)**
Board meeting date(s): Late Apr., late Sept., and as necessary throughout the year
***Final notification:* Mid-Nov**
Officers and Directors:* F. Patrick Doyle,* Pres.; Doug Doyle,* V.P.; Molly Brown,* Secy.; Molly K.D. Glen,* Treas.; Nancy Doyle; Lauren Gunstone; Kathleen MacKinnon; Dan O'Hanlon; Mary Reed Roberts.
Number of staff: 2 part-time professional.
EIN: 880372802

1862
EBV Foundation
38 Grand Corniche Dr.
Henderson, NV 89011-2004
***E-mail:* dani@ebvfoundation.org**; Main URL: http://www.ebvfoundation.org

Established in NV.
Donors: Theodore Lachowicz; Cheryl Lachowicz; Cantor Fitzgerald; Bruce Carusi; Sue Carusi; Tom Foley; Kevin Coyne.
Foundation type: Independent foundation.
Financial data (yr. ended 12/31/12): Assets, $331,739 (M); gifts received, $78,378; expenditures, $593,931; qualifying distributions, $553,150; giving activities include $553,150 for 2 grants (high: $500,000; low: $53,150).
Purpose and activities: Giving primarily to participating veterans to assist in the development of their business plans.
Fields of interest: Social entrepreneurship; Military/veterans.
Limitations: Applications not accepted. Giving primarily in Syracuse, NY; some funding also in Henderson, NV.
Application information: Unsolicited requests for funds not accepted.
Officer: Theodore Lachowicz, Pres.
Board Members: George Bodine; Hon. John C. Cherundolo; Thomas C. Colella; Thomas Foley; Richard L. Haydon; Mark Larsen.
EIN: 263844672

1863
Engelstad Family Foundation
851 S. Rampart Blvd., Ste. 150
Las Vegas, NV 89145-4882 (702) 732-7102

Established in 2002 in NV.
Donors: Richard A. Clyne; Ralph Engelstad; Ralph and Betty Engelstad Trust.
Foundation type: Independent foundation.
Financial data (yr. ended 12/31/12): Assets, $728,328,702 (M); expenditures, $30,737,849; qualifying distributions, $26,338,086; giving activities include $26,338,086 for 100+ grants (high: $3,000,000).
Purpose and activities: Giving primarily to Roman Catholic schools, organizations and churches; funding also for children, youth and social services.
Fields of interest: Education; Human services; Children/youth, services; Catholic agencies & churches.
Limitations: Applications not accepted. Giving primarily in NV, with emphasis on Las Vegas. No grants to individuals.
Application information: Contributes only to pre-selected organizations.
Officers and Trustees:* Betty Engelstad,* Pres.; Kris McGarry,* V.P.; Jeffrey Cooper,* Treas.
EIN: 806008137
Other changes: Owen Nitz is no longer V.P. and Secy.

1864
William H. & Mattie W. Harris Foundation
6655 W. Sahara, Ste. B-118
Las Vegas, NV 89146 (702) 253-1317
Contact: Karen Winnefeld

E-mail: harrisfoundation@lvcoxmail.com; Main URL: http://harrisfoundation-nevada.com/

Established in 2008 in NV.
Foundation type: Independent foundation.
Financial data (yr. ended 12/31/12): Assets, $7,656,711 (M); expenditures, $379,108; qualifying distributions, $277,097; giving activities include $211,160 for 67 grants (high: $19,900; low: $160).
Fields of interest: Arts; Education; Animals/wildlife; Community/economic development.
Limitations: Applications accepted. Giving primarily in AZ, CA, CO, NM, and NV. No grants to individuals.
Application information: See foundation web site for application guidelines. Application form required.
Initial approach: Letter of inquiry
Copies of proposal: 4
Officers: RuthAnne Anderson, Pres.; Haydn Hite, Exec. V.P.; Jessica Hite, Secy.; Marilyn HiteT, Treas.
Director: Cassidy Harrison.
EIN: 262841027

1865
The Jaquish & Kenninger Foundation
P.O. Box 129
Zephyr Cove, NV 89448-0129 (775) 588-4646
***FAX:* (775) 588-2272;**
E-mail: info@jaquishkenningerfoundation.org; Main URL: http://www.jaquishkenningerfoundation.org

Established in 1997 in CA.
Donors: Gail A. Jaquish; Steven C. Kenninger; Ruth L. Kenninger Trust.
Foundation type: Independent foundation.
Financial data (yr. ended 12/31/12): Assets, $7,342,571 (M); expenditures, $204,514; qualifying distributions, $191,700; giving activities include $191,700 for 10 grants (high: $130,000; low: $500).
Purpose and activities: Giving primarily for organizations who support developing excellence in leadership to strengthen Americans' personal and economic freedoms.
Fields of interest: Higher education; Education; Health organizations, association; Human services.
Limitations: Applications accepted. Giving primarily in CA and IN. No grants to individuals.
Application information: Application form required.
Initial approach: Completed application form
Deadline(s): None
Officers: Gail A. Jaquish, Pres.; Steven C. Kenninger, Secy.-Treas.
Directors: R. Taylor Bennett; Stewart L. Hayes; Susan K. Kenninger; Dennis H. Vaughn.
EIN: 330759830

1866
Maddux Foundation
2300 W. Sahara Ave., Ste. 800
Las Vegas, NV **89102-4397**
E-mail: gstunkel@themadduxfoundation.com; Main URL: http://themadduxfoundation.com

Established in 1993 in NV.
Donors: Gregory Maddux; Kathleen Maddux; Personal Management Consultants Inc; Teammates for Kids; David Desantis; Jeffery Overton; James Keller.
Foundation type: Independent foundation.
Financial data (yr. ended 12/31/12): Assets, $377,536 (M); gifts received, $158,200; expenditures, $192,775; qualifying distributions, $57,450; giving activities include $57,450 for 4 grants (high: $30,200; low: $1,000).
Fields of interest: Education; Human services; Children/youth, services.
Limitations: Applications not accepted. Giving primarily in NV. No grants to individuals.
Application information: Contributes only to pre-selected organizations.
Officers and Directors:* Kathleen Maddux,* Pres. and Treas.; Gregory Maddux,* V.P.; Kim Orci,* Secy.; Gene Stunkel, Exec. Dir.; Eddie Orci; Bill Ringer.
EIN: 880300558

1867
Nevada Community Foundation, Inc.
1635 Village Center Circle, Ste. 160
Las Vegas, NV 89134 (702) 892-2326
Contact: Gian Brosco, Pres.
FAX: (702) 892-8580; E-mail: info@nevadacf.org; Main URL: http://www.nevadacf.org
E-Newsletter: http://www.nevadacf.org/eNewsSignup.aspx
Facebook: https://www.facebook.com/NevadaCommunityFoundation
Twitter: https://twitter.com/nvcommunityfdtn

Established in 1988 in NV.
Foundation type: Community foundation.
Financial data (yr. ended 06/30/12): Assets, $29,804,819 (M); gifts received, $5,195,769; expenditures, $3,188,892; giving activities include $2,232,341 for grants.
Purpose and activities: The foundation is committed to improving the lives of southern Nevadans today and for future generations by matching acts of caring to the many needs in the community.
Fields of interest: Arts; Adult/continuing education; Adult education—literacy, basic skills & GED; Education, reading; Education; Environment; Animal welfare; Medical care, rehabilitation; Health care; Substance abuse, services; Mental health/crisis services; Health organizations, association; Cancer; Heart & circulatory diseases; AIDS; Cancer research; Heart & circulatory research; AIDS research; Food services; Youth development, citizenship; Children/youth, services; Family services; Aging, centers/services; Women, centers/services; Minorities/immigrants, centers/services; Homeless, human services; Human services; Economic development; Community/economic development; United Ways and Federated Giving Programs; Government/public administration; Public affairs, citizen participation; Children/youth; Aging; Disabilities, people with; Blind/visually impaired; Minorities; Women; Economically disadvantaged; Homeless.
Type of support: Consulting services; General/operating support; Capital campaigns; Equipment; Emergency funds; Program development; Conferences/seminars; Publication; Seed money; Scholarship funds; Technical assistance; Matching/challenge support.
Limitations: Applications accepted. Giving limited to NV, with an overwhelming emphasis on the southern communities around greater Las Vegas.
Publications: Application guidelines; Annual report; Financial statement; Grants list.
Application information: Visit the foundation's web site for more information on grant programs. Application form required.
Board meeting date(s): Quarterly
Officers and Directors:* Maureen Schafer,* Chair.; **Michael Threet,* Vice-Chair.**; Gian Brosco, Esq.,* Pres.; **Joselyn Cousins,* Secy.**; **Geraldine Tomich,* Treas.**; **Daniel Anderson**; Larry Carter; **Candace Johnson**; Duncan Lee; Michael Morrissey; Charles Silvestri.
Number of staff: 3 full-time professional; 1 part-time professional; 3 full-time support; 1 part-time support.
EIN: 880241420
Other changes: Joselyn Cousins has replaced Chris Wilcox as Secy. Geraldine Tomich has replaced Michael Threet as Treas.
Francisco Aguilar, Jessica Kartzinel, and Shannon West Redwine are no longer directors.

1868
Parasol Tahoe Community Foundation
(formerly Parasol Community Foundation, Inc.)
948 Incline Way
Incline Village, NV 89451 (775) 298-0100
Contact: Megan Weiss, Donor Services Manager
FAX: (775) 298-0099; E-mail: info@parasol.org; Main URL: http://www.parasol.org
Facebook: http://www.facebook.com/pages/Parasol-Tahoe-Community-Foundation/117062444912
Twitter: https://twitter.com/ptcf

Established in 1996 in NV.
Foundation type: Community foundation.
Financial data (yr. ended 06/30/12): Assets, $44,837,817 (M); gifts received, $3,894,221; expenditures, $4,077,131; giving activities include $2,513,155 for 149 grants (high: $50,000), and $3,200 for grants to individuals.
Purpose and activities: The Parasol Tahoe Community Foundation envisions a region known for engaged community. As Tahoe's largest community foundation, they are committed to improving the quality of life throughout the Lake Tahoe basin and empowering donors in meeting their charitable passions. The foundation seeks to serve as a catalyst for a new nonprofit model that will better serve the community.
Fields of interest: Arts; Education; Environment; Human services; Community/economic development.
Type of support: Seed money; Scholarship funds; Matching/challenge support; Capital campaigns; General/operating support; Annual campaigns; Endowments; In-kind gifts.
Limitations: Applications accepted. Giving limited to the Lake Tahoe region of CA and NV.
Publications: Application guidelines; Annual report; Grants list; Newsletter.
Application information: Visit foundation web site application form and guidelines. Application form required.
Initial approach: Submit application form
Copies of proposal: 1
Deadline(s): Early Nov.
Board meeting date(s): Quarterly
Final notification: 4-6 weeks
Officers and Directors:* David Hardie,* Chair.; Dean Meiling,* Co-Vice Chair.; Bridge Stuart,* Co-Vice Chair.; Claudia Anderson,* C.E.O.; George Ashley,* Treas.; Deborah Hackett, C.F.O.; **Ron Alling**; Wayne Cameron; **Colleen Chapman**; Robert Holman; Mary Jurkonis; Aimee LaFayette; Aaron Moore; Janet Pahl; Bill Watson.
Number of staff: 6 full-time professional; 1 part-time professional.
EIN: 880362053
Other changes: Bryan Landaburu is no longer a director.

1869
Donald W. Reynolds Foundation
1701 Village Center Cir.
Las Vegas, NV 89134-6303 (702) 804-6000
Contact: Karina Mayer, Grants Manager
FAX: (702) 804-6099;
E-mail: generalquestions@dwrf.org; Main URL: http://www.dwreynolds.org

Incorporated in 1954 in NV.
Donor: Donald W. Reynolds†.
Foundation type: Independent foundation.
Financial data (yr. ended 12/31/13): Assets, $175,552,668 (M); expenditures, $62,988,267; qualifying distributions, $62,363,024; giving activities include $58,832,495 for 82 grants (high: $14,879,743; low: $200), and $107,436 for 22 employee matching gifts.
Purpose and activities: The foundation seeks to honor the memory of its benefactor, for whom it is named, by filling unmet needs and attempting to gain an immediate, transformational impact in four principal areas of interest: 1) Meeting the greatest needs of communities in Arkansas, Nevada and Oklahoma, primarily through improved facilities for their outstanding local nonprofit organizations; 2) Accelerating the fight against atherosclerosis and atherosclerotic heart disease through cutting-edge, translational research; 3) Improving the quality of life of America's growing elderly population through better training of physicians in geriatrics; and 4) Enhancing the quality and integrity of journalism, focusing particularly on better training of journalists who serve smaller communities and on business journalism. The foundation remains open to consideration of special opportunities in other areas that are consistent with its broad goals. In pursuing its goals, the foundation is committed to the support of nonprofit organizations and institutions that demonstrate sound financial management, efficient operation, program integrity and an entrepreneurial spirit.
Fields of interest: Higher education; Health care; Medical research, institute; Human services; Public affairs.
Type of support: Building/renovation; Equipment; Program development; Research; Employee matching gifts.
Limitations: Applications accepted. Giving primarily in AR, NV, and OK for capital and planning grants. Giving nationally for cardiovascular clinic research and geriatrics training of physicians, and business journalism. No support for elementary or secondary education, or religious institutions or hospitals. No grants to individuals, or for continuing support, program or operating support, or endowment funds.
Publications: Financial statement; Grants list.
Application information: Request guidelines before submitting proposal or visit the foundation's web site. Proposals sent by fax or e-mail not considered. Applicants are encouraged to discuss projects/requests with foundation staff by telephone or in writing. Application form not required.
Initial approach: Letter (1-2 pages)
***Deadline(s):* Varies by program, contact the foundation or visit foundation web site**
Board meeting date(s): Apr. and Oct.
Officers and Trustees:* Fred W. Smith,* Chair.; Wes Smith,* Vice-Chair.; Steven L. Anderson,* Pres.; Lynn Mosier, Exec. V.P. and C.F.O.; Neal R. Pendergraft; Jonathan Smith, O.D.
Number of staff: 11 full-time professional; 2 full-time support; 1 part-time support.
EIN: 716053383
Other changes: Donald E. Pray is no longer Secy. Keith G. Boman, Barbara Smith Campbell and Kathleen Fench are no longer trustees.

1870
Raymond C. Rude Foundation, Inc.
Reno, NV

The foundation terminated in 2011.

1871
The David and Linda Shaheen Foundation, Inc.
P.O. Box 973
Crystal Bay, NV 89402-0973
Contact: David M. Shaheen, Chair.
E-mail: s@eatyourpeas.org; Main URL: http://www.eatyourpeas.org

Established in 2001 in NV.
Donors: David M. Shaheen; Linda F. Shaheen.
Foundation type: Operating foundation.
Financial data (yr. ended 12/31/12): Assets, $8,205,558 (M); expenditures, $526,860; qualifying distributions, $491,700; giving activities include $491,700 for 16 grants (high: $236,200; low: $1,000).
Purpose and activities: Education is the centerpiece of the foundation, with a concentration on three areas: breast cancer prevention and research, AIDS prevention, and higher education for inner city youth.
Fields of interest: Scholarships/financial aid; Breast cancer; AIDS; Breast cancer research; Youth; Economically disadvantaged.
Limitations: Applications accepted. Giving primarily in CA and GA. No grants to individuals.
Application information: Application information available on foundation web site.
Initial approach: E-mail
Deadline(s): None
Officer: David Shaheen, C.E.O. and Pres.
EIN: 582489866

1872
The Charles H. Stout Foundation
1835 Wendy Way
Reno, NV 89509-8208
E-mail: richardmstout@earthlink.net; **Application address: P.O. Box 20733, Reno, NV 89515-0733, tel.: (775) 825-1510**; Main URL: http://www.chstoutfoundation.org

Established in 1982 in NV.
Foundation type: Independent foundation.
Financial data (yr. ended 06/30/13): Assets, $8,120,801 (M); expenditures, $390,640; qualifying distributions, $376,829; giving activities include $369,000 for 28 grants (high: $30,000; low: $2,000).
Fields of interest: Arts; Education; Housing/shelter.
Limitations: Applications accepted. Giving primarily in Siloam Springs, AR, Del Mar, CA, Reno, NV, New York, NY, or in communities where foundation trustees live or visit regularly. No grants to individuals; no loans.
Publications: Application guidelines; Informational brochure (including application guidelines).
Application information: Application form required.
Initial approach: Proposal
Copies of proposal: 1
Deadline(s): June 15
Board meeting date(s): Sept. or Oct.
Final notification: Within one month following board meeting
Officers and Trustees:* Richard M. Stout,* Pres.; Martha Stout Gilweit,* V.P.; **Katherine Gilweit Cartiglia,* Secy.**; **D. Kent Clayburn, Treas.**; Douglas B. McDonald; **Christopher H. Stout.**
EIN: 942797249
Other changes: Katherine Gilweit Cartiglia has replaced Douglas B. McDonald as Secy. D. Kent Clayburn has replaced Ross B. Stout as Treas.

1873
Cyrus Tang Foundation
(formerly Tang Family Foundation)
8960 Spanish Ridge Ave.
Las Vegas, NV 89148-1302 (702) 734-3700
Contact: Stella Liang, Treas.
FAX: (702) 734-6766;
E-mail: tang@tangfoundation.org; Main URL: http://www.tangfoundation.org
Photo Gallieries: http://www.tangfoundation.org/index.php?option=com_content&view=article&id=51&Itemid=97&site=CTF&sub=7

Established in 1996 in NV.
Donors: Cyrus Tang; Tang Industries, Inc.
Foundation type: Independent foundation.
Financial data (yr. ended 12/31/12): Assets, $229,395,891 (M); gifts received, $2,190,010; expenditures, $10,066,869; qualifying distributions, $9,901,184; giving activities include $9,526,333 for grants.
Purpose and activities: Giving primarily to improve the quality of life in disadvantaged communities of China, through effective investments in education and public health, and by fostering community spirit.
Fields of interest: Higher education; Scholarships/financial aid; Education; Human services.
International interests: China.
Type of support: Building/renovation; Scholarship funds; Matching/challenge support.
Limitations: Applications not accepted. Giving primarily in China. No grants to individuals.
Application information: Contributes only to pre-selected organizations. Applications are by invitation only, and are also accepted in Chinese (traditional or simplified).
Officers and Directors:* Cyrus Tang,* Pres.; **Patrick Liang,* V.P.**; Vytas Ambutas, Secy.; Stella Liang,* Treas.
Number of staff: 3 full-time professional.
EIN: 880361180
Other changes: Patrick Liang has replaced Michael Tang as V.P.

1874
Troesh Family Foundation
1370 Jet Stream Dr., Ste. 140
Henderson, NV 89052-4234 **(702) 889-0828**

Donor: Dennis Troesh.
Foundation type: Independent foundation.
Financial data (yr. ended 12/31/12): Assets, $50,001,816 (M); gifts received, $25,446,449; expenditures, $112,461; qualifying distributions, $4,000; giving activities include $4,000 for 1 grant.
Purpose and activities: Giving primarily for higher education, social services and children and youth services, including children's hospitals.
Fields of interest: Higher education; Hospitals (specialty); Human services; YM/YWCAs & YM/YWHAs; Children/youth, services; Christian agencies & churches.
Limitations: Giving in the U.S., with emphasis on CA.

Officers and Directors:* Dennis Troesh,* Pres.; Laurie Mattson,* Secy.; Jeffrey Troesh,* Treas.; **Carol Troesh**; Carrie Troesh; Jon Troesh.
EIN: 330885955
Other changes: At the close of 2012, the fair market value of the grantmaker's assets was $50,001,816, a 758.1% increase over the 2010 value, $5,826,756.

1875
Webb Family Foundation, Inc.
7251 W. Lake Mead Blvd., Ste. 530
Las Vegas, NV 89128-8373
Contact: Lewis M. Webb, Pres.
Application address: 7 Journey, Ste. A, Aliso Viejo, CA 92656

Established in 1998 in NV.
Donors: Lewis M. Webb; Margaret A. Webb.
Foundation type: Independent foundation.
Financial data (yr. ended 06/30/13): Assets, $613,410 (M); expenditures, $175,960; qualifying distributions, $168,821; giving activities include $168,821 for 32 grants (high: $100,000; low: $25).
Fields of interest: Higher education; Hospitals (general); Human services; Children/youth, services; Christian agencies & churches.
Limitations: Applications accepted. Giving primarily in CA and WV.
Application information: Application form required.
Initial approach: Letter
Copies of proposal: 1
Deadline(s): None
Officers: Lewis M. Webb, Pres.; Margaret A. Webb, V.P.; **Robert Underwood, Secy.**
Directors: Karen Webb Armour; Jeremy L. Webb; Lewis M. Webb III.
EIN: 880381296
Other changes: Robert Underwood is now Secy.

1876
Terry Lee Wells Foundation
P.O. Box 70806
Reno, NV 89570-0806 (775) 322-7733
E-mail: info@terryleewellsfoundation.org; Main URL: http://www.terryleewellsfoundation.org
Grants List: http://www.terryleewellsfoundation.org/awards_12.php

Established in 1999 in NV.
Donor: Terry Lee Wells‡.
Foundation type: Independent foundation.
Financial data (yr. ended 12/31/12): Assets, $4,800,790 (M); expenditures, $946,219; qualifying distributions, $814,600; giving activities include $814,600 for grants.
Purpose and activities: Giving to improve the quality of life in northern Nevada by exposing the underprivileged to arts, cultural, economic, and educational opportunities, with a focus on women and children. The foundation also has an interest in addressing the medical needs of northern Nevadans with an emphasis on diabetes.
Fields of interest: Arts; Education; Health care; Diabetes; Human services; Children/youth, services; Adults, women; Economically disadvantaged.
Limitations: Giving to organizations located in any county in NV, except Clark County. No grants to individuals, or for endowments or venture capital.
Publications: Application guidelines; Grants list.
Application information: Application guidelines and form available on foundation web site. Application form required.
Initial approach: 2-4 page narrative
Deadline(s): See application form for current deadline
Board meeting date(s): Between May 1 and June 12, and between Sept. 1 and Oct. 12
Officers and Directors:* Dawn E. Wells,* Chair. and Pres.; Eloise Esser,* V.P.; Sherrie Cartinella,* Secy.; Charlotte McConnell,* Treas. and Exec. Dir.; Lynn Atcheson.
EIN: 880431758

NEW HAMPSHIRE

1877
Alexander Eastman Foundation
75 S. Main St., Unit 7, PMB 250
Concord, NH 03301-4828
Contact: Grants and Admin. Mgr.: Amy Lockwood, Prog. Off.
E-mail: alockwood@alexandereastman.org; **Tel. for grant application inquiries: 1-(888) 228-1821, ext. 80; tel. for scholarship application inquiries: 1-(888) 228-1821, ext. 81**; Main URL: http://www.alexandereastman.org
Grants List: http://www.alexandereastman.org/04pgrants.html

Established in 1983 in NH.
Donor: Leon P. Widger Trust.
Foundation type: Independent foundation.
Financial data (yr. ended 09/30/13): Assets, $11,822,480 (M); gifts received, $76,441; expenditures, $663,475; qualifying distributions, $605,060; giving activities include $507,559 for 14 grants (high: $235,000; low: $5,000), and $23,700 for 12 grants to individuals (high: $2,500; low: $500).
Purpose and activities: Awards grants to improve the quality and availability of health care and to promote good health and well-being for residents of the Derry, Londonderry, Windham, Chester, Hampstead, and Sandown, NH, area; giving also includes scholarship assistance for area residents working in the health care field.
Fields of interest: Education; Health care; Mental health/crisis services; Agriculture/food; Human services; Family services.
Type of support: Seed money; General/operating support; Continuing support; Capital campaigns; Building/renovation; Equipment; Program development; Conferences/seminars; Scholarship funds; Technical assistance; Consulting services; Program evaluation; Scholarships—to individuals.
Limitations: Applications accepted. Giving limited to organizations serving residents of Derry, Londonderry, Windham, Chester, Hampstead and Sandown, NH. No grants to individuals (except for designated scholarship funds); no grants for basic costs that should be covered in municipal budgets.
Publications: Application guidelines; Annual report.
Application information: Online application required; application guidelines and form available on foundation web site. Application form required.
Initial approach: 1st-time applicants: telephone; all other applicants, online-line via foundation web site
Copies of proposal: 1
Deadline(s): Apr. 1 and Oct. 1
Board meeting date(s): May and Nov.
Final notification: May and Nov.
Officers and Trustees:* John Patrick Ahern,* Chair.; William Lonergan,* Vice-Chair.; Cindy Gray,* Secy.; Michael Buckley,* Treas.; Sharyn Findlay; Angela Kouroyen; Angela Loring; Bob McDonald; Earle Rosse; Rebecca Rutter; Larry VanDeventer; Dr. Wayne White.
Number of staff: 2 part-time professional.
EIN: 020222124

1878
Norwin S. and Elizabeth N. Bean Foundation
40 Stark St.
Manchester, NH **03101** (603) 493-7257
E-mail: kcook@beanfoundation.org; Main URL: http://www.beanfoundation.org

Trust established in 1967 in NH; later became an affiliated trust of the New Hampshire Charitable Foundation, of which it is now independent.
Donors: Norwin S. Bean†; Elizabeth N. Bean†.
Foundation type: Independent foundation.
Financial data (yr. ended 12/31/12): Assets, $11,724,970 (M); expenditures, $464,052; qualifying distributions, $402,355; giving activities include $322,979 for 25 grants (high: $22,000; low: $2,287).
Purpose and activities: Giving primarily for human services, including low-income housing programs and youth; support also for education, health associations, the arts, the environment, and the public benefit.
Fields of interest: Arts; Education; Environment; Health care; Health organizations, association; Housing/shelter, development; Human services; Youth, services.
Type of support: General/operating support; Capital campaigns; Building/renovation; Equipment; Program development; Conferences/seminars; Seed money; Consulting services; Program evaluation; Matching/challenge support.
Limitations: Applications accepted. Giving limited to Amherst and Manchester, NH. No support for religious or political organizations. No grants to individuals, or for scholarships, fellowships, or deficit financing.
Publications: Application guidelines; Annual report (including application guidelines); Informational brochure (including application guidelines).
Application information: See foundation web site for application guidelines. Application form required.
Copies of proposal: 2
Board meeting date(s): Feb., Apr., June, Sept. and Dec.
Final notification: 2-3 months
Trustees: John F. Dinkel, Jr.; Thomas J. Donovan; **William H. Dunlap**; William G. Steele, Jr.; **Leslie Stewart**; **Cathryn E. Vaughn**; **Michael Whitney**.
Number of staff: 1 part-time professional.
EIN: 026013381
Other changes: Selma Naccach-Hoff and David Scannell are no longer directors.

1879
The Jack and Dorothy Byrne Foundation, Inc.
c/o Robert E. Snyder
80 S. Main St., Ste. 202
Hanover, NH 03755-2053
Application address: c/o Dorothy Byrne, Pres., 3 Laramie Rd., P.O. Box 599, Etna, NH 03755

Established in 1999 in DE; On Nov. 30, 2007 the foundation absorbed the assets of The Byrne Foundation, Inc.
Donors: Dorothy Byrne; John J. Byrne†.
Foundation type: Independent foundation.
Financial data (yr. ended 12/31/13): Assets, $40,768,342 (M); gifts received, $42,194,187; expenditures, $7,719,533; qualifying distributions, $7,681,994; giving activities include $7,635,799 for 551 grants (high: $500,000; low: $300).
Fields of interest: Higher education, college (community/junior); Cancer research; Philanthropy/voluntarism.
Type of support: General/operating support.
Limitations: Applications accepted. Giving primarily in the upper valley of NH and VT. No grants to individuals.
Application information: No telephone calls.
Initial approach: Letter
Deadline(s): None
Officers and Directors:* Dorothy M. Byrne,* Pres.; Robert E. Snyder,* Secy.-Treas.
EIN: 030363118
Other changes: At the close of 2013, the fair market value of the grantmaker's assets was $40,768,342, a 546.7% increase over the 2012 value, $6,304,465.
John J. Byrne, Donor and V.P., is deceased.

1880
Charter Charitable Foundation
90 N. Main St.
Concord, NH 03301-4915 **(603) 717-8452**
***E-mail:* questions@charterfoundation.org; Application address: c/o Heather A. Dockham, Asst. Secy., P.O. Box 245, Concord, NH 03302, tel.: (603) 545-8277; E-mail: heather@charterfoundation.org**; Main URL: http://charterfoundation.org/

Established in NH.
Donors: K. Malcom Jones; Carol E. Koury; National Securities Corp.; Feminist Women's Health Center; The Butler Foundation.
Foundation type: Independent foundation.
Financial data (yr. ended 12/31/12): Assets, $6,782,894 (M); gifts received, $55,008; expenditures, $444,032; qualifying distributions, $409,400; giving activities include $409,400 for grants.
Fields of interest: Education; Environment; Animals/wildlife; Human services; Women, centers/services.
Limitations: Applications accepted. Giving in the U.S., with emphasis on MA and NH.
Application information: See foundation website for complete application guidelines. Application form required.
***Deadline(s):* Mar. 15 and Oct. 15**
Officers and Directors:* Stephen A. Albrecht,* Chair.; Cynthia Wentworth,* Treas.; Raymond Pinard.
EIN: 200471816
Other changes: The grantmaker now accepts applications.

1881
Taylor Christian Foundation
P.O. Box 457
Wolfeboro, NH **03894**

Established in 2000 in NH.
Foundation type: Independent foundation.
Financial data (yr. ended 09/30/13): Assets, $5,296,483 (M); expenditures, $328,813; qualifying distributions, $285,500; giving activities include $285,500 for 19 grants (high: $130,000; low: $500).
Fields of interest: Children/youth, services; Christian agencies & churches.
Limitations: Applications not accepted. Giving in the U.S., with emphasis on NH and WI; some funding also in Honduras. No grants to individuals.
Application information: Contributes only to pre-selected organizations.
Trustees: G. Robert Lockhart; Romona Lockhart.
EIN: 311745034

1882
The DEKA Foundation
340 Commercial St.
Manchester, NH 03101-1121

Donors: Dean Kamen; HHD, LLC.
Foundation type: Independent foundation.
Financial data (yr. ended 05/31/13): Assets, $10,268,358 (M); gifts received, $5,000,000; expenditures, $1,047,416; qualifying distributions, $1,025,000; giving activities include $1,025,000 for 2 grants (high: $1,000,000; low: $25,000).
Fields of interest: Science; Children.
Limitations: Applications not accepted. Giving primarily in NH and NY.
Application information: Unsolicited requests for funds not accepted.
Directors: Stephen Hazard; Dean Kamen; Maureen Toohey; Robert Tuttle.
EIN: 271188399
Other changes: At the close of 2013, the grantmaker paid grants of $1,025,000, a 318.4% increase over the 2012 disbursements, $245,000.

1883
Endowment for Health, Inc.
1 Pillsbury St., Ste. 301
Concord, NH 03301-3556 (603) 228-2448
FAX: (603) 228-1304;
E-mail: info@endowmentforhealth.org; Application e-mail: applications@endowmentforhealth.org; Main URL: http://www.endowmentforhealth.org
Endowment for Health's Philanthropy Promise: http://www.ncrp.org/philanthropys-promise/who
E-Newsletter: http://www.endowmentforhealth.org/join-our-mailing-list.aspx
Facebook: http://www.facebook.com/pages/Endowment-for-Health/214040860747
Twitter: http://twitter.com/EndowmentHealth

Established in 1999 in NH; converted from Blue Cross/Blue Shield.
Foundation type: Independent foundation.
Financial data (yr. ended 09/30/13): Assets, $82,180,630 (M); expenditures, $3,476,218; qualifying distributions, $3,273,618; giving activities include $1,966,912 for 55 grants (high: $200,000; low: $1,000).
Purpose and activities: The mission of the endowment is to improve the health and reduce the burden of illness of the people of New Hampshire. Giving for oral health, and reducing social-cultural, geographic, and economic barriers to receiving health care.
Fields of interest: Dental care; Health care; Social sciences, public policy.
Type of support: Emergency funds; Program development; Conferences/seminars; Research; Technical assistance.
Limitations: Applications accepted. Giving primarily limited to NH. No support for biomedical research organizations, or for out of state projects. No grants for capital campaigns, lobbying efforts, expensed already incurred, fundraisers, or ongoing expenses.
Publications: Application guidelines; Annual report; Annual report (including application guidelines); Financial statement; Grants list; Informational brochure (including application guidelines); Newsletter; Program policy statement.
Application information: Application form available on foundation web site. Application form required.
Initial approach: Telephone or visit foundation web site
Deadline(s): See web site for current deadlines
Board meeting date(s): Quarterly
Officers and Directors:* Sandra Pelletier, Chair.; Margaret Franckhauser, Vice-Chair.; Steven Rowe, Pres.; Yvonne Goldsberry,* Secy.; Marshall Rowe,* Treas.; Eddie Edwards; Orville Fitch; Randy Foose; **Jody Hoffer Gittell**; Stephen F. Lawlor; Kathleen Murphy; **Ann Peters**; Cindy Rosenwald; Adrienne Rupp; **Jackie Sparks**; **John Wallace**.
Number of staff: 5 full-time professional; 3 part-time professional; 1 full-time support.
EIN: 020512290
Other changes: For the fiscal year ended Sept. 30, 2013, the grantmaker paid grants of $1,966,912, a 66.8% increase over the fiscal 2012 disbursements, $1,178,960.
Karin Caruso, Susan R. Chollet, Cordell Johnston, and Richard Showalter are no longer directors.

1884
The Finlay Foundation
30 Temple St., Ste. 400
Nashua, NH 03060-3449
Main URL: http://www.thefinlayfoundation.org/

Donors: Karin K. Finlay; Robert Finlay.
Foundation type: Independent foundation.
Financial data (yr. ended 12/31/12): Assets, $140,690 (M); gifts received, $288,900; expenditures, $310,853; qualifying distributions, $310,584; giving activities include $310,094 for 35 grants (high: $100,000; low: $200).
Purpose and activities: The Finlay Foundation improves the quality of life for Granite State residents by assisting children and families in need and promoting an array of forward-thinking cultural and educational initiatives.
Fields of interest: Education; Hospitals (general); Housing/shelter; Human services; Children.
Type of support: Advocacy.
Limitations: Applications accepted. Giving primarily in NH.
Application information: Application form required.
Initial approach: Online application form
Deadline(s): None
Officer: Karin K. Finlay, Pres.
Trustee: Robert Finlay.
EIN: 262644613

1885
Foundation for Seacoast Health
100 Campus Dr., Ste. 1
Portsmouth, NH 03801-5892 (603) 422-8200
Contact: Debra S. Grabowski, Exec. Dir.
FAX: (603) 422-8207;
E-mail: ffsh@communitycampus.org; Main URL: http://www.ffsh.org
Facebook: https://www.facebook.com/pages/Foundation-for-Seacoast-Health/431317490236981

Incorporated in 1984 in NH as the Portsmouth Hospital Foundation; converted from the proceeds of the sale of Portsmouth Hospital to Hospital Corporation of America. Name changed in 1986 to Foundation for Seacoast Health.
Foundation type: Independent foundation.
Financial data (yr. ended 12/31/13): Assets, $45,008,431 (M); gifts received, $26,533; expenditures, $2,566,954; qualifying distributions, $1,790,202; giving activities include $693,185 for 10 grants (high: $325,850; low: $500), and $9,500 for 6 grants to individuals (high: $3,500; low: $500).
Purpose and activities: The foundation invests its resources to improve the health and well being of Seacoast citizens. Funding particularly for affordable mental health services, preventative and restorative dental services, affordable child care and after school care, affordable primary medical care, and coordination and dissemination of health information related to identified priority needs.
Fields of interest: Health care, infants; Public health, obesity; Mental health/crisis services; Health organizations; Medical research; Aging, centers/services; Children/youth; Youth; Adults; Disabilities, people with; Physically disabled; Crime/abuse victims; Economically disadvantaged; Homeless; LGBTQ.
Type of support: General/operating support; Technical assistance; Scholarships—to individuals.
Limitations: Applications not accepted. Giving limited to Kittery, Eliot, and York, ME and Portsmouth, Rye, New Castle, Greenland, Newington, and North Hampton, NH. No support for political activities. No grants to individuals (except through the foundation scholarship program), bricks and mortar, deficit financing, travel, lodging, or conferences.
Publications: Annual report; Financial statement; Newsletter.
Application information: The foundation is not considering new grant initiatives at this time.
Board meeting date(s): 3rd Tues. of Jan., Feb., Mar., May, Aug., Sept., Oct., and Nov.; annual meeting, 3rd Tues. in Apr.
Officers and Trustees:* Daniel C. Hoefle,* Chair.; Timothy J. Connors,* Vice-Chair.; Nancy L. Cutter, Secy.; Timothy Driscoll,* Treas.; Debra S. Grabowski, Exec. Dir.; Patricia A. Barbour; Richard Chace, M.D.; Jameson French; John Hebert; Ann Hodsdon; Peter Loughlin; John Lyons; Archie McGowan, M.D.; Amy Schwart; Neal Ouellett; Sharon R. Weston.
Number of staff: 1 full-time professional; 1 part-time professional; 6 full-time support; 2 part-time support.
EIN: 020386319

1886
The Fuller Foundation, Inc.
P.O. Box 479
Rye Beach, NH 03871-0479 **(603) 964-6998**
Contact: John T. Bottomley, Exec. Dir.; Sandi Scagliotti, Prog. Assoc.
FAX: (603) 964-8901; E-mail: ATfuller@aol.com; Main URL: http://www.fullerfoundation.org

Incorporated in 1938 in MA.
Donor: Alvan T. Fuller, Sr.‡.
Foundation type: Independent foundation.
Financial data (yr. ended 12/31/12): Assets, $13,044,053 (M); expenditures, $834,049; qualifying distributions, $668,524; giving activities include $554,817 for grants.
Purpose and activities: The purpose of the foundation is to support non-profit agencies which improve the quality of life for people, animals, and the environment. The foundation also funds the Fuller Foundation of New Hampshire, which supports horticultural and educational programs for the public at Fuller Gardens.
Fields of interest: Arts education; Museums; Performing arts; Arts; Education; Environment, natural resources; Animals/wildlife, preservation/protection; Substance abuse, services; Youth development.
Type of support: General/operating support; Continuing support; Land acquisition; Emergency funds; Program development; Seed money; Scholarship funds; Matching/challenge support.
Limitations: Applications accepted. Giving primarily in the greater Boston, MA, area (inside Rte. 128),

and the immediate seacoast area of NH. There are no geographic limitations for grants for endangered species. No grants to individuals or for capital projects, or conferences; no loans.
Publications: Application guidelines.
Application information: Contact foundation for current guidelines; Faxed or e-mailed requests not accepted. Associated Grant Makers Common Proposal Form accepted, and can be downloaded via foundation web site. Application form required.
Initial approach: Proposal or telephone call
Copies of proposal: 1
Deadline(s): Jan. 15 and June 15
Board meeting date(s): May and Oct.
Final notification: 30 to 60 days
Officers and Trustees:* James D. Henderson II,* Pres.; Peter D. Fuller, Jr.,* Treas.; John T. Bottomley,* Clerk and Exec. Dir.; Miranda Fuller Bocko; Peter Fuller; Peter S. Langley; Corey Fuller MacDonald; Melinda Fuller vanden Heuvel.
Number of staff: 1 full-time professional; 1 part-time support.
EIN: 042241130

1887
Kendal C. & Anna Ham Charitable Foundation, Inc.

P.O. Box 2853
North Conway, NH 03860-2853 (603) 356-3389
***Contact:* Robert J. Murphy, Exec. Dir.**
***FAX:* (603) 356-3334;**
E-mail: thcf@roadrunner.com; Main URL: http://hamcharitablefoundation.org/

Established in 1994.
Foundation type: Independent foundation.
Financial data (yr. ended 12/31/12): Assets, $9,993,860 (M); expenditures, $402,914; qualifying distributions, $351,353; giving activities include $295,300 for 48 grants (high: $52,000; low: $100).
Purpose and activities: Giving to better community life in Bridgton and Fryeburg, ME, and Mount Washington Valley, NH.
Fields of interest: Higher education; Human services.
Type of support: Annual campaigns; Capital campaigns; Building/renovation; Equipment; Land acquisition; Endowments; Debt reduction; Program development; Seed money; Scholarships—to individuals; In-kind gifts; Matching/challenge support.
Limitations: Applications accepted. Giving limited to Bridgton and Fryeburg, ME, and the Mount Washington Valley area of NH.
Publications: Application guidelines; Annual report; Program policy statement.
Application information: Application form required.
Initial approach: Completed application form
Copies of proposal: 1
Deadline(s): 90 days prior to board meeting
Board meeting date(s): Apr. and Oct.
Officers and Directors:* Paul Brigham,* Pres.; Linda Eldridge, V.P.; Robert J. Murphy, Secy.-Treas. and Exec. Dir.; Bruce Chalmers; Dorthea M. Seybold; John H. Stratton.
Number of staff: 1 full-time professional; 1 part-time support.
EIN: 223080012
Other changes: The grantmaker has moved from MA to NH. The grantmaker no longer lists a separate application address.

1888
HNH Foundation, Inc.

49 S. Main St., Ste. 204
Concord, NH 03301-4872 (603) 229-3260
Contact: Patti Baum
***FAX:* (603) 229-3259;**
E-mail: info@hnhfoundation.org; **Letter of Inquiry e-mail: application@hnhfoundation.org (Include "LOI" in subject line, and organization's name and contact in body of e-mail)**; Main URL: http://www.hnhfoundation.org

Established in 1997 in NH, as a result of the merger of the Matthew Thornton Health Plan and Blue Cross/Blue Shield of New Hampshire.
Donor: Matthew Thornton, Inc.
Foundation type: Independent foundation.
Financial data (yr. ended 12/31/12): Assets, $21,440,623 (M); gifts received, $50; expenditures, $959,367; qualifying distributions, $1,042,545; giving activities include $551,234 for 23 grants (high: $217,347; low: $900).
Purpose and activities: Giving primarily to: 1) increase the number of New Hampshire children who have access to health and dental insurance coverage, with a priority on children through age 18; 2) promote preventive oral health care for children through age five and pregnant women, with a priority focus on Coos County, NH; and 3) prevent childhood obesity with a focus on children through age 5.
Fields of interest: Dental care; Public health, obesity; Health care, insurance; Health care; Children/youth, services; Children.
Type of support: General/operating support; Program development; Program-related investments/loans; Matching/challenge support.
Limitations: Applications accepted. Giving limited to NH. No support for sectarian or religious programs. No grants to individuals, or for capital campaigns or expenditures, fundraisers, or bricks and mortar.
Publications: Application guidelines; Annual report; Financial statement; Grants list.
Application information: If the applying organization requires a fiscal sponsor to accept and spend grant funds, the Letter of Inquiry must be submitted by the sponsoring organization, Application form required.
***Initial approach:* Letter of Inquiry (not to exceed 2 pages, submitted via e-mail, and in .pdf format)**
Copies of proposal: 1
***Deadline(s):* See foundation web site for current deadlines**
Officers and Directors:* Martha McLeod,* Chair.; Sandi Van Scoyoc, Pres.; Dr. Steven Paris,* Secy.; Keith R. Ballingall, Treas.; Tyler Brannen; Marc Cullerot; Elaine Van Dyke; **Sandra Mann**; Shannon Mills.
Number of staff: 2 full-time professional; 1 part-time professional.
EIN: 020497577
Other changes: Martha McLeod has replaced Sandra Mann as Chair.
Donald Crandlemire and Anthony Tagliaferro are no longer directors.

1889
Edward C. Johnson Fund

11 Keewaydin Dr., Ste. 100
Salem, NH 03079-2999
Contact: Anne-Marie Soulliere, Pres.

Trust established in 1964 in MA.
Donors: Edward C. Johnson II†; Edward C. Johnson III; Abigail P. Johnson; Edward C. Johnson IV; Elizabeth L. Johnson; Abel Partners; FMR Corp.
Foundation type: Independent foundation.
Financial data (yr. ended 12/31/12): Assets, $333,870,362 (M); gifts received, $6,847,000; expenditures, $52,076,290; qualifying distributions, $54,259,215; giving activities include $49,181,367 for 88 grants (high: $12,102,650; low: $500), and $3,914,799 for foundation-administered programs.
Purpose and activities: Emphasis on museums, historical societies, medical institutions, and some youth programs. Support also for the visual arts, historic preservation, higher education, elementary and secondary schools, and environmental organizations.
Fields of interest: Visual arts; Museums; Performing arts; Historic preservation/historical societies; Arts; Environment; Health care; Medical research, institute; Youth, services.
Type of support: Capital campaigns; Building/renovation; Endowments; Program development; Research.
Limitations: Applications not accepted. Giving limited to the greater Boston, MA, area. No grants to individuals, or for scholarships.
Application information: Unsolicited requests for funds not accepted.
Board meeting date(s): June and Dec.
Officers and Directors:* Edward C. Johnson III,* Chair.; Anne-Marie Soulliere, Pres.; **Desiree Caldwell, V.P.**; Melanie S. Sommer, Secy.; Rupal M. Poltack, Treas.; Abigail P. Johnson; Edward C. Johnson IV; Elizabeth L. Johnson.
EIN: 046108344
Other changes: At the close of 2012, the grantmaker paid grants of $49,181,367, a 67.2% increase over the 2011 disbursements, $29,407,620.

1890
Agnes M. Lindsay Trust

660 Chestnut St.
Manchester, NH 03104-3550 (603) 669-1366
Contact: Susan E. Bouchard, Admin. Dir.
***FAX:* (603) 665-8114;**
E-mail: admin@lindsaytrust.org; Toll-free tel.: (866) 669-1366; Letter of Inquiry e-mail: proposals@lindsaytrust.org; Main URL: http://www.Lindsaytrust.org

Trust established in 1939 in NH.
Donor: Agnes M. Lindsay†.
Foundation type: Independent foundation.
Financial data (yr. ended 12/31/12): Assets, $22,674,725 (M); expenditures, $981,729; qualifying distributions, $728,499; giving activities include $518,958 for 188 grants (high: $15,000; low: $1,000).
Purpose and activities: Support for health and welfare, including services for the blind, deaf and learning disabled, the elderly, children's hospitals, children's homes, youth organizations, youth/family services and summer camperships/summer enrichment programs. The trust also supports colleges, universities, and private secondary schools through scholarship funds administered by the educational institutions to deserving students from rural communities.
Fields of interest: Higher education; Education; Health care; Human services; Children/youth, services; Infants/toddlers; Children/youth; Children; Youth; Young adults; Disabilities, people with; Physically disabled; Blind/visually impaired; Deaf/hearing impaired; Mentally disabled;

Minorities; Asians/Pacific Islanders; African Americans/Blacks; Hispanics/Latinos; Native Americans/American Indians; Adults, women; Adults, men; Substance abusers; AIDS, people with; Crime/abuse victims; Immigrants/refugees; Economically disadvantaged; Homeless.
Type of support: Capital campaigns; Building/renovation; Equipment; Program development; Scholarship funds; Matching/challenge support.
Limitations: Applications accepted. Giving limited to MA, ME, NH, and VT. No support for private foundations, organizations lacking 501(c)(3) status, public entities, libraries, museums, municipalities, or sectarian organizations. No grants to individuals, or for endowments; generally no grants for general operating funds. Capital grants are not awarded to educational institutions.
Publications: Application guidelines; Annual report; Grants list.
Application information: Application form required.
***Initial approach:* Letter of Inquiry via e-mail**
Copies of proposal: 1
Deadline(s): None
Board meeting date(s): Monthly
Trustees: Michael S. DeLucia; Ernest E. Dion; Alan G. Lampert.
Number of staff: 1 full-time professional.
EIN: 026004971

1891
The Mosaic Fund
c/o Colin Cabot
7097 Sanborn Rd.
Loudon, NH 03307-1618

Established in 1994 in NY.
Donors: Clattesad Trust; Clapttrap Trust; Clatpag Trust; Clatscatt Trust; Clattaur Trust; Clattecam Trust.
Foundation type: Independent foundation.
Financial data (yr. ended 12/31/12): Assets, $1,627,436 (M); gifts received, $906,635; expenditures, $740,692; qualifying distributions, $738,455; giving activities include $738,455 for grants.
Purpose and activities: Giving primarily for environmental conservation and protection, including urban parks and gardens, and an equestrian center; some support also for secondary education and the arts.
Fields of interest: Arts; Elementary/secondary education; Environment, natural resources; Environment; Athletics/sports, equestrianism.
Limitations: Applications not accepted. Giving primarily in NY. No grants to individuals.
Application information: Contributes only to pre-selected organizations.
Trustees: F. Colin Cabot; Howard G. Seitz.
EIN: 137045257
Other changes: The grantmaker has moved from NY to NH.
Richard T. Watson is no longer a trustee.

1892
The Panjandrum Foundation
c/o C&S Wholesale Grocers, Inc.
7 Corporate Dr.
Keene, NH 03431-5042
Contact: William Hamlin, Treas.
E-mail: info@panjandrum.org; Main URL: http://www.panjandrum.org
Grants List: http://www.panjandrum.org/pages/past.htm

Established in 1999 in NH.
Donors: Richard B. Cohen; Janet L. Cohen.
Foundation type: Independent foundation.
Financial data (yr. ended 12/31/12): Assets, $3,723,526 (M); gifts received, $300,000; expenditures, $1,518,263; qualifying distributions, $1,510,332; giving activities include $1,508,475 for 4 grants (high: $800,000; low: $15,000).
Purpose and activities: The foundation provides funding to charitable organizations in New Hampshire that are committed to protecting the environment, ending human rights abuses, and supporting women's issues.
Fields of interest: Environment; Civil/human rights; Women.
Type of support: General/operating support; Land acquisition; Program development.
Limitations: Applications not accepted. Giving primarily in NH. No support for religious organizations, or for national health organizations, or organizations with less than 2 years of direct service experience. No grants to individuals, or for multi-year requests, capital requests, endowment drives, mass mailing appeals, sponsorship requests, scholarships, travel expenses or deficit reduction; no loans.
Application information: Unsolicited requests for funds not accepted.
Board meeting date(s): Late spring, late fall
Trustees: Janet L. Cohen; Jill R. Cohen; Perry L. Cohen; Rachel F. Cohen; Richard B. Cohen.
EIN: 036069606

1893
The Penates Foundation
1 Liberty Ln. E., Ste. 100
Hampton, NH 03842-1809 **(603) 926-2369**
Contact: Michele M. Cogan, V.P.

Established in 1984 in NH.
Donors: Paul M. Montrone; Sandra G. Montrone; Prestolite Wire Corp.; Latona Associates Inc.; Chatam, Inc.; Winthrop, Inc.; The Oxford League, Inc.; Fisher Scientific.
Foundation type: Independent foundation.
Financial data (yr. ended 08/31/12): Assets, $11,636,110 (M); gifts received, $24,000; expenditures, $2,011,611; qualifying distributions, $1,904,271; giving activities include $1,865,802 for 104 grants (high: $278,000; low: $100).
Purpose and activities: Giving primarily for the arts, education, medical research, and human services.
Fields of interest: Performing arts centers; Performing arts, opera; Arts; Higher education; Business school/education; Education; Human services; Residential/custodial care, hospices; Christian agencies & churches.
Type of support: Continuing support; Annual campaigns; Capital campaigns; Building/renovation; Land acquisition; Emergency funds; Scholarship funds.
Limitations: Giving primarily in MA, NH, and NY. No grants to individuals.
Application information: Application form not required.
Initial approach: Letter
Copies of proposal: 1
Deadline(s): None
Officers and Directors:* Sandra G. Montrone,* Pres.; Michele M. Cogan,* V.P. and Secy.-Treas.; **Kevin Clark**; **Anthony DiNovi**; Matthew Friel; Angelo Montrone; Jerome Montrone; Paul M. Montrone; **Fred Seigel**.
EIN: 222536075
Other changes: Theodore Kurz and Paul Meister are no longer directors.

1894
The Allan B. & Frances M. Roby Charitable Trust
7 Bliss Ln.
Lyme, NH 03768-3809 (603) 795-2080

Established in 1997 in NH.
Donors: Allan B Roby; Roy Van Vleck; David M. Roby.
Foundation type: Independent foundation.
Financial data (yr. ended 06/30/13): Assets, $3,014,953 (M); expenditures, $304,161; qualifying distributions, $285,706; giving activities include $282,430 for 31 grants (high: $100,100; low: $30).
Fields of interest: Higher education; Law school/education; Environment, natural resources.
Limitations: Applications accepted. Giving primarily in New England, with emphasis on NH and MA. No grants to individuals.
Application information: Application form required.
Initial approach: Letter
Deadline(s): None
Trustees: Barbara Roby; David M. Roby.
EIN: 026106324
Other changes: The grantmaker no longer lists a primary contact.

1895
Marion C. Smyth Trust
1001 Elm St.
Manchester, NH 03101-1828 (603) 623-3420
Contact: Charles S. Goodwin, Tr.

Established in 1946 in NH.
Donor: Marion C. Smyth†.
Foundation type: Independent foundation.
Financial data (yr. ended 12/31/12): Assets, $4,244,573 (M); expenditures, $355,192; qualifying distributions, $316,687; giving activities include $292,200 for 54 grants (high: $44,600; low: $750).
Purpose and activities: The purpose of the trust is to establish and maintain the Frederick Smyth Institute of Music, and to provide funding for musical education, including scholarships, in the city of Manchester, New Hampshire for the cultural benefit of its citizens and to expand their knowledge of the field of music.
Fields of interest: Performing arts, music; Performing arts, orchestras; Performing arts, opera; Arts; Higher education.
Type of support: Continuing support; Equipment; Scholarship funds.
Limitations: Applications accepted. Giving primarily in NH.
Application information: Application form required for student scholarships.
Initial approach: Letter
Copies of proposal: 1
***Deadline(s):* June 1**
Board meeting date(s): As required
Trustees: David H. Bellman; Charles S. Goodwin; Joseph E. Sheehan.
Number of staff: 1 part-time support.
EIN: 026005793

1896
Up The River Endeavors Inc.
90 N. Main St.
Concord, NH 03301-4915

Donors: Kenneth M. Jones; Charter Charitable Foundation.
Foundation type: Independent foundation.

Financial data (yr. ended 12/31/12): Assets, $58,119 (M); gifts received, $269,000; expenditures, $263,853; qualifying distributions, $198,776; giving activities include $179,150 for 10 grants (high: $28,000; low: $1,150).
Fields of interest: Education; Environment; Animals/wildlife.
Limitations: Applications not accepted. Giving primarily in CA, CO, Washington, DC, GA, NY, and WI.
Application information: Unsolicited requests for funds not accepted.
Officer: Steve Albrecht, Exec. Dir.
Directors: David J. Andrews; Mona Cadena; Kenneth M. Jones; Carol E. Koury; Carina Koury-Jones; Cincy Pearson; Amy Parish.
EIN: 272593681
Other changes: The grantmaker no longer lists a URL address.

1897
Gibson Woodbury Charitable Foundation

P.O. Box 406
North Conway, NH 03860-0406 (603) 356-5315
Contact: Mark Butterfield, Exec. Dir.
E-mail: gwcf@gibsonwoodburyfoundation.org; Main URL: http://www.gibsonwoodburyfoundation.org

Established in 2010 in NH.
Donor: Evelyn Woodbury‡.
Foundation type: Operating foundation.
Financial data (yr. ended 06/20/13): Assets, $4,910,772 (M); gifts received, $561; expenditures, $293,985; qualifying distributions, $225,219; giving activities include $212,960 for 34 grants (high: $20,000; low: $700).
Purpose and activities: Giving primarily to enhance the vitality and wellness of organizations and residents of Mount Washington Valley, New Hampshire.
Fields of interest: Performing arts; Arts; Higher education; Education; Medical research; Food banks; Housing/shelter; Human services.
Type of support: Scholarships—to individuals.
Limitations: Applications accepted. Giving primarily in the Mount Washington Valley in Carroll County, NH.
Application information: Application form available on foundation web site. Application form required.
Initial approach: Proposal
***Deadline(s):* May 15 and Nov. 15**
Officer and Trustees:* Mark Butterfield,* Exec. Dir.; Kenneth V. Cargill, Esq.
EIN: 272986345

NEW JERSEY

1898

Ahavat Haim Vachesed

P. O. Box 226
Deal, NJ **07723 (917) 608-5703**
Application address: c/o Rabbi Edmond Nahum, 126 Norwood Ave., Deal, NJ 07723

Established in 2006 in NY.
Donors: Ralph Tawill; David Sitt; Eddie Sitt; Mark Massry; Saul Tawil.
Foundation type: Public charity.
Financial data (yr. ended 06/30/12): Revenue, $181,089; assets, $132,346 (M); gifts received, $181,089; expenditures, $60,258; giving activities include $59,989 for grants.
Fields of interest: Jewish agencies & synagogues.
Limitations: Applications accepted. Giving primarily in NJ. No grants to individuals.
Application information:
Initial approach: Letter
Deadline(s): None
Directors: Eli Braha; Rabbi Edmond Nahum; David Sitt.
EIN: 205293527
Other changes: Ralph Tawil is no longer a member of the governing body.

1899

Alcatel-Lucent Foundation

(formerly Lucent Technologies Foundation)
600 Mountain Ave.
Murray Hill, NJ 07974-2008
Contact: Bishalakhi Ghosh, Exec. Dir.
E-mail: foundation@alcatel-lucent.com; E-mail for Bishalakhi Ghosh: bishalakhi.ghosh@alcatel-lucent.com; Main URL: http://www2.alcatel-lucent.com/foundation/index.php
ConnectEd on Facebook: https://www.facebook.com/ALFConnectEd
Facebook: http://www.facebook.com/AlcatelLucentFoundation
Flickr: https://www.flickr.com/photos/alcatel_lucent_foundation/

Established in 1996.
Donors: Lucent Technologies Inc.; Alcatel-Lucent.
Foundation type: Company-sponsored foundation.
Financial data (yr. ended 12/31/12): Assets, $3,554,752 (M); gifts received, $3,000,000; expenditures, $3,508,868; qualifying distributions, $3,498,868; giving activities include $3,343,300 for 22+ grants (high: $1,057,900).
Purpose and activities: The foundation supports programs designed to promote digital inclusion and sustainability with a focus on underserved communities that enable youth and young women to access education and life skills training.
Fields of interest: Elementary/secondary education; Vocational education; Higher education; Education, e-learning; Education; Employment, training; Disasters, preparedness/services; Youth development, adult & child programs; Big Brothers/Big Sisters; Girl scouts; Youth development, business; Youth development; Youth; Young adults, female; Economically disadvantaged.
Type of support: General/operating support; Continuing support; Program development; Employee volunteer services.
Limitations: Applications not accepted. Giving primarily in areas of company operations, with emphasis on CA, NJ, and NY; giving also to international and national organizations.
Application information: Unsolicited applications are not accepted. Projects must be submitted by employees and supported by senior management.
Board meeting date(s): Bi-annually
Officers and Trustees:* Janet G. Davidson,* Chair.; Barbara Landmann, Vice-Chair.; Sandra D. Motley, V.P.; Alex Yip, Secy. and Legal Counsel; Richard Campbell, Treas.; **Elisabeth Eude, Exec. Dir.**; Frederic Chapelard; Christine Diamente; Radwa Hafez; Marco Malfavon; William Reese; Theodore Sizer.
EIN: 223480423
Other changes: Elisabeth Eude has replaced Bishalakhi Ghosh as Exec. Dir.
George (Gee) Rittenhouse is no longer a director.
Bishalakhi Ghosh is no longer Exec. Dir.

1900

Rita Allen Foundation, Inc.

92 Nassau St., 3rd Fl.
Princeton, NJ 08542-4530 (609) 683-8010
Contact: Elizabeth G. Christopherson, C.E.O. and Pres.
FAX: (609) 683-8025; E-mail: info@ritaallen.org; Main URL: http://www.ritaallen.org
Blog: http://www.ritaallenfoundation.org/investing-in-innovation.htm
E-Newsletter: http://www.ritaallenfoundation.org/index.htm

Incorporated in 1953 in NY.
Donor: Rita Allen Cassel†.
Foundation type: Independent foundation.
Financial data (yr. ended 12/31/12): Assets, $147,522,548 (M); gifts received, $1,836; expenditures, $7,644,660; qualifying distributions, $7,131,007; giving activities include $5,823,826 for 101 grants (high: $250,000; low: $450), and $80,985 for 1 foundation-administered program.
Purpose and activities: The foundation invests in transformative ideas in their earliest stages to leverage their growth and promote breakthrough solutions to significant problems. The foundation's areas of active interest include investing in young leaders in the sciences and social innovation, promoting civil literacy, and building stronger communities. The foundation recognizes that it must be flexible enough to respond to unique challenges, ideas and projects that lie beyond its original program areas.
Fields of interest: Humanities; Arts; Higher education; Health care; Medical research, institute; Agriculture/food; Youth development; Civil/human rights, advocacy; Community/economic development; Jewish federated giving programs; Biology/life sciences; Children/youth; Children; Youth; Adults; Young adults; Minorities; Asians/Pacific Islanders; African Americans/Blacks; Hispanics/Latinos; Native Americans/American Indians; Women; Girls; Adults, women; Young adults, female; Men; Boys; Adults, men; Young adults, male; Economically disadvantaged.
Type of support: Continuing support; Management development/capacity building; Endowments; Emergency funds; Program development; Conferences/seminars; Seed money; Curriculum development; Fellowships; Scholarship funds; Research; Consulting services; Program evaluation.
Limitations: Applications not accepted. Giving on a national basis. No grants to individuals (except university research scientists), or for building funds.
Publications: Annual report; Financial statement; Grants list.
Application information: Unsolicited requests for funds not accepted.
Board meeting date(s): Quarterly and as required
Officers and Directors:* William F. Gadsden,* Chair.; Elizabeth G. Christopherson,* C.E.O. and Pres.; Henry H. Hitch,* Secy.-Treas.; Moore Gates, Jr., Dir. Emeritus; Aristides Georgantas, Dir. Emeritus; **Robert E. Campbell, Dir. Emeritus**; Jon Cummings; Robbert Dijkgraaf, Ph.D.; Landon Y. Jones; Hon. Thomas H. Kean; Sivan Nemovicher; Sam S.H. Wang, Ph. D.
Number of staff: 2 full-time professional; 1 full-time support; 1 part-time support.
EIN: 136116429
Other changes: Robert E. Campbell is now Dir. Emeritus.

1901

Allied Educational Foundation

82 N. Summit St.
Tenafly, NJ 07670-1016 (201) 569-8180
E-mail: info@AlliedEducationalFoundation.org; Main URL: http://alliededucationalfoundation.org/

Established about 1981.
Donors: New York Cardiac Ctr., Inc.; Allied Trades Council; Barton, Babcock & Blair.
Foundation type: Independent foundation.
Financial data (yr. ended 12/31/12): Assets, $6,495,247 (M); gifts received, $100,700; expenditures, $686,228; qualifying distributions, $414,528; giving activities include $300,091 for grants, and $400,680 for 4 foundation-administered programs.
Purpose and activities: Giving primarily in the form of educational seminars and training programs, provision of publications for educational training, and funds directly for education, study, and research.
Fields of interest: Education.
Limitations: Applications not accepted.
Application information: Unsolicited requests for funds not accepted.
Trustees: Benjamin Camadeco; James Crowley; Bertram Gelfand; Herbert Pobiner; Theodore Turitz.
EIN: 136202432
Other changes: George Barasch, Chair., is deceased.

1902

American Friends of Even Yisroel Charitable Foundation

25 Dakota St.
Passaic, NJ 07055-3331
***Contact:* Mitchell Lisker**

Established in 2000 in NY.
Donors: Edgar Billowitz; Ari Coopersmith; Chaim Friedman; Dobert Goodman; Edward Levy; Jacob Levy; Marvin Marmelstein; Jordan Most; Moshe Neurath; Aaron Stopper; Sobel Family Trust; Foundation Jewish Philanthropies of Buffalo; Eastern Union Funding; Stratford Ave. Trust; Agudath Israel of Long Island.
Foundation type: Independent foundation.
Financial data (yr. ended 12/31/12): Assets, $2,572 (M); gifts received, $255,128; expenditures, $259,636; qualifying distributions, $217,126; giving activities include $217,126 for 30 grants to individuals (high: $7,200; low: $7,200).
Fields of interest: Education; Jewish agencies & synagogues.

Type of support: Grants to individuals.
Limitations: Applications not accepted. Giving primarily in CA, MA, OK, and PA.
Application information: Unsolicited requests for funds not accepted.
Trustees: Mitchell Lisker; Solomon Sobel.
EIN: 137173269

1903
Thomas E. and Linda O. Baker Family Foundation
1000 Wychwood Rd.
Westfield, NJ 07090-2357
E-mail: info@bakerfamilyfoundation.org

Established in 1999 in NJ.
Donor: Thomas E. Baker.
Foundation type: Independent foundation.
Financial data (yr. ended 12/31/12): Assets, $1,696,547 (M); expenditures, $1,213,283; qualifying distributions, $1,197,320; giving activities include $1,065,000 for 5 grants (high: $500,000; low: $20,000), and $76,003 for grants to individuals.
Purpose and activities: Scholarships awarded for undergraduate education to individuals with financial need.
Fields of interest: Higher education.
Type of support: General/operating support; Scholarships—to individuals.
Limitations: Applications not accepted. Giving primarily in the NJ and NY area.
Application information: The foundation will no longer be accepting any new applications.
Trustees: Linda O. Baker; Thomas E. Baker.
Number of staff: 1 full-time professional.
EIN: 256611063
Other changes: At the close of 2012, the grantmaker paid grants of $1,141,003, a 362.8% increase over the 2011 disbursements, $246,558.

1904
Banbury Fund, Inc.
c/o Withumsmith & Brown
331 Newman Springs Rd., Ste. 125
Red Bank, NJ 07701-6765

Incorporated in 1946 in NY.
Donors: Marie H. Robertson†; Charles S. Robertson†.
Foundation type: Independent foundation.
Financial data (yr. ended 12/31/12): Assets, $22,786,164 (M); expenditures, $1,103,693; qualifying distributions, $854,421; giving activities include $642,825 for grants.
Purpose and activities: Primary areas of interest include higher and other education, health and medical research, the environment, and marine research and conservation programs.
Fields of interest: Higher education; Education; Environment; Health care; Medical research, institute; Cancer research; Human services; Marine science; Engineering/technology; Biology/life sciences; Science.
Type of support: General/operating support; Continuing support; Annual campaigns; Capital campaigns; Building/renovation; Equipment; Endowments; Debt reduction; Emergency funds; Seed money; Research.
Limitations: Applications not accepted. Giving primarily in CA and NY; funding also in CO, CT, FL, SC and VA. No grants to individuals.
Application information: Contributes only to pre-selected organizations.
Officers and Trustees:* Victoria Linnartz, Pres.; Diana McKibben, Secy.; Andrew McKibben,* Treas.; Katherine R. Ernst; Robert J. Ernst; Anne R. Meier; Walter C. Meier; Geoffrey S. Robertson; Julia Robertson; William S. Robertson.
Number of staff: 4 part-time professional.
EIN: 136062463
Other changes: Timothy Kemper is no longer Exec. Dir.

1905
C. R. Bard Foundation, Inc.
730 Central Ave.
Murray Hill, NJ 07974-1139
Contact: Linda Hrevnack, Mgr., Community Affairs and Contribs.
FAX: (908) 277-8098; **Main URL: http://www.crbard.com/Community_Outreach/C_R__Bard_Foundation,_Inc_.html**

Established in 1987 in NY.
Donor: C.R. Bard, Inc.
Foundation type: Company-sponsored foundation.
Financial data (yr. ended 12/31/12): Assets, $744,663 (M); gifts received, $2,548,000; expenditures, $2,558,565; qualifying distributions, $2,558,299; giving activities include $2,524,458 for 170 grants (high: $100,000; low: $360).
Purpose and activities: The foundation supports organizations involved with education, health, and human services. Special emphasis is directed toward programs designed to promote urology, oncology, vascular, and surgical medicine.
Fields of interest: Education; Health care; Medical specialties; Human services; United Ways and Federated Giving Programs.
Type of support: Employee matching gifts; General/operating support; Program development; Scholarship funds; Sponsorships.
Limitations: Applications accepted. Giving primarily in areas of company operations. No support for private foundations, political parties, fraternal, religious, or sectarian groups, or veterans' organizations. No grants to individuals, or for events that provide a non-charitable benefit to C.R. Bard, or capital campaigns.
Publications: Application guidelines.
Application information: Additional information may be requested at a later date. Site visits may also be encouraged and scheduled before grant awards are made. Application form required.
Initial approach: **Complete online application**
Copies of proposal: 2
Deadline(s): None
Board meeting date(s): Quarterly
Officers: Timothy M. Ring, Pres.; Scott T. Lowry, V.P. and Treas.; John H. Weiland, V.P.; Bronwen K. Kelly, Secy.
EIN: 222840708

1906
The George W. Bauer Family Foundation
616 W. 1st Ave.
Roselle, NJ 07203-1005 (908) 241-2424

Established in 1965 in NJ.
Donor: C.H. Winans Company.
Foundation type: Independent foundation.
Financial data (yr. ended 06/30/13): Assets, $7,662,984 (M); expenditures, $500,646; qualifying distributions, $373,000; giving activities include $373,000 for 20 grants (high: $98,000; low: $2,000).
Fields of interest: Hospitals (general); Health care; Health organizations, association; YM/YWCAs & YM/YWHAs; Foundations (community); Christian agencies & churches.
Limitations: Applications accepted. Giving primarily in NJ. No grants to individuals.
Application information: Application form required.
Initial approach: Letter
Deadline(s): Apr. 30
Board meeting date(s): May or June
Officer: Carol A. Romano, Secy.
Trustees: Betsy Bauer; Thomas B. Boak; John W. Fedor; **Nancy B. Howell.**
EIN: 226069622
Other changes: Robert J. Bauer is no longer a trustee.

1907
The Beer Family Foundation
131 Brayton St.
Englewood, NJ 07631-3101 (800) 937-6782

Established about 1965 in NJ.
Donors: Lovey G. Beer; Murray L. Beer.
Foundation type: Independent foundation.
Financial data (yr. ended 06/30/13): Assets, $585,102 (M); expenditures, $142,528; qualifying distributions, $136,000; giving activities include $130,750 for 48 grants (high: $90,000; low: $20).
Fields of interest: Medical care, rehabilitation; Breast cancer; Human services; Aging, centers/services; Jewish federated giving programs; Jewish agencies & synagogues; Aging.
Type of support: General/operating support; Continuing support; Capital campaigns; Building/renovation; Endowments.
Limitations: Applications accepted. Giving primarily in NJ. No grants to individuals.
Application information: Application form required.
Initial approach: Letter
***Deadline(s):* None**
Trustees: Ingrid Beer; Lovey G. Beer; Murray L. Beer.
Number of staff: 1 part-time professional.
EIN: 226073903

1908
The Russell Berrie Foundation
300 Frank W. Burr Blvd., Bldg. East, 7th Fl.
Teaneck, NJ 07666-6704 (201) 928-1880
Contact: Ruth Salzman, C. E. O
E-mail: inquiry@rbfdtn.org; Main URL: http://www.russellberriefoundation.org
E-Newsletter: http://www.russellberriefoundation.org/getinvolved-enewsletter.php

Established in 1985 in NJ.
Donor: Russell Berrie†.
Foundation type: Independent foundation.
Financial data (yr. ended 12/31/12): Assets, $215,018,834 (M); gifts received, $77,180; expenditures, $21,536,292; qualifying distributions, $20,617,146; giving activities include $18,359,047 for 118 grants (high: $5,160,000; low: $750), and $173,888 for 12 grants to individuals (high: $35,000; low: $5,000).
Purpose and activities: The foundation as created to express the values and passions of Russell Berrie through social investments in innovative ideas designed to: 1) Promote the continuity and enrichment of Jewish communal life; 2) Support advances in medicine focusing on diabetes and humanism in medicine; 3) Fostering the spirit of

religious understanding and pluralism; 4) Recognizing individuals who have made a significant difference to the lives of others; 5) Elevating the profession of sales; and 6) Raising the awareness of terrorism and promoting its prevention.
Fields of interest: Arts; Higher education; Hospitals (general); Health care, clinics/centers; Medical research; Human services; Science, research; Engineering/technology; Jewish agencies & synagogues; Religion, interfaith issues.
Type of support: General/operating support; Continuing support; Management development/capacity building; Emergency funds; Program development; Fellowships; Research; Matching/challenge support.
Limitations: Applications not accepted. Giving primarily in northern NJ, New York City, Israel, and Italy.
Application information: Unsolicited requests for funds not accepted.
Officers and Trustees:* Ruth Salzman, C.E.O. and Exec. Dir.; Angelica Berrie,* Pres.; Scott Berrie,* V.P.; Myron Rosner,* Secy.; Adam Hirsch, C.F.O.; Stephen Seiden,* Treas.; Ilan Kaufthal; Norman Seiden.
Number of staff: 8 full-time professional.
EIN: 222620908

1909
The Corella & Bertram F. Bonner Foundation, Inc.

10 Mercer St.
Princeton, NJ 08540-6808 (609) 924-6663
Contact: Robert Hackett, Pres.
FAX: (609) 683-4626; E-mail: info@bonner.org; Main URL: http://www.bonner.org
Bonner Network Blog: http://bonnernetwork.wordpress.com
Bonner Network Wiki: http://bonnernetwork.pbworks.com/
Facebook: https://www.facebook.com/groups/2204555306
LinkedIn: http://www.linkedin.com/groups?mostPopular=&gid=86257
Slideshare: http://www.slideshare.net/BonnerFoundation/slideshows
Twitter: http://twitter.com/bonnernetwork
YouTube: http://www.youtube.com/user/BonnerNetwork

Established in 1981 in NJ; reactivated in 1989.
Donors: Bertram F. Bonner†; Corella A. Bonner†.
Foundation type: Independent foundation.
Financial data (yr. ended 06/30/13): Assets, $40,080,407 (M); gifts received, $85; expenditures, $6,613,536; qualifying distributions, $5,719,490; giving activities include $5,610,494 for 51 grants (high: $2,500,000; low: $1,250), and $108,996 for foundation-administered programs.
Purpose and activities: Through sustained partnerships with colleges and congregations, the foundation seeks to improve the lives of individuals and communities by helping meet the basic needs of nutrition and educational opportunity. Support primarily for higher education institutions and local anti-poverty and anti-hunger organizations.
Fields of interest: Higher education; Education; Food services; Christian agencies & churches; Religion; Minorities.
Type of support: Continuing support.
Limitations: Applications not accepted. Giving primarily in NJ. No grants to individuals or for capital improvements, endowments, operating budgets, building funds, or renovations.
Publications: Informational brochure.
Application information: Unsolicited requests for funding not accepted. See foundation web site for further information.
Board meeting date(s): Mar., June, Sept., and Dec.
Officers and Trustees:* Kenneth F. Kunzman,* Chair.; Robert Hackett, Pres.; Ariane Hoy, V.P., Prog. and Resource Devel.; William Bush; Carol Clarke; Charles C. Goodfellow; Rev. Dr. John Kuykendall.
Number of staff: 1 full-time professional.
EIN: 222316452

1910
Mary Owen Borden Memorial Foundation

4 Blackpoint Horseshoe
Rumson, NJ 07760-1929 (732) 741-4645
Contact: Quincy A.S. McKean III, Exec. Dir.
FAX: (732) 741-2542; E-mail: qmckean@aol.com;
Main URL: http://fdnweb.org/borden

Incorporated in 1934 in NJ.
Donors: Bertram H. Borden†; Victory Memorial Park Foundation.
Foundation type: Independent foundation.
Financial data (yr. ended 12/31/12): Assets, $12,732,468 (M); expenditures, $796,582; qualifying distributions, $691,653; giving activities include $630,710 for 59 grants (high: $62,500; low: $1,000).
Purpose and activities: The foundation's special focus will be on programs in New Jersey's Mercer and Monmouth counties, addressing the needs of economically disadvantaged youth and their families. This will include health, family planning, education, counseling, child care, substance abuse, and delinquency. Other areas of interest include affordable housing, conservation and the environment, and the arts.
Fields of interest: Arts; Education, early childhood education; Child development, education; Education; Environment, natural resources; Environment; Reproductive health, family planning; Health care; Substance abuse, services; Mental health/crisis services; Health organizations, association; Alcoholism; Crime/violence prevention, youth; Housing/shelter, development; Human services; Children/youth, services; Child development, services; Family services; Women, centers/services; Homeless, human services; Women; Economically disadvantaged; Homeless.
Type of support: General/operating support; Continuing support; Capital campaigns; Building/renovation; Equipment; Program development; Seed money; Matching/challenge support.
Limitations: Applications accepted. Giving limited to Monmouth and Mercer counties, NJ. No grants for scholarships, fellowships, or multi-year grants.
Publications: Application guidelines; Annual report (including application guidelines).
Application information: The foundation only accepts applications from its current grantees. No applications from new applicants will be accepted. Application form required.
Initial approach: Proposal
Deadline(s): None
Board meeting date(s): June and Dec.
Officers: Linda B. McKean, Pres.; Jerri L. Morrison, V.P.; Julie B. Kennedy,* Secy.; Quincy A.S. McKean III, Exec. Dir.
Trustees: Paul McEvily; Vincent Myers.
Number of staff: 1 part-time professional.
EIN: 136137137

1911
The Nicholas J. and Anna K. Bouras Foundation, Inc.

25 De Forest Ave.
Summit, NJ 07901-2140 (908) 918-9400

Established in 1998 in NJ.
Donors: Nicholas J. Bouras; United Steel Deck, Inc.
Foundation type: Independent foundation.
Financial data (yr. ended 12/31/12): Assets, $48,763,565 (M); expenditures, $5,840,268; qualifying distributions, $5,407,344; giving activities include $5,259,051 for 51 grants (high: $1,386,751; low: $5,000).
Purpose and activities: Giving primarily to Greek Orthodox agencies and churches, and to human service organizations which support Greek people.
Fields of interest: Human services; Orthodox agencies & churches.
Limitations: Applications not accepted. Giving in the U.S., with emphasis on NJ and New York, NY. No grants to individuals.
Application information: Contributes only to pre-selected organizations.
Officer and Trustees:* Nicholas J. Bouras,* Pres.; William S. Crane; Andrew J. Stamelman.
EIN: 223591803

1912
The Brookdale Foundation

300 Frank W. Burr Blvd., No. 13
Teaneck, NJ **07666-6703**

Incorporated in 1950 in NY.
Donors: Henry L. Schwartz†; Ramapo Trust.
Foundation type: Independent foundation.
Financial data (yr. ended 06/30/13): Assets, $4,562,407 (M); gifts received, $46,082; expenditures, $174,295; qualifying distributions, $229,714; giving activities include $106,264 for 1 grant.
Fields of interest: Higher education.
Type of support: Program development; Conferences/seminars; Seed money; Research; Matching/challenge support.
Limitations: Applications not accepted. Giving in the U.S., with emphasis on CT, MD, and NY. No grants to individuals, or for operating budgets, continuing support, or annual campaigns; no loans, capital or building campaigns, or deficit financing.
Application information: Unsolicited requests for funds not accepted.
Officers and Directors:* Stephen L. Schwartz,* Pres.; Mary Ann Van Clief,* V.P.; Mary de la Cruz, Secy.; Manuel F. Billena, Treas.; Arthur Norman Field; Andrew M. Schreier; William S. Schreier.
Number of staff: 2 full-time professional; 2 part-time support.
EIN: 136076863

1913
The Brothers Ashkenazi Foundation, Inc.

759 Shrewsbury Ave.
Long Branch, NJ **07740-5027** (732) 574-9000
Contact: Ezra E. Ashkenazi, Tr.

Donors: Isaac Ashkenazi; Ezra E. Ashkenazi; Ronald Ashkenazi; David E. Ashkenazi.
Foundation type: Independent foundation.
Financial data (yr. ended 02/28/13): Assets, $8,611,333 (M); expenditures, $618,391; qualifying distributions, $605,943; giving activities include $605,943 for 1,059 grants (high: $400,000; low: $52).

Purpose and activities: Giving primarily to Jewish agencies, temples, and schools.
Fields of interest: Education; Jewish agencies & synagogues.
Application information: Application form not required.
Initial approach: Letter
Deadline(s): None
Trustees: Ezra E. Ashkenazi; Isaac Ashkenazi; Ronald Ashkenazi.
EIN: 223469592

1914
Fred J. Brotherton Charitable Foundation
(formerly Fred J. Brotherton Foundation, Inc.)
1141 Greenwood Lake Tpke., Ste. C-6
Ringwood, NJ 07456-1433 (973) 728-6100
Contact: Maribeth A. Ligus, Admin. Dir.
E-mail: brothertonfoundation@yahoo.com; Main URL: http://foundationcenter.org/grantmaker/brotherton/

Established in 1995.
Donor: Fred J. Brotherton‡.
Foundation type: Independent foundation.
Financial data (yr. ended 09/30/13): Assets, $14,151,379 (M); expenditures, $850,733; qualifying distributions, $691,029; giving activities include $651,255 for 38 grants (high: $50,000; low: $725).
Purpose and activities: The foundation's major areas of interest are: 1) Educational programs and/or institutions (primarily schools and colleges), with emphasis on, but not limited to, educational programs providing assistance to the needy or disabled; 2) Religion-based programs and/or institutions, with an emphasis on, but not limited to, providing assistance to the needy or disabled, or to benefit a local church in a capital program; 3) Historic Preservation programs and/or institutions (including societies); and 4) Medical and/or Scientific programs and/or their affiliated institutions.
Fields of interest: Historic preservation/historical societies; Education; Medical research; Human services; Children/youth, services; Science, research; Religion.
Type of support: Capital campaigns; Equipment; Endowments; Program development; Conferences/seminars; Seed money; Internship funds; Scholarship funds; Research; Matching/challenge support.
Limitations: Applications accepted. Giving primarily in NJ and NY. No support for environmental programs, or for legal aid programs, advocacy groups, senior citizens programs, soup kitchens or food banks, or for well-endowed institutions or non 501c(3) organizations. No grants to individuals, or for conferences, or for day care programs, documentaries, films or videos, loans, moving expenses, polls or surveys, or for deficit financing.
Publications: IRS Form 990 or 990-PF printed copy available upon request.
Application information: When an organization receives an invitation to submit a full grant proposal, then the full grant proposal guidelines will be provided.
Initial approach: Letter of Inquiry (2 to 3 pages)
Copies of proposal: 4
Deadline(s): None for letter of inquiry; June 1 and Dec. 1 for full grant proposals
Board meeting date(s): Feb. and Aug.
Final notification: Aug. (June 1 cycle); Feb. (Dec. 1 cycle)
Trustees: Wayne A. Brotherton; William P. Brotherton, M.D.
Board of Advisors: Emily Brotherton; John Carrick; Steve Doty; **Gary Jannarone**; Robert H. Neth, Jr.; William Rahal; **Nancy Shade**.
Number of staff: 1 part-time professional.
EIN: 650774706
Other changes: Glen Brothertonm and Tim Burklow are no longer members of the Board of Advisors.

1915
Emil Buehler Perpetual Trust
c/o Boyle & Co., PA
113 Johnson Ave.
Hackensack, NJ 07601-4825
Application address: c/o Gale Sykes, Grants Admin., Wells Fargo Private Bank, 190 River Rd., 2nd Fl., Summit, NJ 07901-1444; **Main URL: https://www.wellsfargo.com/privatefoundationgrants/buehler**

Established in 1984 in NJ.
Donor: Emil Buehler‡.
Foundation type: Independent foundation.
Financial data (yr. ended 11/30/12): Assets, $63,995,532 (M); expenditures, $6,192,886; qualifying distributions, $3,029,696; giving activities include $2,862,598 for 10 grants (high: $666,667; low: $26,500).
Purpose and activities: Giving limited to the research, development, improvement, and promotion of aviation science and technology.
Fields of interest: Museums (science/technology); Higher education; Space/aviation; Engineering/technology; Science.
Type of support: Building/renovation; Equipment; Internship funds; Research; Matching/challenge support.
Limitations: Applications accepted. Giving primarily in southern FL and NJ.
Publications: Informational brochure (including application guidelines).
Application information: See foundation website for complete application guidelines. Application form required.
Initial approach: Letter requesting application form
Copies of proposal: 1
***Deadline(s):* Feb. 1, May 1, Aug. 1, and Nov. 1**
***Board meeting date(s):* Mar., June., Sept., and Dec.**
Trustees: Robert D. Boyle; George Weaver; Wells Fargo Bank, N.A.
EIN: 226395303

1916
The Bunbury Company, Inc.
2 Railroad Pl.
Hopewell, NJ 08525-1818 (609) 333-8800
Contact: Samuel W. Lambert III, Treas.
FAX: (609) 333-8900;
E-mail: grants@bunburycompany.org; Main URL: http://www.bunburycompany.org

Incorporated in 1952 in NY.
Donor: Dean Mathey‡.
Foundation type: Independent foundation.
Financial data (yr. ended 12/31/12): Assets, $20,939,930 (M); expenditures, $1,286,122; qualifying distributions, $1,193,767; giving activities include $1,014,500 for 158 grants (high: $50,000; low: $100).
Purpose and activities: Giving primarily for education, environmental conservation, community building and social services, and the arts.
Fields of interest: Arts; Education; Environment; Youth development; Children/youth, services; Family services.
Type of support: Building/renovation; General/operating support; Capital campaigns; Program development; Matching/challenge support.
Limitations: Giving limited to NJ, with emphasis on Mercer County, as well as Burlington, Camden, Hunterdon, Middlesex, Monmouth, Ocean, and Somerset counties. No support for organizations outside of Mercer county with multiple chapters. No support for sporting activities, outings or events; fraternal or religious organizations, including affiliated schools; summer camps or day care facilities, unless part of a comprehensive aftercare program; nor for specific cultural performances. No grants to individuals, including scholarships and individual fellowships. No support for endowment campaigns, building funds, publications, or surveys.
Publications: Application guidelines; Annual report; Financial statement; Grants list.
Application information: Please follow submission requirements as outlined in guidelines. Application guidelines and forms available on foundation Web site. Faxed or e-mailed applications are not accepted. Application form required.
***Initial approach:* Use electronic application process on foundation web site**
Deadline(s): Varies; see foundation web site for current deadlines
Board meeting date(s): Jan., May, July, and Oct.
Final notification: Within 10 weeks of submission deadline
Officers and Directors:* Jamie Kyte Sapoch,* Pres.; Robert M. Olmsted,* V.P.; **Jeffrey Smith,* Secy.**; William H. Bruett,* Treas.; Elizabeth A. Bankowski; **Frederic Boswell**; William A. Gilbert; Samuel W. Lambert III; Edward J. Zuccaro.
Number of staff: 1 full-time professional; 8 part-time professional.
EIN: 136066172
Other changes: Jeffrey Smith has replaced Elizabeth Bankowski as Secy.

1917
Campbell Soup Foundation
(formerly Campbell Soup Fund)
1 Campbell Pl.
Camden, NJ 08103-1799 (856) 342-4800
Contact: Wendy Milanese, Secy.
E-mail: community_relations@campbellsoup.com; **Main URL: http://www.campbellsoupcompany.com/about-campbell/corporate-responsibility/campbell-soup-foundation**

Incorporated in 1953 in NJ.
Donor: Campbell Soup Co.
Foundation type: Company-sponsored foundation.
Financial data (yr. ended 06/30/13): Assets, $23,579,012 (M); gifts received, $2,000,000; expenditures, $1,831,469; qualifying distributions, $1,673,322; giving activities include $1,673,322 for 278 grants (high: $250,000; low: $100).
Purpose and activities: The foundation supports programs designed to promote community wellbeing; youth empowerment; and economic sustainability initiatives to develop healthy communities.
Fields of interest: Arts; Higher education; Education; Health care; Food services; Nutrition; Recreation, camps; Recreation; Boys & girls clubs; Youth development; Children/youth, services; Human services; Economic development; Community/economic development; United Ways and Federated Giving Programs.

Type of support: Capital campaigns; General/operating support; Building/renovation; Equipment; Program development; Employee volunteer services; Employee matching gifts; Employee-related scholarships; Matching/challenge support.
Limitations: Applications accepted. Giving primarily in areas of company operations in Bakersfield, Davis, Dixon, Emeryville, and Stockton, CA, Bloomfield and Norwalk, CT, Lakeland, FL, Downers Grove, IL, Maxton, NC, New Brunswick and South Plainfield, NJ, Napoleon and Willard, OH, Denver and Downingtown, PA, Paris, TX, Richmond, UT, Everett, WA, and Milwaukee, WI, with emphasis on Camden, NJ. No support for religious organizations not of direct benefit to the entire community, political organizations, or units of government. No grants to individuals (except for employee-related scholarships), or for events or sponsorships; no product donations.
Publications: Application guidelines.
Application information: Letters of intent are accepted during the first week of each grant cycle. Proposals may be requested at a later date. Support is limited to 1 contribution per organization during any given year. Priority is given to applicants who have established an ongoing relationship with the local Campbell or Pepperidge Farm operating facility. Application form not required.
Initial approach: Complete online letter of intent; contact local Campbell or Pepperidge Farm facility for organizations located outside of Camden, NJ
Copies of proposal: 1
Deadline(s): Jan. 1 to Apr. 30 and Sept. 1 to Nov. 30
Board meeting date(s): As required
Final notification: Up to 3 months
Officers and Trustees:* Dave Stangis,* Pres.; Wendy A. Milanese, Secy.; Ashok Madhaven, Treas.; Anthony P. DiSilvestro, Cont.; Mark Cacciatore; Richard Landers; Karen J. Lewis; Joe Spagnoletti; Steve White.
Number of staff: 1 part-time professional; 1 part-time support.
EIN: 216019196

1918
Capozzi Family Foundation
1523 Harding Hwy.
Newfield, NJ 08344-5227

Established in 1996 in DE and NJ.
Donors: Frank Capozzi; Edith Capozzi; Lucy Capozzi†; Mildred Capozzi; Capozzi Farms.
Foundation type: Independent foundation.
Financial data (yr. ended 06/30/13): Assets, $2,422,248 (M); expenditures, $53,647; qualifying distributions, $39,000; giving activities include $39,000 for 2 grants (high: $25,000; low: $14,000).
Fields of interest: Hospitals (general); Medical research, institute; Community/economic development; Religion.
Limitations: Applications not accepted. Giving primarily in NJ. No grants to individuals.
Application information: Unsolicited requests for funds not accepted.
Officers: Frank Capozzi, Pres.; Amelia Capozzi, V.P. and Secy.-Treas.
EIN: 223464762
Other changes: Edith Capozzi is no longer Secy.-Treas.

1919
Catholic Human Services Foundation
P.O. Box 673
Pittstown, NJ 08867-0673 (908) 730-6883
Contact: Maggie Hackett, Grant Prog. Off.
E-mail: chsfoundation@embargmail.com; Main URL: http://www.catholichumanservicesfoundation.org/

Foundation type: Independent foundation.
Financial data (yr. ended 12/31/12): Assets, $12,328,081 (M); expenditures, $897,838; qualifying distributions, $798,990; giving activities include $581,190 for 67 grants (high: $15,000; low: $1,100).
Purpose and activities: Giving primarily to Catholic organizations that provide health and human services, including hospitals, medical research facilities, innovative educational programs and specialized programs for the disabled. Grants are primarily for supplies and equipment.
Fields of interest: Education; Hospitals (general); Health organizations; Housing/shelter; Human services; Religion.
Limitations: Applications accepted. Giving primarily in DE, NJ, and PA. No support for supporting organization having a 509(a)(3) status, non-U.S. based organizations, or to the same organization or project on an ongoing basis. No grants to individuals, or for scholarships, endowments, fellowships, salaries, administrative expenses, matching funds, taxes or shipping and handling charges, demonstration projects or capital campaigns.
Publications: Application guidelines; Grants list.
Application information: Application form required.
Initial approach: Letter of inquiry on organization letterhead
Deadline(s): None
Board meeting date(s): Mar., June, Sept., and Dec.
Officers and Directors:* R. Kevin Hackett,* C.E.O. and Pres.; Maggie Hackett, V.P. and Secy.; Ray Burns; John DeGraaf; Darin Petro.
EIN: 262967521

1920
Dexter & Carol Earle Foundation
c/o Citrin Cooperman & Co., LLP
290 W. Mount Pleasant Ave.
Livingston, NJ **07039**

Established in 1989 in NY.
Donor: Dexter D. Earle.
Foundation type: Independent foundation.
Financial data (yr. ended 01/31/13): Assets, $166,067 (M); expenditures, $226,249; qualifying distributions, $220,450; giving activities include $220,450 for 17 grants (high: $100,000; low: $100).
Fields of interest: Elementary/secondary education; Higher education; Health organizations; Human services.
Limitations: Applications not accepted. Giving primarily in NJ; some funding also in CT and VT. No grants to individuals.
Application information: Contributes only to pre-selected organizations.
Trustees: Carol A. Earle; Dexter D. Earle.
Number of staff: None.
EIN: 133532028

1921
Eisai USA Foundation, Inc.
100 Tice Blvd.
Woodcliff Lake, NJ 07677-8404

Established in 2008 in NJ.
Donor: Easi, Inc.
Foundation type: Independent foundation.
Financial data (yr. ended 03/31/13): Assets, $6,063,098 (M); gifts received, $3,000,000; expenditures, $1,526,716; qualifying distributions, $1,526,550; giving activities include $1,526,550 for 46 grants (high: $920,000; low: $300).
Fields of interest: Higher education; Health organizations, association; Human services; American Red Cross.
Limitations: Applications not accepted. Giving in the U.S., with emphasis on MA and NJ.
Application information: Unsolicited requests for funds not accepted.
Officers: Lonnell Coats, Pres.; Hideo Dan, Exec. V.P. and Secy.; Kenneth Klauser, Treas.
EIN: 770711011

1922
The Eisenreich Family Foundation
c/o David Sussman, Avery Eisenreich
35 Journal Sq., Ste. 1103
Jersey City, NJ **07306-4007**

Established in 1997 in NY.
Donors: Avery Eisenreich; Joel Eisenreich; Toby Eisenreich; Mark Elliot Freund; David Sussman; Mizari Charity Fund; Commercial Security Mortgage Credit, Inc.; SCHI.
Foundation type: Independent foundation.
Financial data (yr. ended 12/31/12): Assets, $44,852,360 (M); gifts received, $48,500; expenditures, $2,616,417; qualifying distributions, $2,341,020; giving activities include $2,338,195 for 21 grants (high: $2,200,000; low: $330).
Purpose and activities: Funding primarily for Jewish agencies and temples; some support also for yeshivas.
Fields of interest: Elementary/secondary education; Jewish agencies & synagogues.
Limitations: Applications not accepted. Giving primarily in New York, NY. No grants to individuals.
Application information: Contributes only to pre-selected organizations.
Trustees: David Sussman; Toby Eisenreich.
EIN: 137118478

1923
The Elias Foundation
P.O. Box 1501, NJ2-130-03-31
Pennington, NJ 08534-1501 (914) 449-6782
FAX: (914) 449-6783;
E-mail: info@eliasfoundation.org; E-mail for questions regarding grantmaking: pwithers@eliasfoundation.org; Main URL: http://www.eliasfoundation.org
Grants List: http://www.eliasfoundation.org/recent_grants/grantees.htm

Established in 1999 in DE.
Donors: Jacqueline Mann; James E. Mann.
Foundation type: Independent foundation.
Financial data (yr. ended 12/31/12): Assets, $6,572,507 (M); gifts received, $1,077,713; expenditures, $824,316; qualifying distributions, $694,510; giving activities include $509,900 for 50 grants (high: $30,000; low: $100).

Purpose and activities: The foundation seeks to promote a more equitable and progressive society by supporting projects that mobilize community leadership and create networks for community change. The foundation values the pursuit of economic equity and social justice, self-directed change led by the experience and wisdom of local communities, community advocacy as a fundamental strategy for progressive action, and community leaders as catalysts, guiding and inspiring future generations.
Fields of interest: Civil/human rights, advocacy; Civil/human rights, minorities; Civil/human rights; Community/economic development; Economically disadvantaged.
Type of support: General/operating support; Management development/capacity building; Research.
Limitations: Applications accepted. Giving primarily in Westchester County, NY. No grants to individuals.
Publications: Application guidelines; Grants list.
Application information: Full proposals will be accepted only following approval of Letter of Intent. Unsolicited full proposals will not be accepted. Guidelines available on foundation Web site.
Initial approach: Letter of Intent
Deadline(s): None
Officers: Jacqueline Mann, Pres.; Alison Mann, V.P.; Anastasia Mann, V.P.; James E. Mann, Secy.; Eldar Shafir, Treas.
EIN: 134092287

1924
Environmental Endowment for New Jersey, Inc.
P.O. Box 3446
Trenton, NJ 08619-0446 (609) 584-1593
Contact: Joan Burkholtz, Secy.
FAX: (609) 584-5341; E-mail: info@eenj.org; Main URL: http://www.eenj.org/
Grants List: http://www.eenj.org/home/grant-list

Established in 1991 in NJ.
Foundation type: Independent foundation.
Financial data (yr. ended 04/30/13): Assets, $5,752,802 (M); expenditures, $331,478; qualifying distributions, $246,386; giving activities include $225,000 for 16 grants (high: $20,000; low: $5,000).
Purpose and activities: The endowment distributes funds from settlements of lawsuits brought to enforce compliance with the federal Clean Water Act. The projects funded must comply with the Court Orders entered in those cases and must have a clear and direct linkage to the waters impacted by the violations underlying the Clean Water Act enforcement cases.
Fields of interest: Environment.
Type of support: Program development; Seed money.
Limitations: Applications accepted. Giving primarily in NJ. No grants to individuals, endowments, or for general operating or capital expenditures.
Application information: Application guidelines available on foundation's web site. Application form required.
Initial approach: Proposal
Copies of proposal: 9
Deadline(s): Dec. 15
Officers and Trustees:* James F. Hall,* Pres.; Cindy Zipf,* V.P.; Joan Burkholtz, Secy.; Ronald Sprague,* Treas.; Sharon Finlayson; Nancy Hedinger; Dena Mottola Jaborska; Eric Stiles.
EIN: 223107878

1925
The Charles Evans Foundation
116 Village Blvd., Ste. 200
Princeton, NJ 08540-5700 (609) 951-2208

Established in 1988 in NY as successor to the Charles Evans Foundation, Inc.
Donor: Charles Evans†.
Foundation type: Independent foundation.
Financial data (yr. ended 12/31/12): Assets, $3,523,295 (M); gifts received, $4,389,089; expenditures, $17,136,653; qualifying distributions, $16,938,559; giving activities include $16,735,810 for 185 grants (high: $1,757,690; low: $500).
Fields of interest: Media, film/video; Education; Health organizations, association; Prostate cancer; Alzheimer's disease; Legal services; Legal services, public interest law; Human services; Jewish agencies & synagogues.
Limitations: Applications not accepted. Giving primarily in New York, NY. No grants to individuals.
Application information: Contributes only to pre-selected organizations.
Officer and Trustees:* Linda J. Munson,* Pres.; Henry M. Buhl; Bonnie L. Pfeifer Evans; Charles Evans, Jr.; Joel M. Pashcow; Alice Shure.
EIN: 136914974
Other changes: At the close of 2012, the grantmaker paid grants of $16,735,810, a 66.1% increase over the 2011 disbursements, $10,075,941.

1926
Ezra Trust Foundation
2 Industrial Way West
Eatontown, NJ **07724**
Contact: Ezra Beyman, Tr.; Debbie Beyman, Tr.

Established in NY.
Donors: Ezra Beyman; Debbie Beyman.
Foundation type: Independent foundation.
Financial data (yr. ended 12/31/12): Assets, $0 (M); expenditures, $0; qualifying distributions, $0.
Purpose and activities: Giving primarily to Jewish agencies, temples, and schools.
Fields of interest: Jewish federated giving programs; Jewish agencies & synagogues.
Limitations: Applications accepted. Giving primarily in Brooklyn, Monsey, and New York, NY.
Application information: Application form required.
Initial approach: Proposal
Deadline(s): None
Trustees: Debbie Beyman; Ezra Beyman; Joseph Seidenberg.
EIN: 206557217
Other changes: The grantmaker no longer lists a phone.

1927
The Fairbanks Family Foundation
319 Lenox Ave.
Westfield, NJ 07090-2137 **(908) 789-7310**
Contact: Steven J. Giacona

Established in 2000 in FL.
Donors: Richard M. Fairbanks III; Shannon A. Fairbanks; Fairbanks Charitable Lead Unitrust.
Foundation type: Independent foundation.
Financial data (yr. ended 12/31/12): Assets, $2,841,853 (M); expenditures, $1,210,345; qualifying distributions, $1,139,235; giving activities include $1,139,235 for 13+ grants (high: $700,000).
Fields of interest: Arts; Education; Human services; International affairs, goodwill promotion.
Limitations: Giving primarily in Washington, DC.
Application information:
Initial approach: Letter or proposal (1-2 pages)
Deadline(s): None
Trustees: Jonathan B. Fairbanks; Richard M. Fairbanks III; Shannon A. Fairbanks; Woods A. Fairbanks.
EIN: 582583288

1928
Feldstein Medical Foundation, Inc.
c/o SMF
855 Valley Rd.
Clifton, NJ 07013-2441
E-mail: questions@feldsteinmedicalfoundation.org; Main URL: http://www.feldsteinmedicalfoundation.org
Grants List: http://www.feldsteinmedicalfoundation.org/PriorFunding.html

Established in 2007 in NJ.
Donors: Creston Electronics, Inc.; George Feldstein.
Foundation type: Independent foundation.
Financial data (yr. ended 05/31/13): Assets, $5,535,029 (M); expenditures, $280,268; qualifying distributions, $240,826; giving activities include $239,592 for 4 grants (high: $60,000; low: $59,592).
Purpose and activities: Giving primarily to fill a void in the funding of medical research involving new areas of research and smaller projects, especially basic science, translation and implementation studies, early clinical research and education.
Fields of interest: Medical school/education; Medical research; Science.
Type of support: Research; Grants to individuals.
Limitations: Applications not accepted. Giving primarily in NJ and NY.
Application information: Unsolicited requests for funds not accepted.
Directors: Anne Baretz; Daniel Feldstein; David Feldstein; Wendy King.
EIN: 260349769

1929
Fenwick Foundation
(formerly Phoenix Family Foundation)
P.O. Box 1501, NJ-2-130-03-31
Pennington, NJ 08534-1501

Established in 1999 in NC.
Donors: Anne Phoenix; Anne and Julius Phoenix Charitable Trust; Anne and Julius Phoenix Charitable Lead Unitrust; Anne and Julius Phoenix Charitable Lead Unitrust No. 2.
Foundation type: Independent foundation.
Financial data (yr. ended 04/30/13): Assets, $6,128,867 (M); gifts received, $165,679; expenditures, $739,937; qualifying distributions, $709,504; giving activities include $508,015 for 97 grants (high: $25,000; low: $300).
Purpose and activities: Giving primarily for the arts, education, and children, youth, and social services.
Fields of interest: Arts; Education; Human services; Children/youth, services.
Limitations: Applications not accepted. Giving primarily in CA and NC. No grants to individuals.
Application information: Contributes only to pre-selected organizations.
Officers: Frank L. Phoenix, Pres.; James E. Phoenix, Secy.; J. Stuart Phoenix, Treas.

Trustees: Joy Phoenix; Kaola Phoenix; Tricia Phoenix.
EIN: 562150323

1930
Focus Autism, Inc.
776 Mountain Blvd., Ste. 202
Watchung, NJ 07069-6269
E-mail: info@focusautisminc.org; Main URL: http://www.focusautisminc.org/
Facebook: https://www.facebook.com/focusautisminc
Twitter: https://twitter.com/FocusAutismInc
YouTube: http://www.youtube.com/watch?v=n8MnzXv3E8E

Established in NJ.
Donors: Barry Segal; Bas Properties, LLC.
Foundation type: Independent foundation.
Financial data (yr. ended 12/31/12): Assets, $7,053,404 (M); gifts received, $2,836,421; expenditures, $1,062,480; qualifying distributions, $738,100; giving activities include $738,100 for grants.
Purpose and activities: The foundation is dedicated to providing information to the public that exposes the cause or causes of the autism epidemic and the rise of chronic illnesses in general, focusing specifically on the role of vaccinations.
Fields of interest: Autism; Medical research, institute; Autism research.
Limitations: Applications not accepted.
Application information: Unsolicited requests for funds not accepted.
Officers and Directors:* Barry Segal, Pres.; Martin Segal,* V.P.; Richard Segal,* Secy.; **Tracey Dupree, Exec. Dir.**; Lisa Green; Brian Hooker; **David Lewis, Ph.D.**; Dolly Segal.
EIN: 273400299

1931
Fortune Education Foundation, Inc.
20 Carbon Pl.
Jersey City, NJ 07305-1125

Donors: Norman Ng; Fortune Metal Group Inc.
Foundation type: Independent foundation.
Financial data (yr. ended 12/31/12): Assets, $880,187 (M); gifts received, $600,000; expenditures, $763,923; qualifying distributions, $757,000; giving activities include $575,000 for 1 grant, and $182,000 for 10 grants to individuals (high: $40,000; low: $6,000).
Fields of interest: Higher education; Hospitals (general).
Limitations: Applications not accepted. Giving primarily in MA.
Application information: Contributes only to pre-selected organizations.
Directors: Chuck Man Ng; John Ng; Norman Ng; Frances Wong.
EIN: 261564290

1932
The Fournier Family Foundation
c/o Pennant Capital Mgmt., LLC
1 DeForest Ave., No. 200
Summit, NJ **07901-2188**

Established in 2004 in NJ.
Donor: Alan P. Fournier.
Foundation type: Independent foundation.
Financial data (yr. ended 12/31/12): Assets, $9,442,566 (M); gifts received, $3,513,029; expenditures, $3,064,482; qualifying distributions, $3,053,655; giving activities include $3,053,655 for 33 grants (high: $1,052,000; low: $250).
Fields of interest: Education; Health organizations, association; Human services.
Limitations: Applications not accepted. Giving primarily in CA, MA, MI, NJ, and NY. No grants to individuals.
Application information: Contributes only to pre-selected organizations.
Officers: Alan P. Fournier, Pres.; H. Norman Bott, V.P.; Jennifer L. Fournier, Secy.-Treas.
EIN: 202015176

1933
Albert and Janice Gamper Foundation
c/o Albert Gamper
475 Holland Rd.
Far Hills, NJ 07931-2642

Established in 2000 in NJ.
Donors: Albert Gamper; Janice Gamper.
Foundation type: Independent foundation.
Financial data (yr. ended 12/31/12): Assets, $565,550 (M); expenditures, $202,928; qualifying distributions, $200,000; giving activities include $200,000 for 1 grant.
Fields of interest: Media, television; Performing arts centers; Higher education, university.
Type of support: General/operating support.
Limitations: Applications not accepted. Giving primarily in NJ. No grants to individuals.
Application information: Unsolicited requests for funds not accepted.
Trustees: Albert R. Gamper, Jr.; Christopher Gamper; Janice Gamper; Jennifer Gamper Meenan.
EIN: 223770735
Other changes: The grantmaker has moved from DE to NJ.

1934
Gibson Family Foundation
3 Royal Oak Dr.
Far Hills, NJ 07931-2569

Established in 2008 in NY.
Donor: Peter Gibson.
Foundation type: Independent foundation.
Financial data (yr. ended 06/30/13): Assets, $73,753 (M); gifts received, $535,064; expenditures, $467,958; qualifying distributions, $457,400; giving activities include $457,400 for 7 grants (high: $150,000; low: $1,000).
Fields of interest: Higher education; Boys & girls clubs; Human services.
Type of support: General/operating support.
Limitations: Applications not accepted. Giving primarily in NJ.
Application information: Unsolicited requests for funds not accepted.
Directors: Dana Gibson; Peter Gibson.
EIN: 261316921
Other changes: The grantmaker has moved from NY to NJ.

1935
Grace Charity Foundation Inc.
11 Edgewood Terr.
Randolph, NJ 07869-2821
E-mail: **jinsoo.kim@graceCfoundation.org**; Main URL: http://www.gracecfoundation.org/

Established in 2006 in NJ.
Foundation type: Independent foundation.
Financial data (yr. ended 12/31/12): Assets, $5,454,719 (M); expenditures, $281,218; qualifying distributions, $230,782; giving activities include $218,042 for 30 grants (high: $53,587; low: $500).
Fields of interest: Scholarships/financial aid; Education.
Limitations: Applications not accepted. Giving primarily in NJ and VA. No grants to individuals.
Application information: Contributes only to pre-selected organizations.
Directors: Jinsoo Kim; Seong Kim; Stephen Kim.
EIN: 208080868

1936
Harbourton Foundation
47 Hulfish St., Ste. 305
Princeton, NJ 08542-3706
Contact: Amy H. Regan, V.P.

Established in 1982 in NJ.
Donor: James S. Regan.
Foundation type: Independent foundation.
Financial data (yr. ended 06/30/13): Assets, $21,639,458 (M); expenditures, $690,188; qualifying distributions, $669,142; giving activities include $491,460 for 31 grants (high: $100,000; low: $1,000).
Purpose and activities: Giving primarily for educational organizations, an international human rights organization, and children and youth services.
Fields of interest: Arts; Education, association; Environment, natural resources; Health organizations; Human services; Children/youth, services; Homeless, human services; International human rights.
Type of support: General/operating support; Capital campaigns; Program development; Technical assistance.
Limitations: Applications not accepted. Giving primarily in NJ, NY and Washington D.C. No grants to individuals.
Application information: Contributes only to pre-selected organizations.
Officers: Amy H. Regan, Pres.; Catherine H. Regan Lawliss, V.P. and Secy.; James S. Regan III, V.P. and Treas.; James S. Regan, V.P.; Patrick H. Regan, V.P.
EIN: 222436112
Other changes: Amy H. Regan is now Pres. James S. Regan, III is now V.P. and Treas. Catherine H. Regan Lawliss is now V.P. and Secy. Steven Smotrich is no longer a V.P. Patrick H. Regan is now a V.P.

1937
Hawthorne Charitable Foundation
c/o Essex Equity
70 S. Orange Ave., Ste. 105
Livingston, NJ 07039-4916 **(908) 988-1090**
***FAX:* (888) 253-4969;**
E-mail: Fax@EssexEquity.com; Main URL: http://hawthornecharitablefoundation.org/

Donor: Basil Maher.

Foundation type: Independent foundation.
Financial data (yr. ended 12/31/12): Assets, $9,291,092 (M); expenditures, $704,604; qualifying distributions, $697,614; giving activities include $697,614 for 4 grants (high: $470,000; low: $25,000).
Fields of interest: Arts; Youth development; Human services.
Limitations: Applications not accepted. Giving primarily in NJ.
Application information: Unsolicited requests for funds not accepted.
Officers and Directors:* Basil Maher,* Chair. and Treas.; Miriam Duffy Maher,* Pres.; Scott Schley,* Secy. and Genl. Counsel.
EIN: 271447633

1938
S. C. Holman Foundation, Inc.
Pennsauken, NJ

The foundation terminated in 2011 and transferred its assets to The Community Foundation of South Jersey.

1939
Richard H. Holzer Memorial Foundation
c/o Chick Master
25 Rockwood Pl., Ste. 335
Englewood, NJ 07631-4959
Contact: Vivian Holzer, Pres.

Established in 1969 in NJ.
Donor: Erich Holzer‡.
Foundation type: Independent foundation.
Financial data (yr. ended 12/31/12): Assets, $6,928,958 (M); expenditures, $448,066; qualifying distributions, $366,000; giving activities include $366,000 for grants.
Purpose and activities: Giving primarily for the arts.
Fields of interest: Performing arts; Performing arts, music; Arts; Higher education; Jewish agencies & synagogues.
Type of support: Continuing support; Annual campaigns; Endowments.
Limitations: Giving primarily in northern NJ.
Application information: Application form not required.
Initial approach: Letter
Deadline(s): None
Board meeting date(s): Biannually
Officers and Directors:* Vivian Holzer,* Pres.; Robert Holzer,* V.P. and Treas.; **Robin Greenbaum, Secy.**; Eva Holzer, Mgr.
Number of staff: 2 part-time professional.
EIN: 237014880
Other changes: Robin Greenbaum has replaced Wally Dietl as Secy.

1940
Horizon Charitable Foundation, Inc.
(doing business as The Horizon Foundation for New Jersey)
3 Penn Plz. E., PP-M2H
Newark, NJ 07105-2258
Contact: Michele L. Berry, Grants Coord.
E-mail: foundation_info@horizonblue.com;
Additional contact: Filomena Machleder, Prog. Off., tel.: (973) 466-8945, e-mail: filomena_machleder@horizonblue.com; Main URL: http://www.horizon-bcbsnj.com/foundation
Healthy U on Facebook: http://www.facebook.com/pages/Healthy-U/109310708427
Healthy U Video: http://www.horizon-bcbsnj.com/foundation/healthyu/Video.html?WT.svl=leftnav

Established in 2003 in NJ.
Donors: Horizon Healthcare Services, Inc.; Parners Investing in Nursing's Future.
Foundation type: Company-sponsored foundation.
Financial data (yr. ended 12/31/12): Assets, $54,029,798 (M); gifts received, $49,000; expenditures, $5,630,937; qualifying distributions, $4,937,763; giving activities include $4,737,030 for 117 grants (high: $455,158; low: $7,500), and $200,733 for employee matching gifts.
Purpose and activities: The foundation supports programs designed to promote health, well-being, and quality of life in New Jersey communities. Special emphasis is directed toward health prevention, education, and program support for chronic diseases; and building vibrant communities through arts and cultural programs.
Fields of interest: Arts, cultural/ethnic awareness; Arts education; Performing arts; Arts; Education; Health care, information services; Health care, clinics/centers; Public health; Public health, obesity; Public health, physical fitness; Health care; Mental health, depression; Mental health/crisis services; Cancer; Heart & circulatory diseases; Diabetes; Nutrition; YM/YWCAs & YM/YWHAs; Children, services; Children; Aging.
Type of support: General/operating support; Continuing support; Program development; Curriculum development; Research; Technical assistance; Employee volunteer services; Sponsorships; Employee matching gifts.
Limitations: Applications accepted. Giving limited to areas of company operations in NJ. No support for hospitals or hospital foundations or political organizations or candidates. No grants to individuals, or for capital campaigns, endowments, or political causes or campaigns.
Publications: Application guidelines; Program policy statement.
Application information: General operating support is only available for art projects. Support is limited to 1 contribution per organization during any given year. Multi-year funding is not automatic. Organizations receiving support are asked to submit a final report. Application form required.
Initial approach: Complete online application form
Copies of proposal: 1
***Deadline(s):* Jan. 8, Apr. 2, July 16, and Oct. 8**
***Board meeting date(s):* Mar. 18, June 10, Sept. 23, and Dec. 16**
Final notification: 90 days
Officers and Directors:* Robert A. Marino,* Pres.; Kevin P. Conlin, V.P.; Linda A. Willet, Secy.; David R. Huber, Treas.; Jonathan R. Pearson, Exec. Dir.
Number of staff: None.
EIN: 200252405
Other changes: Filomena Machleder is now Prog. Off.

1941
The Horner Foundation
c/o Mercadien, PC
P.O. Box 7648
Princeton, NJ 08543-7648
E-mail: HornerEd@gmail.com; Main URL: http://thehornerfoundation.org

Established in 2007 in NJ.
Foundation type: Independent foundation.
Financial data (yr. ended 12/31/12): Assets, $6,298,099 (M); gifts received, $2,576; expenditures, $442,957; qualifying distributions, $354,763; giving activities include $354,763 for 22 grants (high: $63,460; low: $625).
Purpose and activities: Giving primarily for health care and education for youth, with a particular focus on at-risk or vulnerable youth.
Fields of interest: Education; Health care; Youth development.
Limitations: Applications accepted. Giving primarily in southern NJ; Philadelphia, PA; Salt Lake City, UT; Victoria, British Columbia; and central England. No grants to individuals.
Application information: See foundation web site for application information and guidelines.
Officers and Trustees:* **Ann Marie Horner,* Chair.; Tracy Cullen, Exec. Dir.; Carolyn Horner**; Kathryn Horner; Terry Horner; Meghann Horner-Smith; Damon Levy.
EIN: 260697610
Other changes: Jay Cullen is no longer a trustee. Ann Marie Horner is now Chair.

1942
Hudson City Savings Charitable Foundation
(formerly Sound Federal Savings and Loan Association Charitable Foundation)
80 W. Century Rd.
Paramus, NJ 07652-1405 (201) 967-1900
***Contact:* Lisa A. Roberts, Treas.**

Established in 1998 in DE.
Donor: Hudson City Savings Bank.
Foundation type: Company-sponsored foundation.
Financial data (yr. ended 12/31/12): Assets, $2,331,021 (M); expenditures, $193,426; qualifying distributions, $192,000; giving activities include $192,000 for 53 grants (high: $11,000; low: $2,000).
Purpose and activities: The foundation supports organizations involved with arts and culture, education, health, hunger, housing, human services, and community development.
Fields of interest: Health care; Housing/shelter; Human services.
Type of support: General/operating support; Capital campaigns; Building/renovation; Program development; Scholarship funds.
Limitations: Applications accepted. Giving limited to areas of company operations in Fairfield County, CT, NJ, and Rockland and Westchester counties, NY. No grants to individuals.
Application information: Application form not required.
***Initial approach:* Letter**
Deadline(s): None
Officers and Directors:* Ronald E. Hermance,* Pres.; Denis J. Salamane,* Secy.; **Lisa A. Roberts, Treas.**; Donald H. Herthaus.
EIN: 134046178

1943
Hummingbird Foundation, Inc.
c/o David R. Hummel
120 Partree Rd.
Cherry Hill, NJ 08003-2112

Established in 2005 in NJ.
Donor: David R. Hummel.
Foundation type: Independent foundation.
Financial data (yr. ended 02/28/13): Assets, $10,386,441 (M); gifts received, $588,544;

expenditures, $504,717; qualifying distributions, $460,000; giving activities include $460,000 for 8 grants (high: $106,000; low: $10,000).
Fields of interest: Arts; Hospitals (general); Arthritis; Medical research, institute; Food banks; Human services; Children, services.
Type of support: Research.
Limitations: Applications not accepted. Giving primarily in NJ and PA.
Application information: Contributes only to pre-selected organizations.
Officers: David R. Hummel, Pres.; Jane Hummel, V.P.
Trustees: John Blasi; Chad Hummel; **Todd Hummel**; Richard Vestal.
EIN: 593797192

1944
The Hyde and Watson Foundation

31-F Mountain Blvd.
Warren, NJ 07059-5617 (908) 753-3700
FAX: (908) 753-0004;
E-mail: info@hydeandwatson.org; **Main URL: http://fdnweb.org/hydeandwatson**
Grants List: http://fdnweb.org/hydeandwatson/grant-summary/

The Lillia Babbitt Hyde Foundation incorporated in 1924 in NY; The John Jay and Eliza Jane Watson Foundation incorporated in 1949; consolidation of two foundations into Hyde and Watson Foundation in 1983.
Donors: Lillia Babbitt Hyde†; Eliza Jane Watson†.
Foundation type: Independent foundation.
Financial data (yr. ended 12/31/13): Assets, $109,543,399 (M); expenditures, $5,849,375; qualifying distributions, $5,345,577; giving activities include $4,585,500 for 438 grants (high: $125,000; low: $3,000).
Purpose and activities: Support for capital projects such as hard costs related to construction or purchase of new facilities, building renovations and improvements, purchase of capital equipment and furnishings, one-time capital needs, support to limited medical research. Broad fields include health, education, religion, social services, arts, and humanities.
Fields of interest: Performing arts; Humanities; Arts; Education, early childhood education; Child development, education; Elementary school/education; Secondary school/education; Medical school/education; Education; Environment, natural resources; Environment; Hospitals (general); Medical care, rehabilitation; Health care; Substance abuse, services; Mental health/crisis services; Health organizations, association; Cancer; Human services; Children/youth, services; Child development, services; Family services; Aging, centers/services; Minorities/immigrants, centers/services; Homeless, human services; Religion; Infants/toddlers; Children/youth; Children; Youth; Adults; Young adults; Disabilities, people with; Physically disabled; Blind/visually impaired; Deaf/hearing impaired; Mentally disabled; Minorities; African Americans/Blacks; Hispanics/Latinos; Women; Girls; Men; Boys; Substance abusers; AIDS, people with; Crime/abuse victims; Immigrants/refugees; Economically disadvantaged; Homeless; LGBTQ.
Type of support: Capital campaigns; Building/renovation; Equipment; Land acquisition; Debt reduction; Research; Matching/challenge support.
Limitations: Applications accepted. Giving is focused in the five boroughs of New York, NY, and primarily Essex, Union and Morris counties in NJ. No support for projects outside the United States, or for political organizations. No grants to individuals, or for endowments, operating support, benefit fundraisers, annual fund appeals, scholarships, or from fiscal agents.
Publications: Application guidelines; Annual report (including application guidelines); Financial statement; Grants list.
Application information: Due to the large volume of appeals received, it may be impossible to answer all of them; however, every effort will be made to respond. Inquiries by e-mail are not accepted. Supplemental information may be required if proposal is considered by grants committee. The foundation also accepts the New York/New Jersey Area Common Application Form but prefers its own application procedure. See foundation web site for complete application guidelines, instructions, and form. Application form required.
Initial approach: Letter with grant application form, which is available by fax or at the foundation's web site, and attachments
Copies of proposal: 1
Deadline(s): No later than Feb. 15 and Sept. 15
Board meeting date(s): Apr./May and Nov./Dec.
Final notification: After grant or board meeting or preliminary review
Officers and Directors:* Hunter W. Corbin,* Chair.; William V. Engel,* Pres.; Brunilda Moriarty, Exec. V.P.; Robert W. Parsons, Jr.,* Secy.; Thomas W. Berry,* Treas.; H. Corbin Day, Dir. Emeritus; Roger B. Parsons, Dir. Emeritus; Elizabeth R. Curry; Hans Dekker; John W. Holman, Jr.; John W. Holman III; Thomas H. MacCowatt; Anita V. Spivey; Kate B. Wood.
Number of staff: 4 full-time professional; 2 part-time professional.
EIN: 222425725

1945
The Integra Foundation, Inc.

311 Enterprise Dr.
Plainsboro, NJ 08536-3344 (949) 855-7165
Contact: Linda Littlejohns, Pres. and Exec. Dir.
FAX: (949) 595-8703;
E-mail: linda.littlejohns@integralife.com;
Application address: 2 Goodyear #A, Irvine, CA 92618; Main URL: http://www.integra-foundation.org
Grants List: http://www.integra-foundation.org/gh.asp

Established in 2002 in NJ.
Donor: Integra LifeSciences Corp.
Foundation type: Company-sponsored foundation.
Financial data (yr. ended 12/31/12): Assets, $395,073 (M); gifts received, $1,000,000; expenditures, $960,658; qualifying distributions, $915,625; giving activities include $915,625 for 83 grants (high: $100,000; low: $500).
Purpose and activities: The foundation supports programs designed to advance innovative medical and health care research and education, primarily in the areas of neurosurgery, reconstructive surgery, and general surgery, to improve the outcome and quality of life for patients and their communities.
Fields of interest: Medical school/education; Hospitals (general); Health care, clinics/centers; Health care; Neuroscience research; Medical research; Surgery research.
Type of support: Sponsorships; Conferences/seminars; Equipment; Scholarship funds; General/operating support; Program development.
Limitations: Applications accepted. Giving primarily in areas of company operations. No support for political, fraternal, social, veterans', or religious organizations. No grants to individuals, or for programs that directly support marketing or sales objectives of Integra LifeSciences.
Publications: Application guidelines; Grants list; Newsletter.
Application information: Application form required.
Initial approach: Download application form and mail or fax to foundation
Copies of proposal: 1
Deadline(s): None
Board meeting date(s): Feb., May, Aug., and Nov.
Officers and Trustees: Linda Littlejohns, Pres. and Exec. Dir.; Simon Archibald, V.P.; JoAnne Harla, V.P.; Karen March, V.P.; Nora Brennan, Treas.; Stuart Essig; Jack Henneman; Judith O'Grady.
Number of staff: 1 part-time professional.
EIN: 522388679

1946
The International Foundation

1700 Rte. 23N., Ste. 300
Wayne, NJ 07470-7537
Contact: Kathy Gaiser
FAX: (973) 406-3969;
E-mail: info@intlfoundation.org; Main URL: http://www.intlfoundation.org

Incorporated in 1948 in DE.
Foundation type: Independent foundation.
Financial data (yr. ended 12/31/12): Assets, $23,199,362 (M); expenditures, $1,265,083; qualifying distributions, $1,052,732; giving activities include $764,700 for grants.
Purpose and activities: The foundation has supported world-wide development since its founding in 1948. The foundation recognizes the importance of emerging economies and the developmental challenges they face. It supports projects that promote sustainable development in: 1) agriculture: research and production; 2) health: medical, nutrition, and water; 3) education: formal at all levels research; 4) social development: cultural, economic, community, and entrepreneurial activity, and some aid to refugees, and grants for population planning are given; and 5) the environment.
Fields of interest: Education; Environment, natural resources; Health care; Health organizations; Agriculture; Human services; Economic development; Urban/community development; Rural development.
Limitations: Applications accepted. **Giving primarily in Grants limited to U.S.-based 501(c)(3) organizations that design, implement and directly supervise the overseas development program only. No support for overseas adoption, religious organizations, non-profit organizations significantly funded or reimbursed by the U.S. Government, projects in which a U.S.-based organization's (NGO) programs are implemented by an overseas organization that is not a 501 (c)(3) and in which the grant seeker does not have a major management and oversight role.** No grants to individuals, or for endowment funds, operating budgets, capital improvements or construction projects, emergency or disaster aid, service delivery projects, scholarships, fellowships, matching gifts, video productions, or conferences; no loans.
Publications: IRS Form 990 or 990-PF printed copy available upon request.
Application information: Unsolicited requests for funds are not accepted. Grant proposals are by invitation only, upon review of initial Letter of Inquiry. Grants are made once a year, in January, thus applications approved during the first or last quarters of the year will have their grants issued at the same time. See foundation web site for

guidelines. All Letters of Inquiry must be done online on foundation website. Application form required.

Initial approach: Use letter of inquiry form on foundation web site
Copies of proposal: **1**
Deadline(s): Rolling
Board meeting date(s): Jan., Apr., July, and Oct.

Officers and Trustees:* William McCormack, M.D.*, Grants Chair.; Frank Madden,* Pres.; John D. Carrico,* Secy.-Treas.; Gary Dicovitsky,* Investment Chair.; **Letitia K. Butler**; Edward A. Holmes, Ph.D; Douglas Walker.
Number of staff: 1 full-time professional.
EIN: 131962255
Other changes: The grantmaker no longer lists a phone.
At the close of 2012, the fair market value of the grantmaker's assets was $23,199,362 a substantial increase over the 2010 value, $0.

1947
The JM Foundation
116 Village Blvd., Ste. 200
Princeton, NJ 08540-5700 (609) 951-2283
Contact: Carl Helstrom, Exec. Dir.
FAX: (609) 951-2281; Main URL: http://fdnweb.org/jm
Grants List: http://fdnweb.org/jm/grants/year/2013/category/grants-awarded/

Incorporated in 1924 in NY.
Donors: Jeremiah Milbank†; Katharine S. Milbank†.
Foundation type: Independent foundation.
Financial data (yr. ended 12/31/12): Assets, $22,504,960 (M); expenditures, $1,835,581; qualifying distributions, $1,436,065; giving activities include $1,075,000 for 35 grants (high: $100,000; low: $5,000), $116,825 for employee matching gifts, and $41,559 for foundation-administered programs.
Purpose and activities: The foundation has a strong interest in educational activities which strengthen America's pluralistic system of free markets, entrepreneurship, and private enterprise. The foundation's current priorities include: supporting education and research that fosters market-based policy solutions, especially at state think tanks; developing state and national organizations that promote free enterprise, entrepreneurship, and private initiative; and identifying and educating young leaders.
Fields of interest: Children/youth, services; Public policy, research; Children/youth; Adults.
Type of support: Management development/capacity building; Program development; Publication; Fellowships; Internship funds; Research; Employee matching gifts; Matching/challenge support.
Limitations: Applications accepted. Giving on a national basis. No support for the arts, government agencies, public schools, or international activities. No grants to individuals, or for operating expenses, annual fundraising campaigns, equipment, or endowment funds; no loans.
Publications: Application guidelines; Grants list.
Application information: See foundation web site for guidelines. Faxes, e-mails or overnight mail requests not accepted. Application form not required.

Initial approach: Summary letter accompanied by proposal
Copies of proposal: 1
Deadline(s): No firm deadlines. Proposals processed as received. Grant decisions made at board meetings in May and Oct
Board meeting date(s): May and Oct
Final notification: Usually in writing within 30 working days

Officers and Directors:* Jeremiah Milbank III,* Pres.; Jeremiah M. Bogert, V.P.; Peter C. Morse, Secy.; William Lee Hanley, Jr.,* Treas.; Carl Helstrom, Exec. Dir.; Chris Olander, Exec. Dir. Emeritus; Mary Caslin Ross.
Number of staff: 1 full-time professional; 1 part-time professional; 1 part-time support.
EIN: 136068340

1948
Johnson & Johnson Patient Assistance Foundation, Inc.
(formerly Janssen Ortho Patient Assistance Foundation, Inc.)
1 Johnson & Johnson Plz.
New Brunswick, NJ 08933-0001
Contact: Denise Sitarikev, V.P.
FAX: (888) 526-5168; E-mail: dsitarik@jnj.com; Application address: Patient Assistance Program, P.O. Box 221857, Charlotte, NC 28222-1857; Additional tel.: (866) 317-2775, (800) 652-6227; Main URL: http://www.jjpaf.org/

Established as a company-sponsored operating foundation in 1997 in NJ.
Donors: Janssen Pharmaceutica Inc.; Johnson & Johnson; Ortho Biotech Inc.; Ortho-McNeil Pharmaceutical, Inc.; Vistakon Pharmaceutical; Pricara; Ortho Womens Health & Urology; Neurogena; DePuy Mitek, Inc.; Therakos, Inc.
Foundation type: Operating foundation.
Financial data (yr. ended 12/31/12): Assets, $69,921,484 (M); gifts received, $645,062,590; expenditures, $628,527,654; qualifying distributions, $611,680,261; giving activities include $611,680,261 for 152,000 grants to individuals.
Purpose and activities: The foundation provides pharmaceutical products to needy persons who lack prescription drug coverage.
Fields of interest: Health care; Economically disadvantaged.
Type of support: Donated products.
Limitations: Applications accepted. Giving on a national basis, including U.S. territories and the Virgin Islands. No support for religious or political organizations.
Publications: Application guidelines; Informational brochure.
Application information: Application must be completed and signed, and accompanied by proof of income and a HIPAA release form signed by the patient. Applicants may receive free medicines for up to one year. Application form required.

Initial approach: Complete online eligibility quiz and fax or mail application or apply via phone
Deadline(s): None
Board meeting date(s): Third Thursday of each month
Final notification: Within 24 business hours, expedited same day approval possible if needed

Officers and Directors:* Sharon D'Agostino,* Pres.; Denise Sitarik,* V.P.; Michael McCully,* Secy.; Michael Hepburn,* Treas.; Judith Fernandez; Margaret Forrestel; **Robert Inserra**; Gwendolyn Miley; Greg Panico; Louise Weingrod.
Number of staff: 5 full-time professional; 1 full-time support.
EIN: 311520982
Other changes: Irene Infanti is no longer a director.

1949
The Robert Wood Johnson Foundation
College Rd. E. and Rte. 1
P.O. Box 2316
Princeton, NJ 08543-2316 (877) 843-7953
E-mail: mail@rwjf.org; Main URL: http://www.rwjf.org
Culture of Health Blog: http://www.rwjf.org/en/blogs/culture-of-health.html
David C. Colby, V.P., Research & Evaluation on Twitter: https://twitter.com/DavidCColby
E-Newsletter: http://www.rwjf.org/about/newsletterlist.jsp
Facebook: http://www.facebook.com/RobertWoodJohnsonFoundation
Flickr: http://www.flickr.com/photos/rwjf
GiveSmart: http://www.givesmart.org/Stories/Donors/Risa-Lavizzo-Mourey
Grants Database: http://www.rwjf.org/en/grants.html#q/maptype/grants/ll/37.91,-96.38/z/4
Human Capital Blog: http://blog.rwjf.org/humancapital/
Human Capital Twitter: http://twitter.com/RWJF_HumanCap
Knowledge Center: http://www.rwjf.org/pr
NewPublicHealth Blog: http://blog.rwjf.org/publichealth/
Pioneering Ideas Blog: http://www.rwjf.org/en/blogs/pioneering-ideas.html
Quality/Equality Program Twitter: http://twitter.com/RWJF_QualEqual
Risa Lavizzo-Mourey, C.E.O. and Pres. on Twitter: https://twitter.com/risalavizzo
Robert Wood Johnson Foundation Program Teams Twitter List: http://twitter.com/RWJF/rwjf-program-teams
Robert Wood Johnson Foundation's Philanthropy Promise: http://www.ncrp.org/philanthropys-promise/who
RSS Directory: http://www.rwjf.org/global/rss.jsp
The Robert Wood Johnson Foundation Staff: https://twitter.com/RWJF/rwjf-staff-4
Twitter: http://twitter.com/RWJF
Twitter: http://www.twitter.com/rwjf
YouTube: http://youtube.com/rwjfvideo

Incorporated in 1936 in NJ; became a national philanthropy in 1972.
Donor: Robert Wood Johnson†.
Foundation type: Independent foundation.
Financial data (yr. ended 12/31/12): Assets, $9,528,568,196 (M); gifts received, $6,626; expenditures, $473,787,792; qualifying distributions, $393,272,868; giving activities include $292,906,381 for grants, $44,110,441 for foundation-administered programs and $4,158,333 for 2 loans/program-related investments (high: $3,325,000; low: $833,333).
Purpose and activities: The foundation's mission is to improve the health and health care of all Americans. Its efforts focus on fostering environments that promote health and on improving how health care in America is delivered and paid for, and how well it does for patients and their families.
Fields of interest: Child development, education; Medical school/education; Hospitals (general); Public health; Public health, obesity; Public health, physical fitness; Public health, environmental health; Health care, insurance; Health care, cost containment; Palliative care; Nursing care; Health care; Substance abuse, services; Mental health, smoking; Mental health, disorders; Mental health/crisis services; Crime/violence prevention; Children/youth, services; Child development, services; Family services; Aging, centers/services; Homeless, human services; Voluntarism

promotion; Leadership development; Children/youth; Aging; Disabilities, people with; Minorities; Native Americans/American Indians; Homeless.
Type of support: Employee matching gifts; Matching/challenge support; Program development; Program evaluation; Program-related investments/loans; Research; Seed money; Technical assistance.
Limitations: Applications accepted. Giving primarily in the U.S. **No support for political organizations, international activities, programs or institutions concerned solely with specific chronic conditions or basic biomedical research.** No grants to individuals, or for ongoing general operating expenses, endowment funds, capital costs, including construction, renovation, or equipment, or research on unapproved drug therapies or devices, end-of-life care, long-term care or for physical activity for adults age 50 or older.
Publications: Application guidelines; Annual report (including application guidelines); Financial statement; Grants list.
Application information: The foundation awards most grants through calls for proposals connected with its areas of focus. It accepts unsolicited proposals for projects that suggest new and creative approaches to solving health and health care problems. RWJF will continue to accept unsolicited proposals for the Pioneer Portfolio. Pioneer welcomes proposals for unsolicited grants at any time and issues awards throughout the year. There are no deadlines. Check web site for Open Calls for Proposals. Application form required.
Initial approach: Electronic brief proposal
Deadline(s): None
Board meeting date(s): Quarterly
Final notification: 6 to 12 months
Officers and Trustees:* Roger S. Fine,* Chair.; Risa Lavizzo-Mourey, M.D.*, C.E.O. and Pres.; Robin E. Mockenhaupt, Chief of Staff; John R. Lumpkin, M.D., Sr. V.P. and Dir., Health Care Group; James S. Marks, Sr. V.P. and Dir., Health Group; David C. Colby, Ph.D., V.P., Research and Evaluation; Katherine Hatton, V.P., Secy., and Genl. Counsel; Charles "Robin" Hogen, V.P., Communications; David L. Waldman, V.P., Human Resources and Admin.; Albert O. Shar, Ph.D., V.P., Inf. Tech.; Brian S. O'Neil, C.I.O.; Peggi Einhorn, C.F.O. and Treas.; William Roell, Cont.; Linda Burnes Bolton; Allan S. Bufferd; Brenda S. Davis; Charles D. Ellis, Ph.D., M.B.A; William H. Frist, M.D.; Kathryn S. Fuller; Patricia A. Gabow, M.D.; Thomas M. Gorrie, Ph.D; Joann Heffernan Heisen; Jeffrey P. Koplan; Ralph S. Larsen; Robert Litterman; Willard D. Nielsen; Peter R. Orszag; A. Eugene Washington, M.D., M.Sc.; **Phyllis M. Wise.**
Number of staff: 134 full-time professional; 8 part-time professional; 86 full-time support; 3 part-time support.
EIN: 226029397

1950
Blanche & George Jones Fund
c/o Dillon, Bitar and Luther, LLC
P.O. Box 398
Morristown, NJ 07963-0398
Contact: Mary A. Powers Esq.

Established in 1981 in NJ.
Foundation type: Independent foundation.
Financial data (yr. ended 02/28/13): Assets, $2,889,039 (M); expenditures, $180,465; qualifying distributions, $150,583; giving activities include $150,000 for 35 grants (high: $10,000; low: $1,000).
Purpose and activities: Giving primarily for education, health care, and to Christian churches.
Fields of interest: Arts; Secondary school/education; Higher education; Education; Hospitals (general); Mental health, association; Cancer; Cancer research; Boys & girls clubs; Human services; United Ways and Federated Giving Programs; Christian agencies & churches; Buddhism.
Limitations: Applications not accepted. Giving primarily in CA and FL. No grants to individuals.
Application information: Contributes only to pre-selected organizations.
Board meeting date(s): Nov.
Officers: Barbara J. Foreman, Pres.; Gay Osborn, V.P.; Mary A. Powers, Secy.; Peter W. Roome, Treas.
Board Member: Christian Foreman Ellis.
EIN: 136028786
Other changes: Barbara J. Foreman has replaced Phyllis J. Roome as Pres.
Gay Osborn is now V.P.

1951
Fletcher and Lola Kibler Irrevocable Trust
Pennington, NJ

The trust terminated in 2012.

1952
F. M. Kirby Foundation, Inc.
17 DeHart St.
P.O. Box 151
Morristown, NJ 07963-0151 (973) 538-4800
Contact: For application procedure questions: William H. Byrnes, Jr., V.P., Grants
FAX: (973) 538-4801; **Main URL: http://fdnweb.org/kirby**

Incorporated in 1931 in DE.
Donors: F.M. Kirby†; Allan P. Kirby, Sr.†; F.M. Kirby II†.
Foundation type: Independent foundation.
Financial data (yr. ended 12/31/13): Assets, $441,611,886 (M); expenditures, $23,639,874; qualifying distributions, $20,913,526; giving activities include $20,404,834 for 262 grants (high: $1,050,000; low: $2,000).
Purpose and activities: Support for community programs, the arts, historic preservation, social services, conservation, public policy and education organizations, and family planning. Grants are generally limited to organizations associated with the personal interests of present or former family members. Requests to support churches, hospitals, schools and colleges, other than ones attended by or used by members of the family, are not likely to receive favorable consideration.
Fields of interest: Performing arts; Historic preservation/historical societies; Arts; Environment, natural resources; Biomedicine; Medical research, institute; Cancer research; AIDS research; Recreation; Youth development, services; Youth, services; Economics; Public policy, research; Government/public administration; Leadership development; Children/youth; Youth; Aging; Deaf/hearing impaired; Military/veterans; Offenders/ex-offenders; Substance abusers; AIDS, people with; Economically disadvantaged.
Type of support: General/operating support; Continuing support; Annual campaigns; Capital campaigns; Building/renovation; Equipment; Land acquisition; Endowments; Emergency funds; Program development; Conferences/seminars; Research.
Limitations: Applications accepted. Giving primarily in the Raleigh/Durham, NC, area, the Morris County, NJ, area, and eastern PA. Generally no support for churches, hospitals, schools and colleges, other than ones attended by or used by members of the family. No grants to individuals, or for fundraising benefits, dinners, theater, or sporting events; no loans or pledges.
Publications: Informational brochure (including application guidelines).
Application information: Solicitations for grants must contain certain basic information about the applicant, be signed by an official of the applicant and be addressed to the F. M. Kirby Foundation. Unsolicited requests should be in the form of a letter of inquiry. No solicitations by telephone, fax or E-mail are accepted. Application form not required.
Initial approach: Letter of inquiry after checking solicitation guidelines
Copies of proposal: 1
Deadline(s): Proposals received throughout the year; requests received after Oct. 31 are held over to the following year
Board meeting date(s): Three times per year
Final notification: Monthly for positive responses and declinations
Officers and Directors:* S. Dillard Kirby,* Pres. and Dir.; William H. Byrnes, Jr., V.P., Grants; Jefferson W. Kirby,* V.P. and Dir.; **Frank N. Barra, Secy.-Treas.**; Alice Kirby Horton, Asst. Secy. and Dir.; Wilson M. Compton, M.D. M.P.E., Dir.; **Walker D. Kirby, Dir.; Sandra Brown Sherman, Dir.**; Laura H. Virkler, Dir.
Number of staff: 6 full-time support.
EIN: 516017929
Other changes: S. Dillard Kirby has replaced F. M. Kirby as Pres. Jefferson W. Kirby has replaced Walker D. Kirby as V.P.
Frank N. Barra is now Secy.-Treas.

1953
John C. Kish Foundation
(also known as Kish Foundation)
c/o Merrill Lynch Bank & Trust Co.
P.O. Box 1501, NJ2-130-03-31
Pennington, NJ 08534-0671

Donors: John C. Kish; Joan Kish.
Foundation type: Independent foundation.
Financial data (yr. ended 11/30/13): Assets, $33,078,065 (M); gifts received, $3,206,233; expenditures, $1,273,237; qualifying distributions, $1,212,721; giving activities include $1,091,091 for 47 grants (high: $238,697; low: $1,000).
Fields of interest: Education; Animal welfare; Health organizations; Boys & girls clubs; Human services; Christian agencies & churches; Protestant agencies & churches.
Limitations: Applications not accepted. Giving primarily in Henderson and Las Vegas, NV, and Washington, DC. No grants to individuals.
Application information: Contributes only to pre-selected organizations.
Principals: H. Matthew Frazier; Joan Kish; Frank Plevo.
EIN: 731688377

1954
The Charles and Lynne Klatskin Family Charitable Trust
400 Hollister Rd.
Teterboro, NJ 07608-1147

Established in NJ.

Donor: Charles Klatskin.
Foundation type: Independent foundation.
Financial data (yr. ended 06/30/13): Assets, $1,839,290 (M); gifts received, $250,000; expenditures, $1,166,752; qualifying distributions, $1,164,532; giving activities include $1,164,532 for 26 grants (high: $900,000; low: $250).
Fields of interest: Education; Human services; Jewish agencies & synagogues.
Limitations: Applications not accepted. Giving primarily in NJ and NY. No grants to individuals.
Application information: Unsolicited requests for funds not accepted.
Trustees: Charles Klatskin; Deborah Klatskin; Lynne Klatskin; Samuel Klatskin.
EIN: 226831861
Other changes: For the fiscal year ended June 30, 2013, the grantmaker paid grants of $1,164,532, a 234.8% increase over the fiscal 2012 disbursements, $347,790.

1955
Janet H. and C. Harry Knowles Foundation, Inc.
(also known as Knowles Science Teaching Foundation (KSTF))
1000 N. Church St.
Moorestown, NJ 08057-1764 (856) 608-0001
Contact: Angelo Collins Ph.D., Exec. Dir
FAX: (856) 608-0008; E-mail: info@kstf.org; Main URL: http://www.kstf.org
Facebook: http://www.facebook.com/KnowlesScienceTeachingFoundation
Twitter: http://twitter.com/TheKSTF

Established in NJ in 1999.
Donors: Janet H. Knowles; C. Harry Knowles; Paul Kuerbis.
Foundation type: Operating foundation.
Financial data (yr. ended 05/31/12): Assets, $71,700,153 (M); gifts received, $944,134; expenditures, $6,268,425; qualifying distributions, $7,838,386; giving activities include $110,000 for 2 grants (high: $55,000; low: $55,000), $1,057,446 for 193 grants to individuals (high: $18,154; low: $37), and $6,112,956 for 1 foundation-administered program.
Purpose and activities: Giving to increase the number of high quality high school science and mathematics teachers in the United States, and to raise the status of the teaching profession.
Fields of interest: Secondary school/education; Higher education; Teacher school/education; Education; Science; Mathematics; Young adults.
Type of support: Continuing support; Conferences/seminars; Fellowships; Research; Grants to individuals; Scholarships—to individuals.
Limitations: Applications not accepted. Giving limited to the U.S. No support for religious or political organizations, schools or school districts, or university programs. No grants for second career or advanced degrees in any discipline other than education.
Publications: Annual report; Informational brochure; Occasional report.
Application information: Unsolicited requests for funds not accepted.
Board meeting date(s): Three times a year
Officers and Trustees:* C. Harry Knowles,* Chair.; **Edward Viner, M.D.*, Vice-Chair.; William Rulon-Miller,* Pres. and Treas.**; Janet H. Knowles,* Secy.; **Dr. Nicole Gillespie,* Exec. Dir.**; Paul Kuerbis, Ph.D.; Scott McVay; Lawrence Tint; **Dr. Suzanne M. Wilson**.
Number of staff: 9 full-time professional; 1 part-time professional; 5 full-time support; 1 part-time support.
EIN: 010485964
Other changes: Dr. Nicole Gillespie has replaced Angelo Collins as Exec. Dir.
Edward Viner is now Vice-Chair.

1956
The Kovner Foundation
Princeton Plz., Bldg. 2
731 Alexander Rd.
Princeton, NJ 08540-5236 (609) 919-7600

Established in 1986.
Donor: Bruce S. Kovner.
Foundation type: Independent foundation.
Financial data (yr. ended 12/31/12): Assets, $117,443,980 (M); gifts received, $44,365,579; expenditures, $11,414,850; qualifying distributions, $10,452,111; giving activities include $10,452,111 for 18 grants (high: $3,300,000; low: $43,948).
Purpose and activities: Giving primarily for education.
Fields of interest: Arts; Higher education; Education; Public policy, research.
Limitations: Applications not accepted. Giving primarily in Washington, DC New York, NY. No grants to individuals.
Application information: Contributes only to pre-selected organizations.
Officers and Directors:* Bruce S. Kovner,* Pres.; Suzanne F. Kovner, V.P.; Scott B. Bernstein, Secy.; Peter P. D'Angelo,* Treas.; Karen Cross, Cont.; Frank Wohl.
EIN: 223468030
Other changes: At the close of 2012, the fair market value of the grantmaker's assets was $117,443,980, a 51.6% increase over the 2011 value, $77,464,855. For the same period, the grantmaker paid grants of $10,452,111, a 116.4% increase over the 2011 disbursements, $4,830,804.

1957
Charles and Seryl Kushner Charitable Foundation
18 Columbia Tpke.
Florham Park, NJ 07932-2266 (973) 822-0050

Donors: Charles Kushner; Seryl Kushner; G. Gellert.
Foundation type: Independent foundation.
Financial data (yr. ended 12/31/12): Assets, $43,103 (M); gifts received, $3,886,000; expenditures, $3,877,015; qualifying distributions, $3,875,130; giving activities include $3,875,130 for 140 grants (high: $387,500; low: $500).
Purpose and activities: Giving primarily to Jewish organizations; funding also for higher education.
Fields of interest: Elementary/secondary education; Higher education; Jewish federated giving programs; Jewish agencies & synagogues.
Limitations: Applications not accepted. Giving primarily in NJ and NY. No grants to individuals.
Application information: Contributes only to pre-selected organizations.
Officer: Mark Pasquerella, Cont.
Directors: Charles Kushner; Jared Kushner; Josh Kushner; Seryl Kushner; Nicole Meyer; Dara Orbach.
EIN: 223422337
Other changes: At the close of 2012, the grantmaker paid grants of $3,875,130, a 244.9% increase over the 2010 disbursements, $1,123,480.

1958
John C. Lasko Foundation
P.O. Box 1501, NJ2-130-03-31
Pennington, NJ 08534-1501
Contact: Clint Blair
Application address: P.O. Box 339 Belleville, MI 48111; tel.: (734) 699-3400

Established in 1998 MI. Reincorporated in 2010 under a new IRS EI number.
Donors: John C. Lasko†; Republic Die & Tool Co.
Foundation type: Independent foundation.
Financial data (yr. ended 12/31/13): Assets, $117,940,113 (M); expenditures, $5,772,444; qualifying distributions, $5,371,992; giving activities include $4,915,000 for 21 grants (high: $550,000; low: $35,000).
Fields of interest: Protestant agencies & churches.
Type of support: Scholarships—to individuals.
Limitations: Applications not accepted. Giving in the U.S., with some emphasis on MI.
Application information: Unsolicited requests for funds not accepted.
Trustees: Sean H. Cook; Merrill Lynch Trust Co.
EIN: 276173297
Other changes: John C. Lasko, Pres. is deceased. Barbara T. Huston is no longer Secy. Charles Zimmerman is no longer Treas.

1959
The Leavens Foundation, Inc.
P.O. Box 673
Long Valley, NJ 07853
***Contact:* Nancy Leavens, Pres.; Bill Leavens, Secy.**
E-mail: leavensfoundation@gmail.com

Established in 1991 in NJ as successor to The Leavens Foundation.
Foundation type: Independent foundation.
Financial data (yr. ended 12/31/12): Assets, $2,338,513 (M); expenditures, $211,086; qualifying distributions, $186,492; giving activities include $165,000 for 7 grants (high: $40,000; low: $10,000).
Purpose and activities: Giving primarily in the areas of water quality, open space, urban gardening, and family planning and services.
Fields of interest: Environment; Youth development; Human services.
Type of support: Building/renovation; Equipment; Program development; Seed money; Matching/challenge support.
Limitations: Applications not accepted. Giving primarily in Morris and Essex counties, NJ, and in areas where trustees live. No support for religious organizations (unless a board member has a direct affiliation). No grants to individuals.
Application information: Unsolicited requests for funds not accepted.
Board meeting date(s): May and Nov.
Officers: Nancy Leavens, Pres.; Bill Leavens, Secy.; William B. Leavens III, Treas.
EIN: 521754606
Other changes: Nancy Leavens has replaced William Gibson as Pres. Bill Leavens has replaced Nancy Wright as Secy.

1960
Mortimer Levitt Foundation, Inc.
c/o Levitt Properties
106 Quarry Rd., Ste. A
Hamburg, NJ **07419-1341 (973) 823-1140**
***Contact:* Kathy Eberly, Treas.**

Established in 1966 in NY.
Donors: Mortimer Levitt†; The Custom Shops; Farmers Branch.
Foundation type: Independent foundation.
Financial data (yr. ended 02/28/11): Assets, $45,698,803 (M); expenditures, $4,753,509; qualifying distributions, $2,162,219; giving activities include $1,979,192 for 439 grants (high: $75,000; low: $40).
Purpose and activities: Giving primarily for the arts; funding also for health organizations and human services.
Fields of interest: Museums; Performing arts; Arts; Higher education; Health organizations, association; Human services; Children/youth, services; Community/economic development; Foundations (community); Jewish federated giving programs.
Limitations: Giving primarily in New York, NY. No grants to individuals.
Application information:
Initial approach: Letter
Deadline(s): None
Officers: AnneMarie Levitt, Pres.; Elizabeth Levitt-Hirsch, V.P.; Malcolm Chaifetz, Secy. and Gen. Counsel; Kathy Eberly, Treas.
EIN: 136204678
Other changes: The grantmaker no longer lists a separate application address.

1961
The Bradley T. MacDonald Family Foundation, Inc.
(formerly The MacDonald Family Foundation, Inc.)
P.O. Box 1501, NJ2-130-03-31
Pennington, NJ 08534-1501

Established in 2004 in DE.
Donors: Brad MacDonald; Shirley MacDonald; Margaret MacDonald.
Foundation type: Independent foundation.
Financial data (yr. ended 12/31/12): Assets, $3,851,597 (M); expenditures, $170,999; qualifying distributions, $156,838; giving activities include $145,050 for 15 grants (high: $20,600; low: $500).
Fields of interest: Health organizations; Medical research; Human services.
Limitations: Applications not accepted. Giving primarily in FL, MD, OH, PA and TN. No grants to individuals.
Application information: Unsolicited requests for funds not accepted.
Officers and Directors:* Kellie MacDonald Pizzico, V.P. and Fdn. Admin.; Margaret MacDonald, V.P.; Shirley MacDonald,* V.P.
EIN: 200767790

1962
The Mandelbaum Foundation
80 Main St., Ste. 510
West Orange, NJ 07052-5460 (973) 325-0011
Contact: David Mandelbaum, Tr.

Established in 1963.
Donors: David Mandelbaum; Nathan Mandelbaum; Philip Mandelbaum; Davanne Realty Co.; 525 Realty Holding; Clayton Holding Co.; F & E Realty; Nathan Barry Co.; One Twelve Corp.; 450 Corporation.
Foundation type: Independent foundation.
Financial data (yr. ended 09/30/13): Assets, $471,738 (M); gifts received, $105,000; expenditures, $132,762; qualifying distributions, $130,897; giving activities include $129,225 for 86 grants (high: $25,000; low: $25).
Purpose and activities: Giving primarily for education and to Jewish organizations.
Fields of interest: Arts; Higher education; Education; Hospitals (general); Health organizations, association; Jewish federated giving programs; Public affairs; Catholic agencies & churches; Jewish agencies & synagogues.
Type of support: General/operating support.
Limitations: Applications accepted. Giving primarily in NJ and New York, NY. No grants to individuals.
Application information:
Initial approach: Letter on organization stationery
Deadline(s): None
Trustees: Robert Goldberg; David Mandelbaum; Michael Mandelbaum.
EIN: 226060789

1963
Marcon Foundation, Inc.
79 Chestnut St., Ste. 101
Ridgewood, NJ 07450-2533 (201) 447-0185
***Contact:* W.J. Haggerty, Asst. Treas.**

Established in 2003 in NJ.
Donors: Fred R. Marcon; Natalie Marcon.
Foundation type: Independent foundation.
Financial data (yr. ended 12/31/12): Assets, $1,578,470 (M); gifts received, $500,000; expenditures, $1,509,691; qualifying distributions, $1,437,723; giving activities include $1,430,000 for 40 grants (high: $275,000; low: $5,000).
Fields of interest: Health care; Human services; Catholic agencies & churches.
Limitations: Giving primarily in FL and IL. No grants to individuals.
Application information:
Initial approach: Letter
Deadline(s): None
Officer: Fred R. Marcon, Pres.
EIN: 571167051
Other changes: Fred R. Marcon is now Pres.

1964
Joseph and Cheryl Marino Family Foundation, Inc.
70 Grand Ave., Ste. 109
River Edge, NJ **07661-1936**

Established in 2007 in NJ.
Donor: Joseph Marino.
Foundation type: Independent foundation.
Financial data (yr. ended 12/31/12): Assets, $288,902 (M); expenditures, $261,955; qualifying distributions, $261,800; giving activities include $261,800 for 33 grants (high: $40,000; low: $500).
Fields of interest: Education; Health care; Human services; Christian agencies & churches; Jewish agencies & synagogues.
Limitations: Applications not accepted. Giving primarily in NJ. No grants to individuals.
Application information: Unsolicited requests for funds not accepted.
Officers: Joseph Marino, Pres.; Cheryl Marino, V.P.
EIN: 261604015

1965
The MCJ Amelior Foundation
(formerly The MCJ Foundation)
310 South St., 4th Fl.
Morristown, NJ **07960-7301** (973) 540-1946
Contact: Suzanne M. Spero, Exec. Dir.
FAX: (973) 538-8175
GiveSmart: http://www.givesmart.org/Stories/Donors/Ray-Chambers

Established in 1983 in NJ.
Donors: Raymond G. Chambers; Kurt T. Borowsky; Harding Service, LLC.
Foundation type: Independent foundation.
Financial data (yr. ended 12/31/12): Assets, $112,506,314 (M); gifts received, $39,110; expenditures, $8,112,312; qualifying distributions, $8,105,715; giving activities include $6,333,685 for 413 grants (high: $600,000; low: $20).
Purpose and activities: Giving primarily for mentoring and youth initiatives.
Fields of interest: Education, early childhood education; Child development, education; Elementary school/education; Education; Health organizations, association; Crime/violence prevention, gun control; Crime/violence prevention, domestic violence; Human services; Children/youth, services; Youth, pregnancy prevention; Child development, services; Community/economic development; United Ways and Federated Giving Programs; Disabilities, people with; Minorities; Women; AIDS, people with; Economically disadvantaged; Homeless.
Type of support: General/operating support; Seed money; Technical assistance; Matching/challenge support.
Limitations: Applications not accepted. Giving primarily in NJ and NY.
Application information: Contributes only to pre-selected organizations.
Officers and Directors:* Christine Chambers Gilfillan,* Pres.; Donald R. Smith, Secy.; Anthony J. Romano, Treas.; Suzanne M. Spero,* Exec. Dir.; Barbara B. Coleman.
Number of staff: 2 full-time professional; 1 full-time support.
EIN: 222497895

1966
Merck Institute for Science Education, Inc.
P.O. Box 100, WS2F-96
Whitehouse Station, NJ 08889-0100
Contact: Carlo Parravano, Exec. Dir.
E-mail: contactus@mise.org; Additional address: P.O. Box 2000 RY60-215, Rahway, NJ 07065, tel.: (732) 594-3443; fax: (732) 594-3977; **Main URL: http://www.merckresponsibility.com/giving-at-merck/education/**
Grants List: http://www.mise.org/secure/approach/grants.html
Merck Corporate Responsibility Education Website: http://www.merckresponsibility.com/giving-at-merck/education/

Established in 1992 in NJ.
Donor: Merck & Co., Inc.
Foundation type: Company-sponsored foundation.
Financial data (yr. ended 12/31/12): Assets, $0 (M); gifts received, $2,616,833; expenditures, $2,616,833; qualifying distributions, $2,616,833; giving activities include $238,200 for grants.
Purpose and activities: The institute supports programs designed to improve science education; raise levels of science performance in students grades K-12; and provide professional development

for teachers and administrators to enhance their knowledge and skills.
Fields of interest: Education, fund raising/fund distribution; Elementary/secondary education; Higher education; Teacher school/education; Science, formal/general education; Mathematics; Engineering/technology; Science.
Type of support: General/operating support; Management development/capacity building; Program development; Conferences/seminars; Publication; Curriculum development; Fellowships; Internship funds; Research; Scholarships—to individuals.
Limitations: Applications not accepted. Giving limited to NJ and PA.
Application information: Unsolicited grant requests are not accepted. Applicants for the UNCF/Merck Science Initiative should contact the United Negro College Fund. Giving from the MISE is phasing down.
Officers and Directors:* Geralyn S. Ritter, Pres.; Carlo Parravano, Exec. V.P. and Exec. Dir.; Ellen Lambert, V.P.; Celia A. Colbert,* Secy.; Mark E. McDonough, Treas.
EIN: 223208944

1967
Aaron and Rachel Meyer Memorial Foundation, Inc.
c/o Alissa Murphy, Dir.
633 Wyckoff Ave.
Wyckoff, NJ 07481-1485 (201) 891-7007
E-mail: amurphy@armeyerfoundation.org; Main URL: http://www.armeyerfoundation.org

Incorporated in 1964 in NJ.
Donor: Bertram Meyer†.
Foundation type: Independent foundation.
Financial data (yr. ended 03/31/13): Assets, $6,984,493 (M); expenditures, $286,354; qualifying distributions, $236,292; giving activities include $138,000 for 3 grants (high: $130,000; low: $500).
Purpose and activities: Giving primarily for health care, human services, education, animal welfare, and the arts.
Fields of interest: Arts; Education; Animal welfare; Hospitals (general); Health care; Health organizations, association; Human services; Philanthropy/voluntarism.
Limitations: Applications accepted. Giving primarily in Northeast NJ. No grants to individuals.
Application information: Proposals may be submitted electronically, or by U.S. mail. Application information available on foundation web site. Application form required.
Initial approach: **Use Request Application Form on foundation web site**
Deadline(s): Mar. 1 (for Apr. meeting), Sept. 1 (for Oct. meeting)
Board meeting date(s): 7 or 8 times a year
Officers: Philip B. Lowy, Pres.; Janey Lowy, V.P.; Alissa Murphy, Secy.-Treas.
EIN: 226063514
Other changes: The grantmaker no longer lists a separate application address.

1968
Milbank Foundation
(formerly Milbank Foundation for Rehabilitation)
116 Village Blvd., Ste. 200
Princeton, NJ 08540-5700 (609) 951-2283
Contact: Carl Helstrom, Exec. Dir.
FAX: (609) 951-2281; **Main URL: http://fdnweb.org/milbank**
Grants List: http://fdnweb.org/milbank/grants/year/2013/category/grants-awarded/

Established in 1995 in NY; converted through an affiliation between the ICD International Center for the Disabled and the New York Hospital-Cornell Medical Center Network.
Foundation type: Independent foundation.
Financial data (yr. ended 12/31/12): Assets, $27,537,112 (M); expenditures, $1,883,189; qualifying distributions, $1,629,105; giving activities include $1,305,000 for 30 grants (high: $250,000; low: $5,000), and $75,000 for employee matching gifts.
Purpose and activities: The foundation's mission is to integrate people with disabilities into all aspects of American life. Current priorities include, but are not limited to: consumer-focused initiatives that enable people with disabilities to lead fulfilling, independent lives; innovative policy research and education on market-based approaches to health care and rehabilitation; improving and expanding quality health services, especially palliative care, and education and training of allied health and rehabilitation professionals.
Fields of interest: Health care, public policy; Medical care, rehabilitation; Palliative care; Health care; Disabilities, people with.
Type of support: Program development; Conferences/seminars; Publication; Fellowships; Research; Employee matching gifts.
Limitations: Applications accepted. Giving limited to the U.S., with some emphasis on New York, NY. No support for government agencies. No grants to individuals, or for general operating funds, annual appeals, dinners or events, capital campaigns, building funds, direct mailings, solicitations, equipment, music, theater, or campaigns. Usually, the foundation does not make multi-year grants.
Publications: Annual report (including application guidelines); Grants list.
Application information: See web site for guidelines and limitations. Inquiries and proposals are to be sent by regular mail only. Unless requested, please do not send by fax, e-mail, or overnight mail. Application form not required.
Initial approach: Letter or proposal
Copies of proposal: 1
Deadline(s): Proposals processed as received. Grant decisions made at Board Meetings.
Board meeting date(s): May and Oct.
Final notification: Within 1 month of application
Officers and Directors:* Jeremiah M. Bogert,* Chair. and Secy.; Jeremiah Milbank III,* Pres. and Treas.; Carl Helstrom,* Exec. Dir.; Chris Olander, Exec. Dir. Emeritus; Jeremiah M. Bogert, Jr.; Rev. Terence L. Elsberry; Ezra K. Zilkha.
Number of staff: None.
EIN: 115125050

1969
Nandansons Charitable Foundation, Inc
4 Rio Vista Dr.
Edison, NJ 08820-2321 (908) 561-2400
Contact: Ajay Gupta, Pres.

Established in NJ.
Donor: Ajay Gupta.
Foundation type: Independent foundation.
Financial data (yr. ended 06/30/13): Assets, $2,376,082 (M); gifts received, $1,000,000; expenditures, $86,312; qualifying distributions, $81,192; giving activities include $81,192 for 32 grants (high: $26,000; low: $50).
Fields of interest: Education; Health organizations; Human services; Hinduism.
Limitations: Applications accepted. Giving primarily in NJ.
Application information:
***Initial approach:* Brief proposal**
Deadline(s): None
***Final notification:* Within 2 months**
Officers: Ajay Gupta, Pres.; Nutan Gupta, Secy.; Ankur Gupta, Treas.
EIN: 274255136

1970
The Neisloss Family Foundation, Inc.
P.O. Box 1501, NJ2-130-03-31
Pennington, NJ 08534-1501
Application address: c/o James Neisloss, 300 Corporate Plz., Islandia, NY 11749-1519, tel.: (631) 232-2300

Established in 1991 in NY.
Donor: Stanley Neisloss†.
Foundation type: Independent foundation.
Financial data (yr. ended 07/31/13): Assets, $4,342,060 (M); expenditures, $325,975; qualifying distributions, $301,532; giving activities include $283,535 for 21 grants (high: $60,000; low: $250).
Fields of interest: Higher education; Education; Hospitals (general); Health organizations, association; Human services.
Limitations: Applications accepted. Giving primarily in NY; some funding also in CA and NJ. No grants to individuals.
Application information: Application form not required.
***Initial approach:* Proposal**
Deadline(s): None
Officers: Susan Neisloss, Pres.; James Neisloss, V.P.
EIN: 113086865

1971
Newark Charter School Fund, Inc.
60 Park Pl., 17th Fl.
Newark, NJ **07102-5511 (973) 733-2285**
***FAX:* (973) 733-9555**; E-mail: info@ncsfund.org; Main URL: http://ncsfund.org
Facebook: https://www.facebook.com/ncsfund
RSS Feed: http://ncsfund.org/whats-happening/rss
Twitter: https://twitter.com/NCSFund

Established in NJ and DE.
Donors: Doris and Donald Fisher Fund; Bill and Melinda Gates Foundation; Laurene Powell Jobs; Robertson Foundation; Walton Family Foundation.
Foundation type: Operating foundation.
Financial data (yr. ended 12/31/12): Assets, $3,357,948 (M); gifts received, $2,814,492; expenditures, $2,971,992; qualifying distributions, $2,971,592; giving activities include $808,672 for 7 grants (high: $213,300; low: $50,000).
Purpose and activities: NCSF makes grants to charter schools and to nonprofit organizations that support charter schools.
Fields of interest: Elementary/secondary education; Charter schools.
Limitations: Applications not accepted. Giving primarily in NJ, NY and MA. No grants to individuals.
Application information: Unsolicited requests for funds not accepted. The fund works closely with local nonprofit organizations, charter schools,

foundations and stakeholders of various kinds to identity and develop grant prospects.
Officers and Directors:* **Mashea Ashton,*** **C.E.O. and Secy.; Nicole Butler, V.P., Advocacy and Collaboration; Aileen Philbrick, V.P., Quality Schools**; Jim Blew; Phoebe Boyer; Chris Nelson.
EIN: 262224940
Other changes: Mashea Ashton is now C.E.O and Secy. Nicole Butler is now V.P., Advocacy and Collaboration. Adam Porsche and Stacey Rubin are no longer board members. Stig Leschly is no longer Exec. Dir.

1972
The Charlotte W. Newcombe Foundation
35 Park Pl.
Princeton, NJ 08542-6918 (609) 924-7022
Contact: Thomas N. Wilfrid Ph.D., Exec. Dir.
FAX: (609) 252-1773;
E-mail: twilfrid@newcombefoundation.org;
Additional e-mail: info@newcombefoundation.org;
Main URL: http://www.newcombefoundation.org

Trust established in 1979 in PA.
Donor: Charlotte W. Newcombe†.
Foundation type: Independent foundation.
Financial data (yr. ended 12/31/12): Assets, $47,794,700 (M); expenditures, $2,712,532; qualifying distributions, $2,361,526; giving activities include $2,119,725 for 47 grants (high: $743,060; low: $195), and $2,361,526 for foundation-administered programs.
Purpose and activities: Supporting students in pursuit of degrees in higher education.
Fields of interest: Humanities; Higher education; Adult/continuing education; Disabilities, people with; Adults, women; Economically disadvantaged.
Type of support: Endowments; Fellowships; Internship funds; Scholarship funds; Matching/challenge support.
Limitations: Giving for scholarship programs for mature women and students with disabilities is limited to colleges and universities in DE, MD, NJ, PA, Washington, DC, and New York, NY. No grants or scholarships to individuals directly, or for staffing, program development, postdoctoral fellowships, or building funds; scholarships to institutions only; no loans.
Publications: Informational brochure; Program policy statement.
Application information: The foundation accepts inquiries from accredited institutions of higher education within New York City, New Jersey, Pennsylvania, Delaware, Maryland and the District of Columbia. Formal applications are accepted only at the foundation's invitation following institutional inquiry. Application form not required.
Initial approach: Inquire with foundation
Deadline(s): For Newcombe Fellowships: Nov. 15. No deadline for institutional inquiries re scholarship grants.
Board meeting date(s): Feb., Apr., June, Oct., and Dec.
Officer and Trustees:* Thomas N. Wilfrid, Exec. Dir.; Robert M. Adams; **Dale Robinson Anglin**; Elizabeth T. Frank; Louise U. Johnson; J. Barton Luedeke.
Number of staff: 1 full-time professional; 3 part-time professional.
EIN: 232120614
Other changes: Janet A. Fearon, a trustee, is deceased.

1973
Novartis Patient Assistance Foundation, Inc.
1 Health Plz.
USEH 701-441
East Hanover, NJ 07936-1080 (800) 277-2254
Application address: P.O. Box 66531, St. Louis, MO 63166-6556; fax: (866) 470-1750; Main URL: http://www.pharma.us.novartis.com/about-us/our-patient-caregiver-resources/index.shtml
NPC Patient Assistance Web Portal: https://www.npcpapportal.com/

Established in 2008 in NJ.
Donor: Novartis Pharmaceuticals Corp.
Foundation type: Company-sponsored foundation.
Financial data (yr. ended 12/31/12): Assets, $31,616,576 (M); gifts received, $467,999,604; expenditures, $459,661,136; qualifying distributions, $459,661,136; giving activities include $452,745,445 for grants to individuals.
Purpose and activities: The foundation provides medication assistance to patients experiencing financial hardship who have no third party insurance coverage.
Fields of interest: Economically disadvantaged.
Type of support: Donated products; In-kind gifts.
Limitations: Applications accepted. Giving on a national basis.
Publications: Application guidelines.
Application information: Faxed applications must be sent from a physician's office. Application address varies per medication requested. Application form required.
Initial approach: Telephone, complete online application, or download application form and fax or mail to application address
Copies of proposal: 1
Deadline(s): None
Officers and Directors:* Kevin Rigby,* Pres.; Joe Visaggio,* V.P.; Rhoda Crichlow, Secy.; Marc Lewis, Treas.; Alissa Jaffenagler; Barry Rosenfeld.
EIN: 262502555
Other changes: Brandi Robinson is no longer a director.

1974
Onyx and Breezy Foundation
160 Summit Ave.
Montvale, NJ 07645-1750
***Application address:* c/o Mark Shefts, P.O. Box 656, Tuxedo Park, NY 10987, tel.: (201) 782-7400**

Established in 2005 in NY.
Donors: Mark Shefts; Assents LLC; LMB Funding; Penson Financial Services; The NIR Group; Rothstein Rosenfeldt Adler.
Foundation type: Independent foundation.
Financial data (yr. ended 12/31/12): Assets, $394,045 (M); gifts received, $358,194; expenditures, $399,284; qualifying distributions, $383,503; giving activities include $271,766 for 48 + grants (high: $34,407).
Fields of interest: Animal welfare.
Type of support: General/operating support.
Limitations: Applications accepted. Giving primarily in CA, FL and NJ. No grants to individuals.
Application information: Application form required.
Initial approach: Proposal
Deadline(s): None
Trustees: Mark Shefts; Wanda Shefts.
EIN: 137437754

1975
Gustavus and Louise Pfeiffer Research Foundation
P.O. Box 765
Short Hills, NJ 07078-0765 (973) 376-0986
FAX: (973) 376-0987;
E-mail: pfeiffer.research.foundation@gmail.com;
Main URL: http://www.pfeifferfoundation.org

Incorporated in 1942 in NY.
Donors: Gustavus A. Pfeiffer†; Louise F. Pfeiffer†.
Foundation type: Independent foundation.
Financial data (yr. ended 12/31/13): Assets, $26,568,174 (M); expenditures, $840,343; qualifying distributions, $767,270; giving activities include $621,857 for 8 grants (high: $100,000; low: $71,857).
Purpose and activities: The Foundation supports graduate medical scholarship programs and university medical/pharmacy related research projects.
Fields of interest: Medical school/education; Eye research; Ear, nose & throat research; Geriatrics research; Pediatrics research; Medical research; Nutrition.
Limitations: Giving limited to the U.S. No support for national fundraising organizations or publicly financed projects, or for projects involving vivisection or other experiments on animal subjects (excluding insects). No grants to individuals, or for dissertations, tuitions and fees for PhD or Masters programs or individual scholarship requests, or for building or endowment funds; overhead, supplies, equipment, travel, conferences, exhibits, seminars, lectures, workshops, surveys or general purposes, delivery of healthcare services, sabbatical leave, indirect costs, general programs of biomedical research, and projects which are more appropriate for support by other sources, such as pharmaceutical companies for commercial applications of existing products.
Application information: The foundation considers grant applications by invitation only. No other applications will be considered, except institutions with a current grant outstanding may apply for a renewal under the prior application process. Principal investigators with questions must go through their institution's office of sponsored research, which, in turn, will contact the foundation Secretary via email or phone. The foundation does not work directly with principal investigators. If invited, all formal applications must be mailed to the P.O. Box and received by the deadline. Note that courier services do not deliver to the U.S. Post Office. Electronic submissions will not be accepted.
Board meeting date(s): Apr. and Oct.
Officers: Kim Alvarez, Pres. and C.E.O.; H. Robert Herold II, V.P.; Matthew Mayro Keeney, Treas.
Directors: Matthew G. Herold, Jr.; Anne Herold Keeney; Sarah S. P. McCarthy; Patricia Herold Nagle.
Number of staff: None.
EIN: 136086299
Other changes: The grantmaker no longer lists a primary contact.

1976
Pierson Family Foundation, Inc.
(formerly James and Nancy Pierson Foundation)
111 Northfield Ave., Ste. 206
West Orange, NJ 07052-4703
***Application address:* c/o James Pierson, 89 Dodd St., East Orange, NJ 07019, tel.: (973) 673-5000**

Established in NJ.

Donors: James W. Pierson; A & A Fuel Oil Co.; Harry Charlton Co., Inc.; Dixon Bros., Inc.; J.W. Pierson Co.
Foundation type: Operating foundation.
Financial data (yr. ended 06/30/13): Assets, $5,814,127 (M); gifts received, $150,000; expenditures, $238,407; qualifying distributions, $202,862; giving activities include $199,864 for 60 grants (high: $11,050; low: $25).
Fields of interest: Education; Hospitals (general); Health organizations, association; Human services; Religion.
Limitations: Applications accepted. Giving primarily in NJ.
Application information: Application form not required.
Initial approach: **Proposal**
Deadline(s): None
Officers: James W. Pierson, Pres.; Jennifer Pierson, V.P.; Sally Pierson, Secy.; Nancy H. Pierson, Treas.
Trustees: Phoebe Pierson; Gerald Platter.
EIN: 222770138

1977
Point Gammon Foundation

c/o Paseornek & Stimola
140 Rte. 17 N., Ste. 206
Paramus, NJ 07652-2822

Established in 1994 in DE.
Donor: Jane C. Carroll.
Foundation type: Independent foundation.
Financial data (yr. ended 12/31/12): Assets, $11,655,430 (M); gifts received, $309,521; expenditures, $1,253,029; qualifying distributions, $1,246,160; giving activities include $1,246,160 for 48 grants (high: $231,332; low: $250).
Purpose and activities: Giving primarily for the arts, education, and human services.
Fields of interest: Arts, formal/general education; Museums (art); Performing arts; Performing arts, ballet; Higher education; Hospitals (general); Human services; Protestant agencies & churches.
Limitations: Applications not accepted. Giving primarily in New York, NY; funding also in MA and RI.
Application information: Unsolicited requests for funds not accepted.
Directors: Jane C. Carroll; **Jonathan C. Clay**.
EIN: 134049057

1978
Glen and Cynthia Post Foundation

(formerly Post Family Foundation)
P.O. Box 1501, NJ2-130-03-31
Pennington, NJ 08534-1501

Established in 2003 in FL.
Donor: Glen F. Post III.
Foundation type: Independent foundation.
Financial data (yr. ended 05/31/13): Assets, $3,454,177 (M); expenditures, $242,539; qualifying distributions, $219,050; giving activities include $205,523 for 6 grants (high: $100,000; low: $15,000).
Fields of interest: Higher education; Christian agencies & churches.
Type of support: General/operating support.
Limitations: Applications not accepted. Giving primarily in LA, TN and TX. No grants to individuals.
Application information: Unsolicited requests for funds not accepted.
Trustees: Cynthia S. Post; Glen F. Post III.
EIN: 586463580
Other changes: The grantmaker no longer lists a phone.

1979
Princeton Area Community Foundation, Inc.

(formerly The Princeton Area Foundation, Inc.)
15 Princess Rd.
Lawrenceville, NJ 08648-2301 (609) 219-1800
Contact: Nancy W. Kieling, Pres.
FAX: (609) 219-1850; E-mail: info@pacf.org; Main URL: http://www.pacf.org
Twitter: https://twitter.com/princetonareacf

Established in 1991 in NJ.
Foundation type: Community foundation.
Financial data (yr. ended 12/31/12): Assets, $88,395,021 (M); gifts received, $13,087,947; expenditures, $7,565,242; giving activities include $6,078,801 for 209+ grants (high: $471,100), and $145,896 for 39 grants to individuals.
Purpose and activities: The foundation seeks to promote philanthropy across central New Jersey by managing charitable funds created by members of the community, providing competitive discretionary grants to nonprofits, and by making advised grants to nonprofits after consultation with individuals or groups of donors. The foundation also serves as a convener and catalyst, leveraging new funds, and creating partnerships to enable residents to solve community problems.
Fields of interest: Education; Health care; Substance abuse, services; Minorities/immigrants, centers/services; Human services; Community/economic development; Minorities; Economically disadvantaged.
Type of support: Scholarships—to individuals; General/operating support; Continuing support; Emergency funds; Program development; Seed money; Curriculum development; Scholarship funds; Technical assistance.
Limitations: Applications accepted. Giving limited to Mercer County, NJ and surrounding communities in Hunterdon, Somerset, Middlesex, Monmouth and Burlington counties. No support for fraternal and religious activities. No grants for building renovations and new facility construction, capital and endowment campaigns and projects, fundraising appeals and events, field trips (unless part of a larger educational effort), sports activities (unless part of a larger educational effort), or sponsorship of events (sponsorships are occasionally made as part of the foundation's marketing efforts, and solely at the foundation's initiation).
Publications: Application guidelines; Annual report; Grants list; Informational brochure; Newsletter.
Application information: Visit foundation web site for application forms and information. The foundation recommends attending a grant information session before applying for a grant. Application form required.
Initial approach: Submit application form and attachments
Copies of proposal: 1
Deadline(s): Varies
Board meeting date(s): Quarterly
Final notification: 3 months
Officers and Trustees:* David R. Scott,* Chair.; John S. Watson, Jr.,* Vice-Chair.; Nancy W. Kieling,* Pres.; Michelle Cash,* V.P., Grants and Progs.; Elizabeth B. Wagner,* V.P., Devel.; Anne LaBate,* Secy.; Laura J. Longman, C.F.O.; Gordon Danser,* Treas. and Chair., Audit Comm.; William P. Burks, M.D.*, Chair., Asset Building Comm.; Andrew K. Golden,* Chair., Investment Comm.; Samuel W. Lambert III,* Chair., Grants Comm.; John D. Wallace,* Chair., Audit Comm.; Richard Bilotti; Anthony "Skip" Cimino; Sonia Delgado; Liz Erickson; Carol P. Herring; Patricia U. Herst; Eleanor Horne; Meredith C. Moore; Jeffrey F. Perlman; Patrick L. Ryan; Carolyn Sanderson; Lisa Skeete Tatum; Thomas P. Weidner.
Number of staff: 4 full-time professional; 2 full-time support.
EIN: 521746234
Other changes: Ann Reichelderfer is no longer Chair., Comm. on Trustees. Debra Perez is no longer a trustee.

1980
Puffin Foundation, Ltd.

20 Puffin Way
Teaneck, NJ 07666-4167
Contact: Gladys Miller-Rosenstein, Exec. Dir.
Application address: c/o Gladys Miller-Rosenstein, Exec. Dir., 20 Puffin Way, Teaneck, NJ 07666-4111; Main URL: http://www.puffinfoundation.org

Established in 1985 in NY.
Donors: Perry Rosenstein; Brighton-Best Socket Screw Manufacturing, Inc.
Foundation type: Independent foundation.
Financial data (yr. ended 12/31/12): Assets, $12,466,688 (M); gifts received, $1,000,694; expenditures, $2,614,568; qualifying distributions, $2,346,428; giving activities include $1,922,046 for grants.
Purpose and activities: The foundation make grants that encourage emerging artists whose works might have difficulty being aired due to their genre and/or social philosophy. Current areas of interest are video/film, fine arts, dance, and public interest.
Fields of interest: Media, film/video; Performing arts, dance; Arts.
Type of support: Publication; Seed money; Fellowships; Grants to individuals.
Limitations: Applications accepted. Giving on a national basis. No support for religious organizations. No grants for travel, general living expenses, continuing education, or publications.
Publications: Application guidelines.
Application information:
***Initial approach:* Send a S.A.S.E. (#10 business letter sized envelope) to request application form**
***Deadline(s):* See foundation web site for current deadline**
Board meeting date(s): Annually
Officers and Directors:* Perry Rosenstein,* Pres.; Gladys Miller-Rosenstein, Exec. Dir; Carl Rosenstein; Neal Rosenstein.
Number of staff: 6
EIN: 133155489

1981
Ramapo Trust

c/o The Brookdale Foundation Group
300 Frank W. Burr Blvd., Ste. 13
Teaneck, NJ 07666-6703 (201) 836-4602
Contact: For telephone inquiries: Nora O'Brien; For inquiry by mail:: Stephen L. Schwartz, Tr.
FAX: (201) 836-4342;
E-mail: vcb@brookdalefoundation.org; Main URL: http://www.brookdalefoundation.org/

Trust established in 1973 in NY.
Donors: Henry L. Schwartz†; Montebello Trust.
Foundation type: Independent foundation.
Financial data (yr. ended 06/30/13): Assets, $69,803,097 (M); expenditures, $4,148,859; qualifying distributions, $3,595,392; giving activities include $2,684,503 for 45 grants (high: $2,000,000; low: $953).

Purpose and activities: Giving for gerontological and geriatric research and innovative services; support also for health, higher and other education.
Fields of interest: Higher education; Medical school/education; Health care; Health organizations, association; Medical research, institute; Human services; Aging, centers/services; Jewish agencies & synagogues; Aging.
Type of support: Program development; Conferences/seminars; Seed money; Research; Matching/challenge support.
Limitations: Applications not accepted. Giving on a national basis. No grants to individuals, or for capital or building campaigns, operating budgets, continuing support, annual campaigns, media or the arts, or deficit financing; no loans.
Application information: Contributes only to pre-selected organizations.
Board meeting date(s): Quarterly
Trustees: Arthur Norman Field; Karen Schwartz Hart; Stephen L. Schwartz; Rebecca Shaffer; Mary Ann Van Clief.
Number of staff: 3 full-time professional; 2 part-time support.
EIN: 136594279
Other changes: The grantmaker has moved from NY to NJ.
For the fiscal year ended June 30, 2013, the grantmaker paid grants of $2,684,503, a 108.3% increase over the fiscal 2012 disbursements, $1,288,733.

1982
Fannie E. Rippel Foundation
14 Maple Ave., Ste. 200
Morristown, NJ 07960-5451 (973) 540-0101
Contact: Patricia MacBain, Office Mgr.
FAX: (973) 540-0404;
E-mail: info@rippelfoundation.org; Main URL: http://www.rippelfoundation.org
Facebook: https://www.facebook.com/RippelFoundation

Incorporated in 1953 in NJ.
Donor: Julius S. Rippel†.
Foundation type: Independent foundation.
Financial data (yr. ended 04/30/13): Assets, $81,335,353 (M); gifts received, $23,000; expenditures, $5,400,368; qualifying distributions, $4,320,551; giving activities include $317,519 for 17 grants (high: $121,864; low: $150), and $3,221,052 for foundation-administered programs.
Purpose and activities: The core purposes of the foundation are research and treatment related to cancer and heart disease, the health of women and the elderly, and the quality of our nation's hospitals. In today's health environment, the trustees have determined that major advances in these areas will come from substantially new ways of thinking about how we maintain our health, as well as how we define, structure, and deliver healthcare. New paradigms are needed that embrace the wholeness of the individual, the power of science, the globalization of medicine, and the challenging dynamics of our healthcare system. Knowing that purposeful actions can produce significant results, the mission of the foundation is to strategically invest its limited resources to seed innovation, catalyze change, and create model processes that will lead to improvements in health. The goal is to achieve better health, better care and lower costs for all.
Fields of interest: Health care, ethics; Medical care, community health systems; Hospitals (general); Hospitals (specialty); Health care, rural areas; Cancer; Heart & circulatory diseases; Geriatrics; Cancer research; Heart & circulatory research; Geriatrics research; Human services, mind/body enrichment; Gerontology; Aging; Women.
Type of support: Management development/capacity building; Program development; Research.
Limitations: Applications not accepted. Giving on a national basis. No grants to individuals, or for general purposes, operating budgets, continuing support, annual campaigns, deficit financing, scholarships, indirect costs, or building funds, no loans.
Publications: Financial statement; Grants list.
Application information: Unsolicited requests for funds not accepted. Check foundation web site periodically for information.
Board meeting date(s): Approximately 4 times a year
Officers and Trustees:* John D. Campbell,* Chair.; Laura K. Landy,* C.E.O. and Pres.; Chana Fitton, V.P. , Admin. and C.F.O.; Elizabeth G. Christopherson, Secy.; Edward W. Ahart; Elliott S. Fisher; David S. Surrenda.
Number of staff: 4 full-time professional; 2 part-time professional.
EIN: 221559427

1983
Robertson Foundation for Government Inc.
331 Newman Springs Rd.
Red Bank, NJ 07701-5688

Established in 2006 in DE.
Foundation type: Independent foundation.
Financial data (yr. ended 12/31/11): Assets, $1,064,684 (M); gifts received, $1,625,000; expenditures, $1,475,139; qualifying distributions, $1,185,675; giving activities include $563,800 for 8 grants (high: $112,500; low: $5,000).
Fields of interest: Education.
Type of support: Building/renovation.
Limitations: Applications not accepted. Giving primarily in CA, MD, MA, NY and TX.
Application information: Unsolicited request for funds not accepted.
Officers: Katherine R. Ernst, Pres.; Geoffrey S. Robertson, Secy.; John H. Linnartz, Treas.; Timothy Kemper, Exec. Dir.
Board Members: Robert Ernest; Charles R. Meier; William Robertson; Robert Halligan.
EIN: 204630877
Other changes: Geoffrey S. Robertson has replaced Robert Halligan as Secy.
Katherine R. Ernst is now Pres.

1984
Roma Bank Community Foundation, Inc.
2300 Rte. 33
Robbinsville, NJ 08691-1411
Contact: Emma Cartier, Secy. and Tr.

Established in 2006 in NJ.
Donor: Roma Bank.
Foundation type: Operating foundation.
Financial data (yr. ended 12/31/13): Assets, $5,376,358 (M); expenditures, $259,048; qualifying distributions, $257,599; giving activities include $256,150 for 30 grants (high: $20,000; low: $2,500).
Fields of interest: Museums; Education; Housing/shelter; Recreation, community; Human services; Christian agencies & churches.
Limitations: Applications accepted. Giving primarily in NJ.
Application information: Application form not required.
Initial approach: Proposal
Deadline(s): None
Officers: Nicholas Carnivale, Chair.; Peter A. Inverso, Pres.; Sharon L. Lamont, Treas.
Trustees: Robert Cashill; Kevin Cummings; Alfred DeBlasio, Jr.; James Kilgore; Eric Lear; Michele N. Siekerka, Esq.; **William Walsh, Jr.**
EIN: 562582815
Other changes: Emma Cartier is no longer Secy.

1985
The Roscitt Family Foundation
36 Island Dr.
Brick, NJ 08724-4432

Established in 2001 in NY.
Donors: Michelle W. Roscitt; Richard R. Roscitt.
Foundation type: Independent foundation.
Financial data (yr. ended 06/30/13): Assets, $633,737 (M); gifts received, $255,365; expenditures, $16,540; qualifying distributions, $12,850; giving activities include $12,850 for grants.
Fields of interest: Cancer, leukemia; Engineering/technology.
Limitations: Applications not accepted. Giving primarily in NJ, NY, and VA. No grants to individuals.
Application information: Contributes only to pre-selected organizations.
Board meeting date(s): As required
Directors: Michelle W. Roscitt; Richard R. Roscitt.
EIN: 134201736
Other changes: The grantmaker has moved from VA to NJ.

1986
Henry M. Rowan Family Foundation, Inc.
P.O. Box 157
Rancocas, NJ 08073-0157
Application address: c/o Henry M. Rowan, Pres., 10 Indel Ave., Rancocas, NJ 08073

Established in 1999 in NJ.
Donor: Henry M. Rowan.
Foundation type: Independent foundation.
Financial data (yr. ended 12/31/13): Assets, $214,900,561 (M); gifts received, $30,196,522; expenditures, $7,485,867; qualifying distributions, $6,878,000; giving activities include $6,878,000 for 45 grants (high: $1,500,000; low: $5,000).
Fields of interest: Scholarships/financial aid; Education; Environment; Human services.
Limitations: Applications accepted. Giving primarily in NJ and NY.
Application information: Application form not required.
Initial approach: Letter
Deadline(s): None
Officers and Directors:* Henry M. Rowan,* Pres.; Virginia Rowan Smith,* V.P.; Manning J. Smith III,* Secy.-Treas.; Gilbert A. Gehin-Scott; Eleanor Rowan.
EIN: 223655770
Other changes: At the close of 2013, the grantmaker paid grants of $6,878,000, a 70.7% increase over the 2012 disbursements, $4,030,000.

1987
The Charles and Brenda Saka Family Foundation
c/o Charles Saka
195 Carter Dr.
Edison, NJ 08817-2068

Established in 2001 in NJ.
Donor: Sakar International Inc.
Foundation type: Company-sponsored foundation.
Financial data (yr. ended 12/31/12): Assets, $781,007 (M); gifts received, $800,000; expenditures, $1,644,430; qualifying distributions, $1,644,057; giving activities include $1,644,057 for 175 grants (high: $737,500; low: $100).
Purpose and activities: The foundation supports organizations involved with education, children and youth, and Judaism.
Fields of interest: Education; Agriculture/food; Religion.
Type of support: General/operating support.
Limitations: Applications not accepted.
Application information: Contributes only to pre-selected organizations.
Trustees: Charles Saka; Jeffrey Saka; Raymond Saka; Sammy Saka.
EIN: 316650219
Other changes: The grantmaker no longer lists a primary contact.

1988
Sanofi Foundation for North America
(formerly Sanofi-aventis Patient Assistance Foundation)
55 Corporate Dr.
Bridgewater, NJ 08807-2855 (888) 847-4877
FAX: (888) 847-1797; E-mail: nacsr@sanofi.com;
Application address: P.O. Box 222138, Charlotte, NC 28222-2138; Main URL: http://www.sanofifoundation-northamerica.org/
Sanofi Patient Connection Enrollment Form: https://www.visitspconline.com/

Established in 1992.
Donors: Marion Merrell Dow Inc.; Hoechst Marion Roussel, Inc.; Aventis Pharmaceuticals Inc.; Sanofi-Aventis US, LLC; Genzyme Corp.
Foundation type: Company-sponsored foundation.
Financial data (yr. ended 12/31/12): Assets, $2,559,174 (M); gifts received, $286,483,724; expenditures, $284,044,399; qualifying distributions, $284,044,399; giving activities include $3,559,363 for grants, and $280,485,036 for grants to individuals.
Purpose and activities: The foundation provides medication for patients whose incomes are below the federal poverty level and who are not eligible for any third-party medication payments, and supports nonprofit organizations involved with health, human services, education, the environment, and civic and community issues.
Fields of interest: Elementary/secondary education; Higher education; Education; Environment, natural resources; Environment, energy; Environment; Health care; Pediatrics; Youth, services; Family services; Human services; Business/industry; Community/economic development; Economically disadvantaged.
Type of support: General/operating support; Grants to individuals; Donated products.
Limitations: Applications accepted. Giving on a national basis.
Publications: Application guidelines.
Application information: The foundation practices an invitation only process for general grants to organizations. Application form required.
Initial approach: **Download enrollment form or contact foundation for application information**
Deadline(s): None
Officers and Directors:* John Spinnato,* Pres.; Peter Lalli, V.P.; **George Pompetzki, V.P.**; **Sabrina Spitaletta, V.P.**; Martin Travers, Secy.; Edgar Grass, Treas.; **Bernard Armoury**; **Marc Bonnefoi**; **Damian Braga**; **Gregory Irace**; **David Meeker**; Anne Whitaker; Tom Zerzan.
EIN: 431614543

1989
Rueben & Muriel Savin Foundation
P.O. Box 1501, NJ2-130-03-31
Pennington, NJ 08534-1501

Established in 2001 in CA.
Donors: Nathan Savin; Muriel Savin Charitable Lead Trust; Muriel Savin†.
Foundation type: Independent foundation.
Financial data (yr. ended 03/31/13): Assets, $4,803,401 (M); expenditures, $417,985; qualifying distributions, $397,978; giving activities include $324,000 for 23 grants (high: $100,000; low: $1,000).
Fields of interest: Museums; Arts; Higher education, university; Libraries (public); United Ways and Federated Giving Programs; Jewish federated giving programs.
Type of support: General/operating support.
Limitations: Applications not accepted. Giving primarily in CA and IA. No grants to individuals.
Application information: Contributes only to pre-selected organizations.
Directors: Susan Enzle; **Linda Paul**; David L. Peterson; Nathan E. Savin.
EIN: 943399358

1990
The Schumann Fund for New Jersey, Inc.
21 Van Vleck St.
Montclair, NJ 07042-2373 (973) 509-9883
Contact: Barbara Reisman, Exec. Dir.
Main URL: http://foundationcenter.org/grantmaker/schumann/

Established in 1988 in NJ.
Donors: Florence Schumann†; John Schumann†; Florence and John Schumann Foundation.
Foundation type: Independent foundation.
Financial data (yr. ended 12/31/12): Assets, $24,207,433 (M); expenditures, $1,801,399; qualifying distributions, $1,501,340; giving activities include $1,140,500 for 79 grants (high: $50,000; low: $1,000).
Purpose and activities: Support primarily for 1) early childhood development; 2) environmental protection; 3) school innovation; and 4) local activities directed at solving community problems within Essex County.
Fields of interest: Education, early childhood education; Education; Environment; Human services; Children/youth, services; Public affairs; Infants/toddlers; Children/youth; Children.
Type of support: General/operating support; Continuing support; Program development; Seed money.
Limitations: Applications accepted. Giving limited to NJ, with emphasis on Essex County. No support for arts programs. No grants to individuals, or for capital campaigns, annual giving, or endowments.
Publications: Application guidelines; Annual report; Financial statement; Grants list.
Application information: The foundation accepts the New York/ New Jersey Area Common Application Form and the New York/ New Jersey Common Report Form. Program guidelines available on foundation web site. Application form not required.
Initial approach: Proposal
Copies of proposal: 1
Deadline(s): Jan. 15, Apr. 15, July 15, and Oct. 15
Board meeting date(s): Mar., June, Sept., and Dec.
Final notification: 4 to 8 weeks
Officers and Trustees:* Leonard S. Coleman,* Chair.; **Anthony Cicatiello,* Vice-Chair.**; **Roger Pratt,* Secy.-Treas.**; Barbara Reisman, Exec. Dir.; Aubin Z. Ames; Barbara Bell Coleman; Christopher J. Daggett; Martha Bonal Day; **Kenneth Zimmerman.**
Number of staff: 2 full-time professional.
EIN: 521556076
Other changes: Anthony Cicatiello has replaced Christopher Daggett as Vice-Chair. Roger Pratt has replaced Anthony Cicatiello as Secy.-Treas.
The grantmaker now makes its grants list available online.

1991
Schwarz Foundation
200 Central Ave., Ste. 102
Mountainside, NJ 07092-1691 **(908) 654-7010**

Established in 1982 in NJ.
Donors: Steven Schwarz; Henryk Schwarz; Brooklawn Gardens Inc.; East Rock Village, Inc.; Hensyn, Inc.; Greenwood Gardens, Inc.; Oakwood Homes, Inc.; Woodcliff, Inc.
Foundation type: Company-sponsored foundation.
Financial data (yr. ended 06/30/13): Assets, $30,613,944 (M); gifts received, $2,340,000; expenditures, $1,619,340; qualifying distributions, $1,617,500; giving activities include $1,617,500 for 24 grants (high: $1,145,000; low: $1,000).
Purpose and activities: The foundation supports hospitals and organizations involved with children and youth, family services, and Judaism.
Fields of interest: Hospitals (general); Children/youth, services; Family services; Jewish federated giving programs; Jewish agencies & synagogues.
Type of support: General/operating support.
Limitations: Applications not accepted. Giving primarily in NY; some funding in MA. No grants to individuals.
Application information: Contributes only to pre-selected organizations.
Officers: Steven Schwarz, Pres.; Henryk Schwarz, Secy.
EIN: 222430208
Other changes: At the close of 2013, the grantmaker paid grants of $1,617,500, a 94.8% increase over the 2012 disbursements, $830,500.

1992
George & Helen Segal Foundation
136 Davidson's Mill Rd.
North Brunswick, NJ 08902-4747
Contact: Susan Kutliroff, Secy.-Treas.
FAX: (732) 821-5877;
E-mail: segalfoundation@comcast.net; Application address for New Jersey Photographers: 357 Shawn Pl., North Brunswick, NJ 08902; Main URL: http://www.segalfoundation.org

Established in 2000 in NJ.
Donor: George Segal†.
Foundation type: Independent foundation.

Financial data (yr. ended 06/30/13): Assets, $19,085,822 (M); expenditures, $1,861,862; qualifying distributions, $1,294,900; giving activities include $1,294,900 for 6 grants (high: $450,000; low: $6,000).
Purpose and activities: Giving to exhibit and display the works of George Segal, and to award grants to artists for the pursuit of their artistic endeavors. Grants also to NJ photographers who are over the age of 21, and who are not students.
Fields of interest: Visual arts, photography; Museums (art).
Type of support: Grants to individuals.
Limitations: Giving primarily in NJ; funding for photographers is limited to NJ.
Publications: Grants list; Informational brochure.
Application information: The foundation has postponed its grant cycle. Check foundation web site for updates in this matter.
Board meeting date(s): Monthly
Officers: Helen Segal, Pres.; Rena Segal, V.P.; Susan Kutliroff, Secy.-Treas.
Number of staff: 2 full-time professional.
EIN: 223744151

1993
Siemens Foundation
170 Wood Ave. S.
Iselin, NJ 08830-2704 **(877) 822-5233**
FAX: (732) 590-1252;
E-mail: foundation.us@siemens.com; Main URL: http://www.siemens-foundation.org
Facebook: http://www.facebook.com/SiemensFoundation
Siemens STEM Academy on Facebook: http://www.facebook.com/pages/Siemens-STEM-Academy/268535066939?ref=nf
Siemens STEM Academy on Twitter: http://twitter.com/SiemensSTEMAcad
Siemens We Can Change the World Challenge: http://www.facebook.com/WeCanChange
Twitter: http://twitter.com/sfoundation
YouTube: http://www.youtube.com/siemensfoundation

Established in 1998 in NY.
Donor: Siemens Corp.
Foundation type: Company-sponsored foundation.
Financial data (yr. ended 09/30/12): Assets, $54,853,788 (M); gifts received, $6,128,695; expenditures, $7,861,552; qualifying distributions, $7,830,053; giving activities include $831,823 for 12 grants (high: $459,181; low: $1,000), and $745,800 for grants to individuals.
Purpose and activities: The foundation supports programs designed to enhance math and science education.
Fields of interest: Secondary school/education; Higher education; Teacher school/education; Education; Environment; Science, formal/general education; Chemistry; Mathematics; Physics; Engineering/technology; Computer science; Science; Children/youth; Minorities.
Type of support: General/operating support; Scholarship funds; Employee-related scholarships; Scholarships—to individuals.
Limitations: Applications accepted. Giving primarily in GA, IL, NV, TX, and VA; giving on a national basis for Seimens Competition in Math, Science.
Publications: Application guidelines; Program policy statement.
Application information:
Initial approach: Complete online application for Siemens Competition in Math, Science, and Technology and Siemens STARs and Institute; complete online registration for Siemens We Can Change the World Challenge
Copies of proposal: 1
Deadline(s): Oct. 1 for Siemens Competition in Math, Science, and Technology; Feb. 9 for Siemens STARs and Institute; Aug. 24 to Mar. 15 for Siemens We Can Change the World Challenge
Officers and Directors:* Thomas N. McCausland,* Chair.; James Whaley,* Vice-Chair.; **David D. Etzwiler, C.E.O.**; Jeniffer Harper-Taylor, Pres.; Daryl Dulaney; Judy Marks; Michael Panigel; Michael Reitermann; Gergory Sorensen; Eric A. Spiegel; Klaus P. Stegeman; Randy H. Zwirn.
EIN: 522136074
Other changes: Ken Cornelius, Tom Miller, and Peter Y. Solmssen are no longer directors.

1994
Walter H. Simson Foundation, Inc.
Township of Washington, NJ

The foundation terminated in 2011.

1995
The Helen M. Snyder Foundation
3163 Kennedy Blvd.
North Bergen, NJ **07047**

Donor: Richard Snyder.
Foundation type: Independent foundation.
Financial data (yr. ended 06/30/13): Assets, $4,410,226 (M); gifts received, $2,550,465; expenditures, $331,286; qualifying distributions, $246,700; giving activities include $246,700 for 19 grants (high: $100,000; low: $1,000).
Fields of interest: Education; Health organizations, association; Human services; Christian agencies & churches; Protestant agencies & churches.
Limitations: Applications not accepted. Giving primarily in NJ. No grants to individuals.
Application information: Unsolicited requests for funds not accepted.
Directors: Joseph Farrell; Catherine Keens; Edward M. Lombard.
EIN: 223036062
Other changes: Richard Snyder is no longer Pres.

1996
Marisa & Richard Stadtmauer Family Foundation, Inc.
26 Columbia Tpke.
Florham Park, NJ 07932-2266 (973) 822-0220
Contact: Marisa Stadtmauer, V.P.

Established in 1999 in NJ.
Donor: Richard Stadtmauer.
Foundation type: Independent foundation.
Financial data (yr. ended 11/30/12): Assets, $7,085,557 (M); expenditures, $3,519,040; qualifying distributions, $3,512,643; giving activities include $3,512,643 for 79 grants (high: $1,200,000; low: $36).
Purpose and activities: Giving primarily to Jewish agencies, temples, and schools.
Fields of interest: Education; Jewish federated giving programs; Jewish agencies & synagogues.
Limitations: Applications accepted. Giving primarily in NJ and NY.
Application information:
Initial approach: Letter
Deadline(s): None
Officers: Richard Stadtmauer, Pres.; Marisa Stadtmauer, V.P.
EIN: 223645402
Other changes: At the close of 2012, the grantmaker paid grants of $3,512,643, an 89.8% increase over the 2011 disbursements, $1,850,510.

1997
Stechler Foundation, Inc.
563 Winthrop Rd.
Teaneck, NJ **07666-2970**

Established in 1998 in NJ.
Donors: Gail Stechler; Joseph Stechler; Bezalel Aryeh Stechler.
Foundation type: Independent foundation.
Financial data (yr. ended 12/31/12): Assets, $254 (M); expenditures, $165; qualifying distributions, $165; giving activities include $165 for grants.
Fields of interest: Jewish agencies & synagogues.
Limitations: Applications not accepted. Giving primarily in NJ. No grants to individuals.
Application information: Unsolicited requests for funds not accepted.
Trustees: Bezalel Aryeh Stechler; Gail Stechler; Joseph Stechler.
EIN: 223554695

1998
The Summit Area Public Foundation
P.O. Box 867
Summit, NJ 07902-0867 (908) 277-1422
Contact: Barbara Bunting, Treas.
FAX: (908) 277-3042; E-mail: info@sapfnj.org; Grant inquiry e-mail: grants@sapfnj.org; Main URL: http://www.sapfnj.org

Established in 1972 in NJ.
Foundation type: Community foundation.
Financial data (yr. ended 12/31/12): Assets, $13,706,082 (M); gifts received, $229,132; expenditures, $743,899; giving activities include $656,164 for 147+ grants (high: $30,000; low: $32).
Purpose and activities: The Summit Area Public Foundation fosters area-wide philanthropy by identifying local needs and offering donors flexible ways to make a difference in the lives of their neighbors.
Fields of interest: Arts; Education; Health care; Cancer research; Children, services; Community/economic development; Children/youth; Aging; Disabilities, people with.
Type of support: Building/renovation; Equipment; Emergency funds; Program development; Conferences/seminars; Seed money; Scholarship funds; Research; Technical assistance; Matching/challenge support.
Limitations: Applications accepted. Giving limited to the Summit, NJ, area. No support for religious organizations. No grants to individuals (except for scholarships), or for normal annual operating budgets, capital campaigns, or endowments.
Publications: Application guidelines; Grants list; Informational brochure.
Application information: Visit web site for additional application information. Application form required.
Initial approach: Letter
Copies of proposal: 10
Deadline(s): Feb. 15 and Sept. 15
Board meeting date(s): Quarterly
Final notification: June and Dec.

Officers and Trustees:* John W. Cooper,* Pres.; David Dietze,* V.P.; Lyle Brehm,* Secy.; Barbara E. Bunting,* Treas.; Linda B. Hander,* Asst. Treas.; Celine Benet; Sandy Bloom; Reagan Burkholder; Eugene Fox; Jordan Glatt; Baxter Graham; Cary Hardy; Esther Harper; David Hartman; Julie Keenan; Sandra R. Lizza; Frank Macioce; Joanne McDonough; Henry M. Ogden; Mort O'Shea; Gregory Sachs, M.D.
EIN: 221948007
Other changes: Sarah Rosen is no longer a trustee.

1999
Sy Syms Foundation
1 Bridge Plz. N., Ste. 275
Fort Lee, NJ **07024-7586**

Established in 1985 in NJ.
Donor: Sy Syms‡.
Foundation type: Independent foundation.
Financial data (yr. ended 04/30/13): Assets, $40,826,374 (M); expenditures, $1,933,251; qualifying distributions, $1,656,608; giving activities include $1,636,880 for 45 grants (high: $150,000; low: $5,000).
Purpose and activities: Giving primarily for media, Jewish welfare and other Jewish organizations; grants also for higher education and the arts.
Fields of interest: Media, television; Arts; Higher education; Education; Health organizations, association; Human services; Jewish federated giving programs; Jewish agencies & synagogues.
International interests: Israel.
Type of support: General/operating support; Scholarship funds.
Limitations: Applications not accepted. Giving primarily in the U.S., with emphasis on NY. No grants to individuals.
Application information: Contributes only to pre-selected organizations.
Officers and Trustees:* Marcy Syms Merns,* Pres.; Mark Freiberg,* Treas.; Lynn Tamarkin Syms; Robert Syms.
EIN: 222617727

2000
The Henry and Marilyn Taub Foundation
300 Frank W. Burr Blvd., 7th Fl.
Teaneck, NJ 07666-6703 (201) 287-2500

Established in 1967 in DE.
Donors: Henry Taub‡; Marilyn Taub; Endowment Foundation of UJA Federation of Bergen County & North Hudson; Henry Taub Revocable Trust.
Foundation type: Independent foundation.
Financial data (yr. ended 12/31/13): Assets, $171,679,489 (M); expenditures, $8,441,678; qualifying distributions, $7,412,337; giving activities include $6,705,338 for 188 grants (high: $1,175,750; low: $100).
Purpose and activities: Grants largely for Jewish welfare funds; some support for higher and other education, social service and youth agencies, and hospitals.
Fields of interest: Higher education; Education; Hospitals (general); Human services; Children/youth, services; Jewish federated giving programs; Jewish agencies & synagogues.
Limitations: Applications not accepted. Giving primarily in NJ and NY. No grants to individuals.
Application information: Contributes only to pre-selected organizations.
Officers and Directors:* Steven Taub,* Chair. and Pres.; Judith Gold,* V.P. and Secy.; Ira Taub,* V.P. and Treas.; Barbara Lawrence, Exec. Dir.; Marilyn Taub.
EIN: 226100525
Other changes: Fred S. Lafer, Vice-Chair., is deceased.

2001
The Tufenkian Foundation
20 Capitol Dr.
Moonachie, NJ 07074 (201) 221-1055, ext. 367
FAX: (201) 221-1070;
E-mail: akasbarian@tufenkian.com; Main URL: http://www.tufenkianfoundation.org/
Facebook: https://www.facebook.com/TufenkianFoundation

Established in NY.
Donors: James Tufenkian; Adrienne V. Tashjian; Alber K. Karamanoukian; Alex Sarafian; John Kasbarian; K. George Najarian; Tufenkian Import/Export Ventures; Onnik Keshishian; Anahid Mardirosian; George M. Aghjayan; Itsmyseat.com; Kirakos Vapurciyan; Kpaa-Kaiser Permanente; Sara Anjargolian; United Way of NYC; Vahe Nahabetian; Virginia L. Davies; Westpac Banking Corp.
Foundation type: Operating foundation.
Financial data (yr. ended 11/30/12): Assets, $11,431,672 (M); gifts received, $99,539; expenditures, $318,169; qualifying distributions, $318,169; giving activities include $226,979 for 22 grants (high: $70,214; low: $100).
Purpose and activities: Giving primarily for the benefit of Armenian society.
Fields of interest: Education; Human services; Children/youth, services.
Limitations: Applications not accepted. Giving primarily in NY. No grants to individuals.
Application information: Unsolicited requests for funds not accepted.
Officer: James Tufenkian, Pres.
Directors: Diane L. Hodges; David F. Tufenkian.
EIN: 133976159

2002
Turrell Fund
21 Van Vleck St.
Montclair, NJ 07042-2358 (973) 783-9358
Contact: Curtland E. Fields, Pres., C.E.O. and Secy.
FAX: (973) 783-9283; E-mail: turrell@turrellfund.org; Application Contact: Jeneanne Kautzmann, Grants, Mgr.; e-mail: application@turrellfund.org; Main URL: http://www.turrellfund.org

Incorporated in 1935 in NJ.
Donors: Herbert Turrell‡; Margaret Turrell‡.
Foundation type: Independent foundation.
Financial data (yr. ended 12/31/12): Assets, $109,008,610 (M); expenditures, $6,105,840; qualifying distributions, $5,549,448; giving activities include $4,359,610 for 239 grants (high: $325,000; low: $1,000).
Purpose and activities: Grants to organizations dedicated to service or care of children and youth under 12 years of age, with emphasis on the needy, and the disadvantaged; funding also for advocacy and policy involvement.
Fields of interest: Education, early childhood education; Education; Human services; Children/youth, services; Children/youth; Children; Economically disadvantaged.
Type of support: General/operating support; Continuing support; Capital campaigns; Building/renovation; Equipment; Program development; Seed money; Scholarship funds; Matching/challenge support.
Limitations: Applications accepted. Giving limited to Essex, Union, Hudson and Passaic counties, NJ, and VT. No support for lobbying activity, most hospital work, or health delivery services; generally no support for cultural activities. No grants to individuals, or for endowment funds, conferences indirect costs, or research; no loans.
Publications: Application guidelines; Annual report (including application guidelines); Financial statement; Grants list.
Application information: No proposals are to be faxed or sent by e-mail. Organizations applying to the fund for the first time should submit written travel instructions (or a map) along with the proposal in order to facilitate a possible site visit. Online grant transmission only (see foundation web site for guidelines and application). Application form not required.

Initial approach: All applications and proposals must be submitted online
Copies of proposal: 1
Deadline(s): Jan. 1-Feb. 1 (for spring grant cycle), and July 1- Aug. 1 (for fall grant cycle)
Board meeting date(s): May and Nov.
Final notification: Late June and Dec.

Officers and Trustees:* S. Lawrence Prendergast,* Chair.; Curtland E. Fields,* C.E.O., Pres. and Secy.; Sonyia Woloshyn, V.P. and Treas.; Robert E. Angelica; Elizabeth W. Christie; William S. Gannon; Matthew Melmed; Julia A. Miller; Rev. Dr. John P. Mitchell; John Morning; Mark Sustic.
Advisor: Stewart F. Campbell.
Number of staff: 3 full-time professional; 2 full-time support; 1 part-time support.
EIN: 221551936

2003
Unilever United States Foundation, Inc.
c/o Unilever United States, Inc.
800 Sylvan Ave.
Englewood Cliffs, NJ 07632-3113 (201) 894-2450
Contact: Greg Postian, Asst. V.P.
Additional contact: Philip Cohen, tel.: (201) 894-2236; **Main URL: http://www.unileverusa.com/aboutus/foundation/**

Incorporated in 1952 in NY.
Donors: Unilever United States, Inc.; Lever Bros. Co.; Van den Bergh Foods Co.; Unilever Research.
Foundation type: Company-sponsored foundation.
Financial data (yr. ended 12/31/12): Assets, $710,050 (M); gifts received, $2,172,183; expenditures, $1,755,675; qualifying distributions, $1,755,675; giving activities include $1,749,201 for 1,667 grants (high: $796,970; low: $13).
Purpose and activities: The foundation supports programs designed to promote healthier lifestyles for families and children with a focus on good nutrition, active healthy lifestyles, self-esteem, and hunger relief; and environmental issues with a focus on climate change, water conservation, waste and packaging, and environmental preservation.
Fields of interest: Education; Environment, waste management; Environment, climate change/global warming; Environment, natural resources; Environment, water resources; Environment; Public health, physical fitness; Food services; Food banks; Nutrition; Children/youth, services; Human services; Community/economic development.
Type of support: General/operating support; Program development; Scholarship funds; Employee matching gifts; Employee-related scholarships.

Limitations: Applications accepted. Giving primarily in areas of company operations, with emphasis on Washington, DC, IL, NJ, and NY. No support for religious, labor, political, or veterans' organizations. No grants to individuals (except for employee-related scholarships), or for goodwill advertising, fundraising events or testimonial dinners, or capital campaigns; no loans.
Publications: Application guidelines.
Application information: Application form not required.
Initial approach: Proposal
Copies of proposal: 1
Deadline(s): None
Board meeting date(s): May, Oct., and Dec.
Final notification: 1 month following board meetings
Officers and Directors:* Jonathan Atwood,* Pres.; Sharon Rossi,* V.P.; David A. Schwartz, V.P.; Lauren Beck, Secy.; Henry Schirmer,* Treas.
Number of staff: 1 part-time professional.
EIN: 136122117

2004
The Westfield Foundation
301 North Ave. W.
P.O. Box 2295
Westfield, NJ 07091 (908) 233-9787
Contact: Elizabeth B. Chance, Exec. Dir.
FAX: (908) 233-2177;
E-mail: foundation@westfieldnj.com; Main URL: http://www.thewestfieldfoundation.com
RSS Feed: http://thewestfieldfoundation.com/feed/

Incorporated in 1975 in NJ.
Foundation type: Community foundation.
Financial data (yr. ended 12/31/12): Assets, $11,992,816 (M); gifts received, $450,499; expenditures, $383,634; giving activities include $226,094 for 18+ grants (high: $35,000), and $96,400 for 62 grants to individuals.
Purpose and activities: The foundation's mission is to enhance and support the quality of life of the citizens of Westfield, NJ.
Fields of interest: Historic preservation/historical societies; Arts; Education; Health care; Human services; Community/economic development.
Type of support: Management development/capacity building; Building/renovation; Equipment; Emergency funds; Program development; Conferences/seminars; Publication; Seed money; Curriculum development; Research; Technical assistance; Matching/challenge support.
Limitations: Applications accepted. Giving limited to the Westfield, NJ, area. No support for churches, hospitals (except for programs with a strong Westfield orientation), religious organizations for religious activities, or private or parochial schools. No grants to individuals (except for scholarships), or for annual giving, operating expenses, deficit financing, travel, retro-funding, or endowments, unless suggested by the donor of a particular fund.
Publications: Application guidelines; Annual report; Financial statement; Informational brochure; Newsletter.
Application information: Visit foundation web site for application form and guidelines. Application form required.
Initial approach: Submit application form and attachments
Copies of proposal: 1
Deadline(s): Jan. 1, Apr. 1, Aug. 1, and Oct. 1
Board meeting date(s): Feb., May, Sept., and Nov.
Final notification: 1 week after board meeting
Officers and Trustees:* Russell Finestein,* Pres.; Beth Cassie,* V.P.; **Howard Cohen,* Secy.**; Alice Fertig,* Treas.; Elizabeth B. Chance, Exec. Dir.; Claudia Andreski; Jay Boyle; Sal Caruana; Karen Fountain; Robert Gorelick; Ray Kostyack; Michelle Mattessich; Janet Sarkos; Mark Swingle; Darielle Walsh.
Number of staff: 1 part-time professional.
EIN: 222155896
Other changes: Howard Cohen is no longer a member of the governing body.

2005
The Wight Foundation, Inc.
550 Broad St., Ste. 717
Newark, NJ **07102-4516** (973) 824-1195
***Contact:* Rhonda Aususte, Exec. Dir.**
FAX: (973) 824-1199;
E-mail: Wightfoundation@wightfoundation.org;
E-mail for Rhonda Auguste, Exec. Dir.: rauguste@wightfoundation.org; Main URL: http://www.wightfoundation.org

Incorporated in 1986 in NJ.
Donor: Russell Wight, Jr.
Foundation type: Independent foundation.
Financial data (yr. ended 12/31/12): Assets, $13,976,551 (M); expenditures, $1,554,601; qualifying distributions, $1,511,860; giving activities include $147,240 for grants, and $395,921 for grants to individuals.
Purpose and activities: Scholarship awards to seventh-grade students, primarily economically disadvantaged, who attend school in the greater Newark, New Jersey, area.
Fields of interest: Education.
Type of support: General/operating support; Scholarships—to individuals.
Limitations: Applications accepted. Giving limited to the greater Newark, NJ, area.
Publications: Informational brochure (including application guidelines); Newsletter.
Application information: Application guidelines and form available on foundation web site. Application form required.
Initial approach: Complete preliminary application form
Deadline(s): See foundation web site for application deadlines
Board meeting date(s): Bimonthly
Officers and Trustees:* Russell Wight, Jr.,* Pres.; Rhonda Auguste, Exec. Dir.; Bruce Byrne; Yvonne Goyins; Shakirah Miller; Christopher Miller; Alfred Woods.
Number of staff: 1 full-time professional; 2 full-time support.
EIN: 222743349

NEW MEXICO

2006
Albuquerque Community Foundation
624 Tijeras Ave., NW
Albuquerque, NM 87102 (505) 883-6240
Contact: For grants: Nancy Johnson, Prog. Dir.
FAX: (505) 883-3629;
E-mail: foundation@albuquerquefoundation.org;
Mailing address: P.O. Box 25266, Albuquerque, NM 87125-5266; Additional e-mail: njohnson@albuquerquefoundation.org; Main URL: http://www.albuquerquefoundation.org
E-Newsletter: http://visitor.constantcontact.com/manage/optin?v=001EZ1xV5UTY8v4rVPDf6-vAY-_jw1XHvlL
Facebook: http://www.facebook.com/pages/Albuquerque-Community-Foundation/172927816931?ref=ts
Twitter: http://twitter.com/abqfoundation

Established in 1981 in NM.
Foundation type: Community foundation.
Financial data (yr. ended 12/31/12): Assets, $58,483,813 (M); gifts received, $4,523,537; expenditures, $4,336,610; giving activities include $2,896,420 for 161+ grants (high: $800,000), and $131,996 for 126 grants to individuals.
Purpose and activities: The foundation's mission is to build, invest and manage endowment funds to enhance the quality of the community through informed strategic grantmaking.
Fields of interest: Historic preservation/historical societies; Arts; Education; Environment, natural resources; Environment; Health care; Children/youth, services; Human services; Children/youth.
Type of support: Continuing support; General/operating support; Program development; Scholarship funds; Scholarships—to individuals.
Limitations: Applications accepted. Giving primarily in the greater Albuquerque, NM, area. No support for religious purposes, private foundations, or for grantmaking organizations. **Generally, no grants to individuals (except for scholarship funds), or for debt retirement, annual campaigns, capital campaigns, fundraising events, endowments, conferences or symposia, emergency funding or interest or tax payments; no multi-year grants.**
Publications: Annual report (including application guidelines); Financial statement; Grants list; Newsletter.
Application information: Visit foundation web site for application guidelines. Faxed applications are not accepted. Application form not required.
Initial approach: Letter of Intent
Copies of proposal: 8
Deadline(s): Changes annually
Board meeting date(s): Quarterly
***Final notification:* 1 to 2 months**
Officers and Trustees:* Kevin Yearout,* Chair.; Jennifer S. Thomas,* Chair.-Elect.; R. Randall Royster, Esq.,* Pres. and C.E.O.; Glenn Fellows,* Secy.; Julie Weaks Gutierrez,* Treas.; Carl M. Alongi; Karen Bard; Julie Bowdich; William E. Ebel; Terri Giron-Gordon; Mark Gorham; Ted Jorgensen; Steven Keene; William Lang; Kenneth C. Leach; Steve Maestas; Bev McMillan; Marcus Mims, CPA; Diane Harrison Ogawa; Deborah Peacock; Kathleen Raskob; Ron J. Rivera; Jerrald J. Roehl; Chester French Stewart; Peter Touche.
Number of staff: 4 full-time professional; 2 part-time professional; 1 full-time support; 1 part-time support.
EIN: 850295444
Other changes: Kevin Yearout has replaced Ron J. Rivera as Chair. Jennifer S. Thomas has replaced Kevin Yearout as Chair.-Elect. Glenn Fellows has replaced Chester Stewart as Secy. Julie Weaks Gutierrez has replaced Carl Alongi as Treas. R. Randall Royster, Esq. is now Pres. and C.E.O. Nancy Croker, Glenn Fellows, Julie Weaks Gutierrez, and Jennifer Thomas are no longer trustees.

2007
Aurora Foundation
c/o Jeffrey Bronfman
1000 Cordova Pl.
PMB 710
Santa Fe, NM 87505-1825 (505) 988-5924

Established in 1993 in TX and NM.
Donor: Jeffrey Bronfman.
Foundation type: Operating foundation.
Financial data (yr. ended 09/30/12): Assets, $245,369 (M); gifts received, $251,722; expenditures, $661,929; qualifying distributions, $562,762; giving activities include $518,544 for 18 grants (high: $267,298; low: $1,000).
Purpose and activities: Giving for projects that embody strategic efforts for the preservation and protection of planetary ecosystems (i.e. the environment), as well as efforts that secure the perpetuation and practice of indigenous cultures and ancient religious, spiritual and ceremonial traditions (e.g. certain Native American cultures and their religious traditions.).
Fields of interest: Education; Environment.
International interests: Central America; South America.
Limitations: Applications accepted. Giving primarily in NM; some funding also in CA, HI and NY.
Application information:
Deadline(s): None
Officers and Directors:* Jeffrey Bronfman,* Pres. and Treas.; Duncan E. Osborne,* Secy.; Irvin F. Diamond.
EIN: 742660772

2008
B.F. Foundation
c/o David Chase
766 Calle del Resplandor
Santa Fe, NM **87505-5988**
E-mail: dchase@vestor.com

Established in 1965 in AZ.
Donors: Harvey W. Branigar, Jr.‡; Sarah L. Branigar.
Foundation type: Independent foundation.
Financial data (yr. ended 12/31/12): Assets, $4,028,150 (M); gifts received, $134,393; expenditures, $315,782; qualifying distributions, $213,448; giving activities include $178,400 for 32 grants (high: $70,000; low: $50).
Purpose and activities: Giving primarily for education and conservation.
Fields of interest: Museums; Arts; Higher education; Education; Botanical gardens; Environment.
Type of support: General/operating support; Internship funds; Scholarship funds.
Limitations: Applications not accepted. Giving primarily in AZ, CO, and NM. No grants or scholarships to individuals directly.
Application information: Unsolicited requests for funds not accepted.
Officers and Directors:* David D. Chase,* Chair.; Katherin Lee Chase, Pres. and Exec. Dir.; Sara Chase Shaw,* V.P. and Secy.-Treas.; Richard W. Shaw.
Number of staff: 1 full-time professional; 1 part-time professional.
EIN: 366141070

2009
Chase Foundation
510 Texas Ave.
Artesia, NM 88210-2041 (575) 746-4610
Contact: Richard Price, Exec. Dir.
E-mail: richardprice@chasefoundation.com;
Additional e-mail: info@chasefoundation.com;
Additional Contact: Ginny Bush, Assoc. Dir., e-mail: GinnyBush@chasefoundation.com; Main URL: http://www.chasefoundation.com
Facebook: http://www.facebook.com/chasefoundation
Grants List: http://www.chasefoundation.com/index.php/grants-11/historical-funding
Scholarship Recipients: http://www.chasefoundation.com/index.php/scholarships-12/past-recipients/2013

Established in 2006 in NM.
Donors: Gerene Furguson; Mack C. Chase; Marilyn Y. Chase; Chase Oil Co.
Foundation type: Company-sponsored foundation.
Financial data (yr. ended 12/31/12): Assets, $43,095,024 (M); gifts received, $127,370; expenditures, $2,630,880; qualifying distributions, $2,358,770; giving activities include $2,089,375 for 83 grants (high: $800,000; low: $200).
Purpose and activities: The foundation supports organizations involved with pre-school through 12th grade education, higher education, substance abuse, domestic violence, community development, charity infrastructure, youth development, and emergency and critical human services.
Fields of interest: Elementary/secondary education; Higher education; Substance abuse, services; Crime/violence prevention, domestic violence; Youth development; Human services; Community/economic development; Philanthropy/voluntarism.
Type of support: General/operating support; Building/renovation; Program development; Scholarship funds; Employee-related scholarships; Scholarships—to individuals.
Limitations: Applications accepted. Giving primarily in southeastern NM; some giving also in west TX. No support for political or lobbying organizations or international organizations,. No grants to individuals (except for scholarships), or for general operating expenses of established programs, interests or programs detrimental to the oil and gas industry, ticketed events, or projects that do not have sustainability for a 5 year period; no loans.
Publications: Application guidelines; Grants list.
Application information: Application form required.
Initial approach: Compete online application
***Deadline(s):* 4 weeks prior to quarterly board meeting; Apr. 24 for scholarships for graduating AHS students; June 9 for scholarships for 5th year college seniors**
Board meeting date(s): 2nd Tues. of Mar., June, Sept., and Dec.
Officer and Directors: Richard Price,* Exec. Dir.; Deb Chase; Karla Chase; Mack C. Chase; Marilyn Y. Chase; Richard Chase; Robert Chase; Gerene Dianne Chase Ferguson; Johnny Knorr.
Advisor: Brad Bartek.
Trustee: JPMorgan Chase Bank, N.A.
EIN: 367466258
Other changes: The grantmaker no longer publishes an annual report.

2010
Community Foundation of Southern New Mexico
301 S. Church St., Ste. H
Las Cruces, NM 88001 (575) 521-4794
Contact: Luan Wagner Burn Ph.D., Exec. Dir.
E-mail: luan@cfsnm.org; Main URL: http://www.cfsnm.org

Established in 1999 in NM; incorporated in 2000.
Foundation type: Community foundation.
Financial data (yr. ended 12/31/12): Assets, $13,902,672 (M); gifts received, $3,802,476; expenditures, $1,415,729; giving activities include $561,090 for 8+ grants (high: $90,375).
Purpose and activities: The foundation serves as a charitable resource linking donors with community needs.
Limitations: Applications accepted. Giving primarily in Dona Ana, Grant, Hidalgo, Lincoln, Luna, Otero and Sierra counties, NM.
Publications: Annual report; Financial statement.
Application information: Visit foundation for information.
Officers and Directors:* Jeremy Settles,* Pres.; Richard Williams,* V.P.; Diana Seward,* Secy.; Beth Fant,* Treas.; Luan Wagner Burn, Ph.D., Exec. Dir.; **Ken Binkley**; Barrett Brewer; Jennifer Cervantes; **Abel Covarrubias**; Mellow Honek; Many Leatherwood; **Denten Park**.
EIN: 850455682
Other changes: Beth Fant, Diana Seward, Jeremy Settles, and Richard C. Williams are no longer directors.

2011
Con Alma Health Foundation, Inc.
144 Park Ave.
Santa Fe, NM 87501-1833 (505) 438-0776
FAX: (505) 438-6223; E-mail: staff@conalma.org; Main URL: http://www.conalma.org
Con Alma Health Foundation's Philanthropy Promise: http://www.ncrp.org/philanthropys-promise/who
Facebook: http://www.facebook.com/pages/Con-Alma-Health-Foundation/97700599976
Online Application Powerpoint: http://conalma.org/resources_list/online-application-powerpoint/
Online Application Video: http://conalma.org/resources_list/cahf-online-grant-application-introduction-video/
RebelMouse: https://www.rebelmouse.com/ConAlmaHealthFoundation/
Twitter: https://twitter.com/NMhealth
YouTube: http://www.youtube.com/user/ConAlmaNM

The foundation was established in 2001, through the sale of Blue Cross/Blue Shield of New Mexico. The conversion provided charitable assets of $20 million for the foundation.
Donors: Kellogg Foundation; Robert Wood Johnson Foundation; McCune Foundation; Grantmakers in Health.
Foundation type: Independent foundation.
Financial data (yr. ended 12/31/12): Assets, $25,080,623 (M); gifts received, $325,350; expenditures, $1,265,819; qualifying distributions, $993,783; giving activities include $351,208 for 40 grants (high: $15,600; low: $1,500).
Purpose and activities: The foundation is organized to be aware of and respond to the health rights and needs of culturally and demographically diverse peoples and communities of New Mexico. The foundation seeks to address the health needs of underserved populations, to support and strengthen nonprofits that seek to improve the health of the underserved, to encourage leaders in the field, and to inform the development of public policies that promote wellness and access to preventive health care.
Fields of interest: Health care; Infants/toddlers; Children/youth; Youth; Aging; Minorities; Hispanics/Latinos; Native Americans/American Indians; Indigenous peoples; Women; AIDS, people with; Immigrants/refugees; Homeless.
Type of support: General/operating support; Management development/capacity building; Program development; Conferences/seminars; Seed money; Research; Technical assistance; Program evaluation.
Limitations: Applications accepted. Giving limited to NM. No support for lobbying. No grants to individuals, for scholarships/fellowships, or for bricks, mortar, or property.
Publications: Application guidelines; Annual report; Grants list; Informational brochure.
Application information: Application form available on foundation web site. See foundation web site for guidelines and requirements.
Initial approach: **See online application process on foundation web site**
Deadline(s): Varies according to grant cycle
Board meeting date(s): Jan., Apr., July and Oct.
Final notification: Varies
Officers and Trustees:* Erin Bouquin, M.D.*, Pres.; Louis Luna, V.P.; Alfredo Vigil, M.D.*, Secy.; Steve Gaber,* Treas.; Dolores E. Roybal, Exec. Dir.; Jane Batson; Marcie Chavez; Laurel Iron Cloud; **Ardena Orosco**; **Sherrick Roanhorse**; **Valerie Romero-Leggott, M.D.**; **Twila Rutter**; Benny Shendo, Jr.; James Summers; **Richard Tyner**.
Number of staff: 3 full-time professional; 3 part-time professional; 1 full-time support.
EIN: 850484396
Other changes: Erin Bouquin, M.D. has replaced Robert Archuleta as Pres. Louis Luna has replaced Erin Bouquin, M.D. as V.P. Alfredo Vigil, M.D. has replaced Louis Luna as Secy.
Gayle Dine Chacon, Patricia Collins, David Reede, and Juan Vigil are no longer directors.

2012
The Frost Foundation, Ltd.
511 Armijo St., Ste. A
Santa Fe, NM 87501-2899 (505) 986-0208
Contact: Mary Amelia Whited-Howell, Pres.
E-mail: info@frostfound.org; Louisiana grant request fax: (505) 986-0430; Main URL: http://www.frostfound.org

Incorporated in 1959 in LA.
Donor: Virginia C. Frost†.
Foundation type: Independent foundation.
Financial data (yr. ended 12/31/12): Assets, $27,933,056 (M); expenditures, $2,220,527; qualifying distributions, $1,820,036; giving activities include $1,568,768 for 86+ grants (high: $505,000).
Purpose and activities: Focus on the following areas: 1) Social service and humanitarian needs including, but not limited to, violence in the streets, domestic violence, child abuse, specific public health issues such as alcohol and drug abuse, homelessness, and problems of the elderly; 2) Environment - consideration given to programs in research, education, and action to conserve and protect the environment for the well-being and safety of plants, animals, and human beings; and 3) Education - focus on new, innovative, creative, practical programs to address students' and society's needs today, and which recognize our changing sociological structure and concerns.
Fields of interest: Higher education; Business school/education; Education; Environment, natural resources; Environment; Animal welfare; Health care; Substance abuse, services; Mental health/crisis services; Health organizations, association; AIDS; AIDS research; Food services; Human services; Children/youth, services; Family services; Residential/custodial care, hospices; Aging, centers/services; Women, centers/services; Minorities/immigrants, centers/services; Homeless, human services; Aging; Minorities; Native Americans/American Indians; Women; Homeless.
Type of support: Continuing support; Capital campaigns; Equipment; Program development; Conferences/seminars; Publication; Seed money; Curriculum development; Fellowships; Technical assistance; Matching/challenge support.
Limitations: Giving primarily in LA and NM. No support for animal experimentation. No grants to individuals, or for building funds, sponsorships for special events, endowment funds, medical research, or scholarships; no loans.
Publications: Application guidelines; Biennial report.
Application information: Full proposals are by invitation, upon review of initial letter. Faxed submissions are not accepted. Application form not required.
Initial approach: 1-page letter
***Copies of proposal:* 4**
Deadline(s): Dec. 1, for consideration at Mar. meeting, and June 1, for consideration at Sept. meeting
Board meeting date(s): Mar. and Sept.
Final notification: 7 to 10 days
Officers and Directors:* Mary Amelia Whited-Howell,* Pres.; Philip B. Howell,* Exec. V.P.; Taylor Frost Moore,* Secy.-Treas.; Ann Rogers Gerber; John A. LeVan.
Number of staff: 1 full-time professional; 1 part-time professional; 1 full-time support.
EIN: 720520342

2013
Garfield Street Foundation
330 Garfield St.
Santa Fe, NM 87501-2612 **(505) 992-5100**
***Contact:* Robin Smith, V.P.**

Established in 1999 in NM.
Donors: Edward M. Gilbert; BGK Equities II, LLC; BGKP Properties, Inc.; BGK Property Mgmt. LLC; Fresno Clinton Operating Assoc., LP.
Foundation type: Independent foundation.
Financial data (yr. ended 06/30/13): Assets, $243,059 (M); gifts received, $308,215; expenditures, $374,524; qualifying distributions, $302,783; giving activities include $302,783 for 10 + grants (high: $100,000).
Fields of interest: Performing arts, orchestras; Arts; Education; Human services.
Limitations: Applications accepted. Giving primarily in NM, with emphasis on Santa Fe.
Application information: Application form required.
Initial approach: Letter from an agency on behalf of their client
Deadline(s): None
Officer: Robin Smith, V.P.
Directors: Ian Brownlow; Eileen Gabaldon; Steve Love.
EIN: 752830956
Other changes: Katherine Jetter-Burrell is no longer Pres. Edward Gilbert is no longer a director.

2014
J. F Maddox Foundation
P.O. Box 2588
Hobbs, NM 88241-2588 (575) 393-6338
Contact: Robert J. Reid, Secy. and Exec. Dir.
E-mail: bobreid@jfmaddox.org; Main URL: http://www.jfmaddox.org/
Physical address and address for Scholarship applications: 220 W. Broadway St., Ste. 200, Hobbs, NM 88240

Established in 1963 in NM.
Donors: J.F Maddox‡; Mabel S. Maddox‡.
Foundation type: Independent foundation.
Financial data (yr. ended 12/31/12): Assets, $245,058,304 (M); expenditures, $15,582,079; qualifying distributions, $12,123,562; giving activities include $8,465,690 for 266 grants (high: $2,887,390; low: $100), $197,006 for 26 grants to individuals (high: $46,833; low: $75), $366,172 for 4 foundation-administered programs and $1,521,985 for 2 loans/program-related investments (high: $1,468,684; low: $53,301).
Purpose and activities: The mission of the J.F Maddox Foundation is to significantly improve the quality of life in southeastern New Mexico by investing in education, community development, and other social programs. The foundation particularly supports initiatives driven by innovative leadership, designed for substantial impact, and committed to lasting value.
Fields of interest: Performing arts; Elementary/secondary school reform; Higher education; Education; Environment, beautification programs; Substance abuse, services; Youth development; Human services; Children/youth, services; Aging, centers/services; Economic development; Aging.
Type of support: Research; General/operating support; Capital campaigns; Building/renovation; Equipment; Land acquisition; Program development; Seed money; Curriculum development; Program-related investments/loans; Scholarships—to individuals; Matching/challenge support.
Limitations: Applications accepted. Giving primarily in Lea County, NM; scholarships limited to Lea County, NM, residents. No support for private foundations or political organizations. No grants to individuals (except for scholarships), or for endowment funds.
Publications: Grants list.
Application information: Application form required for scholarships. Refer to foundation web site for full application guidelines and requirements. Application form not required.
Initial approach: Letter; telephone for recommended proposal outline
Copies of proposal: 1
Deadline(s): For scholarships: June 30
Board meeting date(s): Quarterly
Final notification: Varies
Officers and Directors:* Don Maddox,* Pres.; James M. Maddox,* Exec. V.P.; **Kerri Frizzell, V.P, Fin. and C.F.O.; Jennifer Grassham, V.P., Grants;** Dennis M. Holmberg, V.P., Special Projects; **Robert J. Reid, Exec. Dir.**; Elaine Agather; Paul Campbell; Benjamin W. Maddox; Catherine M. Maddox; John L. Maddox; Thomas M. Maddox; **Sue Maddox; Susan Maddox**; Ann M. Utterback.
Number of staff: 6 full-time professional; 3 full-time support.
EIN: 756023767
Other changes: Dennis M. Holmberg is now V.P., Special Projects. Jennifer Grassham is now V.P., Grants. Robert J. Reid is now Exec. Dir.

2015
Waite and Genevieve Phillips Foundation
P.O. Box 5726
Santa Fe, NM 87502-5726

Established in 1986 in NM.
Donors: Genevieve Phillips; Waite and Genevieve Phillips Charitable Trust.
Foundation type: Independent foundation.
Financial data (yr. ended 05/31/13): Assets, $11,958,440 (M); expenditures, $699,602; qualifying distributions, $568,324; giving activities include $481,100 for 38 grants (high: $165,300; low: $300).
Fields of interest: Museums (art); Arts; Education; Hospitals (general); Health care; Health organizations, association; Human services; Children/youth, services; United Ways and Federated Giving Programs.
Limitations: Applications not accepted. Giving primarily in NM, OK, and TX. No grants to individuals.
Application information: Unsolicited requests for funds not accepted.
Officers: Julie Phillips Puckett, Chair. and Pres.; **Connie J. Wootton, Sr. V.P. and Secy.-Treas.; Douglas Clay Holcomb, V.P.**; Tom Coker; Lela Phillips Puckett.
EIN: 850335071
Other changes: Virginia Phillips is no longer Secy.-Treas.

2016
Albert I. Pierce Foundation
1110 Pennsylvania N.E. Ste. B
Albuquerque, NM 87110 (505) 883-3114
***Contact:* Debra N. Thrall-Pierce Ph.D, Exec. Dir.**
***FAX:* (505) 881-0645;**
E-mail: aipfound@swcp.com; Main URL: http://www.aipfoundation.org
Grants List: http://www.aipfoundation.org/Pages/Awards2008%20Page.html

Established in 2004 in NM.
Donor: PNM Fund.
Foundation type: Independent foundation.
Financial data (yr. ended 12/31/12): Assets, $1,141,860 (M); expenditures, $164,105; qualifying distributions, $111,830; giving activities include $111,830 for grants.
Purpose and activities: Giving primarily to enrich the cultural life, education and environment in New Mexico.
Fields of interest: Education; Human services; Community/economic development.
Limitations: Applications accepted. Giving primarily in NM; funding in other areas of the U.S are at the discretion of the foundation's Board. No support for religious or political organizations, or for programs or projects that duplicate existing services and/or programs, or construction or acquisition of real property. No grants for dinners, fundraisers, advertising, debt retirement, capital campaigns, endowments, or emergency funding; no loans.
Publications: Application guidelines; Grants list.
Application information: Application form required.
Initial approach: See Web site
Copies of proposal: 2
Deadline(s): Nov. 15th
Officers: Terry S. Pierce, Chair.; Debra Thrall Pierce, Exec. Dir.
Directors: Toby Appel; Lisa Henley; Paul Miko.
EIN: 432032907

2017
Santa Fe Community Foundation
501 Halona St.
Santa Fe, NM 87505 (505) 988-9715
Contact: Brian T. Byrnes, C.E.O. and Pres.; Donor-Advised Funds and Grants Contact: Christa Coggins, V.P., Community Philanthropy
FAX: (505) 988-1829;
E-mail: foundation@santafecf.org; Mailing address: P.O. Box 1827, Sante Fe, NM 87504-1827; Workshop registration e-mail: workshops@santafecf.org; Main URL: http://www.santafecf.org
Facebook: http://www.facebook.com/pages/Santa-Fe-Community-Foundation/108633257617
Santa Fe Community Foundation's Philanthropy Promise: http://ncrp.org/philanthropys-promise/who
Twitter: https://twitter.com/SantaFeCForg
YouTube: http://www.youtube.com/SantaFeCommFound

Incorporated in 1981 in NM.
Foundation type: Community foundation.
Financial data (yr. ended 12/31/12): Assets, $57,212,049 (M); gifts received, $22,330,673; expenditures, $6,325,123; giving activities include $3,916,552 for 149+ grants (high: $137,763).
Purpose and activities: The foundation improves the quality of life for people in Santa Fe and Northern New Mexico, now and for future generations, by: 1) building and managing endowment funds in order to award grants; 2) helping nonprofits operate more effectively; 3) convening area residents to discuss issues of critical importance to the community; and 4) providing leadership for key community initiatives.
Fields of interest: Arts education; Visual arts; Performing arts; Performing arts, music; Humanities; Arts; Education, public education; Child development, education; Elementary school/education; Adult education—literacy, basic skills & GED; Education, drop-out prevention; Education; Environment, natural resources; Environment; Animals/wildlife, preservation/protection; Health care; Substance abuse, prevention; Mental health/crisis services; Health organizations, association; Cancer; AIDS; Alcoholism; Crime/violence prevention, domestic violence; Food services; Housing/shelter; Children/youth, services; Child development, services; Family services, domestic violence; Family services, adolescent parents; Aging, centers/services; Homeless, human services; Human services; Civil/human rights, immigrants; Civil/human rights, minorities; Civil/human rights, disabled; Civil/human rights, women; Civil/human rights, aging; Civil/human rights, LGBTQ; Civil rights, race/intergroup relations; Community development, citizen coalitions; Economic development; Nonprofit management; Community/economic development; Science; Public affairs, citizen participation; Public affairs; Aging; Disabilities, people with; Minorities; Asians/Pacific Islanders; African Americans/Blacks; Hispanics/Latinos; Native Americans/American Indians; Women; AIDS, people with; Immigrants/refugees; Economically disadvantaged; Homeless; LGBTQ.
Type of support: General/operating support; Continuing support; Management development/capacity building; Annual campaigns; Emergency funds; Program development; Publication; Seed money; Scholarship funds; Technical assistance; Matching/challenge support.
Limitations: Applications accepted. Giving limited to northern NM counties, including Los Alamos, Mora, Rio Arriba, San Miguel, Santa Fe and Taos. No support for religious purposes. No grants for capital campaigns, endowments, or technical assistance

grants for travel, conferences, start-up costs, or staff salaries or functions.
Publications: Annual report; Informational brochure (including application guidelines); Newsletter.
Application information: Visit foundation web site for online application and guidelines. Free pre-proposal workshops are offered to assist perspective applicants with information on proposal guidelines and the application/grant process for the foundation's grant cycles; telephone or e-mail to register. Faxed proposals are not accepted. Application form required.
Initial approach: Complete online application
Copies of proposal: 1
***Deadline(s):* Mar. 3 for Spring Grants Cycle covering Economic Opportunity, Education and Environment; Aug. 26 for Fall Grants Cycle covering Arts, Animal Welfare, Health and Human Services**
Board meeting date(s): Bimonthly
Final notification: June 29 and Nov. 15
Officers and Directors:* Hervey A. Juris,* Chair.; Suzanne Ortega Cisneros,* Vice-Chair.; Brian Byrnes, C.E.O. and Pres.; Christa Coggins, V.P., Community Philanthropy; Sarah Sawtell, V.P., Finance and Opers.; Thomas Bustamante; Lisa Enfield; Steve Gaber; Bud Hamilton; Barry Herskowitz; Peggy Hubbard; Dottie Indyke; Jerry G. Jones; Stephanie Kiger; Jennifer Kimball; Sheila Ortega McLaughlin; Beth Moise; Richard Moore; Michael Namingha; Susan Priem; Elizabeth Rice; Kenneth Romero; Patricia Rosenberg.
Number of staff: 7 full-time professional; 7 full-time support.
EIN: 850303044
Other changes: At the close of 2012, the fair market value of the grantmaker's assets was $57,212,049, a 55.5% increase over the 2011 value, $36,780,545. For the same period, the grantmaker paid grants of $3,916,552, a 58.3% increase over the 2011 disbursements, $2,474,606.

2018
The Simon Charitable Foundation
524 Don Gaspar Ave.
Santa Fe, NM 87505-2626 **(505) 982-0733, Ext. 5**
***FAX:* (505) 212-0101; E-mail: susan@simoncf.org**;
Main URL: http://simoncf.org
YouTube: http://www.youtube.com/channel/UC1x2k2mxkngDfoB-I0Kosuw

Established in 2009 in NM.
Donor: Ronald M. Simon Trust.
Foundation type: Independent foundation.
Financial data (yr. ended 06/30/12): Assets, $353,634 (M); gifts received, $1,236,960; expenditures, $1,366,689; qualifying distributions, $1,366,318; giving activities include $176,500 for 20+ grants (high: $25,000; low: $500), $163,586 for grants to individuals, and $1,078,152 for 4 foundation-administered programs.
Purpose and activities: Scholarship awards and stipends to students of the University of New Mexico, Albuquerque, and Santa Fe public schools.
Fields of interest: Arts; Secondary school/education; Higher education, university; Education; Human services.
Type of support: Scholarships—to individuals.
Limitations: Applications not accepted.
Application information: Unsolicited requests for funds not accepted.
Officers and Directors:* Steven Simon,* Chair.; Steven McCarl,* V.P.; J. Alan Marks,* Secy.; Ben Benjamin,* Treas.; Glen Newkirk.
EIN: 273309123

NEW YORK

2019
The 100 Mile Man Foundation Inc.
(formerly The Itzler Family Foundation)
c/o Rothstein Kass Family Office Group
1350 Ave. of the Americas, 15th Fl.
New York, NY 10019-4700 (212) 997-0500
Contact: Jesse Itzler, Pres.
***E-mail:* info@100milegroup.com; Main URL: http://the100mileman.com**
Facebook: https://www.facebook.com/100MileMan
Instagram Profile: http://instagram.com/the100mileman
Twitter: https://twitter.com/the100mileman

Established in 2004 in NY.
Donors: Jesse Itzler; Drew Katz; Stephen L. Gans; Jon Weiner; Richard Santulli; Margaret Santulli; Tor Peterson; Active Network; Student Athletics Inc.
Foundation type: Independent foundation.
Financial data (yr. ended 12/31/12): Assets, $853 (M); gifts received, $36,500; expenditures, $36,549; qualifying distributions, $22,335; giving activities include $22,335 for grants.
Fields of interest: Education, fund raising/fund distribution; Health organizations, association; Medical research, institute; Human services; Foundations (private grantmaking); Jewish agencies & synagogues.
Limitations: Applications accepted. Giving primarily in NY.
Application information: Application form not required.
Initial approach: Proposal
Deadline(s): None
Officers: Jesse Itzler, Pres.; Ellen Itzler, Secy.; Peter Itzler, Treas.
EIN: 200565515

2020
1848 Foundation
c/o Marks, Paneth & Shron, LLP
660 White Plains Rd., Ste. 450
Tarrytown, NY 10591-5173

Established in 1986 in CT.
Donor: Alan Ritter.
Foundation type: Independent foundation.
Financial data (yr. ended 03/31/13): Assets, $7,539,976 (M); expenditures, $506,494; qualifying distributions, $453,819; giving activities include $417,100 for 23 grants (high: $107,600; low: $1,000).
Purpose and activities: Giving primarily to civil rights advocacy groups.
Fields of interest: Crime/violence prevention, child abuse; Children/youth, services; Civil/human rights, advocacy; Civil liberties, advocacy.
Type of support: General/operating support.
Limitations: Applications not accepted. Giving primarily in New York, NY; giving also in CT and GA. No grants to individuals.
Application information: Unsolicited requests for funds not accepted.
Officers: Alan I. Ritter, Pres.; Jonathan Ritter, V.P.; Eileen S. Silverstein, Secy.; Becky Hubbert, Treas.
EIN: 066302129
Other changes: The grantmaker no longer lists a phone.

2021
Abba's Ambassadors, Inc.
P.O. Box 165
South Salem, NY 10590-0165
E-mail: info@abbasambassadors.org; Main URL: http://www.abbasambassadors.org/
Facebook: https://www.facebook.com/AbbasAmbassadors

Established in 2006 in GA.
Donors: John F. Gibson; Cynthia D. Gibson; Daniel Gibson; Jennifer Gibson.
Foundation type: Independent foundation.
Financial data (yr. ended 12/31/12): Assets, $364,514 (M); gifts received, $265,999; expenditures, $248,536; qualifying distributions, $245,738; giving activities include $153,152 for 6 grants (high: $61,178; low: $3,971), and $84,041 for 9 grants to individuals (high: $33,500; low: $1,700).
Fields of interest: Health organizations; Housing/shelter; Religion.
Type of support: General/operating support; Grants to individuals.
Limitations: Giving primarily in WA; with some giving in Israel.
Officers: John F. Gibson, Pres.; Daniel F. Gibson, V.P. and C.F.O.; Cynthia D. Gibson, Secy.
Directors: Elizabeth A. Gibson; Janell M. Gibson; Jennifer L. Gibson; Joel T. Gibson.
EIN: 208043230
Other changes: The grantmaker has moved from SC to NY.

2022
The Abelard Foundation Inc.
c/o Ingram Yuzek
250 Park Ave., 6th Fl.
New York, NY 10177-0001
***Application address for organizations located in the eastern U.S. (east of the Mississippi River):* The Abelard Foundation-East, Att.: Susan Collins, P.O. Box 148, Lincoln, MA 01773, URL: http://www.fdnweb.org/abelardeast; application address for organizations located in the western U.S. (west of the Mississippi River): Common Counsel Foundation, Att.: Grants Administrator, 405 14th St., Ste. 809, Oakland, CA 94612, URL: http://www.commoncounsel.org/Abelard+Foundation+West**
Abelard Foundation's Philanthropy Promise: http://www.ncrp.org/philanthropys-promise/who
Grants List: http://fdnweb.org/abelardeast/grants-approved/

Incorporated in 1958 in NY as successor to Albert B. Wells Charitable Trust established in 1950 in MA. The foundation is split into two groups to handle Eastern and Western applicants separately.
Donors: Ethel B. Wells Trust; and members of the Wells family.
Foundation type: Independent foundation.
Financial data (yr. ended 12/31/12): Assets, $6,615,547 (M); gifts received, $111,000; expenditures, $520,662; qualifying distributions, $440,394; giving activities include $333,105 for 34 grants (high: $11,463; low: $1,000).
Purpose and activities: Giving especially for seed money to new organizations and model projects, with emphasis on protection of civil rights and civil liberties; support for programs designed to achieve social, political, and economic equality for urban and rural poor, including giving them a voice in decisions about their environment.
Fields of interest: Environment, natural resources; Employment, labor unions/organizations; Human services; Civil/human rights, advocacy; Urban/community development; Public affairs.
Type of support: General/operating support; Program development; Publication; Seed money; Technical assistance; Matching/challenge support.
Limitations: Applications accepted. No support for medical, educational, cultural institutions, or government sponsored programs. No grants to individuals, or for building or endowment funds, continuing support, annual campaigns, emergency funds, scholarships, fellowships, research, or video or film production; no loans.
Publications: Grants list; Informational brochure (including application guidelines).
Application information: See foundation websites for complete application guidelines. Application form required.
Initial approach: Letter
Copies of proposal: 1
Deadline(s): None
Board meeting date(s): May and Nov.
Officers: Brian Collins, Pres.; Adele Bernhard, V.P.; **Anna Wells Bernhard, V.P.; Haleryn A. Buck, V.P.**; Susan B. Collins, V.P.; **Lena Neufeld, V.P.**; George B. Wells II, V.P.; Patricia Hewitt, Secy.; **Travis W. Buck, Treas.**
Board Members: Jessica W. Bernhard; Michael Bernhard; Steven Bernhard; Melissa W. Blessing; Shea Breaux-Wells; David B. Magee; **Nancy Doll**; Frances W. Magee; Peter Neufeld; Shane Neufeld; Albert R. Schreck; Celeste W. Schreck; Charles R. Schreck; Christine Schreck; Teresa Juarez Schreck; Mason T. Schreck; Thomas A. Schreck; Albert B. Wells; Kristen Wells; Susan M. Wells.
Number of staff: 1 part-time professional; 2 part-time support.
EIN: 136064580
Other changes: Travis W. Buck has replaced Brian Collins as Treas. Travis W. Buck has replaced Brian Collins as Treas. Brian Collins has replaced Daniel W. Schreck as Pres.
Ashley Collins, Donald Collins and Garrett T. Collins are no longer board members. Anna Wells Bernhard, Haleryn A. Buck and Lena Neufeld are now V.P.s.

2023
The Alexander Abraham Foundation
232 E. 62nd St.
New York, NY 10065-8201
***E-mail:* info@abrahamfoundation.org**; Main URL: http://abrahamfoundation.org/cms/
Facebook: https://www.facebook.com/AbrahamFoundation
Twitter: http://twitter.com/aabrahamfound

Established in 2002 in DE.
Donors: Nancy Abraham; Tiger Conservation Fund.
Foundation type: Independent foundation.
Financial data (yr. ended 11/30/11): Assets, $183,959 (M); gifts received, $553,274; expenditures, $417,644; qualifying distributions, $410,203; giving activities include $375,023 for 36 grants (high: $66,836; low: $100).
Purpose and activities: The foundation is dedicated to conserving the environment and to defending indigenous wildlife with an emphasis on protection of endangered species.
Fields of interest: Animal welfare; Animals/wildlife; Human services.
Limitations: Applications accepted. Giving primarily in Africa and Asia.

Application information: Contributes only to invited organizations upon review of preliminary application form from foundation web site.

Initial approach: Fill out preliminary form from foundation web site if organization is appropriate match for funding

Officers and Directors:* Nancy Abraham,* Pres.; Eleoner Content, Exec. Dir.

EIN: 300139596

2024
Abramson-Clayman Foundation

c/o Marks Paneth and Shron LLP
88 Froehlich Farm Blvd.
Woodbury, NY 11797-2921
***Application address:* c/o Dr. and Mrs. Clayman, 16584 Ironwood Dr., Delray Beach, FL 33445-7048**

Incorporated in 1984 in NJ.

Donors: Edith Abramson Clayman; Melvin Clayman.

Foundation type: Independent foundation.

Financial data (yr. ended 04/30/13): Assets, $2,347,058 (M); expenditures, $347,946; qualifying distributions, $335,615; giving activities include $333,140 for 28 grants (high: $245,000; low: $40).

Purpose and activities: Giving primarily to Jewish organizations, including temples and federated giving programs; support also for health associations, including a cancer hospital, and human services.

Fields of interest: Hospitals (specialty); Health organizations, association; Cancer; Human services; Jewish federated giving programs; Jewish agencies & synagogues.

Limitations: Applications accepted. Giving in the U.S., with emphasis on New York, NY.

Application information: Application form required.

Initial approach: Letter

Deadline(s): Jan. 31

Officers: Edith Abramson Clayman, Pres.; Melvin Clayman, V.P.

Trustees: Andrew Abramson; Caryn Clayman; Anne A. Essig.

EIN: 222641108

Other changes: The grantmaker has moved from NJ to NY.

2025
Access Capital Foundation

c/o Miles and Marcie Stuchin
405 Park Ave., 16th Fl.
New York, NY 10022-9405

Established in 1997 in NY.

Donors: Miles M. Stuchin; First Giving; Marcie Stuchin.

Foundation type: Independent foundation.

Financial data (yr. ended 06/30/13): Assets, $81,325 (M); gifts received, $13,105; expenditures, $101,033; qualifying distributions, $100,833; giving activities include $100,833 for 12 grants (high: $50,000; low: $500).

Fields of interest: Arts; Education; Health organizations; Cancer research.

Type of support: General/operating support.

Limitations: Applications not accepted. Giving primarily in CT and New York, NY. No grants to individuals.

Application information: Unsolicited requests for funds not accepted.

Trustees: Marcie Stuchin; Miles M. Stuchin.

EIN: 367190561

2026
The Achelis Foundation

767 3rd Ave., 4th Fl.
New York, NY 10017-9029 (212) 644-0322
Contact: John B. Krieger, Secy. and Exec. Dir.; Carmel Mazzola, Bookkeeper; Vicki Puluso, Admin. Asst.
FAX: (212) 759-6510;
E-mail: main@achelis-bodman-fnds.org; Main URL: http://www.achelis-bodman-fnds.org
Grants List: http://www.achelis-bodman-fnds.org/grants.html

Incorporated in 1940 in NY.

Donor: Elisabeth Achelis†.

Foundation type: Independent foundation.

Financial data (yr. ended 12/31/12): Assets, $36,714,169 (M); expenditures, $1,748,695; qualifying distributions, $1,540,003; giving activities include $1,400,000 for 55 grants (high: $125,000; low: $2,500).

Purpose and activities: Giving for some social services includes child welfare and disconnected youth, the disabled, substance abusers, ex-offenders and veterans. Education giving includes a preference for K-12 school reform, school choice, and charter schools rather than nonprofits that provide direct services in public schools. The foundation also makes grants to large arts and cultural institutions in New York City. Other interests include voluntarism, entrepreneurship, employment, strengthening the two-parent family, marriage, fatherhood (and father absence), programs that promote self-help and self-reliance, faith-based programs, and prevention and early intervention. The foundation prefers programs that emphasize measurable participant outcomes and program results, innovations and new cost-saving approaches, consumer choice, and parental involvement.

Fields of interest: Humanities; Education, reform; Medical care, rehabilitation; Health care, cost containment; Substance abuse, prevention; Alcoholism; Medical research, institute; Crime/violence prevention, youth; Offenders/ex-offenders, prison alternatives; Employment; Children/youth, services; Family services; International relief; Public policy, research; Welfare policy/reform; Religion; Children/youth; Youth; Disabilities, people with; Physically disabled; Military/veterans; Offenders/ex-offenders; Substance abusers; Economically disadvantaged.

Type of support: General/operating support; Equipment; Program development; Conferences/seminars; Publication; Seed money; Curriculum development; Scholarship funds; Research; Technical assistance; Program evaluation; Matching/challenge support.

Limitations: Applications accepted. Giving primarily in the New York, NY, area. Generally, no support for political organizations, small art, dance, music, or theater groups, national health or mental health organizations, housing, international projects, government agencies, public schools (except charter schools), or nonprofit programs and services significantly funded or wholly reimbursed by the government. No grants to individuals, or for annual appeals, dinner functions, fundraising events, capital campaigns, deficit financing, or film or travel; no loans.

Publications: Financial statement; Grants list.

Application information: Do not send CDs, DVDs, discs or tapes, or proposals through the internet unless requested; see foundation web site for application guidelines and procedures. New York/New Jersey Area Common Grant Application Form accepted. Application form not required.

Initial approach: Letter or short proposal

Copies of proposal: 1

Deadline(s): None

Board meeting date(s): Usually in May, Sept., and Dec.

Final notification: 5 to 6 weeks

Officers and Trustees:* John N. Irwin III,* Chair. and C.E.O.; Russell P. Pennoyer,* Pres.; Peter Frelinghuysen,* V.P.; Mary S. Phipps,* V.P.; John B. Krieger, Secy. and Exec. Dir.; Horace I. Crary, Jr.,* Treas.; Hon. Walter J.P. Curley; Leslie Lenkowsky; Tatiana Pouschine.

Number of staff: 1 full-time professional; 2 part-time support.

EIN: 136022018

2027
Adirondack Foundation

(formerly Adirondack Community Trust)
2284 Saranac Ave.
P.O. Box 288
Lake Placid, NY 12946 (518) 523-9904
Contact: Cali Brooks, Exec. Dir.; For grants: Andrea Grout, Prog. Off.
FAX: (518) 523-9905;
E-mail: info@generousact.org; Grant inquiry e-mail: andrea@generousact.org; Main URL: http://www.generousact.org
Facebook: http://www.facebook.com/pages/Adirondack-Community-Trust/215603083110

Established in 1997 in NY.

Foundation type: Community foundation.

Financial data (yr. ended 06/30/12): Assets, $30,832,731 (M); gifts received, $5,857,264; expenditures, $2,889,127; giving activities include $1,619,597 for 50+ grants (high: $290,800), and $834,868 for 66 grants to individuals.

Purpose and activities: The foundation seeks to unite donors' charitable interests with the needs of the Adirondack region by: 1) building a permanent and flexible endowment that can respond to the most pressing current, and future, needs of the region; 2) working with donors and their advisors to design named endowments that meet the unique and individual charitable objectives of the donor; 3) administering a creative program of grantmaking to give maximum benefit to charitable needs within the area and carry out the wishes of donors; 4) being a prudent manager and faithful steward of philanthropic assets; 5) and being a leader and catalyst focusing attention on the needs of the region.

Fields of interest: Historic preservation/historical societies; Arts; Libraries/library science; Education; Environment; Animal welfare; Health care; Recreation; Children/youth, services; Human services; Community/economic development.

Type of support: General/operating support; Continuing support; Annual campaigns; Capital campaigns; Building/renovation; Land acquisition; Endowments; Program development; Publication; Seed money; Curriculum development; Scholarship funds; Technical assistance; Scholarships—to individuals; Matching/challenge support.

Limitations: Applications accepted. Giving limited to the Adirondack region of NY.

Publications: Annual report; Financial statement; Grants list; Informational brochure; Newsletter.

Application information: Visit foundation web site for application information.

Initial approach: Create online profile

Board meeting date(s): Jan., May, July, and Oct.

Officers and Trustees:* **John Ernst,* Chair.; Nancy Keet,* Vice-Chair.; David Mason,* Vice-Chair.; Susan Waters,* Secy.**; David Heidecorn,* Treas.; Cali Brooks, Exec. Dir.; John Fritzinger; **Barbara**

Linell Glaser; Jerry Hayes; Cathy Johnston; Rich Kroes; Peter Paine; Joe Shaw; Holly Wolff; Cecil Wray.
Number of staff: 2 full-time professional; 1 part-time professional.
EIN: 161535724
Other changes: John Ernst has replaced Adele P. Connors as Co-Chair.
Fred Calder, Nancy Keet, David Mason, and Susan Waters are no longer trustees.

2028
Aequus Institute
P.O. Box 3485
Elmira, NY 14905-0485 (800) 441-1963
Contact: Nancy Padilla

Established in 1990 in CA as successor to Aequus Institute.
Foundation type: Independent foundation.
Financial data (yr. ended 12/31/12): Assets, $3,583,748 (M); gifts received, $160; expenditures, $481,473; qualifying distributions, $398,494; giving activities include $271,500 for 42 grants (high: $50,000; low: $1,000).
Purpose and activities: Giving to promote the teaching of Mary Baker Eddy and the Christian Science Church, and the free market economic system.
Fields of interest: Economics; Political science; Public policy, research; Government/public administration.
Type of support: General/operating support.
Limitations: Applications accepted. Giving primarily in CA; some giving in other states as well. No grants to individuals.
Publications: Informational brochure (including application guidelines).
Application information: Application form required.
Initial approach: Letter
Deadline(s): None
Officers and Directors:* Patrick Parker,* Pres.; David Keyston,* V.P.; Edwin Feulner, Jr., Ph.D.*, Secy.; Larry P. Arnn, Ph.D.*, Exec. Dir.
Number of staff: 2
EIN: 521620982
Other changes: The grantmaker no longer lists a URL address.

2029
AIG Foundation, Inc.
c/o Linda Sabo
175 Water Street, 20th Floor
New York, NY **10038**

Established in 2005 in NY.
Donor: American International Group, Inc.
Foundation type: Company-sponsored foundation.
Financial data (yr. ended 12/31/12): Assets, $3,394 (M); gifts received, $1,728,281; expenditures, $1,728,281; qualifying distributions, $1,728,281; giving activities include $1,461,140 for grants to individuals.
Purpose and activities: The foundation awards college scholarships to dependents of employees of American International Group, Inc.
Fields of interest: Higher education.
Type of support: Employee-related scholarships.
Limitations: Applications not accepted. Giving on a national and international basis in areas of company operations.
Publications: Corporate giving report.
Application information: Contributes only through employee-related scholarships.
Officers: David Herzog, Chair.; Kathleen Shannon, V.P. and Secy.; Brian Schreiber, V.P. and Treas.
EIN: 203713472

2030
Alavi Foundation
650 5th Ave., Ste. 2406
New York, NY **10019-6108** (212) 944-8333
Contact: Hanieh Safakamal, Fin. Mgr.
FAX: (212) 921-0325;
E-mail: info@alavifoundation.org; Main URL: http://www.alavifoundation.org

Incorporated in 1973 in NY.
Foundation type: Independent foundation.
Financial data (yr. ended 03/31/13): Assets, $112,290,806 (M); gifts received, $10,833; expenditures, $4,426,052; qualifying distributions, $3,478,426; giving activities include $1,815,800 for 31 grants (high: $403,000; low: $3,000), $648,690 for foundation-administered programs and $18,754 for loans/program-related investments.
Purpose and activities: A primary aim of the foundation is to promote harmony and understanding among people of different religions. Another of its basic aims is to promote the study of the humanities, arts, and pure and applied sciences. It also gives to organizations that are involved in the teaching of Islamic or Persian culture.
Fields of interest: Arts; Education; Human services; Islam.
Type of support: Continuing support; Building/renovation; Program-related investments/loans; Student loans—to individuals.
Limitations: Applications accepted. Giving on a national basis. No support for political organizations. No grants to individuals, (except for scholarships).
Publications: Grants list; IRS Form 990 or 990-PF printed copy available upon request.
Application information: Student scholarship program has been suspended. Application form not required.
Initial approach: See foundation web site for approach for each individual program
Copies of proposal: 1
Deadline(s): None
Board meeting date(s): Bimonthly
Officers and Directors:* Hoshang Ahmadi, Pres.; Alireza Ebrhamimi,* Secy.; Ali Babiran, Treas.; Hassan Hassani.
Number of staff: 1 full-time professional; 3 full-time support.
EIN: 237345978

2031
Alfiero Family Charitable Foundation
100 Corporate Pkwy., Ste. 130
Amherst, NY 14226-1200
Contact: Salvatore H. Alfiero, Chair.

Established in 1989 in NY.
Donor: Salvatore H. Alfiero.
Foundation type: Independent foundation.
Financial data (yr. ended 12/31/12): Assets, $4,590,993 (M); expenditures, $671,476; qualifying distributions, $664,176; giving activities include $664,176 for 14 grants (high: $250,000; low: $500).
Purpose and activities: Giving primarily for higher education, as well as a heritage organization supporting the Marine Corps, and children, youth, and social services.
Fields of interest: Media/communications; Historical activities; Higher education; Education; Hospitals (specialty); Cancer; Human services; Children/youth, services.
Type of support: General/operating support.
Limitations: Applications not accepted. Giving primarily in NY; some funding also in VA.
Application information: Contributes only to pre-selected organizations.
Managers: Charles C. Alfiero; James J. Alfiero; Salvatore H. Alfiero; Victor S. Alfiero.
EIN: 110036051

2032
Allyn Foundation, Inc.
P.O. Box 22
Skaneateles, NY 13152-0022
Contact: Meg M. O'Connell, Exec. Dir.
E-mail: info@allynfoundation.org; E-mail for questions regarding application: anye@allynfoundation.org; Main URL: http://www.allynfoundation.org
Grants List: http://www.allynfoundation.org/index.php?page=recent-grants

Incorporated in 1956 in NY.
Donors: William Noah Allyn‡; William G. Allyn‡; Welch Allyn, Inc.
Foundation type: Independent foundation.
Financial data (yr. ended 12/31/12): Assets, $27,655,873 (M); gifts received, $200,000; expenditures, $1,926,673; qualifying distributions, $1,672,409; giving activities include $1,445,331 for 157 grants (high: $129,000; low: $150).
Purpose and activities: Giving primarily to improve the quality of life in Central New York. Emphasis placed upon health, human services, education, and youth and families.
Fields of interest: Arts; Higher education; Education; Health care; Human services; Children/youth, services; Family services; Community/economic development; Foundations (community).
Type of support: Annual campaigns; Capital campaigns; Building/renovation; Equipment; Seed money; Scholarship funds; Consulting services; Matching/challenge support.
Limitations: Applications accepted. Giving limited to Onondaga and Cayuga counties in NY. No support for religious programs. No grants to individuals, or for endowment funds for fundraising; no loans.
Publications: Application guidelines; Grants list.
Application information: Application form required.
Initial approach: Application form on foundation web site
Copies of proposal: 1
Deadline(s): Apr. 1, July 1, Sept. 1, and Nov. 1
Board meeting date(s): 4 times per year
Final notification: 1 month following submission deadline
Officers: Dr. Maureen Soderberg, Pres.; William F. Allyn, V.P.; Elsa A. Soderberg, Secy.; Eric Allyn, Treas.; Margaret G. Ogden, Interim Exec. Dir.
Directors: Amy Allyn; David Allyn; Dawn N. Allyn; Janet J. Allyn; Laura A. Allyn; Lew F. Allyn; W. Scott Allyn, M.D.; Dr. Barbara Connor; Richard Newman; Jon Soderberg; Libby Soderberg; Peer Allyn Soderberg, M.D.; Peter H. Soderberg; Thomas Wood.
Number of staff: 1 full-time professional; 1 part-time support.
EIN: 156017723

2033

American Express Charitable Fund

200 Vesey St., 48th Fl.
New York, NY 10285-1000
Application address for organizations located outside of Phoenix, AZ, south FL, and Salt Lake City, UT: 3 World Financial Ctr., M.C. 01-48-04, New York, NY 10285-4804; E-mail for Phoenix, AZ: American Express Co., c/o Community Affairs, PhoenixLOIs@aexp.com; E-mail for south Florida: American Express Co., c/o Community Affairs, FtLauderdaleLOIs@aexp.com; E-mail for Salt Lake City, UT: American Express Co., c/o Community Affairs, SaltLakeCityLOIs@aexp.com; Main URL: http://about.americanexpress.com/csr/e-driven.aspx

Established in 2007 in NY.
Donor: American Express.
Foundation type: Company-sponsored foundation.
Financial data (yr. ended 12/31/12): Assets, $8,426,200 (M); expenditures, $9,950,546; qualifying distributions, $9,950,546; giving activities include $2,836,750 for 254 grants (high: $461,750; low: $500), and $7,042,649 for employee matching gifts.
Purpose and activities: The fund supports programs designed to promote historic preservation; leadership; and community service.
Fields of interest: Arts, cultural/ethnic awareness; Museums; Performing arts; Historic preservation/historical societies; Arts; Higher education; Education; Food services; Disasters, preparedness/services; American Red Cross; YM/YWCAs & YM/YWHAs; Human services; Community/economic development; Foundations (community); United Ways and Federated Giving Programs; Leadership development; Public affairs.
Type of support: General/operating support; Annual campaigns; Building/renovation; Program development; Employee volunteer services; Sponsorships; Employee matching gifts; Employee-related scholarships.
Limitations: Applications accepted. Giving primarily on a national basis in areas of company operations, with emphasis on Phoenix, AZ, Los Angeles and San Francisco, CA, Washington, DC, southern FL, Atlanta, GA, Chicago, IL, Boston, MA, New York, NY, Philadelphia, PA, Dallas and Houston, TX, and Salt Lake City, UT. No support for discriminatory organizations, religious organizations not of direct benefit to the entire community, or political organizations. No grants to individuals (except for employee-related scholarships), or for fundraising, goodwill advertising, souvenir journals, or dinner programs, travel, books, magazines, or articles in professional journals, endowments or capital campaigns, traveling exhibitions, or sports sponsorships.
Publications: Application guidelines; Grants list; Program policy statement.
Application information: A full proposal may be requested at a later date. Historic preservation applications are by invitation only. Leadership applications for youth leadership programs are discouraged. Organizations receiving support of at least $7,500 are asked to provide a final report. Application form required.
Initial approach: **Complete online eligibility quiz and application**
Deadline(s): **None**
Final notification: 3 to 4 months
Officers and Trustees:* Timothy J. McClimon,* Pres.; Mary Ellen Craig, Secy.; David L. Yowan, Treas.; Tammy D. Fried, Counsel; Vernon E. Jordan, Jr.; Frank P. Popoff.
EIN: 261607898

2034

American Express Foundation

World Financial Ctr.
200 Vesey St., 48th Fl.
New York, NY 10285-4804
Main URL: http://about.americanexpress.com/csr/?inav=about_CorpResponsibility
Grants List: http://about.americanexpress.com/csr/docs/2012grantslist.pdf

Incorporated in 1954 in NY.
Donor: American Express Co.
Foundation type: Company-sponsored foundation.
Financial data (yr. ended 12/31/12): Assets, $2,205,372 (M); gifts received, $2,205,372; expenditures, $8,754,117; qualifying distributions, $8,753,670; giving activities include $8,711,000 for 163 grants (high: $1,000,000; low: $4,000).
Purpose and activities: The foundation supports programs designed to promote historic preservation; leadership; and community service.
Fields of interest: Visual arts; Museums; Performing arts; Historic preservation/historical societies; Arts; Higher education; Education; Hospitals (general); Food services; Food banks; Food distribution, meals on wheels; Disasters, preparedness/services; American Red Cross; Children/youth, services; Human services; Economic development; Nonprofit management; Community/economic development; Foundations (community); Voluntarism promotion; Leadership development; Public affairs.
Type of support: General/operating support; Continuing support; Management development/capacity building; Annual campaigns; Emergency funds; Program development; Conferences/seminars.
Limitations: Applications accepted. **Giving on a national and international basis in areas of company operations with emphasis on greater Phoenix, AZ, Los Angeles and San Francisco, CA, Washington, DC, south FL, Atlanta, GA, Chicago, IL, Boston, MA, New York, NY, Philadelphia, PA, Puerto Rico, Houston, TX, Salt Lake City, UT, Argentina, Australia, Canada, China, France, Germany, Hong Kong, India, Italy, Japan, Mexico, Netherlands, Singapore, Spain, Taiwan, and the United Kingdom.** No support for discriminatory organizations, religious organizations not of direct benefit to the entire community, or political organizations. No grants to individuals, or for fundraising, goodwill advertising, souvenir journals, or dinner programs, travel, books, magazines, or articles in professional journals, endowments or capital campaigns, traveling exhibitions, or sports sponsorships.
Publications: Application guidelines; Grants list; Program policy statement.
Application information: A full proposal may be requested at a later date. Historic preservation applications are by invitation only. Leadership applications for youth leadership programs are discouraged. Organizations receiving support of at least $7,500 are asked to provide a final report. Application form required.
Initial approach: **Complete online eligibility quiz and application**
Deadline(s): None
Board meeting date(s): Biannually
Final notification: 3 to 4 months
Officers and Trustees:* Thomas Schick,* Chair.; Timothy J. McClimon, Pres.; Mary Ellen Craig, Compt. and Secy.; Kenneth I. Chenault; Edward P. Gilligan; Daniel T. Henry; Stephen J. Squeri.
EIN: 136123529
Other changes: The grantmaker no longer lists a separate application address.
Judy Tenzer is no longer Secy. Mary Ellen Craig is now Compt. and Secy.

2035

American Friends of the Hebrew University Charitable Common Fund, Inc.

1 Battery Park Plz., 25th Fl.
New York, NY 10004-1405
Main URL: http://www.afhu.org
Facebook: https://www.facebook.com/AmFriendsHU
Twitter: https://twitter.com/AmFriendsHU
YouTube: http://www.youtube.com/user/AmFriendsHU

Established in 1989 in NY.
Donors: Ernest Bogan; Stanley Bogen; Robert Savin; John Steinhardt; Fred S. Lafer; Edward Fein; Jane Zimmerman; Ron Zimmerman; Richard Karp; Jane Karp; American Friends of Hebrew University.
Foundation type: Independent foundation.
Financial data (yr. ended 09/30/12): Assets, $2,232,537 (M); expenditures, $330,170; qualifying distributions, $325,680; giving activities include $325,680 for 34 grants (high: $130,001; low: $100).
Purpose and activities: Support for Jewish agencies, temples, and federated giving programs, the arts, education, and health.
Fields of interest: Arts; Education; Health organizations; Medical research, institute; Jewish federated giving programs; Jewish agencies & synagogues.
Type of support: Continuing support.
Limitations: Applications not accepted. Giving primarily in New York, NY. No grants to individuals.
Application information: Unsolicited requests for funds not accepted.
Trustees: Stanley Bogen; Keith Sachs; Ira Lee Sorkin; Peter Willner.
EIN: 133525587

2036

Anderson-Rogers Foundation, Inc.

(formerly Environmental Data Research Institute)
327 W. 19th St.
New York, NY 10011-3901 (212) 989-9331
Contact: Sarah A. Pope, Pres.
E-mail: **andersonrogersfoundation@gmail.com**; Main URL: http://foundationcenter.org/grantmaker/arfdn/

Established in 2001 as Florida Corp., changed to NY State Corp. in 2004.
Donor: Porter W. Anderson.
Foundation type: Independent foundation.
Financial data (yr. ended 12/31/12): Assets, $8,751,414 (M); expenditures, $445,182; qualifying distributions, $388,500; giving activities include $388,500 for 60 grants (high: $25,000; low: $500).
Purpose and activities: Giving for the support of environmental education and activism, sustainable agriculture, family planning, abortion rights, sex education, the promotion of the separation of church and state, and the dissemination of humanist values.
Fields of interest: Environment, water pollution; Environment, natural resources; Environment, water resources; Environment, land resources; Animal welfare; Animals/wildlife, preservation/protection; Animals/wildlife, endangered species; Animals/wildlife; Reproductive health, family planning; Reproductive health, abortion clinics/services; Reproductive health, sexuality education; Agriculture, sustainable programs; Youth, pregnancy prevention; Civil liberties, reproductive rights; Civil liberties, freedom of religion.

Type of support: General/operating support; Building/renovation; Equipment; Emergency funds; Program development; Publication; Seed money; Curriculum development; Program evaluation.
Limitations: Applications accepted. Giving primarily in No giving limitations within the U.S. but giving primarily in NY state. No support for religious organizations. No grants to individuals, or for scholarships.
Publications: Application guidelines; Grants list.
Application information: Until further notice, the foundation is not accepting applications. See foundation web site for complete information. Application form not required.
Initial approach: Brief letter of inquiry (not more than 2 pages)
Copies of proposal: 1
Board meeting date(s): Annual meeting Oct. 1st. Special meetings 4-6 times a year
Final notification: Within 2 months
Officers and Trustees:* Sarah A. Pope,* Pres. and Treas.; Porter W. Anderson, Jr.,* V.P. and Secy.; Juliette R. Pope; Charles H. Rogers.
Number of staff: 2 part-time professional.
EIN: 223052390

2037
Andor Capital Management Foundation
c/o Andor Capital Mgmt., LLC
4 International Dr., Ste. 100
Rye Brook, NY 10573-1065

Established in 2001 in CT.
Donors: Daniel C. Benton; Douglas Mueller; Aimee Mueller; Peter Streinger; Kevin O'Brien; Jeanine O'Brien; Charlie Hannigan; Katherine Bailon; Julia Dailey; John Levinson; Ellen Levinson; Cheryl Warren; Moshe Metzger; Jose Fernandez; Nancy Fernandez; Walter G. Schendel III; Mark Bertagnolli; Robert Boroujerdi; Michael Fisher; Seth Ostrie.
Foundation type: Independent foundation.
Financial data (yr. ended 08/31/13): Assets, $13,255,291 (M); expenditures, $3,232,260; qualifying distributions, $3,231,390; giving activities include $3,227,000 for 15 grants (high: $1,000,000; low: $5,000).
Purpose and activities: Giving primarily to human service organizations, including organizations which support the families of fallen and/or injured military personnel; funding also for children and family services, as well as for programs and services to families who have lost loved ones on Sept. 11, 2001.
Fields of interest: Hospitals (specialty); Disasters, 9/11/01; Safety/disasters; Human services; Children/youth, services; Family services; Military/veterans.
Limitations: Applications not accepted. Giving primarily in CT, and New York, NY. No grants to individuals.
Application information: Contributes only to pre-selected organizations.
Officers: Stella Buono, Pres.; Kevin O'Brien, Secy.
Director: Daniel Benton.
EIN: 061631047
Other changes: For the fiscal year ended Aug. 31, 2013, the grantmaker paid grants of $3,227,000, a 72.1% increase over the fiscal 2012 disbursements, $1,875,000.
Stella Buono has replaced Julia Dailey as Pres.

2038
Animal Farm Foundation, Inc.
P.O. Box 624
Bangall, NY 12506-0624
***E-mail:* grantsandawards@animalfarmfoundation.org**; Main URL: http://www.animalfarmfoundation.org
Facebook: https://www.facebook.com/animalfarmfoundation
Flickr: https://www.flickr.com/photos/animalfarmfoundation
Pinterest: http://www.pinterest.com/animalfarmfndtn/
Twitter: https://twitter.com/AnimalFarmFndtn
Vimeo: http://vimeo.com/animalfarmfoundation
Wordpress: http://animalfarmfoundation.wordpress.com/

Established in 1985 in NY.
Donors: Jane R. Berkey; Sam Dworkis; Andrew Saul; Denise Saul.
Foundation type: Independent foundation.
Financial data (yr. ended 06/30/13): Assets, $2,537,589 (M); gifts received, $2,893,000; expenditures, $1,856,121; qualifying distributions, $1,792,103; giving activities include $456,324 for 233 grants (high: $16,550; low: $50).
Purpose and activities: Giving primarily to secure equal treatment and opportunity for pit bull dogs.
Fields of interest: Animal welfare.
Type of support: General/operating support.
Limitations: Applications not accepted. Giving primarily in MO. No grants to individuals.
Application information: Unsolicited requests for funds not accepted.
Officers: Jane R. Berkey, Pres.; Peggy Gordijn, V.P.; Donald Cleary, Secy.-Treas.; **Stacey Coleman, Exec. Dir.**
Board Members: Diana M. Gurieva; Andrew Saul; Ledy Vankavage, Esq.
EIN: 222386955

2039
Animal Welfare Trust
141 Halstead Ave., Ste. 301
Mamaroneck, NY 10543-2652 (914) 381-6177
Contact: Brad Goldberg, Pres.
FAX: (914) 381-6176;
E-mail: email@animalwelfaretrust.org; Mailing and application address: P.O. Box 737, Mamaroneck, NY 10543; **Main URL: http://fdnweb.org/awt/**
Grants List: http://fdnweb.org/awt/grants/year/2013/
E-mail for internships: ali@animalwelfaretrust.org

Established in 2001 in NY.
Donors: Bradley Goldberg; Eileen Kay Sterioff‡.
Foundation type: Operating foundation.
Financial data (yr. ended 12/31/13): Assets, $4,277,650 (M); expenditures, $366,962; qualifying distributions, $428,874; giving activities include $238,650 for 13 grants (high: $82,500; low: $650), and $10,500 for 5 grants to individuals (high: $4,000; low: $1,000).
Purpose and activities: The purpose of the trust is to make a difference in the welfare of animals. Its grants program has a particular focus on helping grassroots efforts that have a compelling vision as to how they can make a unique contribution to the animal welfare cause.
Fields of interest: Animal welfare.
Type of support: Grants to individuals; General/operating support.
Limitations: Applications accepted. Giving on a national basis, with some emphasis in Mamaroneck, NY. Generally no support for local animal rescue/shelter and spay/neuter programs, or for wildlife management and conservation projects.
Publications: Application guidelines; Grants list.
Application information: See Trust web site for full application guidelines. Application form not required.
Initial approach: Letter of inquiry by e-mail is encouraged
***Deadline(s):* See Trust web site for deadlines**
Board meeting date(s): Quarterly
Officers and Directors:* Bradley Goldberg,* Pres.; **Mariann Sullivan, Esq.*, Secy.**; **Lilli Lawner, C.S.W.**; Amy Trakinski, Esq.; David Wolfson, Esq.
Number of staff: 1 full-time professional; 1 part-time professional; 3 part-time support.
EIN: 134131408
Other changes: Mariann Sullivan, Esq. has replaced Lilli Goldberg, C.S.W. as Secy.

2040
Arcus Foundation
(formerly Jon L. Stryker Foundation)
44 W. 28th St., 17th Fl.
New York, NY 10001-4212 (212) 488-3000
Contact: Carol Snapp, Comms. Mgr.
FAX: (212) 488-3010; Main URL: http://www.arcusfoundation.org
Arcus Foundation's Philanthropy Promise: http://www.ncrp.org/philanthropys-promise/who
E-Newsletter: http://www.arcusfoundation.org/pages_2/publ.cfm
Grants Database: http://www.arcusfoundation.org/pages_2/funds_n.cfm?

Established in 1997 in MI.
Donor: Jon L. Stryker.
Foundation type: Independent foundation.
Financial data (yr. ended 12/31/12): Assets, $171,196,458 (M); gifts received, $30,107,517; expenditures, $37,150,269; qualifying distributions, $35,910,846; giving activities include $28,596,867 for 260 grants (high: $4,819,747; low: $25).
Purpose and activities: The mission of the foundation is to achieve social justice that is inclusive of sexual orientation, gender identity and race, and to ensure conservation and respect of the great apes.
Fields of interest: Animals/wildlife, endangered species; Animals/wildlife, sanctuaries; Animals/wildlife, special services; Civil/human rights, LGBTQ; Civil/human rights; LGBTQ.
Type of support: General/operating support; Management development/capacity building; Capital campaigns; Building/renovation; Endowments; Program development; Conferences/seminars; Publication; Curriculum development; Technical assistance; Consulting services; Program evaluation; Employee matching gifts; Matching/challenge support.
Limitations: Applications accepted. Giving on a national basis, with some emphasis on MI, especially southwest MI. Giving on an international basis, with emphasis on Africa, the Middle East and Southeast Asia. No support for lobby groups or political campaigns. No grants to individuals, or for religious or political activities, scholarships, or for medical research or film production projects.
Publications: Annual report (including application guidelines); Newsletter.
Application information: Application Process: 1) Please confirm that your organization is an eligible tax-exempt organization under Sec. 501(c)(3) of the IRS regulations (or as a non-US organization, can you demonstrate an equivalent status and a

non-discrimination or EEO policy compliant); 2) Contact appropriate foundation program officer to discuss interest and ideas for your request; 3) Submit a formal Letter of Inquiry to the foundation; and 4) If invited, submit a full proposal. After reviewing your LOI, the foundation will inform you as to whether a full proposal is being invited.
Application form not required.
Initial approach: Contact a foundation program officer and then submit a formal letter of inquiry
Copies of proposal: 4
Deadline(s): Rolling; Once the foundation accepts a Letter of Inquiry and invites a full proposal, a specific deadline for submission of the full proposal will then be provided in the letter of invitation sent by the foundation
Board meeting date(s): Four board meetings annually
Final notification: After board meetings; Grant recipients will receive a Grant Award Letter.
Officers and Directors:* Jon L. Stryker,* Pres.; Annette Lanjouw, V.P., Strategic Initiatives and Great Apes Prog.; Jay Michaelson, V.P., Social Justice Prog.; Thomas W. Nichols, V.P., Finance and Opers.; Cindy Rizzo, V.P., Organizational Learning and Grants Mgmt.; Bryan E. Simmons, V.P., Global Comms.; Arie Weissman, V.P., Finance and Opers.; Linda Ho, Cont.; Kevin Jennings, Exec. Dir.; Stephen Bennett; Jeff Trandahl; Janet Mock; Catherine Pino; Darren Walker.
Number of staff: 21
EIN: 383332791
Other changes: The grantmaker has moved from MI to NY. The grantmaker no longer lists an E-mail address.

2041
The Catherine and Joseph Aresty Foundation Inc.
c/o Alfred Dunner, Inc.
1411 Broadway
New York, NY 10018-3496

Established in 1997 in NY; funded in 2002.
Donors: Joseph Aresty; Catherine Aresty; Steven Aresty.
Foundation type: Independent foundation.
Financial data (yr. ended 07/31/13): Assets, $18,265,001 (M); expenditures, $1,014,241; qualifying distributions, $992,509; giving activities include $902,500 for 27 grants (high: $100,000; low: $7,500).
Fields of interest: Historical activities; Education; Health care; Human services; Christian agencies & churches; Hispanics/Latinos.
Limitations: Applications not accepted. Giving primarily in New York, NY. No grants to individuals.
Application information: Contributes only to pre-selected organizations.
Officers: Catherine Aresty, Chair.; **Joseph Aresty, Vice-Chair.**; Steven Aresty, Secy.-Treas.
EIN: 133962647
Other changes: Joseph Aresty is now Vice-Chair.

2042
Aronson Foundation
35 E. 20th St.
New York, NY 10003
E-mail: JA31628@aol.com

Established in 1992 in MO.
Donors: Adam Aronson†; James Aronson; Judith Aronson; Jonathan Aronson; Joshua Aronson.
Foundation type: Independent foundation.
Financial data (yr. ended 12/31/11): Assets, $3,168,420 (M); gifts received, $41,865; expenditures, $194,526; qualifying distributions, $158,725; giving activities include $157,150 for 10 + grants (high: $36,500).
Purpose and activities: Giving primarily for the arts, art education, and to cultural institutes.
Fields of interest: Arts education; Arts; Young adults.
Type of support: Program development; Curriculum development; Fellowships; Internship funds; Scholarship funds.
Limitations: Applications not accepted. Giving primarily in the St. Louis, MO, metropolitan area. No support for political programs. No grants to individuals, or for "bricks and mortar" or buildings; grants rarely made to capital campaigns.
Application information: Contributes only to pre-selected organizations.
Board meeting date(s): Annually
Trustee: Jonathan Aronson; Joshua Aronson.
Number of staff: None.
EIN: 431616967
Other changes: The grantmaker has moved from MO to NY.
James Aronson is no longer trustee.

2043
Art Matters, Inc.
P.O. Box 311
Prince St. Sta.
New York, NY 10012-0006
Contact: Sacha Yanow, Prog. Dir.
E-mail: info@artmattersfoundation.org; Main URL: http://www.artmattersfoundation.org/
Facebook: https://www.facebook.com/pages/Art-Matters-Foundation/539352129419101

Established in 1985 in NY.
Donors: Good Works Foundation; Laura Donnelley Charitable Lead Trust.
Foundation type: Independent foundation.
Financial data (yr. ended 12/31/12): Assets, $73,996 (M); gifts received, $307,500; expenditures, $289,578; qualifying distributions, $294,869; giving activities include $18,000 for 3 grants (high: $10,000; low: $3,000), and $158,400 for 38 grants to individuals (high: $8,000; low: $300).
Purpose and activities: Giving is provided to encourage exploration of issues and ideas; experimentation in visual arts, media, and performance; and presentation of new art.
Fields of interest: Visual arts.
Type of support: Fellowships; Grants to individuals.
Limitations: Applications not accepted. Giving limited to NY. No support for organizations or individuals working in dance or music, or for individual art studies. No grants for publications.
Application information: The grantmaker considers applications by invitation only. See web site for additional information.
Officers: Laura Donnelley, Chair.; Philip Yenawine, Pres.; Marianne Weems, Exec. V.P.; Cee Brown, V.P.; Laurence Miller, Secy.; Linda Earle, Treas.
Directors: Regine Basha; Mary Beebe; Gai Gherardi; Alex Grey; David Mendoza; Lowery Sims; Bruce Yonemoto.
EIN: 133271577

2044
Artists Fellowship Inc.
c/o Salmagundi Club
47 5th Ave.
New York, NY 10003-4303 **(212) 255-7740, ext. 216**
E-mail: info@Artistsfellowship.org; Main URL: http://artistsfellowship.org

Established in 1859.
Donor: J. B. Lankes†.
Foundation type: Independent foundation.
Financial data (yr. ended 10/31/13): Assets, $4,883,603 (M); gifts received, $76,600; expenditures, $300,738; qualifying distributions, $283,547; giving activities include $234,303 for 66 grants to individuals (high: $23,500; low: $500).
Purpose and activities: Grants for emergency aid to professional fine artists (painters, graphic artists, printmakers, and sculptors), and their families in times of emergency, disability or bereavement. One does not need to be a member of the fellowship to receive assistance, nor does membership in the fellowship entitle one to assistance.
Fields of interest: Visual arts; Aging, centers/services; Aging; Disabilities, people with.
Type of support: Grants to individuals.
Application information: See Fellowship web site for complete application guidelines.
Officers: Wende Caporale, Pres.; Charles Yoder, V.P.; Priscilla McCarthy, Recording Secy.; Joyce Zeller, Corresponding Secy.; Pamela Singleton, Treas.
Trustees: Edith Rae Brown; Terry Brown; Fran Dembitzer; Franklin Feldman; Ira Goldberg; Richard Heinrich; Morton Kaish; Tim Newton; David B. Pena; Claudia Seymour; Sharon Sprung.
EIN: 136122134

2045
The Asen Foundation
224 E. 49th St.
New York, NY 10017-1554
***Contact:* R. Scott Asen**

Established in NY.
Donor: Robert Scott Asen.
Foundation type: Independent foundation.
Financial data (yr. ended 12/31/12): Assets, $1,906,962 (M); expenditures, $358,500; qualifying distributions, $356,750; giving activities include $356,750 for 65 grants (high: $100,000; low: $100).
Fields of interest: Arts; Education; Environment.
Limitations: Applications not accepted. Giving primarily in Washington, DC. No grants to individuals.
Application information: Unsolicited requests for funds not accepted.
Trustee: Robert Scott Asen.
EIN: 207361210

2046
The Assael Foundation
580 5th Ave., 21st Fl.
New York, NY 10036-4701

Established in 1992 in NY.
Donors: Salvador J. Assael; Baruch Assael; Esther Posin; Christina Lang Assael.
Foundation type: Independent foundation.
Financial data (yr. ended 12/31/12): Assets, $4,986,375 (M); gifts received, $2,000,000; expenditures, $2,400,561; qualifying distributions,

$2,378,692; giving activities include $2,366,000 for 7 grants (high: $2,060,000; low: $1,000).
Purpose and activities: Giving primarily for education and the arts.
Fields of interest: Arts, cultural/ethnic awareness; Museums; Performing arts; Arts; Elementary/secondary education; Education, special; Education; Children, services; International development; Jewish agencies & synagogues.
International interests: Israel.
Limitations: Applications not accepted. Giving primarily in NY, with emphasis on the New York metropolitan area. No grants to individuals.
Application information: Contributes only to pre-selected organizations.
Officers and Trustees:* **Christina Lang Assael,* Chair. and Pres.**; **Bandana Kumar, Secy.-Treas.**; Rabbi Marc D. Angel; John D. Block; **Ephraim Propp**; **Benjamin Zucker.**
EIN: 133683069
Other changes: Christina Lang Assael has replaced Salvador J. Assael as Chair. and Pres.
Cyril S. Dwek is no longer a trustee.

2047
Assurant Foundation
(formerly Fortis Foundation)
1 Chase Manhattan Plz., 41st Fl.
New York, NY 10005
Main URL: **http://www.assurant.com/about/corporateresponsibility/assurant_foundation.html**

Established in 1982 in NY.
Donors: Time Insurance Co.; Fortis Insurance Co.; Fortis, Inc.; Fortis Benefits Insurance Co.; Assurant, Inc.
Foundation type: Company-sponsored foundation.
Financial data (yr. ended 12/31/12): Assets, $9,603,401 (M); gifts received, $1,803,071; expenditures, $3,127,494; qualifying distributions, $3,048,367; giving activities include $2,564,540 for 350 grants (high: $351,406; low: $50), and $483,827 for 1 employee matching gift.
Purpose and activities: The foundation supports organizations involved with education, health, nutrition, housing, human services, and community development. Special emphasis is directed toward health and wellness; homes and property; and hometown help.
Fields of interest: Museums (art); Education; Health care; Nutrition; Housing/shelter; Family services; Human services; Community/economic development.
Type of support: General/operating support; Program development; Employee matching gifts.
Limitations: Applications not accepted. Giving primarily in areas of company operations in the New York, NY, metropolitan area. No support for religious or political organizations. No grants to individuals or for lobbying or fundraising.
Trustees: Robert Pollock; Sylvia Wagner; Allen Walker.
EIN: 133156497

2048
The Atlantic Foundation of New York
c/o The Atlantic Philanthropies
75 Varick St., 17th Fl.
New York, NY 10017-1950 (212) 916-7300
E-mail: USA@atlanticphilanthropies.org
Charles F. Feeney's Giving Pledge Profile: http://glasspockets.org/philanthropy-in-focus/eye-on-the-giving-pledge/profiles/feeney

Established in 1989 in NY.
Donors: Atlan Management Corp.; Interpacific Holdings, Inc.; General Atlantic Corp.
Foundation type: Independent foundation.
Financial data (yr. ended 12/31/12): Assets, $6,418,565 (M); expenditures, $1,249,717; qualifying distributions, $1,230,849; giving activities include $1,230,849 for 6 grants (high: $600,000; low: $25,000).
Purpose and activities: The purpose of the foundation is to bring about lasting changes that will improve the lives of disadvantaged and vulnerable people.
Fields of interest: Human services; Native Americans/American Indians.
Limitations: Applications not accepted. Giving in the U.S., with some emphasis on MT. No grants to individuals.
Publications: Financial statement.
Application information: Contributes only to pre-selected organizations.
Officers and Directors:* Gara LaMarche,* Pres.; Colin McCrea, Sr. V.P., Progs.; Deborah R. Phillips, Sr. V.P., Group Svcs. and Eval.; Cynthia Richards,* V.P.; David Sternlieb, Secy.; Philip Coates, C.I.O.; Harvey Dale; Christine V. Downton; Charles F. Feeney; William Hall; Sara Lawrence-Lightfoot; Elizabeth J. McCormack; Thomas N. Mitchell; Cecilia Munoz; Peter Smitham; Frederick A.O. Schwarz, Jr.; Michael I. Sovern; Cummings V. Zuill.
EIN: 133562971
Other changes: At the close of 2012, the grantmaker paid grants of $1,230,849, a 603.3% increase over the 2011 disbursements, $175,000.

2049
The Augustine Foundation
c/o D. Weishselbaum, CPA
147-40 77th Rd.
Queens, NY 11367-3429
Application address: c/o Stephen Greisgraber, 302 Bedford Ave., Brooklyn, NY 11211

Established in 1980 in NY.
Donor: Rose L. Augustine‡.
Foundation type: Independent foundation.
Financial data (yr. ended 06/30/12): Assets, $20,074,962 (M); gifts received, $778,653; expenditures, $3,240,848; qualifying distributions, $2,977,425; giving activities include $2,977,425 for 26 grants (high: $2,500,000; low: $1,500).
Purpose and activities: Giving primarily for the arts and Jewish education.
Fields of interest: Arts; Education; Jewish agencies & synagogues.
Limitations: Applications accepted. Giving in the U.S., with emphasis on NY. No grants to individuals.
Application information: Application form not required.
Initial approach: Letter
Deadline(s): None
Officers: Stephen Greisgraber, Pres.; Leo Mavrovitis, Secy.
Directors: Sharon Isbin; H. Zeisel.
EIN: 132997450
Other changes: The grantmaker has moved from NJ to NY.

2050
The Authors League Fund
31 E. 32nd St., 7th Fl.
New York, NY 10016-5509 (212) 268-1208
Contact: Isabel A. Howe, Exec. Dir.
FAX: (212) 564-5363;
E-mail: staff@authorsleaguefund.org; Main URL: http://www.authorsleaguefund.org
Donors: Joanne Leedom-Ackerman; Priscilla McMillian; Nathan & Dorothy Shainberg Endowment; Winchell Smith‡; The Herman Lissner Foundation; Garrison Keillor; Jenny Lind Nillson; Spencer Johnson.
Foundation type: Independent foundation.
Financial data (yr. ended 12/31/12): Assets, $6,245,062 (M); gifts received, $182,101; expenditures, $335,329; qualifying distributions, $316,636; giving activities include $197,356 for 1 grant, and $172,000 for loans to individuals.
Purpose and activities: The Authors League Fund helps professional writers and dramatists who find themselves in financial need because of medical or health-related problems, temporary loss of income or other misfortune. The fund gives open-ended, interest-free, no-strings-attached loans. These loans are not grants or scholarships meant to subsidize personal writing projects.
Fields of interest: Arts.
Type of support: Loans—to individuals.
Limitations: Applications accepted. Giving primarily in New York, NY.
Publications: Application guidelines.
Application information: See fund web site for complete application procedures and guidelines. Application form required.
Initial approach: **Application available on fund web site**
Deadline(s): None
Officers: Pat Cummings, Pres.; Sidney Offit, V.P.; Marian Seldes, Secy.; Isabel Howe, Exec. Dir.
Directors: Peter Blauner; Georges Borchardt; Gretchen Cryer; Daniel Hoffman; Karen Swenson; Jennifer Egan; Molly Haskell; George J.W. Goodman; Paula Giddings; and 14 additional directors.
EIN: 131966496
Other changes: The grantmaker now publishes application guidelines online.

2051
The AVI CHAI Foundation
(formerly AVI CHAI - A Philanthropic Foundation)
1015 Park Ave.
New York, NY 10028-0904 (212) 396-8850
Contact: Yossi Prager, Exec. Dir., North America
FAX: (212) 396-8833; E-mail: info@avichaina.org;
Additional/mailing address (Israel office): P.O. Box 7617, Jerusalem, 91076 tel.: (02) 621-5300, fax: (02) 621-5331, e-mail: office@avichai.org.il;
Main URL: http://www.avichai.org
Blog: http://avichai.org/blog/
Facebook: https://www.facebook.com/AviChaiFoundation
LinkedIn: http://www.linkedin.com/company/the-avi-chai-foundation/
The Avi Chai Foundation Staff: https://twitter.com/AVICHAIFDN/avichaifdn/members
Twitter: https://twitter.com/AVICHAIFDN

Established in 1984 in NY.
Donor: Zalman C. Bernstein‡.
Foundation type: Independent foundation.
Financial data (yr. ended 12/31/12): Assets, $570,152,807 (M); gifts received, $156,289; expenditures, $43,019,901; qualifying distributions, $50,422,671; giving activities include $35,460,993 for 77 grants (high: $12,258,995; low: $2,500), $75,000 for 1 grant to an individual, $909,756 for foundation-administered programs and $7,342,500 for 10 loans/program-related investments (high: $1,000,000; low: $250,000).

Purpose and activities: The foundation is committed to the perpetuation of the Jewish people, Judaism, and the centrality of the state of Israel to the Jewish people. The objectives of the foundation are to encourage those of the Jewish faith towards greater commitment to Jewish observance and lifestyle by increasing their understanding, appreciation, and practice of Jewish traditions, customs, and laws; and to encourage mutual understanding and sensitivity among Jews of different religious backgrounds and commitments to observance.
Fields of interest: Education; Human services; Youth, services; Jewish federated giving programs.
International interests: Israel.
Type of support: Program development; Conferences/seminars; Curriculum development; Research; Program-related investments/loans.
Limitations: Applications not accepted. Giving primarily in North America and Israel. No grants for building projects or deficits.
Publications: Annual report.
Application information: Unsolicited requests for funds not accepted.
Board meeting date(s): 3 times a year
Officers and Trustees:* Mem Dryan Bernstein,* Chair.; Azriel Novick, C.F.O.; Yossi Prager, Exec. Dir., North America; Eli Silver, Exec. Dir., Israel; Samuel "Buddy" Silberman, Tr. Emeritus; Henry Taub, Tr. Emeritus; Meir Buzaglo; Avital Darmon; Alan R. Feld; Arthur W. Fried; Lauren K. Merkin; George Rohr; Lief D. Rosenblatt; Ruth R. Wisse.
Number of staff: 7 full-time professional; 4 full-time support.
EIN: 133252800
Other changes: Mem Dryan Bernstein has replaced Arthur W. Fried as Chair.
David E. Tadmor is no longer a trustee.

2052
AYN Foundation
c/o Sacks Press & Lacher, PC
600 3rd Ave.
New York, NY 10016-1901
***E-mail:* info@aynfoundation.com**; Main URL: http://www.aynfoundation.com

Established in 1992 in NY.
Donors: Philippa de Menil Friedrich; Heiner Friedrich.
Foundation type: Operating foundation.
Financial data (yr. ended 06/30/12): Assets, $3,281,821 (M); gifts received, $1,500,000; expenditures, $335,390; qualifying distributions, $162,000; giving activities include $142,000 for 1 grant, and $20,000 for 1 grant to an individual.
Fields of interest: Arts.
Type of support: General/operating support.
Limitations: Applications not accepted. Giving primarily in New York, NY.
Application information: Unsolicited requests for funds not accepted.
Officers: Heiner Friedrich, Pres.; Fariha Friedrich, Secy.
EIN: 133692868

2053
Marvin Azrak and Sons Foundation
10 W. 33rd St., Rm. 516
New York, NY 10001-3306 **(212) 947-9600**
Contact: Marvin Azrak, Mgr.

Established in 1994 in NY.
Donors: Adam Azrak; Elliot Azrak; Marvin Azrak; Victor Azrak; members of the Azrak family.
Foundation type: Independent foundation.
Financial data (yr. ended 12/31/12): Assets, $2,629,666 (M); gifts received, $1,029,837; expenditures, $1,027,423; qualifying distributions, $1,000,703; giving activities include $1,000,703 for 160 grants (high: $100,800; low: $18).
Purpose and activities: Giving primarily for Jewish agencies, temples, and schools.
Fields of interest: Education; Jewish federated giving programs; Jewish agencies & synagogues.
Limitations: Giving primarily in NJ, and New York, NY. No grants to individuals.
Application information:
Initial approach: Letter
Deadline(s): None
Officers: Victor Azrak, Pres.; Elliott Azrak, Treas.; Marvin Azrak, Mgr.
Trustees: Adam Azrak.
EIN: 133771410
Other changes: Victor Azrak is now Pres. Elliott Azrak is now Treas.

2054
The Barker Welfare Foundation
P.O. Box 2
Glen Head, NY 11545-0002 (516) 759-5592
Contact: Sarane H. Ross, Pres.
FAX: (516) 759-5497;
E-mail: SusanDeMaio@barkerwelfare.org; Main URL: http://www.barkerwelfare.org

Incorporated in 1934 in IL.
Donor: Mrs. Charles V. Hickox†.
Foundation type: Independent foundation.
Financial data (yr. ended 09/30/13): Assets, $114,149,298 (M); expenditures, $3,788,718; qualifying distributions, $3,361,821; giving activities include $2,951,719 for 320 grants (high: $75,000; low: $500).
Purpose and activities: The mission of the Barker Welfare Foundation is to make grants to qualified charitable organizations whose initiatives improve the quality of life, with an emphasis on strengthening youth and families and to reflect the philosophy of Catherine B. Hickox, the Founder. Grants to established organizations and charitable institutions, with emphasis on youth and families, museums and the fine and performing arts, child welfare and youth agencies, health services and rehabilitation, welfare, aid to the handicapped, family planning, libraries, the environment, recreation, and programs for the elderly.
Fields of interest: Visual arts; Museums; Arts; Libraries/library science; Environment; Health care; Mental health/crisis services; Recreation; Human services; Children/youth, services; Disabilities, people with.
Type of support: General/operating support; Continuing support; Annual campaigns; Capital campaigns; Building/renovation; Equipment.
Limitations: Giving primarily in Chicago, IL, Michigan City, IN, and New York, NY. Requests for funding in Chicago will no longer be accepted unless invited (initiated) by the foundation. No support for political activities, start-up organizations, national health, welfare, or education agencies, institutions or funds, including private or public schools. No grants to individuals, or for endowment funds, seed money, emergency funds, deficit financing, scholarships, fellowships, medical or scientific research, films or videos, or conferences; no loans.
Publications: Application guidelines; Annual report (including application guidelines).
Application information: Proposals must be completed according to the foundation's guidelines and grants process in order to be considered for funding. Grants to Chicago agencies are by invitation only. Proposals sent by fax not considered. Application information available on foundation web site. Application form required.
Initial approach: 2- to 3-page letter of inquiry or online inquiry through web site. A telephone call is also suggested to determine if the applicant falls within the general current policy of the foundation
Copies of proposal: 2
Deadline(s): Feb. 1 and Aug. 1
Board meeting date(s): May and Oct.
Final notification: After board meeting for positive responses; any time for negative responses
Officers and Directors:* Sarane H. Ross,* Pres.; Katrina H. Becker,* V.P.; Danielle H. Moore,* Secy.; Thomas P. McCormick,* Treas.; Diane Curtis; **Frances B. Hickox**; **James A.B. Hickox**; Alline Matheson; Sarane R. O'Connor; Alexander B. Ross; Sarane H. Ross; Stephen B. Ross.
Number of staff: 2 full-time professional; 1 part-time support.
EIN: 366018526
Other changes: Mary Lou Linnen is no longer a director.

2055
Barking Foundation, Inc.
c/o Marks Paneth Shron
685 3rd Ave., 5th Fl.
New York, NY **10017-4024**

Established in 1997 in ME.
Donors: Stephen E. King; Tabitha King.
Foundation type: Independent foundation.
Financial data (yr. ended 12/31/12): Assets, $0 (M); gifts received, $2,340; expenditures, $755,270; qualifying distributions, $748,423; giving activities include $745,193 for 1 grant.
Purpose and activities: Scholarship awards to full or part time undergraduate students at 4 year colleges.
Fields of interest: Education.
Type of support: General/operating support; Scholarships—to individuals.
Limitations: Applications not accepted.
Application information: Unsolicited requests for funds not accepted.
Board meeting date(s): Within 2 months
Officers: Stephen E. King, Pres.; Tabitha King, V.P.; Arthur B. Greene, Secy.
Number of staff: 1 full-time professional.
EIN: 010511020
Other changes: At the close of 2012, the grantmaker paid grants of $745,193, a 364.3% increase over the 2011 disbursements, $160,500.

2056
The Bay and Paul Foundations, Inc.
(formerly Josephine Bay Paul and C. Michael Paul Foundation, Inc.)
17 W. 94th St., 1st Fl.
New York, NY 10025-7116 (212) 663-1115
Contact: Frederick Bay, C.E.O. and Pres.
FAX: (212) 932-0316;
E-mail: info@bayandpaulfoundations.org; Main URL: http://www.bayandpaulfoundations.org

Established in 2005 in NY.
Donors: Josephine Bay Paul†; Charles Ulrick Bay†.
Foundation type: Independent foundation.
Financial data (yr. ended 12/31/12): Assets, $71,635,854 (M); expenditures, $5,489,268; qualifying distributions, $4,559,383; giving

activities include $3,473,026 for 234 grants (high: $200,000; low: $170).
Purpose and activities: Support for organizations demonstrating or developing pre-collegiate educational restructuring; support projects which reinforce the centrality of the arts in pre-collegiate curricula. The foundation also has an interest in projects seeking to sustain the earth's biodiversity. K-12 math and science, arts-in-education: grants are limited to the New York, NY, metropolitan area.
Fields of interest: Arts education; Education, research; Elementary school/education; Secondary school/education; Education; Environment.
Type of support: General/operating support; Continuing support; Program development; Conferences/seminars; Seed money; Research; Technical assistance; Matching/challenge support.
Limitations: Giving limited to the NY metropolitan area for Math/Science and Arts Education; giving on a national basis otherwise. No support for sectarian religious programs, or to other than publicly recognized charities. No grants to individuals, or for building campaigns.
Application information: See foundation web site for the most current application updates and information.
Board meeting date(s): Feb., May, and Nov.
Officers and Directors:* Robert Ashton,* Chair.; Frederick Bay,* C.E.O. and Pres.; Dianne J. Daniels, C.O.O. and Fiscal Off.; Synnova B. Hayes,* V.P., Admin. and Progs, and Treas.; Kenneth D. Hurwitz,* Secy.; Rebecca Adamson; David Bury; Corinne Steel.
Number of staff: 2 full-time professional; 3 part-time professional; 2 full-time support.
EIN: 131991717

2057
B'Chaya Moshe Charitable Trust
3478 Bedford Ave.
Brooklyn, NY **11210-5235**

Established in 2005 in NY.
Donors: Barry Braunstein; Jacqueline Braunstein; Chaya Bleier; Israel Braunstein; Moses & Yetta Charitable Trust.
Foundation type: Independent foundation.
Financial data (yr. ended 12/31/12): Assets, $2,273,734 (M); gifts received, $551,200; expenditures, $493,542; qualifying distributions, $493,192; giving activities include $493,192 for 24 + grants.
Purpose and activities: Giving primarily to Jewish agencies, temples, and schools.
Fields of interest: Elementary/secondary education; Jewish agencies & synagogues.
Limitations: Applications not accepted. Giving primarily in Brooklyn, NY. No grants to individuals.
Application information: Contributes only to pre-selected organizations.
Trustees: Barry Braunstein; Jacqueline Braunstein.
EIN: 206433749

2058
Leo Cox Beach Philanthropic Foundation
P.O. Box 2218
Glens Falls, NY **12801-6218** (518) 792-3146
***Contact:* Deborah Burnham, Dir.**

Established in 1989 in NY.
Donor: Thomas C. Beach, Jr.
Foundation type: Independent foundation.
Financial data (yr. ended 07/31/13): Assets, $3,228,942 (M); expenditures, $214,478; qualifying distributions, $185,000; giving activities include $185,000 for 17 grants (high: $40,000; low: $1,000).
Fields of interest: Media/communications; Museums; Arts; Education; Hospitals (general); Human services.
Limitations: Applications accepted. Giving primarily in NY. No grants to individuals.
Application information: A major portion of funding (90 percent) is committed; the remainder of giving is limited to Washington County, NY. Application form required.
Initial approach: Letter or phone
Deadline(s): None
Directors: Thomas C. Beach, Jr.; Deborah Burnham; Dorothy Jackson; Michael F. Massiano; Pauline E. Palmer; John T. Snell, Esq.; Barbara Velsini.
EIN: 141732259

2059
Robert A. and Renee E. Belfer Family Foundation
c/o Belfer Mgmt., LLC
767 5th Ave., 46th Fl.
New York, NY 10153-0023 **(212) 508-9500**
Contact: Robert A. Belfer, Pres.

Established in 1990 in NY.
Donors: Robert A. Belfer; Jack Resnick & Sons, Inc.; Belfer Two Corp.
Foundation type: Independent foundation.
Financial data (yr. ended 12/31/12): Assets, $16,490,248 (M); gifts received, $1,968,665; expenditures, $9,373,313; qualifying distributions, $9,335,005; giving activities include $9,335,005 for 60 grants (high: $4,000,000; low: $150).
Purpose and activities: Giving primarily for the arts, education, health organizations and Jewish causes.
Fields of interest: Museums (art); Museums (ethnic/folk arts); Performing arts centers; Arts; Elementary/secondary education; Higher education; Medical school/education; Education; Cancer; Health organizations; Medical research, institute; Human services; Jewish federated giving programs; Jewish agencies & synagogues.
Limitations: Applications accepted. Giving primarily in New York, NY; some giving also in Houston, TX. No grants to individuals.
Application information:
Initial approach: Letter
Deadline(s): None
Officer: Robert A. Belfer, Pres. and Secy.
Trustees: Laurence D. Belfer; Renee E. Belfer.
EIN: 136935616
Other changes: At the close of 2012, the grantmaker paid grants of $9,335,005, a 106.2% increase over the 2010 disbursements, $4,527,820.

2060
The Arthur and Rochelle Belfer Foundation, Inc.
(formerly The Belfer Foundation, Inc.)
c/o Belfer Mgmt., LLC
767 5th Ave., 46th Fl.
New York, NY 10153-0023 **(212) 508-9500**
Contact: Robert A. Belfer, V.P.

Incorporated in 1951 in NY.
Donors: Members of the Belfer family; Belfer Corp.
Foundation type: Independent foundation.
Financial data (yr. ended 12/31/12): Assets, $2,003,554 (M); expenditures, $45,557; qualifying distributions, $0.
Purpose and activities: Giving primarily for medical school education; some funding also for Jewish organizations.
Fields of interest: Medical school/education; Jewish agencies & synagogues.
Limitations: Applications not accepted. Giving primarily in NY. No grants to individuals.
Application information: Unsolicited requests for funds not accepted.
Officers and Directors:* Robert A. Belfer,* V.P.; Lawrence Ruben, V.P.; Laurence Belfer,* Secy.; Norman Belfer; Renee E. Belfer; Richard Ruben; Jack Saltz; Dr. Leonard Saltz.
EIN: 136086711

2061
Benmen Fund
48 E. Concord Dr.
Monsey, NY 10952-1719

Established in 1991 in NY.
Donors: Harvey Brecher; Miriam Brecher.
Foundation type: Independent foundation.
Financial data (yr. ended 11/30/13): Assets, $21,161 (M); gifts received, $155,000; expenditures, $140,889; qualifying distributions, $140,889; giving activities include $140,829 for 495 grants (high: $7,500; low: $18).
Purpose and activities: Giving primarily for Jewish organizations.
Fields of interest: Elementary/secondary education; Children, services; Jewish agencies & synagogues.
Limitations: Applications not accepted. Giving primarily in Monsey, NY. No grants to individuals.
Application information: Contributes only to pre-selected organizations.
Officers and Directors:* Harvey Brecher,* Pres. and Treas.; **Miriam Brecher,* V.P. and Secy.**; Yossie Brecher,* V.P.; Malkie Kahn,* V.P.; Eli S. Garber.
EIN: 133620970

2062
The David Berg Foundation, Inc.
16 E. 73rd St., Ste. 1R
New York, NY 10021-4129 (212) 517-8634
Contact: Michele Tocci, Pres.
FAX: (212) 517-8636;
E-mail: mtocci@bergfoundation.org

Established in 1994 in NY.
Donor: David Berg Settlor Trust.
Foundation type: Independent foundation.
Financial data (yr. ended 12/31/12): Assets, $94,343,132 (M); gifts received, $5,131,606; expenditures, $6,655,068; qualifying distributions, $5,505,457; giving activities include $4,711,643 for 94 grants (high: $1,000,000; low: $5,000).
Fields of interest: Museums; Historic preservation/historical societies; Legal services; Jewish agencies & synagogues.
International interests: England; Israel.
Type of support: General/operating support; Continuing support; Annual campaigns; Equipment; Program development; Conferences/seminars; Professorships; Publication; Curriculum development; Fellowships; Scholarship funds; Research; Exchange programs.
Limitations: Applications accepted. Giving primarily in New York, NY. No grants to individuals.
Publications: Application guidelines; Grants list.
Application information: Application form not required.
Initial approach: Letter

Copies of proposal: 1
Deadline(s): Mar. 15 (for June); June 25 (for Nov.); and Nov. 15 (for Feb.)
Board meeting date(s): June, Oct., and Feb.
Officers: Michele C. Tocci, Pres.; William D. Zabel, V.P.; Jerome Zoffer, Secy.-Treas.
Number of staff: 1 full-time professional; 1 part-time professional; 1 part-time support.
EIN: 133753217
Other changes: At the close of 2012, the fair market value of the grantmaker's assets was $94,343,132, a 145.4% increase over the 2010 value, $38,442,481. For the same period, the grantmaker paid grants of $4,711,643, a 116.7% increase over the 2010 disbursements, $2,174,616.

2063
The Eddie and Rachelle Betesh Family Foundation, Inc.

c/o Saramax Apparel
1372 Broadway, 7th Fl.
New York, NY 10018-6107

Established in 1998 in DE and NY.
Donors: Eddie Betesh; Rachelle Betesh.
Foundation type: Independent foundation.
Financial data (yr. ended 12/31/12): Assets, $1,329,484 (M); gifts received, $1,673,600; expenditures, $1,697,457; qualifying distributions, $1,697,142; giving activities include $1,696,621 for 360 grants (high: $227,500; low: $18).
Purpose and activities: Giving primarily to Jewish agencies, temples, and schools.
Fields of interest: Education; Jewish federated giving programs; Jewish agencies & synagogues.
Limitations: Applications not accepted. Giving primarily in NY. No grants to individuals.
Application information: Contributes only to pre-selected organizations.
Officers: Eddie Betesh, Pres.; Rachelle Betesh, Treas.
EIN: 133981963
Other changes: At the close of 2012, the grantmaker paid grants of $1,696,621, a 63.1% increase over the 2011 disbursements, $1,039,970.

2064
The Bikuben Foundation New York, Inc.

36 W. 74th St.
New York, NY 10023-2411
Contact: **Irene Krarup**
E-mail: bg@bikubenfonden.dk; **Application address: c/o Matti Bekkevold, Bikuben Fonden, Fiolstraede 44, 1171 Kobenhaun K, Copenhagen, Denmark, tel.: (453) 377-9385; Danish language URL: http://www.bikubenfonden.dk**

Established in 2003 in DE and NY.
Donor: Bikubenfonden.
Foundation type: Independent foundation.
Financial data (yr. ended 12/31/12): Assets, $18,321,213 (M); expenditures, $724,459; qualifying distributions, $189,159; giving activities include $171,675 for 32 grants to individuals (high: $10,800; low: $3,575).
Purpose and activities: Giving primarily to individuals involved in the arts to enable them to improve or enhance a literary, artistic, musical, scientific, or teaching skill or talent. The foundation also makes a condominium in New York City available to artists, writers, scholars, and researchers in connection with specific projects requiring the presence of the grantee in New York City.
Fields of interest: Arts; Housing/shelter.
Type of support: Scholarships—to individuals.
Limitations: Applications accepted. Giving primarily in NY.
Application information:
Initial approach: Letter
***Deadline(s):* June 15**
Officers and Directors:* Soren Kaare-Andersen,* Pres.; Irene Krarup,* V.P. and Treas.; Peter Hoejland,* Secy.
EIN: 582680849
Other changes: Soren Kaare-Andersen has replaced Michael Metz Morch as Pres.
Irene Krarup is now V.P. and Treas. Henning Skovlund Pedersen is no longer Secy.-Treas.

2065
Harry S. Black & Allon Fuller Fund

c/o U.S. Trust
1 Bryant Park, NY1-100-28-05
New York, NY 10036-6715 (646) 855-1011
Contact: Christine O'Donnell
***Main URL:* https://www.bankofamerica.com/philanthropic/grantmaking.go**

Established in 1930 in NY.
Donor: Harry S. Black.
Foundation type: Independent foundation.
Financial data (yr. ended 12/31/12): Assets, $4,139,510 (M); expenditures, $233,852; qualifying distributions, $184,268; giving activities include $162,500 for 14 grants (high: $20,000; low: $5,000).
Purpose and activities: Grantmaking is focused on the following areas: 1) Health Care: The Fund supports access to health care, health education, and health policy analysis and advocacy; emphasis will be placed on programs serving low-income communities, and 2) Physical Disabilities: The Fund supports access programs for physically disabled individuals, disability policy analysis and advocacy, workforce development programs, and programs that improve quality of life for the disabled.
Fields of interest: Health care; Health organizations, association; Physically disabled.
Type of support: General/operating support; Program development.
Limitations: Giving limited to organizations located in and serving Chicago, IL, and New York, NY. No grants to individuals, or for endowment funds, capital campaigns or research.
Publications: Application guidelines.
Application information: Application guidelines available on Fund web site.
Initial approach: Online via Fund web site
Deadline(s): July 31
Final notification: Dec. 31
Trustee: Bank of America, N.A.
Number of staff: 1 part-time professional; 1 part-time support.
EIN: 136072632

2066
Bloomberg Philanthropies

(formerly The Bloomberg Family Foundation, Inc.)
c/o Geller & Co.
909 3rd Ave., 16th Fl.
New York, NY 10022-4797
Main URL: http://www.bloomberg.org
Blog: http://www.bloomberg.org/blog
Facebook: https://www.facebook.com/bloombergdotorg
Michael Bloomberg's Giving Pledge Profile: http://glasspockets.org/philanthropy-in-focus/eye-on-the-giving-pledge/profiles/bloomberg
Twitter: https://twitter.com/bloombergdotorg

Established in 2006.
Donor: Michael R. Bloomberg.
Foundation type: Independent foundation.
Financial data (yr. ended 12/31/12): Assets, $4,242,746,954 (M); gifts received, $998,378,348; expenditures, $172,928,139; qualifying distributions, $131,969,097; giving activities include $131,263,386 for 41 grants (high: $15,000,000; low: $177,896).
Purpose and activities: The mission is to ensure better, longer lives for the greatest number of people. The organization focuses on five key areas for creating lasting change: public health, environment, education, government innovation and the arts.
Fields of interest: Arts; Education; Environment; Public health; Philanthropy/voluntarism; African Americans/Blacks.
Type of support: Program-related investments/loans.
Limitations: Applications not accepted. Giving primarily in NY and on an international basis, with an emphasis in India and Switzerland. No grants to individuals.
Publications: Annual report.
Application information: Unsolicited requests for funds not accepted.
Officer and Directors:* Patricia E. Harris,* Chair. and C.E.O.; Tenley Albright; Emma Bloomberg; Georgina Bloomberg; Michael R. Bloomberg; Cory A. Booker; David L. Boren; Jeb Bush; Elaine Chao; Kenneth I. Chenault; D. Ronald Daniel; Manny Diaz; Fiona Druckenmiller; Patti E. Harris; Walter Isaacson; Maya Lin; John J. Mack; Joseph McShane, S.J.; Mike Mullen, USN (ret.); Sam Nunn; Samuel J. Palmisano; Hank M. Paulson, Jr.; Alfred Sommer; Martin Sorrell; Anne M. Tatlock; **Dennis Walcott**.
EIN: 205602483

2067
Edith C. Blum Foundation, Inc.

c/o EisnerAmper, LLP
750 3rd Ave.
New York, NY 10017-2703
E-mail: info@ecbfoundation.org; Application address: 396 Washington St., Box 309, Wellesley, MA 02481; tel.: (646) 494-4205

Established in 1990 in NY as successor to the Edith C. Blum Foundation.
Donor: Edith C. Blum Foundation.
Foundation type: Independent foundation.
Financial data (yr. ended 09/30/13): Assets, $18,486,749 (M); expenditures, $1,117,997; qualifying distributions, $1,014,354; giving activities include $922,500 for 45 grants (high: $150,000; low: $5,000).
Purpose and activities: Giving primarily for the arts, education, health, Jewish organizations, and human services, including services for people who are blind.
Fields of interest: Performing arts; Performing arts, theater; Arts; Higher education; Education; Medical research, institute; Human services; Jewish federated giving programs; Jewish agencies & synagogues; Blind/visually impaired.
Limitations: Giving primarily in New York, NY. No grants to individuals.
Application information: Application form not required.
Deadline(s): None

Officers and Directors:* Roy R. Friedman,* Pres. and Treas.; Nancy R. Green,* Secy.; Seth A. Friedman.
EIN: 133564317

2068
The Box of Rain Foundation

c/o Amiel Peretz
17 Mallard Lake Rd.
Pound Ridge, NY 10576-2020

Established in 2001 in NY.
Donor: Amiel M. Peretz.
Foundation type: Independent foundation.
Financial data (yr. ended 11/30/13): Assets, $1,468,329 (M); gifts received, $180,325; expenditures, $173,882; qualifying distributions, $170,367; giving activities include $170,000 for 19 grants (high: $50,000; low: $1,000).
Fields of interest: Higher education; Education; Hospitals (general); Human services; Children/youth, services.
Type of support: General/operating support.
Limitations: Applications not accepted. Giving primarily in NY. No grants to individuals.
Application information: Unsolicited requests for funds not accepted.
Trustees: Amiel M. Peretz; **Dylan M. Peretz**; Michelle Young Peretz; **Taylor M. Peretz**.
EIN: 134157443

2069
B. H. Breslauer Foundation, Inc.

c/o Berge & Assoc., Inc.
25 W. 45th St., Ste. 504
New York, NY 10036 (646) 326-9216
Contact: Ivan S. Rosenblum, Treas.
FAX: (212) 719-3925;
E-mail: bhbreslauerfdn@gmail.com

Established in 2003 in NY.
Donors: Antiquarian Book Foundation; Cambridge in America; University of California-Berkeley; UCLA Foundation; Newberry Library; American Friends for Charities; Art Institute of Chicago; Cotsen Library - Princeton; Ohio State University; University of Virginia; University of Pennsylvania; Grand Valley State University; Georgetown University; Americans for Oxford; McGill University; Morgan Library & Museum; Royal Oak Foundation; Chazen Museum of Art; Grolier Club; National Gallery of Art; Columbia University; Metropolitan Museum of Art; John Carter Brown Library; University of South Carolina; Oberlin College; Friends of The National Libraries; Bidwell Library; National Sporting Library; Johns Hopkins Library; Friends of Milton College; Association du Mecenat de Institut; Staats Bibliotek Berlin; American Antiquarian Society; North American Foundation for University of Manchester; Winterthur.
Foundation type: Independent foundation.
Financial data (yr. ended 12/31/12): Assets, $5,696,855 (M); expenditures, $449,298; qualifying distributions, $383,976; giving activities include $310,310 for 6 grants (high: $100,000; low: $8,000).
Purpose and activities: Funding of acquisitions for rare books and related materials for rare book libraries.
Fields of interest: Arts; Higher education; Philanthropy/voluntarism.
Limitations: Applications accepted. Giving on a national basis. No support for non-501(c)(3) organizations.
Publications: Annual report.
Application information: Application should include a statement of how the material to be acquired is appropriate to the applicant's collection. Application form not required.
Initial approach: Letter or e-mail
Copies of proposal: 3
Deadline(s): None
Final notification: Within 30 days
Officers: Felix Oyens, Pres.; William Voelkle, V.P.; Ivan S. Rosenblum, Secy.-Treas.
Number of staff: None.
EIN: 134076763
Other changes: The grantmaker no longer lists a URL address.

2070
Brillo-Sonnino Family Foundation

350 West Broadway
New York, NY **10013**
***Contact:* Mark D. Sonnino, Tr.**

Established in 2006 in NY.
Donors: Mark D. Sonnino; Lyn Brillo.
Foundation type: Operating foundation.
Financial data (yr. ended 02/28/13): Assets, $5,583,830 (M); expenditures, $304,093; qualifying distributions, $251,150; giving activities include $251,150 for 19 grants (high: $100,000; low: $50).
Fields of interest: Higher education, college; Education; Human services; Family services; Christian agencies & churches.
Limitations: Applications not accepted. Giving primarily in CA and NY. No grants to individuals.
Application information: Contributes only to pre-selected organizations.
Trustee: Mark D. Sonnino.
EIN: 204463571

2071
Broadcasters Foundation of America

(formerly Broadcasters Foundation, Inc.)
125 W. 55th St., 3rd Fl.
New York, NY 10019-5366 **(212) 373-8250**
***Contact:* Grant Admin.**
***FAX:* (212) 373-8254**; E-mail: info@thebfoa.org; Main URL: http://www.broadcastersfoundation.org/

Established in 1942.
Donors: Richard Foreman; Thomas Murphy; Sidney Frank Foundation; Mel Karmazin Foundation; Edward & Patricia McLaughlin Foundation; Broadcasting & Cable; Cambridge Financial Services; Community Foundation; Hearst Argyle Television; Inner City Broadcasting; Saga Communications; Someday Sports; Songwriters Hall of Fame, Inc.; George Stephanopoulos; Howard Stern; Beth Stern; Taishoff Foundation; McHenry Tichenor; Lisa Tichenor; Triton Radio Networks; United Stations Radio Network, Inc.; Univision Communications, Inc.; Wiley Rein & Fielding; Robert Williams.
Foundation type: Independent foundation.
Financial data (yr. ended 12/31/12): Assets, $4,823,818 (M); gifts received, $1,531,382; expenditures, $1,742,209; qualifying distributions, $1,741,697; giving activities include $698,600 for 68 grants to individuals (high: $18,000; low: $1,000).
Purpose and activities: Giving limited to the broadcast industry, including funds for needy members of the industry.
Fields of interest: Media/communications; Human services.
Type of support: Grants to individuals; Scholarships—to individuals.
Limitations: Applications accepted. Giving primarily in CA; some giving nationally.
Publications: Newsletter.
Application information: Contributes only to members of the broadcast industry and their families. Application form required.
Initial approach: Proposal
Deadline(s): None
Officers and Directors:* Philip J. Lombardo,* Chair.; Richard A. Foreman,* Vice-Chair.; Jim Thompson, Pres.; **Peter Doyle, V.P.**; Jeff Haley, V.P.; Steve Lanzano, V.P.; Wade Hargrove,* Secy.; David Barrett; **George G. Beasley**; Philip R. Beuth; Joe Bilotta; Richard J. Bodorff; Rebecca S. Campbell; **Peter Dunn**; Erica Farber; Richard Ferguson; Joseph Field; Skip Finley; Michael J. Fiorile; Alan W. Frank; Mark Gray; Louis Hillelson; **Bill Hoffman**; Paul Karpowicz; N. Scott Knight; **Brian Lawlor**; Jerry Lee; Jerry Levy; **Dan Mason**; Edward F. McLaughlin; **Elizabeth "Beth" Neuhoff**; Deborah Norville; **Mike O'Neill**; William O'Shaughnessy; I. Martin Pompadur; Joseph Reilly; Gordon H. Smith; Jeffrey Smulyan; George Stephanopoulos; Dennis Swanson; Nicholas Verbitsky; Diana Wilkin.
Number of staff: 2 full-time professional; 1 part-time professional.
EIN: 131975618
Other changes: Carl Butrum is no longer a V.P. Joseph Amaturo, Del Bryant, Gary Chapman, Ralph Guild, Sanford Schwartz, Peter Smyth, and Edward Wilson are no longer directors.

2072
The Brock Foundation

c/o Bessemer
630 5th Ave.
New York, NY 10111

Established in 1998 in VA.
Donor: Macon F. Brock, Jr.
Foundation type: Independent foundation.
Financial data (yr. ended 12/31/12): Assets, $3,323,659 (M); expenditures, $148,124; qualifying distributions, $132,850; giving activities include $132,850 for grants.
Fields of interest: Museums; Performing arts; Arts; Education; Environment; Salvation Army; YM/YWCAs & YM/YWHAs; United Ways and Federated Giving Programs; Christian agencies & churches.
Limitations: Applications not accepted. No grants to individuals.
Application information: Unsolicited requests for funds not accepted.
Officers: Macon F. Brock, Jr., Pres.; Joan P. Brock, Secy.
Directors: Macon F. Brock III; Kathryn Brock Everett; Christine Brock Miele.
EIN: 541902235
Other changes: The grantmaker has moved from VA to NY.

2073
The Samuel Bronfman Foundation

(formerly The Edgar M. Bronfman Family Foundation, Inc.)

375 Park Ave., 17th Fl.
New York, NY 10152-0192 **(212) 572-1025**
E-mail: info@thesbf.org; Main URL: http://www.thesbf.org
Edgar M. Bronfman's Giving Pledge Profile: http://glasspockets.org/philanthropy-in-focus/eye-on-the-giving-pledge/profiles/bronfman-edgar
Twitter: http://twitter.com/BronfmanFound

Re-established in 2005 in DE; originally established in 1995 in NY.
Donor: Edgar M. Bronfman, Sr.‡.
Foundation type: Independent foundation.
Financial data (yr. ended 12/31/12): Assets, $326,379 (M); gifts received, $1,627,110; expenditures, $1,600,279; qualifying distributions, $1,524,687; giving activities include $1,150,000 for 12 grants (high: $450,000; low: $20,000).
Purpose and activities: The foundation seeks to inspire a renaissance of Jewish life. The foundation's work is informed by the following four principles: 1) Jewish Renaissance is Grounded in Jewish Learning: through this principal, the foundation seeks to facilitate exploration of Jewish identity and meaningful engagement with Jewish life; 2) Jewish Youth Shape the Future of Jewish People: the foundation indicates that Jewish youth possess exceptional vision and talent, and that they must be empowered to lead the Jewish people and the world community; 3) Vibrant Jewish Communities are Open and Inclusive: the foundation supports a culture of pluralism and mutual respect that celebrates diverse expressions of Jewish life; and 4) All Jews are a Single Family: the foundation affirms the unity of the Jewish people, throughout the world and in Israel.
Fields of interest: Elementary/secondary education; Higher education; Jewish federated giving programs; Jewish agencies & synagogues.
Type of support: General/operating support.
Limitations: Applications not accepted. Giving primarily in Washington, DC and NY, with some giving in UT. No grants to individuals, or for new gifts to endowments.
Application information: Contributes only to pre-selected organizations.
Officers and Directors:* Adam R. Bronfman,* Managing Dir.; Dana Raucher, Exec. Dir.; **Leigh Garofalow, Dir., Fin. and Opers.**
EIN: 141918185
Other changes: Edgar M. Bronfman, Sr., Pres. and Donor, is deceased.

2074
The Andrea and Charles Bronfman Philanthropies, Inc.

110 E. 59th St., 26th Fl.
New York, NY 10022-1327 (212) 931-0100
E-mail: info@acbp.net; Main URL: http://www.acbp.net
Charles Bronfman's Giving Pledge Profile: http://glasspockets.org/philanthropy-in-focus/eye-on-the-giving-pledge/profiles/bronfman-charles
GiveSmart: http://www.givesmart.org/Stories/Donors/Charles-Bronfman

Established in 1998 in DE and NY.
Donors: Charles R. Bronfman; Andrea M. Bronfman‡; Ellen Hauptman; Philippa Cohen; Jeremy Cohen; Andrew Hauptman; Canary/Manitoba Foundation; Edgar Miles Bronfman Trust; Phyllis Lambert Trust; CRB Prize; The CRB Foundations; The Canary Charitable Foundation; The Manitoba Foundation; Judy and Michael Steinhardt Foundation; Charles and Lynn Schusterman Family Foundation; FJC.
Foundation type: Operating foundation.
Financial data (yr. ended 12/31/12): Assets, $10,011,566 (M); gifts received, $5,633,460; expenditures, $8,882,907; qualifying distributions, $8,641,197; giving activities include $4,271,997 for 78 grants (high: $1,563,667; low: $25), and $6,292,071 for 1 foundation-administered program.
Purpose and activities: The organization operates and supports programs in Canada, Israel and the United States to strengthen the unity of the Jewish people, to improve the quality of life in Israel and to promote Canadian heritage. Ultimately, the philanthropies seek to span the separations created by geography, culture, and the requirements of daily life with a bridge built on the willingness of individuals in search of community, identity, and meaning. It operates in a framework of continuing innovation, have an ability to bear risk, and continually emphasizes quality, value creation and building.
Fields of interest: Education; Human services; Jewish agencies & synagogues.
International interests: Canada; Israel.
Type of support: General/operating support; Program development; Conferences/seminars; Seed money; Curriculum development; Research; Technical assistance; Consulting services; Employee matching gifts.
Limitations: Applications not accepted. Giving primarily in NY, Canada, and Israel. No grants to individuals.
Application information: Contributes only to pre-selected organizations.
Officers and Directors:* Charles R. Bronfman,* Chair.; Jeffrey Solomon,* Pres.; John Hoover, Sr. V.P., and C.F.O.; Janet Aviad, Sr. V.P., Israel; Sharna Goldseker, V.P.; **William J. Powers, Secy.**; Richard P. Doyle, Treas.; **William Zabel**.
Number of staff: 9 full-time professional; 3 full-time support.
EIN: 133984936
Other changes: Tzaly Reshef is no longer a director.

2075
Gladys Brooks Foundation

1055 Franklin Ave., Ste. 208
Garden City, NY 11530-2903 **(516) 746-6103**
Contact: Jessica L. Rutledge
***E-mail:* kathy@gladysbrooksfoundation.org**; Main URL: http://www.gladysbrooksfoundation.org
Grants List: http://www.gladysbrooksfoundation.org/annual-report.html

Established in 1981 in NY.
Donor: Gladys Brooks Thayer‡.
Foundation type: Independent foundation.
Financial data (yr. ended 12/31/13): Assets, $37,410,183 (M); expenditures, $1,911,319; qualifying distributions, $1,686,610; giving activities include $1,435,782 for 17 grants (high: $190,000; low: $10,000).
Purpose and activities: The foundation's primary purpose is to provide for the intellectual, moral, and physical welfare of the people of this country by establishing and supporting nonprofit libraries, educational institutions, hospitals, and clinics.
Fields of interest: Higher education; Libraries/library science; Hospitals (general); Health care.
Type of support: Building/renovation; Equipment; Endowments; Scholarship funds.
Limitations: Applications accepted. Giving generally limited to CT, DE, FL, IL, IN, LA, MA, MD, ME, NH, NJ, NY, OH, PA, RI, TN, and VT. No grants to individuals, or for research or salaries.
Publications: Application guidelines; Annual report; Annual report (including application guidelines); Grants list; Program policy statement.
Application information: Electronic submissions are not accepted. The foundation encourages early filing of the application. Application form required.
Initial approach: Use application form on foundation web site, or letter requesting application form
Copies of proposal: 2
Deadline(s): Generally within 45 days from the date of the letter from the foundation furnishing the application to the applicant. See web site for detailed information regarding deadlines
Board meeting date(s): Monthly
Final notification: Dec.
Officers and Governors:* James J. Daly,* Chair.; Thomas Q. Morris, M.D.*, Secy.; Christopher R. Hawkins; Bank of America, N.A.
Number of staff: 1 full-time professional.
EIN: 132955337

2076
Milton V. Brown Foundation

New Hyde Park, NY

The foundation merged into The Eva H. Brown Foundation.

2077
Brownstone Family Foundation

(formerly Lucien & Ethel Brownstone Foundation, Inc.)
350 5th Ave., Ste. 6407
New York, NY 10118-6407

Established in 1953.
Donors: Clyde R. Brownstone; Ethel Brownstone Residuary Trust.
Foundation type: Independent foundation.
Financial data (yr. ended 02/28/13): Assets, $9,862,899 (M); gifts received, $2,759; expenditures, $616,463; qualifying distributions, $510,267; giving activities include $510,267 for 70 grants (high: $62,000; low: $150).
Purpose and activities: Giving primarily for education and human services; funding also for hospitals, the arts, and private grantmaking foundations.
Fields of interest: Arts; Higher education; Libraries (public); Education; Hospitals (general); Public health; Crime/law enforcement, police agencies; Human services; Foundations (private grantmaking).
Limitations: Applications not accepted. Giving primarily in the metropolitan New York, NY, area; giving also in MO. No grants to individuals.
Application information: Contributes only to pre-selected organizations.
Officers: Clyde R. Brownstone, Pres.; Diane Brownstone, V.P.; Jennifer Brownstone, V.P.; Spencer Brownstone, V.P.
EIN: 136138834
Other changes: The grantmaker has moved from NJ to NY.

2078
Buffalo Sabres Alumni Association

c/o Robert Travis
45 Bryant Woods N.
Amherst, NY 14228-3600 (716) 630-2400
Contact: Robert Travis, Treas. and Dir.

Main URL: http://www.sabresalumni.com/
Flickr: https://www.flickr.com/photos/84418649@N04/
Scholarship address: **The Buffalo Sabres Alumni Scholarship Program, c/o Buffalo Sabres Alumni Assoc., First Niagara Ctr., 1 Seymour H. Knox III Plz., Buffalo, NY 14203**

Established in 1989 in NY.
Foundation type: Independent foundation.
Financial data (yr. ended 12/31/12): Assets, $544,185 (M); expenditures, $1,282,422; qualifying distributions, $623,020; giving activities include $623,020 for 44 grants (high: $218,300; low: $280).
Fields of interest: Scholarships/financial aid; Health organizations, association.
Type of support: Scholarships—to individuals; General/operating support; Scholarship funds.
Limitations: Applications accepted. **Giving limited to western NY; scholarships funding includes Southern Ontario, Canada.**
Application information: See foundation web site for scholarship application form. Application form required.
Initial approach: Letter on organization's letterhead
***Deadline(s):* None, for grants; July 1, for scholarships**
Officers and Directors:* Rob Ray,* Pres.; Darryl Shannon,* V.P.; Robert Travis,* Treas.; Cliff Benson; Jay McKee; Craig Muni; Michael Peca; Andrew Peters; Larry Playfair; Ric Seiling; Derek Smith.
EIN: 161356116

2079
The William C. Bullitt Foundation, Inc.
220 5th Ave., 2nd Fl.
New York, NY **10001-7708 (212) 485-6006**
Contact: Christy Pennoyer
E-mail: info@wcbullittfound.org; Main URL: http://www.wcbullittfound.org/
Grants List: http://www.wcbullittfound.org/grants

Established in 2001 in DE.
Donor: Anne M. Bullitt†.
Foundation type: Independent foundation.
Financial data (yr. ended 12/31/12): Assets, $16,475,274 (M); gifts received, $25,039; expenditures, $1,365,935; qualifying distributions, $887,000; giving activities include $887,000 for grants.
Purpose and activities: Giving primarily to organizations that: 1) promote government integrity and protect civil liberties and human rights; 2) help economically and socially disadvantaged children and families achieve the tools necessary to lead independent and productive lives; and 3) protect the natural environment through land conservation and raising public awareness of environmental threats and solutions.
Fields of interest: Environment, land resources; Environment; Human services; Children/youth, services; Civil/human rights; Economically disadvantaged.
Limitations: Applications not accepted. Giving primarily in CT, and the greater New York metropolitan area.
Publications: Grants list.
Application information: Unsolicited requests for funds not accepted.
Officers and Trustees:* Tracy Pennoyer,* Pres.; Sharon Myrie, V.P.; Dana W. Hiscock, Secy.; Robert Pennoyer, Treas.; Christy Pennoyer.
EIN: 134183316

2080
The Burton Foundation
c/o Dorian Alex Vergos & Co., LLC
352 7th Ave.
New York, NY 10001
***Contact:* Burton B. Staniar**

Established in 1997.
Donor: Burton B. Staniar.
Foundation type: Independent foundation.
Financial data (yr. ended 12/31/12): Assets, $1,432,164 (M); gifts received, $103,963; expenditures, $211,719; qualifying distributions, $189,117; giving activities include $189,117 for grants.
Fields of interest: Arts; Higher education; Hospitals (general).
Limitations: Applications not accepted. Giving primarily in NY and VA. No grants to individuals.
Application information: Contributes only to pre-selected organizations.
Trustee: Burton B. Staniar.
EIN: 133975899
Other changes: The grantmaker has moved from NJ to NY.

2081
Butler Conservation Fund, Inc.
(formerly Gilbert & Ildiko Butler Foundation, Inc.)
60 Cutter Mill Rd., Ste. 212
Great Neck, NY **11021-3104 (212) 303-0216**
***FAX:* (516) 466-4795**; Main URL: http://butlerconservationfund.org/
Grants List: http://butlerconservationfund.org/grantees/

Established in 1988 in MA.
Donors: Gilbert Butler; Butler Capital Corp.
Foundation type: Company-sponsored foundation.
Financial data (yr. ended 12/31/12): Assets, $141,229,394 (M); expenditures, $7,972,059; qualifying distributions, $5,722,164; giving activities include $5,284,938 for 40 grants (high: $1,297,275; low: $250).
Purpose and activities: The foundation supports programs designed to conserve, restore, and protect the environment.
Fields of interest: Historic preservation/historical societies; Environment, natural resources; Environment, water resources; Environment, land resources; Botanical gardens; Environmental education; Environment; Animal welfare; Animals/wildlife; Recreation, parks/playgrounds.
Type of support: General/operating support; Capital campaigns; Program development; Research.
Limitations: Applications not accepted. Giving primarily in MA, ME, NY, SC, and VA; giving also to national organizations.
Publications: Financial statement; Grants list; IRS Form 990 or 990-PF printed copy available upon request.
Application information: Unsolicited applications are not accepted.
Officers and Directors:* Gilbert Butler,* Chair., Pres., and Treas.; Anthony P. Grassi,* Vice-Chair.; Dhruvika Patel Amin, V.P., Finance & Admin.; Christopher (Kim) Elliman,* V.P.; Tomer Inbar, Secy.; Dana Beach; Peter Lehner; Kristine McDivitt Tompkins.
EIN: 043032409
Other changes: Dhruvika Patel Amin is now V.P., Finance & Admin. Gilbert Butler is now Chair., Pres., and Treas.

2082
Bydale Foundation
c/o U.S. Trust
114 W. 47th St., NY8-114-10-02
New York, NY 10036
Contact: Christine O'Donnell, Agent
E-mail: christine.l.o'donnell@ustrust.com; **Main URL: http://fdnweb.org/bydale**

Incorporated in 1965 in DE.
Donor: James P. Warburg†.
Foundation type: Independent foundation.
Financial data (yr. ended 12/31/13): Assets, $13,811,191 (M); expenditures, $557,239; qualifying distributions, $536,360; giving activities include $498,500 for 54 grants (high: $30,000; low: $1,000).
Purpose and activities: Giving primarily for the environment, human rights, women's rights, social justice, and poetry.
Fields of interest: Arts; Environment, research; Environment, public policy; Civil/human rights, women; Civil liberties, reproductive rights; Civil/human rights; Women; Economically disadvantaged.
Type of support: General/operating support; Program development; Matching/challenge support.
Limitations: Applications accepted. Giving in Westchester County, NY, NC and Israel. No grants to individuals, or for annual campaigns, emergency funds, deficit financing, endowment funds, demonstration projects, capital funds, scholarships, or fellowships; no loans.
Application information: Unsolicited Inquiry Application Forms are accepted, but the foundation receives many more applications than it funds. Only the foundation's application form is accepted. Application form required.
Initial approach: See foundation web site for details
Copies of proposal: 1
Deadline(s): Aug. 1
Board meeting date(s): Dec.
Final notification: By Dec. 31
Officers and Trustees:* Joan M. Warburg,* Pres.; Frank J. Kick, Treas.; Sarah W. Bliumis-Dunn; James P. Warburg, Jr.; Jennifer Warburg; Philip N. Warburg.
Number of staff: 1 part-time professional; 1 part-time support.
EIN: 136195286

2083
The Canaday Family Charitable Trust
(formerly Canaday Educational and Charitable Trust)
c/o Christine O'Donnell, Bank of America, N.A.
1 Bryant Park
NY1-100-28-05
New York, NY 10036-6715 (646) 855-1011
Contact: Christine O'Donnell, V.P., Bank of America, N.A.
FAX: (646) 855-5463;
E-mail: canaday@ustrust.com; Main URL: http://www.canadayfamily.org/
Grants List: http://www.canadayfamily.org/list.html

Trust established in 1945 in OH.
Donors: Ward M. Canaday†; Mariam C. Canaday†; Doreen Spitzer Trust.
Foundation type: Independent foundation.
Financial data (yr. ended 12/31/12): Assets, $39,195,551 (M); expenditures, $1,958,363; qualifying distributions, $1,655,693; giving activities include $1,613,479 for 71 grants (high: $150,000; low: $300).
Purpose and activities: Giving primarily to organizations that work in Vermont to improve the

lives of children and families, promote environmental education and conservation, and preserve the environment.
Fields of interest: Environment, natural resources; Environmental education; Children/youth, services; Family services; Children; Youth; Young adults.
Type of support: Program development.
Limitations: Applications accepted. Giving primarily in VT. No support for private foundation or organizations lacking 501(c)(3) status. No grants to individuals, or for capital campaigns or endowments.
Publications: Grants list.
Application information: Application guidelines available on foundation web site. Organizations in which the foundation is interested will be contacted and invited to submit a formal grant proposal. Application form not required.
Initial approach: Letter or inquiry, no more than 3 pages; may be submitted in writing or by e-mail
Copies of proposal: 1
Deadline(s): Feb. 1 for letters of inquiry
Board meeting date(s): Annually
Final notification: July
Trustee: Bank of America, N.A.
EIN: 912158408

2084
The Richard E. Capri Foundation
330 Motor Pky., Ste. 202
Hauppauge, NY 11788-5118 **(631) 273-4429**
***FAX:* (631) 273-4451**

Established in 2008 in NY.
Foundation type: Independent foundation.
Financial data (yr. ended 06/30/13): Assets, $12,364,836 (M); expenditures, $389,958; qualifying distributions, $389,958; giving activities include $323,600 for 27 grants (high: $55,000; low: $1,000).
Purpose and activities: The foundation provides funding to organizations researching prevention for chronic diseases and efforts to assist sufferers of cancer, leukemia, and other debilitating diseases.
Fields of interest: Cancer research; Cancer, leukemia research; Medical research.
Type of support: Program development.
Limitations: Applications accepted. Giving primarily in NY.
Application information: Application form required.
Initial approach: Letter
Deadline(s): None
Officers: Edward L. Wolf, Pres.; Steven Wolf, V.P.; Ellen Wolf, Secy.; Jeffrey Wolf, Treas.
EIN: 266445474

2085
Carnegie Corporation of New York
437 Madison Ave.
New York, NY 10022-7003 (212) 371-3200
Contact: Nicole Howe Buggs, Assoc. Corp. Secy. and Dir., Grants Management; Bonnie Rivers, Assoc. Dir., Grants Mgmt.
FAX: (212) 754-4073; E-mail: info@carnegie.org; E-mail for Nicole Howe Buggs: nb@carnegie.org; Main URL: http://www.carnegie.org
Andrew Carnegie Medal of Philanthropy: http://carnegiemedals.org/
E-Newsletter: http://carnegie.org/news/grants-in-action/enews-sign-up/
Facebook: https://www.facebook.com/pages/Carnegie-Corporation-of-New-York/145973965440671
Google Plus: https://plus.google.com/106331518092409117369/posts
Grants Database: http://www.carnegie.org/sub/program/grantsearch.html
iTunes: http://itunes.apple.com/us/podcast/carnegie-corporation-new-york/id275515669?ign-mpt=uo%3D4
LinkedIn: http://www.linkedin.com/company/37222/
Pinterest: http://pinterest.com/carnegiecorp/
RSS Feed: http://carnegie.org/news/rss-subscribe/
Teacher Appreciation: http://greatteaching.carnegie.org/
Twitter: http://www.twitter.com/carnegiecorp
Vimeo: http://vimeo.com/carnegiecorp
Vimeo: http://vimeo.com/channels/ccny/videos
YouTube: http://www.youtube.com/user/carnegiecorpofny

Incorporated in 1911 in NY.
Donor: Andrew Carnegie†.
Foundation type: Independent foundation.
Financial data (yr. ended 09/30/12): Assets, $2,764,431,433 (M); expenditures, $138,902,790; qualifying distributions, $131,578,904; giving activities include $111,116,148 for 436 grants, $512,340 for employee matching gifts, and $1,377,892 for 2 foundation-administered programs.
Purpose and activities: As a grantmaking foundation, Carnegie Corporation of New York seeks to carry out Andrew Carnegie's vision of philanthropy, which he said should aim 'to do real and permanent good in this world.' Currently the foundation's work is focused in two integrated programs: the National Program, which includes support for education as a pathway to citizenship; and the International Program, which addresses international peace and security issues.
Fields of interest: Education, reform; Teacher school/education; Libraries, archives; Education, reading; International peace/security; International affairs, arms control; International affairs, national security; Civil/human rights, immigrants; Civil rights, voter education.
International interests: Africa; China; Russia; Sub-Saharan Africa.
Type of support: General/operating support; Continuing support; Program development; Conferences/seminars; Publication; Curriculum development; Research; Technical assistance; Program evaluation; Employee matching gifts.
Limitations: Applications accepted. Giving primarily for U.S. projects, although some grants are made to selected countries in Sub-Saharan Africa. No support for U.S. libraries, cultural institutions, programs or facilities of community-based educational or human services institutions, churches or religious organizations. No grants directly to individuals for scholarships or fellowships, travel, capital campaigns, or endowments, buildings or fundraising drives, deficits.
Publications: Application guidelines; Annual report; Grants list; Occasional report.
Application information: If the project is judged to be within the current program priorities of the corporation, the applicant will be asked to present the narrative and budget in the corporation's format. Before a grant is made, additional materials would be required, including a formal request from the head of the institution involved.Only full proposals that have been invited will be considered. Application form required.
Initial approach: Online application via grantmaker web site. Submit only one
Copies of proposal: 1
Deadline(s): None
Board meeting date(s): Mar., June, and Sept., and Dec.
Final notification: 4-6 weeks to respond to letter of inquiry
Officers and Trustees:* Thomas H. Kean,* Chair.; Kurt L. Schmoke, Vice-Chair.; Vartan Gregorian,* Pres.; Ellen Bloom, V.P., C.A.O. and Corp. Secy.; Robert J. Seman, V.P. and C.F.O.; Deana Arsenian, V.P., Intl. Prog., and Prog. Dir., Russia and Eurasia; Michele Cahill, V.P., Natl. Prog., and Prog. Dir., Urban Education; Meredith Jenkins, V.P. and Co-C.I.O.; Kim Y. Lew, V.P. and Co-C.I.O.; David Hamburg, Pres. Emeritus; Richard Beattie; Geoffrey T. Boisi; Ralph J. Cicerone; **Jared L. Cohon**; John J. Degioia; Amb. Edward P. Djerejian; John S. Hendricks; Susan Hockfield; Stephen A. Oxman; Don Michael Randel; Louise Richardson; **Janet L. Robinson**; Jorge Sampaio; Anne Tatlock; Ann Claire Williams; James Wolfensohn; **Judy Woodruff**.
Number of staff: 38 full-time professional; 33 full-time support; 1 part-time support.
EIN: 131628151

2086
The Carson Family Charitable Trust
c/o US Trust
114 W. 47th St.
New York, NY 10036-1510

Established in 1990 in NY.
Donors: Russell L. Carson; Judith M. Carson.
Foundation type: Independent foundation.
Financial data (yr. ended 12/31/12): Assets, $26,058,298 (M); gifts received, $15,895,725; expenditures, $19,404,094; qualifying distributions, $18,878,008; giving activities include $18,725,000 for 97 grants (high: $1,000,000; low: $5,000).
Purpose and activities: Funding primarily for poverty relief and community development in New York City.
Fields of interest: Museums (art); Higher education; Environment, natural resources; Public health; Human services; Community/economic development.
Type of support: General/operating support.
Limitations: Applications not accepted. Giving primarily in New York, NY. No grants to individuals.
Application information: Contributes only to pre-selected organizations.
Trustees: Cecily M. Carson; Edward S. Carson; Judith M. Carson; Russell L. Carson; Bank of America, N.A.
EIN: 136957038
Other changes: At the close of 2012, the fair market value of the grantmaker's assets was $26,058,298, a 297.8% increase over the 2011 value, $6,549,798.

2087
Frank & Ruth E. Caruso Foundation
P.O. Box 399
New York, NY 10040-0399
Contact: Lisa Turngren, Pres.
E-mail: laturngren@netscape.net

Established in 2002.
Donors: Frank Caruso†; Ruth Caruso†.
Foundation type: Independent foundation.
Financial data (yr. ended 12/31/12): Assets, $4,672,706 (M); expenditures, $250,642; qualifying distributions, $220,033; giving activities include $150,100 for 14 grants (high: $20,000; low: $2,000).

Purpose and activities: Grants for calendar years 2013-2015 are devoted to the area of sexual violence prevention, funding small (under $1 million operating budget) grassroots community-based organizations in NYC.
Fields of interest: Crime/violence prevention, sexual abuse.
Type of support: General/operating support; Program development.
Limitations: Applications not accepted. Giving primarily in the New York City, New York area. No support for public or private schools, colleges, universities, hospitals, or religious or political organizations. No grants to individuals.
Application information: Does not accept unsolicited proposals, applications, or telephone calls.
Officer: Lisa Turngren, Pres.
EIN: 820581784
Other changes: The grantmaker no longer lists a phone.

2088
The Thomas & Agnes Carvel Foundation
35 E. Grassy Sprain Rd.
Yonkers, NY 10710-4612 (914) 793-7300
***Contact:* Peter Smith, Pres.**

Established in 1976 in NY.
Donors: Thomas Carvel†; Agnes Carvel†; The Agnes Carvel 1991 Trust; Thomas Carvel Unitrust Remainderman.
Foundation type: Independent foundation.
Financial data (yr. ended 11/30/12): Assets, $35,863,248 (M); gifts received, $482,796; expenditures, $2,142,425; qualifying distributions, $1,224,064; giving activities include $1,085,700 for 116 grants (high: $100,000; low: $500).
Purpose and activities: Giving primarily for health care, including hospitals and children's hospitals, funding also for the arts, and children, youth and social services, and for higher education.
Fields of interest: Performing arts, music; Arts; Secondary school/education; Higher education; Hospitals (general); Hospitals (specialty); Health care; Cancer; Human services; Children/youth, services.
Type of support: Scholarship funds; Program development; Building/renovation; Research; Matching/challenge support.
Limitations: Applications accepted. Giving primarily in Westchester County, NY. No support for political and international organizations.
Application information: Application form not required.
Initial approach: Letter
Copies of proposal: 1
Board meeting date(s): Jan., Mar., May, July, and Nov.
Officers: Peter Smith, Pres.; Salvador Molella, V.P.; Marie Holcombe, Treas.
Directors: Brendan Byrne; **Betty Godley**.
Number of staff: 2 part-time professional; 2 full-time support.
EIN: 132879673
Other changes: Peter Smith has replaced William E. Griffin as Pres.

2089
Century 21 Associates Foundation, Inc.
(formerly Gindi Associates Foundation, Inc.)
22 Cortlandt St.
New York, NY 10007-3107

Established in 1982 in NJ.
Donors: Century 21, Inc.; ASG Equities LLC.
Foundation type: Company-sponsored foundation.
Financial data (yr. ended 05/31/13): Assets, $4,783,143 (M); gifts received, $6,500,000; expenditures, $8,043,164; qualifying distributions, $8,027,042; giving activities include $7,967,116 for 1,314 grants (high: $500,000; low: $36).
Purpose and activities: The foundation supports organizations involved with education, human services, and Judaism.
Fields of interest: Higher education; Theological school/education; Education; Human services; Jewish federated giving programs; Jewish agencies & synagogues.
Type of support: General/operating support; Continuing support; Sponsorships.
Limitations: Applications not accepted. Giving primarily in NJ and Brooklyn and New York, NY. No grants to individuals.
Application information: Contributes only to pre-selected organizations.
Trustees: Abraham Gindi; Raymond Gindi; **Sam Gindi.**
EIN: 222412138

2090
Howard and Bess Chapman Charitable Corporation
c/o NBT Financial Group
120 Madison St., Ste. 1800
Syracuse, NY 13202-2807 (315) 475-7595

Established in 1989 in NY.
Foundation type: Independent foundation.
Financial data (yr. ended 10/31/13): Assets, $2,953,957 (M); expenditures, $179,230; qualifying distributions, $146,000; giving activities include $141,000 for 14 grants (high: $60,000; low: $100).
Purpose and activities: Giving primarily for education and for human services.
Fields of interest: Libraries/library science; Education; Human services; YM/YWCAs & YM/YWHAs; Children/youth, services.
Type of support: General/operating support; Building/renovation.
Limitations: Applications accepted. Giving primarily in NY.
Publications: Application guidelines.
Application information: Application form required.
Initial approach: Letter
Copies of proposal: 3
Deadline(s): None
Board meeting date(s): Quarterly
Officers: Robert H. Fearon, Jr., Pres.; Donald H. Dew, V.P.; John E. Haskell, V.P.; Peter M. Dunn, Esq., Secy.; Stephen Schneeweiss, Treas.
Number of staff: 1 part-time professional.
EIN: 161373396

2091
Chautauqua Region Community Foundation, Inc.
418 Spring St.
Jamestown, NY 14701-5332 (716) 661-3390
Contact: Randall J. Sweeney, Exec. Dir.; For grant and scholarship inquiries: Lisa W. Lynde, Prog. Off.
FAX: (716) 488-0387;
E-mail: rsweeney@crcfonline.org; Grant inquiries tel.: (716) 661-3392; Main URL: http://www.crcfonline.org
Facebook: http://www.facebook.com/CRCFOnline
Google Plus: https://plus.google.com/u/0/108261437264599744516/about
RSS Feed: http://crcfonline.org/feed/
YouTube: http://www.youtube.com/crcfonline
Scholarship inquiries e-mail: llynde@crcfonline.org;
Kids First Mini-Grants
e-mail: jdiethrick@crcfonline.org

Incorporated in 1978 in NY.
Foundation type: Community foundation.
Financial data (yr. ended 12/31/12): Assets, $68,078,179 (M); gifts received, $1,330,545; expenditures, $2,830,133; giving activities include $1,305,025 for 285 grants (high: $50,000; low: $25), and $689,119 for 634 grants to individuals.
Purpose and activities: The foundation seeks to enrich the quality of life in the Chautauqua region.
Fields of interest: Arts; Libraries/library science; Education; Housing/shelter, development; Children/youth, services; Human services; Community/economic development; Government/public administration.
Type of support: Program development; General/operating support; Continuing support; Building/renovation; Equipment; Emergency funds; Conferences/seminars; Publication; Seed money; Scholarships—to individuals; Matching/challenge support.
Limitations: Applications accepted. Giving limited to the southern Chautauqua County, NY, area. No support for religious purposes (excluding church related requests supported by the Karl Peterson Fund only). No grants to individuals (except for scholarship grants), or for debt retirement.
Publications: Application guidelines; Annual report (including application guidelines); Informational brochure; Newsletter.
Application information: The foundation is now accepting all grant applications through the www.chautauquagrants.org web site. Please register with the web site and follow the appropriate steps. Application form required.
Initial approach: Create online profile
Deadline(s): Mar. 31, June 30, and Dec. 1 for Community Service grants; last Fri. of each month for Fields-of-Interest grants
Board meeting date(s): Monthly
Final notification: Generally 3-4 months
Officers and Directors:* Jennifer L. Gibson,* Pres.; Pamela D. Noll,* V.P.; Carol S. Hay,* Secy.; Denise R. Jones,* Treas.; Randall J. Sweeney, Exec. Dir.; Michael C. Bird; Christy Brecht; Donald L. Butler; Dr. Ronald W. Kohl; Dana Lundberg; **Peter Stark**; Stephen J. Wright.
Number of staff: 7 full-time professional.
EIN: 161116837

2092
The Chernin Family Foundation, Inc.
c/o Executive Monetary Mgmt.
220 E. 42nd St., 32nd Fl.
New York, NY 10017-5814

Established in 2000 in DE.
Donors: Peter Chernin; Megan Chernin.
Foundation type: Independent foundation.
Financial data (yr. ended 12/31/12): Assets, $468,323 (M); gifts received, $920,308; expenditures, $1,084,943; qualifying distributions, $1,072,530; giving activities include $1,072,530 for 28 grants (high: $500,000; low: $200).
Purpose and activities: Giving primarily for higher education, as well as for health care and the environment.
Fields of interest: Higher education; Education; Environment; Health care; Health organizations, association.

Limitations: Applications not accepted. Giving primarily in NY. No grants to individuals.
Application information: Contributes only to pre-selected organizations.
Officers: Peter Chernin, Pres.; Megan Chernin, V.P. and Treas.
Directors: David Chernin; John Chernin; Margaret Chernin.
EIN: 522281012
Other changes: John D. Dadakis is no longer Secy.

2093
Chesed Foundation of America
c/o Sabr Group
126 E. 56th St., 15th Fl., No. 1520
New York, NY 10022-3613
Contact: Henry Reinhold

Donors: George Karfunkel; Michael Karfunkel; Karfunkel Family Foundation.
Foundation type: Independent foundation.
Financial data (yr. ended 06/30/13): Assets, $292,833,249 (M); gifts received, $15,205,000; expenditures, $11,222,228; qualifying distributions, $11,154,544; giving activities include $11,154,544 for 228 grants (high: $500,000; low: $72).
Purpose and activities: Giving primarily to cover operating expenses for schools and synagogues, as well as for educational scholarships and assistance for the needy.
Fields of interest: Elementary/secondary education; Jewish federated giving programs; Jewish agencies & synagogues.
Limitations: Applications not accepted.
Application information: Unsolicited requests for funds not accepted.
Officers: George Karfunkel, Pres.; Rene Karfunkel, V.P.
Trustee: Ann Karfunkel.
EIN: 133922068
Other changes: For the fiscal year ended June 30, 2013, the grantmaker paid grants of $11,154,544, an 88.0% increase over the fiscal 2012 disbursements, $5,933,850.

2094
The Y.C. Ho/Helen & Michael Chiang Foundation
Park West Finance Sta.
P.O. Box 20845
New York, NY 10025-0013
E-mail: info@hochiangfoundation.org; Main URL: http://hochiangfoundation.org/
Grants List: http://hochiangfoundation.org/grants.html

Established in 2004 in NY.
Donor: Y.C. Ho†.
Foundation type: Independent foundation.
Financial data (yr. ended 04/30/13): Assets, $66,816,163 (M); expenditures, $3,224,312; qualifying distributions, $3,224,187; giving activities include $3,013,496 for 54 grants (high: $250,000; low: $4,275).
Purpose and activities: The mission of The Y.C. Ho/Helen and Michael Chiang Foundation is to improve palliative care and the quality of life for persons of all age groups with serious illnesses.
Fields of interest: Palliative care; Health care.
Type of support: General/operating support.
Limitations: Applications not accepted. Giving primarily in New York, NY. No grants to individuals.
Application information: Contributes only to pre-selected organizations.
Officers and Directors:* Bessie Chiang, M.D.*, Pres. and Treas.; Michael Chiang,* V.P.; Helen Chiang, Secy.; Patricia J. Diaz, Exec. Dir.
EIN: 050613835

2095
Cinereach Ltd.
126 5th Ave., 5th Fl.
New York, NY 10011-5606 (212) 727-3224
FAX: (212) 727-3282;
E-mail: grants@cinereach.org; Reach Film Fellowship e-mail: info@thereachfilmfellowship.org; Additional e-mail: info@cinereach.org; Main URL: http://www.cinereach.org/
Facebook: http://www.facebook.com/pages/Cinereach-Ltd/40157889652?ref=search&sid=1237983244.79003529..1
Organization Blog: http://www.cinereach.org/cinereach-blog
Twitter: http://twitter.com/Cinereach

Established in 2005 in NY.
Donors: Butterfield Trust Bermuda Ltd; San Francisco Film Society.
Foundation type: Operating foundation.
Financial data (yr. ended 06/30/12): Assets, $4,108,680 (M); gifts received, $4,163,507; expenditures, $3,195,200; qualifying distributions, $3,203,370; giving activities include $372,306 for 11 grants (high: $63,830; low: $10,526), and $2,859,694 for foundation-administered programs.
Purpose and activities: Cinereach supports feature-length nonfiction and fiction films that are at the intersection of engaging storytelling, visual artistry, and vital subject matter.
Fields of interest: Media, film/video.
Limitations: Applications accepted. Giving primarily in New York, NY. No support for films under 70 minutes in length (short film applicants should refer to Reach Film Fellowship), or for student films; no organizational support. No grants for capital or endowment campaigns, multi-year grants, individual scholarships for study or travel, or for film outreach and distribution activities.
Publications: Application guidelines; Grants list.
Application information: Application form required.
Initial approach: Use online application center on foundation web site for initial registration and to submit a letter of inquiry, or to view application forms with DVD film sample
Deadline(s): See foundation web site for current deadlines
Officers: Joachim Schuetz, Treas.; **Philipp Engelhorn, Exec. Dir.**
Director: Bruce Rabb.
EIN: 202946241

2096
Frank E. Clark Charitable Trust
(formerly Clark Charitable Fund)
c/o JPMorgan Chase Bank, Philanthropic Svcs.
270 Park Ave., 16th Fl.
New York, NY 10017-2014
Contact: Jonathan G. Horowitz, Prog. Off.
FAX: (212) 464-2304;
E-mail: Jonathan.g.horowitz@jpmchase.com; **Main URL: http://fdnweb.org/feclark**
Grants List: http://fdnweb.org/feclark/grants/year/contributions/

Trust established in 1936 in NY.
Donor: Frank E. Clark†.
Foundation type: Independent foundation.
Financial data (yr. ended 12/31/12): Assets, $5,361,857 (M); expenditures, $338,714; qualifying distributions, $267,684; giving activities include $260,000 for 9 grants (high: $30,000; low: $25,000).
Purpose and activities: Giving primarily (through regional and national denominational bodies) for small churches and services for very low-income adults, including people who are homeless.
Fields of interest: Religion; Economically disadvantaged; Homeless.
Type of support: Program development; Capital campaigns.
Limitations: Applications accepted. Giving limited to New York, NY, for programs serving homeless adults; giving on a national basis for small churches. No support for private foundations. No grants to individuals or private foundations; no matching gifts or loans.
Publications: Application guidelines; Grants list.
Application information: With respect to grants to churches, only solicited proposals are accepted. Complete guidelines available on Trust web site. Application form not required.
Initial approach: Proposal
Copies of proposal: 1
Deadline(s): July 31
Board meeting date(s): Oct.
Final notification: Dec. 31
Trustee: JPMorgan Chase Bank, N.A.
Number of staff: None.
EIN: 136049032
Other changes: The grantmaker has moved from TX to NY.

2097
The Edna McConnell Clark Foundation
415 Madison Ave., 10th Fl.
New York, NY 10017-7949 (212) 551-9100
Contact: Albert Chung, Dir., Comm.
FAX: (212) 421-9325; E-mail: info@emcf.org; Additional e-mail (for Albert Chung): achung@emcf.org; Main URL: http://www.emcf.org
GiveSmart: http://www.givesmart.org/Stories/Donors/Nancy-Roob
Grants Database: http://www.emcf.org/our-grantees/our-grantee-portfolio/
Knowledge Center: http://www.emcf.org/sharing-knowledge/

Incorporated in 1950 in NY and 1969 in DE; the NY corporation merged into the DE corporation in 1974.
Donors: Edna McConnell Clark†; W. Van Alan Clark†.
Foundation type: Independent foundation.
Financial data (yr. ended 09/30/13): Assets, $965,338,606 (M); gifts received, $8,462,163; expenditures, $56,857,041; qualifying distributions, $53,896,375; giving activities include $43,155,001 for 52 grants (high: $6,000,000; low: $8,000), and $6,908,793 for 2 foundation-administered programs.
Purpose and activities: The foundation focuses on strengthening nonprofit youth development organizations so they can better serve more young people with high-quality programs. The foundation's approach to grantmaking is primarily focused on individual institutions. Key to the foundation's approach is a comprehensive, multistage process used to identify promising youth development organizations, assess their overall capabilities, and subsequently invest in the growth of those organizations most capable of benefiting from this kind of support.

Fields of interest: Youth development, services; Youth development; Youth, services; Children/youth; Youth; Young adults; Young adults, female; Young adults, male.
Type of support: Management development/capacity building; General/operating support; Continuing support; Program development; Technical assistance; Consulting services; Program evaluation.
Limitations: Applications not accepted. Giving on a national basis. No grants to individuals, or for capital funds, construction and equipment, endowments, scholarships, fellowships, annual appeals, deficit financing, or matching gifts; no loans to individuals.
Publications: Annual report; Grants list; Occasional report.
Application information: The foundation does not accept unsolicited applications. The foundation invites organizations that think they may qualify for support after reviewing the selection criteria to complete the foundation's online youth organizations Preliminary Application Form.
Board meeting date(s): Mar., June, Sept., and Dec.
Officers and Trustees:* **H. Lawrence Clark,* Chair.**; Nancy Roob, Pres.; **Kelly Fitzsimmons, V.P., Chief Prog. and Strategy Off., Youth Devel. Fund**; Ralph Stefano, V.P., Chief Finance and Admin. Off.; Woodrow C. McCutchen, V.P., Sr. Portfolio Mgr., Youth Devel. Fund; William Moon, Cont.; James McConnell Clark, Tr. Emeritus; James McConnell Clark, Jr.; Alice F. Emerson; Simon Hemus; Kevin W. Kennedy; Janice C. Kreamer; Theodore E. Martin; Joyce Shields.
Number of staff: 21 full-time professional; 7 full-time support.
EIN: 237047034
Other changes: H. Lawrence Clark has replaced Theodore E. Martin as Chair.
James E. Moltz and D. Ellen Shuman are no longer trustees. Kelly Fitzsimmons is now V.P., Chief Prog. and Strategy Off. of Youth Devel. Fund.

2098
Robert Sterling Clark Foundation, Inc.
135 E. 64th St.
New York, NY 10065-7045 (212) 288-8900
Contact: Laura Wolff, Acting Dir.
FAX: (212) 288-1033; E-mail: rscf@rsclark.org; Main URL: http://www.rsclark.org
Grants Database: http://www.rsclark.org/index.php?page=past-grants
Knowledge Center: http://www.rsclark.org/index.php?page=publications
Robert Sterling Clark Foundation's Philanthropy Promise: http://www.ncrp.org/philanthropys-promise/who

Incorporated in 1952 in NY.
Donor: Robert Sterling Clark†.
Foundation type: Independent foundation.
Financial data (yr. ended 10/31/12): Assets, $91,733,173 (M); expenditures, $5,755,574; qualifying distributions, $5,073,793; giving activities include $4,141,485 for 77 grants, and $8,086 for 21 employee matching gifts.
Purpose and activities: The foundation supports projects that: 1) promote international cultural engagement; 2) ensure the effectiveness and accountability of public agencies in New York City and State; and 3) protect access to comprehensive reproductive health through litigation and public policy advocacy in New York State and at the federal level.
Fields of interest: Visual arts; Museums; Performing arts; Performing arts, dance; Performing arts, theater; Performing arts, music; Arts; Environment; Reproductive health, family planning; Human services; Family services; Civil liberties, reproductive rights; Urban/community development; Community/economic development; Public policy, research; Government/public administration; Public affairs; Children/youth; Youth; Aging; Young adults; Women; Adults, women; Economically disadvantaged; Homeless.
International interests: Africa; Global Programs; Latin America; Middle East.
Type of support: Continuing support; Program development; Publication; Research; Employee matching gifts; Exchange programs.
Limitations: Applications accepted. Giving primarily in New York State for the Public Institutions Program; nationally for reproductive rights; and nationally for organizations working in Africa, Latin America, and the Middle East to promote international arts and cultural engagement. No support for religious organizations. No grants to individuals, or for annual campaigns, seed money, emergency funds, deficit financing, capital or endowment funds, general support or scholarships.
Publications: Application guidelines; Annual report (including application guidelines); Grants list; Occasional report; Program policy statement.
Application information: Application form not required.
Initial approach: Proposal (not exceeding 15 pages) and a one-page proposal summary
Copies of proposal: 1
Deadline(s): None
Board meeting date(s): Jan., Apr., July, and Oct.
Final notification: 1 to 6 months
Officers and Directors:* James Allen Smith,* Chair.; Joanna D. Underwood, Secy.; Clara Miller,* Treas.; **Laura Wolff, Acting Exec. Dir.**; Paul R. Dolan; **Philip Li**; Julie Muraco; John Hoyt Stookey.
Number of staff: 2 full-time professional; 1 full-time support.
EIN: 131957792

2099
The Clark Foundation
1 Rockefeller Plz., 31st Fl.
New York, NY 10020-2102 (212) 977-6900
Contact: Doug Bauer, Exec. Dir.

Incorporated in 1931 in NY; merged with Scriven Foundation, Inc. in 1973.
Donor: Members of the Clark family.
Foundation type: Independent foundation.
Financial data (yr. ended 12/31/12): Assets, $471,369,685 (M); gifts received, $500; expenditures, $28,693,172; qualifying distributions, $24,688,706; giving activities include $14,370,421 for 97 grants (high: $500,000; low: $2,250), and $3,140,989 for 1 foundation-administered program.
Purpose and activities: Support for a hospital and museums in Cooperstown, New York; grants also for charitable and educational purposes, including undergraduate scholarships to students residing in the Cooperstown area. The foundation owns and supports the Clark Sports Center, which is located in Cooperstown. Support also for educational, youth, cultural, and community organizations and institutions in New York City.
Fields of interest: Museums; Education; Employment; Human services; Children/youth, services; Young adults; Economically disadvantaged.
Type of support: General/operating support; Continuing support; Management development/capacity building; Capital campaigns; Building/renovation; Program development; Seed money; Technical assistance; Program-related investments/loans.
Limitations: Applications accepted. Giving primarily in New York City and Cooperstown, NY; scholarships restricted to students residing in the Cooperstown, NY, area. No grants to individuals (except as specified in restricted funds), or for deficit financing or matching gifts.
Publications: Application guidelines; Program policy statement.
Application information: The foundation accepts the New York/ New Jersey Area Common Application Form and the New York/ New Jersey Common Report Form. Application form not required.
Initial approach: Letter
Copies of proposal: 1
Deadline(s): Mar. 31, June 30, Sept. 30 and Dec. 31
Board meeting date(s): Mar., June, Oct., and Dec.
Final notification: 2 to 6 months
Officers and Directors:* Jane Forbes Clark,* Pres.; **Gates Helms Hawn,* V.P.**; Doug Bauer, Secy. and Exec. Dir.; Kevin S. Moore,* Treas.; Kent L. Barwick; Felicia H. Blum; William M. Evarts; Terry T. Fulmer; Paul Kellogg; Thomas Q. Morris, M.D.; Anne L. Peretz; **Karl E. Seib**; **Paul C. Shiverick**; Edward W. Stack; John Hoyt Stookey; Clifton R. Wharton, Jr.
Number of staff: 4 full-time professional; 3 part-time professional; 43 full-time support; 20 part-time support.
EIN: 135616528
Other changes: Gates Helms Hawn has replaced Alexander F. Treadwell as V.P.

2100
Coach Foundation, Inc.
c/o Coach, Inc.
516 W. 34th St.
New York, NY 10001-1311
E-mail: coachfoundation@coach.com; Main URL: http://www.coach.com/online/handbags/genWCM-10551-10051-en-/Coach_US/CompanyInformation/CoachFoundation/

Established in 2008 in NY.
Donor: Coach, Inc.
Foundation type: Company-sponsored foundation.
Financial data (yr. ended 06/29/13): Assets, $99,362,321 (M); expenditures, $5,958,809; qualifying distributions, $5,790,010; giving activities include $5,402,959 for 69 grants (high: $2,000,000; low: $2,500), and $387,051 for employee matching gifts.
Purpose and activities: The foundation supports programs designed to empower, educate, and support women and children around the world.
Fields of interest: Secondary school/education; Higher education; Education; Environment; Hospitals (general); Breast cancer; Dispute resolution; Employment, services; Disasters, preparedness/services; American Red Cross; Children, services; Family services; Family services, domestic violence; Women, centers/services; Business/industry; Women.
Type of support: General/operating support; Continuing support; Program development; Scholarship funds; Employee volunteer services; Employee matching gifts.
Limitations: Applications not accepted. Giving primarily in areas of company operations, with some emphasis in New York City; giving also to national organizations.
Publications: Grants list.

Application information: The foundation primarily funds projects recommended by its employees and board members.
Officers and Directors:* Lew Frankfort,* Chair., Pres., and C.E.O.; Jerry Stritzke,* C.O.O.; Todd Kahn,* V.P. and Secy.; Nancy H. Walsh, Treas.; Jane Nielson, C.F.O.; Felice Schulaner, Exec. Dir.; Sarah Dunn; Susan J. Kropf; Jason Weisenfeld.
EIN: 262939018
Other changes: At the close of 2013, the grantmaker paid grants of $5,790,010, a 78.6% increase over the 2012 disbursements, $3,242,525.

2101
The Coby Foundation, Ltd.
511 Avenue of the Americas, No. 387
New York, NY 10011-8436 **(212) 741-7022**
Contact: Ward L.E. Mintz, Exec. Dir.
FAX: (212) 741-6236;
E-mail: cobyfound@nyc.rr.com; Main URL: http://www.cobyfoundation.org

Established in 1994.
Donor: Irene Zambelli Silverman†.
Foundation type: Independent foundation.
Financial data (yr. ended 12/31/12): Assets, $10,425,041 (M); expenditures, $506,713; qualifying distributions, $347,400; giving activities include $347,400 for grants.
Purpose and activities: The foundation funds projects in the textile and needle arts field. Its funding is limited to non-profit organizations in the Mid-Atlantic and New England.
Fields of interest: Visual arts; Visual arts, design; Visual arts, art conservation; Arts.
Type of support: Program development.
Limitations: Applications accepted. Giving in the Mid-Atlantic and northeastern U.S. No grants to individuals, or for operating support, capital projects, or for endowments.
Application information: For complete application information see foundation web site. Application form required.
Initial approach: Letter of inquiry
Copies of proposal: 7
Deadline(s): Six weeks before Jan., May, and Sept. quarterly meetings. Contact Exec. Dir. for exact dates
Board meeting date(s): 3 times per year
Final notification: Within 2 months of application
Officers and Directors:* Leslie Shanken,* Chair.; Rosemarie Garipoli,* Vice-Chair.; Lucille A. Roussin,* Secy.; Lea Paine Highet,* Treas.; Ward L.E. Mintz, Exec. Dir.; Scott L. Fulmer; Martha C. Howell.
Number of staff: 1 part-time professional.
EIN: 133781874

2102
Karen B. Cohen Foundation, Inc.
515 Madison Ave., 29th Fl.
New York, NY **10022-5420**
Contact: Stanley Garber

Donor: Karen B. Cohen.
Foundation type: Independent foundation.
Financial data (yr. ended 12/31/12): Assets, $7,234 (M); gifts received, $206,000; expenditures, $201,530; qualifying distributions, $201,520; giving activities include $201,520 for 20 grants (high: $50,000; low: $95).
Fields of interest: Museums (art); Performing arts, opera; Arts; Libraries/library science; Education; Health organizations, association; Jewish agencies & synagogues.
Limitations: Applications not accepted. Giving primarily in New York, NY. No grants to individuals.
Application information: Contributes only to pre-selected organizations.
Officer: Karen B. Cohen, Pres.
EIN: 133833164

2103
Cohen LD Family Foundation, Inc.
1570 46th St.
Brooklyn, NY 11219-2725
Application address: c/o Mr. Bernat Steinmetz, 18 W. 33rd St., New York, NY 10001, tel.: (212) 563-5733

Established in NY.
Donors: Lea Cohen; Michael Cohen; Sara Cohen; Shrage Brecher; Israel Spiegel; Bernat Steinmetz; Pessie Richard; Micheal Steinmetz; Amy Steinmetz.
Foundation type: Independent foundation.
Financial data (yr. ended 06/30/13): Assets, $3,785,100 (M); gifts received, $70,000; expenditures, $127,020; qualifying distributions, $126,770; giving activities include $126,770 for 33 grants (high: $20,000; low: $360).
Fields of interest: Human services; Jewish federated giving programs; Jewish agencies & synagogues; Religion.
Limitations: Applications accepted. Giving primarily in NY.
Application information: Application form not required.
***Initial approach:* Propossal**
Deadline(s): None
Officers: David Spiegel, Pres.; Sarah Spiegel, V.P.; Michael Steinmetz, Secy.-Treas.
EIN: 300082673

2104
The Chase and Stephanie Coleman Foundation
c/o Tiger Global
101 Park Ave., 48th Fl.
New York, NY 10178-4799

Established in 2006 in NY.
Donors: Charles P. Coleman III; Stephanie A. Coleman.
Foundation type: Independent foundation.
Financial data (yr. ended 12/31/12): Assets, $36,872,714 (M); gifts received, $36,950,000; expenditures, $2,136,160; qualifying distributions, $2,136,160; giving activities include $2,127,650 for 14 grants (high: $1,000,000; low: $5,000).
Fields of interest: Education; Hospitals (general); Foundations (private grantmaking).
Limitations: Applications not accepted. Giving primarily in NY. No grants to individuals.
Application information: Contributes only to pre-selected organizations.
Trustees: Charles P. Coleman III; Stephanie A. Coleman.
EIN: 830451634
Other changes: At the close of 2012, the fair market value of the grantmaker's assets was $36,872,714, a 2,057.1% increase over the 2010 value, $1,709,394. For the same period, the grantmaker paid grants of $2,127,650, a 70.7% increase over the 2010 disbursements, $1,246,600.

2105
Joseph Collins Foundation
c/o Willkie Farr & Gallagher
787 7th Ave.
New York, NY 10019-7099

Incorporated in 1951 in NY.
Donor: Joseph Collins, M.D.†.
Foundation type: Independent foundation.
Financial data (yr. ended 06/30/13): Assets, $23,909,544 (M); expenditures, $1,788,992; qualifying distributions, $1,761,505; giving activities include $1,640,000 for 82 grants to individuals (high: $20,000; low: $20,000).
Purpose and activities: The foundation makes annual grants only to students with inadequate resources, in attendance at medical schools in states east of or contiguous to the Mississippi River, in sums not exceeding $10,000. Grants also for tuition to needy second through fourth year undergraduate medical students on the recommendation of medical school authorities. Students must stand in the upper half of their class, intend to specialize in neurology or psychiatry, or to become a general practitioner, and have outside cultural interests.
Fields of interest: Medical school/education.
Type of support: Grants to individuals.
Limitations: Applications not accepted. Giving limited to students attending accredited medical schools located east of the Mississippi River. No grants for pre-medical or postgraduate medical students.
Publications: Annual report; Program policy statement.
Application information: Unsolicited requests for funds not accepted.
Board meeting date(s): Nov. and as required
Officers and Trustees:* Jack H. Nusbaum,* Pres.; Mark F. Hughes, Jr.,* V.P.; Nora Ann Wallace,* V.P.; Dr. Danielle Lann.
EIN: 136404527
Other changes: Loretta Ippolito is no longer V.P. and Secy.-Treas.

2106
The Commonwealth Fund
1 E. 75th St.
New York, NY 10021-2692
Contact: Andrea C. Landes, V.P., Grants Mgmt.
FAX: (212) 606-3500; E-mail: info@cmwf.org; E-mail for questions from grant applicants: grants@cmwf.org; Main URL: http://www.commonwealthfund.org
Blog: http://www.commonwealthfund.org/Publications/Blog.aspx
E-Newsletter: http://www.commonwealthfund.org/Profile/My-Profile.aspx
Facebook: http://www.facebook.com/pages/The-Commonwealth-Fund/102047517918
Foundation Management and Performance: http://www.commonwealthfund.org/About-Us/Foundation-Management-and-Performance.aspx
Grants Database: http://www.commonwealthfund.org/Grants-and-Programs/Search-Grants.aspx
Innovations: http://www.commonwealthfund.org/Innovations.aspx
iTunes: http://phobos.apple.com/WebObjects/MZStore.woa/wa/viewPodcast?id=284038727
Mobile: http://mobile.commonwealthfund.org/
Multimedia: http://www.commonwealthfund.org/Multimedia-Center.aspx
Podcasts: http://www.commonwealthfund.org/podcasts/

RSS Feed: http://feeds.feedburner.com/TheCommonwealthFund
The Commonwealth Fund Staff: https://twitter.com/commonwealthfnd/fund-staff/members
Twitter: http://twitter.com/commonwealthfnd
YouTube: http://www.youtube.com/CommonwealthFund

Incorporated in 1918 in NY.
Donors: Mrs. Stephen V. Harkness†; Edward S. Harkness†; Mrs. Edward S. Harkness†.
Foundation type: Independent foundation.
Financial data (yr. ended 06/30/13): Assets, $702,204,618 (M); expenditures, $48,738,642; qualifying distributions, $31,674,944; giving activities include $27,183,760 for 248 grants (high: $700,000; low: $98), $2,380,423 for grants to individuals, and $5,121,806 for foundation-administered programs.
Purpose and activities: The mission of the fund is to promote a high performing healthcare system that achieves better access, improved quality, and greater efficiency, particularly for society's most vulnerable, including low-income people, the uninsured, minority Americans, young children, and elderly adults. The fund carries out this mandate by supporting independent research on health care issues and making grants to improve healthcare practice and policy. An international program in health policy is designed to stimulate innovative policies and practices in the United States and other industrialized countries.
Fields of interest: Health care, financing; Health care; Adults; Aging; Disabilities, people with; Minorities.
International interests: Australia; Canada; New Zealand; United Kingdom.
Type of support: Program development; Fellowships; Research; Program evaluation.
Limitations: Applications accepted. Giving on a national basis. No support for religious organizations for religious purposes, or basic biomedical research. No grants to individuals (except through the Commonwealth Fund's fellowship programs), or for scholarships, general planning or ongoing activities, existing deficits, endowment or capital costs, construction, renovation, equipment, conferences, symposia, major media projects, or documentaries (unless they are an out growth of one of the fund's programs).
Publications: Annual report; Annual report (including application guidelines); Financial statement; Grants list; Informational brochure; Newsletter; Occasional report; Program policy statement.
Application information: The fund strongly prefers grant applicants submit letters of inquiry using the online application form, however, letters submitted via regular mail or fax will be accepted. The fund acknowledges letters on receipt; applicants are typically advised of results of initial staff review within two months. Application form not required.
Initial approach: Letter of inquiry
Copies of proposal: 1
Board meeting date(s): Apr., July, and Nov.
Final notification: 4-6 weeks
Officers and Directors:* James R. Tallon,* Chair.; Cristine Russell,* Vice-Chair.; David Blumenthal,* Pres.; John E. Craig, Jr., C.O.O. and Exec. V.P.; Donald Moulds, Exec. V. P., Progs.; **Melinda Abrams, V.P., Delivery System Reform**; **Anne-Marie J. Audet, M.D., M.Sc., V.P., Delivery System Reform and Breakthrough Opportunities**; **Sara Collins, Ph.D., V.P., Health Care Coverage and Access**; Diana Davenport, V.P., Admin.; Michelle M. Doty, V.P., Survey Research and Eval.; Stuart Guterman, V.P., Medicare and Cost Control; Andrea C. Landes, V.P., Grants Mgmt.; Robin Osborn, V.P., and Dir., International Prog., Health Policy and Innovation; Barry Scholl, V.P., Comms. and Publishing; Rachel Nuzum, V.P., Federal and State Health Policy; Jeffry Haber, Cont.; Maureen Bisognano; **Mitchell J. Blutt, M.D.**; Sheila P. Burke, R.N., M.P.A.; Benjamin K. Chu, M.D.; Michael V. Drake, M.D.; Julio Frenk, M.D.; Kathryn Haslanger; Jane E. Henney, M.D.; Robert C. Pozen; Simon Stevens; William Y. Yun.
Number of staff: 28 full-time professional; 21 full-time support.
EIN: 131635260
Other changes: Cathy Schoen is no longer Sr. V.P., Research and Eval. Mary Jane Koren is no longer V.P., Quality of Care for Frail Elders. Edward L. Schor is no longer V.P., State Health Policy and Practice. Samuel C. Fleming and Glen M. Hackbarth are no longer directors. Rachel Nuzum is now V.P., Federal and State Health Policy.

2107
The Community Foundation for South Central New York, Inc.

520 Columbia Dr., Ste. 100
Johnson City, NY 13790-0000 (607) 772-6773
Contact: For grants: Tina Barber, Prog. Off.
FAX: (607) 722-6752;
E-mail: info@donorswhocare.org; Grant inquiry e-mail: tmbarber@stny.rr.com; Main URL: http://www.cfscny.org
Additional URL: http://www.donorswhocare.org/

Established in 1997 in NY.
Foundation type: Community foundation.
Financial data (yr. ended 12/31/12): Assets, $18,120,027 (M); gifts received, $1,124,154; expenditures, $1,292,456; giving activities include $735,440 for grants, $9,000 for 7 grants to individuals (high: $5,000; low: $250), and $116,172 for foundation-administered programs.
Purpose and activities: The foundation seeks to establish and maintain charitable endowments, donor-advised funds and restricted funds for charitable grants and scholarships in Broome, Chenango, Cortland, Delaware and Tioga Counties, NY.
Fields of interest: Humanities; Arts; Higher education; Education; Hospitals (general); Health care; Youth development; Human services; Community/economic development; Infants/toddlers; Children/youth; Children; Youth; Adults; Aging; Young adults; Disabilities, people with; Physically disabled; Mentally disabled; Women; Infants/toddlers, female; Girls; Adults, women; Young adults, female; Men; Infants/toddlers, male; Boys; Adults, men; Young adults, male; Substance abusers; Single parents; Crime/abuse victims; Economically disadvantaged; Homeless.
Type of support: General/operating support; Continuing support; Capital campaigns; Building/renovation; Equipment; Emergency funds; Program development; Conferences/seminars; Seed money; Curriculum development; Scholarship funds; Technical assistance; Consulting services; Program evaluation; Program-related investments/loans; Scholarships—to individuals; Matching/challenge support.
Limitations: Applications accepted. Giving limited to Broome, Chenango, Delaware, Otsego and Tioga counties, NY. No support for religious purposes. No grants to individuals (except for scholarships), or for program deficits, mortgage payments, operating funds, special events, or individual musical theater productions or performances.
Publications: Application guidelines; Annual report; Financial statement; Grants list; Informational brochure; Newsletter.
Application information: Visit foundation web site for application forms and guidelines. Number of copies vary per application attachment. Application form required.
Initial approach: Telephone to confirm project eligibility
Copies of proposal: 16
***Deadline(s):* Mar. 3 and Sept. 2**
Board meeting date(s): Apr. and Oct.
Final notification: Approx. 8 weeks
Officers and Directors:* Keith D. Chadwick,* Chair.; Heather M. Cornell,* Vice-Chair.; Jane L. Zuckerman,* Secy.; John Mirabito,* Treas.; Diane L. Brown,* Exec. Dir.; **James C. Daniels, C.P.A.**; Carolyn Demtrak; Patrick J. Doyle; Elysia M. Gudas; James R. Foley; John W. Foley; Hon. David H. Guy; Jean Levenson; Peter G. Newman; Jon J. Sarra; Catherine M. Scarlett.
Number of staff: 3 full-time professional; 1 full-time support.
EIN: 161512085
Other changes: Garet Livermore and John Mirabito are no longer directors.

2108
The Community Foundation for the Greater Capital Region, Inc.

6 Tower Pl.
Albany, NY 12203-3725 (518) 446-9638
Contact: For grants: Jackie Mahoney, V.P., Progs.
FAX: (518) 446-9708; E-mail: info@cfcr.org; Pre-application submission e-mail: jmahoney@cfgcr.org; Main URL: http://www.cfgcr.org
Facebook: https://www.facebook.com/CFGCR

Incorporated in 1968 in NY.
Foundation type: Community foundation.
Financial data (yr. ended 12/31/12): Assets, $58,388,566 (M); gifts received, $8,839,124; expenditures, $4,971,233; giving activities include $3,902,076 for grants.
Purpose and activities: The mission of the foundation is to strengthen the community by attracting charitable endowments both large and small, maximizing benefits to donors, making effective grants, and providing leadership to address community needs.
Fields of interest: Performing arts, music; Medical school/education; Nursing school/education; Adult education—literacy, basic skills & GED; Environment; Art & music therapy; Health care, home services; Health care; AIDS; Crime/violence prevention, abuse prevention; Employment; Disasters, preparedness/services; Children/youth, services; Aging, centers/services; Homeless, human services; Aging; Disabilities, people with; Blind/visually impaired; Deaf/hearing impaired.
Type of support: General/operating support; Income development; Management development/capacity building; Program development; Seed money; Technical assistance; Employee-related scholarships.
Limitations: Applications accepted. Giving primarily in the ten-county Capital Area region, including Albany, Renssalear, Saratoga, and Schenectady, NY. No support for sectarian religious purposes. No grants to individuals (except for scholarships), endowments or foundations, programs the community foundation will have to operate, research, endowments, travel, conferences and speakers' expenses, advertisements in programs, journals or other publications, special events and

other fundraising events, annual appeals, or membership contributions.
Publications: Application guidelines; Annual report; Financial statement; Informational brochure; Newsletter.
Application information: Visit foundation web site for application guidelines. Based on pre-application questionnaire, the applicant organization will be screened for eligibility and will either be notified of the reason for ineligibility or will be invited to submit an application; the applicant will be supplied with a grant application form and the deadline for submission. Application form required.
Initial approach: E-mail pre-application questionnaire
Copies of proposal: 1
Deadline(s): Feb. 28 for Impact Grants pre-application questionnaire; Apr. for Impact Grants full application; varies for others
Board meeting date(s): Bimonthly
Final notification: Aug. for Impact Grants notification; varies for others
Officers and Directors:* Deborah Onslow,* Chair.; Ellen Sax,* Vice-Chair.; Susan C. Picotte, Esq.,* 2nd Vice-Chair.; Karen Bilowith,* C.E.O. and Pres.; **Jackie Mahoney,* V.P., Progs.**; Christine Standish,* Secy.; Anthony J. Capobianco,* Treas.; Robin Wood,* Asst. Secy.; Jeffrey N. Rosenbaum,* Asst. Treas.; Matthew Bender IV; Gary C. Dake; Gloria DeSole; Mark Eagan; Virginia C. Gregg; Nancy E. Hoffman, Esq.; Paul M. Hohenberg; William Kahn; Steven E. Lobel; **John A. MacAffer**; **Kevin M. O'Bryan**; Amy S. O'Connor, Esq.; Francis Murdock Pitts; Marcus Q. Pryor; Ann M. Sharpe, Esq.; James A. Sidford; Maggie Vinciguerra; C. Wayne Williams.
Number of staff: 5 full-time professional; 2 part-time professional.
EIN: 141505623
Other changes: Jackie Mahoney has replaced Shelly Connolly as V.P., Progs.

2109

The Community Foundation of Elmira-Corning and the Finger Lakes, Inc.

(formerly The Community Foundation of the Chemung County Area and Corning Community Foundation)
301 S. Main St.
Horseheads, NY 14845 (607) 739-3900
Contact: Randi Hewit, Pres.; Sara Palmer, Dir., Grants and Comms.
E-mail: rlh@communityfund.org; Additional e-mail: sep@communityfund.org; Main URL: http://www.communityfund.org
Facebook: http://www.facebook.com/pages/Community-Foundation-of-Elmira-Corning-and-the-Finger-Lakes/404520120537

Established in 1977 in NY as Chemung County; Corning established in 1972 in NY; reincorporated in 1993 under current name after merger of Community Foundation of Chemung County Area and Corning Community Foundation.
Foundation type: Community foundation.
Financial data (yr. ended 06/30/13): Assets, $39,755,545 (M); gifts received, $1,092,363; expenditures, $2,014,843; giving activities include $1,113,956 for 53+ grants (high: $64,421; low: $50), and $213,650 for 96 grants to individuals.
Purpose and activities: The foundation exists in perpetuity to enhance the quality of life in the community. Guided by a board of civic leaders, the foundation provides a continuing source of funding to benefit the community through scholarships and grants to nonprofit organizations.
Fields of interest: Humanities; Arts; Education; Environment; Animal welfare; Health care; Youth development; Human services; Community development, neighborhood development; Women.
Type of support: Grants to individuals; Emergency funds; Management development/capacity building; Capital campaigns; Building/renovation; Equipment; Endowments; Program development; Conferences/seminars; Publication; Seed money; Curriculum development; Scholarship funds; Research; Technical assistance; Consulting services; Program evaluation; Employee-related scholarships; Scholarships—to individuals; Matching/challenge support.
Limitations: Applications accepted. Giving limited to Chemung, Southeast Steuben, Schuyler and Yates counties of New York. No support for religious purposes. No grants for annual campaigns, special event fundraisers, sponsorships, trips, or deficit funding or debt retirement; no loans.
Publications: Application guidelines; Annual report (including application guidelines); Financial statement.
Application information: Visit foundation web site for application forms and guidelines per grant type. Application form required.
Initial approach: Submit letter of intent for Community Grants
Copies of proposal: 5
Deadline(s): Mar. 1 and Aug. 1 for Letter of Intent for Community Grants; Apr. 1 and Sept. 1 for grant application for Community Grants; Feb. 17 for scholarships
Board meeting date(s): Varies
Final notification: Mid-June and mid-Nov. for Community Grants
Officers and Trustees:* Michael Mustico,* Chair.; Thomas Tranter, Jr.,* Vice-Chair.; Randi Hewit,* Pres.; **Clover Drinkwater,* Corporate Secy.**; Michael Eisner,* Treas.; Gail Baity; Paige Christian; Mary Beth Conwell; Kimberly Cutler; **Lou DiFabio**; Chris Fortier; Tom Gough; Carl Hayden; Beth Landin; Judith McInerny; Karen Meriwether; Marc Stemmerman; Douglas Tifft; **Tony Tripeny**; Scott Welliver.
Number of staff: 4 full-time professional.
EIN: 161100837
Other changes: Nancy Van Fleet is now Scholarship Off. and Exec. Asst. Clover Drinkwater is now Corporate Secy.

2110

The Community Foundation of Herkimer & Oneida Counties, Inc.

(formerly Utica Foundation, Inc.)
1222 State St.
Utica, NY 13502-4728 (315) 735-8212
Contact: Margaret O'Shea, C.E.O. and Pres.
FAX: (315) 735-9363;
E-mail: info@foundationhoc.org; Telephone (for grants): 315-735-8212; Main URL: http://www.foundationhoc.org
Facebook: https://www.facebook.com/pages/The-Community-Foundation/201676223188193
Flickr: http://www.flickr.com/photos/foundationhoc/
LinkedIn: http://www.linkedin.com/company/the-community-foundation-of-herkimer-&-oneida-counties
Philanthropy's Promise: http://www.ncrp.org/philanthropys-promise/who
RSS Feed: http://foundationhoc.org/feed/
Twitter: http://www.twitter.com/foundationhoc
YouTube: http://www.youtube.com/user/comfoundation315

Incorporated in 1952 in NY.
Foundation type: Community foundation.
Financial data (yr. ended 12/31/12): Assets, $101,339,408 (M); gifts received, $1,792,966; expenditures, $4,282,999; giving activities include $2,189,578 for 65+ grants (high: $127,090).
Purpose and activities: The foundation provides support for programs and projects that: 1) offer the greatest opportunity for positive and significant change in the community; 2) identify and enhance local strengths to address and provide creative solutions for important existing or emerging community issues; 3) develop organizational and/or individual self-sufficiency; 4) focus on identifiable outcomes that will make a difference; 5) leverage investment of other community resources; 6) and improve the quality or scope of charitable works in the community.
Fields of interest: Arts; Higher education; Libraries/library science; Education; Environment; Hospitals (general); Health care; Children/youth, services; Family services; Aging, centers/services; Human services; Economic development; Public affairs.
Type of support: Management development/capacity building; Capital campaigns; Building/renovation; Equipment; Land acquisition; Endowments; Emergency funds; Program development; Conferences/seminars; Seed money; Curriculum development; Fellowships; Scholarship funds; Technical assistance; Consulting services; Program evaluation; Program-related investments/loans; Matching/challenge support.
Limitations: Applications accepted. Giving limited to Herkimer and Oneida counties, NY. No support for religious purposes. No grants or loans to individuals, or for ongoing operating support, multi-year grants or requests that exceed $100,000; no loans to individuals.
Publications: Application guidelines; Annual report; Financial statement; Newsletter.
Application information: Visit foundation web site for application cover sheet and guidelines. Application form required.
Initial approach: Telephone
Copies of proposal: 16
Deadline(s): None
Board meeting date(s): Grants committee meets 5 to 6 times per year
Final notification: 4 to 8 weeks
Officers and Directors:* Keith Fenstemacher,* Chair.; Peggy O'Shea,* C.E.O. and Pres.; **Judith V. Sweet,* Secy.-Treas.**; Mary Lyons Bradley; Lauren Bull; Richard Callahan; **Laura Casamento**; Linda Cohen; Randy Cuccaro; Burt Danovitz, Ph.D.; L. Michael Fitzgerald; David Jones; Susan G. Matt; Mary Morse; Richard Tantillo; Rev. Robert Umidi; Eve Van de Wal; Randy Van Wagoner; Bonnie Woods.
Number of staff: 6 full-time professional; 1 full-time support; 1 part-time support.
EIN: 156016932
Other changes: Laura Morris is now Exec. Admin. Asst. Judith V. Sweet is now Secy.-Treas. Susan Matt, Ann Marie Murray, and Keith Fenstemacher are no longer directors.

2111

Community Foundation of Orange County, Inc.

(formerly Community Foundation of Orange and Sullivan, Inc.)
30 Scott's Corner Dr., Ste. 202
Montgomery, NY 12549-2262 (845) 769-9393
***Contact:* Karen VanHouten Minogue, C.E.O.**

FAX: (845) 769-9391; E-mail: admin@cfoc-ny.org; Additional e-mail: vanhouten@cfoc-ny.org; Main URL: http://www.cfoc-ny.org
Facebook: http://www.facebook.com/pages/The-Community-Foundation-of-Orange-and-Sullivan/120738087979457
RSS Feed: http://www.yourcommunityfoundations.org/feed

Established in 1999 in NY.
Donors: Mr. R.J. Smith; Mrs. R.J. Smith; Provident Bank Charitable Foundation; Gerry Foundation; James Ottaway Jr. Trust.
Foundation type: Community foundation.
Financial data (yr. ended 06/30/12): Assets, $7,625,870 (M); gifts received, $1,110,006; expenditures, $765,992; giving activities include $268,958 for 10+ grants (high: $72,249), and $95,346 for 82 grants to individuals.
Purpose and activities: The foundation, through effective use of its endowment, seeks to enhance the quality of life for those who live and work within Orange County by encouraging the growth of a permanent charitable endowment to meet the community's immediate and emerging needs, and by providing vehicles for donors with diverse philanthropic interests in a way that makes giving easy, personally satisfying, effective, and lasting.
Fields of interest: Health care; Aging, centers/services.
Type of support: Student loans—to individuals; Scholarships—to individuals; Scholarship funds; Endowments.
Limitations: Applications accepted. Giving primarily in Orange County and Sullivan County, NY.
Publications: Annual report; Financial statement; Grants list; Informational brochure; Newsletter.
Application information: Application form not required.
Initial approach: Contact foundation
Copies of proposal: 1
Deadline(s): None
Board meeting date(s): Every other month
Officers and Directors:* Derrik Wynkoop,* Pres.; Josh Sommers,* V.P., Distribution; Dorothy Fein,* V.P., Devel.; Tim McCausland,* V.P., Devel.; William Bratton,* V.P., Finance; Katharine Fitzgerald,* Secy.; Jack Berkowitz,* Treas.; Michael Bonura,* Asst. Treas.; Karen VanHouten, Exec. Dir.; Jay Anthony; John Davies; Ed Devitt; Eric Fuentes; Philip Guarnieri; Gerald N. Jacobowitz; Dr. Michelle A. Koury; Susan Najork; Bonnie Orr; Andrew Pavloff; Raymond J. Quattrini; Richard Shapiro, Esq.; Gerald J. Skoda; R.J. Smith; Joe Vanderhoof; Todd Whitney; Dr. Michele Winchester-Vega; Wayne Zanetti.
Number of staff: 1 full-time professional; 1 full-time support; 1 part-time support.
EIN: 061551843

2112
Community Foundation of Tompkins County

309 N. Aurora St.
Ithaca, NY 14850-4230 (607) 272-9333
***Contact:* George P. Ferrari, Jr., C.E.O.**
FAX: (607) 272-3030; E-mail: info@cftompkins.org; Grant application e-mail: jcotraccia@communityfoundationoftc.org; Main URL: http://www.cftompkins.org
Facebook: https://www.facebook.com/CFTompkins
LinkedIn: http://www.linkedin.com/pub/george-ferrari/22/a96/46
Twitter: http://twitter.com/comfountc

Established in 2000 in NY.
Foundation type: Community foundation.
Financial data (yr. ended 12/31/12): Assets, $10,808,148 (M); gifts received, $2,879,294; expenditures, $728,571; giving activities include $419,863 for 24+ grants (high: $41,394).
Purpose and activities: The foundation seeks to encourage and develop sustainable philanthropy for a broad range of community efforts by: 1) encouraging the growth of a permanent charitable endowment; 2) making strategic grants as community investments; 3) providing donors with vehicles to make giving easy and effective; and 4) serving as a catalyst and convener.
Fields of interest: General charitable giving.
Type of support: General/operating support; Management development/capacity building; Annual campaigns; Capital campaigns; Building/renovation; Equipment; Emergency funds; Program development; Film/video/radio; Publication; Seed money; Curriculum development; Technical assistance; Consulting services; Program evaluation; Program-related investments/loans; Matching/challenge support.
Limitations: Applications accepted. Giving primarily in Tompkins County, NY. No support for religious organizations.
Publications: Annual report; Financial statement; Grants list; Informational brochure.
Application information: Visit foundation web site for application guidelines. A letter of inquiry must be submitted before applicants are considered for requests that do not match with any grant cycle priority. Application form required.
Initial approach: Submit letter of inquiry
Deadline(s): May 15 and Oct. 15 for letter of inquiry; Varies for applications
Board meeting date(s): 2nd Mon. of each month
Officers and Directors:* Robin Masson,* Chair.; **Richard Banks,* Chair., Devel. and Community Rels.**; **Paula Davis,* Chair., Community Impact**; **Randy Ehrenberg,* Chair., Youth Fund Advisory**; Diane McDonough,* Chair., Financial Admin. and Treas.; Carol Travis,* Chair., Women's Fund Advisory; Linda Wagenet,* Chair., Nominating and Governance; Alan Mathios,* Vice-Chair.; George P. Ferrari, Jr.,* C.E.O.; Mary Berens,* Secy.; Susan Brown; Tom Colbert; Sandy Dhimitri; Ross Feldman; Marcie Finlay; Bob Jewell; Sara Knobel; Tim Little; Philip McPheron; Bill Murphy; Nancy Potter; David Squires; Lucia Tyler; Julie Waters; Baruch Whitehead; Stephanie Wiles.
Number of staff: 1 full-time professional; 1 part-time professional; 1 full-time support.
EIN: 161587553
Other changes: Richard Banks has replaced Jennifer Gabriel as Chair., Devel. Committee and Caroline Cox as Chair., Community Rels. Committee.
George P. Ferrari, Jr. is now C.E.O. Diane McDonough is now Chair., Financial Admin. and Treas. David Squires is no longer Chair., Financial Admin. Comm. and Treas. Paula Davis is now Chair., Community Impact. Carol Travis is now Chair., Women's Fund Advisory. Randy Ehrenberg is now Chair., Youth Fund Advisory. Linda Wagenet is no longer a director. Mickie Sanders-Jauquet is no longer a director.

2113
Community Foundations of the Hudson Valley

80 Washington St., Ste. 201
Poughkeepsie, NY 12601-2316 (845) 452-3077
***Contact:* Andrea L. Reynolds, C.E.O.; For grants: Jennifer Killian, Dir., Progs.**
FAX: (845) 452-3083; E-mail: cfdc@cfdcny.org; **Additional E-mail: areynolds@cfdcny.org; Grant inquiry e-mail: jkillian@cfhvny.org**; Main URL: http://www.cfdcny.org

Established in 1969 in NY.
Donors: McCann Foundation; Lester Freer‡.
Foundation type: Community foundation.
Financial data (yr. ended 06/30/12): Assets, $33,258,296 (M); gifts received, $2,269,557; expenditures, $2,869,704; giving activities include $1,661,301 for grants, and $239,050 for grants to individuals.
Purpose and activities: The foundation strengthens the community by offering donors the means to establish charitable legacies, by making grants, and by providing leadership to address community needs.
Fields of interest: Arts; Education, early childhood education; Elementary school/education; Secondary school/education; Education; Animal welfare; Health care; Human services; Nonprofit management.
Type of support: Management development/capacity building; Equipment; Program development; Seed money; Scholarship funds.
Limitations: Applications accepted. Giving primarily in Dutchess, Putnam, and Ulster counties, NY. No grants to individuals (except through The Area Fund Partnership in Education Grants Program), or for endowment funds, capital campaigns, building funds, land acquisition, matching gifts, deficit financing, operating budgets, or where amount of grant will not make a significant impact on a project; no loans.
Publications: Application guidelines; Annual report; Newsletter; IRS Form 990 or 990-PF printed copy available upon request.
Application information: Visit foundation web site for online application, guidelines, and specific deadlines. Application form required.
Initial approach: Submit application via online application portal
Copies of proposal: 1
Deadline(s): Varies
Board meeting date(s): Jan., Mar., May, Sept., and Nov.
Final notification: Late May and Nov.
Officers and Trustees:* Nancy Rossi Brownell,* Chair.; Bill Brenner,* Vice-Chair., Finance and Treas.; Joseph A. Bonura, Jr.,* Vice-Chair., Dutchess County; John K. Gifford,* Vice-Chair., Audit and Secy.; Matthew Marrone,* Vice-Chair., Putnam; Ann Chambers Meagher,* Vice-Chair., Governance; Arthur R. Upright,* Vice-Chair., Ulster; **Jeff Wood,* Vice-Chair., Grants**; Andrea L. Reynolds, C.E.O. and Pres.; Kevin J. Quilty, V.P., Ulster; Lisette E. Holmes, C.F.O.; Sandy Arteaga; Ellen L. Baker; James F. Davenport; Timothy Dean; Clara Lou Gould; Peter Krulewitch; John E. Mack IV; Thomas J. Murphy; Frederick H. Osborn III; Patrick Page; Lorraine M. Roberts; Sheila E. Scott; Kimberley S. Williams.
Number of staff: 5 full-time professional; 1 full-time support.
EIN: 237026859
Other changes: Jeff Wood has replaced Nancy Rossi Brownell as Vice-Chair., Grants.
Nancy Rossi Brownell is now Chair. Pat Adams, Robert R. Butts, Stephen E. Diamond, Sue Hartshorn, and Michael J. Tomkovitch are no longer trustees.

2114
Berthe M. Cote Foundation Inc.
c/o Fiduciary Trust Company International
600 5th Ave.
New York, NY **10020**

Foundation type: Independent foundation.
Financial data (yr. ended 10/31/13): Assets, $3,242,587 (M); expenditures, $179,051; qualifying distributions, $156,093; giving activities include $143,000 for 10 grants (high: $50,000; low: $5,000).
Fields of interest: Health care; United Ways and Federated Giving Programs.
International interests: Israel.
Limitations: Applications not accepted. Giving primarily in NY. No grants to individuals.
Application information: Unsolicited requests for funds not accepted.
Officers: E. Michael Difabio, Pres.; **Michael D. Difabio, V.P.**; **Linda R. Franciscovich, V.P.**
EIN: 141681452
Other changes: Michael D. Difabio is now V.P. Linda R. Franciscovich is now V.P.

2115
Frederic R. Coudert Foundation
c/o CohnReznick LLP
100 Jericho Quadrangle, No. 223
Jericho, NY **11753-2702**
Application address: **Frederic R. Coudert Foundation, 300 E. 59th St., No. 3102, New York, NY 10022, tel.: (212) 860-0758**

Established in 1999 in NY.
Donor: Frederic R. Coudert III.
Foundation type: Independent foundation.
Financial data (yr. ended 12/31/12): Assets, $10,307,716 (M); gifts received, $1,723,200; expenditures, $599,898; qualifying distributions, $535,635; giving activities include $531,635 for 39 grants (high: $111,000; low: $45).
Fields of interest: Arts; Education; Environment, water resources; Boys & girls clubs; Aging, centers/services.
Limitations: Applications accepted. Giving primarily in NY. No grants to individuals.
Application information:
Initial approach: Letter
Deadline(s): None
Trustees: Cynthia Coudert; Margaret M. Coudert; Sandra Coudert.
EIN: 137180778
Other changes: The grantmaker has moved from NJ to NY.

2116
The Countess Moira Charitable Foundation
P.O. Box 8078
Pelham, NY 10803-8878
Contact: Carolyn Gray, Chair. and Pres.
E-mail: inquiries@countessmoirafdn.org; Main URL: http://www.countessmoirafdn.org

Established in 2000 in NY.
Donors: Edward W.T. Gray III†; Moira Forbes; Countess Moira Forbes Rossi†.
Foundation type: Independent foundation.
Financial data (yr. ended 06/30/13): Assets, $32,838,941 (M); expenditures, $2,116,531; qualifying distributions, $1,760,772; giving activities include $1,744,500 for 24 grants (high: $500,000; low: $7,500).
Purpose and activities: Giving to organizations that provide medical, nutritional and educational programs for children.
Fields of interest: Education; Medical care, in-patient care; Children.
Type of support: Continuing support; General/operating support.
Limitations: Applications not accepted. Giving primarily in NY. No grants to individuals, or for events or fundraisers.
Publications: IRS Form 990 or 990-PF printed copy available upon request.
Application information: Unsolicited requests for funds not accepted.
Officers: Carolyn B. Gray, Chair. and Pres.; Michele J. Le Moal-Gray, Vice-Chair.; Peter G. Gray, V.P. and Secy.; Taylor T. Gray, V.P. and Treas.
Trustees: Donna M. Fitzgerald; Marc E. Garlasco; Kathleen M. Gray.
EIN: 113551993
Other changes: The grantmaker no longer publishes application guidelines.

2117
The Gerald and Daphna Cramer Family Foundation, Inc.
(formerly Gerald B. Cramer Family Foundation, Inc.)
c/o WMKG
185 Crossways Park Dr.
Woodbury, NY **11797-2040** (914) 683-9600
Contact: Gerald Cramer; Christine Stelmack
FAX: (914) 683-9606

Established in 1993 in NY.
Donors: Gerald B. Cramer; Daphna Cramer; Members of the Cramer family.
Foundation type: Independent foundation.
Financial data (yr. ended 12/31/12): Assets, $6,791,627 (M); gifts received, $1,557,000; expenditures, $1,376,205; qualifying distributions, $1,325,857; giving activities include $1,325,857 for 48 grants (high: $408,000; low: $7).
Purpose and activities: Giving primarily for higher education, the arts, hospitals and medical research, and to Jewish organizations.
Fields of interest: Museums; Arts; Higher education; Education; Hospitals (general); Hospitals (specialty); Medical research, institute; Jewish agencies & synagogues.
Limitations: Applications not accepted. Giving primarily in NY. No grants to individuals.
Application information: Contributes only to pre-selected organizations.
Officers: Gerald B. Cramer, Pres.; **Daphna Cramer, V.P.**; **Lauren B. Cramer, Secy.**
Directors: Douglas Cramer; Kimberly Germ-Cramer; Thomas Cramer; **Ron Gallatin**; Roy Raskin; Shelley Raskin; **Arthur Weiss.**
EIN: 133749869
Other changes: Daphna Cramer is now V.P. Lauren B. Cramer is now Secy.

2118
Credit Suisse Americas Foundation
(formerly Credit Suisse First Boston Foundation Trust)
11 Madison Ave., 10th Fl.
New York, NY 10010-3629 (212) 325-2389
Contact: Anne Marie Fell, Dir. of Grantmaking & Comms.
FAX: (212) 538-8347;
E-mail: americas.corporatecitizenship@credit-suisse.com; Additional tel.: (212) 325-5260; Main URL: https://www.credit-suisse.com/citizenship/en/philantropy_americas.jsp
Core Engagement Grantees: https://www.credit-suisse.com/responsibility/doc/core_grantees_2010.pdf
Credit Suisse Americas Foundation Video: https://multimedia.credit-suisse.com/app/player/index.cfm?fuseaction=OpenMultimedia&aoid=355802&coid=268640&lang=EN&popup=true
Education Grantees: https://www.credit-suisse.com/responsibility/doc/education_grantees_2010.pdf

Established in 1959 in MA.
Donors: Credit Suisse First Boston Corp.; Credit Suisse First Boston LLC; Credit Suisse USA.
Foundation type: Company-sponsored foundation.
Financial data (yr. ended 12/31/12): Assets, $29,521,058 (M); gifts received, $4,252,840; expenditures, $6,027,133; qualifying distributions, $5,841,732; giving activities include $5,833,157 for 333 grants.
Purpose and activities: The foundation supports organizations that engage Credit Suisse and create educational opportunities for disadvantaged young people.
Fields of interest: Elementary school/education; Secondary school/education; Teacher school/education; Education; Health care, clinics/centers; Food services; Food banks; Housing/shelter, development; Disasters, preparedness/services; Recreation, parks/playgrounds; Youth development, centers/clubs; Big Brothers/Big Sisters; Youth development, business; American Red Cross; Family services; Human services; Microfinance/microlending; Voluntarism promotion; United Ways and Federated Giving Programs; Youth; Economically disadvantaged.
Type of support: General/operating support; Management development/capacity building; Program development; Employee volunteer services; Matching/challenge support.
Limitations: Applications not accepted. Giving primarily in areas of company operations, with emphasis on New York, NY; giving also in Los Angeles and San Francisco, CA, Washington, DC, Miami, FL, Atlanta, GA, Boston, MA, Baltimore, MD, Chicago, IL, Raleigh-Durham, NC, Princeton, NJ, Conshohocken, PA, Dallas and Houston, TX, and in Nassau, Bahamas, Sao Paulo, Brazil, and Toronto, Canada. No support for religious organizations not of direct benefit to the entire community, veterans', fraternal, or political organizations, private or grantmaking foundations, colleges or universities, or K-12 schools. No grants to individuals, or for scholarships, capital campaigns, endowments, dinners or events, medical research, political causes, or sponsorships; no matching gifts.
Application information: Unsolicited applications are currently not accepted.
Board meeting date(s): Quarterly
Officers and Trustees:* Dean Wilson Ervin,* Chair.; Douglas L. Paul, Vice-Chair.; **Amy Cerciello, Secy.**; Eric Eckholdt, Exec. Dir.; Jim Amine; Nicole Arnaboldi; Rob Basso; Stephen Hilton; Grace J. Koo; Tim O'Hare; Mike Paliotta; Antonio Quintella; D. Neil Radey; Robert S. Shafir; Peter Skoglund; Fred Terrell; Lewis H. Wirshba.
Number of staff: 6 full-time professional.
EIN: 900647568
Other changes: Dean Wilson Ervin has replaced Antonio Quintella as Chair.
Antonio Quintella is no longer Chair. Kathryn M. Quigley is no longer Pres. Marc D. Granetz, Richard P. Zaloom and Kris Klein are no longer directors.

2119
Cricket Island Foundation

(formerly The Cricket Island Foundation)
c/o Elizabeth Sak, Exec. Dir.
25 E. 21st St., 7th Fl.
New York, NY 10010-6207 (212) 782-3730
Contact: Elizabeth Sak, Exec. Dir.; Jenny Peters, Dir., Finance and Opers.; Hana Sun, Prog. Assoc.
FAX: (212) 228-5275;
E-mail: info@cricketisland.org; Additional e-mail: grants@cricketisland.org; Main URL: http://www.cricketisland.org
Blog: http://www.cricketisland.org/news/
Grants List: http://www.cricketisland.org/wp-content/uploads/cricket-island-grant-summary.pdf

Established in 2000 in NY.
Donors: David K. Welles; Georgia E. Welles; Jeffrey F. Welles; David K. Welles, Jr.; Peter C. Welles; Christopher S. Welles; Virginia W. Jordan; Brooke Jordan.
Foundation type: Independent foundation.
Financial data (yr. ended 12/31/12): Assets, $38,007,494 (M); expenditures, $2,234,369; qualifying distributions, $1,973,392; giving activities include $1,442,018 for 59 grants (high: $140,000; low: $1,950).
Purpose and activities: The mission of the foundation is to develop the capacity and commitment of young people to improve their lives, communities and the world around them. The foundation supports organizations that offer meaningful opportunities for young people to contribute to positive societal change.
Fields of interest: Education, public policy; Education, reform; Youth development, alliance/advocacy; Youth development, public policy; Youth development, reform; Civil/human rights, alliance/advocacy; Community/economic development, alliance/advocacy; Community development, citizen coalitions; Youth.
Type of support: General/operating support; Continuing support; Management development/capacity building; Conferences/seminars; Technical assistance; Consulting services.
Limitations: Applications not accepted. Giving primarily in regional cohorts: currently New York, NY and Chicago, IL. No support for general recreational activities or organizations, academic and classroom based training programs, tutoring or job training programs, or for groups that don't involve youth in community change. No grants for scholarships, internships, direct school-based support, individual fellowships, or capital campaigns.
Publications: Grants list.
Application information: Unsolicited requests for funds not accepted. Applications by invitation only; funds currently committed.
Board meeting date(s): Apr. and Nov.
Officers and Directors:* Jeffrey F. Welles,* Chair. and Pres.; Georgia E. Welles,* V.P.; Ginny Jordan, Secy.; Taylor Jordan, Treas.; Elizabeth Sak, Exec. Dir.; Luke Jernagan; Nicole Jordan; Adam Miranda; Cameron Miranda; Berkley Welles; Christopher S. Welles; Hope J. Welles; Maud Welles; Peter Welles; Rene Welles; Ted Welles.
Number of staff: 2 full-time professional; 1 part-time support.
EIN: 341925915

2120
James H. Cummings Foundation, Inc.

120 W. Tupper St., Ste. 201
Buffalo, NY 14201-2170 (716) 874-0040
Contact: Brigid H. Doherty, Secy. and Exec. Dir.
FAX: (716) 854-2659;
E-mail: bdoherty@jameshcummings.com; Main URL: http://www.jameshcummings.com

Incorporated in 1962 in NY.
Donor: James H. Cummings‡.
Foundation type: Independent foundation.
Financial data (yr. ended 05/31/13): Assets, $33,710,899 (M); expenditures, $2,289,524; qualifying distributions, $1,925,691; giving activities include $1,805,821 for 36 grants (high: $500,000; low: $1,000).
Purpose and activities: Giving exclusively for charitable purposes in advancing medical science, research, and education in selected cities in the U.S. and Canada, and for charitable work among underprivileged boys and girls, and aged and infirm persons in designated areas. Priority is given to medical proposals and capital projects, particularly for equipment needs of various kinds.
Fields of interest: Medical school/education; Hospitals (general); Biomedicine; Medical research, institute; Human services; Children/youth, services; Aging, centers/services; Aging; Economically disadvantaged.
International interests: Canada.
Type of support: Capital campaigns; Building/renovation; Equipment; Land acquisition; Seed money; Research; Matching/challenge support.
Limitations: Applications accepted. Giving limited to Toronto, Ontario, Canada, and to Hendersonville, NC, and Buffalo, NY. No support for national health organizations. No grants to individuals, or for annual campaigns, program support, endowment funds, operating budgets, program costs, emergency funds, deficit financing, scholarships, fellowships, publications, conferences, contingency reserves, or continuing support; no loans.
Publications: Annual report (including application guidelines).
Application information: Application form not required.
Initial approach: Preliminary letter (no more than 2 pages) or telephone inquiry is encouraged
Copies of proposal: 6
Deadline(s): 4 weeks prior to board meetings
Board meeting date(s): Quarterly, usually in Feb., May, Sept. and Dec.
Final notification: 1 to 4 weeks
Officers and Directors:* Charles F. Kreiner, Jr., Pres.; Richard C. Bryan, Jr., V.P.; Brigid Doherty, Secy. and Exec. Dir.; **William L. Joyce,* Treas.**; Christopher T. Greene; Robert J.A. Irwin; Theodore I. Putnam, M.D.
Number of staff: 1 part-time professional; 1 part-time support.
EIN: 160864200
Other changes: William L. Joyce has replaced Robert J.A. Irwin as Treas.

2121
The Nathan Cummings Foundation

475 10th Ave., 14th Fl.
New York, NY 10018-9715 (212) 787-7300
Contact: Ernest Tollerson, Interim C.E.O. and Pres.
FAX: (212) 787-7377;
E-mail: contact@nathancummings.org; Main URL: http://www.nathancummings.org
E-Newsletter: http://www.nathancummings.net/news/

Established in 1949 in IL.
Donor: Nathan Cummings‡.
Foundation type: Independent foundation.
Financial data (yr. ended 12/31/12): Assets, $407,948,470 (M); expenditures, $27,252,765; qualifying distributions, $24,330,693; giving activities include $18,799,000 for 286 grants (high: $600,000; low: $500), and $306,347 for foundation-administered programs.
Purpose and activities: The foundation is rooted in the Jewish tradition and committed to democratic values and social justice, including fairness, diversity, and community. It seeks to build a socially and economically just society that values nature and protects the ecological balance for future generations; promotes humane health care; and fosters arts and culture that enriches communities.
Fields of interest: Media/communications; Media, film/video; Media, television; Media, print publishing; Media, radio; Web-based media; Media, journalism; Performing arts (multimedia); Environment, alliance/advocacy; Environment, public policy; Environment, reform; Environment, climate change/global warming; Health care, alliance/advocacy; Health care, administration/regulation; Health care, public policy; Health care, reform; Health care, equal rights; Public health, environmental health; Health organizations, association; Civil/human rights, equal rights; Civil/human rights, advocacy; Civil rights, voter education; Civil liberties, advocacy; Labor rights; Environmental and resource rights; Religion, interfaith issues; Spirituality; African Americans/Blacks; Economically disadvantaged.
International interests: Israel.
Type of support: General/operating support; Management development/capacity building; Program development; Conferences/seminars; Seed money; Fellowships; Research; Program evaluation.
Limitations: Applications not accepted. Giving primarily in the U.S., with some support to work in Israel. No support for specific diseases, Holocaust-related projects, foreign-based organizations, or community based organizations that do not plan to replicate their program(s) regionally or nationally. No grants for scholarships, sponsorships, projects with no plans for replication, endowments or capital campaigns.
Publications: Annual report; Financial statement; Grants list; Newsletter; Occasional report; Program policy statement.
Application information: Unsolicited requests for funds not accepted. 2014 will be a transition year; see foundation web site for updates.
Board meeting date(s): Spring and fall
Officers and Trustees:* Adam N. Cummings,* Chair.; **James K. Cummings,* Vice-Chair.**; Ernest Tollerson,* Interim C.E.O. and Pres.; Bill Dempsey, Sr. V.P., Finance; **Maurine D. Knighton, Sr. V.P., Opers.**; **Jaimie Mayer Phinney,* Secy.**; **Roberta Friedman Cummings,* Treas.**; **Rahman Mohamad, Cont.**; Beatrice Cummings Mayer, Tr. Emeritus; **Hannah Cummings**; **Jason Cummings**; **Rick Cummings**; Ruth Cummings; Sonia Simon Cummings; Danielle Durchslag; **Sophal Ear**; Andrew Lee; **Jane M. Saks**; **Tricia Rose**.
Number of staff: 8 full-time professional; 12 full-time support; 1 part-time support.
EIN: 237093201
Other changes: Adam N. Cummings has replaced James K. Cummings as Chair. James K. Cummings has replaced Adam N. Cummings as Vice-Chair. Jaimie Mayer Phinney has replaced Sonia Simon Cummings as Secy. Roberta Friedman Cummings has replaced Andrew Lee as Treas.
Simon Greer is no longer C.E.O. and Pres. Michael A. Cummings, Ernest Tollerson and Rachel Durchslag are no longer trustees. Caroline L. Williams is no longer Exec. V.P.

2122
The Frances L. & Edwin L. Cummings Memorial Fund
501 5th Ave., Ste. 708
New York, NY 10017-7843 (212) 286-1778
Contact: Elizabeth H. Costas, Exec. Dir.
FAX: (212) 682-9458;
E-mail: info@cummingsfund.org; **All e-mail should be addressed to: Dottye Chew; Main URL: http://fdnweb.org/cummings**
Grants List: http://fdnweb.org/cummings/grants/year/2013/

Established in 1982 in NY.
Donors: Edwin L. Cummings†; Frances L. Cummings†.
Foundation type: Independent foundation.
Financial data (yr. ended 07/31/13): Assets, $34,408,951 (M); expenditures, $1,957,685; qualifying distributions, $1,826,104; giving activities include $1,494,000 for 54 grants (high: $45,000; low: $2,000).
Purpose and activities: The fund's primary interest is in the piloting or expansion of new, innovative programs of organizations operating in New York, NY, and its more urbanized surrounding areas in northeastern NJ (Bergen, Essex, Hudson, Passaic and Union counties). The fund has a particular interest in programs serving young people. Funding interests include 1) Education, especially programs that serve public school children from disadvantaged backgrounds, 2) Social welfare, especially programs addressing issues including child abuse, parent education, juvenile delinquency, teenage pregnancy, housing and homelessness, youth employment and job training, and 3) Health care, particularly for institutions and programs that serve economically and socially disadvantaged people.
Fields of interest: Elementary/secondary education; Elementary/secondary school reform; Vocational education; Adult education—literacy, basic skills & GED; Hospitals (general); Medical care, rehabilitation; Health care; Mental health/crisis services; Crime/violence prevention, youth; Crime/violence prevention, child abuse; Employment, services; Human services; Children/youth, services; Youth, pregnancy prevention; Child development, services; Family services, parent education; Children/youth; Youth; Young adults; Minorities; Economically disadvantaged; Homeless.
Type of support: Program development; Seed money; Technical assistance; Consulting services; Matching/challenge support.
Limitations: Applications accepted. Giving primarily in New York, NY and 5 counties in northeastern NJ (Bergen, Essex, Hudson, Passaic and Union). No support for cultural arts, alcoholism or drug addiction treatment programs, camping programs, day care programs for children and adults, environmental programs, private elementary and secondary schools, programs for senior citizens, soup kitchens and/or food banks, public policy and/or lobbying groups, well-endowed institutions, or legal aid programs. No grants to individuals, or for capital building campaigns, general operating support, moving expenses, conferences, media projects, publications, scholarships, public opinion polls and surveys, annual fundraising campaigns, or research conducted by individuals, soup kitchens and/or food banks, or for equipment.
Publications: IRS Form 990 or 990-PF printed copy available upon request.
Application information: The fund will consider up to 2 different requests at any given time. Proposals should be paginated and then clipped or stapled together, not permanently bound. Faxed or e-mailed proposals are not accepted. Application form not required.
Initial approach: Proposal, (with cover letter and brief executive summary) preferably no more than 7 pages. No more than 10 pages for those organizations submitting two requests. Send either U.S. mail or by messenger
Copies of proposal: 4
Deadline(s): Apr. 1 or Oct. 1
Board meeting date(s): June and Dec.
Final notification: 10 days following board meeting
Officers: Dorothy Riley-Chew, Secy.; Elizabeth Costas, Exec. Dir.
Trustees: J. Andrew Lark, Esq.; The BNY Mellon, N.A.
Board of Advisors: Sean Delany; Julie Floch; Anne Nordeman; Sarah Rosen.
Number of staff: 1 full-time professional; 1 full-time support.
EIN: 136814491
Other changes: Felton Johnson is no longer an advisor.

2123
Cutco Foundation Inc.
1116 E. State St.
Olean, NY 14760-3814
Contact: James M. Stitt, Jr., Treas.

Established in 1995 in NY.
Donors: Cutco Cutlery Corp.; Alcas Corp.; Vector Marketing Corp.; Cutco Cutlery; Mike Lancellot; Cutco Corporation; Cutco Cutlery.
Foundation type: Company-sponsored foundation.
Financial data (yr. ended 12/31/12): Assets, $4,051,417 (M); gifts received, $671,967; expenditures, $440,864; qualifying distributions, $438,620; giving activities include $438,620 for grants.
Purpose and activities: The foundation supports hospitals and community foundations and organizations involved with higher education.
Fields of interest: Higher education; Hospitals (general); Foundations (community).
Type of support: Capital campaigns; Building/renovation; Endowments; Scholarship funds; Matching/challenge support.
Limitations: Applications accepted. Giving primarily in Olean, NY. No grants to individuals.
Application information: Application form required.
Initial approach: Letter
Deadline(s): None
Officers: James E. Stitt, Chair.; John Whelpley, Secy.; James Stitt, Jr., Treas.
Directors: Brent Driscoll; Erick Laine; John Stitt.
EIN: 161491450

2124
Filomena M. D'Agostino Foundation
950 3rd Ave., 32nd Fl.
New York, NY 10022-2717 (212) 486-8615
Contact: David Malkin, V.P.

Established in 1990 in NY.
Donor: Filomena M. D'Agostino Greenberg.
Foundation type: Independent foundation.
Financial data (yr. ended 02/28/13): Assets, $27,116,080 (M); expenditures, $1,396,521; qualifying distributions, $1,317,433; giving activities include $1,312,500 for 25 grants (high: $350,000; low: $2,500).
Purpose and activities: Giving primarily for health organizations and medical research, children, youth and social services, museums, and to a law school.
Fields of interest: Media, television; Museums (art); Museums (natural history); Law school/education; Health organizations, association; Multiple sclerosis; Medical research, institute; Alzheimer's disease research; Human services; Children/youth, services; Blind/visually impaired.
Limitations: Giving primarily in New York, NY. No grants to individuals.
Application information: Application form not required.
***Initial approach:* Letter**
Deadline(s): None
Officers and Directors:* Max D'Agostino,* V.P.; David Malkin,* V.P.; **Lorene A. Corrado,* Co-Secy.-Treas.; Jessica A. Malkin,* Co-Secy.-Treas.**
EIN: 133548660
Other changes: Lorene A. Corrado is now Co-Secy.-Treas. Jessica A. Malkin is now Co-Secy.-Treas.

2125
The Dammann Fund, Inc.
521 5th Ave., 31st Fl.
New York, NY 10175-3300 (212) 956-4118
Contact: Penelope Johnston, Pres.
FAX: (212) 262-9321;
E-mail: df@engelanddavis.com; Main URL: http://www.thedammannfund.com/
Grants List: http://www.thedammannfund.com/jga.html

Incorporated in 1946 in NY.
Donor: Members of the Dammann family.
Foundation type: Independent foundation.
Financial data (yr. ended 11/30/13): Assets, $7,779,491 (M); expenditures, $518,856; qualifying distributions, $455,917; giving activities include $411,375 for 172 grants (high: $30,000; low: $125).
Purpose and activities: Giving primarily for teen parenthood programs and programs to foster independent living skills for the mentally ill.
Fields of interest: Mental health/crisis services; Children/youth, services; Family services.
Type of support: General/operating support; Continuing support; Program development; Seed money.
Limitations: Applications accepted. Giving primarily in the greater metropolitan New York, NY, area, including southern Fairfield County, CT; giving also in Charlottesville, VA. No grants to individuals, or for scholarships, fellowships, or matching gifts; no loans.
Publications: Application guidelines.
Application information: A sample Application Form and an application Checklist along with complete application guidelines are available on fund web site. Applicants are encouraged, although not required, to submit simultaneously, by e-mail, the "project description/funding request" portion of their application package. Application form required.
***Initial approach:* Submit application**
Copies of proposal: 1
***Deadline(s):* June 30 for Joint Gifts program**
Board meeting date(s): May/Jun and Oct./Nov.
***Final notification:* Dec. 1**
Officers and Directors:* Penelope Johnston,* Pres.; Christopher M. Kramer,* V.P.; Daniel R. Kramer, V.P.; John P. Engel, Secy.; Lorraine M. Callaghan, Treas.; Katherine S. Penna.
EIN: 136089896

2126
The Charles A. Dana Foundation, Inc.
(doing business as The Dana Foundation)
505 5th Ave., 6th Fl.
New York, NY 10017-4921
Contact: Burton M. Mirsky, V.P., Finance
FAX: (212) 317-8721; E-mail: danainfo@dana.org; E-mail for grants inquires: grantsinfo@dana.org; Main URL: http://www.dana.org
Blog: http://danapress.typepad.com/
Dana Foundation Blog Feed: http://feeds.feedburner.com/DanaFoundationBlog
E-Newsletter: http://www.dana.org/MemberLogin.aspx?ReturnUrl=%2fmembership%2fSubscriptions.aspx
Facebook: https://www.facebook.com/danafoundation
Knowledge Center: http://www.dana.org/AboutDana/WhatDanaDoes.aspx#Share_Knowledge
Master RSS News Feed: http://www.dana.org/rssfeeds/rssmaster.aspx
Podcasts: http://www.dana.org/podcasts.aspx
Twitter: http://twitter.com/dana_fdn
YouTube: http://www.youtube.com/channel/UC5M4LiJrdoLXelGlgJ0jydg

Incorporated in 1950 in CT.
Donors: Charles A. Dana‡; Eleanor Naylor Dana‡.
Foundation type: Independent foundation.
Financial data (yr. ended 12/31/12): Assets, $230,894,564 (M); expenditures, $22,395,824; qualifying distributions, $21,086,555; giving activities include $16,074,675 for 199 grants (high: $4,750,000; low: $2,500), $26,800 for employee matching gifts, and $4,995,202 for foundation-administered programs.
Purpose and activities: Principal interests are in health and science, particularly neuroscience.
Fields of interest: Neuroscience; Health organizations; Brain research; Medical research; Science.
Type of support: Research; Employee matching gifts.
Limitations: Applications accepted. Giving on a national basis. No grants to individuals, or for annual operating costs, deficit reduction, capital campaigns, or individual sabbaticals.
Publications: Application guidelines; Annual report (including application guidelines); Financial statement; Informational brochure (including application guidelines); Newsletter; Occasional report.
Application information: Please see the program pages on the foundation's web site for each programs application process and deadlines. Application form not required.
Deadline(s): Varies
Board meeting date(s): Apr. Sept., and Dec.
Final notification: Varies
Officers and Directors:* Edward F. Rover,* Chair. and Pres.; **Barbara E. Gill, Exec. V.P., Public Affairs; Burton M. Mirsky, Exec. V.P., Finance; Barbara Rich, Ed.D., Exec. V.P., Comms.**; Brigida C. Gay, Cont.; Edward Bleier; Wallace L. Cook; Charles A. Dana III; Steven E. Hyman, M.D.; Ann McLaughlin Korologos; LaSalle D. Leffall, M.D.; Hildegarde E. Mahoney; Peter A. Nadosy; Herbert J. Siegel.
Number of staff: 46
EIN: 066036761
Other changes: Barbara E. Gill is now Exec. V.P., Public Affairs. Barbara Rich is now Exec. V.P., Comms. Burton M. Mirsky is now Exec. V.P., Finance.

2127
The Daphne Foundation
25 E. 21st St.
New York, NY 10010 (212) 782-3711
Contact: Yvonne L. Moore, Exec. Dir.
FAX: (212) 228-5275;
E-mail: info@daphnefoundation.org; Main URL: http://www.daphnefoundation.org
Grants List: http://www.daphnefoundation.org/domestic-grantees.htm
The Daphne Foundation's Philanthropy Promise: http://www.ncrp.org/philanthropys-promise/who

Established in 1990 in CA and NY.
Donors: Abigail E. Disney; Pierre Hauser II.
Foundation type: Independent foundation.
Financial data (yr. ended 06/30/12): Assets, $8,004,355 (M); expenditures, $762,491; qualifying distributions, $708,530; giving activities include $572,120 for 17 grants (high: $90,000; low: $2,216).
Purpose and activities: The foundation funds programs that confront the causes and consequences of poverty in the 5 boroughs of New York City. The foundation has a particular interest in grassroots and emerging organizations which engage their members in the creation and implementation of long-term solutions to intractable social problems. The foundation believes it should fund in a manner that reinforces and facilitates the work of the programs it funds and that the most inventive and humane solutions to social problems often come from the people most affected by those problems.
Fields of interest: Education, reading; AIDS; Legal services; Children/youth, services; Family services; Women; Economically disadvantaged.
Type of support: Continuing support; General/operating support.
Limitations: Applications accepted. Giving limited to the five boroughs of New York City. No grants to individuals, or for capital campaigns.
Publications: Grants list.
Application information: Visit foundation web site for current application instructions. Application form required.
Board meeting date(s): May and Nov.
Officers and Directors:* Abigail E. Disney,* Co-Pres.; Pierre Hauser II,* Co-Pres.; Deborah S. Howes,* Secy.; Leah Doyle Coleman,* Treas.; Yvonne L. Moore, Exec. Dir.
Number of staff: 1 full-time professional.
EIN: 954288541

2128
The Peter Dartley Charitable Trust
c/o Pequot Capital Mgmt.
77 Bedford Rd.
Katonah, NY 10536-2141

Established in 1986 in CT and NY.
Donor: Peter Dartley.
Foundation type: Independent foundation.
Financial data (yr. ended 12/31/12): Assets, $4,956,158 (M); expenditures, $54,615; qualifying distributions, $45,000; giving activities include $45,000 for grants.
Purpose and activities: Giving primarily for children services, education, health organizations and human services.
Fields of interest: Higher education; Education; Health organizations; Human services; Children/youth, services.
Limitations: Applications not accepted. Giving in the U.S., with emphasis on New York, NY. No grants to individuals.
Application information: Contributes only to pre-selected organizations.
Trustees: Karen Dartley; Peter Dartley.
EIN: 133405097
Other changes: The grantmaker has moved from CT to NY.

2129
Sarah K. de Coizart Article TENTH Perpetual Charitable Trust
(formerly Sarah K. de Coizart Perpetual Charitable Trust)
c/o JPMorgan Private Bank, N.A., Private Foundation Svcs.
270 Park Ave., 16th Fl.
New York, NY 10017-2014
Contact: Casey Castaneda, Prog. Off.; Connie Giampapa, Prog. Off.
***E-mail:* casey.b.castaneda@jpmorgan.com**; E-mail for Connie Giampapa: connie.a.giampapa@jpmorgan.com; **Main URL: http://fdnweb.org/decoizart**
Grants List: http://fdnweb.org/decoizart/grants/year/2012/

Established in 1992 in NY.
Foundation type: Independent foundation.
Financial data (yr. ended 01/31/13): Assets, $33,604,023 (M); expenditures, $1,821,562; qualifying distributions, $1,723,301; giving activities include $1,551,000 for 24 grants (high: $376,000; low: $25,000).
Purpose and activities: Giving primarily for the environment and species conservation and for blindness-related services and research. Additional discretionary grants may be made to specific organizations and program areas that were of interest to Mrs. de Coizart.
Fields of interest: Environment, natural resources; Environmental education; Eye diseases; Eye research.
Type of support: Program development.
Limitations: Applications accepted. Giving primarily in the northeast region of the U.S. No support for organizations lacking 501(c)(3) status. No grants to individuals, or for matching gifts; no loans.
Publications: Application guidelines; Grants list.
Application information: All application materials must be submitted online. Grants range in size from $20,000 to $100,000 per year. See foundation web site for application guidelines and requirements. Application form required.
Initial approach: Proposal
Copies of proposal: 1
Deadline(s): Aug. 15 for proposals
Board meeting date(s): July and Dec.
Final notification: Jan.
Trustees: Richard Bartholome; JPMorgan Chase Bank, N.A.
EIN: 137046581
Other changes: The grantmaker has moved from TX to NY.

2130
Thompson Dean Family Foundation
c/o Regen, Benz & MacKenzie
57 W. 38th St., 3rd Fl.
New York, NY 10018-5500

Established in 1998 in NY.
Donor: Thompson Dean III.

Foundation type: Independent foundation.
Financial data (yr. ended 12/31/12): Assets, $8,568,405 (M); gifts received, $6,378,933; expenditures, $2,122,014; qualifying distributions, $2,120,120; giving activities include $2,090,000 for 19 grants (high: $725,000; low: $5,000).
Fields of interest: Higher education; Education; Human services.
Type of support: General/operating support.
Limitations: Applications not accepted. Giving primarily in MA, NY and VA. No grants to individuals.
Application information: Contributes only to pre-selected organizations.
Officers and Directors:* Thompson Dean III,* Chair.; Caroline W. Dean,* Pres.; Hume R. Steyer, Secy.
EIN: 133942201

2131
The Ira W. DeCamp Foundation

c/o JPMorgan Chase Bank, Fdn. Svcs.
270 Park Ave., 16th Fl.
New York, NY 10017
Contact: Contact for Community Health: Casey Castaneda, Prog. Off.; Contact for Foster Care: Connie Giampapa, Prog. Off.; Contact for Workforce Development: Jonathan Horowitz, Prog. Off
Main URL: **http://fdnweb.org/decamp**
Grants List: http://fdnweb.org/decamp/grants/year/contributions/

Trust established in 1970 in NY.
Donor: Elizabeth DeCamp McInerny‡.
Foundation type: Independent foundation.
Financial data (yr. ended 10/31/12): Assets, $76,099,444 (M); expenditures, $3,217,390; qualifying distributions, $2,924,394; giving activities include $2,565,000 for 31 grants (high: $200,000; low: $40,000).
Purpose and activities: Grants for community-based health care, foster care, and workforce development.
Fields of interest: Health care; Employment; Children, foster care.
Type of support: Capital campaigns; Management development/capacity building; Program development.
Limitations: Applications accepted. Giving primarily in New York, NY. No support for private foundations. No grants to individuals, or for general support, land acquisition, matching gifts, publications, conferences, endowment funds, operating budgets, continuing support, annual campaigns, emergency funds, scholarships, fellowships, or deficit financing; no loans.
Publications: Application guidelines; Grants list.
Application information: All application materials must be submitted online. See foundation web site for full application requirements. Application form not required.
Initial approach: Proposal (3 pages maximum) to be submitted online via foundation web site
Copies of proposal: 1
Deadline(s): Mar. 15
Board meeting date(s): July and Oct.
Final notification: Summer
Trustee: JPMorgan Chase, N.A.
EIN: 510138577

2132
The Deerfield Partnership Foundation

780 3rd Ave., 37th Fl.
New York, NY **10017-2024 (212) 551-1600**
Contact: **Allison Schultz, Secy.**
FAX: **(212) 599-3075;**
E-mail: aschultz@deerfield.com; Main URL: http://www.deerfield.com/Foundation.aspx

Established in 2005 in NY.
Donor: Deerfield Management Company.
Foundation type: Company-sponsored foundation.
Financial data (yr. ended 12/31/12): Assets, $3,856,598 (M); gifts received, $1,919,432; expenditures, $2,721,242; qualifying distributions, $2,522,073; giving activities include $2,502,535 for 15 grants (high: $725,000; low: $13,080).
Purpose and activities: The foundation supports programs designed to invest in healthcare for those in need on a local and a global scale. Special emphasis is directed toward programs that benefit children.
Fields of interest: Secondary school/education; Education; Hospitals (general); Health care, clinics/centers; Health care; Family services; Homeless, human services; Human services; Children.
Type of support: General/operating support; Continuing support; Program development.
Limitations: Applications not accepted. Giving primarily in New York, NY.
Publications: Newsletter.
Application information: Contributes only to pre-selected organizations.
Officers: Alexander Kristofcak, Chair.; Terence Kamal, Pres.; Karen Arnone, V.P.; **Nelson Barriocanal, V.P.; Brian Bizoza, V.P.; Alex Kamal, V.P.**; Allison Schultz, Secy.; Cristina Hohlman, Treas.
EIN: 050618950
Other changes: Alexander Kristofcak has replaced April Tubbs as Chair. Alexander Kristofcak has replaced April Tubbs as Chair.
April Tubbs is no longer Chair. Daniel Glass, Adam Greene, Paul Takats, and Elise Wang are no longer V.P.'s. Jeffrey Kaplan is no longer Secy. Allison Miyake is no longer Treas.

2133
Lydia Collins deForest Charitable Trust

c/o U.S. Trust, Bank of America Private Wealth Mgmt.
1 Bryant Park NY1-100-28-05
New York, NY 10036
Contact: Ken Goody
E-mail: kenneth.l.goody@ustrust.com; **E-mail to discuss application process of for questions: ny.grantmaking@ustrust.com**; Main URL: http://www.bankofamerica.com/grantmaking

Established in 2002 in NJ.
Donor: Lydia Collins deForest‡.
Foundation type: Independent foundation.
Financial data (yr. ended 02/28/13): Assets, $9,598,057 (M); expenditures, $537,226; qualifying distributions, $478,555; giving activities include $430,000 for 19 grants (high: $50,000; low: $5,000).
Purpose and activities: The trust supports organizations that provide services to those who are visually limited, churches and organizations affiliated with the Protestant Episcopal Church in the United States and other religious organizations in union with or recognized by the Episcopal Church, and organizations that provide services to those who are homeless, unemployed, or substance-dependent.
Fields of interest: Education; Substance abuse, services; Employment, services; Human services; Salvation Army; Family services; Protestant agencies & churches; Blind/visually impaired.
Limitations: Applications accepted. Giving primarily in NJ and in the greater New York, NY metropolitan area. No grants to individuals.
Publications: Application guidelines.
Application information:
Deadline(s): **Nov. 30**
Final notification: **Feb. 28**
Trustees: Robert B. Bourne; Jean F. Marano; Bank of America, N.A.
EIN: 030433603

2134
Deutsche Bank Americas Foundation

(formerly BT Foundation)
60 Wall St., NYC60-2312
New York, NY 10005-2858
FAX: (212) 797-2255; Main URL: http://www.db.com/us/content/en/1066.html
Grants List: https://www.db.com/usa/docs/2012_Americas_Philanthropic_Grants_FINAL.pdf
Twitter: http://twitter.com/DBFoundation

Established in 1986 in NY.
Donors: Bankers Trust Co.; BT Capital Corp.; Deutsche Bank Americas Holding Corp.
Foundation type: Company-sponsored foundation.
Financial data (yr. ended 12/31/12): Assets, $26,436,075 (M); gifts received, $11,843,785; expenditures, $12,054,238; qualifying distributions, $13,798,449; giving activities include $8,030,500 for 277 grants (high: $250,000; low: $500), $3,950,285 for 2,652 employee matching gifts, and $1,810,000 for loans/program-related investments.
Purpose and activities: The foundation supports organizations involved with the environment, health, employment, affordable housing, disaster relief, human services, youth, minorities, immigrants, and economically disadvantaged people. Special emphasis is directed toward programs designed to encourage sustainable community development; promote wider access to quality education; and foster the arts to enrich areas where Deutsche Bank does business.
Fields of interest: Visual arts; Museums; Museums (art); Performing arts, music; Arts; Elementary/secondary education; Higher education; Education, services; Education, e-learning; Education; Environment, climate change/global warming; Environment, energy; Environment; Hospitals (general); Optometry/vision screening; Employment, training; Employment; Housing/shelter, development; Housing/shelter; Disasters, preparedness/services; YM/YWCAs & YM/YWHAs; Children/youth, services; Human services, financial counseling; Homeless, human services; Human services; Community development, neighborhood development; Business/industry; Community development, small businesses; Community/economic development; Mathematics; Engineering/technology; Science; Youth; Minorities; Immigrants/refugees; Economically disadvantaged.
International interests: Canada; Latin America.
Type of support: General/operating support; Continuing support; Management development/capacity building; Building/renovation; Program development; Seed money; Curriculum development; Technical assistance; Employee volunteer services; Sponsorships; Program-related investments/loans; Employee matching gifts; Matching/challenge support; Mission-related investments/loans.
Limitations: Applications accepted. Giving on a national basis in areas of company operations with emphasis on NY, Argentina, Brazil, Canada, Chile, Latin America, Mexico, and Peru. No support for

political candidates, veterans', military, or fraternal organizations, United Way agencies not providing a fundraising waiver, professional or trade associations, discriminatory organizations, organizations that employ adversarial and/or confrontational tactics, or organizations that are not in full compliance with anti-terrorism laws. No grants to individuals, or for endowments, capital campaigns, legal advocacy, or religious purposes.
Publications: Application guidelines; Corporate giving report; Newsletter.
Application information: Letters of intent should not exceed 3 pages in length. A full proposal may be requested at a later date. The foundation utilizes a Request for Proposal (RFP) process for most programs. Support is limited to 3 years in length. Application form not required.
Initial approach: Letter of intent
Deadline(s): None
Officers and Directors:* Seth Waugh,* Chair.; Gary S. Hattem,* Pres.; **Nicole Rodriguez Leach, V.P.**; **Sam Marks, V.P.**; Alessandra Digiusto, Secy.-Treas. and C.A.O.; Jorge Arce; Gary Beyer; Jacques Brand; Robert Dibble; Christopher Habig; Frank Kelly; Roelfien Kuijpers; Erich Mauff; Jeffrey Mayer; Joseph Polizzotto; Akbar Poonawala.
Number of staff: 3 full-time professional; 3 full-time support.
EIN: 133321736
Other changes: Richard Walker is no longer a director.

2135
The Robert & Jennifer Diamond Family Foundation
c/o Clarfeld Financial Advisors, Inc.
560 White Plains Rd., 5th Fl.
Tarrytown, NY 10591-5113

Established in 2003 in DE.
Donor: Robert E. Diamond, Jr.
Foundation type: Independent foundation.
Financial data (yr. ended 03/31/13): Assets, $6,382,691 (M); expenditures, $1,506,303; qualifying distributions, $1,432,030; giving activities include $1,432,030 for 12 grants (high: $773,058; low: $20,000).
Fields of interest: Higher education; Education.
Type of support: Continuing support; Annual campaigns; Capital campaigns; Building/ renovation; Fellowships; Scholarship funds.
Limitations: Applications not accepted. Giving in the U.S., with emphasis on ME; some giving also in the U.K. No grants to individuals.
Application information: Contributes only to pre-selected organizations.
Directors: Jennifer Diamond; Nell Diamond; Robert E. Diamond, Jr.; Robert E. Diamond III; Teresa Jane Taylor; Paul Wrobleski.
EIN: 200618456
Other changes: The grantmaker no longer lists a phone.
At the close of 2013, the grantmaker paid grants of $1,432,030, a 568.4% increase over the 2012 disbursements, $214,235.

2136
Irene Diamond Fund
750 3rd Ave.
New York, NY **10017-2703**
Contact: Jane Silver, Pres.

Established in 1994 in NY.
Donor: Irene Diamond†.
Foundation type: Independent foundation.
Financial data (yr. ended 12/31/12): Assets, $45,565,329 (M); expenditures, $55,705,684; qualifying distributions, $52,910,465; giving activities include $52,171,755 for grants.
Purpose and activities: Giving for pre-determined projects in New York, NY, for medical research on HIV/AIDS and immunology, human rights and for the performing arts.
Fields of interest: Arts; Medical research; Civil/ human rights.
Limitations: Applications not accepted. Giving primarily in NY. No grants to individuals.
Application information: Contributes only to pre-selected organizations.
Officers and Board Members:* Jane Silver,* Pres. and Secy,; Peter Kimmelman,* Treas.
Number of staff: 1 full-time professional; 1 part-time professional; 1 full-time support; 1 part-time support.
EIN: 132678431
Other changes: Joseph Polisi is no longer V.P. Yvette Neier is no longer Secy. Jane Silver is now Pres. and Secy, .

2137
The Diller-von Furstenberg Family Foundation
(doing business as The Diller Foundation)
c/o Sarah Knutson, Arrow Investments, Inc.
555 W. 18th St., 2nd Fl.
New York, NY 10011-2822
Barry Diller and Diane von Furstenberg's Giving Pledge Profile: http://glasspockets.org/philanthropy-in-focus/eye-on-the-giving-pledge/profiles/diller

Established in 1986 in CA.
Donors: Barry Diller; Ranger Investments, L.P.
Foundation type: Independent foundation.
Financial data (yr. ended 12/31/12): Assets, $50,016,678 (M); gifts received, $42,389,954; expenditures, $9,735,597; qualifying distributions, $9,617,122; giving activities include $9,597,284 for 91 grants (high: $2,000,000; low: $1,000).
Purpose and activities: Giving primarily for health care and health associations, as well as to hospitals, including children's hospitals; funding also for education, the arts, and children, youth and social services.
Fields of interest: Arts, alliance/advocacy; Media/ communications; Performing arts, theater; Arts; Elementary/secondary education; Higher education; Education; Hospitals (general); Health care; Health organizations, association; Cancer; AIDS; Cancer, leukemia research; Human services; Children/ youth, services; Foundations (private grantmaking).
Type of support: Research.
Limitations: Applications not accepted. Giving primarily in CA and New York, NY. No grants to individuals.
Application information: Contributes only to pre-selected organizations.
Officers and Directors:* Barry Diller,* Pres.; Alexandre Von Furstenberg,* Secy.; **Diane Von Furstenberg; Tatiana Von Furstenberg.**
EIN: 954081892
Other changes: At the close of 2012, the fair market value of the grantmaker's assets was $50,016,678, a 330.3% increase over the 2011 value, $11,622,562. For the same period, the grantmaker paid grants of $9,597,284, a 55.1% increase over the 2011 disbursements, $6,188,746.

2138
The DiMenna Foundation, Inc.
(formerly The DiMenna Family Foundation, Inc.)
10 E. 67th St.
New York, NY 10065-5805

Established in 1998 in CT and NY.
Donor: Joseph A. DiMenna.
Foundation type: Independent foundation.
Financial data (yr. ended 12/31/12): Assets, $23,675,509 (M); expenditures, $1,367,664; qualifying distributions, $1,290,455; giving activities include $1,270,000 for 1 grant.
Fields of interest: Museums; Elementary/ secondary education; Education; Hospitals (general); Human services; Community/economic development.
Limitations: Applications not accepted. Giving primarily in New York, NY; some funding also in Memphis, TN. No grants to individuals.
Application information: Contributes only to pre-selected organizations.
Officers: Joseph A. DiMenna, Pres.; Kevin P. Cannon, Secy.
Director: Diana DiMenna.
EIN: 061534269
Other changes: At the close of 2012, the grantmaker paid grants of $1,270,000, an 81.4% increase over the 2010 disbursements, $700,000.

2139
The Discount Foundation
115 S. Oxford St., No. 569
Brooklyn, NY 11217-1607 (646) 558-6020
Contact: Susan Wefald, Exec. Dir.
E-mail: hallen@discountfoundation.org; Main URL: http://www.discountfoundation.org
Grants Database: http://www.discountfoundation.org/search_grants
The Discount Foundation's Philanthropy Promise: http://www.ncrp.org/philanthropys-promise/who

Established in 1977.
Donors: Jeffrey W. Zinsmeyer; Garfield Trust.
Foundation type: Independent foundation.
Financial data (yr. ended 09/30/12): Assets, $4,425,988 (M); expenditures, $1,314,931; qualifying distributions, $1,268,513; giving activities include $997,500 for 33 grants (high: $40,000; low: $5,000).
Purpose and activities: Giving primarily to improve job opportunities, wages, and benefits for poor and working people, including workfare participants; empower poor and working people by strengthening their collective institutions, specifically community-based organizations, churches and congregations, and labor organizations, and encouraging relationships among these institutions; and advance innovative public policies designed to secure jobs with livable wages, benefits, and career opportunities for poor and working people.
Fields of interest: Employment; Community/ economic development; Public policy, research; Minorities; African Americans/Blacks; Immigrants/ refugees; Economically disadvantaged; Homeless.
Type of support: General/operating support.
Limitations: Applications not accepted. Giving on a national basis. No support for government agencies, schools, or religious programs. No grants to individuals, or for capital campaigns or projects, endowments, publications, research projects, or tours or trips.
Application information: Unsolicited requests for funds are currently not accepted. Refer to foundation web site for updates in this area.

Officers and Directors:* Jeffrey W. Zinsmeyer,* Pres. and Treas.; Thomas R. Asher,* Secy.; Susan Wefald, Exec. Dir.; Deepak Bhargava; Sarita Gupta; Angelica Sala; Margery A. Tabankin; Dorian Warren.
Number of staff: 1 part-time professional.
EIN: 521095120
Other changes: Jeffrey W. Zinsmeyer is now Pres. and Treas. Thomas R. Asher is now Secy.

2140
Dobkin Family Foundation
c/o BCRS Assocs., LLC
77 Water St., 9th Fl.
New York, NY 10005-4401

Established in 1984 in NY.
Donors: Eric S. Dobkin; Barbara Dobkin.
Foundation type: Independent foundation.
Financial data (yr. ended 03/31/13): Assets, $48,752,367 (M); expenditures, $8,272,447; qualifying distributions, $7,046,697; giving activities include $6,740,983 for 196 grants (high: $1,000,000; low: $200).
Purpose and activities: Giving primarily to Jewish organizations and higher education, and for human services.
Fields of interest: Museums; Arts; Higher education; Health organizations, association; Human services; Women, centers/services; Jewish federated giving programs; Jewish agencies & synagogues; Women.
International interests: Israel.
Type of support: General/operating support.
Limitations: Applications not accepted. Giving primarily in New York, NY. No grants to individuals.
Application information: Contributes only to pre-selected organizations.
Trustees: Barbara Dobkin; Eric S. Dobkin; Rachel L. Dobkin.
EIN: 133248042
Other changes: For the fiscal year ended Mar. 31, 2013, the grantmaker paid grants of $6,741,003, an 82.4% increase over the fiscal 2012 disbursements, $3,696,513.

2141
Mike and Evelyn Donatelli Foundation
New York, NY

The foundation terminated in 2013.

2142
The William H. Donner Foundation
520 White Plains Rd., Ste. 500
Tarrytown, NY **10591-5118 (914) 524-0404**
Contact: Deirdre Feeney, Prog. Mgr.
***FAX:* (914) 524-0407**; E-mail: dfeeney@donner.org; Additional tel.: (212) 949-5213; Main URL: http://www.donner.org

Incorporated in 1961 in DC.
Donor: William H. Donner†.
Foundation type: Independent foundation.
Financial data (yr. ended 10/31/12): Assets, $141,834,905 (M); expenditures, $6,827,635; qualifying distributions, $4,920,452; giving activities include $4,380,659 for 138 grants (high: $100,000; low: $1,000).
Purpose and activities: Giving primarily for international development and relief services, education, arts and culture, and public affairs.
Fields of interest: Arts; Elementary/secondary education; Education; Animals/wildlife; Human services; International development; International relief; International affairs; Philanthropy/voluntarism; Public affairs.
Type of support: General/operating support; Program development.
Limitations: Applications not accepted. Giving primarily in CA, CO, Washington, DC and NY, with some giving in VA.
Application information: Only applications invited by the foundation will be considered.
Board meeting date(s): Sept.
Officers and Trustees:* Joseph W. Donner III,* Pres.; **Rebecca D. Winsor,* V.P.; William M. Spencer III,* Secy.; Alexander B. Donner,* Treas.**; Alexander B. Donner, Esq.; David W. Donner; Deborah Donner; Joseph W. Donner, Jr.; Timothy E. Donner; Anita Winsor Edwards; Stephanie K. Hanson; Sharon W. Lainhant; Brittany D. Roy; Dillon Roy; M. Hunter Spencer; Robert D. Spencer; Hon. Curtin Winsor, Jr.; Monica Winsor.
Number of staff: 1 full-time professional; 3 part-time professional; 1 full-time support; 1 part-time support.
EIN: 231611346
Other changes: Rebecca D. Winsor has replaced Cristina S. Winsor as V.P. Alexander B. Donner has replaced Rebecca D. Winsor as Treas. William M. Spencer, III is now Secy. Christopher K. Roosevelt is no longer a trustee.

2143
Dramatists Guild Fund, Inc.
1501 Broadway
New York, NY 10036-5601 **(212) 391-8384**
***Contact:* Rachel Routh, Exec. Dir.**
FAX: (212) 202-4093;
E-mail: rrouth@dramatistsguild.com; Main URL: http://www.dramatistsguildfund.org/

Established in 1962 in NY.
Donors: Charlotte Kesselring†; Sidney S. Kingsley Fund; James Kirkwood†; Loewe Foundation; Howard Lindsay†; Flora Roberts Foundation.
Foundation type: Independent foundation.
Financial data (yr. ended 12/31/11): Assets, $3,237,395 (M); gifts received, $175,279; expenditures, $622,428; qualifying distributions, $226,272; giving activities include $158,050 for 115 grants (high: $5,000; low: $500), and $48,222 for 37 grants to individuals (high: $3,000; low: $400).
Purpose and activities: Support for theater companies and workshops producing new works; also provides loans-in-aid to support playwrights who have had their work produced or published.
Fields of interest: Performing arts, theater; Economically disadvantaged.
Type of support: General/operating support; Emergency funds.
Limitations: Applications accepted. Giving on a national basis.
Publications: Informational brochure.
Application information: Application form required.
Initial approach: Letter or telephone
Copies of proposal: 1
Board meeting date(s): Apr.
Officers and Directors:* Gretchen Cryer, Pres.; Carol Hall,* V.P.; Tina Howe,* Secy.; Paula Wilson,* Treas.; Joe Brerman; Susan Birkenhead; Kirsten Childs; Joan Firestone; Shirley Lauro; Patrick Morrow; Peter Ratray.
Number of staff: 2 full-time professional.
EIN: 136144932

2144
Dreitzer Foundation Inc.
c/o Alan Seget, Esq.
60 E. 42nd St.
New York, NY 10165-0009

Established in 1958 in NY.
Donors: Albert J. Dreitzer†; Mildred H. Dreitzer†.
Foundation type: Independent foundation.
Financial data (yr. ended 12/31/12): Assets, $8,129,058 (M); expenditures, $509,016; qualifying distributions, $450,000; giving activities include $450,000 for 18 grants (high: $100,000; low: $10,000).
Purpose and activities: Giving primarily for the arts, education, and human services.
Fields of interest: Arts; Elementary/secondary education; Education; Human services; Children/youth, services; Homeless, human services; Women.
Type of support: General/operating support.
Limitations: Applications not accepted. Giving primarily in New York, NY.
Application information: Contributes only to pre-selected organizations.
Officers: Judith Wallach, Pres.; Steven Halpern, V.P.; Amy Laff, V.P.; Diane Wallach, V.P.; Alan D. Seget, Secy.-Treas.
EIN: 136162509
Other changes: Sylvan Wallach is no longer a V.P.

2145
Jean and Louis Dreyfus Foundation, Inc.
315 Madison Ave., Ste. 900
New York, NY 10017-5405 (212) 599-1931
Contact: Ms. Edmee de M. Firth, Exec. Dir.
FAX: (212) 599-2956; **E-mail: jk@jldreyfus.org; Main URL: http://www.jldreyfus.org**
Grants List: http://www.jldreyfus.org/recentgrants.html

Incorporated about 1979 in NY.
Donor: Louis Dreyfus†.
Foundation type: Independent foundation.
Financial data (yr. ended 12/31/12): Assets, $15,612,687 (M); expenditures, $888,335; qualifying distributions, $788,441; giving activities include $645,000 for 43 grants (high: $50,000; low: $5,000).
Purpose and activities: Giving primarily for aging, the arts, education and social services.
Fields of interest: Arts; Adult education—literacy, basic skills & GED; Education, reading; Education; Health care; Employment, training; Nutrition; Housing/shelter, homeless; Human services; Children/youth, services; Aging, centers/services; Women, centers/services; Aging; Economically disadvantaged.
Type of support: General/operating support; Capital campaigns; Program development; Matching/challenge support.
Limitations: Giving limited to New York, NY. No grants to individuals.
Publications: Application guidelines; Annual report; Grants list.
Application information: Letters of inquiry are currently only accepted from organizations that have a prior relationship with the foundation. All other inquires will not be accepted at this time. Refer to foundation web site for updates in this area.
Initial approach: Letter of inquiry (1-2 pages) from organizations familiar to the foundation
Deadline(s): Jan. 15 and July 15
Board meeting date(s): May and Nov.

Officers and Directors:* Nicholas L.D. Firth,* Pres.; Katherine V. Firth,* V.P.; Edmee de M. Firth,* Exec. Dir.; Karen L. Rosa; Winthrop Rutherfurd, Jr.
Number of staff: 1 part-time professional; 1 full-time support.
EIN: 132947180

2146
Doris Duke Charitable Foundation
650 5th Ave., 19th Fl.
New York, NY 10019-6108 (212) 974-7000
FAX: (212) 974-7590; Main URL: http://www.ddcf.org
Grants Database: http://www.ddcf.org/Grants/Grant-Recipients/
Twitter: http://twitter.com/DorisDukeFdn

Established in 1996 in NY.
Donor: Doris Duke†.
Foundation type: Independent foundation.
Financial data (yr. ended 12/31/12): Assets, $1,726,653,990 (M); expenditures, $95,724,516; qualifying distributions, $86,576,154; giving activities include $77,659,983 for 230 grants (high: $4,155,000; low: $2,500), and $181,285 for 4 foundation-administered programs.
Purpose and activities: The mission of the foundation is to improve the quality of people's lives through grants supporting the performing arts, environmental conservation, medical research and the prevention of child abuse. In addition to its grantmaking activities, the foundation will support three affiliated operating foundations: Duke Farms Foundation, the Doris Duke Foundation for Islamic Art, and the Newport Restoration Foundation.
Fields of interest: Performing arts; Performing arts, dance; Performing arts, theater; Performing arts, music; Environment, natural resources; Animals/wildlife, preservation/protection; Medical research; Crime/violence prevention, child abuse.
Type of support: Employee matching gifts.
Limitations: Applications accepted. Giving on a national basis. No support for toxic issues, litigation, the visual arts, museums or galleries, or arts programs for rehabilitative or therapeutic purposes. No grants to individuals (except through special foundation programs), or for conferences or publications.
Application information: The foundation staff responds to all letters of inquiry, however, it should be noted that very few grants result from unsolicited letters of inquiry. Do not send binders, books, CDs, videotapes, or audiotapes.
Initial approach: Online Letter of inquiry (2 pages)
Final notification: 2 months for letter of inquiry
Officers and Trustees:* John E. Zuccotti,* Chair.; Anthony S. Fauci, M.D., Vice-Chair.; Peter Simmons, C.O.O.; Edward P. Henry, Pres.; Eileen Oberlander, Cont. and Dir., Finance; Jeffrey Heil, C.I.O.; Marion Oates Charles, Emeritus; Anne Hawley, Emeritus; John J. Mack, Emeritus; Harry B. Demopoulos, M.D.; James F. Gill; Kathy Halbreich; Nannerl O. Keohane; Angela K. Mwanza; Peter A. Nadosy; William H. Schlesinger; Nicholas Scoppetta; Jide Zeitlin.
EIN: 137043679
Other changes: John E. Zuccotti has replaced Nannerl O. Keohane as Chair.
Edward P. Henry is now Pres. Peter Simmons is now C.O.O.

2147
East Hill Foundation
17 Island St.
P.O. Box 547
North Tonawanda, NY 14120-5705 **(716) 204-0204, ext. 201**
Contact: Michele R. Schmidt
***FAX:* (716) 694-6353;**
E-mail: mschmidt@easthillfdn.org; Additional e-mail: info@easthillfdn.org; Main URL: http://www.easthillfdn.org

Established in 1986 in NY.
Donors: Eleanor Greatbatch; Warren Greatbatch.
Foundation type: Independent foundation.
Financial data (yr. ended 12/31/12): Assets, $20,754,241 (M); gifts received, $1,009; expenditures, $1,657,290; qualifying distributions, $1,356,839; giving activities include $916,390 for 59 grants (high: $100,000; low: $1,000), and $250,900 for 1 foundation-administered program.
Purpose and activities: The foundation is currently concentrating on projects that serve basic human needs for the Western New York community.
Fields of interest: Arts; Education; Animal welfare; Health care; Youth development.
Type of support: Building/renovation; Equipment; Program development.
Limitations: Applications accepted. Giving primarily in the eight counties of Allegany, Cattaraugus, Chautauqua, Erie, Genesee, Niagara, Orleans and Wyoming of western NY. No support for religious organizations for direct religious purposes. No grants to individuals, or for endowments, technology, private education, scholarships, salaries or travel expenses.
Publications: Application guidelines; Grants list; Informational brochure (including application guidelines).
Application information: Refer to foundation web site for specific application guidelines which must be followed. Applications sent by fax are not considered. Application form required.
***Initial approach:* Use online application process on foundation web site**
***Deadline(s):* See foundation web site for current deadline**
Board meeting date(s): Semiannually
Officers: Warren D. Greatbatch, Pres.; Ami Greatbatch, V.P.; John E. Siegel, Secy.-Treas.
Directors: Tommie Greatbatch; Marcinda Martin; Jenny Pierce; Julia Spitz.
Number of staff: 1 full-time professional.
EIN: 161441497
Other changes: The grantmaker now publishes application guidelines.

2148
Eastern Star Hall and Home Foundation, Inc.
c/o Pounder Hall
1400 Utica St., P.O. Box 106
Oriskany, NY 13424-0106

Established in 1986 in NY.
Donors: Hilda Brooks†; Mildred Niley†; Althea Julson†; Geraldine Bear†; Lucile Sotherden; Dors S. Bliss†; Natalie Hermann†; Kathryn Martin†; Marilyn Castleman†; Martha Burdick†; Tucker Anthony; Essig Family Trust; Mildred Schneider†; Iris Casey Trust; Helen Bronk; A. Somers Gardner Trust; Anna Mae Stewart†; Order of the Eastern Star; Clifford Scarlett†; Trustees of the Eastern Star Hall; Elia Juchter†; Gladys Hart†; Thelma Seavey Trust; Ann Alsheimen†; John Cole†; J. Bleich Kolhmeir; W.H. Albery Society.
Foundation type: Independent foundation.
Financial data (yr. ended 06/30/13): Assets, $9,303,137 (M); gifts received, $23,380; expenditures, $1,554,907; qualifying distributions, $1,438,535; giving activities include $1,438,535 for grants.
Fields of interest: Human services; Residential/custodial care, senior continuing care; Aging.
Type of support: Endowments.
Limitations: Applications not accepted. Giving primarily in Oriskany, NY. No grants to individuals.
Publications: Annual report.
Application information: Contributes only to pre-selected organizations.
Board meeting date(s): Apr., July, Oct., and Dec.
Officers: Karen Marshall-King, Pres.; **Burniece Herendeen, Recording Secy.**
Directors: John Butcher; Sally Clarke; Ruth Howe; **Isabelle Keuther**; **Ronald Myers.**
EIN: 133458370
Other changes: Lois Carlsen is no longer Chair. Raymond Heim and Linda Angiolillo are no longer directors.

2149
Fred Ebb Foundation
40 W. 20th St., 11th Fl.
New York, NY 10011-4211
E-mail: info@fredebbfoundation.org; Main URL: http://www.fredebbfoundation.org
Application address: c/o Roundabout Theatre, 231 W. 39th St., Ste. 1200, New York, NY 10018

Established in 2005 in NY.
Donor: Fred Ebb†.
Foundation type: Operating foundation.
Financial data (yr. ended 12/31/12): Assets, $27,821,621 (M); expenditures, $1,542,112; qualifying distributions, $1,542,112; giving activities include $1,300,000 for 1 grant, and $50,000 for 1 grant to an individual.
Purpose and activities: The foundation provides an annual award to one or more persons working in the field of musical theater as composers and/or lyricists. Funding also for Broadway Cares/Equity Fights AIDS.
Fields of interest: Performing arts, theater (musical); AIDS.
Type of support: Grants to individuals.
Limitations: Applications accepted. Giving primarily in New York, NY.
Application information: Applications only accepted for musical theater award and are accepted by mail or delivery. See foundation web site for guidelines and application form in this area. Contributes only to pre-selected organizations for grants. Application form required.
***Deadline(s):* Applications accepted June 2-30**
Final notification: Nov.
Officer: Mitchell Bernard, Pres.
EIN: 202184998

2150
Einhorn Family Charitable Trust
c/o Greenlight Capital, Inc.
140 E. 45th St., 24th Fl.
New York, NY 10017-7142
Contact: David Einhorn, Tr.

Established in 2002 in NY.
Donors: David Einhorn; Cheryl Einhorn.
Foundation type: Independent foundation.
Financial data (yr. ended 12/31/12): Assets, $6,508,888 (M); gifts received, $31,352,000;

expenditures, $26,161,878; qualifying distributions, $26,495,144; giving activities include $24,936,333 for 53 grants (high: $4,869,491; low: $100), $2,082 for 17 employee matching gifts, and $333,333 for 1 loan/program-related investment.
Fields of interest: Higher education; International affairs; Foundations (private grantmaking); Jewish agencies & synagogues.
Type of support: Program-related investments/ loans.
Limitations: Applications not accepted. Giving primarily in NY. No grants to individuals.
Application information: Contributes only to pre-selected organizations.
Officers: Harry Bradler, C.F.O.; Jennifer Hoos Rothberg, Exec. Dir.
Trustees: Cheryl Einhorn; David Einhorn.
EIN: 226921358
Other changes: At the close of 2012, the grantmaker paid grants of $24,938,415, a 66.2% increase over the 2011 disbursements, $15,003,812.

2151
EMB Foundation, Ltd.
2621 Ave. N
Brooklyn, NY 11210-5228
Contact: Alex Gonter, Mgr.

Established in 1997 in NY.
Donors: Alex Gonter; Joel Gonter; Mark Gonter; Neil Gonter; Shlomo Gonter; Steven Oppenheimer; Mark Steiger; Sam Tropper.
Foundation type: Independent foundation.
Financial data (yr. ended 12/31/13): Assets, $28,085 (M); gifts received, $141,437; expenditures, $148,037; qualifying distributions, $148,037; giving activities include $148,037 for 1 + grant.
Application information: Application form not required.
Initial approach: **Proposal**
Deadline(s): None
Officer: Alex Gonter, Mgr.
EIN: 113393489

2152
The Eppley Foundation for Research, Inc.
Box 359
244 Madison Ave.
New York, NY 10016
Contact: Ingrid Eisenstadter, Dir. of Grants
***E-mail:* ingrid.e@earthlink.net**; Main URL: http://foundationcenter.org/grantmaker/eppley/

Established in 1947 in RI.
Donor: Marion Eppley†.
Foundation type: Independent foundation.
Financial data (yr. ended 12/31/12): Assets, $2,485,366 (M); gifts received, $181,107; expenditures, $171,118; qualifying distributions, $165,415; giving activities include $150,551 for 6 grants (high: $26,600; low: $24,000).
Purpose and activities: Giving focuses on the following areas of interest: innovative medical investigations, endangered animals and ecosystems, and climate change.
Fields of interest: Environment; Animals/wildlife, research; Biomedicine; Medical research, institute; Medical research; Agriculture; Physical/earth sciences; Chemistry; Biology/life sciences.
Type of support: Research.
Limitations: Applications accepted. No support for social sciences, computer sciences, educational programs, or for research involving AIDS, cancer or heart disease.
Publications: Application guidelines; Informational brochure; Program policy statement.
Application information: Please go to the foundation web site and read the information there before applying. All submissions must start with an emailed Letter of Inquiry, not to exceed four pages, describing the project and qualifications, goals, novelty, and the broader ramifications of the work once completed. It is preferred that the LOI is in the body of the email, but it may also be a Word doc attachment (not docx, not pdf). Full proposals must be accompanied by the foundation's application form and at least two letters of reference from qualified individuals who are familiar with the work proposed. Mail a print copy of the proposal and all attachments to Ingrid Eisenstadter at the foundation address above. Simultaneously, email the proposal, application form and all attachments to Ingrid Eisenstadter at ingrid.e@earthlink.net. Send the proposal and application form as Word docs, not docx, not pdf. (Attachments may be any format.) Grants are made only through recognized education and research organizations with a 501(c)3 US base to receive the funds. Application form required.
***Initial approach:* Letter of inquiry**
***Copies of proposal:* 2**
***Deadline(s):* Letters of Inquiry must be received by Mar. 1 or Sept. 1. If a full proposal is invited, deadlines for receipt are Apr. 15 and Oct. 15**
***Board meeting date(s):* June and Dec.**
Final notification: Within two weeks of board meetings
Officers: Joan Winant, Pres.; Amy S. Saar, Secy.
Directors: Timothy Seldes; John Winant, M.D.
Number of staff: 1 part-time professional; 1 part-time support.
EIN: 050258857

2153
The Bender Family Foundation
111 Washington Ave.
Albany, NY 12210-2214
FAX: (518) 446-9708; E-mail: jmahoney@cfcr.org; Main URL: http://www.cfgcr.org/benderff/
Grants List: http://www.cfgcr.org/benderff/grantmaking.html

Established in 1997 in NY.
Donors: Matthew Bender IV; Matthew Bender Charitable Lead Trust IV.
Foundation type: Independent foundation.
Financial data (yr. ended 12/31/12): Assets, $2,086,314 (M); gifts received, $66,124; expenditures, $221,407; qualifying distributions, $181,150; giving activities include $181,150 for 30 grants (high: $20,000; low: $250).
Purpose and activities: Funding primarily to foster, preserve, and fund the arts, culture, education, history and environment of the New York State Capital Region.
Fields of interest: History/archaeology; Arts; Education; Environment, natural resources; Environment; Youth development.
Type of support: Capital campaigns; Building/ renovation; Equipment; Program development; Seed money.
Limitations: Applications accepted. Giving primarily in Albany County, NY. No support for annual fund drives. No grants to individuals.
Application information: See foundation web site for complete application guidelines.
Officers: Matthew Bender IV, Pres.; Phoebe P. Bender, V.P.
Board Members: M. Christian Bender; Jeffrey P. Bender.
EIN: 161526228
Other changes: The grantmaker now accepts applications.

2154
Max & Marian Farash Charitable Foundation
255 East Ave.
Rochester, NY 14604-2625 (585) 218-9855
FAX: (585) 546-1714;
E-mail: info@farashfoundation.org; Main URL: http://www.farashfoundation.org
Farash Prize for Social Entrepreneurship: http://www.farashfoundation.org/Default.aspx?RD=2275

Established in 1988 in NY.
Foundation type: Independent foundation.
Financial data (yr. ended 12/31/12): Assets, $257,912,246 (M); gifts received, $971,774; expenditures, $43,905,614; qualifying distributions, $10,259,672; giving activities include $6,965,011 for 166 grants (high: $790,000; low: $42).
Purpose and activities: Giving primarily for arts and culture, education, entrepreneurship, and Jewish life.
Fields of interest: Arts; Higher education; Human services; Jewish federated giving programs; Jewish agencies & synagogues.
Type of support: Emergency funds; General/ operating support; Annual campaigns; Capital campaigns; Scholarship funds.
Limitations: Applications accepted. Giving primarily in Monroe and Ontario counties in NY. No grants to individuals directly, or for general operating support.
Publications: Application guidelines.
Application information: Application form not required.
Initial approach: Use application process on foundation web site
Deadline(s): See foundation web site for current deadlines
Officers and Trustees:* Nathan J. Robfogel, Esq.*, Chair.; Hollis S. Budd, Exec. Dir.; Matthew Aroesty; Kenneth D. Bell; Lynn Farash; Edward Hourihan, Jr.; Thomas H. Jackson; Howard Konar; Hoffman Moka Lantum, M.D., Ph.D; Theresa Mazzullo; Alvin L. Ureles, M.D.; **Gregory Wolcott**.
EIN: 222948675
Other changes: The grantmaker now publishes application guidelines.

2155
The Fascitelli Family Foundation
170 East End Ave., Apt. 17 A/B
New York, NY 10128-7681

Established in 1993 in NY.
Donors: Michael D. Fascitelli; Elizabeth Cogan Fascitelli.
Foundation type: Independent foundation.
Financial data (yr. ended 01/31/13): Assets, $19,684,107 (M); gifts received, $3,380,549; expenditures, $1,555,198; qualifying distributions, $1,332,128; giving activities include $1,332,128 for 83 grants (high: $250,000; low: $250).
Purpose and activities: Giving primarily for education, and health associations, including a mental health center for children.

Fields of interest: Arts; Elementary/secondary education; Higher education; Education; Health care; Health organizations, association; Human services.
Limitations: Applications not accepted. Giving primarily in New York, NY; some funding also in NH and RI. No grants to individuals.
Application information: Contributes only to pre-selected organizations.
Officers: Elizabeth Cogan Fascitelli, Treas.; Michael D. Fascitelli, Mgr.
EIN: 133748071
Other changes: For the fiscal year ended Jan. 31, 2013, the fair market value of the grantmaker's assets was $19,684,107, a 159.8% increase over the fiscal 2012 value, $7,578,077.

2156
The Dominic Ferraioli Foundation
60 Railroad Pl., Ste. 300
Saratoga Springs, NY **12866-3048** (518) 736-2911
***Contact:* Mario Papa**
FAX: (518) 736-8165;
E-mail: kratajcz@hodgsonruss.com

Established in 2000 in NY.
Donor: Dominic Ferraioli†.
Foundation type: Independent foundation.
Financial data (yr. ended 06/30/13): Assets, $3,142,287 (M); expenditures, $180,923; qualifying distributions, $148,768; giving activities include $140,000 for 8 grants (high: $54,000; low: $5,000).
Purpose and activities: Giving to further the values and goals of Mr. Ferraioli with particular consideration to aiding and assisting medical facilities.
Fields of interest: Hospitals (general); Health care, clinics/centers; Human services.
Type of support: Technical assistance; Seed money; Research; Program development; Land acquisition; Equipment; Continuing support; Consulting services; Building/renovation.
Application information:
Board meeting date(s): Semi-annually
Trustees: Robert F. Campbell; David L. Evans; Mario J. Papa; Louis M. Papandrea, M.D.; Fred B. Wander.
EIN: 141829814

2157
The Fisher Brothers Foundation, Inc.
c/o Fisher Brothers
299 Park Ave.
New York, NY 10171-0001
***Main URL:* http://www.fisherbrothers.com/about/philanthropies/3**

Established in 1981 in NY.
Donors: Fisher Brothers; Fisher Park Lane Co.; Fisher Capital Assets; 1345 Cleaning Service Co. II LP; 299 Cleaning Service Co. II LP; Plaza Cleaning Service Co. II LP; 605 Cleaning Service Co. II LP; Columbia Cleaning; Fisher 120 Wall; Fisher 92nd St.; FSAR Fee Associates; Rancho Road Development; Park Clipper Leasing Associates; Sandhurst Associates; Zachary & Elizabeth Fisher Charitable Trust.
Foundation type: Company-sponsored foundation.
Financial data (yr. ended 12/31/12): Assets, $44,315 (M); gifts received, $2,900,000; expenditures, $3,123,910; qualifying distributions, $3,096,892; giving activities include $3,086,782 for 54 grants (high: $1,197,600; low: $500).
Purpose and activities: The foundation supports police agencies and fire departments and organizations involved with arts and culture, health, golf, military and veterans, and Judaism.
Fields of interest: Museums; Performing arts centers; Arts; Hospitals (general); Health care; Crime/law enforcement, police agencies; Disasters, fire prevention/control; Athletics/sports, golf; Jewish federated giving programs; Military/veterans' organizations; Jewish agencies & synagogues.
Type of support: Program development; General/operating support; Annual campaigns; Scholarship funds.
Limitations: Applications not accepted. Giving limited to New York, NY. No grants to individuals.
Application information: Contributes only to pre-selected organizations.
Directors: Arnold Fisher; Kenneth Fisher; Winston C. Fisher.
EIN: 133118286

2158
Shirley & William R. Fleischer Foundation, Inc.
7 Penn Plz., Ste. 810
New York, NY **10001-0011**

Established around 1967 in NY.
Donors: Shirley Fleischer; William R. Fleischer†.
Foundation type: Independent foundation.
Financial data (yr. ended 12/31/12): Assets, $5,193,640 (M); gifts received, $50,000; expenditures, $252,143; qualifying distributions, $240,030; giving activities include $240,030 for 15 grants (high: $30,015; low: $15).
Purpose and activities: Giving to Jewish agencies and for human services.
Fields of interest: Higher education; Education; Health organizations; Human services; Jewish federated giving programs; Jewish agencies & synagogues.
Limitations: Applications not accepted. No grants to individuals.
Application information: Unsolicited requests for funds not accepted.
Officers and Trustees:* Shirley Fleischer,* Pres.; Carl Fleischer,* V.P.; Donald Fleischer,* V.P.; Steven Fleischer, V.P.
EIN: 116048777

2159
Flowering Tree
225 E. 57th St., Apt. 18D
New York, NY 10022-2861
E-mail: contactus@floweringtreeinc.org; Main URL: http://www.floweringtreeinc.org
Facebook: https://www.facebook.com/pages/Flowering-Tree-Inc/195773717159535?fref=ts

Established in NY.
Donors: Rajesh Ambasta; Sumita Ambasta; Sansar Capital Foundation.
Foundation type: Operating foundation.
Financial data (yr. ended 12/31/12): Assets, $5,328,420 (M); gifts received, $260,000; expenditures, $268,241; qualifying distributions, $265,356; giving activities include $235,000 for 4 grants (high: $95,000; low: $15,000).
Purpose and activities: The foundation's organization's mission is to support women's development and children's education.
Fields of interest: Education; Children; Women.
International interests: India; Singapore.
Limitations: Applications accepted. Giving primarily in India. No grants to individuals.
Application information: Full proposals accepted by invitation only.
Initial approach: Letter of inquiry
Deadline(s): None
Officers: Sumita Ambasta, Pres.
Directors: Lucy Chuah; Christopher McLeod.
EIN: 352278100

2160
Ford Foundation
320 E. 43rd St.
New York, NY 10017-4801 (212) 573-5000
Contact: Secy.
FAX: (212) 351-3677;
E-mail: secretary@fordfoundation.org; Main URL: http://www.fordfoundation.org
Employment Feed: http://www.fordfoundation.org/feeds/employment
E-Newsletter: http://www.fordfoundation.org/About-Us#sign-up
Facebook: https://www.facebook.com/FordFound
Flickr: http://www.flickr.com/photos/ford-foundation/
Ford Foundation Staff: https://twitter.com/FordFoundation/ford-foundation-staff/members
Ford Foundation's Philanthropy Promise: http://www.ncrp.org/philanthropys-promise/who
Foundation News: http://www.fordfoundation.org/newsroom
GiveSmart: http://www.givesmart.org/Stories/Donors/Darren-Walker
Grantee Perception Report: http://www.fordfoundation.org/pdfs/grants/Ford%20Foundation_Grantee%20Perception%20Report_04-02-13.pdf
Grants Database: http://www.fordfoundation.org/grants/search
Issues Center: http://www.fordfoundation.org/issues
Knowledge Center: http://www.fordfoundation.org/impact
Multimedia: http://www.fordfoundation.org/library/search?contenttype=6
News Feed: http://www.fordfoundation.org/feeds/newsroom
Regional Priorities Center: http://www.fordfoundation.org/regions
Twitter: https://twitter.com/FordFoundation
Vimeo: http://vimeo.com/fordfoundation
YouTube: http://www.youtube.com/fordfoundationTV

Incorporated in 1936 in MI.
Donors: Henry Ford†; Edsel Ford†.
Foundation type: Independent foundation.
Financial data (yr. ended 12/31/12): Assets, $11,238,035,011 (M); expenditures, $768,874,851; qualifying distributions, $739,197,434; giving activities include $593,753,416 for grants, $3,622,444 for 8 foundation-administered programs and $28,863,232 for 12 loans/program-related investments (high: $10,000,000; low: $23,115).
Purpose and activities: The foundation supports visionary leaders and organizations working on the frontlines of social change worldwide. Its goals for more than half a century have been to strengthen democratic values, reduce poverty and injustice, promote international cooperation, and advance human achievement. The foundation focuses on eight issues: 1) Human Rights; 2) Democratic and Accountable Government; 3) Educational Opportunity and Scholarship; 4) Economic Fairness; 5) Metropolitan Opportunity; 6) Sustainable

Development; 7) Freedom of Expression; and 8) Gender, Sexuality and Reproductive Justice.
Fields of interest: Media/communications; Media, film/video; Museums; Performing arts; Performing arts, dance; Performing arts, theater; Performing arts, music; Arts; Education, research; Secondary school/education; Higher education; Education; Environment, natural resources; Environment; Reproductive health; Reproductive health, sexuality education; AIDS; Crime/violence prevention, abuse prevention; Legal services; Employment; Agriculture; Housing/shelter, development; Youth development, research; Human services; Women, centers/services; Minorities/immigrants, centers/services; International economic development; International human rights; International affairs; Civil rights, race/intergroup relations; Civil/human rights; Economic development; Urban/community development; Rural development; Community/economic development; Philanthropy/voluntarism; Social sciences; Economics; Law/international law; Government/public administration; Public affairs, citizen participation; Leadership development; Religion, interfaith issues; Youth; Minorities; Asians/Pacific Islanders; African Americans/Blacks; Hispanics/Latinos; Indigenous peoples; Women; AIDS, people with; Immigrants/refugees; Economically disadvantaged; LGBTQ.
International interests: Africa; Asia; Latin America; Middle East.
Type of support: General/operating support; Continuing support; Management development/capacity building; Endowments; Program development; Program evaluation; Program-related investments/loans; Employee matching gifts.
Limitations: Applications accepted. Giving in the United States, Africa, the Middle East, Asia, Latin America and the Caribbean, and also on a global basis, with a focus on eight core issues. No support for programs for which substantial support from government or other sources is readily available, or for religious sectarian activities. No grants for construction or maintenance of buildings, undergraduate scholarships, or for purely personal or local needs. The vast majority of foundation grants go to organizations. Historically, the foundation has provided a very limited number of fellowship opportunities for individuals, focusing on advanced degrees in areas of interest to the foundation. When available, recipients are selected by universities and other organizations that receive grants from the foundation to support fellowships.
Publications: Annual report; Informational brochure; Occasional report.
Application information: Prospective applicants are advised to carefully review the foundation's initiatives online, and to download and review the Grant Application Guide for additional details about the grant-review process at http://www.fordfoundation.org/pdfs/grants/grant-application-guide.pdf. Application form not required.
Initial approach: After reviewing the Grant Application Guide, submit an inquiry online using the Grant Inquiry Form (http://www.fordfoundation.org/grants/select-country-or-region)
Copies of proposal: 1
Deadline(s): None, grants are made throughout the year
Final notification: Three months from the time a formal proposal is submitted for a potential grant to be fully reviewed
Officers and Trustees:* Kofi Appenteng,* Chair.; Darren Walker, Pres.; Martin Abregu, Vice President for Democracy, Rights and Justice; Eric Doppstadt, Vice President and Chief Investment Officer; Nicholas M. Gabriel, Vice President, Treasurer and Chief Financial Officer; **Samantha Gilbert, Vice President, Talent and HR**; Hilary Pennington, Vice President for Education, Creativity and Free Expression; Marta L. Tellado, Vice President for Communications; Tim Berners-Lee; Martin Eakes; Amy Falls; Juliet V. Garcia; Irene Hirano Inouye; J. Clifford Hudson; Robert S. Kaplan; **Lourdes Lopez**; Thurgood Marshall, Jr.; Paula Moreno; N.R. Narayana Murthy; Peter A. Nadosy; Cecile Richards.
Number of staff: 254 full-time professional; 116 full-time support.
EIN: 131684331
Other changes: Kofi Appenteng has replaced Irene Hirano Inouye as Chair.
Pablo J. Farias is no longer Vice President for Economic Opportunity and Assets. Maya L. Harris is no longer Vice President for Democracy, Rights and Justice. Afsaneh M. Beschloss is no longer a director.

2161
Foundation for Child Development
295 Madison Ave., 40th Fl.
New York, NY 10017-6304 (212) 867-5777
Contact: Mark Bogosian, Comms. and Grants Off.
FAX: (212) 867-5844; E-mail: info@fcd-us.org; Main URL: http://www.fcd-us.org
E-Newsletter: http://www.fcd-us.org/whats-new/subscribe
Grants Database: http://www.fcd-us.org/grants/search
RSS Feed: http://www.fcd-us.org/whats-new
Twitter: http://twitter.com/fcdusorg
Program e-mail: ysp@fcd-us.org

Incorporated as a voluntary agency in 1900 in NY and established as the Association for the Aid of Crippled Children in 1908; current name adopted in 1972, affirming a broader focus on children at risk.
Donors: Milo M. Belding‡; Annie K. Belding‡; and others.
Foundation type: Independent foundation.
Financial data (yr. ended 03/31/13): Assets, $99,997,180 (M); gifts received, $21,000; expenditures, $5,158,021; qualifying distributions, $4,399,367; giving activities include $2,515,945 for 17 grants (high: $726,295; low: $7,500).
Purpose and activities: The Foundation for Child Development (FCD) is a national, private philanthropy dedicated to the principle that all families should have the social and material resources to raise their children to be healthy, educated and productive members of their communities. The foundation seeks to understand children, particularly the disadvantaged, and to promote their well-being. The foundation believes that families, schools, nonprofit organizations, businesses and government at all levels share complementary responsibilities in the critical task of raising new generations.
Fields of interest: Education, reform; Education, early childhood education; Public policy, research; Children; Immigrants/refugees.
Type of support: Fellowships; Endowments; General/operating support; Continuing support; Program development; Conferences/seminars; Publication; Seed money; Research; Technical assistance.
Limitations: Applications not accepted. Giving on a national basis. No support for the direct provision of pre-kindergarten education, child care, or health care. No grants for capital campaigns, endowments, or for the purchase, construction, or renovation of buildings.
Publications: Annual report; Grants list; Informational brochure; Newsletter; Occasional report; Program policy statement.
Application information: Unsolicited requests for funds not accepted.
Board meeting date(s): Mar., June, and Oct.
Officers and Directors:* David Lawrence, Jr.,* Chair.; Margaret Beale Spencer, Ph.D.*, Vice-Chair.; **Jessica Chao, Interim C.E.O. and C.O.O.**; Ruby Takanishi, Ph.D.*, Pres.; **Hirokazu Yoshikawa,* Secy.**; Ellen Berland Gibbs, Treas.; **Eugene E. Garcia**; Walter Giles; **Robert P. Morgenthau**; Andrew D. Racine, M.D., Ph.D.; Margarita Rosa; Joseph Youngblood II.
Number of staff: 5 full-time professional; 1 part-time professional; 1 part-time support.
EIN: 131623901
Other changes: David Lawrence, Jr. has replaced Ruth Ann Burns as Chair. Hirokazu Yoshikawa has replaced Arthur Greenberg as Secy.
David Lawrence, Jr. is now Chair. Hirokazu Yoshikawa is now Secy. Norma Cantu, Michael I. Cohen, John L. Furth, Karen Hill-Scott, and Ian B. MacCallum are no longer directors.

2162
The Regina Bauer Frankenberg Foundation
c/o JPMorgan Chase Bank, N.A., Private Foundation Svcs.
270 Park Ave., 16th Fl.
New York, NY 10017
Contact: Casey Castaneda, Prog. Off.
FAX: (212) 464-2304;
E-mail: casey.b.castaneda@jpmchase.com; **Main URL: http://fdnweb.org/frankenberg**
Grants List: http://fdnweb.org/frankenberg/grants/year/contributions/

Established in 1994 in NY.
Donor: Regina Bauer Frankenberg‡.
Foundation type: Independent foundation.
Financial data (yr. ended 12/31/12): Assets, $20,238,652 (M); expenditures, $1,126,498; qualifying distributions, $921,200; giving activities include $901,600 for 18 grants (high: $150,000; low: $1,600).
Purpose and activities: Giving exclusively for animal welfare, particularly for the protection of endangered wild animals or threatened species by supporting conservation and research, and for strengthening the capacity of organizations working to reduce the homelessness, mistreatment and euthanasia of companion animals through adoption, training, spaying/neutering, and other programs.
Fields of interest: Animal welfare; Animals/wildlife, preservation/protection.
Type of support: Capital campaigns; Management development/capacity building; Program development.
Limitations: Applications accepted. Giving for companion animals limited to New York, NY; giving for wildlife on a national and international scope. No support for private foundations, or for organizations that will engage in or supply animals for vivisection. No grants to individuals, or for matching gifts; no loans.
Publications: Application guidelines; Grants list.
Application information: Application form not required.
Initial approach: Proposal
Copies of proposal: 1
Deadline(s): July 1
Board meeting date(s): Nov.
Final notification: Dec. 31
Trustee: JPMorgan Chase Bank, N.A.

Number of staff: None.
EIN: 133741659

2163
The Freed Foundation
825 3rd Ave., Ste. 224
New York, NY 10022-7519 (212) 520-8399
***Contact:* Grants Committee; Grants Inquiries**
E-mail: freedfoundationnyc@verizon.net

Incorporated in 1954 in Washington, DC.
Donors: Frances W. Freed†; Gerald A. Freed†; Allie S. Freed†.
Foundation type: Independent foundation.
Financial data (yr. ended 12/31/12): Assets, $18,936,917 (M); expenditures, $1,022,261; qualifying distributions, $988,239; giving activities include $806,260 for 17 grants (high: $350,000; low: $1,760).
Purpose and activities: Support for all aspects of animal welfare, and mental health.
Fields of interest: Animal welfare; Animals/wildlife, preservation/protection; Mental health, counseling/support groups; Mental health, disorders; Nutrition; Safety/disasters; Athletics/sports, training; Athletics/sports, school programs.
Type of support: Capital campaigns; Annual campaigns; Building/renovation; Equipment; General/operating support.
Limitations: Applications accepted. Giving primarily in the New York City, NY metropolitan area. **No grants to individuals, or for research, conferences and meetings, and international programs.**
Publications: Grants list.
Application information: Copies of letter should include one by U.S. mail and one by e-mail. Application form not required.
***Initial approach:* E-mail Letter of Inquiry**
***Copies of proposal:* 2**
***Deadline(s):* July 31**
***Board meeting date(s):* Oct.**
***Final notification:* Oct. 31**
Officers and Directors:* Elizabeth Freed,* Pres. and Treas.; **Steven Douenias, Secy.; William Mitchell.**
Number of staff: 1 full-time professional.
EIN: 526047591
Other changes: Steven Douenias has replaced Jane M. Freed as Secy.

2164
Freeman Foundation
c/o Rockefeller Trust Company, N.A.
10 Rockefeller Plz., 3rd Fl.
New York, NY **10020-1903** (212) 549-5270
Contact: George S. Tsandikos
Application address: 499 Taber Hill Rd., Stowe, VT 05672

Established in 1978 in VT.
Donors: Houghton Freeman; Mansfield Freeman†; members of the Freeman family.
Foundation type: Independent foundation.
Financial data (yr. ended 12/31/12): Assets, $301,224,960 (M); expenditures, $16,639,783; qualifying distributions, $14,911,925; giving activities include $13,817,869 for 98 grants (high: $1,560,000; low: $3,500).
Purpose and activities: Support primarily for the promotion of international understanding, farmland preservation projects in the state of VT and special projects in HI.
Fields of interest: Education, public education; Environment, natural resources; International affairs, goodwill promotion; International studies.
International interests: Asia.
Type of support: General/operating support; Land acquisition; Program development; Professorships; Curriculum development; Fellowships; Scholarship funds; Research; Exchange programs; Matching/challenge support.
Limitations: Applications accepted. Giving primarily in VT for conservation and environment grants; Asian studies grants are awarded nationally. No grants to individuals, or for endowments or capital campaigns.
Publications: Annual report.
Application information: Application form not required.
Initial approach: Letter
Copies of proposal: 7
Deadline(s): One month before meetings
Board meeting date(s): Quarterly
Officer and Trustees:* Graeme Freeman, Pres.; Doreen Freeman; George B. Snell.
Number of staff: 4
EIN: 132965090

2165
Marina Kellen French Foundation
c/o JES, LLP
15 Maiden Ln.
New York, NY **10038**

Established in 2001 in NY.
Donors: Michael Kellen French; A.M. & S.M. Kellen Foundation.
Foundation type: Independent foundation.
Financial data (yr. ended 12/31/12): Assets, $10,034,927 (M); expenditures, $1,015,685; qualifying distributions, $593,506; giving activities include $593,506 for grants.
Fields of interest: Arts; Human services.
Limitations: Applications not accepted. No grants to individuals.
Application information: Contributes only to pre-selected organizations.
Officer: Andrew Gundlach, Treas.
Trustee: Marina Kellen French.
EIN: 137270721

2166
The Gerald J. and Dorothy R. Friedman New York Foundation for Medical Research
c/o CohnReznick LLP
1212 6th Ave.
New York, NY 10036-1602

Established in 1999 in NY.
Donors: Dorothy Friedman; Gerald J. Friedman†.
Foundation type: Independent foundation.
Financial data (yr. ended 02/28/13): Assets, $23,122,148 (M); expenditures, $3,234,417; qualifying distributions, $2,981,791; giving activities include $2,838,916 for 8 grants (high: $2,354,916; low: $2,000).
Purpose and activities: Giving primarily to organizations involved in medical research.
Fields of interest: Health care; Health organizations; Medical research.
Limitations: Applications not accepted. Giving primarily in NY; giving also in MA. No grants to individuals.
Application information: Contributes only to pre-selected organizations.
Officers: Jane Friedman, Pres.; Susan Thomases, Exec. V.P.; Judith Kennedy, V.P.; Mark Satlof, V.P.; Lewis Bernstein, Secy.-Treas.
Director: Dorothy Friedman.
EIN: 134034562
Other changes: Jennifer Gerson is no longer a V.P.

2167
Friends of the Congressional Glaucoma Caucus Foundation, Inc.
69-44 76th St.
Middle Village, NY 11379-2829
Contact: S.J. "Bud" Grant, C.E.O
E-mail: RichardGrant716@aol.com; Toll free tel.: (877) 611-4232; Nassau County, NY tel.: (516) 327-2236, fax: (516) 327-0260; Main URL: http://glaucomacongress.org

Established in 2000 in NY.
Donors: Pharmacia & Upjohn, Inc.; Pfizer Inc.; Allergan, Inc.; CDC of Health and Human Services Dept.
Foundation type: Operating foundation.
Financial data (yr. ended 12/31/12): Assets, $136,894 (M); gifts received, $2,044,805; expenditures, $2,201,638; qualifying distributions, $2,372,945; giving activities include $484,456 for 12 grants (high: $225,000; low: $4,500), and $1,871,131 for 1 foundation-administered program.
Purpose and activities: The foundation is dedicated to supporting the activities of the Congressional Glaucoma Caucus, a group of United States Congress members who are dedicated to helping all Americans fight the scourge of glaucoma and other eye diseases. The foundation awards grants to organizations to provide diagnostic screening opportunities and follow up for high risk glaucoma population groups in their home districts across the nation.
Fields of interest: Health care, rural areas; Public health; Eye diseases.
Type of support: Consulting services; Fellowships; Curriculum development; General/operating support.
Limitations: Applications accepted. Giving on a national basis. No grants to individuals.
Application information: See foundation web site for downloading of the Medical School Student Sight Saver Program application form. Application form not required.
Initial approach: Letter or telephone
Copies of proposal: 1
Deadline(s): None
Board meeting date(s): Quarterly
Final notification: 3 months
Officers: Robert J. Bishop, J.D., Chair.; Stanley J. "Bud" Grant, C.E.O. and Pres.; Randall D. Bloomfield, M.D., V.P. and Secy.; **Philip Ragusa, Treas.**
Directors: John J. Abbott, Ph.D.; Judy Collins; Rev. Dr. Floyd Flake; S. Dorothy Anne Fitzgibbons, OP; Edward Greissing; Roger C. Herdman, M.D.; Joseph M. Mattone, J.D.; Hon. Raymond J. McGrath; Carrie Ann Stevens; Robert C. Wertz, J.D.
EIN: 134098767

2168
Marc Galler Research Foundation Inc.
115 Central Park W., Ste. 7-E
New York, NY 10023-2005 **(212) 877-3326**
Contact: Lynne Galler, Pres.

Donor: Beatrice Galler†.
Foundation type: Independent foundation.

Financial data (yr. ended 10/31/13): Assets, $10,812,961 (M); expenditures, $311,123; qualifying distributions, $233,555; giving activities include $233,555 for 9 grants (high: $170,000; low: $400).
Fields of interest: Arts; Religion.
Application information: Application form required.
Initial approach: Letter
Deadline(s): None
Officers: Lynne Galler, Pres.; Hezzy Dattner, Secy.-Treas.
EIN: 237013433

2169
Bruce G. Geary Foundation
c/o Raymond J. Pezzoli, Esq.
698 Forest Ave.
Staten Island, NY 10310-2507

Established in 2007 in NY.
Donor: Bruce G. Geary.
Foundation type: Independent foundation.
Financial data (yr. ended 12/31/12): Assets, $19,661,742 (M); expenditures, $1,247,153; qualifying distributions, $855,736; giving activities include $855,736 for grants.
Fields of interest: Animal welfare; Zoos/zoological societies.
Limitations: Applications not accepted. Giving primarily in NY. No grants to individuals.
Application information: Contributes only to pre-selected organizations.
Officers and Directors:* Raymond J. Pezzoli,* Pres.; Cathy Carlson, V.P.; Mathew Smith, Secy.-Treas.; **John Kosinski**; Herbert Smith III.
EIN: 208075415
Other changes: Raymond J. Pezzoli is now Pres.

2170
Gebbie Foundation, Inc.
215 Cherry St.
Jamestown, NY 14701-5203 (716) 487-1062
***Contact:* Gregory J. Edwards, C.E.O.**
FAX: (716) 484-6401; E-mail: info@gebbie.org; **Email: gedwards@gebbie.org**; Main URL: http://www.gebbie.org
Facebook: https://www.facebook.com/pages/Gebbie-Foundation/318313207852

Incorporated in 1964 in NY.
Donors: Marion B. Gebbie†; Geraldine G. Bellinger†.
Foundation type: Independent foundation.
Financial data (yr. ended 12/31/12): Assets, $72,651,029 (M); expenditures, $3,919,839; qualifying distributions, $3,698,376; giving activities include $3,143,190 for 18+ grants (high: $1,877,019), and $25,000 for 1 employee matching gift.
Purpose and activities: Grants primarily for the arts, children and youth services, community development, education, and human services. The foundation's strategic focus is to rejuvenate downtown Jamestown, New York, through economic development.
Fields of interest: Arts; Education; Human services; Children/youth, services; Community/economic development.
Type of support: General/operating support; Continuing support; Annual campaigns; Capital campaigns; Building/renovation; Equipment; Endowments; Seed money; Scholarship funds; Program-related investments/loans; Matching/challenge support.
Limitations: Applications accepted. Giving primarily in Chautauqua County in western NY, especially the Jamestown, NY, area. No support for sectarian or religious organizations, or for United Way-funded agencies, unless there is a strong link to the foundation's strategic focus. No grants to individuals.
Publications: Application guidelines; Grants list.
Application information: The foundation will accept full proposals from 501(c)(3) organizations that have submitted a Letter of Inquiry and received a written approval in response, or have received an invitation from the foundation. Complete application guidelines available on foundation web site.
Initial approach: Letter of inquiry (1-2 pages)
Copies of proposal: 1
Deadline(s): None
Board meeting date(s): Quarterly
Final notification: 1 to 4 months
Officers and Directors:* Gregory J. Edwards, C.E.O.; Daniel Kathman,* Pres.; Jonathan Taber,* V.P.; Nancy Gleason,* Secy.; Rodney Drake,* Treas.; Dr. Lynn Dunham; Rhoe B. Henderson, III; Tory Irgang; Kristy B. Zabrodsky.
Number of staff: 1 full-time professional; 3 full-time support.
EIN: 166050287
Other changes: Daniel Kathman has replaced Kristy B. Zabrodsky as Pres. Jonathan Taber has replaced Daniel Kathman as V.P. Nancy Gleason has replaced Rhoe B. Henderson, III as Secy. Rodney Drake has replaced Jonathan Taber as Treas. Gregory J. Edwards has replaced John C. Merino as C.E.O.

2171
Leopold R. Gellert Family Trust
750 3rd Ave., Ste. 3300
New York, NY 10017-2703

Established in 1962 in NY.
Donors: Robert J. Gellert; Max E. Gellert†; Donald N. Gellert.
Foundation type: Independent foundation.
Financial data (yr. ended 05/31/13): Assets, $1,124,159 (M); gifts received, $211,631; expenditures, $101,952; qualifying distributions, $87,800; giving activities include $87,800 for 13 grants (high: $60,000; low: $200).
Purpose and activities: Giving primarily for performing arts, education, and human services.
Fields of interest: Performing arts, music; Performing arts, orchestras; Performing arts, opera; Performing arts, education; Higher education; Graduate/professional education; Libraries (public); Education; Human services.
Limitations: Applications not accepted. Giving primarily in NY, PA and WA. No grants to individuals.
Application information: Contributes only to pre-selected organizations.
Trustees: Donald N. Gellert; Robert J. Gellert; Hugh McLoughlin, Jr.; **David B. Spohngellert**.
EIN: 136085289

2172
Gemj Chehebar Foundation
1407 Broadway, Ste. 503
New York, NY 10018-5151
***FAX:* 917-591-7008;**
E-mail: donations@gemchehebar.com; Main URL: http://www.gemjchehebar.com/foundation
Donors: Gabriel A. Chehebar; Ezra A. Chehebar; Skiva International, Inc.; Rainbow USA, Inc.
Foundation type: Independent foundation.
Financial data (yr. ended 12/31/12): Assets, $229,633 (M); gifts received, $320,000; expenditures, $288,100; qualifying distributions, $287,210; giving activities include $287,210 for 195 grants (high: $20,000; low: -$18,802).
Fields of interest: Jewish federated giving programs; Jewish agencies & synagogues.
Limitations: Applications not accepted.
Application information: Unsolicited requests for funds not accepted.
Directors: Ezra A. Chehebar; Gabriel A. Chehebar; Josef A. Chehebar; Michael A. Chehebar.
EIN: 263683879

2173
Genesis Foundation Inc.
505 Park Ave., 4th Fl.
New York, NY 10022-1106 **(212) 421-1185**
***Contact:* Carolina Esquenazi, Pres.; Cristina Gutierrez de Pineres, Exec. Dir.**
E-mail: genesis@genesis-foundation.org; **Additional tel.: (212) 421-1149**; Main URL: http://www.genesis-foundation.org
Facebook: http://www.facebook.com/pages/Genesis-Foundation/227677570578716
Twitter: http://twitter.com/GenesisColombia
Vimeo: http://vimeo.com/genesisfoundation

Established in 2001 in FL.
Donors: Genesis Endowment; ReMax of Georgia; Belive; Daniel Roitman; Edmundo Esquenazi; Greenlight Capital; Jim Marilyn Simons; JPMorgan Chase; Prince Capital; Sources of Hope Foundation; Quadrant Capital; Becky Mayer; Jimmy Mayer; Challenge Me Now.
Foundation type: Independent foundation.
Financial data (yr. ended 12/31/12): Assets, $1,504,623 (M); gifts received, $978,896; expenditures, $1,185,376; qualifying distributions, $745,336; giving activities include $745,336 for grants, and $902,368 for foundation-administered programs.
Purpose and activities: The foundation supports successful programs aimed at enhancing quality education with the purpose of providing underserved Colombian children better opportunities to develop and succeed, contributing to a more equal society.
Fields of interest: Education, management/technical assistance; Education, reform; Education, equal rights; Education, formal/general education; Elementary/secondary education; Education, early childhood education; Secondary school/education; Education, drop-out prevention; Education, reading; Education, community/cooperative; Education, computer literacy/technology training; Education, e-learning; Education; Children/youth.
International interests: Colombia.
Type of support: Management development/capacity building; Equipment; Program development; Curriculum development.
Limitations: Applications not accepted. Giving primarily in Colombia. However, the foundation is willing to consider transferring education methodologies to organizations in other countries.
Publications: Annual report; Grants list; Informational brochure; Newsletter; Occasional report.
Application information: Unsolicited requests for funds not accepted.
Board meeting date(s): May and Nov.

Officers: Carolina Esquenazi-Shaio, Pres.; Herbert Selzer, Secy.; **Cristina Gutierrez de Pineres, Exec. Dir.**
Directors: Jaime Bermudez; Juan Carlos Garcia; Andrea Lawson; **Susie Mayer.**
Number of staff: 6 full-time professional; 1 part-time professional.
EIN: 912120744
Other changes: The grantmaker no longer lists a fax.
Cristina Gutierrez de Pineres has replaced Andrea Lawson as Exec. Dir.
The grantmaker no longer publishes application guidelines.

2174
The Gershwind Family Foundation
152 W. 57th St., 56th Fl.
New York, NY 10019-3310

Established in 1998 in NY.
Donor: Marjorie Gershwind Fiverson.
Foundation type: Independent foundation.
Financial data (yr. ended 12/31/12): Assets, $14,650,843 (M); gifts received, $3,620,500; expenditures, $2,330,566; qualifying distributions, $2,280,609; giving activities include $2,280,609 for 27 grants (high: $1,751,315; low: $250).
Purpose and activities: Giving primarily for education and to Jewish agencies and temples; funding also for a hospital.
Fields of interest: Higher education; Education; Hospitals (general); Health care; Jewish federated giving programs; Jewish agencies & synagogues.
Limitations: Applications not accepted. Giving primarily in NY. No grants to individuals.
Application information: Contributes only to pre-selected organizations.
Officers and Directors:* Marjorie Gershwind Fiverson,* Pres.; Stacey Bennett,* V.P.; Erik Gershwind,* V.P.; J. Robert Small, Secy.-Treas.
EIN: 113359917
Other changes: At the close of 2012, the grantmaker paid grants of $2,280,609, a 55.0% increase over the 2010 disbursements, $1,471,137.
Marjorie Gershwind, Donor and Pres., is now Marjorie Gershwind Fiverson.

2175
The Nomi P. Ghez Foundation
c/o MJSM
P.O. Box 331
Plainview, NY 11803-0331

Established in 1994 in NY.
Donor: Nomi P. Ghez.
Foundation type: Independent foundation.
Financial data (yr. ended 09/30/13): Assets, $3,087,696 (M); gifts received, $989,064; expenditures, $157,284; qualifying distributions, $138,771; giving activities include $138,771 for 21 grants (high: $59,890; low: $100).
Fields of interest: Museums (ethnic/folk arts); Performing arts, opera; Arts; Education; Health care; Jewish federated giving programs; Jewish agencies & synagogues.
Limitations: Applications not accepted. Giving primarily in New York, NY. No grants to individuals; no loans or scholarships.
Application information: Contributes only to pre-selected organizations.
Trustees: Ariana N. Ghez; Nomi P. Ghez.
EIN: 133801608

2176
The Giant Steps Foundation
c/o Rosen, Seymour, Shapps, Martin & Co.
757 3rd Ave., 6th Fl.
New York, NY 10017-2059
E-mail: wendy@giantsteps.org; Main URL: http://www.giantsteps.org

Established in 1998 in CA and DE.
Donors: Jennifer Leeds; Tides Foundation; Liselotte Gerard Leeds.
Foundation type: Independent foundation.
Financial data (yr. ended 11/30/13): Assets, $12,235,052 (M); gifts received, $70,000; expenditures, $362,079; qualifying distributions, $321,319; giving activities include $255,851 for 24 grants (high: $94,101; low: $250).
Purpose and activities: The foundation was created with a desire to spark others to pursue their dreams and to create a kinder, gentler, and healthier world for all living creatures. It does this via three avenues: environmental preservation and education; wildlife advocacy and domestic animal rescue; and human health, fitness, and empowerment activities (with a focus on underserved populations). The foundation strongly encourages those it supports to engage in sustainable, humane, and caring practices.
Fields of interest: Environment; Animal welfare; Human services.
Limitations: Applications not accepted. Giving in the U.S., with emphasis on CA and MN. No grants to individuals.
Application information: Contributes only to pre-selected organizations.
Officers and Directors:* Jennifer Leeds,* Pres.; Richard L. Braunstein, Secy.; Jeffrey J. Sundheim,* Treas.; Lilo J. Leeds.
EIN: 522069841
Other changes: The grantmaker has moved from MA to NY. The grantmaker no longer lists a phone.

2177
The Rosamond Gifford Charitable Corporation
(also known as The Gifford Foundation)
100 Clinton Sq.
126 N. Salina St., 3rd Fl.
Syracuse, NY 13202-1059 (315) 474-2489
Contact: Kathy Goldfarb-Findling, Exec. Dir.
FAX: (315) 475-4983;
E-mail: contact@giffordfoundation.org; Main URL: http://www.giffordfoundation.org
Facebook: http://www.facebook.com/GiffordFoundation?ref=ts
Twitter: https://twitter.com/GiffordCNY

Incorporated in 1954 in NY.
Donor: Rosamond Gifford‡.
Foundation type: Independent foundation.
Financial data (yr. ended 12/31/12): Assets, $20,168,619 (M); gifts received, $99,454; expenditures, $1,652,882; qualifying distributions, $1,458,081; giving activities include $796,730 for 71+ grants (high: $316,506).
Purpose and activities: Giving support for educational, scientific, social, and religious needs in Onondaga, Oswego, and Madison Counties, NY. Particular interest in issues around youth violence, employment for youth, and neighborhood revitalization.
Fields of interest: Arts; Higher education; Hospitals (general); Crime/violence prevention; Youth development; Human services; Children/youth, services; Aging, centers/services.
Type of support: General/operating support; Capital campaigns; Building/renovation; Equipment; Land acquisition; Emergency funds; Program development; Conferences/seminars; Seed money; Curriculum development; Research; Technical assistance; Program evaluation; Matching/challenge support.
Limitations: Giving limited to organizations in or serving Madison, Onondaga and Oswego Counties in NY; the "What If..." Mini Grants program is limited to Syracuse, NY. No grants to individuals, or for endowment funds, continuing support.
Publications: Application guidelines; Annual report; Program policy statement.
Application information: Proposals are by invitation only. Application guidelines available on foundation web site. E-mailed or faxed applications not accepted. Application form not required.
Initial approach: Use Grant Inquiry Form on foundation web site, or telephone foundation
Copies of proposal: 1
Deadline(s): Deadlines are rolling and will be announced at an intake meeting
Board meeting date(s): Monthly
Final notification: 2-3 months
Officers and Trustees:* Laurence G. Bousquet,* Pres.; Ben Walsh,* V.P.; Jaime Alicea,* Secy.; Eric Allyn,* Treas.; Dirk Sonneborn, Exec. Dir.; **Joseph Charles**; Michael Feng; **Monique Fletcher**; Vincent B. Love; Gwyn Mannion; Cynthia B. Morrow, M.D.; Kathy O'Connell; M. Catherine Richardson; **Merike Treier.**
Number of staff: 5 full-time professional; 1 full-time support.
EIN: 150572881
Other changes: Laurence G. Bousquet has replaced Jack H. Webb as Pres. Ben Walsh has replaced Laurence G. Bousquet as V.P.

2178
Sondra & Charles Gilman, Jr. Foundation, Inc.
109 E. 64th St.
New York, NY 10065-7004
Contact: Sondra G. Gonzalez-Falla, Chair.

Established in NY in 1981 as a successor to the Gilman Foundation.
Foundation type: Independent foundation.
Financial data (yr. ended 04/30/13): Assets, $5,790,815 (M); gifts received, $560,000; expenditures, $730,892; qualifying distributions, $311,947; giving activities include $311,947 for 23 grants (high: $171,267; low: $100).
Purpose and activities: Giving primarily for enhancement of the arts.
Fields of interest: Visual arts; Museums (art); Museums (natural history); Performing arts, theater; Arts; Education; Health care; Health organizations, association; Jewish agencies & synagogues.
Type of support: General/operating support; Continuing support; Endowments; Program development.
Limitations: Giving on a national basis, with some emphasis on GA, New York, NY, and TX. No grants to individuals.
Publications: Program policy statement.
Application information: Contributes only to pre-selected organizations.
Board meeting date(s): Quarterly
Officers: Sondra Gilman Gonzalez-Falla, Chair.; Celso M. Gonzalez-Falla, Pres.; Jack Friedland, V.P.; Walter Bauer, Treas.
Directors: Charles Gilman III; Myrna Schatz.
EIN: 133097485
Other changes: The grantmaker no longer lists a phone.

2179

Bernard F. and Alva B. Gimbel Foundation, Inc.
271 Madison Ave., Ste. 605
New York, NY 10016-1001 (212) 684-9110
Contact: Leslie Gimbel, C.E.O. and Pres.
FAX: (212) 684-9114; Main URL: http://www.gimbelfoundation.org
Grants List: http://www.gimbelfoundation.org/grants.html

Incorporated in 1943 in NY.
Donors: Bernard F. Gimbel†; Alva B. Gimbel†.
Foundation type: Independent foundation.
Financial data (yr. ended 12/31/12): Assets, $48,138,858 (M); expenditures, $4,522,523; qualifying distributions, $3,924,835; giving activities include $3,584,250 for 99 grants (high: $125,000; low: $500).
Purpose and activities: Support for education, workforce/economic development, criminal justice, civil legal services, reproductive rights, the environment, and for advocacy in these areas.
Fields of interest: Environment; Legal services; Employment, training; Civil liberties, reproductive rights; Economic development.
Type of support: General/operating support; Continuing support; Program development.
Limitations: Applications accepted. Giving for direct services is limited to New York City programs. No support for individual schools, short-term educational programs or workshops, mentoring, after-school or summer programs, film projects, or direct service programs outside New York City. No grants to individuals.
Publications: Application guidelines; Grants list.
Application information: Applications by fax not accepted. Full proposals accepted by invitation only following review of a Letter of Inquiry. The foundation makes very few new grants each year. For this reason, interested applicants are encouraged to contact the offices before submitting a letter of inquiry. The foundation is no longer accepting requests for funds in the area of education. Application form not required.
Initial approach: Prospective applicants should submit a two- to three-page letter of inquiry through the online system on foundation web site
Copies of proposal: 1
Deadline(s): None, for letters of inquiry; Early Feb. and early Sept. for proposals
Board meeting date(s): June and Dec.
Final notification: Varies
Officers and Directors:* Leslie Gimbel,* C.E.O. and Pres.; Lynn S. Stern,* V.P.; Stephen D. Greenberg,* Treas.; Hope G. Solinger,* Honorary Chairperson; Thomas S.T. Gimbel; Alva G. Greenberg; **Spencer Greenberg**; Judy Mendelsund; Nicholas S.G. Stern.
Number of staff: 2 full-time professional; 1 full-time support.
EIN: 136090843

2180

Gimprich Family Foundation, Inc.
c/o Hebrew Union College
1 W. 4th St.
New York, NY 10012-1105
Contact: Zelda Goldsmith, Exec. Admin.

Established in 1975.
Donor: Marvin Gimprich†.
Foundation type: Independent foundation.
Financial data (yr. ended 05/31/13): Assets, $6,833,070 (M); expenditures, $558,885; qualifying distributions, $558,885; giving activities include $405,000 for 43 grants (high: $20,000; low: $4,000).
Fields of interest: Human services; Children/youth, services; Civil liberties, advocacy; Jewish agencies & synagogues.
International interests: Israel.
Type of support: Seed money.
Limitations: Applications accepted. Giving in the U.S. and internationally, primarily in Israel. No grants to individuals, or for building.
Application information: Application form required.
Initial approach: Letter
Copies of proposal: 1
Deadline(s): None
Officers: David M. Fishman, Pres.; Lila Gimprich d'Adolf, V.P.; Rosalie Dolmatch, Recording Secy.; Eric S. Wittstein, Treas.
Director: Leora Fishman.
Number of staff: 1 part-time professional.
EIN: 510147095
Other changes: The grantmaker no longer lists a URL address.

2181

The Lillian Goldman Charitable Trust
c/o Holland & Knight
31 W. 52 St.
New York, NY 10019-6118
Contact: Donald Goldsmith

Established in 1995 in NY.
Donors: Sol Goldman†; The Sol Goldman Charitable Trust.
Foundation type: Independent foundation.
Financial data (yr. ended 12/31/12): Assets, $26,512,397 (M); expenditures, $7,688,227; qualifying distributions, $7,012,339; giving activities include $6,915,584 for 86 grants (high: $1,000,000; low: $3,662).
Fields of interest: Arts; Higher education; Botanical gardens; Health organizations, association; Human services.
Limitations: Applications not accepted. Giving primarily in New York, NY; funding also in England and Italy. No grants to individuals.
Application information: Contributes only to pre-selected organizations.
Trustees: Sara Goldman Arno; Amy Goldman Fowler; Cary Fowler; Donald A. Goldsmith; Neil Hamilton; **Robin Kemper; Carroll Stevens.**
EIN: 137048279
Other changes: For the fiscal year ended Dec. 31, 2012, the grantmaker paid grants of $6,915,584, a substantial increase over fiscal 2011 disbursements ($1,858,625.)
The grantmaker has changed its fiscal year-end from Apr. 30 to Dec. 31.

2182

Joyce and Irving Goldman Family Foundation, Inc.
(formerly Irving Goldman Foundation, Inc.)
417 5th Ave., Ste. 400
New York, NY 10016-2239 (212) 624-4300
***Contact:* Benjamin Binswanger, Exec. Dir.**
E-mail: jigff@jigff.org

Established in 1984 in NY.
Donors: Goldman Children Trust; Goldman Grandchildren Trust.
Foundation type: Independent foundation.
Financial data (yr. ended 12/31/12): Assets, $149,093,284 (M); gifts received, $4,456,648; expenditures, $6,788,987; qualifying distributions, $6,156,937; giving activities include $5,953,630 for 138 grants (high: $510,000; low: $500).
Purpose and activities: Grants are made in the following three issue areas: Jewish life, medical education and community health in Israel's Negev region, and breast cancer cure/eradication.
Fields of interest: Medical school/education; Cancer; Jewish agencies & synagogues.
Type of support: General/operating support; Continuing support; Program development; Conferences/seminars; Seed money; Research; Program evaluation.
Limitations: Applications accepted. Giving primarily in Israel and the U.S., with special emphasis on NY. No grants to individuals, or for capital requests.
Application information: Consideration for support is primarily through invitation to organizations working in the foundation's areas of interest. Unsolicited letters of inquiry are reviewed; unsolicited proposals are discouraged and should not be submitted unless by invitation from foundation staff. Application form not required.
Initial approach: Letter of inquiry
Copies of proposal: 1
Deadline(s): None
Board meeting date(s): Ongoing
Final notification: Acknowledgment of application immediately; decision within 3-9 months
Officers and Director:* Dorian Goldman,* Pres.; Lloyd Goldman, Secy.; Katja Goldman, Treas.; **Benjamin Binswanger, Exec. Dir.**
Number of staff: 1 full-time professional.
EIN: 133216152
Other changes: Benjamin Binswanger has replaced Sarah E. Meyer as Exec. Dir.

2183

Herman Goldman Foundation
44 Wall St., Ste. 1212
New York, NY 10005-2401 (212) 461-2132
Contact: Richard K. Baron, Exec. Dir.
E-mail: goldfound@aol.com

Incorporated in 1943 in NY.
Donor: Herman Goldman†.
Foundation type: Independent foundation.
Financial data (yr. ended 02/28/13): Assets, $19,274,290 (M); expenditures, $1,582,066; qualifying distributions, $1,196,778; giving activities include $879,000 for 82+ grants.
Purpose and activities: Emphasis on enhancing the quality of life through innovative grants in four main areas: 1) Health - to achieve effective delivery of physical and mental health care services; 2) Social Justice - to develop organizational, social, and legal approaches to aid deprived or handicapped people; 3) Education - for new or improved counseling for effective preschool, vocational and paraprofessional training; and 4) the Arts - to increase opportunities for talented youth to receive training and for less affluent individuals to attend quality presentations; some aid for programs relating to nationwide problems.
Fields of interest: Performing arts; Education, early childhood education; Vocational education; Education; Health care; Mental health/crisis services; Health organizations, association; Crime/law enforcement; Human services; Disabilities, people with; Economically disadvantaged.
Type of support: General/operating support; Continuing support; Annual campaigns; Capital campaigns; Building/renovation; Endowments; Program development; Seed money; Fellowships; Internship funds; Scholarship funds; Research.
Limitations: Applications accepted. Giving primarily in the metropolitan New York, NY, area. No support

for religious organizations. No grants to individuals, or for emergency funds.
Publications: Annual report (including application guidelines).
Application information: NY/NJ Area Common Application Form accepted. Application form not required.
Initial approach: Proposal
Copies of proposal: 1
Deadline(s): None
Board meeting date(s): Monthly; grants considered in Apr., July, and Nov.
Final notification: 2 to 3 months
Officers and Directors:* Alan Michigan,* Pres.; David A. Brauner,* V.P.; **Charles A. Damato,* V.P.; Michael J. Clain,* Secy.; Michael L. Goldstein,* Treas.**; Richard K. Baron, Exec. Dir.; Mel P. Barkan; Jules M. Baron; John H.F. Enteman; Donald Gibson; David R. Kay; Alan Nisselson; Christopher C. Schwabacher; Howard L. Simon; Roy M. Sparber.
Number of staff: 2 full-time professional.
EIN: 136066039
Other changes: Alan Michigan has replaced Alan Michigan as Pres. Michael J. Clain has replaced Charles A. Damato as Secy. Michael L. Goldstein has replaced Michael J. Clain as Secy.
Charles A. Damato is now a V.P.

2184
The Goldstein Family Foundation
c/o Arthur Fox, CPA
420 Lexington Ave., Ste. 1733
New York, NY **10170-1734**

Established in 1984 in NY.
Donor: Jerome Goldstein.
Foundation type: Independent foundation.
Financial data (yr. ended 11/30/13): Assets, $14,490,319 (M); expenditures, $902,147; qualifying distributions, $700,899; giving activities include $683,515 for 75 grants (high: $300,000; low: $115).
Fields of interest: Arts; Higher education; Education; Environment; Hospitals (general); Jewish federated giving programs; Jewish agencies & synagogues.
Limitations: Applications not accepted. Giving primarily in New York, NY; some funding also in NJ. No grants to individuals.
Application information: Contributes only to pre-selected organizations.
Officers: Jerome R. Goldstein, Pres.; Dorothy L. Goldstein, V.P.; Bettina L. Decker, Secy.-Treas.
EIN: 133192220

2185
The B. Thomas Golisano Foundation
c/o Fishers Asset Mgmt.
1 Fishers Rd.
Pittsford, NY 14534-9511 (585) 340-1203
Contact: Ann M. Costello, Dir.
FAX: (585) 340-1204;
E-mail: info@GolisanoFoundation.org; Main URL: http://www.golisanofoundation.org
Facebook: https://www.facebook.com/pages/The-Golisano-Foundation/118294264855416
Grants List: http://www.golisanofoundation.org/grants.html

Established in 1985 in NY.
Donor: B. Thomas Golisano.
Foundation type: Independent foundation.
Financial data (yr. ended 10/31/13): Assets, $28,934,513 (M); expenditures, $1,162,771; qualifying distributions, $1,122,254; giving activities include $927,000 for 26 grants (high: $361,000; low: $5,000).
Purpose and activities: Support for programs that create opportunities for people with developmental disabilities to achieve maximum potential and be active in their communities.
Fields of interest: Disabilities, people with.
Type of support: General/operating support; Capital campaigns; Building/renovation; Equipment; Seed money; Program evaluation; Matching/challenge support.
Limitations: Applications accepted. Giving limited to the greater Rochester, NY area. No support for municipal programs. No grants to individuals, or for fund-raising events, medical research, or for endowments.
Publications: Application guidelines; Annual report; Grants list; Program policy statement.
Application information: Grantmakers Forum of New York's Common Grant Application Form accepted. Application form required.
Initial approach: Telephone or letter of inquiry with application
Copies of proposal: 2
Deadline(s): 4 weeks prior to board meeting
Board meeting date(s): Quarterly; usually 4th Wed. of Jan., Apr., July and Oct.
Final notification: Within 2 weeks after board meeting
Director: Ann M. Costello.
Trustees: G. Thomas Clark; Dr. William Destler; B. Thomas Golisano; **Charles Graham**; Patricia Malgieri; James D. Murray.
Number of staff: 1 part-time professional; 1 part-time support.
EIN: 222692938
Other changes: Nancy N. Koch is no longer a trustee.

2186
Neil and Jane Golub Foundation, Inc.
Schenectady, NY

The foundation terminated on June 29, 2011 and transferred its assets to the William Estelle Neil Jane Golub Family Foundation, Inc.

2187
Adolph and Esther Gottlieb Foundation, Inc.
380 West Broadway
New York, NY 10012-5115 (212) 226-0581
Contact: Sanford Hirsch, Exec. Dir.
FAX: (212) 274-1476;
E-mail: shirsch@gottliebfoundation.org; Main URL: http://www.gottliebfoundation.org

Established in 1976 in NY.
Donors: Adolph Gottlieb†; Esther Gottlieb†; Alice Yamin†; Ann Cooper†.
Foundation type: Independent foundation.
Financial data (yr. ended 06/30/13): Assets, $32,911,466 (M); expenditures, $1,244,487; qualifying distributions, $1,106,168; giving activities include $548,500 for 33 grants to individuals.
Purpose and activities: The foundation maintains two separate grant programs: 1) Individual support program for painters, sculptors, and printmakers who have worked at least 20 years in a mature phase of their art, and are in current financial need; and 2) Emergency assistance program for painters, sculptors, and printmakers who have worked at least 10 years in a mature phase of their art and are in current financial need in excess of and unrelated to their normal economic situation, and which is the result of a recent emergency occurrence such as a fire, flood or medical emergency.
Fields of interest: Visual arts; Visual arts, sculpture; Visual arts, painting; Economically disadvantaged.
Type of support: Emergency funds; Grants to individuals.
Limitations: Giving on a national and international basis. No support for charitable organizations, educational institutions or projects, artists working in crafts, or for dental work, or chronic situations. No grants for capital improvements, or for debt.
Publications: Application guidelines; Informational brochure.
Application information: Application information available on foundation web site. Application form required.
Initial approach: Letter only, requesting application form for Individual Support program; letter or telephone for Emergency Assistance program
Copies of proposal: 1
Deadline(s): Dec. 15 for Individual Support Program grants; none for Emergency Assistance Program
Board meeting date(s): Annually
Final notification: Mar.
Officers and Directors:* Robert Mangold, Pres.; Charlotta Kotik,* V.P.; Gordon Marsh,* V.P.; Sanford Hirsch,* Secy.-Treas. and Exec. Dir.; Lynda Benglis.
Number of staff: 3 full-time professional; 1 part-time professional; 1 part-time support.
EIN: 132853957

2188
Edwin Gould Foundation
55 Exchange Pl., 6th Fl.
New York, NY 10005-3301 (212) 982-5200
Contact: Cynthia Rivera Weissblum, C.E.O. and Pres.
FAX: (212) 982-6886; Main URL: http://www.edwingouldfoundation.org/

Incorporated in 1923 in New York, NY.
Foundation type: Independent foundation.
Financial data (yr. ended 12/31/13): Assets, $42,442,166 (M); gifts received, $75,655; expenditures, $2,629,355; qualifying distributions, $2,114,675; giving activities include $914,004 for 27 grants (high: $508,464; low: $500).
Purpose and activities: The foundation champions innovative organizations that create bold, best-in-class solutions to increase the number of college graduates from under-resourced communities. They seek to accomplish this by seeding and growing educational models that empower motivated, yet underserved students to enter college, graduate and advance society. The foundation seeks to provide educational support where the system leaves off, with a focus on supplemental education initiatives that help students succeed. The foundation has a deep, long-term approach to grantmaking through investment in Gould Partners over the long-term, to provide them with the additional resources and office space needed to work, grow and collaborate.
Fields of interest: Elementary/secondary education; Higher education; Higher education, college; Youth; Young adults; Young adults, female; Young adults, male; Economically disadvantaged.
Type of support: Management development/capacity building; Program development; Seed

money; Curriculum development; Program evaluation.
Limitations: Applications not accepted. Giving primarily in New York, NY, and throughout the U.S. for advocacy. No support for organizations that do not focus on preparation for and persistence to college graduation for motivated yet underserved youth. No grants to individuals, or for building or endowment funds, or matching gifts; no loans.
Application information: Unsolicited requests for funds not accepted.
Officers and Trustees:* Mark Bieler,* Chair.; Cynthia Rivera Weissblum,* C.E.O. and Pres.; Nana Tam, Treas.; Michael W. Osheowitz,* Chair. Emeritus; Steven Brown; Anthony Carnevale; Nicole M. Chestang; Steven Gross; Lofton Holder; Truda Jewitt; Edward A. Lesser; Roszell Mack III; Josh Parker; Alan Weinstein.
Advisors: Marc Porter Magee; Thomas L. Webber.
Number of staff: 5 full-time professional; 1 full-time support.
EIN: 135675642

2189
The Grace and Mercy Foundation, Inc.
c/o Tiger Asia
101 Park Ave., 48th Fl.
New York, NY 10178-4799

Established in 2006 in NY.
Donors: Sung Kook Hwang; Chung Ko; Jensen Ko; Tiger Asia Management; Hwang Donor Advised Fund at Fuller.
Foundation type: Independent foundation.
Financial data (yr. ended 12/31/12): Assets, $68,839,374 (M); gifts received, $23,603; expenditures, $6,981,773; qualifying distributions, $6,938,479; giving activities include $5,648,178 for 61 grants (high: $670,000; low: $250).
Fields of interest: Theological school/education; Education; Health care; Human services; Protestant agencies & churches.
Limitations: Applications not accepted. Giving primarily in New York, NY; funding also in CA. No grants to individuals.
Application information: Contributes only to pre-selected organizations.
Officers and Directors:* Mark W. Shaw, Pres.; Becky Hwang,* V.P.; Jeanne Cox, Secy.; Patrick Halligan, Treas.; Sung Kook Hwang.
EIN: 208050779
Other changes: Mark W. Shaw has replaced Sung Kook Hwang as Pres.

2190
Charles M. & Mary D. Grant Foundation
c/o JPMorgan Chase Bank, Philanthropic Svcs.
270 Park Ave., 16th Fl.
New York, NY 10017-2014
***Contact:* Carolyn O'Brien, Grants Mgr.**
FAX: (212) 464-2304;
E-mail: carolyn.r.obrien@jpmorgan.com; Main URL: http://fdnweb.org/grant
Grants List: http://fdnweb.org/grant/grants/category/contributions/

Established in 1967 in NY.
Donor: Mary D. Grant†.
Foundation type: Independent foundation.
Financial data (yr. ended 12/31/12): Assets, $7,882,604 (M); expenditures, $487,020; qualifying distributions, $400,721; giving activities include $375,000 for 14 grants (high: $40,000; low: $15,000).
Purpose and activities: Support for organizations involved with community and economic development, health and human services, environment, and education.
Fields of interest: Adult education—literacy, basic skills & GED; Education; Environment; Health care; Housing/shelter, development; Human services; Children/youth, services; Economic development; Community/economic development.
Type of support: General/operating support; Program development.
Limitations: Applications accepted. Giving primarily in the southeastern U.S. No support for organizations lacking 501(c)(3) status. No grants to individuals, or for research, endowment funds, or matching gifts; generally no scholarships or fellowships; no loans.
Publications: Application guidelines; Grants list.
Application information: All application materials must be submitted online. See foundation web site for complete application guidelines and requirements. Application form not required.
Copies of proposal: 1
Deadline(s): Apr. 30
Board meeting date(s): Aug.
Trustee: JPMorgan Chase Bank, N.A.
EIN: 136264329

2191
William T. Grant Foundation
570 Lexington Ave., 18th Fl.
New York, NY 10022-6837 (212) 752-0071
Contact: Grants Coord.
FAX: (212) 752-1398; E-mail: info@wtgrantfdn.org; Main URL: http://www.wtgrantfdn.org/
Grants Database: http://www.wtgrantfoundation.org/our_grantees/browse_grants/browse_grants
Knowledge Center: http://www.wtgrantfoundation.org/publications_and_reports

Incorporated in 1936 in DE.
Donor: William T. Grant†.
Foundation type: Independent foundation.
Financial data (yr. ended 12/31/12): Assets, $291,967,654 (M); expenditures, $16,027,377; qualifying distributions, $14,945,698; giving activities include $9,990,715 for 111 grants (high: $567,745; low: $8,315).
Purpose and activities: The mission of the foundation is to help create a society that values young people and enables them to reach their full potential. In pursuit of this goal, the foundation invests in research and in people and projects that use evidence-based approaches. Current grantmaking for research, policy analyses, and evaluations of interventions is restricted to the three interrelated topics that follow: 1) Youth Development: Understanding how youth develop strengths and assets such as the skills and relationships that contribute to their development and well-being; 2) Improving Systems, Organizations, and Programs: Understanding how to improve the quality of youth-serving systems, organizations, and programs; and 3) Adults' Use of Evidence and Their Views of Youth: Understanding how adults who are key constituents (influential policymakers, practitioners, scholars, advocates, and members of the media) view youth, and the policies and services that affect youth. The foundation also supports promising post-doctoral scholars from diverse disciplines through the William T. Grant Scholars Program, and through Youth Service Grants. Support also for local programs in the Tri-State area that actively engage young people and enable them to reach their full potential.
Fields of interest: Education, research; Youth development; Social sciences, research; Psychology/behavioral science; Social sciences, interdisciplinary studies; Social sciences; Public policy, research.
Type of support: Program development; Conferences/seminars; Publication; Fellowships; Research; Program evaluation.
Limitations: Applications accepted. Giving on a national basis; giving limited to NY, NJ, and CT for youth service grants. No grants to individuals or for annual fundraising campaigns, equipment and materials, land acquisition, building or renovation projects, operating budgets, endowments, or scholarships; no loans.
Publications: Application guidelines; Annual report; Financial statement; Grants list; Informational brochure; Informational brochure (including application guidelines).
Application information: Letter of inquiry may be submitted online via foundation web site. The foundation will invite applicants to submit proposals through its web site following review of the letter of inquiry. Application to William T. Grant Scholars Program by nomination only. The foundation accepts the New York/ New Jersey Area Common Application Form. Application form not required.
Initial approach: Letter of inquiry for major grants
Copies of proposal: 6
Deadline(s): See foundation web site for current deadlines
Board meeting date(s): Quarterly
Final notification: Following each quarterly board meeting
Officers and Trustees:* Henry E. Gooss,* Chair.; **Christine James-Brown,* Vice-Chair.**; Adam Gamoran,* Pres.; Deborah E. McGinn, V.P., Finance and Admin.; Vivian Tseng, V.P., Progs.; Russell Pennoyer,* Secy.-Treas.; Margaret R. Burchinal; **Prudence L. Carter**; **Scott Evans**; Olivia Golden; Nancy Gonzales; Andrew C. Porter; Kenneth Prewitt; Judson Reis.
Number of staff: 5 full-time professional; 13 full-time support.
EIN: 131624021
Other changes: Christine James-Brown has replaced Gary Walker as Vice-Chair.
Edward Seidman is no longer Sr. V.P., Progs. J. Lawrence Aber, Kathleen Hall-Jamieson, Lisa Hess, Bridget Macaskill, Melvin Oliver and Sara McLanahan are no longer trustees.

2192
The Greenwall Foundation
420 Lexington Ave., Ste. 2500
New York, NY 10170-0020
Contact: Bernard Lo M.D., C.E.O. and Pres.
E-mail: admin@greenwall.org; Main URL: http://www.greenwall.org
Grants Database: http://www.greenwall.org/grants.php

Incorporated in 1949 in NY.
Donors: Anna A. Greenwall†; Frank K. Greenwall†.
Foundation type: Independent foundation.
Financial data (yr. ended 12/31/12): Assets, $79,848,904 (M); gifts received, $803,701; expenditures, $3,409,701; qualifying distributions, $2,825,615; giving activities include $799,826 for 22 grants (high: $404,195; low: $2,000).
Purpose and activities: Grantmaking will focus solely on building and enriching the Greenwall Faculty Scholars Program in Bioethics.
Fields of interest: Medical care, bioethics.

Type of support: Research.
Limitations: Applications accepted. Giving nationally for bioethics. No grants for building or endowment funds, operating budgets, annual campaigns, deficit financing, or conferences; no loans.
Publications: Financial statement; IRS Form 990 or 990-PF printed copy available upon request.
Application information: See foundation web site for specific application instructions which must be followed. Application form not required.
Initial approach: **Letter of intent to be submitted through link on foundation web site**
Copies of proposal: 1
Deadline(s): **Nov. (See foundation web site for current date)**
Board meeting date(s): May and Nov.
Final notification: After next board meeting
Officers and Directors:* Christine K. Cassel, M.D.*, Chair.; Joseph G. Perpich, M.D., J.D.*, Vice-Chair.; Bernard Lo, M.D.*, Pres.; T. Dennis Sullivan,* Secy. and Treas.; George L. Bunting, Jr.; Jason H. Karlawish, M.D.; Gayle Pemberton, Ph.D.; Richard L. Salzer, Jr., M.D.; James A. Tulsky, M.D.
Number of staff: 1 full-time professional; 2 full-time support.
EIN: 136082277

2193
Gross Foundation, Inc.
P.O. Box 040308
Parkville Sta.
Brooklyn, NY 11204-0308 (718) 851-7724
***Contact:* Dov Gross, Dir.**

Established in 1991 in NY.
Donors: Chaim Gross; Arie Herzog; Pinchus Gross; Esther Gross; Naftali Weiser; Esther Weiser; Shea Rosenfeld; Rachel Rosenfeld; David Spira; Daniel Gross; Robert Kaszovitz.
Foundation type: Independent foundation.
Financial data (yr. ended 02/28/13): Assets, $49,849,931 (M); expenditures, $2,366,263; qualifying distributions, $2,326,767; giving activities include $2,326,767 for grants.
Purpose and activities: Giving primarily for Orthodox Jewish educational and charitable organizations and temples.
Fields of interest: Education; Jewish agencies & synagogues.
Limitations: Applications accepted. Giving primarily in NY. No grants to individuals.
Application information: Application form not required.
***Initial approach:* Letter**
Deadline(s): None
Directors: Dov Gross; Faigie Gross; **Pincus Gross.**
EIN: 113006419
Other changes: Chaim Gross is no longer Pres.

2194
John Simon Guggenheim Memorial Foundation
90 Park Ave.
New York, NY 10016-1302 (212) 687-4470
Contact: Edward Hirsch, Pres.
FAX: (212) 697-3248; E-mail: fellowships@gf.org; Main URL: http://www.gf.org
E-Newsletter: http://list-manage.com/subscribe?u=59d983d0914a509b37f82546c&id=5039a73dec

Incorporated in 1925 in NY.
Donors: Simon Guggenheim†; Mrs. Simon Guggenheim†.
Foundation type: Independent foundation.
Financial data (yr. ended 12/31/12): Assets, $238,109,536 (M); gifts received, $1,030,793; expenditures, $16,867,864; qualifying distributions, $11,924,881; giving activities include $8,069,150 for 325 grants to individuals (high: $55,000; low: $5,000).
Purpose and activities: Fellowships offered to further the development of scholars and artists by assisting them to engage in research in any field of knowledge and creation in any of the arts, under the freest possible conditions and irrespective of race, color, or creed. Fellowships are awarded by the trustees upon nomination by a Committee of Selection. Awards are made to citizens and permanent residents of the U.S., Canada, Latin America, and the Caribbean.
Fields of interest: Visual arts; Humanities; Science; Social sciences.
International interests: Canada; Caribbean; Latin America.
Type of support: Fellowships.
Limitations: Applications accepted. Giving to citizens and permanent residents of the U.S., Canada, Latin America, and the Caribbean. No grants for endowments, operating budgets, special projects, or any other expenses of institutions.
Publications: Application guidelines; Annual report; Financial statement; Informational brochure (including application guidelines).
Application information: Grants are awarded to individuals rather than institutions. Application guidelines available on Web site. Application form required.
Initial approach: Online
Copies of proposal: 1
Deadline(s): **Sept. 19 for U.S. and Canada; Dec. 1 for Latin America and the Caribbean**
Board meeting date(s): Apr., June, and as required
Final notification: Approximately 6 months
Officers and Trustees:* William P. Kelly,* Chair.; Edward Hirsch,* Pres.; Robert A. Caro; Joel Conarroe; Dorothy Tapper Goldman; Michael Hegarty; **Dwight E. Lee**; Joyce Carol Oates; A. Alex Porter; Joseph A. Rice; Richard A. Rifkind; Stacy Schiff; Charles P. Stevenson, Jr.; Waddell W. Stillman; Patrick J. Waide, Jr.; Ellen Taaffe Zwilich.
Number of staff: 8 full-time professional; 12 full-time support.
EIN: 135673173
Other changes: Andre Bernard is no longer V.P. and Secy. Coleen P. Higgins-Jacob is no longer V.P., C.F.O., and Treas.

2195
J. Gurwin Foundation Inc.
40 E. 83rd St., No. 8E
New York, NY **10028-0843**

Incorporated in 1959 in NY.
Donors: Joseph Gurwin; Eric Gurwin; Laura Flug; Kings Point Industries, Inc.; Danielle Flug; Laura Flug.
Foundation type: Independent foundation.
Financial data (yr. ended 07/31/13): Assets, $17,373,028 (M); expenditures, $571,122; qualifying distributions, $511,680; giving activities include $511,680 for 24 grants (high: $112,500; low: $100).
Purpose and activities: Giving primarily for Jewish organizations, schools, and federated giving programs.
Fields of interest: Arts; Education; Human services; Jewish agencies & synagogues.
Limitations: Applications not accepted. Giving primarily in NY. No grants to individuals.
Application information: Contributes only to pre-selected organizations.
Officers: Joseph Gurwin, Pres.; Eric Gurwin, V.P.; Laura Flug, Secy.-Treas.
EIN: 136059258
Other changes: Joseph Gurwin has replaced Laura Flug as Pres.
Danielle Flug is no longer Treas.

2196
Ron and Stacey Gutfleish Foundation
298 Scarborough Rd.
Briarcliff Manor, NY **10510-2065**

Donors: Ron Gutfleish; Stacey Gutfleish.
Foundation type: Independent foundation.
Financial data (yr. ended 06/30/13): Assets, $22,540,399 (M); gifts received, $3,000,000; expenditures, $1,512,006; qualifying distributions, $1,178,950; giving activities include $1,171,500 for 15 grants (high: $400,000; low: $500).
Fields of interest: Higher education; Human services.
Limitations: Applications not accepted. Giving in the U.S., with emphasis on NY and RI. No grants to individuals.
Application information: Contributes only to pre-selected organizations.
Directors: Ron Gutfleish; Stacey Gutfleish.
EIN: 753205276

2197
Stella and Charles Guttman Foundation, Inc.
122 E. 42nd St. Ste. 2010
New York, NY 10168-2101
Contact: Elizabeth Olofson, Exec. Dir.
FAX: (212) 371-8936;
E-mail: eolofson@guttmanfoundation.org; Main URL: http://www.guttmanfoundation.org/

Incorporated in 1959 in NY.
Donors: Charles Guttman†; Stella Guttman†.
Foundation type: Independent foundation.
Financial data (yr. ended 12/31/12): Assets, $50,289,947 (M); expenditures, $3,435,480; qualifying distributions, $2,923,667; giving activities include $2,058,500 for 59 grants (high: $185,000; low: $500).
Purpose and activities: At present, the foundation intends to direct a substantial portion of its grantmaking to programs that serve low income infants, toddlers and preschoolers as they transition to kindergarten. Special emphasis will be placed on programs that improve quality, expand services and create a strong continuum of care for children ages 0-3 in high-need neighborhoods.
Fields of interest: Education, early childhood education.
Type of support: General/operating support; Continuing support; Program development.
Limitations: Applications accepted. **Giving primarily in the five boroughs of New York, NY.** No support for religious organizations for religious purposes, or for public interest litigation or antivivisectionist causes. No grants to individuals, or for foreign travel or foreign study.
Application information: An application form will be provided at the discretion of the foundation.
Initial approach: 2 or 3-page letter of inquiry
Deadline(s): Rolling

Board meeting date(s): Quarterly
Final notification: 4 to 6 weeks
Officers and Directors:* Ernest Rubenstein,* Pres.; Peter A. Herbert,* V.P.; Susan Butler Plum,* Secy.; Robert S. Gassman,* Treas.; Elizabeth Olofson, Exec. Dir.; Patricia L. Fancy; Benjamin Herbert; Paulette LoMonaco.
Number of staff: 4 full-time professional.
EIN: 136103039

2198
The Richard and Mica Hadar Foundation
(formerly The Hadar Foundation)
400 E. 84th St.
New York, NY **10028-5606** (212) 832-9797
Contact: Richard Hadar, Co-Chair.
Main URL: http://www.hadarfoundation.org

Established in 1993 in FL.
Donors: Richard Hadar; The Hadar Charitable Lead Trust.
Foundation type: Operating foundation.
Financial data (yr. ended 12/31/12): Assets, $3,444,519 (M); expenditures, $353,946; qualifying distributions, $176,510; giving activities include $163,450 for 39 grants (high: $28,500; low: $500), and $13,060 for 6 grants to individuals (high: $7,500; low: $40).
Purpose and activities: Giving in support of young artists and scholars, by providing academic scholarships, mentoring, and career guidance.
Fields of interest: Arts education; Arts; Higher education, college; Higher education, university.
Type of support: General/operating support; Scholarships—to individuals.
Limitations: Giving primarily in NY.
Application information: Application form required.
Deadline(s): Jan. 15
Officers: Richard Hadar, Co-Chair.; Mica B. Hadar, Co-Chair.; **Beth Rosenberg, Exec. Dir.**
Director: Ann Feminella.
EIN: 133721350
Other changes: Beth Rosenberg has replaced Ela Bittencourt as Exec. Dir.

2199
Hagedorn Foundation
225 Bryant Ave.
Roslyn Harbor, NY **11576-1153** (516) 767-5754
E-mail: Info@hagedornfoundation.org; Application address: P.O. Box 888, Port Washington, NY 11050-0888; Main URL: http://www.hagedornfoundation.org
Hagedorn Foundation's Philanthropy Promise: http://www.ncrp.org/philanthropys-promise/who

Established in 2007 in NY.
Donors: Horace Hagedorn Foundation; Seedworks.
Foundation type: Independent foundation.
Financial data (yr. ended 12/31/12): Assets, $31,994,459 (M); expenditures, $5,469,061; qualifying distributions, $5,257,037; giving activities include $4,460,823 for 58 grants (high: $665,000; low: $75).
Purpose and activities: Giving primarily to support and promote social equity on Long Island, New York.
Fields of interest: Children, services; Civil/human rights, equal rights.
Limitations: Giving primarily in Long Island, NY. No grants to individuals, or for scholarships, fellowships, deficit reduction, emergency funding, capital campaigns, political programs or endowments.
Publications: Application guidelines.
Application information: If using e-mail, please attach the Concept Paper (as a Word document) to an e-mail with the following subject line: "Concept Paper for HF Funding." Without this subject line, the foundation's online server will reject the e-mail. Full proposals are by invitation only, after review of concept paper. Reports, videos or other attachments are not accepted with the concept paper.
Initial approach: Concept paper (no more than 2 pages) via e-mail or U.S. mail
Deadline(s): None
Officers and Director:* Amy Hagedorn,* Pres.; Lisa O'Beirne, V.P.; Annamarie Quinlan, Secy.; Rob McMahon, Treas.; Darren Sandow, Exec. Dir.
Number of staff: 3 full-time professional; 3 full-time support.
EIN: 260370010

2200
Hagedorn Fund
c/o JPMorgan Chase Bank, N.A., Private Foundation Svcs.
270 Park Ave., 16th Fl.
New York, NY 10017-2014
Contact: Jonathan G. Horowitz, Prog. Off.
FAX: (212) 464-2304;
E-mail: jonathan.g.horowitz@jpmchase.com; **Main URL: http://fdnweb.org/hagedorn**
Grants List: http://fdnweb.org/hagedorn/grants/category/contributions/

Trust established in 1953 in NY.
Donor: William Hagedorn†.
Foundation type: Independent foundation.
Financial data (yr. ended 12/31/12): Assets, $51,167,261 (M); expenditures, $2,584,532; qualifying distributions, $2,345,323; giving activities include $2,136,000 for 70 grants (high: $100,000; low: $1,000).
Purpose and activities: Giving primarily for health (including cancer, HIV/AIDS, blindness), gardens, social services, youth, education, senior services, and housing and community development.
Fields of interest: Education; Botanical gardens; Health care; Cancer; AIDS; Housing/shelter; Youth development; Human services; Community/economic development; Aging; Blind/visually impaired.
Type of support: General/operating support; Capital campaigns; Program development.
Limitations: Applications not accepted. Giving primarily in New York, NY. No support for private foundations. No grants to individuals, or for continuing support, seed money, emergency funds, deficit financing, endowment funds, matching gifts, special projects, publications, or conferences; no loans.
Publications: Grants list.
Application information: Unsolicited proposals are not accepted.
Board meeting date(s): Nov.
Trustees: John J. Kindred III; Malcolm E. Martin; JPMorgan Chase Bank, N.A.
EIN: 136048718

2201
The Hallingby Family Foundation, Inc.
7 Gracie Sq., Ste. 10A
New York, NY 10028-8001
***Contact:* Paul L. Hallingby**

Established in 1998 in CT.
Donor: Paul L. Hallingby.
Foundation type: Operating foundation.
Financial data (yr. ended 04/30/13): Assets, $1,462,732 (M); expenditures, $150,626; qualifying distributions, $149,388; giving activities include $148,300 for 47 grants (high: $50,000; low: $100).
Fields of interest: Higher education; Libraries/library science; Environment; Animal welfare; Hospitals (general); Genetic diseases and disorders; Recreation, parks/playgrounds; Human services; American Red Cross; Civil liberties, reproductive rights; Community/economic development.
Type of support: General/operating support; Capital campaigns.
Limitations: Applications not accepted. Giving primarily in MA and New York, NY. No grants to individuals.
Application information: Contributes only to pre-selected organizations.
Officers: Paul L. Hallingby, Pres.; Julia H. Hallingby, V.P.; Thomas P. Spellane, Secy.-Treas.
EIN: 061516271

2202
The Robert Halper Foundation
(formerly The Robert & Deann Halper Foundation)
271 Central Park W.
New York, NY 10024-3020 (212) 628-6386
Contact: Robert Halper, Pres.

Established in 1991 in NY.
Donors: Deann Halper; Robert Halper.
Foundation type: Independent foundation.
Financial data (yr. ended 12/31/11): Assets, $1,081,159 (M); expenditures, $149,678; qualifying distributions, $145,055; giving activities include $138,500 for 14 grants (high: $40,000; low: $1,000).
Fields of interest: Museums; Arts; Human services; Foundations (private grantmaking); Religious federated giving programs.
Limitations: Applications accepted. Giving primarily in NY.
Application information: Application form required.
Initial approach: Letter
Deadline(s): None
Officers: Robert Halper, Pres.; Murray Halper, Secy.
EIN: 223121072
Other changes: The grantmaker has moved from DE to NY. The grantmaker no longer lists a separate application address.

2203
The Keith Haring Foundation, Inc.
676 Broadway, 5th Fl.
New York, NY 10012-2319
Contact: Julia Gruen, Exec. Dir.
E-mail: jgruen@haring.com; Additional e-mail: fkrieger@haring.com; Main URL: http://www.haring.com/kh_foundation/
Blog: http://www.keithharingfoundationarchives.wordpress.com
Grants List: http://www.haring.com/kh_foundation/grants
Tumblr: http://keithharing.tumblr.com/
Twitter: http://twitter.com/KeithHaring

Established in 1989 in NY.
Donors: Keith Haring†; ACT-UP.
Foundation type: Independent foundation.

Financial data (yr. ended 09/30/12): Assets, $40,731,947 (M); expenditures, $4,170,127; qualifying distributions, $3,253,354; giving activities include $2,203,100 for 48 grants (high: $1,000,000; low: $3,100).
Purpose and activities: Giving primarily to organizations which provide educational opportunities to underprivileged children, and to organizations which engage in research and care with respect to AIDS and HIV infection. The foundation also maintains a collection of art along with archives which facilitate historical research about Keith Haring and the times and places in which he lived and worked. The foundation supports arts and educational institutions by funding exhibitions, educational programs, acquisitions and publications that serve to contextualize and illuminate the artist's work and philosophy.
Fields of interest: Arts education; Health care; AIDS; AIDS research; Children, services; Children/youth; Children; Youth; Minorities; African Americans/ Blacks; Hispanics/Latinos; AIDS, people with; Economically disadvantaged; LGBTQ.
Type of support: Continuing support; Curriculum development.
Limitations: Applications accepted. **Giving primarily in New York, NY.** No support for religious or political organizations. No grants to individuals directly. No grants to organizations lacking 501(c)(3) status.
Publications: Application guidelines; Grants list.
Application information: Application form and guidelines available on foundation web site. Application form required.
Officers: Gilbert Vazquez, Vice-Pres.; David Stark, Secy.; Allen Haring, Treas.; Julia Gruen, Exec. Dir.
Trustees: Judith Cox; Tom Eccles; Kristen Haring.
Number of staff: 4 full-time professional; 3 part-time professional.
EIN: 110249024

2204
The Havens Relief Fund Society

475 Riverside Dr., Rm. 1940
New York, NY 10115-0023
***Contact:* Allison S. McDermott, Exec. Dir.**
***E-mail:* info@havensfund.org**; Main URL: http:// www.havensfund.org

Incorporated in 1870 in NY.
Donors: Charles Gerard Havens†; The Philanthropic Collaborative; The Clarkson Family Foundation.
Foundation type: Operating foundation.
Financial data (yr. ended 12/31/12): Assets, $26,114,200 (M); gifts received, $57,941; expenditures, $1,339,081; qualifying distributions, $1,198,991; giving activities include $753,518 for grants to individuals.
Purpose and activities: Since its founding, the Society's purpose has remained the same: to relieve the suffering caused by a setback in the life of a New York City resident by providing a modest financial boost at a critical time in that person's life. In doing so, the Society's goal is to help the beneficiary overcome an obstacle that stands between him/her and self-sufficiency. The Society works with a network of dedicated individuals called "Almoners" - derived from "the giving of alms" - many of whom work in the New York City's health and social services agencies or serve as religious and community representatives.
Fields of interest: Economically disadvantaged.
Type of support: Grants to individuals.
Limitations: Applications not accepted. Giving limited to New York, NY. No support for institutions, organizations, or agencies.
Application information: Unsolicited requests for funds not accepted.
Board meeting date(s): Feb. and Dec. and May
Officers and Board Members:* Regina S. Peruggi,* Pres.; Paul J. Brignola,* V.P.; Christy Pennoyer,* Secy.; Jose A. Tavares,* Treas.; Allison S. McDermott, Exec. Dir.; Jane Aoyama-Martin, Esq.; Hon. Deborah A. Batts; Hon. P. Kevin Castel; Bayard D. Clarkson, M.D.; David C. Condliffe, Esq.; **Daniel P. Davidson; Abigail Jones Feder; Anna M. Irwin**; Dianne Mack; **Samuel L. Morgan, Ed.D.; Suzanne M. Murphy; Stephanie Nickerson, Ph.D.**; David L. Plimpton, Ph.D.; **David F. Sternleib**; Hon. Laura Taylor Swain; **Hon. Robert W. Sweet**; Jose Tavares; **Thomas D. Thatcher II; George A. von Hassel.**
Number of staff: 2 full-time professional.
EIN: 135562382
Other changes: Regina S. Peruggi has replaced Arthur V. Savage as Pres. Paul J. Brignola has replaced Michael Loening as V.P. Christy Pennoyer has replaced Russell G. O'Oench, III, as Secy. Jose A. Tavares has replaced Paul J. Brignola as Treas. Allison S. McDermott has replaced Joyce R. Willis as Exec. Dir.
JoAnn Delafield, Charles S. Haight, Robert P. Patterson, and Charles P. Sifton are no longer directors.

2205
Heckscher Foundation for Children

123 E. 70th St.
New York, NY 10021-5006 (212) 744-0190
Contact: Heather Sutton, Sr. Prog. Off.
FAX: (212) 744-2761;
E-mail: grants@heckscherfoundation.org; Main URL: http://www.heckscherfoundation.org
Facebook: https://www.facebook.com/ HeckscherFoundation
Instagram: http://www.instagram.com/ heckscherfoundation#
Twitter: https://www.twitter.com/HeckscherFnd

Incorporated in 1921 in NY.
Donor: August Heckscher†.
Foundation type: Independent foundation.
Financial data (yr. ended 12/31/13): Assets, $297,685,633 (M); expenditures, $14,601,444; qualifying distributions, $12,311,347; giving activities include $10,474,429 for 113 grants (high: $500,000).
Purpose and activities: The foundation defines its mission as "leveling the playing field for underserved youth." Its goal is to foster venture philanthropy using three principal funding strategies: 1) Catalytic Giving identifies approaches that have the potential for wide application but which have not reached a scale broad enough to attract investment by larger private foundations or government; 2) Strategic Partnerships promotes collaborations between not for profits, for profits and the public sector toward a common goal; 3) Targeted Problem Solving defines a specific challenge that has a practical solution attainable within a reasonable time and budget, and that encourages creative problem solvers to test that solution. The challenge often addresses barriers to equal opportunity either overlooked or under appreciated.
Fields of interest: Arts education; Health care; Employment; Recreation; Youth, services; Infants/ toddlers; Children/youth; Children; Girls; Boys.
Type of support: Curriculum development; Matching/challenge support; Program development; Program evaluation.
Limitations: Applications not accepted. Giving primarily in the greater New York, NY, area. No grants to individuals, annual campaigns, fundraising events, political efforts, or endowment funds.
Application information: Funding by invitation only. Unsolicited requests for funds not accepted.
Officers and Trustees:* Howard G. Sloane,* Chair. and C.E.O.; Arthur J. Smadbeck,* Vice-Chair. and Treas.; Gail Meyers,* Vice-Chair.; Ourania Vokolos-Zias, V.P., Finance and Admin.; Mark Magowan,* Secy.; Virginia Sloane,* Pres. Emeritus; Hilary Azrael; Mark Beck; Philippe Laub; Kathryn Meyers; Alexander Sloane; Jake Sloan; Nessia Sloane; Jeffrey Smadbeck; Lou Smadbeck; Louis Smadbeck, Jr.; Mark Smadbeck; Paul Smadbeck; David Tillson.
Senior Staff: Indya Hartley, Grants Mgr.; Shelby Marzouk, Prog. Off.; Heather Sutton, Sr. Prog. Off.
Number of staff: 2 full-time professional; 7 full-time support.
EIN: 131820170

2206
Heisman Trophy Trust

111 Broadway, Ste. 103A
New York, NY 10006
***E-mail:* Info@Heisman.com**; Main URL: http:// www.heisman.com/

Established in NY.
Donors: Orange Bowl Committee; Valero Alamo Bowl; Electronic Arts Inc.
Foundation type: Operating foundation.
Financial data (yr. ended 10/30/12): Assets, $11,527,208 (M); gifts received, $160,800; expenditures, $2,482,610; qualifying distributions, $1,047,750; giving activities include $1,047,750 for 114 grants (high: $51,400; low: $500).
Fields of interest: Education; Health organizations, association; Human services; Catholic agencies & churches.
Limitations: Applications not accepted.
Application information: Unsolicited requests for funds not accepted.
Officer: William J. Dockery, Pres.
Directors: Michael Comeford, Esq.; James Corcoran; Anne Fitzpatrick-Donahue; N. Richard Kalikow; Vasili Krishnamurti; Brian Obergfell; Carol Pisano; Sanford Wurmfeld.
EIN: 137052079

2207
The Leona M. and Harry B. Helmsley Charitable Trust

230 Park Ave., Ste. 659
New York, NY 10169-0698 (212) 679-3600
E-mail: grants@helmsleytrust.org; **Additional address: 3130 W. 57th St., Ste. 112, Sioux Falls, SD 57108, tel.: (605) 361-9848**; Main URL: http:// www.helmsleytrust.org/
Grants Database: http://helmsleytrust.org/grants/

Established in 1999 in NY.
Donors: Leona M. Helmsley†; Sierra Towers & Fresh Meadows, LLP; Eastdil Realty, Inc., LLC; Helmsley Enterprises, Inc.
Foundation type: Independent foundation.
Financial data (yr. ended 03/31/13): Assets, $4,241,501,002 (M); gifts received, $97,478,331; expenditures, $242,309,685; qualifying distributions, $222,718,960; giving activities include $210,352,475 for 378 grants (high: $15,018,000; low: $913).

Purpose and activities: The trust aspires to improve lives by supporting effective nonprofits. Grantmaking focuses on four main areas: health and medical research, human services, education, and conservation. The trust, which is administered by four trustees selected by Leona Helmsley, also awards grants in other areas.
Fields of interest: Education; Environment; Hospitals (general); Health care; Digestive diseases; Diabetes; Diabetes research; Medical research; Human services; Philanthropy/voluntarism.
Limitations: Applications not accepted. Giving primarily in NY. No grants to individuals.
Application information: Contributes only to pre-selected organizations.
Officers: John R. Ettinger, C.E.O.; Leigh Bonney, C.F.O.; Nicholas Milowski, Cont.; Rosalind M. Hewsenian, C.I.O.
Trustees: John Codey; Sandor Frankel; David Panzirer; Walter Panzirer.
Investment Committee: Linda B. Strumpf, Chair.; Deborah L. Allinson, Vice Chair.; **Sandor Frankel**; **Howard Marks**; Robert H. Niehaus; **David Panzirer**; **Remy W. Trafelet**.
EIN: 137184401
Other changes: B. Jack Miller and Peter Olson are no longer trustees.

2208
The Joan C. & David L. Henle Foundation
c/o BCRS Assocs., LLC
77 Water St., 9th Fl.
New York, NY 10005-4401

Established in 1996 in NY.
Donor: David L. Henle.
Foundation type: Independent foundation.
Financial data (yr. ended 08/31/13): Assets, $2,363,065 (M); gifts received, $1,106,459; expenditures, $2,198,851; qualifying distributions, $2,185,528; giving activities include $2,183,093 for 49 grants (high: $881,297; low: $50).
Fields of interest: Higher education; Education; Environment, natural resources; Health organizations, association; Human services; Children/youth, services.
Limitations: Applications not accepted. Giving in the U.S., with emphasis on NY. No grants to individuals; no loans or scholarships.
Application information: Contributes only to pre-selected organizations.
Trustees: David L. Henle; Joan C. Henle.
EIN: 137103244
Other changes: For the fiscal year ended Aug. 31, 2013, the grantmaker paid grants of $2,183,093, a 904.4% increase over the fiscal 2012 disbursements, $217,355.

2209
Louis Henry Gross Sponsorship Foundation
1100 Wehrle Dr., 2nd Fl.
Amherst, NY **14221-7748**

Foundation type: Independent foundation.
Financial data (yr. ended 05/31/13): Assets, $4,672,548 (M); expenditures, $168,501; qualifying distributions, $133,000; giving activities include $133,000 for 38 grants to individuals (high: $5,000; low: $3,000).
Fields of interest: Education.
Type of support: Scholarships—to individuals.
Limitations: Applications not accepted. Giving primarily in NY.
Application information: Unsolicited requests for funds not accepted.
Trustee: M&T Bank.
EIN: 276037438

2210
The Jim Henson Foundation
(formerly The Henson Foundation)
37-18 Northern Blvd., Ste. 400
Long Island City, NY 11101-1636 (212) 439-7504
E-mail: info@hensonfoundation.org; Main URL: http://www.hensonfoundation.org
Grants List: http://www.hensonfoundation.org/index.php/grant-awards/2010s/2011
Grants List: http://www.hensonfoundation.org/index.php/grant-awards/2010s/2012
Grants List: http://www.hensonfoundation.org/index.php/grant-awards/2010s/2013-grants
Grants List: http://www.hensonfoundation.org/index.php/grant-awards/2010s/2014-grants

Established in 1982 in NY.
Donors: Jane Henson Foundation; Cheryl Henson; Heather Henson; Jane Henson; James Maury "Jim" Henson‡; members of the Henson Family.
Foundation type: Independent foundation.
Financial data (yr. ended 12/31/12): Assets, $3,005,751 (M); gifts received, $93,391; expenditures, $304,998; qualifying distributions, $286,444; giving activities include $187,000 for 44 grants (high: $10,000; low: $2,000).
Purpose and activities: The mission of the foundation is to develop and encourage the creative art of puppetry in the United States. Emphasis is on contemporary puppet theater for adults, with some focus on new works suitable for family audiences. Grants are awarded for the development of innovative puppet theater by American artists, for American audiences.
Fields of interest: Performing arts.
Type of support: General/operating support; Grants to individuals.
Limitations: Applications accepted. Giving on a national basis. No grants for publications, parades, exhibitions, film or television projects.
Publications: Application guidelines; Grants list.
Application information: Grants only available to American artists. Guidelines and application form are available on foundation web site. Grant awardees will not be allowed to receive new grants the following year. Full proposals will only be accepted by invitation. Application form required.
Initial approach: 1-page letter of intent
Copies of proposal: 1
Deadline(s): Apr. 8 and Sept. 9
Board meeting date(s): June and Nov.
Final notification: No later than Dec. 16
Officers and Directors:* Cheryl Henson,* Pres.; **Richard Termine, V.P.**; **Pam Arciero, Secy.**; Louis Borodinsky, Treas.; Leslee Asch*; **John Farrell**; Kathee Foran; Heather Henson; **Lynn Jeffries**; **Martin Robinson**; **Hanne Tierney**.
Number of staff: 1 part-time support.
EIN: 133133702
Other changes: Richard Termine has replaced Jane Henson as V.P. Pam Arciero has replaced Leslee Asch as Secy.
Bradford Clark, Janie Geiser, and Mark Levenson are no longer directors.

2211
The F. B. Heron Foundation
100 Broadway, 17th Fl.
New York, NY 10005-4506 (212) 404-1800
Contact: John Seidl, Admin. Asst.
FAX: (212) 404-1805; **E-mail: info@heronfdn.org**; Main URL: http://www.fbheron.org/
Facebook: https://www.facebook.com/heronfdn
Knowledge Center: http://fbheron.issuelab.org/home
LinkedIn: http://www.linkedin/company/3006613
Program Review Study: http://www.fbheron.org/review/process.html
Twitter: https://twitter.com/FB

Established in 1992 in DE.
Foundation type: Independent foundation.
Financial data (yr. ended 12/31/12): Assets, $260,548,040 (M); expenditures, $8,830,391; qualifying distributions, $9,279,663; giving activities include $5,266,790 for 100 grants (high: $250,000; low: $100), $174,502 for foundation-administered programs and $2,049,999 for 3 loans/program-related investments.
Purpose and activities: As part of its new strategic plan, the foundation has decided to invest 100 percent of its endowment, as well as other forms of capital, for mission. To advance its mission, the foundation supports organizations that help low-income people to create and preserve wealth to help them take control of their lives and make decisions for themselves and their families. The foundation makes grants to and investments in entities that are engaged in one or more of the following wealth-creation strategies-including emerging opportunities to incorporate sustainable practices within the context of healthy environments-that benefit low- and moderate-income families and communities. The specific wealth-creation and preservation strategies are: 1) Advancing home ownership; 2) Supporting enterprise development; and 3) Increasing access to capital and preserving assets. The foundation will also support research and policy efforts that advance these wealth creation strategies. The foundation makes grants and investments, and commits other foundation resources, to efforts that: 1) Encourage effective practices in philanthropy, specifically to expand social impact through mission-related investing, as well as to promote core support funding, practical means of assessing impact, and high quality customer service to partner grantees and investees. 2) Develop systems and approaches for reliable, credible data, research and technology systems that inform and expand practice and policy in wealth creation. 3) Provide financial or technical assistance to community-based development organizations or coordinate practitioner networks to exchange lessons learned.
Fields of interest: Housing/shelter, home owners; Community development, neighborhood development; Economic development; Foundations (private grantmaking); Financial services.
Type of support: General/operating support; Continuing support; Program development; Technical assistance; Program evaluation; Program-related investments/loans; Employee matching gifts; Matching/challenge support; Mission-related investments/loans.
Limitations: Applications accepted. Giving primarily in New York City, NY, MI, TX, Appalachia and the Mid-South Delta region; some giving also in South Africa. No grants to individuals, or for endowments or capital campaigns.
Publications: Application guidelines; Annual report (including application guidelines); Grants list; Occasional report.

Application information: The foundation will likely not fund new organizations it currently does not support. Information available on the foundation's web site. Videotapes, CDs, DVDs, etc. will not be accepted. Applications not accepted for South Africa grantmaking. Application form not required.

Initial approach: Letter of inquiry (2 - 3 pages)
Copies of proposal: 1
Deadline(s): None
Board meeting date(s): Quarterly
Final notification: 1 week to initial letter of inquiry; 4 weeks max to full proposal, if requested

Officers and Directors:* Buzz Schmidt,* Chair.; Clara Miller,* Pres.; William M. Dietel; Amb. James A. Joseph; William F. McCalpin; John Otterlei.
Number of staff: 5 full-time professional; 1 part-time professional; 3 full-time support; 1 part-time support.
EIN: 133647019

2212
Annette Heyman Foundation, Inc.

c/o 40 North Svcs. LLC
9 W. 57th St., 30th Fl.
New York, NY 10019-2701

Established in 1960.
Donors: Annette Heyman; Samuel J. Heyman; Ronnie F. Heyman; Annette Heyman Family LLC; Larry S. Heyman; Eleanor H. Propp; Jennifer H. Millstone; Elizabeth H. Winter.
Foundation type: Independent foundation.
Financial data (yr. ended 09/30/13): Assets, $2,624,970 (M); gifts received, $575,000; expenditures, $251,712; qualifying distributions, $216,750; giving activities include $181,737 for 29 grants (high: $20,000; low: $250).
Purpose and activities: Giving primarily for the arts, higher education, hospitals and health organizations, social services, and Jewish organizations, including a Jewish museum.
Fields of interest: Museums (ethnic/folk arts); Performing arts centers; Arts; Higher education; Law school/education; Education; Hospitals (general); Health organizations, association; Human services; Jewish federated giving programs; Jewish agencies & synagogues.
Type of support: Annual campaigns; Capital campaigns; Endowments; Professorships; Research.
Limitations: Applications not accepted. Giving primarily in CT and NY, some giving also in FL and MA. No grants to individuals.
Application information: Contributes only to pre-selected organizations.
Officers and Directors:* Ronnie F. Heyman,* Pres.; Lazarus S. Heyman,* V.P. and Secy.; Donald Spiegelman, Treas.; Annette Heyman.
EIN: 066035519

2213
High Five Foundation

c/o Gerald Kaminsky
605 3rd Ave., 43rd Fl.
New York, NY 10158

Established in 1996 in NY.
Donor: Gerald P. Kaminsky.
Foundation type: Independent foundation.
Financial data (yr. ended 10/31/13): Assets, $6,487,306 (M); expenditures, $323,490; qualifying distributions, $311,021; giving activities include $308,181 for 136 grants (high: $25,000; low: $50).
Purpose and activities: Giving primarily for Jewish organizations, health and medical services, and higher education.
Fields of interest: Museums; Arts; Higher education; Health care, information services; Health care; Residential/custodial care, hospices; Jewish agencies & synagogues.
Type of support: General/operating support; Annual campaigns; Capital campaigns; Building/renovation; Endowments; Emergency funds; Curriculum development; Fellowships; Internship funds; Scholarship funds.
Limitations: Applications not accepted. No grants to individuals.
Publications: Annual report.
Application information: Contributes only to pre-selected organizations.
Officers: Gerald P. Kaminsky, Pres.; **Gary J. Kaminsky, V.P. and Treas.**; Jaclyn Kaminsky, Secy.
EIN: 113358107
Other changes: Michael J. Kaminsky is no longer Treas. Gary J. Kaminsky is now V.P. and Treas.

2214
The Hite Foundation, Inc.

c/o Nussbaum Yates Berg Klein & Wolpow, LLP
445 Broadhollow Rd., Ste. 319
Melville, NY 11747-3601
Contact: Arlene Ward
***E-mail:* atward165@gmail.com; Main URL: http://fdnweb.org/hite**

Established in 1987 in NJ.
Donor: Lawrence Hite.
Foundation type: Independent foundation.
Financial data (yr. ended 06/30/13): Assets, $5,968,613 (M); gifts received, $100,000; expenditures, $719,213; qualifying distributions, $337,895; giving activities include $325,300 for 22 grants (high: $50,000; low: $500).
Purpose and activities: The foundation has two primary grant making focus areas: child welfare policy, with special interest in permanency planning, and 19th century British photography.
Fields of interest: Visual arts, photography; Children, services.
Type of support: Program development; Research.
Limitations: Applications not accepted. Giving primarily in the metropolitan New York, NY, area. No grants to individuals.
Application information: Proposals considered by invitation only. Unsolicited proposals not accepted.
Officers: Lawrence D. Hite, Pres.; Simon Levin, Secy.-Treas.
EIN: 222856867

2215
HKH Foundation

New York, NY

The foundation terminated in 2013.

2216
Hochstein Foundation, Inc.

c/o Withumsmith and Brown, P.C.
1411 Broadway, 9th Fl.
New York, NY **10018-3496**

Established in 1960 in NY.
Donor: Bernard Hochstein†.
Foundation type: Independent foundation.
Financial data (yr. ended 12/31/12): Assets, $76,131,722 (M); gifts received, $1,324,515; expenditures, $3,280,079; qualifying distributions, $3,020,600; giving activities include $3,020,500 for 8 grants (high: $2,095,000; low: $3,500).
Purpose and activities: Giving primarily to Jewish agencies, temples, and schools.
Fields of interest: Education; Human services; Jewish federated giving programs; Jewish agencies & synagogues.
Type of support: General/operating support.
Limitations: Applications not accepted. Giving primarily in the metropolitan New York, NY, area. No grants to individuals.
Application information: Contributes only to pre-selected organizations.
Board Members: Michael Hochstein; Miriam Hochstein; Richard Hochstein; Stephen Hochstein.
EIN: 136161765
Other changes: At the close of 2012, the fair market value of the grantmaker's assets was $76,131,722, a 181.7% increase over the 2010 value, $27,028,089. For the same period, the grantmaker paid grants of $3,020,500, a 76.6% increase over the 2010 disbursements, $1,710,500.
Bernard Hochstein, Donor, is deceased. Helen Fuss is no longer a board member.

2217
Hod Foundation

c/o Amtrust Financial
59 Maiden Ln., 6th Fl.
New York, NY 10038-4502 (212) 639-5100
Contact: Henry Reinhold, Tr.

Established in 2000 in NY.
Donors: Michael Karfunkel; Karfunkel Family Foundation.
Foundation type: Independent foundation.
Financial data (yr. ended 06/30/13): Assets, $286,689,211 (M); expenditures, $5,350,896; qualifying distributions, $5,332,300; giving activities include $5,332,300 for 125 grants (high: $3,000,000; low: $500).
Purpose and activities: Giving primarily to Jewish agencies, temples, and schools.
Fields of interest: Elementary/secondary education; Jewish agencies & synagogues.
Limitations: Giving primarily in NY. No grants to individuals.
Application information: Application form not required.

Initial approach: Letter
Deadline(s): None

Directors: Barry Karfunkel; Leah Karfunkel; Michael Karfunkel; **Robert Karfunkel**; Henry Reinhold; Jeffrey Weissmann.
EIN: 133922069

2218
Hoffen Family Foundation

P.O. Box 230568
New York, NY 10023-0010
Contact: Sandra Hoffen, Chair.

Established in 2007 in DE and NY.
Donors: Howard I. Hoffen; Sandra Hoffen.
Foundation type: Independent foundation.
Financial data (yr. ended 12/31/12): Assets, $13,825,268 (M); gifts received, $1,006,620; expenditures, $359,325; qualifying distributions, $349,965; giving activities include $349,965 for grants.

Fields of interest: Arts; Education; Jewish agencies & synagogues.
Limitations: Applications not accepted. Giving primarily in NJ and NY.
Application information: Contributes only to pre-selected organizations.
Officers: Sandra Hoffen, Chair.; Howard I. Hoffen, Treas.
EIN: 261598880

2219
Holmberg Foundation, Inc.

519 Washington St.
Jamestown, NY 14701-4925 (716) 483-0735
Contact: David W. Shepherd, Pres.

Established in 1992 in NY.
Donors: Mr. Holmberg; Mrs. Bessemer; Mary Tilley Bessemer Charitable Reminder Unitrust.
Foundation type: Independent foundation.
Financial data (yr. ended 07/31/13): Assets, $4,974,716 (M); expenditures, $252,711; qualifying distributions, $203,922; giving activities include $201,800 for 16 grants (high: $75,000; low: $1,000).
Purpose and activities: Giving primarily for higher education and youth service programs.
Fields of interest: Higher education; Youth development; Children/youth; Economically disadvantaged.
Limitations: Applications accepted. Giving limited to Southern Chautauqua County, NY. No grants to individuals.
Publications: Application guidelines; Financial statement; Program policy statement (including application guidelines).
Application information: Application form required.
Initial approach: **Use application form at http://www.chautauquagrants.org**
Copies of proposal: 5
Deadline(s): Apr. 15
Board meeting date(s): May and June
Officers: David W. Shepherd, Pres.; Matthew W. Moore, V.P.; Sandra M. Snabl, V.P.; Leslie A. Johnson, Secy.; Joseph C. Johnson, Treas.
Number of staff: None.
EIN: 161426226

2220
The Mr. and Mrs. Raymond J. Horowitz Foundation for the Arts, Inc.

c/o Warren Adelson
823 Park Ave.
New York, NY **10021-2849**

Donor: Margaret Horowitz†.
Foundation type: Independent foundation.
Financial data (yr. ended 12/31/12): Assets, $12,725,436 (M); expenditures, $2,332,406; qualifying distributions, $2,286,202; giving activities include $2,202,500 for 22 grants (high: $250,000; low: $35,000).
Fields of interest: Museums; Museums (art).
Limitations: Applications not accepted. Giving primarily in CT, NY, and PA. No grants to individuals.
Application information: Contributes only to pre-selected organizations.
Officers and Directors:* Warren Adelson,* Pres.; Elaine M. Reich,* V.P.; Michael Simches, Secy.; Steven L. Ingerman,* Treas.; Judith Babcok; Max Berry.
EIN: 133699100
Other changes: At the close of 2012, the grantmaker paid grants of $2,202,500, a 107.5% increase over the 2011 disbursements, $1,061,500.

2221
Stewart W. & Willma C. Hoyt Foundation, Inc.

70 Front St.
Binghamton, NY 13905-4722 (607) 772-0780
Contact: Catherine Schwoeffermann, Exec. Dir.
FAX: (607) 722-0747;
E-mail: hoytfoundation@stny.rr.com; Main URL: http://www.hoytfoundation.org
Grants List: http://www.hoytfoundation.org/grants_13.htm

Established in 1993 in NY as successor to Stewart W. & Willma C. Hoyt Foundation, which was established in 1970; status returned to private foundation in 2006.
Donor: Willma C. Hoyt†.
Foundation type: Independent foundation.
Financial data (yr. ended 12/31/12): Assets, $20,381,435 (M); expenditures, $629,313; qualifying distributions, $488,091; giving activities include $279,482 for 22 grants (high: $100,000; low: $4,000).
Purpose and activities: The foundation aims to use its resources to enhance the quality of life of the people of Broome County, NY, primarily through judicious grantmaking. The foundation focuses broadly on the areas of the arts, humanities, education, health and human services. The foundation is particularly interested in assisting programs that meet an urgent community need, that do not unnecessarily duplicate the work of other organizations, that have explored alternative funding sources, and that have some reasonable assurance of ongoing support.
Fields of interest: Humanities; Arts; Education; Health care; Human services.
Type of support: Capital campaigns; Building/renovation; Equipment; Program development; Curriculum development; Technical assistance; Consulting services; Matching/challenge support.
Limitations: Applications accepted. Giving limited to Broome County, NY. No support for religious purposes, or for economic development projects. No grants to individuals, or for annual campaigns of local chapters of national organizations, deficit financing, general operating, endowments, research, publications, or ongoing maintenance projects.
Publications: Annual report; Financial statement; Grants list.
Application information: A meeting with the Exec. Dir. and approval to submit must precede submission of a full proposal to the foundation. Application form required.
Initial approach: Telephone
Copies of proposal: 1
Deadline(s): Apr. 1 and Sept. 2
Board meeting date(s): Quarterly; grantmaking meetings in June and Nov.
Final notification: 1 to 3 days following board meetings
Officers and Directors:* Marena Gonz,* Chair.; Aubrey Clark,* Vice-Chair.; Gary D. Rein,* Secy.-Treas.; Catherine Schwoeffermann, Exec. Dir.; **Louise Donohue**; Michael J. Gavin; Jeffery T. Smith.
Number of staff: 1 full-time professional; 1 part-time professional; 1 part-time support.
EIN: 223209342
Other changes: Marena Gonz has replaced Aubrey Clark as Chair. Aubrey Clark has replaced Marena Gonz as Vice-Chair. Gary D. Rein has replaced Eugene E. Banick as Secy.-Treas.
David M. Gouldin and Carole Peduto are no longer directors.

2222
Hps Foundation

60 Hewes St.
Brooklyn, NY 11211-7804
***Application address:* c/o Herman Steinmetz, 60 Hewes St., Brooklyn, NY 11206, tel.: (718) 875-9267**

Established in 2000 in NY.
Donors: Herman Steinmetz; Emanuel Clara Steinmetz Trust.
Foundation type: Independent foundation.
Financial data (yr. ended 06/30/13): Assets, $1,168,933 (M); gifts received, $202,500; expenditures, $125,341; qualifying distributions, $122,716; giving activities include $122,716 for 65 grants (high: $25,000; low: $18).
Fields of interest: Jewish agencies & synagogues.
Limitations: Applications accepted. Giving primarily in Brooklyn, NY.
Application information: Application form not required.
Initial approach: Proposal
Deadline(s): None
Trustees: Bluma Steinmetz; Herman Steinmetz.
EIN: 522300814

2223
Hudson River Bancorp, Inc. Foundation

P.O. Box 1189
Hudson, NY 12534-0076 (518) 671-6226
Contact: Holly Rappleyea, Secy.
Main URL: http://www.hrbtfoundation.com

Established in 1998 in NY.
Donors: Hudson River Bank & Trust Co.; Carl Florio.
Foundation type: Company-sponsored foundation.
Financial data (yr. ended 03/31/13): Assets, $13,590,256 (M); expenditures, $881,276; qualifying distributions, $732,671; giving activities include $702,671 for 135 grants (high: $122,500; low: $50).
Purpose and activities: The foundation supports programs designed to address healthcare; community development; education and youth; arts and culture; historic preservation; and environmental protection.
Fields of interest: Historic preservation/historical societies; Arts; Education; Environment, natural resources; Hospitals (general); Health care; Youth, services; Community/economic development.
Type of support: General/operating support; Capital campaigns; Building/renovation; Equipment; Program development; Scholarship funds.
Limitations: Applications accepted. Giving primarily in upstate NY. No support for political groups or religious groups for sectarian purposes. No grants to individuals or for debt liquidation.
Application information: Application form required.
***Initial approach:* Telephone call**
***Deadline(s):* Telephone call**
Officers: Marilyn A. Herrington, Pres.; Tony Jones, V.P.; Holly Rappleyea, Secy.; Carl A. Florio, Treas.
Directors: Joseph Phelan; Sid Richter.
EIN: 223595668
Other changes: The grantmaker no longer lists an E-mail address. The grantmaker no longer lists a fax.

The grantmaker no longer publishes application guidelines.

2224
Geoffrey C. Hughes Foundation, Inc.
c/o Cahill Gordon & Reindel LLP
80 Pine St., Ste. 2133
New York, NY 10005-1702 (212) 701-3400
Contact: John R. Young, Pres.

Established in 1991 in NY.
Donor: Geoffrey C. Hughes†.
Foundation type: Independent foundation.
Financial data (yr. ended 03/31/13): Assets, $30,087,357 (M); expenditures, $1,552,511; qualifying distributions, $1,435,028; giving activities include $1,390,567 for 23 grants (high: $250,000; low: $10,000).
Purpose and activities: Support primarily for environmental protection, opera, and ballet, with preference given to organizations supported by Mr. Hughes during his lifetime.
Fields of interest: Performing arts, ballet; Performing arts, opera; Higher education; Environment, natural resources.
Limitations: Applications accepted. Giving on a national basis. No grants to individuals.
Application information: Application form not required.
Initial approach: Letter of inquiry or telephone
Copies of proposal: 1
Deadline(s): None
Board meeting date(s): As necessary
Final notification: Varies
Officers and Directors:* John R. Young,* Pres.; Ursula Cliff,* V.P. and Secy.; Walter C. Cliff,* V.P. and Treas.
EIN: 133622255
Other changes: Mary K. Young is no longer V.P.

2225
Hultquist Foundation, Inc.
202 N. Main St., 4th Fl.
Jamestown, NY **14701-5208** (716) 664-5210
Contact: Tom Flowers, Pres.

Established in 1965 in NY.
Foundation type: Independent foundation.
Financial data (yr. ended 06/30/13): Assets, $14,993,092 (M); expenditures, $987,821; qualifying distributions, $891,938; giving activities include $882,808 for 17 grants (high: $250,000; low: $4,200).
Purpose and activities: Giving primarily for higher education and human services.
Fields of interest: Higher education; Human services; YM/YWCAs & YM/YWHAs; Human services, mind/body enrichment; United Ways and Federated Giving Programs.
Type of support: General/operating support; Continuing support; Annual campaigns; Capital campaigns; Building/renovation; Equipment; Land acquisition.
Limitations: Applications accepted. Giving limited to Chautauqua County, NY, with emphasis on Jamestown, NY. No grants to individuals.
Application information: Application form required.
Initial approach: Letter
Copies of proposal: 4
Deadline(s): Generally in June and Dec.
Board meeting date(s): Quarterly
Officers: Thomas I. Flowers, Pres.; John K. Plumb, V.P.; **Stephen J. Wright, V.P.**; William L. Wright, V.P.; Robert F. Rohm, Jr., Secy.-Treas.
EIN: 160907729
Other changes: Charles H. Price is no longer V.P.

2226
Hycliff Foundation
c/o Raich, Ende, Malter & Co.
1375 Broadway
New York, NY 10018-7001

Incorporated in 1977 in DE as partial successor to The Bernhard Foundation, Inc.
Donor: The Bernhard Foundation, Inc.
Foundation type: Independent foundation.
Financial data (yr. ended 02/28/13): Assets, $320,903 (M); expenditures, $123,328; qualifying distributions, $115,515; giving activities include $111,550 for 42 grants (high: $50,000; low: $100).
Fields of interest: Museums; Performing arts centers; Arts; Higher education; Hospitals (general); Medical research; Human services; Civil/human rights; United Ways and Federated Giving Programs; Jewish agencies & synagogues; Children.
Type of support: General/operating support; Continuing support; Seed money.
Limitations: Applications not accepted. No grants to individuals or for building funds, endowment funds, scholarships, fellowships, or matching gifts; no loans.
Application information: Unsolicited requests for funds not accepted.
Officers: Robert A. Bernhard, Pres.; Joan M. Bernhard, V.P.; Adele B. Neufeld, Secy.; Michael Bernhard, Treas.
Trustees: Steven G. Bernhard; Susan Bernhard Collins.
EIN: 132893039

2227
IBM International Foundation
(formerly IBM South Africa Projects Fund)
New Orchard Rd.
Armonk, NY 10504-1709
Contact: Judy Chin, Fdn. Mgr.
Main URL: http://www.ibm.com/ibm/responsibility/
IBM Fellowship Grants Website: http://www.ibm.com/developerworks/university/phdfellowship/
KidSmart Early Learning Program Website: http://www.kidsmartearlylearning.org/
E-mail for IBM Fellowship Grants: phdfellow@us.ibm.com

Established in 1985 in NY.
Donor: International Business Machines Corp.
Foundation type: Company-sponsored foundation.
Financial data (yr. ended 12/31/12): Assets, $193,326,732 (M); gifts received, $24,567,673; expenditures, $23,839,105; qualifying distributions, $23,813,698; giving activities include $12,291,100 for grants, and $9,326,905 for employee matching gifts.
Purpose and activities: The foundation supports organizations involved with arts and culture, K-12 education, the environment, health, employment, human services, diversity, science, public policy research, and minorities.
Fields of interest: Arts; Elementary/secondary education; Education, early childhood education; Education, continuing education; Education, reading; Health care; Human services; Civil/human rights, equal rights; Science, formal/general education; Mathematics; Physics; Engineering/technology; Computer science; Engineering; Science; Public policy, research; Disabilities, people with; Minorities.
International interests: Africa; Asia; Canada; Europe; Latin America.
Type of support: Employee matching gifts; Fellowships; General/operating support; Program development.
Limitations: Applications accepted. Giving on a national and international basis, with some emphasis in CA and NY, and in Africa, Asia, Canada, Europe, and Latin America. No support for fraternal, labor, political, or religious organizations or private or parochial schools. No grants to individuals (except for fellowships), or for scholarships, capital campaigns, fundraising, construction or renovation projects, chairs, endowments, conferences, symposia, or sports competitions.
Application information: Proposals should be no longer than 2 pages. Additional information may be requested at a later date. Applicants must be nominated by a faculty member for IBM Fellowship Grants. Application form not required.
Initial approach: Proposal; complete online nomination form for IBM Fellowship Grants
Copies of proposal: 1
Deadline(s): None; Sept. 22 to Nov. 2 for IBM Fellowship Grants
Final notification: 1 month
Officers and Directors:* Samuel J. Palmisano,* Chair.; John C. Iwata,* Vice-Chair.; Stanley S. Litow,* Pres.; **Michelle Browdy, Secy.**; Robert Del Bene, Treas.; Nick D'Anniballe, Cont.; **Jennifer Crozier**; Mark Loughridge.
Number of staff: 1 full-time professional.
EIN: 133267906
Other changes: Michelle Browdy has replaced Andrew Bonzani as Secy.
Andrew Bonzani is no longer Secy. Robin G. Willner is no longer a director.

2228
The IF Foundation
(formerly The Iovino Family Foundation)
26-15 Ulmer St.
College Point, NY 11356-1144 (718) 554-2961
FAX: (718) 554-2799; Main URL: http://www.if-foundation.org
Facebook: https://www.facebook.com/if.foundation
Twitter: https://twitter.com/Theiffoundation

Established in 2001 in NY.
Donors: Michael Capasso; Robert Hood; David Horowitch; Mary Iovino; Thomas Iovino; Mitch Levine; Bernard London; Charles Magrath; Peter Pace; Paul Posillico; Judlau Contracting, Inc.; The Iovino Charitable Lead Annuity Trust; Spearin, Preston and Burrows, Inc.; J-Track LLC; Midland Tech LLC; TC Electric LLC; Grassi and Co.; Posillico Foundation; T and Company Moriarty; Redwood Contracting; Arthur Corwin/Moretrench; St. James Church.
Foundation type: Independent foundation.
Financial data (yr. ended 12/31/12): Assets, $2,572,341 (M); gifts received, $266,478; expenditures, $1,067,735; qualifying distributions, $511,400; giving activities include $511,400 for 2 + grants (high: $300,000).
Purpose and activities: Giving primarily for Episcopal churches, and for higher and other education; funding also for human services.

Fields of interest: Higher education; Education; Human services; Family services; Protestant agencies & churches.
Limitations: Applications not accepted. Giving primarily in NY. No grants to individuals.
Publications: Annual report.
Application information: Contributes only to pre-selected organizations.
Trustees: Thomas Iovino,* Pres.; Frank Cara; Dale Okonow.
EIN: 113619538
Other changes: Thomas Iovino is now Pres. The grantmaker now publishes an annual report.

2229
Imagine 247 Foundation
(formerly Spring Leaf Foundation)
New York, NY

The foundation dissolved on April 30, 2014.

2230
Imago Dei Foundation, Inc.
c/o Emil Woods
140 E. 45th St., Ste. 17C
New York, NY **10017**

Established in 2008.
Donor: Emil Woods.
Foundation type: Independent foundation.
Financial data (yr. ended 06/30/13): Assets, $696,862 (M); expenditures, $301,250; qualifying distributions, $300,000; giving activities include $300,000 for 4 grants (high: $280,000; low: $2,500).
Fields of interest: Higher education; Foundations (private grantmaking).
Limitations: Applications not accepted. Giving in the U.S., with some emphasis on NY.
Application information: Unsolicited requests for funds not accepted.
Trustees: Charles Cascarilla; Emil Woods.
EIN: 263868853

2231
Initial Teaching Alphabet Foundation
P.O. Box 11355
Hauppauge, NY 11788-0991 (631) 813-2991
Contact: Keith Bub, Pres.
Main URL: **http://www.ita-foundation.org**

Incorporated in 1965 in NY.
Donors: Eugene Kelly†; Eugene Kelly Trust.
Foundation type: Operating foundation.
Financial data (yr. ended 12/31/12): Assets, $708,400 (M); gifts received, $800,000; expenditures, $572,637; qualifying distributions, $570,273; giving activities include $362,682 for 9 grants (high: $64,420; low: $12,207), and $134,010 for 1 foundation-administered program.
Purpose and activities: Giving primarily to promote, maintain, and advance education, in all its fields, and in particular, but without limiting the generality of the foregoing, by the development, standardization, propagation, dissemination, teaching, and use of the Initial Teaching Alphabet, with the aim of improving reading and writing skills.
Fields of interest: Education, research; Education, early childhood education; Elementary school/education; Secondary school/education; Higher education, university; Adult/continuing education; Education.
Type of support: Program development; Conferences/seminars; Publication; Research; Technical assistance; Consulting services.
Limitations: Applications accepted. Giving primarily in CA, IL, MN, NY, and TX. No grants to individuals, or for building or endowment funds, general support, scholarships, fellowships, or matching gifts; no loans.
Publications: Application guidelines; Informational brochure; Occasional report; Program policy statement.
Application information: Application form required.
Initial approach: Letter requesting guidelines
Copies of proposal: 2
Deadline(s): Pre-proposal letter by Mar. 15; detailed proposal (by invitation only) deadline Apr. 15
Board meeting date(s): May or June
Final notification: 1 month
Officers: Keith Bub, Pres. and Treas.; Shelly Jerviss, V.P.; Maurice S. Spanbock, Secy.; Carol McKay.
Directors: Betty E. Thompson, Exec. Dir.; Martha Bogart; Dr. Max Bogart; Frank G. Jennings.
Number of staff: 2 full-time professional.
EIN: 112074243

2232
Institute for Depression Studies and Treatment
c/o B. Strauss Assoc. Ltd.
307 5th Ave., 8th Fl.
New York, NY 10016-6517

Donors: George A. Wiegers; Frampton Family Charitable Foundation; Trygve Myrhen; Beth Wood; George Wood; Lori Durham; Brenton Durham; Cannon Harvey; Lydia Harvey; Lydia McKee; His Global Inc.; Reiman Foundation; The Hicks Charitable Foundation; Wiegers Family Foundation.
Foundation type: Independent foundation.
Financial data (yr. ended 06/30/13): Assets, $418,606 (M); gifts received, $167,108; expenditures, $432,481; qualifying distributions, $432,481; giving activities include $223,123 for 4 grants (high: $190,123; low: $1,000).
Fields of interest: Education.
Limitations: Applications not accepted.
Application information: Unsolicited requests for funds not accepted.
Officers and Directors:* George A. Wiegers,* Chair.; Heather Mulvihill,* Vice-Chair.; Peyton F. Perry,* Treas.; Ann Ayers; Susan Drumm; Jack Eck, M.D.; Susan Milhoan; Ann Benson Reidy; Jeannie Ritter; Beth Slifer; Beth Wood.
EIN: 262755241
Other changes: Kris Hoegh Marsh is no longer a director.

2233
Institute for the Study of Aging, Inc.
57 W. 57th St., No. 904
New York, NY 10019-2802 **(212) 901-8000**
FAX: (212) 935-2408; Main URL: http://www.alzdiscovery.org

Established in 1998 in NY.
Donors: Estee Lauder Charitable Trust; Pfizer Inc.; Emisphere Technologies, Inc.; Neurochem, Inc.; Elan Pharmaceuticals, Inc.; Barnhill Family Fund; Elsevier.
Foundation type: Independent foundation.
Financial data (yr. ended 12/31/12): Assets, $5,004,703 (M); gifts received, $4,890,106; expenditures, $3,296,857; qualifying distributions, $3,198,098; giving activities include $177,672 for 2 grants (high: $96,597; low: $81,075).
Purpose and activities: The Institute is a biomedical venture philanthropy whose mission is to catalyze and fund the discovery and development of new therapies to prevent and treat Alzheimer's disease.
Fields of interest: Higher education; Medical school/education; Hospitals (general); Alzheimer's disease; Biology/life sciences.
Type of support: Conferences/seminars; Seed money; Research; Program-related investments/loans.
Limitations: Applications accepted. Giving on a national and international basis. No support for political or religious organizations. No grants to individuals.
Publications: Application guidelines; Annual report; Financial statement; Grants list; Informational brochure (including application guidelines); Occasional report.
Application information: See institute web site for more application information. Application form required.
Initial approach: Electronic letter of intent on institute's web site
Copies of proposal: 1
Deadline(s): None
Final notification: 4-6 months
Officers and Directors:* Leonard A. Lauder,* Co-Pres.; Ronald S. Lauder,* Co-Pres.; Joan Krupskas,* Treas.; Howard Fillit, M.D., Exec. Dir.; Lanny Edelsohn, M.D.; Allan Green, M.D., Ph.D.; Elias K. Michaelis, M.D., Ph.D.
Number of staff: 7 full-time professional; 1 full-time support.
EIN: 134024149

2234
Y. A. Istel Foundation, Inc.
c/o WTAS, LLC
1177 Ave. of the Americas, 18th Fl.
New York, NY **10036-2714**

Established in 1989 in NY.
Donor: Yves-Andre Istel.
Foundation type: Independent foundation.
Financial data (yr. ended 04/30/13): Assets, $307,580 (M); expenditures, $211,047; qualifying distributions, $210,655; giving activities include $206,330 for 57+ grants (high: $25,000).
Fields of interest: Performing arts, theater; Arts; Education; Human services.
Limitations: Applications not accepted. Giving primarily in New York, NY. No grants to individuals.
Application information: Unsolicited requests for funds not accepted.
Officers: Yves Andre Istel, Pres. and Treas.
Directors: Andrea Istel; John Istel.
EIN: 133524729

2235
The Violet Jabara Charitable Trust
c/o Steven J. Wohl, Esq.
445 Hamilton Ave., Ste. 1102
White Plains, NY 10601-1832
E-mail: **info@jabaratrust.org**; Main URL: http://jabaratrust.org

Established in 2007 in NY.
Donor: Linda K. Jacobs.
Foundation type: Independent foundation.
Financial data (yr. ended 12/31/12): Assets, $1,284,527 (M); expenditures, $207,794; qualifying distributions, $185,450; giving activities

include $175,003 for 6 grants (high: $50,000; low: $20,000).
Purpose and activities: The mission of the Trust is two-fold: to help improve the lives of the people in developing countries of the Middle East and to foster greater understanding of Middle Eastern culture in the United States. Consideration will also be given to United States organizations whose purpose is to enhance understanding of Middle Eastern culture and issues.
Fields of interest: Arts, cultural/ethnic awareness; Health care; Women, centers/services; International exchange; International development; International agricultural development; International economic development; Civil/human rights, women; Islam.
Type of support: General/operating support; Program-related investments/loans.
Limitations: Applications accepted. Giving primarily in the Middle East, with emphasis on Lebanon, Jordan, Syria, Iraq, Iran, Palestine, Yemen, Egypt and North Africa; U.S. organizations, whose purpose is to enhance understanding of Middle Eastern culture and issues will also be considered. No grants to individuals.
Application information: Unsolicited full proposals not accepted. If interested after review of letter of inquiry, the Trust will respond with full proposal guidelines.
Initial approach: Letter of inquiry
Trustee: Linda K. Jacobs.
EIN: 137560427

2236
The Jaharis Family Foundation, Inc.
499 Park Ave., 23rd Fl.
New York, NY 10022-1240
Contact: Kathryn Jaharis, Pres.

Established in 1986 in FL.
Donors: Michael Jaharis, Jr.; Mary Jaharis; The 1998 Katina Charitable Trust; The 1998 MJ Trust; The 1998 Katina Charitable Trust No. 2.
Foundation type: Independent foundation.
Financial data (yr. ended 09/30/13): Assets, $229,621,808 (M); expenditures, $17,569,398; qualifying distributions, $14,346,665; giving activities include $14,346,665 for 52 grants (high: $2,250,000; low: $2,000).
Fields of interest: Museums; Arts; Higher education; Medical school/education; Education; Hospitals (general); Human services; Orthodox agencies & churches.
Type of support: Building/renovation; Endowments; Scholarship funds; Research; Matching/challenge support.
Limitations: Giving primarily in FL, IL, NY, MA and PA. No grants to individuals.
Application information: Application form not required.
Deadline(s): None
Officers and Directors:* Kathryn Jaharis,* Pres. and Treas.; Pelagia Sotirhos Nicholson, Secy.; Steven K. Aronoff; Kevin Ferro; Mary Jaharis; Michael Jaharis; Steven Jaharis.
EIN: 592751110

2237
Jewish Foundation for Education of Women
135 E. 64 St.
New York, NY 10065-7045 (212) 288-3931
Contact: Elizabeth Leiman Kraiem, Exec. Dir.
FAX: (212) 288-5798; E-mail: info@jfew.org; Main URL: http://www.jfew.org

Incorporated in 1884 in NY as Hebrew Technical School for Girls.
Donors: Erika Rindler Urbach Living Trust; The Betsy and Alan Cohn Foundation; Sonya Cohen Revocable Trust; Lisbeth Jacobs.
Foundation type: Independent foundation.
Financial data (yr. ended 06/30/13): Assets, $75,814,810 (M); gifts received, $54,066; expenditures, $3,325,416; qualifying distributions, $3,208,474; giving activities include $2,495,453 for 28 grants (high: $206,750; low: $4,032), and $205,500 for 33 grants to individuals (high: $10,000; low: $1,500).
Purpose and activities: The foundation is a New York City-based, non-sectarian organization helping women with financial need to meet their educational and career goals through scholarships and opportunities for professional development. In partnership with schools and non-profits, it fosters a community of women dedicated to education, professional achievement and contributing to society.
Fields of interest: Scholarships/financial aid; Women.
Type of support: Fellowships.
Limitations: Applications accepted. Giving limited to scholarships and related programming for female citizens and permanent residents with demonstrated financial need. The foundation has a strong preference for those living within the lower 8 counties of NY State. No grants for general support, operating budgets, capital or endowment funds, matching gifts, research, special projects, publications, or conferences.
Publications: Newsletter.
Application information: The foundation will consider letters of inquiry for scholarship programs at the Associates, Bachelors and Graduate levels in the following areas: Health Professions; Math, Science and Technology; Aging Society; Public and Communal Service. Letters of inquiry may be up to three pages, plus a budget. They should take into account the characteristics of our programs and include the following information: Selection criteria and process for intended scholarship recipients, which should be consistent with JFEW's eligibility requirements and include a minimum GPA of at least 3.0; Graduation rates of students with these criteria; Job placement rates of students who graduate with these criteria; Profiles of typical students in the program and examples of what they do when they graduate; How the program will create a cohort of scholarship recipients; Proposed programming, summer internships or supportive services for the cohort and how this will contribute to student growth and development; Method of program evaluation. Application information available on foundation web site. Application form not required.
Initial approach: Letter
Copies of proposal: 1
***Deadline(s):* See foundation web site for current deadline**
Board meeting date(s): Quarterly
Final notification: By Jan. 31
Officers and Directors:* Sharon L. Weinberg,* Chair.; Jill W. Smith,* Pres.; Phyllis Korff,* V.P.; Lisa C. Liman,* Secy.; Harold J. Levy, Treas.; Elizabeth Leiman Kraiem, Exec. Dir.; Neil R. Grabois, Dir. Emeritus; Alan R. Kahn, Dir. Emeritus; Irving Kahn, Dir. Emeritus; Ruth Messinger, Dir. Emeritus; James Wood, Dir. Emeritus; Jean G. Bronstein; Alan D. Cohn; Marcia Goldsmith; Suzanne H. Keusch; Reeva S. Mager; Louise Mirrer; Marcy Russo; Susan Schatz; Marion Spanbock; Ann Tanenbaum; Andrew Vogelstein; David Weiner.
Number of staff: 1 full-time professional; 1 full-time support.
EIN: 131860415
Other changes: The grantmaker now makes its newsletter available online.

2238
Jewish Renaissance Foundation Inc.
767 5th Ave.
New York, NY 10153-0110
Established in 1996 in NY.
Donor: Ronald S. Lauder.
Foundation type: Independent foundation.
Financial data (yr. ended 12/31/12): Assets, $7,923,780 (M); gifts received, $80,000; expenditures, $33,484; qualifying distributions, $15,832; giving activities include $20,681 for 1 foundation-administered program.
Purpose and activities: Giving primarily for Jewish educational and cultural heritage programs.
Fields of interest: Jewish federated giving programs; Jewish agencies & synagogues.
Limitations: Applications not accepted. Giving primarily in Miami, FL and New York, NY. No grants to individuals.
Application information: Contributes only to pre-selected organizations.
Officers and Directors:* Ronald S. Lauder,* Pres.; Charles A. Goldstein, V.P. and Secy.; **David Gerson, Treas.**; Malcolm Hoenlein.
EIN: 133906533
Other changes: David Gerson has replaced Kelli Turner as Treas.

2239
Johnson Foundation
(formerly John Alfred & Oscar Johnson Memorial Trust)
c/o Bessemer Trust Co., N.A.
630 5th Ave., Ste. 3425
New York, NY 10111-0100

Established in 1996 in NY.
Foundation type: Independent foundation.
Financial data (yr. ended 01/31/13): Assets, $5,133,929 (M); expenditures, $326,501; qualifying distributions, $297,490; giving activities include $232,965 for 25 grants (high: $100,000; low: $100).
Fields of interest: Education; Environment, natural resources; Medical research, institute; Youth development; Human services; Salvation Army; Children/youth, services; Community/economic development.
Limitations: Giving primarily in Jamestown, NY. No grants to individuals.
Officer: Carol W. Sellstrom, Exec. Dir.
Trustees: John L. Sellstrom; Bessemer Trust Co., N.A.
EIN: 166438291

2240
The Thomas Phillips and Jane Moore Johnson Foundation
(also known as Johnson Family Foundation)
55 Exchange Pl., Ste. 404
New York, NY 10005-2035 (212) 343-1102
Contact: Andrew Lane, Exec. Dir.; Samantha Franklin, Prog. Off.

Main URL: http://www.jffnd.org
Facebook: https://www.facebook.com/pages/Johnson-Family-Foundation/222004264480124
Twitter: https://twitter.com/JohnsonFamFound

Established in 1990 in PA.
Donors: Thomas Phillips Johnson, Sr.‡; Thomas Phillips Johnson, Jr.; James Moore Johnson.
Foundation type: Independent foundation.
Financial data (yr. ended 12/31/12): Assets, $78,449,410 (M); expenditures, $4,293,635; qualifying distributions, $4,005,279; giving activities include $3,200,000 for 59 grants (high: $615,392; low: $5,000).
Purpose and activities: Giving for the development of healthy, vibrant and just communities where individuals, families and the next generation of leaders will thrive. The foundation funds programs to improve the health of our environment; promote equality and social progress; and support education and youth. Its grantmaking is place-based and, in environmental health and LGBT issues, national in scope.
Fields of interest: Arts; Education; Environmental education; Environment; Human services; Civil/human rights, LGBTQ; Public affairs; Children/youth; Youth; Adults; Adults, women; Economically disadvantaged; LGBTQ.
Type of support: Annual campaigns; Continuing support; General/operating support; Management development/capacity building; Matching/challenge support; Program development; Program evaluation; Publication; Research.
Limitations: Applications not accepted. Giving on a national basis; with emphasis on New York City, NY and VT. No grants to individuals.
Publications: Grants list.
Application information: Unsolicited requests for funds not accepted.
Board meeting date(s): Jan. and Aug.
Officers and Trustees:* Thomas P. Johnson, Jr.,* Pres.; James M. Johnson,* Chair.; Asa J. Johnson,* Secy.; Jesse D. Johnson,* Treas.; Andrew Lane, Exec. Dir.
Number of staff: 2 full-time professional.
EIN: 256357015

2241
Willard T. C. Johnson Foundation, Inc.
c/o The Johnson Company, Inc.
610 5th Ave., 2nd Fl.
New York, NY 10020-2403 **(212) 891-4087**
Contact: Robert W. Johnson IV, Pres.

Incorporated in 1979 in NY.
Donors: Willard T.C. Johnson‡; Keith W. Johnson‡.
Foundation type: Independent foundation.
Financial data (yr. ended 12/31/12): Assets, $50,266,449 (M); expenditures, $2,934,925; qualifying distributions, $2,809,425; giving activities include $2,805,000 for 13 grants (high: $1,260,000; low: $15,000).
Fields of interest: Museums; Higher education; Hospitals (general); Hospitals (specialty); Cancer; Medical research, institute; Lupus research; Human services.
Limitations: Applications accepted. Giving primarily in NJ and NY. No grants to individuals.
Application information: Application form not required.
Deadline(s): None
Officers and Directors:* Betty W. Johnson,* Chair.; Robert W. Johnson IV,* Pres.; Christopher W. Johnson,* V.P. and Secy.-Treas.
EIN: 132993310

2242
The JPMorgan Chase Foundation
(formerly The Chase Manhattan Foundation)
270 Park Ave., 4th Fl.
New York, NY 10017-2014 (212) 270-0471
***E-mail address for regional contacts:* Africa, Europe, and the Middle East: bi.x.amosu@jpmorgan.com; Argentina: Maria.S.Urribarri@jpmchase.com; Asia and Pacific: apac.corporate.responsibility@jpmorgan.com; Brazil: rentata.biselli@jpmorgan.com; Canada: renee.l.tremblay@jpmorgan.com; Chile: alejandra.x.gallo@jpmorgan.com; Colombia: ximena.cardenas@jpmorgan.com and andrea.valero@jpmchase.com; Mexico: olivia.zubieta@jpmorgan.com; Multi-Region and Latin America: David.A.Goldberg@jpmchase.com; and Peru: karla.a.stammer@jpmorgan.com**; Main URL: http://www.jpmorganchase.com/corporate/Corporate-Responsibility/corporate-philanthropy.htm

Incorporated in 1969 in NY; name changed in 2001 as a result of the merger of Chase Manhattan Corp. with J.P. Morgan & Co. Inc.
Donors: The Chase Manhattan Bank; JPMorgan Chase Bank, N.A.; Chatham Ventures, Inc.; CMRCC, Inc.; Chemical Investments, Inc.; Bank One Investment Corp.
Foundation type: Company-sponsored foundation.
Financial data (yr. ended 12/31/12): Assets, $328,377,669 (M); gifts received, $169,958,084; expenditures, $116,731,589; qualifying distributions, $115,541,284; giving activities include $115,516,001 for 9,096 grants (high: $2,370,000; low: $1).
Purpose and activities: The foundation supports programs designed to promote affordable housing; economic growth and workforce readiness; and financial capability. Special emphasis is directed toward neighborhoods located in areas of JPMorgan Chase's major operations.
Fields of interest: Arts education; Museums; Museums (art); Arts; Education, reform; Elementary/secondary education; Higher education; Teacher school/education; Adult/continuing education; Education, services; Education, reading; Education; Employment, services; Employment, training; Employment; Food services; Housing/shelter, development; Housing/shelter, home owners; Housing/shelter; Youth development; YM/YWCAs & YM/YWHAs; Children/youth, services; Family services; Human services, financial counseling; Community development, neighborhood development; Economic development; Urban/community development; Community development, small businesses; Microfinance/microlending; Community/economic development; Financial services; Leadership development; Public affairs; Economically disadvantaged.
Type of support: General/operating support; Continuing support; Management development/capacity building; Building/renovation; Program development; Conferences/seminars; Curriculum development; Technical assistance; Employee volunteer services; Sponsorships; Program-related investments/loans; Employee matching gifts.
Limitations: Applications accepted. **Giving in areas of company operations in AZ, CA, CO, Fairfield and New Haven, CT, Washington, DC, DE, FL, Atlanta, GA, ID, IL, IN, KY, LA, Boston, MA, MI, MN, St. Louis and Springfield, MO, NJ, NV, OH, OK, OR, Philadelphia, PA, TX, UT, WA, WI, and WV, with emphasis on NY; giving also to U.S.-based international organizations active in areas of company operations abroad in Africa, Argentina, Asia, Brazil, Canada, Chile, Columbia, Europe, Latin America, Mexico, the Middle East, and Peru.** No support for religious, fraternal, social, or other membership organizations not of direct benefit to the entire community, athletic teams, health or medical-related organizations, discriminatory organizations, parent teacher associations, private schools, public agencies, or volunteer operated organizations. No grants to individuals, or for capital campaigns or endowments, scholarships or tuition assistance, advertising, fundraising, or debt reduction.
Publications: Application guidelines; Corporate giving report; Newsletter.
Application information: A full proposal may be requested at a later date. Grants are administered by Community Relations Officers in each market region. Please visit website for regional contact information. Unsolicited applications from organizations in Europe, the Middle East, and Africa are currently not accepted. Application form required.
Initial approach: Complete online letter of inquiry form; non-U.S.-based organizations should e-mail a short preliminary proposal to regional grants coordinator
Deadline(s): None
Officers: Bruce McNamer, C.E.O.; Dalila Wilson-Scott, Pres.
EIN: 237049738

2243
Max Kade Foundation, Inc.
6 E. 87th St., 5th Fl.
New York, NY 10128-0505 (646) 672-4354
Contact: Lya Friedrich Pfeifer J.D., Pres. and Treas.
Main URL: http://maxkadefoundation.org

Incorporated in 1944 in NY.
Donor: Max Kade‡.
Foundation type: Independent foundation.
Financial data (yr. ended 12/31/12): Assets, $87,533,520 (M); expenditures, $5,795,414; qualifying distributions, $5,769,756; giving activities include $5,146,332 for 201 grants (high: $300,000; low: $1,000).
Purpose and activities: The foundation promotes Germanic studies and transatlantic exchange through the support of existing programs and new indicatives related to German studies which encourage a positive relationship between German-speaking countries and the U.S. The foundation supports initiatives which promote international understanding by sponsoring exchange programs between Germany, Austria and the U.S. such as post-doctoral research exchange programs, visiting faculty exchange programs, and exchange programs of undergraduate and graduate students both in the U.S. and abroad.
Fields of interest: Language/linguistics; Literature; Higher education; Biomedicine; Medical research, institute; Physical/earth sciences; Chemistry; Engineering; Biology/life sciences.
International interests: Austria; Europe; Germany.
Type of support: Program development; Professorships; Exchange programs.
Limitations: Applications accepted. Giving primarily in the U.S. and Europe. No grants to individuals, or for operating budgets, capital funds, development campaigns, or endowment funds; no loans.
Publications: Application guidelines; Occasional report.
Application information:
Initial approach: Letter or proposal
Deadline(s): None
Board meeting date(s): As required

Officers and Directors:* Lya Friedrich Pfeifer,* Pres. and Treas.; Berteline Baier Dale,* Secy.; Reinhard Augustin; Guenter Blobel; Fritz Kade, Jr., M.D.
Number of staff: 4 full-time professional.
EIN: 135658082
Other changes: The grantmaker now publishes application guidelines.

2244
John and Elaine Kanas Family Foundation

c/o Kathleen Hallinan
445 Broadhollow Rd.
Melville, NY 11747-3669
Application address: c/o Capital One Bank, N.A., Attn.: John A. Kanas, Pres., 265 Broadhollow Rd., Melville, NY 11747

Established in 1998 in NY.
Donors: John A. Kanas; Elaine Kanas.
Foundation type: Independent foundation.
Financial data (yr. ended 12/31/12): Assets, $0 (M); gifts received, $1,289,000; expenditures, $5,164,379; qualifying distributions, $5,126,300; giving activities include $5,126,300 for 47 grants (high: $2,000,000; low: $100).
Fields of interest: Secondary school/education; Higher education; Medical school/education; Education; Health organizations; Human services; Christian agencies & churches; Protestant agencies & churches.
Limitations: Giving primarily in NY.
Application information: Application form not required.
Initial approach: Letter
Deadline(s): None
Officers: John A. Kanas, Pres.; Elaine Kanas, V.P.
Directors: Patricia Blake; Kathy Hallinan.
EIN: 113440709
Other changes: At the close of 2012, the grantmaker paid grants of $5,126,300, a 76.5% increase over the 2011 disbursements, $2,904,250.

2245
The J. M. Kaplan Fund, Inc.

261 Madison Ave., 19th Fl.
New York, NY 10016-2303 (212) 767-0630
Contact: Angela Carabine, Grants Mgr.
FAX: (212) 767-0639; E-mail: info@jmkfund.org; Application address for Furthermore Grants in Publishing program:, c/o Ann Birckmayer, Prog. Assoc., P.O. Box 667, Hudson, NY 12534; tel.: (518) 828-8900; Main URL: http://www.jmkfund.org

Incorporated in 1948 in NY as Faigel Leah Foundation, Inc.; The J.M. Kaplan Fund, Inc., a DE corporation, merged with it in 1975 and was renamed The J.M. Kaplan Fund, Inc.
Donor: Members of the J.M. Kaplan family.
Foundation type: Independent foundation.
Financial data (yr. ended 12/31/12): Assets, $134,314,281 (M); expenditures, $10,938,592; qualifying distributions, $7,873,165; giving activities include $6,638,149 for 383 grants (high: $280,000; low: $75).
Purpose and activities: Giving primarily in three areas: environment, historic preservation, and human migrations. The fund offers program-related investments to encourage ventures of particular interest. The fund also has a trustee-initiated grants program that considers grant requests invited by the trustees.
Fields of interest: Historic preservation/historical societies; Environment, natural resources; Environment; Human services; International migration/refugee issues; Community/economic development.
Type of support: General/operating support; Continuing support; Program development; Publication; Seed money; Research; Technical assistance; Program-related investments/loans.
Limitations: Applications accepted. Giving primarily in New York City; cross-borders of North America; and worldwide. No grants to individuals, including scholarships and fellowships, or for construction or building programs, endowment funds, operating budgets of educational or medical institutions, film or video, or sponsorship of books, dances, plays, or other works of art.
Publications: Annual report (including application guidelines).
Application information: Proposals received by fax will not be considered.
Initial approach: 2- to 3-page letter of inquiry
Copies of proposal: 1
Deadline(s): None; requests received after Oct. 1 will be carried over to next year
Board meeting date(s): Quarterly
***Final notification:* Applicants will be notified within approximately 6 weeks of receipt of letter of inquiry if they are to submit a full proposal**
Officers and Trustees:* Peter W. Davidson,* Chair.; William P. Falahee, Cont.; Joan K. Davidson,* Pres. Emeritus; Betsy Davidson; Bradford Davidson; J. Matthew Davidson; Caio Fonseca; Elizabeth K. Fonseca; Isabel Fonseca; Quina Fonseca; Mary E. Kaplan; Richard D. Kaplan.
Number of staff: 4 full-time professional; 1 full-time support.
EIN: 136090286
Other changes: Conn Nugent is no longer Exec. Dir.

2246
Mel Karmazin Foundation

1 Central Park W., Ste. 48B
New York, NY 10023-7703

Established in DE and NY in 1998.
Donors: Melvin Karmazin; Karmazin Trust; Karmazin Trust II.
Foundation type: Independent foundation.
Financial data (yr. ended 12/31/12): Assets, $11,507,391 (M); gifts received, $10,000,000; expenditures, $3,195,328; qualifying distributions, $3,243,350; giving activities include $3,045,880 for 30 grants (high: $793,450; low: $1,000).
Purpose and activities: Giving primarily for medical research, particularly for autism, as well as for children and social services.
Fields of interest: Autism; Medical research, institute; Human services; Children/youth, services.
Limitations: Applications not accepted. Giving primarily in NY. No grants to individuals.
Application information: Contributes only to pre-selected organizations.
Trustees: Dina K. Elkins; Melvin Karmazin.
EIN: 311620186
Other changes: At the close of 2012, the grantmaker paid grants of $3,045,880, an 84.2% increase over the 2011 disbursements, $1,653,500.

2247
The Harvey & Gloria Kaylie Foundation, Inc.

5 Fir Dr.
Kings Point, NY 11024-1528

Established in 1999 in NY.
Donors: Scientific Components Corp.; Harvey Kaylie.
Foundation type: Company-sponsored foundation.
Financial data (yr. ended 12/31/12): Assets, $13,081,848 (M); gifts received, $1,698,800; expenditures, $3,780,767; qualifying distributions, $3,773,134; giving activities include $3,773,134 for 71 grants (high: $865,000; low: $90).
Purpose and activities: The foundation supports organizations involved with education, health, cancer research, human services, and Judaism.
Fields of interest: Secondary school/education; Higher education; Education; Health care; Cancer research; Children, services; Family services; Human services; Jewish federated giving programs; Jewish agencies & synagogues.
Type of support: General/operating support; Matching/challenge support.
Limitations: Applications not accepted. Giving primarily in Brooklyn and New York, NY. No grants to individuals.
Application information: Contributes only to pre-selected organizations.
Officers and Directors:* Harvey Kaylie,* Pres.; Gloria W. Kaylie,* V.P.; Roberta Kaylie,* Secy.; Alicia Kaylie Yacoby,* Treas.
EIN: 113502781

2248
The Ernest and Nancy Keet Foundation

62 Moir Rd.
P.O. Box 1199
Saranac Lake, NY 12983
***E-mail:* Trustee@Keet-Foundation.org; Fax: (208) 275-7423 (Idaho number)**; Main URL: http://www.keet-foundation.org

Established in 1986 in CT.
Donor: Ernest E. Keet.
Foundation type: Independent foundation.
Financial data (yr. ended 12/31/12): Assets, $19,696,172 (M); expenditures, $623,817; qualifying distributions, $553,125; giving activities include $553,125 for 73 grants (high: $100,000; low: $100).
Purpose and activities: Giving primarily for medical research and education, as well as for hunger relief, wilderness preservation, protecting civil liberties, and cultural development.
Fields of interest: Museums (natural history); Arts; Libraries/library science; Education; Environment; Medical research; Disasters, Hurricane Katrina; Human services.
Type of support: General/operating support.
Limitations: Giving primarily in NY, particularly the Adirondack Mountain region. No grants to individuals.
Publications: Application guidelines; IRS Form 990 or 990-PF printed copy available upon request.
Application information: See foundation web site for specific application instructions and Grant Request Form. Application form required.
Trustees: Bonnie Falkenstine Keet; Ernest E. Keet; Nancy R. Keet.
EIN: 222784895
Other changes: The grantmaker now publishes application guidelines online.

2249
The Kekst Family Foundation
895 Park Ave.
New York, NY 10021-0327

Established in 1986 in NY.
Donor: Gershon Kekst.
Foundation type: Independent foundation.
Financial data (yr. ended 12/31/12): Assets, $315,161 (M); gifts received, $10,000; expenditures, $292,355; qualifying distributions, $292,355; giving activities include $292,355 for 6 grants (high: $266,355; low: $2,500).
Purpose and activities: Giving primarily to foster, support, and strengthen the study of Jewish religion, music, art, philosophy, values, traditions, and history, including grants to organizations to enable gifted teachers and students to continue their teaching activities.
Fields of interest: Higher education; Theological school/education; Medical research; Jewish federated giving programs; Jewish agencies & synagogues.
Type of support: Scholarship funds; Research.
Limitations: Applications not accepted. Giving primarily in MA and NY.
Application information: Contributes only to pre-selected organizations.
Officers and Directors:* Gershon Kekst,* Pres.; Carol Kekst,* Secy.-Treas.; David J. Kekst; Joseph Kekst.
EIN: 133382250
Other changes: The grantmaker no longer lists a primary contact.

2250
Anna-Maria & Stephen Kellen Foundation, Inc.
c/o Joel E. Sammet & Co., LLP
15 Maiden Ln., Ste. 500
New York, NY 10038-5117 (212) 269-8628

Established in 1984.
Donors: Stephen M. Kellen†; Anna-Maria Kellen.
Foundation type: Independent foundation.
Financial data (yr. ended 04/30/13): Assets, $558,011,142 (M); gifts received, $85,000,000; expenditures, $29,509,417; qualifying distributions, $19,238,505; giving activities include $18,304,468 for 130 grants (high: $3,578,400; low: $250).
Purpose and activities: Giving primarily for cultural programs, including a music school, a school of design, museums, and performing arts groups; support also for higher and secondary education, Protestant churches, and media and communications.
Fields of interest: Media/communications; Museums; Performing arts, music; Arts; Secondary school/education; Higher education; Medical care, outpatient care; Protestant agencies & churches.
Limitations: Applications not accepted. Giving primarily in New York, NY. No grants to individuals.
Application information: Contributes only to pre-selected organizations.
Officers and Directors:* Michael Kellen,* Pres.; Marina K. French,* V.P.; Andrew Gundlach, Secy.-Treas.; **Nina M. Gorrissen.**
EIN: 133173593

2251
Charles & Lucille King Family Foundation, Inc.
1212 Avenue of the Americas, 7th Fl.
New York, NY 10036-1600 (212) 682-2913
Contact: Michael Donovan, Educational Dir.; Karen E. Kennedy, Asst. Educational Dir.
E-mail: kingscholarships@aol.com; Main URL: http://www.kingfoundation.org
Grants List: http://www.kingfoundation.org/winners.html

Established in 1988 in NJ.
Donors: Diana King; Karen Rabe.
Foundation type: Independent foundation.
Financial data (yr. ended 12/31/12): Assets, $1,207,068 (M); gifts received, $17,996; expenditures, $418,636; qualifying distributions, $251,910; giving activities include $251,910 for 82 grants (high: $50,000; low: $150).
Purpose and activities: Giving primarily for scholarship awards available to junior and senior undergraduate college students of film and television currently attending a four year accredited university in the United States.
Fields of interest: Media/communications; Higher education; Human services.
Type of support: General/operating support; Scholarships—to individuals.
Limitations: Giving on a national basis.
Publications: Application guidelines; Informational brochure (including application guidelines).
Application information: See foundation web site for application guidelines and procedures. Scholarship application forms can only be downloaded from foundation web site between Sept. and Mar. Also, grant guidelines for various programs available on web site.
Initial approach: Letter, telephone, e-mail to request application
Deadline(s): Mar. 15 for the following academic year
Board meeting date(s): Annually
Officers and Directors:* Diana King,* Chair. and Pres.; Charles J. Brucia,* V.P. and Treas.; Eugene V. Kokot,* Secy.; M. Graham Coleman.
Number of staff: None.
EIN: 133489257

2252
The Kleban Foundation, Inc.
c/o Marks Paneth & Shron, LLP
685 3rd Ave.
New York, NY **10017**
Main URL: http://www.newdramatists.org/kleban_award.htm
Application address: c/o Kleban Award Coordinator, New Dramatists, 424 W. 44th St., New York, NY 10036, tel.: (212) 757-6960, ext.75

Established in 1988 in NY.
Donor: Edward L. Kleban†.
Foundation type: Independent foundation.
Financial data (yr. ended 06/30/13): Assets, $3,027,920 (M); expenditures, $347,343; qualifying distributions, $307,854; giving activities include $250,000 for 5 grants to individuals (high: $50,000; low: $50,000).
Purpose and activities: Support for individual theatrical lyricists and librettists.
Fields of interest: Performing arts, theater; Scholarships/financial aid.
Type of support: Grants to individuals.
Limitations: Applications accepted. Giving primarily in New York, NY.
Publications: Application guidelines.
Application information: See foundation web site for complete application information. Application form required.
Initial approach: Written application
Deadline(s): Sept. 15
Officers: Richard Maltby, Jr.,* Pres.; Sheldon Harnick,* V.P.; Sarah Douglas, Secy.; **Richard Terrano,* Treas.**
Directors: Andre Bishop; **Elliot H. Brown**; John Weidman; Maury Yeston.
Number of staff: 1 part-time professional.
EIN: 133490882
Other changes: Richard Terrano has replaced Francis Neuwirth as Treas.
Alan J. Stein is no longer a director.
The grantmaker now publishes application guidelines.

2253
The Conrad and Virginia Klee Foundation, Inc.
84 Court St., Ste. 500
Binghamton, NY 13901-3310 (607) 722-2266
Contact: Judith C. Peckham, Exec. Dir.
FAX: (607) 722-2264;
E-mail: kleefoundation@stny.rr.com; Main URL: http://www.kleefoundation.org
Grants List: http://www.kleefoundation.org/grants/index.html

Incorporated in 1957 in NY.
Donors: Conrad C. Klee†; Virginia Klee†.
Foundation type: Independent foundation.
Financial data (yr. ended 12/31/12): Assets, $16,662,285 (M); expenditures, $1,544,725; qualifying distributions, $1,475,683; giving activities include $1,362,744 for 27 grants (high: $452,000; low: $1,270).
Purpose and activities: Giving primarily for the arts, health care, and human services.
Fields of interest: Arts; Health care; Human services; Children/youth, services.
Type of support: Equipment; Program development; Fellowships.
Limitations: Giving limited to Broome County, NY. No support for religious or political organizations. No grants to individuals.
Publications: Application guidelines; Annual report; Grants list.
Application information: Application form required.
Initial approach: Letter or telephone call
Copies of proposal: 1
Deadline(s): Feb. 15 and Sept. 15
Board meeting date(s): Apr., May, Oct. and Nov.
Final notification: 4-6 weeks
Officers: William J. Orband, Jr., Chair.; Lawrence Anderson, Vice-Chair.; Armond R. George, Secy.-Treas.; Judith C. Peckham, Exec. Dir.
Directors: Ron Akel; Linda Biemer; Gary Holcomb; Patricia Ingraham, Ph.D.; Arthur Orr; Prakash Ramanathan.
Number of staff: 1 part-time professional; 1 part-time support.
EIN: 156019821

2254
The Reb Ephraim Chaim & Miriam Rochel Klein Charitable Foundation
614 Ave. J
Brooklyn, NY 11230-3504

Established in 1989 in NY.
Donors: Abraham Klein; Sarah Dinah Klein; L. Rubin; Abraham Leizirowitz; Stuart Schlesinger; Barbara

Hurwitz; Beach Terrace Care Center; Fairview Nursing Care Center, Inc.; Grandell Rehabilitation; Hyde Park Nursing Home, Inc.; Oceanside Care Center; Park Terrace Care Center; Queens Nassau Nursing Home; Talmide Chidishei Harim.
Foundation type: Independent foundation.
Financial data (yr. ended 12/31/12): Assets, $54,594,452 (M); expenditures, $4,136,444; qualifying distributions, $4,028,631; giving activities include $4,006,981 for 181 grants (high: $1,000,000; low: $100).
Purpose and activities: Giving primarily to Jewish agencies, temples, and schools.
Fields of interest: Elementary/secondary education; Human services; Jewish federated giving programs; Jewish agencies & synagogues; Religion.
International interests: Israel.
Limitations: Applications not accepted. Giving primarily in Brooklyn, NY; some giving nationally, as well as in Israel. No grants to individuals.
Application information: Contributes only to pre-selected organizations.
Directors: Mordechai Klein; Sarah Dinah Klein.
EIN: 223000780
Other changes: At the close of 2012, the grantmaker paid grants of $4,006,981, a 186.7% increase over the 2010 disbursements, $1,397,611.
Abraham Klein is no longer a director.

2255
Klein Family Foundation

c/o Park Terrace Care Ctr.
109-40 Saultell Ave.
Corona, NY 11368-4012
Contact: Abraham N. Klein, Tr.

Established in 1999 in NY.
Donors: Chana Brauner; Abraham Klein; Sarah Dinah Klein; Rifka Green; Bracha Weits; Sara Dina Klein Irrevocable Trust; Lincoln Avenue Realty Co.; Northern Manhattan Nursing; Fairview Nursing Center Inc.; Medford Multicare Center; Beach Terrace Care Center; Grandell Rehabilitation; Queens Nassau Nursing Home; Park Terrace Care Center; Oceanside Care Center; Manhattan Nursing Home Realty Inc.
Foundation type: Independent foundation.
Financial data (yr. ended 12/31/12): Assets, $48,829,688 (M); gifts received, $250,000; expenditures, $2,306,306; qualifying distributions, $2,141,388; giving activities include $2,133,856 for 249 grants (high: $600,000; low: $96).
Purpose and activities: Giving primarily to Jewish agencies, temples, and schools.
Fields of interest: Education; Jewish agencies & synagogues.
Limitations: Applications not accepted. Giving primarily in Brooklyn, NY, and Israel. No grants to individuals.
Application information: Contributes only to pre-selected organizations.
Trustees: Abraham Klein; Sarah Dinah Klein.
EIN: 134092608
Other changes: At the close of 2012, the grantmaker paid grants of $2,133,856, an 89.0% increase over the 2010 disbursements, $1,129,064.

2256
The Esther A. & Joseph Klingenstein Fund, Inc.

125 Park Ave., Ste. 1700
New York, NY 10017-5529 (212) 492-6195
***Contact:* Andrew D. Klingenstein, Pres.; Kathleen Pomerantz, V.P.**
FAX: (212) 492-7007;
E-mail: kathleen.pomerantz@klingenstein.com;
Main URL: http://www.klingfund.org

Incorporated in 1945 in NY.
Donors: Esther A. Klingenstein†; Joseph Klingenstein†; John Klingenstein.
Foundation type: Independent foundation.
Financial data (yr. ended 09/30/13): Assets, $91,013,473 (M); expenditures, $1,726,374; qualifying distributions, $1,079,674; giving activities include $721,681 for 21+ grants (high: $137,106).
Purpose and activities: Primary interests in basic neuroscience research and independent school education.
Fields of interest: Elementary/secondary education; Higher education; Hospitals (general); Medical research, institute; Epilepsy research; Neuroscience research; Civil liberties, first amendment; Public policy, research.
Type of support: General/operating support; Continuing support; Program development; Conferences/seminars; Publication; Seed money; Fellowships; Research; Grants to individuals.
Limitations: Applications accepted. Giving primarily in NY. No grants to individuals (except for Neuroscience Fellowship Program), or for building or endowment funds.
Publications: Informational brochure.
Application information: Online application is required for the Klingenstein Neuroscience Fellowship Awards. Application form not required.
Initial approach: Letter or proposal
Copies of proposal: 1
Deadline(s): See fund web site for current deadline information for the Klingenstein Fellowship Awards
Board meeting date(s): Generally 4 or 5 times a year
Officers and Directors:* Andrew D. Klingenstein,* Pres.; Julie Klingenstein; Patricia D. Klingenstein; Thomas D. Klingenstein; Sally Klingenstein Martell; Nancy Perlman; Nancy K. Simpkins.
Number of staff: 2 full-time professional; 2 part-time professional; 1 full-time support.
EIN: 136028788

2257
Frederick & Sharon Klingenstein Fund

c/o Tanton & Co., LLP
37 W. 57th St., 5th Fl.
New York, NY 10019-3411

Established in 1997 in NY.
Donor: Frederick A. Klingenstein.
Foundation type: Independent foundation.
Financial data (yr. ended 12/31/12): Assets, $18,418,056 (M); expenditures, $980,312; qualifying distributions, $506,977; giving activities include $500,789 for 53 grants (high: $297,661; low: $85).
Purpose and activities: Giving primarily for the arts, particularly museums, as well as for education, with emphasis on a medical school; some funding also for health, children, youth, and social services.
Fields of interest: Museums; Museums (natural history); Arts; Higher education; Medical school/education; Education; Hospitals (general); Human services; Children/youth, services; Community/economic development; Jewish agencies & synagogues.
Limitations: Applications not accepted. Giving primarily in New York, NY.
Application information: Contributes only to pre-selected organizations.
Trustee: Frederick A. Klingenstein.
EIN: 061471980
Other changes: Sharon Klingenstein is no longer a trustee.

2258
The Klingenstein Third Generation Foundation

c/o Tanton Collp
125 Park Ave., Ste. 1700
New York, NY 10017-5529
Contact: Sally Klingenstein Martell, Exec. Dir.
E-mail: info@ktgf.org; **E-mail and telephone for Sally Klingenstein Martell: sally@ktgf.org; (212) 492-6179**; Main URL: http://www.ktgf.org

Established in 1993 in NY.
Donors: Andrew Julie Klingenstein Family; Thomas Klingenstein; Andrew Klingenstein; Esther A. and Joseph Klingenstein Fund; Sarah Martell; Amy Pollinger; Nancy Simpkins.
Foundation type: Independent foundation.
Financial data (yr. ended 09/30/12): Assets, $6,205,413 (M); gifts received, $38,000; expenditures, $416,218; qualifying distributions, $370,274; giving activities include $255,922 for 18 grants (high: $30,000; low: $1,000).
Purpose and activities: Support for programs that strive to improve the lives of families afflicted by depression, with a focus on those that address child and adolescent depression and Attention Deficit Hyperactivity Disorder (ADHD). The foundation operates three funding programs. Two are post-doctoral fellowship programs to fund clinical or basic research. One of these programs supports researchers investigating childhood and adolescent depression. The other supports researchers investigating ADHD in children. Investigators must hold a Ph.D. and/or an M.D. degree, and have completed all research training, including post-doctoral training. The foundation's third funding program supports medical student training programs at a number of institutions. These programs increase students' exposure to the field of child psychiatry. The foundation no longer funds outside the three fellowship programs.
Fields of interest: Medical school/education; Mental health, depression.
Type of support: Fellowships.
Limitations: Applications accepted. Giving on a national basis. No support for direct service programs.
Application information: Complete application guidelines available on foundation web site.
Officers: Andrew Klingenstein, Pres.; Susan Klingenstein, V.P.; Nancy Simpkins, Secy.; Thomas Klingenstein, Treas.; Sally Klingenstein Martell,* Exec. Dir.
Directors: Kathy Klingenstein; Amy Pollinger.
Number of staff: 2 part-time professional.
EIN: 133732439

2259
The Knapp Fund

c/o Silvercrest Asset Mgmt.
1330 Ave. of the Americas
New York, NY 10019-5434

Incorporated in 1917 in NY.
Donor: George O. Knapp†.
Foundation type: Independent foundation.
Financial data (yr. ended 08/31/13): Assets, $3,944,927 (M); expenditures, $201,765; qualifying distributions, $170,500; giving activities include $170,500 for 20 grants (high: $50,000; low: $2,000).
Fields of interest: Elementary/secondary education; Scholarships/financial aid; Education; Environment; Medical research, institute; Human services.
Type of support: Endowments; General/operating support; Continuing support; Annual campaigns; Building/renovation; Program development; Scholarship funds; Research.
Limitations: Applications not accepted. Giving primarily in CT, FL, NY and PA. No grants to individuals, or for matching gifts; no loans.
Application information: Unsolicited requests for funds not accepted.
Officers: George O. Knapp III, Pres.; Anne S. Mauk, V.P. and Treas.; Bart A. Johnston, V.P.; Amber Waugaman, Secy.
Directors: W. Jared Knapp III; Sarah S. Obregon; Louise Knapp Page; F. Russell Sprole.
EIN: 136068384
Other changes: The grantmaker no longer lists a phone. The grantmaker no longer lists a URL address.

2260
Kochov Foundation
c/o Leah Goldberger
4515 18th Ave.
Brooklyn, NY **11204-1292**

Established in 2002 in NY.
Donors: Moses Eilenberg; Leah Goldberger; Yud, Inc.; Abraham Stern.
Foundation type: Independent foundation.
Financial data (yr. ended 12/31/12): Assets, $3,377,980 (M); expenditures, $1,107,208; qualifying distributions, $163,500; giving activities include $162,000 for 3 grants (high: $72,000; low: $36,000).
Fields of interest: Jewish agencies & synagogues.
Limitations: Applications not accepted. Giving primarily in Brooklyn, NY. No grants to individuals.
Application information: Unsolicited requests for funds not accepted.
Trustees: Leah Goldberger; Joseph Leff.
EIN: 300128032

2261
Emily Davie and Joseph S. Kornfeld Foundation
41 Schermerhorn St., Ste. 208
Brooklyn, NY 11201-4802 (718) 624-7969
Contact: Bobye G. List, Exec. Dir.
FAX: (718) 834-1204;
E-mail: office@kornfeldfdn.org; **Main URL: http://kornfeldfdn.org**
Additional URL: http://www.kornfeldfdn.org
Grants List: http://fdnweb.org/kornfeld/recent-grants/

Established in 1979.
Donor: Emily Davie Kornfeld†.
Foundation type: Independent foundation.
Financial data (yr. ended 12/31/12): Assets, $27,697,714 (M); expenditures, $1,732,096; qualifying distributions, $1,541,704; giving activities include $1,274,000 for 28 grants (high: $400,000; low: $2,500).
Purpose and activities: The Foundation supports: 1) Literacy enrichment programs for New York City public school children that focus on arts education and professional development, in collaboration with Columbia University Teachers College Reading and Writing Project; 2) Robert Packard Center for ALS Research at Johns Hopkins Medical School; 3) Grants in palliative care and bioethics, currently focused on the National Palliative Care Research Center at Mount Sinai School of Medicine and the Kornfeld Program in Bioethics and Patient Care, administered by The Greenwall Foundation.
Fields of interest: Education, management/technical assistance; Elementary/secondary education; Medical school/education; Education, reading; Health care, ethics; Palliative care; Health care; Medical research, institute.
Type of support: Program development; Seed money; Curriculum development; Research; Program evaluation.
Limitations: Applications accepted. Giving limited to the continental U.S., with emphasis on New York, NY, for educational grants.
Publications: Annual report (including application guidelines); Grants list.
Application information: The foundation will no longer be accepting grants for after school programs. Bioethics grantmaking now restricted to Kornfeld Program in Bioethics and Patient Care program. Application information available on foundation Web site. The grants listed in current program areas include major ongoing commitments undertaken pursuant to this strategy. Accordingly, only minimal grants to other organizations will be available in the near future. Application form not required.
Initial approach: Letter
Copies of proposal: 1
Deadline(s): Mar. 15, July 15, and Nov. 15
Board meeting date(s): Feb., May, and Oct.
Final notification: Winter, spring, and fall
Officers and Directors:* Christopher C. Angell,* Pres.; Emme L. Deland,* V.P. and Treas.; Barry H. Smith, M.D.*, Secy.; Bobye G. List, Exec. Dir.
Number of staff: 1 full-time professional; 1 part-time support.
EIN: 133042360

2262
Koussevitzky Music Foundation, Inc.
254 W. 31st St., 15th Fl.
New York, NY 10001-2813 (212) 461-6956
Contact: James M. Kendrick, Secy.
FAX: (212) 810-4567;
E-mail: info@koussevitzky.org; Main URL: http://www.koussevitzky.org/
Grants List: http://www.koussevitzky.org/grants.html
Application address: 611 Pennsylvania Ave. S.E., No. 118, Washington, DC 20003-4303, tel.: (202) 707-5503, fax: (202) 707-0621

Established in 1942 in NY.
Donors: Olga Koussevitzky†; Serge Koussevitzky†.
Foundation type: Independent foundation.
Financial data (yr. ended 12/31/12): Assets, $1,310,001 (M); expenditures, $134,248; qualifying distributions, $76,250; giving activities include $76,250 for 10 grants to individuals (high: $12,500; low: $6,250).
Purpose and activities: Grant awards to individual composers for performing arts.
Fields of interest: Performing arts, music.
Type of support: Grants to individuals.
Limitations: Giving on a national basis.
Publications: Application guidelines; Informational brochure (including application guidelines).
Application information: Music Commission procedures will be provided upon request. Application form can be downloaded from foundation web site. Application form required.
Initial approach: Letter
Deadline(s): Mar. 1
Officers and Directors:* Gunther Schuller,* Chair. and Pres.; Fred Lerdahl,* V.P.; James M. Kendrick, Esq., Secy.; Anthony Schmidt, C.P.A.*, Treas.; Phyllis Bryn-Julson; Mario Davidovsky; Lee Hyla; Ursula Oppens; Shulamit Ran; Fred Sherry; Steven Stucky; Olly W. Wilson, Jr.
EIN: 046128361

2263
Samuel H. Kress Foundation
174 E. 80th St.
New York, NY 10075-0439 (212) 861-4993
Contact: Wyman Meers, Prog. Admin.
FAX: (212) 628-3146;
E-mail: wyman.meers@kressfoundation.org; **E-mail for grant and fellowship inquiries: info@kressfoundation.org**; Main URL: http://www.kressfoundation.org

Incorporated in 1929 in NY.
Donors: Samuel H. Kress†; Claude W. Kress†; Rush H. Kress†.
Foundation type: Independent foundation.
Financial data (yr. ended 06/30/13): Assets, $88,824,967 (M); expenditures, $6,751,482; qualifying distributions, $5,206,354; giving activities include $4,111,761 for 237 grants (high: $300,000; low: $49), and $19,442 for 1 foundation-administered program.
Purpose and activities: Giving through five main programs: 1) fellowships for pre-doctoral research in art history; 2) advanced training and research in conservation of works of art; 3) development of scholarly resources in the fields of art history and conservation; 4) conservation and restoration of monuments in Europe; and 5) occasional related projects.
Fields of interest: Visual arts; Museums; History/archaeology; Arts.
International interests: Europe.
Type of support: Conferences/seminars; Professorships; Publication; Fellowships; Internship funds; Research; Employee matching gifts.
Limitations: Applications accepted. Giving primarily in the U.S. and Europe. No support for the purchase of works of art. No grants for living artists, or for operating budgets, continuing support, annual campaigns, endowments, deficit financing, capital funds exhibitions, or films; no loans.
Publications: Application guidelines; Annual report (including application guidelines).
Application information: Application forms required for fellowships in art history and interpretive fellowships. Applications sent by fax not considered. Application form not required.
Initial approach: Proposal
Copies of proposal: 1
Deadline(s): Nov. 30 for research fellowships in art history; Received by Mar. 10 for conservation fellowships, Apr. 1 for interpretive fellowships; Quarterly submission deadlines: Jan. 15, Apr. 1, and Oct. 1
Board meeting date(s): Annually in winter, spring and fall
Final notification: 3 months
Officers and Trustees:* Frederick W. Beinecke,* Chair.; Max Marmor,* Pres.; David Rumsey,

Secy.-Treas.; Elizabeth Eveillard; Carmela Vircillo Franklin; William Higgins; Cheryl Hurley; Barbara A. Shailor; Daniel H. Weiss.
Number of staff: 4 full-time professional; 1 part-time professional.
EIN: 131624176

2264
Laffont Family Foundation

c/o Coatue Management
9 W. 57th St., 25th Fl.
New York, NY 10019-2701

Donors: Philippe Laffont; Laffont 2009 Trust; Coatue Management, LLC.
Foundation type: Independent foundation.
Financial data (yr. ended 12/31/12): Assets, $5,046,665 (M); gifts received, $5,390,651; expenditures, $1,417,031; qualifying distributions, $1,415,476; giving activities include $1,412,170 for 8 grants (high: $1,000,000; low: $10,000).
Fields of interest: Health care; Agriculture/food; Human services.
Limitations: Applications not accepted.
Application information: Unsolicited requests for funds not accepted.
Officers: Philippe Laffont, Pres.; **Ana Luisa Diez De Rivera, Treas.**
EIN: 271517424
Other changes: At the close of 2012, the grantmaker paid grants of $1,412,170, a 643.2% increase over the 2010 disbursements, $190,000. Ana Luisa Diez De Rivera has replaced Thomas Laffont as Treas.

2265
Lake Placid Education Foundation

1992 Saranac Ave.
Crestview Plz., Ste. 3
Lake Placid, NY 12946-1173 (518) 523-4433
Contact: John Lansing

Established in 1922 in NY.
Donor: Melvil Dewey†.
Foundation type: Independent foundation.
Financial data (yr. ended 06/30/13): Assets, $6,097,624 (M); expenditures, $331,194; qualifying distributions, $268,858; giving activities include $240,800 for 33 grants (high: $45,000; low: $500).
Purpose and activities: Giving for public and private schools, the arts, and libraries.
Fields of interest: Arts; Elementary/secondary education; Higher education; Libraries/library science; Education.
Type of support: General/operating support; Continuing support; Equipment; Program development; Conferences/seminars; Seed money; Scholarship funds; Program-related investments/loans; Scholarships—to individuals; Matching/challenge support.
Limitations: Applications accepted. Giving primarily in the northern Adirondack region of NY. No support for political organizations.
Application information: Application form required.
Initial approach: Letter
Copies of proposal: 1
Deadline(s): May 1
Board meeting date(s): June, Dec., and Sept.
Final notification: Two months
Officers: Frederick C. Calder, Pres.; Catherine I. Johnston, V.P.; John Rosenthal, Secy.; Lisa Weibrecht, Treas.; John S. Lansing, Exec. Dir.
Directors: Adele Connors; W. John Friedlander; Sara Kelly Jones; Hilary McDonald; John McMillin; Greg Peacock; Meredith M. Prime.
Number of staff: 1 part-time professional; 1 part-time support.
EIN: 510243919
Other changes: E. Michael O'Connor is no longer a director.

2266
The Randi and Clifford Lane Foundation, Inc.

105 Wilbur Pl.
Bohemia, NY 11716-2426

Established in 2001 in NY.
Donors: Clifford Lane; Randi Lane; ILC Holdings, Inc.; Mildred Lane†.
Foundation type: Independent foundation.
Financial data (yr. ended 12/31/12): Assets, $17,911,525 (M); expenditures, $1,074,132; qualifying distributions, $978,675; giving activities include $978,675 for 39 grants (high: $250,000; low: $225).
Fields of interest: Hospitals (general); Cancer; Medical research, institute; Children/youth, services; Jewish federated giving programs.
Limitations: Applications not accepted. Giving primarily in NY. No grants to individuals.
Application information: Contributes only to pre-selected organizations.
Officers: Clifford Lane, Pres.; Randi Lane, V.P.
Director: Terrence M. Bennett.
EIN: 113635985
Other changes: Kenneth J. Sheedy is no longer Treas.

2267
The Jacob and Valeria Langeloth Foundation

275 Madison Ave., 33rd Fl.
New York, NY 10016-1101 (212) 687-1133
Contact: Andrea Fionda, Prog. Off.
FAX: (212) 687-8877;
E-mail: afionda@langeloth.org; Main URL: http://www.langeloth.org
Facebook: https://www.facebook.com/TheLangelothFoundation
Twitter: https://twitter.com/LangelothFndn

Incorporated in 1915 in NY as the Valeria Home; renamed in 1975.
Donor: Jacob Langeloth†.
Foundation type: Independent foundation.
Financial data (yr. ended 11/30/13): Assets, $97,333,332 (M); expenditures, $5,806,700; qualifying distributions, $4,971,789; giving activities include $4,458,279 for 52 grants (high: $400,000; low: $2,500).
Purpose and activities: The foundation's grantmaking program is centered on the concepts of health and well-being. The foundation's purpose is to promote and support effective and creative programs, practices and policies related to healing from illness, accident, physical, social or emotional trauma and to extend the availability of programs that promote healing to underserved populations, with a focus on justice-involved people. The foundation believes that justice-involved people experience disproportionately higher rates of infectious and chronic diseases, substance abuse, mental illness, and trauma than the general population. As such, jails and prisons represent one of the largest target populations for public health services in America, and are important sites for improving the overall health and well-being of communities. The foundation is interested in projects that seek to improve the physical and mental health of individuals involved in the criminal justice system. Programs focusing on alternatives to incarceration, detention, and reentry will be considered. While the foundation does not support prevention projects, it is interested in programs that seek to reduce recidivism.
Fields of interest: Health care; Adults; Mentally disabled; Minorities; African Americans/Blacks; Hispanics/Latinos; Native Americans/American Indians; Offenders/ex-offenders; Substance abusers; Immigrants/refugees; Economically disadvantaged; Homeless; LGBTQ.
Type of support: Program development; Program evaluation; Matching/challenge support.
Limitations: Applications accepted. Giving primarily in NY and for projects that hold promise of national impact or extensive replication. No support for preventive medicine, or for children or end-of-life issues. No grants to individuals, or for annual campaigns, capital campaigns, building or renovation projects, or budgetary relief.
Publications: Grants list.
Application information: Potential applicants must register project ideas on foundation's web site. Letters of intent and proposals are accepted by invitation only following online project registration. Unsolicited letters of intent or proposals not accepted. Registrations only accepted via foundation's online registration system. Application form required.
Initial approach: Online registration for letter of intent
Copies of proposal: 5
***Deadline(s):* See foundation web site for current deadline**
Board meeting date(s): Apr. and Oct.
Final notification: Varies
Officer: Scott Moyer, Pres.
Number of staff: 3 full-time professional.
EIN: 131773646

2268
Lassalle Fund, Inc.

c/o Norman Foundation
147 E. 48th St.
New York, NY 10017-1223

Established in 1966 in NY.
Donors: The Norman Foundation; Nancy N. Lassalle.
Foundation type: Independent foundation.
Financial data (yr. ended 12/31/12): Assets, $4,169,617 (M); expenditures, $259,347; qualifying distributions, $214,775; giving activities include $210,328 for 32 grants (high: $50,000; low: $2).
Purpose and activities: Giving primarily for ballet, education, and the performing arts.
Fields of interest: Museums (art); Performing arts; Performing arts, ballet; Performing arts, theater; Performing arts, music; Performing arts, opera; Performing arts, education; Arts.
Limitations: Applications not accepted. Giving primarily in NY. No grants to individuals.
Application information: Contributes only to pre-selected organizations.
Officer: Nancy N. Lassalle, Pres.
EIN: 136213551

2269
Lavelle Fund for the Blind, Inc.
307 W. 38th St., Ste. 2010
New York, NY 10018-9507 (212) 668-9801
Contact: Andrew S. Fisher, Exec. Dir.
FAX: (212) 668-9803;
E-mail: afisher@lavellefund.org; Main URL: http://www.lavellefund.org/
Grants List: http://www.lavellefund.org/grants.html

Established in 1999; Converted to an independent foundation in 2003.
Foundation type: Independent foundation.
Financial data (yr. ended 12/31/13): Assets, $122,125,872 (M); expenditures, $5,811,709; qualifying distributions, $6,161,011; giving activities include $4,448,941 for grants, and $1,200,000 for 1 loan/program-related investment.
Purpose and activities: The fund is dedicated to supporting programs that promote the spiritual, moral, intellectual, and physical development of blind and low-vision people of all ages, together with programs that help people avoid vision loss. Priority is given to agencies that concentrate on serving the New York City metropolitan area.
Fields of interest: Eye diseases; Disabilities, people with.
Type of support: General/operating support; Program development; Scholarship funds.
Limitations: Applications accepted. Giving primarily in the New York City metropolitan area. No grants to individuals, or for deficit reduction, emergency funds, medical research programs, conferences or media events (unless an integral part of a broader program of direct service), or advocacy programs; no loans.
Publications: Informational brochure (including application guidelines).
Application information: Application guidelines available on foundation web site. New York/New Jersey Area Common Grant Application Form accepted. Application form not required.
Initial approach: Letter of inquiry on organization's letterhead
Copies of proposal: 1
Deadline(s): None
Board meeting date(s): Quarterly
Final notification: 1 week
Officers and Trustees:* Daniel M. Callahan,* Pres.; John J. Caffrey,* V.P. and Treas.; Andrew S. Fisher, Secy. and Exec. Dir.; Nancy L. Brown; Sr. Mary Flood, M.D., Ph.D.; Michael A. Lemp, M.D.; J. Robert Lunney; Hon. Kevin B. McGrath, Jr.; Jane B. O'Connell; Paul A. Sidoti, M.D.
Number of staff: 2 full-time professional.
EIN: 131740463
Other changes: Thomas A. Galvin is no longer a trustee. Br. James Kearney, F.M.S., and John J. McNally, trustees, are deceased.

2270
Patrick P. Lee Foundation
45 Bryant Woods N.
Amherst, NY 14228-3600 (716) 844-3100
FAX: (716) 844-3117;
E-mail: info@patrickleefoundation.org; Main URL: http://www.patrickpleefoundation.org
All Grants: http://www.patrickpleefoundation.org/work/
Behavioral Health Grants: http://www.patrickpleefoundation.org/work/behavioral-health/
Education Grants: http://www.patrickpleefoundation.org/work/education/
Human and Community Services Grants: http://www.patrickpleefoundation.org/work/human-community-services/
Medical Care and Research Grants: http://www.patrickpleefoundation.org/work/medical-care-research/

Donor: Patrick P. Lee.
Foundation type: Independent foundation.
Financial data (yr. ended 12/31/12): Assets, $26,902,969 (M); gifts received, $308,188; expenditures, $1,627,909; qualifying distributions, $1,520,406; giving activities include $1,388,557 for 63 grants (high: $200,000; low: $500).
Purpose and activities: Giving primarily for behavioral health, education, medical care and research, and human services.
Fields of interest: Higher education; Health care; Human services; Children/youth, services; Family services; Catholic agencies & churches.
Limitations: Applications accepted. Giving primarily in Buffalo, NY. No support for political activities. No grants to individuals or for deficit financing, capacity building funds, seed funds or program-related investments.
Application information: Application guidelines available on foundation web site. Application form required.
Initial approach: Letter of intent
Deadline(s): Jan. 15 for behavioral health; Apr. 15 for education; July 15 for medical care and research; Oct. 15 for human services
Board meeting date(s): Mar. June, Sept., and Dec.
Final notification: Apr. and Oct.
Officers and Directors:* Patrick P. Lee,* Chair.; Mark O'Donnell,* Exec. Dir.; Glenda M. Cadawallader; David C. Hohn, M.D.; David C. Horan; Robert J. Lane, Jr.; Christopher J. Lee; Cynthia R. Lee; Michele R. Lee; Jennifer McNamara; Barbara R. Rhee; John Rhee, M.D.; Lee Wortham.
EIN: 453845576

2271
James T. Lee Foundation Inc.
FDR Station
P.O. Box 606
New York, NY 10150-0606

Incorporated in 1958 in NY.
Donor: James T. Lee†.
Foundation type: Independent foundation.
Financial data (yr. ended 11/30/13): Assets, $3,062,024 (M); expenditures, $337,051; qualifying distributions, $303,857; giving activities include $289,000 for 24 grants (high: $20,000; low: $2,500).
Purpose and activities: Giving primarily for higher and other education, as well as for the arts, health organizations and specialized hospitals, and children, youth, and social services, including a guide dog program for the blind.
Fields of interest: Arts; Education; Human services.
Type of support: Continuing support; Annual campaigns; Debt reduction; Emergency funds; Program development; Scholarship funds; Research.
Limitations: Applications not accepted. Giving primarily in the New York, NY, metropolitan area, including Westchester County. No grants to individuals, or for operating budgets, seed money, capital or endowment funds, publications, or conferences; no loans.
Application information: Contributes only to pre-selected organizations.
Officers and Directors:* Raymond O'Keefe,* Pres.; Delcour S. Potter,* V.P.; Richard W. Wheeless,* Secy.-Treas.; Verne S. Atwater; Leelee Brown; Paul Duffy; Stephen Siegel; Vincent Ziccolella.
EIN: 131878496

2272
Leeds Family Foundation
c/o Lipsky, Goodkin & Co.
120 W. 45th St., 7th Fl.
New York, NY 10036-4041 **(212) 840-6444**
***Contact:* Laurence C. Leeds, Jr., Tr.**

Established in 1999 in NY.
Donors: Laurence C. Leeds, Jr.; Dalia Leeds.
Foundation type: Independent foundation.
Financial data (yr. ended 12/31/12): Assets, $20,949,994 (M); expenditures, $1,314,504; qualifying distributions, $1,083,733; giving activities include $1,080,548 for 60 grants (high: $350,175; low: $75).
Fields of interest: Arts; Higher education; Education; Health care, clinics/centers; Health organizations; Human services.
Limitations: Giving primarily in CT and NY. No grants to individuals.
Application information: Application form not required.
***Initial approach:* Letter of request**
***Deadline(s):* None**
Trustees: Dalia Leeds; Laurence C. Leeds, Jr.
EIN: 137219856

2273
Stephen & May Cavin Leeman Foundation, Inc.
215 W. 92nd St., Ste. 13A
New York, NY 10025-7479 (212) 873-5555
Contact: Cavin P. Leeman, Pres. and Treas.
E-mail: info@leemanfoundation.org; Main URL: http://foundationcenter.org/grantmaker/leeman/
Grants List: http://foundationcenter.org/grantmaker/leeman/grants.html

Established in 1969 in NY.
Donors: Stephen Leeman†; May Cavin Leeman†.
Foundation type: Independent foundation.
Financial data (yr. ended 06/30/13): Assets, $1,992,877 (M); expenditures, $196,925; qualifying distributions, $182,539; giving activities include $141,795 for 16 grants (high: $16,000; low: $500).
Purpose and activities: Giving primarily to relatively small programs serving needy children and youth in New York City.
Fields of interest: Humanities; Arts; Education; Health care; Human services; Children/youth, services; Children/youth.
Limitations: Applications accepted. Giving primarily in New York, NY. No grants to individuals.
Publications: Annual report (including application guidelines).
Application information: Complete application guidelines available on foundation web site. Application form required.
Initial approach: Preliminary letter of interest (not exceeding two pages)
Copies of proposal: 2
Deadline(s): None
Officers: Cavin P. Leeman, M.D., Pres. and Treas.; Diane L. Zimmerman, V.P. and Secy.
Director: Gina Trent.
Number of staff: 1 part-time professional.
EIN: 237057183

2274
Legacy Foundation of Tompkins County
(formerly Tompkins County Foundation, Inc.)
P.O. Box 97
Ithaca, NY 14851-0097
Contact: Scott C. Russell, Dir., Devel.
E-mail: srussell11@twcny.rr.com; Additional Primary Contact: Janet Hewitt, Rec. Secy., email: jhewitt@tompkinstrust.com; Main URL: http://www.tclegacy.org
Grants List: http://www.tclegacy.org/grants.htm

Established in 1945 in NY.
Foundation type: Independent foundation.
Financial data (yr. ended 12/31/12): Assets, $2,241,090 (M); gifts received, $52,018; expenditures, $196,089; qualifying distributions, $156,407; giving activities include $156,407 for 41 grants (high: $12,500; low: $500).
Purpose and activities: Giving for the arts, education, environment, and human services.
Fields of interest: Humanities; Arts; Education; Environment; Health care; Mental health/crisis services; Housing/shelter; Human services; Children/youth, services; Community/economic development.
Type of support: Capital campaigns; Building/renovation; Equipment; Program development; Seed money; Matching/challenge support.
Limitations: Applications accepted. Giving limited to the Tompkins County, NY, area. No support for sectarian organizations or to other foundations. No grants for operating expenses.
Publications: Application guidelines; Annual report; Informational brochure; Newsletter.
Application information: Application form not required.
Initial approach: Proposal on organization letterhead
Copies of proposal: 1
Deadline(s): Apr. 15 and Sept. 15
Board meeting date(s): May and Oct.
Final notification: June 15 and Nov. 15
Officers and Directors:* Greg Hartz,* Pres.; James Brown,* V.P.; Anne DiGiacomo,* Secy.-Treas.; Larry Baum; Robert Cree; Patricia Johnson; Mary Kane; Susan Nohelty; Sean Whittaker.
Number of staff: 2 part-time support.
EIN: 156018481

2275
Levitt Foundation, Inc.
c/o Philanthropic Group
630 5th Ave., 20th Fl.
New York, NY 10111-0100 (212) 501-7785
Contact: Barbara R. Greenberg
***FAX:* (212) 501-7788;**
E-mail: BGreenberg@philanthropicgroup.com; Main URL: http://fdnweb.org/levitt
Grants List: http://fdnweb.org/levitt/grants-approved/

Incorporated in 1949 in NY.
Donors: Levitt and Sons, Inc.; Abraham Levitt†; Alfred Levitt†; William Levitt.
Foundation type: Independent foundation.
Financial data (yr. ended 04/30/13): Assets, $16,930,856 (M); expenditures, $795,137; qualifying distributions, $766,746; giving activities include $675,400 for 54 grants (high: $55,000; low: $1,000).
Purpose and activities: The foundation is interested in youth-powered food justice as it relates to children and youth living in the five boroughs of New York City and Long Island, New York. The foundation funds programs that: enable young people ages 6 to 18 to learn about healthy eating and food systems, and to take action to increase access to affordable fresh foods in their own neighborhoods; provide children and youth with ongoing opportunities to build their confidence and self-esteem, citizenship skills and leadership abilities; and are sponsored by neighborhood and community-based organizations (rather than schools).
Fields of interest: Nutrition; Agriculture/food; Children/youth, services; Community development, neighborhood development.
Type of support: Program development; Internship funds.
Limitations: Applications not accepted. Giving limited to Long Island and New York, NY. No grants to individuals.
Publications: Grants list.
Application information: Unsolicited requests for funds not accepted.
Board meeting date(s): 3 times per year
Officers and Directors:* John M. Brickman,* Pres.; Elaine S. Hutchinson,* Secy.; Carlos Garcia-Tunon,* Treas.; Loren S. Harris; Tracy Green Landauer; Blondel A. Pinnock; Gregg Walker.
EIN: 136128226

2276
The Paul and Karen Levy Family Foundation
c/o Schwartz & Co.
2580 Sunrise Hwy.
Bellmore, NY 11710-3608
Contact: Paul Levy, Tr.

Established in 1997 in NY.
Donors: Paul Levy; Karen Levy.
Foundation type: Independent foundation.
Financial data (yr. ended 12/31/12): Assets, $367,965 (M); gifts received, $1,575,000; expenditures, $1,614,029; qualifying distributions, $1,609,099; giving activities include $1,609,099 for 21 grants (high: $500,000; low: $500).
Purpose and activities: Giving primarily for higher education, as well as for the arts, Jewish organizations, and social services.
Fields of interest: Museums; Arts; Higher education; Law school/education; Human services; Jewish federated giving programs.
Limitations: Giving primarily in NY and PA; some giving nationally.
Application information: Application form not required.
Initial approach: Letter
Deadline(s): None
Trustee: Paul Levy.
EIN: 133982379
Other changes: The grantmaker has changed its fiscal year-end from Nov. 30 to Dec. 31.

2277
The Carol Sutton & William M. Lewis Jr. Charitable Foundation
New York, NY
The foundation terminated in 2011.

2278
The Liberal Do-Gooder Foundation
12A Clinton Ave.
Dobbs Ferry, NY 10522

Established in 2001 in NY.
Donor: Michael Wolkowitz.
Foundation type: Independent foundation.
Financial data (yr. ended 10/31/13): Assets, $410,308 (M); expenditures, $120,793; qualifying distributions, $109,860; giving activities include $105,250 for 8 grants (high: $45,000; low: $2,000).
Fields of interest: Arts; Education; Crime/law enforcement.
Limitations: Applications not accepted. Giving primarily in Washington, D.C. and NY.
Application information: Contributes only to pre-selected organizations.
Trustees: Hope Holiner; Michael Wolkowitz.
EIN: 510450528

2279
Bertha & Isaac Liberman Foundation, Inc.
c/o Jerome Tarnoff, Morrison Cohen LLP
909 3rd Ave.
New York, NY 10022-4731 (212) 735-8632
Contact: Jerome Tarnoff, Pres.

Established in 1947 in NY.
Donor: Isaac Liberman†.
Foundation type: Independent foundation.
Financial data (yr. ended 06/30/13): Assets, $9,317,311 (M); expenditures, $460,246; qualifying distributions, $433,026; giving activities include $392,000 for 22 grants (high: $70,000; low: $500).
Purpose and activities: Giving primarily for the arts, particularly art museums, as well as for education, social services, and Jewish organizations.
Fields of interest: Museums (art); Performing arts; Arts; Higher education; Hospitals (general); Human services; Jewish agencies & synagogues.
Type of support: General/operating support; Capital campaigns; Building/renovation; Program development.
Limitations: Applications accepted. Giving primarily in New York, NY. No grants to individuals.
Application information: Application form not required.
Deadline(s): None
Officers and Directors:* Jerome Tarnoff,* Pres.; Michele Gerber Klein,* V.P.; Karin J. Lundell,* Secy.; David B. Forer,* Treas.; John Moscow.
EIN: 136119056

2280
The Link Foundation
c/o Binghamton University Foundation
P.O. Box 6005
Binghamton, NY **13902-6005**
Contact: Martha J. Gahring
Application address: P.O. Box 6005 Bringhamton, NY 13902-6005; Main URL: http://www.linkfoundation.org

Established in 1953 in NY.
Donors: Edwin A. Link†; Mrs. Edwin A. Link†; Lawrence Clayton; L-3 Link Communications; Link Div. of CAE.
Foundation type: Independent foundation.
Financial data (yr. ended 06/30/13): Assets, $11,044,705 (M); gifts received, $17,390; expenditures, $518,726; qualifying distributions, $452,000; giving activities include $452,000 for grants.
Purpose and activities: The foundation supports programs to foster the theoretical basis, practical knowledge, and application of energy, simulation, and ocean engineering and instrumentation

research, and to disseminate the results of that research through lectures, seminars and publications.
Fields of interest: Environment, energy; Marine science; Space/aviation; Engineering/technology.
Type of support: Continuing support; Fellowships; Research.
Limitations: Applications accepted. Giving primarily in FL and NY. No grants to individuals (except through programs).
Publications: Informational brochure (including application guidelines).
Application information: Application form required.
Initial approach: Letter
Copies of proposal: 1
Deadline(s): Jan. 15
Board meeting date(s): Feb. and June
Final notification: Mar.
Officers and Trustees:* Dr. Thomas F. Kelly,* Chair; Dr. Jimmie Anne Haisley,* Secy.; Douglas R. Johnson,* Treas.; Dr. Andrew M. Clark; **David Gdovin**.
Number of staff: 1 part-time professional.
EIN: 536011109
Other changes: Lee Lynd is no longer a trustee.

2281
Gerda Lissner Foundation, Inc.
15 E. 65th St., 4th Fl.
New York, NY **10065-6501** (212) 826-6100
Contact: Stephen DeMaio, Pres.
FAX: (212) 826-0366;
E-mail: mail@gerdalissner.com; Main URL: http://www.gerdalissner.org
Grants List: http://www.gerdalissner.org/awards.html

Established in 1994 in NY.
Donor: Gerda Lissner†.
Foundation type: Independent foundation.
Financial data (yr. ended 12/31/12): Assets, $9,427,251 (M); expenditures, $911,826; qualifying distributions, $849,263; giving activities include $140,520 for 20 grants (high: $25,000; low: $250), and $185,000 for 50 grants to individuals (high: $15,000; low: $2,000).
Purpose and activities: Giving primarily for awards to assist in the development of world class opera singers.
Fields of interest: Performing arts, opera.
Type of support: General/operating support; Grants to individuals.
Publications: Application guidelines.
Application information: See grantmaker web site for application information and form. Application form required.
Initial approach: Telephone or e-mail
Deadline(s): Mar. 1
Officers: Stephen DeMaio, Pres.; Michael Fornabaro, V.P. and Treas.; Rev. John A. Kamas, Secy.
Trustees: Dorothy Moore; Barbara Ann Testa.
Number of staff: 1 full-time support; 1 part-time support.
EIN: 133566516

2282
The Lucius N. Littauer Foundation, Inc.
220 5th Ave., 19th Fl.
New York, NY **10001** **(212) 697-2677**
***Contact:* Alan Divack, Prog. Off.**
***E-mail:* info@littauerfoundation.org; Main URL: http://littauerfoundation.org/**

Incorporated in 1929 in NY.
Donor: Lucius N. Littauer†.
Foundation type: Independent foundation.
Financial data (yr. ended 12/31/12): Assets, $40,435,321 (M); expenditures, $2,927,273; qualifying distributions, $2,717,723; giving activities include $2,603,900 for 202 grants (high: $150,000; low: $250).
Purpose and activities: Grants for scholarly research on Jewish studies, for the endowment of Judaica book funds at university libraries, for medical ethics and palliative medical care, and NY public projects.
Fields of interest: Humanities; History/archaeology; Language/linguistics; Literature; Higher education; Environment; Medical care, bioethics; Palliative care; Social sciences; Political science; Jewish agencies & synagogues; Religion.
International interests: Israel.
Type of support: Endowments; Program development; Publication; Seed money; Research; Employee matching gifts; Matching/challenge support.
Limitations: Applications accepted. Giving primarily in NY for medical ethics, and environmental related projects. No support for religious programs. No grants to individuals.
Application information: See foundation web site for application guidelines and online application. Application form required.
Board meeting date(s): Annually and as required
Officers and Directors:* Robert D. Frost,* Pres.; **Noah Perlman, Secy.; Geula R. Solomon, Treas.**; Charles Berlin; Berthold Bilski; Mark A. Bilski; George Harris; **Sarah K. Levy**; Henry A. Lowet; Peter J. Solomon.
Number of staff: 1 part-time professional; 1 part-time support.
EIN: 131688027
Other changes: Geula R. Solomon is now Treas. Noah Perlman is now Secy.

2283
The Litwin Foundation, Inc.
1200 Union Tpke.
New Hyde Park, NY 11040-1708
Contact: Leonard Litwin, Pres.

Established in 1989 in NY.
Donors: Leonard Litwin; Woodbourne Foundation.
Foundation type: Independent foundation.
Financial data (yr. ended 12/31/12): Assets, $15,795,814 (M); gifts received, $4,500,000; expenditures, $6,374,849; qualifying distributions, $6,321,663; giving activities include $6,321,663 for grants.
Purpose and activities: Giving primarily for disease research organizations, children's services, human services, education, and the environment.
Fields of interest: Museums; Education; Environment, natural resources; Hospitals (general); Health organizations, association; Medical research, institute; Human services; Children/youth, services; Jewish agencies & synagogues; Aging; Disabilities, people with; Homeless.
Type of support: General/operating support; Research.
Limitations: Applications not accepted. Giving primarily in New York, NY. No grants to individuals.
Application information: Unsolicited requests for funds not accepted.
Officers and Directors:* Leonard Litwin,* Pres.; Diane Miller,* V.P.; Carole Pittelman,* Treas.; **Richard Cohen**; Seymour D. Reich; **Howard Swarzman**.
EIN: 133501980
Other changes: At the close of 2012, the fair market value of the grantmaker's assets was $15,795,814, a 273.9% increase over the 2011 value, $4,224,051.
Morton Sanders is no longer Secy. Ruth Litwin is no longer a director.

2284
Frederick Loewe Foundation, Inc.
c/o Baker Tilly, LLP
1 Penn Plz., Ste. 3000
New York, NY **10119-0032**
Main URL: http://www.frederickloewe.org

Established in 1959 in NY.
Donor: Frederick Loewe†.
Foundation type: Independent foundation.
Financial data (yr. ended 12/31/13): Assets, $9,239,057 (M); expenditures, $601,495; qualifying distributions, $463,924; giving activities include $443,000 for grants.
Purpose and activities: Giving primarily for the arts, particularly theater, and education.
Fields of interest: Arts, association; Arts education; Performing arts; Performing arts, theater; Arts; Higher education; Jewish agencies & synagogues.
Limitations: Applications not accepted. Giving primarily in NY. No grants to individuals.
Application information: Contributes only to pre-selected organizations.
Officers: Emily Altman, Pres. and Treas.; Dara Altman, V.P.
Board Members: Paul Epstein; **Michael Lennon**.
EIN: 136111444
Other changes: Emily Altman is now Pres. and Treas. Jerold L. Couture is no longer Pres. David S. Rhine is no longer Treas.

2285
Theodore Luce Charitable Trust
c/o JPMorgan Chase Bank, N.A., Private Foundation Svcs.
270 Park Ave., 16th Fl.
New York, NY 10017-2014
***Contact:* Connie Giampapa, Prog. Off.**
FAX: (212) 464-2304;
E-mail: connie.a.giampapa@jpmorgan.com; Main URL: http://fdnweb.org/luce
Grants List: http://fdnweb.org/luce/grants/category/contributions/

Established in the 1940s in NY.
Foundation type: Independent foundation.
Financial data (yr. ended 07/31/13): Assets, $13,227,116 (M); expenditures, $808,519; qualifying distributions, $688,584; giving activities include $655,000 for 17 grants (high: $80,000; low: $5,000).
Purpose and activities: Giving primarily to programs that assist young people, ages 8-18, in developing competencies that will enable them to grow, develop their skills and become healthy, responsible and caring youth and adults. The foundation is particularly interested in programs for low-income youth that operate year-round, and address academics, personal and social competence, health and physical well-being, preparation for work, special interests and talents, leadership and citizenship and/or parent involvement. The trust also seeks to support youth development organizations in one of two areas: program enhancement or capacity building.
Fields of interest: Youth development; Children/youth; Youth; LGBTQ.

Type of support: General/operating support; Program development.
Limitations: Applications not accepted. Giving limited to New York, NY. No support for organizations lacking 501(c)(3) status. No grants to individuals, or for matching gifts; no loans.
Publications: Grants list.
Application information: Proposals accepted by invitation only. Invitations will be mailed in Feb. and grant awards will be announced in July.
Board meeting date(s): July
Trustee: JPMorgan Chase Bank, N.A.
EIN: 136029703
Other changes: The grantmaker has moved from TX to NY.

2286
The Henry Luce Foundation, Inc.

51 Madison Ave., 30th Fl.
New York, NY 10010-1603 (212) 489-7700
Contact: Michael Gilligan, Pres.
FAX: (212) 581-9541; E-mail: hlf1@hluce.org; Main URL: http://www.hluce.org

Incorporated in 1936 in NY.
Donors: Henry R. Luce†; Clare Boothe Luce†.
Foundation type: Independent foundation.
Financial data (yr. ended 12/31/12): Assets, $764,393,011 (M); expenditures, $41,694,946; qualifying distributions, $36,450,334; giving activities include $29,663,578 for 240+ grants (high: $1,500,000), $570,535 for grants to individuals, and $424,025 for employee matching gifts.
Purpose and activities: Grants for specific projects in the broad areas of Asian affairs, American art, public policy and the environment, theology, advancement of women in science and engineering, and higher education. The Luce Scholars Program gives a select group of young Americans, not Asian specialists, a year's work experience in East and Southeast Asia. Asia grants support the creation of new scholarly and public resources on East and Southeast Asia as well as innovative cultural and intellectual exchange between the Asia-Pacific and the United States. The Henry R. Luce Professorship Program, which supports innovative programs at private colleges and universities, no longer accepts proposals for new grants. The Clare Boothe Luce Program is designed to enhance the careers of women in science and engineering through scholarships, fellowships, and professorships at invited institutions. Funding in the arts focuses on research, scholarship and exhibitions in American art; direct support for specific projects at major museums and service organizations; dissertation support for topics in American art history through the American Council of Learned Societies. Theology grants are made primarily to seminaries and divinity schools for educational purposes. The Henry Luce III Theology Fellows Program is administered through the Association of Theological Schools. Public Policy grants are to support the development of public leadership and to promote best practices in philanthropy, and the Environment grants are made to support the study of critical issues and environmental training and research.
Fields of interest: Visual arts; Museums; Humanities; Theology; Higher education; Theological school/education; Environment; Engineering/technology; Social sciences; International studies; Public policy, research.
International interests: Eastern Asia; Southeastern Asia.
Type of support: General/operating support; Program development; Professorships; Fellowships; Internship funds; Scholarship funds; Research; Employee matching gifts; Grants to individuals; Matching/challenge support.
Limitations: Applications accepted. Giving on a national and international basis; international activities limited to East and Southeast Asia. No support for medical or healthcare projects. No grants to individuals (except for specially designated programs), or for endowments, domestic building campaigns, annual fund drives; no loans.
Publications: Biennial report (including application guidelines); Grants list; Program policy statement.
Application information: Nominees for Luce Scholars Program accepted from invited institutions only; Clare Boothe Luce Program by invitation to institutions only, individual applications cannot be considered; Luce Fun in American Art requires prior inquiry by Apr.1. Application form not required.
Initial approach: Letter
Copies of proposal: 1
Deadline(s): June 15, for American Art; Nov. 1 for Luce Scholars nominations; all others, no specific deadlines
Board meeting date(s): Mar., June and Nov.
Officers and Directors:* Margaret Boles Fitzgerald,* Chair.; Michael Gilligan,* Pres.; John P. Daley, V.P., Finance and Admin. and Treas.; Toby Volkman, Secy. and Dir., Policy Initiatives; Staci Salomon, Cont.; Robert E. Armstrong, Dir., Emeritus; John C. Evans, Dir., Emeritus; James T. Laney, Dir., Emeritus; Terrence B. Adamson; **Elizabeth Broun**; Mary Brown Bullock; Claire L. Gaudiani; Kenneth T. Jackson; **Debra S. Knopman**; H. Christopher Luce; Thomas L. Pulling; David V. Ragone; George E. Rupp.
Number of staff: 11 full-time professional; 1 part-time professional; 8 full-time support; 2 part-time support.
EIN: 136001282

2287
The M.A.C. AIDS Fund

(formerly The M.A.C. Global Foundation)
130 Prince St., 2th Fl.
New York, NY 10012-3101 (212) 965-6300
***Contact:* Nancy Mahon, Exec. Dir.**
FAX: (212) 372-6171;
E-mail: macaidsf@maccosmetics.com; Main URL: http://www.macaidsfund.org
Twitter: https://twitter.com/macaidsfund

Established in 2000 in NY.
Donors: Make-Up Art Cosmetics Inc.; Estee Lauder Companies, Inc.
Foundation type: Independent foundation.
Financial data (yr. ended 06/30/13): Assets, $23,384,196 (M); gifts received, $23,858,792; expenditures, $23,290,100; qualifying distributions, $22,923,470; giving activities include $21,588,838 for 322 grants (high: $2,683,438; low: $130).
Purpose and activities: Giving primarily to AIDS research, outreach and resource organizations.
Fields of interest: AIDS; Food services; Human services; International affairs.
Limitations: Applications accepted. Giving on a national basis, with some emphasis on CA and NY; giving on an international basis, with some emphasis on Ontario, Canada. No grants to individuals; general operating expenses. deficit reduction; endowments, capital casts, conferences, summits, briefings, research, or multi-year granting.
Publications: Application guidelines.
Application information: See the fund's web site for each program's deadlines and eligibility criteria.
Initial approach: Online application and eligibility quiz
Deadline(s): Varies
Board meeting date(s): Quarterly, usually Mar., June, Sept. and Dec.
Final notification: Varies
Officers and Directors:* John D. Demsey,* Chair.; **Jennifer Balbier,* Secy.**; **Carey Maloney,* Treas.**; Nancy Mahon,* Exec. Dir.; Bruce Hunter,* Exec. Prog. Dir., Canadian Office; Frank Doyle; James Gager; **Peter Jueptner**; **Quarraisha Abdool Karim, Ph.D.**; Nancy M. Louden; **Sara Moss**; Ian Ness; **Jean W. Pape, M.D.**; Charles Richards; Karen Buglisi Weiler; Clyde Williams; **Tracey Travis**; Reggie Van Lee.
EIN: 134144722
Other changes: Jennifer Balbier has replaced Nancy M. Louden as Secy. Carey Maloney has replaced Robert Charles Richards as Treas. Deborah Krulewitch is no longer a director.

2288
Josiah Macy Jr. Foundation

44 E. 64th St.
New York, NY 10065-7306 (212) 486-2424
Contact: George E. Thibault M.D., Pres.; Peter Goodwin M.B.A., C.O.O. and Treas.
FAX: (212) 644-0765;
E-mail: info@macyfoundation.org; Main URL: http://www.macyfoundation.org
LinkedIn: http://www.linkedin.com/groups?home=&gid=4215159
Twitter: http://twitter.com/macyfoundation

Incorporated in 1930 in NY.
Donor: Kate Macy Ladd†.
Foundation type: Independent foundation.
Financial data (yr. ended 06/30/13): Assets, $144,037,503 (M); expenditures, $9,786,597; qualifying distributions, $8,563,244; giving activities include $6,093,628 for 58 grants (high: $325,575; low: $20), $161,710 for employee matching gifts, and $464,352 for foundation-administered programs.
Purpose and activities: Major interest in medicine and health. Support for enhancing and improving health professional and medical education in ways that will better the health of the public. The foundation's grantmaking is focused on projects that: a) Demonstrate or encourage interprofessional education and teamwork among health care professionals;b) Teach principles of patient safety, quality improvement, and system performance;c) Develop new models for clinical education, including community-based models;d)Increase the diversity of the health care professional workforce through career development for underrepresented minorities; and c) Improve education for the care of underserved populations.
Fields of interest: Medical school/education; Nursing school/education; Public health school/education; Health sciences school/education; Health care; Minorities; African Americans/Blacks; Hispanics/Latinos; Native Americans/American Indians; Women; Economically disadvantaged.
Type of support: Program development; Conferences/seminars; Publication; Curriculum development; Fellowships; Program evaluation; Employee matching gifts; Matching/challenge support.
Limitations: Applications accepted. Giving on a national basis. No grants to individuals, or for travel, capital funds, operating budgets, general undesignated support annual fund appeals, financing, construction or renovation projects, research, scholarships, or fellowships; no loans.

Publications: Application guidelines; Annual report; Financial statement; Grants list; Informational brochure; Newsletter; Occasional report; Program policy statement.
Application information: Additional program information is available on the foundation's web site. The foundation no longer accepts submission of applications via mail or e-mail. Application form required.
Initial approach: Letter of inquiry via foundation's web site
Copies of proposal: 1
Deadline(s): None
Board meeting date(s): Jan., May, and Oct.
Final notification: Within 3 months
Officers and Directors:* William H. Wright II,* Chair.; George E. Thibault, M.D.*, Pres.; Peter Goodwin, C.O.O. and Treas.; David Blumenthal, M.D., MPP; George Campbell, Jr., Ph.D.; Linda Cronenwett, Ph.D., R.N.; Harvey V. Fineberg, M.D., Ph.D.; Linda Fried, M.D., MPH; **Terry Fulmer, Ph.D., R.N.**; Henry P. Johnson; Paul G. Ramsey, M.D.; George Rupp, Ph.D; **Steven M. Sayfer, M.D.**; **Gregory H. Warner, M.B.A.**
Number of staff: 2 full-time professional; 1 part-time professional; 3 full-time support.
EIN: 135596895
Other changes: Lawrence K. Altman, John W. Frymoyer, Judith B. Krauss, and Herbert Pardes are no longer directors.

2289
The Marine Society of the City of New York
17 Battery Pl., Ste. 714
New York, NY 10004-1207 **(212) 425-0448**
***FAX:* (212) 425-1117**;
E-mail: info@marinesocietyny.org; Main URL: http://www.marinesocietyny.org

Established in 1770 in NY.
Foundation type: Independent foundation.
Financial data (yr. ended 12/31/12): Assets, $2,774,277 (M); gifts received, $2; expenditures, $334,027; qualifying distributions, $171,430; giving activities include $171,430 for grants.
Purpose and activities: Giving to improve maritime knowledge and for the needs of distressed shipmasters and their widows and orphans.
Fields of interest: Education; Human services; Marine science; Christian agencies & churches.
Type of support: General/operating support; Grants to individuals.
Limitations: Applications not accepted. Giving primarily on the East Coast, with emphasis on NY.
Application information: Unsolicited requests for funds not accepted.
Officers: Timothy Ferrie, Pres.; James McNamara, V.P.; Robert H. Pouch, V.P.; Cynthia J. Roboson, Secy.; Thomas F. Fox, Treas.
EIN: 135643623

2290
The Markle Foundation
(also known as The John and Mary R. Markle Foundation)
10 Rockefeller Plz., 16th Fl.
New York, NY 10020-1903 (212) 713-7600
Contact: Zoe Baird, Pres.
FAX: (212) 765-9690; E-mail: info@markle.org; Main URL: http://www.markle.org/
RSS Feed Directory: http://www.markle.org/stay-connected/rss-feeds
Twitter: http://twitter.com/marklefdn

Incorporated in 1927 in NY.
Donors: John Markle†; Mary Markle†.
Foundation type: Independent foundation.
Financial data (yr. ended 06/30/13): Assets, $143,158,120 (M); expenditures, $11,888,917; qualifying distributions, $10,011,750; giving activities include $1,906,793 for 17 grants (high: $456,859; low: $2,695), and $6,264,603 for 2 foundation-administered programs.
Purpose and activities: The mission of the foundation is to use emerging communication and information technologies to address critical public needs, with emphasis on health, and national and economic security.
Fields of interest: Public policy, research.
Type of support: Endowments.
Limitations: Applications not accepted. Giving primarily in Washington, DC, and New York, NY.
Publications: IRS Form 990 or 990-PF printed copy available upon request.
Application information: The foundation directly supports its work in health and national security.
Officers and Directors:* Lewis B. Kaden,* Chair.; Zoe Baird,* Pres.; Karen Byers, C.F.O. and Secy.-Treas.; Sen. Slade Gorton; Suzanne Nora Johnson; Gilman Louie; Herbert Pardes, M.D.; Edward Rover; Stanley Shulman; Debora Spar.
Number of staff: 15 full-time professional; 4 part-time professional; 2 full-time support; 1 part-time support.
EIN: 131770307
Other changes: John Gage is no longer a director.

2291
Nancy and Edwin Marks Family Foundation
(formerly Marks Family Foundation)
c/o Carl Marks & Co.
900 3rd Ave., 33rd Fl.
New York, NY 10022-4775
Contact: Katherine Liebman, Exec. Dir.

Established in 1986 in NY.
Donors: Edwin S. Marks†; Nancy A. Marks.
Foundation type: Independent foundation.
Financial data (yr. ended 06/30/13): Assets, $16,494,687 (M); expenditures, $610,395; qualifying distributions, $568,286; giving activities include $483,000 for 31 grants (high: $60,000; low: $500).
Purpose and activities: Giving primarily for early childhood education.
Fields of interest: Arts; Human services; Children/youth, services.
Type of support: General/operating support.
Limitations: Giving primarily in New York, NY. No grants to individuals.
Application information:
Initial approach: Proposal
Deadline(s): None
Officers and Directors:* Nancy A. Marks,* Pres. and Secy.; Katherine Liebman, Exec. Dir.; Carolyn Marks; Constance Marks Miller.
EIN: 133385770
Other changes: Linda Marks Katz is no longer a Director.

2292
The Jacob Marley Foundation, Inc.
47 Guilford Rd.
Port Washington, NY 11050-4426 (516) 767-9235
Main URL: http://www.jacobmarley.org

Established in 1993 in NY.
Donors: Christopher Quackenbush†; Traci Quackenbush.
Foundation type: Independent foundation.
Financial data (yr. ended 12/31/12): Assets, $4,244,118 (M); gifts received, $29,725; expenditures, $214,210; qualifying distributions, $150,000; giving activities include $150,000 for 5 grants (high: $65,000; low: $10,000).
Purpose and activities: Giving primarily for education.
Fields of interest: Education; Recreation, camps; Children/youth, services.
Limitations: Giving primarily in New York, NY. No grants to individuals.
Officers & Directors:* Carlton D. Brown,* Pres.; Traci L. Vicklund,* V.P.; Thomas M. O'Brien,* Secy.; James J. Dunne III; William F. Hickey; **Gail Quackenbush**; Michael A. Quackenbush; **Mark Viklund.**
EIN: 113165445
Other changes: Diana L. Holden is no longer Exec. Dir.

2293
Marshall Family Foundation
5810 Lake Bluff Rd.
North Rose, NY 14516-9727 (585) 423-1860

Established in 1995 in NY.
Donors: W. Gilman Marshall†; Ina Marshall.
Foundation type: Independent foundation.
Financial data (yr. ended 10/31/13): Assets, $6,709,130 (M); expenditures, $281,102; qualifying distributions, $220,500; giving activities include $220,500 for 13 grants (high: $132,000; low: $2,000).
Fields of interest: Historic preservation/historical societies; Education; Hospitals (general); AIDS; Health organizations; Youth development, community service clubs; American Red Cross; International affairs, U.N.; Community/economic development; Foundations (community).
Limitations: Applications accepted. Giving primarily in NY. No grants to individuals.
Application information: Application form not required.
***Initial approach:* Letter**
Deadline(s): None
Trustees: Gary Marshall; Kent Marshall.
EIN: 166430502

2294
The G. Harold & Leila Y. Mathers Charitable Foundation
118 N. Bedford Rd., Ste. 203
Mount Kisco, NY 10549-2555 (914) 242-0465
Contact: James H. Handelman, Exec. Dir.
FAX: (914) 242-0665;
E-mail: admin@mathersfoundation.org; Additional e-mail (for James H. Handelman): jh@mathersfoundation.org; Main URL: http://www.mathersfoundation.org

Established in 1975 in NY.
Donors: G. Harold Mathers†; Leila Y. Mathers†.
Foundation type: Independent foundation.
Financial data (yr. ended 12/31/12): Assets, $203,465,494 (M); expenditures, $15,433,353; qualifying distributions, $11,856,322; giving activities include $11,672,561 for 56 grants (high: $1,000,001; low: $5,000).
Purpose and activities: The foundation is primarily interested in supporting fundamental basic research

in the life sciences. Support is provided for specific projects from established researchers at top universities and independent research institutions within the United States.
Fields of interest: Science, research; Biology/life sciences.
Type of support: General/operating support; Research.
Limitations: Applications accepted. Giving on a national basis. No grants to individuals.
Publications: Application guidelines.
Application information: General inquiries can be made via e-mail. Specific detailed queries must be received by mail. Application form not required.
Initial approach: Letter
Copies of proposal: 1
Deadline(s): None
Board meeting date(s): 2 or 3 times per year
Final notification: Within 90 days of submission of request
Officers and Directors:* Donald E. Handelman,* Pres.; William R. Handelman,* V.P.; **John Young,* Secy.**; **Richard Handelman, Treas.**; James H. Handelman, Exec. Dir.; **David Boyle**; William S. Miller.
Number of staff: 1 full-time professional; 1 full-time support.
EIN: 237441901
Other changes: John Young has replaced Don Fizer as Secy. Richard Handelman has replaced Joseph W. Handelman as Treas.

2295
Pierre and Tana Matisse Charitable Foundation
1 E. 53rd St.
New York, NY 10022-4200 **(212) 355-6269**
***Contact:* Sandra Carnielli, Exec. Dir.**

Established in 1995 in DE and NY.
Donors: Maria-Gaetana Matisse; The Maria-Gaetana Matisse Revocable Trust.
Foundation type: Independent foundation.
Financial data (yr. ended 12/31/12): Assets, $216,682,629 (M); expenditures, $3,534,615; qualifying distributions, $3,090,567; giving activities include $1,830,300 for 48 grants (high: $403,000; low: $350), and $260,670 for foundation-administered programs.
Fields of interest: Museums (art); Arts; Education; Foundations (private grantmaking).
Limitations: Giving primarily in New York, NY, some funding also in Phnom Penh, Cambodia. No grants to individuals.
Application information:
***Initial approach:* Letter**
***Deadline(s):* None**
Officers and Directors:* Robert H. Horowitz,* Pres. and Treas.; **Oliver G. Bernier,* V.P. and Secy.**; Janos Farkas,* V.P.; Sandra Carnielli, Exec. Dir.
EIN: 133838457
Other changes: Oliver G. Bernier has replaced Eugene V. Thaw as V.P. and Secy.

2296
The Mayday Fund
c/o SPG
127 W. 26th St., Ste. 800
New York, NY 10001-6869 (212) 366-6970
Contact: Christina Spellman, Exec. Dir.
FAX: (212) 366-6979;
E-mail: inquiry@maydayfund.org; Main URL: http://www.maydayfund.org/
Grants List: http://www.maydayfund.org/maydaygrants.html
Application fax: (301) 654-1589,
e-mail: ghertz@burnesscommunications.com

Established in 1992 in NY.
Donors: Shirley S. Katzenbach‡; John C. Beck; Pamela M. Thye; Caroline N. Sidnam; Harold L. Messenger.
Foundation type: Independent foundation.
Financial data (yr. ended 12/31/13): Assets, $27,149,332 (M); expenditures, $1,339,784; qualifying distributions, $1,310,179; giving activities include $819,434 for 16 grants (high: $200,000; low: $1,950), and $243,927 for 1 foundation-administered program.
Purpose and activities: The foundation is dedicated to the reduction of the profound human problems associated with physical pain and its consequences. The fund is particularly interested in projects that result in clinical interventions to reduce the toll of physical pain, pediatric pain, pain in non-verbal populations, and pain in the context of emergency medicine. The fund also promotes networking between veterinary and human medicine.
Fields of interest: Medical research.
International interests: Canada.
Type of support: Research.
Limitations: Giving on a national basis. No grants to individuals, or generally for endowments, capital projects, equipment, general operating expenses, ongoing activities, or annual fundraising drives.
Publications: Annual report; Financial statement; Grants list.
Application information: Mail and phone contacts only after initial e-mail communications. Application form not required.
Initial approach: E-mail to Exec. Dir.
Copies of proposal: 1
Deadline(s): None
Board meeting date(s): Quarterly
Final notification: 1-6 weeks
Officer: Christina Spellman, Exec. Dir.
Trustees: John C. Beck; Robert D.C. Meeker, Jr.; Caroline N. Sidnam; Pamela M. Thye.
EIN: 133645438

2297
MBIA Foundation, Inc.
113 King St.
Armonk, NY 10504-1611 (914) 765-3834
Contact: Jean McGovern, Secy.
E-mail: Jean.McGovern@mbia.com; Additional tel.: (914) 273-4545; Main URL: http://www.mbia.com/about/about_foundation.html

Established in 2001 in NY.
Donors: Optinuity Alliance Resources Corporation; MBIA Insurance Corp.; John Caouette; Francie Heller; Kathleen Okenica; Kevin D. Silva; Kutak Rock LLP; Richard L. Weil; Moody's Corp.
Foundation type: Company-sponsored foundation.
Financial data (yr. ended 12/31/12): Assets, $10,137,095 (M); gifts received, $3,006,947; expenditures, $2,172,057; qualifying distributions, $2,079,047; giving activities include $2,079,047 for 576 grants (high: $500,200; low: $100).
Purpose and activities: The foundation supports programs designed to serve children and families through education; health services; and human services.
Fields of interest: Museums; Arts; Elementary school/education; Higher education; Law school/education; Education; Health care; Diabetes; Medical research; Food banks; Family services; Family services, parent education; Human services; Community/economic development; Christian agencies & churches; Religion; Children.
Type of support: Continuing support; Building/renovation; Program development; Employee volunteer services; Sponsorships; Employee matching gifts.
Limitations: Applications accepted. Giving primarily in areas of company operations, with emphasis on CT, NJ, NY, and PA. No support for discriminatory organizations, political or lobbying organizations, religious, fraternal, athletic, social, or veterans' organizations not of direct benefit to the entire community, or umbrella agencies such as the United Way. No grants to individuals, or for general operating support, fundraising activities related to individual sponsorship, capital campaigns, endowments, or fundraising events.
Publications: Application guidelines.
Application information: A site visit may be requested. Organizations receiving support are asked to submit a post grant evaluation report. Application form required.
Initial approach: Contact foundation for application form
Deadline(s): Nov. 26
Officers and Directors:* Chuck Chaplin,* Chair.; Williard Hill,* Pres.; Jean McGovern,* Secy.; Joseph Buonadonna,* Treas.; Cliff Corso; **Jennifer C. Cronin**; Bill Fallon; Gail Makode; Rich McKay; **Kimberly Osgood**; Susan A. Voltz.
EIN: 134163899
Other changes: Mitchell Sonkin is no longer a director.

2298
Brian A. McCarthy Foundation, Inc.
c/o O'Connor Davies, LLP
665 5th Ave.
New York, NY 10022-5305
E-mail: brianamccarthyfoundation@gmail.com; Main URL: http://www.brianamccarthy.com
Grants List: http://www.brianamccarthy.com/grants.html

Foundation type: Independent foundation.
Financial data (yr. ended 12/31/12): Assets, $8,832,954 (M); expenditures, $497,139; qualifying distributions, $424,160; giving activities include $415,000 for 8 grants (high: $100,000; low: $25,000).
Purpose and activities: Giving primarily for gay, lesbian, bisexual, and transgender health, education, culture, and well-being with an emphasis on HIV research and prevention, and housing and anti-violence programs for LGBT youth.
Fields of interest: Health care, clinics/centers; AIDS; AIDS research; Neighborhood centers; LGBTQ.
Limitations: Applications not accepted. Giving primarily in the metropolitan New York, NY, area. No grants to individuals.
Publications: Financial statement.
Application information: Contributes only to pre-selected organizations.
Officer and Director:* Brian A. McCarthy,* Pres.
EIN: 262804661

2299
Dextra Baldwin McGonagle Foundation, Inc.
c/o O'Connor Davies, LLP
665 5th Ave.
New York, NY **10022-5305**
Contact: Jonathan G. Spanier, Pres.

Incorporated in 1967 in NY.
Donor: Dextra Baldwin McGonagle†.
Foundation type: Independent foundation.
Financial data (yr. ended 12/31/13): Assets, $19,881,362 (M); expenditures, $1,085,102; qualifying distributions, $909,695; giving activities include $763,938 for 30 grants (high: $130,000; low: $1,000).
Purpose and activities: Primary areas of interest include hospitals, the medical sciences, and medical research, including cancer research; grants also for higher and medical education, social service agencies, and cultural programs.
Fields of interest: Arts; Higher education; Medical school/education; Hospitals (general); Health care; Cancer; Biomedicine; Medical research, institute; Cancer research; Human services; Biology/life sciences; Aging.
Type of support: Annual campaigns; Equipment; Endowments; Seed money; Scholarship funds; Research.
Limitations: Applications accepted. Giving primarily in CA and NY. No grants to individuals, or for matching gifts.
Application information: Application form not required.
Initial approach: 1-page summary of proposal
Copies of proposal: 1
Deadline(s): None
Board meeting date(s): As required
Officers and Directors:* Maury L. Spanier,* Chair.; Jonathan G. Spanier, Pres. and Treas.; David B. Spanier,* V.P. and Secy.
Number of staff: 1 full-time professional; 1 part-time professional; 3 part-time support.
EIN: 136219236

2300
The Donald C. McGraw Foundation, Inc.
c/o Deutsche Trust Co. of NY
P.O. Box 1297
Church St. Sta.
New York, NY 10008-1297

Incorporated in 1963 in NY.
Donors: Donald C. McGraw†; D. McGraw Charitable Trust; Donald C. McGraw Charitable Lead Annuity Trust.
Foundation type: Independent foundation.
Financial data (yr. ended 01/31/13): Assets, $42,192,854 (M); gifts received, $91,600; expenditures, $1,703,731; qualifying distributions, $1,630,353; giving activities include $1,580,000 for 49 grants (high: $250,000; low: $5,000).
Purpose and activities: Giving primarily for health care and medical research, as well as for museums, education, and human services.
Fields of interest: Museums; Elementary/secondary education; Health care; Health organizations, association; Medical research; Human services; Residential/custodial care, hospices.
Limitations: Applications not accepted. Giving primarily to FL and MA. No grants to individuals.
Application information: Contributes only to pre-selected organizations.
Officer: Donald C. McGraw III, Pres.
Directors: J. Patterson Cooper; David W. McGraw; Robert L.W. McGraw.
EIN: 136165603
Other changes: The grantmaker no longer lists a separate application address.

2301
The Clement Meadmore Foundation
(also known as Clement Meadmore 2002 Trust)
246 5th Ave.
New York, NY 10001-7603

Established in NY.
Foundation type: Independent foundation.
Financial data (yr. ended 03/31/13): Assets, $874,150 (M); expenditures, $315,496; qualifying distributions, $55,000; giving activities include $55,000 for 3 grants (high: $25,000; low: $15,000).
Fields of interest: Arts; Education.
Limitations: Applications not accepted.
Application information: Unsolicited request for funds not accepted.
Officer and Trustees:* Ellen Goldberg,* Pres.; **Dan Morgenstern.**
EIN: 206955131

2302
The Andrew W. Mellon Foundation
140 E. 62nd St.
New York, NY 10065-8124 **(212) 838-8400**
***Contact:* Michele S. Warman, V.P., General Counsel and Secy.**
FAX: (212) 752-4306; E-mail: inquiries@mellon.org; Main URL: http://www.mellon.org
Knowledge Center: http://www.mellon.org/news_publications/publications

Trust established in 1940 in DE as Avalon Foundation; incorporated in 1954 in NY; merged with Old Dominion Foundation and renamed The Andrew W. Mellon Foundation in 1969.
Donors: Ailsa Mellon Bruce†; Paul Mellon†.
Foundation type: Independent foundation.
Financial data (yr. ended 12/31/12): Assets, $5,556,152,571 (M); expenditures, $309,839,205; qualifying distributions, $281,427,094; giving activities include $257,085,010 for 571 grants (high: $4,700,000; low: $7,400), $1,020,344 for employee matching gifts, and $634,081 for foundation-administered programs.
Purpose and activities: The foundation's grantmaking philosophy is to build, strengthen and sustain institutions and their core capacities, rather than be a source for narrowly defined projects. As such, it develops thoughtful, long-term collaborations with grant recipients and invests sufficient funds for an extended period to accomplish the purpose at hand and achieve meaningful results. Institutions and programs receiving support are often leaders in fields of foundation activity, but they may also be promising newcomers, or in a position to demonstrate new ways of overcoming obstacles to achieve program goals. The foundation concentrates most of its grantmaking in a few areas: higher education, art history, conservation, museums, performing arts, scholarly communications and information technology.
Fields of interest: Museums; Performing arts; Humanities; Arts; Higher education; Environment; Public affairs.
Type of support: Continuing support; Endowments; Program development; Fellowships; Research; Matching/challenge support.
Limitations: Applications accepted. Giving on a national basis with some international giving, primarily focused on South Africa. No support for primarily local organizations. No grants to individuals (including scholarships); no loans.
Publications: Annual report; Grants list.
Application information: Please direct inquiries to appropriate program officers. Contact should be by writing or e-mail. Unsolicited applications are accepted but most proposals are by invitation. The program officer will provide instructions after reviewing the initial letter. Application form not required.
Initial approach: Letter
***Copies of proposal:* 1**
Deadline(s): None
Board meeting date(s): Mar., June, Sept., and Dec.
Officers and Trustees:* W. Taylor Reveley III,* Chair.; Earl Lewis, Pres.; John E. Hull, V.P., Finance and C.I.O.; Michele S. Warman, V.P., Genl. Counsel and Secy.; Philip E. Lewis, V.P.; Mariet Westermann, V.P.; Danielle S. Allen; Lewis W. Bernard; Richard Brodhead; Katherine G. Farley; Kathryn A. Hall; Paul LeClerc; Glenn D. Lowry; Eric M. Mindich; Sarah E. Thomas.
Number of staff: 55 full-time professional; 17 full-time support; 1 part-time support.
EIN: 131879954
Other changes: W. Taylor Reveley III has replaced Anne M. Tatlock as Chair.
Philip E. Lewis is now V.P. Michele S. Warman is now V.P., Genl. Counsel and Secy. Mariet Westermann is now V.P. Thomas J. Sanders is no longer Cont. and Dir. of Financial Services. Colin Lucas and Lawrence R. Ricciardi are no longer trustees.

2303
The Mendell Family Fund Inc.
(formerly The Ira L. & Margaret P. Mendell Fund, Inc.)
c/o Cbiz M. Cohen, CBIZ MHM, LLC
111 W. 40th St.
New York, NY 10018-1878

Established in 1954 in NY.
Donors: Ira L. Mendell; Thomas G. Mendell.
Foundation type: Independent foundation.
Financial data (yr. ended 11/30/13): Assets, $3,381,064 (M); expenditures, $196,038; qualifying distributions, $153,130; giving activities include $150,000 for 16 grants (high: $35,000; low: $250).
Fields of interest: Arts; Higher education; Cancer research; Recreation, centers; Youth development; Human services; International human rights.
Type of support: Annual campaigns; Endowments; Scholarship funds.
Limitations: Applications not accepted. Giving primarily in Washington, DC, NY, VA, and VT. No grants to individuals.
Application information: Contributes only to pre-selected organizations.
Officers: Thomas G. Mendell, Pres.; James Mendell, V.P. and Secy.; Alice M. Starr, V.P. and Treas.
EIN: 136159009

2304
The Menezes Foundation, Inc.
c/o Victor J. Menezes, U.S. Trust, Bank of America
114 W. 47th St.
New York, NY 10036-1510

Established in 2000 in NY.
Donors: Tara A. Menezes; Victor J. Menezes.
Foundation type: Independent foundation.
Financial data (yr. ended 09/30/13): Assets, $4,271,094 (M); gifts received, $252,000; expenditures, $297,118; qualifying distributions, $277,915; giving activities include $273,865 for 36 grants (high: $44,125; low: $100).
Fields of interest: Higher education; Human services; Catholic federated giving programs; Catholic agencies & churches.
Limitations: Applications not accepted. Giving primarily in NY. No grants to individuals.
Application information: Contributes only to pre-selected organizations.
Officers and Directors:* Victor J. Menezes,* Pres.; Tara A. Menezes,* Secy.; Pia A. Menezes,* Treas.; M. Alia Menezes; Mita N. Menezes.
EIN: 134147704

2305
Mercer Family Foundation
240 Riverside Blvd., Apt. 24A
New York, NY 10069-1024

Established in 2004 in NY.
Donor: Robert Mercer.
Foundation type: Independent foundation.
Financial data (yr. ended 12/31/12): Assets, $37,625,310 (M); gifts received, $4,003,629; expenditures, $11,702,665; qualifying distributions, $11,677,197; giving activities include $11,677,197 for 22 grants (high: $3,000,000; low: $2,905).
Purpose and activities: Giving primarily for human services, public policy organizations, health organizations, and to a media research center.
Fields of interest: Media/communications; Health organizations; Human services; Foundations (private grantmaking); Social sciences, public policy.
Limitations: Applications not accepted. Giving primarily in IL, NY, TX, and VA. No grants to individuals.
Application information: Contributes only to pre-selected organizations.
Director: Rebekah Mercer.
EIN: 201982204
Other changes: At the close of 2012, the grantmaker paid grants of $11,677,197, a 64.3% increase over the 2011 disbursements, $7,105,215.

2306
Mertz Gilmore Foundation
(formerly Joyce Mertz-Gilmore Foundation)
218 E. 18th St.
New York, NY 10003-3694 (212) 475-1137
Contact: Jay Beckner, Pres.
FAX: (212) 777-5226;
E-mail: info@mertzgilmore.org; Main URL: http://www.mertzgilmore.org
Grants List: http://www.mertzgilmore.org/index.php/programs/grants-lists
LinkedIn: http://www.linkedin.com/company/mertz-gilmore-foundation?goback=.cps_1286206604270_1

Incorporated in 1959 in NY.
Donors: Robert Gilmore‡; Joyce Mertz‡.
Foundation type: Independent foundation.
Financial data (yr. ended 12/31/12): Assets, $111,389,466 (M); gifts received, $4,540,000; expenditures, $8,002,861; qualifying distributions, $7,142,557; giving activities include $5,735,905 for 191 grants (high: $250,000; low: $1,000).
Purpose and activities: Current concerns include human rights, the environment, and New York City cultural, social, and civic concerns.
Fields of interest: Performing arts, dance; Environment, energy; Community/economic development, equal rights; Community development, citizen coalitions; Community/economic development.
Type of support: Program-related investments/loans; General/operating support; Continuing support; Program development; Seed money; Technical assistance; Matching/challenge support.
Limitations: Applications accepted. Giving on a national basis for Human Rights; also giving in the Northeast and New York City for Climate Change Solutions, and in New York City for Dance and Communities programs. No support for sectarian religious concerns. No grants to individuals, or for endowments, annual fund appeals, fundraising events, conferences, workshops, publications, film or media projects, scholarships, research, fellowships, or travel.
Publications: Annual report.
Application information: Please submit an online inquiry letter (not a full proposal) of no more than three pages describing the mission of the organization and the purpose of the request. The online inquiry form can be found on foundation web site. Staff will respond to all communications, and, if appropriate, invite a full proposal. Do not submit videos, CDs, audiocassettes, press clippings, books, or other materials unless they are requested. The foundation accepts the New York/ New Jersey Area Common Application Form and the New York/ New Jersey Common Report Form. Application form required.
Initial approach: Online letter of inquiry submission
Copies of proposal: 1
Deadline(s): See web site for current deadlines
Board meeting date(s): Apr. and Nov. for grant decisions
Final notification: Within 2 weeks
Officers and Directors:* Mikki Shepard,* Chair.; Jay Beckner,* Pres.; Lukas Haynes, V.P.; Rini Banerjee,* Treas.; Larry E. Condon,* Chair. Emeritus; Elizabeth Burke Gilmore, Dir. Emeritus; Jared Bernstein; Laura Butzel; **Andrea Sholler.**
Number of staff: 7 full-time professional; 3 full-time support; 3 part-time support.
EIN: 132872722

2307
MetLife Foundation
1095 Ave. of the Americas
New York, NY 10036-6797 (212) 578-6272
Contact: A. Dennis White, C.E.O. and Pres.
FAX: (212) 578-0617;
E-mail: metlifefoundation@metlife.com; **Main URL: https://www.metlife.com/metlife-foundation/**
MetLife Foundation Video Gallery: https://www.metlife.com/metlife-foundation/video/index.html

Incorporated in 1976 in NY.
Donor: Metropolitan Life Insurance Co.
Foundation type: Company-sponsored foundation.
Financial data (yr. ended 12/31/12): Assets, $168,418,066 (M); gifts received, $47,500,000; expenditures, $41,832,441; qualifying distributions, $42,634,812; giving activities include $39,232,310 for 311+ grants (high: $1,000,000), $875,352 for 1,364 employee matching gifts, and $3,512,691 for loans/program-related investments.
Purpose and activities: The foundation supports programs designed to empower communities and bring financial inclusion to low-income individuals and families. Special emphasis is directed toward programs designed to promote access to knowledge; access to services; and access to insights.
Fields of interest: Media, television; Museums (art); Arts; Higher education; Education, services; Education; Public health; Health care; Alzheimer's disease; Alzheimer's disease research; Food banks; Housing/shelter; Youth development, adult & child programs; Youth development, business; Youth development; Children/youth, services; Family services; Human services, financial counseling; Human services; Urban/community development; Social entrepreneurship; Microfinance/microlending; Community/economic development; Financial services; Leadership development; Public affairs; Adults; Aging; Disabilities, people with; Physically disabled; Minorities; Asians/Pacific Islanders; African Americans/Blacks; Hispanics/Latinos; Native Americans/American Indians; Women; Girls; Young adults, female; Men; Boys; Young adults, male; Military/veterans; Economically disadvantaged; Homeless; LGBTQ.
Type of support: General/operating support; Continuing support; Management development/capacity building; Program development; Publication; Scholarship funds; Research; Employee volunteer services; Program evaluation; Program-related investments/loans; Employee matching gifts; Employee-related scholarships; In-kind gifts.
Limitations: Applications accepted. **Giving on a national and international basis, with emphasis in CA, CT, DC, FL, IL, MA, NJ, NY, PA, TX, Brazil, India, Latin America, Mexico, Peru, and South Korea.** No support for private foundations, religious, fraternal, athletic, political, or social organizations, hospitals, local chapters of national organizations, disease-specific organizations, labor groups, organizations primarily engaged in patient care or direct treatment, drug treatment centers, community health clinics, or elementary or secondary schools. **No grants to individuals (except for employee-related scholarships), or for endowments, courtesy advertising, or festival participation.**
Publications: Annual report (including application guidelines); Corporate giving report (including application guidelines); Financial statement.
Application information: Grant requests outside of the financial inclusion priority area are by invitation only. Application form required.
***Initial approach:* Complete online eligibility quiz and application for financial inclusion requests**
Copies of proposal: 1
***Deadline(s):* None for financial inclusion grants**
Officers and Directors:* Michael Zarcone,* Chair.; A. Dennis White,* C.E.O. and Pres.; Phyllis Zanghi, Counsel and Secy.; Jonathan Rosenthal,* Treas.; Robert C. Tarnok, Cont.; Frans Hijkoop; Michel Khalaf; Maria R. Morris; Oscar Schmidt; **Eric Steigerwalt**; Christopher Townsend.
Number of staff: None.
EIN: 132878224

Other changes: Christopher B. Smith is no longer Chair.
The grantmaker now makes its annual report (including application guidelines) available online.

2308
Edwill B. Miller Trust
1100 Wehrle Dr., 2nd Fl.
Amherst, NY 14221-7748

Established in 1977 in PA.
Donors: Edwill B. Miller†; Rachel H. Miller†.
Foundation type: Independent foundation.
Financial data (yr. ended 03/31/13): Assets, $3,010,666 (M); gifts received, $2,087; expenditures, $167,074; qualifying distributions, $138,790; giving activities include $138,790 for 13 grants (high: $21,914; low: $2,922).
Purpose and activities: Giving for hospitals, higher education, Protestant church support, and youth agencies.
Fields of interest: Performing arts, theater; Higher education; Libraries/library science; Hospitals (general); Health care; Youth, services; Community development, service clubs; Protestant agencies & churches.
Limitations: Applications not accepted. Giving primarily in central PA. No grants to individuals.
Application information: Contributes only to pre-selected organizations.
Trustee: M&T Bank.
EIN: 236657558

2309
The Mindich Family Foundation
c/o Rothstein Kass
1350 Ave. of the Americas, 15th Fl.
New York, NY **10019-4700**

Established in 1996 in NY.
Donor: Eric M. Mindich.
Foundation type: Independent foundation.
Financial data (yr. ended 07/31/13): Assets, $3,860,541 (M); expenditures, $81,154; qualifying distributions, $73,537; giving activities include $59,000 for 7 grants (high: $25,000; low: $1,000).
Purpose and activities: Giving primarily for museums, hospitals, education and the arts.
Fields of interest: Museums (art); Performing arts, theater; Education; Hospitals (general); Cancer; Jewish federated giving programs; Jewish agencies & synagogues.
Type of support: General/operating support.
Limitations: Applications not accepted. Giving primarily in New York, NY. No grants to individuals.
Application information: Contributes only to pre-selected organizations.
Trustees: Eric M. Mindich; Stacey B. Mindich.
EIN: 137085272

2310
The Monteforte Foundation, Inc.
c/o Felix Partners
712 5th Ave., 20th Fl.
New York, NY **10019-4108**

Established in 1992 in NJ.
Donors: Willem Kooyker; Judith-Ann Corrente.
Foundation type: Independent foundation.
Financial data (yr. ended 08/31/13): Assets, $23,914,646 (M); gifts received, $7,531,801; expenditures, $13,815,158; qualifying distributions, $13,797,057; giving activities include $13,764,209 for 33 grants (high: $5,000,000; low: $250).
Fields of interest: Arts; Education; Human services.
Type of support: Annual campaigns.
Limitations: Applications not accepted. Giving primarily in NJ and NY. No grants to individuals.
Application information: Contributes only to pre-selected organizations.
Officers and Trustees:* Judith-Ann Corrente,* Pres.; Willem Kooyker,* V.P.; Carmela June Bruno,* Secy.; **Noah Schankler, Treas.**
EIN: 223198329
Other changes: Noah Schankler has replaced Augustine Rossi as Treas.

2311
David and Katherine Moore Family Foundation
c/o D'Arcangelo Co.
800 Westchester Ave., N-400
Rye Brook, NY 10573-1301 (914) 694-4600
***Contact:* Katherine C. Moore, Tr.**
E-mail: pwarner@darcangelo.com

Established in 1997 in NY.
Donors: David E. Moore, Sr.; Katherine C. Moore.
Foundation type: Independent foundation.
Financial data (yr. ended 12/31/12): Assets, $19,523,608 (M); gifts received, $44,598; expenditures, $1,119,477; qualifying distributions, $1,056,462; giving activities include $1,048,250 for 36 grants (high: $350,000; low: $250).
Fields of interest: Reproductive health, family planning; Human services; Foundations (community).
Type of support: General/operating support; Continuing support; Annual campaigns; Capital campaigns; Endowments; Scholarship funds.
Limitations: Applications accepted. Giving primarily in the northeastern U.S., with emphasis on NY.
Application information: The foundation generally does not accept unsolicited requests for funds. Application form not required.
Deadline(s): None
Board meeting date(s): Dec.
Trustees: Katherine C. Moore; **Richard W. Moore.**
EIN: 137103979
Other changes: David E. Moore is no longer a trustee.

2312
Edward S. Moore Family Foundation, Inc.
202 11th St.
Brooklyn, NY 11215-3916

Established in 2005 in NY.
Foundation type: Independent foundation.
Financial data (yr. ended 03/31/13): Assets, $20,872,226 (M); expenditures, $1,099,348; qualifying distributions, $911,200; giving activities include $911,200 for grants.
Purpose and activities: Giving primarily for social services and education.
Fields of interest: Arts; Higher education; Education; Human services; Children/youth, services; Family services.
Limitations: Applications not accepted. Giving primarily in CT and NY.
Application information: Contributes only to pre-selected organizations.
Officers and Directors:* Marion M. Gilbert,* Pres.; Roger Gilbert,* V.P.; Katrina Gilbert Millard,* Secy.; Jeffrey Z. Gilbert,* Treas.; Jane Gilbert; Louisa Gilbert.
EIN: 200249777

2313
Marion Moore Foundation, Inc.
c/o Alston & Bird LLP
90 Park Ave., 12th Fl.
New York, NY 10016-1387

Established in 2004 in CT.
Foundation type: Independent foundation.
Financial data (yr. ended 12/31/12): Assets, $10,961,725 (M); gifts received, $175; expenditures, $1,611,188; qualifying distributions, $1,189,538; giving activities include $845,000 for 53 grants (high: $40,000; low: $2,500).
Fields of interest: Museums; Performing arts, music; Education; Health care; Human services; Children/youth, services.
Limitations: Applications not accepted. Giving primarily in CT and NY. No grants to individuals.
Application information: Contributes only to pre-selected organizations.
Officers and Directors:* John W. Cross III,* Pres.; John F. Baron, Secy.; Cynthia Page Cross; John W. Cross IV; **Gracia T. Willis**; Lois Cross Willis.
EIN: 200249695

2314
The Tom and Judy Moore Foundation
1133 5th Ave.
New York, NY 10128-0123

Established in NY.
Donors: Thomas A. Moore; Judith Livingston Moore.
Foundation type: Independent foundation.
Financial data (yr. ended 12/31/12): Assets, $1,497,309 (M); gifts received, $674,637; expenditures, $2,028,444; qualifying distributions, $2,027,500; giving activities include $2,027,500 for 14 grants (high: $520,000; low: $2,500).
Fields of interest: Elementary/secondary education; Higher education; Law school/education; Human services; Foundations (private grantmaking); Catholic agencies & churches.
Limitations: Applications not accepted. Giving primarily in IN and NY. No grants to individuals.
Application information: Contributes only to pre-selected organizations.
Officers: Thomas A. Moore, Pres.; Judith Livingston Moore, V.P. and Secy.-Treas.
Director: Mary Rose Smith.
EIN: 201258563
Other changes: At the close of 2012, the grantmaker paid grants of $2,027,500, a 69.7% increase over the 2011 disbursements, $1,195,000.

2315
Morgan Stanley Foundation, Inc.
(formerly Morgan Stanley Foundation)
c/o Community Affairs
1585 Broadway, 23rd Fl.
New York, NY **10036-8200 (212) 296-3600**
FAX: (646) 519-5460;
E-mail: whatadifference@morganstanley.com;
E-mail for Richard B. Fisher Scholarship Program: richardbfisherprogram@morganstanley.com; Main URL: http://www.morganstanley.com/globalcitizen/ms_foundation.html

Trust established in 1961 in NY.
Donors: Morgan Stanley Group Inc.; Morgan Stanley & Co. Inc.; Morgan Stanley, Dean Witter, Discover & Co.; Morgan Stanley Dean Witter & Co.; Morgan Stanley.
Foundation type: Company-sponsored foundation.
Financial data (yr. ended 12/31/12): Assets, $55,817,750 (M); gifts received, $4,905,673; expenditures, $9,937,056; qualifying distributions, $9,937,056; giving activities include $9,937,056 for 857 grants (high: $2,500,000; low: $500).
Purpose and activities: The foundation supports programs designed to promote children's health, diversity education, and employee community involvement.
Fields of interest: Elementary/secondary education; Secondary school/education; Higher education; Education; Hospitals (general); Health care, clinics/centers; Health care; Pediatrics; Food services; Food banks; Nutrition; Disasters, preparedness/services; American Red Cross; Human services; Civil/human rights, equal rights; Children; Youth; Disabilities, people with; Minorities; Economically disadvantaged.
Type of support: General/operating support; Continuing support; Program development; Fellowships; Internship funds; Scholarship funds; Employee volunteer services; Scholarships—to individuals.
Limitations: Applications accepted. Giving primarily in areas of company operations, with emphasis on the Phoenix, AZ, Los Angeles and San Francisco, CA, Wilmington, DE, Chicago, IL, MA, New York, NY, Columbus, OH, Philadelphia, PA, Dallas and Houston, TX, and Salt Lake City, UT, metropolitan areas; giving also to national organizations. No support for local organizations with which Morgan Stanley employees are not involved, political candidates or lobbying organizations, religious, fraternal, or professional sports organizations, or individual performing arts organizations. No grants to individuals (except for Morgan Stanley Scholarship Initiatives), or for capital campaigns or endowments, dinners, walks or runs, golf events, political causes or campaigns, or documentaries or productions.
Publications: Application guidelines; Corporate giving report.
Application information: Letters of inquiry should be no longer than 1 to 2 pages. Morgan Stanley initiates the majority of grants. Priority is given to national initiatives and those serving multiple cities across the U.S. Support for local organizations serving only one metropolitan area or state is limited to organizations with which Morgan Stanley employees volunteer and is coordinated through the Volunteer Incentive Program. Application form not required.

Initial approach: Letter of inquiry for Global Alliance for Children's Health or Richard B. Scholars Program

Deadline(s): Varies for Richard B. Scholars Program

Board meeting date(s): Mar., June, Sept., and Dec.

Officers and Trustees:* Carla Harris,* Chair.; Joan E. Steinberg,* Pres.; Matt Berke; Marilyn Booker; Charlie Chasin; Jeff Brodsky; Audrey Choi; Jeanmarie McFadden; Kathleen McCabe; Bill McMahon; Shelley O'Connor; Mary Lou Peters; James A. Rosenthal.
EIN: 261226280
Other changes: Gordon Dean and Josh Connor are no longer trustees.

2316
Mule Family Foundation
c/o BCRS Associates, LLC
77 Water St., 9th Fl.
New York, NY 10005-3801

Established in 1994 in NY.
Donor: Edward A. Mule.
Foundation type: Independent foundation.
Financial data (yr. ended 08/31/13): Assets, $17,616,210 (M); gifts received, $9,919,699; expenditures, $440,735; qualifying distributions, $431,735; giving activities include $429,050 for 37 grants (high: $200,000; low: $200).
Fields of interest: Elementary/secondary education; Higher education; Hospitals (general); Mental health, association; Cancer research; Boys & girls clubs; Human services; Protestant agencies & churches.
Type of support: General/operating support.
Limitations: Applications not accepted. Giving primarily in Greenwich, CT and New York, NY. No grants to individuals.
Application information: Unsolicited requests for funds not accepted.
Trustee: Edward A. Mule.
EIN: 133801234
Other changes: For the fiscal year ended Aug. 31, 2013, the fair market value of the grantmaker's assets was $17,616,210, a 242.8% increase over the 2012 value, $5,138,505.

2317
Mutual of America Foundation
320 Park Ave.
New York, NY 10022-6839 (212) 224-1147
Contact: Thomas Gilliam, Chair. and C.E.O.; Theodore Herman, Vice-Chair.
FAX: (212) 207-3001;
E-mail: thomas.gilliam@mutualofamerica.com;
Main URL: http://www.mutualofamerica.com/cpa/CommunityPartnershipAward
Community Partnership Award Winners: http://www.mutualofamerica.com/about/cpa2010winners.asp?pst=yes

Established in 1989.
Donor: Mutual of America Life Insurance Co.
Foundation type: Company-sponsored foundation.
Financial data (yr. ended 12/31/12): Assets, $332,757 (M); gifts received, $2,677,615; expenditures, $2,642,715; qualifying distributions, $2,642,715; giving activities include $2,077,346 for 1,042 grants (high: $71,030; low: $20).
Purpose and activities: The foundation supports organizations involved with education, and health and human services.
Fields of interest: Secondary school/education; Higher education; Education; Health care, patient services; Health care; Disasters, preparedness/services; Girl scouts; Children/youth, services; Homeless, human services; Human services; United Ways and Federated Giving Programs.
Type of support: Employee matching gifts; General/operating support.
Limitations: Applications accepted. Giving primarily in CA, Washington, DC, GA, IL, NV, TN, TX, and WI.
Publications: Application guidelines; Annual report; Informational brochure (including application guidelines).
Application information: Proposals should be no longer than 3 pages. Application form required.

Initial approach: Download application form and mail proposal and application form to foundation for Community Partnership Award

Copies of proposal: 1

Deadline(s): Apr. 1 for Community Partnership Award

Board meeting date(s): Mar., May, June, Sept., and Nov.

Officers and Directors:* Thomas Gilliam,* Chair. and C.E.O.; Theodore L. Herman,* Vice-Chair.; William S. Conway,* C.O.O.; John R. Greed,* Sr. Exec. V.P. and C.F.O.; James J. Roth,* Exec. V.P., Secy., and Genl. Counsel; George L. Medlin, Exec. V.P. and Treas.; John Corrigan, Exec. V.P. and Internal Auditor; Diane Aramony,* Exec. V.P.; Theodore Herman.
EIN: 133443360

2318
Nakash Family Foundation
c/o Jordache Enterprises Inc.
1400 Broadway, 14th Fl.
New York, NY 10018-5300

Established in 1984 in NY.
Donors: Jordache Ltd.; Jordache Enterprises, Inc.; Nakash Holding LLC.
Foundation type: Company-sponsored foundation.
Financial data (yr. ended 12/31/12): Assets, $1,380,994 (M); gifts received, $950,000; expenditures, $1,159,186; qualifying distributions, $1,086,193; giving activities include $1,086,193 for grants.
Purpose and activities: The foundation supports organizations involved with theological education and Judaism.
Fields of interest: Jewish agencies & synagogues; Religion.
Type of support: General/operating support.
Limitations: Applications not accepted. No grants to individuals.
Application information: Unsolicited requests for funds not accepted.
Officers: Joseph Nakash, Pres.; Avi Nakash, V.P.; Ralph Nakash, Secy.-Treas.
EIN: 133030267

2319
The Naomi Prawer Kadar Foundation, Inc
5 Woodland Ct.
Bedford, NY 10506-2034 (212) 574-6170
E-mail: grants@naomi.org; **Additional email: info@naomi.org**; Main URL: http://www.naomi.org

Established in NY.
Donor: Avraham Kadar.
Foundation type: Independent foundation.
Financial data (yr. ended 06/30/13): Assets, $41,436 (M); gifts received, $1,690,460; expenditures, $1,665,715; qualifying distributions, $1,517,827; giving activities include $1,517,827 for 10 grants (high: $400,000; low: $3,600).
Purpose and activities: The foundation supports Jewish culture, Jewish educational growth and Yiddish-language learning. The foundation also supports the training of the next generation of teachers in all fields and to inspire youth and learners of all ages, as well as it supports medical advances specifically in the field of oncology.
Fields of interest: Teacher school/education; Education; Medical research; Jewish agencies & synagogues.
Application information: Refer to foundation web site for specific application opportunities and deadlines.
Officers: Avraham Kadar, M.D., Pres.; Einat Kadar, V.P.; Maya Kadar, V.P.; Nadav Kadar, V.P.
EIN: 273144255

Other changes: For fiscal year ended June 30, 2013, the grantmaker paid grants of $1,517,827, a 285.2% increase over the fiscal 2012 disbursements, $394,070.

2320
Nash Family Foundation
25 W. 45th St., Ste. 1400
New York, NY 10036-4902
Contact: Judith Ginsberg, Exec. Dir.
E-mail: info@nashff.org; Additional e-mail: judith@nashff.org

Established in 1964 in NY.
Donors: Jack Nash†; Leon Levy†; Helen Nash.
Foundation type: Independent foundation.
Financial data (yr. ended 06/30/13): Assets, $47,164,915 (M); expenditures, $10,733,144; qualifying distributions, $10,295,809; giving activities include $9,591,810 for 253 grants (high: $1,000,000; low: $18).
Purpose and activities: Support primarily for underserved Jewish populations, arts and culture, health care organizations.
Fields of interest: Arts; Elementary/secondary education; Theological school/education; Human services; Jewish agencies & synagogues; Adults; Aging; Young adults; Disabilities, people with; Physically disabled; Mentally disabled; Economically disadvantaged.
International interests: Israel.
Type of support: Program development; General/operating support; Management development/capacity building; Building/renovation; Seed money.
Limitations: Applications accepted. Giving primarily in New York, NY and Israel. No support for political organizations. No grants to individuals or for conferences.
Application information: All doctors, fellows, medical professionals, fiscal sponsors, and other interested parties should please note the discontinuation of the Nash Family Foundation Medical Training Fellowship Program and the Fellowship program. No further applications will be accepted for this program. Application form not required.
Initial approach: Telephone, letter or e-mail
Copies of proposal: 2
Deadline(s): None
Board meeting date(s): Throughout the year
Final notification: 6 months
Officers and Directors:* Helen Nash,* Chair.; Joshua Nash, Pres.; Pamela Rohr, Exec. V.P.; Morris H. Rosenthal, Secy.-Treas.; Judith Ginsberg, Exec. Dir.; Todd Lang, Tr.
Number of staff: 1 full-time professional; 1 part-time professional; 1 full-time support.
EIN: 136168559
Other changes: The grantmaker no longer lists a URL address.
Helen Nash is now Chair. Joshua Nash is now Pres. Pamela Rohr is now Exec. V.P. Morris H. Rosenthal is now Secy.-Treas.

2321
National Fuel Gas Company Foundation
6363 Main St.
Williamsville, NY 14221-5855 (716) 857-7861
Contact: Emily L. Ciraolo
***E-mail:* ciraoloe@natfuel.com**

Established in NY.
Donor: National Fuel Gas Company.
Foundation type: Company-sponsored foundation.
Financial data (yr. ended 09/30/13): Assets, $1,692,896 (M); gifts received, $1,000,025; expenditures, $839,038; qualifying distributions, $839,038; giving activities include $838,782 for 1,627 grants (high: $70,000; low: $25).
Purpose and activities: The foundation matches contributions made by its employees to nonprofit organizations; also a small number of grants on a case by case basis. Special emphasis is directed toward programs that promote community development. Support is limited to areas of company operations in western New York and northwestern Pennsylvania.
Fields of interest: Health organizations; Human services; Community/economic development.
Type of support: Annual campaigns; Capital campaigns; Scholarship funds.
Limitations: Applications accepted. Giving limited to areas of company operations in western NY and northwestern PA. No support for political organizations or candidates, sports teams, or religious or sectarian organizations. No grants to individuals or for lobbying efforts.
Application information: Application form required.
Initial approach: Completed application form
Copies of proposal: 1
Deadline(s): None
Board meeting date(s): Quarterly
Officers and Directors:* David F. Smith,* Pres.; Paula M. Ciprich,* V.P. and Secy.; D.L. DeCarolis,* V.P. and Treas.; A.M. Cellino,* V.P.; Ronald J. Tanski,* V.P.; C.M. Carlotti.
EIN: 201860605

2322
NBC Universal Foundation
(formerly Universal Studios Foundation, Ltd.)
c/o NBC Universal
30 Rockefeller Plz.
New York, NY 10012-0015
Contact: Jennifer Fitzgerald
***Main URL:* http://corporate.comcast.com/our-values/community-investment/philanthropy-partnerships**
Grants List: http://corporate.comcast.com/csr2013/2013-foundation-giving

Incorporated in 1956 in CA.
Donors: Universal Studios, Inc.; NBC Universal, Inc.
Foundation type: Company-sponsored foundation.
Financial data (yr. ended 12/31/13): Assets, $19,111,486 (M); gifts received, $3,000,000; expenditures, $2,449,831; qualifying distributions, $2,442,265; giving activities include $2,310,000 for 57 grants (high: $100,000; low: $25,000).
Purpose and activities: The foundation supports organizations involved with arts and culture, education, the environment, employment, community and economic development, and civic affairs.
Fields of interest: Arts; Secondary school/education; Education; Environment; Employment; Economic development; Community/economic development; Engineering/technology; Public affairs.
Type of support: General/operating support; Program development.
Limitations: Applications accepted. Giving primarily in CA, CT, Washington, DC, Miami, FL, Chicago, IL, New York, NY, Philadelphia, PA, and Dallas and Fort-Worth, TX. No support for private foundations or organizations with overhead expenses exceeding 15 percent of the total project budget. No grants for endowments or major equipment purchases, capital campaigns, annual fundraising events or fund drives, partisan lobbying or political campaigns or activities, individual film or television projects, sponsorship of special events, debt reduction, or religious or sectarian purposes.
Publications: Application guidelines.
Application information: Applications are only accepted for the 21st Century Solutions Initiative in August. Applying organizations must have been in existence for more than two years and have an annual operating budget of more than $300,000. Application form required.
***Initial approach:* Visit local NBC station websites for 21st Century Solutions Initiative**
***Deadline(s):* June 2 to Aug. 8 for 21st Century Solutions Initiative**
***Final notification:* Dec. for 21st Century Solutions Initiative**
Officers and Directors:* Adam Miller,* Pres.; Maren Christensen,* Exec. V.P. and Secy.; Christy Rupert Shibata,* Exec. V.P. and Treas.; **Elizabeth Colleton,* V.P.**; Patricia Fili-Krushel; Cindy Gardner; Charisse Lillie; **Craig P. Robinson**; Valari Staab.
Number of staff: 2 full-time professional.
EIN: 136096061
Other changes: At the close of 2013, the grantmaker paid grants of $2,310,000, a 340.0% increase over the 2012 disbursements, $525,000.
Adam Miller has replaced Ron Meyer as Pres.
Ron Meyer is no longer Pres. Kenneth L. Kahrs is no longer Sr. V.P. Bridget Baker, Bob Corcoran, Susan Haspel, and Lauren Zalaznick are no longer directors.
The grantmaker now publishes application guidelines.

2323
The John and Wendy Neu Family Foundation, Inc.
120 5th Ave., No. 600
New York, NY 10011-5614 (646) 467-6700

Established in 1990 in NY.
Donors: Hugo Neu Corp.; Flynn-Learner.
Foundation type: Independent foundation.
Financial data (yr. ended 12/31/12): Assets, $6,800,594 (M); expenditures, $5,523,248; qualifying distributions, $5,522,250; giving activities include $5,522,250 for 46 grants (high: $1,000,000; low: $250).
Purpose and activities: Giving primarily for animal welfare; support also for hospitals and rehabilitation centers. Some giving for environmental conservation.
Fields of interest: Museums; Education; Environment; Animal welfare; Hospitals (general); Youth development.
Limitations: Applications not accepted. Giving primarily in NJ and NY. No grants to individuals.
Application information: Contributes only to pre-selected organizations.
Officer and Directors:* John L. Neu,* Pres.; Robert T. Neu; Wendy K. Neu.
EIN: 133731089

2324
The New Yankee Stadium Community Benefits Fund, Inc.
199 Lincoln Ave., Ste. 313
Bronx, NY 10454-3707 (347) 591-4767
***Contact:* Veronica Torres**
E-mail: bronxyankeefund@gmail.com; Main URL: http://bronxyankeefund.org/

Established in NY.
Foundation type: Independent foundation.

Financial data (yr. ended 12/31/12): Assets, $145,525 (M); gifts received, $925,998; expenditures, $888,721; qualifying distributions, $754,821; giving activities include $754,821 for 109 grants (high: $15,000; low: $500).
Purpose and activities: Giving primarily to improve the quality of life in the Bronx by addressing civic, socioeconomic and/or educational needs and providing social arts, health, cultural, and recreational opportunities.
Fields of interest: Arts; Education; Health care; Athletics/sports, amateur leagues; Human services; Youth.
Limitations: Applications accepted. Giving primarily in the Bronx section of NY.
Publications: Application guidelines.
Application information: The fund's three different application forms: Large Grants, Small Grants, and Little League, may be downloaded from fund web site. Little League applications are for Bronx little leagues only. Application form required.
Initial approach: Submit appropriate application form via regular U.S. Mail
Deadline(s): See fund web site for current deadlines
Officers: Serafin U. Mariel, Chair.; Ted Jefferson, Secy.; Susan Goldy, Treas.
Board Members: Bishop Ronald Bailey; Robert Crespo; Leo Martinez; Harold Silverman.
EIN: 141979116

2325
The New York Community Trust
909 3rd Ave., 22nd Fl.
New York, NY 10022-4752 (212) 686-0010
Contact: For grant inquiries: Mary Gentile, Exec. Asst., Grants and Special Projects
FAX: (212) 532-8528; E-mail: aw@nyct-cfi.org; Tel. for grant inquiries: (212) 686-0010, ext. 554; **Main URL: http://www.nycommunitytrust.org**
E-Newsletter: http://www.nycommunitytrust.org/tabid/251/default.aspx
Facebook: https://www.facebook.com/pages/The-New-York-Community-Trust/206444912741562?v=wall
GiveSmart: http://www.givesmart.org/Stories/Donors/Lorie-Slutsky
Grants List: http://www.nycommunitytrust.org/GrantSeekers/RecentGrants/tabid/208/Default.aspx
Twitter: http://twitter.com/nycommtrust

Established in 1924 in NY by resolution and declaration of trust.
Foundation type: Community foundation.
Financial data (yr. ended 12/31/13): Assets, $2,443,372,250 (M); gifts received, $145,051,661; expenditures, $156,377,606; giving activities include $144,241,100 for grants.
Purpose and activities: Priority given to applications for projects having particular significance for the New York City area.
Fields of interest: Historic preservation/historical societies; Arts; Education, public education; Child development, education; Education; Environment; Health care; Substance abuse, services; Mental health/crisis services; Health organizations, association; Cancer; AIDS; Biomedicine research; Crime/violence prevention, domestic violence; Legal services; Employment; Food services; Housing/shelter, development; Youth development; Children/youth, services; Family services; Aging, centers/services; Women, centers/services; Homeless, human services; Human services; Civil/human rights, immigrants; Civil/human rights, minorities; Civil/human rights, disabled; Civil/human rights, women; Civil/human rights, aging; Civil/human rights, LGBTQ; Civil liberties, reproductive rights; Community/economic development; Government/public administration; Disabilities, people with; Girls; Young adults, female.
Type of support: Income development; Management development/capacity building; Program development; Publication; Seed money; Fellowships; Scholarship funds; Research; Technical assistance; Consulting services; Program evaluation; Employee matching gifts.
Limitations: Applications accepted. Giving limited to the metropolitan New York, NY, area. No support for religious purposes. No grants to individuals (except for scholarships), or for deficit financing, emergency funds, building campaigns, films, endowment funds, capital projects or general operating support.
Publications: Application guidelines; Annual report; Financial statement; Grants list; Informational brochure (including application guidelines); Newsletter; Occasional report; Program policy statement (including application guidelines).
Application information: Visit foundation web site for application cover sheet and guidelines. Please submit all written materials before calling the foundation to discuss ideas. Faxed or e-mailed proposals are not accepted. The foundation accepts the New York/ New Jersey Area Common Application Form. Application form required.
Initial approach: Submit proposal with cover letter
Copies of proposal: 1
***Deadline(s):* Oct. 15, Feb. 14, and June 13**
Board meeting date(s): Feb., Apr., June, July, Oct., and Dec.
***Final notification:* Apr. 30, Oct. 30, and Dec. 31**
Officers and Directors:* Charlynn Goins,* Chair.; Lorie A. Slutsky,* Pres.; Robert V. Edgar, V.P., Donor Rels.; Mercedes M. Leon, V.P., Admin.; Jenny Patricia, V.P., Grants; Gay Young, V.P., Donor Svcs.; Alan Holzer, C.F.O.; Mary Z. Greenebaum, C.I.O.; Heidi Hotzler, Cont.; Jane L. Wilton, Genl. Counsel; Jamie Drake; Roger Juan Maldonado; Anne Moore, M.D.; Raffiq Nathoo; Valerie S. Peltier; Judith O. Rubin; Barron "Buzz" Tenny; Ann Unterberg; Mary Kay Vyskocil; Jason H. Wright.
Trustee Banks: Bank of America, N.A.; Bessemer Trust Co., N.A.; BNY Mellon, N.A.; Brown Brothers Harriman Trust Co.; Citigroup; Deutsche Bank Americas; Fiduciary Trust Co. International; HSBC Bank USA, N.A.; JPMorgan Chase Bank, N.A.; Lehman Brothers Trust Co., N.A.; Merrill Lynch Trust Co.; Rockefeller Trust Co.; Bank of America, N.A.
Number of staff: 23 full-time professional; 1 part-time professional; 18 full-time support; 1 part-time support.
EIN: 133062214

2326
New York Foundation
10 E. 34th St., 10th Fl.
New York, NY 10016-4327 (212) 594-8009
Contact: Maria Mottola, Exec. Dir.
***E-mail:* info@nyf.org**; Main URL: http://www.nyf.org/
Big Ideas. Locally Grown.: http://nyf.org/category/blog/
Grants Database: http://www.nyf.org/grants-database
Knowledge Center: http://nyf.issuelab.org/
New York Foundation's Philanthropy Promise: http://www.ncrp.org/philanthropys-promise/who
Newsmakers: http://nyf.org/category/newsmakers/
Twitter: https://twitter.com/TheNYFoundation

Incorporated in 1909 in NY.
Donors: Louis A. Heinsheimer†; Alfred M. Heinsheimer†; Lionel J. Salomon†.
Foundation type: Independent foundation.
Financial data (yr. ended 12/31/12): Assets, $58,875,188 (M); gifts received, $34,364; expenditures, $4,806,517; qualifying distributions, $3,418,434; giving activities include $3,418,434 for grants.
Purpose and activities: The New York Foundation is a steadfast supporter of community organizing and advocacy in New York City. It believes that the resilience and vitality of its neighborhoods is the city's greatest resource. Its grants support community-initiated solutions to solve local problems, constituents mobilizing for adequate and equitable resources, and groups organizing a collective voice among those whose voices have not been heard.
Fields of interest: Housing/shelter, development; Youth development, services; Human services; Children/youth, services; Aging, centers/services; Minorities/immigrants, centers/services; Homeless, human services; Civil/human rights, alliance/advocacy; Civil/human rights, immigrants; Civil/human rights, minorities; Civil/human rights, disabled; Civil/human rights, women; Civil/human rights, aging; Civil/human rights, LGBTQ; Civil rights, race/intergroup relations; Civil liberties, reproductive rights; Community/economic development; Youth; Aging; Disabilities, people with; Minorities; African Americans/Blacks; Hispanics/Latinos; AIDS, people with; Immigrants/refugees; Economically disadvantaged; Homeless; Migrant workers; LGBTQ.
Type of support: General/operating support; Continuing support; Management development/capacity building; Program development; Seed money; Technical assistance.
Limitations: Applications accepted. **Giving limited to local programs in the five boroughs of New York City. The foundation does not consider requests outside New York City except from organizations working on statewide issues of concern to youth, the elderly, or the poor. The foundation's charter prohibits it from making grants outside the United States.** No grants to individuals, or for capital campaigns, research studies, films, conferences, or publications (except for those initiated by the foundation).
Publications: Application guidelines; Annual report (including application guidelines); Grants list.
Application information: Fax submissions are not accepted.
***Initial approach:* A simple first step is to complete the Initial Funding Request (a form which can be found on foundation web site), and send via U.S. mail or e-mail to: requests@nyf.org. When request is e-mailed, applicant must save the completed Initial Funding Request as a Word document or PDF and send as an attachment.**
Copies of proposal: 1
Deadline(s): Mar. 1, July 1, and Nov. 1
Board meeting date(s): Feb., June, and Oct.
Final notification: 3 to 6 months
Officers and Trustees:* Seth Borgos,* Chair.; Marlene Provizer,* Vice-Chair.; Denice Williams,* Secy.; Gail Gordon,* Treas.; Maria Mottola, Exec. Dir.; Rose Dobrof, DSW, Tr. Emeritus; Rosa Alfonso-McGoldrick; Kerry-Anne Edwards; Keith Hefner; Stephen Heyman; Wayne Ho; Susan A. Kaplan; Roland Lewis; Lillian Llambelis; Glenn E. Martin; Fitzgerald Miller; Mike Pratt; David Rivel; Aida Rodriguez; Roger Schwed; Dawn Walker; Kyung Yoon.

Number of staff: 3 full-time professional; 2 full-time support.
EIN: 135626345
Other changes: The grantmaker now publishes application guidelines.

2327
New York Jets Foundation, Inc.
c/o The Johnson Co.
610 5th Ave., 2nd Fl.
New York, NY 10020 (973) 549-4800
***Contact:* Brian Friedman, Treas. and Tr.**
***Application address:* c/o New York Jets LLC, 1 Jets Dr., Florham Park, NJ 07932**; Main URL: http://www.newyorkjets.com/community/be-lean-and-green/new-york-jets-foundation.html

Established in 1969.
Donors: Bett Wold Johnson, Inc.; NFL Charities; New York Mercantile Exchange, Inc.; NFL Youth Football Fund; Kraft Total; Paul Tudor Jones.
Foundation type: Company-sponsored foundation.
Financial data (yr. ended 12/31/12): Assets, $3,837,867 (M); gifts received, $826,003; expenditures, $1,182,656; qualifying distributions, $880,552; giving activities include $875,408 for 72 grants (high: $652,097; low: $967).
Purpose and activities: The foundation supports programs designed to promote youth education, fitness, and health with an emphasis on disadvantaged communities.
Fields of interest: Education; Health care; Human services.
Type of support: General/operating support; Program development; Scholarship funds.
Limitations: Applications accepted. Giving primarily in Chicago, IL, NJ, and NY.
Application information: Application form required.
***Initial approach:* Letter**
Deadline(s): None
Officers and Trustees:* Robert Wood Johnson IV,* Chair.; Neil J. Burmeister,* V.P.; Brian Friedman,* Treas.
EIN: 237108291
Other changes: The grantmaker has moved from NJ to NY.
At the close of 2012, the grantmaker paid grants of $875,408, a 235.6% increase over the 2011 disbursements, $260,832.

2328
The Howard and Maryam Newman Family Foundation, Inc.
c/o Maryam Newman
346 Pine Brook Rd.
Bedford, NY 10506-1618

Established in 2005 in NY.
Donor: Howard Newman.
Foundation type: Independent foundation.
Financial data (yr. ended 11/30/13): Assets, $8,664,281 (M); gifts received, $328,165; expenditures, $1,104,015; qualifying distributions, $1,083,390; giving activities include $1,083,390 for 34 grants (high: $250,000; low: $100).
Fields of interest: Arts; Higher education, university; Health organizations; Human services; Biology/life sciences.
Limitations: Applications not accepted. Giving primarily in CA, CT and NY. No grants to individuals.
Application information: Unsolicited requests for funds not accepted.
Officers: Howard H. Newman, Pres.; Zeena M. Meurer, V.P.; Elizabeth V. Newman, Secy.; Maryam R. Newman, Treas.
EIN: 201999992

2329
The Nicholson Foundation
419 E. 50th St.
New York, NY 10022-8074 (212) 953-9200
Contact: Jan Nicholson, Pres.
Main URL: http://www.thenicholsonfoundation-newjersey.org/

Established in 1980 in NJ.
Donor: Marion G. Nicholson.
Foundation type: Independent foundation.
Financial data (yr. ended 12/31/12): Assets, $63,349,238 (M); gifts received, $5,000,874; expenditures, $10,532,584; qualifying distributions, $9,909,079; giving activities include $7,629,439 for 95 grants (high: $734,645; low: $1,000), and $1,710,325 for foundation-administered programs.
Purpose and activities: Giving primarily to address the complex needs of vulnerable populations in New Jersey's urban areas by encouraging the reform of health and human services delivery systems.
Fields of interest: Higher education; Education; Human services; Community/economic development.
Limitations: Applications not accepted. Giving primarily in NJ and NY. No grants to individuals.
Application information: Contributes only to pre-selected organizations.
Officers and Trustees:* Barbara Nicholson McFadyen,* Chair.; Jan Nicholson,* Pres. and Treas.; Marion G. Nicholson,* Secy.
EIN: 222344110

2330
The Robert and Kate Niehaus Foundation
c/o Robert H. Niehaus
770 Park Ave.
New York, NY 10021-4153

Established in 1998 in NY.
Donor: Robert H. Niehaus.
Foundation type: Independent foundation.
Financial data (yr. ended 12/31/12): Assets, $27,929,903 (M); gifts received, $86,400; expenditures, $3,173,673; qualifying distributions, $2,924,676; giving activities include $2,910,024 for 9 grants (high: $1,000,000; low: $24).
Purpose and activities: Giving primarily for a cancer hospital, as well as for education and social entrepreneurship.
Fields of interest: Education; Hospitals (specialty); Social entrepreneurship.
Limitations: Applications not accepted. Giving primarily in New York, NY.
Application information: Contributes only to pre-selected organizations.
Officers: Kate Niehaus, Pres.; Robert H. Niehaus, V.P. and Treas.
Director: Jerome L. Levine.
EIN: 134007527

2331
Northern Chautauqua Community Foundation, Inc.
212 Lake Shore Dr. W.
Dunkirk, NY 14048-1436 (716) 366-4892
Contact: Diane Hannum, Exec. Dir.
FAX: (716) 366-3905;
E-mail: info@nccfoundation.org; Grant application e-mail: grants@nccfoundation.org; Additional e-mail: dhannum@nccfoundation.org; Main URL: http://www.nccfoundation.org
Facebook: https://www.facebook.com/NCCFoundation
Twitter: https://twitter.com/NCCFoundation

Incorporated in 1987 in NY.
Foundation type: Community foundation.
Financial data (yr. ended 12/31/12): Assets, $19,439,061 (M); gifts received, $577,395; expenditures, $585,935; giving activities include $191,699 for 7+ grants (high: $20,000), and $146,423 for grants to individuals.
Purpose and activities: The foundation seeks to enrich the area in which the community lives and works. Primary areas of interest include education, family services, community funds, cultural programs, and other general charitable activities.
Fields of interest: Arts; Higher education; Adult education—literacy, basic skills & GED; Libraries/library science; Education, reading; Education; Environment, public education; Environment, water resources; Environment; Animal welfare; Hospitals (general); Substance abuse, services; Recreation, parks/playgrounds; Recreation; Youth development; Family services; Residential/custodial care, hospices; Aging, centers/services; Economic development; Community/economic development; Voluntarism promotion; Aging.
Type of support: Building/renovation; Equipment; Program development; Seed money; Scholarship funds; Scholarships—to individuals; Matching/challenge support.
Limitations: Applications accepted. Giving limited to northern Chautauqua County, NY. No support for religious organizations. No grants to individuals (except for designated scholarship funds), or for capital campaigns, general operating budgets, publication of books, conferences, or annual fundraising campaigns.
Publications: Application guidelines; Annual report (including application guidelines); Financial statement; Newsletter.
Application information: Visit foundation web site for application form and guidelines. Application form required.
Initial approach: E-mail letter of interest (not to exceed 2 pages)
Copies of proposal: 1
***Deadline(s):* Community Grants Program: Mar. 1 and Sept. 1 for letter of interest; Mar. 19 and Sept. 24 for full proposal**
Board meeting date(s): Quarterly
Final notification: Community Grants Program: Mar. 6 and Sept. 11 for letter of interest determination; Early May and Early Nov. for grant notification
Officers and Directors:* Peter Clark,* Pres.; Elizabeth Booth,* V.P.; John D'Agostino,* Secy.; Daniel Reininga,* Treas.; Diane Hannum, Exec. Dir.; Helen Baran; Jerry Hall; Jim Holton; Priscilla Koch; Blair Koss; Jean Malinoski; Ryan Mourer; Gina Paradis; Pete Ryan; Richard Ryan; Susan L. Wells; Monica White.
Number of staff: 3 full-time professional; 2 part-time professional.
EIN: 161271663

2332
The Greater Norwich Foundation
c/o NBT Bank, N.A.
52 S. Broad St.
Norwich, NY 13815-1646 (607) 337-6193

Established in 1965 in NY.
Donors: Ivory Residual Estate; Kent Barbara Turner; Fred Miers; Charles Burr Charitable Trust; Raymond & Alma Willard Charitable Trust; James Sue Hoy; Peter Smith Laurel Wilt Bank; James Dunne; Weinman Family Foundation; Particia & William Smith Foundation; Thomas Bonie Emerson; Community Foundation of Sarasota; Curran Foundation; W.E. Eaton Charitable Trust; Mary Cattan; Thomas & Esther Flanagan Charitable Trust.
Foundation type: Independent foundation.
Financial data (yr. ended 03/31/13): Assets, $7,244,834 (M); gifts received, $30,285; expenditures, $380,552; qualifying distributions, $350,071; giving activities include $301,879 for 22 grants (high: $60,000; low: $250), and $45,250 for 32 grants to individuals (high: $3,000; low: $500).
Fields of interest: Historic preservation/historical societies; Arts; Higher education; Education; Animal welfare; Hospitals (general); YM/YWCAs & YM/YWHAs; Children/youth, services; Human services.
Type of support: Annual campaigns; Capital campaigns; Building/renovation; Equipment; Program development; Scholarship funds; Scholarships—to individuals.
Limitations: Applications accepted. Giving primarily in the Norwich, NY, area.
Publications: Informational brochure.
Application information: Application form required.
Initial approach: Letter or grant application
Copies of proposal: 1
Deadline(s): Apr. 15 and Oct. 15
Board meeting date(s): May and Nov.
Trustees: James I. Dunne; Jane E. Eaton; Thomas C. Emerson, Esq; Esther C. Flanagan; **Patrick Flanagan**; James A. Hoy; Frederic B. Miers; H. William Smith, Jr.; Peter V. Smith; NBT Bank, N.A.
EIN: 166064927
Other changes: Jacob K. Weinman is no longer a trustee.

2333
Novartis US Foundation
(formerly Sandoz Foundation of America)
230 Park Ave., 21st FL
New York, NY 10169-2403
***Main URL:* http://www.us.novartis.com/novartis-us-foundation/index.shtml**

Incorporated in 1965 in DE; adopted current name in 1997 following a merger with the Ciba Educational Foundation, Inc.
Donors: Sandoz Corp.; Novartis Inc.
Foundation type: Company-sponsored foundation.
Financial data (yr. ended 12/31/12): Assets, $23,093,135 (M); gifts received, $1,012,213; expenditures, $1,443,899; qualifying distributions, $1,393,138; giving activities include $316,000 for 7 grants (high: $100,000; low: $6,000), and $1,077,138 for 1,000 employee matching gifts.
Purpose and activities: The foundation matches contributions made by its employees to nonprofit organizations.
Fields of interest: Education; Public affairs.
Type of support: Employee matching gifts.
Limitations: Applications not accepted. Giving on a national basis, with emphasis on areas of company operations. No support for religious organizations or social, labor, veterans', fraternal, athletic, or alumni organizations.
Application information: Contributes only to pre-selected organizations and through employee matching gifts.
Board meeting date(s): As required
Officer and Trustee:* Robert E. Pelzer,* Chair.; Brenda Blanchard; James Elkin; Brandi Robinson; Meryl Zausner.
EIN: 136193034

2334
NoVo Foundation
(formerly The Spirit Foundation)
535 Fifth Ave., 33rd. Fl.
New York, NY 10017-0051
Contact: Kelly Merryman, Opers. Mgr.
E-mail for Kelly Merryman: Kmerryman@novofoundation.org; Main URL: http://www.novofoundation.org
GiveSmart: http://www.givesmart.org/Stories/Donors/Jennifer-and-Peter-Buffett
NoVo Foundation's Philanthropy Promise: http://www.ncrp.org/philanthropys-promise/who
Warren Buffett's Giving Pledge Profile: http://glasspockets.org/philanthropy-in-focus/eye-on-the-giving-pledge/profiles/buffett

Established in 1999 in NE; classified as a private operating foundation in 2000; reclassified as an independent foundation in 2001.
Donor: Warren E. Buffett.
Foundation type: Independent foundation.
Financial data (yr. ended 12/31/12): Assets, $264,168,686 (M); gifts received, $53,089,976; expenditures, $63,715,651; qualifying distributions, $62,552,448; giving activities include $56,715,829 for 111 grants (high: $10,943,660; low: $2,500), and $1,996,916 for foundation-administered programs.
Purpose and activities: NoVo Foundation seeks to foster a paradigm shift from domination to partnership. Funds are primarily directed toward the empowerment of women and girls, social emotional learning for all, and support for men and boys as their roles transform toward a more balanced society. Strategies include: Education and economic empowerment for young women and girls in the developing world. Ending violence against women and girls. Leadership development for women and men who share our commitment to shifting the paradigm from domination to partnership. Research and advocacy. Advancement of social emotional learning (SEL).
Fields of interest: Youth development, equal rights; Human services, equal rights; Child development, services; Women, centers/services; Civil/human rights, equal rights; Civil/human rights, women; Community/economic development; Women; Girls.
Limitations: Applications not accepted. No grants to individuals.
Publications: Annual report.
Application information: Unsolicited requests for funds not accepted.
Board meeting date(s): May 5 and Nov. 24
Officer and Directors:* Jennifer Buffett,* Co.-Chair., Pres. and Treas.; Peter Buffett,* Co.-Chair.; Aaron Stern, Secy.; **Pamela Shifman, Exec. Dir.**
Number of staff: 7 full-time professional; 2 full-time support.
EIN: 470824753
Other changes: Pamela Shifman is now Exec. Dir.

2335
Jessie Smith Noyes Foundation, Inc.
6 E. 39th St., 12th Fl.
New York, NY 10016-0112 (212) 684-6577
Contact: Victor De Luca, Pres.
FAX: (212) 689-6549; E-mail: noyes@noyes.org; Main URL: http://www.noyes.org
E-Newsletter: http://www.noyes.org/maillist/
Jessie Smith Noyes Foundation's Philanthropy Promise: http://www.ncrp.org/philanthropys-promise/who
Twitter: http://twitter.com/NoyesFoundation

Incorporated in 1947 in NY.
Donor: Charles F. Noyes†.
Foundation type: Independent foundation.
Financial data (yr. ended 12/31/12): Assets, $44,391,249 (M); gifts received, $430,000; expenditures, $3,512,519; qualifying distributions, $3,062,721; giving activities include $1,942,560 for 141 grants (high: $75,000; low: $250), and $12,150 for foundation-administered programs.
Purpose and activities: The foundation envisions a socially just and environmentally sustainable society in which all people are able to gain the knowledge and build the power they need to exercise their rights and participate fully in the economic, social and political decisions that affect their lives and communities. The foundation supports grassroots organizations and movements in the United States, that are working to change environmental, social, economic, and political conditions to bring about a more just, equitable, and sustainable world.
Fields of interest: Environment, toxics; Environment; Agriculture; Civil liberties, reproductive rights; Adults; Minorities; Asians/Pacific Islanders; African Americans/Blacks; Hispanics/Latinos; Native Americans/American Indians; Indigenous peoples; Women; Adults, women; Immigrants/refugees; Economically disadvantaged; Migrant workers.
Type of support: General/operating support; Continuing support; Program development; Seed money; Mission-related investments/loans.
Limitations: Applications accepted. Giving limited to the U.S. No grants to individuals, or for scholarships, fellowships, endowment funds, deficit financing, capital construction funds, or general fundraising drives; generally no support for conferences, research, college and university based programs, or media; no loans.
Publications: Application guidelines; Financial statement; Grants list; Newsletter; Occasional report; Program policy statement.
Application information: Full proposal will be requested after review of letter of intent, background of organization, summary of activities for funding and expected outcome. The foundation encourages requests that address multiple priorities, as well as those that bring together organizations and activists from diverse movements. The foundation prefers to make general support grants and does not limit the number of renewal grants. It believes this helps organizations increase and sustain their effectiveness. The foundation seeks out organizations led by people of color and/or working in low income communities. It supports efforts to develop the leadership skills of, and foster the participation by, low income people and people of color. It encourages requests that address multiple priorities, as well as those that bring together organizations and activists from diverse movements. With first time grants, it tries to bring diverse voices and approaches, and young people into the movements for social change. It makes grants throughout the U.S. in both rural and urban communities. Application form required.

Initial approach: **1- or 2-page web-based letter of inquiry (through foundation web site), including budget estimate**
Copies of proposal: 1
Deadline(s): None
Board meeting date(s): Spring, summer, and fall
Final notification: Within 6 weeks of receipt of letters; within 2 weeks of board meetings for final proposals
Officers and Directors:* Jenifer Getz, Chair.; Martha Matsuoka,* Vice-Chair.; Victor De Luca, Pres.; Wendy Holding,* Secy.; Nicholas Jacangelo,* Treas.; Dorothy Anderson; **Rachel Anderson**; Nikhil Aziz; George Beardsley; Jim Enote; **Steven Godeke**; **Keecha Harris**; **Jaribu Hill**; **Nick Jacangelo**; Joan Lisi; Arlene Rodriguez; **Lenora Suki**; Ann Wiener.
Number of staff: 2 full-time professional; 2 part-time professional; 2 part-time support.
EIN: 135600408
Other changes: Betty Emarita, Bruce Kahn, and Ben Lovell are no longer directors.

2336
NYSE Euronext Foundation, Inc.

(formerly New York Stock Exchange Foundation, Inc.)
20 Broad St., 19th Fl.
New York, NY 10005
***Contact:* Michelle Greene, Exec. Dir.**
FAX: (212) 656-5629; E-mail: foundation@nyx.com; Main URL: http://www.nyx.com/nyse-euronext-foundation

Incorporated in 1983 in NY.
Donors: Charity Folks, Inc., Inc.; New York Stock Exchange LLC; Merrill Lynch, Pierce, Fenner & Smith Inc.
Foundation type: Company-sponsored foundation.
Financial data (yr. ended 12/31/12): Assets, $9,481,200 (M); gifts received, $63,949; expenditures, $2,856,944; qualifying distributions, $2,787,757; giving activities include $2,312,188 for 51 grants (high: $427,516; low: $5,000), and $427,516 for 433 employee matching gifts.
Purpose and activities: The foundation supports programs designed to promote financial literacy; entrepreneurship; economic empowerment; and community.
Fields of interest: Medical care, rehabilitation; Nutrition; Housing/shelter; Youth development; Human services, financial counseling; Human services; Business/industry; Microfinance/microlending; Community/economic development; Economics; Children; Minorities; Economically disadvantaged; Homeless.
Type of support: General/operating support; Annual campaigns; Capital campaigns; Program development; Scholarship funds; Research; Employee volunteer services; Sponsorships; Employee matching gifts.
Limitations: Applications accepted. Giving primarily in areas of company operations in New York, NY. No support for businesses, political, fraternal, or religious organizations, discriminatory organizations, donor advised funds, or private foundations. No grants to individuals, or for tickets to dinners, receptions, or other fundraising events.
Publications: Application guidelines; Annual report (including application guidelines).
Application information: Proposals should be no longer than 3 to 6 pages in length. Organizations receiving support are asked to submit a final report. Application form not required.
Initial approach: Mail grant application cover sheet and proposal to foundation
Copies of proposal: 1
Deadline(s): None
Board meeting date(s): Rolling
Final notification: Varies
Officers and Directors:* Duncan L. Niederauer,* Chair.; **Janet M. McGinness,* Secy.**; Michael S. Geltzeiler,* Treas.; Stephane P. Biehler, Cont.; Michelle D. Greene,* Exec. Dir.; Patrick D. Armstrong; **Mary L. Brienza**; Arthur D. Cashin, Jr.; Dominique Cerruti; **Scott Cutler**; Thomas J. Facchine; Thomas Farley; Scott Hill; Kelly Loeffler; Joseph Mecane; Patrick T. Murphy; David C. O'Day; Richard A. Rosenblatt; Edward G. Schreier; Daniel W. Tandy.
EIN: 133203195
Other changes: Claudia Crowley, Marisa Ricciardi, and Lawrence E. Leibowitz are no longer directors.

2337
Sylvan and Ann Oestreicher Foundation, Inc.

c/o Marks Paneth & Shron, LLP
685 3rd Ave.
New York, NY 10017-4024

Incorporated in 1948 in NY.
Donor: Sylvan Oestreicher†.
Foundation type: Independent foundation.
Financial data (yr. ended 04/30/13): Assets, $4,099 (M); gifts received, $21,271; expenditures, $409,657; qualifying distributions, $381,889; giving activities include $303,000 for 9 grants (high: $100,000; low: $13,000).
Fields of interest: Education; Hospitals (general); Human services; Catholic agencies & churches.
Limitations: Applications not accepted. Giving primarily in New York, NY; funding also in Los Angeles, CA.
Application information: Contributes only to pre-selected organizations.
Officers: Joseph Teklits, Pres.; Annabel Santana, Secy.
EIN: 136085974

2338
Ralph E. Ogden Foundation, Inc.

Pleasant Hill Rd.
P.O. Box 290
Mountainville, NY 10953-0290

Incorporated in 1947 in DE.
Donors: Ralph E. Ogden†; H. Peter Stern; Margaret H. Ogden†.
Foundation type: Independent foundation.
Financial data (yr. ended 12/31/12): Assets, $38,140,275 (M); expenditures, $2,774,606; qualifying distributions, $2,369,590; giving activities include $1,661,190 for 56 grants (high: $1,055,000; low: $1,000).
Purpose and activities: Giving primarily for the arts and education.
Fields of interest: Arts; Education; International affairs.
Limitations: Applications not accepted. Giving primarily in Mountainville and New York, NY. No grants to individuals.
Application information: Contributes only to pre-selected organizations.
Officers: Beatrice Stern, Pres. and Treas.; Elisabeth Ellen Stern, V.P.
Directors: Lucy Cohan; **Peter Erwin**; **Peter Lamb**; **Joan O. Stern**; John Peter Stern.
EIN: 141455902
Other changes: H. Peter Stern is no longer Chair. Colleen Zlock is no longer Secy. Rose Wood is no longer a director.

2339
O'Grady Foundation

140 E. 81St., Ste. 5C
New York, NY 10028-1807 **(212) 744-2713**
Contact: Kathleen C. O'Grady, Pres.
E-mail: info@theogradyfoundation.org; Main URL: http://www.theogradyfoundation.org

Established in 1993 in CT.
Donors: Thomas B. O'Grady†; Kathleen O'Grady.
Foundation type: Independent foundation.
Financial data (yr. ended 12/31/12): Assets, $4,568,816 (M); expenditures, $291,973; qualifying distributions, $246,202; giving activities include $227,500 for 12 grants (high: $50,000; low: $5,000).
Purpose and activities: Giving primarily for technical assistance for arts and cultural organizations with budgets of less than $4 million; also supports arts-in-education programs targeting primary and middle school age children.
Fields of interest: Arts education; Arts.
Type of support: General/operating support; Continuing support; Seed money; Internship funds; Technical assistance; Consulting services; Program evaluation; Matching/challenge support.
Limitations: Applications accepted. Giving primarily in New York, NY. No support for political organizations and religious institutions. No grants to individuals.
Application information: See foundation web site for complete application guidelines. Application form required.
Board meeting date(s): Aug.
Officers and Directors:* Kathleen C. O'Grady,* Pres.; Anne E. Lupica,* Secy.-Treas.
Trustee: Jacqueline P. Beckley.
Number of staff: None.
EIN: 061383651
Other changes: The grantmaker now accepts applications.

2340
The John R. Oishei Foundation

1 Seneca Twr., Ste. 3650
Buffalo, NY 14203-2805 (716) 856-9490
Contact: Robert D. Gioia, Pres.
FAX: (716) 856-9493; **E-mail: info@oishei.org**; Main URL: http://www.oishei.org
CEP Study: http://www.oisheifdt.org/About/mission/GranteePerceptionReport
E-Newsletter: http://www.oisheifdt.org/Home/SignUp
Facebook: https://www.facebook.com/pages/The-John-R-Oishei-Foundation/172658236100389
Grants List: http://www.oisheifdt.org/files/Library/2011GrantmakingRpt.pdf
Knowledge Center: http://www.oisheifdt.org/Home/KnowledgeManagementLibrary
Twitter: https://twitter.com/OisheiFndtn

Incorporated in 1941 in NY.
Donors: Peter C. Cornell Trust; John R. Oishei†; R. John Oishei†; Jean R. Oishei; Oishei Consolidated Trust No. 1; Oishei Consolidated Trust No. 2.
Foundation type: Independent foundation.
Financial data (yr. ended 12/31/12): Assets, $255,827,396 (M); gifts received, $945,977; expenditures, $23,392,259; qualifying distributions, $18,893,957; giving activities include

$17,421,218 for 216 grants (high: $1,007,827; low: $250).
Purpose and activities: The foundation strives to be a catalyst for change to enhance economic vitality and the quality of life for the Buffalo Niagara region.
Fields of interest: Arts; Secondary school/education; Higher education; Health care; Medical research, institute; Human services; Community/economic development; Science, research.
Type of support: Mission-related investments/loans; General/operating support; Management development/capacity building; Program development; Professorships; Seed money; Curriculum development; Scholarship funds; Research; Program evaluation; Program-related investments/loans; Matching/challenge support.
Limitations: Applications accepted. Giving limited to the Buffalo, NY, area. No support for religious organizations for sectarian or propagation of faith purposes. No grants to individuals, organizations which make grants to others, or lobbying or advocacy for specific political candidates or legislation.
Publications: Annual report; Grants list; Informational brochure (including application guidelines).
Application information: Full application guidelines are available on the foundation web site. Application form not required.
Initial approach: Letter of inquiry via online process
Copies of proposal: 1
Deadline(s): None
Board meeting date(s): Bimonthly
Final notification: Within 3 to 6 months
Officers and Directors:* James M. Wadsworth,* Chair.; Mary S. Martino,* Vice-Chair.; Robert D. Gioia, Pres.; **Paul T. Hogan, Exec. V.P.; Blythe T. Merrill, Sr. V.P., Progs.**; Karen Lee Spaulding, V.P., Philanthropic Support; Gayle L. Houck, Secy., Cont., and Grants Mgr.; Edward F. Walsh, Jr.,* Treas.; Robert M. Bennett; Ruth D. Bryant; Florence M. Conti; William G. Giesel, Jr.; Luke T. Jacobs; Ann M. McCarthy.
Number of staff: 4 full-time professional; 1 full-time support.
EIN: 160874319
Other changes: Paul T. Hogan is now Exec. V.P. Blythe T. Merrill is now Sr. V.P. Blythe T. Merrill is now Sr. V.P., Progs. Gayle L. Houck is now Secy., Cont., and Grants Mgr. Thomas E. Baker and Christopher T. Dunstan are no longer directors.

2341
The Ong Family Foundation
c/o Law Office of Deborah Chan, P.C.
401 Broadway, Ste. 1100
New York, NY 10013-3024 (212) 226-8698
E-mail: nlouis@ongfamilyfoundation.org; Main URL: http://www.OngFamilyFoundation.org
Grants List: http://www.ongfamilyfoundation.org/past.html

Established in 1997 in NY.
Donors: Danny O. Yee; Bank of China.
Foundation type: Independent foundation.
Financial data (yr. ended 01/31/13): Assets, $3,778,270 (M); expenditures, $432,478; qualifying distributions, $425,604; giving activities include $418,091 for 26 grants (high: $82,419; low: $350).
Purpose and activities: The foundation seeks to fund programs that are comprehensive, community-based and preventive in nature.
Fields of interest: Arts; Education; Human services; Asians/Pacific Islanders.
Type of support: General/operating support; Management development/capacity building; Capital campaigns; Building/renovation; Equipment; Conferences/seminars; Scholarship funds; Technical assistance; Matching/challenge support.
Limitations: Applications accepted. **Giving primarily in the Greater NY Metropolitan Area.** No support for non-501c(3) organizations, or for foundations or political activities. No grants to individuals or for debt reduction.
Application information: See foundation guidelines for further information.
Initial approach: Letter of intent
Copies of proposal: 1
Deadline(s): Deadlines are set in the 1st quarter of the year
Officer: Nelson Louis, Exec. Dir.
Trustees: Danny O. Yee; Donald Ong Yee; Larry Ong Yee; Stephanie L. Yee.
EIN: 133986239

2342
Ontario Children's Foundation
(formerly Ontario Children's Home)
P.O. Box 82
Canandaigua, NY 14424-0082
Main URL: http://ontariochildrensfoundation.org
Application address for education assistance: c/o Jane Wheeler, 4160 W. Lake Rd., Canadaigua, NY 14424, e-mail: jwheele4@rochester.rr.com

Established in 1863 in NY for civil war orphans.
Foundation type: Independent foundation.
Financial data (yr. ended 09/30/13): Assets, $3,770,687 (M); gifts received, $36,508; expenditures, $198,692; qualifying distributions, $177,680; giving activities include $174,248 for grants.
Purpose and activities: Giving primarily for child welfare including programs for eyeglasses, general dental work and medications, and recreation; support also for student loans. Recipients must be under 21 years of age, reside in Ontario County, New York, and need financial help.
Fields of interest: Education; Dental care; Optometry/vision screening; Recreation; Children/youth, services.
Type of support: Emergency funds; Student loans—to individuals.
Limitations: Giving limited to children in Ontario County, NY.
Application information: Contact high school guidance counselors or school nurses in Ontario County, NY, for application. Application form required.
Initial approach: Letter
Copies of proposal: 1
Deadline(s): None
Board meeting date(s): 2nd Tues. in Oct.
Officers: Richard Hawks, Pres.; Bruce Kennedy, V.P.; **Paul Hudson, Secy.**; **Richard Appel, Treas.**
Trustees: Geoffrey Astles; Randall Farnsworth; **Deborah Wilbur.**
Board of Managers: Jayne Baker; Karen Blazey; Mary Brady; Cynthia Fackler; Nancy Finkle; Linda Marsh; Caroline C. Shipley; and 17 additional managers.
EIN: 166028318
Other changes: Richard Hawks has replaced Richard Appel as Pres. Paul Hudson has replaced Karen Blazey as Secy. Richard Appel has replaced Richard Hawks as Treas.
John McGrath and Michael Shipley are no longer trustees.

2343
Open Society Institute
224 W. 57th St.
New York, NY 10019-3212 (212) 548-0600
Contact: Inquiry Mgr.
FAX: (212) 548-4600; Baltimore, MD office: 201 N. Charles St., Ste. 1300, Baltimore, MD 21201, tel.: (410) 234-1091; Washington, DC office: 1730 Pennsylvania Ave. N.W., 7th fl., Washington, DC 20006, tel.: 202-721-5600; Main URL: http://www.opensocietyfoundations.org/
Blog: http://blog.soros.org/
E-Newsletter: http://www.soros.org/resources/newsletters
Facebook: http://www.facebook.com/OpenSocietyFoundations
Open Society Institute: United States RSS: http://feeds.feedburner.com/OpenSocietyInstituteUnitedStates
Open Society Institute's Philanthropy Promise: http://www.ncrp.org/philanthropys-promise/who
OSI - Baltimore: http://twitter.com/OSIBaltimore
Podcasts: http://www.soros.org/resources/multimedia/podcasts
RSS Directory: http://www.soros.org/feeds
Twitter: http://www.twitter.com/opensociety
YouTube: http://www.youtube.com/opensocietyinstitute

Established in 1993 in NY.
Donor: George Soros.
Foundation type: Operating foundation.
Financial data (yr. ended 12/31/12): Assets, $685,871,435 (M); gifts received, $202,281,105; expenditures, $586,306,761; qualifying distributions, $642,804,792; giving activities include $444,471,445 for 526 grants (high: $245,000,000; low: $600), $9,998,480 for 862 grants to individuals (high: $120,020; low: $79), and $1,393,873 for 419 employee matching gifts.
Purpose and activities: The Open Society Institute (OSI), a private operating and grantmaking foundation, aims to shape public policy to promote democratic governance, human rights, and economic, legal, and social reform. On a local level, OSI implements a range of initiatives to support the rule of law, education, public health, and independent media. At the same time, OSI works to build alliances across borders and continents on issues such as combating corruption and rights abuses. OSI was created in 1993 by investor and philanthropist George Soros to support his foundations in Central and Eastern Europe and the former Soviet Union. Those foundations were established, starting in 1984, to help countries make the transition from communism. OSI has expanded the activities of the Soros foundations network to other areas of the world where the transition to democracy is of particular concern. The Soros foundations network encompasses foundations, offices, initiatives, and grantees in more than 60 countries and regions including: Asia, Southeast Asia, Central Asia, and Caucasus, Latin America and the Caribbean Central and South Eastern Europe, Africa, the Baltics, and North America.
Fields of interest: Media/communications; Arts; Education; Reproductive health; Public health; Palliative care; Crime/law enforcement; International economic development; International human rights; Civil/human rights; Law/international law; Children/youth; Children; Youth; Disabilities, people with; Blind/visually impaired; Mentally disabled; Minorities; African Americans/Blacks; Hispanics/Latinos; Indigenous peoples; Girls; Offenders/ex-offenders; Substance abusers; AIDS, people with; Terminal illness, people with;

Immigrants/refugees; Economically disadvantaged; Migrant workers; LGBTQ.
International interests: Africa; Asia; Caribbean; Central Asia; Eastern Europe; Global Programs; Latin America; Southeastern Asia.
Type of support: General/operating support; Continuing support; Program development; Professorships; Publication; Fellowships; Internship funds; Scholarship funds; Research; Technical assistance; Program-related investments/loans; Employee matching gifts; Grants to individuals; Scholarships—to individuals.
Limitations: Applications accepted. Giving on a national and international basis. No support for political parties or organizations connected to political parties.
Publications: Annual report; Informational brochure; Newsletter; Program policy statement.
Application information: For program application guidelines and deadlines see foundation web site. The site includes a wizard to help determine eligibility and submit an inquiry electronically. Application form not required.
Initial approach: Letter of inquiry, only if grantseeker does not have internet access
Officers and Trustees:* George Soros,* Chair.; Christopher Stone, Pres.; Stewart J. Paperin, Exec. V.P. and Treas.; Annette Laborey, V.P.; Ricardo A. Castro, Secy. and Genl. Counsel; Maija Arbolino, C.F.O.; Leon Botstein; Jonathan Soros.
EIN: 137029285
Other changes: At the close of 2012, the grantmaker paid grants of $455,863,798, a 411.1% increase over the 2011 disbursements, $89,194,831.

2344
The Ostgrodd Foundation, Inc.
c/o McGladrey
1185 Avenue of the Americas
New York, NY **10036**
Contact: Barbara Grodd, Pres. and Treas.

Established in 1995 in NY.
Donor: Barbara Grodd.
Foundation type: Independent foundation.
Financial data (yr. ended 12/31/12): Assets, $1,885,709 (M); expenditures, $201,693; qualifying distributions, $193,350; giving activities include $193,350 for 59 grants (high: $100,000; low: $500).
Purpose and activities: Giving for a range of interests, but there is a focus on small, established community-based organizations that work in challenging neighborhoods, often (but not exclusively) with ex-offender populations.
Fields of interest: Museums; Arts; Higher education; Environment; Reproductive health, family planning; Cancer; Medical research, institute; Offenders/ex-offenders, services; Youth; Women; Men; Offenders/ex-offenders; Economically disadvantaged.
Type of support: General/operating support; Continuing support; Program development.
Limitations: Applications not accepted. Giving primarily in New York, NY. No support for religious or political organizations. No grants to individuals.
Application information: Contributes only to pre-selected organizations.
Officers and Directors:* Barbara Grodd,* Pres. and Treas.; Patricia Grodd Stone,* Secy.; James Grodd.
Number of staff: None.
EIN: 133826884
Other changes: The grantmaker no longer lists a fax. The grantmaker no longer lists a phone.

2345
The Overbrook Foundation
122 E. 42nd St., Ste. 2500
New York, NY 10168-2500 (212) 661-8710
Contact: Nikole LaVelle, Asst. Grants Mgr.
FAX: (212) 661-8664;
E-mail: website@overbrook.org; Main URL: http://www.overbrook.org
The Overbrook Foundation Blog: http://www.overbrook.org/blog/
The Overbrook Foundation's Philanthropy Promise: http://www.ncrp.org/philanthropys-promise/who
Twitter: https://twitter.com/OverbrookFnd

Incorporated in 1948 in NY.
Donors: Frank Altschul†; Helen G. Altschul†; Arthur G. Altschul†; Margaret A. Lang†.
Foundation type: Independent foundation.
Financial data (yr. ended 12/31/12): Assets, $134,264,106 (M); expenditures, $9,789,007; qualifying distributions, $7,215,975; giving activities include $5,807,060 for 134 grants (high: $1,418,500; low: $250).
Purpose and activities: The foundation is a progressive family foundation that supports organizations advancing human rights and conserving the natural environment.
Fields of interest: Environment, natural resources; International human rights; Civil/human rights, advocacy; Civil liberties, advocacy; Civil liberties, reproductive rights; Civil/human rights; Children/youth; Children; Adults; Indigenous peoples; Women; Girls; Young adults, female; LGBTQ.
International interests: Latin America.
Type of support: General/operating support; Program development; Fellowships.
Limitations: Giving primarily in the U.S. and Latin America, with emphasis on Brazil, Mexico, Ecuador and Central America. No grants to individuals.
Publications: Application guidelines; Financial statement; Grants list; Program policy statement.
Application information: The foundation no longer accepts unsolicited requests for new projects or operating support from organizations not currently funded by the foundation. Grant requests are now by invitation only for organizations advancing human rights and the environment.
***Board meeting date(s):* 3 times per year, dates vary**
Officers and Directors:* Stephen F. Altschul,* Chair.; Elizabeth Lindemann,* Vice-Chair. and Secy.; Frances Labaree,* Vice-Chair. and Treas.; Stephen A. Foster, C.E.O. and Pres.; Arthur G. Altschul, Jr.; Serena Altschul; Emily Altschul-Miller; Carolyn J. Cole; Kathryn G. Graham; Robert C. Graham, Jr.; Aaron Labaree; Dinorah Matias-Melendez; Vincent McGee; Isaiah Orozco.
Number of staff: 5 full-time professional; 2 part-time professional.
EIN: 136088860

2346
Overhills Foundation
c/o DAB Management Co., LLC
377 Oak St., No. 405-7
Garden City, NY **11530-6559**

Established in 2000 in DE.
Donors: Omnibus Charitable Trust; Underhill Foundation; Wild Wings Foundation; A.M. Rockefeller Trust; A.R. Rockefeller Charitable Trust; Underhill Charitable Trust.
Foundation type: Independent foundation.
Financial data (yr. ended 11/30/12): Assets, $12,897,170 (M); expenditures, $746,539; qualifying distributions, $673,500; giving activities include $673,500 for grants.
Fields of interest: Arts; Higher education; Education; Environment, formal/general education; Environment, natural resources.
Limitations: Applications not accepted. Giving primarily in CT and NY. No grants to individuals.
Application information: Contributes only to pre-selected organizations.
Officers and Directors:* Ann R. Elliman,* Pres.; Edward H. Elliman,* V.P.; Lucia Brown Evans,* V.P.; Christopher J. Elliman,* Secy.-Treas.
EIN: 133922745

2347
The Palette Fund, Inc.
1201 Broadway, Ste. 504
New York, NY **10001-5405** (646) 861-3292
FAX: (212) 214-0816;
E-mail: info@thepalettefund.org; Main URL: http://www.thepalettefund.org/
Facebook: https://www.facebook.com/thepalettefund
Pinterest: https://www.pinterest.com/palettefund/
RSS Feed: http://www.thepalettefund.org/feed/
Tumblr: http://thepalettefund.tumblr.com/
Twitter: https://twitter.com/PaletteFund
YouTube: http://www.youtube.com/user/ThePaletteFund

Established in NY.
Foundation type: Independent foundation.
Financial data (yr. ended 12/31/12): Assets, $20,912,442 (M); gifts received, $4,201,246; expenditures, $1,670,687; qualifying distributions, $1,493,673; giving activities include $944,205 for 37 grants (high: $172,667; low: $350).
Purpose and activities: Giving primarily for nutrition and wellness, and to LGBT causes.
Fields of interest: Cancer; Health organizations; Nutrition; Human services; LGBTQ.
Limitations: Giving primarily in CA and NY.
Publications: Application guidelines.
Application information: Letters of intent and grant proposals are accepted by invitation only. Complete application guidelines are available online.
***Initial approach:* Email inquiry**
***Deadline(s):* Check foundation web site for current deadlines**
Officers and Directors:* Peter Benassi,* Chair.; Terrence Meck,* Pres. and Exec. Dir.; Kristin Resnansky,* Secy.-Treas.; Todd Sears.
EIN: 262736653
Other changes: The grantmaker now publishes application guidelines.

2348
Pat Palmer Foundation, Inc.
P.O. Box 751149
Forest Hills, NY 11375-8749
Contact: Mark Finkelstein, Pres.

Donor: Pat Palmer Bernard†.
Foundation type: Independent foundation.
Financial data (yr. ended 06/30/13): Assets, $3,011,692 (M); expenditures, $259,240; qualifying distributions, $157,500; giving activities include $157,500 for 7 grants (high: $40,000; low: $7,500).
Fields of interest: Animals/wildlife.
Limitations: Applications accepted. Giving primarily in AZ, MA and TX.

Application information: Application form required.
Initial approach: Letter
Deadline(s): None
Officers: Mark Finkelstein, Pres.; David Walsh, Treas.
Director: Brian Gibson.
EIN: 208559990
Other changes: Matthew Trachtenberg is no longer Secy.

2349
Park Foundation, Inc.
P.O. Box 550
Ithaca, NY 14851-0550 (607) 272-9124
Contact: Jon Jensen, Exec. Dir.
FAX: (607) 272-6057;
E-mail: info@parkfoundation.org; Street Address: 301 E. State St., Ithaca, N.Y., 14850; Main URL: http://www.parkfoundation.org

Established in 1966.
Donors: RHP, Inc.; Roy H. Park‡.
Foundation type: Independent foundation.
Financial data (yr. ended 12/31/12): Assets, $366,405,008 (M); expenditures, $22,168,578; qualifying distributions, $19,736,469; giving activities include $17,814,586 for 380 grants (high: $645,046; low: $20), and $500,000 for 1 loan/program-related investment.
Purpose and activities: Giving primarily for scholarships in higher education, quality public affairs media that heightens public awareness of critical issues, and protection of the environment. In addition to these core program areas, interests include a broad range of charitable giving in communities where the trustees reside.
Fields of interest: Media/communications; Media, television; Media, print publishing; Higher education; Environment, water resources; Animal welfare.
Type of support: Mission-related investments/loans; General/operating support; Continuing support; Management development/capacity building; Program development; Film/video/radio; Scholarship funds; Program-related investments/loans; Employee matching gifts; Matching/challenge support.
Limitations: Applications accepted. Giving limited to the eastern U.S., primarily in central NY, Washington, DC, and NC. No grants to individuals.
Publications: Application guidelines; Grants list; Program policy statement.
Application information: See web site for application requirements. Application form required.
Initial approach: Letter of inquiry, telephone or application (see website)
Copies of proposal: 1
***Deadline(s):* Quarterly: Jan. 3, Apr. 4, July 7 and Sept. 26**
Board meeting date(s): Mar., June, Sept., and Dec.
Final notification: Within 3 months
Officers and Directors:* Adelaide P. Gomer,* Pres.; Alicia P. Wittink,* V.P.; William L. Bondurant,* Secy.-Treas.; Jon Jensen, Exec. Dir.; Jay R. Halfon; Richard G. Robb; Jerome B. Libin.
Number of staff: 7 full-time professional.
EIN: 166071043

2350
Patrina Foundation
901 Pelhamdale Ave.
Pelham, NY **10803-2928** (212) 233-1559
Contact: Kara D'Angelo, Exec. Dir.
E-mail: karadangelo@patrinafoundation.org; Additional tel.: (914) 886-5390; Main URL: http://www.patrinafoundation.org/index.php
Grants Database: http://www.patrinafoundation.org/grants.php

Established in 1990 in NY.
Donor: Lorinda P. de Roulet.
Foundation type: Independent foundation.
Financial data (yr. ended 12/31/12): Assets, $8,366,651 (M); expenditures, $565,612; qualifying distributions, $468,511; giving activities include $358,950 for 55 grants (high: $15,000; low: $500).
Purpose and activities: Giving primarily to improve the lives of girls and women by supporting social and educational nonprofit programming designed to meet the unique needs of girls and women in the greater New York, NY metropolitan area.
Fields of interest: Elementary/secondary education; Women, centers/services; Women; Infants/toddlers, female; Girls; Young adults, female.
Type of support: Continuing support; Program development; Seed money; Curriculum development; Internship funds; Scholarship funds.
Limitations: Applications accepted. Giving primarily in the greater New York, NY, metropolitan area. No grants to individuals, or for advocacy.
Application information: Application guidelines available on foundation web site. Application form required.
Initial approach: E-mail or telephone, followed by proposal
Copies of proposal: 6
Board meeting date(s): Mar., June, and Nov.
Final notification: Within 4 months
Officers and Trustees:* Lorinda P. de Roulet,* Pres.; Whitney Bullock,* Secy.; Daniel C. de Roulet,* Treas.; Kara D'Angelo, Exec. Dir.; Alexandra Bullock; Daniel C. de Roulet, Jr.; Mary Jo McLoughlin; Elizabeth Rainoff.
Number of staff: 1 part-time professional.
EIN: 113035018

2351
Paulson Family Foundation
1251 Ave. of the Americas, 50th Fl.
New York, NY 10020-1104 (212) 350-5151
Contact: John Paulson, Pres. and Treas.

Donor: John Paulson.
Foundation type: Independent foundation.
Financial data (yr. ended 12/31/12): Assets, $490,890,813 (M); gifts received, $24,000,000; expenditures, $27,422,106; qualifying distributions, $27,393,106; giving activities include $27,374,743 for 40 grants (high: $10,050,000; low: $1,000).
Fields of interest: Education; Environment; Human services.
Limitations: Applications accepted. Giving primarily in New York, NY.
Officer and Director:* John Paulson,* Pres. and Treas.
EIN: 263922995
Other changes: At the close of 2012, the grantmaker paid grants of $27,374,743, a 61.9% increase over the 2011 disbursements, $16,912,294.

2352
Alice A. Paxton Charitable Trust
1100 Wehrle Dr., 2nd Fl.
Buffalo, NY **14221**

Established in 2001 in MD.
Donor: Alice A. Paxton Trust.
Foundation type: Independent foundation.
Financial data (yr. ended 11/30/13): Assets, $3,711,080 (M); gifts received, $308,488; expenditures, $197,909; qualifying distributions, $155,000; giving activities include $155,000 for 6 grants (high: $50,000; low: $5,000).
Purpose and activities: Giving for the prevention of cruelty to animals and wildlife preservation.
Fields of interest: Animals/wildlife, alliance/advocacy; Animals/wildlife, preservation/protection.
Type of support: General/operating support.
Limitations: Applications not accepted. Giving primarily in MD and PA. No grants to individuals.
Application information: Contributes only to pre-selected organizations.
Trustee: M&T Bank.
EIN: 016180869

2353
Peale Foundation, Inc.
c/o Elizabeth Allen
665 Old Quaker Hill Rd.
Pawling, NY 12564-3452

Established in 1991 in NY and DE.
Donors: JME II Charitable Lead Trust; JME Charitable Lead Trust; Ruth S. Peale Trust; Schiff, Hardin & Waite; Pawling Charitable Lead Annuity Trust.
Foundation type: Independent foundation.
Financial data (yr. ended 09/30/13): Assets, $6,867,891 (M); expenditures, $567,070; qualifying distributions, $422,293; giving activities include $368,680 for 23 grants (high: $85,000; low: $300).
Purpose and activities: Giving primarily for religion, community and educational programs.
Fields of interest: Education; Community/economic development; Protestant agencies & churches.
Limitations: Applications not accepted. Giving primarily in NY.
Application information: Unsolicited requests for funds not accepted.
Officers and Directors:* Margaret P. Everett,* Pres.; John S. Peale,* V.P.; Elizabeth Peale Allen,* Secy.-Treas.
EIN: 141746478

2354
The PepsiCo Foundation, Inc.
700 Anderson Hill Rd.
Purchase, NY 10577-1401
***Main URL:* http://www.pepsico.com/Purpose/Global-Citizenship**
Grants List: http://www.pepsico.com/Purpose/PepsiCo-Foundation/Contributions.html

Incorporated in 1962 in NY.
Donor: PepsiCo, Inc.
Foundation type: Company-sponsored foundation.
Financial data (yr. ended 12/31/12): Assets, $73,658,150 (M); gifts received, $7,000,000; expenditures, $25,702,202; qualifying distributions, $25,414,950; giving activities include $25,414,950 for 4,360 grants (high: $3,423,930; low: $1).

Purpose and activities: The foundation supports programs designed to promote education, the environment, and health in underserved regions. Special emphasis is directed toward nutrition and safety; safe water and water usage efficiencies; and education and empowerment.
Fields of interest: Higher education; Education; Environment, water pollution; Environment, water resources; Public health; Public health, physical fitness; Public health, clean water supply; Health care; Employment, training; Employment; Food services; Food banks; Nutrition; Agriculture/food; Disasters, preparedness/services; Safety/disasters; Children, services; Civil/human rights, equal rights; Economic development; United Ways and Federated Giving Programs; Minorities; Women; Economically disadvantaged.
International interests: Africa; Asia; Bangladesh; Ghana; India.
Type of support: General/operating support; Continuing support; Management development/capacity building; Program development; Employee volunteer services; Employee matching gifts; Employee-related scholarships; Scholarships—to individuals; In-kind gifts.
Limitations: Applications not accepted. Giving on a national and international basis, with emphasis on Washington, DC, FL, IL, MA, NY, TX, and VA, and in Africa, Asia, Bangladesh, Canada, China, Ghana, India, Mexico, and the United Kingdom. No support for private charities or foundations, religious organizations, political candidates or organizations, discriminatory organizations, or legislative organizations, or for playgrounds, or sports fields. No grants to individuals (except for employee-related and Diamond scholarships), or for political causes or campaigns, endowments or capital campaigns, equipment, film, music, TV, video, or media productions, sports sponsorships, performing arts tours, or association memberships.
Publications: Grants list; Program policy statement.
Application information: Unsolicited letters of inquiry or proposals are currently not accepted. Foundation staff solicits proposals for all major grants over $100,000.
Officers and Directors:* Indra K. Nooyi,* Chair.; Sue Tsokris, V.P.; Christine Griff, Secy.; Tessa Hilado, Treas.; Zein Abdalla; Saad Abdul-Latif; Rich Delaney; Hugh F. Johnston; Donald M. Kendall; Mehmood Khan; Cynthia M. Trudell.
Number of staff: 2 full-time professional; 2 full-time support.
EIN: 136163174

2355
Perelman Family Foundation
35 E. 62nd St.
New York, NY 10065-8014
Ronald Perelman's Giving Pledge Profile: http://glasspockets.org/philanthropy-in-focus/eye-on-the-giving-pledge/profiles/perelman

Established in 1999 in NY.
Donors: R G I Group Incorporated; Ronald O. Perelman.
Foundation type: Independent foundation.
Financial data (yr. ended 12/31/12): Assets, $51,796 (M); gifts received, $10,451,967; expenditures, $10,461,067; qualifying distributions, $10,460,967; giving activities include $10,460,967 for 32 grants (high: $3,125,000; low: $1,000).
Fields of interest: Arts; Hospitals (general); Health organizations, association; Human services; United Ways and Federated Giving Programs; Jewish agencies & synagogues.
Limitations: Applications not accepted. Giving primarily in NY. No grants to individuals.
Application information: Contributes only to pre-selected organizations.
Officers and Directors:* Ronald O. Perelman,* Chair. and C.E.O.; Barry F. Schwartz,* Exec. Vice-Chair. and C.A.O.; **Paul G. Savas, Exec. V.P., Fin.; Michael C. Borofsky, Sr. V.P. and Secy.; Adam F. Ingber, Sr. V.P., Taxation**; Debra G. Perelman,* Sr. V.P.; Christine Taylor, Sr. V.P.; Alison Horowitz, V.P., Treas., and Cont.; **Gary Rozenshteyn, V.P., Taxation**; JoAnne deFreitas, V.P.; Hope G. Perelman, V.P.; Joshua G. Perelman, V.P.; Steven G. Perelman, V.P.
EIN: 134008528
Other changes: Michael C. Borofsky is now Sr. V.P. and Secy. Treas., and Cont. Debra G. Perelman is now Sr. V.P.

2356
The Pershing Square Foundation
c/o Marcum LLP
10 Melville Park Rd.
Melville, NY **11747-3146**
Main URL: http://www.pershingsquarefoundation.org
Bill and Karen Ackman's Giving Pledge Profile: http://glasspockets.org/philanthropy-in-focus/eye-on-the-giving-pledge/profiles/ackman

Established in 2007 in NY.
Donors: William Ackman; Karen Ackman; Nicholas Botta; Roy Katzovicz; Lawrence D. Ackman; Pershing Square Capital Mgmt.
Foundation type: Independent foundation.
Financial data (yr. ended 09/30/13): Assets, $79,862,242 (M); gifts received, $10,000,000; expenditures, $32,498,127; qualifying distributions, $32,341,208; giving activities include $31,135,657 for 80 grants (high: $5,139,426; low: $1,000).
Purpose and activities: Giving primarily for community development, education, the arts, human services, health organizations, and Jewish organizations.
Fields of interest: Historic preservation/historical societies; Arts; Education; Health organizations; Human services; Social entrepreneurship; Community/economic development; Foundations (public); Jewish federated giving programs; Leadership development; Jewish agencies & synagogues.
Limitations: Applications accepted. Giving on a world wide basis with an emphasis on New York, NY and NJ.
Application information: Eligibility includes that applicants should have at least 3 years of experience running their own laboratories and may have up to 10 years of experience. Principal Investigators (PIs) must hold a faculty appointment at an academic research institution in the New York area at the level of Assistant or Associate Professor (or equivalent). The New York area includes New York City and Long Island.
Initial approach: One-page, LOI online application period is open Dec. 2 through Jan. 20.
Deadline(s): By Feb. 17 selected applicants are invited to submit full length proposals. March 31 is the deadline for selected applicants to submit full length proposals.
Final notification: Prize winners notified in May; Projects start in the Summer.
Officers: Paul Bernstein, C.E.O.; **Amy Herskovitz, Exec. V.P.; Olivia Tournay Flatto, Exec. Dir., Pershing Square Sohn Cancer Research Alliance.**
Trustee: Karen Ackman; William Ackman.
EIN: 208068401
Other changes: For the fiscal year ended Sept. 30, 2013, the grantmaker paid grants of $31,135,657, a 59.8% increase over the fiscal 2012 disbursements, $19,482,082.

2357
Peter G. Peterson Foundation
888-C Eighth Ave.
P.O. Box 144
New York, NY 10019-8511 (212) 542-9200
Contact: Rikard Treiber, Dir., Grants Mgmt.
FAX: (212) 542-9250; E-mail: inquiries@pgpf.org; Main URL: http://www.pgpf.org/
Blog: http://www.pgpf.org/blog
E-Newsletter: http://www.pgpf.org/Registration.aspx?ref=/Media/Video/2009/09/Fiscal-Wake-Up-Tour-Online-Dave-Walker.aspx
Facebook: http://www.facebook.com/pages/Peter-G-Peterson-Foundation/15503839732
GiveSmart: http://www.givesmart.org/Stories/Donors/Pete-Peterson
Multimedia: http://www.pgpf.org/Media/Video/2009/09/Fiscal-Wake-Up-Tour-Online-Dave-Walker.aspx
Peter G. Peterson's Giving Pledge Profile: http://glasspockets.org/philanthropy-in-focus/eye-on-the-giving-pledge/profiles/peterson
RSS Feed: http://www.pgpf.org/blog/publicfeed
Twitter: https://twitter.com/pgpfoundation
YouTube: https://www.youtube.com/user/pgpfoundation

Established in 2008.
Donors: Peter G. Peterson; David M. Walker; Warren E. Buffett; Georges Marciano.
Foundation type: Independent foundation.
Financial data (yr. ended 03/31/13): Assets, $484,815,258 (M); expenditures, $18,384,080; qualifying distributions, $16,328,050; giving activities include $8,871,984 for 36 grants (high: $1,546,984; low: $10,000), and $19,234,256 for 3 foundation-administered programs.
Purpose and activities: The mission is to increase public awareness of the nature and urgency of key fiscal challenges threatening America's future and to accelerate action on them. To address these challenges successfully, the foundation works to bring Americans together to find and implement sensible, long-term solutions that transcend age, party lines and ideological divides in order to achieve real results.
Fields of interest: Health care, cost containment; Health care, financing; International affairs, national security; Public affairs, finance; Public affairs, citizen participation.
Type of support: Research; Internship funds; Curriculum development; Conferences/seminars.
Limitations: Applications accepted. Giving limited to the U.S. to nonprofits that are regional or national in scope and have the ability to implement programming nationwide. No support for other private grantmaking foundations, foreign organizations, or for political, social or fraternal organizations. No grants to individuals, or for general operating support, unrestricted purposes, indirect expenses, ongoing funding, capital campaigns, annual appeals, ongoing sponsorships, fundraising events, or to underwrite chairs, endowments or scholarships sponsored by academic or nonprofit institutions.
Publications: Financial statement; Informational brochure; Newsletter; Occasional report.

Application information: The foundation gives only in pre-selected program areas. Application form required.

Initial approach: Submit initial inquiry via inquiries@pgpf.org. If invited, a proposal will be requested

Copies of proposal: 1

Deadline(s): Initial inquiries are accepted throughout the year

Final notification: Varies

Officers and Directors:* Peter G. Peterson,* Chair.; Michael Peterson,* Pres. and C.O.O.; Susan Tanaka, V.P., Policy and Research; Loretta Ucelli, V.P., Comms. and Public Affairs; Moshe Mandelbaum, C.F.O.; Joan Ganz Cooney.

Number of staff: 17 full-time professional; 5 full-time support; 2 part-time support.

EIN: 260316905

Other changes: For the fiscal year ended Mar. 31, 2013, the grantmaker paid grants of $8,871,984, a 59.3% increase over the fiscal 2012 disbursements, $5,570,483.

2358
Carroll Petrie Foundation

c/o RSSM
757 3rd Ave., 6th Fl.
New York, NY 10017-2059

Established in 1996 in DE & NY.

Donor: Carroll M. Petrie.

Foundation type: Independent foundation.

Financial data (yr. ended 12/31/12): Assets, $3,440,983 (M); gifts received, $1,859,893; expenditures, $2,072,333; qualifying distributions, $2,029,440; giving activities include $2,015,000 for 8 grants (high: $1,500,000; low: $10,000).

Fields of interest: Museums (art); Animal welfare.

Limitations: Applications not accepted. Giving primarily in Southampton and New York, NY. No grants to individuals.

Application information: Contributes only to pre-selected organizations.

Board meeting date(s): May

Officers and Directors:* Jay B. Goldberg,* Pres.; William D. Zabel,* Secy.; Camille Manning; Carolina Portago; Theodora Portago.

EIN: 133912203

Other changes: Jay B. Goldberg has replaced Carroll M. Petrie as Pres.
William D. Zabel is now Secy.

2359
Planning and Art Resources for Communities Inc.

P.O. Box 6437
New York, NY **10150-6421**
***FAX:* (646) 383-6999;**
E-mail: info@theparcfoundation.org; Main URL: http://www.theparcfoundation.org

Established in 2006 in NY.

Donor: David Deutsch.

Foundation type: Independent foundation.

Financial data (yr. ended 10/31/12): Assets, $39,497,952 (M); expenditures, $978,852; qualifying distributions, $1,394,522; giving activities include $963,062 for 23 grants (high: $153,962; low: $500).

Purpose and activities: Giving to strengthen communities in need by serving as a catalyst for the development and promotion of contemporary architecture and art.

Fields of interest: Arts.

Type of support: Program-related investments/loans.

Limitations: Applications not accepted. No grants to individuals.

Application information: Contributes only to pre-selected organizations.

Officers and Directors:* David Deutsch,* Chair. and Pres.; Victoria Sambunaris,* Secy.; Megan Wurth,* Fdn. Mgr; Shawn Ganon.

EIN: 134350414

2360
The Kronhill Pletka Foundation

123A W. 69th St.
New York, NY 10023-5127
***E-mail:* info@kronhillpletkafoundation.org**; Application email: LOI@kronhillpletkafoundation.org; Main URL: http://www.kronhillpletkafoundation.org/index.html

Established in 2007 in NY.

Foundation type: Independent foundation.

Financial data (yr. ended 12/31/12): Assets, $5,724,925 (M); expenditures, $316,204; qualifying distributions, $277,057; giving activities include $252,700 for 15 grants (high: $66,975; low: $850).

Fields of interest: Higher education; Jewish agencies & synagogues.

Limitations: Applications accepted. Giving primarily in New York, NY. No grants to individuals.

Publications: Application guidelines.

Application information: The specific project proposal should not exceed 1,000 words. See foundation web site for specific application guidelines.

Initial approach: Letter of intent via e-mail

Deadline(s): 1st Fri. of Feb., May, Aug. and Nov.

Officers and Trustee:* Irene Pletka,* Chair. and Pres.; Peter Pletka, Secy.

EIN: 261466252

2361
The Polisseni Foundation, Inc.

c/o G.P. Associates
1080 Pittsford Victor Dr., Ste. 201
Pittsford, NY **14534-3805 (585) 641-0151**
FAX: (585) 641-0144; E-mail: krohl@pfair.com; Main URL: http://www.polissenifoundation.org

Established in 2001 in NY.

Donor: Wanda Polisseni.

Foundation type: Independent foundation.

Financial data (yr. ended 08/31/13): Assets, $0 (M); gifts received, $500; expenditures, $314,416; qualifying distributions, $266,506; giving activities include $251,500 for 16 grants (high: $150,000; low: $500).

Purpose and activities: Giving to assist organizations and groups in meeting community need and improving quality of life in the areas of education, human services, and civic improvement within upstate New York.

Fields of interest: Hospitals (general); Community/economic development; Foundations (private grantmaking).

Limitations: Applications accepted. Giving primarily in NY; however the foundation accepts applications from anywhere in the U.S. No grants to individuals.

Publications: Application guidelines.

Application information: Application guidelines and form available on foundation web site. Application form required.

Initial approach: Proposal (no more than 2 pages)

Copies of proposal: 1

Deadline(s): 2 weeks prior to board meeting

Board meeting date(s): Jan., May, and Sept. 16

Final notification: 1 week after receipt

Officer: Wanda Polisseni, Pres.

Directors: Glenn Pezzulo; Gary Polisseni; Gregory Polisseni; Valerie Polisseni Wilcox.

Number of staff: 1 full-time professional.

EIN: 161611263

2362
Pollock Foundation

(formerly S. Wilson & Grace M. Pollock Foundation)
1100 Wehrle Dr., 2nd Fl.
Amherst, NY **14221-7748**

Established in 1997 in PA.

Donors: Grace Pollock; S. Wilson Pollock.

Foundation type: Independent foundation.

Financial data (yr. ended 04/30/13): Assets, $8,661,164 (M); gifts received, $35; expenditures, $414,482; qualifying distributions, $375,000; giving activities include $375,000 for 3 grants (high: $250,000; low: $25,000).

Fields of interest: Arts; Libraries/library science; Hospitals (general); Human services; Blind/visually impaired.

Limitations: Applications not accepted. Giving primarily in PA. No grants to individuals.

Application information: Contributes only to pre-selected organizations.

Directors: Lauren P. Cacciamani; Paul A. Cacciamani, Esq.; Courtney P. Gordon; David H. McLane, Ph.D.; Lindsay Kathryn Pollock.

Trustee: M&T Bank.

EIN: 237889770

Other changes: Grace M. Pollock is no longer a director.

2363
The Pollock-Krasner Foundation, Inc.

863 Park Ave.
New York, NY 10075-0380 (212) 517-5400
Contact: Caroline Black, Prog. Off.
FAX: (212) 288-2836; E-mail: grants@pkf.org; E-mail for application-related questions: grantapplication@pkf.org; Main URL: http://www.pkf.org
Grants List: http://www.pkf.org/recent_grantees.html

Established in 1984 in DE.

Donor: Lee Krasner†.

Foundation type: Independent foundation.

Financial data (yr. ended 06/30/12): Assets, $56,416,156 (M); expenditures, $4,502,367; qualifying distributions, $3,444,101; giving activities include $2,039,900 for 143 grants (high: $200,000; low: $5,000).

Purpose and activities: Giving primarily to aid, internationally, those individuals who have worked as artists over a significant period of time. The foundation's dual criteria for grants are recognizable artistic merit and financial need, whether professional, personal or both.

Fields of interest: Visual arts.

Type of support: Grants to individuals.

Limitations: Giving on a national and international basis. No grants for past debt, legal fees, purchase of real estate, tuition reimbursement, moving expenses, costs of installations, commissions or projects ordered by others, or individual grants to students, photographers, commercial,

performance, or video artists, filmmakers or craftsmen.
Publications: Application guidelines; Annual report; Informational brochure (including application guidelines).
Application information: The foundation cannot respond to application requests by telephone or in person; therefore, write, fax or e-mail. Application form required.
Initial approach: Cover letter with application form which can be downloaded on foundation web site
Deadline(s): None
Board meeting date(s): Regularly throughout the year
Final notification: As soon as possible
Officers and Directors:* Charles C. Bergman,* C.E.O. and Chair.; Samuel Sachs II,* Pres.; Kerrie Buitrago, Exec. V.P.
Number of staff: 5 full-time professional; 2 full-time support.
EIN: 133255693

2364
Porticus North America Foundation
(formerly The Humanitas Foundation)
PO Box 1690
New York, NY **10163-1690** (212) 704-2300
FAX: (212) 704-2301;
E-mail: porticusnorthamerica@porticus.com; Canada Address: 1267 Cornwall Rd., Ste. 200, Oakville, Ontario, L6J 7T5; tel.: 905-338-2992; fax: 905-338-1651; Main URL: http://www.porticusna.com

Established in 1979.
Donors: American Retail Group, Inc.; American Retail Properties, Inc.; Argidius Foundation.
Foundation type: Independent foundation.
Financial data (yr. ended 12/31/12): Assets, $574,035 (M); gifts received, $5,340,240; expenditures, $5,717,832; qualifying distributions, $5,717,372; giving activities include $5,717,372 for grants.
Purpose and activities: The foundation is a small, private foundation that supports projects sponsored by Catholic organizations in the United States. Through its grantmaking it seeks to foster church renewal, improve Catholic education, and serve the disadvantaged. It has a sister foundation in Canada known as the Ansgar Charitable Foundation. Grants are only for Roman Catholic organizations within the U.S.
Fields of interest: Catholic agencies & churches.
Type of support: General/operating support; Management development/capacity building; Equipment; Program development; Conferences/seminars; Seed money; Curriculum development; Research; Technical assistance; Consulting services; Matching/challenge support.
Limitations: Applications accepted. Giving on a national basis. No support for individual parishes, schools or colleges not solicited by the foundation. No grants to individuals, or for scholarships, endowments, large construction projects, or capital campaigns.
Publications: Application guidelines.
Application information: See foundation proposal guidelines. Application form required.
Initial approach: Submit a proposal letter no more than two pages
Copies of proposal: 1
Deadline(s): Mar. 30, June 30, Sept. 30 and Dec. 31
Board meeting date(s): Apr. and Oct.
Final notification: Following board meeting
Officer: Anthony P. Mullen, Pres.
Number of staff: 2 full-time professional; 1 full-time support.
EIN: 133005012
Other changes: Suzanne E. Elsesser is no longer Prog. Off.

2365
Ralph B. Post Trust
c/o NBT Bank, N.A.
52 S. Broad St.
Norwich, NY **13815**
Application address: **c/o Post Memorial Scholarship Fund, NBT Bank, N.A., 241 Main St., Ste. 200, Buffalo, NY 14203, tel.: (716) 566-3032**

Established in 1985 in NY.
Foundation type: Independent foundation.
Financial data (yr. ended 09/30/13): Assets, $2,128,388 (M); expenditures, $207,403; qualifying distributions, $191,149; giving activities include $184,274 for 33 grants to individuals (high: $21,323; low: $625).
Purpose and activities: Awards scholarships to female residents of specified geographic areas who are majoring in nursing.
Fields of interest: Nursing school/education.
Type of support: Scholarships—to individuals.
Limitations: Applications accepted. Giving limited to residents of the town of Ballston Spa, the village of Ballston Spa, and the town of Milton, who are majoring in nursing.
Application information: Application form not required.
Deadline(s): None
Trustee: NBT Bank, N.A.
EIN: 146052967

2366
The Pratt-Northam Foundation
P.O. Box 104
Lowville, NY 13367-0104 (315) 771-9889
Contact: Thomas Yousey II, Exec. Dir.
E-mail: prattnortham@frontier.com; Main URL: http://www.prattnortham.org
Grants List: http://www.prattnortham.org/contri.htm

Incorporated in 1962 in NY.
Donor: Hazel Northam†.
Foundation type: Independent foundation.
Financial data (yr. ended 12/31/12): Assets, $4,898,793 (M); expenditures, $256,943; qualifying distributions, $228,331; giving activities include $204,300 for 62 grants (high: $15,000; low: $500).
Purpose and activities: The foundation's mission is to improve the quality of life in the communities of the Black River Valley, New York.
Fields of interest: Arts; Education; Government/public administration.
Type of support: Capital campaigns; Program development; Matching/challenge support.
Limitations: Applications accepted. Giving limited to the Black River Valley region of NY. No grants to individuals.
Application information: Application form required.
***Initial approach:* Contact foundation for application or download application from foundation web site**
Copies of proposal: 1
Deadline(s): None
Board meeting date(s): Bimonthly
Officers and Directors:* Randall Schell,* Pres.; Donald M. Hunt, V.P. and Treas.; James Randall, Secy.; Randolph Myers, Treas.; Thomas Yousey II, Exec. Dir.; Gordon Allen; Roy Hammecker; Don Hunt; Sally Jackson; Chris Lorence; Donna Loucks; Thomas R. Sauter; Jo Ann Ventura.
Number of staff: 1 part-time professional.
EIN: 166088207

2367
The Price Family Foundation, Inc.
(formerly Michael F. Price Foundation, Inc.)
c/o Michael F. Price
667 Madison Ave., 25th Fl.
New York, NY 10065-8025
Contact: Joanne Duhl, Exec. Dir.

Established in 1997 in NJ.
Donor: Michael F. Price.
Foundation type: Independent foundation.
Financial data (yr. ended 11/30/13): Assets, $20,741,090 (M); gifts received, $11,608,875; expenditures, $13,372,507; qualifying distributions, $13,129,905; giving activities include $12,944,208 for 62 grants (high: $7,943,746; low: $500).
Purpose and activities: Giving primarily for higher education, children's services, and hospitals.
Fields of interest: Higher education; Hospitals (general); Children/youth, services; Children/youth; Children; Young adults; Economically disadvantaged.
Limitations: Applications accepted. Giving primarily in NJ and New York City, NY. No grants to individuals.
Publications: Annual report.
Application information: Application form not required.
Initial approach: Letter
Deadline(s): None
Officers: Michael F. Price, Mgr.; Joanne Duhl, Exec. Dir.
Trustees: Martin Bernstein; Claudia Forbs; Jennifer C. Price; Jordan M. Price.
Number of staff: 1 full-time professional.
EIN: 223483367
Other changes: For the fiscal year ended Nov. 30, 2013, the grantmaker paid grants of $12,944,208, an 85.5% increase over the 2012 disbursements, $6,977,936.

2368
Project Home Again Foundation
c/o Bryan Cave LLP
1290 Ave. of the Americas
New York, NY 10104
***Application address:* P.O. Box 851008, New Orleans, LA 70185-1008; tel.: (504) 529-3522**; Main URL: http://www.projecthomeagain.net

Donors: The Riggio Foundation; Greater New Orleans Foundation; New Orleans Redevelopment Authority.
Foundation type: Operating foundation.
Financial data (yr. ended 03/31/12): Assets, $13,529,442 (M); gifts received, $4,695,313; expenditures, $3,489,039; qualifying distributions, $3,357,057; giving activities include $948,320 for 38 grants to individuals (high: $31,600; low: $18,000).
Purpose and activities: Giving to low and moderate income families in New Orleans, LA, who, due to Hurricane Katrina, own homes that are uninhabitable in Gentilly (Planning District 6) in Orleans Parish.

Fields of interest: Housing/shelter; Disasters, Hurricane Katrina; Economically disadvantaged.
Publications: Application guidelines.
Application information: Application form required.
Initial approach: Use Preliminary Application form on foundation web site
Deadline(s): Telephone foundation for deadline
Officers and Directors:* Leonard Riggio,* Pres.; Louise Riggio,* Secy.; **Maria Florez, Treas.**; William Lynch; Carey C. Shea.
EIN: 208733214
Other changes: Maria Florez has replaced Lawrence Zilavy as Treas.

2369
Purple Plume Foundation
(formerly The Whitman-Carlyon Foundation)
240 West End Ave., Apt. 13CD
New York, NY **10023-3602**
Contact: Barbara Whitman, Tr.

Established in 2002 in NY.
Donors: David Carlyon; Barbara Whitman; Martin J. Whitman; Lois Whitman.
Foundation type: Independent foundation.
Financial data (yr. ended 12/31/12): Assets, $4,812,282 (M); expenditures, $118,738; qualifying distributions, $112,500; giving activities include $112,500 for grants.
Fields of interest: Performing arts; Higher education; Higher education, university; Human services.
Limitations: Applications not accepted. Giving primarily in IL, MI and NY. No grants to individuals.
Application information: Unsolicited requests for funds not accepted.
Trustee: Barbara Whitman.
EIN: 571144326
Other changes: David Carlyon is no longer trustee.

2370
The Stephen D. Quinn Foundation
c/o Marks Paneth and Shron LLP
685 3rd Ave., 4th Fl.
New York, NY 10017-6701

Established in 1993 in CT.
Donor: Stephen D. Quinn.
Foundation type: Independent foundation.
Financial data (yr. ended 07/31/13): Assets, $5,918,992 (M); gifts received, $7,213; expenditures, $319,635; qualifying distributions, $314,103; giving activities include $312,330 for 8 grants (high: $286,610; low: $500).
Purpose and activities: Giving primarily to The Church of Jesus Christ of Latter-day Saints; funding also for education and community development.
Fields of interest: Education; Community/economic development; Mormon agencies & churches.
Limitations: Applications not accepted. Giving primarily in UT. No grants to individuals.
Application information: Contributes only to pre-selected organizations.
Trustees: Cydney P. Quinn; Stephen D. Quinn.
EIN: 133789066

2371
F. Rachel Memorial Foundation
c/o Vitaly Pivtorak
3803 Atlantic Ave.
Brooklyn, NY 11224-1208

Established in 1999 in NY.
Donors: Vitaly Pivtorak; Yelena Pavlovsky; Olympia Trust; Pivtorak Family Trust.
Foundation type: Operating foundation.
Financial data (yr. ended 06/30/13): Assets, $8,407,140 (M); gifts received, $102,500; expenditures, $145,195; qualifying distributions, $4,403,811; giving activities include $140,220 for 15 grants (high: $30,900; low: $180).
Fields of interest: Jewish agencies & synagogues.
Limitations: Applications not accepted. No grants to individuals.
Application information: Unsolicited requests for funds not accepted.
Trustees: Yelena Pavlovsky; Vitaly Pivtorak.
EIN: 113498006

2372
Tony Randall Theatrical Fund, Inc.
Ansonia Sta.
P.O. Box 230460
New York, NY 10023-0008
Contact: Heather Randall, Pres.
***E-mail:* tonyrandallfund@gmail.com**; Main URL: http://www.TonyRandallTheatricalFund.org
Blog: http://www.tonyrandalltheatricalfund.org/news-and-updates
Facebook: https://www.facebook.com/tonyrandallfund
Grants List: http://www.tonyrandalltheatricalfund.org/grant-recipients

Established in 1981 in NY.
Donors: Anthony L. Randall†; and the Tony Randall Family.
Foundation type: Independent foundation.
Financial data (yr. ended 06/30/13): Assets, $3,732,439 (M); expenditures, $515,479; qualifying distributions, $346,855; giving activities include $287,650 for 32 grants (high: $62,700; low: $250).
Purpose and activities: Giving primarily to professional non-profit theater organizations in the tri-state area.
Fields of interest: Performing arts, theater; Arts.
Limitations: Applications not accepted. Giving primarily in the CT, NJ, NY tri-state area. No grants to individuals.
Publications: Grants list.
Application information: Contributes only to pre-selected organizations. Applications are currently by invitation only. Check fund web site for latest information.
Officers: Heather Randall, Chair. and Exec. Dir.; Kristie Ashton, V.P.; Scott Gildea, Treas.
Director: Leslie A. Newson.
EIN: 133082489

2373
The Rapoport Family Foundation
9 Barrow St., Apt. 4F
New York, NY 10014-3863 **(917) 226-2592**
Contact: Andrew Rapoport, Exec. Dir.
E-mail: rapoport66@gmail.com; Main URL: http://www.rapoportfamilyfoundation.org

Established in 1987 in NY.
Donor: Ida Rapoport†.
Foundation type: Independent foundation.
Financial data (yr. ended 12/31/12): Assets, $2,804,072 (M); expenditures, $200,369; qualifying distributions, $125,000; giving activities include $125,000 for 11 grants (high: $15,000; low: $10,000).
Purpose and activities: Giving primarily for the community in areas of social services, homeless care, transitional housing, and job outreach.
Fields of interest: Employment, services; Housing/shelter, services; Human services; Homeless.
Type of support: General/operating support; Continuing support; Income development; Management development/capacity building; Equipment; Emergency funds; Program development; Seed money; Technical assistance; Program evaluation; Matching/challenge support.
Limitations: Applications accepted. Giving primarily in Washington, DC. No support for religious organizations (except for those that offer social services) or artistic activities or for medical research. No grants to individuals and no funding for scholarships.
Publications: Application guidelines.
Application information: See foundation web site for complete application policies and guidelines. Application form not required.
Initial approach: Letter
Copies of proposal: 5
Deadline(s): Mar. 1 for June funding, and Sept. 1 for Dec. funding
Officer and Trustee:* Andrew Rapoport,* Pres and Exec. Dir.
Number of staff: 1 part-time professional.
EIN: 133369901
Other changes: Andrew Rapoport has replaced Daniel Rapoport as Pres.

2374
Aishel Rashbi
Brooklyn, NY

Status changed to Public Charity.

2375
V. Kann Rasmussen Foundation
475 Riverside Dr., Ste. 900
New York, NY 10115-0066 **(212) 812-4271**
Contact: Irene Krarup, Assoc. Dir.
FAX: (212) 812-4299; E-mail: ikrarup@vkrf.org; E-mail for Letters of Inquiry: grants@vkrf.org; Main URL: http://www.vkrf.org/

Established in 1991 in MA.
Donor: The Velux Trust.
Foundation type: Independent foundation.
Financial data (yr. ended 06/30/12): Assets, $79,256,505 (M); expenditures, $4,368,546; qualifying distributions, $3,804,562; giving activities include $2,942,955 for 37 grants (high: $500,000; low: $2,205), and $160,000 for 1 foundation-administered program.
Purpose and activities: Giving primarily for the environment. The foundation favors projects that: 1) take stock of the scale of the environmental problems, 2) use a systems approach to achieve change, 3) link policy, advocacy, and practical solution, 4) have international significance and perspective, even if U.S. based, and 5) are based on original thinking and creative ideas. The foundation currently only evaluates projects within the categories of: Ecosystems Resilience, Protection and Restoration, (research and tools of relevance to large scale geographic areas including many countries and continents; natural greenhouse gas sequestration and storage with large scale impact potential, and agro-biodiversity); Framework of Ecological Stability (economic models of living

within global limits and practical implementation of change to a stable global ecosystem, and sustainable production and land use); and Communication and Leadership (communicating value-based living with sustainable use of water, energy, and food resources, new innovative initiatives to enhance international cooperation and knowledge-sharing, and next generation leadership).
Fields of interest: Higher education; Environment, natural resources; Environment; Medical research, institute.
Type of support: General/operating support; Program development; Mission-related investments/loans.
Limitations: Applications accepted. Giving in the U.S., with emphasis on CA, CT, MA, NY, and Washington, DC. No support for general operations of well-established NGO programs, large membership organizations or networks, government organizations, established university research programs, or for organizations whose job it is to re-grant funding received. No grants to individuals, or for scholarships, candidates for political office, conservative projects focused on one single species, book, magazine, or web-based publishing, film, TV, radio, or video projects, medical research, health care, construction or endowment campaigns, U.S. projects with a specific local, state, or regional focus, non-US projects focused on single countries, regions, or specific continents, or for benefits or annual fundraising campaigns.
Publications: Application guidelines; Informational brochure; Occasional report.
Application information: Full proposals are by invitation only. See foundation web site for specific information regarding page restrictions for supplemental information. Application form not required.
Initial approach: Letter of inquiry (2 pages maximum), e-mail only
Copies of proposal: 1
Deadline(s): See foundation web site for current deadlines
Board meeting date(s): Mar./Apr. and Oct./Nov.
Final notification: 30 days or see foundation web site
Officer and Trustees:* Hans Kann Rasmussen,* Chair.; Lois E. H. Smith, Ph.D., M.D.*, Managing Dir.; Irene Krarup, Assoc. Dir.; Anne-Margrete Ogstrup-Pedersen; Astrid Kann Rasmussen; Kristian Kann Rasmussen.
EIN: 223101266

2376
Rauch Foundation
229 7th St., Ste. 306
Garden City, NY 11530-5766 (516) 873-9808
Contact: John McNally
FAX: (516) 873-0708;
E-mail: epitrelli@rauchfoundation.org**; Additional e-mail and e-mail for concept papers: info@rauchfoundation.org**; Main URL: http://www.rauchfoundation.org

Incorporated in 1960 in NY.
Donors: Philip Rauch†; Louis J. Rauch†; Ruth T. Rauch; Philip J. Rauch, Jr.; Nancy R. Douzinas.
Foundation type: Independent foundation.
Financial data (yr. ended 11/30/12): Assets, $77,017,634 (M); gifts received, $14,727,797; expenditures, $4,517,375; qualifying distributions, $4,075,324; giving activities include $2,871,495 for 83 grants (high: $300,000; low: $100).
Purpose and activities: The foundation's mission is to: 1) promote positive outcomes for young children, ages newborn to 6, with particular focus on those with a disadvantaged socio-economic start. The foundation's first priority is to support programs that facilitate systemic change for those children and their families; 2) to protect the environment and improve the quality of life on Long Island, NY, and in MD; and 3) to strengthen the organizational effectiveness of nonprofit institutions that work on these issues through capacity building and leadership development. The foundation focuses its work in the places where Rauch family members have lived and worked— Long Island, NY, and MD.
Fields of interest: Education, early childhood education; Environment; Family services; Community/economic development.
Type of support: General/operating support; Program development; Conferences/seminars; Seed money; Technical assistance; Consulting services; Program evaluation; Matching/challenge support.
Limitations: Applications accepted. Giving primarily in Nassau and Suffolk counties, NY; some giving also in MD. Generally, no grants to individuals, capital expenditures, or emergency funding.
Publications: Application guidelines; Grants list; Occasional report; Program policy statement.
Application information: If a full proposal is requested, applicants may follow the New York/New Jersey Common Application Form. The foundation requests that organizations not send videotapes. Application guidelines available on foundation web site. Application form not required.
Initial approach: Concept paper (no more than 3 pages)
Copies of proposal: 1
Deadline(s): None
Board meeting date(s): Feb., June, and Oct.
Final notification: Within 3 months
Officers and Trustees:* Nancy Rauch Douzinas,* Pres.; Philip J. Rauch, Jr.,* V.P.; **Ruth F. Douzinas**; George W. Frank; **Drew Halevy**; Lance E. Lindblom; Lisa Mars; **David Rauch**; John Trieber; Reginald Tuggle; **Eva D. Veson**; John Wenzel.
Number of staff: 4 full-time professional; 1 part-time professional; 2 full-time support.
EIN: 112001717
Other changes: Gerald I. Lustig and Ruth T. Rauch are no longer trustees.

2377
Regals Foundation
(formerly The Atticus Foundation)
c/o Regals Mgmt., LP
152 W. 57th St.
New York, NY **10019-3386** (212) 256-8489
Contact: David Slager, Managing Dir. and Tr.

Established in 1997 in NY.
Donors: Timothy R. Barakett; Nathaniel Rothschild; Atticus Capital LLC; Matthew J. Edmunds; David Slager; Dilan Siritunga.
Foundation type: Independent foundation.
Financial data (yr. ended 12/31/12): Assets, $1,059,604 (M); expenditures, $5,835,428; qualifying distributions, $5,823,234; giving activities include $5,818,891 for 24 grants (high: $2,280,000; low: $250).
Purpose and activities: Giving primarily for social services, education, health, and Jewish organizations and temples.
Fields of interest: Education; Hospitals (general); Health organizations, association; Medical research, institute; Human services; Children/youth, services; Foundations (private grantmaking); Jewish federated giving programs; Jewish agencies & synagogues.
Type of support: General/operating support.
Limitations: Giving primarily in NY. No grants to individuals.
Application information: Application form not required.
Initial approach: Letter
Deadline(s): None
Officer andTrustees:* David Slager,* Mgr. Dir.; Alexandra Toohey.
EIN: 133981257

2378
The Reich Fund
c/o Seymour Reich
640 Park Ave.
New York, NY 10065

Established in 1975 in NY.
Donor: Seymour Reich.
Foundation type: Independent foundation.
Financial data (yr. ended 10/31/13): Assets, $6,188,876 (M); expenditures, $303,866; qualifying distributions, $253,400; giving activities include $253,080 for 32 grants (high: $145,000; low: $100).
Purpose and activities: Giving primarily to Jewish agencies and temples; also support for educational institutions.
Fields of interest: Higher education; Human services; Jewish federated giving programs; Jewish agencies & synagogues.
Limitations: Applications not accepted. Giving primarily in NY. No grants to individuals.
Application information: Unsolicited requests for funds not accepted.
Trustees: Elizabeth Brimberg; Stanlee Brimberg; Lilian Reich; Seymour Reich.
EIN: 510166322
Other changes: Charles Reich is no longer a trustee.

2379
The Ira M. Resnick Foundation, Inc.
133 E. 58th St., Ste. 705
New York, NY 10022-1236
Contact: Ira M. Resnick, Pres.

Established in 1994 in NY.
Donor: Ira M. Resnick.
Foundation type: Independent foundation.
Financial data (yr. ended 05/31/13): Assets, $1,070,396 (M); gifts received, $1,000,000; expenditures, $1,025,415; qualifying distributions, $890,820; giving activities include $890,820 for grants.
Purpose and activities: Giving primarily for the arts, health associations, children, youth and social services, and to Jewish organizations.
Fields of interest: Museums; Performing arts; Arts; Education; Health organizations, association; Human services; Children/youth, services; Jewish agencies & synagogues.
Limitations: Applications not accepted. Giving primarily in NY.
Application information: Contributes only to pre-selected organizations.
Officers: Ira M. Resnick, Pres.; Gilbert A. Wang, Secy.-Treas.
Director: Paula S. Resnick.
EIN: 133775995
Other changes: The grantmaker no longer lists a phone.

2380
The Jack and Pearl Resnick Foundation
c/o Jack Resnick & Sons Inc.
110 E. 59th St., 37th Fl.
New York, NY 10022-1308

Established in 1989 in NY.
Donors: Jack Resnick; Pearl Resnick‡.
Foundation type: Independent foundation.
Financial data (yr. ended 03/31/13): Assets, $5,594,166 (M); expenditures, $247,878; qualifying distributions, $242,500; giving activities include $239,000 for 12 grants (high: $50,000; low: $10,000).
Purpose and activities: Giving primarily for higher education, including medical education and theology; support also for Jewish agencies.
Fields of interest: Media, film/video; Performing arts, orchestras; Medical school/education; Theological school/education; Jewish agencies & synagogues.
Limitations: Applications not accepted. Giving primarily in Palm Beach, FL and New York, NY. No grants to individuals.
Application information: Unsolicited requests for funds not accepted.
Officers and Directors:* Burton P. Resnick,* Pres.; Marilyn Katz,* V.P. and Secy.; Ira Resnick,* V.P.; Steven J. Rotter.
EIN: 133579145
Other changes: The grantmaker no longer lists a phone.

2381
Lawrence I. & Blanche H. Rhodes Memorial Fund
P.O. Box 7
Wynantskill, NY 12198-0007

Established in 1994 in NY.
Foundation type: Independent foundation.
Financial data (yr. ended 07/31/12): Assets, $1,886,113 (M); expenditures, $210,485; qualifying distributions, $167,656; giving activities include $150,000 for 50 grants (high: $15,000; low: $500).
Purpose and activities: Giving primarily for education and religious organizations.
Fields of interest: Historical activities; Higher education; Dental school/education; Scholarships/financial aid; Education; Health organizations, association; Christian agencies & churches.
Limitations: Applications not accepted. Giving primarily in NY and PA. No grants to individuals.
Application information: Contributes only to pre-selected organizations.
Officers: William J. Dwyer, Pres.; Peter Loomis, Exec. V.P.; **John Smirich, V.P.**; Fred Eckel, Secy.; Barbara Egnot, Treas.; Dennis Marr, Exec. Dir.
EIN: 222159155

2382
Rich Family Foundation
(formerly Rich Foundation)
P.O. Box 245
Buffalo, NY 14240-0245
***Contact:* Robert E. Rich, Jr., Chair.**

Established in 1961.
Donors: Rich Products Corp.; Robert E. Rich, Sr.‡.
Foundation type: Company-sponsored foundation.
Financial data (yr. ended 12/31/12): Assets, $6,693,947 (M); gifts received, $2,200,000; expenditures, $1,284,086; qualifying distributions, $1,269,533; giving activities include $1,254,980 for 97 grants (high: $125,000; low: $100).
Purpose and activities: The foundation supports organizations involved with performing arts, education, health, cancer research, fishing, and business and industry.
Fields of interest: Education; Health care; Human services.
Type of support: General/operating support; Continuing support; Annual campaigns; Sponsorships.
Limitations: Applications accepted. Giving primarily in FL and Buffalo and Cheektowaga, NY.
Application information: Application form required.
***Initial approach:* Letter**
Deadline(s): None
Officers: Robert E. Rich, Jr., Chair.; Melinda Rich, Pres.; **Mary Pat O'Connor, Secy. and Exec. Dir.**; Joseph W. Segarra, Treas.
EIN: 166026199
Other changes: Mary Pat O'Connor is now Secy. and Exec. Dir.

2383
The Rieger Charitable Foundation Trust
c/o Abraham Rieger, Meron Mgmt.
1846 50th St.
Brooklyn, NY 11204-1252 (718) 436-2326

Established in 1998 in NY.
Donors: Abraham Jacob Rieger; Rachel Rieger; A & E Trust; Triangle Trust.
Foundation type: Independent foundation.
Financial data (yr. ended 12/31/12): Assets, $2,118,695 (M); gifts received, $600,000; expenditures, $663,747; qualifying distributions, $663,050; giving activities include $663,050 for 26 grants (high: $297,000; low: $250).
Purpose and activities: Giving primarily to Jewish agencies, temples, and schools.
Fields of interest: Elementary/secondary education; Jewish agencies & synagogues.
Limitations: Giving primarily in Brooklyn, NY.
Application information: Application form not required.
***Initial approach:* Letter**
Deadline(s): None
Directors: Abraham Rieger; David Rieger; Rachel Rieger.
EIN: 116508164

2384
The Ring Foundation, Inc.
212 5th Ave.
New York, NY 10010-2103

Established in 1979 in NY.
Donors: Frank Ring; Leo Ring; Michael Ring; Freda Ring.
Foundation type: Independent foundation.
Financial data (yr. ended 05/31/13): Assets, $4,979,210 (M); gifts received, $9,000; expenditures, $329,763; qualifying distributions, $322,454; giving activities include $322,454 for 24 grants (high: $201,250; low: $50).
Purpose and activities: Support for Jewish religious, cultural, and educational institutions.
Fields of interest: Elementary/secondary education; Higher education; Hospitals (general); Human services; Jewish federated giving programs; Jewish agencies & synagogues.
Type of support: Building/renovation.
Limitations: Applications not accepted. Giving primarily in NY. No grants to individuals.
Application information: Unsolicited requests for funds not considered.
Officers: Frank Ring, Pres.; Michael Ring, Secy.; **Louise Ring, Treas.**
EIN: 133015418

2385
Rivendell Foundation
c/o The Philanthropic Group
630 5th Ave., 20th Fl.
New York, NY 10111-0100 (212) 501-7785
Contact: Barbara R. Greenberg, Fdn. Advisor
FAX: (212) 501-7788;
E-mail: BGreenberg@philanthropicgroup.com; **Main URL: http://fdnweb.org/rivendell**
Grants List: http://fdnweb.org/rivendell/grants-approved/

Established in 1987 in NJ.
Donor: Kenneth J. Goldman.
Foundation type: Independent foundation.
Financial data (yr. ended 12/31/12): Assets, $100,078 (M); gifts received, $195,160; expenditures, $224,352; qualifying distributions, $177,700; giving activities include $177,700 for 11 grants (high: $25,000; low: $10,000).
Purpose and activities: Giving primarily for out-of-school time programming for Newark, NJ, children and youth, and international human rights.
Fields of interest: Neighborhood centers; International human rights; Children/youth.
Type of support: Program development.
Limitations: Applications not accepted. Giving primarily in NJ and NY. No grants to individuals.
Publications: Grants list.
Application information: The foundation considers proposals by invitation only.
Board meeting date(s): 3 times per year
Trustee: Kenneth J. Goldman.
Advisor: Barbara R. Greenberg.
EIN: 222876727

2386
Robbins Foundation
(formerly Larry Robbins Foundation)
c/o Glenview Capital Mgmt.
767 5th Ave., 44th Fl.
New York, NY 10153-0023

Established in 2008 in NY.
Donors: Lawrence Robbins; Mercury Foundation of New York.
Foundation type: Independent foundation.
Financial data (yr. ended 12/31/12): Assets, $47,421,857 (M); gifts received, $130,000; expenditures, $8,167,110; qualifying distributions, $8,104,735; giving activities include $8,053,122 for 38 grants (high: $3,787,500; low: $100).
Fields of interest: Museums (ethnic/folk arts); Education; Hospitals (specialty); Cancer research; Youth development; Jewish federated giving programs.
Limitations: Applications not accepted. Giving primarily in Chicago, IL and New York, NY.
Application information: Contributes only to pre-selected organizations.
Trustee: Lawrence Robbins.
EIN: 261578481

2387
Robinson-Broadhurst Foundation, Inc.
c/o Diane E. Frazee
101 Main St.
P.O. Box 160
Stamford, NY 12167-1140 (607) 652-2508
Contact: Charles K. McKenzie, Pres. and Exec. Dir.
FAX: (607) 652-2453; E-mail: rbfi@stny.rr.com; Main URL: http://www.robinsonbroadhurstfoundationinc.com/

Established in 1984 in NY.
Donors: Anna Broadhurst†; R. Avery Robinson†; Winnie M. Robinson†.
Foundation type: Independent foundation.
Financial data (yr. ended 04/30/13): Assets, $50,643,559 (M); expenditures, $2,717,376; qualifying distributions, $2,328,752; giving activities include $2,128,396 for 94 grants (high: $227,800; low: $600).
Purpose and activities: Giving primarily for local community services.
Fields of interest: Arts; Health care; Community/economic development; Government/public administration.
Type of support: Building/renovation; Equipment; Scholarship funds; Matching/challenge support.
Limitations: Applications accepted. Giving limited to Winchendon, MA; and Stamford and Worcester, NY. No grants to individuals, or for annual operating expenditures or debt reduction.
Publications: Application guidelines; Informational brochure.
Application information: Application form available on foundation web site. Application form required.
Deadline(s): Dec. 31
Board meeting date(s): May
Officers and Trustees:* Charles "Lad" McKenzie,* Pres. and Exec. Dir.; Ralph Beisler,* V.P. and Secy.; Ernest "Bud" Fletcher, Jr.,* Treas.; Martin "Skip" Parks; **Donald VanEtten.**
Number of staff: 1 full-time professional; 1 full-time support.
EIN: 222558699

2388
Edward & Ellen Roche Relief Foundation
c/o U.S. Trust, Philanthropic Solutions
1 Bryant Park, NY1-100-28-05
New York, NY 10036-6715 (646) 743-0425
Contact: Sara Rosen, V.P.
E-mail: sara.rosen@ustrust.com; **Main URL: https://www.bankofamerica.com/philanthropic/grantmaking.go**

Established in 1953.
Donor: Edward Roche†.
Foundation type: Independent foundation.
Financial data (yr. ended 12/31/12): Assets, $4,829,443 (M); expenditures, $279,740; qualifying distributions, $238,594; giving activities include $215,000 for 16 grants (high: $20,000; low: $10,000).
Purpose and activities: The Foundation funds organizations that have a proven track record serving disadvantaged women and youth. Recognizing the diverse array of programs that serve disadvantaged women and youth, the Foundation has chosen to focus its limited resources on projects that address one or more of the following (in no particular order): 1) housing needs of women and families, 2) economic security of low-income women, 3) violence against women, and 4) child welfare.
Fields of interest: Education, early childhood education; Child development, education; Elementary school/education; Health care; Human services; Children/youth, services; Child development, services; Women, centers/services; Minorities; Women; Economically disadvantaged.
Type of support: General/operating support; Program development; Seed money.
Limitations: Giving limited to New York City. Generally, no support for individual schools, after-school programs or childcare centers, organizations with annual budgets in excess of $10 million, or organizations that receive more than 75% of annual revenue from government contracts. Generally, no support for health care or disabilities, for endowment campaigns, capital projects, or research.
Publications: Application guidelines; Financial statement; Program policy statement.
Application information: Complete application guidelines are available on foundation web site.
Initial approach: Online through foundation web site
Deadline(s): July 31
Final notification: Dec. 31
Trustee: Bank of America, N.A.
EIN: 135622067

2389
Rockefeller Brothers Fund, Inc.
475 Riverside Dr., Ste. 900
New York, NY 10115-0066 (212) 812-4200
Contact: Hope Lyons, Program Mgmt.
FAX: (212) 812-4299; E-mail: grantsmgmt@rbf.org; Main URL: http://www.rbf.org
CEP Study: http://www.rbf.org/resource/2010-grantee-and-applicant-perception-reports
David Rockefeller's Giving Pledge Profile: http://glasspockets.org/philanthropy-in-focus/eye-on-the-giving-pledge/profiles/rockefeller
E-Newsletter: http://rbf.us1.list-manage.com/subscribe/post?u=8ced17726d46f75e118db9da7&id=2a6d5fa7b5
Facebook: http://www.facebook.com/pages/Rockefeller-Brothers-Fund/181125435234193
Grants Database: http://www.rbf.org/content/grants-search
Knowledge Center: http://www.rbf.org/news-and-resources
Twitter: http://twitter.com/rockbrosfund/
YouTube: http://www.youtube.com/user/RBFCommunications

Incorporated in 1940 in NY.
Donors: John D. Rockefeller, Jr.†; Martha Baird Rockefeller†; Abby Rockefeller Mauze†; David Rockefeller; John D. Rockefeller III†; Laurance S. Rockefeller†; Nelson A. Rockefeller†; Winthrop Rockefeller†.
Foundation type: Independent foundation.
Financial data (yr. ended 12/31/12): Assets, $800,956,943 (M); gifts received, $8,780,173; expenditures, $49,104,873; qualifying distributions, $42,416,766; giving activities include $29,039,864 for 373 grants (high: $540,000; low: $1,100), $57,619 for 148 employee matching gifts, and $4,651,902 for 3 foundation-administered programs.
Purpose and activities: The Rockefeller Brothers Fund promotes social change that contributes to a more just, sustainable, and peaceful world. Through its grantmaking, the Fund supports efforts to expand knowledge, clarify values and critical choices, nurture creative expression, and shape public policy. The Fund's programs are intended to develop leaders, strengthen institutions, engage citizens, build community, and foster partnerships that include government, business, and civil society. Respect for cultural diversity and ecological integrity pervades the Fund's activities.
Fields of interest: Arts, cultural/ethnic awareness; Arts; Environment, climate change/global warming; Environment, natural resources; Environment; International peace/security.
International interests: Kosovo; China; Montenegro; Serbia.
Type of support: General/operating support; Program development; Conferences/seminars; Seed money; Technical assistance; Consulting services; Employee matching gifts; Matching/challenge support; Mission-related investments/loans.
Limitations: Applications accepted. Giving primarily in the United States and internationally, with an emphasis on three pivotal places: New York City, Southern China and the Western Balkans. No grants to individuals, or for land acquisitions or building funds.
Publications: Annual report; Grants list; Occasional report; IRS Form 990 or 990-PF printed copy available upon request.
Application information: Application guidelines available on foundation web site.
Initial approach: Online letter of inquiry and preliminary grant compatibility quiz. For Pivotal Place: New York City Arts and Culture Grants use online application
Deadline(s): See foundation web site
Board meeting date(s): Mar., June, and Nov.
Final notification: 3 months
Officers and Trustees:* Valerie Rockefeller Wayne,* Chair.; Joseph A. Pierson,* Vice-Chair.; Stephen B. Heintz,* Pres.; Elizabeth C. Campbell, V.P., Progs.; Geraldine F. Watson, V.P., Opers. and Finance; Nancy L. Muirhead, Corp. Secy.; David Rockefeller, Advisory Tr.; Anne Bartley; Nicholas Burns; Wendy Gordon; Miranda M. Kaiser; Daniel Levy; Vali Nasr; Peter M. O'Neill; Timothy O'Neill; Wendy O'Neill; Kavita Ramdas; Justin Rockefeller; Steven C. Rockefeller; Arlene Shuler; Marsha Simms.
Number of staff: 19 full-time professional; 28 full-time support.
EIN: 131760106
Other changes: Valerie Rockefeller Wayne has replaced Richard Rockefeller as Chair. Joseph A. Pierson has replaced Valeri Rockefeller Wayne as Vice-Chair.
Richard G. Rockefeller, Advisory Trustee, is deceased. James E. Moltz and James Gustave Speth are no longer trustees. Jonathan F. Fanton, William H. Luers and Robert B. Oxnam are no longer advisory trustees.

2390
The Rockefeller Foundation
420 5th Ave.
New York, NY 10018-2702 (212) 869-8500
Main URL: http://www.rockefellerfoundation.org/
Centennial Innovation Challenge: http://challenge.rockefellerfoundation.org/
E-Newsletter: http://www.rockefellerfoundation.org/sign-up
Facebook: http://www.facebook.com/rockefellerfoundation
Grants Database: http://www.rockefellerfoundation.org/grants/search
Multimedia: http://www.rockefellerfoundation.org/news/multimedia
RSS Feed: http://www.rockefellerfoundation.org/rockfound.xml
Twitter: https://twitter.com/RockefellerFdn

YouTube: http://www.youtube.com/RockefellerFound

Incorporated in 1913 in NY.
Donor: John D. Rockefeller, Sr.‡.
Foundation type: Independent foundation.
Financial data (yr. ended 12/31/12): Assets, $3,695,617,868 (M); expenditures, $203,195,149; qualifying distributions, $183,007,418; giving activities include $128,785,586 for 634 grants (high: $5,000,000; low: $1,000), $196,989 for 8 grants to individuals (high: $50,000; low: $11,400), $1,674,474 for 350 employee matching gifts, $4,425,698 for 1 foundation-administered program and $3,557,463 for 7 loans/program-related investments (high: $2,000,000; low: $20,132).
Purpose and activities: Operating both within the United States and around the world, the Rockefeller Foundation supports work that expands opportunity and strengthens resilience to social, economic, health and environmental challenges, affirming its pioneering philanthropic mission since 1913 to "promote the well-being" of humanity.
Fields of interest: Environment, climate change/global warming; Health care; International economic development; Community/economic development.
International interests: Global Programs.
Type of support: General/operating support; Continuing support; Program development; Conferences/seminars; Publication; Seed money; Curriculum development; Fellowships; Research; Technical assistance; Program-related investments/loans; Employee matching gifts; Scholarships—to individuals.
Limitations: Applications accepted. Giving primarily in New York City, Africa, North America, and Southeast Asia. No grants to individuals for personal aid, or, except in rare cases, for endowment funds or building or operating funds.
Publications: Annual report (including application guidelines); Financial statement; Grants list.
Application information: Organizations submitting inquiries that foundation staff thinks might contribute to a defined area of work will be asked to submit a full proposal. Please do not send a proposal by mail or e-mail unless invited to do so. See foundation web site for the Ballagio Center application information. Application form not required.
Initial approach: Online funding inquiry form
Copies of proposal: 1
Deadline(s): April 1 for Centennial Innovation Challenge
Board meeting date(s): Apr., Aug., and Dec.
Final notification: 6 to 8 weeks
Officers and Trustees:* David Rockefeller, Jr.,* Chair.; Dr. Judith Rodin,* Pres.; Peter Madonia, C.O.O.; Neill Coleman, V.P., Global Communications; Zia Khan, V.P., Initiatives and Strategy; Shari L. Patrick, Genl. Counsel and Corp. Secy.; Ellen Taus, C.F.O. and Treas.; Donna Dean, C.I.O.; Dominick Impemba, Cont.; Ann M. Fudge; Helene D. Gayle; Alice S. Huang; Martin L. Leibowitz; Yifei Li; Monica Lozano; Strive Masiyiwa; Diana Natalicio; Dr. Ngozi Okonjo-Iweala; Richard D. Parsons; John W. Rowe; **Ravi Venkatesan.**
Number of staff: 171 full-time professional; 2 part-time professional.
EIN: 131659629
Other changes: Heather Grady is no longer V.P., Fdn. Initiatives. Surin Pitsuwan is no longer a trustee. Thomas J. Healey and Sandra Day O'Connor are no trustees.

2391
The Roothbert Fund Inc.
475 Riverside Dr., Rm. 1830
New York, NY 10115-0107 (212) 870-3116
***E-mail:* mail@roothbertfund.org**; Main URL: http://www.roothbertfund.org

Incorporated in 1958 in NY.
Donors: Albert Roothbert‡; Toni Roothbert‡.
Foundation type: Independent foundation.
Financial data (yr. ended 12/31/12): Assets, $4,328,202 (M); gifts received, $3,625; expenditures, $224,746; qualifying distributions, $204,750; giving activities include $145,000 for 50 grants to individuals (high: $4,000; low: $1,500).
Purpose and activities: To assist college or university students who are motivated by spiritual values and have shown distinguished academic achievement, with preference to those considering teaching as a vocation.
Fields of interest: Teacher school/education; Scholarships/financial aid.
Type of support: Scholarship funds.
Limitations: Applications accepted. Giving primarily in the ME to NC corridor, with emphasis on those areas in reasonable commutation distances of New Haven, CT, Washington, DC, New York, NY, and Philadelphia, PA. No grants to individuals directly, or for capital funds, endowment funds, operating budgets, general support, special projects, or matching gifts; no loans.
Publications: Application guidelines; Annual report; Informational brochure.
Application information: Interview with Scholarship Committee is a requirement in the application process; interviews take place in Mar., normally in New York, NY, Washington, DC, Philadelphia, PA, and New Haven, CT. Application form required.
Initial approach: Letter with SASE requesting application after Nov. 1
Copies of proposal: 1
Deadline(s): Submit fund form between Nov. 1 and Jan. 31; deadline Feb. 1
Board meeting date(s): Apr. and Oct.; awards grants annually in Apr.
Final notification: Apr.
Officers and Directors:* Blake T. Newton III,* Pres.; Charles Van Horne,* V.P. and Treas.; Jane Friedman Century,* V.P.; Leonisa Ardizzone; John P. Devlin; Barbara A. Edwards; James G. Heinegg; Donna M. Johnson; Mark Overmyer-Velazquez; Jeffrey K. Pegram; James A. Rosengarten; Vijay R. Varma; Nathalis W. Wamba; Stephen F. Wilder.
Number of staff: 1 part-time professional.
EIN: 136162570

2392
Rose & Kiernan Charitable Foundation, Inc.
99 Troy Rd.
East Greenbush, NY 12061-1027 (518) 244-4245
Contact: Joseph F. Vitale, Dir.
***Main URL:* http://www.rkinsurance.com/Site/384000384/531283200.asp**

Established in 2001 in NY.
Donor: Rose & Kiernan, Inc.
Foundation type: Company-sponsored foundation.
Financial data (yr. ended 12/31/12): Assets, $2,006,540 (M); gifts received, $248,052; expenditures, $153,147; qualifying distributions, $152,495; giving activities include $149,295 for 83 grants (high: $15,000; low: $25).
Purpose and activities: The foundation supports organizations involved with higher education, health, cerebral palsy, and human services.
Fields of interest: Higher education; Hospitals (general); Health care, clinics/centers; Health care; Cerebral palsy; YM/YWCAs & YM/YWHAs; Children/youth, services; Family services; Developmentally disabled, centers & services; Human services; United Ways and Federated Giving Programs.
Type of support: Program development; Scholarship funds; General/operating support.
Limitations: Applications accepted. Giving primarily in areas of company operations in upstate NY.
Application information: Application form required.
Initial approach: Letter
Deadline(s): None
Directors: John F. Murray, Jr.; Joseph F. Vitale; Charles R. Daniels III; Mark C. Nickel.
EIN: 141831866

2393
The Deborah Rose Foundation
200 Madison Ave., 5th Fl.
New York, NY 10016-3912

Established in 1999 in DE.
Donors: Deborah Rose; Sandra P. Rose.
Foundation type: Independent foundation.
Financial data (yr. ended 12/31/12): Assets, $5,849,314 (M); gifts received, $4,648,200; expenditures, $3,972,439; qualifying distributions, $3,933,439; giving activities include $3,933,439 for 41 grants (high: $1,000,000; low: $5,000).
Purpose and activities: Giving primarily for higher education; funding also for human services, and to a scientific research organization.
Fields of interest: Higher education; Education; Human services; Science, research.
Limitations: Applications not accepted. Giving primarily in CT and Washington, DC, and MA. No grants to individuals.
Application information: Contributes only to pre-selected organizations.
Officers and Director:* Deborah Rose,* Pres. and Treas.; John A. Gacinski, Secy.
EIN: 134088811
Other changes: At the close of 2012, the grantmaker paid grants of $3,933,439, a 101.5% increase over the 2011 disbursements, $1,951,852.

2394
The Kim and Ralph Rosenberg Foundation
Bowling Green Sta.
P.O. Box 73
New York, NY 10274-0073

Established in 1999 in NY.
Donor: Ralph Rosenberg.
Foundation type: Independent foundation.
Financial data (yr. ended 10/31/13): Assets, $458 (M); gifts received, $2,720; expenditures, $3,390; qualifying distributions, $0.
Fields of interest: Arts; Higher education; Education; Health care; Human services.
Limitations: Applications not accepted. Giving primarily in NY and RI. No grants to individuals; no loans or scholarships.
Application information: Unsolicited requests for funds not accepted.
Trustees: Kim Rosenberg; Ralph Rosenberg.
EIN: 134052243
Other changes: Stuart Rothenberg is no longer a trustee.

2395
Barbara & William Rosenthal Family Foundation
1 Court Sq., 19th Fl.
Long Island City, NY **11120**

Established in 1998 in NY.
Donors: Dr. William Rosenthal; Mrs. William Rosenthal; Barbara Bakwin Rosenthal Trust; Edward Morris Bakwin.
Foundation type: Independent foundation.
Financial data (yr. ended 06/30/13): Assets, $6,889,829 (M); gifts received, $355,865; expenditures, $332,788; qualifying distributions, $305,375; giving activities include $275,000 for 11 grants (high: $75,000; low: $5,000).
Fields of interest: Education; Hospitals (general); Autism; Recreation; Women, centers/services; Military/veterans' organizations.
Limitations: Applications not accepted. Giving primarily in New York, NY. No grants to individuals.
Application information: Unsolicited requests for funds not accepted.
Trustee: Citibank, N.A.
EIN: 226753977

2396
The Dorothea Haus Ross Foundation
1036 Monroe Ave.
Rochester, NY 14620-1725 (585) 473-6006
Contact: Wayne S. Cook, Fdn. Exec.
FAX: (585) 473-6007;
E-mail: rossfoundation@frontiernet.net; Main URL: http://www.dhrossfoundation.org

Established in 1979 in NY.
Donor: Dorothea Haus Ross‡.
Foundation type: Independent foundation.
Financial data (yr. ended 12/31/12): Assets, $15,826,951 (M); expenditures, $833,392; qualifying distributions, $734,051; giving activities include $458,420 for 48 grants (high: $16,000; low: $1,000).
Purpose and activities: Giving to advance the moral, mental, and physical well-being of children of all races and creeds in all parts of the world; and to aid and assist in providing for the basic needs of food, shelter, and education of such children by whatever means and methods necessary or advisable. The foundation provides direct aid and assistance to vulnerable children between the ages of 0-18, including those who are ill, orphaned, disabled, injured, disfigured, abused and malnourished or have limited access to education.
Fields of interest: Child development, education; Medical care, rehabilitation; Health care; Health organizations, association; Pediatrics; Children/youth, services; Child development, services; Infants/toddlers; Children/youth; Children; Youth; Physically disabled; Blind/visually impaired; Deaf/hearing impaired; Mentally disabled; Native Americans/American Indians; Girls; Boys; Economically disadvantaged.
Type of support: Building/renovation; Equipment; Emergency funds; Program development; Publication; Seed money; Matching/challenge support.
Limitations: Applications accepted. **Giving on a national and international basis (with the following exceptions: Burma, Cuba, Liberia, Libya, North Korea, Sierra Leone, Somalia, Sudan, Nigeria and Zimbabwe). Non-U.S. charities must find a U.S. charity or a Religious Order located near them that has a U.S. affiliate office. No support for day care or public education in America, or to non-U.S. countries where there is war, widespread violence, or where a breakdown of law and order exists or is probable, or to non-U.S. countries where grants are prohibited by the U.S. Department of the Treasury as listed in the Office of Foreign Assets Control Program Summary (OFAC).** No grants to individuals, or for operating budgets, continuing support, annual campaigns, deficit financing, conferences, or fellowships; no loans.
Publications: Application guidelines; Annual report; Grants list.
Application information: Grant proposals are by invitation only, upon review of letter of inquiry. See foundation web site for guidelines. The foundation is less interested in larger projects or capital campaigns that are better left to larger foundations and organizations. Water projects are limited to schools, orphanages and medical centers where children predominate. Organizations applying to the foundation from outside the U.S. should call or e-mail the office for further instructions, or to clarify if whether or not grants are permissible in their country under U.S. law. Application form not required.
Initial approach: **1-2 page letter of inquiry via mail, fax, or e-mail**
Deadline(s): None
Board meeting date(s): Feb., May, Aug., and Nov.
Final notification: Within 3 weeks for letters of inquiry
Officer and Trustees:* Wayne S. Cook, Ph.D.*, Fdn. Exec.; Charles C. Chamberlain; Kathryn C. Chamberlain; Edward C. Radin; Bank of America, N.A.
Number of staff: 1 full-time professional; 1 part-time support.
EIN: 161080458

2397
The Maks & Lea Rothstein Charitable Youth Trust
535 W. 110th St.
New York, NY 10025-2086

Established in 2002.
Donor: Maks Rothstein.
Foundation type: Operating foundation.
Financial data (yr. ended 12/31/12): Assets, $7,694,998 (M); expenditures, $358,165; qualifying distributions, $333,931; giving activities include $258,750 for 55 grants (high: $40,000; low: $1,800).
Fields of interest: Higher education, university; Education; Children/youth, services; Jewish agencies & synagogues.
Type of support: General/operating support.
Limitations: Applications not accepted. No grants to individuals.
Application information: Contributes only to pre-selected organizations.
Officer: Sergio Rothstein, Chair.
EIN: 316652819
Other changes: Maks Rothstein is no longer Pres.

2398
Samuel Rubin Foundation, Inc.
777 United Nations Plz.
New York, NY 10017-3521 (212) 697-8945
Contact: Lauranne Jones, Grants Admin.
FAX: (212) 682-0886;
E-mail: joneslauranne@gmail.com; Main URL: http://www.samuelrubinfoundation.org

Established in 1958 in NY.
Donors: Samuel Rubin‡; Samuel Rubin Foundation, Inc.
Foundation type: Independent foundation.
Financial data (yr. ended 06/30/13): Assets, $11,609,544 (M); expenditures, $847,966; qualifying distributions, $738,987; giving activities include $603,500 for 46 grants (high: $100,000; low: $500).
Purpose and activities: Grants for the pursuit of peace and justice; for an equitable reallocation of the world's resources; and to promote social, economic, political, civil, and cultural rights.
Fields of interest: Higher education; International peace/security; International affairs, arms control; International affairs, foreign policy; International human rights; Civil/human rights; Women.
Type of support: Film/video/radio; General/operating support; Seed money.
Limitations: Applications accepted. Giving on a national and international basis. No grants to individuals, or for endowments, scholarships, or building funds.
Publications: Grants list; Program policy statement.
Application information: Applications sent by e-mail or fax will not be accepted, nor will telephone solicitations. **Application form not required.**
Initial approach: **Proposal (no more than 5 pages)**
Deadline(s): First Fri. in Jan., May, and Sept.
Board meeting date(s): 3 times per year; generally at the end of Feb., June, and Oct.
Final notification: 2 weeks following board meetings
Officers: Cora Weiss, Pres.; Judy Weiss, V.P.; Peter Weiss, Treas.
Directors: Alison R. Bernstein; Daniel Weiss; Tamara Weiss.
Number of staff: 2 full-time professional.
EIN: 136164671

2399
The Shelley & Donald Rubin Foundation, Inc.
17 W. 17th St., 9th Fl.
New York, NY 10011-5510 (646) 839-5911
FAX: (212) 645-3206; E-mail: info@sdrubin.org; Main URL: http://www.sdrubin.org
Grants Database: http://www.sdrubin.org/grants

Established in 1991 in NY.
Donors: Suman Jain; Donald Rubin; Shelley Rubin; Global Leadership Foundation.
Foundation type: Independent foundation.
Financial data (yr. ended 06/30/12): Assets, $13,157,837 (M); gifts received, $55,000; expenditures, $5,821,983; qualifying distributions, $5,770,095; giving activities include $3,244,721 for 18 grants (high: $3,240,521; low: $50).
Purpose and activities: Giving primarily to arts and culture, with a strong commitment to Himalayan art; health and human services; and civil liberty and social justice.
Fields of interest: Arts, cultural/ethnic awareness; Museums (ethnic/folk arts); Arts; Higher education; Adult education—literacy, basic skills & GED; Education; Environment; Children.
Limitations: Giving primarily in the New York City metropolitan area and Himalayan region. No grants to individuals, or for fundraising activities, capital funds, direct services, operating support, scholarships, fellowships, building funds, endowment funds, or for the delivery of direct services.
Publications: Application guidelines.
Application information: The range of funding is between $5,000-$10,000 maximum. The

foundation's grants to educational institutions are for direct program expenses only. No part of such a grant can be used for overhead or indirect costs. Application form not required.
Initial approach: Letter of intent via e-mail
Copies of proposal: 1
Deadline(s): None
Board meeting date(s): Quarterly
Final notification: Within 90 days
Officer and Directors:* **Donald Rubin,*** **Pres. and Exec. Dir.**; Shelley Rubin; Harvey Sigelbaum.
Number of staff: 3 part-time professional.
EIN: 133639542
Other changes: Donald Rubin is now Pres. and Exec. Dir.

2400
Peter B. & Adeline W. Ruffin Foundation, Inc.

1192 Park Ave., Ste. 14A
New York, NY 10128-1314
Contact: Edward G. McAnaney, Pres.

Established in 1964 in NY.
Foundation type: Independent foundation.
Financial data (yr. ended 11/30/13): Assets, $27,656,717 (M); expenditures, $2,512,346; qualifying distributions, $2,260,885; giving activities include $2,251,000 for 66 grants (high: $600,000; low: $500).
Purpose and activities: Support for minority scholarship funds.
Fields of interest: Secondary school/education; Higher education; Education; Human services; Youth; Minorities; Native Americans/American Indians; Economically disadvantaged.
Type of support: Annual campaigns; General/operating support; Capital campaigns; Endowments; Professorships; Scholarship funds.
Limitations: Applications not accepted. Giving primarily in CT, Washington, DC, NJ, NY, PA, and VA. No grants to individuals.
Publications: Annual report.
Application information: Contributes only to pre-selected organizations.
Officer and Trustees:* Edward G. McAnaney,* Pres., Treas., and Mgr.; Sheila K. Kostanecki; Brian T. McAnaney; Kevin G. McAnaney.
Number of staff: 1 part-time professional.
EIN: 136170484
Other changes: For the fiscal year ended Nov. 30, 2013, the grantmaker paid grants of $2,251,000, a 63.8% increase over the fiscal 2012 disbursements, $1,374,500.

2401
S & W Foundation, Inc.

1570 46th St.
Brooklyn, NY 11219-2725 (718) 436-1682
Contact: Abraham Weingarten, Treas.

Established in 2001 in NY.
Donors: David Weingarten; Fay Weingarten; LSM Management; Bernat Steinmetz; Pessie Richard; Sara Cohen.
Foundation type: Independent foundation.
Financial data (yr. ended 06/30/13): Assets, $4,125,546 (M); gifts received, $70,000; expenditures, $98,630; qualifying distributions, $98,400; giving activities include $98,400 for 50 grants (high: $26,000; low: $150).
Fields of interest: Jewish agencies & synagogues.
Limitations: Applications accepted. Giving primarily in NY. No grants to individuals.
Application information: Application form not required.
Initial approach: **Proposal**
Deadline(s): None
Officers: Bernat Steinmetz, Pres.; Fay Weingarten, V.P. and Secy.; Abraham Weingarten, Treas.
EIN: 311732883

2402
Russell Sage Foundation

112 E. 64th St.
New York, NY 10065-7307
Contact: Christopher Brogna, C.F.O.
FAX: (212) 371-4761; E-mail: info@rsage.org; Main URL: http://www.russellsage.org
Blog: http://www.russellsage.org/blog
Facebook: https://www.facebook.com/russellsagefoundation
Twitter: http://www.twitter.com/russellsagefdn
YouTube: http://www.youtube.com/user/RussellSageFdn?feature=mhee

Incorporated in 1907 in NY.
Donor: Mrs. Russell Sage†.
Foundation type: Operating foundation.
Financial data (yr. ended 08/31/13): Assets, $279,298,445 (M); expenditures, $12,911,260; qualifying distributions, $11,342,604; giving activities include $3,614,910 for 70 grants (high: $338,223; low: $429), and $10,483,123 for foundation-administered programs.
Purpose and activities: The foundation is a private operating foundation devoted exclusively to the conduct and dissemination of research in the social sciences. Its current programs include research on the causes and consequences of the decline in demand for low-skilled workers in advanced economies; the adaptation of U.S. immigrants and their children to American society; the social effects of rising economic inequality, efforts by American institutions to accommodate greater racial and ethnic diversity; and a variety of smaller special projects and research initiatives. The foundation sponsors a Visiting Scholar Program in which individual scholars and collaborative groups pursue research and writing projects related to the foundation's interests at its headquarters in New York City for periods of up to one year. The foundation also provides support for scholars at other institutions to pursue research projects that advance the foundation's research interests. The foundation disseminates the resulting research findings through its own book publishing program.
Fields of interest: Social sciences.
Type of support: Program development; Conferences/seminars; Publication; Research; Employee matching gifts.
Limitations: Applications accepted. Giving on a national basis. No grants for capital or endowment funds, independent ongoing activities of other institutions, scholarships, annual campaigns, emergency funds, deficit financing, operating budgets, or continuing support; no loans.
Publications: Application guidelines; Biennial report; Financial statement; Informational brochure (including application guidelines); Newsletter.
Application information: Application information available on foundation's web site. Awards are given to post-Ph.D.'s only. Application form not required.
Initial approach: Letter of inquiry
Copies of proposal: 2
Deadline(s): All major proposals must be submitted 8 weeks prior to board meetings
Board meeting date(s): Feb., June, and Nov.
Final notification: 3 months
Officers and Trustees:* Robert E. Denham,* Chair.; **Sheldon Danziger,*** **Pres.**; Shelley E. Taylor,* Treas.; Christopher Brogna, C.F.O.; **Larry M. Bartels**; Kenneth D. Brody; Karen S. Cook; W. Bowman Cutter III; **Kathryn Edin**; Lawrence F. Katz; Nicholas Lemann; Sara S. McLanahan; Claude M. Steele; Richard H. Thaler.
Number of staff: 10 full-time professional; 19 full-time support; 9 part-time support.
EIN: 131635303
Other changes: Sheldon Danziger has replaced Eric Wanner as Pres.

2403
The Rebecca and Arthur Samberg Foundation

c/o Arthur Samberg
77 Bedford Rd.
Katonah, NY 10536-2141

Established in NY.
Foundation type: Independent foundation.
Financial data (yr. ended 11/30/13): Assets, $826,256 (M); expenditures, $421,712; qualifying distributions, $419,056; giving activities include $416,306 for 17 grants (high: $151,586; low: $1,000).
Fields of interest: Arts; Human services; Children/youth, services.
Limitations: Applications not accepted. Giving primarily in Westchester County, NY.
Application information: Contributes only to pre-selected organizations.
Officers: Rebecca Samberg, Pres. and Treas.; Laura Samberg, V.P. and Secy.
EIN: 542113024

2404
The Sandy Hill Foundation

15 Boulevard
Hudson Falls, NY 12839-1001 (518) 791-3490
Contact: Nancy Juckett Brown, Tr.
Scholarship application address: **P.O. Box 607, Williston, VT 05495, e-mail: njbrown@sandyhillfoundation.org**

Established in 1953.
Donor: J. Walter Juckett.
Foundation type: Independent foundation.
Financial data (yr. ended 08/31/13): Assets, $8,355,434 (M); expenditures, $520,184; qualifying distributions, $483,452; giving activities include $359,779 for 86 grants (high: $100,000; low: $250), and $88,000 for 44 grants to individuals (high: $2,000; low: $2,000).
Purpose and activities: Giving primarily for the arts and culture, higher education, hospitals, health associations, children's and social services, and federated giving programs. Also offers scholarship grants for college education to assist young men and women graduating from designated local area schools.
Fields of interest: Arts; Higher education; Hospitals (general); Health organizations, association; Human services; Children/youth, services; Community/economic development; United Ways and Federated Giving Programs.
Type of support: General/operating support.
Limitations: Applications accepted. Giving primarily in the greater Hudson Falls, NY, area. No grants to individuals directly.
Application information: Application form required.
Initial approach: Proposal
Deadline(s): **Apr. 1 for scholarships**

Trustees: Nancy Juckett Brown; Stephen J. Brown; Timothy S. Brown.
EIN: 146018954

2405
Louisa Stude Sarofim Foundation
c/o WTAS LLC
1177 Ave. of the Americas, 18th Fl.
New York, NY 10036-2714

Established in 1991.
Donor: Louisa Stude Sarofim.
Foundation type: Independent foundation.
Financial data (yr. ended 12/31/12): Assets, $14,212,928 (M); expenditures, $6,551,964; qualifying distributions, $6,350,000; giving activities include $5,350,000 for 3 grants (high: $5,000,000; low: $100,000).
Purpose and activities: Giving primarily for the arts and education; funding also for an animal shelter medical program.
Fields of interest: Performing arts, music; Arts; Elementary/secondary education; Animal welfare.
Limitations: Applications not accepted. Giving primarily in Sante Fe, NM, and Houston, TX. No grants to individuals.
Application information: Contributes only to pre-selected organizations.
Trustees: Mary L. Porter; Allison Sarofim; Christopher Sarofim; Louisa S. Sarofim.
EIN: 760347329
Other changes: At the close of 2012, the grantmaker paid grants of $5,350,000, a 345.8% increase over the 2011 disbursements, $1,200,000.

2406
Schafer Family Foundation
1177 Ave. of the Americas, 18th Fl.
New York, NY **10036-2714** (212) 536-9700

Established in 1986 in NY.
Donor: Oscar S. Schafer.
Foundation type: Independent foundation.
Financial data (yr. ended 12/31/12): Assets, $299,706 (M); gifts received, $52,613; expenditures, $101,749; qualifying distributions, $101,600; giving activities include $101,600 for 7 grants (high: $27,500; low: $100).
Purpose and activities: Giving primarily for social services.
Fields of interest: Museums (art); Education; Hospitals (general); Cancer research; Human services; Jewish agencies & synagogues.
Limitations: Applications not accepted. Giving primarily in the metropolitan New York, NY, area. No grants to individuals.
Application information: Contributes only to pre-selected organizations.
Officer: Oscar S. Schafer, Pres.
Directors: Sigrid U. Schafer; Michael Stein; Paul Stiker.
EIN: 133382931

2407
The Schenectady Foundation
376 Broadway, Fl. 2
Schenectady, NY 12305 (518) 393-9500
Contact: Robert A. Carreau, Secy.
E-mail: info@schenectadyfoundation.org; Grant application e-mail: racarreau@schenectadyfoundation.org; Main URL: http://www.schenectadyfoundation.org

Established in 1963 in NY.
Donors: Eleanor F. Green†; Mabel Birdsall†; Agnes Macdonald†; Laura Ayer†; S. Wells Corbin†; John N. Erbacher†; Kathryn Rice†; Martin Rice†; Willis R. Whitney†; Herman Blumer†; Patrick Garey†; Irving Handelman†; Sara Handelman†; Adelaide Parker†; Alice Stackpole†; Charles W. Carl, Jr.†; Edna Wood†; General Electric Foundation.
Foundation type: Community foundation.
Financial data (yr. ended 12/31/12): Assets, $18,112,931 (M); gifts received, $361,768; expenditures, $1,217,918; giving activities include $1,163,978 for 28+ grants (high: $200,000).
Purpose and activities: The foundation seeks to assist and promote the welfare of Schenectady County, New York and the people who live and/or work there. Support for general charitable purposes; awards scholarships to graduating seniors of Schenectady County, NY, high schools planning to enter the teaching profession.
Fields of interest: Education; Animals/wildlife, preservation/protection; Health care; Youth development; Child development, services; Community/economic development; Engineering/technology; Children.
Type of support: General/operating support; Capital campaigns; Building/renovation; Equipment; Land acquisition; Seed money; Scholarship funds; Research; Matching/challenge support.
Limitations: Applications accepted. Giving limited to Schenectady County, NY. No support for religious organizations for religious purposes. No grants for operating budgets, continuing support, annual campaigns, emergency or deficit financing, general or special endowments, demonstration projects, publications, or conferences or seminars; no loans.
Publications: Application guidelines; Annual report; Grants list; Informational brochure.
Application information: Visit foundation Web site for application guidelines. Application form required.
Initial approach: Letter of Inquiry (no longer than 2 pages)
Copies of proposal: 1
Deadline(s): None
Board meeting date(s): Mar., June, Sept., and Dec.
Officers and Distribution Committee:* Jennifer Kenneally,* Chair.; Robert Bylancik,* Vice-Chair.; **Deborah Mullaney,* Secy.; Robert T. Cushing,* Co-Treas.; Herbert L. Shultz, Jr.,* Co-Treas.**; Michael Ozimek,* Asst. Treas.; Robert A. Carreau, Exec. Dir.; Teresa Little; Joseph Tardi.
Trustee Banks: KeyBank; Trustco Bank.
EIN: 146019650
Other changes: Deborah Mullaney is now Secy. Herbert L. Shultz, Jr. is now Co-Treas. Robert T. Cushing is now Co-Treas. Sarah J. Schermerhorn is no longer a member of the governing body.

2408
Leopold Schepp Foundation
551 5th Ave., Ste. 3000
New York, NY 10176-3201 (212) 692-0191
Main URL: http://www.scheppfoundation.org

Incorporated in 1925 in NY.
Donors: Leopold Schepp†; Florence L. Schepp†.
Foundation type: Independent foundation.
Financial data (yr. ended 02/28/13): Assets, $10,125,550 (M); gifts received, $141,597; expenditures, $862,772; qualifying distributions, $778,534; giving activities include $344,500 for 57 grants to individuals (high: $8,500; low: $1,000).
Purpose and activities: Giving primarily to assist young men and women of character and ability who have insufficient means to complete their vocational or professional education. Undergraduate scholarships to individuals under 30 years of age; graduate scholarships to individuals under 40 years of age; a small number of fellowships for independent study and research to individuals in the arts and literature, medicine, and oceanography.
Fields of interest: Higher education; Education.
Type of support: Fellowships; Grants to individuals; Scholarships—to individuals.
Limitations: Applications accepted. Giving to students on a national basis. No grants for already incurred debt.
Application information: See foundation web site for current information and deadlines.
Board meeting date(s): May and Oct.
Officers and Trustees:* Barbara McLendon,* Pres.; William L.D. Barrett,* V.P.; Kathryn Batchelder Cashman,* V.P.; Sue Ann Dawson,* V.P.; James G. Turino, Treas.; SuzanneClair Guard, Exec. Dir.; Edythe Bobrow; Louise M. Bozorth; Susan Brenner; Anne Coffin; Emily Crawford; Betty David; William G. Gridley, Jr.; Nancy Grossman; Diana P. Hermann; Michele A. Paige; Elizabeth Stone Potter; Bruno A. Quinson; Robert F. Reder, M.D.; Banning Repplier.
Number of staff: 1 full-time professional; 1 full-time support; 2 part-time support.
EIN: 135562353

2409
The Scherman Foundation, Inc.
16 E. 52nd St., Ste. 601
New York, NY 10022-5306 (212) 832-3086
***Contact:* Environment, Arts, Strengthening NYC Communities: Mike Pratt, Pres. and Exec. Dir.; Reproductive Rights and Justice, Strenghtening NYC Communities: Alexis Aviles, Prog. Off.; Help with Electronic Applications: Zabrina Collaza, Prog. Asst.; Admin. and Bookkeeping: Catherine Porter**
FAX: (212) 838-0154; E-mail: info@scherman.org; Additional e-mail address for applications: submissions@scherman.org. Please type SUPPORT REQUEST in the subject line.; Main URL: http://www.scherman.org
The Scherman Foundation's Philanthropy Promise: http://www.ncrp.org/philanthropys-promise/who

Incorporated in 1941 in NY.
Donors: Katharine S. Rosin†; Karen R. Sollins; Members of the Scherman family.
Foundation type: Independent foundation.
Financial data (yr. ended 12/31/12): Assets, $108,620,554 (M); gifts received, $6,103,625; expenditures, $3,702,806; qualifying distributions, $3,196,835; giving activities include $2,415,100 for 70 grants (high: $90,000; low: $2,000), and $3,250 for employee matching gifts.
Purpose and activities: Grants largely for the environment, reproductive rights and services, human rights and liberties, the arts, and social welfare. In the social welfare field, grants are made to New York City organizations concerned with social justice, community organizing, and community development. Arts grants are limited to New York City.
Fields of interest: Performing arts; Performing arts, dance; Performing arts, theater; Performing arts, music; Environment, alliance/advocacy; Environment, natural resources; Environment, water resources; Environment, energy; Environment; Reproductive health, family planning; Legal services; Human services; Civil/human rights,

advocacy; Civil/human rights, minorities; Civil liberties, reproductive rights; Civil/human rights; Community/economic development, alliance/advocacy; Urban/community development; Community/economic development; Minorities; Economically disadvantaged.
Type of support: Annual campaigns; Continuing support; General/operating support; Matching/challenge support; Technical assistance.
Limitations: Applications accepted. Giving in NY and nationally in all areas, except for the arts and social welfare, which is limited to New York City. No support for colleges, universities, or other higher educational institutions. No grants to individuals, or for building or endowment funds, capital campaigns scholarships, fellowships, conferences or symposia, specific media or arts production, medical, science or engineering research.
Publications: Annual report (including application guidelines); Grants list.
Application information: Application guidelines and form available on foundation web site. The foundation does not accept proposals via fax or the Internet. Do not submit video or audio cassettes or CDs, unless requested to do so.
Initial approach: Letter of Intent via foundation web site
Copies of proposal: 1
Deadline(s): Rolling basis for Core Fund and Annual for Rosin Fund (see Grantmaking Programs and Guidelines on foundation web site).
Board meeting date(s): Quarterly
Final notification: Within 8 weeks
Officers and Directors:* Karen R. Sollins,* Chair.; Mike Pratt, Pres.; Susanna Bergtold,* Secy.; Hillary Brown; Miriam Buhl; David R. Jones; Gordon N. Litwin; John J. O'Neil; Marcia Thompson; John Wroclawski.
Number of staff: 2 full-time professional; 2 full-time support.
EIN: 136098464

2410
The Kilian J. and Caroline F. Schmitt Foundation, Inc.
1570 East Ave.
Rochester, NY **14610 (585) 244-4821**
***Contact:* Alfred M. Hallenbeck, Secy.**
***E-mail:* ahallenbeck83@gmail.com**

Established in 1991 in NY as successor to Kilian J. and Caroline F. Schmitt Foundation.
Donors: Kilian J. Schmitt†; Caroline F. Schmitt†.
Foundation type: Independent foundation.
Financial data (yr. ended 02/28/13): Assets, $11,423,577 (M); expenditures, $621,860; qualifying distributions, $567,924; giving activities include $515,086 for 33 grants (high: $215,000; low: $500).
Purpose and activities: Giving primarily for higher education, health care, and human services.
Fields of interest: Performing arts, orchestras; Higher education; Health care; Medical research; Human services; American Red Cross.
Type of support: General/operating support; Annual campaigns; Capital campaigns; Equipment; Endowments.
Limitations: Applications accepted. Giving primarily in the metropolitan Rochester, NY, area. No grants to individuals.
Application information: Application form required.
***Initial approach:* Completed application form**
Deadline(s): None
Officers: Robert H. Fella, Pres.; Alfred M. Hallenbeck, Secy.; Gary J. Lindsay, Treas.
Directors: James R. Dray; Leon Fella; **Megan Henry**; James D. Ryan, Jr.
EIN: 223087449

2411
Adolph & Ruth Schnurmacher Foundation, Inc.
551 5th Ave., Ste. 1210
New York, NY 10176-1299
Contact: Janet Plotkin, Pres.
FAX: (212) 972-2303;
E-mail: arsfoundation@gmail.com; **Additional e-mail: info@arsfoundation.com**; Main URL: http://www.arsfoundation.com

Established in 1977 in NY.
Donors: Adolph Schnurmacher†; Ruth Schnurmacher†.
Foundation type: Independent foundation.
Financial data (yr. ended 12/31/12): Assets, $19,929,811 (M); expenditures, $1,735,724; qualifying distributions, $1,540,515; giving activities include $1,209,251 for 122 grants (high: $56,625; low: $250).
Purpose and activities: The foundation's mission is to make a positive difference in the lives of others. It has a variety of focuses including (but not limited to) human and social services, the arts, children and the elderly, and health care.
Fields of interest: Arts; Education; Health organizations, association; Human services; Public affairs.
Type of support: General/operating support; Continuing support; Annual campaigns; Equipment; Emergency funds; Curriculum development; Scholarship funds; Research; Matching/challenge support.
Limitations: Applications accepted. Giving in the metropolitan New York, NY, area, including Fairfield County, CT. No support for political organizations. No grants to individuals.
Publications: IRS Form 990 or 990-PF printed copy available upon request.
Application information: Applicants should not submit tapes, compact disks or DVDs unless requested to do so. Application form not required.
Initial approach: Letter
Copies of proposal: 1
Deadline(s): None
Board meeting date(s): 6 to 8 times a year
Final notification: None
Officers and Trustees:* Janet Plotkin,* Pres.; Amanda Plotkin,* V.P.; Carolyn Plotkin,* V.P.; Jonathan Plotkin,* V.P.; Fred Plotkin,* Secy.-Treas.
Number of staff: 1 full-time support; 4 part-time support.
EIN: 132938935

2412
The Schumann Media Center, Inc.
(formerly The Schumann Center for Media and Democracy, Inc.)
250 W. 57th St., Ste. 715
New York, NY 10107-0003
Contact: Lynn C. Welhorsky, V.P., Admin.

Incorporated in 1961 in NJ.
Donors: Florence F. Schumann†; John J. Schumann, Jr.†.
Foundation type: Independent foundation.
Financial data (yr. ended 12/31/12): Assets, $29,034,683 (M); expenditures, $4,542,620; qualifying distributions, $4,397,115; giving activities include $2,878,770 for 20 grants (high: $750,000; low: $3,770).
Purpose and activities: Grants for programs in effective governance and the environment.
Fields of interest: Media/communications; Higher education; Public affairs, citizen participation.
Type of support: General/operating support; Continuing support; Program development; Matching/challenge support.
Limitations: Applications not accepted. Giving primarily in New York, NY; some funding nationally. No grants to individuals, or for annual campaigns, capital campaigns, deficit financing, equipment and materials, land acquisition, or endowment funds; no loans.
Application information: Currently, the foundation is not accepting any proposals for consideration.
Board meeting date(s): Feb., June, and Oct.
Officers and Trustees:* Joan Konner,* Chair.; Bill D. Moyers,* Pres.; Lynn C. Welhorsky, V.P., Admin.; Michael J. Johnston,* V.P.; Beth Yingling, Secy.-Treas.; W. Ford Schumann,* Chair. Emeritus; David S. Bate, Trustee Emeritus; Robert M. Herbert; **R. Ford Schumann.**
Number of staff: 2 full-time professional.
EIN: 226044214

2413
Schwartz Family Foundation
c/o Alan Schwartz Guggenheim Partners
330 Madison Ave., 15th Fl.
New York, NY **10017-5032**
Contact: Alan Schwartz, Tr.

Established in 1997 in NY.
Donors: Alan D. Schwartz; Nancy M. Seaman.
Foundation type: Independent foundation.
Financial data (yr. ended 12/31/12): Assets, $20,086,830 (M); gifts received, $2,394,150; expenditures, $1,807,974; qualifying distributions, $1,748,700; giving activities include $1,748,700 for grants.
Purpose and activities: Giving primarily for education, health organizations, social services.
Fields of interest: Higher education; Education; Health organizations, association; Human services; Children/youth, services; Foundations (private grantmaking).
Limitations: Applications not accepted. Giving in the U.S., with strong emphasis on NC and NY. No grants to individuals.
Application information: Contributes only to pre-selected organizations.
Trustees: Alan D. Schwartz; Nancy M. Seaman.
EIN: 137138217

2414
The SDA Foundation
c/o Goldberg Lindsay & Co. LLC
630 5th Ave., 30th Fl.
New York, NY 10111-0001 (212) 651-1100

Established in 2000 in NY.
Donor: Alan E. Goldberg.
Foundation type: Independent foundation.
Financial data (yr. ended 12/31/13): Assets, $7,153 (M); gifts received, $5,520,000; expenditures, $5,513,695; qualifying distributions, $5,499,094; giving activities include $5,498,934 for 32 grants (high: $760,000; low: $1,000).
Purpose and activities: Giving primarily for health care, particularly hospitals and medical research, as well as for Jewish education and to Jewish organizations.

Fields of interest: Higher education; Education; Hospitals (general); Medical research, institute; Cancer research; Human services; Jewish federated giving programs; Jewish agencies & synagogues.
Limitations: Applications accepted. Giving primarily in New York, NY. No grants to individuals.
Application information:
Initial approach: Letter
***Deadline(s):* None**
Trustees: Alan E. Goldberg; Miriam P. Goldberg.
EIN: 137235530

2415
Seneca Foods Foundation
3736 S. Main St.
Marion, NY 14505-9751 (315) 926-8100
Contact: Kraig H. Kayser, C.E.O. and Pres.
E-mail: foundation@senecafoods.com; **Main URL: http://www.senecafoods.com/seneca-foods-foundation**

Established in 1988 in NY.
Donor: Seneca Foods Corp.
Foundation type: Company-sponsored foundation.
Financial data (yr. ended 03/31/13): Assets, $5,415,532 (M); gifts received, $1,000,000; expenditures, $2,260,590; qualifying distributions, $2,249,675; giving activities include $2,239,649 for 231+ grants (high: $2,029,200).
Purpose and activities: The foundation supports programs designed to promote education and employment; and youth development.
Fields of interest: Elementary/secondary education; Education, early childhood education; Higher education; Education, services; Education, drop-out prevention; Education; Crime/violence prevention, abuse prevention; Crime/violence prevention, child abuse; Employment, services; Employment, job counseling; Employment; Youth development, adult & child programs; Youth development; Children/youth, services; United Ways and Federated Giving Programs; Leadership development; Youth.
Type of support: General/operating support; Building/renovation; Program development; Scholarship funds.
Limitations: Applications accepted. **Giving primarily in areas of company operations in Modesto, CA, Sarasota, FL, Buhl and Payette, ID, Princeville, IL, Arlington, Blue Earth, Glencoe, Rochester, and Montgomery, MN, Geneva, Leicester, Marion, and Penn Yan, NY, Lebanon, PA, Dayton, Sunnyside, and Yakima, WA, and Baraboo, Cambria, Clyman, Cumberland, Gillett, Janesville, Maryville, Oakfield, Plainfield, and Ripon, WI.** No support for religious organizations not of direct benefit to the entire community, or legislative organizations. **No grants to individuals, or for endowments, capital campaigns, fundraising events, sponsorships, propaganda, or academic, medical, or scientific research; no product donations.**
Publications: Application guidelines; Program policy statement.
Application information: Grants are limited to organizations with documented performance results. Organizations applying for support must include performance outcomes and performance data to be eligible for funding. Support is limited to 1 contribution per organization during any given year. Priority is given to organizations with Seneca employee or retiree volunteer involvement. Application form required.
Initial approach: Download application form and mail to foundation
Deadline(s): None
Officers and Directors:* Arthur S. Wolcott,* Chair.; Kraig H. Kayser,* C.E.O. and Pres.; Jeffrey L. Van Riper, Secy.; Roland E. Breunig, Treas.; Susan W. Stuart.
EIN: 222996324

2416
The Shalom Ish Foundation
c/o Saul N. Friedman and Company
6201 15th Ave., Apt. 4L
Brooklyn, NY 11219-5441

Established in 1998.
Donors: Ish Shalom‡; Saul N. Friedman; Eva Friedman; Benjamin Friedman; Morris Friedman; Alexander Orenstein; Ish Shalom Trust; Maison Grande Assocs.; Simeon Friedman.
Foundation type: Independent foundation.
Financial data (yr. ended 09/30/13): Assets, $3,354,664 (M); gifts received, $50,000; expenditures, $422,606; qualifying distributions, $408,500; giving activities include $408,500 for 17 grants (high: $55,000; low: $1,800).
Fields of interest: Education; Human services; Jewish agencies & synagogues.
Limitations: Applications not accepted. Giving primarily in NY. No grants to individuals.
Application information: Contributes only to pre-selected organizations.
Director: Saul N. Friedman.
EIN: 113405442

2417
J. D. Shatford Memorial Trust
c/o JPMorgan Chase Bank, N.A.
270 Park Ave., 16th Fl.
New York, NY 10017-2014
E-mail: connie.a.brandeis@JPMorgan.com; Application address: c/o Advisory Committee, P.O. Box 192, Hubbards, Nova Scotia B0J 1T0; e-mail: info@jdshatfordmemorialtrust.org; **Main URL: http://fdnweb.org/shatford**
Grants List: http://fdnweb.org/shatford/recipients/

Trust established in 1955 in NY.
Foundation type: Independent foundation.
Financial data (yr. ended 12/31/12): Assets, $6,613,571 (M); expenditures, $370,363; qualifying distributions, $307,217; giving activities include $288,474 for 27 grants (high: $67,375; low: $2,625).
Purpose and activities: Emphasis on scholarship aid, secondary and higher education, and charities limited to Hubbards, Nova Scotia, Canada, organizations and residents.
Fields of interest: Secondary school/education; Protestant agencies & churches.
International interests: Canada.
Type of support: General/operating support; Scholarships—to individuals.
Limitations: Applications accepted. Giving limited to Hubbards, Nova Scotia, Canada.
Publications: Grants list; Informational brochure.
Application information: Complete application guidelines available on Trust web site. Application form required.
Deadline(s): None
Trustee: JPMorgan Chase Bank, N.A.
EIN: 136029993

2418
Emma A. Sheafer Charitable Trust
c/o JPMorgan Chase Bank, N.A. Private Foundation Services
270 Park Ave., 16th Fl.
New York, NY 10017-2014
Contact: Jonathan Horowitz, Prog. Officer
FAX: (212) 464-2304;
E-mail: jonathan.g.horowitz@jpmchase.com; Main URL: http://fdnweb.org/sheafer
Grants List: http://fdnweb.org/sheafer/grants/category/contributions/

Trust established in 1975 in NY.
Donor: Emma A. Sheafer‡.
Foundation type: Independent foundation.
Financial data (yr. ended 12/31/12): Assets, $5,637,617 (M); expenditures, $346,079; qualifying distributions, $278,636; giving activities include $260,000 for 11 grants (high: $40,000; low: $20,000).
Purpose and activities: Giving primarily for the performing arts in New York City.
Fields of interest: Performing arts.
Type of support: Capital campaigns; Management development/capacity building; Program development.
Limitations: Giving limited to New York, NY. No grants to individuals, or for research, scholarships, matching gifts or fellowships; no loans.
Publications: Application guidelines; Grants list; Informational brochure.
Application information: Organizations may not receive more than 1 grant every 3 years. See foundation web site for full application requirements. Application form not required.
***Initial approach:* Use online application system on trust web site**
Copies of proposal: 1
Deadline(s): May 1
Board meeting date(s): June and Dec.
Final notification: June and Dec.
Trustees: John C. Russell; JPMorgan Chase Bank, N.A.
EIN: 510186114
Other changes: The grantmaker has moved from TX to NY.
The grantmaker now publishes application guidelines online.

2419
Murray G. & Beatrice H. Sherman Foundation
115 Central Park West, Apt. 29F
New York, NY 10023-4198

Established in 1999 in NY.
Foundation type: Independent foundation.
Financial data (yr. ended 12/31/12): Assets, $5,347,247 (M); expenditures, $370,974; qualifying distributions, $316,999; giving activities include $299,673 for 21 grants (high: $50,000; low: $4,000).
Fields of interest: Arts; Libraries (public); Education; Hospitals (general); Human services; Youth, services; International relief; International migration/refugee issues; Community/economic development; United Ways and Federated Giving Programs.
Limitations: Applications not accepted. Giving primarily in New York, NY. No grants to individuals.
Application information: Contributes only to pre-selected organizations.
Trustees: Mary Sherman Mittleman; William S. Sherman.
EIN: 311623371

2420
The Edith Glick Shoolman Children's Foundation
Cherokee Sta.
P.O. Box 20763
New York, NY 10021-0075
E-mail: info@shoolman.org; Main URL: http://www.shoolman.org
Grants List: http://www.shoolman.org/EGSCF/index.php/grantees2/2013-grantees

Established in NY.
Donor: Edith Glick Shoolman†.
Foundation type: Independent foundation.
Financial data (yr. ended 12/31/12): Assets, $22,532,257 (M); expenditures, $1,418,558; qualifying distributions, $1,305,209; giving activities include $1,229,401 for 32 grants (high: $128,401; low: $1,500).
Purpose and activities: Giving to foster the health, education, and well-being of children.
Fields of interest: Child development, education; Child development, services; Children.
Type of support: General/operating support.
Limitations: Giving primarily in the metropolitan New York, NY and Boston, MA, areas. No support for organizations lacking 501(c)(3) status. No grants to individuals, or for pure medical research; also, no funding to endowments, or for annual appeals, or capital improvements other than in connection with the implementation of a specific program being supported; no support for events or outings.
Publications: Application guidelines; Grants list.
Application information: New unsolicited applications for funding will only be accepted from organizations which provide services in the New York City Metropolitan Area. Only online applications are accepted. Please contact the foundation directly for any hardships with online submissions. Application form required.
Initial approach: Letter of inquiry via foundation web site
Deadline(s): None, for letters of inquiry
Officers and Trustees:* Henry L. Berman,* Pres.; Deborah B. Breznay,* Exec. Dir.
EIN: 043414101

2421
The Shoreland Foundation
38 Camel Hollow Rd.
Lloyd Harbor, NY 11743-1604

Established in 1994 in NY.
Donors: Anthony W. Wang; Lulu Wang.
Foundation type: Independent foundation.
Financial data (yr. ended 12/31/12): Assets, $29,979,106 (M); expenditures, $6,024,807; qualifying distributions, $5,698,233; giving activities include $5,642,128 for 41 grants (high: $3,000,000; low: $100).
Purpose and activities: Giving primarily to higher education and the arts, including art and cultural museums.
Fields of interest: Arts, cultural/ethnic awareness; Museums; Museums (art); Higher education.
Type of support: General/operating support; Endowments.
Limitations: Applications not accepted. Giving primarily in NY and MA. No grants to individuals.
Application information: Contributes only to pre-selected organizations.
Officers: Lulu C. Wang, Pres.; Anthony W. Wang, V.P.; Carol-Ann Mealey, Secy.
EIN: 113241828
Other changes: At the close of 2012, the grantmaker paid grants of $5,642,128, a 153.3% increase over the 2011 disbursements, $2,227,796.
Lulu C. Wang has replaced Anthony W. Wang as Pres. Anthony W. Wang has replaced Lulu C. Wang as V.P.
Carol-Ann Mealey is now Secy.

2422
Sidewalk Angels Foundation
P.O. Box 356
Bedford Hills, NY 10507
E-mail: info@sidewalkangelsfoundation.org; Main URL: http://www.sidewalkangelsfoundation.org/
Facebook: https://www.facebook.com/sidewalkangels
Twitter: http://twitter.com/sidewalkangels

Established in 2004 in NY.
Donors: Marisol Thomas; Rob Thomas; New Bidnis Inc.; Music Mastermind Inc.
Foundation type: Operating foundation.
Financial data (yr. ended 12/31/12): Assets, $110,678 (M); gifts received, $248,554; expenditures, $310,558; qualifying distributions, $300,000; giving activities include $300,000 for 19 grants (high: $140,000; low: $2,000).
Purpose and activities: The foundation seeks through its efforts to encourage people to locally address problems such as animals that have been abandoned and abused as well as people who are destitute, homeless, or cannot afford proper medical care.
Fields of interest: Animal welfare; Homeless, human services; Economically disadvantaged; Homeless.
Limitations: Applications not accepted. Giving in the U.S., with emphasis on NY.
Application information: Unsolicited requests for funds not accepted.
Officers: Marisol Thomas, Pres.; Robert Thomas, V.P.; Maria Maldonado, Secy.; Greg Prato, Treas.
Directors: Michael Lippman; Jeff Maldonado; Melissa Lopez Maldonado.
EIN: 200285336

2423
The Simons Foundation
160 5th Ave., 7th Fl.
New York, NY 10010-7037 (646) 654-0066
Contact: Marilyn Simons, Pres.
E-mail: admin@simonsfoundation.org; Main URL: http://www.simonsfoundation.org
James and Marilyn Simons's Giving Pledge Profile: http://glasspockets.org/philanthropy-in-focus/eye-on-the-giving-pledge/profiles/simons
Knowledge Center: https://sfari.org/news-and-opinion
On SFARI Blog: https://sfari.org/news-and-opinion/blog/going-on-sfari
Vimeo: http://vimeo.com/simonsfoundation

Established in 1994 in NY.
Donor: James Simons.
Foundation type: Independent foundation.
Financial data (yr. ended 12/31/12): Assets, $2,083,631,666 (M); gifts received, $150,328,193; expenditures, $218,736,336; qualifying distributions, $185,556,996; giving activities include $184,781,415 for grants, $775,581 for in-kind gifts, and $17,701,081 for foundation-administered programs.
Purpose and activities: The primary mission of the foundation is to advance the frontiers of research in the basic sciences and mathematics.
Fields of interest: Autism research; Science, research; Mathematics.
Type of support: General/operating support; Capital campaigns; Endowments; Professorships; Research.
Publications: Annual report; Financial statement.
Application information: The foundation does not accept proposals outside its established programs. In almost all cases grants are made in response to announced requests for proposals and funding decisions are made through a peer-reviewed proposal process. See foundation web site for requests for applications.
Board meeting date(s): Throughout the year
Officers and Trustees:* James H. Simons, Ph.D.*, Chair.; Marilyn Simons,* Pres.; **Maria Adler, C.F.O. and Treas.**; Marion Greenup, V.P., Admin.; **Patricia Weisenfeld, V.P., Special Initiatives; Fang Han, Cont.**; David Eisenbud; Gerald D. Fischbach; Mark Silber.
Number of staff: 2 part-time professional; 1 full-time support.
EIN: 133794889
Other changes: Maria Adler is now C.F.O. and Treas. James Simons is now Chair. Patricia Weisenfeld is now V.P., Special Initiatives.

2424
The Paul E. Singer Foundation
40 W. 57th St., 4th Fl.
New York, NY 10019-4001

Donor: Paul E. Singer.
Foundation type: Independent foundation.
Financial data (yr. ended 11/30/12): Assets, $195,427,094 (M); expenditures, $13,729,364; qualifying distributions, $13,699,656; giving activities include $13,268,605 for 65 grants (high: $3,700,500; low: $2,500).
Fields of interest: Education; Health care; Cancer; Cancer, leukemia; Human services; Jewish agencies & synagogues.
Limitations: Applications not accepted. Giving primarily in Washington, DC and New York, NY.
Application information: Contributes only to pre-selected organizations.
Officers and Directors:* Paul E. Singer,* Pres. and Treas.; Myron Kaplan,* Secy.
EIN: 272009342
Other changes: The grantmaker has moved from DE to NY.
Paul E. Singer is now Pres. and Treas. Myron Kaplan is now Secy.

2425
Singh Family Foundation
P.O. Box 73
New York, NY **10274-0073** (518) 640-5000

Established in 1999 in NY.
Donor: Dinakar Singh.
Foundation type: Independent foundation.
Financial data (yr. ended 10/31/12): Assets, $43,553 (M); expenditures, $344,362; qualifying distributions, $344,132; giving activities include $344,132 for 4 grants (high: $160,000; low: $25,000).
Fields of interest: Higher education; Genetic diseases and disorders research; Infants/toddlers.
Limitations: Applications not accepted. Giving primarily in New York, NY. No grants to individuals.

Application information: Contributes only to pre-selected organizations.
Trustees: Florence Ann Eng; Dinakar Singh; Ravi Mo Singh.
EIN: 134115900
Other changes: Florence Ann Eng Singh, a trustee, is now Florence Ann Eng.

2426
The Sirus Fund
c/o Susan Helpern, EisnerAmper LLP
750 3rd Ave., 21st Fl.
New York, NY 10017-2703
Contact: Susan U. Halpern, Pres.

Established in 1996 in NY.
Donor: Susan U. Halpern.
Foundation type: Independent foundation.
Financial data (yr. ended 06/30/13): Assets, $13,162,387 (M); gifts received, $20,000; expenditures, $1,216,003; qualifying distributions, $1,116,752; giving activities include $1,067,290 for 55 grants (high: $100,000; low: $300).
Purpose and activities: Giving primarily for services to young children in the metropolitan New York, NY, area.
Fields of interest: Education, early childhood education; Higher education; Child development, services; Family services.
Type of support: General/operating support; Continuing support; Program development.
Limitations: Applications not accepted. Giving primarily in the metropolitan New York, NY, area. No support for religious organizations. No grants to individuals.
Application information: Unsolicited requests for funds not accepted.
Board meeting date(s): June and Sept.
Officer and Trustee:* Susan U. Halpern,* Pres.
Number of staff: None.
EIN: 137100236

2427
Skadden Foundation
(formerly Skadden, Arps, Slate, Meagher & Flom Fellowship Foundation)
360 Hamilton Ave.
White Plains, NY 10601-1811 (212) 735-2956
Contact: Susan Butler Plum, Secy.
FAX: (917) 777-2956;
E-mail: susan.plum@skadden.com; Application address: Skadden Fellowship Program, 4 Times Sq., Rm. 29-218, New York, NY 10036; Main URL: http://www.skaddenfellowships.org/
Fellows: http://www.skaddenfellowships.org/fellows-list

Established in 1988 in NY.
Donor: Skadden, Arps, Slate, Meagher & Flom.
Foundation type: Company-sponsored foundation.
Financial data (yr. ended 12/31/12): Assets, $9,878,610 (M); gifts received, $4,077,400; expenditures, $4,008,674; qualifying distributions, $3,992,696; giving activities include $3,347,701 for 87 grants (high: $129,682; low: $1,713), and $62,373 for 13 grants to individuals (high: $9,148; low: $150).
Purpose and activities: The foundation awards fellowships to graduating law students and outgoing judicial clerks who create projects at public interest organizations designed to provide legal services to the poor, the elderly, the disabled, and those deprived of their civil rights or human rights; and grants to former Skadden Fellows who want to undertake new initiatives on behalf of their clients.
Fields of interest: Law school/education; Civil/human rights, advocacy; Civil/human rights; Leadership development; Aging; Disabilities, people with; Economically disadvantaged.
Type of support: Fellowships; Grants to individuals.
Limitations: Applications accepted. Giving on a national basis, with emphasis on Berkeley, Los Angeles, Oakland, San Diego, and San Francisco, CA, Washington, DC, Chicago, IL, MA, and Bronx, Brooklyn, and New York, NY. No grants to individuals who do not secure a potential position with a sponsoring public interest organization.
Publications: Application guidelines.
Application information: Letters for Flom Memorial Incubator Grants should describe the applicant's career trajectory, the inspiration for the project, and the proposed plan for grant funds. Fellows who have been awarded a FIG must wait two years before reapplying.
Initial approach: Download application form and mail application form and supporting materials for fellowships; letter to foundation for Flom Memorial Incubator Grants
Copies of proposal: 1
***Deadline(s):* Oct. 6 for fellowships; Jan. 15 and July 15 for Flom Memorial Incubator Grants**
***Board meeting date(s):* Dec. 4**
***Final notification:* Dec. 5**
Officers and Trustees: Lauren Aguiar, Pres.; Thomas J. Allingham II, V.P.; C. Benjamin Crisman, Jr., V.P.; Susan Butler Plum, Secy.; Chris Fulton, Treas.; Eric J. Friedman; Barry H. Garfinkel; Hon. Judith S. Kaye; Jose Lozano; Suzanne Mckechnie Klahr; Martha Minow; Michael H. Schill; Kurt Schmoke; Robert C. Sheehan; Solomon Watson IV; Joy Ziegeweid.
Number of staff: 1 full-time professional; 1 part-time support.
EIN: 133455231
Other changes: Alan C. Myers is no longer V.P.

2428
Joseph & Sylvia Slifka Foundation, Inc.
c/o Hecht & Co. PC
350 5th Ave., 68th Fl.
New York, NY **10118-6710**

Established in 1944 in NY.
Donors: Joseph Slifka†; Sylvia Slifka†; Barbara Slifka.
Foundation type: Independent foundation.
Financial data (yr. ended 10/31/13): Assets, $39,580,496 (M); expenditures, $8,721,036; qualifying distributions, $8,466,724; giving activities include $8,443,334 for 34 grants (high: $2,000,000; low: $10,000).
Purpose and activities: Giving primarily for higher education and Jewish activities and philanthropy.
Fields of interest: Museums; Performing arts, ballet; Education; Jewish federated giving programs.
Limitations: Applications not accepted. Giving primarily in the metropolitan New York, NY, area. No grants to individuals.
Application information: Contributes only to pre-selected organizations.
Officers and Trustees:* Barbara S. Slifka,* Pres.; Michael Hecht,* V.P. and Treas.; John J. O'Neil,* Secy.
EIN: 136106433

2429
R. C. Smith Foundation, Inc.
35 W. Main St.
P.O. Box 552
Norwich, NY 13815-0552 (607) 336-5850
Contact: Richard M. Runyan, Exec. Dir.
FAX: (607) 334-8121;
E-mail: rcsmithfoundation@frontiernet.net; Main URL: http://www.rcsmithfoundation.org

Established in 2005 in NY.
Donor: Robert C. Smith†.
Foundation type: Operating foundation.
Financial data (yr. ended 12/31/12): Assets, $17,288,002 (M); gifts received, $43,660; expenditures, $1,004,299; qualifying distributions, $892,588; giving activities include $872,191 for 45 grants (high: $180,000; low: $1,200).
Purpose and activities: Giving primarily for community activities and betterment, as well as for religious agencies.
Fields of interest: Catholic agencies & churches; Religion; Children/youth; Economically disadvantaged.
Type of support: Emergency funds.
Limitations: Applications accepted. Giving primarily in Chenango County, NY.
Publications: Application guidelines; Annual report; Grants list.
Application information: Application guidelines and form available on foundation web site. Application form required.
***Initial approach:* Use application format on foundation web site**
Copies of proposal: 10
Deadline(s): Quarterly: Jan. 1, Apr. 1, July 1, and Oct. 1
Board meeting date(s): Quarterly, in Jan., Apr., July, and Oct.
Officers and Directors:* William Troxell,* Pres.; Betsy Baio,* V.P.; Thomas C. Emerson, Secy.; William Acee,* Treas.; Richard M. Runyon,* Exec. Dir.; Gary Brookins; Mary W. Davis; Pegi LoPresti; Nancy Ritzel.
EIN: 201893940

2430
George D. Smith Fund, Inc.
c/o L.W. Milas & W.B. Norden, Seyfarth Shaw, LLP
620 8th Ave., Ste. 3200
New York, NY 10018-1415 (212) 218-3316
Contact: Lawrence W. Milas, V.P.

Incorporated in 1956 in DE.
Donor: George D. Smith, Sr.†.
Foundation type: Independent foundation.
Financial data (yr. ended 12/31/13): Assets, $112,061,228 (M); expenditures, $16,968,905; qualifying distributions, $16,903,839; giving activities include $16,900,100 for 11 grants (high: $5,000,000; low: $100).
Fields of interest: Media, television; Higher education; Biomedicine; Medical research, institute.
Type of support: Research.
Limitations: Applications not accepted. Giving primarily in CA.
Application information: Unsolicited requests for funds not considered.
Officers: George D. Smith, Jr., Pres. and Secy.-Treas.; Lawrence W. Milas, V.P.; Camilla M. Smith, V.P.
Director: Sarah A. Smith.
EIN: 136138728

2431
Harry E. and Florence W. Snayberger Memorial Foundation
(also known as Snayberger Memorial Foundation)
c/o M&T Bank
1100 Wehrle Dr., 2nd Fl.
Amherst, NY 14221-7748 (716) 842-5506
Contact: Carolyn Bernatonis, Trust Dept.
E-mail: cbernatonis@mtb.com

Established in 1976 in PA.
Donor: Harry E. Snayberger†.
Foundation type: Independent foundation.
Financial data (yr. ended 03/31/13): Assets, $4,259,364 (M); expenditures, $225,626; qualifying distributions, $187,800; giving activities include $35,900 for 47 grants (high: $3,000; low: $400), and $151,900 for 92 grants to individuals (high: $1,700; low: $200).
Purpose and activities: Giving primarily for youth program organizations that benefit the youth of Schuylkill County, PA. Also awards scholarships for higher education, exclusively to Schuylkill County, PA, residents.
Fields of interest: Higher education; Youth development, scouting agencies (general); Children/youth, services.
Type of support: General/operating support; Scholarships—to individuals.
Limitations: Applications accepted. Giving limited to residents of Schuylkill County, PA.
Application information: Scholarship applicants must be no older than 25 years of age. Application form required.
Initial approach: Pick up application at any of the M&T Bank offices located in Schuylkill County, PA, between mid-Dec. and the end of Feb.
Copies of proposal: 1
Deadline(s): Last work day in Feb.
Board meeting date(s): Yearly, or as required
Final notification: Approximately mid-Oct. for scholarships and May for organizations
Trustee: M&T Bank.
Number of staff: None.
EIN: 232056361
Other changes: The grantmaker no longer lists a fax. The grantmaker has moved from PA to NY.

2432
The John Ben Snow Foundation, Inc.
50 Presidential Plz., Ste. 106
Syracuse, NY 13202-2279 **(315) 471-5256**
Contact: Jonathan L. Snow, Pres.
E-mail: johnbensnow@verizon.net; Main URL: http://www.johnbensnow.com/jbsf

Incorporated in 1948 in NY.
Donor: John Ben Snow†.
Foundation type: Independent foundation.
Financial data (yr. ended 12/31/12): Assets, $7,705,414 (M); expenditures, $444,499; qualifying distributions, $384,639; giving activities include $287,900 for 30 grants (high: $25,000; low: $800).
Purpose and activities: The mission of the foundation is to make grants within specific focus areas to enhance the quality of life in central and northern New York state. The focus areas are: arts and culture, community, education, journalism, disabilities, and the environment.
Fields of interest: Media, print publishing; Historic preservation/historical societies; Arts; Higher education; Libraries/library science; Education; Environment, natural resources; Environment; Children/youth, services; Community/economic development; Children/youth; Disabilities, people with.
Type of support: Building/renovation; Equipment; Program development; Publication; Seed money; Fellowships; Scholarship funds; Matching/challenge support.
Limitations: Applications accepted. Giving limited to central NY, with emphasis on Onondaga and Oswego counties. No support for religious organizations or for-profit groups. No grants to individuals, endowment funds, or contingency financing.
Publications: Annual report (including application guidelines); Financial statement.
Application information: Applicants should also include a 1-page executive summary. All inquiries should be made by mail only. Application form not required.
Initial approach: Letter of inquiry
Copies of proposal: 1
Deadline(s): Jan. 1 for letters of inquiry; submit inquiry preferably from July through Dec.; submit application by Apr. 1; submit either a final report after project is completed by Mar. 1 or a progress report by Mar. 1
Board meeting date(s): June
Final notification: July 1
Officers and Directors:* Jonathan L. Snow,* Pres.; David H. Snow,* V.P. and Treas.; Emelie Melton Williams,* Secy.; Angus M. Burton; Valerie A. MacFie.
Number of staff: 1 part-time support.
EIN: 136112704

2433
Valentine Perry Snyder Fund
c/o JPMorgan Chase Pank, N.A. Private Foundation Svcs.
270 Park Ave., 16th Fl.
New York, NY 10017-2014
Contact: Casey Castaneda, Prog. Off.
FAX: (212) 464-2304;
E-mail: casey.b.castaneda@jpmorgan.com; **Main URL: http://fdnweb.org/snyder**
Grants List: http://fdnweb.org/snyder/grants/category/contributions/

Trust established in 1942 in NY.
Donor: Sheba Torbert Snyder†.
Foundation type: Independent foundation.
Financial data (yr. ended 12/31/12): Assets, $8,188,048 (M); expenditures, $507,824; qualifying distributions, $437,544; giving activities include $405,000 for 19 grants (high: $25,000; low: $15,000).
Purpose and activities: Giving primarily for youth and other human services, community workforce development programs, and public affairs.
Fields of interest: Employment, training; Human services; Children/youth, services; Public affairs.
Type of support: General/operating support; Program development.
Limitations: Applications accepted. Giving limited to New York, NY. No support for organizations lacking 501(c)(3) status. No grants to individuals, or for research-related programs, scholarships, fellowships, or matching gifts; no loans.
Publications: Application guidelines; Grants list.
Application information: Organizations must have an annual budget of under $1.5 million to be eligible. See foundation web site for application guidelines and requirements. Application form not required.
Initial approach: Proposal via online application on foundation web site
Copies of proposal: 1
Deadline(s): Sept. 1
Board meeting date(s): Dec.
Final notification: Dec.
Trustee: JPMorgan Chase Bank, N.A.
EIN: 136036765

2434
The Society of the Friendly Sons of Saint Patrick in the City of New York
3 W. 51st St., Rm. 604
New York, NY **10019-6909** (212) 269-1770
Main URL: http://www.friendlysonsnyc.com
Facebook: https://www.facebook.com/pages/The-Society-of-the-Friendly-Sons-of-Saint-Patrick-in-the-City-of-New-York/137611946293243

Established in 1945 in NY.
Foundation type: Independent foundation.
Financial data (yr. ended 03/31/12): Assets, $3,159,297 (M); gifts received, $246,790; expenditures, $882,625; qualifying distributions, $841,114; giving activities include $200,000 for 34 grants (high: $10,000; low: $5,000).
Purpose and activities: Giving primarily to Roman Catholic agencies and services.
Fields of interest: Scholarships/financial aid; Education; Hospitals (general); Recreation; Human services; Catholic agencies & churches; Disabilities, people with.
Limitations: Applications accepted. Giving primarily in NY. No grants to individuals.
Application information:
Initial approach: Letter
Officers: John C. Walton, Pres.; Matthew T. McLaughlin, 1st V.P.; Kevin J. Rooney, 2nd V.P.; John A. Coleman III, Secy.; Thomas H. Sullivan, Treas.
Number of staff: 1 full-time professional; 1 part-time professional.
EIN: 136164757
Other changes: John C. Walton has replaced Mark B. Codd as Pres. Matthew T. McLaughlin has replaced John C. Walton as 1st V.P. Kevin J. Rooney has replaced Matthew T. McLaughlin as 2nd V.P.

2435
Doris and Daniel Solomon Charitable Foundation
North Baldwin, NY

The foundation terminated in 2012 and transferred its assets to The Jewish Federation of Palm Beach County.

2436
Alfred Z. Solomon Testamentary Trust
P.O. Box 108
Saratoga Springs, NY 12866 (518) 584-1500

Established in 2005 in NY.
Donor: Alfred L. Solomon†.
Foundation type: Independent foundation.
Financial data (yr. ended 12/31/12): Assets, $6,885,750 (M); expenditures, $633,558; qualifying distributions, $565,540; giving activities include $565,540 for grants.
Fields of interest: Museums (specialized); Performing arts, theater; Historical activities; Arts; Education; Health care; Food services; American Red Cross; Salvation Army; Jewish agencies & synagogues.

Limitations: Applications accepted. Giving primarily in Saratoga Springs, NY.
Application information: Application form required.
Deadline(s): Nov. 1
Trustees: Victoria Garlanda; Robert E. Ingmire; Harry D. Snyder.
EIN: 137430894

2437
The Elizabeth & Michel Sorel Charitable Organization, Inc.

25 W. 45th St., Ste. 504
New York, NY 10036-4902 (212) 730-3552
***Contact:* Judy Cope, Exec. Dir.**
***E-mail:* Judy@Sorelmusic.org**; Main URL: http://www.sorelmusic.org/

Established in NY.
Donors: Claudette Sorel‡; Ellen Rosenberg.
Foundation type: Independent foundation.
Financial data (yr. ended 12/31/12): Assets, $5,198,178 (M); gifts received, $200; expenditures, $573,773; qualifying distributions, $480,961; giving activities include $199,100 for 13 grants (high: $52,000; low: $2,000).
Purpose and activities: Awards are limited to women composers.
Fields of interest: Performing arts, music; Performing arts, orchestras; Arts; Education; Religion.
Limitations: Giving primarily in NY. No grants to individuals.
Officers and Director:* Berge Avedisian,* Pres.; Walter J. Killmer, Jr., V.P.; Judy Cope, Exec. Dir.
EIN: 133918852
Other changes: The grantmaker has moved from VA to NY.

2438
Soros Charitable Foundation

New York, NY

The foundation terminated on July 18, 2012.

2439
Paul & Daisy Soros Fellowships for New Americans

(formerly Paul & Daisy Soros Foundation)
400 W. 59th St., 4th Fl.
New York, NY 10019-1105 (212) 547-6926
FAX: (212) 548-4623;
E-mail: pdsoros_fellows@sorosny.org; Main URL: http://www.pdsoros.org

Established in 1994 in NY.
Donor: Paul Soros.
Foundation type: Independent foundation.
Financial data (yr. ended 12/31/12): Assets, $48,405,686 (M); gifts received, $331,782; expenditures, $4,382,955; qualifying distributions, $4,168,190; giving activities include $963,239 for 8 grants (high: $300,000; low: $20,000), and $2,401,386 for 86 grants to individuals (high: $57,500; low: $5,000).
Purpose and activities: Grants to new Americans for graduate study. Giving limited to permanent U.S. residents, naturalized U.S. citizens, and U.S.-born applicants who are the children of two naturalized U.S. citizens.
Fields of interest: Education; Adults; Immigrants/refugees.
Type of support: Fellowships; Grants to individuals.
Limitations: Applications accepted. Giving on a national basis. No grants for academic fees other than tuition.
Publications: Application guidelines; Informational brochure; Newsletter.
Application information: Application forms, guidelines, and guidance for recommenders for the Fellowship for New Americans are available on foundation web site. Application form required.
Initial approach: See Web site for details
Deadline(s): Nov. 1 (it is encouraged that materials be submitted prior to this date)
Board meeting date(s): Feb. and Oct. of each year.
Final notification: 2 months from Nov. 1
Director: Yulian Ramos, Deputy Dir.; Stanley J. Heginbotham.
Trustee: Daisy Soros.
Number of staff: 2 full-time professional; 1 full-time support.
EIN: 137057096
Other changes: Yulian Ramos is now Deputy Dir.

2440
Source of Hope Foundation

c/o Stephen Robert, Tr.
667 Madison Ave., Ste. 17B
New York, NY 10065-8029 (212) 583-7002
***E-mail:* gina@sourceofhope.com**; Main URL: http://www.sourceofhope.com/

Established in NY.
Donors: Stephen Robert; Pilar Crespi Robert.
Foundation type: Independent foundation.
Financial data (yr. ended 06/30/13): Assets, $23,929,195 (M); gifts received, $1,100,000; expenditures, $3,694,346; qualifying distributions, $3,681,214; giving activities include $3,426,200 for 26 grants (high: $1,000,000; low: $500).
Purpose and activities: The mission of the foundation is to help people in desperate need through a holistic approach that supplies sustainable aid in the form of food, water, health care, education and micro-finance.
Fields of interest: Housing/shelter, temporary shelter; Human services.
Limitations: Applications not accepted. Giving primarily in NY and OR.
Application information: Unsolicited requests for funds not accepted.
Officers: Stephen Robert, Chair. and Co-C.E.O.; Pilar Crespi Robert, Co-C.E.O. and Pres.
EIN: 264380918

2441
The Sparkplug Foundation

Park West Finance Station
P.O. Box 20956
New York, NY 10025-0016
E-mail: info@sparkplugfoundation.org; Tel./Fax: (877) 866-8285; Main URL: http://www.sparkplugfoundation.org/
Grants Database: http://sparkplugfoundation.org/past-grants

Established in 2003 in NY.
Donors: Felice Gelman; Yoram Gelman; Emmaia Gelman.
Foundation type: Independent foundation.
Financial data (yr. ended 12/31/12): Assets, $6,986,278 (M); gifts received, $14,019; expenditures, $455,869; qualifying distributions, $320,360; giving activities include $319,982 for 43 grants (high: $12,000; low: $2,000).
Purpose and activities: Giving is focused on providing seed money for new organizations, projects or ideas. The foundation makes one-time grants for activities which create sustainable organizing and communities, while recognizing the importance of developing individual cultures by favoring projects that promote diversity. The main areas of focus are music, education, and grassroots organizations, as well as exploring funding projects in the area of alternative and sustainable energies.
Fields of interest: Performing arts, music ensembles/groups; Education; Environment; International human rights; International migration/refugee issues; International affairs; Community/economic development; Science; Young adults; Minorities; Asians/Pacific Islanders; African Americans/Blacks; Hispanics/Latinos; Native Americans/American Indians; Indigenous peoples; Adults, women; AIDS, people with; Immigrants/refugees; LGBTQ.
International interests: East Jerusalem; Israel; West Bank/Gaza (Palestinian Territories).
Type of support: Management development/capacity building; Program development; Conferences/seminars; Publication; Seed money; Curriculum development; Research; Technical assistance; Program evaluation; Grants to individuals.
Limitations: Applications accepted. Giving to every state in the USA. Some giving in Israel for projects that involve Palestinian communities. No support for university-based projects, or for non-secular activities. No grants to non-501(c)(3) organizations unless they have a fiscal sponsor. No grants for performances, tickets or tuitions, equipment, computers or for operating support.
Application information: Complete application guidelines and deadlines available on foundation web site. Application form required.
***Initial approach:* Submit preliminary questionnaire on foundation web site**
Copies of proposal: 1
Board meeting date(s): Within 4 weeks of deadline dates
Final notification: Usually within 1 month
Trustees: Felice Gelman; Yoram Gelman; Emmaia Gelman.
Number of staff: 1 part-time professional.
EIN: 331033952

2442
Spektor Family Foundation, Inc.

c/o CBIZ
1065 Avenue of the Americas
New York, NY **10018**
***Application address:* c/o Mira Spektor, 262 Central Park West, Apt. 14E, New York, NY 10024, tel.: (212) 790-5700**

Established in 1968 in NY.
Donor: Eryk Spektor‡.
Foundation type: Independent foundation.
Financial data (yr. ended 06/30/13): Assets, $3,225,129 (M); expenditures, $162,148; qualifying distributions, $149,416; giving activities include $145,500 for 20 grants (high: $25,000; low: $500).
Purpose and activities: Support primarily for Jewish organizations, arts, community services and education.
Fields of interest: Museums; Higher education; Higher education, university; Human services; Pregnancy centers; Jewish agencies & synagogues.
Type of support: General/operating support; Scholarship funds.

Limitations: Applications accepted. Giving primarily in NY. No grants to individuals.
Application information: Application form required.
Initial approach: Letter
Deadline(s): None
Officer: Mira Spektor, Pres.
EIN: 136277982

2443
The Sperry Fund
99 Park Ave., Ste. 2220
New York, NY 10016-1601
Contact: Thomas L. Parkinson Ph.D., Prog. Dir.
FAX: (610) 625-7919
Scholarship program URL: **http://foundationcenter.org/grantmaker/beinecke/index.html, tel.: (610) 395-5560, e-mail: BeineckeScholarship@earthlink.net**

Established in 1962 in NY.
Foundation type: Independent foundation.
Financial data (yr. ended 06/30/13): Assets, $16,710,206 (M); gifts received, $10,000; expenditures, $1,041,824; qualifying distributions, $963,069; giving activities include $255,000 for 12 grants (high: $25,000; low: $10,000), and $578,274 for grants to individuals.
Purpose and activities: The foundation provides scholarships for the graduate education of young men and women of exceptional promise through the Beinecke Scholarship Program.
Fields of interest: Education.
Type of support: Program development; Scholarships—to individuals.
Limitations: Applications not accepted. Giving primarily in NY.
Publications: Informational brochure.
Application information: College or university must be invited to nominate juniors for scholarship program; completion of application form required for nominees. Applications outside the nomination process not considered. See scholarship web site for guidelines.
Officers and Directors:* Frederick W. Beinecke, Pres.; John B. Beinecke,* V.P.; R. Scott Greathead,* Secy.; Robert J. Barletta, Treas.; William S. Beinecke; Frances Beinecke Elston; Sarah Beinecke Richardson; Melvyn L. Shaffir.
Number of staff: 1 part-time support.
EIN: 136114308

2444
The Seth Sprague Educational and Charitable Foundation
c/o U.S. Trust
114 W. 47th St.
New York, NY 10036-1592 (646) 855-1011
***Contact:* Christine O'Donnell, U.S. Trust**

Trust established in 1939 in NY.
Donor: Seth Sprague†.
Foundation type: Independent foundation.
Financial data (yr. ended 12/31/12): Assets, $65,445,168 (M); expenditures, $3,512,258; qualifying distributions, $3,209,198; giving activities include $3,040,000 for 252 grants (high: $60,500; low: $500).
Purpose and activities: Program priorities in New York, NY, consist of: 1) Arts- priorities include audience engagement for ages 20s to 30s and underserved communities; 2) Education- priorities include professional development and school-day enrichment programs operating in public schools; and 3) Housing and basic needs - priorities include services to support homeless individuals or those at-risk of losing their homes, food distribution and nutrition programs, and comprehensive services for at-risk populations. Program priorities in Boston and Cape Cod, MA, San Diego, CA, and ME include: health care, education, human and social services, environment and the arts.
Fields of interest: Arts; Education; Environment, natural resources; Health care; Food banks; Human services.
Type of support: General/operating support; Program development; Matching/challenge support.
Limitations: Applications accepted. Giving primarily in NY, Boston and Cape Cod, MA, ME, and San Diego, CA. No grants to individuals, or for building funds; no loans.
Application information: Arts in education is no longer a priority of the foundation. Application form not required.
Initial approach: 3-5 page narrative proposal
Copies of proposal: 1
Deadline(s): Apr. 1 and Sept. 1
Board meeting date(s): June and Nov.
Final notification: June and Dec.
Trustees: Rebecca Greenleaf Clapp; Irene de Watteville; Patricia Dunnington.
EIN: 136071886
Other changes: The grantmaker no longer publishes application guidelines.

2445
St. George's Society of New York
216 E. 45th St., Ste. 901
New York, NY 10017-3304 (212) 682-6110
***Contact:* John Shannon, Exec. Dir.; Samantha Hamilton, Dir., Devel. and Membership**
FAX: (212) 682-3465;
E-mail: info@stgeorgessociety.org; Main URL: http://www.stgeorgessociety.org
Facebook: https://www.facebook.com/pages/St-Georges-Society-of-New-York/162723030430738

Established in 1770 in NY.
Donors: Charlotte M. F. Bentley†; British Embassy; DeCoizart Charitable Trust; Andrew MacKenzie Hay†; Florence Davis; Francis Finlay; Richard Grasso; Sir Deryck C. Maughan; Sir Edwin Manton†; William R. Miller; Martin Sullivan; Aetna; Citigroup UK; D'Amato & Lynch; HSBC Bank USA, N.A.; McGraw Hill Companies; Sherman & Sterling; Skaden Arps; JPMorgan Chase Bank, N.A.; Starr Foundation; Revolution Studios; CSFB; Bloomberg; Sony Corp.; AIG; WWP/Young & Rubicam; Hearst Corp.; Sir Howard Stringer; R. Brandon Fradd; Mark C. Pigott; PACCAR, Inc.; Ford Motor Co.
Foundation type: Operating foundation.
Financial data (yr. ended 12/31/12): Assets, $11,798,622 (M); gifts received, $1,074,847; expenditures, $1,662,342; qualifying distributions, $1,477,371; giving activities include $334,633 for 7 grants (high: $155,000; low: $1,000), $499,755 for 91 grants to individuals, and $942,544 for foundation-administered programs.
Purpose and activities: A private operating foundation dedicated to helping men and women from the United Kingdom and the British Commonwealth and their children who find themselves in need, trouble, sickness or other adversity in the New York, NY, area. The Society has two main areas of endeavor, its Beneficiary Program to support the elderly and disabled, and its Scholarship Program to assist outstanding students with university tuition.
Fields of interest: Higher education, university; Health care.
International interests: United Kingdom.
Type of support: Emergency funds; Grants to individuals.
Limitations: Giving limited to the metropolitan New York, NY, area.
Publications: Annual report; Newsletter.
Application information: Applicant must be a native of the United Kingdom or the British Commonwealth, residing in the New York, NY, metropolitan region, with a legal status. Personal interviews and visits from the Society's social worker. Application form not required.
Initial approach: Letter or telephone
Copies of proposal: 1
Deadline(s): None
Board meeting date(s): Quarterly
Final notification: 4-6 weeks
Officers and Directors:* Robert J.K. Titley,* Pres.; Richard Sexton, MBE*, 1st V.P.; Philip Warner, OBE*, 2nd V.P.; Paul Beresford-Hill, MBE, Secy.; Stephen J. Storen, Treas.; Lewis Stetson Allen; **Ceasae Anquillare, JP**; Andrew Booth; **Philippa Cheetham**; **Duncan Edwards**; **June Felix**; **Susan Lopez**; Geneive Brown Metzger; **Jigs Patel**; **Peter Selman**; **Nicholas C. Walsh**; **Stuart Welburn.**
Number of staff: 3 full-time professional; 2 part-time professional; 1 full-time support.
EIN: 237426425
Other changes: John Oden is no longer a director.

2446
St. Simon Charitable Foundation, Inc.
c/o Robert G. Wilmers
350 Park Ave., 6th Fl.
New York, NY 10022-6022

Established in 2001 in DE.
Donor: Robert G. Wilmers.
Foundation type: Independent foundation.
Financial data (yr. ended 06/30/13): Assets, $33,880,094 (M); gifts received, $4,782,725; expenditures, $82,048; qualifying distributions, $60,700; giving activities include $57,500 for 3 grants (high: $37,500; low: $10,000).
Fields of interest: Arts, cultural/ethnic awareness; Performing arts centers.
Limitations: Applications not accepted. Giving primarily in MA and NY. No grants to individuals.
Application information: Contributes only to pre-selected organizations.
Officer: Robert G. Wilmers, Pres.
EIN: 522339484
Other changes: For the fiscal year ended June 30, 2013, the fair market value of the grantmaker's assets was $33,880,094, a 56.1% increase over the fiscal 2012 value, $21,698,073.

2447
Mary Reinhart Stackhouse Foundation
c/o U.S. Trust, Philanthropic Solutions
1 Bryant Park, NY1-100-28-05
New York, NY 10036-6715 (646) 855-0956
Contact: Ken Goody, Senior Vice President
E-mail: kenneth.l.goody@ustrust.com; **Main URL: https://www.bankofamerica.com/philanthropic/grantmaking.go**

Established in 1999 in NJ.
Donor: Mary Stackhouse Trust.
Foundation type: Independent foundation.
Financial data (yr. ended 12/31/12): Assets, $6,746,895 (M); expenditures, $345,886; qualifying distributions, $308,693; giving activities

include $285,000 for 8 grants (high: $85,000; low: $10,000).
Purpose and activities: Giving for environmental and conservation organizations, and to support further education of needy caddies.
Fields of interest: Education; Environment, association; Recreation.
Limitations: Giving primarily in FL and NJ. No grants to individuals.
Application information: Complete application guidelines available on foundation web site.
Initial approach: Online
Deadline(s): Sept. 15
Trustees: Bob McCurdy; Bank of America, N.A.
EIN: 527077828

2448
The Stardust Foundation of Central New York
2 State St.
P.O. Box 798
Auburn, NY 13021-3625 (315) 252-3525
Contact: Guy Cosentino, Exec. Dir.
***FAX:* (315) 252-3646**;
E-mail: info@stardustfoundationcny.org; Main URL: http://stardustfoundationcny.org/

Established in 2007 in NY.
Donors: Gerald Bisgrove; Stardust Foundation of Arizona.
Foundation type: Independent foundation.
Financial data (yr. ended 12/31/13): Assets, $10,409 (M); expenditures, $21,729; qualifying distributions, $0.
Fields of interest: Performing arts, theater; Higher education; Higher education, college (community/junior); Hospitals (general); Human services.
Limitations: Applications accepted. Giving primarily in Auburn, NY.
Application information: Application form not required.
Deadline(s): None
Officers: John Bisgrove, Pres.; Matteo Bartolotta, V.P.; Peter Emerson, Secy.-Treas.; Guy Cosentino, Exec. Dir.
Director: Jerry Bisgrove.
EIN: 208823881

2449
Howard E. Stark Charitable Foundation
53 N. Park Ave., Ste. 50
Rockville Centre, NY 11570-4111 **(516) 678-1927**

Established in NY.
Foundation type: Independent foundation.
Financial data (yr. ended 05/30/13): Assets, $5,282,839 (M); expenditures, $299,956; qualifying distributions, $250,809; giving activities include $215,264 for 17 grants (high: $30,000; low: $224).
Fields of interest: Food services; Housing/shelter; Homeless, human services.
Limitations: Applications accepted. Giving primarily in MA and NY.
Application information: Application form required.
Initial approach: Request formal grant application from foundation
Deadline(s): None
Officer: Jennifer A. Franz, Exec. Dir.
Trustee: Michael T. Pagano.
EIN: 260270223

2450
Jay and Kelly Sugarman Foundation
c/o Jay Sugarman
1114 Ave. of the Americas
New York, NY **10036**

Established in 2004 in NY.
Donors: Jay Sugarman; Kelly Sugarman.
Foundation type: Independent foundation.
Financial data (yr. ended 12/31/12): Assets, $2,280,119 (M); expenditures, $667,990; qualifying distributions, $638,372; giving activities include $598,222 for 26 grants (high: $219,600; low: $1,000).
Purpose and activities: Giving primarily for the arts, education, and human services.
Fields of interest: Performing arts, theater; Arts; Education; Health organizations, association; Human services; Children/youth, services.
Limitations: Applications not accepted. Giving primarily in New York, NY. No grants to individuals.
Application information: Contributes only to pre-selected organizations.
Officers: Jay Sugarman, Pres. and Treas.; Kelly Sugarman, V.P.; Wendy Forshay, Secy.
EIN: 200911399
Other changes: Jay Sugarman is now Pres. and Treas.

2451
The Sulzberger Foundation, Inc.
620 8th Ave., 16th Fl.
New York, NY 10018-1618

Incorporated in 1956 in NY.
Donors: Arthur Hays Sulzberger‡; Iphigene Ochs Sulzberger‡; Marian S. Heiskell; Ruth S. Holmberg; Judith P. Sulzberger; Arthur Ochs Sulzberger‡.
Foundation type: Independent foundation.
Financial data (yr. ended 12/31/12): Assets, $30,758,999 (M); expenditures, $3,041,126; qualifying distributions, $2,759,426; giving activities include $2,689,000 for 2 grants (high: $2,189,000; low: $500,000).
Fields of interest: Museums (specialized); Foundations (public).
Type of support: General/operating support; Continuing support; Annual campaigns; Building/renovation; Endowments; Emergency funds; Program development; Internship funds; Scholarship funds.
Limitations: Applications not accepted. Giving primarily in Cincinnati, OH; some funding also in Washington, DC. No grants to individuals, or for matching gifts; no loans.
Application information: The foundation is not currently accepting applications.
Board meeting date(s): Jan. and as required
Officers: Marian S. Heiskell, Pres.; Ruth S. Holmberg, V.P.
Trustee: Arthur Ochs Sulzberger.
Number of staff: 1 part-time professional; 2 part-time support.
EIN: 136083166
Other changes: At the close of 2012, the grantmaker paid grants of $2,689,000, a 58.2% increase over the 2010 disbursements, $1,700,000.
Judith P. Sulzberger is no longer a V.P.

2452
The John and Jayne Summers Foundation, Inc.
P.O. Box 60620
Rochester, NY 14606-0620

Established in 2000 in NY.
Donors: John M. Summers; Jayne C. Summers‡; Richard Sand; Danny Wegman; John C. Pyles; Steriliz LLC.
Foundation type: Independent foundation.
Financial data (yr. ended 12/31/12): Assets, $11,641,198 (M); gifts received, $1,177,830; expenditures, $1,133,848; qualifying distributions, $778,520; giving activities include $778,520 for 35 grants (high: $125,000; low: $500).
Fields of interest: Higher education; Education; Health organizations, association; Human services.
Limitations: Applications not accepted. Giving primarily in Rochester, NY. No grants to individuals.
Application information: Contributes only to pre-selected organizations.
Officers: John M. Summers, Pres.; Eugene W. Baldino, V.P. and Treas.; Kenneth A. Marvald, V.P.; Susan L. Conrado, Secy.
Directors: Douglas J. Summers; Todd D. Summers.
EIN: 161596923
Other changes: Jayne C. Summers, a director, is deceased.

2453
The Sunrise Klein Foundation Inc.
c/o A. Klein
307 S. Grandview Ave.
Monsey, NY 10952-3305 (845) 426-1214

Established in 2000.
Donors: Julius Klein Diamonds Inc.; Abraham Klein; Sunrise Venture LLC.
Foundation type: Company-sponsored foundation.
Financial data (yr. ended 01/31/13): Assets, $437,040 (M); gifts received, $100; expenditures, $69,603; qualifying distributions, $69,501; giving activities include $69,501 for 3 grants (high: $40,300; low: $7,201).
Purpose and activities: The foundation supports organizations involved with Judaism.
Fields of interest: Jewish agencies & synagogues.
Type of support: General/operating support.
Limitations: Applications accepted. Giving primarily in NY.
Application information: Application form not required.
Initial approach: Proposal
Deadline(s): None
Officers: Abraham Klein, Pres.; Bella Klein, Secy.
EIN: 134097745
Other changes: The grantmaker no longer lists a primary contact.

2454
Surdna Foundation, Inc.
330 Madison Ave., 30th Fl.
New York, NY 10017-5001 (212) 557-0010
Contact: Phillip Henderson, Pres.
FAX: (212) 557-0003; E-mail: grants@surdna.org; Main URL: http://www.surdna.org
E-Newsletter: http://visitor.constantcontact.com/manage/optin/ea?v=001qgl9GeY_mqQM45bpB_NAiA%3D%3D
Grantee Perception Report: http://www.surdna.org/publications-resources/102.html
Grants Database: http://www.surdna.org/what-we-fund/search-our-grants.html

Twitter: http://twitter.com/surdna_fndn

Incorporated in 1917 in NY.
Donor: John E. Andrus‡.
Foundation type: Independent foundation.
Financial data (yr. ended 06/30/13): Assets, $929,596,379 (M); expenditures, $44,766,655; qualifying distributions, $34,643,450; giving activities include $34,643,450 for 501 grants (high: $800,000; low: $100).
Purpose and activities: The foundation seeks to foster just and sustainable communities in the United States guided by principles of social justice and distinguished by healthy environments, strong local economies, and thriving cultures. The foundation focuses on three core areas: 1) Sustainable Environments; 2) Strong Local Economies; and 3) Thriving Cultures.
Fields of interest: Arts, alliance/advocacy; Arts, association; Arts, cultural/ethnic awareness; Arts education; Environment, energy; Environment; Employment; Economic development; Urban/community development; Community/economic development; Public affairs, citizen participation.
Type of support: General/operating support; Continuing support; Management development/capacity building; Program development; Program-related investments/loans; Employee matching gifts.
Limitations: Applications accepted. Giving on a national basis. No support for international projects, or programs addressing direct job training, toxics, hazardous waste, environmental education, sustainable agriculture, or food production. No grants for individuals, endowments/land acquisition, capital campaigns or construction.
Publications: Annual report (including application guidelines); Grants list.
Application information: Online applications encouraged. Applicants should check guidelines and eligibility requirements prior to initiating the application process. The foundation funds the Andrus Family Fund that defines and manages its own grantmaking program and process. For more information see http://www.affund.org. Application form required.
Initial approach: Online at foundation web site
Copies of proposal: 1
Deadline(s): None
Board meeting date(s): Feb., May, and Sept.
Final notification: 90 days for letters of inquiry; approximately 12 weeks for full proposals
Officers and Directors:* Jocelyn Downie,* Chair.; Peter B. Benedict II, Vice-Chair.; Phillip Henderson, Pres.; Marc de Venoge, C.F.O. and C.A.O.; **Lawrence S.C. Griffith, M.D., Secy. and Interim-Treas.**; Bruce Abernethy; Elizabeth H. Andrus; Judy Belk; Carra Cote-Ackah; John F. Hawkins; Kelly D. Nowlin; Tracy Palandjian; Michael S. Spensley; Gwen Walden.
Number of staff: 19 full-time professional; 4 full-time support; 1 part-time support.
EIN: 136108163
Other changes: Lawrence S.C. Griffith is now Secy. and Intrim-Treas.

2455
The Swartz Foundation
6 Light House Point Rd.
Lloyd Harbor, NY **11743-1010**
Main URL: http://www.theswartzfoundation.org
Twitter: http://twitter.com/SwartzCompNeuro

Established in 1995 in NY.
Donors: Dr. Jerome Swartz; JSwartz Charitable Lead Trust.
Foundation type: Independent foundation.
Financial data (yr. ended 10/31/11): Assets, $9,026,185 (M); gifts received, $138,500; expenditures, $2,075,049; qualifying distributions, $1,915,973; giving activities include $1,692,500 for 12 grants (high: $380,000; low: $10,000).
Purpose and activities: The mission of the Swartz foundation is to explore the application of physics, mathematics, and computer engineering principles to neuroscience, as a path to better understanding the brain-mind relationship. Giving primarily to establish research centers devoted to advancing computational neuroscience.
Fields of interest: Higher education; Science, research.
Limitations: Applications not accepted. Giving primarily in CA, CT, MA, NJ, and NY. No grants to individuals.
Application information: Contributes only to pre-selected organizations.
Officer: Paul Kelly, C.F.O.
Trustees: James P. King; Dr. Jerome Swartz.
EIN: 116447242

2456
Lisa and Steven Tananbaum Family Foundation
10 Loden Ln.
Purchase, NY 10577-2310

Donors: Lisa Tananbaum; Steve A. Tananbaum.
Foundation type: Independent foundation.
Financial data (yr. ended 12/31/12): Assets, $13,881,747 (M); gifts received, $1,469,367; expenditures, $886,310; qualifying distributions, $829,411; giving activities include $829,411 for 30 grants (high: $501,000; low: $466).
Purpose and activities: Giving primarily for museums, education, social services, and Jewish organizations.
Fields of interest: Museums (art); Museums (ethnic/folk arts); Elementary/secondary education; Higher education; Human services; Jewish federated giving programs; Jewish agencies & synagogues.
Limitations: Applications not accepted. Giving primarily in New York, NY.
Application information: Contributes only to pre-selected organizations.
Trustees: Lisa Tananbaum; Steve A. Tananbaum.
EIN: 137378428
Other changes: Barry Ritholz is no longer a trustee.

2457
The Doris & Stanley Tananbaum Foundation
c/o D'Arcangelo & Co., LLP
800 Westchester Ave., No. N-400
Rye Brook, NY **10573-1301**

Established in 1998 in NY.
Donors: Doris Tananbaum; Stanley Tananbaum.
Foundation type: Independent foundation.
Financial data (yr. ended 12/31/12): Assets, $13,055,970 (M); expenditures, $46,274; qualifying distributions, $7,728; giving activities include $700 for 3 grants (high: $500; low: $100).
Fields of interest: Health organizations, association; Crime/law enforcement, police agencies; Human services; Jewish federated giving programs.
Type of support: General/operating support.
Limitations: Applications not accepted. Giving primarily in NY. No grants to individuals.
Application information: Unsolicited requests for funds not accepted.
Trustees: Ricki Conway; Doris Tananbaum; Stanley Tananbaum.
EIN: 137161531

2458
Tandon Family Foundation, Inc.
c/o M. Baharestani, CPA
148 Madison Ave., 11th Fl.
New York, NY 10016-6700

Established in NY.
Donors: Chandrika Tandon; Ranjan Tandon.
Foundation type: Independent foundation.
Financial data (yr. ended 12/31/12): Assets, $21,447,258 (M); gifts received, $9,546,766; expenditures, $2,538,193; qualifying distributions, $2,412,490; giving activities include $2,309,653 for 15 grants (high: $1,956,165; low: $500).
Purpose and activities: Giving primarily for U.S.-based organizations and programs concerning India.
Fields of interest: Arts; Education; Hinduism.
International interests: India.
Limitations: Applications not accepted. Giving primarily in New Haven, CT, and New York, NY. No grants to individuals.
Application information: Contributes only to pre-selected organizations.
Directors: Martin Baharestani; **Deven Sharma**; Chandrika Tandon; Lita Tandon; Ranjan Tandon.
EIN: 043744965

2459
The Teagle Foundation
570 Lexington Ave., 38th Fl.
New York, NY 10022-6859 (212) 373-1972
Contact: Sarah Graham, Office Admin.
E-mail: info@teaglefoundation.org; Main URL: http://www.teagle.org
Blog: http://www.teagle.org/liblog/default.aspx
E-Newsletter: http://www.teagle.org/subscription/
Facebook: http://www.facebook.com/pages/The-Teagle-Foundation/164308972617
Grants List: http://www.teagle.org/grantmaking/grantees.aspx
News Feed: http://feeds.rapidfeeds.com/40060/
Podcasts: http://www.teagle.org/learning/podcasts.aspx

Incorporated in 1944 in CT.
Donors: Walter C. Teagle‡; Rowena Lee Teagle‡; Walter C. Teagle, Jr.‡.
Foundation type: Independent foundation.
Financial data (yr. ended 06/30/12): Assets, $141,131,933 (M); gifts received, $500; expenditures, $9,252,640; qualifying distributions, $6,838,338; giving activities include $6,838,338 for grants.
Purpose and activities: The goal of the Teagle Foundation is to mobilize resources, financial and intellectual, to help students "catch fire" intellectually through a challenging, wide-ranging and enriching college education. At this time, the foundation is only focusing on higher education.
Fields of interest: Arts education; Higher education; Children/youth, services.
Type of support: Employee-related scholarships; Continuing support; Program development; Curriculum development; Consulting services; Employee matching gifts; Matching/challenge support.

Limitations: Applications not accepted. Giving limited to the U.S. No grants to community organizations outside New York City. No support for No grants to U.S. organizations for foreign programmatic activities. No loans.
Publications: Annual report.
Application information: Unsolicited proposals are no longer accepted. Please check the foundation's program development and implementation page on its web site for more information.
Board meeting date(s): Feb., May, and Nov.
Officers and Directors:* Walter C. Teagle III,* Chair.; Judith Shapiro,* Pres.; Eli Weinberg, Treas.; Desiree Vazquez, Secy. and Prog. Assoc.; Ann-Marie Buckley, Cont. and Dir., Finance and Operations; **Elizabeth Boylan**; Kenneth P. Cohen; Andrew Delbanco; Blauch Galdenberg; William Chester Jordan; Jayne Keith; Richard J. Light; Philip B. Pool, Jr.; Grant Porter; Barbara Paul Robinson; Brian Rosenberg; Judith R. Shapiro; Cornelia Small; Pauline Yu.
Number of staff: 3 full-time professional; 1 full-time support.
EIN: 131773645
Other changes: Desiree Vazquez is now Secy. and Prog. Assoc.

2460
The Teagle Foundation Incorporated
c/o Jennifer Dale
570 Lexington Ave., 38th Fl.
New York, NY 10022-6837
E-mail: info@teaglefoundation.org; Main URL: http://www.teaglefoundation.org/

Foundation type: Independent foundation.
Financial data (yr. ended 06/30/13): Assets, $146,322,906 (M); gifts received, $1,000; expenditures, $9,499,994; qualifying distributions, $6,909,510; giving activities include $5,814,727 for 194 grants (high: $139,000; low: $50), and $50,489 for foundation-administered programs.
Purpose and activities: The foundation intends to be an influential national voice and a catalyst for change in higher education to improve undergraduate student learning in the arts and sciences.
Fields of interest: Higher education; Human services.
Limitations: Applications not accepted. Giving primarily in New York, NY.
Application information: Unsolicited requests for funds not accepted.
Officers and Directors:* Walter C. Teagle III,* Chair.; Judith R. Shapiro,* Pres.; **Desiree Vazquez, Secy.**; Eli Weinberg, Treas.; Kenneth P. Cohen; Andrew Delbanco; Blanche Goldenburg; William Chester Jordan; Jayne Keith; Richard J. Light; Richard L. Morrill; Philip B. Pool, Jr.; Grant Porter; Barbara Paul Robinson; Cornelia Small; Pauline Yu.
EIN: 201370387
Other changes: Desiree Vazquez has replaced Anne W. Bezbatchenko as Secy.

2461
The Thompson Family Foundation, Inc.
(formerly The Wade F. B. Thompson Charitable Foundation, Inc.)
230 Park Ave., Ste. 1541
New York, NY 10169-1541

Established in 1986 in CT.
Donors: Wade F.B. Thompson†; Wade F.B. Thompson Trust.
Foundation type: Independent foundation.
Financial data (yr. ended 05/31/13): Assets, $453,125,217 (M); gifts received, $200,339,887; expenditures, $13,089,581; qualifying distributions, $11,953,786; giving activities include $11,653,770 for 63 grants (high: $6,356,070; low: $5,000).
Purpose and activities: Giving primarily for historical preservation, health organizations, and human services.
Fields of interest: Museums; Historic preservation/historical societies; Arts; Health organizations, association; Cancer research; Prostate cancer research; Recreation, parks/playgrounds; Human services; Community/economic development.
Type of support: General/operating support; Annual campaigns; Building/renovation; Land acquisition; Seed money.
Limitations: Applications not accepted. Giving primarily in CT and the greater New York, NY, area. No grants to individuals.
Application information: Contributes only to pre-selected organizations.
Officers: Angela E. Thompson, Pres.; Charles A.Y. Thompson, V.P.; Alan Siegel, Secy.; Amanda J.T. Riegel, Treas.
EIN: 061194385
Other changes: For the fiscal year ended May 31, 2013, the fair market value of the grantmaker's assets was $453,125,217, a 179.9% increase over the fiscal 2012 value, $161,866,834. For the same period, the grantmaker paid grants of $11,653,770, a 94.8% increase over the fiscal 2012 disbursements, $5,982,534.

2462
Tick-Borne Disease Alliance
(formerly Turn the Corner Foundation)
New York, NY

Status changed to Public Charity.

2463
The Tiffany & Co. Foundation
200 Fifth Ave.
New York, NY 10010-3302
***Contact:* Anisa Kamadoli Costa, Chair. and Pres.**
E-mail: foundation@tiffany.com; Main URL: http://www.tiffanyandcofoundation.org
Grants Database: http://www.tiffanyandcofoundation.org/grants/
Grants Map: http://www.tiffanyandcofoundation.org/grants/map/

Established in 2000 in NY.
Donor: Tiffany & Co.
Foundation type: Company-sponsored foundation.
Financial data (yr. ended 12/31/12): Assets, $23,440,999 (M); expenditures, $6,001,344; qualifying distributions, $5,820,000; giving activities include $5,820,000 for 32 grants (high: $1,000,000; low: $25,000).
Purpose and activities: The foundation supports programs designed to protect the beauty of nature and the creativity of human nature. Special emphasis is directed toward programs designed to preserve the arts and promote environmental conservation.
Fields of interest: Arts education; Visual arts; Visual arts, design; Museums; Arts; Environment, research; Environment, natural resources; Environment, water resources; Environment, land resources; Botanical/horticulture/landscape services; Environment, beautification programs; Environment; Recreation, parks/playgrounds; Urban/community development; Geology.
Type of support: Continuing support; General/operating support; Program development; Research.
Limitations: Applications accepted. **No support for religious, political, social, or fraternal organizations, or organizations that do not have tax-exempt status under Section 501(c)(3) of the Internal Revenue Code, or the equivalent.** No grants to individuals, or for capital campaigns, fundraising benefits or events, or athletic events; no product donations.
Publications: Application guidelines; Program policy statement.
Application information: Additional information may be requested at a later date. Application form required.
Initial approach: Complete online letter of inquiry
Deadline(s): Rolling
Board meeting date(s): Twice annually
Final notification: 3 months
Officers and Directors:* Anisa Kamadoli Costa,* Chair. and Pres.; Leigh M. Harlan, Secy.; Michael W. Connolly, Treas.; Patrick B. Dorsey; James N. Fernandez; Michael J. Kowalski.
EIN: 134096178
Other changes: The grantmaker no longer lists a fax.

2464
Tiger Foundation
101 Park Ave., 21st Fl.
New York, NY 10178-4799 (212) 984-2565
Contact: Amy Barger, Mgr. Dir.
FAX: (212) 949-9778;
E-mail: info@tigerfoundation.org; **Physical address: 125 Park Ave., 16th Fl., New York, NY 10017**;
Main URL: http://www.tigerfoundation.org
GiveSmart: http://www.givesmart.org/Stories/Donors/Julian-Robertson,-Jr-
Grants List: http://www.tigerfoundation.org/index.php?/our_grantees/
Julian H. Robertson, Jr.'s Giving Pledge Profile: http://glasspockets.org/philanthropy-in-focus/eye-on-the-giving-pledge/profiles/robertson

Established in 1989 in NY.
Donors: Julian H. Robertson, Jr.; Tiger Management LLC employees.
Foundation type: Independent foundation.
Financial data (yr. ended 06/30/13): Assets, $141,389,067 (M); gifts received, $12,920,361; expenditures, $22,226,620; qualifying distributions, $21,921,421; giving activities include $19,280,000 for 95 grants (high: $500,000; low: $10,000), and $1,420,785 for 2 foundation-administered programs.
Purpose and activities: Giving provided to organizations working to break the cycle of poverty in New York City, rather than those which merely alleviate its symptoms. Seeking to provide families with the tools necessary to attain self-sufficiency and build productive lives. To this end, support is to a variety of educational, vocational, and social service and youth development programs designed to catch children and families before they slip into a cycle of poverty and despair, as well as those programs designed to enable individuals to end their dependence on public assistance.
Fields of interest: Education; Employment, services; Youth development, services; Children/youth, services; Family services; Human services; Economically disadvantaged.

Type of support: General/operating support; Continuing support; Management development/ capacity building; Program development; Technical assistance; Program evaluation.
Limitations: Applications accepted. Giving primarily in New York, NY. No support for political organizations or public policy. No grants to individuals, or for endowments, annual or capital campaigns, benefits, legal aid, obligations or debt.
Publications: Application guidelines; Grants list.
Application information: Application form required.
Initial approach: Online application process
Copies of proposal: 1
Deadline(s): None
Board meeting date(s): Quarterly
Officers: Charles Buice, Pres.; Michelle Butynes, Cont.
Number of staff: 8 full-time professional; 1 part-time professional.
EIN: 133555671

2465
The Tikvah Fund
165 E. 65th St., 4th Fl.
New York, NY **10022-6607 (212) 796-1672**
Contact: Roger Hertog, Chair.
FAX: (646) 514-5915; E-mail: info@tikvahfund.org; Main URL: http://tikvahfund.org/
GiveSmart: http://www.givesmart.org/Stories/ Donors/Roger-Hertog

Established in 1992 in NY.
Donor: Zalman C. Bernstein†.
Foundation type: Independent foundation.
Financial data (yr. ended 12/31/12): Assets, $152,877,561 (M); expenditures, $15,759,065; qualifying distributions, $15,174,055; giving activities include $6,337,805 for 41 grants, $212,930 for 13 grants to individuals, and $1,625,514 for foundation-administered programs.
Purpose and activities: Giving primarily for Jewish affairs. Makes grants and program-related investments to companies located in areas of high unemployment or development in Israel, and to companies that are owned by or employ new immigrants or veteran soldiers.
Fields of interest: Religion, public policy; Jewish agencies & synagogues.
International interests: Israel.
Limitations: Applications not accepted. Giving primarily in NY and NJ; some giving in Israel.
Application information: Contributes only to pre-selected organizations.
Officers and Directors:* Roger Hertog,* Chair.; **Maryana Geller, Cont.**; Eric Cohen, Exec. Dir.; **Elliott Abrams**; Mem Dryan Bernstein; **Arthur Fried**; William Kristol; Jay Lefkowitz; Sallai Meridor; Jehuda Reinharz.
EIN: 133676152
Other changes: Arthur W. Fried is no longer C.F.O.

2466
Time Warner Foundation, Inc.
(formerly AOL Time Warner Foundation)
1 Time Warner Ctr.
New York, NY 10019-6038
Contact: Lisa Quiroz, Pres.
***E-mail:* foundation@timewarner.com; Main URL: http://www.timewarnerfoundation.org/**
Time Warner Blog: http://www.timewarner.com/ blog/category/time-warner-foundation
Time Warner Foundation Videos: http:// www.timewarnerfoundation.org/videos

Established in 1997 in VA.
Donors: America Online, Inc.; AOL Time Warner Inc.; Time Warner Inc.
Foundation type: Company-sponsored foundation.
Financial data (yr. ended 12/31/12): Assets, $7,049,490 (M); expenditures, $3,640,000; qualifying distributions, $3,640,000; giving activities include $3,640,000 for 30 grants (high: $500,000; low: $25,000).
Purpose and activities: The foundation supports programs designed to create, develop, and produce work that reflects the voices and experiences of the world, which is critical to sustaining a culturally rich, vibrant and informed community; and promote college access and college advocacy.
Fields of interest: Media/communications; Media, film/video; Media, television; Media, journalism; Museums; Performing arts, theater; Higher education; Education; Disasters, 9/11/01.
Type of support: Capital campaigns; General/ operating support; Building/renovation; Program development.
Limitations: Applications not accepted. Giving primarily in Washington, DC and New York, NY. No support for political, labor, religious, or fraternal organizations or amateur or professional sports groups. No grants to individuals, or for book publication, or film or music production.
Application information: Contributes only to pre-selected organizations.
Officers and Directors:* Lisa Garcia Quiroz,* Pres.; Brenda C. Karickhoff, V.P. and Secy.; Daniel J. Osheyack, V.P.; Rosa Olivares, Treas.; Pascal Desroches, C.F.O.; Philip Sanchez, Assoc. Dir.; Molly Battin; **Sofia Chang**; **Michael Ellenberg**; Sue Fleishman; Gary L. Ginsberg; Lisa Gregorian; Karen Magee; Vinnie Malhotra; **Olaf Olafsson**; Quentin Shaffer; Greg Silverman; Misty Skedgell.
EIN: 541886827
Other changes: Peter Castro, Teri Everett, and Henry McGee are no longer directors.

2467
The Tinker Foundation Inc.
55 E. 59th St., 21st Fl.
New York, NY 10022-1112 (212) 421-6858
Contact: Renate Rennie, Chair. and Pres.
FAX: (212) 223-3326; E-mail: tinker@tinker.org; Main URL: http://www.tinker.org
Grants Database: http://www.tinker.org/grants

Trust established in 1959 in NY; incorporated in 1975 in NY.
Donor: Edward Larocque Tinker†.
Foundation type: Independent foundation.
Financial data (yr. ended 12/31/12): Assets, $80,620,657 (M); expenditures, $5,041,642; qualifying distributions, $4,490,840; giving activities include $3,257,250 for 55+ grants (high: $156,000).
Purpose and activities: The mission of the foundation is to promote the development of an equitable, sustainable, and productive society in Latin America and to enhance the understanding in the U.S. of Latin America and of how U.S. policies may impact the region. Grants are awarded primarily in the areas of democratic governance, education, and sustainable resource management. More limited support is given for projects addressing U.S. policy toward Latin America and Antarctica.
Fields of interest: Education; Environment, natural resources; Environment; International affairs, goodwill promotion; International affairs, foreign policy; International affairs; Marine science; Economics; Political science; Public policy, research; Government/public administration.
International interests: Antarctica; Latin America; Mexico.
Type of support: Program development; Conferences/seminars; Seed money; Research.
Limitations: Applications accepted. Giving limited to projects related to Latin America and Antarctica. No support for projects concerned with health or medical issues or the arts and humanities. No grants to individuals, or for building or endowment funds, equipment, annual campaigns, operating budgets, annual appeals or production costs for film, television, and radio projects.
Publications: Application guidelines; Annual report.
Application information: Application form for Institutional Grants available on foundation web site. Use application guidelines and proposal cover sheet found on the web site or in paper copy, available upon request. Travel to Iberia is no longer supported through Field Research Grants. Application form required.
***Initial approach:* Letter of Inquiry or full proposal via foundation web site for Institutional Grants; download complete application package and forms from foundation web site for Field Research Grants**
Copies of proposal: 2
***Deadline(s):* For Institutional Grants: Mar. 1 and Sept. 15; for Field Research Grants: Oct. 1**
Board meeting date(s): June and Dec.
Final notification: 2 weeks after board meetings
Officers and Directors:* Renate Rennie,* Chair. and Pres.; **Alan Stoga,* Secy.**; Kathleen Waldron,* Treas.; John H. Coatsworth; Sally Grooms Cowal; Arturo C. Porzecanski; Luis Rubio; Susan L. Segal; Bradford K. Smith.
Number of staff: 5 full-time professional; 1 part-time professional; 1 full-time support; 1 part-time support.
EIN: 510175449
Other changes: Alan Stoga has replaced Richard de J. Osborne as Secy.

2468
The Alice M. & Thomas J. Tisch Foundation, Inc.
c/o Mark J. Krinsky
655 Madison Ave., 11th Fl.
New York, NY 10065-8043

Established in 1992 in NY and DE.
Donors: Laurence A. Tisch†; Thomas J. Tisch; Wilma S. Tisch.
Foundation type: Independent foundation.
Financial data (yr. ended 12/31/12): Assets, $59,810,797 (M); gifts received, $16,434,038; expenditures, $27,415,275; qualifying distributions, $27,327,808; giving activities include $27,312,860 for 119 grants (high: $18,792,818; low: $500).
Purpose and activities: Giving primarily for education, arts, health services, youth services, and Jewish agencies and temples.
Fields of interest: Museums (art); Performing arts; Arts; Higher education; Education; Hospitals (general); Health organizations, association; Human services; Children, services; Jewish federated giving programs; Public policy, research; Jewish agencies & synagogues.
Limitations: Applications not accepted. Giving primarily in New York, NY. No grants to individuals.
Application information: Contributes only to pre-selected organizations.
Officers: Thomas J. Tisch, Pres.; Alice M. Tisch, Sr. V.P.; Barry L. Bloom, Secy.-Treas.
EIN: 133693582

Other changes: At the close of 2012, the grantmaker paid grants of $27,312,860, a 193.3% increase over the 2011 disbursements, $9,311,934.
Mark J. Krinsky is no longer V.P.

2469
Tisch Foundation, Inc.
655 Madison Ave., 11th Fl.
New York, NY 10065-8043 (212) 521-2930

Incorporated in 1957 in FL.
Donors: Hotel Americana; Tisch Hotels, Inc.; members of the Tisch family; and closely held corporations.
Foundation type: Independent foundation.
Financial data (yr. ended 12/31/12): Assets, $26,128,605 (M); expenditures, $10,101,637; qualifying distributions, $10,009,151; giving activities include $10,004,951 for 91 grants (high: $6,000,150; low: $15).
Purpose and activities: Emphasis on higher education, including institutions in Israel, and research-related programs; support also for Jewish organizations and welfare funds, museums, and secondary education.
Fields of interest: Museums; Secondary school/education; Higher education; AIDS; Medical research, institute; Human services; Jewish federated giving programs; Jewish agencies & synagogues.
International interests: Israel.
Type of support: Continuing support; Building/renovation; Equipment; Research.
Limitations: Applications not accepted. Giving primarily in NY. No grants to individuals, or for endowment funds, scholarships, fellowships, or matching gifts; no loans.
Application information: Contributes only to pre-selected organizations.
Board meeting date(s): Mar., June, Sept., Dec., and as required
Officers and Directors:* Wilma S. Tisch,* Co-Pres.; Joan H. Tisch,* Co-Pres.; Andrew H. Tisch, V.P.; Daniel R. Tisch, V.P.; James S. Tisch, V.P.; Jonathan M. Tisch, V.P.; Laurie M. Tisch, V.P.; Steven E. Tisch, V.P.; Thomas J. Tisch,* V.P.; Barry L. Bloom,* Secy.-Treas.
EIN: 591002844
Other changes: Mark J. Krinsky is no longer V.P. Thomas M. Steinberg is no longer V.P.

2470
Dan and Sheryl Tishman Family Foundation
100 Park Ave.
New York, NY 10017-5516 **(212) 399-3600**
Contact: Daniel R. Tishman, Dir.; Sheryl C. Tishman, Dir.

Donors: Daniel R. Tishman; Sheryl C. Tishman.
Foundation type: Independent foundation.
Financial data (yr. ended 12/31/12): Assets, $247,944 (M); gifts received, $2,137,785; expenditures, $2,113,254; qualifying distributions, $2,109,000; giving activities include $2,109,000 for grants.
Fields of interest: Education; Health care; Religion.
Limitations: Applications accepted. Giving primarily in New York, NY.
Application information: Application form required.
Initial approach: Letter
Deadline(s): None
Directors: Bob Kerrey; Daniel R. Tishman; Sheryl C. Tishman; John A. Vissicchio; Ed Zukerman.
EIN: 450612382

2471
Touradji Family Foundation
P.O. Box 728
Sagaponack, NY **11962-0728**

Donors: Pejman Touradji; Shannon Touradji.
Foundation type: Independent foundation.
Financial data (yr. ended 12/31/12): Assets, $26,590,452 (M); gifts received, $5,000,000; expenditures, $301,141; qualifying distributions, $300,600; giving activities include $300,000 for 2 grants (high: $250,000; low: $50,000).
Fields of interest: Health organizations; Human services; Foundations (public).
Limitations: Applications not accepted. Giving primarily in New York, NY.
Application information: Contributes only to pre-selected organizations.
Trustees: Pejman Touradji; Shannon Touradji.
EIN: 271533902

2472
The Peter and Elizabeth C. Tower Foundation
2351 N. Forest Rd., Ste. 106
Getzville, NY 14068-1225 (716) 689-0370
Contact: Tracy A. Sawicki, Exec. Dir.
FAX: (716) 689-3716;
E-mail: info@thetowerfoundation.org; Tel. for Donald W. Matteson: (716) 689-0370, ext. 207; Main URL: http://www.thetowerfoundation.org
E-Newsletter: http://www.thetowerfoundation.org/Home/Email
Facebook: https://www.facebook.com/thetowerfoundation
LinkedIn: http://www.linkedin.com/company/the-peter-and-elizabeth-c-tower-foundation?trk=company_logo
RSS Feed: http://www.thetowerfoundation.org/blog
Twitter: https://twitter.com/towerfdn

Established in 1990 in NY.
Donors: Elizabeth C. Tower; Peter Tower; Peter Tower, Inc.; Peter Tower Living Trust.
Foundation type: Independent foundation.
Financial data (yr. ended 12/31/12): Assets, $76,067,758 (M); gifts received, $5,177; expenditures, $4,956,572; qualifying distributions, $4,575,749; giving activities include $3,606,812 for grants (high: $275,377; low: $95).
Purpose and activities: The foundation has four primary funding categories: mental health, substance abuse, learning disabilities, and intellectual disabilities. It also has another category: organizational capacity building, which provides support to eligible organizations that offer programs and services in its primary funding categories.
Fields of interest: Elementary/secondary education; Education, early childhood education; Education; Substance abuse, services; Mental health, treatment; Mental health/crisis services; Children/youth; Youth; Disabilities, people with; Mentally disabled; Substance abusers.
Type of support: Management development/capacity building; Program development; Seed money; Technical assistance; Program evaluation; Matching/challenge support.
Limitations: Giving primarily in Barnstable, Dukes, Essex, and Nantucket counties in MA, and Erie and Niagara counties in NY, and for organizations serving residents of these areas. No support for political campaigns or attempts to influence legislation. No grants to individuals or for general operating support, capital campaigns or capital improvement, or scholarships.
Publications: Application guidelines; Grants list; Program policy statement.
Application information: Application guidelines updated annually; please see foundation web site for current guidelines.
Initial approach: Request for proposal
Board meeting date(s): Quarterly
Officer: Tracy A. Sawicki, Exec. Dir.
Trustees: John N. Blair; Deborah Brayton; John H. Byrnes; Mollie Tower Byrnes; Cynthia Tower Doyle; Robert M. Doyle; Sherif A. Nada; Donna Owens; Joseph J. Rosa; Elizabeth C. Tower; Peter Tower.
Number of staff: 5 full-time professional; 1 full-time support.
EIN: 166350753

2473
Towerbrook Foundation
Park Ave. Tower
65 E. 55th St., 27 Fl.
New York, NY 10022-3362 (212) 699-2200
Contact: Jennifer Glassman, Treas.; Filippo Cardini, Secy.
FAX: (917) 591-9851;
E-mail: contact@towerbrook.com; Additional tel.: (212) 699-2278; **Main URL: http://www.towerbrook.com/towerbrook-foundation/**

Established in 2006 in NY.
Donor: Towerbrook Capital Partners LP.
Foundation type: Company-sponsored foundation.
Financial data (yr. ended 12/31/12): Assets, $8,399,762 (M); expenditures, $1,704,432; qualifying distributions, $1,697,682; giving activities include $1,668,006 for 104 grants (high: $220,000; low: $150).
Purpose and activities: The foundation supports organizations involved with education, health, bone diseases, allergies research, employment, youth development, human services, international development, philanthropy, and military and veterans.
Type of support: General/operating support; Annual campaigns; Equipment; Program development; Scholarship funds.
Limitations: Giving primarily in areas of company operations in CT, MA , and NY, and in Finland, Italy, and the United Kingdom.
Application information:
Initial approach: Contact foundation for application information
Officers and Directors:* Neal Moszkowski,* Co-Chair.; Ramez Sousou, Co-Chair.; Filippo Cardini, Secy.; Jennifer Glassman,* Treas.; Jonathan Bilzin; Robin Esterson; Niclas Gabran; Winston Ginsberg; Hugh Harper; Gordon Holmes; Brian Jacobsen; Michael Karangelen; Adam McLain; Axel Meyersiek; Travis Nelson; Andrew Rolfe; Ian Sacks; Karim Saddi; Patrick Smulders; John Sinik.
EIN: 743182897

2474
The Troy Savings Bank Charitable Foundation, Inc.
32 2nd St.
P.O. Box 598
Troy, NY 12181-0598 (518) 720-0004
Contact: Leslie A. Cheu, Exec. Dir.

FAX: (518) 720-0008;
E-mail: info@tsbfoundation.org; **E-mail for Leslie A. Cheu, Exec. Dir.: lcheu@tsbfoundation.org**; Main URL: http://www.tsbfoundation.org

Established in 1998 in NY as a company-sponsored foundation; status changed to independent foundation in 2004.
Donors: The Troy Savings Bank; Troy Financial Corp.
Foundation type: Independent foundation.
Financial data (yr. ended 12/31/12): Assets, $13,992,883 (M); expenditures, $840,994; qualifying distributions, $734,426; giving activities include $560,080 for grants (average: $5,000–$50,000).
Purpose and activities: The foundation supports organizations involved with arts and culture, community development, and youth development.
Fields of interest: Arts; Housing/shelter; Human services; Children/youth; Youth; Economically disadvantaged; Homeless.
Type of support: Continuing support; Capital campaigns; Equipment; Program development; Curriculum development; Matching/challenge support.
Limitations: Applications accepted. Giving primarily in NY, with emphasis on Albany, Greene, Rensselaer, Saratoga, Schenectady, Schoharie, Warren, and Washington counties. **No support for political, labor or fraternal organizations.** No grants to individuals.
Publications: Application guidelines; Informational brochure.
Application information: See foundation web site for specific application information. Application form required.
Initial approach: Letter (for requests under $1,000), telephone to Exec. Dir. (for requests greater than $1,000)
Deadline(s): Varies. Please contact the Exec. Dir.
Board meeting date(s): Quarterly, with distribution meetings generally held in Jan., Apr., July and Oct.
Final notification: 8 to 10 weeks
Officers and Directors:* Daniel J. Hogarty, Jr.,* Pres.; George H. Arakelian, Secy.; Leslie A. Cheu, Exec. Dir.; Dr. Michael E. Fleming; Willie A. Hammett; Thomas B. Healy; Morris Massry; Edward G. O'Haire.
Number of staff: 2 full-time professional.
EIN: 141813865

2475
Mildred Faulkner Truman Foundation

c/o M&T Bank
1100 Wehrle Dr., 2nd Fl.
Buffalo, NY **14221-7748 (716) 842-5506**
***E-mail:* info@mftf.net**; Main URL: http://www.mftf.net/

Established in 1985 in NY.
Donor: Mildred Faulkner Truman†.
Foundation type: Independent foundation.
Financial data (yr. ended 08/31/13): Assets, $6,852,299 (M); expenditures, $715,730; qualifying distributions, $605,858; giving activities include $605,858 for 38 grants (high: $67,500; low: $1,000).
Purpose and activities: Giving primarily to organizations which enhance the benefit and residents of Tioga County, NY. The foundation wishes to accomplish this mission by encouraging grant requests for critical needs, capital projects, and seed money for new and special projects or programs.
Fields of interest: Historic preservation/historical societies; Higher education; Higher education, college (community/junior); Libraries (public); Education; Athletics/sports, amateur leagues; Human services; Community development, neighborhood development.
Type of support: Capital campaigns; Building/renovation; Equipment; Emergency funds; Program development; Seed money; Scholarship funds; Matching/challenge support.
Limitations: Applications accepted. Giving primarily in Owego and Tioga counties, NY. No grants to individuals.
Publications: Annual report (including application guidelines).
Application information: Completed applications can be mailed or deposited in the drop box located in the basement lobby of M&T Bank at the corner of Front and Church Sts., Owego, NY, during normal banking hours. Application form and guidelines are available on foundation web site. Application form required.
Initial approach: Proposal
Copies of proposal: 11
Deadline(s): 5 weeks prior to board meeting
Board meeting date(s): Jan., Apr., June, Sept.
Final notification: 1 week after board meeting
Officer: Irene C. Graven, Exec. Dir.
Trustee: M&T Bank.
Number of staff: 1 part-time professional.
EIN: 166271201
Other changes: The grantmaker no longer lists a separate application address.
Stephanie Carrigg is no longer Grant Exec.

2476
The Donald J. Trump Foundation

c/o WeiserMazars LLP
60 Crossways Park Dr., No. 301
Woodbury, NY **11797-2018**
Application address: c/o Donald J. Trump, Pres., The Trump Organization, 725 5th Ave., New York, NY 10022

Established in 1987 in NY.
Donors: Donald J. Trump; Alfons J. Schmitt; Maurice R. Povich; Beth Schwartz; Jayson Schwartz; Corinna Jones; Charles Evans; Joel Pashcow; Kinray, Inc.; Trump Park Ave., LLC; Mr. White LLC; NCL America, Inc.; Stark Carpet Corp.; People Magazine; The Charles Evans Foundation; World Wrestling Entertainment.
Foundation type: Independent foundation.
Financial data (yr. ended 12/31/12): Assets, $1,718,511 (M); gifts received, $1,249,746; expenditures, $1,717,394; qualifying distributions, $1,717,394; giving activities include $1,712,089 for 76 grants (high: $200,000; low: $1,000).
Purpose and activities: Giving primarily for health organizations, youth development, and social services.
Fields of interest: Museums; Education; Hospitals (general); Health care; Health organizations; Medical research, institute; Youth development; Human services; Foundations (public).
Limitations: Giving primarily in New York, NY; some funding also in MA.
Application information: Application form not required.
Initial approach: Letter
Deadline(s): None
Officers: Donald J. Trump, Pres.; Allen Weisselberg, Treas.
Directors: Donald J. Trump, Jr.; Eric F. Trump; Ivanka M. Trump.
EIN: 133404773
Other changes: At the close of 2012, the grantmaker paid grants of $1,712,089, a 70.2% increase over the 2011 disbursements, $1,006,150.

2477
Trust for Mutual Understanding

6 W. 48th St., 12th Fl.
New York, NY 10036-1802 (212) 843-0404
Contact: Jennifer P. Goodale, Exec. Dir.; Barbara Lanciers, Dir.
FAX: (212) 843-0344; E-mail: tmu@tmuny.org; Main URL: http://www.tmuny.org
Blog: http://www.tmuny.org/connect/blog
E-Newsletter: http://www.tmuny.org/connect/tmuniverse
Facebook: http://www.facebook.com/pages/Trust-for-Mutual-Understanding/112446932323
Grants Database: http://www.tmuny.org/grantees

Established in 1984 in NY.
Foundation type: Independent foundation.
Financial data (yr. ended 12/31/12): Assets, $36,679,963 (M); expenditures, $2,917,947; qualifying distributions, $2,694,782; giving activities include $1,658,169 for 103 grants (high: $140,000; low: $1,000).
Purpose and activities: Support to American nonprofit organizations for professional exchanges in the arts and environmental fields between the United States, Russia, and Eastern and Central Europe. Support is provided for travel and related expenses for exchange projects that involve direct, in-depth professional interaction, with the potential for sustained collaboration; that show evidence of professional accomplishment and innovation; and/or that respond to social contexts and engage local communities.
Fields of interest: Visual arts; Museums; Performing arts; Performing arts, dance; Performing arts, theater; Performing arts, music; Historic preservation/historical societies; Arts; Environment, natural resources; Environment; Animals/wildlife, preservation/protection; International exchange.
International interests: Albania; Armenia; Azerbaijan; Belarus; Bosnia and Herzegovina; Bulgaria; Croatia; Czech Republic; Estonia; Georgia; Hungary; Kazakhstan; Kosovo; Kyrgyz Republic; Latvia; Lithuania; Macedonia; Montenegro; Moldova; Mongolia; Poland; Romania; Russia; Serbia; Slovenia; Slovakia; Tajikistan; Turkmenistan; Ukraine; Uzbekistan.
Type of support: Exchange programs.
Limitations: Applications accepted. Giving for exchanges between the U.S. and Russia, and Central and Eastern Europe. No support for one-person exhibitions of work by living artists, solo performance tours or youth programs. No grants to individuals, or for fellowships for individual research or academic study, operating expenses, capital campaigns, construction costs, salaries, honoraria or fees, student exchanges, performing or visual arts competitions, literature or publication projects, library acquisitions or equipment purchases, film production, media training, mass communication programs, activities pertaining to arms control or security issues, economic development, medicine, public health, agriculture, activities in which only a single participant is involved, multi-year commitments, retroactive funding, or, except in special circumstances, interregional travel or travel by project participants in their home countries.
Publications: Application guidelines; Annual report; Grants list; Newsletter.
Application information: The trust has recently transitioned to an online application. Grants are made only to tax-exempt organizations in the United

States for exchange projects involving Russia, Central Asia, Mongolia and the Caucasus, and Eastern and Central Europe. Grant funds may only be used for international travel costs. Application form required.

Initial approach: Letter of Inquiry (refer to form on foundation web site); initial contact should be established at least 3 months prior to the application deadline
Copies of proposal: 1
***Deadline(s):* May 1 and Nov. 1 (for initial inquiry); Feb. 1 and Aug. 1 (for full application)**
Board meeting date(s): Spring and fall
***Final notification:* Within 2 weeks (for initial inquiry)**

Director and Trustees:* Jennifer P. Goodale,* Exec. Dir.; Richard S. Lanier; Elizabeth J. McCormack; **Marcia McLean**; Blaire Ruble.
Board of Advisors: Laura Chasin; Wade Greene; William H. Luers; Isaac Shapiro; Arlene Shuler; **Irina Yurna**.
Number of staff: 3 full-time professional; 1 part-time professional; 1 part-time support.
EIN: 133212724
Other changes: Donal C. O'Brien is no longer a director.

2478
Tsadra Foundation
P.O. Box 20192
New York, NY 10014-0710
E-mail: info@tsadra.org; Main URL: http://www.tsadra.org
Advanced Studies Scholarship e-mail: **studyscholarship@tsadra.org, Advanced Contemplative Scholarship e-mail: contemplativescholarship@tsadra.org**

Established in 2000 in NY.
Donors: Eric Colombel; Andrea Soros; Leon Sauke; Trace Foundation.
Foundation type: Independent foundation.
Financial data (yr. ended 12/31/12): Assets, $558,487 (M); gifts received, $2,350,540; expenditures, $2,296,085; qualifying distributions, $1,790,610; giving activities include $604,917 for 31 grants (high: $208,511; low: $4,377), and $875,050 for grants to individuals.
Purpose and activities: Giving primarily for the combined study and practice of Tibetan Buddhism in the west. The foundation also awards scholarships for both advanced Buddhist studies and advanced contemplative training.
Fields of interest: Education; International development; Buddhism.
Type of support: General/operating support; Program development; Fellowships.
Limitations: Applications not accepted. Giving in the U.S., with emphasis on CA, as well as in Canada, France, India and Nepal.
Application information: Unsolicited requests for funds not accepted.
Officers: Eric Colombel, Pres.; **Drupgyu Anthony Chapman, V.P., and Dir., Contemplative Scholarships**.
EIN: 137224970

2479
Isaac H. Tuttle Fund
1155 Park Ave.
New York, NY 10128-1209 (212) 831-0429
Contact: Stephanie A. Raneri, Exec. Dir.
FAX: (212) 426-5684; E-mail: info@tuttlefund.org; Main URL: http://www.tuttlefund.org
Grants List: http://www.tuttlefund.org/grants/2013-grants

Incorporated in 1872 as a public charity; status changed to a private foundation in 2001.
Donors: Martin S. Paine Foundation; Mary Caroline Phelps Trust.
Foundation type: Independent foundation.
Financial data (yr. ended 12/31/12): Assets, $42,805,301 (M); gifts received, $1,149,599; expenditures, $2,267,132; qualifying distributions, $2,159,781; giving activities include $675,000 for grants, $545,312 for grants to individuals, and $1,086,108 for foundation-administered programs.
Purpose and activities: The fund gives direct financial support to elderly individuals (65 years of age or older, unless there are compelling circumstances that merit consideration), and nonprofit community-based organizations that provide services to seniors in the borough of Manhattan in New York City, with the goal of enabling older persons to continue living in their own homes so long as they are physically and mentally able to do so. Applicants must have been productive, contributing members of their communities during their working years.
Fields of interest: Aging, centers/services; Aging.
Type of support: General/operating support; Continuing support; Building/renovation; Equipment; Program development; Technical assistance; Grants to individuals.
Limitations: Applications accepted. Giving limited to applicants residing in the borough of Manhattan in NY.
Publications: Application guidelines; Financial statement.
Application information: Contact Exec. Dir. for grants, or Stipend Prog. Dir. for stipends. Application form required for stipends. Formal proposals are by invitation, only after telephone, e-mail or letter of inquiry contact. Application form required.

Initial approach: Telephone, e-mail or letter of inquiry to Exec. Dir.
Copies of proposal: 1
Deadline(s): 3 months prior to board meetings for grants and stipends
Board meeting date(s): 5 times per year
Final notification: Following board meetings

Officers and Trustees:* Molly O. Parkinson,* Pres.; Kenneth R. Page,* V.P.; Christine Valentine,* Secy.; Anne H. Lindgren,* Treas.; Stephanie A. Raneri, Exec. Dir.; Paul J. Benziger, Jr.; Shirley B. Bresler; Susan P. Cole; William H. Forsyth, Jr.; Charles B. Grace III; John C. Harpole; Martha V. Johns; Ann R. Loeb; K.C. Maurer; The Rev. Edward D. Pardoe III; Oscar S. Straus III; M. Antoinette Thomas.
Number of staff: 6 full-time professional; 1 full-time support.
EIN: 135628325

2480
Unbound Philanthropy
101 Avenue of the Americas, Ste. 1400
New York, NY **10013-1941** (212) 219-1009
FAX: (212) 219-1129;
E-mail: mail@unboundphilanthropy.org; Additional address: 70 Crowcross St., Farrington, London, UK, EC1 M 6EJ; tel.: (020) 7251-9304; Main URL: http://www.unboundphilanthropy.org
Grants List: http://www.unboundphilanthropy.org/grantees.php

Established in 2004 in HI.
Donors: William Huntington Reeves; Deborah K. Berger.
Foundation type: Independent foundation.
Financial data (yr. ended 12/31/12): Assets, $158,488,470 (M); gifts received, $24,100,000; expenditures, $9,543,884; qualifying distributions, $9,355,429; giving activities include $6,850,466 for 70 grants (high: $304,755; low: $10,000).
Purpose and activities: The grantmaker is dedicated to securing justice and opportunity for migrants and refugees.
Fields of interest: Education; Human services; Philanthropy/voluntarism; Children/youth; Women; Immigrants/refugees.
International interests: United Kingdom; Africa.
Limitations: Applications not accepted. Giving on a national basis and in the U.S. and the U.K. No grants to individuals.
Publications: Grants list.
Application information: Contributes only to pre-selected organizations.
Officers and Directors:* Deborah K. Berger,* Pres. and Secy.; Taryn Higashi, Exec. Dir.; Bill Reeves; Hilary Weinstein; Kiki Fordham.
Number of staff: 3 full-time professional.
EIN: 830411606

2481
Union Square Fund
c/o Marks Paneth & Shron LLP
685 3rd Ave.
New York, NY 10017-8408

Established in 1997 in NY.
Foundation type: Independent foundation.
Financial data (yr. ended 12/31/13): Assets, $60,539,693 (M); expenditures, $1,752,747; qualifying distributions, $1,068,174; giving activities include $968,972 for 8 grants (high: $563,972; low: $25,000).
Fields of interest: Education; Health organizations; Nonprofit management.
Limitations: Applications not accepted. Giving primarily in San Francisco, CA; funding also in the Boston, MA, area, and New York, NY. No grants to individuals.
Publications: Informational brochure.
Application information: Contributes only to pre-selected organizations.
Officers: Jeane Ungerleider, Pres.; Steven C. Baum, Secy.-Treas.
Directors: Nan Arons; **Anne Peretz**.
Number of staff: None.
EIN: 311574700

2482
H. van Ameringen Foundation
509 Madison Ave.
New York, NY 10022-5501 (212) 758-6221
Contact: Henry P. van Ameringen, Tr.
H. van Ameringen Foundation's Philanthropy Promise: http://www.ncrp.org/philanthropys-promise/who

Established in 1967 in NY.
Donor: Henry P. van Ameringen.
Foundation type: Independent foundation.
Financial data (yr. ended 12/31/13): Assets, $39,681,377 (M); gifts received, $12,426,733; expenditures, $14,149,324; qualifying distributions, $14,144,708; giving activities include $14,134,000 for 122 grants (high: $4,250,000; low: $1,000).
Purpose and activities: Giving primarily for human service agencies, AIDS programs, health organizations, and civil rights agencies.

Fields of interest: Health care; AIDS; Human services; Civil/human rights, advocacy; AIDS, people with; LGBTQ.
Type of support: General/operating support; Program development; Seed money; Matching/challenge support.
Limitations: Applications accepted. Giving primarily in NY. No support for cultural activities. No grants to individuals or for research.
Application information: Application form not required.
Initial approach: Letter
Copies of proposal: 1
Trustee: Henry P. van Ameringen.
Number of staff: 1 part-time professional.
EIN: 136215329
Other changes: At the close of 2013, the grantmaker paid grants of $14,134,000, a 129.8% increase over the 2012 disbursements, $6,149,991.

2483
van Ameringen Foundation, Inc.
509 Madison Ave.
New York, NY 10022-5501 (212) 758-6221
***Contact:* Kenneth A. Kind, Pres. and Treas.**
FAX: (212) 688-2105;
E-mail: info@vanamfound.org; **Letter of Inquiry e-mail: Letterofinquiry@vanamfound.org**; Main URL: http://www.vanamfound.org/
van Ameringen Foundation's Philanthropy Promise: http://www.ncrp.org/philanthropys-promise/who

Incorporated in 1950 in NY.
Donor: Arnold Louis van Ameringen†.
Foundation type: Independent foundation.
Financial data (yr. ended 12/31/13): Assets, $95,086,433 (M); expenditures, $4,996,823; qualifying distributions, $4,368,793; giving activities include $3,848,500 for 84 grants (high: $250,000; low: $5,000).
Purpose and activities: Grants primarily to promote mental health and social welfare through preventive measures, treatment, and rehabilitation. Support also for the field of psychiatry. Within its broad focus on mental health, the foundation is interested in encouraging and attracting innovative and practical programs in areas which: 1) increase the accessibility of the poor and needy to mental health services; and 2) offer preventative and early intervention strategies.
Fields of interest: Mental health, treatment; Mental health/crisis services; Infants/toddlers; Children/youth; Youth; Aging; Mentally disabled; Hispanics/Latinos; Military/veterans; Offenders/ex-offenders; Crime/abuse victims; Immigrants/refugees; Economically disadvantaged; Homeless.
Type of support: Technical assistance; General/operating support; Management development/capacity building; Program development; Program-related investments/loans; Seed money.
Limitations: Applications accepted. Giving primarily in metropolitan New York, NY, and Philadelphia, PA. No support for international activities and institutions, or for programs for the mentally retarded, the physically handicapped, drug abuse, or alcoholism. No grants or loans to individuals, or for endowments, annual campaigns, deficit financing, emergency funds, capital campaigns, scholarships, or fellowships.
Publications: Application guidelines; Annual report; Financial statement; Grants list.
Application information: Proposals received after a deadline will not be considered for the upcoming meeting. New York/New Jersey Area Common Application accepted but not required. Application form not required.
Initial approach: Letter of inquiry
Copies of proposal: 1
***Deadline(s):* For Letters of Inquiry: Mar. 10 (for June meeting), June 10 (for Nov. meeting), and Nov. 10 (for Mar. meeting)**
Board meeting date(s): Mar., June, and Nov.
Final notification: Within 60 days
Officers and Directors:* Kenneth A. Kind,* Pres. and Treas.; Steadman Westergaard,* V.P. and Secy.; Eleanor K. Sypher, Exec. Dir.; Judith Beck; Alexandra Herzan; Christina Kind; Patricia Kind; Valerie Kind-Rubin; Andrew Kindfuller; Laura K. McKenna; Clarence J. Sundram; Henry P. van Ameringen.
Number of staff: 1 full-time professional; 1 full-time support.
EIN: 136125699
Other changes: Kenneth A. Kind has replaced Henry P. van Ameringen as Pres. and Treas. Steadman Westergaard has replaced George Rowe, Jr. as V.P. and Secy.

2484
The Rachum V'hanun Foundation Inc.
1 W. 34th St., 10th Fl.
New York, NY **10001 (212) 287-9001**
Contact: Salim Alfaks, Dir.

Donors: Chica Bonita, Inc.; Crest Home Designs Inc.; The Fashion Exchange LLC.; Yoki Sports, Inc.; The Fame Fashion House LLC.; Shm Shoes LLC.
Foundation type: Independent foundation.
Financial data (yr. ended 04/30/13): Assets, $27 (M); expenditures, $2,500; qualifying distributions, $0.
Fields of interest: Jewish agencies & synagogues.
Limitations: Applications accepted. Giving primarily in NY.
Application information: Application form not required.
Initial approach: Proposal
Deadline(s): None
Directors: Salim Alfaks; Oni Faks.
EIN: 262726441

2485
The Vidda Foundation
250 W. 57th St., Ste. 1928
New York, NY 10107-1914
Contact: John B. Roberts, Admin.
E-mail: info@vidda.org; Main URL: http://www.vidda.org

Established in 1979 in NY.
Donor: Ursula Corning†.
Foundation type: Independent foundation.
Financial data (yr. ended 05/31/13): Assets, $9,696,188 (M); gifts received, $251; expenditures, $891,192; qualifying distributions, $824,779; giving activities include $751,500 for 40 grants (high: $175,000; low: $2,500).
Purpose and activities: Giving primarily for supporting programs that will have a lasting impact in the areas of conservation, education, health care, human services and the arts.
Fields of interest: Humanities; Arts; Education; Environment, beautification programs; Environment; Animal welfare; Animals/wildlife, preservation/protection; Medical care, in-patient care; Human services; Children/youth, services; Aging, centers/services; Economic development; Community/economic development; Protestant agencies & churches.
Type of support: General/operating support; Continuing support; Annual campaigns; Building/renovation; Endowments; Program development; Seed money; Research.
Limitations: Applications accepted. Giving primarily in NY. No grants to individuals.
Publications: Application guidelines; Financial statement.
Application information: New York/New Jersey Area Common Grant Application Form is required from proposed grantees that receive a positive response to their letter of intent. Please refer to application guidelines on foundation web site; telephone calls, or faxed or e-mailed letters of interest are not accepted. Application form not required.
Initial approach: Letter of interest (2 pages maximum)
Copies of proposal: 1
Deadline(s): None (for letters of interest)
Board meeting date(s): Nov. and May
Final notification: Approximately 3 months
Officer and Trustees:* Gerald E. Rupp,* Chair.; John A. Downey, M.D.; **Stephen Evans**; Helen C. Evarts; Ian H. Fraser; John B. Roberts.
EIN: 132981105

2486
The Vilcek Foundation, Inc.
(formerly The Friderika Fischer Foundation)
167 E. 73rd St.
New York, NY 10021-4160 **(212) 472-2500**
Contact: Rick A. Kinsel, Exec. Dir.
FAX: (212) 472-4720; E-mail: info@vilcek.org; Main URL: http://www.vilcek.org
Facebook: http://www.facebook.com/vilcekfoundation
Grants List: http://www.vilcek.org/about/grants.html
Twitter: https://twitter.com/Vilcek
YouTube: http://www.youtube.com/user/VilcekFoundation

Established in 2000 in NY. Classified as a private operating foundation in 2001.
Donor: Jan Vilcek.
Foundation type: Operating foundation.
Financial data (yr. ended 12/31/12): Assets, $108,974,493 (M); expenditures, $4,121,754; qualifying distributions, $3,350,213; giving activities include $236,333 for 15 grants (high: $62,500; low: $1,000), and $280,000 for 11 grants to individuals (high: $100,000; low: $5,000).
Purpose and activities: The foundation honors foreign-born scientists and artists living in the U.S. who have made outstanding contributions to U.S. society that benefit mankind. Each year the foundation bestows upon certain individuals the Vilcek Prize to honor such achievement in biomedical research and in arts or humanities. Giving primarily for higher education and to fund a research project to develop treatments for chronic inflammatory auto-immune diseases.
Fields of interest: Media, film/video; Arts; Higher education; Medical school/education; Medical research, institute.
Type of support: Conferences/seminars; Research.
Limitations: Applications not accepted. Giving primarily in NY and NM.
Publications: Grants list.
Application information: Unsolicited requests for funds not accepted.
Officers and Directors:* Jan Vilcek, M.D, Ph.D.*, Pres. and Treas.; Marica Vilcek,* V.P. and Secy.; Rick A. Kinsel,* Exec. Dir.; Richard Gaddes; S. Peter

Ludwig; Joan Massague; **Christina Mossaides Strassfield.**
Number of staff: 4 full-time professional.
EIN: 510404790

2487
The Laura B. Vogler Foundation, Inc.
51 Division St., Box. 501
Sag Harbor, NY **11963-3162**
Application address: **P.O. Box 610508, Bayside, N.Y. 11361-0508**

Incorporated in 1959 in NY.
Donors: Laura B. Vogler†; John J. Vogler†.
Foundation type: Independent foundation.
Financial data (yr. ended 10/31/13): Assets, $5,352,284 (M); expenditures, $273,325; qualifying distributions, $246,015; giving activities include $196,770 for 82 grants (high: $3,000; low: $1,500).
Purpose and activities: Awards one-time non-renewable grants for new programs in the areas of health, youth, child welfare, the disadvantaged, the elderly, and other related services.
Fields of interest: Health care; Human services; Religion.
Type of support: Program development; Seed money; Research.
Limitations: Applications accepted. Giving limited to New York City and Long Island, NY. No grants to individuals, or for building or endowment funds, annual fundraising campaigns, or matching gifts; no loans.
Application information: Application form required.
Initial approach: Proposal
Copies of proposal: 1
Deadline(s): Jan. 1, Apr. 1, July 1 and Oct. 1
Officers and Directors:* Lawrence L. D'Amato,* Pres.; Laraine Diamond, Secy.-Treas.; June D'Amato; Max L. Kupferberg; Stephen S. Schwander; Karen M. Yost.
Number of staff: 2 part-time professional.
EIN: 116022241

2488
Voya Foundation
(formerly ING Foundation)
230 Park Ave., 15th Fl.
New York, NY 10169
Contact: Rhoda Mims, Pres.; Chip Wheeler, Dir. Community Rels.
E-mail: **voyafoundation@voya.com**; Main
URL: http://ing.us/about-ing/responsibility

Established in 1990 in MN.
Donors: ReliaStar Financial Corp.; Northern Life Insurance Co.; ReliaStar Bankers Security Life Insurance Co.; ReliaStar United Services Life Insurance Co.; ReliaStar Life Insurance Co.
Foundation type: Company-sponsored foundation.
Financial data (yr. ended 12/31/12): Assets, $2,049,840 (M); gifts received, $5,020,478; expenditures, $2,632,651; qualifying distributions, $2,633,058; giving activities include $2,592,641 for 2,196 grants (high: $569,100; low: $3).
Purpose and activities: The foundation supports programs designed to promote financial literacy and children's education.
Fields of interest: Elementary/secondary education; Education; Disasters, preparedness/ services; Girls clubs; Youth development, business; Children/youth, services; Human services, financial counseling; Economic development; Children/youth; Minorities; Economically disadvantaged.
Type of support: Continuing support; Program development; Conferences/seminars; Scholarship funds; Research; Cause-related marketing; Employee volunteer services; Sponsorships; Program evaluation; Employee matching gifts.
Limitations: Applications accepted. Giving on a national basis in areas of company operations, with emphasis on CA, CO, CT, DE, FL, GA, MA, MN, NY, PA, and TX; giving also to national organizations. No support for religious organizations not of direct benefit to the entire community, private foundations, fraternal organizations, social clubs, labor organizations, lobbying or political organizations, sports teams, or discriminatory organizations. No grants to individuals, or for capital campaigns, endowments, general or administrative costs, institutional, civic, or commemorative advertising, fashion shows, pageants, golf tournaments, athletic events, conferences, workshops, or other meetings, travel, benefits, performances, testimonial dinners, or other fundraising activities.
Publications: Annual report (including application guidelines); Informational brochure.
Application information: Mailed, e-mailed, or hard copy applications are not accepted. Requests under $2,500 are not considered. Additional information may be requested at a later date. Support is limited to 1 contribution per organization during any given year. Multi-year funding is not automatic. Organizations receiving support are asked to submit twice-yearly impact data. Application form required.
Initial approach: Complete online application form
Deadline(s): **May 15, Aug. 29, and Nov. 7**
Board meeting date(s): Feb., May, Aug., and Nov.
Final notification: June 15 and Sept. 14
Officers and Directors:* Rodney O. Martin,* Chair.; Rhoda Mims,* Pres.; **Jennifer Ogren, Secy.**; David S. Pendergrass,* Treas.; Mary E. Beams; Jeffery T. Becker; Donald W. Britton; Bridget M. Healy; Alain Karaoglan; Kevin D. Silva; Michael Smith; Ewout Steenbergen.
Number of staff: None.
EIN: 411682766
Other changes: Jennifer Ogren has replaced Timothy W. Brown as Secy.
Timothy W. Brown is no longer Secy.

2489
Sue and Edgar Wachenheim Foundation
3 Manhattanville Rd.
Purchase, NY 10577-2116
Contact: Edgar Wachenheim III, C.E.O. and Pres.

Established in 1969 in NY.
Donors: Sue W. Wachenheim; Edgar Wachenheim III; Greenhaven Assocs.
Foundation type: Independent foundation.
Financial data (yr. ended 10/31/13): Assets, $207,299,587 (M); expenditures, $7,208,400; qualifying distributions, $7,206,400; giving activities include $7,204,400 for 44 grants (high: $4,000,000; low: $100).
Purpose and activities: Giving primarily for higher education and for health and human services.
Fields of interest: Arts; Higher education; Libraries/ library science; Education; Health care; Human services.
Type of support: Annual campaigns; Capital campaigns; Building/renovation; Scholarship funds.
Limitations: Applications not accepted. Giving primarily in NY. No grants to individuals.
Application information: Contributes only to pre-selected organizations.
Officers and Directors:* Edgar Wachenheim III,* C.E.O. and Pres.; Sue W. Wachenheim,* V.P.; Kim Wachenheim Wagman,* Secy.; Lance R. Wachenheim,* Treas.; **Chris A. Wachenheim.**
Number of staff: None.
EIN: 237011002
Other changes: For the fiscal year ended Oct. 31, 2013, the fair market value of the grantmaker's assets was $207,299,587, an 84.8% increase over the fiscal 2012 value, $112,159,905.
Edgar Wachenheim, III is now C.E.O. and Pres. Sue W. Wachenheim is now V.P.

2490
Wachtell, Lipton, Rosen & Katz Foundation
51 W. 52nd St.
New York, NY 10019-6119

Established in 1981 in NY.
Donor: Wachtell, Lipton, Rosen & Katz.
Foundation type: Company-sponsored foundation.
Financial data (yr. ended 09/30/12): Assets, $9,606,508 (M); expenditures, $750,748; qualifying distributions, $745,920; giving activities include $745,000 for 10 grants (high: $200,000; low: $15,000).
Purpose and activities: The foundation supports medical centers and organizations involved with education, 9/11 memorials, justice, law, Judaism, and people of color.
Fields of interest: Health care; Medical research; Human services.
Type of support: General/operating support; Annual campaigns; Scholarship funds.
Limitations: Applications not accepted. Giving limited to New York, NY. No grants to individuals.
Application information: Contributes only to pre-selected organizations.
Board meeting date(s): As necessary
Officers and Directors:* Martin Lipton,* Pres.; Herbert M. Wachtell,* V.P. and Secy.; Constance Monte, V.P. and Treas.; Edward D. Herlihy,* V.P.; Daniel A. Neff,* V.P.; Jodi D. Schwartz,* V.P.
EIN: 133099901

2491
Rose and Sherle Wagner Foundation
c/o Scialo & Co., C.P.A., PC
4 Executive Blvd., No. 304
Suffern, NY 10901-4173

Established in 1994 in NY.
Donors: Rose Wagner; Sherle Wagner†; Wagner Charitable Lead Trust.
Foundation type: Independent foundation.
Financial data (yr. ended 12/31/12): Assets, $8,688,638 (M); gifts received, $100,000; expenditures, $418,446; qualifying distributions, $395,553; giving activities include $237,500 for 17 grants (high: $20,000; low: $2,500).
Purpose and activities: Giving primarily for grassroots organizing for social and economic justice.
Fields of interest: Student services/organizations; Education; Human services; Youth, services; Civil/ human rights, immigrants; Civil/human rights, minorities; Civil/human rights; Community development, neighborhood development; Minorities; Women; Economically disadvantaged.
Type of support: General/operating support.
Limitations: Applications not accepted. Giving primarily in NY. No grants to individuals.

Application information: Contributes only to pre-selected organizations.
Trustee: Rose Wagner.
Director: Amy Wagner.
Number of staff: 1 full-time professional; 6 part-time support.
EIN: 133738106
Other changes: The grantmaker has moved from NJ to NY.

2492
The Wallace Foundation

(formerly Wallace-Reader's Digest Funds)
5 Penn Plz., 7th Fl.
New York, NY 10001-1837 (212) 251-9700
Contact: Grants Admin.
FAX: (212) 679-6990;
E-mail: grantrequest@wallacefoundation.org; Main URL: http://www.wallacefoundation.org
Facebook: https://www.facebook.com/pages/The-Wallace-Foundation/376102262278
Google Plus: https://plus.google.com/118367860292395448396/posts
Grants Database: http://www.wallacefoundation.org/learn-about-wallace/GrantsPrograms/our-grantees/Pages/default.aspx
Knowledge Center: http://www.wallacefoundation.org/KnowledgeCenter/Pages/default.aspx
Pinterest: http://pinterest.com/wallacefdn/
RSS Feed: http://www.wallacefoundation.org/Pages/rss-feed.aspx
The Wallace Foundation's Philanthropy Promise: http://www.ncrp.org/philanthropys-promise/who
Twitter: http://twitter.com/WallaceFdn
YouTube: http://www.youtube.com/WallaceFdn

The Wallace Foundation is the current manifestation of the philanthropic legacy of DeWitt and Lila Acheson Wallace, who created a series of family foundations in the mid 1950s and 1960s. By 2003, the various foundations had merged and adopted the current name. Immediately prior to this merger, there were two foundations known as the Lila Wallace-Reader's Digest Fund and the DeWitt Wallace-Reader's Digest Fund.
Donors: DeWitt Wallace†; Lila Acheson Wallace†.
Foundation type: Independent foundation.
Financial data (yr. ended 12/31/12): Assets, $1,398,955,579 (M); gifts received, $2,360; expenditures, $78,298,857; qualifying distributions, $71,135,986; giving activities include $57,270,331 for 104 grants (high: $3,750,000; low: $3,000), $13,050 for 34 employee matching gifts, and $2,822,607 for 4 foundation-administered programs.
Purpose and activities: The Wallace Foundation seeks to improve education and enrichment for disadvantaged children. The foundation has an unusual approach: funding projects to test innovative ideas for solving important social problems, conducting research to find out what works and what doesn't and to fill key knowledge gaps; and then communicating the results to help others.
Fields of interest: Arts; Education, services; Education, community/cooperative; Education; Leadership development; Children/youth.
Type of support: General/operating support; Program development; Conferences/seminars; Publication; Research; Technical assistance; Program evaluation; Employee matching gifts.
Limitations: Applications accepted. Giving on a national basis. No support for religious or fraternal organizations; environmental or conservation programs, health, medical or social service programs, international programs, or for private foundations. No grants to individuals, or for annual funds, emergency funds, capital campaigns, historical restorations, or deficit financing.
Publications: Annual report (including application guidelines); Financial statement; Grants list; Occasional report; Program policy statement (including application guidelines).
Application information: Unsolicited proposals are rarely funded. Application guidelines can be found on foundation web site.
Initial approach: **E-mail**
Deadline(s): None
Officers and Directors:* Kevin W. Kennedy,* Chair.; William I. Miller,* Pres.; Kenneth Austin, Sr. Counsel and Corp. Secy.; Mary E. Geras, C.F.O. and Asst. Treas.; Rob D. Nagel, Treas. and C.I.O.; Lawrence T. Babbio, Jr.; Candace K. Beinecke; Linda Darling-Hammond; Augusta Souza Kappner; Susan J. Kropf; Ann S. Moore; Joseph W. Polisi; Amor H. Towles; **Mary Beth West**.
Number of staff: 36 full-time professional; 7 full-time support.
EIN: 136183757

2493
Miriam G. and Ira D. Wallach Foundation

Purchase, NY

The foundation terminated in 2013.

2494
The Andy Warhol Foundation for the Visual Arts

65 Bleecker St., 7th Fl.
New York, NY 10012-2420 (212) 387-7555
Contact: Rachel Bers, Prog. Dir.
FAX: (212) 387-7560;
E-mail: info@warholfoundation.org; E-mail for proposals: deadline@warholfoundation.org; Main URL: http://www.warholfoundation.org
Grants Database: http://www.warholfoundation.org/grant/index.html#/2009

Established in 1987 in NY.
Donor: Andy Warhol†.
Foundation type: Independent foundation.
Financial data (yr. ended 04/30/13): Assets, $327,697,626 (M); expenditures, $21,353,867; qualifying distributions, $15,974,019; giving activities include $12,298,779 for 139 grants (high: $1,500,000; low: $10,000).
Purpose and activities: The foundation's purpose is the advancement of the visual arts. The foundation's principal activities are twofold: it awards grants to nonprofit cultural organizations working in the visual arts; and it has responsibility for all aspects of its collection of Andy Warhol's art.
Fields of interest: Visual arts; Museums; Arts, artist's services; Arts.
Type of support: Fellowships; Program development; Conferences/seminars; Publication; Research.
Limitations: Applications accepted. Giving on a national basis. No grants to individuals.
Publications: Application guidelines; Biennial report; Financial statement; Grants list; Multi-year report.
Application information: Application form not required.
Initial approach: Letter
Copies of proposal: 1
Deadline(s): Mar. 1 and Sept. 1
Board meeting date(s): Apr., June, Oct., and Dec.
Final notification: Jan.1 and July 1
Officers and Directors:* Michael Straus, Chair.; Joel Wachs,* Pres.; **Donald Warhola,* V.P.**; K.C. Maurer, C.F.O. and Treas.; Mark Allen; James Keith Brown; Igor DaCosta; Courtney Fink; Jonathan Lee; Sarah Elizabeth Lewis; Shirin Neshat; Lawrence Rinder; Trevor Schoonmaker; Cindy Sherman; Olga Viso; Carrie Mae Weems; Adam D. Weinberg; Julian Zugazagoitia.
Number of staff: 22 full-time professional; 2 part-time professional.
EIN: 133410749
Other changes: Michael I. Frankel is no longer Secy. Jane Hammond is no longer a director. Donald Warhola is now V.P.

2495
Warwick Savings Foundation

c/o Alario & Associates CPA's PLLC
28 Railroad Ave.
Warwick, NY 10990-1525 **(845) 986-8717**
Contact: Louis Ulatowski, Secy.
Application address: 39 Washington, Rd., Monroe, NY 10950

Established in 1997 in NY.
Donor: Warwick Community Bancorp, Inc.
Foundation type: Company-sponsored foundation.
Financial data (yr. ended 12/31/12): Assets, $5,015,907 (M); expenditures, $269,059; qualifying distributions, $250,442; giving activities include $250,442 for grants.
Purpose and activities: The foundation supports historical societies and organizations involved with education, health, housing development, therapeutic riding, and human services.
Fields of interest: Historic preservation/historical societies; Secondary school/education; Higher education; Education; Hospitals (general); Health care, clinics/centers; Health care; Housing/shelter, development; Athletics/sports, equestrianism; Children/youth, services; Residential/custodial care, hospices; Developmentally disabled, centers & services; Human services.
Type of support: General/operating support.
Limitations: Applications accepted. Giving limited to NY. No grants to individuals.
Application information: Application form required.
***Initial approach:* Letter**
Deadline(s): Sept. 30
Officers and Directors:* John McDermott III,* Pres.; Lois E. Ulatowski, Secy.; R. Michael Kennedy,* Treas.; Frances M. Gorish; Sr. Ann Sakac; Mary Smith; Thomas Sullivan.
EIN: 061504632

2496
Weeden Foundation

35 Adams St., Ground Fl.
Bedford Hills, NY **10507-1819**
Contact: Donald A. Weeden, Exec. Dir.; Gillian Beach, Research Asst.
***FAX:* (914) 864-1377**; E-mail: info@weedenfdn.org; Main URL: http://www.weedenfdn.org
Grants Database: http://www.weedenfoundation.org/Weeden-Foundation-Grantees.php

Established 1963 in CA.
Donors: Frank Weeden†; Alan N. Weeden; Donald E. Weeden; John D. Weeden; William F. Weeden, M.D.; Frank Weeden Fund; Holloman-Price Fdn.

Foundation type: Independent foundation.
Financial data (yr. ended 12/31/12): Assets, $32,894,789 (M); gifts received, $8,586,167; expenditures, $6,109,178; qualifying distributions, $5,136,244; giving activities include $4,497,975 for grants.
Purpose and activities: Giving primarily to environmental organizations working to preserve biological diversity. Program interests also include organizations working to stabilize human population and organizations working to address the over consumption of the earth's resources.
Fields of interest: Environment, natural resources; Environment; Population studies.
International interests: Chile; Russia.
Type of support: General/operating support; Continuing support; Land acquisition; Emergency funds; Program development; Seed money; Program-related investments/loans.
Limitations: Applications accepted. Giving on a national and international basis, primarily in northern CA, the Pacific Northwest, Latin America (Chile), Central Siberia and the Altai Republic in Russia. No grants to individuals, or for multi-year requests; generally no funding for films, conferences, or scientific research.
Publications: Application guidelines; Annual report; Financial statement; Program policy statement.
Application information: The foundation strongly encourages potential applicants to submit a letter of inquiry before presenting a complete proposal. Proposal guidelines available on foundation web site. Application form not required.
Initial approach: Letter of inquiry via e-mail or U.S. mail only
Copies of proposal: 2
Deadline(s): 6 weeks prior to each board meeting; check web site for dates
Board meeting date(s): 3 times a year
Final notification: 8-10 weeks
Officers and Directors:* Norman Weeden, Ph.D.*, Pres.; Tina Roux, V.P.; H. Leslie Weeden,* Secy.; Bob Weeden, Treas.; Donald A. Weeden, Exec. Dir.; Barbara Daugherty; Alan N. Weeden; Donald E. Weeden; Jack D. Weeden; John D. Weeden; William Weeden, M.D.
Number of staff: 2 full-time professional.
EIN: 946109313

2497
The Wegman Family Charitable Foundation
(formerly Robert B. Wegman Charitable Foundation)
1500 Brooks Ave.
P.O. Box 30844
Rochester, NY 14603-0844 (585) 328-2550

Established in 1993 in NY.
Donors: Daniel R. Wegman; Robert B. Wegman†.
Foundation type: Independent foundation.
Financial data (yr. ended 12/31/13): Assets, $56,258,939 (M); expenditures, $24,829,656; qualifying distributions, $24,664,500; giving activities include $24,663,000 for 28 grants (high: $10,000,000; low: $6,000).
Purpose and activities: Giving primarily for human services and education.
Fields of interest: Performing arts centers; Secondary school/education; Education; Hospitals (general); Heart & circulatory diseases; Food banks; Human services; Children, services; Youth, services; Community/economic development; United Ways and Federated Giving Programs; Catholic federated giving programs; Disabilities, people with.
Limitations: Applications not accepted. Giving primarily in Rochester, NY. No grants to individuals.
Application information: Contributes only to pre-selected organizations.
Officers and Directors:* Daniel R. Wegman,* Chair., Pres. and Treas.; Margaret F. Wegman,* V.P.; Paul S. Speranza, Jr.,* Secy.
EIN: 223247037
Other changes: At the close of 2013, the grantmaker paid grants of $24,663,000, a 201.0% increase over the 2012 disbursements, $8,192,500.

2498
Weil, Gotshal & Manges Foundation Inc.
c/o Tax Dept.
767 5th Ave., Ste. 2330
New York, NY 10153-0001 (212) 310-6813
***Contact:* Dennis Foley, Dir.**

Established in 1983 in NY.
Donors: Weil, Gotshal & Manges LLP; Robert Todd Lang; Ira M. Millstein; Harvey R. Miller.
Foundation type: Company-sponsored foundation.
Financial data (yr. ended 12/31/12): Assets, $6,039,530 (M); gifts received, $1,500,000; expenditures, $1,501,013; qualifying distributions, $1,501,013; giving activities include $1,500,633 for 100 grants (high: $327,600; low: $100).
Purpose and activities: The foundation supports museums and organizations involved with education, legal services, disaster relief, children and youth, international relief, civil and human rights, business, and Judaism.
Fields of interest: Education; Human services; Religion.
Type of support: General/operating support; Scholarship funds.
Limitations: Applications accepted. Giving primarily in NJ and NY. No grants to individuals.
Application information: Application form required.
Initial approach: Proposal
Copies of proposal: 1
Deadline(s): Nov. 1
Directors: Joseph Allerhand; Howard Chatzinoff; Dennis Foley; Thomas Roberts.
EIN: 133158325

2499
Kurt Weill Foundation for Music, Inc.
7 E. 20th St., 3rd Fl.
New York, NY 10003-1106 (212) 505-5240
FAX: (212) 353-9663; E-mail: kwfinfo@kwf.org; Main URL: http://www.kwf.org
Grants List: http://www.kwf.org/grants-a-prizes/grant-program/23-kw/88-grants-awarded-1984-2008

Established in 1962.
Donor: Lotte Lenya†.
Foundation type: Operating foundation.
Financial data (yr. ended 12/31/12): Assets, $26,401,692 (M); gifts received, $4,000; expenditures, $1,326,571; qualifying distributions, $1,031,097; giving activities include $77,000 for 19 grants (high: $37,500; low: $500), and $187,350 for 34 grants to individuals (high: $15,000; low: $600).
Purpose and activities: Awards grants to organizations and individuals for projects directly related to Kurt Weill and Lotte Lenya. Applications are accepted in the following categories: Research and Travel, Kurt Weill Dissertation Fellowships, Publication Assistance, Educational Outreach, College/University Performance, Professional Performance, and Broadcasts. In addition, foundation programs include maintenance of a research center and archives, publication of a newsletter and critical editions of Weill's musical works, and production consultation.
Fields of interest: Performing arts, theater; Performing arts, theater (musical); Performing arts, music; Performing arts, opera.
Limitations: Applications accepted. Giving primarily in NY and PA, Germany, and Scotland.
Publications: Application guidelines; Informational brochure; Newsletter.
Application information: Application form and guidelines available on foundation web site. Application form required.
***Initial approach:* Application forms on foundation web site**
Copies of proposal: 1
***Deadline(s):* Nov. 1; June 1 exclusively for College/University Performance grants**
Final notification: Feb. 1
Officers and Trustees:* Kim Kowalke,* Pres.; Milton Coleman,* V.P.; Guy Stern,* Secy.; Philip Getter,* Treas.; Joanne Hubbard Cossa; Paul Epstein; Susan Feder; Walter Hinderer; Welz Kauffman; Julius Rudel.
Director: Carolyn Weber.
Number of staff: 6 full-time professional; 1 full-time support.
EIN: 136139518

2500
The Paul and Harriet Weissman Family Foundation Inc.
(formerly The Paul M. Weissman Family Foundation)
2 Oxford Rd.
White Plains, NY 10605-3603

Established in 1969 in NY.
Donor: Paul M. Weissman.
Foundation type: Independent foundation.
Financial data (yr. ended 02/28/13): Assets, $9,083,908 (M); gifts received, $600,000; expenditures, $1,023,100; qualifying distributions, $1,017,515; giving activities include $1,015,250 for 77 grants (high: $300,000; low: $10).
Purpose and activities: Support primarily for education, the arts, health and social services, and child welfare associations.
Fields of interest: Arts; Elementary/secondary education; Higher education; Education; Hospitals (general); Health care; Human services; Children/youth, services.
Limitations: Applications not accepted. Giving primarily in New York, NY; funding also in White Plains, NY. No grants to individuals.
Application information: Unsolicited requests for funds not accepted.
Officers: Paul M. Weissman, Pres. and Treas.; Harriet L. Weissman, V.P. and Secy.; Michael A. Weissman, V.P.; Peter A. Weissman, V.P.; Stephanie T. Weissman, V.P.
EIN: 237049744
Other changes: For the fiscal year ended Feb. 28, 2013, the grantmaker paid grants of $1,015,250, a 149.2% increase over the fiscal 2012 disbursements, $407,400.

2501
Franklin H. & Ruth L. Wells Foundation
1100 Wehrle Dr., 2nd Fl.
Buffalo, NY **14221-7748**
Contact: Miles J. Gibbons, Jr., Exec. Dir.

E-mail for Miles J. Gibbons, Jr.:
mgibbons989@earthlink.net

Established in 1983 in PA.
Donors: Ruth L. Wells Annuity Trust; Frank Wells Marital Trust.
Foundation type: Independent foundation.
Financial data (yr. ended 05/31/13): Assets, $5,069,708 (M); expenditures, $706,450; qualifying distributions, $691,650; giving activities include $625,250 for 36 grants (high: $70,000; low: $750).
Purpose and activities: Startup funding for new programs in education, human services, community development, health care, and cultural arts.
Fields of interest: Arts; Higher education; Education; Health care; Boys & girls clubs; Girl scouts; Human services; YM/YWCAs & YM/YWHAs; Community/economic development.
Type of support: Equipment; Emergency funds; Program development; Seed money.
Limitations: Applications accepted. Giving primarily in Dauphin, Cumberland, and Perry counties, PA. No support for religious activities. No grants to individuals, or for endowments, debts, or capital campaigns.
Application information: Application form not required.
Initial approach: Letter
Copies of proposal: 1
Board meeting date(s): Apr. and Oct.
Officer: Miles J. Gibbons, Jr.,* Exec. Dir.
Trustee: M & T Trust Co.
Number of staff: 1 full-time professional.
EIN: 222541749

2502
Wenner-Gren Foundation for Anthropological Research, Inc.

470 Park Ave. S., 8th Fl.
New York, NY 10016-6818 **(212) 683-5000**
FAX: (212) 532-1492;
E-mail: inquiries@wennergren.org; Main URL: http://www.wennergren.org
Blog: http://blog.wennergren.org/
Facebook: http://www.facebook.com/wennergrenfoundation
Grants Database: http://www.wennergren.org/grantees
Twitter: http://twitter.com/wennergrenorg

Incorporated in 1941 at The Viking Fund in DE. Later, it was re-named Wenner-Gren Foundation for Anthropological Research, Inc.
Donor: Axel L. Wenner-Gren‡.
Foundation type: Operating foundation.
Financial data (yr. ended 12/31/12): Assets, $162,966,933 (M); gifts received, $52,000; expenditures, $8,487,907; qualifying distributions, $7,271,931; giving activities include $240,280 for 11 grants (high: $52,000; low: $2,000), $4,439,694 for 270 grants to individuals (high: $40,000; low: $603), and $642,589 for 3 foundation-administered programs.
Purpose and activities: A private operating foundation; international support of research in all branches of anthropology including cultural/social anthropology, ethnology, biological/physical anthropology, archaeology, and anthropological linguistics, and in closely related disciplines so far as they pertain to human origins, development, and variation; grants-in-aid for programs of research; subsidies for conferences for anthropologists to promote reporting on results of research; publishes a journal and provides clearinghouse services for anthropological information.
Fields of interest: History/archaeology; Language/linguistics; Anthropology/sociology.
Type of support: Conferences/seminars; Publication; Seed money; Fellowships; Research; Grants to individuals.
Limitations: Applications accepted. Giving on a national and international basis. Individuals from all countries are invited to apply for individual research grants. No support for intermediary funding agencies, nonproject personnel, or institutional overhead or support. No grants for salaries or fringe benefits, tuition or travel to meetings, dissertation write-up or revision, publication subvention, or filmmaking. No publication assistance (outside of the Hunt Post-Doctoral Fellowship).
Publications: Application guidelines; Annual report; Annual report (including application guidelines); Financial statement; Grants list; Informational brochure.
Application information: Application form required.
Initial approach: See Programs Page on foundation web site
Deadline(s): Contact foundation for program deadlines
Board meeting date(s): Apr. and Oct.
Final notification: Approximately 6 months after deadline
Officers and Trustees:* Seth Masters,* Chair.; **Lorraine Sciarra,* Vice-Chair.**; Leslie C. Aiello,* Pres.; **Maugha Kenny, V.P., Fin. and Secy.**; **Lauren Meserve,* Treas.**; Dr. Ira Berlin; Dr. John Immerwahr; and 7 additional trustees.
Number of staff: 13
EIN: 131813827
Other changes: Lorraine Sciarra has replaced Dr. John Immerwahr as Vice-Chair. Lauren Meserve has replaced William L. Cobb, Jr., Treas. Maugha Kenny is now V.P., Fin. and Secy. Joan S. Girgus, Ellen Mickiewicz, William B. Peterson, Darcy Kelley, Ruth Kennedy Sudduth, and Deborah Wadsworth are no longer trustees.

2503
The Western New York Foundation

11 Summer St., 3rd Fl.
Buffalo, NY 14209-2256 (716) 839-4225
Contact: Beth K. Gosch, Exec. Dir.
FAX: (716) 883-1107;
E-mail: bgosch@wnyfoundation.org; Main URL: http://www.wnyfoundation.org
Grants List: http://www.wnyfoundation.org/Tools/Library/frontend/itemlist.asp?reset=1&phase=1&type=1

Incorporated in 1951 in NY as the Wildroot Foundation; present name adopted in 1958.
Donor: Welles V. Moot‡.
Foundation type: Independent foundation.
Financial data (yr. ended 03/31/13): Assets, $13,348,229 (M); gifts received, $193,009; expenditures, $625,493; qualifying distributions, $443,915; giving activities include $443,915 for grants.
Purpose and activities: Grants to nonprofit institutions, with emphasis on capital needs, seed funds for new projects, or expanding services. Support primarily for the fine and performing arts, youth agencies, the natural sciences, and social service agencies; some support also for health services and libraries and other educational institutions.
Fields of interest: Visual arts; Museums; Performing arts; Performing arts, dance; Performing arts, theater; Performing arts, music; Arts; Child development, education; Secondary school/education; Libraries (public); Medical care, rehabilitation; Substance abuse, services; Mental health/crisis services; Alcoholism; Legal services; Crime/law enforcement; Housing/shelter, development; Human services; Children/youth, services; Family services; Residential/custodial care, hospices; Aging, centers/services; Women, centers/services; Community/economic development; Infants/toddlers; Children/youth; Adults; Aging; Disabilities, people with; Mentally disabled; Minorities; Homeless.
Type of support: Income development; Capital campaigns; Building/renovation; Equipment; Land acquisition; Emergency funds; Program development; Conferences/seminars; Publication; Seed money; Technical assistance; Program-related investments/loans; Matching/challenge support.
Limitations: Applications accepted. Giving limited to the 8th Judicial District of NY (Erie, Niagara, Genesee, Wyoming, Allegany, Cattaraugus, and Chautauqua counties). No support for hospitals or religious organizations. No grants to individuals, or for scholarships, fellowships, or generally for operating budgets or deficit financing.
Publications: Annual report (including application guidelines); Informational brochure.
Application information: Application form available on foundation web site. Application form required.
Initial approach: One-and-a-half-page letter
Copies of proposal: 2
Deadline(s): None
Board meeting date(s): 3 or 4 times a year
Final notification: Usually within 3 months
Officers: Jennifer S. Johnson, Chair.; **Ann M. McCarthy, Pres.**; James A.W. McLeod, V.P.; Amey D. Moot, Secy.; Theodore V. Buerger, Treas.; Beth Kinsman Gosch, Exec. Dir.
Trustees: Anthony S. Johnson; Trudy A. Mollenberg; Richard E. Moot; John N. Walsh III.
Number of staff: 1 full-time professional; 2 part-time support.
EIN: 160845962
Other changes: Ann M. McCarthy has replaced Trudy A. Mollenberg as Pres.

2504
Mrs. Giles Whiting Foundation
(also known as Whiting Foundation)

1133 Ave. of the Americas, 22nd Fl.
New York, NY 10036-6710 (212) 336-2138
Contact: Daniel Reid, Exec. Dir.
E-mail: info@whitingfoundation.org; Main URL: http://www.whitingfoundation.org

Incorporated in 1963 in NY.
Donor: Mrs. Giles Whiting‡.
Foundation type: Independent foundation.
Financial data (yr. ended 11/30/12): Assets, $54,247,523 (M); expenditures, $3,018,089; qualifying distributions, $2,682,236; giving activities include $1,717,500 for 32 grants (high: $150,000; low: $1,000), and $400,000 for 16 grants to individuals (high: $25,000; low: $25,000).
Purpose and activities: The foundation is dedicated to the support of the humanities and of literature.
Fields of interest: Humanities; Literature; Higher education.
Limitations: Applications not accepted.
Application information: Unsolicited requests for funds not accepted.
Officers and Trustees:* Antonia M. Grumbach,* Pres.; **John N. Irwin III,* V.P. and Treas.**; **Peter Pennoyer,* V.P.**; Kate Torrey,* V.P.; Robin Krause,* Secy.; Daniel Reid, Exec. Dir.
Number of staff: 2 full-time professional; 1 part-time professional.
EIN: 136154484

Other changes: John N. Irwin, III is now V.P. and Treas. Kate Douglas Torrey and Peter Pennoyer are now V.P.s.
The grantmaker no longer publishes a multi-year report.

2505
The Widgeon Point Charitable Foundation
(formerly The Beinecke Foundation, Inc.)
c/o Coopersmith, Simon and Vogel., C.P.A.s, P.C.
50 Charles Lindbergh Blvd., Ste. 605
Uniondale, NY 11553-3650 (516) 483-5800
Contact: Jeffery Coopersmith, C.F.O.

Incorporated in 1966 in NY as The Kerry Foundation, Inc. and absorbed the Edwin J. Beinecke Trust, NY, in April 1985. The new name for the combined foundations was adopted in Dec. 1985.
Donor: Sylvia B. Robinson†.
Foundation type: Independent foundation.
Financial data (yr. ended 12/31/12): Assets, $58,828,908 (M); gifts received, $53,024; expenditures, $4,053,105; qualifying distributions, $2,945,792; giving activities include $2,292,000 for 145 grants (high: $250,000; low: $100).
Purpose and activities: Giving primarily for education and the arts, particularly museums; funding also for human services.
Fields of interest: Museums (art); Arts; Elementary/secondary education; Higher education; Education; Environment, natural resources; Botanical gardens; Boys clubs; Human services.
Type of support: General/operating support; Capital campaigns; Building/renovation; Equipment; Endowments; Conferences/seminars; Publication.
Limitations: Applications accepted. Giving primarily in CT and NY; some funding also in MA and ME. No grants to individuals; no loans.
Publications: Annual report.
Application information: Application form not required.
Initial approach: Letter
Deadline(s): None
Board meeting date(s): Spring and fall
Officers: John R. Robinson, Pres.; Abigail Phipps Bowers, V.P.; **Jeffrey Coopersmith, C.F.O.**; Rowland P. Robinson, Treas.
Number of staff: 2 full-time professional; 1 full-time support.
EIN: 136201175

2506
Malcolm Hewitt Wiener Foundation, Inc.
c/o The Millburn Corp.
1270 Ave. of the Americas
New York, NY 10020-1700
Contact: Christina Padgett

Incorporated in 1984 in NY.
Donor: Malcolm H. Wiener.
Foundation type: Independent foundation.
Financial data (yr. ended 12/31/12): Assets, $46,612,019 (M); expenditures, $3,524,646; qualifying distributions, $3,059,115; giving activities include $2,776,802 for 86 grants (high: $515,000; low: $2).
Purpose and activities: Giving primarily for international affairs, arts and cultural programs, and higher education. Support also for public affairs.
Fields of interest: Museums (art); Humanities; Higher education; International affairs, goodwill promotion; International peace/security; International affairs, foreign policy.
Limitations: Applications not accepted. Giving primarily in CT, NJ, NY and PA. No grants to individuals.
Application information: Contributes only to pre-selected organizations.
Officers and Directors:* Malcolm H. Wiener,* Pres.; Harvey Beker,* V.P.; **Gregg Buckbinder, Treas.**; George E. Crapple,* V.P.; Martin J. Whitman; Carolyn S. Wiener.
EIN: 133250321
Other changes: Malcolm H. Wiener is now Pres.

2507
The Robert W. Wilson Charitable Trust
c/o Robert W. Wilson
520 83rd St., Ste. 1R
Brooklyn, NY 11209-4520 (718) 748-6113

Established in 2003 in NY.
Donors: Robert W. Wilson†; Bowman Family Foundation.
Foundation type: Independent foundation.
Financial data (yr. ended 12/31/12): Assets, $49,915,996 (M); gifts received, $47,536,194; expenditures, $41,127,773; qualifying distributions, $40,770,618; giving activities include $40,392,341 for 53 grants (high: $5,000,000; low: $50).
Purpose and activities: Giving primarily for art museums, civil rights associations, historic preservation/historical societies, and environmental conservation and protection.
Fields of interest: Museums (art); Historic preservation/historical societies; Environment, natural resources; Environment; Civil/human rights, association.
Type of support: Program-related investments/loans.
Limitations: Applications not accepted. Giving primarily in NY. No grants to individuals.
Application information: Contributes only to pre-selected organizations.
Trustee: Richard Schneidman.
EIN: 516536168
Other changes: Robert W. Wilson, Donor and trustee, is deceased.

2508
Winley Foundation
100 N. Village Ave., Ste. 35
Rockville Centre, NY **11570-3712** (845) 266-3065
Contact: Anna M. Barone, Treas.

Established in NY.
Donor: Amory Winthrop Trust.
Foundation type: Independent foundation.
Financial data (yr. ended 12/31/12): Assets, $18,786,807 (M); gifts received, $141,000; expenditures, $1,511,675; qualifying distributions, $1,400,000; giving activities include $1,400,000 for 13 grants (high: $350,000; low: $10,000).
Purpose and activities: Giving is limited to the benefit of animals.
Fields of interest: Animal welfare; Animals/wildlife, preservation/protection; Animals/wildlife, sanctuaries.
Limitations: Giving primarily in the greater metropolitan Washington, DC, area, including MD and VA; giving also in NY and SC. No grants to individuals.
Application information:
Initial approach: Typewritten letter
Deadline(s): None
Officers: Cathy Liss, Pres.; Heidi Prescott, V.P.; Edward J. Walsh, Jr., Secy.; Anna M. Barone, Treas.
EIN: 521230146
Other changes: Cathy Liss has replaced Tatiana Nagro as Pres.

2509
The Edwin & Shirley Woldar Family Foundation, Inc.
5 Woodbury Farms Dr.
Woodbury, NY 11797-1242
Contact: Paul Woldar, Pres.; Jay Woldar, Secy.-Treas.
***E-mail:* paul.woldar@woldarfamilyfoundation.org**;
Main URL: http://www.woldarfamilyfoundation.org
Grants List: http://www.woldarfamilyfoundation.org/charities.html

Established in 2001 in DE.
Donors: Edwin Woldar†; Shirley Woldar†.
Foundation type: Independent foundation.
Financial data (yr. ended 12/31/12): Assets, $3,074,365 (M); expenditures, $256,014; qualifying distributions, $179,496; giving activities include $179,496 for grants.
Purpose and activities: Giving with emphasis on helping children, funding research for medical advancement, educational institutions and the care for the less fortunate. Also to support the Jewish ideals of Tzedukah.
Fields of interest: Education; Medical research; Human services; Children/youth, services; Jewish agencies & synagogues.
Limitations: Applications not accepted. Giving in the U.S., primarily in NY. No grants to individuals.
Application information: Unsolicited requests for funds not accepted.
Officers: Paul Woldar, Pres.; Jay Woldar, Secy.-Treas.
EIN: 223819532

2510
Louis S. & Molly B. Wolk Foundation
1600 East Ave., Ste. 701
Rochester, NY 14610-1629 (585) 442-6900
Contact: Grants Committee

Established in 1982 in NY.
Donor: Louis S. Wolk†.
Foundation type: Independent foundation.
Financial data (yr. ended 12/31/12): Assets, $28,472,885 (M); expenditures, $1,511,725; qualifying distributions, $1,371,268; giving activities include $1,200,750 for 17+ grants (high: $255,000).
Purpose and activities: Giving primarily to organizations in the greater Rochester, New York area whose goals are focused on health related, educational, geriatric and social issues.
Fields of interest: Health care; Health organizations; Youth development, scouting agencies (general); Human services; Family services, domestic violence; Jewish agencies & synagogues.
Limitations: Applications accepted. Giving primarily in Rochester, NY. No grants to individuals.
Application information: Application form required.
Initial approach: Letter requesting application
Copies of proposal: 2
Deadline(s): None
Board meeting date(s): Monthly
Final notification: Monthly

Officers and Trustees:* Alvin L. Ureles, M.D.*, Chair.; **Marvin L. Wolk, Mgr.**; Michael B. Berger; Harold Samloff; David M. Wolk; Jeremy J. Wolk.
EIN: 222405596
Other changes: Marvin L. Wolk is now Mgr.

2511
Woodcock Foundation
c/o Rock Co.
30 Rockefeller Plz.
New York, NY 10112-0015
Contact: Wendy Goldner
Main URL: http://woodcockfdn.org/

Foundation type: Independent foundation.
Financial data (yr. ended 11/30/12): Assets, $35,962,344 (M); expenditures, $2,981,896; qualifying distributions, $1,992,448; giving activities include $1,668,798 for 16 grants (high: $225,000; low: $10,500), and $221,322 for foundation-administered programs.
Purpose and activities: Giving primarily in the areas of social enterprise, reproductive health and rights, land conservation, media reform and civil society.
Fields of interest: Environment, land resources; Reproductive health, family planning; Human services.
Limitations: Applications not accepted.
Application information: Unsolicited requests for funds not accepted. Applicants who have been invited to submit a proposal should refer to submission process on foundation web site.
Trustees: Olga M. Davidson; Stuart Davidson; Jeremy Guth; Virginia Montgomery; Winthrop Rutherfurd, Esq.; Lindsay D. Shea.
EIN: 341606085

2512
Yashar Foundation, Inc.
3266 Bedford Ave.
Brooklyn, NY 11210-4509
Contact: Michael Kaplan, Exec. Dir.

Established in 2007 in NY.
Donors: Joe and Eileen Sutton Foundation; Yumark Enterprises; Ouyalady Corporation.
Foundation type: Independent foundation.
Financial data (yr. ended 12/31/12): Assets, $3,425,676 (M); gifts received, $3,000,000; expenditures, $1,207,255; qualifying distributions, $1,207,255; giving activities include $1,200,441 for 73 grants (high: $106,000; low: $20).
Fields of interest: Education; Jewish agencies & synagogues.
Limitations: Applications accepted. Giving primarily in NY. No grants to individuals.
Application information: Application form not required.
Deadline(s): None
Officer: Michael Kaplan, Exec. Dir.
Directors: Gizelle Kaplan; Yitzcak Kaplan.
EIN: 260770603
Other changes: At the close of 2012, the grantmaker paid grants of $1,200,441, a 261.0% increase over the 2011 disbursements, $332,488.

2513
Youth Foundation, Inc.
370 Lexington Ave., Ste. 1206
New York, NY 10017-6584
Contact: Johanna M. Lee
***Main URL:* http://fdnweb.org/youthfdn**

Incorporated in 1940 in NY.
Donors: Alexander M. Hadden†; Mrs. Alexander M. Hadden†.
Foundation type: Independent foundation.
Financial data (yr. ended 12/31/12): Assets, $10,444,795 (M); gifts received, $11,150; expenditures, $591,181; qualifying distributions, $506,197; giving activities include $38,500 for 8 grants (high: $4,000; low: $4,000), and $320,365 for 94 grants to individuals (high: $4,300; low: $1,965).
Purpose and activities: Giving primarily for scholarships to exceptionally worthy, financially needy, secondary school seniors for their undergraduate college education.
Fields of interest: Education.
Type of support: General/operating support; Scholarships—to individuals.
Limitations: Applications accepted. Giving on a national basis.
Publications: Application guidelines; Informational brochure; Program policy statement.
Application information: Complete application guidelines are available on foundation web site. Application form required.
***Initial approach:* Letter requesting application (include SASE). No emails or telephone calls accepted**
Copies of proposal: 1
***Deadline(s):* Feb. 28**
Board meeting date(s): 2nd Tues. of every month (except Apr., July, Aug., Oct. and Dec.)
Final notification: May
Officers and Directors:* Pamela S. Fulweiler,* Pres.; Margaret C. Cushing,* V.P.; Mrs. Robert B. Stockman,* V.P.; Guy N. Robinson,* Secy.; S. Scott Nicholls, Jr.,* Treas.; Charles E. Baskett; **Enrico de Allesandrini**; Sven E. Hsia; Mrs. James C. Larmett; E. Timothy McAuliffe; Elizabeth Ann Stribling-Kivlan; Mrs. Vincent S. Villard, Jr.
Number of staff: 1 full-time professional.
EIN: 136093036
Other changes: Pamela S. Fulweiler has replaced Robert W. Radsch as Pres.
Margaret C. Cushing and Mrs. Robert B. Stockman are now V.P. Karen A. Boyd is no longer a director.

2514
Yudelson Foundation
P.O. Box 662
Armonk, NY 10504-0259
***Application address:* c/o Tara Spell, Pres., P.O. Box 2587, Stone Mountain, GA 30085, tel.: (516) 316-5016**

Foundation type: Independent foundation.
Financial data (yr. ended 12/31/12): Assets, $452,216 (M); expenditures, $16,418; qualifying distributions, $7,650; giving activities include $7,650 for grants.
Fields of interest: Youth development; Human services.
Application information: Application form not required.
Initial approach: Proposal
Deadline(s): None
Officer: Tara Spell, Pres. and Treas.
EIN: 263222568
Other changes: The grantmaker has moved from GA to NY.

2515
The Leslie and Daniel Ziff Foundation
(formerly The Daniel M. Ziff Foundation)
c/o ZBI, LLC
350 Park Ave., 4th Fl.
New York, NY 10022-6067

Established in DE.
Donor: Ziff Investment Partnership LP II.
Foundation type: Independent foundation.
Financial data (yr. ended 12/31/13): Assets, $3,555,309 (M); expenditures, $1,233,191; qualifying distributions, $1,230,801; giving activities include $1,229,200 for 12 grants (high: $325,000; low: $2,500).
Fields of interest: Performing arts, dance; Performing arts, ballet; Environment, natural resources; Hospitals (general); Human services.
Limitations: Applications not accepted. Giving primarily in NY. No grants to individuals.
Application information: Contributes only to pre-selected organizations.
Officers: Daniel M. Ziff, Co-Pres.; Leslie Ziff, Co-Pres.; David Gray, V.P. and Secy.; Spencer Lehv, V.P. and Treas.
EIN: 134083253
Other changes: Leslie Ziff is now Co-Pres. Daniel M. Ziff is now Co-Pres.

NORTH CAROLINA

2516
Arthur F. & Alice E. Adams Charitable Foundation
c/o Wells Fargo Bank, N.A.
1525 W. W.T. Harris Blvd., D1114-044
Charlotte, NC 28288-5709
***Application address:* c/o Wells Fargo Bank, N.A., Attn.: Peter Thompson, V.P., tel.: (908) 598-3582; Email: grantadministration@wellsfargo.com; Main URL: https://www.wellsfargo.com/privatefoundationgrants/adams**

Established in 1987 in FL.
Donor: Alice E. Adams†.
Foundation type: Independent foundation.
Financial data (yr. ended 09/30/12): Assets, $15,798,327 (M); expenditures, $1,276,092; qualifying distributions, $993,564; giving activities include $885,000 for 26 grants (high: $250,000; low: $5,000).
Purpose and activities: Giving primarily to organizations benefitting arts, culture, humanities, and education.
Fields of interest: Arts; Education; Human services.
Limitations: Applications accepted. Giving primarily in Miami, FL, New York, NY, and Memphis, TN. No grants to individuals.
Application information: See foundation website for complete application guidelines. Application form required.
Deadline(s): Feb. 15
***Board meeting date(s):* Spring**
Officers: Paul L. Guiabo, Pres.; Renee C. Guiabo, Governor.
Trustees: Arete Warren; Wells Fargo Bank, N.A.
EIN: 656003785

2517
Adams-Mastrovich Family Foundation
c/o Wells Fargo Bank N.A., Trust Tax Dept.
1 W. 4th St., 4th Fl., MAC D4000-041
Winston-Salem, NC 27101-3818
***E-mail:* grantadministration@wellsfargo.com; Main URL: https://www.wellsfargo.com/privatefoundationgrants/adams-mastrovich**

Established in 1957 in MN.
Donor: Mary Adams Balmat†.
Foundation type: Independent foundation.
Financial data (yr. ended 12/31/13): Assets, $26,110,523 (M); expenditures, $1,336,384; qualifying distributions, $1,144,786; giving activities include $1,076,000 for 49 grants (high: $250,000; low: $4,000).
Purpose and activities: Giving primarily for the arts, human services, and Roman Catholic agencies and churches.
Fields of interest: Performing arts; Performing arts, music; Arts; Human services; Catholic agencies & churches; Religion.
Type of support: General/operating support; Continuing support; Building/renovation; Equipment; Program development; Scholarship funds.
Limitations: Applications accepted. Giving limited to Los Angeles County, CA, and SD. No support for political organizations. No grants to individuals, or for conferences or seminars, fundraisers, campaigns, endowments, or for travel.
Application information: See foundation website for complete application guidelines. Application form required.
***Deadline(s):* Aug. 1**
Trustee: Wells Fargo Bank, N.A.
EIN: 416014092
Other changes: The grantmaker has moved from PA to NC.
The grantmaker now accepts applications.

2518
Phil N. Allen Charitable Trust
c/o Wells Fargo Bank, N.A.
1 W. 4th St., 4th Fl., MAC D4000-041
Winston-Salem, NC 27101-3818

Established in 1981 in CA.
Donor: Phil N. Allen†.
Foundation type: Independent foundation.
Financial data (yr. ended 06/30/13): Assets, $2,945,407 (M); expenditures, $33,314; qualifying distributions, $8,574.
Fields of interest: Higher education; Medical research, institute.
Type of support: Research.
Limitations: Applications not accepted. Giving primarily in CA. No grants to individuals.
Application information: Unsolicited requests for funds not accepted.
Trustees: Marvin S. Siegel; Wells Fargo Bank, N.A.
EIN: 956766982
Other changes: The grantmaker has moved from PA to NC.

2519
Anonymous Trust
P.O. Box 31143
Raleigh, NC 27622-1143
Application address: c/o Margaret Turlington, Scholarship Coord., P.O. Box 2087, Clinton, NC 28329; tel.: (910) 385-6716

Established in 2008 in NC.
Donors: Nancy B. Faircloth; Nancy B. Faircloth Trust.
Foundation type: Independent foundation.
Financial data (yr. ended 12/31/13): Assets, $181,220,681 (M); expenditures, $8,866,275; qualifying distributions, $8,416,449; giving activities include $8,175,277 for 37 grants (high: $6,725,464; low: $500), and $176,685 for 33 grants to individuals (high: $26,323; low: $100).
Fields of interest: Higher education.
Limitations: Giving primarily in VA; some giving also in NC and NY. **No grants to.**
Application information: Applicants for the Simple Gifts Scholarships, the Simple Gifts Fund Sampson County Love of Learning Grant Program, and the Simple Gifts Fund Sampson County Teachers Fellowship Program should visit the Simple Gifts Fund web site at http://www.simplegiftsfund.org/.
Initial approach: Letter
Deadline(s): Dec. 1
Trustees: Anne B. Faircloth; Maria M. Lynch.
EIN: 266220561
Other changes: At the close of 2012, the fair market value of the grantmaker's assets was $161,548,132, a 136.5% increase over the 2011 value, $68,318,373.

2520
Stanley & Marty Arkwright Conservation Trust
c/o Wells Fargo Bank, N.A., Trust Tax. Dept.
1 W. 4th St., 4th Flo., MAC D4000-041
Winston-Salem, NC 27101-3818

Established in 2003 in MT as a private foundation; status changed to a supporting organization of the University of Montana Foundation in 2006.
Foundation type: Independent foundation.
Financial data (yr. ended 12/31/12): Assets, $4,153,108 (M); expenditures, $226,680; qualifying distributions, $187,741; giving activities include $176,509 for 1 grant.
Fields of interest: Higher education, university.
Limitations: Applications not accepted. Giving primarily in MT. No grants to individuals.
Application information: Unsolicited requests for funds not accepted.
Trustee: Wells Fargo Bank, N.A.
EIN: 816088061
Other changes: The grantmaker has moved from PA to NC.

2521
Mary Reynolds Babcock Foundation, Inc.
2920 Reynolda Rd.
Winston-Salem, NC 27106-3016 (336) 748-9222
Contact: **David A. Jackson, Exec. Dir.**
FAX: (336) 777-0095; E-mail: info@mrbf.org; Main URL: http://www.mrbf.org
Grants Database: http://mrbf.org/what-and-where-we-fund
Knowledge Center: http://mrbf.org/resources
Mary Reynolds Babcock Foundation's Philanthropy Promise: http://www.ncrp.org/philanthropys-promise/who
Twitter: https://twitter.com/intent/user?screen_name=mrbf_org&original_referer=http://mrbf.org/

Incorporated in 1953 in NC.
Donors: Betsy Babcock†; Charles H. Babcock†; Charles H. Babcock, Jr.†; Mary Reynolds Babcock†.
Foundation type: Independent foundation.
Financial data (yr. ended 12/31/12): Assets, $162,022,145 (M); expenditures, $9,920,905; qualifying distributions, $8,937,803; giving activities include $6,838,514 for 110 grants (high: $250,000; low: $2,600), $115,782 for foundation-administered programs and $325,000 for 3 loans/program-related investments.
Purpose and activities: The foundation supports people in the southeast to build just and caring communities that nurture people, spur enterprise, bridge differences, and foster fairness. Its mission is to help people and places to move out of poverty and achieve greater social and economic justice. The foundation supports organizations and networks that work across race, ethnic, economic and political differences to make possible a brighter future for all.
Fields of interest: Education; Employment; Housing/shelter; Community/economic development; Children/youth; Adults; Minorities; Economically disadvantaged.
Type of support: Mission-related investments/loans; General/operating support; Program-related investments/loans.
Limitations: Applications accepted. Giving in the southeastern U.S., with emphasis on AL, GA, MS, NC, SC, TN, the Gulf Coast regions of AR and LA, and the Appalachian Regions of KY, VA, and WV. No grants to individuals, or for capital improvements,

direct services (such as food or medical assistance), or for satellite operations of organizations outside the southeast.
Publications: Application guidelines; Financial statement; Grants list; Newsletter; Occasional report.
Application information: An Organizational Summary may be completed and submitted online at the Foundation's website. Applications should wait for a response to the summary before submitting a proposal. Application form required.
Initial approach: Organizational summary
Deadline(s): Rolling deadlines
Board meeting date(s): June and Oct.
Officers and Directors:* Wendy S. Johnson,* Pres.; Katherine R. Mountcastle,* V.P.; Dee Davis,* Secy.; Kenneth F. Mountcastle III,* Treas.; David A. Jackson, Exec. Dir.; Bruce M. Babcock; **LaVeeda Battle**; **Chad Berry**; David Dodson; **Jerry Gonzalez**; Derrick Johnson; Barbara B. Millhouse; Dr. James Mitchell; Katharine B. Mountcastle; Laura L. Mountcastle; Mary Mountcastle; Ivan Kohar Parra; Kevin Trapani.
Number of staff: 5 full-time professional; 1 part-time professional; 4 full-time support.
EIN: 560690140
Other changes: Victoria Creed and Carol P. Zippert are no longer directors.

2522
The Bailey Wildlife Foundation
164 Macon Dr.
Littleton, NC 27850-8160

Established in 1987.
Foundation type: Independent foundation.
Financial data (yr. ended 12/31/11): Assets, $4,796,590 (M); expenditures, $284,568; qualifying distributions, $268,987; giving activities include $177,000 for 7 grants (high: $105,000; low: $1,000).
Fields of interest: Education; Environment; Recreation; Human services.
Type of support: General/operating support; Continuing support; Equipment; Land acquisition; Program development; Research; Matching/challenge support.
Limitations: Applications not accepted. Giving primarily in Washington, DC and ME. No grants to individuals.
Application information: Unsolicited requests for funds not accepted.
Officers and Trustees:* H. Whitney Bailey,* Pres.; William H. Bailey,* Secy.; Gordon M. Bailey,* Treas.; John Bailey; Merritt P. Bailey; Mimi Bailey Davis; Mary Whichard.
EIN: 546037402
Other changes: The grantmaker has moved from MA to NC.

2523
Hildegard Balin Charitable Trust
c/o Wells Fargo Bank, N.A.
1 W. 4th St., 4th Fl., MAC D4000-041
Winston-Salem, NC 27101-3818
***E-mail:* grantadministration@wellsfargo.com; Main URL: https://www.wellsfargo.com/privatefoundationgrants/balin**

Established in 1996 in CA.
Foundation type: Independent foundation.
Financial data (yr. ended 12/31/12): Assets, $4,714,952 (M); expenditures, $406,404; qualifying distributions, $272,980; giving activities include $256,000 for 30 grants (high: $22,500; low: $2,000).
Purpose and activities: Support for human services, especially for services benefiting the elderly and the disadvantaged; giving also for animal welfare and health.
Fields of interest: Animal welfare; Animals/wildlife; Health care; Food services; Human services; Children/youth, services; Residential/custodial care, senior continuing care; Aging, centers/services; Aging; Economically disadvantaged.
Limitations: Applications accepted. Giving primarily in CA, with emphasis on Santa Barbara County. No grants to individuals.
Application information: See foundation website for complete application guidelines. Application form required.
***Deadline(s):* July 31**
Trustees: David F. Horton; Wells Fargo Bank, N.A.
EIN: 776132316
Other changes: The grantmaker now accepts applications.

2524
The Bank of America Charitable Foundation, Inc.
401 N. Tryon St., NC1-021-02-20
Charlotte, NC 28255-0001 (800) 218-9946
Main URL: http://www.bankofamerica.com/foundation/index.cfm

Established in 1958; reincorporated in 2004.
Donors: Bank of America Corp.; Bank of America, N.A.; FleetBoston Financial Foundation; The Holden Trust; Merrill Lynch & Co., Inc.
Foundation type: Company-sponsored foundation.
Financial data (yr. ended 12/31/12): Assets, $32,075,548 (M); gifts received, $120,576,140; expenditures, $175,303,789; qualifying distributions, $175,299,789; giving activities include $175,299,789 for 45,820 grants (high: $2,560,503; low: $10).
Purpose and activities: The Bank of America Charitable Foundation provides philanthropic support to address specific needs vital to the health of local communities by focusing on community and economic development initiatives, addressing critical human needs such as hunger, and educating the workforce for 21st century jobs. Special emphasis is directed toward programs supporting low and moderate income communities. Support is given primarily in areas of company operations.
Fields of interest: Arts; Secondary school/education; Higher education; Education; Environment; Hospitals (general); Employment, services; Employment, training; Employment; Food services; Food banks; Nutrition; Housing/shelter, owner/renter issues; Housing/shelter, home owners; Housing/shelter; Youth development, adult & child programs; Youth development; Family services; Human services, financial counseling; Homeless, human services; Human services; Community development, neighborhood development; Community development, small businesses; Community/economic development; United Ways and Federated Giving Programs; Leadership development; Disabilities, people with; Military/veterans; Economically disadvantaged.
Type of support: General/operating support; Continuing support; Management development/capacity building; Program development; Conferences/seminars; Internship funds; Employee volunteer services; Employee matching gifts; Employee-related scholarships.
Limitations: Applications accepted. Giving on a national and international basis in areas of company operations. No support for discriminatory organizations, political, labor, or fraternal organizations, civic clubs, religious organizations not of direct benefit to the entire community, or public or private pre-K-12 schools. No grants to individuals or for fellowships, sports, athletic events or programs, travel-related events, student trips or tours, development or production of books, films, videos, or televisions programs, or memorial campaigns.
Publications: Application guidelines; Program policy statement.
Application information: Support is limited to 1 contribution per organization during any given year. Application form required.
Initial approach: Complete online eligibility quiz and application
***Deadline(s):* Jan. 22 to Feb. 14 for Workforce Development and Education; Apr. 21 to May 9 for Community Development; and July 21 to Aug 8 for Basic Human Services**
Officers and Directors:* Anne M. Finucane,* Chair.; Kerry H. Sullivan, Pres.; Thomas M. Brantley, Sr. V.P., Tax; Dannielle C. Campos, Sr. V.P.; Anna Cowenhoven, Sr. V.P.; **Ximena A. Delgato, Sr. V.P.**; Rena M. DeSisto, Sr. V.P.; Stephen B. Fitzgerald, Sr. V.P.; Robert E. Gallery, Sr. V.P.; Angie Garcia-Lathrop, Sr. V.P.; Charles R. Henderson, Jr., Sr. V.P.; Teresa M. Ingwall, Sr. V.P.; Daniel Letendre, Sr. V.P.; Alexandra C. Liftman, Sr. V.P.; Jennifer Locane, Sr. V.P.; Susan Portugal, Sr. V.P.; Tish Secrest, Sr. V.P.; Michael F. Shriver, Sr. V.P.; Brenda L. Suits, Sr. V.P.; Kristen L. Teskey, Sr. V.P.; Melissa Alpert Anguilla, V.P.; Caitlin M. Bell, V.P.; Abigail Goward, V.P.; Erin M. Hinton, V.P.; Colleen O. Johnson, Secy.; Suzette Finger, Treas.; Keith T. Banks; Amy Woods Brinkley; Walter B. Elcock; Janet W. Lamkin; Andrew D. Plepler; Martin Richards; Purna R. Saggurti.
EIN: 200721133
Other changes: Suzette Finger is now Treas. Helen B. Eggers, Claire A. Huang, and Catherine P. Bessant are no longer directors. Abigail Goward is no longer Sr. V.P.
The grantmaker now publishes application guidelines.

2525
Paul and Merrill Barringer Family Foundation
Weldon, NC

The foundation terminated in 2011 and transferred its assets to Highpoint Community Foundation.

2526
Elizabeth Hurlock Beckman Award Trust
1525 W. WT Harris Blvd. D1114-044
Charlotte, NC 28288-0001
***E-mail:* grantadministration@wellsfargo.com; Main URL: https://www.wellsfargo.com/privatefoundationgrants/beckman**

Foundation type: Independent foundation.
Financial data (yr. ended 12/31/12): Assets, $5,967,444 (M); expenditures, $746,821; qualifying distributions, $673,224; giving activities include $550,000 for 22 grants to individuals (high: $25,000; low: $25,000).
Purpose and activities: Grant awards to current and former academic teachers who have inspired students to make significant contributions for the benefit of the community.

Fields of interest: Education; Community/ economic development; Public affairs.
Type of support: Grants to individuals.
Limitations: Applications accepted. Giving primarily in CA, FL, GA, MA, NY, WA and WI.
Application information: Recipients must be current or former teachers, professors, or instructors at a college, university, junior college, community college, or technical school located in the United States. Preference will be given to educators who teach or who taught in the fields of psychology, medicine, or law. See foundation website for complete application policies and guidelines. Application form required.
Deadline(s): **July 15**
Trustee: Wells Fargo Bank, N.A.
Advisory Committee: Geraldine A. Downey; Karen MaCausland Tidmarsh; Carol Goodheart.
EIN: 371564854
Other changes: The grantmaker now accepts applications.

2527
Frank and Lydia Bergen Foundation
1525 W. WT Harris Blvd., D1114-044
Charlotte, NC 28288-5709
***Wells Fargo Philanthropic Services, 1 W. 4th St., 6th Fl., Winston-Salem, NC 27101, tel:* (855) 739-2920,**
email: grantadministration@wellsfargo.com; Main URL: http://www.wellsfargo.com/privatefoundationgrants/bergen

Incorporated in 1983 in NJ.
Donor: Charlotte V. Bergen‡.
Foundation type: Independent foundation.
Financial data (yr. ended 12/31/12): Assets, $9,317,513 (M); expenditures, $536,490; qualifying distributions, $464,049; giving activities include $437,850 for 28 grants (high: $70,000; low: $1,500).
Purpose and activities: Giving primarily to 1) arrange for musical entertainments, concerts and recitals of a character appropriate for the education and instruction of the public in the musical arts, with paramount consideration given to traditional classical music programs, 2) aid worthy students of music in securing a complete and adequate musical education, and 3) aid organizations in their efforts to present fine music to the public, provided that such organizations are operated exclusively for educational purposes.
Fields of interest: Arts education; Performing arts, music; Arts.
Type of support: Program development; Scholarship funds.
Limitations: Applications accepted. Giving primarily in NJ; some funding also in NY. No grants to individuals, or for endowments or general operating support; fundraising events including dinners, benefits and athletic events; no loans.
Application information: Application form required.
Initial approach: **See foundation web site**
Deadline(s): **Apr. 10 or Aug. 15**
Trustee: Wells Fargo Bank, N.A.
EIN: 226359304

2528
Francis & Monte Bettman Foundation
c/o Wells Fargo Bank N.A., Trust Tax Dept.
1 W. 4th St., 4th Fl., MAC D4000-041
Winston-Salem, NC 27101-3818

Foundation type: Independent foundation.
Financial data (yr. ended 12/31/12): Assets, $3,678,717 (M); expenditures, $238,169; qualifying distributions, $200,925; giving activities include $187,675 for 7 grants (high: $26,811; low: $26,810).
Fields of interest: Health care; Youth development; Human services; Jewish agencies & synagogues.
Type of support: General/operating support.
Limitations: Applications not accepted. Giving primarily in CA, FL, and OR.
Application information: Unsolicited requests for funds not accepted.
Trustee: Wells Fargo Bank, N.A.
EIN: 936033920
Other changes: The grantmaker has moved from PA to NC.

2529
The Mary Duke Biddle Foundation
318 Blackwell St., Ste. 130
PMB 101
Durham, NC **27701-2888** (919) 493-5591
Contact: Douglas C. Zinn, Exec. Dir.
FAX: (919) 489-0118; **E-mail: info@mdbf.org**; Main URL: http://www.mdbf.org
Grants List: http://www.mdbf.org/RecentGrants.html

Trust established in 1956 in NY.
Donors: Mary Duke Biddle‡; Nicholas Duke Biddle 1960 Trust; Nicholas D. Biddle Trust #2.
Foundation type: Independent foundation.
Financial data (yr. ended 12/31/12): Assets, $23,589,154 (M); expenditures, $1,841,124; qualifying distributions, $1,102,759; giving activities include $1,102,759 for 188 grants (high: $132,777; low: $500).
Purpose and activities: Support for private higher and secondary education, specified churches, cultural programs, particularly music, dance and theater, projects in the arts, and aid to the community and to the handicapped; half of the income is committed to Duke University.
Fields of interest: Performing arts, dance; Performing arts, theater; Performing arts, music; Arts; Secondary school/education; Higher education; Education; Community/economic development; Children/youth; Disabilities, people with.
Type of support: Program development; Conferences/seminars; Seed money; Fellowships; Scholarship funds; Matching/challenge support.
Limitations: Applications accepted. Giving limited to NC and New York, NY. No support for public education. No grants to individuals, or for building or endowment funds; generally no operating budgets; no loans.
Publications: Annual report.
Application information: Application guidelines available on foundation web site. Application form not required.
Initial approach: **E-mail brief letter of inquiry**
Copies of proposal: 1
Deadline(s): **See foundation web site for current deadlines**
Board meeting date(s): Mar., June, Sept., and Dec.
Officers and Trustees:* Mary T. Jones,* Chair.; Thomas S. Kenan III,* Vice-Chair. and Secy.; John G. Mebane, Jr.,* Treas.; Mimi O'Brien, Exec. Dir.; C. Russell Bryan; James D.B.T. Semans; Jon E. Zeljo.
Number of staff: 1 full-time professional; 2 part-time support.
EIN: 136068883

2530
Charle & Ruth Billingsley Foundation
c/o Wells Fargo Bank, N.A., Trust Tax. Dept.
1 W. 4th St., 4th Fl., MAC D4000-041
Winston-Salem, NC 27101-3818
E-mail: grantadministration@wellsfargo.com; Main URL: https://www.wellsfargo.com/privatefoundationgrants/billingsley

Established in 1989 in CA.
Donor: U.S. Trust Co.
Foundation type: Independent foundation.
Financial data (yr. ended 12/31/13): Assets, $4,414,963 (M); expenditures, $260,097; qualifying distributions, $208,796; giving activities include $190,495 for grants.
Fields of interest: Museums; Performing arts; Environment; Health care; Youth development, centers/clubs; Human services; Children/youth, services.
Type of support: General/operating support.
Limitations: Applications accepted. Giving primarily in CA. No grants to individuals.
Application information: See foundation website for complete application guidelines. Application form required.
Deadline(s): Apr. 30 and Aug. 31
Trustee: Wells Fargo Bank, N.A.
EIN: 336047988
Other changes: The grantmaker has moved from PA to NC.

2531
The Bolick Foundation
P.O. Box 307
Conover, NC 28613-0307

Established in 1967 in NC.
Donor: Southern Furniture Co. of Conover, Inc.
Foundation type: Company-sponsored foundation.
Financial data (yr. ended 06/30/13): Assets, $9,673,764 (M); expenditures, $495,766; qualifying distributions, $424,100; giving activities include $424,100 for 58 grants (high: $175,000; low: $150).
Purpose and activities: The foundation supports organizations involved with historical activities, education, health, human services, international relief, and Christianity.
Fields of interest: Historical activities; Elementary/secondary education; Higher education; Theological school/education; Education; Health care; Boy scouts; YM/YWCAs & YM/YWHAs; Residential/custodial care, hospices; Human services; International relief; Christian agencies & churches.
Type of support: General/operating support; Annual campaigns; Capital campaigns; Building/renovation.
Limitations: Applications not accepted. Giving primarily in NC. No grants to individuals.
Application information: Contributes only to pre-selected organizations.
Trustees: Jerome W. Bolick; **Judith L. Bolick**; Linda B. Bolick.
EIN: 566086348

2532
Harry H. and Anna Borun Foundation
c/o Wells Fargo Bank, N.A. Trust Tax Dept.
1 W. 4th St., 4th Fl., MAC D4000-041
Winston-Salem, NC 27101-3818
Contact: Bessolos
***Application address:* 1530 3rd Ave., Birmingham, AL 35294, Attn.: Exec. Committee**

Established in 1957 in CA.
Donors: Anna Borun†; Harry Borun†.
Foundation type: Independent foundation.
Financial data (yr. ended 12/31/12): Assets, $7,215,392 (M); expenditures, $352,897; qualifying distributions, $332,312; giving activities include $326,500 for 31 grants (high: $60,000; low: $1,000).
Fields of interest: Higher education, university; Environment, natural resources; Human services; Jewish federated giving programs.
Limitations: Applications accepted. Giving primarily in CA; some giving also in NY. No grants to individuals.
Application information: Application form required.
Initial approach: Letter
***Deadline(s):* May 15**
Trustee: Wells Fargo Bank, N.A.
EIN: 956150362
Other changes: The grantmaker has moved from PA to NC.

2533
Brady Education Foundation, Inc.
(formerly W.H. Brady Foundation, Inc.)
100 Europa Dr., Ste. 351
Chapel Hill, NC 27517-2389
Contact: Elizabeth P. Pungello, Pres.
E-mail: info@bradyeducationfoundation.org; Stage 1 application e-mail: applications@bradyeducationfoundation.org; Main URL: http://bradyeducationfoundation.org/

Incorporated in 1956 in WI.
Foundation type: Independent foundation.
Financial data (yr. ended 06/30/13): Assets, $13,697,228 (M); expenditures, $774,751; qualifying distributions, $627,131; giving activities include $544,575 for 6 grants (high: $142,816; low: $50,000).
Purpose and activities: Giving to close the achievement gap for children at risk for poor school outcomes due to environmental factors associated with living in poverty. The foundation pursues its mission by promoting collaboration between researchers and educators via the funding of research and program evaluations in education.
Fields of interest: Education; Children; Economically disadvantaged.
Type of support: General/operating support; Continuing support; Management development/capacity building; Capital campaigns; Equipment; Program development; Conferences/seminars; Publication; Curriculum development; Scholarship funds; Research; Technical assistance; Program evaluation; Matching/challenge support.
Limitations: Giving in the U.S., with emphasis on NC. No support for sectarian programs or umbrella organizations, or for capital projects, research for children at risk of poor school outcomes due to medical conditions, scaling up programs already found to be effective, or for individual providers who wish to increase their center's Early Childhood Environment Rating Scale score or obtain accreditation. Funding to tax-supported institutions extremely limited. No grants to individuals, or for scholarships or operating costs.
Publications: Application guidelines.
Application information: Stage 2 applications are by invitation only, upon review of Stage 1 applications.
Initial approach: Proposal via e-mail in .pdf format using the foundation's Stage 1 application process which is explained on the foundation's web site
Deadline(s): See foundation web site for current deadlines
Officers and Directors:* Elizabeth P. Pungello,* Pres.; Peter J. Lettenberger,* V.P.; James M. Rauh,* Treas.; Frances Campbell, Ph.D.; Barbara Crockett; **Mark Kuhn**.
Number of staff: 1 part-time support.
EIN: 396064733

2534
Burroughs Wellcome Fund
21 T. W. Alexander Dr.
P.O. Box 13901
Research Triangle Park, NC 27709-3901 (919) 991-5100
Contact: Russell Campbell III, Comms. Off.
FAX: (919) 991-5160; E-mail: info@bwfund.org; Contact info. for Russ Campbell III tel.: (919) 991-5119; fax: (919) 991-5179, e-mail: rcampbell@bwfund.org; Main URL: http://www.bwfund.org
Twitter: https://twitter.com/BWFUND

Incorporated in 1955 in NY.
Donors: Burroughs Wellcome Co.; The Wellcome Trust.
Foundation type: Independent foundation.
Financial data (yr. ended 08/31/13): Assets, $719,935,278 (M); expenditures, $39,319,875; qualifying distributions, $33,322,096; giving activities include $28,407,990 for 699 grants (high: $359,000; low: $500).
Purpose and activities: The fund is an independent private foundation dedicated to advancing the medical sciences by supporting research and other scientific and educational activities. Within this broad mission the Fund has two primary goals: 1) To help scientists early in their careers develop as independent investigators and 2) To advance fields in the basic biomedical sciences that are undervalued or in need of particular encouragement. The fund makes grants primarily to degree-granting institutions on behalf of individual researchers, who must be nominated by their institutions.
Fields of interest: Medical research, institute; Biology/life sciences.
International interests: Canada.
Type of support: Program development; Research.
Limitations: Applications accepted. Giving limited to the U.S. and Canada. No grants to individuals, or for building or endowment funds, equipment, operating budgets, continuing support, annual campaigns, deficit financing, publications, conferences, or matching gifts; no loans.
Publications: Annual report (including application guidelines); Informational brochure (including application guidelines); Newsletter; Occasional report.
Application information: See fund web site for application information. Application form required.
***Initial approach:* All applications must be submitted electronically. Paper applications are not accepted**
Deadline(s): Varies depending on the program. See fund web site for information
Board meeting date(s): Feb., May, July, and Oct.
Final notification: Varies
Officers and Directors:* Carlos J. Bustamante, Ph.D., Chair.; John E. Burris,* Pres.; Steven D. Corman, Hon. Dir.; Philip R. Tracy, J.D., Hon. Dir.; Bruce Alberts; Nancy Andrews; J. Michael Bishop, M.D.; Emery N. Brown, M.D., Ph.D.; Geoff Gerber, Ph.D.; George Langford, Ph.D.; Roderick R. McInnes, M.D., Ph.D.; Carla Shatz; Michael J. Welsh, M.D.; Dyann Wirth, Ph.D.
Number of staff: 17 full-time professional; 4 full-time support; 2 part-time support.
EIN: 237225395
Other changes: Phil Gold, Judith L. Swain and Chris Viehbacher are no longer directors. Jerome F. Strauss, III is no longer Vice-Chair.

2535
Porter B. Byrum Charitable Trust
P.O. Box 11795
Charlotte, NC 28220-1795

Donors: Porter B. Byrum; Park Roads Shopping Centerporter By.
Foundation type: Independent foundation.
Financial data (yr. ended 12/31/12): Assets, $43,132,733 (M); gifts received, $18,471,550; expenditures, $1,372,111; qualifying distributions, $1,062,200; giving activities include $1,062,200 for grants.
Fields of interest: Higher education; Theological school/education; Protestant agencies & churches.
Limitations: Applications not accepted. Giving primarily in NC.
Application information: Contributes only to pre-selected organizations.
Trustee: Porter B. Byrum.
EIN: 266366327
Other changes: At the close of 2012, the fair market value of the grantmaker's assets was $43,132,733, a 146.2% increase over the 2011 value, $17,522,476. For the same period, the grantmaker paid grants of $1,062,200, a 504.5% increase over the 2011 disbursements, $175,705.

2536
Marie Eccles Caine Charitable Foundation
c/o Wells Fargo Bank, N.A.
1 W. 4th St., 4th Fl., MAC D4000-041
Winston-Salem, NC 27101-3818

Established in 1981 in UT.
Donor: Marie Eccles Caine†.
Foundation type: Independent foundation.
Financial data (yr. ended 05/31/13): Assets, $11,865,546 (M); expenditures, $584,515; qualifying distributions, $521,341; giving activities include $507,648 for 13 grants (high: $316,568; low: $3,000).
Fields of interest: Arts; Higher education; Education.
Type of support: General/operating support; Continuing support; Program development; Curriculum development; Scholarship funds.
Limitations: Applications not accepted. Giving primarily in Logan and Salt Lake City, UT. No grants to individuals.
Application information: Contributes only to pre-selected organizations.
Board meeting date(s): Varies
Trustee: Wells Fargo Bank, N.A.
EIN: 942764258
Other changes: The grantmaker has moved from AZ to NC.

2537
Louis J. Christopher Memorial Charity Fund
1525 W. WT Harris Blvd., D1114-044
Charlotte, NC 28262

Established in 2002 in CA.

Foundation type: Independent foundation.
Financial data (yr. ended 12/31/12): Assets, $14,298,938 (M); expenditures, $573,488; qualifying distributions, $496,259; giving activities include $474,306 for 6 grants (high: $144,900; low: $39,510).
Purpose and activities: Giving primarily for higher education and hospitals, particularly to a children's hospital and for orthopedic research.
Fields of interest: Higher education; Hospitals (specialty); Orthopedics; Residential/custodial care, hospices; Foundations (private grantmaking).
Limitations: Applications not accepted. Giving primarily in Los Angeles, CA. No grants to individuals.
Application information: Contributes only to pre-selected organizations.
Trustee: Wells Fargo Bank, N.A.
EIN: 956019838

2538
Community Foundation of Burke County

205 N. King St.
Morganton, NC 28655 (828) 437-7105
Contact: Nancy W. Taylor, Exec. Dir.
FAX: (828) 437-0433;
E-mail: info@cfburkecounty.org; Mailing address: P.O. Box 1156, Morganton, NC 28680; Main URL: http://www.cfburkecounty.org

Established in 1999 in NC.
Foundation type: Community foundation.
Financial data (yr. ended 12/31/12): Assets, $12,835,403 (M); gifts received, $749,401; expenditures, $878,787; giving activities include $605,454 for 143 grants (high: $57,641), and $35,950 for 33 grants to individuals.
Purpose and activities: The foundation seeks to encourage, develop and participate in philanthropy by providing flexible giving opportunities, professional support and responsible stewardship for the benefit of donors and qualified recipients.
Fields of interest: Humanities; Arts; Education, early childhood education; Libraries (public); Education; Environment, association; Environment; Health care; Human services; Economic development; Community/economic development; Protestant agencies & churches; Religion.
Limitations: Applications accepted. Giving primarily in Burke County, NC. No support for religious organizations or purposes. No grants to individuals (except for scholarships), or for annual fund campaigns or capital campaigns, augmenting endowments, or underwriting for fundraising events or performances.
Publications: Annual report; Informational brochure; Newsletter.
Application information: Visit foundation web site for application forms and guidelines. Application form required.
Initial approach: Mail, fax, or e-mail Notification of Intent form
Copies of proposal: 1
***Deadline(s):* June 30 for Letter of Intent, July 25 for application**
Board meeting date(s): 4th Wed. of each month
Officers and Directors:* J. Rountree Collett, Jr.,* Pres.; Edward D. Wall,* V.P.; Martha McMurray-Russ,* Secy.; Phillip E. Church,* Treas.; Nancy W. Taylor, Exec. Dir.; John F. Black, Jr.; William M. Brinkley; Le N. Ervin; Doris Fullwood; Susan L. Haire; Donald J. McCall; Marcus W.H. Mitchell, Jr.; Susan C. Pollpeter; Diana Spangler-Crawford; Benjamin S. Succop; V. Otis Wilson, Jr.

Number of staff: 1 part-time professional; 1 full-time support.
EIN: 562170220

2539
Community Foundation of Henderson County, Inc.

401 N. Main St., 3rd Fl.
P.O. Box 1108
Hendersonville, NC 28792-4915 (828) 697-6224
Contact: McCray V. Benson, C.E.O.; For grants: Kathryn McConnell, V.P., Philanthropy
FAX: (828) 696-4026; E-mail: info@cfhcforever.org; Grant application e-mail: kmcconnell@cfhcforever.org; Main URL: http://www.cfhcforever.org
Facebook: https://www.facebook.com/pages/Community-Foundation-of-Henderson-County/228920600597
LinkedIn: http://www.linkedin.com/company/community-foundation-of-henderson-county?trk=top_nav_home

Incorporated in 1982 in NC.
Foundation type: Community foundation.
Financial data (yr. ended 06/30/12): Assets, $69,187,604 (M); gifts received, $1,866,336; expenditures, $3,698,138; giving activities include $2,265,006 for 60+ grants (high: $283,573), and $125,787 for 122 grants to individuals.
Purpose and activities: The foundation exists to enrich the quality of life in the greater Henderson County, NC, area, through building and increasing endowments in perpetuity.
Fields of interest: Arts; Child development, education; Higher education; Education; Environment; Health care; Disasters, Hurricane Katrina; Child development, services; Aging, centers/services; Homeless, human services; Human services; Community/economic development; Public affairs; Aging; Homeless.
Type of support: Program evaluation; Management development/capacity building; Emergency funds; Equipment; Matching/challenge support; Program development; Scholarships—to individuals; Seed money; Technical assistance.
Limitations: Applications accepted. Giving limited to the Henderson County, NC, area. No support for religious purposes. No grants to individuals (except for scholarships), or for capital campaigns, annual campaigns, fundraising events, or augmenting endowments; no loans.
Publications: Application guidelines; Annual report; Informational brochure; Newsletter.
Application information: Visit foundation Web site for application guidelines. Scholarship availability is announced in November. Application form required.
Initial approach: Letter or telephone
Copies of proposal: 2
Deadline(s): Mar. 1, June 1, Sept. 1, and Dec. 1 for grants; Mar. 1 for scholarships
Board meeting date(s): Monthly
Final notification: 3 months
Officers and Directors:* Randolph Romeo,* Chair.; John Bell, Jr.,* Vice-Chair.; McCray V. Benson,* C.E.O. and Pres.; Kathryn McConnell,* V.P., Community Philanthropy; **Lauretta Cook,* Secy.**; George Bond,* Secy.; Steve Greene,* Treas.; David Marshall,* Asst. Treas.; Les Boyd III; **Cindy Causby**; Keith Dalbec; Tom Darnall; Gary Eblen; Chuck Edwards; Shirley McGee; Kimbela McMinn; Ron Partin; Pam Prather; Charley Rogers; Kaye Youngblood.
Number of staff: 4 full-time professional; 2 full-time support.
EIN: 561330792
Other changes: Lauretta Cook has replaced George Bond as Secy.
Lauretta Sthreshley is no longer Asst. Secy. Jana Humleker and Stan Shelley are no longer directors.

2540
The Community Foundation of Western North Carolina, Inc.

4 Vanderbilt Park Dr., Ste. 300
Asheville, NC 28803 (828) 254-4960
Contact: Diane Crisp, Grants Mgr.
FAX: (828) 251-2258; E-mail: crisp@cfwnc.org; Mailing Address: P.O. Box 1888, Asheville, NC 28802-1888; Main URL: http://www.cfwnc.org
Facebook: http://www.facebook.com/pages/The-Community-Foundation-of-Western-North-Carolina/148250892249
Grants Database: https://www.grantinterface.com/Common/LogOn.aspx?eqs=FzDcrVbouBENQuVFfQC_Gg2
YouTube: http://www.youtube.com/user/cfwnc09

Incorporated in 1978 in NC.
Foundation type: Community foundation.
Financial data (yr. ended 06/30/13): Assets, $211,579,611 (M); gifts received, $16,389,983; expenditures, $11,854,483; giving activities include $8,876,025 for 328+ grants (high: $277,000), and $320,350 for 146 grants to individuals.
Purpose and activities: The Community Foundation of Western North Carolina inspires philanthropy and mobilizes resources to enrich lives and communities in Western North Carolina.
Fields of interest: Arts; Education; Agriculture/food, reform; Children/youth, services; Human services; Nonprofit management; Community/economic development; Infants/toddlers; Children/youth; Women; Girls; Economically disadvantaged.
Type of support: Income development; Management development/capacity building; Equipment; Endowments; Program development; Curriculum development; Scholarship funds; Technical assistance; Program evaluation; Scholarships—to individuals; Matching/challenge support.
Limitations: Applications accepted. Giving limited to Avery, Buncombe, Burke, Cherokee, Clay, Graham, Haywood, Henderson, Jackson, Macon, Madison, McDowell, Mitchell, Polk, Rutherford, Swain, Transylvania, and Yancey counties, NC. No support for religious organizations or sectarian purposes (except from designated funds). No grants to individuals (except for undergraduate student scholarships), or for capital campaigns, endowment funds, start-up funds, or debt retirement.
Publications: Application guidelines; Annual report; Financial statement; Newsletter.
Application information: Visit foundation web site for online application link, guidelines, and specific deadlines. Application form required.
Initial approach: Telephone or e-mail, online letter of intent or application
Copies of proposal: 1
Deadline(s): Varies
Board meeting date(s): Quarterly, 2nd Wed. in Feb., May, Aug., and Nov.
Final notification: Varies
Officers and Directors:* James W. Stickney IV,* Chair.; A.C. Honeycutt, Jr.,* Vice-Chair.; Elizabeth Brazas,* Pres.; Sheryl Aikman, V.P., Devel.; Philip Belcher, V.P., Progs.; Graham Keever, C.F.O.; **Laurence Weiss,* Secy.**; G. Edward Towson II,* Treas.; Maurean B. Adams; **William Clarke**; Jennie

Eblen; Ernest E. Ferguson; Charles Frederick; Howell A. Hammond; Darryl Hart; Susan Jenkins; Stephanie Norris Kiser; Tina McGuire; Lowell R. Pearlman; Ramona C. Rowe; George W. Saenger; Anna S. "Candy" Shivers; Jerry Stone; Sarah Sparboe Thornburg; Stephen Watson; Sharon Kelly West.
Number of staff: 14 full-time professional; 2 part-time professional; 2 full-time support.
EIN: 561223384
Other changes: James W. Stickney IV has replaced Ernest E. Ferguson as Chair. Laurence Weiss has replaced Terry Van Duyn as Secy.
A.C. Honeycutt, Jr. is now Vice-Chair. Marla T. Adams, Louise W. Baker, David S. Dimling, Thomas Lee Finger, and T. Wood Lovell are no longer directors.

2541
Cumberland Community Foundation, Inc.

308 Green St.
P.O. Box 2345
Fayetteville, NC 28301-1703 (910) 483-4449
Contact: Mary M. Holmes, Exec. Dir.
FAX: (910) 483-2905;
E-mail: info@cumberlandcf.org; Additional e-mail: mary@cumberlandcf.org; Main URL: http://www.cumberlandcf.org
Knowledge Center: http://www.cumberlandcf.org/ccf_news.php

Established in 1980 in NC by Dr. Lucile Hutaff.
Donor: Lucile Hutaff†.
Foundation type: Community foundation.
Financial data (yr. ended 06/30/13): Assets, $65,791,812 (M); gifts received, $4,888,330; expenditures, $4,147,096; giving activities include $3,090,452 for 44+ grants, and $204,750 for grants to individuals.
Purpose and activities: The foundation exists to foster creative change, to encourage and test new ideas, and to work for the common good of all citizens of Cumberland County and the surrounding area by: 1) promoting local philanthropy and its rewards; 2) building and maintaining a permanent endowment for the benefit of the community; 3) providing a flexible vehicle for prospective donors with varied charitable interests and abilities to give; and 4) developing solutions to changing community needs through effective grantmaking.
Fields of interest: Museums; Performing arts; Humanities; History/archaeology; Language/linguistics; Literature; Arts; Child development, education; Vocational education; Higher education; Adult/continuing education; Libraries/library science; Education; Environment, natural resources; Environment; Animals/wildlife, preservation/protection; Reproductive health, family planning; Medical care, rehabilitation; Health care; Substance abuse, services; Mental health/crisis services; AIDS; Crime/violence prevention, youth; Employment; Nutrition; Housing/shelter, development; Recreation; Youth development, services; Children/youth, services; Child development, services; Family services; Residential/custodial care, hospices; Aging, centers/services; Women, centers/services; Minorities/immigrants, centers/services; Homeless, human services; Human services; Civil rights, race/intergroup relations; Civil/human rights; Economic development; Rural development; Community/economic development; Voluntarism promotion; Population studies; Military/veterans' organizations; Leadership development; Children/youth; Youth; Disabilities, people with; Blind/visually impaired; Minorities; Native Americans/American Indians; Women; Economically disadvantaged; Homeless.
Type of support: General/operating support; Income development; Management development/capacity building; Program development; Conferences/seminars; Publication; Seed money; Scholarship funds; Technical assistance; Program evaluation; Scholarships—to individuals; In-kind gifts; Matching/challenge support.
Limitations: Applications accepted. Giving limited to Cumberland County, NC. No support for religious purposes. No grants to individuals (except for scholarships), or for annual campaigns, special event fundraisers or sponsorships, capital campaigns, endowments, trips for schools or clubs, membership dues, or deficit funding or debt retirement.
Publications: Application guidelines; Annual report; Financial statement; Grants list; Informational brochure; Newsletter; Occasional report; Program policy statement.
Application information: Visit foundation web site for application guidelines. Based on the letter of intent and data form, the foundation's Grants Committee will consider all eligible requests and determine what organizations/projects will be invited to submit a full grant application. Application form required.

Initial approach: **Attend Grant Overview Session**
Copies of proposal: 1
***Deadline(s):* Aug. 15 for Community Grants**
Board meeting date(s): 2nd Thurs. of every other month
***Final notification:* Complete review process takes approx. 15 weeks**

Officers and Directors:* S. Lynn Legatski,* Pres.; James R. Konneker,* V.P.; Mary M. Holmes, Exec. Dir.; Mary Anne Brooks, C.F.O.; John S. Ayers; Cathy J. Blackwell; Jesse H. Byrd, Jr.; Libby Stanfield Daniel; Dr. Loleta Wood Foster; **Ashton L. Fox;** Rakesh Gupta, M.D.; Elaine Bryant Hayes; John Healy; Lucy H. Jones; Elizabeth Marler Keeney; O. Raymond Manning, Jr.; Lonnie J. McAllister; Dan K. McNeill; Sandra W. Monroe; Barbara B. Richardson; Emily K. Schaefer; Ole M. Sorensen; Eva C. Williams.
Number of staff: 5 full-time professional; 1 full-time support; 1 part-time support.
EIN: 581406831
Other changes: S. Lynn Legatski has replaced Raymond O. Manning Jr. as Pres. James R. Konneker has replaced Lynn S. Legatski as V.P. Chrysoula Bantsolas is now Donor Srvs. Mgr. S. Lynn Legatski and James R. Konneker are no longer directors. Ron Matthews and Ellen K. Parker are no longer directors.

2542
Dalton-Brand Foundation, Inc.

(formerly Harry L. Dalton Foundation, Inc.)
112 S. Tryon St., Ste. 805
Charlotte, NC 28284-1106 **(704) 332-5380**
FAX: (704) 332-1972;
E-mail: brand0598@gmail.com

Established about 1954 in NC.
Foundation type: Independent foundation.
Financial data (yr. ended 07/31/13): Assets, $5,294,966 (M); expenditures, $583,108; qualifying distributions, $532,500; giving activities include $532,500 for 33 grants (high: $181,800; low: $200).
Purpose and activities: Giving primarily for education, including higher education; support also for the arts, including a museum, performing arts center and cultural programs; giving also for a Presbyterian church.
Fields of interest: Museums; Arts; Higher education; Education; Human services; Children/youth, services; Community/economic development; Protestant agencies & churches.
Type of support: Capital campaigns; Building/renovation; Endowments.
Limitations: Applications accepted. Giving primarily in Mecklenburg County, NC.
Publications: Annual report.
Application information:

***Deadline(s):* None**
Board meeting date(s): Quarterly

Officers and Director:* Elizabeth D. Brand, Pres. and Treas.; R. Alfred Brand III, V.P.; Deeda M. Coffey,* Secy.
Number of staff: 1 part-time support.
EIN: 566061267
Other changes: The grantmaker now accepts applications.

2543
Davie Community Foundation, Inc.

107 N. Salisbury St.
P.O. Box 546
Mocksville, NC 27028-2322 **(336) 753-6903**
***Contact:* Jane Simpson, Pres. and C.E.O.**
FAX: (336) 753-6904;
E-mail: info@daviefoundation.org; Main URL: http://www.daviefoundation.org
Facebook: http://www.facebook.com/daviefoundation
Flickr: http://www.flickr.com/photos/daviefoundation
Twitter: http://twitter.com/daviefoundation
YouTube: http://www.youtube.com/user/daviefoundation

Established in 1988 in NC; reorganized in 2003.
Foundation type: Community foundation.
Financial data (yr. ended 12/31/12): Assets, $10,753,669 (M); gifts received, $697,124; expenditures, $588,151; giving activities include $362,359 for 85+ grants (high: $81,081).
Purpose and activities: The foundation promotes the well being of the people of Davie County and is operated exclusively for civic, educational, cultural, religious and charitable purposes.
Fields of interest: Education, reading; Children/youth; Youth.
Type of support: General/operating support; Management development/capacity building; Program development; Scholarship funds; Scholarships—to individuals; Matching/challenge support.
Limitations: Applications accepted. Giving limited to Davie County, NC.
Publications: Application guidelines; Annual report; Financial statement; Grants list; Informational brochure; Newsletter.
Application information: Visit foundation web site for application forms and guidelines. If applicants notification of intent form falls within the requirements and interest of the foundation, a grant application will be sent for completion. Application form required.

Initial approach: Mail, fax, or e-mail notification of intent form
Copies of proposal: 1
***Deadline(s):* Feb. 1. for full grant application; Mar. 12 for scholarships**
Board meeting date(s): 2nd Mon. of each month
Final notification: 1 week for full application invitation; June for grant determination

Officers and Directors:* Phillip Fuller,* Chair.; George Webb,* Vice-Chair.; Jane Simpson,* Pres. and C.E.O.; **Marlene Shamel,* Secy.**; Joan Woodard,* Treas.; J. Chad Bomar; Joel Edwards, M.D.; Christopher Owens, O.D.; **Mike Owen**; **Henry P. VanHoy**; **Dr. Richard Williams**; Zach Wright.
Number of staff: 1 full-time professional; 1 part-time professional; 1 part-time support.
EIN: 581850531
Other changes: Marlene Shamel has replaced Gladys Scott as Secy.
Jane Simpson is now Pres. and C.E.O. Patsy Crenshaw, Pat Newman, and Marlene Shamel are no longer directors.

2544
Elmer R. Deaver Foundation, IDT
1525 W. WT Harris Blvd., D1114-044
Charlotte, NC 28288-5709
***Application address:* c/o Wells Fargo Bank, 1 W. 4th St., D4000-062, Winston-Salem NC 27101-3818, tel.: (855) 739-2920**

Established in 1996 in PA.
Donor: Delema Deaver Foundation.
Foundation type: Independent foundation.
Financial data (yr. ended 12/31/13): Assets, $12,643,034 (M); gifts received, $281,011; expenditures, $866,521; qualifying distributions, $787,540; giving activities include $683,080 for 22 + grants (high: $147,443).
Purpose and activities: Giving scholarships for descendants of employees of Quaker City Life Insurance Company, including spouses and dependent children.
Fields of interest: Higher education.
Type of support: Scholarships—to individuals; Endowments.
Limitations: Applications accepted. Giving primarily in PA.
Application information: Refer to https://www.csascholars.org/deaver/index.php for scholarship application information. Application form required.
Deadline(s): **Scholarship applicants: see foundation web page for current deadlines**
Trustee: Wells Fargo Bank, N.A.
EIN: 237830263

2545
Samuel C. Dobbs Trust
c/o Wells Fargo Bank, N.A.
1 W. 4th St., 4th Fl., MAC D4000-041
Winston-Salem, NC 27101-3818

Foundation type: Independent foundation.
Financial data (yr. ended 09/30/13): Assets, $15,592,024 (M); expenditures, $880,832; qualifying distributions, $741,991; giving activities include $710,636 for 2 grants (high: $700,636; low: $10,000).
Fields of interest: Higher education.
Limitations: Applications not accepted. Giving primarily in GA.
Application information: Contributes only to pre-selected organizations.
Trustee: Wells Fargo Bank, N.A.
EIN: 586026550
Other changes: The grantmaker has moved from PA to NC.

2546
Duke University Medical School and Hospital Trust
c/o Wells Fargo Bank, N.A.
1 W. 4th St., 4th Fl., MAC D4000-041
Winston-Salem, NC 27101-3818

Foundation type: Independent foundation.
Financial data (yr. ended 08/31/13): Assets, $14,842,338 (M); expenditures, $769,173; qualifying distributions, $659,825; giving activities include $628,100 for 1 grant.
Fields of interest: Higher education.
Limitations: Applications not accepted. Giving primarily in Durham, NC.
Application information: Contributes only to pre-selected organizations.
Trustee: Wells Fargo Bank, N.A.
EIN: 566036456
Other changes: The grantmaker has moved from PA to NC.

2547
John G. Duncan Trust
c/o Wells Fargo Bank, N.A.
1 W. 4th St., 4th Fl., MAC D4000-041
Winston-Salem, NC 27101-3818
Contact: Jim Luensmann; Colleen Lynch
***Application address:* c/o Wells Fargo Bank, N.A., 1740 Broadway, MAC C7300-483, Denver, CO 80274, tel.: (720) 947-6732; E-mail for Colleen Lynch: colleen.f.lynch@wellsfargo.com**; Main URL: https://www.wellsfargo.com/privatefoundationgrants/duncan

Trust established in 1955 in CO.
Donor: John G. Duncan†.
Foundation type: Independent foundation.
Financial data (yr. ended 12/31/12): Assets, $6,540,205 (M); expenditures, $385,514; qualifying distributions, $317,620; giving activities include $296,300 for 107 grants (high: $7,000; low: $1,000).
Fields of interest: Arts; Education; Health care; Human services; Religion.
Type of support: Capital campaigns; Building/renovation; Equipment; Emergency funds; Program development; Seed money; Research.
Limitations: Applications accepted. Giving limited to CO. No support for other grantmaking organizations. No grants to individuals, or for general operating expenses or endowments.
Publications: Application guidelines.
Application information: Application form required.
Initial approach: Telephone or e-mail
Copies of proposal: 1
Deadline(s): **Contact foundation for current deadline**
Board meeting date(s): Feb., May, Aug. and Nov.
Final notification: Month following board meeting
Trustee: Wells Fargo Bank, N.A.
Number of staff: None.
EIN: 846016555
Other changes: The grantmaker has moved from CO to NC.

2548
Eddy Foundation
(formerly Eddy Foundation Charitable Trust)
c/o Wells Fargo Bank, N.A.
1 W. 4th St., 4th Fl., MAC D4000-041
Winston-Salem, NC 27101-3818
Application addresses: For University of Minnesota-Duluth students: Dept. of Communication Sciences and Disorders, University of Minnesota, 221 Bohannon Hall, 10 University Dr., Duluth, MN 55812-2496; For non-University students and special situations: Edwin H. Eddy Foundation Scholarship, Northwest Bank Minnesota North, N.A., Trust Dept., P.O. Box 488, Duluth, MN 55801-0488

Established in 1982 in MN.
Donor: Edwin H. Eddy, Jr.†.
Foundation type: Independent foundation.
Financial data (yr. ended 06/30/13): Assets, $3,228,582 (M); expenditures, $218,513; qualifying distributions, $179,886; giving activities include $164,631 for 2 grants (high: $160,131; low: $4,500).
Purpose and activities: Grants for research into and treatment of individuals with speech or hearing disorders. Also awards scholarships for students studying in the field of communication disorders: 1st priority for Duluth, MN, area residents at the University of Minnesota, Duluth; 2nd priority for area residents at other institutions; and 3rd priority for non-residents at the University of Minnesota, Duluth.
Fields of interest: Education, special; Speech/hearing centers; Medical research, institute; Disabilities, people with.
Type of support: Continuing support; Conferences/seminars; Professorships; Curriculum development; Internship funds; Scholarship funds; Research; Technical assistance; Grants to individuals; Scholarships—to individuals; Matching/challenge support.
Limitations: Applications accepted. Giving limited to the Duluth, MN, area. No grants for capital improvements or salaries.
Publications: Application guidelines; Informational brochure (including application guidelines); Program policy statement.
Application information: Application form required for scholarships.
Initial approach: Proposal
Copies of proposal: 8
Deadline(s): July 10 for scholarships
Trustees: Rodney Edwards; Elizabeth Simonson; Barbara A. Spencer; Wells Fargo Bank, N.A.
EIN: 416242226
Other changes: The grantmaker has moved from PA to NC.

2549
Emma Barnsley Foundation
c/o Wells Fargo Bank, N.A., Trust Tax Dept.
1 W. 4th St., 4th Fl., MAC D4000-041
Winston-Salem, NC 27101-3818
***E-mail:* grantadministration@wellsfargo.com**; Application address: c/o Wells Fargo Bank, N.A., 4101 JBS Pkwy., Odessa, TX 79762, tel.: (432) 498-4400; **Main URL: https://www.wellsfargo.com/privatefoundationgrants/barnsley**
Donor: Emma Barnsley†.
Foundation type: Independent foundation.
Financial data (yr. ended 12/31/12): Assets, $2,163,135 (M); gifts received, $491,133; expenditures, $263,668; qualifying distributions, $219,622; giving activities include $203,837 for 8 grants (high: $115,000; low: $3,837).
Fields of interest: Education; Environment; Animal welfare.

Limitations: Applications accepted. Giving primarily in TX.
Application information: See foundation website for complete application guidelines. Application form required.
Initial approach: Proposal
***Deadline(s):* Aug. 31**
Trustee: Wells Fargo Bank, N.A.
EIN: 264785578
Other changes: The grantmaker has moved from PA to NC.

2550
Herschel H. & Cornelia N. Everett Foundation
c/o Wells Fargo Bank N.A., Trust Tax Dept.
1 W. 4th St., 4th Fl., MAC D4000-041
Winston-Salem, NC 27101-3818

Established in 2001 in NC.
Foundation type: Independent foundation.
Financial data (yr. ended 06/30/13): Assets, $4,503,830 (M); expenditures, $204,406; qualifying distributions, $160,406; giving activities include $148,000 for 8 grants (high: $33,000; low: $2,000).
Fields of interest: Theological school/education; Education; Christian agencies & churches.
Type of support: General/operating support.
Limitations: Applications not accepted. Giving primarily in NC; some funding also in VA. No grants to individuals.
Application information: Contributes only to pre-selected organizations.
Trustees: Paul B. Wyche; Wells Fargo Bank, N.A.
EIN: 566093697

2551
Freeman E. Fairfield - Meeker Charitable Trust
c/o Wells Fargo Bank, N.A.
1 W. 4th St., 4th Fl., MAC D4000-041
Winston-Salem, NC 27101-3818
Application address: c/o Diane Dunham, P.O. Box 2302, Meeker, CO 81641-2302, tel.: (702) 878-4466

Trust established in 1969 in CO.
Donor: Freeman E. Fairfield†.
Foundation type: Independent foundation.
Financial data (yr. ended 11/30/13): Assets, $4,397,241 (M); expenditures, $222,417; qualifying distributions, $187,348; giving activities include $158,642 for 31 grants (high: $50,000; low: $800).
Purpose and activities: Support for programs within Meeker and Rio Blanco County, Colorado, and scholarships for graduates of Meeker High School.
Fields of interest: Historic preservation/historical societies; Education; Human services; Government/public administration; Jewish agencies & synagogues.
Type of support: General/operating support; Scholarships—to individuals.
Limitations: Applications accepted. Giving limited to Meeker and Rio Blanco County, CO.
Application information: Scholarship application form available from the Trust and from the Meeker High School guidance counselor. Scholarships are available only to graduates of Meeker High School. Application form required.
Initial approach: Letter
Copies of proposal: 6
Deadline(s): For grants more than $1500: Oct. 1 and Apr. 1
Board meeting date(s): As necessary
Trustee: Wells Fargo Bank, N.A.
EIN: 846068906
Other changes: The grantmaker has moved from PA to NC.

2552
Percy B. Ferebee Endowment
1525 W. WT Harris Blvd., D1114-044
Charlotte, NC 28288
***Main URL:* https://www.wellsfargo.com/privatefoundationgrants/ferebee**

Established in 1973 in NC.
Donor: Percy Ferebee†.
Foundation type: Independent foundation.
Financial data (yr. ended 12/31/12): Assets, $3,144,300 (M); expenditures, $174,167; qualifying distributions, $145,527; giving activities include $125,000 for 9 grants (high: $75,000; low: $4,000).
Purpose and activities: Giving primarily for scholarships available to high school seniors attending a 4 year public or private college or university located in North Carolina.
Fields of interest: Arts; Scholarships/financial aid; Education; Government/public administration.
Type of support: Annual campaigns; Building/renovation; Equipment; Land acquisition; Emergency funds; Seed money; Scholarship funds; Scholarships—to individuals.
Limitations: Applications accepted. Giving primarily in Cherokee, Clay, Graham, Jackson, Macon, and Swain counties, NC, and the Cherokee Indian Reservation. No grants to individuals (except for scholarships), or for operating budgets.
Publications: Informational brochure (including application guidelines).
Application information: See foundation website for complete application guidelines. Application form required.
Copies of proposal: 1
***Deadline(s):* Sept. 30**
Board meeting date(s): May and Nov.
Committee Members: Frela Owl Beck; Jim Carringer; James Conley; Max Holland; Patsy Ingram; Betty Sandlin; Janet Stiles.
Trustee: Wells Fargo Bank, N.A.
EIN: 566118992

2553
Ed & Claude Fortson Charitable Trust
c/o Wells Fargo Bank, N.A.
1 W. 4th St., 4th Fl.
Winston-Salem, NC 27101-3818

Established in 1987 in GA.
Donor: Edred Fortson†.
Foundation type: Independent foundation.
Financial data (yr. ended 12/31/12): Assets, $7,594,767 (M); expenditures, $360,375; qualifying distributions, $360,375; giving activities include $246,700 for 13 grants (high: $42,000; low: $5,000).
Purpose and activities: Giving primarily for education, health care, health associations, and human services.
Fields of interest: Education; Health care; Cancer; Medical research, association; Recreation, camps; Human services; Christian agencies & churches.
Limitations: Applications not accepted. Giving primarily in Henry County, GA. No grants to individuals.
Application information: Unsolicited requests for funds not accepted.
Advisory Committee: James L. Henderson, Jr.; J.W. Martin; Keith McBrayer.
Trustee: Wells Fargo Bank, N.A.
EIN: 586201850
Other changes: The grantmaker has moved from PA to NC.

2554
Samuel & Katharine French Fund
(formerly Samuel H. French III and Katharine Weaver French Fund)
c/o Wells Fargo Bank, N.A., Trust Tax Dept.
1 W. 4th St., 4th Fl., MAC D4000-041
Winston-Salem, NC 27101-3818
E-mail: grantadministration@wellsfargo.com; Main URL: https://www.wellsfargo.com/privatefoundationgrants/french

Established in 1986 in CA.
Donor: French Charitable Remainder Unitrust f/b/o J & B Megroz.
Foundation type: Independent foundation.
Financial data (yr. ended 12/31/13): Assets, $11,433,735 (M); expenditures, $659,943; qualifying distributions, $555,818; giving activities include $528,111 for 56 grants (high: $100,000; low: $150).
Purpose and activities: Support for underprivileged children and the elderly.
Fields of interest: Hospitals (general); Health organizations, association; YM/YWCAs & YM/YWHAs; Children/youth, services; Aging, centers/services; Children; Aging.
Type of support: Building/renovation; Equipment; Program development; Conferences/seminars; Scholarship funds; Research; Matching/challenge support.
Limitations: Applications accepted. Giving limited to San Diego County, CA. No support for start-up organizations. No grants to individuals, or for salaries.
Application information: See foundation website for complete application guidelines. Application form required.
Deadline(s): Apr. 30, Aug. 31, and Dec. 31
Trustee: Wells Fargo Bank, N.A.
EIN: 954111082
Other changes: The grantmaker has moved from PA to NC.

2555
The Fund for Democratic Communities
620 S. Elm St., Ste. 355
Greensboro, NC 27406-1398
E-mail: info@f4dc.org; Main URL: http://www.f4dc.org
Blog: http://f4dc.org/blog/
Facebook: https://www.facebook.com/Fund4DemocraticCommunities
Flickr: https://www.flickr.com/photos/f4dc/
Google Plus: https://plus.google.com/+F4dcOrg/posts
Grants List: http://f4dc.org/programs/grassroots-matching-grants/
Twitter: http://twitter.com/f4dc

Donors: Stephen Johnson; Marnie Thompson; W. Hayden Thompson†; William H. Thompson.
Foundation type: Independent foundation.

Financial data (yr. ended 12/31/12): Assets, $7,975,284 (M); gifts received, $848,712; expenditures, $625,917; qualifying distributions, $575,906; giving activities include $226,096 for 32 grants (high: $120,000; low: $250), and $575,906 for 1 foundation-administered program.
Purpose and activities: Supports groups that engage in participatory democracy to further their social change objectives; convenes groups and individuals committed to social and economic justice through deepening democratic practice; conducts research; and produces materials to nurture the growth of authentic democracy.
Type of support: General/operating support; Matching/challenge support.
Limitations: Applications accepted. Giving primarily in GA and NC.
Publications: Application guidelines.
Application information: Application form and complete application guidelines available on fund web site. Application form required.
Deadline(s): None
***Final notification:* 4 weeks**
Managing Directors: Marnie Thompson, Co-Managing Director; Ed Whitfield, Co-Managing Director.
EIN: 260344869
Other changes: Marnie Thompson and Ed Whitfield are now Co-Managing Directors.
The grantmaker now publishes application guidelines.

2556
Gambrill Foundation
1525 W. WT Harris Blvd., D1114-044
Charlotte, NC 28262-8522 (336) 747-8002
***E-mail:* grantadministration@wellsfargo.com; Main URL: https://www.wellsfargo.com/privatefoundationgrants/gambrill**

Established in 1967.
Donor: Anne J. Gambrill†.
Foundation type: Independent foundation.
Financial data (yr. ended 12/31/12): Assets, $4,285,253 (M); expenditures, $228,479; qualifying distributions, $201,258; giving activities include $173,000 for 16 grants (high: $28,000; low: $2,500).
Fields of interest: Performing arts, music; Historic preservation/historical societies; Higher education; Engineering school/education; Libraries/library science; Education; Health care; Pediatrics; Food services; Human services; Salvation Army; Residential/custodial care, hospices; United Ways and Federated Giving Programs; Religion, interfaith issues.
Limitations: Applications accepted. Giving primarily in SC. No grants to individuals.
Application information: See foundation website for complete application guidelines. Application form required.
Initial approach: Proposal
***Deadline(s):* Apr. 1 and Sept. 15**
Trustees: Lia F. Albergotti; Fred L. Foster, Jr.; Ann D. Herbert; Robert M. Rainey; F. McKinnon Wilkinson; Wells Fargo Bank, N.A.
EIN: 576029520

2557
Garrow Family Charitable Foundation
c/o Wells Fargo Bank, N.A., Trust Tax Dept.
1 W. 4th St., 4th Fl., MAC D4000-041
Winston-Salem, NC 27101-3818

Established in 2009 in OR.
Foundation type: Independent foundation.
Financial data (yr. ended 12/31/12): Assets, $1,641,520 (M); expenditures, $193,585; qualifying distributions, $172,565; giving activities include $165,399 for 6 grants (high: $27,567; low: $27,566).
Fields of interest: Education; Health organizations; Religion.
Limitations: Applications not accepted.
Application information: Unsolicited requests for funds not accepted.
Trustee: Wells Fargo Bank, N.A.
EIN: 326099554
Other changes: The grantmaker has moved from PA to NC.

2558
William & Marian Ghidotti Foundation
c/o Wells Fargo Bank, N.A., Trust Tax Dept.
1 W. 4th St., 4th Fl., MAC D4000-041
Winston-Salem, NC 27101-3818
***Application address:* c/o Wells Fargo Bank, N.A., P.O. Box 63954, MAC A 0330-011, San Francisco, CA 94163, tel.: (800) 352-3705**

Established in 1969 in CA.
Donors: William Ghidotti; Marian Ghidotti†.
Foundation type: Independent foundation.
Financial data (yr. ended 12/31/12): Assets, $10,711,937 (M); expenditures, $646,700; qualifying distributions, $595,784; giving activities include $61,504 for grants, and $516,729 for grants to individuals.
Purpose and activities: Awards student scholarships to graduating seniors residing in and attending Nevada County, CA, high schools; some support also for the arts, education, health care, human services, and community programs.
Fields of interest: Arts; Education; Health care; Human services; Children/youth, services.
Type of support: Equipment; Scholarships—to individuals.
Limitations: Applications accepted. Giving limited to residents of Nevada County, CA.
Application information: Scholarship applicants should submit Std. Scholarship APF/Transcript of grades, student and family income, and resume. Application form required.
Initial approach: Proposal
Deadline(s): Feb. for new scholarships; Aug. for renewals
Trustees: Erica Erickson; Wells Fargo Bank, N.A.
EIN: 946181833
Other changes: The grantmaker has moved from PA to NC.

2559
Glass Foundation, Inc.
(formerly Glass Family Foundation, Inc.)
2 Town Square Blvd., Ste. 310
Asheville, NC **28803-8814**
E-mail: lnolletti@glassfoundation.org; Main URL: http://www.glassfoundation.org

Established in 2000 in NC.
Donors: Kenneth E. Glass; TECT.
Foundation type: Independent foundation.
Financial data (yr. ended 12/31/12): Assets, $13,535,602 (M); gifts received, $1,420,249; expenditures, $830,606; qualifying distributions, $675,337; giving activities include $675,337 for grants.
Purpose and activities: The foundation believes in helping the Western North Carolina region thrive as a whole community educationally, environmentally, and culturally and offer a distinctive quality of life. The overall vision of the foundation is to enable Western North Carolina to realize a vision of itself as a premier place to both live and work by making the region a center of high quality educational opportunity; helping to preserve a diverse array of natural resources; and by maintaining a rich cultural and historical heritage.
Fields of interest: Education; Environment, natural resources; Health organizations, association; Human services; United Ways and Federated Giving Programs; Children/youth; Youth.
Type of support: Capital campaigns; Building/renovation; Equipment; Land acquisition; Conferences/seminars; Matching/challenge support.
Limitations: Applications accepted. Giving primarily in NC. No grants to individuals.
Publications: Application guidelines.
Application information: Complete application policies and guidelines available on foundation web site. Application form not required.
***Initial approach:* Submit proposal or e-mail a summary of the project to ensure compatibility prior to submitting proposal**
***Deadline(s):* None**
Officers and Directors:* Kenneth E. Glass,* Chair.; Lara Nolletti,* Pres.; **Nancy J. Glass,* Secy.**; **David Nolletti**; **Bernard Stanek.**
Number of staff: 1 part-time professional.
EIN: 562196225
Other changes: The grantmaker now accepts applications.
Nancy J. Glass is now Secy.
The grantmaker now publishes application guidelines.

2560
The Carrie E. and Lena V. Glenn Foundation, Inc.
1552 Union Rd., Ste. D
Gastonia, NC 28054-5582 (704) 867-0296
Contact: Barbara H. Vourhees
FAX: (704) 867-4496;
E-mail: glennfnd@bellsouth.net; Main URL: http://www.theglennfoundation.org/

Established in 1971 in NC.
Donors: Carrie Eugenia Glenn†; Lena Viola Glenn†.
Foundation type: Independent foundation.
Financial data (yr. ended 06/30/13): Assets, $6,797,001 (M); expenditures, $427,522; qualifying distributions, $384,170; giving activities include $315,000 for 28 grants (high: $65,000; low: $2,450).
Purpose and activities: To promote and support the charitable spirit of the Glenn sisters by helping people in need through grants for religious, health, educational and community needs.
Fields of interest: Arts; Elementary/secondary education; Environment; Human services; Children/youth, services; Christian agencies & churches; Infants/toddlers; Children/youth; Children; Youth; Adults; Aging; Young adults; Disabilities, people with; Physically disabled; Mentally disabled; Minorities; African Americans/Blacks; Hispanics/Latinos; Women; Infants/toddlers, female; Girls; Adults, women; Men; Infants/toddlers, male; Boys; Adults, men; Substance abusers; AIDS, people with; Single parents; Crime/abuse victims; Terminal illness, people with; Economically disadvantaged; Homeless.

Type of support: General/operating support; Building/renovation; Equipment; Program development; Seed money; Matching/challenge support.
Limitations: Applications accepted. Giving only to Gaston County, NC, or to out-of-county organizations whose programs benefit citizens of Gaston County, NC. No multi-year grants, planning grants, or fund-raising campaigns; no grants to individuals; no grants for scholarships.
Application information: Complete application guidelines available on foundation web site.
Initial approach: Request application form by using form on foundation web site
Board meeting date(s): Quarterly
Officers and Directors:* Julia M. Shovelin,* Chair.; H. Timothy Efird II,* Vice-Chair.; Emily C. Craig,* Secy.; Charles W. Gallman,* Treas.; Robert H. Collis; John L. Frye; Laura G. Lineberger.
Number of staff: 1 part-time professional.
EIN: 201808211
Other changes: Julia M. Shovelin has replaced Martha D. Eddins as Chair. H. Timothy Efird II has replaced Patrick H. Perryman as Vice-Chair. Emily C. Craig has replaced Jane T. Sumner as Secy. Charles W. Gallman has replaced Timothy T. Paschall as Treas.
Richard K. Craig, Richard E. Rankin, and Malinda B. Lowery are no longer directors.

2561
Goodrich Foundation
(formerly The Goodrich Foundation, Inc.)
4 Coliseum Centre
2730 W. Tyvola Rd.
Charlotte, NC 28217-4578 (704) 423-7489
***Contact:* Cynthia Forbes, Mgr., Community Rels.**
FAX: (704) 423-7011;
E-mail: cynthia.forbes@utas.utc.com; Main URL: http://utcaerospacesystems.com/Company/Pages/goodrich-foundation.aspx

Established in 1989 in OH.
Donors: The B.F.Goodrich Co.; Goodrich Corp.
Foundation type: Company-sponsored foundation.
Financial data (yr. ended 12/31/12): Assets, $5,325,236 (M); expenditures, $2,172,872; qualifying distributions, $2,138,687; giving activities include $2,121,687 for 57 grants (high: $799,433; low: $1,562).
Purpose and activities: The foundation supports programs designed to advance K-12 and higher education science, technology, engineering, and math initiatives focused on the next generation of engineering scientists; promote vibrant communities through community revitalization, health and social services, and arts and culture; and build sustainable cities through environmental sustainable practices, projects, and urban green space.
Fields of interest: Museums (science/technology); Arts; Education, reform; Elementary/secondary education; Higher education; Adult/continuing education; Education, services; Education; Environment; Health care; Disasters, preparedness/services; Human services; Community/economic development; United Ways and Federated Giving Programs; Space/aviation; Mathematics; Engineering/technology; Science.
Type of support: General/operating support; Continuing support; Management development/capacity building; Annual campaigns; Program development; Scholarship funds; Research; Employee volunteer services; Use of facilities; Sponsorships; Employee matching gifts; Employee-related scholarships; In-kind gifts; Matching/challenge support.
Limitations: Applications accepted. Giving on a national basis in areas of company operations, with emphasis on Charlotte, NC. No support for private foundations, churches, fraternal, social, labor groups with high fundraising or administrative expenses, political parties or candidates, discriminatory organizations, organizations primarily funded through municipal, country, state, or federal dollars, individual United Way agencies already supported by Goodrich, and international organizations. No grants to individuals, or for endowments, religious programs, lobbying activities, travel, tours, exhibitions, trips, local athletics, sports programs, equipment, courtesy advertising benefits, tables, or tickets.
Publications: Application guidelines.
Application information: Multi-year funding is not automatic. Multi-year funding requests should not exceed 5 years. Telephone calls are not encouraged. Application form required.
Initial approach: Complete online application form
Deadline(s): Mar. 1 and Aug. 1
Board meeting date(s): Quarterly
Final notification: 90 days
Officers: Terrence G. Linnert, Pres.; Jack Carmola, V.P.; Scott Kuechle, Treas.
Number of staff: 1 full-time professional; 1 full-time support.
EIN: 261195329
Other changes: Kelly Chopus is no longer Secy.

2562
The Jeff Gordon Children's Foundation
(formerly The Jeff Gordon Foundation)
7575 West Winds Blvd. N.W., Ste., C
Concord, NC **28027-3328 (980) 255-8508**
Contact: Grant Program
E-mail: foundation@jgiracing.com; Main URL: http://www.jeffgordonchildrensfoundation.org
ebay: http://cgi3.ebay.com/ws/eBayISAPI.dll?ViewUserPage&userid=jeffgordon4cure
E-Newsletter: http://www.jeffgordonchildrensfoundation.org/site/c.5oIDJRPyGfISF/b.5968399/k.991E/eNewsletter.htm
Facebook: http://www.facebook.com/JGChildrensFoundation?ref=ts
Pinterest: https://www.pinterest.com/jeffgordon4cure/
RSS Feed: http://www.jeffgordonchildrensfoundation.org/site/apps/nl/rss2.asp?c=5oIDJRPyGfISF&b=5968491
Twitter: https://twitter.com/#!/JeffGordon4Cure
YouTube: http://www.youtube.com/user/JeffGordon4Cure

Established in 1999 in NC.
Donors: American Book Wholesale; Greg Biffle; Bristol Motor Speedway; Clarian Health; El DuPont DE Nemours Co.; Eldora Speedway, Inc.; Elkhorn Auto Services LLC; Fox Channel Services LLC; Jeffrey M. Gordon; Jeff Gordon, Inc.; HGJ Licensing LLC; Hendrick Gordon Leasing; Hendrick Motorsports; Rebecca Hoover; ICAP Securities USA LLC; IJO; Int'l Merchandising Corp.; Jimmie Johnson Foundation; Just Marketing, Inc.; Just Rite Acoustics, Inc.; Rebecca Kasten; Kraft Foods Global, Inc.; Lowes; Marcus Pointe Baptist Church; Midwest Maintenance and Construction; Motorsports Authentics; Motorsports Charities; Motorsports Marketing; Music Today LLC; The Nexxus Group; Nicorette; One America; Pacific Technical Resources; Pepsico; Penguin Group; Perfection Products, Inc.; Julian Rawl; RCI North American; Schwan's Home Services; Kiros Sistevans; Speedway Children's Charities; Sprint Nextel; Brad Swaback; Mitchell Swaback Charities, Inc.; Tracie Thompson; Village Pantry; Paul Wellnitz; Rhonda Zamora.
Foundation type: Independent foundation.
Financial data (yr. ended 12/31/12): Assets, $404,026 (M); gifts received, $1,297,726; expenditures, $1,924,804; qualifying distributions, $1,811,789; giving activities include $1,335,544 for 11+ grants (high: $300,000).
Purpose and activities: The foundation supports children battling cancer by funding programs that improve patients' quality of life, treatment programs that increase survivorship and pediatric medical research dedicated to finding a cure. Additionally, the foundation provides support to the Jeff Gordon Children's Hospital in Concord, NC, which serves children in the community by providing a high level of primary and specialty pediatric care.
Fields of interest: Hospitals (specialty); Health care; Cancer; Pediatrics; Medical research, institute; Cancer research; Human services; Children/youth, services; Family services.
Limitations: Giving in the U.S., with emphasis on NC; funding also in IN, MA, and MN. No grants to individuals, or for endowment funds.
Publications: Application guidelines; Annual report; Grants list; Informational brochure.
Application information: Must submit proposal with the Jeff Gordon Foundation grant application form which can be downloaded from foundation web site. Application form required.
Initial approach: Submit application form
Copies of proposal: 1
Deadline(s): Usually in Aug. See foundation web site for current deadline date
Final notification: Dec. 31
Officers and Director:* Jeffrey M. Gordon, Pres.; John S. Bickford, Sr., V.P. and Secy.; Ryan Hutcheson, C.F.O.; **Dianne Chipps Bailey**; **Jeffrey W. Chell, M.D.**; **Wade Clapp, M.D.**; **Rick Hendrick**; **James Reichard**; **Glenn Schineller**.
Number of staff: 1 full-time professional.
EIN: 562174163
Other changes: The grantmaker no longer lists a fax.
Patricia Kriger is no longer a director.

2563
The Griffin Endowment
1850 E. Third St., Ste. 205
Charlotte, NC **28204-3297**
Contact: Haynes G. Griffin, Secy.-Treas.

Established in 1990 in NC.
Donors: Clarence A. Griffin‡; Elizabeth S. Griffin.
Foundation type: Independent foundation.
Financial data (yr. ended 06/30/13): Assets, $3,505,099 (M); expenditures, $200,664; qualifying distributions, $166,112; giving activities include $166,112 for 13 grants (high: $40,000; low: $200).
Purpose and activities: Giving primarily for education and human services.
Fields of interest: Elementary school/education; Secondary school/education; Reproductive health, family planning; Nursing care; Agriculture; Food services; Human services; Protestant agencies & churches.
Type of support: General/operating support.
Limitations: Applications accepted. Giving primarily in Charlotte, NC. No grants to individuals.
Application information:
Initial approach: Letter

Deadline(s): None
Board meeting date(s): Quarterly
Officers and Directors:* Clarence A. Griffin III,* Pres.; Jeffrey Griffin, V.P.; Haynes G. Griffin, Secy.-Treas.
Number of staff: 1 part-time support.
EIN: 561687879

2564
James and Pauline Hackbarth Foundation, Inc.

6654 Castlebrook Way
Ocean Isle Beach, NC 28469-5620

Established in 2005 in NJ.
Donor: James P. Hackbarth†.
Foundation type: Independent foundation.
Financial data (yr. ended 06/30/13): Assets, $5,279,003 (M); expenditures, $521,738; qualifying distributions, $470,838; giving activities include $394,250 for 5 grants (high: $368,750; low: $2,500).
Fields of interest: Libraries (public); Education.
Limitations: Applications not accepted. Giving primarily in NJ. No grants to individuals.
Application information: Contributes only to pre-selected organizations.
Officers: James Hackbarth, Chair. and Pres.; Leonard Lesniak, Vice-Chair. and Treas.; Marc Keane, Secy.; **Joe Englert, Treas.**
Trustee: Mona Rodriguez.
EIN: 200521089
Other changes: Joe Englert has replaced Mona Rodriguez as Treas.

2565
The John W. and Anna H. Hanes Foundation

c/o Wachovia Bank N.A.
1525 W. WT Harris Blvd., D1114-044
Charlotte, NC 28288-5709
Contact: Christopher W. Spaugh, V.P., Wachovia Bank, N.A.
***Main URL:* https://www.wellsfargo.com/privatefoundationgrants/hanes**

Trust established in 1947 in NC.
Foundation type: Independent foundation.
Financial data (yr. ended 12/31/12): Assets, $27,551,153 (M); expenditures, $1,713,896; qualifying distributions, $1,451,150; giving activities include $1,377,633 for 38 grants (high: $140,000; low: $2,500).
Purpose and activities: Giving primarily for the arts and higher education.
Fields of interest: Historic preservation/historical societies; Arts; Higher education; Environment, natural resources; Environment; Health care; Human services; Children/youth, services.
Type of support: Annual campaigns; Capital campaigns; Building/renovation; Equipment; Land acquisition; Endowments; Emergency funds; Program development; Seed money; Matching/challenge support.
Limitations: Applications accepted. Giving limited to NC, with emphasis on Forsyth County. No grants to individuals, or for operating expenses.
Publications: Application guidelines; Program policy statement.
Application information: Application form required.
Initial approach: Telephone or letter
Copies of proposal: 1
Deadline(s): 15th day of month preceding board meeting
Board meeting date(s): Jan., Apr., July, and Oct.
Final notification: 10 days following board meeting
Trustees: Frank B. Hanes, Sr.; F. Borden Hanes, Jr.; R. Philip Hanes, Jr.; Mrs. Drewry H. Nostitz; Ralph H. Womble; Wells Fargo Bank.
EIN: 566037589

2566
Harvest Charities

(formerly Belk-Simpson Foundation)
1525 W. WT Harris Blvd., D1114-044
Charlotte, NC 28288-1161 **(864) 255-8231**
***Application address:* c/o Wells Fargo, P.O. Box 969, M.C. D3310-026, Greenville, SC 29602**

Trust established in 1944 in SC.
Donors: Belk-Simpson Co.; J. A. Kuhn.
Foundation type: Company-sponsored foundation.
Financial data (yr. ended 12/31/12): Assets, $10,127,564 (M); expenditures, $510,798; qualifying distributions, $454,341; giving activities include $439,500 for 29 grants (high: $150,000; low: $1,000).
Purpose and activities: The foundation supports museums and organizations involved with education, health, human services, and religion.
Fields of interest: Arts; Higher education; Education; YM/YWCAs & YM/YWHAs; United Ways and Federated Giving Programs; Christian agencies & churches; Religion.
Type of support: General/operating support; Capital campaigns; Program development; Scholarship funds.
Limitations: Applications accepted. Giving primarily in Greenville, SC. No grants to individuals.
Application information: Application form not required.
***Initial approach:* Letter**
***Deadline(s):* Apr. 1 and Oct. 1**
Board meeting date(s): May 1 and Nov. 1
Trustee: Wells Fargo Bank, N.A.
Advisory Board: Claire Efird; John A. Kuhn; Lucy S. Kuhn; William D.S. Kuhne; Nell M. Rice; Caroline Schmitt; Katherine Sullivan.
EIN: 576020261
Other changes: The grantmaker no longer lists a primary contact.
The grantmaker now accepts applications.

2567
Weston Havens Foundation

c/o Wells Fargo Bank, N.A.
1 W. 4th St., 4th Fl., MAC D4000-041
Winston-Salem, NC 27101-3818

Established in 2005 in CA.
Donor: Westen Havens Living Trust.
Foundation type: Independent foundation.
Financial data (yr. ended 06/30/13): Assets, $28,238,837 (M); expenditures, $1,599,178; qualifying distributions, $1,419,349; giving activities include $1,350,000 for 3 grants (high: $450,000; low: $450,000).
Fields of interest: Higher education.
Limitations: Applications not accepted. Giving primarily in CA. No grants to individuals.
Application information: Contributes only to pre-selected organizations.
Trustee: Wells Fargo Bank, N.A.
EIN: 306051962
Other changes: The grantmaker has moved from PA to NC.

2568
H. T. Helb Trust

c/o Wells Fargo Bank, N.A.
1 W. 4th St., 4th Fl., MAC D4000-041
Winston-Salem, NC 27101-3818

Established in 2004 in PA.
Foundation type: Independent foundation.
Financial data (yr. ended 10/31/13): Assets, $4,340,167 (M); expenditures, $215,949; qualifying distributions, $178,012; giving activities include $164,593 for 4 grants (high: $65,837; low: $24,689).
Fields of interest: Hospitals (general); Health organizations; Salvation Army; United Ways and Federated Giving Programs; Protestant agencies & churches.
Type of support: General/operating support.
Limitations: Applications not accepted. Giving primarily in PA. No grants to individuals.
Application information: Contributes only to pre-selected organizations.
Trustee: Wells Fargo Bank, N.A.
EIN: 236278588
Other changes: The grantmaker has moved from PA to NC.

2569
William G. & Helen C. Hoffman Foundation

1525 W. WT Harris Blvd., D1114-044
Charlotte, NC 28288 (888) 234-1999
***E-mail:* grantadministration@wellsfargo.com; Main URL: https://www.wellsfargo.com/privatefoundationgrants/hoffman**

Established in 1998 in NJ.
Foundation type: Independent foundation.
Financial data (yr. ended 12/31/12): Assets, $4,741,619 (M); expenditures, $294,721; qualifying distributions, $238,639; giving activities include $226,495 for 16 grants (high: $30,000; low: $3,000).
Purpose and activities: Giving primarily for the blind and medical research for the prevention of blindness.
Fields of interest: Elementary/secondary education; Libraries (public); Education; Hospitals (general); Eye research; Children/youth, services; Christian agencies & churches; Blind/visually impaired; Economically disadvantaged.
Limitations: Applications accepted. **Giving primarily in NJ and NY.** No grants to individuals.
Application information: See foundation website for complete application guidelines. Application form required.
Deadline(s): Jan. 15 and Aug. 22
***Board meeting date(s):* Mar. and Oct.**
Trustee: Wells Fargo Bank, N.A.
EIN: 237981677

2570
The Howe Foundation, Inc.

P.O. Box 227
Belmont, NC 28012-0227 (704) 825-5372
Contact: Henry Howe, Dir.

Established in 1966 in NC.
Donors: Knitcraft, Inc.; Beltax Corp.
Foundation type: Company-sponsored foundation.
Financial data (yr. ended 10/31/13): Assets, $2,493,862 (M); expenditures, $298,547; qualifying distributions, $268,450; giving activities include $268,450 for 45 grants (high: $200,000; low: $200).

Purpose and activities: The foundation supports organizations involved with arts and culture, education, human services, Christianity, and people with mental disabilities.
Fields of interest: Arts; Elementary/secondary education; Higher education; Education; Human services; Christian agencies & churches; Mentally disabled.
Type of support: General/operating support.
Limitations: Applications accepted. Giving limited to the Belmont, NC, area. No grants to individuals.
Application information: Application form required.
Initial approach: Letter
Deadline(s): None
Officer: H.T. Howe, Treas.
Directors: Dave Hall; Dave Howe; H.R. Howe.
EIN: 566070727
Other changes: G.M. Howe is no longer a member of the governing body.

2571
James Daniel Humphrey Foundation

c/o Wells Fargo Bank, N.A.
1525 W. WT Harris Blvd., D1114-044
Charlotte, NC 28288-0001

Established in MN; supporting organization of AFS-USA Inc., St. Paul Area American Red Cross, Bennington College, Camp Fire Boys & Girls, MN Council, National Camp Fire Boys & Girls, Carleton College, Children's Home Society of MIN, Christ Episcopal Church, Social Service League of La Jolla, First Church of Christ Scientist, First Congressional United Church of Christ, First Congregational Church - Rockport, Hamline University, House of Hope Presbyterian Church, Mary Institute, United Way of St. Paul, Mother Church, Presbyterian Homes, Princeton University, St. Paul Academy & Summit School, Presbyterian Church Foundation, Vassar College, Wayzata Community Church Foundation, La Jolla YMCA, YMCA of Greater St. Paul.
Foundation type: Independent foundation.
Financial data (yr. ended 03/31/13): Assets, $31,746,062 (M); expenditures, $1,631,784; qualifying distributions, $1,387,440; giving activities include $1,387,440 for grants.
Fields of interest: Higher education; Human services; YM/YWCAs & YM/YWHAs; Protestant agencies & churches.
Limitations: Applications not accepted. Giving in the U.S., with emphasis on MN.
Application information: Unsolicited requests for funds not considered or acknowledged.
Trustees: Joann "Joan" E. Aalfs; Marvin J. Pertzik; Wells Fargo Bank Minnesota, N.A.
EIN: 416263553
Other changes: The grantmaker has moved from MN to NC. The grantmaker no longer lists a phone.

2572
C. Giles Hunt Charitable Trust

c/o Wells Fargo Bank N.A.
1 W. 4th St., 4th Fl., MAC D4000-41
Winston-Salem, NC 27101-3818
Contact: David A. Frosaker, V.P. and Trust Off., Wells Fargo Bank Northwest, N.A.
Grant request e-mail address: pcsgrantrequest@wellsfargo.com; Main URL: https://www.wellsfargo.com/privatefoundationgrants/hunt

Trust established in 1974 in OR.
Donor: C. Giles Hunt‡.
Foundation type: Independent foundation.
Financial data (yr. ended 12/31/12): Assets, $5,873,583 (M); expenditures, $352,126; qualifying distributions, $295,135; giving activities include $276,999 for 53 grants (high: $20,000; low: $850).
Purpose and activities: Giving primarily for education, including for public libraries.
Fields of interest: Secondary school/education; Libraries/library science; Human services; Children/youth, services; Government/public administration.
Type of support: General/operating support; Capital campaigns; Building/renovation; Equipment.
Limitations: Giving primarily in Douglas County, OR. No grants to individuals.
Publications: Application guidelines.
Application information: Application form required.
Initial approach: Online application only. E-mail to request the link to the application. Hard copy not accepted.
Copies of proposal: 1
Deadline(s): Submit proposal in Jan. or Feb.; deadline Feb. 28
Board meeting date(s): Mar. and Apr.
Final notification: June or July
Trustee: Wells Fargo Bank Northwest, N.A.
EIN: 237428278
Other changes: The grantmaker has moved from OR to NC. The grantmaker no longer lists a phone.

2573
Estelle Hunter Charitable Trust

c/o Wells Fargo Bank, N.A., Trust Tax Dept.
1 W. 4th St., 4th Fl., MAC D4000-041
Winston-Salem, NC 27101-3818

Foundation type: Independent foundation.
Financial data (yr. ended 12/31/12): Assets, $10,784,790 (M); expenditures, $552,869; qualifying distributions, $456,843; giving activities include $428,307 for 4 grants (high: $160,615; low: $53,538).
Purpose and activities: Giving primarily for higher education, and for human services, including a children's home.
Fields of interest: Higher education; Human services; Residential/custodial care; Children.
Limitations: Applications not accepted. Giving primarily in Denver, CO.
Application information: Unsolicited requests for funds not accepted.
Trustee: Wells Fargo Bank, N.A.
EIN: 846016605
Other changes: The grantmaker has moved from PA to NC.

2574
Jimmie Johnson Foundation

c/o Alan R. Miller
4325 Papa Joe Hendrick Blvd.
Charlotte, NC 28262-5701 **(704) 586-2996**
***FAX:* (704) 561-3333; *E-mail:* jjf@jjracinginc.com**; Main URL: http://jimmiejohnsonfoundation.org/
E-Newsletter: http://jimmiejohnsonfoundation.org/news/enewsletters_new/

Established in 2005 in MI.
Donors: Kevin DeLana Harvick; Euler Hermes; Barbara Cooper; Harry You; Mrs. Harry You; Bruce Kennedy; Lesa Kennedy; Well's Dairy Inc.; Hubbard Foundation; Eisen Family Foundation; Teammates for Kids Foundation; Tdub LLC; Stock Car Steel Aluminum Inc.; Stallings Foundation; San Diego Habitat for Humanity; PepsiCola North America; Nascar; Music Today LLC; McKinsey Company; Jewish Communal Fund; HGJ Licensing.
Foundation type: Independent foundation.
Financial data (yr. ended 12/31/12): Assets, $279,212 (M); gifts received, $1,207,541; expenditures, $1,333,964; qualifying distributions, $1,177,381; giving activities include $873,851 for 36 grants (high: $72,407; low: $500).
Purpose and activities: The foundation is dedicated to assisting children, families and communities in need throughout the United States.
Fields of interest: Human services; Community/economic development; Children/youth.
Limitations: Applications not accepted. Giving limited to the U.S. No grants to individuals.
Application information: Contributes only to pre-selected organizations.
Officers: Jimmie Johnson, Pres.; Chandra Jenway Johnson, V.P. and Treas.; Allan R. Miller, Secy.; **Mary Gallivan, Exec. Dir.**
EIN: 202387645

2575
Louis J. & Golda I. Kanitz Scholarship Memorial Fund

c/o Wells Fargo Bank, N.A., Trust Tax Dept.
1 W. 4th St., 4th Fl., MAC D4000-041
Winston-Salem, NC 27101-3818

Established in 1994 in CA.
Foundation type: Independent foundation.
Financial data (yr. ended 12/31/12): Assets, $5,507,443 (M); expenditures, $324,907; qualifying distributions, $262,541; giving activities include $250,910 for 6 grants (high: $84,488; low: $8,227).
Purpose and activities: Giving primarily for education and Roman Catholic churches.
Fields of interest: Secondary school/education; Higher education; Scholarships/financial aid; Education; Catholic agencies & churches.
Limitations: Applications not accepted. Giving primarily in CA and MI.
Application information: Unsolicited requests for funds not accepted.
Trustee: Wells Fargo Bank, N.A.
EIN: 946665743
Other changes: The grantmaker has moved from PA to NC.

2576
H.L. Katz Foundation

(formerly Harry Katz Memorial Fund)
c/o Wells Fargo Bank, N.A.
1 W. 4th St., 4th Fl., MAC D4000-041
Winston Salem, NC 27101-3818
E-mail: reginald.middleton@wachovia.com; Main URL: https://www.wellsfargo.com/privatefoundationgrants/katz

Established in 1955 in NJ.
Foundation type: Independent foundation.
Financial data (yr. ended 12/31/13): Assets, $3,868,053 (M); expenditures, $240,173; qualifying distributions, $191,264; giving activities include $175,731 for 5 grants (high: $60,000; low: $20,000).
Purpose and activities: Support primarily for Jewish organizations, including education and community and family services.
Fields of interest: Education; Family services; Jewish agencies & synagogues.

Type of support: General/operating support; Capital campaigns; Equipment; Program development.
Limitations: Applications accepted. Giving primarily in Atlantic County, NJ. No grants to individuals.
Application information: See foundation website for complete application guidelines. Application form required.
Deadline(s): Oct. 1
Trustee: Wells Fargo Bank, N.A.
Number of staff: 1 full-time professional; 1 full-time support.
EIN: 510171174
Other changes: Florence K. Bernstein is no longer trustee.

2577
William R. Kenan, Jr. Charitable Trust
Kenan Center
P.O. Box 3858
Chapel Hill, NC 27515-3858
Contact: Richard M. Drasno, Exec. Dir.; Douglas Zinn, Asst. Exec. Dir.

Established in 1965 in NY.
Donor: William R. Kenan, Jr.‡.
Foundation type: Independent foundation.
Financial data (yr. ended 06/30/13): Assets, $570,678,087 (M); expenditures, $27,549,785; qualifying distributions, $24,765,664; giving activities include $22,754,797 for 76 grants (high: $1,996,667; low: $10,000).
Purpose and activities: To support the advancement of education in a broad sense, giving first priority to programs that have the potential to fundamentally improve educational opportunities throughout the United States. In particular, to seek out institutions, programs and activities that hold exceptional promise to become models or guides for more general and lasting value to American society.
Fields of interest: Secondary school/education; Higher education; Education.
Type of support: Endowments; Seed money; Matching/challenge support.
Limitations: Applications not accepted. Giving in the U.S., primarily in states where William R. Kenan, Jr. and his family have had significant interests: FL, KY, NC, and NY. No grants to individuals, or for capital projects (except under special circumstances).
Publications: Annual report.
Application information: Unsolicited requests for funds not accepted.
Board meeting date(s): As required
Officer: Richard M. Krasno, Exec. Dir.; Douglas Zinn, Asst. Exec. Dir.
Trustees: James G. Kenan III; Thomas S. Kenan III; JPMorgan Chase Bank, N.A.
EIN: 136192029
Other changes: For the fiscal year ended June 30, 2013, the grantmaker paid grants of $22,754,797, a 78.6% increase over the fiscal 2012 disbursements, $12,742,492.

2578
Catherine Kennedy Home Foundation
P.O. Box 4782
Wilmington, NC 28406-1782

Established in 2001 in NC.
Donors: The Catherine Kennedy Home, Inc.; Allie Morriss Fetchig Charitable Remainder Unitrust.
Foundation type: Independent foundation.
Financial data (yr. ended 06/30/11): Assets, $3,575,348 (M); expenditures, $152,059; qualifying distributions, $142,534; giving activities include $141,000 for 21 grants (high: $15,000; low: $2,000).
Fields of interest: Food distribution, meals on wheels; YM/YWCAs & YM/YWHAs; Family services, domestic violence; Residential/custodial care, hospices; Aging, centers/services; Developmentally disabled, centers & services; Christian agencies & churches; Aging.
Limitations: Applications accepted. Giving primarily in Wilmington, NC.
Application information: Application form required.
Initial approach: Written application
Deadline(s): Feb. 28
Officers and Directors:* Ann Parker, Chair.; Anita Liebscher, Secy.; Anna P. Erwin, Treas.; Martha Clark; Garry A. Garris; **Linda Hundley; Mrs. Chris Johnson; Besty Leonard; Jane Maloy; Ned Marable; Anne Murchison.**
EIN: 522282843
Other changes: Walter G. Craven is no longer director.

2579
Mary C. Kistler Trust
c/o Wells Fargo Bank, N.A.
1 W. 4th St., 4th Fl., MAC D4000-041
Winston-Salem, NC 27101-3818

Donor: Wachovia Bank, N.A.
Foundation type: Independent foundation.
Financial data (yr. ended 09/30/13): Assets, $10,240,727 (M); expenditures, $478,806; qualifying distributions, $407,759; giving activities include $381,967 for 5 grants (high: $152,787; low: $57,295).
Fields of interest: Elementary/secondary education; Hospitals (general); Children/youth, services; Family services.
Type of support: General/operating support.
Limitations: Applications not accepted. Giving primarily in NC.
Application information: Contributes only to pre-selected organizations.
Trustee: Wells Fargo Bank, N.A.
EIN: 566049771
Other changes: The grantmaker has moved from PA to NC.

2580
Harry L. & Janet M. Kitselman Foundation
c/o Wells Fargo Bank, N.A., Trust Tax Dept.
1 W. 4th St., 4th Fl., MAC D4000-041
Winston-Salem, NC 27101-3818

Established in 2001 in MN.
Donor: Janet M. Kitselman.
Foundation type: Independent foundation.
Financial data (yr. ended 12/31/12): Assets, $3,599,463 (M); expenditures, $225,160; qualifying distributions, $181,329; giving activities include $170,000 for 22 grants (high: $68,000; low: $250).
Fields of interest: Arts; Education; Human services; Community/economic development; Foundations (community).
Limitations: Applications not accepted. Giving primarily in MN. No grants to individuals.
Application information: Contributes only to pre-selected organizations.
Trustee: Wells Fargo Bank, N.A.
EIN: 416491134
Other changes: The grantmaker has moved from PA to NC.

2581
Harry Kramer Memorial Fund
1 W. 4th St., D4000-041
Winston-Salem, NC 27101
***E-mail:* grantadministration@wellsfargo.com; Main URL: https://www.wellsfargo.com/privatefoundationgrants/kramer**

Established in 1982 in FL.
Foundation type: Independent foundation.
Financial data (yr. ended 12/31/12): Assets, $5,790,976 (M); expenditures, $383,305; qualifying distributions, $312,117; giving activities include $234,000 for 29 grants (high: $32,300; low: $2,100).
Fields of interest: Education; Health care; Human services; International affairs; Jewish federated giving programs; Jewish agencies & synagogues.
International interests: Israel.
Type of support: Capital campaigns; Building/renovation; Program development; Seed money; Scholarship funds.
Limitations: Applications accepted. Giving primarily in FL and NY. No grants to individuals or for operating budgets or continuing support.
Application information: See foundation website for complete application guidelines. Application form required.
***Deadline(s):* June 30**
Trustees: Leslie J. August; Wells Fargo Bank, N.A.
EIN: 596644290
Other changes: The grantmaker now accepts applications.

2582
Anna Pitzl and J. Fred Krost Charitable Trust No. 2
c/o Wells Fargo Bank, N.A.
1 W. 4th St., 4th Fl., MAC D4000-041
Winston-Salem, NC 27101-3818

Foundation type: Independent foundation.
Financial data (yr. ended 04/30/13): Assets, $4,088,425 (M); expenditures, $246,050; qualifying distributions, $200,925; giving activities include $187,226 for 10 grants (high: $36,844; low: $12,287).
Fields of interest: Education; Health care; Religion.
Limitations: Applications not accepted. Giving primarily in MN. No grants to individuals.
Application information: Unsolicited requests for funds not accepted.
Trustee: Wells Fargo Bank, N.A.
EIN: 416268462
Other changes: The grantmaker has moved from AZ to NC.

2583
John and Maria Laffin Trust
c/o Wells Fargo Bank, N.A., Trust Tax Dept.
1 W. 4th St., 4th Fl., MAC D4000-041
Winston-Salem, NC 27101-3818
Main URL: https://www.wellsfargo.com/privatefoundationgrants/laffin

Established around 1989.
Foundation type: Independent foundation.
Financial data (yr. ended 12/31/13): Assets, $4,988,613 (M); expenditures, $275,246; qualifying distributions, $215,988; giving activities include $200,000 for 29 grants (high: $28,000; low: $2,000).
Purpose and activities: The foundation priorities are as follows: 30 percent of any periodic distribution

amount shall be granted to animal welfare organizations or foundations within Los Angeles City and County that are demonstrably dedicated to the preservation and humane placement of abandoned and/or homeless small domesticated animals even when no homes for such animals are readily or immediately available; 25 percent of any periodic distribution amount shall be granted to medical research organizations that do not arbitrarily exclude from consideration any alternative or seemingly radical and/or controversial treatment that the American Medical Association may currently oppose; 25 percent of any periodic distribution amount shall be granted to humanitarian organizations that establish, to the trustee's satisfaction, that 80 percent or more of their proceeds are in fact used to alleviate human misery, suffering, and starvation, whenever and wherever these may occur in any part of the world; 20 percent of any periodic distribution amount shall be granted to educational institutions at the college and university level in the Los Angeles City and County areas that are dedicated to maintaining and raising the standards of scholastic excellence rather than to the proliferation of mediocrity.
Fields of interest: Education; Animal welfare; Medical research; Human services.
Type of support: General/operating support; Scholarship funds; Research.
Limitations: Applications accepted. Giving primarily in CA for education and animal welfare; worldwide giving for humanitarian and medical research. No grants to individuals.
Application information: See foundation website for complete application guidelines. Application form required.
Deadline(s): May 31 and Oct. 31
Board meeting date(s): June 30 and Dec. 31
Trustee: Wells Fargo Bank, N.A.
EIN: 946609731
Other changes: The grantmaker has moved from PA to NC.

2584
The Leon Levine Foundation
6000 Fairview Rd., Ste. 1525
Charlotte, NC 28210-2212 (704) 817-6502
Contact: Thomas W. Lawrence III, Treas.
FAX: (704) 817-6515; E-mail for Thomas W. Lawrence: tlawrence@leonlevinefoundation.org; Main URL: http://www.leonlevinefoundation.org/

Established in 1981 in NC.
Donors: Leon Levine; Howard Levine.
Foundation type: Independent foundation.
Financial data (yr. ended 06/30/13): Assets, $338,429,517 (M); expenditures, $17,886,018; qualifying distributions, $15,491,964; giving activities include $14,946,318 for 244 grants (high: $2,000,000; low: $125).
Purpose and activities: Giving primarily to improve and advance the human condition in four major areas: Education, Healthcare, Jewish Religion and Human Services. The foundation exists to support individuals and institutions seeking to accomplish the following: 1) Supporting the physically, mentally or emotionally ill through medical assistance and scientific research; 2) Pursuing academic excellence and providing access for disadvantaged and deserving individuals; 3) Building Jewish identity and strengthening Jewish Communities locally and worldwide; 4) Eliminating homelessness, alleviating personal crisis, improving the lives of families, children and the elderly and supporting cultural activities; 5) Responding to other emerging issues which could have a significant impact on society.
Fields of interest: Arts; Education; Health care; Human services; Foundations (community); Jewish agencies & synagogues.
Type of support: Capital campaigns; Endowments; Matching/challenge support.
Limitations: Applications accepted. Giving primarily in Charlotte, NC. No support for foreign organizations or 509(a)(3) supporting organizations. No grants to individuals.
Application information: Upon review of the letter of intent, an applicant may be invited to submit a formal proposal. See the foundation's web site for additional information.
Initial approach: Online letter of intent
Deadline(s): For proposals: Apr. 1 for grants made in June; Oct. 1 for grants made in Dec. However, applicants are not guaranteed consideration for that cycle depending on the number of requests already under consideration.
***Board meeting date(s):* June, Sept., and Dec.**
Final notification: 30 days for confirmation of receipt of proposal and in which cycle the foundation expects to consider the application. Successful applicants normally are notified of the board's funding decision within 30-60 days after the decision.
Officers and Directors:* Leon Levine,* Chair. and Pres.; Sandra P. Levine,* V.P. and Secy.; Lidnsey O'Neil, Cont.; Thomas W. Lawrence III,* Treas. and Exec. Dir.; **Larry Polsky**; Michael Richardson.
EIN: 581427515

2585
James B. Linsmayer Foundation Trust
1 W. 4th St., D4000-041
Winston Salem, NC 27101 (612) 667-9010
***E-mail:* grantadministration@wellsfargo.com; Main URL: https://www.wellsfargo.com/privatefoundationgrants/linsmayer**

Established in 2010 in MN.
Donor: James B. Linsmayer Revocable Trust.
Foundation type: Independent foundation.
Financial data (yr. ended 12/31/12): Assets, $1,243,191 (M); gifts received, $1,988,118; expenditures, $396,592; qualifying distributions, $315,221; giving activities include $310,000 for 18 grants (high: $50,000; low: $10,000).
Fields of interest: Arts; Animal welfare; Health care; Health organizations; Human services.
Limitations: Applications accepted. Giving primarily in Minneapolis, MN. **No grants to individuals.**
Application information: See foundation website for complete application guidelines. Application form required.
Initial approach: Letter
***Deadline(s):* Aug. 1**
Trustee: Wells Fargo Bank, N.A.
EIN: 356791172

2586
Edith H. Lynum Trust
c/o Wells Fargo Bank, N.A., Trust Tax Dept.
1 W. 4th St., 4th Fl., MAC D4000-041
Winston-Salem, NC 27101-3818

Supporting organization of the University of Wisconsin River Falls, MPLS Medical Research Foundation, Regents of the University of Minnesota McNamara Alumni Center, Mayo Foundation, and University of Wisconsin Madison.
Foundation type: Independent foundation.
Financial data (yr. ended 12/31/12): Assets, $2,231,929 (M); expenditures, $175,704; qualifying distributions, $150,905; giving activities include $142,546 for 6 grants (high: $70,273; low: $2,000).
Fields of interest: Education; Health care; Medical research.
Limitations: Applications not accepted. Giving primarily in MN and WI. No grants to individuals.
Application information: Unsolicited requests for funds not accepted.
Trustee: Wells Fargo Bank, N.A.
EIN: 416013654
Other changes: The grantmaker has moved from PA to NC.

2587
Edward N. and Margaret G. Marsh Foundation
c/o Wells Fargo Bank N.A., Trust Tax Dept.
1 W. 4th St., 4th Fl., MAC D4000-041
Winston-Salem, NC 27101-3818
Application address: c/o Wells Fargo Bank, N.A., Attn.: Linda Jex, Trust Off., P.O. Box 9502, Las Vegas, NV 89102, tel.: (902) 765-3967; Main URL: https://www.wellsfargo.com/privatefoundationgrants/marsh

Foundation type: Independent foundation.
Financial data (yr. ended 12/31/13): Assets, $4,465,662 (M); expenditures, $260,267; qualifying distributions, $212,213; giving activities include $195,000 for 4 grants (high: $100,000; low: $10,000).
Fields of interest: Education; Animals/wildlife; Health care.
Application information: Application form required.
Initial approach: Letter
Deadline(s): June 30th
Trustee: Wells Fargo Bank, N.A.
EIN: 270974165
Other changes: The grantmaker has moved from PA to NC.

2588
George Henry Mayr Trust
c/o Wells Fargo Bank, N.A., Trust Tax Dept.
1 W. 4th St., 4th Fl., MAC D4000-041
Winston-Salem, NC 27101-3818

Trust established in 1949 in CA.
Donor: George Henry Mayr†.
Foundation type: Independent foundation.
Financial data (yr. ended 12/31/12): Assets, $22,216,426 (M); expenditures, $1,239,910; qualifying distributions, $924,064; giving activities include $823,285 for 97 grants (high: $16,285; low: $1,000).
Purpose and activities: Grants to California private schools for scholarships to students who have completed the 8th grade and reside in the state.
Fields of interest: Secondary school/education; Higher education; Education; Minorities.
Type of support: Scholarship funds.
Limitations: Applications not accepted. Giving limited to CA. No support for medical education other than dentistry. No grants to individuals.
Application information: Contributes only to pre-selected organizations.
Board meeting date(s): Quarterly
Officer and Directors:* Natalie Haden O'Connor,* Secy.; Michele McGarry Crahan; Catherine Grier Olson.
Trustee: Wells Fargo Bank, N.A.

Number of staff: 1 part-time support.
EIN: 956062009
Other changes: The grantmaker has moved from PA to NC.

2589
Alexander McCausland Charitable Trust
1525 W. WT Harris Blvd., D1114-044
Charlotte, NC 28288-0001
Application address: c/o Wells Fargo Philanthropic Services, One W. 4th St., Winston-Salem, NC 27101, tel.: (888) 234-1999; **Main URL: https://www.wellsfargo.com/privatefoundationgrants/mccausland**

Donor: Alexander Mccausland†.
Foundation type: Independent foundation.
Financial data (yr. ended 12/31/12): Assets, $15,885,440 (M); expenditures, $935,529; qualifying distributions, $777,917; giving activities include $733,751 for 21 grants (high: $100,000; low: $5,000).
Fields of interest: Animals/wildlife; Human services.
Limitations: Applications accepted. Giving in the U.S., with emphasis on VA. No grants to individuals.
Application information: Application form required.
Initial approach: Complete online application form
Deadline(s): Sept. 30
Trustee: Wells Fargo Bank, N.A.
EIN: 376437195

2590
John N. McNeil and Stella McNeil Scholarship Trust
c/o Wells Fargo Bank, N.A., Trust Tax Dept.
1 W. 4th St., 4th Fl., MAC D4000-041
Winston-Salem, NC 27101-3818
Application address: c/o Kingsford High School, Att.: Rita Edberg, 431 Hamilton Ave., Kingsford, MI 49802, tel.: (906) 776-2670

Supporting organization of Kingsford High School.
Foundation type: Independent foundation.
Financial data (yr. ended 12/31/13): Assets, $4,913,026 (M); expenditures, $247,005; qualifying distributions, $191,552; giving activities include $177,000 for 43 grants (high: $28,500; low: $1,500).
Purpose and activities: The organization provides scholarships to graduating seniors of Kingsford High School.
Fields of interest: Higher education.
Type of support: Scholarships—to individuals.
Limitations: Applications accepted. Giving primarily in MI.
Application information: Application form not required.
***Initial approach:* Proposal**
Deadline(s): Mar.
Trustee: Wells Fargo Bank, N.A.
EIN: 386788691
Other changes: The grantmaker has moved from PA to NC.

2591
Bette M. Merrick Medical Equip. Trust
c/o Wells Fargo Bank, N.A., Trust Tax Dept.
1 W. 4th St., 4th Fl., MAC D4000-041
Winston-Salem, NC 27101-3818

Established in 2003 in WY; supporting organization of United Medical Center.
Foundation type: Independent foundation.
Financial data (yr. ended 12/31/12): Assets, $6,095,924 (M); expenditures, $461,324; qualifying distributions, $354,120; giving activities include $333,347 for 1 grant.
Fields of interest: Hospitals (general).
Limitations: Applications not accepted. Giving primarily in Cheyenne, WY.
Application information: Contributes only to pre-selected organizations.
Trustee: Wells Fargo Bank, N.A.
EIN: 836027064
Other changes: The grantmaker has moved from PA to NC.

2592
Albert & Helen C. Meserve Memorial Fund
c/o Wells Fargo Bank, N.A.
1 W. 4th St., 4th Fl., MAC D4000-041
Winston-Salem, NC 27101-3818
Application address: c/o Fairfield County FDN, 523 Danbury Rd., Wilton, CT 06897; tel.: 203-834-9393; Main URL: https://www.wellsfargo.com/privatefoundationgrants/meserve

Established in 1983 in CT; grant program administered through the Fairfield County Community Foundation.
Donors: Albert W. Meserve†; Helen C. Meserve†.
Foundation type: Independent foundation.
Financial data (yr. ended 08/31/13): Assets, $3,819,880 (M); expenditures, $234,625; qualifying distributions, $185,567; giving activities include $164,000 for 29 grants (high: $65,000; low: $1,000).
Fields of interest: Historic preservation/historical societies; Arts; Higher education; Scholarships/financial aid; Education; Human services; Children/youth, services; Aging, centers/services; Urban/community development; Philanthropy/voluntarism.
Type of support: Program development; Conferences/seminars; Seed money; Scholarship funds; Technical assistance; Consulting services; Matching/challenge support.
Limitations: Applications accepted. Giving primarily in Bethel, Bridgewater, Brookfield, Danbury, New Fairfield, New Milford, Newton, Redding, Ridgefield, and Sherman, CT. No support for religious or sectarian organizations, political activities, or groups desiring to benefit their own membership. No grants to individuals directly, or endowment or general fund drives, operating budgets of United Way agencies, or deficit financing.
Application information:
Initial approach: Proposal
Deadline(s): Apr. 1st for June and Oct. 1st for Dec.
Trustees: David C. Murphy; Wells Fargo Bank, N.A.
Number of staff: 2 part-time professional; 1 part-time support.
EIN: 066254956
Other changes: The grantmaker has moved from PA to NC.

2593
Melba Bayers Meyer Charitable Trust
1525 W. WT Harris Blvd., D1114-044
Charlotte, NC 28288-5709
Application address: c/o Wells Fargo Bank Philanthropic Service, 1 W. 4th St., 6th Fl., Winston Salem, NC 27101-3818, tel.: (336) 747-8184; **Main URL: https://www.wellsfargo.com/privatefoundationgrants/meyer2**

Established in 1995 in PA.
Donor: Melba Bayers Meyer†.
Foundation type: Independent foundation.
Financial data (yr. ended 05/31/13): Assets, $6,768,031 (M); expenditures, $393,959; qualifying distributions, $332,013; giving activities include $312,821 for 16 grants (high: $100,000; low: $7,500).
Fields of interest: Animal welfare; Health care; Human services; Children/youth, services; Native Americans/American Indians.
Limitations: Applications accepted. **Giving primarily in AL, and Pensacola, FL.** No grants to individuals.
Application information: See foundation website for complete application guidelines. Application form required.
Initial approach: Proposal
Deadline(s): May 1
Trustee: Wells Fargo Bank, N.A.
EIN: 656192782

2594
Milton and Sophie Meyer Fund
c/o Wells Fargo Bank, N.A., Trust Tax Dept.
1 W. 4th St., 4th Fl., MAC D4000-041
Winston-Salem, NC 27101-3818
E-mail: grantadministration@wellsfargo.com; Main URL: https://www.wellsfargo.com/privatefoundationgrants/meyer3

Established in 1980 in CA.
Donor: Milton Meyer†.
Foundation type: Independent foundation.
Financial data (yr. ended 12/31/13): Assets, $3,624,533 (M); expenditures, $220,371; qualifying distributions, $177,953; giving activities include $164,000 for 30 grants (high: $15,000; low: $1,000).
Purpose and activities: Giving limited to Jewish charities.
Fields of interest: Education; Jewish federated giving programs; Jewish agencies & synagogues.
Type of support: General/operating support; Continuing support; Annual campaigns; Capital campaigns; Building/renovation; Endowments; Emergency funds; Seed money; Scholarship funds; Research.
Limitations: Applications accepted. Giving primarily in the San Francisco Bay Area, CA. No grants to individuals.
Application information: See foundation website for complete application guidelines. Application form required.
Deadline(s): Jan. 31, May 31, Sept. 30, and Nov. 30
Trustee: Wells Fargo Bank, N.A.
Directors: Steven R. Lowenthal; Sander Stadtler.
EIN: 946480997
Other changes: The grantmaker has moved from PA to NC.

2595
O. Leonard Moretz Foundation Trust, Inc.
c/o Wells Fargo Bank, N.A., Trust Tax Dept.
1 W. 4th Fl., MAC D4000-041
Winston-Salem, NC 27101-3818

Established in 1980 in NC.
Foundation type: Independent foundation.
Financial data (yr. ended 07/31/13): Assets, $3,119,703 (M); expenditures, $185,482; qualifying distributions, $166,967; giving activities include $160,000 for 14 grants (high: $65,000; low: $1,000).

Fields of interest: Higher education, college; Education; Youth development, scouting agencies (general); Human services; YM/YWCAs & YM/YWHAs; Children/youth, services; Family services; Residential/custodial care, hospices; Science; Christian agencies & churches.
Limitations: Applications not accepted. Giving primarily in NC. No grants to individuals.
Application information: Contributes only to pre-selected organizations.
Trustee: Wells Fargo Bank, N.A.
EIN: 580012117

2596
Morgan Creek Foundation
301 W. Barbee Chapel Rd., Ste. 100
Chapel Hill, NC 27517-8834
FAX: (919) 933-4048;
E-mail: info@morgancreekfoundation.org; Main URL: http://www.morgancreekfoundation.org/index.html

Established in 2005 in NC.
Donor: Mark W. Yusko.
Foundation type: Independent foundation.
Financial data (yr. ended 12/31/12): Assets, $3,553,548 (M); gifts received, $251,500; expenditures, $340,148; qualifying distributions, $331,000; giving activities include $331,000 for grants.
Purpose and activities: The foundation's mission is to help educate disadvantaged children and youth and give them the opportunity to develop the skills necessary to become successful.
Fields of interest: Education, reading; YM/YWCAs & YM/YWHAs; Children/youth, services.
Limitations: Applications not accepted. Giving primarily in NC. No grants to individuals.
Application information: Contributes only to pre-selected organizations.
Officers and Directors:* Mark W. Yusko,* Pres.; Stacey Yusko,* V.P.; Wendy L. Ruggiero, Treas.; **Michael P. Hennessy; Andrea Szigethy; Joshua Tilley.**
EIN: 203999739
Other changes: William M. Watts is no longer Secy.

2597
Robert Sidney Needham Foundation
1525 W. W.T. Harris Blvd., D1114-044
Charlotte, NC 28288-1161 (855) 739-2920
E-mail: grantadministration@wellsfargo.com; **Main URL: https://www.wellsfargo.com/privatefoundationgrants/needham**

Donor: Dorothy E. Needham†.
Foundation type: Independent foundation.
Financial data (yr. ended 12/31/12): Assets, $7,753,436 (M); gifts received, $461,984; expenditures, $404,589; qualifying distributions, $340,499; giving activities include $293,200 for 32 grants (high: $50,000; low: $4,000).
Purpose and activities: Grant awards to individuals through New Jersey colleges and universities supporting the Robert Sydney Needham Memorial Scholarship Program.
Fields of interest: Higher education, college; Higher education, university.
Type of support: Scholarship funds.
Limitations: Applications accepted. **Giving limited to NJ. No grants to individuals (directly).**
Application information: See foundation website for complete application guidelines. Application form required.
Initial approach: Email
Deadline(s): Apr. 1
Trustees: John B. Newman, Esq.; Nina Stack; Wells Fargo Bank, N.A.
EIN: 300562220

2598
Leo Niessen, Jr. Charitable Trust
c/o Wells Fargo Bank, N.A., Trust Tax Dept.
1 W. 4th St., 4th Fl., MAC D4000-041
Winston-Salem, NC **27101-3818**
1-888-234-1999
***FAX:* 1-877-746-5889;**
E-mail: grantadministration@wellsfargo.com; Main URL: https://www.wellsfargo.com/privatefoundationgrants/niessen

Established in 1994 in PA.
Donor: Leo Niessen, Jr.†.
Foundation type: Independent foundation.
Financial data (yr. ended 06/30/13): Assets, $3,559,856 (M); expenditures, $236,691; qualifying distributions, $205,989; giving activities include $192,000 for 19 grants (high: $35,000; low: $2,000).
Fields of interest: Arts; Secondary school/education; Higher education; Education; Human services; Children/youth, services; Religion; Women.
Type of support: General/operating support; Scholarship funds.
Limitations: Applications accepted. **Giving primarily in NJ and PA.**
Application information: Applications must be submitted through the online grant application form or alternative accessible application designed for assistive technology users. See Trust web site for complete application information. Application form required.
Initial approach: Complete online application form on trust web site
***Deadline(s):* Apr. 30**
Trustees: William R. Sasso, Esq.; Wells Fargo Bank, N.A.
EIN: 227723097

2599
North Carolina Community Foundation
4601 Six Forks Rd., Ste. 524
Raleigh, NC 27609-5286 (919) 828-4387
Contact: Jennifer Tolle Whiteside, Pres.; For grants: Sally Migliore, Dir., Community Leadership
FAX: (919) 828-5495;
E-mail: info@nccommunityfoundation.org; Additional tel.: (800) 201-9533; Main URL: http://www.nccommunityfoundation.org
Blog: http://www.nccommunityfoundation.org/blog
Facebook: http://www.facebook.com/pages/North-Carolina-Community-Foundation/55963655306
Flickr: http://www.flickr.com/photos/nccommunityfoundation/
LinkedIn: http://www.linkedin.com/company/2079728?trk=tyah
Twitter: https://twitter.com/NCCF
YouTube: http://www.youtube.com/user/nccommunityfoundatio

Established in 1988 in NC.
Foundation type: Community foundation.
Financial data (yr. ended 03/31/13): Assets, $171,218,139 (M); gifts received, $9,919,407; expenditures, $9,454,598; giving activities include $5,847,110 for 1,058+ grants (high: $157,982; low: $100).
Purpose and activities: The foundation's mission is to inspire North Carolinians to make lasting and meaningful contributions to their communities.
Fields of interest: Humanities; Arts; Education; Environment; Animals/wildlife; Health care; Youth development; Human services; Public affairs; Religion; Children/youth; Youth; Adults; Aging; Young adults; Disabilities, people with; Physically disabled; Blind/visually impaired; Deaf/hearing impaired; Mentally disabled; Minorities; Asians/Pacific Islanders; African Americans/Blacks; Hispanics/Latinos; Native Americans/American Indians; Indigenous peoples; Women; Military/veterans; Offenders/ex-offenders; Substance abusers; AIDS, people with; Single parents; Crime/abuse victims; Terminal illness, people with; Immigrants/refugees; Economically disadvantaged; Homeless.
Type of support: Capital campaigns; Building/renovation; Conferences/seminars; Consulting services; Continuing support; Curriculum development; Emergency funds; Employee-related scholarships; Endowments; Equipment; Fellowships; General/operating support; Management development/capacity building; Program development; Program evaluation; Publication; Research; Scholarship funds; Scholarships—to individuals; Technical assistance.
Limitations: Applications accepted. Giving primarily in NC.
Publications: Application guidelines; Annual report; Financial statement; Grants list; Informational brochure; Newsletter.
Application information: Visit foundation web site for application information per affiliate foundation. Application form required.
Initial approach: Submit online application
Copies of proposal: 1
Deadline(s): Varies
Board meeting date(s): Quarterly
Final notification: Varies
Officers and Directors:* Stuart B. Dorsett,* Chair.; Linda J. Staunch,* Vice-Chair.; Jennifer Tolle Whiteside,* C.E.O. and Pres.; Beth Boney Jenkins, V.P., Devel.; James Bell Black,* Chair., Governance; Rodney E. Martin,* Chair., Grants; Ken G. Reece, Chair., Resource Devel.; Dean E. Painter, Jr.,* Secy.; John Berngartt, C.F.O.; W. Trent Ragland, Jr.,* Treas.; Sandi Matthews, Cont.; James W. Narron,* Immediate Past-Chair.; Annabelle L. Fetterman, Dir. Emeritus; Henry E. Frye, Dir. Emeritus; Martha Guy, Dir. Emeritus; John R. Jordan, Jr., Dir. Emeritus; Sherwood H. Smith, Jr., Dir. Emeritus; Juan Austin; Robert E. Barnhill, Jr.; Laura Beasley; Dr. John Cameron; J. Keith Crisco; Brian C. Crutchfield; Sarah Belk Gambrell; Frank B. Gibson, Jr.; Katharine Harrison Hardin; Clyde P. Harris, Jr.; H. Kel Landis; James M. Parrott, Jr.; C. Ron Scheeler; Karen Stiwinter; Elizabeth Hobgood Wellons; Billy T. Woodard.
Number of staff: 23 full-time professional.
EIN: 581661700

2600
The North Carolina GlaxoSmithKline Foundation, Inc.
(formerly The Glaxo Wellcome Foundation)
5 Moore Dr.
P.O. Box 13398
Research Triangle Park, NC 27709-3398 (919) 483-2140
Contact: Marilyn E. Foote-Hudson, Exec. Dir.
FAX: (919) 315-3015;
E-mail: info@ncgskfoundation.org; Contact for

Ribbon of Hope: Jesse Rainey, tel.: (303) 632-5590, e-mail: jrainey@mcrel.org or RibbonOfHope@mcrel.org; Main URL: http://www.ncgskfoundation.org/index.html
Additional URL: http://www.mcrel.org/GSKRibbonOfHope
Ribbon of Hope Recipients: http://www2.mcrel.org/NCGSKFRibbonOfHope/recipients13.asp
Traditional Grants Recipients: http://www.ncgskfoundation.org/cp.html
Twitter: https://twitter.com/NCGSKFound

Established in 1986 in NC.
Donors: Glaxo Wellcome Americas Inc.; GlaxoSmithKline Holdings (Americas) Inc.
Foundation type: Company-sponsored foundation.
Financial data (yr. ended 12/31/12): Assets, $59,837,197 (M); gifts received, $163,913; expenditures, $3,915,088; qualifying distributions, $3,755,357; giving activities include $2,950,845 for 25 grants (high: $537,920; low: $2,714).
Purpose and activities: The foundation supports programs designed to promote education, health, and science.
Fields of interest: Museums; Museums (art); Elementary/secondary education; Higher education; Higher education, college (community/junior); Education, reading; Education; Health care, association; Public health; Health care; Children/youth, services; Science; Children/youth; Adults; Minorities.
Type of support: Professorships; Matching/challenge support; Curriculum development; Capital campaigns; Internship funds; Program development; Scholarship funds; Seed money.
Limitations: Applications accepted. Giving primarily in NC. No support for religious, political, or international organizations. No grants to individuals, or for construction, restoration projects, or for general operating costs.
Publications: Annual report (including application guidelines); Grants list.
Application information: Proposals for Ribbon of Hope should be no longer than 10 pages. Support is limited to 1 contribution per organization during any given year. Organizations receiving support are asked to provide interim reports and a final report. Application form not required.
Initial approach: Proposal for Traditional Grants; download application form and e-mail or mail proposal and application form for Ribbon of Hope
Copies of proposal: 1
Deadline(s): Jan. 1, Apr. 1, July 1, and Oct. 1 for Traditional Grants; Apr. 1 and Oct. 1 for Ribbon of Hope
Board meeting date(s): Mar., June, Sept., and Dec.
Final notification: Within 15 days following board meetings for Traditional Grants; Apr. and Nov. for Ribbon of Hope
Officers and Directors:* Robert A. Ingram,* Chair.; Margaret B. Dardess,* Pres.; Paul A. Holcombe, Jr.,* Secy.; Marilyn E. Foote-Hudson, Exec. Dir.; **Adrianna Carter, Legal Counsel**; Diedre P. Connelly; W. Robert Connor; Shirley T. Frye; Thomas R. Haber; Charles A. Sanders, M.D.; Mark Werner; Janice M. Whitaker.
Number of staff: 2 full-time professional; 1 part-time professional; 1 full-time support.
EIN: 581698610
Other changes: Adrianna Carter has replaced Mark Werner as Legal Counsel.
Mark Werner is no longer Legal Counsel. Julius L. Chambers is no longer a director.

2601
Nucor Foundation
1915 Rexford Rd.
Charlotte, NC **28211-3465 (704) 367-8662**
***FAX:* (704) 943-7199;**
E-mail: scholarshipsupport@nucor.com; Main URL: https://scholarshipapply.nucor.com/

Established in 1973 in NC.
Donor: Nucor Corp.
Foundation type: Company-sponsored foundation.
Financial data (yr. ended 12/31/13): Assets, $109,614 (M); gifts received, $1,800,000; expenditures, $1,848,254; qualifying distributions, $1,848,254; giving activities include $1,847,100 for 725 grants to individuals (high: $6,000; low: $36).
Purpose and activities: The foundation awards undergraduate and vocational education scholarships to children and stepchildren of employees of Nucor Corporation and scholarships to students pursuing degrees in engineering and metallurgy form communities where Nucor operates.
Fields of interest: Vocational education; Higher education; Education.
Type of support: Employee-related scholarships; Scholarships—to individuals.
Limitations: Applications accepted. Giving primarily in areas of company operations.
Application information: Application form required.
***Initial approach:* Complete online application**
***Deadline(s):* Mar. 1**
Directors: Daniel R. Dimicco; James D. Frias; Daniel W. Krug.
EIN: 237318064

2602
Robert S. & Helen P. Odell Fund
(formerly Robert Stewart and Helen Pfeiffer Odell Fund)
c/o Wells Fargo Bank, N.A., Trust Tax. Dept.
1 W. 4th St., 4th Fl., MAC D4000-041
Winston-Salem, NC 27101-3818
Application address: c/o Wells Fargo Bank, Attn.: Eugene Ranchiasci, 420 Montgomery St., 5th Fl., San Francisco, CA 94104-1207, tel.: (412) 396-3215; Main URL: https://www.wellsfargo.com/privatefoundationgrants/odell

Established in 1967 in CA.
Donors: Robert Stewart Odell†; Helen Pfeiffer Odell†.
Foundation type: Independent foundation.
Financial data (yr. ended 12/31/13): Assets, $39,973,745 (M); expenditures, $1,954,096; qualifying distributions, $1,590,789; giving activities include $1,495,000 for 43 grants (high: $100,000; low: $10,000).
Purpose and activities: Giving primarily to education, the performing arts, human services and Catholic agencies.
Fields of interest: Performing arts; Arts; Elementary/secondary education; Higher education; Health organizations, association; Human services; Children/youth, services; Catholic agencies & churches.
Limitations: Giving primarily in the San Francisco Bay Area, CA. No grants to individuals.
Application information: Application form not required.
Initial approach: Letter
Copies of proposal: 1
Deadline(s): None
Board meeting date(s): Quarterly
Trustees: James P. Conn; Paul Fay III; Wells Fargo Bank, N.A.
EIN: 946132116
Other changes: The grantmaker has moved from PA to NC.

2603
Olin Corporation Charitable Trust
1525 W. WT Harris Blvd., D1114-044
Charlotte, NC 28288-5709 (618) 258-2961
Contact: Susan Dona
***Application address:* 427 N. Shamrock St., East Alton, IL 62024, Tel.: (618) 258-2961**

Established in 1945 in MO.
Donor: Olin Corp.
Foundation type: Company-sponsored foundation.
Financial data (yr. ended 06/30/13): Assets, $1,092,389 (M); gifts received, $500,000; expenditures, $365,421; qualifying distributions, $353,456; giving activities include $344,468 for 87 grants (high: $88,000; low: $50).
Purpose and activities: The foundation supports fire departments and organizations involved with arts and culture, education, health, youth development, human services, business promotion, and mining.
Fields of interest: Arts; Elementary school/education; Higher education; Education; Health care, patient services; Health care; Disasters, fire prevention/control; Youth development, business; Salvation Army; Children/youth, services; Human services; Community development, business promotion; United Ways and Federated Giving Programs; Geology.
Type of support: General/operating support; Continuing support; Annual campaigns; Capital campaigns; Building/renovation; Equipment; Program development; Curriculum development; Scholarship funds; Research; Employee matching gifts.
Limitations: Applications accepted. Giving primarily in areas of company operations in AL, IL, MO, SC, TN, and WA. No grants to individuals or for endowments; no loans.
Application information: Application form not required.
Initial approach: Proposal
Copies of proposal: 1
Deadline(s): None
Officers: Brenda M. Pantalone, Secy.; Thomas J. Fitgerald, Admin.
Trustees: Dennis R. MGough; George H. Pain; Wells Fargo Bank, N.A.
Number of staff: 1 full-time professional; 1 part-time support.
EIN: 436022750
Other changes: The grantmaker no longer lists an E-mail address. The grantmaker no longer lists a fax.

2604
Outer Banks Community Foundation, Inc.
13 Skyline Rd.
Southern Shores, NC 27949 (252) 261-8839
Contact: Lorelei Costa, Exec. Dir.
FAX: (252) 261-0371; E-mail: info@obcf.org; Main URL: http://www.obcf.org
E-Newsletter: http://www.obcf.org/news-updates/e-newsletter/
Facebook: https://www.facebook.com/pages/Outer-Banks-Community-Foundation/131828147548
YouTube: http://www.youtube.com/channel/UCy8W-OVykhp_jyMPQOOwpug

Incorporated in 1982 in NC.
Foundation type: Community foundation.
Financial data (yr. ended 12/31/12): Assets, $9,997,620 (M); gifts received, $464,748; expenditures, $714,510; giving activities include $487,985 for 19+ grants (high: $40,000).
Purpose and activities: The foundation seeks to enhance the quality of life in the Outer Banks community by providing leadership and opportunities through the development and utilization of donor funds.
Fields of interest: Historic preservation/historical societies; Arts; Education; Environment; Health care; Disasters, preparedness/services; Youth development; Human services; Community/ economic development.
Type of support: Building/renovation; Equipment; Endowments; Emergency funds; Program development; Conferences/seminars; Film/video/ radio; Publication; Seed money; Scholarship funds; Technical assistance; Consulting services; Scholarships—to individuals; Matching/challenge support.
Limitations: Applications accepted. Giving limited to the Outer Banks, NC, area. No grants to individuals (except through designated scholarship funds), or for annual operating expenses.
Publications: Application guidelines; Annual report; Financial statement; Grants list; Informational brochure; Newsletter.
Application information: Visit foundation web site for online application and guidelines. Application form required.
Initial approach: **Contact foundation**
Deadline(s): Feb. 7, May 2, Aug. 1, Oct. 31
Board meeting date(s): First Thurs. of Mar., June, Sept., and Dec.
Officers and Directors:* Sharon Elliott,* Pres.; Ed Olsen,* V.P.; Avery Harrison,* Secy.; Bob Muller,* Treas.; John Graham; Deloris Harrell; Mike Kelly; Dorothy Killingsworth; Scott Leggat; Loretta Michael; Teresa Osbourn; Chris Seawell.
Number of staff: 1 full-time professional; 1 full-time support.
EIN: 581516313

2605
Jerome & Mildred Paddock Foundation
c/o Wells Fargo Bank, N.A.
1 W. 4th St., D4000-041
Winston-Salem, NC 27101
E-mail: grantadministration@wellsfargo.com; **Wells Fargo Philanthropic Services: Toll-free tel.: 1-(888) 234-1999; tel. for technical questions about online application: 1-(888) 235-4351; fax: 1-(877) 746-5889; Application address: Paddock Foundation, 1819 Main St., No. 230, Sarasota, FL 34236, tel.: (941) 361-5803**; Main URL: https://www.wellsfargo.com/privatefoundationgrants/paddock

Established in 1967.
Foundation type: Independent foundation.
Financial data (yr. ended 05/31/13): Assets, $4,819,344 (M); expenditures, $238,470; qualifying distributions, $183,158; giving activities include $165,500 for 25 grants (high: $15,000; low: $2,000).
Purpose and activities: Giving primarily for disadvantaged children and the elderly.
Fields of interest: Health care; Human services; Children/youth, services; Aging; Economically disadvantaged.
Limitations: Applications accepted. Giving primarily in Sarasota County, FL. No grants to individuals, or for endowments, debt reduction, operating expenses, conferences or seminars, workshops, travel, surveys, advertising, research, fund raising or for annual campaigns or capital campaigns.
Publications: Grants list.
Application information: Application guidelines and form available on foundation web site. Application form required.
Copies of proposal: 6
Deadline(s): Jan. 15
Final notification: Mar. 15
Trustee: Wells Fargo Bank, N.A.
EIN: 596200844
Other changes: The grantmaker has moved from FL to NC.

2606
Clifford A. and Lillian C. Peeler Family Foundation, Inc.
1816 E. Innes St.
Salisbury, NC **28145-2153**

Established in 1997 in NC.
Donor: Clifford Peeler†.
Foundation type: Independent foundation.
Financial data (yr. ended 06/30/13): Assets, $3,058,660 (M); expenditures, $204,199; qualifying distributions, $167,711; giving activities include $167,711 for 11 grants (high: $55,904; low: $4,659).
Fields of interest: Education, services; Salvation Army; Children/youth, services; Protestant agencies & churches; Aging; Women.
Limitations: Applications not accepted. Giving primarily in NC. No grants to individuals.
Application information: Unsolicited requests for funds not accepted.
Officers: Larry Peeler, Pres. and Treas.; Shirley Ritchie, Secy.
EIN: 562060988
Other changes: The grantmaker no longer lists a phone.

2607
Sylvia Perkin Perpetual Charitable Trust
c/o Wells Fargo IM&T Fid. Tax, SVCMAC D4000-04
1 W. 4th St., 4th Fl.
Winston-Salem, NC 27101
***Main URL:* https://www.wellsfargo.com/ privatefoundationgrants/perkin**

Established in 1986 in PA.
Donor: Sylvia Perkin†.
Foundation type: Independent foundation.
Financial data (yr. ended 04/30/13): Assets, $7,087,157 (M); expenditures, $381,587; qualifying distributions, $336,679; giving activities include $324,500 for 39 grants (high: $60,000; low: $1,000).
Purpose and activities: Giving primarily for Jewish agencies and federated giving programs, education, human services, and arts and culture.
Fields of interest: Historic preservation/historical societies; Arts; Higher education; Education; Human services; Children/youth, services; Jewish federated giving programs; Jewish agencies & synagogues.
Type of support: General/operating support; Scholarship funds.
Limitations: Applications accepted. Giving limited to Lehigh Valley, Allentown, PA. No grants to individuals.
Application information: See foundation website for complete application guidelines. Application form not required.
Initial approach: Proposal
***Deadline(s):* Feb. 1**
Trustees: James D. Christie; Jed Rapoport; Wells Fargo Bank, N.A.
EIN: 236792999
Other changes: The grantmaker has moved from PA to NC. The grantmaker no longer lists a separate application address.

2608
John W. Plansoen Trust
1525 W. WT Harris Blvd.
Charlotte, NC 28288-5709

Established in NJ.
Foundation type: Independent foundation.
Financial data (yr. ended 12/31/12): Assets, $4,138,854 (M); expenditures, $213,685; qualifying distributions, $183,694; giving activities include $173,476 for 14 grants (high: $35,000; low: $4,358).
Fields of interest: Hospitals (general); Salvation Army; Protestant agencies & churches.
Limitations: Applications not accepted. Giving primarily in FL and MA. No grants to individuals.
Application information: Contributes only to pre-selected organizations.
Trustees: Hector L. Plansoen; **Johanna Young**; Wells Fargo Bank, N.A.
EIN: 226020281
Other changes: John L. Plansoen is no longer trustee.

2609
The Polk County Community Foundation, Inc.
255 S. Trade St.
Tryon, NC 28782-3707 (828) 859-5314
Contact: Elizabeth Nager, Exec. Dir.; Cathie Campbell, Grants Mgr.
FAX: (828) 859-6122;
E-mail: foundation@polkccf.org; Additional E-mail: ccampbell@polkccf.org; Main URL: http://www.polkccf.org

Incorporated in 1975 in NC.
Foundation type: Community foundation.
Financial data (yr. ended 12/31/12): Assets, $43,582,773 (M); gifts received, $3,308,704; expenditures, $2,025,760; giving activities include $1,026,115 for 26+ grants (high: $211,494), and $160,698 for 79 grants to individuals.
Purpose and activities: The foundation seeks to improve the quality of life in Polk County, NC, and Landrum, SC.
Fields of interest: Humanities; Arts; Education; Environment, natural resources; Health care; Human services; Community/economic development.
Type of support: General/operating support; Continuing support; Capital campaigns; Building/ renovation; Equipment; Program development; Conferences/seminars; Publication; Seed money; Curriculum development; Internship funds; Scholarship funds; Scholarships—to individuals; Matching/challenge support.
Limitations: Applications accepted. Giving limited to Polk County, NC, and Landrum, SC. No grants to individuals (except for scholarships), or for debt reduction, medical research, courtesy advertising, benefit tickets, or telephone solicitations.

Publications: Application guidelines; Annual report; Financial statement; Informational brochure (including application guidelines); Occasional report.
Application information: Visit foundation web site for application form, guidelines, and specific deadlines. Faxed or incomplete applications are not accepted. Application form required.
Initial approach: Submit application form and attachments
Copies of proposal: 1
Deadline(s): Varies
Board meeting date(s): Mar., May, June, Sept., Oct., and Nov.
Final notification: Approx. 3 months
Officers and Directors:* Marcy Wright,* Chair.; Donald A. Eifert,* Vice-Chair.; Elizabeth Nager,* Pres. and C.E.O.; Frank Cannon,* Secy.; Sally McPherson,* Treas.; **Melanie Campbell-Cobb**; Norma Powers; **Marilyn Ochs**; Kathy Taft; Lois Tirre; Sherril L. Wingo.
Number of staff: 1 full-time professional; 2 part-time professional; 1 full-time support.
EIN: 510168751
Other changes: Frank Cannon, Sally McPherson, and Roger Traxler are no longer directors.

2610
John William Pope Foundation
4601 Six Forks Rd., Ste. 300
Raleigh, NC 27609-5271 **(919) 861-6445**
Contact: James Arthur Pope, Pres.
FAX: (919) 790-9526; E-mail: info@jwpf.org; Main URL: http://www.jwpf.org/
Facebook: https://www.facebook.com/PopeFoundation
Twitter: https://twitter.com/PopeFoundation
YouTube: http://www.youtube.com/user/PopeFoundation

Established in 1986 in NC.
Donor: Members of the Pope family.
Foundation type: Independent foundation.
Financial data (yr. ended 06/30/13): Assets, $145,867,004 (M); expenditures, $10,544,990; qualifying distributions, $9,841,966; giving activities include $9,704,808 for 146 grants (high: $1,000,000; low: $2,500).
Fields of interest: Education; Public policy, research.
Limitations: Applications accepted. Giving primarily in Washington, DC, NC, and VA. No grants to individuals.
Application information: Application guidelines available on foundation web site. Application form not required.
***Initial approach:* Online application**
Deadline(s): Jan. 1
Officers and Directors:* James Arthur Pope,* Chair.; Amanda Joyce Pope,* Vice-Chair.; **David W. Riggs, Exec. V.P.**; Joyce W. Pope; David Stover.
EIN: 581691765
Other changes: David W. Riggs is now Exec. V.P.

2611
Reidsville Area Foundation
124 S. Scales St.
Reidsville, NC **27320-3834**
Contact: R. Craig Cardwell, Exec. Dir.
E-mail: rafoundation@bellsouth.net; Main URL: http://www.rafoundation.org
Flickr: https://www.flickr.com/photos/40088270@N08/

Established in 2001 in NC.
Foundation type: Independent foundation.
Financial data (yr. ended 09/30/13): Assets, $32,850,850 (M); gifts received, $6,150; expenditures, $1,875,111; qualifying distributions, $1,773,809; giving activities include $1,518,149 for 73 grants (high: $635,000; low: $250).
Purpose and activities: The foundation provides financial support to programs and initiatives which improve the health, wellness, education, and quality of life of Rockingham County, North Carolina citizens.
Fields of interest: Education; Health care; Infants/toddlers; Children/youth; Youth; Adults; Aging; Young adults; Disabilities, people with; Physically disabled; Mentally disabled; African Americans/Blacks; Hispanics/Latinos; Women; Men; Adults, men; Offenders/ex-offenders; Substance abusers; Single parents; Crime/abuse victims; Terminal illness, people with; Economically disadvantaged; Homeless.
Type of support: Technical assistance; Program evaluation; Continuing support; Consulting services; Capital campaigns; General/operating support; Management development/capacity building; Building/renovation; Equipment; Emergency funds; Program development; Matching/challenge support.
Limitations: Applications accepted. Giving limited to Rockingham County, NC. No support for individual religious or political organizations. No grants to individuals, or for medical research.
Publications: Application guidelines; Grants list.
Application information: Full grant applications are by invitation, only after review of initial Letter of Interest. Application guidelines and forms available on foundation web site. Application form required.
Initial approach: Use Letter of Interest form on foundation web site, or e-mail or telephone for form
Copies of proposal: 1
Deadline(s): Feb. 15 for Letter of Interest; Apr. 1 for Grant Application
Board meeting date(s): June
Final notification: June
Officers: Donna Rothrock, Chair.; Jacob Balsley III, Vice-Chair.; Lafayette Judkins, DDS, Secy.; J. Wayne Keeling, M.D., Treas.; R. Craig Cardwell, Exec. Dir.
Directors: Victor Armstrong; James L. Burston, Ph.D.; Malcolm N. Clark, CPA; **Jonathan W. Craig, Jr.**; **Leon Niegelsky, Jr.**; Kenneth G. Norman; J. Scottie Penn; Joe M. Walker, Jr.; **Ann D. Willis**; Edwin G. Wilson, Jr.
Number of staff: 2 full-time professional.
EIN: 562255809
Other changes: Donna Rothrock has replaced James L Burston, Ph.D. as Chair. Jacob Balsley III has replaced Donna S. Rothrock as Vice-Chair. Mary R. Fagan and Kathleen Halm are no longer directors.

2612
John Rex Endowment
712 W. North St.
Raleigh, NC 27603-1419 (919) 838-1110
Contact: Kevin Cain, C.E.O. and Pres.
E-mail: info@rexendowment.org; Main URL: http://www.rexendowment.org

Established in 2000 in NC; converted from the result of an acquisition of Rex Healthcare.
Foundation type: Independent foundation.
Financial data (yr. ended 12/31/12): Assets, $71,066,233 (M); expenditures, $4,021,206; qualifying distributions, $3,334,715; giving activities include $2,346,986 for 27 grants (high: $371,563; low: $9,570).
Purpose and activities: Giving primarily for healthy weight, injury prevention, mental health, social and emotional well-being, and nonprofit capacity building for children and families in the Wake County, NC, area.
Fields of interest: Health care; Children/youth.
Type of support: Management development/capacity building; Program development; Seed money; Technical assistance; Program evaluation.
Limitations: Applications accepted. Giving limited to Wake, NC and surrounding counties.
Publications: Application guidelines; Annual report; Grants list; Occasional report.
Application information: Application form required.
***Initial approach:* Use online Grant Management System on foundation web site**
Board meeting date(s): Jan., July, and Oct.
Officers and Directors:* Sherry Worth,* Chair.; Jill Wright, M.D.*, Vice-Chair.; Kevin M. Cain,* C.E.O. and Pres.; **Virginia Parker,* Secy.**; Larry D. Barbour,* Treas.; Linda Butler, M.D.; **Janet Cowell**; **Dick Daugherty**; **Jill Wells Heath**; Tom McGuire; **Cathy Moore**; **Deborah Nelson**; George Reed; Ramon Rojano; **Jimmy Talton**.
Number of staff: 3 full-time professional; 1 part-time professional.
EIN: 311678223
Other changes: Sherry Worth has replaced Hon. Robert B. Rader as Chair. Jill Wright, M.D. has replaced Sherry Worth as V.P. Virginia Parker has replaced Orage Quarles, III as Secy.
Marvin Connelly, Steven C. Lilly, and Donald Rosenblitt are no longer directors.

2613
Reynolds American Foundation
(formerly R. J. Reynolds Foundation)
Plaza Bldg., 15th Fl.
P.O. Box 891
Winston-Salem, NC 27102-2959 (336) 741-0106
Contact: Alan Caldwell, Exec. Dir.
E-mail: caldwea1@rjrt.com; Main URL: http://www.rjrt.com/fndnguide.aspx

Established in 1986 in NC.
Donors: RJR Nabisco Holdings Corp.; R.J. Reynolds Tobacco Co.; Nabisco Brands, Inc.; Planters LifeSavers Co.; RJR Tobacco Intl.; RJR Acquisition Corp.; Reynolds American.
Foundation type: Company-sponsored foundation.
Financial data (yr. ended 12/31/12): Assets, $65,885,114 (M); expenditures, $4,461,067; qualifying distributions, $4,125,057; giving activities include $3,633,835 for 42 grants (high: $1,252,142; low: $358), and $465,667 for 397 employee matching gifts.
Purpose and activities: The foundation supports organizations involved with arts and culture, education, community development, and economically disadvantaged people.
Fields of interest: Arts councils; Arts; Child development, education; Elementary school/education; Higher education; Education; American Red Cross; YM/YWCAs & YM/YWHAs; Community/economic development; United Ways and Federated Giving Programs; Economically disadvantaged.
Type of support: Continuing support; Annual campaigns; Capital campaigns; Program development; Scholarship funds; Employee matching gifts; Employee-related scholarships.
Limitations: Applications accepted. Giving primarily in areas of company operations in KY and NC. No support for churches or religious organizations not of direct benefit to the entire community, political

candidates or organizations, individual day-care centers, or discriminatory organizations. No grants to individuals (except for employee-related scholarships), or for endowments, general operating support, travel expenses, or sponsorships.
Publications: Application guidelines.
Application information: Proposals should be no longer than 5 pages. Support is limited to 1 contribution per organization during any given year. Application form not required.
Initial approach: Proposal
Deadline(s): Feb. 1, May 1, Aug. 1, and Nov. 1
Board meeting date(s): Quarterly
Final notification: Mar. 31, June 30, Sept. 30, and Dec. 31
Officers and Directors: John S. (Tripp) Wilson, Pres.; William Nance, V.P.; Fred W. Franklin, Secy.; Dan A. Fawley, Treas.; Alan L. Caldwell, Exec. Dir.; **Robert H. Dunham**; Nancy H. Hawley; Nancy G. Sturgeon.
Number of staff: 1 full-time professional; 1 full-time support.
EIN: 581681920

2614
Kate B. Reynolds Charitable Trust
(also known as KBR Charitable Trust)
128 Reynolda Village
Winston-Salem, NC 27106-5123 (336) 397-5500
Contact: Karen McNeil-Miller, Pres.; Allen Smart, Dir., Health Care Div.; Joe Crocker, Dir., Poor and Needy Div.
FAX: (336) 723-7765; Toll free tel.: 1-800-485-9080; E-mail for Joe Crocker: joe@kbr.org, e-mail for Allen Smart: Allen@kbr.org; Main URL: http://www.kbr.org
Facebook: https://www.facebook.com/KateBReynoldsTrust
Google Plus: https://plus.google.com/107849778428160345243/about
Kate B. Reynolds Charitable Trust's Philanthropy Promise: http://www.ncrp.org/philanthropys-promise/who
Twitter: http://twitter.com/KateBReynolds

Established in 1947 in NC.
Donor: Kate B. Reynolds†.
Foundation type: Independent foundation.
Financial data (yr. ended 08/31/13): Assets, $532,506,481 (M); expenditures, $28,180,298; qualifying distributions, $25,613,545; giving activities include $22,753,821 for 222 grants (high: $773,728; low: $5,000), and $549,926 for foundation-administered programs.
Purpose and activities: To improve the quality of life and quality of health for the financially needy of North Carolina. The trust accomplishes its work through its two divisions. The Health Care Division and The Poor and Needy Division.
Fields of interest: Education, early childhood education; Middle schools/education; Education; Health care, clinics/centers; Health care, rural areas; Public health, obesity; Health care; Health care, insurance; Substance abuse, services; Mental health, treatment; Mental health/crisis services; Housing/shelter; Human services; Community/economic development.
Type of support: Capital campaigns; Building/renovation; Equipment; Program development; Seed money; Technical assistance; Program evaluation; Matching/challenge support.
Limitations: Applications accepted. Giving limited to NC; Poor and Needy Division limited to Forsyth County; Health Care Division, statewide. No grants to individuals, or for endowment funds or medical research; grants on a highly selective basis for construction of facilities or purchase of equipment.
Publications: Application guidelines; Financial statement; Grants list; Newsletter; Occasional report; Program policy statement.
Application information: Applicants should contact the trust staff to discuss the proposal prior to submitting a written application. Advance consultation is required before an application can be accepted for consideration. Applications will only be accepted online. Application form required.
Initial approach: Telephone inquiry, then in-person advance consult. For the Poor and Needy Division, call to schedule a meeting with a program officer. For the Health Care Division, contact the program associate to discuss your idea and determine if an advance consultation makes sense
Copies of proposal: 1
Deadline(s): 2nd Tues. in Feb. and in Aug.
Final notification: May and Nov.
Trustee: Wells Fargo Bank, N.A.
Officers: Karen McNeil-Miller, Pres.; Allen J. Smart, V.P., Progs.
Number of staff: 11 full-time professional; 1 part-time professional; 3 full-time support.
EIN: 566036515
Other changes: Allen J. Smart is now V.P., Progs.

2615
Dorothy N. Ribenack Charitable Trust
c/o Wells Fargo Bank, N.A.
1 W. 4th St., 4th Fl., MAC D4000-041
Winston-Salem, NC 27101-3818

Supporting organization of the Aftenro Society, the Board of Social Ministry Lakeshore Lutheran Home, Polinsky Fund of Miller-Dwan Foundation, Trustees of Duluth Community Chest, and Young Men's Christian Association of Duluth.
Foundation type: Independent foundation.
Financial data (yr. ended 10/31/13): Assets, $7,886,514 (M); expenditures, $362,317; qualifying distributions, $299,378; giving activities include $276,962 for 5 grants (high: $55,393; low: $55,392).
Fields of interest: Medical care, rehabilitation; Nursing care; YM/YWCAs & YM/YWHAs.
Limitations: Applications not accepted. Giving primarily in Duluth, MN.
Application information: Unsolicited requests for funds not accepted.
Trustee: Wells Fargo Bank, N.A.
EIN: 416054248
Other changes: The grantmaker has moved from PA to NC.

2616
Richmond Community Foundation, Inc.
220 N. Tryon St.
Charlotte, NC 28202-2137 (704) 973-4500

Established in 2001 in NC.
Donors: Richmond Memorial Hospital Foundation; First Union National Bank.
Foundation type: Independent foundation.
Financial data (yr. ended 12/31/12): Assets, $26,929,111 (M); expenditures, $2,047,887; qualifying distributions, $1,933,219; giving activities include $1,800,000 for 7 grants (high: $1,400,000; low: $10,000).
Fields of interest: Education; Health care; Children/youth, services.
Limitations: Applications accepted. Giving primarily in the Richmond County, NC, area. No grants to individuals.
Application information: Application form required.
Deadline(s): Varies
Officers and Directors:* Russell E. Bennett, Jr.,* Chair.; John J. Jackson,* Secy.; Betty Dorsett; Robert E. Hutchinson; Franklin Clay Jenkins; Paul R. Smart; Roger Staley; Bruce Stanback.
EIN: 562168849
Other changes: At the close of 2012, the grantmaker paid grants of $1,800,000, a 106.4% increase over the 2011 disbursements, $872,000.

2617
Percival Roberts, Jr. Trust
1 W. 4th St., D4000-041
Winston Salem, NC 27101-5709
E-mail: **grantadministration@wellsfargo.com; Main URL: https://www.wellsfargo.com/privatefoundationgrants/roberts**

Established in PA.
Foundation type: Independent foundation.
Financial data (yr. ended 12/31/12): Assets, $14,482,479 (M); expenditures, $632,437; qualifying distributions, $527,923; giving activities include $500,000 for 2 grants (high: $250,000; low: $250,000).
Purpose and activities: Giving primarily to children's causes, including children's hospitals; funding also for higher education.
Fields of interest: Higher education; Hospitals (specialty); Children.
Limitations: Applications accepted. Giving primarily in Tampa, FL, and Philadelphia, PA. **No grants to individuals.**
Application information: See foundation website for complete application guidelines. Application form required.
Deadline(s): **Apr. 1**
Trustee: Wells Fargo Bank, N.A.
EIN: 236219291
Other changes: The grantmaker now accepts applications.

2618
Florence Rogers Charitable Trust
P.O. Box 36006
Fayetteville, NC 28303 (910) 484-2033
Contact: Connie Sessoms; Joann Stancil

Trust established in 1961 in NC.
Donor: Florence L. Rogers†.
Foundation type: Independent foundation.
Financial data (yr. ended 03/31/13): Assets, $6,091,785 (M); expenditures, $473,045; qualifying distributions, $299,301; giving activities include $238,480 for grants.
Purpose and activities: Support for music and the arts, education, recreation, hunger programs, youth and child welfare, nursing and hospices, wildlife, and the general quality of life in the area. Preference is given to seed money for new ideas.
Fields of interest: Museums; Arts; Elementary/secondary education; Higher education; Nursing school/education; Botanical gardens; Human services; Protestant agencies & churches.
Type of support: General/operating support; Equipment; Emergency funds; Program development; Conferences/seminars; Publication; Seed money; Scholarship funds; Research; Matching/challenge support.

Limitations: Applications accepted. Giving primarily in Cumberland County, Fayetteville, and southeastern NC. No grants to individuals, or for building or endowment funds, scholarships, or fellowships; no loans.
Publications: Informational brochure (including application guidelines).
Application information: Application form required.
Initial approach: **Grant application form**
Copies of proposal: 1
Deadline(s): **None**
Board meeting date(s): Monthly
Trustees: J. William Lambert; **Jessie Tally.**
Number of staff: 2 full-time professional; 1 part-time professional; 2 full-time support; 1 part-time support.
EIN: 566074515

2619
E. K. Rose Pf F/B/O Asia Connection
c/o Wells Fargo Bank N.A., Trust Tax Dept.
1 W. 4th St., 4th Fl., MAC D4000-041
Winston-Salem, NC 27101-3818

Foundation type: Independent foundation.
Financial data (yr. ended 12/31/12): Assets, $1,259,437 (M); expenditures, $443,300; qualifying distributions, $425,939; giving activities include $416,198 for 1 grant (high: $416,198).
Fields of interest: Human services.
Limitations: Applications not accepted. Giving primarily in FL.
Application information: Unsolicited requests for funds not accepted.
Trustee: Wells Fargo Bank, N.A.
EIN: 453570784
Other changes: The grantmaker has moved from PA to NC.

2620
Caroline J. S. Sanders Charitable Trust No. II
c/o Wells Fargo Bank, N.A.
1 W. 4th St., 4th Fl., MAC D4000-041
Winston-Salem, NC 27101-3818

Established in 1990 in PA.
Donor: Caroline J.S. Sanders†.
Foundation type: Independent foundation.
Financial data (yr. ended 09/30/13): Assets, $3,635,566 (M); expenditures, $195,047; qualifying distributions, $156,611; giving activities include $144,000 for 36 grants (high: $10,000; low: $2,000).
Fields of interest: Arts; Education; Health care; Human services; Children/youth.
Type of support: General/operating support; Equipment; Program development; Scholarship funds.
Limitations: Applications accepted. Giving primarily in NJ and PA. No support for churches or athletic events. No grants to individuals, or for fundraising, or endowment or general operating funds; no loans.
Application information: See foundation website for complete application guidelines. Application form required.
Deadline(s): Mar. 1 and Sept. 1
Board meeting date(s): Apr. and Oct.
Trustee: Wells Fargo Bank, N.A.
EIN: 232676889

2621
Kurt Sandt Trust
c/o Wells Fargo Bank, N.A., Trust Tax Dept.
1 W. 4th St., 4th Fl., MAC D4000-041
Winston-Salem, NC 27101-3818

Foundation type: Independent foundation.
Financial data (yr. ended 12/31/12): Assets, $2,692,865 (M); expenditures, $234,823; qualifying distributions, $187,634; giving activities include $177,049 for 3 grants (high: $175,000; low: $49).
Fields of interest: Higher education.
Limitations: Applications not accepted. Giving primarily in MN.
Application information: Unsolicited requests for funds not accepted.
Trustee: Wells Fargo Bank, N.A.
EIN: 466088034
Other changes: The grantmaker has moved from PA to NC.

2622
The Milton and Leonore Schmuhl Scholarship Fund Trust
c/o Wells Fargo Bank, N.A., Trust Tax Dept.
1 W. 4th St., 4th Fl., MAC D4000-041
Winston-Salem, NC 27101-3818

Foundation type: Independent foundation.
Financial data (yr. ended 06/30/12): Assets, $3,105,321 (M); expenditures, $193,493; qualifying distributions, $150,074; giving activities include $138,650 for 83 grants to individuals (high: $2,950; low: $900).
Fields of interest: Higher education; Education.
Type of support: Scholarships—to individuals.
Limitations: Applications not accepted.
Application information: Unsolicited requests for funds not accepted.
Trustee: Wells Fargo Bank, N.A.
EIN: 201291627
Other changes: The grantmaker has moved from PA to NC.

2623
The Bill & Susan Sherrard Foundation
c/o Wells Fargo Bank, N.A.
1 W. 4th St., 4th Fl., MAC D4000-041
Winston-Salem, NC 27101-3818
E-mail: grantadministration@wellsfargo.com; Main URL: https://www.wellsfargo.com/privatefoundationgrants/sherrard

Established in 1993 in IL.
Donor: William Sherrard†.
Foundation type: Independent foundation.
Financial data (yr. ended 06/30/13): Assets, $5,673,321 (M); expenditures, $223,654; qualifying distributions, $177,246; giving activities include $165,832 for 9 grants (high: $74,500; low: $832).
Purpose and activities: Giving primarily to organizations benefiting residents of Henry County, Illinois, in the areas of education, historic preservation and nursing care.
Fields of interest: Education; Foundations (community); Protestant agencies & churches.
Type of support: General/operating support.
Limitations: Applications accepted. Giving primarily IA and Henry County, IL. No grants to individuals.
Application information: See foundation website for complete application guidelines. Application form required.
Deadline(s): Oct. 15
Trustee: Wells Fargo Bank, N.A.
EIN: 363918216
Other changes: The grantmaker has moved from PA to NC.

2624
Newton B. Shingleton Trust
1525 W. WT Harris Blvd., D1114-044
Charlotte, NC 28288-1161
Application address: **c/o Kevin Grogan, 1 W. 4th St., 2nd Fl., Winston-Salem, NC 27101, tel.: (855) 739-2920**; Main URL: https://www.wellsfargo.com/privatefoundationgrants/shingleton

Established in 1990 in VA.
Foundation type: Independent foundation.
Financial data (yr. ended 04/30/13): Assets, $4,609,099 (M); expenditures, $267,857; qualifying distributions, $223,379; giving activities include $205,821 for 76 grants (high: $60,000; low: $264).
Purpose and activities: Giving primarily to Christian churches and for education.
Fields of interest: Higher education; Libraries/library science; Education; Disasters, fire prevention/control; Human services; Christian agencies & churches; Blind/visually impaired.
Type of support: General/operating support.
Limitations: Applications accepted. Giving primarily in VA. No grants to individuals.
Application information: Application form required.
Initial approach: Contact Trust for application
Deadline(s): Dec. 31
Trustee: Wells Fargo Bank, N.A.
EIN: 546329857

2625
Shelton H. Short, Jr. Trust
c/o Wells Fargo Bank, N.A.
1525 W. WT Harris Blvd., D1114-044
Charlotte, NC 28288-1114
Application address: c/o Kevin Grogan, Wells Fargo Bank, 1 W. 4th St., D400-062, Winston-Salem, NC 27101-3818, tel.: (336) 747-8173; **Main URL: https://www.wellsfargo.com/privatefoundationgrants/short**

Established in VA.
Donor: Jean R. Short†.
Foundation type: Independent foundation.
Financial data (yr. ended 12/31/12): Assets, $28,740,300 (M); expenditures, $1,521,365; qualifying distributions, $1,253,816; giving activities include $1,200,000 for 31 grants (high: $250,000; low: $5,000).
Purpose and activities: Giving primarily for higher education, human services, and to a golf association.
Fields of interest: Higher education; Recreation, association; Human services.
Limitations: Applications accepted. Giving primarily in southeast VA. No grants to individuals.
Application information: See foundation website for complete application guidelines. Application form required.
Deadline(s): May 15 and Oct. 15
Trustee: Wells Fargo Bank, N.A.
EIN: 546140127

2626
The Simpson Foundation
1525 W. WT Harris Blvd., D1114-044
Charlotte, NC 28288-5709 (864) 255-8231
***E-mail:* grantadministration@wellsfargo.com; Main URL: https://www.wellsfargo.com/privatefoundationgrants/simpson**

Trust established in 1956 in SC.
Donors: W.H.B. Simpson†; Mrs. W.H.B. Simpson; Jack Kuhne; Lucy Kuhne.
Foundation type: Independent foundation.
Financial data (yr. ended 12/31/12): Assets, $28,296,993 (M); expenditures, $1,573,942; qualifying distributions, $1,403,313; giving activities include $1,372,500 for 33 grants (high: $382,000; low: $1,000).
Purpose and activities: Giving primarily for education, human services, health organizations, and to Presbyterian churches.
Fields of interest: Higher education; Education; Animal welfare; Health organizations; Human services; Protestant agencies & churches.
Type of support: Capital campaigns; Matching/challenge support.
Limitations: Applications accepted. Giving primarily in Greenville County, SC. No support for educational purposes. No grants to individuals, or for scholarships; no loans.
Application information: See foundation website for complete application guidelines. Application form required.
Initial approach: Letter or Proposal
Copies of proposal: 2
Deadline(s): Apr. 1 and Oct. 1
Board meeting date(s): Middle of May and Nov.
Trustee: Wells Fargo Bank, N.A.
EIN: 576017451

2627
Sites Designated Charities Trust
(formerly Venette and Mabel Sites Foundation)
c/o Wells Fargo Bank, N.A., Trust Tax Dept.
1 W. 4th St., 4th Fl., MAC D4000-041
Winston-Salem, NC 27101-3818

Established in 1969; supporting organization of the World Council of Churches, Evangelical Lutheran Church, Fort Wayne Educational Foundation, Heifer Project International, Salvation Army National Headquarters, Trinity English Lutheran Church, and Church Women United.
Foundation type: Independent foundation.
Financial data (yr. ended 12/31/12): Assets, $5,780,870 (M); expenditures, $340,644; qualifying distributions, $289,660; giving activities include $272,974 for 8 grants (high: $88,830; low: $5,119).
Fields of interest: Education; Salvation Army; Christian agencies & churches; Protestant agencies & churches.
Type of support: General/operating support.
Limitations: Applications not accepted. Giving primarily in IL, IN, NY and VA.
Application information: Unsolicited requests for funds not accepted.
Trustee: Wells Fargo Bank, N.A.
EIN: 356018382
Other changes: The grantmaker has moved from PA to NC.

2628
Carole C. and O. Temple Sloan, Jr. Foundation
4900 Falls of Neuse Rd., Ste. 150
Raleigh, NC **27609-5490**
Contact: Cheryl Ligon, Tr.

Established in 1994 in NC.
Donors: O. Temple Sloan, Jr.; O. Temple Sloan, Jr. Charitable Lead Trust; St. Andrews Presbyterian College.
Foundation type: Independent foundation.
Financial data (yr. ended 12/31/12): Assets, $16,364,599 (M); gifts received, $250,005; expenditures, $1,216,140; qualifying distributions, $1,089,127; giving activities include $1,089,127 for 108 grants (high: $132,600; low: $194).
Purpose and activities: Giving primarily for education, hospitals, and religious organizations.
Fields of interest: Higher education; Hospitals (general); United Ways and Federated Giving Programs; Christian agencies & churches; Protestant agencies & churches.
Type of support: Capital campaigns; Scholarships—to individuals.
Limitations: Giving primarily in NC; some funding also in MT.
Application information: Application form required.
***Initial approach:* Letter**
Deadline(s): None
Trustees: Cheryl P. Ligon; Malcolm C. Graham; Carson S. Henline; W. Gerald Thornton; George C. Turner.
EIN: 561870844

2629
Ethel Sergeant Clark Smith Memorial Fund
c/o Wells Fargo Bank
1525 W. WT Harris Blvd., D1114-044
Charlotte, NC 28288-1161 (888) 234-1999
Contact: Kyle J. Quinlivan, Trust Admin.
FAX: (877) 746-5889;
E-mail: grantsadministration@wellsfargo.com; Main URL: https://www.wellsfargo.com/privatefoundationgrants/smith

Established in 1977 in PA.
Donor: Ethel Sergeant Clark Smith†.
Foundation type: Independent foundation.
Financial data (yr. ended 05/31/13): Assets, $13,548,313 (M); expenditures, $683,222; qualifying distributions, $519,067; giving activities include $463,000 for 38 grants (high: $120,000; low: $1,000).
Purpose and activities: Giving for health associations and hospitals, education, including early childhood and secondary schools, child welfare and development, social service organizations, libraries, fine and performing arts groups and culture, museums and historical buildings, recreation, music and drama facilities, and programs for women, the handicapped and exceptional persons, and community reinvestment.
Fields of interest: Visual arts; Museums; Performing arts; Performing arts, theater; Performing arts, orchestras; Historic preservation/historical societies; Arts; Education, early childhood education; Child development, education; Secondary school/education; Higher education; Libraries/library science; Education; Speech/hearing centers; Mental health/crisis services; Health organizations, association; Recreation; Human services; Children/youth, services; Child development, services; Women, centers/services; Community/economic development; Disabilities, people with; Women.
Type of support: General/operating support; Capital campaigns; Building/renovation; Equipment; Emergency funds; Program development; Seed money; Research; Technical assistance; Exchange programs; Matching/challenge support.
Limitations: Applications accepted. Giving limited to southeastern PA, with emphasis on Delaware County. No support for single-disease organizations. No grants to individuals, or for deficit financing, construction or renovations to real estate not owned by the charitable entity, salaries, professional fundraiser fees, scholarships, or fellowships; no gifts longer than 3 years consecutively; no loans.
Publications: Application guidelines; Informational brochure (including application guidelines).
Application information: Application form required.
***Initial approach:* Apply online via foundation web site**
Copies of proposal: 1
Deadline(s): Mar. 1 and Sept. 1
Board meeting date(s): May and Nov. (Advisory Committee)
Final notification: 2 months after trustee meets with advisory committee
Trustee: Wells Fargo Bank, N.A.
EIN: 236648857

2630
Southern Bank Foundation
P.O. Box 729
Mount Olive, NC 28365-0729 **(919) 658-7025**
***Contact:* John L. Heeden, Secy.**

Established in 1996 in NC.
Donors: Southern Bank & Trust Co.; Southern Bancshares, Inc.
Foundation type: Company-sponsored foundation.
Financial data (yr. ended 12/31/12): Assets, $12,203,795 (M); gifts received, $4,081; expenditures, $610,250; qualifying distributions, $610,250; giving activities include $610,250 for 70 grants (high: $100,000; low: $200).
Purpose and activities: The foundation supports hospitals and organizations involved with education, human services, community development, and Christianity.
Fields of interest: Higher education; Libraries (public); Education; Hospitals (general); Health care; Health organizations; Salvation Army.
Type of support: General/operating support; Annual campaigns; Capital campaigns; Building/renovation; Equipment; Debt reduction; Program development; Scholarship funds.
Limitations: Applications accepted. Giving primarily in eastern NC. No grants to individuals.
Application information: Application form required.
***Initial approach:* Request application form**
Deadline(s): None
Officers: Frank B. Holding, Pres.; **William H. Bryan, V.P.; J. Grey Morgan, V.P.; John L. Heeden, Secy.;** David A. Bean, Treas.
EIN: 562002871
Other changes: John L. Heeden has replaced John E. Pegram, Jr. as Secy.
Hope Holding Connell is no longer a member of the governing body. Charles L. Revelle is no longer a member of the governing body.

2631

Joseph H. Stahlberg Foundation

c/o Wells Fargo Bank, N.A., Trust Tax Dept.
1 W. 4th St., 4th Fl., MAC D41000-041
Winston-Salem, NC 27101-3818
E-mail: grantadministration@wellsfargo.com; Main URL: https://www.wellsfargo.com/privatefoundationgrants/stahlberg

Foundation type: Independent foundation.
Financial data (yr. ended 12/31/12): Assets, $1,918,302 (M); expenditures, $173,654; qualifying distributions, $148,480; giving activities include $140,000 for grants.
Fields of interest: Brain disorders; Alzheimer's disease; Health organizations; Autism research.
Type of support: General/operating support.
Limitations: Applications accepted. Giving primarily in CA. No grants to individuals.
Application information: See foundation website for complete application guidelines. Application form required.
Deadline(s): Aug. 31
Trustee: Wells Fargo Bank, N.A.
EIN: 263456559
Other changes: The grantmaker has moved from PA to NC.

2632

State Employees' Credit Union Foundation

(doing business as SECU Foundation)
P.O. Box 27665
Raleigh, NC 27611-7665 **(919) 839-5000**
Contact: G. Mark Twisdale, Exec. Dir.
E-mail: secufoundation@ncsecu.org; **Toll free tel.: (800) 438-1104**; Main URL: http://www.ncsecufoundation.org

Established in 2001 in NC; funding initiated in 2004.
Foundation type: Operating foundation.
Financial data (yr. ended 06/30/13): Assets, $33,023,474 (M); gifts received, $11,229,681; expenditures, $7,088,139; qualifying distributions, $12,181,062; giving activities include $3,095,342 for 8 grants (high: $1,000,000; low: $15,000), $3,955,000 for 1,685 grants to individuals (high: $2,500; low: $750), and $5,094,105 for 5 loans/program-related investments (high: $2,431,770; low: $49,379).
Purpose and activities: The purpose of the foundation is to help identify and address community issues that are beyond the normal scope of State Employees' Credit Union. The foundation will promote local community development primarily through high impact projects in the areas of education, health, and human services.
Fields of interest: Higher education; Education; Health care; Human services.
Type of support: Capital campaigns; Building/renovation; Scholarships—to individuals.
Limitations: Applications accepted. Giving limited to NC. No grants for operational budgets, debt reduction, sponsorship or events.
Publications: Application guidelines; Annual report; Multi-year report.
Application information: There is no formal application process for scholarships; individual recipients are chosen by local area scholarship selection committees. Scholarship eligibility guidelines available on foundation web site. Application form required.
Initial approach: Letter of Interest for grant requests available on foundation's web site
Copies of proposal: 1
Deadline(s): Varies
Board meeting date(s): Quarterly
Officers and Directors:* McKinley Wooten,* Chair.; **Jim Johnson,* Vice-Chair.**; **Cynthia Jolly, Secy.-Treas.**; Mark Twisdale, Exec. Dir.; Jim Barber*; Shirley Bell; Bob Brinson; Karan Bunn; Michael Clements; Olson Huff; David King; Tom King; Robert S. Parker; Jo Anne Sanford; Marilyn Sheerer.
EIN: 562255292
Other changes: Jim Johnson has replaced McKinley Wooten as Vice-Chair. Cynthia Jolly has replaced Jim Johnson as Secy.-Treas.

2633

Strowd Roses, Inc.

P.O. Box 3558
Chapel Hill, NC 27515-3558
Contact: Jennifer B. Boger
FAX: (919) 929-1990;
E-mail: jenniferb@strowdroses.org; Contact for applicants affiliated with the Chapel Hill-Carrboro City Schools: Exec. Dir., Public School Foundation, P.O. Box 877, Carrboro, NC 27510, tel.: (919) 968-8819, e-mail: psf@chccs.k12.nc.us; Main URL: http://www.strowdroses.org
Grants List: http://strowdroses.org/PastGrantRecipList.html

Established in 2001 in NC.
Donors: Irene H. Strowd‡; Gladis H. Adams Charitable Trust; Community Action Network.
Foundation type: Independent foundation.
Financial data (yr. ended 12/31/12): Assets, $6,975,225 (M); gifts received, $1,000; expenditures, $335,824; qualifying distributions, $302,718; giving activities include $294,111 for 62 grants (high: $48,801; low: $700).
Purpose and activities: Giving to support programs and projects which improve the quality of life for citizens of Chapel Hill and Carrboro, North Carolina. The foundation also makes an annual bloc grant to cover funding requests from programs operating under the auspices of the Chapel Hill-Carrboro City Schools. This grant is administered by the Public School Foundation of Chapel-Hill Carrboro.
Fields of interest: Arts; Elementary/secondary education; Environment; Health care; Recreation; Children/youth, services; Children/youth; Youth; Aging; Physically disabled; Mentally disabled; African Americans/Blacks; Hispanics/Latinos; Women; Girls; Immigrants/refugees; Economically disadvantaged; Homeless.
Type of support: General/operating support; Continuing support; Management development/capacity building; Capital campaigns; Building/renovation; Equipment; Endowments; Debt reduction; Program development; Conferences/seminars; Seed money; Internship funds; Program evaluation; Grants to individuals; Matching/challenge support.
Limitations: Applications accepted. Giving limited to Chapel Hill and Carrboro, NC.
Publications: Application guidelines; Grants list; Informational brochure.
Application information: Application guidelines and form available on foundation web site. Application form required.
Initial approach: Letter requesting application
Copies of proposal: 1
Deadline(s): Jan. 31, Apr. 30, and July 31
Board meeting date(s): Mid-Mar., mid-June, and mid-Sept.
Final notification: Four weeks following board meeting
Officers and Directors:* Edward A. Norfleet,* Pres.; Sydenham B. Alexander,* V.P.; Stephen B. Miller,* Secy.
Board Members: Frederick H. Black; Jennifer B. Boger; Rosemary Waldorf.
Number of staff: None.
EIN: 562241874

2634

Stuart George and Jeanette Charitable Trust

c/o Wells Fargo Bank N.A., Trust Tax Dept.
1 W. 4th St., 4th Fl., MAC D4000-041
Winston-Salem, NC 27101-3818

Foundation type: Independent foundation.
Financial data (yr. ended 12/31/12): Assets, $9,081,746 (M); expenditures, $468,706; qualifying distributions, $309,456; giving activities include $280,000 for 6 grants (high: $100,000; low: $20,000).
Fields of interest: Performing arts, music; Arts; Health care; Human services; Children.
Type of support: General/operating support.
Limitations: Applications not accepted.
Application information: Unsolicited requests for funds not accepted.
Trustee: Wells Fargo Bank, N.A.
EIN: 270522116
Other changes: The grantmaker has moved from PA to NC.

2635

Walter and Louise Sutcliffe Foundation

1 W. 4th St., 2nd Fl.
Winston Salem, NC 27101-3818 336 747-8203
***E-mail:* grantadministration@wellsfargo.com; Main URL: https://www.wellsfargo.com/privatefoundationgrants/sutcliffe**

Established in 1990 in NJ as successor to the Walter and Louise Sutcliffe Foundation.
Donor: Louise Sutcliffe‡.
Foundation type: Independent foundation.
Financial data (yr. ended 12/31/12): Assets, $4,819,642 (M); expenditures, $233,307; qualifying distributions, $184,740; giving activities include $165,000 for 10 grants (high: $30,000; low: $10,000).
Purpose and activities: The foundation provides grants to institutions for nursing education and cancer research.
Fields of interest: Nursing school/education; Cancer; Medical research, institute; Cancer research.
Type of support: Program development; Scholarship funds; Research.
Limitations: Applications accepted. Giving primarily in NJ. No grants to individuals, or for endowments, general operating support, or fundraising events, including dinners, benefits, or athletic events; no loans.
Publications: Application guidelines.
Application information: See foundation website for complete application guidelines. Application form required.
Initial approach: Proposal
Copies of proposal: 1
Deadline(s): Feb. 15th and Sept. 1st
***Board meeting date(s):* Apr. and Nov.**
Trustee: Wells Fargo Bank, N.A.
EIN: 521720225

2636
F. W. Symmes Foundation
1525 W. WT Harris Blvd., D1114-044
Charlotte, NC 28288-5709 (888) 234-1999
***E-mail:* grantadministration@wellsfargo.com**; Main URL: https://www.wellsfargo.com/privatefoundationgrants/symmes

Established in 1954 in SC.
Donor: F.W. Symmes†.
Foundation type: Independent foundation.
Financial data (yr. ended 12/31/12): Assets, $13,999,531 (M); expenditures, $707,631; qualifying distributions, $619,701; giving activities include $578,000 for 26 grants (high: $50,000; low: $5,000).
Purpose and activities: Giving primarily for the arts and social services, including a Catholic agency.
Fields of interest: Arts; Education; Human services; YM/YWCAs & YM/YWHAs; Children/youth, services; Catholic agencies & churches.
Limitations: Applications accepted. Giving primarily in the Greenville, SC, area. No grants to individuals.
Application information: Application form required.
Initial approach: Online application form
Deadline(s): Mar. 15 and Sept. 1
Board meeting date(s): May and Oct.
Trustees: O. Perry Earle III; Eleanor Welling; F. McKinnon Wilkinson; Wells Fargo Bank, N.A.
EIN: 576017472

2637
Tannenbaum-Sternberger Foundation, Inc.
(formerly Sigmund Sternberger Foundation, Inc.)
324 W. Wendover Ave., Ste. 118
Greensboro, NC 27404-8438 (336) 274-5761
Contact: Robert O. Klepfer, Jr., Exec. Dir.
FAX: (336) 274-5763;
E-mail: bobklepfer@tsfoundation.com; Mailing address: P.O. Box 41199, Greensboro, NC 27404-1199; Main URL: http://www.TSFoundation.com

Incorporated in 1955 in NC.
Donors: Sigmund Sternberger†; Leah Louise B. Tannenbaum†; Rosa Sternberger Williams†.
Foundation type: Independent foundation.
Financial data (yr. ended 03/31/13): Assets, $16,378,440 (M); expenditures, $984,473; qualifying distributions, $804,001; giving activities include $697,534 for 55 grants (high: $112,500; low: $2,500).
Purpose and activities: Support for higher education, including scholarship funds, and individual scholarships for children and grandchildren of members of the Revolution Masonic Lodge in Greensboro, NC; grants also to 501(c)(3) organizations for purposes benefiting residents of Guilford County, NC.
Fields of interest: Historic preservation/historical societies; Arts; Higher education; Health care; Human services; Community/economic development.
Type of support: Program evaluation; Land acquisition; General/operating support; Management development/capacity building; Capital campaigns; Building/renovation; Equipment; Emergency funds; Program development; Conferences/seminars; Seed money; Internship funds; Scholarship funds; Scholarships—to individuals; Matching/challenge support.
Limitations: Applications accepted. Giving primarily in Guilford County, NC. Generally, no grants to endowment funds.
Publications: Application guidelines; Grants list.
Application information: Application must be submitted online. Application form required.
Initial approach: Letter, e-mail or telephone
Copies of proposal: 1
Deadline(s): Approx. 6 weeks prior to board meeting
Board meeting date(s): Usually in Mar., July, Nov. and as required
Final notification: Within 3 weeks of Board meeting at which grant proposals are considered
Officers and Directors:* Susan M. Tannenbaum,* Chair.; Sigmund I. Tannenbaum, M.D.*, Vice-Chair. and Secy.; Nancy B. Tannenbaum,* Vice-Chair.; John T. Warmath, Jr., Treas.; Robert O. Klepfer, Jr., Exec. Dir.; Edward F. Cone; Michael L. Diamond; Jeanne L. Tannenbaum, M.D.
Number of staff: 1 part-time professional; 1 part-time support.
EIN: 566045483
Other changes: Susan M. Tannenbaum has replaced Jeanne L. Tannenbaum, M.D. as Chair.

2638
Curtis Templin Charitable Trust
c/o Wells Fargo Bank, N.A., Trust Tax Dept.
1 W. 4th St., 4th Fl., MAC D4000-041
Winston-Salem, NC 27101-3818

Foundation type: Independent foundation.
Financial data (yr. ended 12/31/12): Assets, $1,317,325 (M); expenditures, $953,379; qualifying distributions, $888,075; giving activities include $882,314 for 15 grants (high: $58,850; low: $58,762).
Fields of interest: Health care; Eye diseases; Eye research; Human services; Salvation Army; Children/youth, services; Children, foster care; Children, services; Christian agencies & churches.
Limitations: Applications not accepted. Giving primarily in WY; some giving also in CA, IL, and NY.
Application information: Contributes only to pre-selected organizations.
Trustee: Wells Fargo Bank, N.A.
EIN: 836011358
Other changes: The grantmaker has moved from PA to NC.

2639
Roland R. and Hazel C. Todd Foundation
c/o Wells Fargo Bank, N.A.
1 W. 4th St., 4th Fl., MAC D4000-041
Winston-Salem, NC 27101-3818

Established in CA.
Donor: Ronald and Hazel Todd.
Foundation type: Independent foundation.
Financial data (yr. ended 06/30/13): Assets, $9,080,213 (M); expenditures, $487,920; qualifying distributions, $426,062; giving activities include $406,000 for 1 grant.
Fields of interest: Foundations (community).
Limitations: Applications not accepted. Giving primarily in Santa Rosa, CA.
Application information: Unsolicited requests for funds not accepted.
Trustee: Wells Fargo Bank, N.A.
EIN: 272969468
Other changes: The grantmaker has moved from PA to NC.

2640
The Toleo Foundation
(formerly The Kaplan Family Foundation)
445 Dolley Madison Rd., Ste. 208
Greensboro, NC 27410-5169
FAX: (336) 851-0410; E-mail: Toleo@toleo.net

Established in 1982 in NC.
Donors: Leonard J. Kaplan; Tobee W. Kaplan.
Foundation type: Independent foundation.
Financial data (yr. ended 12/31/12): Assets, $59,320 (M); gifts received, $5,000; expenditures, $6,627; qualifying distributions, $6,625; giving activities include $6,625 for grants.
Fields of interest: Education; Human services; United Ways and Federated Giving Programs; Jewish federated giving programs; Jewish agencies & synagogues.
Limitations: Applications not accepted. Giving primarily in NC. No grants to individuals.
Application information: Contributes only to pre-selected organizations.
Officers: Leonard J. Kaplan, Pres. and Treas.; Tobee W. Kaplan, V.P. and Secy.
Number of staff: 1 full-time professional; 1 part-time support.
EIN: 581496345
Other changes: At the close of 2011, the grantmaker paid grants of $4,375,652, a 2127.0% increase over the 2010 disbursements, $196,481.

2641
C. E. Towne Scholarship Fund
c/o Wells Fargo Bank, N.A.
1 W. 4th St., 4th Fl., MAC D4000-041
Winston-Salem, NC 27101-3818
Application address: c/o California Masonic Foundation, 111 California St., San Francisco, CA 94108-2284, tel.: (414) 292-9196

Foundation type: Independent foundation.
Financial data (yr. ended 06/30/13): Assets, $5,942,362 (M); gifts received, $72; expenditures, $357,879; qualifying distributions, $286,825; giving activities include $268,666 for 107 grants to individuals (high: $6,667; low: $1,000).
Purpose and activities: Scholarship awards primarily to children of Masonic families.
Fields of interest: Higher education.
Type of support: Scholarships—to individuals.
Application information: Applications are to be requested from the California Masonic Foundation. Application form required.
Deadline(s): Feb. 28
Trustee: Wells Fargo Bank, N.A.
EIN: 946700587
Other changes: The grantmaker has moved from PA to NC.

2642
The VF Foundation
105 Corporate Center Blvd.
Greensboro, NC 27408-3194
Main URL: http://www.vfc.com/corporate-responsibility/social/vf-in-the-community

Established in 2002 in NC.
Donor: V.F. Corp.
Foundation type: Company-sponsored foundation.
Financial data (yr. ended 12/31/13): Assets, $6,582,577 (M); expenditures, $1,749,574; qualifying distributions, $1,806,271; giving activities include $1,743,341 for 174 grants (high: $400,000; low: -$550,000).

Purpose and activities: The foundation supports organizations involved with arts and culture, education, conservation, diabetes, human services, and economic development.
Fields of interest: Museums; Museums (science/technology); Performing arts, theater; Arts; Education; Environment, natural resources; Diabetes; American Red Cross; Children, services; Family services; Residential/custodial care, hospices; Human services; Economic development; Community/economic development.
Type of support: General/operating support; Capital campaigns; Employee volunteer services; Employee matching gifts.
Limitations: Applications not accepted. Giving primarily in areas of company operations in Greensboro, NC. No support for religious or political organizations. No grants to individuals.
Application information: Contributes only to pre-selected organizations.
Officers and Directors:* Eric C. Wiseman,* Chair.; **Patrick Guido, V.P.; Laura Meagher,* Secy.**; Susan McDonald,* Treas.
EIN: 562322084

2643
Ralph J. Wann Foundation

c/o Wells Fargo Bank N.A., Trust Tax Dept.
1 W. 4th St., 4th Fl., MAC D4000-041
Winston-Salem, NC 27101-3818

Foundation type: Independent foundation.
Financial data (yr. ended 12/31/12): Assets, $4,585,470 (M); expenditures, $240,509; qualifying distributions, $207,952; giving activities include $196,264 for 1 grant.
Purpose and activities: Giving primarily to support a humane society.
Fields of interest: Animal welfare; Human services; Disabilities, people with.
Type of support: General/operating support.
Limitations: Applications not accepted. Giving primarily in CO.
Application information: Unsolicited requests for funds not accepted.
Trustee: Wells Fargo Bank, N.A.
EIN: 846022561
Other changes: The grantmaker has moved from PA to NC.

2644
Margaret C. Woodson Foundation, Inc.

225 N. Main St.
Salisbury, NC 28144-0829
***Application address:* c/o Foundation of the Carolinas, 220 N. Tryon St., Charlotte, NC 28202; tel.: (704) 973-4500**

Incorporated in 1954 in NC.
Donors: Margaret C. Woodson†; Margaret C. Woodson Trust.
Foundation type: Independent foundation.
Financial data (yr. ended 12/31/12): Assets, $475,081 (M); gifts received, $819,484; expenditures, $572,295; qualifying distributions, $568,150; giving activities include $490,000 for 39 grants (high: $95,000; low: $1,100).
Purpose and activities: Giving primarily for education and human services, with designated funds for Davidson College, Mary Baldwin College and Barium Springs Childrens Home.
Fields of interest: Museums; Arts; Higher education; Theological school/education; Human services; YM/YWCAs & YM/YWHAs; Children/youth, services.
Type of support: General/operating support.
Limitations: Giving primarily in Davie and Rowan counties, NC. No grants for research.
Application information: Application form not required.
Initial approach: Letter
Deadline(s): Mar. 1
Officers and Directors:* William G. Johnson,* Pres.; Mary Holt Woodson Murphy,* V.P.; John B.E. Cunningham,* Secy.; Donald D. Sayers,* Treas.; Paul Leake Bernhardt; Charlotte Davis; Robert P. Shay, Jr.; Paul B. Woodson, Jr.
EIN: 566064938

2645
Leopold Edward Wrasse Trust

c/o Wells Fargo Bank, N.A.
1 W. 4th St., 4th Fl, MAC D4000-041
Winston Salem, NC 27101-3818

Established in CA.
Foundation type: Independent foundation.
Financial data (yr. ended 11/30/11): Assets, $4,718,319 (M); expenditures, $383,934; qualifying distributions, $233,104; giving activities include $233,104 for 1 grant.
Fields of interest: Vocational education, post-secondary.
Limitations: Applications not accepted. Giving primarily in San Luis Obispo, CA.
Application information: Unsolicited requests for funds not accepted.
Trustee: Wells Fargo Bank, N.A.
EIN: 946070629
Other changes: The grantmaker has moved from TX to NC.

2646
Wyly Scholarship Fund

c/o Wells Fargo Bank N.A., Trust Tax Dept.
1 W. 4th St., 4th Fl., MAC D4000-041
Winston-Salem, NC 27101-3818
Application address: **c/o Walhalla High School, Attn.: John Hostetler, 151 Razorback Ln., Walhalla, SC 29691**

Established in 1976 in SC.
Foundation type: Independent foundation.
Financial data (yr. ended 07/31/13): Assets, $1,682,672 (M); expenditures, $94,480; qualifying distributions, $76,559; giving activities include $63,700 for 1 grant.
Purpose and activities: Support for Clemson University and Winthrop University, including scholarships to students in the area served by Walhalla High School, South Carolina.
Fields of interest: Education.
Type of support: Scholarship funds; Scholarships—to individuals.
Limitations: Applications accepted. Giving limited to SC.
Application information: Application form required.
Initial approach: Proposal
Deadline(s): Feb. 15
Trustee: Wells Fargo Bank, N.A.
EIN: 570640726
Other changes: The grantmaker has moved from PA to NC.

2647
The Zelnak Private Foundation

c/o PNC Bank, N.A.
409 Drummond Dr.
Raleigh, NC 27609-7033
Contact: Stephen P. Zelnak, Jr., Tr.

Established in 1998 in NC.
Donor: Stephen P. Zelnak, Jr.
Foundation type: Independent foundation.
Financial data (yr. ended 12/31/12): Assets, $3,128,444 (M); expenditures, $515,778; qualifying distributions, $500,000; giving activities include $500,000 for 1 grant.
Purpose and activities: Giving primarily for education and religious organizations.
Fields of interest: Salvation Army.
Type of support: General/operating support.
Limitations: Applications not accepted. Giving primarily in NC. No grants to individuals.
Application information: Contributes only to pre-selected organizations.
Trustees: Judy D. Zelnak; Stephen P. Zelnak, Jr.
EIN: 562115096

NORTH DAKOTA

2648
Community Foundation of Grand Forks, East Grand Forks and Region

(formerly The Greater Grand Forks Community Foundation)
620 DeMers Ave.
Grand Forks, ND 58201-4531 (701) 746-0668
Contact: Kristi Mishler, Exec. Dir.
FAX: (701) 772-3018;
E-mail: communityfoundation@gofoundation.org;
Main URL: http://www.gofoundation.org
Blog: http://gofoundation.org/blog/
Facebook: http://www.facebook.com/pages/Community-Foundation-of-Grand-Forks-East-Grand-Forks-Region/301984133722
YouTube: http://www.youtube.com/user/CommunityFoundationG

Established in 1997 in ND.
Foundation type: Community foundation.
Financial data (yr. ended 12/31/12): Assets, $6,611,620 (M); gifts received, $1,113,005; expenditures, $1,128,148; giving activities include $892,886 for 23+ grants (high: $264,250).
Purpose and activities: The foundation seeks to manage and develop diverse endowments that generate funding to address the quality of life in the Grand Forks, ND, area.
Fields of interest: Arts; Education; Children/youth, services; Human services; Community/economic development.
Type of support: Endowments; Conferences/seminars; Publication; Curriculum development; Scholarship funds; Research.
Limitations: Applications accepted. Giving limited to northwest MN and northeast ND. No support for religious organizations for religious purposes. No grants to individuals, or for non-program operating expenses, annual appeals or capital campaigns.
Publications: Annual report; Informational brochure (including application guidelines).
Application information: Visit foundation web site for application form and guidelines. Application form required.
Initial approach: **Contact foundation**
Board meeting date(s): Quarterly in Mar., June, Sept., and Dec.
Final notification: Quarterly
Officers and Directors:* Kristin Shea,* Pres.; Jim Satrom,* V.P.; Marilynn Ogden,* Secy.-Treas.; Kristi Mishler, Exec. Dir.; **Sandy Crary**; David Evenson; **Cathi Feeley**; Mary Dale Hansen; Joan Hawthorne; **Derrick Johnson**; **Curt Kreun**; Bill Lee; Dr. Lee Lipp; John Marchell; Gerard Neil; Margaret Tweten; Barry Wilfahrt.
Number of staff: 2 full-time professional; 1 full-time support.
EIN: 450448088
Other changes: Rohinee Damle, Marilynn Ogden, Jim Satrom, and Kristin Shea are no longer directors.

2649
Fargo-Moorhead Area Foundation

502 1st Ave. N., Ste. 202
Fargo, ND 58102-4804 (701) 234-0756
Contact: For grants and scholarships: Cher Hersrud, Prog. Off.; Darcy Putnam, Admin. Asst.
FAX: (701) 234-9724;
E-mail: lexi@areafoundation.org; Additional grant and scholarship info.: cher@areafoundation.org;
Main URL: http://www.areafoundation.org

Established in 1960 in ND.
Foundation type: Community foundation.
Financial data (yr. ended 12/31/12): Assets, $55,942,700 (M); gifts received, $2,643,911; expenditures, $3,143,377; giving activities include $2,213,801 for grants.
Purpose and activities: The foundation seeks to enrich the quality of life of the people in the Clay County, MN, and Cass County, ND, area by encouraging philanthropy and developing permanent endowment, assessing and responding to emerging and changing community needs, providing flexibility for donors with varied interests and levels of giving capabilities, and serving as a resource and catalyst for other organizations.
Fields of interest: Arts; Education; Environment; Animals/wildlife; Health care; Health organizations, association; Employment; Agriculture/food; Housing/shelter; Safety/disasters; Recreation; Youth development; Children/youth, services; Human services; Community/economic development; Government/public administration; Public affairs; Youth.
Type of support: Scholarships—to individuals; Management development/capacity building; Capital campaigns; Building/renovation; Equipment; Emergency funds; Program development; Scholarship funds; Technical assistance; In-kind gifts; Matching/challenge support.
Limitations: Applications accepted. Giving limited to Clay County, MN, and Cass County, ND. No support for religious purposes. No grants to individuals (except for scholarships), or for operating expenses (except for limited experimental or start-up periods), annual appeals or membership drives, capital debt reduction, or organizations which have outstanding reports from previous Fargo-Moorhead Foundation grants.
Publications: Application guidelines; Annual report; Newsletter; Program policy statement.
Application information: Visit foundation web site for application form and guidelines. Application form required.
Initial approach: Submit application form and attachments
Copies of proposal: 1
***Deadline(s):* Apr. 18**
Board meeting date(s): Quarterly
Final notification: 6 weeks
Officers and Directors:* Carol Schlossman,* Chair.; Morrie Lanning,* Vice-Chair.; Laine Brantner,* Secy.; Dorwin Marquardt,* Treas.; Tim Beaton, Exec. Dir.; Tom Dawson; **Corey Elmer**; Bruce Furness; Thomas Jefferson; **Susan E. Johnson-Drenth**; Neil Jordheim; Dr. Joel Jorgenson; **Joan Justesen**; Matthew Mohr; Lisa Vatnsdal.
Trustee Banks: Alerus Financial; Bank of the West; Bremer Bank, N.A.; Heartland Trust Co.; State Bank & Trust Co.; U.S. National Bank; Wells Fargo Bank, N.A.
Number of staff: 3 full-time professional; 1 full-time support; 1 part-time support.
EIN: 456010377
Other changes: Carol Schlossman has replaced Joan Justesen as Chair. Morrie Lanning has replaced Kate Haugen as Vice-Chair. Laine Brantner has replaced Corey Ekmer as Secy. Laine Branter, Morrie Lannin, Thomas Schaffer, and Carol Schlossman are no longer directors.

2650
Edson & Margaret Larson Foundation

406 Main Ave.
Fargo, ND 58126-0002
***E-mail:* grantadministration@wellsfargo.com; Main URL: https://www.wellsfargo.com/privatefoundationgrants/larson**

Established in ND.
Donor: Margaret Larson.
Foundation type: Independent foundation.
Financial data (yr. ended 12/31/12): Assets, $16,062,665 (M); expenditures, $756,433; qualifying distributions, $858,612; giving activities include $588,000 for 5 grants (high: $380,000; low: $25,000).
Fields of interest: Performing arts, education; Higher education; Community/economic development; Public affairs.
Limitations: Applications accepted. Giving primarily in ND. **No grants to individuals.**
Application information: See foundation website for complete application guidelines. Application form required.
***Deadline(s):* Sept. 30**
Officers: Douglas A. Christensen, Pres.; Andrew B. Kjos, Secy.-Treas.
Trustees: Julie A. Barner; Harold Newman; Drew Wrigley.
EIN: 271507358
Other changes: The grantmaker now accepts applications.

2651
C.F. Martell Memorial Foundation

c/o 1st International Trust Dept.
P.O. Box 1088
Williston, ND 58802-1088
***Application address:* P.O. Box 546, Watford City, ND 58854, tel.: (701) 774-8321**

Established in 1962 in ND.
Foundation type: Independent foundation.
Financial data (yr. ended 07/31/13): Assets, $941,326 (M); expenditures, $22,575; qualifying distributions, $17,289; giving activities include $12,000 for 4 grants to individuals (high: $3,000; low: $3,000).
Purpose and activities: Student loans to residents of Williams and McKenzie counties, North Dakota, for study at trade, technical, or professional schools and colleges in the U.S. Support also for two local charities.
Fields of interest: Arts; Education.
Type of support: Student loans—to individuals.
Limitations: Applications accepted. Giving limited to residents of Williams and McKenzie counties, ND.
Application information: Application form required.
Initial approach: Application form with references
Deadline(s): July 1
Board meeting date(s): July
Officers: William McLees, Chair.; Linda Svihovec, Secy.
Directors: Steve Holen; Fr. Russell Kovash; Karen Leiseth; David W. Nelson.
Trustee: 1st International Trust Dept.
EIN: 456010183

2652
MDU Resources Foundation

P.O. Box 5650
Bismarck, ND 58506-5650
Contact: Rita O'Neill, Fdn. Mgr.

FAX: (701) 530-1737;
E-mail: rita.o'neill@MDUResources.com; **Main URL: http://www.mdu.com/integrity/foundation**

Established in 1983 in ND.
Donors: MDU Resources Group, Inc.; WBI Energy, Inc.; Knife River Corp.; Montana Dakota Utilities Co.; WBI Energy Transmission, Inc.; MDU Construction Services Grp.; Fidelity Exploration & Production Co.; Great Plains Natural Gas Co.; Cascade Natural Gas Corp.; Intermountain Gas Co.; WBI Energy Midstream, LLC.
Foundation type: Company-sponsored foundation.
Financial data (yr. ended 12/31/13): Assets, $5,012,090 (M); gifts received, $1,613,244; expenditures, $1,658,953; qualifying distributions, $1,657,953; giving activities include $1,652,570 for 593 grants (high: $50,000; low: $50).
Purpose and activities: The foundation supports organizations involved with arts and culture, education, the environment, health, human services, community development, civic affairs, and senior citizens.
Fields of interest: Arts councils; Museums; Performing arts, theater; Arts; Secondary school/education; Higher education; Business school/education; Libraries (public); Education; Environment, natural resources; Environment; Hospitals (general); Health care; Youth, services; Human services; Community/economic development; Aging.
Type of support: General/operating support; Continuing support; Annual campaigns; Capital campaigns; Building/renovation; Equipment; Program development; Scholarship funds; Employee volunteer services; Employee matching gifts; Employee-related scholarships.
Limitations: Applications accepted. Giving primarily in areas of company operations. No support for athletic, labor, fraternal, political, lobbying, organizations or regional or national organizations without local affiliation. **No grants to individuals (except for employee-related scholarships), or for economic development; no loans or venture capital requests.**
Publications: Application guidelines; Annual report; Program policy statement.
Application information: Application form required.
Initial approach: Download application form and mail to local MDU Resources office
Copies of proposal: 1
Deadline(s): Oct. 1
Board meeting date(s): Jan,
Officers and Directors:* Cynthia J. Norland,* Pres.; Paul K. Sandness,* V.P.; Rita R. O'Neill, Secy. and Mgr.; Douglas A. Mahowald,* Treas.; Steven L. Bietz; Nancy K. Christenson; **K. Frank Morehouse**; Thomas D. Nosbusch; J. Kent Wells.
Number of staff: 1 full-time professional.
EIN: 450378937
Other changes: David L. Goodin is no longer a director.

2653
North Dakota Community Foundation

(also known as NDCF)
309 N. Mandan St., Ste. 2
P.O. Box 387
Bismarck, ND 58502-0387 (701) 222-8349
Contact: Kevin J. Dvorak, C.E.O.; Kara Geiger, Devel. Dir.-West; Jordan J. Neufeld, Admin. and Acct.
E-mail: jordan@ndcf.net; Grand Forks Office: P.O. Box 5155, Grand Forks, ND 58206-5155; Additional e-mails: amy@ndcf.net, kara@ndcf.net, and jordan@ndcf.net; Main URL: http://www.ndcf.net
Facebook: http://www.facebook.com/NDCommunityFoundation

Established in 1977 in ND.
Foundation type: Community foundation.
Financial data (yr. ended 12/31/12): Assets, $46,925,453 (M); gifts received, $3,991,052; expenditures, $2,464,185; giving activities include $1,420,836 for 47 grants (high: $146,045), and $471,784 for 306 grants to individuals.
Purpose and activities: The foundation seeks to improve the quality of life for North Dakota's citizens through charitable giving and promoting philanthropy. Unrestricted funds largely for aid to the elderly and disadvantaged; support also for health services, including mental health, youth agencies, parks and recreation, and arts and cultural programs in ND.
Fields of interest: Arts; Higher education; Education; Environment; Health care; Mental health/crisis services; Recreation; Children/youth, services; Aging, centers/services; Human services; Community/economic development; Children/youth; Youth; Aging; Economically disadvantaged; Homeless.
Type of support: General/operating support; Annual campaigns; Building/renovation; Equipment; Endowments; Program development; Conferences/seminars; Publication; Seed money; Scholarship funds; Research; Scholarships—to individuals; Matching/challenge support.
Limitations: Applications accepted. Giving primarily in North Dakota and organizations supporting North Dakota. No support for sectarian projects or national organizations (generally). No grants to individuals (except for scholarships), or for multi-year commitments.
Publications: Application guidelines; Annual report; Annual report (including application guidelines); Financial statement; Grants list; Informational brochure; Informational brochure (including application guidelines); Newsletter; Occasional report.
Application information: Visit foundation web site for application guidelines. If the foundation's board is interested in additional information, formal application materials are sent in late September. Requests not continuing through the process will be notified by the first of October. Grants do not exceed $5,000. Application form not required.
Initial approach: Letter of Inquiry (not exceeding 2 pages)
Copies of proposal: 1
Deadline(s): Aug. 15 for letter of inquiry
Board meeting date(s): Mid-Sept.
Final notification: End of Dec.
Officers and Directors:* Aaron Schmit,* Chair.; Kevin J. Dvorak,* C.E.O. and Pres.; **Jordan J. Neufeld,* C.F.O.**; Nancy Johnson; Dawn Keeley; **Christie Obenauer**; Donald Oppegard; **Steve Ottmar**; Chad Peterson; Diane Peyerl; Douglass Prchal; Jennifer Rasch; Scott Swenson; Becky Thatcher-Keller; David Trottier; LouAnn Waliser.
Number of staff: 3 full-time professional; 1 full-time support.
EIN: 450336015
Other changes: Jordan Neufeld is now Admin. and Cont. and Acct.

OHIO

2654
The Abington Foundation
c/o Foundation Mgmt. Svcs., Inc.
1422 Euclid Ave., Ste. 966
Cleveland, OH 44115-2001 (216) 621-2901
Contact: Cristin Slesh, Consultant
FAX: (216) 621-8198;
E-mail: abington@fmscleveland.com; Main URL: http://www.fmscleveland.com/abington
Grants List: http://www.fmscleveland.com/abington/grants.cfm

Established in 1983 in OH.
Donors: David Knight Ford†; Elizabeth Brooks Ford†.
Foundation type: Independent foundation.
Financial data (yr. ended 12/31/12): Assets, $26,751,169 (M); expenditures, $1,437,119; qualifying distributions, $1,358,017; giving activities include $1,163,418 for 73 grants (high: $100,000; low: $3,500).
Purpose and activities: The foundation was established to support organizations that promote education, health care, economic independence and cultural activities in Cuyahoga County, Ohio. The current priority is urban education.
Fields of interest: Education; Health care; Human services; Children/youth; Youth; Aging; Economically disadvantaged.
Type of support: Management development/capacity building; Capital campaigns; Building/renovation; Program development.
Limitations: Applications accepted. Giving primarily in Cuyahoga County, OH. No grants to individuals; no support for endowments, sponsorships, seminars, or general operating support.
Application information: The foundation has adopted an online application form for all grant requests. Application guidelines and procedures available on foundation web site. Mass mailings not accepted. Application form required.
Initial approach: Use online application form on foundation web site
Deadline(s): May 1, Sept. 1, and Dec. 1. When a deadline falls on a weekend or a holiday, the proposal must be submitted by 4:00 p.m. the following business day. See foundation web site for any updates on deadlines
Board meeting date(s): Jan., June, and Nov.
Final notification: 2 weeks after board meeting
Officers: Allen H. Ford, Pres.; Charles Ford, V.P.
Trustees: Alex Ford; Allen Ford; Charles K. Ford; David Ford, Jr.; David Kingsley Ford; Lise Ford; Ned Ford; Sarah Ford Whitener.
EIN: 341404854

2655
Akron Community Foundation
195 S. Main St., Ste. 300
Akron, OH **44308** (330) 376-8522
Contact: John T. Petures, Jr., C.E.O.
FAX: (330) 376-0202;
E-mail: acfmail@akroncommunityfdn.org; Main URL: http://www.akroncf.org/
Facebook: http://www.facebook.com/pages/Akron-Community-Foundation/107558384403
Twitter: https://twitter.com/AkronCF

Incorporated in 1955 in OH.
Foundation type: Community foundation.
Financial data (yr. ended 03/31/12): Assets, $140,719,939 (M); gifts received, $9,921,568; expenditures, $8,425,897; giving activities include $5,983,252 for 947 grants (high: $497,500; low: $100).
Purpose and activities: To improve the quality of life in greater Akron by building permanent endowments and providing philanthropic leadership that enables you to make a lasting investment in the community. To fulfill this mission, the foundation is committed to: 1) serving Akron and surrounding areas with creative, visionary and sensitive grants that address the evolving needs of an area experiencing rapid economic and social change; 2) devoting special emphasis to programs that enrich the community in the following distinct areas: arts and culture, education, health and human services, and civic affairs; 3) advising fundholders in areas of charitable concern and helping them achieving the highest likelihood of beneficial results; and 4) demonstrating community leadership by designing innovative programs and acting as a catalyst in identifying problems and sharing information with other funders.
Fields of interest: Media, film/video; Museums; Performing arts; Historic preservation/historical societies; Arts; Education; Environment; Health care; Mental health/crisis services; Health organizations, association; Medical research, institute; Medical research; Employment; Disasters, fire prevention/control; Disasters, Hurricane Katrina; Recreation; Children/youth, services; Children, day care; Family services; Aging, centers/services; Human services; Civil/human rights, advocacy; Community/economic development; Consumer protection; Public affairs; Aging; Disabilities, people with; African Americans/Blacks; Women; AIDS, people with; Immigrants/refugees; Economically disadvantaged; Homeless; LGBTQ.
Type of support: Program development; Seed money; Scholarship funds; Research; Matching/challenge support.
Limitations: Applications accepted. Giving primarily in Summit County, OH. No support for religious organizations for religious purposes. No grants for endowment funds, capital campaigns, or fellowships; no loans.
Publications: Application guidelines; Annual report (including application guidelines); Newsletter.
Application information: Visit foundation web site for online pre-application form and application guidelines. The foundation accepts full proposals based on pre-application form. No more than 1 grant to an organization in a 12-month period. Application form required.
Initial approach: Complete online pre-application form
Deadline(s): Full proposals are due: Apr. 1 for Arts and Culture, July 1 for Civic Affairs, and Oct. 1 for Health and Human Services and Dec. 15 for Education and Early Education
Board meeting date(s): Generally Feb., May, Aug., and Nov.
Final notification: 8 weeks
Officers and Trustees:* Mark Allio,* Chair.; Steven Cox,* Vice-Chair.; John T. Petures, Jr., C.E.O. and Pres.; Tina Boyes, V.P., Mktg. and Comms.; John Garofalo, V.P., Community Investment; Margaret Medzie, V.P., Devel. and Donor Engagement; **Steven Schloenbach, V.P. and C.F.O.; Rev. Sandra F. Selby,* Secy.; Paul Belair,* Treas.**; Dennis Jansky, Cont.; Virginia Albanese; F. Steven Albrecht; Nick Browning; Tommy Bruno; Marilyn Myers Buckey; Ellen Burg; Robert Cooper; Olivia Demas; Samuel DeShazior; Edward Eliopoulos; Rick Fedorovich; Sarah Friebert, M.D.; Tom Knoll; Dale Koblenzer; Rob Malone; Hon. Carla Moore; Vivian Neal; Robert Reffner; Steve Strayer; Mike Sweeney.
Trustee Banks: Brandes Investment Partners; Clover Capital Mgmt.; FirstMerit Bank, N.A.; Frontier Capital Mgmt.; JPMorgan Chase Bank, N.A.; National City Bank; Oak Assocs.; Osprey Investment Partners.
Number of staff: 4 full-time professional; 1 part-time professional; 3 full-time support.
EIN: 341087615
Other changes: Mark Allio has replaced Mike Sweeney as Vice-Chair. Steven Cox has replaced Mark Allio as Vice-Chair.
Steven Schloenbach is now V.P. and C.F.O. Rev. Sandra F. Selby is now Secy. Paul Belair is now Treas. Diane Schumaker is now Devel. and Donor Engagement Off. Melinda Boyce is now Database and Grants Admin. and Jr. System Admin. Bill Feth, Susan Kinnamon, and Sandra Selby are no longer trustees.

2656
American Electric Power Foundation
1 Riverside Plz.
Columbus, OH **43215** (614) 716-1000
***Contact:* Beth Smail**
***E-mail:* Educate@aep.com**; Additional application addresses: Ronn Robinson, c/o Kentucky Power, 101 Enterprise Dr., P.O. Box 5190, Frankfort, KY 40602, e-mail: rgrobinson@aep.com; Tina Salazar, c/o AEP Texas, 539 N. Carancahua, 17th FL, Corpus Christi, TX 78478, e-mail: tmsalazar@aep.com; Linda Riddle, c/o PSO, 1601 N.W. Expressway, Ste. 1400, Oklahoma City, OK 73118, e-mail: lkriddle@aep.com; Jeri Matheney, c/o Appalachian Power, P.O. Box 1986, Charleston, WV 25327, e-mail: jhmatheney@aep.com; Brian Bond c/o SWEPCO, 428 Travis St., Shreveport, LA 71101, e-mail: tbbond@aep.com; Jim Riggle, c/o Indiana Michigan Power, 110 East Waye St., Fort Wayne, IN 46802, e-mail: jariggle@aep.com; Main URL: http://www.aep.com/community/AEPFoundation/

Established in 2005 in OH.
Donor: American Electric Power Service Corp.
Foundation type: Company-sponsored foundation.
Financial data (yr. ended 12/31/12): Assets, $59,741,496 (M); expenditures, $9,330,746; qualifying distributions, $9,259,799; giving activities include $9,259,799 for 25+ grants (high: $1,000,000).
Purpose and activities: The foundation supports programs designed to improve lives through education from early childhood through higher education; protect the environment; provide basic human services in the areas of hunger, housing, health, and safety; and enrich the quality of life of communities through art, music, and cultural heritage.
Fields of interest: Arts, cultural/ethnic awareness; Museums (art); Performing arts, music; Arts; Elementary/secondary education; Education, early childhood education; Higher education; Education; Environment, natural resources; Environmental education; Environment; Hospitals (general); Health care; Food services; Food banks; Housing/shelter, development; Housing/shelter; Safety/disasters; Boys & girls clubs; Big Brothers/Big Sisters; Human services; Community/economic development.
Type of support: General/operating support; Continuing support; Capital campaigns; Building/renovation; Endowments; Program development; Scholarship funds.
Limitations: Applications not accepted. Giving primarily in areas of company operations in AR, IN, KY, LA, MI, OH, OK, TN, TX, VA, and WV. No support for religious, fraternal, athletic or veterans' organizations. No grants to individuals.

Application information: Online application by invitation only. Proposals should be submitted using organization letterhead and should include an executed IRS Form W-9. Proposals for multi-state or national projects should be limited to a one-page synopsis and submitted in Microsoft Word format to Educate@AEP.com. Visit website for local AEP regional utility addresses.
Trustees: Nicholas K. Akins; Carl L. English; Teresa L. McWain; Michael G. Morris; Robert M. Powers; Brian X. Tierney; Susan Tomasky; Dennis E. Welch.
EIN: 203886453

2657
The American Electric Power System Educational Trust Fund
c/o AEP Tax Dept.
1 Riverside Plz.
Columbus, OH **43215-2373 (614) 716-1000**
Scholarship address: AEP, Human Resources, 1 Riverside Plaza, Columbus, OH 43215

Donors: American Electric Power Co., Inc.; Columbus Southern Power Co.; Ohio Power Co.; CSW Foundation.
Foundation type: Company-sponsored foundation.
Financial data (yr. ended 02/28/13): Assets, $5,271,398 (M); expenditures, $316,144; qualifying distributions, $301,406; giving activities include $295,000 for 125 grants to individuals (high: $4,500; low: $2,000).
Purpose and activities: The foundation awards college scholarships to children of AEP employees.
Fields of interest: Higher education.
Type of support: Employee-related scholarships.
Limitations: Applications not accepted. Giving primarily in areas of company operations, including IN, OH, and VA.
Publications: Program policy statement.
Application information: Contributes only through employee-related scholarships.
Trustees: Joe Cisneros; Venita McCellon-Allen; Robert P. Powers.
EIN: 237418083
Other changes: Carl L. English is no longer a member of the governing body.

2658
William P. Anderson Foundation
c/o PNC Advisors, Ohio
P.O. Box 1198
Cincinnati, OH 45273-9631
Contact: Phyllis Wahl
***Application address:* 620 Liberty Ave., Pittsburgh, PA 15222-2705, tel.: (412) 768-7716**

Incorporated in 1941 in OH.
Foundation type: Independent foundation.
Financial data (yr. ended 10/31/13): Assets, $6,443,262 (M); expenditures, $357,783; qualifying distributions, $308,492; giving activities include $291,425 for 60 grants (high: $12,000; low: $1,000).
Purpose and activities: Giving primarily for the arts, health care and for AIDS research.
Fields of interest: Visual arts; Performing arts; Arts; Education; Environment, natural resources; Hospitals (general); Health care; AIDS; AIDS research; Crime/violence prevention, youth; Children/youth, services; United Ways and Federated Giving Programs.
Type of support: Annual campaigns; Capital campaigns; Building/renovation; Equipment; Seed money.
Limitations: Applications accepted. Giving primarily in Cincinnati, OH. No grants to individuals.
Application information: Application form required.
Initial approach: Letter
Copies of proposal: 1
Deadline(s): Oct. 1
Board meeting date(s): Nov.
Officers and Trustees:* William P. Anderson V,* Pres.; **Michael A. Coombe,* V.P.**; Harry W. Whittaker,* V.P.; **Phyllis C. Wahl,* Secy.**; Grenville Anderson,* Treas.; Nicholas R. Anderson; **John L. Campbell**; Will Claflin; Tucker J. Coombe; James A. Myers; **David Whittaker**; Polly W. Whittaker.
EIN: 316034059
Other changes: Phyllis C. Wahl has replaced Tucker J. Coombe as Secy.
Michael A. Coombe is now V.P.

2659
The Andrews Foundation
3401 Enterprise Pkwy., Ste. 340
Beachwood, OH 44122-7340 (216) 766-5784
Contact: Laura Baxter-Heuer, Pres.
E-mail: andrewsfdn@aol.com

Incorporated in 1951 in OH.
Donor: Mrs. Matthew Andrews†.
Foundation type: Independent foundation.
Financial data (yr. ended 12/31/12): Assets, $7,328,686 (M); expenditures, $515,269; qualifying distributions, $401,118; giving activities include $370,000 for 15 grants (high: $50,000; low: $10,000).
Purpose and activities: Giving primarily for education.
Fields of interest: Performing arts; Secondary school/education; Higher education; Alcoholism.
Type of support: General/operating support; Annual campaigns; Capital campaigns; Endowments.
Limitations: Applications accepted. Giving limited to OH. No grants to individuals.
Application information: Application form not required.
Initial approach: E-mail is preferred method for initial contact
Copies of proposal: 1
Deadline(s): None
Board meeting date(s): Spring and fall
Officers and Trustees:* Laura Baxter-Heuer,* Pres.; Michael A. Heuer,* V.P.
Number of staff: 1 full-time professional.
EIN: 346515110
Other changes: Ann Garson is no longer Secy.-Treas.

2660
The Angels on Track Foundation
8286 Clover Rd. N.E.
Salineville, OH 43945-9418
E-mail: info@angelsontrack.org; Main URL: http://www.angelsontrack.org
E-Newsletter: http://www.angelsontrack.org/newsletter.html

Established in 1997 in OH.
Foundation type: Independent foundation.
Financial data (yr. ended 12/31/12): Assets, $3,373,438 (M); gifts received, $47,348; expenditures, $233,507; qualifying distributions, $163,535; giving activities include $162,582 for 1 grant.
Purpose and activities: The foundation's mission is to provide the financial backing needed to improve railroad crossing safety throughout Ohio, and to educate local highway authorities on the various programs available through state and federal funding.
Fields of interest: Safety, education.
Type of support: General/operating support.
Limitations: Applications not accepted. Giving limited to OH.
Application information: Unsolicited requests for funds not accepted.
Trustees: Dennis F. Moore; Vicky L. Moore.
EIN: 311549790

2661
Ar-Hale Family Foundation, Inc.
(formerly Ar-Hale Foundation, Inc.)
P.O. Box 210
Lima, OH 45802-0210
Contact: Arlene F. Hawk, Pres.
***E-mail:* dprueter@cox.net; Application address: P.O. Box 210, Lima, OH 45802-0210**

Established in 1990 in OH.
Donors: Superior Metal Products, Inc.; American Trim.
Foundation type: Company-sponsored foundation.
Financial data (yr. ended 12/31/12): Assets, $1,863,502 (M); gifts received, $1,457,587; expenditures, $403,940; qualifying distributions, $369,848; giving activities include $369,848 for 61 grants (high: $55,000; low: $250).
Purpose and activities: The foundation supports philanthropic and religious initiatives that personally impact the lives of families and children. Support is given primarily to communities where American Trim does business and in the communities where American Trim shareholders reside.
Fields of interest: Performing arts, orchestras; Secondary school/education; Higher education; Education; Health care; Athletics/sports, baseball; YM/YWCAs & YM/YWHAs; Family services; Human services; Christian agencies & churches; Catholic agencies & churches.
Type of support: General/operating support; Continuing support; Management development/capacity building; Annual campaigns; Capital campaigns; Building/renovation; Endowments; Emergency funds; Program development; Film/video/radio; Seed money; Curriculum development; Fellowships; Technical assistance; Consulting services; Scholarships—to individuals; Matching/challenge support.
Limitations: Applications accepted. **Giving primarily in communities where the foundation shareholders reside, with emphasis on Louisville, KY; Allen, Auglaize, and Shelby counties, and the cities of Dayton and Lima, OH, Shawnee, OK, and Erie, PA. No support for political organizations.** No grants to individuals (except for scholarships).
Application information: Application form required.
***Initial approach:* Proposal; e-mail dprueter@cox.net for application and information regarding next meeting date**
Copies of proposal: 2
Deadline(s): None
***Board meeting date(s):* Last Sunday in July; others as necessary**
***Final notification:* within 1 week after board meeting**
Officers: Bryan Hawk,* Chair.; Arlene F. Hawk,* Pres.; **Timothy Hawk,* V.P.**; Beverly Prueter, Secy. and Exec. Dir.; Mark McKinley, Treas.
Number of staff: 1 part-time professional.
EIN: 341644337
Other changes: The grantmaker no longer lists a phone.

Beverly Prueter is now Secy. and Exec. Dir. Dennis Gallant is no longer Treas.

2662
Athens Foundation

2 S. Court St., 2nd Fl.
P.O. Box 366
Athens, OH 45701-0366 (740) 594-6061
Contact: Susan Urano, Exec. Dir.
FAX: (740) 594-6061;
E-mail: susan@athensfoundation.org; Additional e-mail: susan@athensfoundation.org; Main URL: http://www.athensfoundation.org
Blog: http://www.athensfoundation.blogspot.in/
Facebook: https://www.facebook.com/pages/The-Athens-Foundation/312616252558
Twitter: http://twitter.com/AthensFDN

Established in 1980 in OH; reincorporated in 1999.
Donors: Deluxe Corp.; Thelma Sheridan†.
Foundation type: Community foundation.
Financial data (yr. ended 09/30/13): Assets, $4,333,317 (M); gifts received, $321,769; expenditures, $418,967; giving activities include $195,847 for 9+ grants (high: $15,000).
Purpose and activities: The foundation's mission is to enhance the quality of life for the people of the Athens region through building endowments, awarding grants, and providing leadership on key community issues now and for generations to come.
Fields of interest: Humanities; Arts; Education; Environment, natural resources; Environment; Animal welfare; Hospitals (general); Health care; Mental health/crisis services; Recreation; Human services; Public affairs; Children; Disabilities, people with.
Type of support: Continuing support; Management development/capacity building; Capital campaigns; Program development; Conferences/seminars; Curriculum development; Research; Technical assistance; Consulting services.
Limitations: Applications accepted. Giving limited to Athens County, OH. No support for religious or political purposes, or for legislative action groups. No grants to individuals, or for endowments, budget deficits, scholarships, or annual fund raising drives.
Publications: Application guidelines; Annual report; Financial statement; Grants list; Informational brochure; Newsletter; Program policy statement.
Application information: Visit foundation web site for grant guidelines, pre-eligibility screening questions, and online application. Application form required.
Initial approach: Contact foundation
***Deadline(s):* Mar. 17 For Spring Grant., Sept. 15 For Fall Grant.**
Board meeting date(s): Last Tues. of every month
Final notification: May
Officers and Board Members:* Dr. Tom Davis,* Chair., Governance; **Dr. Vipin Koshal,* Chair., Devel.**; Judith Millesen,* Chair., Community Leadership; **Paul Wiehl,* Chair., Grants Comm.**; **Michael Carpenter,* Pres.**; Kristina Gerig,* Secy.; **Scott Robe,* Treas.**; Susan Urano, Exec. Dir.; Ada Woodson Adams; Dr. James Gaskell; Thomas Kostohryz; Jim McDonald; Kerry Pigman; Andrea Reik; Scott Robe; David Sharp; Mark Snider; Wendy Weiser.
Number of staff: 1 full-time professional; 2 part-time professional.
EIN: 311040215
Other changes: Paul Wiehl has replaced Wendy Jakmas as Chair., Grants Comm.
Carol Kuhre is no longer a board member.

2663
Austin-Bailey Health and Wellness Foundation

2719 Fulton Dr. N.W., Ste. D
Canton, OH 44718-3519 (330) 580-2380
Contact: Don A. Sultzbach, Exec. Dir.
FAX: (330) 580-2381; E-mail: abfdn@sbcglobal.net;
Main URL: http://fdnweb.org/austinbailey
Grants List: http://fdnweb.org/austinbailey/grant-awards/

Established in 1996 in OH.
Foundation type: Independent foundation.
Financial data (yr. ended 06/30/13): Assets, $7,410,543 (M); gifts received, $1,475; expenditures, $493,186; qualifying distributions, $324,058; giving activities include $324,058 for 30 grants (high: $30,000; low: $1,479).
Purpose and activities: The purpose of the foundation is to support programs that promote the physical and mental well-being of citizens of Holmes, Stark, Tuscarawas and Wayne counties, OH. The foundation emphasizes healthcare affordability concerns of people who are uninsured and underinsured, economically disadvantaged, children, single parents and the aging. The foundation also advocates programs that speak to the mental health needs of individuals and families.
Fields of interest: Dental care; Public health; Health care, insurance; Health care; Mental health/crisis services; Human services; Family services.
Type of support: General/operating support; Continuing support; Equipment; Emergency funds; Program development; Conferences/seminars; Seed money; Curriculum development; Scholarship funds; Employee matching gifts; Matching/challenge support.
Limitations: Applications accepted. Giving limited to Holmes, Stark, Tuscarawas, and Wayne counties, OH. No support for religious organizations for overtly religious purposes. No grants to annual and capital campaigns, membership drives, fundraising, advertising, or endowment funds.
Publications: Application guidelines; Financial statement; Grants list; Informational brochure; Informational brochure (including application guidelines).
Application information: Application form required.
Initial approach: Telephone call to request grant guidelines
Copies of proposal: 6
***Deadline(s):* See foundation web site for current deadlines**
Board meeting date(s): 2nd Thurs. in Jan., Mar., June, and Sept.
Final notification: 14 days after board meeting in Mar. and Sept.
Officers and Trustees:* Frederick W. Rohrig,* Chair.; Charles R. Conklin, D.O.*, Vice-Chair.; Virginia Neutzling, RN, BS, M.Ed*, Secy.; Peter Kopko,* Treas.; Don A. Sultzbach, Exec. Dir.; Daniel J. Fuline; Diane K. Jarrett; Elton D. Lehman, D.O.; David A. Miller; Daniel N. Moretta, D.O.; John L. Muhlbach, Jr.; Scott P. Sandrock; Eugene A. Thorn III; Thomas F. Turner.
Number of staff: 2 part-time professional; 1 part-time support.
EIN: 341845584

2664
Barberton Community Foundation

460 W. Paige Ave.
Barberton, OH 44203-2564 (330) 745-5995
Contact: Larry Lallo, Exec. Dir.
FAX: (330) 745-3990;
E-mail: jstephenson@barbertoncf.org; Main URL: http://www.barbertoncf.org
Facebook: https://www.facebook.com/barbertoncommunityfoundation
Flickr: http://www.flickr.com/photos/bcfcharity/
LinkedIn: http://www.linkedin.com/company/barberton-community-foundation

Established in 1996 in OH.
Foundation type: Community foundation.
Financial data (yr. ended 12/31/12): Assets, $86,017,062 (M); gifts received, $211,232; expenditures, $4,819,465; giving activities include $3,536,884 for grants.
Purpose and activities: The foundation supports projects that benefit the citizens of Barberton, OH.
Fields of interest: Education; Health organizations, association; Recreation; Urban/community development.
Type of support: Capital campaigns; Building/renovation; Equipment; Land acquisition; Program development; Conferences/seminars; Curriculum development; Scholarship funds; Technical assistance; Program-related investments/loans; Matching/challenge support.
Limitations: Applications accepted. Giving limited to Barberton, OH. No support for religious organizations for religious purposes. No grants to individuals (except for scholarships), or for debt reduction, deficits or previous obligations, annual fundraising drives, ongoing operational expenses, sabbatical leaves or scholarly research, or for endowments housed at institutions other than the foundation.
Publications: Application guidelines; Annual report; Financial statement; Grants list; Informational brochure; Informational brochure (including application guidelines); Newsletter; Quarterly report.
Application information: Visit foundation web site for application forms and additional guidelines per grant type; number of copies vary per grant type. The Small Grants program accepts applications for grants of up to $1,000. Application form required.
Initial approach: Letter or telephone
Copies of proposal: 10
Deadline(s): Jan. 2, Apr. 1, July 1, and Oct. 1 for quarterly program; last Fri. of each month for small grants program
Board meeting date(s): 3rd Thurs. of each month
Final notification: Within 3 to 4 weeks for Small Grants program; within 7 to 8 weeks for quarterly grants
Officers and Trustees:* Thomas Harnden,* Chair.; **Michael Chisnell,* Vice-Chair.**; Mary Jo Goss,* Secy.; Ryan Pendleton,* Treas.; Jim Stonkus,* Exec. Dir.; Thomas Anders; Edna Boyle; **Josh Gordon**; **Brett Haverlick**; William Judge; Steve Kelleher; Tina Linton; Frederick Maurer; Bruce May; Michael Vinay; Richard R. Wiley.
Number of staff: 5 full-time professional; 1 full-time support.
EIN: 341846432
Other changes: Michael Chisnell has replaced Thomas L. Harnden as Vice-Chair.
Dennis Liddle, Jr. is no longer Co-Chair. Michael Chisnell, Lois Matney, and Kimberly Karson are no longer trustees.

2665
The John C. Bates Foundation

2401 Front St.
Toledo, OH 43605-1145

Established in 1993 in OH.
Donors: Heidtman Steel Products, Inc.; Centaur, Inc.; HS Processing, LP.

Foundation type: Company-sponsored foundation.
Financial data (yr. ended 03/31/13): Assets, $1,376,365 (M); gifts received, $158,100; expenditures, $157,491; qualifying distributions, $156,740; giving activities include $153,558 for 22 grants (high: $33,333; low: $75).
Purpose and activities: The foundation supports zoological societies, community foundations, and organizations involved with education, health, human services, and Christianity.
Fields of interest: Elementary/secondary education; Higher education; Education; Zoos/zoological societies; Health care; Cancer; Family services; Human services; Foundations (community); Christian agencies & churches.
Type of support: Capital campaigns; Program development; Scholarship funds.
Limitations: Applications not accepted. Giving primarily in IN, MI, and OH. No grants to individuals.
Application information: Contributes only to pre-selected organizations.
Officers and Trustees:* Darlene B. Dotson,* Pres.; John M. Carey,* Secy.; Mark E. Ridenour,* Treas.; **John C. Bates**; **John C. Bates, Jr.**; Sarah J. Bates; Debra A. Shinkle.
EIN: 341749094

2666
The Benedict Foundation for Independent Schools
224 W. Thruston Blvd.
Dayton, OH 45419-3334
Contact: Peter B. Benedict II, Pres.
Main URL: http://thebenedictfoundation.org/
Grants List: http://www.thebenedictfoundation.org/previous-grantees

Established in 1983 in DE.
Donor: Peter B. Benedict.
Foundation type: Independent foundation.
Financial data (yr. ended 12/31/12): Assets, $5,182,547 (M); gifts received, $325,000; expenditures, $334,494; qualifying distributions, $334,494; giving activities include $305,000 for 16 grants (high: $30,000; low: $10,000).
Purpose and activities: Giving for independent secondary schools that have been members of the National Association of Independent Schools for ten consecutive years. Challenge grants are preferred for purposes of improving academic programs, scholarship aid, building programs, faculty salaries, faculty summer workshops, or other programs to improve the quality of the school's educational activities.
Fields of interest: Secondary school/education; Education.
Type of support: Building/renovation; Scholarship funds; Matching/challenge support.
Limitations: Applications accepted. Giving on a national basis. No grants to individuals, or for endowment funds or operating costs; or multi-year grants; no loans.
Publications: Informational brochure (including application guidelines).
Application information: After receipt of letter, BFIS sends a brochure and cover letter specifying requirements. Complete application guidelines available on foundation web site. Application form required.
Initial approach: Letter
Copies of proposal: 6
Deadline(s): Applications should be received between Jan. 1 and Mar. 31
Board meeting date(s): June
Final notification: July
Officers and Directors:* Peter B. Benedict II,* Pres.; Davis M. Benedict,* V.P. and Treas.; Randall D. Corwin,* Secy.; Nancy H. Benedict; Peter B. Benedict.
Number of staff: None.
EIN: 592383209

2667
Ralph L. & Florence A. Bernard Foundation
1735 S. Hawkins, Ste. 3
Akron, OH **44320**
***Application address:* c/o Ralph L. Bernard, Jr., P.O. Box 8176, Akron, OH 44320-0176, tel.: (330) 836-9306**

Established in 1998 in OH.
Donor: Ralph L. Bernard.
Foundation type: Independent foundation.
Financial data (yr. ended 04/30/13): Assets, $4,686,746 (M); expenditures, $297,460; qualifying distributions, $195,650; giving activities include $195,650 for 10 grants (high: $50,750; low: $250).
Fields of interest: Education; Health care; Human services; Catholic agencies & churches.
Limitations: Applications accepted. Giving primarily in OH. No grants to individuals.
Application information: Application form not required.
Initial approach: Proposal
Deadline(s): None
Trustees: Ralph L. Bernard, Jr.; Regina A. Dain.
EIN: 341867382

2668
The William Bingham Foundation
1111 Superior Ave., Ste. 700
Cleveland, OH 44114-2540 (216) 344-5200
Contact: Laura H. Gilbertson, Chief Admin.
E-mail: info@WBinghamFoundation.org; **Additional contact: Daniel L. Horn, Secy., tel.: (216) 781-7800, e-mail: hornoffice@att.net**; Main URL: http://www.wbinghamfoundation.org

Incorporated in 1955 in OH.
Donor: Elizabeth B. Blossom†.
Foundation type: Independent foundation.
Financial data (yr. ended 12/31/12): Assets, $19,210,267 (M); expenditures, $1,219,892; qualifying distributions, $998,726; giving activities include $820,604 for 29 grants (high: $99,000; low: $750).
Purpose and activities: The foundation furthers the philanthropic intent of its founder, Elizabeth Bingham Blossom. It supports organizations in the fields of education, science, health and human services, and the arts. It works for a world that is environmentally self-sustaining; seeks to strengthen civil society and its institutions; educates family members and others in the values and practice of philanthropy, community service, and stewardship; and it seeks to build a sense of community.
Fields of interest: Education; Environment; Health care; Human services.
Type of support: General/operating support; Continuing support; Management development/capacity building; Capital campaigns; Building/renovation; Equipment; Endowments; Program development; Conferences/seminars; Curriculum development; Technical assistance; Matching/challenge support.
Limitations: Giving on a national basis, with focus on areas in which the foundation trustees reside; see foundation web site. No support for foreign organizations. No grants to individuals; no loans.
Publications: Application guidelines; Financial statement; Grants list.
Application information: Unsolicited applications not accepted unless specific focus is posted on web site. Applications generally are accepted by invitation only. The foundation issues an RFP approximately once per year for organizations with which it does not have a relationship. Application form is provided to invited applicants. Application form required.
Initial approach: See foundation web site for current submission policy
Copies of proposal: 1
Deadline(s): Varies, see foundation web site for current deadline
Board meeting date(s): Usually Feb. and Aug.
Final notification: Varies.
Officers and Trustees:* C. Perry Blossom,* Pres.; Virginia Blossom Kruntorad,* V.P.; Daniel L. Horn,* Secy.; **C. Bingham Blossom,* Treas.**; David B. Blossom; Jonathan B. Blossom; Laurel Blossom; Robin Dunn Blossom; James B. Heffernan; Elizabeth B. Meers.
Number of staff: 1 full-time professional.
EIN: 346513791
Other changes: C. Perry Blossom has replaced Elizabeth Meers as Pres. Virginia Blossom Kruntorad has replaced Jonathan B. Blossom as V.P. C. Bingham Blossom has replaced C. Perry Blossom as Treas.

2669
Boles Family Foundation
Columbus, OH

The foundation terminated in 2011. The remaining assets were given to the Columbus Foundation.

2670
Brentwood Foundation
30799 Pinetree Rd., Ste. 274
Cleveland, OH 44124-5903 (216) 328-9294
Contact: Christine Gibbons, Dir.
FAX: (216) 328-9219;
E-mail: brentfoundation@sbcglobal.net; Tel. for information regarding South Pointe Hospital grant application process: (216) 491-7234 or (216) 491-7461; Main URL: http://www.brentwood-foundation.org/

Established in 1994 in OH; converted following the merger of Brentwood Hospital, which was an osteopathic hospital, with Meridia Suburban Hospital.
Foundation type: Independent foundation.
Financial data (yr. ended 12/31/12): Assets, $20,489,092 (M); expenditures, $1,000,938; qualifying distributions, $928,410; giving activities include $807,663 for 3 grants (high: $504,663; low: $3,000).
Purpose and activities: Giving to enhance osteopathic medicine, research and patient care by: 1) providing educational opportunities designed to strengthen the capabilities of students and practitioners, (including interns and residents), 2) supporting research efforts which focus upon the acquisition, advancement, and dissemination of knowledge in this field, 3) educating the public about osteopathic services and trends, and 4) initiating activities designed to advance and improve patient care in osteopathic hospitals and in the community.

Fields of interest: Medical school/education; Hospitals (general).
Type of support: General/operating support; Continuing support; Equipment; Program development; Conferences/seminars; Curriculum development; Research; Consulting services; Matching/challenge support.
Limitations: Applications accepted. Giving primarily in OH, particularly Northeast OH. The foundation will consider funding requests outside of OH if they directly impact OH or Northeast OH. No support for activities which are in direct competition with the osteopathic education and medical activities being conducted within the Cleveland Clinic Health System. No grants to individuals.
Publications: Application guidelines; Annual report; Annual report (including application guidelines); Financial statement; Grants list; Informational brochure (including application guidelines).
Application information: Grant requests submitted from South Pointe Hospital and other hospitals or programs within the Cleveland Clinic Health System must follow South Pointe Hospital's grant application procedures. See web site for application guidelines and Grant Cover Sheet.
Initial approach: Letter of inquiry
Copies of proposal: 2
Deadline(s): Apr. 1 or Sept. 1 (If a deadline date falls on a weekend or a holiday, the following Mon. will be considered the deadline date)
Board meeting date(s): June and Nov.
Officers and Trustees:* Roger F. Classen,* Chair.; Raymond J. Grabow, Vice-Chair.; Michael F. Killeen,* Secy.; George Kappos, Jr.,* Treas.; Richard Barone; Vincent F. DeCrane; **Rick A. Gemma**; David Krahe, D.O.; Gregory P. Kurtz; Michael McClain, D.O.; Michael Merriman; Lucille Reed Narducci; Brenda R. Saridakis; Jeffrey A. Stanley, D.O.
Director: Christine Gibbons.
Number of staff: 1 full-time professional.
EIN: 341783117

2671
The Robert H. Brethen Foundation
40 N. Main St., Ste. 2560
Dayton, OH 45423-1730 (937) 224-1730
Contact: Robert H. Brethen, Pres. and Treas.

Established in 1988 in OH.
Donors: Robert H. Brethen; Celstar Group, Inc.
Foundation type: Independent foundation.
Financial data (yr. ended 10/31/13): Assets, $4,305,496 (M); expenditures, $366,128; qualifying distributions, $341,090; giving activities include $341,090 for 42 grants (high: $75,000; low: $50).
Fields of interest: Health care; Human services; Salvation Army; Residential/custodial care, hospices; Homeless, human services; Christian agencies & churches; Youth.
Type of support: General/operating support.
Limitations: Applications accepted. Giving primarily in the greater Dayton, OH, area. No grants to individuals.
Application information: Application form not required.
Initial approach: Letter
Deadline(s): None
Officers and Trustees:* Robert H. Brethen, Pres. and Treas.; David M. Brethen,* Secy.; Karen B. Johns.
EIN: 311213173

2672
Warren Brown Family Foundation
6475 Perimeter Dr.
P.O. Box 163
Dublin, OH 43016-8459
Contact: Jan Brown, Pres.
E-mail: wbff@bellsouth.net

Established in 1996 in OH.
Donor: D. Warren Brown†.
Foundation type: Independent foundation.
Financial data (yr. ended 12/31/12): Assets, $3,066,065 (M); expenditures, $218,073; qualifying distributions, $203,500; giving activities include $203,500 for grants.
Purpose and activities: Giving primarily for youth, education, church/ministry, health, and the Marion, Ohio, community.
Fields of interest: Arts; Education; Children/youth, services; United Ways and Federated Giving Programs.
Type of support: General/operating support; Continuing support; Annual campaigns; Capital campaigns; Building/renovation; Equipment; Emergency funds; Professorships; Scholarship funds; Research.
Limitations: Applications accepted. Giving primarily in Marion, OH. No grants to individuals.
Application information: Application form required.
Initial approach: Letter (no more than 3 pages)
Copies of proposal: 5
Deadline(s): Sept. 1
Board meeting date(s): Bi-annually
Final notification: Dec. 31
Officers: Janice J. Brown, Pres.; Douglas W. Brown, Secy.; Joe D. Donithen, Treas.
Trustees: Katherine B. Shepherd; James H. Wyland.
EIN: 341811779
Other changes: The grantmaker has moved from GA to OH.

2673
Brush Foundation
25350 Rockside Rd., 3rd Fl.
Bedford Heights, OH **44146-3704 (216) 961-8804 x1250**
***Contact:* Judy Wright, Prog. Off.**
E-mail: brushfoundation@hotmail.com; **Main URL: http://fdnweb.org/brush/**
Grants List: http://fdnweb.org/brush/project-grants/

Established in 1928 in OH.
Donors: Charles F. Brush†; Maurice Perkins†; Rufus S. Day, Jr. Trust.
Foundation type: Independent foundation.
Financial data (yr. ended 12/31/12): Assets, $6,445,347 (M); expenditures, $359,057; qualifying distributions, $340,894; giving activities include $290,400 for 16 grants (high: $35,000; low: $2,900).
Purpose and activities: To ensure that family planning worldwide becomes acceptable, available, accessible, affordable, effective and safe. Funding is focused, nationally and internationally, on those organizations with innovative projects which will: 1) Protect and enhance people's ability to manage their reproductive health; 2) Carry out public policy analysis and/or public education in areas related to reproductive behavior and its social implications; and 3) Advance the knowledge and purposeful behavior of young people regarding sexuality within both a social and health context. The current major interests of the foundation are adolescent sexuality and the control of adolescent pregnancy, preservation of the freedom of choice of women to plan the spacing and number of children, how laws and regulations may control population growth, and pilot family planning programs in Third World countries. Grants range from $5,000 to $25,000.
Fields of interest: Reproductive health, family planning; Civil liberties, reproductive rights; Youth; Adults; Young adults; Women; Girls; Adults, women; Young adults, female; Young adults, male.
International interests: Developing Countries.
Type of support: Scholarships—to individuals; General/operating support; Program development.
Limitations: Applications accepted. Giving in the U.S., with some emphasis on northeast OH; giving also on an international basis. No grants for capital endowment funds, operating support, or fellowships; no loans.
Publications: Application guidelines.
Application information: See foundation website for complete application guidelines. Application form required.
Officers: Jacqueline Darroch, Ph.D, Pres.; Abigail English, Pres.; Elizabeth Stites, Secy.; Ellen Rome, M.D., Treas.
Board of Managers: Barbara Brush-Wright; Daphne Byers; Cindie Carroll-Pankhurst, PhD; Henry C. Doll; Stacey Easterling; Gita P. Gidwani, M.D.; Dan Pellegrom; Gordon Weir, M.D.
Trustee: KeyBank, N.A.
Number of staff: 1 part-time professional.
EIN: 346000445
Other changes: The grantmaker no longer lists a separate application address.

2674
Bryan Area Foundation, Inc.
516 E. High St.
P.O. Box 651
Bryan, OH 43506-1316 (419) 633-1156
Contact: Ralph W. Gallagher, Chair.
***FAX:* (419) 633-9262**;
E-mail: foundation@bryanareafoundation.org; Main URL: http://www.bryanareafoundation.org

Established in 1969 in OH.
Foundation type: Community foundation.
Financial data (yr. ended 06/30/12): Assets, $17,130,361 (M); gifts received, $639,266; expenditures, $626,839; giving activities include $140,403 for 6+ grants (high: $25,000; low: $8,176), and $106,625 for grants to individuals.
Purpose and activities: The foundation seeks to enhance the quality of life for all citizens of the Bryan, OH area, now and for generations to come by building community endowment, addressing needs through grantmaking, and serving as a leader, catalyst and resource for charitable giving. Focus areas include historic preservation, higher education, health care, agriculture, recreation, children and youth services, community development and religion.
Fields of interest: Historic preservation/historical societies; Arts; Higher education; Education; Environment, beautification programs; Environment; Health care; Agriculture; Recreation, parks/playgrounds; Recreation; Youth development, adult & child programs; Youth development, scouting agencies (general); Youth development, agriculture; Aging, centers/services; Community/economic development; Religion.
Type of support: Capital campaigns; Building/renovation; Equipment; Program development; Curriculum development; Research; Technical assistance; Scholarships—to individuals; Matching/challenge support.
Limitations: Applications accepted. Giving limited to the Bryan, OH, area. No support for religious or

sectarian purposes. No grants to individuals (except for scholarships), or for endowments, make-up of operating deficits, post-event, or after-the-fact situations.
Publications: Application guidelines; Newsletter; Occasional report.
Application information: Visit foundation web site for application form and guidelines. All applicants must schedule a meeting with the Exec. Dir. at least 30 days in advance of the grant deadline. Application form required.
Initial approach: **Contact foundation**
Copies of proposal: 10
Deadline(s): Mar. 31, June 30, Sept. 30, and Dec. 29
Board meeting date(s): Quarterly
Final notification: Mar., June, Sept., and Dec.
Officers and Trustees:* Ralph W. Gallagher,* Chair.; James C. Wood III,* Vice-Chair.; Jack E. Brace,* C.E.O. and Pres.; Michael A. Shaffer,* Secy.; George H. Gardner,* Treas.; Julie A. Brown; Christopher Cullis; Laura Eckhardt; William G. Martin; **Mark Miller**; Glen L. Newcomer; E. Clifford Oberlin III; Pamela B. Steel.
Members: James R. Bard; **Jason Beals**; Bruce O. Benedict; George Brown; Wayne Carlin; **Michael Culler**; **Emily Ebaugh**; Philip L. Ennen; Diana Moore Eschhofen; Betty Franks; Karen K. Gallagher; David Gorzelanczyk; Thomas M. Herman; Stephen Hess; Beth Hollabaugh; Albert Horn, Jr.; Jason Kunsman; Bruce Manett; Nancy Merillat; David C. Newcomer; William Pepple; **Diana Savage**; David Schumm; Carolyn Sharrock-Dorsten; C. Gregory Spangler; Dean L. Spangler; Art Spletzer, Jr.; William Steel; George E. Stockman; Mary Thaman; Constance M. Tipton; John G. Toner; Tom Turnbull; Kirkland Vashaw; Thomas A. Voigt; Ann Vreeland; Richard C. Wright.
Number of staff: 1 full-time professional; 2 part-time professional.
EIN: 237041310
Other changes: James C. Wood is no longer a trustee. Michael Culler, Emily Ebaugh, James R. Bard, David B. Brown, Allen Dean, Mark Miller, and E. Clifford Oberlin are no longer trustees.

2675
Building Healthy Lives Foundation
625 Eden Park Dr., Ste. 200
Cincinnati, OH 45202-6057 (513) 419-6587
Contact: Dianne Dunkelman, Pres.
***FAX:* (513) 241-2888;**
E-mail: kclark@clevercrazes.com; Main URL: http://www.clevercrazes.com/

Donors: Duke Energy; Carol Ann and Ralph V. Haile Jr. Foundation; JRO Charitable Lead Annuity Trust; The Kurzrok Foundation; National Speaking of Women's Health; The Selz Foundation, Inc.; Jodi Geiser.
Foundation type: Independent foundation.
Financial data (yr. ended 12/31/12): Assets, $43,945,859 (M); gifts received, $341,883; expenditures, $3,107,664; qualifying distributions, $430,425; giving activities include $430,425 for grants.
Fields of interest: Health care; Youth development; Human services.
Limitations: Applications accepted. Giving primarily in Cincinnati, OH.
Application information: Application form required.
Initial approach: Proposal
Deadline(s): None
Officers: Dianne Dunkelmann, Pres.; Lorrence Kellar, Secy.
Directors: Guy M. Hild; Sandra Lobert; Patricia Smitson.
EIN: 300214078

2676
Kenneth L. Calhoun Charitable Trust
4900 Tiedeman Rd., OH-01-49-0150
Brooklyn, OH 44144-2302
***Application address:* c/o Brian L. Cherkala, 219 S. Main St., Akron, OH 44308, tel.: (330) 258-4044**

Established in 1982 in OH.
Donor: Kenneth Calhoun†.
Foundation type: Independent foundation.
Financial data (yr. ended 07/31/13): Assets, $6,151,713 (M); expenditures, $315,920; qualifying distributions, $283,344; giving activities include $271,347 for 66 grants (high: $12,000; low: $1,250).
Purpose and activities: Giving primarily for the arts; as well as education, health organizations, and human services.
Fields of interest: Arts; Higher education; Education; Health organizations, association; Human services; Children/youth, services; Community/economic development.
Limitations: Applications accepted. Giving primarily in the greater Akron, OH, area with emphasis on Summit County. No grants to individuals.
Application information: Application form required.
Initial approach: Letter
Deadline(s): June 30
Trustee: KeyBank N.A.
EIN: 341370330

2677
Cardinal Health Foundation
c/o Community Rels.
7000 Cardinal Pl.
Dublin, OH 43017-1091 (614) 757-7481
Contact: Dianne Radigan, Dir., Community Rels.
E-mail: communityrelations@cardinalhealth.com; E-mail for Dianne Radigan: Dianne.Radigan@cardinalhealth.com; Main URL: http://www.cardinal.com/
Facebook: http://www.facebook.com/CardinalHealthFoundation
You Are Essential to Community: http://www.cardinal.com/us/en/community/documents/video/index.html

Established in 2000 in OH.
Donors: The Baxter Allegiance Foundation; Cardinal Health, Inc.; World Reach.
Foundation type: Company-sponsored foundation.
Financial data (yr. ended 06/30/13): Assets, $56,596,715 (M); gifts received, $4,000,000; expenditures, $8,505,722; qualifying distributions, $8,388,505; giving activities include $7,109,580 for 472 grants (high: $250,000; low: $63), and $829,342 for employee matching gifts.
Purpose and activities: The foundation supports healthcare programs designed to improve efficiency, enhance quality, and enable cost-effectiveness; increase awareness of prescription drug abuse; and build healthy communities.
Fields of interest: Education; Medical care, community health systems; Hospitals (general); Health care, clinics/centers; Pharmacy/prescriptions; Public health; Public health, physical fitness; Health care, patient services; Health care; Disasters, preparedness/services; Safety/disasters; Children; Youth; Aging.
Type of support: Continuing support; Program development; Conferences/seminars; Scholarship funds; Research; Employee volunteer services; Employee matching gifts; Employee-related scholarships; Donated products; In-kind gifts; Matching/challenge support.
Limitations: Applications accepted. Giving primarily in areas of company operations, with emphasis on Little Rock, AR, northern Chicago, Lake, and McHenry County, IL, Radcliff, KY, Albuquerque, NM, central OH, LaVergne, TN, El Paso, TX, PR, Kenosha County, WI; giving also to national organizations and internationally in China, Dominican Republic, and Mexico. No support for fraternal, athletic, or social clubs, member-based organizations, including chambers of commerce, rotary clubs, or IRS 501(c)(4) legions or associations, municipalities, including fire departments or police departments, organizations classified as IRS 509(a)(3), discriminatory organizations, organizations with divisive or litigious public agendas, religious organizations not of direct benefit to the entire community, sport teams, veterans', labor, or political organizations, private foundations or deferred giving trusts, marching bands, or youth clubs. No grants to individuals (except for employee-related scholarships), or for advertising, capital campaigns outside of Ohio, endowments, general operating support, debt reduction, political campaigns, athletic competitions, memberships, subscriptions, club dues, or travel; no loans.
Publications: Application guidelines; IRS Form 990 or 990-PF printed copy available upon request; Program policy statement.
Application information: Organizations receiving E3 Grants are asked to submit a mid-year progress report and a final report. Organizations receiving support for Prescription Drug Abuse and Misuse Prevention Grant Program are asked to participate in webinars or conference calls, submit a program/project evaluation, and submit a year-end summary report. Application form not required.
***Initial approach:* Complete online proposal for E3 Grants, Prescription Drug Abuse and Misuse Prevention Grant Program, and Essential to Wellness Grants**
***Deadline(s):* Dec. 7 for E3 Grants; Apr. 25 for Prescription Drug Abuse and Misuse Prevention Grant Program; Jan. 17 for Essential to Wellness Grants**
***Final notification:* Apr. for E3 Grants; May for Prescription Drug Abuse and Misuse Prevention Grant Program; Apr. for Essential to Wellness Grants**
Officers and Directors:* Shelley Bird,* Chair.; Tony Caprio,* Vice-Chair.; Stephen Falk,* Secy.; **Sam Samad, Treas.**; Lisa Ashby; Jon Giacomin; **Jorge Gomez**; Carole Watkins; Connie Woodburn.
EIN: 311746458
Other changes: Sam Samad has replaced Jorge Gomez as Treas.
Kelly Stover is no longer Sr. Grants Specialist.

2678
Charities Foundation
c/o Kathleen Matzinger
1 Michael Owens Way Plz. 1, 3rd Fl.
Perrysburg, OH 43551-2999

Established in 1937 in OH.
Donors: Owens-Illinois, Inc.; William E. Levis†; Harold Boeschenstein†.
Foundation type: Company-sponsored foundation.
Financial data (yr. ended 12/31/12): Assets, $157,500 (M); gifts received, $1,895,724; expenditures, $2,041,701; qualifying distributions,

$2,040,390; giving activities include $2,026,779 for 199 grants (high: $529,604; low: $25).
Purpose and activities: The foundation supports organizations involved with arts and culture, education, the environment, health, and human services.
Fields of interest: Visual arts; Museums (art); Performing arts, orchestras; Arts; Secondary school/education; Higher education; Scholarships/financial aid; Education, reading; Education; Environment, natural resources; Environment, beautification programs; Health care, clinics/centers; Health care; Children/youth, services; Homeless, human services; Human services; United Ways and Federated Giving Programs.
Type of support: General/operating support; Scholarship funds; Employee matching gifts; Matching/challenge support.
Limitations: Applications not accepted. Giving primarily in OH, with emphasis on Toledo. No grants to individuals, or for scholarships.
Application information: Contributes only to pre-selected organizations.
Officer: Catherine Neel, Treas.
Trustees: Jim Baehren; Stephen Bramlage.
Number of staff: 1 part-time support.
EIN: 346554560
Other changes: The grantmaker no longer lists a phone. The grantmaker no longer lists a primary contact.

2679
The Greater Cincinnati Foundation
200 W. 4th St.
Cincinnati, OH 45202-2775
Contact: For grants: Kay Pennington, Community Investment Coord.; Shiloh Turner, V.P., Community Investment
E-mail: info@gcfdn.org; Grant application e-mail: penningtonk@gcfdn.org; Main URL: http://www.gcfdn.org
Facebook: http://www.facebook.com/pages/The-Greater-Cincinnati-Foundation/107439465485
Flickr: http://www.flickr.com/photos/14141531@N08/sets/
LinkedIn: http://www.linkedin.com/companies/the-greater-cincinnati-foundation
Pinterest: http://www.pinterest.com/gcfdn/pins/
Twitter: http://twitter.com/GrCinciFdn/
YouTube: http://www.youtube.com/user/GCFonline

Established in 1963 in OH by bank resolution and declaration of trust.
Foundation type: Community foundation.
Financial data (yr. ended 12/31/13): Assets, $539,645,114 (M); gifts received, $75,478,707; expenditures, $76,142,312; giving activities include $69,133,479 for grants.
Purpose and activities: Grants for a broad range of existing activities in general categories of arts and culture, community progress, environmental needs, education, health, and social and human services, including youth agencies. The foundation actively seeks to promote access, equity and diversity, and to end discrimination based on race, ethnicity, gender, disability and age.
Fields of interest: Arts; Education, early childhood education; Education; Environment; Health care; Housing/shelter, home owners; Disasters, Hurricane Katrina; Children/youth, services; Human services; Community/economic development; Voluntarism promotion; Children/youth; Children; Youth; Adults; Aging; Young adults; Disabilities, people with; Physically disabled; Blind/visually impaired; Deaf/hearing impaired; Mentally disabled; Minorities; African Americans/Blacks; Hispanics/Latinos; Women; Men; Economically disadvantaged; Homeless.
Type of support: Capital campaigns; Building/renovation; Equipment; Emergency funds; Program development; Seed money; Technical assistance; Matching/challenge support.
Limitations: Applications accepted. Giving limited to southeastern IN, northern KY, and the greater Cincinnati, OH area. **No support for private or parochial religious purposes, units of government or government agencies, schools, hospitals, nursing homes, playgrounds, sports teams, or sports activities, or retirement centers.** No grants to individuals (except for scholarships), or for operating budgets, fundraising drives, event sponsorship, or underwriting, equipment, stand-alone publications or videos, annual campaigns, deficit financing, endowments, travel, fellowships, internships, exchange programs, or scholarly or medical research; no loans.
Publications: Application guidelines; Annual report (including application guidelines); Grants list; Informational brochure (including application guidelines); Newsletter.
Application information: Visit foundation web site for online application and guidelines per grant type. Application form required.
Initial approach: Visit web site or telephone
Copies of proposal: 1
Deadline(s): Varies
Board meeting date(s): Mar., June, Sept., and Dec.
Final notification: Varies
Officers and Governing Board:* Peter S. Strange,* Chair.; Dianne M. Rosenberg,* Vice-Chair.; Kathryn E. Merchant, C.E.O. and Pres.; Elizabeth Reiter Benson, V.P., Comms. and Mktg.; Amy L. Cheney, V.P., Giving Strategies; J. Scott McReynolds, V.P., Finance and Admin.; Shiloh Turner, V.P., Community Investment; Janis Holloway, Cont.; **Ronald C. Christian, Legal Counsel**; Calvin D. Buford; Neil Comber; Alva Jean Crawford; Thomas D. Croft; David Ellis III; Linda C. Fath; Christopher L. Fister; Wijdan Jreisat; Dr. Molly Katz; Janet B. Reid, Ph.D.; Ryan M. Rybolt; Charles R. Scheper; Ann M. Schwister; Patricia Mann Smitson.
Trustee Banks: Fifth Third Bank; The Huntington National Bank; JPMorgan Chase Bank, N.A.; KeyBank N.A.; LCNB National Bank; North Side Bank & Trust Co.; PNC Bank, N.A.; The Provident Bank; U.S. Bank, N.A.
Number of staff: 19 full-time professional; 10 full-time support; 1 part-time support.
EIN: 310669700
Other changes: Ronald C. Christian has replaced Daniel J. Hoffheimer as Legal Counsel.
Lori A. Beiler is now Sr. Grants Mgr. Melissa Krabbe is now Mgr., Acctg. Teri L. List-Stoll and Joseph P. Tomain are no longer members of the governing board.

2680
The Cincinnati Foundation for the Aged
2100 4th and Vine Twr.
5 W. 4th St.
Cincinnati, OH 45202-3604 (513) 381-6859
Contact: Heather Jansen

Established in 1891 in OH.
Donors: Oscar Cohrs†; Otto Luedeking†; William Meyer†; Oscar Cohrs Trust.
Foundation type: Independent foundation.
Financial data (yr. ended 03/31/13): Assets, $26,201,744 (M); gifts received, $260,420; expenditures, $1,187,341; qualifying distributions, $1,137,283; giving activities include $1,117,020 for 15 grants (high: $300,000; low: $4,000).
Purpose and activities: The sole purpose of the foundation is to assist indigent persons in the greater Cincinnati, OH, area, to gain admission to nonprofit nursing homes.
Fields of interest: Aging, centers/services; Aging.
Limitations: Giving primarily in the greater Cincinnati, OH, area; some funding also in KY. No grants to individuals.
Application information: Disbursements limited to the foundation's single mission described in Purpose & Activities; funding requests for studies or any other activity not eligible for consideration. Application form required.
Deadline(s): None
Board meeting date(s): Mar., June, Sept., and Dec.
Officers and Trustees:* Robert Porter III,* Pres.; Sr. Jean Marie Hoffman, 1st V.P.; **Gene Weber,* 2nd V.P.**; Heather Jansen, Secy.-Treas.; Jon Blohm; Boyd Colglazier; Thomas L. Finn; Jack Greer; Richard Hoefinghoff; Vince Hopkins; James Kemp; Robert C. Porter, Jr.; William H. Strietmann.
Number of staff: 1 full-time support.
EIN: 310536971
Other changes: Gene Weber has replaced Thomas Finn as 2nd V.P.

2681
The Cliffs Foundation
(formerly The Cleveland-Cliffs Foundation)
200 Public Sq., Ste. 3300
Cleveland, OH 44114-2315 (216) 694-5700
Contact: Kimberly Regan, Mgr., Public Affairs
E-mail: kimberly.regan@cliffsnr.com; **Main URL: http://www.cliffsnaturalresources.com/EN/CorpResponsibility/philanthropy/Pages/default.aspx**

Established in 1962 in OH.
Donors: Cleveland-Cliffs Inc.; Tilden Mining Co.; Empire Iron Mining Partnership; Hibbing Taconite Co.; Northshore Mining Co.; Cliffs Natural Resources.
Foundation type: Company-sponsored foundation.
Financial data (yr. ended 12/31/13): Assets, $4,927,062 (M); gifts received, $1,500,000; expenditures, $1,958,284; qualifying distributions, $1,958,284; giving activities include $1,903,276 for 122 grants (high: $200,000; low: $500), and $54,274 for 42 employee matching gifts.
Purpose and activities: The foundation supports programs designed to promote healthy communities and vibrant communities through economic development, environmental stewardship, community services, and arts and culture. Special emphasis is directed toward education programs associated with mining and related technology.
Fields of interest: Museums (science/technology); Performing arts, theater; Performing arts, orchestras; Arts; Secondary school/education; Higher education; Education; Hospitals (general); Health care; Boys & girls clubs; American Red Cross; Children/youth, services; Human services; United Ways and Federated Giving Programs; Geology; Engineering/technology; Public affairs; Economically disadvantaged.
Type of support: General/operating support; Annual campaigns; Capital campaigns; Building/renovation; Scholarship funds; Employee matching gifts; Employee-related scholarships.

Limitations: Applications accepted. Giving primarily in areas of company operations, with emphasis on northwest AL, the upper MI peninsula, northeastern MN, Cleveland, OH, and southern WV. No support for political candidates or organizations, for-profit organizations, or discriminatory organizations. No grants to individuals, or for membership drives, or travel; no loans.
Publications: Application guidelines.
Application information: No solicitations made by telephone or in person will be accepted. Organizations receiving support are asked to submit interim reports and a final report. Support is limited to 1 contribution per organization during any given year. Application form not required.
Initial approach: Download application form and mail or e-mail application and proposal to foundation or local public affairs representative
Copies of proposal: 1
Deadline(s): June 1
Board meeting date(s): Annually
Officers and Trustees:* P. Kelly Tompkins,* Pres.; Raga S. Elim, V.P.; Traci L. Forrester, Secy.-Treas.; Gary B. Halverson; James R. Michaud.
EIN: 346525124

2682
Community Foundation for Crawford County
(formerly Bucyrus Area Community Foundation)
254 E. Mansfield St.
Bucyrus, OH 44820 **(419) 562-3958**
E-mail: info@cfcrawford.org; Main URL: http://cfcrawford.org/
E-Newsletter: http://cfcrawford.org/newsletter
Facebook: https://www.facebook.com/bacfoundation
Twitter: http://twitter.com/bacfoundation
YouTube: http://www.youtube.com/user/bucyrusfoundation

Established in 1985 in OH.
Foundation type: Community foundation.
Financial data (yr. ended 12/31/12): Assets, $12,582,798 (M); gifts received, $334,518; expenditures, $913,709; giving activities include $518,263 for 24 grants (high: $190,972), and $5,700 for 6 grants to individuals.
Purpose and activities: As a catalyst, the foundation works to enhance the quality of life for all residents of Crawford County by: 1) offering a flexible vehicle that assures donors' charitable interests and goals are realized; 2) offering support (financial, expert/technical assistance) in response to emerging community needs; and 3) standing ready to partner with community organizations and collaboratives in support of promising innovations.
Fields of interest: Arts; Education; Environment; Health care; Recreation; Family services; Residential/custodial care, hospices; Human services; Community/economic development; Computer science; Youth.
Type of support: Annual campaigns; Building/renovation; Equipment; Emergency funds; Program development; Scholarship funds; Scholarships—to individuals; Matching/challenge support.
Limitations: Applications accepted. Giving limited to the Crawford County, OH, area (except for the Galion area including Polk Township). No support for sectarian religious purposes (except for designated grants). No grants to individuals (including graduate fellowships and travel grants to individuals, except for designated grants), or for operating funds, annual campaigns, research, or endowment programs; no loans.
Publications: Annual report; Financial statement; Grants list; Informational brochure (including application guidelines); Multi-year report.
Application information: Applications also available in Word format to be downloaded and e-mailed to foundation; visit foundation web site for application and guidelines. Application form required.
Initial approach: Complete online grant application
***Deadline(s):* Dec. 31 and Aug. 20**
Board meeting date(s): 6 times a year
Final notification: Mar. and Oct.
Officers and Trustees:* Tim Stenson,* Chair.; Janet P. Pry,* Pres.; Valerie Sanderson,* V.P.; Michael Dostal,* Secy.; Roger Miller,* Treas.; Annie Carter; Bob Hiltbrand; Janel Hord; **Justin McMullen**; Rick Niese; Mike Romanoff; Judi Saurers; Brad Starkey.
Number of staff: 1 part-time professional; 1 part-time support.
EIN: 341465822
Other changes: Tim Stenson is now Chair.

2683
The Community Foundation of Lorain County
(formerly The Community Foundation of Greater Lorain County)
9080 Leavitt Rd.
Elyria, OH 44035 (440) 984-7390
Contact: Brian R. Frederick, C.E.O.; For grants: Linda Ong Styer, Sr. Prog. Off.
FAX: (440) 984-7399;
E-mail: info@peoplewhocare.org; Additional e-mail: bfrederick@peoplewhocare.org; Grant inquiry e-mail: lsyter@peoplewhocare.org; Main URL: http://www.peoplewhocare.org
Facebook: http://www.facebook.com/pages/Community-Foundation-of-Lorain-County/260644913281
Flickr: http://www.flickr.com//photos/peoplewhocare/
LinkedIn: http://www.linkedin.com//company/community-foundation-of-lorain-county
Twitter: https://twitter.com/connectcarematr
YouTube: http://www.youtube.com/user/ConnectCareMatter

Incorporated in 1980 in OH.
Foundation type: Community foundation.
Financial data (yr. ended 12/31/12): Assets, $88,644,009 (M); gifts received, $3,250,810; expenditures, $4,514,514; giving activities include $4,500,728 for grants.
Purpose and activities: The foundation seeks to improve the quality of life and to instill a greater sense of unity in the Greater Lorain County community by mobilizing individuals to become active partners in building a better community; providing a permanent instrument for receiving and managing charitable gifts and bequests; supporting innovative programs and acting as a catalyst in identifying problems and sharing information with individuals, other foundations, corporations, and organizations; and exercising and promoting leadership in meeting the changing needs and opportunities of the entire community.
Fields of interest: Arts; Education; Environment; Health care; Health organizations, association; Human services; Community development, neighborhood development; Economic development; Children/youth; Youth; Asians/Pacific Islanders; African Americans/Blacks; Hispanics/Latinos; Women.
Type of support: General/operating support; Program development; Seed money; Scholarship funds; Technical assistance; Scholarships—to individuals; Matching/challenge support.
Limitations: Applications accepted. Giving primarily in Lorain County, OH. No support for religious purposes, street repair, government services, public or non-public school services required by law, or self-help clubs that meet the needs of a small population. No grants to individuals (except for scholarships), or for annual campaigns, medical research, deficit financing, membership fees, tickets for benefits, tours, equipment, group travel, or capital campaigns; no loans.
Publications: Application guidelines; Annual report (including application guidelines); Financial statement; Informational brochure (including application guidelines); Newsletter; Program policy statement.
Application information: Grantseekers should contact the Sr. Prog. Off. to discuss the proposal before submitting an application. Visit foundation web site for application form and guidelines. Application form required.
Initial approach: Letter or telephone
Copies of proposal: 2
Deadline(s): Feb. 1 and July 1 for general grants
Board meeting date(s): Bimonthly
Final notification: July and Dec. for general grants
Officers and Directors:* Jim Vandemark,* Chair.; Tim Harris,* Vice-Chair.; Brian R. Frederick,* C.E.O. and Pres.; Sandhya Subramanian,* Secy.; Susan J. Bowers,* Treas.; Cheryl McKenna,* C.F.O.; Farnaz Ansari-Berna,* Chair., Grants Comm.; Sharon Furcron,* Chair., Governance Comm.; Karen Wells,* Chair., Advancement Comm.; Joel Arrendondo; J. Lawry Babitt; Raymond L. Cushing; Chris Bellamy; Kevin Donovan; Joseph F. Miclat; Ruth Miller; Morgan Parsons; Kris Putnam-Walkerly; Margarita Quinones; Samuel Speck III; Eric Woidke.
Number of staff: 7 full-time professional; 3 full-time support.
EIN: 341322781
Other changes: Thomas Biery is no longer a member of the governing body.

2684
The Community Foundation of Shelby County
(formerly The Community Foundation of Sidney and Shelby County)
100 S. Main Ave., Ste. 202
Sidney, OH 45365-2771 (937) 497-7800
Contact: Marian Spicer, Exec. Dir.
FAX: (937) 497-7799;
E-mail: mspicer@commfoun.com; Additional e-mail: info@commfoun.com; Main URL: http://www.commfoun.com
Facebook: https://www.facebook.com/CommunityFoundationofShelbyCountyOhio

Incorporated in 1952 in OH.
Foundation type: Community foundation.
Financial data (yr. ended 12/31/12): Assets, $18,404,283 (M); gifts received, $1,602,410; expenditures, $1,102,001; giving activities include $757,889 for 30+ grants (high: $119,911), and $111,590 for 134 grants to individuals.
Purpose and activities: The foundation seeks to cultivate, administer, and distribute legacy gifts for the benefit of the community. Primary areas of giving include: Arts and Culture, Family and Community, Education, Environment, and Health.
Fields of interest: Arts; Education; Environment, natural resources; Environment, beautification programs; Environment; Health care; Health organizations, association; Recreation; Family

services; Human services; Community/economic development.
Type of support: Capital campaigns; Equipment; Program development; Seed money; Scholarship funds; Scholarships—to individuals.
Limitations: Applications accepted. Giving limited to Shelby County, OH, and surrounding areas. No support for religious organizations for religious purposes. No grants to individuals (except for scholarships), or for endowments, fundraising campaigns from existing organizations, specific scientific, medical, or academic research, or general operating expenses.
Publications: Annual report; Informational brochure; Newsletter.
Application information: Visit foundation web site for preliminary grant proposal form and guidelines. Preliminary grant proposal form and proposals will not be accepted if applicant has not discussed grant request with foundation staff. Application form required.
Initial approach: Telephone
Copies of proposal: 7
***Deadline(s):* Mar. 20 for preliminary grant proposal and scholarships; May 15 for full proposal**
Board meeting date(s): Bimonthly
Final notification: June
Officers and Trustees:* Priscilla Wilt,* Chair.; Rudy Keister,* Vice-Chair.; Ken Monnier,* Secy.; Andy Counts,* Treas.; Marian Spicer, Exec. Dir.; Carol Bennett; **Doug Borchers**; Jerry Doerger; **Aaron Koenig**; Mardie Milligan; Norm Smith.
Number of staff: 1 part-time professional; 1 part-time support.
EIN: 346565194
Other changes: Keith Daniel is no longer a trustee.

2685
Community Foundation of the Mahoning Valley
201 E. Commerce St., Ste. 150
Youngstown, OH 44503 (330) 743-5555
Contact: Shari Harrell, Pres.
FAX: (330) 743-1802; E-mail: info@cfmv.org; Additional e-mail: sharrell@cfmv.org; Main URL: http://www.cfmv.org

Established in 1999 in OH.
Foundation type: Community foundation.
Financial data (yr. ended 06/30/12): Assets, $12,398,670 (M); gifts received, $2,198,898; expenditures, $1,238,615; giving activities include $967,635 for 54+ grants (high: $100,000).
Purpose and activities: The mission of the foundation is to attract and invest permanent resources, with the purpose of enhancing the quality of life for the residents of the Mahoning Valley and future generations, in accordance with the charitable intentions of its donors.
Fields of interest: Humanities; Historic preservation/historical societies; Arts; Education; Environment; Animals/wildlife; Health care; Recreation; Children/youth, services; Aging, centers/services; Human services; Economic development; Science, research; Religion.
Type of support: General/operating support; Continuing support; Capital campaigns; Building/renovation; Equipment; Endowments; Program development; Technical assistance; Matching/challenge support.
Limitations: Applications accepted. Giving limited to Mahoning County and Trumbull County, OH.
Publications: Application guidelines; Annual report; Financial statement; Grants list; Informational brochure; Newsletter.
Application information: Visit foundation web site for additional information. Application form required.
***Initial approach:* Create online profile**
Deadline(s): Jan. 1, Apr. 1, July 1, and Oct. 1
Board meeting date(s): Mar., June, Sept., and Dec.
Final notification: 2 months
Officers and Directors:* Shelley Taylor Odille,* Chair.; Jerry Bryan,* Vice-Chair.; Shari Harrell, Pres.; Julie Scarsella, V.P.; **Gordon B. Wean,* Secy.**; Trinette Simon,* Treas.; **Bruce R. Beeghly**; Gloria Cagigas; Kevin Y.T. Chiu; **Brian R. Corbin**; Phillip Dennison; Hon. Douglas Franklin; David J. Kostolansky; Patrice Kouvas; Diane Sauer; Hon. Diane S. A. Vettori.
Number of staff: 3 part-time professional; 1 full-time support.
EIN: 341904353
Other changes: Shelley Taylor Odille has replaced Phillip Dennison as Chair. Jerry Bryan has replaced Shelley Taylor Odille as Vice-Chair. Gordon B. Wean has replaced Thomas Humphries as Secy. Trinette Simon is now Treas.

2686
Coshocton Foundation
220 S. 4th St.
P.O. Box 55
Coshocton, OH 43812-2019 (740) 622-0010
Contact: Kathy Thompson, Exec. Dir.
FAX: (740) 622-1660;
E-mail: kthompson@coshoctonfoundation.org; Main URL: http://www.coshoctonfoundation.org

Established in 1966 in OH.
Donors: Adolph Golden†; Fred Johnston; Edward E. Montgomery†; Edith Schooler†; Seward Schooler†; Mary F. Taylor; Robert M. Thomas; Willard Baughman†; Willard S. Breon; James E. Wilson†; Herbert E. Carlson†; Ralph Wisenburg; Richard Barthebaug; Mrs. Richard Barthebaug; Ed Mulligan; Marion Mulligan Sutton.
Foundation type: Community foundation.
Financial data (yr. ended 09/30/12): Assets, $25,437,563 (M); gifts received, $1,716,723; expenditures, $779,241; giving activities include $341,955 for grants, and $197,524 for grants to individuals.
Purpose and activities: The mission of the foundation is to provide a community controlled organization dedicated to the betterment and long term development of Coshocton County's natural, community, and human resources.
Fields of interest: Museums; Performing arts, dance; Arts; Child development, education; Secondary school/education; Higher education; Education; Hospitals (general); Health care; Substance abuse, services; Mental health/crisis services; Alcoholism; Crime/law enforcement; Safety/disasters; Athletics/sports, water sports; Youth development, services; Youth development, citizenship; Children/youth, services; Child development, services; Community/economic development; Government/public administration; Public affairs, citizen participation; Leadership development.
Type of support: Continuing support; Capital campaigns; Building/renovation; Equipment; Program development; Conferences/seminars; Seed money; Curriculum development; Scholarship funds; Employee matching gifts; Scholarships—to individuals; Matching/challenge support.
Limitations: Applications accepted. Giving limited to Coshocton County, OH.
Publications: Application guidelines; Annual report; Financial statement; Informational brochure (including application guidelines); Newsletter; Occasional report.
Application information: Visit foundation web site for application form, guidelines, and specific deadlines. Application form required.
Initial approach: Complete online application
Copies of proposal: 7
Deadline(s): One week before quarterly meeting
Board meeting date(s): Quarterly
Final notification: 45 days after receipt
Officers and Trustees:* Catherine Miller,* Pres.; Joe Skelton,* V.P.; Beccy Porteus,* Secy.; Kathy Thompson,* Treas. and Exec. Dir.; Sally Bullens; **Barbara Brooks Emmons**; Bruce Wallace.
Distribution Committee: William Brown, Chair., Distrib. Comm.; Greg Coffman; Steve Foster; Lisa Gibson; Rex Snyder.
Investment Committee: Steve Nelson, Chair., Investment Comm.; Preston Bair; Michael Baker; Richard Tompkins; Tim Vance.
Number of staff: 1 full-time professional; 1 full-time support.
EIN: 316064567
Other changes: William Brown has replaced Rick Davis as Chair., Distrib. Comm. Steve Nelson has replaced Richard Baker as Chair., Investment Comm.

2687
Charles H. Dater Foundation, Inc.
302 Gwynne Bldg.
602 Main St., Ste. 302
Cincinnati, OH 45202-2534 (513) 241-2658
Contact: Bruce A. Krone, Secy.
FAX: (513) 241-2731;
E-mail: info@DaterFoundation.org; **E-mail for Grants Coordinator, Beth Broomall: bb@DaterFoundation.org**; Main URL: http://www.daterfoundation.org
E-Newsletter: http://www.daterfoundation.org/newsletter.php

Established in 1985 in OH.
Donor: Charles H. Dater†.
Foundation type: Independent foundation.
Financial data (yr. ended 08/31/13): Assets, $44,474,427 (M); expenditures, $2,091,994; qualifying distributions, $1,893,762; giving activities include $1,501,026 for 111 grants (high: $50,000; low: $1,000).
Purpose and activities: The foundation makes grants to private, nonprofit organizations and public agencies in Greater Cincinnati, Ohio, for programs that benefit children in the region in the areas of arts/culture, education, health care, social services and other community needs.
Fields of interest: Historic preservation/historical societies; Arts; Child development, education; Higher education; Libraries/library science; Education; Hospitals (general); Medical care, rehabilitation; Crime/violence prevention, youth; Recreation; Human services; Children/youth, services; Child development, services; Family services; Christian agencies & churches; Disabilities, people with; Economically disadvantaged.
Type of support: General/operating support; Continuing support; Annual campaigns; Building/renovation; Equipment; Program development; Seed money; Scholarship funds; Consulting services.
Limitations: Giving primarily in the greater Cincinnati, OH, area. No grants to individuals, or for scholarships, debt reduction, or for capital projects.

Publications: Application guidelines; Annual report; Multi-year report.
Application information: Application guidelines and form available on foundation web site. Application form required.
Initial approach: Refer to online application process on foundation web site
Copies of proposal: 6
Deadline(s): None
Board meeting date(s): Monthly
Final notification: Within 2 months
Officers and Directors:* Bruce A. Krone,* Pres. and Secy.; Roger L. Ruhl,* V.P.; Stanley J. "Jack" Frank, Jr.,* Treas.; Dorothy G. Krone, Dir. Emeritus; Amanda Prebble Lenhart.
EIN: 311150951
Other changes: John D. Silvati is no longer a V.P. The grantmaker now makes its application guidelines available online.

2688
The Dayton Power and Light Company Foundation

1065 Woodman Dr.
Dayton, OH 45432-1423 (937) 259-7925
Main URL: http://www.dpandl.com/about-dpl/who-we-are/community-investments/

Established in 1985 in OH.
Donor: The Dayton Power and Light Co.
Foundation type: Company-sponsored foundation.
Financial data (yr. ended 12/31/12): Assets, $27,084,620 (M); expenditures, $1,275,644; qualifying distributions, $1,244,380; giving activities include $1,190,295 for 95 grants (high: $135,000; low: $50).
Purpose and activities: The foundation supports food banks and festivals and organizations involved with arts and culture, health, human services, community economic development, civic affairs, and youth.
Fields of interest: Performing arts; Arts; Secondary school/education; Higher education; Education; Health care; Food banks; Recreation, fairs/festivals; Big Brothers/Big Sisters; Boy scouts; Girl scouts; American Red Cross; Salvation Army; Human services; Community development, business promotion; Community/economic development; United Ways and Federated Giving Programs; Public affairs; Youth.
Type of support: General/operating support; Continuing support; Program development; Employee volunteer services.
Limitations: Applications accepted. Giving in areas of company operations in west central OH. No support for religious, fraternal, labor, or veterans' organizations, national organizations, or sports leagues. No grants to individuals, or for capital campaigns, endowments or development campaigns, general operating support for hospitals, or telephone or mass mail solicitations.
Publications: Application guidelines; Informational brochure (including application guidelines).
Application information: Application form not required.
Initial approach: Proposal
Copies of proposal: 1
Deadline(s): None
Board meeting date(s): Quarterly
Officers and Directors:* Daniel J. McCabe, Pres.; Joe Mulpas, Treas.; Tom Raga, Exec. Dir.; Paul R. Bishop; Scott J. Kelly; Tim Rice; Ned J. Sifferlen.
Number of staff: 1 full-time professional.
EIN: 311138883
Other changes: The grantmaker no longer lists a fax.

2689
Delaware County Foundation

(formerly Community Fdn. of Delaware County)
3954 N. Hampton Dr.
Powell, OH 43065-8430 (614) 764-2332
FAX: (614) 764-2333;
E-mail: foundation@delawarecf.org; Main URL: http://www.delawarecf.org
Facebook: https://www.facebook.com/pages/Delaware-County-Foundation/191663982236
Flickr: http://www.flickr.com/photos/communityfoundationofdelawarecounty/

Established in 1995 in OH.
Foundation type: Community foundation.
Financial data (yr. ended 12/31/12): Assets, $8,169,147 (M); gifts received, $573,841; expenditures, $934,567; giving activities include $493,440 for 8 grants (high: $354,137), and $159,300 for 94 grants to individuals.
Purpose and activities: The foundation seeks to provide for various charitable, cultural, educational and community purposes in Delaware County, OH. Also provides scholarships to college students.
Fields of interest: Arts; Scholarships/financial aid; Education; Environment; Health care; Human services; Community/economic development; Public affairs.
Type of support: Continuing support; Capital campaigns; Building/renovation; Equipment; Program development; Seed money; Scholarship funds; Scholarships—to individuals; Matching/challenge support.
Limitations: Applications accepted. Giving limited to Delaware County, OH. No support for religious purposes. **No grants to individuals (except for scholarships), or for deficit reduction, internships, operating expenses, or special fundraising events.**
Publications: Application guidelines; Financial statement; Grants list; Informational brochure; Newsletter; Occasional report.
Application information: Visit foundation web site for grant application Cover Sheet and guidelines. Application form required.
Initial approach: Letter and proposal
Copies of proposal: 2
Deadline(s): Sept. 3 for grants; Mar. and June for scholarships
Board meeting date(s): 2nd Wed. of every other month
Final notification: 60-90 days
Officers and Directors:* Michael Tarullo,* Chair.; Skip Weiler,* Vice-Chair.; Marlene A. Casini,* C.E.O. and Pres.; Jane Martin,* Secy.; Rev. Dr. Norman Dewire,* Treas.; Stephen D. Martin, Emeritus; E. Jane Van Fossen, Emeritus; Mark Bergstedt; Susan Hatcher; Wayne Jenkins, Esq.; Rockwell Jones; Thomas Louden; Sue Mahler; Traci Martinez, Esq.; Susan Robenalt; David Smith, M.D.; Matt Weller.
Number of staff: 1 full-time professional; 2 part-time support.
EIN: 311450786

2690
Roderick H. Dillon, Jr. Foundation

Columbus, OH

The foundation terminated in 2011.

2691
Corinne L. Dodero Trust for the Arts and Sciences

P.O. Box 127
Rome, OH **44085-0127**

Established in 1998 in FL.
Donor: Samuel J. Frankino.
Foundation type: Independent foundation.
Financial data (yr. ended 03/31/13): Assets, $10,630,715 (M); expenditures, $661,929; qualifying distributions, $547,489; giving activities include $475,730 for 92 grants (high: $75,000; low: $75).
Purpose and activities: Giving primarily for health organizations and human services; funding also for education, and children and youth services.
Fields of interest: Arts; Secondary school/education; Education; Hospitals (general); Health organizations, association; Medical research, institute; Human services; American Red Cross; Children/youth, services.
Type of support: General/operating support; Building/renovation; Program development; Research.
Limitations: Applications not accepted. No grants to individuals.
Application information: Contributes only to pre-selected organizations.
Trustees: Corinne L. Dodero; Lorraine C. Dodero; William Dodero.
EIN: 656239071

2692
The Eaton Charitable Fund

c/o Eaton Corp.
1111 Superior Ave.
Cleveland, OH 44114-2584 (216) 523-4944
Contact: William B. Doggett, Sr. V.P., Public and Community Affairs
FAX: (216) 479-7013;
E-mail: barrydoggett@eaton.com; Main URL: http://www.eaton.com/Eaton/OurCompany/Sustainability/SustainablePractices/Community/index.htm
RSS Feed: http://www.eaton.com/EatonCom/OurCompany/NewsandEvents/NewsList/index.htm?category=Community

Trust established in 1953 in OH.
Donor: Eaton Corp.
Foundation type: Company-sponsored foundation.
Financial data (yr. ended 12/31/12): Assets, $1,768,286 (M); gifts received, $7,000,000; expenditures, $7,675,417; qualifying distributions, $7,673,629; giving activities include $7,667,833 for 1,528 grants (high: $200,000; low: $25).
Purpose and activities: The fund supports organizations involved with arts and culture, education, health, cancer, housing, disaster relief, human services, and community development. Special emphasis is directed toward organizations with which employees of Eaton are involved.
Fields of interest: Museums (art); Performing arts, theater; Performing arts, orchestras; Arts; Secondary school/education; Higher education; Education; Hospitals (general); Health care, patient services; Health care; Cancer; Housing/shelter, development; Housing/shelter; Disasters, preparedness/services; Youth development, business; American Red Cross; Salvation Army; YM/YWCAs & YM/YWHAs; Children/youth, services; Family services; Human services; Community/economic development; United Ways and Federated Giving Programs.

Type of support: General/operating support; Continuing support; Capital campaigns; Building/renovation; Equipment; Program development; Scholarship funds; Employee volunteer services; Employee matching gifts; In-kind gifts; Matching/challenge support.
Limitations: Applications accepted. Giving on a national and international basis in areas of company operations. No support for religious organizations not of direct benefit to the entire community; fraternal or labor organizations. No grants to individuals, or for endowments, medical research, general operating support for United Way agencies or hospitals, or debt reduction, fundraising events, or sponsorships; no loans.
Publications: Application guidelines; Corporate giving report; Informational brochure (including application guidelines).
Application information: Cover letter should be submitted using organization letterhead. Proposals should be no longer than 1 to 3 pages. Support is limited to 1 contribution per organization during any given year. Multi-year funding is not automatic. Video and audio submissions are not encouraged. Application form not required.
***Initial approach:* Cover letter and proposal to nearest company facility or human resources manager**
Copies of proposal: 1
Deadline(s): None
Board meeting date(s): Bimonthly
Final notification: 2 to 3 months
Directors: Cynthia Brabander; William B. Doggett; Trent M. Meyerhoefer.
Trustee: KeyBank N.A.
Number of staff: None.
EIN: 346501856
Other changes: James W. McGill and Kurt B. McMakens are no longer directors.

2693
The Cyrus Eaton Foundation
The Heights Rockefeller Bldg.
2475 Lee Blvd., Ste. 2B
Cleveland Heights, OH 44118-1214 (216) 320-2285
FAX: (216) 320-2287;
E-mail: cyrus.eaton.foundation@deepcove.org; Main URL: http://www.deepcove.org
Grants List: http://www.deepcove.org/Grants/pastyeargrants.html

Established in 1955 in DE.
Foundation type: Independent foundation.
Financial data (yr. ended 12/31/12): Assets, $3,076,983 (M); expenditures, $187,867; qualifying distributions, $180,731; giving activities include $144,675 for 51 grants (high: $3,500; low: $1,000).
Purpose and activities: Giving primarily to support non-profit organizations in Cleveland and northeast Ohio whose programs enhance the quality of life in the area, and whose aims are in accord with Cyrus Eaton, the founder of the foundation.
Fields of interest: Arts; Education; Environment, natural resources; Environment; Human services; International peace/security; Community/economic development; Public affairs.
International interests: Canada.
Type of support: General/operating support; Endowments; Program development; Seed money.
Limitations: Applications accepted. Giving primarily in OH, with emphasis on Cleveland. No support for municipalities or organizations lacking 501(c)(3) status. No grants to individuals, or for tickets or tables for events.
Application information: See foundation web site for complete guidelines. Application form required.
Initial approach: Cover letter (no more than 2 pages)
Copies of proposal: 1
***Deadline(s):* Oct. 31**
Board meeting date(s): Oct.
Final notification: Following board meeting
Officers and Trustees:* Raymond Szabo,* Pres.; Catherine I. Eaton,* V.P.; Alice J. Gulick,* Secy.; Henry W. Gulick,* Treas.; Ralph P. Higgins; Pamela Niedes.
Number of staff: 1 part-time support.
EIN: 237440277

2694
The Thomas J. Emery Memorial
200 W. 4th St.
Cincinnati, OH 45202-2775 (513) 241-2880
Contact: Jennie Geisheimer
Facebook: http://www.facebook.com/gcfdn
RSS Feed: http://www.gcfdn.org/DesktopModules/DNNArticle/DNNArticleRSS.aspx?moduleid=691&tabid=163&categoryid=4
Twitter: http://twitter.com/grcincifdn

Incorporated in 1925 in OH.
Donor: Mary Muhlenberg Emery‡.
Foundation type: Independent foundation.
Financial data (yr. ended 12/31/12): Assets, $24,955,238 (M); expenditures, $1,097,284; qualifying distributions, $955,780; giving activities include $861,000 for 59 grants (high: $80,000; low: $500).
Purpose and activities: The purpose of the foundation is to secure a citizenry which shall be more sane, sound and effective because of more satisfactory initial conditions of environment and education. The foundation is used for the physical, social, civic and educational betterment of individuals.
Fields of interest: Performing arts; Arts; Elementary/secondary education; Higher education; Health care; Human services.
Type of support: Equipment; Capital campaigns; Building/renovation; Program development.
Limitations: Applications accepted. Giving primarily in the greater Cincinnati area, including Hamilton, Butler, Clermont and Warren counties in OH, and Boone, Campbell and Kenton counties in KY. No support for non 501(c)(3) organizations. No grants to individuals, or for continuing support or conferences; no loans.
Publications: Application guidelines.
Application information: For application information, see the Memorial page on The Greater Cincinnati Foundation web site www.gcfdn.org. Application form required.
Board meeting date(s): Apr. and Nov.
Officers and Trustees:* Lee A. Carter,* Pres.; John F. Barrett,* V.P.; Michael A. Hirschfeld,* Secy.; Thomas L. Williams,* Treas.; John T. Lawrence III.
EIN: 310536711

2695
The Thomas J. Evans Foundation
36 N. 2nd St.
Newark, OH 43055-5610
***Contact:* Sarah R. Wallace**

Established in 1965 in OH.
Donors: Thomas J. Evans‡; Dan Evans; Peggy Evans.
Foundation type: Independent foundation.
Financial data (yr. ended 10/31/13): Assets, $24,842,322 (M); gifts received, $350; expenditures, $562,658; qualifying distributions, $734,719; giving activities include $300,000 for 2 grants (high: $250,000; low: $50,000).
Purpose and activities: Giving primarily for education.
Fields of interest: Higher education; Education; Human services.
Type of support: Capital campaigns; General/operating support; Building/renovation; Seed money; Scholarship funds.
Limitations: Applications accepted. Giving primarily in the Licking County, OH, area. No grants to individuals.
Application information: Application form not required.
Initial approach: Letter
Deadline(s): None
Board meeting date(s): Quarterly
Officers: J. Gilbert Reese, Chair. and C.E.O.; Sarah Wallace, Pres. and Secy.; Louella H. Reese, V.P. and Treas.
Trustees: Sally W. Heckman; Gilbert H. Reese; John H. Wallace.
EIN: 316055767

2696
Fairfield County Foundation
162 E. Main St.
P.O. Box 159
Lancaster, OH 43130-3712 (740) 654-8451
Contact: Amy Eyman, Exec. Dir.
FAX: (740) 654-3971;
E-mail: aeyman@fairfieldcountyfoundation.org; Main URL: http://www.fairfieldcountyfoundation.org
Scholarship inquiry e-mail: mfarrow@fairfieldcountyfoundation.org

Established in 1989 in OH.
Foundation type: Community foundation.
Financial data (yr. ended 12/31/12): Assets, $32,393,126 (M); gifts received, $2,442,473; expenditures, $1,888,542; giving activities include $652,471 for 32+ grants (high: $46,200), and $505,342 for 280 grants to individuals.
Purpose and activities: The foundation was created to receive and administer charitable gifts that will provide long-term, continuing benefits to Fairfield County and its residents by supporting educational, scientific, cultural, social, environmental, medical and other charitable purposes.
Fields of interest: Arts; Education, early childhood education; Elementary/secondary school reform; Education, continuing education; Education; Environment, beautification programs; Environment; Hospitals (general); Health care; Mental health/crisis services; Health organizations, association; Employment; Housing/shelter; Recreation; Children/youth, services; Aging, centers/services; Human services; Community/economic development; Infants/toddlers; Children/youth; Children; Youth; Adults; Aging; Young adults; Disabilities, people with; Physically disabled; Blind/visually impaired; Deaf/hearing impaired; Mentally disabled; Minorities; Women; Infants/toddlers, female; Girls; Adults, women; Young adults, female; Men; Infants/toddlers, male; Boys; Adults, men; Young adults, male; Military/veterans; Substance abusers; Single parents; Crime/abuse victims; Terminal illness, people with; Economically disadvantaged; Homeless.
Type of support: Management development/capacity building; Land acquisition; General/operating support; Endowments; Employee-related scholarships; Emergency funds; Continuing support;

Capital campaigns; Building/renovation; Equipment; Program development; Publication; Seed money; Curriculum development; Scholarship funds; Technical assistance; Scholarships—to individuals; Matching/challenge support.
Limitations: Applications accepted. Giving limited to Fairfield County, OH. No support for religious organizations for religious purposes, or for specific scientific, medical or academic research. No grants to individuals (except for scholarships), or for general operating expenses of existing organizations, endowments, annual fundraising campaigns, debt retirement, or vehicles.
Publications: Application guidelines; Annual report; Financial statement; Grants list; Informational brochure; Informational brochure (including application guidelines); Newsletter.
Application information: Visit foundation web site for preliminary grant proposal form and guidelines. Based on the preliminary application, the foundation's Grants Committee will confirm if project fits within the foundation's guidelines and invite the applicant to submit a full proposal. Applications submitted by e-mail or fax not accepted. Application form required.
Initial approach: Telephone
Copies of proposal: 3
Deadline(s): 2nd Mon. in Mar. or Aug. for preliminary application; 2nd Mon. in May or Oct. for full proposal
Board meeting date(s): 3rd Thurs. in Jan., Mar., May, July, Sept., and Nov.
Final notification: 2 weeks for preliminary application response
Officers and Trustees:* Judy Root,* Chair.; James Barrett, M.D.*, Vice-Chair.; Matthew E. Johnson,* Secy.; Sheila Heath,* Treas.; Amy Eyman, Exec. Dir.; John Baughman; Jonathan Clark; Terry McGhee; **Andrew Ogilvie**; Brian Shonk; Kamilla Sigafoos; James Smith; Howard Sniderman; Gary Taylor; Richard Warner; Penny Wasem.
Number of staff: 1 full-time professional; 2 part-time professional; 1 part-time support.
EIN: 341623983
Other changes: James Barrett and Matthew E. Johnson are no longer trustees.

2697

Ferro Foundation

6060 Parkland Blvd.
Mayfield Heights, OH 44124 (216) 641-8580
***Main URL:* http://www.ferro.com/**

Incorporated in 1959 in OH.
Donor: Ferro Corp.
Foundation type: Company-sponsored foundation.
Financial data (yr. ended 04/30/13): Assets, $40,080 (M); gifts received, $200,000; expenditures, $186,434; qualifying distributions, $183,284; giving activities include $183,284 for 31 grants (high: $45,000; low: $1,000).
Purpose and activities: The foundation supports organizations involved with arts and culture, education, health and welfare, and community development. Special emphasis is directed toward programs designed to promote human services and civic development.
Fields of interest: Arts; Higher education; Education; Health care; Human services; Community/economic development; United Ways and Federated Giving Programs; Public affairs.
Type of support: Program development; General/operating support; Annual campaigns; Capital campaigns; Building/renovation.
Limitations: Applications accepted. Giving primarily in areas of company operations, with emphasis on the greater Cleveland, OH area. No support for religious, political, lobbying, or labor organizations. No grants to individuals.
Publications: Application guidelines.
Application information: Application form required.
***Initial approach:* Letter**
Deadline(s): None
Officers: James F. Kirsch, Pres.; Don E. Katchman, V.P.; M. Abood, Secy.; D. R. Knapp, Treas.
Trustees: Mark H. Duesenberg; Ann E. Killian.
EIN: 346554832

2698

Fibus Family Foundation

P.O. Box 470
Niles, OH 44446-0470

Established in 1982 in OH.
Donors: Steel City Corp.; C. Kenneth Fibus; M. Fibus†; Dinesol Plastics, Inc.; Fibus Family Properties, LLC.
Foundation type: Independent foundation.
Financial data (yr. ended 05/31/13): Assets, $2,213,921 (M); gifts received, $250,000; expenditures, $217,115; qualifying distributions, $201,328; giving activities include $201,328 for 51 grants (high: $126,000; low: $100).
Purpose and activities: Giving primarily for health organizations and Jewish agencies.
Fields of interest: Higher education, university; Cancer; Multiple sclerosis; Diabetes; Human services; Jewish federated giving programs; Jewish agencies & synagogues.
Limitations: Applications not accepted. No grants to individuals.
Application information: Unsolicited requests for funds not accepted.
Trustee: C. Kenneth Fibus.
EIN: 341340458
Other changes: Stuart A. Strasfeld and Robert Wagmiller are no longer trustees.

2699

The Fifth Third Foundation

38 Fountain Square Plz., M.D. 1090CA
Cincinnati, OH 45263 (513) 534-4397
Contact: Heidi B. Jark, Managing Dir.
FAX: (513) 534-0960; Additional tel.: (513) 534-7001; Main URL: https://www.53.com/site/about/in-the-community/

Trust established in 1948 in OH.
Donor: Fifth Third Bank.
Foundation type: Company-sponsored foundation.
Financial data (yr. ended 09/30/13): Assets, $9,652,581 (M); gifts received, $3,000,000; expenditures, $4,010,330; qualifying distributions, $3,940,154; giving activities include $3,912,253 for 599 grants (high: $500,000; low: $25).
Purpose and activities: The foundation supports organizations involved with arts and culture, education, health, human services, and community development.
Fields of interest: Arts; Higher education; Business school/education; Education; Health care; Housing/shelter; American Red Cross; Family services; Human services; Community/economic development; United Ways and Federated Giving Programs.
Type of support: General/operating support; Continuing support; Management development/capacity building; Annual campaigns; Capital campaigns; Building/renovation; Equipment; Program development; Scholarship funds; Employee-related scholarships.
Limitations: Applications accepted. Giving primarily in areas of company operations in FL, GA, IL, IN, KY, MI, MO, NC, OH, PA, TN, and WV. **No support for individual churches or publicly-supported organizations or government agencies; generally, no support for elementary or middle schools; no support for United Way and Fine Arts Funds.** No grants to individuals (except for employee-related scholarships), or for start-up funds.
Publications: Application guidelines; Corporate giving report.
Application information: Visit website for nearest company facility address. A full proposal may be requested. A site visit may be requested. Support is limited to 1 contribution per organization during any given year. Applicants seeking multi-year funding must meet additional requirements. A waiting period of three years is required for prior grant recipients receiving $10,000 or more. Organizations receiving support are asked to submit a written evaluation. Application form not required.
Initial approach: Letter of inquiry to nearest company facility; contact foundation for major campaign requests
Deadline(s): None
Board meeting date(s): Jan., Mar., June, and Sept.
Final notification: 6 months
Trustee: Fifth Third Bank.
EIN: 316024135

2700

The Findlay Hancock County Community Foundation

101 W. Sandusky St., Ste. 207
Findlay, OH 45840-3276 (419) 425-1100
***Contact:* Katherine Kreuchauf, Pres.; Karen Smith, C.F.O.**
FAX: (419) 425-9339;
E-mail: info@community-foundation.com; Main URL: http://www.community-foundation.com
Blog: http://community-foundation.com/category/blog/
Facebook: http://www.facebook.com/pages/The-Findlay-Hancock-County-Community-Foundation/109824349061442
Twitter: https://twitter.com/tcffindlay
YouTube: https://www.youtube.com/channel/UCJIHzLdDjENjIYARTzvfDQg
Scholarship tel.: **419-425-1100; Scholarship e-mail: sjoseph@community-foundation.com**

Established in 1992 in OH as a supporting organization of the Cleveland Foundation; became a community foundation independent of the Cleveland Foundation in Feb. 1999.
Foundation type: Community foundation.
Financial data (yr. ended 12/31/12): Assets, $70,959,790 (M); gifts received, $3,145,824; expenditures, $3,033,930; giving activities include $1,296,218 for 40+ grants (high: $107,952), and $3,400 for grants to individuals.
Purpose and activities: The foundation is dedicated to improving the quality of life in the Hancock County area through collaborative leadership, responsible grantmaking, and development of philanthropic giving. The foundation seeks to facilitate philanthropic efforts through the development and stewardship of donor funds. The foundation builds permanent endowed funds contributed by individuals, corporations and institutions, provides grants and assistance to develop and strengthen organizations located in the community, encourages partnerships with other foundations, businesses

and government entities to increase funds distributed to the community, and inspires philanthropic and community involvement.
Fields of interest: Arts; Adult education—literacy, basic skills & GED; Education; Health care; Youth development; Human services; Economic development; Public affairs.
Type of support: General/operating support; Endowments; Management development/capacity building; Capital campaigns; Building/renovation; Program development; Seed money; Scholarship funds; Technical assistance; Consulting services; Program evaluation; Program-related investments/loans.
Limitations: Applications accepted. Giving limited to the greater Hancock County, OH, area. No support for religious organizations for religious purposes, community services such as the police and fire protection, or for staff positions for government agencies. **No grants to individuals (except for scholarships), or for endowment campaigns. Generally no grants for ongoing operating expenses, annual appeals or membership drives, sponsoring or attending conferences, fundraising projects or advertisements, travel, existing obligations, debts or liabilities, or for the printing of publications, audiovisual projects or video productions. Support for capital requests are seldom considered.**
Publications: Application guidelines; Annual report; Financial statement; Informational brochure; Informational brochure (including application guidelines).
Application information: Visit foundation web site for application forms and requirements. Proposals submitted by fax or e-mail are not accepted. Application form required.
Initial approach: Submit letter of intent
Copies of proposal: 2
Deadline(s): 1st Fri. of Jan., Apr., July and Oct. for letter of intent; 1st Fri. of Mar., June, Sept. and Dec. for full proposal
Board meeting date(s): Feb., Apr., May, July, Sept., and Nov.
Final notification: Within 3 months
Officers and Trustees:* Patricia J. Brown,* Chair.; Michael S. Needler,* Vice-Chair.; Katherine Kreuchauf,* Pres.; Sherri Garner Brumbaugh,* Secy.; Garry L. Peiffer,* Treas.; Karen Smith, C.F.O.; Gwen Kuenzli; J. Alec Reinhardt; Ralph D. Russo; Gene Stevens; Gary Wilson.
Number of staff: 6 full-time professional; 1 full-time support.
EIN: 341713261

2701
Donald J. Foss Memorial Employees Trust
604 Madison Ave.
Wooster, OH 44691-4764 **(330) 264-4440**
***Contact:* Allan K. Rodd, Tr.**

Established in 1956 in OH.
Donors: Donald J. Foss†; Mrs. Donald J. Foss†; Walter R. Foss†.
Foundation type: Independent foundation.
Financial data (yr. ended 04/30/13): Assets, $7,159,613 (M); expenditures, $358,215; qualifying distributions, $357,766; giving activities include $145,000 for 2 grants (high: $125,000; low: $20,000), and $212,766 for 28 grants to individuals (high: $8,300; low: $120).
Purpose and activities: Grants awarded primarily to employees of the Wooster Brush Co. or members of their immediate families in time of sickness, death, or other unfortunate circumstances; some additional charitable giving.
Fields of interest: Higher education; American Red Cross; United Ways and Federated Giving Programs; Economically disadvantaged.
Type of support: General/operating support; Grants to individuals.
Limitations: Applications accepted. Giving primarily in Wooster, OH.
Application information: Application form required.
Deadline(s): None
Trustees: William Fagert; Allan K. Rodd; Thomas W. Zook.
EIN: 346517801
Other changes: Woodrow J. Zook is no longer a trustee.

2702
The Foundation for Appalachian Ohio
36 Public Sq.
P.O. Box 456
Nelsonville, OH 45764-1133 (740) 753-1111
Contact: Cara Dingus Brook, Pres. and C.E.O.
FAX: (740) 753-3333; E-mail: mwanczyk@ffao.org; Additional e-mail: cbrook@ffao.org; Main URL: http://www.appalachianohio.org
E-Newsletter: http://www.appalachianohio.org/contact/index.php?section=256&page=356

Established in 1998 in OH.
Foundation type: Community foundation.
Financial data (yr. ended 12/31/12): Assets, $12,140,667 (M); gifts received, $2,517,485; expenditures, $1,296,084; giving activities include $152,235 for 111+ grants, and $173,186 for 53 grants to individuals.
Purpose and activities: Enriches the current and future quality of life in the 32 counties of Appalachian Ohio by fostering access to opportunity.
Fields of interest: Scholarships/financial aid; Children/youth, services; Family services; Economic development; Community/economic development; Leadership development.
Type of support: General/operating support; Continuing support; Income development; Endowments; Emergency funds; Program development; Conferences/seminars; Publication; Curriculum development; Scholarship funds; Technical assistance; Consulting services.
Limitations: Applications accepted. Giving limited to 32 county Appalachian Ohio region, including Adams, Ashtabula, Athens, Belmont, Brown, Carroll, Clermont, Columbiana, Coshocton, Gallia, Guernsey, Harrison, Highland, Hocking, Holmes, Jackson, Jefferson, Lawrence, Mahoning, Meigs, Monroe, Morgan, Muskingum, Noble, Perry, Pike, Ross, Scioto, Trumbull, Tuscarawas, Vinton and Washington. No grant for capital requests for buildings or renovations.
Publications: Informational brochure.
Application information: Visit foundation's website for current grant opportunities.
Deadline(s): Varies
Officers and Trustees:* Mike Workman,* Chair.; Joy Padgett,* Vice-Chair.; Cara Dingus Brook,* Pres. and C.E.O.; Holly Shelton,* V.P., Admin. and Advancement; Belinda Jones,* Secy.; Mike Carey,* Treas.; TJ Conger; Ron Cremeans; Matt Elli; Barbara Hansen; Gordon Litt; Jennifer Simon; B.J. Smith.
EIN: 311620483

2703
The Char and Chuck Fowler Family Foundation
(formerly Charles and Charlotte Fowler Family Foundation)
c/o Cornerstone Family Offices
5885 Landerbrook Dr., Ste. 300
Mayfield Heights, OH 44124-4031 (440) 460-0460
FAX: (440) 460-0420;
E-mail: grants@fowlerfamilyfdn.org; Main URL: http://fowlerfamilyfdn.org/

Established in 2003 in OH.
Donors: Charles D. Fowler; Charlotte Fowler; Grandsand LLC; Chaolley Limited Partnership.
Foundation type: Independent foundation.
Financial data (yr. ended 12/31/12): Assets, $48,719,265 (M); gifts received, $4,250,000; expenditures, $3,270,796; qualifying distributions, $3,002,800; giving activities include $3,002,800 for 18 grants (high: $650,000; low: $5,000).
Purpose and activities: Giving primarily for education, health and the arts.
Fields of interest: Arts; Education; Health care.
Type of support: Program development; Management development/capacity building; General/operating support; Equipment; Curriculum development; Continuing support; Building/renovation.
Limitations: Applications accepted. Giving primarily in the greater Cleveland, OH, area. No support for political groups, annual fund raising events or event sponsorships. No grants to individuals.
Application information: See foundation web site for online letter of intent form. Application form required.
Initial approach: Online letter of intent
***Deadline(s):* Spring Grant Cycle: Feb. 10 for LOI, April 11 for application; Fall Grant Cycle: Aug. 29 for LOI, Oct. 20 for application**
***Board meeting date(s):* Twice yearly**
***Final notification:* Spring Grant Cycle: May 12; Fall Grant Cycle: Nov. 17**
Officers and Trustees:* Charlotte A. Fowler,* Pres.; Chann Fowler-Spellman,* Secy.; **Charles D. Fowler, Treas.**; Holley Fowler Martens.
EIN: 900035660
Other changes: Charlotte A. Fowler has replaced Charles D. Fowler as Pres. Charlotte A. Fowler has replaced Charles D. Fowler as Pres.
Charles D. Fowler is now Treas. .

2704
Walter Henry Freygang Foundation
2794 Forestview Dr.
Akron, OH 44333-2785

Incorporated in 1949 in NJ.
Donors: Walter Henry Freygang†; Marie A. Freygang†.
Foundation type: Independent foundation.
Financial data (yr. ended 08/31/13): Assets, $8,911,593 (M); expenditures, $431,873; qualifying distributions, $379,089; giving activities include $379,089 for 56 grants (high: $27,199; low: $1,200).
Fields of interest: Higher education; Education; Hospitals (specialty); Health organizations; Food distribution, meals on wheels; Human services; Children/youth, services.
Limitations: Applications not accepted. Giving primarily in NJ, NY, OH and MA. No grants to individuals.
Application information: Contributes only to pre-selected organizations.
Board meeting date(s): Oct.
Officers: Dale G. Freygang, Pres. and Treas.; **James Drennan, V.P.**; Katherine A. Freygang, Secy.
Trustees: Joseph A. Drennan; Antje Freygang; David B. Freygang; W. Nicholas F. Freygang.
EIN: 226027952

2705

Gardner Foundation
10 W. 2nd St., 26th Fl.
Dayton, OH 45402-1971
Application address: c/o Eugenie Campbell, 1424 Black Horse Run, Lebanon, OH 45036

Incorporated in 1952 in OH.
Foundation type: Independent foundation.
Financial data (yr. ended 05/31/13): Assets, $4,456,589 (M); expenditures, $237,573; qualifying distributions, $209,000; giving activities include $209,000 for grants.
Purpose and activities: Giving to organizations that disburse scholarships to Middletown and Cincinnati, Ohio, students.
Fields of interest: Education; Foundations (community).
Type of support: General/operating support; Scholarships—to individuals.
Limitations: Applications accepted. Giving limited to Middletown and Cincinnati, OH. No grants to individuals (except for limited scholarship program).
Publications: Application guidelines; Program policy statement.
Application information: Application form required.
Initial approach: Proposal
Deadline(s): None
Board meeting date(s): June 18 and 19
Officers and Trustees:* Lee H. Gardner,* Pres.; Eugenie Campbell,* V.P., Opers.; **Edward T. Gardner III,* Co-V.P., Finance**; Robert Gardner III,* Co-V.P., Finance; Tina Evans,* Secy.; Susanah A. Gardner,* Treas.; **Mimi Gardner Gates**.
EIN: 316050604
Other changes: Lee H. Gardner has replaced Edward T. Gardner, III as Pres. Edward T. Gardner III has replaced Lee H. Gardner as Co-V.P., Finance.

2706

The Frank Hadley Ginn and Cornelia Root Ginn Charitable Trust
(also known as The Ginn Foundation)
13940 Cedar Road
Box 239
University Heights, OH 44118
Contact: Walter Ginn, Pres. and Trustee
E-mail: info@ginnfoundation.org; Main URL: http://www.ginnfoundation.org/
Grants List: http://www.ginnfoundation.org/grants2013.html
Grants List: http://www.ginnfoundation.org/grants2012.html
Grants List: http://www.ginnfoundation.org/grants2011.html

Established in 1991 in OH.
Donor: Alexander Ginn‡.
Foundation type: Independent foundation.
Financial data (yr. ended 12/31/13): Assets, $3,202,000 (M); expenditures, $181,000; qualifying distributions, $170,000; giving activities include $170,000 for 27 grants (high: $15,000; low: $2,500).
Purpose and activities: The foundation seeks to address education and community-based health care needs of low-income individuals through supporting effective programs and services that bring about long-term solutions for individuals and the community, principally in Cuyahoga County, OH. The foundation will also consider assisting nonprofits in building internal capacity to meet their goals in areas such as fundraising, technology, infrastructure, and staff development.
Fields of interest: Arts education; Education; Medical care, community health systems; Public health; Health care.
Type of support: General/operating support; Income development; Management development/capacity building; Program development; Program evaluation.
Limitations: Applications accepted. Giving primarily in Cuyahoga County, OH; support also for trustee-sponsored proposals for organizations in Washington, DC, Chicago, IL, and the metropolitan Minneapolis-St. Paul, MN, area. No grants to individuals, or for endowment, capital, or annual fund campaigns, or special events or attendance at conferences or symposia.
Application information: Applications submitted by fax not considered. Application form not required.
Initial approach: Proposal
Copies of proposal: 1
Deadline(s): Mar. 15 and Sept. 15
Board meeting date(s): Early May and Nov.
Final notification: Immediately following Board meetings
Trustees: Meredith G. Carr; Patricia G. Feeney; Ann L. Ginn; Mary C. Ginn; Walter P. Ginn; Tara F. VanWynkel.
EIN: 346953379

2707

Greene County Community Foundation
(doing business as Greene Giving)
25 Greene St.
Xenia, OH 45385-3101 (937) 562-5550
Contact: Edward Marrinan, Exec. Dir.
FAX: (937) 562-5556;
E-mail: emarrinan@co.greene.oh.us; Main URL: http://www.greenegiving.org

Established in 2001 in OH.
Foundation type: Community foundation.
Financial data (yr. ended 12/31/11): Assets, $8,270,135 (M); gifts received, $2,107,284; expenditures, $1,353,204; giving activities include $837,001 for 14+ grants (high: $57,059), and $349,828 for grants to individuals.
Purpose and activities: The foundation seeks to promote philanthropy and provide stewardship and leadership to enhance the use of regional resources to meet charitable needs.
Fields of interest: Arts; Education, public education; Health care; Agriculture; Recreation; Family services; Aging, centers/services; Community development, neighborhood development; Economic development.
Type of support: Building/renovation; Equipment; Scholarship funds.
Limitations: Applications accepted. Giving limited to Greene County, OH.
Publications: Informational brochure.
Application information: Application form required.
Initial approach: Letter, telephone, or e-mail
Copies of proposal: 1
Board meeting date(s): Bi-monthly
Officers and Directors:* Mark Schutter,* Pres.; Anne Gerard,* Secy.; **Greg Devilbiss,* Treas.**; Robert Baird; David Bartlett; Chuck Bechtel; Phil Cunningham; Michael Cusak; John Dautel; Paul Dillaplain; Jack Gayheart; Mark Guess; Joe Harkleroad; Jamie Hensley; Don Hollister; Gussie Jones; **Shannon Martin**; Herman N. Menapace; Paul Newman; Jane Newton; Shaun Nicholson; Mary Nutter; Fran O'Shaughnessy; Matt Pauley; Jerry Pfeifer; Dennis Phillips.
EIN: 311751001
Other changes: Greg Devilbiss is now Treas. Shannon Martin, Ed Phillips, Fred Pumroy, Dennis Phillips, Dona Seger-Lawson, John Siehl, Joe Stadniear, Stephanie Stephan, and Julie Vann are no longer directors.

2708

The George Gund Foundation
1845 Guildhall Bldg.
45 Prospect Ave. W.
Cleveland, OH 44115-1018 (216) 241-3114
Contact: David T. Abbott, Exec. Dir.; For Fellowships:: Robert B. Jaquay, Assoc. Dir.
FAX: (216) 241-6560; E-mail: info@gundfdn.org; Main URL: http://www.gundfdn.org
CEP Study: http://gundfoundation.org/forms-resources/2010-grantee-perception-report/
E-Newsletter: http://www.gundfoundation.org/contact-us/join-our-email-list
Grants Database: http://gundfoundation.org/grants-awarded/search-grants-archives/

Incorporated in 1952 in OH.
Donor: George Gund‡.
Foundation type: Independent foundation.
Financial data (yr. ended 12/31/12): Assets, $454,005,114 (M); expenditures, $28,632,663; qualifying distributions, $24,020,582; giving activities include $21,472,643 for 290 grants (high: $2,000,000; low: $1,000).
Purpose and activities: Priority to education projects, with emphasis on new concepts and methods of teaching and learning, and on increasing educational opportunities for the disadvantaged; programs advancing economic revitalization and job creation; projects promoting neighborhood development; projects for improving human services, employment opportunities, housing for minority and low-income groups; support also for ecology, civic affairs, and the arts. Preference is given to pilot projects and innovative programs which present prospects for broad replication.
Fields of interest: Arts; Education, research; Education, early childhood education; Elementary school/education; Secondary school/education; Higher education; Education; Environment, natural resources; Environment; AIDS; AIDS research; Crime/law enforcement; Employment; Housing/shelter, development; Human services; Children/youth, services; Women, centers/services; Minorities/immigrants, centers/services; Civil rights, race/intergroup relations; Urban/community development; Community/economic development; Government/public administration; Public affairs; Minorities; Women; Economically disadvantaged.
Type of support: General/operating support; Continuing support; Land acquisition; Emergency funds; Program development; Conferences/seminars; Publication; Seed money; Internship funds; Scholarship funds; Research; Technical assistance; Program-related investments/loans; Matching/challenge support.
Limitations: Applications accepted. Giving primarily in northeastern OH and the greater Cleveland, OH, area. No support for political groups, services for the physically, mentally or developmentally disabled, or the elderly. Generally, no grants to individuals, or for building or endowment funds, political campaigns, debt reduction, equipment, renovation projects, or to fund benefit events. No capital grants to projects that have not adopted green building principles.
Publications: Grants list; Newsletter; Quarterly report.
Application information: The foundation has moved to an online proposal process. Mailed grant requests will not be considered. Application form required.

Initial approach: Following review of eligibility on foundation web site, complete online application process
Copies of proposal: 1
***Deadline(s):* Mar. 15, July 15 and Nov. 15**
Board meeting date(s): Feb., July and Nov.
Final notification: Generally three months
Officers and Trustees:* Geoffrey Gund,* Pres. and Treas.; **Ann L. Gund,* V.P.; Catherine Gund, Secy.**; David T. Abbott, Exec. Dir.; George Gund IV; Zachary Gund; Randell McShepard; Robyn Minter Smyers; Anna Traggio.
Number of staff: 8 full-time professional; 4 full-time support.
EIN: 346519769
Other changes: Ann L. Gund has replaced Llura A. Gund as V.P. Catherine Gund has replaced Ann L. Gund as Secy.
David Goodman is no longer a trustee.

2709
Carol & Ralph Haile, Jr./U.S. Bank Foundation

(formerly Carol & Ralph Haile, Jr. Foundation)
c/o U.S. Bank, N.A.
425 Walnut St., CN-OH-W11F
Cincinnati, OH 45202-3956
***E-mail:* chad.mccarter@haileusb.org**; Main URL: http://www.haileusb.org

Established in 2003 in OH.
Donors: Ralph V. Haile; Ralph V. Haile Trust.
Foundation type: Independent foundation.
Financial data (yr. ended 12/31/12): Assets, $229,104,157 (M); expenditures, $13,669,608; qualifying distributions, $12,253,011; giving activities include $10,842,887 for 199 grants (high: $3,000,000; low: $500).
Purpose and activities: Giving primarily for arts and culture, community development, education, and human services.
Fields of interest: Performing arts; Higher education; Education; Health organizations; Cancer research; Human services; YM/YWCAs & YM/YWHAs; Community/economic development; Foundations (community); United Ways and Federated Giving Programs.
Limitations: Applications not accepted. Giving primarily in the Greater Cincinnati, OH, area, including Dearborn and Franklin in IN, and Boone, Campbell and Kenton in KY. No grants to individuals.
Application information: Contributes only to pre-selected organizations.
Officers: Timothy Maloney, C.E.O. and Pres.; Leslie Maloney, Sr. V.P., Prog. Mgr., Education; Christine A. Bochenek, V.P., Operations and Sr. Prog. Mgr.; **Eric Avner, V.P. and Sr. Prog. Mgr., Community Devel.**
Advisory Committee: Jennie P. Carlson; Terry K. Crilley; Richard K. Davis; Leslie P. Maloney.
Trustee: U.S. Bank, N.A.
EIN: 542135984
Other changes: Eric Avner is now V.P. and Sr. Prog. Mgr., Community Devel.

2710
The Hamilton Community Foundation, Inc.

319 N. 3rd St.
Hamilton, OH 45011-1624 (513) 863-1717
Contact: John J. Guidugli, C.E.O.
FAX: (513) 863-2868;
E-mail: info@hamiltonfoundation.org; Main URL: http://www.hamiltonfoundation.org
Facebook: http://www.facebook.com/pages/Hamilton-Community-Foundation-OH/119062244714

Incorporated in 1951 in OH.
Foundation type: Community foundation.
Financial data (yr. ended 12/31/12): Assets, $76,188,512 (M); gifts received, $5,472,589; expenditures, $7,776,126; giving activities include $5,006,428 for 65+ grants (high: $800,000), and $515,883 for 329 grants to individuals.
Purpose and activities: Entrusted with the responsibility to improve quality of life, the foundation has a four-part mission: 1) to serve as a leader, catalyst, and resource for philanthropy; 2) to build and permanently hold a growing endowment for the community's changing needs and opportunities; 3) to strive for excellence through strategic grant-making in such fields as the arts, education, housing, social services, civic beautification, community development, and recreation; and 4) to provide a flexible and cost-effective way for donors to improve their community now and in the future.
Fields of interest: Arts; Elementary school/education; Education; Environment, beautification programs; Health care; Substance abuse, services; Health organizations, association; Alcoholism; Housing/shelter, development; Recreation; Children/youth, services; Human services; Community/economic development.
Type of support: Emergency funds; Program development; Conferences/seminars; Seed money; Scholarship funds; Program-related investments/loans.
Limitations: Applications accepted. Giving limited to Butler County, OH. No support for individual religious organizations, including churches and parochial schools. No grants to individuals (except for scholarships), or for operating budgets, continuing support, annual campaigns, deficit financing, capital or endowment funds, matching gifts, research, demonstration projects, equipment, or publications; no loans (except for program-related investments).
Publications: Application guidelines; Annual report; Informational brochure (including application guidelines); Newsletter.
Application information: Visit foundation web site for application form and guidelines. Application form not required.
Initial approach: Telephone
Copies of proposal: 12
Deadline(s): Jan. 1, Mar. 1, May 1, Sept. 1, and Nov. 1 for general grantmaking program; May 1 for capital grants; varies for scholarships
Board meeting date(s): Feb., Apr., June, Oct., and Dec.
Final notification: Immediately following each Board meeting for general grantmaking program; Following June Board meeting for capital grants
Officers and Trustees:* Kathleen Klink,* Chair.; Herman R. Sanders,* Vice-Chair.; John J. Guidugli,* C.E.O. and Pres.; Katie E. Braswell,* V.P.; Betsy Hope,* V.P., Comms.; **Daniel J. Sander,* V.P., Finance**; Craig Wilks,* Secy.; Heather Lewis,* Treas.; Cynthia V. Parrish, Exec. Dir.; Lee H. Parrish, Legal Counsel; David L. Belew, Tr. Emeritus; Sara P. Carruthers; **Michael P. Dingeldein**; James K. Fitton; Scott Hartford; Butch Hubble; Thomas Rentschler, Jr.; Steve Timmer.
Trustee Banks: First Financial Bank; U.S. Bank, N.A.
Number of staff: 2 full-time professional; 2 part-time professional; 2 full-time support; 1 part-time support.
EIN: 316038277
Other changes: Michael P. Dingeldein is no longer a trustee.

2711
The Hershey Foundation

10229 Prouty Rd.
Concord Township, OH 44077-2104 (440) 256-6003
Contact: Debra Hershey Guren, Pres.
FAX: (440) 256-0233;
E-mail: thehersheyfoundation@gmail.com; **Main URL: http://fdnweb.org/hershey**
Grants List: http://fdnweb.org/hershey/grants-awarded/

Established in 1986 in OH.
Donors: Jo Hershey Selden†; Loren W. Hershey; Debra Hershey Guren; Carole Hershey Walters.
Foundation type: Independent foundation.
Financial data (yr. ended 12/31/12): Assets, $18,494,890 (M); expenditures, $1,366,514; qualifying distributions, $1,236,700; giving activities include $1,236,700 for 45 grants (high: $110,000; low: $1,500).
Purpose and activities: The foundation is dedicated to providing children in northeastern Ohio, from all socio-economic and cultural backgrounds, with special opportunities for personal growth and development. Support from the foundation helps schools, museums, cultural institutions, and other non-profit organizations develop and implement innovative programs that make the future brighter for children by improving quality of life, building self-esteem, enhancing learning, increasing exposure to other cultures and ideas, and encouraging the development of independent thinking and problem-solving skills.
Fields of interest: Arts education; Education, early childhood education; Child development, education; Elementary school/education; Education; Children/youth, services; Child development, services; Infants/toddlers; Children; Infants/toddlers, female; Girls; Infants/toddlers, male; Boys.
Type of support: Capital campaigns; Building/renovation; Equipment; Endowments; Program development; Seed money; Curriculum development.
Limitations: Applications accepted. Giving primarily in northeastern OH. No grants to individuals, or for annual campaigns, operating budgets, computer systems, technology or research, or feasibility studies.
Publications: Application guidelines; Annual report; Grants list; Informational brochure (including application guidelines); Multi-year report.
Application information: See foundation Web site for application guidelines and procedures. Application form not required.
Initial approach: 1-page letter or telephone
Copies of proposal: 1
Deadline(s): Dec. 1 and June 1
Board meeting date(s): Feb. and Aug.
Final notification: Feb. and Aug.
Officers and Trustees:* Debra Hershey Guren,* C.E.O. and Pres.; Adam M. Guren,* V.P. and Treas.; Carole Hershey Walters,* Secy.; Georgia A. Froelich; Loren W. Hershey.
Number of staff: None.
EIN: 341525626

2712
Home is the Foundation
1751 N. Barron St.
Eaton, OH 45320-9277 (937) 472-0500
Contact: Bill Hutton
***FAX:* (937) 472-0501**; Main URL: http://www.hitfoundation.org/

Established in 2003 in OH. Classified as a private operating foundation in 2004.
Donors: Franklin Steet; Mary Bullen.
Foundation type: Operating foundation.
Financial data (yr. ended 12/31/12): Assets, $1,461,328 (M); gifts received, $866,074; expenditures, $918,742; qualifying distributions, $763,357.
Fields of interest: Housing/shelter.
Application information: Application form required.
Initial approach: Apply in person or contact foundation for application form
Deadline(s): None
Officers: Mary Bullen, Pres.; Chip Christman, Treas.; Billy J. Hutton, Jr., Exec. Dir.
Directors: Joan Kreitzer; Teresa McCown; Sharon Shute; Mike Simpson.
EIN: 421580792

2713
K. Huntingdon, Jr. Charitable Trust
Cincinnati, OH

The trust terminated on Feb. 28, 2013 and transferred its assets to The Dayton Foundation.

2714
Johnson Family Foundation
c/o U.S. Bank, N.A.
P.O. Box 1118, ML CN-OH-W10X
Cincinnati, OH 45201-1118

Established in 1997 in OH.
Donors: Arlyn T. Johnson; Samuel J. Johnson IV.
Foundation type: Independent foundation.
Financial data (yr. ended 04/30/13): Assets, $7,410,530 (M); gifts received, $350,000; expenditures, $358,853; qualifying distributions, $300,204; giving activities include $293,800 for 15 grants (high: $40,000; low: $7,500).
Purpose and activities: Giving primarily for education and human services.
Fields of interest: Education; Human services; Children/youth, services; Residential/custodial care, hospices; Disabilities, people with; Homeless.
Limitations: Applications not accepted. Giving primarily in KY, MA, and OH; some giving in New York, NY. No grants to individuals.
Application information: Contributes only to pre-selected organizations.
Directors: Terry K. Crilley; **Lauren Lipcon Dale**; David B. Hamilton; Gwendolyn Kess Johnson; Johanna Johnson; **Zachary Johnson**; Charlotte Johnson Lilly; Jesse Lipcon; Patricia L. Johnson Lipcon; **Scott Lipcon**; Todd Lipcon; Crosley Johnson Sigmon.
EIN: 311542859

2715
Robert T. Keeler Foundation
425 Walnut St., Ste. 1800
Cincinnati, OH 45202-3957

Established in 2001 in OH.
Donor: Robert T. Keeler†.
Foundation type: Independent foundation.
Financial data (yr. ended 12/31/12): Assets, $25,701,729 (M); gifts received, $3,989,654; expenditures, $1,005,647; qualifying distributions, $632,500; giving activities include $632,500 for grants.
Fields of interest: Arts; Education; Hospitals (specialty); Health care; Children.
Limitations: Applications not accepted. Giving primarily in CA and OH. No grants to individuals.
Application information: Contributes only to pre-selected organizations.
Officers and Trustees:* Peter P. Mithoefer,* Pres.; Heather M. Mithoefer,* V.P.; Mary L. Rust,* Secy.-Treas.
Number of staff: None.
EIN: 311420552
Other changes: The grantmaker no longer lists a primary contact.
At the close of 2011, the fair market value of the grantmaker's assets was $20,381,076, a 106.5% increase over the 2010 value, $9,867,518.
Mary L. Rust is now Secy.-Treas.

2716
The Virginia W. Kettering Foundation
1480 Kettering Twr.
Dayton, OH 45423 (937) 228-1021
Contact: Judith M. Thompson, Exec. Dir.
E-mail: info@ketteringfamilyphilanthropies.org; Main URL: http://vwk.cfketteringfamilies.com/
Grants List: http://kff.cfketteringfamilies.com/vwk/grants-history

Established in 2003 in OH.
Donors: Virginia W. Kettering†; 1988 Kettering Tower Trust.
Foundation type: Independent foundation.
Financial data (yr. ended 12/31/12): Assets, $26,697,560 (M); expenditures, $1,361,981; qualifying distributions, $1,212,983; giving activities include $1,187,500 for 48 grants (high: $125,000; low: $2,000).
Purpose and activities: Giving to support charitable activities within Montgomery County, Ohio and counties contiguous to it. The foundation's primary areas of support are arts, culture and humanities, education, the environment, medical and health, human services and programs that benefit the public and society.
Fields of interest: Arts; Education; Environment; Health care; Human services.
Type of support: General/operating support; Management development/capacity building; Annual campaigns; Capital campaigns; Equipment; Program development; Scholarship funds; Research.
Limitations: Applications accepted. Giving primarily in Butler, Clark, Darke, Greene, Miami, Montgomery, Preble, and Warren counties in OH. No support for religious organizations for religious purposes or for individual public elementary or secondary schools or public school districts. No grants or loans to individuals or for multi-year grants, tickets, advertising or sponsorship of fundraising events.
Publications: Application guidelines; Financial statement; Grants list.
Application information: Full proposals are by invitation only, upon review of request summary. All applications are to be submitted through the web site's on-line process. Faxed, mailed or hand-delivered request summaries and full proposals will not be accepted except under unusual circumstances, and solely at the discretion of foundation staff.
Initial approach: Create (or return to) online account on foundation web site, then access online request summary form. The foundation strongly recommends that applicants contact the office to discuss the proposed program before the application process begins
Copies of proposal: 1
Deadline(s): Jan. 31 and July 31 for request summary
Board meeting date(s): Spring and fall
Final notification: 3 weeks after submission of request summary
Officer: Judith Thompson, Exec. Dir.
Trustee: JPMorgan Chase Bank, N.A.
EIN: 316570701

2717
KeyBank Foundation
(formerly Key Foundation)
800 Superior Ave., 1st Fl.
M.C. OH-01-02-0126
Cleveland, OH 44114-2601 (216) 828-7349
Contact: Lorraine Vega, Sr. Prog. Off.
FAX: (216) 828-7845;
E-mail: key_foundation@keybank.com;
Philanthropic Contacts: Civic, Health, and Human Services: Lorraine, Vega, tel.: (216) 828-7402, e-mail: Lorraine_Vega@KeyBank.com; Education: Eric S. Brown, tel.: (216) 828-7396, e-mail eric_s_brown@keybank.com; Arts and Culture and sponsorships: Karen White, tel.: (216) 828-8539, e-mail: Karen_A_White@KeyBank.com; Main URL: https://www.key.com/about/community/key-foundation-philanthropy-banking.jsp

Established about 1969 in OH.
Donors: Society Corp.; Society Capital Corp.; KeyBank N.A.; KeyCorp.
Foundation type: Company-sponsored foundation.
Financial data (yr. ended 12/31/12): Assets, $37,019,359 (M); gifts received, $9,250,000; expenditures, $12,936,466; qualifying distributions, $12,839,816; giving activities include $12,839,816 for 4,468 grants (high: $1,000,000; low: $25).
Purpose and activities: The foundation supports organizations involved with arts and culture, education, health, human services, and civic affairs. Special emphasis is directed toward programs designed to enhance economic self-sufficiency through financial education, workforce development, and diversity.
Fields of interest: Arts; Vocational education; Education; Health care; Employment, services; Employment, training; Employment; Human services, financial counseling; Human services; Civil/human rights, equal rights; Community development, small businesses; United Ways and Federated Giving Programs; Public affairs; Physically disabled; Minorities; Economically disadvantaged; LGBTQ.
Type of support: General/operating support; Continuing support; Annual campaigns; Capital campaigns; Program development; Curriculum development; Scholarship funds; Employee volunteer services; Sponsorships; Employee matching gifts; Matching/challenge support.
Limitations: Applications accepted. Giving primarily in areas of company operations in AK, CO, ID, IN, KY, ME, MI, NY, OH, OR, UT, VT, and WA; giving also to national organizations. **No support for organizations outside geographic footprint, athletic teams, fraternal organizations, or discriminatory organizations.** No grants to individuals, or for memberships, lobbying or political activities, or advertising.

Publications: Application guidelines; Corporate report; Occasional report.
Application information: Full proposals must include a proposal summary form. Proposals are evaluated by funding committees in KeyBank district offices. Visit website for nearest district office address. Organizations receiving support are asked to provide a final report 3 months after the completion of the project.
Initial approach: Letter of inquiry, proposal summary form, or telephone for preliminary inquiries; full proposals to foundation for organizations located in northeast OH; full proposal to closest key district office for organizations located outside of northeast, OH
Copies of proposal: 1
Deadline(s): None
Board meeting date(s): Quarterly
Final notification: Within 3 months
Officers and Trustees:* Margot James Copeland,* Chair.; Christopher M. Gorman, Pres.; James Hoffman, V.P.; Paul N. Harris, Secy.; Mark Whitham, Treas.; Cindy P. Crotty; Bruce D. Murphy; Elizabeth J. Oliver.
Number of staff: 4 full-time professional.
EIN: 237036607

2718
The Knight Family Foundation
Cleveland, OH

The foundation terminated on Aug. 16, 2011 and transferred its assets to The Illinois Foundation.

2719
Miriam G. Knoll Charitable Foundation
300 High St.
Hamilton, OH 45011-6078
Application address: c/o First Financial Bank-WRG, 815 S. Breiel Blvd., Middletown, OH 45042, tel.: (513) 425-7532

Established in 1985 in OH.
Foundation type: Independent foundation.
Financial data (yr. ended 10/31/13): Assets, $6,664,638 (M); expenditures, $255,245; qualifying distributions, $235,265; giving activities include $175,200 for 15 grants (high: $42,000; low: $1,000).
Purpose and activities: Giving primarily to Ohio community foundations; support also for the arts and human services, including services for people with disabilities.
Fields of interest: Performing arts; Arts; Higher education; Housing/shelter; Youth development; Human services; Community/economic development; Foundations (community); Protestant agencies & churches.
Type of support: General/operating support; Building/renovation; Scholarship funds.
Limitations: Applications accepted. Giving limited to OH, primarily in Middletown. No grants to individuals.
Application information: Application form not required.
Initial approach: Proposal
Deadline(s): None
Advisors: Roland P. Ely, Jr.; **Joseph Lyons**; John D. Sawyer; William H. Shaefer.
Trustee: First Financial Bank.
Officer: John Peterson, Exec. Dir.
EIN: 316282842

2720
Austin E. Knowlton Foundation Inc.
414 Walnut St., Ste. 1205
Cincinnati, OH 45202-3957 (513) 381-2400
Contact: **Sherri L. Calk, C.A.O.**
***FAX:* (513) 381-7666; E-mail address for Sherri L. Calk, C.A.O.: scalk@aekfoundation.org; Main URL: http://www.aekfoundation.org**

Established in 1982 in OH.
Donor: Austin E. Knowlton‡.
Foundation type: Independent foundation.
Financial data (yr. ended 12/31/12): Assets, $161,151,522 (M); gifts received, $128,550,541; expenditures, $7,277,411; qualifying distributions, $7,273,261; giving activities include $6,735,000 for 28 grants (high: $2,000,000; low: $5,000).
Fields of interest: Higher education.
Type of support: General/operating support.
Limitations: Applications accepted. Giving primarily in IL and OH. No grants to individuals.
Application information: Application form not required.
Initial approach: Proposal
Copies of proposal: 1
Deadline(s): None
Officers: John C. Lindberg, Pres.; Eric V. Lindberg, V.P.; **Sherri L. Calk, C.A.O.**
Trustees: Edward D. Diller; Robert A. Pitcairn, Jr.
EIN: 311044475
Other changes: Charles D. Lindberg, Secy.-Treas., is deceased.

2721
Kulas Foundation
50 Public Sq., Ste. 600
Cleveland, OH 44113-2267 (216) 623-4770
Contact: Nancy W. McCann, Pres.
FAX: (216) 623-4773; **Main URL: http://fdnweb.org/kulas**

Incorporated in 1937 in OH.
Donors: Fynette H. Kulas‡; E.J. Kulas‡.
Foundation type: Independent foundation.
Financial data (yr. ended 12/31/13): Assets, $40,326,384 (M); expenditures, $3,027,838; qualifying distributions, $2,830,370; giving activities include $2,379,700 for 100 grants (high: $210,000; low: $200).
Purpose and activities: Grants largely to music institutions and for higher education; support also for local performing arts and social services.
Fields of interest: Museums; Performing arts; Performing arts, music; Arts; Education, association; Education, fund raising/fund distribution; Higher education; Education; Human services.
Type of support: General/operating support; Continuing support; Annual campaigns; Capital campaigns; Building/renovation; Equipment; Land acquisition; Program development; Conferences/seminars; Professorships; Research; Consulting services; Matching/challenge support.
Limitations: Applications not accepted. Giving limited to Cuyahoga County, OH, and its contiguous counties. No support for mental health organizations. No grants to individuals, or for endowment funds; no loans or scholarships.
Publications: Financial statement.
Application information: The foundation currently is not accepting applications from new grantseekers. See foundation web site for further details.
Board meeting date(s): 4 times per year
Officers and Trustees:* Richard W. Pogue,* Chair. and V.P.; Nancy W. McCann,* Pres. and Treas.; Richard J. Clark, V.P. and Secy.; Patrick F. McCartan, Esq.*, V.P.; Ellen E. Halfon, Esq.
Number of staff: 1 full-time professional; 2 full-time support.
EIN: 340770687

2722
The Lerner Foundation
26500 Curtiss Wright Pkwy.
Highland Heights, OH 44143-1438 (440) 891-5000
Contact: Douglas C. Jacobs

Established in 1993 in OH.
Donors: Alfred Lerner‡; Norma Lerner.
Foundation type: Independent foundation.
Financial data (yr. ended 12/31/13): Assets, $12,072,851 (M); expenditures, $2,309,121; qualifying distributions, $2,287,431; giving activities include $2,285,231 for 33 grants (high: $625,000; low: $100).
Purpose and activities: Support primarily for medical care, Jewish agencies and temples and Jewish federated giving programs.
Fields of interest: Museums (art); Higher education; Health care, single organization support; Hospitals (general); Jewish federated giving programs; Jewish agencies & synagogues.
Limitations: Applications accepted. Giving primarily in NY, OH and VA. No grants to individuals.
Application information: Application form not required.
Initial approach: Letter
Deadline(s): None
Officers and Trustees:* Norma Lerner,* Pres. and Treas.; Nancy Fisher,* V.P.; Randolph Lerner,* V.P.; James H. Berick,* Secy.
EIN: 341744726

2723
Licking County Foundation
30 N. Second St.
P.O. Box 4212
Newark, OH 43058-4212 (740) 349-3863
Contact: Connie Hawk, Dir.
FAX: (740) 322-6260;
E-mail: lcf@thelcfoundation.org; Grant Inquiry Form e-mail: grants@thelcfoundation.org; Main URL: http://www.thelcfoundation.org
Scholarship inquiry e-mail: scholarships@thelcfoundation.org

Established in 1956 in OH.
Foundation type: Community foundation.
Financial data (yr. ended 12/31/11): Assets, $48,755,346 (M); gifts received, $959,288; expenditures, $3,031,979; giving activities include $2,186,126 for grants.
Purpose and activities: The foundation seeks to improve the quality of life for the citizens of Licking County, OH. Giving primarily for arts, education, health care, recreation, human services, and children and youth services.
Fields of interest: Performing arts, music; Arts; Education; Environment, beautification programs; Health care; Mental health/crisis services; Medical research, institute; Diabetes research; Recreation; Children/youth, services; Human services; Children/youth; Disabilities, people with; Blind/visually impaired.
Type of support: Capital campaigns; Building/renovation; Equipment; Conferences/seminars; Seed money; Curriculum development; Scholarship funds; Matching/challenge support.

Limitations: Applications accepted. Giving limited to Licking County, OH. No support for religious or sectarian purposes. No grants to individuals (except for scholarships), or for annual campaigns, debt retirement or restructuring, national fundraising drives or events, feasibility studies, tickets for benefits, regranting organizations, or endowments.
Publications: Application guidelines; Annual report; Informational brochure; Newsletter.
Application information: Visit foundation web site for Grant Inquiry Form and application guidelines. Application form required.
Initial approach: E-mail Grant Inquiry Form
Copies of proposal: 5
Deadline(s): Aug. 21 for Grant Inquiry Form; Oct. 16 for Full Grant Proposal
Board meeting date(s): Feb., May, Aug., and Nov.
Final notification: Early Dec.
Officers and Governing Committee:* David Trautman,* Chair.; Frank Murphy,* Chair., Emeritus; J. Gilbert Reese,* Chair., Emeritus; **Jeff Cox,* Vice-Chair.**; **Judy Pierce,* Secy.-Treas.**; **Mike Cantlin**; Eschol Curl; **Michael Kennedy**; Jerry McClain; William McConnell; Cynthia Menzer; Sue Moore; Janine Mortellaro; Stu Parsons.
Trustee Banks: Merrill Lynch Trust Co.; National City Bank; The Park National Bank.
Number of staff: 2 full-time professional; 1 part-time professional.
EIN: 316018618
Other changes: David Trautman has replaced Mike Cantlin as Chair. Jeff Cox has replaced David Trautman as Chair. Judy Pierce has replaced Jeff Cox as Secy.-Treas.
Judy Pierce is no longer a member of the governing body. Ann Fryman is no longer a member of the governing body.

2724
The G.R. Lincoln Family Foundation
30195 Chagrin Blvd., Ste. 250
Cleveland, OH 44124-5719

Established in OH.
Donors: G. Russell Lincoln; Laura Heath Irrevocable Trust; Constance P. Lincoln.
Foundation type: Independent foundation.
Financial data (yr. ended 12/31/12): Assets, $5,154,136 (M); gifts received, $248,036; expenditures, $285,815; qualifying distributions, $237,400; giving activities include $237,200 for 25 grants (high: $60,000; low: $50).
Fields of interest: Arts; Higher education; Education; Environment, natural resources; Hospitals (general).
Limitations: Applications not accepted. Giving primarily in Cleveland, OH. No grants to individuals.
Application information: Unsolicited requests for funds not accepted.
Advisory Committee: G. Russell Lincoln, Pres.; Christopher Horsburgh; Brinton C. Lincoln; Constance P. Lincoln; James D. Lincoln.
EIN: 383471702
Other changes: G. Russell Lincoln is now Pres. Samuel P. Lincoln is no longer a member of the advisory committee.

2725
The Llewellyn Foundation
c/o Cynthia Barnett
P.O. Box 1488
Springfield, OH 45501-1488
Main URL: http://llewellynfoundation.org/

Established in 1997 in OH.
Donor: Sarah H. Lupfer.
Foundation type: Independent foundation.
Financial data (yr. ended 02/28/13): Assets, $13,383,699 (M); expenditures, $708,697; qualifying distributions, $636,250; giving activities include $636,250 for 42 grants (high: $50,000; low: $5,000).
Fields of interest: Higher education; Education; Human services; Children/youth, services.
Limitations: Giving in the U.S., with emphasis on MA. No grants to individuals.
Application information: The foundation will only request more information from an applicant upon consideration of initial contact form. Application form required.
***Initial approach:* Use contact form on foundation web site**
***Deadline(s):* Apr. 30 and Sept. 30, for new inquires via foundation web site; May 31 and Oct. 31, for invited grants**
Board meeting date(s): Varies
Officers and Trustees:* Sarah H. Lupfer,* Pres.; Caroline Lupfer Kurtz,* Secy.; Jonathan B. Lupfer,* Treas.; Willis O. Kurtz.
EIN: 311534056

2726
Macy's Foundation
(formerly Federated Department Stores Foundation)
c/o Macy's Corp. Svcs., Inc.
7 W. 7th St.
Cincinnati, OH 45202-2424 (513) 579-7000
FAX: (513) 579-7185; Main URL: http://www.federated-fds.com/community/

Established in 1995 in OH.
Donors: Federated Department Stores, Inc.; The May Department Stores Foundation.
Foundation type: Company-sponsored foundation.
Financial data (yr. ended 02/02/13): Assets, $1,177,534 (M); gifts received, $9,790,000; expenditures, $12,538,100; qualifying distributions, $12,550,604; giving activities include $12,325,533 for 5,367 grants (high: $912,590; low: $25).
Purpose and activities: The foundation supports programs designed to promote arts and culture, education, the environment, HIV/AIDS, and women issues and domestic violence.
Fields of interest: Arts; Education; Environment; Breast cancer; AIDS; AIDS research; Food services; Food banks; Youth development, intergenerational programs; Aging, centers/services; United Ways and Federated Giving Programs; Minorities; Women.
Type of support: General/operating support; Continuing support; Annual campaigns; Capital campaigns; Program development; Seed money; Scholarship funds; Employee volunteer services; Employee matching gifts; Employee-related scholarships; Matching/challenge support.
Limitations: Applications accepted. Giving on a national basis in areas of company operations, with emphasis on CA, FL, GA, MO, NY, and OH. **No support for private foundations, fraternal organizations, political or advocacy groups, athletic teams, religious organizations not of direct benefit to the entire community, charities whose focus and operations are primarily international, or fiscal agents or other umbrella organizations providing funding to nonprofit organizations.** No grants to individuals, or for event or program sponsorships, or salaries for nonprofit staffing.
Publications: Application guidelines; Program policy statement.
Application information: The foundation utilizes an invitation only process for general corporate grants. My Macy's District Grants are reviewed by local District Grants Committee's. Application form not required.
***Initial approach:* Complete online eligibility quiz and application for My Macy's District Gants**
Copies of proposal: 1
***Deadline(s):* None for My Macy's District Gants**
Board meeting date(s): Quarterly
***Final notification:* 4 to 8 weeks**
Officers and Trustees:* Jim Sluzewski,* Pres.; Ann Munson Steines, Secy.; Matt Stautberg, Treas.; **Timothy Adams**; David W. Clark; Julie Greiner; Karen M. Hoguet; Ron Klein.
EIN: 311427325
Other changes: The grantmaker has changed its fiscal year-end from Jan. 28 to Feb. 2.

2727
The Milton and Tamar Maltz Family Foundation
3333 Richmond Rd., Ste. 460
Beachwood, OH 44122-4199
Contact: Jason Fishman, Exec. Dir.
E-mail: jfishman@maltzfamilyfoundation.org; Main URL: http://maltzfoundation.org/

Established in 1989 in FL.
Donors: Milton S. Maltz; Tamar Maltz; Daniel Maltz; David Maltz; Julie E. Konigsberg.
Foundation type: Independent foundation.
Financial data (yr. ended 12/31/12): Assets, $82,623,120 (M); gifts received, $6,027,978; expenditures, $3,908,804; qualifying distributions, $3,398,010; giving activities include $3,398,010 for 90 grants (high: $360,000; low: $1,000).
Purpose and activities: The foundation supports programs in the areas of the arts, health and human services, medical research, education, and the environment.
Fields of interest: Arts; Education; Environment, natural resources; Environment; Animals/wildlife; Health care; Medical research; Human services.
International interests: Israel.
Type of support: General/operating support; Management development/capacity building; Annual campaigns; Capital campaigns; Building/renovation; Land acquisition; Endowments; Professorships; Scholarship funds; Research; Matching/challenge support.
Limitations: Applications not accepted. Giving on a national basis, with emphasis on AZ, FL, and Cleveland, OH. No support for lobbying. No grants to individuals.
Application information: Contributes only to pre-selected organizations. Unsolicited proposals, grant requests, or letters of inquiry are not accepted.
Officers: Milton S. Maltz, Pres.; Julie E. Konigsberg, V.P.; Daniel Maltz, V.P.; Tamar Maltz, Secy.; David Maltz, Treas.
Number of staff: 2 full-time professional.
EIN: 650164300

2728
The Joseph and Florence Mandel Family Foundation
(formerly The Joseph and Florence Mandel Foundation)
1000 Lakeside Ave. E.
Cleveland, OH 44114-1117 (216) 875-6523
Contact: JoAnn White, Tr.

FAX: (216) 875-6550; Main URL: http://www.mandelfoundation.org

Established in 1963 in OH.
Donors: Florence Mandel†; Joseph C. Mandel.
Foundation type: Independent foundation.
Financial data (yr. ended 12/31/12): Assets, $124,452,068 (M); expenditures, $8,459,360; qualifying distributions, $5,910,979; giving activities include $5,271,696 for 319+ grants (high: $3,042,712; low: $15).
Purpose and activities: Giving primarily to a Jewish community fund and other Jewish organizations, including Jewish museums.
Fields of interest: Museums (art); Museums (ethnic/folk arts); Arts; Higher education; Health organizations; United Ways and Federated Giving Programs; Jewish federated giving programs; Jewish agencies & synagogues.
Type of support: General/operating support.
Limitations: Giving primarily in OH; giving also in FL and NY. No grants to individuals.
Application information: Application form not required.
Initial approach: Proposal
Deadline(s): None
Officers and Trustees:* Bradley S. Smith,* Pres.; Karen A. Vereb, Secy.; **JoAnn White, Treas.**; Michele Beyer; Morton L. Mandel; Penni M. Weinberg.
EIN: 346546419
Other changes: JoAnn White has replaced Anthony J. Pishkula as Treas.

2729
The Morton and Barbara Mandel Family Foundation

(formerly Morton and Barbara Mandel Foundation)
1000 Lakeside Ave.
Cleveland, OH **44114-1117 (216) 875-6523**
***Contact:* JoAnn White, Tr.**
FAX: (216) 875-6550; **Israel office: 15 Graetz St., Jerusalem 93111, Israel; tel.: (972) (2) 539-9666; fax: (972) (2) 566-2837**; Main URL: http://www.mandelfoundation.org

Established in 1963 in OH.
Donors: Morton L. Mandel; Barbara A. Mandel.
Foundation type: Independent foundation.
Financial data (yr. ended 12/31/12): Assets, $159,702,295 (M); gifts received, $5,389,892; expenditures, $11,086,752; qualifying distributions, $7,832,412; giving activities include $7,150,073 for 179+ grants (high: $150,000).
Purpose and activities: Support primarily for leadership, management of nonprofits, higher education, Jewish education and continuity, and for urban neighborhood renewal.
Fields of interest: Higher education; Education; Urban/community development; Nonprofit management; Community/economic development; United Ways and Federated Giving Programs; Jewish federated giving programs; Leadership development; Jewish agencies & synagogues.
International interests: Israel.
Type of support: General/operating support.
Limitations: Applications not accepted. Giving primarily in Cleveland, OH; and the U.S. & Israel. No grants to individuals.
Application information: Contributes only to pre-selected organizations.
Officers and Trustees:* Morton L. Mandel,* Pres.; Barbara A. Mandel,* V.P.; Karen A. Vereb, Secy.; **JoAnn White, Treas.**; Amy C. Mandel; Stacy L. Mandel; Thomas A. Mandel; Bradley S. Smith.
Number of staff: 1 full-time professional; 1 part-time professional; 2 full-time support.
EIN: 346546420
Other changes: JoAnn White has replaced Anthony J. Pishkula as Treas.

2730
Jack, Joseph, and Morton Mandel Foundation

(formerly Jack N. and Lilyan Mandel Foundation)
1000 Lakeside Ave.
Cleveland, OH **44114-1117** (216) 875-6523
FAX: (216) 875-6570; **Additional address: 15 Graetz St., Jerusalem 93111, Israeltel.: (972) (2) 539-9669fax: (972) (2) 566-2837**; Main URL: http://www.mandelfoundation.org

Established in 1963 in OH.
Donors: Jack N. Mandel†; Lilyan Mandel†.
Foundation type: Independent foundation.
Financial data (yr. ended 12/31/12): Assets, $347,274,968 (M); gifts received, $26,077,303; expenditures, $23,152,602; qualifying distributions, $16,295,588; giving activities include $15,656,109 for 93+ grants (high: $15,145,150).
Purpose and activities: Giving primarily to Jewish agencies, temples and schools.
Fields of interest: Elementary/secondary education; Jewish federated giving programs; Jewish agencies & synagogues.
Limitations: Applications accepted. Giving primarily in Cleveland, OH. No grants to individuals.
Application information: Application form not required.
Initial approach: Proposal
Deadline(s): None
Officers and Trustees:* Morton L. Mandel,* Pres.; JoAnn White, Treas.; Karen A. Vereb, Secy.; Joseph C. Mandel; Bradley Smith.
EIN: 346546418
Other changes: JoAnn White has replaced Anthony J. Pishkula as Treas.
Morton L. Mandel is now Pres.

2731
Marafiki Global Aids Ministry

(formerly Rafiki Aids Ministry)
P.O. Box 4074
Dublin, OH **43016-0563**
E-mail: marafikiglobalaidsministry@yahoo.com

Established in 1996 in OH.
Donors: Robert Karaffa; Tracee Karaffa; Betty Jane Ford; St. Paul's Episcopal Church Outreach Grant Council; Fee Mission Council; Mark Galantowicz; Barbara Galantowicz; Jack Shuter; Pat Shuter; Newark Rotary Club; Upper Arlington Senior Fund; Rotary Club of Upper Arlington; Rotary Club of Columbus; Terry Davis; Barbara Davis.
Foundation type: Operating foundation.
Financial data (yr. ended 12/31/12): Assets, $10,311 (M); gifts received, $203,208; expenditures, $222,436; qualifying distributions, $222,436; giving activities include $180,009 for 1 grant, and $13,126 for 1 grant to an individual.
Purpose and activities: Giving to provide food, shelter, medical care, education, a safe Christian living environment, and loving support to children worldwide who have been orphaned by HIV/AIDS.
International interests: Kenya.
Limitations: Applications not accepted. Giving primarily in Kikuyu, Kenya and Nassau, Bahamas.
Application information: Contributes only to pre-selected organizations.
Officers: John Nganga, Chair. and C.E.O.; Susan Munga, Vice-Chair.; Patti Chapman, Secy.; Molapo Kgabo, Treas.
EIN: 311586466

2732
Marietta Community Foundation

100 Putnam St.
P.O. Box 77
Marietta, OH 45750-0077 (740) 373-3286
***Contact:* Carol B. Wharff, Pres. and C.E.O.**
FAX: (740) 373-3937;
E-mail: info@mariettacommunityfoundation.org; Additional e-mail: carol@mcfohio.org; Main URL: http://www.mariettacommunityfoundation.org
Facebook: https://www.facebook.com/mcfohio

Established in 1974 in OH.
Donors: Lillian Strecker Smith†; Mrs. William Mildren, Sr.†; William Mildren, Sr.†; Carl L. Broughton†; Susan Marsch; Jane McCoy Peterson†; Ida Zimmer.
Foundation type: Community foundation.
Financial data (yr. ended 12/31/12): Assets, $14,799,613 (M); gifts received, $600,877; expenditures, $864,192; giving activities include $523,836 for 27+ grants (high: $24,650), and $38,940 for 25 grants to individuals.
Purpose and activities: The foundation is committed to building a strong foundation for the community and making life better for all citizens of Washington County, OH and the surrounding communities. The foundation seeks to respond to a wide variety of needs in the community.
Fields of interest: Arts; Education; Health care; Children/youth, services; Aging, centers/services; Community/economic development.
Type of support: General/operating support; Building/renovation; Equipment; Endowments; Program development; Conferences/seminars; Seed money; Scholarship funds; Research; Technical assistance; Program-related investments/loans; Grants to individuals; Scholarships—to individuals; Matching/challenge support.
Limitations: Applications accepted. Giving limited to the Marietta, OH, area, including Washington County, OH, and Wood County, WV. No grants for annual funds or continuing support.
Publications: Application guidelines; Annual report; Grants list; Informational brochure (including application guidelines); Newsletter.
Application information: Visit foundation web site for application form and guidelines. Application form required.
Initial approach: Telephone
Copies of proposal: 1
Deadline(s): Feb. 7, June 7, and Oct. 7
Board meeting date(s): 3rd Tues. of each month
Final notification: 60 to 90 days following deadlines
Officers and Directors:* Eric Erb,* Chair.; Jonathan Dehmlow,* Vice-Chair.; Carol B. Wharff,* C.E.O. and Pres.; **Arlene Archer,* Secy.**; Doug Robinson,* Treas.; Jennifer Christy; Dr. Bret Frye; Louise Holmes; **Karen Osborne**; Mark Schwendeman; Marcy Wesel; Teri Ann Zide.
Number of staff: 1 full-time professional; 1 part-time professional; 2 part-time support.
EIN: 743054287
Other changes: Arlene Archer has replaced Mary S. Broughton as Secy.
Arlene Archer and Tawni Love are no longer directors.

2733
Marion Community Foundation, Inc.
(formerly Ohio MedCenter Foundation, Inc.)
504 S. State St.
Marion, OH 43302-5036 (740) 387-9704
Contact: Bradley C. Bebout, C.E.O.
FAX: (740) 375-0665;
E-mail: marionlegacy@frontier.com; Main
URL: http://www.marioncommunityfoundation.org

Established in 1998 in OH; converted from the sale of MedCenter Hospital.
Foundation type: Community foundation.
Financial data (yr. ended 06/30/12): Assets, $37,433,438 (M); gifts received, $937,643; expenditures, $1,483,626; giving activities include $914,765 for 25 grants (high: $179,854).
Purpose and activities: The foundation is dedicated to enhancing the quality of life for the greater Marion area through fostering philanthropy consistent with community values by providing a vehicle for planned giving through acceptance management and distribution of endowed funds in accordance with the wishes of their donors.
Fields of interest: Public health, obesity; Health care; Eye diseases; Arthritis; Parkinson's disease; Food services; Food banks; Recreation, adaptive sports; Youth development; Human services, transportation; Disabilities, people with; Economically disadvantaged; Homeless.
International interests: Dominican Republic.
Type of support: General/operating support; Annual campaigns; Capital campaigns; Building/renovation; Equipment; Endowments; Program development; Conferences/seminars; Publication; Seed money; Curriculum development; Scholarship funds; Research; Technical assistance; Program evaluation; Scholarships—to individuals.
Limitations: Applications accepted. Giving limited to the greater Marion County, OH, area.
Publications: Application guidelines; Annual report; Financial statement; Grants list; Informational brochure; Newsletter.
Application information: Visit foundation web site for application forms and guidelines. Application form required.
Initial approach: Submit application form and attachments
Copies of proposal: 1
Deadline(s): July 26
Board meeting date(s): Monthly
Officers and Trustees:* **Susie Brown,* Chair.; Dr. Charles Garvin,* Vice-Chair.; Dean L. Jacob,* C.E.O. and Pres.; Nicole Workman,* Secy.; Megan Queen,* Treas.; Dr. James Barney; John C. Bartram; Larry Geissler**; Ted Graham; **Kathy Goodman**; Hon. Thomas K. Jenkins; Rev. Daniel Kiger; Rex Parrott; Dr. Kimberly Stark; Lowell Thurston; Dr. Scott Yancey.
Number of staff: 1 full-time professional; 1 part-time professional; 1 full-time support.
EIN: 314446189
Other changes: Susie Brown has replaced Sue Jacob as Chair. Dr. Charles Garvin has replaced De. James Barney as Vice-Chair. Dean L. Jacob has replaced Bradley C. Benout as C.E.O. and Pres. Nicole Workman has replaced Susie Brown as Secy. Megan Queen has replaced Charles Garvin as Treas.
Lori Stevenson is now Mktg. and Public Rels. Julie Prettyman is now Prog. Mgr. Diana Rinesmith is now Off. Mgr. Ronald D. Cramer, Doug Ford, Tom Johnston, Megan Queen, and Nicole Workman are no longer trustees.

2734
Mathile Family Foundation
6450 Sand Lake Rd., Ste. 100
Dayton, OH 45414-2679 **(937) 264-4600**
***Contact:* Emily Lewis, Opers. Coord.**
FAX: (937) 264-4805;
E-mail: mffinfo@mathilefamilyfoundation.org; **E-mail for letter of inquiry: grants@mathilefamilyfoundation.org**; Main
URL: http://www.mathilefamilyfoundation.org/
E-Newsletter: http://
www.mathilefamilyfoundation.org/contact/

Established in 1989 in OH.
Donors: Clayton Lee Mathile; MaryAnn Mathile.
Foundation type: Independent foundation.
Financial data (yr. ended 11/30/12): Assets, $299,902,107 (M); gifts received, $348,500; expenditures, $30,721,253; qualifying distributions, $24,589,296; giving activities include $22,830,077 for 182 grants (high: $9,100,000; low: $2,000).
Purpose and activities: The mission of the foundation is transforming the lives of children and its vision is sharing God's blessings by perpetuating a multi-generational foundation committed to philanthropic excellence. The foundation believes in fostering hope and inspiring change, impacting children in need, the strength of family, and being a servant of God's work.
Fields of interest: Education; Food services; Children/youth, services; Family services; Homeless, human services; Infants/toddlers; Children/youth; Children; Youth; Economically disadvantaged.
Type of support: General/operating support; Equipment; Program development; Matching/challenge support.
Limitations: Applications accepted. Giving primarily in the Dayton and Montgomery County, OH, areas. No support for political organizations. **No grants to individuals or for sponsorships, endowment funds, advertising for fundraising events/tickets, or mass appeals for funding.**
Publications: Application guidelines; Annual report (including application guidelines).
Application information: See foundation web site for more application information. **Application form required.**
***Initial approach:* Letter of inquiry must be e-mailed. Proposal must be submitted online**
Copies of proposal: 1
Deadline(s): Feb. 1, May 1, Aug. 1, and Nov. 1
***Final notification:* Within 100 days after the deadline**
Officers and Trustees:* **MaryAnn Mathile,* Chair., C.E.O., and Treas.**; Clayton Lee Mathile,* Pres.; Richard J. Chernesky,* Secy.; **Gregory Edwards, Exec. Dir.**; Francis J. Butler; Timothy Mathile; John C. Vatterott; Mary E. Walsh.
Number of staff: 8 full-time professional.
EIN: 311257219
Other changes: MaryAnn Mathile is now Chair., C.E.O., and Treas. Catherine Mathile Laden and Michelle Mathile are no longer trustees.

2735
Manuel D. & Rhoda Mayerson Foundation
312 Walnut St., Ste. 3600
Cincinnati, OH 45202-4029 (513) 621-7500
***Contact:* Jeff Seibert, Grants Off.**
FAX: (513) 621-2864; **E-mail for Jeff Seibert, Grants Off.: jeffs@mayersonfoundation.org; additional e-mail: info@mayersonfoundation.org**; Main
URL: http://www.mayersonfoundation.org

Established in 1986 in FL.
Donors: Manuel D. Mayerson†; Rhoda Mayerson; Manuel D. Mayerson Charitable Annuity Lead Trust; The 2002 Arlene and Neal Mayerson Charitable Lead Trust.
Foundation type: Independent foundation.
Financial data (yr. ended 10/31/12): Assets, $30,008,134 (M); gifts received, $347,935; expenditures, $3,446,513; qualifying distributions, $2,907,915; giving activities include $2,907,915 for 78 grants (high: $945,178; low: $25).
Purpose and activities: Giving primarily for Judaism, health and well-being, basic needs, inclusion, civic engagement, and the arts.
Fields of interest: Arts; Health care; Human services; Jewish federated giving programs; Jewish agencies & synagogues.
Type of support: General/operating support; Management development/capacity building; Annual campaigns; Capital campaigns; Building/renovation; Emergency funds; Program development; Seed money; Technical assistance; Matching/challenge support.
Limitations: Applications accepted. **Giving primarily in the Greater Cincinnati, OH, area, with limited grantmaking in other areas where foundation trustees reside, and at the initiative of those trustees.** No support for political organizations. No grants to individuals, or for travel or study.
Publications: Grants list; Informational brochure (including application guidelines); Multi-year report.
Application information: Letters of intent or full proposals are by invitation only, after initial correspondence with Jeff Seibert. Application form required.
***Initial approach:* Tel. or e-mail Jeff Seibert, Grants Off. to determine eligibility**
Copies of proposal: 1
Deadline(s): Ongoing
Board meeting date(s): Quarterly
Final notification: One quarter after full proposal is received
Officers and Trustees:* Neal H. Mayerson, Ph.D.*, Pres. and Treas.; Arlene B. Mayerson,* V.P.; Donna Mayerson, Ph.D.*, Secy.; Frederic H. Mayerson, J.D.; Rhoda Mayerson.
Number of staff: 3 full-time professional; 2 part-time professional; 1 full-time support.
EIN: 311310431

2736
The McGregor Foundation
c/o Foundation Management Svcs.
1422 Euclid Ave., Ste. 627
Cleveland, OH 44115-1952 (216) 621-2901
Contact: Susan O. Althans
FAX: (216) 621-8198;
E-mail: info@fmscleveland.com; Main URL: http://
www.mcgregorfoundation.org

Established in 2003 in OH from an initial endowment from The A.M. McGregor Home.
Donors: Robert Rhodes†; Mary B. Donahue†.
Foundation type: Independent foundation.
Financial data (yr. ended 04/30/13): Assets, $21,720,117 (M); gifts received, $100; expenditures, $1,148,635; qualifying distributions, $979,576; giving activities include $784,860 for 37 grants (high: $60,000; low: $3,000).
Purpose and activities: The foundation's Board of Directors favors grant requests that meet the needs of the economically disadvantaged and frail elderly in the following priority areas: 1) Home and community based care, particularly programs such as affordable housing with services; 2) Workforce development, especially related to providing

ongoing educational and training opportunities for workers engaged in direct contact with, or providing services for, seniors in home and community based settings; and 3) Total quality of life programming for seniors in all settings.
Fields of interest: Geriatrics; Human services; Residential/custodial care, hospices; Aging, centers/services; Aging.
Limitations: Applications accepted. Giving limited to Cuyahoga County, OH, with emphasis on the areas served by the A.M. McGregor Home. No support for long-term residential care facilities (for capital projects). **No grants to individuals, or for scholarships, debt reduction, annual funds, research, symposia, fundraising events, or for endowments.**
Publications: Application guidelines; Annual report; Grants list.
Application information: First time applicants and returning applicants should refer to foundation web site for specific application instructions and forms. Application form not required.
Initial approach: **Submit application online via foundation web site**
Deadline(s): Feb. 1 and Sept. 1
Board meeting date(s): Apr. and Nov.
Officers and Directors:* Jane K. Meyer,* Chair.; R. Robertson Hilton,* Secy.; William D. Buss II; Marcia Egbert; Andrew L. Fabens III; David P. Handke, Jr.; Sharon Milligan, Ph.D; Bruce D. Murphy; D. Kirk Neiswander; David N. Smith; Linda M. Warren.
EIN: 352166848

2737
Middletown Community Foundation

300 N. Main St., Ste. 300
Middletown, OH 45042 (513) 424-7369
Contact: T. Duane Gordon, Exec. Dir.
FAX: (513) 424-7555;
E-mail: info@mcfoundation.org; Main URL: http://www.mcfoundation.org/

Incorporated in 1976 in OH.
Foundation type: Community foundation.
Financial data (yr. ended 12/31/11): Assets, $23,345,511 (M); gifts received, $1,680,810; expenditures, $2,717,241; giving activities include $1,003,578 for 48+ grants, and $843,380 for 350 grants to individuals.
Purpose and activities: The mission of the foundation is to: 1) serve as a leader, catalyst and resource for philanthropy; 2) serve as a permanent and growing endowment for the community's changing needs and opportunities; 3) strive for excellence through strategic grantmaking in the areas of the arts, education, health, social services, recreation and community development; 4) provide a flexible and cost-effective way for donors to improve their community.
Fields of interest: Performing arts; Arts; Elementary/secondary education; Education, early childhood education; Elementary school/education; Higher education; Libraries/library science; Education; Health care; Recreation; Youth development, services; Youth development, citizenship; Youth, services; Family services; Human services; Community/economic development; Public affairs, citizen participation; Leadership development; Aging.
Type of support: Capital campaigns; Building/renovation; Equipment; Emergency funds; Program development; Seed money; Curriculum development; Scholarship funds; Employee matching gifts; Scholarships—to individuals; Matching/challenge support.
Limitations: Applications accepted. Giving limited to the greater Middletown, OH area. No support for religious organizations other than religious schools, medical or other research organizations, or national or regional organizations (unless program addresses local needs). No grants to individuals (except for scholarships), or for endowments or general operating budgets of established organizations.
Publications: Application guidelines; Annual report; Financial statement; Informational brochure (including application guidelines); Newsletter.
Application information: Visit foundation web site for application guidelines. Common Grant Application may be submitted for grant requests. Application form not required.
Initial approach: Submit application form and attachments
Copies of proposal: 1
Deadline(s): Mar. 1 and Sept. 1 for Recreation, Arts, Festivals, and Community Devel. grants and June 1 and Dec. 1 for Education and Human Needs grants; varies for scholarships
Board meeting date(s): Quarterly
Final notification: 60 to 90 days
Officers and Trustees:* Cathie Mulligan,* Pres.; **Richard Isroff,* V.P. and Pres.-Elect.**; Robin Dennis,* Secy.; John Venturella,* Treas.; T. Duane Gordon, Exec. Dir.; Cathy Bishop-Clark; Kee Edwards; Karen Halsey; Wendy Kissel; Gina Miltenberger; Hon. Larry Mulligan; Rick Pearce; G. Michael Pratt; Tom Scott; Carole Schul; Terrence Sherrer; Andy Singer; Verlena Stewart; Joan Stonitsch; Mike Wallner; Tom Wiley; Scott Zollett; and 6 additional trustees.
Number of staff: 1 full-time professional; 1 full-time support.
EIN: 310898380
Other changes: Richard Isroff is now V.P. and Pres.-Elect. Ron Ely is no longer Tr. Emeritus. Tim Carlson, Robin Dennis, Patricia Miller Gage, and Kathleen Dobrozki Romans are no longer trustees.

2738
Mirolo Charitable Foundation
(formerly Mirolo Foundation)

c/o Bloomfield & Kempf
175 S. 3rd St., Ste. 505
Columbus, OH 43215-5134

Established in 1994 in OH.
Donor: Amelita Mirolo.
Foundation type: Independent foundation.
Financial data (yr. ended 12/31/12): Assets, $2,849,216 (M); expenditures, $208,082; qualifying distributions, $148,000; giving activities include $148,000 for grants.
Fields of interest: Museums (art); Higher education.
Limitations: Applications not accepted. Giving primarily in OH. No grants to individuals.
Application information: Unsolicited requests for funds not accepted.
Officers and Directors:* David S. Bloomfield,* Chair.; Christopher J. Kempf,* Vice-Chair.; Paul Bloomfield,* Treas.
EIN: 311375646

2739
Morgan Family Foundation

130 Glen St., Unit 6
P.O. Box 561
Yellow Springs, OH 45387-1844 (937) 767-9208
Contact: Lori Kuhn, Exec. Dir.
FAX: (937) 767-9308;
E-mail: info@morganfamilyfdn.org; Main URL: http://www.morganfamilyfdn.org

Established in 2003 in OH.
Donors: Lee M. Morgan; Victoria A. Morgan.
Foundation type: Independent foundation.
Financial data (yr. ended 12/31/12): Assets, $45,447,366 (M); expenditures, $2,321,577; qualifying distributions, $2,321,577; giving activities include $2,072,446 for grants (high: $250,000; low: $1,000; average: $33,000–$44,329).
Purpose and activities: The foundation will be a vehicle of change and instill hope for a bright future by fostering individual human potential and the desire of communities to seek out and optimize that potential, and a movement toward a healthier, more just, more caring and sustainable society.
Fields of interest: Media, radio; Performing arts; Elementary/secondary education; Higher education; Environment; Housing/shelter, development; Youth development; Human services; Foundations (community); Children/youth; Youth; Minorities; Women.
Type of support: General/operating support; Income development; Management development/capacity building; Capital campaigns; Building/renovation; Equipment; Program development; Technical assistance; Matching/challenge support.
Limitations: Applications accepted. **Giving primarily in Yellow Springs OH, and St. Cloud, MN. Through 2015, the foundation will consider unsolicited grant requests only from the St. Cloud, MN area, and will also award grants to pre-selected public charities in Yellow Springs, OH and Portland, OR.** Generally, no support for medical research, animal rights, animal welfare causes or to promote any particular religious doctrine. No grants to individuals.
Publications: Application guidelines; Grants list.
Application information: Full applications are by invitation only, upon review of Letter of Inquiry and narrative. Application form required.
Initial approach: Letter of Inquiry on foundation web site, and a 1-page narrative via e-mail
Copies of proposal: 2
Deadline(s): Jan. and Aug.
Board meeting date(s): Apr. and Nov.
Final notification: Within three weeks of board meeting
Officers and Directors:* Lee M. Morgan,* Pres.; Victoria A. Morgan,* V.P. and Treas.; Lori Kuhn, Exec. Dir.; Stephen T. Williams, C.F.O.; Karla Morgan; Asha Morgan Moran; Marty Moran.
Number of staff: 1 full-time professional; 1 full-time support; 1 part-time support.
EIN: 300205024

2740
The Burton D. Morgan Foundation

22 Aurora St.
Hudson, OH 44236-2947 (330) 655-1660
Contact: Deborah D. Hoover, Pres.
FAX: (330) 655-1673;
E-mail: admin@bdmorganfdn.org; Contact for application guidelines: Leslie Nelson, email: lnelson@bdmorganfdn.org; Main URL: http://www.bdmorganfdn.org
e-Spirit Newsletter: http://www.bdmorganfdn.org/espirit
Flickr: https://www.flickr.com/photos/burtondmorgan/
Grants List: http://www.bdmorganfdn.org/grants-awarded
Twitter: http://twitter.com/bdmorganfdn

Venture Adventure Newsletter: http://www.bdmorganfdn.org/venture-adventure

Established in 1967 in OH.
Donor: Burton D. Morgan†.
Foundation type: Independent foundation.
Financial data (yr. ended 12/31/13): Assets, $152,371,400 (M); expenditures, $6,956,900; qualifying distributions, $4,752,000; giving activities include $4,752,000 for grants.
Purpose and activities: Giving to strengthen the free enterprise system by investing in organizations and institutions that foster the entrepreneurial spirit. The foundation is interested in supporting projects that nurture creativity, invention, entrepreneurship, and innovation. The foundation seeks to support educational programs and projects at the adult, collegiate, and youth levels that are designed to build competencies in entrepreneurship, free enterprise, and innovation; nonprofit organizations and programs that directly assist entrepreneurs in business planning, start-up and acceleration, and access to capital; and selected initiatives aimed at rejuvenating economic competitiveness within Northeast Ohio.
Fields of interest: Higher education; Business school/education; Education; Economics.
Type of support: General/operating support; Endowments; Program development; Conferences/seminars; Seed money; Curriculum development; Internship funds; Scholarship funds; Matching/challenge support.
Limitations: Applications accepted. Giving primarily in northeastern OH. No support for non 501(c)(3) public charities, or for governmental units, or to organizations or institutions that are primarily taxpayer-supported including state universities. No giving for arts or social services organizations outside of Hudson, OH. No grants to individuals or for multi-year grants or annual fund drives.
Publications: Application guidelines; Annual report (including application guidelines); Grants list; Newsletter.
Application information: Before submitting a full proposal, organizations should submit a letter of inquiry to the foundation regarding a request. The Pres. will then determine if the organization should proceed with a formal grant application. Organizations may only submit one grant proposal within a 12-month period. Please visit the foundation web site for additional information. Application form not required.
Initial approach: Letter of inquiry (1 page)
Copies of proposal: 1
Deadline(s): Sept. 1, Feb. 1 and May 1 for Letter of Inquiry; Oct. 1, Mar. 1 and June 1 for grant requests
Board meeting date(s): Jan., June, and Sept.
Officers: Deborah D. Hoover, C.E.O. and Pres.; **Denise M. Griggs, C.F.O.**
Trustees: Keith A. Brown; J. Martin Erbaugh; **Patrick T. Finley**; **J. Michael Hochwender**; Stanley C. Gault; Mark D. Robeson; Richard N. Seaman.
Number of staff: 3 full-time professional; 3 part-time professional; 2 full-time support.
EIN: 346598971
Other changes: Deborah D. Hoover is now C.E.O. and Pres. John V. Frank is no longer a trustee. The grantmaker now makes its newsletter available online.

2741
The Margaret Clark Morgan Foundation
10 W. Streetsboro St., Ste. 200
Hudson, OH 44236-2851 (330) 655-1366
Contact: Rick Kellar, Pres.
FAX: (330) 655-1696; E-mail: inquiry@mcmfdn.org; Main URL: http://www.mcmfdn.org
Grants List: http://www.mcmfdn.org/past-grants
Twitter: https://www.twitter.com/mcmfoundation
YouTube: http://www.youtube.com/user/MCMFFDN

Established in 2001 in OH.
Donors: Margaret Clark Morgan†; Burton D. Morgan†.
Foundation type: Independent foundation.
Financial data (yr. ended 12/31/12): Assets, $77,796,920 (M); gifts received, $86,285; expenditures, $4,680,090; qualifying distributions, $3,671,827; giving activities include $3,039,902 for 64 grants (high: $500,000; low: $2,500), and $161,853 for 4 foundation-administered programs.
Purpose and activities: Giving to improve the lives of people with serious mental illness by investing in innovative projects in Northeast Ohio having national transformational impact.
Fields of interest: Arts; Education; Mental health/crisis services.
Type of support: General/operating support; Continuing support; Management development/capacity building; Program development; Conferences/seminars; Curriculum development; Fellowships; Technical assistance; Consulting services; Program evaluation; Program-related investments/loans; Matching/challenge support.
Limitations: Applications accepted. Giving primarily in northeast OH counties: Ashland, Ashtabula, Carroll, Columbiana, Cuyahoga, Geauga, Holmes, Jefferson, Lake, Lorain, Mahoning, Medina, Portage, Stark, Summit, Trumbull, Tuscarwas and Wayne. No grants to individuals, or for lobbying or legislative activities.
Publications: Annual report; Grants list.
Application information: See foundation Web site for application guidelines and procedures. Application form required.
Initial approach: 1-page letter
Copies of proposal: 1
Deadline(s): Letter of inquiry deadlines: Nov. 1 and May 1
Board meeting date(s): Varies
Final notification: June and Nov.
Officers and Trustees:* A. William McGraw,* Chair.; Rick Kellar, Pres.; Jeffrey Knoll, Secy.; Jonathan Pavloff, Treas.; William H. Fellows,* Tr. Emeritus; Penelope Frese; Bob Kallstrom; Suzanne Morgan; **Theresa Proenza**; Keith Riley.
Number of staff: 5 full-time professional; 1 part-time professional.
EIN: 341948246
Other changes: Lois Margaret Nora is no longer a trustee.

2742
Morino Institute
(formerly Morino Foundation)
c/o Mario M. Morino
19111 Detroit Rd., Ste. 101
Rocky River, OH 44116-1740 **(440) 895-2950**
***FAX:* (440) 895-2951;**
E-mail: feedback@morino.org; Main URL: http://www.morino.org
GiveSmart: http://www.givesmart.org/Stories/Donors/Mario-Morino

Established in 1992 in VA.
Donor: Mario M. Morino.
Foundation type: Independent foundation.
Financial data (yr. ended 12/31/13): Assets, $659,195 (M); gifts received, $270,252; expenditures, $112,623; qualifying distributions, $112,623; giving activities include $25,000 for 1 grant.
Purpose and activities: Giving for initiatives and programs that seek to achieve positive educational, economic, and social change in four areas of focus: understanding the Internet and society, closing social divides, stimulating New Economy entrepreneurship and advancing a more effective philanthropy. Funding is typically "program directed" and is used to help evolve concepts or programs that are advancing or incubating around its focus areas.
Fields of interest: Economic development; Business/industry; Nonprofit management; Philanthropy/voluntarism; Social sciences; Public policy, research; Public affairs, citizen participation; Electronic communications/Internet.
Limitations: Applications not accepted. Giving primarily in Washington, DC. No grants to individuals.
Application information: The institute does not accept unsolicited proposals. Grants are self-directed, done in partnership, and must be closely aligned to the institute's mission.
Officers: Mario M. Morino, Chair.; Dana S. Morino, Vice-Chair.; Matthew Morino, Secy.; Rich T. McDonnell, Treas.
EIN: 541643112

2743
Grant Munro Scholarship Trust
c/o PNC Bank, N.A.
P.O. Box 94651
Cleveland, OH 44101-4651

Established in 1995.
Donor: Grant Munro.
Foundation type: Independent foundation.
Financial data (yr. ended 05/31/13): Assets, $6,349,339 (M); expenditures, $100,989; qualifying distributions, $86,102; giving activities include $72,553 for grants to individuals.
Fields of interest: Medical school/education; Theological school/education.
Type of support: Scholarships—to individuals.
Limitations: Applications not accepted. Giving primarily to residents of Fairfield County, OH.
Application information: Unsolicited requests for funds not accepted.
Trustee: PNC Bank, N.A.
EIN: 316517313
Other changes: The grantmaker no longer lists a URL address.

2744
The Murphy Family Foundation
29325 Chagrin Blvd., Ste. 103
Pepper Pike, OH 44122-4600 (216) 831-7320
Contact: Karen Rogers
FAX: (216) 831-2296; E-mail: mff@apk.net; Main URL: http://www.murphyfamilyfoundation.org
Grants List: http://www.murphyfamilyfoundation.org/grants.cfm

Established in 1986 in OH.
Donor: Members of the Murphy family.
Foundation type: Independent foundation.
Financial data (yr. ended 12/31/12): Assets, $8,109,603 (M); gifts received, $5,054,484; expenditures, $297,297; qualifying distributions, $253,700; giving activities include $253,700 for 53 grants (high: $15,000; low: $100).
Purpose and activities: The foundation considers its primary mission to be the support of viable

programs addressing the problems of poverty in the greater Cleveland, OH, area. Grantmaking is primarily to those organizations providing food for the hungry, shelter for the homeless and educational opportunities for the disadvantaged.
Fields of interest: Education; Food services; Housing/shelter, development; Human services; Children/youth, services; Homeless, human services; Economically disadvantaged; Homeless.
Type of support: General/operating support; Continuing support; Annual campaigns; Capital campaigns; Building/renovation; Equipment; Endowments; Emergency funds; Program development; Scholarship funds; Matching/challenge support.
Limitations: Applications accepted. Giving primarily in the greater Cleveland, OH, area. Generally no support for health or disability-related programs, or the arts. No grants to individuals.
Publications: Application guidelines; Annual report; Grants list.
Application information: Application information and application form available on foundation web site. Application form not required.
Copies of proposal: 1
Deadline(s): Feb. 28, June 30 and Sept. 30
Board meeting date(s): May, Aug. and Dec.
Final notification: May 15, Sept. 15 and Dec. 15
Officers and Trustees:* Melody Murphy Thomas, Pres.; Paul J. Murphy,* V.P. and Secy.-Treas.; Rita Murphy Carfagna; Brian F. Murphy; Murlan J. Murphy, Jr.; Raymond M. Murphy.
EIN: 341526161

2745
John P. Murphy Foundation

Terminal Tower
50 Public Sq., Ste. 600
Cleveland, OH 44113-2203 (216) 623-4770
Contact: Richard J. Clark, Exec. V.P.
FAX: (216) 623-4773;
E-mail: rclark@johnpmurphy.org; Additional tel.: (216) 623-4771; **Main URL: http://fdnweb.org/jpmurphy**

Incorporated in 1960 in OH.
Donor: John P. Murphy†.
Foundation type: Independent foundation.
Financial data (yr. ended 12/31/13): Assets, $51,014,926 (M); expenditures, $3,729,455; qualifying distributions, $3,387,861; giving activities include $2,694,000 for 128 grants (high: $150,000; low: $500).
Purpose and activities: Giving primarily for higher education, civic affairs, the performing arts, community development and health; support also for social services and youth. The foundation's board identified the subject of economic development in Northeastern Ohio as a special interest.
Fields of interest: Visual arts; Museums; Performing arts; Performing arts, dance; Performing arts, theater; History/archaeology; Historic preservation/historical societies; Arts; Vocational education; Higher education; Libraries/library science; Education; Hospitals (general); Medical care, rehabilitation; Nursing care; Health care; Health organizations, association; Alcoholism; Youth development, services; Human services; Children/youth, services; Women, centers/services; Urban/community development; Community/economic development; United Ways and Federated Giving Programs; Economics; Government/public administration; Leadership development; Public affairs; Disabilities, people with; Women.
Type of support: General/operating support; Continuing support; Annual campaigns; Capital campaigns; Building/renovation; Equipment; Program development; Publication; Curriculum development; Research; Consulting services; Program-related investments/loans; Exchange programs; Matching/challenge support.
Limitations: Applications not accepted. Giving primarily in Cuyahoga County, OH, and the surrounding counties. No support for K-12 education or mental health. No grants to individuals, scholarships, or for endowment funds; no loans (except for program-related investments).
Publications: Financial statement; Informational brochure.
Application information: The grantmaker is not accepting applications from new grant seekers. See foundation web site for latest application updates.
Board meeting date(s): 4 times a year
Officers and Trustees:* Nancy W. McCann,* Pres. and Treas.; Richard J. Clark,* Exec. V.P. and Secy.; Robert R. Broadbent,* V.P.; Patricia Brownell,* V.P.; John F. O'Brien,* V.P.; Leslie Resnik,* V.P.; Frederick G. Stueber,* V.P.
Number of staff: 1 full-time professional; 2 full-time support.
EIN: 346528308

2746
T. R. Murphy Residuary Trust

422 Main St.
Zanesville, OH 43701-3515
Application address: c/o Scott D. Eickelberger, 50 N. 4th St., Zanesville, OH 43701, tel.: (750) 454-2591

Established in 1985.
Foundation type: Independent foundation.
Financial data (yr. ended 06/30/13): Assets, $3,195,472 (M); expenditures, $197,903; qualifying distributions, $197,903; giving activities include $41,367 for grants, and $114,486 for 362 grants to individuals (high: $800; low: $200).
Purpose and activities: Awards scholarships to worthy graduates of Muskingum County, OH, high schools; also supports operating expenses of local area Catholic schools.
Fields of interest: Elementary/secondary education; Scholarships/financial aid; Catholic agencies & churches.
Type of support: General/operating support; Scholarships—to individuals.
Limitations: Applications accepted. Giving limited to Muskingum County, OH.
Application information: Application form required for scholarships.
Deadline(s): May 1 for scholarships
Committee Members: Scott D. Eickelberger; **Jennifer Mallett**; Perry Robinson; **Jeff Zellers; Mark Ulbrich.**
EIN: 316285970

2747
Muskingum County Community Foundation

534 Putnam Ave.
Zanesville, OH 43701-4933 (740) 453-5192
Contact: David P. Mitzel, Exec. Dir.; For scholarships: Heather Sands, Dir., College Access Progs.
FAX: (740) 453-5734; E-mail: giving@mccf.org; Main URL: http://www.mccf.org
Facebook: http://www.facebook.com/pages/Muskingum-County-Community-Foundation/80469432596
Scholarship Central tel.: (740) 453-5192

Established in 1985 in OH.
Foundation type: Community foundation.
Financial data (yr. ended 12/31/12): Assets, $22,308,503 (M); gifts received, $939,979; expenditures, $2,401,011; giving activities include $1,621,540 for grants.
Purpose and activities: The mission of the Muskingum County Community Foundation.
Fields of interest: Performing arts; Performing arts, music; Arts; Elementary/secondary education; Libraries/library science; Education; Animal welfare; Animals/wildlife, preservation/protection; Hospitals (general); Health care; Recreation; Youth development, services; Children/youth, services; Residential/custodial care, hospices; Human services; Community/economic development; Leadership development; Aging.
Type of support: General/operating support; Capital campaigns; Building/renovation; Equipment; Land acquisition; Endowments; Program development; Conferences/seminars; Publication; Seed money; Fellowships; Internship funds; Scholarship funds; Research; Technical assistance; Consulting services; Program-related investments/loans; Scholarships—to individuals; In-kind gifts; Matching/challenge support.
Limitations: Applications accepted. Giving limited to Muskingum County, OH.
Publications: Application guidelines; Annual report; Grants list; Informational brochure; Newsletter.
Application information: Visit foundation web site for application form and guidelines. Application form required.
Initial approach: Submit application and attachments
Copies of proposal: 11
Deadline(s): Mar. 1 and Nov. 1 for grant proposals
Board meeting date(s): 4th Wed. of Jan., Apr., July, and Oct.
Final notification: Within 30 days
Officers and Trustees:* Tim McLain,* Pres.; Greg Adams,* V.P.; Steven G. Randles,* Secy.; Michael Steen,* Treas.; David P. Mitzel, Exec. Dir.; Jamie Thomas, Cont.; Thomas Holdren; Monica Martinelli; Susan Montgomery McDonald; Michael Micheli; D. Scott Moyer; Dr. Doug Ramsay; Dan Sylvester; Beth Upton; Brian Wagner.
Number of staff: 2 full-time professional; 1 full-time support; 1 part-time support.
EIN: 311147022
Other changes: Juliet Lacy is now Dir., Donor Srvs. and Community Youth Foundation Advisor. Matthew Elli, Melanie Imlay, Jim Lepi, Ryan Moyer, Patrick Nash, Alana Ryan, Susan Stubbins, and Geraldine Zylinsky are no longer trustees.

2748
National Machinery Foundation Inc.

P.O. Box 747
Tiffin, OH 44883-0747 **(419) 443-2306**
***Contact:* Larry F. Baker, Pres.**
FAX: (419) 443-2184

Incorporated in 1948 in OH.
Donors: National Machinery Co.; National Machinery LLC.
Foundation type: Company-sponsored foundation.
Financial data (yr. ended 12/31/12): Assets, $15,089,753 (M); expenditures, $706,859; qualifying distributions, $611,634; giving activities include $611,634 for grants.
Purpose and activities: The foundation supports organizations involved with theater, education, health, child welfare, housing development, animal welfare, human services, and community development; and awards grants for good

citizenship to high school students and relief assistance to needy individuals in Seneca County, OH.
Fields of interest: Performing arts, theater; Elementary/secondary education; Higher education; Education; Animal welfare; Hospitals (general); Health care; Crime/violence prevention, child abuse; Housing/shelter, development; Salvation Army; YM/YWCAs & YM/YWHAs; Youth, services; Human services; Community/economic development; United Ways and Federated Giving Programs.
Type of support: General/operating support; Annual campaigns; Capital campaigns; Equipment; Emergency funds; Program development; Scholarship funds; Sponsorships; Employee-related scholarships; Grants to individuals; Scholarships—to individuals.
Limitations: Applications accepted. Giving limited to the Seneca County, OH, area.
Application information: Application form required.
Initial approach: **Letter**
Deadline(s): None
Officer: Larry F. Baker, Pres.
Number of staff: 1 part-time professional.
EIN: 346520191
Other changes: The grantmaker no longer lists an E-mail address.

2749
The Needmor Fund
42 S. St. Clair St.
Toledo, OH 43604-8736 (419) 255-5560
Contact: Mary Sobecki, Grants Mgr.
FAX: (419) 255-5561;
E-mail: msobecki@needmorfund.org; **Additional e-mail: moreinfo@needmorfund.org**; Main URL: http://www.needmorfund.org/
Online insructional application video: https://www.youtube.com/watch?v=_oPaOE3V7uU
The Needmor Fund's Philanthropy Promise: http://www.ncrp.org/philanthropys-promise/who

Trust established in 1956 in OH.
Donor: Members of the Stranahan family.
Foundation type: Independent foundation.
Financial data (yr. ended 12/31/12): Assets, $23,974,238 (M); gifts received, $857,103; expenditures, $2,419,588; qualifying distributions, $2,210,648; giving activities include $1,559,769 for 74 grants (high: $40,000; low: $250).
Purpose and activities: The mission of The Needmor Fund is to work with others to bring about social justice. It supports groups that work together to change the social, economic, or political conditions that bar access to participation in a democratic society. Needmor has identified grassroots community organizing as the most effective process by which low- and moderate-income people can build power, address the systemic barriers to the practice of democracy, hold public and corporate officials accountable for their actions, and begin to participate in shaping public policy. Its grantmaking is focused exclusively on providing support for multi-issue, democratically controlled, membership-based community organizations.
Fields of interest: Community development, citizen coalitions.
Type of support: General/operating support.
Limitations: Applications accepted. Giving limited to the U.S. No support for public or private schools. No grants to individuals, or for capital or endowment funds, scholarships, fellowships, matching gifts, deficit financing, operating support for traditional community services, replacement of lost government funding, land acquisition, purchase of buildings or equipment, or publications, media, computer projects or research.
Publications: Application guidelines; Biennial report (including application guidelines); Financial statement; Grants list.
Application information: Application form required.
Initial approach: **Use online grantmaking system on foundation web site**
Deadline(s): **See foundation web site for current deadlines**
Board meeting date(s): May and Nov.
Officers and Directors:* Abby Stranahan,* Chair.; Ken Rolling,* Vice-Chair.; Daniel Stranahan, Secy.-Treas.; Frank I. Sanchez, Exec. Dir.; Susan Chinn; Louis Delgado; James Dickson; Ana Guerrero; Virginia Parry; Ann Stranahan; Mary C. Stranahan; Patti Stranahan.
Number of staff: 3 full-time professional; 1 full-time support.
EIN: 346504812

2750
New Albany Community Foundation
220 Market St., Ste. 205
New Albany, OH 43054-9031 (614) 939-8150
***Contact:* J. Craig Mohre, Exec. Dir.**
FAX: (614) 939-8155;
E-mail: craigmohre@newalbanyfoundation.org; Main URL: http://www.newalbanyfoundation.org
Facebook: http://www.facebook.com/pages/The-New-Albany-Community-Foundation/111921911896
YouTube: https://www.youtube.com/user/newalbanycf?feature=watch

Established in 1994 in OH.
Foundation type: Community foundation.
Financial data (yr. ended 06/30/13): Assets, $10,677,162 (M); gifts received, $3,022,775; expenditures, $2,050,023; giving activities include $1,232,440 for 15 grants (high: $180,000; low: $600).
Purpose and activities: The foundation's mission is to assist donors and others in strengthening and improving New Albany, OH, for the benefit of all of its residents. The scope of the foundation's charitable grantmaking includes both capital and program grants.
Fields of interest: Humanities; Arts; Education; Environment; Health care; Human services; Community/economic development.
Limitations: Applications accepted. Giving limited to New Albany, OH. No support for religious organizations or religious purposes. No grants to individuals (except for scholarships), or for operating expenses, deficit financing for programs or capital expenditures, endowment funds, annual appeals, membership contributions, conferences, or recognition events.
Publications: Application guidelines; Annual report.
Application information: Visit foundation web site for application form and guidelines. Application form required.
Initial approach: Contact foundation
Copies of proposal: 3
Board meeting date(s): Apr., July, and Oct.
Officers and Trustees:* Michael J. DeAscentis, Jr.,* Chair.; Dennis E. Welch,* Vice-Chair.; J. Craig Mohre,* Pres.; Patti Steinour,* Secy.; **Kirt A. Walker,* Treas.**; J. Craig Mohre, Exec. Dir.; Keith R. Berend, M.D.; Scott Bracale; Philip Heit, Ph.D.; Cindy Hilsheimer; Richard P. Lavin; Michael Marx; Ira Sharfin; Sanjay Singh.
Number of staff: 1 full-time professional; 1 part-time support.
EIN: 311409264
Other changes: At the close of 2013, the grantmaker paid grants of $1,232,440, a 249.8% increase over the 2012 disbursements, $352,299.
Michael J. DeAscentis, Jr. has replaced Cindy Hilsheimer as Chair. Dennis E. Welch has replaced Michael J. DeAscentis Jr. as Vice-Chair. Kirt A. Walker has replaced Ira Sharfin as Treas.
Jonathan Ramsden is no longer a member of the governing body. Rich Ramsey is no longer a member of the governing body. Yaromir Steiner is no longer a member of the governing body. Kirt A. Walker is no longer a member of the governing body. Dennis E. Welch is no longer a member of the governing body.
The grantmaker now publishes application guidelines.

2751
L. and L. Nippert Charitable Foundation, Inc.
c/o The Randolph Co.
8255 Spooky Hollow Rd.
Cincinnati, OH **45242-6518**
Contact: Carter Randolph Ph.D., V.P.
E-mail: info@lnlcharitable.org; **Contact for grantmaking process: Peggy Schatz, tel.: (513) 891-4227**; Main URL: http://www.lnlcharitable.org

Established in 1992 in OH as successor to L. and L. Nippert Charitable Foundation.
Donors: Louis Nippert‡; Louise D. Nippert‡; Louise Dieterle Nippert Trust.
Foundation type: Independent foundation.
Financial data (yr. ended 12/31/12): Assets, $18,680,682 (M); gifts received, $5,526,007; expenditures, $741,432; qualifying distributions, $631,982; giving activities include $630,000 for 16 grants (high: $120,000; low: $5,000).
Purpose and activities: Giving primarily for education, human services, and to a children's hospital as well as a YMCA.
Fields of interest: Education; Hospitals (specialty); Human services; YM/YWCAs & YM/YWHAs; Children/youth, services.
Type of support: General/operating support; Continuing support; Annual campaigns; Capital campaigns; Building/renovation; Program development; Curriculum development; Internship funds; Scholarship funds; Research.
Limitations: Giving primarily in the greater Cincinnati, OH area; some funding also in MO and TN. **No grants to individuals, or for endowments.**
Publications: Application guidelines; IRS Form 990 or 990-PF printed copy available upon request.
Application information: Applicants must use 12-point type and 1 inch margins all around. Applicants may use the Ohio Common Grant Application Short Form (which can be downloaded from foundation web site) to submit a proposal. All applications must be received on a USB flash drive in Microsoft Word format with one original hard copy. The Summary of Grant Request and application should be separate files on the disk. See foundation web site for additional application information. Application form required.
Initial approach: **Use Summary of Grant Request (which can be downloaded from foundation web site) and an application**
Deadline(s): Sept. 15
Board meeting date(s): Annual
Officers and Directors:* Dr. Carter Randolph,* V.P. and Treas.; Lawrence Kyte, Secy.; Marie Eberhard;

Dr. Timothy Johnson; Guy Randolph, Jr.; **Jane R. Randolph**; Nancy Walker.
EIN: 311351011
Other changes: The grantmaker now publishes application guidelines.

2752
NiSource Charitable Foundation
(formerly Columbia Gas Foundation)
200 Civic Center Dr.
Columbus, OH 43215-4138 **(219) 647-6209**
Contact: Jennifer L. Moench, Exec. Dir.
E-mail: jmoench@nisource.com; **Additional address: NiSource Corp. Citizenship, 801 E. 86th Ave., Merrillville, IN 46410-6271**; Main URL: http://www.nisource.com/en/sustainability/communities/corporate-giving.aspx

Established in 1990 in DE.
Donors: The Columbia Gas System, Inc.; Columbia Energy Group; Columbia Gas of Ohio, Inc.; NiSource Corporate Services Co.
Foundation type: Company-sponsored foundation.
Financial data (yr. ended 12/31/12): Assets, $19,821,130 (M); expenditures, $2,780,036; qualifying distributions, $2,702,789; giving activities include $2,702,789 for 210 grants (high: $1,004,700; low: $50).
Purpose and activities: The foundation supports programs designed to promote community vitality and development; environmental and energy sustainability; learning and science education; and public safety and human services.
Fields of interest: Education; Environment, energy; Environment; Safety/disasters; Salvation Army; Human services; Community/economic development; United Ways and Federated Giving Programs; Science, formal/general education; Science.
Type of support: Continuing support; Annual campaigns; Building/renovation; Program development.
Limitations: Applications accepted. Giving on a national basis in areas of company operations, with some emphasis on IN and OH. No support for religious organizations, political candidates or organizations, or discriminatory organizations. No grants to individuals, or for sports sponsorships, goodwill advertising, fundraising benefits, or program books.
Publications: Application guidelines.
Application information: Application form required.
Initial approach: **Contact local community relations representative or e-mail foundation for application form**
Copies of proposal: 1
Deadline(s): Varies
Board meeting date(s): May and Oct.
Officers and Trustees:* Robert E. Smith, Secy.; David J. Vadja, Treas.; Julie Wozniak, Cont.; Jennifer L. Moench,* Exec. Dir.; Robert D. Campbell; **Joseph Hamrock**; Christopher A. Helms; Carrie J. Hightman; Glen L. Kettering; Kathleen O'Leary; Robert C. Skaggs, Jr.; S Stephen P. Smith; Jimmy D. Staton; Jim L. Stanley.
EIN: 510324200
Other changes: Gary W. Pottorff is no longer Secy. Susanne M. Taylor is no longer Cont.

2753
Donald and Alice Noble Foundation, Inc.
(formerly Donald E. and Alice M. Noble Charitable Foundation, Inc.)
1061 Venture Blvd.
Wooster, OH **44691-9358 (330) 264-8066**
Contact: David D. Noble, Pres.
FAX: (330) 264-8083

Established in 1990 in OH.
Donors: Donald E. Noble†; Alice M. Noble.
Foundation type: Independent foundation.
Financial data (yr. ended 12/31/12): Assets, $37,611,595 (M); expenditures, $3,978,777; qualifying distributions, $2,481,548; giving activities include $2,276,494 for 81 grants (high: $501,300; low: $50).
Purpose and activities: Giving for education and human services.
Fields of interest: Education, public education; Secondary school/education; Human services; Foundations (community); Children/youth; Youth; Economically disadvantaged.
International interests: Ghana; Honduras; Kenya; Namibia; Nicaragua; South Africa.
Type of support: General/operating support; Capital campaigns; Program development.
Limitations: Giving primarily in Wooster, OH and in Ghana and Honduras. No grants to individuals.
Application information: Application form not required.
Initial approach: Letter
Copies of proposal: 1
Deadline(s): None
Board meeting date(s): Spring and fall
Final notification: 2 weeks
Officer: David D. Noble, Pres.
Trustees: Nancy L. Holland; Steve Matthew; Donald Noble II; Matthew Noble; Chris Schmid.
Number of staff: 1 full-time professional; 1 full-time support.
EIN: 341665641

2754
The Nord Family Foundation
747 Milan Ave.
Amherst, OH 44001-1310 (440) 984-3939
Contact: John Mullaney, Exec. Dir.
FAX: (440) 984-3934; E-mail: johnm@nordft.org; Additional tel.: (800) 745-8946; E-mail: info@nordff.org or execdir@nordff.org; Main URL: http://www.nordff.org
Grants Database: http://www.nordff.org/meet_grantees

Trust established in 1952 in OH; reorganized in 1988 under current name.
Donors: Walter G. Nord†; Mrs. Walter G. Nord†; Nordson Corp.
Foundation type: Independent foundation.
Financial data (yr. ended 12/31/12): Assets, $114,162,559 (M); gifts received, $25,000; expenditures, $6,432,613; qualifying distributions, $5,925,174; giving activities include $4,924,413 for 445 grants (high: $100,000; low: $25), and $219,457 for 3 foundation-administered programs.
Purpose and activities: Emphasis on projects to assist the disadvantaged and minorities, including giving for early childhood, secondary, and higher education, social services, health, cultural affairs, and civic activities. Initiatives included a project to establish a common agenda to address factors which inhibit social and economic progress within the county and a program to strengthen nonprofit organizations which address family issues.
Fields of interest: Arts; Education, early childhood education; Child development, education; Secondary school/education; Higher education; Education; Environment; Health care; Health organizations, association; Human services; Children/youth, services; Child development, services; Minorities/immigrants, centers/services; Urban/community development; Children/youth; Children; Youth; Minorities; Economically disadvantaged; Homeless.
Type of support: General/operating support; Continuing support; Capital campaigns; Building/renovation; Program development; Conferences/seminars; Publication; Seed money; Technical assistance; Program-related investments/loans; Employee matching gifts; Matching/challenge support.
Limitations: Applications accepted. Giving primarily in the Lorain and Cuyahoga County, OH, areas; also gives secondarily in Denver, CO, Boston, MA, and Columbia, SC. No support for religious or political organizations. No grants to individuals, or for deficit financing, research, capital campaigns, tickets, or advertising for fundraising activities.
Publications: Application guidelines; Annual report (including application guidelines); Financial statement; Grants list; Informational brochure (including application guidelines); Occasional report.
Application information: Colorado Common Grant Application form accepted. Application form required.
Initial approach: **Online grant application and eligibility quiz on foundation web site**
Copies of proposal: 1
Deadline(s): Apr. 1, Aug. 1, and Dec. 1
Board meeting date(s): Feb., June, and Oct.
Final notification: 1 to 3 months
Officers and Trustees:* Kathleen Nord Peterson,* Pres.; Virginia Barbato,* V.P.; Brian Ignat,* Secy.; Joseph Ignat,* Treas.; Sharon White, Cont.; John J. Mullaney, Exec. Dir.; J. Mac Bennett; Caprice Bragg; **T.K. McClintock**; **Cindy Nord**; Eric Charles Nord; Shannon Nord; Donald Sheldon*; Allyson Wandtke.
Number of staff: 3 full-time professional; 1 part-time professional; 1 full-time support; 1 part-time support.
EIN: 341595929
Other changes: Kathleen Nord Peterson has replaced Elizabeth Bausch as Pres. Eric Barbato is no longer a trustee.

2755
The Nordson Corporation Foundation
28601 Clemens Rd.
Westlake, OH 44145-1119 (440) 892-1580
Contact: Cecilia H. Render, Exec. Dir.
E-mail: crender@nordson.com; **Contact for Lorain County, OH: Kathy Ladiner, Grants Mgr., e-mail: kladiner@nordson.com; Mahoning County, OH and PA: Johanna Friedrich, e-mail: j.friedrich@us.xaloy.com; GA: Cindy Baumgardner, Prog. Off., tel.: (770) 497-3672, e-mail: cindy.baumgardner@nordson.com; CO: Marcus Kincaid, tel.: (970) 2675200, e-mail: marcus.kincaid@nordson.com; CA: Ray McHenry, Dir., HR, tel.: (760) 930-7258, e-mail: ray.mchenry@nordson.com; NJ: Jennifer Kuhn, tel.: (609) 772-8462, e-mail: jennifer.kuhn@nordson.com; RI and southern MA: Shannon Aiton, Exec. Asst., tel.: (401) 431-7094; and WI: Wendy Crotteau, e-mail: wcrotteau@extrusiondies.com**; Main URL: http://www.nordson.com/en-us/about-nordson/community/Pages/NordsonCorporationFoundationWelcomePage1.aspx
Grants List: http://www.nordson.com/en-us/about-nordson/community/Pages/2008-Foundation-Annual-Report.aspx

Established in 1988 in OH as successor to the Nordson Foundation, established in 1952.
Donor: Nordson Corp.
Foundation type: Company-sponsored foundation.
Financial data (yr. ended 10/31/13): Assets, $23,678,161 (M); gifts received, $12,425,394; expenditures, $4,180,899; qualifying distributions, $4,087,865; giving activities include $4,087,865 for 217 grants (high: $560,000; low: $2,100).
Purpose and activities: The foundation supports organizations involved with education. Special emphasis is directed toward programs that cultivate educational curriculum and experiences that foster self-sufficiency, job readiness, and goals to aspire to higher education.
Fields of interest: Arts, cultural/ethnic awareness; Visual arts; Performing arts; Historic preservation/historical societies; Arts; Education, reform; Elementary/secondary education; Education, reading; Education; Environment; Employment, training; Housing/shelter; Human services, alliance/advocacy; Human services, reform; Children/youth, services; Family services; Human services, personal services; Human services; Economic development; Voluntarism promotion; Science, formal/general education; Mathematics; Public affairs, citizen participation; Accessibility/universal design; Public affairs; Youth; Economically disadvantaged; Homeless.
Type of support: Continuing support; Annual campaigns; Capital campaigns; Building/renovation; Equipment; Emergency funds; Seed money; Curriculum development; Scholarship funds; Technical assistance; Employee volunteer services; Employee matching gifts.
Limitations: Applications accepted. Giving primarily in areas of company operations, with emphasis on North San Diego County, CA, Larimer County, CO, Dawson County, Gwinnett County, and Emanuel County, GA, Mahoning County, OH, southeastern, MA, Mercer County, NJ, Lawrence County, PA, Providence, RI, VA, Chippewa County, WI. No support for political organizations or candidates or discriminatory organizations. No grants to individuals (except for Nordson BUILDS Scholarships), or for loans, endowments, membership drives, or travel.
Publications: Application guidelines; Annual report; Grants list; Program policy statement.
Application information: Applicants are encouraged to contact the Foundation staff member who represents their geographic area before applying. Organizations receiving support are asked to provide a final report. Application form required.
Initial approach: Complete online application
Copies of proposal: 1
Deadline(s): Feb. 15 for Mahoning County, OH, PA, and VA; Feb. 15, and May 15 for CA; Feb. 15, May 15, Aug. 15, and Nov. 15 for Lorain County, OH; May 15 for CO; Aug. 15 for NJ and RI; Aug. 15, May 15, and Nov. 15 for GA; and Nov. 15 for WI
Board meeting date(s): Feb., Apr., July, and Oct.
Final notification: Within 3 months of application
Officers and Directors:* Michael F. Hilton, Pres. and C.E.O.; John J. Keane, Sr. V.P.; Peter Lambert, Sr. V.P.; Doug Bloomfield, V.P.; Shelly Peet, V.P.; Greg Thaxton, C.F.O.; Beverly J. Coen,* Chief Tax and Risk Off.; Cecilia H. Render, Exec. Dir.
Number of staff: 3 full-time professional; 1 full-time support.
EIN: 341596194
Other changes: Joan Szczepanik is now Prog. Off. James DeVries is no longer a director. Ray McHenry is now Dir., Human Resources, CA. Stephanie Shaw is no longer Mgr., Human Resources, RI.

2756
The Ohio National Foundation
1 Financial Way
Cincinnati, OH 45242-5851 (513) 794-6100
Contact: Anthony G. Esposito, Tr.
***Main URL:* https://www.ohionational.com/portal/site/client/ON_Foundation/**

Established in 1987 in OH.
Donors: The Ohio National Life Insurance Co.; Ohio National Financial Svcs.
Foundation type: Company-sponsored foundation.
Financial data (yr. ended 12/31/12): Assets, $3,769,784 (M); gifts received, $300,000; expenditures, $1,216,871; qualifying distributions, $1,215,860; giving activities include $1,215,860 for 94 grants (high: $184,500; low: $50).
Purpose and activities: The foundation supports hospitals and organizations involved with arts and culture, education, housing development, and human services.
Fields of interest: Arts, association; Museums; Museums (art); Performing arts, orchestras; Performing arts, opera; Arts; Education, early childhood education; Higher education; Libraries (public); Education; Hospitals (general); Housing/shelter, development; Boy scouts; American Red Cross; Children/youth, services; Residential/custodial care; Aging, centers/services; Developmentally disabled, centers & services; Human services; United Ways and Federated Giving Programs.
Type of support: General/operating support; Annual campaigns; Capital campaigns; Building/renovation; Sponsorships; Employee matching gifts.
Limitations: Applications accepted. Giving primarily in Cincinnati, OH. No grants to individuals.
Application information: Application form required.
Initial approach: Proposal
Deadline(s): None
Trustees: Howard C. Becker; Joseph Campanella; Christopher A. Carlson; Ronald J. Dolan; Anthony G. Esposito; Diane S. Hagenbuch; Gary T. Huffman; David B. O'Maley.
EIN: 311230164

2757
The Ohio Valley Foundation
c/o Fifth Third Bank
P.O. Box 630858
Cincinnati, OH **45263-0858**
Contact: Heidi B. Jark, V.P. and Mgr., Fifth Third Bank
***Application address:* c/o Fifth Third Bank Foundation, 38 Fountain Sq. Plz. M/D 1090CA, Cincinnati, OH 45263, tel.: (513) 534-4397**

Incorporated in 1946 in OH.
Donors: John J. Rowe†; L. McGrath†; John W. Warrington†.
Foundation type: Independent foundation.
Financial data (yr. ended 09/30/13): Assets, $6,972,130 (M); expenditures, $384,232; qualifying distributions, $322,521; giving activities include $304,000 for 16 grants (high: $25,000; low: $4,000).
Fields of interest: Museums; Arts; Education; Youth development, community service clubs; Human services; YM/YWCAs & YM/YWHAs.
Type of support: Capital campaigns; Building/renovation.
Limitations: Applications accepted. Giving primarily in the greater Cincinnati, OH, area. No support for religious organizations. No grants to individuals, or for endowment funds or operating budgets.
Publications: Application guidelines; Annual report.
Application information: Organizations will be given an Ohio Common Grant Application Form by invitation from the foundation. Application form required.
Initial approach: Letter
Copies of proposal: 1
Deadline(s): None
Board meeting date(s): Jan., Mar., June, and Sept.
Final notification: Immediately after meeting
Officers and Board Members:* Thomas Shiller,* Chair.; Phillip C. Long, Secy.-Treas.; Mitchel D. Livingston, Ph.D.; Mike Michael; Carolyn McCoy; Leigh Prop; Jann Seidenfaden; Dudley S. Taft.
EIN: 316008508
Other changes: George A. Schaefer is no longer a trustee. Thomas Shiller is now Chair. Phillip C. Long is now Secy.-Treas.

2758
Omnicare Foundation
900 Omnicare Ctr.
201 E. 4th St.
Cincinnati, OH 45202 (513) 719-2600
***Contact:* Donna M. Lecky**

Established in 1993 in KY.
Donors: Omnicare, Inc.; Thomas R. Isgrig.
Foundation type: Company-sponsored foundation.
Financial data (yr. ended 12/31/12): Assets, $756,859 (M); gifts received, $898,500; expenditures, $148,572; qualifying distributions, $148,144; giving activities include $130,500 for 16 grants (high: $35,000; low: $1,000).
Purpose and activities: The foundation supports organizations involved with education, health, children and youth, and Judaism. Special emphasis directed toward programs designed to benefit the geriatric population.
Fields of interest: Education; Health care; Religion.
Type of support: General/operating support; Capital campaigns; Program development; Research; Sponsorships.
Limitations: Applications accepted. Giving primarily in IL, NY, and OH, and in Israel. No grants to individuals.
Application information: Application form required.
Initial approach: Letter of inquiry
Deadline(s): None
Officers and Trustees :* Andrea R. Lindell,* Chair.; Erin Ascher, Vice-Chair.; Alexander Kayne, Secy.; Regis T. Robbins, Treas.; **Rocky Kraft**; Nitin Sahney; John L. Workman.
EIN: 311389112

2759
OMNOVA Solutions Foundation, Inc.
175 Ghent Rd.
Fairlawn, OH 44333-3300 (330) 869-4289
Contact: Theresa Carter, Pres.
Main URL: http://www.omnova.com/about/community/community.aspx

Established in 1999 in OH.
Donor: GenCorp Foundation Inc.
Foundation type: Company-sponsored foundation.
Financial data (yr. ended 11/30/12): Assets, $23,346,058 (M); expenditures, $1,886,964; qualifying distributions, $1,826,544; giving activities include $1,674,415 for 545 grants (high: $118,000; low: -$1,000).
Purpose and activities: The foundation supports programs designed to create educational opportunities; connect people to health and social

services; energize civic pride; and create access to the arts.
Fields of interest: Arts, cultural/ethnic awareness; Performing arts; Arts; Elementary/secondary education; Adult education—literacy, basic skills & GED; Education, services; Education, reading; Education; Hospitals (general); Crime/violence prevention; Disasters, preparedness/services; Safety/disasters; Family services, parent education; Human services; Economic development; Urban/community development; Mathematics; Science; Public affairs.
International interests: Canada; China; France; India; Thailand.
Type of support: General/operating support; Continuing support; Annual campaigns; Capital campaigns; Building/renovation; Endowments; Program development; Scholarship funds; Employee volunteer services; Employee matching gifts; Employee-related scholarships; In-kind gifts.
Limitations: Applications accepted. **Giving primarily in areas of company operations in GA, MA, MS, NC, OH, PA, SC, WI, and in Canada, China, France, India, and Thailand; giving on a limited basis to national organizations.** No support for private foundations, fraternal, social, labor, or veterans' organizations, discriminatory organizations, organizations not of direct benefit to the entire community, political parties or candidates, organizations posing a conflict of interest with OMNOVA, or churches or religious organizations. No grants to individuals (except for employee-related scholarships), or for lobbying activities, local athletic or sports programs or sports equipment, travel, advertising, benefits, raffles, or similar fundraising events, or research or conferences.
Publications: Application guidelines; Annual report.
Application information: Multi-year funding is not automatic. Telephone solicitations will not be considered. Application form not required.
Initial approach: **Proposal**
Copies of proposal: 1
Deadline(s): None
Board meeting date(s): As required
***Final notification:* 4 to 6 weeks**
Officers: Michael E. Hicks, Chair.; S. Theresa Carter, Pres.; Kristine G. Syrvalin,* Secy.; Frank P. Robers,* Treas.
Trustees: Sandi Noah; Nick Triantafillopoulos.
Number of staff: 1 full-time professional; 1 part-time support.
EIN: 341909350
Other changes: The grantmaker no longer lists a fax. The grantmaker no longer lists an E-mail address.

2760
The William J. and Dorothy K. O'Neill Foundation, Inc.

30195 Chagrin Blvd., Ste. 106
Cleveland, OH 44124-5703 (216) 831-4134
Contact: Leah S. Gary, Pres. and C.E.O.; Cynthia Drennan, Grants Mgr.; Catherine T. Abbott, Dir.
FAX: (216) 378-0594;
E-mail: info@oneill-foundation.org; Contact for letter of inquiry: Timothy M. McCue, Sr. Prog. Off., tel.: (216) 831-4136, e-mail: mccuetmm@oneill-foundation.org; For questions regarding the application process or submission of application form: Symone McClain, Mgr. Grants and Office Opers., tel.: (216) 831-4135, e-mail: smcclain@oneill-foundation.org; Main URL: http://www.oneillfdn.org
Facebook: https://www.facebook.com/oneillfoundation
Twitter: https://twitter.com/oneillfdn

Established in 1987 in OH.
Donor: Dorothy K. O'Neill†.
Foundation type: Independent foundation.
Financial data (yr. ended 12/31/12): Assets, $78,967,608 (M); gifts received, $103,969; expenditures, $4,599,449; qualifying distributions, $3,606,582; giving activities include $3,019,893 for 179 grants (high: $150,000; low: $100).
Purpose and activities: The foundation's philosophy is rooted in the shared values, sentiments and beliefs of members of the O'Neill family. The foundation exists to serve our fellow human beings. The foundation believes they can best serve by maximizing all their resources and deploying them under well thought-out strategies, developed in partnership with others, in important areas of large beneficial impact. The foundation's vision is for strong communities where families thrive. The foundation's mission is to partner with nonprofits to improve the quality of life for families and communities, in places where O'Neill family members live.
Fields of interest: Family services; Children/youth; Children; Youth; Adults; Aging; Young adults; Disabilities, people with; Physically disabled; Blind/visually impaired; Deaf/hearing impaired; Mentally disabled; Minorities; Asians/Pacific Islanders; African Americans/Blacks; Hispanics/Latinos; Women; Girls; Adults, women; Young adults, female; Men; Boys; Adults, men; Young adults, male; Offenders/ex-offenders; Substance abusers; Single parents; Crime/abuse victims; Terminal illness, people with; Economically disadvantaged; Homeless.
Type of support: Income development; Management development/capacity building; Program development; Conferences/seminars; Curriculum development; Technical assistance; Consulting services; Program evaluation; Matching/challenge support.
Limitations: Applications accepted. **Giving primarily in areas where family members reside: the Washington, DC metropolitan area (including Prince George and Montgomery counties in MD), Bonita Springs, Greater Orlando, and Naples, FL, Big Island, HI, Annapolis, Anne Arundel, and Baltimore City, MD, New York, NY, Cleveland, Columbus, and Licking County, OH, Austin and Houston, TX, and Alexandria, Arlington, Richmond and Virginia Beach, VA.** No support for organizations operating outside the U.S., or for agencies engaging in lobbying or evangelization. No grants to individuals, or for annual campaigns, general operating costs, debt retirement, fundraising events, lobbying activities, capital campaigns or scholarships.
Publications: Application guidelines; Annual report (including application guidelines); Financial statement; Grants list; Occasional report.
Application information: Application form required.
Initial approach: Letter of inquiry via form on foundation web site
Copies of proposal: 3
Deadline(s): See foundation web site for current deadlines
Board meeting date(s): Mar. 13, July 17 and Oct. 30
Final notification: By e-mail and letter
Officers and Trustees:* Kelly Sweeney McShane,* Chair.; Dennis W. Bower,* Chair., Grantmaking Comm.; Leah S. Gary,* C.E.O. and Pres.; Sara O'Neill Sullivan, Secy.; Robert W. Donahey,* Treas.; William J. O'Neill, Jr., Tr. Emeritus; Linda M. Clifford; John H. O'Neill.
Number of staff: 3 full-time professional.
EIN: 341560893

2761
Robert O. and AnnaMae Orr Family Foundation

1817 Brookwood Dr.
Akron, OH 44313-5061
Contact: Karen Murray, Exec. Dir.
E-mail: karenmurray45@yahoo.com; Main URL: http://www.orrfamilyfoundation.org

Established in 1998 in OH.
Donor: Robert O. Orr†.
Foundation type: Independent foundation.
Financial data (yr. ended 12/31/12): Assets, $8,467,791 (M); gifts received, $25; expenditures, $774,441; qualifying distributions, $610,424; giving activities include $510,276 for 37 grants (high: $70,000; low: $300).
Fields of interest: Arts; Education; Youth development; Human services; Community/economic development; Christian agencies & churches.
Type of support: General/operating support; Equipment; Program development.
Limitations: Applications accepted. **Giving limited to Summit and Stark counties, OH, with emphasis on Akron.** No support for political organizations. No grants to individuals.
Publications: Application guidelines.
Application information: Application form required.
***Initial approach:* Complete application form on foundation web site or request form from foundation**
Copies of proposal: 1
Deadline(s): None
Officer and Board Members:* Karen Murray,* Exec. Dir.; Kate Baker; Karen Stevens; Mary Stark; Michael Stark.
Number of staff: 1 part-time professional.
EIN: 341867983

2762
Osteopathic Heritage Foundations

1500 Lake Shore Dr., Ste. 230
Columbus, OH 43204-3800 (614) 737-4370
Contact: Richard Vincent, Pres.
***FAX:* (614) 737-4371**;
E-mail: heritage@ohf-ohio.org; Toll-free tel.: (866) 737-4370; Main URL: http://www.osteopathicheritage.org/
E-Newsletter: http://www.osteopathicheritage.org/News/eNewsletter.aspx
Grants Database: http://www.osteopathicheritage.org/FundingPriorities/fundingawards.aspx
Knowledge Center: http://www.osteopathicheritage.org/newsandreports.aspx

Redesigned in 1998 in OH.
Donors: Doctors Hospital; The Columbus Foundation and Affiliated Organizations.
Foundation type: Independent foundation.
Financial data (yr. ended 12/31/12): Assets, $228,414,402 (M); gifts received, $2,410; expenditures, $13,774,808; qualifying distributions, $11,863,738; giving activities include $9,902,690 for 31 grants (high: $6,400,000).
Purpose and activities: Comprised of two private foundations that share a common mission and vision, while maintaining separate boards and funding concentration: 1) the Osteopathic Heritage Foundation supports community health and quality of life - primarily in central Ohio - as well as osteopathic medical education and research throughout the nation, and 2) the Osteopathic Heritage Foundation of Nelsonville directs its

funding support primarily to improving community health and quality of life in southeastern Ohio. The foundations' focus on health and quality of life is broad and concentrated primarily on mission-related, target priorities, including the following: improving access to oral health care; reducing the prevalence of overweight/obesity in central Ohio; resolving healthcare workforce shortages; enhancing access to healthcare services; enhancing osteopathic medical education; and medical research. In addition, the foundations have made reducing homelessness a recent funding priority.
Fields of interest: Health care, information services; Health care, formal/general education; Medical care, community health systems; Public health; Health care; Housing/shelter, homeless; Homeless, human services; Homeless.
Type of support: Management development/ capacity building; Endowments; Program development.
Limitations: Applications not accepted. Giving primarily in the following OH counties: Athens, Delaware, Fairfield, Fayette, Franklin, Hocking, Jackson, Knox, Licking, Madison, Meigs, Morgan, Perry, Pickaway, Ross, Union, Vinton, and Washington.
Publications: Informational brochure.
Application information: Unsolicited requests for funds generally not accepted. Grant requests are considered through a Request for Proposals (RFP) process. See foundation web site for RFP summary and application forms.
Officers and Directors:* Robert A. Palma, D.O.*, Chair., Osteopathic Heritage Fdn.; Frederick L. Oremus,* Chair., Osteopathic Heritage Fdn. of Nelsonville; **Jane W. Cunningham,* Vice-Chair., Osteopathic Heritage Foundation**; Joseph A. Holtel, D.O.*, Vice-Chair., Osteopathic Heritage Fdn. of Nelsonville; Richard A. Vincent,* C.E.O. and Pres.; **Terri Donlin Huesman, V.P., Progs.**; George O. Faerber, D.O.*, Secy., Osteopathic Heritage Fdn.; Mark R. Seckinger,* Secy., Osteopathic Heritage Fdn. of Nelsonville; Richard A. Mitchell,* Treas.; Theodore M. Ofat, Cont.; Thomas M. Anderson, D.O.; J. Michael Brooks; Steven E. Cox; Rebecca deVillers, D.O.; Susan L. Hunter; Jeffrey Hutchison, D.O.; Peter E. Johnston, D.O.; Kathy Krendl, Ph.D.; Edward Schreck, D.O.
Other changes: Jane W. Cunningham has replaced I. Robert Amerine as Vice-Chair., Osteopathic Heritage Foundation.
John C. Auseon and George W. Hairston are no longer directors. Terri Donlin Huesman is now V.P., Progs.

2763
The Piqua Community Foundation
126 W. High St.
P.O. Box 226
Piqua, OH 45356-2310 (937) 615-9080
Contact: Karen S. Wendeln, Exec. Dir.
FAX: (937) 615-9981;
E-mail: kwendeln@piquacommunityfoundation.org;
Main URL: http://
www.piquacommunityfoundation.org

Established in 1993 in OH.
Foundation type: Community foundation.
Financial data (yr. ended 12/31/12): Assets, $7,030,230 (M); gifts received, $668,772; expenditures, $823,451; giving activities include $677,526 for 14+ grants (high: $314,185), and $46,500 for 37 grants to individuals.
Purpose and activities: The foundation encourages charitable giving to benefit the citizens of Piqua, and provides a variety of methods for donors to help fulfill their charitable giving wishes.
Fields of interest: Arts; Secondary school/ education; Education; Health care; Cystic fibrosis; Health organizations; Athletics/sports, school programs; Human services; Community/economic development; United Ways and Federated Giving Programs; Science; Christian agencies & churches.
Type of support: Capital campaigns; Building/ renovation; Equipment; Program development; Seed money; Scholarships—to individuals.
Limitations: Applications accepted. Giving limited to the greater Piqua, OH, area. No grants for general operating support or wages and salaries.
Publications: Application guidelines; Annual report; Grants list; Informational brochure; Newsletter.
Application information: Visit foundation web site for application information. Faxed or e-mailed applications are not accepted. Applicants are invited to contact the executive director with any questions or concerns, at Piquacf@sbcglobal.net. Application form required.
Initial approach: Letter, telephone, or e-mail
Copies of proposal: 8
***Deadline(s):* Mar. 31 and Sept. 30 for Standard Grants; Mar. 15 and Sept. 15 for mini-grants**
Board meeting date(s): Varies
Final notification: Within 30 days of deadline
Officers and Directors:* Daniel E. Ramer,* Pres.; L. Edward Fry,* V.P.; Neill H. Haas,* Secy.-Treas.; Karen S. Wendeln,* Exec. Dir.; Jack L. Neuenschwander, Legal Counsel; John S. Alexander; Cheryl L. Burkhardt; Mimi A. Crawford; Daniel P. French; David K. Galbreath, Jr.; Michael E. Gutmann; Christine J. Hulme; Nancy K. Johnston; Craig M. Mullenbrock; Kathryn M. Patten; Stacy P. Scott; Steven K. Staley; Tony Wendeln; Michael P. Yannucci.
Number of staff: 1 part-time professional.
EIN: 311391908

2764
The Progressive Insurance Foundation
6300 Wilson Mills Rd.
Mayfield Village, OH 44143-2109
Main URL: http://www.progressive.com/ progressive-insurance/foundation.aspx

Established in 2001 in OH.
Donors: Progressive Specialty Insurance Company; Progressive Casualty Insurance Co.
Foundation type: Company-sponsored foundation.
Financial data (yr. ended 12/31/12): Assets, $1,174,769 (M); gifts received, $5,338,851; expenditures, $5,362,880; qualifying distributions, $5,312,387; giving activities include $5,268,930 for 2,601 grants (high: $1,957,554; low: $16).
Purpose and activities: The foundation supports the Insurance Institute for Highway Safety to reduce human traumas and the economic cost of auto accidents; and matches employee giving to nonprofit organizations.
Fields of interest: Safety, automotive safety.
Type of support: General/operating support; Annual campaigns; Employee matching gifts.
Limitations: Applications not accepted. Giving primarily in areas of company operations, with emphasis on OH and VA.
Application information: Contributes only to a pre-selected organization and through employee-matching gifts.
Officers and Trustees:* Glenn M. Renwick, Pres.; Brian Domeck, V.P.; Michael J. Moroney, Secy.; James Kusmer, Treas.; W. Thomas Forrester; R. Steven Kestner.
EIN: 300013138

Other changes: Charles E. Jarrett is no longer Secy.

2765
The Reinberger Foundation
30000 Chagrin Blvd., No. 300
Cleveland, OH 44124-5721 (216) 292-2790
Contact: Karen L. Hooser, Pres.; Sara Dyer, V.P.
FAX: (216) 292-4466;
E-mail: info@reinbergerfoundation.org; **E-mail for Letters of Inquiry: request@reinbergerfoundation.org**; Main URL: http://www.reinbergerfoundation.org

Established in 1968 in OH.
Donors: Clarence T. Reinberger†; Louise F. Reinberger†.
Foundation type: Independent foundation.
Financial data (yr. ended 12/31/12): Assets, $64,895,938 (M); expenditures, $3,475,723; qualifying distributions, $3,039,558; giving activities include $2,738,068 for 114 grants (high: $125,000; low: $1,000).
Purpose and activities: Support for the arts, social service, education, and health care.
Fields of interest: Media/communications; Visual arts; Museums; Performing arts; Humanities; Arts; Elementary/secondary education; Education, early childhood education; Higher education; Adult education—literacy, basic skills & GED; Libraries/ library science; Education; Zoos/zoological societies; Hospitals (general); Health care, home services; Health care; Substance abuse, prevention; Substance abuse, treatment; Mental health, treatment; Medical research; Offenders/ ex-offenders, rehabilitation; Employment, vocational rehabilitation; Food banks; Housing/shelter, temporary shelter; Recreation; Youth development; Children/youth, services; Family services, domestic violence.
Type of support: Management development/ capacity building; General/operating support; Annual campaigns; Capital campaigns; Building/ renovation; Equipment; Program development; Research; Matching/challenge support.
Limitations: Applications accepted. Giving primarily in Columbus and in northeastern OH. No grants to individuals, or for seed money, emergency funds, land acquisition, demonstration projects, or conferences; no loans.
Publications: Informational brochure (including application guidelines).
Application information: The foundation does not accept unsolicited full proposals, after review of the letter of inquiry the foundation will request a proposal if desired. Application form not required.
***Initial approach:* Letter of inquiry (2 pages maximum), via U.S. Mail, e-mail, or through the online application process on foundation web site**
Copies of proposal: 1
***Deadline(s):* See foundation web site for current deadlines**
Board meeting date(s): Feb., May, Aug., and Nov.
Final notification: Within 1 month of deadline
Officers and Trustees:* Karen R. Hooser,* Pres.; Sara R. Dyer,* V.P. and Treas.; Richard H. Oman,* Secy.; William C. Reinberger.
Number of staff: 1 full-time professional.
EIN: 346574879

2766
Renner Foundation
1120 Chester Ave., Ste. 470
Cleveland, OH 44114-3521

Incorporated in 1947 in OH as Renner Clinic Foundation.
Donor: R. Richard Renner, M.D.‡.
Foundation type: Independent foundation.
Financial data (yr. ended 05/31/13): Assets, $3,490,961 (M); expenditures, $209,728; qualifying distributions, $163,000; giving activities include $163,000 for 2 grants (high: $86,500; low: $76,500).
Fields of interest: Arts; Higher education; Health organizations; Religion.
Type of support: Endowments; Scholarship funds.
Limitations: Applications not accepted. Giving primarily in OH and WV. No grants to individuals.
Application information: Unsolicited requests for funds not accepted.
Officers: Karen Renner Sargent, Pres.; Debra Renner, V.P.; Jennie Renner-Yeomans, Secy.; Steven Renner, Treas.
Trustees: Brett Percy; **David Percy**; Jennifer Percy-Falls; Kevin Percy; Daniel S. Renner; John W. Renner; J. Robert Renner; Mary Renner; Reid Renner; Richard R. Renner; Robert Renner; Tamara Renner; Tara Renner; Ann Stillwater.
Number of staff: None.
EIN: 340684303
Other changes: The grantmaker no longer lists an E-mail address.

2767
Richland County Foundation
(formerly The Richland County Foundation of Mansfield, Ohio)
24 W. 3rd St., Ste. 100
Mansfield, OH 44902-1209 (419) 525-3020
Contact: Bradford Groves, Pres.
FAX: (419) 525-1590;
E-mail: info@rcfoundation.org; Additional e-mail: bgroves@rcfoundation.org; Main URL: http://www.richlandcountyfoundation.org/
E-Newsletter: http://www.richlandcountyfoundation.org/surveys/newsletter-signup
Facebook: https://www.facebook.com/RichlandCountyFoundation

Incorporated in 1945 in OH.
Foundation type: Community foundation.
Financial data (yr. ended 12/31/12): Assets, $105,910,279 (M); gifts received, $17,647,939; expenditures, $3,133,178; giving activities include $2,123,934 for 44+ grants (high: $238,801), and $346,308 for 397 grants to individuals.
Purpose and activities: The foundation seeks to improve and enhance the quality of life in Richland County through strategic philanthropy and community leadership. The foundation accomplishes this mission by: 1) providing leadership and acting as a catalyst in identifying and addressing emerging community needs; 2) distributing grants for charitable purposes in the areas of Health, Economic Development, Basic Human Needs, Education, Cultural Activities, Environment, and Community Services; 3) prudently managing the Foundation's resources to achieve the maximum benefit for Richland County in perpetuity; 4) identifying and cultivating donors of all economic means and charitable interests; and 5) assisting donors in establishing funds to meet community needs and distribute proceeds in accordance with the donor's intent.
Fields of interest: Historic preservation/historical societies; Arts; Education, early childhood education; Child development, education; Elementary school/education; Secondary school/education; Vocational education; Higher education; Adult/continuing education; Adult education—literacy, basic skills & GED; Libraries/library science; Education, reading; Education; Environment; Hospitals (general); Health care; Substance abuse, services; Mental health/crisis services; Health organizations, association; Employment; Children/youth, services; Child development, services; Family services; Aging, centers/services; Women, centers/services; Human services; Civil rights, race/intergroup relations; Economic development; Community/economic development; Government/public administration; Children/youth; Children; Aging; Disabilities, people with; Physically disabled; Minorities; Women; Girls; Economically disadvantaged.
Type of support: General/operating support; Management development/capacity building; Capital campaigns; Building/renovation; Equipment; Land acquisition; Endowments; Emergency funds; Program development; Seed money; Scholarship funds; Technical assistance; Program-related investments/loans; Scholarships—to individuals; Matching/challenge support.
Limitations: Applications accepted. Giving primarily in Richland County, OH. No support for sectarian religious purposes. No grants to individuals (except for scholarships), or annual campaigns, operating expenses, computer systems, fellowships, highly technical or specialized research, maintenance funds, travel, debt, or medical, scientific or academic research.
Publications: Application guidelines; Annual report (including application guidelines); Informational brochure; Newsletter.
Application information: Visit foundation web site for grant guidelines; scholarship applications also available on web site. Application form required.
Initial approach: Telephone for appointment
Copies of proposal: 1
***Deadline(s):* Jan. 3, Apr. 11, Aug. 22, and Oct. 17 for Competitive Grants**
Board meeting date(s): 2nd Mon. of Feb., Apr., June, Aug., Oct., and Dec.; annual meeting in May
Final notification: Feb. 10, June 9, Oct. 13, and Dec. 8
Officers and Trustees:* John C. Roby,* Chair.; Beth DeLaney,* Chair.-Elect; Bradford Groves,* Pres.; Mark Masters,* Secy.; Bruce Cummins,* Treas.; Chris E. Harris,* Treas.; Patricia Addeo; Glenna Cannon; Michael Bennett; David D. Carto; Michael Chambers; Bruce Jackson, M.D.; Jason B. Murray; Justin Marotta; W. Chandler Stevens; Cathy Stimpert; Sam VanCura.
Number of staff: 4 full-time professional; 1 full-time support.
EIN: 340872883
Other changes: Maura Teynor is now Dir. Donor Srvs. and Comms. Robert Barrett is now V.P., Opers. and Finance. Don Mitchell and Betty E. Preston are no longer trustees.

2768
Roggecora Memorial Foundation
P.O. Box 425
Zanesville, OH **43702-0425**

Established in OH.
Foundation type: Independent foundation.
Financial data (yr. ended 12/31/12): Assets, $11,474,029 (M); expenditures, $628,121; qualifying distributions, $561,536; giving activities include $545,507 for 13 grants (high: $99,044; low: $1,000).
Fields of interest: Elementary/secondary education; Higher education; Community/economic development; Catholic agencies & churches.
Limitations: Applications not accepted. Giving primarily in Zanesville, OH. No grants to individuals.
Application information: Unsolicited requests for funds not accepted.
Trustee: PNC Bank, N.A.
EIN: 316183600

2769
The Albert J. Ryan Foundation
225 W. Court St.
Cincinnati, OH **45202-1012 (513) 721-5525**
***Contact:* Robert H. Mitchell Esq., Co-Trustee**
FAX: (516) 721-4268; **E-mail for Robert H. Mitchell, Esq.: rhm@manleyburke.com**; Main URL: http://www.albertjryanfoundation.org/
Grants List: http://www.albertjryanfoundation.org/fellows.cfm

Established in 1967 in OH; supporting organization of Dartmouth College, Harvard University, and the University of Cincinnati.
Foundation type: Independent foundation.
Financial data (yr. ended 12/31/12): Assets, $2,398,012 (M); expenditures, $250,834; qualifying distributions, $195,000; giving activities include $195,000 for grants.
Fields of interest: Higher education, university; Medical school/education.
Type of support: Scholarship funds; Research.
Limitations: Applications not accepted. Giving limited to MA, NH, and OH.
Application information: Contributes only to pre-selected organizations; participating colleges select scholars to receive scholarships from foundation.
Officer and Trustees:* Michael J. Bohman,* V.P.; Robert H. Mitchell; Manley Burke, LPA; U.S. Bank, N.A.
EIN: 316066371
Other changes: Michael J. Bohman is now V.P. Robert Manley is no longer a trustee.

2770
Saint Luke's Foundation of Cleveland, Ohio
11327 Shaker Blvd., Ste. 600 W.
Cleveland, OH **44104** (216) 431-8010
***Contact:* Denise S. Zeman, Pres.**
FAX: (216) 431-8015;
E-mail: dzeman@saintlukesfoundation.org; Main URL: http://www.saintlukesfoundation.org/
Facebook: http://www.facebook.com/pages/Saint-Lukes-Foundation/130812285054?ref=ts
Flickr: http://www.flickr.com/photos/27371974@N04/
Saint Luke's Foundation of Cleveland, Ohio's Philanthropy's Promise: http://www.ncrp.org/philanthropy-promise/who
Twitter: http://www.twitter.com/saintlukesfdn
Video Presentation: http://www.saintlukesfoundation.org/focus-and-funding/grantmaking-philosophy/
YouTube: http://www.youtube.com/user/saintlukesfoundation

Established in 1997 in OH; converted from the Saint Luke's Medical Center.
Foundation type: Independent foundation.
Financial data (yr. ended 12/31/12): Assets, $173,547,118 (M); gifts received, $135,995; expenditures, $12,645,544; qualifying

distributions, $12,046,088; giving activities include $10,184,154 for 79 grants (high: $1,561,503; low: $2,500).
Purpose and activities: The foundation reinvests its resources to provide leadership and support for the improvement and transformation of the health and well-being of individuals, families and communities of Greater Cleveland. grantmaking revolves around three core areas: 1) Healthy People; 2) Strong Communities; 3) Resilient Families.
Fields of interest: Health care; Family services; Human services; Community development, neighborhood development; Infants/toddlers; Children; Youth; Adults; Aging; Young adults; Disabilities, people with; Physically disabled; Deaf/hearing impaired; Mentally disabled; Minorities; African Americans/Blacks; Hispanics/Latinos; Women; Substance abusers; AIDS, people with; Crime/abuse victims; Terminal illness, people with; Economically disadvantaged; Homeless.
Type of support: General/operating support; Management development/capacity building; Capital campaigns; Building/renovation; Equipment; Emergency funds; Program development; Publication; Seed money; Curriculum development; Scholarship funds; Research; Technical assistance; Consulting services; Program evaluation; Program-related investments/loans; Matching/challenge support.
Limitations: Applications accepted. Giving limited to northeastern OH. No support for for-profit organizations or for religious purposes. No grants to individuals or fundraising events, endowments, biomedical research, lobbying, or debt retirement.
Publications: Application guidelines; Annual report; Annual report (including application guidelines); Grants list; Informational brochure; Informational brochure (including application guidelines).
Application information: See web site for additional application information. Application form required.
Initial approach: Online proposal
Copies of proposal: 1
Deadline(s): Apr. 1, July 1 and Oct. 1
Board meeting date(s): Mar., June, Sept. and Dec.
Final notification: 3 months after receipt of application
Officers and Trustees:* Douglas Wang,* Chair.; **Arthur Lavin, M.D.,* Vice-Chair.; Anne Goodman,* C.E.O. and Pres.**; LaTida Smith, V.P., Program, Outcomes and Learning; Belva Denmark Tibbs, Secy.; **Robert Monitello, C.F.O.**; John P. O'Brien, Treas. and Chair., Finance/Aud. Comm.; Francis Afram-Gyening; **April Miller Boise**; Janet E. Burney; Geraldine H. Burns; **Luis Cartagena; Diana Centeno-Gomez**; John R. Corlett; Colleen M. Cotter; Claudia J. Coulton; Edgar B. Jackson, M.D.; Sandra Kiely Kolb; J. Christopher Manners; George Mateyo; Lori McClung; **Ann O'Brien**; Ashley Basile Oeken; Ken Okeson; Sally J. Staley.
Number of staff: 6 full-time professional; 2 part-time professional; 2 full-time support.
EIN: 340714513
Other changes: Anne Goodman has replaced Denise S. Zeman as C.E.O. and Pres. Robert Monitello has replaced Daniel Harrington as C.F.O. Arthur Lavin, M.D. is now Vice-Chair. Francis H. Beam, Jr., a trustee is deceased. Thomas A. Rathbone is no longer a trustee.

2771
Salem Community Foundation, Inc.
P.O. Box 553
Salem, OH 44460-2911 (330) 332-4021
Contact: John E. Tonti, Pres.
FAX: (330) 332-4021;
E-mail: Info@salemcommunityfoundation.org; Main URL: http://www.salemcommunityfoundation.org

Established in 1966 in OH.
Donors: Joseph Sedzmak; Donna Sedzmak; A. Franklin Hubert†; Albert Morris Family; Bernice Melitschka; Corinne Mackall†.
Foundation type: Community foundation.
Financial data (yr. ended 12/31/12): Assets, $16,427,389 (M); gifts received, $1,005,214; expenditures, $851,898; giving activities include $778,789 for 8+ grants (high: $504,550).
Purpose and activities: The foundation seeks to improve the quality of life in Salem, OH, and the immediate area. The foundation, through special grants, supports charitable, educational, scientific, literary, artistic, and civic efforts, as well as public safety, welfare, and recreational programs in Salem.
Fields of interest: Arts; Education; Children/youth, services; Government/public administration; Disabilities, people with; Economically disadvantaged.
Type of support: Continuing support; Annual campaigns; Building/renovation; Equipment; Land acquisition; Scholarship funds.
Limitations: Applications accepted. Giving primarily in Salem City and Perry Township, OH. No support for religious purposes or to federal agencies. No grants to individuals (except for scholarships), or for operating budgets of established organizations or programs, budget deficits, endowments, conferences, or scholarly research.
Publications: Application guidelines; Annual report; Newsletter; Quarterly report.
Application information: Visit foundation web site for application form and guidelines. Application form required.
Initial approach: Submit application form and attachments
Copies of proposal: 2
Deadline(s): 1 month prior to quarterly board meeting
Board meeting date(s): Quarterly
Final notification: Immediately following quarterly board meetings
Officers and Directors:* John E. Tonti,* Pres.; Rob McCulloch III,* V.P.; Salvatore C. Apicella, M.D.*, Secy.; Gary E. Moffett,* Treas.; **Steven J. Bailey**; Larry G. Cecil; Rev. Meta S. Cramer; **Mark C. Equizi**; Karl Getzinger; George W.S. Hays; Joseph Julian; Deb McCulloch; Frederic E. Naragon; Audrey C. Null; Lou Ramunno; Connie Rowe; Joseph P. Sedzmak.
Number of staff: 1 part-time support.
EIN: 341001130
Other changes: Thomas Bratten, Michael J. Sevilla, and Gary E. Moffett are no longer directors.

2772
Samaritan Foundation
P.O. Box 97
Haviland, OH 45851-0097 (419) 622-4611
***Contact:* Todd Stoller, Secy.-Treas.; Craig Stoller, V.P.**

Established in 2002 in OH.
Donor: Haviland Plastic Products Co.
Foundation type: Company-sponsored foundation.
Financial data (yr. ended 12/31/12): Assets, $5,353,507 (M); gifts received, $1,245,510; expenditures, $1,213,541; qualifying distributions, $1,211,754; giving activities include $1,211,754 for grants.
Purpose and activities: The foundation supports food banks and organizations involved with education, patient services, disaster relief, human services, and Christianity; awards grants and loans to indigent individuals in economic distress; and awards college scholarships to students located in Paulding County, Ohio.
Fields of interest: Secondary school/education; Education; Health care, patient services; Food banks; Disasters, preparedness/services; American Red Cross; Children/youth, services; Human services; Christian agencies & churches; Economically disadvantaged.
Type of support: General/operating support; Grants to individuals; Scholarships—to individuals; Loans—to individuals.
Limitations: Applications accepted. Giving primarily in IN, KY, and OH.
Publications: Application guidelines.
Application information: An application form is required for scholarships. **Application form required.**
***Initial approach:* Completed application form**
Deadline(s): None
Officers: Russell Stoller, Pres.; Craig Stoller, V.P.; Todd Stoller, Secy.-Treas.
EIN: 341957355

2773
Sandusky/Erie County Community Foundation
135 E. Washington Row
Sandusky, OH 44870-2609 (419) 621-9690
***Contact:* Anna J. Oertel, Exec. Dir.; For grants: Randall J. Wagner, Dir., Finance**
FAX: (419) 621-8420;
E-mail: info@sanduskyfoundation.org; **Grant application email: executivedirector@sanduskyfoundation.org; Grant inquiry email: randyw@eriefoundation.org**; Main URL: http://www.sanduskyfoundation.org
E-Newsletter: http://www.sanduskyfoundation.org/contact-us/newsletter-signup/
Facebook: http://www.facebook.com/pages/SanduskyErie-County-Community-Foundation/145979392120013
Twitter: https://twitter.com/erieccf

Established in 1996 in OH.
Foundation type: Community foundation.
Financial data (yr. ended 12/31/12): Assets, $14,934,755 (M); gifts received, $611,629; expenditures, $758,620; giving activities include $349,429 for 12+ grants (high: $39,107), and $65,897 for 49 grants to individuals.
Purpose and activities: The mission of the foundation is to develop a permanent endowment to identify and respond to community needs, and to facilitate charitable giving.
Fields of interest: Arts; Education; Environment; Health care; Human services; Economic development; Community/economic development; Children/youth.
Type of support: Management development/capacity building; Capital campaigns; Building/renovation; Equipment; Program development; Seed money; Scholarship funds; Program evaluation; Matching/challenge support.
Limitations: Applications accepted. Giving limited to Erie County, OH. No support for sectarian religious purposes, or medical or other research organizations. No grants to individuals (except for scholarships), or for advertising or sponsorships, annual campaigns, debt reduction, salaries/benefits of organization staff, or tickets or advertising for fundraising events.

Publications: Application guidelines; Annual report; Financial statement; Grants list; Informational brochure; Newsletter.
Application information: Visit foundation web site for application form and guidelines per grant type. Incomplete applications, faxed applications, or applications submitted after the deadline will not be considered. Application form required.
Initial approach: Submit application form and attachments
Copies of proposal: 15
Deadline(s): Feb. 1 and Aug. 1 for Community Grants
Board meeting date(s): Apr., June, Sept., and Dec.
Final notification: Within 60 days for Community Grants
Officers and Directors:* Mary Jane Hill,* Chair.; Paula J. Rengel,* Vice-Chair.; Roger Gundlach,* Secy.; Eugene A. Koby,* Treas.; Thomas M. Wolf,* Investment Adv.; Anna J. Oertel, Exec. Dir.; Jeanette Henry, Dir. Emeritus; M.J. Stauffer, Dir. Emeritus; John O. Bacon; Laurence A. Bettcher; **Richard R. Brady**; Eileen Bulan; Faith Denslow; Marcia Goff; Judith Kinzel; Donald G. Koch; Carole Kuhns; Darlene Lowery; George L. Mylander; Ruth F. Parker; Charles W. Rainger; Patrecia Sizemore; J. William Springer; Sparky Weilnau; Andy White.
Number of staff: 2 full-time professional; 1 full-time support; 1 part-time support.
EIN: 341792862

2774
The Schiewetz Foundation, Inc.
3110 Kettering Blvd.
Dayton, OH 45439-1924

Established in 2001 in OH.
Donor: Richard F. Schiewetz†.
Foundation type: Independent foundation.
Financial data (yr. ended 12/31/12): Assets, $69,901,143 (M); gifts received, $17,760,864; expenditures, $3,251,963; qualifying distributions, $2,704,978; giving activities include $2,585,492 for 16 grants (high: $916,242; low: $2,500).
Fields of interest: Historic preservation/historical societies; Arts; Education; Boy scouts; YM/YWCAs & YM/YWHAs; Youth, services.
Limitations: Applications not accepted. Giving primarily in Dayton, OH. No grants to individuals.
Application information: Contributes only to pre-selected organizations.
Officers: Richard W. Schwartz, Pres.; Amy C. Kress, V.P.; Jennifer L. Schmidt, Secy.-Treas.
Director: Jane R. Schwartz.
EIN: 311812245
Other changes: At the close of 2012, the fair market value of the grantmaker's assets was $69,901,143, a 58.1% increase over the 2011 value, $44,222,869.
Richard F. Schiewetz, Donor, is deceased.

2775
Charlotte R. Schmidlapp Fund
(formerly C. Schmidlapp Fund)
c/o Fifth Third Bank, N.A.
P.O. Box 630858
Cincinnati, OH **45263-0858**
***Application address:* Fifth Third Bank Foundation Office, 38 Fountain Square Plz., MD1090CA, Cincinnati, OH 45263, tel.: (513) 534-4397**

Trust established in 1908 in OH.
Donor: Jacob G. Schmidlapp†.
Foundation type: Independent foundation.
Financial data (yr. ended 09/30/13): Assets, $26,252,517 (M); gifts received, $100; expenditures, $439,936; qualifying distributions, $257,326; giving activities include $205,000 for 5 grants (high: $100,000; low: $10,000).
Purpose and activities: The fund supports initiatives that empower and assist women and girls in achieving self sufficiency. Grants for the relief of sickness, suffering, and distress, and for the care of young children, the aged, or the helpless and afflicted. Also giving for the promotion of education, to improve living conditions and/or the good and welfare of the state/nation in emergencies. Funding also for YWCAs.
Fields of interest: Higher education; Human services; YM/YWCAs & YM/YWHAs; Women, centers/services.
Type of support: Program development; Seed money.
Limitations: Applications accepted. Giving primarily in Cincinnati, OH.
Publications: Application guidelines; Annual report.
Application information: Application form required.
***Initial approach:* Request application form**
Copies of proposal: 1
***Deadline(s):* Available on request**
Trustee: Fifth Third Bank, N.A.
EIN: 310532641

2776
Schooler Family Foundation
P.O. Box 6137
Columbus, OH 43206
Contact: Heather L. Schooler, Mgr., Grants & Communications
E-mail: schoolerfamilyfoundation@gmail.com

Established in 1985 in Ohio.
Donors: Seward D. Schooler†; Edith Schooler†.
Foundation type: Independent foundation.
Financial data (yr. ended 12/31/13): Assets, $6,006,699 (M); expenditures, $343,326; qualifying distributions, $310,881; giving activities include $248,000 for 10 grants (high: $100,000; low: $500).
Purpose and activities: Support for a broad range of charitable programs.
Limitations: Giving primarily in Ohio, with emphasis on central and east central Ohio, and elsewhere in the U.S. No support for research using, or conducted on, animals. No grants to individuals.
Application information: Proposals invited only after review of initial letter of inquiry. Grants awarded in two funding cycles each year.
Initial approach: Letter of inquiry
***Deadline(s):* July 1 and Feb. 1**
Board meeting date(s): As required
Officers and Trustees:* David R. Schooler,* Pres.; Heather L. Schooler,* Secy. and Mgr., Grants and Communications; Dean Schooler, Treas.; Steven Barr; C. Fenning Pierce; Deana Puls; Matthew Schooler; Wesley Schooler.
Number of staff: 3 part-time professional.
EIN: 311157433

2777
The Jay and Jean Schottenstein Foundation
(formerly Jay L. Schottenstein Foundation)
c/o Charles Spicer Inc.
4300 E. Fifth Ave.
Columbus, OH 43219-1816 (614) 449-4253

Established in OH.
Donors: Jay Schottenstein; Jeffrey Schottenstein; Jonathan Schottenstein; Joseph Schottenstein.
Foundation type: Independent foundation.
Financial data (yr. ended 12/31/12): Assets, $15,243,035 (M); gifts received, $1,646,089; expenditures, $9,775,925; qualifying distributions, $9,728,096; giving activities include $9,728,096 for 69 grants (high: $2,750,000; low: $54).
Purpose and activities: Support only for Jewish agencies, temples, and schools.
Fields of interest: Elementary/secondary education; Theological school/education; Jewish federated giving programs; Jewish agencies & synagogues.
Type of support: General/operating support.
Limitations: Applications not accepted. Giving limited to NY and OH. No grants to individuals.
Application information: Contributes only to pre-selected organizations.
Officer: Jay Schottenstein, Pres.
EIN: 311111955
Other changes: Geraldine Schottenstein Hoffman is no longer V.P.

2778
Saul Schottenstein Foundation C
c/o Arshot Investment Corp.
107 S. High St., 3rd Fl.
Columbus, OH 43215-3456 (614) 463-9730
Contact: Thomas H. Schottenstein, Pres.

Foundation type: Independent foundation.
Financial data (yr. ended 12/31/12): Assets, $5,892,991 (M); gifts received, $1,000; expenditures, $557,479; qualifying distributions, $463,469; giving activities include $463,469 for grants.
Fields of interest: Jewish agencies & synagogues.
Application information: Application form required.
Initial approach: Letter
Deadline(s): None
Officer: Thomas H. Schottenstein, Pres.
EIN: 270167574
Other changes: The grantmaker no longer lists a URL address.

2779
Scotford Foundation
211 S. Main St.
Poland, OH 44514-2026 (330) 757-3761
Contact: John P. Scotford, Jr., Tr.

Established in 1978 in OH.
Donors: John P. Scotford; Judy Scotford; John Scotford, Jr.; Laura Scotford; Stephen L. Scotford.
Foundation type: Independent foundation.
Financial data (yr. ended 12/31/13): Assets, $4,402,413 (M); gifts received, $251,354; expenditures, $222,843; qualifying distributions, $202,965; giving activities include $201,990 for 30 grants (high: $65,000; low: $200).
Purpose and activities: Giving primarily to Protestant agencies and churches and for education.
Fields of interest: Elementary/secondary education; Higher education; Youth development; Protestant agencies & churches.
Type of support: General/operating support; Annual campaigns; Capital campaigns; Building/renovation; Land acquisition; Endowments; Matching/challenge support.
Limitations: Applications accepted. Giving primarily in FL, OH and WA. No grants to individuals.
Application information: Application form required.

Initial approach: Letter
Deadline(s): None
Board meeting date(s): Varies

Trustees: John P. Scotford; John P. Scotford, Jr.; Laura L. Scotford; Stephen L. Scotford.
EIN: 341278622
Other changes: E. Judith Scotford is no longer a trustee.

2780
Scripps Howard Foundation

P.O. Box 5380
312 Walnut St., 28th Fl.
Cincinnati, OH 45201 (513) 977-3035
Contact: Patty Cottingham, V.P., Admin.; Mike Philipps, C.E.O. and Pres.
FAX: (513) 977-3800;
E-mail: mike.philipps@scripps.com; Contact for Roy W. Howard Scripps Howard Competition, National Journalism Awards and Internships: Susan J. Porter, V.P., Progs., tel.: (800) 888-3000, ext. 3030, e-mail: sue.porter@scripps.com. See Web site for information on specific foundation programs.; Main URL: http://www.scripps.com/foundation
Facebook: https://www.facebook.com/scrippshowardfoundation
Scripps Howard Awards: http://www.shawards.org
Scripps Howard Foundation Wire: http://www.shfwire.com/
YouTube: https://www.youtube.com/watch?v=CRNS9n2DIBc

Incorporated in 1962 in OH.
Donors: The E.W. Scripps Co.; Jack R. Howard Trust; Robert P. Scripps; Robert A. Buzzelli; Julia & Robert Heidt; Alan & Beverley Horton Fund; Ken Lowe; George & Mary Ann Sanchez; Nackey & Robert Scagliotti; Cindy J. Scripps; Edward W. & Christy Scripps; Henry R. Scripps; William H. & Kathryn Scripps; Donna & Ed Spray; Felicia & Virginia Vasquez.
Foundation type: Company-sponsored foundation.
Financial data (yr. ended 12/31/12): Assets, $65,198,617 (M); gifts received, $3,405,998; expenditures, $6,300,234; qualifying distributions, $4,618,992; giving activities include $4,250,384 for 832 grants (high: $500,000; low: $25), and $368,608 for 92 grants to individuals (high: $35,000; low: $500).
Purpose and activities: The foundation strives to advance the cause of a free press through support of excellence in journalism, quality journalism education, and professional development. The foundation helps build healthy communities and improve the quality of life through support of sound educational programs, strong families, vital social services, enriching arts and culture, and inclusive civic affairs, with emphasis on areas of company operations.
Fields of interest: Media, print publishing; Arts; Journalism school/education; Education, reading; Education; Environment; Family services; Human services; Civil liberties, first amendment; Public affairs; General charitable giving.
Type of support: Emergency funds; General/operating support; Capital campaigns; Building/renovation; Equipment; Endowments; Program development; Conferences/seminars; Professorships; Seed money; Curriculum development; Fellowships; Internship funds; Research; Technical assistance; Employee volunteer services; Employee matching gifts; Employee-related scholarships; Grants to individuals; Scholarships—to individuals; Matching/challenge support.
Limitations: Applications accepted. Giving on a national basis, with emphasis on areas of company operations. No support for religious organizations not of direct benefit to the entire community, political causes or candidates, anti-business organizations, discriminatory organizations, private foundations, or veterans', fraternal, or labor organizations. No grants for courtesy advertising.
Publications: Application guidelines; Annual report.
Application information: See Foundation website for contact information on specific programs. Application form not required.
Initial approach: Send Community Fund (including Literacy Grant) proposals to your local Scripps executive; Greater Cincinnati Fund proposals to Patty Cottingham and Journalism Fund proposals to Mike Philipps
Copies of proposal: 1
Deadline(s): None
Board meeting date(s): Semiannually
Final notification: 90 days

Officers and Trustees:* Mike Philipps,* C.E.O. and Pres.; Patty Cottingham, V.P., Admin.; Susan J. Porter, V.P., Progs.; E. John Wolfzorn, Treas.; Charles Barmonde; Rebecca Scripps Brickner; Robin A. Davis; Eduardo Fernandez; Julia Scripps Heidt; Jack Howard-Potter; Lisa A. Knutson; Brian G. Lawlor; Margaret Scripps Klenzing; Paul K. Scripps; Virginia Scripps Vasquez; Timothy E. Stautberg; Adam Symson; Ellen Weiss; Timothy M. Wesolowski.
Members: Richard A. Boehne; Kelly Conlin; Anne M. La Dow; John W. Hayden; Roger Ogden; Mary Peirce; Mike Philipps; J. Marvin Quin; Paul K. Scripps; Kim Williams.
Number of staff: 6 full-time professional.
EIN: 316025114

2781
The Sears-Swetland Family Foundation

(formerly The Sears-Swetland Foundation)
13003 Lake Shore Blvd.
Bratenahl, OH 44108-1144
Contact: Ruth Swetland Eppig, Pres.
E-mail: sears.swetland.fdn@gmail.com; E-mail for Ruth Swetland Eppig: rseppig@aol.com; Main URL: http://www.searsswetlandfoundation.wordpress.com
Grants List: http://searsswetlandfoundation.wordpress.com/who-we-fund/

Trust established in 1949 in OH.
Donors: Anna L. Sears†; Lester M. Sears†; Ruth P. Sears†; Mary Ann Swetland†; David W. Swetland†; David Sears Swetland; Ruth Swetland Eppig; Polly Swetland Jones.
Foundation type: Independent foundation.
Financial data (yr. ended 12/31/12): Assets, $3,360,264 (M); gifts received, $16,469; expenditures, $233,503; qualifying distributions, $176,222; giving activities include $160,900 for 30 grants (high: $30,000; low: $1,000).
Purpose and activities: Support for smart growth, conservation, urban revitalization and fair access, education and environmental health in the greater Cleveland, Ohio, area.
Fields of interest: Arts; Education; Environment; Health organizations; Medical research; Employment; Housing/shelter; Youth development; Civil/human rights; Economic development; Community/economic development; Philanthropy/voluntarism.
Type of support: General/operating support; Continuing support; Management development/capacity building; Annual campaigns; Capital campaigns; Building/renovation; Equipment; Land acquisition; Program development; Seed money; Curriculum development; Internship funds; Scholarship funds; Research; Matching/challenge support.
Limitations: Applications accepted. Giving primarily in the Cleveland, OH, area. No grants to individuals.
Publications: Application guidelines; Grants list; Program policy statement.
Application information: Application form not required.
Initial approach: E-mail
Deadline(s): Submit proposal preferably before Nov.; annual fund proposals before June
Board meeting date(s): As needed
Final notification: 60 days

Officers: Ruth Swetland Eppig, Pres.; Marianne E. Eppig, Secy.
Trustees: Lydia L. Harrington; David Sears Swetland.
Number of staff: 1 part-time professional.
EIN: 346522143

2782
Murray and Agnes Seasongood Good Government Foundation

15 E. 8th St., Ste. 200W
Cincinnati, OH 45202-2087 (513) 721-2180
Contact: D. David Altman
***E-mail:* info@seasongoodfoundation.com; Main URL: http://www.seasongoodfoundation.com/**
Grants List: http://www.seasongoodfoundation.com/projects.html

Established in 1987 in OH.
Foundation type: Independent foundation.
Financial data (yr. ended 12/31/12): Assets, $6,015,261 (M); expenditures, $400,617; qualifying distributions, $367,760; giving activities include $297,950 for 34 grants (high: $40,320; low: $900).
Fields of interest: Media/communications; Higher education, university; Education; Environment; Legal services; Human services; Community development, neighborhood development; Community development, citizen coalitions; Foundations (community); Government/public administration.
Type of support: Program development; Internship funds; Research.
Limitations: Applications accepted. Giving primarily in Cincinnati, OH.
Publications: Informational brochure.
Application information: See foundation website for complete application guidelines. Application form required.
Copies of proposal: 15
Deadline(s): At least two weeks before a board meeting
Board meeting date(s): Feb., May, Aug. and Nov.

Officers: Marjorie Davies, Pres.; David Mann, V.P.; Dean Jay Chatterjee, Secy.; Melaine Moody, Jr., Treas.
Trustees: Mary Asbury; William Bahlman; David Mann; Jerry Newfarmer; Julie Olberding; Myrtis Powell; Fanon Rucker; David Singleton; Henry Winkler.
Number of staff: 1 part-time professional.
EIN: 311220827

2783
William M. Shinnick Educational Fund

3608 Maple Ave.
Zanesville, OH 43701-3771 (740) 452-2273
***Contact:* William M. Shinnick, Admin. Asst.**

Established in 1923 in OH.
Donors: William M. Shinnick; Eunice Hale Buckingham.
Foundation type: Independent foundation.
Financial data (yr. ended 06/30/13): Assets, $4,393,437 (M); gifts received, $102,400; expenditures, $365,631; qualifying distributions, $317,614; giving activities include $280,000 for 150 grants to individuals (high: $2,000; low: $1,000).
Purpose and activities: Scholarship awards and loans to students who are residents of Muskingum County, Ohio.
Fields of interest: Higher education.
Type of support: Scholarships—to individuals; Student loans—to individuals.
Limitations: Applications accepted. Giving limited to residents of Muskingum County, OH.
Publications: Application guidelines; Informational brochure.
Application information: Application form required.
Initial approach: Telephone
Deadline(s): June 30
Board meeting date(s): Varies
Officers: Thomas Price, Pres.; Barbara Cornell, Secy.
Trustees: William S. Barry; C. Trafford Dick; William D. Joseph; Norma Littick.
Number of staff: 1 full-time professional.
EIN: 314394168

2784
Skyler Foundation
P.O. Box 145496
Cincinnati, OH 45250-5496
***Application address:* c/o Charles Schiff, 3457 Observatory Pl., Cincinnati, OH 45208, tel.: (513) 870-2580**

Established in 1994 in OH.
Donor: John J. Schiff, Jr.
Foundation type: Independent foundation.
Financial data (yr. ended 09/30/13): Assets, $8,258,973 (M); gifts received, $1,445,587; expenditures, $323,975; qualifying distributions, $286,200; giving activities include $286,000 for 18 grants (high: $40,000; low: $2,000).
Fields of interest: Arts, formal/general education; Arts; Elementary/secondary education; Higher education; Education; Hospitals (specialty); Dental care; Children/youth, services; Astronomy.
Type of support: General/operating support; Program development.
Limitations: Applications accepted. Giving primarily in Cincinnati, OH. No grants to individuals.
Application information:
Initial approach: 1-page letter
Deadline(s): None
Board meeting date(s): Annually
Trustees: Marguerite Gieske; Charles O. Schiff; John J. Schiff III.
EIN: 311420623

2785
The Slemp Foundation
c/o Patricia L. Durbin, U.S. Bank, N.A. Trust Division
P.O. Box 5208, Loc. CN-OH-W7PT
Cincinnati, OH **45201-5208**
***Grant and scholarship application address:* c/o Patricia L. Durbin, Tr. Off., U.S. Bank, N.A., Trust Div., P.O. Box 5208, ML CN-OH-W7PT, Cincinnati, OH 45201-5208; tel.: (513) 762-8878**; Main URL: http://www.slempfoundation.org
Grants List: http://www.slempfoundation.org/grants/pastgrantees.aspx

Trust established in 1943 in VA.
Donors: C. Bascom Slemp‡; Mary Virginia Edmonds Charitable Remainder Trust.
Foundation type: Independent foundation.
Financial data (yr. ended 06/30/13): Assets, $21,778,722 (M); expenditures, $1,391,111; qualifying distributions, $1,270,720; giving activities include $872,454 for 34 grants (high: $204,100; low: $500), and $320,000 for 130 grants to individuals (high: $2,500; low: $1,250).
Purpose and activities: Giving primarily for education and the arts for the benefit of residents of Lee and Wise counties, VA. Giving also for scholarships to residents of Lee and Wise counties, VA, and to descendants of a resident thereof.
Fields of interest: Arts; Education; Recreation, parks/playgrounds; Youth development, centers/clubs.
Type of support: Building/renovation; Equipment; Endowments; Emergency funds; Seed money; Curriculum development; Scholarship funds; Scholarships—to individuals.
Limitations: Giving primarily in Lee and Wise counties, VA.
Publications: Application guidelines.
Application information: See foundation web site for application guidelines and procedures, and downloading of scholarship application form. Application form required.
Initial approach: Letter
Copies of proposal: 1
Deadline(s): Oct. 15 for first time scholarship applicants; Jul. 1 for continuing education applicants; no deadlines for grants
Board meeting date(s): Apr., July, and Nov.
Trustees: Pamela S. Edmonds; Melissa Smith Jensen; James Campbell Smith; Nancey Edmonds Smith.
Agent: U.S. Bank, N.A.
EIN: 316025080

2786
Spirit Services, Inc.
5700 Lombardo Center Dr.
Rock Run - North, Ste. 215
Seven Hills, OH 44131-6912 (216) 447-1380
Contact: Jean Takacs, Secy. and Exec. Dir.
FAX: (216) 447-1386;
E-mail: jeantakacs@spiritservices.org; Main URL: http://spiritservices.org/

Established in 2006 in OH.
Foundation type: Independent foundation.
Financial data (yr. ended 06/30/11): Assets, $3,131 (M); gifts received, $16,198; expenditures, $1,224,334; qualifying distributions, $1,220,123; giving activities include $965,051 for grants.
Purpose and activities: Giving primarily to serve and support Catholic elementary schools in providing children access to a quality Catholic education.
Fields of interest: Education; Catholic agencies & churches.
Limitations: Applications accepted. **Giving primarily in the Akron, Cleveland, and Lorain areas of the Diocese of Cleveland in OH.** No grants to individuals.
Publications: Application guidelines.
Application information: See web site for application policies, guidelines and forms. Application form required.
Officers and Advisors:* Ronald Trzcinski, Pres. and Treas.; Jean Takacs, Secy. and Exec. Dir.; Fr. Gary Chmura; Margaret Lyons; Fr. John McNulty; Sr. Carol Anne Smith; Sr. Karen Somerville; Sr. Rosario Vega.
EIN: 050604676

2787
The Springfield Foundation
333 N. Limestone St., Ste. 201
Springfield, OH 45503 (937) 324-8773
Contact: Ted Vander Roest, Exec. Dir.; For grant application: Joan Elder, Prog. Off.
FAX: (937) 324-1836;
E-mail: info@springfieldfoundation.org; Additional E-mail: joan@springfieldfoundation.org; Main URL: http://www.springfieldfoundation.org
Facebook: http://www.facebook.com/pages/Springfield-Foundation/181879671843571

Incorporated in 1948 in OH.
Foundation type: Community foundation.
Financial data (yr. ended 12/31/12): Assets, $46,413,526 (M); gifts received, $3,455,945; expenditures, $2,917,480; giving activities include $2,173,863 for grants.
Purpose and activities: The foundation raises, strengthens, and distributes permanent charitable funds to benefit Clark County, OH.
Fields of interest: Arts; Education; Environment; Health care; Human services; Public affairs; Infants/toddlers; Children/youth; Youth; Disabilities, people with; Physically disabled; Blind/visually impaired; Deaf/hearing impaired; Mentally disabled; African Americans/Blacks; Crime/abuse victims; Homeless.
Type of support: General/operating support; Equipment; Program development; Publication; Seed money; Curriculum development; Research; Technical assistance; Program evaluation; Scholarships—to individuals.
Limitations: Applications accepted. Giving limited to Clark County, OH. No support for sectarian worship, instruction, or proselytizing, fraternal, labor, athletic, and social or veterans' groups, or private or parochial schools. No grants to individuals (except for designated scholarships), or for annual memberships or dues, grants management or consultant fees, debt retirements, deficit financing, annual fund drives or fundraising activities, or school bands and school choral groups, drill teams, or color guards.
Publications: Application guidelines; Annual report; Financial statement; Grants list; Informational brochure (including application guidelines); Newsletter; Program policy statement.
Application information: Visit foundation web site for online application. Application form required.
Initial approach: Submit online application
Deadline(s): Aug. 15 for discretionary grant letters of inquiry; Mar. 1 for scholarship applications
Board meeting date(s): Mar., June, Sept., and Dec.
Final notification: Approx. 6 weeks for initial response; Mid-Dec. for grant determination
Officers and Trustees:* Andy Bell,* Pres.; Plato Pavlatos,* V.P.; Randall Comer,* Secy.; Kim Nedelman Fish,* Treas.; Ted Vander Roest, Exec. Dir.; Tamimi Angle; Dean Blair; Bill Brougher; Bob Burton; Lula Cosby; Cathy Crompton; William Fralick; Gus Geil; Debbie Hill; Robyn Koch-Schumaker; Edward Leventhal; Tom Loftis; Mel Marsh; Maureen Messaro; Dan O'Keefe; David Sanders; Bill Scarff; Jagdish Singh; Les Smithers; Michelle Sweeney.
Number of staff: 5 full-time professional.
EIN: 316030764
Other changes: Steve Neely and Rob Rue are no longer trustees.

2788
Stark Community Foundation
(formerly The Stark County Foundation, Inc.)
400 Market Ave. N., Ste. 200
Canton, OH 44702-2107 (330) 454-3426
Contact: Mark J. Samolczyk, Pres.; For scholarship inquiries: Jackie Gilin, Donor Svcs./Prog. Off.
FAX: (330) 454-5855; E-mail: info@starkcf.org; Scholarship inquiries: jgilin@starkcf.org; Main URL: http://www.starkcf.org/
E-Newsletter: http://www.starkcf.org/news/newsletters
Facebook: http://www.facebook.com/pages/Stark-Community-Foundation/381913043984
YouTube: http://www.youtube.com/user/starkcomfoundation

Established in 1963 in OH by resolution and declaration of trust.
Foundation type: Community foundation.
Financial data (yr. ended 12/31/12): Assets, $182,082,860 (M); gifts received, $17,643,996; expenditures, $8,526,030; giving activities include $6,835,359 for grants.
Purpose and activities: The foundation seeks to enhance the sound health and general welfare of Stark County, OH, citizens through support for civic improvement programs and educational institutions. Primary areas of interest include the arts, education, community development, health and wellness, youth, and social services.
Fields of interest: Visual arts; Performing arts; Historic preservation/historical societies; Arts; Education, early childhood education; Child development, education; Elementary school/education; Higher education; Business school/education; Law school/education; Education; Environment, natural resources; Environment; Health care; Substance abuse, services; AIDS; AIDS research; Crime/law enforcement; Food services; Housing/shelter, development; Recreation; Youth development, services; Children/youth, services; Child development, services; Family services; Aging, centers/services; Minorities/immigrants, centers/services; Homeless, human services; Human services; Urban/community development; Community/economic development; Government/public administration; Leadership development; Youth; Aging; Disabilities, people with; Minorities; Homeless.
Type of support: In-kind gifts; General/operating support; Capital campaigns; Building/renovation; Equipment; Land acquisition; Emergency funds; Program development; Seed money; Scholarship funds; Research; Technical assistance; Consulting services; Scholarships—to individuals; Matching/challenge support; Student loans—to individuals.
Limitations: Applications accepted. Giving limited to Stark County, OH. No support for religious organizations for religious purposes. **No grants for endowment funds, operating expenses of well-established organizations, continuing support, endowments, vehicles, annual appeals or membership contributions, publications, conferences or deficit financing; no grants or loans to individuals (except to college students who are permanent residents of Stark County, OH).**
Publications: Application guidelines; Annual report (including application guidelines); Financial statement; Grants list; Informational brochure; Newsletter; Program policy statement.
Application information: Visit foundation web site for application cover sheet and guidelines per grant type. Application form required.
Initial approach: Submit proposal and attachments
Copies of proposal: 1
Deadline(s): **Mar. 7 and Sept. 5 for discretionary grants**
Board meeting date(s): 8 to 10 times per year
Final notification: **May and Nov. for discretionary grants**
Officers and Board of Trustees:* Thomas W. Schervish,* Chair.; E. Lang D'Atri,* Vice-Chair.; Mark J. Samolczyk, Pres.; Bridgette Neisel, V.P., Advancement; Patricia C. Quick, V.P. and C.F.O.; William Cook; Charles Dix II; Thomas V. Ferrero; Nancy Gessner; Gregory W. Luntz; Stephen A. Perry; Nancy A. Varian.
Trustee Banks: FirstMerit Bank, N.A.; The Huntington National Bank; KeyBank N.A.; PNC Bank; Premier Bank.
Number of staff: 12 full-time professional; 1 part-time professional; 3 full-time support; 1 part-time support.
EIN: 340943665
Other changes: Thomas W. Schervish has replaced Robert DeHoff as Chair.
E. Lang D'Atri is now Vice-Chair.

2789
Robert & Christine Steinmann Family
2011 Madison Rd.
Cincinnati, OH 45208
Contact: Hugh Campbell
E-mail: **kfister@rocketmail.com**; Main URL: http://www.steinmannfoundation.org

Established in 2003 in OH.
Donors: Robert P. Steinmann; Steinmann Pharmacy, Inc.
Foundation type: Independent foundation.
Financial data (yr. ended 12/31/12): Assets, $4,196,431 (M); expenditures, $208,097; qualifying distributions, $177,998; giving activities include $177,998 for 13 grants (high: $25,000; low: $4,450).
Purpose and activities: Giving primarily for the support of Judeo/Christian organizations, educational scholarships in pharmacy and nursing, aid and medical care for the elderly and needy, and cancer research, with a focus in the greater Cincinnati, Ohio, area.
Fields of interest: Nursing school/education; Geriatrics; Cancer research; Aging, centers/services; Christian agencies & churches.
Type of support: Scholarship funds; Endowments.
Limitations: Applications accepted. Giving primarily in OH. No support for political or conduit or for-profit organizations. No grants for overhead operating needs, funds to service debt, travel or group trips or for video productions.
Application information: See foundation website for complete application guidelines. Application form required.
Deadline(s): **Varies**
Directors: Bruce Fister; Kent D. Fister; Carolyn Rose; Robert Stretch.
EIN: 200166460
Other changes: The grantmaker now accepts applications.

2790
Stranahan Foundation
4169 Holland-Sylvania Rd., Ste. 201
Toledo, OH 43623-2590 (419) 882-5575
Contact: Pamela G. Roberts, Grants Mgr.
FAX: (419) 882-2072;
E-mail: proberts@stranahanfoundation.org;
Additional e-mail: mail@stranahanfoundation.org;
Main URL: http://www.stranahanfoundation.org

Trust established in 1944 in OH.
Donors: Robert A. Stranahan‡; Frank D. Stranahan‡; Ms. Troubetzkoy Trust.
Foundation type: Independent foundation.
Financial data (yr. ended 12/31/12): Assets, $86,475,864 (M); gifts received, $51,000; expenditures, $6,008,584; qualifying distributions, $5,402,351; giving activities include $4,869,327 for 70 grants (high: $568,087; low: $2,775).
Purpose and activities: Giving primarily for: 1) Education, particularly to support initiatives that will increase the quality of education for students at the pre-school, primary and secondary levels, and/or promote access to quality educational programs; learning institutions that value independent thinking, artistic appreciation, cultural, economic and ethnic diversity, and community service; provide access to programs that offer alternatives to traditional educational opportunities (e.g.: career-oriented or vocational training, etc.); and small manageable programs within institutions of higher learning; 2) Physical and Mental Health, particularly programs that create better access to care, educate people to take better care of themselves and their families, as well as support alternative care methods, preventive measures, and research to eradicate health crises; 3) Ecological Well-Being, particularly programs that preserve or return to healthy, sustainable communities for both current and future generations, conserve and restore the natural environment, as well as educate community members about the natural environment; 4) Arts and Culture, particularly programs that communicate, delight and educate, motivate and build self esteem, build and reinforce communities, and have therapeutic value; and 5) Human Services, particularly programs that offer disadvantaged families and individuals of all ages access to services that meet basic human needs, opportunities to work, recreate and fully participate in community life, and provide avenues for achieving self-sufficiency and making positive contributions to their community.
Fields of interest: Arts; Education; Human services; Youth, services; Community/economic development.
Type of support: Continuing support; Program development; Program evaluation; Matching/challenge support; Mission-related investments/loans.
Limitations: Giving in Toledo and northwestern OH; giving in other regions is by invitation only. No support for religious purposes, projects located outside the U.S., or government sponsored or controlled projects. No grants to individuals.
Publications: Annual report; Grants list.
Application information: Unsolicited requests for funds accepted only from Toledo, OH, area applicants; giving in other geographic areas is by invitation only. Before an applicant begins their letter of inquiry, they must select a grant type from the choices in the Application Instructions on foundation web site. Full applications are by invitation only, upon review of initial letter of inquiry. E-mailed, faxed or mailed inquires are not accepted. Application information and form available on foundation web site. Application form required.
Initial approach: **Letter of inquiry (no more than 2 pages) to be submitted online, via foundation's e-grant system on web site**
Deadline(s): See foundation web site for current deadlines
Board meeting date(s): May and Nov.
Final notification: 3 weeks after board meetings
Officers and Trustees:* Pam Howell, C.E.O.; Patrick Stranahan,* Pres.; Robert Stranahan,* V.P.; Page Armstrong,* Secy.; William Foster,* Treas.; Paget Ferrell; Timothy Foster; Trevor Foster; Julie Higgins;

Easter Page; Frances Parry; Mark Stranahan; Sarah Stranahan.
Number of staff: 1 full-time professional; 1 full-time support; 3 part-time support.
EIN: 346514375

2791
Nelson Talbott Foundation
37070 Shaker Blvd.
Chagrin Falls, OH **44022-6644**

Established in 1947 in OH.
Donor: Nelson S. Talbott.
Foundation type: Independent foundation.
Financial data (yr. ended 09/30/13): Assets, $4,085,284 (M); expenditures, $242,848; qualifying distributions, $199,235; giving activities include $199,235 for 120 grants (high: $35,000; low: $50).
Purpose and activities: Giving primarily for conservation programs and local charities.
Fields of interest: Arts; Higher education; Environment, natural resources; Environment; Human services.
Limitations: Applications not accepted. Giving primarily in Washington, DC, and Cleveland, OH. No grants to individuals.
Application information: Contributes only to pre-selected organizations.
Trustees: A.L. Fabems; E. P. Talbott; Nelson S. Talbott.
EIN: 316039441
Other changes: The grantmaker no longer lists a primary contact.

2792
Third Federal Foundation
7007 Broadway Ave.
Cleveland, OH 44105-1441 (216) 641-7270
Contact: Kurt Karakul, Pres. and Exec. Dir.

Established in 2007 in OH.
Donors: Third Federal Savings and Loan Association, MHC; TFS Financial Corp.
Foundation type: Company-sponsored foundation.
Financial data (yr. ended 12/31/12): Assets, $41,752,855 (M); gifts received, $500; expenditures, $2,714,633; qualifying distributions, $2,337,555; giving activities include $2,337,555 for 80 grants (high: $300,000; low: $91).
Purpose and activities: The foundation supports nonprofit organizations involved with education and community development. Special emphasis is directed toward programs designed to raise the aspirations of students in the community and enhance knowledge of specific areas, including economics, communications, business, and public speaking.
Fields of interest: Elementary school/education; Secondary school/education; Higher education; Business school/education; Boys & girls clubs; Youth development; Community development, neighborhood development; Economic development; Community/economic development; Economics; Economically disadvantaged.
Type of support: General/operating support; Program development.
Limitations: Applications accepted. Giving primarily in areas of company operations in OH, with emphasis on Cleveland. No grants to individuals.
Application information: Application form not required.
Initial approach: Proposal
Deadline(s): None
Final notification: Following review
Officers and Directors:* Marc A. Stefanski,* C.E.O.; Kurt Karakul, Pres. and Exec. Dir.; Ralph M. Betters, Secy.-Treas.; Robert A. Fiala; John Marino.
EIN: 208467212
Other changes: Meredith Weil is no longer V.P. and Treas. Ralph M. Betters is now Secy.-Treas.

2793
The Tiffin Charitable Foundation
68 S. Washington St.
Tiffin, OH 44883-2350 (419) 448-1791
E-mail: adm@tiffinfoundation.org; Main URL: http://www.tiffinfoundation.org

Established in 1983 in OH.
Foundation type: Community foundation.
Financial data (yr. ended 12/31/12): Assets, $12,637,005 (M); gifts received, $134,633; expenditures, $960,784; giving activities include $877,902 for grants to individuals.
Purpose and activities: The foundation supports charitable purposes that promote the well-being of the citizens of the city of Tiffin and Seneca County, Ohio.
Fields of interest: Arts, cultural/ethnic awareness; Humanities; Arts; Higher education; Education; Environment; Animals/wildlife; Health care; Human services.
Type of support: Annual campaigns; Capital campaigns; Conferences/seminars; Emergency funds; Equipment; Matching/challenge support; Program development; Scholarship funds; Technical assistance.
Limitations: Applications accepted. Giving limited to the Tiffin and Seneca County, OH, area. No support for religious or sectarian purposes. No grants to individuals (except for scholarships), or for construction projects for routine maintenance, normal operating expenses, loan payments, endowments, multi-year funding, or re-granting in any of the next three year if the original grant was $10,000 or more.
Publications: Application guidelines; Annual report; Financial statement; Informational brochure; Newsletter.
Application information: Visit foundation web site for application guidelines. Application form required.
Initial approach: Telephone, e-mail, or online
Copies of proposal: 1
***Deadline(s):* Mar. 12, Jun. 4, Sept. 3, and Dec. 3**
Board meeting date(s): Quarterly
Final notification: 1 to 3 months
Directors: Laura Brickner; Jeannine Curns; Charles Ervin; Thomas J. Gordon; Dr. Robert H. Huntington; Allen Schultz; Dr. Lillian Schumacher; Eric Shook; Jerry Weininger.
Number of staff: 1 full-time professional.
EIN: 341405286

2794
The Troy Foundation
216 W. Franklin St.
Troy, OH 45373-2846 (937) 339-8935
Contact: Melissa A. Kleptz, Exec. Dir.
FAX: (937) 339-8992;
E-mail: info@thetroyfoundation.org; Main URL: http://thetroyfoundation.org/

Established in 1924 in OH by bank resolution and declaration of trust.
Donors: Nannie Kendall†; A.G. Stouder†; J.M. Spencer†.
Foundation type: Community foundation.
Financial data (yr. ended 12/31/12): Assets, $68,331,999 (M); gifts received, $3,423,295; expenditures, $3,060,585; giving activities include $2,024,831 for 229 grants (high: $155,204; low: $75), and $331,976 for 57 grants to individuals.
Purpose and activities: The foundation seeks to improve the quality of life for the community served by promoting philanthropy and stewardship for a better tomorrow.
Fields of interest: Museums; Historic preservation/historical societies; Arts; Elementary/secondary education; Child development, education; Elementary school/education; Vocational education; Business school/education; Libraries/library science; Education; Environment, natural resources; Environment; Hospitals (general); Health care; Substance abuse, services; Recreation; Children/youth, services; Child development, services; Residential/custodial care, hospices; Human services; Community/economic development; Youth.
Type of support: Capital campaigns; Building/renovation; Equipment; Emergency funds; Program development; Seed money; Curriculum development; Scholarship funds; Matching/challenge support.
Limitations: Applications accepted. Giving limited to the Troy City, OH. No support for religious organizations. No grants to individuals (except for scholarships), or for endowment funds, operating budgets, continuing support, deficit financing, research, demonstration projects, publications, conferences, or fellowships; no loans.
Publications: Application guidelines; Annual report; Informational brochure; Informational brochure (including application guidelines); Newsletter.
Application information: Visit foundation web site for application form and guidelines. Application form required.
Initial approach: Submit grant application and attachments
Copies of proposal: 7
Deadline(s): 15th of the month preceding board meeting
Board meeting date(s): 3rd Thurs. of Mar., June, Sept., and Dec.
Final notification: Within 10 days of the grant review meeting
Officers and Trustees:* Wanda C. Lukens,* Pres.; Brian R. Williamson,* V.P.; Robert N. Schlemmer,* Secy.; Melissa A. Kleptz, Exec. Dir.; Susan J. Behm; Mark Douglas; David J. Dippold; William J. Fulker; Judith K. Hartman; James M. Johnson; Thomas E. Robinson; David Selsor; Craig E. Wise.
Number of staff: 2 full-time professional.
EIN: 316018703
Other changes: Beth Alexander is now Admin. Asst. Susan J. Behm, Brent J. Black, Mark A. Douglas, Ozzie Haddad, Ted Mercer, and David K. Selsor are no longer trustees.

2795
Tuscarawas County Community Foundation
1323 4th St. NW
New Philadelphia, OH **44663-1205** (330) 602-6264
Contact: Scott Robinson, Exec. Dir.
***E-mail:* info@tuscfoundation.com; Main URL: http://tuscfoundation.com/**
Grant Awardees: http://tuscfoundation.com/grant-awardees/

Scholarship Awardees: http://tuscfoundation.com/scholarship-awardees/

Established in 2001 in OH.
Foundation type: Independent foundation.
Financial data (yr. ended 12/31/12): Assets, $8,442,357 (M); gifts received, $5,350; expenditures, $456,526; qualifying distributions, $398,925; giving activities include $322,236 for 26 grants (high: $55,000; low: $250).
Purpose and activities: The foundation's mission is to enhance the quality of life in the Tuscarawas County community through the strengthening of its educational, economic, social, and cultural fabrics by: 1) making charitable grants of investment income; 2) educating the community regarding the ways the needs of local citizens can be served; 3) attracting and investing endowment resources; and 4) being accountable for grantmaking and financial reporting to the community.
Fields of interest: Humanities; Arts; Education; Environment; Health care; Human services; Community/economic development.
Type of support: Continuing support; Management development/capacity building; Annual campaigns; Capital campaigns; Building/renovation; Equipment; Scholarship funds; Grants to individuals; Scholarships—to individuals.
Limitations: Applications accepted. Giving primarily limited to Tuscarawas County, OH, area. No support for religious organizations. No grants to individuals (except through scholarship funds), operating expenses of well-established organizations, deficit financing, endowment funds, annual appeals, or conference or recognition events.
Publications: Application guidelines; Financial statement; Grants list; Informational brochure; Occasional report.
Application information: Application form required.
Initial approach: Personal contact by letter or telephone
Copies of proposal: 6
Deadline(s): June 15
Board meeting date(s): Every 3 months
Final notification: July
Officers and Directors:* **Robert R. Gerber,*** **Pres.**; Karen Jenkins,* V.P.; **Renee Brown Parker,*** **Secy.**; Janine Garber, Treas.; Scott Robinson, Exec. Dir.; **Alan Bambeck**; **John Beitzel**; Blair A. Hillyer; **John Maxwell**; **Kent Watson**.
Number of staff: 1 part-time support.
EIN: 341930804
Other changes: Robert R. Gerber has replaced Scott Robinson as Pres. Renee Brown Parker has replaced Elizabeth W. Stephenson as Secy. David Hanhart, Matthew Mullen and Michael Noretto are no longer directors.

2796
Tuscora Park Health & Wellness Foundation
460 W. Paige Ave.
Barberton, OH 44203-2564 (330) 753-4607
FAX: (330) 745-3990;
E-mail: tuschealthfdn@yahoo.com; **Main URL: http://www.barbertoncf.org/tphwf**
Blog: http://www.barbertoncf.org/tphwf-news
Scholarship application address: c/o Barbara Berlin, Nursing Office, Summa Barberton Hospital, Nursing Scholarship Comm., 155 5th St. N.E., Barberton, OH 44203, tel.: (330) 745-1611, ext. 3352

Established in 1996 in OH; converted from the merger of the Barberton Citizens Auxiliary and the Barberton Citizens Hospital Foundation.
Foundation type: Independent foundation.
Financial data (yr. ended 12/31/12): Assets, $4,348,368 (M); expenditures, $253,465; qualifying distributions, $196,642; giving activities include $196,642 for grants.
Purpose and activities: Supports activities that promote wellness and extend health care, medical and educational services, and opportunities to residents of Summit County, OH, and surrounding counties. Also provides nursing scholarships.
Fields of interest: Nursing school/education; Education; Health care; Human services.
Type of support: Equipment; Program development; Conferences/seminars; Scholarships—to individuals.
Limitations: Applications accepted. Giving primarily in southern Summit County, OH, and surrounding communities. No support for religious organizations. No grants for membership drives, endowments, lobbying activities, deficits, or operating expenses.
Application information: See web site for application policies, guidelines and forms or contact the foundation for application guidelines and materials. Application form required.
Initial approach: Proposal
Copies of proposal: 6
Deadline(s): Jan. 2, Apr. 1, July 1, and Oct. 1
Board meeting date(s): Feb., May, Aug., and Nov.
Final notification: Within 1 week of board meeting
Officers: Willard Roderick, Chair.; Patrick S. Roberts, Vice-Chair.; Laurette Bradnick, Secy.; Michael Moldvay, Treas.
Trustees: Leonard Foster; Michael Frank; John Hall; Duane Isham; Kathy Jobe; Lawrence G. Lauter; Aaron Lepp; Lucy Majorkiewicz; Patrick McGrath; Jim Stonkus; Pat Taylor; Emil Voelz; Daniel G. Warder.
Number of staff: 3 full-time professional.
EIN: 341193807

2797
The Veale Foundation
(formerly V and V Foundation)
30195 Chagrin Blvd., Ste. 310-N
Pepper Pike, OH 44124-5703 (216) 255-3179
***Contact:* Cynthia L. Bailie, Exec. Dir.**
FAX: (216) 514-0064;
E-mail: vealefoundation@vealefound.org

Established in 1965 in OH.
Donors: Tinkham Veale II†; Harriet Ernst Veale†.
Foundation type: Independent foundation.
Financial data (yr. ended 12/31/12): Assets, $56,622,977 (M); gifts received, $7,637,999; expenditures, $3,068,542; qualifying distributions, $2,713,200; giving activities include $2,713,200 for 52 grants (high: $2,000,000; low: $1,200).
Fields of interest: Elementary/secondary education; Higher education; Education; Health care; Human services; International affairs, foreign policy; United Ways and Federated Giving Programs; Christian agencies & churches.
Type of support: General/operating support.
Limitations: Applications not accepted. Giving primarily in OH, with emphasis on Cleveland. No grants to individuals.
Application information: Contributes only to pre-selected organizations.
Officers and Trustees:* Daniel P. Harrington,* Chair.; Jane Kober,* Vice-Chair.; Richard K. Harr,* Secy.; William J. Culbertson.
Number of staff: 1 full-time professional.
EIN: 346565830

2798
Wayne County Community Foundation
(formerly Greater Wayne County Foundation, Inc.)
517 N. Market St.
Wooster, OH 44691-3405 (330) 262-3877
Contact: Sara L. Patton, Exec. Dir.
FAX: (330) 262-8057; E-mail: wccf@sssnet.com; Additional e-mail: gwcf@gwcf.net; Main URL: http://www.waynecountycommunityfoundation.org
E-Newsletter: http://www.waynecountycommunityfoundation.org/about-us/wccf-newsletters
Facebook: http://www.facebook.com/pages/Wayne-County-Community-Foundation/328152980611795

Established in 1978 in OH.
Foundation type: Community foundation.
Financial data (yr. ended 06/30/12): Assets, $48,947,071 (M); gifts received, $11,596,370; expenditures, $4,525,111; giving activities include $3,717,414 for 53+ grants (high: $1,025,462), and $309,279 for grants to individuals.
Purpose and activities: The foundation seeks to: 1) encourage individuals who have prospered in Wayne County to leave part of their estates for the good of the community in which they lived; 2) assist community nonprofit organizations in the creation and management of endowments to meet future financial needs; and 3) provide oversight of investment and disbursement of funds devoted to charitable purposes.
Fields of interest: Humanities; Arts; Education; Environment; Health care; Human services; Community/economic development.
Type of support: Continuing support; Management development/capacity building; Capital campaigns; Building/renovation; Equipment; Land acquisition; Endowments; Emergency funds; Program development; Seed money; Scholarship funds; Research; Matching/challenge support.
Limitations: Applications accepted. Giving limited to Wayne County, OH. No support for religious organizations for religious purposes. No grants for deficit financing, endowment funds, annual appeals or membership contributions, conferences, field trips, travel, recognition events, or general operating expenses of well-established organizations including computers and office equipment.
Publications: Application guidelines; Annual report; Financial statement; Informational brochure (including application guidelines).
Application information: Application process has moved entirely online. Visit foundation web site for online application and guidelines. Application form required.
Initial approach: Create online profile
Copies of proposal: 1
Deadline(s): Mar. 1 and Sept. 1
Board meeting date(s): Quarterly
Final notification: June 1 and Dec. 1
Officers and Trustees:* J.C. Johnston III,* Pres.; Steve Matthew,* V.P.; Mark A. Auble,* Secy.; Mary Alice Streeter,* Treas.; Sara L. Patton, Exec. Dir.; Michael D. Agnoni; Marlene Barkheimer; Maribeth Burns; William J. DeRodes; Glenda Lehman Ervin; Cheryl M. Kirkbride; Larry Markley; William J. Robertson; Stephen L. Shapiro; Rod Steiger; Brent Steiner; Deanna Troutman; Bala Venkataraman; Howard Wenger.
Number of staff: 1 full-time professional; 1 full-time support; 1 part-time support.
EIN: 341281026
Other changes: Lacie Neal is now Prog. Mgr.

2799
The Raymond John Wean Foundation
147 W. Market St.
Warren, OH 44481-1022 (330) 394-5600
***Contact:* Jennifer Roller, Pres.**
FAX: (330) 394-5601; E-mail: info@rjweanfdn.org; Main URL: http://www.rjweanfdn.org
E-Newsletter: http://www.rjweanfdn.org/ContactUs.aspx
The Raymond John Wean Foundation's Philanthropy Promise: http://www.ncrp.org/philanthropys-promise/who

Established in 1949 in OH.
Donor: Raymond John Wean, Sr.†.
Foundation type: Independent foundation.
Financial data (yr. ended 12/31/13): Assets, $80,350,284 (M); gifts received, $10,000; expenditures, $3,858,666; qualifying distributions, $3,257,142; giving activities include $2,227,560 for 174 grants (high: $425,000; low: $500).
Purpose and activities: To enhance community well-being and vitality in the Mahoning Valley through strategic grant making intended to support people living in the Valley's economically disadvantaged communities and neighborhoods in adherence to the following principles: to explore new innovative approaches to addressing issues, to seek inclusion and broad community involvement; to build on the considerable assets of the Mahoning Valley; to strive for equity and support social justice; to leverage additional resources, partners and ideas; to support the development of human assets and capital; to cultivate leadership in the community; and to provide support to people and communities which are often overlooked or insufficiently funded.
Fields of interest: Education, early childhood education; Child development, services; Community/economic development.
Type of support: Income development; Management development/capacity building; Program development; Technical assistance; Program evaluation; Program-related investments/loans.
Limitations: Applications accepted. Giving limited to the Mahoning and/or Trumbull Counties in OH. No support for sectarian religious activities, veterans' or fraternal organizations, or local or national offices of organizations combating a particular disease or family of diseases. No grants to individuals; or for endowment funds, debt reduction, foreign operations, national fundraising campaigns or film or video production.
Publications: Application guidelines; Annual report; Financial statement; Grants list.
Application information: Applications accepted only after letter of inquiry. Letter of inquiry form is available of foundation's web site. The foundation also accepts the Ohio Grantmakers Forum's letter of inquiry, application and final evaluation forms. Application form required.
Initial approach: Complete letter of inquiry form
Copies of proposal: 2
Deadline(s): See foundation web site for current deadlines
Board meeting date(s): Mar., Jun., Sept. and Dec.
Final notification: Following board meeting
Officers and Administrators:* Gordon B. Wean,* Chair.; **Jennifer Roller, Pres.**; Germaine Bennett; Don Emerson; Suzanne Fleming; Paul Hagman; Pastor Michael Harrison; William Mullane; John L. Pogue; Janis Sanfrey.
Trustee: The Glenmede Trust Company.
Number of staff: 4 full-time professional; 1 full-time support.
EIN: 346505038
Other changes: Jennifer Roller has replaced Jeffrey M. Glebocki as Pres.

2800
The Thomas H. White No. 1 Trust
(also known as Thomas H. White Foundation)
c/o Foundation Mgmt. Svcs., Inc.
1422 Euclid Ave., Ste. 966
Cleveland, OH 44115-1952 **(216) 621-2901**
Contact: Susan Althans, Consultant
FAX: (216) 621-8198;
E-mail: salthans@fmscleveland.com**; Additional e-mail: info@fmscleveland.com**; Main URL: http://www.fmscleveland.com/thomaswhite/

Trust established in 1913 in OH; became active in 1939.
Donor: Thomas H. White†.
Foundation type: Independent foundation.
Financial data (yr. ended 12/31/13): Assets, $24,308,433 (M); expenditures, $1,274,212; qualifying distributions, $1,214,786; giving activities include $1,112,548 for 90 grants (high: $30,000; low: $2,500).
Purpose and activities: The foundation will consider requests from tax-exempt, non-profit charitable and educational institutions located within Cuyahoga County, Ohio, if such organizations and their services and facilities primarily serve residents of the city of Cleveland. The foundation will focus its grantmaking on two major areas: education and human services. Specifically, the foundation is interested in supporting programs that address three critical areas: Workforce readiness: programs that emphasize science and technology education, adequate employment preparation, support systems, and the relationship to earning potential. School retention: programs that emphasize the critical transition issues that occur during early teenage years and affect family relationships and school attendance. Early childhood enrichment: programs that enhance the learning environment; provide support, training, and ancillary services to parents; and/or the recruitment and training of daycare providers. Organizations and programs that contribute generally to the quality of life in Greater Cleveland may also be considered at the foundation's discretion.
Fields of interest: Education, early childhood education; Elementary school/education; Secondary school/education; Education; Crime/violence prevention, domestic violence; Employment; Human services; Children/youth, services; Family services; Homeless, human services; Disabilities, people with; Minorities; Women; AIDS, people with; Economically disadvantaged; Homeless.
Type of support: Capital campaigns; Building/renovation; Equipment; Emergency funds; Program development; Seed money.
Limitations: Applications accepted. Giving limited to nonprofit charitable organizations located within Cuyahoga County, OH, if such organizations, and their services and facilities, primarily serve residents of the City of Cleveland. No grants to individuals, or for annual campaigns, general operating support, scholarships, endowments, research, symposia, seminars, deficit financing, or land acquisition; no loans.
Publications: Application guidelines; Annual report (including application guidelines); Financial statement.
Application information: Mass mailings not accepted. All applications must be submitted online. Application guidelines and form available on trust's website. Application form required.
Initial approach: Proposal
Copies of proposal: 1
Deadline(s): Apr. 1, Aug. 1, and Dec. 1
Board meeting date(s): Distribution Committee meets in Jan., May, and Sept.
Final notification: Within several weeks
Distribution Committee: Margot James Copeland; Robin Cottingham; Jan Culver; Michael S. Galland; Catherine O'Malley Kearney.
Trustee: KeyBank N.A.
EIN: 346505722

2801
Woodruff Foundation
1422 Euclid Ave., Ste. 966
Cleveland, OH 44115-2001 (216) 566-1853
Contact: Allison Rand, Consultant
FAX: (216) 621-8198;
E-mail: arand@fmscleveland.com; Main URL: http://www.fmscleveland.com/woodruff
Grants List: http://www.fmscleveland.com/woodruff/grants.cfm

Established in 1986 in OH; converted with proceeds from the sale of Woodruff Hospital.
Foundation type: Independent foundation.
Financial data (yr. ended 12/31/12): Assets, $10,934,594 (M); expenditures, $555,316; qualifying distributions, $507,943; giving activities include $382,000 for 20 grants (high: $40,000; low: $2,000).
Purpose and activities: Giving primarily to support the development and delivery of mental health services in Cuyahoga County, OH. Specifically, the foundation seeks to fund projects that will foster and enhance: the treatment of persons affected by mental disorders and chemical dependency; educational programs related to mental health, the coordination of mental health resources in the community; research into the causes, nature and recurrence of mental illness. High priority areas of interest include encouraging the implementation of innovative prevention and treatment programs and strengthening the effectiveness of existing service delivery systems.
Fields of interest: Substance abuse, services; Mental health/crisis services; Alcoholism.
Type of support: Emergency funds; Program development; Seed money; Research.
Limitations: Applications accepted. Giving limited to Cuyahoga County, OH. No grants for scholarships or fellowships, operating expenses, endowments, or annual fundraising campaigns.
Publications: Application guidelines; Financial statement; Grants list.
Application information: Online applications are available 1 month prior to deadlines. See foundation web site for necessary application details. Mass mailings are not accepted. Application form required.
Initial approach: Use online application process
Deadline(s): Jan. 1, May 1, and Sept. 1
Board meeting date(s): Feb., June, and Oct.
Officers: Ann Reischman, Pres.; Richard A. Paulson, V.P.; Valerie Bradley Hicks, Secy.-Treas.
Trustees: Mark Bonhard; Frank Fecser; Franklin J. Hickman; Valerie Raines; Robert J. Ronis.
EIN: 237425631

2802
The Wyler Family Foundation
401 Milford Pkwy., Ste. A
Milford, OH **45150-9119** (513) 752-7450
Main URL: http://www.wylerfamilyfoundation.org/Index.asp

Donors: Agency Serv. Consolidated, Inc.; Katz, Teller, Brant & Hild; Turnbull-wahlert Construction, Inc.; Jeff Wyler Eastgate, Inc.; Jeff Wyler Florence, Inc.; Jeff Wyler Colerain, Inc.
Foundation type: Independent foundation.
Financial data (yr. ended 12/31/12): Assets, $1,831,114 (M); gifts received, $1,173,785; expenditures, $350,231; qualifying distributions, $350,231; giving activities include $349,231 for 30 grants (high: $113,000; low: $100).
Fields of interest: Health care; Youth development; Community/economic development.
Limitations: Applications accepted. Giving primarily in OH. **No support for sports, athletic events, or athletic programs; travel-related events, including students trips or tours; development or production of books, films, videos, or television programs; memorial campaigns; individuals, including those seeking scholarships or fellowships assistance.**
Application information: Requests can be most easily made via the foundation web site. Application form not required.
Initial approach: Proposal
Deadline(s): None
Officers: Jeffrey L. Wyler, C.E.O.; J. David Wyler, Pres.; W. Scott Bristow, V.P.; Linda Wyler, Secy.; Julie Bristow, Treas.
EIN: 264396121

2803
The Hugo H. and Mabel B. Young Foundation
120 N. Water St.
Loudonville, OH 44842-1249
Contact: Michael C. Bandy, Secy.-Treas.
***Application address:* c/o Michael C. Bandy, P.O. Box 63, Loudonville, OH 44842, email: hugomabelyoung@gmail.com**

Incorporated in 1963 in OH.
Foundation type: Independent foundation.
Financial data (yr. ended 04/30/13): Assets, $5,711,936 (M); expenditures, $329,123; qualifying distributions, $274,421; giving activities include $264,247 for 15 grants (high: $53,200; low: $3,000).
Fields of interest: Performing arts, orchestras; Libraries (public); Education; Recreation; Human services; Community/economic development; Foundations (community); Christian agencies & churches.
Type of support: Capital campaigns; Building/renovation; Equipment; Scholarship funds; Matching/challenge support.
Limitations: Applications accepted. Giving primarily in Ashland and Holmes counties, OH. No grants to individuals, or for general purposes or matching gifts; no loans.
Publications: Application guidelines.
Application information: Application form required.
Initial approach: Letter
Copies of proposal: 7
Deadline(s): Apr. 1
Board meeting date(s): 3rd Tues. in May
Final notification: Late May or early June
Officers and Trustees: Barb Burd, Pres.; Jon H. Cooperrider II, V.P.; Michael C. Bandy,* Secy.-Treas.; James J. Dudte; William B. LaPlace; James S. Lingenfelter; **Ronny Portz**; Phillip A. Ranney.
EIN: 346560664
Other changes: Barb Burd has replaced James S. Lingenfelter as Pres. Jon H. Cooperrider II has replaced James J. Dudte as V.P.

2804
The Youngstown Foundation
P.O. Box 1162
Youngstown, OH 44501-1162 (330) 744-0320
Contact: Janice E. Strasfeld, Exec. Dir.
FAX: (330) 744-0344;
E-mail: info@youngstownfoundation.org; Additional e-mail: jan@youngstownfoundation.org; Main URL: http://www.youngstownfoundation.org

Established in 1918 in OH by bank resolution.
Foundation type: Community foundation.
Financial data (yr. ended 12/31/11): Assets, $79,603,847 (M); gifts received, $3,318,745; expenditures, $4,227,220; giving activities include $3,681,041 for 150 grants.
Purpose and activities: The foundation seeks to support local charitable and educational agencies for the betterment of the community; grants for capital purposes, with emphasis on aid to crippled children, community funds, youth agencies, music and cultural programs, and hospitals.
Fields of interest: Visual arts; Museums; Performing arts; Performing arts, music; Historic preservation/historical societies; Arts; Education, association; Child development, education; Education; Environment; Health care; Alcoholism; Recreation; Youth development, services; Children/youth, services; Child development, services; Family services; Residential/custodial care, hospices; Human services; Urban/community development; Leadership development; Children/youth; Children; Youth; Adults; Aging; Disabilities, people with; Physically disabled; Mentally disabled; Girls; Military/veterans; Single parents; Crime/abuse victims; Economically disadvantaged.
Type of support: General/operating support; Management development/capacity building; Capital campaigns; Building/renovation; Equipment; Emergency funds; Program development.
Limitations: Applications accepted. Giving limited to Youngstown, OH and vicinity. No support for religious groups for religious purposes. No grants to individuals (except for scholarships), or for endowment funds, seed money, deficit financing, land acquisition, demonstration projects, publications, fellowships, travel, tours or trips, underwriting of conferences, debt reduction, projects normally the responsibility of government, sabbatical leaves, scholarly research organizations not tax exempt, or matching gifts.
Publications: Application guidelines; Annual report; Financial statement; Grants list; Informational brochure.
Application information: Visit foundation web site for application guidelines. Application form not required.
Initial approach: Proposal
Copies of proposal: 3
Deadline(s): Jan. 25, Apr. 26, July 26, and Oct. 18
Board meeting date(s): Mar., June, Sept., and Dec.
Final notification: 6 weeks
Officers and Distribution Committee:* George Berlin,* Chair.; Jude Nohra,* Vice-Chair.; Janice E. Strasfield, Exec. Dir.; Eugenia Atkinson; **Dr. Randy J. Dunn**; John MacIntosh; **Jeffrey Simon**.
Number of staff: 2 part-time professional; 1 part-time support.
EIN: 346515788
Other changes: Lisa Dickson and Dave Turner are no longer directors.

2805
YSI Foundation Inc.
P.O. Box 279
Yellow Springs, OH 45387-0279 **(937) 767-7241**
E-mail: smiller@ysi.com

Established in 1990 in OH.
Donor: YSI Inc.
Foundation type: Company-sponsored foundation.
Financial data (yr. ended 12/31/12): Assets, $4,334 (M); gifts received, $58,000; expenditures, $110,639; qualifying distributions, $109,104; giving activities include $107,529 for 81 grants (high: $20,000; low: $25).
Purpose and activities: The foundation supports organizations involved with arts and culture, education, disaster relief, human services, community development, and life sciences. Special emphasis is directed to programs designed to promote global environmental stewardship.
Fields of interest: Arts; Education; Environment.
Type of support: Continuing support; Capital campaigns; Building/renovation; Equipment; Endowments; Emergency funds; Program development; Publication; Seed money; Curriculum development; Scholarship funds; Technical assistance; Employee matching gifts; Employee-related scholarships; Scholarships—to individuals; Matching/challenge support.
Limitations: Applications not accepted. Giving primarily in OH. Generally, no support for large national or local organizations. No grants for general operating support or annual campaigns.
Application information: Unsolicited requests for funds not accepted.
Officer: Deb Stottlemyer, Treas.
Trustees: Anita Brown; Michael Fields; Tim Finegan; Christopher McIntire; Charlene Miller; Susan Miller; Fred Tolliver; **Christopher McIntire**; **Charlene Miller**.
EIN: 311292180
Other changes: The grantmaker no longer lists a primary contact.
The grantmaker no longer publishes application guidelines.

OKLAHOMA

2806
The Judith and Jean Pape Adams Charitable Foundation

7030 S. Yale Ave., Ste. 600
Tulsa, OK 74136-5749 (830) 997-7347
Contact: Marcia Manhart, Exec. Dir.
FAX: (830) 997-9888;
E-mail: mmanhart@jjpafoundation.com; Main URL: http://www.jjpafoundation.com/
ALS Research Grants: http://www.adamsfoundation.org/annual-report/recently-awarded-als-grants/
Tulsa Grants: http://www.adamsfoundation.org/annual-report/recently-awarded-tulsa-grants/

Established in 2003 in OK.
Donor: Jean Pape Adams Trust.
Foundation type: Independent foundation.
Financial data (yr. ended 12/31/12): Assets, $17,275,638 (M); expenditures, $1,700,072; qualifying distributions, $1,322,654; giving activities include $1,189,760 for 76 grants (high: $200,000; low: $500).
Purpose and activities: One-third of giving is reserved for national ALS research. Two-thirds of giving is reserved for Tulsa-area grants for arts/culture, social services, education and health.
Fields of interest: Arts; Education; Environment; Health organizations; ALS research; Human services.
Type of support: General/operating support; Annual campaigns; Capital campaigns; Building/renovation; Program development; Research; Matching/challenge support.
Limitations: Applications accepted. Giving limited to the Tulsa, OK area, except for ALS grants, which are made on a national basis. No support for political organizations. No grants to individuals.
Publications: Application guidelines; Annual report.
Application information: Application guidelines available on foundation web site. Application form not required.

Initial approach: **Use online application process on foundation web site**
Copies of proposal: 1
Deadline(s): See foundation web site for current deadline
Board meeting date(s): May and Nov. or as needed
Final notification: Mid-Dec.

Officer and Trustees:* Marcia Y. Manhart,* Exec. Dir.; Katherine G. Coyle; INTRUST Bank, N.A.
Number of staff: 1 full-time professional; 1 part-time support.
EIN: 200189630

2807
Grace & Franklin Bernsen Foundation

15 W. 6th St., No. 1308
Tulsa, OK 74119-5407 (918) 584-4711
Contact: Trustees
FAX: (918) 584-4713; E-mail: info@bernsen.org; E-mail for grant application correspondence: gfbernsen@aol.com; Main URL: http://www.bernsen.org

Established 1968.
Donors: Grace Bernsen†; Franklin Bernsen†.
Foundation type: Independent foundation.
Financial data (yr. ended 09/30/12): Assets, $28,932,838 (M); expenditures, $2,141,807; qualifying distributions, $2,042,084; giving activities include $1,776,700 for 64 grants (high: $500,000; low: $2,500).
Purpose and activities: Giving primarily for the arts, education, health, children and youth services, and to Protestant churches. Elementary or secondary education institutions will be considered if they involve programs for at-risk, handicapped or learning-disabled children, or if they are innovative and apply to all schools in the system.
Fields of interest: Arts; Higher education; Mental health/crisis services; Health organizations, association; Human services; Children/youth, services; Protestant agencies & churches.
Type of support: Capital campaigns; Building/renovation; Equipment; Emergency funds; Program development; Conferences/seminars; Matching/challenge support.
Limitations: Applications accepted. Giving limited to within the city of Tulsa, OK. No support for continuing or additional support for the same programs (although a single grant may cover a period of several years). No grants to individuals, or for debt reduction.
Publications: Application guidelines; Annual report; Grants list; Informational brochure (including application guidelines).
Application information: Application guidelines available on foundation web site. Applicants should not use paragraph subtitles in their summary, or it will be returned. Proposals submitted in plastic covers, binders or sheet protectors will not be considered. Do not include DVDs, CDs, bound books or bulky leaflets, or letters of support. OK tax documents, certificate of incorporation or Bylaws are also not needed with application. Application form not required.

Initial approach: **Letter (no more than 3 pages with type no smaller than 10.5 point); a copy of the letter must also be e-mailed in Word format immediately to application correspondence address and received in the foundation's office before the grant request is received. (Only letter should be e-mailed, not the full grant request)**
Copies of proposal: 1
Deadline(s): 12th of each month
Board meeting date(s): Monthly
Final notification: Generally within 1-week following board meeting

Officers and Trustees:* W. Bland Williamson,* Secy.; **Barbara H. Pray**; Donald E. Pray; John D. Strong, Jr.
Number of staff: 1 full-time professional.
EIN: 237009414

2808
H. A. and Mary K. Chapman Charitable Trust

c/o Chapman Foundations Management, LLC
6100 S. Yale Ave., Ste. 1816
Tulsa, OK 74136-1928 (918) 496-7882
Contact: J. Jerry Dickman, Tr.; Donne W. Pitman, Tr.; Andrea Doyle, Prog. Off.
FAX: (918) 496-7887;
E-mail: grants@chapmantrusts.com; **E-mail for Letters of inquiry: grants@chapmantrusts.com; Contact for general inquiries regarding grant programs and procedures, Andie Doyle, Prog. Off., tel.: (719) 465-5977, ext. 3, e-mail: andie@chapmantrusts.com. Additional address: c/o Chapman Foundations Management, LLC, 121 S. Tejon St., Ste. 1105, Colorado Springs, CO 80903; fax: (719) 465-5979; e-mail for Jerry Dickman, Tr.: jerry@chapmantrusts.com; e-mail for Donne Pitman, Tr.: donne@chapmantrusts.com**; Main URL: http://www.chapmantrusts.org

Trust established in 1976 in OK.
Donors: H.A. Chapman†; Mary K. Chapman†.
Foundation type: Independent foundation.
Financial data (yr. ended 12/31/12): Assets, $84,436,134 (M); expenditures, $5,087,569; qualifying distributions, $4,510,183; giving activities include $4,287,000 for 77 grants (high: $500,000; low: $1,000).
Purpose and activities: Grants largely for education, particularly higher education, health, social services, and cultural programs.
Fields of interest: Arts; Higher education; Education; Environment; Animals/wildlife; Health care; Health organizations, association; Human services.
Type of support: General/operating support; Annual campaigns; Capital campaigns; Building/renovation; Program development; Research; Program evaluation; Matching/challenge support.
Limitations: Applications accepted. Giving primarily in OK, AR, and TX for colleges and universities and in OK for elementary and secondary education and for health care. No support for political campaigns, religious programs of religious organizations, or purposes normally funded by taxation or governmental agencies. No grants to individuals, or for endowments, scholarships, deficit financing, debt retirement, projects for which the foundation would be the sole source of support, for travel, conferences, conventions, group meetings, seminars, or camp programs and other seasonal activities.
Publications: Application guidelines; IRS Form 990 or 990-PF printed copy available upon request.
Application information: Application guidelines available on foundation web site. Proposal form will be sent upon approval of letter of inquiry. Application form required.

Initial approach: E-mail letter of inquiry, no more than 3 pages and in .pdf format to Prog. Off.
Copies of proposal: 3
Deadline(s): None for Letters of Inquiry; 1st day of the month preceding quarterly meeting for invited proposal
Board meeting date(s): March, June, Sept. and Dec.

Trustees: J. Jerry Dickman; Donne W. Pitman.
Number of staff: None.
EIN: 736177739

2809
Cherokee Strip Community Foundation

(formerly Enid Community Foundation, Inc.)
114 S. Independence, Ste. 140
Enid, OK 73701 (580) 234-3988
***Contact:* Mary M. Stallings, Exec. Dir.**
FAX: (580) 234-3311; Mailing address: P.O. Box 263, Enid, OK 73702; Main URL: http://www.cherokeestripcf.com

Established in 2000 in OK.
Donors: Harold Hamm; Sue Hamm; St. Mary's Hospital; Helen Garriott; Owen Garriott.
Foundation type: Community foundation.
Financial data (yr. ended 12/31/12): Assets, $12,553,203 (M); gifts received, $318,801; expenditures, $500,849; giving activities include $412,673 for 9+ grants (high: $124,352).
Purpose and activities: The foundation seeks to distribute resources to the community, particularly in the areas of arts and culture, health and human services, recreation and neighborhoods, economic development, and education and the environment.

Fields of interest: Arts; Education; Environment; Health care; Health organizations; Recreation; Human services; Economic development; Community/economic development.
Type of support: Management development/ capacity building; Equipment; Endowments; Program development; Conferences/seminars; Curriculum development; Technical assistance; Consulting services; Program evaluation; Matching/ challenge support.
Limitations: Applications accepted. Giving primarily in the Cherokee Strip Region, OK. No support for sectarian or religious purposes. No grants to individuals, or for operating or maintenance expenses, medical or scholarly research, membership fees, ticket sales for charitable fundraising events, travel for groups, or capital debt reductions.
Publications: Application guidelines; Annual report; Financial statement; Grants list; Informational brochure (including application guidelines); Newsletter.
Application information: Visit foundation web site for application form and guidelines. Before a grant proposal is requested by the foundation, a letter of intent must be submitted for consideration. Faxed letters of intent and proposals are not accepted. Application form required.
Initial approach: Letter of Intent (no longer than 2 pages)
Copies of proposal: 12
Deadline(s): July 31 for Letter of Intent; Sept. 1 for grant proposal
Board meeting date(s): Feb., May, Aug., and Nov.
Final notification: Within 6 weeks for full grant proposal invitation; Nov. Board meeting for grants
Officers and Trustees:* David Grissett,* Pres.; Richard DeVaughn,* V.P.; Amber Fitzgerald,* Secy.; Linda Record,* Treas.; **Mary M. Stallings, Exec. Dir.**; **Pamela Ballard**; Kyle Brownlee; **Brad Boeckman**; **Cheryl Bryan**; **Lewis Cunningham**; Peter Dillingham; Todd Earl; Phil Edwards; Willa Jo Fowler; Don Gaston; Aaron Harmon; Dr. Marcie Mack; **Clark McKeever**; Brad Mendenhall; Marcy Price; Dr. David Russell; Walter P. Scheffe; Bill Shewey; Steve Whitfill; John Wynne.
Number of staff: 1 full-time professional.
EIN: 731547637
Other changes: Mary M. Stallings has replaced Ashley M. Ewbank as Exec. Dir.
Mike Bigheart, Gary L. Brown, Sean Byrne, John Cromwell, Richard DeVaughn, Amber Fitzgerald, and Jeff Funk are no longer trustees.

2810
The Dolese Foundation
P.O. Box 677
Oklahoma City, OK 73101-0677

Established in 1979 in OK.
Donor: Roger M. Dolese.
Foundation type: Independent foundation.
Financial data (yr. ended 03/31/13): Assets, $138,380 (M); gifts received, $5,007; expenditures, $118,141,315; qualifying distributions, $118,056,788; giving activities include $118,056,788 for 5 grants (high: $58,430,380; low: $2,500).
Fields of interest: Education; Health care; Human services.
Limitations: Applications not accepted. Giving primarily in Oklahoma City, OK. No grants to individuals.
Application information: Contributes only to pre-selected organizations.
Trustees: James H. Allen, Jr.; Tony Basolo III; Mark Helm; Dwight Journey; Edward Moler; William Schlittler.
EIN: 731074447
Other changes: For the fiscal year ended Mar. 31, 2013, the grantmaker paid grants of $118,056,788, a 140.2% increase over the fiscal 2012 disbursements, $49,151,992.

2811
Ethics & Excellence in Journalism Foundation
210 Park Ave., Ste. 3150
Oklahoma City, OK 73102-5604 (405) 604-5388
Contact: Nancy Hodgkinson, Sr. Prog. Off.
FAX: (405) 604-0297;
E-mail: nancy.hodgkinson@journalismfoundation.org; Main URL: http://www.journalismfoundation.org
Grants Database: http://www.journalismfoundation.org/grants.htm

Established in 1982 in OK.
Donor: Edith Kinney Gaylord†.
Foundation type: Independent foundation.
Financial data (yr. ended 06/30/13): Assets, $100,278,358 (M); expenditures, $6,184,250; qualifying distributions, $3,750,823; giving activities include $3,240,500 for 78 grants (high: $100,000; low: $25,000), $58,346 for 62 employee matching gifts, and $11,995 for 2 foundation-administered programs.
Purpose and activities: The foundation invests in the future of journalism by building the ethics, skills and opportunities needed to advance principled, probing news and information.
Fields of interest: Media/communications; Journalism school/education.
Type of support: Capital campaigns; Program development; Conferences/seminars; Seed money; Curriculum development; Technical assistance.
Limitations: Applications accepted. Giving on a national basis, with some emphasis on OK. No support for international organizations, equipment, book publishing, literacy programs or documentaries. No grants to individuals or for scholarships, endowments, or personal research projects.
Publications: Grants list.
Application information: The foundation has a two-stage application process. Submit a Letter of Inquiry through the foundation's web site (use Application button on the home page). Link to online application provided for those invited to apply. Applications accepted from media institutions and journalism schools nationwide, primarily in the areas of investigative reporting, professional development, youth education and special opportunities. Within these areas, particular emphasis is placed on ethics and new media. Application form required.
Initial approach: Letters of Inquiry submitted online through the foundation's web site
Deadline(s): May 15 and Nov. 15 for letters of inquiry; June 15 and Dec. 15 for approved applications
Board meeting date(s): Jan. and July
Final notification: 2 months
Officers and Directors:* William J. Ross,* Chair.; Robert J. Ross,* C.E.O. and Pres.; **Richard A. Davis, C.F.O.**; David O. Hogan; Andrew W. Roff; J. Hugh Roff, Jr.; Patrick T. Rooney.
Advisory Committee Members: John A. Rieger, Chair.; Andrew C. Barth; Janet Cromley; Marian Cromley; Kay Dyer; John T. Greiner, Jr.; Ed Kelley; Jan Schaffer; Vivian Vahlberg.
Number of staff: 6 full-time professional; 3 full-time support.
EIN: 731167175

2812
Freese Family Foundation, Inc.
(formerly 307 Brady Foundation)
2021 S. Lewis Ave., Ste. 660
Tulsa, OK 74104-5731
Application address: c/o John Markam Freese, 3411 E. 62nd St., Tulsa, OK 74136, tel.: (918) 749-9331

Donor: John Markham Freese.
Foundation type: Independent foundation.
Financial data (yr. ended 12/31/12): Assets, $864,992 (M); gifts received, $864,992; expenditures, $179,469; qualifying distributions, $151,300; giving activities include $151,300 for 15 grants (high: $78,300; low: $2,500).
Fields of interest: Arts; Recreation; Human services.
Limitations: Applications accepted. Giving primarily in IL and OK.
Application information: Application form not required.
Initial approach: Letter
Deadline(s): None
Directors: John Markham Freese; Patricia A. Freese.
EIN: 263617644

2813
E. L. and Thelma Gaylord Foundation
6305 Waterford Blvd., Ste. 350
Oklahoma City, OK 73118-1176
Contact: Christy Gaylord Everest, Tr.
***Email address for Linda Walker Brown, Dir. Admin.:* lbrown@gaylordfoundation.org**; Main URL: http://www.gaylordfoundation.org/

Established in 1994 in OK.
Donors: Edward L. Gaylord; Thelma F. Gaylord.
Foundation type: Independent foundation.
Financial data (yr. ended 12/31/12): Assets, $215,847,570 (M); gifts received, $8,943,158; expenditures, $7,140,059; qualifying distributions, $6,762,330; giving activities include $6,516,447 for 91 grants (high: $1,000,000; low: $300).
Purpose and activities: Funding primarily for education. Some funding also for the Red Cross, and arts and culture.
Fields of interest: Museums (history); Arts; Elementary/secondary education; Higher education; Education; Medical research, institute; Human services; American Red Cross; Christian agencies & churches.
Type of support: Building/renovation.
Limitations: Applications accepted. **Giving primarily in the greater metropolitan Oklahoma City, OK area.** No grants to individuals.
Application information: Application form required.
Initial approach: Online letter of inquiry
Copies of proposal: 1
Deadline(s): Jan. 15 and July 15
Board meeting date(s): Mar., June, Sept. and Dec.
Trustees: Louise Gaylord Bennett; Christine Gaylord Everest; David O. Hogan; Mary Gaylord McClean.
EIN: 731463569

2814

The Hardesty Family Foundation, Inc.
c/o United States Aviation Bldg.
4141 N. Memorial Dr.
Tulsa, OK 74115-1400
Contact: Michelle Hardesty, Exec. Dir.
E-mail: mhardesty@hardestyco.com; **Additional contact: Dana Wilkes, Grants Mgr., tel.: (918) 560-9260, e-mail: dana@hardestyco.com**; Main URL: http://www.hardestyfamilyfoundation.org

Established in OK.
Donor: F. Roger Hardesty.
Foundation type: Independent foundation.
Financial data (yr. ended 11/30/13): Assets, $109,273,129 (M); gifts received, $7,900,000; expenditures, $1,613,086; qualifying distributions, $4,493,965; giving activities include $1,065,194 for 44 grants (high: $500,000; low: $50), and $3,233,058 for 2 loans/program-related investments.
Fields of interest: Humanities; Education; Health organizations, association; Human services; Children/youth, services; Infants/toddlers; Children/youth; Children; Youth; Adults; Young adults; Disabilities, people with; Physically disabled; Blind/visually impaired; Deaf/hearing impaired; Mentally disabled; Minorities; Women; Infants/toddlers, female; Girls; Adults, women; Young adults, female; Men; Infants/toddlers, male; Boys; Adults, men; Young adults, male; Military/veterans; Offenders/ex-offenders; Substance abusers; Single parents; Terminal illness, people with; Economically disadvantaged; Homeless.
Type of support: Research; Program evaluation; Program development; Matching/challenge support; Equipment; Capital campaigns; Program-related investments/loans.
Limitations: Applications not accepted. Giving primarily in Tulsa, OK. No support for religious organizations. No grants to individuals.
Application information: Applications are by invitation only. See foundation web site for information.
Board meeting date(s): Quarterly
Officers and Directors:* F. Roger Hardesty,* Pres.; Donna J. Hardesty,* V.P.; Marilyn Cox,* Secy.; **Alan Lister, Cont.**; Michelle Hardesty, Exec. Dir.; Alex Cristo.
Number of staff: 2 full-time professional; 1 full-time support.
EIN: 204094088

2815

Pearl M. & Julia J. Harmon Foundation
P.O. Box 52568
Tulsa, OK 74152-0568
Main URL: http://www.harmonfound.org

Established in 1962 in OK.
Donors: Claude C. Harmon†; Julia J. Harmon†.
Foundation type: Independent foundation.
Financial data (yr. ended 05/31/13): Assets, $60,561,534 (M); expenditures, $613,386; qualifying distributions, $3,319,574; giving activities include $173,779 for 38 grants (high: $20,000; low: $500), $128,043 for 2 foundation-administered programs and $3,000,000 for loans/program-related investments.
Purpose and activities: Giving primarily for low-interest loans to charitable organizations.
Fields of interest: Education; Human services; Christian agencies & churches.
Type of support: General/operating support; Program-related investments/loans.
Limitations: Applications accepted. Giving limited to AR, KS, NM, OK and TX, with preference given to northeastern OK. No support for medical research or evangelical organizations. No grants or loans to individuals or for-profit businesses.
Publications: Application guidelines.
Application information: All available funds are being directed toward the foundation's operating program; the foundation does not expect to solicit proposals over the next several years. However, applications are being accepted for program-related investment loans. Application form available on foundation web site. Application form required.
Deadline(s): None
Board meeting date(s): As necessary
Officer and Trustees:* George L. Hangs, Jr.,* Exec. Dir.; Cathey Frederick; **G. E. Holmes**; Jean M. Kuntz; Mary Grant Wendl.
EIN: 736095893
Other changes: Bryan Lee is no longer a trustee.

2816

Hille Family Charitable Foundation
624 S. Boston Ave., Ste. 710
Tulsa, OK 74119-1222
Contact: Margaret Hille Yar, Exec. Dir.
FAX: (918) 592-4185;
E-mail: smartin@hillefoundation.org; Main URL: http://www.hillefoundation.org
Grants List: http://www.hillefoundation.org/2013grants.html

Established in 1997 in OK.
Donors: Jo Bob Hille†; Mary Ann Hille.
Foundation type: Independent foundation.
Financial data (yr. ended 12/31/12): Assets, $51,385,235 (M); expenditures, $3,121,289; qualifying distributions, $1,957,507; giving activities include $1,571,570 for 67 grants (high: $200,000; low: $75).
Purpose and activities: The foundation was born out of the Christian principle that it is a privilege to serve others. Raising the educational, spiritual, and physical well-being of those helpless or ignored in society and promoting projects which benefit and revitalize the Tulsa, Oklahoma community at large are primary aims of the foundation. Consideration is also given to funding research and programs aimed at those affected by Alzheimer's disease and juvenile diabetes.
Fields of interest: Education; Environment; Alzheimer's disease research; Diabetes research; Recreation, camps; Human services; Children, services; Community/economic development; Infants/toddlers; Children/youth; Children; Youth; Adults; Aging; Young adults; Disabilities, people with; Physically disabled; Blind/visually impaired; Deaf/hearing impaired; Mentally disabled; Minorities; African Americans/Blacks; Hispanics/Latinos; Indigenous peoples; Women; Girls; Men; Infants/toddlers, male; Boys; Offenders/ex-offenders; Substance abusers; AIDS, people with; Terminal illness, people with; Immigrants/refugees; Economically disadvantaged; Homeless; LGBTQ.
Type of support: Consulting services; General/operating support; Continuing support; Management development/capacity building; Annual campaigns; Capital campaigns; Building/renovation; Equipment; Land acquisition; Endowments; Emergency funds; Program development; Curriculum development; Fellowships; Scholarship funds; Research; Technical assistance; Matching/challenge support.
Limitations: Giving primarily in the Tulsa, OK, area. No grants to individuals.
Publications: Application guidelines; Grants list; Program policy statement (including application guidelines).
Application information: Please check foundation web site for updated funding opportunities.
Copies of proposal: 1
Board meeting date(s): Feb., July, and Oct.
Officers and Trustees:* Mary Ann Hille,* Pres.; Margaret Hille Yar,* Exec. Dir.; Leslie Hille Hamrick,* Grant Report Off.; Sheila Hille Lequerica,* Grant Report Off.; Shirley Moyers Martin,* Grant Off.
Number of staff: 2 full-time professional; 1 part-time professional; 1 full-time support; 2 part-time support.
EIN: 731521975

2817

Fred Jones Family Foundation
(formerly The Fred and Mary Eddy Jones Foundation)
9225 Lake Hefner Pkwy., Ste. 200
Oklahoma City, OK 73120-2061 (405) 231-2415
Contact: Wendy Smith, V.P.
***FAX:* (405) 231-2406;**
E-mail: wsmith@fredjonesfamilyfoundation.com; Main URL: http://www.fredjonesfamilyfoundation.com
Grants List: http://www.fredjonesfamilyfoundation.com/grant_history.html

Donors: Fred Jones†; Mary Eddy Jones†; Hall Capital, LLC.
Foundation type: Independent foundation.
Financial data (yr. ended 06/30/13): Assets, $10,872,752 (M); expenditures, $631,986; qualifying distributions, $558,100; giving activities include $526,525 for 129 grants (high: $75,000; low: $200), and $31,575 for 5 employee matching gifts.
Purpose and activities: The foundation is dedicated to supporting organizations that increase the quality of life in central Oklahoma through projects dedicated to cultural growth and beautification.
Fields of interest: Arts; Education; Community/economic development; Christian agencies & churches.
Limitations: Applications accepted. Giving primarily in central OK.
Application information: Application form required.
Initial approach: Letter
Deadline(s): None
Officers and Directors:* Kirkland Hall,* Chair. and Pres.; Brooks Hall, Jr.,* V.P.; Fred Jones Hall,* V.P.; Wendy Smith, V.P.; Vicki Schilling, Secy.; Debra Melott, Treas.; Marilyn Upsher.
EIN: 203110536

2818

E. Phil and Roberta Kirschner Foundation
P.O. Box 1866
Muskogee, OK 74402-1866 (918) 682-3151

Established in 1984 in OK.
Donors: E. Phil Kirschner†; Roberta L. Kirschner†.
Foundation type: Independent foundation.
Financial data (yr. ended 05/31/13): Assets, $7,969,258 (M); expenditures, $419,282; qualifying distributions, $316,349; giving activities include $282,700 for 60 grants (high: $30,000; low: $500).
Purpose and activities: Giving to education and training of orphans and the handicapped.

Fields of interest: Arts; Education; Public affairs.
Type of support: Continuing support; Endowments; Scholarship funds.
Limitations: Applications accepted. Giving primarily in OK. No support for single-disease foundations. No grants to individuals, or for routine public education expenses, office or computer equipment, tables or tickets, or sponsored sports events.
Publications: Application guidelines; Annual report; Financial statement.
Application information: Some special consideration given to students of the Jewish faith. Application form not required.

Initial approach: **Proposal**
Copies of proposal: 1
Deadline(s): Sept. 1
Board meeting date(s): Sept. or Oct.
Final notification: Dec. 1

Officer and Trustees:* **Miriam Freedman,* Mgr.**; Pauli Loeffler; Robert C. Freedman; **Jermaine Wheeler.**
Number of staff: 1 part-time professional; 1 part-time support.
EIN: 731164196
Other changes: The grantmaker no longer lists a primary contact.
Miriam Freedman is now Mgr.

2819
Robert Clay Liddell Foundation
3000 Berry Rd.
Norman, OK 73072-7472 (405) 310-3103

Established in 2004 in OK.
Donors: Richard D. Liddell; Kelly Rose; Suzanne Rose; Commercial Brick Corp.; Doris Dahl.
Foundation type: Company-sponsored foundation.
Financial data (yr. ended 12/31/12): Assets, $1 (M); gifts received, $556,050; expenditures, $558,676; qualifying distributions, $553,534; giving activities include $553,534 for grants.
Fields of interest: Mental health, addictions; Residential/custodial care; Christian agencies & churches.
Application information: Application form required.

Initial approach: Letter
Deadline(s): None

Officers: Richard D. Liddell, Pres.; Larry Pruitt, Secy.
Director: Lloyd R. Trenary.
EIN: 200420550

2820
The McGee Foundation, Inc.
P.O. Box 18127
Oklahoma City, OK 73154-0127

Incorporated in 1903 in OK.
Donor: Dean A. McGee‡.
Foundation type: Independent foundation.
Financial data (yr. ended 06/30/13): Assets, $11,962,961 (M); expenditures, $589,292; qualifying distributions, $579,000; giving activities include $577,000 for 18 grants (high: $120,000; low: $5,000).
Fields of interest: Historic preservation/historical societies; Arts; Education; Reproductive health, family planning; Foundations (community).
Type of support: General/operating support; Annual campaigns; Capital campaigns; Building/renovation; Equipment; Land acquisition; Endowments; Professorships; Scholarship funds; Research; Matching/challenge support.
Limitations: Applications accepted. Giving primarily in CA and Oklahoma City, OK. No grants to individuals.
Application information: Application form not required.

Initial approach: Proposal
Deadline(s): None
Board meeting date(s): Early May

Officers and Directors:* Marcia McGee Bieber,* Pres.; Patricia McGee Maino,* V.P.; Charles Bieber, M.D.*, Secy.-Treas.; **Paula Love.**
Number of staff: 1 part-time support.
EIN: 736099203
Other changes: Jerry Love is no longer a director.

2821
The Merrick Foundation
2932 N.W. 122nd St., Ste. D
Oklahoma City, OK 73120-1955
E-mail: fwmerrick@foundationmanagementinc.com;
Main URL: http://www.foundationmanagementinc.com/foundations/merrick-foundation/

Trust established in 1948 in OK; incorporated in 1968.
Donor: Mrs. Frank W. Merrick‡.
Foundation type: Independent foundation.
Financial data (yr. ended 12/31/12): Assets, $10,208,683 (M); expenditures, $579,549; qualifying distributions, $510,945; giving activities include $412,000 for grants.
Purpose and activities: The mission of the foundation is to enhance the quality of life of Oklahomans and their communities with primary emphasis on South Central Oklahoma. With this goal in mind, the foundation trustees are committed to furthering the philanthropic vision of Ward S. Merrick, Sr. by awarding grants to charitable organizations that foster independence and achievement, and that stimulate educational, economic and cultural growth. The foundation's major areas of interest are education, health and medical research, arts and humanities, and social services.
Fields of interest: Arts; Higher education; Medical research, institute; Human services; Youth, services.
Type of support: General/operating support; Annual campaigns; Capital campaigns; Building/renovation; Program development; Seed money; Research; Technical assistance; Program evaluation; Matching/challenge support.
Limitations: Applications accepted. Giving primarily in OK, with emphasis on south central OK. No grants to individuals, or for endowment funds.
Publications: Annual report; Informational brochure.
Application information: Application guidelines available on foundation web site. Application form required.

Initial approach: **Online application process on foundation web site. All correspondence will be done through e-mail**
Copies of proposal: 1
Board meeting date(s): May and Nov.

Officers and Trustees:* Ross M. Coe,* Pres.; Frank W. Merrick,* V.P.; Valda M. Buchanan,* Secy.; Laura Clay; Charles R. Coe, Jr.; Ross M. "Rick" Coe; Ward I. Coe; Michael McCauley; Frank W. Merrick; Frank W. "Will" Merrick, Jr.; Ward S. Merrick III; Jessie Nance.
EIN: 736111622

2822
The Samuel Roberts Noble Foundation, Inc.
2510 Sam Noble Pkwy.
P.O. Box 2180
Ardmore, OK 73401-2124 (580) 223-5810
Contact: William Buckner, C.E.O. and Pres.
FAX: (580) 224-6212;
E-mail: Admin-Granting@noble.org; Main URL: http://www.noble.org
Grants Database: http://www.noble.org/WebApps/GrantHistory/GrantHistorySearch.aspx
Pinterest: http://pinterest.com/noblefoundation/
RSS Feed: http://www.noble.org/rss/index.html

Trust established in 1945 in OK; incorporated in 1952.
Donor: Lloyd Noble‡.
Foundation type: Independent foundation.
Financial data (yr. ended 12/31/12): Assets, $1,172,213,441 (M); gifts received, $1,360; expenditures, $66,439,961; qualifying distributions, $48,154,942; giving activities include $653,835 for 178 grants (high: $59,626; low: $25), $313,750 for 82 grants to individuals (high: $6,250; low: $1,250), $38,748 for 1 employee matching gift, and $43,947,356 for 3 foundation-administered programs.
Purpose and activities: The Noble Foundation conducts its operations through the work of three operating divisions: 1) Agricultural Division - assists more than 1,700 regional farmers and ranchers in achieving their individual financial, production, stewardship and quality-of life goals; 2) Plant Biology Division - conducts basic biochemical, genetic and genomic plant research for the purpose of improving crop productivity and value, and enhancing animal and human health; and 3) Forage Improvement Division - translates basic plant science research into tangible plant varieties. Within the institution, the Forage Improvement Division serves as a link between the discoveries in the laboratory and the field, where such discoveries are intended to enhance agricultural outcomes in Oklahoma and around the world. Through its grantmaking program, the Noble Foundation assists community service, health research and delivery systems, educational and other nonprofit organizations through grants and employee involvement. The foundation also administers a matching gift program for employees of the Samuel Roberts Noble Foundation, Noble Corporation and Noble Energy, Inc.
Fields of interest: Higher education; Health care; Medical research, institute; Human services.
Type of support: General/operating support; Capital campaigns; Building/renovation; Equipment; Professorships; Seed money; Research; Employee matching gifts; Employee-related scholarships; Matching/challenge support.
Limitations: Applications accepted. Giving primarily in OK. No grants to individuals (except through the Noble Educational Fund and the Sam Noble Scholarship Program).
Publications: Application guidelines; Annual report; Grants list; Informational brochure; Quarterly report.
Application information: Application guidelines available on foundation web site. Application form required.

Initial approach: Letter of inquiry
Copies of proposal: 1
Deadline(s): Mar. 1, June 1, Sept. 1 and Dec.1
Board meeting date(s): Jan., Apr., July, Oct. and Dec.
Final notification: 2 weeks after board meetings

Officers and Trustees:* William Buckner,* C.E.O. and Pres.; Billy Cook,* Sr. V.P. and Dir., Agricultural Division; Michael Udvardi, Sr. V.P. and Dir., Plant Biology; Steven Rhines, V.P., General counsel and

Dir. of Public Affairs; Diane Pinsker, V.P., Business Development; Jill Wallace, V.P. and C.F.O.; Elizabeth A. Aldridge, Corp. Secy.; Sarah Richardson, Cont.; Ginger DuBose, Advisory Tr.; Cody Noble, Advisory Tr.; D. Randolph Brown, Jr.; Susan Brown; James C. Day; Sam Dubose; Vivian N. Dubose; William R. Goddard, Jr.; Shelley Dru Mullins; Jessie Nance; Russell Noble; Marianne Rooney; **Patrick Rooney**; Stephen F. Young.
Number of staff: 272 full-time professional; 1 part-time professional; 99 full-time support; 46 part-time support.
EIN: 730606209
Other changes: William G. Thurman is no longer a trustee.

2823
Oklahoma Gas and Electric Company Foundation, Inc.
(also known as OGE Energy Corp. Foundation)
P.O. Box 321, M.C. 1100
Oklahoma City, OK 73101-0321 (405) 553-3203
Contact: Peter B. Delaney, Pres.
Additional tel.: (405) 553-3397; Main URL: http://www.oge.com/community/OGEFoundation/Pages/OGEFoundation.aspx

Incorporated in 1957 in OK.
Donor: Oklahoma Gas and Electric Co.
Foundation type: Company-sponsored foundation.
Financial data (yr. ended 12/31/12): Assets, $13,993,934 (M); gifts received, $3,000,110; expenditures, $1,996,482; qualifying distributions, $1,939,465; giving activities include $1,929,313 for 127 grants (high: $249,973; low: $30).
Purpose and activities: The foundation supports organizations involved with arts and culture, human services, and community development. Special emphasis is directed toward early education, primarily math and science.
Fields of interest: Museums (art); Arts; Elementary/secondary education; Higher education; Education; Recreation; Salvation Army; Human services; United Ways and Federated Giving Programs; Mathematics; Science.
Type of support: General/operating support; Continuing support; Annual campaigns; Building/renovation; Equipment; Program development; Scholarship funds; Sponsorships; Employee matching gifts.
Limitations: Applications accepted. Giving limited to areas of company operations in OK. No support for religious or faith-based organizations not of direct benefit to the entire community or political parties or candidates. No grants to individuals or families, or for sporting events, golf tournaments, dinners, luncheons, or other forms of indirect support, or capital campaigns; no loans.
Publications: Application guidelines.
Application information: Grants range from $500 to $5,000. Organizations receiving support are asked to submit a final report. Application form not required.
Initial approach: Proposal
Copies of proposal: 1
Deadline(s): Mar. 15, June 15, Sept. 15, and Dec. 15
Board meeting date(s): Mar., June, Sept., and Dec.
Final notification: 30 days
Officers and Directors:* Peter B. Delaney,* Pres.; Susie White, Secy.-Treas.; **Brian Alford**; **Max Myers.**
EIN: 736093572

Other changes: Danny P. Harris is no longer V.P. Paul Renfrow is no longer a director.

2824
Robert A. Parman Foundation
c/o Trust Company of Oklahoma
6307 Waterford Blvd., Ste. 215
Oklahoma City, OK **73118**
***Application address:* c/o The Law Office of Tom A. Hemry, P.C., Att.: Jerry Hemry, P.O. Box 22486, Oklahoma City, OK, 73123, tel.: (405) 602-2053**
Trust established in 1962 in OK.
Donor: Robert A. Parman†.
Foundation type: Independent foundation.
Financial data (yr. ended 08/31/13): Assets, $4,204,485 (M); expenditures, $399,162; qualifying distributions, $287,108; giving activities include $264,500 for 14 grants (high: $60,000; low: $1,000).
Purpose and activities: Support primarily for higher education; grants also to social service organizations.
Fields of interest: Higher education; Health organizations, association; Kidney diseases; Arthritis; Food banks; Human services; American Red Cross; Salvation Army.
Limitations: Applications accepted. Giving primarily in OK. No grants to individuals.
Application information:
Initial approach: Letter
Deadline(s): None
Trustees: J.W. Lanier; **Richard Metheny**; Jerry M. Thomason.
EIN: 736098053

2825
Madalynne L. Peel Foundation
116 S. Main St.
Newkirk, OK 74647-4512
Contact: Jack De McCarty, Pres.

Established in 1997.
Donor: Madalynne L. Peel.
Foundation type: Independent foundation.
Financial data (yr. ended 09/30/13): Assets, $4,741,662 (M); expenditures, $137,113; qualifying distributions, $117,658; giving activities include $115,158 for 13 grants (high: $50,000; low: $600).
Fields of interest: Girl scouts; Children/youth, services; Christian agencies & churches.
Limitations: Applications accepted. Giving primarily in OK.
Application information: Application form not required.
***Initial approach:* Proposal**
Deadline(s): None
Officers: Jack De McCarty, Pres.; Thomas M. Rigdon, Secy.-Treas.
Directors: Philip A. Ross; Betty J. Scott; Marybeth Glass.
EIN: 731526716
Other changes: The grantmaker no longer lists a phone.

2826
Presbyterian Health Foundation
655 Research Pkwy., Ste. 500
Oklahoma City, OK 73104-3603 (405) 319-8150
FAX: (405) 319-8168; **E-mail: tgray@phfokc.com**; Main URL: http://www.phfokc.com

Established in 1985 in OK; converted from the proceeds of the sale of Presbyterian Hospital to HCA.
Donor: Nicole Barr.
Foundation type: Independent foundation.
Financial data (yr. ended 09/30/12): Assets, $169,672,044 (M); gifts received, $1,285; expenditures, $12,095,434; qualifying distributions, $2,108,071; giving activities include $394,111 for 3 grants (high: $200,000; low: $97,055).
Purpose and activities: Support primarily for health, including medical research and medical education, clinical pastoral education, resource development through medical technology transfer, community health-related programs and to Oklahoma Health Center Institutions.
Fields of interest: Medical school/education; Theological school/education; Medical care, community health systems; Medical research, institute; Engineering/technology.
Type of support: Equipment; Endowments; Program development; Professorships; Research; Program-related investments/loans.
Limitations: Applications not accepted. Giving primarily in OK. No grants to individuals.
Application information: Applications are accepted by invitation only.
Board meeting date(s): Quarterly
Officers and Trustees:* Carl Edwards,* Chair.; Michael D. Anderson, Ph.D.*, C. E. O. and Pres.; Dennis McGrath,* V.P. and C. F. O.; J.R. Caton, V.P., Research Park; William M. Beard,* Treas.; Stanton L. Young,* Chair., Emeritus; William F. Barnes, M.D.; Robert S. Ellis, M.D.; Michael Joseph; David Rainbolt; Harry B. Tate, M.D.; Jerry B. Vannata, M.D.; Rainey Williams.
Number of staff: 2 full-time professional; 2 full-time support.
EIN: 730709836

2827
ROI Community, Inc.
(formerly Center for Leadership Initiatives, Inc.)
110 W. 7th St., Ste. 2000
Tulsa, OK **74119-1076**
Canada address: 425 W. 8th Ave., Ste. 324, Vancouver, British Columbia, Canada V5Y 3Z5, tel.: (604) 737-3676, fax: (604) 737-3686. Israel address: 1 Ben-Maimon St., Jerusalem, Israel 92262, tel.: 972-2-566-7772, fax: 972-2-566-6744 Facebook: http://www.facebook.com/group.php?gid=5319338077&ref=nf

Donors: Lynn Schusterman; Aaron Edelheit; LJS Revocable Trust; Morris B. Squire Trust; Samburg Family Foundation; Russell Berrie Foundation; Dallas Jewish Community Foundation; Howard & Leslie Schultz Family Foundation; Jewish Funders Network; The David and Minnie Meyerson Foundation.
Foundation type: Operating foundation.
Financial data (yr. ended 12/31/12): Assets, $10,566 (M); gifts received, $5,266,245; expenditures, $5,269,259; qualifying distributions, $3,659,721; giving activities include $3,379,471 for grants, and $894,500 for foundation-administered programs.

Purpose and activities: Giving for the development of Jewish leaders and promoting managerial excellence throughout the Jewish community.
Fields of interest: Jewish federated giving programs; Jewish agencies & synagogues.
Limitations: Applications not accepted. Giving primarily in CA, and Jerusalem, Israel. No grants to individuals.
Publications: Newsletter.
Application information: Contributes only to pre-selected organizations.
Officers and Directors:* Mira Oreck,* Chair.; Sanford Cardin,* Pres.; Victoria Smith,* Secy.; Adam D. Grossman,* Treas.; Rabbi Yonatan Gordis, Managing Dir.; Jonathan Gordis; Lynn Schusterman; Stacy Schusterman.
EIN: 205344753
Other changes: The grantmaker no longer lists an e-mail address or a URL address.
At the close of 2012, the grantmaker paid grants of $3,379,471, a 140.7% increase over the 2011 disbursements, $1,404,084.

2828
Sarkeys Foundation

530 E. Main St.
Norman, OK 73071-5823 (405) 364-3703
FAX: (405) 364-8191; E-mail: sarkeys@sarkeys.org;
E-mail contact for questions: Angela Holladay, Dir., Grants Mgmt., angela@sarkeys.org; Main URL: http://www.sarkeys.org
E-Newsletter: http://www.sarkeys.org/pages/newsletter
Facebook: http://www.facebook.com/#!/pages/Norman-OK/Sarkeys-Foundation/139638042731774?ref=search
RSS Feed: http://www.sarkeys.org/blogs/in_the_news/feed

Established in 1962 in OK.
Donor: S.J. Sarkeys†.
Foundation type: Independent foundation.
Financial data (yr. ended 11/30/13): Assets, $104,421,489 (M); expenditures, $5,051,576; qualifying distributions, $4,321,285; giving activities include $3,169,704 for grants, and $184,610 for foundation-administered programs.
Purpose and activities: Giving primarily to improve the quality of life in Oklahoma.
Fields of interest: Arts; Education; Health care; Medical research; Human services.
Type of support: Consulting services; Management development/capacity building; Capital campaigns; Building/renovation; Equipment; Endowments; Emergency funds; Program development; Professorships; Scholarship funds; Research; Technical assistance; Program evaluation; Matching/challenge support.
Limitations: Applications accepted. Giving limited to OK. No support for direct-to-government agencies or individual public or private elementary or secondary schools, unless they are serving the needs of a special population which are not met elsewhere; generally, no support for hospitals or local programs appropriately financed within the community or for religious institutions and their subsidiaries, or for out of state institutions. No grants to individuals, or for operating support, permanent financing, profitmaking programs, grants which trigger expenditure responsibility, direct mail solicitations, start-up funding for new organizations, feasibility studies, vehicles or for annual campaigns.
Publications: Application guidelines; Annual report (including application guidelines).
Application information: See foundation web site for application information. Application form required.
Initial approach: **Telephone a foundation program officer and inquire about submitting a Letter of Inquiry. Successful applicants will receive a password for the online application**
Deadline(s): **See foundation web site for current Letter of Inquiry deadlines. Feb. 1 and Aug. 1, for proposals**
Board meeting date(s): Jan., Apr., July, and Oct.; grants considered at Apr. and Oct. meetings
Final notification: Varies
Officers and Trustees:* Fred Gipson,* Pres.; Dan Little, V.P.; Joseph W. Morris, Secy.-Treas.; Kim Henry, Exec. Dir.; Teresa B. Adwan; **Elizabeth Base**; **Dr. John Bell**; **Clay Christensen**; **Jim Loftis**; Terry W. West.
Number of staff: 4 full-time professional; 4 full-time support.
EIN: 730736496
Other changes: The grantmaker now publishes application guidelines.

2829
Charles and Lynn Schusterman Family Foundation

P.O. Box 51
Tulsa, OK 74101-0051 (918) 879-0209
Contact: Sanford "Sandy" R. Cardin, Pres.
***Additional address:* Washington, DC Office: 1250 Eye St., Ste. 700, Washington, DC 20005**; Main URL: http://www.schusterman.org
Blog: http://www.schusterman.org/category/blog
Facebook: http://www.facebook.com/schustermanfamilyfoundation?ref=sgm
Flickr: http://www.flickr.com/photos/schustermanfoundation/
Knowledge Center: http://www.schusterman.org/resources
LinkedIn: http://www.linkedin.com/company/charles-and-lynn-schusterman-family-foundation?goback=.cps_1286207986738_1
Lynn Schusterman's Giving Pledge Profile: http://glasspockets.org/philanthropy-in-focus/eye-on-the-giving-pledge/profiles/schusterman
Multimedia: http://www.schusterman.org/resources/videos-gallery
RSS Feed: http://www.schusterman.org/feed
Twitter-DC: http://www.twitter.com/schustermanfoun
Twitter-Tulsa: http://twitter.com/clsff
YouTube: http://www.youtube.com/user/SchustermanFoun

Established in 1987 in OK.
Donors: Charles Schusterman†; Lynn Schusterman; LJS Revocable Trust.
Foundation type: Independent foundation.
Financial data (yr. ended 12/31/12): Assets, $2,208,464,518 (M); gifts received, $6,413,710; expenditures, $48,270,919; qualifying distributions, $46,909,322; giving activities include $42,632,056 for 232 grants (high: $7,370,286; low: $118).
Purpose and activities: The foundation is dedicated to helping the Jewish people flourish by supporting programs throughout the world that spread Jewish living, giving and learning. The foundation also provides assistance to non-sectarian charitable organizations dedicated to enhancing the quality of life in Tulsa, Oklahoma, especially in the areas of education, child development, and community service.
Fields of interest: Arts; Education; Crime/violence prevention, child abuse; Human services; Children/youth, services; Voluntarism promotion.
International interests: Israel.
Type of support: General/operating support; Continuing support; Annual campaigns; Capital campaigns; Building/renovation; Emergency funds; Program development; Conferences/seminars; Professorships; Publication; Seed money; Curriculum development; Fellowships; Internship funds; Scholarship funds; Research; Technical assistance; Consulting services; In-kind gifts; Matching/challenge support.
Limitations: Applications not accepted. Giving primarily to nonsectarian organizations in OK; giving on a local, national, and international basis for Jewish organizations. No grants to individuals, or for endowment funds, deficit funds, media based projects, or programs that require expenditure responsibility.
Publications: Grants list.
Application information: Unsolicited requests for funds not accepted.
Officers and Directors:* Lynn Schusterman,* Co-Chair.; **Stacy H. Schusterman,* Co-Chair.**; Sanford "Sandy" R. Cardin, Pres.; **Gaila Gross, C.F.O., Israel**; Alana Hughes, C.O.O., Tulsa.
Number of staff: 5 full-time professional.
EIN: 731312965
Other changes: Stacy H. Schusterman is now Co-Chair. Lynn Schusterman is now Co-Chair.

2830
Sam Viersen Family Foundation, Inc.

c/o Lisa R. Rhynes
P.O. Box 702708
Tulsa, OK 74170-2708 (918) 742-1979
FAX: (918) 742-1670

Established in 1988 in OK.
Donor: Sam K. Viersen, Jr.†.
Foundation type: Independent foundation.
Financial data (yr. ended 12/31/12): Assets, $21,090,064 (M); expenditures, $1,354,285; qualifying distributions, $1,130,356; giving activities include $1,054,564 for grants.
Fields of interest: Arts; Higher education; Libraries/library science; Education; Human services; YM/YWCAs & YM/YWHAs; Children/youth, services.
Type of support: General/operating support; Continuing support; Management development/capacity building; Capital campaigns; Building/renovation; Equipment; Land acquisition; Endowments; Emergency funds; Program development.
Limitations: Applications accepted. Giving limited to Tulsa and Okmulgee counties, OK. No support for religious or tax funded organizations. No grants to individuals.
Application information: Application form not required.
Initial approach: Telephone
Copies of proposal: 1
Deadline(s): None
Board meeting date(s): Apr. and Oct.
Officers and Directors:* Maralynn V. Sant,* Pres.; Lisa Rhynes, Mgr.; Robert English; Brian C. Johnson; Jill Johnson; Jennifer Miller; Margaret Robinson; Leo M. Sant; Julie Schenk.
Number of staff: 1 full-time professional.
EIN: 731295358

2831
The William K. Warren Foundation
P.O. Box 470372
Tulsa, OK 74147-0372
***Contact:* M. Ross, Secy.**

Incorporated in 1945 in OK.
Donors: William K. Warren†; Mrs. William K. Warren†; N.W. Bryant; P.W. Swindle.
Foundation type: Independent foundation.
Financial data (yr. ended 12/31/12): Assets, $386,617,179 (M); gifts received, $670,376; expenditures, $25,371,275; qualifying distributions, $19,886,547; giving activities include $19,264,130 for 30 grants (high: $11,885,874; low: $500), and $165,615 for 1 loan/ program-related investment.
Purpose and activities: Grants for local Catholic healthcare facilities, education, and social services; substantial support for a medical research program.
Fields of interest: Education; Health care; Medical research, institute; Human services; Catholic federated giving programs.
Type of support: Program-related investments/ loans; General/operating support; Building/ renovation; Endowments; Program development; Research.
Limitations: Applications accepted. Giving primarily in OK. No grants to individuals.
Application information: Application form not required.
Initial approach: Letter
Deadline(s): None
Board meeting date(s): Semiannually
Officers and Directors:* John-Kelly C. Warren,* Chair. and C.E.O.; W.R. Lissau,* Vice-Chair.; Stephen K. Warren,* Sr. V.P.; **M. Ross, Secy.**; M.A. Buntz, C.F.O. and Treas.; L. Glenn, Cont.; W.K. Warren, Jr.,* Chair. Emeritus; **Peter P. Aran**; Elizabeth Warren Blankenship; John A. Gaberino, Jr.; J. Frederick McNeer, M.D.; Jean M. Warren.
Number of staff: 10
EIN: 730609599
Other changes: M. Ross has replaced David B. Whitehill as Secy.

2832
Wisdom Family Foundation, Inc
P.O. Box 37
Alva, OK **73717-0037** (580) 327-2215
Contact: Jim Pfeiffer, Exec. Dir.

Donor: Grace Wisdom†.
Foundation type: Independent foundation.
Financial data (yr. ended 02/28/13): Assets, $18,601,103 (M); expenditures, $914,913; qualifying distributions, $775,000; giving activities include $775,000 for grants.
Fields of interest: Foundations (private grantmaking).
Application information: Application form required.
Initial approach: Letter
Deadline(s): Sept. 30
Directors: Lee Brandt; Robert Boeckman; Nancy Hall; Jeanne Anne King; Ken Schultz; Douglas Voth; Peggy Wisdom; Jim Pfeiffer.
EIN: 262151892

2833
Zarrow Families Foundation
401 S. Boston Ave., Ste. 900
Tulsa, OK 74103-4012 **(918) 295-8004**
***Contact:* Bill Major, Exec. Dir.**
FAX: (918) 295-8049; E-mail: bmajor@zarrow.com;
Main URL: http://www.zarrow.com/zff.htm

Established in 1987 in OK.
Donors: Henry H. Zarrow; Jack C. Zarrow.
Foundation type: Independent foundation.
Financial data (yr. ended 12/31/13): Assets, $10,437,637 (M); expenditures, $2,970,045; qualifying distributions, $2,925,596; giving activities include $2,885,738 for grants.
Purpose and activities: Giving primarily for Jewish causes and charities' fundraising events.
Fields of interest: Arts; Elementary/secondary education; Health care; Mental health/crisis services; Health organizations, association; Human services; Youth, services; United Ways and Federated Giving Programs.
Type of support: General/operating support; Conferences/seminars.
Limitations: Applications not accepted. Giving primarily in the Tulsa, OK, area. No grants to individuals.
Publications: Financial statement; Grants list.
Application information: Contributes only to pre-selected organizations.
Board meeting date(s): May and Nov.
Trustees: Judy Kishner; Gail Richards; Stuart Zarrow.
Number of staff: 1 full-time professional.
EIN: 731332141
Other changes: At the close of 2013, the grantmaker paid grants of $2,885,738, a 507.5% increase over the 2012 disbursements, $475,003.

2834
The Anne and Henry Zarrow Foundation
401 S. Boston Ave., Ste. 900
Tulsa, OK 74103-4012 (918) 295-8004
Contact: Bill Major, Exec. Dir.
FAX: (918) 295-8049; E-mail: Bmajor@zarrow.com;
Main URL: http://www.zarrow.com/ anne-henry-zarrow-foundation/

Established in 1986 in OK.
Donor: Henry H. Zarrow†.
Foundation type: Independent foundation.
Financial data (yr. ended 12/31/13): Assets, $103,996,854 (M); gifts received, $2,681,800; expenditures, $8,298,958; qualifying distributions, $7,970,895; giving activities include $7,703,138 for 316 grants (high: $600,000; low: $500).
Purpose and activities: Giving primarily for education, social services, Jewish causes, health programs, medical research and mental health programs. The foundation is also very interested in helping to provide food, clothing, and shelter for the challenged, disadvantaged and homeless. The foundation also funds scholarships at selected universities in OK.
Fields of interest: Arts; Education; Health care; Human services; Aging, centers/services; United Ways and Federated Giving Programs; Disabilities, people with.
Type of support: General/operating support; Annual campaigns; Scholarship funds.
Limitations: Applications accepted. Giving primarily in the Tulsa, OK, area. No grants to individuals.
Publications: Application guidelines.
Application information: See foundation's web site for detailed application information and guidelines.The foundation will no longer take scholarship applications from students who are not already receiving scholarship assistance from the foundation. Application form not required.
Initial approach: Letter
Copies of proposal: 1
Deadline(s): Jan. 15, Apr. 15, Aug. 15, and Oct. 15 for grants.
Board meeting date(s): Feb., Apr., Sept., and Nov.
Officers and Directors:* Judith Z. Kishner,* Pres.; Stuart A. Zarrow,* V.P.; Bill Major, Exec. Dir.; Julie W. Cohen; Jay Wohlgemuth; Edward Zarrow.
Number of staff: 1 full-time professional; 2 part-time professional.
EIN: 731286874
Other changes: Henry H. Zarrow, Donor, and Secy. is deceased.

OREGON

2835
Benton County Foundation
660 N.W. Harrison Blvd.
Corvallis, OR **97330** (541) 753-1603
***Contact:* Dick Thompson, Exec. Dir.**
E-mail: bcf@peak.org; Mailing address: P.O. Box 911, Corvallis, OR 97339-0911; Main URL: http://bentoncountyfoundation.org
Scholarship e-mail: sue@bentoncountyfoundation.org

Established in 1953 in OR.
Foundation type: Community foundation.
Financial data (yr. ended 12/31/11): Assets, $14,168,886 (M); gifts received, $157,049; expenditures, $503,331; giving activities include $294,948 for 8+ grants (high: $49,745), and $69,464 for grants to individuals.
Purpose and activities: The foundation provides a service to individuals, families, and organizations to establish endowments, manage the funds received, and distribute a portion of the earnings each year to benefit the youth and community.
Fields of interest: Performing arts; Arts; Education, reading; Education; Health care; Health organizations, association; Athletics/sports, water sports; Recreation; Youth, services; Aging, centers/services; Community/economic development; Children/youth; Youth; Disabilities, people with; Physically disabled; Mentally disabled; Minorities; Hispanics/Latinos; Native Americans/American Indians; Military/veterans; Economically disadvantaged; Homeless.
Type of support: General/operating support; Continuing support; Annual campaigns; Capital campaigns; Building/renovation; Equipment; Endowments; Internship funds; Scholarship funds; Scholarships—to individuals.
Limitations: Applications accepted. Giving limited to Benton County, OR.
Publications: Application guidelines; Annual report; Grants list; Informational brochure; Newsletter.
Application information: Visit foundation web site for grant application form. Application form required.
Initial approach: Submit application form and attachments
Copies of proposal: 1
Deadline(s): Mar. 14
Board meeting date(s): 3rd Thurs. of each month
Officers and Directors:* Peter Sekermestrovich,* Pres.; Diana Simpson-Godfrey,* V.P.; Larry Holcomb,* Secy.; Joy Ragsdale,* Treas.; Dick Thompson, Exec. Dir.; Scott Fewel; **Robert Gardner**; **Jim Jordan**; **Glenn Plemmons**; Mike Rainbolt; Susan Schmidt; Lark Wysham.
Number of staff: 1 part-time professional; 1 part-time support.
EIN: 936022916
Other changes: David Gazeley is no longer a director.

2836
Braemar Charitable Trust
P.O. Box 25442
Portland, OR 97298-0442
Contact: Martha B. Cox, Tr.
E-mail: MaryL@trustmanagementservices.net; Application address: c/o Mary Lanthrum, Trust Mgmt. Svcs., P.O. Box 1990, Waldport, OR 97394-1990, tel.: (541) 563-7279; fax: (541) 563-7216

Established in 1993 in OR.
Donors: Hobart M. Bird; Marian A. Bird.
Foundation type: Independent foundation.
Financial data (yr. ended 09/30/13): Assets, $20,693,810 (M); expenditures, $799,328; qualifying distributions, $643,865; giving activities include $526,314 for 64 grants (high: $10,000; low: $2,802).
Fields of interest: Arts; Education; Human services; Children/youth, services.
Type of support: General/operating support; Building/renovation; Equipment; Program development; Curriculum development.
Limitations: Applications accepted. Giving limited to OR. No support for political organizations. No grants to individuals; or for scholarships, capital campaigns, endowments or debt retirement.
Publications: Application guidelines.
Application information: Applications sent by fax are not accepted. Application form required.
Initial approach: Request application guidelines from Waldport address, or download from web site: http://www.trustmanagementservices.net
Copies of proposal: 1
Deadline(s): Varies by region, refer to web site: http://www.trustmanagementservices.net. Applications should not be submitted more than 30 days prior to deadline date
Trustees: Hobart M. Bird; Martha B. Cox; Melanie A. Dawson.
EIN: 936272124
Other changes: Marian A. Bird is no longer a trustee.

2837
The Burning Foundation
715 S.W. Morrison St., Ste. 901
Portland, OR **97205** **(503) 419-8454**
***Contact:* Sybil Ackerman-Munson, Fdn. Advisor**
FAX: (206) 784-5987;
E-mail: BurningFoundation@gmail.com; **Main URL: http://fdnweb.org/burning**
Grants List: http://fdnweb.org/burning/grant-examples/

Established in 1997 in WA.
Donor: David Weise.
Foundation type: Independent foundation.
Financial data (yr. ended 12/31/12): Assets, $10,917,074 (M); expenditures, $515,960; qualifying distributions, $481,301; giving activities include $473,000 for 37 grants (high: $20,000; low: $8,000).
Purpose and activities: Giving primarily to organizations whose environmental programs address issues in WA and OR. Priority areas include protecting threatened rivers and forests, nurturing native fish populations, and conserving land and open space for ecological and recreational purposes. Preference will be given to requests from local groups working to improve their immediate environment and from statewide groups addressing general conservation and protection issues, rather than national organizations with projects in the Pacific Northwest. The foundation also supports teen pregnancy prevention projects which may include school-based health and education programs, mentoring projects, and community clinic programs providing information and services on birth control, choice, and sex education.
Fields of interest: Environment, natural resources; Environment, water resources; Environment, land resources; Environment, forests; Environmental education; Animals/wildlife, fisheries; Youth, pregnancy prevention; Youth, services.
Type of support: General/operating support; Program development.
Limitations: Giving limited to OR and WA for environmental requests, and the Puget Sound area for conservation programs for youth and teen pregnancy prevention programs. No support for private schools, universities, gardening programs, the creation or renovation of community parks, environmental education programs, or for programs related to energy conservation, alternative energy, nuclear waste, toxics, or global warming. No grants to individuals for research or scholarships, or for capital campaigns for building construction or renovations, computer, software, or office equipment purchases, or book, video, film, or home-page productions, unless the production is an essential component of the funded project.
Publications: Application guidelines; Grants list.
Application information: See foundation web site for complete application guidelines.
Deadline(s): Spring cycle: 3rd Wed. of Jan. for letter, 1st Wed. of Mar. for invited proposal; fall cycle: 3rd Wed. of Aug for letter, 1st Wed. of Oct. for invited proposal
Final notification: 1st Wed. of May and 4th Wed. of Nov.
Officers: David N. Weise, Pres.; Daniel W. Weise, V.P.; Alisa K. F. Weise, Secy.
EIN: 911815335

2838
Caddock Foundation, Inc.
17271 N. Umpqua Hwy.
Roseburg, OR 97470-9422
***Application address:* c/o Sue E. Brinkman, Secy.-Treas., 1717 Chicago Ave., Riverside, CA 92507-2208, tel.: (541) 672-1716**

Incorporated in 1968 in CA.
Foundation type: Independent foundation.
Financial data (yr. ended 12/31/12): Assets, $1,806,388 (M); expenditures, $813,383; qualifying distributions, $810,782; giving activities include $810,782 for 13 grants (high: $610,000; low: $1,600).
Purpose and activities: Grants to Evangelical Christian religious associations and activities, including Bible studies.
Fields of interest: Christian agencies & churches.
Type of support: General/operating support; Continuing support; Program evaluation.
Limitations: Applications accepted. Giving primarily in CA, IL, TX and OR. No grants to individuals.
Application information:
Initial approach: Letter
Deadline(s): None
Officers: John B. Caddock, Pres.; **Richard E. Caddock, Jr., V.P.; Sue E. Brinkman, Secy.-Treas.**
EIN: 952559728
Other changes: Richard E. Caddock, Jr. has replaced James C. Caddock as V.P.
Sue E. Brinkman is now Secy.-Treas.

2839
Castle Foundation
c/o U.S. Bank, N.A.
P.O. Box 3168
Portland, OR 97208-3168
Contact: Carolyn O'Malley
***Application address:* c/o U.S. Bank, N.A., Attn.: Michael I. Poulter or Songa Corbin, 170 S.**

Main St., Ste. 600, Salt Lake City, UT 84101, Portland, OR tel.: (503) 275-4327

Established in 1953 in UT.
Foundation type: Independent foundation.
Financial data (yr. ended 06/30/13): Assets, $3,471,830 (M); expenditures, $228,338; qualifying distributions, $192,164; giving activities include $183,120 for 76 grants (high: $5,000; low: $1,000).
Fields of interest: Arts; Elementary/secondary education; Higher education; Health care; Human services; Children/youth, services.
Type of support: General/operating support; Equipment; Program development; Scholarship funds.
Limitations: Applications accepted. Giving primarily in UT.
Publications: Application guidelines.
Application information: Application form required.
Initial approach: Letter
Copies of proposal: 4
Deadline(s): None
Board meeting date(s): May and Nov.
Final notification: 3 weeks after board meeting
Trustee: U.S. Bank, N.A.
EIN: 876117177

2840
Robert and Frances Chaney Family Foundation
P.O. Box 840
Jacksonville, OR 97530-0840 (541) 899-9199
Contact: Carrie Hanson, Exec. Dir.
FAX: (541) 899-9679;
E-mail: chanson.familyfoundation@gmail.com; Main URL: http://www.familyfoundationchaney.org

Established in 2006 in OR.
Donors: Robert Chaney; Frances Chaney.
Foundation type: Independent foundation.
Financial data (yr. ended 05/31/13): Assets, $8,760,636 (M); expenditures, $497,619; qualifying distributions, $399,013; giving activities include $327,464 for 69 grants (high: $15,000; low: $500).
Purpose and activities: Giving primarily to organizations to build a better future by granting funds for educational purposes, human services, charitable and faith-based groups, and other purposes focusing on benefiting children, families and public safety personnel.
Fields of interest: Higher education; Human services.
Limitations: Applications accepted. Giving limited to organizations whose projects or programs exclusively benefit the residents of Jackson & Josephine Counties, OR; Barry County, MO; and Cabell County, WV. No support for visual and performing arts programs. No grants to individuals or for endowments, annual fund drives, overhead expenses, fundraising events, or for property acquisition.
Application information: Application guidelines available on foundation web site. Application form required.
Initial approach: Contact foundation website for application form
Deadline(s): Jan 31 and July 31
Officers and Trustees:* Frances Chaney, Pres.; **Robin Whitzel,* V.P.; Susan Krammer,* Secy.-Treas.**; Jason Anderson; **Brenda Green**; **Cerise Stephens**.
EIN: 205052365
Other changes: Robin Whitzel has replaced Susan Krammer as V.P. Susan Krammer has replaced Robin Whitzel as Secy.-Treas.

2841
The Coit Family Foundation
111 S.W. 5th Ave., Ste. 1500
Portland, OR **97204-3619**
***Contact:* Peter Duffy**

Established in 1997 in OR.
Donor: Barbara E. Coit.
Foundation type: Independent foundation.
Financial data (yr. ended 12/31/12): Assets, $4,003,457 (M); gifts received, $176,247; expenditures, $222,261; qualifying distributions, $163,933; giving activities include $163,933 for grants.
Fields of interest: Media/communications; Arts; Education; Animal welfare; Food banks; Human services.
Limitations: Applications not accepted. Giving primarily in Portland, OR. No grants to individuals.
Application information: Contributes only to pre-selected organizations.
Officers: Barbara Coit Yeager, Pres.; Ann Coit Goss, V.P.; Susan Coit, Secy.; William E. Coit, Treas.
EIN: 911806333

2842
Collins Medical Trust
1618 S.W. 1st Ave., Ste. 500
Portland, OR 97201-5706 (503) 227-1219
Contact: Nancy L. Helseth, Admin.
FAX: (503) 227-5349;
E-mail: nhelseth@collinsmedicaltrust.org; Tel. for applications: (503) 471-2223; Main URL: http://www.collinsmedicaltrust.org

Established in 1956 in OR.
Donor: Truman W. Collins†.
Foundation type: Independent foundation.
Financial data (yr. ended 09/30/13): Assets, $8,190,870 (M); expenditures, $435,431; qualifying distributions, $431,355; giving activities include $429,538 for 13 grants (high: $70,000; low: $29,760).
Purpose and activities: Grants limited to medical research and medical education within the state of Oregon.
Fields of interest: Higher education; Medical school/education; Nursing school/education; Cancer; Biomedicine; Medical research, institute; Cancer research.
Type of support: Equipment; Program development; Seed money; Scholarship funds; Research; Matching/challenge support.
Limitations: Applications accepted. Giving limited to OR.
Publications: Application guidelines; Annual report.
Application information: Complete application guidelines available on trust web site. Application form not required.
Initial approach: Letter or e-mail (e-mail preferred)
***Copies of proposal:* 2**
***Deadline(s):* Last business day of the month preceding board meetings**
Board meeting date(s): Jan., May, and Sept.
Officers: Timothy R. Bishop, Treas.; Nancy L. Helseth, Admin.
Trustees: Truman W. Collins, Jr.; Elizabeth Eckstrom, M.D., M.P.H.; Walter J. McDonald, M.D.
EIN: 936021895
Other changes: The grantmaker now makes its application guidelines available online.

2843
Coon Family Foundation
2939 N.W. 53rd Dr.
Portland, OR 97210-1067
Main URL: http://coonfamilyfoundation.org/
Grants List: http://coonfamilyfoundation.org/grants.html

Established in OR.
Donors: James S. Coon; Cheryl F. Coon.
Foundation type: Independent foundation.
Financial data (yr. ended 12/31/12): Assets, $1,127,951 (M); gifts received, $550,000; expenditures, $171,722; qualifying distributions, $170,307; giving activities include $168,900 for 9 grants (high: $61,400; low: $5,000).
Purpose and activities: Support for the environment, poverty, healthcare and arts.
Fields of interest: Environment.
Limitations: Applications not accepted. Giving primarily in Portland, OR.
Application information: Contributes only to pre-selected organizations.
Officers: James S. Coon, Pres.; Eli Coon, Secy.; Cheryl F. Coon, Exec. Dir.
EIN: 270756406

2844
Bernard Daly Educational Fund
P.O. Box 351
Lakeview, OR 97630-0123 (541) 947-2196

Established in 1922 in OR.
Donors: Bernard Daly†; Jess and Alta Roberts Trust; Charles Bogner Trust.
Foundation type: Independent foundation.
Financial data (yr. ended 05/31/13): Assets, $5,719,677 (M); expenditures, $426,150; qualifying distributions, $381,633; giving activities include $377,000 for 51 grants to individuals (high: $7,800; low: $2,600).
Purpose and activities: Giving primarily for financial aid for study at technical schools and colleges in OR.
Fields of interest: Vocational education.
Type of support: Scholarships—to individuals.
Limitations: Applications accepted. Giving primarily in Lake County, OR.
Application information: Application form required.
Initial approach: Contact Foundation
Copies of proposal: 2
Deadline(s): None
Officers: Alan Parks, Chair.; Melinda Howard, Vice-Chair.; **Dave Vandenberg, Secy.-Treas.**
Trustee: Mike Sabin.
EIN: 936025466
Other changes: Dave Vandenberg has replaced James C. Lynch as Secy.-Treas.

2845
Flowerree Foundation
P.O. Box 8098
Portland, OR **97207-8098**

Established in 1961 in OR.
Donors: Robert E. Flowerree; Elaine D. Flowerree; Flowerree Residuary Marital Trust.
Foundation type: Independent foundation.
Financial data (yr. ended 12/31/12): Assets, $7,405,389 (M); expenditures, $283,479;

qualifying distributions, $195,206; giving activities include $193,550 for 51 grants (high: $25,000; low: $100).
Fields of interest: Higher education; Education; Environment, natural resources; Botanical gardens; Human services; Community/economic development; Christian agencies & churches; Religion.
Type of support: Annual campaigns; Capital campaigns; Seed money; Employee matching gifts.
Limitations: Applications not accepted. Giving primarily in CA, LA, and OR. No grants to individuals.
Application information: Unsolicited requests for funds not accepted.
Officers and Directors:* Ann D. Flowerree,* Pres.; David R. Flowerree,* V.P.; Elaine D. Flowerree,* V.P.; John H. Flowerree,* V.P.; David M. Munro,* Secy.
EIN: 936034207

2846
The Ford Family Foundation
1600 N.W. Stewart Pkwy.
Roseburg, OR 97471-1957 (541) 957-5574
***Contact:* Anne C. Kubisch, Pres.**
FAX: (541) 957-5720; E-mail: info@tfff.org; Main URL: http://www.tfff.org
Scholarship application address: **The Ford Family Foundation Scholarship Office, 440 E. Broadway, Ste., 200, Eugene, OR 97401, tel.: (541) 485-6211, toll free: (877) 864-2872, e-mail: fordscholarships@tfff.org, fax: (541) 485-6223**

Incorporated in 1957 in OR.
Donors: Kenneth W. Ford†; Hallie E. Ford†.
Foundation type: Independent foundation.
Financial data (yr. ended 12/31/12): Assets, $721,115,314 (M); gifts received, $120,420; expenditures, $38,571,212; qualifying distributions, $35,851,252; giving activities include $14,970,124 for 543 grants (high: $1,900,000; low: $50), $11,189,835 for 1,370 grants to individuals (high: $36,825; low: $162), and $5,320,930 for 2 foundation-administered programs.
Purpose and activities: The foundation makes grants to public charities that pre-dominantly benefit small communities in rural Oregon and Siskiyou County, California. It is committed to investing in the capacities of individuals and communities through scholarships, grants and the Ford Institute of Community Building.
Fields of interest: Arts, administration/regulation; Visual arts; Libraries/library science; Health care, clinics/centers; Dental care; Crime/violence prevention, child abuse; Youth development; Children/youth, services; Community/economic development; Infants/toddlers; Children/youth; Children; Youth; Infants/toddlers, female.
Type of support: General/operating support; Management development/capacity building; Capital campaigns; Building/renovation; Equipment; Program development; Fellowships; Technical assistance; Employee matching gifts; Scholarships—to individuals; Matching/challenge support.
Limitations: Applications accepted. Giving primarily in rural OR, with special interest in Douglas and Coos counties; giving also in Siskiyou County, CA, or for populations less than 30,000 not adjacent to or part of an urban area. No support for projects or programs that are indirectly funded through a fiscal agent, or for lobbying or propaganda. No grants to individuals (except for scholarships or fellowships), or for endowment/reserve funds, general fund drives, debt retirement, deficits, or for indirect or overhead expenses.
Publications: Informational brochure (including application guidelines); Newsletter.
Application information: The foundation only accepts requests for funding through an on-line application process. Full proposals are accepted by invitation only. Application form required.
Initial approach: Review application guidelines to determine eligibility
Copies of proposal: 1
Deadline(s): None for responsive and technical assistance grants
Board meeting date(s): Four times per year
Final notification: 3-4 weeks
Officers and Directors:* Karla S. Chambers,* Chair.; Toby Luther,* Vice-Chair.; Anne Kubisch, C.E.O. and Pres.; Allyn C. Ford,* Secy.-Treas.; **Deborah Millsap, C.F.O.**; Dr. Knute Buehler; Joe Robertson; Wesley Sand; Carrie Thompson.
Number of staff: 7 full-time professional; 11 full-time support.
EIN: 936026156
Other changes: Karla S. Chambers has replaced Ronald C. Parker as Chair. Toby Luther has replaced Karla Chambers as Vice-Chair. David B. Frohnmayer and Joseph P. Kearns are no longer directors. Deborah Millsap is now C.F.O.

2847
Glory Foundation
c/o Robert J. Preston, Esq.
707 S.W. Washington St., Ste. 1500
Portland, OR 97205-3532

Donor: Katherine A. Eiting.
Foundation type: Independent foundation.
Financial data (yr. ended 12/31/12): Assets, $2,772,743 (M); gifts received, $630,580; expenditures, $1,681,948; qualifying distributions, $1,637,187; giving activities include $1,636,187 for 38 grants (high: $255,000; low: $1,197).
Fields of interest: Education; Health care; Human services; Children, services; Catholic federated giving programs.
Limitations: Applications not accepted. Giving primarily in CA, OH, OR, and VA; some funding also in MD.
Application information: Contributes only to pre-selected organizations.
Officers and Directors:* Katherine A. Eiting,* Pres.; Robert J. Preston,* Secy.-Treas.
EIN: 721574570
Other changes: The grantmaker no longer lists a separate application address.

2848
The Bill Healy Foundation
P.O. Box 4525
Portland, OR 97208-4525 (503) 222-1899
Contact: Diane Hall, Exec. Dir.
FAX: (503) 222-1861;
E-mail: info@billhealyfoundation.org; **Office address: 721 N.W. 9th Ave., Ste. 229, Portland, OR 97209**; Main URL: http://www.billhealyfoundation.org
Grants List: http://www.billhealyfoundation.org/recipients2013.html

Established in 1995 in OR.
Donor: Cameron Healy.
Foundation type: Independent foundation.
Financial data (yr. ended 12/31/12): Assets, $26,618,748 (M); gifts received, $200; expenditures, $1,430,558; qualifying distributions, $1,295,783; giving activities include $940,039 for 70+ grants (high: $50,000).
Purpose and activities: Giving primarily for environmental conservation and the well-being of children. The foundation is committed to responsible grant making through thoughtful choices by recognizing the fragile interdependence between the environment and human beings.
Fields of interest: Education; Environment; Children.
Limitations: Applications accepted. Giving primarily in HI and OR. No grants to individuals.
Publications: Application guidelines.
Application information: See foundation web site for application policies and form. Application form required.
Initial approach: Submit grant consideration application
Deadline(s): See foundation web site for current deadlines
Officers: Cameron Healy, Chair.; Diane Hall, Exec. Dir.
Directors: Marc Cramer; Christine Hart; Tim Healy; Susan Snow.
EIN: 931208721

2849
Hedinger Family Foundation
1750 N.W. NAITO Pkwy., Ste. 106
Portland, OR 97209-2532

Established in 1998 in OR.
Donor: American Industries, Inc.
Foundation type: Company-sponsored foundation.
Financial data (yr. ended 12/31/12): Assets, $487,243 (M); gifts received, $1,000,000; expenditures, $1,774,909; qualifying distributions, $1,757,847; giving activities include $1,757,847 for 46 grants (high: $200,000; low: $500).
Purpose and activities: The foundation supports science museums and organizations involved with education, animals and wildlife, health, cancer, youth development, and human services.
Fields of interest: Education; Animals/wildlife; Youth development.
Type of support: General/operating support; Building/renovation; Program development; Scholarship funds.
Limitations: Applications not accepted. Giving primarily in the greater Portland, OR, area. No grants to individuals.
Application information: Contributes only to pre-selected organizations.
Directors: Hillary Hedinger Guelfi; Blake H. Hedinger; Howard H. Hedinger.
EIN: 931255431
Other changes: The grantmaker no longer lists a fax. The grantmaker no longer lists a primary contact.

2850
I Have a Dream Foundation - Oregon
2916 N.E. Alberta St., Ste. D
Portland, OR 97211-7069 (503) 287-7203
FAX: (503) 287-0539;
E-mail: info@dreamoregon.org; Main URL: http://www.dreamoregon.org/
Facebook: http://www.facebook.com/ihaveadreamoregon
Flickr: https://www.flickr.com/photos/ihaveadreamoregon/
LinkedIn: http://www.linkedin.com/company/i-have-a-dream-foundation—oregon

Twitter: https://twitter.com/IHaveaDreamOR
YouTube: http://www.youtube.com/user/IHaveaDreamFdnOregon

Established in 1990 in OR.
Donor: The Oregon Community Foundation.
Foundation type: Operating foundation.
Financial data (yr. ended 06/30/12): Assets, $2,890,173 (M); gifts received, $1,417,277; expenditures, $1,657,108; qualifying distributions, $1,617,599; giving activities include $180,327 for 130 grants to individuals (high: $6,000; low: $100).
Purpose and activities: Scholarship awards to children from low-income areas to assist in their education and achieve their career goals by providing a long-term program of mentoring, tutoring, and enrichment with an assured opportunity for higher education.
Fields of interest: Education, services; Economically disadvantaged.
Type of support: Grants to individuals.
Limitations: Applications accepted. Giving primarily in Portland, OR.
Application information: Scholarship application form available on foundation web site. Application form required.
Officers: Rose Hartwig, Chair; Markland Fountain, Vice-Chair.; Mark Langseth, Pres. and C.E.O.; Jim Schlachter, Secy.; Nancy Horton, Treas.
Board Members: Julie Ball; Diane Boly; Eve Callahan; Betsy Cramer; Sarah Curtiss; Johnnie Driessner; Julie Frantz; Greg Friedman; Dan Goldman; Kay Hall; Dwayne Johnson; Terry Michaelson; Josh Reynolds; Mark Stevenson.
EIN: 931037323

2851
The Jackson Foundation

P.O. Box 3168
Portland, OR 97208-3168 (503) 275-6564
Main URL: http://www.thejacksonfoundation.com

Trust established in 1960 in OR; Philip Ludwell Jackson Charitable and Residual Trusts were merged into The Jackson Foundation in 1981.
Donor: Maria C. Jackson†.
Foundation type: Independent foundation.
Financial data (yr. ended 06/30/13): Assets, $12,875,185 (M); expenditures, $718,831; qualifying distributions, $542,500; giving activities include $542,500 for grants.
Purpose and activities: Giving primarily for the arts, education, health, and children, youth and social services.
Fields of interest: Performing arts; Arts; Education; Health care; Human services; Children/youth, services.
Type of support: Continuing support; Capital campaigns; Endowments; Research.
Limitations: Applications accepted. **Giving limited to OR, with emphasis on Portland; requests for projects located outside the Portland metropolitan area are accepted, provided that the project is of statewide appeal, rather than of local concern.** No support for churches or temples. No grants to individuals, or for matching gifts, scholarships, fellowships, or building or equipment funds for religious organizations; no loans to individuals.
Publications: Application guidelines; Annual report.
Application information: Refer to foundation web site for specific application information. Telephone calls are not accepted. Application form required.
Initial approach: **Use application form on foundation web site**
Deadline(s): Mar. 31, June 30, Sept. 30, and Dec. 31
Board meeting date(s): Jan., Apr., July, and Oct.
***Final notification:* Approximately 2-3 weeks after Board meeting date**
Trustees: Julie Vigeland; U.S. Bank, N.A.
Number of staff: 3 part-time professional.
EIN: 936020752

2852
The Jeld-Wen Foundation

(formerly Jeld-Wen, Wenco Foundation)
3250 Lakeport Blvd.
Klamath Falls, OR 97601-1036 (541) 880-2185
Contact: Robert Kingzett, Exec. Dir.
Klamath Falls Office: 3250 Lakeport Blvd., Klamath Falls, OR 97601, tel.: (541) 880-2185; Main URL: http://www.jeld-wenfoundation.org/

Established in 1969.
Donors: Jeld-Wen, Inc.; Jeld-Wen Fiber Products, Inc. of Iowa; Jeld-Wen Co. of Arizona; Wenco, Inc. of North Carolina; Wenco, Inc. of Ohio; Jeld-Wen Holding, Inc.
Foundation type: Company-sponsored foundation.
Financial data (yr. ended 12/31/12): Assets, $19,261,341 (M); gifts received, $500,000; expenditures, $1,637,209; qualifying distributions, $1,595,091; giving activities include $1,375,960 for 47 grants (high: $200,000).
Purpose and activities: The foundation supports organizations involved with arts and culture, education, health, human services, community development, and civic affairs. Special emphasis is directed toward programs designed to strengthen families, improve neighborhoods, and build better communities.
Fields of interest: Humanities; Arts; Education; Hospitals (general); Health care; Human services; Community/economic development; United Ways and Federated Giving Programs; Public policy, research; Public affairs.
Type of support: Matching/challenge support; General/operating support; Capital campaigns; Building/renovation; Equipment; Endowments; Program development; Scholarship funds.
Limitations: Applications accepted. Giving on a national basis in areas of company operations, with emphasis on OR. No support for private or religious schools. No grants to individuals, or for religious activities or programs that duplicate services provided by other government or private agencies; no annual support.
Publications: Application guidelines.
Application information: The foundation requests that applicants involve a Jeld-Wen manager in the application process. A site visit may be requested. Support is limited to 1 contribution per organization during any given year. Application form required.
Initial approach: Contact foundation or nearest general manager for application form
Deadline(s): Varies, but are scheduled around quarterly meetings
Board meeting date(s): Quarterly
Officers and Trustees:* Roderick C. Wendt,* Secy.; Robert Kingzett, Exec. Dir.; W. B. Early; Robert F. Turner; Nancy J. Wendt.
EIN: 936054272
Other changes: The grantmaker no longer lists a fax.

2853
Jubitz Family Foundation

221 N.W. 2nd Ave., Ste. 204
Portland, OR **97209-3982** (503) 274-6255
Contact: Raymond Jubitz, Exec. Dir.
FAX: (503) 274-6256; **E-mail: info@jubitz.org**; Main URL: http://www.jubitzff.org

Established in 2001 in OR.
Donors: Jubitz Investments, LP; Saybrook, Inc.; M. Albin Jubitz, Jr.; Mike Caruso.
Foundation type: Independent foundation.
Financial data (yr. ended 12/31/12): Assets, $12,594,716 (M); gifts received, $20,000; expenditures, $758,565; qualifying distributions, $667,427; giving activities include $494,200 for 83 grants (high: $20,000; low: $2,000).
Purpose and activities: The foundation supports projects and organizations that enhance the communities in which its officers live by strengthening families, by respecting the natural environment, and by fostering peace. Areas of interest include early childhood development and education, with an emphasis on children at-risk; environmental stewardship, with an emphasis on rivers and their watershed ecosystems; and peacemaking activities, with an emphasis on teaching peace and conflict resolution.
Fields of interest: Elementary/secondary education; Higher education; Education; Environment, natural resources; Environment; Animals/wildlife; Youth development; Human services; Children/youth, services; Family services.
Limitations: Applications accepted. Giving primarily in OR. No grants for capital expenditures.
Publications: Application guidelines; Grants list.
Application information: See foundation web site for application guidelines and procedures, and application form. Application form required.
Initial approach: First time applicants: 1-page letter of request to Exec. Dir. via form on foundation web site; previously funded applicants should submit a grant request via foundation web site
Deadline(s): First time applicants: Jan 1 (for Apr. 1 grant deadline), and July 1 (for Oct. 1 grant deadline); for previously funded applicants: Apr. 1 and Oct. 1
Officers: M. Albin Jubitz, Jr., Pres.; Elizabeth Jubitz Sayler, V.P.; Katherine H. Jubitz, Secy.; Sarah C. Jubitz, Treas.; Raymond G. Jubitz, Exec. Dir.
EIN: 931324016

2854
Knight Foundation

c/o Lisa McKillips
1 Bowerman Dr.
Beaverton, OR 97005-0979 (503) 671-3500
Contact: Lisa Mckillips

Established in 1997 in OR.
Donors: Philip H. Knight; Phight LLC.
Foundation type: Independent foundation.
Financial data (yr. ended 12/31/12): Assets, $208,747,724 (M); gifts received, $75,000,014; expenditures, $5,574,105; qualifying distributions, $5,008,576; giving activities include $5,000,000 for 1 grant.
Purpose and activities: Giving primarily for higher and other education, including a graduate school of business.
Fields of interest: Higher education; Health care; Medical research.
Limitations: Applications not accepted. Giving primarily in Portland, OR. No grants to individuals.

Application information: Contributes only to pre-selected organizations.
Officers and Director:* Philip H. Knight, Pres. and Treas.; Penelope P. Knight,* V.P.; Travis A. Knight, Secy.
EIN: 911791788
Other changes: At the close of 2012, the fair market value of the grantmaker's assets was $208,747,724, a 55.9% increase over the 2011 value, $133,881,136.

2855
Lamb Foundation
P.O. Box 1705
Lake Oswego, OR 97035-0575 (503) 635-8010
FAX: (503) 635-6544;
E-mail: lambfnd@thelambfoundation.org; Main URL: http://www.thelambfoundation.org
Grants List: http://www.lambfoundation.org/past-grants/

Established in 1971 in OR.
Donor: Members of the Lamb family.
Foundation type: Independent foundation.
Financial data (yr. ended 12/31/12): Assets, $5,872,366 (M); expenditures, $335,491; qualifying distributions, $294,693; giving activities include $232,700 for 58 grants (high: $20,000; low: $100).
Purpose and activities: Support for a wide range of creative programs to improve the quality of the human experience.
Fields of interest: Arts; Environment; Children/youth, services; Children/youth.
Type of support: Program development; Seed money; Matching/challenge support.
Limitations: Applications accepted. Giving limited to the Pacific Northwest, with emphasis on OR and WA. No grants to individuals, or for scholarships or for proposals submitted to individual directors.
Publications: Financial statement; Grants list; Informational brochure; Program policy statement.
Application information: Application form required.
Initial approach: Letter
Deadline(s): Mar. 30 and Sept. 30
Officers and Directors:* Barbara Lamb,* Pres.; Frank Lamb,* V.P.; Dorothy Lamb,* Secy.; Jim Lamb,* Treas.; Anita Lamb Bailey; Dustin Bailey; Gayle Horton; Brenda Lamb; Paula Lamb; Rick Lamb, Jr.
Number of staff: 1 part-time professional.
EIN: 237120564

2856
The Lazar Foundation
715 S.W. Morrison St., Ste. 901
Portland, OR 97205-3105 (503) 225-0265
***Contact:* Sybil Ackerman, Exec. Dir.**
FAX: (503) 225-9620;
E-mail: info@lazarfoundation.org; Sybil Ackerman's e-mail: sybil@lazarfoundation.org; **Main URL: http://fdnweb.org/lazar**
Grants List: http://fdnweb.org/lazar/grant-examples/

Incorporated in 1956 in DE.
Donors: Jack Lazar†; Helen B. Lazar†.
Foundation type: Independent foundation.
Financial data (yr. ended 12/31/12): Assets, $22,489,000 (M); gifts received, $197,420; expenditures, $1,281,604; qualifying distributions, $1,088,135; giving activities include $826,845 for 50 grants (high: $100,000; low: $1,000).
Purpose and activities: The foundation focuses on preservation of biological diversity and ecosystems; broadening the environmental movement, and message development.
Fields of interest: Environment.
Type of support: General/operating support; Program development; Seed money.
Limitations: Giving primarily in ID, OR, and WA. No support for environmental education, civic projects, urban issues, suburban projects, or conservation-based scientific research, unless it directly supports a project that the foundation is currently funding. No grants to individuals, or for endowments, land acquisition, film or video projects, capital campaigns or for computer-related expenses.
Publications: Application guidelines; Grants list.
Application information: Full proposal is by invitation only, upon review of initial letter. Telephone calls are not accepted. Application form required.
Initial approach: Letter only (no more than 1-page) via e-mail to Sybil Ackerman with "LOI" in the subject bar
Copies of proposal: 1
Deadline(s): Feb. 15, June 15, and Oct. 15
Board meeting date(s): Mar., July, and Nov.
Final notification: Applicants who do not receive a reply to their LOI within 1-month will not be asked to submit a proposal
Officers and Trustees:* William B. Lazar,* Pres.; Jeanne L. Morency,* Secy.; Sybil Ackerman, Exec. Dir.; Michael Morency.
Number of staff: 1 part-time professional; 1 part-time support.
EIN: 136088182

2857
The Lemelson Foundation
45 S.W. Ankeny St., Ste. 200
Portland, OR **97204-3500** (503) 827-8910
E-mail: webmaster@lemelson.org; Main URL: http://www.lemelson.org/
E-Newsletter: http://lemelson.us1.list-manage.com/subscribe?u=de855f63e59f43c6bce8afdd2&id=eb6afc211b
Facebook: http://www.facebook.com/TheLemelsonFoundation?ref=ts
Twitter: http://twitter.com/LemelsonFdn
YouTube: http://www.youtube.com/lemelsonfoundation

Established in 1994 in NV.
Donors: Dorothy Lemelson; Eric Lemelson; Jerome Lemelson†; Robert B. Lemelson.
Foundation type: Independent foundation.
Financial data (yr. ended 12/31/12): Assets, $343,785,771 (M); expenditures, $18,986,244; qualifying distributions, $16,602,891; giving activities include $11,940,587 for 36 grants (high: $1,626,840; low: $1,000), and $1,188,703 for 2 loans/program-related investments.
Purpose and activities: The foundation uses the power of invention to improve lives, by inspiring and enabling the next generation of inventors and invention based enterprises to promote economic growth in the U.S. and social and economic progress for the poor in developing countries. Established by prolific U.S. inventor Jerome Lemelson and his wife Dorothy in 1992. To date the foundation has provided or committed more than $175 million in grants and PRIs in support of its mission.
Fields of interest: Higher education; Economic development; Business/industry; Engineering/technology.
International interests: Developing Countries.
Type of support: Program-related investments/loans.
Limitations: Applications not accepted. Giving primarily in the United States and internationally in Africa, Asia and Latin America. No grants to individuals.
Application information: Contributes only to pre-selected organizations.
Officers and Directors:* Dorothy Lemelson,* Chair and Pres.; Robert Lemelson, Ph.D.*, V.P. and Secy.; Eric Lemelson,* V.P. and Treas.; Philip Varnum, C.F.O. and C.A.O.; Carol Dahl, Exec. Dir.; Jennifer Bruml Lemelson; Susan Morse.
EIN: 880391959

2858
Red and Gena Leonard Foundation
P.O. Box 1024
Hermiston, OR 97838-3024 (541) 564-9177
Contact: Tracy Gammell, Exec. Dir.
FAX: (541) 567-5358;
E-mail: rglfoundation@qwestoffice.net; Main URL: http://www.leonardfoundation.org

Established in 1997.
Donor: Gena Leonard & Related Trusts.
Foundation type: Independent foundation.
Financial data (yr. ended 06/30/13): Assets, $5,507,536 (M); expenditures, $226,196; qualifying distributions, $188,027; giving activities include $158,811 for grants.
Purpose and activities: Giving to improve the educational opportunities of average students of good character with poor financial circumstances who have a desire to seek further educational opportunities.
Fields of interest: Higher education; Higher education, college (community/junior); Nursing school/education.
Type of support: Scholarships—to individuals.
Limitations: Applications accepted. Giving limited to Gilliam, Grant, Morrow, Umatilla, and Wheeler counties, OR.
Application information: See web site for complete application policies, guidelines and application form. Students must complete the application form, provide official transcripts, a completed FAFSA form, a completed SAR form, and have two letters of recommendation. Application form required.
Initial approach: Complete application form
Copies of proposal: 2
Deadline(s): Mar. 15
Officers: Glenn S. Chowning, Pres.; Larry Mills, V.P.; Ron Daniels, Secy.; Nellie Madison, Treas.; Tracy Gammell, Exec. Dir.
Director: Nancy Mabry.
EIN: 931232272

2859
Maybelle Clark Macdonald Fund
P.O. Box 1496
Bend, OR 97709-1496
***E-mail:* information@mcmfundgiving.org; Main URL: http://www.mcmfundgiving.org/**

Established in 1970 in OR.
Donor: Maybelle Clark Macdonald†.
Foundation type: Independent foundation.
Financial data (yr. ended 06/30/13): Assets, $127,198,117 (M); expenditures, $5,694,362; qualifying distributions, $4,645,510; giving activities include $4,350,829 for 142 grants (high: $350,000; low: $1,000).

Purpose and activities: The mission of the foundation is to relieve the misfortune and promote the well being of mankind. Grantmaking priorities are: 1) Cultural Arts; 2) Education; 3) Human Services; 4) Medical Research; and 5) Public Benefit.
Fields of interest: Arts; Elementary/secondary education; Health care; Medical research; Human services; Aging, centers/services.
Type of support: General/operating support; Annual campaigns; Capital campaigns; Building/renovation; Endowments; Internship funds; Scholarship funds; Matching/challenge support.
Limitations: Applications accepted. Giving primarily in OR. No grants to individuals.
Application information: Full proposals by invitation after review of LOI.
Initial approach: **Online letter of inquiry through foundation web site**
Deadline(s): Letter of inquiry: Feb. 15 and Aug. 15
Officers and Directors:* Clark C. Munro, Sr.,* Chair.; Monique M. McCleary,* Pres.; Maurie M. Munro,* Secy.; Gary R. Branden; Gene d'Autremont; Janeen McAninch; Christopher R. Munro; Clark C. Munro, Jr.; Warner R. Munro.
Number of staff: 1 part-time professional; 1 full-time support; 1 part-time support.
EIN: 237108002

2860
The Leightman Maxey Foundation

P.O. Box 907
Medford, OR 97501-0272 (541) 734-9322
Contact: Dee Ann Harris, Exec. Dir.
Email for Dee Ann Harris: daharris@leightmanmaxeyfoundation.org; Main URL: http://www.leightmanmaxeyfoundation.org
Facebook: http://www.facebook.com/pages/Leightman-Maxey-Foundation/249161328490310
Grants List: http://www.leightmanmaxeyfoundation.org/?page_id=35

Established in 2003 in OR.
Foundation type: Independent foundation.
Financial data (yr. ended 12/31/12): Assets, $6,252,659 (M); expenditures, $378,431; qualifying distributions, $287,764; giving activities include $160,649 for 16 grants (high: $16,500; low: $500).
Purpose and activities: Giving to provide educational experiences related to careers, finance and nutrition for individuals to encourage and enable them to be self-reliant, productive members of society.
Fields of interest: Education.
Limitations: Applications accepted. Giving primarily in Jackson, Josephine, Klamath and Curry counties, OR. No support for projects seeking to influence elections or promote legislation. No grants to individuals or for political candidates.
Publications: Application guidelines.
Application information: See grantmaker web site for complete application policies, guidelines and application form. Application form required.
Initial approach: **Follow link to application system on foundation web site**
Copies of proposal: 1
Deadline(s): Mar. 1 and Sept. 1
Final notification: 10-12 weeks after each deadline
Trustee and Director:* Dee Ann Harris, Exec. Dir.
EIN: 476261291
Other changes: The grantmaker now publishes application guidelines.

2861
Meyer Memorial Trust

(formerly Fred Meyer Charitable Trust)
425 N.W. 10th Ave., Ste. 400
Portland, OR 97209-3128 (503) 228-5512
Contact: Doug Stamm, C.E.O.
E-mail: mmt@mmt.org; Main URL: http://www.mmt.org
Connectipedia: http://connectipedia.org
E-Newsletter: http://www.mmt.org/newsletters
Flickr: http://www.flickr.com/photos/meyermemorialtrust/
Foundation Blogs: http://www.mmt.org/blogs
Grants Database: http://www.mmt.org/awards
Knowledge Center: http://www.mmt.org/program-analysis
LinkedIn: http://www.linkedin.com/companies/meyer-memorial-trust
Meyer Discussion Forums: http://www.mmt.org/forum
Meyer Memorial Trust's Philanthropy Promise: http://www.ncrp.org/philanthropys-promise/who
Multimedia: http://www.mmt.org/stories
PRI Awards: http://www.mmt.org/awards-by-program/14
Slideshare: http://www.slideshare.net/MeyerMT
Twitter: http://www.twitter.com/meyermt
YouTube: http://www.youtube.com/meyertrust

Trust established by will in 1978; obtained IRS status in 1982 in OR.
Donor: Fred G. Meyer‡.
Foundation type: Independent foundation.
Financial data (yr. ended 03/31/13): Assets, $714,334,616 (M); expenditures, $34,648,570; qualifying distributions, $35,307,836; giving activities include $26,329,963 for 329 grants, $215,157 for employee matching gifts, and $4,850,000 for 6 loans/program-related investments.
Purpose and activities: The trust works with and invest in organizations, communities, ideas and efforts that contribute to a flourishing and equitable Oregon.
Fields of interest: Performing arts; Humanities; Arts; Child development, education; Higher education; Education; Environment, natural resources; Environment; Health care; Crime/violence prevention, youth; Housing/shelter, development; Human services; Children/youth, services; Child development, services; Family services; Aging, centers/services; Community/economic development.
Type of support: Emergency funds; Building/renovation; Capital campaigns; Employee matching gifts; Equipment; General/operating support; Income development; Management development/capacity building; Matching/challenge support; Mission-related investments/loans; Program development; Program-related investments/loans; Seed money; Technical assistance.
Limitations: Applications accepted. Giving limited to programs operating in the state of OR and Clark County, WA. No support for sectarian or religious organizations for religious purposes, for animal welfare organizations, animal-assisted therapy programs, or projects that primarily benefit students of a single K-12 school (unless the school is an independent alternative school primarily serving low-income and/or special needs populations). No grants to individuals or for endowment funds, annual campaigns, general fund drives, special events, sponsorships, direct replacement funding for activities previously supported by federal, state, or local public sources, deficit financing, acquisition of land for conservation purposes (except through Program Related Investments), or hospital capital construction projects (except through Program Related Investments).
Publications: Application guidelines; Financial statement; Grants list; Newsletter.
Application information: All applications online using GrantIS, an application system developed by MMT. Responsive Grants/PRIs use two-step process: Online Initial Inquiry with online Full Proposal if invited. Grassroots Grants program is a one-step online proposal process. Applications at this time are invited only from the state of OR and Clark County, WA. Please see the foundation's web site for additional details. Application form required.
Initial approach: Online application form
Deadline(s): None for Responsive Grants and PRIs; Grassroots Grants program: Mar. 15, July 15, Oct. 15
Board meeting date(s): Monthly
Final notification: 4 to 6 months for Responsive Grants proposals that pass first screening; 1 to 2 months for those that do not; 3 to 4 months for Grassroots Grants
Officers and Trustees:* Debbie F. Craig, Chair.; Doug Stamm, C.E.O.; **Brenda Hodges, Cont.**; **Rukaiyah Adams, C.I.O.**; George J. Puentes; John Emrick; Orcilla Zuniga Forbes; Charles Wilhoite.
Number of staff: 15 full-time professional; 1 part-time professional; 9 full-time support.
EIN: 930806316
Other changes: Debbie F. Craig has replaced George J. Puentes as Chair.
Wayne G. Pierson is no longer C.F.O. and Treas.

2862
Herbert I. and Elsa B. Michael Foundation

c/o U.S. Bank, N.A.
P.O. Box 3168
Portland, OR 97208
***Application address:* c/o U.S. Bank, N.A., Att.: Michael I. Polter/Songa Corbin, P.O. Box 3058, Portland, OR 97204, tel.: (801) 534-6045**

Established in 1950 in UT.
Donor: Elsa B. Michael‡.
Foundation type: Independent foundation.
Financial data (yr. ended 09/30/13): Assets, $7,008,659 (M); expenditures, $374,455; qualifying distributions, $315,290; giving activities include $300,500 for 59 grants (high: $15,000; low: $2,000).
Purpose and activities: Giving primarily for cultural programs and higher and secondary education. Some giving for hospitals and social service agencies.
Fields of interest: Arts; Higher education; Education; Hospitals (general); Human services; Children/youth, services.
Type of support: General/operating support; Scholarship funds; Matching/challenge support.
Limitations: Applications accepted. Giving primarily in the greater Salt Lake City, UT, area. No support for sectarian religious activities.
Publications: Application guidelines.
Application information: Application form not required.
***Initial approach:* Letter**
Copies of proposal: 6
***Deadline(s):* None**
Board meeting date(s): Apr. and Oct.
Trustee: U.S. Bank, N.A.
Advisory Committee: Christine M. Durham; Matthew Durrant; Keith Odendahl; Tracy D. Smith; Michael K. Young.
EIN: 876122556
Other changes: The grantmaker has moved from UT to OR.

2863
Mission Increase Foundation
7357 S.W. Beveland St., Ste. 200
Tigard, OR 97223-9074
FAX: (503) 210-0283;
E-mail: info@missionincrease.org; Main URL: http://www.missionincrease.org
Blog: http://www.missionincrease.org/blog/
Grants List: http://www.missionincrease.org/index.cfm?action=general.grantHistory

Established 2001 in OR.
Donors: Fidelity Charitable Gift Fund; Pearson Financial Group; Northwest Christian Community Foundation; The Christian Foundation of the Triangle; Marketplace One Foundation; Sacred Harvest Foundation.
Foundation type: Operating foundation.
Financial data (yr. ended 12/31/12): Assets, $30,240,393 (M); gifts received, $12,725; expenditures, $1,815,641; qualifying distributions, $1,580,619; giving activities include $1,502,265 for 57 grants (high: $100,000; low: $1,000).
Purpose and activities: Provides grants and targeted training to Christian ministries in the Portland, OR, Seattle, WA, Phoenix, AZ, Los Angeles and San Francisco, CA, and Denver, CO, metropolitan areas, and Raleigh, NC, Dallas, TX, Kansas City, KS, and Springfield and Columbus, OH.
Fields of interest: Human services; Children/youth, services; Christian agencies & churches; Religion.
Type of support: General/operating support; Income development; Management development/capacity building; Capital campaigns; Equipment; Program development; Consulting services; Employee matching gifts; Matching/challenge support.
Limitations: Applications not accepted. Giving primarily in the greater metro areas of Phoenix AZ, Los Angeles and San Francisco CA, Denver CO, Kansas City, KS, Raleigh, NC, Columbus and Springfield, OH, Portland OR, Dallas, TX, and Seattle WA. No grants to individuals.
Publications: Grants list; Informational brochure.
Application information: Contributes only to pre-selected organizations.
Board meeting date(s): Quarterly
Officers and Board Members:* Dale R. Stockamp,* Chair.; David Farquhar, Pres.; Ron Post,* Secy.; Daniel Davis, C.F.O.; Gail Stockamp.
Number of staff: 15 full-time professional; 1 part-time professional; 3 full-time support; 3 part-time support.
EIN: 810618279

2864
Morris Family Foundation
839 Alder Creek Dr.
Medford, OR 97504-8900
Application address: c/o Gary Rosenberger, Pres., 437 De Barr Ave., Medford, OR 97501-1661, tel.: (541) 779-1869

Established in 1998 in OR.
Donor: Earl W. Morris.
Foundation type: Independent foundation.
Financial data (yr. ended 06/30/13): Assets, $9,033,606 (M); expenditures, $561,209; qualifying distributions, $466,534; giving activities include $444,715 for 1 grant.
Purpose and activities: Scholarship awards to students in Jackson County, Oregon, School Districts No. 6, No. 35, No. 91 and No. 9, who are enrolled at Rogue Community College, Oregon, and are engaged in technical vocational education programs; giving also for orphans and victims of disasters.
Fields of interest: Education.
Type of support: General/operating support; Scholarship funds.
Limitations: Applications accepted. Giving limited to residents of Jackson County, OR.
Application information: Application form required.
Initial approach: **Letter or scholarship application form**
Deadline(s): None
Officers: Gary Rosenberger, Pres.; Jean Miller, V.P.; Erick Lieder, Secy.; Richard Entinger, Treas.; Pam Murphy, Exec. Dir.
EIN: 931230039

2865
NIKE Foundation
(formerly NIKE P.L.A.Y. Foundation)
1 Bowerman Dr.
Beaverton, OR 97005-6453
E-mail: nike.foundation@nike.com; E-mail for the Girl Effect: info@girleffect.org; Main URL: http://nikeinc.com/pages/the-nike-foundation
The Girl Effect on Facebook: http://www.facebook.com/girleffect
The Girl Effect on Twitter: http://twitter.com/girleffect
The Girl Effect on YouTube: http://www.youtube.com/girleffect

Established in 1994 in OR.
Donors: NIKE, Inc.; NoVo Foundation.
Foundation type: Company-sponsored foundation.
Financial data (yr. ended 05/31/13): Assets, $71,495,610 (M); gifts received, $6,775,807; expenditures, $30,028,172; qualifying distributions, $26,861,625; giving activities include $10,143,661 for 37 grants (high: $1,997,970; low: $15,000), and $1,997,970 for foundation-administered programs.
Purpose and activities: The foundation supports programs designed to empower adolescent girls in the developing world. Special emphasis is directed toward programs directed at reducing early marriage and delayign first birth; ensuring health and safety; secondary school completion and transitions to employment; and expanding direct access to economic assets.
Fields of interest: Secondary school/education; Education; Health care; Employment; Safety/disasters; Youth development, adult & child programs; Human services, financial counseling; Economic development; Social entrepreneurship; Microfinance/microlending; Girls; Economically disadvantaged.
International interests: Africa; Brazil; Developing Countries; India.
Type of support: General/operating support; Management development/capacity building; Program development; Seed money.
Limitations: Applications not accepted. Giving primarily in CA, Washington, DC, NY; giving on an international basis in Africa, Bangladesh, Brazil, India, Kenya, Nigeria, Paraguay, Tanzania, Uganda, and Zambia. No support for discriminatory organizations. No grants to individuals, or for general operating support for established programs, research or travel, films, television, or radio programs that are not an integral part of a project, religious programs, endowments or fundraising campaigns, lobbying or political activities, or depreciation or debt reduction.
Application information: Contributes only to pre-selected organizations. The foundation utilizes an invitation only Request for Proposal (RFP) process.
Officers and Directors:* Maria S. Eitel,* C.E.O. and Pres.; Collette Hemmings, C.O.O.; Howard Taylor, V.P. and Managing Dir.; Donald W. Blair; Trevor Edwards; Hannah Jones; Hilary Krane.
EIN: 931159948
Other changes: At the close of 2013, the fair market value of the grantmaker's assets was $71,495,610, a 80.1% increase over the 2012 value, $39,698,757.
Jennifer Buffett, Peter Buffett, Mark Parker, Charlie D. Denson, and Gary DeStefano are no longer directors.

2866
PacificSource Foundation for Health Improvement
(doing business as Pacific Source Health Plan)
(formerly PacificSource Charitable Foundation, Inc.)
P.O. Box 7068
Eugene, OR 97401-0068 **(541) 684-5221**
E-mail: CharitableFoundation@pacificsource.com; **Toll-free tel.: (800) 624-6052; Main URL: http://www.pacificsource.com/CharitableFoundation/**

Established in 1992 in OR.
Donors: Pacific Hospital Assn.; PacificSource Health Plans.
Foundation type: Independent foundation.
Financial data (yr. ended 12/31/12): Assets, $5,734,552 (M); gifts received, $600,000; expenditures, $910,226; qualifying distributions, $903,410; giving activities include $902,702 for 42 grants (high: $51,602; low: $10,000).
Fields of interest: Public health; Health care; Human services.
Type of support: General/operating support.
Limitations: Applications accepted. Giving limited to OR and ID.
Application information: Application form available on foundation web site. Applications are only accepted electronically. Application form required.
Initial approach: See foundation web site for guidelines and forms
Copies of proposal: 1
Deadline(s): At least 1 month prior to board meetings
Board meeting date(s): Semi-annually
Officers: Kenneth Provencher, Pres.; Marian Blankenship, Exec. Dir.
Trustees: David Abel, M.D.; Patricia Buchanan, M.D.; Fletcher Little; Mary McCauley-Burrows.
EIN: 931100080

2867
PGE Foundation
(formerly PGE-Enron Foundation)
One World Trade Center, 3rd Fl.
121 W. Salmon St.
Portland, OR 97204-2901 (503) 464-8818
Contact: Melissa Sircy, Grant Admin.
FAX: (503) 464-2929;
E-mail: pgefoundation@pgn.com; Additional contact: Rachel DeRosia, Prog. Off., tel.: (503) 464-8599, e-mail: rachel.derosia@pgn.com; Main URL: http://www.pgefoundation.org/

Established in 1994 in OR.
Donor: Portland General Electric Co.
Foundation type: Company-sponsored foundation.
Financial data (yr. ended 12/31/12): Assets, $22,884,117 (M); gifts received, $97,129; expenditures, $1,027,729; qualifying distributions,

$1,001,495; giving activities include $874,933 for 113 grants (high: $85,133; low: $200).
Purpose and activities: The foundation supports programs designed to promote education, healthy families, and arts and culture. Special emphasis is directed toward education programs and basic needs services.
Fields of interest: Arts education; History/archaeology; Arts; Elementary/secondary education; Higher education; Education, drop-out prevention; Education, reading; Education; Health care; Employment; Food services; Food banks; Children/youth, services; Family services; Family services, parent education; Family services, domestic violence; Aging, centers/services; Developmentally disabled, centers & services; Homeless, human services; Human services; United Ways and Federated Giving Programs; Mathematics; Engineering/technology; Science; Minorities.
Type of support: General/operating support; Continuing support; Program development; Curriculum development; Scholarship funds; Sponsorships.
Limitations: Applications accepted. Giving primarily in areas of company operations in OR. No support for political entities or candidates for political office, discriminatory organizations, or fraternal, sectarian, or religious organizations not of direct benefit to the entire community. No grants to individuals, or for bridge grants, debt retirements, or operational deficits, endowments, general operating support, annual campaigns, ballot measure campaigns, travel, conferences, symposiums, festivals, events, team sponsorships, or user fees, or salaries of employees (unless costs relate directly to the funded project); generally no capital campaigns that include building improvements, equipment purchases, or anything considered an asset of the organization.
Publications: Application guidelines; Annual report.
Application information: Grants range from $2,500 to $10,000. A full application may be requested at a later date. Support is limited to 1 contribution per organization during any given year. Organizations receiving support are asked to submit a final report. Application form not required.
Initial approach: Complete online letter of inquiry
***Deadline(s):* Feb. 7, May 3, and Nov. 21**
***Board meeting date(s):* May, Sept., and Feb.**
Final notification: 30 days
Officers and Directors:* Gwyneth Gamble-Booth,* Chair.; Carole E. Morse, Pres.; Rosalie Duron, Secy.; **James Lobdell, Treas.**; David K. Carboneau; Carol Dillin; Peggy Y. Fowler; Randolph L. Miller; James J. Piro; David Robertson; DeAngeloa Wells.
EIN: 931138806
Other changes: James Lobdell has replaced Maria M. Pope as Treas.
Maria M. Pope is no longer Treas.

2868
Portland Women's Foundation
(also known as Battered Women's Foundation)
(formerly Portland Women's Union Foundation)
P.O. Box 4901
Portland, OR 97207-1032

Established as a foundation in 1983 in OR.
Donors: Andy Bryant; Nancy Kay Bryant; Candace Clark Beber; Clark Lewis Family Foundation.
Foundation type: Independent foundation.
Financial data (yr. ended 04/30/13): Assets, $3,145,073 (M); gifts received, $40,505; expenditures, $226,793; qualifying distributions, $198,755; giving activities include $191,303 for 24 grants (high: $35,000; low: $5,000).
Purpose and activities: Giving primarily to benefit women in the areas of housing and education for self-sufficiency.
Fields of interest: Education; Housing/shelter, development; Human services; Women, centers/services; Women; Economically disadvantaged.
Type of support: Annual campaigns; Technical assistance; In-kind gifts.
Limitations: Applications accepted. Giving limited to the Tri-County area of Multnomah, including Clackamas and Washington counties, OR. No support for research projects, or resource or data banks, services that do not directly benefit women, or for childcare. No grants to individuals, or for start up costs.
Publications: Application guidelines.
Application information: Copies of financial statements for the past two years are required. Application form required.
***Initial approach:* Completed application form**
Copies of proposal: 1
Deadline(s): Nov. 15
Board meeting date(s): Sept., Oct., Nov., Jan. and Mar.
Officers: Mary Roberts, Pres.; Cynthia Griffin,* Secy.; Marcella McGee, Treas.
Board Members: Verna Bailey; **Lynne Bangsund**; Alice Bergman; **Cobi Jackson**; Martha Gazley; **Nicole Deering**; Cathie Glennon; Gundrun Granholm; Stephanie Knight; Karen Nelson; Anne Noell; Dana Plautz; Dianne Redd; Kimberlee Sheng; Christy Stockton; Jeanne Teisher; Megan Wentworth; Sonia Worcel.
EIN: 930386905
Other changes: Mary Roberts has replaced Lynne Bangsund as Pres.

2869
The Renaissance Foundation
(formerly The Levin Family Foundation)
P.O. Box 80516
Portland, OR 97280-1516
Main URL: http://www.trfwebsite.org
Application address: Renaissance Scholarship Applications, Attn: The Renaissance Foundation, 8405 SW Nimbus Ave., Ste. D, Beaverton, OR 97008, tel.: (971) 722-6119, e-mail: josh.laurie@pcc.edu

Established in 2000 in OR.
Donors: Irving J. Levin; Frenda Levin.
Foundation type: Independent foundation.
Financial data (yr. ended 12/31/12): Assets, $12,705,246 (M); expenditures, $670,570; qualifying distributions, $593,010; giving activities include $589,400 for 60 grants (high: $124,217; low: $500).
Purpose and activities: Giving primarily for education, human services, and the environment. The foundation also offers a renewable scholarship awarded to first generation college freshmen and sophomores who demonstrate financial need, a passion for their field of study, and who have shown academic achievement. Scholarships are renewable for up to 4 years provided the recipient maintains a 3.0 GPA or better and completes 12 or more credits each term.
Fields of interest: Arts; Higher education; Education; Environment; Human services; Children/youth, services; Jewish agencies & synagogues.
Type of support: General/operating support; Scholarship funds.
Limitations: Giving primarily in Portland, OR. **No grants to individuals (directly).**
Publications: Application guidelines.
Application information: See foundation web site for scholarship application information. Scholarships paid directly to educational institutions.
Initial approach: For first-time applicants: Letter of Inquiry (no more than 2 pages in font size 12); for previous grant recipients: proposal
Final notification: Within 3-6 months for proposals
Trustees: Stephanie J. Fowler; Diana Hoff; Irving J. Levin.
EIN: 931306116

2870
Anne & Eli Shapira Charitable Foundation
7327 S.W. Barnes Rd., No. 124
Portland, OR 97225-6119 **(877) 586-9416**
Contact: Robert Thompson, Grant Admin.
***FAX:* (877) 586-9416;**
E-mail: robbt@shapirafoundation.org; Main URL: http://www.shapirafoundation.org
Grants List: http://www.shapirafoundation.org/newsinfo.html

Established in 2000 in OR.
Donor: Elijahu Shapira.
Foundation type: Independent foundation.
Financial data (yr. ended 12/31/12): Assets, $2,262,122 (M); expenditures, $299,854; qualifying distributions, $291,586; giving activities include $235,006 for 22 grants (high: $50,000; low: $948).
Purpose and activities: The focus of the foundation is to provide strong family support including tutoring, mentoring and counseling services to disadvantaged families and individuals, to improve educational opportunities for disadvantaged and/or disabled individuals, and to enhance the healthy development of individuals faced with disadvantages or disabilities that may hinder their quality of life.
Fields of interest: Language (foreign); Education, special; Scholarships/financial aid; Human services; Youth, services.
Limitations: Giving primarily in OR. No support for athletic teams, or political or religious organizations. No grants to individuals, or for capital campaigns, fundraisers, debt reduction drives, or lobbying activities.
Application information: After letter of inquiry is reviewed, foundation will invite full applications. Unsolicited full applications will not be accepted. See foundation web site for additional policies and guidelines. Application form required.
Initial approach: Letter of inquiry (1-2 pages)
Copies of proposal: 1
Trustees: Anne L. Shapira; Elijahu Shapira.
EIN: 931306729

2871
Simple Actions Family Foundation
8045 N.W. Skillings Dr.
Corvallis, OR 97330-2724
Main URL: http://simpleactionsfamilyfoundation.org/
Grants List: http://www.simpleactionsfamilyfoundation.org/archive

Established in 2008 in OR.
Donors: Eric Helpenstell; Bonnie Helpenstell.
Foundation type: Independent foundation.
Financial data (yr. ended 12/31/12): Assets, $915,410 (M); gifts received, $480,000; expenditures, $343,120; qualifying distributions,

$336,450; giving activities include $336,450 for grants.
Fields of interest: Education; Mental health/crisis services; Housing/shelter.
Limitations: Applications not accepted. Giving primarily in OR.
Application information: Unsolicited requests for funds not accepted.
Officers: Bonnie Helpenstell, Pres.; Lily Helpenstell, V.P.; Emily Helpenstell, Secy.; Eric Helpenstell, Treas.
EIN: 263209131

2872
Storms Family Foundation
PMB 325, 25 N.W. 23rd Pl., Ste. 6
Portland, OR 97210-5580
Main URL: http://www.stormsfamilyfoundation.org
Grants List: http://www.stormsfamilyfoundation.org/past-grants/2013.aspx
Grants List: http://www.stormsfamilyfoundation.org/past-grants/2012.aspx
Grants List: http://www.stormsfamilyfoundation.org/past-grants/2011.aspx

Foundation type: Independent foundation.
Financial data (yr. ended 12/31/12): Assets, $7,776,222 (M); expenditures, $528,177; qualifying distributions, $476,896; giving activities include $399,706 for 23 grants (high: $42,000; low: $2,500).
Purpose and activities: The focus of the foundation is respect for life.
Fields of interest: Human services; Family services.
Limitations: Applications accepted. Giving primarily in OR; with some giving to AZ.
Application information: Application guidelines available on foundation web site. Application form required.
Officers: Suzanne Storms Millis, Pres.; Rosemary Storms Montgomery, Secy.; Anna Storms Ingram, Treas.
EIN: 262020553

2873
TeamCFA Foundation
311B Ave., Ste. M
Lake Oswego, OR 97034
***Main URL:* http://teamcfa.org/**
Twitter: https://twitter.com/teamcfa

Donors: Challenge Foundation, Inc.; Louis Calder Foundation; Kenneth Levy.
Foundation type: Operating foundation.
Financial data (yr. ended 12/31/12): Assets, $558,166 (M); gifts received, $2,609,439; expenditures, $2,067,949; qualifying distributions, $1,772,381; giving activities include $871,200 for 11 grants (high: $187,618; low: $3,900).
Fields of interest: Secondary school/education.
Limitations: Applications not accepted.
Application information: Unsolicited requests for funds not accepted.
Officers and Directors:* **Alfred C. Eckert III, Chair.**; Joseph A. Maimone,* Pres.; Joan Lange, Secy.; William M. Steinbrook, Jr.,* Treas.; **Ruppert Reinstadler**; **Ryan Stowers**; **Abigail Thernstrom**.
EIN: 262778821

2874
Herbert A. Templeton Foundation
0650 S.W. Gaines St., Ste. 1102
Portland, OR 97239 (503) 223-0036
Contact: Ruth B. Richmond, Pres.

Incorporated in 1955 in OR.
Donors: Herbert A. Templeton†; Herbert A. Templeson Trust for robert Templeson.
Foundation type: Independent foundation.
Financial data (yr. ended 12/31/13): Assets, $23,594,796 (M); expenditures, $1,277,809; qualifying distributions, $1,117,637; giving activities include $1,013,850 for 135 grants (high: $25,000; low: $1,900).
Purpose and activities: Grants for youth, cultural, and social service organizations operating in Oregon, or having programs significantly affecting Oregon residents; present emphasis on program and direct services.
Fields of interest: Arts; Education, early childhood education; Human services; Children/youth, services; Children/youth; Youth.
Type of support: General/operating support; Continuing support; Emergency funds; Program development; Seed money.
Limitations: Applications accepted. Giving limited to OR. No support for medical services, the aged, or parochial education. No grants to individuals, or for fellowships, building or endowment funds, scientific research or technology, matching gifts, or medical or medically-related programs; no loans or program-related investments.
Publications: Application guidelines; Program policy statement.
Application information: Application form required.
Initial approach: Letter
Copies of proposal: 1
Deadline(s): Mar. 15 and Sept. 15 (no later than 5:00pm on deadline days)
Board meeting date(s): Feb., May, Sept. and Nov.
Officers and Trustees:* Ruth B. Richmond,* Pres.; Henry R. Richmond,* V.P.; Terrence R. Pancoast,* Secy.; **Jimmie Perkins,* Treas.**; Margaret Eickmann; Linda McKinley Girard; Christian T. Richmond.
Number of staff: 2 part-time professional.
EIN: 930505586
Other changes: Jimmie Perkins has replaced Loren L. Wyss as Treas.

2875
Merle S. & Emma J. West Scholarship Fund
(also known as West Scholarship Fund)
c/o U.S. Bank, N.A.
P.O. Box 3168
Portland, OR 97208-3168 **(541) 883-3857**
***Contact:* Rebecca Bibleheimer, Trust Off.**
***E-mail for Rebecca Bibleheimer:* rebecca.bibleheimer@usbank.com**; Main URL: http://www.merlewestscholarship.com

Established around 1984 in OR.
Foundation type: Independent foundation.
Financial data (yr. ended 12/31/12): Assets, $3,525,285 (M); gifts received, $200; expenditures, $212,154; qualifying distributions, $166,047; giving activities include $157,641 for grants.
Purpose and activities: Giving primarily for scholarship funds available to graduates of Klamath County, Oregon, high schools.
Fields of interest: Education.
Type of support: Scholarship funds.
Limitations: Applications accepted. Giving limited to residents of Klamath County, OR.
Publications: Application guidelines.
Application information: Application form available on fund web site. See fund's web site for complete application guidelines.
***Initial approach:* Submit application online or by mail**
***Deadline(s):* Varies**
Trustee: U.S. Bank, N.A.
EIN: 936160221
Other changes: The grantmaker now publishes application guidelines.

2876
Western Lane Community Foundation
(formerly Western Lane County Foundation)
1525 W. 12th St., Ste. 18
P.O. Box 1589
Florence, OR 97439-8482 (541) 997-1274
***Contact:* Gayle Waiss, Exec. Dir.**
FAX: (541) 997-1274; E-mail: wlcf@oregonfast.net; Main URL: http://www.wlcfonline.org/
E-Newsletter: http://www.wlcfonline.org/newsletter.html

Established in 1974.
Foundation type: Community foundation.
Financial data (yr. ended 12/31/12): Assets, $5,046,814 (M); gifts received, $36,139; expenditures, $282,457; giving activities include $185,195 for grants, and $24,309 for grants to individuals.
Purpose and activities: The foundation seeks to improve life in Western Lane County, OR, and promote effective philanthropy.
Fields of interest: Arts; Education; Health care; Community development, neighborhood development; Science.
Type of support: Building/renovation; Equipment; Endowments; Program development; Seed money; Scholarships—to individuals.
Limitations: Applications accepted. Giving limited to Western Lane County, OR, defined as the Mapleton and Siuslaw school districts. No support for sectarian religious purposes. No grants to individuals (except for scholarships), or for emergency funding, travel to or in support of conferences, debt retirement or operational deficits, or annual fund drives or operation expenses (except during a start up period not to exceed three years).
Publications: Application guidelines; Annual report; Informational brochure; Newsletter; Program policy statement.
Application information: Visit foundation web site for application form and guidelines. Application form required.
Initial approach: Submit application
Copies of proposal: 11
Deadline(s): Jan. 15
Board meeting date(s): Monthly
Officers and Directors:* Cindy Cable,* Pres.; Dr. Ray Mans,* V.P.; Pat Stewart,* Secy.; Roger McCorkle,* Treas.; Gayle Waiss, Exec. Dir.; **Tom Bassett**; **Lis Farm**; Dee Osborne; Vicki Sieber-Benson; **Nancy Walker**.
EIN: 237438503
Other changes: Dan Gilday and Ray Mans are no longer directors.

2877
The Woodard Family Foundation
(also known as Woodard Family Foundation)

P.O. Box 10666
Eugene, OR 97440 **(541) 343-9402**
Contact: Tyson Woodard, Dir.
***FAX:* (541) 343-0122;**
E-mail: wffstaff@woodardff.com; Main URL: http://www.woodardff.com

Incorporated in 1952 in OR.
Donors: Walter A. Woodard†; Carlton Woodard.
Foundation type: Independent foundation.
Financial data (yr. ended 06/30/13): Assets, $8,676,276 (M); expenditures, $783,509; qualifying distributions, $636,675; giving activities include $636,675 for grants.
Purpose and activities: It is the desire of the foundation to assist charitable organizations in developing the internal capacity to meet present and future needs; not to remove responsibilities from people.
Fields of interest: Arts; Higher education; Business school/education; Education; Human services; Community/economic development.
Type of support: General/operating support; Annual campaigns; Capital campaigns; Building/renovation; Land acquisition; Program development; Professorships; Seed money; Consulting services.
Limitations: Applications accepted. Giving limited to local organizations in the greater Cottage Grove/Eugene, OR, area.
Publications: Application guidelines.
Application information: See foundation web site for complete application guidelines. Application form required.
Initial approach: Letter request, or contact foundation for application form
Copies of proposal: 1
Board meeting date(s): Quarterly
Officers and Directors:* Tod Woodard,* Pres.; Andrew Woodard,* V.P. and Treas.; Pepper Woodard Bridgens,* Secy.; Dena Woodard McCoy; Carlton Woodard; Joy Woodard; Kim Woodard; Kristen A. Woodard; Tyson Woodard.
Number of staff: 1 part-time professional; 1 part-time support.
EIN: 936026550

2878
The Wyss Foundation
620 S.W. 5th Ave., Ste. 1010
Portland, OR 97204-1424
E-mail: lwyss@aol.com

Established in 1989 in OR.
Donors: Judith Wyss; Loren L. Wyss.
Foundation type: Independent foundation.
Financial data (yr. ended 04/30/13): Assets, $5,921,848 (M); expenditures, $198,462; qualifying distributions, $197,702; giving activities include $169,800 for 67 grants (high: $6,000; low: $1,000).
Fields of interest: Arts; Education; Environment; Animals/wildlife, association; Human services.
International interests: United Kingdom.
Type of support: General/operating support; Program development.
Limitations: Applications not accepted. Giving primarily in CA, and the Portland, OR, area. No support for political causes, medical research or for lobbying groups. No grants to individuals.
Application information: Unsolicited requests for funds not accepted.
Officer: Judith Wyss, Pres. and Treas.
Directors: James Damis; Edmund J. Wyss; Emily A. Wyss; Isabel J. Wyss; Jennifer A. Wyss-Jones.
Number of staff: None.
EIN: 931010019
Other changes: Judith Wyss has replaced Loren L. Wyss as Pres. and Treas.

PENNSYLVANIA

2879
100 Acre Wood Foundation
201 S. Hellertown Ave.
Quakertown, PA **18951-1768**

Established in 2000 in PA.
Donors: Kenneth F. Brown; Pamela H. Brown.
Foundation type: Independent foundation.
Financial data (yr. ended 04/30/13): Assets, $789,719 (M); expenditures, $206,382; qualifying distributions, $201,240; giving activities include $201,240 for 7 grants (high: $126,870; low: $1,250).
Purpose and activities: Giving primarily to a YMCA, as well as for human services.
Fields of interest: Human services; YM/YWCAs & YM/YWHAs; Child development, services.
Limitations: Applications not accepted. Giving primarily in Quakertown, PA. No grants to individuals.
Application information: Unsolicited requests for funds not accepted.
Trustees: Kenneth F. Brown; Pamela H. Brown; Shawn P. Brown.
EIN: 256714457

2880
ACE Charitable Foundation
(formerly ACE INA Foundation)
436 Walnut St., WA 08G
Philadelphia, PA 19106-3786
Contact: Eden Kratchman, Exec. Dir.
E-mail: acecharitablefoundation@acegroup.com; Main URL: http://www.acegroup.com/About-ACE/Philanthropy/Philanthropy.html

Established in 2007 in PA.
Donor: ACE American Insurance Co.
Foundation type: Company-sponsored foundation.
Financial data (yr. ended 12/31/12): Assets, $2,961,688 (M); gifts received, $1,370,441; expenditures, $1,950,246; qualifying distributions, $1,940,651; giving activities include $1,379,674 for 66 grants (high: $250,000; low: $75), and $560,977 for 1,104 employee matching gifts.
Purpose and activities: The foundation supports organizations involved with education, poverty and health, and the environment. Special consideration is given to opportunities where ACE employees' time and expertise can be utilized in addition to financial support.
Fields of interest: Museums; Higher education; Education; Environment, water resources; Environment, land resources; Environment; Health care; Food services; Food banks; Disasters, preparedness/services; American Red Cross; International development; International relief; United Ways and Federated Giving Programs; Economically disadvantaged.
Type of support: Scholarship funds; General/operating support; Program development; Employee volunteer services; Employee matching gifts.
Limitations: Giving on a national and international basis in areas of company operations (outside of Bermuda), with some emphasis on Philadelphia, PA.
Application information:
Initial approach: E-mail foundation for application guidelines
Deadline(s): None
Officers and Directors:* **Evan Greenberg,* Chair. and C.E.O.**; Brian Dowd,* Exec. V.P.; John Keogh,* Exec. V.P.; Lori Samson,* V.P.; Kathryn Schneider, Secy.; Joseph Jordan, Treas.; Eden M. Kratchman, Exec. Dir.; Robert Hernandez.
EIN: 262456949
Other changes: Evan Greenberg is now Chair. and C.E.O.

2881
Adams Foundation Inc.
c/o Abarta, Inc.
1000 Gamma Dr., 5th Fl
Pittsburgh, PA 15238-2929 (412) 963-1087
Contact: **Shelley M. Taylor, Pres. and Tr.**

Incorporated in 1955 in PA.
Donors: Rolland L. Adams†; ABARTA Inc.
Foundation type: Company-sponsored foundation.
Financial data (yr. ended 12/31/12): Assets, $1,905,422 (M); expenditures, $178,395; qualifying distributions, $176,250; giving activities include $176,250 for grants.
Purpose and activities: The foundation supports food banks and civic centers and organizations involved with arts and culture, education, mental health, and arthritis.
Fields of interest: Performing arts, ballet; Performing arts, theater; Arts; Higher education; Education; Mental health/crisis services; Arthritis; Food banks; Community development, civic centers.
Type of support: General/operating support.
Limitations: Applications accepted. Giving primarily in Ithaca, NY and Pittsburgh, PA. No grants to individuals.
Application information: Application form required.
Initial approach: **Letter**
Copies of proposal: 1
Deadline(s): None
Officers and Trustees:* Shelley M. Taylor,* Pres.; Mary R. Hudson,* Secy.; James A. Taylor,* Treas.
EIN: 240866511
Other changes: Shelley M. Taylor has replaced Nancy A. Taylor as Pres. Mary R. Hudson has replaced Shelley A. Taylor as Secy.

2882
Alcoa Foundation
Alcoa Corporate Ctr.
201 Isabella St.
Pittsburgh, PA 15212-5858
Main URL: http://www.alcoa.com/global/en/community/foundation.asp
E-Newsletter: http://www.alcoa.com/global/en/community/foundation/info_page/newsletters.asp
Facebook: http://www.facebook.com/alcoamonthofservice
Grants Database: http://www.alcoa.com/global/en/community/foundation/grants.asp
Twitter: https://twitter.com/alcoafoundation
YouTube: http://www.youtube.com/alcoatv

Trust established in 1952 in PA; incorporated in 1964.
Donors: Alcoa Corp.; Aluminum Co. of America; Alcoa Inc.
Foundation type: Company-sponsored foundation.
Financial data (yr. ended 12/31/12): Assets, $460,142,329 (M); gifts received, $500,000; expenditures, $24,816,126; qualifying distributions, $23,143,326; giving activities include $21,517,932 for 1,070 grants.
Purpose and activities: The foundation supports programs designed to engage people to improve the environment, educate tomorrow's leaders, and enhance communities where Alcoa operates around the world.
Fields of interest: Higher education; Teacher school/education; Adult/continuing education; Education, services; Education; Environment, public policy; Environment, pollution control; Environment, waste management; Environment, recycling; Environment, climate change/global warming; Environment, natural resources; Environment, water resources; Environment, land resources; Environment, energy; Environment, forests; Environmental education; Environment; Employment, services; Employment, training; Employment; Disasters, preparedness/services; Safety/disasters; Recreation, parks/playgrounds; Girl scouts; Youth development, business; Youth development; American Red Cross; Children/youth, services; Urban/community development; Mathematics; Engineering/technology; Science; Transportation; Minorities; Women; Girls.
International interests: Africa; Asia; Australia; Caribbean; Central America; Europe; Mexico; South America.
Type of support: Continuing support; Management development/capacity building; Annual campaigns; Building/renovation; Equipment; Emergency funds; Program development; Conferences/seminars; Curriculum development; Scholarship funds; Research; Employee volunteer services; Sponsorships; Employee matching gifts; Employee-related scholarships; Matching/challenge support.
Limitations: Applications accepted. Giving on a national and international basis in areas of company operations, with emphasis on New York, NY, Pittsburgh, PA, Africa, Asia, Australia, Brazil, Canada, Caribbean, China, Central America, Europe, Mexico, Russia, and South America. No support for political or lobbying organizations, sectarian or religious organizations not of direct benefit to the entire community, discriminatory organizations, social clubs or organizations, sports teams, private foundations, or trust funds. No grants to individuals (except for employee-related scholarships), or for endowments, capital campaigns, debt reduction, operating costs or reserves, indirect or overhead costs, fundraising events or sponsorships including walks/runs, golf tournaments, tickets, tables, benefits, raffles, souvenir programs, advertising, or fundraising dinners, trips, conferences, seminars, festivals, one-day events, documentaries, videos, or research projects/programs.
Publications: Application guidelines; Corporate giving report; Grants list; Newsletter; Program policy statement.
Application information: The minimum grant request is $15,000. Selected applicants will be invited to submit an online application. Organizations receiving support are asked to submit interim reports and a final report.
Initial approach: Proposal to nearest company facility
Copies of proposal: 1
Deadline(s): Contact nearest company facility
Board meeting date(s): Monthly
Officers and Directors:* Esra Ozer,* Pres.; Dean Will, Cont. and Business Mgr.; Micheal T. (Mike) Barriere; John (Jack) D. Bergen; Alan Cransberg; Franklin L. (Frank) Feder; Shauna Huang; Lysane Martel; Tim D. Myers; William J. O'Rourke; William F. (Bill) Oplin; Shannon Parks; Rosa Garcia Pineiro; **Vitaliy V. Rusakov**; Maxim Smirnov.
Corporate Trustee: The Bank of New York Mellon, N.A.
Number of staff: 6 full-time professional; 1 full-time support.
EIN: 251128857

Other changes: Esra Ozer has replaced Paul Davis as Pres.
Nicholas J. Ashooh and no longer and Chris L. Ayers are no longer directors. Paula Davis is no longer Pres.

2883
Allegheny Foundation
1 Oxford Ctr.
301 Grant St., Ste. 3900
Pittsburgh, PA 15219-6401 (412) 392-2900
Contact: Matthew A. Groll, Exec. Dir.
Main URL: http://www.scaife.com/alleghen.html

Incorporated in 1953 in PA.
Donor: Richard M. Scaife†.
Foundation type: Independent foundation.
Financial data (yr. ended 12/31/12): Assets, $55,943,723 (M); gifts received, $1,000,000; expenditures, $3,319,075; qualifying distributions, $3,025,162; giving activities include $2,568,000 for 40 grants (high: $210,000; low: $3,000).
Purpose and activities: Giving primarily for historic preservation, education, and community development.
Fields of interest: Historic preservation/historical societies; Education; Youth development; Community development, neighborhood development.
Type of support: General/operating support; Program development; Seed money.
Limitations: Applications accepted. Giving primarily in western PA, with emphasis on Pittsburgh. No grants to individuals, or for endowment funds, event sponsorship, capital campaigns, renovations, government agencies, scholarships, or fellowships; no loans.
Publications: Application guidelines; Annual report.
Application information: Application form not required.
Initial approach: Letter
Copies of proposal: 1
Deadline(s): None
Board meeting date(s): Nov.
Final notification: 4-6 weeks
Officers and Trustees:* Matthew A. Groll, Exec. Dir.; Joanne B. Beyer; Ralph H. Goettler; Doris O'Donnell; Jane Roesch; George Weymouth; Arthur P. Ziegler, Jr.
Number of staff: 1 part-time professional; 1 full-time support.
EIN: 256012303
Other changes: Richard M. Scaife, Chair. and Donor, is deceased.

2884
Harriett Ames Charitable Trust
c/o PNC Bank, N.A.
1600 Market St., 29th Fl.
Philadelphia, PA 19103-7240

Trust established in 1952 in NY.
Donor: Harriett Ames†.
Foundation type: Independent foundation.
Financial data (yr. ended 12/31/12): Assets, $2,185,455 (M); expenditures, $3,478,840; qualifying distributions, $3,459,915; giving activities include $3,459,915 for 39 grants (high: $3,009,615; low: $1,000).
Purpose and activities: Giving primarily for the arts, particularly to art museums, education, and health.
Fields of interest: Museums; Museums (art); Arts; Higher education; Education; Animal welfare; Hospitals (general); Health organizations, association; Human services; Jewish agencies & synagogues.
Type of support: General/operating support; Annual campaigns.
Limitations: Applications not accepted. Giving primarily in the metropolitan New York, NY, area and in Philadelphia, PA. No grants to individuals.
Application information: Contributes only to pre-selected organizations. Unsolicited requests for funds not considered.
Board meeting date(s): Varies
Trustee: Steven Ames.
EIN: 236286757
Other changes: At the close of 2012, the grantmaker paid grants of $3,459,915, a 375.6% increase over the 2011 disbursements, $727,500.

2885
Arkema Inc. Foundation
(formerly Atofina Chemicals, Inc. Foundation)
900 First Ave.
King of Prussia, PA 19406-1308 (215) 419-7735
Contact: Diane Milici, Admin.
E-mail: diane.milici@arkema.com; **Main URL: http://www.arkema-americas.com/en/social-responsibility/local-programs/arkema-inc.-foundation/index.html**

Trust established in 1957 in PA.
Donors: Elf Atochem North America, Inc.; Atofina Chemicals, Inc.; Arkema Inc.
Foundation type: Company-sponsored foundation.
Financial data (yr. ended 12/31/12): Assets, $280,820 (M); gifts received, $190,000; expenditures, $278,312; qualifying distributions, $272,562; giving activities include $240,062 for 67 grants (high: $33,200; low: $500), and $32,500 for 66 grants to individuals (high: $500; low: $300).
Purpose and activities: The foundation supports organizations involved with arts and culture, education, and civic affairs. Special emphasis is directed toward programs designed to advance elementary school science education.
Fields of interest: Media/communications; Museums; Arts; Elementary school/education; Higher education; Education; United Ways and Federated Giving Programs; Science; Public affairs.
Type of support: General/operating support; Continuing support; Annual campaigns; Building/renovation; Equipment; Emergency funds; Employee matching gifts; Employee-related scholarships; Matching/challenge support.
Limitations: Applications accepted. Giving primarily in areas of company operations, with some emphasis on the Philadelphia, PA, area; giving in Axis, AL, Calvert City, Carrollton, and Louisville, KY, Blooming Prairie, MN, Geneseo, NY, Birdsboro, PA, Memphis, TN, and Beaumont, Crosby, and Houston, TX for the Science Teacher Program. No support for veterans', fraternal, labor, or sectarian religious organizations, or sports teams. No grants to individuals (except for employee-related scholarships), or for endowments, special projects, research, publications, conferences, courtesy advertising, entertainment promotions, event sponsorships, public education, athletic competitions, or political causes or campaigns; no loans.
Publications: Application guidelines.
Application information: Letters of inquiry should be no longer than 2 pages. Application form not required.
Initial approach: Letter of inquiry; download application form and mail to nearest participating company facility for Science Teacher Program
Copies of proposal: 1
Deadline(s): None
Board meeting date(s): Mar., June, Sept., and Dec.
Final notification: 1 to 3 months
Trustees: Ryan Dirkx; Chris Giangrasso; Bernard Roche.
Number of staff: 1 part-time professional.
EIN: 236256818

2886
Dexter F. and Dorothy H. Baker Foundation
3440 Lehigh St.
P.O. Box 290
Allentown, PA **18103-7001 (610) 533-2837**
Contact: Ellen B. Ghelardi, Exec. Dir.
FAX: (610) 481-5450; **E-mail: baker1ebb@aol.com**

Established in 1986 in PA.
Donors: Dexter F. Baker; Dorothy H. Baker.
Foundation type: Independent foundation.
Financial data (yr. ended 12/31/12): Assets, $16,978,703 (M); expenditures, $880,132; qualifying distributions, $853,672; giving activities include $783,375 for 35 grants (high: $125,000; low: $500).
Purpose and activities: Giving primarily for arts and culture, youth, education, and social service initiatives.
Fields of interest: Arts education; Visual arts; Performing arts; Higher education; Social entrepreneurship; United Ways and Federated Giving Programs; Youth.
Type of support: General/operating support; Continuing support; Management development/capacity building; Annual campaigns; Capital campaigns; Equipment; Program development; Conferences/seminars; Film/video/radio; Curriculum development; Scholarship funds; Technical assistance; Matching/challenge support.
Limitations: Applications accepted. Giving primarily in Lehigh, and Northampton counties, PA, trustee endorsed grants in Collier, County FL, Hilton Head, SC, Syracuse, NY, Dallas, TX, San Francisco, CA, and Philadelphia, PA, only. No support for non-Presbyterian religious organizations, for government or for political organizations. No grants to individuals, or for endowment funds or for debt reduction.
Publications: Application guidelines.
Application information: Application form required.
***Initial approach:* Contact Ellen Baker Ghelardi to request guidelines**
Copies of proposal: 1
Deadline(s): Letter of intent deadline: Mar. 15th; Invited applicants, July 15th
Board meeting date(s): Nov.
Final notification: Dec. 1
Officers and Trustees:* Dorothy H. Baker,* Chair.; Leslie Baker Boris,* Secy.; Ellen Baker Ghelardi,* Exec. Dir.; Carolyn Baker; Susan B. Royal.
Number of staff: 1 full-time professional; 1 part-time support.
EIN: 232453230
Other changes: Dorothy H. Baker has replaced Dexter F. Baker as Chair.
Dexter F. Baker, Chair., is deceased.

2887
Barra Foundation, Inc.
200 W. Lancaster Ave., Ste. 202
Wayne, PA 19087-4046 (610) 964-7601
Contact: Kristina Wahl, Pres.
***FAX:* (610) 964-0155**;
E-mail: kwahl@barrafoundation.org; E-mail address for Kristi Poling, Prog. Off.: kpoling@barrafoundation.org; e-mail address for Kate Houstoun, Prog. Off.: khoustoun@barrafoundation.org; e-mail address for Stephanie Mullen, Admin. Asst.: smullen@barrafoundation.org; Main URL: http://www.barrafoundation.org/

Incorporated in 1963 in DE.
Donor: Robert L. McNeil, Jr.
Foundation type: Independent foundation.
Financial data (yr. ended 12/31/12): Assets, $88,047,212 (M); gifts received, $1,853,507; expenditures, $5,172,006; qualifying distributions, $4,768,145; giving activities include $4,241,196 for 423 grants (high: $800,000; low: $1,000).
Purpose and activities: The foundation seeks to support and encourage innovation, a key element to discovering new and more effective ways to serve the ever-changing needs in communities. It funds organizations and projects that enable the foundation to achieve greater social impact in the Philadelphia five-county region through strategic grantmaking in the areas of arts and culture, education, health, and human services. The foundation pursues two goals in its grantmaking: 1) to advance the health, education, well-being, achievement, and life prospects of low-income, underserved individuals and communities, and 2) to enrich the quality of life for all by promoting the sustainability of a vibrant arts and cultural community.
Fields of interest: Arts; Education; Human services.
Type of support: General/operating support; Management development/capacity building; Program development; Consulting services; Program evaluation.
Limitations: Applications accepted. **Giving limited to organizations in the 5 county Philadelphia, PA, area (Bucks, Chester, Delaware, Montgomery and Philadelphia).** No support for religious organizations, or for environmental or preservation groups. No grants to individuals, or for annual or capital campaigns, building or endowment funds, operating budgets, deficit drives, scholarships, fellowships, ongoing programs, publications, catalogues or exhibitions; no loans.
Application information: See foundation web site for complete policies, guidelines and application form. Application form required.
Initial approach: Proposal
Copies of proposal: 1
Deadline(s): None
Board meeting date(s): Dec. and as appropriate
Final notification: 3 to 6 months
Officers and Directors:* Seymour S. Preston III,* Chair.; Kristina Wahl, Pres.; Victoria M. LeVine,* Secy.; Eric C. Andersen; Patrick P. Coyne; A. Louis Denton; William Harral III; Frazierita D. Klasen; Joanna M. Lewis; Collin F. McNeil; Robert L. McNeil III.
Number of staff: 3 full-time professional; 1 part-time support.
EIN: 236277885

2888
Bayer USA Foundation
(formerly Bayer Foundation)
100 Bayer Rd.
Pittsburgh, PA 15205-9741 (412) 777-2000
Contact: Sarah Toulouse, Exec. Dir.
Main URL: http://www.bayerus.com/Foundation/Foundation_Home.aspx

Established in 1985 in PA.
Donor: Bayer Corp.
Foundation type: Company-sponsored foundation.
Financial data (yr. ended 12/31/12): Assets, $42,552,317 (M); gifts received, $9,145,127; expenditures, $6,825,690; qualifying distributions, $6,768,060; giving activities include $6,456,590 for 137 grants (high: $3,000,000; low: $100).
Purpose and activities: The foundation supports programs designed to promote education and workforce development; and the environment and sustainability.
Fields of interest: Museums; Museums (science/technology); Arts; Higher education; Engineering school/education; Education; Environment, energy; Environmental education; Environment; Cancer; Diabetes; Employment, services; Food banks; Housing/shelter; American Red Cross; Youth, services; Human services; Economic development; Community/economic development; Mathematics; Engineering/technology; Science; Youth; Minorities; Women.
Type of support: Continuing support; Capital campaigns; Equipment; Program development; Conferences/seminars; Curriculum development; Scholarship funds.
Limitations: Applications accepted. Giving primarily in areas of company operations in Berkeley and northern CA, Shawnee, KS, Kansas City, MO, Raleigh-Durham, NC, northern NJ, Newark, OH, Allegheny county and Pittsburgh, PA, and Baytown and Houston, TX; giving also to national organizations. No support for discriminatory, political, or religious organizations, primary or secondary schools, or organizations outside of the U.S. No grants to individuals, or for general operating support for United Way affiliated organizations, endowments, debt reduction or operating reserves, charitable dinners, events, sponsorships, conferences, or seminars, community or event advertising, research projects, student trips or exchange programs, athletic sponsorships or scholarships, or telephone solicitations.
Publications: Application guidelines; Program policy statement.
Application information: A full proposal may be requested at a later date. The Bayer USA Foundation application follows the Common Grant application process. Collateral materials including books, binders, videos, CDs, DVDs, programs, brochures, etc. will not be accepted unless specifically requested by the foundation. Application form not required.
Initial approach: Complete online application
Copies of proposal: 1
Deadline(s): None
Board meeting date(s): Feb. and Oct.
Final notification: Following board meetings
Officers and Directors:* Richard K. Heller, V.P., Tax; Robert J. Koch, Secy.; James Martin, Treas.; Sarah Toulouse, Exec. Dir.; Lars Benecke; Andrew J. Diana; Micheal J. McDonald; Elizabeth Roden.
EIN: 251508079
Other changes: Claudio Abreu and Jack Boyne are no longer directors.

2889
Beacon Foundation Inc.
(formerly The Giant Eagle Foundation)
c/o Giant Eagle, Inc.
101 Kappa Dr.
Pittsburgh, PA 15238-2809 (412) 963-6200
Contact: David S. Shapira, Dir.

Established in PA.
Donor: Giant Eagle, Inc.
Foundation type: Company-sponsored foundation.
Financial data (yr. ended 06/30/13): Assets, $46,287,856 (M); expenditures, $517,074; qualifying distributions, $395,494; giving activities include $395,494 for 1 grant.
Purpose and activities: The foundation supports organizations involved with education and Judaism.
Fields of interest: Higher education; Theological school/education; Education; Jewish federated giving programs; Jewish agencies & synagogues.
Type of support: General/operating support; Continuing support; Program development.
Limitations: Applications accepted. Giving primarily in Pittsburgh, PA.
Application information: Application form not required.
Initial approach: Letter of inquiry
Deadline(s): None
Directors: Gerald Chait; Edward Moravitz; Louis Plung; Charles Porter; David S. Shapira; Norman Weizenbaum.
EIN: 202734721

2890
The Beaver County Foundation
P.O. Box 569
Beaver, PA 15009-0569 (724) 728-1331
Contact: Charles O'Data, Pres.
E-mail: cnodata@aol.com; Main URL: http://www.beavercountyfoundation.com

Established in 1992 in PA.
Foundation type: Community foundation.
Financial data (yr. ended 12/31/12): Assets, $6,957,038 (M); gifts received, $380,472; expenditures, $543,916; giving activities include $328,972 for 74+ grants (high: $133,359), and $51,500 for 35 grants to individuals.
Purpose and activities: The mission of the Beaver County Foundation is to create an atmosphere for and an understanding of philanthropy, the love of humankind, in order to preserve and encourage the development of organizations and programs that meet human needs. This has been accomplished by enabling individuals and organizations to build endowments, which, in turn, produce revenues designed to strengthen programs, and events which serve to benefit the people of Beaver County and the surrounding geographic region.
Fields of interest: Arts; Education; Health care; Human services; Community development, neighborhood development; Economic development; Christian agencies & churches; Children/youth; Children.
Type of support: General/operating support; Program development; Scholarship funds; Research; Scholarships—to individuals.
Limitations: Applications accepted. Giving limited to Beaver County, PA; support for pharmacological research or addiction interdiction given nationwide. No grants to individuals (except for scholarships).
Publications: Informational brochure.
Application information: Visit the foundation's web site for more information. Application form required.
Initial approach: Contact foundation by letter, phone or e-mail
Copies of proposal: 1
***Deadline(s):* Apr. 1 and Oct. 1**

Board meeting date(s): May, July, Oct., and Dec.
***Final notification:* generally during the last week of April and the last week of October.**
Officers and Directors:* Charles N. O'Data,* Chair. and Pres.; Yvonne Connor,* Vice-Chair.; **Toni L. Sadecky,* Treas.**; **Theresa M. Laderer, Exec. Dir.**; Jessica Briggs, Genl. Counsel; **Joseph Bauman**; **Richard Blackwood**; **Thomas J. Bryan**; George Juba; Thomas Reed; Richard Shaw; Melvin H. Steals, Ph.D.; Paul Sweeney; Kimberly D. Tomaino; Joseph N. Tosh II; Keith M. Wing.
Number of staff: 1 part-time professional.
EIN: 251660309
Other changes: Toni L. Sadecky has replaced Richard Canonge as Treas. Theresa M. Laderer has replaced Gloria Cheshier as Exec. Dir.
Charles N. O'Data is now Chair. and Pres. Robert J. Campbell, Charles Copeland, Toni Sadecky, and Alex Sebastian are no longer directors.

2891
A.H. Bee Irrevocable Trust

(formerly The Anna and Albert Bee Scholarship Fund)
Philadelphia, PA

The trust terminated in 2012 and transferred its assets to Alexander Bee Scholarship Fund.

2892
Claude Worthington Benedum Foundation

223 4th Ave.
1400 Benedum-Trees Bldg.
Pittsburgh, PA 15222-1713 (412) 288-0360
Contact: William P. Getty, Pres.
FAX: (412) 288-0366; E-mail: info@benedum.org;
Tel. for Grants Admin.: (412) 246-3636; Main URL: http://www.benedum.org
Grants Database: http://www.benedum.org/grants/grants.shtml
Knowledge Center: http://www.benedum.org/pages.cfm?id=17

Incorporated in 1944 in PA.
Donors: Michael Late Benedum†; Sarah N. Benedum†.
Foundation type: Independent foundation.
Financial data (yr. ended 12/31/12): Assets, $348,280,507 (M); expenditures, $18,401,160; qualifying distributions, $16,599,817; giving activities include $14,262,325 for 163 grants (high: $500,000; low: $4,000), $25,000 for foundation-administered programs and $325,000 for 2 loans/program-related investments (high: $200,000; low: $125,000).
Purpose and activities: The foundation makes grants in three program areas that spans its geographic areas of interest, West Virginia, and in Southwestern Pennsylvania: education, civic engagement, and economic development. In addition, the Foundation supports community development and health & human services grants programs in West Virginia, and in Southwestern Pennsylvania supports the major performing arts organizations within the cultural district. The Foundation recognizes that economic regions do not follow political boundaries, and therefore, the foundation both encourages projects that cross state lines, and supports economic initiatives that benefit the multi-state economy centered on Pittsburgh.
Fields of interest: Education; Health care; Human services; Economic development; Community/economic development.
Type of support: Management development/capacity building; Program development; Seed money; Technical assistance; Matching/challenge support.
Limitations: Applications accepted. Giving limited to southwestern PA and WV. No support for biomedical research, national organizations, or individual elementary or secondary schools. No grants to individuals, or for student aid, fellowships, travel, ongoing operating expenses, annual appeals, membership drives, conferences, films, books, or audio-visual productions (unless an integral part of a foundation supported program), or for construction, equipment, religious activities or endowments.
Publications: Annual report (including application guidelines).
Application information: Applicants should submit applications using the foundation's online grant application process found on the foundation's web site.If one does not have the ability to submit online, please contact the Grants Admin. Application form not required.
Initial approach: Online application
Copies of proposal: 1
Deadline(s): None
Board meeting date(s): Mar., June, Sept., and Dec.
Final notification: Within 60 days
Officers and Trustees:* Lloyd G. Jackson II,* Chair.; William P. Getty,* Pres.; Dwight M. Keating, V.P. and C.I.O.; James V. Denova, V.P.; Rose A. McKee, Secy. and Dir., Admin.; Lori Lordo, Treas.; Ralph J. Bean, Jr., Tr. Emeritus; Gaston Caperton, Honorary Tr.; L. Newton Thomas, Tr. Emeritus; G. Randolph Worls, Tr. Emeritus; Esther L. Barazzone; G. Nicholas Beckwith III; Paul G. Benedum, Jr.; Thomas A. Heywood; Parween S. Mascari; Robert B. Walker, M.D.
Number of staff: 7 full-time professional; 2 part-time professional; 3 full-time support.
EIN: 251086799
Other changes: Lloyd G. Jackson II has replaced Paul G. Benedum Jr. as Chair.

2893
Berks County Community Foundation

237 Court St.
Reading, PA 19601 (610) 685-2223
***Contact:* Kevin K. Murphy, Pres.; For grants: Heidi Williamson, V.P., Grantmaking and Comms.**
FAX: (610) 685-2240; E-mail: info@bccf.org; **Grant program e-mail: heidiw@bccf.org; Finance e-mail: frankia@bccf.org**; Main URL: http://www.bccf.org
E-Newsletter: http://www.bccf.org/index.php?option=com_content&view=article&id=371&Itemid=248
LinkedIn: http://www.linkedin.com/companies/berks-county-community-foundation
YouTube: http://www.youtube.com/user/bccfor

Established in 1994 in PA.
Foundation type: Community foundation.
Financial data (yr. ended 06/30/12): Assets, $51,964,330 (M); gifts received, $11,000,038; expenditures, $4,661,722; giving activities include $2,329,465 for 68 grants (high: $260,000; low: $100), $567,020 for 287 grants to individuals (high: $24,474), $31,499 for 7 loans to individuals (high: $5,000; low: $1,458), $906,760 for foundation-administered programs and $2,132,020 for 10 loans/program-related investments (high: $500,000; low: $9,600).
Purpose and activities: The mission of the foundation is to promote philanthropy and improve the quality of life for the residents of Berks County, PA.
Fields of interest: Arts, cultural/ethnic awareness; Historic preservation/historical societies; Arts; Higher education; Education; Environment; Animals/wildlife; Health care; Youth development; Community development, neighborhood development; Economic development; Community/economic development; Aging.
Type of support: Fellowships; Capital campaigns; Program development; Conferences/seminars; Seed money; Scholarship funds; Research; Consulting services; Program-related investments/loans; Employee-related scholarships; Grants to individuals; Scholarships—to individuals; Matching/challenge support.
Limitations: Applications accepted. Giving limited to Berks County, PA for discretionary funds. No support for religious organizations from discretionary funds. No grants for operational support.
Publications: Application guidelines; Annual report; Financial statement; Grants list; Newsletter.
Application information: Visit foundation web site for additional information. Application form required.
Initial approach: Telephone or e-mail
Copies of proposal: 1
Deadline(s): Varies
Board meeting date(s): Feb., Apr., June, Aug., Oct., and Dec.
Officers and Directors:* J. William Widing III, Esq.*, Chair.; P. Sue Perrotty,* Vice-Chair.; Kevin K. Murphy,* Pres.; **Frances A. Aitken,* Sr. V.P., Finance and Opers. and Treas.**; Heidi Williamson, V.P., Comms. and Grantmaking; Jay R. Wagner, Esq.,* Secy.; Latisha Bernard Schuenemann,* Asst. Treas.; James S. Boscov; **Eric Burkey**; **P. Michael Ehlerman**; James A. Gilmartin; Charles Haddad, Esq.; Kathleen D. Herbein; Thomas D. Leidy, Esq.; Chris Pruitt, CPA; Al Weber.
Number of staff: 3 full-time professional; 2 part-time professional; 4 full-time support.
EIN: 232769892
Other changes: J. William Widing III, Esq. has replaced Kathleen D. Herbein as Chair.
Daniel Boyer, John Dever, Mary Ann Chelius Smith, and Mary Ann Ullman are no longer directors.

2894
Charles G. Berwind Foundation, Inc.

3000 Centre Sq. W.
1500 Market St.
Philadelphia, PA 19102-2100
Contact: Eileen P. Moore, Secy.

Donor: Berwind Corporation.
Foundation type: Independent foundation.
Financial data (yr. ended 09/30/13): Assets, $7,365,387 (M); expenditures, $420,596; qualifying distributions, $350,994; giving activities include $342,394 for 45 grants to individuals (high: $14,250; low: $1,500).
Purpose and activities: Scholarship awards to students to attend accredited institutions of higher learning in the U.S.
Fields of interest: Higher education.
Type of support: Scholarships—to individuals.
Limitations: Applications accepted. Giving primarily to residents of PA.
Application information: Application form required.
***Initial approach:* Scholarship application**
Deadline(s): Varies; contact foundation
Officers: C. Graham Berwind, Pres.; Joanna B. Creamer, V.P.; Eileen P. Moore, Secy.; Bruce J. McKenney, Treas.

Selection Committee: Walter Arader; Sandra Berwind; Michelle M. Mancini; Constance McSherry.
EIN: 203039970

2895
Theodora B. Betz Foundation
c/o B. Little
1600 Market St., Ste. 3600
Philadelphia, PA **19103-7212**

Established in 1989 in PA.
Foundation type: Independent foundation.
Financial data (yr. ended 04/30/13): Assets, $3,577,327 (M); expenditures, $245,076; qualifying distributions, $203,623; giving activities include $190,000 for 3 grants (high: $100,000; low: $40,000).
Fields of interest: Higher education; Hospitals (general); Health organizations, association; ALS; Cancer research.
Type of support: Research.
Limitations: Applications not accepted. Giving primarily in PA. No grants to individuals.
Application information: Contributes only to pre-selected organizations.
Trustees: Henry Kwiecinski; George Nofer.
EIN: 236965187

2896
The Birmingham Foundation
Brashear Ctr.
2005 Sarah St., 2nd Fl.
Pittsburgh, PA 15203-2021 (412) 481-2777
Contact: Chris Mason, Admin. Asst.; Mark Stephen Bibro, Exec. Dir.
FAX: (412) 481-2727; E-mail: info@bfpgh.org; Main URL: http://www.birminghamfoundation.org
Grants List: http://foundationcenter.org/grantmaker/birminghamfdn/awarded.html

Established in 1996 in PA; converted with assets from the sale of The South Side Hospital.
Foundation type: Independent foundation.
Financial data (yr. ended 06/30/13): Assets, $22,181,519 (M); gifts received, $11,581; expenditures, $1,602,653; qualifying distributions, $1,433,948; giving activities include $1,192,850 for 53 grants (high: $105,000; low: $500).
Purpose and activities: The foundation is dedicated to health and human services, and serves as a change agent for improved health and wellness in South Pittsburgh, PA, through the dynamic use of resources such as grantmaking, information-sharing, partnering and leveraging of assets. Funding priorities include health access and education, strengthening children's well being, enhancing senior safety and health, building the capacity of local organizations, and improving community life by addressing violence, substance abuse and mental health. Within these priorities, the foundation has streamlined it focus on programs that 1) deal with issues of violence, especially youth violence, 2) deal with safety net issues such as food banks and utility assistance, 3) deal with school youth, including programs that decrease drop out rates, are high quality out-of-school programs, and improve reading and educational opportunities, and 4) deal with healthcare improvements for vulnerable and underserved populations.
Fields of interest: Health care; Human services; Infants/toddlers; Children/youth; Youth; Adults; Aging; Young adults; Disabilities, people with; Minorities; African Americans/Blacks; Women; Girls; Men; Boys; Substance abusers; Crime/abuse victims; Economically disadvantaged.
Type of support: General/operating support; Program development; Technical assistance.
Limitations: Applications accepted. Giving limited to the South Pittsburgh, PA, area served by the following zip codes: 15203 (South Side), 15210 (Mt. Oliver and Hilltop), and 15211 (Mt. Washington), including in particular the neighborhoods of Allentown, Arlington, Arlington Heights, Beltzhoover, Bon Air, Carrick, Duquesne Heights, Knoxville, Mt. Oliver, Mt. Washington, St. Clair Village, and the South Side Flats and Slopes. No grants to individuals, or for operating budgets, deficits, fund-raising, general research, overhead, scholarships, political campaigns; no loans.
Publications: Application guidelines; Biennial report; Financial statement; Grants list; Multi-year report; IRS Form 990 or 990-PF printed copy available upon request.
Application information: The foundation now has an online grant application system. Application information available on foundation web site. Grantmakers of Western Pennsylvania's Common Grant Application Format accepted; see URL: http://www.gwpa.org for copies. Application form required.
Initial approach: Complete letter of intent on foundation web site
Copies of proposal: 1
Deadline(s): 2 months prior to board meetings
Board meeting date(s): Apr. and Nov.
Final notification: Letters of approval mailed following board meetings
Officers and Directors:* Terrence L. Wirginis,* Chair.; William T. Simmons, Esq.*, Vice-Chair.; Carey A. Harris,* Chair., Grants; Eileen O. Smith,* Secy.; H. Don Gordon,* Treas.; Jane H. Roesch, Dir., Emeritus; Mark S. Bibro, Exec. Dir.; Roberta Smith, Dir., Emeritus; Maurita J. Bryant; Hugo Churchill; Betty Kripp; Beth Marcello; Mihai Marcu; Kenneth McCrory; Duane Swager II.
Number of staff: 1 full-time professional; 1 full-time support.
EIN: 250965572

2897
Elizabeth S. Black Charitable Trust
c/o PNC Bank, N.A.
P.O. Box 609
Pittsburgh, PA 15230-9738
***Application address:* c/o PNC Bank, N.A., Att.: Brian Dornseif, 1900 E. 9th St., 13th Fl., Cleveland, OH 44114, tel.: (216) 222-2799**

Foundation type: Independent foundation.
Financial data (yr. ended 10/31/13): Assets, $10,125,979 (M); expenditures, $412,015; qualifying distributions, $362,487; giving activities include $322,318 for 12 grants (high: $89,000; low: $1,579).
Fields of interest: Arts; Elementary/secondary education; Higher education; Education, services; Youth development, services; Human services; YM/YWCAs & YM/YWHAs; Children/youth, services; Foundations (community); Protestant agencies & churches.
Type of support: General/operating support.
Limitations: Applications accepted. Giving primarily in the Oil City, PA area. No grants to individuals.
Application information: Application form required.
Deadline(s): None
Trustee: PNC Bank, N.A.
EIN: 043731472
Other changes: The grantmaker has moved from OH to PA.

2898
The Dietrich W. Botstiber Foundation
200 E. State St., Ste. 306-A
Media, PA 19063-3434 (610) 566-3375
Contact: Carlie Numi, Grants Mgr.
FAX: (610) 566-3376;
E-mail: varapis@botstiber.org; E-mail for Carlie Numi: Cnumi@botstiber.org; Main URL: http://www.botstiber.org/

Established in 1995 in PA.
Donors: Dietrich W. Botstiber†; Dietrich W. Botstiber Charitable Lead Annuity Trust.
Foundation type: Independent foundation.
Financial data (yr. ended 08/31/12): Assets, $29,001,749 (M); gifts received, $790,000; expenditures, $1,625,230; qualifying distributions, $1,438,006; giving activities include $329,766 for 8 grants (high: $259,066; low: $2,600), and $891,607 for 12 grants to individuals (high: $25,000; low: $1,400).
Purpose and activities: Giving in 3 major areas: 1) scholarships; 2) Austrian-U.S.A. relations; and 3) prevention of cruelty to humans and animals.
Fields of interest: Higher education, university; International affairs.
Type of support: Scholarships—to individuals; Professorships; Scholarship funds.
Limitations: Giving primarily in PA, and Vienna, Austria.
Publications: Financial statement; IRS Form 990 or 990-PF printed copy available upon request.
Application information: Unsolicited requests for funds not accepted, except for grant requests to the Botstiber Institute for Austrian-American Studies.
Board meeting date(s): Bimonthly
Trustees: Dorothy Boylan; Terrance A. Kline.
Number of staff: 1 part-time professional.
EIN: 237807828

2899
Cora L. Brooks Foundation
P.O. Box 5453
Bethlehem, PA 18015-0453 (610) 954-7737
Contact: Michael J. Cox, Dir.; Laura Herzog Kaplus, Assoc. Dir.
FAX: (610) 954-5591;
E-mail: clbf@foundationoffices.org; Main URL: http://www.foundationoffices.org

Established in 1999 in IL.
Donor: Susan Hurd Cumings.
Foundation type: Independent foundation.
Financial data (yr. ended 12/31/12): Assets, $9,519,114 (M); gifts received, $199,758; expenditures, $433,869; qualifying distributions, $397,231; giving activities include $288,640 for 27 grants (high: $15,000; low: $1,500).
Purpose and activities: The foundation's primary interest is environmental conservation or restoration within the watersheds of the Delaware and Susquehanna Rivers, with particular emphasis on environmental protection issues relating to clean water and water related ecologies. The foundation prefers to support organizations whose annual revenue is $5 million or less.
Fields of interest: Environment, management/technical assistance; Environment, research; Environment, public policy; Environment, single organization support; Environment, water pollution; Environment, toxics; Environment, natural resources; Environment, water resources; Environment, land resources; Environment, forests; Environment, plant conservation; Environment, beautification programs; Environment; Animals/wildlife, preservation/

protection; Animals/wildlife, endangered species; Animals/wildlife, bird preserves; Animals/wildlife, fisheries; Animals/wildlife; Agriculture, farmlands.
Type of support: Equipment; Emergency funds; Program development; Research; Technical assistance; Matching/challenge support.
Limitations: Applications not accepted. Giving within watersheds of the Delaware and Susquehanna Rivers, an area that includes 5 states. Please ensure that the project falls within this geographic area. No support for political organizations, or organizations whose revenue is greater than $5,000,000 (as shown on the organization's Form 990.). No grants to individuals, or for naming opportunities, multi-year pledges, school or public education programs or any education-related request, or for ongoing support.
Application information: The foundation is not accepting grant applications.
Board meeting date(s): Annual
Directors: Michael J. Cox, Dir.; Laura Herzog Kaplus, Assoc. Dir.
Trustees: Elizabeth Bray; Susan Cumings; Douglas Law; Bank of America, N.A.
Number of staff: 2 full-time professional; 1 part-time professional.
EIN: 367256643

2900
Bucks County Foundation
60 E. Court St.
P.O. Box 2073
Doylestown, PA 18901 (215) 997-8566
Contact: Linda Goodwin, Exec. Dir.
FAX: (215) 997-8564;
E-mail: lg@buckscountyfoundation.org; Main URL: http://www.buckscountyfoundation.org

Established in 1979 in PA.
Foundation type: Community foundation.
Financial data (yr. ended 12/31/12): Assets, $11,313,113 (M); gifts received, $45,777; expenditures, $536,957; giving activities include $341,526 for 18+ grants (high: $34,000).
Purpose and activities: The foundation seeks to enhance the quality of life for residents of the county by stimulating philanthropic opportunity and developing long-term financial assets to meet a wide range of the community's charitable needs.
Fields of interest: Arts; Higher education; Environment; Health care; Human services; Community/economic development.
Type of support: Scholarship funds; Publication; Program development; Matching/challenge support; Management development/capacity building; General/operating support; Equipment; Endowments; Conferences/seminars; Capital campaigns; Building/renovation; Annual campaigns.
Limitations: Applications accepted. Giving limited to the Bucks County, PA area. No support for religious purposes. No grants for deficit financing, advertising publications, or research.
Publications: Application guidelines; Annual report; Financial statement; Informational brochure.
Application information: Delaware Valley Grantmakers Common Grant Application Form accepted. Visit foundation web site for application guidelines. Application form required.
Initial approach: Submit application form and attachments
Copies of proposal: 1
Deadline(s): Jan. 15 and July 15
Board meeting date(s): Mar., July, Sept., and Dec.
Final notification: 60 days
Officers and Distribution Committee Members:* Grace Deon, Esq.,* Pres.; Ron Bolig, Esq.,* Treas.; Linda Goodwin, Exec. Dir.; Frederick Breitenfeld, Jr.; John Detweiler; Donna Farrington; **Lawrence Grim, Esq.**; Jere Hohmann; Jeffrey Sprowles; Peter Van Dire, J.D.
Trustees: First National Bank and Trust of Newtown; First Savings Bank of Perkasie; **Mellon**; PNC; Univest; Wachovia.
EIN: 239031005

2901
The Buhl Foundation
City Centre Tower
650 Smithfield St., Ste. 2300
Pittsburgh, PA 15222-3912 (412) 566-2711
Contact: Linda Weaver, Office Mgr.
FAX: (412) 566-2714;
E-mail: buhl@buhlfoundation.org; Main URL: http://www.buhlfoundation.org/

Established as a trust in 1927 in PA; reincorporated in 1992.
Donors: Henry Buhl, Jr.†; Henry C. Frick†.
Foundation type: Independent foundation.
Financial data (yr. ended 06/30/13): Assets, $83,120,429 (M); expenditures, $4,816,758; qualifying distributions, $4,217,319; giving activities include $3,638,772 for 138 grants (high: $500,000; low: $1,500), and $80,253 for foundation-administered programs.
Purpose and activities: Emphasis on developmental or innovative grants to regional institutions, with special interest in education, particularly K-12, and in regional concerns, particularly those related to problems of children and youth.
Fields of interest: Elementary/secondary education; Child development, education; Libraries/library science; Education; Children/youth, services; Child development, services; Economic development; Engineering/technology; Science; Children/youth; Minorities; Economically disadvantaged.
Type of support: Management development/capacity building; Program development; Seed money; Curriculum development; Research; Technical assistance; Program evaluation; Program-related investments/loans; Employee matching gifts.
Limitations: Applications accepted. Giving primarily in southwestern PA, with emphasis on the Pittsburgh area. No support for religious or political activities, or nationally funded organizations. No grants to individuals, or for building funds, overhead costs, accumulated deficits, operating budgets, scholarships, fellowships, fundraising campaigns; no loans (except for program-related investments).
Publications: Annual report; Informational brochure (including application guidelines).
Application information: Submit final proposal upon invitation only. Grantmakers of Western Pennsylvania's Common Grant Application Format accepted. Application form not required.
Initial approach: Letter of inquiry required prior to submitting a proposal. Letter of inquiry may be unsolicited but generally only invited proposals accepted.
Copies of proposal: 1
Deadline(s): If a letter of inquiry is approved, and a formal proposal invited, the proposal is due typically, at least 1 month prior to particular Board meeting
Board meeting date(s): 6 times a year (usually in Feb., Apr., June., Sept., Oct., and Dec.)
Final notification: Approximately 6 weeks
Officers and Directors:* Peter F. Mathieson,* Chair.; Saleem H. Ghubril,* Vice-Chair.; Frederick W. Thieman, Esq.*, Pres.; Diana Bucco, V.P.; **Kim Tillotson Fleming, Secy.-Treas.**; Jean A. Robinson; **Lara E. Washington.**
Number of staff: 2 full-time professional; 1 part-time professional; 1 full-time support; 1 part-time support.
EIN: 250378910
Other changes: Peter F. Mathieson has replaced Jean A. Robinson as Chair. Saleem H. Ghubril has replaced Peter F. Mathieson as Vice-Chair. Kim Tillotson Fleming is now Secy.-Treas.

2902
Jack Buncher Foundation
(formerly Buncher Family Foundation)
Penn Liberty Plz. I
1300 Penn Ave., Ste. 300
Pittsburgh, PA 15222-4211 (412) 422-9900
Contact: Bernita Buncher, Pres.

Established in 1974 in PA.
Donors: Jack G. Buncher†; The Buncher Co.; Buncher Rail Car Service Co.; Jack G. Buncher Trust.
Foundation type: Independent foundation.
Financial data (yr. ended 11/30/13): Assets, $270,089,243 (M); expenditures, $25,556,755; qualifying distributions, $25,508,994; giving activities include $25,296,164 for 240 grants (high: $3,757,174; low: $15).
Purpose and activities: Giving primarily to encourage the pursuit of ideas and innovations that unlock the potential of individuals and communities, and that enrich people's lives.
Fields of interest: Arts; Education; Health care; Medical research, institute; Human services; Jewish federated giving programs; Jewish agencies & synagogues.
Type of support: Scholarship funds; Program development; Matching/challenge support; General/operating support; Capital campaigns; Building/renovation; Annual campaigns.
Limitations: Applications accepted. Giving primarily in PA, with emphasis on Pittsburgh. No grants to individuals.
Application information: Grantmakers of Western Pennsylvania's Common Grant Application Format accepted. Application form required.
Initial approach: Letter
Deadline(s): None
Final notification: Within 3 months from receipt
Officers: Bernita Buncher, Pres.; Thomas Balestrieri, V.P.; Joseph M. Jakovic, Secy.; H. William Doring, Treas.
Number of staff: 1 part-time professional; 1 part-time support.
EIN: 237366998
Other changes: For the fiscal year ended Nov. 30, 2013, the grantmaker paid grants of $25,296,164, a 56.7% increase over the fiscal 2012 disbursements, $16,140,532.

2903
Ralph L. & Florence R. Burgess Trust
c/o Wells Fargo Bank, N.A.
101N Independence Mall E., MACY1372-062
Philadelphia, PA 19106-2112

Established in 1985 in CO.
Foundation type: Independent foundation.
Financial data (yr. ended 01/31/13): Assets, $2,999,221 (M); expenditures, $165,286; qualifying distributions, $132,174; giving activities

include $121,975 for 37 grants (high: $5,500; low: $1,800).
Fields of interest: Performing arts.
Type of support: General/operating support; Continuing support.
Limitations: Applications not accepted. Giving limited to the city and county of Denver, CO. No grants to individuals.
Application information: Contributes only to pre-selected organizations.
Board meeting date(s): Apr. and Oct.
Trustee: Wells Fargo Bank, N.A.
EIN: 742383505
Other changes: The grantmaker has moved from AZ to PA.

2904
Stephen G. Calvert Memorial Merit Scholarship Foundation
5 Tower Bridge, 300 Barr Harbor Dr., Ste. 600
West Conshohocken, PA 19428-2998

Established in 1996 in PA.
Donors: Keystone Foods Corp.; Keystone Foods LLC.
Foundation type: Company-sponsored foundation.
Financial data (yr. ended 10/31/13): Assets, $16,327 (M); gifts received, $200,000; expenditures, $198,100; qualifying distributions, $177,000; giving activities include $177,000 for 36 grants (high: $8,600; low: $2,000).
Purpose and activities: The foundation awards college scholarships to dependents of employees of Keystone Foods.
Fields of interest: Higher education.
Type of support: Employee-related scholarships.
Limitations: Applications accepted. Giving limited to areas of company operations.
Application information: Application form required.
Initial approach: Letter
Deadline(s): None
Officers: Edward M. Delate, Pres.; Donna Curtis, Secy.; **Frank Pelone, Treas.**
Director: Charles Wallace.
EIN: 232816413

2905
The Cardiovascular Medical Research and Education Fund, Inc.
510 Walnut St., Ste. 500
Philadelphia, PA 19106-3601 (215) 413-2414
Contact: Patricia A. Wolf, Exec. Dir.
E-mail: patt.wolfe@ipahresearch.org; Main URL: http://www.ipahresearch.org/

Established in 2003 in PA.
Foundation type: Independent foundation.
Financial data (yr. ended 12/31/12): Assets, $15,250,201 (M); expenditures, $3,756,722; qualifying distributions, $3,641,703; giving activities include $3,612,675 for 15 grants (high: $697,021; low: $30,000).
Purpose and activities: The fund's mission is to support research to uncover the etiology and pathogenesis of idiopathic pulmonary arterial hypertension (IPAH, or PPH), in pursuit of the ultimate goal of its treatment and cure.
Fields of interest: Heart & circulatory research.
Type of support: Research; Grants to individuals.
Limitations: Giving on a national basis.
Publications: Application guidelines; Annual report.
Application information: Submit letter of intent in electronic format. The fund will respond within four weeks if a full application will be requested. Complete application guidelines are available on the fund web site. Application form required.
***Initial approach:* Online Letter of Intent (not exceeding 2 pages)**
Officers and Directors:* John H. Newman, M.D.*, Pres.; Patricia A. Wolfe, Exec. Dir.; Michael Fishbein, Esq.; Peter Pantaleo, Esq.
Research Advisory Committee: Stuart Rich, M.D.
EIN: 050579911
Other changes: Robyn Barst, MD, is deceased. The grantmaker now publishes application guidelines.

2906
Carnegie Hero Fund Commission
436 7th Ave., Ste. 1101
Pittsburgh, PA 15219-1841
Contact: Jeffrey A. Dooley, Investigations Mgr.
FAX: (412) 281-5751;
E-mail: carnegiehero@carnegiehero.org; Toll free tel.: (800) 447-8900; Main URL: http://www.carnegiehero.org/
Awardees database: http://carnegiehero.org/search-awardees/

Established in 1904 in PA.
Donor: Andrew Carnegie‡.
Foundation type: Operating foundation.
Financial data (yr. ended 12/31/12): Assets, $38,278,724 (M); gifts received, $620; expenditures, $1,775,175; qualifying distributions, $1,755,068; giving activities include $920,544 for grants to individuals.
Purpose and activities: A private operating foundation established to recognize, with the award of medals and sums of money, heroism voluntarily performed by civilians within the U.S. and Canada in saving or attempting to save the lives of others; and to grant monetary assistance, including scholarship aid, to awardees and to the dependents of those who have lost their lives or who have been disabled in such heroic manner.
Fields of interest: Human services; Voluntarism promotion.
International interests: Canada.
Type of support: Continuing support; Grants to individuals; Scholarships—to individuals.
Limitations: Applications accepted. Giving primarily in the U.S.; some giving also in Canada.
Publications: Annual report; Informational brochure; Newsletter.
Application information: Awards by nomination only. Refer to the commission web site for complete nominating guidelines and form. Application form required.
Initial approach: Use online nomination form on foundation web site, or contact the Commission to request a nomination form. Nominations may also be made by letter
Copies of proposal: 1
Deadline(s): Within 2 years of the act for nominations
Board meeting date(s): Mar., June, Sept., and Dec.
Final notification: Following board meetings
Officers and Trustees:* **Mark Laskow,* Chair.; Walter F. Rutkowski, Pres. and Secy.**; Priscilla J. McCrady,* V.P.; Dan D. Sandman,* Treas.; Albert H. Burchfield III; **Robert J. Cindrich**; **Robert M. Hernandez**; Thomas J. Hilliard, Jr.; David McL. Hillman; Linda T. Hills; Peter J. Lambrou; **Natalie Lemieux**; Christopher R. McCrady; Ann M. McGuinn; Nancy L. Rackoff; Frank Brooks Robinson; Arthur M. Scully III; **Michael A. Thompson**; Sybil P. Veeder, Ph.D.; Joseph C. Walton; Susanne C. Wean; Thomas L. Wentling, Jr.
Number of staff: 5 full-time professional; 2 part-time professional; 2 full-time support; 1 part-time support.
EIN: 251062730
Other changes: Mark Laskow is now Chair. Walter F. Rutkowski is now Pres. and Secy. Elizabeth H. Genter, Alfred W. Wishart, and Carol A. Word are no longer trustees.

2907
Central Pennsylvania Community Foundation
(formerly Blair County Community Endowment)
1330 11th Ave.
Altoona, PA 16601-3302 (814) 944-6102
Contact: Jodi Cessna, Exec. Dir.
FAX: (814) 381-7104;
E-mail: cessna@centralpacf.org; Main URL: http://centralpagives.org/

Established in 1995 in PA.
Foundation type: Community foundation.
Financial data (yr. ended 12/31/11): Assets, $7,452,953 (M); gifts received, $1,329,922; expenditures, $1,392,095; giving activities include $1,204,347 for 42+ grants (high: $155,714).
Purpose and activities: The foundation seeks to provide a permanent trust that will help the local community in the future by providing a perpetual fund to aid civic and charitable projects.
Fields of interest: Performing arts, music; Arts; Education; Health organizations, association; Recreation; Community/economic development; Science, research; Religion.
Type of support: Fellowships.
Limitations: Applications accepted. Giving limited to Blair County, PA. No grants to individuals.
Publications: Application guidelines; Informational brochure; Newsletter.
Application information: Visit foundation web site for application cover sheet and guidelines.
Initial approach: Contact foundation
Copies of proposal: 9
Deadline(s): Last business day of Apr.
Board meeting date(s): Mar., June, Sept., and Dec.
Final notification: 4 weeks
Officers and Directors:* John Kazmaier,* Chair.; Allan G. Hancock,* Pres.; Nancy Devorris,* V.P.; Randy Tarpey,* Secy.; Fred Imler, Sr.,* Treas.; Jodi Cessna, Exec. Dir.; Len Whiting, Dir. Emeritus; Gerald Wolf, Dir. Emeritus; Larry Claton; John E. Eberhardt, Jr.; **Matt Garber**; Michele Haas; Barry Halbritter; Ray Hess; Joseph D. Hurd, Jr.; Gail H. Irwin; Craig Kilmer; Michael Kranich, Sr.; Astride McLanahan; James Moran; Neil Port; April Ressler; Steve Sloan; Maureen Smithe.
Number of staff: 1 full-time professional.
EIN: 251761379

2908
Central Susquehanna Community Foundation
(formerly Administers of the Berwick Health and Wellness Fund)
725 West Front St.
Berwick, PA 18603 (570) 752-3930
Contact: Eric DeWald, C.E.O.; For grants: Kara Seesholtz, Prog. Off.
FAX: (570) 752-7435;
E-mail: edewald@csgiving.org; Additional e-mail: kseesholtz@csgiving.org; Main URL: http://www.csgiving.org

Established in 1999 in PA; converted from the sale of Berwick Hospital.
Foundation type: Community foundation.
Financial data (yr. ended 12/31/12): Assets, $38,016,293 (M); gifts received, $1,135,926; expenditures, $3,024,033; giving activities include $1,948,857 for 45+ grants (high: $522,226), and $157,024 for 29 grants to individuals.
Purpose and activities: The foundation seeks to improve the quality of life for citizens of the Central Susquehanna Region.
Fields of interest: Arts; Education; Health care; Mental health/crisis services; Human services.
Type of support: General/operating support; Continuing support; Building/renovation; Equipment; Program development; Seed money; Technical assistance; Consulting services; Program-related investments/loans; Scholarships—to individuals; Matching/challenge support.
Limitations: Applications accepted. Giving limited to Columbia, Lower Luzerne, Montour, Northumberland, and Snyder counties, PA. No support for religious purposes. No grants to individuals (except for scholarships).
Publications: Application guidelines; Annual report; Financial statement; Grants list; Informational brochure; Newsletter; Occasional report (including application guidelines).
Application information: Visit foundation web site for application guidelines. Application form required.
Initial approach: Telephone
Copies of proposal: 2
Deadline(s): Varies
Board meeting date(s): Quarterly
Final notification: Within 2 months
Officers and Trustees:* M. Holly Morrison,* Chair.; Kendra Aucker,* Vice-Chair.; Eric Dewald,* C.E.O. and Pres.; Roger S. Haddon, Jr.,* Secy.; **Dr. John E. DeFinnis,* Treas.**; **Al Meale, Cont.**; Timothy Apple; Roger J. Davis; **JoAnne Ferentz**; **Peggy Fullmer**; Thomas R. Harlow; James Kishbaugh; John S. Mulka; John B. Parker; Joseph Scopelliti; Rhonda Seebold; J. Donald Steele, Jr.; Connie Tressler; Kevin D. Woodeshick.
Number of staff: 2 full-time professional; 3 part-time professional.
EIN: 232982141
Other changes: Dr. John E. DeFinnis has replaced Kevin D. Woodeshick as Treas.
John E. DeFinnis is no longer a member of the governing body. Michael F. Flock is no longer a member of the governing body. Michael P. Goresh is no longer a member of the governing body. Andreae K. Hoosty is no longer a member of the governing body. David Saracino is no longer a member of the governing body. Kevin Tanribilir is no longer a member of the governing body. Pamela L. White is no longer a member of the governing body.

2909
Centre County Community Foundation, Inc.

2601 Gateway Dr., Bristol II, Ste. 175
P.O. Box 648
State College, PA 16804-0648 (814) 237-6229
Contact: Molly Kunkel, Exec. Dir.
FAX: (814) 237-2624;
E-mail: Email:info@centre-foundation.org; Additional e-mail: mkunkel@centrecountycf.org; Main URL: http://www.centrecountycf.org
Blog: http://centrefoundation.wordpress.com/
Facebook: http://www.facebook.com/pages/Centre-County-Community-Foundation/108336539198975
LinkedIn: http://www.linkedin.com/company/centre-county-community-foundation
Twitter: http://twitter.com/CentreFNDN

Established in 1981 in PA.
Foundation type: Community foundation.
Financial data (yr. ended 12/31/11): Assets, $22,480,265 (M); gifts received, $1,408,745; expenditures, $1,433,401; giving activities include $891,841 for 499+ grants (high: $17,731; low: $4).
Purpose and activities: The foundation's mission is to improve the quality of life in Centre County by providing enduring support to community charities from the invested gifts of visionary donors.
Fields of interest: Arts; Education; Environment; Health care; Human services; Community/economic development.
Type of support: General/operating support; Income development; Annual campaigns; Capital campaigns; Building/renovation; Equipment; Emergency funds; Program development; Conferences/seminars; Publication; Seed money; Internship funds; Scholarship funds; Research; Technical assistance; Matching/challenge support.
Limitations: Applications accepted. Giving limited to PA, predominately in Centre County; limited funding also to immediate surrounding counties. No support for religious organizations for sectarian purposes, or government or educational entities with taxing authority. No grants for payment of debt, travel or accommodation services, or event ads or sponsorships.
Publications: Application guidelines; Annual report (including application guidelines); Informational brochure; Occasional report; Quarterly report.
Application information: Visit foundation web site for specific application forms and guidelines per grant type. Application form required.
Initial approach: Visit foundation web site to create online profile and complete eligibility quiz
Deadline(s): July 17 and Oct. 30
Board meeting date(s): 3rd Wed. of Feb., May, Aug., and Nov.
Final notification: May and Dec.
Officer and Directors:* Molly Kunkel,* Exec. Dir.; Patrick Bisbey; John Conroy; Desiree Fralick; Blake Gall; Tammy Gentzel; Amos Goodall; R. Riggs Griffith; Kelly Grimes; Jack Infield; Oscar Johnston; Terrell Jones; Bill Keough; Heddy Kervandjian; Kay Kustanbauter; Heidi Nicholas; Rabbi David Ostrich; Carmine Prestia; Bob Ricketts; Todd Sloan; Chuck Witmer; Ted Ziff II; Jane Zimmerman.
Number of staff: 2 full-time professional; 1 full-time support.
EIN: 251782197
Other changes: Sarah Sciabica is now Grant and Scholarship Coord. Irene Miller is now Devel. & Events Coord. Emily Gette-Doyle is no longer a director.

2910
Michele and Agnese Cestone Foundation, Inc.

c/o Bruce Bickel, PNC Private Foundation
1 PNC Plz.
249 5th Ave., 3rd Fl.
Pittsburgh, PA 15222 (412) 762-3502
Contact: Bruce Bickel; Cynthia Hamorsky; Yhezzi Owen
FAX: (412) 762-4160;
E-mail: bruce.bickel@pnc.com

Established in 1990 in NJ.
Foundation type: Independent foundation.
Financial data (yr. ended 12/31/12): Assets, $17,615,368 (M); expenditures, $1,029,703; qualifying distributions, $989,473; giving activities include $874,000 for 50 grants (high: $170,000; low: $3,000).
Purpose and activities: Giving primarily for the care and welfare of animals.
Fields of interest: Animal welfare.
Type of support: General/operating support; Continuing support; Capital campaigns; Building/renovation; Equipment; Emergency funds; Program development; Seed money; Curriculum development; Scholarship funds; Research; Technical assistance; Matching/challenge support.
Limitations: Applications accepted. Giving on the East Coast of the U.S., with some emphasis on NJ and NY.
Publications: Application guidelines.
Application information: Application form required.
Initial approach: Letter
Copies of proposal: 1
Deadline(s): Contact foundation for deadlines
Board meeting date(s): June and Nov.
Final notification: 30 days
Officers and Trustees:* Michele J. Cestone,* Pres.; Maria A. Cestone II,* Secy.
Number of staff: 2 full-time professional.
EIN: 521720903

2911
Julius & Ray Charlestein Foundation

1710 Romano Dr.
Plymouth Meeting, PA 19462-2822 **(610) 239-6000**
Contact: Ellyn Phillips, Exec. Dir.

Established in 1963 in PA.
Donors: Morton L. Charlestein; Premier Dental Products Co.; Premier Medical Co.
Foundation type: Company-sponsored foundation.
Financial data (yr. ended 06/30/13): Assets, $3,123,813 (M); gifts received, $310,000; expenditures, $388,592; qualifying distributions, $335,193; giving activities include $335,193 for 42 grants (high: $62,000; low: $250).
Purpose and activities: The foundation supports organizations involved with education, ALS, human services, and Judaism.
Fields of interest: Secondary school/education; Theological school/education; Education; ALS; Human services; United Ways and Federated Giving Programs; Jewish federated giving programs; Jewish agencies & synagogues.
Type of support: General/operating support; Annual campaigns; Program development; Scholarship funds.
Limitations: Applications accepted. Giving primarily in the Philadelphia, PA, area. No grants to individuals.
Application information: Application form not required.
Initial approach: Proposal
Deadline(s): None
Officers: Gary Charlestein, Secy.-Treas.; Ellyn Phillips, Exec. Dir.
EIN: 232310090
Other changes: Morton L. Charlestein is no longer Pres.

2912
The Charter Foundation
640 Narcisi Ln.
Wayne, PA 19087-2238 **(610) 688-9055**
***E-mail:* info@thecharterfoundation.com**; Main URL: http://thecharterfoundation.com/

Donor: The McLean Contributionship.
Foundation type: Independent foundation.
Financial data (yr. ended 12/31/12): Assets, $13,161,929 (M); gifts received, $15,000; expenditures, $717,228; qualifying distributions, $634,410; giving activities include $592,000 for 23 grants (high: $200,000; low: $2,000).
Purpose and activities: Giving primarily for education, healthcare, medical research, and other human services.
Fields of interest: Education; Hospitals (general); Health care; Human services.
Limitations: Applications accepted. **Giving primarily in the Greater Philadelphia, PA, area. No grants for annual appeals, or annual event sponsorship.**
Publications: Application guidelines; Grants list.
Application information: Application form required.
Initial approach: **Take eligibility quiz on foundation web site to determine eligibility**
Deadline(s): See foundation web site for current deadlines
Officers and Trustees:* Joseph K. Gordon, Esq.*, Pres.; **Leila Gordon,* V.P. and Exec. Dir.**; C. Scott Gordon; Hunter R. Gordon.
EIN: 271234570
Other changes: Leila Gordon is now V.P. and Exec. Dir.
The grantmaker now publishes application guidelines.

2913
Alice P. Chase Trust
c/o BNY Mellon, NA
P.O. Box 185
Pittsburgh, PA 15230-0185

Trust established in 1956 in MA.
Donor: Alice P. Chase†.
Foundation type: Independent foundation.
Financial data (yr. ended 08/31/13): Assets, $6,164,415 (M); expenditures, $339,313; qualifying distributions, $313,344; giving activities include $300,000 for 11 grants (high: $50,000; low: $15,000).
Purpose and activities: Giving primarily for education, youth services, and homeless support.
Fields of interest: Education; Housing/shelter; Human services; Youth, services; Family services, domestic violence; Community/economic development; Disabilities, people with; Blind/visually impaired.
Type of support: General/operating support; Capital campaigns; Building/renovation; Equipment; Program development; Technical assistance.
Limitations: Applications not accepted. Giving limited to the greater Boston, MA, area. No grants to individuals or for matching gifts; no loans.
Application information: Contributes only to pre-selected organizations.
Trustee: BNY Mellon, N.A.
EIN: 046093897

2914
C.C. Chenault, Jr. Agricultural Foundation
c/o PNC Bank, N.A.
P.O. Box 609
Pittsburgh, PA 15230-9738

Established in 1976; supporting organization of the Bath County Board of Education, KY.
Foundation type: Independent foundation.
Financial data (yr. ended 08/31/13): Assets, $3,297,113 (M); expenditures, $185,632; qualifying distributions, $170,061; giving activities include $157,273 for 1 grant.
Fields of interest: Education.
Type of support: General/operating support.
Limitations: Applications not accepted. Giving limited to KY.
Application information: Contributes only to pre-selected organizations.
Trustee: PNC Bank, N.A.
EIN: 616102245
Other changes: The grantmaker has moved from OH to PA.

2915
Chester County Community Foundation
The Lincoln Bldg.
28 W. Market St.
West Chester, PA 19382-3020 (610) 696-8211
Contact: Karen A. Simmons, C.E.O.; For grants: Beth Harper Briglia, V.P., Grants and Donor Svcs.
FAX: (610) 696-8213; E-mail: info@chescocf.org; Additional e-mail: karen@chescocf.org; Grant application e-mail: grants@chescocf.org; Main URL: http://www.chescocf.org
Blog: http://chescocf.wordpress.com
Facebook: http://www.facebook.com/pages/Chester-County-Community-Foundation/89750399079
Twitter: http://twitter.com/ChesCoCF

Established in 1994 in PA.
Foundation type: Community foundation.
Financial data (yr. ended 06/30/13): Assets, $39,530,395 (M); gifts received, $8,038,150; expenditures, $2,833,778; giving activities include $1,205,733 for 26+ grants (high: $120,000), and $188,761 for 154 grants to individuals.
Purpose and activities: Grow legacy philanthropy via those who live, work and enjoy Chester County, connecting people who care with causes that matter now and forever.
Fields of interest: Arts; Libraries/library science; Scholarships/financial aid; Education, drop-out prevention; Education; Environment; Health care; Youth development; Human services; Community development, neighborhood development; Economic development.
Type of support: General/operating support; Management development/capacity building; Capital campaigns; Building/renovation; Endowments; Program development; Conferences/seminars; Scholarship funds; Research; Consulting services; Program evaluation; Scholarships—to individuals.
Limitations: Applications accepted. Giving primarily in Chester County, PA. No grants to individuals (except for scholarships).
Publications: Application guidelines; Annual report; Financial statement; Informational brochure; Newsletter.
Application information: Visit foundation web site for application form and guidelines. Proposals submitted by Sept. 15 will receive priority consideration under all grantmaking funds. Delaware Valley Grantmakers Common Grant Application Form accepted. Application form required.
Initial approach: E-mail grant Summary Sheet and proposal
Copies of proposal: 1
Deadline(s): Sept. 15 for Fund for Chester County Initiative; none for Donor-Advised and Field-of-Interest funds
Board meeting date(s): Feb., May., Sept., and Nov.
Final notification: 2 months
Officers and Directors:* L. Peter Temple, Esq.,* Chair.; J. Stoddard Hayes, Jr., Esq.,* Vice-Chair.; Meghan McVety,* Vice-Chair.; Karen A. Simmons,* C.E.O. and Pres.; Beth Harper Briglia,* V.P., Donor Svcs. and Grantmaking; Cynthia Sineath Ray,* Corp. Secy.-Treas.; Carol Clark; John H. Diederich; David Elderkin; Carl Francis; William J. Gallagher, Esq.; Sara D. Harris; Ann Hutton; **Michael B. Karwic**; Stacey Willits McConnell, Esq.; Anthony Morris, Esq.; Robert E. Rigg; Karen Simmons.
Number of staff: 4 full-time professional; 1 part-time professional; 8 part-time support.
EIN: 232773822
Other changes: James McCormick is no longer Cont.

2916
Child Development Foundation
(also known as Child Development Foundation)
(formerly Child Development Center)
2500 DeKalb Pike, Ste. 100
Norristown, PA 19401-2007 **(610) 277-4000**
***Contact:* Trish Ewing, Exec. Asst.**
***E-mail:* ewing@childdevelopmentfoundation.org**; Main URL: http://www.childdevelopmentfoundation.org

Established in 1987 in PA.
Foundation type: Independent foundation.
Financial data (yr. ended 06/30/13): Assets, $7,706,939 (M); gifts received, $120; expenditures, $468,421; qualifying distributions, $372,592; giving activities include $350,985 for 39 grants (high: $35,000; low: $2,000).
Purpose and activities: Giving limited to organizations aiding disabled or handicapped children.
Fields of interest: Child development, education; Children/youth, services; Child development, services; Infants/toddlers; Children/youth; Youth; Disabilities, people with; Physically disabled; Blind/visually impaired; Mentally disabled; Infants/toddlers, female; Girls; Young adults, female; Infants/toddlers, male; Boys; Young adults, male.
Type of support: General/operating support; Equipment; Program development.
Limitations: Applications accepted. Giving limited to Montgomery County, PA. No grants to individuals, or for capital campaigns, debt service, or multi-year commitments.
Publications: Application guidelines; Financial statement; Informational brochure (including application guidelines).
Application information: Application form required.
Initial approach: Request application
Copies of proposal: 13
Deadline(s): Mar. 31
Board meeting date(s): Varies
Final notification: Mid-June
Officers and Directors:* Joseph M. Dimino,* Pres.; R. Kurtz Holloway, Esq.*, V.P.; Sandra Zuchero,* Secy.-Treas.; **Joanne E. Bryers**; Matthew Cappelletti, Jr.; Mark Constable; Wendy Davis; J. David Farrell, Esq.; Christine P. Wiegand, Esq.; Deborah Young, M.D.
Number of staff: 1 part-time support.
EIN: 231539361
Other changes: Sheila M. Darden is no longer a director.

2917
CIGNA Foundation
1601 Chestnut St., TL15C
Philadelphia, PA 19192-1540 (215) 761-4328
***Contact:* David Figliuzzi, Exec. Dir.**
E-mail: CommunityService@Cigna.com; Application address: CIGNA Grant Program, P.O. Box 2248, Princeton, NJ 08543-2248, tel.: 866) 865-5277; Main URL: http://www.cigna.com/about-us/corporate-responsibility/cigna-foundation

Incorporated in 1962 in PA.
Donor: CIGNA Corp.
Foundation type: Company-sponsored foundation.
Financial data (yr. ended 12/31/12): Assets, $3,669,331 (M); gifts received, $6,687,846; expenditures, $3,940,974; qualifying distributions, $3,939,478; giving activities include $3,853,023 for 1,006 grants (high: $500,000; low: $25).
Purpose and activities: The foundation supports programs designed to enable individuals and family to take responsibility for their own wealth; make heath information and services available through expanded opportunities; leverage education and life experiences to promote personal and professional growth; and encourage shared approaches to issues of local and global concern.
Fields of interest: Elementary school/education; Higher education; Education; Environment; Health care, equal rights; Health care, clinics/centers; Public health; Health care, patient services; Health care; Genetic diseases and disorders; Breast cancer; Recreation, parks/playgrounds; American Red Cross; YM/YWCAs & YM/YWHAs; Children/youth, services; Family services; Developmentally disabled, centers & services; Human services; Civil/human rights, equal rights; Civil/human rights, advocacy; Community/economic development; Foundations (public); Public policy, research; Leadership development.
Type of support: Capital campaigns; General/operating support; Annual campaigns; Program development; Conferences/seminars; Scholarship funds; Employee volunteer services; Employee matching gifts.
Limitations: Applications accepted. Giving primarily in Hartford, CT, Washington, DC, and Philadelphia, PA; giving also to national organizations. No support for fraternal organizations, social or political organizations, faith-based organizations not of direct of the entire community, or discriminatory groups. No grants to individuals, or for capital campaigns, or discriminatory projects.
Publications: Application guidelines; Annual report; Corporate giving report (including application guidelines).
Application information: Support is generally limited to 1 contribution per organization during any given year. Support for capital campaigns is extremely selective. Application form required.
Initial approach: Complete online application form
Deadline(s): None, but Oct. 15 is encouraged
Board meeting date(s): Biannually
Final notification: All funds distributed on an annual basis by Nov. 30
Officers and Directors:* John M. Murabito,* Chair.; Margaret M. Fitzpatrick,* Pres.; Thomas A. McCarthy, V.P.; David Figliuzzi, Exec. Dir.; David M. Cordani.
EIN: 236261726
Other changes: Gianna S. Jackon is no longer Exec. Dir.

2918
Claneil Foundation, Inc.
2250 Hickory Rd., Ste. 450
Plymouth Meeting, PA 19462-1074 (610) 941-1131
Contact: Mailee Walker, Exec. Dir.
FAX: (610) 828-6405**; For questions about Letter of Intent process or online application system, contact Karen Race, Grants Mgr. and Exec. Asst., tel.: (610) 941-1143**; Main URL: http://www.claneil.org

Incorporated in 1968 in DE.
Donors: Henry S. McNeil‡; Claneil Enterprises, Inc.
Foundation type: Independent foundation.
Financial data (yr. ended 12/31/12): Assets, $62,657,909 (M); expenditures, $3,265,741; qualifying distributions, $3,221,780; giving activities include $3,221,720 for 167 grants (high: $350,000; low: $1,500).
Purpose and activities: Giving to create healthy communities by supporting organizations that make a difference in the lives of individuals, families and the institutions that support them, and to develop an informed, educated and engaged citizenry, and increase the understanding and appreciation of natural, built and cultural assets.
Fields of interest: Visual arts; Performing arts; Historic preservation/historical societies; Arts; Education, early childhood education; Secondary school/education; Environment, natural resources; Environment, beautification programs; Environment; Reproductive health, family planning; Health care; Crime/violence prevention, domestic violence; Crime/violence prevention, child abuse; Housing/shelter; Youth development; Human services; Family services; Civil liberties, reproductive rights; Community/economic development; Women; Economically disadvantaged.
Type of support: General/operating support; Continuing support; Management development/capacity building; Capital campaigns; Building/renovation; Equipment; Land acquisition; Endowments; Program development; Conferences/seminars; Publication; Seed money; Curriculum development; Scholarship funds; Research; Technical assistance; Consulting services; Program evaluation; Matching/challenge support.
Limitations: Applications accepted. Giving primarily in southeastern PA, with emphasis on Chester, Delaware, Montgomery and Philadelphia counties. No support for religion-based programming. No grants to individuals.
Publications: Application guidelines; Informational brochure (including application guidelines).
Application information: Under the Community Grant Program, organizations that received funding in the past 3 years may submit a grant proposal without a letter of intent. The Emerging Leaders Fund and the Proactive Grant Program are invitation-only grant programs, unsolicited inquiries are not accepted in these areas. Only electronic submissions are accepted. See foundation web site for additional information. Application form required.
Initial approach: Letter of intent via online application system on foundation web site only
Copies of proposal: 1
***Deadline(s):* For Letters of Intent: June 30 (for fall cycle), and Dec. 1 (for spring cycle). Special Project Fund letters are accepted for consideration in the spring cycle only**
Board meeting date(s): Nov. and June
Officers and Directors:* Marjorie M. Findlay, Chair.; Gretchen Menzies, Vice-Chair.; Jennifer McNeil, Secy.; Langhorne B. Smith,* Treas.; Mailee Walker, Exec. Dir.; Hathaway F. Jade; Geoffrey T. Freeman; Barbara M. Jordan; Duncan McFarland; Robert D. McNeil.
Number of staff: 1 full-time professional; 1 full-time support.
EIN: 236445450

2919
The Clareth Fund: The Philadelphia Association of Zeta Psi Fraternity
30 S. 17th St.
Philadelphia, PA 19103-4196
Contact: Frank G. Cooper, Esq.

Foundation type: Independent foundation.
Financial data (yr. ended 12/31/13): Assets, $5,454,669 (M); expenditures, $300,114; qualifying distributions, $237,297; giving activities include $40,000 for 2 grants (high: $20,000; low: $20,000), and $183,250 for 39 grants to individuals (high: $7,000; low: $250).
Fields of interest: Graduate/professional education.
Type of support: General/operating support; Scholarships—to individuals; Student loans—to individuals.
Limitations: Applications not accepted. Giving limited to PA.
Application information: Contributes only to pre-selected organizations.
Officers and Directors:* McBee Butcher,* Pres.; Peter B. Pakradooni, V.P.; Gregory E. McElroy,* Secy.; James P. Bodine, Treas.; **Andrew Biros**; **R. Carter Caldwell**; **Richard L. Guest**; **Dr. Kenneth Kazahaya**; **Dr. Masayuki Kazahaya**; David L. Sims; **Jonathan R. Stott**.
EIN: 232092500
Other changes: Peter F. Arfaa, Marc C. Ganzi, Charles L. Ingersoll, Roger Jones, Eric Lombardini, Christopher Rice and Michael A. Walsh are no longer directors.

2920
Clark Foundation, Inc.
80 Dillon Dr.
Youngsville, PA 16371-1602 **(814) 563-4601**
Contact: David G. Clark, Secy.-Treas.

Established in PA.
Donors: Robert J. Clark; Judy M. Clark; David G. Clark; Christine M. Clark; Jay D. Curtis; Julie L. Curtis.
Foundation type: Independent foundation.
Financial data (yr. ended 06/30/13): Assets, $406,692 (M); gifts received, $42,000; expenditures, $59,943; qualifying distributions, $59,750; giving activities include $59,750 for 2 grants (high: $45,750; low: $14,000).
Fields of interest: Christian agencies & churches.
Limitations: Applications accepted. Giving primarily in PA. No grants to individuals.
Application information: Application form required.
Initial approach: Letter
Deadline(s): None
Officers: Robert J. Clark, Pres.; Judy M. Clark, V.P.; David G. Clark, Secy.-Treas.
Director: Christine M. Clark.
EIN: 251411319

2921
The Comcast Foundation
1 Comcast Ctr., 48th Fl.
Philadelphia, PA 19103-2838 (215) 286-1700
Contact: William D. Black, V.P. and Exec. Dir.
E-mail for Leaders and Achievers Scholarships: comcast@applyists.com; Main URL: http://www.comcast.com/corporate/about/inthecommunity/foundation/comcastfoundation.html
ComcastVoices: http://corporate.comcast.com/comcast-voices?category=community-investment
Facebook: https://www.facebook.com/WePowerDreams
Leaders and Achievers Scholarship Program on Facebook: http://www.facebook.com/ComcastLeadersandAchievers?ref=mf
Twitter: https://twitter.com/comcastdreambig

Established in 1999 in DE.
Donors: Comcast CICG, LP; Comcast QVC, Inc.; MOC Holdco II, Inc.
Foundation type: Company-sponsored foundation.
Financial data (yr. ended 12/31/12): Assets, $4,508,591 (M); expenditures, $16,196,745; qualifying distributions, $16,170,519; giving activities include $14,228,519 for 1,202 grants (high: $525,000; low: $250), and $1,942,000 for 1,790 grants to individuals (high: $10,000; low: $1,000).
Purpose and activities: The foundation supports programs designed to expand digital literacy; promote community service; and build tomorrow's leaders; and awards college scholarships to high school seniors.
Fields of interest: Education, reading; Education, computer literacy/technology training; Education, e-learning; Education; Employment, training; Boys & girls clubs; Big Brothers/Big Sisters; Youth development, services; YM/YWCAs & YM/YWHAs; Children/youth, services; Voluntarism promotion; United Ways and Federated Giving Programs; Computer science; Military/veterans' organizations; Leadership development; Economically disadvantaged.
Type of support: General/operating support; Continuing support; Program development; Conferences/seminars; Publication; Scholarship funds; Employee volunteer services; Sponsorships; Scholarships—to individuals.
Limitations: Applications accepted. Giving on a national basis in areas of company operations, with emphasis on CA, MA, and PA. No support for discriminatory organizations, donor-advised funds, private foundations, political candidates or organizations, or Type III Non-Supporting organizations as defined by the IRS. No grants to individuals (except for scholarships), or for marketing sponsorships, sporting events, trips or tours, capital campaigns, endowments, research studies, or lobbying campaigns.
Publications: Application guidelines.
Application information: Contributes only to individuals nominated by high school principals for scholarships. Unsolicited applications for grants or sponsorships are not accepted. Local Comcast systems and employees identify non-profit organizations as potential grant recipients. Application form required.
Initial approach: Principals should e-mail foundation to verify school eligibility status and request nomination form for scholarships
Deadline(s): Dec. 7 for Comcast Leaders and Achievers Scholarship Program
Officers and Directors:* David L. Cohen,* Co-Chair.; Ralph J. Roberts,* Co-Chair.; Charisse Lillie, Pres.; Kristine A. Dankenbrink,* Sr. V.P. and Secy.; Jospeh F. Ditrolio,* Sr. V.P. and Treas.; Tracy J. Baumgartner, Sr. V.P.; William E. Dordelman, Sr. V.P.; William D. Black, V.P. and Exec Dir.; **Frederick J. Maahs, V.P.**; Dave R. Breidinger; Julian A. Brodsky; Kevin M. Casey; William Connors; **Elizabeth A. Colleton**; Thomas J. Donnelly; A. Melissa Maxfield; Adam L. Miller; David A. Scott; Steven A. White.
EIN: 510390132

2922
The Community Foundation for the Alleghenies
(also known as The Community Foundation of Greater Johnstown)
116 Market St., Ste. 4
Johnstown, PA 15901-1644 (814) 536-7741
Contact: Michael Kane, Pres.
FAX: (814) 536-5859;
E-mail: info@cfalleghenies.org; Main URL: http://www.cfalleghenies.org
Facebook: http://www.facebook.com/pages/Johnstown-PA/Community-Foundation-for-the-Alleghenies/369858724479?ref=search

Established in 1990 in PA.
Foundation type: Community foundation.
Financial data (yr. ended 06/30/13): Assets, $54,986,653 (M); gifts received, $4,328,398; expenditures, $7,932,893; giving activities include $3,767,341 for grants.
Purpose and activities: The foundation seeks to obtain permanent endowments to provide benefits to individuals and organizations located in Bedford, Cambria, Indiana and Somerset counties, PA.
Fields of interest: Humanities; Arts; Education; Environment, natural resources; Health care; Health organizations, association; Disasters, Hurricane Katrina; Children/youth, services; Human services; Community/economic development; Public affairs; Religion; Children/youth.
Type of support: Continuing support; Equipment; Program development; Program-related investments/loans; Scholarships—to individuals.
Limitations: Applications accepted. Giving primarily in Bedford, Cambria, Indiana and Somerset counties, PA.
Publications: Annual report; Annual report (including application guidelines); Grants list; Informational brochure; Newsletter.
Application information: Visit foundation Web site for application form and guidelines; accepts Grantmakers of Western Pennsylvania Common Grant Application Format. Application form required.
Initial approach: Submit application form and attachments
Copies of proposal: 2
Deadline(s): Last Fri. in Jan. and last Fri. in Aug.
Board meeting date(s): Every 2 months
Final notification: Mid-Apr. and Mid-Nov.
Officers and Directors:* Mark E. Pasquerilla,* Chair.; Michael Kane,* Pres. and Exec. Dir.; Gary C. Horner, Esq.,* Secy.; Terry K. Dunkle,* Treas.; Robert Allen, Exec. Dir., Emeritus; Michelle Beener; John Blackburn III; **Allan Cashaw**; **Lori Copley**; Raymond DiBattista; Robert J. Eyer; Hon. Linda Rovder Fleming; Daniel Glosser; William L. Glosser, Esq.; Jerry Hudson; Sue Kiniry; John M. Kriak; Richard H. Mayer; Robin Quillon; Bill Rice; Michael Sahlaney, Esq.; Sara Ann Sargent; Thomas C. Slater; Rev. Robert Swanson; Michelle Tokarsky, Esq.; Dr. Donato Zucco.
Number of staff: 3 full-time professional; 1 part-time professional; 1 full-time support; 1 part-time support.
EIN: 251637373
Other changes: Linda Rovder Fleming is no longer a director.

2923
Community Foundation of Fayette County
2 W. Main St., Ste. 101
Uniontown, PA 15401-3450 (724) 437-8600
Contact: Marilyn J. McDaniel, C.E.O.
FAX: (724) 438-3856;
E-mail: cpascoe@cffayettepa.org; Main URL: http://cffayettepa.org
Facebook: https://www.facebook.com/pages/The-Community-Foundation-of-Fayette-County/126870187383560

Established in 1999 in PA.
Donor: Emmanuel Osagie, Ph.D.‡.
Foundation type: Community foundation.
Financial data (yr. ended 12/31/11): Assets, $8,218,402 (M); gifts received, $1,712,924; expenditures, $793,448; giving activities include $417,051 for grants.
Purpose and activities: The foundation helps define charitable needs, connects donors with causes that matters to them, supports nonprofit organizations, and invests charitable assets to make the community a better place to live.
Fields of interest: Historic preservation/historical societies; Arts; Education; Environment; Health care; Health organizations, association; Human services; Economic development; Economic development, visitors/convention bureau/tourism promotion; Community/economic development.
Type of support: Annual campaigns; Capital campaigns; Building/renovation; Equipment; Emergency funds; Program development; Scholarship funds; Technical assistance; Scholarships—to individuals.
Limitations: Applications accepted. Giving limited to the Fayette County, PA, area.
Publications: Application guidelines; Annual report; Grants list; Informational brochure; Newsletter.
Application information: Visit foundation web site for summary request form and application guidelines. Based on information provided in the letter, selected organizations may be requested additional information that could assist in making a decision. Grantmakers of Western Pennsylvania's Common Grant Application Format accepted. Application form required.
Initial approach: Letter (2 to 3 pages)
Copies of proposal: 1
Deadline(s): Feb. 28
Board meeting date(s): Jan., Apr., July, and Oct.
Officers and Directors:* James R. Foutz,* Chair.; W. David Kerr,* Vice-Chair.; Marilyn J. McDaniel,* C.E.O.; **Beth Casteel,* Secy.**; David M. Callahan,* Treas.; Robin Bubarth; Joseph F. Ferens, Esq.; David R. Hughes; Joy Huston; Philip S. Rishel; John A. Sunyecz, M.D.; Joshua Swimmer; Lynda S. Waggoner; Charles W. Watson, Esq.
Number of staff: 2 full-time professional; 1 part-time professional.
EIN: 251851158
Other changes: Beth Casteel has replaced David M. Callahan as Secy.
Jean B. Braun is no longer a director.

2924
Community Foundation of Greene County, Pennsylvania

108 E. High St.
P.O. Box 768
Waynesburg, PA 15370 (724) 627-2010
Contact: Bettie B. Stammerjohn, Exec. Dir.; An'Etta Neff, Admin. Asst.
FAX: (724) 627-2011; E-mail: cfgcpa@gmail.com; Main URL: http://www.cfgcpa.org

Established in December 2000 in PA.
Foundation type: Community foundation.
Financial data (yr. ended 12/31/12): Assets, $3,253,473 (M); gifts received, $372,498; expenditures, $519,964; giving activities include $160,674 for 7+ grants (high: $30,000), and $137,048 for 132 grants to individuals.
Purpose and activities: The foundation seeks to strengthen Greene County, PA by building charitable endowments, maximizing benefits to donors, making effective grants, and providing leadership to address community needs.
Fields of interest: Arts; Education; Environment; Health care; Food services; Food banks; Recreation; Children/youth, services; Women, centers/services; Human services; Community development, neighborhood development; Economic development; Nonprofit management.
Type of support: Building/renovation; Equipment; Program development; Conferences/seminars; Publication; Seed money; Curriculum development; Research; Technical assistance; Program evaluation; Scholarships—to individuals; Matching/challenge support.
Limitations: Applications accepted. Giving primarily in Greene County, PA. No support for political organizations. No grants to individuals (except for scholarships), or for debt reduction, or capital campaign funds; no multi-year grants.
Publications: Application guidelines; Annual report; Financial statement; Grants list; Informational brochure; Newsletter; Occasional report; Program policy statement.
Application information: See web site www.cfgcpa.org for additional information. Application form required.
Initial approach: Telephone
Copies of proposal: 1
Deadline(s): Feb. 27 for Homeless Fund; June 15 and Oct. 1 for Discretionary Grants; year-round for EITC Innovation Curriculum Grants
Board meeting date(s): 3rd Thurs. of alternating months, beginning in Jan.
Final notification: 6 weeks to 2 months
Officers and Directors:* Nancy I. Davis,* Chair.; Connie Grimes,* Vice-Chair.; **Thelma Szarell,* Secy.**; **Thomas G. Milinovich,* Treas.**; **Jeffrey Widdup, Asst. Treas.**; Bettie B. Stammerjohn, Exec. Dir.; Mark Carlson; **Linda Corfront**; Kim Grimes; Morris Harper, M.D.; Jessica Johnson; Goldie Saesan; Chad Sethman, Ph.D.; Dolly Throckmorton; Jim Zalar.
Number of staff: 1 full-time professional; 1 full-time support.
EIN: 251881899
Other changes: Thelma Szarell has replaced Margaret E. Rock as Secy. Thomas G. Milinovich has replaced James R. O'Connell as Treas. Jeffrey Widdup is now Asst. Treas. Leonard Brown, Lucy Northrop Corwin, Robert Willison, and Laural Ziemba are no longer directors.

2925
Community Foundation of Western Pennsylvania and Eastern Ohio

(formerly Shenango Valley Foundation)
7 W. State St.
Sharon, PA 16146-2713 (724) 981-5882
Contact: Lawrence E. Haynes, Exec. Dir.; For grants: Amy Atkinson, Assoc. Dir.
FAX: (724) 983-9044;
E-mail: info@comm-foundation.com; Additional tel.: (866) 901-7204; Grant inquiry e-mail: amy@comm-foundation.org; **Main URL: http://comm-foundation.org/**
Facebook: https://www.facebook.com/TCFWPEO
YouTube: http://www.youtube.com/user/tcfwpeo?feature=watch

Established in PA in 1981.
Donors: Paul O'Brien; Tina O'Brien.
Foundation type: Community foundation.
Financial data (yr. ended 12/31/12): Assets, $51,748,231 (M); gifts received, $9,066,461; expenditures, $4,411,730; giving activities include $2,350,183 for 59+ grants (high: $100,000), and $847,543 for 791 grants to individuals.
Purpose and activities: The foundation is a public, non-profit charitable organization designed to attract and invest permanent endowment resources, with the purpose of enhancing the quality of life for the residents of western Pennsylvania and eastern Ohio, in accordance with the charitable intentions of its donors who wish to leave a legacy. To fulfill this mission, the foundation will: 1) identify and support community-based charitable purposes in the areas of health, education, economic development, human services, historical, cultural and environmental activities; 2) help to shape responses to community needs through philanthropic leadership, commitment, and compassion; and 3) demonstrate accountability and integrity in the management of resources.
Fields of interest: Education, early childhood education; Higher education; Medical care, rehabilitation; Food services; Homeless, human services; Community/economic development; Aging; Disabilities, people with; Economically disadvantaged.
Type of support: General/operating support; Building/renovation; Equipment; Emergency funds; Program development; Curriculum development; Scholarship funds; Employee-related scholarships; Grants to individuals; Scholarships—to individuals; Matching/challenge support; Student loans—to individuals.
Limitations: Applications accepted. Giving limited to the Shenango Valley area, including Trumbull and Mahoning counties, OH, and Mercer and Lawrence counties, PA. No support for sectarian religious activities or fire departments. No grants for program ads, fundraising events, more than half the cost of a vehicle, start-up organizations, school playgrounds, endowments, field trips, internships, or indirect costs.
Publications: Application guidelines; Annual report; Informational brochure.
Application information: Visit foundation web site for application information. The foundation will request full proposals based on letters of inquiry. Application form required.
Initial approach: Letter of inquiry
Copies of proposal: 1
Deadline(s): None
Board meeting date(s): Quarterly
Officers and Directors:* James A. O'Brien, Esq.,* Pres.; Karen Winner Sed,* V.P.; Ronald R. Anderson,* Secy.; James E. Feeney,* Treas.; Shelly R. Mason, C.F.O.; Lawrence E. Haynes, Exec. Dir.; Robert C. Jazwinski, Dir. Emeritus; Mel Grata; Paul E. O'Brien; Albert R. Puntureri; William J. Strimbu; James T. Weller, Sr.; Donna Winner.
Number of staff: 1 full-time professional; 2 part-time professional.
EIN: 251407396
Other changes: Sandy Anderson Baker is now Prog. Coord.

2926
Connelly Foundation

100 Front St.
1 Tower Bridge, Ste. 1450
West Conshohocken, PA **19428-2873** (610) 834-3222
Contact: E. Ann Wilcox, Assoc. V.P., Admin.
FAX: (610) 834-0866; E-mail: info@connellyfdn.org; Main URL: http://www.connellyfdn.org
Grants Database: http://www.connellyfdn.org/searchgrants.aspx

Incorporated in 1955 in PA.
Donors: John F. Connelly†; Josephine C. Connelly†.
Foundation type: Independent foundation.
Financial data (yr. ended 12/31/12): Assets, $223,101,276 (M); gifts received, $98,863; expenditures, $17,072,600; qualifying distributions, $10,915,696; giving activities include $9,199,737 for 552 grants (high: $750,000; low: $100).
Purpose and activities: The foundation seeks to foster learning and to improve the quality of life in the Greater Philadelphia area. The foundation supports local non-profit organizations in the fields of education, health and human services, arts and culture, and civic enterprise.
Fields of interest: Arts; Elementary/secondary education; Education, early childhood education; Child development, education; Elementary school/education; Secondary school/education; Higher education; Adult/continuing education; Education; Health care; Substance abuse, services; Alcoholism; Employment, training; Youth development, citizenship; Human services; Children/youth, services; Child development, services; Aging, centers/services; Women, centers/services; Homeless, human services; Community/economic development; Protestant agencies & churches; Catholic agencies & churches; Infants/toddlers; Children/youth; Children; Youth; Adults; Aging; Young adults; Disabilities, people with; Physically disabled; Blind/visually impaired; Deaf/hearing impaired; Mentally disabled; Minorities; Hispanics/Latinos; Women; Girls; Immigrants/refugees; Economically disadvantaged; Homeless.
Type of support: Technical assistance; General/operating support; Continuing support; Capital campaigns; Building/renovation; Equipment; Program development; Scholarship funds; Employee matching gifts; Matching/challenge support.
Limitations: Applications accepted. Giving in Philadelphia, and surrounding counties of Bucks, Chester, Delaware and Montgomery, PA, and in Camden, NJ. No support for political or national organizations, or for public or charter schools, environmental programs, re-granting organizations, or for national organizations focused on a single disease. No grants to individuals, or for research, annual appeals advocacy, conferences, feasibility or planning studies, general solicitations, or for historic preservation projects.
Publications: Application guidelines; Financial statement.
Application information: Delaware Valley Grantmakers Common Grant Application Form and the Delaware Valley Grantmakers Common Report Form accepted. To access these forms (along with

two other specific application instructions) please go to the "Downloadable Forms" section of the foundation website. Application form required.

Initial approach: Proposal
Copies of proposal: 1
Deadline(s): None
Board meeting date(s): Jan., Apr., Aug., Nov.
Final notification: 3 months

Officers and Trustees:* Josephine C. Mandeville,* Chair., C.E.O., and Pres.; Victoria K. Flaville,* C.O.O. and Sr. V.P., Progs.; Emily C. Riley,* Exec. V.P.; Lewis W. Bluemle,* Sr. V.P.; Thomas A. Riley, V.P., Planning; Amy M. Snyder,* C.F.O. and Treas.; Joseph D. Frangiosa, Cont.; Ira Brind; Craig R. Carnaroli; Christine C. Connelly; Daniele M. Connelly; Stephan T. Connelly; Thomas S. Connelly; Eleanor L. Davis; Brendan Delany; Mary G. Duden; James P. Gallagher; Scott M. Jenkins; Caroline Mandeville; Amelia Q. Riley; Barbara W. Riley.
Number of staff: 6 full-time professional; 6 part-time professional; 3 full-time support; 2 part-time support.
EIN: 236296825

2927
The Cooper-Siegel Family Foundation
c/o BNY Mellon, N.A.
P.O. Box 185
Pittsburgh, PA 15230-0185

Established in 1996 in PA.
Donors: Eric C. Cooper; Cooper-Siegel Foundation Charitable Lead Trusts; Eric C. Cooper Charitable Lead Trust; Naomi L. Siegel Charitable Lead Trust.
Foundation type: Independent foundation.
Financial data (yr. ended 04/30/13): Assets, $2,851,008 (M); gifts received, $841,528; expenditures, $928,285; qualifying distributions, $911,000; giving activities include $911,000 for grants.
Fields of interest: Education; Health organizations; Diabetes research; Human services; Children/youth, services; Jewish federated giving programs.
Limitations: Applications not accepted. Giving primarily in Pittsburgh, PA; some giving in NY. No grants to individuals.
Application information: Contributes only to pre-selected organizations.
Trustee: E. David Margolis.
EIN: 311537177

2928
Copernicus Society of America
1 Reiffs Mill Rd.
Ambler, PA 19002-4280

Established in 1972 in PA.
Donors: Edward J. Piszek, Sr.†; James A. Michener†.
Foundation type: Independent foundation.
Financial data (yr. ended 06/30/13): Assets, $4,868,807 (M); gifts received, $3,262,744; expenditures, $1,968,757; qualifying distributions, $1,880,516; giving activities include $1,842,263 for 34 grants (high: $1,686,000; low: $100).
Purpose and activities: Giving primarily for the support and advancement of the Polish culture and heritage. Giving also for education and Roman Catholic organizations.
Fields of interest: Higher education, university; Education; Catholic agencies & churches.
International interests: Poland.
Type of support: Continuing support; Endowments; Conferences/seminars; Publication.
Limitations: Applications not accepted. Giving primarily in PA. No grants to individuals, or for special projects, operating budgets, annual campaigns, seed money, emergency funds, deficit financing, building funds, equipment and materials, land acquisition, matching gifts, scholarships, fellowships, or research; no loans.
Application information: Unsolicited requests for funds not accepted.
Officers: Helen P. Nelson, Pres.; Francis Keenan, V.P.; Edward J. Piszek, Jr., V.P.; George W. Piszek, V.P.; William P. Piszek, V.P.; P. Erik Nelson, Exec. Dir.
Number of staff: 1 full-time professional; 3 part-time support.
EIN: 237184731
Other changes: For the fiscal year ended June 30, 2013, the grantmaker paid grants of $1,842,263, a 1145.0% increase over the 2012 disbursements, $147,978.

2929
Rebecca Davis Trust
c/o PNC Bank, N.A.
P.O. Box 609
Pittsburgh, PA 15230-9738

Foundation type: Independent foundation.
Financial data (yr. ended 12/31/12): Assets, $12,118,469 (M); expenditures, $653,082; qualifying distributions, $590,461; giving activities include $531,533 for 11 grants (high: $100,991; low: $15,946).
Fields of interest: Higher education; Education; Health care; Jewish agencies & synagogues; Religion.
Limitations: Applications not accepted. Giving primarily in New York, NY.
Application information: Unsolicited requests for funds not accepted.
Trustee: PNC Bank, N.A.
EIN: 256104864
Other changes: The grantmaker has moved from OH to PA.

2930
Mirrel Davis Trust for Charity
c/o PNC Bank, N.A.
P.O. Box 609
Pittsburgh, PA 15230-9738

Foundation type: Independent foundation.
Financial data (yr. ended 12/31/12): Assets, $9,857,947 (M); expenditures, $544,992; qualifying distributions, $490,353; giving activities include $438,505 for 11 grants (high: $83,316; low: $13,155).
Fields of interest: Education; Health care; Community/economic development; Jewish agencies & synagogues.
Limitations: Applications not accepted.
Application information: Unsolicited requests for funds not accepted.
Trustee: PNC Bank, N.A.
EIN: 256064855
Other changes: The grantmaker has moved from OH to PA.

2931
The 1994 Charles B. Degenstein Foundation
c/o BNY Mellon, N.A.
P.O. Box 185
Pittsburgh, PA 15230-0185
Application address: 43 S. 5th St., Sunbury, PA 17801-2896, tel.: (570) 286-1582; Main URL: http://www.deg-fdn.org/

Established in 1996 in PA.
Foundation type: Independent foundation.
Financial data (yr. ended 06/30/12): Assets, $86,906,153 (M); expenditures, $5,290,075; qualifying distributions, $4,527,638; giving activities include $4,178,377 for 120 grants (high: $1,000,000; low: $1,000).
Purpose and activities: Special consideration is given to unique, innovative, and creative projects that benefit children, promote education, improve health care, encourage business, culture, conservation of nature resources, and protection of the environment.
Fields of interest: Arts; Libraries (public); Education; Health care; Disasters, fire prevention/control; Human services; YM/YWCAs & YM/YWHAs; Children, services; Community/economic development; United Ways and Federated Giving Programs; Christian agencies & churches.
Type of support: Capital campaigns; Equipment; Program development; Matching/challenge support.
Limitations: Applications accepted. Giving within a 75-mile radius of Sunbury, PA. No support for religious or political activities. No grants to individuals, or for scholarships, annual campaigns, endowment funds, operating budgets, emergency needs, or mass mailings; no loans.
Publications: Application guidelines.
Application information: Application form pages must be stapled with one staple in the upper left corner. Do not use notebooks, folders, or bind pages together. All information submitted to the foundation shall be on recycled paper and stapled with ease of recycling in mind. Videos, cassettes, or applications submitted by fax or e-mail are not accepted. See instructions on application form for exact number of copies which need to be submitted. Application form required.

Initial approach: 1-page cover letter along with 2-page application form which can be found on foundation web site
Deadline(s): None

Trustee: BNY Mellon, N.A.
EIN: 237792979

2932
Delaware County Community Foundation
P.O. Box 496
Wayne, PA 19087 (610) 994-9856
Contact: John A. Durso, Jr., Exec. Dir.
FAX: (610) 540-0190; E-mail: info@delcocf.org; Main URL: http://www.delcocf.org/

Established in 2002 in PA.
Foundation type: Community foundation.
Financial data (yr. ended 12/31/12): Assets, $1,638,656 (M); gifts received, $246,491; expenditures, $332,196; giving activities include $215,932 for 6+ grants (high: $37,000).
Purpose and activities: The foundation aims to encourage local philanthropy by assisting donors with their charitable objectives through lasting legacies that improve the quality of life for residents of Delaware County.
Fields of interest: Arts; Education; Environment; Animals/wildlife; Health care; Crime/law

enforcement; Children/youth, services; Family services; Human services; Community/economic development; Children/youth.
Limitations: Applications accepted. Giving primarily in Delaware County, VA.
Application information: Visit web site for application and guidelines per grant type. Application form required.
Deadline(s): Varies
Officers and Directors:* Grant Gegwich,* Chair.; Joe Costigan, C.F.A.*, Vice-Chair.; David A. Stitely,* Chair. Emeritus; David Kauffman,* Secy.; Marc Simmons, CPA*, Treas.; John A. Dusro, Jr., Exec. Dir.; Carmen P. Belefonte, Esq.; Peter J. Berol; Edward P. Caine, CPA; Stephen Carroll, Esq.; Anthony J. Cavaliere; Barbara A. Denczi; **Steven R. Derby**; Leo A. Hackett, Esq.; Joseph E. Lastowka, Jr., Esq.; Donna F. Tait; James E. Turner; Randolph B. Winton.
Board of Advisors: James C. Brennan, Esq.; Bruce M. Brown; **Fred Dewey**; Brian T. Hannon; Jack Holefelder, Jr.; **Lydia Holiat**; **Kim Landry**; Robert E. Latshaw; Hollie McDonald; Colleen P. Morrone; Laura Otten, Ph.D.; Joseph Pew; David L. Phillips, Ed.D.; Louis E. Prevost; Gwendolyn A. Smith; Rev. Dr. Larry V. Smoose; Laura Solomon, Esq.; Dennis Woody, Esq.; Florence F. Wright, Esq.
EIN: 611419515
Other changes: Joe Costigan, David Kauffman, Arthur R. Lewis, and Marc Simmons are no longer directors.

2933
Donahue Family Foundation, Inc.

1001 Liberty Ave., Ste. 850
Pittsburgh, PA 15222-3718
Contact: William Donahue, Pres.
E-mail: bdonahue@thebeechwood.com

Established around 1990 in PA.
Donors: John F. Donahue; Rhodora J. Donahue.
Foundation type: Independent foundation.
Financial data (yr. ended 12/31/12): Assets, $6,669,318 (M); expenditures, $1,959,386; qualifying distributions, $1,949,289; giving activities include $1,861,570 for 49 grants (high: $806,359; low: $500), and $87,719 for foundation-administered programs.
Purpose and activities: Giving primarily for education and Roman Catholic organizations.
Fields of interest: Education; Human services; Catholic agencies & churches.
Limitations: Applications accepted. Giving primarily in Pittsburgh, PA. No grants to individuals.
Application information: CGAF Common Grant Application Format accepted. Application form not required.
Initial approach: 1-page letter
Copies of proposal: 2
Deadline(s): May 1
Board meeting date(s): June and Dec.
Final notification: 60 days
Officers and Directors:* John F. Donahue,* Chair.; William J. Donahue,* Pres.; James Bougher,* Secy.-Treas.; **Benjamin P. Barton**; Dick K. Barton; **James C. Donahue**; Rhodora J. Donahue; **Kathleen M. Donahue-Wallach**; Richard S. Donley; **Thomas M. Freyvogel III**; Patrick K. Moore; Rhodara Freyvogel Noethling; **Rainey D. Redd**.
Number of staff: 1 full-time professional.
EIN: 251619351

2934
The Alfred And Mary Douty Foundation

(also known as The Alfred and Mary Douty Foundation)
Philadelphia, PA

The foundation terminated in 2013.

2935
Peter C. Dozzi Family Foundation

(also known as Eugene Dozzi Charitable Foundation)
2000 Lincoln Rd.
Pittsburgh, PA 15235-1129

Established in 1969 in PA.
Donors: Domenic P. Dozzi; Peter C. Dozzi; Dwight E. Kuhn; Petrina A. Lloyd; Thomas J. Murphy; EPIC Metals Corp.; Jendoco Construction Corp.; Theresa K. Dozzi; Plum Corp.; Theresa K. Dozzi.
Foundation type: Independent foundation.
Financial data (yr. ended 04/30/13): Assets, $5,376,231 (M); gifts received, $103,500; expenditures, $234,070; qualifying distributions, $226,195; giving activities include $216,655 for 83 grants (high: $50,000; low: $100).
Fields of interest: Museums (natural history); Historic preservation/historical societies; Arts; Higher education; Hospitals (general); Health care; Health organizations, association; Human services; Jewish agencies & synagogues.
Type of support: General/operating support.
Limitations: Applications not accepted. Giving primarily in Pittsburgh, PA. No grants to individuals.
Application information: Unsolicited requests for funds not accepted.
Officer and Trustees:* Petrina A. Lloyd,* Mgr.; Domenic P. Dozzi; Peter C. Dozzi; Theresa K. Dozzi.
EIN: 237023479
Other changes: Dwight E. Kuhn is no longer a trustee.

2936
Drueding Foundation

c/o Mrs. James J. Stokes, III
669 Dodds Ln.
Gladwyne, PA 19035-1514

Established in 1986 in PA.
Foundation type: Independent foundation.
Financial data (yr. ended 06/30/13): Assets, $7,184,352 (M); expenditures, $328,213; qualifying distributions, $301,550; giving activities include $299,500 for 24 grants (high: $20,000; low: $1,000).
Purpose and activities: Giving primarily to hospitals and health organizations; funding also for human services.
Fields of interest: Hospitals (general); Health care; Health organizations, association; Cancer research; Medical research; Human services; Children/youth, services; Women; Homeless.
Limitations: Applications not accepted. Giving primarily in PA. No grants to individuals.
Application information: Contributes only to pre-selected organizations.
Officers: Mary Beth Lopiccolo, Pres.; Nanny G. Gifford, V.P.; James Drueding, Secy.; Patricia D. Stokes, Treas.
Trustees: Richard Drueding; Lizanne Michener; Diana D. Stewart; Caroline M. Stokes.
EIN: 232418214

2937
DSF Charitable Foundation

(formerly Scaife Charitable Foundation)
5840 Ellsworth Ave., Ste. 200
Pittsburgh, PA 15232-1727 (412) 362-6000
Contact: J. Nicholas Beldecos, Exec. Dir.
FAX: (412) 362-6600; E-mail: info@dsfcf.org; Main URL: http://www.dsfcf.org

Established in 2000 in PA.
Foundation type: Independent foundation.
Financial data (yr. ended 12/31/12): Assets, $94,403,850 (M); expenditures, $4,001,702; qualifying distributions, $3,392,828; giving activities include $2,765,230 for 25 grants (high: $1,100,000; low: $15,000).
Purpose and activities: Giving primarily for human services, health, and education.
Fields of interest: Higher education; Education; Health care; Biomedicine; Neuroscience; Medical research; Human services; Children/youth, services; Residential/custodial care, senior continuing care.
Type of support: General/operating support; Building/renovation; Equipment; Program development; Seed money; Research; Program evaluation; Matching/challenge support.
Limitations: Applications accepted. Giving primarily in southwestern PA, particularly in Pittsburgh. No grants to individuals, or for endowments.
Publications: Application guidelines.
Application information: Accepts the Common Grant Application Format of Grantmakers of Western Pennsylvania. See foundation web site for application information and guidelines. Though not required, all material may be submitted in electronic format (PDF preferred). Application form not required.
Initial approach: Letter of inquiry (with supporting material not to exceed 5 pages)
Copies of proposal: 1
Deadline(s): None
Board meeting date(s): Varies
Final notification: Following board meeting
Officers and Trustees:* David N. Scaife,* Chair.; Sanford B. Ferguson,* Vice-Chair.; Sara D. Scaife,* Secy.; Edward J. Goncz,* Treas.; J. Nicholas Beldecos, Exec. Dir.; Donald A. Collins; Frances G. Scaife.
Number of staff: 1 full-time professional; 2 part-time professional; 1 full-time support.
EIN: 251847237
Other changes: Joseph C. Walton is no longer a trustee.

2938
Lola G. Duff & William H. Duff II Scholarship Fund

P.O. Box 609
Pittsburgh, PA 15230-9738

Foundation type: Independent foundation.
Financial data (yr. ended 03/31/13): Assets, $89,618,949 (M); expenditures, $3,857,943; qualifying distributions, $3,479,987; giving activities include $3,257,108 for grants.
Fields of interest: Scholarships/financial aid.
Type of support: Scholarship funds.
Limitations: Applications not accepted. Giving primarily in PA. No grants to individuals.
Application information: Unsolicited requests for funds not accepted.
Trustee: PNC Bank, N.A.
EIN: 611467176
Other changes: The grantmaker has moved from OH to PA.

2939

Elk County Community Foundation

(doing business as Community Foundation of North Central Pennsylvania)
32 S. St.Marys St.
P.O. Box 934
Saint Marys, PA 15857 (814) 834-2125
Contact: Paula Fritz Eddy, Exec. Dir.
FAX: (814) 834-2126; E-mail: eccf@windstream.net; Main URL: http://www.elkcountyfoundation.com
Facebook: https://www.facebook.com/elkcountycommunityfoundation

Established in 2000 in PA.
Foundation type: Community foundation.
Financial data (yr. ended 12/31/12): Assets, $6,072,186 (M); gifts received, $202,555; expenditures, $402,895; giving activities include $218,223 for 17+ grants (high: $38,964), and $84,076 for 106 grants to individuals.
Purpose and activities: The foundation provides a vehicle that will enable citizens of Elk County to achieve their philanthropic expectations and in so doing strengthen the quality of life in the region.
Fields of interest: Arts; Higher education; Education; Environment; Health care; Health organizations, association; Children/youth, services; Human services; Economic development; Aging.
Type of support: Building/renovation; Equipment; Program development; Scholarship funds; Program-related investments/loans; Scholarships—to individuals; Matching/challenge support.
Limitations: Applications accepted. Giving primarily in Elk County, PA. No grants for ongoing operational support or event sponsorship.
Publications: Application guidelines; Annual report; Grants list; Informational brochure; Informational brochure (including application guidelines); Newsletter.
Application information: Visit foundation web site for application form and guidelines. Application form required.
Initial approach: Mail application form and attachments
Copies of proposal: 1
Deadline(s): Jan. 15 and July 15
Board meeting date(s): Mar., May, Aug., and Nov.
Officers and Directors:* Donald Valone,* Pres.; James A. Meyer,* V.P.; Rich Smith,* Secy.; J.M. Hamlin Johnson,* Treas.; Paula Fritz Eddy, Exec. Dir.; Gennaro Aiello; Paul Bierly; William Conrad; Charles Constable; John Dippold III; Barb Duffy; Frtiz Lecker; Judy Manno Stager; Charlie Steger; Dan Straub.
Number of staff: 1 part-time professional; 1 part-time support.
EIN: 251859637

2940

EQT Foundation, Inc.

(formerly Equitable Resources Foundation, Inc.)
1 PNC Plaza
249 Fifth Ave., 3rd Fl.
Pittsburgh, PA 15222 (412) 762-3502
Contact: Bruce Bickel, Exec. Dir.
E-mail: bruce.bickel@pncadvisors.com; **Main URL: http://www.eqt.com/ourcommunities/eqt-foundation.aspx**
ASPIRE on Facebook: https://www.facebook.com/pages/ASPIRE-Area-Students-Participating-in-Rewarding-Education/214494945406237
ASPIRE Website: http://www.aspireprogram.org/
Application address: 625 Liberty Ave., Pittsburgh, PA 15222, e-mail: aspire@egt.com

Established in 2003 in PA.
Donors: Equitable Production Co.; EQD Holdings Co., LLC.
Foundation type: Company-sponsored foundation.
Financial data (yr. ended 12/31/12): Assets, $24,337,308 (M); expenditures, $3,156,514; qualifying distributions, $2,922,822; giving activities include $2,888,936 for 353 grants (high: $146,162; low: $100).
Purpose and activities: The foundation supports programs designed to promote education for children and adults; encourage the development of safe and livable communities; promote the environment and preservation of local natural resources; and foster understanding and appreciation of culture and heritage.
Fields of interest: Arts, cultural/ethnic awareness; Museums; Performing arts; Arts; Elementary/secondary education; Higher education; Adult/continuing education; Libraries (public); Education, reading; Education; Environment, recycling; Environment, natural resources; Environment, energy; Horticulture/garden clubs; Environmental education; Animal welfare; Employment, services; Housing/shelter, development; Recreation, fairs/festivals; Youth development, adult & child programs; Youth development, business; Business/industry; Community/economic development; Voluntarism promotion; Mathematics; Engineering/technology; Science; Aging; Economically disadvantaged.
Type of support: Program development; Seed money; Scholarship funds; Employee volunteer services; Sponsorships; Scholarships—to individuals; In-kind gifts; Matching/challenge support.
Limitations: Applications accepted. Giving primarily in areas of company operations in KY, Pittsburgh, PA, VA, and WV. No support for churches or religious organizations, political parties, candidates, or public policy advocates, for-profit businesses or associations, tax-supported entities (except for public schools), or fraternal, social, union, or hobby/recreational clubs or organizations. No grants to individuals (except for ASPIRE), or for capital campaigns, endowments, new construction or building renovations, mortgage/rent/insurance/utility costs, vehicle purchases or repairs, infrastructure improvements, sporting events including golf outings, travel to conferences, workshops, seminars, competitions, or emergency or stop-gap funding.
Publications: Application guidelines.
Application information: Proposals should be no longer than 6 pages. Application form required.
Initial approach: Download application form and mail proposal and application form to foundation; complete application form during enrollment period for ASPIRE
Copies of proposal: 1
Deadline(s): Feb. 1, May 1, Aug. 1, and Nov. 1; Varies for ASPIRE
Board meeting date(s): Mar., June, Sept., and Dec.
Officers and Directors:* Charlene G. Petrelli,* Pres.; Natalie Cox, V.P., Public Affairs; Ellen Donnelly, V.P., Community Rels.; Patrick J. Kane, V.P., Finance; Christopher T. Akers, V.P.; Kenneth C. Kirk, V.P.; John H. Obrist, Secy.; Thomas E. Quinlan, Treas.; Bruce Bickel, Exec. Dir.; Martin A. Fritz, Esq.; M. Elise Hyland; Lewis B. Gardner; Steven T. Schlotterbeck.
EIN: 043747289
Other changes: James E. Crockard, III is no longer Treas. Pamela Coates is no longer V.P., Community Rels. John Kevin West is no longer V.P., Public Affairs.

2941

The Moses Feldman Family Foundation

8 Tower Bridge
161 Washington St, Ste. 410
Conshokocken, PA **19428-2043**

Established in 2005 in PA.
Donors: The Feldman Foundation; Jacob Feldman Marital Trust; Jacob Feldman Charitable Lead Trust.
Foundation type: Independent foundation.
Financial data (yr. ended 12/31/12): Assets, $29,778,600 (M); gifts received, $7,228,020; expenditures, $1,286,489; qualifying distributions, $1,103,169; giving activities include $1,002,500 for 43 grants (high: $110,000; low: $5,000).
Purpose and activities: Giving primarily for Jewish organizations, higher education, and the environment, specifically an arboretum and an environmental club.
Fields of interest: Higher education; Botanical gardens; Animals/wildlife, clubs; Jewish federated giving programs; Public policy, research; Jewish agencies & synagogues.
Type of support: General/operating support.
Limitations: Applications not accepted. Giving primarily in MA, NY, PA, and Washington, DC. No grants to individuals.
Application information: Contributes only to pre-selected organizations.
Trustees: Moses Feldman; Susan Feldman.
EIN: 202086533
Other changes: Robert Pozen is no longer an officer.

2942

Samuel S. Fels Fund

1528 Walnut St., Ste. 1002
Philadelphia, PA 19102-3627 (215) 731-9455
Contact: Helen Cunningham, Exec. Dir.
FAX: (215) 731-9457; **tel: (215) 731-9455**; Main URL: http://www.samfels.org

Incorporated in 1935 in PA.
Donor: Samuel S. Fels†.
Foundation type: Independent foundation.
Financial data (yr. ended 12/31/12): Assets, $45,828,790 (M); expenditures, $2,088,564; qualifying distributions, $1,942,017; giving activities include $1,459,250 for 151 grants (high: $125,000; low: $1,000).
Purpose and activities: Grants for projects and organizations that help to prevent, lessen, or resolve contemporary social problems, or that seek to provide permanent improvements in the provision of services for the improvement of daily life; to increase the stability of arts organizations and enrich the cultural life of the city of Philadelphia, PA.
Fields of interest: Arts; Education; Community/economic development.
Type of support: General/operating support; Continuing support; Equipment; Program development; Seed money; Curriculum development; Internship funds; Technical assistance; Matching/challenge support.
Limitations: Applications accepted. Giving limited to the City of Philadelphia, PA. No support for national organizations, day or after-school care programs, routine social services or counseling, drug and alcohol addiction programs, religious education, private schools, hospitals, programs for animals, or summer recreation programs. No grants for endowment or building funds, travel, research, publications, deficit financing, scholarships, fellowships, purchase of tickets, tables, ads or sponsorships, parties, conferences, fairs and festivals, or disease research.

Publications: Application guidelines; Annual report (including application guidelines); Grants list.
Application information: Applicant must request guidelines before submitting proposals; the fund accepts Delaware Valley Grantmakers Common Grant Application and Common Report forms. Proposal Cover Sheet is available on foundation web site. Application form required.
Initial approach: Proposal or telephone requesting guidelines
Copies of proposal: 1
***Deadline(s):* For Arts and Humanities projects: by 5:00 p.m. on Jan. 15 or May 15; None for others**
Board meeting date(s): Rolling application review, board meets 7 times a year
Final notification: Usually one or two months
Officers and Directors:* Valerie Clayton,* Pres.; Beverly Coleman,* V.P.; Helen Cunningham,* Secy. and Exec. Dir.; **John Rice,* Treas.;** Ida K. Chen; Sandra Featherman; Phoebe A. Haddon; Len Rieser; David H. Wice.
Number of staff: 1 full-time professional; 1 full-time support; 1 part-time support.
EIN: 231365325
Other changes: Valerie Clayton has replaced Mindy M. Posoff as Pres. Beverly Coleman has replaced Valerie Clayton as V.P. John Rice has replaced Beverly Coleman as Treas.

2943
The Female Association of Philadelphia
c/o Haverford Trust Company
3 Radnor Corp. Ctr.
Radnor, PA 19087-4580

Established in 1800 in PA.
Foundation type: Independent foundation.
Financial data (yr. ended 09/30/13): Assets, $3,069,628 (M); gifts received, $1,415; expenditures, $176,011; qualifying distributions, $144,650; giving activities include $144,650 for 359+ grants.
Purpose and activities: Modest, individual grants awarded only to women 60 years of age or older, who reside in the Philadelphia, PA, area with a per annum income under $12,000, and who do not receive Supplemental Security Income (SSI).
Fields of interest: Aging; Women; Economically disadvantaged.
Type of support: Grants to individuals.
Limitations: Applications not accepted. Giving primarily in PA.
Application information: Unsolicited requests for funds not accepted.
Officers and Trustees:* Rodney D. Day III,* Pres.; Jack M. Maxwell III,* V.P.; Anne Pringle III,* Secy.; Ellen G. Anderson III,* Treas.; **Pierce Archer; William L. Hires;** Robert B. Hobbs, Jr.; Pamela W. Leighton; **Brian J. Linz; Marg Macdonald; David Maxey.**
EIN: 236214961
Other changes: Jack M. Maxwell III has replaced Rodney D. Day, III as V.P. Rodney D. Day III has replaced B. Graeme Frazier, III as Pres.
Carla P. Childs, John N. Childs, Marda Donner, and Morris A. Stout are no longer trustees.

2944
Ferree Foundation
229 N. Duke St.
Lancaster, PA 17602-2709 **(717) 735-8288, ext. 109**
Contact: Phillip L. Calhoun, Exec. Dir.
FAX: (717) 735-8291;
E-mail: pcalhoun@ferree-foundation.org; Main URL: http://www.ferree-foundation.org

Established in 2004 in PA.
Foundation type: Independent foundation.
Financial data (yr. ended 12/31/12): Assets, $15,269,673 (M); gifts received, $770,044; expenditures, $1,379,614; qualifying distributions, $1,287,084; giving activities include $1,227,500 for 34 grants (high: $200,000; low: $1,000).
Purpose and activities: The foundation is dedicated to promoting and supporting excellence in the arts, culture and history, education, youth engagement, health, human services, and local economic and community development.
Fields of interest: Performing arts; Historical activities; Higher education; Education; Health care; Children/youth, services.
Type of support: Building/renovation; Endowments; Program development; Capital campaigns; Technical assistance; Research; General/operating support; Annual campaigns.
Limitations: Applications accepted. Giving primarily in Lancaster County and southeastern PA. No grants to individuals; no loans.
Publications: Application guidelines; Financial statement; Grants list; Program policy statement (including application guidelines).
Application information: Application guidelines available on foundation web site. Full proposals accepted by invitation only, following positive ruling on letter of inquiry. Delaware Valley Grantmakers Common Grant Application Form accepted.
Application form not required.
***Initial approach:* Letter of inquiry (1-page maximum)**
Copies of proposal: 1
Deadline(s): Oct. 15th
Board meeting date(s): Bi-annually
Final notification: Ruling on letter of inquiry within 1 month
Officers and Directors:* Paul W. Ware,* Pres.; Ron Frederick, V.P.; Phillip L. Calhoun, Exec. Dir.; Judy S. Ware.
Number of staff: 1 part-time professional; 1 part-time support.
EIN: 201060557

2945
Joseph and Marie Field Family Environmental Foundation
30 Valley Stream Pkwy.
Malvern, PA 19355-1462
***Contact:* E.R. Boynton**

Donors: Joseph M. Field; Marie H. Field.
Foundation type: Independent foundation.
Financial data (yr. ended 07/31/13): Assets, $8,030,417 (M); gifts received, $1,224,804; expenditures, $414,693; qualifying distributions, $400,000; giving activities include $400,000 for 10 grants (high: $200,000; low: $10,000).
Fields of interest: Environment; International affairs.
Limitations: Applications not accepted. Giving primarily in NY and Arlington, VA.
Application information: Unsolicited requests for funds not accepted.
Officers and Directors:* Joseph M. Field,* Pres. and Treas.; Marie H. Field,* V.P. and Secy.; Nancy E. Field,* V.P.; David J. Field,* V.P.; Jaimie Field; **Michael Schulder.**
EIN: 263923674

2946
J. B. Finley Charitable Trust
c/o PNC Charitable Trusts
249 Fifth Ave.
1 PNC Plz., 20th Fl.
Pittsburgh, PA 15222 **(412) 762-3413**
E-mail: charitabletrusts@pnc.com

Trust established in 1919 in PA.
Donor: J.B. Finley†.
Foundation type: Independent foundation.
Financial data (yr. ended 09/30/13): Assets, $3,709,254 (M); expenditures, $219,883; qualifying distributions, $182,186; giving activities include $164,514 for 14 grants (high: $25,000; low: $5,000).
Fields of interest: Arts; Education; Human services; Christian agencies & churches.
Type of support: General/operating support; Building/renovation; Equipment; Program development; Seed money; Matching/challenge support.
Limitations: Applications accepted. Giving primarily in PA. No support for political organizations, or for labor, fraternal, or advocacy organizations. No grants to individuals, or for events or general operating costs.
Application information: Application form required.
Initial approach: Letter of inquiry or telephone
Copies of proposal: 1
Trustee: PNC Bank, N.A.
EIN: 256024443

2947
First Community Foundation Partnership of Pennsylvania
(formerly Williamsport-Lycoming Foundation)
330 Pine St., Ste. 401
Williamsport, PA 17701-6242 (570) 321-1500
Contact: For grants and scholarships: Betty Gilmour, Dir., Grantmaking
FAX: (570) 321-6434;
E-mail: jenniferw@fcfpartnership.org; Additional tel.: (866) 901-2372; Grant and scholarship inquiry e-mail: bettyg@fcfpartnership.org; Main URL: http://www.fcfpa.org

Established in 1916 in PA by bank resolution.
Foundation type: Community foundation.
Financial data (yr. ended 12/31/11): Assets, $61,777,189 (M); gifts received, $1,537,045; expenditures, $3,681,242; giving activities include $2,038,943 for 136+ grants (high: $189,614).
Purpose and activities: The foundation serves Central and Northcentral PA by helping donors make a difference in the community and making grants to nonprofit organizations in support of their charitable work.
Fields of interest: Historic preservation/historical societies; Arts; Higher education; Education; Environment, natural resources; Environment; Health care; Recreation; Youth development; Youth, services; Family services; Human services; Economic development; Community/economic development.
Type of support: Computer technology; General/operating support; Continuing support; Capital campaigns; Building/renovation; Equipment; Land acquisition; Program development; Conferences/seminars; Seed money; Scholarship funds; Program-related investments/loans; Matching/challenge support.
Limitations: Applications accepted. Giving primarily in Central and Northcentral PA. No support for sectarian religious programs, clubs, sports teams, cemeteries, school districts, or fire companies. No

grants to individuals (except for scholarships), or generally for endowment funds, annual campaigns, event sponsorships, debt reduction, fellowships, honorary awards, travel grants, or ongoing operating support; no loans to individuals.
Publications: Application guidelines; Annual report; Financial statement; Informational brochure; Program policy statement.
Application information: Visit foundation web site for application guidelines per grant type. Based on letter of intent, nonprofit organizations will be notified of whether they will be invited to submit a full grant application or whether their proposal has been denied. Application form required.
Initial approach: Submit letter of intent
Copies of proposal: 1
Deadline(s): Varies
Board meeting date(s): Monthly
Final notification: Varies
Officers and Directors:* Marshall Welch III,* Chair.; Frank Pellegrino,* Vice-Chair.; Jennifer D. Wilson,* C.E.O. and Pres.; Dawn M. Linn,* V.P., Planned Philanthropy.; Jack Willoughby,* C.F.O.; Timothy D. Fitzgerald,* Secy.; Jay B. Alexander; Lise M. Barrick; Thomas Charles; **Ronald Cimini**; Davie Jane Gilmour, Ph.D.; **Tim Karr**; Daniel A. Klingerman; Keith S. Kuzio; George E. Logue, Jr.; Grace M. Mahon; Trisha G. Marty; Teri MacBride; R. Jack McKernan, Jr.; Gary Peck; **Ted Strosser**; Leslie P. Temple; Alice Trowbridge; Tammy A. Weber; Bob Wayne; Jennifer Wilson; Sue Young.
Number of staff: 4 full-time professional; 1 part-time professional; 1 full-time support; 1 part-time support.
EIN: 246013117

2948
The First Hospital Foundation
230 S. Broad St., Ste. 402
Philadelphia, PA 19102-4108 (215) 546-4290
Contact: Ann Marie Healy, Exec. Dir.; Julia Boerth, Prog. Off.
FAX: (215) 546-4291;
E-mail: amhealy@firsthospitalfdn.org; Main URL: http://www.firsthospitalfdn.org
Blog: http://firsthospitalfdn.org/news-events/
Grants List: http://firsthospitalfdn.org/grantees/

Established in 1997 in PA.
Foundation type: Independent foundation.
Financial data (yr. ended 12/31/12): Assets, $39,661,545 (M); expenditures, $1,919,299; qualifying distributions, $1,821,321; giving activities include $1,484,067 for 50 grants (high: $140,000; low: $1,650).
Purpose and activities: The foundation seeks to provide funding support for the health needs of the underserved in the communities served by the Pennsylvania Hospital.
Fields of interest: Health care; Crime/violence prevention, abuse prevention; Human services; Community/economic development; Children; Youth; Adults; Aging; Disabilities, people with; Physically disabled; Blind/visually impaired; Deaf/hearing impaired; Mentally disabled; Minorities; Asians/Pacific Islanders; African Americans/Blacks; Hispanics/Latinos; Native Americans/American Indians; Women; Substance abusers; AIDS, people with; Single parents; Terminal illness, people with; Economically disadvantaged; Homeless; LGBTQ.
Type of support: Program evaluation; Program development; Matching/challenge support; Management development/capacity building; General/operating support; Equipment; Continuing support.
Limitations: Applications accepted. Giving primarily in the greater Philadelphia region, preference to Philadelphia County. No support for fraternal organizations, political parties, candidates, veterans, labor or local civic groups, groups engaged in influencing legislation. No grants for capital campaigns or costs associated with foundation fundraising; major building projects (minor renovations that relate directly to the effectiveness of the program may be considered); no scholarships, fellowships, grants to individuals.
Publications: Application guidelines; Financial statement; Grants list; IRS Form 990 or 990-PF printed copy available upon request.
Application information: Faxed applications are not accepted. Application form required.
Initial approach: Submit application form from foundation web site via e-mail or U.S. Mail
Deadline(s): July 31
Board meeting date(s): Apr., Oct. and Dec.
Officers and Directors:* Julia Dutton, Ph.D.*, Chair.; Jane G. Pepper,* Vice-Chair.; Suzanne Sheehan Becker, Secy.; Keith Kasper, MBA*, Treas.; Ann Marie Healy, Exec. Dir.; R. Michael Buckley, Jr., M.D.; Helen L. Coons, Ph.D., ABPP; Joanne R. Denworth; Bruce W. Herdman, M.B.A., Ph.D.; Natalie Levkovich; Sueyun Pyo Locks; Lawrence T. Mangan; A. Scott McNeal, DO; Susan E. Phillips; Pamela A. Strisofksy.
Number of staff: 1 full-time professional.
EIN: 232904262

2949
Clara Helen Firth Charitable Trust
(formerly Clara Helen Firth Testamentary Trust)
c/o Wells Fargo Bank, N.A.
101N Independence Mall E., MACY1372-062
Philadelphia, PA 19106-2112

Established in 1981; supporting organization of the Massachusetts Society for the Prevention of Cruelty to Animals, the Humane Society of the United States, American Humane Association, the Salvation Army, and Haven Humane Society, Inc.
Foundation type: Independent foundation.
Financial data (yr. ended 02/28/13): Assets, $5,931,814 (M); expenditures, $364,973; qualifying distributions, $303,470; giving activities include $285,820 for 5 grants (high: $200,074; low: $14,291).
Fields of interest: Animal welfare; Salvation Army; Human services.
Limitations: Applications not accepted. Giving on a national basis.
Application information: Unsolicited requests for funds not accepted.
Trustee: Wells Fargo Bank, N.A.
EIN: 956698210
Other changes: The grantmaker has moved from CA to PA.

2950
FISA Foundation
535 Smithfield St., Ste. 170
Pittsburgh, PA 15222-2393 (412) 456-5550
Contact: Kristy Trautmann, Exec. Dir.
FAX: (412) 456-5551;
E-mail: info@fisafoundation.org; Main URL: http://www.fisafoundation.org/
Facebook: http://www.facebook.com/fisafoundation
FISA Foundation's Philanthropy Promise: http://www.ncrp.org/philanthropys-promise/who
Grants Database: http://fisafoundation.org/grants/grants-awarded/
YouTube: http://www.youtube.com/user/fisafoundation/feed?feature=context

Established in 1996 in PA; converted from proceeds received through the sale of Harmaville Rehabilitation Center to HEALTHSOUTH Corporation.
Foundation type: Independent foundation.
Financial data (yr. ended 06/30/13): Assets, $39,993,295 (M); gifts received, $8,676; expenditures, $2,227,332; qualifying distributions, $1,992,522; giving activities include $1,591,837 for 79 grants (high: $53,751; low: $200).
Purpose and activities: The foundation's mission is to build a culture of respect and improve the quality of life for three populations in southwestern Pennsylvania: women, girls, and people with disabilities.
Fields of interest: Medical care, rehabilitation; Health care; Mental health/crisis services, rape victim services; Mental health/crisis services; Autism; Crime/violence prevention, domestic violence; Crime/violence prevention, sexual abuse; Employment, vocational rehabilitation; Employment, sheltered workshops; Recreation; Girl scouts; Human services; Family services, domestic violence; Family services, adolescent parents; Women, centers/services; Human services; Civil/human rights, disabled; Civil/human rights; Disabilities, people with; Mentally disabled; Women; Girls.
Type of support: General/operating support; Continuing support; Capital campaigns; Building/renovation; Equipment; Program development; Conferences/seminars; Seed money; Technical assistance; Program evaluation; Matching/challenge support.
Limitations: Applications accepted. Giving limited to a 10-county area of southwestern PA, including: Allegheny, Armstrong, Beaver, Butler, Greene, Fayette, Indiana, Lawrence, Washington, and Westmoreland counties. No support for organizations that lack tax-exempt status, or for religious purposes. No grants to individuals, or for scholarships, endowments, travel, or study.
Publications: Application guidelines; Annual report; Financial statement; Occasional report.
Application information: Unsolicited inquiries accepted, but unsolicited proposals are not. Full proposal is by invitation only; Grantmakers of Western Pennsylvania's Common Grant Application Format accepted. Application form required.
***Initial approach:* Letter of inquiry along with foundation application form (which can be downloaded from foundation web site), via U.S. mail or e-mail**
Copies of proposal: 1
Deadline(s): 3-4 months prior to board meeting
Board meeting date(s): Feb., June and Oct.
Final notification: Within 2 weeks
Officers and Board Members:* Susan L. Chase,* Pres.; **Linda Beerbower Burke, Esq.*, V.P.**; Margaret Mary Kimmel, Ph.D.*, Secy.; **Margaret Mary Kanaan,* Treas.**; Kristy Trautmann, Exec. Dir.; Tina Calabro; Kulsum G. Davidson; Susan Davis; **Susan Kirsch**; Deborah W. Linhart; Carol S. MacPhail; **Rosa Copeland Miller**; **Cheryl A. Parzych**; Evelyn D. Savido; Janet Simon, Ph.D.; Bernadette Eyler Smith; **Ellen Srodes**; Tamiko L. Stanley; Andrea M. Williams; **Elise Roby Yanders**.
Number of staff: 2 full-time professional; 1 full-time support.
EIN: 250965388
Other changes: Linda Beerbower Burke, Esq. has replaced Chaton T. Turner as V.P. Margaret Mary Kanaan has replaced Jane C. Burger as Treas.

Debora S. Foster, Gabriela Gavrila, and Mary M. Unkovic are no longer directors.

2951
The Fishman Family Foundation
(formerly Bernard and Annabelle Fishman Family Foundation)
Bryn Mawr, PA

The foundation dissolved as of Dec. 31, 2013.

2952
The Foundation for Enhancing Communities
(formerly The Greater Harrisburg Foundation)
200 N. 3rd St., 8th Fl.
P.O. Box 678
Harrisburg, PA 17108-0678 (717) 236-5040
Contact: Janice R. Black, C.E.O.; For grants: Jennifer Doyle, Dir., Devel. and Community Investment
FAX: (717) 231-4463; E-mail: janice@tfec.org; Grant application e-mail: jkuntche@tfec.org; Main URL: http://www.tfec.org
Scholarship inquiry e-mail: allison@tfec.org

Established in 1920 in PA; assets first acquired in 1940; grants first made in the mid-1940's.
Foundation type: Community foundation.
Financial data (yr. ended 12/31/12): Assets, $54,117,886 (M); gifts received, $5,116,513; expenditures, $6,037,174; giving activities include $3,335,675 for 157 grants (high: $187,500), $294,538 for 218 grants to individuals, and $1,466,961 for 89 foundation-administered programs.
Purpose and activities: The foundation seeks to stimulate philanthropy and enhance the quality of life in the community through accumulating, managing and disbursing financial assets, and to serve as a catalyst and neutral convener to meet a wide range of community needs in the south central Pennsylvania counties of Cumberland, Dauphin, Franklin, Lebanon, and Perry, and also in the Dillsburg area.
Fields of interest: Humanities; Arts; Education; Environment; Health care; Health organizations, association; Human services; Community/economic development; Religion.
Type of support: General/operating support; Equipment; Program development; Publication; Seed money; Scholarship funds; Technical assistance; Scholarships—to individuals; Matching/challenge support.
Limitations: Applications accepted. Giving primarily in Cumberland, Dauphin, Franklin, Lebanon, and Perry counties, PA. No support for religious organizations for religious purposes (except from Donor-Advised or Restricted funds), or for private foundations or discretionary funds. No grants to individuals (except for scholarships).
Publications: Application guidelines; Annual report (including application guidelines); Financial statement; Grants list; Informational brochure (including application guidelines); Newsletter; Program policy statement.
Application information: Call Prog. Off. for current application guidelines or visit foundation web site; copies of application vary per regional fdn.; faxed applications are not accepted. Application form required.
Initial approach: Contact Prog. Off.
Copies of proposal: 13
Deadline(s): Varies
Board meeting date(s): Jan., Mar., June, Sept., and Nov.
Final notification: Approx. 8 weeks after proposal submission
Officers and Directors:* David Schankweiler,* Chair.; Kathy Pape,* Vice-Chair.; Janice R. Black,* C.E.O. and Pres.; Neal S. West, Esq.,* Secy.; Steven M. Hoffman,* Treas.; Kirk C. Demyan,* C.F.O.; David B. Skerpon,* Asst. Secy.; Cynthia Tolsma,* Asst. Treas.; Marilynn R. Abrams; Michael R. Gillepsie; Nancy J. Glen; David M. Kleppinger; Kenneth E. Lehman; L. Jeffrey Mattern; Karen F. Snider; and 3 additional directors.
Trustee Banks: BNY Mellon, N.A.; Bryn Mawr Trust Company; Citizens Bank of Southern Pennslyvania; Farmers Trust of Carlisle; Financial Trust Services; First National Bank & Trust of Waynesboro; First National Bank of Greencastle; Fulton Financial Advisors, N.A.; GHF, Inc.; Hershey Trust Co.; Juniata Valley Bank; M&T Bank; PNC Bank, N.A.; Pennsylvania State Bank; Sentry Trust Co.; Susquehanna Bank; Valley Bank & Trust Co.; Wachovia Bank, N.A.; Wells Fargo.
Number of staff: 9 full-time professional; 1 part-time professional; 2 full-time support.
EIN: 010564355
Other changes: Jim Martin is now Sr. Financial Advisor. Robert J. Dolan, Miles J. Gibbons, Alan Krasner, Stephen C. MacDonald, and Nancy Dering Mock are no longer directors.

2953
Fourjay Foundation
2300 Computer Ave., Bldg. G, Ste. 1
Willow Grove, PA 19090-1753 (215) 830-1437
Contact: Ann T. Bucci, Grants Coord.
FAX: (215) 830-0157; E-mail: info@fourjay.org; Main URL: http://www.fourjay.org

Established in 1988 in PA.
Donors: Eugene W. Jackson‡; Springhouse Realty Co.
Foundation type: Independent foundation.
Financial data (yr. ended 12/31/13): Assets, $16,851,922 (M); expenditures, $1,143,271; qualifying distributions, $962,794; giving activities include $828,950 for 161 grants (high: $50,000; low: $200).
Purpose and activities: The foundation supports education and human services. Its directors believe these two areas of human endeavor offer people the greatest help; education enables people to make the most of their abilities; human services offer a helping hand to the afflicted, the socially disadvantaged, and the financially handicapped.
Fields of interest: Higher education; Adult education—literacy, basic skills & GED; Medical care, rehabilitation; Nursing care; Health care; Substance abuse, services; Mental health/crisis services; Health organizations, association; Cancer; Eye diseases; Ear, nose & throat diseases; Food services; Human services; Children/youth, services; Family services; Residential/custodial care, hospices; Aging, centers/services; Homeless, human services; Disabilities, people with; Economically disadvantaged; Homeless.
Type of support: General/operating support; Continuing support; Building/renovation; Equipment; Endowments; Emergency funds; Program development; Publication; Seed money; Scholarship funds; Matching/challenge support.
Limitations: Applications accepted. Giving limited to Philadelphia, Bucks, and Montgomery counties, PA. **No support for political or religious organizations, museums, musical groups, theaters, or cultural organizations, athletic groups, civic associations, alumni associations, elementary or secondary schools, foreign organizations, public broadcasting, libraries, the United Way, or the YMCA.** No grants to individuals or multi-year grants.
Publications: Application guidelines; Grants list.
Application information: Telephone calls accepted. Submit 1 complete proposal and 7 copies of cover proposal letter; only 1 application per organization accepted per year. Grant requests lacking appropriate financial information will not be accepted. All requests for foundation guidelines should be submitted in writing on the grant seeking organization's letterhead, with the appropriate return mailing and contact information provided. Copies of current guidelines can be downloaded from the foundation web site. Unannounced or impromptu visits are not entertained. Delaware Valley Grantmakers Common Grant Application Form accepted. Application form not required.
Initial approach: Proposal and separate 1-page cover letter on organization letterhead
Deadline(s): See foundation web site for current deadlines
Board meeting date(s): Mar. 15, June 15, Sept. 15, and Dec. 15
Final notification: Generally within 90 days of proposal receipt
Officer and Directors:* Susan Jackson Tressider, Exec. Dir. and Managing Tr.; Geoffrey W. Jackson,* Managing Tr.; Sean E. Brinda; Diana Loukedis Doherty; **Marie-Louise Jackson**; Daniel O'Connell, Esq.; Jean Robinson.
Number of staff: 1 part-time professional; 1 part-time support.
EIN: 232537126

2954
Freas Foundation, Inc.
2201 Ridgewood Rd., Ste. 180
Wyomissing, PA 19610-1190
Contact: David M. Trout, Mgr.

Established in 1951.
Foundation type: Independent foundation.
Financial data (yr. ended 12/31/12): Assets, $3,496,916 (M); expenditures, $184,408; qualifying distributions, $162,337; giving activities include $162,337 for 29 grants (high: $15,000; low: $1,000).
Purpose and activities: Giving primarily for the arts, education, and human services.
Fields of interest: Arts; Higher education; Human services; Children/youth, services.
Type of support: General/operating support; Annual campaigns; Capital campaigns; Program development; Scholarship funds; Matching/challenge support.
Limitations: Applications not accepted. Giving primarily in PA. No grants to individuals.
Application information: Contributes only to pre-selected organizations.
Officers: Donald Freas, Pres.; Nancy Pratt, V.P.; Susan Magargee, Secy.; Lawrence Freas, Treas.
EIN: 221714810
Other changes: The grantmaker has moved from CT to PA.
Donald Freas has replaced Arthur K. Freas as Pres. Margery H. Freas is no longer V.P.

2955
The Eugene Garfield Foundation
c/o Glenmede Trust Co.
1650 Market St., Ste. 1200
Philadelphia, PA 19103-7391 (215) 419-6000
Contact: Eugene Garfield, Chair., Pres. and Treas.

Established in 1988 in PA.
Donors: Eugene Garfield; Catheryne Stout.
Foundation type: Independent foundation.
Financial data (yr. ended 11/30/13): Assets, $3,694,264 (M); expenditures, $784,466; qualifying distributions, $766,064; giving activities include $761,500 for 25 grants (high: $300,000; low: $500).
Purpose and activities: Giving primarily for higher education and human services; funding also for the arts.
Fields of interest: Performing arts; Higher education; Medical school/education; Education; Human services.
Limitations: Applications accepted. Giving primarily in CA, NY, and PA. No grants to individuals.
Application information: Application form required.
Initial approach: Letter
Deadline(s): None
Officers: Eugene Garfield, Chair., Pres., and Treas.; Joshua Garfield, V.P. and Secy.
Director: Robert S. Bramson.
EIN: 232553258
Other changes: At the close of 2013, the grantmaker paid grants of $761,500, a 454.1% increase over the 2012 disbursements, $137,442.

2956
Anne & Philip Glatfelter III Family Foundation
c/o Bryn Mawr Trust Co.
1 E. Chocolate Ave., Ste. 1E
Hershey, PA **17033-1314**
***Application address:* c/o Lisa Piergallini, V.P., Bryn Mawr Trust, 1 W. Chocolate Ave., Ste. 200, Hershey, PA 17033, tel.: (717) 534-3225**
Established in 2001 in PA.
Donor: Anne M. Glatfelter Charitable Lead Trust.
Foundation type: Operating foundation.
Financial data (yr. ended 12/31/12): Assets, $14,101,159 (M); gifts received, $1,100,376; expenditures, $581,578; qualifying distributions, $543,081; giving activities include $539,122 for 38 grants (high: $37,500; low: $1,500).
Fields of interest: Arts; Higher education; Education.
Limitations: Giving limited to southeastern PA. No grants to individuals.
Application information: Application form required.
***Initial approach:* Contact foundation for application form**
Copies of proposal: 3
***Deadline(s):* Refer to application form for deadlines**
Board meeting date(s): Apr. and Oct.
Officers: Elizabeth Glatfelter, Pres.; Patricia G. Foulkrod, Secy.
EIN: 233094915

2957
GlaxoSmithKline Foundation
(formerly SmithKline Beecham Foundation)
5 Crescent Drive, NY0200
Philadelphia, PA **19112**
Established in 1967 in DE.
Donors: GlaxoSmithKline LLC F.K.A. SmithKline; SmithKline Beecham Corp.
Foundation type: Company-sponsored foundation.
Financial data (yr. ended 12/31/12): Assets, $264,653 (M); gifts received, $3,387,589; expenditures, $3,294,843; qualifying distributions, $3,294,843; giving activities include $500,000 for 1 grant, and $2,794,843 for 10,501 employee matching gifts.
Purpose and activities: The foundation matches contributions made by part-time and full-time employees, directors, and retirees of GlaxoSmithKline to nonprofit organizations.
Fields of interest: General charitable giving.
Type of support: Employee matching gifts.
Limitations: Applications not accepted. Giving primarily in Philadelphia, PA. No grants to individuals.
Application information: Contributes only through employee matching gifts.
Officers and Directors:* Lewsley A. Tewnion,* Chair.; Mary Linda Andrews,* Secy.-Treas.; Robert W. Carr; M. Judith Lynch; Nancy K. Pekarek.
EIN: 232120418

2958
Golden Slipper Club Uptown Home for the Aged
2655 Philmont Ave.
Huntingdon Valley, PA 19006
***Contact:* Herbert Weinstein**

Foundation type: Independent foundation.
Financial data (yr. ended 06/30/13): Assets, $3,629,754 (M); expenditures, $270,697; qualifying distributions, $259,750; giving activities include $259,750 for 1 grant.
Fields of interest: Aging, centers/services.
Limitations: Applications not accepted. Giving limited to Bala Cynwyd, PA.
Application information: Unsolicited requests for funds not accepted.
Officer: Norman Zarwin, Pres. and Secy.
Directors: Neal Grabell; Michael Hare; M. Douglas Kosmin; William Landsburg; **Herb Weinstein.**
EIN: 231401542
Other changes: Norman Zarwin is now Pres. and Secy.

2959
Goshen Hill Foundation, Inc.
c/o BNY Mellon Trust of Delaware
P.O. Box 185
Pittsburgh, PA 15230-0185

Foundation type: Independent foundation.
Financial data (yr. ended 06/30/13): Assets, $3,171,808 (M); expenditures, $174,229; qualifying distributions, $165,767; giving activities include $162,500 for 13 grants (high: $30,000; low: $2,500).
Fields of interest: Animal welfare; Food services; Athletics/sports, equestrianism; Human services; United Ways and Federated Giving Programs.
Type of support: General/operating support.
Limitations: Applications not accepted. Giving primarily in Washington, DC, NC and PA. No grants to individuals.
Application information: Unsolicited requests for funds not accepted.
Trustee: BNY Mellon Trust of Delaware, N.A.
Director: Caroline A. Moran.
EIN: 412160007

2960
The Mary E. Groff Surgical and Medical Research and Education Charitable Trust
5 Radnor Corporate Ctr.
100 Malsonford Rd., Ste. 450
Radnor, PA 19087-4526

Established in 1999 in PA.
Donor: Mary E. Groff†.
Foundation type: Independent foundation.
Financial data (yr. ended 12/31/12): Assets, $4,114,027 (M); expenditures, $241,480; qualifying distributions, $189,680; giving activities include $162,495 for 4 grants (high: $42,500; low: $25,000).
Purpose and activities: Giving primarily for higher education.
Fields of interest: Higher education; Hospitals (general).
Limitations: Applications not accepted. Giving primarily in PA. No grants to individuals.
Application information: Unsolicited requests for funds not accepted.
Trustees: Adam Burkey, M.D.; Fatema E.F. Burkey, Esq.; Coryell Urban.
EIN: 232725113
Other changes: Manucher Fellahnejad and Anne M. Cusack are no longer trustees.

2961
The M. S. Grumbacher Foundation
c/o Cozen O'Connor
1900 Market St.
Philadelphia, PA 19103-3508 (215) 665-4117
Contact: David Glyn, Dir.

Established around 1992 in PA.
Donor: M.S. Grumbacher.
Foundation type: Independent foundation.
Financial data (yr. ended 08/31/13): Assets, $6,271,616 (M); expenditures, $339,767; qualifying distributions, $286,119; giving activities include $266,000 for 19 grants (high: $55,000; low: $1,000).
Fields of interest: Performing arts centers; Arts; Higher education; Education; Health care; Health organizations; Alzheimer's disease; Human services; YM/YWCAs & YM/YWHAs; Children/youth, services; Community/economic development; Foundations (community); Jewish agencies & synagogues.
Limitations: Applications accepted. Giving limited to PA, with emphasis on the York area. No grants to individuals.
Application information: Application form required.
Initial approach: Letter
Deadline(s): Submit application between Nov. 1 and Apr. 30
Officer: Joshua G. Schultz, Pres.
Directors: David R. Glyn; Susan Gregory; Mary Jo Grumbacher; **Rowan Shultz.**
EIN: 232697348

2962
The Grundy Foundation
680 Radcliffe St.
Bristol, PA 19007-5136 (215) 788-5460
Contact: Eugene J. Williams, Exec. Dir.
FAX: (215) 788-0915;
E-mail: info@grundyfoundation.com; Main URL: http://www.grundyfoundation.com
Philanthropic Endeavors: http://www.grundyfoundation.com/content/philanthropy

Established in 1961 in PA.
Donor: Joseph R. Grundy‡.
Foundation type: Independent foundation.
Financial data (yr. ended 12/31/12): Assets, $56,658,631 (M); gifts received, $133; expenditures, $2,525,774; qualifying distributions, $2,407,177; giving activities include $220,545 for 16 grants (high: $100,545; low: $1,000), and $1,552,513 for 2 foundation-administered programs.
Purpose and activities: Grants for civic affairs and community planning, social service and youth agencies, a community fund, the arts, higher education, and health. Giving restricted to organizations supported by Mr. Grundy during his lifetime.
Fields of interest: Arts; Higher education; Hospitals (general); Children/youth, services; Community/economic development; Government/public administration.
Type of support: General/operating support; Building/renovation; Equipment; Land acquisition; Program development.
Limitations: Applications accepted. Giving limited to Bucks County, PA. No support for religious organizations. No grants to individuals, or for endowment funds, research, scholarships, or fellowships; no loans.
Publications: Application guidelines; Informational brochure (including application guidelines).
Application information: Application and guidelines available on foundation web site. Delaware Valley Grantmakers Common Grant Application Form accepted. Application form not required.
Initial approach: Letter
Copies of proposal: 1
Deadline(s): None
Board meeting date(s): Monthly except in Aug.
Trustees: Frederick J.M. LaValley; Bonnie J. O'Boyle; Thomas F. Praiss; Leonard N. Snyder; Wells Fargo Bank.
Number of staff: 2 full-time professional.
EIN: 231609243

2963
The Halloran Foundation

100 Four Falls Corporate Ctr., Rm. 215
West Conshohocken, PA 19428-2974
***E-mail:* info@halloranphilanthropies.org**; Main URL: http://www.halloranphilanthropies.org

Established in 2005 in PA.
Donors: Harry Halloran, Jr.; American Refining Bio-Chemical, Inc.
Foundation type: Independent foundation.
Financial data (yr. ended 12/31/12): Assets, $3,519,745 (M); gifts received, $1,091,230; expenditures, $1,304,264; qualifying distributions, $1,220,567; giving activities include $1,042,134 for 4 foundation-administered programs.
Fields of interest: Environment, energy; Human services; Social sciences, public policy.
Limitations: Applications not accepted. No grants to individuals.
Application information: Unsolicited requests for funds not accepted.
Officer: J. Anthony Carr, Exec. Dir.
Trustee: Harry Halloran, Jr.
EIN: 256885444

2964
William Stucki Hansen Foundation

(formerly Hansen Foundation)
432 Green St.
Sewickley, PA **15143-1563** (412) 771-7300

Established in 1984 in PA.
Donors: William Gregg Hansen‡; Hansen, Inc.
Foundation type: Independent foundation.
Financial data (yr. ended 12/31/12): Assets, $28,354,389 (M); expenditures, $1,451,976; qualifying distributions, $1,289,250; giving activities include $1,289,250 for 25 grants (high: $250,000; low: $1,000).
Fields of interest: Arts; Higher education; Education; Family services.
Type of support: General/operating support; Endowments; Program-related investments/loans.
Limitations: Giving primarily in Pittsburgh and Sewickley, PA. No grants to individuals.
Application information: Application form not required.
***Initial approach:* Letter**
Deadline(s): None
Directors: Gretchen Hansen; Nancy K. Hansen; David W. Lendt.
EIN: 251483674

2965
The Morris and Gertrude Harris Foundation

c/o PNC Bank, N.A.
P.O. Box 609
Pittsburgh, PA 15230-9738
***Application address:* c/o PNC Bank, N.A., Att.: John Montoya, 2 PNC Plz., 7th Fl., 620 Liberty Ave., Pittsburgh, PA 15222, tel.: (412) 768-8538**

Established in 1994 in PA.
Donor: Blanche H. Abrams‡.
Foundation type: Independent foundation.
Financial data (yr. ended 10/31/13): Assets, $3,798,102 (M); expenditures, $205,916; qualifying distributions, $163,460; giving activities include $137,665 for 1 grant.
Purpose and activities: Support primarily for scholarship funds benefiting medical students of the Jewish religion who are attending the University of Pittsburgh School of Medicine.
Fields of interest: Education.
Type of support: General/operating support; Scholarship funds.
Limitations: Applications accepted. Giving primarily in Pittsburgh, PA. No grants to individuals directly.
Application information: Application forms are available from The University of Pittsburgh School of Medicine, Office of Financial Aid. Application form required.
***Deadline(s):* Sept. 1**
Trustees: Bruce F. Rudoy; PNC Bank, N.A.
EIN: 256508058
Other changes: The grantmaker no longer lists a URL address.
The grantmaker now accepts applications.

2966
The Heinz Endowments

30 Dominion Twr.
625 Liberty Ave., 30th Fl.
Pittsburgh, PA 15222-3115 (412) 281-5777
Contact: Robert F. Vagt, Pres.
FAX: (412) 281-5788; E-mail: info@heinz.org; Main URL: http://www.heinz.org
Environmental health initiative: http://breatheproject.org/
Grants Database: http://www.heinz.org/grants_recipients.aspx
Knowledge Center: http://www.heinz.org/library.aspx

The Heinz Endowments was formed in 2007 from the Howard Heinz Endowments, established in 1941, and the Vira I. Heinz Endowment, established in 1986.
Donors: Howard Heinz; Vira I. Heinz.
Foundation type: Independent foundation.
Financial data (yr. ended 12/31/12): Assets, $1,466,928,593 (M); expenditures, $74,387,539; qualifying distributions, $68,704,307; giving activities include $61,124,899 for 554 grants (high: $2,500,000; low: $1,000), and $500,661 for 4 foundation-administered programs.
Purpose and activities: The Heinz Endowments is based in Pittsburgh, where it uses its region as a laboratory for the development of solutions to challenges that are national in scope. Although the majority of its giving is concentrated within southwestern Pennsylvania, it does work wherever necessary, including statewide and nationally, to fulfill its mission. That mission is to help the Endowments' region thrive as a whole community, economically, ecologically, educationally and culturally, while advancing the state of knowledge and practice in the fields in which it works. Its fields of emphasis include philanthropy in general and the disciplines represented by its five grant-making programs: Arts & Culture; Children, Youth & Families; Community & Economic Development; Education; and Environment.
Fields of interest: Arts; Education; Environment; Children/youth, services; Family services; Economic development; Children/youth; Young adults; African Americans/Blacks; Girls; Boys; Economically disadvantaged.
Type of support: Continuing support; General/operating support; Management development/capacity building; Program development; Program evaluation; Technical assistance.
Limitations: Applications accepted. Giving primarily to southwestern PA. Funding for projects outside the Commonwealth of Pennsylvania is generally only at specific request of the foundation. No support for for-profit organizations. No grants to individuals.
Publications: Annual report; Financial statement; Grants list; Occasional report.
Application information: Supporting materials can be uploaded electronically to the application. Please do not send any other paper materials unless requested by endowments' staff. Application form not required.
Initial approach: Prospective applicants should review carefully the guidelines for the grant-making program from which they anticipate seeking support.Inquiries regarding funding should demonstrate a familiarity with the program's goals and strategies. Review the eligibility requirements. Create an account and submit application online. No paper applications accepted.
Deadline(s): Mar. 1 (for spring board meeting), and Aug. 1 (for fall board meeting)
Board meeting date(s): May and Oct.
Final notification: Within several weeks of board meeting
Officers and Directors:* Teresa F. Heinz,* Chair.; James M. Walton,* Vice-Chair.; **Grant Oliphant, Pres.; Edward Kolano, V.P., Finance and Admin. and C.F.O.**; Ann C. Plunkett, Cont. and Dir., Payroll/Benefits Admin.; Drue Heinz, Dir. Emeritus; Damon Aherne; Carol R. Brown; Jared L. Cohon; Judith Davenport; Franco Harris; Andre T. Heinz; Christopher Heinz; H. John Heinz, IV; Sasha Heinz; Wendy Mackenzie; Shirley M. Malcom; James Rohr.
Number of staff: 20 full-time professional; 4 part-time professional; 10 full-time support.
EIN: 251721100

Other changes: Grant Oliphant has replaced Robert F. Vagt as Pres. Edward Kolano has replaced Jack E. Kime as V.P., Finance and Admin. and C.F.O.

2967
Henkels Foundation

985 Jolly Rd.
Blue Bell, PA 19422-0900

Established in 1956 in DE and PA.
Donors: Henkels & McCoy, Inc.; Liberty Mutual Group.
Foundation type: Company-sponsored foundation.
Financial data (yr. ended 06/30/13): Assets, $913,813 (M); gifts received, $2,037,598; expenditures, $1,751,078; qualifying distributions, $1,748,751; giving activities include $1,720,554 for 82 grants (high: $269,424; low: $200).
Purpose and activities: The foundation supports organizations involved with education, family planning, human services, and Christianity.
Fields of interest: Education; Health care; Human services.
Type of support: General/operating support; Program development; Scholarship funds.
Limitations: Applications not accepted. Giving primarily in PA. No grants to individuals.
Application information: Contributes only to pre-selected organizations.
Officers: Barbara B. Henkels, Pres.; Christopher B. Henkels, V.P.; Paul M. Henkels, Jr., V.P.; Angela Henkels Dale, Secy.-Treas.
EIN: 236235239
Other changes: The grantmaker no longer lists a phone.

2968
Highmark Foundation

120 5th Ave., Ste. 1733
Pittsburgh, PA 15222-3001 (866) 594-1730
FAX: (412) 544-6120;
E-mail: info@highmarkfoundation.org; Additional tel.: (866) 594-1730; Main URL: http://www.highmarkfoundation.org/
Additional URL: http://www.highmarkhealthyhigh5.org/index.shtml
Grants List: http://www.highmarkfoundation.org/grants/11_5_2013_HM_Foundation_Grants.pdf
Highmark Healthy High 5: http://www.highmarkhealthyhigh5.org
School Grants Program Grants List: http://www.highmarkfoundation.org/about_us/2013%20Creating%20a%20Healthy%20School%20Environment%20Website.pdf

Established in 2000 in PA.
Donors: Highmark West Virginia, Inc.; Highmark Inc.
Foundation type: Company-sponsored foundation.
Financial data (yr. ended 12/31/12): Assets, $21,908,655 (M); expenditures, $6,947,160; qualifying distributions, $5,765,267; giving activities include $4,507,735 for 66 grants (high: $598,000; low: $500).
Purpose and activities: The foundation supports programs designed to address chronic disease, family health, service delivery systems, and healthy communities. Special emphasis is directed toward programs designed to address bullying prevention; childhood obesity; and schools.
Fields of interest: Elementary/secondary education; Education; Health care, equal rights; Hospitals (general); Health care, clinics/centers; Dental care; Reproductive health, prenatal care; Public health; Public health, obesity; Public health, physical fitness; Health care, patient services; Health care; Mental health, grief/bereavement counseling; Mental health/crisis services; Cancer; Heart & circulatory diseases; Nerve, muscle & bone diseases; Diabetes; Health organizations; Crime/violence prevention, youth; Nutrition; Family services; Children; Youth; Aging; Disabilities, people with; Minorities; Economically disadvantaged.
Type of support: General/operating support; Continuing support; Management development/capacity building; Equipment; Program development; Curriculum development; Matching/challenge support.
Limitations: Applications accepted. Giving primarily in PA. No support for fraternal or civic groups, discriminatory organizations, or sports teams. No grants to individuals, or for annual fundraising campaigns, capital campaigns, endowment funds, lobbying or political causes or campaigns, debt reduction, sponsorships, clinical research, scholarships, routine operational costs, or overhead costs or direct financial subsidies of health services.
Publications: Application guidelines; Informational brochure (including application guidelines); Program policy statement.
Application information: Unsolicited proposals are considered on rare occasions. The foundation utilizes invited proposals and a request for proposals (RFP) process.
Initial approach: Proposal
Deadline(s): None
Board meeting date(s): Mar., June, Sept., and Dec.
Officers and Directors:* Doris Carson Williams,* Vice-Chair.; Yvonne Cook, Pres.; Melissa M. Anderson,* Treas.; C. Michael Blackwood; **James B. Bramson**; Janine Colinear; **Evan S. Frazier**; Don Onorato; Judy Sjostedt.
EIN: 251876666
Other changes: Thomas J. Rohner is no longer a director.

2969
Hillman Family Foundations

(formerly Henry L. Hillman Foundation)
310 Grant St., Ste. 2000
Pittsburgh, PA 15219-2309 (412) 338-3466
Contact: David K. Roger, Pres.
FAX: (412) 338-3463;
E-mail: foundation@hillmanfo.com; Main URL: http://hillmanfamilyfoundations.org/

Donors: Henry L. Hillman; J.H. Hillman, Jr.
Foundation type: Independent foundation.
Financial data (yr. ended 12/31/12): Assets, $357,584,648 (M); gifts received, $9,985,926; expenditures, $19,513,079; qualifying distributions, $18,704,422; giving activities include $17,093,300 for 588 grants (high: $2,000,000; low: $500), and $500,000 for 1 loan/program-related investment.
Purpose and activities: Hillman Family Foundations acts as the umbrella for the individual foundations listed. Prospective applicants should address grants inquiries to the appropriate individual foundations. Each foundation retains its own grantmaking focus and eligibility criteria. 1) Hillman Foundation: Arts and culture, health and medicine, education, economic development, human services, and conservation; 2) Henry L. Hillman Foundation: Arts and culture (focus on visual arts), health and medicine (research focused), education (focus on higher education), economic development, human services, conservation, and technology ; 3) Elsie L. Hillman Foundation: Education, human services (women-focused), religion, arts and culture, and community development with emphasis on civic affairs; 4) Mary Hillman Jennings Foundation: Healthcare, human services (focus on disabilities) and education; 5) Polk Foundation: Human services for individuals with intellectual and developmental disabilities; 6) Audrey Hillman Fisher Foundation: Human services (focus on woman and children), healthcare, conservation, education, arts ; 7) Juliet Lea Hillman Simonds Foundation: Arts and culture ; 8) Henry Lea Hillman, Jr. Foundation: Education, arts and culture, human services, community development, conservation, health and medicine; 9) William Talbott Hillman Foundation: Arts and culture, education, environment/conservation and human services ; 10) Dylan Todd Simonds Foundation: Environment/conservation (focus on sustainable development) arts and culture, education; 11) Talbott and Carter Simonds Foundation: Health and medicine, arts/culture, education, youth programs (focus on social enterprise and entrepreneurship); 12) Henry John Simonds Foundation: Arts/culture (focus on artist development in visual and performing arts) civic affairs, community development, education, conservation and environment; 13) Justin Brooks Fisher Foundation: Conservation/environment (focus on animal health and veterinary medicine), education, arts/culture; 14) Matthew Hillman Fisher Foundation: Arts/culture, human services, education, conservation/environment; 15) Nina Baldwin Fisher Foundation: Human services (focus on women and children) education (focus on culinary training), environment/conservation and arts/culture; 16) Lilah Hilliard Fisher Foundation: Human services (focus on early childhood development. adolescents, women and reproductive rights), education, arts/culture and environment/conservation ; 17) Juliet Ashby Hillman Foundation: Animal welfare, education and human services; 18) Summer Lea Hillman Foundation: Animal welfare, education and human services.
Fields of interest: Arts; Education; Environment; Health care; Human services.
Type of support: Program-related investments/loans; Continuing support; Capital campaigns; Endowments.
Limitations: Applications accepted. Giving primarily in the following areas: Hillman Foundation: Pittsburgh and Southwestern PA; Henry L. Hillman Foundation: Pittsburgh and Southwestern PA; Mary Hillman Jennings Foundation: Pittsburgh and Southwestern PA; Elsie H. Hillman Foundation: Pittsburgh and Southwestern PA; Polk Foundation: Pittsburgh, PA; Juliet Lea Simonds Foundation: Pittsburgh, PA and New York City, NY; Audrey Hillman Fisher Foundation: Pittsburgh, PA, Santa Barbara, CA, and central NH; Henry Lea Hillman, Jr. Foundation: Portland, OR; William Talbott Hillman Foundation: Pittsburgh, PA and New York City, NY; Dylan Todd Simonds Foundation: San Francisco, CA and Pittsburgh, PA; Talbott & Carter Simonds Foundation: New York City, NY and Pittsburgh, PA; Henry John Simonds Foundation: New York City, NY and Pittsburgh, PA; Justin Brooks Fisher Foundation: Boulder, CO and Pittsburgh, PA; Matthew Hillman Fisher Foundation: Pittsburgh, PA, New York City, NY and Los Angeles, CA; Lilah Hilliard Fisher Foundation: New York City, NY and Pittsburgh, PA; Nina Baldwin Fisher Foundation: Pittsburgh, PA, Juliet Ashby Hillman Foundation: Portland, OR, Summer Lea Hillman Foundation: Portland, OR. No grants to individuals, or for deficit financing, publications, or conferences.
Application information: Prospective applicants should address grant requests and inquiries to one of the individual foundations.
***Initial approach:* Online**
Board meeting date(s): Apr., June, Oct. and Dec.

Officers and Directors:* Henry L. Hillman,* Chair.; David K. Roger,* Pres.; C.G. Grefenstette,* V.P.; Bruce I. Crocker,* Secy.; Lisa R. Johns, Treas. and Prog. Mgr.; Elsie H. Hillman; Juliet L. Hillman Simonds.
Number of staff: 5
EIN: 256065959

2970
Lynne & Harold Honickman Foundation
210 W. Rittenhouse Sq., Ste. 3303
Philadelphia, PA 19103-5780 (215) 790-1710
Contact: Lynne Honickman, Tr.
Main URL: http://www.honickmanfoundation.org/
Facebook: https://www.facebook.com/pages/The-Honickman-Foundation/232318940115941?sk=wall

Established in 1988 in PA.
Donors: Lynne Honickman; Pepsi Cola & National Brand Beverage.
Foundation type: Independent foundation.
Financial data (yr. ended 12/31/12): Assets, $10,179,870 (M); gifts received, $25,000; expenditures, $510,462; qualifying distributions, $471,485; giving activities include $415,569 for 153 grants (high: $106,181; low: $50).
Purpose and activities: Giving primarily to support projects that promote the arts, education, health, social change, and heritage.
Fields of interest: Museums (art); Arts; Education; Health care; Family services; Jewish federated giving programs.
Type of support: General/operating support; Grants to individuals.
Limitations: Applications accepted. Giving primarily in Philadelphia, PA, and the surrounding 5 counties.
Publications: Grants list.
Application information: Application form not required.
Initial approach: Proposal
Deadline(s): None
Officers: Lynne Honickman, Pres.; Kathy H. Ruyak, V.P.
Number of staff: 1 full-time professional.
EIN: 232513138
Other changes: Lynne Honickman is now Pres.

2971
Roy A. Hunt Foundation
1 Bigelow Sq., Ste. 630
Pittsburgh, PA 15219-3030 (412) 281-8734
Contact: Tony Macklin, Exec. Dir.
FAX: (412) 255-0522; E-mail: info@rahuntfdn.org; Main URL: http://www.rahuntfdn.org
Grants Mapping feature: http://batchgeo.com/map/bcabb381cdea3bad436c568c7a723411
LinkedIn: http://www.linkedin.com/company/roy-a.-hunt-foundation
RSS Feed: http://feeds.feedburner.com/RoyAHuntFoundation

Established in 1966 in PA.
Donor: Roy A. Hunt‡.
Foundation type: Independent foundation.
Financial data (yr. ended 05/31/13): Assets, $72,611,597 (M); expenditures, $3,663,843; qualifying distributions, $3,468,301; giving activities include $3,021,000 for 395 grants (high: $100,000; low: $1,000).
Purpose and activities: Giving to improve the quality of life through grants for education, the arts and cultural programs, social services, the environment, health services, community development, and youth violence prevention.
Fields of interest: Arts; Elementary/secondary education; Higher education; Environment; Health care; Crime/violence prevention, youth; Human services; Community/economic development; Public affairs; Religion.
Type of support: Continuing support; Program evaluation; Program development; General/operating support; Annual campaigns; Capital campaigns; Building/renovation; Endowments.
Limitations: Giving primarily in the Boston, MA, and Pittsburgh, PA, areas, also in CA, ID, NH, ME, and OH. No grants to individuals.
Publications: Application guidelines; Grants list.
Application information: Applicants are encouraged to use the foundation's on-line grant-making system. Organizations that are new to the foundation complete a narrative using the Charting Impact questions and attach: past and current financials, board list, key staff list, and other optional materials. Previous Grant Recipients complete a streamlined proposal. Special Initiative Proposals require a 6-question narrative and a project budget, past financials, board and staff list. Once invited to submit a proposal, applicants will receive detailed instructions from the foundation on how to submit their proposal via the on-line system. Organizations that have received a general grant in the past three years do not need to submit a letter of inquiry, the foundation will send e-mail instructions to apply to all invited organizations in late summer. Organizations that have never received funding and special initiative applicants are required to submit a letter of inquiry and should review the "Applying for a Grant" page on the foundation's web site for more guidance.
Initial approach: Letter of inquiry via the foundation's online grantmaking system
***Deadline(s):* Special Initiatives: Letter of Inquiry, Jan. 20 (for June meeting), and June 23 (for Nov. meeting), Invited Proposal: Mar. 10 (for June meeting) and Aug. 11 (for Nov. meeting); For General Grants: Letter of Inquiry, Mar 31. (for June meeting), and Aug. 20 (for Nov. meeting), Invited Proposal: Apr. 15 (for June meeting), and Sept. 15 (for Nov. meeting)**
Board meeting date(s): June and Nov.
Final notification: 30 days for a letter of inquiry and 1 week after board meeting for full proposal
Officer: Tony Macklin, Exec. Dir.
Trustees: Marion M. Badiner; Helen Hunt Bouscaren; Cathryn Hunt Graybill; Susan Hunt Hollingsworth; A. James Hunt; Alexandra K. Hunt; Andrew McQ. Hunt; Avery S. Hunt; Bonnie B.K. Hunt; Christopher M. Hunt; Daniel K. Hunt; Edward M. Hunt; Elizabeth H. Hunt; Evan McMasters Hunt; John B. Hunt; Lila C. Hunt; Richard M. Hunt; Roy A. Hunt III; Torrence M. Hunt, Jr.; Torrence W.B. Hunt; Tyler B. Hunt; William E. Hunt; Rachel Hunt Knowles; Joan Hunt Scott Maxwell; Caroline Hunt Zaw-Mon.
Number of staff: 1 full-time professional; 1 full-time support.
EIN: 256105162

2972
Horace C. Hunt Memorial Foundation
(formerly Horace C. Hunt Foundation)
c/o BNY Mellon, N.A.
P.O. Box 185
Pittsburgh, PA 15230-0185

Foundation type: Independent foundation.
Financial data (yr. ended 10/31/13): Assets, $4,289,039 (M); expenditures, $220,524; qualifying distributions, $196,555; giving activities include $180,000 for 8 grants (high: $35,000; low: $10,000).
Fields of interest: Health organizations, association; Cancer; Human services; American Red Cross; Salvation Army; Family services; Christian agencies & churches.
Limitations: Applications not accepted. Giving primarily in the Boston, MA, area. No grants to individuals.
Application information: Contributes only to pre-selected organizations.
Trustees: Robert G. Bannish; Ronald Garmey; BNY Mellon, N.A.
EIN: 046171963

2973
The Huston Foundation
900 W. Valley Rd., Ste. 204
Wayne, PA 19087-1849 **(610) 832-4955**
FAX: (610) 832-4960; E-mail: hustonfndn@aol.com; For secular information contact: Susan B. Heilman, Exec. Asst., tel.: (610) 832-4955, ext. 1; for Protestant Evangelical Christian information contact: Patricia A. Jones, tel.: (610) 832-4955, ext. 4; Main URL: http://www.hustonfoundation.org

Incorporated in 1957 in PA.
Donors: Charles L. Huston, Jr.‡; Ruth Huston‡.
Foundation type: Independent foundation.
Financial data (yr. ended 12/31/12): Assets, $24,168,890 (M); expenditures, $1,543,057; qualifying distributions, $1,383,328; giving activities include $856,288 for 132 grants (high: $60,000; low: $400).
Purpose and activities: Giving primarily to Protestant evangelical ministries, health organizations, and human service organizations. Also some support for education and the arts.
Fields of interest: Arts; Education; Health care; Human services; Public policy, research; Christian agencies & churches; Protestant agencies & churches.
International interests: Italy; Africa.
Type of support: General/operating support; Annual campaigns; Equipment; Emergency funds; Program development; Seed money; Research; Technical assistance; Matching/challenge support.
Limitations: Giving primarily in southeastern PA; some funding nationally. No grants to individuals, or for research programs, endowments, fellowships, capital campaigns or salaries; no loans.
Publications: Application guidelines; Annual report.
Application information: See foundation web site for complete application guidelines. Application form required.
Initial approach: Letter of request or telephone call
Copies of proposal: 1
***Deadline(s):* Jan. 1 and Mar. 15 for spring, July 1 and Sept. 15 for Fall**
Board meeting date(s): May and Nov.
Officers and Directors:* Elinor Huston Lashley,* Chair.; Charles L. Huston III,* C.E.O. and Pres.; Nancy Huston Hansen,* V.P.; Rebecca H. Mathews,* Secy.; Charles L. Huston IV,* Treas.; Scott G. Huston; **Patricia A. Jones.**
Number of staff: 4 full-time professional; 1 part-time professional.
EIN: 236284125
Other changes: Charles B. Chadwick is no longer a director.

2974
II-VI Foundation
(formerly II-VI Incorporated Foundation)
1370 Washington Pike, Ste. 404
Bridgeville, PA 15017-2826 (412) 206-0580
Contact: Richard W. Purnell, Exec. Dir.
FAX: (412) 206-0583;
E-mail: info@ii-vifoundation.com; Main URL: http://ii-vifoundation.com/index.html
Facebook: https://www.facebook.com/pages/II-VI-Foundation/425726714117561

Established in 2007 in PA.
Donors: Carl J. Johnson; Margot A. Johnson.
Foundation type: Independent foundation.
Financial data (yr. ended 12/31/12): Assets, $26,833,332 (M); gifts received, $1,038; expenditures, $3,537,129; qualifying distributions, $3,452,806; giving activities include $2,488,029 for 35 grants (high: $167,856; low: $1,000), and $501,837 for 56 grants to individuals (high: $10,000; low: $2,247).
Purpose and activities: Scholarship awards to graduating high school students in the areas where II-VI, Inc. maintains a facility. The overall mission of the foundation is to encourage and enable students to pursue a career in engineering, science and mathematics while maintaining a standard of excellence in that pursuit.
Fields of interest: Higher education.
Type of support: Scholarships—to individuals.
Limitations: Giving primarily in areas where II-VI, Inc. maintains a plant or a manufacturing facility.
Application information: Application information and forms available on foundation web site. Application form required.
Deadline(s): See application form for current deadlines
Officers and Directors:* Carl J. Johnson,* Chair.; Robert D. German, Secy.; Richard W. Purnell, Exec. Dir.; Marc Y.E. Pelaez; Peter Sognefast.
EIN: 208824719

2975
Independence Blue Cross Foundation
1901 Market St., 37 Fl
Philadelphia, PA **19103-1480** (855) 422-3386
***Contact:* Marie Lange, Prog. Anaylst**
***E-mail:* ibxfoundation@ibx.com; E-mail and tel. for Marie Lange: marie.lange@ibx.com; (215) 241-2817**; Main URL: http://www.ibxfoundation.org/
Blue Safety Net Grant Recipients: http://www.ibxfoundation.org/grants/grantees/blue_safety_net.html
Building Healthier Communities Grant Recipients: http://www.ibxfoundation.org/grants/grantees/healthy_communities.html
Nurses for Tomorrow Grant Recipients: http://www.ibxfoundation.org/grants/grantees/nurses_for_tomorrow.html
Twitter: https://twitter.com/ibxfdn

Donor: Independence Blue Cross.
Foundation type: Company-sponsored foundation.
Financial data (yr. ended 12/31/12): Assets, $57,319,736 (M); gifts received, $15,000,000; expenditures, $5,068,145; qualifying distributions, $4,028,399; giving activities include $4,018,599 for 66 grants (high: $231,690; low: $2,226).
Purpose and activities: The foundation supports programs designed to care for the most vulnerable; enhance health care delivery; and build healthier communities.
Fields of interest: Nursing school/education; Health care, clinics/centers; Public health; Public health, obesity; Public health, physical fitness; Health care; Nutrition; Children; Economically disadvantaged.
Type of support: General/operating support; Management development/capacity building; Program development; Internship funds; Scholarship funds.
Limitations: Applications accepted. **Giving primarily in southeastern PA, with emphasis on Bucks, Chester, Montgomery, and Philadelphia County.** No support for political causes, candidates, organizations, or capital campaigns;. **No grants to individuals or for endowments, award dinners, sponsorships or fundraising events, capital construction, conferences, seminars, trips or camps.**
Publications: Application guidelines.
Application information: A site visit may be conducted.
***Initial approach:* Complete online application for Blue Safety Net and Building Healthier Communities**
***Deadline(s):* Varies for Blue Safety Net; Apr. 9 and June 20 for Building Healthier Communities**
Officers and Directors:* Patrick B. Gillespie,* Chair.; Lorina L. Marshall-Blake, Pres.; Lilton R. Taliaferro, Jr., Esq., Secy.; Alan Krigstein, Treas.; Chistopher Cashman; Joan Hilferty; Plato A. Marinakos; Paul A. Tufano, Esq.; I. Steven Udvarhelyi, M.D.
EIN: 364685801
Other changes: The grantmaker now publishes application guidelines.

2976
Independence Foundation
200 S. Broad St., Ste. 1101
Philadelphia, PA 19102-3802 (215) 985-4009
Contact: Susan E. Sherman, C.E.O. and Pres.
FAX: (215) 985-3989; Main URL: http://independencefoundation.org/about-us/

Established in 1932 as International Cancer Research Foundation; incorporated as Donner Foundation in 1945 in DE; divided in 1961 into Independence Foundation and a newly formed William H. Donner Foundation.
Donor: William H. Donner†.
Foundation type: Independent foundation.
Financial data (yr. ended 12/31/12): Assets, $65,788,302 (M); expenditures, $5,344,409; qualifying distributions, $4,814,409; giving activities include $3,440,547 for 286 grants (high: $165,000; low: $6), and $88,600 for 12 grants to individuals (high: $10,000; low: $6,200).
Purpose and activities: The foundation's mission is to support organizations that provide services to people who do not ordinarily have access to them. The current funding agenda includes the following areas of interest: nurse managed health care, culture and the arts, public interest legal services, and health and human services, with special focus on food distribution, housing for the homeless, and services which help people with disabilities to lead independent lives. The foundation also has two special initiatives: Public Interest Law Fellowships and Fellowships for Visual and Performing Artists.
Fields of interest: Visual arts; Performing arts; Arts; Nursing school/education; Nursing care; Health care; Legal services; Legal services, public interest law; Human services; Children; Aging; Disabilities, people with; Physically disabled; Women; Immigrants/refugees; Economically disadvantaged; Homeless; Migrant workers.
Type of support: General/operating support; Professorships; Fellowships; Scholarship funds; Matching/challenge support.
Limitations: Applications accepted. Giving primarily in Philadelphia, PA, and Bucks, Chester, Delaware, and Montgomery counties. No grants to individuals (except for art fellowships), or for building and development funds, travel, research, publications, or matching gifts.
Publications: Application guidelines; Annual report; Grants list; Occasional report.
Application information: Unsolicited proposals are not accepted. Application form required.
***Initial approach:* 2-page Letter of Inquiry**
Copies of proposal: 10
Deadline(s): Contact foundation for deadline dates
Board meeting date(s): Varies
Final notification: Varies
Officers and Directors:* Hon. Phyllis W. Beck,* Chair. and Treas.; Susan E. Sherman,* C.E.O. and Pres.; Andre Dennis,* V. P.; Barton M. Silverman,* V.P.; Andrea L. Mengel, Ph.D.*, Secy.; Pedro Ramos.
Number of staff: 5 full-time professional; 2 full-time support.
EIN: 231352110

2977
Kevy K. & Hortense M. Kaiserman Foundation
201 S. 18th St., Ste. 300
Philadelphia, PA 19103-5921

Established in 1980 in PA.
Donors: Hortense M. Kaiserman; Kenneth S. Kaiserman; Ronald L. Kaiserman; Kevy K. Kaiserman Marital Trust; Constance K. Robinson; Kaiserman Enterprises, LP.
Foundation type: Independent foundation.
Financial data (yr. ended 06/30/11): Assets, $619,186 (M); gifts received, $350,000; expenditures, $348,078; qualifying distributions, $342,928; giving activities include $340,000 for 2 grants (high: $330,000; low: $10,000).
Fields of interest: Arts; Higher education; Jewish federated giving programs; Jewish agencies & synagogues.
Limitations: Applications not accepted. Giving primarily in Waltham, MA and Philadelphia, PA. No grants to individuals.
Application information: Contributes only to pre-selected organizations.
Board meeting date(s): Apr. and Oct.
Trustees: Ronald L. Kaiserman; Constance K. Robinson; **Homer Robinson**.
EIN: 232299921
Other changes: Kenneth S. Kaiserman is no longer trustee.

2978
KL Felicitas Foundation
(formerly Kleissner Family Foundation)
c/o Febert & Assocs., LLC
707 Grant St., Ste. 1140
Pittsburgh, PA 15219-1909
Contact: Lisa Kleissner, Pres.
***E-mail:* info@klfelicitasfoundation.org**; Main URL: http://www.klfelicitasfoundation.org/

Established in 2000 in CA.
Donors: Karl Kleissner; Lisa Kleissner; KD Primus Trust.
Foundation type: Independent foundation.

Financial data (yr. ended 12/31/12): Assets, $9,937,705 (M); expenditures, $525,227; qualifying distributions, $463,034; giving activities include $231,134 for 13 grants (high: $80,000; low: $39).
Purpose and activities: Giving to enable social entrepreneurs worldwide to develop and grow economically sustainable, scalable enterprises with high measurable social impact and to empower rural communities and families through sustainable economic and social change.
Fields of interest: Environment; Community/economic development.
International interests: Brazil; India; Sri Lanka.
Type of support: Mission-related investments/loans; General/operating support; Income development; Management development/capacity building; Annual campaigns; Capital campaigns; Building/renovation; Endowments; Program development; Seed money; Curriculum development; Research; Technical assistance; Consulting services; Program-related investments/loans; Matching/challenge support.
Limitations: Applications not accepted. Giving in the U.S., as well as in Brazil, India, and Sri Lanka. No support for religious organizations. No grants to individuals.
Application information: Contributes only to pre-selected organizations.
Board meeting date(s): Jan. 2, June 12-13, and Oct. 30-31
Officers: Lisa Kleissner, Pres.; Alex Kleissner, V.P.; Karl Kleissner, Secy.; Andrea Kleissner, Treas.
EIN: 770539366

2979
The Kohelet Foundation
822 Montgomery Ave., Ste. 201
Narbeth, PA 19072-1937 (484) 278-1328
Contact: Nancy Bonner, Office Mgr.
FAX: (484) 589-4638;
E-mail: info@koheletfoundation.org; E-mail address for Nancy Bonner, Office Mgr.: nancy@koheletfoundation.org; Main URL: http://www.koheletfoundation.org/
Blog: http://www.koheletfoundation.org/blog
Facebook: https://www.facebook.com/koheletfoundation

Donors: David M. Magerman; Kohelet Yeshiva High School.
Foundation type: Independent foundation.
Financial data (yr. ended 12/31/12): Assets, $304,595 (M); gifts received, $5,121,333; expenditures, $5,119,448; qualifying distributions, $5,005,332; giving activities include $4,019,824 for 49 grants (high: $577,134; low: $335), and $465,422 for foundation-administered programs.
Purpose and activities: Giving primarily for the healthy development of Jewish identity and the observance of Jewish laws and traditions. The foundation's interests are to: 1) promote access to Jewish education at all levels as the path to cultivating a strong Jewish identity; 2) ease the financial obstacles to families committed to day school education; 3) reinforce the value of family learning to strengthen the impact of Jewish day school education; 4) unify the educational messages at school and at home so that Jewish living and learning are fortified; and 5) inspire life-long learning and the conviction that the Jewish person's pursuit of learning, questioning and refining is never complete.
Fields of interest: Education; Jewish agencies & synagogues.
Limitations: Applications accepted. Giving primarily in the greater Philadelphia, PA, region. No support for organizations outside the U.S. No grants to individuals, or for capital campaigns, construction, debt, or endowments.
Application information:
***Initial approach:* Letter**
***Final notification:* Four weeks**
Officers: David Magerman, Pres.; Holly B. Cohen, Exec. Dir.
Advisors: Michael Bohnen; Lester Lipschutz; Sam Moed; Yossi Prager.
EIN: 263773063
Other changes: The grantmaker now accepts applications.

2980
John Crain Kunkel Foundation
225 Market St., 2nd Fl.
Harrisburg, PA 17101-0658 (717) 902-9817
Contact: Nancy W. Bergert, Tr.
***E-mail:* info@kunkelfoundation.org**; Main URL: http://www.kunkelfoundation.org

Established in 1965 in PA.
Foundation type: Independent foundation.
Financial data (yr. ended 12/31/12): Assets, $12,127,870 (M); expenditures, $732,682; qualifying distributions, $686,041; giving activities include $549,685 for 21 grants (high: $100,000; low: $2,500).
Purpose and activities: Giving primarily for human services, health care, and to a museum.
Fields of interest: Museums (specialized); Health care; Human services; YM/YWCAs & YM/YWHAs; United Ways and Federated Giving Programs.
Type of support: General/operating support.
Limitations: Applications accepted. Giving primarily in Harrisburg, PA.
Application information: See foundation website for complete application guidelines. Application form required.
Initial approach: Letter
Trustees: Nancy W. Bergert; Elizabeth K. Davis; Deborah L. Facini; John C. Kunkel II; Paul A. Kunkel; Jay W. Stark; John K. Stark; Jennifer R. Wright; William T. Wright II.
EIN: 237026914

2981
The Lancaster County Community Foundation
(formerly The Lancaster County Foundation)
24 W. King St., Ste. 201
Lancaster, PA 17603 (717) 397-1629
Contact: Samuel J. Bressi, C.E.O.
FAX: (717) 397-6877;
E-mail: info@lancastercountyfoundation.org; Main URL: http://www.lancfound.org/
Blog: http://lancfound.org/blog/
Facebook: http://www.facebook.com/pages/Lancaster-County-Community-Foundation/61365582396
LinkedIn: http://www.linkedin.com/companies/lancaster-community-foundation
Twitter: https://twitter.com/lancfound

Established in 1924 in PA.
Foundation type: Community foundation.
Financial data (yr. ended 12/31/12): Assets, $71,604,558 (M); gifts received, $2,399,242; expenditures, $5,147,466; giving activities include $3,502,168 for grants.
Purpose and activities: The foundation advances the vitality and well-being of the people of Lancaster County by inspiring generosity and by being responsible stewards of gifts for today and tomorrow.
Fields of interest: Arts; Education; Environment; Health care; Housing/shelter, home owners; Children/youth, services; Human services; Community/economic development; Disabilities, people with.
Type of support: Management development/capacity building; Endowments; Program development; Scholarship funds; Mission-related investments/loans.
Limitations: Applications accepted. Giving limited to Lancaster County, PA. No support for governmental agencies, umbrella organizations for purposes of re-granting funds, cemetery associations, or sectarian religious purposes. No grants to individuals (except for scholarships), or for operating budgets, continuing support, annual campaigns, deficit financing, land acquisition, fellowships, consulting services, fundraising events, solicitations, multi-year funding for bricks and mortar projects, conferences, trips, or seminars.
Publications: Application guidelines; Annual report; Grants list; Informational brochure; Newsletter.
Application information: The foundation accepts applications on a yearly basis. Applications are posted and accepted online. Visit foundation Web site to sign up for our e-newsletter and learn about our grant opportunities. Application form required.
Initial approach: Complete online application
Copies of proposal: 1
Deadline(s): Rolling
Board meeting date(s): 6 times annually
Final notification: Within a few weeks after proposal deadline
Officers and Directors:* Samuel J. Bressi,* C.E.O. and Pres.; Tracy Cutler,* V.P., Comms. and Donor Cultivation; Lisa Hostler,* V.P., Finance and Investments; Melody Keim,* V.P., Progs. and Initiatives; Kim Shorter,* V.P., Opers. and Donor Support; Vance Antonacci; Benjamin Atwater; Jan Bergen; **Joe Byorick**; Jennifer Craighead; Steve Geisenberger; Elizabeth Krapp; Francine McNairy; Rod Messick; Lisa Riggs; Tim Rochel, Sr.; Kim Smith; Linda Porr Sweeney.
Number of staff: 7 full-time professional; 1 full-time support; 1 part-time support.
EIN: 200874857
Other changes: Vance Antonacci is no longer a director. David Koser is now Prog. Off. Jill Carson and Elizabeth Dunlap are no longer directors.

2982
R.K. Laros Foundation
134 Pine Top Trail
Bethlehem, PA **18017-1728 (610) 390-6016**
***Contact:* Sharon Zondag, Exec. Dir.**
***E-mail:* larosfoundation@gmail.com**; Main URL: http://www.larosfoundation.org

Trust established in 1952 in PA.
Donor: Russell K. Laros†.
Foundation type: Independent foundation.
Financial data (yr. ended 12/31/12): Assets, $3,478,953 (M); gifts received, $6,823; expenditures, $180,870; qualifying distributions, $160,640; giving activities include $139,400 for 6 grants (high: $50,000; low: $8,400).
Fields of interest: Education; Hospitals (general); Human services; YM/YWCAs & YM/YWHAs; Children, services; Community/economic development; Hispanics/Latinos.

Type of support: Capital campaigns; Building/renovation; Equipment; Seed money.
Limitations: Applications not accepted. Giving primarily in PA.
Application information: Unsolicited requests for funds not accepted.
Officers and Directors:* Russell K. Laros, Jr.,* Pres.; George Mowrer,* Secy.; **Sharon Zondag, Exec. Dir.**; Michael A. Abgott; Robert W. Bilheimer; Diane Donaher; Ronald Donchez; Laurie Gostley-Hackett; Robert Huth, Jr.; Russell K. Laros III; Gordon B. Mowrer; Robert H. Young, Jr.
Number of staff: 1 full-time support.
EIN: 236207353

2983
The John Lazarich Foundation
704 Haywood Dr.
Exton, PA 19341-1136 **(610) 458-1090**
Contact: William Kronenberg III, Tr.; James Sacchetta, Tr.

Established in 1997 in PA.
Donor: William Kronenberg III.
Foundation type: Independent foundation.
Financial data (yr. ended 11/30/13): Assets, $7,267,077 (M); expenditures, $563,247; qualifying distributions, $490,725; giving activities include $408,505 for 29 grants (high: $160,329; low: $500).
Fields of interest: Secondary school/education; Education; Big Brothers/Big Sisters; Human services; Community/economic development; Children/youth; Disabilities, people with; Physically disabled; Economically disadvantaged.
Type of support: Annual campaigns; Capital campaigns; Scholarships—to individuals.
Limitations: Applications accepted. Giving primarily in Phoenixville, PA. No support for religious or political organizations.
Application information: Application form required.
Initial approach: Letter
Deadline(s): None
Trustees: Alex Kronenberg; Dorothy Kronenberg; William Kronenberg III; Lenoard R. Olsen, Jr.; James Sacchetta.
EIN: 237918137

2984
Jerry Lee Foundation
c/o Webb FM Radio Inc.
225 City Ave.
Bala Cynwyd, PA 19004-1704 **(610) 538-1225**
***Contact:* Heather Crosby**
E-mail for Heather Crosby:
HeatherC@JerryLeeFoundation.org; Main URL: http://jerryleefoundation.com/default.asp

Established in 1996 in PA.
Donors: David Kurtz‡; Jerry Lee; Gearld Lee.
Foundation type: Independent foundation.
Financial data (yr. ended 12/31/12): Assets, $6,980 (M); gifts received, $96,929; expenditures, $364,634; qualifying distributions, $349,630; giving activities include $349,630 for grants.
Purpose and activities: Giving limited for research in education and criminology.
Fields of interest: Education, research; Crime/law enforcement, research.
Type of support: Research.
Limitations: Applications not accepted. Giving primarily in the U.S., with some emphasis on Philadelphia, PA, and the greater metropolitan Washington, DC, area. No grants to individuals.
Application information: Contributes only to pre-selected organizations.
Director: Gerald Lee.
EIN: 232867684

2985
The Leeway Foundation
The Philadelphia Bldg.
1315 Walnut St., Ste. 832
Philadelphia, PA 19109-1025 (215) 545-4078
FAX: (215) 545-4021; E-mail: info@leeway.org; Main URL: http://www.leeway.org/
Blog: http://www.leeway.org/blog/
Facebook: http://www.facebook.com/leewayfoundation
Flickr: https://www.flickr.com/photos/leewayfoundation/
Foundation's Instagram Profile: http://instagram.com/leewayfound
Grants List: http://www.leeway.org/grantees/
Twitter: http://twitter.com/leewayfound
Vimeo: http://vimeo.com/leeway

Established in 1993 in PA.
Donors: Helen Berman Alter‡; Linda L. Alter; Bertha Dagan Berman‡.
Foundation type: Independent foundation.
Financial data (yr. ended 12/31/12): Assets, $16,849,379 (M); gifts received, $2,000; expenditures, $874,986; qualifying distributions, $805,284; giving activities include $214,360 for 74 grants to individuals (high: $15,000; low: $100).
Purpose and activities: The foundation supports individual women and transgender artists in order to help them achieve individual and community transformation in Camden County, New Jersey and the Philadelphia, Pennsylvania, 5-county area.
Fields of interest: Arts; Women.
Type of support: Grants to individuals.
Limitations: Applications accepted. Giving to residents in the Delaware Valley area.
Publications: Application guidelines; Annual report; Grants list.
Application information: Complete guidelines and application form available on foundation web site. Application form required.
Initial approach: Letter, telephone or e-mail inquiry
Copies of proposal: 1
Deadline(s): See foundation web site for current deadlines
Board meeting date(s): Six times per year
Final notification: 60 days after deadline
Officers: Amandee Braxton, Pres.; Gretjen Clausing, Treas.; Denise Brown, Exec. Dir.
Board Members: Carolyn Chernoff; Tina Morton; Patience Rage; Virginia P. Sikes, Esq.
Number of staff: 3 full-time professional; 1 full-time support; 1 part-time support.
EIN: 232727140
Other changes: Sabina Neem is no longer Secy. Naima Lowe and Alison Roh Park are no longer directors.

2986
Lehigh Valley Community Foundation
(formerly Bethlehem Area Foundation)
968 Postal Rd., Ste. 100
Allentown, PA 18109-9301 (610) 266-4284
Contact: Bernard J. Story, C.E.O.; For grants: Ron Horvath, Fiscal Mgr.
FAX: (610) 266-4285;
E-mail: lvcf@lvcfoundation.org; Grant inquiry e-mail: ron@lvcfoundation.org; Main URL: http://www.lehighvalleyfoundation.org/
Facebook: https://www.facebook.com/Lehighvalleycommunityfoundation
Twitter: https://twitter.com/LVCF1

Established in 1967 in PA.
Foundation type: Community foundation.
Financial data (yr. ended 06/30/12): Assets, $33,471,791 (M); gifts received, $1,656,466; expenditures, $2,457,612; giving activities include $1,798,825 for 80 grants (high: $114,400), and $3,210 for grants to individuals.
Purpose and activities: The foundation enables donors, including individuals, families, businesses, private foundations and nonprofit agencies, to establish funds which will serve their charitable intentions temporarily or in perpetuity by providing grants to nonprofit organizations and programs. Giving for arts, culture, and heritage, community development, education, environment and science, health care, and human services.
Fields of interest: Historic preservation/historical societies; Arts; Education; Environment; Health care; Children, services; Human services; Community/economic development; Science.
Type of support: Management development/capacity building; Capital campaigns; Building/renovation; Equipment; Emergency funds; Program development; Publication; Seed money; Scholarship funds; Matching/challenge support.
Limitations: Applications accepted. Giving limited to Lehigh, Monroe, Northampton, and Upper Bucks counties, PA. No support for sectarian religious purposes. No grants for operating budgets, continuing support, annual campaigns, deficit financing, endowments, foundation scholarships, or research; no loans.
Publications: Application guidelines; Annual report; Grants list; Program policy statement.
Application information: Visit foundation web site for application form guidelines and specific deadlines. Faxed or e-mailed applications are accepted. Capital funding: must submit invoice copies when requesting release of funds. Site visits may be made. Final reports required. Application form required.
Initial approach: Complete application form
Deadline(s): Varies
Board meeting date(s): Quarterly
Officers and Board of Governors:* Denise M. Blew,* Chair.; Michael Stershic,* Vice-Chair.; Bernard J. Story,* Pres. and C.E.O.; Trisha R. Higgins,* V.P. and C.F.O.; Kamran Afsar, Ph.D.; **Geoffrey B. Borda**; Beth Williams Boyer; Greg L. Butz; **Thomas L. Campbell**; Bonnie S. Coyle, M.D.; Cynthia Lambert Durham; W. Beal Fowler, Ph.D.; Robert E. Gadomski; Karen R. Green; Raymond B. Holton; David Lobach; Jennifer L. Mann; L. Charles Marcon; James Margolis, Ph.D.; **Robert Moffett, Esq.**; William K. Murphy, Esq.; Bruce A. Palmer; Martha Phelps; Ann Haggerty Raines; Matthew R. Sorrentino, Esq.; Melinda Stumpf; J. Marshall Wolff.
Investment Management: BNY Mellon, N.A.; Comerica; Merrill Lynch Trust Co.; Morgan Stanley Smith Barney; Vanguard Group; Wells Fargo.
Number of staff: 3 full-time professional; 1 part-time professional; 1 full-time support.
EIN: 231686634
Other changes: Corrina Passaro is now Mktg. and Grants Mgr. Trisha R. Higgins is now V.P. and C.F.O. Shelley Brown is no longer a governor. Alan Abraham, David K. Bausch, Gregory E. Grim, and David Rabaut are no longer governors.

2987
Mabelle McLeod Lewis Memorial Fund
c/o Wells Fargo Bank, N.A.
101N Independence Mall E., MACY1372-062
Philadelphia, PA 19106-2112
Application address: P.O. Box 3730, Stanford, CA 94305

Established in 1968 in CA.
Donor: Donald McLeod Lewis†.
Foundation type: Operating foundation.
Financial data (yr. ended 03/31/13): Assets, $4,955,806 (M); expenditures, $283,530; qualifying distributions, $247,412; giving activities include $217,185 for 9 grants to individuals (high: $35,306; low: $3,404).
Purpose and activities: Grants to scholars in the humanities affiliated with northern CA universities and colleges to bring about the completion of a scholarly dissertation on which a substantial amount of work has already been completed; also awards grants to doctoral candidates who are in their last year of study.
Fields of interest: Humanities.
Type of support: Fellowships; Research; Scholarships—to individuals.
Limitations: Applications accepted. Giving limited to northern CA.
Publications: Application guidelines; Program policy statement.
Application information: Submit application by mail only. Application form required.
Initial approach: Letter
Deadline(s): Jan. 15
Board meeting date(s): Feb. or Mar.
Trustees: Robert M. Raymer; Wells Fargo Bank, N.A.
Number of staff: 1
EIN: 237079585
Other changes: The grantmaker has moved from CA to PA.

2988
Christopher Ludwick Foundation
(formerly The Ludwick Institute)
16 N. Bryn Mawr Ave.
P.O. Box 1313
Bryn Mawr, PA 19010-3379
Contact: Trina Vaux, Secy.
E-mail: info@ludwickfoundation.org; Main URL: http://www.ludwickfoundation.org

Established in 1799 in PA.
Donor: Christopher Ludwick†.
Foundation type: Independent foundation.
Financial data (yr. ended 04/30/13): Assets, $5,123,906 (M); expenditures, $223,582; qualifying distributions, $220,945; giving activities include $207,500 for 40 grants (high: $20,000; low: $500).
Purpose and activities: Giving primarily for the education of poor youth in Philadelphia, Pennsylvania. For a list of recent grants, see foundation web site.
Fields of interest: Museums; Arts; Secondary school/education; Botanical gardens; Children/youth, services; Children; Youth; Young adults; Minorities; Economically disadvantaged.
Type of support: Program development.
Limitations: Applications accepted. Giving limited to the City of Philadelphia, PA. **No support for political organizations or programs targeted at children with disabilities for which other funding sources exist.** No grants to individuals, or for building campaigns, endowments, equipment, or general operating support.
Publications: Application guidelines; Grants list.
Application information: 2 paper copies of proposal should be submitted (along with email). Application form required.
Initial approach: Use application form on foundation web site
***Deadline(s):* Applications accepted between Feb. 1 and Feb. 28**
Board meeting date(s): May and Oct.
***Final notification:* Approx. June 15**
Officers: Susan W. Catherwood, Pres.; William M. Davison IV, V.P. and Treas.; Rhonda Cohen, V.P.; Trina Vaux, Secy.; and 9 directors and trustees.
Number of staff: 1 part-time support.
EIN: 236256408

2989
The M.E. Foundation
P.O. Box 363
Lampeter, PA 17537-0363
Contact: David Aungst, Dir.
VA tel.: (703) 478-0100

Established in 1966 in NY.
Donors: Margaret Brown Trimble†; Frances Carroll Brown†; Carol Brown†.
Foundation type: Independent foundation.
Financial data (yr. ended 12/31/11): Assets, $1,327,915 (M); expenditures, $1,512,633; qualifying distributions, $1,485,747; giving activities include $1,467,000 for 62 grants (high: $470,000; low: $1,000).
Purpose and activities: Grants to organizations in the U.S. and abroad for evangelistic missionary work and Bible studies.
Fields of interest: Christian agencies & churches.
Limitations: Applications not accepted. Giving on a national and international basis. No support for political organizations. No grants to individuals.
Application information: New grants proposals are not accepted. Only currently supported organizations may apply.
Board meeting date(s): Oct.
Officer and Directors:* Charles W. Colson,* Chair. and Pres.; **David Aungst**; Sharon Berry, M.D.; Calvin E. Howe; Daniel D. Smith.
EIN: 136205356

2990
The Martin Family Foundation
Horsham, PA

The foundation terminated in 2012.

2991
George & Miriam Martin Foundation
1818 Market St., 35th Fl.
Philadelphia, PA 19103-3636 (215) 587-8400
Contact: George Martin, Tr.
E-mail: gmteam@paworkinjury.com; Main URL: http://www.themartinfoundation.org
Grants List: http://www.themartinfoundation.org/grantHistory.htm

Established in 1996 in PA.
Donors: George Martin; Carol Martin Strange; Matthew Wilson; Lawrence Strange.
Foundation type: Independent foundation.
Financial data (yr. ended 12/31/12): Assets, $7,316,224 (M); gifts received, $401,000; expenditures, $442,016; qualifying distributions, $404,500; giving activities include $404,500 for grants.
Purpose and activities: Grants are given for charitable river or watershed protection activities, including trails, conservation easements, and wetland protection.
Fields of interest: Environment, research; Environment, water resources.
Type of support: General/operating support; Continuing support; Annual campaigns; Capital campaigns; Land acquisition; Seed money; Matching/challenge support.
Limitations: Applications accepted. Giving primarily in southeast PA.
Publications: Application guidelines; Grants list.
Application information: See foundation web site for application guidelines and procedures. Application form not required.
Initial approach: Letter
Copies of proposal: 1
Deadline(s): None
Board meeting date(s): Mar.
Directors: Glenn Emery; Christy Martin; George Martin; **Rebecca Martin**; Maura Shuey; Carol Martin Strange; H. Lawrence Strange.
Number of staff: None.
EIN: 232828201

2992
The Matthews Fund
Paoli, PA

The fund terminated on Dec. 31, 2011.

2993
McCune Foundation
3 PPG Pl., Ste. 400
Pittsburgh, PA **15222-5411** (412) 644-8779
Contact: Henry S. Beukema, Exec. Dir.
E-mail: info@mccune.org; Main URL: http://www.mccune.org
Grants Database: http://www.mccune.org/foundation:Website,mccune,grants

Established in 1979 in PA.
Donor: Charles L. McCune†.
Foundation type: Independent foundation.
Financial data (yr. ended 09/30/12): Assets, $343,318,226 (M); expenditures, $105,111,515; qualifying distributions, $104,240,252; giving activities include $102,414,440 for 147 grants (high: $8,017,944; low: $1,000).
Purpose and activities: The mission of the foundation is to enable communities and nonprofit institutions to improve the quality and circumstances of life for present and future generations. In meeting these challenges, the foundation employs flexible approaches and innovative strategies that are responsive to changing needs and new opportunities. The goal is to stimulate long-lasting and sustainable progress, which contributes to community vitality and economic growth.
Fields of interest: Museums; Performing arts; Historic preservation/historical societies; Arts; Higher education; Adult education—literacy, basic skills & GED; Libraries/library science; Health care; Medical research, institute; Employment; Housing/shelter, development; Youth development, services; Human services; Economic development; Urban/community development.
Type of support: Income development; Management development/capacity building; Capital campaigns; Building/renovation; Equipment; Land acquisition; Endowments; Program development; Seed money;

Technical assistance; Program-related investments/loans; Employee matching gifts.
Limitations: Applications accepted. Giving primarily in western PA, with emphasis on the Pittsburgh area. No grants to individuals.
Publications: Application guidelines; Financial statement; Grants list.
Application information: Applicants can be submitted via foundation's web site. Applicants are encouraged to wait at least 3 years after receiving a grant before reapplying. Funding is concentrated in Southwestern PA, mainly the Pittsburgh area. Unsolicited proposals from outside this region are not accepted. Application form required.
Initial approach: Inquiry letter (2 - 3 pages)
Copies of proposal: 1
Deadline(s): None
Board meeting date(s): Mar., June, Sept., and Dec.
Final notification: Minimum 90 days
Officers and Distribution Committee:* Michael M. Edwards,* Chair.; Henry S. Beukema, Exec. Dir.; **Ronald R. Davenport, Jr.; Adam B. Edwards**; John H. Edwards; **Laura E. Ellsworth**; Sarah McCune Losinger; **James C. Roddey**.
Trustee: National City Bank.
Number of staff: 4 full-time professional; 2 full-time support.
EIN: 256210269
Other changes: John R. McCune is no longer a member of the distribution committee.

2994
Lalitta Nash McKaig Foundation
c/o PNC Advisors
620 Liberty Ave., 10th Fl.
Pittsburgh, PA 15222-2705
***Application address:* Gregory H. Getty, Esq., Admin, c/o Geppert, McMullen, Paye & Getty, 21 Prospect Sq., Cumberland, MD, 21502, tel.: (301) 777-1515**

Established in 1973 in PA.
Foundation type: Independent foundation.
Financial data (yr. ended 09/30/13): Assets, $11,639,782 (M); expenditures, $626,023; qualifying distributions, $551,225; giving activities include $488,650 for grants to individuals.
Fields of interest: Higher education; Higher education, university.
Type of support: Scholarships—to individuals.
Limitations: Applications accepted. Giving limited to residents who graduated from high schools in Allegany and Garrett counties, MD, Bedford and Somerset counties, PA, and Mineral and Hampshire counties, WV.
Publications: Application guidelines.
Application information: Application forms can be obtained from high school guidance offices in the Cumberland, MD, area, financial aid offices of Frostburg State College and Allegany Community College, the foundation's office in Cumberland, MD, or PNC Bank, N.A. Application form required.
Deadline(s): May 30
Board meeting date(s): June
Trustee: PNC Bank, N.A.
EIN: 256071908

2995
Virginia A. McKee for the Poor Fund
c/o PNC Bank, N.A.
620 Liberty Ave., 10th Fl.
Pittsburgh, PA 15222-2705
***Application address:* c/o PNC Bank, N.A., Attn.: Trust Grant Review C, 1 PNC Plz., 249 5th Ave., 20th Fl., Pittsburgh, PA 15222, tel.: (412) 762-3413**

Trust established in 1929 in PA.
Donor: Virginia A. McKee†.
Foundation type: Independent foundation.
Financial data (yr. ended 09/30/13): Assets, $3,093,968 (M); expenditures, $116,718; qualifying distributions, $92,233; giving activities include $78,406 for 6 grants (high: $20,000; low: $7,744).
Purpose and activities: Giving for the benefit of the poor.
Fields of interest: Education; Human services; Christian agencies & churches; Economically disadvantaged.
Type of support: Emergency funds.
Limitations: Applications accepted. Giving primarily in Pittsburgh, PA. No support for private foundations, or for political organizations, fraternal organizations, labor organizations, or for advocacy groups. No grants to individuals, or for building or endowment funds, research, scholarships, events, general operating support, fellowships, or matching gifts; no loans.
Application information:
Initial approach: Letter
Deadline(s): None
Board meeting date(s): May and Nov.
Trustee: PNC Bank, N.A.
EIN: 256023292
Other changes: The grantmaker no longer lists a primary contact.

2996
William V. and Catherine A. McKinney Charitable Foundation
c/o PNC Bank, N.A.
P.O. Box 609
Pittsburgh, PA 15230-9738

Established in 1990 in PA.
Donor: Catherine A. McKinney†.
Foundation type: Independent foundation.
Financial data (yr. ended 03/31/13): Assets, $10,879,391 (M); expenditures, $557,087; qualifying distributions, $502,890; giving activities include $433,117 for grants.
Purpose and activities: Giving limited to organizations in western PA whose activities aid the elderly, disadvantaged youth and/or the disabled and support the arts.
Fields of interest: Arts; Human services; Public affairs.
Type of support: General/operating support; Capital campaigns; Endowments; Program development; Matching/challenge support.
Limitations: Applications not accepted. Giving limited to western PA. No grants to individuals.
Application information: Contributes only to pre-selected organizations.
Board meeting date(s): 3 times per year
Trustee: PNC Bank.
EIN: 251641619
Other changes: The grantmaker has moved from OH to PA.

2997
The McLean Contributionship
230 Sugartown Rd., Ste. 30
Wayne, PA **19087-6001 (610) 989-8090**
Contact: Sandra L. McLean, Exec. Dir.
***Main URL:* http://fdnweb.org/mclean**
Arts, Culture and Humanities Grants: http://fdnweb.org/mclean/grants-arts/
Education Grants: http://fdnweb.org/mclean/grants-education/
Environment and Animal Welfare Grants: http://fdnweb.org/mclean/grants-environment-animals/
Health Grants: http://fdnweb.org/mclean/grants-health/
Human Services Grants: http://fdnweb.org/mclean/grants-human-services/

Trust established in 1951 in PA.
Donors: William L. McLean, Jr.†; Robert McLean†; William L. McLean III†; William Clarke Mason†; William L. McLean IV; Sandra McLean; Lisa McLean; Elizabeth P. McLean; Elizabeth R. McLean; Wendy McLean; Richard Bove; Bulletin Co.; Independent Publications, Inc.; Independence Communications, Inc.
Foundation type: Independent foundation.
Financial data (yr. ended 12/31/12): Assets, $39,541,579 (M); gifts received, $183,851; expenditures, $2,191,169; qualifying distributions, $2,063,075; giving activities include $1,937,156 for 111 grants (high: $100,000; low: $1,000).
Purpose and activities: The grantmaker supports understanding and preservation of the environment, compassionate and cost effective health care and improving the quality of life through capital and other projects. Trustees prefer special projects rather than continuing programs and focus on capital projects: bricks and mortar, endowment, or will provide seed money for purposes falling within the contributorship's guidelines.
Fields of interest: Museums; Performing arts; Historic preservation/historical societies; Libraries/library science; Education; Environment, natural resources; Environmental education; Hospitals (general); Nursing home/convalescent facility; Health care, home services; Youth development, services; Children/youth, services; Aging, centers/services; Children/youth; Youth; Aging.
Type of support: Capital campaigns; Building/renovation; Equipment; Land acquisition; Endowments; Program development; Publication; Seed money; Research; Matching/challenge support.
Limitations: Applications accepted. Giving primarily in the greater Philadelphia, PA, area. No grants to individuals.
Publications: Application guidelines; Financial statement; Grants list; Informational brochure; Informational brochure (including application guidelines).
Application information: Philanthropy Network Greater Philadelphia Common Grant Application Form accepted, and can be downloaded via grantmaker web site. Preference is for applications to be submitted online. See foundation web site for application guidelines and procedures. Application form not required.
Initial approach: Use online application system on grantmaker web site
Copies of proposal: 1
Deadline(s): See grantmaker web site for current deadlines
Board meeting date(s): Quarterly: Mar., June, Sept., and Dec.
Officers and Trustees:* William L. McLean IV,* Chair.; Sandra L. McLean, Vice-Chair., Secy. and Exec. Dir.; Susannah McLean, Advisory Trustee;

Jean G. Bodine, Trustee Emeritus; John F. Bales III; Diana McLean Liefer; Carolyn M. Raymond.
Number of staff: None.
EIN: 236396940
Other changes: The grantmaker no longer lists a fax.

2998
Richard King Mellon Foundation
BNY Mellon Ctr.
500 Grant St., 41st Fl., Ste. 4106
Pittsburgh, PA 15219-2502 (412) 392-2800
Contact: Scott Izzo, Dir.
FAX: (412) 392-2837; Main URL: http://fdncenter.org/grantmaker/rkmellon
Grants List: http://foundationcenter.org/grantmaker/rkmellon/grantlist2010.html

Trust established in 1947 in PA; incorporated in 1971 in PA.
Donor: Richard K. Mellon†.
Foundation type: Independent foundation.
Financial data (yr. ended 12/31/12): Assets, $2,060,318,008 (M); expenditures, $99,659,922; qualifying distributions, $89,683,343; giving activities include $84,211,046 for 195 grants (high: $11,000,000; low: $1,500), and $3,000,000 for 1 loan/program-related investment.
Purpose and activities: Local grant programs emphasize conservation, education, families and youth, regional economic development, system reform; support also for conservation of natural areas and wildlife preservation elsewhere in the United States.
Fields of interest: Education, early childhood education; Education; Environment, natural resources; Environment; Youth development, services; Human services; Children/youth, services; Family services; Urban/community development; Community/economic development; Infants/toddlers; Children/youth; Youth; Adults; Young adults; Economically disadvantaged.
Type of support: Technical assistance; General/operating support; Continuing support; Capital campaigns; Building/renovation; Equipment; Land acquisition; Program development; Seed money; Research; Program evaluation; Program-related investments/loans; Matching/challenge support.
Limitations: Applications accepted. Giving primarily in Southwestern PA. No grants to individuals, or for fellowships or scholarships, or conduit organizations.
Publications: Annual report (including application guidelines); Grants list.
Application information: Grantmakers of Western Pennsylvania's Common Grant Application Format accepted. Application form required.
Initial approach: Proposal or letter of inquiry
Copies of proposal: 1
Deadline(s): None
Board meeting date(s): Varies
Final notification: 1 - 6 months
Officers and Trustees:* Seward Prosser Mellon,* Chair. and C.E.O.; **W. Russell G. Byers, Jr.,* Pres.**; Douglas L. Sisson, V.P. and Treas.; Lisa Kuzma, Secy. and Sr. Prog. Off.; Scott D. Izzo,* Dir.; John J. Turcik,* Cont.; Richard P. Mellon, Chair. and Tr. Emeritus; Lawrence S. Busch; Alison M. Byers; Catharine Mellon Cathey; Bruce King Mellon Henderson; Constance Elizabeth Mellon Kapp; Armour N. Mellon; Richard A. Mellon.
Number of staff: 1 full-time support.
EIN: 251127705
Other changes: W. Russell G. Byers, Jr. has replaced Bruce King Mellon Henderson as Pres.

2999
Solomon & Sylvia Mendel Charitable Trust
c/o PNC Bank, N.A.
620 Liberty Ave., 10th Fl.
Pittsburgh, PA 15222-2705

Established in 1986 in PA.
Foundation type: Independent foundation.
Financial data (yr. ended 07/31/13): Assets, $4,681,011 (M); expenditures, $246,935; qualifying distributions, $206,026; giving activities include $184,312 for 15 grants (high: $20,000; low: $7,500).
Fields of interest: Museums (history); Higher education; Education; Hospitals (specialty); Jewish federated giving programs; Jewish agencies & synagogues; Blind/visually impaired.
Type of support: General/operating support.
Limitations: Applications not accepted. Giving primarily in Pittsburgh, PA. No grants to individuals.
Application information: Contributes only to pre-selected organization.
Trustee: PNC Bank, N.A.
EIN: 256271818
Other changes: J. Quint Salmon is no longer a trustee.

3000
Merchants Fund
1616 Walnut St., Ste. 802
Philadelphia, PA 19103-5308 (215) 339-1339
Contact: Patricia Blakely
FAX: (215) 399-1440;
E-mail: info@merchantsfund.org; Main URL: http://www.merchantsfund.org/
Grants List: http://www.merchantsfund.org/grantee-awards.html

Established Jan. 21, 1854 in PA.
Donors: Lewis Elkins Fund; Lewis Elkins Trust; Charles Fearon†.
Foundation type: Independent foundation.
Financial data (yr. ended 12/31/12): Assets, $14,108,714 (M); expenditures, $610,427; qualifying distributions, $577,819; giving activities include $281,495 for 32 grants (high: $11,071; low: $2,750).
Purpose and activities: The Merchants Fund is committed to providing for the economic needs of the merchant community by making modest grants to small businesses. Merchants must do business in Philadelphia, Pennsylvania and have conducted business for a minimum of three years. Grant-making areas include: stabilization grants, loan matches, and emergency grants,.
Fields of interest: Community development, business promotion; Community development, small businesses; Economically disadvantaged.
Type of support: Emergency funds; Technical assistance; Grants to individuals.
Limitations: Applications accepted. Giving primarily in Philadelphia, PA. No support for home businesses, or businesses holding an off-premise liquor license. No grants for new business ventures.
Publications: Application guidelines; Grants list.
Application information: See foundation Web site for guidelines and latest news. Application form required.
Initial approach: E-mail, telephone or letter
Copies of proposal: 1
Deadline(s): Feb., May, and Oct. Refer to foundation Web site for details
Board meeting date(s): Feb., May, Sept., and Dec.
Final notification: 6-8 weeks
Officers and Directors:* Bruce Hotaling,* Pres.; John W. Gould, Treas.; Fernando Chang-Muy, Secy.; Patricia Blakely, Exec. Dir.; Henry Winsor, Emeritus; Kira Baker-Doyle; Steven King, Sr.; Suzanne Cunningham; Elbert Sampson; Andrew Toy.
Number of staff: 1 full-time professional.
EIN: 231584975

3001
The Mylan Charitable Foundation
1500 Corporate Dr., Ste. 400
Canonsburg, PA 15317-8580
Contact: Christina Matluck, Exec. Admin.
E-mail: christina.matluck@mylanfoundation.org

Established in 2002 in PA and WV.
Donors: Mylan Laboratories Inc.; Mylan Pharmaceuticals.
Foundation type: Company-sponsored foundation.
Financial data (yr. ended 12/31/12): Assets, $10,200,441 (M); expenditures, $943,036; qualifying distributions, $862,500; giving activities include $862,500 for 11 grants (high: $250,000; low: $25,000).
Purpose and activities: The foundation supports organizations involved with education, health, human services, and community development.
Fields of interest: Arts; Education; Health care.
Type of support: General/operating support; Building/renovation.
Limitations: Applications accepted. Giving primarily in PA and WV as well as Rockford, IL, Sugar Land, TX, and St. Albans, VT. No grants to individuals.
Application information:
***Copies of proposal:* 1**
Deadline(s): Varies
Officers and Directors: Rodney L. Piatt, Chair.; C. B. Todd, Secy.; Brian Byala, Treas.; Heather Bresch; Robert J. Coury.
Number of staff: 1 full-time professional.
EIN: 431954390
Other changes: The grantmaker no longer publishes application guidelines.

3002
Naylor Family Foundation
100 Boxwood Ln.
York, PA 17402-9305

Established in 2004 in PA.
Donors: Irvin S. Naylor; Leah R. Naylor; Sarah R. Naylor.
Foundation type: Independent foundation.
Financial data (yr. ended 12/31/12): Assets, $1,878,263 (M); expenditures, $1,078,687; qualifying distributions, $1,076,500; giving activities include $1,075,000 for 3 grants (high: $1,000,000; low: $25,000).
Fields of interest: Higher education; Education; Athletics/sports, equestrianism.
Limitations: Applications not accepted. Giving primarily in MD. No grants to individuals.
Application information: Contributes only to pre-selected organizations.
Officers: Diane G. Naylor, Pres.; Irvin S. Naylor, V.P.; Albert G. Blakey III, Secy.; **Brad Leber, Secy.**; Scott W. Romberger, Treas.
Director: S. Chester Naylor II.
EIN: 421640416

3003
Grace S. & W. Linton Nelson Foundation

150 N. Radnor Chester Rd., Ste. F200
Radnor, PA **19087 (610) 977-2488**
Contact: Gloria Feldman, Exec. Admin.
***FAX:* (610) 977-0043**;
E-mail: nelson.info@nelsonfoundationpa.org; Main URL: http://nelsonfoundationpa.org

Established in 1984 in PA.
Donors: ADM. W. Linton Nelson†; Grace Nelson†; William P. Brady; Delaware Management Co.
Foundation type: Independent foundation.
Financial data (yr. ended 12/31/12): Assets, $18,953,822 (M); expenditures, $842,909; qualifying distributions, $763,312; giving activities include $502,656 for 51 grants (high: $198,906; low: $1,000).
Purpose and activities: Giving for: 1) the unmet needs of children and youth in the areas of shelter, day care, preschool, education, health care, child and drug abuse prevention, after school and summer programs, child advocacy, parenting, and foster care and adoption; 2) The Nelson Foundation Scholarship Program at the Wharton School; and 3) programs fostering leadership and citizenship in youth.
Fields of interest: Child development, education; Youth development, citizenship; Children/youth, services; Child development, services.
Type of support: General/operating support; Equipment; Program development; Seed money.
Limitations: Applications accepted. Giving primarily in Philadelphia, PA, and the surrounding counties, including Bucks, Chester, Delaware, Montgomery and Philadelphia. No support for national or umbrella organizations, religious education, public, private or charter schools, routine social services or counseling, individual daycare, disease research, hospitals or programs for animals. No grants to individuals directly, or for tickets, tables, ads, sponsorships, parties, conferences, fairs and fundraising events, fellowships, travel, or public policy research or advocacy.
Publications: Application guidelines.
Application information: Application form required.
Initial approach: Proposal cover sheet (which can be downloaded from foundation web site)
Copies of proposal: 1
Deadline(s): 6 weeks before board meetings in Jan., Apr., July, and Oct.
Board meeting date(s): 2nd week of every month; grants reviewed quarterly in Jan., Apr., July, and Oct.
Officers and Directors:* Alexandra A. Aldridge,* Pres.; Fred C. Aldridge, Jr.,* Treas.; Beth A. Coyne; Richard J. Flannery.
Number of staff: 2 part-time professional.
EIN: 222583922

3004
Florence Nesh Charitable Trust

c/o PNC Bank
620 Liberty Ave., 10th Fl.
Pittsburgh, PA 15222-2705
Application address: c/o PNC Charitable Trust Grant Review Committee, 1 PNC Plz., 249 Fifth Ave., 20th Fl., Pittsburgh, PA 15222-2705, tel.: (412) 768-7716

Established in 2006 in DC.
Donor: Florence Nesh†.
Foundation type: Independent foundation.
Financial data (yr. ended 06/30/13): Assets, $5,550,377 (M); expenditures, $321,356; qualifying distributions, $269,973; giving activities include $245,000 for 3 grants (high: $90,000; low: $75,000).
Fields of interest: Higher education, university; Nursing school/education; Hospitals (specialty); Children.
Limitations: Applications accepted. Giving primarily in Washington, DC, MD and VA.
Application information: Application form required.
Initial approach: See website
Deadline(s): See website
Trustee: PNC Bank, N.A.
EIN: 206758590
Other changes: The grantmaker no longer lists a URL address or an E-mail address.

3005
John H. Noll Foundation

c/o PNC Bank, N.A.
P.O. Box 609
Pittsburgh, PA 15230-9738
***Application address:* c/o PNC Bank, N.A., Attn.: Jane Kleinsmith, 1900 E. 19th St., Cleveland, OH 44114, tel.: (216) 222-9815**

Established in 1967 in IN.
Foundation type: Independent foundation.
Financial data (yr. ended 09/30/13): Assets, $3,892,279 (M); expenditures, $189,912; qualifying distributions, $169,590; giving activities include $152,698 for grants to individuals.
Purpose and activities: Scholarship awards to graduating seniors of Fort Wayne, Indiana, community high schools, Bishop Dwenger, Bishop Luers, and Concordia high schools, and the Homestead High School.
Fields of interest: Education.
Type of support: Scholarships—to individuals.
Limitations: Applications accepted. Giving limited to residents of IN.
Application information: Application forms are available from guidance counselors at participating Fort Wayne, IN, high schools. Application form required.
Initial approach: Proposal
Deadline(s): Mar. 31
Trustee: PNC Bank, N.A.
EIN: 237082877
Other changes: The grantmaker has moved from OH to PA.

3006
North Penn Community Health Foundation

2506 N. Broad St., Ste. 206
Colmar, PA 18915-9439 (215) 716-5400
Contact: Russell Johnson, C.E.O. and Pres.
FAX: (215) 716-5410; E-mail: jpedroni@npchf.org; Toll-free tel.: (888) 412-0314; Main URL: http://www.npchf.org

Established in 2002; converted from the sale of North Penn Hospital. Converted to a private foundation in 2008.
Foundation type: Independent foundation.
Financial data (yr. ended 06/30/13): Assets, $44,792,336 (M); gifts received, $527,370; expenditures, $2,027,666; qualifying distributions, $1,463,854; giving activities include $486,118 for 24 grants (high: $65,875; low: $100), and $941,880 for foundation-administered programs.
Purpose and activities: The foundation provides support to health and human service organizations that serve the residents living in the service community. The foundation is interested in building collaborative relationships with providing organizations. By establishing and strengthening these relationships, the foundation intends to identify, select and invest in programs and organizations that will improve the health, welfare and quality of life of children and families, adults and senior citizens, people with disabilities and other disadvantaged populations residing the foundation's service community.
Fields of interest: Health care, reform; Public health; Health care, patient services; Health care; Food services; Nutrition; Housing/shelter, reform; Housing/shelter, homeless; Housing/shelter, services; Housing/shelter; Human services; Aging; Disabilities, people with; Physically disabled; Mentally disabled; Economically disadvantaged; Homeless.
Type of support: Management development/capacity building; Program development; Technical assistance; Consulting services; Matching/challenge support.
Limitations: Applications accepted. Giving in Montgomery County and the North Penn region, PA. Montgomery County is a suburban county of the Philadelphia metropolitan region, in the southeastern portion of the state. The North Penn region is defined by the boundaries of the North Penn, Souderton Area, and Wissahickon School Districts. No support for No support to for-profit organizations, disease-specific charities, religious congregations, fraternal, political, or civic groups, or recreational clubs. No grants to individuals, or for fundraising, endowments, debt reduction, replacement of lost government funds, supplementation of groups, private/public insurance, clinical or academic research, student projects, athletic, or alumni activities, equipment, or publications (unless such publications are an integral component for a specific grant initiative).
Publications: Application guidelines; Annual report; Financial statement; Grants list; Occasional report.
Application information: The foundation has an online application format. Do not submit videos or electronic media unless directly related to the nature of the grant request. Do not use ringed binders or other elaborate document fasteners. Faxed or e-mailed applications are not accepted.
Initial approach: The foundation prefers to receive a phone call or letter of inquiry prior to full application
Deadline(s): Generally 6-8 weeks before board meetings
Board meeting date(s): Varies (refer to foundation web site for current dates)
Final notification: Approximately 1-week after board meeting following receipt of application
Officers and Directors:* Russel R. Hensel, Ph.D.*, Chair.; Nancy Alba Dunleavy, Vice-Chair.; Russell Johnson,* C.E.O. and Pres.; **Alfredo de la Pena,* Secy.; Kenneth Amey,* Treas.**; David Crosson; George E. Marks, AIA; Paul W. Pocalyko, CPA/CFF, CFE; William C. Stevens III; R. John Stubbs, Ph.D.; Elizabeth Styer; Sandra C. Vasoli.
Number of staff: 4 full-time professional.
EIN: 231352175
Other changes: Russel R. Hensel, Ph.D. has replaced R. John Stubbs as Chair. Alfredo de la Pena has replaced David Crosson as Secy. Kenneth Amey has replaced Alfredo de la Pena as Treas. Nancy Alba Dunleavy is now Vice-Chair. Kathleen Fitzgerald is no longer a director.

3007
O'Brien-Veba Scholarship Trust

c/o PNC Bank, N.A.
P.O. Box 609
Pittsburgh, PA 15230-9738

Established in 1991 in IL.
Foundation type: Independent foundation.
Financial data (yr. ended 09/30/13): Assets, $3,588,500 (M); expenditures, $196,373; qualifying distributions, $176,823; giving activities include $156,800 for grants to individuals.
Purpose and activities: Giving for higher education, primarily to individuals of Roman Catholic faith.
Fields of interest: Higher education; Catholic agencies & churches.
Type of support: General/operating support; Scholarship funds; Scholarships—to individuals.
Limitations: Applications not accepted. Giving primarily to residents of IA, IL, IN, MI, and WI.
Application information: Unsolicited requests for funds not accepted.
Directors: John Bass; Thomas C. Brady; Ann Hupert; Harvey Share; Cindy Summers.
Trustee: PNC Bank, N.A.
EIN: 376277500
Other changes: The grantmaker has moved from OH to PA. The grantmaker no longer lists a URL address.
James R. Doyle is no longer a director.

3008
Horace B. Packer Foundation Inc.
P.O. Box 732
Wellsboro, PA 16901-0732 (570) 724-1800
FAX: (570) 723-1490;
E-mail: michelle@owlettlewis.com

Incorporated in 1951 in PA.
Donors: Horace B. Packer‡; Horace B. Packer Trust.
Foundation type: Independent foundation.
Financial data (yr. ended 12/31/12): Assets, $191,160 (M); gifts received, $192,000; expenditures, $261,550; qualifying distributions, $261,520; giving activities include $253,150 for 17 grants (high: $60,000; low: $500).
Purpose and activities: Giving for services to benefit the youth of Tioga County, PA, and to educational institutions for scholarships to students residing in the county.
Fields of interest: Libraries (public); Education; Hospitals (general); Health care; Recreation, parks/playgrounds; Athletics/sports, Special Olympics; Children/youth, services; Community/economic development; Christian agencies & churches.
Type of support: Capital campaigns; Scholarship funds.
Limitations: Applications accepted. Giving limited to the Tioga County, PA, area.
Application information: Application form required.
Initial approach: Letter
Copies of proposal: 1
Board meeting date(s): 3rd Mon. in Apr., Aug., and Dec.
Officers: Eugene Seelye, Pres.; R. James Dunham, V.P.; Robert F. Cox, Jr., Secy.; Rhonda Litchfield, Treas.
Directors: Jeffrey A. Fetzer; **Thomas Freeman**; Gregory P. Hinton.
Number of staff: None.
EIN: 236390932
Other changes: The grantmaker no longer lists a primary contact.
Edward H. Owlett is no longer a director.

3009
A. J. & Sigismunda Palumbo Charitable Trust
c/o PNC Bank, N.A.
620 Liberty Ave. N., 10th Fl.
Pittsburgh, PA 15222-2705
Application address: c/o John W. Kowach, 1659 Rt. 228, Ste. 4, Cranberry Township, PA 16066-5319; tel.: (814) 788-5093

Established in 1974 in PA.
Donors: A.J. Palumbo; Antonio J. Palumbo‡.
Foundation type: Independent foundation.
Financial data (yr. ended 03/31/13): Assets, $50,268,656 (M); gifts received, $7,558,000; expenditures, $2,746,503; qualifying distributions, $2,488,024; giving activities include $2,281,614 for 60 grants (high: $200,000; low: $5,000).
Fields of interest: Higher education; Hospitals (general); Human services; Catholic agencies & churches.
Limitations: Giving primarily in western PA.
Application information: Application form required.
Initial approach: Letter requesting application procedure
***Deadline(s):* Dec. 31**
Board meeting date(s): Mar. 1
Trustees: Donald Fleming; Rex Knisley; Robert Y. Kopf, Jr.; John W. Kowach; Donald W. Meredith; **Robert Ordiway**; Joseph Palumbo; P.J. Palumbo; David A. Ricchuito; PNC Bank, N.A.
Number of staff: 1 part-time support.
EIN: 256168159

3010
W. I. Patterson Charitable Fund
1 Oxford Ctr., Ste. 2100
Pittsburgh, PA 15219-1400
***Application address:* c/o Timothy F. Burke, Jr., Nancy L. Rackoff, or Robert B. Wolf, 301 Grant St., 20th Fl., Pittsburgh, PA 15219, tel.: (412) 281-5580**

Trust established in 1955 in PA.
Donor: W.I. Patterson‡.
Foundation type: Independent foundation.
Financial data (yr. ended 07/31/13): Assets, $5,436,173 (M); expenditures, $272,315; qualifying distributions, $252,501; giving activities include $222,689 for 57 grants (high: $44,538; low: $1,000).
Fields of interest: Museums (children's); Performing arts, ballet; Performing arts, theater; Performing arts, opera; Performing arts, music (choral); Historic preservation/historical societies; Arts; Higher education; Libraries (public); Education; Hospitals (general); Health organizations, association; Food banks; Recreation, camps; Big Brothers/Big Sisters; Human services; Children/youth, services; Civil liberties, reproductive rights; Blind/visually impaired.
Type of support: General/operating support; Continuing support; Annual campaigns; Capital campaigns; Building/renovation; Equipment; Land acquisition; Debt reduction; Emergency funds; Publication; Seed money; Research.
Limitations: Applications accepted. Giving limited to Allegheny County, PA. No grants to individuals or for endowment funds, scholarships, fellowships, or matching gifts; no loans.
Application information:
***Initial approach:* Letter**
Copies of proposal: 1
***Deadline(s):* Trustees review applications quarterly for consideration within the fund's fiscal year**
Trustees: Timothy F. Burke, Jr.; Nancy L. Rackoff; Robert B. Wolf.
EIN: 256028639

3011
The William Penn Foundation
2 Logan Sq., 11th Fl.
100 N. 18th St.
Philadelphia, PA 19103-2757 (215) 988-1830
Contact: Helen Davis Picher, Interim Pres.; Laura Sparks, V.P., Phil. Prog(s)
FAX: (215) 988-1823;
E-mail: grants@williampennfoundation.org; Main URL: http://www.williampennfoundation.org
Grants Database: http://www.williampennfoundation.org/Search.aspx
Knowledge Center: http://www.williampennfoundation.org/Strategy.aspx
Twitter: https://twitter.com/WilliamPennFdn

Incorporated in 1945 in DE.
Donors: John C. Haas‡; Otto Haas‡; Phoebe W. Haas‡; Otto Haas & Phoebe W. Haas Charitable Trusts.
Foundation type: Independent foundation.
Financial data (yr. ended 12/31/12): Assets, $2,019,462,152 (M); expenditures, $101,970,000; qualifying distributions, $86,500,000; giving activities include $79,563,172 for 236 grants (high: $15,000,000; low: $6,000), and $111,828 for 174 employee matching gifts.
Purpose and activities: The foundation is dedicated to improving the quality of life in the Greater Philadelphia region through efforts that close the achievement gap for low-income children, ensure a sustainable environment, foster creativity that enhances civic life, and advance philanthropy in the Philadelphia region. In partnership with others, the foundation works to advance opportunity, ensure sustainability, and enable effective solutions.
Fields of interest: Performing arts; Arts; Child development, education; Elementary school/education; Secondary school/education; Elementary/secondary school reform; Environment, natural resources; Environment, beautification programs; Environment; Economically disadvantaged.
Type of support: Building/renovation; Capital campaigns; Consulting services; Employee matching gifts; Equipment; General/operating support; Land acquisition; Management development/capacity building; Matching/challenge support; Program development; Program evaluation; Program-related investments/loans; Research; Seed money; Technical assistance.
Limitations: Applications accepted. Giving limited to the greater Philadelphia region. (An expanded region for some environmental grants may be viewed on the foundation web site). No support for sectarian religious activities, political lobbying or legislative activities, or for-profit organizations. No support for institutions that discriminate on the basis of race, ethnicity, creed, gender, or sexual orientation in policy or practice. No grants to individuals, or for debt reduction, hospital capital projects, medical research, programs that replace lost government support, housing construction or rehabilitation, scholarships, or fellowships; no loans (except for program-related investments).
Publications: Application guidelines; Annual report; Grants list.
Application information: Letters of inquiry are not accepted by fax. If the LOI indicates a potential fit with the foundation's criteria, applicants will be invited to submit a formal and complete proposal.

Those applicants encouraged to submit a full proposal will be directed to the appropriate site section for information on preparing a complete proposal. Unsolicited complete grant proposals are no longer accepted. Please see the foundation Web site for additional information. Application form required.

Initial approach: Complete a general inquiry form. Review program guidelines on the foundation's website and confirm that the proposed work aligns with the foundation's strategic priorities. Once an idea has been submitted, foundation staff will review the submission and notify the organization of next steps, which could include a request for more information, a request to discuss the idea further, or notification from the foundation that the idea is ineligible or not aligned with the foundation's strategic priorities

Copies of proposal: 1

Deadline(s): Deadlines have been imposed for funding through Increasing Arts Education and Advancing Arts and Cultural Organizations. Please see the foundation web site for further information

Board meeting date(s): Four times per year (Jan., Apr., July and Nov.)

Final notification: 30 days

Officers and Directors:* David W. Haas,* Chair.; Janet Haas, M.D.*, Vice-Chair.; Frederick R. Haas,* Secy.; Laura Sparks, Exec. Dir.; MaDoe Htun, C.I.O.; Judith Freyer; James Gately; Andrew Haas; Christina Haas; Katherine Haas; Leonard C. Haas; Thomas W. Haas; Daniel Meyer, M.D.; Howard Meyers.

Number of staff: 24 full-time professional; 3 part-time professional; 6 full-time support.

EIN: 231503488

Other changes: Helen Davis Picher is no longer Interim Pres.

3012
Raymond & Ruth Perelman Education Foundation

1 Bala Ave., Ste. 310
Bala Cynwyd, PA 19004-3210

Established in 1995 in PA.

Foundation type: Independent foundation.

Financial data (yr. ended 04/30/13): Assets, $44,034,977 (M); expenditures, $1,349,305; qualifying distributions, $602,800; giving activities include $602,800 for 10 grants (high: $250,000; low: $200).

Fields of interest: Higher education; Medical school/education; Human services.

Limitations: Applications not accepted. Giving primarily in PA. No grants to individuals.

Application information: Contributes only to pre-selected organizations.

Trustee: Raymond G. Perelman.

EIN: 232819735

Other changes: At the close of 2013, the fair market value of the grantmaker's assets was $44,034,977, a 52.7% increase over the 2012 value, $28,831,052.

3013
Jennie Perelman Foundation

1 Bala Ave., Ste. 310
Bala Cynwyd, PA 19004-3210

Established in 1985 in PA.

Donor: General Refractories Co.

Foundation type: Independent foundation.

Financial data (yr. ended 02/28/13): Assets, $2,566,543 (M); expenditures, $239,648; qualifying distributions, $231,880; giving activities include $231,880 for 11 grants (high: $107,250; low: $20).

Fields of interest: Museums; Arts; Higher education; Cancer; Eye diseases; Children, services; Community/economic development; Jewish federated giving programs; Jewish agencies & synagogues.

Limitations: Applications not accepted. Giving primarily in PA. No grants to individuals.

Application information: Unsolicited requests for funds not accepted.

Trustee: Raymond G. Perelman.

EIN: 236251650

Other changes: Ruth Perelman is no longer a trustee.

3014
Phoenixville Community Health Foundation

821 Gay St.
Phoenixville, PA 19460-4410 (610) 917-9890
Contact: Louis J. Beccaria, C.E.O. and Pres.
FAX: (610) 917-9861; E-mail: pchf1@pchf1.org; Main URL: http://www.pchf1.org/
Blog: http://pchf1.blogspot.com/

Established in 1997 in PA; converted from Phoenixville Hospital.

Foundation type: Independent foundation.

Financial data (yr. ended 06/30/13): Assets, $50,203,434 (M); gifts received, $11,960; expenditures, $2,390,260; qualifying distributions, $2,180,044; giving activities include $1,624,118 for 185 grants (high: $528,500; low: $50), $45,000 for 24 grants to individuals (high: $3,000; low: $1,000), and $17,800 for 1 loan/program-related investment.

Purpose and activities: The foundation seeks to improve the health and quality of life in the greater Phoenixville, PA community.

Fields of interest: Medical care, community health systems; Optometry/vision screening; Public health; Health care; Mental health/crisis services; Housing/shelter; Children, services; Youth, services; Human services; Children/youth; Children; Youth; Adults; Aging; Young adults; Disabilities, people with; Physically disabled; Blind/visually impaired; Deaf/hearing impaired; Mentally disabled; Hispanics/Latinos; Women; Girls; Adults, women; Young adults, female; Men; Adults, men; Young adults, male; Military/veterans; Substance abusers; Single parents; Crime/abuse victims; Terminal illness, people with; Economically disadvantaged; Homeless.

Type of support: General/operating support; Continuing support; Management development/capacity building; Capital campaigns; Building/renovation; Equipment; Endowments; Program development; Seed money; Technical assistance; Program evaluation; Scholarships—to individuals; Matching/challenge support.

Limitations: Applications accepted. Giving primarily in the greater Phoenixville, PA, area. No support for fraternal organizations, political parties, or veterans, labor, or civic groups. No grants for benefits, operating deficits, or publications.

Publications: Application guidelines; Annual report; Financial statement; Grants list; Informational brochure (including application guidelines); Newsletter; Occasional report; Program policy statement.

Application information: Based on the initial telephone call or meeting, a grant request will be accepted if the proposed initiative fits within the foundation's guidelines. Application information and forms available on foundation web site. Application form required.

Initial approach: Telephone or office visit

Copies of proposal: 1

***Deadline(s):* See foundation web site for current deadlines**

Board meeting date(s): Jan., Apr., and Sept.

Final notification: 8 weeks

Officers and Directors:* Robert Ryan,* Chair.; Maria Schwab, Ed.D.*, Vice-Chair.; Louis J. Beccaria, Ph.D.*, C.E.O. and Pres.; **Carol Poinier, V.P., Admin.; Lynn Pike Hartman, V.P., Progs.; Charles Henry, Jr.,* Secy.; David Gautreau, Treas.**; Frank J. Cirone; Timothy Durkin; **Kathryn Evans; Anna Mae Galbraith**; R. John Giannone; **Anita Guzman; Andrea Hanaway, M.D.; James Kovaleski; Kenneth Krenicky; Rev. Dr. Koshy Mathews.**

Number of staff: 3 full-time professional; 1 full-time support.

EIN: 232912035

Other changes: Robert Ryan has replaced Amy Barto as Chair. Maria Schwab, Ed.D. has replaced Frank J. Cirone as Vice-Chair. Charles Henry, Jr. has replaced Karen Coldwell as Secy. David Gautreau has replaced Travis Eubanks-Bey as Treas.

Robert Ryan is now Chair. Robb Frees, Richard Kirkner, Cynthia Krommes, Marian Moskowitz, Joseph Oliva, Graciela Prolet, and Kenneth Winston are no longer directors.

3015
The Leo and Peggy Pierce Family Foundation

(formerly The L. W. Pierce Family Foundation)
2 Tower Bridge, Ste. 410
1 Fayette St.
Conshohocken, PA 19428-4133 (610) 862-2105
Contact: Constance Buckley, Pres.
FAX: (610) 862-2120;
E-mail: lwpiercefamilyfoundation@yahoo.com; Main URL: http://www.lwpiercefamilyfoundation.org

Established in 1997 in FL.

Donors: Leo W. Pierce, Sr.; Marjorie L. Pierce‡; Mary Pierce; Sarah Quinn.

Foundation type: Independent foundation.

Financial data (yr. ended 12/31/12): Assets, $16,832,542 (M); gifts received, $745,825; expenditures, $947,864; qualifying distributions, $771,708; giving activities include $683,700 for 52 grants (high: $100,000; low: $2,000).

Purpose and activities: Giving primarily for activities that address hunger and food insecurity through direct service program and/or advocacy efforts.

Fields of interest: Food services; Human services; Aging.

Type of support: General/operating support; Capital campaigns; Building/renovation; Endowments.

Limitations: Applications accepted. **Giving primarily in the 5-county Philadelphia, PA, area.** No grants to individuals.

Publications: Application guidelines; Grants list.

Application information: Faxed requests will not be considered. Application form not required.

Initial approach: Letter

***Copies of proposal:* 2**

***Deadline(s):* Jan. 15 and July 15**

Board meeting date(s): Apr. and Oct.

Final notification: 2 weeks following board meetings

Officers and Trustees:* Constance Buckley,* Chair. and Pres.; **Molly Pierce, V.P. and Secy.**; Michael Pierce,* Treas.; Kathryn Cox; Eve Pierce; J. Peter Pierce; Kathleen F. Pierce; Leo W. Pierce, Jr.; Barbara Quinn.
EIN: 597109847
Other changes: Leo W. Pierce, Sr. , Chair., is deceased. Molly Pierce is now V.P. and Secy.

3016
The Pilgrim Foundation
P.O. Box 155
East Earl, PA **17519-0155 (610) 314-1967**
Contact: Gary L. Pilgrim, Pres.
E-mail: info@thepilgrimfoundation.org; Main URL: http://www.thepilgrimfoundation.org
Blog: http://thepilgrimfoundation.org/blog/

Established in 1998 in PA.
Donor: Gary L. Pilgrim.
Foundation type: Independent foundation.
Financial data (yr. ended 06/30/13): Assets, $16,488,668 (M); gifts received, $1,433,195; expenditures, $814,879; qualifying distributions, $773,105; giving activities include $636,000 for 29 grants (high: $70,000; low: $5,000).
Purpose and activities: Giving primarily to Christian organizations and churches, and to Evangelical Christian organizations benefiting women and children, primarily in Chester County, PA.
Fields of interest: Education; Reproductive health; Family services; Women, centers/services; Christian agencies & churches; Infants/toddlers; Children/youth; Children; Youth; Minorities; Women; Infants/toddlers, female; Girls; Infants/toddlers, male; Boys; Single parents; Economically disadvantaged.
International interests: India; Zimbabwe.
Type of support: General/operating support; Scholarship funds.
Limitations: Applications not accepted. Giving primarily in Chester County, PA. No grants to individuals.
Application information: Unsolicited requests for funds not accepted.
Board meeting date(s): No set dates
Officers: Gary L. Pilgrim, Pres.; **Karen Pennell, Exec. Dir.**
Director: Suzanne T. Daniel.
Number of staff: 1 part-time support.
EIN: 232955610

3017
Pottstown Area Health & Wellness Foundation
152 E. High St., Ste. 500
Pottstown, PA 19464-5400 **(610) 323-2006**
Contact: Anna Brendle, Prog. Off.
FAX: (610) 323-0047;
E-mail: rosecrews@pottstownfoundation.org;
Contact for large event, grant-related requests: Ashley Pultorak, e-mail: apultorak@pottstownfoundation.org; Main URL: http://pottstownfoundation.org

Established in 2003 in PA; supporting organization of PMMC Over Corp.
Foundation type: Independent foundation.
Financial data (yr. ended 06/30/13): Assets, $78,446,123 (M); gifts received, $44,192; expenditures, $4,150,299; qualifying distributions, $3,566,515; giving activities include $2,583,859 for 62 grants (high: $466,700; low: $2,500).
Purpose and activities: Giving primarily to enhance the health and wellness of area residents, providing education, funding and programs that motivate people to adopt healthy lifestyles.
Fields of interest: Education; Medical care, community health systems; Public health; Public health, physical fitness; Health care; YM/YWCAs & YM/YWHAs.
Type of support: General/operating support; Management development/capacity building; Annual campaigns; Building/renovation; Program development; Conferences/seminars; Curriculum development; Research; Consulting services; Matching/challenge support.
Limitations: Applications accepted. Giving limited to Pottstown, PA. No support for for-profit organizations, disease-related charities, art programs, or economic development. No grants to individuals, or for endowments, debt reduction, or alumni activities; no loans.
Publications: Application guidelines; Annual report; Grants list.
Application information: Application form required.
Initial approach: Letter of intent
Copies of proposal: 12
***Deadline(s):* See foundation web site for current deadlines**
Board meeting date(s): 4th Tues. of every month
Final notification: 1-2 months
Officers and Directors:* Kenneth E. Picardi, Esq.*, Pres.; **Arthur Green,* V.P.; Myra Gehert Forrest, Ed.D.*, Secy.; Matthew Cappelletti, Jr., C.P.A.*, Treas.**; Laura DeFlavia, Cont.; Dave Kraybill,* Exec. Dir.; Todd Alderfer; Robert W. Boyce; James R. Bush; Philip I. Cook, M.D., J.D.; D. Scott Detar, C.P.A.; **Linda Flederbach, MSW, LSW**; Milton D. Martyny; Charles F. Palladino; Rev. Kerry Pidcock-Lester; Donald Silverson; William Taddonio, M.D.; **B. Douglas Trainer**; Sharon L. Weaver.
Number of staff: 3 full-time professional; 1 part-time professional; 1 full-time support; 1 part-time support.
EIN: 232344729
Other changes: Arthur Green has replaced Charles Palladino as V.P. Myra Gehert Forrest, Ed.D. has replaced Arthur Green as Secy. Matthew Cappelletti, Jr., C.P.A. has replaced Robert Boyce as Treas.
Ashia Cooper, Jonathan Corson, Keith W. Harrison, Phyllis L. Harwood, Linda D. Lignelli, and Robert H. Moses are no longer directors.

3018
PPG Industries Foundation
1 PPG Pl., Ste. 7E
Pittsburgh, PA 15272-0001
Contact: Sue Sloan, Exec. Dir.
E-mail: foundation@ppg.com; Main URL: http://www.ppg.com/en/ppgfoundation/Pages/default.aspx

Incorporated in 1951 in PA.
Donor: PPG Industries, Inc.
Foundation type: Company-sponsored foundation.
Financial data (yr. ended 12/31/12): Assets, $9,337,618 (M); gifts received, $5,000,000; expenditures, $5,255,340; qualifying distributions, $5,185,281; giving activities include $4,582,454 for 301+ grants (high: $500,000), and $381,297 for employee matching gifts.
Purpose and activities: The foundation supports organizations that enhance the quality of life in communities where PPG has a presence. Special emphasis is directed toward programs designed to promote educational opportunities and access to community services.
Fields of interest: Arts, equal rights; Museums (science/technology); Performing arts; Arts; Elementary/secondary education; Higher education; Libraries (public); Scholarships/financial aid; Education; Environmental education; Zoos/zoological societies; Aquariums; Disasters, preparedness/services; Youth development, adult & child programs; American Red Cross; YM/YWCAs & YM/YWHAs; Human services, financial counseling; Human services; Economic development; Community/economic development; United Ways and Federated Giving Programs; Science, formal/general education; Chemistry; Mathematics; Engineering/technology; Science; Public affairs; Disabilities, people with; Minorities; African Americans/Blacks; Women; Economically disadvantaged.
Type of support: General/operating support; Continuing support; Annual campaigns; Capital campaigns; Building/renovation; Equipment; Emergency funds; Program development; Scholarship funds; Employee volunteer services; Employee matching gifts; Employee-related scholarships.
Limitations: Applications accepted. Giving on a national basis in areas of company operations in AL, AR, CA, CT, DE, GA, KY, IA, IL, LA, MI, NC, NV, OH, SC, TX, WA, WI, and WV, with emphasis on Pittsburgh, PA; giving also to national organizations and in Africa, Asia, Europe, and the Middle East for the Global Charitable Contributions Program. No support for lobbying organizations, political organizations, or religious organizations not of direct benefit to the entire community. No grants to individuals (except for scholarships), or for advertising or sponsorships, endowments, projects that would directly benefit PPG, special events or telephone solicitation, or general operating support for United Way-supported organizations.
Publications: Application guidelines; Annual report (including application guidelines); Financial statement.
Application information: Organizations located in the Pittsburgh area and organizations of national scope should direct inquiries to the Executive Director of the foundation. Additional information may be requested at a later date. Application form required.
Initial approach: Complete online application
Deadline(s): None
Board meeting date(s): Usually in June and Dec.
Final notification: Following board meetings
Officers and Directors:* Charles E. Bunch,* Chair. and Pres.; David B. Navikas, Vice-Chair.; **Glenn E. Bost II,* V.P. and Genl. Counsel**; J. Craig Jordan,* V.P.; Lynn D. Schmidt, V.P.; Daniel Fayock, Secy.; Aziz S. Giga, Treas. and Cont.; Sue Sloan, Exec. Dir.
Number of staff: 1 full-time professional; 1 part-time professional; 1 part-time support.
EIN: 256037790
Other changes: David B. Navikas is now Vice-Chair. Donna Lee Walker is no longer V.P. J. Craig Jordan is now V.P. Glenn E. Bost, II is now V.P. and Genl. Counsel.

3019
The Presser Foundation
385 Lancaster Ave., No. 205
Haverford, PA 19041-1576 (610) 658-9030
Contact: Mariel Frank, Exec. Dir.
E-mail: mfrank@presserfoundation.org; Main URL: http://www.presserfoundation.org

Founded in 1916; incorporated in 1939 in PA.
Donors: Theodore Presser‡; Theodore Presser Foundation.

Foundation type: Independent foundation.
Financial data (yr. ended 06/30/13): Assets, $61,712,301 (M); gifts received, $1,879,221; expenditures, $2,965,871; qualifying distributions, $2,911,914; giving activities include $1,615,134 for grants, and $1,092,800 for grants to individuals.
Purpose and activities: Giving primarily to: 1) promising undergraduate and graduate students of music through grants to accredited institutions in the U.S.; 2) enhance music education and performance by supporting the acquisition of musical equipment and instruments and the construction and renovation of suitable buildings for musical instruction and performance; 3) advance the study and appreciation of music by aiding the promotion of formal musical programs and projects; and 4) provide financial relief to worthy teachers of music in distress.
Fields of interest: Arts education; Performing arts, music; Higher education.
Type of support: Building/renovation; Equipment; Program development; Seed money; Fellowships; Scholarship funds; Grants to individuals; Matching/challenge support.
Limitations: Giving primarily to organizations located in DE, MD NJ, and PA, and are within a 100-mile radius of Philadelphia.
Publications: Application guidelines.
Application information: Application forms available for financial aid to needy music teachers and for scholarships. The participating institutions select the students to receive the awards. The foundation does not give awards directly to individuals. Faxed or e-mailed applications are not considered. Application form required.

***Initial approach:* Use online application process on foundation web site**
Deadline(s): See foundation web site for deadline information

Officers and Trustees:* Robert Capanna, Pres.; Jeffrey Cornelius,* V.P.; Lucinda Landreth,* Secy.; William M. Davison IV,* Treas.; Mariel Frank, Exec. Dir.; Leon Bates; Peter Burwasser; Anthony P. Checchia; Robert W. Denious, Esq.; Martin A. Heckscher, Esq.; Thomas M. Hyndman, Jr., Esq.; William B. McLaughlin III; Corey R. Smith; Sharon L. Sorokin; Michael Stairs; Henderson Supplee III; Radclyffe F. Thompson; Mark Wait; Vera Wilson.
Number of staff: 1 full-time professional.
EIN: 232164013
Other changes: D. James Baker is no longer a trustee.

3020
Norman Raab Foundation
P.O. Box 657
Holicong, PA 18928-0657 (215) 794-5640
Contact: Stephen Raab, Tr.
FAX: (215) 794-5642;
E-mail: info@raabfoundation.org; E-mail for Letters of Inquiry: inquiries@raabfoundation.org; Main URL: http://raabfoundation.org

Established in PA in 1968.
Donors: Norman Raab‡; Stephen Raab; Whitney Raab; Sara Raab.
Foundation type: Independent foundation.
Financial data (yr. ended 09/30/13): Assets, $21,194,757 (M); expenditures, $1,531,424; qualifying distributions, $1,222,218; giving activities include $1,222,218 for 77 grants (high: $64,500; low: $500).
Purpose and activities: Giving primarily for education, health and research, and human services.
Fields of interest: Education; Health care; Human services.
Type of support: General/operating support; Research.
Limitations: Applications accepted. **Giving primarily in CA, MD, NY, PA, and WA.** No support for political organizations. No grants to individuals.
Publications: Application guidelines.
Application information: All submissions must be filed electronically. Grant requests are by invitation only, upon review of letter of inquiry. Application form not required.

***Initial approach:* Letter of Inquiry via the foundation's online grant management system**
Copies of proposal: 3
***Deadline(s):* See foundation web site for current deadlines**
Board meeting date(s): Jan. 25 and Apr. 30

Officer and Trustees:* Stephen Raab,* Chair.; Stephen A. Bleyer; Marie Brickley-Raab; Emily Raab; Isabel Raab; Sara Raab; Whitney Raab.
Number of staff: 1 part-time support.
EIN: 237006390
Other changes: Jennie Raab is no longer a director.

3021
Charity Randall Foundation
6031 Wallace Rd., Ext., Ste. 202
Wexford, PA 15090 (724) 799-8680
Contact: Robert P. Randall, Pres.

Established in 1978.
Donors: Earl R. Randall; Three Rivers Aluminum Co.
Foundation type: Independent foundation.
Financial data (yr. ended 06/30/13): Assets, $5,097,997 (M); expenditures, $258,986; qualifying distributions, $233,425; giving activities include $233,425 for 7 grants (high: $100,000; low: $4,725).
Purpose and activities: Grants primarily for higher education and to encourage literary and environmental conservation endeavors; also giving for fine arts, social service and community development.
Fields of interest: Museums; Performing arts, theater; Literature; Arts; Higher education; Libraries (special); Education; Botanical gardens; Environment; Zoos/zoological societies; Animals/wildlife; Recreation, parks/playgrounds.
Type of support: General/operating support; Scholarship funds.
Limitations: Applications accepted. Giving primarily in Pittsburgh, PA.
Application information: Individuals should submit a resume of academic qualifications, and, in the case of research grants, an outline of the proposed investigation and a proposed budget. Organizations must use the foundation's standard grant application. Application form required.

***Initial approach:* Letter**
Deadline(s): Apr. 30th
Final notification: Within 1 month

Officers and Directors: Robin S. Randall, Chair.; Robert P. Randall,* Pres.; Adam Randall, Treas.; Brett Randall; Chris Randall; Rita Randall.
EIN: 251329778

3022
John G. Rangos Charitable Foundation
1301 Grandview Ave., Ste. 230
Pittsburgh, PA 15211-1288 **(412) 871-6120**
Main URL: http://www.rangosfoundation.org/
Google Plus: https://plus.google.com/113826762632597248016/

Established in 1987 in PA.
Donor: John G. Rangos, Sr.
Foundation type: Independent foundation.
Financial data (yr. ended 06/30/12): Assets, $2,161,828 (M); gifts received, $47,218; expenditures, $506,945; qualifying distributions, $469,178; giving activities include $336,764 for 12 grants (high: $150,000; low: $200).
Purpose and activities: The foundation is dedicated to providing children with a springboard to knowledge through education and good health, so that they may build a blueprint for life.
Fields of interest: Higher education; Health care; Pediatrics; Medical research; Youth development; Children/youth, services; Christian agencies & churches; Children.
Type of support: Annual campaigns; Program development.
Limitations: Giving primarily in MD and PA. No grants to individuals.
Application information: Application form not required.

Deadline(s): None

Trustees: Alexander Rangos; Jenica Rangos; Jill Rangos; John G. Rangos, Sr.; John G. Rangos, Jr.
Number of staff: 1 full-time professional.
EIN: 251599198

3023
Respironics Sleep and Respiratory Research Foundation
1010 Murry Ridge Ln.
Murrysville, PA 15668-8525

Established in 2003 in PA.
Donor: Respironics, Inc.
Foundation type: Company-sponsored foundation.
Financial data (yr. ended 06/30/13): Assets, $52,899 (M); expenditures, $5,244; qualifying distributions, $5,244.
Purpose and activities: The foundation supports programs designed to conduct sleep medicine and respiratory research.
Fields of interest: Higher education; Medical school/education; Hospitals (general); Lung research.
Type of support: General/operating support; Professorships.
Limitations: Applications not accepted. Giving primarily in MA, NJ, NY, and OH, and in Australia, Canada, Denmark, Germany, and Sweden. No grants to individuals.
Application information: Contributes only to pre-selected organizations.
Officers and Directors:* John Frank,* V.P.; Priscilla Johnson,* Secy.
EIN: 522421348
Other changes: David White is no longer Pres.

3024
Rider-Pool Foundation
1050 S. Cedar Crest Blvd., Ste. 202
Allentown, PA 18103-5454 (610) 770-9346
Contact: Edward F. Meehan, Exec. Dir.
FAX: (610) 770-9361; E-mail: drpool@ptd.net; Additional contact: Bridget I. Rassler, Admin. Mgr.;

Main URL: http://www.pooltrust.com/rpf/default.html

Established in 1957 in PA.
Donor: Dorothy Rider-Pool†.
Foundation type: Independent foundation.
Financial data (yr. ended 12/31/12): Assets, $10,336,166 (M); gifts received, $5,620; expenditures, $484,936; qualifying distributions, $457,215; giving activities include $331,500 for 80 grants (high: $20,000; low: $1,000).
Purpose and activities: The foundation's purpose is to serve as a means to improve the quality of life in the community, to build on the community's strengths and add to its vitality, and to increase the capacity of the community to serve the needs of all its citizens.
Fields of interest: Museums (art); Arts; Education; Health care; Boys & girls clubs; Salvation Army; Community/economic development.
Type of support: General/operating support; Continuing support; Program development.
Limitations: Applications accepted. Giving primarily in the Lehigh Valley, PA, area. No support for fraternal organizations or organizations outside the U.S. or its territories; generally no support for sectarian institutions, religious organizations for religious purposes, hospitals, or United Way member agencies. No grants to individuals, or for fundraising or related advertising, testimonial dinners, subsidization of books, mailings, or articles in professional journals.
Publications: Application guidelines; Biennial report; Financial statement; Grants list; Informational brochure (including application guidelines).
Application information: Requests for funds are accepted through an electronic application process described on foundation web site. See foundation web site for application guidelines and procedures. Application form not required.
Copies of proposal: 1
***Deadline(s):* Aug. 15**
Board meeting date(s): May and Oct.
Trustees: Denise M Gargan; Leon C. Holt, Jr.; John P. Jones III; John E. McGlade; **Edward F. Meehan**; **J. Scott Pidcock**.
EIN: 236207356
Other changes: Edward Donley is no longer a trustee.

3025
The Riverside Foundation Charitable Trust
P.O. Box 363
Lampeter, PA 17537-0363
Contact: David Aungst, Dir.

Established in 1998.
Donor: The Trimble Revocable Living Trust.
Foundation type: Independent foundation.
Financial data (yr. ended 12/31/11): Assets, $3,881,566 (M); expenditures, $2,107,667; qualifying distributions, $2,070,775; giving activities include $2,048,725 for 44 grants (high: $624,973; low: $2,000).
Purpose and activities: The trust supports organizations that participate in evangelical religious ministry to the handicapped community.
Fields of interest: Human services; Civil/human rights, disabled; Religion.
Limitations: Applications not accepted. Giving on a national basis. No support for political organizations. No grants to individuals.
Application information: New applications are not accepted. Only currently supported organizations may apply.
Board meeting date(s): Oct.
Officers and Directors:* Daniel D. Smith,* Pres.; Sharon R. Berry,* V.P.; Charles W. Colson,* Treas.; **David Aungst**; Joni Eareckson Tada; Ralph D. Veerman.
EIN: 546417931
Other changes: Calvin Howe is no longer a director.

3026
The Kelly Rooney Foundation
265 Abrahams Ln.
Villanova, PA **19085-1102** (610) 745-2002
Contact: Sean Rooney, Tr.
***E-mail:* info@kellyrooney.org**; Main URL: http://kellyrooney.org/
Facebook: https://www.facebook.com/kellyrooneyfoundation
Twitter: https://twitter.com/KellyRooneyFdn

Established in 2006 in PA.
Donors: Save 2nd Base; Kevin Connor; Gail Connor; Jenn Sims; Carter Sims; John Rooney; Joann Rooney; ARAMARK; Comcast Spectator; INFOR; Thomas & Jane Dooner; IMX; Tom & Jill Nerney; American Ireland Fund; Charles O'Brein; Mari O'Brein; Nearney Family Foundation; Davis Foundation; Palm Beach Kennel Club; Pittsburgh Steelers; Sean Rooney; Adernaline Lacrosse; Steve Siegfried; Thomas Dooner; Jane Dooner; PNC.
Foundation type: Independent foundation.
Financial data (yr. ended 12/31/12): Assets, $180,976 (M); gifts received, $53,166; expenditures, $358,383; qualifying distributions, $218,310; giving activities include $218,310 for 7 + grants (high: $100,000).
Fields of interest: Higher education, university; Education; Breast cancer; Health organizations.
Limitations: Applications accepted. Giving primarily in PA. No grants to individuals.
Application information: Application form not required.
Initial approach: Proposal
Deadline(s): None
Trustee: Sean Rooney.
EIN: 207003413

3027
Ross Family Fund
(formerly Lynn & George M. Ross Foundation)
c/o Cozen O'Connor
1900 Market St.
Philadelphia, PA 19103-3527

Established in 1977.
Donors: George M. Ross†; Merry Ross; Patrick Zimski; Michael Ross.
Foundation type: Independent foundation.
Financial data (yr. ended 02/28/13): Assets, $1,860,346 (M); expenditures, $8,041,041; qualifying distributions, $7,955,186; giving activities include $7,866,205 for 111 grants (high: $7,500,000; low: $100).
Fields of interest: Museums; Arts; Higher education; Education; Health organizations, association; Cancer; Human services; Jewish federated giving programs; Jewish agencies & synagogues.
Limitations: Applications not accepted. Giving primarily in FL and PA. No grants to individuals.
Application information: Contributes only to pre-selected organizations.
Director: Lyn M. Ross.
EIN: 232049592
Other changes: The grantmaker has moved from NY to PA.

For the fiscal year ended Feb. 28, 2013, the grantmaker paid grants of $7,886,205, a 385.2% increase over the fiscal 2012 disbursements, $1,625,282.

3028
Rossin Foundation
(formerly Dynamet Foundation)
P.O. Box 1225
McMurray, PA 15317-4225 (412) 746-3401
***Contact:* Viola G. Taboni**

Established in 1989 in PA.
Donors: Dynamet Inc.; Peter C. Rossin; Ada E. Rossin.
Foundation type: Company-sponsored foundation.
Financial data (yr. ended 12/31/12): Assets, $17,416,308 (M); gifts received, $753,143; expenditures, $390,299; qualifying distributions, $183,646; giving activities include $183,646 for grants.
Purpose and activities: The foundation supports hospitals and organizations involved with arts and culture, patient services, and senior citizens.
Fields of interest: Museums (art); Arts; Hospitals (general); Health care, patient services; YM/YWCAs & YM/YWHAs; Aging, centers/services.
Type of support: Building/renovation; General/operating support; Program development; Research.
Limitations: Applications accepted. Giving primarily in PA, with some emphasis on Pittsburgh. No grants to individuals.
Application information: Application form required.
***Initial approach:* Letter**
Deadline(s): None
Officers and Trustees:* Joan R. Stephans,* Chair.; Peter N. Stephans,* Pres.; **John Campbell Harmon,* Secy.**; Elizabeth Stephans Baker,* Treas.; Katherine Dec.
EIN: 256327217
Other changes: Joan R. Stephans has replaced Ada E. Rossin as Chair.

3029
The Saramar Charitable Fund
951 Frazier Rd.
Rydal, PA 19046-2407
Contact: Marjorie Honickman, Tr.
***Application address:* 8275 N. US Rte. 130, Pennsauken, NJ 08110-1435**

Established in 2003 in PA.
Donors: Manhattan Beer Distributors, LLC; Marjorie Honickman.
Foundation type: Company-sponsored foundation.
Financial data (yr. ended 12/31/12): Assets, $3,634,739 (M); gifts received, $250,000; expenditures, $174,197; qualifying distributions, $171,549; giving activities include $171,549 for grants.
Purpose and activities: The foundation supports organizations involved with arts and culture, education, cancer, human services, and Judaism.
Fields of interest: Museums (art); Performing arts; Arts; Elementary school/education; Secondary school/education; Higher education; Education; Hospitals (general); Health care; Cancer; Aging, centers/services; Human services; Jewish federated giving programs; Jewish agencies & synagogues.
Type of support: General/operating support; Program development; Scholarship funds.
Limitations: Applications accepted. Giving primarily in Philadelphia, PA. No grants to individuals.

Application information: Application form not required.
Initial approach: Proposal
Deadline(s): None
Trustees: Jeffrey A. Honickman; Marjorie Honickman.
EIN: 256839698

3030
Scattergood Behavioral Health Foundation
4641 Roosevelt Blvd.
Philadelphia, PA 19124-2399 (215) 831-3000
Contact: Joe Pyle, Pres.
FAX: (215) 831-3028;
E-mail: info@scattergoodfoundation.org; **Additional address: Thomas Scattergood Behavioral Health Foundation at Friends Center, 1501 Cherry St., Philadelphia, PA 19102**; Main URL: http://www.scattergoodfoundation.org/
Facebook: https://www.facebook.com/pages/The-Thomas-Scattergood-Foundation/354334557958051
Twitter: https://twitter.com/ScattergoodFdn

Donors: Joseph Gaskill; Philadelphia Foundation.
Foundation type: Independent foundation.
Financial data (yr. ended 06/30/13): Assets, $21,529,249 (M); gifts received, $182,271; expenditures, $1,428,041; qualifying distributions, $1,219,202; giving activities include $691,811 for 59 grants (high: $50,000; low: $99).
Purpose and activities: This Quaker-based foundation is committed to the improvement of the system through which behavioral healthcare is delivered in the Philadelphia, PA, region.
Fields of interest: Education; Mental health/crisis services.
Publications: Application guidelines; Grants list.
Application information: Unsolicited requests for funds are not considered. Applications are by invitation only. Invited applicants should follow guidelines on foundation web site. Innovation Award nominations may be made through foundation web site.
Deadline(s): See foundation web site for Innovation Awards nomination deadlines
Officer: Joe Pyle, Pres.
Directors: Cindy Baum-Baicker, Ph.D.; David R. Fair; Bruce S. Haines, Esq.; Anne H. Matlack; N. Chiyo Moriuchi; Samuel V. Rhoads; David Roby, M.D.; Antonio Valdes; **Molly Kreider Viscardi**; **Catherine Williams**.
EIN: 231352178
Other changes: Carol Ashton-Hergenhan and Katie Perch are no longer directors.

3031
The Scranton Area Foundation, Inc.
615 Jefferson Ave., Ste. 102
Scranton, PA 18510 (570) 347-6203
Contact: Laura J. Ducceschi, C.E.O.; For grants: Cathy Fitzpatrick, Donor Svcs. and Comms. Assoc.
FAX: (570) 347-7587; E-mail: safinfo@safdn.org; Grant inquiry e-mail: cathyf@sadfn.org; Main URL: http://www.safdn.org
Facebook: https://www.facebook.com/ScrantonAreaCommunityFoundation

Established in 1954 in PA by resolution and declaration of trust; reorganized in 1998.
Foundation type: Community foundation.
Financial data (yr. ended 12/31/11): Assets, $25,450,403 (M); gifts received, $812,119; expenditures, $1,666,132; giving activities include $643,736 for 12 grants (high: $100,000), and $359,520 for 73 grants to individuals.
Purpose and activities: The foundation's mission is to enhance the quality of life for all people in Lackawanna County through the development of organized philanthropy. The foundation strives to carry out this mission as a steward by developing and managing permanent endowment funds, as a grant maker by awarding grants and support to enable the community to respond to emerging and changing needs and opportunities, as a charitable resource by encouraging and educating donors and providing a flexible vehicle for individual donors, non-profit organizations and the community-at-large, and as a catalyst by mobilizing community leadership in response to issues.
Fields of interest: Historic preservation/historical societies; Arts; Child development, education; Vocational education; Higher education; Libraries/library science; Education; Environment, natural resources; Environment; Animal welfare; Health care; Mental health/crisis services; Health organizations, association; Housing/shelter; Youth development, services; Children/youth, services; Child development, services; Human services; International human rights; Community/economic development; Voluntarism promotion; Leadership development; Public affairs; Religion; Aging.
Type of support: General/operating support; Continuing support; Program development; Conferences/seminars; Publication; Seed money; Curriculum development; Scholarship funds; Research; Technical assistance; Consulting services; Matching/challenge support.
Limitations: Applications accepted. Giving limited to Lackawanna County and Scranton, PA, area. No grants for building funds, annual campaigns, deficit financing, or emergency funds.
Publications: Application guidelines; Annual report; Annual report (including application guidelines); Grants list; Informational brochure; Informational brochure (including application guidelines); Newsletter; Occasional report.
Application information: Visit foundation web site for application guidelines. The foundation strongly recommends submission of letter of intent; immediate response as to the potential for the project will be provided. Application forms may be requested by calling the foundation. Application form required.
Initial approach: Submit letter of intent (1-2 pages maximum)
Copies of proposal: 1
Deadline(s): Varies
Board meeting date(s): Feb., May, Sept., and Dec.
Final notification: Applications are reviewed quarterly
Officers and Governors:* Kathleen Graff,* Chair.; David Hawk,* Vice-Chair.; Laura J. Ducceschi, M.B.A.*, C.E.O. and Pres.; William J. Calpin, Jr.,* Secy.; John P. Kearney,* Treas.; Rosemary Broderick; **Ida Castro**; **James F. Clemente**; Matthew E. Haggerty, Esq.; Cathy Ann Hardaway; Alan F. Hughes; James Gillotti, Esq.; Paula Mackarey; Jane Oppenheim; Ann Lavelle Powell, Esq.; Maryla Scranton; Mary Ann Sorokanich; Jack Tighe; Cynthia Yevich.
Investment Managers: Penn Security Bank & Trust Co.; PNC Advisors.
Number of staff: 1 full-time professional; 3 full-time support.
EIN: 232890364
Other changes: Eileen G. Crimi is now Finance Mgr. Cathy Fitzpatrick is now Grants Admin. James B. Baker, Dante A. Cancelli, Amy Clegg, Kathleen Graff, David Hawk, John P. Kearney, James A. Ross, Arianne Naismith Slocum, and Thomas G. Speicher are no longer governors.

3032
The Sedwick Foundation
c/o Kirby J. Campbell
1 Armstrong Pl.
Butler, PA 16001-1951

Established in 1986 in PA.
Donors: Armstrong Utilities, Inc.; Jay L. Sedwick; Linda Sedwick; Armstrong Communications, Inc.; Armstrong Telephone Co. of West Virginia; Armstrong Telephone Co. of Maryland; Guardian Protection Services, Inc.
Foundation type: Company-sponsored foundation.
Financial data (yr. ended 06/30/13): Assets, $40,125,857 (M); gifts received, $6,113,280; expenditures, $2,155,869; qualifying distributions, $1,953,418; giving activities include $1,953,418 for 51 grants (high: $100,000; low: $1,000).
Purpose and activities: The foundation supports camps and medical centers and organizations involved with higher education, human services, public policy, and Christianity.
Fields of interest: Higher education; Health care, clinics/centers; Recreation, camps; YM/YWCAs & YM/YWHAs; Human services; Public policy, research; Christian agencies & churches.
Type of support: General/operating support.
Limitations: Applications not accepted. Giving primarily in Butler, PA. No grants to individuals.
Application information: Contributes only to pre-selected organizations.
Trustees: Kirby J. Campbell; Dru A. Sedwick; Jay L. Sedwick; William C. Stewart.
EIN: 256284774
Other changes: The grantmaker no longer lists a phone.

3033
Frances Seebe Trust
c/o Wells Fargo Bank, N.A.
101N Independence Mall E., MACY1372-062
Philadelphia, PA 19106-2112

Established in 1983 in CA.
Foundation type: Independent foundation.
Financial data (yr. ended 01/31/13): Assets, $4,225,940 (M); expenditures, $274,036; qualifying distributions, $222,492; giving activities include $212,657 for 11 grants (high: $43,245; low: $5,000).
Purpose and activities: Giving primarily for wildlife research and animal protection; support also for medical research.
Fields of interest: Education; Animal welfare; Animals/wildlife, preservation/protection; Animals/wildlife; Cancer research; Arthritis research.
Limitations: Applications not accepted. Giving primarily in Los Angeles, CA, Washington, DC, GA, and NM. No grants to individuals.
Application information: Contributes only to pre-selected organizations.
Trustee: Wells Fargo Bank, N.A.
EIN: 956795278
Other changes: The grantmaker has moved from CA to PA.

3034
Adam and Maria Sarah Seybert Institution for Poor Boys and Girls
(also known as Seybert Institution)
P.O. Box 1286
Doylestown, PA 18901-0100 (215) 696-9336
Contact: Diana Loukedis Doherty, Mgr.
E-mail: admin@seybertfoundation.org; Main URL: http://seybertfoundation.org/index.html

Incorporated in 1914 in PA.
Donor: Henry Seybert†.
Foundation type: Independent foundation.
Financial data (yr. ended 12/31/12): Assets, $6,044,786 (M); expenditures, $259,678; qualifying distributions, $230,186; giving activities include $178,000 for 62 grants (high: $5,000; low: $1,500).
Purpose and activities: Support for projects and services for disadvantaged children in Philadelphia, Pennsylvania, primarily through community-based organizations.
Fields of interest: Education, early childhood education; Child development, education; Elementary school/education; Education; Human services; Children/youth, services; Child development, services; Family services; Minorities; Economically disadvantaged.
Type of support: Program development; Seed money; Matching/challenge support.
Limitations: Giving limited to Philadelphia, PA. No grants to individuals, or for building or endowment funds; low priority given to capital expenditures.
Publications: Annual report (including application guidelines).
Application information: Applicants limited to 1 request per calendar year; accepts Delaware Valley Grantmakers Common Grant Application and Common Report Form. For regular programs submit 1 original and 10 copies of proposal, 3 copies of the most recent audited annual financial report and 1 copy of the tax-exempt determination letter. See web site for additional application policies and guidelines and for application forms for all programs. Application form required.
Initial approach: Proposal (no more than 6 pages)
Copies of proposal: 10
Deadline(s): Mar. 15 and Sept. 15
Board meeting date(s): Last Wed. in Jan., Apr., and Oct.
Final notification: Feb. 15, May 15 and Nov. 15
Officers and Directors:* Dwayne Wharton,* Pres.; Aishah Miller, V.P.; Julie Cousler-Emig, Ph.D., Secy.; Dario Bellot, Treas.; Obinna Abara, Esq.; Sara S. Moran; Deepa Vasudevan; **Linda White**.
EIN: 236260105
Other changes: C. Richard Cox and Dee Hillas are no longer directors.

3035
Shaffer Family Charitable Trust
1588 Weyhill Cir.
Bethlehem, PA **18015-5253 (610) 867-7568**
Contact: David N. Shaffer, Tr.

Established in 1987 in PA.
Donors: David Shaffer; Susan Shaffer; Jack M. Shaffer†; Cecile Shaffer; Rose Shaffer.
Foundation type: Independent foundation.
Financial data (yr. ended 12/31/12): Assets, $10,601,634 (M); gifts received, $134,268; expenditures, $1,220,271; qualifying distributions, $1,119,450; giving activities include $1,119,450 for 39 grants (high: $250,000; low: $3,000).
Purpose and activities: Support for capital operations and special projects not funded through normal income sources to social service agencies serving the at-risk population in the Lehigh Valley, PA, area.
Fields of interest: Human services; Children/youth, services; Aging, centers/services.
Type of support: General/operating support; Capital campaigns; Endowments; Seed money.
Limitations: Applications not accepted. Giving primarily in Lehigh Valley, PA. No grants to individuals.
Application information:
Board meeting date(s): Quarterly
Trustees: David Shaffer; Rose Shaffer; Susan Shaffer.
EIN: 232502319
Other changes: Joshua H. Shaffer and Samantha J. Shaffer are no longer trustees.

3036
The Robbins Shuman Scholarship Fund Trust
P.O. Box 3215
Lancaster, PA 17604-3216
***Application address:* FNB Bank, c/o Fulton Financial Advisors, 344 Mill St., Danville, PA 17821, tel.: (717) 291-2523**

Established in 2005 in PA.
Foundation type: Independent foundation.
Financial data (yr. ended 04/30/13): Assets, $3,135,161 (M); expenditures, $186,877; qualifying distributions, $160,650; giving activities include $160,650 for 54 grants to individuals (high: $3,500; low: $700).
Purpose and activities: Giving only to full time students who are residents of Columbia County, Pennsylvania, and who have a 3.0 GPA.
Fields of interest: Education.
Type of support: Scholarships—to individuals.
Limitations: Applications accepted. Giving primarily to residents of PA.
Application information: Application form required.
Deadline(s): None
Trustee: Fulton Bank, N.A.
EIN: 256857939

3037
Frank J. Smith Foundation
c/o PNC Bank, N.A.
P.O. Box 609
Pittsburgh, PA 15230-9738

Established in 1994 in IN.
Donors: Frank J. Smith; Geraldine Schmidt Trust.
Foundation type: Independent foundation.
Financial data (yr. ended 01/31/13): Assets, $3,723,229 (M); expenditures, $210,914; qualifying distributions, $189,939; giving activities include $170,861 for 25 grants (high: $29,283; low: $976).
Fields of interest: Elementary/secondary education; Human services; Protestant agencies & churches; Catholic agencies & churches.
Limitations: Applications not accepted. Giving primarily in Fort Wayne, IN. No grants to individuals.
Application information: Contributes only to pre-selected organizations.
Trustee: PNC Bank, N.A.
EIN: 356598564
Other changes: The grantmaker no longer lists a primary contact, separate application address or a phone. The grantmaker has moved from OH to PA.

3038
Dorothy Melcher Sneath Trust
c/o BNY Mellon, N.A.
P.O. Box 185
Pittsburgh, PA 15230-0185

Established in MA.
Foundation type: Independent foundation.
Financial data (yr. ended 08/31/13): Assets, $5,181,957 (M); expenditures, $287,228; qualifying distributions, $257,274; giving activities include $240,000 for 9 grants (high: $55,000; low: $15,000).
Purpose and activities: Giving primarily to provide scholarship funds to independent private preparatory schools in New England with preference to the following schools in MA: Winsor School, Beaver County Day School, Milton Academy, Noble and Greenough School, Middlesex School, and Brooks School.
Fields of interest: Secondary school/education; Education.
Type of support: Scholarship funds.
Limitations: Applications not accepted. Giving limited to MA. No grants to individuals directly.
Application information: Contributes primarily to pre-selected private preparatory schools in New England.
Trustees: Ronald Garmey, Esq.; BNY Mellon, N.A.
EIN: 046093840

3039
Snee-Reinhardt Charitable Foundation
470 Streets Run Rd., Ste. 401
Pittsburgh, PA 15236-2075 (412) 884-3626
Contact: Jill M. Oluszak, Exec. Asst.; Christina Heasley-Treadwell, Chair. and Fdn. Mgr.
FAX: (412) 881-4636;
E-mail: info@snee-reinhardt.org; Main URL: http://www.snee-reinhardt.org

Established in 1987 in PA.
Donor: Katherine E. Snee†.
Foundation type: Independent foundation.
Financial data (yr. ended 12/31/12): Assets, $19,087,626 (M); gifts received, $125,000; expenditures, $1,138,768; qualifying distributions, $773,697; giving activities include $773,697 for grants.
Purpose and activities: The foundation believes that life is like that of an oak tree; strong and beautiful and should be given every chance to grow. As a family foundation in Pittsburgh, PA, the foundation's philanthropic traditions are well rooted in its continued support of organizations that foster transformative programs which best serve the local community as a whole in the areas of arts and culture, education, environmental, health and medical, human services, and religion.
Fields of interest: Arts; Libraries/library science; Education; Environment; Health care; Substance abuse, services; Health organizations, association; Cancer; Children/youth, services; Aging, centers/services; Community/economic development; Christian agencies & churches; Aging.
Type of support: Building/renovation; Equipment; Program development.
Limitations: Applications accepted. Giving primarily in southwestern PA, secondly in northern WV, northern MD, and PA; some giving also throughout the U.S. No support for sectarian or religious organizations or for programs that promote, research or support the prevention of life, abortion, the practice of euthanasia, or cruelty to animals, or highly specialized health or medical programs that do not have a specific impact on the community. No

grants to individuals, or for capital campaigns, endowment funds, or general operating expenses, including salaries and fringe benefits, chairs or professorships.
Publications: Application guidelines; Grants list.
Application information: Application guidelines and procedures are available on foundation web site. The amount being requested should not exceed $50,000. A request for a greater amount or a request that would be payable over a multiple-year period should not be submitted without first contacting the foundation office. All proposals should be printed single-sided, unbound, and unstapled. Do not mail proposals with signature required for receipt. Application form required.
Initial approach: Letter of inquiry or telephone call to the office.
Copies of proposal: 1
Deadline(s): Apr. 1 and Aug. 1. (If deadline falls on a weekend then deadline is prior Friday).
Board meeting date(s): Grant review on the second Tues. of May and Sept., and annual meeting on the second Tues. of Nov.
Final notification: 2 weeks after board meeting
Officer and Directors:* Christina Heasley-Treadwell,* Chair. and Mgr.; **Jeff Flick**; Karen Heasley; Lucas Heasley.
Trustee: PNC Bank, N.A.
Number of staff: 1 full-time support.
EIN: 256292908

3040
Society for Analytical Chemists of Pittsburgh
300 Penn Ctr. Blvd., Ste. 332
Pittsburgh, PA 15235-5503 **(412) 825-3220 ext. 204**
Contact: Valerie Daugherty, Admin. Asst.
FAX: (412) 825-3224; E-mail: sacpinfo@pittcon.org;
E-mail for Valerie Daughtery: daugherty@pittcon.org; Main URL: http://www.sacp.org/
Facebook: https://www.facebook.com/SocietyForAnalyticalChemistsOfPittsburgh
LinkedIn: http://www.linkedin.com/groups/Society-Analytical-Chemists-Pittsburgh-4823656?gid=4823656&trk=hb_side_g

Established in 1971.
Donors: James L. Waters Fund; PGH Conf. on Analytical Chemistry and Applied Spectroscopy.
Foundation type: Independent foundation.
Financial data (yr. ended 06/30/12): Assets, $179,167 (M); gifts received, $521,424; expenditures, $527,035; qualifying distributions, $513,517; giving activities include $391,859 for 152 grants (high: $40,000; low: $50).
Purpose and activities: Giving primarily for education and research projects in the field of analytical chemistry and applied spectroscopy.
Fields of interest: Education; Physical/earth sciences.
Type of support: General/operating support; Conferences/seminars; Internship funds; Scholarship funds; Research; Scholarships—to individuals.
Limitations: Giving primarily in the Pittsburgh, PA, area.
Publications: Informational brochure.
Application information: See foundation web site for application policies, guidelines, and form. Application form required.
Deadline(s): Varies
Officers: Fu-Tyan Lin, Chair.; Dr. James Manner, Chair.-Elect; Heather Juzwa, Secy.; Robert LaCount, Treas.
EIN: 256072976

3041
Graham and Thelma Somerville Charitable Trust
c/o PNC Bank, N.A.
P.O. Box 609
Pittsburgh, PA 15230-9738

Established in 1983 in IN; supporting organization of the Arthritis Foundation, American Cancer Society, American Lung Association, Turnstone Center, Inc., League for the Blind and Disabled, Scan Inc., Ft. Wayne Children's Home, Alzheimer's Disease and Related Disorders, St. Mary's Catholic Church, Junior Achievement of Fort Wayne, and Fort Wayne Rescue Mission.
Foundation type: Independent foundation.
Financial data (yr. ended 10/31/13): Assets, $3,459,530 (M); expenditures, $232,323; qualifying distributions, $213,163; giving activities include $198,165 for 11 grants (high: $35,670; low: $2,972).
Fields of interest: Cancer; Lung diseases; Arthritis; Alzheimer's disease; Health organizations; Human services; Children, services; Catholic agencies & churches.
Limitations: Applications not accepted. Giving limited to IN.
Application information: Contributes only to pre-selected organizations; unsolicited requests for funds not considered or acknowledged.
Trustee: PNC Bank, N.A.
EIN: 356547211
Other changes: The grantmaker has moved from OH to PA.

3042
Stackpole-Hall Foundation
44 S. St. Marys St.
St. Marys, PA 15857-1667 (814) 834-1845
FAX: (814) 834-1869;
E-mail: stackpolehall@windstream.net; Main URL: http://www.stackpolehall.org/

Trust established in 1951 in PA.
Donors: Lyle G. Hall, Sr.‡; J. Hall Stackpole‡; Harrison C. Stackpole‡; Lyle G. Hall, Jr.; Adelaide Stackpole‡; Stackpole Carbon Co.
Foundation type: Independent foundation.
Financial data (yr. ended 12/31/12): Assets, $23,673,512 (M); expenditures, $1,186,301; qualifying distributions, $1,051,338; giving activities include $782,983 for 69 grants (high: $40,799; low: $500).
Purpose and activities: Support for higher and secondary education, and literacy and vocational projects; Christian agencies and churches; social services, including youth and child welfare agencies; the arts and cultural programs; health services, including mental health and drug abuse issues; and community development, including civic affairs and leadership development, conservation concerns, rural development, and voluntarism.
Fields of interest: Education, fund raising/fund distribution; Secondary school/education; Vocational education; Higher education; Adult/continuing education; Adult education—literacy, basic skills & GED; Libraries/library science; Education, reading; Education; Substance abuse, services; Mental health/crisis services; Alcoholism; Youth development, services; Human services; Children/youth, services; Rural development; Community/economic development; Voluntarism promotion; Leadership development; Protestant agencies & churches; Catholic agencies & churches; Disabilities, people with.
Type of support: Annual campaigns; Capital campaigns; Building/renovation; Equipment; Program development; Seed money; Matching/challenge support.
Limitations: Applications accepted. Giving primarily in Elk County, PA, and communities in which the foundation's donors, donors' families and trustees reside. No grants to individuals, or for scholarships or fellowships; generally, no grants for operating budgets or endowment funds; no loans.
Publications: Application guidelines; Annual report (including application guidelines); Financial statement; Grants list.
Application information: Grantmakers of Western Pennsylvania's Common Grant Application Format accepted; application guidelines available on foundation web site. Application form not required.
Initial approach: E-mailed grant requests preferred; supporting documentation maybe sent via U.S. mail
Copies of proposal: 1
Deadline(s): None
Board meeting date(s): Quarterly
Officers and Trustees:* R. Dauer Stackpole,* Chair.; J.M. Hamlin Johnson,* Vice-Chair.; William C. Conrad,* Exec. Dir.; Heather L. Conrad; Douglas R. Dobson; Francis Grandinetti; **Lyle G. Hall**; Megan Hall; Richard Masson; Deborah Pontzer; John I. Saalfield; Alexander Sheble-Hall; Laurey Stackpole Turner; Lawrence E. Whiteman.
Number of staff: 1 full-time professional; 1 full-time support; 1 part-time support.
EIN: 256006650
Other changes: Dennis Bonanno is no longer Secy.-Treas.

3043
Thomas F. Staley Foundation
c/o Diane S. Bernard
520 Frutchey Hill Rd.
Easton, PA 18040-7109

Trust established in 1943 in MI.
Donors: Thomas F. Staley‡; Shirley H. Hunter‡.
Foundation type: Independent foundation.
Financial data (yr. ended 12/31/12): Assets, $4,848,102 (M); expenditures, $452,306; qualifying distributions, $384,233; giving activities include $303,195 for 47 grants (high: $30,000; low: $250).
Fields of interest: Education; Children/youth, services; Family services; Christian agencies & churches; Protestant agencies & churches.
Type of support: Curriculum development.
Limitations: Applications not accepted. Giving primarily in PA. No grants to individuals.
Publications: Informational brochure; Program policy statement.
Application information: Contributes only to pre-selected organizations.
Board meeting date(s): June
Officers: Stuart Staley, Chair.; Robert G. Howard, Treas.
Trustees: Diane Staley Bernard; Susan H. Canada; Janet Howard; Catherine Staley; Sarah H. Wichert.
Number of staff: 1 full-time professional.
EIN: 136071888
Other changes: The grantmaker has moved from NY to PA.

Stuart Staley is now Chair. Thomas F. Staley, Jr. is no longer Pres.

3044
Staunton Farm Foundation
650 Smithfield St., Ste. 210
Pittsburgh, PA 15222-3907 (412) 281-8020
Contact: Joni Schwager, Exec. Dir.
FAX: (412) 232-3115;
E-mail: jschwager@stauntonfarm.org; **E-mail for letter of inquiry or questions regarding application process: office@stauntonfarm.org**; Main URL: http://www.stauntonfarm.org
Facebook: https://www.facebook.com/stauntonfarm

Incorporated in 1937 in PA.
Donor: Mathilda Staunton Craig McCready†.
Foundation type: Independent foundation.
Financial data (yr. ended 12/31/12): Assets, $52,975,123 (M); expenditures, $2,819,294; qualifying distributions, $2,600,575; giving activities include $2,154,122 for 58 grants (high: $147,000; low: $75).
Purpose and activities: The foundation is dedicated to improving the lives of people who suffer from mental illness. It works to enhance mental health treatment and support by advancing the best practices through grant making to non profit organizations in the 10 southwestern Pennsylvania counties of Allegheny, Armstrong, Beaver, Butler, Fayette, Greene, Indiana, Lawrence, Washington, and Westmoreland. Current priorities include: 1) rural behavioral health: applicants for this grant will provide services to people in at least one rural area and will describe how the approach used will reach and engage people who face the challenges of distance and stigma; 2) access to behavioral health services and support for underserved populations: applicants for this grant will make the case that the population they are targeting does not now receive services at an expected rate and that their project will reach and engage the underserved individuals more effectively; and 3) Criminal Justice Diversion. Applicants for this grant will propose a program in collaboration with the criminal justice system that will divert youth or adults with behavioral health issues from arrest/jail to treatment and support in the community.
Fields of interest: Substance abuse, services; Substance abuse, prevention; Substance abuse, treatment; Mental health, treatment; Mental health/crisis services; Crime/violence prevention, domestic violence; Human services; Children/youth, services; Family services; Family services, counseling; Psychology/behavioral science; Infants/toddlers; Children/youth; Children; Youth; Adults; Young adults; Disabilities, people with; African Americans/Blacks; Women; Girls; Men; Military/veterans; Substance abusers; Crime/abuse victims; Homeless; LGBTQ; Lesbians.
Type of support: Management development/capacity building; Program development; Conferences/seminars; Seed money; Curriculum development; Program evaluation; Matching/challenge support.
Limitations: Giving limited to a ten-county area in southwestern PA: Allegheny, Armstrong, Beaver, Butler, Fayette, Greene, Indiana, Lawrence, Washington, and Westmoreland counties.
Publications: Application guidelines; Annual report; Grants list.
Application information: Application guidelines available on foundation web site. SWPA Common Grant Application accepted. Application form required.
Initial approach: **Use letter of inquiry format and online application process on foundation web site**
Copies of proposal: 1
Deadline(s): Refer to foundation web site for latest deadlines
Board meeting date(s): Quarterly
Final notification: Immediately following board meetings
Officers and Directors:* Robert B. Ferree IV, Pres.; Margaret Weaver,* V.P.; Paul "Stoney" Griffiths III, Secy.; Joni S. Schwager, Exec. Dir.; Bonni Dunlap, Ph.D.; Philip G. Gulley.
Number of staff: 3 full-time professional; 1 part-time professional.
EIN: 250965573

3045
Stoneleigh Foundation
(formerly A. Stoneleigh Research and Education Center Serving Children and Youth)
123 S. Broad St., Ste. 1130
Philadelphia, PA 19109-1019 (215) 735-7080
Contact: Cathy M. Weiss, Exec. Dir.
FAX: (215) 735-7089;
E-mail: info@stoneleighfoundation.org; Main URL: http://www.stoneleighfoundation.org
Blog: http://stoneleighfoundation.org/blog
E-Newsletter: http://stoneleighfoundation.org/news/newsletters
Facebook: https://www.facebook.com/StoneleighFdn?ref=hl
LinkedIn: http://www.linkedin.com/company/stoneleigh-foundation
RSS Feed: http://stoneleighfoundation.org/blog/rss.xml
Twitter: http://twitter.com/StoneleighFdn
Vimeo: http://www.vimeo.com/user3587811
YouTube: http://www.youtube.com/user/StoneleighFoundation

Established in 2006 in PA.
Donors: John C. Haas; Chara C. Haas.
Foundation type: Operating foundation.
Financial data (yr. ended 06/30/12): Assets, $12,478,280 (M); gifts received, $1,638,587; expenditures, $1,612,904; qualifying distributions, $1,354,496; giving activities include $830,315 for 15 grants (high: $113,625; low: $135), $75,076 for 1 grant to an individual, and $1,353,989 for foundation-administered programs.
Purpose and activities: Giving to improve life outcomes for most vulnerable youth (those in child welfare and juvenile justice systems).
Fields of interest: Children/youth.
Type of support: Fellowships.
Limitations: Applications accepted. Giving primarily in the Philadelphia, PA, area. No support for projects. No grants for direct service support.
Publications: Application guidelines.
Application information: Faxed or incomplete proposals not accepted. Application form not required.
Initial approach: Letter of inquiry
Deadline(s): None
Board meeting date(s): Mar., June, Sept. and Dec.
Final notification: 1-month
Officers and Directors:* Carole Haas Gravagno,* Chair.; **Darlyne Bailey, Ph.D., Secy.; Morrison C. Huston, Jr., Treas.; Ronnie L. Bloom, Esq., Exec. Dir.**; Paul DiLorenzo; Katherine Hanrahan; Frazierita D. Klasen; David M. Rubin, M.D.; Larry Steinberg.
Number of staff: 2 full-time professional; 1 full-time support.
EIN: 371526458
Other changes: Darlyne Bailey, Ph.D. has replaced Elizabeth Werthen as Secy. Morrison C. Huston, Jr. has replaced David W. Haas as Treas. Ronnie L. Bloom, Esq. has replaced Cathy M. Weiss as Exec. Dir.

3046
The Sunoco Foundation
1735 Market St., Ste. LL
Philadelphia, PA 19103-7583
***Main URL:* https://online.foundationsource.com/public/home/sunoco**

Established in 2005 in PA.
Donor: Sunoco, Inc.
Foundation type: Company-sponsored foundation.
Financial data (yr. ended 12/31/12): Assets, $29,488,917 (M); expenditures, $2,275,066; qualifying distributions, $2,256,146; giving activities include $2,208,045 for 43 grants (high: $289,235; low: $316).
Purpose and activities: The foundation supports programs designed to promote projects that educate and develop skills for the workforce; promote environmental stewardship and responsibility; and help communities become better places to live and work.
Fields of interest: Education; Agriculture/food; Human services.
Type of support: Program development.
Limitations: Applications accepted. Giving primarily in areas of company operations, with emphasis on Philadelphia, PA. No support for athletic teams, bands, or choirs, religious organizations, pass-through organizations, discriminatory organizations, political parties, candidates, or partisan-political groups, fraternal or war veteran organizations, or private schools. No grants to individuals, or for fundraising events or sponsorships, single diseases or disease related causes, equipment (unless part of a community outreach program), athletic events, memorial grants, or travel.
Publications: Application guidelines.
Application information: Application form required.
Initial approach: Complete online application
Deadline(s): None
Officers and Directors:* Dennis Zeleny, Chair.; Ruth A. Clauser, Pres.; **John J. DiRocco, Jr., Secy.**; Charmian Uy,* Treas.; **Anne-Marie Ainsworth**; **Cynthia A. Archer**; **Kathleen Shea-Ballay**; David C. Webster.
EIN: 203459268
Other changes: The grantmaker no longer lists an E-mail address. The grantmaker no longer lists a fax. The grantmaker no longer lists a phone. The grantmaker no longer lists a primary contact.

3047
John Templeton Foundation
300 Conshohocken State Rd., Ste. 500
West Conshohocken, PA 19428-3801 (610) 941-2828
Contact: Grant Admin.
FAX: (610) 825-1730; E-mail: info@templeton.org; Main URL: http://www.templeton.org/
Facebook: http://www.facebook.com/TempletonFoundation
Twitter: http://twitter.com/templeton_fdn
YouTube: http://www.youtube.com/user/TempletonFoundation

Established in 1988 in TN.

Donors: Sir. John Marks Templeton†; Templeton Religious Trust; Templeton World Charity Foundation.
Foundation type: Independent foundation.
Financial data (yr. ended 12/31/12): Assets, $2,555,855,497 (M); gifts received, $65,303,327; expenditures, $135,931,727; qualifying distributions, $126,124,827; giving activities include $105,248,596 for grants, and $2,429,016 for foundation-administered programs.
Purpose and activities: The John Templeton Foundation serves as a philanthropic catalyst for discoveries relating to the Big Questions of human purpose and ultimate reality. It supports research on subjects ranging from complexity, evolution, and infinity to creativity, forgiveness, love, and free will. It encourages civil, informed dialogue among scientists, philosophers, and theologians and between such experts and the public at large, for the purposes of definitional clarity and new insights. Its vision is derived from the late Sir John Templeton's optimism about the possibility of acquiring "new spiritual information" and from his commitment to rigorous scientific research and related scholarship. The foundation's motto, "How little we know, how eager to learn," exemplifies its support for open-minded inquiry and its hope for advancing human progress through breakthrough discoveries.
Fields of interest: Health care; Youth development; Economic development; Science; Leadership development; Religion.
Type of support: Program development; Conferences/seminars; Publication; Curriculum development; Fellowships; Research; Grants to individuals; Matching/challenge support.
Limitations: Applications accepted. Giving on a national and international basis. No support for the development of new business ventures or the creation of for-profit companies. No grants for academic scholarships for individuals or groups, endowment funds, building funds, real estate holdings, capital campaigns, or artistic productions; no grants for the purchase of equipment, unless deemed a vital and necessary component of a larger research project falling within the foundation's funding purposes; and no grants for general operating support to universities, institutions, or organizations.
Publications: Annual report; Financial statement; Informational brochure; Newsletter.
Application information: The foundation has established a new online grantmaking process for its Core Funding and Funding Priorities areas. Grants to individuals are a tiny portion of its grant-making because the foundation focuses on making grants in its area of interest. The foundation will award a grant to an applicant, whether an individual or an organization, if the applicant establishes an ability to make a contribution in one of the foundation's areas of interest. Generally, individual applicants must be associated with a 501 (c) (3) organization and the grant will be made to the organization. Full proposals will be accepted by invitation only. Application form required.

Initial approach: Submit online funding inquiry form
***Deadline(s):* Deadlines for inquiries: Feb. 3 - Apr. 1 and Aug.1 - Oct. 1**
Board meeting date(s): Varies
***Final notification:* May 2 and Nov. 5**

Officers and Trustees:* John Marks Templeton, Jr., M.D.*, Chair. and Pres.; Douglas W. Scott, Exec. V.P. and C.A.O.; Dawn Bryant, Exec. V.P. and General Counsel; Michael J. Murray, Exec. V.P., Progs.; Barnaby Marsh, Sr. V.P., Management and Strategic Initiatives; Kimon Howland Sargeant, Ph.D., V.P., Human Sciences; Paul K. Wason, Ph.D., V.P., Life Sciences and Genetics; **Earl D. Whipple, V.P., Comms. and Public Affairs**; Harvey M. Templeton III,* Secy.; Valerie K. Martin, C.F.O.; Denis R. Alexander; Heather Templeton Dill; Nidhal Guessoum; Rory Knight; Stephen G. Post; Eric Priest; Jeffrey P. Schloss; John W. Schott, M.D.; Jane M. Siebels, Ph.D.; Josephine "Pina" Templeton.
Number of staff: 12 full-time professional; 6 full-time support.
EIN: 621322826
Other changes: John D. Barrow, David G. Myers and Gail Zimmerman are no longer trustees. Mauro De Lorenzo is no longer V.P., Freedom and Free Enterprise. Kent Hill is no longer V.P. Character Devel. Judith Marchand is no longer V.P., Special Projects. Pamela Thompson is no longer V.P., Comms. Anne Templeton Cameron is no longer Treas.

3048
Edith L. Trees Charitable Trust

c/o PNC Bank, N.A.
620 Liberty Ave., 10th Fl.
Pittsburgh, PA 15222-2705 (412) 762-4133
***Contact:* M. Bradley Dean, V.P., PNC Bank, N.A.; J. Murray Egan Esq., Tr.**

Established around 1976.
Donor: Edith L. Trees Trust.
Foundation type: Independent foundation.
Financial data (yr. ended 12/31/13): Assets, $192,327,199 (M); gifts received, $38,000,000; expenditures, $7,511,307; qualifying distributions, $6,282,746; giving activities include $6,176,351 for 106 grants (high: $500,000; low: $5,000).
Purpose and activities: Giving solely for the care and welfare of children with mental retardation.
Fields of interest: Children/youth, services; Youth, services; Mentally disabled.
Type of support: General/operating support; Equipment; Endowments; Debt reduction.
Limitations: Applications accepted. Giving primarily in PA. No grants to individuals.
Application information: Application form not required.

Initial approach: Proposal
Deadline(s): Oct. 1

Trustees: J. Murray Egan; PNC Bank, N.A.
EIN: 256026443

3049
Harry C. Trexler Trust

33 S. 7th St., Ste. 205
Allentown, PA 18101-2406
Contact: Janet E. Roth, Exec. Dir.
FAX: (610) 437-5721; Main URL: http://www.TrexlerTrust.org

Trust established in 1934 in PA.
Donors: Harry C. Trexler†; Mary M. Trexler†.
Foundation type: Independent foundation.
Financial data (yr. ended 03/31/13): Assets, $114,463,040 (M); expenditures, $5,261,597; qualifying distributions, $4,120,080; giving activities include $3,741,975 for 104 grants (high: $1,039,598; low: $1,000).
Purpose and activities: The trust provides that one-fourth of the income shall be added to the corpus, one-fourth paid to the city of Allentown for park purposes, and the remainder distributed to such charitable organizations and objects as shall be of the most benefit to humanity, but limited to Allentown and Lehigh County, Pennsylvania, particularly for hospitals, churches, institutions for the care of the crippled and orphans, youth agencies, social services, cultural programs, and support of ministerial students at two named Pennsylvania institutions.
Fields of interest: Arts; Higher education; Education; Food banks; Recreation; Human services; Children/youth, services; Aging, centers/services; Disabilities, people with; Economically disadvantaged.
Type of support: General/operating support; Continuing support; Capital campaigns; Building/renovation; Equipment; Land acquisition; Program development; Matching/challenge support.
Limitations: Applications accepted. Giving limited to Lehigh County, PA. No grants to individuals, or for endowment funds, research, scholarships, or fellowships; no loans.
Publications: Application guidelines; Annual report; Grants list; Occasional report.
Application information: Prospective grantees are welcome to request a meeting with staff well in advance of the Dec. 1 deadline to discuss the grant application process. Questions may be directed to Janet E. Roth, Exec. Dir., at the trust office. Application form and guidelines available on foundation web site. Application form required.

Initial approach: Letter no more than 3 pages
Copies of proposal: 1
Deadline(s): Dec. 1 for consideration at annual fund distribution
Board meeting date(s): Monthly; grant distribution takes place annually after Mar. 31
Final notification: June 1

Officer: Janet E. Roth, Exec. Dir.
Trustees: Barnet H. Fraenkel; Fr. Daniel G. Gambet; Malcolm J. Gross; L. Charles Marcon; Jamie P. Musselman.
Number of staff: 1 full-time professional; 1 part-time professional; 1 full-time support.
EIN: 231162215

3050
Tuttleman Family Foundation

23 Tettemer Rd.
Erwinna, PA 18920-9259
Contact: Jan S. Tuttleman, Tr.
FAX: (858) 457-7790; E-mail: jtuttleman@gmail.com

Established in 1993 in PA.
Donor: Members of the Tuttleman family.
Foundation type: Independent foundation.
Financial data (yr. ended 12/31/12): Assets, $4,557,413 (M); expenditures, $276,499; qualifying distributions, $246,500; giving activities include $246,500 for grants.
Purpose and activities: The mission of the foundation is to support programs that enrich the quality of life for Jewish and secular children, their families, and the elderly in the Philadelphia, PA, area who are underprivileged, disadvantaged, or at risk. The foundation also supports medical research for Type II diabetes.
Fields of interest: Arts; Education; Health organizations, association; Human services; Children/youth, services; Children, services; Women, centers/services; Urban/community development; Jewish federated giving programs.
Type of support: Technical assistance; Curriculum development; General/operating support; Emergency funds; Program development; Conferences/seminars; Seed money; Internship funds; Research.
Limitations: Applications not accepted. Giving primarily in Philadelphia, PA. No support for capital campaigns. No grants to individuals.

Application information: Contributes only to pre-selected organizations.
Trustees: David Z. Tuttleman; Edna S. Tuttleman; Jan S. Tuttleman; Steven M. Tuttleman.
EIN: 237715836
Other changes: The grantmaker has moved from CA to PA.

3051
Union Benevolent Association
c/o Kasey Thompson
1528 Walnut St., Ste. 1002
Philadelphia, PA **19102-3627** (215) 763-7670
E-mail: info@uba1831.org; Main URL: http://www.uba1831.org
Facebook: https://www.facebook.com/UBA1831
Grants List: http://uba1831.org/index.php/about-our-grants/recent-recipients/

Founded in 1831 in PA.
Foundation type: Independent foundation.
Financial data (yr. ended 12/31/12): Assets, $4,128,441 (M); gifts received, $1,036; expenditures, $226,800; qualifying distributions, $202,552; giving activities include $177,675 for 100 grants (high: $4,875; low: $250).
Fields of interest: Child development, education; Adult education—literacy, basic skills & GED; Education, reading; Education; Reproductive health, family planning; Substance abuse, services; AIDS; AIDS research; Crime/law enforcement; Housing/shelter, development; Human services; Child development, services; Homeless, human services; Civil rights, race/intergroup relations; Community/economic development; Minorities; Economically disadvantaged; Homeless.
Type of support: General/operating support; Continuing support; Building/renovation; Equipment; Emergency funds.
Limitations: Applications accepted. Giving limited to Philadelphia, PA. No support for national organizations, religious organizations for religious purposes, or government agencies. No grants to individuals, or for capital renovations.
Publications: Annual report (including application guidelines).
Application information: Delaware Valley Grantmakers Common Application Form (including coversheet, summary, narrative and budget) required. The Association will only fund an organization for three years (not necessarily consecutive) out of five. Application form required.
Initial approach: Letter
Copies of proposal: 1
Deadline(s): Apr. 30 and Sept. 30
Officers: Phyllis Martino, Pres.; Diane-Louise Wormley, V.P.; Nia Ngina Meeks, Secy.; William J. Burke, Jr., Treas.
Board Members: Daniel Gerber; Will Gonzalez; Luz Hernandez; Jon Herrmann; Michael Hinson; Sigrid Lundby; Heseung Ann Song.
EIN: 231360861

3052
United Space Alliance Foundation
c/o Bank of New York Mellon Corp.
P.O. Box 535007
Pittsburgh, PA **15253-5007**
Contact: Eileen A. Groves Esq., Dir.
Application address: 1150 Gemini St., Houston, TX 77058-2708

Established in 2001 in AL, DE, FL, and TX.
Donor: United Space Alliance, LLC.
Foundation type: Company-sponsored foundation.
Financial data (yr. ended 12/31/12): Assets, $62,727 (M); gifts received, $132,000; expenditures, $142,340; qualifying distributions, $142,340; giving activities include $142,340 for 100 grants (high: $20,000; low: $25).
Purpose and activities: The foundation supports museums and community foundations and organizations involved with education, human services, and space and aviation.
Fields of interest: Education; Youth development; Human services.
Type of support: General/operating support; Scholarship funds.
Limitations: Applications accepted. Giving primarily in AL, FL, and TX.
Application information: Application form required.
Initial approach: Contact foundation for application information
***Deadline(s):* Contact foundation for deadline**
Officer: Vanessa Rincones, Secy.
Directors: Meghan Allen; Virginia Barnes; William Capel; Rochelle Cooper; Kari Fluegel; Scott Hartwig; Sherri Lee; Mark Nappi.
EIN: 760668924
Other changes: Eileen Groves, Esq. is no longer Co-Secy. Vanessa Rincones is now Secy. Daniel C. Brandenstein is no longer a member of the governing body. Kim Doering is no longer a member of the governing body. Norm Gookins is no longer a member of the governing body. Kate B. Kronmiller is no longer a member of the governing body.

3053
Valentine Foundation
409 Merion Hill Ln.
West Conshohocken, PA 19428 (610) 525-7200
Contact: Alexandra V.A. Frazier, Exec. Dir.
E-mail: info@valentinefoundation.org; Main URL: http://www.valentinefoundation.org
Facebook: https://www.facebook.com/pages/The-Valentine-Foundation/127542280618958
Grants List: http://www.valentinefoundation.org/2013-grantees/grantees/

Established in 1985 in PA.
Donors: Susan Garrison; Walter R. Garrison; Pam Phelan; Phoebe V. Valentine†; The Hess Foundation.
Foundation type: Independent foundation.
Financial data (yr. ended 11/30/13): Assets, $3,613,726 (M); gifts received, $104,931; expenditures, $244,717; qualifying distributions, $199,149; giving activities include $176,319 for 23 grants (high: $12,000; low: $500).
Purpose and activities: The foundation makes grants to organizations or programs that empower women and girls to recognize and develop their full potential or that work to change established attitudes that discourage them from recognizing their potential. Grants will be given for endeavors to effect fundamental change - to change attitudes, policies, or social patterns. The trustees commit a minimum of half of their grants to programs for girls and the balance to programs for women. The programs for women must include advocacy for social change.
Fields of interest: Education; Women, centers/services; Women; Girls.
Type of support: General/operating support; Continuing support; Program development; Seed money.
Limitations: Applications not accepted. Giving primarily in the Philadelphia, PA, area. No support for capital campaigns, religious organizations for religious purposes or political organizations for political purposes, and no support for international initiatives. No grants to individuals, or for scholarships, endowments, or capital campaigns.
Application information: Unsolicited requests for funds not accepted.
Trustees: Peggy Curchack; Nancy J. Kirby; Barbara J. Silzle; Shawn Towey; Tracy Tripp; Linda A. White.
Officers: Alexandra Samuels, Chair.; Alexandra V. A. Frazier, Exec. Dir.
Number of staff: 1 part-time professional.
EIN: 236806061

3054
Washington County Community Foundation, Inc.
331 S. Main St.
Washington, PA 15301 (724) 222-6330
Contact: Betsie Trew, C.E.O.
FAX: (724) 222-7960; E-mail: info@wccf.net;
Additional e-mail: brtrew@wccf.net; Main URL: http://www.wccf.net
Facebook: https://www.facebook.com/pages/Washington-County-Community-Foundation/221252694651719
RSS Feed: http://www.wccf.net/rss
Twitter: https://twitter.com/washcocommfdtn

Established in 1993 in PA.
Foundation type: Community foundation.
Financial data (yr. ended 12/31/12): Assets, $14,796,203 (M); gifts received, $5,231,530; expenditures, $878,387; giving activities include $600,971 for 26+ grants (high: $100,000).
Purpose and activities: The foundation fosters philanthropy by offering charitable gifting opportunities to donors. Its purpose includes helping donors accomplish their goals by professionally managing funds entrusted to it for today and for the future, and by distributing these funds as directed by the donor or the Board of Trustees in the areas of arts, education, the environment, health, human needs, and religion.
Fields of interest: Arts education; Visual arts; Performing arts; Humanities; Arts; Education; Environment, pollution control; Environment; Animal welfare; Health care; Human services; Community development, neighborhood development; Economic development; Urban/community development; Religion.
Type of support: Film/video/radio; Publication; Program development; General/operating support; Equipment; Continuing support; Capital campaigns; Building/renovation; Annual campaigns; Scholarship funds; Scholarships—to individuals.
Limitations: Applications accepted. Giving primarily in Washington County, PA. No support for private charities. **No grants to individuals (except for scholarships), or for routine or land acquisition projects, or endowment funds; no loans.**
Publications: Application guidelines; Annual report; Financial statement; Informational brochure; Newsletter.
Application information: Visit foundation web site for application forms and guidelines. Application form required.
Initial approach: Application
Copies of proposal: 1
Deadline(s): Sept. 1 for discretionary fund grants; varies for others
Board meeting date(s): 4th Thurs. of each month; annual meeting in June
Final notification: Varies
Officers and Trustees:* Deborah E. Takach,* Chair.; **Edward C. Morascyzk,* Vice-Chair.**; Betsie

Trew,* Pres. and C.E.O.; **Jarol A. DeVoge,* Secy.**; **Sandra Guthrie,* Treas.**; Mark A. Campbell; **William M. Campbell**; Thomas Gladden; Tammy Hardy; Thomas Hart; Thomas F. Hoffman; Geraldine M. Jones; Charles C. Keller; William M. Kline III; John McCarthy; Barron P. McCune, Jr.; James McCune; Andrew M. McIlvaine; Thomas P. Northrup; Alex E. Paris, III; Kurt Salvatori; Gwen Simmons; Brian J. Smith; Lynne Stout; Dorothy Tecklenburg; Thomas Uram; Richard L. White.
Number of staff: 1 full-time professional; 2 part-time support.
EIN: 251726013
Other changes: Edward C. Morascyzk has replaced Deborah E. Takach as Vice-Chair. Jarol A. DeVoge has replaced Edward C. Morascyzk as Secy. Sandra Guthrie has replaced William G. Stough Treas.
Neil Bassi and Kenneth Donahue are no longer trustees.

3055
Wells Fargo Regional Foundation

(formerly Wachovia Regional Foundation)
123 S. Broad St.
MAC Y1379-030
Philadelphia, PA 19109-1029 (215) 670-4300
Contact: Denise McGregor Armbrister, Exec. Dir.
FAX: (215) 670-4313;
E-mail: communityaffairs@wachovia.com; Contact for Neighborhood Implementation and Planning Grants: Kimberly Allen, Prog. Off., tel.: (215) 670-4307, Crystal Dundas, Prog. Off., tel.: (215) 670-4311; Main URL: https://www.wellsfargo.com/about/regional-foundation/index
Grants List: https://www.wellsfargo.com/downloads/pdf/about/WFRF_Active_Grantee_Portfolio.pdf

Established in 1998.
Donors: CoreStates Financial Corp; First Union Corp.; Wachovia Corp.
Foundation type: Company-sponsored foundation.
Financial data (yr. ended 12/31/12): Assets, $77,675,043 (M); expenditures, $5,250,455; qualifying distributions, $4,974,479; giving activities include $4,861,350 for 118 grants (high: $110,000; low: $1,500).
Purpose and activities: The foundation supports organizations involved with neighborhood planning and development.
Fields of interest: Employment, job counseling; Employment, training; Housing/shelter, development; Housing/shelter; Children, services; Family services; Community development, neighborhood development; Economic development; Urban/community development.
Type of support: Equipment; Program development; Technical assistance; Program evaluation.
Limitations: Applications accepted. Giving primarily in Kent, New Castle, and Sussex, DE, Atlantic, Bergen, Burlington, Camden, Cape May, Cumberland, Essex, Hudson, Hunterdon, Gloucester, Mercer, Middlesex, Monmouth, Morris, Ocean, Passaic, Salem, Somerset, Sussex, Union, and Warren, NJ, and Adams, Berks, Bradford, Bucks, Carbon, Centre, Chester, Clinton, Columbia, Cumberland, Dauphin, Delaware, Juniata, Lackawanna, Lancaster, Lebanon, Lehigh, Lycoming, Luzerne, Mifflin, Monroe, Montgomery, Montour, Northampton, Northumberland, Perry, Philadelphia, Pike, Potter, Schuylkill, Snyder, Sullivan, Susquehanna, Tioga, Union, Wayne, Wyoming, and York, PA. No support for political organizations or national or international organizations; generally, no support for K-12 private schools, colleges or universities, veterans' or fraternal organizations, arts or cultural organizations, hospitals or medical centers, or health- or disease-related organizations. No grants to individuals, or for general operating support, strategic or business plans, "bricks and mortar" projects, political causes, endowments, capital campaigns, debt reduction, or special events; generally, no grants for religious programs or activities.
Publications: Application guidelines; Grants list; Program policy statement.
Application information: Neighborhood Planning and Implementation Grants have two phases. Phase two of the application process is by invitation only. A site visit may be requested. Application form required.
Initial approach: Complete online eligibility quiz and application form
***Deadline(s):* Sept. 5 for phase one and Oct. 13 for phase two for Neighborhood Planning Grants; Apr. 11 and Oct. 24 for phase one and June 23 and Jan. 16 for phase two for Neighborhood Implementation Grants**
Board meeting date(s): Jan., Apr., July, and Oct.
Final notification: Jan. 31 for Neighborhood Planning Grants; Nov. 1 and Apr. 30 for Neighborhood Implementation Grants
Officers and Directors:* Austin J. Burke, Chair.; **Robert Torres, Esq., Vice-Chair.**; Denise McGregor Armbrister, Sr. V.P. and Exec. Dir.; Lois W. Greco, Sr. V.P. and Evaluation Off.; Kimberly Allen, V.P. and Sr. Prog. Off.; Fernando Chang-Muy, Esq.; **Shinjoo Choo**; Lucia Gibbons; Tom Hanlon; Stacy Holland; Maria Matos; Gabriella Morris; Greg Redden; Ralph Smith, Esq.; John Thurber, Esq.
Number of staff: 4 full-time professional; 1 full-time support.
EIN: 222625990
Other changes: Austin J. Burke has replaced C. Kent McGuire, Ph.D. as Chair. Robert Torres, Esq. has replaced Austin J. Burke as Vice-Chair. Kimberly Allen is now V.P. and Sr. Prog. Off. Susanne Svizeny is no longer Pres. John Petillo is no longer a director. C. Kent McGuire is no longer Chair.

3056
Widener Memorial Foundation in Aid of Handicapped Children

4060 Butler Pike, Ste. 225
Plymouth Meeting, PA 19462-1554 **(215) 825-8900**
Contact: Edith R. Dixon, Treas.

Incorporated in 1912 in PA.
Donors: Peter A.B. Widener†; Widener Memorial Foundation 2; Widener Memorial School Endowment.
Foundation type: Independent foundation.
Financial data (yr. ended 12/31/12): Assets, $7,413,784 (M); gifts received, $645,052; expenditures, $1,006,230; qualifying distributions, $961,808; giving activities include $961,808 for grants.
Purpose and activities: Support for research into the causes, treatment, and prevention of diseases and conditions which handicap children orthopedically; to aid and assist public and private charitable institutions and associations in the care, education, and rehabilitation of children so handicapped.
Fields of interest: Orthopedics; Medical research, institute; Children/youth, services; Disabilities, people with.
Type of support: Building/renovation; Equipment; Program development; Seed money; Research.
Limitations: Giving limited to the Delaware Valley area, with emphasis on Philadelphia, PA. No support for private foundations or for organizations lacking 501(c)(3) status. No grants to individuals, or for endowment funds, scholarships, fellowships, or matching gifts; no loans.
Application information: Application form not required.
Initial approach: Letter
Copies of proposal: 1
Deadline(s): Apr. 15 and Oct. 15
Board meeting date(s): May and Nov.
Final notification: Immediately after board meetings
Officers and Trustees:* Edith D. Miller,* Pres.; Peter M. Mattoon,* V.P.; **George W. Dixon,* Secy.**; **Edith R. Dixon,* Treas.**; Bruce L. Castor; Michael Clancy, M.D.; Mark S. DePillis; **Linda Grobman**; **John Keleher.**
EIN: 236267223
Other changes: Edith D. Miller has replaced Edith R. Dixon as Pres.
Ellin Dixon Miller is no longer a trustee.

3057
Willary Foundation

P.O. Box 283
Scranton, PA 18501 (570) 961-6952
***FAX:* (570) 961-7269; E-mail: info@willary.org**;
Main URL: http://www.willary.org

Established in 1968 in PA.
Donors: William W. Scranton; Mary L. Scranton.
Foundation type: Independent foundation.
Financial data (yr. ended 12/31/12): Assets, $4,577,325 (M); expenditures, $234,061; qualifying distributions, $213,688; giving activities include $192,486 for 10 grants (high: $25,000; low: $3,400).
Purpose and activities: The foundation wishes to promote the special qualities of the people of northeastern Pennsylvania, and is particularly interested in projects that support leadership and the development of leadership in business, the economy, education, human services, government, the arts, media and research.
Fields of interest: Education; Human services; Community/economic development.
Type of support: Program development; Matching/challenge support.
Limitations: Applications accepted. Giving primarily in Lackawanna and Luzerne counties, PA. No grants to individuals, or for capital campaigns or annual drives; no loans.
Publications: Application guidelines; Grants list.
Application information: Application guidelines and form available on foundation web site. Application form required.
Copies of proposal: 6
***Deadline(s):* Mar. 10 for the spring board meeting; Aug. 27 for the winter board meeting**
Trustees: Susan Scranton Dawson; Joseph C. Scranton; Mary L. Scranton; Peter K. Scranton; S. Caitlin Scranton; William W. Scranton; William W. Scranton III; Elizabeth S. Valosek.
EIN: 237014785
Other changes: The grantmaker no longer lists a separate application address.

3058
Edward M. Wilson Family Foundation
c/o PNC Bank, N.A.
P.O. Box 609
Pittsburgh, PA 15230-0609
Application address: c/o Jocy Muya PNC Bank, 101 W. Washington St., Ste. 600E, Indianapolis, IN 46204-3494, tel.: (216) 222-3226

Established around 1980 in IN.
Donor: William Telfer.
Foundation type: Independent foundation.
Financial data (yr. ended 09/30/13): Assets, $32,532,224 (M); expenditures, $1,591,900; qualifying distributions, $1,482,591; giving activities include $1,381,200 for 87 grants (high: $85,000; low: $1,500).
Purpose and activities: Giving primarily for arts and culture, education, children, youth and social services, and to Christian organizations.
Fields of interest: Museums (art); Arts; Education; Human services; American Red Cross; YM/YWCAs & YM/YWHAs; Children/youth, services; Foundations (private grantmaking); Christian agencies & churches.
Type of support: General/operating support.
Limitations: Giving primarily in Fort Wayne, IN. No grants to individuals.
Application information:
Initial approach: Proposal
Deadline(s): None
Distribution Committee: Janet C. Chrzan; Hon. William Lee; Tom Quirk; Thomas Shoaff; Don A. Wolf.
Trustee: PNC Bank, N.A.
EIN: 310976337
Other changes: The grantmaker has moved from OH to PA.

3059
The Wyomissing Foundation, Inc.
960 Old Mill Rd.
Wyomissing, PA 19610-2522 (610) 376-7494
Contact: Paul R. Roedel, Treas.
FAX: (610) 372-7626; E-mail: wfbbec@nnl.com

Incorporated in 1929 in DE.
Donors: Ferdinand Thun‡; and family.
Foundation type: Independent foundation.
Financial data (yr. ended 12/31/12): Assets, $23,882,320 (M); expenditures, $1,810,386; qualifying distributions, $1,503,535; giving activities include $1,224,101 for 37 grants (high: $150,000; low: $3,936).
Purpose and activities: Giving primarily for the arts, education, and human services.
Fields of interest: Arts; Higher education; Environment, natural resources; Human services; United Ways and Federated Giving Programs.
Type of support: General/operating support; Continuing support; Annual campaigns; Capital campaigns; Building/renovation; Equipment; Endowments; Emergency funds; Seed money; Matching/challenge support.
Limitations: Giving primarily in Reading, PA. No grants to individuals, or for deficit financing, land acquisition, publications, conferences, scholarships, or fellowships; no loans.
Publications: Application guidelines; Program policy statement.
Application information: Application form not required.
Initial approach: Letter
Board meeting date(s): Mar., June, Sept., and Dec.
Officers and Trustees:* John P. Weidenhammer,* Pres.; Alexena Frazee,* V.P.; Eliza Lake,* Secy.; **Christopher Pruitt, Treas.**; Karen Rightmire, Exec. Dir.; Tom Beaver; Arthur Grim; **Leslie Karasin**; Glenn E. Moyer; Peter Thun; Anna Weitz; Christian Willauer.
Number of staff: 1 full-time support; 1 part-time support.
EIN: 231980570
Other changes: Christopher Pruitt has replaced Paul R. Rodel as Treas.
Michael Fromm and Daniel Scheffey are no longer trustees.

3060
Zeldin Family Foundation
2039 Delancey St.
Philadelphia, PA **19103-6509**

Established in 1986 in PA.
Donors: Martex Fiber Southern Corp.; Claudia Zeldlin; Martin Zeldin; Stephanie Zeldin.
Foundation type: Independent foundation.
Financial data (yr. ended 11/30/12): Assets, $3,413,744 (M); gifts received, $225,590; expenditures, $177,011; qualifying distributions, $172,815; giving activities include $172,000 for 88 grants (high: $21,428; low: $200).
Purpose and activities: Giving primarily for education, youth and children's services, and for women's interests.
Fields of interest: Arts; Higher education; Education; Health organizations, association; Children/youth, services; Women, centers/services; International relief.
Type of support: General/operating support; Annual campaigns; Capital campaigns; Emergency funds; Program development; Scholarship funds; Matching/challenge support.
Limitations: Applications not accepted. Giving on a national basis. No support for religious or political organizations. No grants to individuals.
Application information: Unsolicited requests for funds will not be accepted.
Board meeting date(s): Nov.
Trustees: Claudia Zeldin; Jessica Zeldin; Martin Zeldin; Stephanie Zeldin; Sybille Zeldin; Marc Williamson.
Number of staff: None.
EIN: 236861835

PUERTO RICO

3061

Puerto Rico Community Foundation, Inc.

1719 Ponce de Leon Ave.
San Juan, PR 00909-1905 (787) 721-1037
Contact: Juan J. Reyes, Admin.
FAX: (787) 982-1673; E-mail: fcpr@fcpr.og; Mailing address: PO Box 70362, San Juan, PR 00936-8362; Main URL: http://www.fcpr.org

Incorporated in 1984 in PR; began operations in 1985.
Foundation type: Community foundation.
Financial data (yr. ended 12/31/12): Assets, $26,002,495 (M); gifts received, $1,502,087; expenditures, $3,020,007; giving activities include $1,079,139 for grants, and $288,226 for grants to individuals.
Purpose and activities: The foundation seeks to develop the capacities of communities in Puerto Rico to accomplish their social transformation and economic self-sufficiency, stimulating investment in the communities and maximizing the yield of each contribution. The scope of the foundation's program areas, which reflect the area of interest and opportunities available to the community, are community economic development, community development and housing, education, youth, arts and health.
Fields of interest: Education; Housing/shelter; Community/economic development; Economically disadvantaged.
Type of support: General/operating support; Continuing support; Management development/ capacity building; Equipment; Emergency funds; Program development; Conferences/seminars; Professorships; Publication; Curriculum development; Research; Technical assistance; Consulting services; Program-related investments/ loans; Scholarships—to individuals; In-kind gifts; Matching/challenge support.
Limitations: Applications accepted. Giving limited to PR. No support for religious organizations for sectarian or proselytizing purposes. No grants for capital or trust funds, operational expenses of an already established organization, operational deficit, annual fundraising, membership fees for associations, galas, special events, travel expenses, or building funds.
Publications: Application guidelines; Annual report; Biennial report; Financial statement; Informational brochure (including application guidelines); Newsletter; Occasional report; Program policy statement.
Application information: Visit foundation web site for application guidelines. Application form required.
Initial approach: Letter
Copies of proposal: 2
Deadline(s): None
Board meeting date(s): Mar., June, Sept., Dec.
Final notification: Within 2 weeks after board meetings
Officers and Directors:* Rene Pinto Lugo,* Pres.; Dr. Nelson I. Colon,* Exec. Pres.; Cesar A. Rey-Hernandez,* V.P.; Mary A. Gabino,* Inst. Devel. V.P.; Aida Torres Cruz,* Secy.; Carlos H. del Rio,* Sub-Treas.; Antonio Escudero Viera,* Treas.; Juan J. Reyes, Admin.; Justo Mendez Aramburu; Maria D. Fernos; Victor Rivera Hernandez; Angel L. Saez Lopez; Dr. Manuel A. Morales; Roberto Pagan; Ruben Morales Rivera; Sandra D. Rodriguez; Victor Garcia San Inocencio.
Number of staff: 10 full-time professional; 4 full-time support.
EIN: 660413230
Other changes: Antonio Escudero Viera is no longer a director.

RHODE ISLAND

3062
Helene and Bertram Bernhardt Foundation
55 Dorrance St., Ste. 400
Providence, RI **02903 (401) 861-2900**
***Contact:* Samuel D. Zurier Esq.**

Established in 2007 in RI.
Donor: The Bertram L. Bernhardt Trust.
Foundation type: Independent foundation.
Financial data (yr. ended 04/30/13): Assets, $11,655,208 (M); expenditures, $580,861; qualifying distributions, $554,069; giving activities include $388,319 for 20 grants (high: $199,319; low: $100), and $20,000 for 1 employee matching gift.
Fields of interest: Jewish federated giving programs; Jewish agencies & synagogues.
Type of support: Capital campaigns.
Limitations: Applications accepted. Giving primarily in Providence, RI.
Application information: Application form required.
Initial approach: Letter
Deadline(s): None
Officer: Samuel D. Zurier, Esq., Secy.
Trustees: Leslie Gutterman; Robert G. Huckins.
EIN: 342053837
Other changes: Samuel D. Zurier, Esq. has replaced Melvin Zurier as Secy.

3063
Biogen Idec Foundation Incorporated
(formerly Biogen Foundation, Inc.)
P.O. Box 1802
Providence, RI 02901-1802
FAX: (617) 679-3223;
E-mail: foundation@biogenidec.com**; Additional address: 133 Boston Post Rd., Weston, MA 02493; Main URL: http://www.biogenidec.com/foundation.aspx?ID=20552**

Established in 2002 in MA.
Donor: Biogen idec Foundation, Inc.
Foundation type: Company-sponsored foundation.
Financial data (yr. ended 12/31/12): Assets, $25,074,770 (M); gifts received, $2,000,000; expenditures, $1,743,921; qualifying distributions, $1,613,874; giving activities include $1,403,070 for 208 grants (high: $200,000; low: $25).
Purpose and activities: The foundation supports programs designed to improve quality of life for communities in which Biogen operates. Special emphasis is directed toward programs designed to promote science literacy and encourage young people to consider careers in science.
Fields of interest: Museums; Museums (science/technology); Arts; Middle schools/education; Secondary school/education; Higher education; Education; Youth, services; Human services; Mathematics; Science.
Type of support: General/operating support; Continuing support; Annual campaigns; Program development; Sponsorships; Employee matching gifts.
Limitations: Applications accepted. Giving primarily in areas of company operations in San Diego, CA, Cambridge and Greater Boston, MA, and Durham and Raleigh, NC. No support for discriminatory, religious, or political organizations, or government agencies. No grants to individuals, or for political candidates, special events, fundraising, or capital campaigns.
Publications: Application guidelines.
Application information: Application form required.
***Initial approach:* Complete eligibility quiz and application**
Deadline(s): None
Board meeting date(s): Quarterly
Officers and Directors:* Tony Kingsley,* Chair. and Pres.; Robert Light, Secy.; Michael Dambach,* Treas.; Daniel McIntyre; Machelle Sanders; Jo Ann Taormina; Jo Viney.
Number of staff: 1 full-time professional.
EIN: 161636254
Other changes: The grantmaker no longer lists a phone. The grantmaker has moved from MA to RI. Tony Kingsley has replaced Esther Alegria as Chair.

3064
Lizzie & Edward V. Bird Trust
P.O. Box 1802
Providence, RI 02901-1802
Application address: **c/o Susan Morrissey, Dept. of Social Svcs., Massachusetts General Hospital, 15 Parkman St., Boston, MA 02114-3117**

Established in MA.
Foundation type: Independent foundation.
Financial data (yr. ended 02/28/13): Assets, $5,362,729 (M); expenditures, $228,484; qualifying distributions, $198,120; giving activities include $179,358 for 1 grant.
Purpose and activities: Provides medical aid, through Massachusetts General Hospital, to needy individuals.
Fields of interest: Hospitals (general); Health care.
Limitations: Applications accepted. Giving limited to MA.
Application information: Application forms available only at Massachusetts General Hospital. Application form required.
Deadline(s): None
Trustee: Bank of America, N.A.
EIN: 046020389
Other changes: The grantmaker no longer lists a fax. The grantmaker no longer lists a phone. The grantmaker has moved from MA to RI.

3065
Frederick S. Bliss Estate Trust
P.O. Box 1802
Providence, RI 02901-1802

Foundation type: Independent foundation.
Financial data (yr. ended 08/31/13): Assets, $9,476,678 (M); expenditures, $460,372; qualifying distributions, $423,482; giving activities include $401,231 for 7 grants (high: $143,300; low: $9,553).
Fields of interest: Hospitals (general); Human services.
Limitations: Applications not accepted. Giving primarily in CT.
Application information: Contributes only to pre-selected organizations.
Trustee: Bank of America, N.A.
EIN: 066027343
Other changes: The grantmaker has changed its fiscal year-end from Dec. 31 to Aug. 31.

3066
Harry E. Chamberlain & Adrienne S. Chamberlain Memorial Fund
c/o Bank of America, N.A.
P.O Box 1802
Providence, RI 02901-1802

Established in 1986; supporting organization of the Animal Welfare League, Illinois Masonic Children's Home, The Salvation Army, Union League Foundation for Boys Club, Seeing Eye, Inc., and Damon-Runyon-Walter Winchell Cancer Fund.
Foundation type: Independent foundation.
Financial data (yr. ended 04/30/13): Assets, $14,479,414 (M); expenditures, $989,277; qualifying distributions, $895,160; giving activities include $895,160 for grants.
Fields of interest: Animal welfare; Cancer; Boys clubs; Salvation Army; Children/youth, services.
Limitations: Applications not accepted. Giving primarily in Long Beach, CA, Charlestown, Chicago and Chicago Ridge, IL, Morristown, NJ, and New York, NY. No grants to individuals.
Application information: Contributes only to pre-selected organizations.
Trustee: Bank of America, N.A.
EIN: 366836133
Other changes: The grantmaker has moved from IL to RI.

3067
Citizens Charitable Foundation
10 Tripps Ln.
Riverside, RI 02915-7995
Main URL: http://www.citizensbank.com/community/corporate/grants.aspx

Established in 1967 in RI; reincorporated in 2005.
Donors: Citizens Savings Bank; Citizens Trust Co.; Citizens Bank of Rhode Island; Cambridgeport Bank; Charter One Bank; The Citizens Bank Mid-Atlantic Charitable Foundation; Citizens Charitable Foundation; RBS Citizens, N.A.
Foundation type: Company-sponsored foundation.
Financial data (yr. ended 12/31/12): Assets, $9,154,163 (M); gifts received, $7,164,104; expenditures, $11,248,600; qualifying distributions, $11,218,067; giving activities include $11,186,774 for 3,114 grants (high: $150,000; low: $25).
Purpose and activities: The foundation supports organizations involved with affordable housing, hunger programs, economic development activities, and financial education.
Fields of interest: Employment; Nutrition; Agriculture/food; Housing/shelter, development; Housing/shelter; Human services; Economic development; Community/economic development; Economically disadvantaged.
Type of support: Employee matching gifts; Employee volunteer services; General/operating support; Program development; Public relations services; Scholarship funds; Sponsorships.
Limitations: Applications accepted. Giving on a national basis in areas of company operations, with emphasis on CT, DE, IL, MA, MI, NH, NJ, NY, OH, PA, RI, and VT. No support for discriminatory organizations, single disease/issue information or research organizations, religious organizations, labor, fraternal, or veterans' organizations, political organizations, governmental or quasi-governmental public agencies or organizations, grantmakers, or public or private educational institutions. No grants to individuals, or for annual campaigns, political projects, debt reduction, conferences or seminars, endowments, trips or tours, advertising or

fundraising activities, or historic preservation; no loans.
Publications: Application guidelines; Informational brochure.
Application information: Prospective applicants must take the charitable grant eligibility quiz on the foundation's website. A site visit and additional information may be requested at a later date. Application form not required.
Initial approach: Complete online application or submit proposal to nearest Public Relations Department
Copies of proposal: 1
Deadline(s): None
Board meeting date(s): Monthly
Final notification: 8 weeks
Officers and Directors: Robert Matthews, Pres.; Denise Leyhe, V.P.; Reza Aghamirzadeh; Heidi Brooks; Cindy Erikson; Bruce Figueroa; Quincy Miller; Tony Moscrop; Kevin Walsh.
Trustee: RBS Citizens, N.A.
Number of staff: 4 full-time professional.
EIN: 202302039
Other changes: The grantmaker has moved from MA to RI.
Robert Matthews is now Pres. Denise Leyhe is now V.P.

3068
CVS Caremark Charitable Trust, Inc.
(formerly CVS/pharmacy Charitable Trust, Inc.)
1 CVS Dr.
Woonsocket, RI 02895-6146 **(401) 770-2898**
Contact: Joanne Dwyer, Dir., Corporate Comms. & Community Relas.
E-mail: Joanne.Dwyer@cvscaremark.com; General Community Rels. Inquiries: CommunityMailbox@cvscaremark.com; Main URL: http://www.cvscaremark.com/community/our-impact/charitable-trust
All Kids Can Blog: http://info.cvscaremark.com/community/our-giving-focus/kids/all-kids-can-blog
All Kids Can CREATE Website: http://www.kennedy-center.org/education/vsa/programs/vsa_create.cfm
Charitable Trust Featured Recipients: http://info.cvscaremark.com/healthier-communities/charitable-trust-featured-grantees
CVS Caremark Charitable Trust Video: http://info.cvscaremark.com/node/2084
RSS Feed: http://info.cvscaremark.com/newsroom/press-releases/community/feed

Established in 1992 in DE and MA.
Donors: Melville Corp.; CVS Corp.; CVS Pharmacy, Inc.
Foundation type: Company-sponsored foundation.
Financial data (yr. ended 12/31/12): Assets, $45,651,274 (M); expenditures, $5,830,000; qualifying distributions, $5,779,242; giving activities include $5,665,193 for 487 grants (high: $375,994; low: $500).
Purpose and activities: The trust supports programs designed to promote access to health care; wellness and prevention initiatives to help people achieve their best health; and programs designed to help all kids in their path to better health.
Fields of interest: Higher education; Medical school/education; Health care, equal rights; Medicine/medical care, public education; Hospitals (general); Health care, clinics/centers; Medical care, rehabilitation; Physical therapy; Art & music therapy; Pharmacy/prescriptions; Public health, physical fitness; Health care, patient services; Health care; Heart & circulatory diseases; Asthma; Diabetes; Pediatrics; Disasters, preparedness/services; Recreation, camps; Recreation, parks/playgrounds; Athletics/sports, school programs; Recreation; Youth development; Family services, parent education; Independent living, disability; Assistive technology; Children; Disabilities, people with; Economically disadvantaged.
Type of support: Continuing support; Management development/capacity building; Building/renovation; Program development; Scholarship funds; Employee volunteer services; Employee-related scholarships.
Limitations: Applications not accepted. Giving primarily in areas of company operations in the U.S. and Puerto Rico. No grants for general operating support, direct healthcare services, staff salaries (unless it's needed to create or enhance a program or increase the number of people or geographic areas served), fundraising events, sponsorships, scholarships (except for employee-related and pharmacy scholarships), endowments, or capital campaigns.
Publications: Grants list; Program policy statement.
Application information: Unsolicited applications are currently not accepted. Giving is by invitation only.
Officers and Directors:* Eileen Howard Boone,* Pres.; David M. Denton,* V.P. and Treas.; Carol A. DeNale, V.P.
EIN: 223206973
Other changes: The grantmaker no longer publishes application guidelines.

3069
Decedric Charitable Trust
535 Atwood Ave.
Cranston, RI **02920-5324**

Established in 2005 in RI.
Foundation type: Operating foundation.
Financial data (yr. ended 06/30/13): Assets, $165,116 (M); expenditures, $137,875; qualifying distributions, $121,450; giving activities include $107,500 for 8 grants (high: $14,700; low: $10,000).
Fields of interest: Arts; Education; Health care.
Limitations: Applications not accepted. Giving primarily in RI. No grants to individuals.
Application information: Contributes only to pre-selected organizations.
Trustees: Dorothy Desaulniers; **Susan Richardson**.
EIN: 206188907

3070
Elmer Hobson DeLoura Trust for Scholarships
(formerly The DeLoura Family Trust)
P.O. Box 1802
Providence, RI 02901-1802
Contact: Susanna Posteo-Castillo
FAX: (617) 434-7567
Application address: c/o Scholarship America, Inc., P.O. Box 297, St. Peter, MN 56802

Established in TX.
Foundation type: Independent foundation.
Financial data (yr. ended 01/31/13): Assets, $4,445,651 (M); expenditures, $263,957; qualifying distributions, $201,439; giving activities include $156,000 for 1 grant.
Purpose and activities: Giving primarily for scholarship funds for graduates of Martha's Vineyard, Massachusetts schools.
Fields of interest: Education.
Type of support: Scholarship funds.
Limitations: Applications accepted. Giving limited to Martha's Vineyard, MA. No grants to individuals directly.
Application information: Applications available at the guidance office of Martha's Vineyard, MA, schools. Application form required.
Deadline(s): Mar. 15
Board meeting date(s): None
Trustee: Bank of America, N.A.
EIN: 046460749
Other changes: The grantmaker has moved from MA to RI.

3071
Dorot Foundation
401 Elmgrove Ave.
Providence, RI 02906-3451 (401) 351-8866
Contact: Michael Hill, Exec. V.P.
FAX: (401) 351-4975; E-mail: dorotinfo@dorot.org; Main URL: http://www.dorot.org
Fellowship e-mail: **dfi@dorot.org**

Incorporated in 1958 in NY as Joy and Samuel Ungerleider Foundation.
Donors: Joy G. Ungerleider-Mayerson†; D.S. and R.H. Gottesman Foundation; Yesod Fund.
Foundation type: Independent foundation.
Financial data (yr. ended 03/31/13): Assets, $46,511,324 (M); gifts received, $2,012,273; expenditures, $3,519,963; qualifying distributions, $3,049,378; giving activities include $1,647,691 for 44 grants (high: $175,000; low: $3,000), and $566,930 for 10 grants to individuals (high: $57,240; low: $56,140).
Purpose and activities: Grants primarily for informal education, the Dorot Fellowship in Israel, cultural organizations with which the foundation has an existing relationship, and organizations supporting adult education for democratic participation in Israel.
Fields of interest: Arts, cultural/ethnic awareness; Education; International affairs; Public affairs, citizen participation.
International interests: Israel.
Type of support: General/operating support; Continuing support; Program development; Publication; Seed money; Fellowships; Internship funds; Technical assistance; Program evaluation; Matching/challenge support.
Limitations: Applications not accepted. Giving primarily in Washington, DC, MA, NY, and Israel. No support for acquisitions for museums or excavation phase of archaeological work. No grants for endowments, capital campaigns, equipment, debt reduction, consultants or technical assistance, or events.
Publications: Financial statement; Grants list.
Application information: Unsolicited requests for funds not accepted. See foundation web site for Fellowship application guidelines.
Board meeting date(s): Apr./May and Oct./Nov.
Officers and Director:* Dr. Ernest S. Frerichs,* Pres.; Michael Hill, Exec. V.P.; Steven M. Jackson, V.P. Strategy.
Number of staff: 3 full-time professional; 1 part-time professional.
EIN: 136116927

3072
The Elms Foundation
244 Gano St.
Providence, RI 02906-4027

Established in 1989 in RI.
Donors: Stanley P. Goldstein; Merle F. Goldstein; JPMorgan Chase Bank, N.A.; First Republic Bank.
Foundation type: Independent foundation.
Financial data (yr. ended 12/31/12): Assets, $11,785,202 (M); expenditures, $475,518; qualifying distributions, $397,100; giving activities include $378,700 for 40 grants (high: $50,000; low: $1,000).
Purpose and activities: Funding primarily for education; some giving also for health care and the arts.
Fields of interest: Arts; Education; Health care; Community/economic development; Jewish federated giving programs; Jewish agencies & synagogues.
Limitations: Applications not accepted. Giving primarily in RI.
Application information: Unsolicited requests for funds not accepted.
Officers and Directors:* Stanley P. Goldstein,* Pres. and Treas.; Merle R. Goldstein,* Secy.; Eugene S. Goldstein; Larry M. Goldstein; Peter Karoff.
EIN: 050450051
Other changes: The grantmaker has moved from NC to RI.

3073
Estate Of Elizabeth Straut
P.O. Box 1802
Providence, RI 02901-1802

Foundation type: Independent foundation.
Financial data (yr. ended 04/30/13): Assets, $4,445,302 (M); expenditures, $308,827; qualifying distributions, $273,401; giving activities include $257,916 for 3 grants (high: $85,972; low: $85,972).
Fields of interest: Environment; Youth development; Religion.
Type of support: General/operating support.
Limitations: Applications not accepted. Giving primarily in IL.
Application information: Unsolicited requests for funds not accepted.
Trustee: Bank of America, N.A.
EIN: 366038536
Other changes: The grantmaker has moved from IL to RI.

3074
Dr. Ralph and Marian Falk Medical Research Trust
c/o US Trust Tax Svcs.
P.O. Box 1802
Providence, RI 02901-1802 (888) 866-3275
***Application address:* c/o George Thorn, Bank of America, N.A., 231 S. LaSalle St., Chicago, IL 60604, tel.: (312) 828-6763**

Established in 1991 in IL.
Donor: Marian Citron Falk Trust.
Foundation type: Independent foundation.
Financial data (yr. ended 11/30/13): Assets, $150,326,031 (M); expenditures, $7,019,141; qualifying distributions, $6,311,716; giving activities include $5,692,403 for 15 grants (high: $787,403; low: $50,000).
Purpose and activities: Support for medical research in the area of diseases for which no definite cure is known.
Fields of interest: Medical research, institute.
Limitations: Applications accepted. Giving primarily in IL. No grants to individuals.
Application information: Application form not required.
Initial approach: Proposal
Deadline(s): None
Trustee: Bank of America, N.A.
EIN: 366975534
Other changes: The grantmaker has moved from IL to RI.

3075
June M. Farrington Charitable Trust
Providence, RI

The trust terminated in 2013.

3076
Maurice R. & Meta G. Gross Foundation
c/o Bank of America, N.A.
P. O. Box 1802
Providence, RI 02901-1802
***Application address:* c/o Bank of America, Attn.: George R. Thorn, 231 S. LaSalle, Chicago, IL 60697, tel.: (312) 828-6763**

Established in 1992 in IL.
Donor: Meta G. Gross Irrevocable Trust.
Foundation type: Independent foundation.
Financial data (yr. ended 11/30/13): Assets, $6,919,515 (M); expenditures, $395,249; qualifying distributions, $338,854; giving activities include $295,920 for 45 grants (high: $50,000; low: $1,000).
Purpose and activities: Giving primarily for museum support, higher education, and youth programs.
Fields of interest: Museums; Arts; Higher education; Medical research, institute; Children/youth, services; Jewish federated giving programs.
Limitations: Applications accepted. Giving primarily in AZ and IL. No grants to individuals, or for building or capital campaigns.
Publications: Application guidelines.
Application information: Application form not required.
Initial approach: Telephone
Copies of proposal: 2
***Deadline(s):* None**
Board meeting date(s): Oct.
Trustee: Bank of America, N.A.
EIN: 367013665
Other changes: The grantmaker has moved from IL to RI.
John D. Marshall is no longer trustee.

3077
Hasbro Children's Fund, Inc.
(formerly Hasbro Charitable Trust, Inc.)
c/o Hasbro, Inc.
1027 Newport Ave.
Pawtucket, RI 02861-2539 (401) 727-5429
Contact: Karen Davis, V.P., Community Rels.
E-mail: kdavis@hasbro.com; **Main URL: http://www.hasbro.com/corporate/en_US/community-relations/childrens-fund.cfm**
Grants List: http://www.hasbro.com/corporate-2/en_US/community-relations/upload/2013-Local-Grantees-for-Internet-pdf.pdf

Established in 1984 in RI.
Donor: Hasbro, Inc.
Foundation type: Company-sponsored foundation.
Financial data (yr. ended 12/30/12): Assets, $4,728,634 (M); gifts received, $109,843; expenditures, $4,052,490; qualifying distributions, $4,052,475; giving activities include $3,991,841 for 114 grants (high: $1,104,134; low: $25).
Purpose and activities: The fund supports programs designed to provide hope to children who need it most; play for children who otherwise would not be able to experience that joy; and empowerment of youth through service.
Fields of interest: Elementary/secondary education; Zoos/zoological societies; Hospitals (general); Health care; Mental health/crisis services; Pediatrics; Food services; Food banks; Disasters, preparedness/services; Recreation, parks/playgrounds; Recreation; Philanthropy/voluntarism; Children; Economically disadvantaged.
Type of support: General/operating support; Continuing support; Capital campaigns; Building/renovation; Program development; Employee matching gifts.
Limitations: Applications not accepted. Giving primarily in Los Angeles, CA, Springfield, MA, RI, and Renton, WA; giving also to regional, national, and U.S.-based international organizations through strategic partnership program. No support for religious organizations, political organizations, or schools. No grants to individuals, or for research, scholarships, travel, endowments, advertising, sponsorship of recreational activities, fundraisers, or auctions; no loans; no cash-free grants.
Publications: Corporate giving report.
Application information: The fund awards grants through an RFP process. Visit website for updated guidelines. Unsolicited requests from regional, national, and U.S.-based international organizations are not accepted.
Board meeting date(s): Oct./Nov.
Officers: David D.R. Hargreaves, C.O.O.; Brian Goldner, Pres.; Barbara Finigan, Sr. V.P. and Secy.; Deborah Thomas, Sr. V.P. and C.F.O.; Martin Trueb, Sr. V.P. and Treas.; Jeffrey Barkan, Sr. V.P and Cont.
Number of staff: 3 full-time professional; 1 full-time support; 1 part-time support.
EIN: 222538470
Other changes: The grantmaker no longer publishes application guidelines.

3078
Leslie L. & Mary B. Hecht Memorial Fund
P.O. Box 1802
Providence, RI 02901-1802

Established in 1983; supporting organization of the Salvation Army, American Cancer Society, and Shriners Hospital for Children.
Foundation type: Independent foundation.
Financial data (yr. ended 03/31/13): Assets, $5,672,040 (M); expenditures, $294,785; qualifying distributions, $258,470; giving activities include $240,111 for 3 grants (high: $80,037; low: $80,037).
Fields of interest: Hospitals (specialty); Cancer; Salvation Army.
Limitations: Applications not accepted. Giving limited to Tampa, FL, Chicago, IL, and Oklahoma City, OK.
Application information: Contributes only to pre-selected organizations.
Trustee: Bank of America, N.A.
EIN: 366774670

Other changes: The grantmaker no longer lists a phone. The grantmaker has moved from IL to RI.

3079
Horace A. Kimball and S. Ella Kimball Foundation
23 Broad St.
Westerly, RI 02891-1879
***Application address:* c/o Thomas F. Black, III, Pres., 130 Woodville Rd., Hope Valley, RI 02832-2423, tel.: (401) 364-7799**; Main URL: http://www.hkimballfoundation.org

Incorporated in 1956 in DE.
Donor: H. Earle Kimball‡.
Foundation type: Independent foundation.
Financial data (yr. ended 10/31/13): Assets, $9,291,649 (M); expenditures, $568,951; qualifying distributions, $537,056; giving activities include $490,325 for 48 grants (high: $50,000; low: $1,500).
Purpose and activities: Giving broadly in the areas of human services, the environment, and health care.
Fields of interest: Arts; Secondary school/education; Education; Environment, natural resources; Environment; Animal welfare; Hospitals (general); Health care; Health organizations, association; Food banks; Boys clubs; Human services; YM/YWCAs & YM/YWHAs; Children/youth, services; Aging, centers/services; Homeless, human services; Aging; Disabilities, people with; Economically disadvantaged; Homeless.
Type of support: General/operating support; Capital campaigns; Building/renovation; Emergency funds; Seed money; Matching/challenge support.
Limitations: Applications accepted. Giving primarily in RI. No support for religious organizations. No grants to individuals, or for feasibility studies, capital projects or multi-year commitments.
Publications: Financial statement; Grants list.
Application information: Application form and guidelines available on foundation web site; online application preferred. Application form required.
Copies of proposal: 3
Deadline(s): None, but preferably by July 15
Board meeting date(s): Mar., June, Aug., and Oct.
Officers and Trustees:* Thomas F. Black III,* Pres.; Norman D. Baker, Jr.,* Secy.-Treas.; **Edward C. Marth**.
Number of staff: 1 part-time support.
EIN: 056006130
Other changes: Paul D. Lynch is no longer a trustee.

3080
Cornelius L. King Foundation
P.O. Box 1802
Providence, RI 02901-1802 **(646) 855-1011**
***Contact:* Christine O'Donnell**
***Application address:* c/o Bank of America, N.A., 1 Bryant Park, New York, NY 10036, tel.: (646) 855-1011**

Established in 2003 in NY.
Donor: Cornelius L. King Charitable Trust.
Foundation type: Independent foundation.
Financial data (yr. ended 09/30/13): Assets, $64,198 (M); expenditures, $121,466; qualifying distributions, $120,428; giving activities include $120,000 for 34 grants (high: $25,000; low: $500).
Fields of interest: Education; Environment; Religion.
International interests: Israel.
Limitations: Applications accepted. Giving primarily in NY; some giving in CT, NJ, and VT. No grants to individuals.
Application information: Application form required.
Initial approach: Letter
Deadline(s): None
Trustees: Bruce Alter; Bank of America, N.A.
EIN: 137425372

3081
The Koffler Bornstein Family Foundation
(formerly The Koffler Family Foundation)
c/o The Koffler Group
10 Memorial Blvd., Ste. 901
Providence, RI 02903-1152

Established in 1978 in RI.
Donors: The Koffler Corp.; Lillian Koffler; Richard J. Bornstein.
Foundation type: Independent foundation.
Financial data (yr. ended 07/31/13): Assets, $5,354,764 (M); gifts received, $250,000; expenditures, $404,394; qualifying distributions, $307,860; giving activities include $307,860 for 41 grants (high: $50,000; low: $200).
Purpose and activities: Giving primarily to Jewish organizations, including welfare funds, congregations, and yeshivas; support also for higher education and hospitals.
Fields of interest: Elementary/secondary education; Higher education; Hospitals (general); Jewish federated giving programs; Jewish agencies & synagogues.
Limitations: Applications not accepted. Giving primarily in RI, with emphasis on Providence; some giving in FL. No grants to individuals.
Application information: Contributes only to pre-selected organizations.
Trustees: Richard Bornstein; Sandra Bornstein; Jo-An Kaplan; Ben Pastor.
EIN: 050376269

3082
Edward K. Love Conservation Foundation
P.O. Box 1802
Providence, RI 02901-1802
***Application address:* c/o Andrew S. Love, Jr., 414 Olive St., Ste. 1400, St. Louis, MO 63101, tel.: (314) 621-1200**

Established in MO.
Foundation type: Independent foundation.
Financial data (yr. ended 09/30/13): Assets, $7,996,941 (M); expenditures, $364,487; qualifying distributions, $334,270; giving activities include $319,026 for 9 grants (high: $95,000; low: $15,000).
Purpose and activities: Giving is limited to recipients who aid in the protection and conservation of wildlife in Missouri.
Fields of interest: Higher education; Environment, natural resources; Animals/wildlife, preservation/protection.
Limitations: Applications accepted. Giving limited to MO.
Application information:
Initial approach: Proposal
Deadline(s): None
Board of Governors: Andrew Sproule Love, Jr.; Daniel Spoule Love; Stephen C. Bradford; Scott Schnuck.
Trustee: Bank of America, N.A.
EIN: 436022352

Other changes: The grantmaker has moved from IL to RI.

3083
Masonic Grand Lodge Charities of Rhode Island, Inc.
222 Taunton Ave.
East Providence, RI 02914-4556 (401) 435-4650
Contact: Wyman P. Hallstrom, Jr., Secy.

Established in 1912 in RI.
Donors: Edward M. Docherty Memorial Fund; W. Farnum Residual Charity Trust.
Foundation type: Independent foundation.
Financial data (yr. ended 10/31/12): Assets, $6,232,608 (M); gifts received, $174,598; expenditures, $676,867; qualifying distributions, $330,704; giving activities include $330,704 for grants.
Purpose and activities: Giving for the benefit of those with a Masonic affiliation or who have been a Rhode Island resident for at least five years.
Fields of interest: Higher education; Education; Human services.
Type of support: General/operating support; Scholarships—to individuals.
Limitations: Applications accepted. Giving primarily in RI.
Application information: Application form required.
Deadline(s): Apr. 18
Officers: Russell R. Davis, Jr., Pres.; Wyman P. Hallstrom III, V.P.; Wyman P. Hallstrom, Jr., Secy.; Michael J. Barboza, Treas.
Directors: Raymond E. Hassell; James Lapostora; David Lavery; Manuel M. Lewis; Kenneth B. Phillips; and 5 additional directors.
EIN: 056014340
Other changes: Russell R. Davis, Jr. has replaced Leon G. Knusden as Pres. Wyman P. Hallstrom III has replaced Douglas E. Connell as V.P. Richard Andrews, James W. Bethel and Gilbert J. Fontes are no longer directors.

3084
McCabe Catholic Charities
c/o Bank of America, N.A.
P.O. Box 1802
Providence, RI 02901-1802

Established in 1983; supporting organization of Diocese of Mobile, Dominican Fathers Priory, Franciscan Friars, Franciscan Friars of Atonement, Glenmary Home Missionaries, Immaculate Heart Missions, Josephite Fathers, Missionary Servants of the Most Holy Trinity, Passionist Missionaries, Priests of the Sacred Heart, Sacred Heart Monastery, Society of the Propagation of Faith, St. Anthony's Guild, and St. Gabriel's Monastery.
Foundation type: Independent foundation.
Financial data (yr. ended 06/30/13): Assets, $5,254,237 (M); expenditures, $398,915; qualifying distributions, $366,869; giving activities include $344,988 for 13 grants (high: $49,284; low: $24,642).
Fields of interest: Catholic agencies & churches.
Limitations: Applications not accepted.
Application information: Unsolicited requests for funds not accepted.
Trustee: Bank of America, N.A.
EIN: 366774682

3085
Frederick McDonald Trust
c/o Bank of America, NA
P.O. Box 1802
Providence, RI 02901-1802
Contact: Sara J. Rosen
E-mail: christine.l.o'donnell@ustrust.com; **Main URL: https://www.bankofamerica.com/philanthropic/grantmaking.go**

Established in 1950 in NY.
Donor: Frederick McDonald†.
Foundation type: Independent foundation.
Financial data (yr. ended 12/31/12): Assets, $3,049,196 (M); expenditures, $175,233; qualifying distributions, $152,788; giving activities include $140,000 for 15 grants (high: $15,000; low: $5,000).
Purpose and activities: Giving to promote quality educational, human services, and health care programming for underserved populations in Albany, New York.
Fields of interest: Education; Health care; Youth development.
Type of support: General/operating support; Annual campaigns; Capital campaigns; Equipment; Program development; Curriculum development.
Limitations: Applications accepted. Giving limited to Albany, NY. No grants to individuals.
Application information: Application guidelines are available on the trust's website. Application form required.
Initial approach: Apply online
Deadline(s): May 1
Trustee: Bank of America, N.A.
EIN: 146014233

3086
Colonel Stanley R. McNeil Foundation
P.O. Box 1802
Providence, RI 02901-1802
E-mail: ilgrantmaking@ustrust.com; Main URL: http://www.bankofamerica.com/grantmaking

Established in 1993 in IL.
Donor: Stanley McNeil.
Foundation type: Independent foundation.
Financial data (yr. ended 11/30/13): Assets, $20,532,998 (M); expenditures, $1,000,939; qualifying distributions, $914,243; giving activities include $776,000 for 40 grants (high: $125,000; low: $2,500).
Purpose and activities: Giving primarily for children's causes, healthcare, and to start-up initiatives within the human services or arts and cultural arenas.
Fields of interest: Arts; Education; Health care; Human services; Children/youth, services.
Type of support: General/operating support; Building/renovation; Equipment; Program development; Curriculum development; Scholarship funds; Research; Matching/challenge support.
Limitations: Giving primarily in the Chicago, IL, area. No grants to individuals, or for endowments, capital projects, or multi-year funding requests.
Publications: Application guidelines.
Application information: The foundation will consider requests for general operations only if the organization's operating budget is less than $1 million. Application form not required.
Copies of proposal: 1
Deadline(s): Feb. 1 and June 1
Final notification: June 30 (for the Feb. deadline), Nov. 30 (for the June deadline)
Trustee: Bank of America, N.A.
Number of staff: 1 full-time professional; 3 full-time support.
EIN: 367016333
Other changes: The grantmaker has moved from IL to RI.

3087
Newport Fed Charitable Foundation
Newport, RI

The foundation terminated.

3088
John W. Parmelee Foundation
c/o Bank of America, N.A.
P.O. Box 1802
Providence, RI 02901-1802

Foundation type: Independent foundation.
Financial data (yr. ended 04/30/13): Assets, $3,214,751 (M); expenditures, $150,508; qualifying distributions, $127,915; giving activities include $112,000 for 3 grants (high: $41,000; low: $30,000).
Fields of interest: Salvation Army; Family services; Human services; Christian agencies & churches; Religion.
Limitations: Applications not accepted. Giving primarily in IL.
Application information: Unsolicited requests for funds not accepted.
Trustee: Bank of America, N.A.
EIN: 366038529
Other changes: The grantmaker has moved from IL to RI.

3089
The Rhode Island Foundation
(also known as The Rhode Island Community Foundation)
1 Union Station
Providence, RI 02903-1746 (401) 274-4564
FAX: (401) 331-8085;
E-mail: nsteinberg@rifoundation.org; Main URL: http://www.rifoundation.org
Facebook: http://www.facebook.com/rhodeislandfoundation?ref=mf
RSS Feed: http://www.rifoundation.org/DefaultPermissions/Home/tabid/36/moduleid/927/RSS.aspx
Video Directory: http://www.rifoundation.org/AboutUs/VideosOurWorkintheCommunity/tabid/509/Default.aspx

Incorporated in 1916 in RI (includes The Rhode Island Community Foundation in 1984).
Foundation type: Community foundation.
Financial data (yr. ended 12/31/12): Assets, $678,230,790 (M); gifts received, $38,467,685; expenditures, $36,048,030; giving activities include $28,267,948 for grants.
Purpose and activities: The foundation seeks to promote philanthropic activities that will improve the living conditions and well-being of the inhabitants of Rhode Island.
Fields of interest: Performing arts; Historic preservation/historical societies; Arts; Libraries/library science; Education; Environment, natural resources; Environment; Animal welfare; Health care; Health organizations, association; AIDS; Legal services; Housing/shelter; Children/youth, services; Family services; Human services, emergency aid; Minorities/immigrants, centers/services; Homeless, human services; Human services; Nonprofit management; Community/economic development; Voluntarism promotion; Government/public administration; Leadership development; Public affairs.
Type of support: General/operating support; Management development/capacity building; Capital campaigns; Building/renovation; Equipment; Land acquisition; Emergency funds; Program development; Conferences/seminars; Film/video/radio; Publication; Seed money; Fellowships; Scholarship funds; Technical assistance; Consulting services; Program evaluation; Program-related investments/loans; Grants to individuals; Scholarships—to individuals; Matching/challenge support.
Limitations: Applications accepted. Giving through discretionary funds limited to RI. No support for religious organizations for sectarian purposes (except as specified by donors). No grants for endowment funds, research, hospital equipment, capital needs of health organizations, annual campaigns, deficit financing, or educational institutions for general operating expenses.
Publications: Application guidelines; Annual report (including application guidelines); Financial statement; Grants list; Informational brochure; Informational brochure (including application guidelines); Newsletter; Occasional report; Program policy statement.
Application information: Visit foundation web site for application guidelines as well as scholarship information. Application form required.
Initial approach: Letter of intent
Copies of proposal: 1
Deadline(s): Varies
Board meeting date(s): Varies
Final notification: Varies
Officers and Directors:* Frederick K. Butler,* Chair.; Neil Steinberg,* C.E.O. and Pres.; Jessica David, V.P., Strategy and Public Affairs; Daniel Kertzner, V.P., Grants Progs.; Kathleen Malin, V.P., Technology and Opers. Mgmt.; Jill Pfitzenmayer, Ph.D., V.P., Initiative for Nonprofit Excellence; James Sanzi, V.P., Devel.; Jennifer Reid, Cont.; **Michael K. Allio**; Mary W.C. Daly; Jorge O. Elorza; Patricia J. Flanagan, M.D.; Ned Handy; Marie J. Langlois; Mary F. Lovejoy; H. Ronald K. Machtley; Cynthia Reed; Hon. Ernest C. Torres.
Number of staff: 30 full-time professional; 4 part-time professional; 11 full-time support.
EIN: 222604963
Other changes: Lorne Adrian is no longer a director.

3090
F. A. O. Schwarz Family Foundation
P.O. Box 1802
Providence, RI 02901-1802

Established in 1991 in NY.
Donors: Dorothy S. Hines; Alex Millard; Eric Schwarz; Frederick A.O. Schwarz III; H. Marshall Schwarz.
Foundation type: Independent foundation.
Financial data (yr. ended 04/30/13): Assets, $2,699,434 (M); expenditures, $506,011; qualifying distributions, $488,877; giving activities include $410,750 for 52 grants (high: $50,000; low: $500).
Fields of interest: Museums; Higher education; Education; Hospitals (general); Health care; Youth development; Human services; American Red Cross; Children, services; United Ways and Federated Giving Programs.

Limitations: Applications not accepted. Giving primarily in Gainesville, FL; Boston, MA; and New York, NY. No grants to individuals.
Application information: Contributes only to pre-selected organizations.
Trustees: Alex Millard; **Peter Schastny**; Eliza Ladd Schwarz; Frederick A.O. Schwarz III; Rae Paige Schwarz; Molly Wing-Berman; Bank of America, N.A.
EIN: 136986221
Other changes: Eric Schwarz is no longer a trustee.

3091
George Dudley Seymour Trust
c/o Bank of America, N.A., Fdn. and Philanthropic Svcs.
P.O. Box 1802
Providence, RI 02901-1802
***Application Address:* c/o Bank of America, Attn.: Carmen Britt, 200 Glastonbury Blvd., Glastonbury, CT 06033**

Established in 1986 in CT.
Foundation type: Independent foundation.
Financial data (yr. ended 07/31/13): Assets, $6,000,674 (M); expenditures, $521,030; qualifying distributions, $479,878; giving activities include $459,000 for 1 grant.
Purpose and activities: Grants are made primarily for purchase of lands within the state of Connecticut to be delivered as recreational centers in the towns, and secondarily for the preservation of the history of Connecticut and its cities and towns.
Fields of interest: Public affairs.
Type of support: General/operating support; Land acquisition.
Limitations: Applications accepted. Giving limited to CT. No grants to individuals.
Publications: Application guidelines.
Application information: Application form required.
Initial approach: Letter
Deadline(s): None
Board meeting date(s): June
Trustee: Bank of America, N.A.
EIN: 066021772

3092
Shaw's Supermarket Charitable Foundation
(formerly Shaw's Market Trust Fund)
P.O. Box 1802
Providence, RI 02901-1802

Trust established in 1959 in ME.
Donor: Shaw's Supermarkets, Inc.
Foundation type: Company-sponsored foundation.
Financial data (yr. ended 07/31/13): Assets, $6,306 (M); expenditures, $268,880; qualifying distributions, $268,064; giving activities include $267,600 for 18 grants (high: $160,000; low: $300).
Purpose and activities: The foundation supports organizations involved with health, cancer, housing accessibility modifications, human services, and military and veterans.
Fields of interest: Health care, clinics/centers; Health care; Cancer; Home accessibility modifications; YM/YWCAs & YM/YWHAs; United Ways and Federated Giving Programs; Military/veterans' organizations.
Type of support: General/operating support; Capital campaigns; Building/renovation.
Limitations: Applications accepted. Giving limited to areas of company operations in MA, southern ME, and southern NH. No grants to individuals.
Application information: Application form not required.
Initial approach: Proposal
Deadline(s): None
Trustee: Bank of America, N.A.
EIN: 016008389
Other changes: The grantmaker no longer lists a separate application address.

3093
The Textron Charitable Trust
c/o Textron Inc.
40 Westminster St.
Providence, RI **02903-2525 (401) 457-3573**
Contact: Karen Warfield, Mgr., Community Affairs
***E-mail:* kwarfield@textron.com**; Main URL: http://www.textron.com/about/commitment/corp-giving/

Trust established in 1953 in VT.
Donors: Textron Inc.; Cessna Foundation, Inc.
Foundation type: Company-sponsored foundation.
Financial data (yr. ended 12/31/12): Assets, $19,727,812 (M); expenditures, $2,927,600; qualifying distributions, $2,874,575; giving activities include $1,901,262 for 111 grants (high: $350,000; low: $1,000), and $838,611 for 1,895 employee matching gifts.
Purpose and activities: The foundation supports organizations involved with arts and culture, education, the environment, animals and wildlife, health, workforce development, hunger, housing, youth development, human services, community revitalization, minorities, women, and low-income individuals.
Fields of interest: Arts; Education, early childhood education; Higher education; Education, ESL programs; Education, services; Education, reading; Education; Environment; Animals/wildlife; Hospitals (general); Public health; Health care; Employment, training; Employment; Food services; Food banks; Housing/shelter; Youth development, adult & child programs; Youth development; Family services; Homeless, human services; Human services; Economic development; Community/economic development; United Ways and Federated Giving Programs; Engineering/technology; Minorities; Women; Economically disadvantaged.
Type of support: Sponsorships; General/operating support; Continuing support; Capital campaigns; Building/renovation; Equipment; Program development; Internship funds; Scholarship funds; Technical assistance; Employee matching gifts; Employee-related scholarships; Matching/challenge support.
Limitations: Applications accepted. Giving on a national basis in areas of company operations, with emphasis on Washington, DC, KS, NJ, RI, and VA. No support for political, fraternal, or veterans' organizations, religious institutions, or discriminatory organizations. No grants to individuals (except for employee-related scholarships), or for endowments, land acquisition, debt reduction, or demonstration projects; no loans.
Publications: Application guidelines; Program policy statement.
Application information: Proposals should be no longer than 5 pages. The Associated Grant Makers (AGM) Common Proposal Form is also accepted. Support is limited to 1 contribution per organization during any given year. Multi-year commitments will be considered but are limited. Application form required.
Initial approach: Download application form and mail proposal and application form to foundation
Copies of proposal: 1
Deadline(s): Mar. 1 and Sept. 1
Board meeting date(s): Quarterly
Charitable Contributions Committee: John D. Butler; Terry O' Donnell; Deborah Imondi; Jim Walters; Richard Yates.
Trustees: Robert Rowland; Adele J. Suddes; Keith Watson; State Street Bank & Trust Co.
Number of staff: 1 full-time professional.
EIN: 256115832

3094
van Beuren Charitable Foundation, Inc.
130 Bellevue Ave., Ste. 304
Newport, RI 02840-3291 (401) 619-5910
Contact: Elizabeth R. Lynn, Exec. Dir.
FAX: (401) 619-5917;
E-mail: kdame@vbcfoundation.org; Contact for questions regarding grant application: Kim Dame, Grants Mgr., tel.: (401) 619-5910; Main URL: http://www.vbcfoundation.org
Facebook: https://www.facebook.com/pages/Van-Beuren-Charitable-Foundation/153747571340286
Grants List: http://vbcfoundation.org/recent-recipients/
Twitter: https://twitter.com/vbcfoundation

Established in 1986 in RI.
Donor: Members of the van Beuren family.
Foundation type: Independent foundation.
Financial data (yr. ended 12/31/12): Assets, $200,930,376 (M); gifts received, $6,640,947; expenditures, $4,517,003; qualifying distributions, $3,882,263; giving activities include $3,345,963 for 146 grants (high: $261,000; low: $100), and $28,241 for foundation-administered programs.
Purpose and activities: The primary mission of the foundation is to build community value by protecting and preserving Newport County's unique quality of place, and improving the quality of life for its residents. Program areas include Health, Education, Land Use and Conservation, and for Historic Preservation.
Fields of interest: Historic preservation/historical societies; Education; Environment, land resources; Health care; Human services.
Type of support: General/operating support; Capital campaigns; Building/renovation; Land acquisition; Endowments; Program development.
Limitations: Applications accepted. Giving primarily in Newport County, RI. No grants to individuals.
Publications: Application guidelines; Annual report (including application guidelines); Grants list.
Application information: Application form required.
Initial approach: Use online application process on foundation web site
Copies of proposal: 1
Deadline(s): See foundation web site for current deadline date
Board meeting date(s): Fall
Officers and Directors:* Hope Hill van Beuren,* Chair.; **Archbold D. van Beuren,* Pres.**; Leonard B. Boehner, Secy.; **Stephen L. Glascock, Treas.**; Elizabeth R. Lynn,* Exec. Dir.; Roger E. Kass; Andrea van Beuren; Barbara van Beuren; Helene B. van Beuren.
Number of staff: 2 full-time support.
EIN: 222773769
Other changes: Archbold D. van Beuren has replaced Barbara van Buren as Pres.
Stephen L. Glascock is now Treas.

3095
The Washington Trust Charitable Foundation
c/o The Washington Trust Co.
23 Broad St.
Westerly, RI 02891-1879 (401) 348-1207
Contact: Dennis L. Algiere, Dir., Community Affairs
Main URL: http://www.washtrust.com/home/about/community

Established in 1994 in RI.
Donor: The Washington Trust Co.
Foundation type: Company-sponsored foundation.
Financial data (yr. ended 12/31/12): Assets, $2,759,713 (M); gifts received, $400,000; expenditures, $347,399; qualifying distributions, $340,233; giving activities include $340,233 for 86 grants (high: $53,000; low: $200).
Purpose and activities: The foundation supports programs designed to promote affordable housing and revitalization; business and economic development; youth and family services; health and human services; arts and culture; colleges, universities, and libraries; and conservation and the environment.
Fields of interest: Museums; Arts; Higher education; Libraries (public); Education; Environment, natural resources; Environment; Hospitals (general); Health care; Housing/shelter; YM/YWCAs & YM/YWHAs; Youth, services; Family services; Human services; Business/industry; Community/economic development; United Ways and Federated Giving Programs.
Type of support: General/operating support; Continuing support; Capital campaigns; Building/renovation; Program development.
Limitations: Applications accepted. Giving primarily in areas of company operations in southeastern CT, MA, and RI. No grants to individuals.
Publications: Application guidelines.
Application information: Application form required.
Initial approach: Letter
Copies of proposal: 1
Deadline(s): Oct. 1
Trustee: The Washington Trust Co.
EIN: 050477294

SOUTH CAROLINA

3096
The Bailey Foundation
c/o TD Bank, N.A.
P.O. Box 494
Clinton, SC 29325-0494 (864) 938-2632
Contact: Robert S. Link, Jr., Admin.
FAX: (864) 938-2669

Trust established in 1951 in SC. Classified as a company-sponsored operating foundation in 1999.
Donors: M.S. Bailey & Son, Bankers; Clinton Investment Co.
Foundation type: Operating foundation.
Financial data (yr. ended 08/31/13): Assets, $4,435,587 (M); gifts received, $10,000; expenditures, $310,935; qualifying distributions, $278,510; giving activities include $209,100 for 32 grants (high: $50,000; low: $1,500), $40,000 for 10 grants to individuals (high: $5,000; low: $2,500), and $29,410 for 13 employee matching gifts.
Purpose and activities: The foundation supports health clinics and organizations involved with education, human services, community development, and Christianity and awards college scholarships to students graduating from public high schools in Laurens County, South Carolina.
Fields of interest: Higher education; Education; Health care, clinics/centers; YM/YWCAs & YM/YWHAs; Children/youth, services; Residential/custodial care, senior continuing care; Human services; Community/economic development; United Ways and Federated Giving Programs; Christian agencies & churches.
Type of support: Annual campaigns; Capital campaigns; Building/renovation; Endowments; Scholarship funds; Employee matching gifts; Scholarships—to individuals; Matching/challenge support.
Limitations: Applications accepted. Giving limited to Laurens County, SC. No grants to individuals (except for scholarships), or for general operating support.
Publications: Annual report; Informational brochure (including application guidelines).
Application information: An application form is required for scholarships.
Initial approach: Proposal; contact guidance counselor at Clinton High School or Laurens High School for application form for scholarships
Copies of proposal: 1
Deadline(s): Oct. 1; Apr. 15 of applicant's senior year in high school for scholarships
Board meeting date(s): Periodically
Final notification: May 15
Advisory Committee: George H. Cornelson IV, Chair.; Martin S. Cornelson; C. Bailey Dixon; Norman W. Dixon; Walter S. Montgomery, Sr.; **Fleming Patterson**; James L. Switzer, Jr.; Toccoa W. Switzer; Virginia G. Vance.
Trustee: TD Bank, N.A.
EIN: 576018387

3097
Mary Black Foundation, Inc.
349 E. Main St., Ste. 100
Spartanburg, SC 29302-1917 (864) 573-9500
Contact: Kathy Dunleavy, Pres.
FAX: (864) 573-5805; Main URL: http://www.maryblackfoundation.org
Blog: http://www.maryblackfoundation.org/blog
Facebook: http://www.facebook.com/pages/Spartanburg-SC/Mary-Black-Foundation/50398562097
Grants List: http://www.maryblackfoundation.org/grantmaking/grant-history
Twitter: http://twitter.com/MaryBFoundation
YouTube: http://www.youtube.com/user/MaryBFoundation

Established in 1986 in SC; converted from the proceeds from the sale of Mary Black Memorial Hospital in 1996.
Foundation type: Independent foundation.
Financial data (yr. ended 12/31/12): Assets, $74,873,952 (M); expenditures, $3,893,556; qualifying distributions, $3,749,026; giving activities include $1,450,913 for 41 grants (high: $250,000; low: $100), and $3,739,390 for foundation-administered programs.
Purpose and activities: The foundation's mission is to improve the health and wellness of the people and communities of Spartanburg County, South Carolina. Funding priorities are Healthy Eating and Active Living and Early Childhood Development.
Fields of interest: Public health; Health care; Health organizations, public education.
Type of support: General/operating support; Continuing support; Management development/capacity building; Program development; Seed money; Technical assistance; Program evaluation.
Limitations: Applications accepted. Giving primarily in Spartanburg County, SC. No support for political organizations or for proselytizing religious work. No grants to individuals or for general fundraising solicitations.
Publications: Application guidelines; Annual report; Financial statement; Grants list; Informational brochure (including application guidelines); Occasional report.
Application information: See foundation web site for application guidelines and procedures: www.maryblackfoundation.org. Application form required.
Initial approach: Grant Consultation is required for Healthy Eating and Active Living and Early Childhood Development applications.
Copies of proposal: 1
Deadline(s): Quarterly (Mar. 1, June 1, Sept. 1, and Dec. 1)
Board meeting date(s): 3rd Tues. of Feb., March, April, Aug., Sep., Nov., and Dec.
Final notification: Generally within 90 days
Officers and Trustees:* Ruth L. Cate,* Chair.; Kathy Dunleavy, C.E.O. and Pres.; Molly Talbot-Metz, V.P., Progs.; Ethan Burroughs; William M. Coker; Anna Converse; A. Tony Fisher; Colleen Perry Keith, Ph.D.; Dr. James A. Littlefield; Jack McBride; D. Byrd Miller III; Betsy Teter; Doris H. Tidwell.
Number of staff: 4 full-time professional; 2 full-time support.
EIN: 570843135

3098
The Byerly Foundation
P.O. Drawer 1925
Hartsville, SC 29551-1925 **(843) 383-2400**
Contact: Richard A. Puffer, Exec. Dir.
***FAX:* (843) 383-0661; E-mail for Richard A. Puffer: rapuffer@byerlyfoundation.org**; Main URL: http://www.byerlyfoundation.org
Facebook: https://www.facebook.com/ByerlyFoundation
YouTube: https://www.youtube.com/channel/UCENOFjTAKZKuVtaNLiPOR8Q

Established in 1995 in SC; converted from the sale of local hospital.
Foundation type: Independent foundation.
Financial data (yr. ended 09/30/12): Assets, $21,345,719 (M); expenditures, $946,606; qualifying distributions, $790,692; giving activities include $682,810 for 17 grants (high: $453,450; low: $1,000).
Purpose and activities: The mission of the foundation is to improve the quality of life in Hartsville, SC.
Fields of interest: Education; Economic development; Community/economic development.
Type of support: Curriculum development; General/operating support; Continuing support; Capital campaigns; Building/renovation; Equipment; Program development; Seed money; Technical assistance; Consulting services; Program evaluation; Matching/challenge support.
Limitations: Giving primarily in Hartsville, SC. No support for sectarian religious programs, or intermediate organizations. No grants to individuals, or for debt and existing obligations, lobbying or political campaigns, technical or specialized research, fundraising, teams or special events, advertising, or memorials.
Publications: Application guidelines; Annual report; Financial statement; Grants list; Occasional report.
Application information: Application form required.
***Initial approach:* Telephone or brief letter of inquiry**
Copies of proposal: 1
Board meeting date(s): Monthly, on the last Tues.
Officer: Richard A. Puffer, Exec. Dir.
Directors: Steve Avant; Monty Bell; **Harris DeLoach**; **Brianna Douglas**; Alvin T. Heatley; **Nancy McGee**; **Jerome Reyes**; Barry Saunders; **Todd Shifflett**; Johnna Shirley; Rob Tiede.
Number of staff: 1 part-time professional; 1 part-time support.
EIN: 570324909
Other changes: Flossie Hopkins and Anthony Floyd are no longer directors.
The grantmaker now publishes application guidelines.

3099
Community Foundation of Greenville, Inc.
630 E. Washington St., Ste. A
Greenville, SC 29601 (864) 233-5925
Contact: Robert W. Morris, Pres.
FAX: (864) 242-9292;
E-mail: rmorris@cfgreenville.org; Main URL: http://www.cfgreenville.org
Facebook: http://www.facebook.com/pages/Community-Foundation-of-Greenville/77607907249
Scholarship inquiry e-mail: dcooper@cfgreenville.org

Established in 1956 in SC; incorporated in 1970.
Foundation type: Community foundation.
Financial data (yr. ended 12/31/12): Assets, $41,548,322 (M); gifts received, $5,738,535; expenditures, $7,879,235; giving activities include $6,933,642 for 155+ grants (high: $485,550).
Purpose and activities: The foundation exists to enhance the quality of life of citizens of Greater Greenville, SC by linking philanthropic leadership, charitable resources and civic influence with needs and opportunities in the community.
Fields of interest: Arts; Education, early childhood education; Higher education; Education; Environment; Health care; Children/youth, services;

Human services; United Ways and Federated Giving Programs; Christian agencies & churches.
Type of support: Equipment; Emergency funds; Program development; Conferences/seminars; Seed money; Internship funds; Scholarship funds; Technical assistance; In-kind gifts; Matching/challenge support.
Limitations: Applications accepted. Giving limited to Greenville County, SC. No grants to individuals (except for scholarships), or for general operational expenses or existing debts; no multi-year grants.
Publications: Application guidelines; Annual report; Informational brochure; Newsletter; Program policy statement.
Application information: Visit foundation web site for application forms and guidelines. Application form required.
Initial approach: Telephone or letter
***Deadline(s):* Varies**
Board meeting date(s): Jan., Mar., May, July, Sept., and Nov.
***Final notification:* Varies**
Officers and Board Members:* Harriet Goldsmith,* Chair.; Dick Wilkerson,* Vice-Chair.; Robert W. Morris, Pres.; Susan Priester,* Secy.; Sharon Gibbs, C.F.O.; Doug Kroske,* Treas.; J. Tod Hyche, Legal Counsel; Perry Gilreath, Asst. Secy.; Bill Bridges, Asst. Treas.; Ann Bryan; Ben Clauss; Mark Cooter; Mark Crocker; Jon Good; Todd Harward; Lesa Kastler; Adela Mendoza; Marie Monroe; Rob Morgan; Travis Olmert; Frances Patterson; Magaly Penn; Michelle Seaver; Steve Spinks; Ralph Sweeney; Brenda Thames; Wendy Walden; Angela Webb.
Number of staff: 5 full-time professional; 1 part-time professional.
EIN: 576019318
Other changes: Tracy Hardaway, Emilyn Sanders, Joe Sullivan, and Terri Wilfong are no longer board members.

3100
Community Foundation of the Lowcountry
(formerly Hilton Head Island Foundation, Inc.)
4 Northridge Dr., Ste. A
P.O. Box 23019
Hilton Head Island, SC 29925-3019 (843) 681-9100
Contact: Denise K. Spencer, C.E.O.
FAX: (843) 681-9101;
E-mail: foundation@cf-lowcountry.org; Main URL: http://www.cf-lowcountry.org
Facebook: http://www.facebook.com/pages/Community-Foundation-of-the-Lowcountry/77341029228
Twitter: http://twitter.com/cflowcountry
YouTube: http://www.youtube.com/user/CFLowcountry

Established in 1983 in SC; converted to a community foundation in 1994 from the proceeds of the sale of Hilton Head Hospital to AMI.
Foundation type: Community foundation.
Financial data (yr. ended 06/30/12): Assets, $57,525,194 (M); gifts received, $20,680,838; expenditures, $5,922,592; giving activities include $4,234,331 for grants.
Purpose and activities: The foundation strengthens the community by connecting people, resources and needs.
Fields of interest: Arts; Education; Environment; Health care; Human services; Community development, neighborhood development; Community/economic development.
Type of support: Management development/capacity building; Building/renovation; Equipment; Program development; Seed money; Curriculum development; Technical assistance; Consulting services; Program evaluation; Scholarships—to individuals; Matching/challenge support.
Limitations: Applications accepted. Giving limited to Beaufort, Colleton, Hampton and Jasper counties, SC. No support for sectarian or religious activities. No grants to individuals (except for scholarships), or for capital campaigns, endowments, or special events or fundraisers.
Publications: Application guidelines; Annual report; Financial statement; Grants list; Informational brochure; Informational brochure (including application guidelines); Newsletter.
Application information: Visit foundation Web site for application forms and guidelines. Application form required.
Initial approach: Telephone or letter
Copies of proposal: 11
Deadline(s): Apr. 1, Aug. 1, and Dec. 1
Board meeting date(s): Jan., Mar., May, July, Sept., and Nov.
Final notification: Approximately 3 months after deadline
Officers and Trustees:* Perry Washington,* Chair.; Denise K. Spencer,* C.E.O. and Pres.; Carl L. Conklin,* V.P., Finance and Admin.; Emmy Rooney,* V.P., Devel. and Donor Svcs.; Cynthia Smith, Ph.D.*, V.P., Grantmaking and Community Leadership; Carolyn Torgersen,* V.P., Mktg. and Comms.; Donna Bafundo; Rabbi Brad Bloom; Denis Bonnett; **Jeff Bradley**; Marva J. Brooks; Ethel Denmark; Berryman W. Edwards; Eric Esquivel; Jeff Evans; J. Dudley King, Jr.; Helen S. Mavrogordato; Elizabeth B. Mayo; Joyce Patterson; William Stinnett III; John Weymouth; J. Eric Woods.
Number of staff: 6 full-time professional; 3 part-time professional; 1 full-time support.
EIN: 570756987
Other changes: Perry Washington has replaced Ernst W. Bruderer as Chair.
Perry L. Washington is no longer a trustee.

3101
Daniel-Mickel Foundation
(formerly The Daniel Foundation of South Carolina)
P.O. Box 9278
Greenville, SC 29604-9278 (864) 271-7503
Contact: Tamara Lawson, Asst.
E-mail: tamara@thelewiscompany.org; Main URL: http://www.daniel-mickel-foundation.org

Established in 1978 in SC as partial successor to The Daniel Foundation.
Donors: Daniel International Corp.; Charles E. Daniel†.
Foundation type: Independent foundation.
Financial data (yr. ended 12/31/12): Assets, $15,980,461 (M); expenditures, $894,402; qualifying distributions, $807,677; giving activities include $783,000 for 92 grants (high: $100,000; low: $100).
Purpose and activities: Giving primarily for higher education, art, healthcare, and upstate SC community development.
Fields of interest: Performing arts, orchestras; Higher education; Hospitals (general); Human services.
Type of support: Continuing support; Management development/capacity building; Capital campaigns; Building/renovation; Equipment; Endowments; Program development; Seed money; Curriculum development; Program evaluation; Matching/challenge support.
Limitations: Applications accepted. Giving primarily in SC. No grants to individuals, or for scholarships.
Publications: Annual report; Program policy statement.
Application information:
***Initial approach:* Use application system on foundation web site**
Copies of proposal: 1
Deadline(s): None
Board meeting date(s): May, Aug., Nov., and Feb.
Final notification: 4 months
Officers and Trustees:* Minor M. Shaw,* Chair. and Pres.; Buck A. Mickel,* V.P.; Charles Mickel,* V.P.; **Tamara S. Lawson, EA*, Secy.-Treas.**
EIN: 570673409
Other changes: Tamara S. Lawson, EA has replaced Ken Lewis as Secy.-Treas.
Ken Lewis, Secy.-Treas., is deceased.

3102
Foothills Community Foundation
907 N. Main St.
P.O. Box 1228
Anderson, SC 29621-5526 (864) 222-9096
Contact: Robert M. Rainey, Pres.
FAX: (864) 222-9727;
E-mail: info@foothillsfoundation.org; Main URL: http://www.foothillscommunityfoundation.org

Established in 1999 in SC.
Foundation type: Community foundation.
Financial data (yr. ended 06/30/13): Assets, $11,421,408 (M); gifts received, $609,118; expenditures, $984,550; giving activities include $671,128 for 23+ grants (high: $65,285).
Purpose and activities: The foundation seeks to retain and nurture the charitable wealth of the community for the perpetual benefit of all in the foundation's service area.
Fields of interest: Arts; Education, public education; Higher education, college; Education; Health care; Recreation; Youth, services; Community/economic development; Foundations (community); United Ways and Federated Giving Programs.
Type of support: Continuing support; Capital campaigns; Scholarship funds.
Limitations: Applications accepted. Giving primarily in Abbeville, Anderson, Oconee, and Pickens counties, SC.
Publications: Annual report; Financial statement; Occasional report.
Application information: Visit foundation web site for application information.
Initial approach: Telephone
Officer and Directors:* Robert M. Rainey, Pres.; Lamar Bailes; James T. Boseman; Glenn D. Buddin, Jr.; Irvin L. Cauthen; **Fred L. Foster**; Ann D. Herbert; F. Stevon Kay; Theresa G. Knopp, M.D.; John A. Miller, Jr.; Jane W. Mudd; William B. Pickens; Edward A. Spitz; **D. Gray Suggs**; **Joseph J. Turner, Jr.**; **Robert W. Wilkes**; S. Smith Wham.
Number of staff: 1 full-time professional; 1 part-time support.
EIN: 582453349

3103
The Graham Foundation
531 S. Main St., Ste. ML-7
Greenville, SC 29601-2500
Contact: William A. Bridges, Managing Tr.
FAX: (864) 233-3667;
E-mail: bill@thegrahamfoundation.org; **Additional e-mails: Eleanor B. Dunlap: eleanor@thegrahamfoundation.org, Stephen J. Lambert, Tr.: steve@thegrahamfoundation.org**; Main URL: http://www.thegrahamfoundation.org

Established in 1985 in SC.
Donors: Allen J. Graham†; Frances G. MacIlwinen†; Allen J. Graham Marital Trust.
Foundation type: Independent foundation.
Financial data (yr. ended 08/31/13): Assets, $52,090,586 (M); gifts received, $5,065,500; expenditures, $2,866,639; qualifying distributions, $2,442,188; giving activities include $2,014,125 for 105 grants (high: $210,000; low: $1,000).
Purpose and activities: Giving to organizations that make a significant difference for the betterment of residents of Greenville and upstate, South Carolina, and are focused on needs that are specific and contained. The primary areas of focus are the arts, children, community welfare, education, the environment, and religion.
Fields of interest: Performing arts; Historic preservation/historical societies; Arts; Elementary/secondary education; Education; Health care; Human services; Community/economic development; Children.
Type of support: Capital campaigns; Building/renovation; Equipment; Endowments; Matching/challenge support.
Limitations: Applications accepted. Giving primarily in Greenville and upstate, SC. No support for political purposes. No grants to individuals or for scholarships.
Publications: Application guidelines.
Application information: Application guidelines, procedures, deadlines, application form available on foundation web site. Application form required.
Initial approach: Letter or telephone, or e-mail
Copies of proposal: 3
Deadline(s): See application page on foundation web site for current deadline
Board meeting date(s): Feb., May, Aug. and Nov.
Final notification: Generally within 30 days after the end of the month following the board meeting dates.
Trustees: William A. Bridges; Stephen J. Lambert; Susan R. Lambert.
Agent: Bank of America, N.A.
EIN: 570805774

3104
The Joanna Foundation
P.O. Box 308
Sullivans Island, SC 29482-0308 (843) 883-9199
Contact: Margaret P. Schachte, V.P.
E-mail: info@joannafoundation.org; Main URL: http://www.joannafoundation.org
Grants List: http://joannafoundation.org/grants/recipients/

Established in 1945 in SC.
Donor: Marquette Charitable Organization.
Foundation type: Independent foundation.
Financial data (yr. ended 12/31/12): Assets, $3,647,126 (M); expenditures, $216,641; qualifying distributions, $176,556; giving activities include $132,650 for 44 grants (high: $25,000; low: $500).
Purpose and activities: Primary areas of interest include higher education, youth, the environment, community development, the arts, health, and public benefit.
Fields of interest: Historic preservation/historical societies; Arts; Higher education; Environment; Health care; Human services; Children/youth, services; Community/economic development; Public affairs.
Type of support: Capital campaigns; General/operating support; Building/renovation; Program development; Matching/challenge support.
Limitations: Applications accepted. Giving primarily in Berkeley, Charleston, Dorchester, Laurens and Newberry counties, SC. No grants for debt reduction, research projects, recurring expenses, conferences, symposia or publications or for tickets, tables, advertising, or for fundraising events.
Publications: Grants list; Informational brochure (including application guidelines).
Application information: See foundation website for complete application guidelines. Application form required.
Initial approach: Letter
Copies of proposal: 8
Board meeting date(s): Feb., June, and Nov.
Officers: Walter C. Regnery,* Pres.; Margaret P. Schachte,* V.P.; Charles E. Menefee, Jr.,* Secy.-Treas.
Trustees: Mary Beth Greenslade; Yonge R. Jones; Eugene J. Parker; Eugenie F. Regnery; Particia L. Regnery.
Number of staff: 1 part-time professional.
EIN: 570314444

3105
Clarence H. and Anna E. Lutz Foundation
1373 West End Rd.
Chester, SC 29706-8030 (803) 385-5357
Contact: Dewey G. Guyton, Pres.; Joan L. Guyton, V.P. and Treas.
E-mail: dguyton@lutzfoundation.org; Main URL: http://www.lutzfoundation.org/
Grants List: http://www.lutzfoundation.org/index.php?location=Grants2011

Established in 1996 in NC and SC.
Foundation type: Independent foundation.
Financial data (yr. ended 02/28/13): Assets, $5,903,301 (M); expenditures, $321,318; qualifying distributions, $270,000; giving activities include $270,000 for 20 grants (high: $30,000; low: $3,000).
Purpose and activities: The purpose of the foundation is to help fund various religious and community needs, as well as educational, health and welfare programs.
Fields of interest: Performing arts, theater; Arts; Higher education; Education; Food services; YM/YWCAs & YM/YWHAs; Family services; Residential/custodial care, hospices; Community/economic development; Utilities; Protestant agencies & churches; Children/youth; Adults; Economically disadvantaged.
Type of support: Continuing support; Capital campaigns; Building/renovation; Equipment; Program development.
Limitations: Applications accepted. Giving primarily in Chester County, SC, and the surrounding areas. No support for political organizations. No grants to individuals, or for scholarships, general operating expenses, or general fund campaigns.
Publications: Application guidelines; Annual report; Annual report (including application guidelines); Grants list; Program policy statement.
Application information: Application form required.
Initial approach: Letter (on letterhead) of no more than 2 pages
Copies of proposal: 2
Deadline(s): Nov. 30
Board meeting date(s): Jan. and July, plus meetings as needed
Officers and Directors:* Dewey G. Guyton,* Pres.; Joan L. Guyton,* V.P. and Treas.; Susan L. Stephenson,* V.P., Public Rels.; Mary S. Jolly,* V.P., Tech.
Number of staff: None.
EIN: 570940342

3106
Ellison S. and Noel P. McKissick Foundation
(formerly Alice Manufacturing Company, Inc. Foundation)
P.O. Box 369
Easley, SC 29641-0369 **(864) 859-6323**

Established in 1983.
Donors: Alice Manufacturing Co., Inc.; Trust A U/A of Ellison S. Mckissick, Jr.
Foundation type: Company-sponsored foundation.
Financial data (yr. ended 06/30/13): Assets, $17,214,462 (M); expenditures, $856,011; qualifying distributions, $805,000; giving activities include $762,000 for 26 grants (high: $265,000; low: $1,000).
Purpose and activities: The foundation supports museums and organizations involved with education, land conservation, medical care, children, and Christianity.
Fields of interest: Museums; Elementary/secondary education; Higher education; Business school/education; Education; Environment, land resources; Medical care, rehabilitation; Boys & girls clubs; American Red Cross; Children, services; United Ways and Federated Giving Programs; Christian agencies & churches.
Type of support: Scholarship funds; General/operating support.
Limitations: Applications not accepted. Giving primarily in NC and SC. No grants to individuals.
Application information: Contributes only to pre-selected organizations.
Officer: Robert H. Thomas, Treas.
Directors: Elizabeth M. Fauntleroy; Ellison Smyth McKissick III; Caroline McKissick Young.
EIN: 570739969

3107
The Mark Elliott Motley Foundation Inc.
P.O. Box 1014
Charleston, SC 29402-1014
***Contact:* Jennifer Alphonse, V.P.**
Main URL: http://www.motleyfoundation.org

Established in 2002 in SC.
Donors: Ronald L. Motley; Motley Rice, LLC; John Herrick.
Foundation type: Independent foundation.
Financial data (yr. ended 06/30/13): Assets, $3,011,425 (M); gifts received, $17,980; expenditures, $166,338; qualifying distributions, $137,000; giving activities include $137,000 for 14 grants (high: $45,000; low: $500).
Purpose and activities: Giving primarily to tax-exempt public charities located in the Charleston, SC, area, which focus on improving the health, education and welfare of children and young adults.
Fields of interest: Recreation, camps; Youth development, services; Human services; Children/youth, services; Children.
Limitations: Applications accepted. Giving primarily in Charleston, SC. No grants to individuals.
Publications: Grants list.
Application information: See foundation web site for complete application guidelines. Application form required.
Initial approach: Letter
Copies of proposal: 2
Deadline(s): Mar. 1
Officers and Directors:* Ronald L. Motley,* Chair.; Douglas D. Kugley,* Pres. and Treas.; Jennifer B. Alphonse,* V.P. and Secy.
EIN: 270013752

Other changes: The grantmaker no longer lists a phone.

3108
Singing for Change
(also known as SFC Charitable Foundation)
P.O. Box 729
Sullivans Island, SC 29482-0729 (843) 388-7730
Contact: Judith Ranger Smith, Exec. Dir.
E-mail: info@singingforchange.com; **Main URL: http://www.singingforchange.org**
Grants List: http://www.singingforchange.org/previous_grants.html

Established in 1995.
Donors: Jimmy Buffett; Live Nation Worldwide, Inc.
Foundation type: Independent foundation.
Financial data (yr. ended 12/31/12): Assets, $534,540 (M); gifts received, $704,244; expenditures, $563,103; qualifying distributions, $359,230; giving activities include $359,230 for 28 grants (high: $100,000; low: $1,530).
Purpose and activities: Funding primarily for children and families, the environment, and disenfranchised groups.
Fields of interest: Education; Environmental education; Human services; Children/youth, services.
Type of support: General/operating support; Continuing support.
Limitations: Applications accepted. Giving in the U.S., with emphasis on FL and LA. No support for religious organizations, public or private schools, or for medical research or disease treatment organizations. No grants to individuals, or for art, music, or recreational purposes.
Publications: Application guidelines; Annual report; Grants list.
Application information: Full proposals are by invitation only, upon review of letter of interest. Unsolicited full proposals are not considered. See foundation web site for additional information.
Initial approach: 1-page letter of interest via e-mail or USPS
Deadline(s): None
Board meeting date(s): Quarterly
Officers and Trustees:* Howard Kaufman,* Pres.; Joel A. Katz,* Secy.; Irwin L. Rennert,* Treas.
Number of staff: 1 full-time professional.
EIN: 650565248

3109
J.M. Smith Foundation
101 W. St. John St., Ste. 305
Spartanburg, SC 29306-5150

Established in 1996 in SC.
Donor: J M Smith Corp.
Foundation type: Company-sponsored foundation.
Financial data (yr. ended 02/28/13): Assets, $435,242 (M); gifts received, $2,982,337; expenditures, $2,854,492; qualifying distributions, $2,854,492; giving activities include $2,854,090 for 392 grants (high: $146,660; low: $200).
Purpose and activities: The foundation supports organizations involved with education, hunger, human services, and Christianity.
Fields of interest: Secondary school/education; Higher education; Education; Food services; Food distribution, meals on wheels; Boys & girls clubs; YM/YWCAs & YM/YWHAs; Human services; United Ways and Federated Giving Programs; Christian agencies & churches.
Type of support: Equipment; General/operating support; Continuing support; Program development; Scholarship funds.
Limitations: Applications not accepted. Giving primarily in SC; giving also in AR, FL, GA, KY, NC, PA, and VA. No grants to individuals.
Application information: Contributes only to pre-selected organizations.
Officers: Kenneth R. Couch, Pres.; Tammy Devine, Secy.; James C. Wilson, Jr., Treas.
Directors: Henry D. Smith; Mike Webb; Russ Webber.
EIN: 571046595

3110
The Spartanburg County Foundation
424 E. Kennedy St.
Spartanburg, SC 29302-1916 (864) 582-0138
***Contact:* Troy M. Hanna, C.E.O.; For grants: Ashley Thomason, Prog. Assoc.**
FAX: (864) 573-5378; E-mail: info@spcf.org;
Additional e-mail: thanna@spcf.org; Grant inquiry e-mail: athomason@spcf.org; Main URL: http://www.spcf.org
Facebook: https://www.facebook.com/pages/The-Spartanburg-County-Foundation/130298439113
LinkedIn: http://www.linkedin.com/company/the-spartanburg-county-foundation
Twitter: https://twitter.com/spcountyfdn
YouTube: http://www.youtube.com/user/SpartanburgCntyFndn?feature=mhee

Incorporated in 1943 in SC.
Foundation type: Community foundation.
Financial data (yr. ended 12/31/12): Assets, $109,237,666 (M); gifts received, $20,973,574; expenditures, $10,850,318; giving activities include $8,696,555 for grants.
Purpose and activities: The foundation seeks to provide for the mental, moral, intellectual and physical improvement, assistance and relief of the inhabitants of Spartanburg County. Primary areas of interest include local projects in higher and other education, community development, recreation, and health.
Fields of interest: Humanities; Historic preservation/historical societies; Arts; Higher education; Adult/continuing education; Education; Environment; Health care; Health organizations, association; Recreation; Children/youth, services; Human services; Community/economic development; Children/youth.
Type of support: Continuing support; Building/renovation; Equipment; Emergency funds; Conferences/seminars; Seed money; Curriculum development; Scholarship funds; Consulting services; Employee-related scholarships; Scholarships—to individuals; In-kind gifts; Matching/challenge support.
Limitations: Applications accepted. Giving limited to the Spartanburg County, SC, area. No support for religious organizations for sectarian purposes. No grants to individuals (except designated scholarship funds), or for operating budgets, annual campaigns, deficit financing, land acquisition, film projects, publication of books or reports, or endowment funds; no loans.
Publications: Application guidelines; Annual report (including application guidelines); Informational brochure; Newsletter.
Application information: Visit foundation web site for application guidelines. Application form required.
Copies of proposal: 1
***Deadline(s):* Spring and Fall**
Board meeting date(s): Monthly
Officers and Trustees:* Robert E. Gregory, Jr.,* Chair.; **John S. Poole,* Vice-Chair.; Troy M. Hanna, C.E.O. and Pres.**; Mary L. Thomas, C.O.O.; Dr. John Stockwell,* Secy.; Andrew J. Falatok,* Treas.; James W. Shaw, Genl. Council and Asst. Secy.; **John E. Bauknight**; Terry L. Cash; Dr. Kay E. Woodward.
Number of staff: 8 full-time professional.
EIN: 570351398
Other changes: John S. Poole has replaced Dr. Kay E. Woodward as Vice-Chair. Troy M. Hanna has replaced John B.H. Dargan as C.E.O. and Pres. Thomas R. Young is no longer a trustee.

3111
The Springs Close Foundation, Inc.
(formerly Springs Foundation, Inc.)
951 Market St., Ste. 205
Fort Mill, SC 29708-6529 (803) 548-2002
Contact: Angela H. McCrae, Pres.
FAX: (803) 548-1797;
E-mail: amccrae@springsfnd.com; **Lancaster, SC, office address: 201 W. Gay St., Lancaster, SC 29720, tel.: (803) 286-2197, fax: (803) 416-4626; Chester, SC, office address: 109 Gadsden St., Chester, SC 29706, tel.: (803) 581-7874, fax: (803) 581-2431**; Main URL: http://www.thespringsclosefoundation.org

Incorporated in 1942 in DE.
Donors: Elliott W. Springs†; Anne Springs Close; Frances Ley Springs†; members of the Springs and Close families.
Foundation type: Independent foundation.
Financial data (yr. ended 12/31/12): Assets, $41,344,751 (M); gifts received, $17,100; expenditures, $1,568,189; qualifying distributions, $1,490,971; giving activities include $1,115,166 for grants.
Purpose and activities: In response to high unemployment rates and growing economic distress, the foundation shifted its charitable efforts toward helping local citizens who need basic and emergency needs, such as shelter, food, and medical assistance.
Fields of interest: Education, early childhood education; Health care; Family services; Aging, centers/services; Community/economic development; Christian agencies & churches; Economically disadvantaged.
Type of support: General/operating support; Annual campaigns; Capital campaigns; Building/renovation; Equipment; Endowments; Program development; Seed money; Matching/challenge support; Student loans—to individuals.
Limitations: Applications accepted. Giving limited to Chester, Lancaster and York Counties, SC. No grants to individuals (except for student loans), or for travel expenses.
Publications: Application guidelines; Annual report; Annual report (including application guidelines); Grants list.
Application information: Applications should be mailed or delivered to the Fort Mill, SC, office. Applications may be faxed as well to the foundation's 1797 number, or scanned and e-mailed to the foundation's main e-mail address. Application form required.
***Initial approach:* Use application form on foundation web site; applicants are strongly encouraged to contact foundation Pres., Angela McCrae to discuss proposals prior to submission**
Copies of proposal: 1
Deadline(s): Mar. 1 and Oct. 1; none for grant requests of up to $2,500

Board meeting date(s): Apr. and Nov.
Final notification: 3 months
Officers and Directors:* Anne Springs Close,* Chair.; Angela H. McCrae, Pres.; Harry B. Emerson, Secy.; William G. Taylor,* Treas.; Chantay Bouler; Crandall C. Bowles; Bruce A. Brumfield; Derick S. Close; Elliott S. Close; Frances A. Close; H.W. Close; Katherine A. Close; M. Scott Close; **Nancy Coleman**; W. Dehler Hart; Robert Holcombe, Jr.
Number of staff: 1 full-time professional; 2 part-time professional; 1 full-time support.
EIN: 570426344
Other changes: Charles A. Bundy is no longer a director.

3112
Waccamaw Community Foundation

3655 S. Hwy. 17 Bus.
Murrells Inlet, SC 29576-6178 (843) 357-4483
Contact: Kif Cook, Exec. Dir.
FAX: (843) 357-4457; E-mail: kif@mywcf.org; Main URL: http://www.waccamawcf.org
Facebook: https://www.facebook.com/WaccamawCF

Established in 1997 in SC as an affiliate of the Foundation For The Carolinas; became an independent community foundation in 1999.
Foundation type: Community foundation.
Financial data (yr. ended 12/31/10): Assets, $18,438,645 (M); gifts received, $2,341,464; expenditures, $2,795,338; giving activities include $2,182,876 for grants.
Purpose and activities: The foundation uses distributions from various funds to award grants to many of the humanitarian, educational and cultural organizations in the community.
Fields of interest: Arts; Education; Environment; Animal welfare; Community/economic development; Children.
Type of support: Scholarship funds.
Limitations: Applications accepted. Giving limited to Georgetown and Horry, SC.
Publications: Application guidelines; Annual report; Financial statement; Informational brochure; Newsletter.
Application information: Visit foundation web site for application information and guidelines. Application form required.
Initial approach: Submit Concept Letter
Officers and Board Members:* G. David Bishop,* Chair.; Scott W. Hutto,* Vice-Chair.; Muriel Ward O'Tuel, Ph.D.*, Secy.; Ruell L. Hicks, Jr.,* Treas.; Kathryn M. Cook, Exec. Dir.; Clyde W. Port, Emeritus; Cheryl Adamson; Frank J. Bullard III; John Draughn; William F. Drew, Jr.; Dr. Hal Holmes, Jr.; Otis Allen Jeffcoat III; Dennis Wade.
EIN: 562121992
Other changes: Angela Bare is now Finance and Admin. Asst. J. Carson Benton and J. Robert Calliham are no longer board members.

3113
The WebbCraft Family Foundation, Inc.

938 Simpson Rd.
Belton, SC 29627-8970 (864) 338-9734
Contact: Jerri Lynn Sharpe, Exec. Dir.
FAX: (864) 338-9737; E-mail: info@webbcraft.org; Main URL: http://www.webbcraft.org/

Established in 2000 in SC.
Donor: Joy Craft Malcolm.
Foundation type: Independent foundation.
Financial data (yr. ended 12/31/12): Assets, $3,100,433 (M); gifts received, $6,000; expenditures, $282,681; qualifying distributions, $262,493; giving activities include $170,700 for 13 grants (high: $70,000; low: $250).
Purpose and activities: The foundation supports education and the development of individuals in the Belton and Honea Path, South Carolina, areas.
Fields of interest: Arts education; Museums; Arts; Secondary school/education; Higher education; Education.
Limitations: Applications accepted. Giving primarily in SC. No grants to individuals.
Application information: Application guidelines and form available on foundation web site. Application form required.
Initial approach: Applicants must contact the foundation prior to submitting an application
***Deadline(s):* Apr. 1 and Oct. 1**
Officers and Directors:* Jerri Lynn Craft Sharpe,* Chair.; Joy Craft,* Vice-Chair.; Jana Craft Burdette,* Secy.; Michael Pascuzzi,* Treas.; Julie Kay Bell; Jimmy Craft; **Lindy Craft Fullbright**; Jane Craft Kay; Faye Staton.
EIN: 571111833
Other changes: Jerri Lynn Craft Sharpe has replaced Joy Craft as Chair.
Joy Craft is now Vice-Chair. Michael Pascuzzi is now Treas. Jana Craft Burdette is now Secy.

SOUTH DAKOTA

3114
Blythe Brenden-Mann Foundation
(formerly Brenden-Mann Foundation)
401 E. 8th St., Ste. 319
Sioux Falls, SD 57103-7031
Main URL: http://www.blythebrendenmannfdn.org/
Facebook: https://www.facebook.com/blythebrendenmannfdn
LinkedIn: http://www.linkedin.com/company/3155222

Established in 2005 in SD.
Donor: The Tedd & Roberts Mann Foundation of Minnesota.
Foundation type: Independent foundation.
Financial data (yr. ended 12/31/12): Assets, $24,461,369 (M); expenditures, $1,447,104; qualifying distributions, $1,311,332; giving activities include $1,174,865 for 19 grants (high: $268,500; low: $465).
Fields of interest: Arts; Hospitals (general).
Limitations: Applications not accepted.
Application information: Unsolicited requests for funds not accepted.
Trustee: Dorsey & Whitney Trust Co., LLC.
EIN: 416546887

3115
Chiesman Foundation for Democracy, Inc.
1641 Deadwood Ave.
P.O. Box 8288
Rapid City, SD 57709-8288
FAX: (605) 344-3902

Established in 1995 in SD.
Donor: Allene R. Chiesman.
Foundation type: Operating foundation.
Financial data (yr. ended 12/31/12): Assets, $2,460,369 (M); gifts received, $121,900; expenditures, $354,326; qualifying distributions, $810,228; giving activities include $120,000 for 1 grant, and $825,447 for 2 foundation-administered programs.
Purpose and activities: Giving primarily for education, youth services, and social sciences.
Fields of interest: Education; Children/youth, services; Social sciences.
Limitations: Applications not accepted. Giving primarily in SD. No grants to individuals.
Application information: Contributes only to pre-selected organizations.
Officers: Morris Hallock, Chair.; **Joyce Hazeltine, Vice-Chair.**; **Helen Usera, Pres.**; **Catherine Murschel, Secy.**; James Borszich, Treas.
Directors: Tom Hills; Richard Brown; Deborah Gates; Merton Tice, Jr.
EIN: 460438703
Other changes: Helen Usera has replaced John J. Usera as Pres. Catherine Murschel has replaced Tom Hills as Secy.
Joyce Hazeltine is now Vice-Chair. William Clark, Ted Muenster and Barry Vickrey are no longer directors.

3116
The Hatterscheidt Foundation Inc.
c/o Dacotah Bank Trust
P.O. Box 1210
Aberdeen, SD **57402-1210**
***Application address:* c/o Tyler DeBoer, 204 S. 1st St., P.O. Box 849, Aberdeen, SD 57402-0849, tel.: (605) 229-8223**

Incorporated in 1947 in DE.
Donors: Ruth K. Hatterscheidt†; F.W. Hatterscheidt Trusts.
Foundation type: Independent foundation.
Financial data (yr. ended 12/31/12): Assets, $4,436,799 (M); expenditures, $298,153; qualifying distributions, $240,513; giving activities include $232,000 for 33 grants (high: $65,500; low: $500).
Purpose and activities: Giving primarily to assist graduating seniors from South Dakota high schools with a 3.0 GPA or better for their freshman year of college in the state; some support also for local charitable organizations.
Fields of interest: Higher education.
Type of support: Scholarship funds; Scholarships—to individuals.
Limitations: Applications accepted. Giving primarily in SD. No grants for matching gifts; no loans.
Application information: Application form required.
Initial approach: Proposal
Copies of proposal: 1
Deadline(s): None
Board meeting date(s): Apr. and Nov.
Officers: Jack Thompson, Pres.; Harvey Jewett, Secy.-Treas.
Trustees: Dennis Kraft; Dorothy O'Keefe.
Number of staff: None.
EIN: 466012543
Other changes: Harry Jasinski is no longer V.P.

3117
Edward L. Schwab Memorial Foundation
c/o Dacotah Bank
P.O. Box 1210
Aberdeen, SD 57402-1210 (605) 229-7122
***Contact:* Tom Appletoft**

Established in 1996 in SD.
Foundation type: Operating foundation.
Financial data (yr. ended 08/31/13): Assets, $3,202,604 (M); expenditures, $240,723; qualifying distributions, $184,169; giving activities include $175,000 for 5 grants (high: $58,950; low: $4,500).
Fields of interest: Higher education.
Type of support: Scholarship funds.
Limitations: Applications accepted. Giving limited to residents of Henry, Willow Lake, Clark, Florence and Hamlin counties, school districts, SD.
Application information: Application form required.
Initial approach: Contact foundation
Deadline(s): 180 days after publication notice
Officers: Kevin Wegehaupt, Pres.; Marci Caster, V.P.; **Tom Labrie, Secy.-Treas.**
Directors: Henry Desnoyers; Gary Neuberger.
Trustee: Dacotah Bank, N.A.
EIN: 911770168
Other changes: Tom Labrie has replaced Ralph Kusler as Secy.-Treas.

3118
South Dakota Education Access Foundation
115 1st Ave. S.W.
Aberdeen, SD 57401-4124 **(888) 502-5902, ext. 3035**
FAX: (800) 354-7070; E-mail: cwold@glhec.org; Main URL: http://www.sdeducationaccess.org

Established in 2009 in SD.
Donor: Great Lakes Higher Education Guaranty Corporation.
Foundation type: Independent foundation.
Financial data (yr. ended 12/31/12): Assets, $41,365,841 (M); gifts received, $431,203; expenditures, $2,170,775; qualifying distributions, $1,952,478; giving activities include $1,845,900 for 29 grants (high: $371,800; low: $900).
Purpose and activities: The foundation seeks to provide scholarships for postsecondary education and to donate to programs at higher education institutions and other nonprofit agencies that help people access the same.
Fields of interest: Higher education; Education.
Type of support: Scholarship funds.
Limitations: Giving limited to SD. No support for religious or political activities. No grants for capital campaigns, endowments, equipment, corporate sponsorships or fundraising events.
Publications: Application guidelines.
Application information:
Initial approach: SD colleges and universities may submit a proposal
Officers: Rod Fouberg, Co-Pres.; Clark Wold, Co-Pres.; Kae McNeil, Secy. - Treas.
Directors: Mike Duch; **Kristen Fauth**; Dennis Hagny; **Chris Jung**; Patti Mesmer; Cindi Walsh.
EIN: 263941129
Other changes: Jack Thompson is no longer a director.

TENNESSEE

3119
Alumni Achievement Awards, Inc.
7201 Shallowford Rd., Ste. 200
Chattanooga, TN 37421-2780 (423) 308-1855
Contact: Melanie Litchfield
***E-mail:* info@alumniawards.org; Main URL: http://alumniawards.org**
Facebook: https://www.facebook.com/AlumniAwardsFoundation

Established in 2004 in TN.
Donors: I.M. Feldkemp; Arpad Soo; Gary Wilt; George T. Herding; Versa Cace Inc.; McKee Foods Corp.; Byron DeFoor; Dr. C.H. Dehaan; Dave Briscoe.
Foundation type: Operating foundation.
Financial data (yr. ended 06/30/13): Assets, $131,084 (M); gifts received, $1,041,171; expenditures, $990,551; qualifying distributions, $723,796; giving activities include $505,000 for 2 grants (high: $285,833; low: $219,167), and $40,000 for 20 grants to individuals (high: $2,000; low: $2,000).
Purpose and activities: Giving to inspire and reward excellence in Adventist K-12 schools, educators and alumni.
Fields of interest: Education.
Type of support: General/operating support; Scholarships—to individuals.
Limitations: Applications not accepted. Giving primarily in AZ.
Application information: Unsolicited requests for funds not accepted.
Officers: Dr. Robert B. Summerour, M.D., Chair.; Dave Briscoe, Treas.
Board Members: Dr. Joan Coggin; Byron DeFoor; Dr. Greg Gerard; Jeff Londis; John O'Brien; Kathy Proffitt; Arpad Soo; Keith White; Gary Wilt.
Director: Melanie Litchfield.
EIN: 592413171

3120
The Assisi Foundation of Memphis, Inc.
(formerly Assisi Foundation)
515 Erin Dr.
Memphis, TN 38117-4211 (901) 684-1564
Contact: Jan Young, Exec. Dir.
FAX: (901) 684-1997;
E-mail: jyoung@assisifoundation.org; Main URL: http://www.assisifoundation.org/

Established in 1994 in TN; converted from the sale of St. Francis Hospital.
Foundation type: Independent foundation.
Financial data (yr. ended 12/31/13): Assets, $228,227,005 (M), expenditures, $12,107,971; qualifying distributions, $10,444,883; giving activities include $9,780,971 for 63+ grants (high: $550,250).
Purpose and activities: The foundation supports health, lifelong learning, social justice and responsible use of resources with respect and compassion for all.
Fields of interest: Education; Health care; Human services; Community/economic development; Social sciences, ethics; Social sciences, equal rights.
Type of support: General/operating support; Management development/capacity building; Capital campaigns; Equipment; Endowments; Emergency funds; Program development; Conferences/seminars; Publication; Curriculum development; Research; Technical assistance; Consulting services; Program evaluation; Matching/challenge support.
Limitations: Applications accepted. Giving primarily in the Greater Memphis area of Shelby, Fayette and Tipton Counties, TN; Crittenden County, AR and Desoto County, MS. No grants to individuals, fundraising, tickets for benefits, lobbying, budget deficits, or for tournament fees and/or travel for athletic competitions, scholarships or for replacement of government funding cuts.
Publications: Application guidelines.
Application information: See foundation's web site for additional information. Application form required.
Copies of proposal: 8
Deadline(s): Feb. 13, May 15, Aug. 14 and Nov. 13
Board meeting date(s): 4th Thurs. of Jan., Apr., July, and Oct.
Final notification: First week of Apr., July., Oct. and Jan.
Officers and Directors:* Lee J. Chase III,* Chair.; Martin F. Thompson,* Vice-Chair; Ronald Belz, Secy.; Gary Joffe, C.F.O.; William L. Zoccola, Treas.; Dr. Jan Young, Exec. Dir.; Dr. Susan M. Aguillard; Jack A. Belz; **Michael J. Bruns**; Fred L. Davis; Joseph Evangelisti; William E. Frulla; James J. Gattas; Art Gilliam; Harry Goldsmith; Robert D. Gooch III; Forrest N. Jenkins; Nancy C. Lanigan; Deborah O. Schadt, Ph.D.; Charles D. Schaffler; **Thomas W. Scherer**; Peggy I. Veeser, Ed.D.; C. Thomas Whitman; Philip R. Zanone, Jr.
Number of staff: 4 full-time professional; 1 part-time professional; 1 full-time support; 1 part-time support.
EIN: 621558722
Other changes: Susan Mack Aguillard, Franklin P. "Pepper" Allen, and Thomas K. Corona are no longer directors.

3121
Ayers Foundation
450 Tennessee Ave., Ste. 101
P.O. Box 217
Parsons, TN 38363-4615 (731) 847-4962
Contact: Janet Ayers, Pres.

Established in 1999 in TN.
Donors: James W. Ayers; Nancy Sharon Ayers; Jon Ayers; Sarah K. Givens; Tennessee Higher Education Assn.; Oasis Center.
Foundation type: Independent foundation.
Financial data (yr. ended 12/31/12): Assets, $192,771 (M); gifts received, $2,310,598; expenditures, $3,916,164; qualifying distributions, $3,418,626; giving activities include $3,418,626 for 55 grants (high: $1,197,761; low: $100).
Fields of interest: Higher education; Human services; Foundations (community).
Limitations: Applications accepted. Giving limited to Decatur and Henderson counties, TN. No grants to individuals.
Application information: Application form not required.
Initial approach: Letter
Deadline(s): None
Officers: James W. Ayers, Chair.; Janet Ayers, Pres.; Clay Petrey, Secy.
Directors: Jon Ayers; Kristy Ayers; Agenia Clark; Lee Ann Ingram; Cassie Lynn; Joann Lynn.
EIN: 621773033
Other changes: Michael Price is no longer V.P.

3122
Baptist Healing Hospital Trust
(also known as Baptist Healing Trust)
2928 Sidco Dr.
Nashville, TN 37204-3758 (615) 284-8271
Contact: Kristen Keely-Dinger, V.P., Progs. & Grants
FAX: (615) 284-2683;
E-mail: info@healinghospital.org; Main URL: http://www.baptisthealingtrust.org
LinkedIn: http://www.linkedin.com/company/baptist-healing-trust

Established in 2002; converted from the sale of the Baptist Hospital System to Ascension Health Systems.
Foundation type: Independent foundation.
Financial data (yr. ended 12/31/12): Assets, $117,384,024 (M); expenditures, $5,115,661; qualifying distributions, $5,710,997; giving activities include $3,961,350 for 144 grants (high: $323,860; low: $100).
Purpose and activities: The trust supports organizations that offer a holistic and loving approach to health care. It seeks to increase the access of underprivileged populations to appropriate and affordable health care and to support and enhance the success of the nonprofit organizations it funds by offering funding and consulting to organizations to promote cultures centered on compassionate care.
Fields of interest: Holistic medicine; Health care; Mental health/crisis services; Infants/toddlers; Children/youth; Youth; Adults; Aging; Young adults; Disabilities, people with; Physically disabled; Deaf/hearing impaired; Mentally disabled; Minorities; African Americans/Blacks; Hispanics/Latinos; Native Americans/American Indians; Military/veterans; Offenders/ex-offenders; Substance abusers; AIDS, people with; Crime/abuse victims; Terminal illness, people with; Immigrants/refugees; Economically disadvantaged; Homeless.
Type of support: General/operating support; Continuing support; Emergency funds; Program development; Technical assistance.
Limitations: Applications accepted. **Giving limited to middle TN, and serve at least one of the forty counties in Middle TN (list of counties available on foundation web site).** No support for fraternal organization or political parties. No grants to individuals.
Publications: Application guidelines; Grants list; Informational brochure.
Application information: Application form required.
***Initial approach:* New applicants are required to attend an introduction workshop. See foundation web site for specific details**
Deadline(s): Jan., Apr., July, and Oct.
Board meeting date(s): June and Dec.
Final notification: 2 months
Officers: Catherine Self, P.T., Ph.D., C.E.O. and Pres.; Kristen Keely-Dinger, V.P., Progs. and Grants; Matt Deeb, C.F.O.
Number of staff: 6 full-time professional.
EIN: 522362225

3123
Benwood Foundation, Inc.
736 Market St., Ste. 1600
Chattanooga, TN 37402-4807
Contact: Sarah H. Morgan, Pres.
FAX: (423) 267-9049;
E-mail: smorgan@benwood.org; Main URL: http://www.benwood.org
Facebook: http://www.facebook.com/pages/Chattanooga-TN/The-Benwood-Foundation/35114638807

Gaining Ground Facebook: http://www.facebook.com/pages/Gaining-Ground-Chattanooga/403992784713
Gaining Ground Twitter: http://twitter.com/GainGroundCHA
Grants List: http://www.benwood.org/pages/Grants-Awarded/

Incorporated in 1944 in DE, and 1945 in TN.
Donor: George Thomas Hunter†.
Foundation type: Independent foundation.
Financial data (yr. ended 12/31/12): Assets, $105,162,018 (M); expenditures, $6,583,538; qualifying distributions, $5,934,381; giving activities include $4,209,144 for 129 grants (high: $1,000,000; low: $1,000).
Purpose and activities: The foundation seeks to stimulate creative and innovative efforts to build and strengthen the Chattanooga, TN community.
Fields of interest: Performing arts; Humanities; Arts; Education, early childhood education; Secondary school/education; Environment; Economic development; Urban/community development.
Type of support: Program-related investments/loans; Management development/capacity building; Land acquisition; Continuing support; Capital campaigns; Building/renovation; Equipment; Program development; Conferences/seminars; Seed money; Scholarship funds; Technical assistance; Matching/challenge support.
Limitations: Applications not accepted. Giving primarily in the Chattanooga, TN, area. No support for political organizations or causes. No grants to individuals, financial deficits, fundraising, or endowments, no loans (except for program-related investments).
Application information: Contributes only to selected organizations.
Board meeting date(s): Jan., Apr., July, and Oct.
Officers and Trustees:* **Robert J. Sudderth, Jr.,* Chair.; Sebert Brewer, Jr.,* Vice-Chair.**; Sarah H. Morgan, Pres.; **Martha T. Robinson,* Secy.; Paul K. Brock, Jr.,* Treas.**; William H. Chapin.
Number of staff: 4 full-time professional; 2 full-time support.
EIN: 620476283
Other changes: Robert J. Sudderth, Jr. is now Chair. Sebert Brewer, Jr. is now Vice-Chair. Martha T. Robinson is now Secy. Paul K. Brock, Jr. is now Treas.

3124
Thomas W. Briggs Foundation, Inc.
c/o The Cresent Ctr.
6075 Poplar Ave., Ste. 330
Memphis, TN 38119-0114 (901) 680-0276
***Contact:* Margaret Craddock, Exec. Dir.**
E-mail: twbriggs@aol.com; Main URL: http://www.thomaswbriggsfoundation.com

Established in 1957.
Donors: Thomas W. Briggs Residuary Trust; Isabell Bateman†.
Foundation type: Independent foundation.
Financial data (yr. ended 09/30/13): Assets, $15,531,145 (M); expenditures, $984,190; qualifying distributions, $775,245; giving activities include $688,025 for 47 grants (high: $75,000; low: $25).
Purpose and activities: The focus of the foundation's funding includes youth projects and programs, education, social services, arts and cultural organizations and civic organizations that promote quality of life.
Fields of interest: Museums; Museums (children's); Arts; Education; Human services; Children/youth, services.
Type of support: General/operating support; Capital campaigns; Building/renovation.
Limitations: Applications accepted. Giving primarily in the Memphis, TN, area. No support for nationally affiliated organizations, or for public and private schools, or churches and synagogues. **No grants for seminars or special events.**
Publications: Application guidelines.
Application information: The information that is to be included in the initial letter, must appear in the order indicated on foundation web site. New applicants and those that have not received funding from the foundation in the past 10 years, must arrange for a site visit by the foundation's Exec. Dir., well in advance of the funding deadlines. Application form not required.
Initial approach: **Letter (no more than 3 pages, and typed in a 12 point font)**
Copies of proposal: 1
Deadline(s): Aug. 1 and Feb. 1
Board meeting date(s): Spring and fall
Final notification: May and Nov.
Officers and Directors:* James D. Witherington, Jr.,* Chair.; Lawrence Jenson,* Pres.; Gwen P. Owen,* V.P.; Hunter Witherington,* Treas.; **Margaret Craddock, Secy. and Exec. Dir.**; Kathleen D. Blair; **V. Lynn Evans**; Bernice H. Hussey; Dr. Kenneth S. Robinson; Spence Wilson.
Number of staff: 1 full-time professional.
EIN: 626039986
Other changes: James D. Witherington, Jr. has replaced Buzzy Hussey as Chair. Lawrence Jenson has replaced James D. Witherington, Jr. as Pres. Gwen P. Owen has replaced Stephen H. Rhea, Jr. as V.P. Margaret Craddock has replaced Jo Anne Tilly as Secy. and Exec. Dir.

3125
Chattanooga Ophthalmological Foundation
605 Chestnut St., Ste. 1700
Chattanooga, TN **37450-0019**

Established in 2007 in TN.
Foundation type: Independent foundation.
Financial data (yr. ended 06/30/13): Assets, $3,950,469 (M); expenditures, $208,033; qualifying distributions, $160,948; giving activities include $123,954 for 1 grant (high: $123,954), and $6,038 for 5 grants to individuals (high: $2,194; low: $125).
Fields of interest: Health organizations; Foundations (community); United Ways and Federated Giving Programs.
Limitations: Applications not accepted. Giving primarily in TN. No grants to individuals.
Application information: Unsolicited requests for funds not accepted.
Officers and Directors:* Molly R. Seal, M.D., Pres.; George M. Clark III,* V.P.; E. Stephen Jett,* Secy.-Treas.; Charles A. Kirby, M.D.; Ira M. Long, M.D.; W. Luther Masingill; Gloria McConnel; Thomas M. Reynolds, M.D.; Camden B. Scearce.
EIN: 237038515

3126
The C.A.T.S. Foundation (Checotah Animal, Town, and School Foundation)
c/o Haber
1920 Adelcia St., No. 300
Nashville, TN 37212-2231
Main URL: http://www.thecatsfoundation.com/

Donor: Carrie Underwood.
Foundation type: Independent foundation.
Financial data (yr. ended 12/31/12): Assets, $95,783 (M); gifts received, $129,880; expenditures, $137,174; qualifying distributions, $126,000; giving activities include $126,000 for 1 grant.
Fields of interest: Animal welfare.
Limitations: Applications not accepted. Giving primarily in Checotah, OK.
Application information: Unsolicited requests for funds not accepted.
Officers and Directors:* Carrie Underwood,* Chair.; Carole Underwood, Pres.; Ann Edelblute,* Secy.; Gary Haber,* Treas.; **Rick Fisher; Dawn Nepp**; Kate Paris; Judee Ann Williams.
EIN: 800367499

3127
CIC Foundation, Inc.
139 Lake Harbor Dr.
Hendersonville, TN 37075 (615) 386-2296
***Main URL:* http://www.cicfoundationinc.org/**

Established in 2003 in TN.
Donor: Credit Bureau of Nashville, Inc.
Foundation type: Company-sponsored foundation.
Financial data (yr. ended 12/31/12): Assets, $0 (M); expenditures, $6,355,437; qualifying distributions, $5,493,203; giving activities include $3,268,121 for 61 grants (high: $350,000; low: -$185,000), and $2,211,300 for 254 grants to individuals (high: $60,000; low: $1,250).
Purpose and activities: The foundation supports organizations involved with health, substance abuse, human services, and Christianity and awards college scholarships to students located in Kentucky and Tennessee.
Fields of interest: Education; Human services; Religion.
Type of support: General/operating support; Building/renovation; Program development; Scholarship funds; Scholarships—to individuals.
Limitations: Applications accepted. Giving primarily in KY and TN.
Application information: Application form required.
Initial approach: Contact foundation for scholarship application
Deadline(s): Apr. 1 for scholarships
Officers: William D. Maxfield, Chair.; Garry V. Forsythe, Pres.; Charles C. Martin, Secy.; Donna Tilley, Treas.
Directors: Leslie B. Enoch II; W. Dale Maxfield, Sr.; J. Terry Olive; M. Terry Turner.
EIN: 562348880
Other changes: The grantmaker no longer lists a primary contact.
At the close of 2012, the grantmaker paid grants of $5,479,421, a 192.8% increase over the 2011 disbursements, $1,871,502.

3128
The Clayton Family Foundation
520 W. Summit Hill Dr., Ste. 801
Knoxville, TN 37902-2006
Contact: Grant Officer

E-mail: CFF.mail@Clayton.org; **E-mail for grant requests: Grant.Request@Clayton.org; E-mail to request copy of application process: Grants@Clayton.org**; Main URL: http://www.clayton.org

Established in 1991 in TN.
Donor: James L. Clayton.
Foundation type: Independent foundation.
Financial data (yr. ended 12/31/12): Assets, $91,816,291 (M); expenditures, $4,946,625; qualifying distributions, $4,634,350; giving activities include $4,634,350 for 287 grants (high: $850,000; low: $500).
Purpose and activities: Giving primarily for higher education, health associations, youth development, the arts, health organizations, social services, and Protestant churches.
Fields of interest: Arts; Elementary/secondary education; Higher education; Education; Health care; Health organizations, association; Boys & girls clubs; Human services; YM/YWCAs & YM/YWHAs; Children/youth, services; Community/economic development; Foundations (public); United Ways and Federated Giving Programs; Protestant agencies & churches.
Limitations: Giving limited to areas of company operations, particularly where Clayton Banks and other family businesses are located in TN. No support for private or supporting foundations, non-US charities, or political activities. No grants to individuals, or for fundraisers, social or sporting events, advertising, conferences, trips, tours, or seed money.
Publications: Application guidelines; IRS Form 990 or 990-PF printed copy available upon request.
Application information: One grant request per calendar year. Resumes or staff bios, letters of support, photographs, news articles, videos or DVDs, or 990 forms should not be initially sent with application. Incomplete grant requests will not be processed. See foundation web site for application information. Application form not required.
Deadline(s): None
Final notification: Up to 3 months following receipt of grant request
Officers and Directors:* James L. Clayton,* Pres.; Janice K. Clayton,* V.P.; Jeanne C. Campbell,* Secy.-Treas. and Managing Dir.; Kay Clayton, Exec. Dir.; B. Joe Clayton; Kevin T. Clayton.
EIN: 581970851

3129
Community Foundation of Middle Tennessee, Inc.

(formerly Nashville Community Foundation, Inc.)
3833 Cleghorn Ave., No. 400
Nashville, TN 37215-2519 (615) 321-4939
Contact: Ellen E. Lehman, Pres.
FAX: (615) 327-2746; E-mail: mail@cfmt.org; Additional tel.: (888) 540-5200; Main URL: http://www.cfmt.org
E-Newsletter: http://www.cfmt.org/newsletter/subscribe/
Facebook: http://www.facebook.com/pages/Nashville-TN/The-Community-Foundation-of-Middle-Tennessee/55356141327
Google+: https://plus.google.com/106900481091008609401/posts
Grants List: http://www.cfmt.org/request/grants/grantees/
LinkedIn: http://www.linkedin.com/companies/the-community-foundation-of-middle-tennessee
Twitter: http://twitter.com/CFMT

Established in 1991 in TN.
Foundation type: Community foundation.
Financial data (yr. ended 12/31/12): Assets, $360,123,135 (M); gifts received, $34,943,501; expenditures, $78,005,653; giving activities include $70,695,058 for 332+ grants, and $2,010,613 for 407 grants to individuals.
Purpose and activities: The foundation is dedicated to enriching the quality of life in middle Tennessee. It serves as a leader, catalyst and resource for philanthropy, and strives to build a permanent endowment for the community for now and all time.
Fields of interest: Humanities; Historic preservation/historical societies; Arts; Education; Environment, natural resources; Environment; Animal welfare; Animals/wildlife; Health care; Health organizations, association; Employment; Housing/shelter, development; Aging, centers/services; Human services; Community development, neighborhood development; Community/economic development; Aging.
Type of support: Program development.
Limitations: Applications accepted. Giving limited to serving the 40 counties comprising the middle TN area. No support for private foundations, religious or sectarian purposes, private schools, biomedical or clinic studies (other than those related to breast cancer), or fundraising feasibility studies. **No grants for fundraising events, debt retirement, annual and capital campaigns, endowment campaigns, equipment and technology for general operations, fundraising events, receptions, advertising, sponsorships, trips, conferences, computers or equipment.**
Publications: Annual report; Informational brochure; Newsletter.
Application information: Visit foundation web site for application forms and guidelines. Faxed or e-mailed applications are not accepted. Application form required.
Initial approach: Create online profile
Deadline(s): Aug. 1 for grants; Mar. 15 for scholarships
Board meeting date(s): Feb., Apr., June, Sept., Nov., and Dec.
Final notification: Mid-Nov. for grants; Mid-May for scholarships
Officers and Directors:* Jerry B. Williams,* Chair.; Kerry Graham,* Vice-Chair.; Ellen E. Lehman,* Pres.; **Leilani S. Boulware,* Secy.**; Charles W. Cook, Jr.,* Treas.; Melisa Currey, Compt.; Ronald L. Corbin; Jana J. Davis; Rod Essig; Irwin E. Fisher; Dr. Stephen F. Flatt; Jay L. Frank; Ben G. Freeland; Gary A. Garfield; Hon. Alberto R. Gonzales; Jose D. Gonzalez; Mark R. Gwyn; Carl T. Haley; Henry B. Hicks, III; Carol Hudler; Decosta E. Jenkins; Hon. William C. Koch, Jr.; Robert S. Lipman; Don MacLachlan; Bert Mathews; Stephen F. Moore; Joelle J. Phillips; Deborah Taylor Tate; Dr. Stephanie H. Walker; Kevin J. Wheeler; David Williams II.
Trustees: Judy Liff Barker; Jack O. Bovender, Jr.; Ben Cundiff; Kitty Moon Emery; Richard J. Eskind; Farzin Ferdowsi; John D. Ferguson; Dr. Thomas F. Frist, Jr.; Joel C. Gordon; Francis Guess; James S. Gulmi; Mr. Aubrey B. Harwell, Jr.; Catherine T. Jackson; Kevin P. Lavender; Dr. John E. Maupin, Jr.; Ralph W. Mosley; Donna D. Nicely; Ben R. Rechter; Michael D. Shmerling; Susan W. Simons; Howard L. Stringer; Charles A. Trost; Deborah F. Turner; Jack B. Turner; Betsy Walkup.
Number of staff: 20 full-time professional.
EIN: 621471789
Other changes: Jerry B. Williams has replaced Francis Guess as Chair. Kerry Graham has replaced Jerry B. Williams as Vice-Chair. Leilani S. Boulware has replaced Kitty Moon Emery as Secy. Laundrea Lewis is now Grants Mgr. Brittany Mori is now Creative Svcs. Coord. Benja Whitelaw is now Prog. Mgr. Agenia W. Clark, George N. Bullard, Charles O. Frazier, and Kerry Graham are no longer members of the governing body.

3130
Joe C. Davis Foundation

3022 Vanderbilt Pl.
Nashville, TN **37212-2516**
***Contact:* Angela Moretti Goddard, Assoc. Dir.**
***E-mail:* agoddard@joecdavisfoundation.org; Main URL: http://www.joecdavisfoundation.org**

Established in 1976 in TN.
Donor: Joe C. Davis†.
Foundation type: Independent foundation.
Financial data (yr. ended 09/30/13): Assets, $121,660,795 (M); expenditures, $6,147,616; qualifying distributions, $4,772,964; giving activities include $4,700,000 for 55 grants (high: $1,501,000; low: $2,500).
Purpose and activities: Support for all levels of education; grants also for health, medical research, and human services.
Fields of interest: Education, early childhood education; Elementary school/education; Education; Health care; Substance abuse, services; Health organizations, association; Cancer; Alcoholism; Medical research, institute; Cancer research; Housing/shelter, development.
Type of support: Program development; Seed money; Scholarship funds; Research; Matching/challenge support.
Limitations: Applications accepted. Giving primarily in the Nashville, TN, area; funding also in Boston, MA. No grants to individuals.
Publications: Application guidelines.
Application information: Organizations may only submit one grant request per calendar year. Requests should not exceed $25,000 for the Feb./Mar. grant cycle. Application form not required.
Initial approach: Letter (2-3 pages) sent via e-mail
Copies of proposal: 1
Deadline(s): Feb. 15 and Aug. 1
Board meeting date(s): Mar. 20 and Sept. 20
Final notification: Mar. 31 and Sept. 30
Trustees: Nancy Graves Beveridge; Delta Anne Davis; William R. DeLoache, Jr.; Frances D. Ellison.
Number of staff: 1 part-time support.
EIN: 626125481

3131
The Terry D. and Rosann B. Douglass Foundation

Knoxville, TN

The foundation terminated in 2011.

3132
Dugas Family Foundation, Inc.

138 2nd Ave. N., Ste. 200
Nashville, TN 37201-1927 (615) 846-2053
Contact: Cabot Pyle

Donors: Laura Jo Dugas; Wayne F. Dugas, Sr.
Foundation type: Independent foundation.
Financial data (yr. ended 12/31/12): Assets, $23,798,078 (M); gifts received, $1,278,000; expenditures, $3,983,740; qualifying distributions, $3,646,934; giving activities include $3,580,051 for 24 grants (high: $615,000; low: $5,000).

Fields of interest: Education; Environment, natural resources; Human services; Children/youth, services.
Limitations: Applications accepted. Giving primarily in FL. No grants to individuals, or for travel, seminars, dinner events, or telethons; no loans.
Application information: Application form required.
Initial approach: **Letter requesting application form**
Deadline(s): **None**
Officers: Laura Jo Dugas, Pres.; Wayne F. Dugas, Sr., V.P.; **Lynn King Dugas, Secy.**; Stephen H. Dugas, Treas.
Directors: Pam Dugas; Wayne F. Dugas, Jr.
EIN: 263847853
Other changes: At the close of 2012, the grantmaker paid grants of $3,580,051, a 147.1% increase over the 2010 disbursements, $1,448,908.
Lynn King Dugas has replaced Wayne F. Dugas, Jr. as Secy.

3133
Eastman Chemical Company Foundation, Inc.

c/o Bank One Trust Co.
P.O. Box 511
Kingsport, TN 37662-5075 (423) 229-1413
Contact: Paul Montgomery, Dir.
Application address: Pennsylvania: Gerald Kuhn, Jefferson Site Mgr., Eastman Chemical Co., P.O. Box 567, West Elizabeth, PA 15088, fax: (412) 384-7311, e-mail: gkuhn@eastman.com; Tennessee and National Organizations: Angie Jobe, Eastman Chemical Co., P.O. Box 431, Kingsport, TN 37662, fax: (423) 229-8280, e-mail: angieb@eastman.com; and Texas: Sally Azbell, Eastman Chemical Co., P.O. Box 7444, Longview, TX 75607, fax: (903) 237-5799, e-mail: sazbell@eastman.com; **Main URL: http://www.eastman.com/Company/Sustainability/Social_Responsibility/communities/Eastman_Foundation/Pages/Eastman_Foundation.aspx**

Established in 1996 in TN.
Donor: Eastman Chemical Co.
Foundation type: Company-sponsored foundation.
Financial data (yr. ended 12/31/13): Assets, $4,146,343 (M); gifts received, $929,900; expenditures, $2,641,149; qualifying distributions, $2,625,324; giving activities include $2,625,324 for 393 grants (high: $400,000; low: $300).
Purpose and activities: The foundation supports programs designed to promote arts and culture, education, health, human services, community development, and civic affairs. Special emphasis is directed toward programs designed to improve the quality of life in communities where Eastman employees live and work.
Fields of interest: Arts councils; Performing arts; Arts; Higher education; Education, reading; Health care; Human services; Community development, neighborhood development; Business/industry; Community/economic development; United Ways and Federated Giving Programs; Mathematics; Engineering/technology; Science; Public affairs.
Type of support: General/operating support; Continuing support; Capital campaigns; Endowments; Program development; Scholarship funds.
Limitations: Applications accepted. Giving in areas of company operations, with emphasis on PA, TN and TX; giving also to national organizations. No support for athletic teams, choirs, bands, drill teams, labor, veterans', fraternal, social, or political organizations, United Way-supported agencies (except for capital fund drives), discriminatory organizations, or religious organizations not of direct benefit to the entire community. No grants to individuals, or for travel, student trips, or tours.
Publications: Application guidelines.
Application information: Multi-year funding is not automatic. Support is limited to 1 contribution per organization during any given year. Multi-year funding is not automatic. Application form required.
Initial approach: Complete online application or download application form and mail or fax to nearest application address
Deadline(s): July 31
Final notification: 12 weeks
Officers and Directors:* David Golden,* Pres.; Etta Clark,* V.P.; Elizabeth Twomey, Secy.; Mary Hall,* Treas.; Paul Montgomery; Perry Stuckey.
EIN: 621614800

3134
Elgin Foundation

4624 Chambliss Ave., Ste. 200
Knoxville, TN 37919-5118

Established in 2003 in TN.
Donor: The B.R. Thompson Charitable Trust.
Foundation type: Independent foundation.
Financial data (yr. ended 06/30/13): Assets, $33,719,156 (M); expenditures, $1,733,535; qualifying distributions, $1,385,344; giving activities include $1,267,395 for 8 grants (high: $642,943; low: $400).
Fields of interest: Education; Human services; Christian agencies & churches.
Limitations: Applications not accepted. Giving primarily in GA and TN. No grants to individuals.
Application information: Contributes only to pre-selected organizations.
Officers and Directors:* B. Ray Thompson, Jr.,* Pres.; Sarah T. Tarver,* Secy.; Rebekah T. Palmer; Adella S. Thompson; B. Ray Thompson III; Juanne J. Thompson; C. Vance Thompson.
EIN: 200337919
Other changes: At the close of 2013, the grantmaker paid grants of $1,267,395, a 227.6% increase over the 2012 disbursements, $386,879.

3135
First Horizon Foundation

(formerly First Tennessee Foundation)
c/o First Horizon National Corp.
165 Madison Ave., 8th. Fl.
Memphis, TN 38103-2723 **(901) 523-4207**
***Contact:* Melissa Duong, Mgr.**
FAX: (901) 523-4354;
E-mail: MDuong@FirstTennessee.com; Contact for Leadership Grants Program: Erica Wilkins, e-mail: EEWilkins@firsthorizon.com; Additional tel.: (901) 523-4291; Contact for Award for Innovation in the Arts: Lizzy Haymond, Corp. Comms., tel.: (901) 523-4291, e-mail: emhaymond@firsthorizon.com; Main URL: http://www.firsttennesseefoundation.com/

Established in 1993 in TN.
Donors: First Tennessee National Corp.; First Horizon National Corp.
Foundation type: Company-sponsored foundation.
Financial data (yr. ended 12/31/12): Assets, $46,311,463 (M); expenditures, $5,454,714; qualifying distributions, $5,228,724; giving activities include $5,228,724 for 1,035 grants (high: $391,000; low: $25).
Purpose and activities: The foundation supports programs designed to promote arts and culture; education and youth; financial literacy and economic development; and health and human services.
Fields of interest: Visual arts; Museums; Performing arts, orchestras; Arts; Elementary/secondary education; Higher education; Education; Environment, natural resources; Environment, land resources; Environment; Hospitals (general); Health care, clinics/centers; Health care; Athletics/sports, amateur leagues; Salvation Army; Youth, services; Human services, financial counseling; Human services; Economic development; United Ways and Federated Giving Programs.
Type of support: General/operating support; Annual campaigns; Capital campaigns; Building/renovation; Equipment; Endowments; Program development; Conferences/seminars; Professorships; Scholarship funds; Employee volunteer services; Sponsorships; Employee matching gifts.
Limitations: Applications accepted. Giving primarily in areas of company operations in TN. No support for bank clearinghouse organizations, charities sponsored solely by a single civic organization, pass through organizations, religious, veterans', social, or fraternal organizations, or political organizations. No grants to individuals, or for trips or tours, or debt reduction.
Publications: Application guidelines.
Application information:
Initial approach: E-mail or mail cover letter and proposal to nearest community investment manager
Deadline(s): Nov. 1
Final notification: End of Feb.
Officers and Directors:* **Charles G. Burkett, Chair.**; Gregg I. Lansky,* Pres., C.F.O, and Treas.; Clyde A. Billings, Jr.,* V.P. and Secy.; Kimberley C. Cherry; **Charles T. Tuggle, Jr.**; William C. Losch III.
EIN: 621533987
Other changes: Charles G. Burkett has replaced Charles T. Tuggle, Jr. as Chair.
Herbert H. Hilliard is no longer a director.

3136
The Dorothy Cate & Thomas F. Frist Foundation

(formerly The Frist Medical Foundation)
95 White Bridge Rd., Ste. 505
Nashville, TN **37205**
E-mail: dctffoundation@bellsouth.net

Established in 1989 in TN.
Donors: Dr. Thomas F. Frist, Sr.‡; Dorothy Cate Frist‡.
Foundation type: Independent foundation.
Financial data (yr. ended 11/30/13): Assets, $46,643,026 (M); expenditures, $2,246,589; qualifying distributions, $1,945,125; giving activities include $1,875,000 for 327 grants (high: $375,000; low: $100).
Fields of interest: Education; Human services.
Type of support: Annual campaigns; Capital campaigns; Building/renovation; Scholarship funds; Research.
Limitations: Applications not accepted. Giving primarily in TN. No grants to individuals.
Application information: Contributes only to pre-selected organizations.
Board meeting date(s): Mar. and Oct.
Officers: Thomas F. Frist, Jr., M.D., Pres.; Mary F. Barfield, V.P.; Dorothy Cate Frist, V.P.; Robert A. Frist, M.D., V.P.; William H. Frist, M.D., Secy.

Number of staff: 1 part-time professional.
EIN: 621103568

3137
Helen and Jabie Hardin Charitable Trust
4385 Poplar Ave.
Memphis, TN 38117-3715 **(901) 681-2349**
***Contact:* Leigh Lawler**

Established in 2009 in TN.
Donor: Helen E. Hardin Trust.
Foundation type: Independent foundation.
Financial data (yr. ended 10/31/13): Assets, $15,259,900 (M); expenditures, $6,615,541; qualifying distributions, $6,550,103; giving activities include $6,502,500 for 18 grants (high: $4,300,000; low: $2,500).
Fields of interest: Higher education; Education; Health care.
Limitations: Applications accepted. Giving primarily in TN.
Application information:
***Initial approach:* Letter**
***Deadline(s):* None**
Trustee: First Tennessee Bank.
EIN: 266754597
Other changes: For the fiscal year ended Oct. 31, 2013, the grantmaker paid grants of $6,502,500, a 710.3% increase over the fiscal 2012 disbursements, $802,500.
The grantmaker now accepts applications.

3138
The Haslam 3 Foundation, Inc.
(formerly The Sycamore Foundation, Inc.)
P.O. Box 10573
Knoxville, TN **37919-0573 (865) 384-4178**
Contact: Susan B. Haslam, Pres.

Established in 2001 in TN.
Donors: James A. Haslam III; Susan B. Haslam.
Foundation type: Independent foundation.
Financial data (yr. ended 12/31/12): Assets, $5,006,925 (M); gifts received, $771,000; expenditures, $1,279,544; qualifying distributions, $1,155,580; giving activities include $1,145,309 for 31 grants (high: $312,500; low: $1,000).
Fields of interest: Arts; Higher education; Education; Human services; United Ways and Federated Giving Programs; Christian agencies & churches.
Limitations: Giving primarily in Knoxville, TN.
Application information:
Initial approach: Letter
Deadline(s): June 30 and Dec. 31
Officers and Directors:* Susan B. Haslam,* Pres.; James A. Haslam III,* V.P.; **James E. Oakley III,* Secy.-Treas.**; Cynthia Haslam Arnholt; Whitney H. Johnson.
EIN: 621867421
Other changes: James E. Oakley III has replaced J. Todd Ellis as Secy.-Treas.

3139
The HCA Foundation
(formerly Columbia/HCA Healthcare Foundation, Inc.)
1 Park Plz., 4th Fl. East
Nashville, TN 37203-6527 (615) 344-2390
Contact: Lois Abrams, Grants Mgr.
FAX: (615) 344-5722;
E-mail: lois.abrams@hcahealthcare.com; Tel.: (615) 344-2343; e-mail: Corp.FoundationsGifts@HCAHealthcare.com; **Main URL: http://hcacaring.org/**
Grants List: http://hcacaring.org/supporting/agency-list.dot

Established in 1992 in KY.
Donors: Columbia/HCA Healthcare Corp.; HCA—The Healthcare Co.; HCA Inc.
Foundation type: Company-sponsored foundation.
Financial data (yr. ended 12/31/12): Assets, $76,555,046 (M); expenditures, $5,238,547; qualifying distributions, $4,753,498; giving activities include $4,650,965 for 756 grants (high: $300,000; low: $1).
Purpose and activities: The foundation supports organizations involved with education, health, mental health, hunger, housing, family services, and economic development. Special emphasis is directed toward programs designed to promote health and well-being; support childhood and youth development; and foster the arts in middle Tennessee.
Fields of interest: Arts education; Visual arts; Performing arts, opera; Historical activities; Arts; Education; Health care, clinics/centers; Health care; Food services; Housing/shelter, development; Housing/shelter; Youth development, community service clubs; Youth development, business; Youth development; YM/YWCAs & YM/YWHAs; Family services; Economic development; United Ways and Federated Giving Programs.
Type of support: General/operating support; Annual campaigns; Capital campaigns; Building/renovation; Equipment; Program development; Scholarship funds; Employee volunteer services; Employee matching gifts; Matching/challenge support.
Limitations: Applications accepted. Giving primarily in middle TN. No support for political organizations, individual churches or schools, organizations established less than 3 years ago, or research, sports, environmental, wildlife, civic or international affairs organizations. No grants to individuals, or for advertising or sponsorships or social events or similar fundraising activities.
Publications: Corporate giving report; Grants list; Newsletter.
Application information: Letters of inquiry should be no longer than 1 to 2 pages. A full application may be requested at a later date. Organizations must have a full updated GivingMatters.com profile to be considered for funding. General operations and program grants range from $1,500 - $25,000. Basic need and primary health grants range from $25,000 - $50,000.Organizations receiving support of $5,000 or more are asked to submit semi-annual and final progress reports. Application form not required.
Initial approach: Letter of inquiry to foundation for new applicants; complete online application for returning grantees
***Deadline(s):* Mar. 14, June 13, Sept. 12, and Dec. 13**
***Board meeting date(s):* Mar., May, Aug., and Nov.**
Officers and Directors:* Richard M. Bracken,* Chair.; R. Milton Johnson, Vice-Chair.; Joanne Pulles,* Pres.; Gary Pack, Secy.; David G. Anderson, Treas.; Peter F. Bird, Jr.; Jana Davis; Ray Monroe; Bruce Moore, Jr.; Cheryl Read; John M. Steele; John Steakley; Noel Brown Williams.
Number of staff: 1 full-time professional; 1 full-time support.
EIN: 611230563

3140
Orion L. & Emma B. Hurlbut Memorial Fund
701 Market St.
Chattanooga, TN 37402-4828
Application address: c/o Kathy Wood, 975 E. 3rd St., Chattanooga, TN 37403-2147; tel.: (423) 778-7503

Established in 1937 in TN.
Foundation type: Independent foundation.
Financial data (yr. ended 04/30/13): Assets, $21,088,208 (M); expenditures, $747,071; qualifying distributions, $721,179; giving activities include $581,429 for 2 grants (high: $550,000; low: $31,429).
Purpose and activities: Giving primarily to a tumor clinic; support also for treatment of indigent cancer patients outside of Hamilton County, TN.
Fields of interest: Cancer; Cancer research; Foundations (community); Economically disadvantaged.
Type of support: Grants to individuals.
Limitations: Giving primarily in Chattanooga, TN.
Application information: Applicants should include physicians' detailed expense voucher.
Initial approach: Letter
Deadline(s): None
Directors: Dr. John F. Boxell; Dr. Frank C. Kimsey; Harold G. Robertson.
Trustee: First Tennessee Bank, N.A.
EIN: 626034546
Other changes: Mary Lou Drazech is no longer a director.

3141
Hazel Montague Hutcheson Foundation
c/o John L. Hutcheson, IV
1237 Browns Ferry Rd.
Chattanooga, TN **37419-1531**
***Application address:* c/o Brooks, Moore & Assoc., Inc., Att.: Ricky Moore, 3905 St. Elmo Ave., Chattanooga, TN 37409, tel.: (423) 756-8628**

Established in 1962 in TN.
Donor: Hazel G.M. Montague†.
Foundation type: Independent foundation.
Financial data (yr. ended 06/30/13): Assets, $5,664,277 (M); expenditures, $335,693; qualifying distributions, $311,872; giving activities include $292,000 for 81 grants (high: $37,000; low: $300).
Fields of interest: Education; Human services; Children, services; Protestant agencies & churches.
Type of support: General/operating support; Annual campaigns.
Limitations: Applications accepted. Giving primarily in TN. No grants for scholarships; no loans.
Application information: Application form required.
Initial approach: Letter
Deadline(s): None
Board meeting date(s): Varies
Trustees: John Banks; Hazel H. Bell; John L. Hutcheson IV; Theodore M. Hutcheson, Jr.
EIN: 626045925

3142
International Paper Company Foundation
6400 Poplar Ave.
Memphis, TN 38197-0100 (800) 236-1996
Contact: Deano C. Orr, Exec. Dir.
E-mail: IPFoundation@ipaper.com; E-mail for Coins 4 Kids Program: coins4kids@ipaper.com; Main URL: http://www.internationalpaper.com/US/EN/Company/IPGiving/IPFoundation.html

Incorporated in 1952 in NY.
Donor: International Paper Co.
Foundation type: Company-sponsored foundation.
Financial data (yr. ended 12/31/12): Assets, $55,611,033 (M); expenditures, $2,913,305; qualifying distributions, $2,654,995; giving activities include $2,654,995 for 484 grants (high: $600,000; low: $30).
Purpose and activities: The foundation supports organizations involved with literacy, environmental education, and critical community needs.
Fields of interest: Museums; Education, ESL programs; Education, reading; Education; Environment, air pollution; Environment, water pollution; Environment, recycling; Environment, forests; Environmental education; Food services; Human services; Science; Children; Youth.
International interests: Africa.
Type of support: General/operating support; Equipment; Program development; Seed money; Curriculum development; Employee volunteer services; Employee matching gifts; In-kind gifts.
Limitations: Applications accepted. Giving on a national basis in areas of company operations, with some emphasis on Memphis, TN; giving also in Africa through the World Food Program. No support for veterans' or labor groups, religious or political groups, lobbying organizations, discriminatory organizations, or private foundations. No grants to individuals, or for scholarships, salaries, stipends, or other forms of compensation, mortgage, rent, or utilities, endowments, capital campaigns, multi-year commitments, sponsorships, advertising, travel or lodging expenses, national conferences, sporting events, or other one-time events; no loans.
Publications: Application guidelines; Corporate giving report; IRS Form 990 or 990-PF printed copy available upon request; Program policy statement.
Application information: All applications are routed to a local IP facility. Please contact the facility for local submission deadlines. Multi-year funding is not automatic. Application form required.
Initial approach: Complete online eligibility quiz and application
Copies of proposal: 1
***Deadline(s):* Varies per location, but generally reviewed Feb. 1, Apr. 1, Aug. 1, and Oct. 1**
Board meeting date(s): Sept.
Officers and Directors:* Patricia Neuhoff, Pres.; Marla Adair, Secy.; Carol Tusch, Treas.; Deano C. Orr, Exec. Dir.; Terri Herrington; Paul J. Karre; Franz Marx; Carol L. Roberts; Mark Sutton; Fred Towler.
Number of staff: 3 full-time professional; 1 part-time support.
EIN: 136155080
Other changes: Chandra Towler is now Comms. Specialist .

3143
Robert E. and Jenny D. Kirkland Foundation
624 E. Reelfoot Ave.
Union City, TN 38261-5739

Established in 2003 in TN.
Donors: Robert Kirkland; Kirkland 2004 Charitable Trust; Kirkland 2005 Charitable Trust; Kirkland 2007 Charitable Trust.
Foundation type: Independent foundation.
Financial data (yr. ended 12/31/12): Assets, $82,447,043 (M); gifts received, $7,539,195; expenditures, $1,912,503; qualifying distributions, $1,826,566; giving activities include $1,756,214 for 23 grants (high: $1,665,773; low: $100).
Fields of interest: Elementary/secondary education; Children/youth, services.
Type of support: Scholarship funds.
Limitations: Applications not accepted. Giving primarily in TN. No grants to individuals.
Application information: Contributes only to pre-selected organizations.
Officers and Directors:* Jenny D. Kirkland,* Pres.; Christopher Kirkland,* Secy.; Bedford F. Kirkland; Macy D. Swensson.
EIN: 134228589
Other changes: At the close of 2012, the fair market value of the grantmaker's assets was $82,447,043, an 80.0% increase over the 2011 value, $45,808,137.

3144
The Bill and Carol Latimer Charitable Foundation
201 W. Main St., Ste. E
Union City, TN 38261-2132 **(731) 885-2888**
Contact: **William H. Latimer III, Pres.**
FAX: (731) 885-3888;
E-mail: bill@latimerfoundation.org; Main URL: http://www.latimerfoundation.org/

Established in 2005 in TN.
Donor: William H. Lattimer III.
Foundation type: Independent foundation.
Financial data (yr. ended 12/31/12): Assets, $133,188,510 (M); expenditures, $11,949,503; qualifying distributions, $11,949,503; giving activities include $11,490,129 for 29+ grants (high: $7,000,000), and $26,705 for 8 loans to individuals (high: $9,259; low: $427).
Purpose and activities: Giving primarily to Christian churches and organizations, including a seminary, as well as for human services; student loans also available to students graduating from Obion, Weakly and Lake County, TN, high schools to secure a college or technical education.
Fields of interest: Theological school/education; Education; Human services; Christian agencies & churches.
Type of support: Student loans—to individuals.
Limitations: Applications not accepted.
Application information: Unsolicited requests for funds not accepted.
Officers and Trustees:* John L. Warner, Jr.,* Chair.; William H. Latimer III,* Pres.; Carol Rogers Latimer,* Secy.; Al Creswell; Barry Duncan; John Harney; Douglas N. Latimer; Mark M. Layne; Alan G. Oliver.
EIN: 203450991
Other changes: The grantmaker no longer lists a separate application address.
At the close of 2012, the grantmaker paid grants of $11,516,834, a 103.0% increase over the 2011 disbursements, $5,672,183.

3145
Lyndhurst Foundation
517 E. 5th St.
Chattanooga, TN 37403-1826 (423) 756-0767
Contact: Benic M. Clark III, Pres.
FAX: (423) 756-0770; E-mail for proposals: Krudolph@lyndhurstfoundation.org; Main URL: http://www.lyndhurstfoundation.org
Grants List: http://www.lyndhurstfoundation.org/page/grant-list/

Incorporated in 1938 in DE.
Donors: T. Cartter Lupton†; Central Shares Corp.
Foundation type: Independent foundation.
Financial data (yr. ended 12/31/12): Assets, $109,622,109 (M); expenditures, $4,900,181; qualifying distributions, $4,114,537; giving activities include $3,079,267 for 30 grants (high: $750,000; low: $2,500).
Purpose and activities: The mission of the foundation is to invest in initiatives, institutions, people and programs that contribute to the long-term livability and resilience of the greater Chattanooga region. It will accomplish this by focusing its efforts on education, conservation, arts, culture, economy, urban design and development, neighborhood revitalization, and physical health.
Fields of interest: Arts; Elementary school/education; Secondary school/education; Environment; Housing/shelter, development; Community/economic development.
Type of support: General/operating support; Continuing support; Capital campaigns; Building/renovation; Land acquisition; Program development; Seed money; Technical assistance; Employee matching gifts; Matching/challenge support.
Limitations: Applications not accepted. Giving primarily in the metropolitan Chattanooga, TN, area and the surrounding three-state region. No support for political organizations. No grants to individuals.
Publications: Financial statement; Grants list.
Application information: Unsolicited requests for funds not accepted.
Board meeting date(s): Feb., May, Aug., and Nov.
Officers and Trustees:* Robert C. Taylor, Jr., Chair.; Benic M. Clark III, Pres. and Treas.; **Katherine N. Currin,* Secy.**; Margaret Stakely, Cont.; Stephen A. Culp; Kathlee S. Hunt, M.D.; James O. Kennedy; Alison G. Lebovitz; James J. McGinness; Robert K. Mills; Margaret W. Townsend.
Number of staff: 4 full-time professional; 1 full-time support.
EIN: 626044177
Other changes: Katherine N. Currin is now Secy. Monique P. Berke is no longer a trustee.

3146
The Maclellan Foundation, Inc.
820 Broad St., Ste. 300
Chattanooga, TN 37402-2604 (423) 755-1366
Contact: Hugh O. Maclellan, Jr., Pres.
FAX: (423) 755-1640; E-mail: info@maclellan.net;
Additional e-mail: support@maclellan.net; Main URL: http://www.maclellan.net/family-foundations/maclellan

Incorporated in 1945 in DE; reincorporated in TN in 1992.
Donors: Robert J. Maclellan†; and members of the Maclellan family.
Foundation type: Independent foundation.
Financial data (yr. ended 12/31/12): Assets, $318,069,563 (M); expenditures, $34,369,148; qualifying distributions, $25,962,233; giving activities include $21,013,152 for 2+ grants (high: $17,660,000).
Purpose and activities: The purpose of the foundation in the Chattanooga area is to provide financial and leadership resources to foster biblical Christian values in the community and meet practical and spiritual needs. This is primarily accomplished through faith-based ministries. On a national basis, the foundation's vision is to see strong families worshipping in healthy churches, influencing culture, and seeking to serve God above all else. The focus is on nationwide strategies that deliver faith-based solutions.On an international basis, the foundation's vision is to see a vibrant, disciplined, reproducing church. The focus is on establishing and strengthening the church, discipleship and leadership development,

promoting community transformation, and increasing access to Scripture.
Fields of interest: Religion, association; Christian agencies & churches; Protestant agencies & churches; Children; Youth; Adults; Young adults; Hispanics/Latinos; Indigenous peoples.
International interests: Africa; Asia; Eastern Europe; Middle East.
Type of support: Consulting services; Matching/challenge support; Program development; Program evaluation.
Limitations: Applications accepted. Giving nationally, with emphasis on the Chattanooga, TN, area; giving internationally in Asia, Africa, Europe and Eurasia and the Middle East. No grants to individuals, or for emergency funds, deficit financing, land acquisition, endowment funds, health services, medical research, publications scholarships, or for renovations.
Application information: See foundation's website for granting guidelines, LOI, and explanation of application process. Only online LOI's will be considered. Application form not required.
Initial approach: Online application required
Copies of proposal: 1
Deadline(s): Ongoing through out the year.
Board meeting date(s): 3-4 times per year
Final notification: Within 60 days of LOI submission
Officers and Trustees:* Hugh O. Maclellan, Jr.,* Exec. Chair. and Treas.; Robert H. Maclellan,* Vice-Chair.; Sandy Barber, Compt.; David Denmark, Exec. Dir.; Tom Lowe, C.I.O.; Mrs. R.L. Maclellan, Tr. Emeritus; Ronald W. Blue; Mrs. Catherine Maclellan Heald; Christopher Maclellan; A.S. Pat MacMillan; Niel Nielson, Ph.D.; Laurence Powell; W. Miller Welborn.
Number of staff: 17 full-time professional; 5 full-time support.
EIN: 626041468

3147
Weldon F. Osborne Foundation, Inc.
Krystal Bldg.
1 Union Sq., Ste. 210
Chattanooga, TN 37402-2501 **(423) 267-0931**
***Contact:* Barbara Marter, Exec. Dir.**
***FAX:* (423) 402-8040;**
E-mail: wosborne@comcast.net; Main URL: http://www.wfosbornefoundation.org/
Grants List: http://www.wfosbornefoundation.org/grant-history/

Established in 1959.
Donors: Osborne Enterprises, Inc.; Osborne Building Corp.
Foundation type: Independent foundation.
Financial data (yr. ended 06/30/13): Assets, $18,534,890 (M); expenditures, $1,545,008; qualifying distributions, $1,122,362; giving activities include $998,024 for 116 grants (high: $100,000; low: $500).
Purpose and activities: Giving for civic, community, education and youth services.
Fields of interest: Education; Human services; Children/youth, services; Foundations (community); United Ways and Federated Giving Programs; Christian agencies & churches.
Type of support: Capital campaigns; Building/renovation; Seed money; Scholarship funds; Matching/challenge support.
Limitations: Giving primarily in the Chattanooga and Hamilton County, TN, areas. No grants to individuals.
Publications: Application guidelines; Annual report; Financial statement.
Application information: Application video tutorials and application policies and guidelines available on foundation web site. Application form required.
***Initial approach:* Letter of Inquiry to be submitted online through foundation web site after creating a user ID and password**
***Deadline(s):* Nov. 1 - Jan. 31 (for Feb. meeting); Mar. 1 - May 31 (for June meeting); and July 1 - Sept. 30 (for Oct. meeting)**
Board meeting date(s): 2nd Tues. each quarter; after annual meeting 2nd Tues. in June
Final notification: After next board meeting
Officers and Directors:* Glenn C. Stophel,* Pres.; H.E. "Gene" Burnett,* V.P., Progs.; Arch E. Trimble III,* Secy.; **Barbara J. Marter, Exec. Dir.**; C. Duffy Franck, Jr.; W. Scott Mattice; Dr. Christine B. Smith.
Number of staff: 1 part-time professional.
EIN: 626026442
Other changes: The grantmaker no longer lists a separate application address.
The grantmaker now makes its application guidelines available online.

3148
The Pedigree Foundation
(formerly The Pedigree Adoption Drive Foundation)
315 Cool Spring Blvd.
Franklin, TN 37067-1632
***E-mail:* info@pedigreefoundation.org**; Main URL: http://www.pedigreefoundation.org/
Facebook: https://www.facebook.com/pedigreefoundation
Pinterest: http://www.pinterest.com/Pedigreefou/
Twitter: https://twitter.com/PedigreeFound
YouTube: https://www.youtube.com/channel/UC8TDVpJsdXzxcGURtj5w6wQ

Established in 2007 in TN.
Donors: Lisa Liewald; Mars Petcare; Jacqueline Autry; Meryl Hartsband; Omnicom Group; Pedigree Brand; Linda Mars; Angelici Estate; Atlas Bass Fund.
Foundation type: Independent foundation.
Financial data (yr. ended 12/31/12): Assets, $984,314 (M); gifts received, $1,033,634; expenditures, $450,683; qualifying distributions, $450,433; giving activities include $342,805 for 162 grants (high: $25,000; low: $1,000).
Fields of interest: Animal welfare.
Limitations: Applications not accepted. Giving in the U.S.
Application information: Unsolicited requests for funds not accepted.
Officers and Directors:* Debra Fair,* Pres.; Bo Segers,* Secy.; Denise Battaglini,* Treas.; **Julie Duke, Exec. Dir.**; Steve Capitani; Chris Hamilton; Chris Mondzelewski.
EIN: 261121498
Other changes: Linda Mars and Angel May are no longer directors.

3149
Louie M. & Betty M. Phillips Foundation
4400 Harding Pike, Ste. 310
Nashville, TN 37205-2314
Application address: c/o Mr. Louie P. Buntin, C.E.O., 3334 Powell Ave., P.O. Box, 40788, Nashville, TN 37204-0788, tel.: (615) 385-5949, FAX: (615) 385-2507
Grants List: http://www.phillipsfoundation.org/gran2010.asp

Established in 1978 in TN.
Donors: Betty M. Phillips†; Louie M. Phillips†.
Foundation type: Independent foundation.
Financial data (yr. ended 12/31/12): Assets, $5,940,648 (M); expenditures, $708,538; qualifying distributions, $579,176; giving activities include $385,135 for 57 grants (high: $35,000; low: $500).
Purpose and activities: Giving primarily for health, human services, civic affairs, education and the arts.
Fields of interest: Arts; Education; Health care; Human services; Community/economic development.
Type of support: General/operating support; Continuing support; Annual campaigns; Capital campaigns; Building/renovation; Equipment; Endowments; Debt reduction; Seed money; Scholarship funds; Matching/challenge support.
Limitations: Applications accepted. Giving generally limited to the greater Nashville, TN, area. No support for disease-specific organizations, or for biomedical or clinical research. No grants to individuals, or for advertising or sponsorships.
Publications: Application guidelines; Grants list; Informational brochure (including application guidelines).
Application information: Application form required.
Initial approach: Letter
Copies of proposal: 1
Deadline(s): June 1 and Nov. 1
Board meeting date(s): June and Nov.
Officer: Louie P. Buntin, C.E.O.
Trustees: Equitable Trust Company; Trustmark National Bank.
Number of staff: 1 full-time professional.
EIN: 581326615
Other changes: The grantmaker no longer lists a URL or E-mail address.

3150
Promethean Foundation
206 E. Reelfoot Ave., Ste. 23
Union City, TN 38261-5739 (731) 884-0088
FAX: (888) 884-0237;
E-mail: promethean@bellsouth.net; Application address: c/o Cathy Waggoner, 115 W. Main St., Union City, TN 38261-3223; **Main URL: http://www.unioncityrotary.org/serviceProjects/promethean.asp**

Established in 2004 in TN.
Donor: Robert E. & Jenny D. Kirkland Foundation.
Foundation type: Independent foundation.
Financial data (yr. ended 12/31/12): Assets, $149,179 (M); gifts received, $1,665,773; expenditures, $1,713,377; qualifying distributions, $1,543,454; giving activities include $1,543,454 for grants.
Purpose and activities: The foundation provides scholarships for qualifying day care to newborns throughout school age, with the requirement that their progress be monitored throughout their school years. The applicants must live in Obion County, Tennessee, and scholarships are only paid to day cares which are approved and monitored by the foundation. The qualifying daycare facility must meet the moral, social, and educational values that the foundation feels are necessary to provide an excellent background for a successful life.
Fields of interest: Children, day care.
Type of support: Scholarship funds.
Limitations: Giving limited to Obion County, TN.
Application information: Application form required.
Initial approach: Letter or telephone requesting application form
Deadline(s): Prior to the birth of the child for which the scholarship is being requested

Officers and Directors:* Henry Clay Woods III,* Chair.; **Todd Stone,* Vice-Chair.**; **Gary Houston,* Secy.**; **Clint Joiner,* Treas.**; **David Huss**; Robert E. Kirkland; Martin Sisco.
EIN: 201690784
Other changes: Todd Stone has replaced Gary Houston as Vice-Chair. Gary Houston has replaced Martin Sisco as Secy. Clint Joiner has replaced Chuck Doss as Treas.
Vincent Bell, Dan Boykin, and Roger Williams are no longer trustees.

3151
Regal Foundation
7132 Regal Ln.
Knoxville, TN 37918-5803 (865) 925-9435
Main URL: http://www.regmovies.com/About-Regal/Community-Affairs

Established in 2003.
Donor: Regal Entertainment Group.
Foundation type: Company-sponsored foundation.
Financial data (yr. ended 12/31/12): Assets, $7,450,049 (M); gifts received, $5,226,353; expenditures, $3,561,793; qualifying distributions, $3,561,362; giving activities include $3,339,671 for 179 grants (high: $1,006,950; low: $100).
Purpose and activities: The foundation supports food banks and organizations involved with arts and culture, education, health, cancer, multiple sclerosis, diabetes, child welfare, human services, and children. Special emphasis is directed toward programs designed to benefit economically disadvantaged people or persons suffering economic, social, physical, or educational hardship.
Fields of interest: Media, film/video; Museums (art); Performing arts, theater; Arts; Secondary school/education; Higher education; Education; Hospitals (general); Health care, patient services; Health care; Cancer; Multiple sclerosis; Diabetes; Crime/violence prevention, child abuse; Food banks; Boys & girls clubs; American Red Cross; YM/YWCAs & YM/YWHAs; Human services, gift distribution; Human services; United Ways and Federated Giving Programs; Children; Economically disadvantaged.
Type of support: Capital campaigns; General/operating support; Program development; Scholarship funds; Sponsorships; In-kind gifts.
Limitations: Applications not accepted. Giving primarily in areas of company operations in CA and Knoxville, TN. No support for political or discriminatory organizations. No grants for travel, operating, or advertising expenses.
Officers and Directors: Michael L. Campbell,* Pres.; **Richard S. Westerling, Secy.**; Gregory W. Dunn; Neal D. Pinsker; Amy E. Miles; Raymond L. Smith, Jr.
EIN: 134249812

3152
Scarlett Family Foundation
4117 Hillsboro Pike, Ste. 103255
Nashville, TN 37215-2728
Contact: Tom Parrish, Exec. Dir.
E-mail: tomparrish@scarlettfoundation.org; Main URL: http://www.scarlettfoundation.org/
E-Newsletter: https://app.e2ma.net/app2/audience/signup/1744548/1726359/?v=a
Facebook: https://www.facebook.com/pages/Scarlett-Family-Foundation/165267570180614
LinkedIn: http://www.linkedin.com/company/scarlett-family-foundation?goback=.cps_1290558041631_1&trk=co_search_results
Twitter: https://twitter.com/ScarlettFndt
Scholarship application address: **c/o International Scholarship Tuition Services, Inc., 1321 Murfreesboro Rd., Ste. 800, Nashville, TN 37217, tel.: (615) 777-3750, fax: (615) 320-3151, e-mail: info@applyists.com**

Established in 2004 in TN.
Donor: Joseph H. Scarlett, Jr.
Foundation type: Independent foundation.
Financial data (yr. ended 06/30/13): Assets, $53,260,252 (M); gifts received, $24,730,551; expenditures, $2,221,891; qualifying distributions, $1,863,333; giving activities include $1,314,891 for 27 grants (high: $260,000; low: $4,576), and $397,204 for 57 grants to individuals (high: $15,000; low: $2,462).
Purpose and activities: Giving primarily for education, including scholarship awards to high school seniors and college freshmen, sophomores, and juniors from Middle Tennessee for full-time enrollment in a 4-year not-for-profit business studies program at a college or university within the U.S. Grants to Middle Tennessee-based organizations that support education for students of all ages.
Fields of interest: Higher education; Education; Children; Adults; Young adults; Girls; Boys.
Type of support: General/operating support; Continuing support; Management development/capacity building; Program development; Seed money; Curriculum development; Internship funds; Program evaluation; Scholarships—to individuals.
Limitations: Giving primarily in middle TN (the 39 counties are available on foundation web site). No support for political programs or purposes. No grants to individuals (except for scholarships), or for news letters or magazines, tickets to charitable events or dinners, sponsor special events, productions, or performances, legislative lobbying or to retire debt.
Publications: Application guidelines; Grants list.
Application information: Application form required for scholarships and grants. Grant applications are accepted by invitation only. See web site for application information. Application form required.
Initial approach: E-mail
Copies of proposal: 1
Board meeting date(s): Four times a year.
Officers and Directors:* Tara Anne Scarlett, Pres.; Jennifer Scarlett, Secy.; Andrew S. Scarlett, Treas.; Tom Parrish, Exec. Dir.; Dorothy F. Scarlett; Joseph H. Scarlett, Jr.
Number of staff: 1 part-time professional.
EIN: 201980932
Other changes: For the fiscal year ended June 30, 2013, the fair market value of the grantmaker's assets was $53,260,252, a 132.9% increase over the fiscal 2012 value, $22,871,394.

3153
William E. Schmidt Foundation, Inc.
3712 Central Ave., Ste. 500
Nashville, TN 37205
***Application address for Schmidt Youth Vocal Competition:* c/o Linda McAlister, Coor., 109 Presser Hall, 501 S. Patterson Ave., Miami University, Oxford, OH 45056, tel.: (513) 529-3046**; Main URL: http://www.schmidtfoundation.org/
Grants List: http://www.schmidtfoundation.org/grants.shtml

Established in 1993 in IN.
Donor: William E. Schmidt.
Foundation type: Independent foundation.
Financial data (yr. ended 12/31/12): Assets, $3,467,374 (M); gifts received, $1,250; expenditures, $312,650; qualifying distributions, $277,450; giving activities include $253,650 for 16 grants (high: $171,000; low: $100).
Purpose and activities: Giving to support youth in the musical arts and through education.
Fields of interest: Performing arts, opera; Higher education; Education; Boys & girls clubs; Christian agencies & churches; Young adults.
Type of support: Annual campaigns; Capital campaigns; Matching/challenge support.
Limitations: Applications accepted. Giving primarily in Evansville, IN, KY and FL.
Application information: See foundation web site for complete application guidelines. Application form required.
Officers: William E. Schmidt, Pres.; Sarah E. Schmidt, V.P.; Chester Schmidt, Secy.; Richard W. Shymanski, Treas.
Board Members: David F. Hamilton; Elizabeth Hamilton; John Hamilton; Chad Schmidt; Douglas M. Schmidt; Steven Schmidt; Lea Schmidt-Rogers.
EIN: 351884241
Other changes: The grantmaker has moved from IN to TN.

3154
The Sparks Foundation
775 Ridge Lake Blvd., Ste. 450
Memphis, TN 38120-9473 **(901) 766-4412**
Contact: Robert D. Sparks, Tr.
FAX: (901) 766-8133

Established in 2001 in TN.
Donors: Willard D. Sparks; Gerard Miller.
Foundation type: Independent foundation.
Financial data (yr. ended 12/31/12): Assets, $12,441,821 (M); expenditures, $601,959; qualifying distributions, $538,745; giving activities include $538,745 for 38 grants (high: $200,000; low: $350).
Purpose and activities: Giving primarily for the arts, education, causes for the handicapped, and religion.
Fields of interest: Education; Human services; Religion.
Limitations: Applications accepted. Giving limited to MS, OK and TN. No grants to individuals, or for federated campaigns.
Application information: Application form required.
Initial approach: Proposal
Deadline(s): Mar. 31 and Oct. 31
Board meeting date(s): Apr. and Nov.
Final notification: Within 30 days
Trustee: Robert D. Sparks.
EIN: 237029788
Other changes: The grantmaker no longer lists a URL address.

3155
Stuttering Foundation of America, Inc.
(also known as The Stuttering Foundation)(formerly Speech Foundation of America)
1805 Moriah Woods Blvd., Ste. 3
Memphis, TN 38117-7121 (800) 992-9392
Contact: Jane Fraser, Pres.
FAX: (901) 761-0484;
E-mail: info@stutteringhelp.org; Mailing address: Stuttering Foundation of America, Inc., c/o Jane Fraser, Pres., P.O. Box 11749, Memphis, TN

38111-0749; Main URL: http://www.stutteringhelp.org
E-Newsletter: http://www.stutteringhelp.org/newsletters
Facebook: https://www.facebook.com/stutteringhelp
Pinterest: http://www.pinterest.com/stutteringfdn/
Podcasts: http://www.stutteringhelp.org/podcasts
RSS Feed: http://feeds.feedburner.com/blogspot/CLLc
Twitter: http://twitter.com/stutteringfdn
YouTube: http://www.youtube.com/user/stutteringfdn
Established in 1947 in TN.
Donors: Members of the Fraser family; Jane Fraser.
Foundation type: Operating foundation.
Financial data (yr. ended 12/31/12): Assets, $24,966,597 (M); gifts received, $348,282; expenditures, $1,794,623; qualifying distributions, $1,570,519; giving activities include $250,000 for 1 grant (high: $250,000), and $4,375 for 35 grants to individuals (high: $125; low: $125).
Purpose and activities: Giving for foundation-initiated programs in therapy and the prevention of stuttering.
Type of support: Conferences/seminars; Publication; Grants to individuals.
Limitations: Applications not accepted.
Publications: Annual report; Informational brochure; Newsletter.
Application information: Unsolicited requests for funds not accepted.
Board meeting date(s): May
Officers: Jane Fraser, Pres.; Joe Fulcher, V.P.; Joseph Walker, Secy.; Donald Edwards, Treas.
Directors: Frances Cook; Dennis Drayna; Jean Fraser Gruss; Robert M. Kurtz, Jr.; Donald Lineback; Alan Rabinowitz.
Number of staff: 1 full-time professional; 3 full-time support; 2 part-time support.
EIN: 626047678

3156
Tucker Foundation
600 Krystal Bldg.
100 W. MLK Blvd.
Chattanooga, TN 37402-2514 **(423) 756-1202**
Contact: M. Hayne Hamilton, Pres.
E-mail: hhamilton@johnsouth.com; Additional e-mail: amoore@johnsouth.com; **Main URL: http://www.thetuckerfoundation.org/**
Established in 1996.
Donor: S.K. Johnston, Jr.
Foundation type: Independent foundation.
Financial data (yr. ended 12/31/12): Assets, $27,908,308 (M); expenditures, $1,683,378; qualifying distributions, $1,334,145; giving activities include $1,201,230 for 53 grants (high: $290,003; low: $200).
Purpose and activities: The primary objective of The Tucker Foundation is to provide financial support to non-profit organizations to produce in young people the character and skills required to live a productive and happy life. It also supports organizations that conserve essential elements of our natural environment forever.
Fields of interest: Arts, public education; Performing arts, education; Humanities; Education; Environment; Human services.
Type of support: Scholarship funds; Program-related investments/loans; Land acquisition; Internship funds; General/operating support; Endowments; Capital campaigns; Building/renovation; Annual campaigns.
Limitations: Applications accepted. Giving primarily in the Chattanooga/Hamilton County metro area and the Cleveland/Bradley County, area, TN, Sheridan County and Johnson County, WY, and Palm Beach County, FL. No support for political or lobbying activities, churches and purely religious activities, start-ups or organizations without 501 (c) (3) status. No grants to individuals, or for seed money, capacity building, film, video, or radio or for institutional startup or reorganization, marketing and public relations activities or for requests containing any benefit to family members, trustees, and officers of the foundation.
Application information: Application form not required.
Initial approach: Online application process
Copies of proposal: 1
Deadline(s): Apr. 15th for June meeting; Oct. 15th for Dec. meeting
Board meeting date(s): June and Dec.
Final notification: July and Dec.
Officers and Trustees:* M. Hayne Hamilton,* Pres.; Pamela K. Cuzzort,* Treas.; Andrew G. Cope; Gillian Johnston; Lavinia Johnston; Robert T. Johnston; Katherine J. Tudor.
Number of staff: 2 full-time professional.
EIN: 621603398

3157
The Kemmons Wilson Family Foundation
8700 Trail Lake Dr., Ste. 300
Memphis, TN 38125-8205 (901) 328-5037
Contact: Lauren Wilson-Young, Exec. Dir.
FAX: (901) 396-3570; E-mail: lyoung@kwilson.com; Additional e-mail for Lee Morris: lmorris@kwilson.com, e-mail for Libby Wilson, Dir., Comm.: lwilson@kwilson.com; Main URL: http://www.kwilsonff.com
Established about 1961 in TN.
Foundation type: Independent foundation.
Financial data (yr. ended 12/31/12): Assets, $34,870,623 (M); gifts received, $9,436; expenditures, $1,832,025; qualifying distributions, $1,795,600; giving activities include $1,595,741 for 153 grants (high: $55,000; low: $100).
Purpose and activities: The foundation intends to positively impact and transform the Memphis, Tennessee community through grantmaking in the following categories: community outreach, and development advancement of youth, enriching education, faith-based ministries, and health and research related organizations.
Fields of interest: Museums; Elementary/secondary education; Higher education; Hospitals (general); Children/youth, services; Community/economic development; United Ways and Federated Giving Programs; Protestant agencies & churches; Infants/toddlers; Children/youth; Children; Youth; Adults; Aging; Young adults; Disabilities, people with; Physically disabled; Deaf/hearing impaired; Mentally disabled; Minorities; African Americans/Blacks; Women; Infants/toddlers, female; Girls; Adults, women; Young adults, female; Men; Infants/toddlers, male; Boys; Adults, men; Young adults, male; Military/veterans; Substance abusers; Single parents; Crime/abuse victims; Terminal illness, people with; Economically disadvantaged; Homeless.
Type of support: General/operating support; Continuing support; Annual campaigns; Capital campaigns; Building/renovation; Endowments; Emergency funds; Program development; Seed money; Curriculum development; Scholarship funds; Research; Program evaluation; Matching/challenge support.
Limitations: Applications accepted. Giving primarily in the greater Memphis area, TN. No grants to individuals.
Publications: Application guidelines.
Application information: Complete application guidelines available on foundation web site. Application form required.
***Initial approach:* Use grant application system on foundation web site**
Copies of proposal: 1
***Deadline(s):* Jan. 15 and Aug. 15**
Board meeting date(s): Mar., Aug. and Nov.
Officers and Directors:* Spence L. Wilson,* Pres.; Charles K. Wilson, Jr.,* V.P.; Robert A. Wilson,* V.P.; Elizabeth Wilson-Moore; Carol Wilson-West.
Number of staff: 3 part-time professional.
EIN: 626046687
Other changes: The grantmaker now publishes application guidelines.

TEXAS

3158
A Glimmer of Hope Foundation
3600 N. Capital of TX Hwy, Bldg. B, Ste. 330
Austin, TX 78746-3209 (512) 328-9944
Contact: Michael O'Keefe, Comms. Dir.
FAX: (512) 328-8872;
E-mail: inquiries@aglimmerofhope.org; Main URL: http://www.aglimmerofhope.org
A Glimmer of Hope Foundation's Philanthropy's Promise: http://www.ncrp.org/philanthropys-promise/who
Facebook: http://www.facebook.com/pages/A-Glimmer-of-Hope-Foundation/102487557749
Founder's Blog: http://aglimmerofhopefoundation.blogspot.com/
Multimedia: http://www.aglimmerofhope.org/success-stories
Twitter: http://twitter.com/aglimmerofhope
Vimeo: http://www.vimeo.com/aglimmerofhope
YouTube: http://www.youtube.com/aglimmerofhopeorg

Established in 2000 in TX.
Donors: Donna Berber; Philip Berber; Eric Schmidhauser; Lucie Schmidhauser; Leslie Moore; Kathy Moore; Neil Webber; Ronnie Morgan; Bill Parrish; Margaret Parrish; Neil Webber; Ernst & Young; Tim Brosnan; Tony Gannon; Berberfam, Ltd.; Operation Days Work; Berberfam, Ltd.; Austin Ethiopian Women Assn.; Lee Portnoi; Mark Stryker; Oregon Ethiopian Community Organization; Robert Epstein; Preston Ctr.; The Andrew S. Roddick Foundation.
Foundation type: Independent foundation.
Financial data (yr. ended 12/31/12): Assets, $50,557,929 (M); gifts received, $10,250,911; expenditures, $11,950,582; qualifying distributions, $11,560,671; giving activities include $8,738,503 for 14 grants (high: $5,750,412; low: $9,926).
Purpose and activities: The foundation serves to ease some of the pain and suffering on the planet. It currently operates a national aid program in Ethiopia as well as programs for excluded youth in the U.S. and the U.K.
Fields of interest: Business school/education; Human services; Children/youth, services; International relief; International affairs; Economically disadvantaged.
International interests: Ireland; England; Ethiopia.
Limitations: Applications not accepted. Giving primarily in Austin, TX, London, England, and Ethiopia.
Application information: Contributes only to pre-selected organizations.
Officers: Donna Berber, Co-Chair.; Philip Berber, Co-Chair.; Brian Cooper, C.E.O.; **Stephanie Fast, C.F.O.**; David Porter III, Exec. Dir.; Carla Power, Cont.
EIN: 311758218

3159
A Glimmer of Hope Foundation - Austin
3600 N. Capital of Texas Hwy., Bldg. B., Ste. 330
Austin, TX 78746-3314 (512) 328-9944
***FAX:* (512) 328-8872**;
E-mail: austinprojects@aglimmerofhope.org; Main URL: http://www.aglimmerofhopeaustin.org/
Facebook: https://www.facebook.com/aglimmerofhopeaustin
Twitter: https://twitter.com/glimmeraustin

Donors: Ross Garber; A Glimmer of Hope Foundation; Silverton Foundation; Austin Athletic Scholarship Foundation; Cumberland Continental; Wells Fargo Bank, N.A.; Mydna Media, Inc.; The Andrew S. Roddick Foundation.
Foundation type: Independent foundation.
Financial data (yr. ended 12/31/12): Assets, $405,532 (M); gifts received, $339,642; expenditures, $394,399; qualifying distributions, $394,343; giving activities include $378,413 for 44 grants (high: $20,128; low: $250).
Purpose and activities: A Glimmer of Hope in Austin is committed to improving the lives of young people (up to age 25), who suffer from exclusion, social injustices, and educational disadvantages. Projects selected for funding empower youth, prepare them for success in life, and help them to make positive choices. One-year grants are awarded to organizations serving youth in the following areas: 1) After-school and Education, 2) Life and Job Skills, 3) Health and Nutrition, 4) Arts and Dance, and 5) Safety and Security.
Fields of interest: Children/youth, services.
Limitations: Applications accepted. Giving primarily in East and South Austin, TX, with the following boundaries: North (Rundberg Ln.), South (Slaughter Ln.), East (Decker Ln./Hwy. 183 Corridor), and West (IH 35 Corridor). The following postal codes are also eligible to apply: 78751, 78752, 78757, and 78758. No support for cultural exchange programs. No grants to individuals, or for travel or scholarship assistance, general operating funds, construction projects, hardware upgrades or labs, fundraising events, mass mailings, advertising projects, conferences or symposia, out-of-state performances or competition expenses, or for academic or scientific research.
Application information: Application guidelines available on foundation web site.
Officers: Donna Berber, Pres.; Philip Berber, V.P.; Ryan Berber, Secy.-Treas.
EIN: 200733502

3160
Abell-Hanger Foundation
P.O. Box 430
Midland, TX 79702-0430
Contact: David L. Smith, Exec. V.P. and Exec. Dir.
FAX: (432) 684-4474;
E-mail: AHF@abell-hanger.org; Main URL: http://www.abell-hanger.org

Incorporated in 1954 in TX.
Donors: George T. Abell†; Gladys H. Abell†.
Foundation type: Independent foundation.
Financial data (yr. ended 06/30/13): Assets, $155,772,456 (M); expenditures, $8,871,669; qualifying distributions, $8,701,554; giving activities include $6,702,316 for 186 grants (high: $1,500,000; low: $85), and $407,647 for 157 employee matching gifts.
Purpose and activities: Support primarily for higher education, youth activities, cultural programs, health services, the handicapped, and social welfare agencies.
Fields of interest: Arts; Higher education; Business school/education; Nursing school/education; Nursing care; Health care; Substance abuse, services; Human services; Children/youth, services; Family services; Aging, centers/services; Community/economic development; Voluntarism promotion; Government/public administration; Children/youth; Young adults; Disabilities, people with; Physically disabled; Blind/visually impaired; Deaf/hearing impaired; Mentally disabled; Hispanics/Latinos; Substance abusers; AIDS, people with; Crime/abuse victims; Economically disadvantaged; Homeless; Migrant workers.
Type of support: General/operating support; Continuing support; Annual campaigns; Capital campaigns; Building/renovation; Equipment; Program development; Seed money; Scholarship funds; Research; Employee matching gifts; Matching/challenge support.
Limitations: Applications accepted. Giving limited to West TX, especially the Midland and Ector counties. No support for individuals, or for individual scholarships or fellowships; no loans.
Publications: Annual report (including application guidelines); Financial statement; Grants list.
Application information: The foundation supplied grant application forms are required. The foundation does not acknowledge the receipt of proposals, and only grants interviews with applicants at the final stage of the application process. Application form required.
Copies of proposal: 1
***Deadline(s):* Feb., May, Aug., and Nov. 15.**
Board meeting date(s): Mar., June, Sept., and Dec.
Final notification: 1 month
Officers and Trustees:* Tevis Herd,* Pres.; David L. Smith,* Exec. V.P. and Exec. Dir.; Herbert L. Cartwright, V.P., Secy.-Treas., and Comp.; John D. Bergman; Jake Harper; Robert C. Leibrock; Elaine Magruder; Clarence Scharbauer III; Wes Perry; James C. Trott; Charles M. Younger, M.D.
Number of staff: 4 full-time professional; 1 full-time support.
EIN: 756020781

3161
Alcon Cares, Inc.
6201 S. Freeway
Fort Worth, TX 76134-2001 (817) 293-0450
Contact: Don Doyle, Pres.
Main URL: http://www.alcon.com/en/corporate-responsibility/alcon-foundation.asp

Donor: Alcon Laboratories, Inc.
Foundation type: Operating foundation.
Financial data (yr. ended 12/31/12): Assets, $0 (M); gifts received, $222,638; expenditures, $222,638; giving activities include $222,638 for grants.
Purpose and activities: The foundation provides medications to individuals who cannot afford their medication and to those who lack prescription insurance coverage; and provides access to eye care medication for U.S. medical facilities serving large numbers of Medicare and Medicaid patients.
Fields of interest: Eye diseases; Eye research; Human services; Economically disadvantaged.
Type of support: Grants to individuals; Donated products; In-kind gifts.
Limitations: Applications accepted. Giving on a national basis and to communities in which Alcon has a facility. No support for religious, fraternal, labor, political or veteran programs. No support for non 501(c)(3) designated organizations, or for individual or family requests for scholarships, or for fellowship assistance, endowments, or capital and building campaigns outside of community-aligned grants, or for matching gifts, private schools K-12, books, research papers, or articles in professional journals, or for travel expenses.
Publications: Application guidelines.
Application information: Application form required.
***Initial approach:* Completed application form**
Deadline(s): None
Officers: Don Doyle, Pres.; Becky Walker, Secy.; Carol Duval, Treas.

Directors: Eduardo Blas; **David Malenfant**; John Reding.
EIN: 204118713

3162
The Alcon Foundation, Inc.
6201 S. Freeway
Fort Worth, TX 76134-2099 (800) 222-8103
Contact: Matthew Head, Dir., Corp. Giving
***FAX:* (817) 615-3811**; Main URL: http://www.alcon.com/en/corporate-responsibility/alcon-foundation.asp

Established in 1962 in TX.
Donor: Alcon Laboratories, Inc.
Foundation type: Company-sponsored foundation.
Financial data (yr. ended 12/31/12): Assets, $30,000 (M); gifts received, $6,379,485; expenditures, $6,398,990; qualifying distributions, $6,398,990; giving activities include $6,379,485 for 155 grants (high: $600,000; low: $677).
Purpose and activities: The Alcon Foundation supports programs designed to improve the quality of eye care and patient access to eye care; advance eye health education, research, and awareness; and enhance and create sound communities where Alcon has a facility presence.
Fields of interest: Medical school/education; Education; Hospitals (specialty); Optometry/vision screening; Eye diseases; Eye research; Human services; Community/economic development; Blind/visually impaired; Economically disadvantaged.
Type of support: Management development/capacity building; Program development; Curriculum development; Research.
Limitations: Applications accepted. Giving primarily in areas of company operations in Irvine, CA, Atlanta, GA, Sinking Spring, PA, Fort Worth and Houston, TX, and Huntington, WV. No support for fraternal, labor, political, or veterans' organizations, discriminatory organizations, or private K-12 schools. No grants to individuals, or for family requests for scholarships, fellowships, religious activities, endowments, capital or building campaigns, matching gifts, university administrative, management, or indirect fees, golf tournaments, athletic events, league or team sponsorships, school-affiliated orchestras, bands, choirs, student trips or tours, unrestricted grants, books, research papers, articles in professional journals, travel, fundraising activities, or advertising sponsorships.
Publications: Application guidelines; Corporate giving report.
Application information: Application form required.
Initial approach: Complete online eligibility quiz and application
Deadline(s): None; Feb. 1 to July 31 for requests of $50,000 or more
Board meeting date(s): 4th quarter
Final notification: Final notification for large grant requests is 1st quarter of the following year.
Officers and Directors:* Kevin J. Buehler,* Chair.; Bettina Maunz, Pres.; Christina Ackerman; Robert Kim; Merrick McCracken; Steven Wilson.
EIN: 200166600
Other changes: At the close of 2012, the grantmaker paid grants of $6,379,485, a 60.5% increase over the 2011 disbursements, $3,975,157.

3163
Amarillo Area Foundation, Inc.
801 S. Fillmore, Ste. 700
Amarillo, TX 79101-3537 (806) 376-4521
Contact: For grants: Kathie Grant, Grants Coord.
FAX: (806) 373-3656; E-mail: haf@aaf-hf.org; Grant application e-mail: kathie@aaf-hf.org; Main URL: http://www.amarilloareafoundation.org
E-Newsletter: http://www.amarilloareafoundation.org/page.aspx?pid=528

Established as a trust in 1957 in TX.
Foundation type: Community foundation.
Financial data (yr. ended 12/31/12): Assets, $205,986,892 (M); gifts received, $8,409,849; expenditures, $9,851,923; giving activities include $5,378,320 for 174+ grants (high: $479,621), and $827,475 for 783 grants to individuals.
Purpose and activities: The foundation seeks to improve the quality of life in the TX Panhandle through effective philanthropic efforts. The foundation is currently focused on four areas of particular priority: 1) Education; 2) Health; 3) Human Services; and 4) Youth and Families.
Fields of interest: Arts; Education; Health care; Disasters, preparedness/services; Recreation, centers; Recreation; Children/youth, services; Family services; Aging, centers/services; Human services; Youth; Economically disadvantaged.
Type of support: Management development/capacity building; Building/renovation; Equipment; Land acquisition; Emergency funds; Program development; Seed money; Scholarship funds; Matching/challenge support.
Limitations: Applications accepted. Giving limited to the 26 northernmost counties of the Texas Panhandle region. No support for private or parochial schools, national, state, or local fundraising activities, or religious activities or programs that serve or appear to serve specific religious groups, or denominations. No grants to individuals (except for the scholarship program), or generally for operating budgets, annual campaigns, deficit financing, endowment funds, publications, conferences, travel, research projects, or historic preservation; no loans.
Publications: Annual report; Informational brochure; Newsletter.
Application information: Visit foundation web site for application form and guidelines. Proposals should be submitted a minimum of 3-4 months before funds are needed. Application form required.
Initial approach: Mail or e-mail application form and attachments
Copies of proposal: 1
Deadline(s): None
Board meeting date(s): Feb., Apr., June, Aug., Oct., and Dec.; Exec. Comm. meets bimonthly: Mar., May, July, Sept., and Nov.
Officers and Directors:* Julie Mitchell,* Chair.; Cliff Bickerstaff,* 1st Vice-Chair.; Puff Niegos,* 2nd Vice-Chair.; Clay Stribling,* C.E.O. and Pres.; Angela Lust,* Sr. V.P.; Charlotte Rhodes,* V.P., Regional Svcs.; **Linda Rasor,* Secy.; Jason Herrick,* Treas.**; Roy Bara; **Jeri Bezner**; Vanessa Buzzard; Terry Caviness; Paul Clark; Kathy Cornett; LeRayne Donelson; Mike Engler; Steve Hoard; Steve Hoard; Larry Johnson; Ken Kelley; Sharon Miner; Alice O'Brien; Jackie Pearson; Dyke Rogers; Rod Schroder; Edward Scott; Nancy Seliger; Caroline Smith; Roy Urrutia.
Number of staff: 10 full-time professional.
EIN: 750978220
Other changes: Julie Mitchell has replaced Mike Engler as Chair. Cliff Bickerstaff has replaced Julie Mitchell as 1st Vice-Chair. Puff Niegos has replaced Cliff Bickerstaff as 2nd Vice-Chair. Linda Rasor has replaced Caroline Smith as Secy. Jason Herrick has replaced Puff Niegos as Treas.
Brent Allen and Chris Matthews are no longer directors.

3164
Robert A. and Kathey K. Anderson Foundation
10100 Reunion Pl., Ste. 635
San Antonio, TX 78216-4128 (210) 377-0669
Contact: Robert A. Anderson, Pres.

Established in 2001 in TX.
Donor: Robert A. Anderson.
Foundation type: Independent foundation.
Financial data (yr. ended 08/31/13): Assets, $6,995,825 (M); expenditures, $327,873; qualifying distributions, $307,450; giving activities include $307,450 for 46 grants (high: $74,000; low: $500).
Fields of interest: Higher education; Human services; Salvation Army; Protestant agencies & churches.
Type of support: General/operating support.
Limitations: Applications accepted. Giving primarily in TX, with emphasis on San Antonio. No grants to individuals.
Application information: Application form required.
***Initial approach:* Proposal**
***Deadline(s):* None**
Officers: Robert A. Anderson, Pres.; Kathey K. Anderson, V.P.; Thomas L. Keller, Secy.-Treas.
EIN: 743015784

3165
Martha Jane & James Edward Anthony Foundation, Inc.
Granbury, TX

The foundation terminated in 2011.

3166
Nina Heard Astin Charitable Trust
c/o Wells Fargo Bank, N.A., Trust Dept.
P.O. Box 913
Bryan, TX 77805-0913
***E-mail:* grantadministration@wellsfargo.com**; Application address: c/o Wells Fargo Bank, N.A., Trust Dept., 3000 Briarcrest, Bryan, TX 77805, tel.: (979) 776-3267; **Main URL: https://www.wellsfargo.com/privatefoundationgrants/astin**
Scholarship application addresses: c/o Bryan High School Counselors, 3401 E. 29th St., Bryan, TX 77802, tel.: (979) 774-3276; c/o A&M Consolidated High School, 701 West Loop S., Bryan, TX 77840, tel.: (979) 696-0544

Established around 1975 in TX.
Foundation type: Independent foundation.
Financial data (yr. ended 03/31/13): Assets, $7,837,833 (M); expenditures, $338,603; qualifying distributions, $249,136; giving activities include $227,750 for 22 grants (high: $50,000; low: $750).
Purpose and activities: Scholarships limited to graduating seniors attending Bryan High School or A&M Consolidated High School, TX; also giving for the arts, youth services, and Presbyterian agencies and churches.
Fields of interest: Arts; Education; Health care; Health organizations, association; Protestant

federated giving programs; Protestant agencies & churches.
Type of support: General/operating support; Program development; Scholarships—to individuals.
Limitations: Applications accepted. Giving primarily in TX.
Application information: Application form required for scholarships.
Initial approach: Letter
Deadline(s): May 1 for scholarships; no set deadline for other grant proposals
Trustee: Wells Fargo Bank, N.A.
EIN: 741721901

3167
AT&T Foundation
(formerly SBC Foundation)
208 S. Akard, Ste. 100
Dallas, TX 75202-4206
***Additional e-mail:* questions@aspirerfp.com**; Main URL: http://www.att.com/gen/landing-pages?pid=7735
AT&T Aspire Local Impact Initiative Recipients: http://www.att.com/gen/press-room?pid=23079
AT&T Aspire on Twitter: https://twitter.com/attaspire/
AT&T Aspire on YouTube: https://www.youtube.com/playlist?list=PL804D2528577ACFAC
AT&T Aspire RFP website: http://www.aspirerfp.com
AT&T Military/Veterans Program Funding Inquiry: http://about.att.com/content/csr/home/people/serving-our-communities/supporting-our-troops/at-t-military-veterans-program-survey.html
RSS Feed: http://www.att.com/gen/press-room?pid=21287
The People| Planet| Possibilities Blog: http://about.att.com/content/csr/home/blog.html

Established in 1984 in MO.
Donors: Southwestern Bell Corp.; SBC Communications Inc.; AT&T Inc.; Network for Good.
Foundation type: Company-sponsored foundation.
Financial data (yr. ended 12/31/12): Assets, $9,768,836 (M); gifts received, $261,703; expenditures, $11,312,889; qualifying distributions, $11,464,285; giving activities include $8,745,039 for 57 grants (high: $1,124,494; low: $10,000), $153,200 for 753 grants to individuals (high: $3,000; low: $100), and $2,114,471 for 452 employee matching gifts.
Purpose and activities: The foundation supports programs designed to advance education. Through its community initiatives, AT&T has a long history of investing in projects that create learning opportunities; promote academic and economic achievement; or address community needs.
Fields of interest: Arts; Secondary school/education; Higher education; Scholarships/financial aid; Education, drop-out prevention; Education; Health care; Employment, training; Employment; Disasters, preparedness/services; Human services; Community development, neighborhood development; Community/economic development; Mathematics; Engineering/technology; Science; Leadership development; Public affairs; Children/youth; Youth; Young adults; Minorities; Military/veterans; Economically disadvantaged.
Type of support: Curriculum development; Employee matching gifts; Employee volunteer services; Matching/challenge support; Program development; Scholarship funds.
Limitations: Applications accepted. **Giving on a national basis in areas of company operations.** No support for religious organizations not of direct benefit to the entire community, or for political, discriminatory, or disease-specific organizations, or medical clinics or research. No grants to individuals (except for employee-related disaster grants) or for capital campaigns, endowment funds, goodwill ads, ticket or dinner purchases, sports programs or events, or cause-related marketing; no product donations.
Publications: Corporate giving report; Program policy statement.
Application information: Company facility addresses can be found on the 990. Multi-year funding is not automatic. AT&T Aspire applications are accepted on an invitation-only basis. Visit website for RFP announcements.
***Initial approach:* Contact nearest statewide facility for general funding; proposal to application address for general national funding; complete online pre-qualification for AT&T Aspire RFP**
***Copies of proposal:* 1**
***Deadline(s):* None for general funding; Jan. 17 for AT&T Aspire RFP**
Board meeting date(s): Twice per year
***Final notification:* Mid-June for AT&T Aspire, 4-6 weeks for all other applications**
Officers and Directors:* James W. Cicconi,* Chair.; **Nicole Anderson, Pres. and Exec. Dir., Philanthropy**; Thomas R. Giltner, V.P. and Secy.; Jonathan P. Klug, V.P. and Treas.; Charlene Lake, V.P.; William A. Blase, Jr.; Catherine Coughlin; Ralph De La Vega; John Stephens; Wayne Watts.
Number of staff: 11 full-time professional; 1 full-time support.
EIN: 431353948
Other changes: The grantmaker no longer lists a separate application address. The grantmaker no longer lists a fax.
Carissa Cassin is now Dir., AMA & Volunteerism.
Nicole Anderson is now Pres. and Exec. Dir., Philanthropy. Beth Shiroishi is no longer Pres.

3168
The Marilyn Augur Family Foundation
(formerly The Marilyn Augur Foundation)
6060 N. Central Expy., Ste. 616
Dallas, TX **75206-5236**
***Contact:* Tracey Frattaroli, Exec. Dir.**
FAX: (214) 526-0253; E-mail: maff@maugur.com; Main URL: http://www.maugur.org/

Established in 1990 in TX; funded in 1991.
Donor: Marilyn H. Augur.
Foundation type: Independent foundation.
Financial data (yr. ended 12/31/12): Assets, $6,478,495 (M); expenditures, $399,319; qualifying distributions, $330,139; giving activities include $215,740 for 72 grants (high: $48,000; low: $250).
Purpose and activities: Giving primarily for basic human needs (defined by the MAFF Board as food, shelter, clothing, health, and education aimed at transforming lives of those living in poverty or prison). The foundation funds non-profits which provide services for those who are economically, physically, emotionally and spiritually needy as it seeks to accomplish the mission stated in Matthew 25:35-40.
Fields of interest: Hospitals (general); Human services; Children/youth, services; Christian agencies & churches.
Type of support: General/operating support; Continuing support; Annual campaigns; Capital campaigns; Emergency funds; Program development; Scholarship funds.
Limitations: Applications not accepted. Giving primarily in Dallas, TX. No support for arts and culture. No grants to individuals.
Application information: Unsolicited requests for funds not accepted. Check foundation web site for updates.
Board meeting date(s): Spring and fall
Officers and Trustees:* Marilyn H. Augur,* Pres.; Nancy Elizabeth Roberts, V.P.; Elizabeth T. Jones Turner,* V.P.; P. Mike McCullough,* Secy.; Margaret M. Augur Hancock,* Treas.; Tracey Frattaroli, Exec. Dir.
Number of staff: 1 part-time support.
EIN: 752358239

3169
The B.E.L.I.E.F. Foundation
(formerly Janet Jarie Jensen Foundation)
130 E. John Carpenter Fwy.
Irving, TX 75062-2708 (972) 999-4564
FAX: (972) 999-4568;
E-mail: info@thebelieffoundation.com; Main URL: http://www.thebelieffoundation.org
Grants List: http://www.thebelieffoundation.org/recipients.php

Established in 1996 in TX.
Donor: Janet Jarie Jensen.
Foundation type: Independent foundation.
Financial data (yr. ended 12/31/12): Assets, $9,326,007 (M); expenditures, $792,077; qualifying distributions, $637,712; giving activities include $637,712 for grants.
Purpose and activities: The philosophy of the B.E.L.I.E.F. Foundation's Scholarship Program is to give financial assistance to deserving college, vocational or technical school students as well as provide encouragement and support to the students and their families.
Fields of interest: Higher education; Scholarships/financial aid; Education; Youth.
Type of support: Scholarship funds.
Limitations: Applications not accepted. Giving limited to 22 zip codes within the Dallas, TX area. No grants to individuals.
Application information: Contributes only to pre-selected organizations.
Trustee: Janet Jarie Jensen.
EIN: 752707934

3170
Baker Hughes Foundation
P.O. Box 3045
Houston, TX 77253-3045 **(713) 439-8662**
***Contact:* Sandra E. Alford, Secy.-Treas. and Exec. Dir.**
***E-mail:* bakerhughesfoundation@bakerhughes.com; Main URL: http://www.bakerhughes.com/company/corporate-social-responsibility/people-and-society/**

Established in 1994 in TX.
Donor: Baker Hughes Inc.
Foundation type: Company-sponsored foundation.
Financial data (yr. ended 12/31/12): Assets, $5,311,235 (M); gifts received, $3,768,532; expenditures, $3,105,045; qualifying distributions, $3,103,447; giving activities include $3,095,122 for 311 grants (high: $1,051,650; low: $100).

Purpose and activities: The foundation supports nonprofit organizations on a case by case basis in areas of company operations.
Fields of interest: Arts; Education; Health care; Youth, services; Human services.
Type of support: Scholarship funds; Employee matching gifts.
Limitations: Applications accepted. Giving in areas of company operations in the greater Tulsa, OK, and Houston, TX, areas; and on an international basis in Angola. No support for religious or political organizations or secondary schools.
Application information: Application form required.
***Initial approach:* E-mail or mail proposal**
Copies of proposal: 1
Deadline(s): None
Officers and Trustees:* Chad C. Deaton,* Chair. and Pres.; Didier Charreton,* V.P.; Alan R. Crain, Jr.,* V.P.; **Martin Craighead,* V.P.**; Peter A. Ragauss,* V.P.; Sandra E. Alford, Secy.-Treas. and Exec. Dir.
Number of staff: 1 full-time professional.
EIN: 760441292
Other changes: At the close of 2012, the grantmaker paid grants of $3,095,122, a 83.6% increase over the 2011 disbursements, $1,685,820.
Sandra E. Alford is now Secy.-Treas. and Exec. Dir.
Martin Craighead is now V.P.

3171
Baron & Blue Foundation

P.O. Box 25464
Dallas, TX **75225-1464** (214) 692-5789
***E-mail:* info@baronandbluefoundation.org**; Main URL: http://www.baronandbluefoundation.org
Facebook: https://www.facebook.com/pages/The-Baron-and-Blue-Foundation/316486968410248
Twitter: https://twitter.com/baronbluefdn

Established in 2001 in TX.
Donors: Frederick M. Baron†; Lisa A. Blue Baron.
Foundation type: Independent foundation.
Financial data (yr. ended 12/31/12): Assets, $4,417,706 (M); expenditures, $726,368; qualifying distributions, $587,883; giving activities include $587,883 for grants.
Purpose and activities: The foundation strives to enhance the function of non-profit organizations in the Dallas, TX community by assisting to maintain existing programs and further opportunities for grassroots organizations focusing on homelessness, transitional housing and the needs of the underserved.
Fields of interest: Education; Housing/shelter; Human services; Family services; Homeless.
Type of support: Program development; General/operating support.
Limitations: Applications accepted. Giving limited to Dallas County, TX.
Publications: Application guidelines.
Application information: Application form required.
Initial approach: Submit online form via foundation web site
Deadline(s): Apr. 1st and Oct. 1st
Officers and Directors:* Lisa A. Blue Baron,* Pres. and Treas.; Robert M. Greenberg,* V.P. and Secy.; Lara Ashmore, Exec. Dir.; Robert M. Greenberg; Laura Miller.
Number of staff: 1 full-time professional.
EIN: 752965720

3172
Harry W. Bass, Jr. Foundation

4809 Cole Ave., Ste. 250
Dallas, TX 75205-3553 (214) 599-0300
Contact: F. David Calhoun, Exec. Dir.
FAX: (214) 599-0405; E-mail: dcalhoun@hbrf.org; **Grant correspondence should be addressed to: Grants Dept.**; Main URL: http://www.harrybassfoundation.org

Established in 1983 in TX.
Donor: Harry W. Bass, Jr.†.
Foundation type: Independent foundation.
Financial data (yr. ended 12/31/12): Assets, $62,258,334 (M); expenditures, $1,749,855; qualifying distributions, $1,431,273; giving activities include $1,145,262 for 57 grants (high: $700,000; low: $50).
Purpose and activities: Primary focus is in the areas of youth and education.
Fields of interest: Arts education; Museums; Performing arts centers; Arts; Education, early childhood education; Child development, education; Secondary school/education; Education; Environment, public education; Botanical gardens; Animals/wildlife; Health care; Medical research; Crime/violence prevention, abuse prevention; Food banks; Food distribution, meals on wheels; Human services; American Red Cross; YM/YWCAs & YM/YWHAs; Children/youth, services; Children, services; Youth, services; Child development, services; Family services; Aging, centers/services; Science; Infants/toddlers; Children/youth; Children; Youth; Adults; Aging; Physically disabled; Women; Infants/toddlers, female; Girls; Adults, women; Young adults, female; Infants/toddlers, male; Boys; Adults, men; Young adults, male; Economically disadvantaged.
Type of support: General/operating support; Continuing support; Building/renovation; Equipment; Program development; Research; Matching/challenge support.
Limitations: Applications accepted. Giving exclusively in the greater Dallas, TX area. No support for seminaries or private foundations. No grants to individuals, or for capital campaigns, fundraisers or conferences.
Publications: Application guidelines; Financial statement; Grants list.
Application information: Application form not required.
***Initial approach:* Letter with full grant application via e-mail followed by a printed copy**
Copies of proposal: 1
Deadline(s): None
Board meeting date(s): Quarterly
Final notification: 3 months
Officers and Trustees:* Doris L. Bass,* Pres.; Michael Calhoun,* V.P.; F. David Calhoun,* Secy. and Exec. Dir.; J. Michael Wylie.
Number of staff: 1 full-time professional; 1 part-time support.
EIN: 751876307
Other changes: The grantmaker now publishes application guidelines.

3173
The Baxter Trust

c/o Private Foundation Services, Inc.
4265 San Felipe, Ste. 1100
Houston, TX 77027-2913
Contact: Lynn Stanley

Donors: Murphy H. Baxter; Murphy Baxter†.
Foundation type: Independent foundation.
Financial data (yr. ended 12/31/12): Assets, $42,446,305 (M); gifts received, $15,268; expenditures, $2,014,117; qualifying distributions, $1,745,834; giving activities include $1,678,523 for 41 grants (high: $120,000; low: $5,000).
Fields of interest: Mental health/crisis services, suicide; Children, services; Christian agencies & churches; Children/youth; Children; Aging; Disabilities, people with; Deaf/hearing impaired; Mentally disabled; Economically disadvantaged; Homeless.
Limitations: Applications not accepted. Giving primarily in TX. No grants to individuals.
Application information: Contributes only to pre-selected organizations.
Trustees: Blair Baxter; Thomas G. Hambrick, Jr.; **David Hessel**; Heidi Kelsey; Tobias T. Mongan; David Welsh; David D. Welsh.
Number of staff: 1 part-time professional.
EIN: 760174893
Other changes: Ashley E. Baxter and Sidney S. Lindley are no longer trustees.

3174
The Beal Foundation

104 S. Pecos
Midland, TX **79701-5021 (432) 682-3753**
***Contact:* Spencer E. Beal**

Incorporated in 1962 in TX.
Donors: Carlton Beal; Keleen H. Beal; W.R. Davis; Barry Beal, Jr.
Foundation type: Independent foundation.
Financial data (yr. ended 12/31/12): Assets, $19,785,503 (M); expenditures, $1,866,925; qualifying distributions, $1,434,000; giving activities include $1,434,000 for grants.
Fields of interest: Education; Human services; Children/youth, services.
Type of support: General/operating support.
Limitations: Applications accepted. Giving primarily in the Midland, TX, area.
Application information: First time applicants must complete longer application form. Application form required.
Initial approach: Request application
***Deadline(s):* 1 month prior to board meetings**
Board meeting date(s): Apr. 1 and Nov. 1
Officers: Carlton Beal, Jr., Chair.; Bryan Limmer, Secy.-Treas.
Trustees: Barry Beal, Jr.; Kelly S. Beal; Spencer E. Beal; Stuart Beal; Larry Bell; Elizabeth Beal Davenport; Karlene Beal Garber; Steven C. Hofer; Ray Poage; Laura Buckner.
EIN: 756034480

3175
Theodore and Beulah Beasley Foundation, Inc.

3811 Turtle Creek Blvd., Ste. 940
Dallas, TX 75219-4490

Incorporated in 1957 in TX.
Donors: Theodore P. Beasley; Mary Evans Beasley†.
Foundation type: Independent foundation.
Financial data (yr. ended 12/31/13): Assets, $30,754,217 (M); expenditures, $1,622,187; qualifying distributions, $1,292,433; giving activities include $1,178,738 for 48 grants (high: $225,000; low: $1,500).
Fields of interest: Arts; Education; Health care; Human services; YM/YWCAs & YM/YWHAs; Children/youth, services.

Type of support: General/operating support; Capital campaigns; Building/renovation.
Limitations: Applications not accepted. Giving primarily in the Dallas, TX, area. No grants to individuals.
Application information: Contributes only to pre-selected organizations.
Officers: Robert R. Beasley, Pres. and Treas.; Vicki Vanderslice, V.P. and Secy.
Directors: Samuel Dashefsky; Linda Tinney; Michael Vanderslice.
EIN: 756035806
Other changes: Robert R. Beasley is now Pres. and Treas. Vicki Vanderslice is now V.P. and Secy.

3176
Behmann Brothers Foundation

P.O. Box 271486
Corpus Christi, TX 78427-1486 **(361) 438-1589**
Contact: Charles L. Kosarek, Jr., Pres.
***E-mail:* info@behmannbrothersfoundation.org**;
Main URL: http://behmannbrothersfoundation.org/

Established in 1979.
Donors: Arno W. Behmann†; Herman W. Behmann†.
Foundation type: Independent foundation.
Financial data (yr. ended 06/30/13): Assets, $6,798,027 (M); expenditures, $429,347; qualifying distributions, $321,490; giving activities include $310,232 for 61 grants (high: $30,000; low: $250).
Purpose and activities: Giving primarily for agricultural research and education, schools, youth groups, health care and service organizations.
Fields of interest: Higher education; Education; Health organizations, association; Agriculture, farmlands; Human services; Children/youth, services; Community/economic development; Christian agencies & churches.
Type of support: Program development.
Limitations: Applications accepted. Giving limited to TX, with an emphasis on the counties of Aransas, Bee, Kleberg, Live Oak, Nueces, San Patricio, Refugio, and Jim Wells. No support for political organizations. No grants to individuals.
Application information: See web site for application policies, guidelines and forms. Application form required.
Initial approach: Proposal
Copies of proposal: 1
Deadline(s): May 1
Board meeting date(s): June
Final notification: June, positive replies only
Officers and Directors:* Charles L. Kosarek, Jr.,* Pres.; **T. Mark Anderson, V.P.**; Sherry Kosarek, Secy.; Willie J. Kosarek, Treas.; John Lloyd Bluntzer.
EIN: 742146739
Other changes: T. Mark Anderson has replaced Karen K. Clark as V.P.
Jeffrey D. Clark is no longer director.

3177
The Belo Foundation

(formerly A. H. Belo Corporation Foundation)
Dallas, TX

The foundation terminated.

3178
Bickel & Brewer Foundation

(formerly Bickel & Brewer Legal Foundation)
4800 Comerica Bank Tower
1717 Main Street
Dallas, TX 75201 **(214) 653-4026**
***Contact:* Andrea Burnett**
E-mail: aburnett@bickelbrewer.com; Main URL: http://www.bickelbrewer.com/#/thefoundation

Established in 1995 in TX.
Donor: Bickel & Brewer.
Foundation type: Company-sponsored foundation.
Financial data (yr. ended 12/31/12): Assets, $43,928 (M); gifts received, $3,016,008; expenditures, $2,967,334; qualifying distributions, $2,992,334; giving activities include $758,098 for 33 grants (high: $132,348; low: $500), and $1,731,426 for 3 foundation-administered programs.
Purpose and activities: The foundation supports organizations involved with health, community reinvestment, and public policy. Special emphasis is directed toward programs designed to promote law and education.
Fields of interest: Higher education; Law school/education; Education; Health care; Legal services; Crime/law enforcement; Community/economic development; Public policy, research.
Type of support: General/operating support; Annual campaigns; Program development; Scholarship funds.
Limitations: Applications accepted. Giving primarily in New York, NY, and TX, with some emphasis on the Dallas area. No grants to individuals.
Publications: Application guidelines.
Application information: Application form not required.
***Initial approach:* Download application form and mail to foundation**
Copies of proposal: 1
Deadline(s): None
Officers: William A. Brewer III, Chair.; John W. Bickel II, Pres.; James S. Renard, Secy.; Mike McCormack, Treas.; **Travis J. Carter, Exec. Dir.**
EIN: 752625364
Other changes: William A. Brewer, III is now Chair. William A. Brewer, III is no longer Chair. James S. Renard is now Secy. Kat Sewers is no longer Exec. Dir.

3179
Simon Bolivar Foundation, Inc.

P.O. Box 4689
Houston, TX 77210-4689
***Contact:* Dario Merchan, Pres.**
E-mail: sbf@citgo.com; **Additional address: 1293 Eldridge Pkwy, N5033, Houston, TX 77077**; Main URL: http://www.simonbolivarfoundation.org/

Established in 2007 in TX.
Donor: CITGO Petroleum Corporation.
Foundation type: Company-sponsored foundation.
Financial data (yr. ended 12/31/12): Assets, $4,540,592 (M); expenditures, $8,461,223; qualifying distributions, $8,354,459; giving activities include $2,815,141 for 39 grants (high: $2,000,000; low: $7,500), and $5,338,616 for 3 foundation-administered programs.
Purpose and activities: The foundation supports programs designed to expand access to healthcare to underprivileged individuals who are affected by critical illness and poverty.
Fields of interest: Environment; Hospitals (general); Health care, clinics/centers; Speech/hearing centers; Health care, support services; Health care, organ/tissue banks; Health care, patient services; Health care; Disasters, preparedness/services; Human services; Economically disadvantaged.
International interests: Venezuela.
Type of support: Building/renovation; Equipment; Program development.
Limitations: Applications accepted. Giving primarily in Washington, DC, New York, NY, Argentina, Italy, and Venezuela.
Publications: Application guidelines; Program policy statement.
Application information: Application form required.
Initial approach: Complete online application for medical assistance and Bronx Social Programs
***Deadline(s):* None for medical assistance; Mar. 27 for Bronx Social Programs**
Officers and Directors:* Maritza Rojas de Villanueva,* Chair.; Dario Merchan, Pres.; Arnaldo Arcay, Secy.; Fatima Romero, Treas.; **David Diaz; Richard Gooley; Orestes Parilli; Eladio Perez; Fernando Valera.**
EIN: 205787382
Other changes: Patricia Milano is no longer V.P. Daniel Cortez and Brian O'Kelly are no longer directors.

3180
Booth Ferris Foundation

c/o JPMorgan Private Bank, Philanthropic Svcs.
P.O. 227237 TX1-2963
Dallas, TX 75222-7237
Contact: Contact for Parks and Gardens, Arts and Culture: Jonathan Horowitz, Prog. Off.; Contact for Education: Casey Castaneda, V.P. and Prog. Off.; Contact for Strengthening NYC's Nonprofit Sector: Connie Giampapa, Prog. Off.
FAX: (212) 464-2304;
E-mail: jonathan.g.horowitz@jpmorgan.com; E-mail for jonathan.g.horowitz@jpmchase.com; e-mail for Connie Giampapa: connie.a.giampapa@jpmorgan.com; e-mail for Casey Castaneda: casey.b.castaneda@jpmchase.com; **Main URL: http://fdnweb.org/boothferris**

Trusts established in 1957 and 1958 in NY; merged in 1964.
Donors: Chancie Ferris Booth†; Willis H. Booth†.
Foundation type: Independent foundation.
Financial data (yr. ended 12/31/12): Assets, $207,825,957 (M); expenditures, $10,684,936; qualifying distributions, $9,438,622; giving activities include $9,093,600 for grants.
Purpose and activities: Grants primarily for education, smaller colleges, and independent secondary schools; limited support also for urban programs, social service agencies, and cultural activities.
Fields of interest: Museums; Arts; Education, association; Secondary school/education; Higher education; Adult education—literacy, basic skills & GED; Education, reading; Education; Human services; Children/youth, services; Community/economic development; Government/public administration; Public affairs.
Type of support: Management development/capacity building; Capital campaigns.
Limitations: Applications accepted. Giving limited to the New York, NY, metropolitan area for the arts, K-12 education, and civic and urban affairs; a broader geographic scope for higher education. No support for federated campaigns, community chests, social services and cultural institutions from outside the New York metropolitan area, or for work with specific diseases or disabilities. No grants to

individuals, or for research; generally no grants to educational institutions for scholarships, fellowships, or unrestricted endowments; no loans.
Publications: Annual report; Annual report (including application guidelines).
Application information: Interviews will not be granted prior to the submission of a proposal. After proposals are received interviews will be granted only in those cases in which the trustees feel it will be helpful to their decision. The foundation will make every effort to inform applicants promptly if their proposal will not be successful. At least three years must pass between grant awards. Proposals from social services and cultural institutions from outside the metropolitan New York area will not be considered. Do not mail applications. Only submit information online at http://www.jpmorgan.com/pages/jpmorgan/private_banking/foundations/online_grant_application/guidelines_to_apply. Application form not required.
Initial approach: Proposals for funding should be submitted to the appropriate contact person
Copies of proposal: 1
Deadline(s): Feb. 1 for Strengthening NYC, Education and Arts/Culture grants; May 31, Parks Gardens grants
Board meeting date(s): Approximately 4 times per year
Final notification: 5 months
Trustee: JPMorgan Chase Bank, N.A.
EIN: 136170340

3181
BP Foundation, Inc.
(formerly BP Amoco Foundation, Inc.)
501 Westlake Park Blvd., 25th Fl
Houston, TX 77079-2604
***Main URL:* http://www.bp.com/en/global/corporate/sustainability/society/Supporting-development-in-societies-where-we-work/community-investment.html**

Incorporated in 1952 in IN.
Donors: Amoco Corp.; BP Amoco Corp.; BP Corp. North America Inc.; BP America Inc.; Amoco Production Co.; Atlantic Richfield Co.; BP Products North America, Inc.
Foundation type: Company-sponsored foundation.
Financial data (yr. ended 12/31/13): Assets, $25,714,939 (M); expenditures, $19,230,326; qualifying distributions, $19,211,498; giving activities include $18,152,126 for 32 grants (high: $7,714,444; low: $38,565).
Purpose and activities: The foundation supports programs designed to promote science, engineering, and math education, economic development, practical approaches to environmental need, and provide humanitarian relief.
Fields of interest: Higher education; Education; Environment, natural resources; Environment; Disasters, preparedness/services; American Red Cross; Human services; International relief; Community/economic development; Foundations (community); Mathematics; Engineering/technology; Science; Economically disadvantaged.
Type of support: General/operating support; Emergency funds; Program development; Scholarship funds; Research; Employee volunteer services; Sponsorships; Employee matching gifts.
Limitations: Applications not accepted. Giving primarily in AK, AL, CA, Washington, DC, GA, Chicago, IL, IN, NY, and OH; giving also in Australia, China, Europe, Germany, Japan, Philippines and the United Kingdom. No support for religious, fraternal, political, social, or athletic organizations; generally, no support for organizations already receiving general operating support through the United Way. No grants to individuals, or for endowments, medical research, publications, or conferences.
Application information: Contributes only to pre-selected organizations.
Board meeting date(s): Apr., July, and Nov.
Officers and Directors:* Andrew P. Hopwood,* Chair.; Ray C. Dempsey,* Pres.; Don Eldred,* C.F.O.; Mark E. Thompson, Treas.; Hans Boas, Legal Counsel; Lori Wittlin, Genl. Tax Off.; Sherry L. Strasner, Assoc. Dir.; Benjamin E. Cannon, Exec. Dir.; Iris M. Cross; Elodie Grant Goodey; Anshul Mathur; Luis Sierra; Marta Vasel.
Number of staff: 4 full-time professional; 1 full-time support.
EIN: 366046879

3182
George W. Brackenridge Foundation
700 N. Saint Mary's St., Ste. 875
San Antonio, TX **78205-3507 (210) 693-0819**
Contact: Karen Matyear, Opers. Mgr.
FAX: (210) 226-1715;
E-mail: info@brackenridgefoundtion.org; Main URL: http://www.brackenridgefoundation.org

Trust established in 1920 in TX.
Donor: George W. Brackenridge†.
Foundation type: Independent foundation.
Financial data (yr. ended 12/31/12): Assets, $26,541,299 (M); expenditures, $1,552,251; qualifying distributions, $1,319,772; giving activities include $829,550 for 15 grants (high: $515,550; low: $5,000).
Purpose and activities: The foundation's current focus is assisting best-in-class CMOs (charter management organizations) to create high performing public charter schools in the San Antonio, TX, area.
Fields of interest: Charter schools; Education.
Type of support: Endowments; Program development; Scholarship funds; Research.
Limitations: Giving primarily in San Antonio, TX, and the surrounding area. No grants to individuals, or for general purposes, continuing support, seed money, emergency funds, land acquisition, renovation projects, building funds, operating budgets, annual campaigns, deficit financing, or matching gifts; no loans.
Application information: Applications are currently by invitation only. See foundation web site for updates in this area.
Board meeting date(s): Mar., June, Sept., and Dec.
Officer and Trustee:* Victoria B. Rico,* Chair.; Randy J. Boatright; **David H.O. Roth.**
EIN: 746034977
Other changes: Stephanie Shearer is no longer a trustee.

3183
The Brown Foundation, Inc.
2217 Welch Ave.
Houston, TX 77019-5617 (713) 523-6867
Contact: Nancy Pittman, Exec. Dir.
FAX: (713) 523-2917;
E-mail: bfi@brownfoundation.org; Application address: P.O. Box 130646, Houston, TX 77219-0646; Main URL: http://www.brownfoundation.org

Incorporated in 1951 in TX.
Donors: Herman Brown†; Margarett Root Brown†; George R. Brown†; Alice Pratt Brown†.
Foundation type: Independent foundation.
Financial data (yr. ended 06/30/13): Assets, $1,183,267,396 (M); expenditures, $58,442,675; qualifying distributions, $54,115,912; giving activities include $51,943,531 for 640 grants (high: $4,231,356; low: $1,000), and $870,417 for 162 employee matching gifts.
Purpose and activities: Support principally for the encouragement of and assistance to education, the arts and community service. The projects selected for funding most likely will have the potential for long-lasting significant impact in the community. The foundation's current emphasis is in the field of public education at the primary and secondary levels. It will focus on finding and supporting nontraditional and innovative approaches designed to improve public education primarily within the state of Texas. Other areas of interest continue to be the visual and performing arts, and also include community service projects focused upon the needs of children and youth, especially in the Houston area.
Fields of interest: Arts; Education; Human services; Science; Public affairs.
Type of support: General/operating support; Continuing support; Annual campaigns; Capital campaigns; Building/renovation; Land acquisition; Program development; Professorships; Curriculum development; Scholarship funds; Research; Employee matching gifts; Matching/challenge support.
Limitations: Applications accepted. Giving primarily in TX, with emphasis on Houston. No support for political organizations, private foundations, or religious organizations for religious purposes. No grants to individuals, or for operating deficits, debt retirement, testimonial dinners, marketing or fundraising events; no loans.
Publications: Application guidelines; Annual report (including application guidelines); Informational brochure (including application guidelines).
Application information: Grant proposal guidelines and proposal summary form are available upon request. Will consider one grant proposal per 12-month period from an organization. See foundation web site for downloadable proposal summary form. Application form required.
Initial approach: Proposal should be submitted a minimum of 4 months before funds are needed
Copies of proposal: 1
Deadline(s): None
Board meeting date(s): Feb., May, Sept., and Nov.
Final notification: 3 months
Officers and Trustees:* Nancy Brown Negley,* Chair.; Herman L. Stude,* Pres.; Louisa Stude Sarofim,* V.P. and Secy.; William N. Mathis,* Treas.; **Jacklyn Tatge, C.F.O.; Carla Knobloch, C.I.O.; Nancy Abendshein**; Holbrook Dorn; John O'Connor; Elisa Stude Pye; Christopher B. Sarofim.
Number of staff: 3 full-time professional; 2 part-time professional; 4 full-time support.
EIN: 746036466
Other changes: Nancy Brown Negley has replaced Isabel Brown Wilson as Chair.
Isabel Brown Wilson, Chair., and Maconda Brown O'Connor, V.P., are deceased.

3184
Burch Family Foundation
784 Drifting Wind Run
Dripping Springs, TX 78620-4463
Contact: Berkely Burch-Martinez, Tr.

Established in 1984 in CA.

Donor: Robert D. Burch.
Foundation type: Independent foundation.
Financial data (yr. ended 05/31/13): Assets, $6,865,161 (M); expenditures, $404,368; qualifying distributions, $336,371; giving activities include $336,371 for 28 grants (high: $100,000; low: $1,000).
Purpose and activities: Giving primarily for higher and other education, and for social services.
Fields of interest: Education; Human services; Public affairs.
Type of support: General/operating support; Continuing support; Annual campaigns; Endowments; Program development; Professorships.
Limitations: Applications accepted. Giving primarily in CA; some funding also in Washington, DC, and Arlington, VA. No grants to individuals.
Application information: Application form not required.
Initial approach: Proposal
Deadline(s): None
Trustees: Barry B. Burch; Berkeley Burch-Martinez.
EIN: 953924403
Other changes: The grantmaker has moved from CA to TX.

3185
The Burnett Foundation

(formerly The Burnett-Tandy Foundation)
801 Cherry St., Ste. 1585
Fort Worth, TX 76102-6881 (817) 877-3344
Contact: V. Neils Agather, Exec. Dir.

Established in 1978 in TX.
Donors: Anne Burnett Tandy†; Dee Kelly Foundation.
Foundation type: Independent foundation.
Financial data (yr. ended 12/31/12): Assets, $269,560,726 (M); expenditures, $22,842,105; qualifying distributions, $16,372,549; giving activities include $15,989,810 for 28 grants (high: $10,000,000; low: $7,500), and $6,561 for 1 foundation-administered program.
Purpose and activities: Support primarily for major museum projects and other cultural institutions, social service agencies, community development groups, and educational institutions.
Fields of interest: Museums; Arts; Education; AIDS; Human services; Community development, neighborhood development.
Type of support: General/operating support; Capital campaigns; Program development; Seed money; Technical assistance; Program-related investments/loans.
Limitations: Applications not accepted. Giving primarily in the Fort Worth, TX, area.
Application information: Unsolicited requests not accepted.
Board meeting date(s): Generally in June and Nov.
Officers and Trustees:* Anne W. Marion,* Pres.; **Edward R. Hudson, Jr.,* V.P. and Secy.; V. Neils Agather, V.P. and Treas.**; Benjamin J. Fortson,* V.P.; **John L. Marion,* V.P.**; Anne W. Grimes.
Number of staff: 1 full-time professional; 2 full-time support.
EIN: 751638517
Other changes: V. Neils Agather is now V.P. and Treas. Edward R. Hudson, Jr. is now V.P. and Secy. Benjamin J. Fortson is now V.P. John L. Marion is now V.P.

3186
C.I.O.S.

P.O. Box 20815
Waco, TX 76702-0815 (254) 752-5551

Incorporated about 1952 in TN; corporation liquidated into a charitable trust in 1987.
Donors: Paul P. Piper, Sr.; Mrs. Paul P. Piper; Paul P. Piper, Jr.; Piper Industries, Inc.
Foundation type: Independent foundation.
Financial data (yr. ended 06/30/13): Assets, $112,535,310 (M); gifts received, $2,725; expenditures, $7,088,124; qualifying distributions, $6,483,075; giving activities include $6,094,462 for 47 grants (high: $500,000; low: $1,000), and $25,000 for 1 loan/program-related investment.
Purpose and activities: Grants for Protestant church support and religious programs, including Christian education, evangelism, welfare, and support for foreign missions.
Fields of interest: Theological school/education; Human services; Christian agencies & churches; Protestant agencies & churches.
Type of support: Program-related investments/loans.
Limitations: Applications not accepted. Giving primarily in TX. No grants to individuals.
Application information: Contributes only to pre-selected organizations.
Board meeting date(s): Monthly
Trustees: Jill Piper Lawrence; Lynn Piper; Paul Piper, Jr.; Shirley Piper; Polly Piper Rickard.
EIN: 742472778
Other changes: Mary J. Piper is no longer a trustee.

3187
The Cailloux Foundation

(also known as Floyd A. & Kathleen C. Cailloux Foundation)
P.O. Box 291276
Kerrville, TX 78029-1276 (830) 895-5222
Contact: Barbara Gaither, Exec. Asst.
FAX: (830) 895-5212;
E-mail: info@caillouxfoundation.org; Main URL: http://www.caillouxfoundation.org

Established in 1994 in TX.
Donors: Floyd A. Cailloux†; Kathleen C. Cailloux†.
Foundation type: Independent foundation.
Financial data (yr. ended 12/31/12): Assets, $91,478,316 (M); gifts received, $48,503; expenditures, $6,761,357; qualifying distributions, $6,274,160; giving activities include $5,131,257 for 61 grants (high: $2,429,388; low: $2,500).
Purpose and activities: Giving primarily to civic, community service, cultural, educational, child development, health and rehabilitation and animal welfare organizations.
Fields of interest: Education; Animal welfare; Health care; Health organizations; Children/youth, services; Family services; Community/economic development.
Type of support: General/operating support; Continuing support; Annual campaigns; Capital campaigns; Building/renovation; Equipment; Land acquisition; Emergency funds; Program development; Seed money; Scholarship funds; Technical assistance; Program evaluation; Matching/challenge support.
Limitations: Applications accepted. Giving limited to Kerr County, TX, and its surrounding communities of Bandera, Edwards, Gillespie, Kimble and Real counties for grants. Giving is limited to residents of selected Texas Hill Country communities for scholarships. No support for seminaries for construction, projects normally funded by governmental entities or church-related entities that do not meet foundation guidelines. No grants to individuals, or for fund raisers, conferences, membership drives or competitions; no loans.
Publications: Application guidelines; Financial statement; Program policy statement (including application guidelines).
Application information: The foundation only reviews grant proposals from applicants whose online letter of inquiry has been approved. Application available on foundation web site. Application form required.
Initial approach: Use letter of inquiry form on foundation web site
Copies of proposal: 1
Deadline(s): None for grants; see web site for Scholarship Program
Board meeting date(s): Quarterly
Final notification: Within 4 weeks
Officers and Directors:* Kenneth F. Cailloux,* Chair. and Pres.; Robert Andresakis,* V.P.; Paula Heilemann,* V.P.; Sandra Cailloux,* Secy. and Exec. Dir.; Hon. Steve Ables; **Summer Andresakis**; Blackie Heilemann; David Jackson; Cori Modisett; Leslie Modisett; Mark Moore.
Number of staff: 3 full-time professional; 1 part-time professional; 1 full-time support.
EIN: 746422979

3188
The Effie and Wofford Cain Foundation

(doing business as The Cain Foundation)
4131 Spicewood Springs Rd., Ste. A-1
Austin, TX 78759-8658 (512) 346-7490
Contact: Lynn Fowler, Secy.-Treas. and Exec. Dir.
FAX: (512) 346-7491;
E-mail: info@cainfoundation.org

Incorporated in 1952 in TX.
Donors: Effie Marie Cain†; R. Wofford Cain†.
Foundation type: Independent foundation.
Financial data (yr. ended 10/31/13): Assets, $124,295,893 (M); expenditures, $6,085,119; qualifying distributions, $5,393,355; giving activities include $4,711,700 for 98 grants (high: $1,000,000; low: $300).
Purpose and activities: Giving primarily to scientific, medical, and educational institutions.
Fields of interest: Elementary/secondary education; Secondary school/education; Higher education; Health care; Medical research, institute; Protestant agencies & churches.
Type of support: Endowments; Professorships; Scholarship funds; Research.
Limitations: Applications not accepted. Giving primarily in TX. No grants to individuals or organizations on behalf of specific individuals.
Application information: The foundation provides grants and contributions, on a highly selective basis, primarily to scientific, medical, and educational institutions. Substantially all of the grants and contributions are dedicated for purposes that fulfill the foundation's philanthropic goals and are made to organizations with which the foundation has an existing historical relationship. The foundation's general policy is to not accept unsolicited grant applications and no grants are made to or for the benefit of specific individuals.
Board meeting date(s): Oct. (annual meeting); 6 to 8 interim meetings (dates vary)
Officers and Directors:* Franklin W. Denius,* Pres.; John C. Cain,* V.P.; F. Wofford Denius,* V.P.; **Charmaine D. McGill,* V.P. and Grants Admin.**; Lynn Fowler, Secy.-Treas. and Exec. Dir.
Number of staff: 3 full-time professional.
EIN: 756030774

Other changes: Charmaine D. McGill is now V.P. and Grants Admin.

3189
The Mary H. Cain Foundation
8 Greenway Plz., Ste. 606
Houston, TX 77046-0801 (713) 840-7896
Contact: Margaret W. Weaver, Chair. and Pres.

Established in 2007 in TX.
Foundation type: Independent foundation.
Financial data (yr. ended 12/31/12): Assets, $14,667,448 (M); expenditures, $805,848; qualifying distributions, $725,551; giving activities include $725,551 for 17 grants (high: $175,000; low: $1).
Fields of interest: Education; Human services; Foundations (private grantmaking).
Limitations: Applications accepted. Giving primarily in Houston, TX. No grants to individuals.
Application information: Proposals in binders, report covers, or folders are not accepted. Application form required.
Initial approach: Formal proposal
***Deadline(s):* Nov. 1 for Dec. board meeting**
***Board meeting date(s):* Dec.**
Officers and Directors:* Margaret W. Weaver,* Chair. and Pres.; **Pam Woods, Secy.**; John M. Sullivan,* Treas.
EIN: 208483925
Other changes: Gordon D. Oehmig is no longer a director.

3190
Amon G. Carter Foundation
201 Main St., Ste. 1945
Fort Worth, TX 76102-3114 (817) 332-2783
Contact: John H. Robinson, Exec. V.P., Grant Admin.
FAX: (817) 332-2787; E-mail: jrobinson@agcf.org; Application address: P.O. Box 1036, Fort Worth, TX 76101; Main URL: http://www.agcf.org/
Grants List: http://www.agcf.org/documents/Grants_2009.pdf

Incorporated in 1945 in TX.
Donors: Amon G. Carter‡; N.B. Carter‡; Star-Telegram Employees Fund; Carter Foundation Production Co.
Foundation type: Independent foundation.
Financial data (yr. ended 12/31/12): Assets, $524,045,898 (M); gifts received, $60,000; expenditures, $29,312,759; qualifying distributions, $24,495,763; giving activities include $21,264,454 for 194 grants (high: $8,118,244; low: $1,500).
Purpose and activities: Grants primarily for arts, education, health care and medical services, social service and youth agencies, programs for youth and the elderly, and civic and community endeavors that enhance the quality of life. The foundation sponsors and largely supports the Amon Carter Museum.
Fields of interest: Museums; Performing arts; Arts; Higher education; Education; Hospitals (general); Health care; Human services; Youth, services; Aging, centers/services; Government/public administration; Aging.
Type of support: General/operating support; Continuing support; Annual campaigns; Capital campaigns; Building/renovation; Equipment; Land acquisition; Endowments; Emergency funds; Program development; Professorships; Seed money; Scholarship funds; Research; Matching/challenge support.
Limitations: Applications accepted. Giving largely restricted to Fort Worth and Tarrant County, TX. No grants to individuals, or for ongoing operating budgets, deficit financing, publications, or conferences; no loans.
Publications: Application guidelines; Financial statement; Grants list; Program policy statement.
Application information: Grants outside local geographic area usually initiated by board. The foundation does not currently accept grant applications via e-mail. Application form not required.
Initial approach: Letter
Copies of proposal: 1
Deadline(s): None
Board meeting date(s): Feb., May and Nov.
Final notification: Within 10 days of board meeting
Officers and Directors:* Mark L. Johnson,* Pres.; W. Patrick Harris, Exec. V.P., Investments; John H. Robinson, Exec. V.P., Grant Admin.; Robert W. Brown, M.D.*, V.P.; Sheila B. Johnson,* Secy.; **Kate Johnson,* Treas.**; Kathy A. King, Cont.
Number of staff: 3 full-time professional; 2 full-time support.
EIN: 756000331
Other changes: Mark L. Johnson has replaced Ruth Carter Stevenson as Pres. Kate Johnson has replaced Mark L. Johnson as Treas.

3191
CEMEX Foundation
(formerly Southdown Foundation)
c/o Cemex Inc.
P.O. Box 1500
Houston, TX 77251-1500 (713) 650-6200
Application address: c/o CEMEX Inc., 929 Gessner Rd., Ste. 1900, Houston, TX 77024

Established in 1993.
Donors: Medusa Corp.; CEMEX Corp.
Foundation type: Company-sponsored foundation.
Financial data (yr. ended 12/31/12): Assets, $6,145,404 (M); expenditures, $505,057; qualifying distributions, $497,888; giving activities include $497,888 for 16+ grants (high: $105,000).
Purpose and activities: The foundation supports organizations involved with education, birth defects, human services, and the masonry trade.
Fields of interest: Education; Human services.
Type of support: General/operating support.
Limitations: Applications accepted. Giving primarily on FL, NY, and OH. No grants to individuals.
Application information: Application form required.
***Initial approach:* Letter**
Deadline(s): None
Officers: Karl H. Watson, Jr., Chair. and Pres.; Mike F. Egan, Secy.; Frank E. Angelle, Treas.
EIN: 346505254
Other changes: Karl H. Watson, Jr. has replaced Gilberto Perez as Chair. and Pres.
Frank E. Angelle is now Secy. Frank E. Angelle is now Treas. R. Frank Craddock is no longer a member of the governing body. Andrew M. Miller is no longer a member of the governing body.

3192
The Chasdrew Fund
130 E. John Carpenter Fwy.
Irving, TX 75062
Facebook: https://www.facebook.com/sharer/sharer.php?u=http%3A%2F%2Fchasdrew.org%2Fcontact%2F&t=Contact
Twitter: http://twitter.com/intent/tweet?source=webclient&text=Contact+-+http%3A%2F%2Fchasdrew.org%2Fcontact%2F

Established in 1997 in MD.
Donor: Julie Jensen.
Foundation type: Operating foundation.
Financial data (yr. ended 12/31/11): Assets, $3,325,472 (M); expenditures, $940,000; qualifying distributions, $920,767; giving activities include $750,830 for 7+ grants (high: $455,000).
Fields of interest: Human services; LGBTQ.
Type of support: Technical assistance.
Limitations: Applications not accepted. No grants to individuals.
Publications: Occasional report; Program policy statement.
Application information: Contributes only to pre-selected organizations.
Officer and Trustees:* Julie Jensen,* Chair.; Scott Letier; Jane Smith.
Number of staff: None.
EIN: 526854447
Other changes: The grantmaker no longer lists a URL address.

3193
The Chisholm Trail Communities Foundation
(formerly The Georgetown Area Community Foundation)
116 W. 8th St., Ste. 105
P.O. Box 1060
Georgetown, TX 78626-5847 (512) 863-4186
Contact: Mike Weir, Managing Dir.
FAX: (866) 348-8033;
E-mail: friends@chisholm-trail.org; Main URL: http://www.chisholm-trail.org/
Facebook: https://www.facebook.com/CTCFoundation
LinkedIn: http://www.linkedin.com/company/2460698
Twitter: http://twitter.com/chisholmtrail

Established in 1998 in TX.
Foundation type: Community foundation.
Financial data (yr. ended 12/31/12): Assets, $2,160,491 (M); gifts received, $697,171; expenditures, $652,540; giving activities include $279,367 for 11+ grants (high: $45,000), and $11,000 for grants to individuals.
Purpose and activities: The foundation grants funds for projects and programs that address community needs in the areas of community development and community services, education and training, arts and culture, health, and human services.
Fields of interest: Arts; Education; Health care; Human services; Community/economic development.
Limitations: Applications accepted. Giving primarily in the greater Georgetown, TX area. No support for religious organizations for religious purposes. No grants to individuals (except for scholarships).
Publications: Application guidelines.
Application information: Visit foundation web site for application form and guidelines. Application form required.
Initial approach: Full proposal, e-mail, or telephone
***Copies of proposal:* 5**
Deadline(s): Feb. 1, May 1, Aug. 1, and Nov. 1
Board meeting date(s): Quarterly
Final notification: Within 2 weeks after quarterly board meeting
Officers and Directors:* Doug Groves,* Chair.; Nelson Avery; Ray Barron; **Dr. Barbara Brightwell**;

Karen Cole; Howard Faske; Ron Greening; Hayden Johnson; Lynne Moore; Gary Newman; Bill Sattler.
EIN: 742786718

3194
Chrest Foundation, Inc.
(formerly J. Jensen Family Foundation, Inc.)
130 E. John Carpenter Freeway
Irving, TX 75062-2708 (972) 999-4514
Contact: Lou Anne King Jensen, Pres.
FAX: (972) 999-4502;
E-mail: administrator@chrestfoundation.org; Main URL: http://www.chrestfoundation.org
Grants List: http://www.chrestfoundation.org/EN/grantsawarded.asp

Established in 1999 in TX.
Donors: Jeffrey J. Jensen; Gladys Margaret Jensen.
Foundation type: Independent foundation.
Financial data (yr. ended 12/31/12): Assets, $7,814,412 (M); gifts received, $20,648; expenditures, $407,671; qualifying distributions, $320,220; giving activities include $320,220 for grants.
Purpose and activities: The foundation believes that social action and civic participation contribute to the creation of a more equitable and tolerant society. The foundation concentrates its resources on civil society organizations in Turkey that focus on increasing gender equality and fostering communication and dialogue through arts and culture.
Fields of interest: Children; Youth; Women; Adults, women.
International interests: Turkey.
Type of support: Emergency funds; Film/video/radio; Management development/capacity building; Matching/challenge support; Program development; Program evaluation; Program-related investments/loans; Research; Technical assistance.
Limitations: Applications accepted. Giving primarily in Turkey, with occasional support to Cyprus and the Caucasus. No grants to individuals.
Publications: Application guidelines; Grants list; Program policy statement; Program policy statement (including application guidelines).
Application information: Application guidelines available on foundation web site. Application form required.
Initial approach: E-mail, telephone, or grant inquiry form on foundation web site
Copies of proposal: 1
Deadline(s): None
Board meeting date(s): Two times per year
Final notification: Ranges from days to eight weeks
Officers and Directors:* Lou Anne King Jensen, Pres.; Jeffrey J. Jensen,* V.P.; Haley Barb,* Secy.; Julie J. Jensen,* Treas.
Number of staff: 1 full-time professional; 1 part-time support.
EIN: 752840026

3195
The Clements Family Foundation
4710 Kinsey Dr., Ste. 200
Tyler, TX **75703-1009**

Donors: Michael Clements; Clements Charitable Trust.
Foundation type: Independent foundation.
Financial data (yr. ended 09/30/13): Assets, $6,421,901 (M); gifts received, $1,772,452; expenditures, $427,919; qualifying distributions, $427,919; giving activities include $395,572 for 9 grants (high: $131,000; low: $1,250).
Fields of interest: Boys & girls clubs; Christian agencies & churches.
Limitations: Applications not accepted. Giving primarily in TX. No grants to individuals.
Application information: Contributes only to pre-selected organizations.
Officers: Michael Clements, Pres.; Donna Clements, Secy.; Megan Tarrant, Treas.
EIN: 261770695

3196
Coastal Bend Community Foundation
615 N. Upper Broadway, Ste. 1950
Corpus Christi, TX **78401** (361) 882-9745
Contact: Karen W. Selim, C.E.O.
FAX: (361) 882-2865;
E-mail: kselim@cbcfoundation.org; Main URL: http://www.cbcfoundation.org
Scholarship inquiry e-mail: kwesson@cbcfoundation.org

Established in 1981 in TX.
Foundation type: Community foundation.
Financial data (yr. ended 12/31/12): Assets, $52,932,112 (M); gifts received, $5,811,192; expenditures, $4,643,473; giving activities include $1,944,927 for 80 grants (high: $91,130), and $1,034,507 for 997 grants to individuals.
Purpose and activities: The foundation seeks to help meet the charitable and educational needs and enhance and improve the quality of life in the Coastal Bend area of Texas through grants to charitable organizations; serve a wide variety donors by providing a vehicle for the establishment of various types of funds designed to serve their charitable wishes; exercise leadership on charitable issues and advance the cause of philanthropy throughout the area; and solicit others to partner with the foundation to provide for increased giving to address the ever-growing needs of the Coastal Bend.
Fields of interest: Museums; History/archaeology; Arts; Higher education; Adult education—literacy, basic skills & GED; Libraries/library science; Education, reading; Education; Environment; Animal welfare; Zoos/zoological societies; Hospitals (general); Health care, patient services; Health care; Substance abuse, services; Alcoholism; Diabetes; Food services; Food banks; Housing/shelter; Disasters, preparedness/services; Safety/disasters; Recreation, parks/playgrounds; Children/youth, services; Family services; Aging, centers/services; Homeless, human services; Human services; Community/economic development; Children/youth; Aging; Economically disadvantaged; Homeless.
Type of support: General/operating support; Equipment; Program development; Seed money; Fellowships; Scholarship funds.
Limitations: Applications accepted. Giving limited to Aransas, Bee, Jim Wells, Kleberg, Nueces, Refugio, and San Patricio counties, TX. No support for religious purposes, athletic teams, school groups, school districts, or academic or scientific research projects. No grants to individuals (except for scholarships), or for annual fund drives, social or special events, debt retirement, travel expenses, office or playground equipment (unless for efficiency or safety), or trips.
Publications: Application guidelines; Annual report; Grants list; Informational brochure.
Application information: Visit foundation web site for application guidelines. Application form required.
Initial approach: Complete application online
Copies of proposal: 1
Deadline(s): June 15
Board meeting date(s): Feb., May, Aug., and Nov.
Officers and Directors:* Dr. Robert Furgason,* Chair.; Jean Claire Turcotte,* Vice-Chair.; **Karen W. Selim,* Pres. and C.E.O.**; Leah Pagan Olivarri,* Secy.; Kathleen M. White,* Treas.; Larry D. Aduddell; Jan G. Anderson; Judge Bobby Galvan; Ralph Gomez; Joe Henkel; Jonathan M. Hornblower; Susan E. Hutchinson; Nancy Bellows Johnson; Rumaldo Z. Juarez, Ph.D.; Omar J. Leal; Robert W. Maxwell; Lou Adele May; Laura M. Miller; Fred J. Nemec; Henry Nuss; Karen O'Connor Urban; Jon Whatley; William B. Whitworth; Clare Atkinson Wonders; Jack W. Wright.
Number of staff: 3 full-time professional; 1 part-time professional; 1 full-time support.
EIN: 742190039
Other changes: Karen W. Selim has replaced Kent Williams as C.E.O. and Pres.

3197
Elizabeth Huth Coates Charitable Foundation of 1992
P.O. Box 17001
San Antonio, TX 78217-0001
***Main URL:* http://broadwaybank.com/wealthmanagement/FoundationElizabethHuthCoates.html**

Established in 1993 in TX.
Donor: Elizabeth Huth Coates‡.
Foundation type: Independent foundation.
Financial data (yr. ended 12/31/12): Assets, $35,238,082 (M); expenditures, $1,779,761; qualifying distributions, $1,686,364; giving activities include $1,645,400 for 48 grants (high: $263,700; low: $4,900).
Purpose and activities: Giving primarily for the arts and education.
Fields of interest: Museums; Arts; Higher education; Education; Zoos/zoological societies; Medical research, institute; Protestant agencies & churches; Catholic agencies & churches.
Type of support: General/operating support; Continuing support; Annual campaigns; Capital campaigns; Building/renovation; Program development; Curriculum development; Research.
Limitations: Applications accepted. Giving primarily in San Antonio, TX. No grants to individuals.
Application information: See foundation website for complete application guidelines. Application form required.
Board meeting date(s): Feb.
Distribution Committee: Betty Ann Stieren Kelso; Amy Stieren.
Trustee: Broadway National Bank.
Number of staff: 2
EIN: 746399782
Other changes: The grantmaker now accepts applications.

3198
College First Foundation
130 E. John Carpenter Freeway
Irving, TX 75062-2708 (972) 999-4560
Contact: Toppy Cantrell, Admin.
FAX: (972) 999-4559

Established in 1996 in TX.
Donors: Ronald L. Jensen; Alliance for Affordable Healthcare Association, Inc.; Alliance For Affordable Services, Inc.; Americans for Financial Security; B.E.L.I.E.F. Foundation; UGSC; Health Markets.

Foundation type: Independent foundation.
Financial data (yr. ended 12/31/12): Assets, $560,235 (M); gifts received, $365,956; expenditures, $395,105; qualifying distributions, $389,457; giving activities include $325,000 for 191 grants to individuals (high: $5,000; low: $1,000).
Purpose and activities: The foundation seeks to improve the quality of life of well deserving students by promoting higher education though scholarship programs for children of active employees or agents of participating companies and associations.
Fields of interest: Scholarships/financial aid.
Type of support: Scholarships—to individuals.
Limitations: Applications not accepted. Giving primarily to residents of TX.
Application information: Contributes only to pre-selected organizations.
Officers and Directors:* Jeff Jensen,* Pres.; Lou Anne Jensen,* V.P.; Janet Jensen,* Secy.-Treas.
EIN: 752638941

3199
Calvert K. Collins Family Foundation, Inc.
(formerly Calvert K. Collins Foundation, Inc.)
c/o Kuprion-Thomas, PC
8510 N. Central Expwy., Ste. 1900
Dallas, TX **75206**
E-mail: sthomas@kuprionthomas.com; Main URL: http://www.calvertkcollins.com

Incorporated in 1962 in TX.
Donor: Carr P. Collins.
Foundation type: Independent foundation.
Financial data (yr. ended 12/31/12): Assets, $16,644,807 (M); expenditures, $985,673; qualifying distributions, $831,687; giving activities include $686,551 for 34 grants (high: $246,551; low: $200), and $116,492 for foundation-administered programs.
Purpose and activities: Giving primarily to federated giving programs and for philanthropy; funding also for the arts, education, and children, youth, and social services. The foundation also has an investment in an 1872 registered historic property, the House of the Seasons, in Jefferson, TX. The foundation is involved in preserving this historic property, promoting and increasing the visibility of Jefferson, TX, and other historic homes, buildings and monuments, while providing information and education to the public regarding the historic city of Jefferson.
Fields of interest: Historic preservation/historical societies; Arts; Elementary/secondary school reform; Higher education; Human services; Children/youth, services; Community/economic development.
Type of support: General/operating support; Building/renovation; Research.
Limitations: Applications not accepted. Giving primarily in Dallas, TX; some funding also in Jefferson, TX. No grants to individuals.
Application information: Contributes only to pre-selected organizations.
Board meeting date(s): April
Officers and Directors:* Calvert K. Collins,* Pres.; Sandra R. Kuprion-Thomas, V.P. and Secy.; Richard H. Collins,* V.P. and Treas.
Number of staff: 1 full-time professional.
EIN: 756011615
Other changes: Calvert K. Collins is now Pres. Richard H. Collins is now V.P. and Treas. Sandra R. Kuprion-Thomas is now V.P. and Secy.

3200
Community Hospital Foundation
13301 East Freeway, Ste. 307
Houston, TX 77015-5815

Incorporated in 1986 in TX.
Foundation type: Independent foundation.
Financial data (yr. ended 05/31/13): Assets, $2,842,686 (M); expenditures, $319,243; qualifying distributions, $294,030; giving activities include $257,500 for 31 grants (high: $5,000; low: $1,000).
Purpose and activities: Giving primarily for higher and other education, as well as for health care, youth and social services, and to recognized religious, nonprofit affiliations.
Fields of interest: Higher education; Education; Health care; Human services; Youth, services; Protestant agencies & churches; Catholic agencies & churches.
Type of support: General/operating support; Capital campaigns; Building/renovation; Equipment; Scholarship funds.
Limitations: Applications not accepted. No support for organizations without 501(c)(3) status. No grants to individuals.
Application information: Contributes only to pre-selected organizations.
Officers: Loren Rohr, Pres.; Gerald Cobb, C.F.O.; John Ward, V.P.; Kay Howard, Secy.-Treas.
Director: Patsy Simon.
Number of staff: 1 part-time support.
EIN: 741470290
Other changes: Kay Howard is no longer Fin. Clerk.

3201
Gene Conley Foundation
P.O. Box 41629
Austin, TX 78704-9926
Application address: c/o Wells Fargo Bank, N.A., Attn.: J. Scott Tucker, V.P., 2301 Kell Blvd., Wichita Falls, TX 76308, tel.: (940) 766-8312; **Main URL: https://www.wellsfargo.com/privatefoundationgrants/conley**

Established in 1989 in TX.
Foundation type: Independent foundation.
Financial data (yr. ended 12/31/12): Assets, $8,942,955 (M); expenditures, $551,372; qualifying distributions, $380,322; giving activities include $339,198 for 28 grants (high: $95,000; low: $1,000).
Fields of interest: Education; Health organizations; Boys & girls clubs; Boy scouts; Human services; Children/youth, services; Science.
Limitations: Applications accepted. Giving primarily in North TX. No grants to individuals.
Application information: See foundation website for complete application guidelines. Application form required.
Initial approach: Proposal
Copies of proposal: 8
Deadline(s): May 1
Final notification: July 31
Trustee: Wells Fargo Bank Texas, N.A.
Advisory Board Members: Mac Cannedy; Bill Daniel; Mike Elyea; Steve McSpadden; Terry Pence; Barry Plaxco; Rhonda Poirot; David I. Ramsey; Joseph N. Sherrill, Jr.; Chris Travelstead.
EIN: 752224430

3202
The Constantin Foundation, Inc.
4809 Cole Ave., LB 127, Ste. 346
Dallas, TX 75205-3654 **(214) 522-9300**
Contact: Angie Burch, Exec. Dir.
FAX: (214) 521-7025;
E-mail: constantinfdn@sbcglobal.net

Trust established in 1947 in TX; reincorporated under current IRS identification number in 2007.
Donors: E. Constantin, Jr.‡; Mrs. E. Constantin, Jr.‡.
Foundation type: Independent foundation.
Financial data (yr. ended 12/31/12): Assets, $48,403,289 (M); expenditures, $2,674,188; qualifying distributions, $2,251,273; giving activities include $2,224,000 for 10 grants (high: $609,000; low: $1,750).
Purpose and activities: Emphasis on higher and other education; some support for cultural programs, social service and youth agencies, and hospitals and health, including alcohol and drug abuse programs.
Fields of interest: Museums; Humanities; Arts; Secondary school/education; Vocational education; Higher education; Adult/continuing education; Libraries/library science; Education; Hospitals (general); Medical care, rehabilitation; Health care; Substance abuse, services; Crime/violence prevention, youth; Housing/shelter, development; Human services; Children/youth, services; Children/youth; Youth; Disabilities, people with; Economically disadvantaged.
Type of support: Capital campaigns; Building/renovation; Equipment; Land acquisition; Endowments; Program development; Scholarship funds; Matching/challenge support.
Limitations: Applications accepted. Giving limited to Dallas County, TX. No support for tax-supported institutions, theater groups, churches, debt retirement, political organizations or second party requesters. **No grants to individuals, or for debt retirement, operations, research, special events, fundraisers, or second party requests; no loans.**
Publications: Application guidelines.
Application information: Application form not required.
Initial approach: Letter (up to 3 pages)
Copies of proposal: 1
Deadline(s): Sept. 15 for letters of inquiry; grants reviewed at quarterly meetings; grant meeting in Dec.
***Board meeting date(s):* Feb., May, Aug., and Dec.**
***Final notification:* Following Dec. meeting, and only if applicant is a recipient of a grant**
Officers: Roy Gene Evans, Chair.; Gene H. Bishop, Pres.; **Patrick McEvoy, Secy.-Treas.**; Angie Burch, Exec. Dir.; Joel T. Williams, Jr., Chair. Emeritus.
Directors: Harvey Berryman Cash; Joseph Boyd Neuhoff.
Number of staff: 1 full-time professional.
EIN: 205150433
Other changes: Roy Gene Evans has replaced Joel T. Williams, Jr. as Chair. Patrick McEvoy has replaced Roy Gene Evans as Secy.-Treas.

3203
Cooper Industries Foundation
Houston, TX

The foundation terminated.

3204
Cornerstones for Kids
Houston, TX

The foundation terminated on Dec. 7, 2010.

3205
Faye L. and William L. Cowden Charitable Foundation
c/o Broadway National Bank, Trust Dept.
P.O. Box 17001
San Antonio, TX 78217-0001 (210) 283-6500
Contact: David White, Trust Off., Broadway National Bank
***Main URL:* http://broadwaybank.com/wealthmanagement/FoundationFayeLWilliamLCowden.html**

Established in 1988 in TX.
Foundation type: Operating foundation.
Financial data (yr. ended 03/31/12): Assets, $12,095,743 (M); expenditures, $589,599; qualifying distributions, $520,381; giving activities include $512,000 for 47 grants (high: $25,000; low: $1,500).
Purpose and activities: Giving to Texas organizations which direct their activities toward the health, medical care and treatment of children, the education of children and young adults, the prevention of cruelty to children or animals, and the protection and preservation of wildlife and natural areas.
Fields of interest: Arts; Education; Human services; Children/youth, services.
Limitations: Applications accepted. Giving limited to TX, with emphasis on San Antonio. No grants to individuals.
Application information: See foundation website for complete application guidelines. Application form required.
Initial approach: Letter
Deadline(s): None
Trustee: Broadway National Bank.
EIN: 746359520

3206
The Crain Foundation
P.O. Box 2146
Longview, TX 75606-2146 (903) 758-8276
Contact: Ann Lacy Crain, Pres.

Established in 1997 in TX.
Donors: Lacy Holdings Ltd.; Crain Resources.
Foundation type: Independent foundation.
Financial data (yr. ended 12/31/12): Assets, $30,167,203 (M); gifts received, $1,500,000; expenditures, $1,429,537; qualifying distributions, $1,351,510; giving activities include $1,285,740 for 100 grants (high: $200,000; low: $50), and $65,770 for 9 employee matching gifts.
Fields of interest: Secondary school/education; Education; Health care; Children/youth, services; Protestant agencies & churches.
Limitations: Applications accepted. Giving primarily in TX, with emphasis on Houston and Longview.
Application information:
Initial approach: Proposal
Deadline(s): None
Final notification: Within 2 months of request
Officers and Directors:* Ann Lacy Crain,* Pres.; Rogers L. Crain,* V.P. and Secy.; Susan Mincey, V.P. and Treas.; Ann Lacy Crain II,* V.P.; B. Walter Crain III,* V.P.; **Darren Croce, V.P.; Terri Downing, Cont.**
EIN: 752698267

3207
W.A. Criswell Foundation, Inc.
2000 McKinney Ave., Ste. 975
Dallas, TX 75201-2084

Donors: Blake Pogue; Ann Pogue; Jack Brady; Dan Hall; Evelyn Johnson; W.A. Criswell†; Clifford E. Winkler; Don Hodges; Harriet Miers; The Pogue Foundation; Virginia Fay Gross Trust; The Simpson Charitable Trust; Premier Designs.
Foundation type: Independent foundation.
Financial data (yr. ended 12/31/12): Assets, $25,646,985 (M); gifts received, $165,460; expenditures, $1,935,583; qualifying distributions, $1,747,907; giving activities include $1,428,487 for 8 grants (high: $1,338,707; low: $713), and $319,420 for foundation-administered programs.
Purpose and activities: Giving primarily for education, including support for a Southern Baptist theological seminary, and to a Christian radio station.
Fields of interest: Media, radio; Elementary/secondary education; Higher education; Theological school/education; Christian agencies & churches; Protestant agencies & churches.
Limitations: Applications not accepted. Giving primarily in Arlington and Dallas, TX.
Application information: Contributes only to pre-selected organizations.
Officers and Directors:* Jack Pogue,* Chair.; Darrell Lafitte,* Pres.; Curtis Baker; Randy Bradley; Jack Brady; Dean Childress; Brian Hermes; Don Hodges; Garry Kinder; **Michael Lafitte**; Blake Pogue; Dr. Steve Washburn.
EIN: 237226473
Other changes: Calvin Wittman is no longer a director.

3208
Cruz-Diez Foundation
c/o UHY Advisors TX, LLC
2929 Allen Pkwy., 20th Fl.
Houston, TX **77019-7101**
***France address:* 23 rue Pierre Semard, 75009 Paris, France**; Main URL: http://www.cruz-diezfoundation.org
Facebook: https://www.facebook.com/pages/Cruz-Diez-Foundation/134333933285231
Twitter: https://twitter.com/cruzdiezfound

Established in TX.
Donors: Carlos Cruz-Diez; Jorge Cruz Delgado; Brad Bucher; Luis Campos, M.D.; Jose Tomas Duarte.
Foundation type: Independent foundation.
Financial data (yr. ended 12/31/12): Assets, $10,059,254 (M); gifts received, $1,077,569; expenditures, $516,253; qualifying distributions, $473,566; giving activities include $83,303 for 1 grant, and $380,133 for foundation-administered programs.
Fields of interest: Museums (art).
Limitations: Applications not accepted. Giving primarily in Houston, TX.
Application information: Unsolicited requests for funds not accepted.
Officers: Nicole Schindler, C.E.O.; David Ayers, Secy.
Directors: Luis Benshimol; Joel Bracho; Brad Bucher; Luis Campos, M.D.; Carlos Cruz Delgado; Jorge Cruz Delgado; Jose Tomas Duarte; Gabriel Cruz Mendoza.
EIN: 204405884

3209
The Dallas Foundation
Reagan Place at Old Parkland
3963 Maple Ave., Ste. 390
Dallas, TX 75219 (214) 741-9898
***Contact:* Mary M. Jalonick, Pres.; For grants: Laura J. Ward, Dir., Community Philanthropy**
FAX: (214) 741-9848;
E-mail: info@dallasfoundation.org; Additional e-mail: mjalonick@dallasfoundation.org; Grant request e-mail: lward@dallasfoundation.org; Main URL: http://www.dallasfoundation.org
Facebook: http://www.facebook.com/dallasfoundation

Established in 1929 in TX.
Foundation type: Community foundation.
Financial data (yr. ended 12/31/12): Assets, $237,683,349 (M); gifts received, $39,607,136; expenditures, $34,447,583; giving activities include $33,204,208 for grants.
Purpose and activities: The foundation serves as a resource, leader, and catalyst for philanthropy by providing donors with flexible means of making gifts to charitable causes that enhance the community.
Fields of interest: Arts; Education; Animal welfare; Health care; Health organizations, association; Crime/violence prevention, child abuse; Recreation, parks/playgrounds; Human services; Community development, neighborhood development; Infants/toddlers; Aging; Disabilities, people with; Physically disabled; Blind/visually impaired; Deaf/hearing impaired; Mentally disabled; African Americans/Blacks; Military/veterans; AIDS, people with; Crime/abuse victims; Immigrants/refugees; Economically disadvantaged; Homeless; LGBTQ.
Type of support: General/operating support; Management development/capacity building; Capital campaigns; Building/renovation; Equipment; Emergency funds; Program development; Scholarship funds; Employee-related scholarships; Matching/challenge support.
Limitations: Applications accepted. Giving primarily to the City and County of Dallas, TX. No support for religious purposes from discretionary funds. No grants to individuals from discretionary funds, or for endowments, research, operating budgets, annual fund campaigns, debt retirement, or underwriting of fundraising events or marketing campaigns; generally no multi-year grants.
Publications: Application guidelines; Annual report; Financial statement; Grants list; Newsletter.
Application information: Visit foundation web site for application guidelines per grant type. Application form required.
Initial approach: Attend Grantmaking Seminar
Copies of proposal: 1
***Deadline(s):* Aug. 1 for letters of inquiry for full proposals for Community Impact grants; Mar. 3 for Field-of-Interest fund grants; rolling basis for Safety Net Fund grants**
Board meeting date(s): Mar., June, Sept., and Dec.
Final notification: Mid-Dec. for Unrestricted fund grants; Mid-June for Field-of-Interest fund grants; within 30 days for Safety Net fund grants
Officers and Governors:* John P. Puckett III,* Chair.; Anne B. Motsenbocker,* Vice-Chair.; Mary M. Jalonick, Pres.; **Nita Clark,* Secy.**; William T. Solomon, Jr., C.F.O.; Torrey B. Littleton, Cont.; Liz Cedillo-Perez; **David R. Corrigan**; Don W. Crisp;

Valerie Freeman; Stephanie E. Hunt; Carol Levy; James M. "Jim" Moroney III; Amirali Rupani; Jere W. Thompson, Jr.; W. Kelvin Walker.
Trustee Banks: Bank of America, N.A.; Compass Bank.
Number of staff: 7 full-time professional; 5 full-time support.
EIN: 752890371
Other changes: John P. Puckett III has replaced David R. Corrigan as Chair. Anne B. Motsenbocker has replaced John P. Puckett III as Vice-Chair. Nita Clark has replaced Anne B. Motsenbocker as Secy. Larry J. Haynes and Douglas S. Lang are no longer governors.

3210
Katrine Menzing Deakins Charitable Trust
c/o U.S. Trust, Bank of America, N.A.
500 W. 7th St., 15th Fl., TX-1-497-15-08
Fort Worth, TX 76102-4700 (817) 390-6028
Contact: Mark J. Smith, Philanthropic Rels. Mgr.
E-mail: tx.philanthropic@ustrust.com; **Main URL: https://www.bankofamerica.com/philanthropic/grantmaking.go**

Established in 1987 in TX.
Foundation type: Independent foundation.
Financial data (yr. ended 03/31/13): Assets, $6,637,392 (M); expenditures, $434,664; qualifying distributions, $393,834; giving activities include $364,950 for 20 grants (high: $62,000; low: $2,500).
Fields of interest: Performing arts; Arts; Education; Health care; Health organizations, association; Human services.
Type of support: General/operating support.
Limitations: Applications accepted. Giving limited to TX. No grants to individuals.
Publications: Annual report (including application guidelines).
Application information:
Initial approach: Consult online guidelines on Trust web site
Deadline(s): Mar. 31 and Sept. 30
Trustee: Bank of America, N.A.
EIN: 756370503

3211
DeBusk Foundation
207 E. Virginia St., Ste. 205
McKinney, TX 75069-4374 (972) 542-0811
E-mail: director@debuskfoundation.org; Main URL: http://www.debuskfoundation.org
Grants List: http://www.debuskfoundation.org/fundedprograms.html

Established in 1979.
Foundation type: Independent foundation.
Financial data (yr. ended 12/31/12): Assets, $4,357,971 (M); expenditures, $251,594; qualifying distributions, $169,000; giving activities include $169,000 for 8 grants (high: $44,000; low: $9,000).
Purpose and activities: The DeBusk Foundation makes grants to educational organizations for the purpose of providing financial assistance to gifted students 12 years of age and under who are classified as elementary students. Grants will be limited to the state of Texas and priority will be given to established organizations.
Fields of interest: Elementary/secondary education; Elementary school/education.
Type of support: Scholarship funds.
Limitations: Applications accepted. Giving limited to TX.
Publications: Application guidelines.
Application information: Application guidelines available on foundation web site. Application form required.
Copies of proposal: 8
Deadline(s): Oct. 15
Board meeting date(s): Feb., May, Aug., and Nov.
Final notification: Within 8-10 weeks of the deadline
Officers and Directors:* Patricia McNutt,* Pres.; Diane Cooper,* V.P.; Kari Kolber,* Secy.; Keith Belcher,* Treas.; **Mike Tibbals**; Marty Webb.
EIN: 751671193

3212
The Patricia Dedman Family Foundation
5956 Sherry Ln., Ste. 1800
Dallas, TX 75225-8029

Established in 2007 in TX.
Donor: Nancy Dedman.
Foundation type: Independent foundation.
Financial data (yr. ended 12/31/12): Assets, $4,333,689 (M); expenditures, $214,669; qualifying distributions, $174,762; giving activities include $174,762 for 23 grants (high: $77,737; low: $64).
Purpose and activities: Giving primarily for the arts, education, and human services.
Fields of interest: Visual arts; Performing arts; Education; Botanical gardens; Human services; Community/economic development; Foundations (community); Protestant agencies & churches.
Limitations: Applications not accepted. Giving primarily in Aspen, CO, and TX, with emphasis on Dallas.
Application information: Contributes only to pre-selected organizations.
Directors: Patricia Brown Dedman; **Christina Dedman Dietz**; Jonathan Dedman Dietz.
EIN: 260209206
Other changes: Robert H. Dedman, Jr. is no longer Pres.

3213
The Michael and Susan Dell Foundation
P.O. Box 163867
Austin, TX 78716-3867
***FAX:* (512) 600-5501**; E-mail: info@msdf.org; Main URL: http://www.msdf.org/
Blog: http://www.msdf.org/blog/
Facebook: http://www.facebook.com/dellfamilyfoundation?v=info
Grants Database: http://www.msdf.org/Grants/Master_Grant_List.aspx
Twitter: http://twitter.com/msdf_foundation

Established in 1999 in TX.
Donors: Michael Dell; Susan Dell.
Foundation type: Independent foundation.
Financial data (yr. ended 12/31/12): Assets, $803,631,256 (M); gifts received, $24,883,148; expenditures, $118,834,622; qualifying distributions, $115,965,743; giving activities include $80,821,766 for 419 grants (high: $4,342,107; low: $1,000), $10,620,485 for 4 foundation-administered programs and $3,050,376 for 3 loans/program-related investments.
Purpose and activities: The foundation's mission is to fund initiatives that seek to foster active minds, healthy bodies and a safe environment where children can thrive. It proactively seeks out opportunities to support or develop programs that address five essential focus areas: children's health, education, safety, youth development and early childhood care.
Fields of interest: Elementary/secondary education; Elementary/secondary school reform; Education; Health care, HMOs; Health care, clinics/centers; Health care, infants; Health care; Health care, patient services; Crime/violence prevention, abuse prevention; Crime/violence prevention, child abuse; Youth development; Children/youth, services; Children, day care; Community/economic development.
Limitations: Applications accepted. Giving on a local (central TX) , regional, national and international basis (international emphasis is on India). No support for medical research. **No grants to individuals except for scholarship program, or for fundraisers, sponsorships, lobbying or endowments.**
Publications: Grants list.
Application information: See foundation web site for guidelines and requirements. To begin, use the foundation's "Check Your Eligibility" section on its web site.
Initial approach: Submit preliminary grant request online
Officers and Directors:* Michael Dell,* Pres.; Susan Dell,* 1st V.P.; Alexander Dell,* 2nd V.P.; Marc Lisker, Secy.; **Lorenzo Tellez, C.F.O.**; Janet Mountain, Exec. Dir.
Number of staff: 35
EIN: 364336415
Other changes: Tricia Teegardin is no longer Treas. Lorenzo Tellez is now C.F.O.

3214
DeSantis Family Foundation
600 Travis St., Ste. 7450
Houston, TX 77002-3022

Established in 2006 in CA.
Donors: Robert J. DeSantis; Ann Ranae DeSantis.
Foundation type: Independent foundation.
Financial data (yr. ended 06/30/13): Assets, $6,836,710 (M); gifts received, $4,313; expenditures, $255,613; qualifying distributions, $133,483; giving activities include $133,483 for 21 grants (high: $25,000; low: $250).
Fields of interest: Education; Environment; Human services.
Limitations: Applications not accepted. Giving primarily in CA and RI. No grants to individuals.
Application information: Contributes only to pre-selected organizations.
Trustee: Ann Ranae DeSantis.
EIN: 207114699
Other changes: Robert J. DeSantis is no longer director.

3215
Lucille and John B. Dougherty Trust
c/o Wells Fargo Bank, N.A.
P.O. Box 913
Bryan, TX 77805-0913 (979) 776-3267
***E-mail:* grantadministration@wellsfargo.com; Main URL: https://www.wellsfargo.com/privatefoundationgrants/dougherty**

Established in 2008 in TX.
Foundation type: Independent foundation.
Financial data (yr. ended 12/31/12): Assets, $5,263,745 (M); expenditures, $306,118; qualifying distributions, $240,437; giving activities

include $216,750 for 16 grants (high: $40,000; low: $1,000).
Fields of interest: Education; Health care; Christian agencies & churches.
Limitations: Applications accepted. Giving primarily in Bryan, The Woodlands, College Station, TX.
Application information: See foundation website for complete application guidelines. Application form required.
Initial approach: Proposal
Deadline(s): July 31
Trustees: William S. Thornton; Wells Fargo Bank, N.A.
EIN: 261444071

3216
John S. Dunn Research Foundation
3355 W. Alabama St., Ste. 990
Houston, TX 77098-1863 (713) 626-0368
***Contact:* Donna Nasso, Office Mgr.**
***FAX:* (713) 626-3866; E-mail: jsdrf@swbell.net; Main URL: http://johnsdunnfoundation.org/**

Established in 1985 in TX.
Donor: John S. Dunn, Sr.‡.
Foundation type: Independent foundation.
Financial data (yr. ended 12/31/12): Assets, $88,488,650 (M); expenditures, $6,137,912; qualifying distributions, $5,278,584; giving activities include $5,010,250 for 32 grants (high: $400,000; low: $35,000).
Purpose and activities: Giving limited to institutions in the State of Texas and the foundation's grants are generally approved for nursing programs, healthcare clinics for the underserved, mental health programs, and medical research and education in the greater Houston, TX, area.
Fields of interest: Hospitals (general); Health care; Health organizations, association; Cancer; Medical research, institute; Cancer research; Biology/life sciences.
Type of support: Endowments; Matching/challenge support; Professorships; Research.
Limitations: Applications accepted. Giving generally limited to TX. No grants to individuals, or for multi-year or seed money grants.
Publications: Application guidelines; Informational brochure (including application guidelines).
Application information: Application form not required.
Initial approach: Letter
Copies of proposal: 1
Deadline(s): None
***Board meeting date(s):* Full board meets monthly and quarterly; 4th Wed. of each month**
Final notification: Written notice 1 week following meeting
Officers and Trustees:* J. Dickson Rogers,* Pres.; Dan S. Wilford,* 1st V.P.; John S. Dunn, Jr.,* V.P. and Secy.-Treas.; Mrs. Dagmar Dunn Pickens Gipe,* V.P.; **David G. Key,* V.P.; Charles M. Lusk III,* V.P.**; John R. Wallace,* V.P.
Number of staff: 1 full-time professional; 2 full-time support.
EIN: 741933660
Other changes: Charles W. Hall is no longer V.P. C. Harold Wallace is no longer V.P.

3217
Devary Durrill Foundation, Inc.
615 S. Upper Broadway
Corpus Christi, TX 78401-3432
Contact: Marcia Kelly
Main URL: http://devarydurrillfoundation.org/

Established in 1984 in TX.
Donor: William R. Durrill.
Foundation type: Independent foundation.
Financial data (yr. ended 12/31/12): Assets, $9,548,534 (M); gifts received, $7,265; expenditures, $1,305,441; qualifying distributions, $495,131; giving activities include $457,239 for 29 grants (high: $137,254; low: $500).
Purpose and activities: Giving primarily for higher education.
Fields of interest: Higher education, university; Human services.
Limitations: Giving primarily in the Corpus Christi, TX, area. **No grants to individuals, or for debt.**
Publications: Application guidelines.
Application information: Application form required.
Initial approach: Refer to guidelines on foundation web site
Officer: William R. Durrill, Pres.
Directors: Ginger Durrill; Melissa Durrill; Michele Durrill; William R. Durrill, Jr.
EIN: 742370613

3218
J. E. S. Edwards Foundation
P.O. Box 122297
Fort Worth, TX **76121-2297** (817) 737-6924
Contact: Jareen E. Schmidt, Pres.

Established in 1976 in TX.
Donors: Jareen E. Schmidt; Jareen E. Schmidt Irrevocable Charitable Lead Annuity Trust; Jareen E. Schmidt Revocable Trust.
Foundation type: Independent foundation.
Financial data (yr. ended 07/31/13): Assets, $15,132,723 (M); gifts received, $589,778; expenditures, $724,909; qualifying distributions, $621,000; giving activities include $621,000 for 41 grants (high: $50,000; low: $2,350).
Purpose and activities: Grants largely for social services, including programs for women, hunger, the disadvantaged, and child welfare; support also for health and at-risk youth agencies, and Christian missionary programs.
Fields of interest: Child development, education; Adult/continuing education; Health care; Cancer; Medical research, institute; Cancer research; Food services; Human services; Youth, services; Child development, services; Women, centers/services; Christian agencies & churches; Religion; Women; Economically disadvantaged.
Type of support: Technical assistance; General/operating support; Capital campaigns; Equipment; Emergency funds; Research; Matching/challenge support.
Limitations: Applications accepted. Giving primarily in Fort Worth, TX. No support for individual churches. No grants to individuals, or for scholarships.
Application information: Application form required.
Initial approach: Letter
Copies of proposal: 1
Deadline(s): May 31
Board meeting date(s): June
Officers: Jareen E. Schmidt, Pres.; Stace Sewell, V.P.; Sheryl E. Bowen, Secy.-Treas.
Director: Stan Sewell.
EIN: 510173260

3219
Kirk Edwards Foundation
4201 Bluff View Dr.
Granbury, TX 76048-5013

Established in 1966 in TX.
Donor: A.B. Kirk Edwards‡.
Foundation type: Independent foundation.
Financial data (yr. ended 10/31/13): Assets, $3,393,283 (M); expenditures, $203,995; qualifying distributions, $161,484; giving activities include $152,000 for 18 grants (high: $40,000; low: $1,500).
Fields of interest: Higher education, university; Education; Hospitals (specialty); Medical care, rehabilitation; Boys & girls clubs; Youth development; Human services; Children/youth, services; Catholic agencies & churches; Children/youth; Disabilities, people with.
Type of support: General/operating support; Scholarship funds.
Limitations: Applications not accepted. Giving in TX, primarily in Dallas, Henrietta, Houston, and Wichita Falls. No grants to individuals.
Application information: Contributes only to pre-selected organizations.
Officers and Trustees:* Carolyn Sullivan,* Pres.; George Slagle,* V.P.; Elizabeth Young,* Secy.; David J. Walch,* Treas.; **Henry Medaris; Wilson Scaling; Edwin Taegel.**
EIN: 756054922

3220
J. A. and Isabel M. Elkins Foundation
c/o Paraffine Management
1001 Fannin St., Ste. 1001
Houston, TX **77002-6708**
***Contact:* Larry Medford**

Established in 1956 in TX.
Foundation type: Independent foundation.
Financial data (yr. ended 08/31/13): Assets, $5,210,478 (M); expenditures, $288,057; qualifying distributions, $240,000; giving activities include $240,000 for grants.
Purpose and activities: Grants primarily for religious, charitable, scientific, or educational agencies, institutions, and corporations. General focus on churches and religious associations; child welfare, hospitals, and health agencies; scientific organizations sponsoring research; and schools and universities.
Fields of interest: Higher education; Education; Hospitals (general); Health organizations, association; Medical research, institute; Children/youth, services; Engineering/technology; Science; Religion.
Type of support: Capital campaigns; Building/renovation; Equipment; Endowments; Emergency funds; Program development; Research.
Limitations: Applications accepted. Giving primarily in TX, with emphasis on the metropolitan Houston area. No grants to individuals, or for deficit financing; generally no grants for continuing operating support.
Application information:
***Initial approach:* Letter**
***Deadline(s):* None**
Trustees: Margaret Elise Elkins Joseph; **William L. Medford**; Leslie Keith Elkins Sasser.
EIN: 746047894
Other changes: The grantmaker now accepts applications.
J.A. Elkins is no longer trustee.

3221
The Elkins Foundation
(formerly Margaret & James A. Elkins, Jr. Foundation)

1166 First City Twr.
1001 Fannin St.
Houston, TX 77002-6706
Contact: Larry Medford

Established in 1956 in TX.
Donor: Elkins Family Charitable Lead Annuity Trust.
Foundation type: Independent foundation.
Financial data (yr. ended 10/31/13): Assets, $209,160,859 (M); gifts received, $3,540,031; expenditures, $9,639,997; qualifying distributions, $8,660,000; giving activities include $8,660,000 for 54 grants (high: $2,150,000; low: $5,000).
Purpose and activities: Giving primarily for charitable, religious, scientific, or educational and literacy programs, including public safety testing, and the prevention of cruelty to children and animals.
Fields of interest: Child development, education; Higher education; Medical school/education; Education; Hospitals (general); Health organizations, association; Medical research, institute; Safety/disasters; Children/youth, services; Child development, services; Engineering/technology; Biology/life sciences; Science; Christian agencies & churches; Religion.
Type of support: Capital campaigns; Building/renovation; Equipment; Endowments; Emergency funds; Program development; Research.
Limitations: Applications accepted. Giving primarily in the metropolitan Houston, TX area, support also in Princeton, NJ. No grants to individuals, or for deficit financing; generally no grants for continuing operating support.
Application information: Application form not required.
Initial approach: Letter
Copies of proposal: 1
Deadline(s): None
Board meeting date(s): Varies
Officers and Trustees:* Leslie E. Sasser,* Pres.; Elise E. Joseph,* V.P.; William L. Medford, Secy.-Treas.; **Virginia A. Elkins.**
EIN: 746051746
Other changes: For the fiscal year ended Oct. 31, 2013, the grantmaker paid grants of $8,660,000, a 146.7% increase over the fiscal 2012 disbursements, $3,510,000.

3222
Embrey Family Foundation
3625 N. Hall St., Ste. 720
Dallas, TX 75219-5106 (214) 206-3577
Contact: Jackie Robertson, Grants Admin.
FAX: (214) 599-9203;
E-mail: jrobertson@embreyfdn.org; E-mail for Jackie Robertson: jrobertson@embreyfdn.org; Main URL: http://www.embreyfdn.org
Facebook: https://www.facebook.com/EmbreyFamilyFoundation
Twitter: https://twitter.com/embreyfdn
WordPress: http://www.embreyfoundation.wordpress.com
YouTube: http://www.youtube.com/user/EmbreyFoundation

Established in 2004.
Donor: James L. Embrey, Jr.†.
Foundation type: Independent foundation.
Financial data (yr. ended 12/31/12): Assets, $24,216,297 (M); gifts received, $2,318,294; expenditures, $5,479,684; qualifying distributions, $4,956,292; giving activities include $4,300,436 for 40+ grants (high: $500,000), and $28,268 for loans/program-related investments.
Purpose and activities: The foundation's mission champions the well-being and rights of all people by supporting programs that advance human rights, healthy communities, the environment, education, and creativity.
Fields of interest: Arts; Education; Animal welfare; Human services; Civil/human rights; Community/economic development; Infants/toddlers; Children/youth; Adults; Aging; Minorities; Hispanics/Latinos; Women; Girls; Adults, women; Young adults, female; Adults, men; AIDS, people with; Single parents; Crime/abuse victims; Immigrants/refugees; Economically disadvantaged; Homeless.
Type of support: General/operating support; Continuing support; Capital campaigns; Building/renovation; Equipment; Emergency funds; Program development; Seed money; Matching/challenge support.
Limitations: Applications not accepted. Giving primarily in the North TX area. No support for religious, political or medical organizations, or for youth sports programs and activities. No grants to individuals or for individual scholarship awards, or for operating deficits, debt retirement, research, media production or publications, conferences, school trips or other educational events.
Application information: All grant requests are via invitation only. If you believe your program aligns with the foundation's priorities, please contact the foundation to discuss the possibility of receiving an invitation.
Board meeting date(s): Jan., Apr., July, and Oct.
Officers and Directors:* Lauren Embrey,* Chair., C.E.O., and Pres.; Gayle Embrey,* Vice-Chair. and V.P.; Ben Ablon,* Secy.; Michael Magers,* Treas.; Bobbie Embrey; Jeffery Harwell, Jr.; Bryan Marquis.
EIN: 200215399
Other changes: At the close of 2012, the fair market value of the grantmaker's assets was $24,216,297, a 168.7% increase over the 2011 value, $9,012,420.
Gayle Embrey is now Vice-Chair. and V.P. Lauren Embrey is now Chair., C.E.O, and Pres.

3223
Paul F. and Virginia J. Engler Foundation
P.O. Box 2010
Amarillo, TX **79105-2010**

Established in 1990 in TX.
Donors: Members of the Engler family; Paul F. Engler.
Foundation type: Independent foundation.
Financial data (yr. ended 12/31/12): Assets, $36,585,508 (M); gifts received, $134,243; expenditures, $2,490,145; qualifying distributions, $2,044,281; giving activities include $2,044,281 for 38 grants (high: $2,000,000; low: $37).
Fields of interest: Higher education; Education; Health organizations, association; Human services.
Limitations: Applications not accepted. Giving primarily in Lincoln, NE, and TX. No grants to individuals.
Application information: Contributes only to pre-selected organizations.
Officers and Directors:* Paul F. Engler,* Chair.; Peggy McGuire, Exec. Dir.; Jerry D. Miller; Richard C. Ware III.
EIN: 752356449
Other changes: Cathleen May is no longer Secy.-Treas. Sara Engler Cody, Mike Engler, Caroline M. Fauks, and Claudia M. Gilson are no longer directors.

3224
Erol Foundation
800 Gessner, Ste. 1260
Houston, TX 77024-4273
***FAX:* (415) 358-8233;**
E-mail: info@erolfoundation.org; Main URL: http://www.erolfoundation.org/
Facebook: https://www.facebook.com/ErolFoundation
Twitter: https://twitter.com/ErolFoundation

Established in 2007 in TX.
Donor: Normandy Trust.
Foundation type: Independent foundation.
Financial data (yr. ended 12/31/12): Assets, $85,361 (M); expenditures, $447,620; qualifying distributions, $235,000; giving activities include $235,000 for 4 grants (high: $100,000; low: $10,000).
Fields of interest: Education; Economically disadvantaged.
Type of support: General/operating support.
Limitations: Applications accepted. Giving primarily in CA.
Application information: See foundation website for complete application guidelines.
Officers and Directors:* Julie Lepinard,* Pres. and Treas.; Sebastien Lepinard,* V.P.; Marvin A. Wurzer, Secy.; Delphine Doron.
EIN: 261382214
Other changes: The grantmaker now accepts applications.

3225
Esping Family Foundation
2828 Routh St., Ste. 500
Dallas, TX 75201-1438 **(214) 849-9808**
Contact: Heather H. Esping, Pres.
FAX: (214) 849-9807;
E-mail: hesping@espingfamilyfoundation.org; Main URL: http://www.espingfamilyfoundation.org

Established in 1997 in TX.
Donor: Perry E. Esping†.
Foundation type: Independent foundation.
Financial data (yr. ended 12/31/12): Assets, $9,435,311 (M); expenditures, $587,952; qualifying distributions, $472,673; giving activities include $397,900 for 18 grants (high: $50,000; low: $10,000).
Purpose and activities: Giving to help others help themselves by supporting active programs with strong leadership and entrepreneurial activity. Grants are made in four categories: education, human services, health, and arts and culture. Within these categories, the foundation gives priority to projects that target 3 primary program areas: improving the education outcomes of Texas children (K-12), children and families, and youth development.
Fields of interest: Arts; Elementary/secondary education; Education; Health care; Youth development; Human services; Children/youth, services; Family services.
Type of support: Continuing support; Equipment; Program development; Curriculum development; Scholarship funds; Research.
Limitations: Applications accepted. Giving limited to the Dallas-Fort Worth, TX, Metroplex, with most of its grant resources going to organizations helping those in the Dallas area. No support for school sports or bands, church or seminary construction, or single artistic events or performances. No grants for individual scholarships, underwriting for charity balls or fundraising events, endowment or permanent funds, professional conferences and symposia

(unless directly related to the foundation's areas of high interest), travel, or capital campaigns; no loans.
Publications: Grants list.
Application information: See foundation website for complete application guidelines. Application form required.
Initial approach: Proposal
Copies of proposal: 1
Board meeting date(s): May and Nov.
Officers and Directors:* William P. Esping, Chair.; Heather H. Esping,* Pres.; Jennifer E. Kirtland,* V.P. and Secy.; Julie E. Blanton,* V.P. and Treas.; Darren Blanton; John E. Kirtland; Kathryn Esping Woods; Rodney Woods.
Number of staff: 2 part-time support.
EIN: 752702676

3226
Ezekiel Foundation, Inc.
5380 Old Bullard Rd.
Tyler, TX **75703-3607**

Donors: Jeff Bishop; Nic Lesmeister.
Foundation type: Independent foundation.
Financial data (yr. ended 12/31/12): Assets, $139,967 (M); gifts received, $152,000; expenditures, $236,514; qualifying distributions, $188,517; giving activities include $188,517 for 20 grants (high: $54,000; low: $25).
Fields of interest: Human services; Protestant agencies & churches.
Limitations: Applications not accepted. Giving primarily in Grand Prairie, TX.
Application information: Unsolicited requests for funds not accepted.
Officers and Directors:* Jeff Bishop,* Pres.; Elias Reyes,* V.P. and Treas.; Nic Lesmeister,* Secy.; Melissa Bishop.
EIN: 273165690

3227
I. D. & Marguerite Fairchild Foundation
517 S. First St.
Lufkin, TX 75901-3867
Application address: c/o Phil Medford, Pres., P.O. Box 150143, Lufkin, TX 75915, tel.: (936) 632-6661

Established in 1977 in TX.
Donor: Marguerite Fairchild†.
Foundation type: Independent foundation.
Financial data (yr. ended 06/30/13): Assets, $5,650,234 (M); expenditures, $264,897; qualifying distributions, $247,124; giving activities include $235,000 for 7 grants (high: $90,000; low: $10,000).
Fields of interest: Museums; Arts; Education; Zoos/zoological societies.
Type of support: General/operating support; Endowments; Program development; Scholarship funds.
Limitations: Applications accepted. Giving primarily in the Angelina County, TX, area. No grants to individuals.
Application information: Application form not required.
Initial approach: Letter
Deadline(s): None
Board meeting date(s): June
Officers: Phil Medford, Pres.; Hilda Mitchell, V.P.; Mary Duncan, Secy.
Directors: Bob Flournoy; C. James Haley, Jr.; Jay Shands; Ellen Temple; George Thannisch.
EIN: 751572514
Other changes: Jack Hicks is no longer a director.

3228
The William Stamps Farish Fund
1100 Louisiana St., Ste. 2200
Houston, TX 77002-5245
Contact: William Stamps Farish, Pres.

Incorporated in 1951 in TX.
Donor: Libbie Rice Farish†.
Foundation type: Independent foundation.
Financial data (yr. ended 06/30/13): Assets, $238,930,758 (M); expenditures, $12,258,871; qualifying distributions, $11,959,581; giving activities include $11,800,000 for 111 grants (high: $500,000; low: $10,000).
Purpose and activities: Giving primarily for basic education and basic medical research.
Fields of interest: Education; Medical research; Human services.
Type of support: Equipment; Program development; Research.
Limitations: Applications accepted. Giving primarily in Houston, TX. No support for political organizations. No grants to individuals, or for annual campaigns, deficit financing, operating budgets, exchange programs, consulting services, or endowment funds; no loans.
Publications: Application guidelines.
Application information: Application form not required.
Initial approach: Proposal
Copies of proposal: 1
Deadline(s): July 1- Apr. 1
Board meeting date(s): Annually
Final notification: 1 year
Officers and Trustees:* William Stamps Farish,* Pres.; **Larry L. Shryock, V.P. and Treas.**; Laura Farish Chadwick, V.P.; Cornelia Gerry Corbett, V.P.; Caroline P. Rotan, Secy.
Number of staff: 1 full-time professional.
EIN: 746043019
Other changes: Laura Farish Chadwick is now V.P. Cornelia Gerry Corbett is now V.P. Terry W. Ward is no longer Treas.

3229
The Fasken Foundation
P.O. Box 2024
Midland, TX 79702-2024 **(432) 683-5401**
***Contact:* Jeff Alsup, Exec. Dir.**
FAX: (432) 683-5402;
E-mail: jeff@faskenfoundation.org; Main URL: http://www.faskenfoundation.org

Incorporated in 1955 in TX.
Donors: Andrew A. Fasken†; Helen Fasken House†; Vickie Mallison†; Howard Marshall Johnson†; Ruth Shelton†.
Foundation type: Independent foundation.
Financial data (yr. ended 12/31/12): Assets, $17,332,770 (M); expenditures, $1,550,314; qualifying distributions, $960,206; giving activities include $774,546 for 66 grants (high: $110,000; low: $1,000), and $95,514 for 39 grants to individuals (high: $3,300; low: $289).
Purpose and activities: Giving primarily for youth, health, human services, and education, including scholarships to the Texas students of: Midland High School, Midland Robert Lee High School, Midland Greenwood High School, and Ft. Stockton High School. Also, nursing educational scholarships are available through Midland College.
Fields of interest: Arts; Hospitals (general); Health organizations; Human services; Children/youth, services.
Type of support: General/operating support; Program development; Curriculum development; Scholarship funds; Scholarships—to individuals; Matching/challenge support.
Limitations: Applications accepted. Giving limited to TX. Eighty percent of the giving is in the Midland area; 20 percent of the giving is to communities where foundation directors reside. No support for political or religious organizations. No grants to individuals (except scholarships limited to graduates of Midland County, TX, public high schools and junior college); no loans.
Publications: Application guidelines.
Application information: Application form required.
Initial approach: Letter, with appropriate application forms
Copies of proposal: 1
Deadline(s): None
Board meeting date(s): Jan., Apr., July, and Oct.
Officers and Directors:* Steve Fasken,* Pres.; John W. Wilkins, Jr.,* V.P.; Paula Fasken,* Secy.-Treas.; Jeff Alsup, Jr.,* Exec. Dir.; Tracy Elms*; Susan F. Hartin; Tevis Herd; Bobby Jones; Thomas E. Kelly.
Number of staff: 1 full-time professional; 1 part-time support.
EIN: 756023680
Other changes: Jeff Alsup, Jr. has replaced Gerald C. Nobles, Jr. as Exec. Dir. Jeff Alsup, Jr. has replaced Gerald C. Nobles, Jr. as Exec. Dir. John W. Wilkins, Jr. is now V.P. Paula Fasken is now Secy.-Treas. Stephen P. Fasken is no longer director.

3230
The Feldman Family Foundation
1431 Greenway Dr., No. 360
Irving, TX 75038-2442
Contact: Robert L. Feldman, V.P.

Established in 2005 in TX as successor foundation to The Feldman Foundation.
Donor: The Feldman Foundation.
Foundation type: Independent foundation.
Financial data (yr. ended 12/31/12): Assets, $65,564,413 (M); gifts received, $26,092,819; expenditures, $1,983,561; qualifying distributions, $1,736,823; giving activities include $1,339,180 for 37 grants (high: $250,000; low: $1,680).
Fields of interest: Education; Human services; Jewish federated giving programs; Jewish agencies & synagogues.
International interests: Israel.
Limitations: Applications accepted. Giving primarily in CA and TX.
Application information: Application form not required.
Initial approach: Letter
Copies of proposal: 1
Deadline(s): None
Board meeting date(s): Late summer/early fall
Officers and Directors:* Daniel E. Feldman,* Pres.; Robert L. Feldman,* V.P.
Number of staff: 1 part-time support.
EIN: 202098529
Other changes: At the close of 2012, the fair market value of the grantmaker's assets was $65,564,413, an 83.1% increase over the 2011 value, $35,810,700.

3231
Fifth Age Of Man Foundation
4211 Long Champ Dr.
Austin, TX 78746-1161
Main URL: http://www.5thage.org/
Facebook: https://www.facebook.com/pages/Fifth-Age-of-Man-Foundation/180777262003582

Foundation type: Independent foundation.
Financial data (yr. ended 12/31/12): Assets, $5,694,303 (M); expenditures, $456,534; qualifying distributions, $298,817; giving activities include $298,817 for 17 grants (high: $50,000; low: $1,000).
Fields of interest: Education.
Application information: Application form required.
Deadline(s): **None**
Officers: A. Chandler, Pres.; C. Vitlin, V.P.; M. Vitlin, V.P.; V. Vitlin, Treas.
EIN: 352403651

3232
Ben & Maytee Fisch Foundation
P.O. Box 6905
Tyler, TX 75711-6905
Contact: Dawn Franks, Exec. Dir.
E-mail: info@fischfoundation.org; Main URL: http://www.fischfoundation.org

Established in 1997 in TX.
Donors: Ben Fisch†; Maytee R. Fisch†.
Foundation type: Independent foundation.
Financial data (yr. ended 12/31/12): Assets, $59,763,662 (M); gifts received, $191,577; expenditures, $3,409,443; qualifying distributions, $2,773,198; giving activities include $2,762,629 for 83 grants (high: $250,000; low: $500).
Purpose and activities: The foundation is focused on human needs and strives to help people help themselves.
Fields of interest: Higher education; Adult education—literacy, basic skills & GED; Education; Mental health/crisis services; Food banks; Housing/shelter; Human services; Children/youth, services; Residential/custodial care, hospices.
Type of support: General/operating support; Continuing support; Annual campaigns; Capital campaigns; Building/renovation; Equipment; Program development; Scholarship funds; Matching/challenge support.
Limitations: Applications accepted. **Giving primarily in East TX; national organizations with significant operations in or providing material benefits to the citizens of East Texas will be considered based on the degree of benefits.** No support for public or private elementary or secondary schools. No grants for debt retirement, reserve funding, endowments or conferences.
Publications: Application guidelines.
Application information: Application form required.
Initial approach: On-line application
Copies of proposal: 1
Deadline(s): Check for deadlines
Board meeting date(s): 3 times per year.
Final notification: 60-90 days
Officers: Martee F. Fuerst, Pres.; Stephanie Fisch, V.P.; Mandy Fuerst, Secy.
Directors: Sandra Fisch; Stephanie Fisch; David Fuerst; Jan F. Fuerst.
Number of staff: 1 part-time support.
EIN: 752732192

3233
Ray C. Fish Foundation
2001 Kirby Dr., Ste. 1005
Houston, TX 77019-6081
Contact: Catherine Daniel Kaldis, Pres.
FAX: (713) 529-4033;
E-mail: sarahg.young@outlook.com; Main URL: http://www.raycfishfoundation.org

Incorporated in 1957 in TX.
Donors: Raymond Clinton Fish†; Mirtha G. Fish†; Ray C. Fish and Mirtha G. Fish Trust.
Foundation type: Independent foundation.
Financial data (yr. ended 06/30/13): Assets, $22,985,967 (M); gifts received, $69,998; expenditures, $1,831,781; qualifying distributions, $1,463,109; giving activities include $1,180,430 for 71 grants (high: $250,000; low: $1,000).
Purpose and activities: Giving to support, establish or advance educational, scientific or other charitable activities.
Fields of interest: Performing arts; Arts; Higher education; Libraries (special); Education; Hospitals (general); Medical research, institute; Human services; Children/youth, services.
Type of support: General/operating support; Continuing support; Annual campaigns; Capital campaigns; Building/renovation; Endowments; Program development; Professorships; Seed money; Scholarship funds; Research; Matching/challenge support.
Limitations: Giving primarily in TX, with emphasis on Houston. No grants to individuals.
Publications: Application guidelines; Informational brochure (including application guidelines).
Application information: See foundation web site for updates regarding grantmaking procedures.
Board meeting date(s): Quarterly
Officers and Trustees:* Catherine Daniel Kaldis, Pres.; Robert J. Cruikshank,* V.P. and Treas.; Christopher J. Daniel,* V.P.; James L. Daniel, Jr.,* V.P.; Paula Hooton,* Secy.
Number of staff: 1 full-time professional; 1 part-time professional.
EIN: 746043047

3234
Louis & Elizabeth Nave Flarsheim Charitable Foundation
c/o Bank of America, N.A.
P.O. Box 831041
Dallas, TX 75283-1041 (816) 292-4300
Contact: Spence Heddens, Market Pres.
E-mail: spence.heddens@ustrust.com; Application Address: P.O. Box 219119, Kansas City, MO 64121-9119; **Main URL: https://www.bankofamerica.com/philanthropic/grantmaking.go**

Established in 1980.
Donors: Louis Flarsheim; Elizabeth Flarsheim.
Foundation type: Independent foundation.
Financial data (yr. ended 12/31/12): Assets, $3,152,122 (M); expenditures, $190,163; qualifying distributions, $160,919; giving activities include $144,600 for 12 grants (high: $25,000; low: $1,000).
Purpose and activities: Established to support and promote quality educational, cultural, human services, and health care programming that serve the residents of Kansas City, MO.
Fields of interest: Arts; Education; Health care.
Type of support: General/operating support; Program development; Seed money.
Limitations: Applications accepted. Giving primarily in Kansas City, MO. No grants for capital support.
Application information: Application form required.
Initial approach: Letter
Copies of proposal: 2
Deadline(s): None
Board meeting date(s): Varies
Trustee: Bank of America, N.A.
Number of staff: 1 full-time professional.
EIN: 436223957

3235
The Fluor Foundation
6700 Las Colina Blvd.
Irving, TX 75039-2902 (469) 398-7000
***Contact:* Terence H. Robinson, Pres.**
E-mail: community.relations@fluor.com; Main URL: http://www.fluor.com/sustainability/community/Pages/default.aspx

Incorporated in 1952 in CA.
Donor: Fluor Corp.
Foundation type: Company-sponsored foundation.
Financial data (yr. ended 12/31/12): Assets, $12,476,435 (M); gifts received, $3,158,038; expenditures, $4,348,321; qualifying distributions, $4,327,953; giving activities include $4,327,951 for 443 grants (high: $544,943; low: $50).
Purpose and activities: The foundation supports programs designed to promote education; social services; community and economic development; and the environment.
Fields of interest: Elementary/secondary education; Middle schools/education; Higher education; Business school/education; Engineering school/education; Education; Environment, natural resources; Environmental education; Environment; Employment, services; Employment, training; Employment, retraining; Food services; Housing/shelter; Disasters, preparedness/services; Youth development, adult & child programs; Youth, services; Family services; Human services, emergency aid; Homeless, human services; Human services; Economic development; Community/economic development; Science, formal/general education; Mathematics; Engineering/technology; Science; Crime/abuse victims; Homeless.
Type of support: General/operating support; Annual campaigns; Capital campaigns; Building/renovation; Equipment; Endowments; Program development; Curriculum development; Scholarship funds; Research; Employee volunteer services; Employee matching gifts; Employee-related scholarships.
Limitations: Applications accepted. Giving primarily in areas of company operations, with some emphasis on AK, Aliso Viejo, CA, FL, KY, MS, NM, Greenville, SC, Irving and Sugar Land, TX, and Richland, WA. No support for sectarian or denominational religious organizations, political organizations or candidates, fraternal or labor organizations, or school-related bands. No grants to individuals (except for employee scholarships), or for entertainment events, school-related events, freelance films, video tapes, or audio productions, or courtesy advertising, program books, or yearbooks.
Publications: Application guidelines; Financial statement; Informational brochure; IRS Form 990 or 990-PF printed copy available upon request; Program policy statement.
Application information: Proposals should be no longer than 2 to 3 pages. Additional information may be requested at a later date. Application form not required.
Initial approach: Proposal to nearest company facility
Copies of proposal: 1

Deadline(s): None
Board meeting date(s): Apr. and Oct.
Final notification: Within 2 months
Officers and Directors:* **David T. Seaton, Chair.**; Torrence H. Robinson, Pres.; **Carlos M. Hernandez, Secy.**; E. J. Kowalchuk, Treas.; Ray F. Barnard; S. B. Dobbs; Glenn C. Gilkey; Kirk Grimes; Biggs C. Porter; Dwayne A. Wilson.
EIN: 510196032
Other changes: Clif Webb is no longer Pres. Leann Taylor is no longer Community Relations, Richland. Judy Connell is no longer a director. Carlos M. Hernandez is now Secy. David T. Seaton is now Chair.

3236
Fort Worth Burn Foundation
Fort Worth, TX

The foundation terminated on Dec. 31, 2012.

3237
Forte American Heroes Fund
909 Lake Carolyn Pkwy., Ste. 775
Irving, TX 75039-4001

Donors: Roger Soape; Carrington Coleman; Chesapeake Energy Corporation; Freeman; Keeton Hay Group; Noble Royalties, Inc.; Riomax, Ltd.; Shell Offshore, Inc.; The American Oil Gas Reporter; Roger A. Soape, Inc.; TFC Services, Inc.
Foundation type: Independent foundation.
Financial data (yr. ended 06/30/13): Assets, $126 (M); gifts received, $2,450; expenditures, $7,250; qualifying distributions, $7,250; giving activities include $7,250 for grants.
Fields of interest: Animals/wildlife; Human services.
Limitations: Applications not accepted. Giving primarily in CA and TX.
Application information: Unsolicited requests for funds not accepted.
Directors: M. Craig Clark; Robin Forte; **Christy Payne**; **Chelsea Petty**.
EIN: 203912597
Other changes: Roger Soape is no longer a director.

3238
The Frees Foundation
1770 St. James Pl., Ste. 616
Houston, TX 77056-3500 **(713) 623-0515**
***FAX:* (713) 623-6509**;
E-mail: nancy@freesfoundation.org; Main URL: http://www.freesfoundation.org
Grants List: http://www.freesfoundation.org/index_files/granthistoryff.htm

Established in 1983 in TX.
Donors: C. Norman Frees†; Shirley B. Frees.
Foundation type: Independent foundation.
Financial data (yr. ended 12/31/12): Assets, $11,318,466 (M); expenditures, $838,771; qualifying distributions, $774,698; giving activities include $542,650 for 40 grants (high: $50,000; low: $1,000).
Purpose and activities: The grantmaker's mission is to assist vulnerable and underserved populations in achieving self-sufficiency.
Fields of interest: Education; Health care; Housing/shelter, development; Children/youth, services; Family services; Aging, centers/services; Community/economic development; Aging; Minorities; Hispanics/Latinos; Women; Girls; Immigrants/refugees; Economically disadvantaged; Homeless.
Type of support: General/operating support; Continuing support; Program development.
Limitations: Applications not accepted. Giving primarily in Houston, TX. No support for art programs, the environment, animals, and political organizations. No grants to individuals, or for deficit financing, endowments, capital campaigns, or fundraising events.
Application information: Unsolicited requests for funds not accepted.
Board meeting date(s): Apr. 15 and Oct. 15
Officers: Edmund M. Fountain, Jr., Pres. and Treas.; Esther M. Perrine, V.P.; Nancy Frees Fountain, Managing Dir.
Number of staff: 1 full-time professional; 1 full-time support.
EIN: 760053200

3239
The Alfred S. Gage Foundation
P.O. Box 12170
San Antonio, TX **78212-0170** (210) 229-1975
E-mail: tina.pawelek@paisanocattle.com

Established in 1989 in TX.
Donor: Roxana Gage Catto†.
Foundation type: Independent foundation.
Financial data (yr. ended 06/30/13): Assets, $3,219,443 (M); expenditures, $156,389; qualifying distributions, $125,585; giving activities include $111,967 for 34 grants (high: $10,000; low: $100).
Fields of interest: Arts; Education; Animals/wildlife.
Type of support: General/operating support; Capital campaigns; Building/renovation.
Limitations: Applications accepted. Giving primarily in San Antonio, the Texas Hill Country, and Brewster and Presidio counties, TX. No grants to individuals.
Publications: Application guidelines.
Application information: Application form not required.
Initial approach: Letter
Copies of proposal: 1
Deadline(s): None
Board meeting date(s): Quarterly
Officers: Joan Negley Kelleher, Pres. and Treas.; Roxana Catto Hayne, V.P. and Secy.
Directors: Nancy E. Hayne; Julie K. Stacy.
EIN: 742553574

3240
The Galtney Foundation
820 Gessner, Ste. 1000
Houston, TX 77024-4274 (713) 932-5304
Contact: Ronda Wright

Established in 1995 in TX.
Donor: William F. Galtney, Jr.
Foundation type: Independent foundation.
Financial data (yr. ended 12/31/12): Assets, $126,053 (M); gifts received, $125,000; expenditures, $175,130; qualifying distributions, $175,000; giving activities include $175,000 for 1 grant.
Fields of interest: Health care.
Limitations: Applications accepted. Giving primarily in TX. No grants to individuals.
Application information: Application form required.
Initial approach: Proposal
Deadline(s): Nov. 1
Final notification: Within 1-3 months
Officers: William F. Galtney, Jr., Pres.; Joseph L. Moore, Treas.
Director: Robert F. Galtney.
EIN: 760489358
Other changes: The grantmaker no longer lists a URL address.

3241
The Goldsbury Foundation
P.O. Box 460567
San Antonio, TX **78246-0567** **(210) 582-2074**
Contact: Suzanne Mead Feldmann, Exec. Dir.
FAX: (210) 930-2482;
E-mail: info@goldsbury-foundation.org; Main URL: http://www.goldsbury-foundation.org

Established in 1996 in TX.
Donors: Christopher Goldsbury, Jr.; Goldsbury Charitable Trust.
Foundation type: Independent foundation.
Financial data (yr. ended 12/31/12): Assets, $49,135,190 (M); gifts received, $24,861,108; expenditures, $3,295,032; qualifying distributions, $3,246,461; giving activities include $3,010,756 for 36 grants (high: $1,000,000; low: $100).
Purpose and activities: The foundation is committed to providing meaningful philanthropic support that stimulates positive and lasting change for the children and families of San Antonio, Texas. Reflecting its historic funding focus on the prevention of substance abuse, the foundation remains strongly committed to providing positive healthy and transformational experiences and opportunities for the children and families of San Antonio. On a going forward basis, it is specifically interested in addressing the issues contributing to young people dropping out of school in its community.
Fields of interest: Arts; Elementary/secondary education; Education; Substance abuse, prevention; Heart & circulatory research; Crime/violence prevention, child abuse; Children/youth, services; Homeless, human services.
Type of support: General/operating support; Program development; Matching/challenge support.
Limitations: Applications not accepted. Giving primarily in San Antonio, TX. No support for research, or for political or religious organizations. No grants to individuals, or for capital campaigns, conferences, dinners, special events, sponsorships, or advertising.
Publications: Grants list.
Application information: Unsolicited requests for funds are currently not accepted.
Board meeting date(s): Quarterly
Officers and Directors:* Christopher Goldsbury, Jr.,* Pres.; Angela Aboltin Goldsbury,* V.P.; William Scanlan, Jr.,* Secy.; Suzanne Mead Feldmann, Exec. Dir.
Number of staff: 1 part-time professional.
EIN: 742780083
Other changes: At the close of 2012, the fair market value of the grantmaker's assets was $49,135,190, an 87.6% increase over the 2011 value, $26,192,243.

3242
Goodman-Abell Foundation
1721 Hollister St.
Houston, TX **77055-3126**

Established in 1998 in TX.

Donors: G. Hughes Abell; Betsy G. Abell; Nelson Abell Foundation.
Foundation type: Independent foundation.
Financial data (yr. ended 02/28/13): Assets, $20,645,379 (M); gifts received, $1,995,153; expenditures, $1,374,558; qualifying distributions, $1,374,558; giving activities include $1,169,981 for 42 grants (high: $261,968; low: $250).
Fields of interest: Museums; Arts; Elementary/secondary education; Children/youth, services; United Ways and Federated Giving Programs.
Type of support: General/operating support.
Limitations: Applications not accepted. Giving primarily in Austin, TX. No grants to individuals.
Application information: Contributes only to pre-selected organizations.
Officers: Betsy G. Abell, Pres.; G. Hughes Abell, V.P.
EIN: 742869876

3243
The W. K. Gordon, Jr. Foundation
Fort Worth, TX

The foundation terminated on Dec. 30, 2011 and transferred its assets to Tarleton State University.

3244
The Greentree Fund
5130 Green Tree
Houston, TX 77056-1406

Established in 1968 in TX.
Donor: Nancy C. Allen.
Foundation type: Independent foundation.
Financial data (yr. ended 06/30/13): Assets, $6,291,769 (M); expenditures, $333,410; qualifying distributions, $257,697; giving activities include $254,100 for 54 grants (high: $50,000; low: $100).
Purpose and activities: Giving primarily for education and the arts.
Fields of interest: Museums; Arts; Elementary/secondary education; Higher education; Hospitals (general); Health organizations, association; Human services; Christian agencies & churches.
Limitations: Applications not accepted. Giving primarily in Austin and Houston, TX. No grants to individuals.
Application information: Unsolicited requests for funds not accepted.
Trustees: Edward R. Allen III; Nancy C. Allen; **Wilson G. Allen.**
EIN: 237065240
Other changes: Fayez Sarofim is no longer a trustee.

3245
Gulf Coast Medical Foundation
P.O. Box 30
Wharton, TX 77488-0030
E-mail: mburnham@gulfcoastmedfndn.org; **Tel./fax: (979) 532-0904**; Main URL: http://www.gulfcoastmedfndn.org

Established in 1983 in TX; converted from Caney Valley Memorial Hospital and Gulf Coast Medical Center.
Foundation type: Independent foundation.
Financial data (yr. ended 12/31/12): Assets, $15,849,059 (M); expenditures, $1,001,947; qualifying distributions, $760,530; giving activities include $681,379 for 34 grants (high: $110,000; low: $79).
Purpose and activities: The Gulf Coast Medical Foundation is a private foundation which aims to make a meaningful and significant difference in the quality of life for residents of Fort Bend, Matagorda, and Wharton counties in Texas. To achieve this aim, grants are awarded to qualified non-profit organizations primarily in the following areas: medical/health, human services, education, civic and arts & culture with priority given to medical/health projects.
Fields of interest: Higher education; Medical school/education; Nursing care; Health care; Mental health/crisis services; Children/youth, services.
Type of support: General/operating support; Capital campaigns; Building/renovation; Equipment; Endowments; Program development; Matching/challenge support.
Limitations: Applications accepted. Giving primarily in Fort Bend, Matagorda and Wharton counties, TX. No support for national fundraising organizations. **No grants to individuals; no loans.**
Publications: Application guidelines; Grants list.
Application information: Application form required.
Initial approach: **Use online application process on foundation web site**
Copies of proposal: 1
Deadline(s): Dec. 15, Mar. 15, June 15, and Sept. 15
Board meeting date(s): Quarterly
Officers: Jeffrey D. Blair, Pres.; Melissa M. Burnham, Exec. V.P.; Robert Michael Farrell, V.P.; Jack Moore,* Secy.; Charles Davis, Treas.
Directors: Laurance H. Armour III; Sam Golden; **Joe Gurecky**; Kent Hill; Janet Peden; Clive Runnells III; Guy F. Stovall III; **Robert M. Taylor.**
Number of staff: 1 part-time professional.
EIN: 741285242

3246
D. D. Hachar Charitable Trust Fund
2200 Post Oak Blvd., 19th Fl.
Houston, TX 77056-4700 (956) 764-2811
FAX: (956) 764-1592; **Application address: c/o BBVA Compass Bank, 700 San Bernardo Ave., Laredo, TX 78042, tel.: (956) 727-9311**

Established in 1980 in TX.
Donor: Lamar Bruni Vergara Trust.
Foundation type: Independent foundation.
Financial data (yr. ended 04/30/13): Assets, $25,257,202 (M); expenditures, $1,626,472; qualifying distributions, $1,344,391; giving activities include $1,306,818 for 17 grants (high: $268,250).
Purpose and activities: Giving primarily for higher education, particularly scholarships to financially needy residents (of at least 3 years) of Laredo, Webb County, and surrounding counties in TX, who must maintain a GPA of 2.75. Students planning to attend a technical or vocational school will be considered on an individual basis as far as grade point average is concerned.
Fields of interest: Higher education.
Type of support: General/operating support; Scholarships—to individuals; Student loans—to individuals.
Limitations: Giving limited to Laredo and Webb County, TX, and surrounding areas.
Publications: Application guidelines; Annual report; Informational brochure; Program policy statement.
Application information: Application form required for scholarships. Grants to organizations are limited. Application form required.
Initial approach: Letter or telephone requesting application guidelines
Deadline(s): Refer to application guidelines
Trustee: BBVA Compass Bank.
Number of staff: 2 full-time professional.
EIN: 742093680

3247
The Ewing Halsell Foundation
711 Navarro St., Ste. 737
San Antonio, TX 78205-1711 (210) 223-2640
Contact: Jackie Moczygemba, Mgr.

Foundation type: Independent foundation.
Financial data (yr. ended 06/30/13): Assets, $159,426,713 (M); expenditures, $9,365,869; qualifying distributions, $8,058,932; giving activities include $7,816,000 for 29 grants (high: $2,000,000; low: $5,000).
Fields of interest: Museums; Arts; Education; Biomedicine research; Agriculture/food; Human services; Children/youth, services.
Limitations: Giving primarily in TX.
Application information:
Initial approach: **Telephone foundation mgr. to discuss project/program and set up a meeting, then submit 1-5 page proposal letter.**
Officer: Jackie Moczygemba, Fdn. Mgr.
Directors: Edward H. Austin, Jr.; Hugh A. Fitzsimons, Jr.; William Harte; William Scanlan.
EIN: 300654055

3248
George and Mary Josephine Hamman Foundation
3336 Richmond, Ste. 310
Houston, TX 77098-3022 (713) 522-9891
Contact: D. Troy Derouen CPA, Exec. Dir.
FAX: (713) 522-9693;
E-mail: HammanFdn@aol.com; Main URL: http://www.hammanfoundation.org

Incorporated in 1954 in TX.
Donors: Mary Josephine Hamman†; George Hamman†.
Foundation type: Independent foundation.
Financial data (yr. ended 12/31/12): Assets, $91,354,903 (M); expenditures, $5,397,175; qualifying distributions, $4,868,916; giving activities include $3,502,750 for grants, and $924,750 for grants to individuals.
Purpose and activities: Giving for construction and operation of hospitals, medical treatment, and research organizations and programs; grants to churches and affiliated religious organizations (nondenominational); grants to building programs or special educational projects at colleges and universities, mostly local; contributions also to cultural programs, social services, youth agencies, and ecological causes. Each spring, the foundation also awards 70 scholarships to Houston area high school seniors for undergraduate study. The award is $16,000, disbursed over 4 years. Applicants must have a minimum SAT score of 1,000 (on the Math and Critical Reading portions combined), and/or ACT score of 21. The recipient may select any major at any four year college or university.
Fields of interest: Arts; Higher education; Education; Hospitals (general); Health care; Medical research, institute; Human services; Children/youth, services; Religion.
Type of support: General/operating support; Continuing support; Annual campaigns; Capital

campaigns; Building/renovation; Equipment; Scholarship funds; Research; Scholarships—to individuals; Matching/challenge support.
Limitations: Applications accepted. Giving only in the state of TX for grants. Scholarships to high school seniors is limited to the immediate Houston area, particularly Brazoria, Chambers, Fort Bend, Galveston, Harris, Liberty, Montgomery and Waller counties. No support for postgraduate education. No grants to individuals (except for scholarships).
Publications: Application guidelines; Financial statement; Grants list.
Application information: Grant Application form and Grant follow-up reports must be completed for grantseekers. Application and financial qualification statement must be completed for scholarships. Forms can also be downloaded from foundation web site. Requests by fax or e-mail will not be accepted. For applicants who have received a prior grant from the foundation, complete the one-page "Follow-up Report" on the prior grant. Do not expand beyond the foundation's 1-page report. Application form required.
Initial approach: Application
Copies of proposal: 1
Deadline(s): Feb. 22 for scholarships, none for grants
Board meeting date(s): Bi-monthly
Final notification: 60 days
Officers and Directors:* Henry R. Hamman,* Pres.; Anne H. Shepherd,* Secy.; Charles D. Milby, Jr.,* Treas.; D. Troy Derouen, CPA, Exec. Dir.; Russell R. Hamman; Mary J. Milby.
Number of staff: 1 full-time professional; 1 full-time support.
EIN: 746061447

3249
Donald D. Hammill Foundation
8700 Shoal Creek Blvd.
Austin, TX 78757-6816 (512) 451-3246
Contact: Judith K. Voress, Exec. Dir.
FAX: (512) 451-1888;
E-mail: jvoress@hammillfoundation.org; Main URL: http://www.hammillfoundation.org
Grants List: http://www.hammillfoundation.org/projects.html

Established in 1987 in TX.
Donor: Donald D. Hammill.
Foundation type: Independent foundation.
Financial data (yr. ended 12/31/12): Assets, $12,697,226 (M); expenditures, $581,641; qualifying distributions, $410,350; giving activities include $410,350 for grants.
Purpose and activities: Giving limited to nonprofit organizations providing assistance to financially disadvantaged, disabled, or elderly individuals in the greater Austin, TX area.
Fields of interest: Education, research; Education, special; Human services; Aging; Disabilities, people with; Economically disadvantaged.
Type of support: Annual campaigns; Emergency funds.
Limitations: Applications accepted. Giving limited to the Austin TX, area. No support for religious or political organizations, businesses, non-501(c)(3) organizations, or 509(a)(3) organizations. No grants to public schools, colleges or universities.
Publications: Application guidelines; Grants list.
Application information: Application form not required.
Initial approach: Letter or e-mail
Copies of proposal: 1
Deadline(s): Mar. 15
Board meeting date(s): Feb.
Final notification: 2 weeks
Officers and Directors:* Donald D. Hammill,* Pres.; Nils Pearson,* Secy.; Cindy Thigpen, Treas.; Judith Voress,* Exec. Dir.; Phyllis Newcomer; Jim Patton.
EIN: 742499947

3250
The Haraldson Foundation
25025 I-45 N., Ste. 410
The Woodlands, TX 77380-3034 **(281) 362-9909**
Contact: Dale A. Dossey, Dir.
***FAX:* (281) 476-7045;**
E-mail: ndossey@haraldsonfoundation.org; Main URL: http://www.haraldsonfoundation.org

Established in 1993 in TX.
Donor: Beulah M. Haraldson†.
Foundation type: Operating foundation.
Financial data (yr. ended 09/30/13): Assets, $6,174,859 (M); expenditures, $469,278; qualifying distributions, $244,400; giving activities include $244,400 for 3 grants (high: $225,600; low: $4,700).
Purpose and activities: To encourage individual students to become Texas leaders for the 21st century, by providing scholarships for study at the University of Texas.
Fields of interest: Education.
Type of support: Scholarship funds; Scholarships—to individuals.
Limitations: Applications accepted. Giving limited to TX.
Publications: Application guidelines; Annual report; Grants list; Informational brochure (including application guidelines); Newsletter.
Application information: Application form and guidelines available on foundation web site. Application form required.
Initial approach: Telephone or letter
Deadline(s): Dec. 1
Board meeting date(s): After Jan. 1
Officers and Directors:* Karen Sue Emami,* Chair.; Betty Jean Cook,* Vice-Chair.; Dale A. Dossey,* Secy.; John Emami; Scott Emami; Tiffany Emami.
Number of staff: 1 part-time professional.
EIN: 760420758

3251
Harte Charitable Foundation
20742 Stone Oak Pkwy., Ste. 107
San Antonio, TX 78258-7538

Established in 2002 in TX.
Donor: Edward Harte.
Foundation type: Independent foundation.
Financial data (yr. ended 06/30/13): Assets, $5,168,183 (M); expenditures, $801,213; qualifying distributions, $756,895; giving activities include $592,284 for 3 grants (high: $322,284; low: $25,000).
Fields of interest: Higher education, university.
Limitations: Applications not accepted. Giving primarily in TX. No grants to individuals.
Application information: Contributes only to pre-selected organizations.
Officers and Directors:* William S. Harte,* Co-Pres.; Julia H. Widdowson,* Co-Pres.; David L. Sinak,* Secy.-Treas.; Christopher M. Harte; Elizabeth H. Owens.
EIN: 450489907
Other changes: William S. Harte is now Co-Pres. Julia H. Widdowson is now Co-Pres.

3252
The Gordon Hartman Family Foundation
c/o Gordon Hartman Family Foundation
1202 W. Bitters Bldg. 1, Ste. 1200
San Antonio, TX 78216-7851 **(210) 479-2811**
FAX: (210) 493-7828;
E-mail: becky@gordonhartman.com; Main URL: http://hartmansa.org
E-Newsletter: http://hartmansa.org/About/newsletter-sign-up.asp
Facebook: http://www.facebook.com/HartmanFoundation
Grants List: http://www.hartmansa.org/grants/previously-awarded
Twitter: http://twitter.com/GHFF

Established in 2005 in TX.
Donors: Gordon Hartman; RAD Investments Inc.; Meh Holding Company, Ltd; Margaret M. Hartman; Ruth Eaton; Joseph Eaton.
Foundation type: Independent foundation.
Financial data (yr. ended 12/31/12): Assets, $10,757,911 (M); gifts received, $486,513; expenditures, $1,050,924; qualifying distributions, $621,972; giving activities include $621,972 for grants.
Purpose and activities: The foundation supports programs, projects and collaborative efforts of Bexar County, TX, organizations that serve individuals with cognitive and physical disabilities, with a particular focus on serving children's needs in this area.
Fields of interest: Children; Disabilities, people with; Physically disabled; Mentally disabled.
Limitations: Giving limited to the Bexar County, TX, area. No support for for-profit organizations, or for religious organizations for sectarian purposes. No grants to individuals, or for economic development, annual fund drives, events, fundraisers or sponsorships.
Publications: Application guidelines.
Application information: Applications are by invitation only, upon the selection committee's review of the Letter of Inquiry. Complete application guidelines and policies are available on foundation web site.
***Initial approach:* Letter of Inquiry**
***Deadline(s):* See foundation web site for current deadlines**
Officers: Gordon V. Hartman, Pres.; Margaret M. Hartman, Secy.-Treas.
EIN: 203537281
Other changes: The grantmaker now publishes application guidelines.

3253
Gary & Diane Heavin Community Fund
(formerly The Curves Community Fund, Inc.)
c/o Ronnie Glaesmann
100 Ritchie Rd.
Waco, TX 76712-8544

Established in 2001 in TX.
Donors: Curves International, Inc.; Gary Heavin; Diane Heavin.
Foundation type: Company-sponsored foundation.
Financial data (yr. ended 12/31/12): Assets, $36,099,714 (M); gifts received, $20,000,000; expenditures, $1,943,814; qualifying distributions, $1,754,886; giving activities include $1,754,886 for 53 grants (high: $263,271; low: $250).
Purpose and activities: The fund supports organizations involved with television, radio, education, health, human services, and Christianity.
Fields of interest: Media, television; Media, radio; Higher education; Education; Hospitals (general); Health care; Salvation Army; Family services; Family

services, domestic violence; Aging, centers/services; Developmentally disabled, centers & services; Human services; Christian agencies & churches.
Type of support: General/operating support.
Limitations: Applications not accepted. Giving primarily in Waco, TX.
Application information: Contributes only to pre-selected organizations.
Officers: Gary H. Heavin, Pres.; Diane Heavin, V.P.
EIN: 743003293
Other changes: At the close of 2012, the fair market value of the grantmaker's assets was $36,099,714, a 101.2% increase over the 2011 value, $17,946,615.

3254
Robert A. and Virginia Heinlein Prize Trust

3106 Beauchamp St., 2nd Fl.
Houston, TX 77019-7206 **(713) 861-3600**
Contact: Arthur Dula, Dir.
FAX: (713) 861-3620;
E-mail: info@heinleinprize.com; Main URL: http://www.heinleinprize.com
RSS Feed: http://www.heinleinprize.com/?feed=rss2

Foundation type: Independent foundation.
Financial data (yr. ended 12/31/12): Assets, $12,059,641 (M); expenditures, $653,484; qualifying distributions, $294,120; giving activities include $268,520 for 12 grants (high: $118,970; low: $2,500), $25,600 for grants to individuals, and $240,545 for foundation-administered programs.
Purpose and activities: The purpose of the Heinlein Prize is to encourage and reward progress in commercial space activities that advances the dream of humanity's future in space.
Fields of interest: Space/aviation.
Type of support: Program-related investments/loans; Grants to individuals.
Application information: Application form required.
Initial approach: Letter
Deadline(s): None
Directors: Art Dula; Buckner Hightower; James M. Vaughn, Jr.
EIN: 766079186

3255
Henderson-Wessendorff Foundation

611 Morton St.
Richmond, TX 77469-3083 **(281) 342-2044**
Application address: c/o Joe D. Robinson, P.O. Box 669, Richmond, TX 77469, tel.: (281) 762-5205

Established in 1956 in TX.
Donor: Loise J. Henderson†.
Foundation type: Independent foundation.
Financial data (yr. ended 12/31/12): Assets, $186,538,479 (M); gifts received, $74,383,631; expenditures, $7,856,638; qualifying distributions, $5,163,832; giving activities include $3,485,461 for 44 grants (high: $1,000,000; low: $200).
Fields of interest: Elementary/secondary education; Theological school/education; Animal welfare; Hospitals (general); Mental health/crisis services; Health organizations, association; Human services; Protestant agencies & churches; Religion; Women.
Limitations: Applications accepted. Giving primarily in TX. No grants to individuals.
Application information:
Initial approach: Letter
Deadline(s): None
Officers: Charles Pat McDonald, C.E.O. and Pres.; Ben Jones, C.F.O.; Jack Moore,* Secy.
Directors: Barbara R. Bleil; Seth Deleery; Will Robertson; Lane Ward.
EIN: 746047149
Other changes: At the close of 2012, the fair market value of the grantmaker's assets was $186,538,479, a 2097.8% increase over the 2010 value, $8,487,486. For the same period, the grantmaker paid grants of $3,485,461, a 2434.0% increase over the 2010 disbursements, $137,550. Jack Felps is no longer a director.

3256
Albert & Ethel Herzstein Charitable Foundation

6131 Westview Dr.
Houston, TX 77055-5421 (713) 681-7868
Contact: L. Michael Hajtman, Pres.
FAX: (713) 681-3652;
E-mail: mail@herzsteinfoundation.org; Main URL: http://www.herzsteinfoundation.org
Grants List: http://www.herzsteinfoundation.org/Grant_History.html

Established in 1965 in TX.
Donors: Albert H. Herzstein†; Ethel Avis Herzstein†; Sadie Herzstein Smith†; and members of the Herzstein family.
Foundation type: Independent foundation.
Financial data (yr. ended 12/31/12): Assets, $97,836,563 (M); expenditures, $5,337,202; qualifying distributions, $4,499,365; giving activities include $4,046,550 for 258 grants (high: $500,000; low: $1,000).
Purpose and activities: The trust was organized and shall be operated exclusively for religious, charitable, scientific, literary and/or educational purposes.
Fields of interest: Historic preservation/historical societies; Arts; Education, community/cooperative; Education; Environment; Health care; Youth development; Human services; Community development, civic centers; Community/economic development.
Type of support: General/operating support; Continuing support; Annual campaigns; Capital campaigns; Building/renovation; Equipment; Land acquisition; Endowments; Debt reduction; Scholarship funds.
Limitations: Applications accepted. Giving primarily in TX, with emphasis on the greater Houston-Galveston area. No grants to individuals.
Publications: Application guidelines; Annual report; Grants list; Informational brochure (including application guidelines).
Application information: Only one proposal may be submitted in any twelve month period. All proposals must be submitted via U.S. mail, and must be unbound. E-mails are not accepted. Application form not required.
Initial approach: Letter or proposal
Copies of proposal: 1
Deadline(s): None
Final notification: 90 days
Officers and Directors:* George W. Strake,* Chair.; L. Michael Hajtman,* Pres.; Steven Goodman; Richard Loewenstern; Bryan Miller; Nathan H. Topek, M.D.
Number of staff: 1 full-time professional; 3 full-time support.
EIN: 746070484
Other changes: George W. Strake has replaced Nathan H. Topek, M.D. as Chair.
Steven Sheldon and Michael Viator are no longer directors.

3257
Hext Family Foundation, Inc.

5704 Ponderosa
Odessa, TX 79762-9431 (432) 561-5063
Contact: Jane Hext, Pres.

Established in 1998 in TX.
Donors: Jane Hext; Hext Management, LLC; Mark Palmer; Susan Palmer; Melinda Spencer; Tim Spencer.
Foundation type: Independent foundation.
Financial data (yr. ended 12/31/12): Assets, $2,669,047 (M); expenditures, $171,407; qualifying distributions, $149,000; giving activities include $149,000 for grants.
Purpose and activities: Giving primarily for cancer research, vocational education, and religious charities in the Permian Basin area.
Fields of interest: Vocational education; Cancer research; Human services; Christian agencies & churches.
Type of support: General/operating support; Capital campaigns; Building/renovation; Equipment; Land acquisition; Emergency funds; Program development; Conferences/seminars; Publication; Seed money; Scholarship funds; Research; Technical assistance; Consulting services; Matching/challenge support.
Limitations: Giving primarily in the Permian Basin, TX area.
Publications: Application guidelines; Grants list; Informational brochure (including application guidelines); Program policy statement.
Application information: Application form required.
Initial approach: Letter
Copies of proposal: 1
Deadline(s): Annually
Final notification: Mar. 15
Officers: Jane Hext, Pres.; Melinda Spencer, V.P.
Trustee: Tim Spencer.
EIN: 752754667
Other changes: The grantmaker no longer lists a URL address.

3258
Hildebrand Foundation

P.O. Box 1308
Houston, TX 77251-1308 (713) 965-9177
FAX: (713) 622-2732;
E-mail: myrawilliams@hilhouse.com; Application address: c/o John Larsen, 1201 Louisiana St., Houston, TX 77002-5606; Main URL: http://www.hildebrandfoundation.com

Established in 2001 in TX.
Donors: Jeffrey D. Hildebrand; Melinda B. Hildebrand.
Foundation type: Independent foundation.
Financial data (yr. ended 12/31/12): Assets, $170,794,069 (M); gifts received, $93,668,628; expenditures, $9,640,754; qualifying distributions, $9,335,306; giving activities include $9,329,848 for 82 grants (high: $2,000,000; low: $1,000).
Purpose and activities: Giving for the poor and needy through faith-based organizations.
Fields of interest: Religion.
Limitations: Applications accepted. Giving primarily in Houston, TX. No support for trips for school-related organizations or amateur sports teams. No grants to individuals, or for the purchase of uniforms, or equipment; no loans.
Application information: Application form not required.
Initial approach: Written request on organization's letterhead
Copies of proposal: 1

Deadline(s): Ongoing
Board meeting date(s): Several times each year
Final notification: Two weeks after board meeting
Officers: Jeffrey D. Hildebrand, Pres.; Melinda B. Hildebrand, V.P.
Director: Jean-Paul Budinger.
EIN: 760699250
Other changes: At the close of 2012, the fair market value of the grantmaker's assets was $170,794,069, a 131.2% increase over the 2011 value, $73,863,032. For the same period, the grantmaker paid grants of $9,329,848, a 212.1% increase over the 2011 disbursements, $2,989,784.

3259
Hill Country Community Foundation
P.O. Box 848
Burnet, TX 78611 (512) 756-8211
Contact: Pat Williams
***E-mail:* pwilliams200@austin.rr.com**; Additional e-mail: support@thehccf.com; Main URL: http://www.thehccf.org
Facebook: https://www.facebook.com/pages/Hill-Country-Community-Foundation/117940184977074
YouTube: https://www.youtube.com/user/BurnetHCCF

Established in 1982 in TX.
Foundation type: Community foundation.
Financial data (yr. ended 12/31/12): Assets, $5,515,008 (M); gifts received, $388,506; expenditures, $341,339; giving activities include $59,455 for 9 grants (high: $26,000), and $254,532 for 193 grants to individuals.
Purpose and activities: The foundation, by investing endowment money to earn income, provides funding for certain local benefits. Specifically, the foundation seeks to advance the following goals: 1) grant multi-year scholarships to college freshman and sophomore students who are pursuing collegiate or other advanced educations; and 2) aid a variety of local youth and health organizations.
Fields of interest: Health care; Youth development; Family services; Community development, neighborhood development; Economic development; Young adults.
Type of support: Endowments; Scholarships—to individuals.
Limitations: Giving limited to residents of the Texas Hill Country area.
Publications: Annual report.
Application information: The foundation does not accept unsolicited grant applications.
Initial approach: Submit letter
Board meeting date(s): Bi-monthly
Officers and Directors:* Mike Lucksinger,* Pres.; Ken Graham,* V.P.; Dennis Hoover,* Secy.; Glen Bible,* Treas.; **Dale Hill**; John Hoover; Cary Johnson; Sallye Long; Keith McBurnett; T.J. Reed; **Michael Rockafellow**; Kyle Stripling.
Number of staff: 1 part-time support.
EIN: 742452519

3260
The Margaret and Al Hill Family Foundation
(formerly Hill Foundation)
2001 Ross Ave., Ste. 4600
Dallas, TX 75201-8007 **(214) 922-1100**
Contact: Lyda Hill, Pres.

Established in CO and TX.
Donor: Margaret Hunt Hill†.
Foundation type: Independent foundation.
Financial data (yr. ended 02/28/13): Assets, $4,647,048 (M); expenditures, $248,953; qualifying distributions, $149,596; giving activities include $149,461 for 12 grants (high: $45,000; low: $300).
Fields of interest: Reproductive health, family planning; Health organizations; Human services; Residential/custodial care, hospices.
Type of support: General/operating support; Annual campaigns; Capital campaigns; Building/renovation; Scholarship funds.
Limitations: Applications accepted. Giving primarily in CO, with emphasis on Colorado Springs. No grants to individuals.
Application information: Application form required.
Initial approach: Letter
Deadline(s): None
Officers and Trustees:* Lyda Hill, Chair. and Pres.; Al G. Hill, Jr.,* V.P.; Alinda H. Wikert,* V.P.; Heather H. Washburne,* Secy.-Treas.; Elisa Hill Summers; Cody M. Wikert; Margretta H. Wikert; Michael B. Wisenbaker, Jr.; Wesley Hill Wisenbaker.
EIN: 756010533

3261
Hillcrest Foundation
c/o US Trust, Philanthropic Solutions
901 Main St., 19th Fl., TX1-492-19-11
Dallas, TX 75283-1041 (214) 209-1965
Contact: David T. Ross, US Trust, Philanthropic Solutions
***E-mail for David T. Ross:* david.ross@baml.com; Additional e-mail for Debi Allen: debi.allen@baml.com; additional e-mail for questions about the application process or the foundation: tx.philanthropic@ustrust.com (indicate the foundation name in e-mail subject line)**; Main URL: http://www.bankofamerica.com/grantmaking

Trust established in 1959 in TX.
Donor: Mrs. W.W. Caruth, Sr.†.
Foundation type: Independent foundation.
Financial data (yr. ended 05/31/13): Assets, $143,498,239 (M); expenditures, $7,036,684; qualifying distributions, $6,481,981; giving activities include $5,947,000 for 151 grants (high: $250,000; low: $1,000).
Purpose and activities: To relieve poverty, advance education, and promote health; support for higher and other education, health and hospitals, social services, including programs for youth and child welfare, drug abuse, rehabilitation and housing. Grant requests for capital and program support are strongly encouraged.
Fields of interest: Secondary school/education; Vocational education; Higher education; Business school/education; Adult/continuing education; Education; Hospitals (general); Dental care; Medical care, rehabilitation; Health care; Substance abuse, services; Health organizations, association; Cancer; Medical research, institute; Food services; Housing/shelter, development; Human services; Children/youth, services; Aging, centers/services; Aging; Disabilities, people with.
Type of support: Capital campaigns; Building/renovation; Equipment; Land acquisition; Program development; Matching/challenge support.
Limitations: Applications accepted. Giving limited to TX, with emphasis on Dallas County. No grants to individuals or for general operating support; no loans.
Publications: Application guidelines; Informational brochure (including application guidelines).
Application information: The majority of grants are 1 year in duration. On occasion, multi-year support is awarded. An organization that receives a one-year grant must skip a year before submitting a subsequent application. An organization that receives a multi-year grant is not eligible to apply until one year after the close of its grant cycle. Application form required.
Initial approach: Letter
Copies of proposal: 2
Deadline(s): Rolling for proposals; Applications: Feb. 28, July 31 and Nov. 30
Board meeting date(s): As required, usually 3 times annually; Feb., May, and Oct.
Final notification: Feb. deadline applicants will be notified by June 30; July applicants will be notified by Nov. 30; Nov. applicants will be notified by Mar. 31 of the following year
Trustees: George W. Bramblett, Jr.; D. Harold Byrd, Jr.; W.W. Caruth III; Sandra Estess; Charles P. Storey; Bank of America, N.A.
Number of staff: 1 part-time professional; 2 part-time support.
EIN: 756007565

3262
Hoblitzelle Foundation
5556 Caruth Haven Ln., Ste. 200
Dallas, TX 75225-8146 (214) 373-0462
Contact: Paul W. Harris, C.E.O. and Pres.
FAX: (214) 750-7412;
E-mail: pharris@hoblitzelle.org; **E-mail address for Kathy Shannon Stone for general inquiries: kstone@hoblitzelle.org**; Main URL: http://www.hoblitzelle.org

Trust established in 1942 in TX; incorporated in 1953.
Donors: Karl St. John Hoblitzelle†; Esther T. Hoblitzelle†; Karl Hoblitzelle Trust.
Foundation type: Independent foundation.
Financial data (yr. ended 04/30/13): Assets, $119,487,983 (M); gifts received, $38,717; expenditures, $5,700,717; qualifying distributions, $5,448,155; giving activities include $5,142,049 for 87 grants (high: $425,000; low: $500).
Purpose and activities: Grants for higher, secondary, vocational, scientific and medical education, hospitals and health services, youth agencies, cultural programs, social services, and community development.
Fields of interest: Visual arts; Performing arts; Historic preservation/historical societies; Arts; Secondary school/education; Vocational education; Higher education; Medical school/education; Adult/continuing education; Adult education—literacy, basic skills & GED; Education, reading; Education; Hospitals (general); Medical care, rehabilitation; Health care; AIDS; Alcoholism; Housing/shelter, development; Human services; Children/youth, services; Aging, centers/services; Community/economic development; Science; Children/youth; Youth; Aging; Disabilities, people with; Mentally disabled; Minorities; Substance abusers; Economically disadvantaged; Homeless.
Type of support: Capital campaigns; Building/renovation; Equipment; Land acquisition; Program development; Seed money; Matching/challenge support.
Limitations: Applications accepted. Giving limited to TX, primarily within the Dallas Metroplex. No support for religious organizations (except for sectarian purposes). No grants to individuals; only occasional board-initiated support for operating budgets, debt reduction, research, scholarships, media

productions, publications, or endowments; no loans (except for program-related investments).
Publications: Application guidelines; Annual report (including application guidelines); Grants list; Newsletter; Program policy statement.
Application information: Submitted application material must be unbound without folders or binders. Application form not required.
Initial approach: Letter
Copies of proposal: 1
Deadline(s): Dec. 15, Apr. 15 and Aug. 15
Board meeting date(s): Latter part of Jan, May, and Sept.
Final notification: After next board meeting
Officers and Directors:* William T. Solomon,* Chair.; Caren H. Prothro,* Vice-Chair.; Paul W. Harris, C.E.O. and Pres.; J. McDonald Williams,* Treas.; Rafael M. Anchia; Linda P. Custard; John Dayton; **Karen L. Shuford**; Deedie Rose; **Jere W. Thompson, Jr.**; Kern Wildenthal, M.D., Ph.D.
Number of staff: 1 full-time professional; 1 full-time support.
EIN: 756003984

3263
The Hoglund Foundation
5910 N. Central Expwy., Ste. 255
Dallas, TX 75206-1106 (214) 987-3605
Contact: Kelly H. Compton, Secy.-Treas.
FAX: (214) 363-6507;
E-mail: info@hoglundfoundation.org; Main URL: http://www.hoglundfoundation.org
Grants List: http://www.hoglundfoundation.org/grants_prior.html

Established in 1989 in TX.
Donor: Forrest E. Hoglund.
Foundation type: Independent foundation.
Financial data (yr. ended 12/31/12): Assets, $57,296,509 (M); gifts received, $10,301; expenditures, $3,722,052; qualifying distributions, $3,479,748; giving activities include $3,109,045 for 129 grants (high: $500,000; low: $695).
Purpose and activities: The primary focus of the foundation is to promote interests and entities in education, health science and services, social services and children's health and development.
Fields of interest: Education; Health care; Health organizations, association; Human services; Child development, services; Infants/toddlers; Children/youth; Adults; Young adults; Mentally disabled; Adults, women; Adults, men; Single parents; Crime/abuse victims; Economically disadvantaged.
Type of support: General/operating support; Annual campaigns; Capital campaigns; Building/renovation; Equipment; Endowments; Program development; Scholarship funds; Research; Matching/challenge support.
Limitations: Applications accepted. Giving primarily to organizations that are located in and focused on the city of Dallas, TX. No grants to individuals.
Publications: Application guidelines.
Application information: Inclusion of videos or CDs with application is discouraged. See foundation web site for specific application guidelines. Application form not required.
Initial approach: Letter
Copies of proposal: 1
Deadline(s): 75 days prior to meeting date.
Board meeting date(s): Apr., Aug., and Dec.
Final notification: Within 4 months
Officers and Trustees:* Forrest E. Hoglund,* Chair. and Pres.; Sally R. Hoglund,* V.P.; Kelly H. Compton,* Secy.-Treas. and Exec. Dir.; Shelly H. Dee; Kristy H. Robinson.
Number of staff: 2 full-time professional; 1 part-time professional; 1 part-time support.
EIN: 752300978
Other changes: The grantmaker now makes its application guidelines available online.

3264
The Graham and Carolyn Holloway Family Foundation
P.O. Box 989
Colleyville, TX 76034-0989
Contact: Valerie Holloway Skinner, V.P.
E-mail: valerie@hollowayfamilyfoundation.org; Main URL: http://www.hollowayfamilyfoundation.org
Grants List: http://www.hollowayfamilyfoundation.org/grants.htm

Established in 1994 in TX.
Donors: E. Graham Holloway‡; Carolyn G. Holloway.
Foundation type: Independent foundation.
Financial data (yr. ended 12/31/12): Assets, $4,237,974 (M); gifts received, $18,132; expenditures, $241,108; qualifying distributions, $200,500; giving activities include $200,500 for 52 grants (high: $10,000; low: $1,000).
Purpose and activities: Giving primarily to aid the elderly, individuals with developmental and/or physical disabilities, the chronically or terminally ill, and disadvantaged children.
Fields of interest: Arts; Education; Hospitals (general); AIDS; Alzheimer's disease; Human services; Youth, services; Children; Aging; Disabilities, people with; Physically disabled; Mentally disabled; AIDS, people with; Terminal illness, people with; Economically disadvantaged; Homeless.
Type of support: General/operating support; Program development; Research.
Limitations: Applications accepted. Giving primarily in NC, TN and TX. No support for churches or political interest groups. No grants to individuals and no loans; no international giving.
Publications: Application guidelines; Financial statement; Grants list.
Application information: See grantmaker web site for application policies and guidelines. Application form not required.
***Initial approach:* Create account on foundation web site**
Copies of proposal: 1
***Deadline(s):* See foundation web site for current deadlines**
Board meeting date(s): May and Nov.
Officer and Trustees:* Valerie Holloway Skinner,* V.P.; **Elizabeth Holloway Heinburger**; Carolyn G. Holloway; Susan Holloway Ward.
Number of staff: 1 part-time support.
EIN: 752569765
Other changes: Elizabeth Holloway Heinburger is no longer Secy.

3265
The Holthouse Foundation for Kids
1800 West Loop S., Ste. 1875
Houston, TX 77027-3209 (713) 626-5511
Contact: Lisa Holthouse, Dir.
E-mail: lisa@holthouse.net**; Additional e-mail: info@holthouse.net**; Main URL: http://www.holthousefoundationforkids.org
Blog: http://blog.hffk.org/
Twitter: http://twitter.com/holthouseffk

Established in 2000 in TX.
Donors: Colleen Holthouse; Michael H. Holthouse.
Foundation type: Independent foundation.
Financial data (yr. ended 12/31/12): Assets, $18,978,733 (M); expenditures, $1,119,030; qualifying distributions, $977,051; giving activities include $911,677 for 68 grants (high: $185,000; low: $250).
Purpose and activities: The foundation engages in proactive initiatives to improve opportunities for at-risk children, by developing and implementing programs that will teach them set goals, build character, become self-reliant, and establish positive direction in their lives.
Fields of interest: Education; Health organizations, association; Boys & girls clubs; Human services; Children/youth, services; Family services.
Limitations: Applications accepted. Giving primarily in Houston, TX. No support for political or legislative causes. No grants to individuals, or for lobbying, or debt.
Application information: Proposals are by invitation, only after consideration of initial letter of inquiry. The foundation will not grant funds to the same organization for more than 5 consecutive years. Application guidelines available on foundation web site.
Initial approach: Letter of inquiry (no more than 3 pages)
Deadline(s): None
Board meeting date(s): Jan., Apr., July, and Oct.
Final notification: 1 month (for letter)
Officers and Directors:* Michael H. Holthouse,* Pres.; Lisa Holthouse,* V.P.; Richard H. Stein,* Secy.-Treas.; Colleen M. Holthouse.
EIN: 760620426

3266
Greater Houston Community Foundation
5120 Woodway Dr., Ste. 6000
Houston, TX 77056 (713) 333-2200
Contact: Linda Gardner, Dir., Opers.; Nelson Hernandez, Acct. Mgr.
FAX: (713) 333-2220; E-mail: lgardner@ghcf.org; Main URL: http://www.ghcf.org
E-Newsletter: http://www.ghcf.org/Resources/News/Publications/
Facebook: http://www.facebook.com/pages/Greater-Houston-Community-Foundation/147438280341

Established in 1971 in TX.
Foundation type: Community foundation.
Financial data (yr. ended 12/31/13): Assets, $438,701,314 (M); gifts received, $118,518,630; expenditures, $108,171,184; giving activities include $98,934,435 for grants.
Purpose and activities: The foundation grows effective philanthropy by connecting donors to the causes they care about, provides excellent stewardship of assets entrusted to them, and convenes resources to address important community needs.
Fields of interest: Arts; Education; Environment; Health care; Human services; Public affairs; Religion.
Type of support: General/operating support; Continuing support; Income development; Management development/capacity building; Annual campaigns; Capital campaigns; Building/renovation; Equipment; Land acquisition; Endowments; Debt reduction; Emergency funds; Program development; Conferences/seminars; Professorships; Film/video/radio; Publication; Seed money; Curriculum development; Fellowships; Internship funds; Scholarship funds; Research; Technical assistance; Consulting services; Program evaluation; Program-related investments/loans;

Employee matching gifts; Employee-related scholarships; Exchange programs; In-kind gifts; Matching/challenge support.
Limitations: Applications not accepted. Giving primarily in Houston, TX. Also gives nationally and internationally. No grants to individuals (except for disaster relief funds).
Publications: Annual report; Financial statement; Grants list; Informational brochure; Newsletter; Occasional report; IRS Form 990 or 990-PF printed copy available upon request.
Application information: The foundation does not issue requests for proposals or take grant applications.
Board meeting date(s): 4 times a year
Officers and Directors:* Bruce R. Bilger,* Chair.; Stephen D. Maislin, C.E.O. and Pres.; Renee Wizig-Barrios, V.P. and Chief Philanthropy Off.; Ed Padar, Cont.; William J. Bryan; Ric Campo; Martha Carnes; Ernie D. Cockrell II; Michael R. Dumas; Rob Galtney; Melanie Gray; Terri Lacy; Leo Linbeck III; Barry H. Margolis; Gasper Mir III; Dave Pruner; Gavin H. Smith; Elizabeth A. Tilney.
Number of staff: 12 full-time professional; 10 full-time support.
EIN: 237160400
Other changes: Bruce R. Bilger has replaced Steven L. Miller as Chair.
Gus H. Comiskey, Jeffery D. Hildebrand, Steven L. Miller, and Thomas L. Ryan are no longer directors.

3267
Houston Endowment Inc.

600 Travis, Ste. 6400
Houston, TX 77002-3003 (713) 238-8100
***Contact:* Lydia Hickey, Grant Mgr.**
FAX: (713) 238-8101;
E-mail: info@houstonendowment.org; **E-mail and tel. for Lydia Hickey: online@houstonendowment.org; (713) 238-8134**;
Main URL: http://www.houstonendowment.org
Grants Database: http://www.houstonendowment.org/GrantHistory/Search.aspx

Incorporated in 1937 in TX.
Donors: Jesse H. Jones†; Mrs. Jesse H. Jones†.
Foundation type: Independent foundation.
Financial data (yr. ended 12/31/12): Assets, $1,545,616,901 (M); expenditures, $108,357,045; qualifying distributions, $83,787,053; giving activities include $73,981,079 for 419 grants (high: $5,200,000; low: $5,000), $4,337,166 for 1,348 grants to individuals (high: $9,400; low: $300), and $399,805 for 257 employee matching gifts.
Purpose and activities: Support primarily for nonprofit organizations and educational institutions that improve life for the people of the greater Houston, TX area. Funding for programs in the arts, community enhancement, education, health, human services, the environment and neighborhood development.
Fields of interest: Arts; Education; Environment; Health care; Human services; Community development, neighborhood development.
Type of support: General/operating support; Continuing support; Annual campaigns; Capital campaigns; Building/renovation; Equipment; Land acquisition; Endowments; Program development; Conferences/seminars; Publication; Curriculum development; Fellowships; Scholarship funds; Research; Employee matching gifts.
Limitations: Applications accepted. Giving primarily in the greater Houston, TX area, with some funding throughout the state for projects central to TX history. No support for religious organizations for religious purposes, or organizations that are the responsibility of the government. No grants to individuals (except for scholarships); or generally for fundraising activities including galas, lobbying or for individual memorials, or for scholarship programs other than the Jones Scholars.
Publications: Application guidelines; Annual report; Financial statement; Grants list; Informational brochure (including application guidelines).
Application information: The foundation has recently implemented a comprehensive online Grant Management System. Applicants should go to the program area that matches their request, select the result area and type of investment that matches their request. The foundation will contact applicants to request any additional information needed. In some cases, organizations will need to complete a pre-application. Scholarship applicants should contact their high school college counselor for an application. Application form not required.
Initial approach: Online submission
Copies of proposal: 1
Deadline(s): None
Board meeting date(s): 9 to 10 times per year
Final notification: Online submissions receive e-mail response within 2 weeks
Officers and Directors:* Linnet F. Deily,* Chair.; Ann B. Stern,* Pres.; Sheryl L. Johns, Exec. V.P.; Lisa Hall, V.P., Prog(s).; Anne S. Chao; **Anthony Chase**; Douglas L. Foshee; Anthony W. Hall, Jr.; Jesse H. Jones II; David Louis Mendez; Paul B. Murphy, Jr.
Number of staff: 16 full-time professional; 10 full-time support.
EIN: 746013920
Other changes: Anna B. Leal is no longer V.P. and Grant Dir.

3268
Laverne and Thomas Howell Foundation

P.O. Box 2003
Rockport, TX 78381-2003 (361) 729-3441
E-mail: info@howellfoundationtx.org; **Letter of Inquiry e-mail: grantrequests@HowellFoundationTx.org**; Main URL: http://www.howellfoundationtx.org/public/

Established in 2003 in TX.
Donor: Laverne Howell†.
Foundation type: Independent foundation.
Financial data (yr. ended 12/31/12): Assets, $11,516,480 (M); expenditures, $610,079; qualifying distributions, $541,373; giving activities include $479,655 for 18 grants (high: $147,000; low: $10,000).
Purpose and activities: Giving primarily for Christian religious activities, impoverished individuals in need of financial or health care assistance, or other similar charitable purposes.
Fields of interest: Health organizations, association; Human services; Christian agencies & churches; Economically disadvantaged.
Limitations: Giving limited to Nueces County, TX. No grants to individuals.
Application information: Full proposals are by invitation only, upon review of Letter of Inquiry.
***Initial approach:* Letter of Inquiry (1-2 pages) via U.S. mail or e-mail**
***Deadline(s):* May 1**
Officers and Directors:* Martin C. Davis,* Mgr.; Sandra L. Garrison,* Mgr.; Gary B. Pearce.
EIN: 460501821

3269
International Medical Outreach, Inc.

915 Gessner Rd., Ste. 620
Houston, TX 77024-2551 (713) 935-9057
Contact: Todd Price, C.E.O. and Pres.
Main URL: http://www.imoutreach.com
Twitter: https://twitter.com/imoutreach

Established in 1997 in TX.
Donors: Todd Price, M.D.; William Lee; Donna Greer; Ingrid Sharon, M.D.; Leticia J. Dizov; Lakewood Church; Christian Alliance for Humanitarian Aid; Medical Bridges, Inc.; Feed the Children.
Foundation type: Operating foundation.
Financial data (yr. ended 12/31/12): Assets, $788,111 (M); gifts received, $249,408,395; expenditures, $247,561,196; qualifying distributions, $247,416,601; giving activities include $247,416,601 for 12 grants (high: $120,248,725; low: $1,100).
Purpose and activities: The grantmaker provides health care for those in need on a worldwide basis. It concentrates on efforts towards the relief of infectious diseases, including malaria, HIV/AIDS, tuberculosis, pneumonia, and diarrhea in addition to other diseases. It also establishes and assists existing medical clinics, orphanages, feeding centers, drug rehabilitation projects and teaching centers among other humanitarian efforts.
Fields of interest: Health care, clinics/centers; Health care, support services; Public health; Health care; Substance abuse, treatment; AIDS; Diseases (rare); Food services; Children, adoption; Children, services; International relief.
Type of support: General/operating support.
Limitations: Giving primarily on an international basis.
Application information: Applicants must also include the need for medical supplies and equipment, as well as the Christian-related organization with which they are affiliated.
Initial approach: Letter
Deadline(s): None
Officers: Todd Price, M.D., C.E.O. and Pres.; **Andrew Francis Price, C.O.O.**; Susan Price, V.P. and Exec. Dir.
EIN: 760392915
Other changes: At the close of 2012, the grantmaker paid grants of $247,416,601, a 468.1% increase over the 2011 disbursements, $43,554,412.
Todd Price is now C.E.O. and Pres. Susan Price is now V.P. and Exec. Dir. Robert Liken is no longer Secy. Justin Osteen is no longer Treas.

3270
Jiv Daya Foundation

5420 Lyndon B. Johnson Fwy., Ste. 410
Dallas, TX **75240-6279 (214) 593-0500**
Contact: Sarah Hunt Oswald, Grants Coord.
FAX: (214) 593-1902;
E-mail: coordinators@jivdayafound.org; Tel. for Sarah Hunt Oswald: (214) 360-7484; e-mail: shoswald@jivdayafound.org. Additional fax: (214) 593-1902; Main URL: http://www.jivdayafound.org
Facebook: https://www.facebook.com/pages/Jiv-Daya-Foundation/100438146673008
Twitter: http://twitter.com/JivDaya

Established in 2002 in TX.
Donors: Vinay K. Jain; Kanika Virmani Jain.
Foundation type: Independent foundation.
Financial data (yr. ended 12/31/12): Assets, $80,889,120 (M); gifts received, $1,464,421; expenditures, $4,240,565; qualifying distributions,

$4,189,370; giving activities include $3,784,340 for 79 grants (high: $3,000,000; low: $495).
Purpose and activities: Giving primarily for pediatric oncology, palliative care, amputee assistance, kala-azar/tropical disease eradication, and maternal and neonatal health.
Fields of interest: Education; Reproductive health; Palliative care; Health care; Tropical diseases; Pediatrics; Human services; Foundations (public).
International interests: India.
Limitations: Giving primarily in MA and India.
Publications: Application guidelines.
Application information:
Initial approach: Letter via form on foundation web site
Officers and Directors:* Vinay K. Jain,* Pres. and Treas.; Kanika Virmani Jain,* V.P. and Secy.; Yash Paul Virmani.
EIN: 320045123

3271
The Willard and Ruth Johnson Charitable Foundation
P.O. Box 27727
Houston, TX **77227-7727**

Established in 1992 in TX.
Donors: Ruth Johnson‡; Willard Johnson‡.
Foundation type: Independent foundation.
Financial data (yr. ended 12/31/12): Assets, $22,268,275 (M); expenditures, $1,290,225; qualifying distributions, $1,095,050; giving activities include $1,095,050 for 66 grants (high: $200,000; low: $200).
Purpose and activities: Giving primarily for education, children and youth services, social services, and to a United Methodist church.
Fields of interest: Elementary/secondary education; Higher education; Education; Human services; Children/youth, services; Protestant agencies & churches.
Limitations: Applications not accepted. Giving primarily in Houston and Midland, TX. No grants to individuals.
Application information: Contributes only to pre-selected organizations.
Officers: John W. Johnson, Pres.; David M. Johnson, V.P.; Steven J. Lindley, V.P.; Christopher B. Johnson, Secy.
EIN: 760386599

3272
Walter S. and Evan C. Jones Testamentary Trust
c/o Bank of America, N.A.
P.O. Box 831041
Dallas, TX 75283-1041
Application address: c/o James J. Mueth, Trust Off., Bank of America, N.A., P.O. Box 219119, Kansas City, MO 64121-9119, tel.: (816) 292-4342

Established in KS and MO.
Foundation type: Independent foundation.
Financial data (yr. ended 06/30/13): Assets, $86,864,091 (M); expenditures, $7,082,103; qualifying distributions, $6,336,861; giving activities include $6,042,910 for 23 grants (high: $2,282,500; low: $5,000).
Purpose and activities: Giving for the improvement of recreational or governmental services to the public in the cities, towns, and other government subdivisions within Lyon, Coffey, and Osage Counties, Kansas.
Fields of interest: Arts councils; Higher education; Education; Health care; Youth development, centers/clubs; Foundations (private grantmaking).
Limitations: Giving limited to Lyon, Coffey and Osage counties, KS. No grants to individuals.
Application information: Application form not required.
Initial approach: Letter, no more than 3 pages
Deadline(s): None
Board meeting date(s): 2nd Tues. quarterly
Advisory Committee: Gregory A. Bachman; Max Stewart, Jr.; Thomas D. Thomas.
Trustee: Bank of America, N.A.
EIN: 480674648
Other changes: For the fiscal year ended June 30, 2013, the grantmaker paid grants of $6,042,910, a 67.5% increase over the fiscal 2012 disbursements, $3,607,443.

3273
KDK-Harman Foundation
1000 Westbank Dr., Bldg. 3
Austin, TX 78746-6687 (512) 328-9400
FAX: (512) 328-9402;
E-mail: info@kdk-harman.org; Main URL: http://www.kdk-harman.org
Blog: http://www.kdk-harman.org/blog
Facebook: http://www.facebook.com/KDKHarman
Grants Database: http://www.kdk-harman.org/index.php?option=com_content&view=article&id=65&Itemid=66
Knowledge Center: http://www.kdk-harman.org/index.php?option=com_content&view=article&id=67&Itemid=213
Twitter: http://twitter.com/KDKHarman
YouTube: http://www.youtube.com/user/KDKHarman

Established in 2004 in Austin, TX.
Donor: Janet E. Harman.
Foundation type: Independent foundation.
Financial data (yr. ended 12/31/12): Assets, $24,477,125 (M); gifts received, $500,000; expenditures, $1,235,783; qualifying distributions, $1,137,740; giving activities include $928,000 for 27 grants (high: $60,000; low: $10,000).
Purpose and activities: The foundation's mission is to break the cycle of poverty through education in Central Texas. It focuses strictly on academic education. The foundation funds educational programs across the age spectrum from pre-kindergarten through adult. Its program interests include early and family literacy, college access, GED certification, academically rigorous out-of-school-time programs, traditional pre-K-12 education, and postsecondary education. It also supports workforce development programs that are academically rigorous, allow individuals to obtain college credit, and open doors for them to acquire living-wage jobs. In addition, KDK-Harman will favor those programs in the areas of science, technology, engineering, and math (STEM).
Fields of interest: Education, public policy; Education, formal/general education; Education, services; Science, formal/general education; Economically disadvantaged.
Type of support: Mission-related investments/loans; General/operating support; Continuing support; Management development/capacity building; Program development; Technical assistance.
Limitations: Applications accepted. Giving primarily in central TX: Travis, Williamson, Hays, Bastrop, Caldwell, Burnet, and Llano counties. No support for arts or athletic education, tax-generating entities for services, political campaigns, or pregnancy prevention programs. No grants to individuals, or for loans to individuals, research, scholarships, purchase of tickets for events, or school fundraisers.
Publications: Application guidelines; Annual report; Financial statement; Grants list.
Application information: Electronic application is required. Upon review of letter of inquiry, the foundation will send an e-mail either inviting an application, or declining the request. Following approval of application by the board, the grant contract and evaluation is developed. Once executed, the grant funds are released. This process takes 30-45 days after the board meeting. Central Texas Education Funders Common Application Form accepted. Application form required.
Initial approach: Letter of inquiry. Instructions, grant guidelines and form available on foundation web site.
Deadline(s): Throughout the year
Board meeting date(s): Apr., Sept., and Nov.
Final notification: Applications approved by the board are notified within a week of the board meeting
Officers and Trustees:* Janet E. Harman,* Pres.; Eugene Sepulveda,* V.P.; **Mark Williams,* Secy.-Treas.**; **Melanie Moore, Exec. Dir.**; **Kent Mayes.**
Number of staff: 2 part-time professional; 1 full-time support.
EIN: 611478157
Other changes: Mark Williams has replaced Jo Ivester as Secy.-Treas.

3274
Kinder Foundation
(formerly Richard D. Kinder Foundation, Inc.)
P.O. Box 130776
Houston, TX 77219-0776
Contact: Nancy G. Kinder, Pres.
Main URL: http://www.kinderfoundation.org
Richard D. and Nancy Kinder's Giving Pledge Profile: http://glasspockets.org/philanthropy-in-focus/eye-on-the-giving-pledge/profiles/kinder

Established in 1994 in TX.
Donors: Richard D. Kinder; Nancy G. Kinder.
Foundation type: Independent foundation.
Financial data (yr. ended 12/31/13): Assets, $138,622,283 (M); gifts received, $69,816,443; expenditures, $33,993,241; qualifying distributions, $33,374,261; giving activities include $33,214,714 for 83 grants (high: $9,899,042; low: $500).
Purpose and activities: Giving primarily for the arts, education, health associations, social services, children services, including a children's hospital, community development and federated giving programs.
Fields of interest: Museums; Arts; Education; Environment; Hospitals (specialty); Health organizations, association; Human services; Children, services; Community/economic development; Catholic agencies & churches.
Type of support: Matching/challenge support; Scholarship funds; Emergency funds; Land acquisition; General/operating support; Continuing support; Annual campaigns; Capital campaigns; Building/renovation; Endowments; Program development; Professorships.

Limitations: Applications not accepted. **Giving primarily in TX, with emphasis on the Greater Houston area.** No grants to individuals.
Application information: Contributes only to pre-selected organizations.
Board meeting date(s): Unscheduled
Officers and Board Members:* Richard D. Kinder,* Chair.; **Nancy G. Kinder, Pres. and Treas.; James V. Derrick, Jr., Secy.; Gary C. Dudley; David D. Kinder; Roxann S. Neumann; Kara K. Vidal.**
Advisory Board: Todd V. Adam; Ginger A. Corley; Polly K. Whittle.
Number of staff: None.
EIN: 760519073
Other changes: At the close of 2013, the fair market value of the grantmaker's assets was $138,622,283, a 69.4% increase over the 2012 value, $81,842,619.
Nancy G. Kinder is now Pres. and Treas. Katherine Kinder Howes is no longer V.P. and Secy.-Treas.

3275
Carl B. and Florence E. King Foundation
2301 Cedar Springs Rd., Ste. 330
Dallas, TX 75201-7886 (214) 750-1884
Contact: Michelle D. Monse, Pres.
FAX: (214) 750-1651;
E-mail: michellemonse@kingfoundation.com; Main URL: http://www.kingfoundation.com
Grants List: http://www.kingfoundation.com/Grants/Grants-By-Year.aspx

Incorporated in 1966 in TX.
Donors: Carl B. King†; Florence E. King†; Dorothy E. King†.
Foundation type: Independent foundation.
Financial data (yr. ended 12/31/13): Assets, $74,556,988 (M); expenditures, $3,470,958; qualifying distributions, $2,847,528; giving activities include $2,135,561 for 90 grants (high: $100,000; low: $5,000), and $40,951 for 1 foundation-administered program.
Purpose and activities: The foundation is committed to the highest standards of philanthropy and to honoring the intent of the founders, Carl B. and Florence E. King. The foundation's work is guided by the following principles: commitment to high ethical standards, adherence to strict financial guidelines, selection of appropriate and mission-focused grantees, evaluation and assessment of the grants, and clear and timely communications with all constituents. Grants are made in defined areas of Texas and Arkansas in the following areas: aging; arts, culture, and history; children and youth; education; the indigent; and nonprofit capacity, including nonprofit management.
Fields of interest: Arts education; Performing arts; Historical activities; Arts; Education, early childhood education; Child development, education; Adult education—literacy, basic skills & GED; Libraries (public); Education; Health care, clinics/centers; Health care, rural areas; AIDS; Alzheimer's disease; Crime/violence prevention, abuse prevention; Crime/violence prevention, domestic violence; Crime/violence prevention, child abuse; Employment, job counseling; Food banks; Food distribution, groceries on wheels; Food services, congregate meals; Agriculture/food; Housing/shelter; Youth development; Children/youth, services; Family services; Aging, centers/services; Human services; Rural development; Nonprofit management; Children/youth; Aging; Economically disadvantaged; Homeless.
Type of support: Management development/capacity building; Building/renovation; Equipment; Program development.
Limitations: Applications accepted. **Giving in 28 counties in eastern and southern Arkansas, 5 counties in the Dallas-Fort Worth area, and 38 counties in West Texas; please see foundation web site for a list of the specific counties. No support for religious organizations, or to non-exempt organizations. The foundation will, however, support social service programs conducted by faith-based organizations. No grants to individuals directly, or for construction of churches or seminaries, or for religious programs (except for social service programs available to the community at large) or for ongoing operating expenses or funds to offset operating losses. No grants for loan financing; endowments; professional conferences or symposia; or balls, events, or for galas benefiting charitable organizations.**
Publications: Financial statement; Grants list.
Application information: Effective in 2015, the foundation will change its North Texas grantmaking to focus on a small number of issues via an RFP process. Details of that change are still being decided, but should be announced by September 20, 2014, on the foundation's web site. Proposals will be invited only after a letter of inquiry has been submitted and approved. Application form required.
***Initial approach:* Letter of inquiry to be submitted online. The foundation no longer accepts applications in hard copy**
Deadline(s): Fall cycle: letter of inquiry due June 15; invited proposals due Aug. 31. Spring cycle: letter of inquiry due Dec. 15; invited proposals due Feb. 28. If the deadline falls on a weekend or holiday, the deadline rolls to the next business day.
Board meeting date(s): June and Dec.
Final notification: 6 weeks for letters of inquiry; 3-4 months for proposals.
Officers and Directors:* John Martin Davis, Chair.; Robert E. Weiss, Vice-Chair.; Michelle D. Monse, Pres.; Kimberly H. Evans,* V.P.; Robert I. Fernandez,* V.P.; Michael Phillips, V.P.; Patricia A. Porter, V.P.; Teresa D. Wilkinson,* V.P.; Ann C. Fielder, Secy.
Number of staff: 4 full-time professional.
EIN: 756052203

3276
Caesar Kleberg Foundation for Wildlife Conservation
P.O. Box 911
Kingsville, TX 78364-0911 (361) 592-8501
***Contact:* Stephen J. Kleberg, Tr.**
FAX: (210) 223-3657

Trust established about 1951 in TX.
Donor: Caesar Kleberg†.
Foundation type: Independent foundation.
Financial data (yr. ended 12/31/12): Assets, $53,268,834 (M); gifts received, $4,000; expenditures, $2,726,988; qualifying distributions, $2,244,849; giving activities include $2,113,000 for 3 grants (high: $2,098,000; low: $5,000).
Purpose and activities: Giving primarily for wildlife conservation and studies.
Fields of interest: Higher education; Animals/wildlife, research; Animals/wildlife, preservation/protection.
Limitations: Giving in the U.S., with emphasis on TX. No grants to individuals, or for building or endowment funds, scholarships, fellowships, or matching gifts; no loans.
Application information: Application form not required.
Initial approach: Letter on organization's letterhead
Copies of proposal: 3
Deadline(s): None
Board meeting date(s): As required
Final notification: 3 months
Trustees: Chris Kleberg; Stephen J. Kleberg; Dr. Duane M. Leach.
EIN: 746038766
Other changes: Leroy G. Denman is no longer a trustee.

3277
Kleinheinz Family Endowment for the Arts
209 W. 2nd St., No. 308
Fort Worth, TX 76102-3021 (682) 747-5656
***Contact:* James K. Phillips, C.F.O.**

Established in TX.
Donor: John B. Kleinheinz.
Foundation type: Independent foundation.
Financial data (yr. ended 12/31/12): Assets, $78,469,035 (M); gifts received, $10,945,085; expenditures, $2,100,170; qualifying distributions, $1,183,201; giving activities include $1,027,926 for 5 grants (high: $647,926; low: $30,000).
Fields of interest: Arts, cultural/ethnic awareness; Higher education, university; Education; Catholic agencies & churches.
Limitations: Applications accepted. Giving primarily in OR and TX. No grants to individuals.
Application information:
Initial approach: Proposal
Deadline(s): June 1 and Nov. 1
Officers and Directors:* Marsha Kleinheinz,* Pres.; Peter Philpott,* V.P.; James K. Phillips, C.F.O.; **Jay Herd; Peter Mesrobian.**
EIN: 261631057
Other changes: Andrew J. Rosell is no longer Secy.

3278
L. P. McCuistion Sanitarium Foundation
228 S.E. 6th St.
Paris, TX 75460-5908

Foundation type: Independent foundation.
Financial data (yr. ended 06/30/13): Assets, $107,188 (M); expenditures, $62,348; qualifying distributions, $50,000; giving activities include $50,000 for 1 grant.
Fields of interest: Foundations (private grantmaking).
Limitations: Applications not accepted. Giving primarily in Paris, TX.
Application information: Unsolicited requests for funds not accepted.
Trustees: Richard M. Amis; **Brad Hutchison**; Frank Ray.
EIN: 756015315

3279
Martha, David & Bagby Lennox Foundation
P.O. Box 188
Paris, TX **75461-0188**
Contact: William P. Streng, Pres.
***Application email:* submit@mdblf.org**; Main URL: http://www.mdblf.org

Established in 1985 in TX.
Donors: Martha Lennox†; David Lennox†; Bagby Lennox†.
Foundation type: Independent foundation.

Financial data (yr. ended 12/31/12): Assets, $15,612,997 (M); expenditures, $906,363; qualifying distributions, $608,018; giving activities include $530,661 for 27 grants (high: $113,500; low: $5,000).
Purpose and activities: Giving primarily for education, the environment, and children, youth and social services.
Fields of interest: Higher education; Education; Environment, natural resources; Human services; Children/youth, services.
Limitations: Applications accepted. Giving primarily in the northeast TX area. No grants to individuals.
Publications: Application guidelines.
Application information: See foundation web site for complete application guidelines. Application form required.
Initial approach: **Letter or e-mail**
Deadline(s): **Oct. 31**
Board meeting date(s): Varies
Officers and Directors:* William P. Streng,* Pres. and Treas.; Sam L. Hocker,* V.P. and Secy.; Mary W. Clark, V.P.
EIN: 760157945
Other changes: The grantmaker no longer lists a separate application address.
William P. Streng is now Pres. and Treas. Sam L. Hocker is now V.P. and Secy. Mary W. Clark is now V.P.

3280
The Levant Foundation
c/o JPMorgan Chase Twr.
600 Travis St., Ste. 6800
Houston, TX 77002-3010 **(713) 222-6900**
***FAX:* (713) 222-1614; Main URL: http://www.thelevantfoundation.org/**

Established in 1999 in TX.
Donors: Jamal Daniel; Rania Daniel.
Foundation type: Independent foundation.
Financial data (yr. ended 12/31/12): Assets, $36,495 (M); gifts received, $2,975,000; expenditures, $2,962,266; qualifying distributions, $2,771,075; giving activities include $2,771,075 for grants.
Fields of interest: Arts, cultural/ethnic awareness; Higher education, university; Education; Foundations (community).
Limitations: Applications not accepted. Giving primarily in Washington, DC and Houston, TX; some giving in Geneva, Switzerland. No grants to individuals.
Application information: Contributes only to pre-selected organizations.
Officers and Directors:* Pamela E. Powers,* Chair. and Pres.; Michelle Upton, V.P.; Bernice Holland, Secy.; Deb Loscuito, Treas.; Sonny Hudson, Exec. Dir.; Toufic Chahine; John M. Howland.
EIN: 311637973

3281
Jack H. & William M. Light Charitable Trust
P.O. Box 17001-Trust
San Antonio, TX 78217-0001
***Main URL:* http://broadwaybank.com/wealthmanagement/FoundationWilliamMLight.html**

Established in 1998 in TX.
Donors: Jack H. Light†; William M. Light†; William M. Light Community Property Trust.
Foundation type: Independent foundation.
Financial data (yr. ended 12/31/12): Assets, $9,730,605 (M); expenditures, $547,514; qualifying distributions, $499,296; giving activities include $460,000 for 42 grants (high: $35,000; low: $2,500).
Purpose and activities: Giving primarily for health and human services for the benefit of children.
Fields of interest: Human services.
Type of support: Continuing support; Annual campaigns; Capital campaigns; Building/renovation; Equipment; Endowments; Emergency funds; Program development; Curriculum development; Research.
Limitations: Applications accepted. Giving primarily in Houston and San Antonio, TX. No grants to individuals.
Application information: See foundation website for complete application guidelines. Application form required.
***Deadline(s):* Apr. 30 and Oct. 31**
***Final notification:* June and Dec.**
Trustee: Broadway National Bank, N.A.
EIN: 742874941
Other changes: The grantmaker now accepts applications.

3282
Larry Lightner Sams Foundation, Inc.
16800 Dallas Pkwy., Ste. 218
Dallas, TX 75248-6796 (972) 458-8811
Contact: Larry Lightner, Tr.

Established in 1994 in TX.
Foundation type: Independent foundation.
Financial data (yr. ended 12/31/12): Assets, $12,385,955 (M); expenditures, $796,840; qualifying distributions, $621,653; giving activities include $505,580 for 42 grants (high: $40,000; low: $500).
Fields of interest: Education; Health organizations, association; Medical research, institute; Human services; Children/youth, services; Community/economic development; Children/youth; Aging; Women.
Type of support: General/operating support; Annual campaigns; Capital campaigns; Building/renovation; Equipment; Debt reduction; Program development; Research; Matching/challenge support.
Limitations: Applications not accepted. Giving primarily in Dallas, TX. No support for political organizations. No grants to individuals, or for fundraisers.
Application information: Unsolicited requests for funds not accepted; applications are by trustee invitation only.
Board meeting date(s): Late Mar., late July, and late Nov.
Trustees: Charles Derek Adleta; Larry Lightner; Sue B. Lightner; Kamala Lightner Scammahorn.
Number of staff: 1 full-time professional; 1 part-time professional; 1 full-time support.
EIN: 752555622

3283
Helen Irwin Littauer Educational Trust
c/o Bank of America, N.A.
P.O. Box 831041
Dallas, TX 75283-1041
Contact: Mark J. Smith
E-mail: tx.philanthropic@ustrust.com; Main URL: http://www.bankofamerica.com/grantmaking

Established in 1969 in TX.
Foundation type: Independent foundation.
Financial data (yr. ended 04/30/13): Assets, $8,692,417 (M); expenditures, $688,688; qualifying distributions, $644,126; giving activities include $585,000 for 25 grants (high: $75,000; low: $5,000).
Purpose and activities: The trust is particularly interested in, but not limited to charitable organizations that focus on: scholarships that enable needy, but worthy boys and girls and young adults to attend school, college, or university, with a particular emphasis on making scholarships available for attending schools of journalism; promotion of art, education, and good citizenship; alleviating human suffering; medical care and treatment for all needy persons, including hospitals and clinics; providing care, education, recreation and/or physical training for needy, orphaned or disabled children; care of needy persons who are sick, aged or disabled; and improvement of living and working conditions of all persons.
Fields of interest: Performing arts; Performing arts, opera; Arts; Education; Health care; Housing/shelter; Youth development; Human services; Children/youth, services.
Type of support: General/operating support; Income development; Building/renovation; Program development; Matching/challenge support.
Limitations: Applications accepted. Giving primarily in Tarrant County, TX. No grants to individuals.
Application information: Application guidelines on Trust web site. Application form required.
Deadline(s): Mar. 31 and Sept. 30
Trustee: Bank of America, N.A.
EIN: 237029857
Other changes: The grantmaker no longer lists a phone.

3284
Lockheed Martin Vought Systems Employee Charity Fund
P.O. Box 650003, M/S: PT 42
Dallas, TX 75265-0003 (972) 603-0587
***Contact:* Hannah Stone, V.P. and Treas.**

Established in 1994 in TX.
Donors: Lockheed Martin Corp.; Lockheed Martin Vought Systems.
Foundation type: Company-sponsored foundation.
Financial data (yr. ended 12/31/12): Assets, $406,890 (M); gifts received, $527,469; expenditures, $388,576; qualifying distributions, $388,570; giving activities include $388,570 for 55 grants (high: $50,000; low: $500).
Purpose and activities: The fund supports hospitals and organizations involved with patient services, cancer, hunger, children and youth, human services, and military and veterans and awards emergency grants to employees of Lockheed Martin Missiles and Fire Control for accidents, illness, or other catastrophes.
Fields of interest: Health care; Agriculture/food; Human services.
Type of support: General/operating support; Continuing support; Annual campaigns; Emergency funds; Research; Grants to individuals.
Limitations: Applications accepted. Giving primarily in Camden, AR and Arlington, Dallas, Fort Worth, and Lufkin, TX.
Application information: Application form required.
***Initial approach:* Letter**
Copies of proposal: 1
Deadline(s): None

Officers and Directors:* James F. Berry,* Pres.; **Hannah Stone,* V.P. and Treas.**; Donald Remenapp,* Secy.; **Craig Vanbebber**.
EIN: 752528901
Other changes: Hannah Stone is now V.P. and Treas. Julia Novikoff is no longer a member of the governing body.

3285
The Long Foundation
(formerly The Joe and Teresa L. Long Foundation for the Arts)
40 N. I-H 35, Ste. 7C2
Austin, TX 78701-4359 (512) 479-4080
Contact: Mitchell Long, Secy.-Treas.
***FAX:* (512) 479-4182;**
E-mail: mitchell@longfoundation.org; Main URL: http://www.longfoundation.org/content/nav_lf.html
Grants List: http://www.longfoundation.org/content/history.html

Established in 1999 in TX.
Donor: Joe R. Long.
Foundation type: Independent foundation.
Financial data (yr. ended 12/31/12): Assets, $9,044,254 (M); expenditures, $551,231; qualifying distributions, $395,077; giving activities include $333,000 for 19 grants (high: $100,000; low: $5,000).
Purpose and activities: Giving primarily for education and youth services, particularly Texas Hispanic youth.
Fields of interest: Higher education; Education, drop-out prevention; Education, reading; Education; Health care, clinics/centers; Children, services; Community/economic development; Hispanics/Latinos.
Type of support: General/operating support; Program development; Scholarship funds; Matching/challenge support.
Limitations: Applications accepted. Giving primarily in TX. No support for religious programs or environmental organizations. No grants to individuals.
Application information: Application form required.
Initial approach: See website
Deadline(s): See website
Officers: Joe R. Long, Pres.; Teresa L. Long, V.P.; Mitchell Long, Secy.-Treas. and Exec. Dir.
Director: Ruby Long.
EIN: 742916682

3286
Harry Wilson Loose Trust
c/o Bank of America, N.A.
P.O. Box 831041
Dallas, TX 75283-1041
***Application address:* c/o Greater Kansas City Community Foundation, Attn.: Harry Wilson Loose Trust, 1055 Broadway, Ste. 130, Kansas City, MO 64105, tel.: (816) 842-0944**

Trust established in 1927 in MO.
Donor: Harry Wilson Loose†.
Foundation type: Independent foundation.
Financial data (yr. ended 12/31/12): Assets, $5,115,036 (M); expenditures, $243,612; qualifying distributions, $194,160; giving activities include $150,000 for 1 grant.
Fields of interest: Arts; Health care; Health organizations, association; Human services; Community/economic development; Foundations (community); Government/public administration.
Limitations: Applications accepted. Giving limited to Kansas City, MO.
Application information: Visit www.gkccf.org for complete application guidelines. Application form required.
Trustee: Bank of America, N.A.
Number of staff: 43
EIN: 446009245

3287
Lubbock Area Foundation, Inc.
2509 80th St.
Lubbock, TX 79423 (806) 762-8061
***Contact:* For grants: Michelle Tosi-Stephens, Dir., Grants and Scholarships**
FAX: (806) 762-8551;
E-mail: contact@lubbockareafoundation.org; **Grant inquiry e-mail: michelle@lubbockareafoundation.org**; Main URL: http://www.lubbockareafoundation.org
Facebook: http://www.facebook.com/pages/Lubbock-Area-Foundation/171261678910
Google Plus: https://plus.google.com/+LubbockAreaFoundationOrg/about?hl=en
Pinterest: http://www.pinterest.com/LubbockAreaFdn/
Twitter: https://twitter.com/LubbockAreaFdn
YouTube: https://www.youtube.com/channel/UCwjoh29CMtmkUvfoWhZPSzA/feed

Incorporated in 1980 in TX.
Foundation type: Community foundation.
Financial data (yr. ended 12/31/12): Assets, $28,748,043 (M); gifts received, $2,526,048; expenditures, $1,239,684; giving activities include $582,028 for 38+ grants (high: $70,000), and $109,613 for 64 grants to individuals.
Purpose and activities: The foundation is a permanent charitable institution dedicated to the South Plains community. Giving primarily for education, arts, environment, health, civic affairs, and social services.
Fields of interest: Historic preservation/historical societies; Arts; Adult education—literacy, basic skills & GED; Education, reading; Education; Environment; Animal welfare; Health care; Health organizations, association; Children/youth, services; Family services; Human services; Community/economic development.
Type of support: General/operating support; Continuing support; Capital campaigns; Building/renovation; Equipment; Emergency funds; Program development; Seed money; Scholarship funds; Matching/challenge support.
Limitations: Applications accepted. Giving limited to Lubbock, TX, and the surrounding South Plains counties. No grants to individuals (except for scholarships), or for debt retirement; no loans.
Publications: Application guidelines; Annual report; Financial statement; Grants list; Informational brochure; Newsletter.
Application information: Visit foundation web site for application form and guidelines. Application form required.
Initial approach: Submit application form
Copies of proposal: 12
Deadline(s): Feb. 1, May 1, Sept. 1 and Nov. 1 for Community Fund grants
Board meeting date(s): Jan., Mar., May, July, Sept., and Nov.
Final notification: 2 months
Officers and Directors:* Jim Phillips,* Chair.; Jeff Klotzman,* Chair.-Elect.; Sheryl Cates,* Pres.; Martha Ann McDonald,* V.P., Donor Rels.; Sherry Boyles, V.P., External Affairs and Devel.; John Tye,* Secy.-Treas.; Bronson Blodgett; **Rodney Cates**; Linda Gaither; Chad Grant; Nita Kiesling; Robert Kollman; Jerry Kolander; Bill Lowell; Eric McDonald; Elaine McNair; Mark Meurer; Carlos Morales; Mack Owen; Norval Pollard; Don Rushing; Ted Rushing; Tim Sampson; Ray Thornton; Laura Vinson; Cindy Whitehead; Diann Windham.
Number of staff: 2 full-time professional; 2 part-time professional.
EIN: 751709180
Other changes: Sheryl Cates has replaced Nita Kiesling as Pres.
Martha Ann McDonald is now V.P., Donor Rels.
Suzie Baker and Lisa Flathers are no longer directors.

3288
T. C. Lupton Family Foundation
3811 Turtle Creek Blvd., No. 480
Dallas, TX 75219-4474

Established in 1994 in TX.
Donors: T.C. Lupton, Jr.; Carolyn C. Lupton.
Foundation type: Independent foundation.
Financial data (yr. ended 06/30/13): Assets, $4,654,131 (M); expenditures, $239,547; qualifying distributions, $220,895; giving activities include $220,895 for 44 grants (high: $30,702; low: $500).
Purpose and activities: Giving primarily for youth services and education.
Fields of interest: Libraries (special); Education; Youth development, adult & child programs; Children/youth, services; Human services; Religion.
Limitations: Applications not accepted. Giving primarily in Dallas, TX. No grants to individuals.
Application information: Contributes only to pre-selected organizations.
Officers: T.C. Lupton, Jr., Chair.; Carol L. Huckin, Pres.; Carolyn C. Lupton, Secy.; Tavenner C. Lupton III, Treas.
Director: Laurie L. Liedtke.
EIN: 752549244
Other changes: The grantmaker no longer lists a phone.

3289
W. P. & Bulah Luse Foundation
c/o U.S. Trust, Philanthropic Solutions
901 Main St., 19th Fl., TX1-492-19-11
Dallas, TX 75202-3714
Contact: David T. Ross, Sr. V.P.
E-mail: tx.philanthropic@ustrust.com; **Main URL: https://www.bankofamerica.com/philanthropic/grantmaking.go**

Established in 1947 in TX.
Donors: Bulah Luse†; W.P. Luse†.
Foundation type: Independent foundation.
Financial data (yr. ended 12/31/12): Assets, $9,407,819 (M); expenditures, $461,136; qualifying distributions, $327,546; giving activities include $267,000 for 51 grants (high: $10,000; low: $5,000).
Purpose and activities: Giving to support and promote quality education, human services, and health care programming for underserved populations.
Fields of interest: Medical school/education; Education; Health organizations, association; Human services.
Type of support: General/operating support; Continuing support; Annual campaigns; Capital campaigns; Building/renovation; Equipment; Scholarship funds.

Limitations: Applications accepted. Giving limited to Dallas County, TX. No support for political or religious organizations. No grants to individuals.
Publications: Application guidelines.
Application information: Complete application guidelines are available on foundation web site.
Initial approach: Online through foundation web site
Deadline(s): June 30 and Dec. 31
Trustees: James P. Bevans; Karen Shuford; Kelly Watson; Bank of America, N.A.
EIN: 756007639

3290
Douglas B. Marshall, Jr. Family Foundation
600 Jefferson St., Ste. 310
Houston, TX 77002-7324 (713) 651-8806
Contact: Robert Carter, Secy.
FAX: (713) 651-2387;
E-mail: rcarter@legacytrust.com; Main URL: http://www.dbmjr.org

Established in 2001 in TX.
Donors: Douglas B. Marshall, Jr.†; Douglas B. Marshall III.
Foundation type: Independent foundation.
Financial data (yr. ended 12/31/12): Assets, $29,836,157 (M); expenditures, $1,654,558; qualifying distributions, $1,366,873; giving activities include $1,342,464 for 19 grants (high: $400,000; low: $2,000).
Purpose and activities: The mission of the foundation is to support education and research on all levels. This includes supporting cutting edge research at universities, laboratories, and other such institutions. It also includes the support of basic education, especially in areas of literacy, numeracy, and science. Since education and research are impossible without food, shelter, clothing, or medicine, it is within the bounds of the foundation's mission to provide these when necessary.
Fields of interest: Education; Human services; Poverty studies.
Type of support: General/operating support; Continuing support; Income development; Annual campaigns; Capital campaigns; Building/renovation; Equipment; Emergency funds; Program development; Seed money; Curriculum development; Scholarship funds; Research; In-kind gifts; Matching/challenge support.
Limitations: Applications not accepted. Giving on a national basis. No grants to individuals.
Application information: Grant applications are by invitation only.
Board meeting date(s): As necessary
Officers and Directors:* Douglas B. Marshall III,* Pres.; Robert T. Arnold,* V.P.; Robert Carter, Secy.; Carla Chaney, Treas.; J.K. Jones; Wilhelmina B. Traylor.
EIN: 760664812

3291
The Guadalupe and Lilia Martinez Foundation
361 Pine Valley Dr.
Fairview, TX 75069-1915 (972) 549-1605
Contact: Shirley S. Gonzalez, Pres.
E-mail: glmfoundation@grandecom.net; Main URL: http://www.glmfoundation.org

Established in 2001 in TX.
Donors: Guadalupe Martinez†; Lilia Martinez†; Guadalupe Martinez 2001 Trust.
Foundation type: Independent foundation.
Financial data (yr. ended 12/31/12): Assets, $40,060,461 (M); gifts received, $5,009; expenditures, $2,448,359; qualifying distributions, $1,902,830; giving activities include $1,902,830 for 36 grants (high: $260,000; low: $1,000).
Purpose and activities: Giving primarily for charitable and religious organizations and for scientific testing for public safety, literacy, health, and education primarily for the benefit of the people of Webb and Zapata counties in Texas.
Fields of interest: Elementary/secondary education; Higher education; Human services; Christian agencies & churches.
Type of support: General/operating support; Continuing support; Annual campaigns; Capital campaigns; Building/renovation; Equipment; Program development; Scholarship funds.
Limitations: Applications accepted. Giving primarily in Webb and Zapata counties in TX. No grants to individuals.
Application information: Application form not required.
***Initial approach:* Letter of request (1 or 2 pages, via U.S. mail or e-mail)**
Copies of proposal: 1
Deadline(s): None
Board meeting date(s): 3-4 times annually, as determined by board
Final notification: After the next board meeting
Officers and Directors:* Shirley Gonzalez,* Pres.; Robert J. Gonzalez, Jr., V.P.; Larry Sandlin,* V.P.; Maria Louisa Sandlin,* V.P.; Ana A. Wasielewski,* Secy.; Robert Gonzalez,* Treas.
EIN: 743005930

3292
Oliver Dewey Mayor Foundation
P.O. Box 1088
Sherman, TX 75091-1088
Contact: Regina D. Pruitt, Asst. V.P.
FAX: (903) 813-5121;
E-mail: rpruitt@bankoftexas.com

Established in 1983 in TX.
Donor: Oliver Dewey Mayor†.
Foundation type: Independent foundation.
Financial data (yr. ended 06/30/13): Assets, $14,856,306 (M); expenditures, $1,545,113; qualifying distributions, $900,632; giving activities include $793,695 for 25 grants (high: $337,750; low: $364).
Purpose and activities: Support for education, community development, and youth and social services.
Fields of interest: Education; Human services; Youth, services; Community/economic development.
Type of support: General/operating support; Building/renovation; Research; Matching/challenge support.
Limitations: Applications accepted. Giving limited to Mayes County, OK and Grayson County, TX. No grants to individuals.
Publications: Application guidelines.
Application information: Application form required.
Initial approach: Proposal
Copies of proposal: 9
Deadline(s): Mar. 15, June 15, Sept. 15 and Dec. 15
Board meeting date(s): Mar. 15, Jun. 15, Sept. 15, and Dec. 15
Board of Governors: Tracey L. Dean; Samuel W. Graber; Nash Lamb; Dr. James E. Pledger; Marion Stinson; **Gail Utter**; Vickie White.
Trustee: Bank of Texas, N.A.
EIN: 751864630
Other changes: Regina D. Pruitt is no longer a member of the Board of Governors.

3293
The Eugene McDermott Foundation
3808 Euclid Ave.
Dallas, TX 75205-3102 (214) 521-2924
Contact: Mary McDermott Cook, Pres.

Incorporated in 1972 in TX; absorbed The McDermott Foundation in 1977.
Donors: Eugene McDermott†; Mrs. Eugene McDermott.
Foundation type: Independent foundation.
Financial data (yr. ended 08/31/13): Assets, $91,279,437 (M); expenditures, $6,353,496; qualifying distributions, $6,090,917; giving activities include $6,000,500 for 65 grants (high: $1,000,000; low: $1,500).
Purpose and activities: Support primarily for cultural programs, higher and secondary education, health, and general community interests.
Fields of interest: Museums; Historic preservation/historical societies; Arts; Education, early childhood education; Elementary school/education; Secondary school/education; Higher education; Education; Hospitals (general); Health care; Health organizations, association; Medical research, institute; Children/youth, services; International human rights; Community/economic development; United Ways and Federated Giving Programs; Government/public administration; Children/youth; Children; Youth; Adults; Aging; Young adults; Disabilities, people with; Physically disabled; Blind/visually impaired; Deaf/hearing impaired; Mentally disabled; Minorities; African Americans/Blacks; Hispanics/Latinos; Native Americans/American Indians; Indigenous peoples; Women; Girls; Young adults, female; Men; Boys; Young adults, male; Substance abusers; AIDS, people with; Single parents; Crime/abuse victims; Terminal illness, people with; Economically disadvantaged; Homeless.
Type of support: General/operating support; Continuing support; Annual campaigns; Capital campaigns; Building/renovation; Equipment; Land acquisition; Endowments; Program development; Professorships; Seed money; Curriculum development; Scholarship funds; Research; Matching/challenge support.
Limitations: Applications accepted. Giving primarily in Dallas, TX. No grants to individuals.
Application information: No printed material available. Application form not required.
Initial approach: Letter
Copies of proposal: 1
Deadline(s): None
Board meeting date(s): Quarterly
Final notification: Prior to Aug. 31
Officers and Trustees:* Mary McDermott Cook,* Pres.; J.H. Cullum Clark; Mrs. Eugene McDermott.
Agent: Bank of America, N.A.
Number of staff: 2 part-time professional.
EIN: 237237919
Other changes: Patricia Brown is no longer Secy. Liza Lee and Sam Self are no longer trustees.

3294
Shirley & William S. McIntyre Foundation
c/o William S. McIntyre, V.P.
12222 Merit Dr., Ste. 1450
Dallas, TX 75251-3212

Established in 2000 in TX.
Donors: Shirley C. McIntyre; William S. McIntyre; International Risk Management; McIntyre Financial Svcs.; American Contractors Insurance Group.
Foundation type: Independent foundation.
Financial data (yr. ended 06/30/13): Assets, $2,293,223 (M); gifts received, $1,381,397; expenditures, $670,348; qualifying distributions, $591,354; giving activities include $585,292 for 46 grants (high: $200,000; low: $50).
Fields of interest: Performing arts; Arts; Hospitals (general); Human services.
Limitations: Applications not accepted. Giving primarily in Dallas, TX. No grants to individuals.
Application information: Contributes only to pre-selected organizations.
Officers: Shirley C. McIntyre, Pres.; William S. McIntyre, V.P.
EIN: 752910339

3295
Robert E. and Evelyn McKee Foundation
5835 Cromo Dr., Ste. 1
El Paso, TX 79912-5501 (915) 581-4025
Contact: Louis B. McKee, Pres.
FAX: (915) 833-3714;
E-mail: mckeefoundation@att.net; Application address: P.O. Box 220599, El Paso, TX 79913-2599; Main URL: http://www.mckeefoundation.org
Grants List: http://www.mckeefoundation.org/Donation%20List%202014.pdf

Incorporated in 1952 in TX.
Donors: Robert E. McKee†; Evelyn McKee†; Robert E. McKee, Inc.; The Zia Co.
Foundation type: Independent foundation.
Financial data (yr. ended 12/31/12): Assets, $7,429,493 (M); gifts received, $500; expenditures, $490,989; qualifying distributions, $354,622; giving activities include $328,161 for 52 grants (high: $60,000; low: $250).
Purpose and activities: Emphasis on local hospitals, community funds, and rehabilitation and the handicapped; grants also for religious organizations, higher and other education, youth agencies, child welfare, and medical research.
Fields of interest: Higher education; Education; Hospitals (general); Medical care, rehabilitation; Medical research, institute; Children/youth, services; United Ways and Federated Giving Programs; Christian agencies & churches; Disabilities, people with.
Type of support: General/operating support; Continuing support; Annual campaigns; Capital campaigns; Building/renovation; Equipment; Emergency funds; Program development; Conferences/seminars; Seed money; Scholarship funds; Research; In-kind gifts.
Limitations: Applications accepted. Giving primarily in TX, with emphasis on El Paso. No support for organizations limited by race or ethnic origin, other private foundations (except for a local community foundation), religious organizations (except local Episcopal churches), or attempts to influence legislation. No grants or loans to individuals, or for endowment funds or deficit financing.
Publications: Application guidelines; Annual report (including application guidelines); Program policy statement.
Application information: Application guidelines available on foundation web site. Application form not required.
Initial approach: Proposal
Copies of proposal: 1
Deadline(s): Dec. 15
Board meeting date(s): June
Final notification: After Feb. 15
Officers and Trustees:* Louis B. McKee,* Pres. and Treas.; Helen Lund Yancey,* V.P. and Secy.; Margaret McKee Lund, Sr. V.P.; Charlotte McKee Cohen,* V.P.; Sharon Hays Herrera,* V.P.; F. James McKee, V.P.; James T. McKee,* V.P.; Philip Russell McKee,* V.P.; Susan J. McKee, V.P.; Linda Hays Gunter; C. Steven McKee; R. Brian McKee; Robert E. McKee IV; H.A. Woods.
Number of staff: 1 part-time professional; 1 part-time support.
EIN: 746036675

3296
The Meadows Foundation, Inc.
Wilson Historic District
3003 Swiss Ave.
Dallas, TX 75204-6049 (214) 826-9431
Contact: Bruce H. Esterline, V.P., Grants
FAX: (214) 827-7042;
E-mail: webgrants3003@mfi.org; Additional tel.: (800) 826-9431; Main URL: http://www.mfi.org
Customer Feedback Study: http://www.mfi.org/display.asp?link=ETMA0D
Grants Database: http://www.mfi.org/display.asp?link=GSRCH1

Incorporated in 1948 in TX.
Donors: Algur Hurtle Meadows†; Virginia Meadows†.
Foundation type: Independent foundation.
Financial data (yr. ended 12/31/12): Assets, $706,427,734 (M); expenditures, $40,132,177; qualifying distributions, $30,528,487; giving activities include $19,866,071 for 622 grants (high: $3,000,000; low: $2,500), $276,762 for 203 employee matching gifts, $621 for in-kind gifts, $695,362 for 2 foundation-administered programs and $884,096 for 3 loans/program-related investments (high: $250,000; low: $50,000).
Purpose and activities: The foundation strives to exemplify the principles of its founder in addressing basic human needs by working toward the elimination of ignorance, hopelessness and suffering, protecting the environment, providing cultural enrichment, encouraging excellence and promoting understanding and cooperation among people. It exists to assist people and institutions of Texas improve the quality and circumstances of life for themselves and future generations.
Fields of interest: Media/communications; Visual arts, architecture; Museums; Humanities; History/archaeology; Historic preservation/historical societies; Arts; Education, public education; Education, early childhood education; Child development, education; Medical school/education; Adult/continuing education; Adult education—literacy, basic skills & GED; Libraries/library science; Education, reading; Education; Environment, natural resources; Environment; Animals/wildlife, preservation/protection; Dental care; Medical care, rehabilitation; Nursing care; Health care; Substance abuse, services; Mental health/crisis services; AIDS; Alcoholism; AIDS research; Crime/violence prevention, abuse prevention; Crime/violence prevention, domestic violence; Crime/violence prevention, child abuse; Crime/law enforcement; Employment; Agriculture; Nutrition; Housing/shelter, development; Housing/shelter, homeless; Safety/disasters; Recreation; Youth development, services; Human services; Children/youth, services; Child development, services; Family services; Residential/custodial care, hospices; Aging, centers/services; Homeless, human services; Civil rights, race/intergroup relations; Urban/community development; Rural development; Community/economic development; Voluntarism promotion; Government/public administration; Transportation; Leadership development; Public affairs; Aging; Economically disadvantaged; Homeless.
Type of support: General/operating support; Continuing support; Income development; Management development/capacity building; Capital campaigns; Building/renovation; Equipment; Land acquisition; Debt reduction; Emergency funds; Program development; Film/video/radio; Publication; Seed money; Curriculum development; Research; Technical assistance; Consulting services; Program evaluation; Program-related investments/loans; Employee matching gifts; Matching/challenge support.
Limitations: Applications accepted. Giving limited to TX. No grants to individuals; generally, no grants for annual campaigns, fundraising events, professional conferences and symposia, travel expenses for groups to perform or compete outside of TX, construction of churches and seminaries, scholarships, or support of single artistic events or performances.
Publications: Application guidelines; Annual report (including application guidelines); Financial statement.
Application information: An online grant application form is available on the foundation's web site. Please do not attempt to attach files to online applications. Please mail attachments and grant correspondence to the foundation main address. Applications are acknowledged within a week, but are usually processed within three to four months. Grants staff is available by phone or email to respond to inquiries at any time and may schedule pre-grant interviews with applicants as time permits. After receiving an application, a face-to-face meeting may be scheduled as needed. Applicants seeking funding for construction and renovations should review the foundation's Green Building Guidelines, and for projects incorporating human-animal connection they should see the foundation's Animal Welfare Plan. Application form not required.
Initial approach: Proposal
Copies of proposal: 1
Deadline(s): None
Board meeting date(s): Grants review committee meets monthly; full board meets 2 or 3 times a year
Final notification: 3 to 4 months
Officers and Directors:* Robert A. Meadows,* Chair. and V.P.; Linda P. Evans,* C.E.O. and Pres.; Paula Herring, V.P. and Treas.; **Tom Gale, V.P. and C.I.O.**; Bruce H. Esterline, V.P., Grants; John W. Broadfoot, Dir. Emeritus; Judy Broadfoot Culbertson, Dir. Emeritus; Sally R. Lancaster, Dir. Emeritus; Curtis W. Meadows, Jr., Dir. Emeritus; Sally Cheney Miller, Dir. Emeritus; Eloise Meadows Rouse, Dir. Emeritus; Dorothy Cheney Wilson, Dir. Emeritus; Holli Leigh Broadfoot; John Broadfoot, Jr.; Daniel H. Chapman; Linda P. Evans; John A. Hammack; Virginia Hanson; P. Mike McCullough; Karen L. Meadows; Julie Lancaster Morris; William A. Nesbitt; Jason Ritzen; Dudley L. Rouse, Jr.; Elizabeth Meadows Rouse; Amy Whiting.
Number of staff: 25 full-time professional; 1 part-time professional; 18 full-time support; 2 part-time support.
EIN: 756015322
Other changes: Tom Gale has replaced Gregory C. Dowell as V.P. and C.I.O.
Robert E. Weiss is no longer V.P., Admin. Chere St. Clair is no longer Corp. Secy. Olin Lancaster, Margaret Macdonald, Peter Miller, Kimberly C.

Morris and Jean B. Silvertooth are no longer directors and/or trustess.

3297
The Cynthia & George Mitchell Foundation
P.O. Box 8937
The Woodlands, TX 77387-8937 (713) 377-5060
Contact: Katherine Lorenz, Pres.; Marilu Hastings, Dir., Sustainability Prog.
***Main URL:* http://www.cgmf.org/p/home.html**
Cynthia and George Mitchell Foundation Blog: http://www.cgmf.org/blog/rss.php
Facebook: https://www.facebook.com/MitchellFoundation
George Mitchell's Giving Pledge Profile: http://glasspockets.org/philanthropy-in-focus/eye-on-the-giving-pledge/profiles/mitchell
Google Plus: https://www.plus.google.com/111250604816631864539/posts
Twitter: https://twitter.com/MitchFound
YouTube: https://www.youtube.com/user/CGMFoundation

Established in 1981 in TX.
Donors: Cynthia W. Mitchell†; George P. Mitchell†.
Foundation type: Independent foundation.
Financial data (yr. ended 12/31/12): Assets, $133,156,145 (M); gifts received, $24,700,630; expenditures, $14,855,243; qualifying distributions, $15,092,777; giving activities include $12,871,500 for 128 grants (high: $2,500,000; low: $500).
Purpose and activities: The foundation is a mission-driven grantmaking foundation that seeks innovative, sustainable solutions for human and environmental problems. The foundation works as an engine of change in both policy and practice in Texas, supporting high-impact projects at the nexus of environmental protection, social equity, and economic vibrancy.
Fields of interest: Science; Science.
Limitations: Giving limited to TX. No support for political candidates or support to influence legislation, or for research, development, commercialization or demonstration of technology, and no support for demonstration projects or local community projects. No grants for for-profit organizations and generally no support for general operating support.
Application information: The foundation does not review unsolicited proposals. If you are confident that your project fits within the priorities of a particular foundation program, you may complete the online Letter of Inquiry form available on foundation website without discussing your project with foundation staff.
Initial approach: Online letter of inquiry
Officers and Directors:* **Katherine Lorenz,* Pres. and Treas.**; Carleton Grant Mitchell,* V.P. and Secy.; Meredith Mitchell Dreiss,* Pres. Emeritus; Meredith Heimburger; Pamela Mitchell Maguire; Brian Gregory Mitchell; George Scott Mitchell; John Kirk Mitchell; Mark Douglas Mitchell; Michael Kent Mitchell; Sarah Scott Mitchell.
EIN: 742170127
Other changes: Katherine Lorenz has replaced Meredith Mitchell Dreiss as Pres. and Treas. Adrienne Dreiss Ropp is no longer a dir. George P. Mitchell, Chair. and Donor, is deceased. Carleton Grant Mitchell is now V.P. and Secy. Jeffrey Todd Mitchell is no longer a director.

3298
The Moody Foundation
2302 Post Office St., Ste. 704
Galveston, TX 77550-1936 (409) 797-1500
***Contact:* Allan Matthews, Grants Dir.**
FAX: (409) 763-5564; E-mail: info@themoodyf.org; **Additional tel. (for Dallas office): (866) 742-1133. E-mail for Allan Matthews: Amatthews@moodyf.org**; Main URL: http://www.moodyf.org
For scholarships: **Samantha Seale, Scholarship Admin., tel.: (409) 797-1511, e-mail: Samanthas@moodyf.org**

Trust established in 1942 in TX.
Donors: William Lewis Moody, Jr.†; Libbie Shearn Moody†.
Foundation type: Independent foundation.
Financial data (yr. ended 12/31/12): Assets, $1,241,224,220 (M); gifts received, $24,222,000; expenditures, $56,639,329; qualifying distributions, $53,348,689; giving activities include $49,635,746 for 62 grants (high: $12,000,000; low: $5,000), and $371,325 for grants to individuals.
Purpose and activities: Funds to be used for historic restoration projects, performing arts organizations, and cultural programs; promotion of health, science, and education; community and social services; and the field of religion.
Fields of interest: Performing arts; Arts; Medical school/education; Education; Environment; Health care; AIDS; Medical research, institute; AIDS research; Youth development; Human services; Community/economic development; Engineering/technology; Science; Religion; Aging; Disabilities, people with; Economically disadvantaged.
Type of support: Capital campaigns; Building/renovation; Equipment; Land acquisition; Program development; Conferences/seminars; Publication; Seed money; Scholarship funds; Research; Technical assistance; Matching/challenge support.
Limitations: Applications accepted. Giving limited to TX, with a primary emphasis on foundation-initiated projects in Galveston. No grants to individuals (except for students covered by scholarship programs in Galveston and Dallas Counties), or for operating budgets (except for start-up purposes), continuing support, annual campaigns, or deficit financing; no loans or program-related investments.
Publications: Application guidelines; Annual report; Grants list.
Application information: Foundation will send application guidelines if project is of interest. For scholarship application form and submission deadlines contact Samantha Seale, Scholarship Admin. Application form required.
Initial approach: Letter of inquiry or through web site on an ongoing basis
Copies of proposal: 1
Deadline(s): 6 weeks prior to board meetings
Board meeting date(s): Quarterly
Final notification: 3 weeks after board meetings
Officers and Trustees:* Robert L. Moody, Sr.,* Chair.; Garrick Addison, C.F.O.; Frances A. Moody-Dahlberg,* Exec. Dir.; Ross R. Moody.
Number of staff: 10 full-time professional; 4 full-time support.
EIN: 741403105

3299
Allen Lovelace Moore and Blanche Davis Moore Foundation
(doing business as The Blanche Davis Moore Foundation)
700 Everhart Rd., Ste. J-21
Corpus Christi, TX 78411-1941 (361) 814-6700
***Contact:* Gary J. Leach**
FAX: (361) 814-6701; Main URL: http://www.moorefoundationcc.com

Established in 1993 in TX.
Donor: Blanche Davis Moore†.
Foundation type: Independent foundation.
Financial data (yr. ended 12/31/12): Assets, $13,198,480 (M); expenditures, $1,193,429; qualifying distributions, $677,627; giving activities include $677,627 for 53 grants (high: $150,000; low: $127).
Purpose and activities: Support primarily for projects benefiting children and youth under 18 years of age, in Neuces County, TX, and the immediately surrounding counties.
Fields of interest: Higher education; Athletics/sports, training; Human services; Salvation Army; YM/YWCAs & YM/YWHAs; Children/youth, services; Christian agencies & churches; Infants/toddlers; Children/youth; Children; Youth; Young adults; Disabilities, people with; Physically disabled; Blind/visually impaired; Deaf/hearing impaired; Mentally disabled; Minorities; African Americans/Blacks; Hispanics/Latinos; Infants/toddlers, female; Girls; Young adults, female; Infants/toddlers, male; Boys; Young adults, male; Substance abusers; Crime/abuse victims; Immigrants/refugees; Economically disadvantaged; Homeless.
Type of support: General/operating support; Continuing support; Annual campaigns; Equipment; Emergency funds; Program development; Conferences/seminars; Film/video/radio; Publication; Scholarship funds; Research; Technical assistance.
Limitations: Applications accepted. Giving primarily in the Corpus Christi, TX area. No grants to individuals.
Publications: Application guidelines; Grants list.
Application information: Application form and complete application guidelines available on foundation web site. Application form required.
Initial approach: Fax or mail application
Deadline(s): July 1
Board meeting date(s): Oct.
Officer and Directors:* Rev. J. Homer Davis,* Chair.; Gary J. Leach,* Pres.; Paul Davis,* Treas.; **Robyn Abernathy**; Ira Gillum; **Brandon Leach.**
Number of staff: 1 full-time professional; 1 full-time support.
EIN: 742675281

3300
Wayne & Jo Ann Moore Charitable Foundation
403 N. Marienfeld St.
Midland, TX 79701-7323

Established in 2006 in TX.
Donor: Lee Wayne Moore†.
Foundation type: Independent foundation.
Financial data (yr. ended 12/31/12): Assets, $36,998,743 (M); gifts received, $728,000; expenditures, $2,903,970; qualifying distributions, $1,985,419; giving activities include $1,910,633 for 84 grants (high: $135,000; low: $5,000).
Fields of interest: Human services.

Limitations: Applications not accepted. Giving primarily in TX, with emphasis on Midland. No grants to individuals.
Application information: Contributes only to pre-selected organizations.
Officer: Tom Moore, Pres. and Exec. Dir.
Directors: Emily Gilmer; Stuart Gilmer; Dauphen Jackson; Ann Jensen; James Moore.
EIN: 204808454
Other changes: At the close of 2012, the grantmaker paid grants of $1,910,633, a 97.4% increase over the 2011 disbursements, $968,000.

3301
Morgan Foundation
11 Greenway Plz., Ste. 2000
Houston, TX 77046

Established in 2002 in TX.
Donor: Portcullis Partners, L.P.
Foundation type: Company-sponsored foundation.
Financial data (yr. ended 12/31/12): Assets, $20,093,555 (M); expenditures, $1,748,421; qualifying distributions, $1,600,000; giving activities include $1,600,000 for 2 grants (high: $1,400,000; low: $200,000).
Purpose and activities: The foundation supports community foundations and organizations involved with folk arts, secondary and higher education.
Fields of interest: Arts, folk arts; Secondary school/education; Higher education; Foundations (community).
Type of support: Scholarship funds; General/operating support; Program development.
Limitations: Applications not accepted. Giving limited to CA and Houston, TX. No grants to individuals.
Application information: Contributes only to pre-selected organizations.
Officers and Directors:* William V. Morgan,* Pres. and Treas.; Sara S. Morgan,* V.P. and Secy.; Catherine A. Morgan; Christine R. Morgan; Michael C. Morgan.
Number of staff: None.
EIN: 223886549
Other changes: The grantmaker no longer lists a primary contact.

3302
The Mundy Family Foundation
11150 S. Wilcrest Dr., Ste. 300
Houston, TX 77099-4343 **(281) 530-8711**
***Contact:* John Mundy**

Established in 1996 in TX.
Donors: Joe S. Mundy; John T. Mundy; David Mundy; Shane Burden.
Foundation type: Independent foundation.
Financial data (yr. ended 12/31/12): Assets, $6,542,451 (M); expenditures, $160,827; qualifying distributions, $110,000; giving activities include $110,000 for 2 grants (high: $100,000; low: $10,000).
Purpose and activities: Giving primarily to a Church of Christ church and to a residential facility for disabled adults.
Fields of interest: Arts; Education; Human services; Residential/custodial care; Developmentally disabled, centers & services; Protestant agencies & churches.
Limitations: Applications accepted. Giving primarily in TX. No grants to individuals.
Application information:
Initial approach: Letter
Deadline(s): None
Trustees: John T. Mundy; Marion E. Mundy; Sue E. Mundy.
EIN: 760520888

3303
Music Doing Good, Inc.
(formerly Divas World Productions, Inc.)
4203 Yoakum Boulevard, Ste. 200
Houston, TX 77006-5455 (713) 900-3468
FAX: (713) 524-2898; Main URL: http://www.musicdoinggood.org/
Facebook: https://www.facebook.com/MusicDoingGood
Philanthropy's Promise: http://www.pinterest.com/musicdoinggood/
RSS Feed: http://www.musicdoinggood.org/rss.html?p=news
Twitter: https://twitter.com/musicdoinggood
YouTube: http://www.youtube.com/user/MusicDoingGood

Donors: Marie Bosarge; The Leopard Delaware Trust.
Foundation type: Independent foundation.
Financial data (yr. ended 08/31/12): Assets, $11,626,104 (M); gifts received, $1,003,703; expenditures, $1,226,110; qualifying distributions, $1,143,157; giving activities include $168,810 for 5+ grants (high: $150,000), and $1,143,157 for 2 foundation-administered programs.
Purpose and activities: The foundation's purpose is to inspire and transform lives through innovative, music-based and educational community outreach programs and concert events and also awarding scholarships in music development.
Fields of interest: Performing arts; Arts; Education.
Limitations: Applications accepted. Giving primarily in Houston, TX.
Application information: See foundation web site for application form and guidelines. Application form required.
Initial approach: Letter
Deadline(s): Varies
Officers and Directors:* Marie Bosarge, Pres.; Alexis Breeding, Secy.; Darla Tollefson, Treas.; Wilbur Edwin Bosarge, Jr.; David Eagleman; Anita Kruse; Daniel Karp; Delfeayo Marsalis.
EIN: 262377013

3304
Harvey E. Najim Family Foundation
613 N.W. Loop 410, Ste. 875
San Antonio, TX 78216-5507 (210) 369-0666
Contact: Melissa Bauman, Exec. Dir.
FAX: (210) 918-1860;
E-mail: melissa.bauman@najimfoundation.org;
E-mail for Stephanie Sanders, Grants Admin.: stephanie.sanders@najimfoundation.org, tel.: (210) 255-8435, ext. 18002; Main URL: http://www.najimfoundation.org/
Facebook: http://www.facebook.com/pages/San-Antonio-TX/The-Harvey-E-Najim-Family-Foundation/83493988379

Established in 2006 in TX.
Donor: Harvey E. Najim.
Foundation type: Independent foundation.
Financial data (yr. ended 12/31/12): Assets, $71,843,534 (M); gifts received, $16,000; expenditures, $4,766,339; qualifying distributions, $4,448,271; giving activities include $4,448,271 for grants.
Purpose and activities: The foundation's mission is to help 501(c)(3) public charities in the greater San Antonio, Texas, area to advance children's education, children's medical treatment, medical research for illnesses and diseases affecting children, and other children's charitable purposes.
Fields of interest: Education; Health care; Medical research; Crime/violence prevention, child abuse; Youth development, services; Children/youth, services; Children; Disabilities, people with.
Limitations: Applications accepted. Giving primarily in the greater San Antonio, TX area. No support for organizations lacking 501(c)(3) status. No grants to individuals, or for multi-year projects.
Application information: Once the Letter of Inquiry and IRS determination letter have been completed and uploaded to the foundation web site, applicants must e-mail Stephanie Sanders, Grants Admin., stating that these materials have been uploaded. See foundation web site for full guidelines and requirements. A letter of inquiry (no more than 3 pages), must be submitted to the foundation for consideration to be invited for a full application. Articles, reports, videos, or other material are to be submitted upon the request of the foundation if needed.
Initial approach: Online Letter of Inquiry format on foundation web site
Copies of proposal: 9
Deadline(s): See funding schedule on foundation web site for current deadlines
Board meeting date(s): Apr., July, and Oct.
Final notification: Within 60 days following deadline dates
Directors: Don Harris; Jim House; Carrie N. Matthiesen; Nancy May; Harvey E. Najim; Christine N. Ray; Roy Terracina.
EIN: 208060391

3305
Navarro County Educational Foundation
401 N. 14th St.
Corsicana, TX 75110-4509
Application address: c/o Navarro College, 3200 W. 7th Ave., Corsicana, TX 75110, tel.: (903) 874-6501

Established in 1988 in TX.
Foundation type: Independent foundation.
Financial data (yr. ended 12/31/13): Assets, $4,527,176 (M); expenditures, $216,661; qualifying distributions, $183,010; giving activities include $174,823 for 1 grant.
Purpose and activities: Support only for Navarro College, TX, through a scholarship fund.
Fields of interest: Higher education.
Type of support: Scholarship funds.
Limitations: Applications accepted. Giving primarily in TX.
Application information: Application form required.
***Initial approach:* Completed application form**
***Deadline(s):* See application form for current deadline**
Officers: C. David Campbell, M.D., Pres.; Barbara Moe, Secy.-Treas.
Directors: Don Denbow; Mike Gage; Mickey Hillock; Larry Morrison.
EIN: 752227788
Other changes: Oliver Albritton is no longer V.P.

3306

Mary Moody Northen Endowment

2618 Broadway
Galveston, TX 77550-4427 (409) 765-9770
Contact: Betty Massey, Exec. Dir.
FAX: (409) 762-7055;
E-mail: b.massey@northenendowment.org; Main URL: http://www.northenendowment.org

Established in 1964.
Donor: Mary Moody Northen†.
Foundation type: Independent foundation.
Financial data (yr. ended 12/31/12): Assets, $64,110,632 (M); gifts received, $400,000; expenditures, $3,616,215; qualifying distributions, $1,739,773; giving activities include $501,800 for 8 grants (high: $405,000; low: $1,800), and $945,899 for foundation-administered programs.
Purpose and activities: Support for educational institutions, community development and civic affairs, and wildlife and the environment. The foundation has completed restoration of the W.L. Moody residence and currently operates it as a house museum. The foundation also conducts research of the history of 20th century Texas, and gives to an organization that provides affordable space for artists and art organizations.
Fields of interest: Museums; History/archaeology; Historic preservation/historical societies; Arts, artist's services; Arts; Education, research; Education; Environment, natural resources; Environment; Animals/wildlife, preservation/protection; Community/economic development.
Type of support: General/operating support; Continuing support; Capital campaigns; Building/renovation; Program development; Curriculum development; Consulting services.
Limitations: Applications accepted. Giving limited to TX and VA.
Publications: Grants list.
Application information: The foundation is currently not considering grants. See web site for updates in this matter.
Board meeting date(s): Monthly
Officers and Directors:* Edward L. Protz,* Pres.; G. William Rider,* V.P. and Treas.; Robert L. Moody,* Secy.; Betty Massey, Exec. Dir.
Number of staff: 1 full-time professional; 2 full-time support.
EIN: 751171741

3307

NuStar Foundation

19003 IH-10 W.
San Antonio, TX 78257-9518 **(210) 918-2000**
Contact: Cynthia Pena
Application address: c/o Cynthia Pena, P.O. Box 781609, San Antonio, TX 78269, tel.: (210) 918-2000

Donor: NuStar Logistics, L.P.
Foundation type: Company-sponsored foundation.
Financial data (yr. ended 12/31/12): Assets, $1,435,877 (M); gifts received, $5,025,440; expenditures, $3,622,891; qualifying distributions, $3,174,988; giving activities include $3,174,988 for 557 grants (high: $450,000; low: $48).
Purpose and activities: The foundation supports organizations involved with arts and culture, education, medical research, golf, youth development, human services, and community development.
Fields of interest: Arts education; Arts; Higher education; Education; Heart & circulatory diseases; Medical research; Athletics/sports, golf; Youth development; Homeless, human services; Human services; Community/economic development; United Ways and Federated Giving Programs.
Type of support: Employee matching gifts; General/operating support.
Limitations: Applications accepted. Giving in the U.S., primarily in TX; with some emphasis on San Antonio.
Application information: Application form required.
Initial approach: Proposal
Deadline(s): None
Directors: Curtis V. Anastasio; Mary Rose Brown; William E. Greehey.
EIN: 260629473

3308

Oldham Little Church Foundation

24 Greenway Plz., Ste. 1202
Houston, TX 77046-2445 (713) 275-1050
Contact: Paul Sanders
FAX: (713) 275-1051; E-mail: info@oldhamlcf.org; Main URL: http://www.oldhamlcf.org/

Trust established in 1949 in TX.
Donor: Morris Calvin Oldham†.
Foundation type: Independent foundation.
Financial data (yr. ended 12/31/12): Assets, $27,214,075 (M); expenditures, $1,331,421; qualifying distributions, $1,042,149; giving activities include $660,328 for 98 grants (high: $13,000; low: $800).
Purpose and activities: Giving limited to small Protestant churches and organizations with emphasis on Baptist churches.
Fields of interest: Protestant agencies & churches.
Type of support: Building/renovation; Equipment; Program development.
Limitations: Applications accepted. Giving primarily in the U.S., with some emphasis on TX; very limited funding internationally. No grants to individuals, or for operating budgets, endowments, or deficit financing; no loans.
Publications: Application guidelines.
Application information: Applications sent by U.S. mail, fax or e-mail are not accepted. Application form required.
Initial approach: Use online application process on foundation web site
Copies of proposal: 1
Deadline(s): See foundation web site for current deadlines
Officers and Directors:* Stewart Morris, Jr.,* Chair.; Paul Sanders,* C.E.O. and Pres.; **Rev. Garry Blackmon,* V.P.**; Louis E. "Ed" Finlay,* V.P.; Ralph Hull,* V.P.; Kay Parker,* V.P.; David Stutts,* V.P.; David Taylor,* V.P.; Stewart Morris, Sr.,* Secy.
Number of staff: 1 part-time professional; 1 full-time support; 1 part-time support.
EIN: 760465633

3309

Waldon H. and Adele Orr Charitable Trust

c/o Wells Fargo Bank, N.A.
P.O. Box 41629
Austin, TX 78704-9926 (979) 776-3237
***E-mail:* grantadministration@wellsfargo.com; Main URL: https://www.wellsfargo.com/privatefoundationgrants/orr**

Established in 2003 in TX.
Donors: Adele S. Orr†; Waldon H. Orr†.
Foundation type: Independent foundation.
Financial data (yr. ended 12/31/12): Assets, $4,815,827 (M); expenditures, $257,947; qualifying distributions, $213,446; giving activities include $199,500 for 18 grants (high: $35,000; low: $1,500).
Fields of interest: Museums (ethnic/folk arts); Youth development; Human services; United Ways and Federated Giving Programs; Protestant agencies & churches.
Limitations: Applications accepted. Giving primarily in TX. No grants to individuals.
Application information: See foundation website for complete application guidelines. Application form required.
Initial approach: Letter
***Deadline(s):* July 31**
Trustee: Wells Fargo Trust Dept.
EIN: 746523535

3310

Genevieve and Ward Orsinger Foundation

(formerly Genevieve McDavitt Orsinger Foundation)
P.O. Box 90987
San Antonio, TX 78209-9094
Contact: Linda McDavitt, C.E.O. and Pres.
E-mail: lmcd@orsingerfoundation.org; Tel./fax: (210) 590-0535; mobile phone: (210) 378-6614; Main URL: http://www.orsingerfoundation.org

Established in 1997 in TX.
Donor: Genevieve McDavitt Orsinger†.
Foundation type: Independent foundation.
Financial data (yr. ended 12/31/13): Assets, $11,237,576 (M); expenditures, $812,879; qualifying distributions, $745,400; giving activities include $657,238 for 71 grants (high: $100,000; low: $250).
Purpose and activities: Giving in Bexar County includes: 1) programs related to early childhood that emphasize health and wellness, the fine arts, outdoor activities and/or literacy; 2) community service learning projects planned and operated by youth; 3) programs for adults that support self-sufficiency and/or enhance their capacity to care for their families; and 4) programs for elderly persons that use the fine arts to enhance quality of life and/or support health and wellness. Giving in the Central Texas counties of Comal, Guadalupe, Hays, Kendall and Travis consists of programs delivered to children ages 0 to 5 years old that utilize fine arts in curriculum.
Fields of interest: Arts; Education; Human services; Infants/toddlers; Children/youth; Children; Youth; Adults; Aging; Young adults; Disabilities, people with; Physically disabled; Mentally disabled; Minorities; Indigenous peoples; Women; Infants/toddlers, female; Girls; Adults, women; Men; Boys; Adults, men; Military/veterans; Offenders/ex-offenders; Substance abusers; Single parents; Terminal illness, people with; Economically disadvantaged; Homeless.
Type of support: General/operating support; Continuing support; Management development/capacity building; Equipment; Program development; Curriculum development; Technical assistance; Program evaluation; Program-related investments/loans; Matching/challenge support.
Limitations: Applications accepted. **Giving primarily in Bexar County, TX; outside Bexar County, the foundation will only consider requests for programs in Comal, Guadalupe, Hays, Kendall and/or Travis Counties delivered to children aged 0 to 5 years old that utilize fine arts in the curriculum.** No support for political organizations. **No grants to individuals; no grants for start up funds or seed money, capital campaigns, endowments, fundraising events or sponsorships, long term commitments, salaries, reduction of debts or scholarships.**

Publications: Application guidelines; Grants list; IRS Form 990 or 990-PF printed copy available upon request.
Application information: Must submit letter of inquiry first and then be asked to submit a full application. Letter of inquiry and application available on foundation web site. Strong preference will be given to existing programs/projects or general operating support that have funding from other sources, rather than new programs or the expansion of existing programs. Application form required.
Initial approach: Electronic letter of inquiry from foundation web site
Copies of proposal: 1
***Deadline(s):* See foundation web site for current deadline**
Board meeting date(s): Mid-Mar.
Final notification: Letter of inquiry response by Dec. 1 to ask for full application. Grants reviewed results by Apr. 1
Officers and Directors:* Linda McDavitt, C.E.O. and Pres.; Clarence Bray, Secy.-Treas.; Nancy May; Patricia Meyer; Megan Kromer.
Number of staff: 1 part-time professional.
EIN: 742832873

3311
The P Twenty-One Foundation
c/o Joseph W. Ryan
P.O. Box 27883
Houston, TX 77227-7883 (832) 228-8974

Established in 2000 in TX.
Donors: Joseph W. Ryan; Yolanda V. Ryan.
Foundation type: Independent foundation.
Financial data (yr. ended 11/30/13): Assets, $3,247,437 (M); expenditures, $155,629; qualifying distributions, $148,000; giving activities include $148,000 for 15 grants (high: $25,000; low: $2,000).
Purpose and activities: Giving primarily for public health and ecological activities.
Fields of interest: Performing arts, orchestras; Elementary/secondary education; Environment; Animals/wildlife; Public health; Health care; Mental health, clinics; Catholic agencies & churches.
Type of support: General/operating support; Capital campaigns.
Limitations: Applications accepted. Giving primarily in CA, GA, NY and TX.
Application information: Application form required.
Initial approach: Letter
Deadline(s): None
Officers and Directors:* Joseph W. Ryan,* Pres. and Treas.; Yolanda V. Ryan,* V.P. and Secy.; Noralisa Villarreal, M.D.
EIN: 760628482

3312
Paso del Norte Health Foundation
221 N. Kansas St., Ste. 1900
El Paso, TX 79901-1428 (915) 544-7636
Contact: Myrna Deckert, C.E.O. and Pres.
FAX: (915) 544-7713; E-mail: health@pdnhf.org; Additional E-mail: mdeckert@pdnhf.org; Main URL: http://www.pdnhf.org
Blog: http://www.pdnhf.org/Blog.asp
Facebook: https://www.facebook.com/PdNHFoundation
Grants Database: http://www.pdnhf.org/searchgrantdb.asp
RSS Feed: http://www.pdnhf.org/index.php?option=com_content&view=category&id=60&Itemid=83&lang=us
Twitter: https://twitter.com/PdNHFoundation
YouTube: https://www.youtube.com/user/PDNHFoundation?feature=CEgQwRs%3D

Established in 1995 in TX; converted from sale of the assets of Providence Memorial Hospital.
Foundation type: Independent foundation.
Financial data (yr. ended 12/31/12): Assets, $204,802,919 (M); gifts received, $1,460; expenditures, $6,928,522; qualifying distributions, $5,527,498; giving activities include $3,373,607 for 66 grants (high: $331,709; low: $1,500), and $254,223 for 1 foundation-administered program.
Purpose and activities: The foundation's mission is to promote health and prevent disease in the region through leadership in health education, research, and advocacy.
Fields of interest: Education, public education; Health care, support services; Health care; Mental health/crisis services; Nutrition; Youth development; Human services; Children/youth; Children; Youth; Hispanics/Latinos.
International interests: Mexico.
Type of support: Technical assistance; Program evaluation; Program development.
Limitations: Applications not accepted. **Giving limited to Dona Ana, Luna, and Otero Counties in Southern NM, Hudspeth and El Paso Counties in West TX, and Ciudad Juarez, Chihuahua, Mexico.** No support for political organizations. No grants to individuals, or for building/renovation, capital campaigns, or research.
Publications: Annual report.
Application information: Unsolicited applications not accepted. However, when launching a new request for proposals, a grant workshop will be hosted by the foundation for nonprofit organizations so that they may better understand the purpose of the initiative and how to respond to the Request For Proposal (RFP).
Board meeting date(s): Jan., Mar., May, July, Sept., and Nov.
Officers and Directors:* Robert Ash,* Chair.; Carolyn Mora,* Vice-Chair.; Myrna Deckert, C.E.O. and Pres.; Marcela Garcia, C.F.O.; John Law, C.O.O.; Alan Abbott; Sandra Sanchez Almanzan; Sharon Butterworth; Allan Goldfarb; Christopher Lopez; Michael Miles; Jose Prieto, M.D.; **Hector Retta; Judy Robinson**; Benjamin Torres-Barron.
Number of staff: 11 full-time professional; 3 full-time support.
EIN: 741143071
Other changes: Robert Ash has replaced Allan Goldfarb as Chair.
Carolyn Mora is now Vice-Chair. Tilahun Adera and Eduardo Sanchez are no longer directors.

3313
Peine Charitable Foundation for Manhattan Fund
c/o Bank of America, N.A.
P.O. Box 831041
Dallas, TX 75283-1041
***Application address:* c/o Bank of America, N.A., Attn.: Trust Off., Ref.: Manhattan Community Fdn., P.O. Box 1127, Manhattan, KS 66505, tel.: (785) 587-8995; Main URL: http://peinefoundation.org/**

Established in 2005 in TX.
Donor: Caroline F. Peine‡.
Foundation type: Independent foundation.
Financial data (yr. ended 08/31/13): Assets, $8,258,384 (M); expenditures, $490,197; qualifying distributions, $449,185; giving activities include $407,612 for 18 grants (high: $125,000; low: $1,000).
Purpose and activities: Giving to organizations that improve the quality of life in the city of Manhattan, Kansas, including, but not limited to, parks and recreation, arts and theater, historical preservation, and human services.
Fields of interest: Arts; Education; Health care; Recreation; Boys & girls clubs; Community/economic development; Foundations (community).
Type of support: General/operating support.
Limitations: Applications accepted. Giving limited to Manhattan, KS. No support for industrial development, organized athletics, or church or religious purposes. No grants to individuals.
Application information: Application form required.
***Initial approach:* See web site**
***Deadline(s):* See web site**
Final notification: Accepted applicants only by May 26
Distribution Committee: Diana Chapel; Geri Simon; Bruce C. Snead; Stan Ward.
Trustee: Bank of America, N.A.
EIN: 597250365

3314
Penland Foundation
6550 Tram Rd.
Beaumont, TX 77713-8703 (409) 722-4594
Contact: Joe Penland Sr., Pres.

Established in 2007 in TX.
Donors: Joe Penland, Sr.; Tram Road Partners, LP.
Foundation type: Independent foundation.
Financial data (yr. ended 09/30/13): Assets, $2,842,264 (M); gifts received, $385,200; expenditures, $311,878; qualifying distributions, $303,912; giving activities include $303,912 for 8 grants (high: $100,000; low: $6,912).
Fields of interest: Education; Health care; Cancer; Human services; Children/youth, services; Christian agencies & churches.
Limitations: Applications accepted. Giving primarily in TX.
Application information: Application form not required.
***Initial approach:* Proposal**
Deadline(s): None
Officers: Joe Penland, Sr., Pres.; Linda Penland, V.P.
Director: Joe C. Vernon.
EIN: 205692339
Other changes: Banker Phares is no longer a member of the governing body.

3315
J. C. Penney Company Fund, Inc.
6501 Legacy Dr., MS 1205
Plano, TX 75024-3612 (972) 431-1431
Contact: Jodi Gibson, Pres. and Exec. Dir.
FAX: (972) 431-1355; **Main URL: http://www.jcpenney.com/jsp/browse/marketing/promotion.jsp?&pageId=pg40037900007**

Established in 1984 in NY.
Donors: J.C. Penney Co., Inc.; J.C. Penney Corp., Inc.
Foundation type: Company-sponsored foundation.
Financial data (yr. ended 02/02/13): Assets, $10,355,909 (M); gifts received, $3,505,362; expenditures, $4,847,149; qualifying distributions, $4,847,149; giving activities include $4,846,275 for grants.

Purpose and activities: The fund supports organizations involved with arts and culture, education, health and welfare, cancer, disaster relief, youth development, human services, the retail industry, and civic betterment.
Fields of interest: Arts; Elementary/secondary education; Higher education; Scholarships/financial aid; Education; Health care; Cancer; Disasters, preparedness/services; Youth development, business; Youth development; American Red Cross; Developmentally disabled, centers & services; Human services; Business/industry; United Ways and Federated Giving Programs; Public affairs.
Type of support: General/operating support; Annual campaigns; Equipment; Program development; Scholarship funds; Employee volunteer services; Sponsorships; Grants to individuals.
Limitations: Applications accepted. Giving on a national basis in areas of company operations. No support for individual K-12 schools lacking a community partnership with J.C. Penney, PTO's or PTA's, higher education institutions lacking a business or recruiting relationship with J.C. Penney, or membership, religious, political, labor, or fraternal organizations. No grants to individuals (except for disaster relief grants), or for door prizes, gift certificates, or other giveaways, fundraising or special events, proms or graduations, scholarships for colleges lacking a recruiting relationship with J.C. Penney, conferences or seminars, capital campaigns, multi-year or long-term support, or film or video projects or research projects; no merchandise donations; no employee matching gifts.
Publications: Application guidelines; Corporate giving report.
Application information: Additional information may be requested at a later date. Telephone calls are not encouraged. Application form not required.
Initial approach: Letter of inquiry
Copies of proposal: 1
Deadline(s): None
Final notification: 6 to 8 weeks
Officers and Directors: Jodie Gibson, Pres. and Exec. Dir.; Darcie Brossart, V.P.; Brandy Treadway, Secy.; Windon Chau, Treas.; Susan Fournier, Cont.; Michael Dastugue; Janet Dhillon; Kenneth Hannah; Michael Kramer; Daniel Walker.
EIN: 133274961
Other changes: Charlotte Thacker is no longer Secy. Roger Peterson is no longer Co.-Cont. Robert B. Cavanaugh, Thomas M. Nelson, Michael W. Texter, and Michael T. Theilmann are no longer directors.
The grantmaker has changed its fiscal year-end from Jan. 28 to Feb. 2.

3316
Permian Basin Area Foundation

200 N. Loraine St., Ste. 500
Midland, TX 79701-4711 (432) 617-3213
Contact: Guy McCrary, C.E.O.
FAX: (432) 617-0151; E-mail: gmccrary@pbaf.org; Main URL: http://www.pbaf.org

Incorporated in 1989 in TX.
Foundation type: Community foundation.
Financial data (yr. ended 12/31/12): Assets, $91,907,173 (M); gifts received, $13,460,945; expenditures, $9,006,646; giving activities include $7,093,640 for 96+ grants (high: $1,580,000), and $277,530 for 266 grants to individuals.
Purpose and activities: The foundation seeks to provide a vehicle through which donors may make gifts for charitable, religious, scientific, and educational uses. The ultimate goals are to improve the quality of life of the communities' residents, promote equality of opportunity, and assist those in need or at risk in the Permian Basin.
Fields of interest: Humanities; Arts; Education; Health care; Housing/shelter; Human services; Community/economic development; Public affairs; Aging.
Type of support: Emergency funds; Program development; Seed money; Scholarship funds; Matching/challenge support.
Limitations: Applications accepted. Giving primarily in the Permian Basin area of western TX, with consideration to southeastern NM. No grants to individuals (except for scholarships), or for ongoing operating expenses, basic research, endowment funds, deficit financing, or fundraising campaigns; generally no multi-year grants.
Publications: Application guidelines; Annual report; Newsletter.
Application information: Visit foundation web site for application form and guidelines. Based on Pre-Application Summary form, applicants will be notified that they are encouraged to submit a full application or that their project is unlikely to be funded. Application form required.
Initial approach: Submit Pre-Application Summary form
Copies of proposal: 1
Deadline(s): Apr. 1 and Oct. 1 for pre-application summary
Board meeting date(s): Feb., Apr., June, Aug., Oct., and Dec.
Final notification: Approx. 30 days from pre-application submission for full application request; July and Dec. for grant determination
Officers and Governors:* Mike Canon,* Chair.; Trey Grafa,* Vice-Chair.; Guy McCrary,* C.E.O. and Pres.; Mark Nicholas,* Secy.; Stacey Gerig,* Treas.; Kathy Clark; **Cathy Eastham**; **Larry Edgerton**; **Cal Hendrick**; Patty Herd; Scott Kidwell; Jerry Morales; Carolyn Stone.
Number of staff: 6 full-time professional; 3 full-time support.
EIN: 752295008
Other changes: Stacey Gerig, Trey Grafa, and Larry Edgerton are no longer governors.

3317
The Perot Foundation

P.O. Box 269014
Plano, TX 75026-9014 (972) 535-1900
Contact: Carolyn P. Rathjen, V.P.

Established in 1969 in TX.
Donor: H. Ross Perot.
Foundation type: Independent foundation.
Financial data (yr. ended 12/31/12): Assets, $75,553,806 (M); gifts received, $20,182,921; expenditures, $13,354,276; qualifying distributions, $13,256,753; giving activities include $12,925,084 for 204 grants (high: $2,000,000; low: $100).
Purpose and activities: Support primarily for higher education, a Salvation Army training school, and a Presbyterian church.
Fields of interest: Higher education; Human services; Religious federated giving programs; Protestant agencies & churches.
Type of support: Grants to individuals.
Limitations: Applications accepted. Giving primarily in TX.
Application information:
***Initial approach:* Letter**
Officers and Directors:* H. Ross Perot,* Pres.; Carolyn P. Rathjen,* V.P. and Exec. Dir.; J. Thomas Walter,* Secy.; J.Y. Robb III, Treas.; Katherine P. Reeves; Suzanne P. McGee; Nancy P. Mulford; Bette Perot; H. Ross Perot, Jr.; Margot B. Perot.
EIN: 756093258
Other changes: The grantmaker now accepts applications.

3318
Hal & Charlie Peterson Foundation

P.O. Box 293870
Kerrville, TX 78029-3871
Contact: Brian Oehler, Gen. Mgr.
FAX: (830) 896-2283;
E-mail: info@hcpetersonfoundation.org; **Additional address: 515 Jefferson St., Kerrville, TX 78028**;
Main URL: http://www.hcpetersonfoundation.org/

Established in 1944 in TX.
Donors: Hal Peterson†; Charlie Peterson†.
Foundation type: Independent foundation.
Financial data (yr. ended 12/31/12): Assets, $52,906,400 (M); gifts received, $9,195; expenditures, $1,630,383; qualifying distributions, $1,443,405; giving activities include $1,196,870 for 50 grants (high: $100,000; low: $425).
Purpose and activities: Giving primarily for education and health care.
Fields of interest: Elementary school/education; Secondary school/education; Higher education; Health care.
Type of support: General/operating support; Building/renovation; Equipment; Seed money; Matching/challenge support.
Limitations: Applications accepted. Giving limited to Kerr, Bandera, Edwards, Gillespie, Kendall, Kimble and Real counties, TX, and to state or national organizations with a local chapter in this area. No support for religious purposes. No grants to individuals, or for operating budgets, debt retirement, media productions, lobbying, publications, or endowments; no loans.
Publications: Application guidelines; Informational brochure (including application guidelines); Program policy statement.
Application information: Application form required.
Initial approach: Letter or telephone requesting application form
Copies of proposal: 1
Deadline(s): See foundation web site for current deadlines
Board meeting date(s): Monthly
Officers and Directors:* Scott Parker,* Pres.; W.H. Cowden, Jr.,* V.P.; John Mosty,* Secy.-Treas.; Lynn Lemeilleur; Nowlin McBryde; Kyle Priour; James Stehling.
Number of staff: 1 full-time professional; 1 full-time support.
EIN: 741109626

3319
The Philecology Foundation

201 Main St., Ste. 2300
Fort Worth, TX 76102-3137

Established in 2007 in TX.
Donors: Edward P. Bass; Fine Line, LP.
Foundation type: Independent foundation.
Financial data (yr. ended 06/30/13): Assets, $41,505,701 (M); gifts received, $149,236; expenditures, $294,902; qualifying distributions, $275,000; giving activities include $275,000 for 3 grants (high: $200,000; low: $25,000).
Fields of interest: Environment.
Limitations: Applications not accepted. Giving in the U.S., with emphasis on Washington, DC.

Application information: Contributes only to pre-selected organizations.
Officers and Directors:* Edward P. Bass,* Pres.; Thomas W. White,* V.P. and Treas.; Gary Reese, V.P.; Dee Steer,* Secy.
EIN: 208987808
Other changes: The grantmaker no longer lists a phone.

3320
The PHM Foundation
4817 N FM 1417
Sherman, TX 75092-6605
Main URL: http://phmfoundation.org/

Established in 2006 in TX.
Donors: Care Now; Dura Medical Inc.; Primary Health Management, Ltd.; Primary Health, Inc.
Foundation type: Operating foundation.
Financial data (yr. ended 12/31/12): Assets, $7,202,529 (M); gifts received, $8,100,000; expenditures, $6,166,778; qualifying distributions, $6,166,091; giving activities include $6,151,549 for 14 grants (high: $2,145,000; low: $20,000).
Purpose and activities: The foundation supports religious ministries and organizations involved with print publishing, reproductive health, and youth. The foundation also operates an economic development program to promote entrepreneurship and development in developing countries.
Fields of interest: Media, print publishing; Reproductive health; Youth, services; International economic development; Social entrepreneurship; Christian agencies & churches; Jewish agencies & synagogues; Religion, interfaith issues; Religion.
International interests: Developing Countries.
Type of support: General/operating support; Program-related investments/loans.
Limitations: Applications not accepted. Giving primarily in CA, Washington, DC, FL, MO, NM, NV, and TX; giving also to developing countries through program-related investments. No grants to individuals.
Application information: Unsolicited applications are not accepted. The foundation utilizes an invitation only process for giving.
Officers and Directors:* David Walter,* Pres.; Jennifer L. Walter,* Secy.; Daniel E. Walter,* Exec. Dir.
EIN: 204948182

3321
The T. Boone Pickens Foundation
8117 Preston Rd., Ste. 260 W.
Dallas, TX 75225-6321
Main URL: http://www.tboonepickensfoundation.org
T. Boone Pickens's Giving Pledge Profile: http://glasspockets.org/philanthropy-in-focus/eye-on-the-giving-pledge/profiles/pickens

Established in 2006 in TX.
Donors: T. Boone Pickens; Dick Grant.
Foundation type: Independent foundation.
Financial data (yr. ended 12/31/12): Assets, $328,709 (M); gifts received, $1,453,650; expenditures, $1,137,153; qualifying distributions, $1,134,903; giving activities include $1,125,000 for 6 grants (high: $600,000; low: $10,000).
Purpose and activities: The foundation improves lives through grants supporting education, medical research/development and services, athletics and corporate wellness, at-risk youths, the entrepreneurial process, conservation and wildlife programs and a wide range of public policy initiatives.
Fields of interest: Environment, natural resources; Health care; Medical research; Human services.
Limitations: Applications not accepted. **Giving primarily in OK and TX.**
Application information: Contributes only to pre-selected organizations.
Officers: T. Boone Pickens, Chair.; Ronald D. Bassett, Pres.; Robert L. Stillwell, V.P. and Secy.-Treas.; Andrew Littlefair, V.P.; **Marti Carlin, Mgr., Community Rels.**
EIN: 205892962

3322
Gilbert & Thyra Plass Charitable Trust
c/o Wells Fargo Bank, N.A.
P.O. Drawer 913
Bryan, TX 77805-0913 (979) 776-3267
***E-mail:* grantadministration@wellsfargo.com; Main URL: https://www.wellsfargo.com/privatefoundationgrants/plass**

Established in 2005 in TX.
Donor: Thyra Plass†.
Foundation type: Independent foundation.
Financial data (yr. ended 12/31/12): Assets, $2,323,231 (M); expenditures, $167,766; qualifying distributions, $145,221; giving activities include $135,000 for 14 grants (high: $30,000; low: $1,000).
Fields of interest: Performing arts, orchestras; Higher education, college; Health care; Housing/shelter; Christian agencies & churches.
Limitations: Applications accepted. Giving limited to the Brazos County, TX, area. No grants to individuals.
Application information: See foundation website for complete application guidelines. Application form required.
Deadline(s): July 31
Trustee: Wells Fargo Bank, N.A.
EIN: 203705169

3323
Potts and Sibley Foundation
P.O. Box 8907
Midland, TX 79708-8907 (432) 686-7051
Main URL: http://www.amcguire.com/

Established in 1967 in TX.
Donor: Effie Potts Sibley Irrevocable Trust.
Foundation type: Independent foundation.
Financial data (yr. ended 07/31/13): Assets, $7,728,688 (M); expenditures, $457,461; qualifying distributions, $334,671; giving activities include $321,000 for 6 grants (high: $100,000; low: $9,000).
Fields of interest: Museums; Performing arts, orchestras; Higher education; Environment, natural resources; Hospitals (general); Mental health, association; Medical research, institute; Human services; Salvation Army; Pregnancy centers; Residential/custodial care, hospices; Protestant agencies & churches.
Limitations: Applications accepted. Giving primarily in TX. No support for private foundations. No grants to individuals.
Application information: Application form and guidelines available at http://www.amcguire.com, under the Foundations link. Application form required.
***Initial approach:* Request application form**
Deadline(s): None
Board meeting date(s): Jan. and July
Officers and Trustee:* Hiram Sibley, Chair.; Robert W. Bechtel,* Mgr.; Allen G. McGuire.
Director: Tom Scott.
EIN: 756081070
Other changes: The grantmaker no longer lists a primary contact.

3324
The Powell Foundation
2121 San Felipe, Ste. 110
Houston, TX 77019-5600 (713) 523-7557
Contact: Caroline J. Sabin, Exec. Dir.
FAX: (713) 523-7553;
E-mail: info@powellfoundation.org; Main URL: http://www.powellfoundation.org

Established in 1967 in TX.
Donors: Ben H. Powell, Jr.†; Kitty King Powell.
Foundation type: Independent foundation.
Financial data (yr. ended 12/31/12): Assets, $25,363,545 (M); gifts received, $600,000; expenditures, $1,248,991; qualifying distributions, $1,099,530; giving activities include $962,685 for 133 grants (high: $25,000; low: $200).
Purpose and activities: The foundation distributes funds for public charitable purposes, principally for the support, encouragement, and assistance to education, health, conservation, and the arts with a direct impact within the foundation's geographic zone of interest: Harris, Travis, and Walker counties in TX.
Fields of interest: Arts; Education, public education; Education, early childhood education; Environment; Health care; Human services; Children/youth; Children; Youth; Minorities; Economically disadvantaged.
Type of support: General/operating support; Management development/capacity building; Program development; Curriculum development; Scholarship funds; Matching/challenge support.
Limitations: Applications accepted. Giving primarily in Harris, Travis and Walker counties, TX. No support for private foundations, or religious organizations for religious purposes. No grants to individuals or for testimonial dinners, building funds, fundraising events, advertising, or for debt retirement or operating deficits.
Publications: Application guidelines; Annual report (including application guidelines); Grants list.
Application information: See foundation web site for complete application policies and guidelines. Application form required.
Initial approach: Proposal
Copies of proposal: 1
Deadline(s): None
Board meeting date(s): Spring and fall
Officers and Directors:* Nancy Powell Moore,* Pres. and Treas.; Albert S. Tabor,* V.P. and Secy.; Ben H. Powell V,* V.P.; Caroline J. Sabin, Exec. Dir.; Kitty King Powell, Founding Dir.; **Charles F. Caldwell**; **Marian M. Casey**; Marian P. Harrison; Katherine P. Hill; **Ben H. Powell VI**; **Jan L. Redford**; Katherine Osborn Valdez.
Number of staff: 1 full-time professional; 1 part-time professional; 1 part-time support.
EIN: 746104592
Other changes: Molly N. Kidd and Harvin C. Moore are no longer directors.
The grantmaker now makes its application guidelines available online.

3325
Hahl Proctor Charitable Trust
c/o U.S. Trust, Bank of America, N.A.
500 W. 7th St., 15th Fl., TX1-497-15-08
Fort Worth, TX 76102-4700 (817) 390-6028
Contact: Mark J. Smith, Philanthropic Relationship Mgr.
E-mail: tx.philanthropic@ustrust.com; Application address: P.O. Box 270, Midland, TX 79702-0270;
Main URL: https://www.bankofamerica.com/philanthropic/grantmaking.go

Established in 1987 in TX.
Foundation type: Independent foundation.
Financial data (yr. ended 04/30/13): Assets, $5,510,178 (M); expenditures, $298,092; qualifying distributions, $266,231; giving activities include $240,000 for 15 grants (high: $40,000; low: $4,500).
Purpose and activities: Giving primarily for youth development and education, including education and services for children who are mentally or physically disabled; funding also for other children, youth, and social services and for the performing arts.
Fields of interest: Performing arts; Education, special; Education; Youth development, services; Human services; Children/youth, services; Residential/custodial care; Developmentally disabled, centers & services; Physically disabled.
Limitations: Applications accepted. Giving primarily in Midland, TX. No grants to individuals.
Application information: Application form required.
Initial approach: Online proposal via Trust web site
Deadline(s): May 15
Committee Members: Bob Elliott; Sean Low; Jeff Morton; David Smith; Mark Smith; Lisa Van der Zanden.
EIN: 756382699

3326
Professional Contract Services Inc.
(formerly Physically Challenged Services Industries, Inc.)
718 W. FM 1626, Bldg. 100
Austin, TX 78748 (512) 358-8887
***Contact:* Carroll Schubert, Pres. and C.E.O.**
***FAX:* (512) 358-8890; Main URL: https://www.pcsi.org/**
LinkedIn: https://www.linkedin.com/company/professional-contract-services-incorporated

Established in 1996 in TX. Classified as a private operating foundation in 1997.
Donor: National Institute for the Severely Handicapped (NISH).
Foundation type: Public charity.
Financial data (yr. ended 06/30/12): Revenue, $89,666,710; assets, $47,410,503 (M); gifts received, $89,445,774; expenditures, $83,079,001; program services expenses, $75,736,982; giving activities include $233,250 for 10 grants (high: $50,000; low: $7,500).
Fields of interest: Education; Community/economic development; United Ways and Federated Giving Programs.
Limitations: Applications accepted. Giving primarily in TX. No grants to individuals.
Application information: Application form required.
Initial approach: Letter
Deadline(s): None
Officers and Directors:* E. Craig Lusk,* Chair.; Carroll W. Schubert,* Pres. and C.E.O.; Eric Barbosa,* V.P. and Genl. Counsel; Trina Baumgarten,* V.P. and C.F.O.; Kevin Cloud,* V.P., Contract Admin. and IT; Keith Walker,* V.P., Opers. and Bus. Devel.; James Hill; Greg Oveland; Carroll Schubert; J.E. Ward.
EIN: 742786094
Other changes: Carroll W. Schubert has replaced Ace L. Burt as Pres. and C.E.O. Eric Barbosa has replaced Carroll W. Schubert as Exec. V.P. and Genl. Counsel. Trina Baumgarten has replaced Trina Baumgarten as C.F.O.
Kevin Cloud is now V.P., Contract Admin. and IT. Keith Walker is now V.P., Opers. and Bus. Devel.

3327
The Psalm 25:10 Foundation
P.O. Box 6808
Fort Worth, TX 76110-0808

Established in 2006 in TX.
Donor: Cellular City, Ltd.
Foundation type: Independent foundation.
Financial data (yr. ended 12/31/12): Assets, $34,137,812 (M); gifts received, $2,094,658; expenditures, $775,611; qualifying distributions, $119,682; giving activities include $119,000 for 4 grants (high: $100,000; low: $1,000).
Fields of interest: Protestant agencies & churches.
Limitations: Applications not accepted. Giving primarily in TX. No grants to individuals.
Application information: Contributes only to pre-selected organizations.
Officer: David Shanks, Pres.
Directors: Glenn Hodge; Derek Holmes.
EIN: 204128717
Other changes: At the close of 2012, the fair market value of the grantmaker's assets was $34,137,812, a 116.9% increase over the 2010 value, $15,738,903.

3328
The QuadW Foundation
(also known as What Would Willie Want Foundation)
100 Crescent Ct., Ste. 700
Dallas, TX 75201-2112 (214) 459-3330
Contact: Lisa Tichenor, Tr.
E-mail: info@QuadW.org; Main URL: http://www.quadw.org
Facebook: https://www.facebook.com/pages/QuadW-Foundation/195619433811221

Established in 2006 in TX.
Donor: McHenry "Taylor" T. Tichenor III.
Foundation type: Independent foundation.
Financial data (yr. ended 12/31/12): Assets, $10,303,578 (M); gifts received, $310,492; expenditures, $739,912; qualifying distributions, $672,220; giving activities include $567,240 for 13 grants (high: $203,867; low: $1,000).
Purpose and activities: Giving primarily for higher education, sarcoma research, and transforming mission experiences.
Fields of interest: Higher education; Cancer research; Spirituality.
Type of support: Internship funds; Research; Program development; General/operating support; Fellowships; Scholarship funds.
Publications: Application guidelines; Multi-year report.
Application information: Application guidelines available for each program on foundation web site. Application form required.
Initial approach: E-mail
Deadline(s): 1 month before each board meeting
Board meeting date(s): Aug. and Dec.
Officer: McHenry "Mac" T. Tichenor, Jr., Exec. Dir.
Directors: Bret Alexander; Charlie Haggard; Laureen Hayden; Johnny Peters; Elizabeth Trieu; Ross Vick; Mary Katherine Vigness.
Trustees: Lisa Tichenor; Taylor Tichenor.
EIN: 204750916

3329
Ed Rachal Foundation
500 N. Shoreline Blvd., Ste. 606
Corpus Christi, TX 78401-0323
Contact: Paul D. Altheide, C.E.O.
FAX: (361) 881-9885; E-mail: info@edrachal.org; Main URL: http://www.edrachal.org

Established in 1965 in TX.
Donor: Ed Rachal†.
Foundation type: Independent foundation.
Financial data (yr. ended 08/31/13): Assets, $208,323,946 (M); expenditures, $12,703,386; qualifying distributions, $11,608,756; giving activities include $9,321,508 for 154 grants (high: $2,000,000; low: $500), and $683,665 for foundation-administered programs.
Purpose and activities: The combination of commitments to education and youth, and to the land and its resources, is the cornerstone of the foundation.
Fields of interest: Higher education; Libraries/library science; Health organizations, association; Human services; Children/youth, services; Christian agencies & churches.
Type of support: General/operating support; Capital campaigns; Building/renovation; Equipment; Emergency funds; Employee matching gifts.
Limitations: Applications accepted. Giving limited to TX. No grants to individuals, or for multi-year commitments.
Publications: Application guidelines; Annual report; Grants list.
Application information: Applications sent by fax will not be accepted. It is not necessary to place application in folder or binder. Application guidelines available on foundation web site. Application form required.
Initial approach: Use application form on foundation web site
Copies of proposal: 1
Deadline(s): None
Board meeting date(s): Jan., Apr., July, and Oct.
Officers and Directors:* John D. White,* Chair.; Robert L. Walker,* Vice-Chair.; Paul D. Altheide,* C.E.O. and Secy.; Richard Schendel,* Treas.; David Hoyer; John J. Johnson; Ken W. Trawick.
Number of staff: 1 full-time professional; 1 full-time support.
EIN: 741116595
Other changes: For the fiscal year ended Aug. 31, 2013, the fair market value of the grantmaker's assets was $208,323,946, an 82.9% increase over the fiscal 2012 value, $113,876,058.

3330
The Radler Foundation
3131 W. 7th St., Ste. 400
Fort Worth, TX 76107-8702 (817) 632-5200
***Contact:* Casey Leiber**
***E-mail:* info@radlerfoundation.org**; Main URL: http://www.radlerfoundation.org

Established in 2009 in TX.
Donors: Michael G. Radler; Chief Oil & Gas, LLC; Christ Church; Drop in the Bucket; Radler 2000; The Water Project, Inc.; Helfen Wir; Jeremiah Project; Lenexa Baptist Church; Neverthirst; Villages of Hope

Africa; Salinas Valley Community Church; A to Z Mud Co., Inc.; Alliance for the Lost Boys of Sudan; Aqua-Africa; Baker Hughes; Brooke Point High School; Covenant Church of Pittsburgh; Diq Deep; Frost Bank; Geoff Radler; Rosario Garcia; Greg Garcia; Jeff Jordan; Leon Laubscher; Loadcraft Industries, Ltd.; Nikki Mildren; Matt Mildren; Radler 2000 Limited Partnership; Randy Wolsey; Tim Ellsworth; U. S. Trust; Villages of Hope Africa; Mary Frank.
Foundation type: Independent foundation.
Financial data (yr. ended 12/31/12): Assets, $1,329,637 (M); gifts received, $453,970; expenditures, $3,546,689; qualifying distributions, $3,211,417; giving activities include $3,184,059 for 24 grants (high: $2,618,767; low: $538).
Purpose and activities: The foundation is a private, Christian foundation that supports organizations serving the local community and around the world, with a special focus on East Africa.
Fields of interest: Education; Health organizations; Housing/shelter.
Limitations: Applications not accepted. Giving primarily in TX; with some giving in Eastern Africa and South Sudan.
Application information: Unsolicited requests for funds not accepted.
Officers and Directors:* Michael G. Radler,* Pres.; Graham C. Radler,* Secy.; Michael Evan Radler,* Treas.; Gail Andrae-Pianta, Cont.; B.J. Goergen; Reinke Radler.
EIN: 264582178

3331
Bernard and Audre Rapoport Foundation

5400 Bosque Blvd., Ste. 304
Waco, TX 76710-4446 (254) 741-0510
***Contact:* Tom Stanton, Exec. Dir.**
FAX: (254) 741-0092;
E-mail: tom@rapoportfdn.org; Additional e-mail: Casey, Foundation Coord.: casey@rapoportfdn.org; Main URL: http://www.rapoportfdn.org
Grants Database: http://www.rapoportfdn.org/grants.php

Established in 1986 in TX.
Donors: Audre Rapoport; Bernard Rapoport; Patricia Rapoport; Ronald B. Rapoport.
Foundation type: Independent foundation.
Financial data (yr. ended 12/31/12): Assets, $50,557,422 (M); expenditures, $3,372,034; qualifying distributions, $2,665,483; giving activities include $2,378,462 for 34 grants (high: $200,000; low: $4,300).
Purpose and activities: To meet basic human needs while building individual and social resiliency.
Fields of interest: Arts; Education; Health care; Civil/human rights; Community/economic development; Jewish federated giving programs.
Type of support: General/operating support; Equipment; Program development; Seed money; Matching/challenge support.
Limitations: Applications accepted. Giving primarily within a 30 mile radius of Waco, TX. No support for political or religious organizations. No grants to individuals.
Publications: Annual report.
Application information: Application form required.
Initial approach: Use online application form on foundation web site
Board meeting date(s): Three times per year
Officers and Trustees:* Ronald B. Rapoport,* Chair.; Audre Rapoport,* Pres.; William A. Nesbitt, Secy.-Treas.; Tom Stanton, Exec. Dir.; Rick Battistoni; James D. Chesney; Lyndon Olson, Jr.; Emily Rapoport; Patricia Rapoport; Joel Schwartz.
Number of staff: 2 full-time professional.
EIN: 742479712

3332
RDM Positive Impact Foundation

81 N. Bay Blvd.
The Woodlands, TX 77380-1069

Established in 2005 in CA.
Donors: Ronald J. Mittelstaedt; Darin Mittelstaedt.
Foundation type: Independent foundation.
Financial data (yr. ended 12/31/12): Assets, $1,612,927 (M); gifts received, $131,434; expenditures, $296,382; qualifying distributions, $286,675; giving activities include $286,675 for 11 grants (high: $100,000; low: $3,000).
Fields of interest: Medical research; Human services; Children/youth, services; Protestant agencies & churches.
Limitations: Applications not accepted. Giving primarily in CA. No grants to individuals.
Application information: Contributes only to pre-selected organizations.
Officers: Ronald J. Mittelstaedt, C.E.O.; Darin Mittelstaedt, Secy.
EIN: 203502111
Other changes: The grantmaker has moved from CA to TX.

3333
The Reilly Family Foundation

1017 S. FM Rd. 5
Aledo, TX 76008-4558 (817) 265-2364
Contact: Michael A. Reilly, Chair.; Beverly A. Reilly, V.P.

Established in 1996 in TX.
Donors: John C. Franklin; Stars for Children; Peter Baldwin; Reilly Parkway; Beverly A. Reilly; Michael A. Reilly.
Foundation type: Independent foundation.
Financial data (yr. ended 12/31/12): Assets, $1,913,661 (M); expenditures, $413,672; qualifying distributions, $327,748; giving activities include $323,119 for 49 grants (high: $52,500; low: $100), and $4,629 for 1 grant to an individual.
Purpose and activities: Giving primarily for education, including scholarships to high school graduates pursuing higher education.
Fields of interest: Higher education; Education; Health care; Human services; International development; Christian agencies & churches.
Type of support: General/operating support; Scholarship funds; Scholarships—to individuals.
Limitations: Applications accepted. Giving in the U.S., primarily in the Dallas-Fort Worth, TX, area.
Application information: An application and list of information required to be submitted will be mailed or faxed to the applicant upon such request. Application form required.
Initial approach: Letter of telephone
Deadline(s): None
Officers and Directors:* Michael A. Reilly,* Chair.; Richard D. Trubitt,* V.P. and Secy.-Treas.; Beverly A. Reilly,* V.P.; Robert Barnes; Anson Reilly; Asher Reilly; Atlee Reilly; Austin Reilly; Axton Reilly.
EIN: 752366809

3334
Sid W. Richardson Foundation

309 Main St.
Fort Worth, TX 76102-4006 (817) 336-0494
Contact: Pete Geren, Pres.
FAX: (817) 332-2176;
E-mail: cjohns@sidrichardson.org; E-mail for Pete Geren: pgeren@sidrichardson.org; Main URL: http://www.sidrichardson.org

Established in 1947 in TX.
Donors: Sid W. Richardson†; and associated companies.
Foundation type: Independent foundation.
Financial data (yr. ended 12/31/12): Assets, $500,659,658 (M); gifts received, $35,752; expenditures, $17,245,208; qualifying distributions, $15,030,024; giving activities include $11,843,286 for 152 grants (high: $1,000,000; low: $1,500), and $1,628,820 for 1 foundation-administered program.
Purpose and activities: Giving primarily for education, health, the arts, and social service programs.
Fields of interest: Performing arts; Arts; Higher education; Education; Health care; Health organizations, association; Human services.
Type of support: Program-related investments/loans; General/operating support; Continuing support; Building/renovation; Equipment; Land acquisition; Endowments; Program development; Conferences/seminars; Publication; Seed money; Research; Matching/challenge support.
Limitations: Applications accepted. Giving limited to TX, with emphasis on Fort Worth for the arts and human services, and statewide for health and education. No support for religious organizations. No grants to individuals, or for scholarships or fellowships; no loans (except for program-related investments).
Publications: Annual report (including application guidelines); Financial statement; Grants list.
Application information: Formal proposals are by invitation, only after review of letter. Application form required.
Initial approach: Letter
Copies of proposal: 1
Deadline(s): Jan. 15
Board meeting date(s): Spring and fall
Final notification: Varies
Officers and Directors:* Edward P. Bass,* Chair.; **Pete Geren, C.E.O. and Pres.**; Lee M. Bass,* V.P.; Sid R. Bass,* V.P.
Number of staff: 5 full-time professional.
EIN: 756015828
Other changes: Pete Geren is now C.E.O. and Pres. Dee Steer is no longer Secy. Nancy Bass is no longer V.P. Emeritus.

3335
Anne S. Richardson Fund

(formerly Anne S. Richardson Charitable Trust)
c/o JPMorgan Chase Bank, Philanthropic Svcs.
P.O. Box 227237 TX1-2963
Dallas, TX 75222-7237
Contact: Ms. Casey Castaneda, Prog. Off.
FAX: (212) 464-2305;
E-mail: casey.b.castaneda@jpmchase.com; Main URL: http://fdnweb.org/richardson
Grants List: http://fdnweb.org/richardson/grants/year/2013-contributions/

Trust established in 1965 in CT.
Donor: Anne S. Richardson†.
Foundation type: Independent foundation.

Financial data (yr. ended 07/31/12): Assets, $11,279,538 (M); expenditures, $695,241; qualifying distributions, $581,572; giving activities include $571,000 for 23 grants (high: $65,000; low: $5,000).
Purpose and activities: Funding interests include: 1) eight organizations recommended by the donor; 2) programs in Ridgefield, Connecticut, that assist lower-income people or that are of broad interest to the community; and 3) programs in Fairfield County, Connecticut, that promote the independence of women, support the lesbian and gay community, foster youth development, or enhance the natural beautification of communities through parks or gardens.
Fields of interest: Botanical/horticulture/landscape services; Recreation, parks/playgrounds; Youth development; Children/youth, services; Women; LGBTQ.
Type of support: General/operating support; Capital campaigns; Program development.
Limitations: Giving primarily in CT, with emphasis on the town of Ridgefield and Fairfield County. No support for private foundations or organizations lacking 501(c)(3) status. No grants to individuals; no loans.
Publications: Application guidelines; Grants list.
Application information: Application guidelines available on foundation web site.
Initial approach: Use proposal format on foundation web site
Deadline(s): Mar. 2
Final notification: July 31
Trustee: JPMorgan Chase Bank, N.A.
Number of staff: None.
EIN: 136192516

3336
Sid Richardson Memorial Fund

309 Main St.
Fort Worth, TX 76102-4006 (817) 336-0494
Contact: Peggy Laskoski, Coord.
FAX: (817) 332-2176;
E-mail: plaskoski@sidrichardson.org; Main URL: http://www.sidrichardson.org
Grants Database: http://www.sidrichardson.org/grants/prior/

Incorporated in 1965 in TX.
Donor: Sid W. Richardson†.
Foundation type: Independent foundation.
Financial data (yr. ended 12/31/12): Assets, $6,855,304 (M); expenditures, $411,025; qualifying distributions, $338,708; giving activities include $268,750 for 64 grants to individuals (high: $9,000; low: $750).
Purpose and activities: Giving limited to scholarships for direct descendants of donor's employees.
Fields of interest: Higher education.
Type of support: Employee-related scholarships.
Limitations: Applications accepted. Giving primarily in TX. No grants for capital or endowment funds, operating budgets, general purposes, special projects, research, or matching gifts; no loans.
Application information: Application form required.
Initial approach: Letter, telephone, or fax
Copies of proposal: 1
Deadline(s): Submit application between Jan. and Mar.; deadline Mar. 31
Board meeting date(s): Sept./Oct.; selection committee meets annually in May
Final notification: 2 months
Officers and Directors:* John Hogg,* Pres.; Peggy Laskoski, Secy.; Cynthia K. Alexander, Treas.; Robert E. Kolba; Valleau Wilkie, Jr.
EIN: 751220266

3337
Adam Richter Charitable Trust

c/o Bank of America, N.A.
P.O. Box 831041
Dallas, TX 75283-1041
***Application address:* c/o Bank of America, N.A., Att.: Constance Morrow, 901 Main St., 9th Fl., Dallas, TX 75202-3714, tel.: (866) 461-7281**

Established in 1994 in CA.
Foundation type: Independent foundation.
Financial data (yr. ended 09/30/13): Assets, $4,092,533 (M); expenditures, $289,125; qualifying distributions, $209,883; giving activities include $207,859 for 21 grants (high: $24,250; low: $2,000).
Fields of interest: Arts; Higher education; Environment; Animal welfare; Hospitals (general); Health organizations, association; Human services; Christian agencies & churches.
Limitations: Applications accepted. Giving primarily in CA. No grants to individuals.
Application information: Application form required.
Initial approach: Letter
Deadline(s): None
Trustee: Bank of America, N.A.
EIN: 956978793

3338
Rockwell Fund, Inc.

770 S. Post Oak Ln., Ste. 525
Houston, TX 77056-6660 (713) 629-9022
Contact: Judy Ahlgrim, Grants Admin.
FAX: (713) 629-7702; E-mail: info@rockfund.org; Main URL: http://www.rockfund.org

Trust established in 1931; incorporated in 1949 in TX; merged with Rockwell Brothers Endowment, Inc. in 1981.
Donor: Members of the James M. Rockwell family.
Foundation type: Independent foundation.
Financial data (yr. ended 12/31/12): Assets, $77,281,547 (M); gifts received, $500; expenditures, $4,807,273; qualifying distributions, $4,008,087; giving activities include $3,058,952 for 44 grants (high: $575,000; low: $1).
Purpose and activities: The foundation's grantmaking priorities focus on tackling issues in a comprehensive and coordinated manner to provide the best outcomes for low-income individuals, families and communities. Its current Issue Areas are: Education: Dropout prevention strategies that target the intermediate and middle school years; Health: Community-based health services, including physical, mental and behavioral health; Housing: Supportive housing, defined as affordable housing coupled with on-site support services needed to achieve self-sufficiency; Workforce Development: Job training/placement and jobs creation/small business development opportunities.
Fields of interest: Secondary school/education; Public health; Mental health/crisis services, association; Mental health, treatment; Mental health, counseling/support groups; Mental health, disorders; Employment, services; Employment, training; Housing/shelter, services; Human services; Children/youth, services; Family services; Community development, neighborhood development; Nonprofit management; Community/economic development; Children/youth; Children; Youth; Adults; Young adults; Mentally disabled; Minorities; Hispanics/Latinos; Women; Girls; Adults, women; Young adults, female; Men; Boys; Adults, men; Young adults, male; Single parents; Economically disadvantaged; Homeless.
Type of support: Continuing support; Curriculum development; General/operating support; Income development; Management development/capacity building; Matching/challenge support; Program development; Program evaluation; Program-related investments/loans; Seed money; Technical assistance.
Limitations: Giving primarily in Houston, TX. No support for houses of worship, organizations that target a specific disease, or for parochial, private primary or secondary schools. No grants to individuals or for medical or scientific research projects, underwriting benefits, dinners, galas, golf tournaments, and fundraising special events, or mass appeal solicitations.
Publications: Application guidelines; Financial statement; Grants list.
Application information: Ann on-line letter of inquiry must be submitted first. Please refer to the foundation web site. Applicants should not submit more than 1 proposal per year. Application form required.
Initial approach: On-line inquiry form
Copies of proposal: 1
Deadline(s): None
Board meeting date(s): Quarterly
Final notification: After each quarterly meeting
Officers and Trustees:* R. Terry Bell,* C.E.O. and Pres.; **Margaret E. McConn,* V.P., C.F.O., and C.I.O.**; Barbara W. Bellatti,* Secy.; Whitney Randolph, Treas.; Domingo Barrios; Sharon Edwards; William "Billy" Granville III.
Number of staff: 4 full-time professional; 2 full-time support.
EIN: 746040258
Other changes: Margaret E. McConn is now V.P., C.F.O., and C.I.O.

3339
The Rogers Foundation

P.O. Box 8799
Tyler, TX **75711-8799**
***Application address:* c/o Robyn Rogers, C.E.O., 2335 Oak Alley, Tyler, TX 75703, tel.: (903) 561-4041**

Established in 1986 in TX.
Donors: Robert M. Rogers†; Rogers Children's Heritage Trust One; Rogers Children's Heritage Trust Two; Rogers Granchildren's Heritage Trust.
Foundation type: Independent foundation.
Financial data (yr. ended 12/31/12): Assets, $43,779,751 (M); gifts received, $60,000; expenditures, $1,636,457; qualifying distributions, $1,358,622; giving activities include $1,271,490 for 67 grants (high: $100,000; low: $1,000).
Purpose and activities: Giving to promote education by providing funds for schools, educational programs, scholarships, and scholarship funds; support also for Protestant organizations.
Fields of interest: Arts; Education, fund raising/fund distribution; Elementary/secondary education; Elementary school/education; Higher education; Health care; Protestant agencies & churches; Religion.
Type of support: General/operating support; Building/renovation; Scholarship funds; Matching/challenge support.
Limitations: Applications accepted. Giving primarily in ID and TX. No grants to individuals.

Publications: Informational brochure (including application guidelines).
Application information: Application form required.
Initial approach: Letter
Copies of proposal: 1
Deadline(s): Oct. 1
Officers and Directors:* Robyn M. Rogers,* C.E.O. and Pres.; Sheryl Rogers Palmer,* V.P.; Paul W. Powell,* Secy.-Treas.
Number of staff: 1 part-time professional.
EIN: 752143064

3340
The Rosewood Foundation
2101 Cedar Springs Rd., Ste. 1600
Dallas, TX 75201-7861

Established in 2000 in TX.
Donor: The Rosewood Corp.
Foundation type: Independent foundation.
Financial data (yr. ended 12/31/12): Assets, $23,297 (M); gifts received, $554,033; expenditures, $533,081; qualifying distributions, $533,081; giving activities include $533,081 for 286 grants (high: $35,000; low: $50).
Fields of interest: Performing arts; Arts; Higher education; Education; Environment; Youth development; Human services; Children/youth, services.
Type of support: General/operating support; Continuing support; Annual campaigns; Capital campaigns; Building/renovation; Program development; Research; Program evaluation; Employee matching gifts; Matching/challenge support.
Limitations: Applications not accepted. Giving primarily in TX. No support for direct funding of churches or schools. No grants to individuals.
Application information: Contributes only to pre-selected organizations.
Board meeting date(s): Quarterly
Officers and Trustees:* Patrick B. Sands,* Pres.; Don W. Crisp,* V.P. and Treas.; Laurie Sands Harrison,* V.P.; **Haven S. Heinrichs,* V.P.; J. Clayton Sands,* V.P.; Stephen Sands,* Secy.;** Schuyler B. Marshall IV.
Number of staff: 1 part-time professional.
EIN: 752827470

3341
Saint Susie Charitable Foundation
800 Navarro St., Ste. 210
San Antonio, TX 78205-1877 (210) 226-9249
Contact: John R. Hannah, Tr.
***Main URL:* http://www.saintsusie.org**

Established in 2004 in TX.
Foundation type: Independent foundation.
Financial data (yr. ended 12/31/12): Assets, $9,988,846 (M); gifts received, $2,000; expenditures, $562,484; qualifying distributions, $488,750; giving activities include $488,750 for 35 grants (high: $90,000; low: $1,250).
Purpose and activities: The foundation's goal is to support organizations that contribute to medicine, education and religion.
Fields of interest: Arts; Education; Health care; Human services; Children/youth, services; Family services.
Limitations: Applications accepted. Giving primarily in San Antonio, TX. No grants to individuals.
Publications: IRS Form 990 or 990-PF printed copy available upon request.
Application information:
Initial approach: Concise proposal via U.S. mail
Deadline(s): None
Trustees: Dr. Fernando Guerra; John R. Hannah.
EIN: 200404671

3342
Earl C. Sams Foundation, Inc.
101 N. Shoreline Dr., Ste. 602
Corpus Christi, TX 78401-2824 (361) 888-6485
Contact: Bruce S. Hawn, Pres. and C.E.O.
E-mail: sueo@ecsams.org; Main URL: http://www.ecsams.org

Incorporated in 1946 in NY; reincorporated in 1988 in TX.
Donor: Earl C. Sams†.
Foundation type: Independent foundation.
Financial data (yr. ended 12/31/12): Assets, $22,360,480 (M); expenditures, $1,443,810; qualifying distributions, $1,116,393; giving activities include $768,782 for 3 grants (high: $768,344; low: $33).
Purpose and activities: Giving support for health care, youth and community development, and the environment.
Fields of interest: Environment; Health care; Children/youth, services; Community/economic development.
Type of support: General/operating support; Continuing support; Annual campaigns; Building/renovation; Equipment; Program development; In-kind gifts; Matching/challenge support.
Limitations: Applications accepted. Giving primarily in southern TX. No grants to individuals.
Publications: Application guidelines; Grants list; Program policy statement (including application guidelines).
Application information: Electronic submissions are preferred. Application should be scanned and e-mailed in PDF format. Application form required.
***Initial approach:* Use application form on foundation web site**
Copies of proposal: 1
Deadline(s): Mar., June, Nov.
Board meeting date(s): Mar., June, and Nov.
Officers and Directors:* Susan G. Hawn,* Chair. and V.P.; Bruce Sams Hawn,* C.E.O. and Pres.; Susan Ohnmacht, Secy.; Candace Coutinho; **Caitlyn J. Hawn**; Nancy E. Hawn; Sydney E. Thames; Michael T. Yuras.
Number of staff: 4 full-time professional.
EIN: 741463151
Other changes: The grantmaker now makes its grants list and application guidelines available online.

3343
San Angelo Health Foundation
P.O. Box 3550
San Angelo, TX 76902-3550 (325) 486-0185
Contact: Tom Early, Pres.; Vicki Ford, Admin. Off.
FAX: (325) 486-1125;
E-mail: tomearly@sahfoundation.org; Main URL: http://www.sahfoundation.org

Established in 1995 in TX.
Foundation type: Independent foundation.
Financial data (yr. ended 12/31/12): Assets, $56,684,841 (M); expenditures, $2,540,148; qualifying distributions, $2,085,982; giving activities include $1,752,969 for 34 grants (high: $492,144; low: $1,500).
Purpose and activities: The foundation seeks to enhance the quality of life for the people of the San Angelo, TX, area.
Fields of interest: Arts; Education; Health care; Human services; Community/economic development.
Type of support: Consulting services; General/operating support; Management development/capacity building; Capital campaigns; Building/renovation; Equipment; Land acquisition; Emergency funds; Program development; Conferences/seminars; Seed money; Research; Technical assistance; Program evaluation; Matching/challenge support.
Limitations: Applications accepted. Giving limited to San Angelo and the Concho Valley, TX, area. No support for religious organizations for religious purposes. No grants to individuals, or for fundraising events, operating deficits or debt retirement.
Publications: Application guidelines; Annual report.
Application information: See foundation web site for application guidelines. Application form not required.
Initial approach: Proposal
Copies of proposal: 2
Deadline(s): 3 to 4 months prior to when funds are needed
Board meeting date(s): Quarterly
Final notification: 1 to 3 months
Officers: Mike Boyd, Chair.; Marilyn Aboussie, Vice-Chair.; Tom Early, Pres.; **Mary Jane Steadman, Secy.; David Lupton, Treas.**
Trustees: Devin Bates; Jim Cummings; Rick DeHoyos; Sande Vincent Harrison; T. Richey Oliver; Robert S. Patyrak, M.D.; Karen Pfluger; Joanne Rice; Hugh Lamar Stone III; Joe B. Wilkinson, M.D.
Number of staff: 2 full-time professional.
EIN: 751315145
Other changes: Marilyn Aboussie has replaced Mike Boyd as Vice-Chair. Mary Jane Steadman has replaced Marilyn Aboussie as Secy. David Lupton has replaced Jim Cummings as Treas. Mike Boyd is now Chair.

3344
Saxena Foundation Inc
67 St. Stephens School Rd.
Austin, TX 78746 (512) 347-8484
Contact: Shubhada Saxena, Pres.
***E-mail:* info@saxenafoundation.org**; Main URL: http://www.saxenafoundation.org

Donors: Manoj Saxena; Shubhada Saxena.
Foundation type: Independent foundation.
Financial data (yr. ended 12/31/11): Assets, $137,013 (M); gifts received, $285,229; expenditures, $214,878; qualifying distributions, $143,500; giving activities include $143,500 for 1 grant.
Fields of interest: Education, drop-out prevention; Youth development, services.
Limitations: Applications accepted. Giving primarily in TX.
Application information: Application form not required.
Initial approach: Proposal
Deadline(s): Grant applications can be submitted throughout the year
Officers: Shubhada Saxena, Pres.; Avinash Saxena, Secy.; Manoj Saxena, Treas.
EIN: 263328292

3345
Scharbauer Foundation Inc
300 N. Marienfeld St., Ste. 850
Midland, TX 79701-4387 (432) 683-2222
Contact: Grant A. Billingsley, Exec. Dir.
E-mail: gbillingsley@scharbauerfoundation.org;
Main URL: http://www.scharbauerfoundation.org

Established in TX.
Donor: Clarence Scharbauer, Jr.
Foundation type: Independent foundation.
Financial data (yr. ended 12/31/12): Assets, $122,917,413 (M); gifts received, $27,457,297; expenditures, $3,146,657; qualifying distributions, $2,289,002; giving activities include $2,204,000 for 16 grants (high: $1,000,000; low: $1,500).
Fields of interest: Arts; Education; Health care; Human services; Public affairs; Religion.
Limitations: Applications accepted. Giving primarily in TX, with emphasis on Midland, the Permian Basin region, and the Panhandle region. No support for lobbying organizations. No grants or loans to individuals.
Publications: Application guidelines; Grants list.
Application information: Pre-applications are not generally considered out-of-cycle. Only hard-copy Pre-application forms will be accepted and no electronic, fax, or handwritten Pre-application forms will be accepted. Pre-applications must be received by the foundation by 5:00 p.m. on the day of the deadline. Pre-application form and guidelines available on foundation web site.
Initial approach: Pre-application
Deadline(s): See foundation web site for current deadlines
Officers: Clarence Scharbauer, Jr., Pres.; Clarence Scharbauer, III, V.P.; James M. Alsup, V.P.; Allen McGuire, Treas.; Cynthia Y. Benson, Cont.; Grant Billingsley, Exec. Dir.
EIN: 262527362
Other changes: At the close of 2012, the fair market value of the grantmaker's assets was $122,917,413, a 121.5% increase over the 2011 value, $55,488,020. For the same period, the grantmaker paid grants of $2,204,000, a 68.2% increase over the 2011 disbursements, $1,310,000.
The grantmaker now publishes application guidelines.

3346
The Schissler Foundation
(formerly Schissler Charitable Foundation)
c/o Nancy Lynn Red
P.O. Box 272805
Houston, TX 77277-2805 (713) 626-3890
Contact: Richard P. Schissler, Pres.

Established in 1983 in TX.
Donors: Chifton Ltd Co.; Nancy R. Schissler; Richard P. Schissler.
Foundation type: Independent foundation.
Financial data (yr. ended 03/31/13): Assets, $242,922 (M); gifts received, $200,000; expenditures, $189,663; qualifying distributions, $182,850; giving activities include $181,250 for 14 grants (high: $100,000; low: $500).
Purpose and activities: Giving primarily for education and human services, including a YMCA.
Fields of interest: Performing arts, orchestras; Performing arts, opera; Higher education; Graduate/professional education; Education; Recreation, community; Human services; YM/YWCAs & YM/YWHAs; Jewish federated giving programs.
Limitations: Applications accepted. Giving primarily in Houston, TX. No grants to individuals.
Application information: Application form not required.
Initial approach: Proposal
Deadline(s): None
Officers and Trustees:* Richard P. Schissler,* Pres.; Richard P. Schissler III, V.P.; Nancy Lynn Red, Secy.-Treas.; Laura Lee Jenkins; Nancy R. Schissler.
EIN: 760056884

3347
Semmes Foundation, Inc.
800 Navarro St., Ste. 210
San Antonio, TX 78205-1877
Contact: Thomas R. Semmes, Pres.
Main URL: http://www.semmesfoundation.org
Grants List: http://www.semmesfoundation.org/recipients.htm

Incorporated in 1952 in TX.
Donors: Douglas R. Semmes†; Julia Yates Semmes†.
Foundation type: Independent foundation.
Financial data (yr. ended 12/31/12): Assets, $36,777,271 (M); gifts received, $45,739; expenditures, $2,831,082; qualifying distributions, $2,092,573; giving activities include $2,050,145 for 16 grants (high: $550,000; low: $1,500).
Purpose and activities: Support for museums and nonprofit organizations involved with education and health.
Fields of interest: Museums; Education; Health care.
Limitations: Applications accepted. Giving primarily in the San Antonio, TX, area. No grants to individuals; no loans.
Publications: IRS Form 990 or 990-PF printed copy available upon request.
Application information: Application guidelines available on foundation web site. The overwhelming majority of grants are initiated by the directors of the foundation. Application form not required.
Initial approach: Proposal via regular mail
Copies of proposal: 1
Deadline(s): None
Board meeting date(s): Annually, and as required
Final notification: Within 6 months
Officers and Directors:* Thomas R. Semmes,* Pres.; Douglas R. Semmes, Jr.,* V.P.; Carol Duffell, Secy.-Treas.; **John R. Hannah**; Patricia A. Semmes.
Number of staff: 1 part-time professional.
EIN: 746062264
Other changes: Lucian L. Morrison is no longer a director.

3348
Shell Oil Company Foundation
(formerly Shell Companies Foundation, Inc.)
1 Shell Plz., P.O. Box 4749
Houston, TX 77210-4749
FAX: (713) 241-3329;
E-mail: scofoundation@shellus.com

Incorporated in 1953 in NY.
Donors: Shell Oil Co.; Shell Exploration & Production; Motiva.
Foundation type: Company-sponsored foundation.
Financial data (yr. ended 12/31/12): Assets, $127,428,662 (M); gifts received, $226,754; expenditures, $3,060,299; qualifying distributions, $2,319,879; giving activities include $2,319,879 for 1,138 grants (high: $88,147; low: $25).
Purpose and activities: The foundation supports organizations involved with community development and through an employee matching gift program.
Fields of interest: Community/economic development; United Ways and Federated Giving Programs.
Type of support: General/operating support; Employee matching gifts.
Limitations: Applications not accepted. Giving primarily in areas of company operations with emphasis on Houston, TX. No support for religious organizations not of direct benefit to the entire community, fraternal or labor organizations, private foundations, or organizations located outside the U.S. No grants to individuals, or for endowments, capital campaigns, or general operating support, or conferences and seminars.
Application information: Contributes only to pre-selected organizations.
Officers and Directors: Bruce Culpepper, Pres.; Frazier Wilson, V.P.; Lynn S. Borgmeier, Secy.; Anothy M. Nolte, Cont. and Treas.; Cynthia A. P. Deere; **Christopher B. Rice**.
Number of staff: 7
EIN: 136066583
Other changes: Marvin E. Odum is no longer Co-Pres..Smith Deborah is no longer Cont. Tom N. Smith, M. Quartemain, S. P. Methvin, William C. Lowery, Lisa A. Davis, Randy Braud, and Curtis R. Frasier is no longer directors.

3349
Shelter Golf, Inc.
4318 Abbott Ave.
Dallas, TX **75205-4306**

Established in 1990 in TX.
Donor: Ewing Autohaus.
Foundation type: Operating foundation.
Financial data (yr. ended 12/31/11): Assets, $10,047 (M); gifts received, $373,500; expenditures, $367,052; qualifying distributions, $367,052; giving activities include $300,000 for 2 grants (high: $290,000; low: $10,000).
Purpose and activities: Grants awarded to provide assistance to homeless individuals and families.
Fields of interest: Family services, domestic violence; Homeless, human services; Women.
Type of support: General/operating support.
Limitations: Applications not accepted. Giving limited to Dallas, TX. No grants to individuals.
Application information: Contributes only to pre-selected organizations.
Officers and Trustees:* Tom C. Davis,* Co-Pres.; William C. Duvall,* Co-Pres.; S. Finley Ewing III,* V.P.; Donald Steen,* V.P.; A. Starke Taylor, Jr.,* V.P.; Charles W. Griege, Jr.; J. Lanny Wadkins.
EIN: 752340289

3350
Shelton Family Foundation
P.O. Box 2791
Abilene, TX 79604-2791 (325) 676-7724
Contact: David L. Copeland, Pres.

Established in 1997 in TX.
Donor: Andrew B. Shelton†.
Foundation type: Independent foundation.
Financial data (yr. ended 06/30/13): Assets, $44,220,598 (M); expenditures, $2,148,057; qualifying distributions, $2,011,338; giving activities include $1,777,122 for 76 grants (high: $327,622; low: $250).
Purpose and activities: Giving primarily for the arts, education, health, children, youth and social services, and to Christian and Protestant organizations.

Fields of interest: Arts; Higher education; Education; Health organizations, association; Human services; Salvation Army; Children/youth, services; Foundations (private grantmaking); Christian agencies & churches; Protestant agencies & churches.
Limitations: Applications accepted. Giving primarily in the west central TX area. No grants to individuals.
Application information: Application form not required.
Initial approach: Letter requesting guidelines
Deadline(s): None
Officers and Directors:* David L. Copeland,* Pres. and Treas.; C. Christine Nicols, Advisory Dir.; Andrew D. Durham; David R. Durham; Sindy Shelton Durham; Wendy H. Durham; Leonard R. Hoffman; Shay Shelton Hoffman; Ruby W. Shelton.
EIN: 752655885
Other changes: Stanley P. Wilson is no longer V.P.

3351
The Sikh Spirit Foundation, Inc.
24902 Miranda Ridge
Boerne, TX 78006-8439
Contact: Simran Jeet Singh, Exec. Dir.
E-mail: simran.singh@sikhspiritfoundation.org;
E-mail to request application information: info@sikhspiritfoundation.org; Additional e-mail: ideas@sikhspiritfoundation.org; Main URL: http://www.sikhspiritfoundation.org

Established in 2004 in TX.
Donor: Gurvinder P. Singh.
Foundation type: Operating foundation.
Financial data (yr. ended 12/31/12): Assets, $5,648,638 (M); gifts received, $19,500; expenditures, $199,945; qualifying distributions, $191,800; giving activities include $171,378 for 20 grants (high: $66,000; low: $75).
Purpose and activities: Giving primarily for Sikh and Punjabi education and civil rights. The foundation embraces all positive possibilities and hope that this open approach inspires all potential grantees to conceive of fresh and imaginative projects. At the same time, the Sikh Spirit Foundation feels that positive change ought to be rooted in a firm educational foundation. Educational projects are viewed most favorably and given highest priority in the grant-making process. The foundation sincerely believes that it has a responsibility to ensure that those dedicated to serving the community should not be hindered by financial obstacles, and this conviction compels us to seriously consider any and all projects that will provide real benefits to the Sikh community.
Fields of interest: Education; Civil/human rights; Religion.
Type of support: Program development; Publication; Seed money; Research; Grants to individuals; Scholarships—to individuals; Matching/challenge support.
Limitations: Giving primarily in CA, NY, and TX. No grants for equipment or construction.
Application information: Funds are allocated with the intention to stimulate maximum impact and growth for the Sikh community. Project proposals may receive funding from a minimum of $500 to a maximum of $25,000. Each proposal should be confined to a single project, although applicants are welcome to submit multiple project proposals.
Initial approach: Request application guidelines via e-mail
Copies of proposal: 1
Deadline(s): June 1 and Oct. 1
Officers: Gurvinder P. Singh, Pres.; Parvinder Kaur, V.P.; Gurpaul Singh, Secy.
EIN: 870723170

3352
The Simmons Foundation
109 N. Post Oak Ln., Ste. 220
Houston, TX 77024-7750 (713) 268-8099
Contact: Linda K. May, Pres.
FAX: (713) 580-1850;
E-mail: kdavis@thesimmonsfoundation.org;
Additional e-mail: info@thesimmonsfoundation.org; Main URL: http://www.thesimmonsfoundation.org
Facebook: https://www.facebook.com/TheSimmonsFdn
LinkedIn: http://www.linkedin.com/groups?trk=hb_side_g&gid=4709034
Twitter: https://twitter.com/TheSimmonsFdn

Established in 1993 in TX.
Donors: Gay A. Roane; Marjorie S. Gray†.
Foundation type: Independent foundation.
Financial data (yr. ended 12/31/12): Assets, $8,681,270 (M); expenditures, $3,888,786; qualifying distributions, $3,840,907; giving activities include $3,433,465 for 213 grants (high: $37,500; low: $236).
Purpose and activities: The foundation's mission is to invest in the community so lives can be improved by helping people help themselves. The foundation focuses its funding in one of 5 areas: health, education, civic/community, capacity building, and humans services. In each quarter the foundation pays particular attention to the following: advocacy, empowering vulnerable communities, prevention and intervention, and women and children.
Fields of interest: Education; Health care; Human services; Children/youth, services; Women, centers/services; Community/economic development.
Type of support: General/operating support; Continuing support; Management development/capacity building; Capital campaigns; Building/renovation; Equipment; Emergency funds; Program development; Seed money; Technical assistance; Employee-related scholarships; Matching/challenge support.
Limitations: Applications accepted. **Giving primarily in Harris County and the Greater Houston, TX area; the foundation may fund in other TX cities when the purpose of the grant directly benefits and/or affects Greater Houston. No support for religious organizations for religious purposes, (though the foundation funds faith-based organizations, unless they require clients to participate in religious worship or practices as a condition of service), major arts organizations, political organizations, major medical research projects, international organizations, local, national or international organizations' annual giving or holiday campaigns, 509(a)(3) Type III supporting organizations, disease-related organizations, or adoption agencies. No grants for individual scholarships (except for The Simmons Foundation/Redstone Scholarship Program), or for galas/social fundraisers, annual giving campaigns, luncheons, medical research, seniors, substance abuse, people with disabilities, or endowments.**
Publications: Application guidelines; Annual report; Grants list.
Application information: Proposals are by invitation only, upon review of Letter of Inquiry.
***Initial approach:* Letter of Inquiry to be submitted through online application system on foundation web site**
Copies of proposal: 1
***Deadline(s):* See foundation web site for current deadlines**
Board meeting date(s): Quarterly
Final notification: Within 10 business days for letters of inquiry
Officers and Directors:* Linda K. May,* Pres. and Exec. Dir.; Bob Henricksen,* V.P.; Amanda Cloud, Secy.; John Durie; Gay A. Roane; Betty K. Mathis; Jim T. Mills.
Number of staff: 2 full-time professional; 1 full-time support.
EIN: 760398915

3353
Clara Blackford Smith & W. Aubrey Smith Charitable Foundation
c/o US Trust, Philanthropic Solutions
901 Main St., 19th Fl., TX1-492-19-11
Dallas, TX 75202-3714
Contact: David T. Ross, Sr. V.P.
E-mail: tx.philanthropic@ustrust.com; Main URL: http://www.bankofamerica.com/grantmaking

Established in 1985 in TX.
Donor: Clara Blackford Smith†.
Foundation type: Independent foundation.
Financial data (yr. ended 06/30/13): Assets, $15,848,598 (M); expenditures, $1,052,332; qualifying distributions, $977,982; giving activities include $865,425 for 78 grants (high: $157,925; low: $500).
Purpose and activities: The foundation was established to support and promote quality education, health care, and human services programming for underserved populations. Special consideration is given to charitable organizations that serve the people of Grayson County, TX.
Fields of interest: Elementary school/education; Higher education; Health care; Youth development; Human services; Children/youth, services; Community/economic development; Economically disadvantaged.
Type of support: Capital campaigns; Building/renovation; Equipment; Program development.
Limitations: Giving primarily in Grayson County, TX, and its surrounding areas.
Publications: Application guidelines.
Application information: Application form required.
***Initial approach:* See foundation web site**
Copies of proposal: 6
Deadline(s): Mar. 1, June 1, Sept. 1 and Dec. 1
Board meeting date(s): Quarterly
Final notification: June 30, Sept. 30, Dec. 31 and Mar. 31
Directors: Ronnie Cole; Jerry Culpepper; Wayne E. Delaney, M.D.; Jack B. Lilley.
Trustee: Bank of America, N.A.
EIN: 756314114

3354
The Mary Alice Smith Charitable Foundation
c/o Harrison Interests Ltd.
712 Main St., Ste. 1900
Houston, TX 77002-3220 **(713) 632-1300**
***Contact:* Brenda Straube**

Established in 2003 in TX.
Foundation type: Independent foundation.
Financial data (yr. ended 05/31/13): Assets, $15,275,003 (M); expenditures, $752,148; qualifying distributions, $710,000; giving activities

include $710,000 for 8 grants (high: $455,000; low: $10,000).
Fields of interest: Historic preservation/historical societies; Health care; Alzheimer's disease; Aging, centers/services.
Limitations: Giving primarily in TX.
Application information: Application form not required.
Initial approach: **Letter**
Deadline(s): **None**
Director and Trustee:* Dan J. Harrison III*.
EIN: 200532337

3355
The Smith Foundation
(formerly The Lester and Sue Smith Foundation)
c/o Sharin A. Scott, Secy.
1001 Fannin St., Ste. 3850
Houston, TX 77002-6706

Established in 2002 in TX.
Donor: Lester H. Smith.
Foundation type: Independent foundation.
Financial data (yr. ended 12/31/12): Assets, $4,830,157 (M); gifts received, $11,259,425; expenditures, $7,559,999; qualifying distributions, $7,453,995; giving activities include $7,149,847 for 75 grants (high: $1,500,000; low: $98).
Purpose and activities: Giving primarily for education and medical research; funding also for the arts, social services, and Jewish temples.
Fields of interest: Museums; Arts; Higher education; Education; Hospitals (specialty); Health organizations, association; Medical research, institute; Cancer research; Breast cancer research; Human services; Jewish agencies & synagogues.
Limitations: Applications not accepted. Giving primarily in Houston, TX. No grants to individuals.
Application information: Contributes only to pre-selected organizations.
Board meeting date(s): Annually in May
Officers and Trustees:* Lester H. Smith,* Pres.; **Trish Morille, Exec. V.P.**; Sue A. Smith,* V.P.; Karla Neal, Secy.; Jill McDonald,* Treas.; M.S. Hendry; S.M. Smith.
EIN: 270040023
Other changes: At the close of 2012, the grantmaker paid grants of $7,149,847, a 167.1% increase over the 2010 disbursements, $2,676,582.

3356
South Plains Foundation
511 Ave. K
Lubbock, TX 79408-1800 (806) 747-9009
Contact: Sue Hudson, Exec. Dir.
FAX: (806) 762-8622; **E-mail: sueh24@gmail.com**; Main URL: http://www.southplainsfoundation.com

Established in 1989 in TX.
Foundation type: Independent foundation.
Financial data (yr. ended 06/30/13): Assets, $5,099,421 (M); expenditures, $286,422; qualifying distributions, $203,535; giving activities include $203,535 for grants.
Purpose and activities: Giving primarily for innovative programs providing effective health care services and in-service training in schools, institutions, and agencies in west Texas; giving also for a research grant program which encourages medical and behavioral science research focused on health care.
Fields of interest: Higher education, university; Medical school/education; Adult/continuing education; Medical care, rehabilitation; Health care; Mental health/crisis services; Health organizations, association; Medical research, institute; Kidney research; Food banks; Food distribution, meals on wheels.
Type of support: Program development; Seed money; Scholarship funds; Research; Grants to individuals; Matching/challenge support.
Limitations: Applications accepted. Giving limited to the Lubbock, TX, area.
Application information: See foundation website for complete application guidelines. Application form required.
Initial approach: Proposal
Deadline(s): **Varies**
Officers: Max Ince, Pres.; Sandy Ogletree, V.P.; Jim Moore, Secy.; Sue Hudson, Exec. Dir.
Board Member: Bill Miller.
Number of staff: 1 part-time professional.
EIN: 752294100

3357
Nelda C. and H. J. Lutcher Stark Foundation
P.O. Drawer 909
Orange, TX 77631-0909
Contact: Grant Dept.
Address for physical delivery: 601 W. Green Ave. Orange, TX 77630-5718; Main URL: http://www.starkfoundation.org/
E-Newsletter: http://www.starkfoundation.org/sign-up/

Incorporated in 1961 in TX.
Donors: H.J. Lutcher Stark†; Nelda C. Stark†.
Foundation type: Operating foundation.
Financial data (yr. ended 12/31/12): Assets, $564,419,643 (M); gifts received, $32,477; expenditures, $21,014,634; qualifying distributions, $17,020,580; giving activities include $2,851,945 for 16 grants (high: $1,905,000; low: $5,000), $49,500 for 21 grants to individuals (high: $6,500; low: $1,500), and $12,798,239 for foundation-administered programs.
Limitations: Applications not accepted. No grants to individuals (except local contest award winners), or for endowment funds or operating budgets.
Publications: Annual report.
Application information: Contributes only to pre-selected organizations. Unsolicited requests for funds not accepted. The foundation makes infrequent grants, and they are at the sole discretion of the Board of Directors.
Board meeting date(s): Quarterly
Officers and Directors:* Deborah L. Hughes,* Chair.; R. Frederick Gregory, M.D.*, Vice-Chair.; Walter G. Riedel III,* C.E.O. and Pres.; Clyde V. McKee III,* V.P., C.F.O, and Treas.; Elizabeth C. Turley, V.P., C.C.O. and Gen. Counsel; James R. Dunaway,* Secy.; Roy S. Wingate,* Dir. Emeritus; Laurence R. David; John Cash Smith; Ruby J. Wimberley.
Number of staff: 13 full-time professional; 3 part-time professional; 45 full-time support; 37 part-time support.
EIN: 746047440
Other changes: Deborah L. Hughes has replaced John Cash Smith as Chair. R. Frederick Gregory, M.D. has replaced Debbie Hughes as Vice-Chair.

3358
Sterling-Turner Foundation
(formerly Turner Charitable Foundation)
5850 San Felipe St., Ste. 125
Houston, TX 77057-3292 (713) 237-1117
Contact: Patricia Moser Stilley, Exec. Dir.
FAX: (713) 223-4638; **Email: pstilley@stfdn.org; additional contact: Jeannie Arnold, Exec. Asst., email: Jeannie.arnold@stfdn.org**; Main URL: http://sterlingturnerfoundation.org

Incorporated in 1960 in TX.
Donors: Isla Carroll Turner†; P.E. Turner†.
Foundation type: Independent foundation.
Financial data (yr. ended 12/31/12): Assets, $59,245,389 (M); expenditures, $2,948,250; qualifying distributions, $2,859,813; giving activities include $2,709,500 for 55 grants (high: $500,000; low: $2,000).
Purpose and activities: Giving for higher and secondary education, social services, youth, the elderly, fine and performing arts groups and other cultural programs, Catholic, Jewish, and Protestant church support and religious programs, hospitals, health services, AIDS research, hospices, programs for women and children, minorities, the homeless, the handicapped, urban and community development, civic and urban affairs, libraries, and conservation programs.
Fields of interest: Visual arts; Museums; Performing arts; Performing arts, theater; Historic preservation/historical societies; Arts; Education, association; Education, research; Education, fund raising/fund distribution; Elementary/secondary education; Child development, education; Secondary school/education; Higher education; Adult education—literacy, basic skills & GED; Libraries/library science; Education, reading; Education; Environment, natural resources; Hospitals (general); Medical care, rehabilitation; Health care; Substance abuse, services; Mental health/crisis services; Cancer; Heart & circulatory diseases; AIDS; Cancer research; Heart & circulatory research; AIDS research; Crime/violence prevention, domestic violence; Food services; Recreation; YM/YWCAs & YM/YWHAs; Children/youth, services; Child development, services; Family services; Residential/custodial care, hospices; Minorities/immigrants, centers/services; Homeless, human services; Community development, business promotion; Community/economic development; Protestant agencies & churches; Catholic agencies & churches; Jewish agencies & synagogues; Religion; Children; Youth; Aging; Minorities; African Americans/Blacks; Hispanics/Latinos; Women; AIDS, people with; Homeless.
Type of support: General/operating support; Annual campaigns; Capital campaigns; Building/renovation; Equipment; Land acquisition; Endowments; Debt reduction; Emergency funds; Program development; Conferences/seminars; Professorships; Publication; Seed money; Curriculum development; Fellowships; Scholarship funds; Research; Matching/challenge support.
Limitations: Applications accepted. Giving limited to Travis, Harris, Kerr, Fort Bend, and Tom Greene counties, TX. No grants to individuals.
Publications: Application guidelines; Financial statement.
Application information: Select application form on foundation web site depending on geographic county. In addition to emailing the application form, mail necessary documents to foundation. Application form and complete list of necessary documents available on foundation web site. Application form required.
Initial approach: On-line application
Copies of proposal: 1
Deadline(s): **Mar. 1 at 5:00 PM; if Mar. 1 falls on Saturday or Sunday proposals will be accepted until the following Monday by noon**
Board meeting date(s): First Tues. in Apr.

Officers and Trustees:* T.R. Reckling III,* Pres.; L. David Winston,* V.P.; Christiana R. McConn,* Secy.; Isla C. Reckling,* Treas.; Patricia Moser Stilley, Exec. Dir.; Carroll R. Goodman; Chaille W. Hawkins; Isla C. Jornayvaz; James S. Reckling; John B. Reckling; Stephen M. Reckling; T.R. "Cliff" Reckling IV; Thomas K. Reckling; E. Carroll Schuler; Bert F. Winston III; Blake W. Winston.
Number of staff: 2 full-time professional.
EIN: 741460482
Other changes: At the close of 2012, the fair market value of the grantmaker's assets was $59,245,389, a 37143.7% increase over the 2011 value, $159,075. For the same period, the grantmaker paid grants of $2,709,500, a 60.8% increase over the 2011 disbursements, $1,685,000.

3359
Stevens Family Charitable Trust
123 W. Mills Ave., Ste. 600
El Paso, TX 79901-1577

Established in 2009 in TX.
Donors: Jeff Allan Stevens; Sharon A. Sayre.
Foundation type: Independent foundation.
Financial data (yr. ended 12/31/12): Assets, $13,170,885 (M); expenditures, $5,763,957; qualifying distributions, $5,755,000; giving activities include $5,755,000 for 10 grants (high: $4,400,000; low: $5,000).
Fields of interest: Higher education.
Limitations: Applications not accepted. Giving primarily in AZ, TX, and WA.
Application information: Contributes only to pre-selected organizations.
Trustees: Timothy Allan Demore; Kevin Michael Reis; William Wallace Sheely; Alexandra Marie Stevens; **Colin Michael Stevens**; Jeff Allan Stevens; Sharon Ann Stevens.
EIN: 266824259

3360
Roy & Christine Sturgis Charitable Trust
c/o US Trust, Philanthropic Solutions
901 Main St., 19th Fl.
Dallas, TX 75202-3707 (214) 209-1965
Contact: David T. Ross, Sr. V.P.
E-mail: tx.philanthropic@ustrust.com; Main URL: http://www.bankofamerica.com/grantmaking

Established in 1981 in AR.
Donor: Christine Sturgis†.
Foundation type: Independent foundation.
Financial data (yr. ended 09/30/13): Assets, $43,386,583 (M); expenditures, $2,457,377; qualifying distributions, $2,041,845; giving activities include $1,858,000 for 61 grants (high: $200,000; low: $4,000).
Purpose and activities: The trust supports and promotes quality educational, cultural, human services, and health care programming for all people.
Fields of interest: Arts; Libraries/library science; Education; Hospitals (general); Health care; Health organizations, association; Medical research, institute; Food services; Human services; Homeless, human services; Engineering/technology; Science; Economically disadvantaged; Homeless.
Type of support: General/operating support; Capital campaigns; Building/renovation; Equipment; Endowments; Program development; Scholarship funds; Research; Matching/challenge support.
Limitations: Applications accepted. Giving primarily in AR and the Dallas, TX, area. No grants to individuals or for seminars; no loans.
Publications: Application guidelines; Program policy statement.
Application information: See trust web site for application form, guidelines and requirements, including specific grantmaking procedures for Texas applicants. Application form required.
Initial approach: **Use application form on foundation web site**
Deadline(s): **Mar. 1**
Board meeting date(s): Apr.
Final notification: Prior to June 30
Trustee Bank: Bank of America, N.A.
Number of staff: 1 part-time professional; 1 part-time support.
EIN: 756331832
Other changes: The grantmaker no longer lists a separate application address.
The grantmaker now makes its application guidelines available online.

3361
The Summerlee Foundation
5556 Caruth Haven Ln.
Dallas, TX 75225-8146 (214) 363-9000
Contact: John W. Crain, Pres.
FAX: (214) 363-1941; E-mail: info@summerlee.org; **Animal Protection Program address: c/o Melanie K. Anderson, Prog. Dir., 6660 Delmonico Dr., Ste. D429, Colorado Springs, CO 80919-1856, tel.: (800) 256-7515 or (719) 266-5460, fax: (719) 266-5459, e-mail: mal3@summerlee.org; Texas History Program contact: John W. Crain, Prog. Dir. at the foundation's Dallas, TX, address, tel., and fax, e-mail: jwcrain@summerlee.org**; Main URL: http://www.summerlee.org/

Established in 1988 in TX.
Donor: Annie Lee Roberts†.
Foundation type: Independent foundation.
Financial data (yr. ended 06/30/13): Assets, $67,026,636 (M); gifts received, $427; expenditures, $3,049,026; qualifying distributions, $2,964,007; giving activities include $1,823,580 for 83 grants (high: $500,000; low: $750).
Purpose and activities: Giving limited to 1) the alleviation of pain and suffering and the prevention of cruelty to animals; and 2) for the study, promotion, preservation, and documentation of all facets of TX history.
Fields of interest: History/archaeology; Historic preservation/historical societies; Animal welfare; Animals/wildlife, preservation/protection.
International interests: Canada; Mexico.
Type of support: Capital campaigns; Building/renovation; Equipment; Land acquisition; Program development; Conferences/seminars; Professorships; Film/video/radio; Publication; Seed money; Curriculum development; Fellowships; Internship funds; Research; Technical assistance; Matching/challenge support.
Limitations: Applications accepted. Giving primarily in TX for history programs; National and international giving for animal welfare program. No support for religious purposes. No grants to individuals.
Publications: Application guidelines; Grants list.
Application information: See foundation web site for programs, and application guidelines including deadlines and procedures. Faxed, e-mailed or incomplete applications will not be accepted. Application form not required.
Initial approach: Telephone, letter, e-mail
Copies of proposal: 1
Deadline(s): Deadlines vary every year. See foundation web site.
Board meeting date(s): Quarterly
Final notification: 3 months
Officers and Directors:* John W. Crain,* Pres. and Prog. Dir., TX history; Melanie Anderson,* V.P. and Prog. Dir., Animal Protection; Hon. David D. Jackson,* V.P.; Hon. Nikki DeShazo,* Secy.; Martha Benson, Treas.; Michael H. Collins; Ron Tyler, Ph.D.
Number of staff: 2 full-time professional; 1 full-time support.
EIN: 752252355

3362
The J. T. and Margaret Talkington Foundation
5010 University Ave., No. 433
Lubbock, TX 79413-4429 **(806) 792-1014**
***Contact:* Charlotte Park, Secy.-Treas.**
***E-mail:* info@talkingtonfoundation.com; Main URL: http://www.talkingtonfoundation.com**

Established in TX.
Donor: Margaret K. Talkington†.
Foundation type: Operating foundation.
Financial data (yr. ended 03/31/13): Assets, $93,767,793 (M); gifts received, $59,694,580; expenditures, $46,708,903; qualifying distributions, $40,598,144; giving activities include $40,534,645 for 44 grants (high: $12,500,000; low: $10,000).
Purpose and activities: Giving primarily for (but not limited to) arts and culture, community-based education, youth services, and other areas of community improvement.
Fields of interest: Arts; Higher education; Education; Human services; Youth, services.
Type of support: General/operating support.
Limitations: Giving primarily in Hockley and Lubbock counties, TX. No grants to individuals.
Publications: Application guidelines.
Application information: See foundation web site for specific application guidelines. Application form required.
Initial approach: **Summary Request Form which is available on foundation web site**
Copies of proposal: **6**
Officers and Directors:* Norton Baker,* C.E.O. and Pres.; Dr. Kitty S. Harris,* V.P.; **Alan Henry,* V.P.; Myrna Verner,* V.P.**; Charlotte Park,* Secy.-Treas.
EIN: 752733220
Other changes: For the fiscal year ended Mar. 31, 2013, the fair market value of the grantmaker's assets was $93,767,793, a 443.6% increase over the fiscal 2012 value, $17,249,856. For the same period, the grantmaker paid grants of $40,534,645, a 1719.5% increase over the fiscal 2012 disbursements, $2,227,812.
Dr. Kitty S. Harris, Alan Henry, and Myrna Verner are now V.P.s. Norton Baker is now C.E.O. and Pres.
The grantmaker now publishes application guidelines.

3363
Task Force Dagger Foundation
5900 S. Lake Forest Dr., Ste. 200
McKinney, TX 75070-2199
E-mail: info@taskforcedagger.org; Main URL: http://www.taskforcedagger.org/
Facebook: https://www.facebook.com/TaskForceDaggerFoundation
Flickr: https://www.flickr.com/photos/tfdaggerfoundation

YouTube: http://www.youtube.com/user/TFDaggerFoundation

Donors: Robert Mizell; Richard Downs; Raythoen; Jeffrey Herman; Markel Corporation.
Foundation type: Independent foundation.
Financial data (yr. ended 06/30/12): Assets, $86,360 (M); gifts received, $210,780; expenditures, $204,456; qualifying distributions, $193,107; giving activities include $180,228 for 15 + grants (high: $76,235; low: $248), and $12,879 for 7 grants to individuals (high: $3,962; low: $1,100).
Fields of interest: Recreation.
Type of support: Grants to individuals.
Limitations: Applications accepted. Giving primarily in TX.
Application information: Application form required.
Initial approach: Proposal
Deadline(s): None
Trustees: Frank Antenori; Benjamin Bethke; Charles Keith David; Rick L. Walker.
EIN: 800439987

3364
The Texas Area Fund Foundation, Inc.
207 W. Spring St.
P.O. Box 283
Palestine, TX 75802-0283 (903) 729-6048
***Contact:* Connie Fain, Admin.**
Main URL: http://www.txareafundfoundation.org
Facebook: https://www.facebook.com/pages/The-Action-Fund/507995375943228
Picasa Album: https://picasaweb.google.com/115520342924674979263

Established in 1999 in TX.
Foundation type: Community foundation.
Financial data (yr. ended 12/31/12): Assets, $1,374,956 (M); gifts received, $184,739; expenditures, $208,736; giving activities include $93,544 for 2+ grants (high: $35,100), and $57,250 for 15 grants to individuals.
Purpose and activities: The foundation seeks to help Palestine and Anderson County, TX, become a better place through directed funds and projects in these areas: Community Pride, Education, Recreation, Health Care, and Culture and the Arts.
Fields of interest: Arts; Higher education; Education; Environment, beautification programs; Environment; Health care; Recreation; Human services; Community/economic development.
Type of support: Scholarship funds; Grants to individuals; Scholarships—to individuals.
Limitations: Applications not accepted. Giving limited to Palestine and Anderson County, TX.
Application information:
Board meeting date(s): Monthly
Officers and Directors:* Jackson Hanks,* Pres.; David Barnard,* V.P., Governance; Cad Williams,* V.P.; Russ Gideon,* Secy.; Cecil Staples,* Treas.; Danice Brumley; Linda Dickens; Alan George; Allyson Mitchell; Freta Parkes; Dorenda Smith; Ahnise Summers; Jeff Watson.
EIN: 752834546

3365
Texas Pioneer Foundation
3911 Moores Ln.
Texarkana, TX **75503-2193**

Established in TX.
Donors: SASL; CTFSC.
Foundation type: Independent foundation.
Financial data (yr. ended 06/30/13): Assets, $50,566,418 (M); expenditures, $2,619,148; qualifying distributions, $2,432,960; giving activities include $1,973,392 for 80 grants (high: $115,740; low: $500), and $153,358 for 1 foundation-administered program.
Fields of interest: Higher education; Education.
Limitations: Applications not accepted. Giving primarily in TX. No grants to individuals.
Application information: Contributes only to pre-selected organizations.
Officers: Fred J. Markham, Pres.; Cliff Bandy, V.P.; Dick Cummins, V.P.; Margaret Lindsey, Secy.-Treas.
Director: Mary Borm, C.P.A.
EIN: 741966306

3366
The Thirteen Foundation
10235 Interstate 20
Eastland, TX 76448-5643

Donors: Farris Wilks; JoAnn Wilks.
Foundation type: Independent foundation.
Financial data (yr. ended 12/31/12): Assets, $97,579,811 (M); gifts received, $2,501,000; expenditures, $13,375,996; qualifying distributions, $13,170,445; giving activities include $12,841,324 for 47 grants (high: $2,242,857; low: $3,000).
Fields of interest: Christian agencies & churches.
Limitations: Applications not accepted. Giving primarily in TX.
Application information: Contributes only to pre-selected organizations.
Officer: Jonathan Francis, Exec. Dir.
Trustees: Farris C. Wilks; JoAnn Wilks.
EIN: 276977311
Other changes: At the close of 2012, the grantmaker paid grants of $12,841,324, a 203.4% increase over the 2011 disbursements, $4,232,680.

3367
Jim and Angela Thompson Foundation
(also known as The James and Angela Thompson Foundation)
6125 Luther Ln., No. 386
Dallas, TX **75225-6202**
***Contact:* Angela M. Thompson, Pres.**
Main URL: http://www.jatf.us

Established in 2006 in TX.
Donors: James R. Thompson; Clifford M. Weiner.
Foundation type: Independent foundation.
Financial data (yr. ended 12/31/12): Assets, $1,053,341 (M); gifts received, $1,540,000; expenditures, $730,811; qualifying distributions, $729,310; giving activities include $710,112 for 24 grants (high: $425,000; low: $100).
Purpose and activities: Giving primarily for children and family services, education, general aviation, free speech and animal services.
Fields of interest: Education; Animal welfare; Health organizations; Medical research; Children/youth, services; Family services; Space/aviation.
Limitations: Applications not accepted. Giving primarily in TX, with some emphasis on Dallas. No grants to individuals.
Application information: Contributes only to pre-selected organizations.
Officers: James R. Thompson, Chair.; Angela M. Thompson, Pres.; Andrew P. Lester, Secy.
Director: Kathleen E. Collisson.
EIN: 205856025

3368
Tingari-Silverton Foundation, Inc.
(also known as Silverton Foundation)
1000 Rio Grande St.
Austin, TX 78701-2014 (512) 782-0005
Contact: Andrea Crow
FAX: (512) 597-8518;
E-mail: info@silvertonfoundation.org; Main URL: http://www.silvertonfoundation.org

Established in 2000 in TX.
Donors: William P. Wood; Pamela M. Ryan; Silverton Partners, LP.
Foundation type: Independent foundation.
Financial data (yr. ended 12/31/12): Assets, $11,727,985 (M); expenditures, $562,401; qualifying distributions, $505,732; giving activities include $461,000 for 5 grants (high: $225,000; low: $1,000).
Purpose and activities: Giving primarily for disadvantaged and underserved populations, specifically for programs that provide services related to health, education, social services, and economic development.
Fields of interest: Education; Human services; Economic development.
Limitations: Applications accepted. Giving in Australia, East Timor, and the U.S., with primary emphasis on central TX. No grants to individuals, or for endowments, capital campaigns, ongoing operating expenses, existing deficits or lobbying.
Publications: Application guidelines; Annual report (including application guidelines); IRS Form 990 or 990-PF printed copy available upon request.
Application information: Full proposals are by invitation only, upon review of 1-page summary. Application form not required.
Initial approach: 1-page summary via regular mail or e-mail (preferred)
Deadline(s): None
Officers: Pamela M. Ryan, Chair.; **Karen Skelton, Pres.; Melissa D. Abel, Secy.**
EIN: 742936881
Other changes: Karen Skelton has replaced William P. Wood as Pres. Melissa D. Abel has replaced Andrew S. White as Secy.

3369
Tocker Foundation
3814 Medical Pkwy.
Austin, TX 78756-4002 (512) 452-1044
Contact: Darryl Tocker, Exec. Dir.
FAX: (512) 452-7690; E-mail: grants@tocker.org; Main URL: http://www.tocker.org

Established in 1964 in TX.
Donors: Phillip Tocker‡; Mrs. Phillip Tocker‡.
Foundation type: Independent foundation.
Financial data (yr. ended 11/30/12): Assets, $28,637,955 (M); expenditures, $1,766,085; qualifying distributions, $1,354,874; giving activities include $1,202,841 for 138 grants (high: $50,000; low: $165).
Purpose and activities: Giving primarily for the support, encouragement of and assistance to, small, rural libraries in Texas, which serve populations of 12,000 or less.
Fields of interest: Libraries/library science.
Type of support: Management development/capacity building; Equipment; Program development; Conferences/seminars.
Limitations: Applications accepted. Giving primarily in TX. **No grants to individuals, or for debt service, endowment funds, salaries, employee benefits, normal operating expenses, construction, electrical, flooring, phones or other items**

supported by the municipality, or e-books or membership fees to e-book providers.
Publications: Application guidelines; Informational brochure (including application guidelines).
Application information: Application form available on foundation web site. Application form required.
Initial approach: **Applicants are encouraged to contact the foundation's Director of Grants Mgmt., Karin Gerstenhaber, to discuss their project and provide a preliminary grant review**
Copies of proposal: 1
Deadline(s): **Jan. 15 and June 1for Library Grants (short extensions can be obtained by contacting the foundation via fax, letter, or e-mail); none for Library Automation Upgrade Program**
Final notification: 45-60 days after the application deadline
Officers and Directors:* Robert Tocker,* Chair.; Darryl Tocker, Exec. Dir.; Beth Fox; Mel Kunze; Barbara Tocker; Terry Tocker.
Number of staff: 1 full-time professional; 1 full-time support.
EIN: 756037871

3370
Toma Foundation
1415 Lavaca St.
Austin, TX 78701-1634 (512) 708-8662
Contact: Robert J. Tessen, Exec. Dir.
FAX: **(512) 708-1415**; Main URL: http://www.txosteo.org

Established in TX.
Donors: TMF Health Quality Institute; University of North Texas Health Science Center.
Foundation type: Independent foundation.
Financial data (yr. ended 12/31/11): Assets, $133,015 (M); gifts received, $26,145; expenditures, $410,135; qualifying distributions, $410,135; giving activities include $192,293 for 2 grants (high: $159,975; low: $32,318).
Fields of interest: Health organizations, association.
Limitations: Applications accepted. Giving primarily in TX. No grants to individuals.
Application information: Application form required.
Initial approach: Contact foundation for application form
Deadline(s): None
Officers: Jim W. Czewski, Pres.; Robert J. Tessen, Exec. Dir.
Directors: David Armbruster; Jobey D. Claborn; Robert C. Deluca; Steven Gates; Arthur J. Speece; Rodney Wiseman.
EIN: 752221904

3371
Max and Minnie Tomerlin Voelcker Fund
c/o Banks Smith
112 E. Pecan St., Ste. 3000
San Antonio, TX 78205-1516
Contact: **Emily Harrison Lijenwall**
FAX: (210) 224-7983;
E-mail: voelckerfund@scs-law.com; **Email for Emily Harrison Lijenwall: eliljenwall@scs-law.com**; Main URL: http://www.voelckerfund.org

Foundation type: Independent foundation.
Financial data (yr. ended 06/30/13): Assets, $68,276,438 (M); expenditures, $3,917,679; qualifying distributions, $3,038,689; giving activities include $2,954,275 for 22 grants (high: $344,528; low: $5), and $58,844 for 1 foundation-administered program.
Purpose and activities: The foundation funds charitable organizations engaged in medical research with emphasis on awarding grants to be given to research to find cures for cancer, heart disease, arthritis, muscular dystrophy, retinitis, and/or emasculative degeneration of the retina.
Fields of interest: Cancer research; Eye research; Heart & circulatory research; Medical research.
Type of support: Seed money; Matching/challenge support.
Limitations: Applications accepted. Giving primarily in San Antonio and Bexar County, TX, area. No grants to individuals, or for administrative costs, debt reduction, or fund-raising efforts.
Publications: Application guidelines; Grants list.
Application information: Full grant proposals are by invitation only, after review of LOI. Application guidelines available on fund web site.
Initial approach: Letter of inquiry (no longer than 4 pages)
Deadline(s): None
Trustees: David P. Berndt; Banks M. Smith; Forrester M. Smith III.
EIN: 742985834

3372
Topfer Family Foundation
(formerly The Morton & Angela Topfer Family Foundation)
3600 N. Capital of TX Hwy., Bldg. B, No. 310
Austin, TX 78746-3314 (512) 329-0009
Contact: Erica Gustafson, Prog. Off., Austin
FAX: (512) 329-6462;
E-mail: info@topferfoundation.org; Toll free tel.: (866) 897-0298; application e-mail: application@topferfoundation.org; Main URL: http://www.topferfamilyfoundation.org

Established in 2000 in TX.
Donors: Angela Topfer†; Morton Topfer.
Foundation type: Independent foundation.
Financial data (yr. ended 12/31/12): Assets, $42,845,219 (M); expenditures, $3,767,929; qualifying distributions, $3,500,778; giving activities include $3,246,651 for 245 grants (high: $250,000; low: $10).
Purpose and activities: The foundation is committed to helping people connect to the tools and resources needed to build self-sufficient and fulfilling lives.
Fields of interest: Education, drop-out prevention; Health care, infants; Pediatrics; Crime/violence prevention, child abuse; Employment, services; Employment, job counseling; Employment, training; Housing/shelter, aging; Youth development; Children/youth, services; Family services, parent education; Family services, adolescent parents; Economically disadvantaged.
Type of support: General/operating support; Continuing support; Capital campaigns; Building/renovation; Program development; Matching/challenge support.
Limitations: Applications accepted. Giving primarily in the greater metropolitan areas of Chicago, IL (particularly to organizations serving Cook and DuPage counties), and Austin, TX. No support for political campaigns or purposes, academic or scientific research. No grants to individuals, advertising, dinner, gala, or raffle tickets, school fundraisers or events; no loans.
Publications: Application guidelines.
Application information: The foundation has suspended accepting unsolicited proposals for the Chicago metropolitan area for the foreseeable future. If the applicant's supporting documents are too large to submit with the online application, please submit them as an e-mail attachment addressed to the application e-mail. Attachments that cannot be submitted electronically may be mailed. Applications available on foundation web site. Application form required.
Initial approach: Online grant application with required documents
Copies of proposal: 1
Deadline(s): None
Board meeting date(s): Mar., June, Sept., and Dec.
Officers and Directors:* Mort Topfer,* Chair. and Pres.; Alan Topfer,* V.P. and Treas.; Richard Topfer,* Secy.; Patricia Hayes, Ph.D.; Jacqueline Hynek; Steven L. Hynek; Bonnie Vozar.
Number of staff: 2 full-time professional; 1 part-time professional.
EIN: 742961304

3373
The Trull Foundation
404 4th St.
Palacios, TX 77465-4812 (361) 972-5241
Contact: E. Gail Purvis, Exec. Dir.
FAX: (361) 972-1109;
E-mail: gpurvis@trullfoundation.org; Main URL: http://www.trullfoundation.org

Established in 1967 in TX. Originally established in 1948 as The B.W. Trull Foundation.
Donors: R.B. Trull†; Florence M. Trull†; Gladys T. Brooking; Jean T. Herlin†; Laura Shiflett.
Foundation type: Independent foundation.
Financial data (yr. ended 12/31/12): Assets, $23,877,448 (M); expenditures, $2,445,834; qualifying distributions, $2,158,787; giving activities include $2,071,300 for 300 grants (high: $60,000; low: $500).
Purpose and activities: The foundation's grant focus areas include: concern for needs of the Palacios and Matagorda County, where the foundation has its roots; concern for children, channeling lives away from abuse, neglect, hunger, and poverty; concern for those persons and families devastated by the effects of substance abuse; concern for the coastal Texas environment, recognizing and including water issues, estuaries, birds, agriculture, and aquaculture.
Fields of interest: Museums; Elementary/secondary education; Child development, education; Elementary school/education; Secondary school/education; Higher education; Theological school/education; Adult education—literacy, basic skills & GED; Libraries/library science; Education; Environment; Substance abuse, services; Food services; Human services; Children/youth, services; Child development, services; Family services; Minorities/immigrants, centers/services; Homeless, human services; International relief; Community/economic development; Religion; Children/youth.
Type of support: Annual campaigns; Continuing support; Equipment; General/operating support; Management development/capacity building; Matching/challenge support; Program development; Publication; Scholarship funds; Seed money; Technical assistance.
Limitations: Applications accepted. Giving primarily in TX, with emphasis on the rural TX, south TX, and the Palacios and Matagorda County areas. No grants to individuals directly, or for capital building campaigns, endowment funds; no loans.
Publications: Application guidelines; Biennial report (including application guidelines); Grants list; IRS

Form 990 or 990-PF printed copy available upon request.
Application information: Proposals submitted by fax or e-mail not considered. Telephone inquiries about proposals and grants will be answered Mon.-Fri., from 8:00am-12:00pm. Application guidelines and proposal fact sheet available on foundation web site. Please do not send 990s, audits, CDs, videos, information concerning staff, Board of Dirs., plaques or certificates of appreciation. Application form required.
Initial approach: Download foundation's fact sheet from foundation web site
Copies of proposal: 1
Deadline(s): See foundation web site for application deadlines
Board meeting date(s): Usually twice a year; contributions committee 10 times per year and as required
Final notification: 1-2 months
Officers and Trustees:* **R. Scott Trull,* Chair.**; Cara P. Herlin,* Vice-Chair.; **Craig A. Wallis, Secy.-Treas.**; E. Gail Purvis, Exec. Dir.; Kristan Olfers, Advisory Tr.; Colleen Claybourn; Sarah H. Olfers.
Number of staff: 1 full-time professional; 1 full-time support.
EIN: 237423943
Other changes: R. Scott Trull has replaced Colleen Claybourn as Chair. Craig A. Wallis has replaced R. Scott Trull as Secy.-Treas.
Susan Herlin is no longer an Advisory Tr.

3374
Charles B. and Patricia A. Tubbs Charitable Trust
6642 Sewanee Ave.
West University Place, TX 77005-3750 (713) 666-8292
Contact: Patricia A. Tubbs, Tr.

Established in 2001 in TX.
Donors: Charles B. Tubbs; Patricia A. Tubbs.
Foundation type: Independent foundation.
Financial data (yr. ended 12/31/12): Assets, $15,964,386 (M); expenditures, $123,925; qualifying distributions, $16,335; giving activities include $16,335 for 1 grant.
Fields of interest: Higher education.
Limitations: Giving primarily in TX, with emphasis on Houston.
Application information: Application form not required.
***Initial approach:* Letter**
Deadline(s): None
Trustees: Maria L. Opalenik; Patricia A. Tubbs.
EIN: 766169925
Other changes: Leonor C. Torres is no longer a trustee.

3375
Tyler Foundation
c/o Tyler Technologies Inc.
5101 Tennyson Pkwy.
Plano, TX 75024 (972) 713-3700
Contact: Terri L. Alford, Secy.

Established in 1971 in TX.
Donors: Tyler Corp.; Tyler Technologies, Inc.
Foundation type: Company-sponsored foundation.
Financial data (yr. ended 12/31/12): Assets, $2,960,486 (M); expenditures, $197,529; qualifying distributions, $178,858; giving activities include $178,858 for 59 grants (high: $15,000; low: $75).
Purpose and activities: The foundation supports hospitals and services clubs and organizations involved with education, patient services, cystic fibrosis, breast cancer, diabetes, housing development, golf, and human services.
Fields of interest: Education; Health organizations; Youth development.
Type of support: General/operating support.
Limitations: Applications accepted. Giving primarily in areas of company operations, with emphasis on ME and Dallas, TX. No grants to individuals, or for scholarships or fellowships; no loans; no matching gifts.
Application information: Application form not required.
Initial approach: Proposal
Copies of proposal: 1
Deadline(s): None
Board meeting date(s): As required
Officers and Trustee:* John M. Yeaman,* Pres.; **Brian K. Miller, C.F.O. and Treas.**; Terri L. Alford, Secy.
EIN: 237140526

3376
Lamar Bruni Vergara Trust
106 Del Ct.
Laredo, TX 78041-2276 (956) 712-9190
Contact: J.C. Martin III, Tr.

Established in 1990 in TX.
Donor: Lamar Bruni Vergara†.
Foundation type: Independent foundation.
Financial data (yr. ended 12/31/12): Assets, $73,626,388 (M); expenditures, $2,070,586; qualifying distributions, $1,195,394; giving activities include $1,195,394 for grants.
Purpose and activities: Giving primarily for education; funding also for children, youth and social services.
Fields of interest: Higher education; Education; Human services; Children/youth, services; Christian agencies & churches.
Limitations: Giving primarily in Laredo, TX. No grants to individuals.
Trustees: J.C. Martin III; Pearl Assocs., LC.
EIN: 746374699
Other changes: Solomon Casseb is no longer a trustee.

3377
VHA Foundation, Inc.
(formerly The VHA Health Foundation, Inc.)
290 E. John Carpenter Freeway
Irving, TX **75062 (877) 847-1450**
FAX: (972) 830-0332;
E-mail: vhahealthfoundation@vha.com; Main URL: https://www.vha.com/sustainability2011/community.htm
VHA Foundation Celebrating 10 Years Video: http://vhatv.vha.com/media/2008/vha/hf/hf-full.asx

Donors: VHA Inc.; VHA Gulf States; Blessing Hospital Foundation; Parrish Medical Center; VHA Southeast; Aspirus Wausau Hospital; Carolina East Medical Center; Center Care Health; Cox Health; Doblin Group, Inc.; Fairmont Olympic Hotel; FMOL Health System; Grand View Hospital; Health East Care Bethesda Hospital; Karla Strange; Marion General Hospital; Maritan Memorial Hospital; Stormont-Vail Foundation; The Queen's Medical; University Hospital od Eastern Carolina; Yale New Haven Health.
Foundation type: Company-sponsored foundation.
Financial data (yr. ended 12/31/12): Assets, $822,475 (M); gifts received, $280,310; expenditures, $423,643; qualifying distributions, $401,943; giving activities include $397,643 for 12 grants (high: $292,000; low: $1,250).
Purpose and activities: The foundation supports programs designed to improve individual and community health. Special emphasis is directed toward programs designed to promote patient safety and provide disaster relief.
Fields of interest: Health care.
Type of support: General/operating support; Program development; Grants to individuals.
Limitations: Applications not accepted. Giving on a national basis.
Publications: Financial statement; Grants list.
Application information: Contributes only to pre-selected organizations.
Board meeting date(s): Feb. 19, Apr. 15, Oct. 16, and Dec. 11
Officers and Director: Curt Nonomaque, Chair.; **Colleen M. Risk,* Secy.**; Franco Dooley, Treas.
Number of staff: 1 full-time professional; 1 part-time professional.
EIN: 222710552

3378
Waco Foundation
1227 N. Valley Mills Dr., Ste. 231
Waco, TX 76710 (254) 754-3404
Contact: Ashley Allison, Exec. Dir.; Grantmaking: Nicole Wynter, Dir., Grants and Capacity Building
FAX: (254) 753-2887;
E-mail: info@wacofoundation.org; Additional tel.: (254) 752-9457; Grant inquiry e-mail: nwynter@wacofoundation.org; Main URL: http://www.wacofoundation.org
MAC College Money Program: https://www.facebook.com/wacomac
MAC College Money Program: https://twitter.com/wacomac

Established in 1958 in TX.
Foundation type: Community foundation.
Financial data (yr. ended 03/31/13): Assets, $67,828,605 (M); gifts received, $4,448,223; expenditures, $5,414,376; giving activities include $3,660,722 for 43 grants (high: $397,040), and $255,380 for 240 grants to individuals.
Purpose and activities: The foundation seeks to make a positive difference in the lives and future of the people in Waco and McLennan County through grantmaking, promotion of community philanthropy, and support of the nonprofit sector.
Fields of interest: Arts; Education; Environment; Animals/wildlife; Health care; Mental health/crisis services; Medical research, institute; Children/youth, services; Children, day care; Family services; Women, centers/services; Human services; Community/economic development; Infants/toddlers; Children; Youth; Disabilities, people with; Women; Economically disadvantaged; Homeless.
Type of support: Management development/capacity building; Capital campaigns; Building/renovation; Equipment; Program development; Seed money; Scholarship funds; Technical assistance; Matching/challenge support.
Limitations: Applications accepted. Giving limited to McLennan County, TX. **No support for religious activities or for medical or scholarly research. No grants to individuals (except for scholarships), or for annual campaigns, continuing support,**

membership fees, deficit financing, endowments, or student loans.
Publications: Application guidelines; Annual report; Financial statement; Grants list; Informational brochure; Newsletter.
Application information: Initial questions may be emailed or telephoned; visit foundation web site for application form and guidelines. Application form required.
Initial approach: Online submission
***Deadline(s):* Jan. 12, Apr. 1, June 1, Aug. 1, Sept. 12, and Nov. 1**
Board meeting date(s): 4th Wed. of each month
Final notification: Mid-June and mid-Nov.
Officers and Trustees:* Jim Haller,* Chair.; David Dickson,* Vice-Chair.; Cara Chase,* Secy.-Treas.; Ashley Allison, Exec. Dir.; Sam Allison; Betty Bauer; Steve Cates; Kyle Deaver; Lisa Jaynes; Kris Kaiser Olson; Maggie Stinnett.
Number of staff: 10 full-time professional; 3 part-time professional; 6 part-time support.
EIN: 746054628

3379
Crystelle Waggoner Charitable Trust
c/o U.S. Trust, Bank of America, N.A.
500 W. 7th St., 15th Fl.
Fort Worth, TX 76102-4772 (817) 390-6028
Contact: Mark J. Smith, Philanthropic Rels. Mgr.
E-mail: tx.philanthropic@ustrust.com

Established in 1982 in TX.
Donor: Crystelle Waggoner†.
Foundation type: Independent foundation.
Financial data (yr. ended 06/30/13): Assets, $18,550,443 (M); expenditures, $3,345,194; qualifying distributions, $3,004,634; giving activities include $2,939,405 for 42 grants (high: $250,000; low: $1,000).
Purpose and activities: Giving to Texas charitable organizations in existence before Jan. 24, 1982, including health organizations, the arts, and children, youth and social services.
Fields of interest: Arts; Education; Botanical gardens; Health organizations, association; Human services; Children/youth, services; Catholic federated giving programs.
Type of support: General/operating support; Continuing support; Annual campaigns; Capital campaigns; Building/renovation; Equipment; Endowments; Emergency funds; Program development; Professorships; Publication; Seed money; Curriculum development; Scholarship funds; Research.
Limitations: Applications accepted. Giving limited to TX. No support for organizations not in existence before Jan. 24, 1982. No grants to individuals, or for consulting services, deficit financing, or conferences; no loans.
Publications: Annual report (including application guidelines).
Application information: Application form required.
Initial approach: Letter
Copies of proposal: 1
Deadline(s): Mar. 31 and Sept. 30
Trustee: Bank of America, N.A.
EIN: 751881219
Other changes: For the fiscal year ended June 30, 2013, the grantmaker paid grants of $2,939,405, a 57.8% increase over the fiscal 2012 disbursements, $1,862,153.

3380
Richard Wallrath Educational Foundation
P.O. Box 1249
Centerville, TX 75833-1249
Application addresses: c/o Texas FFA, 614 E. 12th St., Austin, TX 78701, tel.: (512) 480-8045; c/o Texas 4-H, 2473 TAMU, College Station, TX 77843-2473, tel.: (979) 845-1213

Established in 2005 in TX.
Donor: Richard Wallrath.
Foundation type: Independent foundation.
Financial data (yr. ended 12/31/12): Assets, $6,902,886 (M); expenditures, $1,026,102; qualifying distributions, $955,803; giving activities include $952,875 for 73 grants (high: $391,875; low: $625).
Fields of interest: Higher education; Education.
Type of support: Scholarship funds.
Limitations: Applications accepted. Giving primarily in TX. No grants to individuals.
Application information: Consult Texas FFA and Texas 4-H for application guidelines. Application form required.
Officers: Robert Adam, Pres.; Richard Wallrath, V.P.; Patsy Murphy, Secy.; Pamela Dolenz, Treas.
EIN: 204091122

3381
Mamie McFaddin Ward Heritage Foundation
c/o Capital One Bank, N.A.
P.O. Box 3928
Beaumont, TX 77704-3928 **(409) 880-1415**

Established in 1976 in TX.
Donor: Mamie McFaddin Ward†.
Foundation type: Independent foundation.
Financial data (yr. ended 12/31/12): Assets, $38,533,906 (M); expenditures, $2,069,237; qualifying distributions, $1,580,262; giving activities include $1,580,262 for 21 grants (high: $816,542; low: $4,800).
Purpose and activities: Support for the McFaddin-Ward House historical site and other cultural programs, education, and human services.
Fields of interest: Museums; Historic preservation/historical societies; Education; Human services; Children/youth, services; Family services; Protestant agencies & churches.
Type of support: Capital campaigns; Building/renovation; Equipment; Seed money.
Limitations: Giving limited to southeast TX. No grants to individuals.
Publications: Application guidelines.
Application information: Application form provided by Capital One, N.A. Application form required.
Initial approach: Letter requesting application form
Copies of proposal: 9
Deadline(s): Aug. 31
Final notification: Nov.
Trustees: Eugene H.B. McFaddin; Ida M. Pyle; Rosine M. Wilson; Capital One Bank, N.A.
EIN: 746260525
Other changes: The grantmaker no longer lists a separate application address.

3382
Cecilia Young Willard Helping Fund
c/o Broadway National Bank
P.O. Box 17001
San Antonio, TX 78217-0001
Main URL: http://broadwaybank.com/wealthmanagement/FoundationCeciliaYoungWillard.html

Established in 1987 in TX.
Donor: Cecilia Young Willard Trust.
Foundation type: Independent foundation.
Financial data (yr. ended 05/31/13): Assets, $5,041,295 (M); expenditures, $260,651; qualifying distributions, $216,360; giving activities include $216,360 for grants.
Purpose and activities: Giving primarily for health organizations, and children, youth and social services.
Fields of interest: Performing arts, orchestras; Education; Health organizations; Human services; Children/youth, services.
Type of support: General/operating support; Continuing support; Annual campaigns; Capital campaigns; Building/renovation; Emergency funds; Curriculum development; Research.
Limitations: Applications accepted. Giving primarily in MD, NC, PA, and TX. No grants to individuals.
Application information: See foundation website for complete application guidelines. Application form required.
***Deadline(s):* May 31**
Trustee: Broadway National Bank.
EIN: 746350893
Other changes: The grantmaker now accepts applications.

3383
Lester and Beatrice Williams Foundation
168 Butler St.
Onalaska, TX 77360-7317 (936) 646-3335
***Contact:* Beverly Elliott, Dir.**
E-mail: info@thewilliamsfoundation.org; Main URL: http://www.thewilliamsfoundation.org

Established in 1997 in TX.
Donor: Beatrice Williams†.
Foundation type: Operating foundation.
Financial data (yr. ended 12/31/12): Assets, $4,883,039 (M); expenditures, $652,789; qualifying distributions, $522,425; giving activities include $291,310 for 5 grants (high: $150,000; low: $1,310).
Purpose and activities: A private operating foundation, giving primarily for education and community organizations.
Fields of interest: Education; Food services; Children/youth, services; Community/economic development; Protestant agencies & churches.
Limitations: Applications accepted. Giving primarily in Cameron, TX. No grants, loans or scholarships to individuals or for annual funds, galas, and fundraising activities, debt reduction, emergency or disaster relief efforts, administrative and operating expenses or for conferences, seminars or workshops.
Application information: Generally contributes to pre-selected organizations. Application information available on foundation web site. Application form not required.
Initial approach: Letter, fax or e-mail
Copies of proposal: 3
Deadline(s): None
Directors: Beverly Elliott; William Elliott; Amy Poe; Charles S. Poe.
EIN: 742847229

Other changes: The grantmaker no longer lists a separate application address. The grantmaker has moved from NJ to TX.

3384
Wilson-Lyon Family Foundation
Fort Worth, TX

The foundation terminated in 2011.

3385
Orien and Dr. Jack Woolf Charitable Foundation
612 Forest Bend Dr.
Plano, TX 75025-6105

Established in TX.
Donor: Orien Levy Woolf†.
Foundation type: Independent foundation.
Financial data (yr. ended 11/30/13): Assets, $4,154,390 (M); expenditures, $261,188; qualifying distributions, $203,050; giving activities include $203,050 for 6 grants (high: $60,700; low: $350).
Fields of interest: Arts; Education; Human services.
Limitations: Applications not accepted. Giving primarily in Dallas, TX.
Application information: Unsolicited requests for funds not accepted.
Officers: Roberta Shapiro, Pres.; Michelle Devereux, V.P.; John Broude, Secy.
Trustees: Katy Crowe; **Barbara Devereux**.
EIN: 272113885

3386
Lola Wright Foundation
c/o U.S. Trust
515 Congress Ave., 10th Fl.
Austin, TX 78701 (512) 397-2001
Contact: Amber Carden
E-mail: amber.carden@ustrust.com; **Main URL: http://fdnweb.org/lolawright**

Incorporated in 1954 in TX.
Donor: Johnie E. Wright†.
Foundation type: Independent foundation.
Financial data (yr. ended 12/31/12): Assets, $23,913,424 (M); expenditures, $1,352,702; qualifying distributions, $1,163,198; giving activities include $1,128,780 for 83 grants (high: $100,000; low: $1,600).
Purpose and activities: Giving to support arts and culture, children and youth, community development, education, health, religion, social and human services, and sports and recreation.
Fields of interest: Media/communications; Visual arts; Museums; Performing arts; Arts; Education, early childhood education; Child development, education; Higher education; Adult education—literacy, basic skills & GED; Education, reading; Education; Environment; Medical care, rehabilitation; Health care; Substance abuse, services; Health organizations, association; Heart & circulatory diseases; AIDS; Alcoholism; Legal services; Human services; Children/youth, services; Child development, services; Family services; Residential/custodial care, hospices; Aging, centers/services; Minorities/immigrants, centers/services; Homeless, human services; United Ways and Federated Giving Programs; Infants/toddlers; Children/youth; Adults; Aging; Disabilities, people with; Minorities; Economically disadvantaged; Homeless.
Type of support: Continuing support; Building/renovation; Equipment; Program development.
Limitations: Applications accepted. Giving limited to within a 50-mile radius of Austin, TX. No grants to individuals; generally no support for operating budgets.
Publications: Application guidelines; Program policy statement (including application guidelines).
Application information: Application guidelines and forms available on foundation web site. Application form required.
Initial approach: Use grant application following the proposal guidelines
Copies of proposal: 9
Deadline(s): Feb. 28 and Aug. 31
Board meeting date(s): May and Nov.
Final notification: May 15 and Nov. 15
Officers and Directors:* Wilford Flowers,* Pres.; Paul Hilgers,* V.P.; Ron Oliveira,* Secy.; Adrian Rhae Fowler; Carole Keeton Strayhorn; **Jay Stewart**.
EIN: 746054717
Other changes: James R. Meyers and Anita Motloch are no longer directors.

3387
The Zachry Foundation
P.O. Box 33240
San Antonio, TX **78265-3240** (210) 258-2663
FAX: (210) 258-2199;
E-mail: foundation@zachry.com; Main URL: http://www.zachryfoundation.org

Incorporated in 1960 in TX.
Donors: H.B. Zachry Co.; Zachry Construction Corp.; Capitol Aggregates.
Foundation type: Independent foundation.
Financial data (yr. ended 12/31/12): Assets, $10,992,185 (M); expenditures, $1,611,329; qualifying distributions, $1,546,803; giving activities include $1,535,000 for 10 grants (high: $1,000,000; low: $10,000).
Purpose and activities: The areas of primary interest include: education, arts and humanities, and health and social services throughout San Antonio, TX.
Fields of interest: Humanities; Arts; Elementary/secondary education; Higher education; Health care; Human services; Engineering/technology.
Type of support: Annual campaigns; Capital campaigns; Building/renovation; Equipment; Program development; Matching/challenge support.
Limitations: Giving limited to San Antonio, TX, except for higher education grants, which are made only in Texas. No grants to individuals, or for endowments.
Publications: Application guidelines.
Application information: The foundation is not currently accepting unsolicited requests for funds.
Board meeting date(s): Early summer
Officers and Trustees:* J.P. Zachry,* Pres.; H.B. Zachry, Jr.,* V.P.; Murray L. Johnston, Jr.,* Secy.; Charles Ebrom,* Treas.; Ellen Zachry Carrie; Cathy Obriotti Green; Anne Zachry Rochelle; David S. Zachry; John B. Zachry; Mollie Steves Zachry.
Number of staff: 1 full-time professional.
EIN: 741485544

UTAH

3388
The Ashton Family Foundation
199 N. 290 W., No. 100
Lindon, UT 84042-1810 (801) 226-1266
***Contact:* Dave Harkness**
FAX: (801) 443-2310; E-mail: dee@bessmark.com

Established in 1993 in UT.
Donor: Alan C. Ashton.
Foundation type: Independent foundation.
Financial data (yr. ended 12/31/12): Assets, $12,222,807 (M); expenditures, $889,146; qualifying distributions, $819,344; giving activities include $819,344 for 93 grants (high: $120,000; low: $1,500).
Purpose and activities: Support for religious institutions, as well as education, the arts and health.
Fields of interest: Arts; Education; Health organizations, association; Mormon agencies & churches.
Type of support: Program development; Equipment; General/operating support.
Limitations: Applications accepted. Giving primarily in UT.
Publications: Application guidelines.
Application information: Application form required.
Initial approach: Letter
Copies of proposal: 1
Deadline(s): 15th of month prior to meeting
Board meeting date(s): Quarterly
Final notification: Varies
Officer: Ralph Rasmussen, Exec. Dir.
Trustees: Adam Ashton; Alan C. Ashton; Annalura Ashton; Brigham Ashton; Elizabeth Ashton; Erin Ashton; Karen Ashton; Melissa Ashton; Morgan Ashton; Samuel Ashton; Spencer Ashton; Stephanie Ashton; Stephen Ashton; Traci Ashton; Emily Ann Eddington; Paul Eddington; Allison Norton; Toby Norton; Heath Westfall; Rebekah Westfall; Amy Jo Young; Chad Young.
Number of staff: 1 part-time support.
EIN: 870480108

3389
Ruth Eleanor Bamberger and John Ernest Bamberger Memorial Foundation
136 S. Main St., Ste. 418
Salt Lake City, UT 84101-1690 (801) 364-2045
Contact: Eleanor Roser, Chair.
E-mail: bambergermemfdn@qwestoffice.net; Main URL: http://www.ruthandjohnbambergermemorialfdn.org

Incorporated in 1947 in UT.
Donors: Ernest Bamberger†; Eleanor F. Bamberger†.
Foundation type: Independent foundation.
Financial data (yr. ended 12/31/12): Assets, $20,566,629 (M); expenditures, $1,465,329; qualifying distributions, $1,339,736; giving activities include $1,260,112 for 89 grants (high: $202,000; low: $2,000).
Purpose and activities: Giving primarily for secondary education, especially undergraduate scholarships for student nurses, and for schools, hospitals and health agencies, youth and child welfare agencies and a natural history museum.
Fields of interest: Museums (natural history); Elementary/secondary education; Higher education; Medical school/education; Nursing care; Health care; Human services; Children/youth, services.
Type of support: General/operating support; Continuing support; Equipment; Scholarship funds; Scholarships—to individuals.
Limitations: Giving limited to UT. No grants to individuals, except for scholarships to local students (which are not paid directly to the individual), or for endowment or building funds, research, or matching gifts.
Application information: The foundation is not accepting requests from new organizations at this time. Application form not required.
***Initial approach:* Letter to Ellie Roser, Chair.**
Copies of proposal: 6
Deadline(s): Application deadlines available on foundation web site; application deadlines vary from year to year.
Board meeting date(s): Biannually
Final notification: 2 months
Officer and Members:* Eleanor Roser,* Chair.; Julie Barrett; Clark P. Giles; Carol Olwell; Harris Simmons.
Number of staff: None.
EIN: 876116540

3390
Dialysis Research Foundation
5575 S. 500 E.
Ogden, UT 84405-6907 (801) 479-0351
FAX: (801) 476-1766

Established in 1984.
Foundation type: Independent foundation.
Financial data (yr. ended 12/31/12): Assets, $0 (M); gifts received, $500; expenditures, $1,002,587; qualifying distributions, $760,890; giving activities include $760,890 for 5 grants (high: $707,000; low: $8,364).
Purpose and activities: Giving limited to renal disease research and treatment, and for non-profit kidney disease foundations.
Fields of interest: Medical research, institute.
Type of support: Research.
Limitations: Giving primarily in UT.
Application information: The foundation no longer awards grants to individual patients.
Initial approach: Letter
Deadline(s): None
Officers and Board Members:* Fred Galvez,* Pres.; Mardee Hagen,* Secy. and Exec. Dir.; Todd Schenck,* Treas.; Adhish Agarwal; **Allen Berrett**; Neal Berube; Pam Corbridge; Kelvin Jackson; Lee L. Miles; Harry Senekjian, M.D.
EIN: 942819009

3391
Earth Stewardship Foundation
P.O. Box 369
Springville, UT 84663-0369
***Application address:* c/o Thomas W. Mower, 1325 W. Industrial Cir., Springville, UT 84663, tel.: (801) 704-6121**

Established in 2004 in UT.
Donor: Thomas E. Mower.
Foundation type: Operating foundation.
Financial data (yr. ended 12/31/12): Assets, $5,852,129 (M); gifts received, $20,304; expenditures, $360,657; qualifying distributions, $225,733; giving activities include $16,739 for 1 grant, and $208,994 for 3 foundation-administered programs.
Fields of interest: Environment; Animal welfare; Children.
Limitations: Applications accepted. Giving primarily in Los Angeles, CA.
Application information: Application form not required.
Initial approach: Proposal
Deadline(s): None
Directors: Richard L. Hill; Darick E. Mower; Thomas W. Mower.
EIN: 206511102

3392
Willard L. Eccles Charitable Foundation
P.O. Box 58198
Salt Lake City, UT 84158-0198 (801) 582-4483
Contact: Stephen Eccles Denkers, Exec. Dir.
FAX: (801) 582-2955; E-mail: steve@wleccles.org; Main URL: http://www.wleccles.org

Established in 1981 in UT.
Foundation type: Independent foundation.
Financial data (yr. ended 03/31/13): Assets, $31,210,202 (M); expenditures, $1,833,552; qualifying distributions, $1,702,980; giving activities include $1,354,321 for 54 grants (high: $690,000; low: $900).
Purpose and activities: Grants primarily for education, the environment, social services, basic science, and healthcare for the underserved.
Fields of interest: Higher education; Education; Environment; Health care; Human services.
Type of support: General/operating support; Capital campaigns; Building/renovation; Equipment; Land acquisition; Fellowships; Scholarship funds; Research; Matching/challenge support.
Limitations: Giving primarily in UT, with emphasis on Salt Lake City. No grants to individuals.
Application information:
***Initial approach:* Use online application process on foundation web site**
***Deadline(s):* Applications are accepted only in the 3-month window prior to the committee meeting Apr., May and June**
Board meeting date(s): Quarterly
Officer and Committee Members:* Stephen E. Denkers,* Exec. Dir.; **William E. Coit, M.D., Secy.**; Susan Coit; Julie Denkers; Stephen G. Denkers; Susan E. Denkers; Ann C. Goss; Barbara Coit Yeager.
Trustee: Wells Fargo Bank Northwest, N.A.
Number of staff: 1 full-time support.
EIN: 942759395
Other changes: William E. Coit is now Secy.

3393
Henry W. & Leslie M. Eskuche Charitable Foundation
c/o U.S. Bank, N.A.
170 S. Main St., Ste. 600
Salt Lake City, UT 84101-3600 **(801) 534-6045**
Contact: Michael Poulter; Songa Corbin

Established in 1978.
Donor: Leslie M. Eskuche†.
Foundation type: Independent foundation.
Financial data (yr. ended 02/28/13): Assets, $6,494,613 (M); expenditures, $393,447; qualifying distributions, $321,090; giving activities include $303,000 for 73 grants (high: $70,000; low: $1,000).
Purpose and activities: Giving primarily for education and health care.
Fields of interest: Elementary/secondary education; Higher education; Education; Hospitals (general); Health care; Human services; Children/

youth, services; Community/economic development; Christian agencies & churches.
Type of support: General/operating support; Capital campaigns; Building/renovation; Equipment; Scholarship funds.
Limitations: Applications accepted. Giving primarily in UT. No grants to individuals.
Publications: Application guidelines.
Application information: Application form required.
Initial approach: Proposal
Copies of proposal: 4
***Deadline(s):* None**
Board meeting date(s): Jan., May, and Sept.
Advisory Committee: Michael S. Bassis; Paula Julander; **Brian Levin-Stankevich**; Tracy D. Smith.
Trustee: U.S. Bank, N.A.
EIN: 876179296

3394
Val A. Green and Edith D. Green Foundation

c/o Val J. Green
4660 McKinney Ct.
Park City, UT 84098-8515 **(801) 560-9326**
***Main URL:* http://fdnweb.org/green**

Established in 1997 in UT.
Donors: Edith D. Green; Val A. Green.
Foundation type: Independent foundation.
Financial data (yr. ended 03/31/13): Assets, $8,227,625 (M); expenditures, $441,105; qualifying distributions, $423,449; giving activities include $259,500 for 17 grants (high: $70,000; low: $1,500).
Purpose and activities: The foundation's mission is to fund health care, medical research, local and higher education, and community projects in UT.
Fields of interest: Arts; Elementary/secondary education; Higher education; Health care, clinics/centers; Health care; Eye diseases; Medical research; Recreation, parks/playgrounds; YM/YWCAs & YM/YWHAs; Community/economic development.
Type of support: Capital campaigns; Equipment; Scholarship funds.
Limitations: Applications accepted. Giving limited to UT, with emphasis placed along the Wasatch Front. No support for foreign organizations. No grants to individuals.
Application information: See foundation web site for full application guidelines and requirements, including downloadable application form. Application form required.
Initial approach: Summary letter and application form
***Deadline(s):* Dec. 31**
Final notification: Within 30 to 60 days
Officer and Trustees:* Val J. Green,* Pres.; Edith D. Green; Brody Hamblin; Holly Hamblin; Kenlon Reeve.
EIN: 841407030

3395
The Alan and Jeanne Hall Foundation

5929 S. Fashion Pt. Dr., Ste. 300
Ogden, UT 84403-4684
***E-mail:* support@hallfoundation.com**; Main URL: http://www.hallfoundation.com/
Grants List: http://www.hallfoundation.com/grants/

Established in 1999 in UT.
Donors: Alan E. Hall; Jeannie Hall; Betty Nowak; Henry Nowak; Hall Family Investments, LLC.
Foundation type: Independent foundation.
Financial data (yr. ended 12/31/12): Assets, $13,973,811 (M); gifts received, $1,666,410; expenditures, $1,035,465; qualifying distributions, $956,968; giving activities include $956,968 for 25 grants (high: $241,183; low: $700).
Fields of interest: Arts; Education; Human services; Children/youth, services; Mormon agencies & churches.
Limitations: Applications accepted. Giving primarily in Ogden and Salt Lake City, UT. No grants to individuals.
Application information: See foundation web site for complete application guidelines.
***Initial approach:* E-mail**
Officer: Alan E. Hall, Pres.
Trustees: Curtis Funk; Megan Funk; Aaron Hall; Adam Hall; Annette Hall; Cami Hall; Christian Hall; Emily Hall; Eric Hall; Jeannie Hall; Kim Hall; Laura West; Matt West.
EIN: 870644251
Other changes: The grantmaker now accepts applications.

3396
The Richard K. and Shirley S. Hemingway Foundation

P.O. Box 11026
Salt Lake City, UT 84147-0026 (801) 363-5227
Contact: Brianne Johnson, Admin.
FAX: (801) 863-6157;
E-mail: briannej@xmission.com; Main URL: http://www.HemingwayFoundation.org

Established in 1987 in UT.
Donors: Richard Keith Hemingway†; Shirley Stranquist Hemingway†.
Foundation type: Independent foundation.
Financial data (yr. ended 12/31/12): Assets, $17,207,025 (M); gifts received, $9,000; expenditures, $1,053,111; qualifying distributions, $877,125; giving activities include $751,562 for 85 grants (high: $79,024; low: $500).
Purpose and activities: Giving primarily for the development of the arts; educational and developmental programs fostering positive values and behaviors relating to children, youth and family issues; the preservation, protection and enhancement of the environment; and educational and developmental programs fostering the implementation of healthier lifestyles. The foundation gives preference to programs, which have a direct and substantial human benefit over funding of capital campaigns or ordinary operations and focuses their resources upon projects that serve communities in the states of ID and UT.
Fields of interest: Arts; Education; Environment; Children/youth, services; Family services; Government/public administration.
Type of support: General/operating support; Continuing support; Building/renovation; Equipment; Emergency funds; Program development; Conferences/seminars; Curriculum development; Research; Consulting services; In-kind gifts.
Limitations: Applications accepted. Giving limited to ID and UT. No support for religious organizations. No grants to individuals, or for general operating expenses or building funds.
Application information: 2 copies of all additional forms/info. See foundation web site for application information and exact submission requirements. Failure to include necessary requirements will be grounds to reject application. The foundation does not accept hand-delivered applications. Application form required.
Initial approach: Letter or telephone for application form or download from web site
Copies of proposal: 2
Deadline(s): Mar. 1 and Sept. 1
Board meeting date(s): Apr. and Oct.
Officers and Trustees:* Ann Hemingway,* Chair., Investments; Helen Hemingway Cardon,* Pres.; Henry S. Hemingway,* Secy.; Jane Hemingway Mason.
Number of staff: 1 full-time professional.
EIN: 876205846

3397
The McCarthey Dressman Education Foundation

610 E. South Temple St., Ste. 110
Salt Lake City, UT 84102-1208 (801) 578-1260
FAX: (801) 578-1261;
E-mail: info@mccartheydressman.org; Main URL: http://www.mccartheydressman.org/
Blog: http://mccartheydressman.org/blog/
Facebook: https://www.facebook.com/MDLearningNetwork
Flickr: http://www.flickr.com/groups/1983862@N21/
Grants List: http://mccartheydressman.org/grant-recipients/
Twitter: http://twitter.com/MDLearning

Established in 1999 in UT. Classified as a private operating foundation in 2000.
Donor: Sarah McCarthey, Ph.D.
Foundation type: Operating foundation.
Financial data (yr. ended 12/31/12): Assets, $22,125 (M); gifts received, $51,285; expenditures, $248,061; qualifying distributions, $247,495; giving activities include $152,824 for 23 grants to individuals (high: $11,000; low: $680).
Purpose and activities: The foundation's mission is to serve as a catalyst in maximizing the skills and creativity of educators at the k-12 levels and in cultivating pioneering approaches to teaching that result in dynamic student learning. The foundation sponsors proposals that enhance student learning and educational quality, paying particular attention to those that best serve the at-risk and under-funded.
Fields of interest: Secondary school/education; Higher education; Education, services.
Limitations: Applications accepted. Giving primarily in UT; some giving in WV, AZ, GA, and OK.
Application information: See foundation web site. Application form required.
Deadline(s): Application deadlines available on foundation web site
Officers and Trustees:* Sarah McCarthey, Ph.D.*, Pres.; Mark Dressman, Ph.D.*, V.P.; Judy Abbott, Ph.D.; Jane Abe, MS; Michael Borish, MBA; Carmen Gonzales, Ph.D.; Carolyn Schubach, MA; Patrick Scott, Ph.D.; Kip Tellez, Ph.D.; Jo Worthy, Ph.D.
EIN: 870646265

3398
The Holly and Bronco Mendenhall Foundation

(formerly The Fully Invested Foundation)
11672 N. Pennbrooke Ln.
Highland, UT 84003

Donor: Bronco Mendenhall.
Foundation type: Independent foundation.
Financial data (yr. ended 12/31/12): Assets, $118,361 (M); gifts received, $240,769; expenditures, $190,141; qualifying distributions,

$89,746; giving activities include $89,746 for grants.
Fields of interest: Housing/shelter; Religion.
Limitations: Applications not accepted. Giving primarily in UT.
Application information: Unsolicited requests for funds not accepted.
Trusteees: Bronco Mendenhall; Holly Mendenhall; Paul Mendenall; C. Stephen King; Dan Van Woerkom.
EIN: 263144586
Other changes: The grantmaker no longer lists a URL address.

3399
Morrell Family Charities
3448 S. 5700 W.
Wellsville, UT 84339-9204 (801) 450-9021

Established in 2005 in UT.
Foundation type: Independent foundation.
Financial data (yr. ended 12/31/12): Assets, $738 (M); gifts received, $185,211; expenditures, $197,262; qualifying distributions, $196,029; giving activities include $127,623 for 17 grants (high: $25,000; low: $345), and $74,736 for 4 foundation-administered programs.
Purpose and activities: The objectives of the foundation are: 1) To alleviate poverty and suffering worldwide, but with special emphasis on children; 2) to support individuals with supplies, expenses, and a small stipend in efforts to travel to various destinations to perform service to the poor and needy; and 3) to provide donations to LDS Church and other charities to help with various efforts including missionary work.
Fields of interest: Mormon agencies & churches; Children; Economically disadvantaged.
Limitations: Applications accepted. Giving primarily in UT.
Application information: Application form required.
Deadline(s): None
Officers and Trustees:* Cherish Newman,* Chair.; Katie Yanguez,* Pres.; Heidi Brown, Secy.; Amy Summy, Secy.; Kelly D. Newman, Treas.
EIN: 204153684
Other changes: The grantmaker no longer lists an E-mail address or a URL address.

3400
Original Sorenson Legacy Foundation
(formerly The Sorenson Legacy Foundation)
Salt Lake City, UT

The foundation terminated on Dec. 28, 2012 and distributed its assets to Sorenson Legacy Foundation and Sorenson Impact Foundation.

3401
The Park City Foundation
1790 Bonanza Dr., Ste. 250
Park City, UT 84060 (435) 214-7475
***Contact:* For grants: Katie Wright, Exec. Dir.**
FAX: (435) 214-7489;
E-mail: katie@theparkcityfoundation.org;
Application address: P.O. Box 681499, Park City, UT 84068; Grant application e-mail: katie@theparkcityfoundation.org; Main URL: http://www.theparkcityfoundation.org
Facebook: https://www.facebook.com/parkcitycommunityfoundation

Established in 2003 in UT.
Donor: Bradley A. Olch.
Foundation type: Community foundation.
Financial data (yr. ended 12/31/11): Assets, $3,164,645 (M); gifts received, $934,363; expenditures, $798,286; giving activities include $321,307 for 109 grants (high: $37,000), and $53,235 for 6 grants to individuals.
Purpose and activities: The foundation works to connect private philanthropy with the greater Park City community by optimizing the impact of each charitable gift. As a community foundation, it seeks to offer strategies and services for donors, and support to strengthen local nonprofits for the betterment of the community.
Fields of interest: Arts; Education; Environment; Animals/wildlife; Health care; Recreation; Human services; Community/economic development; Foundations (community); Public affairs.
Limitations: Applications accepted. Giving primarily in the greater Park City region of Summit County, UT. No support for grants that further political or religious doctrine, or political campaigns. No grants to individuals (except for scholarships), or for debt reductions or retiring past operating deficits, fellowships, litigation, endowment funds, or graduate or post-graduate research; no loans.
Application information: Visit foundation web site for application guidelines; qualified nonprofit organizations will be asked to submit a full application based on proposal. Application form required.
Initial approach: Submit proposal (300-400 words or less) via e-mail
***Deadline(s):* Apr. 4**
Officers and Directors:* Jack Mueller,* Chair.; Katie Wright, Exec. Dir.; John D. Cumming, Dir. Emeritus; Hon. Judith M. Billings; William H. Coleman; Christopher M. Conabee; J. Taylor Crandall; Mark J. Fischer; **Diane Foster**; Jody Gross; **Thomas Grossman**; Cathy Hill; Jolie Iacobelli; Becky Kearns; Robert M. La Forgia; Elizabeth Lockette; Hank Louis; Jon Monk; Franklin L. Morton; Emily Scott Pottruck; Sydney Reed; Bob Richer; Mike Ruzek; Stephen R. Sloan; Stephen A. Tyler; Linda Warren.
EIN: 300171971
Other changes: Jack Mueller has replaced John D. Cumming as Chair.
Katie Wright is now Exec. Dir. John D. Cumming is now Dir. Emeritus. Susan Graham Mayo, Emily Scott Pottruck, and Christa Riepe are no longer directors.

3402
S. J. & Jessie E. Quinney Foundation
P.O. Box 45385
Salt Lake City, UT 84145-0385
Contact: Herbert C. Livsey, Dir.

Established about 1982 in UT.
Donor: S.J. Quinney†.
Foundation type: Independent foundation.
Financial data (yr. ended 12/31/12): Assets, $43,809,176 (M); gifts received, $5,000; expenditures, $1,743,556; qualifying distributions, $1,191,921; giving activities include $1,137,500 for 24 grants (high: $530,000; low: $1,000).
Purpose and activities: Giving primarily for higher and other education; support also for social services and cultural programs, including the performing arts.
Fields of interest: Performing arts; Arts; Higher education; Education; Human services.
Type of support: General/operating support.
Limitations: Applications not accepted. Giving primarily in UT. No grants to individuals.
Application information: Contributes only to pre-selected organizations.
Directors: Frederick Q. Lawson; Peter Q. Lawson; Stephen B. Nebeker; **Ellen E. Rossi**.
Trustees: Clark P. Giles; Charles H. Livsey; Herbert C. Livsey; David E. Quinney; David E. Quinney III.
EIN: 870389312
Other changes: Ellen S. Erlingsson is no longer a director.

3403
Theodore & Elizabeth Schmidt Family Foundation
2115 Connor Park Cove
Salt Lake City, UT 84109-2468

Established in 1998 in CA.
Donors: Elizabeth Schmidt; Theodore Schmidt, Jr.
Foundation type: Independent foundation.
Financial data (yr. ended 07/31/13): Assets, $4,361,423 (M); expenditures, $297,148; qualifying distributions, $254,150; giving activities include $254,150 for 43 grants (high: $50,000; low: $300).
Purpose and activities: Giving primarily for education and hospitals; funding also for human services.
Fields of interest: Performing arts; Arts; Higher education; Education; Hospitals (general); Cancer research; Human services; American Red Cross; YM/YWCAs & YM/YWHAs; United Ways and Federated Giving Programs; Christian agencies & churches; Mormon agencies & churches.
Limitations: Applications not accepted. Giving primarily in CA and UT. No grants to individuals.
Application information: Contributes only to pre-selected organizations.
Officers: Theodore Schmidt, Pres.; Sandefur Schmidt, Treas.
EIN: 680422838
Other changes: The grantmaker no longer lists a phone.

3404
Semnani Family Foundation
(formerly Semnani Foundation)
P.O. Box 11623
Salt Lake City, UT 84147-0623 (801) 321-7725
Contact: Khosrow B. Semnani, Dir.
E-mail: info@semnanifamilyfoundation.org; **E-mail for foundation program inquiries: programs@semnanifamilyfoundation.org**; Main URL: http://www.semnanifamilyfoundation.org

Established in 1991 in UT.
Donor: Khosrow B. Semnani.
Foundation type: Independent foundation.
Financial data (yr. ended 12/31/12): Assets, $58,272,444 (M); gifts received, $1,978,553; expenditures, $2,735,327; qualifying distributions, $2,430,674; giving activities include $2,428,280 for 55 grants (high: $1,500,000; low: $250).
Purpose and activities: Giving primarily for promoting health, education, and disaster relief for marginal communities in the United States and around the world. Given the importance of religion to the life of many immigrant communities and refugees, the foundation has worked closely with religious communities and leaders to promote interfaith dialogue, understanding and integration. It has helped immigrant and refugee communities build houses of worship, extend and expand social services, and fight prejudice. The foundation's program interests include: social issues, health,

children, women, disaster relief, Iranian-American issues, religious tolerance and interfaith dialogue, and advancing health, education and welfare of the people of UT.
Fields of interest: Arts, cultural/ethnic awareness; Higher education; Education; Health care, clinics/centers; Health organizations, association; Medical research, institute; Human services; International relief; Foundations (private grantmaking); Foundations (public); Islam; Religion, interfaith issues.
Limitations: Giving primarily in UT, with emphasis on Salt Lake City; some funding also in PA. No grants to individuals.
Application information: Application form not required.
Initial approach: Letter
Deadline(s): None
Directors: Nolan Karras; Shirin Kia; Ghazelah Semnani; Khosrow Semnani; Taymour Semnani.
EIN: 742639794

3405
Utah Medical Association Foundation
310 E. 4500 S.
Salt Lake City, UT 84107-4250 (801) 747-3500
Contact: Michelle S. McOmber, Secy.-Treas.
E-mail: **michelle@utahmed.org; Main URL: http://www.utahmed.org/WCM/Health_Promotion/UMA_Foundation/wcm/_HealthPromotion/Foundation3.aspx**

Foundation type: Independent foundation.
Financial data (yr. ended 12/31/12): Assets, $4,105,319 (M); gifts received, $4,650; expenditures, $323,263; qualifying distributions, $263,437; giving activities include $250,033 for 28 grants (high: $30,000; low: $2,500).
Fields of interest: Education; Animals/wildlife; Health care.
Limitations: Applications accepted. Giving primarily in UT.
Application information: See foundation website for complete application guidelines. Application form required.
Initial approach: Proposal
Deadline(s): Apr. 15, Oct. 15
Officers: Scott A. Leckman, M.D., Chair.; Michelle S. McOmber, Secy.-Treas.
Directors: Stewart E. Barlow, M.D.; George W. Cannon, M.D.; F. James Cowan; John Gates; Richard Home; Val B. Johnson, M.D.; Richard J. Sperry, M.D.
EIN: 876122299

3406
Yamagata Foundation
1250 E. 200 S., Ste. 2D
Lehi, UT **84043-1483** (801) 326-3500
Contact: John Nitta, Dir.

Established in 2004 in UT.
Donor: Gene H. Yamagata.
Foundation type: Independent foundation.
Financial data (yr. ended 12/31/12): Assets, $43,030 (M); gifts received, $415,042; expenditures, $577,081; qualifying distributions, $568,720; giving activities include $568,720 for grants.
Fields of interest: Higher education; Mormon agencies & churches.
Limitations: Applications accepted. Giving primarily in HI and UT.
Application information: Application form not required.
Deadline(s): None
Directors: Matt Hawkins; John Nitta; Rick Nitta; Scott Oelkers; David M. Senior.
EIN: 201078807

VERMONT

3407
Ben & Jerry's Foundation, Inc.
30 Community Dr.
South Burlington, VT 05403-6828 (802) 846-1500
Contact: Lisa Pendolino, Managing Dir.
E-mail: info@benandjerrysfoundation.org; Main URL: http://www.benandjerrysfoundation.org
Grants List: http://www.benandjerrysfoundation.org/grantees.html
Philanthropy's Promise: http://www.ncrp.org/philanthropys-promise/who

Established in 1985 in NY.
Donors: Ben & Jerry's Homemade, Inc.; Ben & Jerry's Corp.; Bennett Cohen.
Foundation type: Company-sponsored foundation.
Financial data (yr. ended 12/31/12): Assets, $5,184,496 (M); gifts received, $2,272,896; expenditures, $2,252,045; qualifying distributions, $2,216,996; giving activities include $2,016,922 for 568 grants (high: $100,000).
Purpose and activities: The foundation promotes progressive social change by supporting grassroots organizations that utilize community organizing strategies to advance social and environmental justice.
Fields of interest: Environment, natural resources; Environment; Agriculture, community food systems; Youth, services; Human services; Civil/human rights, immigrants; Civil rights, race/intergroup relations; Labor rights; Civil/human rights; Community/economic development; Public policy, research; Public affairs, citizen participation; Minorities; Economically disadvantaged.
Type of support: General/operating support; Management development/capacity building; Program development; Employee matching gifts.
Limitations: Applications accepted. Giving on a national basis, with emphasis on St. Albans, South Burlington, and Waterbury, VT. No support for schools, colleges or universities, state agencies, businesses or business associations, other foundations or regranting organizations, organizations and programs that are focused or based outside of the United States, or organizations with annual budgets over $500,000. No grants to individuals, or for scholarship programs, advocacy programs, discretionary or emergency funds, research projects, capital campaigns, religious programs, international or foreign-based programs, government sponsored programs, social service programs, or arts and media programs.
Publications: Application guidelines; Annual report; Grants list; IRS Form 990 or 990-PF printed copy available upon request; Program policy statement.
Application information: A full proposal may be requested at a later date for the Grassroots Organizing for Social Change Program. Additional information and a site visit may be requested for Vermont Capacity Building Grant Program. Support is limited to 1 contribution per organization during any given year. Application form required.
Initial approach: **Complete online letter of interest for Grassroots Organizing for Social Change Program; complete online application for Vermont Capacity Building Grant Program, Vermont Economic Justice Grant Program, and Vermont Community Action Teams Grant Program**
Deadline(s): **Mar. 21 and Oct. 15 for Grassroots Organizing for Social Change Program; May 5 for Vermont Capacity Building Grant Program; July 3 for Vermont Economic Justice Program; None for Vermont Community Action Teams**
Board meeting date(s): Monthly
Final notification: **Oct. for Vermont Capacity Building Grant Program**
Officers and Trustees:* Jerry Greenfield,* Pres.; Elizabeth Bankowski,* Secy.; Jeffrey Furman,* Treas.; Anuradha Mittal.
Number of staff: 2 part-time professional; 1 full-time support.
EIN: 030300865

3408
Better and Better Foundation
(formerly Green Mountain Coffee Roasters Foundation)
Burlington, VT

The foundation terminated June 28, 2013 and transferred its assets to the Stiller Family Foundation.

3409
Harris & Frances Block Foundation Inc.
c/o Betsy Chodorkoff
491 Ennis Hill Rd.
Marshfield, VT 05658-8250 **(802) 426-2026**
E-mail: info@blockfound.org; Main URL: http://www.blockfound.org

Established in 2001 in VT.
Donor: Carol Maurer†.
Foundation type: Independent foundation.
Financial data (yr. ended 12/31/12): Assets, $6,682,260 (M); gifts received, $470,000; expenditures, $453,845; qualifying distributions, $359,000; giving activities include $359,000 for grants.
Purpose and activities: Giving primarily in the areas of economic justice, environmental protection, arms control, community development, and historic preservation.
Fields of interest: Historic preservation/historical societies; Environment, natural resources; International affairs, arms control; Civil/human rights; Economic development.
Limitations: Applications accepted. Giving in the U.S., primarily in VT; giving also in CT, MA, NC, and VA.
Application information: Complete application guidelines available on foundation web site. Application form required.
Initial approach: Letter of inquiry
Deadline(s): None
Officers: Nancy M. Sluys, V.P.; Diane Maurer Schatz, Secy.; Betsy M. Chodorkoff, Treas.
EIN: 311784246

3410
General Education Fund, Inc.
(doing business as The Curtis Fund)
c/o Merchants Trust Co.
P.O. Box 8490
Burlington, VT 05402-8490
Contact: Dan Stanyon
***E-mail:* jboutin@thecurtisfund.org**; Main URL: http://www.thecurtisfund.org/
E-Newsletter: http://www.thecurtisfund.org/e-newsletter/
Facebook: http://www.facebook.com/pages/The-Curtis-Fund/176700985676729
Twitter: http://twitter.com/thecurtisfund
Application address: General Education Fund (GEF), Inc. Scholarship - NEW, VSAC Scholarship Programs, 10 E. Allen St., P.O. Box 2000, Winooski, VT, 05404-2601

Incorporated in 1918 in VT.
Donors: Emma Eliza Curtis†; Lorenzo E. Woodhouse†.
Foundation type: Independent foundation.
Financial data (yr. ended 07/30/13): Assets, $31,262,653 (M); gifts received, $1,901; expenditures, $1,715,252; qualifying distributions, $1,565,638; giving activities include $1,512,494 for grants to individuals, and $52,874 for foundation-administered programs.
Purpose and activities: Provides undergraduate scholarships to Vermont high school graduates, who are nominated by a Vermont Student Assistance Corporation (VSAC) outreach counselor, who will attend an accredited postsecondary school approved for federal Title IV funding, who are enrolled in an undergraduate associate's or bachelor's degree program, and who demonstrate financial need.
Fields of interest: Higher education.
Type of support: Scholarships—to individuals.
Limitations: Giving limited to VT residents. No grants for building or endowment funds, operating budgets, or special projects.
Publications: Newsletter.
Application information: The foundation does not accept direct applications from students. The Vermont Student Assistance Corporation (VSAC) determines, through its Outreach program, which students meet the criteria for assistance. See foundation web site for additional information.
Initial approach: Contact the Vermont Student Assistance Corporation (VSAC)
Trustees: Joseph Boutin; Mike Breen; J. Churchill Hindes, Ph.D.; Spencer Knapp; Amy Mellencamp.
EIN: 036009912

3411
Philip S. Harper Foundation
P.O. Box 96
Weston, VT 05161-0086

Incorporated in 1953 in IL.
Donors: Philip S. Harper; Harper-Wyman Co.
Foundation type: Independent foundation.
Financial data (yr. ended 09/30/13): Assets, $6,817,838 (M); expenditures, $365,384; qualifying distributions, $331,828; giving activities include $304,500 for 170 grants (high: $15,000; low: $250).
Fields of interest: Media/communications; Arts; Elementary/secondary education; Higher education; Environment, natural resources; Health care; Health organizations, association; Medical research, institute; Legal services; Human services; Children/youth, services; Family services; Public affairs; Christian agencies & churches; Protestant agencies & churches; Women; Girls; Economically disadvantaged.
Limitations: Applications not accepted. Giving primarily in CA, CO, Washington, DC, FL, Atlanta, GA, IA, Chicago, IL, MA, MI, New York, NY, VA, and VT. No grants to individuals.
Application information: Unsolicited requests for funds not accepted.
Officers: Lamar Williams, Pres.; Kirk Harper William, V.P.; Andrew Harper, Secy.-Treas.
Director: Steven Palumbo.
EIN: 366049875
Other changes: Lamar Williams has replaced Anne Harper as Pres.

3412
Lintilhac Foundation
886 N. Gate Rd.
Shelburne, VT 05482-7211 (802) 985-4106
Contact: Crea S. Lintilhac, Dir.
FAX: (802) 985-3725; E-mail: lint@together.net; Main URL: http://www.lintilhacfoundation.org
Grants List: http://www.lintilhacfoundation.org/biennialreport.html

Established in 1975.
Donors: Claire Malcolm Lintilhac†; Claire D. Lintilhac Annuity Trust I; Claire D. Lintilhac Annuity Trust II.
Foundation type: Independent foundation.
Financial data (yr. ended 06/30/12): Assets, $19,055,816 (M); gifts received, $329,446; expenditures, $1,193,777; qualifying distributions, $1,053,649; giving activities include $968,558 for 129 grants (high: $100,000; low: $100).
Purpose and activities: The foundation's central purpose is to support organizations that are making sustainable, positive change for Vermont's environment and its people and providing Vermonters the information and resources they need to control their environmental destinies and strong traditions of democratic engagement.
Fields of interest: Arts; Education; Environment; Health care; Community/economic development; Science, research.
Type of support: General/operating support; Continuing support; Capital campaigns; Land acquisition; Program development; Conferences/seminars; Professorships; Seed money; Fellowships; Scholarship funds; Research; Matching/challenge support.
Limitations: Applications accepted. Giving limited to VT. No support for religious organizations. No grants to individuals.
Publications: Biennial report; Biennial report (including application guidelines); Grants list.
Application information: Applicants must submit proposals using the online application system found on the foundation website. Hard copy proposals will not be accepted. Application guidelines available on foundation web site.
Initial approach: Proposal
Deadline(s): See foundation web site for current deadlines
Final notification: 1-3 months
Officers and Directors:* Louise S. Lintilhac,* Pres.; William S. Lintilhac,* V.P.; Philip M. Lintilhac,* Secy.-Treas.; Raeman P. Sopher, Dir. Emeritus; **Crea S. Lintilhac**; Paul S. Lintilhac.
Number of staff: 1 full-time support.
EIN: 510176851
Other changes: Louise S. Lintilhac has replaced Philip M. Lintilhac as Pres. William S. Lintilhac has replaced Louise S. Lintilhac as V.P. Philip M. Lintilhac has replaced Crea S. Lintilhac as Secy.-Treas.

3413
McKenzie Family Charitable Trust
P.O. Box 285
Putney, VT 05346-0285
Contact: J. Michael McKenzie, Tr.
***E-mail:* torin.koester@gmail.com; Main URL: http://mckenziefamilycharitabletrust.org/**

Established in 1993 in VT.
Donor: J. Michael McKenzie.
Foundation type: Independent foundation.
Financial data (yr. ended 12/31/12): Assets, $12,757,944 (M); gifts received, $650,000; expenditures, $744,787; qualifying distributions, $543,435; giving activities include $448,698 for 11 grants (high: $205,129; low: $2,000).
Purpose and activities: Giving to public education, with an emphasis on music.
Fields of interest: Arts education; Performing arts, music; Performing arts, education; Higher education; Children/youth, services; Science.
Type of support: General/operating support; Scholarship funds.
Limitations: Applications not accepted. Giving primarily in MA and VT. No grants to individuals.
Application information: Contributes only to pre-selected organizations.
Trustees: Torin S. Koester, Managing Tr.; J. Michael McKenzie.
EIN: 226596096

3414
Merchants Bank Foundation, Inc.
275 Kennedy Dr.
South Burlington, VT 05403-6785 (802) 865-1627
Contact: Stephanie Macaskill, Secy.

Established in 1967 in VT.
Donors: Merchants Bancshares, Inc.; Merchants Bank.
Foundation type: Company-sponsored foundation.
Financial data (yr. ended 08/31/12): Assets, $1,341,750 (M); gifts received, $100,000; expenditures, $190,896; qualifying distributions, $179,287; giving activities include $179,287 for 120 grants (high: $30,000; low: $50).
Purpose and activities: The Foundation provides funding to organizations for programs and services that support general education, human services, or community enrichment for all Vermonters for purposes of advancing education, household self-sufficiency, sustainable independence, and viable community development.
Fields of interest: Arts; Education; Hospitals (general); Human services; Family services.
Type of support: Capital campaigns; Building/renovation; Equipment; Program development; Curriculum development; Scholarship funds.
Limitations: Applications accepted. Giving primarily in VT. No grants to individuals.
Publications: Application guidelines.
Application information: Application form required.
***Initial approach:* Completed application form**
Copies of proposal: 1
***Deadline(s):* Jan. 15, Apr. 15, July 15, Oct. 15**
Officers: Martha Davis, Chair. and Pres.; Pamela Matweecha, V.P.; Erinn Perry, Secy.; Stephanie Macaskill, Treas.
Trustees: Kevin Farley; Diane Gagnon; Sean Houghton; Kathryn Leech; Jessica Rohde.
EIN: 036016628

3415
The Rowland Foundation Inc.
P.O. Box 88
South Londonderry, VT 05155-0088 (802) 824-6400
Contact: Charles Scranton, Exec. Dir.
E-mail: info@therowlandfoundation.org; Main URL: http://www.therowlandfoundation.org/
diigo: https://groups.diigo.com/group/rowland_foundation
Facebook: https://www.facebook.com/Rowland.Foundation

Established in 2008 in VT.
Donors: Benjamin A. Rowland, Jr.; Wendy G. Rowland.
Foundation type: Independent foundation.
Financial data (yr. ended 06/30/13): Assets, $12,152,100 (M); gifts received, $1,020,000; expenditures, $723,406; qualifying distributions, $695,927; giving activities include $475,000 for 5 grants (high: $100,000; low: $75,000).
Purpose and activities: The foundation provides Vermont secondary school educators with a unique professional development and leadership opportunity, and the resources to positively affect the culture and climate of their respective schools.
Fields of interest: Elementary/secondary education; Teacher school/education; Education.
Type of support: Fellowships; Scholarships—to individuals.
Limitations: Applications accepted. Giving limited to VT.
Publications: Application guidelines.
Application information: Application information and form available on foundation web site. Application form required.
***Initial approach:* 1-page cover letter, plus proposal (3 pages maximum)**
***Copies of proposal:* 4**
***Deadline(s):* Dec. 31**
Officers and Trustees:* Benjamin A. Rowland, Jr., Pres. and Treas.; Wendy G. Rowland, Secy.; Charles W. Scranton,* Exec. Dir.; Heidi Lynn; James C. Mooney; Daniel B. Rowland; John A. Shepard, Jr.
EIN: 262698626

3416
Richard E. and Deborah L. Tarrant Foundation, Inc.
(formerly Richard E. Tarrant Foundation, Inc.)
P.O. Box 521
Winooski, VT 05404-0521 (802) 857-0495
Contact: Lauren A. Curry, Exec. Dir.
FAX: (802) 857-0496;
E-mail: lcurry@tarrantfoundation.org**; Additional e-mail: info@tarrantfoundation.org**; Main URL: http://www.tarrantfoundation.org
Twitter: https://twitter.com/TarrantGiving

Established in 1997 in VT.
Donor: Richard E. Tarrant.
Foundation type: Independent foundation.
Financial data (yr. ended 12/31/12): Assets, $12,047,735 (M); expenditures, $1,455,464; qualifying distributions, $1,315,907; giving activities include $1,144,660 for 61 grants (high: $250,000; low: $250).
Purpose and activities: Giving to enrich the quality of life and communities throughout Vermont.
Fields of interest: Higher education; Human services; Community/economic development.
Type of support: General/operating support; Annual campaigns; Capital campaigns; Building/renovation; Equipment; Program development; Scholarship funds.
Limitations: Applications accepted. Giving limited to VT. **No support for political organizations, or for research, lobbying activities, environmental, arts or medical health programs, schools, classrooms, or school-based clubs/activities. No grants to individuals, or for endowments, events or fundraisers, debt retirement, or multi-year grants.**
Publications: Application guidelines.
Application information: Full applications are by invitation only, upon review of initial letter. Application form required.
***Initial approach:* Letter (no more than 2 pages) via e-mail (to Lauren A. Curry, Exec. Dir.) or U.S. Mail**

Copies of proposal: 1
Deadline(s): Jan. 1, Apr. 1, July 1 or Oct. 1
Board meeting date(s): Quarterly
Officer: Lauren A. Curry, Exec. Dir.
Directors: Ronald L. Roberts; Deborah L. Tarrant; **Richard E. Tarrant**; **Kevin S. Veller**.
Number of staff: 1 part-time professional.
EIN: 030364509

3417
Vermont Community Foundation
3 Court St.
Middlebury, VT 05753 (802) 388-3355
Contact: For questions about grants: Jen Peterson, V.P., Program and Grants; For questions about accounting and finance: Debra Rooney, V.P., Finance and C.F.O.; For media inquiries or questions about publications: Felipe Rivera, V.P., Communications
FAX: (802) 388-3398; E-mail: info@vermontcf.org; Main URL: http://www.vermontcf.org
Facebook: http://www.facebook.com/vermontcf
LinkedIn: http://www.linkedin.com/company/the-vermont-community-foundation
Philanthropy's Promise: http://www.ncrp.org/philanthropys-promise/who
President's Blog: What's Stu-ing?: http://www.vermontcf.org/AboutUs/PresidentsBlogWhatsStu-ing.aspx
RSS Feed: http://www.vermontcf.org/DesktopModules/DNNArticle/DNNArticleRSS.aspx?portalid=0&moduleid=412&tabid=95&categoryid=2&cp=False&uid=1
Twitter: http://twitter.com/vermontcf
YouTube: http://www.youtube.com/user/vermontcf?feature=watch

Established in 1986 in VT.
Foundation type: Community foundation.
Financial data (yr. ended 12/31/12): Assets, $167,245,557 (M); gifts received, $16,537,381; expenditures, $16,608,412; giving activities include $12,603,915 for grants.
Purpose and activities: To build philanthropy in order to sustain healthy and vital Vermont communities.
Fields of interest: Humanities; Historic preservation/historical societies; Arts; Education, early childhood education; Child development, education; Elementary school/education; Secondary school/education; Higher education; Adult/continuing education; Libraries/library science; Education; Environment, natural resources; Environment; Reproductive health, family planning; Health care; Substance abuse, services; Mental health/crisis services; AIDS; Alcoholism; Health organizations; Food services; Housing/shelter; Children/youth, services; Youth, services; Child development, services; Family services; Minorities/immigrants, centers/services; Homeless, human services; Human services; Civil/human rights; Economic development; Community/economic development; Public affairs.
Type of support: Program-related investments/loans; Grants to individuals; Film/video/radio; Building/renovation; General/operating support; Income development; Management development/capacity building; Equipment; Emergency funds; Program development; Publication; Seed money; Curriculum development; Technical assistance; Consulting services; Program evaluation; Mission-related investments/loans.
Limitations: Applications accepted. Giving limited to VT. No support for religious purposes. No grants for capital campaigns, continuing support, debt reduction, or general endowments.
Publications: Application guidelines; Annual report; Financial statement; Grants list; Newsletter; Occasional report.
Application information: Visit foundation web site for application, additional guidelines per grant type, and specific deadlines. Application form required.
Initial approach: Online application only
Deadline(s): Varies
Board meeting date(s): 4 times annually
Final notification: Varies
Officers and Directors:* A. Jay Kenlan,* Chair.; Tim Volk,* Vice-Chair.; Stuart Comstock-Gay, C.E.O. and Pres.; **Patrick H. Berry, V.P., Philanthropy**; Jen Peterson, V.P., Progs. and Grants; Felipe Rivera, V.P., Comms.; Debbie Rooney, V.P., Finance and C.F.O.; James G. Wheeler, Jr.,* Secy.; Deb Brighton,* Treas.; Lisa Cashdan; Staige Davis; John Killacky; Peter Kinder; Michael Metz; Julie Peterson; Betsy Rathbun-Gunn; Margaret Seely.
Number of staff: 14 full-time professional; 4 part-time professional; 3 full-time support; 1 part-time support.
EIN: 222712160
Other changes: Peter Espenshade is no longer V.P., Community Philanthropy. David F. Finney is no longer a director.

3418
The Windham Foundation, Inc.
P.O. Box 70
Grafton, VT 05146-0070 (802) 843-2211
FAX: (802) 843-2205;
E-mail: info@windham-foundation.org; Main URL: http://www.windham-foundation.org
LinkedIn: http://www.linkedin.com/company/the-windham-foundation
Scholarship e-mail address: scholarships@windham-foundation.org

Incorporated in 1963 in VT.
Donors: The Bunbury Co., Inc.; Dean Mathey‡.
Foundation type: Operating foundation.
Financial data (yr. ended 03/31/12): Assets, $46,600,541 (M); gifts received, $68,714; expenditures, $9,511,790; qualifying distributions, $8,869,069; giving activities include $242,789 for 63 grants (high: $23,600; low: $50), $11,600 for 18 grants to individuals (high: $2,500; low: $150), and $3,419,134 for 2 foundation-administered programs.
Purpose and activities: The Windham Foundation, one of the largest foundations chartered in the state, is a nonprofit organization located in Grafton, Vermont. The foundation was established in 1963 to promote the vitality of Grafton and Vermont's rural communities through its philanthropic and educational programs and its subsidiaries whose operations contribute to these endeavors. Funding interests are in agriculture and food systems, land use, social services, disadvantaged youth, arts and culture, and historic preservation and education.
Fields of interest: Historic preservation/historical societies; Arts; Education; Environment, plant conservation; Agriculture/food; Community/economic development; Social sciences.
Type of support: Annual campaigns; Building/renovation; Capital campaigns; Conferences/seminars; Consulting services; Curriculum development; General/operating support; Matching/challenge support; Program development; Scholarships—to individuals; Seed money; Technical assistance.
Limitations: Applications accepted. Giving limited to VT. No support for playgrounds or daycare centers, or religious or political organizations. No grants to individuals (except for undergraduate college scholarship program for residents of Windham County, VT), or for endowment funds; no loans.
Publications: Application guidelines; Annual report; Informational brochure; Informational brochure (including application guidelines); Newsletter.
Application information: E-mail or fax requests will not be accepted. Application form and guidelines available on foundation web site. Only 1 application accepted annually from an organization. Application form required.
Initial approach: Letter or telephone for application and guidelines
Copies of proposal: 5
Deadline(s): See foundation web site for grant and scholarship application deadlines
Board meeting date(s): Quarterly
Final notification: 10-12 weeks
Officers and Trustees:* Edward R. Zuccaro,* Chair.; Bob Allen,* Pres. and C.E.O.; Elizabeth Bankowski,* V.P.; Daniel Nornamdeau, V.P.; William A. Gilbert, Secy.; Robert M. Olmsted, Treas.; William H. Bruett; Samuel W. Lambert; Jamie Kyte Sapoch.
Number of staff: 8 full-time professional.
EIN: 136142024

VIRGIN ISLANDS

3419

Community Foundation of the Virgin Islands

(also known as CFVI)
5600 Royal Dane Mall, Ste. 19
Charlotte Amalie, VI 00802-6410 (340) 774-6031
Contact: Dee Baecher-Brown, Pres.
FAX: (340) 774-3852; E-mail: general.info@cfvi.net; **Mailing Address: P.O. Box 11790, Charlotte Amalie, VI 00801-4790; Additional e-mail: dbrown@cfvi.net**; Main URL: http://www.cfvi.net/
Facebook: http://www.facebook.com/CFVirginIslands

Established in 1990 in the U.S. Virgin Islands.
Foundation type: Community foundation.
Financial data (yr. ended 12/31/11): Assets, $6,944,548 (M); gifts received, $1,775,169; expenditures, $2,106,788; giving activities include $1,096,614 for 10+ grants, and $561,480 for 482 grants to individuals.
Purpose and activities: The Community Foundation of the Virgin Island (CFVI) was created to serve both donors and nonprofit organizations of the Virgin Islands that want to ensure the highest quality of life for both present and future generations. Its primary goal is to build a growing collection of permanent funds, the income from which will be used to enhance the educational, physical, social, cultural and environmental well-being of the islands' people.
Fields of interest: Education; Environment; Health care; Children/youth, services; Child development, services; Family services; Aging, centers/services; Community/economic development.
Type of support: Grants to individuals.
Limitations: Applications accepted. Giving limited to St. Croix, St. John, St. Thomas, and Water Island, VI.
Publications: Financial statement; Newsletter.
Application information: Visit the foundation web site for full application guidelines, specific deadlines, and requirements, including forms for the mini-grants program and scholarships. Application form required.
Initial approach: Submit application form
Deadline(s): Varies
Board meeting date(s): Monthly
Officers and Directors:* George H. T. Dudley,* Chair.; Alda Monsanto,* 1st Vice-Chair.; Victoria B. Sanders,* 2nd Vice-Chair.; **Ricardo J. Charaf, Chair. Emeritus**; Dee Baecher-Brown,* Pres.; Trudie J. Prior,* Secy.; William L. Graham, Treas.; Scott Barber; Filippo Cassinelli; Vivek A. Daswani; William L. Graham; Letty Hulsman; Lawrence Kupfer; Catherine L. Mills; Trudie J. Prior; Mark Robertson; Margaret Sprauve-Martin; Claire Starkey.
Number of staff: 1 part-time professional.
EIN: 660470703
Other changes: Leah George is no longer C.F.O. Denaullia Rouse is now Acct. Asst.

VIRGINIA

3420
AMERIGROUP Foundation
P.O. Box 62509
Virginia Beach, VA 23466-2509 (757) 490-6900
FAX: (757) 222-2360;
E-mail: wellpoint.foundation@wellpoint.com; Main URL: http://www.amerigroup.com/about-amerigroup/amerigroup-foundation

Donor: AMERIGROUP Corp.
Foundation type: Company-sponsored foundation.
Financial data (yr. ended 12/31/12): Assets, $1,647,802 (M); gifts received, $134,423; expenditures, $3,075,181; qualifying distributions, $3,075,181; giving activities include $2,837,610 for grants, $4,793 for grants to individuals, and $194,602 for employee matching gifts.
Purpose and activities: The foundation supports programs designed to foster access to healthcare; encourage safe and healthy children and families; and promote community improvement and healthy neighborhoods. Special emphasis is directed toward programs designed to serve the financially disadvantaged, seniors, and people with disabilities.
Fields of interest: Higher education; Health sciences school/education; Education; Health care, research; Reproductive health; Reproductive health, prenatal care; Public health; Health care, insurance; Health care; Food services; Nutrition; Recreation; YM/YWCAs & YM/YWHAs; Children/youth, services; Children, services; Family services; Aging, centers/services; Developmentally disabled, centers & services; Independent living, disability; Community/economic development; United Ways and Federated Giving Programs; Aging; Disabilities, people with; Economically disadvantaged.
Type of support: General/operating support; Continuing support; Building/renovation; Program development; Research; Sponsorships; Employee matching gifts.
Limitations: Applications accepted. **Giving primarily in AZ,CA, CO, CT, FL, GA, IN, KS, KY, LA, MA, MD, ME, MO, NH, NJ, NM, NV, NY, OH, SC, TN, TX, WV, and WI with emphasis on VA.** No support for private foundations, fraternal, social, athletic, labor, or veterans' organizations, political parties or candidates, for profit-entities including start-up businesses, or for organizations not of direct benefit to the entire community. No grants to individuals, or for tickets, tables, benefits, raffles, souvenir programs, fundraising dinners, golf outings, trips, tours, or similar events.
Publications: Application guidelines; Program policy statement.
Application information: Visit website for additional application information. Foundation grants will be administered by Wellpoint. Telephone calls are not encouraged during the application process. Application form required.
Initial approach: Complete online application
***Deadline(s):* Varies**
***Final notification:* 4 to 6 months**
Officers: John E. Littel, Pres.; Scott W. Anglin, V.P.; Richard C. Zoretic, V.P.
EIN: 542014061
Other changes: At the close of 2012, the grantmaker paid grants of $3,037,005, a 63.5% increase over the 2011 disbursements, $1,858,046.
Nicholas J. Pace is no longer V.P. and Secy. James G. Carlson is no longer V.P.

3421
Arlington Community Foundation
818 N. Quincy St., Ste. 103
Arlington, VA 22203 (703) 243-4785
Contact: Wanda L. Pierce, Exec. Dir.
FAX: (703) 243-4796; E-mail: info@arlcf.org; Grant inquiry e-mail: grants@arlcf.org; Main URL: http://www.arlcf.org
E-Newsletter: http://arlcf.org/index.cfm/newsletter
Facebook: http://www.facebook.com/pages/Arlington-Community-Foundation/130015137014
LinkedIn: http://www.linkedin.com/companies/arlington-community-foundation
Twitter: http://twitter.com/Arlcf

Established in 1991 in VA.
Foundation type: Community foundation.
Financial data (yr. ended 06/30/12): Assets, $9,008,913 (M); gifts received, $1,414,877; expenditures, $1,192,951; giving activities include $431,364 for 23+ grants (high: $58,052), and $326,210 for 142 grants to individuals.
Purpose and activities: The foundation is an independent charitable organization that actively promotes, protects and improves the quality of life for those who live or work in Arlington. The foundation provides philanthropic leadership and raises capital for grants and scholarships to address community needs now and in the future.
Fields of interest: Performing arts; Humanities; Arts; Adult education—literacy, basic skills & GED; Education, reading; Education; Environment; Health care; Food services; Housing/shelter; Disasters, Hurricane Katrina; Safety/disasters; Children/youth, services; Aging, centers/services; Minorities/immigrants, centers/services; Human services; Community/economic development; Government/public administration; Aging; Minorities; Native Americans/American Indians; Women; Economically disadvantaged.
Type of support: Scholarships—to individuals; General/operating support; Continuing support; Management development/capacity building; Emergency funds; Program development; Seed money; Curriculum development; Scholarship funds; Technical assistance; Consulting services; Grants to individuals.
Limitations: Applications accepted. Giving limited to the Arlington, VA, area. No support for religious purposes. No grants to individuals (except for scholarships or specific awards by nomination), or for endowments, capital campaigns or for debts.
Publications: Application guidelines; Annual report; Financial statement; Grants list; Informational brochure; Multi-year report; Newsletter; Program policy statement.
Application information: Visit foundation web site for application forms and guidelines. Application form required.
Initial approach: Letter or telephone
Copies of proposal: 1
Deadline(s): Varies
Board meeting date(s): Feb., Apr., June, Aug., Oct., and Dec.
Final notification: 1 week
Officers and Trustees:* Julian Fore,* Pres.; Vicki Foster,* V.P.; Hon. Mary Margaret Whipple,* Secy.; David W. Briggs,* Treas.; R.B. Anderson,* Asst. Treas.; Wanda L. Pierce, Exec. Dir.; Hon. William T. Newman, Jr., Pres. Emeritus; Hon. David A. Bell; Jeanne Broyhill; Billy Buck; Patricia Connally; Bradford R. Coyle; Susan S. Duke; Leni Gonzalez; Dr. Leonard L. Hamin, Sr.; Deborah T. Johnson; Artemis McDonald; Lola C. Reinsch; Peggy Richardson; Libby Ross; Dr. Matthew D. Shank; John G. Shooshan; Nancy Snell; Marion Spraggins; Brian J. Steffan; Michael Timpane; Jim Whittaker.
Number of staff: 1 full-time professional; 2 part-time professional.
EIN: 541602838
Other changes: John P. Andelin, Robert H. Hawthorne, Fernanda S. Howard, Jonathan C. Kinney, and Christine T. Milliken are no longer trustees.

3422
Blue Moon Fund, Inc.
(formerly W. Alton Jones Foundation, Inc.)
222 W. South St.
Charlottesville, VA 22902-5041 (434) 295-5160
FAX: (434) 295-6894;
E-mail: info@bluemoonfund.org**; Additional address: 2000 Florida Ave. NW, Ste. 100, Washington, DC 20009**; Main URL: http://www.bluemoonfund.org
Grants Database: http://www.bluemoonfund.org/grantmaking/search/

Incorporated in 1944 in NY as W. Alton Jones Foundation.
Donor: W. Alton Jones‡.
Foundation type: Independent foundation.
Financial data (yr. ended 12/31/12): Assets, $158,546,880 (M); expenditures, $15,682,446; qualifying distributions, $13,007,784; giving activities include $9,984,260 for 112 grants, and $81,487 for foundation-administered programs.
Purpose and activities: The fund supports initiatives that work to build human and natural resilience to a changing and warming world. It uses natural, social, and financial capital to implement new models in high-diversity regions around the world.
Fields of interest: Environment, climate change/global warming; Environment, natural resources; Environment, energy; Economic development.
Type of support: General/operating support; Program development; Program-related investments/loans; Matching/challenge support; Mission-related investments/loans.
Limitations: Applications accepted. Giving in Asia, primarily in China, the Greater Mekong region, and the Himalayas, in North America primarily in the Chesapeake, Appalachian and Gulf Coast regions, and in the Tropical Americas, primarily in the Andes-Amazon, the Eastern Amazon, and the Mesoamerica regions. No grants for lobbying, advertising, dissertations, thesis and other academic work.
Application information: The fund is an initiative-based organization and generally does not take unsolicited proposals. Staff selects organizations to fund that have the skills to further the projects developed by the staff. Organizations may also submit letters of inquiry through the foundation's web site. LOI's are reviewed periodically by staff who may invite full proposals.
Initial approach: Eligibility quiz on foundation web site
Board meeting date(s): Typically, five times annually
Officers and Trustees:* Diane Edgerton Miller,* C.E.O. and Pres.; Adrian Forsyth, Ph.D., V.P., Progs.; Ji-Qiang Zhang, V.P., Progs.; Diane Schmidt, C.F.O.; Jasem Green, C.I.O.
EIN: 136034219
Other changes: Beverly Lamb is no longer Compt.

3423
Leonard X. Bosack and Bette M. Kruger Charitable Foundation, Inc.
8458 W. Main St.
Marshall, VA 20115-3231

Re-established in 2002 in MA.
Donors: Leonard Bosack; Sandy Lerner; The Leonard X. Bosack & Bette M. Kruger Foundation.
Foundation type: Independent foundation.
Financial data (yr. ended 12/31/12): Assets, $6,858,294 (M); expenditures, $1,937,144; qualifying distributions, $1,867,080; giving activities include $1,714,726 for 28 grants (high: $168,809; low: $500).
Purpose and activities: Funding specifically in support of scientific education and the promotion of animal welfare, with a special emphasis on the welfare of captive wildlife, humane alternatives in veterinary education, collaborative spay and neuter programs, and protection of wild carnivores; funding also for the preservation and study of works by 17th, 18th, and early 19th century women writers.
Fields of interest: Higher education; Libraries/library science; Animal welfare; Engineering/technology; Science.
Type of support: Building/renovation; Equipment; Emergency funds; Program development; Conferences/seminars; Research.
Limitations: Applications not accepted. Giving primarily in the U.S.; some giving in the UK. No grants to individuals, or for operating budgets.
Application information: Contributes only to pre-selected organizations.
Board meeting date(s): Varies
Officers and Directors:* Sandy Lerner,* Pres.; Leonard Bosack,* Secy.; Brook Middleton,* Treas.; Alicia Falsetto; Robert Liebscher.
Number of staff: 1 part-time professional.
EIN: 753089497
Other changes: The grantmaker has moved from DE to VA.

3424
Ron Brown Scholar Fund
(formerly CAP Charitable Foundation USA)
1160 Pepsi Pl., Ste. 206
Charlottesville, VA 22901-0807 (434) 964-1588
***Contact:* Michael A. Mallory, Pres. and Exec. Dir.**
FAX: (434) 964-1589; E-mail: info@ronbrown.org; Main URL: http://www.ronbrown.org

Established in 1986 in DE.
Donors: CAP Properties Ltd.; The Clinton Family Foundation; Patton Boggs, LLP; Oak Foundation; DLA Piper US LLP; Donald Orkand; Kim Orkand; State Farm; Verizon Business Community Relation; Sonjia Smith; Terri Dean; The Ruffin Foundation; MTV Networks; The Community Foundation; Werner Family Foundation; RFI Foundation Inc.; CareFirst Blue Cross Blue Shield; Catalyst Foundation, Inc.; The Cochran Firm; Jordon Goldberg; Archura, LLC; Christopher Pilaro; Phobe Pilaro; Consumer Electronics Association; Black Entertainment TV; CMGRP, Inc.; Lockheed Martin; Office of Commissioner of Baseball; The Helping Hand Sales Inc.; The Reginald F. Lewis Foundation; Eddie Brown; Carmen Brown; Marva Smalls, Coastal Community Foundation; Annette Lerner; NY Community Trust; Theodore Lerner; Stuart Pape; Michael Ryan; Siemens; Elsie Thompson; Kathy Thorton-Bias; RBS Alumini Association.
Foundation type: Independent foundation.
Financial data (yr. ended 12/31/12): Assets, $12,211,717 (M); gifts received, $2,235,847; expenditures, $1,319,616; qualifying distributions, $1,236,088; giving activities include $250,896 for 49 grants to individuals (high: $10,000; low: $900).
Purpose and activities: Giving primarily college scholarships to African-American high school seniors through a scholarship program. Students must be U.S. citizens or have a permanent resident Visa card, attend a 4-year college or university in the U.S., and demonstrate financial need.
Fields of interest: Young adults; African Americans/Blacks.
Type of support: Scholarships—to individuals.
Limitations: Applications accepted. Giving to qualified individuals nationwide.
Publications: Application guidelines; Informational brochure; Newsletter.
Application information: Application form required.
***Initial approach:* Use application on foundation web site**
Deadline(s): Jan. 9 of senior year in high school
Officers and Trustees:* Michael A. Mallory, Pres. and Exec. Dir.; Christopher Pilaro,* V.P.; Anita Whelan, Secy.
Number of staff: 2 full-time professional; 1 full-time support; 1 part-time support.
EIN: 541832314
Other changes: Michael A. Mallory is now Pres. and Exec. Dir.

3425
The Robert G. Cabell III and Maude Morgan Cabell Foundation
901 E. Cary St., Ste. 1402
Richmond, VA 23219-4037 (804) 780-2050
Contact: Jill A. McCormick, Exec. Dir.
FAX: (804) 780-2198;
E-mail: Cabell.foundation@gmail.com

Incorporated in 1957 in VA.
Donors: Robert G. Cabell III†; Maude Morgan Cabell†.
Foundation type: Independent foundation.
Financial data (yr. ended 12/31/13): Assets, $114,578,332 (M); expenditures, $5,951,192; qualifying distributions, $5,444,350; giving activities include $5,444,350 for 28 grants (high: $500,000; low: $23,000).
Purpose and activities: Grants primarily for higher education, health care, historic preservation, the arts and cultural projects, community development, and social welfare.
Fields of interest: Historic preservation/historical societies; Arts; Higher education; Human services; Community/economic development.
Type of support: Capital campaigns; Building/renovation; Equipment; Endowments; Matching/challenge support.
Limitations: Applications accepted. Giving limited to VA with emphasis on the Metro Richmond region. No support for special interest groups or for religious organizations for exclusive use of its membership. No grants to individuals, or for operating programs, or research projects.
Publications: Application guidelines; Informational brochure (including application guidelines).
Application information: Application form not required.
Initial approach: Telephone or letter
Copies of proposal: 1
Deadline(s): Mar. 1st and Sept. 1st.
Board meeting date(s): Mar., May, and Nov.
Final notification: Promptly following spring and fall board grant review meetings
Officers and Directors:* J. Read Branch, Jr.,* Pres.; Patteson Branch, Jr.,* V.P.; Charles L. Cabell,* Pres.; **John Branch Cabell, Secy.**; **Elizabeth Cabell Jennings,* Treas.**; Jill A. McCormack, Exec. Dir.; Patteson Branch III; Mary Z. Zeugner.
Number of staff: 1 part-time professional; 1 part-time support.
EIN: 546039157
Other changes: J. Read Branch, Jr. has replaced Charles L. Cabell as Pres. Patteson Branch, Jr. has replaced J. Read Branch, Jr. as V.P. John Branch Cabell has replaced Elizabeth Cabell Jennings as Secy.
Elizabeth Cabell Jennings is now Treas.

3426
Capital One Foundation
(formerly North Fork Foundation)
1680 Capital One Dr.
McLean, VA 22102-3407 (804) 284-2118
Contact: Mary Johnson Fain, Sr. Mgr., Opers.
E-mail: communityaffairs@capitalone.com; Main URL: http://www.capitalone.com/about/corporate-citizenship/partnerships/

Established in 1994 in NY.
Donors: GreenPoint Bank; Capital One.
Foundation type: Company-sponsored foundation.
Financial data (yr. ended 12/31/12): Assets, $46,759,574 (M); gifts received, $6,500,000; expenditures, $6,375,406; qualifying distributions, $6,124,000; giving activities include $6,010,000 for 130 grants (high: $345,000; low: $5,000).
Purpose and activities: The foundation supports programs designed to promote safe and affordable housing; financial literacy; workforce and economic development; social improvement; and early childhood education.
Fields of interest: Elementary/secondary education; Education, early childhood education; Education, services; Education, reading; Education; Employment, services; Employment, training; Housing/shelter, home owners; Housing/shelter; Youth development; Children, day care; Human services, financial counseling; Community development, small businesses; Community/economic development.
Type of support: General/operating support; Continuing support; Management development/capacity building; Program development; Employee matching gifts.
Limitations: Applications accepted. Giving primarily in Washington, DC, greater New Orleans, LA, MD, northern and central NJ, New York City and Long Island, NY, the greater Dallas and Houston, TX, areas, and Fairfax County, VA; giving also to national organizations. No support for political, labor, fraternal organizations, or civic clubs, religious organizations not of direct benefit of the entire community, or health-related organizations. No grants to individuals, or for fundraising or fellowships, advertising or marketing activities, sports, athletic events, or athletic programs, travel-related events including student trips or tours, development or production of books, films, videos, or television programs, or memorial campaigns.
Publications: Application guidelines; Corporate giving report.
Application information:
Initial approach: Complete online letter of inquiry form
Deadline(s): None
Officers and Directors:* John G. Finneran, Jr.,* Chair.; Richard A. Woods, Vice-Chair.; Carolyn S. Berkowitz,* Pres.; Amy D. Cook, Secy.; Andrew D. Labenne, Treas.; Guenet M. Beshah; Dorothy

Broadman; Heather M. Cox; Kenneth Kido; Robert J. Magnano; Michael C. Siocum.
EIN: 113276603
Other changes: At the close of 2012, the grantmaker paid grants of $6,010,000, a 86.9% increase over the 2011 disbursements, $3,216,171.
John G. Finneran, Jr. is now Chair. Richard A. Woods is now Vice-Chair.
The grantmaker has changed its fiscal year-end from Sept. 30 to Dec. 31.

3427
The CarMax Foundation

12800 Tuckahoe Creek Pkwy.
Richmond, VA 23238-1115
Contact: Leslie Parpart, Mgr., Community Rels. and CarMax Fdn.
FAX: (804) 935-4516;
E-mail: kmxfoundation@carmax.com; Main URL: http://www.carmaxcares.com
Twitter: http://twitter.com/CarMaxCares

Established in 2003 in VA.
Donors: CarMax Auto Superstores, Inc.; CarMax Business Services, LLC.
Foundation type: Company-sponsored foundation.
Financial data (yr. ended 02/28/13): Assets, $9,398,303 (M); gifts received, $4,000,000; expenditures, $3,676,154; qualifying distributions, $3,676,154; giving activities include $2,896,380 for 721 grants (high: $661,200; low: -$1,500), and $490,170 for 453 employee matching gifts.
Purpose and activities: The foundation supports programs designed to promote education; youth leadership; and wellness in communities where CarMax associates live and work.
Fields of interest: Arts education; Elementary/secondary education; Vocational education; Education, drop-out prevention; Education; Public health, obesity; Food services; Nutrition; Recreation, camps; Recreation, parks/playgrounds; Recreation; Youth development, adult & child programs; Youth development; Family services; Family services, domestic violence; Human services; Mathematics; Engineering/technology; Science; Leadership development; Children/youth; Economically disadvantaged.
Type of support: Continuing support; Program development; Employee volunteer services; Employee matching gifts.
Limitations: Applications accepted. Giving primarily in areas of company operations, with emphasis on the greater Richmond, VA, area; giving also to national organizations. No support for discriminatory organizations, organizations posing a conflict of interest with CarMax's mission, goals, programs, or products, fraternal, athletic, social, labor, or political organizations. No grants for debt reduction, political campaigns, or capital campaigns, endowments, event sponsorships, or scholarships; no vehicle donations.
Publications: Application guidelines; Annual report; IRS Form 990 or 990-PF printed copy available upon request.
Application information: Letters of inquiry should include a statement describing the project; and indicate the approximate date when an application will be submitted. Application form required.
Initial approach: For Richmond, VA only, letter of intent by Oct. 15; invitations for full proposals by Feb. 15.
Copies of proposal: 1
Deadline(s): Feb. 15 for Richmond Giving Program
***Board meeting date(s):* Mar., June, Sept., and Dec.**
Final notification: Mar. 31 for Richmond Giving Program
Officers and Directors:* Lynn Mussatt,* Pres.; Ron Bevers, V.P.; Dan Bickett,* V.P.; Natalie Wyatt, Treas.; Alice Heinz; Bill McCrystal.
Number of staff: 2 full-time professional.
EIN: 383681796

3428
Charlottesville Area Community Foundation

(formerly Charlottesville-Albemarle Community Foundation)
114 4th St. S.E.
P.O. Box 1767
Charlottesville, VA 22902-1767 (434) 296-1024
Contact: Brennan Gould, Dir., Grants and Strategic Initiatives
FAX: (434) 296-2503; E-mail: cacf@cacfonline.org; **Additional e-mail: bgould@cacfonline.org; Grant application e-mail: communityendowment@cacfonline.org**; Main URL: http://www.cacfonline.org

Established in 1967 in VA.
Foundation type: Community foundation.
Financial data (yr. ended 12/31/12): Assets, $103,891,600 (M); gifts received, $7,068,463; expenditures, $8,751,857; giving activities include $6,861,487 for 203+ grants (high: $470,000; low: $100), and $400,096 for 102 grants to individuals.
Purpose and activities: The mission of the foundation is to improve the quality of life for those living and working in the city of Charlottesville, VA and the surrounding counties of Albemarle, Buckingham, Fluvanna, Greene, Louisa, Nelson, and Orange.
Fields of interest: Humanities; Arts; Education; Environment; Health care; Human services; Community/economic development.
Type of support: General/operating support; Seed money; Scholarship funds; Matching/challenge support.
Limitations: Applications accepted. Giving limited to the Charlottesville, VA, area, including the City of Charlottesville and the counties of Albemarle, Greene, Orange, Louisa, Fluvanna, Buckingham, and Nelson east of the Blue Ridge Mountains. No support for religious programs. No grants to individuals (except for scholarships), or for endowments, deficit reduction, fundraising events, or annual appeals of well-established organizations.
Publications: Application guidelines; Annual report; Newsletter.
Application information: Full proposals will be solicited from organizations under consideration for funding based in letter of inquiry (staff recommendations are submitted to the Community Endowment Grants Committee, which is comprised of members of the Foundation's Governing Board and other community members). Visit foundation web site for complete application guidelines. Application form required.
***Initial approach:* Contact foundation**
Deadline(s): Community Endowment: Apr. 1 for letters of inquiry for grant requests of $10,000 to $100,000; Oct. 1 for letters of inquiry for grant requests of $10,000 or less
Board meeting date(s): Twice annually
Officers and Board of Governors:* Lawrence J. Martin,* Chair.; Louise M. Dudley,* Vice-Chair.; John R. Redick,* Pres.; Constance Waite, Sr. V.P., Finance and Admin.; Kathleen Bowman,* Secy.; Peter A. Agelasto; Julian M. Bivins, Jr.; O. Whitfield Broome, Jr.; Alan N. Culbertson; Joe H. Gieck; James L. Jessup, Jr.; Eric S. Johnson; Meghan Murray; Kelli E. Palmer; Susan K. Payne; Joseph W. "Rick" Richmond, Jr.; Joseph T. Samuels, Jr.; Leonard W. Sandridge, Jr.; Frederic W. Scott, Jr.; Elizabeth H. Woodard; Bruce Woodzell.
Number of staff: 2 full-time professional; 1 part-time professional; 2 full-time support.
EIN: 541506312

3429
The Community Foundation of the Central Blue Ridge

(doing business as Staunton Augusta Waynesboro Community Foundation)
117 S. Lewis St.
P.O. Box 815
Staunton, VA 24402 (540) 231-2150
***Contact:* For grants: Susan Lendermon, Dir., Nonprofit Srvs.**
FAX: (540) 242-3387;
E-mail: info@communityfoundationcbr.org; Grant inquiry e-mail: slendermon@communityfoundationcbr.org; Grant inquiry tel.: 540-213-2150; Main URL: http://www.communityfoundationcbr.org
Additional URL: http://www.communityfoundationCBR.org
Facebook: https://www.facebook.com/pages/Community-Foundation-of-the-Central-Blue-Ridge/249542215372
LinkedIn: http://www.linkedin.com/company/608279?goback=.fcs_*2_Community+Foundation+of+Central+Blue+Ridge_*2_*2_*2_*2_*2_*2_*2_*2_*2_*2_*2&trk=ncsrch_hits
Twitter: http://twitter.com/CommFdn_CBR

Established in 1992 in VA.
Donor: H.D. "Buz" Dawbarn‡.
Foundation type: Community foundation.
Financial data (yr. ended 12/31/12): Assets, $13,643,841 (M); gifts received, $1,011,346; expenditures, $725,820; giving activities include $303,776 for 51+ grants (high: $28,790), and $143,175 for 33 grants to individuals.
Purpose and activities: The foundation's mission is to enhance the quality of life by meeting needs and inspiring philanthropy in the community.
Fields of interest: Historic preservation/historical societies; Arts; Education; Environment; Health care; Safety/disasters; Recreation; Youth, services; Family services; Human services; Community development, neighborhood development.
Type of support: General/operating support; Equipment; Endowments; Program development; Curriculum development; Scholarship funds; Consulting services; Program evaluation.
Limitations: Applications accepted. Giving limited to Augusta County, Highland County, Nelson County, Staunton, and Waynesboro, VA. No support for sectarian, fraternal, or religious organizations. No grants for general annual fund appeals, deficit reduction, capital campaigns or endowments, fundraising or celebration events or start-up funds.
Publications: Application guidelines; Annual report; Financial statement; Grants list; Informational brochure; Newsletter.
Application information: Visit foundation web site for application form and guidelines. Applications must be submitted electronically. Application form required.
Initial approach: E-mail application and attachments

Copies of proposal: 1
***Deadline(s):* Mar. 6**
Board meeting date(s): 4th Tues. of each month
Final notification: Apr.

Officers and Directors:* Ronald Denney, Esq.*, Chair.; Steve Elkins,* Vice-Chair.; Dan Layman,* Pres. and C.E.O.; Carl Rosberg,* Secy. - Treas.; **Lewis M. Coiner, Emeritus**; **Harold C. Cook, Emeritus**; Ken Boward; Laura-Jean Brand, M.D.; Cary Dahl; Perry Fridley; David T. Gauldin II; Dinah Gottschalk; William Larry Harrell, M.D.; John R. Higgs; Becky Kelly; Jan Mangun; Deborah T. Metz; John W. Sills III; Butch Smiley; Travis Tysinger; Wilson F. Vellines, Jr.
Number of staff: 1 full-time professional; 3 part-time professional; 1 full-time support.
EIN: 541647385
Other changes: Menieka K. Garber is now Dir., Opers. and Donor Srvs.

3430
Community Foundation of the Dan River Region

(formerly DPC Community Foundation)
541 Loyal St.
Danville, VA 24541 (434) 793-0884
Contact: Debra L. Dodson, Exec. Dir.
FAX: (434) 793-6489; E-mail: info@cfdrr.org; Additional e-mail: cfdrr@gamewood.net; Main URL: http://www.cfdrr.org

Established in 1996 in VA.
Foundation type: Community foundation.
Financial data (yr. ended 06/30/12): Assets, $23,702,340 (M); gifts received, $926,761; expenditures, $2,168,918; giving activities include $827,073 for 99+ grants (high: $114,000), and $150,552 for 68 grants to individuals.
Purpose and activities: The foundation helps donors meet community needs through endowment funds.
Fields of interest: Arts; Education; Human services.
Type of support: Scholarship funds; Scholarships—to individuals.
Limitations: Applications accepted. Giving primarily in Caswell County, NC, and Danville and Pittsylvania County, VA, as well as southern VA and northern NC.
Publications: Application guidelines; Annual report; Financial statement; Grants list; Informational brochure; Newsletter.
Application information: Visit foundation web site for application guidelines. Organizations wishing to be added to the foundation's mailing list for grant applications should contact the foundation's office. Application forms for scholarships are sent to guidance offices of public high schools in early spring. Application form required.
Initial approach: Preliminary grant request letter
Copies of proposal: 10
Deadline(s): July
Board meeting date(s): Quarterly
Final notification: Jan.

Officers and Directors:* F. Lawrence McFall,* Pres.; Peter K. Howard,* V.P.; Margaret Scott,* Secy.; William S. Woods,* Treas.; Debra L. Dodson, Exec. Dir.; Gerald Adcock; Lamar Barr; Scott Batson; Brenda Blair; P. Niles Daly, Jr.; Gail Gunn; Harry T. Kolendrianos; Donald Nodtvedt; T. Wayne Oakes; Rev. Ed Pope; Dora Pradhan; **Paul W. Thompson, Jr.**; Lewis Wall; Verla Wall; Stuart Watlington; Logan Young.
Number of staff: 3 full-time professional.
EIN: 541823141

3431
The Community Foundation of the New River Valley

50 N. Franklin St., 2nd Fl.
P.O. Box 6009
Christiansburg, VA 24068-6009 (540) 381-8999
Contact: Jessica Wirgau, Exec. Dir.
FAX: (540) 381-1406; E-mail: cfnrv@cfnrv.org; Additional e-mail: jessicawirgau@cfnrv.org; Main URL: http://www.cfnrv.org

Established in 1994 in VA.
Foundation type: Community foundation.
Financial data (yr. ended 12/31/12): Assets, $7,349,535 (M); gifts received, $1,287,570; expenditures, $510,379; giving activities include $192,394 for 8+ grants (high: $44,095), and $36,536 for grants to individuals.
Purpose and activities: The mission of the Community Foundation of the New River Valley is to enrich the community by providing professional management services to donors for their charitable causes, awarding visionary grants and scholarships, and nurturing collaborations in the local community.
Fields of interest: Arts, cultural/ethnic awareness; Museums; Historic preservation/historical societies; Arts; Libraries/library science; Education; Environment, natural resources; Animals/wildlife; Health care; Youth development, citizenship; Human services; Community development, neighborhood development; Community/economic development; Government/public administration; Religion.
Type of support: General/operating support; Continuing support; Equipment; Publication; Seed money; Scholarship funds; Matching/challenge support.
Limitations: Applications accepted. Giving primarily in the City of Radford and Floyd, Giles, Montgomery, and Pulaski counties, VA. No grants for "bricks and mortar" projects (generally).
Publications: Application guidelines; Annual report; Financial statement; Grants list; Informational brochure; Newsletter.
Application information: Applicants are invited to submit a full application at the invitation of the foundation after reviewing Intent to Apply Forms. Faxed or e-mailed full applications are not accepted. Visit foundation website for more information. Application form required.
***Initial approach:* Submit Intent to Apply Form**
***Copies of proposal:* 1**
***Deadline(s):* Apr. 4 for Intent to Apply Form, July 18 for Full Application**
Board meeting date(s): 4th Tues. of each month

Officers and Directors:* **Courtney Grohs,* Pres.**; **Ed Lawhorn,* V.P.**; **Terri Fisher,* Secy.**; Katy Kirk,* Treas.; Jessica Wirgau, Exec. Dir.; C.J. Carter; Belva Collins; Peggy Eaton; Nancy Eiss; **Ginny Gardner**; Gary Hancock; Pat Huber; Hugh Jenkins; Dwayne Kittle; Mike Larrowe; Carlotta Lewis; Hing-Har Lo; Barbara Michelsen; Sam Minner; John Muffo; Andrew Warren.
Number of staff: 1 full-time professional; 1 full-time support; 1 part-time support.
EIN: 541740455
Other changes: Courtney Grohs has replaced Reed Kennedy as Pres. Ed Lawhorn has replaced Barbara Michelsen as V.P. Terri Fisher has replaced Ginny Gardner as Secy.
Sara Bohn is no longer a director.

3432
Community Foundation of Western Virginia

(doing business as Foundation for Roanoke Valley)
611 S. Jefferson St., Ste. 8
Roanoke, VA 24011 (540) 985-0204
Contact: For grants and scholarships: Michelle Eberly, Prog. Off.
FAX: (540) 982-8175; E-mail: info@foundationforroanokevalley.org; Mailing address: P.O. Box 1159, Roanoke, VA 24006; Grant inquiry e-mail: programs@foundationforroanokevalley.org; Main URL: http://www.foundationforroanokevalley.org
Facebook: http://www.facebook.com/foundationforroanokevalley

Established in 1988 in VA; funded in 1990.
Foundation type: Community foundation.
Financial data (yr. ended 06/30/12): Assets, $49,375,293 (M); gifts received, $4,618,498; expenditures, $4,546,828; giving activities include $3,047,196 for 109+ grants (high: $445,379).
Purpose and activities: The foundation seeks to foster positive change on behalf of the community by: 1) enabling donors to carry out their charitable intent through prudently administered permanent endowment funds; 2) offering a comprehensive array of services to encourage, advance and educate concerning effective philanthropy; 3) making creative grants to meet continuing and emerging community needs and opportunities; and 4) providing leadership in identifying and assessing community issues and acting as a catalyst to initiate specific responses.
Fields of interest: Arts; Education; Health care; Health organizations, association; Children/youth, services; Family services; Human services.
Type of support: General/operating support; Equipment; Emergency funds; Program development; Seed money; Scholarship funds.
Limitations: Applications accepted. Giving primarily in the greater Roanoke Valley, VA, area, with emphasis on Roanoke, Botetourt, Craig, Franklin and Rockbridge counties, VA. No support for sectarian, religious, or fraternal organizations. No grants to individuals (except for scholarships), or for deficit reduction, capital campaigns or endowments, fundraising events, or celebration events.
Publications: Annual report; Financial statement; Informational brochure; Newsletter.
Application information: Visit foundation web site for online application and guidelines. LOIs will be reviewed to determine if the project meets current grantmaking priorities and guidelines. If the LOI is selected for further consideration, the foundation's staff will notify the organization of the application deadline and additional materials required. Application form required.
Initial approach: Create online account
Copies of proposal: 1
Deadline(s): Varies
Board meeting date(s): Quarterly

Officers and Governors:* Melinda T. Chitwood,* Chair.; Susan K. Still,* Vice-Chair.; A. Damon Williams,* Treas.; Alan E. Ronk, Exec. Dir.; Rita D. Bishop; Lucy R. Ellett; William D, Elliot; Russell H. Ellis; Robert P. Fralin; Maryellen Goodlatte; Jim McAden; Stephen A. Musselwhite; Debbbie Oelschlager; Kathryn Krisch Oelschlager; Randall R. Rhea, M.D.; Cynthia M. Shelor; Cleo Simms; Kenneth Tuck; Jim Wade.
Number of staff: 2 full-time professional; 1 part-time professional.
EIN: 541959458
Other changes: Carrie Hurd is now Acct. Dir. Robert A. Archer, Maryellen F. Goodlatte, Cynthia

D. Lawrence, Charlotte K. Porterfield, and Kenneth D. Tuck are no longer governors.

3433

The Community Foundation Serving Richmond & Central Virginia

(formerly Greater Richmond Community Foundation)
7501 Boulders View Dr., Ste. 110
Richmond, VA 23225-4047 (804) 330-7400
Contact: Darcy S. Oman, C.E.O.; For grants: Susan Hallett, V.P., Progs.; For grants: Elaine Summerfield, V.P., Progs.
FAX: (804) 330-5992; E-mail: info@tcfrichmond.org; Additional e-mail: doman@tcfrichmond.org; Grant application e-mails: shallett@tcfrichmond.org and esummerfield@tcfrichmond.org; Main URL: http://www.tcfrichmond.org
Facebook: http://www.facebook.com/tcfrichmond
Twitter: http://twitter.com/giverichmond
Scholarship e-mail: skeeley@tcfrichmond.org

Established in 1968 in VA.
Foundation type: Community foundation.
Financial data (yr. ended 12/31/12): Assets, $497,636,734 (M); gifts received, $31,809,626; expenditures, $36,662,325; giving activities include $32,429,867 for grants.
Purpose and activities: The foundation serves and inspires people to build philanthropy for the region and to engage in the local community. The foundation works closely with donors and community partners to fulfill this mission by: 1) promoting a regional perspective; 2) developing and sharing community knowledge; 3) collaborating towards common goals; 4) demonstrating inclusiveness and respect; and 5) achieving transparency, accountability and efficiency.
Fields of interest: Arts; Education; AIDS; Housing/shelter, development; Youth development; Children/youth, services; Community/economic development.
Type of support: General/operating support; Continuing support; Equipment; Emergency funds; Program development; Seed money; Technical assistance; Grants to individuals; Scholarships—to individuals; Matching/challenge support.
Limitations: Applications accepted. Giving limited to residents of metropolitan Richmond, the tri-cities area, including Hopewell, Colonial Heights, and Petersburg, and Chesterfield, Hanover, and Henrico counties, VA. No grants for annual campaigns, deficit financing, land acquisition, or building funds.
Publications: Application guidelines; Annual report; Biennial report.
Application information: Visit foundation web site for additional guidelines per grant type. The foundation will invite organizations to submit a full proposal based on their letter of intent. Faxed or e-mailed letters of intent are not accepted. Application form required.
Initial approach: Preliminary letter of intent (no more than 2 pages)
Copies of proposal: 2
***Deadline(s):* May 5 and Nov. 5 for letter of intent; Jan. 6 and July 7 for proposals**
Board meeting date(s): Quarterly
Final notification: May 19 and Nov. 19 for full proposal invitation; 3rd week of Mar. and Sept. for grant decision
Officers and Board of Governors:* Farhad Aghdami,* Chair.; Thomas N. Chewning,* Vice-Chair.; Darcy S. Oman,* C.E.O. and Pres.; Susan Brown Davis, Sr. V.P., Community Leadership Initiatives; Karen Hand, Sr. V.P., Finance & Admin.; Robert Thalhimer, Sr. V.P., Philanthropic Svcs. and Donor Engagement; Molly Dean Bittner, V.P., Philanthropic Svcs.; Susan H. Hallett, V.P., Progs.; Michelle A. Nelson, V.P., Finance; Lisa Pratt O'Mara, V.P., Donor Engagement; Kimberly Russell, V.P., Comms.; Elaine Summerfield, V.P., Progs.; Lissy S. Bryan,* Secy.; Thomas G. Snead, Jr.,* Treas.; Maureen C. Ackerly; Karen Booth Adams; Austin Brockenbrough IV; Thomas D. Byer; Thomas S. Gayner; Iris E. Holliday; John A. Luke, Jr.; Dee Ann Remo; Dianne L. Reynolds-Cane, M.D.; Pamela J. Royal, M.D.; Stuart C. Siegel; Mark P. Sisisky; Robert C. Sledd III; T. Kirk Tattersall; Christopher H. Williams.
Number of staff: 10 full-time professional; 1 part-time professional; 4 full-time support.
EIN: 237009135

3434

William A. Cooke Foundation

P.O. Box 462
Louisa, VA 23093-0462 (540) 967-0881
Contact: Wallace L. Tingler C.P.A., Pres.
FAX: (540) 967-0711;
E-mail: rltingler1@gmail.com; Main URL: http://wacookefoundation.com/
Grants List: http://wacookefoundation.com/pages/grants

Donors: William A. Cooke, Incorporated; William A. Cooke Trust.
Foundation type: Independent foundation.
Financial data (yr. ended 12/31/12): Assets, $9,141,972 (M); gifts received, $2,448,757; expenditures, $442,649; qualifying distributions, $209,231; giving activities include $8,100 for 3 grants (high: $5,000; low: $200), and $135,000 for 57 grants to individuals (high: $5,000; low: $500).
Fields of interest: Arts; Education; Health care.
Limitations: Applications accepted. Giving limited to Louisa and Orange counties, VA.
Application information: Application form required.
Initial approach: Proposal
Deadline(s): None
Officers: Wallace L. Tingler, C.P.A., Pres.; Randall L. Tingler, V.P.; Rebecca B. Cavanaugh, Secy.
Directors: Dean P. Agee; C. Champian Bowles; Gloria G. Layne; Linda J. Parker; Deborah Pettit.
EIN: 542012726

3435

Helen Pumphrey Denit Charitable Trust

(formerly The Helen Pumphrey Denit Trust for Charitable and Educational Purposes)
c/o U.S. Trust, Bank of America, N.A.
1111 E. Main St., VA2-300-12-92
Richmond, VA 23219 (804) 788-2673
Contact: Sarah Kay, V.P.
E-mail: sarah.kay@ustrust.com; **Main URL: https://www.bankofamerica.com/philanthropic/grantmaking.go**

Established in 1989 in DC and MD.
Donor: Helen P. Denit†.
Foundation type: Independent foundation.
Financial data (yr. ended 06/30/13): Assets, $6,756,210 (M); expenditures, $424,877; qualifying distributions, $331,453; giving activities include $298,500 for 22 grants (high: $50,000; low: $5,000).
Purpose and activities: Giving to support charitable organizations that promote quality education, culture, human service, health service, and arts opportunities.
Fields of interest: Museums (art); Arts; Higher education; Theological school/education; Hospitals (general); Human services.
Limitations: Applications accepted. Giving primarily in Washington, DC and Baltimore, MD. No grants to individuals.
Application information:
Initial approach: Online via Trust web site
Deadline(s): Feb. 1
Trustee: Bank of America, N.A.
EIN: 526401248

3436

Leifur Eiriksson Foundation

c/o University of Virginia Foundation
P.O. Box 400222
Charlottesville, VA **22904-4222 (434) 982-4849**
Contact: Margo Eppard, Treas.
E-mail: mde5c@virginia.edu; **Application address: c/o Karen Torgersen, Coordinator, 1209 Redbud Rd., Blacksburg, VA 24060, tel.: (434) 981-2061, e-mail: eiriksson.foundation@gmail.com; Additional contact: c/o Susan G. Harris, Secy., e-mail: sgh4c@virginia.edu**; Main URL: http://www.leifureiriksson foundation.org/

Foundation type: Independent foundation.
Financial data (yr. ended 06/30/12): Assets, $5,002,938 (M); gifts received, $25; expenditures, $238,970; qualifying distributions, $209,922; giving activities include $162,500 for 7 grants to individuals (high: $25,000; low: $12,500).
Purpose and activities: The foundation funds a graduate fellowship exchange program between Iceland and the United States.
Fields of interest: Education.
International interests: Iceland.
Type of support: Fellowships.
Application information: See foundation web site for complete application guidelines. Application form required.
Initial approach: Email or complete online application form
Deadline(s): Applications by Dec. 2; supporting documents by Dec. 13
Officers: John T. Casteen III, Chair.; Susan G. Harris, Secy.; Margo D. Eppard, Treas.
Trustees: Thrainn Eggertsson; Joan Fry; Halla Tomasdottir; Richard S. Williams, Jr.
EIN: 542056415

3437

The Flagler Foundation

(formerly The Clisby Charitable Trust)
Richmond, VA

The foundation terminated in 2012.

3438

Foundation of the Pierre Fauchard Academy

11654 Plaza American Dr., Ste. 901
Reston, VA 20190 (703) 217-1480
***Contact:* Jennifer Teale, Exec. Dir.**
***E-mail:* information@foundationpfa.org; Email for completed applications: jteale@foundationpfa.org; Main URL: http://www.foundationpfa.org**

Established in 1986 in CA.
Foundation type: Independent foundation.

Financial data (yr. ended 12/31/12): Assets, $6,530,970 (M); gifts received, $52,006; expenditures, $403,802; qualifying distributions, $294,794; giving activities include $122,800 for 20 grants (high: $10,000; low: $2,500), and $81,000 for 54 grants to individuals (high: $1,000; low: $1,000).
Purpose and activities: Support primarily for dental schools and for the study and research of dentistry. Support also for programs that support dental care for the underserved world wide.
Fields of interest: Dental school/education; Human services.
Type of support: General/operating support; Scholarships—to individuals.
Limitations: Applications accepted. Giving on a national basis.
Application information: See Academy web site for application information for grants and scholarships.
Board meeting date(s): Oct.
Officers: Dr. Kevin L. Roach, Pres.; Dr. Gary Lowder, V.P.; Dr. Michael J. Perpich, Treas.; Dr. Howard Mark, Grants Chair.; Jennifer Teale, Exec. Dir.
Trustees: Dr. Malcolm David Campbell; Dr. Charles G. Eller; Dr. James A. Englander; **Dr. Steven Hedlund; William B. Kort; Hubert Pierre Ouvrard.**
EIN: 770120371
Other changes: Dr. Kevin L. Roach has replaced Dr. Malcolm David Campbell as Pres. Dr. Gary Lowder has replaced Dr. C.F. Larry Barrett as V.P. Dr. Michael J. Perpich has replaced William B. Kort as Treas.
Jennifer Teale is now Exec. Dir.

3439
The William and Eva Fox Foundation
P.O. Box 1408
McLean, VA 22101-1408
Main URL: http://www.tcg.org/fox/index.htm
Grants List: http://www.tcg.org/fox/fellows_past.htm

Established in 1987 in DE; funded in 1994.
Donor: Belle Fox‡.
Foundation type: Independent foundation.
Financial data (yr. ended 06/30/12): Assets, $5,084,127 (M); expenditures, $264,620; qualifying distributions, $255,375; giving activities include $255,000 for 2 grants (high: $200,000; low: $55,000).
Purpose and activities: The foundation's mission is committed to the artistic development of theatre actors as a strategy to strengthen live theatre.
Fields of interest: Performing arts; Performing arts, theater.
International interests: United Kingdom.
Type of support: Fellowships.
Limitations: Giving on a national basis and in England.
Publications: Grants list.
Application information: Application guidelines and form available on foundation web site.
Officer and Director:* Robert P. Warren,* Pres.
EIN: 133497192

3440
Helen G. Gifford Foundation
(formerly The Lee A. & Helen G. Gifford Foundation)
1004 Witch Point Trail
Virginia Beach, VA 23455-5645 (757) 412-1467
FAX: (757) 412-1468; E-mail: WHearst@cox.net

Established in 1997 in VA.
Donor: Helen G. Gifford‡.
Foundation type: Independent foundation.
Financial data (yr. ended 06/30/13): Assets, $4,131,459 (M); expenditures, $505,980; qualifying distributions, $400,140; giving activities include $393,500 for 52 grants (high: $115,000; low: $1,000).
Purpose and activities: Funding primarily for Jewish agencies, temples, and federated giving programs. Funding also for arts and culture, and human services.
Fields of interest: Museums; Performing arts; Arts; Human services; United Ways and Federated Giving Programs; Jewish agencies & synagogues.
Limitations: Applications not accepted. Giving primarily in Hampton Roads, VA. No support for political organizations. No grants to individuals.
Application information: Unsolicited requests for funds not accepted.
Board meeting date(s): Quarterly
Officers and Directors:* William A. Hearst,* Pres.; Zelma G. Rivint,* Exec. V.P.; Patricia M. Rowland,* 1st V.P.; Jennifer Rosenberg,* 2nd V.P.; Michael E. Barney,* Secy.; Joseph B. Hearst,* Treas.
EIN: 541850266
Other changes: The grantmaker has changed its fiscal year-end from Feb. 28 to June 30.

3441
Greensville Memorial Foundation
(formerly Greensville Memorial Hospital)
P.O. Box 1015
Emporia, VA 23847-1015 (434) 336-9822
Contact: Jill Slate, Exec. Dir.

Established in VA.
Foundation type: Independent foundation.
Financial data (yr. ended 08/31/13): Assets, $13,704,862 (M); expenditures, $854,455; qualifying distributions, $384,991; giving activities include $326,098 for 14 grants (high: $127,708; low: $160).
Purpose and activities: Giving primarily to community organizations for equipment procurement; some funding for education, particularly a nursing program, social services, and to a YMCA.
Fields of interest: Nursing school/education; Safety/disasters, volunteer services; Disasters, fire prevention/control; Human services; YM/YWCAs & YM/YWHAs.
Limitations: Applications accepted. Giving restricted to areas serviced by the Greensville Memorial Hospital, Greensville, VA.
Application information: Application form required.
Initial approach: Proposal
***Deadline(s):* Aug. 1 for fall grant cycle and Feb. 1 for spring grant cycle**
Officers: Michael S. Anderson, M.D., Chair.; Robert Grizzard, Jr., Vice-Chair.; Angela B. Wilson, M.D., Secy.; Frank E. Kientz, Treas.; Jill Slate, Exec. Dir.
Board Members: Theopolis Gilliam; Brian K. Roberts; James C. Saunders.
EIN: 540645217
Other changes: Elfren A. Quitiquit, Robert G. O'Hara and Raymond A. Thomas are no longer board members.

3442
Richard and Caroline T. Gwathmey Memorial Trust
c/o U.S. Trust, Philanthropic Solutions
1111 E. Main St., VA2-300-12-92
Richmond, VA 23219-3531
Contact: Sarah Kay, V.P., U.S. Trust
FAX: (804) 788-2673;
E-mail: sarah.kay@ustrust.com**; E-mail to discuss application process and for questions: va.grantmaking@ustrust.com. (Foundation name should be indicated in subject line)**; Main URL: http://www.bankofamerica.com/grantmaking

Established in 1981 in VA.
Donor: Elizabeth G. Jeffress‡.
Foundation type: Independent foundation.
Financial data (yr. ended 06/30/13): Assets, $14,084,461 (M); expenditures, $786,575; qualifying distributions, $693,695; giving activities include $616,450 for 36 grants (high: $39,000; low: $5,000).
Purpose and activities: Giving primarily to the arts, cultural institutions, and for education.
Fields of interest: Museums; Historic preservation/historical societies; Arts; Education; Human services.
Type of support: Capital campaigns; Building/renovation; Equipment; Program development; Matching/challenge support.
Limitations: Applications accepted. Giving limited to VA. No support for active churches. No grants to individuals or for operating expenses.
Publications: Application guidelines; Informational brochure (including application guidelines).
Application information: Application form not required.
Initial approach: Letter requesting guidelines
Copies of proposal: 1
Deadline(s): Mar. 1 and Sept. 1
Board meeting date(s): Nov. and May
***Final notification:* June 15 (for Mar. deadline), and Dec. 31 (for Sept. deadline)**
Advisor: Sarah Kay.
Allocations Committee: Richard Hamprick, M.D.; Ernest R. Lail; Carolyn A. White, Esq.; Raphael Witorsch, Ph.D.; David L. Yarter.
Trustee: Bank of America, N.A.
Number of staff: 1 part-time professional; 1 part-time support.
EIN: 546191586

3443
The Harvest Foundation of the Piedmont
1 Ellsworth St.
P.O. Box 5183
Martinsville, VA 24112-2845 (276) 632-3329
Contact: Allyson Rothrock, Pres.
FAX: (276) 632-1878;
E-mail: info@theharvestfoundation.org; Main URL: http://www.theharvestfoundation.org
Facebook: https://www.facebook.com/pages/Harvest-Foundation-Piedmont/137147119666676

Established in 2002 in VA; converted from the sale of Memorial Health System to Province Healthcare of Brentwood, TN.
Foundation type: Independent foundation.
Financial data (yr. ended 12/31/12): Assets, $197,359,569 (M); expenditures, $13,936,843; qualifying distributions, $12,540,567; giving activities include $11,227,042 for 34 grants (high: $4,394,230; low: $8,425), and $251,295 for 1 foundation-administered program.
Purpose and activities: The foundation researches and responsibly invests in programs and initiatives

to address local challenges in health, education, and community vitality.
Fields of interest: Education; Health care; Community/economic development.
Limitations: Applications accepted. Giving limited to Martinsville and Henry County, VA. No support for institutions that discriminate on the basis of race, creed, gender, or sexual orientation; international programs; sectarian religious activities; political lobbying; profit-making enterprises; or direct replacement of discontinued government support. No grants to individuals, or for scholarships, fellowships, debt reduction, medical research, emergency funding or extreme time-sensitive requests, or endowment funds.
Publications: Application guidelines; Annual report.
Application information: Program staff invites selected applying organizations to submit full proposals. Program Staff performs due diligence on possible applicants. As appropriate, program staff will present full proposals to the Board of Directors for consideration. The Board of Directors will make all final decisions to approve or decline requests. (Grant seekers are strongly discouraged from lobbying Board Members.) If approved, the applying Organization will receive, sign, and return a copy of the Letter of Agreement to the foundation. No organization should make commitments or expenditures until the full proposal has been approved by the Board of Directors and the Letter of Agreement has been signed and executed. Application form required.
Initial approach: Online application form required. Applying organizations should first review the foundation's funding priorities and guidelines and then, if appropriate, complete and submit online Program Summary.
Deadline(s): There are no specific deadlines for document submission. Funding requests are reviewed by the foundation's Board of Directors two times per year. As a rule, the foundation does not accept emergency or out-of-cycle proposals.
Final notification: The foundation's staff commits to keeping applying organizations continually informed throughout the Grants Application Process.
Officers and Directors:* James McClain II,* Chair.; W. Christopher Beeler,* Vice-Chair.; Allyson Rothrock, Pres.; **Martha W. Medley,* Secy.**; Eugene C. Madonia, M.D.*, Treas.; Georgia Compton, Cont.; Leanna B. Blevins, Ph.D.; Paul R. Eason, M.D.; Virginia W. Hamlet; F. Dewitt House, Jr.; Cynthia Ingram, Ed.D.; Amy P. Lampe; James K. Muehleck, D.D.S.; David L. Stone, Jr.; E. Larry Ryder.
Number of staff: 7 full-time professional.
EIN: 311496872
Other changes: At the close of 2012, the grantmaker paid grants of $11,227,042, a 64.7% increase over the 2011 disbursements, $6,816,485.
Martha W. Medley has replaced Gracie R. Agnew as Secy.

3444
Thomas F. and Kate Miller Jeffress Memorial Trust
c/o US Trust, Philanthropic Solutions
1111 E. Main St., VA2-300-12-92
Richmond, VA 23219-3573
Contact: Sarah Kay, V.P.
E-mail: sarak.kay@ustrust.com; **Tel. for information regarding the application process for Jeffress Trust Awards Program in Interdisciplinary Research: (617) 279-2240, ext. 709; Main URL: http://www.bankofamerica.com/grantmaking**

Established in 1981 in VA.
Donor: Robert M. Jeffress†.
Foundation type: Independent foundation.
Financial data (yr. ended 06/30/13): Assets, $31,370,851 (M); expenditures, $1,084,268; qualifying distributions, $880,536; giving activities include $671,450 for 14 grants (high: $120,000; low: $10,000).
Purpose and activities: Giving primarily to VA colleges and universities for basic research in chemical, medical, and other scientific research.
Fields of interest: Biomedicine; Medical research, institute; Science; Physical/earth sciences; Chemistry.
Type of support: Research.
Limitations: Applications accepted. Giving limited to VA. No support for clinical research, maintenance for institutionally-owned equipment, or instrument computer time. No grants to individuals, or for fringe benefits, indirect costs, common supplies and services, secretarial services, academic stipends or salaries, or for travel.
Publications: Application guidelines; Informational brochure (including application guidelines).
Application information: Application guidelines and form available on foundation web site. Application form required.
***Deadline(s):* Jan. 15**
Board meeting date(s): May and Nov.
Officer: Sarah Kay, Secy.
Trustee: Bank of America, N.A.
Advisor: Richard B. Brandt, Ph.D.
Allocations Committee: James K. Cluverius, Esq.; Dr. Richard Hamrich; Gregory B. Robertson; Dr. Rafael Witorsch; David L. Yarter.
Number of staff: 1 part-time professional; 1 part-time support.
EIN: 546094925

3445
Charles B. Keesee Educational Fund, Inc.
P.O. Box 431
Martinsville, VA 24114-0431 (276) 632-2229
Contact: Mrs. Vernie W. Lewis, Secy.-Treas.
E-mail: cbkeesee@earthlink.net; Main URL: http://www.cbkeesee.com

Established in 1941 in VA.
Donors: Patricia Pilcher; Floyd Smith Charitable Remainder Unitrust.
Foundation type: Independent foundation.
Financial data (yr. ended 01/31/13): Assets, $68,042,090 (M); gifts received, $37,775; expenditures, $3,194,353; qualifying distributions, $2,546,306; giving activities include $550,000 for 4 grants, and $1,817,129 for grants to individuals.
Purpose and activities: The fund's purpose is to provide funds through grants to students of its supported organizations. Applicant must be a resident of NC, SC or VA for a minimum of 12 months prior to entering school. Applicant must be preparing to enter the Baptist ministry or religious work in the Baptist denomination, and must be a member of a Baptist church, and enrolled in a Master's degree program.
Fields of interest: Education; Religion, formal/general education.
Limitations: Applications accepted. Giving limited to NC, SC and VA.
Application information: Application guidelines and form available on foundation web site. Application form required.
***Initial approach:* Application via U.S. mail**
***Deadline(s):* Apr. 1 for Seminaries and Divinity Schools; Oct. 1 for second semester only grants**
Officers and Trustees:* David D. Burhans,* Pres.; Douglas T. Ramsey,* V.P.; Vernie W. Lewis, Secy.-Treas.; Frank R. Campbell; **Georgia Compton**; G. Paul Fletcher; **John T. Fulcher**; Dick Hensley; Martha W. Medley; Betty Lou Pigg.
EIN: 540490435

3446
The Kellar Family Foundation
P.O. Box 3547
Manassas, VA **20108-0964**

Established in 1997 in VA.
Donors: Arthur Kellar; Elizabeth Kellar†; Kellar Family Charitable Lead Trust.
Foundation type: Independent foundation.
Financial data (yr. ended 02/28/13): Assets, $44,900,133 (M); gifts received, $1,980,507; expenditures, $2,524,916; qualifying distributions, $2,223,302; giving activities include $2,200,014 for 2 grants (high: $2,200,000; low: $4).
Purpose and activities: Giving primarily for the arts, animal welfare, human services, and health organizations.
Fields of interest: Arts; Higher education; Education; Animal welfare; Health care; Health organizations, association; Human services.
Limitations: Applications not accepted. Giving primarily in Cincinnati, OH. No grants to individuals.
Application information: Contributes only to pre-selected organizations.
Officers: Mary K. Kellar, Pres.; Judith C. Kellar Box, V.P.; **Anne Ridgway, Secy.-Treas.**
EIN: 522026425
Other changes: Casey Box is no longer Treas. Anne Ridgway is now Secy.-Treas.

3447
Ruth and Hal Launders Charitable Trust
c/o Jeffrey J. Fairfield, P.C.
459 Herndon Pkwy., No. 14
P.O. Box 546
Herndon, VA 20170-6222
E-mail: jeff@jjfpc.com; Main URL: http://www.rhlct.org

Established in 2007 in VA.
Donor: Ruth C. Launders Marital Trust.
Foundation type: Independent foundation.
Financial data (yr. ended 04/30/13): Assets, $28,226,123 (M); expenditures, $2,396,219; qualifying distributions, $1,711,684; giving activities include $1,618,187 for 56 grants (high: $861,187; low: $2,500).
Fields of interest: Elementary/secondary education; Higher education; Human services; Community/economic development; Homeless.
Limitations: Applications not accepted. **Giving in the U.S., with emphasis on FL, NY and VA.** No grants to individuals.
Application information: Contributes only to pre-selected organizations.
Trustees: Jeffrey J. Fairfield, Esq.; Rebecca Fehrs; L. Farnum Johnson, Jr.; Jerome L. Lonnes; Eugenie W. Maine; John H. Webb; Catherine P. Whelan.
EIN: 020703907
Other changes: For the fiscal year ended Apr. 30, 2013, the grantmaker paid grants of $1,618,187, an 82.2% increase over the fiscal 2012 disbursements, $888,284.

3448
Lee-Jackson Educational Foundation
(formerly The Lee-Jackson Foundation)
P.O. Box 8121
Charlottesville, VA 22906-8121
Contact: Stephanie P. Leech, Secy.
***E-mail:* leejacksonfoundation@yahoo.com; Main URL: http://www.lee-jackson.org**

Established in 1953 in VA.
Donors: Jay W. Johns; Civil War Preservation Trust.
Foundation type: Independent foundation.
Financial data (yr. ended 03/31/13): Assets, $0 (M); expenditures, $260,054; qualifying distributions, $231,661; giving activities include $155,000 for 20 grants (high: $25,000; low: $1,000), and $30,000 for 16 grants to individuals (high: $10,000; low: $1,000).
Purpose and activities: The foundation works to increase educational opportunities for Virginia's youth with scholarships awarded through an essay competition; an applicant must be a junior or senior in a Virginia public or private high school who is a resident of Virginia. Funding also for museums and historical activities, secondary schools, and higher education.
Fields of interest: Museums (specialized); Historic preservation/historical societies; Secondary school/education; Higher education; Foundations (private grantmaking).
Type of support: General/operating support; Scholarships—to individuals.
Limitations: Applications accepted. **Giving limited to residents of VA.**
Application information: See foundation web site for complete application guidelines. Application form required.
Initial approach: Proposal
***Deadline(s):* Mid-Feb.**
Officers: John P. Ackerly III, Pres.; William W. Bergen, V.P.; Stephanie Leech, Secy.; Robert R. Humphris,* Treas.
Directors: Adm. Thomas E. Bass III; Richard H. Britton; Claude P. Foster; Gary W. Gallagher; Donovan E. Hower, Sr.; Robert K. Krick; Richard Bland Lee V; Alexander C. Von Thelen; David M. West.
EIN: 540581000
Other changes: The grantmaker no longer lists a phone.

3449
The Lincoln-Lane Foundation
c/o Edith Grandy
207 Granby St., Ste. 302
Norfolk, VA 23510-1825 (757) 622-2557
FAX: (757) 623-2698;
E-mail: contact@lincolnlanefoundation.org; Main URL: http://www.lincolnlanefoundation.org

Incorporated in 1928 in VA.
Donor: John H. Rogers†.
Foundation type: Independent foundation.
Financial data (yr. ended 07/31/13): Assets, $7,152,364 (M); gifts received, $26,000; expenditures, $588,447; qualifying distributions, $521,592; giving activities include $377,000 for 147 grants to individuals (high: $4,000; low: $250).
Purpose and activities: Giving limited to awards for college scholarships to individuals.
Fields of interest: Higher education.
Type of support: Scholarships—to individuals.
Limitations: Applications accepted. Giving limited to permanent residents of the Tidewater, VA, area. No grants for endowment or building programs, operating budgets, special projects, or annual fundraising campaigns; no loans.
Publications: Application guidelines; Program policy statement.
Application information: Application form required.
Initial approach: Letter requesting application form
Copies of proposal: 1
Deadline(s): Sept. 1 through Oct. 15. Letters requesting applications must be postmarked no later than Oct. 15
Board meeting date(s): Apr., May, Oct., and Dec.
***Final notification:* Early April**
Officers: Ruth P. Acra, Pres.; Walter M. Moore IV, V.P.; Edith G. Grandy, Secy.-Treas.
Directors: John M. Ankerson; Patricia J. Shotton.
Number of staff: 1 part-time professional; 1 part-time support.
EIN: 540601700
Other changes: Patricia Patten is no longer a director.
The grantmaker now makes its application guidelines available online.

3450
The Jesse and Rose Loeb Foundation, Inc.
P.O. Box 803
Warrenton, VA 20188-0803 (540) 428-1960
Contact: Thomas H. Kirk, Exec. Dir.
***E-mail:* kirk@loebfoundation.org**; Main URL: http://www.loebfoundation.org

Established in 1991 in VA.
Donor: Rose Loeb.
Foundation type: Independent foundation.
Financial data (yr. ended 09/30/13): Assets, $9,756,847 (M); expenditures, $518,866; qualifying distributions, $500,253; giving activities include $347,500 for 19 grants (high: $52,000; low: $1,500), and $55,000 for 11 grants to individuals (high: $5,000; low: $5,000).
Purpose and activities: Giving primarily for human services and community development. Funding also for scholarships to student graduates of Liberty High School in Fauquier County, Virginia, who are pursuing higher education in the state of Virginia.
Fields of interest: Arts; Education; Public health; Human services; Community/economic development.
Limitations: Applications accepted. Giving limited to the Fauquier County, VA, region. No grants to.
Publications: Application guidelines.
Application information: Application guidelines available on foundation web site. Application form required.
Copies of proposal: 5
Deadline(s): Between Feb. 1 and Apr. 30; mid-Apr. for scholarship applications
Officer: Thomas H. Kirk, Exec. Dir.
Directors: G. Wayne Eastham; Sue Ann Meek; Richard Monahan; Donald R. Yowell.
EIN: 541604839

3451
Longview Foundation for Education in World Affairs and International Understanding, Inc.
1069 W. Broad St., Ste. 801
Falls Church, VA 22046-4610
Contact: Jennifer Manise, Exec. Dir.
E-mail: globaled@longviewfdn.org; Main URL: http://www.longviewfdn.org/
Grants Database: http://www.longviewfdn.org/grants-grantees/grants-awarded/
LinkedIn: http://www.linkedin.com/company/the-longview-foundation
Twitter: https://twitter.com/LongviewGlobal

Established in 1966 in MD.
Donor: William L. Breese†.
Foundation type: Independent foundation.
Financial data (yr. ended 09/30/13): Assets, $6,487,045 (M); expenditures, $466,144; qualifying distributions, $398,237; giving activities include $241,359 for 11 grants (high: $32,377; low: $4,550).
Purpose and activities: Giving to foster greater awareness of world affairs and international understanding within American schools at the K-12 grade level.
Fields of interest: Education, association; Education, public policy; Teacher school/education; Education.
Type of support: Program development; Conferences/seminars; Publication; Seed money; Curriculum development; Research; Technical assistance; Matching/challenge support.
Limitations: Applications accepted. Giving on a national basis. No support for individual schools or foundations. No grants to individuals or for indirect costs not directly related to a project.
Publications: Application guidelines; Grants list; Occasional report.
Application information: Proposals are accepted by invitation only. Guidelines available on web site. Electronic submissions required. Application form required.
Initial approach: E-mail inquiry form
Copies of proposal: 1
Deadline(s): See foundation web site for deadlines
Board meeting date(s): Apr. and Oct.
Final notification: May 15 and Nov. 15
Officers and Trustees:* Lois Adams-Rodgers,* Pres.; Anthony Jackson, V.P.; Susan Sclafani, Secy.; Yvonne Chan, Treas.; John Friedland; Breese McIlvaine; Caryn Stedman; Ron Thorpe; John Wilson.
Number of staff: 1 part-time professional.
EIN: 526070327

3452
Davis Love, III Foundation
c/o HRH CPA
808 Moorefield Park Dr.
Richmond, VA 23236
LinkedIn: http://www.linkedin.com/company/davis-love-foundation
Twitter: http://twitter.com/love3d

Established in 2005 in GA.
Donor: Davis M. Love III.
Foundation type: Independent foundation.
Financial data (yr. ended 12/31/11): Assets, $674,821 (M); gifts received, $307,278; expenditures, $5,893,109; qualifying distributions, $428,852; giving activities include $428,852 for 32 grants (high: $100,000; low: $70).
Purpose and activities: Giving for the well-being and progress of society by supporting both national and community-based programs that focus on children and their families.
Fields of interest: Education; Human services; Community/economic development; Protestant agencies & churches; Children/youth.
Limitations: Applications not accepted. Giving primarily in GA, ID, and NC.

Application information: Unsolicited requests for funds not accepted.
Directors: Davis M. Love III; Robin B. Love.
EIN: 202920597

3453
The Loyola Foundation, Inc.

10335 Democracy Ln., No. 202
Fairfax, VA 22030-2527 (571) 435-9401
Contact: Albert G. McCarthy III; Christine M. Rice
FAX: (571) 435-9402;
E-mail: info@loyolafoundation.org; Main URL: http://www.loyolafoundation.org/

Incorporated in 1957 in DC.
Donor: Members of the Albert Gregory McCarthy, Jr. family.
Foundation type: Independent foundation.
Financial data (yr. ended 10/31/13): Assets, $40,777,011 (M); expenditures, $1,916,290; qualifying distributions, $1,533,392; giving activities include $1,204,695 for 201 grants (high: $50,000; low: $250), and $1,533,392 for foundation-administered programs.
Purpose and activities: Grants primarily for basic overseas Roman Catholic missionary work and other Catholic activities of special interest to the trustees. Primary interest in nonrecurring requests for capital improvements in the missionary area, which are self-sustaining after completion; special consideration given to requests where there are matching contributions from the missionary area, itself.
Fields of interest: Catholic agencies & churches.
International interests: Africa; Developing Countries; Latin America; Asia.
Type of support: Building/renovation; Equipment; Matching/challenge support.
Limitations: Applications accepted. Giving primarily in Third World developing nations. Grants made in the U.S. only to institutions or organizations of special interest to the trustees. No support for minor seminaries. **No grants to individuals, or for annual budgets, endowment funds, research, continuing support, operating expenses, emergency funds, deficit financing, publications, conferences, scholarships, tuitions, fellowships, travel and meetings, or for used or reconditioned vehicles; no loans.**
Publications: Application guidelines; Financial statement; Multi-year report.
Application information: All requests must be in English. Applicants should only proceed with the application form after they have received the foundation's confirmation that their initial submission of the grant request is eligible for consideration. Application form available on foundation web site. For requests for projects whose cost is in excess of $50,000, applications cannot be accepted until at least 75 percent of the total funds needed for the project have been secured from other sources. The foundation acknowledges receipt of proposals and grants interviews with applicants upon request.
Application form required.
Initial approach: Letter
Copies of proposal: 1
Deadline(s): Mar. 31 and Sept. 30
Board meeting date(s): June and Dec.
Final notification: Jan. and July
Officers and Trustees:* Andrea M. Hattler-Bramson,* Pres.; John N. Malyska,* V.P.; Amy Hattler Page,* Treas.; A. Gregory McCarthy IV,* Secy. and Exec. Dir.; Daniel J. Altobello; Rev. William J. Byron, S.J.; Kathleen D.H. Carr; William J. Fiore; Denise M. Hattler; Hillary A. Hattler; Cardinal Theodore E. McCarrick; Diana Hattler McDonough; Raymond W. Merritt.
Number of staff: 2 full-time professional; 1 part-time professional.
EIN: 520781255

3454
Greater Lynchburg Community Trust

101 Paulette Circle, Ste. B
Lynchburg, VA 24504 (434) 845-6500
Contact: Stuart C. Fauber, C.E.O.
FAX: (434) 845-6530; E-mail: challglct@verizon.net; Additional e-mail: sfauberglct@verizon.net; Main URL: http://www.lynchburgtrust.org

Established as a community trust in 1972 in VA.
Foundation type: Community foundation.
Financial data (yr. ended 06/30/12): Assets, $29,622,750 (M); gifts received, $2,354,627; expenditures, $1,626,217; giving activities include $1,301,172 for 75+ grants (high: $282,700), and $30,114 for 40 grants to individuals.
Purpose and activities: The principal mission of the Community Trust is to enhance the quality of life in the communities served by establishment of permanent endowments for the cities of Lynchburg and Bedford and the counties of Amherst, Appomattox, Bedford and Campbell, with income distributed annually to charitable organizations within the community. Needs served are broad in scope including education, health, the arts, the humanities, and human services to children, youth, the needy, and the elderly.
Fields of interest: Humanities; Arts; Libraries/library science; Education; Health care; Food services; Youth development, services; Children/youth, services; Family services; Aging, centers/services; Women, centers/services; Homeless, human services; Human services; Nonprofit management; Community/economic development; Social sciences; Youth; Aging; Disabilities, people with; Women; Economically disadvantaged; Homeless.
Type of support: Capital campaigns; Building/renovation; Equipment; Emergency funds; Program development; Seed money; Scholarship funds; Technical assistance; Employee-related scholarships; Scholarships—to individuals; Matching/challenge support.
Limitations: Applications accepted. Giving limited to Lynchburg and Bedford City, and Amherst, Bedford, and Campbell counties, VA. No support for religious organizations for sectarian or religious purposes. No grants to individuals (except for designated scholarship funds), or for routine operating expenses or deficit financing.
Publications: Application guidelines; Annual report; Informational brochure; Newsletter; Program policy statement.
Application information: Visit foundation web site for grant application information sheet and guidelines. Application form required.
Initial approach: Submit grant information sheet and attachments
Copies of proposal: 10
Deadline(s): Mar. 15 and Sept. 15
Board meeting date(s): June, Sept., Dec., Feb., and Apr.
Final notification: June and Dec.
Officers and Directors:* Stuart C. Fauber,* C.E.O. and Pres.; John R. Alford, Jr.; Mary Jane Dolan; Robert Finch, Jr.; John M. Flippin; Ernie T. Guill, Jr.; David A. Herrick; Hylan T. Hubbard; Ellen P. Jamerson; Wallace G. McKenna, Jr.; Ellen Nygaard; Augustus A. Petticolas, Jr.; James R. Richards; Marc A. Schewel; Massie G. Ware, Jr.; Charles B. White; James W. Wright.
Trustee Banks: Bank of America, N.A.; BB&T; SunTrust Bank; Wachovia Bank, N.A.
Number of staff: 1 full-time professional; 1 part-time professional; 1 part-time support.
EIN: 546112680
Other changes: Kenneth S. White and Elliot S. Schewel are no longer directors.

3455
MAIHS Foundation

1209 Riverside Dr.
Newport News, VA 23606-2830

Established in VA.
Donors: Richard F. Abbitt†; Carolyn S. Abbitt.
Foundation type: Independent foundation.
Financial data (yr. ended 07/31/13): Assets, $6,194,784 (M); expenditures, $290,373; qualifying distributions, $256,507; giving activities include $256,507 for 40 grants (high: $130,000; low: $250).
Fields of interest: Museums; Higher education, university; Education, services; Education; Aquariums; Autism; Protestant agencies & churches.
Limitations: Applications not accepted. Giving primarily in VA. No grants to individuals.
Application information: Contributes only to pre-selected organizations.
Officer: Carolyn S. Abbitt, Pres.
Directors: Matthew M. Abbitt; **Stephen M. Abbitt.**
EIN: 521441636

3456
J. T. - Minnie Maude Charitable Trust

223 Riverview Dr., Ste. G
Danville, VA 24541-3435 (434) 797-3330
Contact: Fred K. Webb, Jr., Exec. Dir.
FAX: (434) 797-3343; Main URL: http://www.jtmm.org
RSS Feed: http://jtmm.org/?feed=rss2

Established in 2007 in VA.
Donor: James T. Emerson†.
Foundation type: Independent foundation.
Financial data (yr. ended 12/31/12): Assets, $48,934,020 (M); expenditures, $2,662,880; qualifying distributions, $1,812,858; giving activities include $1,812,858 for grants.
Purpose and activities: Scholarship awards to residents of the Danville/Pittsylvania, VA, area, and surrounding counties in NC.
Fields of interest: Elementary/secondary education; Higher education; Human services.
Type of support: Scholarships—to individuals.
Limitations: Applications accepted. **Giving limited to the Danville/Pittsylvania, VA, area, and in Caswell and Rockingham counties, NC, including all towns and cities located therein.**
Publications: Application guidelines.
Application information: At this time, due to the trust's own existing scholarship program, the trust is not funding grants which provide or establish scholarship programs. See foundation web site for additional application information.
***Initial approach:* Letter on corporate letterhead**
Deadline(s): See foundation web site for current deadlines
Officers: Katherine Emerson, C.F.O.; Fred K. Webb, Jr., Exec. Dir.

Trustees: Earl K. Emerson, Jr.; John D. Lovelace; Sarah E. Lovelace; Harry Sakellaris; Lessie E. Webb.
EIN: 260771142
Other changes: The grantmaker now publishes application guidelines online.

3457
MAXIMUS Foundation, Inc.
1891 Metro Ctr. Dr.
Reston, VA 20190-5207 **(800) 629-4687**
***Contact:* John Boyer, Chair.**
***E-mail:* maximuscharitablefoundation@maximus.com; Main URL: http://www.maximus.com/foundation**
Facebook: https://www.facebook.com/MAXIMUS501c3
Google Plus: https://plus.google.com/111357399481224373881/posts
Grants List: https://www.maximusfoundation.org/our-grant-recipients/
MAXIMUS Foundation Blog: http://www.maximusfoundation.org/
Twitter: https://twitter.com/MAXIMUS501c3

Established in 2000 in VA.
Donor: MAXIMUS, Inc.
Foundation type: Company-sponsored foundation.
Financial data (yr. ended 09/30/13): Assets, $248,291 (M); gifts received, $665,818; expenditures, $683,244; qualifying distributions, $682,930; giving activities include $682,930 for 168 grants (high: $50,000; low: $250).
Purpose and activities: The foundation supports programs designed to promote growth and self-sufficiency through improved health, augmented child and family development, and community development. Special emphasis is directed toward programs designed to serve disadvantaged populations and underserved communities.
Fields of interest: Arts; Education, reading; Education; Health care, home services; Health care; AIDS; Crime/violence prevention, child abuse; Employment, services; Employment, training; Food services; Nutrition; Disasters, preparedness/services; Children/youth, services; Family services; Developmentally disabled, centers & services; Homeless, human services; Human services; Community/economic development; Youth; Economically disadvantaged.
Type of support: General/operating support; Program development.
Limitations: Applications accepted. Giving primarily in CA, Washington, DC, GA, IL, MA, NY, TN, TX, and VA. No support for political candidates. No grants to individuals, or for advertising, ticket events, or dinners, political causes, endowments, or capital campaigns.
Publications: Application guidelines; Annual report; Grants list; Informational brochure (including application guidelines).
Application information: Support is limited to 1 contribution per organization during any given year. Application form required.
Initial approach: **Completed application form**
Deadline(s): Jan. 31 and Aug. 31
Officers and Directors:* John F. Boyer,* Chair.; David R. Francis, Secy.; David Casey; **Benjamin R. Coss**; Mark Elvin; Christine Vaughn Graham; Awilda L. Martinez-Rodriguez; Melinda Metteauer; Paula Wales.
EIN: 541993677
Other changes: The grantmaker no longer lists a fax.
John F. Boyer is now Chair.

3458
Memorial Foundation for Children
P.O. Box 18488
Richmond, VA **23226-8488 (804) 221-1994**
***Contact:* Michelle Thomson, Grants Chair.**
***E-mail:* MFCRichmond@gmail.com; Main URL: http://fdnweb.org/mfc**

Established about 1934 in VA.
Donors: Alexander S. George†; Elizabeth Strother Scott†.
Foundation type: Independent foundation.
Financial data (yr. ended 12/31/13): Assets, $16,522,432 (M); expenditures, $783,956; qualifying distributions, $726,983; giving activities include $726,983 for grants.
Purpose and activities: Aid to nonprofit groups for the care and education of Richmond, VA, area children 18 years of age and under.
Fields of interest: Arts; Child development, education; Education; Human services; Children/youth, services; Child development, services; Infants/toddlers; Children/youth; Children; Disabilities, people with; Blind/visually impaired; Deaf/hearing impaired; Crime/abuse victims; Economically disadvantaged.
Type of support: General/operating support; Equipment; Program development; Seed money; Curriculum development; Scholarship funds.
Limitations: Applications accepted. Giving limited to the Richmond, VA, area, including Chesterfield, Goochland, Hanover and Henrico counties. No support for the Hopewell and Petersburg county, VA, areas. No grants to individuals, or for capital or endowment funds, annual campaigns, emergency funds, deficit financing, matching gifts, publications, conferences, scholarships, or fellowships; no loans.
Publications: Informational brochure (including application guidelines).
Application information: Application form required.
Initial approach: Letter
Copies of proposal: 2
Deadline(s): May 31
Board meeting date(s): Mar., May, Oct., and Nov.
Officers: Wendy Schultz, Pres.; Prem Hall, V.P.; Jean Oakey, Treas.; Missy Chase, Recording Secy.; Sallie Thalhimer, Corresponding Secy.
Number of staff: 1 part-time support.
EIN: 540536103

3459
Metropolitan Health Foundation, Inc.
4132 Innslake Dr.
Glen Allen, VA 23060-3344 (804) 346-2626
Contact: Charles P. Winkler M.D., Pres.

Established in 1984 in VA.
Foundation type: Independent foundation.
Financial data (yr. ended 12/31/13): Assets, $2,195,078 (M); expenditures, $162,263; qualifying distributions, $145,170; giving activities include $140,000 for 21 grants (high: $31,000; low: $1,000).
Purpose and activities: Giving for health education through nursing scholarships, and for public welfare support.
Fields of interest: Nursing school/education; Health care; Health organizations, association; Aging, centers/services.
Type of support: General/operating support.
Limitations: Applications accepted. Giving primarily in Richmond, VA.
Application information: Application form required.
Initial approach: Letter
Deadline(s): None
Officers: Charles P. Winkler, M.D., Pres.; **Michael A. Lormand, V.P.**; Malcolm E. Ritsch, Jr., Secy.-Treas.
Number of staff: 1 part-time support.
EIN: 510186144
Other changes: Michael A. Lormand has replaced Edmond A. Hooker, Jr., M.D. as V.P.
Malcolm E. Ritsch, Jr. is now Secy.-Treas. William E. Holland is no longer director.

3460
The MLG Foundation
0 Court Sq.
Charlottesville, VA 22902-5144 (434) 244-3317
Contact: Emily Erwin
Main URL: http://www.mlgfound.org/

Foundation type: Independent foundation.
Financial data (yr. ended 12/31/12): Assets, $4,174,071 (M); gifts received, $710,000; expenditures, $775,988; qualifying distributions, $747,512; giving activities include $727,850 for 18 grants (high: $181,000; low: $750).
Purpose and activities: Giving primarily for hunger, health and nutrition, children and families, education, and the betterment of the Charlottesville, VA, community.
Fields of interest: Education; Nutrition; Family services; Children.
Limitations: Applications accepted. **Giving primarily in Charlottesville, VA.**
Publications: Application guidelines.
Application information: Application form required.
Initial approach: Online grant application form
***Deadline(s):* See foundation web site for current deadlines. Foundation will review grant applications 2 times per year**
Trustees: Ellen A. Geismar; Michael S. Geismar.
EIN: 263934845
Other changes: The grantmaker now publishes application guidelines.

3461
The Claude Moore Charitable Foundation
11350 Random Hills Rd., Ste. 520
Fairfax, VA 22030-7429 (703) 934-1147
Contact: K. Lynn Tadlock, Deputy Exec. Dir., Giving
FAX: (703) 273-0152;
E-mail: claudemoorefoundation@claudemoore.org;
Main URL: http://www.claudemoorefoundation.org

Established in 1987 in VA.
Donor: Claude Moore†.
Foundation type: Independent foundation.
Financial data (yr. ended 12/31/12): Assets, $125,332,896 (M); expenditures, $5,910,777; qualifying distributions, $4,388,286; giving activities include $1,742,064 for 56 grants (high: $500,000; low: $300).
Purpose and activities: The mission of the foundation is to enhance educational opportunities, including higher education, for young people in the Commonwealth of Virginia and elsewhere.
Fields of interest: Museums (specialized); Higher education; Medical school/education; Nursing school/education; Teacher school/education; Adult education—literacy, basic skills & GED; Education; Health care, formal/general education; Boy scouts.
Type of support: General/operating support; Continuing support; Program development; Conferences/seminars; Scholarship funds; Matching/challenge support.
Limitations: Applications not accepted. Giving primarily in VA. No grants to individuals.

Application information: Unsolicited requests for funds not accepted.
Board meeting date(s): Monthly
Officer: J. Hamilton Lambert, Exec. Dir.
Trustees: Peter A. Arntson; **Gary W. Brown**; Guy M. Gravett; Leigh B. Middleditch, Jr.
EIN: 521558571
Other changes: Jesse B. Wilson is no longer a trustee.

3462
Moran Family Foundation
1489 Chain Bridge Rd., Ste. 200
McLean, VA 22101-5743
***E-mail:* moranfamfdn@aol.com; Main URL: http://fdnweb.org/moran/**

Established in 2003 in VA.
Donors: William A. Moran; Suzanne S. Moran.
Foundation type: Independent foundation.
Financial data (yr. ended 12/31/13): Assets, $9,581,963 (M); expenditures, $501,404; qualifying distributions, $400,025; giving activities include $400,000 for 2 grants (high: $250,000; low: $150,000).
Purpose and activities: The foundation supports innovative programs that promote healthy development of at-risk children and at-risk families whose lives are impacted by the challenges of poverty. The foundation invests in community-based organizations that work to empower at-risk youth and their families to enhance the opportunity for each child to achieve their full potential.
Fields of interest: Children/youth, services; Family services.
Limitations: Applications not accepted. **Giving primarily in the Greater Washington D.C. area as well as the Greater Cleveland, Ohio region.** No support for organizations lacking 501(c)(3) status or for projects that are sectarian in nature. No grants to individuals.
Application information: Unsolicited requests for funds not accepted. Invited organizations may use the "Common Grant Letter of Intent" and the "Common Grant Application" via the Washington Regional Association of Grantmakers; www.washingtongrantmakers.org.
Directors: Patrick Michael Moran; Suzanne S. Moran; Katherine Mary McGovern Moran Pinho.
EIN: 200500658

3463
Marietta McNeill Morgan & Samuel Tate Morgan, Jr. Trust
c/o US Trust, Philanthropic Solutions
1111 E. Main St. VA2-300-12-92
Richmond, VA 23219-3531 (804) 788-2673
***E-mail:* va.grantmaking@ustrust.com**; Main URL: http://www.bankofamerica.com/grantmaking

Trust established in 1967 in VA.
Donors: Marietta McNeill Morgan†; Samuel T. Morgan, Jr.†.
Foundation type: Independent foundation.
Financial data (yr. ended 06/30/13): Assets, $20,325,052 (M); expenditures, $1,149,631; qualifying distributions, $973,075; giving activities include $850,150 for 35 grants (high: $45,000; low: $10,000).
Fields of interest: Museums; Historic preservation/historical societies; Arts; Higher education; Education; Health care; Food banks; Human services.
Type of support: Building/renovation; Equipment; Matching/challenge support.
Limitations: Applications accepted. Giving limited to VA. No support for private foundations or individual churches or congregations. No grants to individuals, or for scholarships, endowment funds, multi-year grants, production of videos, movies, radio or TV programs, or for any purposes except capital projects; no loans.
Publications: Informational brochure (including application guidelines).
Application information: The foundation only makes grants for specific capital expenditures. Guidelines available on foundation web site. Application form not required.
Initial approach: Letter preferred
Copies of proposal: 1
Deadline(s): May 1 and Nov. 1
Board meeting date(s): Feb. and June
Final notification: June 30 and Feb. 28
Advisor: Elizabeth Seaman.
Trustee: Bank of America, N.A.
EIN: 546069447

3464
Northern Piedmont Community Foundation
P.O. Box 182
Warrenton, VA 20188 (540) 349-0631
Contact: M. Cole Johnson, Exec. Dir.
FAX: (540) 349-0633; E-mail: info@npcf.org; Main URL: http://www.npcf.org
Facebook: https://www.facebook.com/northernpiedmontcommunityfoundation

Established in 2000 in VA.
Foundation type: Community foundation.
Financial data (yr. ended 06/30/13): Assets, $6,104,597 (M); gifts received, $299,970; expenditures, $492,450; giving activities include $284,794 for 16+ grants (high: $40,000), and $27,850 for 23 grants to individuals.
Purpose and activities: The foundation seeks to build philanthropic capital to enhance and preserve the quality of life in Culpepper, Fauquier, Rappahannock and Madison counties, and to strengthen the region's nonprofit organizations.
Fields of interest: Arts; Higher education; Education; Environment; Health care; Family services; Human services; Community/economic development.
Type of support: Management development/capacity building; Building/renovation; Equipment; Program development; Publication; Research; Program evaluation.
Limitations: Applications accepted. Giving primarily in Culpeper, Fauquier, Madison, and Rappahannock counties, VA. No support for religious purposes, or national or international organizations. No grants to individuals (except for scholarships), or for ongoing operating support or annual fund drives, endowment, debt or operating deficit reduction, scholarly research, or fellowships or travel.
Publications: Application guidelines; Annual report; Informational brochure; Newsletter.
Application information: Visit foundation web site for application cover sheet and guidelines. Faxed or e-mailed applications are not accepted. Application form required.
Initial approach: Letter or telephone
Copies of proposal: 5
***Deadline(s):* Oct. 15 for Community Fund**
Board meeting date(s): Monthly
Final notification: 3 months
Officers and Directors:* John W. McCarthy, III*, Chair.; Robin C. Gulick,* Pres.; Molly F. Sanford,* Secy.; Thomas D. Gillespie,* Treas.; M. Cole Johnson, Exec. Dir.; Robert C. Dart, M.D.; Marshall deF. Doeller; Trice Gravatte, M.D.; **Susan S. Griffin, D.D.S.**; Michael T. Leake; Nina McKee; **Merrill P. Strange**; **Carlton M. Yowell**.
Number of staff: 2 part-time professional.
EIN: 311742955
Other changes: Carlton M. Yowell and Eugene F. Triplett are no longer directors.

3465
The Northrop Grumman Foundation
(formerly Foundation of the Litton Industries)
2980 Fairview Park Dr.
Falls Church, VA 22042
Contact: Carlene Beste, Secy. and Mgr.
E-mail: ngfoundation@ngc.com.; **E-mail for Carlene Beste: carleen.beste@ngc.com**; Main URL: http://www.northropgrumman.com/CorporateResponsibility/CorporateCitizenship/Philanthropy/Pages/Foundation.aspx

Incorporated in 1954 in CA.
Donors: Litton Industries, Inc.; Northrop Grumman Corp.
Foundation type: Company-sponsored foundation.
Financial data (yr. ended 12/31/12): Assets, $29,021,558 (M); gifts received, $10,000,000; expenditures, $10,726,229; qualifying distributions, $10,598,527; giving activities include $9,809,518 for 91 grants (high: $1,750,000; low: $1,000), and $763,809 for 774 employee matching gifts.
Purpose and activities: The foundation supports programs designed to provide educational opportunities for youth and educators. Special emphasis is directed toward programs designed to promote science, technology, engineering and mathematics (STEM) for students and teachers.
Fields of interest: Elementary/secondary education; Higher education; Education, reading; Education; Mathematics; Engineering/technology; Science; Youth.
Type of support: Employee matching gifts; Program development; Scholarship funds.
Limitations: Giving on a national basis for STEM programming. No support for campus student organizations, fraternities, sororities, honor societies, religious schools or colleges with a primary focus on religious beliefs, athletic teams or athletic support organizations, or choirs, bands, or drill teams. No grants to individuals (except for employee-related scholarships), or for fundraising events, advertising or underwriting expenses, capital campaigns, endowments, or tuition.
Publications: Annual report; Newsletter.
Application information: The foundation is no longer accepting requests for 2014 funding. Visit website for 2015 announcements.
Board meeting date(s): Annually
Officers and Directors:* Sandra Evers-Manly,* Pres.; Carleen Beste, Secy. and Mgr.; Silva Thomas,* Treas.; Shelia Cheston; Frank Flores; Darryl M. Fraser; Denise Peppard.
EIN: 956095343

3466
Oak Hill Fund
P.O. Box 1624
Charlottesville, VA 22902-1624
Contact: Jeff Adams, C.F.O
E-mail: info@oakhillfund.org; Main URL: http://www.oakhillfund.org

Established in 2002 in VA as part of the restructure of the W. Alton Jones Foundation (now known as Blue Moon Fund).
Donor: Blue Moon Fund, Inc.
Foundation type: Independent foundation.
Financial data (yr. ended 12/31/12): Assets, $89,125,277 (M); expenditures, $7,836,246; qualifying distributions, $5,983,157; giving activities include $4,774,339 for 150 grants (high: $316,880; low: $50).
Purpose and activities: The mission of the fund is to promote the well-being of mankind through effective and inspiring grantmaking. The fund currently has three programs: 1) to focus on the promotion of the principles of sustainable development into the design of affordable construction, with a primary focus on residential housing; 2) women's reproductive health and rights, and 3) a local program that addresses quality of life issues within the greater Charlottesville community, including the areas of health and safety, grassroots environment.
Fields of interest: Environment, natural resources; Reproductive health; Housing/shelter, development; Safety, education; Community development, neighborhood development; Women.
Limitations: Applications accepted. Giving limited to the southeastern U.S., including AL, DE, FL, GA, KY, MD, MS, NC, TN, SC, VA, WV, and Washington, DC. The fund's local program is limited to the Thomas Jefferson Planning District, in the foothills of central VA's Blue Ridge Mountains; the district includes the city of Charlottesville and the counties of Albemarle, Greene, Louisa, Fluvanna, and Nelson. No support for organizations lacking 501(c)(3) status. No grants to individuals, or for capital campaigns, endowments, bricks and mortar projects, books, or films; no general operating support or support for research.
Publications: Application guidelines.
Application information: See fund web site for application guidelines and requirements. Application form not required.
Initial approach: **Use Letter of Inquiry process on the fund's web site**
Copies of proposal: 1
Deadline(s): None
Board meeting date(s): Monthly
Final notification: 30 days from receipt
Officers: William A. Ederton, Pres.; Liza T. Ederton, V.P.; Robert W. Hurst, Exec. Dir.; Jeff Adams, C.F.O.
Number of staff: 5 full-time professional; 6 part-time professional.
EIN: 311810011

3467
Obici Healthcare Foundation, Inc.
(formerly Obici Foundation, Inc.)
106 W. Finney Ave.
Suffolk, VA 23434-5265 (757) 539-8810
Contact: Lisa Kelch, Grants Assoc.
FAX: (757) 539-8887; E-mail: lkelch@obicihcf.org; Main URL: http://www.obicihcf.org/
Grants List: http://www.obicihcf.org/recipients.asp

Established in VA; reincorporated in 2006 as a private foundation.
Donor: Sentara Healthcare.
Foundation type: Independent foundation.
Financial data (yr. ended 03/31/13): Assets, $105,585,269 (M); expenditures, $6,116,116; qualifying distributions, $5,102,164; giving activities include $4,136,138 for 132 grants (high: $250,000; low: $85).
Purpose and activities: Giving to improve the health status of people in the Suffolk, VA, and surrounding communities, by addressing the unmet needs of the medically indigent and uninsured, and by supporting programs that have the primary purpose of preventing and reducing illness and disease.
Fields of interest: Health care; Human services; Youth, services; Family services, domestic violence; Residential/custodial care; Economically disadvantaged.
Limitations: Giving primarily in the cities of Suffolk and Franklin, VA, as well as Boykins, Courtland, Dendron, Elberon, Isle of Wright County, Ivor, Newsoms, Sedley, Surry, Wakefield and Waverly, VA; and in Gates County, NC. No grants to individuals, including patient assistance funds, or for lobbying or political activities, biomedical, clinical or educational research, meetings and conferences, unless they are essential to a larger project, scholarships, endowments, annual fund drives, or direct funding for direct medical or social services that already are funded through existing third-party reimbursement sources.
Publications: Application guidelines; Annual report; Financial statement; Grants list; Newsletter.
Application information: Full proposals are by invitation only, upon consideration of concept paper. Application form required.
Initial approach: Follow concept paper guidelines on foundation web site
Deadline(s): See foundation web site for current deadlines
Officers and Directors:* George Y. Birdsong,* Chair.; J. Samuel Glasscock,* Vice-Chair.; Robert M. Hayes,* Secy.-Treas.; Michael Hammond, C.F.O.; Gina L. Pitrone, Exec. Dir.
EIN: 510249728
Other changes: The grantmaker now publishes an annual report.

3468
The George and Carol Olmsted Foundation
80 E. Jefferson St., Ste. 300B
Falls Church, VA 22046-3566
FAX: (703) 536-5020;
E-mail: scholars@olmstedfoundation.org; Toll-free tel.: (877) 656-7833; Main URL: http://www.olmstedfoundation.org

Incorporated in 1960 in VA.
Donor: George Olmsted‡.
Foundation type: Independent foundation.
Financial data (yr. ended 12/31/12): Assets, $41,309,729 (M); gifts received, $9,950; expenditures, $2,168,169; qualifying distributions, $1,793,529; giving activities include $397,250 for 10 grants (high: $110,000; low: $250), and $514,022 for grants to individuals.
Purpose and activities: The primary objective of the foundation is to support programs designed to contribute to the nation's security by providing potential leaders with a comprehensive education, knowledge and depth of understanding of the political, economic and military factors involved in international relations. To this end, the foundation funds the Olmsted Scholar Program, through which career officers are awarded grants for study in a foreign country. The foundation supports active duty regular line officers, service academy cadets, and ROTC cadets. The foundation does not support civilian personnel.
Fields of interest: Education; Military/veterans' organizations.
Type of support: General/operating support; Scholarships—to individuals.
Limitations: Giving on a national basis. No grants to individuals (except for Olmsted Scholars).
Publications: Annual report; Informational brochure; IRS Form 990 or 990-PF printed copy available upon request.
Application information: Qualified military officers apply through their respective Military Service. Applicants are encouraged to take the candidate qualifications survey, which is available on the foundation web site.
Initial approach: Grant requests should be sent to the foundation for forwarding to the Board of Directors. Requests for grants considered when initiated by a member of the Board of Directors
Board meeting date(s): Mar. and Nov.
Officers and Directors:* William "Doug" D. Crowder,* Chair.; Maj. Genl. Bruce K. Scott,* C.E.O. and Pres.; Col. David G. Estep,* Exec. V.P.; Capt. Joseph McManus, Secy.-Treas.; Genl. John P. Abizaid; George "Tom" T. Donovan; Lt. Genl. Emerson "Emo" N. Gardner; **Kathryn "Kathy" L. Gauthier**; Brig. Genl. Silvanus "Taco" Gilbert; Dr. Christopher "Chris" B. Howard; Edward "Ed" L. Jeep; Deborah A. Loewer; Alexander "Alec" R. Mackenzie; Col. Robert "Bob" A. Stratton; Angela "Angie" W. Suplisson.
Number of staff: 3 full-time professional; 1 part-time professional; 1 full-time support.
EIN: 546049005
Other changes: William "Doug" D. Crowder has replaced Genl. Henry "Butch" Viccellip, Jr. as Chair.

3469
The O'Shaughnessy-Hurst Memorial Foundation
602 S. King St., Ste. 200
Leesburg, VA 20175-3919

Established in VA.
Donors: Mary Hurst O'Shaughnessy‡; M. O'Shaughnessy‡.
Foundation type: Independent foundation.
Financial data (yr. ended 12/31/12): Assets, $7,947,146 (M); expenditures, $525,581; qualifying distributions, $369,520; giving activities include $369,520 for grants.
Fields of interest: Education; Human services.
Limitations: Applications not accepted. Giving primarily in VA. No grants to individuals.
Application information: Unsolicited requests for funds not accepted.
Officers: William Soza, Chair.; Deborah Dech Piland, Pres.; Richard Piland, V.P.; Stephanie Marsh, Secy.; Kurt Pfluger, Treas.
EIN: 541394736
Other changes: The grantmaker no longer lists a URL address.

3470
The Mary Morton Parsons Foundation
901 E. Cary St., Ste. 1404
Richmond, VA 23219-4037 **(804) 780-2183**
Contact: Amy P. Nisenson, Exec. Dir.
***FAX:* (804) 915-2737**;
E-mail: mmparsons.foundation@gmail.com; Main URL: http://www.mmparsonsfoundation.org

Established in 1988 in VA.
Donor: Mary Morton Parsons‡.
Foundation type: Independent foundation.
Financial data (yr. ended 12/31/12): Assets, $93,223,709 (M); expenditures, $5,098,279; qualifying distributions, $4,609,000; giving

activities include $4,609,000 for 55 grants (high: $200,000; low: $8,000).
Purpose and activities: Support primarily for museums and historical groups, institutions concerned with education, and social services or welfare.
Fields of interest: Museums; Historic preservation/historical societies; Arts; Education; Environment; Human services.
Type of support: Capital campaigns; Building/renovation; Equipment.
Limitations: Applications accepted. Giving primarily in VA, with an emphasis on Richmond. No grants to individuals, or for debt reduction, endowments, research, or general operating expenses.
Publications: Informational brochure (including application guidelines).
Application information: Proposals submitted without contacting the foundation's Executive Director before the grant deadlines will not receive priority consideration. Faxed or e-mail proposals are not accepted. Application form not required.
Initial approach: **Letter; the foundation encourages telephone inquiries**
Copies of proposal: 1
Deadline(s): Mar. 15 and Sept. 15
Board meeting date(s): May and Nov.
Officers and Directors:* Thurston R. Moore,* Pres.; Charles F. Witthoefft,* V.P. and Secy.; Mrs. Palmer P. Garson,* Treas.; Amy P. Nisenson, Exec. Dir.
Number of staff: 1 part-time professional.
EIN: 541530891

3471
Potomac Health Foundation
2296 Opitz Blvd., Ste. 200
Woodbridge, VA 22191-3352 (703) 523-0630
Contact: Sheri Warren, Dir., Grant Progs.
FAX: (571) 542-9964;
E-mail: info@potomachealthfoundation.org; Main URL: http://potomachealthfoundation.org/
RSS Feed: http://feeds.feedburner.com/potomachealthfoundation.org/OGpU
Twitter: https://twitter.com/@phfound
YouTube: http://www.youtube.com/user/PHFound

Established in VA in Dec. 2009.
Foundation type: Independent foundation.
Financial data (yr. ended 10/31/13): Assets, $101,321,082 (M); expenditures, $4,869,776; qualifying distributions, $4,428,924; giving activities include $4,046,570 for 49 grants (high: $266,058; low: $10,500).
Purpose and activities: Giving limited to community-based, population health projects.
Fields of interest: Health care.
Type of support: Scholarship funds; Program development; Matching/challenge support; General/operating support; Building/renovation.
Limitations: Applications accepted. Giving primarily in eastern Prince William County, VA, and the immediately adjacent communities in eastern Fairfax and Stafford counties, including Aquia, Dale City, Dumfries, Garrisonville, Lake Ridge, Lorton, Manassas, Montclair, Quantico, Southbridge, Triangle and Woodbridge, VA.
Publications: Application guidelines; Financial statement; Grants list.
Application information: Application form required.
Initial approach: Submit letter of intent online via foundation web site
Deadline(s): See foundation web site for current deadline
Officers and Directors:* Marion M. Wall,* Chair.; Carol S. Shapiro, M.D.*, Vice-Chair.; Michael D. Lubleley,* Secy.; R. Michael Sorensen,* Treas.; Stephen V. Batsche, Exec. Dir.; Howard L. Greenhouse; Donnie Hylton; Deborah Johnson; Kenneth Krakaur; Wayne Mallard; William M. Moss; Sarah Pitkin, Ph.D.
Number of staff: 2 full-time professional.
EIN: 521340920

3472
Theodore H. & Nancy Price Foundation, Inc.
c/o Theodore W. Price
P.O. Box 85678
Richmond, VA 23285-5678

Established around 1980.
Donors: Theodore W. Price; Gail Trust.
Foundation type: Independent foundation.
Financial data (yr. ended 03/31/13): Assets, $701,754 (M); gifts received, $95,506; expenditures, $182,234; qualifying distributions, $171,700; giving activities include $171,700 for 21 grants (high: $64,000; low: $500).
Fields of interest: Museums (natural history); Performing arts, ballet; Performing arts, theater; Historic preservation/historical societies; Elementary/secondary education; Higher education; Foundations (public); United Ways and Federated Giving Programs.
Limitations: Applications not accepted. Giving primarily in VA; giving also in Paris, France. No grants to individuals.
Application information: Unsolicited requests for funds not accepted.
Officers: Theodore W. Price, Pres. and Treas.; Gail P. Messiqua, V.P.; Carol B. Price, Secy.
EIN: 136199406

3473
The Pruden Foundation
6464 Hampton Blvd.
Norfolk, VA 23508 (757) 425-3011
***Contact:* Peter D. Pruden III, Pres.**

Established in 1972 in VA.
Donors: Peter D. Pruden, Jr.; Peter D. Pruden, Sr.‡.
Foundation type: Independent foundation.
Financial data (yr. ended 02/28/13): Assets, $3,001,885 (M); expenditures, $178,169; qualifying distributions, $152,500; giving activities include $152,500 for 20 grants (high: $20,000; low: $2,500).
Fields of interest: Arts; Education; Health care; Housing/shelter; Human services.
Type of support: General/operating support; Continuing support; Annual campaigns; Capital campaigns; Building/renovation; Equipment; Emergency funds; Program development; Scholarship funds.
Limitations: Applications accepted. Giving primarily in VA.
Application information: Application form not required.
Copies of proposal: 1
Board meeting date(s): Mar., Sept., and Dec.
Officers: Peter D. Pruden III, Pres.; Thomas F. Hofler, V.P.; Jonathan E. Pruden, Secy.-Treas.
Directors: J. Brooke Pruden III; Bobby L. Ralph; Whitney G. Saunders; Vernon Towler.
EIN: 540923448
Other changes: The grantmaker no longer lists a separate application address.

3474
The RECO Foundation
P.O. Box 25189
Richmond, VA 23260-5189 (804) 644-2800
***Contact:* Robert C. Courain, Jr., Pres. and Treas.**
Application address: 720 Hospital St., Richmond, VA 23219

Donors: RECO Constructors, Inc.; RECO Industries, Inc.; Virginia American Industries, Inc.; Robert C. Courain, Jr.
Foundation type: Company-sponsored foundation.
Financial data (yr. ended 09/30/12): Assets, $5,399,848 (M); gifts received, $211,000; expenditures, $296,217; qualifying distributions, $255,950; giving activities include $255,950 for 96 grants (high: $131,500; low: $200).
Purpose and activities: The foundation supports food banks and health clinics and organizations involved with historic preservation, education, cancer, temporary housing, youth, and family services.
Fields of interest: Education; Health organizations; Human services.
Type of support: General/operating support; Annual campaigns; Capital campaigns; Program development; Scholarship funds; Research.
Limitations: Applications accepted. Giving primarily in Richmond, VA. No grants to individuals.
Application information: Application form not required.
Initial approach: Proposal
Deadline(s): None
Officers and Directors:* Robert C. Courain, Jr.,* Pres. and Treas.; Ruth D. Courain,* V.P.; William M. Richardson,* Secy.; Jennifer R. Courain; Robert C. Courain III; Allen C. Goolsby III; Frank G. Louthan, Jr.; Lauren C. Luke.
EIN: 546039609

3475
C. E. Richardson Benevolent Foundation
P.O. Box 1120
Pulaski, VA 24301-1120
***Application address:* c/o Ruth S. Looney, 202 N. Washington Ave., Pulaski, VA 24301-1120, tel.: (540) 980-6628**

Established in 1979 in VA.
Foundation type: Independent foundation.
Financial data (yr. ended 05/31/13): Assets, $4,221,983 (M); expenditures, $170,134; qualifying distributions, $161,307; giving activities include $146,000 for 43 grants (high: $10,000; low: $1,000).
Purpose and activities: Support for programs for needy children, women, aged people, and indigent or handicapped persons; support also for private colleges and universities.
Fields of interest: Higher education; Education; Health care; Human services; Community/economic development; United Ways and Federated Giving Programs.
Limitations: Applications accepted. Giving limited to VA. No grants to individuals.
Publications: Application guidelines; Program policy statement.
Application information: Application form required.
***Initial approach:* Completed application form**
Copies of proposal: 1
***Deadline(s):* Sept. 15**
Board meeting date(s): Oct.
Trustees: James D. Miller; James C. Turk.
Directors: Betty S. King; Ruth S. Looney.
Number of staff: 1 part-time support.
EIN: 510227549

3476
Richmond Memorial Health Foundation
1801 Bayberry Ct., Ste. 104
Richmond, VA 23226-3771 (804) 282-6282
FAX: (804) 282-6255;
E-mail: info@rmhfoundation.org; Main URL: http://www.rmhfoundation.org

Donors: Arthur Glasgow Trust; Partners Investing in Nursing's Future.
Foundation type: Independent foundation.
Financial data (yr. ended 06/30/13): Assets, $182,490,207 (M); gifts received, $32,691; expenditures, $4,186,541; qualifying distributions, $3,277,802; giving activities include $2,220,292 for 77 grants (high: $400,000; low: $150), and $551,182 for 3 foundation-administered programs.
Purpose and activities: Giving to improve health care and wellness in Richmond and central Virginia. Some giving will be for Bon Secours Memorial Regional Medical Center.
Fields of interest: Nursing school/education; Health care; Alzheimer's disease; Geriatrics; Pediatrics.
Limitations: Giving primarily in Richmond and central VA.
Publications: Application guidelines; Annual report; Financial statement.
Application information: Full applications are by invitation, upon review of concept proposal. See foundation web site for complete application guidelines. Application form required.
Initial approach: Concept proposal
Copies of proposal: 3
***Deadline(s):* For concept proposals: noon, the first Wed. in Jan. for Winter Grant Cycle; and noon, the first Wed. in July for Summer Grant Cycle**
Officers and Trustees:* Michele A.W. McKinnon, Esq.*, Chair.; Dee Ann Remo,* Vice-Chair.; Jeffrey S. Cribbs, Sr., C.E.O. and Pres.; **Sheryl L. Garland, Secy.**; Harry A. Thurton, Jr.,* Treas.; **Danny TK Avula, M.D., MPH**; **A. Dale Cannady**; Reginald E. Gordan, Esq.; **Richard L. Grier, Esq.**; **JR Hipple**; John W. Martin; William R. Nelson, M.D., MPH; **Joe Schilling**; Robert L. Thalhimer; Deborah L. Ulmer, RN, Ph.D.
EIN: 510211020
Other changes: Michele A.W. McKinnon, Esq. has replaced Sheryl L. Garland as Chair. Dee Ann Remo has replaced Michele A.W. McKinnon, Esq. as Vice-Chair. Sheryl L. Garland has replaced Claudia N. MacSwain as Secy.
Christopher M. Carney, Alexander M. Macaulay, Michael B. Matthews, and Thomas A. Silvestri are no longer trustees.
The grantmaker now publishes an annual report.

3477
Robins Foundation
10 S. 3rd St.
Richmond, VA **23219-3702 (804) 523-1144**
Contact: Martha Loving, Office Mgr.
***FAX:* (804) 523-1150**; E-mail for Martha Loving: martha.loving@robinsfdn.org; Main URL: http://www.robinsfdn.org
Grants List: http://www.robinsfdn.org/what-we-fund/

Established in 1957 in VA.
Donor: E. Claiborne Robins†.
Foundation type: Independent foundation.
Financial data (yr. ended 12/31/12): Assets, $139,242,814 (M); expenditures, $8,714,366; qualifying distributions, $6,932,586; giving activities include $5,875,785 for 130 grants, and $447,647 for 1 loan/program-related investment.
Purpose and activities: Gives to a broad range of causes in the Richmond, VA, area.
Fields of interest: Children/youth, services.
Type of support: General/operating support; Income development; Management development/capacity building; Capital campaigns; Building/renovation; Equipment; Land acquisition; Endowments; Program development; Consulting services; Program evaluation; Program-related investments/loans.
Limitations: Applications not accepted. Giving primarily in Richmond, VA; the foundation does not accept unsolicited proposals from organizations outside of the Richmond metropolitan area. No grants to individuals, or for annual funds or special events.
Publications: Grants list.
Application information: The foundation is not accepting unsolicited grant proposals at this time. See foundation web site for updated application information.
Officers and Directors:* Sheryl Robins Nolt,* Pres.; **Robin R. Shield, V.P.**; **Kelly Chopus, Exec. Dir.**; Reginald N. Jones,* Treas.; Lewis T. Booker; E. Bruce Heilman; Ann Carol Marchant; Robert E. Marchant; Betty Robins Porter; **E. Claiborne Robins, Jr.**; Gregory C. Robins; Juliet E. Shield-Taylor.
Number of staff: 5 full-time professional; 1 part-time professional; 1 full-time support.
EIN: 540784484
Other changes: Sheryl Robins Nolt has replaced Betty Robins Porter as Pres. Robin R. Shield has replaced Sheryl Robins Nolt as V.P.
E. Claiborne Robins, Jr. is now Secy.
The grantmaker no longer publishes application guidelines.

3478
Samberg Family Foundation
2107 Wilson Blvd., Suite 750
Arlington, VA **22201-3077** (703) 351-9405
Contact: Laura J. Samberg, Co-Dir.
Main URL: http://www.sambergfdn.org

Established in 1996.
Donor: Arthur Samberg.
Foundation type: Independent foundation.
Financial data (yr. ended 11/30/12): Assets, $67,420,879 (M); expenditures, $6,839,727; qualifying distributions, $6,550,632; giving activities include $6,200,402 for 26 grants (high: $1,000,000; low: $5,000).
Purpose and activities: Giving primarily for children, youth and families; health; and Jewish issues.
Fields of interest: Museums; Education; Health care; Youth development, services; Children/youth, services; Family services; Jewish federated giving programs.
International interests: Israel.
Type of support: General/operating support; Continuing support; Management development/capacity building; Program development; Seed money; Curriculum development; Research; Technical assistance; Program evaluation; Matching/challenge support.
Limitations: Applications not accepted. Giving primarily in NY. No grants to individuals.
Publications: Grants list.
Application information: Unsolicited requests for funds not accepted.
Officer: Gerald D. Levine, Pres.
Director: Laura Samberg Faino; **Sue Ellen Madden**.
Trustees: Arthur Samberg; Rebecca Samberg.
Number of staff: 3 full-time professional.
EIN: 066439895

3479
Charles E. Smith Family Foundation
2345 Crystal Dr., 11th Fl.
Arlington, VA 22202-4801 (703) 769-1023

Established in 1963 in VA.
Donors: Charles E. Smith†; Robert H. Smith; Robert P. Kogod; Charles E. Smith Trust.
Foundation type: Independent foundation.
Financial data (yr. ended 02/28/13): Assets, $28,382,509 (M); expenditures, $5,606,125; qualifying distributions, $5,353,719; giving activities include $5,350,167 for 18 grants (high: $1,300,000; low: $10,000).
Purpose and activities: Support primarily for a Jewish welfare fund and other Jewish organizations.
Fields of interest: Human services; Jewish federated giving programs; Jewish agencies & synagogues.
Limitations: Applications not accepted. Giving primarily in the greater Washington, DC, area, MD, VA, NJ, and NY. No grants to individuals.
Application information: Contributes only to pre-selected organizations.
Officers: Robert P. Kogod, Pres.; David B. Smith, V.P.; Clarice R. Smith, Secy.; Arlene R. Kogod, Treas.
EIN: 311570183

3480
Stafford Foundation
(formerly The Stafford Family Foundation)
P.O. Box 2665
Reston, VA **20195-0665 (703) 689-9849**
***E-mail:* info@thestaffordfoundation.org; Main URL: https://www.thestaffordfoundation.org/**
Facebook: https://www.facebook.com/pages/The-Stafford-Foundation/83603224718
Flickr: https://www.flickr.com/photos/thestaffordfoundation/
RSS Feed: https://www.thestaffordfoundation.org/feed/
Twitter: https://twitter.com/staffordfnd

Established in 2002 in DE and VA; funded in 2008.
Donors: Earl W. Stafford, Sr.; Amanda Stafford.
Foundation type: Independent foundation.
Financial data (yr. ended 12/31/12): Assets, $646,011 (M); gifts received, $43,280; expenditures, $470,110; qualifying distributions, $444,725; giving activities include $152,490 for 24 grants (high: $50,000; low: $9).
Fields of interest: Christian agencies & churches.
Type of support: General/operating support.
Limitations: Applications accepted. Giving primarily in DC and VA.
Application information: Application form required.
Initial approach: Letter
Deadline(s): None
Officer: Earl W. Stafford, Sr., Chair.; Adam Grotke, C.F.O.; Robin F. Patterson, Secy.
Director: Heidi J. Everett.
EIN: 753072793

3481
Hattie M. Strong Foundation
6551 Loisdale Ct., Ste. 160
Springfield, VA 22150-1820 (703) 313-6791
FAX: (703) 313-6793;
E-mail: hmsf@hmstrongfoundation.org; Main URL: http://www.hmstrongfoundation.org/

Incorporated in 1928 in DC.
Donors: Hattie M. Strong†; L. Corrin Strong†.

Foundation type: Independent foundation.
Financial data (yr. ended 08/31/13): Assets, $32,458,699 (M); gifts received, $2,113; expenditures, $1,537,651; qualifying distributions, $1,382,242; giving activities include $825,000 for 64 grants (high: $25,000; low: $5,000), and $150,000 for 15 grants to individuals (high: $10,000; low: $10,000).
Purpose and activities: The foundation administers two distinct programs: 1) a scholarship program aimed at college students enrolled in teacher-training programs at selected partnering institutions in addition to collecting outstanding student loans from previous student loan program. 2) A grant program, with the foundation's current priority aiming to assist organizations that provide out-of-school time (OST) programming during the after-school hours, Saturdays, and summers. Preference is given to programs that support, reinforce, and enrich the core academic objectives of the DC Public Schools, as well as character development, community service, good citizenship, and appreciation of the performing and visual arts.
Fields of interest: Elementary/secondary education; Adult education—literacy, basic skills & GED; Education, reading; Education; Infants/toddlers; Children/youth; Children; Minorities.
Type of support: General/operating support; Program development; Curriculum development; Scholarship funds.
Limitations: Applications not accepted. Giving limited to the Washington, DC, area for grant program. No support for programs of national or international scope. No grants to individuals, or for building or endowment funds, research, fellowships, equipment, conferences, special events or benefits, or projects designed to educate the general public.
Application information: Unsolicited requests for funds not accepted.
Board meeting date(s): Fall, spring, and summer
Officers and Directors:* Henry L. Strong,* Chair. and Pres.; Sigrid S. Reynolds,* V.P.; Robin C. Tanner, Secy.-Treas. and Exec. Dir.; Judith B. Cyphers; John M. Lynham, Jr.; Richard S.T. Marsh; H. Gregory Platts; **C. Lockwood Reynolds**; Carol L. Schwartz; Bente Strong.
Number of staff: 2 full-time professional; 1 full-time support; 1 part-time support.
EIN: 530237223

3482
Truland Foundation
1900 Oracle Way, Ste. 700
Reston, VA 20190-4733 (703) 464-3000
Contact: Robert W. Truland, Pres.

Established in 1954 in VA.
Donor: Truland Systems Corp.
Foundation type: Company-sponsored foundation.
Financial data (yr. ended 03/31/13): Assets, $196,885 (M); gifts received, $546,186; expenditures, $298,486; qualifying distributions, $514,417; giving activities include $514,417 for 26 grants (high: $230,000; low: $250).
Purpose and activities: The foundation supports maritime museums and organizations involved with education, health, cystic fibrosis, cancer, heart disease, and Christianity.
Fields of interest: Museums (marine/maritime); Historic preservation/historical societies; Elementary/secondary education; Higher education; Education; Hospitals (general); Health care; Cystic fibrosis; Cancer; Heart & circulatory diseases; Christian agencies & churches.
Type of support: Capital campaigns; General/operating support.
Limitations: Applications accepted. Giving primarily in Washington, DC, MD, and VA; some giving in Bermuda. No grants to individuals.
Application information: Application form required.
***Initial approach:* Letter**
Deadline(s): None
Officers and Directors:* Robert W. Truland,* Pres.; Ingrid A. Moini, Secy.; Mary W. Truland.
EIN: 546037172
Other changes: The grantmaker no longer lists an E-mail address.

3483
The Twinkling Eyes Foundation
7857 Heritage Dr., Ste. 300
Annandale, VA 22003-5350
***Contact:* Curry Uflacker**
***E-mail:* curry@twinklingeyes.org**; Main URL: http://www.twinklingeyes.org/

Foundation type: Independent foundation.
Financial data (yr. ended 12/31/12): Assets, $6,573,906 (M); expenditures, $520,472; qualifying distributions, $255,500; giving activities include $255,500 for 5 grants (high: $240,000; low: $2,000).
Fields of interest: Food services; Children.
Type of support: General/operating support.
Limitations: Applications not accepted. Giving primarily in VA.
Application information: Unsolicited requests for funds not accepted.
Officers: Denise Medved, Chair. and C.E.O.; William Medved, V.P. and Secy.
Directors: Edward Kratovil; Steve Perraud; Curry Uflacker.
EIN: 261098195

3484
The United Company Charitable Foundation
(formerly United Coal Company Charitable Foundation)
1005 Glenway Ave.
Bristol, VA 24201-3473 (276) 645-1458
***Contact:* Jane Arnold, Admin. Asst.**
FAX: (276) 645-1420;
E-mail: jarnold@unitedco.net; Main URL: http://www.uccharitable.com/
Scholarship address: Rose Hurley, Mountain Mission School, 1760 Edgewater Dr., Grundy VA 24614, tel.: (276) 791-1514, e-mail: rhurley@unitedco.net

Established in 1986 in VA.
Donors: United Coal Co., Inc.; Burton Fletcher; The Summit Fund, LLC.
Foundation type: Company-sponsored foundation.
Financial data (yr. ended 12/31/12): Assets, $40,590,587 (M); expenditures, $3,070,412; qualifying distributions, $2,828,050; giving activities include $2,054,844 for 101 grants (high: $400,000; low: $100), and $649,217 for 3 foundation-administered programs.
Purpose and activities: The foundation supports organizations involved with arts and culture, education, health, hunger, human services, and the economically disadvantaged.
Fields of interest: Museums (art); Arts; Higher education; Libraries (public); Education; Health care, clinics/centers; Health care; Food services; Food banks; Boys & girls clubs; Boy scouts; Salvation Army; YM/YWCAs & YM/YWHAs; Children/youth, services; Human services.
Type of support: General/operating support; Capital campaigns; Building/renovation; Program development; Scholarship funds; Sponsorships; Scholarships—to individuals.
Limitations: Applications accepted. Giving primarily in TN and VA. No grants to individuals (except for scholarships) or for political or related causes; no loans.
Application information: Application form not required.
Initial approach: Contact foundation for application information for grants; contact foundation for application form for scholarships
***Deadline(s):* July 1 and Dec. 1 for scholarships**
Final notification: 3 to 4 weeks for scholarships
Officers and Directors:* James W. McGlothlin,* Chair.; Martha McGlothlin-Gayle,* Pres.; Nicholas D. Street,* Secy.; Lois A. Clarke,* Treas.; Frances G. McGlothlin; David A. Street; Fay H. Street.
EIN: 541390453

3485
The Volgenau Foundation
8300 Greensboro Dr., Ste. 1025
McLean, VA 22102-3621
***E-mail:* maryanna@volgenaufoundation.org**; Main URL: http://www.volgenaufoundation.org
Grants List: http://www.volgenaufoundation.org/grants1

Established in 1994 in VA.
Donors: Ernst Volgenau; Sara Lane Volgenau; The Fuller Foundation.
Foundation type: Operating foundation.
Financial data (yr. ended 12/31/12): Assets, $1,515,004 (M); gifts received, $597,287; expenditures, $807,438; qualifying distributions, $837,605; giving activities include $400,467 for 24 grants (high: $25,000; low: $5,000).
Fields of interest: Arts; Education; Environment.
Limitations: Applications not accepted. No grants to individuals.
Publications: Occasional report.
Application information: Contributes only to pre-selected organizations.
Officers: Ernst Volgenau, Pres.; Sara Lane Volgenau, Secy.-Treas.; Maryanna L. Kieffer, Exec. Dir.
Directors: Lauren Volgenau Knapp; Lisa Volgenau; Jennifer Volgenau Wiley.
Number of staff: 1 part-time professional.
EIN: 541738281
Other changes: The grantmaker has changed its fiscal year-end from June 30 to Dec. 31.

3486
WestWind Foundation
204 E. High St.
Charlottesville, VA 22902-5177 **(434) 977-5762 x 24**
FAX: (434) 977-3176;
E-mail: info@westwindfoundation.org; Main URL: http://www.westwindfoundation.org

Established in 1987 in DC.
Donors: Edward M. Miller; WWF, Ltd.
Foundation type: Independent foundation.
Financial data (yr. ended 12/31/12): Assets, $45,928,289 (M); expenditures, $3,989,059; qualifying distributions, $3,790,573; giving activities include $3,790,573 for 125 grants (high: $356,000; low: $500).

Purpose and activities: The foundation is dedicated to protecting the integrity of natural ecosystems and the health of human communities through its grantmaking programs. WestWind tends to provide more general support grants, but the foundation will also provide grants for project or program specific requests.
Fields of interest: Education; Environment, land resources; Environment, forests; Environment; Reproductive health, family planning; Youth development; Human services; Youth; Young adults.
International interests: Caribbean; Latin America.
Type of support: General/operating support; Continuing support; Land acquisition; Program development; Conferences/seminars; Matching/challenge support.
Limitations: Giving on a national level, with emphasis on the Southeast, for environment program. Giving is primarily targeted toward benefiting Latin America and the Caribbean for Reproductive Health and Rights program, although domestic support is available. No support for religious organizations. No grants to individuals, or for capital campaigns, endowments or brick and mortar projects.
Publications: Application guidelines; Grants list.
Application information: Current application guidelines and deadlines available on foundation web site.
Board meeting date(s): May, Sept., and Nov.
Trustees: Janet H. Miller; Edward M. Miller.
Number of staff: 1 full-time support.
EIN: 526358830
Other changes: The foundation no longer lists a primary contact.

3487
Williamsburg Community Health Foundation

4801 Courthouse St., Ste. 200
Williamsburg, VA **23188-2678** (757) 345-0912
Contact: Jeanne Zeidler, C.E.O. and Pres.
FAX: (757) 345-0913;
E-mail: info@williamsburghealthfoundation.org;
Main URL: http://www.wchf.com

Established in 1996 in VA; converted from the partnership between the Williamsburg Community Hospital and Sentara Health System.
Foundation type: Independent foundation.
Financial data (yr. ended 12/31/12): Assets, $117,781,000 (M); expenditures, $5,627,000; qualifying distributions, $5,300,000; giving activities include $4,531,000 for 61 grants (high: $554,000; low: $500), and $124,000 for 5 foundation-administered programs.
Purpose and activities: Giving to improve the health of people living in Williamsburg, VA, and surrounding counties by strengthening access to quality health services and promoting responsible health practices. At present, the foundation is continuing to focus on challenges to the healthcare safety net, including challenges posed by the economic downturn and the resulting rise in citizens who are medically underserved. Grant consideration is also given to programs that strengthen health care for all citizens in the greater Williamsburg area by emphasizing wellness, offering preventive care, providing health-oriented educational programs and/or increase access to high-quality, cost-effective healthcare.
Fields of interest: Medical care, community health systems; Health care; Substance abuse, services; Infants/toddlers; Children/youth; Youth; Adults; Aging; Disabilities, people with; Substance abusers; Economically disadvantaged.
Type of support: Research; General/operating support; Continuing support; Management development/capacity building; Program development; Program evaluation.
Limitations: Applications accepted. Giving primarily to organizations and programs serving the cities of Williamsburg and Poquoson and the counties of James City, York, and Gloucester, VA. No support for organizations limiting services to an exclusive membership or to political organizations. No grants to individuals or for lobbying activities, annual appeals and fundraisers, real estate acquisition, or restoration of funds cut by government or other organizations; no multi-year grants.
Publications: Application guidelines; Annual report; Grants list; Program policy statement.
Application information: For application guidelines see foundation web site. Application form required.
Initial approach: Online letter of intent
Copies of proposal: 1
Deadline(s): First and Second annual grant cycles
Board meeting date(s): Quarterly
Final notification: Approximately 4 months
Officers and Trustees:* Douglas Myers,* Chair.; Jeffrey O. Smith,* Vice-Chair.; Jeanne Zeidler, Secy.; James R. Golden,* Treas.; Stephen R. Adkins; Catherine Allport; David C. Anderson; David E. Bush; Hon. Cressondra B. Conyers; Randall Foskey; F. Brian Hiestand; Dr. Joyce M. Jarrett; Laura J. Loda; Virginia L. McLaughlin; Stephen Montgomery; Richard H. Rizk; Lois F. Rossiter; Richard Schreiber; Richard G. Smith; Marshall N. Warner; Jonathan V. Weiss; Clarence A. Wilson; Kimberly Zeuli.
Number of staff: 6 full-time professional; 2 full-time support.
EIN: 541822359

3488
Greater Williamsburg Community Trust

(also known as Williamsburg Community Foundation)
424 Scotland St.
Williamsburg, VA **23185** (757) 259-1660
***Contact:* Nancy Cote Sullivan, Exec. Dir.**
FAX: (757) 259-1227;
E-mail: office@williamsburgcommunityfoundation.org; Mailing Address: P.O. Box 2821, Williamsburg, VA 23187; Additional e-mail: ncsullivan@williamsburgcommunityfoundation.org; Main URL: http://www.williamsburgcommunityfoundation.org/
Facebook: http://www.facebook.com/WilliamsburgCommunityFoundation
LinkedIn: http://www.linkedin.com/company/williamsburg-community-foundation?trk=top_nav_home

Established in 1999 in VA.
Foundation type: Community foundation.
Financial data (yr. ended 01/31/13): Assets, $4,746,769 (M); gifts received, $927,522; expenditures, $600,308; giving activities include $299,078 for 16+ grants (high: $29,305), and $132,097 for 95 grants to individuals.
Purpose and activities: The foundation connects people who care with causes that matter in the local community. The foundation pursues this mission by: 1) helping donors respond to emerging and changing community needs; 2) building a permanent, flexible endowment; 3) providing effective stewardship of charitable funds; and 4) serving as a resource, catalyst and coordinator for charitable activities.
Fields of interest: Historic preservation/historical societies; Arts; Education; Health care; Human services; Community/economic development.
Limitations: Applications accepted. Giving primarily in Williamsburg, VA.
Publications: Annual report; Newsletter.
Application information: Visit foundation web site for application form and guidelines per grant type. Application form required.
Initial approach: Contact foundation
Board meeting date(s): Sept. and Dec.
Officers and Trustees:* Michael D. Maddocks,* Chair.; Margaret Beck Pritchard,* Vice-Chair.; Kendall S. Kerby,* Secy.; Robert G. Topping,* Treas.; Nancy Sullivan, Exec. Dir.; James N. Allburn; Betsy C. Anderson; Carol S. Beers; Joseph R. Burkart; John R. Curtis, Jr.; Margaret M. Driscoll; Paul Gerhardt; Susanna B. Hickman; Kathy Hornsby; Karen Jamison; Mark Monroe; Bill Morrison; Randy W. Myers; Joe Poole, III; William L. Roberts, Jr.; Roger E. Schultz, M.D.; Craig Stambaugh; Alfred L. Woods.
EIN: 541927558

WASHINGTON

3489
Ginger and Barry Ackerley Foundation
4111 E. Madison St., No. 210
Seattle, WA 98112-3241 **(206) 624-2888**
Contact: Kimberly Cleworth, Exec. Dir.
FAX: (206) 623-7853;
E-mail: info@ackerleyfoundation.org; Main URL: http://www.ackerleyfoundation.org
RSS Feed: http://ackerleyfoundation.org/feed

Established in 1997 in WA.
Donors: Barry A. Ackerley; Gail A. Ackerley.
Foundation type: Independent foundation.
Financial data (yr. ended 12/31/12): Assets, $15,646,268 (M); gifts received, $499,445; expenditures, $1,232,828; qualifying distributions, $1,053,116; giving activities include $900,054 for 12 grants (high: $251,500; low: $6).
Purpose and activities: Grants to public and private institutions around Puget Sound that sponsor core programs enhancing the education of young learners. Support opportunities such as skills support, literacy development, mentoring relationships and programs that connect school and home.
Fields of interest: Education, early childhood education; Secondary school/education; Education; Children/youth; Economically disadvantaged.
Type of support: Capital campaigns; Building/renovation; Endowments; Program development; Curriculum development; Matching/challenge support.
Limitations: Applications not accepted. Giving limited to the greater Puget Sound, WA region. No support for religious organizations. No grants to individuals, or for debt retirement, operating deficits, team sponsorship, individual athletic endeavors, travel expenses, or annual fund drives; no loans.
Publications: Grants list; Informational brochure.
Application information: Unsolicited requests for funds not accepted.
Board meeting date(s): 1st and 3rd quarters
Officers: Kim Cleworth, Pres. and Exec. Dir.; Christopher Ackerley, V.P.; Edward Ackerley, V.P.
Directors: Barry A. Ackerley; Gail A. Ackerley.
Number of staff: 1 full-time professional.
EIN: 911800463

3490
The Paul G. Allen Family Foundation
505 5th Ave. S., Ste. 900
Seattle, WA 98104-3821 (206) 342-2030
Contact: Lisa Arnold, Grants Mgr.
FAX: (206) 342-3030;
E-mail: info@pgafamilyfoundation.org; Additional contact inf. for Lisa Arnold, e-mail: lisaa@pgafamilyfoundation.org, fax: (206) 342-3085; Main URL: http://www.pgafamilyfoundation.org
Grants Database: http://www.pgafamilyfoundation.org/TemplateGranteeList.aspx?contentId=21
Paul G. Allen's Giving Pledge Profile: http://glasspockets.org/philanthropy-in-focus/eye-on-the-giving-pledge/profiles/allen

Established in 2005 in WA. In 2004, The Paul G. Allen Charitable Foundation, along with The Allen Foundation for the Arts, The Paul G. Allen Foundation for Medical Research, The Paul G. Allen Forest Protection Foundation, The Allen Foundation for Music, and The Paul G. Allen Virtual Education Foundation, were consolidated into a new foundation, The Paul G. Allen Family Foundation.
Donors: Paul G. Allen; The Paul G. Allen Foundation for Medical Research; The Paul G. Allen Virtual Education Foundation; The Allen Foundation for Music.
Foundation type: Independent foundation.
Financial data (yr. ended 12/31/12): Assets, $286,858,712 (M); expenditures, $19,444,808; qualifying distributions, $18,578,965; giving activities include $18,570,900 for 237 grants (high: $3,000,000; low: $539).
Purpose and activities: The mission of the foundation is to transform lives and strengthen communities by fostering innovation, creating knowledge, and promoting social programs. The foundation advances its mission through focusing on the following key areas: arts and culture, asset building, basic needs, libraries, innovations in science and technology and youth education.
Fields of interest: Museums; Performing arts; Arts; Libraries (public); Education; Human services; Youth, services; Science; Children/youth; Native Americans/American Indians; Economically disadvantaged.
Type of support: Income development; Management development/capacity building; Capital campaigns; Building/renovation; Emergency funds; Program development; Research; Technical assistance; Program evaluation; Matching/challenge support.
Limitations: Giving primarily in the Pacific Northwest, including AK, ID, MT, OR and WA. No support for sectarian or religious organizations whose principle activity is for the benefit of their own members or adherents, or for organizations whose policies or practices discriminate on the basis of ethnic, origin, gender, race, religion, or sexual orientation. No grants to individuals or for general operating support, annual appeals, federated campaigns, general fund drives, scholarships, special events or sponsorships, or for projects not aligned with the foundation's specified program areas; no loans.
Publications: Application guidelines; Grants list; Multi-year report; Occasional report.
Application information: Unsolicited letters of inquiry and proposals are not accepted. Full proposals are by invitation. Although foundation's process is by invitation, applicants are encouraged to contact the staff through the foundation's web site if their projects are aligned with the foundation's programs.
Copies of proposal: 1
Board meeting date(s): Spring and fall
Final notification: 7 months
Officers and Directors:* Paul G. Allen,* Chair.; Jo Lynn Allen,* Pres.; Susan Drake, V.P.; Allen D. Israel, Secy.
Number of staff: 8 full-time professional.
EIN: 943082532
Other changes: Susan M. Coliton is no longer V.P.

3491
Almi Foundation, Inc.
(formerly The M.A.C.H. Foundation)
601 Union St., Ste. 3300
Seattle, WA 98101-4024

Established in 1989 in DE and CA; named Rafael Foundation; first name change in 1999 to The Mach Foundation; second name changed in 2007 to Almi Foundation, Inc.
Donor: Yolande L. Jurzykowski.
Foundation type: Independent foundation.
Financial data (yr. ended 12/31/12): Assets, $14,348,620 (M); expenditures, $3,780,215; qualifying distributions, $3,600,361; giving activities include $3,600,361 for 4 grants (high: $1,858,686; low: $25,000).
Fields of interest: Philanthropy/voluntarism; Buddhism.
Limitations: Applications not accepted. Giving primarily in CA; some giving also in AZ. No grants to individuals.
Application information: Contributes only to pre-selected organizations.
Officers: Yolande L. Jurzykowski, Pres.; Robyn Doecke, Secy.
EIN: 680203129
Other changes: At the close of 2012, the grantmaker paid grants of $3,600,361, a 102.6% increase over the 2011 disbursements, $1,777,149.

3492
Anderson Foundation
537 10th Ave. W.
Kirkland, WA 98033-4839

Established in 1952 in WA.
Donors: Charles M. Anderson‡; Dorothy I. Anderson; William Anderson; Barbara A. Lawrence.
Foundation type: Independent foundation.
Financial data (yr. ended 06/30/13): Assets, $26,707,593 (M); expenditures, $1,856,800; qualifying distributions, $1,800,000; giving activities include $1,800,000 for 37 grants (high: $400,000; low: $2,500).
Purpose and activities: Giving primarily for education, social services, medical research, hospitals, including a children's hospital, as well as for other children and youth services.
Fields of interest: Higher education; Education; Hospitals (general); Hospitals (specialty); Medical research, institute; Human services; Children/youth, services.
Type of support: Building/renovation; Equipment; Professorships; Scholarship funds; Research.
Limitations: Applications not accepted. Giving primarily in WA, with emphasis on Seattle. No grants to individuals, or for endowment funds or matching gifts; no loans.
Application information: Contributes only to pre-selected organizations.
Board meeting date(s): Annually
Officers: Katharine L. Murray, Pres.; Charlie Anderson, V.P.; David Murray, Secy.
Number of staff: 2 part-time support.
EIN: 916031724
Other changes: Charlie Anderson has replaced Barbara A. Lawrence as V.P.
Katherine C. Murray is no longer Secy.-Treas.

3493
Arise Charitable Trust
P.O. Box 1014
Freeland, WA 98249-1014 **(360) 331-5792**
E-mail: info@arisecharitabletrust.org; Main URL: http://www.arisecharitabletrust.org

Established in 1986 in WA.
Donor: Judith P. Yeakel.
Foundation type: Independent foundation.
Financial data (yr. ended 09/30/13): Assets, $4,670,278 (M); expenditures, $245,098; qualifying distributions, $208,095; giving activities include $95,620 for 7 grants (high: $30,000; low:

$3,000), and $94,842 for 56 grants to individuals (high: $3,500; low: $194).
Purpose and activities: Giving limited to aid programs benefiting local women in the form of scholarships to individuals and grants to social service agencies.
Fields of interest: Human services; Women, centers/services; Women.
Type of support: General/operating support; Scholarships—to individuals.
Limitations: Applications accepted. Giving limited to residents of the South Whidbey, WA, area.
Publications: Informational brochure.
Application information: See trust web site for complete application guidelines. Application form required.
Copies of proposal: 1
Board meeting date(s): Varies
Officer and Trustees:* Charles W. Edwards,* Mgr.; Carolyn Cliff; Anne Pettit; Barbara Yeakel; Judith P. Yeakel.
EIN: 911350780

3494
Bainbridge Community Foundation
(formerly Bainbridge Island Community Endowment)
221 Winslow Way W., No. 305
Bainbridge Island, WA 98110-4918 (206) 842-0433
Contact: Jim Hopper, Exec. Dir.; For grants: Debbie Kuffel, Funds and Grants Admin.
E-mail: info@bainbridgecf.org; Additional address: 149 Finch Place SW, Suite 4, Bainbridge Island, WA 98110; Additional e-mail: jhopper@bainbridgecommunityfoundation.org; Grant inquiry e-mail: grants@bainbridgecf.org; Grant inquiry tel.: 206-842-0814; Main URL: http://www.bainbridgecommunityfoundation.org
Facebook: http://www.facebook.com/pages/Bainbridge-Community-Foundation/214785191915998
Twitter: http://twitter.com/investinbcf

Established in 2001 in WA.
Donors: Sada Ross Fund; Harold Hurlen Fund; H. Clay and Sherry Roberts Fund; Barry Peters; Channice Peters; The Mathurin Fund; The Emile Fund; Class of 1961 Fund.
Foundation type: Community foundation.
Financial data (yr. ended 12/31/11): Assets, $6,971,255 (M); gifts received, $447,965; expenditures, $1,058,842; giving activities include $768,987 for 30+ grants (high: $362,500).
Purpose and activities: The foundation seeks to encourage philanthropy and build a stronger community on Bainbridge Island, Washington.
Fields of interest: Arts; Education; Environment; Animals/wildlife; Health care; Housing/shelter; Youth development; Human services; Science; Engineering/technology; Social sciences, public policy; Social sciences.
Type of support: General/operating support; Income development; Capital campaigns; Building/renovation; Equipment; Scholarship funds.
Limitations: Applications accepted. Giving limited to the Bainbridge Island, WA, area. No support for religious organizations (unless for secular purposes). No grants to individuals, or for fundraising events, debt reduction, items purchased or activities completed prior to grant decision; no multi-year grants.
Publications: Application guidelines; Annual report; Informational brochure; Occasional report.
Application information: Visit foundation web site online grant application and additional guidelines. Application form required.
Initial approach: Complete online application
Deadline(s): Mar. 10
Board meeting date(s): Six times annually
Final notification: June
Officer and Trustees:* Jim Hopper, Exec. Dir.; Lynn Agnew; Len Beil; Paul Carroll; Colleen Chupik; Jola Greiner; Shel Klasky; Cynthia Massa; Carl Middleton; Wendy O'Connor; Tom Seifert; Chris Snow; Elaine VonRosenstiel.
Number of staff: 2 part-time professional.
EIN: 912155208
Other changes: Mary Kerr, Mark Lund, and Larry Mills are no longer trustees.

3495
The Bamford Foundation
(formerly The Globe Foundation)
P.O. Box 2274
Tacoma, WA 98401-2274 **(253) 620-4743**
***Contact:* Holly Bamford Hunt**
***E-mail:* info@bamfordfoundation.org**; Main URL: http://bamfordfoundation.org/
Grants List: http://bamfordfoundation.org/Bamford%20Foundation%20Grants%202012.pdf

Established in 1990 in WA.
Donors: Calvin D. Bamford, Jr.; JoAnne W. Bamford.
Foundation type: Independent foundation.
Financial data (yr. ended 11/30/12): Assets, $4,244,060 (M); gifts received, $1,605,753; expenditures, $702,079; qualifying distributions, $691,129; giving activities include $661,850 for 52 grants (high: $81,000; low: $1,000).
Purpose and activities: Giving primarily to improve the quality of life of individuals and to strengthen their communities, primarily in Tacoma, Washington and the South Puget Sound area of the Pacific Northwest.
Fields of interest: Museums; Higher education; Education; Human services; YM/YWCAs & YM/YWHAs; United Ways and Federated Giving Programs; Protestant agencies & churches.
Limitations: Applications not accepted. Giving primarily in Tacoma, WA. No grants to individuals.
Application information: Contributes only to pre-selected organizations.
***Board meeting date(s):* Quarterly**
Officers and Directors:* Calvin D. Bamford, Jr., Pres. and Treas.; Joanne W. Bamford,* V.P.; Holly Bamford Hunt,* Secy.; Drew Bamford; Heather Bamford.
EIN: 911504193

3496
Sheri & Les Biller Family Foundation
(formerly Sheri & Les Biller Family Foundation)
1420 5th Ave., Ste. 2625
Seattle, WA 98101-4049 (206) 687-7909
E-mail: inquiries@billerfamilyfoundation.org; Main URL: http://www.billerfamilyfoundation.org
Facebook: http://www.facebook.com/pages/The-Sheri-and-Les-Biller-Family-Foundation/122644051043
Twitter: http://twitter.com/BillerFamFdtn
YouTube: http://www.youtube.com/user/billerfamfoundation

Established in 2001 in CA.
Donors: Les Biller; Sheri Biller.
Foundation type: Independent foundation.
Financial data (yr. ended 12/31/12): Assets, $8,616,370 (M); gifts received, $1,434,688; expenditures, $1,475,635; qualifying distributions, $1,335,373; giving activities include $932,632 for 93 grants (high: $175,000; low: $56).
Purpose and activities: Giving to enhance the quality of life in the community through support of: 1) women's organizations which relieve suffering, defend rights, and improve living conditions of women in areas of abuse, health, vocational, legal assistance and family planning; 2) higher education for children of immigrants, in which the foundation funds, through a third party organization candidate selection process, the higher education expenses of children of immigrants, immigrant (resident) children, and naturalized citizen children; 3) disadvantaged youth programs which focus on education, mentoring, developing leadership skills, encouraging community services and building self-esteem; and 4) theater arts programs in general education, the opera, theatrical arts, and in particular, youth performing arts that serve the needs of disadvantaged youth.
Fields of interest: Performing arts, theater; Arts; Higher education; Education; Medical research, institute; Cancer research; Human services; Children/youth; Women; Immigrants/refugees; Economically disadvantaged.
Limitations: Applications not accepted. Giving primarily in Los Angeles, CA, and WA. No support for projects outside the stated areas of interest, pilot or seed programs unless the Founding Trustee is actively involved, or for organizations determined to be unhealthy or financially unstable. No grants to individuals, or for requests less than $1,000, or for more than directed by the Trust document.
Application information: Unsolicited requests for funds not accepted.
Officer: Sarah Lyding, Exec. Dir.; **Howard Behar.**
Trustees: Yvonne Bell; Les Biller; Sheri Biller; **Alexander Cappello; Lindsey C. Kozberg; John R. Ohanesian.**
EIN: 841608504
Other changes: The grantmaker has moved from CA to WA.

3497
Blakemore Foundation
1201 3rd Ave., Ste. 4900
Seattle, WA 98101-3095 (206) 359-8778
Contact: For all inquiries: Cathy Scheibner, Exec. Asst.
FAX: (206) 359-9778;
E-mail: blakemorefoundation@gmail.com; Additional e-mail: blakemore@perkinscoie.com; Main URL: http://www.blakemorefoundation.org
Facebook: http://www.facebook.com/pages/Blakemore-Foundation/79550692938
Grants List: http://www.blakemorefoundation.org/Recent%20Grants/Recent%20Grants.htm

Established in 1990 in WA.
Donors: Thomas L. Blakemore‡; Frances L. Blakemore‡; Eugene H. Lee; Freeman Foundation; Tokyo Club; Worldbridge LLC.
Foundation type: Independent foundation.
Financial data (yr. ended 12/31/12): Assets, $8,720,160 (M); gifts received, $502,095; expenditures, $988,047; qualifying distributions, $888,447; giving activities include $35,282 for 1 grant, and $768,278 for 31 grants to individuals (high: $54,036; low: $400).
Purpose and activities: Grants to individuals pursuing academic, business, or professional careers involving East or Southeast Asia for advanced study of East or Southeast Asian languages in Asia. Grants to museums, universities and other educational or art-related institutions in

the United States for exhibitions and internships to broaden and deepen the understanding of Asian art in the United States.
Fields of interest: Museums; Language (foreign); Arts; Higher education.
Type of support: Fellowships; Scholarships—to individuals.
Publications: Application guidelines; Annual report; Grants list; Informational brochure.
Application information: Application form, instructions, and grant guidelines for Language Grants to individuals are available on foundation web site. Asian Art Grant applications are by invitation only. See foundation web site for further information.
Initial approach: See foundation web site for forms and eligibility requirements
Copies of proposal: 1
Deadline(s): Postmarked by Dec. 30 for language grants (or Dec. 31 if the 30th falls on a postal holiday)
Board meeting date(s): Biannually, usually June and Dec.
Final notification: Late Mar. or early Apr. for Language Grants
Officer and Board Members:* Mimi Gardner Gates,* Chair.; Eugene H. Lee, Trustee; Griffith Way, Trustee Emeritus; Paul Atkins; Therese Caouette; **Lorri Hagman**; Darryl M. Johnson; Robert A. Kapp; Joseph Massey; Haicheng Wang.
EIN: 911505735

3498
Blue Mountain Community Foundation
(formerly Blue Mountain Area Foundation)
22 E. Poplar St., Ste. 206
P.O. Box 603
Walla Walla, WA **99362** (509) 529-4371
***Contact:* Kari Isaacson, Exec. Dir.**
FAX: (509) 529-5284;
E-mail: bmcf@bluemountainfoundation.org; Main URL: http://www.bluemountainfoundation.org
Blog: http://www.bluemountainfoundation.org/?feed
Facebook: http://www.facebook.com/pages/Blue-Mountain-Community-Foundation/298194080507
LinkedIn: http://www.linkedin.com/company/1498208
RSS Feed: http://www.bluemountainfoundation.org/feed/
YouTube: http://www.youtube.com/user/BMCFoundation

Incorporated in 1984 in WA.
Foundation type: Community foundation.
Financial data (yr. ended 06/30/13): Assets, $34,182,386 (M); gifts received, $2,023,327; expenditures, $2,263,906; giving activities include $1,334,521 for 63+ grants (high: $63,934), and $410,233 for 76 grants to individuals.
Purpose and activities: The foundation promotes effective philanthropy by fostering private charitable giving, providing management of funds, and financially supporting students and charitable organizations to improve the quality of life in the community.
Fields of interest: Visual arts; Performing arts; Humanities; Historic preservation/historical societies; Arts; Higher education; Adult education—literacy, basic skills & GED; Education; Environment; Animal welfare; Reproductive health, family planning; Health care; Children/youth, services; Child development, services; Family services; Residential/custodial care, hospices; Aging, centers/services; Homeless, human services; Human services; Community development, neighborhood development; Economic development.
Type of support: General/operating support; Continuing support; Management development/capacity building; Equipment; Endowments; Program development; Curriculum development; Fellowships; Internship funds; Technical assistance; Scholarships—to individuals.
Limitations: Applications accepted. Giving limited to Umatilla County, OR, and Columbia, Garfield, and Walla Walla counties, WA. No support for sectarian religious programs. No grants for seed money, multi-year grants, operating expenses, annual fund drives, field trips, or travel to or in support of conferences.
Publications: Application guidelines; Annual report; Grants list; Informational brochure; Newsletter.
Application information: Visit foundation web site for application form and guidelines. Grants are only made to 501(c)(3) organizations in the Foundation's service area. Application form required.
Initial approach: Submit application summary and attachments
Copies of proposal: 10
Deadline(s): July 1 for grants; Mar. 1 for scholarships
Board meeting date(s): Quarterly
Final notification: Oct. for grants; June 1 for scholarships
Officers and Trustees:* Dan Reid,* Pres.; Craig Sievertsen,* V.P.; Leslie Brown,* Secy.; Shannon Bergevin,* Treas.; Kari Isaacson, Exec. Dir.; Tony Billingsley; Sandi Blackaby; Sherilee Coffey; Carol Varga Morgan; Keith Olson; Norm Passmore; Laure Quaresma; Anne-Marie Zell Schwerin; Larry Siegel; Anne Walsh; Richard M. Wylie.
Number of staff: 3 full-time professional; 1 part-time support.
EIN: 911250104

3499
Casey Family Programs
2001 8th Ave., Ste. 2700
Seattle, WA 98121-2641 (206) 282-7300
FAX: (206) 282-3555; New York Field Office address: 165 Broadway, 1 Liberty Plz., New York, N.Y., 10006, tel.: (212) 863-4860, Managing Dir., Zeinab Chahine; Main URL: http://www.casey.org
Google Plus: https://plus.google.com/+CaseyOrg/posts
Twitter: https://twitter.com/CaseyPrograms
YouTube: http://www.youtube.com/CaseyFamilyPrograms

Established in 1966. Classified as a private operating foundation in 1972.
Foundation type: Operating foundation.
Financial data (yr. ended 12/31/12): Assets, $2,061,764,408 (M); gifts received, $2,328,759; expenditures, $124,132,155; qualifying distributions, $111,763,619; giving activities include $3,528,325 for 104 grants (high: $1,690,000; low: $50), and $110,074,262 for foundation-administered programs.
Purpose and activities: The foundation serves children, youth, and families. Its primary focus is on children who cannot live safely within their own home.
Fields of interest: Substance abuse, services; Mental health/crisis services; Children, foster care.
Type of support: General/operating support; Continuing support; Program development; Scholarship funds; Research; Technical assistance; Program evaluation.
Limitations: Applications not accepted. Giving primarily in the U.S., with emphasis on Washington, DC, and WA. No grants to individuals.
Publications: Informational brochure.
Application information: Unsolicited requests for funds will not be accepted.
Officers and Trustees:* Robert A. "Bob" Watt,* Chair.; Joan B. Poliak,* Vice-Chair.; William C. Bell, C.E.O. and Pres.; Dave Danielson,* Exec. V.P., Admin. and C.F.O.; Marva Hammons,* Exec. V.P., Child and Family Svcs.; Alexandra McKay,* Exec.V.P. and Chief Prog. Counsel; Laura Sagen, Exec. V.P., Comms. and Human Resources; David Sanders, Exec. V.P., Systems Improvement; Joseph A. Boateng, C.I.O.; America Bracho,* Secy.; Sharon L. McDaniel,* Treas.; Shelia Evans-Tranum; Norm B. Rice.
Number of staff: 273 full-time professional; 6 part-time professional; 71 full-time support; 29 part-time support.
EIN: 910793881
Other changes: At the close of 2012, the grantmaker paid grants of $3,528,325, a 92.1% increase over the 2011 disbursements, $1,836,328.
Robert A. "Bob" Watt has replaced Shelia Evans-Tranumn as Chair.

3500
Marguerite Casey Foundation
(formerly Casey Family Grants Program)
1425 4th Ave., Ste. 900
Seattle, WA 98101-2222 (206) 691-3134
Contact: Kathleen Baca, Dir., Comms.
FAX: (206) 286-2725; E-mail: info@caseygrants.org; TTY: (206) 273-7395; Main URL: http://www.caseygrants.org/
E-Newsletter: http://www.caseygrants.org/pages/misc/misc_pubsignup.asp
Equal Voice America's Family Story: http://www.equalvoiceforfamilies.org/#
Equal Voice for America's Families Blog: http://equalvoiceforamericafamilies.blogspot.com/
Equal Voice for America's Family: http://www.facebook.com/EqualVoiceNews
Equal Voice News: http://twitter.com/equalvoicenews
Flickr: http://www.flickr.com/photos/caseygrants/
Grants Database: http://www.caseygrants.org/pages/equalvoice/equalvoice_ourgrantees.asp
Knowledge Center: http://www.caseygrants.org/pages/resources/resources_reportsandpubs.asp#opendialogue
Marguerite Casey Foundation's Philanthropy Promise: http://www.ncrp.org/philanthropys-promise/who
YouTube: http://www.youtube.com/user/caseygrants

Established in 2001 in WA.
Donor: Casey Family Programs.
Foundation type: Independent foundation.
Financial data (yr. ended 12/31/12): Assets, $619,185,416 (M); expenditures, $30,307,888; qualifying distributions, $27,840,161; giving activities include $21,514,332 for 263 grants (high: $750,000; low: $200), and $1,373,400 for foundation-administered programs.
Purpose and activities: The foundation makes grants that encourage low-income families to strengthen their voices and mobilize their communities in order to build a more just and equitable society for all. Its grantmaking is informed and guided by the following goals and objectives: engage low-income parents in efforts to improve conditions for their families, connect grantee

organizations within and across regions and disciplines for movement-building, and enhance the capacity and effectiveness of cornerstone organizations in low-income communities. The grantmaking is focused on three areas: education, advocacy and activism.
Fields of interest: Youth development; Children/youth, services; Family services; Economic development; Community/economic development; Disabilities, people with.
Type of support: General/operating support; Income development; Management development/capacity building; Program development; Research; Technical assistance; Program evaluation; Employee matching gifts.
Limitations: Applications not accepted. Giving primarily in four regions of the U.S.: CA; the Southwest, including the U.S./Mexico border; the Deep South; the Midwest, beginning in Chicago, IL; and WA state. No support for religious purposes. No grants to individuals, or for capital campaigns, endowments, fundraising drives, litigation, or film and video production.
Publications: Annual report; Financial statement; Grants list; Informational brochure; Program policy statement.
Application information: The foundation does not accept unsolicited proposals or letters of intent.
Board meeting date(s): Quarterly
Officers and Directors:* Freeman A. Hrabowski III,* Chair.; Patricia Schroeder,* Vice-Chair.; Luz Vega-Marquis, C.E.O. and Pres.; Douglas X. Patino,* Secy.; **Joyce Lee, C.F.O.**; David Villa,* Treas.; **Melody Barnes**; Angela Diaz, M.D.; William H. Foege.
Number of staff: 7 full-time professional; 8 full-time support; 1 part-time support.
EIN: 912062197
Other changes: Joyce Lee has replaced Stephen Sage as C.F.O.
America Bracho, Lynn Huntle, Joan B. Poliak and Ruth W. Massinga are no longer directors.

3501
Children's Chance for Life
20720 Snag Island Dr.
Lake Tapps, WA 98391-8712
E-mail: teeter@attglobal.net; Main URL: http://www.ccfl-online.org
Blog: http://ccfl-online.org/category/blog/
Facebook: https://www.facebook.com/ChildrensChanceForLife
RSS Feed: http://ccfl-online.org/comments/feed/
Twitter: https://twitter.com/CCFLfoundation

Established in 2002 as a public charity; reclassified as an independent foundation in 2007.
Donors: Roger Teeter; Jennifer Teeter; Timothy Moore; Vicky Moore.
Foundation type: Independent foundation.
Financial data (yr. ended 12/31/12): Assets, $231,798 (M); gifts received, $291,117; expenditures, $156,754; qualifying distributions, $154,000; giving activities include $154,000 for grants.
Purpose and activities: Giving primarily for children that are raised by Christian foster mothers and currently have the choice to attend Faith-way, a Christian school, or one of the other schools in town.
Fields of interest: Human services; Christian agencies & churches.
Limitations: Applications not accepted. Giving primarily in South Africa. No grants to individuals.
Application information: Contributes only to pre-selected organizations.
Officers: Roger C. Teeter, Pres.; Ann Rylie Teeter, V.P.; Jennifer M. Teeter, Secy.-Treas.
EIN: 450490401

3502
College Spark Washington
190 Queen Anne Ave. N., Ste. 260
Seattle, WA 98109-4926 (206) 461-5374
Contact: Rachel Clements, Prog. Off.
FAX: (206) 461-7208;
E-mail: info@collegespark.org; E-mail for Rachel Clements, Prog. Off: rachel@collegespark.org; Main URL: http://www.collegespark.org/
Facebook: https://www.facebook.com/CollegeSparkWashington
Twitter: https://twitter.com/CollegeSparkWA

Foundation type: Independent foundation.
Financial data (yr. ended 09/30/12): Assets, $117,438,042 (M); expenditures, $6,618,100; qualifying distributions, $6,472,282; giving activities include $5,349,361 for 62 grants (high: $665,300; low: $100).
Purpose and activities: Giving to organizations with a staffed and physical presence in Washington State that can demonstrate successful experience in reaching and serving low-income students. Students are considered low-income if they are eligible for Pell Grants or Washington State Need Grants, or from families eligible for one of the following public assistance programs: Food Stamps, Free and Reduced Price Lunch, or Temporary Assistance to Needy Families. The foundation is especially interested in projects that allow it to learn more about strategies identified as promising practices for improving Community Grants Program outcome indicators.
Fields of interest: Education.
Limitations: Applications accepted. Giving primarily in WA.
Application information: Application guidelines and form available on foundation web site. Application form required.
Initial approach: Letter of interest
Copies of proposal: 2
Deadline(s): See foundation website for application deadline
Officers and Trustees:* Steven C. Pumphrey,* Chair.; John Rose,* Secy.; Dr. Deborah J. Wilds,* Treas.; Christine A. McCabe, Exec. Dir.; Chio Flores; Bob Gilb; Trevor Greene; Dr. Jean Hernandez; Jesus Hernandez; Kris Lambright, CPA; Faith Li Pettis; Chris Reykdal; Barb Richardson; Dr. Ed Taylor; Bernie Thomas.
EIN: 911215725
Other changes: Dr. Brian Benzel is no longer Vice-Chair. Christie Querna and Denny Hurtado are no longer trustees.

3503
Community Foundation of North Central Washington
(formerly Greater Wenatchee Community Foundation)
9 South Wenatchee Ave.
Wenatchee, WA 98807 (509) 663-7716
***Contact:* Beth A. Stipe, Exec. Dir.; For grants: Denise Sorom, Dir., Community Philanthropy**
FAX: (888) 317-8314; E-mail: info@cfncw.org;
Additional e-mails: beth@cfncw.org; Grant inquiry e-mail: denise@cfncw.org; Main URL: http://www.cfncw.org
Facebook: https://www.facebook.com/cfncw
Twitter: http://twitter.com/cfncw
YouTube: http://www.youtube.com/cfncw
Scholarship application e-mail: scholarships@cfncw.org

Incorporated in 1986 in WA.
Foundation type: Community foundation.
Financial data (yr. ended 06/30/13): Assets, $48,156,037 (M); gifts received, $3,921,516; expenditures, $3,886,063; giving activities include $2,702,911 for 46+ grants (high: $267,550), and $360,597 for 244 grants to individuals.
Purpose and activities: The foundation makes a difference by serving as a bridge between donors and the broader community. Primary areas of interest include the arts, education, the environment, and the disadvantaged, with emphasis on child welfare and the elderly.
Fields of interest: Media/communications; Visual arts; Museums; Performing arts; Performing arts, theater; Performing arts, music; Humanities; History/archaeology; Historic preservation/historical societies; Arts; Education, early childhood education; Child development, education; Elementary school/education; Higher education; Adult/continuing education; Adult education—literacy, basic skills & GED; Libraries/library science; Education, reading; Education; Environment, natural resources; Environment; Animal welfare; Animals/wildlife, preservation/protection; Hospitals (general); Reproductive health, family planning; Medical care, rehabilitation; Health care; Substance abuse, services; Mental health/crisis services; AIDS; Alcoholism; Food services; Housing/shelter, development; Safety/disasters; Recreation; Children/youth, services; Child development, services; Family services; Residential/custodial care, hospices; Aging, centers/services; Women, centers/services; Minorities/immigrants, centers/services; Homeless, human services; Human services; Community development, neighborhood development; Community/economic development; Voluntarism promotion; Children/youth; Aging; Disabilities, people with; Minorities; Women; Economically disadvantaged; Homeless.
Type of support: General/operating support; Management development/capacity building; Building/renovation; Equipment; Land acquisition; Endowments; Program development; Seed money; Technical assistance; Scholarships—to individuals; Matching/challenge support.
Limitations: Applications accepted. Giving limited to north central WA: Chelan, Douglas, and Okanogan counties. No support for religious sectarian purposes. No grants to individuals (except for scholarships), or for debt retirement or budget deficits, tuition, annual campaigns, fundraising campaigns or events, or purchases or activities that occur prior to grant decisions.
Publications: Application guidelines; Annual report; Grants list; Informational brochure; Informational brochure (including application guidelines); Newsletter; Occasional report.
Application information: Visit foundation web site for application information and guidelines. Application form not required.
Initial approach: Telephone or letter
Copies of proposal: 1
Deadline(s): Varies
Board meeting date(s): 6 times annually
Final notification: Within 90 days
Officers and Trustees:* Katie Kavanaugh Pauly,* Chair.; Ken Marson,* Vice-Chair.; Gil Sparks,* Secy.-Treas.; Beth A. Stipe, Exec. Dir.; Judy A. Cleveland, Cont.; Diane Carson; Bart Clennon; Lisa Day; Claudia DeRobles; Emira Forner; Jane Gilbertsen; Deborah Hartl; Craig Homchick; Ken Jackson; Mary Lou Johnson; Hank Manriquez; Danielle Marchant; Steve Robinson; Peter

Rutherford, M.D.; Eliot Scull; Ron Skagen; Mark Spurgeon; Mike Stancil; Mike Steele; Kris Taylor; Nevio Tontini; Peter Valaas; Darci Waterman; David Weber, M.D.; Anne White.
Number of staff: 1 full-time professional; 1 part-time professional; 2 full-time support.
EIN: 911349486
Other changes: Katie Kavanaugh Pauly has replaced Kris Taylor as Chair. Ken Marson has replaced Katie Kavanaugh Pauly as Vice-Chair. Gil Sparks has replaced Ken Marson as Secy.-Treas.

3504
The Community Foundation of South Puget Sound
(formerly Greater Thurston County Community Foundation)
212 Union Ave. S.E., Ste. 102
Olympia, WA 98501-1302 (360) 705-3340
Contact: Norma Schuiteman, Exec. Dir.
FAX: (360) 705-2656;
E-mail: legacy@thecommunityfoundation.com; Main URL: http://www.thecommunityfoundation.com
Facebook: https://www.facebook.com/thecommunityfoundationsouthsound

Established in 1989 in WA.
Foundation type: Community foundation.
Financial data (yr. ended 12/31/12): Assets, $15,332,050 (M); gifts received, $2,764,218; expenditures, $1,326,127; giving activities include $673,263 for 84 grants (high: $43,500; low: $300).
Purpose and activities: The mission of the foundation is to encourage the growth and responsible distribution of charitable resources to build stronger communities.
Fields of interest: Arts; Education; Environment; Health care; Human services; Community/economic development.
Type of support: General/operating support; Emergency funds; Program development; Scholarship funds; Consulting services; In-kind gifts; Matching/challenge support.
Limitations: Applications accepted. Giving limited to Lewis, Mason and Thurston counties, WA. No support for religious organizations for religious purposes. No grants to individuals (except from scholarship funds), or for annual campaigns, debt reduction, capital campaigns, endowment funds, direct mail, special events, or for multiple year commitments.
Publications: Application guidelines; Annual report; Grants list; Informational brochure.
Application information: Visit foundation web site for application form and guidelines. Application form required.
Initial approach: Submit application form and attachments
Copies of proposal: 5
***Deadline(s):* Sept. 19**
Board meeting date(s): Every 4th Thurs.
Officers and Directors:* Lori Drummond,* Chair.; Bob Buhl,* Vice-Chair.; Stefani Parsons,* Secy.; Sue Vickerman,* Treas.; Norma Schuiteman, Exec. Dir.; Patti Case; Marty Juergens; Joe Lynch; **Jim Morrell**; Stacie-Dee Motoyama; Thomas L. Purce, Ed.D.; Greg Rhodes; Rebecca Staebler; Melanie Stewart; Brian Vance; Mary Williams; Robert Wubbena; Rodney Youckton.
Number of staff: 2 full-time professional; 1 part-time professional.
EIN: 943121390
Other changes: Mike Barnard, Pat McClain, and Gordon Shewfelt are no longer directors.

3505
Corvias Foundation
(formerly Our Family for Families First, Inc.)
210 5th Ave. S., Ste. 202
Edmonds, WA 98020-3625 (401) 228-2836
Contact: Maria Montalvo, Exec. Dir.
FAX: (401) 336-2505;
E-mail: info@corviasfoundation.org; E-mail for Maria Montalvo: Maria.montalvo@corviasfoundation.org; Main URL: http://www.corviasfoundation.org
Grants List: http://corviasfoundation.org/?id=charitable-giving

Established in 2006 in RI.
Donors: John C. Picerne; Brian Beauregard; USI Insurance; Armstrong; Severn Plumbing; Armstrong Wood Products; Armstrong World; Associated Materials; Bank of America; Barclays; Brian Beauregard; Brickman Group; Ch2M Hill; Builders First Choice; Cigna; Goebel; HD Supply; HB Communications; J. McDonald; Konica Minolta; L Stanley Shaw; John G P I Cerne; Kcs Landscaping; Kimley-Horn; Master Brand; Michael Steiner; MOEN; Sherwin Williams; Picerne Real Estate Group; Real Page; Seagull Lighting; Tony Freedman; USI Insurance; Westrope; Winslow Tech Group; Yardi.
Foundation type: Independent foundation.
Financial data (yr. ended 12/31/12): Assets, $69,000 (M); gifts received, $901,346; expenditures, $944,794; qualifying distributions, $683,578; giving activities include $625,112 for 127 grants (high: $60,000; low: $20), and $58,466 for 17 grants to individuals (high: $5,000; low: $214).
Purpose and activities: Giving to support Army families in the pursuit of higher education, establishing a tradition of community service, and encouraging professional career paths through education, internships, and mentoring programs.
Fields of interest: Education; Heart & circulatory diseases; Community/economic development.
Type of support: General/operating support; Scholarships—to individuals.
Limitations: Applications accepted. Giving limited to a child or a spouse of an active-duty Army Soldier stationed at one of the following U.S. Army installations: Fort Rucker, AL, Fort Riley, KS, Fort Polk, LA, Aberdeen Proving Ground and Fort Meade, MD, Fort Bragg, NC and Fort Sill, OK.
Publications: Application guidelines.
Application information: Complete application guidelines available on foundation web site.
***Initial approach:* See foundation web site**
Officers and Directors:* John G. Picerne,* Pres.; Maria Montalvo,* Secy.; Claude Levesque,* Treas.; Janet G. Colantuono; Lynn Fossum.
EIN: 204848228
Other changes: The grantmaker now accepts applications.
The grantmaker now publishes application guidelines.

3506
The Dimmer Family Foundation
1019 Pacific Ave., Ste. 916
Tacoma, WA 98402-4492 (253) 572-4607
***Contact:* Diane C. Dimmer, Exec. Dir.**
FAX: (253) 572-4647;
E-mail: info@dimmerfoundation.org; Main URL: http://www.dimmerfoundation.org
Facebook: https://www.facebook.com/DimmerFamilyFoundation?skip_nax_wizard=true#

Established in 1994 in WA.
Donor: John C. Dimmer.
Foundation type: Independent foundation.
Financial data (yr. ended 12/31/12): Assets, $14,244,087 (M); expenditures, $970,180; qualifying distributions, $610,894; giving activities include $521,480 for 125 grants (high: $57,750; low: $100).
Purpose and activities: Giving primarily for the arts, education, and for health care and human services.
Fields of interest: Museums; Museums (children's); Arts; Higher education; Education; Animal welfare; Hospitals (general); Health care; Medical research, institute; Youth development, centers/clubs; Human services.
Type of support: General/operating support; Continuing support; Annual campaigns; Capital campaigns; Building/renovation; Equipment; Endowments; Program development; Scholarship funds; Research; Matching/challenge support.
Limitations: Applications accepted. Giving primarily in Tacoma, WA.
Publications: Grants list; Informational brochure.
Application information: Application form required.
Initial approach: Proposal
Deadline(s): None
Board meeting date(s): 4-6 weeks after each deadline
Officers: John C. Dimmer, Pres.; Carolyn Dimmer, V.P.; Marilyn Dimmer, V.P.; Diane C. Dimmer, Secy. and Exec. Dir.; John B. Dimmer, Treas.
Number of staff: 1 part-time professional.
EIN: 911622059

3507
Discuren Charitable Foundation
1201 3rd Ave., Ste. 4900
Seattle, WA 98101-3095 (206) 359-8574
Contact: F. Jean Watson, Secy.-Treas.

Established in 2004 in WA.
Donor: Blue Heron Trust.
Foundation type: Independent foundation.
Financial data (yr. ended 12/31/12): Assets, $15,520,160 (M); expenditures, $1,510,327; qualifying distributions, $1,361,775; giving activities include $1,224,818 for 36 grants (high: $86,286; low: $8,500).
Purpose and activities: Giving to organizations that address the needs of literacy, basic education, drop-out prevention, and provide teaching and learning environments for children.
Fields of interest: Elementary/secondary education; Higher education; Education, drop-out prevention; Education; YM/YWCAs & YM/YWHAs; Children/youth, services; Family services.
Limitations: Giving limited to WA.
Application information: Application form required.
Initial approach: Letter or telephone requesting application form
***Deadline(s):* Quarterly**
Officers: Colonel F. Betz, Pres.; Robert S. Mucklestone, V.P.; F. Jean Watson, Secy.-Treas.
Directors: Martha Ashenfelter; Greg Coy; Polly M. Olsen.
EIN: 202046554

3508
Echo Bay Foundation
c/o Anders Berglund
7055 Beach Dr. S.W.
Seattle, WA **98136**

Established in 2005 in WA.
Donors: Anders Berglund; Janet Berglund.
Foundation type: Independent foundation.

Financial data (yr. ended 09/30/13): Assets, $7,071,691 (M); expenditures, $350,186; qualifying distributions, $325,587; giving activities include $310,000 for 12 grants (high: $100,000; low: $5,000).
Fields of interest: Performing arts; Scholarships/financial aid; Education; Children/youth, services.
Limitations: Applications not accepted. Giving primarily in CA and WA. No grants to individuals.
Application information: Contributes only to pre-selected organizations.
Trustees: Anders Berglund; Janet Berglund.
EIN: 201985227

3509
Eggnog Latte Foundation
(doing business as Renee and Jeff Harbers Family Foundation)
P.O. Box 298
Medina, WA 98039-0298
Main URL: http://www.harbersfoundation.org/

Established in WA.
Donor: Renee W. Harbers.
Foundation type: Operating foundation.
Financial data (yr. ended 11/30/12): Assets, $5,390,362 (M); gifts received, $1,602,228; expenditures, $1,412,381; qualifying distributions, $1,410,692; giving activities include $1,139,338 for 11 grants (high: $500,000; low: $491), and $703,773 for 4 foundation-administered programs.
Purpose and activities: The foundation brings human and environmental issues into focus by setting the aperture for inspiring and motivating visual narratives. Working with some of the world's leading photographers and visual storytellers, it creates exceptional visual narratives that represent the diverse initiatives of cutting edge non-profits and NGOs around the world, focusing on global conservation issues and humanitarian need.
Fields of interest: Arts; Environment; Health care; Human services.
Limitations: Applications not accepted.
Application information: Unsolicited requests for funds not accepted.
Officers: Renee W. Harbers, C.E.O.; Gretchen Huizinga, Exec. Dir.
Trustees: Geoff Cowper; Mark Kroese.
EIN: 261616837
Other changes: Renee W. Harbers is now C.E.O.

3510
Empire Health Foundation
P.O. Box 244
Spokane, WA **99210-0244** (509) 315-1323
E-mail: brian@empirehealthfoundation.org; Main URL: http://www.empirehealthfoundation.org
Blog: http://www.empirehealthfoundation.org/blog
E-Newsletter: http://www.empirehealthfoundation.org/mailing-list
Grants List: http://www.empirehealthfoundation.org/grants-awarded
RSS Feed: http://empirehealthfoundation.org/news/rss.xml
Twitter: http://twitter.com/empirehealth

Established in 2008 in WA.
Donors: Empire Health Services; Boone Foundation; Woodrow Foundation; Grant Makers in Health.
Foundation type: Independent foundation.
Financial data (yr. ended 12/31/12): Assets, $64,983,909 (M); gifts received, $177,515; expenditures, $3,057,765; qualifying distributions, $8,018,223; giving activities include $1,331,614 for 90 grants (high: $150,579; low: $100), and $7,973,223 for foundation-administered programs.
Purpose and activities: The foundation works to improve the health of communities in eastern Washington. The foundation seeks to design and implement a strategic vision for impact, and establish itself as a catalyst and convener in the region.
Fields of interest: Arts; Education; Agriculture/food.
Limitations: Applications accepted. Giving primarily in Ferry, Stevens, Pend Oreille, Lincoln, Spokane, Adams and Whitman counties, WA. No grants to individuals.
Application information: Application form required.
Initial approach: E-mail
Officers and Trustees:* Garman Lutz,* Chair.; Sue Lanai W. Madsen,* Vice-Chair.; **Antony Chiang, Pres.; Kristen West, V.P., Grant Progs.**; Anne C. Cowles,* Secy.; Dave Luhn, C.F.O.; Matthew Layton,* Treas.; Lisa Brown; Craig Dias; Deb Harper; Todd Koyama; Teressa Martinez; Michael Nowling; Theresa Sanders; Mary C. Selecky; Sam Selinger, M.D.; Gary Stokes.
EIN: 263375286
Other changes: Brian Benzel and Michael A. Senske are no longer trustees.

3511
The Greater Everett Community Foundation
2823 Rockefeller Ave.
P.O. Box 5549
Everett, WA 98201-3524 **(425) 212-4056**
***Contact:* Maddy Metzger-Utt, Pres. and C.E.O.; Karri Matau**
FAX: (425) 212-4059;
E-mail: maddy@greatereverettcf.org; Mailing address: P.O. Box 5549, Everett, WA 98206-5549; Additional e-mail: info@greatereverettcf.org; Grant inquiry tel. 425-212-4056; Main URL: http://www.greatereverettcf.org

Established in 2001 in WA.
Foundation type: Community foundation.
Financial data (yr. ended 12/31/12): Assets, $10,525,375 (M); gifts received, $714,245; expenditures, $866,736; giving activities include $414,719 for 23+ grants (high: $25,840), and $28,200 for 16 grants to individuals.
Purpose and activities: The foundation works in partnership with donors to strengthen communities in greater Everett and Snohomish County, WA, by building permanent charitable funds, connecting donors to the causes they care about, making effective grants, and providing leadership to address community issues.
Fields of interest: Arts; Education; Environment; Health care; Youth development, adult & child programs; Developmentally disabled, centers & services; Human services; Children; Youth; Mentally disabled.
Type of support: General/operating support; Annual campaigns; Equipment; Endowments; Program development; Scholarship funds; Employee matching gifts; Scholarships—to individuals.
Limitations: Applications accepted. Giving primarily in Snohomish County, WA.
Publications: Application guidelines; Annual report.
Application information: Visit foundation web site for application forms and guidelines per grant type. Application form required.
Initial approach: Submit application form
Copies of proposal: 1
***Deadline(s):* Apr. 30 for Spring Grants and Oct. 31 for Fall Grants**
Board meeting date(s): 4th Wed. of every other month
Final notification: 60 days
Officers and Directors:* Melinda Grout,* Chair.; Bill Neumeister,* Vice-Chair.; **Maddy Metzger-Utt,* Pres. and C.E.O.; Karri Matau,* V.P., Grantmaking and Partnerships; Elena Pullen-Venema,* V.P., Devel.**; Martha Dankers,* Secy.; Scott Murphy,* Treas.; Judy Baker; Patty DeGroodt; Sarah Duncan; Bonnie Eckley; Carlton Gipson; Mary Hale; Kelly Johnson; John Middleton; Ross Rettenmier.
Number of staff: 1 full-time professional; 2 part-time professional.
EIN: 943188703
Other changes: Maddy Metzger-Utt has replaced Ross Rettenmier as Pres.
Karri Matau is no longer V.P., Philanthropic Svcs.
Sarah Duncan is no longer a director.

3512
Fales Foundation Trust
c/o Union Bank, N.A.
2825 Colby Ave.
Everett, WA 98201-3554 **(206) 781-3472**
Contact: J. Thomas McCully, Trust Off., Union Bank, N.A.
E-mail: OgleFounds@aol.com; **Main URL: http://fdnweb.org/fales**
Grants List: http://fdnweb.org/fales/grants/year/2013/

Established in 1985 in WA.
Donor: Gilbert R. Fales‡.
Foundation type: Independent foundation.
Financial data (yr. ended 01/31/13): Assets, $4,365,209 (M); expenditures, $265,823; qualifying distributions, $225,978; giving activities include $199,500 for 72 grants (high: $10,000; low: $1,000).
Purpose and activities: Giving primarily to programs serving the homeless and hungry, and to arts and culture (primarily community-based arts programs related to issues of homelessness and hunger, providing arts opportunities for underserved constituencies).
Fields of interest: Arts; Education; Food services; Housing/shelter, homeless; Human services.
Type of support: General/operating support; Annual campaigns; Program development.
Limitations: Applications accepted. Giving limited to Seattle, WA. No grants to individuals, or for film/video, computers, office equipment, or software.
Publications: Application guidelines.
Application information: Application form required.
Initial approach: Proposal
Copies of proposal: 1
Deadline(s): Apr. 1
Board meeting date(s): May and Dec.
Final notification: Following board meetings
Trustee: Union Bank, N.A.
Number of staff: 1 part-time professional.
EIN: 916087669

3513
The Hugh and Jane Ferguson Foundation
6723 Sycamore Ave. NW
Seattle, WA 98117-4849 **(206) 781-3472**
Contact: Therese Ogle, Fdn. Advisor
E-mail: OgleFounds@aol.com; Main URL: http://fdnweb.org/ferguson
Alaska Grants: http://fdnweb.org/ferguson/grants/category/alaska-groups/
Cultural Grants: http://fdnweb.org/ferguson/grants/category/cultural-projects/

Oregon Environmental Grants: http://fdnweb.org/ferguson/grants/category/oregon-environmental-groups/
Washington Environmental Grants: http://fdnweb.org/ferguson/grants/category/washington-environmental-groups/

Established in 1986 in WA.
Donors: Hugh S. Ferguson; Jane Avery Ferguson†.
Foundation type: Independent foundation.
Financial data (yr. ended 09/30/12): Assets, $479,281 (M); gifts received, $175,000; expenditures, $390,477; qualifying distributions, $362,296; giving activities include $346,900 for 39 grants (high: $100,000; low: $300).
Purpose and activities: The foundation is dedicated to the preservation and restoration of nature, including wildlife and their required habitats. It also supports the institutions that present nature and the cultural heritage of the greater Puget Sound area to the public—museums, libraries, aquariums, zoos and public media.
Fields of interest: Museums; Higher education; Libraries (public); Education; Environment, natural resources; Zoos/zoological societies; Aquariums; Animals/wildlife; Human services; United Ways and Federated Giving Programs.
Type of support: General/operating support; Continuing support; Capital campaigns; Land acquisition; Program development; Seed money; Technical assistance.
Limitations: Applications not accepted. Giving primarily in AK, OR, and WA, with emphasis on WA. No support for social service agencies, schools or government agencies or collaborations between nonprofits and government agencies in which the government provides majority funding or leadership. No grants to individuals or for research projects, book publications, web or video/film productions, capital campaigns, curriculum development, or scholarships.
Publications: Grants list.
Application information: The foundation is not accepting unsolicited proposals.
Board meeting date(s): Mar. and Sept.
Officers and Directors:* Hugh S. Ferguson,* Pres.; Ellen Lee Ferguson,* Secy.
EIN: 911357603

3514
First Financial Northwest Foundation
c/o Joann E. Lee
201 Wells Ave. S.
Renton, WA 98057-2131

Established in 2007 in WA.
Donor: First Financial Northwest, Inc.
Foundation type: Company-sponsored foundation.
Financial data (yr. ended 12/31/12): Assets, $11,222,517 (M); expenditures, $479,330; qualifying distributions, $453,550; giving activities include $431,801 for 3 grants (high: $261,801; low: $20,000).
Purpose and activities: The foundation supports community foundations and organizations involved with human services.
Fields of interest: Human services; Community/economic development.
Type of support: General/operating support.
Limitations: Applications not accepted. Giving primarily in Renton, WA. No grants for individuals.
Application information: Contributes only to pre-selected organizations.
Officers: Charles J. Delaurenti II, Chair.; Gary F. Faull, Secy.; JoAnn E. Lee, Treas.; Gary F. Kohlwes, Exec. Dir.
Trustee: Harry A. Blencoe.
EIN: 261421623

3515
Foundation for the Future
16150 N.E. 85th St., Ste. 119
Redmond, WA 98052-3542

Established in 1996 in WA as a private operating foundation.
Donor: Walter P. Kistler.
Foundation type: Independent foundation.
Financial data (yr. ended 12/31/12): Assets, $7,673,106 (M); expenditures, $3,693,619; qualifying distributions, $3,443,074; giving activities include $1,377,908 for 13 grants (high: $1,000,000; low: $5,000), $7,500 for 1 grant to an individual, and $98,643 for foundation-administered programs.
Purpose and activities: The mission of the foundation is to increase and diffuse knowledge concerning the long-term future of humanity. It conducts a broad range of programs and activities to promote an understanding of the factors in the social, genetic, biological, medical, psychological, physiological, cultural, technological, and ecological fields that may have an impact on human life.
Fields of interest: Education.
Type of support: Continuing support; Program development; Seed money; Research.
Limitations: Applications not accepted. Giving primarily in VA; funding also in India and Peru.
Application information: Unsolicited requests for funds not accepted.
Board meeting date(s): Quarterly
Officers and Trustees:* Walter Kistler,* Pres.; Sesh Velamoor,* Exec. Dir.; Donna Hines; **Sylvia Thompson**; Milton Woods.
Number of staff: 5 full-time professional; 1 part-time professional; 1 full-time support; 1 part-time support.
EIN: 911732102
Other changes: The grantmaker no longer lists a phone.
At the close of 2012, the grantmaker paid grants of $1,385,408, an 87.9% increase over the 2011 disbursements, $737,433.
Charles Murray, Barry Swartz, and Crispin Tickell are no longer trustees.

3516
Bill & Melinda Gates Foundation
(formerly William H. Gates Foundation)
P.O. Box 23350
Seattle, WA 98102-0650 **(206) 709-3100**
Contact: Inquiry Admin.
E-mail: info@gatesfoundation.org; **For grant inquiries: (206) 709-3140. East Coast Office address: P.O. Box 6176, Benjamin Franklin Station, Washington, DC 20044, tel.: (202) 662-8130**; Main URL: http://www.gatesfoundation.org
Bill & Melinda Gates Foundation Staff: https://twitter.com/gatesfoundation/team
Bill and Melinda Gates and Warren Buffett's Giving Pledge Profile: http://glasspockets.org/philanthropy-in-focus/eye-on-the-giving-pledge/profiles/gates
E-Newsletter: http://www.gatesfoundation.org/Pages/subscribe-email-rss.aspx
Facebook: http://www.facebook.com/billmelindagatesfoundation?v=info
Flickr: http://www.flickr.com/photos/gatesfoundation/
GiveSmart: http://www.givesmart.org/Stories/Donors/Melinda-Gates
Grand Challenges in Global Health: http://www.grandchallenges.org/Pages/Default.aspx
Grantee Perception Report: http://www.gatesfoundation.org/How-We-Work/Resources/Grantee-Perception-Report-Summary-2013
Grants Database: http://www.gatesfoundation.org/How-We-Work/Quick-Links/Grants-Database
Impatient Optimists: http://www.impatientoptimists.org/
Knowledge Center: http://www.gatesfoundation.org/learning/Pages/overview.aspx
Pinterest: http://pinterest.com/gatesfoundation/
Twitter: http://www.twitter.com/gatesfoundation
YouTube: http://www.youtube.com/GatesFoundation

Established in 1994 in WA as the William H. Gates Foundation. The William H. Gates Foundation, focused on global health, was created in 1994 by Microsoft co-founder William H. "Bill" Gates, III and his wife, Melinda French Gates. Three years later, he and Melinda created the Gates Library Foundation, which worked to bring public access computers with Internet connections to libraries in the United States. Its name changed to the Gates Learning Foundation in 1999 to reflect its focus on ensuring that low-income minority students are prepared for college and have the means to attend. In 2000, to increase efficiency and communication, the two organizations merged into the Bill & Melinda Gates Foundation. In 2006, Warren Buffett, founder of Berkshire Hathaway Inc., pledged 10 million shares of Berkshire Hathaway B stock (valued at approximately $31 billion) to the Bill & Melinda Gates Foundation. Each year, 5 percent of the remaining pledged shares will be transferred to the asset trust, and starting in 2008, the total value of the previous year's gift must be spent. In 2007, the foundation restructured and created a separate organization, the Bill & Melinda Gates Foundation Trust, to oversee the foundation's assets. The trust will include the annual installments of Warren Buffett's gift to the foundation and in turn, will fund the program foundation. Bill and Melinda Gates will be the sole trustees of the asset trust. The original entity, the Bill & Melinda Gates Foundation, conducts the foundation's programmatic and grantmaking activities. Based in Seattle, Washington, the foundation also has offices in Washington, D.C.; Beijing, China; Delhi, India; and London, United Kingdom. The foundation plans to close 50 years after the deaths of its three current trustees - Bill and Melinda Gates, and Warren Buffett. Separately from the foundation, Bill and Melinda Gates and Warren Buffett have made a commitment to The Giving Pledge, an effort to invite the wealthiest individuals and families to give the majority of their wealth to philanthropic causes during their lifetime or after their death.
Donors: William H. "Bill" Gates III; Melinda French Gates; Warren E. Buffett.
Foundation type: Independent foundation.
Financial data (yr. ended 12/31/12): Assets, $37,176,776,438 (M); gifts received, $3,875,024,893; expenditures, $3,858,588,368; qualifying distributions, $3,896,896,800; giving activities include $3,178,235,962 for grants, $229,934,413 for foundation-administered programs and $38,474,529 for loans/program-related investments.
Purpose and activities: Guided by the belief that every life has equal value, the Bill & Melinda Gates

Foundation works to help all people lead healthy, productive lives. In developing countries, it focuses on improving people's health and giving them the chance to lift themselves out of hunger and extreme poverty. In the United States, it seeks to ensure that all people-especially those with the fewest resources-have access to the opportunities they need to succeed in school and life.
Grantmaking areas are: 1) Global Development: to help the world's poorest people lift themselves out of hunger and poverty; 2) Global Health: to harness advances in science and technology to save lives in developing countries; and 3) U.S. Division: to improve U.S. high school and postsecondary education and support vulnerable children and families in Washington State.
Fields of interest: Education, public education; Elementary/secondary education; Middle schools/education; Elementary school/education; Secondary school/education; Higher education, college (community/junior); Libraries/library science; Education; Health care, infants; Reproductive health, family planning; Public health; Public health, clean water supply; Public health, sanitation; Health care; AIDS; Parasitic diseases research; Immunology research; Agriculture; Nutrition; Safety/disasters; Human services; International development; Economic development; Community/economic development; Philanthropy/voluntarism, alliance/advocacy; Financial services; Infants/toddlers; Children/youth; Children; Youth; Adults; Young adults; Women; Infants/toddlers, female; Girls; Adults, women; Young adults, female; Men; Infants/toddlers, male; Boys; Adults, men; Young adults, male; AIDS, people with; Economically disadvantaged; Homeless.
International interests: Africa; Asia; Developing Countries; Europe.
Type of support: General/operating support; Continuing support; Annual campaigns; Program development; Publication; Scholarship funds; Research; Technical assistance; Program-related investments/loans; Employee matching gifts.
Limitations: Applications accepted. **Giving on a national and international basis. No support for projects addressing health problems in developed countries, nor for projects that exclusively serve religious purposes. No direct donations or grants to individuals, and no funding for building or capital campaigns, or for political campaigns and legislative lobbying efforts.**
Publications: Application guidelines; Annual report; Financial statement; Grants list; Informational brochure; Newsletter; Occasional report; Program policy statement.
Application information: In general, the foundation directly invites proposals by directly contacting organizations. Review funding guidelines and eligibility overview on foundation's web site before initial contact with foundation. No mail-in applications are accepted. Application form required.

- ***Initial approach:* Online letter of inquiry not exceeding 4 pages only accepted for Global Health; submit formal funding proposal upon invitation from foundation**
- *Deadline(s):* Generally none

Officers and Trustees:* Melinda French Gates,* Co-Chair.; William H. "Bill" Gates III,* Co-Chair.; William H. Gates, Sr., Co-Chair.; **Susan Desmond-Hellmann, M.D., M.P.H., C.E.O.; Leigh Morgan, C.O.O.; Christopher Elias, Pres., Global Devel.**; Allan C. Golston, Pres., U.S. Prog.; Trevor Mundel, Pres., Global Health Prog.; Mark Suzman, Pres., Global Policy & Advocacy; Connie Collingsworth, Secy. and Genl. Counsel; **Jim Bromley, C.F.O.**; Dale Christian, C.I.O.; Susan Byrnes, Interim Chief Comms. Off.; Kurt Fischer, Chief HR Off.; Warren E. Buffett.
Global Health Scientific Advisory Committe: John Bell, Chair.; Alan Bernstein, Ph.D., FRSC; M.K. Bhan, M.D.; Zulfiqar A. Butta, Ph.D.; Tumani Corrah, M.D., Ph.D.; Yvonne Greenstreet, M.D., M.B.A.; H. Robert Horvitz, Ph.D.; Salim S. Abdool Karim, Ph.D.; Shabir A. Madhi, Ph.D.; Francine Ntoumi, Ph.D.; Harold Varmus, M.D.; Timothy Wright, M.D.; Elias A. Zerhouni, M.D.
U.S. Program Advisory Board: Ann Fudge, Chair.; Christopher Edley; Edward Glaeser; Jim Nussle; Margaret Spellings.
Number of staff: 1211
EIN: 562618866
Other changes: The grantmaker no longer lists a fax.
Jim Bromley has replaced Richard Henriques as C.F.O. Christopher Elias has replaced Sylvia Mathews Burwell as Pres., Global Devel. Prog.
Susan Desmond-Hellmann, M.D., M.P.H. has replaced Jeff Raikes as C.E.O.
Martha Choe is no longer C.A.O.

3517
Glaser Progress Foundation
(formerly The Glaser Foundation)
1601 2nd Ave., Ste. 1080
Seattle, WA 98101-3526
Contact: Melessa Rogers, Operations Mgr.
FAX: (206) 728-1123;
E-mail: grants@glaserprogress.org; E-mail for application questions:
melessa@glaserprogress.org; Main URL: http://www.glaserprogress.org

Established in 1993 in WA.
Donor: Robert D. Glaser.
Foundation type: Independent foundation.
Financial data (yr. ended 12/31/12): Assets, $7,645,227 (M); expenditures, $1,764,122; qualifying distributions, $1,750,631; giving activities include $1,289,950 for 15 grants (high: $999,950; low: $1,000).
Purpose and activities: The foundation focuses on four program areas: 1) Measuring Progress: build a more equitable and sustainable world by improving our understanding and measurement of human progress, 2) Animal Advocacy: make animal treatment a crucial consideration in business, policy and personal decision-making, 3) Independent Media: strengthen democracy by making independent voices heard (the foundation has also launched a Progress Education Project which will influence all grant awards in this area), and 4) Global HIV/AIDS: to identify and implement programs that provide support for and fulfillment of the goals of the Global Fund to Fight AIDS, tuberculosis, and malaria.
Fields of interest: Media/communications; Animal welfare; International economic development.
Type of support: General/operating support; Program development; Conferences/seminars; Technical assistance.
Limitations: Applications accepted. Giving on a national basis. No support for political organizations. No grants to individuals.
Publications: Application guidelines; Grants list; IRS Form 990 or 990-PF printed copy available upon request.
Application information: Unsolicited grant proposals for the Global HIV/AIDS program are not accepted. Please do not include supporting materials (videos, CDs, newsletters, reports, books) at the early stage of the application process. Application form not required.

- ***Initial approach:* Letter via U.S. Mail, e-mail, or fax (choose only one option)**
- *Copies of proposal:* 1
- *Deadline(s):* None
- *Board meeting date(s):* Approx. 6 months after receipt of application letter to staff and board review
- ***Final notification:* Approx. 6 months**

Officer: Martin Collier, Exec. Dir.
Trustee: Robert D. Glaser.
Number of staff: 3 full-time professional.
EIN: 911626010

3518
The Goodman Foundation
2801 Alaskan Way, Ste. 310
Seattle, WA 98121-1136
***Contact:* Teresa Beattie**
E-mail for Teresa Beattie:
teresa@goodmanfound.org; Main URL: http://www.goodmanfound.org

Established in 2005 in WA.
Donors: John Goodman; Shawn Goodman.
Foundation type: Independent foundation.
Financial data (yr. ended 12/31/12): Assets, $2,072 (M); gifts received, $257,300; expenditures, $258,592; qualifying distributions, $257,440; giving activities include $255,600 for 12 grants (high: $75,000; low: $600).
Purpose and activities: The foundation's mission is to fund organizations that support children and their families.
Fields of interest: Education; Boys & girls clubs; Human services; American Red Cross; Children, services; Family services; Christian agencies & churches.
Limitations: Applications not accepted. No grants to individuals.
Application information: Unsolicited requests for funds not accepted.
Officers and Directors:* John A. Goodman,* Pres. and Treas.; Shawn Goodman,* Secy.
EIN: 203215663

3519
The Atsuhiko and Ina Goodwin Tateuchi Foundation
c/o Foundation Mgmt. Group, LLC
1000 2nd Ave., 34th Fl.
Seattle, WA 98104-1022
E-mail: info@tateuchi.org; Main URL: http://www.tateuchi.org
Grants List: http://www.tateuchi.org/grants.html

Established in 2000 in Japan and then in 2006 in WA.
Donors: Atsuhiko Tateuchi; Ina Tateuchi.
Foundation type: Independent foundation.
Financial data (yr. ended 12/31/12): Assets, $12,458,476 (M); expenditures, $1,569,028; qualifying distributions, $1,540,698; giving activities include $1,498,850 for 23 grants (high: $520,000; low: $500).
Purpose and activities: The foundation's mission seeks to promote and improve international understanding, knowledge, and the quality of relations between Japan and the United States.
Fields of interest: Arts, cultural/ethnic awareness; Museums (ethnic/folk arts); Higher education, university; Botanical gardens; Foundations (community).

Type of support: General/operating support; Capital campaigns; Seed money; Matching/challenge support.
Limitations: Applications accepted. Giving primarily in CA and WA; some giving also in Japan.
Application information: Application guidelines available on foundation web site.
Initial approach: 1-2 page concise letter or e-mail of inquiry
Deadline(s): None
Final notification: Within 30 days of the conclusion of the grant review process
Officers and Director:* Ina Tateuchi,* Pres., V.P., and Treas.; Laura Hurdelbrink, Secy.
EIN: 912090773

3520
Grays Harbor Community Foundation
707 J St.
P.O. Box 615
Hoquiam, WA 98550-3624 (360) 532-1600
Contact: Jim Daly, Exec. Dir.; For grants: Cassie Lentz, Prog. Off.
FAX: (360) 532-8111; E-mail: info@gh-cf.org; Additional e-mail: cassie@gh-cf.org; Main URL: http://www.gh-cf.org
Facebook: http://www.facebook.com/GraysHarborCommunityFoundation

Established in 1994 in WA.
Foundation type: Community foundation.
Financial data (yr. ended 12/31/12): Assets, $37,380,788 (M); gifts received, $4,061,246; expenditures, $1,746,455; giving activities include $1,010,514 for 31+ grants (high: $164,750), and $379,034 for 237 grants to individuals.
Purpose and activities: The foundation aims to improve the quality of life in communities throughout Grays Harbor County by: 1) promoting philanthropy at all levels of giving; 2) seeking permanent endowment funds and other contributions from a diverse and ever-widening group of donors; 3) helping donors achieve their charitable and financial goals by offering services that make charitable giving easy, effective and satisfying; 4) providing responsible and effective financial management; 5) distributing earnings from investments according to community needs and donor intent; and 6) championing good works in every community served. Grantmaking priorities include arts and culture, education, health, human services, and community development.
Fields of interest: Historic preservation/historical societies; Arts; Adult education—literacy, basic skills & GED; Student services/organizations; Education; Health care; Mental health/crisis services; Agriculture/food; Homeless, human services; Human services; Community/economic development; Children/youth.
Type of support: General/operating support; Income development; Management development/capacity building; Capital campaigns; Building/renovation; Equipment; Land acquisition; Emergency funds; Program development; Conferences/seminars; Seed money; Curriculum development; Scholarships—to individuals; In-kind gifts; Matching/challenge support.
Limitations: Applications accepted. Giving primarily to residents of Grays Harbor County, WA, area. No support for religious organizations for religious purposes. No grants to individuals (except for scholarships), or for endowments, debt retirement, fundraising events, advertising, or attending conferences.
Publications: Application guidelines; Annual report; Grants list; Informational brochure; Informational brochure (including application guidelines); Newsletter.
Application information: Visit foundation web site for grant application cover sheet and guidelines. The foundation welcomes phone calls and letters of inquiry at all times. Application form required.
Initial approach: Submit application cover sheet and attachments
Copies of proposal: 7
Deadline(s): Jan. 1, Apr. 1, July 1, and Oct. 1
Board meeting date(s): 3rd Thurs. of alternating months
Final notification: Quarterly
Officers and Directors:* Tom Quigg,* Chair.; Jon Parker,* Vice-Chair.; Dr. David Westby,* Secy.; Bob Preble,* Treas.; Jim Daly, Exec. Dir.; Dr. Donald J. Arima; Barbara Bennett-Parsons; Tom Brennan; David Burnett; Ron Caufman; George Donovan; Martin Kay; Todd Lindley; Dennis Long; John Mertz; Wes Peterson; Stan Pinnick; Randy Rust; Bill Stewart; Mike Stoney; Rich Vroman; John Warring; Maryann Welch.
Number of staff: 2 full-time professional; 1 full-time support.
EIN: 911607005
Other changes: Dick Warren is no longer a director.

3521
Joshua Green Foundation
1425 4th Ave., Ste. 420
P.O. Box 21829
Seattle, WA **98101-2218** (206) 622-0420
Contact: Sandra Spurlock, Secy.
***FAX:* (206) 467-1176;**
E-mail: sandras@joshuagreencorp.com; Main URL: http://www.joshuagreencorp.com/
Grants List: http://new.joshuagreencorp.com/foundation/

Established in 1956 in WA.
Donors: Joshua Green†; Mrs. Joshua Green†; Charles P. Burnett III; Joshua Green III; Jennifer Carter; Frances Davidson; Laura Gowen; Herbert Gowen; William C. Gowen; Louisa Gowen; Shirley Burnett; William Burnett; Vivian Burnett; William Burnett, Jr.; Shannon Hoffer; Laura Brisbane; Louisa Malatos; Sarah Burnett; Leslie Hawkins; Jean Tannehill; David Burnett; Leah Holser; Paige Dunn; William Burnett; Vivian Burnett; William Burnett, Jr.; Jean Tannehill; Rocky Tannehill; Robert Burnett; Joshua Green Corporation; H. Gowen II; Reagam Dunn.
Foundation type: Independent foundation.
Financial data (yr. ended 12/31/12): Assets, $41,985,032 (M); gifts received, $832,850; expenditures, $1,644,707; qualifying distributions, $1,479,126; giving activities include $1,477,800 for 157 grants (high: $150,000; low: $50).
Fields of interest: Arts; Elementary/secondary education; Higher education; Health care; Human services; Family services; Christian agencies & churches.
Type of support: Capital campaigns; Building/renovation; Land acquisition; Emergency funds.
Limitations: Applications accepted. Giving primarily in the King County, WA, area. No grants to individuals, or for scholarships or fellowships; no loans.
Publications: Application guidelines.
Application information: See foundation web site for complete application guidelines. Application form required.
***Initial approach:* Letter or E-mail**
Copies of proposal: 1
Deadline(s): None
Officers: Joshua Green III, Pres.; Charles P. Burnett III, V.P.; Stanley P. McCammon, V.P.; Sandra Spurlock, Secy.
Trustees: Jennifer Carter; Louisa Malatos; Charles E. Riley.
EIN: 916050748

3522
Albert Haller Foundation
P.O. Box 2739
Sequim, WA 98382-2739

Established in 1992 in WA.
Donor: Albert G. Haller†.
Foundation type: Independent foundation.
Financial data (yr. ended 12/31/12): Assets, $10,087,409 (M); expenditures, $537,911; qualifying distributions, $497,727; giving activities include $411,958 for 63 grants (high: $68,958; low: $600), and $78,000 for 20 grants to individuals (high: $4,000; low: $2,000).
Purpose and activities: Funding primarily to projects that provide food, housing, clothing, medical care and other programs that may enhance and enrich the lives of the poor and needy of Clallam County, WA. Special attention is given to distributing food to those in need, and clothing and other necessities to children who lack the essentials to progress in school.
Fields of interest: Education; Health care; Food services; Recreation; Human services; Community/economic development; United Ways and Federated Giving Programs.
Type of support: General/operating support; Scholarships—to individuals.
Limitations: Applications accepted. Giving limited to Clallam County, WA.
Publications: Informational brochure (including application guidelines).
Application information: Application form required.
Initial approach: Scholarships: Contact Superintendents of public high schools, Grants: Contact United way for application form
Copies of proposal: 1
Deadline(s): Scholarships: Jan., Grants: June
Board meeting date(s): At least 4 times per year
Officers: Gary Smith, Pres.; Richard Schneider, V.P.; David Blake, Secy.-Treas.
Directors: Jane Pryne; **Patrick Kelly Shea.**
EIN: 911556810
Other changes: Bill Bentley is no longer a director.

3523
The Nick and Leslie Hanauer Foundation
The Highlands
179 N.W. Cascade Dr.
Shoreline, WA **98177-8000**

Established in 2007 in WA.
Donors: Nick Hanauer; Leslie Hanauer; Gerald Hanauer†.
Foundation type: Independent foundation.
Financial data (yr. ended 12/31/12): Assets, $8,386,581 (M); expenditures, $786,213; qualifying distributions, $722,545; giving activities include $722,545 for grants.
Fields of interest: Performing arts, opera; Environment.
Limitations: Applications not accepted. Giving primarily in Seattle, WA. No grants to individuals.
Application information: Contributes only to pre-selected organizations.
Directors: Leslie Hanauer; Nick Hanauer.
EIN: 261593306

3524
Harder Foundation
401 Broadway, Ste. 303
Tacoma, WA **98402-3904** (253) 593-2121
Contact: Mary G. Martin, Off. Mgr.
FAX: (253) 593-2122;
E-mail: info@theharderfoundation.org; Main URL: http://www.theharderfoundation.org
Grants List: http://theharderfoundation.org/2013-grantees/

Incorporated in 1955 in MI.
Donor: Delmar S. Harder†.
Foundation type: Independent foundation.
Financial data (yr. ended 12/31/12): Assets, $31,898,986 (M); gifts received, $71,600; expenditures, $1,709,689; qualifying distributions, $1,531,800; giving activities include $1,095,000 for 39 grants (high: $130,000; low: $2,500).
Purpose and activities: The foundation is dedicated to the preservation of an American quality of life that includes clean air and drinking water, unpolluted lakes and rivers, and healthy forests, parks, and wildland. It has a special concern for the protection of wildlife populations and the habitats on which they depend. Projects funded by the foundation typically involve efforts to achieve long-term protection of specific public forests and wildlands, rivers, near shore marine ecosystems, and estuaries.
Fields of interest: Environment, natural resources; Environment.
Type of support: General/operating support; Continuing support; Annual campaigns; Endowments; Seed money; Matching/challenge support.
Limitations: Applications not accepted. Giving limited to AK, CO, FL, ID, MT, OR, WA, and WY. No grants to individuals, or for deficit financing, building funds, equipment, renovation projects, scholarships, fellowships, research, publications, or conferences; no loans.
Publications: Annual report; Grants list.
Application information: Unsolicited requests for funds not accepted; proposals accepted by invitation only.
Board meeting date(s): Feb.
Officers and Trustees:* Del Langbauer,* Pres.; **John Driggers, V.P.**; Robert Langbauer,* Treas.; Kay Treakle, Exec. Dir.
Number of staff: 3 full-time professional; 1 full-time support; 1 part-time support.
EIN: 386048242
Other changes: John Driggers is now V.P. Jay A. Herbst is no longer Secy. William H. Langbauer is no longer director.

3525
Howard Charitable Foundation
4616 25th Ave. NE, PMB 617
Seattle, WA 98105-4183 (760) 730-7342
Contact: Richard D. Newell, Secy.-Treas.

Established in 1999 in WA.
Donor: Robert S. Howard.
Foundation type: Independent foundation.
Financial data (yr. ended 12/31/13): Assets, $15,232,160 (M); expenditures, $3,687,164; qualifying distributions, $3,134,890; giving activities include $2,992,300 for 30 grants (high: $1,000,000; low: $2,000).
Purpose and activities: Giving primarily to health care, educational, and domestic humanitarian charities.
Fields of interest: Education; Health care; Human services.
Limitations: Applications accepted. Giving primarily in San Diego, CA and Washington, DC. No grants to individuals.
Application information: Application form required.
Initial approach: Letter requesting application form
Deadline(s): None
Officer: Richard D. Newell, Secy.-Treas.
EIN: 911952040
Other changes: The grantmaker has moved from CA to WA.

3526
Inland Northwest Community Foundation
(formerly Foundation Northwest)
421 West Riverside Ave., Ste. 606
Spokane, WA 99201-0405 (509) 624-2606
Contact: Mark Hurtubise, C.E.O.
E-mail: admin@inwcf.org; Additional tel.: (888) 267-5606; Additional e-mail: mhurtubise@inwcf.org; Main URL: http://www.inwcf.org
LinkedIn: http://www.linkedin.com/companies/inland-northwest-community-foundation

Incorporated in 1974 in WA.
Foundation type: Community foundation.
Financial data (yr. ended 06/30/12): Assets, $68,641,267 (M); gifts received, $5,511,200; expenditures, $5,039,253; giving activities include $3,385,654 for grants.
Purpose and activities: The foundation seeks to foster vibrant and sustainable communities in the Inland Northwest. Primary areas of interest include the arts, humanities, education, community development, and human services.
Fields of interest: Humanities; Historic preservation/historical societies; Arts; Education; Environment; Animals/wildlife; Health care; Youth, services; Aging, centers/services; Human services; Community development, neighborhood development; Economic development; Community/economic development; Aging.
Type of support: General/operating support; Management development/capacity building; Capital campaigns; Building/renovation; Equipment; Program development; Seed money; Technical assistance; Program evaluation.
Limitations: Applications accepted. Giving limited to the Inland Northwest: Benewah, Bonner, Boundary, Clearwater, Idaho, Kootenai, Latah, Lewis, Nez Perce, and Shoshone counties, ID, and Adams, Asotin, Columbia, Ferry, Garfield, Lincoln, Pend Oreille, Spokane, Stevens, and Whitman counties, WA. No support for sectarian religious purposes, chambers of commerce, or programs addressing specific disease or health conditions. No grants to individuals (except for scholarship awards), or for deficit financing, debt reduction, conferences (including travel), endowments, publications and film production, private or parochial education, academic or scientific research, one-time fundraising events or campaigns, or replacement of government funding.
Publications: Application guidelines; Annual report; Financial statement; Newsletter.
Application information: Visit foundation Web site for grant program guidelines per grant type and online application. Application form required.
Initial approach: Complete online grant application
Copies of proposal: 1
Deadline(s): Varies
Board meeting date(s): Sept. through June
Final notification: 3 to 6 months
Officers and Directors:* Robert A. Larson,* Chair.; Dale N. Schuman,* Vice-Chair.; Mark Hurtubise,* C.E.O. and Pres.; Shelley L. Bennett,* Secy.; Michael Bibin; Bob Bishopp; **William O. Bouten; K. Duane Brelsford**; Scott K. Jones; Patricia McRae; Charles R. Nipp; Christie R. Querna; William A. Simer; Betsy Wilkerson.
Number of staff: 5 full-time professional; 2 full-time support; 1 part-time support.
EIN: 910941053
Other changes: Shelley L. Bennett and Dale N. Schuman are no longer directors.

3527
Intermec Foundation
(formerly The UNOVA Foundation)
6001 36th Ave. W.
Everett, WA 98203-1264
***Main URL:* http://www.seattlefoundation.org/intermec/Pages/IntermecFoundation.aspx**

Established in 1993 in CA.
Foundation type: Independent foundation.
Financial data (yr. ended 06/30/13): Assets, $16,454,423 (M); expenditures, $1,106,606; qualifying distributions, $1,040,692; giving activities include $989,998 for 212 grants (high: $72,760; low: $500).
Purpose and activities: The foundation focuses on educational, food banks, art and cultural programs, health and wellness organizations and on occasion, community relief causes.
Fields of interest: Arts; Education; Health care; Food banks.
Type of support: Equipment; Employee volunteer services; Employee matching gifts; Employee-related scholarships.
Limitations: Applications not accepted. Giving primarily in IA, OH, and WA.
Application information: Unsolicited requests for funds not accepted. Employees of Intermec apply for foundation grants on behalf of nonprofit organizations. See foundation web site for specific eligibility requirements.
Officers: Sue Taylor, Pres.; **Frank McCallick, V.P. and Treas.; Scott Anderson, V.P.; Paula A. Bauert, V.P.; Nancy Gallup, V.P.; Ronald Kubera, V.P.;** Constance Chapman, Secy.
Directors: Robert Driessnack; Douglas Stubsten.
EIN: 954453230
Other changes: Frank McCallick is now V.P. and Treas.

3528
The Ji Ji Foundation
2730 Westlake Ave. N.
Seattle, WA 98109-1916 (206) 328-2393
Contact: Anne McEnany
E-mail: anne@jiji.org; Main URL: http://www.jiji.org

Established in 1994 in WA.
Donors: Alan B. Harper; Louise G. Harper Charitable Lead Annuity Trust.
Foundation type: Independent foundation.
Financial data (yr. ended 09/30/12): Assets, $2,853,487 (M); gifts received, $323,750; expenditures, $643,612; qualifying distributions, $604,296; giving activities include $521,598 for 57 grants (high: $55,500; low: $1,000), and $79,822 for 4 grants to individuals (high: $67,522; low: $2,000).
Purpose and activities: Giving primarily to support conservation, research, and public education on environmental issues.

Fields of interest: Education; Environment, research; Environment, natural resources.
Type of support: General/operating support; Land acquisition; Conferences/seminars; Publication; Seed money; Curriculum development; Research; Grants to individuals.
Limitations: Applications accepted. Giving primarily in CA, and Baja California, Mexico. No grants for endowments.
Publications: Application guidelines; Grants list.
Application information: Applications are also accepted for small conservation grants ($1,000-3,000) for field research related to coastal sage scrub, chaparral, and desert ecosystems in Baja California, Mexico. Any application for a small conservation grant must demonstrate how the project is directly related to the goals of the foundation for Baja California, Mexico. The foundation will not be funding any work in island ecosystems or on the Gulf of California coastline at this time. See foundation web site for specific application guidelines. Application form required.

Initial approach: Letter of request (for grants between $3,000-10,000) or a letter of inquiry (for grants between $10,000-50,000). A cover sheet (which can be downloaded from foundation web site) should also be included
Copies of proposal: 1
Deadline(s): See foundation web site for current deadlines
Board meeting date(s): Quarterly

Officers: Alan B. Harper, Pres.; Carol J. Baird, Secy.; Margo Reich, Treas.
Trustee: Bruce Sherman.
Number of staff: None.
EIN: 911664723

3529
Margery Jones Charitable Trust
9115 Fortuna Dr., Apt. 6412
Mercer Island, WA 98040-3158

Established in 2010.
Donor: Margery M. Jones†.
Foundation type: Independent foundation.
Financial data (yr. ended 09/30/13): Assets, $7,252,787 (M); expenditures, $375,684; qualifying distributions, $352,548; giving activities include $335,000 for 10 grants (high: $55,000; low: $10,000).
Fields of interest: Arts; Education; Human services.
Limitations: Applications not accepted. Giving primarily in CA and WA.
Application information: Unsolicited requests for funds not accepted.
EIN: 276589503

3530
The Herbert B. Jones Foundation
c/o Key Private Bank
601 108th Ave. N.E., Ste. 260
Bellevue, WA 98004-8606 (206) 285-1729
Main URL: http://www.hbjfoundation.com
Grants Database: http://www.hbjfoundation.com/grant_history.html

Established in 1989 in WA.
Donor: Herbert B. Jones.
Foundation type: Independent foundation.
Financial data (yr. ended 08/31/12): Assets, $10,969,352 (M); expenditures, $535,841; qualifying distributions, $526,806; giving activities include $468,796 for 19 grants (high: $85,000; low: $5,000).
Purpose and activities: The foundation promotes small-business and entrepreneurism through programs managed by post-secondary educational institutions.
Fields of interest: Higher education; Business school/education; Education.
Type of support: Program development; Conferences/seminars; Seed money; Curriculum development.
Limitations: Applications accepted. Giving limited to WA. No grants to individuals, or for equipment, capital projects, gifts, endowments or food costs.
Publications: Application guidelines.
Application information: Refer to foundation web site for complete guideline information. Application form required.

***Initial approach:* Proposal (2 pages maximum, with a minimum font size of 11)**
Copies of proposal: 6
***Deadline(s):* First Mon. in Apr.**
Board meeting date(s): May
Final notification: Within 8 weeks

Trustees: Michael R. Bauer; Tom Crha; Bill Erwert; Tammy Miller; Terry Smith; Janet Woods.
Number of staff: None.
EIN: 943124801

3531
Kawabe Memorial Fund
(also known as Harry S. Kawabe Trust)
c/o Bank of America, Philanthropic Mgmt.
P.O. Box 3977, WA1-501-33-23
Seattle, WA **98124-2477**
Contact: Nancy Atkinson, V.P.
E-mail: nancy.l.atkinson@baml.com; Toll-free tel.: 1-800-848-7177; **Main URL: http://fdnweb.org/kawabe**
Grants List: http://fdnweb.org/kawabe/grants/year/2011/

Trust established in 1971 in WA.
Donors: Tomo Kawabe†; Harry Kawabe†.
Foundation type: Independent foundation.
Financial data (yr. ended 12/31/12): Assets, $3,970,274 (M); gifts received, $100; expenditures, $211,628; qualifying distributions, $185,268; giving activities include $137,100 for 52 grants (high: $5,000; low: $500), and $21,000 for 9 grants to individuals (high: $3,400; low: $1,750).
Purpose and activities: Giving to support and promote quality human services programming for the economically disadvantaged, children and the elderly. Some giving also as capital grants to churches, as well as scholarships to support teachers and the clergy. The Fund typically supports organizations serving the people of the Puget Sound area.
Fields of interest: Theological school/education; Human services; Children/youth, services; Aging, centers/services; Aging; Economically disadvantaged.
Type of support: General/operating support; Continuing support; Building/renovation; Equipment; Program development; Seed money; Scholarships—to individuals.
Limitations: Giving primarily to organizations serving the people of the Puget Sound area.
Publications: Application guidelines.
Application information: Complete application guidelines available on Fund web site.

Initial approach: Online through Fund web site
Deadline(s): Second Fridays of Jan. (spring cycle), April (summer cycle) and Aug. (fall cycle)

Allocation Committee: Yasue Brevig; Paul Hosoda; Thomas M. Ikeda; Aizo Kosai; Rev. Hoshu Y. Matsubayashi; Takashi Matsui; Tsuyoshi Nakano; Toru Sakahara; Katsumi Tanino; Warren Yasutake.
Trustee: Bank of America, N.A.
EIN: 916116549

3532
Korum for Kids Foundation
P.O. Box 538
Puyallup, WA 98371 (253) 927-0966
***Contact:* Sophia Hall, Mgr.**

Established in 1994 in WA.
Donors: Korum Automotive Group, Inc.; Jerry Korum Investments; Jerome Korum; Korum Family Limited Partnership.
Foundation type: Company-sponsored foundation.
Financial data (yr. ended 12/31/12): Assets, $6,996,532 (M); gifts received, $1,000,000; expenditures, $365,695; qualifying distributions, $256,584; giving activities include $256,584 for grants.
Purpose and activities: The foundation supports programs designed to promote and improve the health, welfare, and future of young people.
Fields of interest: Arts; Education; Health care; Recreation; Human services; Children/youth.
Type of support: General/operating support; Capital campaigns; Building/renovation; Equipment; Program development; Scholarship funds; Sponsorships; Matching/challenge support.
Application information: Application form required.

Initial approach: Contact foundation for application form
Copies of proposal: 3
Deadline(s): None

Officer and Trustees:* Sophia Hall,* Mgr.; Germaine R. Korum; Jerry Korum.
EIN: 916528752

3533
Wayne D. & Joan E. Kuni Foundation
1053 Officers Row
Vancouver, WA 98661 (360) 694-2550
E-mail: lynne_siegel@kunifoundation.org; Main URL: http://www.kunifoundation.org
Grants List: http://www.kunifoundation.org/grant_awards.htm

Established in 2005 in WA.
Donors: Wayne D. Kuni†; Joan E. Kuni; Wayne D. Kuni Trust; Andersen Construction Co.
Foundation type: Independent foundation.
Financial data (yr. ended 12/31/12): Assets, $30,850,913 (M); gifts received, $4,431,400; expenditures, $3,689,053; qualifying distributions, $2,657,965; giving activities include $2,657,965 for grants.
Purpose and activities: Giving for medical research, especially for the diagnosis and treatment of cancer, and to support and enhance the lives of mentally disabled adults.
Fields of interest: Medical research, institute; Cancer research; Mentally disabled.
Limitations: Applications accepted. Giving primarily in WA. No grants to individuals.
Application information: Application form required.

Initial approach: See website for application form
Deadline(s): See website for deadline

Officer: Lynne F. Siegel, Exec. Dir.
Trustee: Washington Trust Bank.
EIN: 616316804

3534

Paul Lauzier Charitable Foundation
P.O. Box 1230
117 Basin St. N.W.
Ephrata, WA 98823-1230 (509) 754-3209
***Contact:* Michael Rex Tabler, Tr.**
FAX: (509) 754-8481; E-mail: ck.lauzuer@nwi.net; Main URL: http://www.lauzier.org/charitable-foundation

Established in 1997 in WA.
Donor: Paul Lauzier†.
Foundation type: Independent foundation.
Financial data (yr. ended 12/31/12): Assets, $8,380 (M); gifts received, $452,558; expenditures, $454,599; qualifying distributions, $450,600; giving activities include $450,600 for 18 grants (high: $130,000; low: $100).
Purpose and activities: Giving primarily for higher and other education, as well as for health care, and children, youth and social services.
Fields of interest: Higher education; Education; Health care; Health organizations; Agriculture; Human services; Children/youth, services; Community development, neighborhood development; Catholic agencies & churches.
Type of support: Capital campaigns; Equipment.
Limitations: Giving primarily in rural communities located in central and eastern WA, with emphasis on Grant County. No support for political campaigns. No grants to individuals, or for salaries, debt retirement, or tuition assistance.
Publications: Application guidelines.
Application information: Complete application guidelines available on foundation web site. Application form not required.
Initial approach: Proposal (not exceeding 5 pages)
Deadline(s): See foundation web site for current deadline
Trustee: Michael Rex Tabler.
EIN: 911701539

3535

Paul Lauzier Scholarship Foundation
117 Basin St. N.W.
P.O. Box 1230
Ephrata, WA 98823-1623 (509) 754-3209
E-mail: ck.lauzier@nwi.net; Main URL: http://www.lauzier.org/scholarship-foundation
Hand delivered address: 117 Basin St. N.W., Ephrata, WA

Established in 1997.
Donor: Paul Lauzier†.
Foundation type: Independent foundation.
Financial data (yr. ended 12/31/12): Assets, $3,058 (M); gifts received, $425,000; expenditures, $442,216; qualifying distributions, $438,200; giving activities include $438,200 for 195 grants to individuals (high: $5,000; low: $1,000).
Purpose and activities: Scholarships to graduates of Grant County, WA, high schools who attend a college or vocational school (full time) within the State of Washington. Students pursuing graduate degrees are also eligible for scholarship awards. Applicants must reside in Grant County for a minimum of 2 years prior to high school graduation.
Fields of interest: Higher education.
Type of support: Scholarships—to individuals.
Limitations: Applications accepted. Giving limited to residents of Grant County, WA. **No grants for salaries, debt retirement, or tuitions assistance.**
Publications: Application guidelines.
Application information: Application forms available on foundation web site. There are two different application forms: one for graduating seniors, and another for students who are out of high school. Applicants should make sure they complete the appropriate form. All applications must be typed. Handwritten applications, as well as faxed or e-mailed applications will not be considered. Applicants should not use folders, binders, covers, or double-sided copies, or staple any material. Application form required.
Deadline(s): See application form for current deadlines
Trustee: Michael Rex Tabler.
EIN: 911701545

3536

The Lochland Foundation
P.O. Box 327
Medina, WA 98039 (425) 548-3482
***Contact:* Katherine Binder, Secy.-Treas.**
***Application address:* 90 Cascade Key, Bellevue, WA 98006, Tel.: (425) 548-3482**

Established in 2002 in WA.
Donors: Phyllis Lindsey; Exotic Metals Forming Co., LLC; Mark Lindsey; Katherine A. Binder.
Foundation type: Company-sponsored foundation.
Financial data (yr. ended 12/31/12): Assets, $9,457,603 (M); gifts received, $3,555,000; expenditures, $219,880; qualifying distributions, $219,240; giving activities include $210,500 for 9 grants (high: $70,000; low: $2,500).
Purpose and activities: The foundation supports flight museums and organizations involved with education, animal welfare, and Christianity and awards college scholarships to high school students in the Seattle area.
Fields of interest: Arts; Education; Religion.
Type of support: General/operating support; Scholarship funds; Scholarships—to individuals.
Limitations: Applications accepted. Giving primarily in WA.
Application information: Application form required.
***Initial approach:* Letter**
***Deadline(s):* None**
Officers: Phyllis Lindsey, Pres.; Mark Lindsey, V.P.; Katherine A. Binder, Secy.-Treas.
EIN: 510420961

3537

Luke 12:48 Foundation
c/o Heather Tuininga, Exec. Dir.
333 108th Ave., N.E., Ste. 2010
Bellevue, WA 98004-5777 (425) 974-3755
E-mail: heather@luke1248.org; Main URL: http://www.luke1248.org
Grants List: http://luke1248.org/grant-making/grantees/

Established in 2007 in WA.
Donors: Michael Johnston; Marybeth Johnston.
Foundation type: Independent foundation.
Financial data (yr. ended 12/31/12): Assets, $826,312 (M); expenditures, $836,970; qualifying distributions, $834,519; giving activities include $555,427 for 19 grants (high: $47,500; low: $80), and $43,578 for foundation-administered programs.
Purpose and activities: The vision of the foundation is to serve as witness to the realness of Jesus and His relentless, transforming love by supporting organizations that: 1) make fishers of men, 2) transform communities, 3) promote justice, and 4) care for the least of these.
Fields of interest: Human services; Children/youth, services; Community/economic development; Christian agencies & churches.
International interests: Uganda.
Limitations: Applications not accepted. Giving primarily in the Pacific Northwest and Uganda, Africa.
Publications: Grants list.
Application information: Contributes only to pre-selected organizations.
Board meeting date(s): Quarterly
Officers: Marybeth Johnston, Pres. and Treas.; J. Michael Johnston, V.P. and Secy.; Heather Tuininga, Exec. Dir.
Number of staff: 1 full-time professional.
EIN: 261110518

3538

Peter R. Marsh Foundation
1101 S.E. Tech Center Dr., Ste. 160
Vancouver, WA 98683-5521
Main URL: http://www.prmfoundation.org/

Established in 2004 in OR.
Donor: Peter R. Marsh.
Foundation type: Independent foundation.
Financial data (yr. ended 12/31/12): Assets, $1,697,436 (M); expenditures, $96,104; qualifying distributions, $77,500; giving activities include $77,500 for 2 grants (high: $57,500; low: $20,000).
Purpose and activities: The foundation's mission is to better society by cultivating Servant First Leadership. The foundation believes that great leadership has the power to make the world a better place, and the foundation exists to offer leaders in the Pacific Northwest region the training, resources and support they need to experience both practical success and personal fulfillment in their leadership. The foundation provides quality training opportunities for leaders to develop their skills and receive valuable insights that will enhance their success. Training seminars and workshops are offered throughout the Pacific Northwest region on a variety of leadership topics. The foundation also produces articles and podcasts that address some of the pressing issues leaders face today.
Fields of interest: Leadership development.
Limitations: Applications not accepted. Giving primarily in WA. No grants to individuals.
Application information: Unsolicited requests for funds not accepted.
Officers: Thomas O. Reese, Chair.; Cindy Robert, Secy.; R. Russell Walker, Treas.
Directors: Byron Van Kley; Jack Schwartz; John Upton.
EIN: 201524353

3539

Edmund F. Maxwell Foundation
c/o David G. Johansen
P.O. Box 55548
Seattle, WA **98155-0548**
E-mail: admin@maxwell.org; Main URL: http://www.maxwell.org
Grants List: http://www.maxwell.org/awardrecipients.aspx

Established in 1992 in WA.
Foundation type: Independent foundation.
Financial data (yr. ended 12/31/12): Assets, $8,035,674 (M); expenditures, $400,108; qualifying distributions, $329,792; giving activities

include $256,271 for 57 grants to individuals (high: $5,000; low: $1,981).
Purpose and activities: Scholarships for residents of western Washington attending accredited independent colleges or universities. Grants are dependent on financial need, as determined by the college or university attended.
Fields of interest: Higher education.
Type of support: Scholarships—to individuals.
Limitations: Applications accepted. Giving limited to students residing in western WA attending accredited private colleges and universities. No grants to individuals directly.
Application information: Complete application guidelines available on foundation web site. Application form required.
Deadline(s): Varies
Board meeting date(s): Varies
Trustees: David G. Johansen; David D. Lewis; John Morton.
Number of staff: 2 part-time professional.
EIN: 916181008

3540
The Craig and Susan McCaw Foundation
P.O. Box 2908
Kirkland, WA 98083-2908 (425) 828-8000

Established in 1998 in WA.
Donor: Craig O. McCaw.
Foundation type: Independent foundation.
Financial data (yr. ended 12/31/12): Assets, $36,590,205 (M); gifts received, $7,852,325; expenditures, $3,769,775; qualifying distributions, $3,663,626; giving activities include $3,657,050 for 22 grants (high: $2,000,000; low: $500).
Fields of interest: Higher education; Human services.
Limitations: Applications accepted. Giving primarily in CA and WA. No grants to individuals.
Application information:
Initial approach: Letter or telephone
Deadline(s): None
Officers and Directors:* Craig O. McCaw,* Pres.; Susan R. McCaw,* V.P.; **Amit Mehta, V.P.**; Teresa Mason, Secy.; Cindy Hegge, Treas.; Ben Wolf.
EIN: 911943269

3541
D. V. & Ida McEachern Charitable Trust
(formerly Ida J. McEachern Charitable Trust)
c/o McEachern Trust, Union Bank, Personal Trust
P.O. Box 3123
Seattle, WA 98114-3123 (206) 781-3472
Contact: Therese Ogle, Grants Consultant
E-mail: OgleFounds@aol.com; Physical address: 1201 3rd Ave., Ste. 900, Seattle, WA 98101; **Main URL: http://fdnweb.org/mceachern**
Grants List: http://fdnweb.org/mceachern/grants/year/2013/

Trust established in 1966 in WA.
Donors: Ida J. McEachern†; D.V. McEachern†.
Foundation type: Independent foundation.
Financial data (yr. ended 08/31/13): Assets, $17,885,771 (M); expenditures, $979,504; qualifying distributions, $830,709; giving activities include $797,022 for 72 grants (high: $80,000; low: $250).
Purpose and activities: Giving exclusively for capital funding of youth agencies serving children under the age of 18, where the purpose is to give a better start in life, both physically and mentally, to all children. The trust prefers organizations in existence at least five years and whose operational funding comes generally from a non-tax-based source.
Fields of interest: Performing arts; Education; Health organizations, association; Recreation; Human services; Children/youth, services.
Type of support: Capital campaigns; Building/renovation; Equipment.
Limitations: Giving limited to the Puget Sound area of WA, particularly King, Pierce, and Snohomish counties. Generally no support for organizations established less than five years (absent indications of community leadership and reputation, offering unique enrichment programs for children), or for religious institutions. No grants to individuals, or for endowment funds, scholarships, fellowships, operating budgets, continuing support, annual campaigns, seed money, deficit financing, publications, conferences, research programs, or matching gifts; no loans.
Publications: Application guidelines; Grants list.
Application information: See foundation web site for full application guidelines. Application form not required.
Initial approach: Proposal (narrative not to exceed 4 pages)
Copies of proposal: 1
Deadline(s): Mar. 8, Sept. 8, and Dec. 8
Board meeting date(s): Usually in May and Oct.
Trustee: Union Bank, N.A.
EIN: 916063710

3542
Medina Foundation
801 2nd Ave., Ste. 1300
Seattle, WA 98104-1517 (206) 652-8783
***Contact:* Aana Lauckhart, Prog. Off.**
FAX: (206) 652-8791;
E-mail: info@medinafoundation.org; Main URL: http://www.medinafoundation.org
Grants Database: http://www.medinafoundation.org/index.php?p=Our_Grantees&s=4

Incorporated in 1947 in WA.
Foundation type: Independent foundation.
Financial data (yr. ended 12/31/12): Assets, $91,169,947 (M); expenditures, $4,615,485; qualifying distributions, $4,120,285; giving activities include $3,573,715 for 143 grants (high: $200,000; low: $3,100), and $9,367 for foundation-administered programs.
Purpose and activities: The Medina Foundation is a family foundation that works to foster positive change in the Greater Puget Sound region of Washington State. In honoring the vision of its founder, Norton Clapp, the foundation aspires to improve lives by funding human service organizations that provide direct support to Puget Sound residents. Areas of interest include: housing and homelessness, youth development, hunger, education, family support, and economic development.
Fields of interest: Education; Housing/shelter; Family services; Homeless, human services; Economic development.
Type of support: General/operating support; Management development/capacity building; Building/renovation; Program development; Program evaluation; Matching/challenge support.
Limitations: Applications accepted. Giving limited to the greater Puget Sound, WA, area, including the counties of Clallam, Grays Harbor, Island, Jefferson, King, Kitsap, Mason, Pacific, Pierce, San Juan, Skagit, Snohomish, Thurston, and Whatcom.
Publications: Application guidelines; Grants list.
Application information: The foundation will provide a grant application online if the Letter of Inquiry is accepted. If your organization received funding from the foundation within the last year, please wait at least twelve months from receipt of last grant before submitting another letter of inquiry. Application form required.
Initial approach: Online letter of inquiry on foundation web site
Deadline(s): None
Board meeting date(s): Monthly
Final notification: 30 to 60 days
Officers and Trustees:* Piper Henry-Keller,* Pres.; Gail Gant,* V.P.; Patricia Henry,* Secy.; Jean Gardner,* Treas.; **Jennifer Teunon, Exec. Dir.**; Haleh Clapp; James N. Clapp II; Margaret Clapp; Matthew N. Clapp, Jr.; Tamsin O. Clapp; Steve Gant; Jill Gardner; **Marion Clapp Rawlinson**; Elizabeth Williams.
EIN: 910745225
Other changes: Jennifer Teunon has replaced Adrienne Quinn as Exec. Dir.

3543
Gary E. Milgard Family Foundation
(formerly Gary & Carol Milgard Family Foundation)
1701 Commerce St.
Tacoma, WA 98402-3207 (253) 274-0121
Contact: Christine Zemanek, C.E.O.
FAX: (253) 274-0478; Christine Zemanek, C.E.O., e-mail: chris@milgardfamily.com, tel.(253) 572-9330; Main URL: http://www.garymilgardfamilyfoundation.org

Established in 2000 in WA.
Foundation type: Independent foundation.
Financial data (yr. ended 12/31/12): Assets, $256,231,051 (M); expenditures, $13,883,996; qualifying distributions, $12,680,782; giving activities include $11,722,969 for 113 grants (high: $1,000,000; low: $20).
Purpose and activities: The goal of the foundation is to support the work of a wide variety of organizations that serve our community. The foundation believes this is a way for the family to give back and continue to educate their descendants in the value of community service.
Fields of interest: Education; Health care; Human services; Children/youth, services.
Type of support: Matching/challenge support; Scholarship funds; Program development; Equipment; Endowments; Capital campaigns; Building/renovation; Annual campaigns; General/operating support.
Limitations: Applications accepted. Giving primarily in Pierce County and the greater Puget Sound, WA, area. No support for political organizations or religious organizations where funds would be used to further a religious purpose. No grants for deficit reduction.
Publications: Grants list.
Application information: For applicants who do not have internet access, contact foundation. Application form required.
Initial approach: Online application
Copies of proposal: 1
Deadline(s): 4:00pm on the last business day of each month
Board meeting date(s): Jan., Apr., July, and Oct.
Final notification: 60 days
Officers: Christine Zemanek, C.E.O. and Pres.; Jim Sheehan, Exec. Dir.
Directors: Cari Milgard-DeGoede; Lori Milgard-Rivera; Mark Milgard.
EIN: 912074073

Other changes: Christine Zemanek is now C.E.O. and Pres.

3544
Hazel Miller Foundation

1000 2nd. Ave., 34th Fl.
Seattle, WA 98104-1022 (206) 667-0300
FAX: (206) 682-1874;
E-mail: info@hazelmillerfoundation.org; Main URL: http://hazelmillerfoundation.org

Established in WA.
Donor: Hazel Miller Trust.
Foundation type: Independent foundation.
Financial data (yr. ended 12/31/12): Assets, $12,603,512 (M); gifts received, $454,267; expenditures, $557,875; qualifying distributions, $487,970; giving activities include $465,470 for 27 grants (high: $97,200; low: $2,500).
Fields of interest: Arts, cultural/ethnic awareness; Education; Housing/shelter; Recreation, parks/playgrounds; Children/youth, services; Community development, civic centers; Religion.
Limitations: Applications accepted. Giving primarily in Edmonds and South Snohomish County, WA.
Application information: See foundation web site for guidelines and application form. Application form required.
Initial approach: Letter
***Deadline(s):* Jan. 31, Apr. 4, July 11, and Oct. 10**
Officers and Trustees:* **Renee Mcrae,* Chair.**; Leigh Bennett,* Vice-Chair.; **Patrick Shields,* Secy.**; **Jack Loos,* Treas.**; Maria Montalvo; Diana White; **Dick Ellis.**
EIN: 271173049
Other changes: Renee Mcrae has replaced Jack Loos as Chair. Patrick Shields has replaced Renee Mcrae as Secy. Jack Loos has replaced Patrick Shields as Treas.

3545
Moccasin Lake Foundation

1405 42nd Ave. E.
Seattle, WA 98112-3807 (206) 329-8899
Contact: Lisa P. Anderson
E-mail: mlfoundation@moccasinlake.org; Main URL: http://www.moccasinlake.org

Established in 1991 in WA.
Donors: James C. Pigott; Gaye T. Pigott; Maureen Pigott; Paul Pigott; Mark Kranwinkle; Sara Kranwinkle; Lisa Anderson; Michael Anderson; Julie Gould; Frederick Beau Gould; James C. Pigott 2005 Charitable Lead Annuity Trust; James C. Pigott 2005 Charitable Lead Unitrust.
Foundation type: Independent foundation.
Financial data (yr. ended 12/31/12): Assets, $2,868,497 (M); gifts received, $3,893,951; expenditures, $4,491,350; qualifying distributions, $4,489,644; giving activities include $4,489,590 for 123 grants (high: $1,010,833; low: $200).
Purpose and activities: The foundation is a private not-for-profit organization founded in 1991 as a long-term philanthropic program. The foundation has been established with broad charitable purposes so that its grant making policies may always reflect the diverse interests of the Moccasin Lake Foundation and its individual board members. Currently the Moccasin Lake Foundation has developed a special focus on the Methow Valley in the State of Washington.
Fields of interest: Arts; Education; Environment, natural resources; Animals/wildlife, preservation/protection; Hospitals (general); Reproductive health, family planning; Cancer; Multiple sclerosis; Human services; Religion.
Limitations: Applications accepted. Giving primarily in WA, with a special focus on the Methow Valley. No grants to individuals.
Application information: Application guidelines and concept paper available on foundation web site. Submission of full proposals is by request only, after concept paper has been reviewed. Proof of tax exemption status will only be asked for if a full proposal is requested.
Initial approach: Concept paper (no more than 3 pages)
Deadline(s): None
Board meeting date(s): Quarterly
Final notification: 6 months
Officers and Directors:* Frederick Beau Gould,* Pres.; Julie Gould,* V.P.; Mark Kranwinkle,* Secy.; James C. Pigott,* Treas.; Lisa Anderson; Michael Anderson; Gaye T. Pigott; Maureen "Dina" Pigott; Paul Pigott.
EIN: 911545081

3546
Northwest Fund for the Environment

1904 3rd Ave., Ste. 615
Seattle, WA 98101-3326 (206) 386-7220
Contact: Pamela Fujita-Yuhas, Fdn. Dir.; For Aquatic Ecosystem Proposal: Zoe Rothchild, Fdn. Dir.
FAX: (206) 386-7223; E-mail: staff@nwfund.org; E-mail for Pamela Fujita-Yuhas: pamf@nwfund.org; e-mail for Zoe Rothchild: zoer@nwfund.org; Main URL: http://www.nwfund.org
Grants List: http://www.nwfund.org/charitable-grants-2009/
Grants List: http://www.nwfund.org/charitable-grants-2010/
Grants List: http://www.nwfund.org/2011-charitable-grants/
Grants List: http://www.nwfund.org/2012-standard-grants/
Grants List: http://www.nwfund.org/2013-charitable-grants/

Established in 1971 in WA.
Donor: Helen May Marcy Johnson‡.
Foundation type: Independent foundation.
Financial data (yr. ended 12/31/12): Assets, $6,037,300 (M); expenditures, $397,424; qualifying distributions, $315,840; giving activities include $218,050 for 26 grants (high: $20,000; low: $1,550).
Purpose and activities: Giving for environmental purposes, including grants for protection of wildlife habitats, water quality, and shoreline and wetland environments, enforcement of environmental regulations, and capacity building for conservation organizations.
Fields of interest: Environment, alliance/advocacy; Environment, natural resources; Environment, water resources; Animals/wildlife, preservation/protection.
Type of support: General/operating support; Program development; Seed money; Matching/challenge support.
Limitations: Applications accepted. Giving limited to WA. No support for partisan political activities or purely educational programs, art projects, Web page development, youth groups, museum displays, government agencies, or field research. No grants to individuals, or for academic research, endowment funds, land acquisition, or capital projects or debt reduction; no loans.
Publications: Annual report.
Application information: Call the Fund office to discuss project. If staff determines that the project meets guidelines and criteria, they will e-mail a cover letter and guidelines for the Letter of Inquiry. Unsolicited Letter of Inquiry or applications will not be accepted. Complete application guidelines are available on Fund web site. Application form required.
Initial approach: Telephone to discuss project
Deadline(s): See Fund web site for deadlines
Final notification: Within 3 weeks
Officers and Trustees:* **Jennifer Dold,* Pres.**; David Harrison, V.P.; **Susan Markey, Secy.**; **Jim Harless, Treas.**; Helmut Golde; **Rick Moore**; Claudia Newman; **Janna Rolland**; Annette Sommers.
Number of staff: 2 part-time professional.
EIN: 237134880
Other changes: Jennifer Dold has replaced Sandra D. Moore as Pres. Susan Markey has replaced Jennifer Dold as Secy.
Doug Lawrence is no longer trustee.

3547
OneFamily Foundation

(formerly Wood Family Foundation)
6723 Sycamore Ave. N.W.
Seattle, WA 98117-4849 (206) 781-3472
Contact: Therese Ogle
E-mail: OgleFounds@aol.com; **Main URL: http://fdnweb.org/onefamily**
Grants List: http://fdnweb.org/onefamily/grants/year/2014/

Established in 1997 in WA.
Donors: Bill Morgan; Sara Morgan; Brenda K. Wood.
Foundation type: Independent foundation.
Financial data (yr. ended 12/31/13): Assets, $11,707,113 (M); gifts received, $183; expenditures, $713,540; qualifying distributions, $635,478; giving activities include $590,250 for 59 grants (high: $150,000; low: $750), and $33,183 for 3 foundation-administered programs.
Purpose and activities: The goals of the foundation are to provide resources to enhance the lives of women living in poverty and at-risk youth, to support services for abused women, and to aid efforts to end violence and sexual assault against women and children.
Fields of interest: Education; Health care; Human services; Children/youth, services; Family services, domestic violence; Women, centers/services; Christian agencies & churches; Economically disadvantaged.
Type of support: General/operating support.
Limitations: Applications accepted. Giving limited to King and Snohomish counties, WA, and the Olympic Peninsula. No support for schools, summer camps, low-income housing or shelter programs (unless they are specifically focused on serving women), or groups that have been declined three times. No grants to individuals, or for capital grants, scholarships, research, multi-year grants, athletic events, video or film projects, website development, or book publications.
Publications: Application guidelines; Grants list.
Application information: After receiving three grants, a group must wait two years before re-applying. Incomplete applications will be forwarded to the next funding cycle pending receipt of any missing materials.
Initial approach: Proposal (not exceeding 3 pages)
Copies of proposal: 2
Deadline(s): 2nd Fri. in Mar. and Aug.
***Final notification:* 1st Mon. in May and Oct.**
Officers: Brenda K. Wood, Pres.; Donald R. Wood III, V.P.; Brandon C. Wood, Secy.-Treas.
EIN: 911722889

3548
Charles Pankow Foundation
P.O. Box 820631
Vancouver, WA 98682-0014 (360) 326-3767
***Contact:* Mark Perniconi P.E., Exec. Dir.**
***E-mail:* info@pankowfoundation.org; E-mail for Mark Perniconi, P.E., Exec. Dir.: mperniconi@pankowfoundation.org**; Main URL: http://www.pankowfoundation.org

Established in 2002 in CA.
Donors: Charles J. Pankow†; Pankow Family Trust of 1976; Foundation of Integrated Services.
Foundation type: Independent foundation.
Financial data (yr. ended 12/31/12): Assets, $26,232,274 (M); expenditures, $1,423,449; qualifying distributions, $1,304,521; giving activities include $925,000 for 38 grants (high: $169,000; low: $1,000).
Purpose and activities: The foundation exists to advance innovations in building design and construction through research, so as to provide the public with buildings of improved quality, efficiency, and value.
Fields of interest: Housing/shelter, research; Engineering.
Type of support: Research.
Limitations: Giving primarily in CA. No grants to individuals.
Publications: Application guidelines; Annual report.
Application information: See foundation web site for Research Need Statement guidelines.
***Initial approach:* Submit a Research Need Statement (not more than 2 pages)**
***Deadline(s):* None, for Research Need Statement**
Officers and Directors:* Richard M. Kunnath, P.E.*, Pres.; Timothy P. Murphy, Esq.*, Secy. and C.F.O.; **Mark J. Perniconi, P.E., Exec. Dir.**; Ron Klemencic, P.E.
Number of staff: 1 part-time professional.
EIN: 710919052
Other changes: The grantmaker no longer lists a fax. The grantmaker has moved from CA to WA. Mark J. Perniconi, P.E. has replaced Robert K. Tener as Exec. Dir.
The grantmaker now publishes an annual report and application guidelines.

3549
PEMCO Foundation, Inc.
325 Eastlake Ave. E.
Seattle, WA 98109-5407
Contact: Stan W. McNaughton, Pres. and Treas.

Established in 1965 in WA.
Donors: Gladys McLaughlin†; PEMCO Corp.; Washington School Employees Credit Union; Evergreen Bank, N.A.; Evergreen Bancorp, Inc.; Teachers Foundation; PEMCO Technology Services, Inc.; School Employees Credit Union of Washington; PEMCO Mutual Insurance Co.; PCCS, Inc.
Foundation type: Company-sponsored foundation.
Financial data (yr. ended 06/30/13): Assets, $2,127,892 (M); gifts received, $166,980; expenditures, $636,613; qualifying distributions, $636,613; giving activities include $634,670 for 345 grants (high: $94,100; low: $25).
Purpose and activities: The foundation supports organizations involved with television, education, crime and violence prevention, youth development, human services, and business and awards college scholarships to high school students located in Washington.
Fields of interest: Media, television; Secondary school/education; Higher education; Education; Crime/violence prevention; Boys & girls clubs; Camp Fire; Youth development, business; Youth development; American Red Cross; Children, services; Human services; Business/industry; United Ways and Federated Giving Programs.
Type of support: General/operating support; Program development; Scholarship funds; Scholarships—to individuals.
Limitations: Applications accepted. Giving primarily in WA, with emphasis on Seattle; giving limited to WA for scholarships.
Application information: Application form not required.
***Initial approach:* Letter**
Deadline(s): None
Final notification: 2 months for scholarships
Officers and Trustees:* Stan W. McNaughton,* Pres. and Treas.; Sandra M. Kurack,* V.P.; Denice M. Town, Secy.; Gayle C. Grass; Brian R. McNaughton; Astrid I. Thompson.
EIN: 916072723

3550
James D. and Sherry Raisbeck Foundation Trust
7536 Seward Park Ave. S.
Seattle, WA 98118-4247
***Main URL:* http://www.raisbeck.com/about/raisbeckfoundation**

Established in 1999 in WA.
Donors: James D. Raisbeck; Sherry L. Raisbeck.
Foundation type: Company-sponsored foundation.
Financial data (yr. ended 12/31/12): Assets, $27,283,556 (M); expenditures, $1,626,177; qualifying distributions, $1,535,028; giving activities include $1,527,988 for 12 grants (high: $1,459,750; low: $778).
Fields of interest: Arts; Human services; United Ways and Federated Giving Programs.
Limitations: Applications not accepted. **Giving primarily in Seattle, WA.** No grants to individuals.
Application information: Contributes only to pre-selected organizations.
Trustees: James D. Raisbeck; Sherry L. Raisbeck.
EIN: 916478077

3551
The REI Foundation
P.O. Box 1938
Sumner, WA 98390-0800
Main URL: http://www.rei.com/stewardship/report/community/rei-foundation.html

Established in 1993 in WA.
Donor: Recreational Equipment Inc.
Foundation type: Company-sponsored foundation.
Financial data (yr. ended 12/31/12): Assets, $10,205,543 (M); gifts received, $3,227; expenditures, $324,050; qualifying distributions, $275,000; giving activities include $275,000 for grants.
Purpose and activities: The foundation supports programs designed to ensure that tomorrow's outdoor enthusiasts and conservation stewards reflect the diversity of America.
Fields of interest: Environment, natural resources; Environment, land resources; Recreation; American Red Cross; YM/YWCAs & YM/YWHAs; Youth, services.
Type of support: General/operating support.
Limitations: Applications not accepted. Giving primarily in CA.
Application information: Contributes only to pre-selected organizations.
Officers and Directors: Michael Collins, Pres.; David Jayo, V.P.; Catherine Walker, Secy.; Rick Palmer, Treas.; Sally Jewell; Tom Vogl.
EIN: 911577992
Other changes: The grantmaker no longer lists a phone. The grantmaker no longer lists a primary contact.

3552
Renton Community Foundation
1101 Bronson Way N.
P.O. Box 820
Renton, WA 98057 (425) 282-5199
Contact: Lynn Bohart, Exec. Dir.
FAX: (425) 282-5889;
E-mail: lbohart@rentonfoundation.org; Main URL: http://www.rentonfoundation.org
E-Newsletter: http://www.rentonfoundation.org/e-connections-newsletter.html
YouTube: http://www.youtube.com/user/rentonfoundation?feature=watch

Established in 1999 in WA.
Foundation type: Community foundation.
Financial data (yr. ended 12/31/12): Assets, $6,608,122 (M); gifts received, $614,042; expenditures, $556,136; giving activities include $420,371 for 5+ grants (high: $238,028).
Purpose and activities: The foundation manages a group of individual charitable funds for a broad array of community services such as the arts, health care, pet care, education, emergency services and more.
Fields of interest: Arts education; Museums; Performing arts; Historic preservation/historical societies; Arts; Education, early childhood education; Child development, education; Adult/continuing education; Adult education—literacy, basic skills & GED; Education, continuing education; Education; Environment; Animals/wildlife; Health care; Mental health, counseling/support groups; Crime/violence prevention, domestic violence; Crime/violence prevention, child abuse; Food banks; Housing/shelter; Disasters, fire prevention/control; Safety/disasters; Recreation; Youth development; Neighborhood centers; Children, services; Residential/custodial care, hospices; Aging, centers/services; Homeless, human services; Human services; Community/economic development.
Type of support: Equipment; Building/renovation; General/operating support; Continuing support; Endowments; Program development; Scholarship funds.
Limitations: Applications accepted. Giving primarily in greater Renton, WA, area.
Publications: Annual report; Grants list; Newsletter.
Application information: Visit foundation web site for application forms and guidelines. Application form required.
Initial approach: Telephone
Copies of proposal: 2
Deadline(s): Varies
Officers and Directors:* Rich Wagner,* Pres.; Gene Sens,* V.P.; Marlene Winter,* Secy.; Vicki Faull,* Treas.; Lynn Bohart, Exec. Dir.; Karyn Beckley; **Kim Browne**; Robert Cugini; **Mark Gropper**; Steve Hanson; J. Michael Hardy, D.D.S.; Dave Kroeger; Jim Medzegian; Marilyn Milne; Valerie O'Halloran; Vicky Persson; Jim Poff; Brian Quint; Bob Raphael; Dr. Merri Rieger; Judi Schafer; **Lynn Wallace.**
Number of staff: 1 full-time professional.
EIN: 237069988

Other changes: Ahmad Attallah, Char Baker, Rebecca Holverson Cherney, Charlie Conner, Vicky Persson, Gene Sens are no longer directors.

3553
M. Valeria Richardson Irrevocable Trust

c/o Wells Fargo Bank, N.A.
P.O. Box 21927
Seattle, WA 98111-3927
Application addresses: University of Wyoming, 1000 E. University Ave., Laramie, WY 82071, tel.: (307) 766-1121; Casper College, 125 College Dr., Casper, WY 82601, tel.: (307) 268-2713

Established in WY.
Foundation type: Independent foundation.
Financial data (yr. ended 06/30/13): Assets, $26,327,148 (M); expenditures, $1,235,407; qualifying distributions, $1,135,561; giving activities include $1,052,370 for 2 grants (high: $679,512; low: $372,858).
Fields of interest: Higher education.
Limitations: Applications accepted. Giving primarily in Casper and Laramie, WY.
Application information: Application form required.
Initial approach: **Letter**
Deadline(s): None
Trustee: Wells Fargo Private Client Services.
EIN: 836003603

3554
Safeco Insurance Fund

1001 4th Ave., Safeco Plaza, Ste. 1800
Seattle, WA 98154-1117 (206) 473-5745
Contact: Paul Hollie, Fdn. Dir.
E-mail: Safeco.Foundation@libertymutual.com; Main URL: http://www.safeco.com/about-safeco/community/foundation

Established in 2006 in WA.
Donors: Safeco Corp.; Safeco Insurance Co.
Foundation type: Company-sponsored foundation.
Financial data (yr. ended 12/31/12): Assets, $56,927,367 (M); expenditures, $3,260,417; qualifying distributions, $3,100,025; giving activities include $3,100,000 for 682 grants (high: $200,000; low: $3).
Purpose and activities: The foundation supports nonprofit organizations involved with arts and culture, hunger, human services, youth, the disabled, economically disadvantaged people, and the homeless. Special emphasis is directed toward programs designed to promote education and health and safety.
Fields of interest: Performing arts; Arts; Elementary school/education; Vocational education; Libraries (public); Education, services; Education, reading; Education; Health care, clinics/centers; Health care; Food services; Safety/disasters; YM/YWCAs & YM/YWHAs; Family services; Developmentally disabled, centers & services; Homeless, human services; Human services; United Ways and Federated Giving Programs; Youth; Disabilities, people with; Economically disadvantaged; Homeless.
Type of support: Curriculum development; General/operating support; Continuing support; Capital campaigns; Program development; Employee matching gifts.
Limitations: Applications accepted. Giving primarily in areas of company operations OR and WA. No support for grantmaking agencies, fraternal, social, labor, or political organizations. No grants to individuals, or for sectarian activities, trips, tours, or transportation, deficit spending or debt liquidation, conferences, forums, or special events.
Publications: Application guidelines; Grants list; Program policy statement.
Application information: Visit website for Education Initiative and Basic Services Initiative Request for Proposals (RFP) announcement. Support is limited to 1 contribution per organization during any given year. Application form required.
Initial approach: Complete online application
Deadline(s): None
Final notification: 10 weeks
Officers and Directors:* David H. Long,* Chair.; Michael H. Hughes,* Pres.; Dexter K. Legg, V.P. and Secy.; Dennis J. Langwell,* V.P., C.F.O., and Treas.; A. Alexander Fontanes,* V.P. and C.I.O.; Christopher C. Mansfield,* V.P. and Genl. Counsel; Melissa M. MacDonnell, V.P.; Gary J. Ostrow, V.P.; Mathew D. Nickerson.
EIN: 204894146

3555
San Juan Island Community Foundation

P.O. Box 1352
Friday Harbor, WA 98250-1352 (360) 378-1001
E-mail: info@sjicf.org; Additional e-mail: grants@sjicf.org; Main URL: http://www.sjicf.org
Grants List: http://sjicf.org/category/news/recent-grants/
RSS Feed: http://www.sjicf.org/feed/
Scholarship e-mail: scholarships@sjicf.org

Established in 1994 in WA.
Donors: Barry A. Ackerley; David Bayley.
Foundation type: Community foundation.
Financial data (yr. ended 12/31/11): Assets, $7,458,254 (M); gifts received, $3,577,823; expenditures, $2,413,044; giving activities include $2,061,755 for 10+ grants (high: $1,900,000), and $141,377 for 29 grants to individuals.
Purpose and activities: The mission of the foundation is to enhance the quality of life on San Juan Island, WA, by encouraging philanthropy, growing an endowment for purposeful grants to community charitable organizations, and building partnerships that effectively connect donors with island nonprofit organizations.
Fields of interest: Arts; Education; Environment; Animals/wildlife; Children/youth, services; Human services; Community/economic development.
Type of support: Capital campaigns; Building/renovation; Scholarship funds; In-kind gifts; Matching/challenge support.
Limitations: Applications accepted. Giving limited to San Juan Island, WA. No support for religious organizations for religious purposes. No grants for operating expenses, or endowments.
Publications: Application guidelines; Annual report; Grants list; Informational brochure; Informational brochure (including application guidelines); Newsletter.
Application information: Visit foundation web site for application Cover Sheet and guidelines. Application form required.
Initial approach: Letter or telephone
Copies of proposal: 1
Deadline(s): Quarterly
Board meeting date(s): Quarterly, varies
Final notification: 6 weeks
Officers and Directors:* Charles Anderson,* Chair.; Lauren Levinson,* Vice-Chair.; Barbara Cable,* Secy.; Barbara Von Gehr,* Treas.; **Susan Matthews, Exec. Dir.**; Jim Barnhart; Scott Boden; Tom Cable; Maude Cumming; Jan Cyre; Peg Gerlock; Pamela Gross; Rebecca Pohlad.
Number of staff: 1 full-time professional.
EIN: 911648730
Other changes: George Swindells is no longer a director.

3556
Satterberg Foundation

825 Securities Bldg.
1904 3rd Ave.
Seattle, WA 98101-1126 (206) 441-3045
Contact: Peter F. Helsell, Treas.
FAX: (206) 374-9336; E-mail: info@satterberg.org; Main URL: http://www.satterberg.org
Grants List: http://www.satterberg.org/open_grants/current_grantees
Grants List: http://www.satterberg.org/capacity_building_grants/past_grantees

Established in 1990 in WA.
Donors: Virginia S. Helsell†; Judy P. Swenson; William A. Helsell.
Foundation type: Independent foundation.
Financial data (yr. ended 12/31/12): Assets, $2,495,877 (M); expenditures, $459,724; qualifying distributions, $441,071; giving activities include $399,100 for 46 grants (high: $20,000; low: $1,000).
Purpose and activities: The mission of the foundation is to maintain and enjoy the interconnection of its family and to provide funds to non-profit organizations that enrich and support its communities.
Fields of interest: Education; Health care; Housing/shelter, development; Youth development, centers/clubs; Human services; Children/youth, services; Family services.
Type of support: Income development; Management development/capacity building.
Limitations: Applications accepted. Giving primarily in CA and WA. No support for evangelical groups. No grants to individuals.
Application information: Application guidelines for capacity-building only, may be obtained by writing to the foundation or from the web site. Application form required.
Initial approach: Letter or e-mail
Copies of proposal: 1
Deadline(s): Available on request
Board meeting date(s): Quarterly
Final notification: Quarterly
Officers and Directors:* Ben Lazarus,* Pres.; Katherine Lazarus, Secy.; Peter F. Helsell,* Treas.; Mary Pigott,* Exec. Dir.; Frank P. Helsell; J. David Lazarus; Judy Pigott; Michael J. Pigott; Amy Shamah.
Trustee: Bank of America, N.A.
EIN: 911501066

3557
Schultz Family Foundation

4209 21st Ave. W., Ste. 401
Seattle, WA 98199-1254 (206) 623-9395
Contact: Loren D. Hostek CPA, Tr.

Established in 1996 in WA.
Donors: Howard D. Schultz; Sheri K. Schultz.
Foundation type: Independent foundation.
Financial data (yr. ended 06/30/13): Assets, $52,117,140 (M); gifts received, $10,650,000; expenditures, $3,758,098; qualifying distributions, $3,748,098; giving activities include $3,716,335 for 46 grants (high: $3,039,978; low: $1,000).
Fields of interest: Education; Health organizations, association; Human services; Children/youth,

services; United Ways and Federated Giving Programs; Jewish federated giving programs.
Limitations: Giving primarily in Seattle, WA. No grants to individuals.
Application information:
Initial approach: Letter
Deadline(s): None
Trustees: Loren D. Hostek; Sheri Kersch-Schultz; Mathew McCutchen; Howard D. Schultz.
EIN: 911746414
Other changes: For the fiscal year ended June 30, 2013, the grantmaker paid grants of $3,716,335, a 67.6% increase over the fiscal 2012 disbursements, $2,217,937.

3558
The Seattle Foundation
1200 5th Ave., Ste. 1300
Seattle, WA 98101-3151 (206) 622-2294
Contact: Ceil Erickson, Dir., Community Progs.
FAX: (206) 622-7673;
E-mail: info@seattlefoundation.org; **Grant application e-mail: grantmaking@seattlefoundation.org; Main URL: http://www.seattlefoundation.org**
Facebook: http://www.facebook.com/TheSeattleFoundation
Giving Center: http://www.seattlefoundation.org/givingcenter/Pages/default.aspx
Grants List: http://www.seattlefoundation.org/nonprofits/grantmaking/Pages/RecentGrants.aspx
Twitter: http://twitter.com/TheSeattleFdn/

Incorporated in 1946 in WA.
Foundation type: Community foundation.
Financial data (yr. ended 12/31/12): Assets, $690,275,245 (M); gifts received, $66,099,895; expenditures, $79,222,798; giving activities include $67,353,039 for grants.
Purpose and activities: The foundation seeks to foster powerful and rewarding philanthropy to make King County a stronger, more vibrant community for all.
Fields of interest: Media, film/video; Media, radio; Visual arts; Performing arts, dance; Performing arts, music; Humanities; Literature; Historic preservation/historical societies; Arts; Education, early childhood education; Adult/continuing education; Education, ESL programs; Libraries (public); Education, reading; Education; Environment, public education; Environment, air pollution; Environment, water pollution; Environment; Animals/wildlife; Health care; Mental health/crisis services; Health organizations, association; Medical research; Agriculture/food; Housing/shelter; Recreation, parks/playgrounds; Recreation; Youth development; Children/youth, services; Homeless, human services; Human services; Economic development; Community development, small businesses; Community/economic development; Public affairs.
Type of support: General/operating support; Capital campaigns; Building/renovation; Equipment; Mission-related investments/loans.
Limitations: Applications accepted. Giving limited to King County, WA. No support for religious purposes. No grants for endowment funds, debt reduction, fundraising events, fundraising feasibility projects, conferences or seminars, film or video production, publications, first year organizations, or operating expenses for public or private elementary and secondary schools, colleges, and universities.
Publications: Annual report; Financial statement; Grants list; Informational brochure; Newsletter; Program policy statement.
Application information: Seattle Foundation will no longer offer a traditional annual grantmaking program. Grants will be provided via targeted, multi-year community leadership initiatives, and programs that connect donors to King County nonprofit organizations. Visit foundation web site for more information. Application form required.
Initial approach: Telephone or e-mail
Deadline(s): Varies
Board meeting date(s): Mar., June, Sept., and Dec.
Officers and Trustees:* Martha Choe,* Chair.; Ann Watson,* 1st Vice-Chair.; Tay Yoshitani,* 2nd Vice-Chair.; **Tony Mestres,* C.E.O. and Pres.**; Jared Watson, Sr. V.P.; Jane Repensek, Sr. V.P., Finance and Opers.; Michael Brown, V.P., Community Leadership; Fidelma McGinn, V.P., Philanthropic Svcs.; Mary Grace Roske, V.P. and Dir., Comms.; Jeanette Lodwig,* Secy.; Pete Shimer,* Treas.; Kareen Holmquist, Cont.; Libby Armintrout; Fraser Black; Nathaniel T. "Buster" Brown; Carolyn Corvi; Jean Enersen; Bob Flowers; Marcia Fujimoto; Joe Gaffney; Mark Gibson; Steve Hill; Gary S. Kaplan, M.D.; Linda Park, Ph.D.; Mary Pugh; Chris Rivera; Scott Shapiro; Brad Smith; John Stanton; Kevin Washington; Jan Whitsitt; James Williams; Grace T. Yuan.
Number of staff: 17 full-time professional; 1 part-time professional; 8 full-time support; 1 part-time support.
EIN: 916013536
Other changes: Tony Mestres has replaced Norman Rice as C.E.O. and Pres.
Ceil Erickson is now Dir., Community Progs. Allison Peake Parker is now Sr. Philanthropic Advisor. Aaron Robertson is now Community Progs. Off. Jennifer Sorensen is now Dir., Treasury. Cherlyn Cloy is now Sr. Assoc., Gift Planning. Caroline Maillard is now Sr. Off., Community Progs. Jennifer Martin is now Dir., Center for Community Partnerships. Allison Peake Parker is now Sr. Philanthropic Advisor. Christine Stansfield is now Community Progs. Assoc.
The grantmaker no longer publishes application guidelines.

3559
Sequoia Foundation
1250 Pacific Ave., Ste. 870
Tacoma, WA 98402-4334
Contact: Amy Rose; Bickley Barich, Office Admin.
FAX: (253) 627-6249;
E-mail: grants@grantmakerconsultants.com; Main URL: http://www.sequoiafound.org/

Established in 1982 in WA.
Donors: W. John Driscoll; C. Davis Weyerhaeuser†; F.T. Weyerhaeuser; William T. Weyerhaeuser.
Foundation type: Independent foundation.
Financial data (yr. ended 10/31/13): Assets, $32,738,979 (M); gifts received, $2,053,621; expenditures, $6,334,271; qualifying distributions, $6,072,437; giving activities include $5,665,526 for 116 grants (high: $1,000,000; low: $1,500), and $30,000 for 1 loan/program-related investment.
Purpose and activities: The foundation is committed to strengthening and enriching the quality of life in Tacoma and Pierce County, WA, and to enhancing environmental and economic outcomes in the Pacific Northwest.
Limitations: Applications not accepted. Giving primarily in Pierce County, WA.
Application information: The foundation solicits proposals at its sole discretion. Unsolicited proposals are not considered.
Officers and Directors:* William T. Weyerhaeuser,* Pres. and Treas.; Gail T. Weyerhaeuser,* V.P.; Nicholas C. Spika, Secy.; Brian F. Boyd, Exec. Dir.; Benjamin D. Weyerhaeuser; W. Drew Weywrhaeuser.
Number of staff: None.
EIN: 911178052
Other changes: Annette B. Weyerhaeuser, a director, is deceased.

3560
Alfred & Tillie Shemanski Testamentary Trust
c/o Bank of America, N.A.
800 5th Ave. WA1-501-33-23
Seattle, WA 98104-3176
E-mail: wa.grantmaking@ustrust.com; **Main URL: https://www.bankofamerica.com/philanthropic/grantmaking.go**

Trust established in 1974 in WA.
Donors: Alfred Shemanski†; Tillie Shemanski†.
Foundation type: Independent foundation.
Financial data (yr. ended 12/31/12): Assets, $7,641,435 (M); expenditures, $447,484; qualifying distributions, $391,697; giving activities include $340,000 for 25 grants (high: $50,000; low: $1,000).
Purpose and activities: Giving primarily to: 1) Improve the capacity of and cooperation among Jewish congregations in the City of Seattle, Washington; 2) Support interfaith tolerance and understanding; 3) Provide scholarship assistance, primarily to the University of Washington and Seattle University; 4) Support and promote quality educational, human services, and health care programming for economically disadvantaged individuals and families.
Fields of interest: Higher education; Hospitals (general); Health organizations, association; Human services; Children/youth, services; Youth, services; Jewish federated giving programs; Jewish agencies & synagogues; Religion.
Limitations: Giving primarily in the greater Seattle, WA, area. No grants to individuals.
Application information: Application guidelines available on Trust web site.
Initial approach: Online through Trust web site
Deadline(s): Oct. 15
Trustee: Bank of America, N.A.
EIN: 916196855

3561
Sherwood Trust
P.O. Box 1855
Walla Walla, WA 99362-0035
Contact: George M. Edwards, Pres.
Tel./fax: (509) 529-2791

Established in 1991 in WA.
Foundation type: Independent foundation.
Financial data (yr. ended 12/31/12): Assets, $29,932,130 (M); expenditures, $1,714,157; qualifying distributions, $1,465,393; giving activities include $1,422,055 for 38 grants (high: $235,000; low: $500).
Purpose and activities: The foundation's purpose is to serve the Walla Walla Valley as a catalyst to build the community's capacity and will to achieve in appreciation of its originators, Donald and Virginia Sherwood.
Fields of interest: Performing arts; Higher education, college; Education, services; Human services; Community/economic development; Economically disadvantaged.

Type of support: Matching/challenge support; Management development/capacity building; Capital campaigns; Building/renovation; Land acquisition; Endowments; Technical assistance.
Limitations: Applications accepted. Giving limited to the Walla Walla, WA, area. No support for religious or political organizations. No grants to individuals.
Publications: Application guidelines; Program policy statement.
Application information: Application form not required.
Initial approach: Telephone or letter
Copies of proposal: 2
Deadline(s): Mar. 1
Board meeting date(s): Monthly
Final notification: 1-2 months from receipt for final approval or rejection
Officers and Directors:* Larry Mulkerin,* Chair.; George M. Edwards,* Pres.; **Peggy Sanderson,* V.P.**; Leona M. Clarno, Secy.-Treas.; Allan Gillespie; Robert Zagelow.
Number of staff: 1 full-time support; 1 part-time support.
EIN: 916337526

3562
Charles and Lisa Simonyi Fund for Arts and Sciences

(formerly Charles Simonyi Fund for Arts and Sciences)
P.O. Box 85900
Seattle, WA 98145-1900 (206) 522-7000
Contact: Susan Hutchison, Exec. Dir.
E-mail: susan@simonyifund.org; Main URL: http://www.simonyifund.org/

Established in 2003 in WA.
Donor: Charles Simonyi.
Foundation type: Independent foundation.
Financial data (yr. ended 12/31/12): Assets, $3,564,830 (M); gifts received, $5,391,200; expenditures, $7,035,853; qualifying distributions, $6,941,064; giving activities include $6,341,179 for 30 grants (high: $2,050,000; low: $214).
Purpose and activities: The foundation distributes funds to worthy organizations that demonstrate excellence in the arts, sciences and education.
Fields of interest: Arts; Education; Science, public education; Science.
Limitations: Applications not accepted. Giving primarily in Seattle, WA. No grants to individuals.
Application information: Contributes only to pre-selected organizations.
Officer: Susan Hutchison, Exec. Dir.
Director: Charles Simonyi; **Lisa Simonyi**.
EIN: 550846712

3563
Singh Family Foundation

2609 Evergreen Point Rd.
Medina, WA 98039-1528
E-mail: Gopal@Singhfoundation.com; Main URL: http://singhfamilyfoundation.com/
E-Newsletter: http://singhfamilyfoundation.com/about-us/newsletter

Established in 2006 in MI.
Donors: Gopal Singh; Kamala Singh; Rajeev Singh; Jill Singh; Thomas Despasquale; Mahendra Amin; Saroj Amin; Rajat Bhargava; Dean Morehouse.
Foundation type: Independent foundation.
Financial data (yr. ended 12/31/11): Assets, $5,440,696 (M); gifts received, $117,244; expenditures, $307,374; qualifying distributions, $302,800; giving activities include $302,800 for 13 grants (high: $119,000; low: $1,000).
Purpose and activities: The foundation's mission provides: 1) Quality middle and high school education to young rural girls, 2) Urgently needed medical care to the elderly, and 3) Community outreach programs designed to meet basic needs.
Fields of interest: Health care; Girls; Economically disadvantaged.
Limitations: Applications not accepted. Giving primarily in WA and Jaunpur, India. No grants to individuals.
Application information: Unsolicited requests for funds not accepted.
Officers: Gopal Singh, Pres.; Kamala Singh, Secy.
Board Member: Sudhir Singh.
EIN: 300360186

3564
The Lester M. Smith Foundation

P.O. Box 3010
Bellevue, WA 98009-3010

Established in 1981 in WA.
Donor: Lester M. Smith.
Foundation type: Independent foundation.
Financial data (yr. ended 10/31/13): Assets, $5,215,335 (M); expenditures, $312,915; qualifying distributions, $279,900; giving activities include $275,312 for 49 grants (high: $40,000; low: $100).
Fields of interest: Arts; Education; Health organizations; Medical research; United Ways and Federated Giving Programs.
Type of support: General/operating support.
Limitations: Applications not accepted. Giving primarily in WA. No grants to individuals.
Application information: Contributions only to pre-selected organizations.
Directors: Alexander M. Smith; Bernice R. Smith.
EIN: 911156087
Other changes: Lester M. Smith is no longer director.

3565
The Starbucks Foundation

c/o Starbucks Corp.
2401 Utah Ave. S.
Seattle, WA 98134-1436
E-mail: foundationgrants@starbucks.com; Main URL: http://www.starbucks.com/responsibility/community
Youth Leadership Grant Recipients: http://globalassets.starbucks.com/assets/a3e82bc037324a238bebd95184e25a18.pdf

Established in 1997 in WA.
Donors: Starbucks Corp.; Starbucks Coffee Co.; Pepsico; Schultz Family Foundation.
Foundation type: Company-sponsored foundation.
Financial data (yr. ended 09/30/12): Assets, $12,586,900 (M); gifts received, $1,907,486; expenditures, $15,449,043; qualifying distributions, $15,441,914; giving activities include $12,327,813 for 3,679 grants (high: $664,160; low: $20).
Purpose and activities: The foundation supports programs designed to support young people creating change in local communities; water projects through the Ethos Water Fund; and social investments in countries where Starbuck buys coffee, tea, and cocoa.
Fields of interest: Education; Environment, water resources; Public health, clean water supply; Public health, sanitation; Health care; Agriculture; Nutrition; Disasters, preparedness/services; Youth development; International economic development; Social entrepreneurship; Microfinance/microlending; Community/economic development; Children/youth.
International interests: Africa; Asia; Canada; China; Europe; Latin America; Middle East; United Kingdom.
Type of support: Seed money; General/operating support; Continuing support; Emergency funds; Program development; Employee volunteer services; Employee matching gifts.
Limitations: Giving on a national and international basis in areas of company operations and in countries where the company buys coffee, tea, and cocoa. No support for private foundations, political, labor, or fraternal organizations, religious organizations not of direct benefit to the entire community, hospitals or medical research institutions, universities or academic research institutions, individual schools or parent teacher associations, or sporting teams. No grants to individuals, or for neighborhood clean-ups or tree plantings, wildlife conservation projects, capital campaigns, capital expenditures or land acquisition, school bands or orchestras or non-literacy art programs, fundraising events, one-time events or programs, event sponsorships, trips or travel, league sports programs, scholarships or fellowships, expeditions, political campaigns, the production of marketing material promoting Starbucks, the production of products to sell in Starbucks stores, endowments, conferences or symposia, contests, festivals, or parades, advertising, tickets to events, or supply drives.
Publications: Application guidelines; Grants list.
Application information: A full proposal may be requested at a later date for Youth Leadership Grants. Priority funding is given to organizations that can demonstrate sustainability. Unsolicited requests are currently not accepted for the Ethos Water Fund and Social Investments in Coffee, Tea, & Cocoa Communities.
Initial approach: Complete online letter of inquiry for Youth Leadership Grants
Deadline(s): Nov. 1 to Dec. 15 for Youth Leadership Grants
***Final notification:* Feb. for Youth Leadership Grants**
Officers and Directors:* Orin Smith,* Pres.; Donna Brooks, Treas.; Rodney Hines, Exec. Dir.; Cliff Burrows; John Culver; Michelle Gass; Lucy Helm; Vivek Varma.
Number of staff: 3 part-time professional; 1 part-time support.
EIN: 911795425

3566
Bruce and Mary Stevenson Foundation, Inc.

(formerly Mary Hoyt Stevenson Foundation, Inc.)
2507 2nd Ave. N.
Seattle, WA **98109-1806**

Established in 1986 in OR.
Donors: Mary H. Stevenson†; Leslie Stevenson Campbell.
Foundation type: Independent foundation.
Financial data (yr. ended 09/30/13): Assets, $10,502,403 (M); gifts received, $25; expenditures, $549,389; qualifying distributions, $459,379; giving activities include $459,379 for 32 grants (high: $160,000; low: $100).
Fields of interest: Museums (art); Museums (natural history); Arts; Medical school/education.

Limitations: Applications not accepted. Giving primarily in OR and WA. No grants to individuals.
Application information: Contributes only to pre-selected organizations.
Officer: Laura Stevenson Cheney, Pres.
Directors: Leslie Stevenson Campbell; Anne Stevenson.
Number of staff: None.
EIN: 943028591

3567
The Greater Tacoma Community Foundation
950 Pacific Ave., Ste. 1100
P.O. Box 1995
Tacoma, WA 98402-4423 (253) 383-5622
Contact: For grants and scholarships: Sherrana Kildun, Dir., Community Progs.
FAX: (253) 272-8099; E-mail: info@gtcf.org; Main URL: http://www.gtcf.org
Blog: https://www.gtcf.org/blog/
Facebook: http://www.facebook.com/?sk=ff#!/pages/The-Greater-Tacoma-Community-Foundation/236157808732
Fund for Women and Girls: http://twitter.com/fundwomengirls
RSS Feed: https://www.gtcf.org/news/rss.php
Twitter: http://twitter.com/GreaterTacoma

Incorporated in 1977 in WA.
Foundation type: Community foundation.
Financial data (yr. ended 06/30/12): Assets, $79,793,561 (M); gifts received, $5,840,692; expenditures, $6,312,848; giving activities include $2,704,965 for grants.
Purpose and activities: The foundation fosters generosity by connecting people who care with causes that matter, forever enriching the community.
Fields of interest: Arts education; Museums; Performing arts; Performing arts, theater; Humanities; Historic preservation/historical societies; Arts; Child development, education; Higher education; Adult/continuing education; Libraries/library science; Education; Environment, natural resources; Environment; Animal welfare; Hospitals (general); Health care; Substance abuse, services; Mental health/crisis services; Health organizations, association; AIDS; AIDS research; Food services; Housing/shelter, development; Recreation; Youth development, services; Children/youth, services; Child development, services; Family services; Residential/custodial care, hospices; Aging, centers/services; Homeless, human services; Human services; Community/economic development; Voluntarism promotion; Government/public administration; Leadership development; Children/youth; Aging; Disabilities, people with; Women; Girls; Economically disadvantaged; Homeless.
Type of support: General/operating support; Continuing support; Management development/capacity building; Equipment; Land acquisition; Emergency funds; Program development; Seed money; Technical assistance; Consulting services; Program evaluation; Program-related investments/loans; Scholarships—to individuals; Matching/challenge support.
Limitations: Applications accepted. Giving limited to Pierce County, WA. No support for religious organizations for sacramental/theological purposes. No grants to individuals (except for scholarships), or for annual campaigns, fellowships, seminars, meetings or travel, fundraising events or fundraising feasibility projects, endowments or debt reduction, or publications, unless specified by donor.
Publications: Application guidelines; Annual report; Financial statement; Informational brochure; Informational brochure (including application guidelines); Newsletter.
Application information: Visit foundation web site for application forms and guidelines per grant type. A letter of intent is required prior to submitting a full grant request. Faxed or e-mailed applications are not accepted. Application form required.
Initial approach: Letter of intent (1 page)
Deadline(s): Jan. 15 and July 15 for letter of intent for Vibrant Community grants; varies for others
Board meeting date(s): 6 times yearly
Final notification: Within 10 days for letter of intent determination and June and Dec. for grant determination for Vibrant Community grants; varies for others
Officers and Directors:* T. Gary Connett,* Chair.; **Ed Grogan, Vice-Chair.**; Rose Lincoln Hamilton,* C.E.O. and Pres.; Katherine Severson,* Secy.; **Sheri Tonn,* Treas.**; Gary Brooks; Maro Imirizian; Laurie Jinkins; John Korsmo; Scott Limoli; Lamont Loo; Joe Mayer; Carla Pelster; Patricia Talton; Cindy Thompson; Dwight Williams.
Number of staff: 9 full-time professional; 1 full-time support.
EIN: 911007459
Other changes: Sheri Tonn has replaced John Wiborg as Treas.
Carol Park is now Grants Admin. Debra Friedman, Ed Grogan, and Timothy Tucci are no longer directors.

3568
Three Rivers Community Foundation
1333 Columbia Park Trail, Ste. 310
Richland, WA 99352 (509) 735-5559
***Contact:* Carrie Green, Secy. and Exec. Dir.**
E-mail: carrie@3rcf.org; Main URL: http://www.3rcf.org

Established in 1999 in WA.
Foundation type: Community foundation.
Financial data (yr. ended 12/31/11): Assets, $1,736,176 (M); gifts received, $512,968; expenditures, $555,646; giving activities include $321,073 for 42+ grants (high: $125,000), and $52,429 for 12 grants to individuals.
Purpose and activities: The Three Rivers Community Foundation is a community endowment whose mission is to strengthen and improve the quality of life in the Three Rivers Community by supporting and enhancing philanthropy and charitable activities.
Fields of interest: General charitable giving.
Limitations: Giving primarily in Benton or Franklin counties, WA.
Publications: Grants list.
Application information: Visit foundation web site for application guidelines. The foundation accepts draft proposals for review prior to formal application.
Initial approach: Telephone or e-mail
Copies of proposal: 1
Officers and Advisory Board:* Tim Anderson,* Chair.; Matt Hammer,* Vice-Chair.; Carrie Green,* Secy. and Exec. Dir.; Dale Burgeson,* Treas.; Keith Christensen; John Crook; Jim Dillman; David Lippes; Jeanne McPherson; Bill Moffitt; Sheri Noland; Greg Oberg; Erik Pielstik; Rella Reimann; Anne Schur; Muriel Templeton; Mel Wicks.
EIN: 912049302

3569
The Tudor Foundation
411 University St., Ste. 1200
Seattle, WA 98101-2519
Contact: Roger Rieger

Established in 1996 in WA.
Donors: E. Annette Rieger; Roger A. Rieger.
Foundation type: Operating foundation.
Financial data (yr. ended 12/31/12): Assets, $1,153,010 (M); gifts received, $14,916; expenditures, $238,632; qualifying distributions, $238,632; giving activities include $57,092 for 7 grants (high: $25,096; low: $1,000), and $177,304 for grants to individuals.
Fields of interest: Education.
Type of support: Scholarship funds; Grants to individuals; Scholarships—to individuals.
Limitations: Applications not accepted. Giving primarily in Seattle, WA.
Application information: Unsolicited requests for funds not accepted.
Officers: Roger A. Rieger, Pres.; **Erin R. Baranick, V.P.**; E. Annette Rieger, Secy.
EIN: 911708176

3570
Washington Research Foundation
2815 Eastlake Ave. E., Ste. 300
Seattle, WA 98102-3086
Contact: Amy McCormick, Office Mgr.
FAX: (206) 336-5615;
E-mail: amccormi@wrfseattle.org; Main URL: http://www.wrfseattle.org

Established in 1981 in WA.
Foundation type: Independent foundation.
Financial data (yr. ended 06/30/13): Assets, $276,893,961 (M); expenditures, $76,099,649; qualifying distributions, $6,081,810; giving activities include $5,452,718 for 35 grants (high: $1,250,000; low: $250), and $569,162 for foundation-administered programs.
Purpose and activities: The foundation's mission is to capture and enhance the value of intellectual property, arising from Washington State research institutions, to support research and scholarship.
Fields of interest: Higher education; Science, research.
Type of support: Seed money; Research; Program-related investments/loans.
Limitations: Applications not accepted. Giving limited to research institutions in Seattle, WA. No grants to individuals.
Publications: Annual report; Informational brochure.
Application information: Contributes only to pre-selected organizations.
Board meeting date(s): Jan., Apr., July, and Oct.
Officers and Directors:* C. Kent Carlson, Chair.; **Thomas J. Cable,* Vice-Chair.**; Ronald S. Howell,* C.E.O. and Pres.; Jeff Eby,* C.F.O.; Emer Dooley, Ph.D.; Barry Forman, D. Phil.; David Galas, Ph.D.; Sally Narodick; Brooks Simpson; George I. Thomas, M.D.; James R. Uhlir.
Number of staff: 8 full-time professional; 3 full-time support.
EIN: 911160492
Other changes: Thomas J. Cable is now Vice-Chair.

3571
Whatcom Community Foundation
119 Grand Ave., Ste. A
Bellingham, WA 98225-4400 (360) 671-6463
Contact: Mauri Ingram, C.E.O. and Pres.

FAX: (360) 671-6437; E-mail: wcf@whatcomcf.org; Main URL: http://www.whatcomcf.org
Facebook: https://www.facebook.com/WhatcomCommunityFoundation
YouTube: http://www.youtube.com/user/whatcomcf

Established in 1996 in WA.
Foundation type: Community foundation.
Financial data (yr. ended 06/30/12): Assets, $15,285,379 (M); gifts received, $2,424,193; expenditures, $3,008,783; giving activities include $2,135,238 for 417 grants (high: $632,000; low: $100; average: $2,000–$10,000), $84,843 for grants to individuals, $588,237 for 5 foundation-administered programs and $25,000 for 1 loan/program-related investment.
Purpose and activities: Mission - To enhance philanthropy to strengthen Whatcom County by linking people who care with causes that matter. Vision - A community working together, giving generously and moving forward. Core Values - Operate with integrity, include new people and new ideas, encourage collaboration, creative solutions and action.
Fields of interest: Arts; Education; Environment; Mental health/crisis services; Children/youth, services; Family services; Foundations (community).
Type of support: General/operating support; Management development/capacity building; Program development; Scholarship funds; Technical assistance; Consulting services; In-kind gifts.
Limitations: Applications accepted. Giving primarily in Whatcom County, WA. No support for religious activities or for-profit organizations. No grants to individuals (except for post-secondary education scholarships), or for capital requests (bricks and mortar), endowment funds, debt retirement, memberships, courtesy advertising, tickets for benefits, or fundraising events.
Publications: Application guidelines; Annual report; Financial statement; Grants list; Informational brochure; Newsletter.
Application information: Visit foundation web site for complete grant round information. Application to be submitted online. Application form required.
Initial approach: One stage grant round process in January
Copies of proposal: 1
Deadline(s): Jan. 27
Board meeting date(s): 4th Wed. of each month
Final notification: Late Apr.
Officers and Directors:* Bob Trunek,* Chair.; Sati Mookherjee,* Vice-Chair.; Mauri Ingram,* C.E.O. and Pres.; Kevin DeYoung,* Secy.-Treas.; Jennifer Hine; Brenda-Lee Karasik; Cheryl Macpherson; Fred Miller; Joyce Pedlow; Chuck Robinson; Steve Swan.
Number of staff: 1 full-time professional; 3 part-time professional; 1 full-time support; 4 part-time support.
EIN: 911726410
Other changes: Missy Belles is now Asst. to the C.E.O. Rachel Myers is now Devel. and Prog. Mgr. Shannon Elmendorf is now Projects Asst. Erin Schlichting is no longer a member of the governing body.

3572
The Wilburforce Foundation
2034 NW 56th St., Ste. 300
Seattle, WA **98107-3127**
Contact: Timothy Greyhavens, Secy. and Exec. Dir.
FAX: (206) 632-2326;
E-mail: grants@wilburforce.org; Additional address (Montana office): P.O. Box 296, Bozeman, MT 59771-0296, tel.: (406) 586-9796, fax: (406) 586-3076, e-mail: jennifer@wilburforce.org; Additional tel.: (800) 201-0148 (Seattle office), (800) 317-8180 (Montana office); Main URL: http://www.wilburforce.org
Grants Database: http://www.wilburforce.org/grant-history

Established in 1990 in WA.
Donors: James Letwin; Rosanna W. Letwin.
Foundation type: Independent foundation.
Financial data (yr. ended 12/31/12): Assets, $12,590,012 (M); gifts received, $12,861,310; expenditures, $12,999,102; qualifying distributions, $12,761,557; giving activities include $10,152,145 for 283 grants (high: $871,250; low: $500), and $30,000 for 3 grants to individuals (high: $10,000; low: $10,000).
Purpose and activities: The foundation is dedicated to protecting nature's richness and diversity through funding programs that help to preserve our remaining wild places. The foundation focuses on increasing the amount of protected critical wildlife habitat, assuring the quality and extent of key connective land between core habitat areas, lessening immediate threats to critical wildlife habitat, improving management programs that preserve the ecological integrity of existing or proposed protected areas, increasing knowledge of wildlife populations and/or improving managements plans that ensure the viability of local species in a region and building the capacity of organizations working to protect priority areas.
Fields of interest: Environment, natural resources; Environment.
International interests: Canada.
Type of support: General/operating support; Continuing support; Management development/capacity building; Capital campaigns; Equipment; Program development; Seed money; Research; Technical assistance; Consulting services; Program evaluation; Matching/challenge support.
Limitations: Applications accepted. Giving primarily in the western U.S. and western Canada, particularly AK, AZ, MT, NM, OR, UT, WA, British Columbia, and the Yellowstone to Yukon region of U.S.-Canada. No support for schools or universities, governmental agencies, agricultural issues, air quality or other clean air programs, energy-related programs; environmental education, environmental justice programs, habitat restoration, marine or other water-only programs, pollution prevention on other pollution-related projects, salmon recovery programs, sustainable development or other economically based programs, sprawl or other growth management programs, transportation-related programs, wildlife rehabilitation programs or youth education programs. No grants to individuals (except for Leadership Awards), or for fellowships or scholarships, endowment funds, operating budgets, deficit financing or indirect costs, annual meetings, conferences or symposia, or land acquisition and/or stewardship; no loans.
Publications: Application guidelines; Grants list.
Application information: Applicants who are interested in submitting a grant proposal must contact the appropriate staff member prior to developing a proposal. Please do not submit a full proposal without first contacting a program officer. When contacting a program officer regarding the possibility of a grant, be sure to specify the dollar level of your request. Grant Application Form will be sent to an organization only after it has received approval to submit a full proposal. Application form required.
Initial approach: Telephone
Copies of proposal: 1
Deadline(s): See web site for details
Board meeting date(s): Feb., Mar., July and Nov.
Final notification: Grants of more than $25,000: Quarterly; Six to eight weeks for grants of $25,000 or less
Officers and Directors:* Rosanna W. Letwin,* Pres.; Timothy Greyhavens, Secy. and Exec. Dir.; **Stephanie Nichols-Young,* Treas.**
Number of staff: 11 full-time professional.
EIN: 943137894
Other changes: Rosanna W. Letwin has replaced Stephanie Nichols-Young as Pres.
Stephanie Nichols-Young is now Treas.

3573
Catherine Holmes Wilkens Charitable Foundation
(formerly Wilkins Charitable Foundation)
c/o Bank of America, N.A., Philanthropic Solutions
P.O. Box 24565, WA1-501-33-23
Seattle, WA **98124-0565** (206) 781-3472
Contact: Nancy Atkinson, V.P.
E-mail for Nancy Atkinson:
nancy.l.atkinson@baml.com; Main URL: http://fdnweb.org/wilkins

Established in 1986.
Donor: Catherine Wilkins‡.
Foundation type: Independent foundation.
Financial data (yr. ended 08/31/13): Assets, $4,141,951 (M); expenditures, $225,755; qualifying distributions, $188,970; giving activities include $157,500 for 45 grants (high: $5,000; low: $2,000).
Purpose and activities: Giving primarily to medical and academic centers conducting research and training in areas such as cancer, heart disease, and mental illness, community nonprofit agencies providing direct social services to people with physical disabilities or mental illness, and community-based programs providing immediate support to the needy, with particular emphasis on services for abused women and children.
Fields of interest: Education; Hospitals (general); Medical research, institute; Human services; Physically disabled; Mentally disabled.
Limitations: Applications accepted. Giving limited to the greater Seattle, WA area (Tacoma to Everett). No grants to individuals, or for scholarships, or debt retirement.
Publications: Application guidelines; Grants list.
Application information: Application guidelines available on foundation web site. Application form required.
Initial approach: Proposal
Copies of proposal: 4
Deadline(s): None
Board meeting date(s): Quarterly
Officers: Brian Comstock, Chair.; Bob Bunting, Vice-Chair.; Loy D. Smith, Secy. and Mgr.
Trustee: Bank of America, N.A.
EIN: 916277933

3574
Bagley and Virginia Wright Foundation
(formerly The Bagley Wright Family Fund)
407 Dexter Ave. N.
Seattle, WA 98109-4704
Contact: Jan Day

Established in 2001 in WA.
Donor: Bill True.
Foundation type: Independent foundation.
Financial data (yr. ended 12/31/12): Assets, $15,746,949 (M); expenditures, $9,095,210;

qualifying distributions, $8,970,329; giving activities include $8,824,000 for 16 grants (high: $4,059,000; low: $2,000).
Purpose and activities: Giving primarily for arts and culture.
Fields of interest: Museums (art); Performing arts centers; Performing arts, theater; Arts.
Type of support: Capital campaigns.
Limitations: Applications not accepted. Giving primarily in Seattle, WA. No grants to individuals.
Application information: Contributes only to pre-selected organizations.
Trustees: Robin Wright Moll; Charles B. Wright III; Merrill Wright; Prentice "Bing" Wright; Virginia B. Wright.
EIN: 916526097
Other changes: At the close of 2012, the grantmaker paid grants of $8,824,000, an 828.8% increase over the 2011 disbursements, $950,000.

3575
Julie Ann Wrigley Foundation, Inc.

c/o Peterson Sullivan LLP
601 Union St., Ste. 2300
Seattle, WA 98101-2345

Established in 2001 in WI.
Donor: Julie A. Wrigley.
Foundation type: Independent foundation.
Financial data (yr. ended 12/31/12): Assets, $59,355 (M); gifts received, $1,300,000; expenditures, $1,271,937; qualifying distributions, $1,270,698; giving activities include $1,269,430 for 19 grants (high: $922,093; low: $500).
Fields of interest: Higher education; Animal welfare; Health care; Human services.
Limitations: Applications not accepted. Giving primarily in AZ and Washington, DC; funding also in CA and ID. No grants to individuals.
Application information: Contributes only to pre-selected organizations.
Officers: Julie Ann Wrigley, Pres.; **Peter Teutsch, V.P.**; Brian D. Collins, Secy.-Treas.
EIN: 030395312

3576
Yakima Valley Community Foundation

111 S. University Pkwy., Ste. 103
Yakima, WA 98901-1471 (509) 457-7616
FAX: (509) 457-7625; E-mail: emilym@yvcf.com; Grant application e-mail: grants@yvcf.org; Main URL: http://www.yvcf.com/

Established in 2004 in WA.
Foundation type: Community foundation.
Financial data (yr. ended 12/31/11): Assets, $46,798,207 (M); gifts received, $1,789,023; expenditures, $2,587,410; giving activities include $1,302,013 for grants.
Purpose and activities: The foundation seeks to improve the cultural, economic, social, health and educational quality of life for residents of Yakima County, WA, with special attention to unmet needs, and to help donors achieve their philanthropic goals.
Fields of interest: Arts, folk arts; Media/communications; Visual arts; Performing arts; Literature; Arts; Elementary/secondary education; Education, early childhood education; Vocational education; Higher education; Adult/continuing education; Libraries/library science; Education, services; Education; Environment, natural resources; Environment; Health care; Mental health/crisis services; Housing/shelter; Youth development; Family services, parent education; Human services; Economic development; Community/economic development; Philanthropy/voluntarism; Aging.
Type of support: Equipment.
Limitations: Applications accepted. Giving primarily in Yakima County, WA. No support for academic or scientific research, individual school classrooms and individual schools, colleges and universities, or religious organizations for religious purposes. No grants to individuals, or for operating support, capital expenditures (real estate/bricks and mortar), debt retirement or reduction, conferences, workshops, or symposia, travel, endowments, publications, video, or film, special fundraising events, or annual campaign appeals.
Publications: Annual report; Financial statement.
Application information: Visit foundation web site for application format and guidelines. Based on the letters of intent, applicants selected for further consideration will be asked to provide additional information and materials about the project and submitting organization. Faxed and e-mailed applications are not accepted. Application form not required.
Initial approach: Submit Letter of Intent (limited to 3 pages)
Copies of proposal: 5
Deadline(s): June 1 for Letter of Intent
Officers and Directors:* Dave Edler,* Chair.; Minerva Morales,* Vice-Chair.; Linda G. Moore,* Pres. and C.E.O.; **Mary Rita Rohde,* Secy.; Ann Hittle,* Treas.; David Abeyta; Crystal Bass**; Michele Besso; Gina Gamboa; Ricardo Garcia; Hank Heffernan; Leah Holbrook; Ester Huey; Paul Larson; Elizabeth McGree; Jessie Randhawa.
EIN: 200697012
Other changes: Dave Edler has replaced Bill Douglas as Chair. Minerva Morales has replaced Dave Edler as Vice-Chair. Mary Rita Rohde has replaced Elizabeth McGree as Secy. Ann Hittle has replaced Ann O'Brien as Treas.
Mary Rita Rohde is no longer a member of the governing body. Minerva Morales is no longer a member of the governing body. Dave Edler is no longer a member of the governing body.

WEST VIRGINIA

3577
Beckley Area Foundation, Inc.
129 Main St., Ste. 203
Beckley, WV 25801-4615 (304) 253-3806
***Contact:* Susan S. Landis, Exec. Dir.**
FAX: (304) 253-7304; E-mail: info@bafwv.org; Main URL: http://www.bafwv.org/

Established in 1985 in WV.
Foundation type: Community foundation.
Financial data (yr. ended 03/31/13): Assets, $31,560,282 (M); gifts received, $1,609,941; expenditures, $974,282; giving activities include $668,387 for 178 grants (high: $31,385), and $4,456 for grants to individuals.
Purpose and activities: The foundation focuses its grantmaking on the arts, health and human services, public recreation, education, and civic beautification in specific geographic areas of southern West Virginia.
Fields of interest: Arts; Education; Environment, beautification programs; Health organizations, association; Recreation; Human services; Community development, neighborhood development.
Type of support: Capital campaigns; Building/renovation; Equipment; Program development; Conferences/seminars; Seed money; Scholarship funds; Technical assistance; Consulting services; Matching/challenge support.
Limitations: Applications accepted. Giving limited to the Beckley and Raleigh County, WV, area for Discretionary grant program; designated funds support a number of counties in WV. No support for sectarian religious programs. No grants for ongoing maintenance and operating expenses, annual campaigns, debt reduction, or endowments.
Publications: Application guidelines; Annual report; Financial statement; Grants list; Informational brochure; Informational brochure (including application guidelines); Newsletter; Occasional report; Program policy statement (including application guidelines).
Application information: Visit foundation web site for application form and guidelines. Faxed or e-mailed applications are not accepted. Application form required.
Initial approach: Mail grant request form and proposal
Copies of proposal: 1
Deadline(s): Dec. 16 for grants; Oct. 1 for "Student's First" mini-grants
Board meeting date(s): Mar., Apr., June, Sept., and Dec.
Final notification: Mar. for grants; Oct. 31 for "Student's First" mini-grants
Officers and Directors:* William H. File,* Pres.; Michael Cavendish,* V.P.; Rachel Abrams Hopkins,* Secy.; Jon Calfee,* Treas.; Dena Cushman,* C.F.O.; Susan S. Landis, Exec. Dir.; Bill Baker; Hazel Burroughs; Dawn Dayton; Dan Doman; Dr. Brett Eckley; Deborah Songer Gray; Bill O'Brien; Susan Pietrantozzi; Linda Polly; Yvonne D. Seay; William L. Turner.
Number of staff: 3 full-time professional.
EIN: 311125328

3578
The Warren and Betty Burnside Foundation, Inc.
300 W. Pike St.
Clarksburg, WV 26301-2710 (304) 623-3668
Contact: James C. West, Jr.
***E-mail:* burnsidefoundation@frontier.com**; Main URL: http://www.burnsidefoundation.org

Established in 1991 in WV.
Donors: Warren Burnside; Betty Burnside.
Foundation type: Independent foundation.
Financial data (yr. ended 01/31/13): Assets, $6,668,370 (M); gifts received, $65,290; expenditures, $318,728; qualifying distributions, $309,794; giving activities include $213,000 for grants to individuals.
Purpose and activities: Scholarships for higher education only to deserving and achieving students from Harrison County, WV.
Fields of interest: Higher education.
Type of support: Scholarships—to individuals.
Limitations: Applications accepted. Giving limited to residents of Harrison County, WV.
Application information: See foundation web site for application information. Application form required.
Officers and Directors:* James C. West, Jr.,* Pres.; John L. Westfall,* V.P.; Dean C. Ramsey,* Secy.; Kathryn K. Allen,* Treas.; Jean Hardesty; Robert Kittle; Harry Murray, Jr.; Robert Tolley; Tim Whalen; Becky Wilson.
EIN: 550709158

3579
Community Foundation for the Ohio Valley, Inc.
(also known as CFOV)
1310 Market St.
Wheeling, WV 26003-0085 (304) 242-3144
Contact: Susie Nelson, Exec. Dir.
FAX: (304) 234-4753; E-mail: info@cfov.org; Mailing address: P.O. 670, Wheeling, WV 26003-0085; Additional e-mail: director@cfov.org; Main URL: http://www.cfov.org

Established in 1972 in WV.
Foundation type: Community foundation.
Financial data (yr. ended 06/30/12): Assets, $26,123,744 (M); gifts received, $731,299; expenditures, $1,366,250; giving activities include $1,057,073 for 40+ grants (high: $226,112).
Purpose and activities: To increase a permanent endowment that can respond to the current and future needs of the Upper Ohio Valley. The foundation accomplish this mission via several ways: 1) works with donors and their financial advisors to provide a flexible, efficient and lasting way for them to benefit their community; 2) is a faithful steward and prudent manager of philanthropic assets; 3) initiates responses that focus on the needs within the community; 4) makes grants that will have a significant impact upon the recipients.
Fields of interest: Historic preservation/historical societies; Arts; Education; Health care; Human services; Economic development; Community/economic development; Children/youth; Youth; Women; Girls; Economically disadvantaged.
Type of support: Building/renovation; Conferences/seminars; Consulting services; Equipment; Matching/challenge support; Program development; Scholarship funds; Seed money; Technical assistance.
Limitations: Applications accepted. Giving in the Upper Ohio Valley area: Brooke, Jefferson, Marshall, Ohio, Tyler and Wetzel counties, WV, and Belmont, Guernsey and Monroe counties, OH. No support for sectarian religious purposes. No grants to individuals (except for scholarships), or for endowment campaigns, or general operating or maintenance expenses for established organizations; no loans.
Publications: Application guidelines; Annual report; Annual report (including application guidelines); Grants list; Informational brochure; Newsletter; Program policy statement.
Application information: Visit foundation web site for required pre-application form and guidelines. Application form required.
Initial approach: Telephone or letter
Copies of proposal: 1
Deadline(s): Pre-application due Apr. 15; full application due May 31
Board meeting date(s): Jan., Apr., July, and Oct.
Final notification: Determination in early May to submit full application. Final determination in July.
Officers and Directors:* Sue Seibert Farnsworth,* Pres.; Bob Robinson,* V.P.; David B. Dalzell, Jr.,* Secy.; Edward Gompers,* Treas.; Susie Nelson, Exec. Dir.; **Joseph W. Boutaugh, Emeritus**; Mark C. Ferrell; Beri Fox; Joseph Glaub; Jay Goodman; Christine Hargrave; Carlos Jimenez, M.D.; Dr. H. Lawrence Jones; Charles J. Kaiser, Jr.; Mark A. McKeen; Tulane Mensore; William O. Nutting; Elsie Reyes; Fredrick Dean Rohrig; James G. Squibb, Jr.; Joan Corson Stamp; Will Turani; William J. Yaeger, Jr.
Trustee Banks: Huntington Bank; Monteverde Group; Premier Bank and Trust; Security National Trust Co.; United Bank; WesBanco Trust & Investment Services, Inc.
Number of staff: 1 full-time professional; 1 full-time support; 1 part-time support.
EIN: 310908698
Other changes: Joseph W. Boutaugh is now Emeritus. Brent Bush is no longer a director.

3580
Eastern West Virginia Community Foundation
229 E. Martin St., Ste. 4
Martinsburg, WV 25401-4307 (304) 264-0353
Contact: Michael Whalton, Exec. Dir.
FAX: (888) 507-8375; E-mail: info@ewvcf.org; Main URL: http://www.ewvcf.org
Facebook: http://www.facebook.com/pages/Eastern-West-Virginia-Community-Foundation/130566868758

Established in 1995 in WV.
Foundation type: Community foundation.
Financial data (yr. ended 12/31/12): Assets, $16,684,886 (M); gifts received, $477,846; expenditures, $1,198,615; giving activities include $840,439 for 18+ grants (high: $602,000), and $56,920 for 46 grants to individuals.
Purpose and activities: The foundation seeks to build and sustain endowment growth in the West Virginia's Eastern panhandle to benefit charitable programs and activities.
Fields of interest: Arts education; Performing arts, theater; Arts; Education; Environment; Health care; Substance abuse, services; Recreation; Children/youth, services; Family services; Community development, neighborhood development; Economic development; Infants/toddlers; Children/youth; Children; Youth; Disabilities, people with; Homeless.

Type of support: General/operating support; Continuing support; Management development/capacity building; Annual campaigns; Capital campaigns; Building/renovation; Equipment; Land acquisition; Endowments; Program development; Seed money; Curriculum development; Internship funds; Scholarships—to individuals; Matching/challenge support.
Limitations: Applications accepted. Giving primarily in Berkeley, Hardy, Hampshire, Jefferson, and Morgan counties, WV.
Publications: Application guidelines; Annual report; Financial statement; Grants list; Informational brochure; Newsletter.
Application information: Visit foundation web site for application cover forms and guidelines. Application form required.

Initial approach: Telephone or submit application cover form and proposal
Copies of proposal: 11
Deadline(s): Varies
Board meeting date(s): Varies
Final notification: Varies

Officers and Directors:* Scott Roach,* Pres.; Darlene Truman,* V.P.; **Diane Dailey,* Secy.**; **Lisa Welch,* Treas.**; **Tia McMillan,* Asst. Treas.**; Michael Whalton, Exec. Dir.; Jeff Boehm; **Alan Brill**; Dick Hamblin; Conrad Hammann; **Chip Hensell**; Tiffany Hine; Jim Keel; Diane Melby; Taylor Perry; Ruth Pritchard; R.B. Seem; Terry Walker; Jan Wilkins.
Number of staff: 3 full-time professional.
EIN: 550742377
Other changes: Diane Dailey has replaced Lisa Welch as Secy. Lisa Welch has replaced Tia McMillan As Treas.
Felicia Fuller is now Finance and Admin. Mgr. Amy Pancake is now Affiliate Dir. and Scholarship/Grants Mgr. Betsy Coffey, Diane Dailey, Doug Roach, and Betty Russell are no longer directors.

3581
Fenton Foundation Inc.

700 Elizabeth St.
Williamstown, WV 26187-1028 **(304) 375-6122**
Contact: Thomas K. Fenton, Pres. and Treas.

Established in 1955 in WV.
Donors: Fenton Art Glass Co.; Fenton Gift Shops, Inc.; Thomas K. Fenton; Harold Swartz; Neva Swartz; Martin Land Co.
Foundation type: Company-sponsored foundation.
Financial data (yr. ended 12/31/12): Assets, $3,397,105 (M); expenditures, $191,065; qualifying distributions, $160,524; giving activities include $160,499 for 48 grants (high: $18,000; low: $50).
Purpose and activities: The foundation supports organizations involved with arts and culture, elementary and higher education, health, human services, community development, and Christianity.
Fields of interest: Arts; Education; Human services.
Type of support: General/operating support; Capital campaigns.
Limitations: Applications accepted. Giving primarily in the William County, OH and Williamstown, WV, area. No grants to individuals.
Application information: Application form not required.

***Initial approach:* Letter**
Copies of proposal: 1
Deadline(s): None

Officers: Thomas K. Fenton, Pres. and Treas.; Randall R. Fenton, V.P.; Lynn F. Erb, Secy.
Directors: David C. Fenton; Michael D. Fenton.
EIN: 556017260

3582
Five Promises for Children Foundation, Inc.

P.O. Box 1468
Charleston, WV 25325-1468 (304) 346-0441
Contact: Brooke Manchin
***E-mail:* info@5promiseswv.org**; Main URL: http://www.5promiseswv.org

Established in WV.
Donor: Committee to Re-elect Joe Manchin.
Foundation type: Independent foundation.
Financial data (yr. ended 12/31/12): Assets, $88,045 (M); expenditures, $179,743; qualifying distributions, $179,537; giving activities include $153,900 for 51 grants (high: $7,500; low: $1,000).
Fields of interest: Arts; Education; Youth development.
Limitations: Applications accepted. Giving primarily in WV.
Application information: Application form required.

Initial approach: Proposal
Deadline(s): May 1 for first session and Nov. 1 for second session

Officers: Jack Rossi, Chair.; Richard Donovan, Secy.
Directors: Linda Hickman; Ann Starcher; Diane Strong-Treister.
EIN: 264542011

3583
The Arthur B. Hodges Center, Inc.

Charleston, WV

The foundation terminated in 2011 and transferred its assets to Edgewood Summit, Inc.

3584
Maier Foundation, Inc.

(formerly Sarah & Pauline Maier Foundation)
P.O. Box 6190
Charleston, WV 25362-0190
Contact: Brad M. Rowe, Pres.
Main URL: http://www.maierfoundation.org
Grants List: http://www.maierfoundation.org/granthistory.php

Established in 1958 in WV.
Donors: William J. Maier, Jr.‡; Pauline Maier‡; General Corporation.
Foundation type: Independent foundation.
Financial data (yr. ended 10/31/13): Assets, $27,212,043 (M); expenditures, $1,677,486; qualifying distributions, $1,162,126; giving activities include $1,161,000 for 23 grants (high: $250,000; low: $1,000).
Purpose and activities: Giving for higher education in West Virginia and other educationally-related pursuits in Kanawha County, West Virginia.
Fields of interest: Higher education; Education.
Type of support: General/operating support; Annual campaigns; Capital campaigns; Building/renovation; Equipment; Endowments; Program development; Professorships; Scholarship funds; Matching/challenge support.
Limitations: Applications accepted. Giving limited to WV. No support for religious or political organizations, or primary or secondary educational institutions. No grants to individuals.
Publications: Application guidelines; Program policy statement.
Application information: Application form required.

Initial approach: Letter
Copies of proposal: 11
Deadline(s): Oct. 1
Board meeting date(s): 1st Fri. in Dec.
Final notification: Dec. 31

Officers and Board Members:* Edward H. Maier,* Chair.; Bradley M. Rowe,* Pres.; Sandra D. Thomas,* Secy.; Sara M. Rowe,* Treas.; John T. Copenhaver; Charles I. Jones, Jr.; J. Holmes Morrison; Thomas W. Rowe; J. Randy Valentine.
Number of staff: None.
EIN: 556023833

3585
Robert W. McCormick Scholarship Fund

c/o Bank of Charles Town
P.O. Drawer 40
Charles Town, WV 25414-0040 (304) 728-2435

Established in 1994 in WV.
Donor: Robert W. McCormick.
Foundation type: Independent foundation.
Financial data (yr. ended 04/30/13): Assets, $4,363,924 (M); expenditures, $225,066; qualifying distributions, $169,005; giving activities include $38,240 for 1 grant, and $130,765 for 14 grants to individuals (high: $21,617; low: $1,100).
Purpose and activities: Giving primarily for education; scholarships are available only to students graduating from a high school in the Jefferson County, West Virginia, area, who will attend a public college or university in West Virginia.
Fields of interest: Education.
Type of support: General/operating support; Scholarships—to individuals.
Limitations: Applications accepted. Giving limited to residents of Jefferson County, WV.
Application information: Students must graduate with a "B" average from a high school located in Jefferson County, West Virginia. Application form required.

Deadline(s): Feb. 20

Trustees: F. Samuel Byrer; Bank of Charles Town.
EIN: 550734149

3586
Bernard McDonough Foundation, Inc.

311 4th St.
Parkersburg, WV 26101-5315 (304) 424-6280
FAX: (304) 424-6281; Main URL: http://www.mcdonoughfoundation.org/

Incorporated in 1961 in WV.
Donor: Bernard P. McDonough‡.
Foundation type: Independent foundation.
Financial data (yr. ended 12/31/12): Assets, $34,419,357 (M); expenditures, $1,614,855; qualifying distributions, $1,492,957; giving activities include $1,153,632 for 102 grants (high: $80,000; low: $100).
Purpose and activities: Giving primarily for 1) Health and Medical (support of hospitals, clinics and other health related charities); 2) Social Welfare (those organizations whose primary function is to serve the general welfare requirements of people whose circumstances in life require that they receive financial or social aid to improve their quality of life); and 3) Civic and Community Enterprises (organizations and municipalities whose projects need financial

support to enhance the economic growth and general welfare of the community).
Fields of interest: Health care; Human services; Community/economic development.
Type of support: General/operating support; Annual campaigns; Capital campaigns; Building/renovation; Equipment; Emergency funds; Program development; Employee matching gifts; Matching/challenge support.
Limitations: Applications accepted. **Giving primarily in Washington County, OH, and WV; applicants whose services extend to the residents of the primary geographical area, but whose location may be just outside the primary geographical area are accepted.** No support for religious or political organizations, or for public or private school clubs, extra-curricular organizations, or facilities used primarily for athletics or athletic events. No grants to individuals, or for sports, travel or start-up operations.
Publications: Application guidelines.
Application information: Application form not required.
Initial approach: Letter
Copies of proposal: 1
Deadline(s): None
Board meeting date(s): Feb., May, Aug. and Oct.
Final notification: 2 to 4 weeks
Officers and Directors:* Robert W. Stephens, Ed.D.*, Pres.; Mary Riccobene,* V.P.; Katrina A. Valentine, Secy.; Francis C. McCusker,* Treas.; Robert S. Boone; Dale A. Knight.
Number of staff: 2 full-time professional.
EIN: 556023693
Other changes: The grantmaker now makes its application guidelines available online.

3587
Parkersburg Area Community Foundation

(also known as Our Community's Foundation)
1620 Park Ave.
P.O. Box 1762
Parkersburg, WV 26102-1762 (304) 428-4438
Contact: Judy Sjostedt, Exec. Dir.; Marian Clowes, Prog. and Devel. Off.
FAX: (304) 428-1200; E-mail: info@pacfwv.com; Additional tel.: (866) 428-4438; Additional e-mail: marian.clowes@pacfwv.com; Main URL: http://www.pacfwv.com
Facebook: https://www.facebook.com/pages/Our-Communitys-Foundation/94685606425
YouTube: http://www.youtube.com/user/PACFWV?feature=creators_cornier-http%253A%2F%2Fs.ytimg.com%2Fyt%2Fimg%2Fcreators_corner%2FYouTube%2Fyoutube_32x32.png

Established in 1963 in WV.
Donors: Albert Wolfe; The Keystone Foundation.
Foundation type: Community foundation.
Financial data (yr. ended 06/30/11): Assets, $28,536,938 (M); gifts received, $2,272,062; expenditures, $2,245,062; giving activities include $1,505,215 for grants, and $293,055 for grants to individuals.
Purpose and activities: The foundation serves the people of region by providing leadership and inspiring people to build permanent resources for the betterment of their communities through the foundation.
Fields of interest: Museums; Historic preservation/historical societies; Arts; Child development, education; Higher education; Adult education—literacy, basic skills & GED; Libraries/library science; Education, reading; Education; Animal welfare; Health care; Mental health/crisis services; Recreation; Children/youth, services; Child development, services; Family services; Human services; Economic development; Community/economic development.
Type of support: Management development/capacity building; Capital campaigns; Building/renovation; Equipment; Emergency funds; Program development; Seed money; Scholarship funds; Scholarships—to individuals; Matching/challenge support.
Limitations: Applications accepted. Giving limited to the Mid-Ohio Valley communities of Calhoun, Doddridge, Gilmer, Jackson, Mason, Pleasants, Ritchie, Roane, Wirt, and Wood counties, WV, and Washington County, OH. No support for sectarian religious purposes. Generally no grants for annual campaigns, endowments, sectarian religious purposes, retiring existing obligations, debts or liabilities, student travel or student participation in meetings, seminars or study exchange programs.
Publications: Application guidelines; Annual report; Informational brochure; Newsletter.
Application information: Visit the foundation's web site to access information about grantmaking programs, guidelines, and the online application form. May also e-mail, telephone, or send letter for guidelines. Application form required.
Initial approach: Application process is online
Deadline(s): Mar. 1 and Sept. 1; emergency and mini-grants may be considered at other times
Board meeting date(s): 3rd Fri. in Jan., Mar., May, July, Sept., and Nov.
Final notification: May and Nov.
Officers and Governors:* Ann Beck,* Chair.; Marie Caltrider,* Vice-Chair.; Dr. Usha Vasan,* Secy.; Curtis Miller,* Treas.; Judy Sjostedt,* Exec. Dir.; **James Bennett**; Cynthia Brown; Gwen Bush; Becky Deem; Randy Dick; Beau Ellison; Michael L. Fleak; Rob Fouss; Linda Gerrard; Larry Hancock; Greg Herrick; Paul Hicks; Bob Kent; Dr. Mansoor Matcheswalla; John Ralsten; Missi Scraberry; Donna Smith; Jim Strader; John Tebay; Tom Whaling; Daniel B. Wharton.
Number of staff: 2 full-time professional; 2 part-time professional; 1 full-time support.
EIN: 556027764
Other changes: Fred Rader is no longer a member of the governing body.

3588
The Ross Foundation Inc.

200 Star Ave., Ste. 212
Parkersburg, WV 26101-5459 (304) 865-7294
E-mail: apply@therossfoundation.org; Main URL: http://www.therossfoundation.org

Established in 2006 in WV.
Donors: Ross Tailwind; Samuel B. Ross II; Samuel B. Ross III.
Foundation type: Independent foundation.
Financial data (yr. ended 12/31/12): Assets, $16,008,951 (M); expenditures, $753,327; qualifying distributions, $699,415; giving activities include $575,329 for 38 grants (high: $100,000; low: $500).
Purpose and activities: Giving primarily for education, arts and culture, programs for people with disabilities, animals, temporary assistance and community initiatives.
Fields of interest: Education; Animals/wildlife; Human services; Community/economic development; Disabilities, people with.
Limitations: Applications accepted. Giving primarily in WV, with emphasis on the five counties of Doddridge, Jackson, Pleasants, Ritchie, and Wood. No grants to individuals.
Publications: Grants list.
Application information: A staff member of the foundation will be available to provide guidance to nonprofits on what each section of the online application requires and why. A conference call with a staff member will be available to all applicants for 1-hour on the second Monday of the first month of the grant period if enough nonprofits wish to be part of it. If not enough nonprofits wish to be part of the conference call, then one on one contact with the few nonprofits asking about that process will be available. Application form required.
***Initial approach:* See foundation web site for application form**
Deadline(s): Application should be submitted during the first month of a given grant cycle
Officers: Samuel B. Ross II, Chair.; Samuel B. Ross III, Exec. Dir.
Board Members: Mellisa Ross; Spencer B. Ross; Susan S. Ross.
EIN: 204652067

3589
Tucker Community Foundation

501 Chestnut St.
P.O. Box 491
Parsons, WV 26287 (304) 478-2930
Contact: Robert A. Burns, Exec. Dir.
FAX: (304) 478-9966; E-mail: tcf1@frontiernet.net; Main URL: http://www.tuckerfoundation.net
Facebook: https://www.facebook.com/tucker.commfound?

Established in 1988 in WV.
Foundation type: Community foundation.
Financial data (yr. ended 12/31/11): Assets, $18,556,022 (M); gifts received, $825,276; expenditures, $881,758; giving activities include $610,073 for 8+ grants, and $36,350 for 54 grants to individuals.
Purpose and activities: The foundation seeks to build a permanent pool of endowed funds to serve the broad charitable needs of the community, to manage these funds responsibly, and to use them efficiently in responding to the community's changing needs and opportunities. Scholarships for local community services, including playgrounds, art and cultural programs, and for fire and medical services.
Fields of interest: Visual arts; Performing arts; Libraries/library science; Education; Health care; Recreation.
Type of support: General/operating support; Continuing support; Endowments; Program development; Seed money; Curriculum development; Scholarship funds; Technical assistance; Employee-related scholarships; Scholarships—to individuals.
Limitations: Applications accepted. Giving limited to Barbour, Grant, Pocahontas, Preston, Randolph, and Tucker counties, WV, and Garrett County, MD. No support for annual fund campaigns, deficit financing or debt retirement, fraternal organizations, religious organizations for sectarian purposes, scientific research, or political organizations or campaigns. No grants to individuals, except for selected scholarships.
Publications: Annual report; Grants list; Newsletter.
Application information: Visit foundation web site for application guidelines per grant size. Application form required.
Initial approach: Letter or telephone
***Deadline(s):* 3rd Fri. in Sept. for grant requests over $500; grant requests under $500 accepted anytime**
Board meeting date(s): Jan., May, July, and Oct.
Final notification: May and Oct.

Officers and Directors:* David Cooper,* Pres.; Jim Cooper, III*, V.P.; David Moran,* Secy.; Marvin Parsons,* Treas.; Robert A. Burns, Exec. Dir.; Shannon Anderson; Amy Barb; Diane Beall; Dan Bucher; Beth Clevenger; Rachelle Davis; Mark Doak; Nancy K. Dotson; Sam Goughnour; Lyndsey Nestor; Milan Nypl; Donna Patrick; Kelly Stadleman.
Number of staff: 1 full-time professional.
EIN: 550687098

3590
Arthur and Joan Weisberg Family Foundation, Inc.
2010 2nd Ave.
P.O. Box 5346
Huntington, WV 25703-1108

Established in 1995 in WV.
Donors: Arthur Weisberg; Joan Weisberg; Arthur & Joan Weisberg Charitable Lead Trust.
Foundation type: Independent foundation.
Financial data (yr. ended 08/31/13): Assets, $1,663,397 (M); gifts received, $722,500; expenditures, $676,280; qualifying distributions, $676,226; giving activities include $676,226 for 35 grants (high: $402,000; low: $100).
Fields of interest: Education; Science; Jewish agencies & synagogues; Blind/visually impaired.
Type of support: General/operating support.
Limitations: Applications not accepted. Giving primarily in Washington, DC, New York, NY, TX and Huntington, WV. No grants to individuals.
Application information: Unsolicited requests for funds not accepted.
Officers: Joan Weisberg, Chair. and Pres.; Martha Weisberg Barvin, Vice-Chair. and V.P.; Pamela Weisberg, Secy.; Charles Weisberg, Treas.
EIN: 550746517
Other changes: Pamela Weisberg is now Secy. Charles Weisberg is now Treas. Louis Weisberg and Seth Weisberg are no longer directors.

3591
Your Community Foundation, Inc.
(formerly Greater Morgantown Community Trust, Inc.)
111 High St.
P. O. Box 409
Morgantown, WV 26505 (304) 296-3433
Contact: Beth Fuller, Pres.
E-mail: beth@ycfwv.org; Main URL: http://www.ycfwv.org/
Facebook: https://www.facebook.com/pages/Your-Community-Foundation-YCF/154019484631226?ref=ts&fref=ts
Twitter: https://twitter.com/YCF_Morgantown?refsrc=email
YouTube: http://www.youtube.com/channel/UCZdLI7tlFwpKJsOhsPoYq1A?feature=watch

Established in 2001 in WV.
Foundation type: Community foundation.
Financial data (yr. ended 12/31/12): Assets, $9,023,414 (M); gifts received, $1,772,178; expenditures, $899,105; giving activities include $583,479 for 9+ grants (high: $50,000), and $81,194 for 58 grants to individuals (high: $4,684; low: $500).
Purpose and activities: The foundation enables people with philanthropic interests to easily and effectively support the issues they care about, immediately, or through their will.
Fields of interest: Arts; Education; Health care; Recreation; Youth, services; Family services; Human services.
Type of support: Emergency funds; Program development; Equipment; Endowments; Seed money; Scholarship funds; Matching/challenge support.
Limitations: Applications accepted. Giving primarily in North Central, WV. No grants for operational expenses, ongoing programs, existing obligations, debts or liabilities, conferences, seminars, annual campaigns, endowments, travel, or work training.
Publications: Annual report; Informational brochure.
Application information: Visit foundation web site for application form and guidelines. Faxed and e-mailed applications are also accepted. Application form required.
Initial approach: Mail application form and attachments
Deadline(s): Mar. 31
Board meeting date(s): Quarterly
Final notification: June 1
Officers and Directors:* Gerry Schmidt,* Chair.; Barbara Alexander McKinney,* Vice-Chair.; Beth Fuller,* Pres.; Billy Atkins,* Secy.; Mike DeProspero,* Treas.; Billy L. Coffindaffer; Judy Collett; Steve Decker; Robert Greer; James Griffin; Ranjit Majumder; M.L. Quinn; Scott Rotuck; Ginna Royce; Ian Rudick; Tara Stevens.
Number of staff: 1 full-time professional; 2 part-time professional.
EIN: 275249383

WISCONSIN

3592
Alliant Energy Foundation, Inc.
(formerly Wisconsin Power and Light Foundation, Inc.)
4902 N. Biltmore Ln., Ste. 1000
Madison, WI **53718-2148** (608) 458-4483
Contact: Julie Bauer, Exec. Dir.
FAX: (608) 458-4820;
E-mail: foundation@alliantenergy.com; Additional tel.: (866) 769-3779; contact for Community Service Scholarships: Dawn Lehtinen, Prog. Mgr., tel.: (507) 931-0482, e-mail: dlehtinen@scholarshipamerica.org; Main URL: http://www.alliantenergy.com/CommunityInvolvement/index.htm
Community Service Scholarship Recipients: http://www.alliantenergy.com/CommunityInvolvement/CharitableFoundation/Programs/ssLINK/026251
Facebook: http://www.facebook.com/AlliantEnergyFoundation
Grants List: http://www.alliantenergy.com/wcm/groups/wcm_internet/@int/documents/document/mdaw/mdi2/~edisp/026251.pdf

Established in 1984 in WI.
Donors: Wisconsin Power and Light Co.; Alliant Energy Corp.; Interstate Power and Light Co.
Foundation type: Company-sponsored foundation.
Financial data (yr. ended 12/31/12): Assets, $12,563,716 (M); gifts received, $1,000,000; expenditures, $3,949,204; qualifying distributions, $3,885,399; giving activities include $2,543,140 for 682+ grants (high: $100,000), and $1,023,918 for 3,550 employee matching gifts.
Purpose and activities: The foundation supports organizations involved with arts and culture, education, the environment, health, employment, housing, safety, human services, community development, civic affairs, and minorities.
Fields of interest: Humanities; Arts; Higher education; Libraries (public); Education; Environment, natural resources; Environmental education; Environment; Health care; Crime/law enforcement, police agencies; Employment, training; Employment; Housing/shelter; Disasters, preparedness/services; Disasters, fire prevention/control; Safety/disasters; Boys & girls clubs; Youth development, business; YM/YWCAs & YM/YWHAs; Human services; Civil/human rights, equal rights; Economic development; Community/economic development; United Ways and Federated Giving Programs; Leadership development; Public affairs; Minorities.
Type of support: Continuing support; Annual campaigns; Building/renovation; Equipment; Emergency funds; Program development; Conferences/seminars; Seed money; Scholarship funds; Research; Employee volunteer services; Employee matching gifts; Employee-related scholarships; Scholarships—to individuals; Matching/challenge support.
Limitations: Applications accepted. Giving limited to areas of company operations in IA, MN, and WI. No support for athletes or teams, fraternal or social clubs, third party funding groups, religious organizations not of direct benefit to the entire community, or discriminatory organizations. No grants to individuals (except for scholarships), or for advertising, door prizes, raffle tickets, dinner tables, golf outings or sponsorships of organized sports teams or activities, sporting events or tournaments, endowments, registration fees or participation fees, books, magazines or professional journal articles, political activities, salaries, facilities costs or general operating expenses, capital campaigns, or "bricks and mortar" projects.
Publications: Application guidelines; Annual report (including application guidelines); Grants list; Informational brochure (including application guidelines); Program policy statement.
Application information: Additional information may be requested at a later date. Support is limited to 1 contribution per organization during any given year. Organizations receiving support are asked to provide a final report. Application form required.
Initial approach: Complete online eligibility quiz and application for Community Grants and Community Service Scholarships; download application form and mail to foundation for Hometown Challenge Grant
Copies of proposal: 1
Deadline(s): Jan. 15, May 15, and Sept. 15 for Community Grants; Feb. 15 for Community Service Scholarships; none for Hometown Challenge Grant
Board meeting date(s): Quarterly
***Final notification:* Apr. 1, Aug. 1, and Dec. 1 for Community Grants; 15 days for Hometown Challenge Grant**
Officers and Directors:* Thomas L. Aller,* Pres.; Patricia L. Kampling,* V.P.; Julie Bauer, Secy. and Exec. Dir.; Colleen Thomas, Treas.; Robert J. Bartlett; John O. Larsen.
Number of staff: 3 full-time professional; 3 part-time professional.
EIN: 391444065

3593
The Victor and Christine Anthony Foundation, Inc.
P.O. Box 385
Waupaca, WI 54981-1958 (715) 258-2587
***Application address:* c/o Victor or Christine Anthony, 134 Shadow Lake Dr., Waupaca, WI 54981; tel.: (715) 258-2587**

Established in 2007 in WI.
Foundation type: Independent foundation.
Financial data (yr. ended 12/31/12): Assets, $19,355,740 (M); expenditures, $1,060,748; qualifying distributions, $981,382; giving activities include $975,700 for 56 grants (high: $100,000; low: $500).
Fields of interest: Food services; Safety/disasters; Human services; American Red Cross; Salvation Army; Family services.
Limitations: Applications accepted. Giving primarily in IL and WI.
Application information:
Initial approach: Telephone or letter
Deadline(s): None
Officers: Victor W. Anthony, Jr., Pres. and Treas.; Christine A. Anthony, V.P. and Secy.
Directors: Carol C. Anthony; Katherine A. Anthony; Karen A. Gabler.
EIN: 260851891
Other changes: Mark J. Bradley is no longer a director.

3594
Ariens Foundation, Ltd.
655 W. Ryan St.
Brillion, WI 54110-1072
***Contact:* Leone M. Pahl, V.P.**

Established in 1967 in WI.
Donors: Ariens Corp.; Francis Ariens Memorial; Ariens Co.; Ariens Company.
Foundation type: Company-sponsored foundation.
Financial data (yr. ended 06/30/13): Assets, $402,498 (M); gifts received, $158,775; expenditures, $201,691; qualifying distributions, $201,691; giving activities include $191,485 for 35 grants (high: $108,775; low: $60), and $9,750 for grants to individuals.
Purpose and activities: The foundation supports community foundations and organizations involved with secondary and higher education, the environment, homeless shelters, athletics, civil liberties, and human services and awards scholarships to individuals.
Fields of interest: Secondary school/education; Higher education; Environmental education; Environment; Housing/shelter, homeless; Athletics/sports, amateur leagues; Youth development, business; Human services; Civil liberties, right to life.
Type of support: Building/renovation; General/operating support; Scholarship funds; Scholarships—to individuals.
Limitations: Applications accepted. Giving primarily in northeastern WI, with emphasis on Brillion.
Application information: Application form required.
Initial approach: Proposal
Deadline(s): None
Officers: Mary M. Ariens, Pres.; **Leone M. Pahl, V.P.; Stephen Letourneaux, Secy.**; H. James Jensen, Treas.
EIN: 396102058

3595
Baird Foundation, Inc.
(formerly Robert W. Baird and Company Foundation, Inc.)
777 E. Wisconsin Ave.
Milwaukee, WI 53202-5302 **(414) 298-1722**
***Contact:* Audrey Warner**
***E-mail:* awarner@rwbaird.com; Additional contact: Margaret Welch, Fdn. Assoc., mmwelch@rwbaird.com, tel.: (414) 298-6197**; Main URL: http://www.rwbaird.com/about-baird/culture/baird-foundation.aspx

Established in 1967 in WI.
Donor: Robert W. Baird and Co.
Foundation type: Company-sponsored foundation.
Financial data (yr. ended 12/31/12): Assets, $28,940,737 (M); gifts received, $13,521,249; expenditures, $2,632,066; qualifying distributions, $2,604,861; giving activities include $2,604,861 for 1,832 grants (high: $75,000; low: $5).
Purpose and activities: The foundation supports programs designed to promote education; health and human services; the arts; and diversity and organizations with which Baird associates are actively engaged in order to maximize the impact on those organizations and communities.
Fields of interest: Museums (art); Performing arts; Performing arts, ballet; Performing arts, opera; Arts; Secondary school/education; Higher education; Education; Hospitals (general); Health care; Mental health, grief/bereavement counseling; Cystic fibrosis; Boys & girls clubs; Boy scouts; American Red Cross; YM/YWCAs & YM/YWHAs; Children/youth, services; Human services; Civil/human rights, equal rights; Community/economic development; United Ways and Federated Giving Programs.
Type of support: General/operating support; Annual campaigns; Capital campaigns; Program

development; Employee volunteer services; Employee matching gifts.
Limitations: Applications not accepted. Giving on a national basis, with emphasis on WI; giving also to national and international organizations. No grants to individuals.
Publications: Annual report.
Application information: Contributes only to pre-selected organizations.
Officers: James D. Bell, Jr.,* Chair.; Paul E. Purcell, Pres.; Leslie H. Dixon, V.P.; Peter S. Kies, V.P.; C.H. Randolph Lyon, V.P.; Mary Ellen Stanek, V.P.; Glen F. Hackmann, Secy.; Dominick P. Zarcone, Treas.
EIN: 396107937
Other changes: At the close of 2012, the fair market value of the grantmaker's assets was $28,940,737, a 76.0% increase over the 2011 value, $16,447,495.
Leonard M. Rush is no longer Treas. Margaret Welch is now Fdn. Assoc.

3596
Pat and Jay Baker Foundation, Inc.
c/o Peter M. Sommerhauser
780 N. Water St.
Milwaukee, WI 53202-3512

Established in 1993 in WI.
Donors: Jay H. Baker; Jay Baker Living Trust.
Foundation type: Independent foundation.
Financial data (yr. ended 12/31/12): Assets, $23,839,777 (M); gifts received, $19,042,000; expenditures, $4,781,500; qualifying distributions, $4,780,500; giving activities include $4,771,000 for 15 grants (high: $3,000,000; low: $1,000).
Purpose and activities: Giving primarily for the performing arts, education and health care.
Fields of interest: Museums; Performing arts; Arts; Business school/education; Health care; Human services.
Limitations: Applications not accepted. Giving primarily in NY and Naples, FL; some giving also in PA. No grants to individuals.
Application information: Contributes only to pre-selected organizations.
Officers and Directors:* Jay H. Baker,* Pres. and Treas.; Pat Good Baker,* V.P. and Secy.; Peter M. Sommerhauser.
EIN: 391776268
Other changes: At the close of 2010, the fair market value of the grantmaker's assets was $17,282,070, a 220.7% increase over the 2009 value, $5,388,492.

3597
BayCare Clinic Foundation, Ltd.
164 N. Broadway
Green Bay, WI 54303-2728 (920) 405-5382
Contact: Ann Seidl, Dir.
***FAX:* (920) 405-8004**; Main URL: http://www.baycare.net/about-us/baycare-clinic-foundation

Established in 2000 in WI.
Donors: BayCare Health Systems, LLC; Dr. Ahmet Dervish; Dr. Richard Harrison; Joseph Hodgson, M.D.; Dr. John Lee; Bruce Neal, M.D.; Dr. Alex Roitstein; Dr. Christopher Sorrells; Paul Summerside, M.D.; Dr. Kevin Wienkers; Mrs. Kevin Wienkers; Dr. Per Anderas; Dr. Scott Gage; Dr. Stephen Brada.
Foundation type: Independent foundation.
Financial data (yr. ended 12/31/12): Assets, $210,248 (M); gifts received, $217,272; expenditures, $197,970; qualifying distributions, $197,909; giving activities include $197,688 for 167 grants (high: $20,003; low: $20).
Purpose and activities: Giving to promote the health and well-being of residents within Green Bay, Northeast Wisconsin and Michigan's Upper Peninsula.
Fields of interest: Arts; Education; Health organizations, association; Human services; Children/youth, services; Christian agencies & churches; Religion.
Type of support: General/operating support; Grants to individuals.
Limitations: Applications accepted. Giving primarily in Green Bay, WI.
Application information: Application form required.
Initial approach: Proposal
Deadline(s): Jan. 14, Apr. 14, July 14, and Oct. 13
Officers and Directors:* Joseph Hodgson, M.D.*, Pres.; Bruce Neal, M.D.*, V.P.; Paul Summerside,* Secy.,-Treas.; Dianna Bordewick, M.D.; John Lee; Ann Seidl; Christopher Sorrells, M.D.
EIN: 392000503

3598
Bemis Company Foundation
One Neenah Ctr., 4th Fl.
P.O. Box 669
Neenah, WI 54957-0669 (920) 527-5300
***Contact:* Kim Wetzel, Fdn. Consultant**
***E-mail:* kwetzel@bemis.com**; Application contact and address: Kim Wetzel, Fdn. Consultant, tel.: (920) 734-2707, e-mail: kwetzel@bemis.com; Main URL: http://www.bemis.com/citizenship/

Trust established in 1959 in MO.
Donor: Bemis Co., Inc.
Foundation type: Company-sponsored foundation.
Financial data (yr. ended 12/31/12): Assets, $62,971 (M); gifts received, $3,410,000; expenditures, $3,370,726; qualifying distributions, $3,370,726; giving activities include $3,304,829 for 1,397 grants (high: $700,000; low: $25).
Purpose and activities: The foundation supports programs designed to encourage through basic needs and emergency assistance; empower through basic education and health and fitness; and elevate through higher education and arts and culture.
Fields of interest: Performing arts, dance; Performing arts, theater; Historic preservation/historical societies; Arts; Higher education; Education; Environment, natural resources; Animal welfare; Public health, physical fitness; Health care; Food services; Food banks; Athletics/sports, school programs; Recreation, fairs/festivals; Recreation; Youth development; Salvation Army; Youth, services; Human services; United Ways and Federated Giving Programs; Mathematics; Engineering/technology; Science; Public affairs.
Type of support: General/operating support; Continuing support; Annual campaigns; Capital campaigns; Building/renovation; Program development; Employee matching gifts; Employee-related scholarships.
Limitations: Applications accepted. **Giving limited to areas of company operations in Crossett and Russellville, AR, Centerville, Clinton, and Des Moines, IA, Batavia and Bellwood, IL, Columbus and Terre Haute, IN, Shelbyville, KY, West Monroe, LA, Mankato and Minneapolis, MN, Joplin, MO, Edgewood, NY, Akron, Fremont, and Stow, OH, Pauls Valley, OK, Lebanon, Philadelphia, Scranton, and West Hazleton, PA, Shelbyville, TN, and Appleton, Boscobel, Lancaster, Menasha, Neenah, New London, and Oshkosh, WI.** No support for religious, lobbying, or political organizations, hospitals, or other foundations. No grants to individuals (except for employee-related scholarships), or for endowments, research, educational capital campaigns, or trips or tours; no loans.
Publications: Application guidelines.
Application information: Grants are limited to 3 years in length. Telephone calls during the application process are not encouraged. Application form required.
***Initial approach:* Complete online eligibility quiz and application for Small Grants; letter of inquiry for Community Support Grants Program**
Copies of proposal: 1
***Deadline(s):* None for Small Grants; Dec. 12 for Basic Needs Emergency Assistance, Mar. 18 for Basic Education Health & Wellness, and June 17 for Higher Education and Arts & Culture**
Board meeting date(s): Mar. 15, June 15, Sept. 15, and Dec. 15
***Final notification:* 4 weeks for Small Grants**
Trustees: Timothy S. Fliss, Jr.; Jerry Krempa; Scott B. Ullem.
Number of staff: 2 part-time professional.
EIN: 416038616
Other changes: Stanley A. Jaffy is no longer a director.

3599
Blooming Prairie Foundation, Inc.
c/o Willy St. Grocery Co-op
1882 E. Main St.
Madison, WI **53704-5288 (608) 556-3055**
Contact: Sverre D. Roang, Dir.
E-mail: bpfinfo@yahoo.com; **Main URL: http://www.bloomingprairiefoundation.org/**

Established in 2003 in WI.
Foundation type: Independent foundation.
Financial data (yr. ended 06/30/13): Assets, $1,864,704 (M); expenditures, $301,048; qualifying distributions, $278,785; giving activities include $270,000 for 2 grants (high: $250,000; low: $20,000).
Purpose and activities: The foundation makes grants to non-profit, charitable organizations that conduct any of the following activities: 1) developmental, research, and educational efforts in the organic industry and the cooperative community; 2) the development of organic and natural products; or 3) cooperative development in the natural products industry.
Fields of interest: Education, community/cooperative; Environmental education; Agriculture, farm cooperatives; Agriculture, sustainable programs; Nutrition.
Type of support: Debt reduction; Program development; Scholarship funds; Matching/challenge support.
Limitations: No support for organizations lacking 501(c)(3) status. No grants to individuals.
Application information: See foundation web site for current application guidelines.
Officers and Directors:* Anya Firszt,* Chair.; Leslie Campbell,* Secy.; Allan Gallant; Pam Kringlund; Sheila Phillips-Hawkins; Sverre David Roang.
Number of staff: 2 part-time support.
EIN: 450511132
Other changes: Leslie Campbell is now Secy.

3600

John C. Bock Foundation

411 E. Wisconsin Ave., Ste. 700
Milwaukee, WI 53202-4497 (414) 276-1122
Contact: Sally C. Merrell Esq.
FAX: (414) 978-8877; E-mail for Sally C. Merrell: smerrell@vonbriesen.com; Main URL: http://www.bockfoundation.com
Grants List: http://www.bockfoundation.com/bock/testimonials_and_portfolio.htm

Established in 2002 in WI.
Donor: John C. Bock Revocable Trust.
Foundation type: Independent foundation.
Financial data (yr. ended 12/31/12): Assets, $6,158,809 (M); expenditures, $284,935; qualifying distributions, $145,360; giving activities include $145,360 for grants.
Purpose and activities: Giving for the preservation, maintenance and enhancement of land areas in their natural or undeveloped state that support woodlands and old-growth forests, principally those proximate to Lake Mendota, WI, and generally in the state of WI.
Fields of interest: Higher education, college; Environment, legal rights; Environment, natural resources; Environmental education.
Limitations: Applications accepted. Giving primarily in WI.
Application information: Application form required.
Initial approach: See website for application form and details
Deadline(s): May 31
Trustees: Carl J. Bock; Sharon L. Bock; Albert Goldstein; Luke Seggelink; Jeremy C. Shea.
EIN: 266014448

3601

The Lynde and Harry Bradley Foundation, Inc.

1241 N. Franklin Pl.
Milwaukee, WI 53202-2901 (414) 291-9915
Contact: Daniel P. Schmidt, V.P., Progs.
FAX: (414) 291-9991; Main URL: http://www.bradleyfdn.org
Grants Database: http://www.bradleyfdn.org/2008_grantees.asp
Twitter: https://twitter.com/bradleyfdn

Incorporated in 1942 in WI as the Allen-Bradley Foundation, Inc.; adopted present name in 1985.
Donors: Harry L. Bradley†; Caroline D. Bradley†; Margaret B. Bradley†; Margaret Loock Trust; Allen-Bradley Co.; Michael Keiser; Mrs. Michael Keiser.
Foundation type: Independent foundation.
Financial data (yr. ended 12/31/12): Assets, $640,390,126 (M); gifts received, $26,382,000; expenditures, $45,284,936; qualifying distributions, $40,380,856; giving activities include $34,340,138 for 627 grants (high: $3,000,000; low: $500), and $157,756 for 2 foundation-administered programs.
Purpose and activities: Support for projects that cultivate a renewed, healthier, and more vigorous sense of citizenship, at home and abroad. Projects will reflect the assumption that free men and women are genuinely self-governing, personally responsible citizens, able to run their daily affairs without the intrusive therapies of the bureaucratic, social service state. Consequently, they will seek to reinvigorate and revive the authority of the traditional institutions of civil society - families, schools, churches, neighborhoods, and entrepreneurial enterprises - that cultivate and provide room for the exercise of citizenship, individual responsibility, and strong moral character. Projects reflecting this view of citizenship and civil society may be demonstrations with national significance; public policy research in economics, politics, culture, or foreign affairs; or media and public education undertakings. Local support is directed toward cultural programs, education, social services, medical and health programs, and public policy research.
Fields of interest: Humanities; History/archaeology; Arts; Education, research; Higher education; Education; Youth development, citizenship; International affairs, foreign policy; International affairs; Economics; Political science; Public policy, research; Public affairs, citizen participation; Public affairs.
Type of support: General/operating support; Continuing support; Annual campaigns; Building/renovation; Equipment; Program development; Conferences/seminars; Professorships; Publication; Curriculum development; Fellowships; Internship funds; Scholarship funds; Research; Program-related investments/loans; Matching/challenge support.
Limitations: Applications accepted. Giving primarily in Milwaukee, WI; giving also on a national and international basis. No support for strictly denominational projects. No grants to individuals (except for Bradley Prizes), or for endowment funds.
Publications: Application guidelines; Annual report; Grants list; Occasional report (including application guidelines).
Application information: If the foundation determines the project to be within the current program interests as determined by its Board of Directors, the applicant will be invited to submit a formal proposal. Application form not required.
Initial approach: Letter of inquiry
Copies of proposal: 1
Deadline(s): Feb. 1, May 1, Aug. 1 and Nov. 1
Board meeting date(s): Feb., May or June, Aug., and Nov.
Final notification: 3 to 5 months
Officers and Directors:* **Dennis J. Kuester,* Chair.**; David V. Uihlein, Jr.,* Vice-Chair.; Michael W. Grebe,* C.E.O. and Pres.; Cynthia K. Friauf, V.P., Finance and Treas.; Terri L. Farmer, V.P., Admin.; R. Michael Lempke, V.P., Investments; Robert E. Norton II, V.P., Donor Relations; Daniel P. Schmidt, V.P., Progs.; **Cleta Mitchell, Secy.**; Mandy L. Hess, Cont.; Terry Considine; Richard W. Graber; Robert P. George; Diane M. Hendricks; San W. Orr, Jr.; **James Arthur Pope**; Thomas L. Smallwood; Shelby Steele; George F. Will.
Number of staff: 9 full-time professional; 8 full-time support; 3 part-time support.
EIN: 396037928
Other changes: Dennis J. Kuester has replaced Terry Considine as Chair. Cleta Mitchell has replaced Thomas L. Smallwood as Secy. Cleta Mitchell has replaced Thomas L. Smallwood as Secy.
Bob Smith is no longer a director.

3602

The Robert and Susan Brown Family Foundation Inc.

P.O. Box 201
Neenah, WI 54957-0201 (920) 727-1137
Contact: Melinda S. Brown
***E-mail:* info@red-canoe.org**; Main URL: http://red-canoe.org/

Established in 2009 in WI.
Donors: Robert W. Brown; Susan T. Brown.
Foundation type: Independent foundation.
Financial data (yr. ended 12/31/12): Assets, $2,159,352 (M); expenditures, $179,055; qualifying distributions, $159,293; giving activities include $158,500 for 28 grants (high: $25,000; low: $500).
Fields of interest: Education; Housing/shelter; Human services.
Application information: The foundation has decided not to accept any grant applications for 2014.
Officers: Daniel T. Brown, Pres.; Robert W. Brown, V.P. and Secy.; Susan T. Brown, Treas.
EIN: 260743538

3603

CBM Credit Education Foundation, Inc.

c/o William Wilcox
P.O. Box 105
Belleville, WI **53508-0105**

Established in 1999 in WI.
Donors: CBM of Madison, Inc.; CBM Cos., Inc.
Foundation type: Independent foundation.
Financial data (yr. ended 12/31/12): Assets, $4,265,162 (M); expenditures, $398,499; qualifying distributions, $326,868; giving activities include $111,536 for 8 grants (high: $30,974; low: $1,500).
Purpose and activities: Giving primarily for consumer services and financial literacy.
Fields of interest: Education; Consumer protection.
Limitations: Applications not accepted. Giving primarily in Dane County, WI; some giving in Washington, DC, and MD. No support for mental health programs. No grants to individuals or for operating expenses, endowments, debt retirement, lobbying, annual campaigns, scholarships, and fundraising functions.
Application information: Unsolicted requests for funds not accepted.
Officers and Directors:* Douglas Timmerman,* Chair.; William Wilcox,* Pres. and Secy.-Treas.; Gary Switzky,* V.P.; Mark Timmerman.
Number of staff: 1 full-time professional.
EIN: 391974526

3604

The Center for Life Transitions Inc.

2719 S. Shore Dr.
Milwaukee, WI 53207-2323 (414) 394-9347
Contact: Thomas Bachhuber Ed.D., Pres.
Main URL: http://www.centerforlifetransitions.net/
Blog: http://www.centerforlifetransitions.net/blog/transpirations/
LinkedIn: http://www.linkedin.com/groups/Center-Life-Transitions-3873112
Twitter: https://www.twitter.com/center4lifetran

Established in 2003 in NJ.
Donor: Ethel Kienz†.
Foundation type: Independent foundation.
Financial data (yr. ended 06/30/13): Assets, $257,323 (M); expenditures, $68,381; qualifying distributions, $36,639; giving activities include $39,212 for foundation-administered programs.
Purpose and activities: The Center for Life Transitions is dedicated to serving people at "crossroads" in their work/career lives. It develops and delivers leading personal, print, and web solutions for work/career transitions across the lifespan -internships/college through retirement -which are integrated with opportunities for spiritual exploration and growth.

Fields of interest: Community/economic development; Christian agencies & churches.
Type of support: Scholarship funds.
Limitations: Applications accepted. Giving primarily in Bridgewater, NJ.
Publications: Informational brochure.
Application information: Application form not required.
Initial approach: Proposal
Deadline(s): None
Officers: Thomas Bachhuber, Ed.D., Pres.; Charles D. Hays, V.P.; Connie Popp, Ed.D., Secy.; John Glaser, Treas.
Directors: Nadya Fouad, Ph.D.; Angela Knight; Bill Sneck, Ph.D.
EIN: 300118835

3605
Chipstone Foundation

c/o Foley & Lardner LLP
777 E. Wisconsin Ave., Ste. 3600
Milwaukee, WI 53202-5306
Main URL: http://www.chipstone.org/
Facebook: https://www.facebook.com/pages/Chipstone-Foundation/142603039504
Foundation's ArtBabble Profile: http://www.artbabble.org/partner/chipstone
Foundation's Instagram Profile: http://instagram.com/chipstone_org
Twitter: https://twitter.com/chipstone_org

Established in 1966.
Donors: Stanley Stone†; Ivor Noel Hume; Mrs. Ivor Noel Hume; I. Stanley Stone Charitable Trust; Carol Hume.
Foundation type: Operating foundation.
Financial data (yr. ended 12/31/12): Assets, $70,385,776 (M); gifts received, $1,032,111; expenditures, $4,157,251; qualifying distributions, $3,732,670; giving activities include $243,282 for 20 grants (high: $127,324; low: $500).
Purpose and activities: Giving to institutions dedicated to the study and preservation of American material culture and related activities, and education.
Fields of interest: Museums; Historic preservation/historical societies; Higher education; Human services; Children, services; United Ways and Federated Giving Programs.
Type of support: General/operating support.
Limitations: Applications not accepted. Giving primarily in Madison and Milwaukee, WI. No grants to individuals.
Application information: Contributes only to pre-selected organizations.
Officers and Directors:* W. David Knox II,* Chair., Pres. and Treas.; Ted D. Kellner,* Vice-Chair.; Jacquelyn A. Sarich, V.P., Admin.; L. Elizabeth Beetz, Secy.; Jonathan Prown, Exec. Dir.; Edward S. Cook, Jr.; Charles F. Hummel; Peter M. Kenny; John S. McGregor; Alison Stone; Stanley Stone III; Gustavus F. Taylor.
Number of staff: 2 full-time professional.
EIN: 396096593

3606
Community Foundation of Central Wisconsin, Inc.

(formerly Community Foundation of Portage County, Inc.)
1501 Clark St.
P.O. Box 968
Stevens Point, WI 54481-0968 (715) 342-4454
Contact: Terry Rothmann, Exec. Dir.
FAX: (715) 342-5560;
E-mail: foundation@cfcwi.org; Additional E-mail: terryr@cfpcwi.org; **Main URL: http://www.cfcwi.org/**
Blog: http://cfcwi.blogspot.com/
Facebook: https://www.facebook.com/cfcwi
Grants List: http://www.cfcwi.org/receive/grant-award-listing.html

Established in 1982 in WI.
Foundation type: Community foundation.
Financial data (yr. ended 06/30/12): Assets, $12,921,089 (M); gifts received, $4,509,355; expenditures, $1,020,130; giving activities include $693,009 for 7+ grants (high: $30,000), and $138,800 for 154 grants to individuals.
Purpose and activities: The foundation seeks to help make the Portage County community a better place to grow, work, play, and retire by helping people, enhancing education, enriching arts and culture, contributing to wellness, and improving the environment through financial management of gifts and grants from individuals and organizations.
Fields of interest: Arts; Education; Environment; Health care; Human services; Women; Economically disadvantaged.
Type of support: General/operating support; Continuing support; Building/renovation; Equipment; Land acquisition; Program development; Conferences/seminars; Seed money; Curriculum development; Scholarship funds; Research; Matching/challenge support.
Limitations: Applications accepted. Giving limited to Portage and Waushara County, WI. No support for sectarian causes. No grants to individuals (except for scholarships), or for annual fund drives, capital campaigns, debt retirement, endowment funds, or operation losses.
Publications: Application guidelines; Annual report; Grants list; Informational brochure.
Application information: Visit foundation web site for application form and guidelines. Application form required.
Initial approach: Telephone or e-mail
Copies of proposal: 10
Deadline(s): Aug. 15
Board meeting date(s): Monthly
Final notification: Oct.
Officers and Directors:* Jim Koziol,* Pres.; **Rob Manzke,* Pres.-Elect.**; Bev Laska,* V.P.; Carie Winn,* Secy.; Tom Klismith,* Treas.; Terry Rothman, Exec. Dir.; Trish Baker; Jim Canales; Soua Cheng; Michele Dufresne; Rick Flugaur; Sharon Jakusz; Vicki Jenks; Nancy Moore; Katy Olson; Craig Reinking; Jim Robinson; Ted Schlafke; Dave Williams; Jennifer Young.
Number of staff: 1 part-time professional; 1 part-time support.
EIN: 390827885
Other changes: Rob Manzke has replaced Jim Koziol as Pres.-Elect.
Jim Koziol, Rob Manzke, and Tom Klismith are no longer directors.

3607
Community Foundation of Southern Wisconsin, Inc.

(formerly United Community Foundation, Inc.)
26 S. Jackson St.
Janesville, WI 53548-3838 (608) 758-0883
***Contact:* Sue S. Conley, Exec. Dir.; For grants: Lindsey Hulstrom, Grants and Scholarships Mgr.**
FAX: (608) 758-8551; E-mail: info@cfsw.org;
Additional tel.: (800) 995-CFSW; Grant inquiry e-mail: lindsey@cfsw.org; Additional e-mail: sueconley@cfsw.org; Main URL: http://www.cfsw.org
Facebook: http://www.facebook.com/pages/Community-Foundation-of-Southern-Wisconsin-Inc/105619273962
Twitter: https://twitter.com/cfsw2014

Established in 1991 in Wisconsin.
Foundation type: Community foundation.
Financial data (yr. ended 06/30/13): Assets, $35,220,164 (M); gifts received, $4,445,221; expenditures, $3,112,179; giving activities include $1,604,930 for 46 grants (high: $84,498), and $532,263 for 385 grants to individuals.
Purpose and activities: The foundation primarily supports the arts, the environment, education, health, human services, and historic preservation in Crawford, Grant, Green, Iowa, Lafayette, Rock, Sauk, Vernon and Walworth counties, WI.
Fields of interest: Historic preservation/historical societies; Arts; Education; Environment; Health care; Safety/disasters; Recreation; Human services; Asians/Pacific Islanders; African Americans/Blacks; Hispanics/Latinos; Native Americans/American Indians; Women; Girls; Single parents.
Type of support: General/operating support; Management development/capacity building; Capital campaigns; Building/renovation; Equipment; Endowments; Emergency funds; Program development; Conferences/seminars; Seed money; Curriculum development; Internship funds; Scholarship funds; Technical assistance; Program evaluation; Scholarships—to individuals; In-kind gifts; Matching/challenge support.
Limitations: Applications accepted. Giving limited to Crawford, Grant, Green, Iowa, Lafayette, Rock, Sauk, Vernon and Walworth counties, WI. No grants to individuals (except for scholarships), or for endowments.
Publications: Application guidelines; Annual report; Financial statement; Informational brochure (including application guidelines); Newsletter.
Application information: Visit foundation web site for application guidelines per grant type. Application form required.
Initial approach: Letter of inquiry or telephone
Copies of proposal: 2
Deadline(s): Varies
Board meeting date(s): Quarterly
Final notification: Varies
Officers and Directors:* Steve Sheiffer,* Pres.; **Ronald Spielman,* V.P.**; Dick Jaeger,* Secy.; Steve Olsen,* Treas.; Tina Lorenz, C.F.O.; Sue S. Conley, Exec. Dir.; **Larry Barton**; Roberta Bernet; Laura Carney; **Jim Finley**; Carol Hatch; Cheryl Mader; William McDaniel; Joseph Nemeth; Dawn Ripkey; Cindy Tang.
Number of staff: 1 full-time professional; 5 part-time professional; 3 part-time support.
EIN: 391711388
Other changes: Steve Sheiffer has replaced James Finley as Chair. Ronald Spielman has replaced Steve Sheiffer as Vice-Chair.
Sharon Kennedy is no longer a director.

3608
Cornerstone Foundation of Northeastern Wisconsin Inc.

111 N. Washington St., Ste. 450
Green Bay, WI 54301-4208 (920) 490-8290
Contact: Sheri R. Prosser, V.P. & Secy.
FAX: (920) 490-8620

Incorporated in 1953 in WI.
Foundation type: Independent foundation.

Financial data (yr. ended 12/31/12): Assets, $25,266,531 (M); expenditures, $1,268,582; qualifying distributions, $978,571; giving activities include $824,438 for 76 grants (high: $75,000; low: $100).
Purpose and activities: Emphasis on education, cultural programs, and social service and youth agencies; support also for healthcare facilities.
Fields of interest: Education, association; Adult education—literacy, basic skills & GED; Health care; Human services; Youth, services; Children/youth; Disabilities, people with; Blind/visually impaired; Mentally disabled; Substance abusers; AIDS, people with; Crime/abuse victims; Economically disadvantaged; Homeless.
Type of support: General/operating support; Continuing support; Annual campaigns; Capital campaigns; Building/renovation; Equipment; Endowments; Debt reduction; Emergency funds; Program development; Matching/challenge support.
Limitations: Applications accepted. Giving primarily in Brown County, WI. No support for religious or political organizations. No grants to individuals.
Publications: Application guidelines.
Application information: Application form required.
Initial approach: Telephone
Copies of proposal: 12
Deadline(s): None
Board meeting date(s): Feb. and Oct.
Officers and Directors:* Paul J. Schierl,* C.E.O.; Sheri R. Prosser,* V.P. and Secy.; James J. Schoshinski,* V.P. and Treas.; **Tim Day,* V.P.**; John W. Hickey,* V.P.; Mark J. McMullen,* V.P.; **Thomas L. Olson,* V.P.**; Carol A. Schierl,* V.P.; Michael J. Schierl,* V.P.; Mary G. Schaupp; Susan P. Watts.
Number of staff: 1 full-time professional; 1 part-time support.
EIN: 362761910

3609
Door County Community Foundation, Inc.
228 N. 3rd Ave.
Sturgeon Bay, WI 54235 **(920) 746-1786**
***Contact:* Bret Bicoy, Pres. and C.E.O.**
FAX: (920) 473-2066;
E-mail: bret@doorcountycommunityfoundation.org; Mailing Address: P.O. Box 802 Sturgeon Bay, WI 54235; Main URL: http://www.doorcountycommunityfoundation.org
Facebook: https://www.facebook.com/doorcountycommunityfoundation

Established in 1999 in WI.
Foundation type: Community foundation.
Financial data (yr. ended 06/30/12): Assets, $7,273,204 (M); gifts received, $1,677,022; expenditures, $654,581; giving activities include $463,083 for 12 grants (high: $123,401), and $12,500 for grants to individuals.
Purpose and activities: The foundation seeks to enhance the quality of life in Door County by perpetually serving the charitable needs of the community, and encouraging the continued and expanded philanthropic activities of citizens.
Fields of interest: Arts; Environment; Animals/wildlife, preservation/protection; Human services.
Type of support: General/operating support; Program development.
Limitations: Applications accepted. Giving primarily in Door County, WI. No support for religious purposes. No grants to individuals (except for scholarships), or for debt retirement, normal operating expenses, annual campaigns, or endowments.
Publications: Informational brochure; Newsletter.
Application information: Visit foundation web site for application form and guidelines per grant type. Application form required.
Initial approach: Telephone, e-mail, or letter
Deadline(s): Varies
Final notification: 6 to 8 weeks
Officers and Directors:* John L. Herlache,* Chair.; David Eliot,* Vice-Chair.; Bret Bicoy,* C.E.O. and Pres.; Polly Alberts,* Secy.; Michael Felhofer,* Treas.; Bill Boettcher; Michael Brecke; Jacinda Duffin; **Dick Egan**; Dick Hauser; Mark Jinkins; Linda Laarman; **Michael McCoy**; Arvid W. Munson; Kaaren Northrop; Marcia Peterson; Nancy Sargent; Jane Stevenson.
Number of staff: 1 part-time professional.
EIN: 391980685
Other changes: Ruth Baldwin Barker is no longer a director.

3610
Dudley Foundation Inc.
500 1st St., Ste. 2
Wausau, WI 54403-4881 (715) 849-5729

Established in 2000 in WI.
Donor: Richard D. Dudley.
Foundation type: Independent foundation.
Financial data (yr. ended 06/30/13): Assets, $5,538,109 (M); expenditures, $272,881; qualifying distributions, $250,427; giving activities include $215,750 for 26 grants (high: $50,000; low: $500).
Purpose and activities: Support for organizations benefiting WI, with emphasis on Marathon County, WI.
Fields of interest: Arts; Education; Environment; Health care, home services; Housing/shelter; Safety/disasters, public education; Safety/disasters; Recreation; Human services; Children, services; Economic development.
Type of support: General/operating support; Capital campaigns; Building/renovation; Equipment; Land acquisition; Emergency funds; Program development; Seed money; Technical assistance; Program evaluation; Matching/challenge support.
Limitations: Applications accepted. Giving primarily in WI, with emphasis on Marathon County, WI. No grants to individuals or private businesses.
Application information: Application form required.
Initial approach: Proposal
Copies of proposal: 8
Deadline(s): 1 month before board meeting
Board meeting date(s): Mar., June, Sept., and Dec.
Final notification: 2 months from receipt
Officers: Richard D. Dudley, Chair.; Ann Dudley Shannon, Pres.; John D. Dudley, V.P.; Paul C. Schlindwein II, Secy.; Gary W. Freels, Treas.
Directors: Mary C. Dudley; Robert J. Dudley II; **Chad D. Kane.**
Number of staff: None.
EIN: 392003427

3611
Eau Claire Community Foundation
(formerly Eau Claire Area Foundation)
306 S. Barstow, Ste. 104
P.O. Box 511
Eau Claire, WI 54702-0511 (715) 552-3801
Contact: For grants: Sue Bornick, Exec. Dir.
FAX: (715) 552-3802;
E-mail: info@eccommunityfoundation.org; Additional e-mail: suebornick@eccommunityfoundation.org; Main URL: http://www.eccommunityfoundation.org
Facebook: https://www.facebook.com/eccommunityfoundation

Established in 1997 in WI.
Donors: Interfaith Hospitality; Roger & Sue Tietz.
Foundation type: Community foundation.
Financial data (yr. ended 12/31/12): Assets, $7,932,962 (M); gifts received, $921,385; expenditures, $361,570; giving activities include $166,207 for 13+ grants (high: $35,928).
Purpose and activities: The foundation strengthens the community by offering donors opportunities to establish charitable legacies, by making grants, and by serving as a catalyst to address community needs.
Fields of interest: Arts; Education; Environment; Recreation; Human services.
Type of support: Capital campaigns; Building/renovation; Equipment; Program development; Seed money; Research; Technical assistance; Program evaluation; Matching/challenge support.
Limitations: Applications accepted. Giving limited to the greater Eau Claire, WI, area. No support for sectarian causes. **No grants to individuals, or for annual campaigns, capital campaigns, debt retirement, endowments, lobbying, or routine operating expenses.**
Publications: Annual report; Financial statement; Grants list; Informational brochure (including application guidelines); Newsletter.
Application information: Visit foundation web site for application form and guidelines. Full proposals sent by fax or e-mail are not accepted. The foundation strongly encourages applicants to attend one of the orientation sessions prior to submitting an application. Application form required.
Initial approach: Contact foundation
Copies of proposal: 16
Deadline(s): 1 month prior to grant deadline for Letter of Intent; Feb. 8 for full grant application
Board meeting date(s): Monthly
Final notification: 90 days
Officers and Trustees:* Jane Lokken,* Chair.; Mark Faanes,* Vice-Chair.; Laura Talley,* Secy.; Lois Krause,* Treas.; Sue Bornick, Exec. Dir.; Suzanne Ashley; Jill Barland; Thomas Dow; Joe Fesenmaier; Dave Frederikson; Charlie Grossklaus; Jeff Halloin; Betsy Kell; Nicole Lasker; Leland Meyer, M.D.; Wayne Peters; Pat Quinn.
Number of staff: 1 full-time professional; 3 part-time support.
EIN: 391891064

3612
Ebling Charitable Trust
Neenah, WI

The foundation terminated on June 25, 2013.

3613
Einhorn Family Foundation Inc.
(formerly Einhorn Family Charitable Trust)
8205 N. River Rd.
Milwaukee, WI 53217-2546 (414) 351-3169
Contact: Nancy Einhorn, Pres.
E-mail: info@einhornfamilyfoundation.org; Main URL: http://www.einhornfamilyfoundation.org

Established in 1996.
Donors: Stephen Einhorn; Nancy Einhorn.
Foundation type: Independent foundation.
Financial data (yr. ended 12/31/12): Assets, $3,409,830 (M); gifts received, $100,010;

expenditures, $312,687; qualifying distributions, $312,632; giving activities include $306,500 for 28 grants (high: $50,000; low: $1,000).
Purpose and activities: Giving primarily for the arts and education.
Fields of interest: Museums (art); Performing arts, ballet; Arts; Higher education; Education.
Type of support: General/operating support.
Limitations: Applications accepted. Giving limited to the greater Milwaukee, WI area. No grants to individuals, or for annual campaigns or endowments.
Application information: Application forms are by invitation only, upon review of initial proposal. Application form required.
Initial approach: **Short proposal via U.S. mail or e-mail**
Deadline(s): None
Officers: Nancy Einhorn, Pres.; Stephen Einhorn, V.P.
EIN: 396643717

3614
The Elmwood Foundation, Inc.
2004 Kramer St.
La Crosse, WI 54603-2365 **(608) 781-0850**
Contact: Daniel Gelatt, Pres.; Margaret Berg, Secy.-Treas.

Incorporated in 1954 in WI.
Donors: Charles D. Gelatt; Northern Engraving and Manufacturing Co.
Foundation type: Independent foundation.
Financial data (yr. ended 06/30/13): Assets, $1,925,767 (M); gifts received, $25,000; expenditures, $117,112; qualifying distributions, $117,056; giving activities include $117,000 for 7 grants (high: $40,000; low: $5,000).
Fields of interest: Arts; Higher education; Youth development; YM/YWCAs & YM/YWHAs; Children/youth, services; United Ways and Federated Giving Programs.
Type of support: General/operating support; Continuing support; Annual campaigns; Building/renovation; Matching/challenge support.
Limitations: Applications accepted. Giving primarily in WI, with emphasis on the La Crosse area. No grants to individuals, or for seed money, emergency or endowment funds, deficit financing, equipment, land acquisition, scholarships, fellowships, research, special projects, publications, or conferences; no loans.
Application information: Application form not required.
Initial approach: Letter or telephone
Deadline(s): None
Officers: Daniel Gelatt, Pres.; Roberta K. Gelatt, V.P.; Margaret Berg, Secy.-Treas.
EIN: 396044165

3615
Fond du Lac Area Foundation
384 N. Main St., Ste. 4
Fond du Lac, WI 54935-2310 (920) 921-2215
Contact: Sandi Roehrig, Exec. Dir.
FAX: (920) 921-1036;
E-mail: info@fdlareafoundation.com; Main URL: http://www.fdlareafoundation.com
Facebook: https://www.facebook.com/pages/Fond-du-Lac-Area-Foundation/160412896964

Established as a trust in 1975 in WI.
Foundation type: Community foundation.
Financial data (yr. ended 12/31/12): Assets, $25,537,562 (M); gifts received, $693,703; expenditures, $1,571,343; giving activities include $1,130,037 for 507+ grants (high: $150,000; low: $25).
Purpose and activities: The foundation's purpose is to accept, manage, and distribute charitable contributions that will fulfill the needs and enhance the present and future quality of life within the Fond du Lac, WI, community.
Fields of interest: Arts; Education; Environment; Health care; Youth, services; Human services; Community/economic development.
Type of support: Program development; Seed money; Scholarship funds.
Limitations: Applications accepted. Giving limited to Fond du Lac, WI and the surrounding area. No support for religious organizations for religious purposes. No grants to individuals (except for scholarships), or for ongoing operating expenses or building funds, capital campaigns, endowments, debt reduction, scholarly research, fund drives, or for travel.
Publications: Application guidelines; Annual report (including application guidelines); Financial statement; Grants list; Informational brochure (including application guidelines); Newsletter.
Application information: Visit foundation Web site for application guidelines; contact the foundation to receive an application form. Application form required.
Initial approach: Telephone or letter
Copies of proposal: 1
Deadline(s): Jan. 15 and July 31
Board meeting date(s): Quarterly
Final notification: June 30 and Dec. 4
Officers and Directors:* Tom Herre,* Chair.; Steve Peterson,* Vice-Chair.; Patricia A. Miller,* Secy.; Stephen L. Franke,* Treas.; Sandi Roehrig, Exec. Dir.; Steven Cramer; Steven J. Dilling; Carol Hyland; Steven G. Millin; Paul Rosenfeldt; Mimi M. Sager; Jack E. Twohig; Scott Wittchow; Karen A. Wuest.
Number of staff: 3 full-time professional.
EIN: 510181570
Other changes: Mimi M. Sager is no longer a director.

3616
Fort Atkinson Community Foundation
244 N. Main St.
Fort Atkinson, WI 53538-1829 (920) 563-3210
Contact: For grants: Sue Hartwick, Prog. Admin.
E-mail: facf@fortfoundation.org; Main URL: http://fortfoundation.org/

Established in 1973 in WI.
Foundation type: Community foundation.
Financial data (yr. ended 06/30/12): Assets, $20,004,392 (M); gifts received, $527,691; expenditures, $655,268; giving activities include $260,418 for grants, and $266,717 for grants to individuals.
Purpose and activities: The mission of the foundation is to receive donations for educational, cultural, charitable, or benevolent purposes and use them to benefit residents and enhance the quality of life in the Fort Atkinson area.
Fields of interest: Arts; Education; Environment, beautification programs; Recreation; Human services; Community/economic development.
Type of support: General/operating support; Scholarships—to individuals.
Limitations: Applications accepted. Giving limited to the Fort Atkinson, WI, area. No support for sectarian or religious purposes. No grants to individuals (except through award or pre-established scholarship fund), or for endowment funds, debt retirement, wages or salary, or operating expenses (in response to annual fund drives or to eliminate previously incurred deficits).
Publications: Annual report.
Application information: Visit foundation web site for application guidelines. Application form required.
Initial approach: Contact foundation for application form
Deadline(s): Mar. 15, June 15, Sept. 15, and Dec. 15 for grants; varies for scholarships
Board meeting date(s): Jan., Apr., July, and Oct.
Final notification: Following board meetings
Officers and Directors:* Beth McLaughlin,* Chair.; W. Phil Niemeyer,* Vice-Chair.; James J. Vance,* Secy. and Legal Counsel; **Mary Behling**; Dean Brown; Christopher Rogers.
Trustee: Rod Ellenbecker; Ann Herdendorf; Premier Bank, N.A.
EIN: 396220899
Other changes: Phil Niemeyer is no longer a member of the governing body.

3617
Fund for Wisconsin Scholars, Inc.
(formerly Fund for Wisconsin Scholarship, Inc.)
P.O. Box 5506
Madison, WI 53705-0506 (608) 238-2400
Contact: Mary Gulbrandsen, Exec. Dir.
FAX: (608) 238-0044;
E-mail: mgulbrandsen@ffws.org; Main URL: http://www.ffws.org
GiveSmart: http://www.givesmart.org/Stories/Donors/Tashia-and-John-Morgridge
Tashia and John Morgridge's Giving Pledge Profile: http://glasspockets.org/philanthropy-in-focus/eye-on-the-giving-pledge/profiles/morgridge

Established in 2007 in WI.
Donors: John P. Morgridge; Tashia Morgridge; Ted Kellner; Mary Kellner.
Foundation type: Independent foundation.
Financial data (yr. ended 06/30/13): Assets, $159,913,107 (M); gifts received, $21,145,000; expenditures, $9,784,723; qualifying distributions, $8,195,192; giving activities include $7,861,579 for 2 grants (high: $7,038,353; low: $823,226), and $25,000 for 50 grants to individuals.
Purpose and activities: The fund provides need-based grants to support the access to and completion of college, to graduates of Wisconsin public high schools who are attending Wisconsin public colleges. The Fund for Wisconsin Scholars will help reduce the financial barriers to college and lighten the debt that many Wisconsin students incur during their college years by providing need-based grants.
Fields of interest: Higher education.
Type of support: Scholarships—to individuals.
Limitations: Applications not accepted. Giving limited to WI.
Publications: Annual report.
Application information: Unsolicited requests for funds not accepted. Students do not apply to the fund for grants. Recipients are randomly selected from a group of eligible students. Refer to the fund's web site for eligibility guidelines.
Officers and Directors:* John P. Morgridge,* Chair. and Pres.; David Ward,* V.P.; Ted Kellner,* Treas.; Mary W. Gulbrandsen,* Exec. Dir.; John Daniels, Jr.; Tashia F. Morgridge.
EIN: 261412296
Other changes: John P. Morgridge is now Chair. and Pres.

3618
Dudley and Constance Godfrey Foundation Inc.

P.O. Box 510260
Milwaukee, WI 53203-0054

Established in 1986 in WI.
Donors: Dudley J. Godfrey, Jr.; Constance P. Godfrey; D. Godfrey Jr. Charitable Lead Trust.
Foundation type: Independent foundation.
Financial data (yr. ended 12/31/13): Assets, $138,654 (M); gifts received, $393,400; expenditures, $652,439; qualifying distributions, $652,439; giving activities include $650,300 for 3 grants (high: $650,000; low: $100).
Fields of interest: Education.
Limitations: Applications not accepted. Giving primarily in WI. No grants to individuals.
Application information: Contributes only to pre-selected organizations.
Officers and Directors:* Constance P. Godfrey,* Pres. and Treas.; **J. Gardner Govan,* V.P. and Secy.**; Sue E. Christensen.
EIN: 391562846
Other changes: J. Gardner Govan has replaced Andrew R. Lauritzen as V.P. and Secy.

3619
Greater Green Bay Community Foundation, Inc.

310 W. Walnut St., Ste. 350
Green Bay, WI 54303-2734 (920) 432-0800
Contact: David Z. Pamperin, C.E.O.; For grants: Martha Ahrendt, V.P., Progs.
FAX: (920) 432-5577; E-mail: ggbcf@ggbcf.org; Grant inquiry e-mail: martha@ggbcf.org; Grant inquiry tel.: 920-432-0800; Main URL: http://www.ggbcf.org
Twitter: http://twitter.com/ggbcfoundation

Established in 1991 in WI.
Foundation type: Community foundation.
Financial data (yr. ended 06/30/12): Assets, $66,121,412 (M); gifts received, $4,747,123; expenditures, $4,580,878; giving activities include $4,035,684 for grants.
Purpose and activities: The foundation seeks to inspire and encourage charitable giving in northeastern Wisconsin by connecting caring people with solutions that strengthen the local community: 1) serving donors by providing a flexible and responsive vehicle for their charitable interests; 2) using resources wisely and efficiently through sensitive and creative grants addressing the emerging and changing needs of the community in the areas of the arts, education, health and human services, the youth and elderly, and resource conservation and preservation; 3) demonstrating community leadership by acting as a catalyst in identifying community needs and opportunities and sharing information with other foundations, corporations and organizations, both private and non-profit, to shape effective responses to those needs; and 4) acting as a responsible solicitor and prudent manager of philanthropic assets created by charitable gifts and bequests.
Fields of interest: Arts, cultural/ethnic awareness; Historic preservation/historical societies; Arts; Education; Environment; Health care; Alzheimer's disease; Diabetes; Youth development; Residential/custodial care, hospices; Human services; Community development, neighborhood development; Community/economic development; Infants/toddlers; Children/youth; Children; Adults; Aging; Young adults; Disabilities, people with; Physically disabled; Blind/visually impaired; Mentally disabled; Minorities; African Americans/Blacks; Hispanics/Latinos; Native Americans/American Indians; Military/veterans; Substance abusers; AIDS, people with; Single parents; Crime/abuse victims; Terminal illness, people with; Economically disadvantaged; Homeless.
Type of support: Continuing support; Management development/capacity building; Equipment; Computer technology; Emergency funds; Program development; Seed money; Curriculum development; Scholarship funds; Technical assistance; Program evaluation; Scholarships—to individuals; Matching/challenge support.
Limitations: Applications accepted. Giving limited to Brown, Door, Kewaunee, and Oconto counties, WI. No support for religious programs for religious purposes. No grants to individuals (except scholarships), or for annual or capital campaigns, endowments, capital improvement requests, fundraising activities or events, or debt retirement.
Publications: Application guidelines; Annual report; Financial statement; Informational brochure; Occasional report.
Application information: Visit foundation web site for grant application forms and guidelines per grant type. Faxed applications are not accepted. Application form required.
Initial approach: Contact foundation
Copies of proposal: 1
Deadline(s): Apr. 1 and Oct. 1 for Funds for Greater Green Bay grants; varies for others
Board meeting date(s): Mar., June, Sept., and Dec.
Final notification: Within 5 weeks of application deadline for Funds for Greater Green Bay grants
Officers and Board Members:* Tim Weyenberg,* Chair.; Mark McMullen,* Vice-Chair.; David Z. Pamperin,* C.E.O. and Pres.; Martha Ahrendt, Ph.D.*, V.P., Progs.; Christine Woleske,* Secy.; Mike Simmer,* Treas.; Jonathan J. Kubick, C.F.O.; Terry Fulwiler; Mark Kaspar; Charles Lieb; Gary Lofquist; Gail McNutt; Betsy Mitchell; Sue Olmsted; Therese Pandl; Mark Skogen; Adrian Ulatowski; and 7 additional board members.
Number of staff: 3 full-time professional; 3 part-time professional; 2 part-time support.
EIN: 391699966
Other changes: Janet Bonkowski, Dan Gulling, Michael Meeuwsen, Thomas Olson, Robert Rupp, and Chris Woleske are no longer board members.

3620
B.A. and Esther Greenheck Foundation

500 1st St., Ste. 2200
Wausau, WI 54403-4871

Established in WI.
Donors: Esther M. Greenheck Survivor's Trust; Bernard A. Greenheck Marital Trust.
Foundation type: Independent foundation.
Financial data (yr. ended 12/31/12): Assets, $44,483,702 (M); gifts received, $403,272; expenditures, $1,860,913; qualifying distributions, $1,498,751; giving activities include $1,232,917 for 59 grants (high: $128,086; low: $450).
Fields of interest: Education; Health care; Human services; Foundations (community); United Ways and Federated Giving Programs.
Limitations: Applications not accepted. Giving primarily in WI. No grants to individuals.
Application information: Unsolicited requests for funds not accepted.
Officer and Trustees:* Brian Gumness,* Exec. Dir.; Mark J. Bradley; Barb Brown; Pamela A. Coenen; Donald L. Grade; Sandra L. Gumness; **Eben Jackson**; Jon A. Jackson; Peter D. Jackson; Jean C. Tehan; Bob Weirauch.
EIN: 391937735
Other changes: At the close of 2012, the grantmaker paid grants of $1,232,917, a 317.8% increase over the 2011 disbursements, $295,102. Dave Johnson is no longer a trustee.

3621
Harley-Davidson Foundation, Inc.

3700 W. Juneau Ave.
P.O. Box 653
Milwaukee, WI 53208-2818 (414) 343-4001
Contact: Mary Ann Martiny, Secy. and Mgr.
E-mail: foundationapplications@Harley-Davidson.com; **Main URL: http://www.harley-davidson.com/en_US/Content/Pages/Company/Sustainability/Foundation/foundation.html?locale=en_US&bmLocale=en_US**
Grants List: http://www.harley-davidson.com/en_US/Media/downloads/Foundation/Grant-Recipients-2013.pdf

Established in 1994 in WI.
Donors: Harley-Davidson, Inc.; Karl Eberle; John Mink.
Foundation type: Company-sponsored foundation.
Financial data (yr. ended 12/31/12): Assets, $23,180,070 (M); gifts received, $2,000,135; expenditures, $2,637,159; qualifying distributions, $2,501,385; giving activities include $2,501,385 for 268 grants (high: $283,499; low: $30).
Purpose and activities: The foundation supports programs designed to meet basic needs of the community; improve the lives of Harley-Davidson stakeholders; and encourage social responsibility. Special emphasis is directed toward education programs within the public school systems located in areas of Harley-Davidson operations.
Fields of interest: Arts education; Arts; Elementary/secondary education; Education; Environment, natural resources; Botanical/horticulture/landscape services; Environmental education; Environment; Public health; Health care; Mental health/crisis services; Food services; Youth development; Human services; Community development, neighborhood development; Community/economic development; United Ways and Federated Giving Programs; Military/veterans' organizations.
Type of support: Capital campaigns; Program development; Conferences/seminars; Curriculum development; Scholarship funds; Employee volunteer services; Employee matching gifts.
Limitations: Applications accepted. **Giving primarily in areas of company operations in Mohave County and Yucca, AZ, Chicago, IL, Kansas City, MO, Valley View, OH; York, PA, Plano, TX, and Milwaukee, Menomonee Falls, Tomahawk, and Wauwatosa, WI; giving also to national organizations.** No support for political candidates, athletic teams, or religious organizations not of direct benefit to the entire community. No grants to individuals, or for political causes, general operating, or endowment funds.
Publications: Application guidelines; Corporate giving report; Grants list; IRS Form 990 or 990-PF printed copy available upon request.
Application information: National organizations or organizations requesting conference or capital campaign support must e-mail a letter of intent to the foundation. Application form required.
Initial approach: Complete online eligibility quiz and application

Copies of proposal: 1
***Deadline(s):* Mar. 7, July 11, Oct. 10, and Dec. 12**

Officers and Directors:* Tonit M. Calaway,* Pres.; John A. Olin,* V.P. and C.F.O.; J. Darrell Thomas, V.P. and Treas.; Mary Anne Martiny, Secy.; John P. Baker; Joanne M. Bischmann; Matthew S. Levatich; Patrick Smith.
EIN: 391769946

3622
The Eric D. & Steven D. Hovde Foundation
122 W. Washington Ave., Ste. 350
Madison, WI 53703-2758 (608) 255-5175, ext. 35
Contact: Jeffrey Boyd, Exec. Dir.
E-mail: jboyd@hovdefoundation.org; Main URL: http://www.hovdefoundation.org
Facebook: https://www.facebook.com/hovdefoundation

Established in 1998 in IL.
Donors: Eric D. Hovde; Steven D. Hovde; Curt Sidden; Jennifer Sidden; Hovde Financial, Inc.; Banco Popular North America; Hovde Capital I, LLC; The Lili Claire Foundation, Inc.; Ellis Management Svcs., Inc.
Foundation type: Independent foundation.
Financial data (yr. ended 12/31/12): Assets, $11,479,492 (M); gifts received, $483,950; expenditures, $1,275,397; qualifying distributions, $1,159,261; giving activities include $901,619 for 22 grants (high: $230,749; low: $500).
Purpose and activities: Giving to find a cure for Multiple Sclerosis (MS), and to help people in crisis situations, especially homeless children.
Fields of interest: Medical research, institute; Multiple sclerosis research; Human services; International development; Christian agencies & churches.
Limitations: Applications not accepted. Giving in the U.S., with emphasis on Washington, DC, and NY. No grants to individuals.
Application information: Contributes only to pre-selected organizations.
Officers: Jeffrey Cashdin, C.F.O.; Jeffrey Boyd, Exec. Dir.
Trustees: Eric D. Hovde; Steven D. Hovde; Richard J. Perry, Jr.
EIN: 522107093
Other changes: The grantmaker has moved from DC to WI.

3623
Incourage Community Foundation, Inc.
(formerly Community Foundation of Greater South Wood County, Inc.)
478 E. Grand Ave.
Wisconsin Rapids, WI 54494 (715) 423-3863
Contact: Kelly Ryan, C.E.O.; For grants: Dawn Vruwink, V.P., Community Resources
FAX: (715) 423-3019;
E-mail: hello@incouragecf.org; Grant request E-mail: dvruwink@incouragecf.org; Main URL: http://www.incouragecf.org
Blog: http://kellyincourage.blogspot.com
Facebook: https://www.facebook.com/incouragecf
LinkedIn: http://www.linkedin.com/company/incourage-community-foundation?trk=tyah
RSS Feed: http://incouragecf.org/feed/
Twitter: https://twitter.com/incouragecf
YouTube: http://www.youtube.com/incouragecf

Established in 1993 in WI.
Foundation type: Community foundation.
Financial data (yr. ended 12/31/13): Assets, $34,601,113 (M); gifts received, $908,742; expenditures, $3,069,105; giving activities include $665,661 for grants.
Purpose and activities: The foundation is a not-for-profit community foundation incorporated under the laws of the State of Wisconsin in 1993. Its primary mission is to promote strategic philanthropy, build social capital, and leverage community resources for the common good. The foundation's vision is a resilient, thriving community that embraces and supports all people. It receives and maintains funds to be utilized for philanthropic activities that meet the requirements of the foundation's governing documents.
Fields of interest: Museums (art); Performing arts; Performing arts, theater; Historic preservation/historical societies; Arts; Elementary/secondary education; Higher education; Education; Hospitals (general); Health care; Health organizations; Disasters, preparedness/services; Boys & girls clubs; Youth development; Children/youth, services; Family services; Aging, centers/services; Human services; Community/economic development.
Type of support: Management development/capacity building; Building/renovation; Equipment; Emergency funds; Program development; Seed money; Scholarship funds; Research; Technical assistance; Program-related investments/loans; Scholarships—to individuals; Matching/challenge support.
Limitations: Applications accepted. Giving limited to south Wood County, WI, and the Town of Rome. No support for religious organizations for sectarian purposes. No grants to individuals (except for scholarships), or for debt retirement, deficit financing, fundraising activities, endowment funds, operating expenses for United Way agencies, routine operating needs, annual fundraising, capital fund drives, or for umbrella funding.
Publications: Application guidelines; Financial statement; Informational brochure; Newsletter.
Application information: Visit foundation web site for application form and guidelines. Application form required.
Initial approach: Telephone, e-mail, or letter of inquiry
Copies of proposal: 1
Deadline(s): None
Board meeting date(s): At least quarterly
Final notification: 4 to 6 weeks
Officers and Directors:* Helen Jungwirth,* Chair.; Carl Wartman,* Vice-Chair.; Kelly Ryan,* C.E.O. and Pres.; Dawn Vruwink,* V.P., Community Resources; Mary Wirtz,* V.P., Donor Svcs.; Dawn Neuman,* C.F.O. and C.O.O.; Kirk Willard,* Secy.; **Dale Bikowski; Paul Liebherr; Kristie Rauter**.
Number of staff: 11 full-time professional; 2 part-time professional; 3 full-time support; 4 part-time support.
EIN: 391772651
Other changes: Sandra Hughes is no longer a director.

3624
Jeffris Family Foundation, Ltd.
P.O. Box 1160
Janesville, WI 53547-1160 (608) 757-1039
Contact: Thomas M. Jeffris, Pres.
FAX: (608) 757-2352;
E-mail: info@jeffrisfoundation.org; Main URL: http://www.jeffrisfoundation.org/

Established in 1977 in WI.
Donor: Thomas M. Jeffris.
Foundation type: Independent foundation.
Financial data (yr. ended 12/31/12): Assets, $23,838,926 (M); gifts received, $100; expenditures, $2,277,655; qualifying distributions, $2,059,427; giving activities include $1,814,463 for 20 grants (high: $350,000; low: $1,000).
Purpose and activities: Giving primarily to: 1) support the preservation of history and culture and the unique sense of place in small towns and cities; 2) develop significant historic sites in eight Midwestern states; 3) assure sustainability and quality restoration through good research and planning; and 4) inspire and motivate community leaders and local families to support historic preservation in their towns.
Fields of interest: Historic preservation/historical societies.
Type of support: Building/renovation; Matching/challenge support.
Limitations: Giving primarily in IA, IL, IN, MI, MN, MO, OH, and WI. No grants to individuals, or for endowments, maintenance projects, acquisition, debt, operating budgets, or compensation.
Publications: Application guidelines; Informational brochure.
Application information:
Initial approach: Use preliminary request form on foundation web site
Copies of proposal: 4
Board meeting date(s): Fall
Officers and Directors:* Thomas M. Jeffris,* Pres.; Roman Vetter; Royce Yeater.
EIN: 391281879
Other changes: At the close of 2012, the grantmaker paid grants of $1,814,463, a 56.6% increase over the 2011 disbursements, $1,158,492.
Peggy Sheridan is no longer V.P. and Secy. Henry E. Fuldner is no longer V.P.

3625
SC Johnson Giving, Inc.
(formerly SC Johnson Fund, Inc.)
1525 Howe St.
Racine, WI 53403-2237
***E-mail:* USCommu@scj.com**; Main URL: http://www.scjohnson.com/en/commitment/focus-on/creating/giving-back.aspx

Incorporated in 1959 in WI.
Donors: S.C. Johnson & Son, Inc.; JohnsonDiversey, Inc.
Foundation type: Company-sponsored foundation.
Financial data (yr. ended 06/28/13): Assets, $12,694,284 (M); gifts received, $8,353,831; expenditures, $3,120,447; qualifying distributions, $3,076,928; giving activities include $3,049,510 for 105 grants (high: $886,693; low: $25).
Purpose and activities: The foundation supports organizations involved with arts and culture, education, the environment, health, social services, and community development.
Fields of interest: Museums; Performing arts; Humanities; Historic preservation/historical societies; Arts; Elementary/secondary education; Higher education; Education; Environment, pollution control; Environment, natural resources; Environment, energy; Environment, beautification programs; Environment; Animal welfare; Employment, training; Athletics/sports, amateur leagues; Youth, services; Family services, domestic violence; Homeless, human services; Human services; Community/economic

development; United Ways and Federated Giving Programs; Economically disadvantaged.
Type of support: General/operating support; Management development/capacity building; Annual campaigns; Capital campaigns; Building/renovation; Equipment; Endowments; Program development; Seed money; Scholarship funds; Sponsorships; Employee matching gifts; Employee-related scholarships.
Limitations: Applications accepted. Giving primarily in areas of company operations in Racine, WI. No support for political, religious, social, athletic, veterans', labor, or fraternal organizations, United Way-supported organizations, or national health organizations. **No grants to individuals (except for scholarships) or for staff or administrative payrolls.**
Publications: Application guidelines; Corporate giving report.
Application information: Support is limited to 1 contribution per organization during any given year. Additional information may be requested at a later date. Organizations receiving grants of more than $5,000 are expected to submit an outcome report at the end of the project or program year. Application form not required.
Initial approach: **Complete online application**
Copies of proposal: 1
Deadline(s): **None**
Board meeting date(s): Feb., June, and Oct.
Final notification: **90 to 120 days**
Officers and Trustees:* H. Fisk Johnson III,* Chair. and C.E.O.; Kelly M. Semrau, Vice-Chair. and Pres.; **Gregory L. Anderegg, V.P. and Secy.**; Steven M. Carter, V.P. and Treas.
Number of staff: 2 full-time professional; 2 part-time professional; 2 part-time support.
EIN: 396052089
Other changes: Gregory L. Anderegg is now V.P. and Secy. Jeffrey M. Waller is no longer V.P. and Treas.
The grantmaker now makes its application guidelines available online.

3626
J. J. Keller Foundation, Inc.

(formerly Keller Foundation, Inc.)
3003 Breezewood Ln.
P.O. Box 368
Neenah, WI 54957-0368 (920) 720-7872
Contact: Mary Harp-Jirschele, Exec. Dir.
FAX: (920) 727-7503;
E-mail: mharp-jirschele@jjkeller.com; Main URL: http://www.jjkellerfoundation.org
Grants List: http://www.jjkellerfoundation.org/grants/grant-recipients/

Established in 1990 in WI.
Donors: J.J. Keller & Associates, Inc.; John J. and Ethel D. Keller†.
Foundation type: Independent foundation.
Financial data (yr. ended 12/31/12): Assets, $66,098,662 (M); expenditures, $3,545,149; qualifying distributions, $3,545,149; giving activities include $3,495,095 for grants, and $50,054 for 139 employee matching gifts.
Purpose and activities: The foundation supports programs designed to positively impact lives in the greater Fox Valley community, including the homeless, disadvantaged, elderly, children, and youth. Special emphasis is directed toward initiatives designed to promote physical and mental health and healing; human services; education programs; preventative programs; and critical community needs.
Fields of interest: Health care; Mental health/crisis services; Aging, centers/services; Homeless, human services; Human services; Aging; Mentally disabled; Economically disadvantaged.
Type of support: Employee matching gifts; General/operating support; Matching/challenge support; Program development.
Limitations: Applications accepted. Giving primarily in Fox Valley, WI. **No support for political organizations or for youth, adult sports programs, or schools.** No grants to individuals, or for raffle tickets or door prizes, endowments, or capital campaigns.
Publications: Application guidelines; Annual report; Grants list.
Application information: Additional information may be requested at a later date. A site visit may be requested. Organizations receiving support are asked to submit a final report. Application form required.
Initial approach: **Complete eligibility quiz on foundation web site**
Copies of proposal: 1
Deadline(s): None; small requests reviewed monthly; large requests reviewed in Mar., June, Sept., and Dec.
Board meeting date(s): Quarterly
Final notification: 30 days for grants of $15,000 or less; 120 days for grants larger than $15,000
Officers and Directors:* Robert L. Keller,* Pres.; James J. Keller,* V.P. and Treas.; Marne Keller-Krikava, Secy.; Mary Harp-Jirschele, Exec. Dir.; Brian Keller.
Number of staff: 1 full-time professional.
EIN: 391683437

3627
The Kern Family Foundation, Inc.

W305 S4239 Brookhill Rd.
Waukesha, WI 53189-9126 **(262) 968-6838**
E-mail: info@kffdn.org; Main URL: http://www.kffdn.org/

Established in 1998 in WI.
Donors: Robert D. Kern; Patricia E. Kern.
Foundation type: Independent foundation.
Financial data (yr. ended 12/31/12): Assets, $627,060,713 (M); gifts received, $200; expenditures, $32,062,515; qualifying distributions, $32,020,538; giving activities include $27,197,469 for 236 grants (high: $3,000,000; low: $190), $338,434 for 2 foundation-administered programs and $1,000,000 for 1 loan/program-related investment.
Purpose and activities: The foundation's purpose is to seek to enhance and encourage religious values, family and community competitive educational structures, and moral and ethical values in society. The foundation supports the promotion of religious values in religious ministry and promotes the study and enhancement of competitive educational structures in the U.S.
Fields of interest: Education; Youth development; Protestant agencies & churches.
Type of support: Program development; Scholarship funds.
Limitations: Applications not accepted. Giving primarily in the Midwest. No support for individual public or private K-12 schools. No grants to individuals, or for endowments, indirect costs as part of the grant request, debt reduction, or annual fund drives for sustaining support.
Application information: Unsolicited proposals are not accepted.
Board meeting date(s): Jan., Apr., July, and Oct.
Officers and Directors:* Marcia Peterson,* Chair.; James Rahn,* Pres.; **Daniel Kelly, V.P.**; Robert D. Kern,* V.P.; Richard A. Van Deuren, Secy.; Michael Senske, C.F.O. and Treas.; Rick Graber; Deborah Kern; Patricia E. Kern; William (Chip) H. Mellor; Dawn Tabat; Hermann Viets.
Number of staff: 4 full-time professional; 1 full-time support.
EIN: 391923558

3628
John & Ruth Kloss Charitable Trust

c/o US Bank N.A.
P.O. Box 2043
Milwaukee, WI 53201-9668
Application address: **c/o U.S. Bank, N.A. Foundation Team, 777 E. Wisconsin Ave., MK-WI-TWPT, Milwaukee, WI 53202, tel.: (414) 765-5672**

Established in 2006 in WI.
Foundation type: Independent foundation.
Financial data (yr. ended 05/31/13): Assets, $8,937,208 (M); expenditures, $524,453; qualifying distributions, $426,074; giving activities include $414,000 for 34 grants (high: $48,000; low: $2,000).
Fields of interest: Education; Animal welfare; Human services.
Limitations: Applications accepted. Giving primarily in southeastern WI, with emphasis on Kenosha County.
Application information: Application form required.
Initial approach: Letter requesting application form
Deadline(s): None
Board Members: Bryan Albrecht; John Antaramian; Jane Harrington-Heide; Mary Plunkett.
Trustee: U.S. Bank, N.A.
EIN: 396790033

3629
Kohler Foundation, Inc.

725 Woodlake Rd., Ste. X
Kohler, WI 53044-1354 (920) 458-1972
Contact: Terri Yoho, Exec. Dir.
FAX: (920) 458-4280;
E-mail: terri.yoho@kohler.com; Main URL: http://www.kohlerfoundation.org
Facebook: https://www.facebook.com/kohlerfoundation
Twitter: https://twitter.com/KohlerFdn

Incorporated in 1940 in WI.
Donors: Herbert V. Kohler†; Marie C. Kohler†; Evangeline Kohler†; Lillie B. Kohler†; O.A. Kroos†.
Foundation type: Independent foundation.
Financial data (yr. ended 12/31/12): Assets, $201,620,916 (M); expenditures, $8,845,567; qualifying distributions, $8,757,756; giving activities include $262,001 for 60 grants (high: $100,000; low: $400), $356,771 for 98 grants to individuals (high: $15,000; low: $1,250), $6,068,992 for 21 in-kind gifts, and $1,301,981 for 2 foundation-administered programs.
Purpose and activities: Supports education and the arts in WI. Annual program funds provide scholarships for students graduating from Sheboygan County high schools. All scholarship recipients are chosen by their schools. The Distinguished Guest Series, a performing arts series, is presented as a cultural benefit to the community.
Fields of interest: Visual arts; Performing arts; Arts; Higher education; Education.

Type of support: Program development; Seed money; Scholarships—to individuals.
Limitations: Applications accepted. Giving limited to WI, primarily in Sheboygan County. No support for health care or medical programs. No grants to individuals (except for scholarships in Sheboygan County), or for operating budgets, capital campaigns, or annual fundraising drives; no loans.
Application information: See foundation web site for additional application information.
Initial approach: Online application form
Copies of proposal: 1
Deadline(s): Mar. 15th and Sept. 15th
Board meeting date(s): June, Dec. and as required
Final notification: 1 week after contributions meetings
Officers and Directors:* Natalie A. Black,* Pres.; Jeffrey P. Cheney,* V.P. and Treas.; Paul H. Ten Pas,* Secy.; Terri Yoho, Exec. Dir.
Number of staff: 5 full-time professional; 1 part-time support.
EIN: 390810536

3630
The John E. Kuenzl Foundation Inc.
c/o Cliftolarsonallen LLP
P.O. Box 2886
Oshkosh, WI 54903-2886 (920) 231-5890
Contact: Gerald J. Stadtmueller, Dir.

Established in 2000 in WI.
Donors: Sheboygan Beverage, Inc.; Gambrinus Enterprises; John E. Kuenzl†.
Foundation type: Company-sponsored foundation.
Financial data (yr. ended 12/31/12): Assets, $21,362,444 (M); expenditures, $1,159,083; qualifying distributions, $1,079,172; giving activities include $1,071,400 for 45 grants (high: $175,000; low: $1,000).
Purpose and activities: The foundation supports museums, fire departments, and community foundations and organizations involved with performing arts, hunger, housing development, and human services.
Fields of interest: Agriculture/food; Human services; Community/economic development.
Type of support: General/operating support.
Limitations: Applications accepted. Giving primarily in WI. No grants to individuals.
Application information: Application form required.
***Initial approach:* Letter**
Deadline(s): Dec. 1
Directors: Norma Kuenzl; Gerald Stadtmueller; James J. Williamson.
EIN: 391998578

3631
La Crosse Community Foundation
300 2nd St. N., Ste. 320
La Crosse, WI 54601-2001 (608) 782-3223
Contact: Sheila Garrity, Exec. Dir.
FAX: (608) 782-3222;
E-mail: lacrosscommfoundation@centurytel.net;
Main URL: http://www.laxcommfoundation.com
E-Newsletter: http://visitor.constantcontact.com/manage/optin/ea?v=0011QHrsLot1-fGgHBL9f8nDtZNIU9IU3pFQc49_C5NhtUsUdxyXr_IyY1QuOLXRS0qychke9acyjLwfe-17tK0lg%3D%3D
Facebook: http://www.facebook.com/pages/La-Crosse-Community-Foundation/148545897282

Established in 1930 in WI.
Foundation type: Community foundation.
Financial data (yr. ended 12/31/12): Assets, $54,458,678 (M); gifts received, $4,120,016; expenditures, $3,583,541; giving activities include $2,563,512 for 60+ grants (high: $353,974), and $195,645 for 186 grants to individuals.
Purpose and activities: The purpose of the foundation is to enrich the quality of life in the greater La Crosse area by: 1) attracting charitable gifts promoting community philanthropy; 2) serving as a steward for entrusted funds and using these precious resources wisely and efficiently; 3) supporting programs and activities of economic, educational, social and cultural nonprofit organizations; 4) providing leadership by serving as a convenor/catalyst in identifying problems and opportunities and shaping effective responses to them; and 5) being a community resource and providing services to donors, nonprofit agencies and the community-at-large.
Fields of interest: Arts; Higher education; Education; Health care; Recreation; Children/youth, services; Family services; Human services; Government/public administration; Children/youth; Youth; Adults; Aging; Young adults; Disabilities, people with; Physically disabled; Blind/visually impaired; Deaf/hearing impaired; Minorities; Asians/Pacific Islanders; African Americans/Blacks; Women; Substance abusers; Single parents; Immigrants/refugees; Economically disadvantaged; Homeless; LGBTQ.
Type of support: General/operating support; Continuing support; Capital campaigns; Equipment; Program development; Seed money; Curriculum development; Scholarship funds; Scholarships—to individuals; Matching/challenge support.
Limitations: Applications accepted. Giving primarily in La Crosse County, WI, and surrounding area. No support for sectarian or religious purposes. No grants to individuals (except for scholarships), or for operating expenses of well-established organizations, deficit financing, endowment funds, travel, land acquisition, consulting services, or technical assistance; no loans.
Publications: Annual report (including application guidelines).
Application information: Visit foundation web site for application information; contact foundation for initial application form and guidelines. Application form required.
Initial approach: Telephone
Deadline(s): Submit proposal by the 15th of Jan., Apr., July, and Oct.
Board meeting date(s): Feb., May, Aug., and Nov.
Final notification: Within 1 month of committee meetings
Officers and Directors:* Sue Christopherson,* Chair.; Sandy Brekke,* Vice-Chair.; Barb Erickson,* Secy.; Sheila Garrity, Exec. Dir.; T.J. Brooks; Larry Kirch; Julie S. Nordeen; Todd Poss; Tom Sleik; **Brent Smith**; Randy Smith; Gina Yang.
Trustee: North Central Trust Co.
Number of staff: 1 full-time professional; 2 part-time professional; 1 part-time support.
EIN: 396037996
Other changes: Barb Erickson and Roger Le Grand are no longer directors.

3632
The Manitowoc Company Foundation
(formerly Welbilt Corporation Foundation)
2400 S. 44th St.
Manitowoc, WI 54220-5846
Contact: S. Powers

Established in 1972 in MI.
Donors: Kysor Industrial Corp.; Manitowoc Company.
Foundation type: Company-sponsored foundation.
Financial data (yr. ended 05/31/12): Assets, $1,880,972 (M); gifts received, $158,525; expenditures, $163,310; qualifying distributions, $156,322; giving activities include $151,525 for 40 grants (high: $75,000; low: $100).
Purpose and activities: The foundation supports organizations involved with education, health, cancer, and human services.
Fields of interest: Higher education; Libraries (public); Education; Health care, patient services; Health care; Cancer; Boys & girls clubs; Big Brothers/Big Sisters; American Red Cross; YM/YWCAs & YM/YWHAs; Children/youth, services; Human services; United Ways and Federated Giving Programs.
Type of support: General/operating support; Continuing support; Capital campaigns; Building/renovation; Publication; Research.
Limitations: Applications not accepted. Giving primarily in areas of company operations in CO, GA, LA, MD, PA, and TX; giving also to national organizations. No support for political organizations, religious organizations not of direct benefit to the entire community, or national or international organizations. No grants to individuals or for political campaigns.
Application information: Contributes only to pre-selected organizations.
Officers: Michael J. Kachner, Pres.; Maurice D. Jones, V.P. and Secy.; Carl J. Laurino, V.P. and Treas.; W. David Wrench,* V.P.
EIN: 237199469
Other changes: John G. Oros is no longer V.P. and Treas. Irwin M. Shur is no longer Secy.

3633
Marshfield Area Community Foundation
P.O. Box 456
Marshfield, WI 54449-0456 (715) 384-9029
Contact: Amber Kigins-Leifheit, Exec. Dir.
FAX: (715) 384-9229;
E-mail: macf@marshfieldareacommunityfoundation.org; Main URL: http://marshfieldareacommunityfoundation.org/

Established in 1993 in WI.
Donors: Harry Chronquist†; Gladys Chronquist†; G. Stanley Custer†; Violet Custer†; Leonard L. Hartl†; Margaret Quirt Heck†; Melvin A. Hintz†; LaVerne R. Kohs†; Patrice LeGrand†; J.P. Leonard†; George Mac Kinnon†; Anne Adler; Bette Adler; Joseph Lang†; Floyd Hamus; Pat Hamus; Margaret B. King†; Dennis DeVetter; Roberta DeVetter.
Foundation type: Community foundation.
Financial data (yr. ended 06/30/13): Assets, $5,639,442 (M); gifts received, $380,383; expenditures, $287,600; giving activities include $131,405 for 6+ grants (high: $27,355), and $51,802 for grants to individuals.
Purpose and activities: The purpose of the foundation is to receive and accept property exclusively for educational, recreational, artistic/cultural, conservation, community development, charitable or benevolent purposes for the benefit and improvement of residents of the Marshfield, WI, area.
Fields of interest: Arts; Education; Environment; Animals/wildlife; Recreation; Community development, neighborhood development; Community/economic development; Religion; Infants/toddlers; Children/youth; Children; Youth; Adults; Aging; Young adults; Physically disabled; Mentally disabled; Minorities; Hispanics/Latinos;

Women; Infants/toddlers, female; Girls; Adults, women; Young adults, female; Men; Infants/ toddlers, male; Boys; Adults, men; Young adults, male; Military/veterans; Single parents; Crime/ abuse victims; Immigrants/refugees; Economically disadvantaged; Migrant workers.
Type of support: General/operating support; Continuing support; Management development/ capacity building; Annual campaigns; Equipment; Endowments; Program development; Conferences/ seminars; Publication; Scholarship funds; Technical assistance; Grants to individuals; Scholarships—to individuals; In-kind gifts; Matching/challenge support.
Limitations: Applications accepted. Giving limited to Marshfield, WI and surrounding areas. No grants for capital campaigns or debt reduction.
Publications: Application guidelines; Annual report; Financial statement; Grants list; Informational brochure; Informational brochure (including application guidelines); Newsletter.
Application information: Visit foundation web site for application form and guidelines. Application form required.
Initial approach: Submit application form and attachments
Copies of proposal: 8
***Deadline(s):* June 2**
Board meeting date(s): Third Tues. in Jan., Feb., Apr., May, Sept., Oct., and Nov.
Final notification: Following Sept. board meeting
Officers and Trustees:* Marty Reinhart,* Chair.; Pat Saucerman,* Vice-Chair.; Amber Kiggens-Leifheit, Exec. Dir.; Kathleen Anderson; **Ed Englehart**; **Bill Heiting**; Paula Jero; Scott Larson; Graham Olson; Pete Schmeling; Patricia Stuhr; Ron Wilczek; Don Zais.
Number of staff: 1 part-time professional; 1 part-time support.
EIN: 396578767
Other changes: William Berry, Alan L. Billings, Amanda Lang, Pat Saucerman, and Tim Schultz are no longer trustees.

3634
Faye McBeath Foundation
101 W. Pleasant St., Ste. 210
Milwaukee, WI 53212-3963
Contact: Scott E. Gelzer, Exec. Dir.
FAX: (414) 272-6235;
E-mail: info@fayemcbeath.org; Main URL: http://www.fayemcbeath.org

Trust established in 1964 in WI.
Donor: Faye McBeath†.
Foundation type: Independent foundation.
Financial data (yr. ended 12/31/12): Assets, $2,453,272 (M); gifts received, $1,564; expenditures, $1,342,734; qualifying distributions, $1,185,659; giving activities include $997,854 for 47 grants (high: $65,000; low: $250).
Purpose and activities: Giving to benefit the people of Wisconsin by providing homes and care for elderly persons, promoting education in medical science and public health, providing medical, nursing, and hospital care for the sick and disabled, promoting the welfare of children, and promoting research in civics and government, directed towards improvement in the efficiency of local government.
Fields of interest: Education, early childhood education; Elementary school/education; Secondary school/education; Medical school/ education; Dental care; Nursing care; Health care; Substance abuse, services; Mental health/crisis services; Health organizations, association; AIDS; Alcoholism; Biomedicine; Nutrition; Youth development, citizenship; Human services; Children/youth, services; Child development, services; Family services; Residential/custodial care, hospices; Aging, centers/services; Public policy, research; Government/public administration; Public affairs, citizen participation; Aging.
Type of support: General/operating support; Continuing support; Program development; Seed money; Technical assistance; Matching/challenge support.
Limitations: Applications not accepted. Giving limited to WI, with emphasis on the greater Milwaukee area, including Milwaukee, Ozaukee, Waukesha and Washington counties. No grants to individuals, or for annual campaigns, capital projects, scholarships, fellowships, or specific medical or scientific research projects; grants rarely for emergency funds; no loans.
Publications: Annual report; Grants list; Informational brochure; Program policy statement.
Application information: Unsolicited requests for funds not accepted.
Board meeting date(s): Feb., May, Sept., Dec.
Officers and Trustees:* P. Michael Mahoney,* Chair.; Mary T. Kellner,* Vice-Chair.; Gregory Wesley,* Secy.; Scott E. Gelzer, Exec. Dir.; Sara E. Aster; Steven J. Smith.
Number of staff: 1 part-time professional; 1 part-time support.
EIN: 396074450

3635
McDonough Foundation
c/o Chris Noyes
780 N. Water St.
Milwaukee, WI 53202-3590
***Application address:* 230 Northgate St., Ste. 304, Lake forest, IL 60045**

Established in 1987 in WI.
Donors: John J. McDonough; Midwest Dental Products Corp.; Marilyn N. McDonough.
Foundation type: Independent foundation.
Financial data (yr. ended 09/30/13): Assets, $16,364 (M); gifts received, $195,000; expenditures, $194,236; qualifying distributions, $193,475; giving activities include $191,450 for 16 grants (high: $50,000; low: $100).
Purpose and activities: Giving primarily for diabetes organizations.
Fields of interest: Arts; Higher education, university; Education; Health care, clinics/centers; Health organizations, association; Diabetes; Human services; Catholic agencies & churches.
Type of support: General/operating support.
Limitations: Applications not accepted. Giving primarily in FL and IL. No grants to individuals.
Application information: Contributes only to pre-selected organizations.
Officers and Directors:* Allison McDonough,* Pres.; Marilyn N. McDonough,* Secy.; John J. McDonough,* Treas.
EIN: 391627844

3636
Menasha Corporation Foundation
P.O. Box 367
Neenah, WI 54957-0367 (920) 751-2036
Contact: Kevin Schuh, Treas.
Main URL: http://www.menasha.com/Foundation

Established in 1953 in WI.
Donor: Menasha Corp.
Foundation type: Company-sponsored foundation.
Financial data (yr. ended 12/31/13): Assets, $2,369,799 (M); gifts received, $1,493,000; expenditures, $917,596; qualifying distributions, $905,537; giving activities include $802,047 for 464 grants (high: $56,250; low: $50), $66,000 for 44 grants to individuals (high: $1,500; low: $1,500), and $37,490 for 84 employee matching gifts.
Purpose and activities: The foundation supports programs designed to promote safe and healthy citizens; an educated society; community betterment; and environmental sustainability.
Fields of interest: Arts; Higher education; Education; Health care.
Type of support: General/operating support; Employee volunteer services; Employee matching gifts; Scholarships—to individuals.
Limitations: Applications accepted. Giving primarily in areas of company operations in Neenah, WI. No grants to individuals (except for employee-related scholarships).
Application information: Application form not required.
Initial approach: Proposal
Copies of proposal: 1
Deadline(s): None
Board meeting date(s): Mar., June, Sept. and Dec.
Officers and Directors:* Jim Kotek, Chair.; Mike Waite,* Pres.; Tom Rettler,* V.P.; Angie Burns, Secy.; Kevin Schuh, Treas.; Andy Gansner; Pierce Smith; Bill Ash.
EIN: 396047384

3637
Greater Milwaukee Foundation
(formerly Milwaukee Foundation)
101 W. Pleasant St., Ste. 210
Milwaukee, WI 53212 (414) 272-5805
FAX: (414) 272-6235;
E-mail: info@greatermilwaukeefoundation.org; Main URL: http://www.greatermilwaukeefoundation.org
Facebook: http://www.facebook.com/GreaterMilwaukeeFoundation
Twitter: http://twitter.com/grmkefdn

Established in 1915 in WI by declaration of trust.
Foundation type: Community foundation.
Financial data (yr. ended 12/31/12): Assets, $612,115,000 (M); gifts received, $28,421,000; expenditures, $36,659,000; giving activities include $30,050,000 for 3,414 grants.
Purpose and activities: Present funds include many discretionary funds and some funds designated by the donors to benefit specific institutions or for special purposes, including educational institutions, arts and cultural programs, community development, social services, and health care; support also for conservation and historic preservation.
Fields of interest: Visual arts; Performing arts; Performing arts, dance; Historic preservation/ historical societies; Arts; Education, early childhood education; Child development, education; Elementary school/education; Secondary school/ education; Higher education; Adult/continuing education; Education; Environment, natural resources; Environment; Animal welfare; Reproductive health, family planning; Health care; Substance abuse, services; Mental health/crisis services; Health organizations, association; Parkinson's disease; AIDS; Nerve, muscle & bone research; Multiple sclerosis research; Diabetes research; Lupus research; Medical research; Crime/ violence prevention, youth; Legal services; Employment, training; Employment; Food services; Nutrition; Housing/shelter, development;

Recreation; Youth development; Children/youth, services; Child development, services; Family services; Aging, centers/services; Women, centers/services; Homeless, human services; Human services; Civil rights, race/intergroup relations; Urban/community development; Community/economic development; Public policy, research; Government/public administration; Children/youth; Youth; Adults; Aging; Young adults; Disabilities, people with; Minorities; Girls; Military/veterans; Offenders/ex-offenders; AIDS, people with; Economically disadvantaged; Homeless; LGBTQ.
Type of support: Continuing support; Management development/capacity building; Capital campaigns; Building/renovation; Equipment; Land acquisition; Emergency funds; Program development; Seed money; Fellowships; Scholarship funds; Research; Technical assistance; Program evaluation; Scholarships—to individuals; Matching/challenge support.
Limitations: Applications accepted. Giving primarily in Milwaukee, Ozaukee, Washington, and Waukesha counties, WI. No support for 501(c)(4)s or 501(c)(6) s. No support for the general use of churches or for sectarian religious purposes, except from donor advised and designated funds. **No grants to individuals (except for established awards), or for ongoing operating expenses, debt reduction, or agency endowments.**
Publications: Application guidelines; Annual report; Financial statement; Grants list; Informational brochure; Newsletter; Program policy statement.
Application information: Visit foundation web site for online letter of inquiry and application guidelines. The foundation's staff will invite selected applicants to submit full proposals based on letter of inquiry. Application form required.
Initial approach: Set up and complete an organizational profile on Philanthropy Online
Copies of proposal: 1
Deadline(s): Quarterly
Board meeting date(s): Mar., June, Sept., Dec., and as needed
Final notification: 1 week after board meetings
Officers and Directors:* Thomas L. Spero,* Chair.; David J. Lubar,* Vice-Chair.; Ellen M. Gilligan,* C.E.O. and Pres.; Kathryn Dunn, V.P., Community Investment; **Timothy Larson, V.P., Philanthropic Svcs.; Susan M. Smith, V.P., Mktg. and Comms.**; Marcus White, V.P., Civic Engagement; Patti Dew,* C.F.O., V.P., Finance and Admin., Secy., and Treas.; Wendy Ponting, Cont.; **Wendy Reed Bosworth**; Peter W. Bruce; Ness Flores; Janine P. Geske; Cecelia Gore; Jacqueline Herd-Barber; Paul J. Jones; Judy Jorgenson; David J. Kundert; Gregory S. Marcus; Cory L. Nettles.
Number of staff: 22 full-time professional; 4 part-time professional; 9 full-time support; 1 part-time support.
EIN: 396036407
Other changes: Thomas L. Spero has replaced Peter W. Bruce as Chair. David J. Lubar has replaced Thomas L. Spero as Vice-Chair. David J. Lubar is now Vice-Chair. Marcus White is now V.P., Civic Engagement. Timothy Larson is now V.P., Philanthropic Svcs. Rafael J. Acevedo, Jr. is now Philanthropic Advisor. Marybeth Budisch is now Philanthropic Advisor. Will Janisch is now Philanthopic Adviser. John W. Daniels and Mary B. Read are no longer directors.

3638
Harry and Virginia Murray Foundation
c/o U.S. Bank, N.A.
P.O. Box 2043
Milwaukee, WI 53201-9116
***Application address:* c/o U.S. Bank, N.A., 201 Jefferson St., Burlington, IA 52601-5250, tel.: (319) 753-8761**

Established in IA.
Foundation type: Independent foundation.
Financial data (yr. ended 12/31/12): Assets, $8,499,936 (M); gifts received, $58,231; expenditures, $456,441; qualifying distributions, $371,692; giving activities include $364,000 for 18 grants (high: $100,000; low: $1,000).
Fields of interest: Historic preservation/historical societies; Education; Health organizations; Salvation Army; Human services; Protestant agencies & churches.
Type of support: Capital campaigns.
Limitations: Applications accepted. Giving limited to Des Moines County, IA. No grants to individuals.
Application information:
Initial approach: Letter
Deadline(s): None
Trustee: U.S. Bank, N.A.
EIN: 426291207

3639
Neese Family Foundation, Inc.
2870 Riverside Dr.
Beloit, WI 53511-1506 (608) 368-1200

Incorporated in 1986 in IL.
Donors: Margaret L. Neese 1957 Trust; Robert H. Neese Trust of 1954.
Foundation type: Independent foundation.
Financial data (yr. ended 06/30/13): Assets, $2,663,181 (M); gifts received, $3,131; expenditures, $500,979; qualifying distributions, $493,868; giving activities include $487,858 for 5 grants (high: $417,858; low: $2,000).
Fields of interest: Higher education; Libraries (public); Hospitals (general); Human services; YM/YWCAs & YM/YWHAs; United Ways and Federated Giving Programs.
Type of support: Endowments; Annual campaigns; General/operating support; Capital campaigns; Building/renovation; Scholarship funds.
Limitations: Applications accepted. Giving primarily in WI. No grants to individuals.
Application information: Application form not required.
Initial approach: Letter
Deadline(s): None
Board meeting date(s): Varies
Officers: Margaret L.N. Brooks, Pres.; Robert H. Neese, V.P.; Gary G. Grabowski, Secy.-Treas.
Director: Wendy L. Neese.
EIN: 363473918

3640
Victor & Mary D. Nelson Scholarship Fund
c/o BMO Harris Bank, N.A.
P.O. Box 2980
Milwaukee, WI 53201-2980
Scholarship address: **c/o William Retinstrand, Superior Senior High School, 2600 Catlin Ave., Superior, WI 54880, tel.: (715) 384-0271**

Established in 1973 in WI.
Donor: Mary D. Nelson†.
Foundation type: Independent foundation.
Financial data (yr. ended 06/30/13): Assets, $4,802,303 (M); expenditures, $273,483; qualifying distributions, $229,316; giving activities include $209,833 for grants.
Purpose and activities: Awards scholarships for higher and vocational education to graduates of Superior High School in WI.
Fields of interest: Vocational education; Higher education; Education.
Type of support: Scholarships—to individuals.
Limitations: Applications accepted. Giving limited to Superior, WI.
Application information: Application form required.
Initial approach: Contact WM Retinstrand Superior Senior High School Counseling Office for application form
Deadline(s): Apr. 15
Trustee: BMO Harris Bank, N.A.
EIN: 396184729

3641
The New Richmond Area Community Foundation
421 S. Green Ave.
P.O. Box 96
New Richmond, WI 54017 (715) 246-3999
E-mail: nracfoundation@gmail.com; Main URL: http://www.nracfoundation.com

Established in 2002 in WI.
Foundation type: Community foundation.
Financial data (yr. ended 06/30/13): Assets, $210,419 (M); gifts received, $24,532; expenditures, $105,740.
Purpose and activities: The foundation is the center point for service-based philanthropy, creating collaborative partnerships that identify needs in the communities it serves. They develop strategies to provide citizens in these communities with diverse opportunities to meet these needs through their commitment and the giving of time and financial resources.
Fields of interest: Arts; Education; Environment; Health care; Autism research; Recreation; Family services; Human services; Leadership development; Youth; Adults; Disabilities, people with; Minorities; Economically disadvantaged.
Type of support: Equipment; Publication; Seed money.
Limitations: Applications accepted. Giving primarily in the New Richmond and St. Croix County, WI area. No grants to individuals, or for routine operating expenses and annual campaigns, endowments, regranting,.
Publications: Application guidelines; Annual report; Grants list; Informational brochure.
Application information: Visit foundation web site for grant application form and guidelines. Application form required.
Initial approach: Contact foundation
Copies of proposal: 1
***Deadline(s):* May 30**
Board meeting date(s): 3rd Tues. of each month
Officers and Directors:* Paul Mayer,* Chair.; Tim O'Brien,* Vice-Chair.; Jean Needham,* Secy.; Jesse Kvitek,* Treas.; Darian Blattner; **Troy Boe**; Bill Buell; **Marie Gremore; Mary Hailey; Heather McAbee**; Tom Mews; Trish Moberg; Steve Skoglund; JoAnn Wrich.
Number of staff: 1 part-time support.
EIN: 391392267
Other changes: Paul Mayer has replaced Heather McAbee as Chair. Tim O'Brien has replaced Paul Mayer as Vice-Chair. Jean Needham has replaced Stephen Skoglund as Secy. Jesse Kvitek has replaced Jean Needham as Treas.

Joe Earley and Dave Schleh are no longer directors.

3642

Oshkosh Area Community Foundation

(formerly Oshkosh Foundation)
230 Ohio St., Ste. 100
Oshkosh, WI 54902 (920) 426-3993
Contact: Diane Abraham, C.E.O.; For grants: Amy Putzer, Dir., Progs.
FAX: (920) 426-6997;
E-mail: info@oshkoshareaf.org; Additional e-mail: diane@oshkoshareacf.org; Grant inquiry e-mail: amy@oshkoshareacf.org; Main URL: http://www.oshkoshareacf.org
E-Newsletter: http://www.oshkoshareacf.org/signup.cfm
Facebook: http://www.facebook.com/OshkoshFoundation
Flickr: http://www.flickr.com/photos/oshkoshareacf
Twitter: http://twitter.com/OACF
YouTube: http://www.youtube.com/user/oshfdn

Established in 1928 in WI by declaration of trust.
Foundation type: Community foundation.
Financial data (yr. ended 06/30/13): Assets, $87,475,004 (M); gifts received, $5,358,462; expenditures, $4,707,217; giving activities include $4,057,085 for grants.
Purpose and activities: The foundation seeks to address community needs by providing leadership through grantmaking and fund development.
Fields of interest: Arts; Higher education; Education; Recreation; Children/youth, services; Community/economic development; Children/youth; Youth; Aging; Women; Girls.
Type of support: Management development/capacity building; General/operating support; Continuing support; Capital campaigns; Building/renovation; Equipment; Endowments; Emergency funds; Program development; Conferences/seminars; Seed money; Scholarship funds; Program-related investments/loans; Scholarships—to individuals; Matching/challenge support.
Limitations: Applications accepted. Giving limited to Green Lake, Waushara, and Winnebago, counties, WI. No grants to individuals (except for scholarships), or for deficit financing, research, or publications; no loans.
Publications: Application guidelines; Annual report; Financial statement; Informational brochure; Newsletter.
Application information: Visit foundation web site for application forms, guidelines, and specific deadlines. Applications not accepted unless service area requirements and funding guidelines are met. Application form required.
Initial approach: Submit application form and attachments
Copies of proposal: 1
Deadline(s): Varies
Board meeting date(s): 8 times a year
Final notification: 12 weeks
Officers and Board of Governors:* Beth Wyman,* Pres.; Mark Lasky,* V.P.; **Diane Abraham,* Pres. and C.E.O.**; Jason Hirschberg,* Secy.; Cathy Luther,* Treas.; Nancy Albright, Dir. Emeritus; **John Bermingham, Dir. Emeritus**; **Larry Bittner, Dir. Emeritus**; Mike Castle, Dir. Emeritus; **Marcy Coglianese, Dir. Emeritus**; **Bob Hergert, Dir. Emeritus**; **Tom Harenburg, Dir. Emeritus**; **Ginna Nelson, Dir. Emeritus**; **Jack Schloesser, Dir. Emeritus**; **Pat Seubert, Dir. Emeritus**; **Sam Sundet, Dir. Emeritus**; **Jack Sullivan, Dir. Emeritus**; **Bill Wyman, Dir. Emeritus**; Gary Yakes, Dir. Emeritus; Dave Elbing; Peter Lang; Jim Malczewski; Sylvia McDonald; Kate Pfaendtner; Peter Prickett; Bruce Rounds; Steve Sorenson; Carol Sullivan; Jeff Trembly.
Trustees: Advisory Small Cap Value; Artisan International Value; Associated Banc-Corp; BMO Harris Bank; Capital Counsel; Colchester Global Bond; Forester Offshore; Gryphon International Growth; JPMorgan Chase Bank, N.A.; McClain Select Value; PIMCO; Post Traditional High Yield Fund; Reinhart Partners; TIFF ARP III; UBP/Smith Barney; Vanguard.
Number of staff: 5 full-time professional; 1 part-time professional; 1 full-time support; 1 part-time support.
EIN: 392034571
Other changes: Diane Abraham is now Pres. and C.E.O. Dawn Clark is now Admin. Asst. Kate Salter is now Devel. and Comms. Mgr. Kate Salter is now Devel. and Comms. Asst.

3643

Oshkosh Corporation Foundation, Inc.

(formerly Oshkosh Truck Foundation, Inc.)
P.O. Box 2566
Oshkosh, WI 54903-2566 (920) 233-9206
Contact: Jana C. Heft, Secy.

Incorporated in 1960 in WI.
Donors: Oshkosh Corp.; Oshkosh Truck Corp.
Foundation type: Company-sponsored foundation.
Financial data (yr. ended 09/30/12): Assets, $2,048,460 (M); expenditures, $409,333; qualifying distributions, $402,005; giving activities include $396,100 for 25 grants (high: $102,600; low: $200).
Purpose and activities: The foundation supports community foundations and firefighters and organizations involved with education, health, hunger, housing development, youth development, and human services. Special emphasis is directed toward programs designed to address basic needs and cultural development.
Fields of interest: Arts; Housing/shelter, development; Big Brothers/Big Sisters; Youth development; Salvation Army; YM/YWCAs & YM/YWHAs; Community/economic development; Foundations (community); United Ways and Federated Giving Programs.
Type of support: General/operating support; Continuing support; Annual campaigns; Program development.
Limitations: Applications accepted. Giving primarily in areas of company operations in Oshkosh and the Winnebago County, WI, area. No grants for start-up needs, debt reduction, land acquisition, special projects, research, publications, conferences, or endowments; no loans; no matching gifts.
Application information: Application form required.
***Initial approach:* Letter**
Copies of proposal: 1
Deadline(s): None
Officers and Trustees:* Charles L. Szews,* Pres.; David M. Sagehorn,* V.P. and Treas.; Bryan J. Blankfield,* V.P.; Wilson R. Jones,* V.P.; Michael K. Rohrkaste,* V.P.; Jana C. Heft, Secy.
EIN: 396062129

3644

Pamida Foundation

P.O. Box 19060
Green Bay, WI 54307-9060 (920) 429-2211

Established in 1983 in NE.
Donor: Pamida, Inc.
Foundation type: Company-sponsored foundation.
Financial data (yr. ended 01/31/13): Assets, $714,576 (M); gifts received, $622,944; expenditures, $818,478; qualifying distributions, $804,024; giving activities include $767,436 for 546 grants (high: $37,155; low: $9).
Purpose and activities: The foundation supports programs designed to encourage and educate youth; help families in need; and enhance quality of life for senior citizens.
Fields of interest: Education; Health care; Food banks; Family services; Aging, centers/services; Youth; Aging; Economically disadvantaged.
Type of support: General/operating support; Program development; Sponsorships; Matching/challenge support.
Limitations: Applications accepted. Giving limited to areas of company operations in IA, IL, IN, KS, KY, MI, MN, MO, MT, ND, NE, OH, SD, TN, WI, and WY. No support for religious organizations, for-profit businesses, school cubs, athletic teams, political, labor, or fraternal organizations, or discriminatory organizations. No grants to individuals, or for sports events, advertising in event programs or yearbooks, or mass solicitations by national or international organizations.
Application information: Proposals should be submitted using organization letterhead. Additional information may be requested at a later date. Support is limited to 1 contribution per organization during any given year. Application form not required.
Initial approach: Proposal
Copies of proposal: 1
Deadline(s): None
Officers: Michael J. Bettiga, Pres.; Chad Frazell, Secy.; Mary Meixelsperger, Treas.
EIN: 470656225
Other changes: The grantmaker has moved from NE to WI.
Michael J. Bettiga has replaced W. Paul Jones as Pres.
Jessica Strohman is no longer Exec. Dir. W. Paul Jones is no longer Pres.

3645

Jane Bradley Pettit Foundation

(formerly Jane and Lloyd Pettit Foundation, Inc.)
1200 N. Mayfair Rd., Ste. 430
Wauwatosa, WI 53226-3282 (414) 982-2880
Contact: Kara A. Nehring, Dir., Admin.
FAX: (414) 982-2889;
E-mail: knehring@staffordlaw.com; **Tel. for Kara Nehring, Dir., Admin.: (414) 982-2875**; Main URL: http://www.jbpf.org

Incorporated in 1986 in WI.
Donor: Jane Bradley Pettit†.
Foundation type: Independent foundation.
Financial data (yr. ended 12/31/13): Assets, $21,625,553 (M); expenditures, $3,394,147; qualifying distributions, $3,394,147; giving activities include $2,928,400 for 97 grants (high: $300,000).
Purpose and activities: The foundation will provide funds to initiate and sustain projects in the Greater Milwaukee, WI, community. The foundation will focus on programs and projects that serve low-income and disadvantaged individuals, women, children and the elderly. The foundation will support charitable organizations that address these concerns through arts and culture, community and social development, education and health.
Fields of interest: Arts; Secondary school/education; Higher education; Education; Hospitals (general); Health care; Health organizations, association; Human services; Children/youth,

services; Children, services; Aging, centers/services; Women, centers/services; Community/economic development; Children/youth; Adults; Disabilities, people with; Economically disadvantaged; Homeless.
Type of support: General/operating support; Annual campaigns; Capital campaigns; Building/renovation; Program development; Research.
Limitations: Applications accepted. Giving primarily in the greater Milwaukee, WI, area. No grants to individuals.
Publications: Application guidelines.
Application information: The foundation will not consider requests for additional support for the period in which an organization currently has a grant in effect. Requests for capital projects will only be considered in the Jan. 15 grant cycle.
Initial approach: **Use online application system on foundation web site**
Copies of proposal: 1
Deadline(s): Jan. 15, May 15, and Sept. 15
Board meeting date(s): Quarterly
Final notification: May, Sept., and Dec.
Officers and Directors:* Francis R. Croak,* Pres.; Margaret T. Lund,* V.P.; JoAnn C. Youngman,* Secy.-Treas.
EIN: 391574123
Other changes: The grantmaker now makes its application guidelines available online.

3646
Melitta S. Pick Charitable Trust
c/o George A. Dionisopoulos
777 E. Wisconsin Ave.
Milwaukee, WI 53202-5306 (414) 297-5750

Established in 1972 in WI.
Donor: Melitta S. Pick†.
Foundation type: Independent foundation.
Financial data (yr. ended 01/31/13): Assets, $21,361,100 (M); gifts received, $1,211,255; expenditures, $1,917,659; qualifying distributions, $1,742,439; giving activities include $1,699,000 for 45 grants (high: $600,000; low: $1,000).
Purpose and activities: Giving primarily for the arts and human services.
Fields of interest: Museums; Performing arts; Performing arts, orchestras; Arts; Human services; Youth, services.
Type of support: General/operating support; Annual campaigns; Capital campaigns; Building/renovation; Endowments; Emergency funds.
Limitations: Giving primarily in Milwaukee, WI. No grants to individuals.
Application information: Application form not required.
Initial approach: Letter
Deadline(s): None
Board meeting date(s): Usually quarterly
Trustees: George A. Dionisopoulos; **Richard S. Gallagher**; Joan M. Pick.
EIN: 237243490

3647
Pritchett Foundation
c/o BMO Harris Bank, N.A.
P.O. Box 2980
Milwaukee, WI 53201-2977
Application address: c/o Traci Williams, 1251 N.W. Briarcliff Pkwy., Ste. 140, Kansas City, MO 64116, tel.: (816) 584-4009

Established in 1994 in KS.
Donor: First State Bank & Trust Co.
Foundation type: Independent foundation.
Financial data (yr. ended 05/31/13): Assets, $9,081,452 (M); expenditures, $491,701; qualifying distributions, $400,119; giving activities include $399,358 for 39 grants (high: $50,000; low: $600).
Purpose and activities: The foundation's mission is to improve the quality of life in Pittsburg and Crawford County, KS, by strengthening children, youth, and families, and by supporting projects that serve these populations.
Fields of interest: Elementary/secondary education; Higher education; Education; Human services; Children/youth, services; Youth, services; Family services; Foundations (community).
Limitations: Applications accepted. Giving limited to Crawford County and Pittsburg, KS. No grants to individuals.
Application information: All documents must be submitted on 8 1/2 x 11 inch sheets of paper printed on one side. Do not bind papers or set them in bulky notebooks; the complete proposal and its 1-page synopsis must be submitted at the same time.
Initial approach: Complete proposal, and a 1-page synopsis thereof
Copies of proposal: 1
Deadline(s): Jan. 2
Final notification: End of Feb.
Trustee: BMO Harris Bank, N.A.
EIN: 481210113

3648
Racine Community Foundation, Inc.
(formerly Racine County Area Foundation, Inc.)
245 Main St., Garden Level
Racine, WI 53403-1034 (262) 632-8474
Contact: Mary Beth Mikrut, Exec. Dir.
FAX: (262) 632-3739;
E-mail: info@racinecommunityfoundation.org; Main URL: http://www.racinecommunityfoundation.org
Facebook: https://www.facebook.com/RacineCommunityFoundation
LinkedIn: http://www.linkedin.com/company/racine-community-foundation?trk=hb_tab_compy_id_1224926

Incorporated in 1975 in WI.
Foundation type: Community foundation.
Financial data (yr. ended 12/31/12): Assets, $44,646,488 (M); gifts received, $2,962,726; expenditures, $1,846,117; giving activities include $1,429,610 for 69+ grants (high: $119,062).
Purpose and activities: The mission of the foundation is to encourage and provide opportunities for charitable giving, to manage and distribute the funds in a responsible manner, and to enhance the quality of life for the people of Racine County, WI.
Fields of interest: Arts; Education; Environment; Health care; Human services; Community/economic development; Youth; Aging; Disabilities, people with; Mentally disabled; Economically disadvantaged.
Type of support: Equipment; Endowments; Program development; Conferences/seminars; Seed money; Scholarships—to individuals; Matching/challenge support.
Limitations: Applications accepted. Giving limited to Racine County, WI. No support for church or missionary groups unless for entire community benefit, grantmaking foundations, or social, athletic, veterans', labor, or fraternal organizations. No grants to individuals (except for donor directed scholarships), or for capital expenditures, including building funds, endowment funds, research, travel, or publications.
Publications: Application guidelines; Annual report; Financial statement; Informational brochure; Newsletter.
Application information: Visit foundation web site for application guidelines. Application form required.
Initial approach: Telephone
Copies of proposal: 16
Deadline(s): Jan. 15, Apr. 15, July 15, and Oct. 15
Board meeting date(s): Mar., June, Sept., and Dec.
Final notification: By letter after meeting in which proposal was discussed (2 months after deadline)
Officers and Directors:* Steen Sanderhoff,* Pres.; Sheila R. Bugalecki,* V.P., Grants; **Roger Dower,* V.P., Mktg.**; Jose Martinez,* V.P., Donor Rels.; **Russell C. Weyers,* V.P., Investments; Tracy Short,* Secy.; Ted Hart,* Treas.**; Chris Greco, Cont.; **Jill Heller, Co-Exec. Dir.; Liz Powell, Co-Exec. Dir.**; Bryan D. Albrecht; David C. Easley; R. David Foster; Danice C. Griffin; April Johnson-Howell; Brian Lauer; David Novick; Eric Olesen; Robert F. Siegert, M.D.; James Small; Michael P. Staeck; GeorgAnn Stinson; Ernest C. Styberg, Jr.
Number of staff: 2 full-time professional; 2 part-time professional.
EIN: 510188377
Other changes: Steen Sanderhoff has replaced Elizabeth A. Powell as Pres. Roger Dower has replaced Steen Sanderhoff as Pres.-Elect. and V.P., Mktg. Russell C. Weyers has replaced James C. Small as V.P., Finance and Investments and Treas. Tracy Short has replaced Jill Heller as Secy. Ted Hart has replaced James C. Small as Treas. Jill Heller has replaced Mary Beth Mikrut as Exec. Dir. Tracy Middlebrook is now Prog. Off. Roger Dower, Camela M. Meyer, Tracy K. Short are no longer directors.

3649
Raibrook Foundation
30 N. 18th Ave., Unit 4
Sturgeon Bay, WI 54235-3207 (920) 746-2995
FAX: (920) 746-2996; Application e-mail: julie@raibrookfoundation.com; Main URL: http://www.raibrookfoundation.com

Established in 1990 in WI.
Donor: George R. Brooks†.
Foundation type: Independent foundation.
Financial data (yr. ended 12/31/12): Assets, $27,069,836 (M); gifts received, $2,521; expenditures, $2,907,624; qualifying distributions, $2,164,251; giving activities include $1,629,826 for 67 grants (high: $221,788; low: $282).
Purpose and activities: The foundation is dedicated to providing support to local nonprofit organizations which strive to improve the communities it serves and to assist projects that reflect the philosophy of its founder. The foundation funds projects which address community needs in the areas of education, history and recreation.
Fields of interest: Museums; Historic preservation/historical societies; Elementary/secondary education; Education; Human services; YM/YWCAs & YM/YWHAs; Family services; Community/economic development.
Limitations: Applications accepted. Giving limited to Door County, WI, with emphasis on Nasewaupee, Sevastopol and Sturgeon Bay. No support for businesses, for-profit organizations, or projects of organizations whose policies or practices discriminate on the basis of ethnic origin, gender, race, religion or sexual orientation. No grants to

individuals, or for general operating support for ongoing activities, debt retirement, endowment funds, annual appeals, general fund drives, special events, or sponsorships; no loans.
Publications: Application guidelines.
Application information: Application form available on foundation web site. Proposals sent by mail or fax are not accepted. Late applications will be considered, but not until the following month. Application form required.
Deadline(s): 1st of each month
Final notification: Applications are reviewed monthly
Officer and Board Members:* Julie LaLuzerne,* Grant Prog. Mgr.; Mike Madden; Karl May; Roger Wood; Cap Wulf.
EIN: 391683091

3650
Reiman Foundation, Inc.
(formerly Reiman Charitable Foundation, Inc.)
115 S. 84th St., Ste. 221
Milwaukee, WI 53214-1474 (414) 456-0600
Contact: Michael J. Hipp, Secy.
FAX: (414) 456-0606;
E-mail: reimanfoundation@hexagoninc.com; Main URL: http://www.reimanfoundation.org

Established in 1986 in WI.
Donors: Roy J. Reiman; Roberta M. Reiman; Scott J. Reiman; Joni R. Winston; Cynthia A. Lambert; Julia M. Ellis; Terrin S. Riemer.
Foundation type: Independent foundation.
Financial data (yr. ended 12/31/12): Assets, $121,589,825 (M); gifts received, $6,000,000; expenditures, $14,147,671; qualifying distributions, $11,839,852; giving activities include $11,839,852 for 168 grants (high: $1,000,000; low: $100).
Purpose and activities: Giving primarily for education, health care, and children's initiatives.
Fields of interest: Education; Health care; Children, services; Children.
Limitations: Applications accepted. Giving primarily in WI; giving also in CO, GA, IA, MO, and NY. No grants to individuals.
Publications: Application guidelines.
Application information: The foundation will acknowledge receipt of application. See foundation web site for further details. Application form not required.
Initial approach: Letter
Deadline(s): None
Officers and Directors:* Scott J. Reiman,* Pres.; Brian F. Fleischmann,* V.P.; Roberta M. Reiman,* V.P.; Roy J. Reiman,* V.P.; Michael J. Hipp,* Secy.; Julia M. Ellis; Troy G. Hildebrandt.
EIN: 391570264
Other changes: At the close of 2012, the grantmaker paid grants of $11,839,852, a 169.2% increase over the 2011 disbursements, $4,397,779.

3651
RITE-HITE Corporation Foundation Inc.
8900 N. Arbon Dr.
Milwaukee, WI 53223-2451 (414) 355-2600
***Contact:* Mark S. Kirkish, Treas.**

Established in 1984.
Donors: RITE-HITE Corp.; RITE-HITE Holding Corp.
Foundation type: Company-sponsored foundation.
Financial data (yr. ended 12/31/12): Assets, $45,159 (M); gifts received, $100,000; expenditures, $80,010; qualifying distributions, $80,000; giving activities include $80,000 for 20 grants (high: $20,000; low: $250).
Purpose and activities: The foundation supports museums and organizations involved with performing arts, higher education, legal aid, youth development, and children and youth.
Fields of interest: Museums; Performing arts; Higher education; Health care; Legal services; Boys & girls clubs; YM/YWCAs & YM/YWHAs; Youth, services; United Ways and Federated Giving Programs.
Type of support: General/operating support.
Limitations: Applications accepted. Giving primarily in Milwaukee, WI.
Application information: Application form not required.
Initial approach: Proposal
Deadline(s): None
Officers and Directors:* Michael H. White,* Pres.; **Paul J. Maly, V.P.; Antonio P. Catalano, Secy.;** Mark S. Kirkish,* Treas.
EIN: 391522057
Other changes: Paul J. Maly has replaced Mark G. Petri as V.P.
Mark G. Petri is no longer V.P.

3652
Pleasant T. Rowland Foundation, Inc.
3415 Gateway Rd., Ste. 200
Brookfield, WI 53045-5111
Contact: Grants Mgr.
Application address: 6120 University Ave., Middletown, WI 53562, tel.: (608) 729-2811

Established in 1997 in WI.
Donor: Pleasant T. Rowland.
Foundation type: Independent foundation.
Financial data (yr. ended 12/31/12): Assets, $52,822,527 (M); expenditures, $4,952,694; qualifying distributions, $3,934,960; giving activities include $3,934,960 for 88 grants (high: $1,600,000; low: $100).
Purpose and activities: Giving primarily for arts, education and historic preservation.
Fields of interest: Historic preservation/historical societies; Arts; Education.
Type of support: Program development; Matching/challenge support.
Limitations: Applications accepted. Giving primarily in WI, with emphasis on Dane County. No support for religious or political organizations. No grants to individuals.
Publications: Application guidelines.
Application information: Application form required.
Initial approach: Telephone
Copies of proposal: 1
Deadline(s): June 30 and Nov. 30
Board meeting date(s): Apr., July, Oct., and Dec.
Final notification: 4 - 6 weeks
Officers and Directors: Pleasant T. Rowland, Pres.; Rhona E. Vogel, Secy.; Barbara Thiele Carr; Walter Jerome Frautschi; Valerie Tripp; **Catharine B. Waller.**
Number of staff: 1 full-time professional.
EIN: 391868295

3653
Rylander Memorial Library Trust
Milwaukee, WI

The trust terminated in 2012 and transferred its assets to Friends of The Rylander Memorial Library.

3654
Sand County Foundation, Inc.
c/o David Allen
16 N. Carroll St., Ste 450
Madison, WI 53703-2784 (608) 663-4605
FAX: (608) 663-4617; E-mail: info@sandcounty.net; Main URL: http://www.sandcounty.net
Blog: http://sandcounty.net/category/newsroom/
E-Newsletter: http://sandcounty.net/newsletter/
Facebook: https://www.facebook.com/SandCountyFoundation
LinkedIn: http://www.linkedin.com/groups?gid=2956944
RSS Feed: http://sandcounty.net/category/newsroom/feed/
Twitter: http://twitter.com/sandcountyfdn/
YouTube: http://www.youtube.com/user/SandCountyFdn

Classified as a private operating foundation in 1987.
Donors: Nash Williams†; Wisconsin Dept. of Natural Resources; Norman Basset Foundation; U.S. Fish and Wildlife Service; Ed Warner; Wisconsin Dept. of Transportation; Lynde & Harry Bradley Foundation.
Foundation type: Operating foundation.
Financial data (yr. ended 12/31/12): Assets, $8,093,988 (M); gifts received, $1,943,840; expenditures, $2,412,229; qualifying distributions, $2,225,228; giving activities include $311,000 for 16 grants (high: $85,000; low: $1,000).
Purpose and activities: Giving to advance the use of ethical and scientifically sound land management practices and partnerships for the benefit of people and the ecological landscape.
Fields of interest: Education; Environment, water resources; Environment, land resources.
International interests: Southern Africa.
Type of support: General/operating support; Program development; Conferences/seminars; Research.
Limitations: Applications not accepted. No grants to individuals.
Publications: Annual report; Newsletter.
Application information: Contributes only to pre-selected organizations.
Board meeting date(s): Feb., June, Sept., and Dec.
Officers and Directors:* Reed Coleman,* Chair.; David J. Hanson,* Vice-Chair. and Secy.; Kevin McAleese, Exec. V.P.; Brent M. Haglund,* Pres.; Tina Y. Buford; Dr. Ingrid "Indy" Burke; Dr. Stephen F. Hayward; George Kennedy; Charlie Potter; Dr. Stanley A. Temple; Ed Warner.
Number of staff: 6 full-time professional; 1 full-time support.
EIN: 396089450

3655
W. R. and Floy A. Sauey Family Foundation
715 Lynn Ave.
Baraboo, WI 53913-2488 **(608) 356-2130**
Contact: Alison Martin, Pres.
***Application address:* c/o Nordic Group, 414 Broadway, Baraboo, WI 53913**; Main URL: http://www.saueyfamily.org/

Established in 1998 in WI.
Donors: Flambeau, Inc.; Seats Inc.; Nordic Group of Cos., Ltd.
Foundation type: Company-sponsored foundation.
Financial data (yr. ended 12/31/12): Assets, $975,435 (M); gifts received, $127,238; expenditures, $89,246; qualifying distributions,

$69,000; giving activities include $69,000 for grants.
Purpose and activities: The foundation supports programs designed to promote education; preserve and increase participation in the free market system; and promote quality of life in local communities with emphasis on child and family issues.
Fields of interest: Higher education; Education, reading; Education; Children/youth, services; Family services; Family services, domestic violence; Homeless, human services; Human services; Community/economic development.
Type of support: General/operating support; Annual campaigns; Employee-related scholarships.
Limitations: Applications accepted. Giving primarily in areas of company operations, with emphasis on MN and WI.
Publications: Informational brochure.
Application information: Application form required.
Initial approach: **Request application form**
Deadline(s): None
Officers: Alison Martin, Pres.; Floy A. Sauey, Secy.; William Hans, Treas.
Directors: Charles Frank; Todd L. Sauey; William R. Sauey.
EIN: 391934775

3656
Oscar C. & Augusta Schlegel Foundation
c/o BMO Harris Bank, N.A.
P.O. Box 2980
Milwaukee, WI 53201-2980

Established in 1987 in WI.
Foundation type: Independent foundation.
Financial data (yr. ended 03/31/13): Assets, $7,748,544 (M); expenditures, $386,154; qualifying distributions, $348,300; giving activities include $348,300 for 28 grants (high: $85,000; low: $1,000).
Fields of interest: Arts; Secondary school/education; Hospitals (general); Recreation, parks/playgrounds; Girl scouts; Human services; YM/YWCAs & YM/YWHAs; Youth, services.
Limitations: Applications not accepted. Giving limited to WI. No grants to individuals.
Application information: Contributes only to pre-selected organizations.
Officers: Marilyn L. Holmquist, Chair.; Roger T. Stephenson, Vice-Chair.; Kim Palleon, Secy.
Trustee: BMO Harris Bank, N.A.
EIN: 391586544
Other changes: The grantmaker no longer lists a phone.

3657
Sentry Insurance Foundation, Inc.
(formerly Sentry Foundation, Inc.)
1800 N. Point Dr.
Stevens Point, WI 54481-1283 (715) 346-6000
Main URL: **https://www.sentry.com/sentry-insurance-foundation.aspx**

Incorporated in 1963 in WI.
Donor: Sentry Insurance.
Foundation type: Company-sponsored foundation.
Financial data (yr. ended 12/31/13): Assets, $9,112,510 (M); gifts received, $1,573,971; expenditures, $2,895,472; giving activities include $1,421,500 for 73 grants (high: $822,087; low: $500), and $456,190 for 211 employee matching gifts.
Purpose and activities: The foundation supports organizations involved with fine arts and community services. Special emphasis is directed toward educational initiatives.
Fields of interest: Visual arts; Performing arts; Arts; Higher education; Education, reading; Education; Boys & girls clubs; YM/YWCAs & YM/YWHAs; Children, services; Community/economic development; United Ways and Federated Giving Programs.
Type of support: Employee-related scholarships; General/operating support; Continuing support; Scholarship funds; Sponsorships; Employee matching gifts.
Limitations: Applications accepted. Giving primarily in areas of company operations in WI. No support for religious organizations.
Application information: Application form required.
Initial approach: Letter
Copies of proposal: 1
Deadline(s): None
Officers and Directors:* James J. Weishan, Chair. and Pres.; **Peter G. McParland,* V.P.**; Kenneth J. Erier, Secy.; Carol P. Sanders, Treas.; Michael J. Williams.
EIN: 391037370
Other changes: Peter G. McParland has replaced Daniel L. Revai as V.P.
Daniel L. Revai is no longer V.P. William M. O'Reilly is no longer Secy. William James Lohr is no longer Treas.

3658
Seramur Family Foundation Inc.
2026 County Rd., Ste. HH
Plover, WI 54467-2653

Established in 1994 in WI.
Donor: John C. Seramur.
Foundation type: Independent foundation.
Financial data (yr. ended 09/30/13): Assets, $5,518,853 (M); gifts received, $500,005; expenditures, $229,646; qualifying distributions, $193,850; giving activities include $193,850 for 17 grants (high: $100,000; low: $250).
Purpose and activities: Giving primarily for educational and community oriented programs; funding also for medical research, and to a Roman Catholic church.
Fields of interest: Museums (children's); Higher education; Education; Medical research, institute; Catholic agencies & churches.
Type of support: Equipment.
Limitations: Applications not accepted. Giving primarily in WI. No grants to individuals.
Application information: Contributes only to pre-selected organizations.
Officers: John C. Seramur, Pres.; Gary T. Pucci, V.P.; Joan Seramur, Secy.-Treas.
Directors: Brian Seramur; Brenda S. Thompson.
EIN: 391806609

3659
Siebert Lutheran Foundation, Inc.
300 N. Corporate Dr., Ste. 200
Brookfield, WI 53045-5862 (262) 754-9160
Contact: Ronald D. Jones, Pres.
FAX: (262) 754-9162;
E-mail: contactus@siebertfoundation.org; Main URL: http://www.siebertfoundation.org

Incorporated in 1952 in WI.
Donors: A.F. Siebert†; Reginald L. Siebert†.
Foundation type: Independent foundation.
Financial data (yr. ended 12/31/13): Assets, $96,400,186 (M); expenditures, $4,997,289; qualifying distributions, $4,238,960; giving activities include $3,891,187 for 87 grants (high: $257,000; low: $1,200).
Purpose and activities: The Siebert Lutheran Foundation, using its resources, stewardship and relationships, enables the Lutheran community to be more collaborative, creative, and effective in sharing the Word of God, educating and instilling Christian values in youth, and serving people in need. The foundation's areas of interest include sharing the Gospel through Lutheran Churches and Organizations, Breaking the Poverty Cycle through Faith-Based Education, and Supporting Bible-Based Human Services. Special grants are made to seminary students who are members of Lutheran churches in Wisconsin.
Fields of interest: Elementary/secondary education; Education, early childhood education; Child development, education; Secondary school/education; Higher education; Education; Youth development, religion; Human services; Child development, services; Protestant federated giving programs; Protestant agencies & churches; Religion; Minorities; Economically disadvantaged.
Type of support: Program development; Seed money; Consulting services; Matching/challenge support.
Limitations: Applications accepted. Giving primarily in WI. **No support for one hundred percent of a project. No grants to individuals directly, or for endowment funds, trusts, scholarships or fellowships; no loans.**
Publications: Application guidelines; Annual report.
Application information: On-line grant application required. Grantees are required to sign Grant Agreement Form. Grantees are required to submit a final report after project completion. Application form not required.
Initial approach: Letter of Inquiry part of on-line grant application.
Deadline(s): Feb. 1, Aug. 1, and Nov. 1
Board meeting date(s): Jan., Apr., July, and Oct.
Final notification: 1 week after board meeting
Officers and Directors:* Knute Jacobson,* Chair.; Brenda Skelton,* Vice-Chair.; Ronald D. Jones, Pres.; Kurt Bechtold,* Secy.; Kurtiss R. Krueger,* Treas.; David W. Romoser; John Sellars; Julie Van Cleave; John Zimdars.
Number of staff: 1 full-time professional; 2 full-time support.
EIN: 396050046

3660
C. D. Smith Foundation Inc.
c/o Gary Smith
889 Johnson St.
Fond du Lac, WI 54936-2933

Established in 1999 in WI.
Donor: C.D. Smith Construction, Inc.
Foundation type: Company-sponsored foundation.
Financial data (yr. ended 12/31/12): Assets, $860,843 (M); expenditures, $790; qualifying distributions, $0.
Purpose and activities: The foundation provides charitable donations to the Fond Du Lac Family YMCA in Wisconsin.
Fields of interest: YM/YWCAs & YM/YWHAs.
Type of support: General/operating support.
Limitations: Applications not accepted. Giving limited to WI. No grants to individuals.
Application information: Contributes only to a pre-selected organization.

Officers: Gary M. Smith, Pres.; Thomas J. Baker, V.P.; Patrick S. Smith, Secy.; Robert Baker, Treas.
Directors: Thomas D. Baker; Mike P. Fortune; Justin Smith; Mary Lou Smith.
EIN: 391972533

3661
Nancy Woodson Spire Foundation, Inc.
602 First American Ctr.
Wausau, WI 54403 (715) 845-9201
Contact: San W. Orr, Jr., Pres.
***Application address:* c/o Wilmington Trust Co., 1100 N. Market St., Wilmington, DE 19801-1289; tel.: (302) 651-8159**

Established in WI.
Foundation type: Independent foundation.
Financial data (yr. ended 06/30/13): Assets, $29,604,387 (M); expenditures, $1,426,556; qualifying distributions, $1,257,505; giving activities include $1,207,500 for 5 grants (high: $450,000; low: $1,000).
Fields of interest: Museums (art); Historic preservation/historical societies; YM/YWCAs & YM/YWHAs.
Limitations: Giving primarily in Wausau, WI; some funding also in Washington, DC, and VA.
Application information: Application form not required.
***Initial approach:* Letter**
Deadline(s): None
Officers and Directors:* San W. Orr, Jr.,* Pres.; John P. Garniewski, Jr., V.P.; Thomas J. Howatt; Charles M. Rombach.
EIN: 391367383
Other changes: Ann M. Dubore is no longer Secy.-Treas.

3662
St. Croix Valley Foundation
516 2nd St., Ste. 214
Hudson, WI 54016 (715) 386-9490
Contact: Jane Hetland Stevenson, Pres.; For grants: Jill A. Shannon, Dir., Community Partnerships
FAX: (715) 386-1250;
E-mail: info@scvfoundation.org; Additional E-mail: jstevenson@scvcfoundation.org; Grant inquiry E-mail: jshannon@scvfoundation.org; Main URL: http://www.scvfoundation.org/

Established in 1995 in WI and MN.
Foundation type: Community foundation.
Financial data (yr. ended 06/30/12): Assets, $28,405,554 (M); gifts received, $2,578,478; expenditures, $1,650,721; giving activities include $1,017,405 for grants.
Purpose and activities: The foundation's mission is to advance the quality of life in the St. Croix Valley of WI and MN.
Fields of interest: Arts; Education; Environment; Health care; Human services; Community/economic development; Children; Youth; Adults.
Type of support: Technical assistance; Seed money; Scholarships—to individuals; Scholarship funds; Program evaluation; Matching/challenge support; Management development/capacity building; General/operating support; Endowments; Consulting services; Conferences/seminars.
Limitations: Applications accepted. Giving primarily in Chisago and Washington counties, MN and Pierce, Polk and St. Croix counties, WI.
Publications: Application guidelines; Annual report; Financial statement; Informational brochure.
Application information: Visit foundation web site for application forms and additional guidelines per grant type. Application form required.
Initial approach: Letter
Copies of proposal: 8
Deadline(s): Varies
Board meeting date(s): 2nd Tues. of each month
Final notification: Within 2 months of submission
Officers and Directors:* Marty Harding,* Chair.; **Todd Gillingham,* Vice-Chair.**; Jane Hetland Stevenson,* Pres.; **Jennifer Anderson**; **Chuck Arneson**; Ann Brookman; Suzann Brown; Jill Burchill; **Dwight Cummins**; **Sue Gerlach**; Andy Kass; Andy Kubiak; Katrina Larsen; Jim Lutiger; **David Palmer**; Lisa Rinde; Rod Rommel; Steve Schroeder; Linda Skoglund; Gretchen Stein; Jeanne Walz; David Wettergren; Steven Wilcox.
Number of staff: 3 full-time professional; 1 full-time support; 1 part-time support.
EIN: 411817315
Other changes: Todd Gillingham is now Vice-Chair. Charles Arnason, Chris Galvin, Marty Harding, Michael Johnson, Katrina Larson, and Mark Vanasse are no longer directors.

3663
The Stateline Community Foundation
(formerly The Greater Beloit Community Foundation)
690 3rd St., Ste. 110
Beloit, WI 53511-6210 (608) 362-4228
Contact: Tara Jean Tinder, Exec. Dir.
FAX: (608) 362-0056; E-mail: statelinecf@aol.com; Additional E-mail: tara@statelinecf.com; Main URL: http://www.statelinecf.org
Facebook: http://www.facebook.com/StatelineCommunityFoundation

Established in 1986 in WI.
Foundation type: Community foundation.
Financial data (yr. ended 12/31/12): Assets, $9,741,658 (M); gifts received, $202,690; expenditures, $653,284; giving activities include $184,717 for 14+ grants (high: $15,291), and $132,514 for grants to individuals.
Purpose and activities: The foundation seeks to provide for the betterment of the greater Beloit, WI, Stateline area and the enhancement of the quality of life for all of its citizens.
Fields of interest: Performing arts; Arts; Education, early childhood education; Higher education; Education; Environment; Health organizations, association; Recreation; Youth development, services; Children/youth, services; Homeless, human services; Human services; Urban/community development; Community/economic development; Leadership development; Youth; Aging; Disabilities, people with; Minorities; Homeless.
Type of support: Equipment; Emergency funds; Program development; Seed money; Curriculum development; Scholarship funds; Program evaluation; Matching/challenge support.
Limitations: Applications accepted. Giving limited to the greater Stateline area encompassing Rock County, WI, and northern Winnebago County, IL. **No support for scholarly research.** No grants to individuals (except for designated scholarship funds), or for ongoing operating expenses, building funds or capital campaigns, endowments and debt reduction, annual fundraising drives or travel grants.
Publications: Application guidelines; Annual report; Grants list; Informational brochure; Newsletter.
Application information: Visit foundation web site for application guidelines. Selected organizations will be notified of their status within 10 days following submission of their letter of inquiry for the Community Needs Grant Program. Application form required.
Initial approach: Submit online Letter of Inquiry
Deadline(s): Jan. 1 for Community Needs Grant Program full proposal; None for Discretionary grants; Jan. 21, Apr. 21, July. 21, Oct. 21 For J.E.T. Grants and Destination Grants. Oct. 31 for Teachers Mini-Grant.
Final notification: 6 to 8 weeks for Community Needs Grant Program
Officers and Directors:* Bill Lock,* Chair.; Martha Mitchell,* 1st Vice-Chair.; J. Marc Perry,* Secy.; Don Huebschen,* Treas.; Tara Jean Tinder, Exec. Dir.; Joanne Acomb; **Francisca Amadore**; Heidi Eldred; William Flanagan; Jeff Johnson; Sarah Kruse; Bruce Lans; Kay Nightingale; Lynee Tourdot; Mike Wickiser; Cecil Youngblood.
Number of staff: 2 full-time professional.
EIN: 391585271
Other changes: Bill Lock has replaced Hagan Harker as Chair. Martha Mitchell has replaced Francisca Amadore as 1st Vice-Chair.
J. Marc. Perry is now Secy. Nancy Boutelle and Judy Kaplan are no longer directors.

3664
The Stone Foundation, Inc.
c/o National Exchange Bank, Trust Dept.
130 S. Main St.
Fond du Lac, WI 54935-4210
***Application address:* c/o Eric Stone or Dale Brooks, P.O. Box 988, Fond du Lac, WI 54936-0988; tel.: (920) 921-7700**

Established in WI.
Donors: Peter E. Stone; NEB Corp.; American Bank.
Foundation type: Independent foundation.
Financial data (yr. ended 12/31/12): Assets, $36,133,969 (M); gifts received, $445,000; expenditures, $1,632,019; qualifying distributions, $1,559,333; giving activities include $1,551,300 for 61 grants (high: $500,000; low: $250).
Purpose and activities: Giving primarily for human services.
Fields of interest: Substance abuse, treatment; Human services; Children/youth, services; Community/economic development; Foundations (community).
Limitations: Giving primarily in Fond du Lac, WI. No grants to individuals.
Application information:
***Initial approach:* Letter**
***Deadline(s):* None**
Officers and Directors:* Peter E. Stone,* Pres. and Treas.; Dale G. Brooks,* V.P.; Eric P. Stone,* V.P.; S. Adam Stone,* V.P.; Barbara S. Stone,* Secy.; Michael L. Burch; James R. Chatterton.
EIN: 391597843

3665
U.S. Venture/Schmidt Family Foundation, Inc.
(formerly U.S. Oil/Schmidt Family Foundation, Inc.)
425 Better Way
Appleton, WI 54915-6192
***Contact:* Cathy Mutschler, Dir. of Giving**
***E-mail for Cathy Mutschler:* cmutschler@usventure.com; tel. for Cathy Mutschler: (920) 243-5798**; Main URL: http://www.usventure.com/Community/Pages/Foundation.aspx

Established in 1984 in WI.

Donors: Raymond Schmidt; Arthur J. Schmidt; William Schmidt; Thomas A. Schmidt; U.S. Oil Co., Inc.; U.S. Venture, Inc.
Foundation type: Independent foundation.
Financial data (yr. ended 07/31/12): Assets, $3,846,027 (M); gifts received, $450,000; expenditures, $837,559; qualifying distributions, $802,214; giving activities include $802,214 for 182 grants (high: $250,000; low: $25).
Purpose and activities: Giving primarily for education, international relief, health, human services, community development, arts and culture, and environmental stewardship.
Fields of interest: Arts; Education; Environment, natural resources; Health organizations, association; Human services; Community/economic development.
Type of support: General/operating support; Continuing support; Annual campaigns; Building/renovation; Equipment; Land acquisition; Emergency funds; Publication; Seed money; Employee matching gifts; Matching/challenge support.
Limitations: Giving primarily in WI. No support for government-sponsored programs (where 50 percent or more of an organization's budget is obtained from government contracts or initiatives). No grants to individuals, or for conferences.
Publications: Application guidelines.
Application information: The foundation may request additional information if the applying organization's work coincides with the foundation's goals. Contact information must also be e-mailed along with letter of intent. Complete application guidelines available on foundation web site.
Initial approach: **E-mail or call Dir. of Giving**
Officers: Arthur J. Schmidt, Pres.; William J. Schmidt, V.P.; Raymond E. Schmidt, Secy.-Treas.
Director: Thomas A. Schmidt.
Number of staff: 1 part-time professional; 2 part-time support.
EIN: 391540933

3666
The Wagner Foundation, Ltd.
(formerly R. H. Wagner Foundation, Ltd.)
P.O. Box 307
Lyons, WI 53148-0307

Established in 1981 in WI.
Donors: Richard H. Wagner; Roberta L. Wagner; Ken Essman; Marcy Essman; Bob O'Neil; Julie O'Neil; S. Heekin; Molly Carl; Roger Ringelman; Burlington Rotary Club; Robert W. Baird Foundation; The Word at Work Foundation; Rotary Club of Elmbrook; Kikkoman Foods Foundation.
Foundation type: Independent foundation.
Financial data (yr. ended 06/30/13): Assets, $13,460,955 (M); gifts received, $293,000; expenditures, $549,680; qualifying distributions, $545,032; giving activities include $476,522 for 23 grants (high: $85,000; low: $1,500).
Purpose and activities: Giving primarily for humanitarian aid in Central America and Africa; support also for education, including Roman Catholic schools, and human services.
Fields of interest: Education; Human services; Children/youth, services; International relief; Catholic agencies & churches.
International interests: Bolivia; Belize; Bermuda; Central America; Philippines.
Type of support: Equipment; Scholarship funds; Grants to individuals.
Limitations: Applications not accepted. Giving in the U.S. and in Africa, Central America and South America.
Application information: Unsolicited requests for funds not accepted.
Officers: Richard H. Wagner, Pres.; Roberta L. Wagner, V.P.
Directors: Melissa Doyle; **Paul B. Edwards, CPA**; **Abbey Essman**; Adam Essman; Ken Essman; Marcy Essman; Emily LaBadie; Bob O'Neill; Julie O'Neill; Meghan O'Neill; Molly O'Neill; Marci Rueter.
EIN: 391311452
Other changes: Emily Essman is no longer a director.

3667
The Wanek-Vogel Foundation, Ltd.
c/o Ashley Furniture Industries, Inc.
1 Ashley Way
Arcadia, WI 54612-1218 (608) 323-6249
Contact: Paulette Rippley

Established in WI.
Donor: Ashley Furniture Industries.
Foundation type: Company-sponsored foundation.
Financial data (yr. ended 12/31/12): Assets, $34,559,816 (M); gifts received, $20,000,000; expenditures, $3,002,306; qualifying distributions, $2,973,564; giving activities include $2,973,564 for 44 grants (high: $2,173,927; low: $100).
Purpose and activities: The foundation supports arts councils and organizations involved with secondary education, health, human services, and community development.
Fields of interest: Arts councils; Secondary school/education; Health care, clinics/centers; Health care; Residential/custodial care, hospices; Human services; Community development, business promotion; Community/economic development.
Type of support: General/operating support.
Limitations: Applications accepted. Giving primarily in WI. No grants to individuals.
Application information: The letter of inquiry should have a margin of 1 inch on all sides and type not smaller than 10 point. Support is limited to 1 contribution per organization during any given year. Application form not required.
Initial approach: Letter of inquiry
Deadline(s): None
Final notification: 12 weeks
Directors: Benjamin Charles Vogel; Charles H.E. Vogel; Ronald G. Wanek; Todd R. Wanek.
EIN: 391948289
Other changes: At the close of 2012, the fair market value of the grantmaker's assets was $34,559,816, a 104.6% increase over the 2011 value, $16,890,476.

3668
Windhover Foundation, Inc.
N61 W23044 Harry's Way
Sussex, WI **53089-9807**
***E-mail:* contact@windhoverfoundation.org; Main URL: https://www.windhoverfoundation.org/**

Established in 1983.
Donors: Quad/Graphics, Inc.; Harry V. Quadracci 1998 Trust.
Foundation type: Company-sponsored foundation.
Financial data (yr. ended 12/31/12): Assets, $82,336,076 (M); gifts received, $3,239,638; expenditures, $3,526,150; qualifying distributions, $3,230,885; giving activities include $2,922,885 for 114 grants (high: $485,925; low: $10), and $308,000 for 188 grants to individuals (high: $2,500; low: $1,000).
Purpose and activities: The foundation supports parks and playgrounds and organizations involved with arts and culture, education, health, hunger, sports, and human services. Special emphasis is directed toward projects designed to meet unfilled social needs.
Fields of interest: Museums (art); Arts; Elementary/secondary education; Higher education; Libraries (public); Education; Hospitals (general); Reproductive health, family planning; Health care; Food services; Food banks; Recreation, parks/playgrounds; American Red Cross; Children/youth, services; Residential/custodial care, hospices; Women, centers/services; Human services; United Ways and Federated Giving Programs; Christian agencies & churches.
Type of support: General/operating support; Continuing support; Annual campaigns; Employee matching gifts; Employee-related scholarships.
Limitations: Applications accepted. Giving primarily in areas of company operations in Milwaukee, WI. No support for religious organizations or teams or leagues. No grants to individuals (except for employee-related scholarships), or for sponsorships, fundraising events, competitions, or contests.
Publications: Application guidelines.
Application information: Application form not required.
Initial approach: Complete online application
Copies of proposal: 1
Deadline(s): None
Officers and Directors: Elizabeth E. Quadracci, Pres.; Elizabeth Quadracci Harned, V.P.; John C. Fowler, Secy.-Treas.; Kathryn Q. Flores; J. Joel Quadracci.
EIN: 391482470

3669
Windway Foundation, Inc.
P.O. Box 897
Sheboygan, WI 53081 (920) 457-8600
Contact: Terry Kohler, Pres.
Application address: c/o Windway Capital, 630 Riverfront Dr., Ste. 200, Sheboygan, WI 53081

Donors: The Vollrath Co., LLC; Windway Capital Corp.
Foundation type: Company-sponsored foundation.
Financial data (yr. ended 09/30/13): Assets, $49,478 (M); gifts received, $180,000; expenditures, $165,196; qualifying distributions, $165,196; giving activities include $164,200 for 32 grants (high: $20,000; low: $500).
Purpose and activities: The foundation supports organizations involved with arts and culture, education, human services, civil rights, and civic affairs.
Fields of interest: Arts; Higher education; Education; Youth, services; Human services; Civil/human rights; Public affairs.
Type of support: Equipment; Program development; Scholarship funds; Research; In-kind gifts.
Limitations: Applications accepted. Giving primarily in areas of company operations. No grants to individuals.
Application information: Application form required.
Initial approach: Letter
Deadline(s): None
Officers and Directors:* Terry J. Kohler,* Pres.; Mary S. Kohler,* V.P.; **Mary Theune,* Secy.**; **Roland M. Neumann,* Treas.**
EIN: 396046987

3670
Joseph J. and Vera Zilber Family Foundation
710 N. Plankinton Ave., Ste. 1200
Milwaukee, WI 53203-2404 (414) 274-2447
E-mail: info@zilberfamilyfoundation.org; Main URL: http://www.zilberfamilyfoundation.org

Established in 1962 in WI.
Donors: Joseph J. Zilber‡; Vera J. Zilber; Zilber, Ltd.
Foundation type: Independent foundation.
Financial data (yr. ended 06/30/13): Assets, $24,806,020 (M); gifts received, $23,500; expenditures, $5,249,765; qualifying distributions, $5,070,092; giving activities include $4,370,697 for 87 grants (high: $1,000,000; low: $32).
Purpose and activities: Giving primarily for human services and neighborhood development.
Fields of interest: Museums (specialized); Higher education; Environment; Health organizations, association; Boys & girls clubs; Human services; Community development, neighborhood development; Jewish federated giving programs.
Type of support: Program evaluation; Program development; Matching/challenge support; Management development/capacity building; General/operating support; Employee matching gifts; Capital campaigns.
Limitations: Giving primarily in WI, with emphasis on Milwaukee. No support for political or religious organizations. No grants to individuals, or for endowments, annual appeals, conferences, workshops, fundraising events, scholarships, fellowships, research, loans, travel, athletic events, or film or media projects.
Publications: Application guidelines.
Application information: Full proposals are by invitation only, after review of initial letter of inquiry. Videos, CDs, press clippings or books are not accepted (unless they are requested).
Initial approach: Letter of inquiry (preferably sent via e-mail)
Final notification: Within 30 days
Officers and Directors:* Marcy Zilber Jackson,* Pres.; James F. Janz,* V.P.; Stephan J. Chevalier,* Secy.-Treas.; Susan Lloyd, Ph.D., Exec. Dir.; Melissa S.A. Jackson; Shane M. Jackson; Michael P. Mervis; John K. Tsui; Marilyn Zilber.
Number of staff: 4 full-time professional.
EIN: 396077241
Other changes: James F. Janz has replaced Marcy Zilber Jackson as V.P.
Marcy Zilber Jackson is now Pres. Stephan J. Chevalier is now Secy.-Treas.

WYOMING

3671
Christian Mission Concerns of Tennessee, Inc.
3125 Tucker Ranch Rd.
Wilson, WY 83014-9703 **(307) 733-8112**
***Contact:* Paul P. Piper, Jr.**
Application telephone: (307) 733-8112

Established in TN.
Donors: Mary Piper; Paul P. Piper.
Foundation type: Independent foundation.
Financial data (yr. ended 12/31/12): Assets, $17,366,588 (M); expenditures, $1,084,256; qualifying distributions, $910,031; giving activities include $816,500 for 7 grants (high: $400,000; low: $500).
Purpose and activities: Giving primarily to Christian programs and projects. In addition, the grantmaker runs a childcare center that provides daytime child care and education in a Christian environment. As part of their education, children are taught Bible stories on a weekly basis.
Fields of interest: Performing arts, music (choral); Education, early childhood education; Theological school/education; Children, day care; Christian agencies & churches; Protestant agencies & churches.
Limitations: Giving primarily in Washington, FL, GA, TX, and WY.
Application information:
Initial approach: Concept letter (not exceeding 3 pages)
Deadline(s): None
Officers: Paul Piper, Pres.; Ronald K. Piper, V.P.
Director: Lynn Piper.
EIN: 582021971
Other changes: Tom L. Maschmeyer, Jr. is no longer Secy.

3672
Cody Medical Foundation
1108 14th St., No. 422
Cody, WY 82414-3423 **(307) 250-0454**
Contact: Marty Coe, Exec. Dir.
Main URL: http://codymedicalfoundation.org

Established about 1940.
Foundation type: Independent foundation.
Financial data (yr. ended 06/30/13): Assets, $1,466,747 (M); expenditures, $133,461; qualifying distributions, $79,595; giving activities include $65,571 for 19 grants (high: $20,000; low: $371).
Purpose and activities: Giving to enhance health care for residents of the West Park Hospital district, including the towns of Cody and Meeteetse. The foundation also administers a scholarship program for students majoring in medicine or nursing who reside, or whose parents reside, in the West Park Hospital district.
Fields of interest: Hospitals (general); Health care; Health organizations, association; Cancer; Recreation.
Type of support: General/operating support; Grants to individuals; Scholarships—to individuals.
Limitations: Applications accepted. Giving limited to the West Park Hospital district, Park County, WY.
Publications: Application guidelines.
Application information: Application guidelines available on foundation web site.
Initial approach: Letter
Deadline(s): None
Board meeting date(s): 3rd Wed. of each month
Officers: Henry H.R. Coe, Jr., Pres.; Edward Webster, V.P.; Marty Coe, Exec. Dir.
Trustees: Henry H.R. Coe III; Kathleen Divencenzo; Anne Hayes; Doug McMillan; Carol Roberts; Peggy Rohrbach; Steve Simonton; Joe Tilden.
Number of staff: 1
EIN: 836006491

3673
The Carine and Jacques Dubois Family Foundation
(formerly The Jacques & Lucille Dubois Charitable Foundation)
P.O. Box 10100
Jackson, WY 83002-0100

Established in 1998 in CT.
Donor: Jacques E. Dubois.
Foundation type: Independent foundation.
Financial data (yr. ended 06/30/13): Assets, $5,480,359 (M); gifts received, $60; expenditures, $217,676; qualifying distributions, $158,480; giving activities include $155,000 for 3 grants (high: $100,000; low: $25,000).
Fields of interest: Higher education; Education; Boy scouts; Human services; Foundations (community).
Limitations: Applications not accepted. Giving primarily in CT, NM, RI, and WY. No grants to individuals.
Application information: Contributes only to pre-selected organizations.
Officers: Carine R. Klein, Chair.; Jacques E. Dubois, Pres.
EIN: 061529842
Other changes: The grantmaker no longer lists a primary contact.

3674
Furrer Foundation
c/o John Furrer, Dir.
P.O. Box 10849
Jackson, WY 83002-0849
Contact: John Furrer

Established in 1986 in IL.
Donor: John R. Furrer.
Foundation type: Independent foundation.
Financial data (yr. ended 06/30/13): Assets, $289,303 (M); expenditures, $595; qualifying distributions, $0.
Fields of interest: Hospitals (general); Religion.
Limitations: Applications not accepted. Giving primarily in Vero Beach, FL, and Jackson Hole, WY. No grants to individuals.
Application information: Unsolicited requests for funds not accepted.
Directors: Annie W. Furrer; Blake Furrer; John R. Furrer; Kimberly Van Nortwick.
EIN: 363496954

3675
Marine Ventures Foundation, Inc.
P.O. Box 14390
Jackson, WY 83002
***E-mail:* info@marineventures.org**; Main URL: http://www.marineventures.org
Blog: http://www.marineventures.org/blog/

Established in 2001 in DC.
Donor: John Thomas McMurray.
Foundation type: Independent foundation.
Financial data (yr. ended 12/31/12): Assets, $3,338,601 (M); expenditures, $187,255; qualifying distributions, $151,625; giving activities include $142,500 for 3 grants (high: $100,000; low: $17,500).
Purpose and activities: Giving to fund new conservation efforts to ensure healthy fish populations in the world's rivers and oceans. The grantmaker's vision is to shift the cultural focus of short-term wealth extraction of our limited natural resources in the world's river and marine ecosystems, to long-term stewardship for the benefit of the rivers and oceans and all of us who depend on them.
Fields of interest: Education; Animals/wildlife, fisheries; Animals/wildlife; Human services.
Limitations: Applications not accepted. No grants to individuals.
Application information: Contributes only to pre-selected organizations.
Officer: Tom McMurray, C.E.O. and Pres.
Directors: Carson Reid McMurray; John Thomas McMurray; McCain Jay McMurray; Brandon C. White.
EIN: 522297698

3676
The McMurry Foundation
P.O. Box 2016
Casper, WY 82602-2016
***Contact:* Trudi McMurry, Fdn. Dir.**
FAX: (307) 234-4631; E-mail: trudi@mcmurry.net; Additional e-mail: Jaci Schoup, Asst. Dir., Jschoup@mcmurry.net; Main URL: http://www.mcmurryfoundation.org/

Established in 1998 in WY.
Donors: Neil A. McMurry; Susie McMurry.
Foundation type: Independent foundation.
Financial data (yr. ended 12/31/12): Assets, $51,047,665 (M); gifts received, $500,000; expenditures, $5,075,313; qualifying distributions, $4,280,314; giving activities include $4,032,628 for 129 grants (high: $1,000,000; low: $250).
Purpose and activities: The foundation places special emphasis on the areas of education, religion, children and advocacy for children, health and human services, the arts and humanities, and a favorable business environment. In carrying out its work, the foundation is guided by the values of excellence and compassion. The foundation invests in innovative ventures as well as established community programs that have the potential to make a lasting difference. It provides seed money to start new programs as well as general funds to expand or improve services offered by established agencies. The foundation also helps organizations within its community become more self-sufficient and efficient through strategic planning, increasing management capacity and board development, in order to better serve community needs.
Fields of interest: Humanities; Arts; Education; Human services; Children/youth, services; Religion; Infants/toddlers; Children/youth; Children; Adults; Aging; Disabilities, people with.
Type of support: Scholarship funds; General/operating support; Continuing support; Capital campaigns; Building/renovation; Equipment; Endowments; Emergency funds; Program development; Seed money; Technical assistance.
Limitations: Applications accepted. Giving primarily in WY, with special emphasis on Natrona County. No grants to individuals.
Publications: Application guidelines.

Application information: See web site for application guidelines. Application form required.
Initial approach: Online letter of inquiry
Copies of proposal: 1
Deadline(s): See web site for current deadlines
Board meeting date(s): Quarterly
Final notification: Within 2 months
Officers and Directors:* Mick McMurry,* Pres.; Susie McMurry,* Secy.; George Bryce,* Treas.
Number of staff: 1 full-time professional; 2 part-time professional.
EIN: 830323982

3677
Willard H. Moyer Foundation
P.O. Box 801
Powell, WY 82435-0801 (307) 754-2962

Established in 1988 in WY.
Foundation type: Operating foundation.
Financial data (yr. ended 12/31/12): Assets, $2,163,779 (M); expenditures, $31,910; qualifying distributions, $20,633; giving activities include $13,327 for 4 grants (high: $5,000; low: $1,327).
Fields of interest: Boys & girls clubs; Big Brothers/Big Sisters; Human services; Community/economic development.
Type of support: Equipment; Land acquisition; Matching/challenge support.
Limitations: Giving primarily in Powell, WY. No grants to individuals.
Publications: Application guidelines.
Application information: Application form required.
Initial approach: Letter or proposal
Deadline(s): None
Board meeting date(s): Quarterly
Directors: Mindy Christiansen; S. Joseph Darrah; **Cheryl Elliott**; Wesley J. Metzler; John Max Stutzman.
EIN: 742480676
Other changes: Nicholas W. Morris and David R. Reetz are no longer directors.

3678
B. F. & Rose H. Perkins Foundation
45 E. Loucks St., Ste. 110
Sheridan, WY **82801-6329** (307) 674-8871
FAX: (307) 674-8803;
E-mail: bfperkin@fiberpipe.net; Main URL: http://www.perkinsfoundation.org/

Established in 1933 in WY.
Donor: Benjamin F. Perkins†.
Foundation type: Independent foundation.
Financial data (yr. ended 12/31/12): Assets, $9,428,191 (M); expenditures, $829,199; qualifying distributions, $1,014,578; giving activities include $590,500 for 5 grants (high: $550,000; low: $3,500), $79,843 for 67 grants to individuals, $238,540 for 50 loans to individuals, and $32,263 for foundation-administered programs.
Purpose and activities: Medical and educational assistance to individuals under the age of 21; recipients of educational loans must be graduates of a Sheridan County, Wyoming, high school.
Fields of interest: Higher education; Youth, services; Economically disadvantaged.
Type of support: General/operating support; Grants to individuals; Student loans—to individuals.
Limitations: Applications accepted. Giving limited to residents of Sheridan County, WY.
Publications: Application guidelines; Informational brochure.
Application information: Minimum 1 year residency in Sheridan County, WY. Application form required.
Initial approach: Letter
Copies of proposal: 1
Deadline(s): June 1 for fall registration; 1st of each month for other educational grants and for medical grants
Board meeting date(s): Third Tues. or second to last Tues. of each month
Officers and Trustees:* Victor Garber,* Chair.; Paddy Bard,* Vice-Chair.; Stephen D. Carroll,* Treas.; George P. Fletcher; Michael Pilch.
Number of staff: 1 full-time professional; 5 full-time support; 2 part-time support.
EIN: 830138740

3679
Homer A. & Mildred S. Scott Foundation
P.O. Box 2007
Sheridan, WY 82801-2007 (307) 672-1448
Contact: Jenny Craft, Exec. Dir.
FAX: (307) 672-1443; E-mail: jenny.craft@fib.com;
Foundation office telephone: (307) 672-1440;
Main URL: http://www.scottfoundation.org
Grants List: http://www.scottfoundation.org/grant-recipients/

Established in 1982 in WY.
Donors: Homer A. Scott†; Mildred S. Scott†.
Foundation type: Independent foundation.
Financial data (yr. ended 02/28/14): Assets, $27,616,227 (M); expenditures, $1,228,922; qualifying distributions, $1,120,378; giving activities include $969,335 for 274 grants (high: $125,000; low: $25).
Purpose and activities: The trustees will look favorably upon grant requests that are designed to intervene in and prevent the problems of young people; build public awareness of early childhood and youth issues particularly in Sheridan County, WY; and promote coordination and communication among programs and agencies serving young people and the larger community. The trustees also encourage grants that support community development and improvement.
Fields of interest: Humanities; Arts; Education; Health care; Human services; Children/youth, services; Community/economic development; Infants/toddlers; Children/youth; Children.
Type of support: General/operating support; Continuing support; Management development/capacity building; Program development; Curriculum development; Scholarship funds; Employee matching gifts; Matching/challenge support.
Limitations: Applications accepted. Giving within a 35-mile radius of Sheridan, WY, and in specific areas of MT. No grants to individuals.
Publications: Application guidelines; Grants list; Program policy statement.
Application information: Application form required.
***Initial approach:* Telephone or e-mail for guidelines**
Copies of proposal: 1
Deadline(s): Varies, contact office for dates
Board meeting date(s): Quarterly
Final notification: 1 week after board meeting
Officer and Trustees:* Jenny Craft, Exec. Dir.; Jay M. McGinnis; Tom S. Heyneman; Mark Kinner; Lynette Scott; Michelle Sullivan; Sandra Scott Suzor; Arin Waddell.
Number of staff: 1 full-time professional.
EIN: 742250381
Other changes: The grantmaker now makes its application guidelines and grants list available online.

3680
Seven Pillars Foundation
P.O. Box 2091
Sheridan, WY 82801-2091 (307) 675-5098
Contact: Hannah Barnes, Secy.

Foundation type: Independent foundation.
Financial data (yr. ended 12/31/12): Assets, $1,749,094 (M); gifts received, $1,419,496; expenditures, $2,257,725; qualifying distributions, $2,247,105; giving activities include $2,223,105 for 16 grants (high: $1,000,000).
Purpose and activities: Giving primarily to Christian organizations to spread the word of Jesus Christ.
Fields of interest: Christian agencies & churches.
Limitations: Giving in the U.S., with emphasis on WY.
Application information:
Initial approach: Proposal
Deadline(s): None
***Final notification:* Within 6 weeks**
Officers: Casey H. Osborn, Pres.; Susan J. Osborn, V.P. and Treas.; Hannah Barnes, Secy.
EIN: 263174574
Other changes: At the close of 2012, the grantmaker paid grants of $2,223,105, a 76.8% increase over the 2011 disbursements, $1,257,173.

3681
Harry & Thelma Surrena Memorial
P.O. Box 603
Sheridan, WY 82801-0603
Application address: P.O. Box 27, Buffalo, WY 82834-0027, tel.: (307) 684-5574

Established in 1973 in WY.
Foundation type: Independent foundation.
Financial data (yr. ended 10/31/13): Assets, $5,378,062 (M); expenditures, $297,259; qualifying distributions, $262,691; giving activities include $248,500 for 23 grants (high: $45,000; low: $500).
Fields of interest: Education; Human services; YM/YWCAs & YM/YWHAs; Children, services; Protestant agencies & churches.
Limitations: Applications accepted. Giving primarily in WY. No grants to individuals.
Application information:
Initial approach: Letter
Deadline(s): None
Trustees: John Pradere; Ralph C. Robinson; **Robert Wyatt**.
EIN: 237435554

3682
William E. Weiss Foundation, Inc.
P.O. Box 14270
Jackson, WY 83002-4270
Contact: Liz D. Hutchinson
FAX: (307) 733-7545

Incorporated in 1955 in NY.
Donors: William E. Weiss, Jr.†; Helene K. Brown†.
Foundation type: Independent foundation.
Financial data (yr. ended 03/31/13): Assets, $7,226,931 (M); expenditures, $429,942; qualifying distributions, $339,775; giving activities include $339,500 for 26 grants (high: $44,500; low: $1,500).
Purpose and activities: Giving primarily to museums and for arts and cultural programs.
Fields of interest: Arts; Education; Environment.

Type of support: General/operating support; Continuing support; Capital campaigns; Building/renovation; Program development.
Limitations: Applications not accepted. Giving primarily in CA, MO, NY, TN and WY. No grants to individuals.
Application information: Contributes only to pre-selected organizations.
Officers: Monte Brown, Pres.; William U. Weiss, V.P.; Katrina W. Ryan, Secy.; Dwyer Brown, Treas.
Number of staff: 1 part-time support.
EIN: 556016633

3683
Whitney Benefits, Inc.

P.O. Box 5085
Sheridan, WY 82801-1385 (307) 674-7303
Contact: Patrick Henderson, Exec. Dir.
FAX: (307) 674-4335;
E-mail: assistant@whitneybenefits.org; Physical address: 145 N. Connor St., Ste. 1, Sheridan, WY 82801; Main URL: http://www.whitneybenefits.org

Incorporated in 1927 in WY.
Donors: Edward A. Whitney‡; Scott Foundation; Sheridan County YMCA.
Foundation type: Independent foundation.
Financial data (yr. ended 06/30/13): Assets, $127,739,290 (M); expenditures, $7,152,788; qualifying distributions, $8,474,350; giving activities include $6,181,888 for 7 grants (high: $5,716,739; low: $2,207), and $1,872,505 for loans/program-related investments.
Purpose and activities: Giving primarily for the township of Sheridan, WY. The foundation also provides interest-free student loans to men and women with modest financial assistance, so they may pursue undergraduate academic and vocational studies. Applicants should either be graduates of high schools in Sheridan and Johnson counties, WY, GED recipients from Sheridan County, WY, or individuals who have had at least seven years of continuous residency in Sheridan or Johnson County immediately prior to applying for a loan.
Fields of interest: Higher education; Community/economic development.
Type of support: General/operating support; Program-related investments/loans; Student loans—to individuals.
Limitations: Applications accepted. Giving limited to Sheridan County, WY.
Publications: Annual report.
Application information: Applications accepted for loan program only. Application form required.
Initial approach: Request loan application
Board meeting date(s): Monthly
Officers and Directors:* Tom Kinnison,* Pres.; Roy Garber,* V.P.; Tom Belus,* Secy.; Stephen Holst,* Treas.; Patrick Henderson, Exec. Dir.; Maureen Humphrys; Kim Love; Everett McGlothlin; **Lori McMullen**; **Lynie Phipps**; **Tom Pilch**; **Robert Prusak**; Peter Schoonmaker; Sam Scott.
Number of staff: 1 full-time professional; 1 full-time support.
EIN: 830168511
Other changes: Val Burgess, Jack P. Chase, David J. Withrow and Samuel S. Street are no longer directors.

3684
Wyoming Community Foundation

1472 N. 5th St., Ste. 201
Laramie, WY 82072 (307) 721-8300
Contact: For grants: Samin Dadelahi, C.O.O.
FAX: (307) 721-8333; E-mail: wcf@wycf.org; Additional tel.: (866) 708-7878; Grant inquiry e-mail: samin@wycf.org; Main URL: http://www.wycf.org
Facebook: https://www.facebook.com/pages/Wyoming-Community-Foundation/138109556202547
YouTube: http://www.youtube.com/wyomingcf

Incorporated in 1989 in WY.
Foundation type: Community foundation.
Financial data (yr. ended 12/31/12): Assets, $87,725,830 (M); gifts received, $4,276,752; expenditures, $5,607,489; giving activities include $2,483,836 for grants, and $114,770 for 112 grants to individuals.
Purpose and activities: The foundation seeks to foster the community and enhance the quality of life for Wyoming residents through asset building, grantmaking and increased civic engagement, participation and leadership. Current statewide areas of need from the foundation's unrestricted funds are children and youth and civic projects.
Fields of interest: Arts; Education; Environment, natural resources; Health care; Health organizations, association; Children/youth, services; Human services; Community development, public/private ventures; Rural development; Community/economic development; Voluntarism promotion.
Type of support: General/operating support; Continuing support; Management development/capacity building; Program development; Conferences/seminars; Seed money; Technical assistance; Program evaluation; Scholarships—to individuals; Matching/challenge support.
Limitations: Applications accepted. Giving primarily in WY. No grants to individuals (except for scholarships), or generally for block grants, capital campaigns, annual campaigns, or debt retirement.
Publications: Application guidelines; Annual report; Grants list; Informational brochure (including application guidelines); Newsletter; Program policy statement.
Application information: Visit foundation web site for online account access, application forms and guidelines. Application form required.
Initial approach: Create online account
Copies of proposal: 11
Deadline(s): Mar. 1, July 1, and Nov. 1
Board meeting date(s): Quarterly
Final notification: June 15, Sept. 15, and Mar. 15
Officers and Directors:* Diane Harrop,* Chair.; Billie Addleman,* Vice-Chair.; Craig R. Showalter,* C.E.O. and Pres.; Samin Dadelahi, C.O.O.; **Misty Gehle, C.F.O.**; Connie Brezik,* Secy.; Jim Gersack,* Treas.; John Andrikopoulos; Robert B. Betts, Jr.; Kathryn Boswell; Carolyn Bing; **Affie Ellis**; Joan Evans; Greg Irwin; Arne Jorgensen; Cathy MacPherson; George McIlvaine; Douglas McLaughlin; Anna Moscicki; Lollie Benz Plank; Jim Rice; Kent Richins; Kathy Tomassi; Sandra Wallop.
Number of staff: 7 full-time professional; 2 full-time support; 1 part-time support.
EIN: 830287513
Other changes: Affie Ellis is no longer a director.

INDEX TO DONORS, OFFICERS, TRUSTEES

1345 Cleaning Service Co. II LP, 2157
1988 Kettering Tower Trust, 2716
1998 Katina Charitable Trust No. 2, The, 2236
1998 Katina Charitable Trust, The, 2236
1998 MJ Trust, The, 2236
1st International Trust Dept., 2651

299 Cleaning Service Co. II LP, 2157

3510 LLC, 1379
3M Co., 1676

450 Corporation, 1962

525 Realty Holding, 1962

605 Cleaning Service Co. II LP, 2157

8101 Sepulveda LLC, 116

A & A Fuel Oil Co., 1976
A & E Trust, 2383
A Glimmer of Hope Foundation, 3159
A to Z Mud Co., Inc., 3330
A&R Enterprises, 130
A.F. and A.M Grand Lodge of Colorado, 482
Aalfs, Joann "Joan" E., 2571
Aamodt, Patsy, 28
Aamoth, Gordon M., 1734
Aaron, Patrice, 1625
AARP, 186
Abara, Obinna, Esq., 3034
ABARTA Inc., 2881
Abbitt, Carolyn S., 3455
Abbitt, Matthew M., 3455
Abbitt, Richard F., 3455
Abbitt, Stephen M., 3455
Abbott, Alan, 3312
Abbott, Clara, 954
Abbott, David T., 2708
Abbott, Herschel L., Jr., 1299
Abbott, James W., 662
Abbott, John, 1581
Abbott, John J., 2167
Abbott, Judy, 3397
Abbott, Julie, 1200
Abbs, David J., 1662
Abbs, Jim, 1179
Abdalla, Zein, 2354
Abdul-Latif, Saad, 2354
Abe, Jane, 3397
Abel Partners, 1889
Abel, David, 2866
Abel, Melissa D., 3368
Abell Foundation, Nelson, 3242
Abell, Betsy G., 3242
Abell, G. Hughes, 3242
Abell, George T., 3160
Abell, Gladys H., 3160
Abels, Kathy Simon, 410
Abelsen, James, 1677
Abendshein, Nancy, 3183
Abernathy, Chad, 1010
Abernathy, Maggie E., 1768
Abernathy, Robyn, 3299
Abernathy, Tom, 867
Abernethy, Bruce, 768, 2454
Abernethy, Todd, 726
Abeyta, David, 3576
Abgott, Michael A., 2982
Abizaid, John P., Genl., 3468
Ableidinger, Esther, 1587
Ables, Steve, Hon., 3187
Ablon, Ben, 3222
Abney, Kim, 1131
Abood, M., 2697
Aboussie, Marilyn, 3343
Abplanalp, Dean, 1163
Abraham, Diane, 3642
Abraham, Jane, 1410
Abraham, Nancy, 2023
Abraham, Stephen H., 1410
Abramowitz, Kenneth, 548
Abramowitz, Nira, 548
Abrams, Blanche H., 2965
Abrams, Donald, 65
Abrams, Elliott, 2465
Abrams, Marilynn R., 2952
Abrams, Melinda, 2106
Abrams, Orin, 83
Abramson, Andrew, 2024
Abregu, Martin, 2160
Abreu Trust, Francis, 846
Abreu, Claire, 846
Abreu, Katherine M., 846
Abreu, Michael, 846
Abreu, Peter M., 846
Absey, Julie, 309
Abshire, Jennifer, 912
Acamovic, Millie, 1722
ACE American Insurance Co., 2880
Ace Beverage Co., 85
Ace Endowment Fund, 797
Acee, William, 2429
Aceves, Ann N., 593
Achelis, Elisabeth, 2026
Acheson, James C., 1571
Ackerley, Barry A., 3489, 3555
Ackerley, Christopher, 3489
Ackerley, Edward, 3489
Ackerley, Gail A., 3489
Ackerly, John P., III, 3448
Ackerly, Maureen C., 3433
Ackerman, Barbara Berkman, 1434
Ackerman, Christina, 3162
Ackerman, Sybil, 2856
Ackley, Carlyle, 1289
Ackley, Tom, 1848
Ackman, Karen, 2356
Ackman, Lawrence D., 2356
Ackman, William, 2356
Acomb, Joanne, 3663
Acone, Tony, 488
Acosta Sales & Marketing, 952
Acra, Ruth P., 3449
ACT-UP, 2203
Active Network, 272, 2019
Acton, Pam W., 1137
Acuff, A. Marshall, Jr., 1645
Adair, Marla, 3142
Adam, Diane, 394
Adam, Milton F., 945
Adam, Robert, 3380
Adam, Todd V., 3274
Adams Charitable Trust, Gladis H., 2633
Adams Trust, Jean Pape, 2806
Adams, Ada Woodson, 2662
Adams, Aileen, 456
Adams, Alice E., 2516
Adams, Allan B., 508
Adams, Brett, 1146
Adams, Caroline J., 1423
Adams, Charles E., 1423
Adams, Deborah, 525
Adams, Elizabeth Helms, 247
Adams, Ellen H., 549
Adams, Frederick M., Jr., 1588
Adams, Greg, 2747
Adams, Holmes S., 1767
Adams, James W., 549
Adams, Jean, 1717
Adams, Jeff, 3466
Adams, John, 484
Adams, Jonna, 909
Adams, Karen, 549
Adams, Karen Booth, 3433
Adams, Marjorie Carr, 956
Adams, Maurean B., 2540
Adams, Megan, 1524
Adams, Nathan, 1186
Adams, Peter D., 76
Adams, Rebecca B., 76
Adams, Robert M., 1972
Adams, Rolland L., 2881
Adams, Rukaiyah, 2861
Adams, Timothy, 2726
Adams, Warren, 1524
Adams, William James "will.i.am", Jr., 259
Adams, William L., 1345
Adams-Rodgers, Lois, 3451
Adamson, Cheryl, 3112
Adamson, Katharine J., 613
Adamson, Rebecca, 2056
Adamson, Terrence B., 2286
Adcock, Gerald, 3430
Adcock, Louis N., Jr., 801
Addeo, Patricia, 2767
Adderley, Terence E., 1588
Addington, Susan, 1265
Addison, Garrick, 3298
Addison, Loveanne, 900
Addleman, Billie, 3684
Adelson, Miriam, Dr., 1424
Adelson, Sheldon G., 1424
Adelson, Warren, 2220
Aderhold, John E., 918
Adkins, Lisa, 1282
Adkins, Stephen R., 3487
Adler, Anne, 3633
Adler, Bette, 3633
Adler, Constance, 1336
Adler, Les K., Dr., 462
Adler, Maria, 2423
Adler, Rothstein Rosenfeldt, 1974
Adleta, Charles Derek, 3282
Aduddell, Larry D., 3196
Advisory Small Cap Value, 3642
Advocate and Greenwich Times Holiday Fund, The, 613
Adwan, Teresa B., 2828
AEGON Transamerica Foundation, 1228
Aetna, 2445
Aetna Health Inc., 550
Aetna Inc., 550
Aetna Life Insurance Company, 550
Afram-Gyening, Francis, 2770
Afsar, Kamran, 2986
Aft, David, 868
Agarwal, Adhish, 3390
Agarwal, Sunil, 216
Agather, Elaine, 2014
Agather, V. Neils, 3185
Agee, Dean P., 3434
Agee, Robert D., 628
Agelasto, Peter A., 3428
Agency Serv. Consolidated, Inc., 2802
Aghamirzadeh, Reza, 3067
Aghdami, Farhad, 3433
Aghjayan, George M., 2001
Agli, Andria, 31
Agnew, Lynn, 3494
Agnoni, Michael D., 2798
Agouron Institution, 559
AGR Trust, The, 1086
Agresta, Maurice, 1353
Agudath Israel of Long Island, 1902
Aguiar, Lauren, 2427
Aguilar, Don, 408
Aguilar, Francisco, 54
Aguilo, Elizabeth, 1564
Ahart, Edward W., 1982
Ahearn, Gayle S., 38
Ahearn, Michael J., 38
Ahern, John Patrick, 1877
Aherne, Damon, 2966
Ahmadi, Hoshang, 2030
Ahmanson, Howard F., 77
Ahmanson, Howard F., Jr., 77
Ahmanson, Robert H., 77
Ahmanson, William H., 77
Ahmanson, William Howard, 77
Ahmed, Mohammed Raheemuddin, 78
Ahrendt, Martha, 3619
Ahrens, Barbara, 503
Ahrens, Chad W., 1210
Ahrens, Claude W., 1210
Ahrens, Edward D., 941
Ahrens, Lydia, 992
Ahuja, Namrata, 37
Ahuja, Natasha, 37
Ahyakak, Eddie, 28
Aicher Trust, Paul J., The, 1323
Aicher, Paul J., 1323
Aicher, Peter, 1323
Aidikoff, Uhl & Bakhtiari, 368
Aids Institute, Inc., The, 797

America Online, Inc., 2466
American Antiquarian Society, 2069
American Bank, 3664
American Book Wholesale, 2562
American Contractors Insurance Group, 3294
American Electric Power Co., Inc., 2657
American Electric Power Service Corp., 2656
American Express, 2033
American Express Co., 2034
American Flange & Manufacturing Co., Inc., 796
American Friends for Charities, 2069
American Friends of Hebrew University, 2035
American Homecare Federation, Inc., 560
American Industries, Inc., 2849
American International Group, Inc., 2029
American Ireland Fund, 3026
American Livestock Insurance Co., 1101
American Mutual Life Insurance Co., 1211
American National Bank & Trust Co., 532
American Oil Gas Reporter, The, 3237
American Refining Bio-Chemical, Inc., 2963
American Retail Group, Inc., 2364
American Retail Properties, Inc., 2364
American Trading and Production Corp., 1349, 1409
American Trim, 2661
American United Life Insurance Co., 1183
Americans for Financial Security, 3198
Americans for Oxford, 2069
AmeriCorps, 1090
AMERIGROUP Corp., 3420
AmerUs Group Co., 1211
Ames, Aubin Z., 1990
Ames, Brooks A., 1449
Ames, Harriett, 2884
Ames, Kathryn, 1346
Ames, Marshall, 778
Ames, Steven, 2884
Amestoy, Jay, 313
Amey, Kenneth, 3006
Amin, Dhruvika Patel, 2081
Amin, Mahendra, 3563
Amin, Saroj, 3563
Amine, Jim, 2118
Amis, Richard M., 3278
Ammer, Katrina, 543
Ammerman, Don, 800
Amoco Corp., 28, 3181
Amoco Production Co., 3181
Amonette, Tracy L., 514
Amor, Jack, 830
Amoroso Construction, 102
Amos Charitable Lead Trust, Olivia D., 849
Amos Trust, Jean, 848
Amos Trust, Paul, 848
Amos Trust, Paul S. and Jean R., 848
Amos, Daniel P., 848
Amos, Olivia D., 849
AmSouth Bancorporation, 19
AmSouth Bank, 19
Amundson, Diane, 1753
AMVESCAP, 847
Amzak Corp., 766
Anastasio, Curtis V., 3307
Anchia, Rafael M., 3262
Anchorage Times Publishing Co., 29
Anderas, Per, Dr., 3597
Anderegg, Gregory L., 3625
Anders, Betty, 1224
Anders, Jay, 1647
Anders, Thomas, 2664
Andersen Construction Co., 3533
Andersen Corp., 1678
Andersen, Anne Heller, 246
Andersen, Eric C., 2887
Andersen, Fred C., 1702
Andersen, Katherine B., 1702
Andersen, Mark, 545
Anderson Foundation, Rose-Marie and Jack R., 1356
Anderson, Alice Childs, 559
Anderson, Annette, 386
Anderson, Betsy C., 3488
Anderson, Bradford L., 207
Anderson, Charles, 3555
Anderson, Charles M., 3492
Anderson, Charlie, 3492
Anderson, Christina S.T., 991
Anderson, Claudia, 1868
Anderson, Daniel, 1867
Anderson, David C., 3487
Anderson, David G., 3139
Anderson, Dennis, 1699
Anderson, Diana, 1740
Anderson, Dorothy, 2335
Anderson, Dorothy I., 3492
Anderson, Douglas K., 611
Anderson, Edwin A., 1699
Anderson, Ellen G., III, 2943
Anderson, Ethel D., 867
Anderson, Frederic, 562
Anderson, Gerard M., 1588, 1638
Anderson, Grant A., 250
Anderson, Grenville, 2658
Anderson, Jan G., 3196
Anderson, Jason, 2840
Anderson, Jennifer, 3662
Anderson, Jim, 257
Anderson, John E., 85
Anderson, John E., Jr., 85
Anderson, John T., 1040
Anderson, Judith, 43
Anderson, Julie, 34
Anderson, Kathey K., 3164
Anderson, Kathleen, 3633
Anderson, Kathy, 1731
Anderson, Keith, 1699
Anderson, Ken, 1487
Anderson, Kerry, 442
Anderson, Kerry K., 26
Anderson, Lawrence, 2253
Anderson, Lisa, 3545
Anderson, Loren, 36
Anderson, Lorraine W., 531
Anderson, Lyn, 638
Anderson, Marion, 85
Anderson, Martha, 1567
Anderson, Matt, 484
Anderson, Melanie, 3361
Anderson, Melissa M., 2968
Anderson, Michael, 3545
Anderson, Michael D., 2826
Anderson, Michael K., 877, 915
Anderson, Michael S., 3441
Anderson, Michael W., 102
Anderson, Millicent, 415
Anderson, Nicholas R., 2658
Anderson, Nicole, 288, 3167
Anderson, Peg, 1241
Anderson, Peyton Tooke, Jr., 850
Anderson, Porter W., 2036
Anderson, Porter W., Jr., 2036
Anderson, R.B., 3421
Anderson, Rachel, 2335
Anderson, Raymond E., 531
Anderson, Rob, 1845
Anderson, Robert, 505
Anderson, Robert A., 3164
Anderson, Ronald R., 2925
Anderson, RuthAnne, 1864
Anderson, S. Eric, 260
Anderson, Scott, 3527
Anderson, Scott P., 1726
Anderson, Shannon, 3589
Anderson, Steven L., 1869
Anderson, Susan A., 33
Anderson, T. Mark, 3176
Anderson, Terri, 1822
Anderson, Thomas, 1060
Anderson, Thomas M., 2762
Anderson, Tim, 3568
Anderson, Tom, 1723
Anderson, Warrenn, 1751
Anderson, William, 3492
Anderson, William P., V, 2658
Anderson, William S., 85
Andover Publishing Co., 1536
Andrae-Pianta, Gail, 3330
Andreas, David, 1679
Andreas, Lowell W., 1679
Andresakis, Robert, 3187
Andresakis, Summer, 3187
Andrew Julie Klingenstein Family, 2258
Andrew, Anne, 538
Andrew, Robert, 1124
Andrews, Christie F., 506
Andrews, Daryl, 1203
Andrews, David J., 1896
Andrews, Edward, Jr., 866
Andrews, June, 1837
Andrews, Mary Linda, 2957
Andrews, Matthew, Mrs., 2659
Andrews, Nancy, 2534
Andrews, Nathan, 569
Andrews, Paul R., 574
Andrews, Renee Elise, 506
Andrews, Richard J., 506
Andrikopoulos, John, 3684
Andringa, Mary Vermeer, 1624
Andrus, Elizabeth H., 2454
Andrus, John E., 2454
Anfang, Stuart, 1479
Angel, Marc D., Rabbi, 2046
Angeles, Fatima, 140
Angelica, Robert E., 2002
Angelici Estate, 3148
Angell, Charles T., 962
Angell, Christopher C., 1538, 2261
Angell, James S ., 962
Angell, Michael T., 962
Angelle, Frank E., 3191
Angle, Tamimi, 2787
Anglin, Dale Robinson, 1972
Anglin, Scott W., 3420
Angner, Dennis P., 1622
Angoff, Walter, 1467
Anguilla, Melissa Alpert, 2524
Anheuser-Busch Cos., Inc., 1774
Anjargolian, Sara, 2001
Ankerson, John M., 3449
Annegers, Clarice, 574
Annenberg Foundation, The, 87
Annenberg, Wallis, 86, 87
Annenberg, Walter H., Hon., 86
Annis, John, 727
Anquillare, Ceasae, 2445
Ansara, Karen, 1464
Ansari-Berna, Farnaz, 2683
Anschuetz, Sara, 1065
Anschutz Foundation, The, 478
Ansin, Edmund N., 689
Ansley, Nancy, 697
Anstine, Mary K., 508
Antaramian, John, 3628
Antenori, Frank, 3363
Antes, Shirley M., 1257
Anthem Health Plans of New Hampshire, Inc., 1206
Anthem Insurance Cos., Inc., 1206
Anthem, Inc., 1156, 1206
Anthony, Carol C., 3593
Anthony, Christine A., 3593
Anthony, E. Jean, 1395
Anthony, Jay, 2111
Anthony, Joseph M., 1395
Anthony, Katherine A., 3593
Anthony, Mary, 547
Anthony, Rebecca R., 361
Anthony, Tucker, 2148
Anthony, Victor W., Jr., 3593
Antion, Kathleen, 150
Antiquarian Book Foundation, 2069
Antle, Tonya, 157
Anton, Mary, 1030
Anton, Raymond, Jr., 1344
Antonacci, Vance, 2981
Antonatos, Julia, 1001
Antongiovanni, A.J., 279
AOL Time Warner Inc., 2466
Aon Corp., 963
Aoyama-Martin, Jane, 2204
Apex Settlement, 368
Apfel, Derek, 1837
Apicella, Salvatore C., 2771
Appel, Daniel, 1190, 1204
Appel, Daniel C., 1145
Appel, Richard, 2342
Appel, Toby, 2016
Appenteng, Kofi, 2160
Apple, Timothy, 2908
Applebaum, Alan T., 690
Applebaum, Joseph, 690
Applebaum, Leila, 690
Applied Materials, Inc., 88
Aqua-Africa, 3330
Aquino, David, 43
Arader, Walter, 2894
Aragon, Andrea, 492
Arakelian, George H., 2474
ARAMARK, 3026
Aramburu, Justo Mendez, 3061
Aramony, Diane, 2317
Aran, Peter P., 2831
Aratani, George T., 89
Aratani, Linda Y., 89
Aratani, Sakaye I., 89
Arbella, Inc., 1426
Arbolino, Maija, 2343
Arbury, Julie Carol, 1597
Arbut, Ed, 1616
Arcana Foundation, The, 676
Arcay, Arnaldo, 3179
Arce, Jorge, 2134
ArcelorMittal USA, Inc., 964
Archdiocese of St. Louis, 1815
Archer, Arlene, 2732
Archer, Cynthia A., 3046
Archer, David, 1189

Archer, Galen, 493
Archer, Jessica, 1137
Archer, Keith, 1189
Archer, Pierce, 2943
Archibald, Anne G., 1427
Archibald, John L.G., 1427
Archibald, Simon, 1945
Archura, LLC, 3424
Arciero, Pam, 2210
Arctic Slope Regional Corp., 28
Ardisana, Lizabeth, 1645, 1666
Ardizzone, Leonisa, 2391
Arellano, Daniel, 43
Arellano, Michelle, 356
Arentz, Richard, 379
Aresty, Catherine, 2041
Aresty, Joseph, 2041
Aresty, Steven, 2041
Argidius Foundation, 2364
Aria Foundation, 678
Ariens Co., 3594
Ariens Company, 3594
Ariens Corp., 3594
Ariens Memorial, Francis, 3594
Ariens, Mary M., 3594
Arima, Donald J., Dr., 3520
Arison, Cassie, 691
Arison, David, 691
Arison, Jason, 691
Arison, Marilyn, 691
Arizona Public Service Co., 39
Arkema Inc., 2885
Arkin, Harry L., 479
Arlen, Alice, 678
Arloma Corp., 389
Armagno, Valerie S., 832
Arman, Kambiz, 260
Armann, Claudia, 320
Armbrister, Denise McGregor, 3055
Armbruster, David, 3370
Armendariz, Jim, 1268
Armintrout, Libby, 3558
Armknecht, Leila B., 625
Armour, Karen Webb, 1875
Armour, Laurance H., III, 3245
Armoury, Bernard, 1988
Armstrong, 3505
Armstrong Communications, Inc., 3032
Armstrong Telephone Co. of Maryland, 3032
Armstrong Telephone Co. of West Virginia, 3032
Armstrong Utilities, Inc., 3032
Armstrong Wood Products, 3505
Armstrong World, 3505
Armstrong, Bob, 1663
Armstrong, Carol, 538
Armstrong, Dick, 1158
Armstrong, Elaine, 1214
Armstrong, Gary, 1185
Armstrong, Jeffrey R., 510
Armstrong, Meta, 1837
Armstrong, Mike, 538
Armstrong, Page, 2790
Armstrong, Patrick D., 2336
Armstrong, R. Stephen, 1726
Armstrong, Robert E., 2286
Armstrong, Sidney O'Malley, 1823
Armstrong, Victor, 2611
Armstrong, Waymon, 724
Arnaboldi, Nicole, 2118
Arnall, Daniel M., 164
Arnall, Dawn, 92
Arnall, Roland, 92
Arneson, Chuck, 3662
Arneson, Jerry, 1751
Arnhold, Henry H., 337
Arnhold, John P., 337
Arnholt, Cynthia Haslam, 3138
Arnn, Larry P., 2028
Arno, Sara Goldman, 2181
Arnold, Andy, 543
Arnold, Clair (Yum), 917
Arnold, Jeni, 1753
Arnold, Julie Keeton, 867
Arnold, Kay Kelley, 1308
Arnold, Kay Kelly, 1763
Arnold, Lauren, 502
Arnold, Patricia, 1683
Arnold, Robert T., 3290
Arnone, Karen, 2132
Arntson, Peter A., 3461
Arntz Builders Inc., 93
Arntz, Donald M., 93
Arntz, Eugene S., 93
Arntz, K. Allan, 93
Arntz, Thomas E., 93
Aroesty, Matthew, 2154
Aronoff, Steven K., 2236
Arons, Nan, 2481
Aronson, Adam, 2042
Aronson, Ami Becker, 652
Aronson, James, 2042
Aronson, Jonathan, 2042
Aronson, Joshua, 2042
Aronson, Judith, 2042
Arp, Dave, 347, 397
Arrendondo, Joel, 2683
Arreola, Enrique, 159
Arsenian, Deana, 2085
Art Institute of Chicago, 2069
Arteaga, Sandy, 2113
Arthur Patricia Price Family Trust, 374
Arthur, William J., 398
Artisan International Value, 3642
ARYZ Corp., 390
Asam, Claire L., Dr., 929
Asbill, Richard M., 900
Asbury, Mary, 2782
Asch, Leslee, 2210
Ascher, Erin, 2758
Asen, Robert Scott, 2045
ASG Equities LLC, 2089
Ash, Bill, 3636
Ash, Jeff, 900
Ash, Robert, 3312
Ashby, Lisa, 2677
Ashby, Norma, 1823
Ashcraft, Alyce, 378
Ashenfelter, Martha, 3507
Asher, Jane, 653
Asher, John D., 111
Asher, Laura, 1067
Asher, Robert, 653
Asher, Thomas R., 2139
Ashford, Brytain, 138
Ashkenazi, David E., 1913
Ashkenazi, Ezra E., 1913
Ashkenazi, Isaac, 1913
Ashkenazi, Ronald, 1913
Ashley Furniture Industries, 3667
Ashley, George, 1868
Ashley, Suzanne, 3611
Ashmore, Lara, 3171
Ashton, Adam, 3388
Ashton, Alan C., 3388
Ashton, Annalura, 3388
Ashton, Brigham, 3388
Ashton, Elizabeth, 3388
Ashton, Eric A., Jr., 162
Ashton, Erin, 3388
Ashton, Karen, 3388
Ashton, Kristie, 2372
Ashton, Laurie, 394
Ashton, Mashea, 360, 1971
Ashton, Melissa, 3388
Ashton, Morgan, 3388
Ashton, Robert, 2056
Ashton, Samuel, 3388
Ashton, Spencer, 3388
Ashton, Stephanie, 3388
Ashton, Stephen, 3388
Ashton, Traci, 3388
Ashur, George, 1509
Askren, Stan A., 1223
Aspacher, Derek, 308
Aspirus Wausau Hospital, 3377
Assad, Lia Iacocca, 1487
Assael, Baruch, 2046
Assael, Christina Lang, 2046
Assael, Salvador J., 2046
Assents LLC, 1974
Assistance League of Stockton, 161
Associated Banc-Corp, 3642
Associated Materials, 3505
Association du Mecenat de Institut, 2069
Assurance Dimensions, 826
Assurant, Inc, 2047
Aster, Sara E., 3634
Astles, Geoffrey, 2342
AstraZeneca Pharmaceuticals LP, 623
AT&T Inc., 3167
Atcheson, Lynn, 1876
Atherton, Frank C., 925
Atherton, John, 1769
Atherton, Juliette M., 925
Atherton, Liz, 117
Atkins, Billy, 3591
Atkins, C. Richard, 1302
Atkins, George W.P., 896
Atkins, Paul, 3497
Atkins, Steve, 1218
Atkinson, Carol, 1832
Atkinson, Esther M., 1551
Atkinson, Eugenia, 2804
Atkinson, Harold S., 861
Atkinson, Herbert J., 1551
Atkinson, Terry, 378
Atlan Management Corp., 2048
Atlantic Foundation, The, 811
Atlantic Richfield Co., 3181
Atlantic Trust Co., N.A., 622, 636
Atlas Bass Fund, 3148
Atlas Realty Co., 215
Atlas, Lezlie, 96
Atlas, Richard S., 96
Atnip, Janice Pierce, 494
Atofina Chemicals, Inc., 2885
Attal, Charles A., 830
Attaway, John, 792, 804
Atticus Capital LLC, 2377
Atwater, Benjamin, 2981
Atwater, Verne S., 2271
Atwood, Elaine, 29
Atwood, Henry, 1720
Atwood, Jonathan, 2003
Atwood, Nicholas, 1720
Atwood, Robert B., 29
Atwood, Tom, 1720
Au, Carlton K.C., 929
Aubin, Nicole, 64
Auble, Mark A., 2798
Auburn Construction, 1517
Auchenpaugh, Faye, 1723
Aucker, Kendra, 2908
Audet, Anne-Marie J., 2106
Auer Irrevocable Trust, Ione Breeden, 1120
Auerbach, John M., 1366
Auerbach, Wally, 441
Augur, Marilyn H., 3168
August, Leslie J., 2581
August, Lourie, 1540
Auguste, Rhonda, 2005
Augustin, Reinhard, 2243
Augustine, Rose L., 2049
Ault, James F., 1175
Aungst, David, 2989, 3025
Aurora Chamber of Conference, 498
Aust, Bruce E., 1401
Austen, Christopher M., 771
Austgen, Dave, 1171
Austin Athletic Scholarship Foundation, 3159
Austin Ethiopian Women Assn., 3158
Austin, Edward H., Jr., 3247
Austin, Juan, 2599
Austin, Kenneth, 2492
Automatic Service Corp., 1388
Autry, Jacqueline, 3148
Auyang, Angela, 2
Auyang, Eric, 2
Auyang, Sunny, 2
Avant, Steve, 3098
Avedisian, Berge, 2437
Aventis Pharmaceuticals Inc., 1988
Avera, Mark, 725
Avery, Karen, 1124
Avery, Nelson, 3193
Aviad, Janet, 2074
Aviles, Jesus, 1216
Avis, Greg, 264
Aviva Life and Annuity Co., 1211
Avner, Eric, 2709
Avner, Marcia, 650
Avula, Danny TK, 3476
Awaya, Alvin, 1416
Axel, Joan U., 1217
Axelrad, Bertram, 828
Axelrod, Emily, 1441
Aycock, James M., 7
Ayer, Gordon C., 1341
Ayer, Laura, 2407
Ayer, Susan, 1341
Ayers, Ann, 2232
Ayers, David, 3208
Ayers, James W., 3121
Ayers, Janet, 3121
Ayers, John S., 2541
Ayers, Jon, 3121
Ayers, Kristy, 3121
Ayers, Nancy Sharon, 3121
Ayotte, Mark, 1687
Ayres, Nuri Delacruz, 728
Azar, Joe, 1760
Azeez, Anne, 694
Azeez, Kathleen, 694
Azeez, Michael, 694
Aziz, Nikhil, 2335
Azrael, Hilary, 2205
Azrak, Adam, 2053
Azrak, Elliot, 2053
Azrak, Elliott, 2053
Azrak, Marvin, 2053
Azrak, Victor, 2053

B.E.L.I.E.F. Foundation, 3198
B.F.Goodrich Co., The, 2561
B.P.O.E., 628
Baas, Janet Heldt, 1182
Baba, Gwendolyn, 117
Babbio, Lawrence T., Jr., 2492
Babcock, Betsy, 2521
Babcock, Bruce M., 2521
Babcock, Charles H., 2521
Babcock, Charles H., Jr., 2521
Babcock, John E., 1703
Babcock, John J., 1703
Babcock, Mary Reynolds, 2521
Babcock, Tim, 1207
Babcok, Judith, 2220
Babicka, Jerry, 574
Babicka, Jonathan, 574
Babicka, Lynn P., 574
Babicka, Missy, 574
Babiran, Ali, 2030
Babitt, J. Lawry, 2683
Babson, Averill, 1429
Babson, Deborah E., 1429
Babson, James A., 1429, 1430
Babson, Katherine L., 1430
Babson, Katherine L., Jr., 1429
Babson, Paul T., 1430
Babson, Richard L., 1429
Babson, Susan, 1429
Babylon, Caroline, 1357
Bach, Nathan, 988
Bachhuber, Thomas, 3604
Bachman, Dale S., 932
Bachman, Greg, 1262
Bachman, Gregory A., 3272
Bachman, Shannon, 1428
Bachmann, Bruce R., 1075
Bacigalupi, Tracy, 1578
Back Home Again Foundation, 1156
Backus, Curt, 1663
Backus, Lisa, Dr., 168
Bacon, John O., 2773
Badiner, Marion M., 2971
Baecher-Brown, Dee, 3419
Baehren, Jim, 2678
Baer, Timothy R., 1744
Bafundo, Donna, 3100
Bafunno, Norm, 1205
Bagby, Alyson M., 16
Bagget, Art, Jr., 354
Baggett, Art, 354
Bagley, Diane M., 949
Bagley, Martha R., Esq., 1460
Bagley, Nicole, 911
Bagley, Ralph R., Esq., 1460
Baharestani, Martin, 2458
Bahena, Jorge, 757
Bahl, Felicia V., 1681
Bahl, Roy W., 1503
Bahl, Tracy L., 1681
Bahlman, William, 2782
Bahr, Adam, 1241
Bahr, Bahr, 1268
Baiardi, Angelo, 1577
Baiardi, Chris A., 1577
Baiardi, Cindy J., 1577
Baiardi, Kristen L., 1577
Baiardi, Suzanne M., 1577
Baier, Jon, 1214
Baig, Mirza, 78
Baig, Patricia, 78
Bailes, Jacqueline H., 759
Bailes, Lamar, 3102
Bailey & Son, Bankers, M.S., 3096
Bailey, Andrew C., 1523
Bailey, Anita Lamb, 2855
Bailey, Charles D., Jr., 798
Bailey, Darlyne, 3045
Bailey, Dianne Chipps, 2562
Bailey, Dustin, 2855
Bailey, Gordon M., 2522
Bailey, H. Whitney, 2522
Bailey, Jackie, 1759
Bailey, John, 2522
Bailey, Judith, 160
Bailey, Merritt P., 2522
Bailey, Patricia B., 1426
Bailey, Penny, 1681
Bailey, Rich, 1847
Bailey, Robert, 564
Bailey, Ronald, Bishop, 2324
Bailey, Steven J., 2771
Bailey, Tammy, 1614
Bailey, Verna, 2868
Bailey, William H., 2522
Bailon, Katherine, 2037
Bain, Kevin, 1205
Bainum, Barbara, 1356
Bainum, Bruce, 1356
Bainum, Jane, 1356
Bainum, Roberta, 1356
Bainum, Stewart, Sr., 1356
Baio, Betsy, 2429
Bair, Jack, 1225
Bair, Preston, 2686
Baird and Co., Robert W., 3595
Baird Foundation, Robert W., 3666
Baird, Carol J., 3528
Baird, Dee, 1222
Baird, Mark, 1198
Baird, Pat, 1228
Baird, Patrick, 1228
Baird, Rob, 1805
Baird, Robert, 2707
Baird, William F., 1766
Baird, Zoe, 2290
Baity, Gail, 2109
Bakely, Claudia, 1263
Baker and Daniels, LLP, 1156
Baker Hughes Inc., 3170
Baker Lewis, David, 1666
Baker Living Trust, Jay, 3596
Baker, Ann, 1852
Baker, Bill, 3577
Baker, Brian, 1176
Baker, Carolyn, 2886
Baker, Clark A., 853
Baker, Curtis, 3207
Baker, Dexter F., 2886
Baker, Dorothy H., 2886
Baker, Douglas, 1181
Baker, Edward D., III, 98
Baker, Elizabeth Stephans, 3028
Baker, Ellen L., 2113
Baker, Howard H., Jr., 662
Baker, Jack, 564
Baker, James A., III, 276
Baker, Jay H., 3596
Baker, Jayne, 2342
Baker, Jeffrey B., 1726
Baker, John C., 479
Baker, John P., 3621
Baker, Judy, 3511
Baker, Kate, 2761
Baker, Larry F., 2748
Baker, Linda O., 1903
Baker, Marjorie Montgomery Ward, 1111
Baker, Martha, 722
Baker, Michael, 2686
Baker, Nichole D., 137
Baker, Norman D., Jr., 3079
Baker, Norton, 3362
Baker, Pat Good, 3596
Baker, Richard W., 824
Baker, Robert, 3660
Baker, Robert G., Jr., 536
Baker, Rosemary Boccio, 98
Baker, Thomas D., 3660
Baker, Thomas E., 1903
Baker, Thomas J., 3660
Baker, Tracy A., 1611
Baker, Trish, 3606
Baker, W. K., 837
Baker-Doyle, Kira, 3000
Bakken, Eric A., 1732
Bakwin, Edward Morris, 2395
Balbier, Jennifer, 2287
Balch, Alan F., 1296
Baldaeus, Gary, 901
Baldini, Tom, 1636
Baldino, Eugene W., 2452
Baldridge, Bill, 372
Baldwin, Dan, 157
Baldwin, Dennis E., 485
Baldwin, Edward, 926
Baldwin, Fred, 926
Baldwin, H. Furlong, 1401
Baldwin, Jeremy C., 926
Baldwin, Kathleen, 122
Baldwin, Kitt, 930
Baldwin, Kittredge A., Dr., 929
Baldwin, Peter, 3333
Bales, Carol, 1259
Bales, John F., III, 2997
Bales, Mayuli, 1703
Balestrieri, Thomas, 2902
Balfour, L.G., 1431
Balka, Don, 1176
Ball, Christi, 1847
Ball, Deborah Lowenberg, 1098
Ball, Edmund B., 1121
Ball, Edmund F., 1121
Ball, Frank C., 1121
Ball, George A., 1121
Ball, Julie, 2850
Ball, Lucius L., 1121
Ball, Lynne, 1482
Ball, Nancy Elitharp, 53
Ball, Virginia B., 1121
Ball, William A., 1121
Ball-Rokeach, Sandra, 320
Ballantine, Christopher, 474
Ballantine, David, 474
Ballantine, Elizabeth, 474
Ballantine, Jeri, 1178
Ballantine, Morley C., 474
Ballantine, Richard G., 474
Ballard, Christopher, 1630
Ballard, Pamela, 2809
Ballingall, Keith R., 1888
Ballou, E. Spencer Pardoe, 1522
Balloun, Julie W. Lanier, 891
Balmat, Mary Adams, 2517
Balsam, Cheryl, 990
Balsley, Jacob, III, 2611
Baltimore Gas and Electric Co., 1407
Baltoland Inc., 1388
Balzar, Rick, 288
Bamattre, William, 359
Bambeck, Alan, 2795
Bamberger, Eleanor F., 3389
Bamberger, Ernest, 3389
Bamford, Calvin D., Jr., 3495
Bamford, Drew, 3495
Bamford, Heather, 3495
Bamford, JoAnne W., 3495
Banaka, Jerry, 1268
Banco Popular North America, 3622
Bancroft, John, 1842
Bancroft, William N., 1539
Bandy, Cliff, 3365
Bandy, Michael C., 2803
Bane, Richard C., 1461
Banerjee, Rini, 2306
Banet, Gary, 1136
Bang, Dolores, 1836
Bangsund, Lynne, 2868
Bank of America, 3505
Bank of America Corp., 2524
Bank of America Merrill Lynch, 601, 1440, 1566
Bank of America, N.A., 575, 579, 583, 584, 588, 590, 600, 609, 695, 743, 801, 813, 853, 859, 875, 879, 880, 955, 966, 967, 977, 982, 1032, 1038, 1111, 1423, 1425, 1431, 1437, 1446, 1448, 1465, 1480, 1484, 1506, 1511, 1520, 1521, 1526, 1527, 1533, 1551, 1777, 1795, 1809, 1813, 1821, 2065, 2075, 2083, 2086, 2133, 2325, 2388, 2396, 2447, 2524, 2899, 3064, 3065, 3066, 3070, 3073, 3074, 3076, 3078, 3080, 3082, 3084, 3085, 3086, 3088, 3090, 3091, 3092, 3103, 3209, 3210, 3234, 3261, 3272, 3283, 3286, 3289, 3293, 3313, 3337, 3353, 3360, 3379, 3435, 3442, 3444, 3454, 3463, 3531, 3556, 3560, 3573
Bank of Charles Town, 3585
Bank of China, 2341
Bank of Hawaii, 925, 938, 940
Bank of New York Mellon, N.A., The, 2882
Bank of Texas, N.A., 3292
Bank of the West, 2649
Bank One Investment Corp., 2242
Bank, Premier, 2788
Banke, Barbara R., 266
Banke, Kathleen, 364
Banker, Alex, 301
Bankers Trust Co., 2134
Bankowski, Elizabeth, 3407, 3418
Bankowski, Elizabeth A., 1916
Banks, Betsy, 676
Banks, Dennis, 1129
Banks, Greg, 676
Banks, Jerry, 1235
Banks, John, 3141
Banks, Keith T., 2524
Banks, Richard, 2112
Bannigan, Patrick, 523
Bannish, Robert G., 2972
Bannister, Michael E., 1588
Bannon, Alexandra Laboutin, 113
Bannon, Mel B., 113
Bannon, Robert D., 113
Baptist Community Ministries, 1299
Baptist, Megan, 808
Bar Harbor Trust Svcs., 1335
Bara, Roy, 3163
Barabino, John, 502
Baradaran, Sharon, 341
Barakett, Timothy R., 2377
Baran, Helen, 2331
Baranick, Erin R., 3569
Barazzone, Esther L., 2892

Barb, Amy, 3589
Barb, Haley, 3194
Barbato, Virginia, 2754
Barber, Jim, 2632
Barber, Sandy, 3146
Barber, Scott, 3419
Barbieri, Barbara, 1207
Barbosa, Eric, 3326
Barbour, Larry D., 2612
Barbour, Margaret Sewall, 1339
Barbour, Patricia A., 1885
Barboza, Michael J., 3083
Barclay, Gilian R., 550
Barclays, 3505
Bard, C.R., Inc., 1905
Bard, James R., 2674
Bard, Karen, 2006
Bard, Paddy, 3678
Bare, John, 856
Barefield, Lun Ye Crim, 1012
Barens, Kristi, 283
Baretz, Anne, 1928
Barfield, Mary F., 3136
Barfield, Thomas J., 1432
Barhrambeygui, Sherry, 373
Barkan, Jeffrey, 3077
Barkan, Mel P., 2183
Barker, Chelsea, 1260
Barker, Dick, 1395
Barker, Jeff, 866
Barker, John, 540
Barker, Jonathan, 1282
Barker, Judy Liff, 3129
Barker, Peter K., 270, 276
Barker, Robert W. "Bob", 184
Barkheimer, Marlene, 2798
Barksdale, David, 1316
Barksdale, James L., 1768
Barksdale, Kathleen M., 909
Barksdale, Sally M., 1768
Barland, Jill, 3611
Barletta, Robert J., 2443
Barley, Harold W., 842
Barlow, David S., 140, 429
Barlow, Ed, 538
Barlow, Stewart E., 3405
Barmonde, Charles, 2780
Barna, Janet, 1848
Barnard Trust, George D., 1428
Barnard, Bryn, 667
Barnard, David, 3364
Barnard, Judith A., 990
Barnard, June, 1003
Barnard, Ray F., 3235
Barner, Julie A., 2650
Barnes, Bill, 1133, 1257
Barnes, Brett W., 1101
Barnes, Bruce, 468
Barnes, Chris, 1101
Barnes, Hannah, 3680
Barnes, Janet, 776
Barnes, Kenneth W., 1101
Barnes, Melody, 3500
Barnes, Robert, 1663, 3333
Barnes, Ron, 1764
Barnes, Virginia, 3052
Barnes, William F., 2826
Barnett, Albert E., 260
Barnett, Carol, 804
Barnett, Crawford F., Jr., 923
Barnett, Harvey J., 1083
Barnett, Hoyt, 804
Barnett, Janet, 1129
Barnett, Kathleen M., 1082
Barney, James, Dr., 2733
Barney, Michael E., 3440
Barnhart, Jim, 3555
Barnhill Family Fund, 2233
Barnhill, Robert E., Jr., 2599
Barnholt, Edward W., 357
Barnsley, Emma, 2549
Baron, Frederick M., 3171
Baron, Jason, 666
Baron, John F., 2313
Baron, Jules M., 2183
Baron, Lisa A. Blue, 3171
Baron, Richard K., 2183
Barone, Anna M., 2508
Barone, Richard, 2670
Barr, Edward S., 1285
Barr, Garland H., III, 1282
Barr, John F., 1360
Barr, Lamar, 3430
Barr, Lynn E., 102
Barr, Nicole, 2826
Barr, Steven, 2776
Barra, Frank N., 1952
Barra, Lori, 79
Barrak, Marion L., 585
Barranda, Michael, 1127
Barrera, Joel, 1515
Barreto, Lucy, 176
Barrett, Ann Dobson, 361
Barrett, Bill, 1845
Barrett, Clint, 1620
Barrett, David, 2071
Barrett, David O., 1150
Barrett, Jacqueline, 1150
Barrett, James, 2696
Barrett, John, 1620
Barrett, John F., 2694
Barrett, John P., 1359
Barrett, Julie, 3389
Barrett, Laura K., 1092
Barrett, William L.D., 2408
Barrett, Yvonne, 1742
Barrick, Lise M., 2947
Barrientos, Robert, 1808
Barriere Construction Company, 1736
Barriere, Micheal T. (Mike), 2882
Barringer, Phil, 830
Barriocanal, Nelson, 2132
Barrionnuevo, Helen J., 784
Barrios, Domingo, 3338
Barron, Patricia C., 59
Barron, Ray, 3193
Barrs, W. Craig, 877
Barry, John, 1113
Barry, Linda, 1113
Barry, Michael J., 1489
Barry, William S., 2783
Barsalou, Judy, 659
Barsophy, Jan, 1187
Bartek, Brad, 2009
Bartell, James R., 1069
Bartelmo, Thomas, 769
Bartels, Larry M., 2402
Bartenbach, Jennifer K., 1126
Barter, Davida D., 1340
Barth, Andrew C., 2811
Barth, Andrew F., 461
Barth, Aneila, 101
Barth, Eugene F., 101
Barthebaug, Richard, 2686
Barthebaug, Richard, Mrs., 2686
Bartholome, Richard, 2129
Bartholomew, Lesley M., 1240
Bartle, Barbara, 1847
Bartlett, Barbara, 1415
Bartlett, David, 2707
Bartlett, Robert J., 3592
Bartley, Anne, 650, 2389
Bartner, Beverly D.N., 696
Bartner, Nicole, 696
Bartner, Robert G., 696
Barto, JJ, 67
Bartolotta, Joseph, 1505
Bartolotta, Matteo, 2448
Barton, Babcock & Blair, 1901
Barton, Benjamin P., 2933
Barton, Cliff, 1300
Barton, Dick K., 2933
Barton, Florence Lucille, 40
Barton, Larry, 3607
Bartram, John C., 2733
Barvin, Martha Weisberg, 3590
Barwick, Kent L., 2099
Barz, Richard J., 1622
Bas Properties, LLC, 1930
Basant LTDA, 1524
Bascom, Roxanne, 1842
Basden, Mildred V., 436
Base, Elizabeth, 2828
Basha, Regine, 2043
Bashor, Beth, 484
Basile, Vincent D., 1517
Baskerville, H.M., Jr., 1733
Baskett, Charles E., 2513
Baskin, Caleb, 163
Baskin, Richard, 428
Basolo, Tony, III, 2810
Bass, Angela, 360
Bass, Crystal, 3576
Bass, Doris L., 3172
Bass, Edward P., 3319, 3334
Bass, Gary D., 650
Bass, Harry W., Jr., 3172
Bass, John, 3007
Bass, John T., 487
Bass, Lee M., 3334
Bass, Sid R., 3334
Bass, Thomas E., III, Adm., 3448
Basset Foundation, Norman, 3654
Bassett, David, 770
Bassett, Ronald D., 3321
Bassett, Tom, 2876
Bassingthwaite, Dwight, 1695
Bassis, Michael S., 3393
Basso, Rob, 2118
Bastean, Todd A., 1779
Bastian, Jill, 1791
Bastian, Melanie, 58
Basye, Matthew J., 1240
Batali, Mario, 1314
Batchelor Enterprises, 697
Batchelor, George E., 697
Batchelor, Jon, 697
Batchelor-Robjohns, Anne O., 697
Bate, David S., 2412
Bateman, Isabell, 3124
Bates, Devin, 3343
Bates, Janet Fleishhacker, 199
Bates, Jeanne, 1793
Bates, John C., 2665
Bates, John C., Jr., 2665
Bates, Jon, 990
Bates, Leon, 3019
Bates, Sarah J., 2665
Bath, Paquita, 441
Baton, Bob, 221
Batsche, Stephen V., 3471
Batson, Jane, 2011
Batson, Scott, 3430
Battaglini, Denise, 3148
Battey, Jane, 408
Battin, Molly, 2466
Battistoni, Rick, 3331
Battle, LaVeeda, 2521
Batts, Deborah A., Hon., 2204
Battye, Kenneth S., 1348
Battye, Susan A., 1348
Bauer Foundation, Evalyn M., 145
Bauer, Betsy, 1906
Bauer, Betty, 3378
Bauer, Brad, 553
Bauer, Carol, 553
Bauer, Doug, 2099
Bauer, Gary W., 1205
Bauer, George P., 553
Bauer, Janet, 1603
Bauer, Jocelyn, 553
Bauer, Julie, 3592
Bauer, Laurie, 1678
Bauer, Michael R., 3530
Bauer, Walter, 2178
Bauer-Farr, Gudrun, 147
Bauerly, Rick, 1703
Bauert, Paula A., 3527
Baughman, John, 2696
Baughman, Willard, 2686
Bauknight, John E., 3110
Baum, Charles, 1410
Baum, Dale, 1573
Baum, Larry, 2274
Baum, Marc, 1401
Baum, Steven C., 204, 2481
Baum-Baicker, Cindy, 3030
Bauman, Jessica, 650
Bauman, Joseph, 2890
Bauman, Lionel R., 650
Bauman, Patricia, 650
Bauman, Steve, 71
Baumbach, Martha, 1730
Baumgardner, Christine, 1587
Baumgarten, Trina, 3326
Baumgartner, Tracy J., 2921
Baxter Allegiance Foundation, The, 2677
Baxter, Blair, 3173
Baxter, John, 1764
Baxter, Mike, 746
Baxter, Murphy, 3173
Baxter, Murphy H., 3173
Baxter, Richard, 65
Baxter-Heuer, Laura, 2659
Bay Area Primary Care, 797
Bay, Charles Ulrick, 2056
Bay, Frederick, 2056
Bay, Mogens, 1835
Bay, Mogens C., 1843
BayCare Health Systems, LLC, 3597
Bayer Corp., 2888
Bayley, David, 3555
Baylor, Tim, 1717
Bayne, Betsy, 1832
Bayne, Robin, 718
BB&T, 3454
BBVA Compass Bank, 3246
BDI Capital Mgmt., 809
Beach Terrace Care Center, 2254, 2255
Beach, Dana, 2081
Beach, Marianna, 1250
Beach, Ross, 1250
Beach, Stewart, 1007
Beach, Thomas C., Jr., 2058
Beacon, Owen, 971
Beaird, Carolyn W., 1301

Beaird, Charles T., Dr., 1301
Beaird, John B., 1301
Beaird, Susan, 1301
Beal, Barry, Jr., 3174
Beal, Carlton, 3174
Beal, Carlton, Jr., 3174
Beal, Keleen H., 3174
Beal, Kelly S., 3174
Beal, Spencer E., 3174
Beal, Stuart, 3174
Beale, David A., 699
Beall, Diane, 3589
Beall, Dorothy M., 823
Beall, Kenneth S., Jr., 840
Beall, Lisa A., 918
Bealmear, Michael, 255
Beals, Jason, 2674
Beam, Robert M., 1612
Beaman, Phillip, 1136
Beams, Mary E., 2488
Bean, David A., 2630
Bean, Elizabeth N., 1878
Bean, Norwin S., 1878
Bean, Ralph J., Jr., 2892
Bean, Robert R., 933
Bear, Diane, 1241
Bear, Geraldine, 2148
Bear, Julie, 1848
Beard, Anson H., 834
Beard, Anson McCook, Jr., 834
Beard, Debra, 834
Beard, James M., 834
Beard, Laurie F., 1615
Beard, Veronica M., 834
Beard, Veronica S., 834
Beard, William M., 2826
Bearden, Steven W., 1672
Beardsley, George, 2335
Beardsley, Lyda, 440
Beasley, Charles E., 1299
Beasley, George G., 2071
Beasley, Laura, 2599
Beasley, Mary Evans, 3175
Beasley, Robert R., 3175
Beasley, Theodore P., 3175
Beaton, Tim, 2649
Beattie, Arthur P., 915
Beattie, Richard, 2085
Beattie, Scott, 161
Beatty, Eunice, 1282
Beatty, John, 1132
Beatty, Scott, 1395
Beaulieu, Carole, 667
Beaulieu, Jo-Ann, 1428
Beaumont Investments, Ltd., 473
Beauregard, Brian, 3505
Beaver, Tom, 3059
Beavers, Inc., The, 102
Beber, Candace Clark, 2868
Beccaria, Louis J., 3014
Becerra, M. Isabel, 140
Bechard, Kristin, 1797
Bechdol, Matthew A., 1144
Becher, Richard, 377
Bechler River Partners, LLC, 1524
Bechtel, Chuck, 2707
Bechtel, Cynthia, 1515
Bechtel, Elizabeth H., 103
Bechtel, Elizabeth Hogan, 104
Bechtel, Robert W., 3323
Bechtel, S.D., Jr., 104
Bechtel, Stephen D., Jr., 103
Bechtold, Kurt, 3659
Beck, Ann, 3587
Beck, Carol Morley, 1644
Beck, Frela Owl, 2552
Beck, John C., 2296
Beck, Judith, 2483
Beck, Karen, 296
Beck, Laura, 427
Beck, Lauren, 2003
Beck, Lynne, 538
Beck, Mark, 2205
Beck, Maureen Bazinet, 1717
Beck, Melissa, 574
Beck, Phyllis W., Hon., 2976
Beck, Sue, 1241
Beck, Ted, 523
Beck, Thomas C., 1565
Beck, Wayne, 1154
Becker, Carol R., Dr., 1360
Becker, Douglas L., 648
Becker, Greg, 407
Becker, Howard C., 2756
Becker, Jeffery T., 2488
Becker, Jennifer, 1237
Becker, Katrina H., 2054
Becker, Laura Lee Baskerville, 1733
Becker, Margaret, 1438
Becker, Paul, 1272
Becker, Richard C., 1088
Becker, Shawn, 652
Becker, Steve, 235
Becker, Suzanne Sheehan, 2948
Becker, Terry R., 1733
Beckley, Jacqueline P., 2339
Beckley, Karyn, 3552
Beckman, Arnold O., 105
Beckman, Mabel M., 105
Beckner, Jay, 2306
Beckner, Thomas, 979
Beckort, Paul, 1155
Beckos, Barbara J., 619
Beckos, Dean J., 619
Beckos-Wood, Georgia, 619
Beckwith, F. William, 1213
Beckwith, G. Nicholas, III, 2892
Beckwith, Leola I., 1213
Beckwith, Page, 717
Bedard, Daniel L., 564
Bedard, Kipp A., 950
Bedel, Elaine, 1126
Bedke, Michael A., 523
Bedner, Mark, 866
Bedolfe, Herbert M., 310
Bedward, Royce, 1034
Beebe, Frederick S., 663
Beebe, Mary, 2043
Beeghly, Bruce R., 2685
Beeler, W. Christopher, 3443
Beeman, Tom, 1175
Beemer, Michael G., 961
Beene, Steve, 1760
Beener, Michelle, 2922
Beer Institute, 1344
Beer, Ingrid, 1907
Beer, Lovey G., 1907
Beer, Murray L., 1907
Beers, Carol S., 3488
Beetz, L. Elizabeth, 3605
Behar, Howard, 3496
Behling, Mary, 3616
Behm, Susan J., 2794
Behmann, Arno W., 3176
Behmann, Herman W., 3176
Behnke, Karen, 1129
Behrens, Bobbette, 1235
Beil, Len, 3494
Beim, John, 1270
Beim, N.C., 1683
Beim, Raymond N., 1683
Beinecke Foundation, The, 667
Beinecke, Candace K., 2492
Beinecke, Frederick W., 2263, 2443
Beinecke, John B., 2443
Beinecke, William S., 2443
Beinhaker, Mitchell, 2004
Beisler, Ralph, 2387
Beitzel, John, 2795
Bejcek, Kim, 1652
Bekavac, Nancy, 400
Beker, Harvey, 2506
Bekolo, Jean-Pierre, 176
Belair, Paul, 2655
Belanger, Beth A., 1590
Belcher, Anne, 1156
Belcher, Keith, 3211
Belcher, Philip, 2540
Beldecos, J. Nicholas, 2937
Belding, Annie K., 2161
Belding, Milo M., 2161
Belefonte, Carmen P., Esq., 2932
Belew, David L., 2710
Belfer Corp., 2060
Belfer Two Corp., 2059
Belfer, Laurence, 2060
Belfer, Laurence D., 2059
Belfer, Norman, 2060
Belfer, Renee E., 2059, 2060
Belfer, Robert A., 2059, 2060
Belgard, Donald A., 1089
Belisle, Barbara J., 22
Belitz, K.C., 1851
Belive, 2173
Belk, Judy, 140, 2454
Belk-Simpson Co., 2566
Bell Family Trust, 107
Bell, Andy, 2787
Bell, Ben H., Jr., 482
Bell, Caitlin M., 2524
Bell, Charles H., 1680
Bell, Constance L., 698
Bell, David A., Hon., 3421
Bell, Diane Fisher, 577
Bell, Eileen, 631
Bell, Garrett, 631
Bell, Hazel H., 3141
Bell, James D., Jr., 3595
Bell, James E., 698
Bell, James R., 1489
Bell, John, 3516
Bell, John, Dr., 2828
Bell, John, Jr., 2539
Bell, Judith M., 492
Bell, Julie Kay, 3113
Bell, Kenneth D., 2154
Bell, Larry, 3174
Bell, Laura, 1634
Bell, Martha A., 107
Bell, Monty, 3098
Bell, R. Terry, 3338
Bell, Samuel P., 270
Bell, Shirley, 2632
Bell, Stephen Helms, 247
Bell, Steve, 364
Bell, Stuart M., 698
Bell, Tom, 1257
Bell, Vance D., 868
Bell, William C., 3499
Bell, Yvonne, 3496
Bell-Flynn, Kathleen, 107
Bell-Rose, Stephanie, 771
Bellamy, Chris, 2683
Bellanca, Rose B., Dr., 1576
Bellange, Debbie, 30
Bellatti, Barbara W., 3338
Belles, Lawrence L., 981
Bellinger, Geraldine G., 2170
Bellizzi, John, 425
Bellman, David H., 1895
Bellmore, Chris J., 1024
Bellot, Dario, 3034
Bellotti, Frances X., 1426
Belshaw-Jones, Sharon, 207
Belsky, Shenyu, 301
Beltax Corp., 2570
Belton, John, 1315
Belton, Marc, 1697
Beltran-del Olmo, Magdalena, 140
Belus, Tom, 3683
Belz, Jack A., 3120
Belz, Ronald, 3120
Bemis Co., Inc., 3598
Ben & Jerry's Corp., 3407
Ben & Jerry's Homemade, Inc., 3407
Benassi, Peter, 2347
Benbow, Robert, 1122
Bender Charitable Lead Trust, Matthew, IV, 2153
Bender, Beth, 1796
Bender, Florence H., 554
Bender, George A., 447
Bender, Jeffrey P., 2153
Bender, M. Christian, 2153
Bender, Matthew, IV, 2108, 2153
Bender, Morris, 554
Bender, Phoebe P., 2153
Bendon, Dorothy, 1859
Bendon, James A., 1859
Bendon, John James, 1859
Bendon, Susan Kaylor, 1859
Bene, Robert Del, 2227
Benecke, Lars, 2888
Benedict, Bruce O., 2674
Benedict, Davis M., 2666
Benedict, Nancy H., 2666
Benedict, Peter B., 2666
Benedict, Peter B., II, 2454, 2666
Benedum, Michael Late, 2892
Benedum, Paul G., Jr., 2892
Benedum, Sarah N., 2892
Benet, Celine, 1998
Bengier, Brooke N., 109
Bengier, Cynthia S., 109
Bengier, Gary F., 109
Benglis, Lynda, 2187
Benike, John, 1735
Benjamin, Ben, 2018
Benjamin, Clarence, 397
Benjamin, Claude, 699
Benjamin, John F., 1083
Benkert, Jerome A., Jr., 1202
Bennett, Carol, 2684
Bennett, Craig, Rev., 1382
Bennett, Elizabeth, 247
Bennett, Elizabeth A., 1592
Bennett, Germaine, 2799
Bennett, Gloria K., 9
Bennett, J. Mac, 2754
Bennett, James, 3587
Bennett, Joanna, 1507
Bennett, John T., Jr., 705
Bennett, Justin, 1097
Bennett, Leigh, 3544
Bennett, Linda, 1205
Bennett, Louise Gaylord, 2813

Bennett, Mary E. Frey, 1609
Bennett, Michael, 2767
Bennett, Pat, 1188
Bennett, R. Taylor, 1865
Bennett, Robert M., 2340
Bennett, Robert W., 1081
Bennett, Russell E., Jr., 2616
Bennett, Shelley L., 3526
Bennett, Stacey, 2174
Bennett, Stephen, 138, 2040
Bennett, Terrence M., 2266
Bennett, Tony, 328
Bennett, Vera, 408
Bennett, Wayne, 1
Bennett-Parsons, Barbara, 3520
Bennon, Rhonda, 26
Benoit, John, 1336
Bensema, Marian, 1289
Benshimol, Luis, 3208
Benson, Andrew, 1664
Benson, Barbara F., 1664
Benson, Cliff, 2078
Benson, Cynthia Y., 3345
Benson, Dave, 1593
Benson, Elizabeth Reiter, 2679
Benson, Martha, 3361
Benson, McCray V., 2539
Benson, Roger, 989
Benson-Valavanis, Alexa, 346
Bentinck-Smith, Elizabeth, 1752
Bentley, Charlotte M. F., 2445
Benton, Daniel, 2037
Benton, Daniel C., 2037
Benton, Margaret, 768
Benton, Pam, 1636
Bentzen, Michael P., 1372
Benz, Eric, 1191
Benz, Norman E., 827
Benziger, Paul J., Jr., 2479
Berardesco, C. A., 1407
Berber, Donna, 3158, 3159
Berber, Philip, 3158, 3159
Berber, Ryan, 3159
Berberfam, Ltd., 3158
Berberich, Bill, 707
Berckmann, Warren, 30
Berend, Keith R., 2750
Berendt, Barbara, 1112
Berens, Mary, 2112
Berenson, Jeffrey L., 1482
Beresford-Hill, Paul, 2445
Bereuter, Douglas, Hon., 1851
Berg Settlor Trust, David, 2062
Berg, Bill, 948
Berg, Margaret, 3614
Bergart, Jeff, 1505
Bergen, Charlotte V., 2527
Bergen, Jan, 2981
Bergen, John (Jack) D., 2882
Bergen, Todd M., 1222
Bergen, William W., 3448
Berger, Deborah, 933
Berger, Deborah K., 2480
Berger, Michael B., 2510
Bergert, Nancy W., 2980
Bergevin, Shannon, 3498
Berghorst, Linda E., 1650
Berghorst, Linda Ellen, 1650
Berghorst, Ryan, 1650
Berglund, Anders, 3508
Berglund, Janet, 3508
Bergman, Alan, 328
Bergman, Alice, 2868
Bergman, Charles C., 2363
Bergman, Jessica, 1136
Bergman, John D., 3160
Bergman, Kevin, 1738
Bergman, Marilyn, 428
Bergmann, Joan Heymann, 1313
Bergmann, Paul A., 1240
Bergmeyer, John, 1847
Bergquist, Scott, 407
Bergstedt, Mark, 2689
Bergstrom Climate Systems, Inc., 965
Bergstrom Inc., 965
Bergstrom Manufacturing Co., Inc., 965
Bergtold, Susanna, 2409
Berick, James H., 2722
Berinstein, Henry W., 552
Berke, Jacqueline, 1845
Berke, Matt, 2315
Berkey, Jane R., 2038
Berkley, Mark, 1274
Berkley, Scott, 1155
Berkman, Allen H., 1434
Berkman, James S., 1434
Berkman, Richard L., 1434
Berkman, Selma W., 1434
Berkowitz, Carolyn S., 3426
Berkowitz, Jack, 2111
Berkowitz, Judy, 543
Berkshire Hathaway Inc., 473
Berkshire, Sharlene, 1209
Berktold, Daniel J., 823
Berktold, Jane H., 823
Berlin, Charles, 2282
Berlin, George, 2804
Berlin, Ira, Dr., 2502
Berlin, Thomas, 1596
Berlow, Alan, 1350
Berman, Bertha Dagan, 2985
Berman, Henry L., 2420
Bermas, Stephen, 565
Bermingham, John, 3642
Bermudez, Jaime, 2173
Bernacki, Mark, 563
Bernard, Diane Staley, 3043
Bernard, Lewis W., 2302
Bernard, Mitchell, 2149
Bernard, Pat Palmer, 2348
Bernard, Ralph L., 2667
Bernard, Ralph L., Jr., 2667
Berndt, David P., 3371
Bernel, Elizabeth, 1201
Berners-Lee, Tim, 2160
Bernet, Roberta, 3607
Berngartt, John, 2599
Bernhard Foundation, Inc., The, 2226
Bernhard, Adele, 2022
Bernhard, Anna Wells, 2022
Bernhard, Jessica W., 2022
Bernhard, Joan M., 2226
Bernhard, Michael, 2022, 2226
Bernhard, Robert A., 2226
Bernhard, Steven, 2022
Bernhard, Steven G., 2226
Bernhardt Trust, Bertram L., The, 3062
Bernhardt, James, 807
Bernhardt, Paul Leake, 2644
Bernier, John, 1340
Bernier, Oliver G., 2295
Berniger, Michael, 525
Berns, Michael W., 106
Bernsen, Franklin, 2807
Bernsen, Grace, 2807
Bernstein, Adam K., 652
Bernstein, Alan, 3516
Bernstein, Alison R., 2398
Bernstein, Baron John, 652
Bernstein, Boruch, Rabbi, 652
Bernstein, Heleina, 612
Bernstein, Jared, 2306
Bernstein, Joshua B., 672
Bernstein, Leo M., 652
Bernstein, Lewis, 2166
Bernstein, Martha, 564
Bernstein, Martin, 2367
Bernstein, Mem Dryan, 2051, 2465
Bernstein, Paul, 2356
Bernstein, Richard, 652
Bernstein, Scott B., 1956
Bernstein, Stuart, Amb., 652
Bernstein, Tara, 652
Bernstein, Zalman C., 2051, 2465
Berol, Peter J., 2932
Beronio, Janet, 1860
Berresford, Susan, 1734
Berresford, Susan V., 138
Berrett, Allen, 3390
Berrie Foundation, Russell, 2827
Berrie, Angelica, 1908
Berrie, Russell, 1908
Berrie, Scott, 1908
Berriz, Albert M., 1588
Berry, Beryl, 823
Berry, Bill, 110
Berry, Chad, 2521
Berry, Derek W., 110
Berry, Elizabeth, 670
Berry, James F., 3284
Berry, Joanne, 110
Berry, Leah, 992
Berry, Lowell W., 111
Berry, Margie, 1783
Berry, Mark, 878
Berry, Max, 2220
Berry, Nella F., 110
Berry, Patrick H., 3417
Berry, Sharon, 2989
Berry, Sharon R., 3025
Berry, Thomas W., 1944
Berry, Viveca Ann S., 211
Berry, William F., 110
Berryman, Hunt, 792
Bersted, Alfred, 966
Bersted, Grace A., 967
Bertacchi, Gary, 996
Bertagnolli, Mark, 2037
Bertch, David, 1200
Berteau, John T., 798
Bertman, Lori, 1317
Bertolini, Mark T., 550
Bertrando, Cindy, 623
Berube, Neal, 3390
Berwick, Donald M., 1538
Berwind Corporation, 2894
Berwind, C. Graham, 2894
Berwind, Sandra, 2894
Berylson, Amy Smith, 1546
Berylson, James, 1546
Berylson, John G., 1546
Beshah, Guenet M., 3426
Besio, Gregory J., 963
Besole, Cindy, 25
Bess, Barry R., 1613
Bessemer Charitable Reminder Unitrust, Mary Tilley, 2219
Bessemer Trust Co., N.A., 2239, 2325
Bessemer, Mrs., 2219
Besso, Michele, 3576
Best Buy, 272
Best Buy Co., Inc., 1685
Best Fertilizer Co. of Texas, The, 111
Beste, Carleen, 3465
Betesh, Eddie, 2063
Betesh, Rachelle, 2063
Bethel, Jim, 868
Bethke, Benjamin, 3363
Bethscheider, Alan, 496
Betley, Leonard J., 1145, 1190, 1204
Bett Wold Johnson, 2327
Bettcher, Laurence A., 2773
Betters, Ralph M., 2792
Bettiga, Michael J., 3644
Bettinelli, William, 268
Bettis, Harry, 946
Bettis, Harry L., 946
Bettis, Laura MacGregor, 946
Betts, Benji, 1163
Betts, Richard, 538
Betts, Robert B., Jr., 3684
Betz, Colonel F., 3507
Beukema, Henry S., 2993
Beumer, Kathy, 1135
Beuth, Philip R., 2071
Bevans, James P., 3289
Beveridge, Nancy Graves, 3130
Bevers, Ron, 3427
Bevers, Susan, 1132
Beyer, Gary, 2134
Beyer, Joanne B., 2883
Beyer, Michele, 2728
Beyman, Debbie, 1926
Beyman, Ezra, 1926
Beynon, Kathryne, 113
Beyster, John Robert, 203
Beyster, John Robert, Dr., 203
Beyster, Mary Ann, 203
Bezner, Jeri, 3163
BGK Equities II, LLC, 2013
BGK Property Mgmt. LLC, 2013
BGKP Properties, Inc., 2013
Bhan, M.K., 3516
Bhargava, Deepak, 650, 2139
Bhargava, Rajat, 3563
Bianchi, Michelle, 1620
Bianco, Mary, 308
Bias, Alfred, 1197
Bias, Wendell, 1200
Biastre Trust, 116
Bibbs, Katie, 100
Bibin, Michael, 3526
Bible, Glen, 3259
Bibro, Mark S., 2896
Bickart, Wendy, 802
Bickel & Brewer, 3178
Bickel, Bruce, 2940
Bickel, John W., II, 3178
Bickerstaff, Cliff, 3163
Bickett, Dan, 3427
Bickford, John S., Sr., 2562
Bicoy, Bret, 3609
Bicum, Truman, 1616
Biddiscombe, John S., 592
Biddle 1960 Trust, Nicholas Duke, 2529
Biddle Trust #2, Nicholas D., 2529
Biddle, Mary Duke, 2529
Biddy, Ralph L., 1814
Bidwell Library, 2069
Bieber, Charles, 2820
Bieber, Marcia McGee, 2820
Biehl-Owens, Amy, 1845
Biehler, Stephane P., 2336
Biehn, Brian V., 1163
Bieker, Dennis L., 1273
Bieler, Mark, 2188

Biemann, Betsy, 1339
Biemer, Linda, 2253
Bierbaum, Rosina, 333
Bierbower, William J., 682
Bierly, Paul, 2939
Biermann, Janet, 1065
Bieser, Jerry, 288
Biester, Edward G., Jr., 679
Bietz, Steven L., 2652
Biffle, Greg, 2562
Big Y Foods, Inc., 1456
Bigelow, Peggy, 961
Bigg, Susan, 1842
Bikoff, Mary E. "Betsy", 1145
Bikowski, Dale, 3623
Bikubenfonden, 2064
Bildner, James L., 1631
Bildstein, Lars, 291
Bilezikian, Charles G., 1435
Bilezikian, Doreen, 1435
Bilezikian, Gregory C., 1435
Bilezikian, Jeffrey D., 1435
Bilger, Bruce R., 3266
Bilheimer, Robert W., 2982
Billard, Thomas D., 355
Billena, Manuel F., 1912
Biller, Les, 3496
Biller, Sheri, 3496
Billings, Clyde A., Jr., 3135
Billings, John, 1489
Billings, Judith M., Hon., 3401
Billingsley, Grant, 3345
Billingsley, Tony, 3498
Billington, Marcy, 999
Billowitz, Edgar, 1902
Bilodeau, Ken, 1589
Bilotta, Joe, 2071
Bilotti, Richard, 1979
Bilowith, Karen, 2108
Bilski, Berthold, 2282
Bilski, Mark A., 2282
Bilzin, Jonathan, 2473
Binda, Guido A., 1579
Binda, Robert, 1579
Binder, Katherine A., 3536
Binder, Leslie E., 328
Bineth-Horowitz, Michal, 1537
Bing, Carolyn, 3684
Bing, Dave, 1638
Binger, Anne, 1715
Binger, Erika L., 1715
Binger, James H., 1715, 1734
Binger, Patricia S., 1714
Binger, Virginia M., 1715
Bingham McHale, LLP, 1156
Bingham, Sallie, 1292
Bingham, Wade, 347, 397
Binkley, Ken, 2010
Binns, David, 203
Binswanger, Ben, 412
Binswanger, Benjamin, 2182
Biogen idec Foundation, Inc., 3063
Biotronik SE & Co. KG, 757
Birch, Edward E., 335
Birch, Suzanne, 335
Bird, Hobart M., 2836
Bird, Kai, 678
Bird, Marian A., 2836
Bird, Mary Lynne, 667
Bird, Michael C., 2091
Bird, Peter F., Jr., 3139
Bird, Shelley, 2677
Birdsall, Mabel, 2407
Birdsong, George Y., 3467
Birkenhead, Susan, 2143
Birkholz, Jeff, 371
Biros, Andrew, 2919
Bisbey, Patrick, 2909
Bischmann, Joanne M., 3621
Bisesi, James T., 1150
Bisgrove Foundation, 63
Bisgrove, Debra, 63
Bisgrove, Gerald, 63, 2448
Bisgrove, Jerry, 2448
Bisgrove, John, 2448
Bisher, Branden, 1620
Bisher, Sharon E., 1620
Bishop, Andre, 2252
Bishop, G. David, 3112
Bishop, Gene H., 3202
Bishop, Hayden L.H., 1153
Bishop, Ivan, 1
Bishop, J. Michael, 2534
Bishop, Jeff, 3226
Bishop, Julie, 1464
Bishop, Melissa, 3226
Bishop, Paul R., 2688
Bishop, Rita D., 3432
Bishop, Robert J., 2167
Bishop, Suzy, 1180
Bishop, Timothy R., 2842
Bishop-Clark, Cathy, 2737
Bishopp, Bob, 3526
Bisognano, Maureen, 2106
Bissett, Hallie, 33
Bissinger, Hans, 347, 397
Bitterman, Mary G.F., 933
Bittner, Larry, 3642
Bittner, Molly Dean, 3433
Bittner, R. Richard, 1212
Bivins, Julian M., Jr., 3428
Bixler, Susie, 1163
Bizoza, Brian, 2132
BJP Ventures, LLC, 1524
Black Entertainment TV, 3424
Black Lance, Charles, 1703
Black, Bill, 1162
Black, Chris, 1286
Black, Dameron, III, 873, 898
Black, Dameron, IV, 873
Black, Fraser, 3558
Black, Frederick H., 2633
Black, Harry S., 2065
Black, James Bell, 2599
Black, James Floyd, 873
Black, Jane Cocke, 873
Black, Janice R., 2952
Black, Jerry, 1823
Black, John E., 534
Black, John F., Jr., 2538
Black, Linda C., 1443
Black, Lynne, 1615
Black, Natalie A., 3629
Black, Noel, 544
Black, Paula Cooper, 545
Black, Sherry Salway, 666
Black, Sophie C., 1443
Black, Thomas F., III, 3079
Black, William D., 2921
Blackaby, Sandi, 3498
Blackburn, John, III, 2922
Blackburn, Joseph D., 11
Blackhurst, Jan Jones, 1860
Blackman, Linda, 868
Blackman, Radha, 241
Blackmon, Elaine O., 854
Blackmon, Garry, Rev., 3308
Blackstone, Lisa, 1296
Blackstone, Richard, 1317
Blackwell, Cathy J., 2541
Blackwell, Mike, 1200
Blackwell, William, 482
Blackwood, C. Michael, 2968
Blackwood, Richard, 2890
Blackwood, Sandra, 15
Blahnik, Richard J., 1110
Blair, Brenda, 3430
Blair, Dean, 2787
Blair, Donald W., 2865
Blair, Edward McCormick, Jr., 1081
Blair, Gregg, 1357
Blair, Jeffrey D., 3245
Blair, Jill, 462
Blair, Jim, 1802
Blair, John N., 2472
Blair, Kathleen D., 3124
Blake, David, 3522
Blake, Patricia, 2244
Blake, Patrick, 321
Blake, Susan, 1307
Blake, Veronica, 371
Blakely, Matt, 1066
Blakely, Patricia, 3000
Blakemore, Frances L., 3497
Blakemore, Thomas L., 3497
Blakeslee, Bill, 1358
Blakeway, Nigel, 1070
Blakey, Albert G., III, 3002
Blanc, Gene, 1063
Blanchard, Andre, 211
Blanchard, Ashley Snowdon, 664
Blanchard, Bill, 1012
Blanchard, Brenda, 2333
Blanchard, Lisa G., 1656
Blanchard, Marcelle, 211
Blanchard, Mark, 1316
Blanchard, William R., 849
Blanco, Pat, 729
Blandin Foundation, 1699, 1723
Blank, Arthur M., 856
Blank, Kenny, 856
Blank, Michael, 856
Blank, Nancy, 856, 1200
Blankenship, Elizabeth Warren, 2831
Blankenship, Marian, 2866
Blankfield, Bryan J., 3643
Blanksteen, David, 701
Blanksteen, Goldie, 701
Blanton, Darren, 3225
Blanton, Hilda Sutton, 702
Blanton, Jean, 1128
Blanton, Julie E., 3225
Blanton, Larry, Hon., 1184
Blanz, Dennis, 831
Blas, Eduardo, 3161
Blase, William A., Jr., 3167
Blaser, Chip, 1256
Blasetto, James W., 623
Blasi, John, 1943
Blasius, Louise, 1663
Blass, Gus, III, 71
Blatnick, Gary, 257
Blattner, Darian, 3641
Blatz, Kathleen, 1734
Blau, Helen M., 191
Blauner, Peter, 2050
Blaustein, Jacob, 1349
Blaustein, Jeanne P., 1350
Blaustein, Mary Jane, 1350
Blaustein, Morton K., 1350
Blaustein, Susan B., 1350
Blazek-White, Doris D., 668
Blazer, Cedric, 978
Blazer, Mark, 978
Blazey, Karen, 2342
Bleier, Chaya, 2057
Bleier, Edward, 2126
Bleil, Barbara R., 3255
Blencoe, Harry A., 3514
Blessing Hospital Foundation, 3377
Blessing, Linda J., 44
Blessing, Melissa W., 2022
Blevins, Kerrie, 1688, 1745
Blevins, Leanna B., 3443
Blew, Denise M., 2986
Blew, Jim, 1971
Bleyer, Stephen A., 3020
Blickhan, Gary L., 992
Blickhan, Jill Arnold, 992
Bliss, Aden, 114
Bliss, Dors S., 2148
Blitt, Chela, 440
Blitt, Irwin, 440
Blitt, Rita, 440
Bliumis-Dunn, Sarah W., 2082
Blizzard, Mel, 1357
Blobel, Guenter, 2243
Block, Andrew K., 1083
Block, David R., 30
Block, Diane M., 30
Block, Herbert L., 653
Block, Jennifer Berylson, 1546
Block, John D., 2046
Block, Jonathan, 1546
Block, Judith S., 1014
Block, Patrick, 30
Block, Richard L., 30
Blodgett, Bronson, 3287
Blodgett, Gary, 1242
Blohm, Jon, 2680
Bloom, Barry L., 2468, 2469
Bloom, Brad, Rabbi, 3100
Bloom, Bruce, 1580
Bloom, Ellen, 2085
Bloom, Peter, 633
Bloom, Ronnie L., 3045
Bloom, Sandy, 1998
Bloomberg, 2445
Bloomberg, Emma, 2066
Bloomberg, Georgina, 2066
Bloomberg, Michael R., 2066
Bloomfield, David S., 2738
Bloomfield, Doug, 2755
Bloomfield, Paul, 2738
Bloomfield, Randall D., 2167
Blossom, C. Bingham, 2668
Blossom, C. Perry, 2668
Blossom, David B., 2668
Blossom, Elizabeth B., 2668
Blossom, Jonathan B., 2668
Blossom, Laurel, 2668
Blossom, Robin Dunn, 2668
Blount, Reginald, Rev., 1031
Blue Cross and Blue Shield of Alabama, Inc., 7
Blue Cross and Blue Shield of Florida, Inc., 744
Blue Cross and Blue Shield of Georgia, Inc., 886
Blue Cross and Blue Shield of Iowa, 1246
Blue Cross and Blue Shield of South Dakota, 1246
Blue Cross Blue Shield of Louisiana, 1302
Blue Cross of Idaho Health Service, Inc., 950

Blue Heron Trust, 3507
Blue Hills Bank, 1436
Blue Moon Fund, Inc., 3466
Blue, Ronald W., 3146
Bluemle, Lewis W., 2926
Bluhm, Leslie, 982
Blum Foundation, Edith C., 2067
Blum Trust, 1083
Blum, Felicia H., 2099
Blum, James A., 1123
Blum, John S., 342
Blum, Kenneth, 342
Blum, Kenneth J., 307
Blum, Richard C., 115
Blumenfeld, Jack, 637
Blumenstein, Penny B., 1588
Blumenthal, David, 2106, 2288
Blumer, Herman, 2407
Bluntzer, John Lloyd, 3176
Blutt, Mitchell J., 2106
BMC West, 484
BMO Harris Bank, 3642
BMO Harris Bank, N.A., 982, 1117, 3640, 3647, 3656
BNY Mellon, 1534
BNY Mellon Trust of Delaware, N.A., 2959
BNY Mellon, N.A., 843, 2325, 2913, 2931, 2952, 2972, 2986, 3038
BNY Mellon, N.A., The, 2122
Boak, Thomas B., 1906
Boardman, Shirley, 1124
Boas, Hans, 3181
Boateng, Joseph A., 3499
Boatman, Dennis L., 1222
Boatright, Randy J., 3182
Boazman, Dianne C., 1299
Bobb, Jay, 1541
Bobb, John G., 714
Boben, Linda, 1691
Bobilya, David A., 1147
Bobrow, Edythe, 2408
Bocanegra, Juanita, 1591
Boccalatte, John L., 592
Bochenek, Christine A., 2709
Bock Revocable Trust, John C., 3600
Bock, Carl J., 3600
Bock, Sharon L., 3600
Bocko, Miranda Fuller, 1886
Boden, Scott, 3555
Bodenheimer, Henry, 1310
Bodenmiller, Jim, 1130
Bodfish, Paul, Sr., 28
Bodine, George, 1862
Bodine, James P., 2919
Bodine, Jean G., 2997
Bodman, Ralph L., 1665
Bodorff, Richard J., 2071
Boe, Troy, 3641
Boeckman, Brad, 2809
Boeckman, Robert, 2832
Boeckmann, Herbert F., II, 116
Boeckmann, Jane, 116
Boeckmann, Jane F., 116
Boehm, Jeff, 3580
Boehne, Richard A., 2780
Boehner, Leonard B., 3094
Boeing Co., The, 498
Boesch, Donald, 1413
Boeschenstein, Harold, 2678
Boesen, Theodore J., Jr., 1246
Boettcher, Bill, 3609
Boettcher, Irene, 484
Boettcher, Richard, 484
Bogan, Ernest, 2035
Bogart, Gary, 770
Bogart, Martha, 2231
Bogart, Max, Dr., 2231
Bogen, Andrew E., 456
Bogen, Stanley, 2035
Boger, Jennifer B., 2633
Bogert, Jeremiah M., 1947, 1968
Bogert, Jeremiah M., Jr., 1968
Bogigian, Bob, 1154
Bogle, Peter C., 1453
Bogner Trust, Charles, 2844
Boh, Robert S., 1316
Bohart, Holly, 574
Bohart, James, Jr., 574
Bohart, Lynn, 3552
Bohm, Pete, 1275
Bohman, Michael J., 2769
Bohnen, Michael, 1479, 2979
Bohnett, David C., 117
Bohnsack, Rob, 1225
Boise, April Miller, 2770
Boisi, Geoffrey T., 2085
Bok, Elliot P., 555
Bok, Roxanne, 555
Bok, Scott L., 555
Boklund, Mary Lee, 221
Bokor, Peter, 1350
Bold, William, 376
Boldt, Dana, 388
Bolen, Pamela A., 62
Bolger, Heidi A., 1662
Bolick, Jerome W., 2531
Bolick, Judith L., 2531
Bolick, Linda B., 2531
Bolig, Ron, Esq., 2900
Boling, Karen, 1168
Bolinger, Martha, 1746
Bolker, Cynthia Taper, 433
Boll, Marlene, 543
Bolles, Larry D., 999
Bollier, Barbara, 1255
Bollier, John E., 102
Bolling, Landrum R., 661
Bollinger, Brad, 197
Bollinger, Lee C., 1631
Bollman, Milton W., 485
Bolsen, Barbara, Rev., 968
Bolser, Benjamin, 1587
Bolton, Linda Burnes, 1949
Bolton, Marilyn, 1260
Boly, Diane, 2850
Boman, Ryan, 1693
Bomar, J. Chad, 2543
Bon, Lauren, 86
Bon, Lauren A., 87
Bonaparte, Shane, 1128
Bonard, Glenn R., 671
Bonbright, Lisa, 457
Boncher, Heidi, 1100
Boncher, Kristen, 1100
Bond, A.D., III, 1790
Bond, Christopher S., 1790
Bond, George, 2539
Bond, Reva, 484
Bond, Richard, 484
Bond, Tory, 472
Bondenmann, Linda, 1453
Bondurant, William L., 2349
Bondy, Richard C., 796
Bongi, Anne, 407
Bongiovanni, Lisa Marie, 312
Bonhard, Mark, 2801
Bonieskie, Raymond, 653
Bonifaz, John, 1422
Bonn, Bernard, III, 1462
Bonn, Kelley R., 608
Bonnefoi, Marc, 1988
Bonner, Bertram F., 1909
Bonner, Clark J., 118
Bonner, Corella A., 1909
Bonner, Elizabeth Snowdon, 664
Bonner, Nancy S., 118
Bonner, Sarah L., 738
Bonness, Barbara, 1185
Bonnet, Esther, 1391
Bonnett, Denis, 3100
Bonney, Leigh, 2207
Bonta, Diana, 90
Bonta, Diana M., 1353
Bontrager, Mahlon, 1170
Bonura, Joseph A., Jr., 2113
Bonura, Michael, 2111
Boogaard, Marcia, 1415
Boogaard, Thomas, 1415
Booker, Claude, 866
Booker, Cory A., 2066
Booker, Lewis T., 3477
Booker, Marilyn, 2315
Boone Foundation, 3510
Boone, Eileen Howard, 3068
Boone, Robert S., 3586
Boone, Thomas H., 1830
Booth, Alex E., Jr., 704
Booth, Andrew, 2445
Booth, Beth A., 638
Booth, Chancie Ferris, 3180
Booth, Debbie, 716
Booth, Elizabeth, 2331
Booth, Katherine, 704
Booth, Willis H., 3180
Booth-Barbarin, Ann V., 623
Boothroyd, Lorna, 161
Borchardt, Georges, 2050
Borcheck, Teresa W., 762
Borcherding, Lori, 1241
Borchers, Doug, 2684
Borda, Geoffrey B., 2986
Borden, Alice, 1470
Borden, Bertram H., 1910
Borden, Debra S., Esq., 1358
Bordern, Elizabeth, 559
Borders, Lisa M., 864
Bordewick, Dianna, 3597
Borek, John M., Jr., 876
Borel, George E., CPA, 1576
Boren, David L., 2066
Borenin, Jessica, 27
Borgen, Bjorn Erik, 543
Borger, Judy, 690
Borges, Francisco L., 771
Borgmeier, Lynn S., 3348
Borgos, Seth, 2326
Bories, Robert, 1316
Boris, Leslie Baker, 2886
Borish, Michael, 3397
Borlinghaus, Scott R., 1788
Borm, Mary, 3365
Borman, Adam, 1325
Borman, Cornelius H., 1325
Borman, Donald, 1325
Borman, Kate, 1325
Borman, Matthew, 1325
Borman, Robert, 1325
Borman, Robert, Jr., 1325
Borne, Dan, 1302
Borner, Thomas, 562
Bornheimer, Deborah Hill, 1461
Bornick, Sue, 3611
Bornstein, Richard, 3081
Bornstein, Richard J., 3081
Bornstein, Rita, 842
Bornstein, Sandra, 3081
Borodinsky, Louis, 2210
Borofsky, Michael C., 2355
Boroujerdi, Robert, 2037
Borowsky, Kurt T., 1965
Borszich, James, 3115
Borthwick, Maribeth A., 447
Borthwick, Paul, 487
Boruff, Joy, 1063
Borun, Anna, 2532
Borun, Harry, 2532
Bosack & Bette M. Kruger Foundation, Leonard X., The, 3423
Bosack, Leonard, 3423
Bosarge, Marie, 3303
Bosarge, Wilbur Edwin, Jr., 3303
Boschwitz, Nancy Zellerbach, 471
Boscov, James S., 2893
Bose McKinney, Attorneys, 1156
Boseman, James T., 3102
Boserup, Viggo, 268
Boskofsky, Peter, 36
Boss, Hugh M., 394
Boss, LaVerne H., 1579
Boss, W. Andrew, 1686
Bosse, James F., 1382
Bossler, Victoria, 69
Bost, Glenn E., II, 3018
Boston Scientific, 757
Bostyancic, Derek, 1699
Boswell, Frederic, 1916
Boswell, Kathryn, 3684
Bosworth, Susan M., 1236
Bosworth, Wendy Reed, 3637
Botham, Lydia, 1710
Bothin, Ellen Chabot, 120
Bothin, Henry E., 120
Botkin, Patricia, 1589
Botstein, Leon, 2343
Botstiber Charitable Lead Annuity Trust, Dietrich W., 2898
Botstiber, Dietrich W., 2898
Bott, H. Norman, 1932
Botta, Nicholas, 2356
Bottomley, John T., 1886
Bottoms, Roger G., 1040
Bou, Edward C., 654
Bou, Stephen A., 654
Bougher, James, 2933
Bouler, Chantay, 3111
Boulier, Charles J., 564
Boulware, Leilani S., 3129
Bouquin, Erin, 2011
Bouras, Nicholas J., 1911
Bourke, Anita, 1261
Bourland, Jill, 1647
Bourne, Robert B., 2133
Bourque, Katleen, 1547
Bousa, Edward, 1487
Bouscaren, Helen Hunt, 2971
Bousquet, Laurence G., 2177
Boutaugh, Joseph W., 3579
Bouten, William O., 3526
Bouterse, Mary, 807
Boutin, Joseph, 3410
Bouton, William W., III, 595
Boutrous, Theodore J., Jr., 220
Bouwman, Laurie, 1573
Bouwman, Laurie G., 1653
Bovard, Tami, 1141
Bove, Richard, 2997
Bovender, Jack O., Jr., 3129

Briggs Residuary Trust, Thomas W., 3124
Briggs, David W., 3421
Briggs, Jessica, 2890
Briggs, Karen, 1200
Brigham, Paul, 1887
Brighton, Deb, 3417
Brighton-Best Socket Screw Manufacturing, Inc., 1980
Brightwater Trust, The, 557
Brightwell, Barbara, Dr., 3193
Briglia, Beth Harper, 2915
Brignola, Paul J., 2204
Brill, Alan, 3580
Brill, Betsy, 994, 1050
Brill, Debra, 448
Brilliant, Larry, 412, 413
Brillo, Lyn, 2070
Briman, Steve, 1279
Brimberg, Elizabeth, 2378
Brimberg, Stanlee, 2378
Brin, Sergey, 231
Brind, Ira, 2926
Brinda, Sean E., 2953
Brinkerhoff, Elizabeth, 1428
Brinkley, Amy Woods, 2524
Brinkley, William M., 2538
Brinkman, Sue E., 2838
Brinson, Bob, 2632
Brinton, William D., 722
Brisbane, Laura, 3521
Briscoe, Chuck, 1281
Briscoe, Dave, 3119
Briscoe, Robert B., 1755
Brisson, Katie G., 1588
Bristol Bay Native Corp., 31
Bristol Motor Speedway, 2562
Bristow, Julie, 2802
Bristow, W. Scott, 2802
British Embassy, 2445
Britt, Wayman P., 1615
Brittingham, Ella, 128
Brittingham, Scott, 128
Britton, Donald W., 2488
Britton, Richard H., 3448
Brlas, Laurie, 2681
Broach, Theresa, 562
Broad, Edythe L., 129
Broad, Eli, 129
Broadbent, Robert R., 2745
Broadcasting & Cable, 2071
Broadfoot, Holli Leigh, 3296
Broadfoot, John W., 3296
Broadfoot, John, Jr., 3296
Broadhurst, Anna, 2387
Broadman, Dorothy, 3426
Broadnax, Marcus, 746
Broadrup, Robert E., 1358
Broadway Cares, 1156
Broadway National Bank, 3197, 3205, 3382
Broadway National Bank, N.A., 3281
Brocchini Farms, Inc., 130
Brocchini, Kristine, 130
Brocchini, Robert, 130
Brocchini, Stephen, 130
Brock, Charles M., 954
Brock, Joan P., 2072
Brock, Macon F., III, 2072
Brock, Macon F., Jr., 2072
Brock, Paul K., Jr., 3123
Brock-Wilson, Jane, 1482
Brockenbrough, Austin, IV, 3433
Brockmeier, Judy, 1851
Brockway, Eleanor, 1512
Broder, Sherry, 1327
Broderick, Michael, 933
Broderick, Rosemary, 3031
Brodersen, Ellen H., 448
Brodeur, Lawrence, 1471
Brodhead, Richard, 2302
Brodrick, James W., Jr., 1547
Brodsky, Jeff, 2315
Brodsky, Julian A., 2921
Brody, Kenneth D., 2402
Brody, Mike, 1012
Brody, William R., 276
Brogna, Christopher, 2402
Broidy, Steven D., 456
Brokas, Erich, 658
Brokehuizen, Elsa D. Prince, 1658
Broker, William K., 911
Bromley, Jim, 3516
Bronfman Trust, Edgar Miles, 2074
Bronfman, Adam R., 2073
Bronfman, Andrea M., 2074
Bronfman, Charles R., 2074
Bronfman, Edgar M., Sr., 2073
Bronfman, Jeffrey, 2007
Bronk, Helen, 2148
Bronner, Jim, 545
Bronstein, Jean G., 2237
Brook, Cara Dingus, 2702
Brooke Point High School, 3330
Brooke, Deborah, 1428
Brooke, Dell S., 24
Brooking, Gladys T., 3373
Brookins, Gary, 2429
Brooklawn Gardens Inc., 1991
Brookman, Ann, 3662
Brooks, Alvin, 1808
Brooks, Blake, 1616
Brooks, Brian, 762
Brooks, Cali, 2027
Brooks, Conley, 1713
Brooks, Conley, Jr., 1713
Brooks, Dale G., 3664
Brooks, Denise M., 1590
Brooks, Donna, 3565
Brooks, Edward, 1713
Brooks, Gary, 3567
Brooks, George R., 3649
Brooks, Harold, 1440
Brooks, Hattie H., 131
Brooks, Heidi, 3067
Brooks, Hilda, 2148
Brooks, J. Michael, 2762
Brooks, James E., 1439
Brooks, Jim, 235
Brooks, Margaret L.N., 3639
Brooks, Mark A., 77
Brooks, Markell C., 1713
Brooks, Marva J., 3100
Brooks, Mary Anne, 2541
Brooks, Mary C., 1439
Brooks, Robert A., 44
Brooks, Stephen B., 1713
Brooks, Sunshine, 131
Brooks, T.J., 3631
Brooks, Tom, 762
Broome, O. Whitfield, Jr., 3428
Broome, Paul, 1817
Brophy, John, 1569
Brosco, Gian, Esq., 1867
Brosnan, Betsy K., 1008
Brosnan, Daniel, 1540
Brosnan, Tim, 3158
Brossart, Darcie, 3315
Brotherhood Mutual Insurance Co., 1123
Brothers, Kelly, 278
Brotherton, Emily, 1914
Brotherton, Fred J., 1914
Brotherton, Wayne A., 1914
Brotherton, William P., 1914
Broude, John, 3385
Brougher, Bill, 2787
Broughton, Carl L., 2732
Broun, Elizabeth, 2286
Broussard, David M., 1300
Browdy, Candace A., 1090
Browdy, Michelle, 2227
Brown Brothers Harriman Trust Co., 2325
Brown Group Inc., Charitable Trust, Inc., 707
Brown Library, John Carter, 2069
Brown Shoe Co., Inc., 707
Brown Trust, Patricia A., 132
Brown, Alice Pratt, 3183
Brown, Alma, 988
Brown, Anita, 2805
Brown, Ann, 157
Brown, Barb, 3620
Brown, Barbara, 568
Brown, Bennett A., III, 625
Brown, Bruce M., 2932
Brown, Calvin, 1010
Brown, Carlton D., 2292
Brown, Carmen, 3424
Brown, Carol, 2989
Brown, Carol L., 982
Brown, Carol R., 2966
Brown, Cedric, 273
Brown, Cee, 2043
Brown, Charles S., 954
Brown, Charles S., Mrs., 954
Brown, Christian T., 1316
Brown, Cuyler, 1068
Brown, Cynthia, 3587
Brown, D. Randolph, Jr., 2822
Brown, D. Warren, 2672
Brown, Daniel T., 3602
Brown, David A., 1174
Brown, Dawn, 1129
Brown, Dean, 3616
Brown, Deirdre A., 830
Brown, Denise, 2985
Brown, Diane L., 2107
Brown, Diane Solomon, Dr., 1355
Brown, Douglas W., 2672
Brown, Drew M., 44
Brown, Dwyer, 3682
Brown, Eddie, 3424
Brown, Edith Rae, 2044
Brown, Elizabeth A., 478
Brown, Elliot H., 2252
Brown, Emery N., 2534
Brown, Forrest C., 776
Brown, Frances Carroll, 2989
Brown, Frank D., 903
Brown, Gary W., 3461
Brown, George, 2674
Brown, George R., 3183
Brown, George W., 448
Brown, Gloria, 408
Brown, Hank, 488
Brown, Harmon, 538
Brown, Heidi, 3399
Brown, Helene K., 3682
Brown, Herman, 3183
Brown, Hillary, 2409
Brown, J. Graham, 1283
Brown, J. Stokes, 5
Brown, Jake F., II, 1445
Brown, James, 2274
Brown, James Keith, 2494
Brown, Jane, 1369
Brown, Janice J., 2672
Brown, Joanne, 538
Brown, John E., III, 75
Brown, John Seely, 1056
Brown, Judy L., 1655
Brown, Julie A., 2674
Brown, Keith A., 2740
Brown, Kenneth F., 2879
Brown, Kris Nolan, 1837
Brown, Leelee, 2271
Brown, Leslie, 3498
Brown, Lisa, 3510
Brown, Lynn A., 132
Brown, M. Dolores, 1000
Brown, Margarett Root, 3183
Brown, Mary Rose, 3307
Brown, Meghan Binger, 1715
Brown, Michael, 3558
Brown, Molly, 1861
Brown, Monte, 3682
Brown, Nancy Juckett, 2404
Brown, Nancy L., 2269
Brown, Nathaniel T. "Buster", 3558
Brown, Pamela H., 2879
Brown, Patricia J., 2700
Brown, Peter A., 1468
Brown, Rachel, 59
Brown, Randal L., 1206
Brown, Raymond, 1764
Brown, Richard, 3115
Brown, Rita O., 8
Brown, Robert W., 1316, 3190, 3602
Brown, Russell, 1267
Brown, Scott, 1214
Brown, Shawn P., 2879
Brown, Shona, 231
Brown, Stephen J., 2404
Brown, Steven, 2188
Brown, Stuart, 1355
Brown, Susan, 2112, 2822
Brown, Susan T., 3602
Brown, Susie, 2733
Brown, Suzann, 3662
Brown, Suzi, 83
Brown, Terry, 2044
Brown, Timothy H., 1001
Brown, Timothy S., 2404
Brown, Virginia Sory, 5
Brown, William, 2686
Brownback, Mary, 1279
Browne, Chuck, 235
Browne, Kim, 3552
Brownell, Nancy Rossi, 2113
Brownell, Patricia, 2745
Browning, Nick, 2655
Browning, Steve, 1823
Brownlee, Kyle, 2809
Brownlow, Ian, 2013
Brownstone Residuary Trust, Ethel, 2077
Brownstone, Clyde R., 2077
Brownstone, Diane, 2077
Brownstone, Jennifer, 2077
Brownstone, Spencer, 2077
Broyhill, Jeanne, 3421
Broyles, Mike, 1158
Brubaker, Jeffrey R., 153
Bruce, Ailsa Mellon, 2302
Bruce, Peter W., 3637

Brucia, Charles J., 2251
Bruckner, Sandra, 269
Bruer, John T., 1800
Bruett, William H., 1916, 3418
Bruffey, Mike, 1764
Bruga, Richard D., 226
Bruininks, Robert, 1715, 1738
Brumbaugh, Sherri Garner, 2700
Brumfield, Bruce A., 3111
Brumley, Danice, 3364
Brummond, J.C., 102
Bruncati Charitable Lead Remainder Trust, 368
Bruner, James D., 57
Bruner, John, 1215
Bruner, Joshua E., 1441
Bruner, Martha, 1441
Bruner, Paula, 1141
Bruner, R. Simeon, 1441
Bruner, Rudy, 1441
Bruni, Michael, 993
Brunner, Alice, 1020
Bruno, Carmela June, 2310
Bruno, Tommy, 2655
Brunoehler Scholarship Fund, Carl J., 842
Bruns, Andy, 1360
Bruns, Michael J., 3120
Brunson, Philip, 569
Brunst, Robert, 297
Brunswick, Lewis, 133
Brush, Charles F., 2673
Brush, Ed, 868
Brush-Wright, Barbara, 2673
Bruski, Kate, 1587
Bryan, Ann, 3099
Bryan, Ashley, 1764
Bryan, C. Russell, 2529
Bryan, Cheryl, 2809
Bryan, J.F., IV, 808
Bryan, Jeff, 808
Bryan, Jerry, 2685
Bryan, Lissy S., 3433
Bryan, Peggy, 722
Bryan, Richard C., Jr., 2120
Bryan, Thomas J., 2890
Bryan, William H., 2630
Bryan, William J., 3266
Bryant, Andy, 2868
Bryant, Christine, 381
Bryant, David J., 1042
Bryant, Dawn, 560, 3047
Bryant, Helen, 1136
Bryant, John Landrum, Jr., 650
Bryant, Maurita J., 2896
Bryant, N.W., 2831
Bryant, Nancy Kay, 2868
Bryant, Rachelle, 1842
Bryant, Ruth D., 2340
Bryant, William, 704
Bryce, George, 3676
Bryce, James D., 748
Bryers, Joanne E., 2916
Bryn Mawr Trust Company, 2952
Bryn-Julson, Phyllis, 2262
Bryson, John E., 276
Bryson, Louis Henry, 137
Brzozowski, John, 1603
BT Capital Corp., 2134
BTIG, LLC, 647
Bub, Keith, 2231
Bubarth, Robin, 2923
Bucaro, Thomas, 958
Buccaneer L.P., 750
Bucco, Diana, 2901
Buchanan, Leslie, 738
Buchanan, Patricia, 2866
Buchanan, Valda M., 2821
Buchele, Ken, 1257
Bucher, Brad, 3208
Bucher, Dan, 3589
Bucher, Trent, 1207
Bucholtz, Gary A., 828
Buck, 1997 Trust No. 1, Alexander K., Jr., 1331
Buck, 1997 Trust No. 2, Alexander K., Jr., 1331
Buck, Alexander K., Jr., 1331
Buck, Alexander K., Sr., 1331
Buck, Anne E., 1331
Buck, Billy, 3421
Buck, Haleryn A., 2022
Buck, Jan G., 66
Buck, Jason, 260
Buck, John Garner, 66
Buck, N. Harrison, 1331
Buck, Nancy B., 1331
Buck, Richard E., 66
Buck, Sara L., 1331
Buck, Travis W., 2022
Buckbinder, Gregg, 2506
Buckey, Marilyn Myers, 2655
Buckingham, Eunice Hale, 2783
Buckingham, Greg, 351
Buckius, Richard, 1190
Buckles, Donna J., 1224
Buckley, Andre, 1662
Buckley, Ann-Marie, 2459
Buckley, Constance, 3015
Buckley, Jean C., 1104
Buckley, John, 693
Buckley, Marie L., 1240
Buckley, Michael, 1877
Buckley, Peter, 165
Buckley, R. Michael, Jr., 2948
Buckmaster, James, 169
Buckmaster, Raleigh D., 1230
Buckner, Laura, 3174
Buckner, Walker G., Jr., 1554
Buckner, William, 2822
Budd, Hollis S., 2154
Budd, Laura, 1691
Buddin, Glenn D., Jr., 3102
Budganowitz, Sheila, 528
Budinger, Jean-Paul, 3258
Budnik, Shaun L., 569
Buehler, Emil, 1915
Buehler, Kevin J., 3162
Buehler, Knute, Dr., 2846
Buell, Bill, 3641
Buell, Mark, 134
Buell, Stephanie, 1845
Buell, Susie R. Tompkins, 134
Buerger, Theodore V., 2503
Bufferd, Allan S., 1949
Buffett, Devon G., 975
Buffett, Doris, 1500
Buffett, Howard G., 975
Buffett, Howard W., 975, 1500
Buffett, Jennifer, 2334
Buffett, Jimmy, 3108
Buffett, Katherine, 1488
Buffett, Peter, 2334
Buffett, Peter A., 1833
Buffett, Susan A., 1833
Buffett, Susan T., 975, 1833
Buffett, Thomas M., 1488
Buffett, Warren E., 975, 1833, 2334, 2357, 3516
Buffett, Wendy O., 1488
Buffett, William N., 1488
Buffett-Kennedy, Noah E., 1488
Buffoni, Brad, 1228
Buford, Calvin D., 2679
Buford, Tina Y., 3654
Bugalecki, Sheila R., 3648
Buhl, Bob, 3504
Buhl, Henry M., 1925
Buhl, Henry, Jr., 2901
Buhl, Miriam, 2409
Buhl, Thomas C., 1588
Buhler, John, 537
Buhler, Shelly, 1263, 1279
Buice, Charles, 2464
Buick, Kevin, 999
Builders, 1388
Builders First Choice, 3505
Buitrago, Kerrie, 2363
Buku, Michele, 1634
Bulan, Eileen, 2773
Bull, Belitje B., 854
Bull, George, III, 309
Bull, Lauren, 2110
Bullard, Frank J., III, 3112
Bullard, Ginger, 73
Bullard, Peter, 1453
Bullen, Mary, 2712
Bullens, Sally, 2686
Buller, Mary, 1836
Bulletin Co., 2997
Bullington, Roger, 1837
Bullitt, Anne M., 2079
Bullock, Alexandra, 2350
Bullock, Mary Brown, 2286
Bullock, Michelle, 360
Bullock, Whitney, 2350
Bumgardner, Brad C., 1186
Bump, Benjamin, 1547
Bump, Kirsten, 533
Bunbury Co., Inc., The, 3418
Bunch and Assocs., Inc., 715
Bunch, Charles E., 3018
Bunch, Cynthia L., 715
Bunch, Herb, 1158
Bunch, James D., 715
Buncher Co., The, 2902
Buncher Rail Car Service Co., 2902
Buncher Trust, Jack G., 2902
Buncher, Bernita, 2902
Buncher, Jack G., 2902
Bunegar, James, 1119
Bunge North America, Inc., 1779
Bunn, Karan, 2632
Bunnell, Terry, 1286
Buntin, Louie P., 3149
Bunting Family Foundation, The, 1402
Bunting, Anne R., 1402
Bunting, Barbara E., 1998
Bunting, Bob, 3573
Bunting, Christopher L., 1352, 1402
Bunting, George L., Jr., 1402, 2192
Bunting, Marc, 1402
Bunting, Mary Catherine, 1352, 1402
Bunting, Rebekah S., 1402
Buntz, M.A., 2831
Bunzl Mid Atlantic Region, 952
Buonadonna, Joseph, 2297
Buono, Stella, 2037
Buquet, James J., III, 1316
Burbage, Todd E., 1359
Burch, Angie, 3202
Burch, Barry B., 3184
Burch, Kevin, 1155
Burch, Michael L., 3664
Burch, Robert D., 3184
Burch-Martinez, Berkeley, 3184
Burcham, David W., 242
Burchfield, Albert H., III, 2906
Burchill, Jill, 3662
Burchinal, Margaret R., 2191
Burd, Barb, 2803
Burd, Karen, 484
Burden, Shane, 3302
Burdette, Jana Craft, 3113
Burdick, Christopher, 1498
Burdick, Lalor, 1498
Burdick, Martha, 2148
Buresh, Ernie, 1222
Buretta, Sheri D., 32
Burg, Ellen, 2655
Burger, Ernest P., 162
Burgeson, Dale, 3568
Burgess, Ruth, 371
Burgess, Shari L., 1632
Burggraf, Steve, 1699
Burgio, Rosemary, 827
Burhans, David D., 3445
Burk Trust, Henrietta Lange, 977
Burk, Amy, 1616
Burkart, Joseph R., 3488
Burke, Austin J., 3055
Burke, Bill, 869
Burke, Bruce, 54
Burke, Christine, 351
Burke, Ingrid "Indy", Dr., 3654
Burke, James D., 1789
Burke, John, 351, 1549
Burke, Linda Beerbower, 2950
Burke, Sandra, 1753
Burke, Sharon, 943
Burke, Sheila P., 2106
Burke, Sheryl A., 550
Burke, Thomas C., 859
Burke, Timothy, 1124
Burke, Timothy F., Jr., 3010
Burke, William J., Jr., 3051
Burke, Yvonne B., 287
Burkett, Charles G., 3135
Burkey, Adam, 2960
Burkey, Eric, 2893
Burkey, Fatema E.F., Esq., 2960
Burkhardt, Cheryl L., 2763
Burkhardt, David, 1192
Burkholder, Reagan, 1998
Burkholtz, Joan, 1924
Burks, Jami Lynn, 937
Burks, Lewis G., Jr., 22
Burks, William P., 1979
Burlington Rotary Club, 3666
Burmeister, Neil J., 2327
Burn, Luan Wagner, 2010
Burnes, Richard M., Jr., 1366
Burnes, Rick, 1514
Burnett, Bill, Dr., 1162
Burnett, Bruce K., 708
Burnett, Charles P., III, 3521
Burnett, Charles, III, 1760
Burnett, David, 3520, 3521
Burnett, H.E. "Gene", 3147
Burnett, H.L., 800
Burnett, Ipek S., 357
Burnett, J. Albert, 708
Burnett, Jason K., 357
Burnett, Lynn, 1807
Burnett, Mary Elise, 989
Burnett, Nancy, 332
Burnett, Nancy L., 708
Burnett, Nancy Packard, 357

Burnett, R. Kenneth, 1807
Burnett, Rebecca, 1596
Burnett, Robert, 3521
Burnett, Sarah, 3521
Burnett, Shirley, 3521
Burnett, Vivian, 3521
Burnett, William, 3521
Burnett, William, Jr., 3521
Burnette, Leah B., 808
Burnetti, Dean, 709
Burnetti, Denise L., 709
Burnetti, Douglas K., 709
Burnetti, Patricia A., 709
Burney, Janet E., 2770
Burnham, Deborah, 2058
Burnham, Melissa M., 3245
Burns, Angie, 3636
Burns, Ann, 1717
Burns, Donald A., 710
Burns, Emily Wilson, 556
Burns, Fritz B., 136
Burns, Geraldine H., 2770
Burns, Hilda, 1131
Burns, Laurie, 732
Burns, Lucy, 1125
Burns, Maribeth, 2798
Burns, Nicholas, 2389
Burns, Ray, 1919
Burns, Robert A., 3589
Burns, Susan T., 135
Burns, Tim, 1215
Burns, Tori A., 135
Burns, Truman, 354
Burnside, Betty, 3578
Burnside, Warren, 3578
Burr Charitable Trust, Charles, 2332
Burris, John E., 2534
Burroughs Wellcome Co., 2534
Burroughs, Ethan, 3097
Burroughs, Hazel, 3577
Burrows, Cliff, 3565
Burston, James L., 2611
Burt's Bees, 626
Burt, F.R., 479
Burt, N.B., 479
Burt, Stephen M., 1008
Burton Industries, Wm. T., Inc., 1303
Burton, Angus M., 2432
Burton, Bob, 2787
Burton, Davis S., 11
Burton, Kevin, 651
Burton, Lynda, 1391
Burton, Tamara L., 1153
Burton, William T., 1303
Burwasser, Peter, 3019
Burwell, Sylvia Mathews, 74
Bury, David, 2056
Busam, Ray, 988
Busby, Gail, 498
Busch, Lawrence S., 2998
Busch, Paul B., 1689
Buse, John B., 623
Busey Trust Co., 1106
Bush, Antoinett "Toni" Cook, 672
Bush, Carol, 526
Bush, David E., 3487
Bush, Edyth Bassler, 712
Bush, Gwen, 3587
Bush, James R., 3017
Bush, Jeb, 2066
Bush, Lori, 1591
Bush, William, 1909
Bush, William L., 1611
Bushinger, Lynn, 1703
Bushner, Stanley, C.P.A., 1232
Busick, Brett, 1184
Busot, Aldo C., 783
Buss, William D., II, 2736
Busse, Keith E., 1196
Bussell, Diane, 1178
Busselle, Chris, 231
Bustamante, Carlos J., 2534
Bustamante, Thomas, 2017
Buster, Walter L., Ed.D., 138
Bustillo, Rafael, 3
Butcher, James R., 1370
Butcher, Jeanne D., 1370
Butcher, John, 2148
Butcher, McBee, 2919
Butler Capital Corp., 2081
Butler Foundation, J.E. and Z.B., 655
Butler Foundation, The, 1880
Butler Manufacturing Co., 1780
Butler, Aimee Mott, 1688
Butler, Ashley Novak, 1293
Butler, Brigid M., 1688
Butler, Carol W., 13
Butler, Catherine C., 1688
Butler, Cathy, 988
Butler, Donald L., 2091
Butler, Francis J., 2734
Butler, Frederick K., 3089
Butler, Gilbert, 2081
Butler, Gregory B., 598
Butler, John D., 3093
Butler, John K., 1688
Butler, Letitia K., 1946
Butler, Linda, 2612
Butler, Nathaniel, 1564
Butler, Nicole, 1971
Butler, Patricia M., 1688
Butler, Patrick, 1688
Butler, Patrick, Jr., 1688
Butler, Paul S., 1688
Butler, Peter M., 1688
Butler, Rex, 942
Butler, Sandra K., 1688
Butler, Steven, 667
Butler, Susan Storz, 1854
Butler, Thomas, 165
Butt, Patricia, 1132
Butta, Zulfiqar A., 3516
Butterfield Trust Bermuda Ltd, 2095
Butterfield, Frank, 897
Butterfield, John, 1623
Butterfield, Mark, 1897
Butterworth, Gary, 492
Butterworth, Sharon, 3312
Buttram, Susan, 1260
Butynes, Michelle, 2464
Butz, Greg L., 2986
Butzel, Laura, 2306
Buxton, Henry, 1663
Buzaglo, Meir, 2051
Buzzard, Vanessa, 3163
Buzzelli, Robert A., 2780
Byala, Brian, 3001
Byer, Thomas D., 3433
Byers, Alison M., 2998
Byers, Daphne, 2673
Byers, Karen, 2290
Byers, W. Russell G., Jr., 2998
Bylancik, Robert, 2407
Bynum, Bill, 1763
Byorick, Joe, 2981
Byram, Jennifer, 340
Byrd, D. Harold, Jr., 3261
Byrd, Daryl G., 1316
Byrd, Edward R., 355
Byrd, Jesse H., Jr., 2541
Byrd, Julie A., 1589
Byrer, F. Samuel, 3585
Byrne, Brendan, 2088
Byrne, Bruce, 2005
Byrne, Dorothy, 1879
Byrne, Dorothy M., 1879
Byrne, Gary, 159
Byrne, Gary D., 1849
Byrne, John J., 1879
Byrne, Kevin, 918
Byrne, Rebecca, 10
Byrnes, Brian, 2017
Byrnes, John H., 2472
Byrnes, Mollie, 1464
Byrnes, Mollie Tower, 2472
Byrnes, Susan, 3516
Byrnes, William H., Jr., 1952
Byron, Larry, 1569
Byron, William J., Rev., 3453
Byrski, Mary, 718
Byrum, D. Michael, 700
Byrum, Porter B., 2535

C&A Industries, Inc., 1844
Cabe, Charles L., Jr., 67
Cabe, Charles Lee "Sandy", 67
Cabe, Horace C., 67
Cabe, Thomas H., 67
Cabell, Charles L., 3425
Cabell, John Branch, 3425
Cabell, Maude Morgan, 3425
Cabell, Robert G., III, 3425
Cable, Barbara, 3555
Cable, Cindy, 2876
Cable, Thomas J., 3570
Cable, Tom, 3555
Cabot 1986 Conduit Trust, Thomas D., 1443
Cabot 1994 Charitable Lead Unitrust, Thomas D., 1443
Cabot 1996 Charitable Lead Unitrust, Virginia W., 1443
Cabot Revocable Trust, Virginia W., 1443
Cabot, Alexis, 1443
Cabot, Amiel, 1443
Cabot, Bradford W., 1443
Cabot, Elizabeth C., 1443
Cabot, F. Colin, 1891
Cabot, Godfrey L., 1442
Cabot, James W., 1443
Cabot, John G.L., 1442
Cabot, Thomas D., Jr., 1443
Cabrera, Phillip R., 1008
Cacciamani, Lauren P., 2362
Cacciamani, Paul A., 2362
Cacciatore, Mark, 1917
Cadawallader, Glenda M., 2270
Caddell Construction Co., Inc., 6
Caddell, Cathy L., 6
Caddell, Christopher P., 6
Caddell, Jeffrey P., 6
Caddell, John A., 6
Caddell, John K., 6
Caddell, Joyce K., 6
Caddell, Michael A., 6
Caddie Homes, Inc., 1364
Caddock, John B., 2838
Caddock, Richard E., Jr., 2838
Cade, Martha, 634
Cade, Mary, 634
Cadena, Mona, 1896
Cadiente, Katherine, 641
Cadle, John P., 979
Caesars Entertainment Operating Company, Inc., 1860
Caffrey, John J., 2269
Cafritz Foundation, Morris and Gwendolyn, 676
Cafritz, Anthony W., 656
Cafritz, Calvin, 656
Cafritz, Elliot S., 656
Cafritz, Gwendolyn D., 656
Cafritz, Jane Lipton, 656
Cafritz, Morris, 656
Cagigas, Gloria, 2685
Cahill, Becky, 630
Cahill, Michele, 2085
Cahill, Robert V., 150
Cahill, William, 268
Cahillane, Mary J., 1098
Cahn, Judy, 754
Cailloux, Floyd A., 3187
Cailloux, Kathleen C., 3187
Cailloux, Kenneth F., 3187
Cailloux, Sandra, 3187
Cain, Douglas M., 497
Cain, Edmund J., 251
Cain, Effie Marie, 3188
Cain, Jeffrey J., 389
Cain, John C., 3188
Cain, Jonathan, 434
Cain, Kevin M., 2612
Cain, R. Wofford, 3188
Caine, Edward P., 2932
Caine, Marie Eccles, 2536
Cajun Constructors, Inc., 1312
Calabrese, Alex, 410
Calabro, Tina, 2950
Calaway, Tonit M., 3621
Calciano, Marilyn, 163
Calder Foundation, Louis, 2873
Calder, Frederick C., 2265
Calder, Louis, 558
Calder, Peter D., 558
Calderon-Rosado, Vanessa, 1472
Calderwood Trust, Stanford, 1444
Calderwood, Stanford M., 1444
Caldwell, Alan L., 2613
Caldwell, Bob, 1847
Caldwell, Charles F., 3324
Caldwell, Christopher, 117
Caldwell, Desiree, 1889
Caldwell, Kevin, 257
Caldwell, R. Carter, 2919
Caldwell, Stacy, 441
Calfee, Jon, 3577
Calhoun, Cheryl A., 395
Calhoun, F. David, 3172
Calhoun, Ken, 1257
Calhoun, Kenneth, 2676
Calhoun, Michael, 3172
Calhoun, Phillip L., 2944
California Physicians' Service Agency Inc., 114
California Wellness Foundation, The, 244
Calinski, Rick, 1187
Calk, Sherri L., 2720
Call, Bradley C., 444
Callaghan, Lorraine M., 2125
Callahan, Christopher M., 1145
Callahan, Daniel M., 2269
Callahan, David M., 2923
Callahan, Eve, 2850
Callahan, Kevin, 181
Callahan, Michael A., 15
Callahan, Richard, 2110

Callahan, Sandra W., 830
Callas, Darcy, 1063
Calle, 37
Callen, C.J., 462
Calloway, W. Harold, 1205
Calone Law Group, 161
Calonge, Ned, M.D., 483
Calpin, William J., Jr., 3031
Caltrider, Marie, 3587
Calvo, Jose, 729
Camadeco, Benjamin, 1901
Cambell, Catherine, 1022
Cambone, Steve, Dr., 679
Cambridge Financial Services, 2071
Cambridge in America, 2069
Cambridgeport Bank, 3067
Camden, Andrew L., 1588
Cameron, Brenda, Hon., 1277
Cameron, John, Dr., 2599
Cameron, Wayne, 1868
Camlin, Dean, 1357
Cammett, Richard, 1562
Camp, John M., Jr., 861
Camp, Ruth Turner, 777
Camp, Tom R., 182
Campanella, Joseph, 2756
Campau, Anne E., 1623
Campbell Soup Co., 1917
Campbell, Alex G., Jr., 1285
Campbell, Ardis, 1519
Campbell, Barbara, 1154
Campbell, Brian P., 1576
Campbell, C. David, 3305
Campbell, Cayman, 1679
Campbell, D. Keith, 142
Campbell, Davis, 429
Campbell, Elizabeth C., 2389
Campbell, Eugene, 724
Campbell, Eugenie, 2705
Campbell, Frances, 2533
Campbell, Frank R., 3445
Campbell, George, Jr., 2288
Campbell, J. Bulow, 860
Campbell, Jack D., 1834
Campbell, Jan, 394
Campbell, Jeanne C., 3128
Campbell, John D., 1982
Campbell, John L., 2658
Campbell, Keith, 142
Campbell, Kirby J., 3032
Campbell, Laura, 1187
Campbell, Leslie, 3599
Campbell, Leslie Stevenson, 3566
Campbell, Malcolm David, Dr., 3438
Campbell, Margie, 391
Campbell, Mark A., 3054
Campbell, Michael L., 3151
Campbell, Pat, 537
Campbell, Paul, 2014
Campbell, Rebecca S., 2071
Campbell, Richard, 1899
Campbell, Robert D., 2752
Campbell, Robert E., 1900
Campbell, Robert F., 2156
Campbell, Robert L., 983
Campbell, Samantha, 142
Campbell, Stewart F., 2002
Campbell, Thomas L., 2986
Campbell, William M., 3054
Campbell-Cobb, Melanie, 2609
Campion, Jane, 1735
Campo, Ric, 3266
Campos, Dannielle C., 2524
Campos, Luis, 3208
Canada, Susan H., 3043
Canaday, Mariam C., 2083
Canaday, Ward M., 2083
Canale, Brad, 1636
Canale, Mark, 1636
Canales, James, 1433
Canales, Jim, 3606
Canary Charitable Foundation, The, 2074
Canary/Manitoba Foundation, 2074
Cane, Karen Marie, 423
Canepa, Patricia, 439
Canfield, William W., 1781
Canida, Ben, Dr., 1133
Cannady, A. Dale, 3476
Cannedy, Mac, 3201
Canning, Richard, 1507
Cannom, David M., M.D., 444
Cannon Manufacturing Co., 232
Cannon, Benjamin E., 3181
Cannon, Frank, 2609
Cannon, George W., 3405
Cannon, Glenna, 2767
Cannon, Kevin P., 2138
Cannon, Sally, 1578
Cannon, Ted, 1853
Cano, Andres, 43
Canon, Mike, 3316
Canoose, Jean, 64
Cansfield, Michael J., 1590
Cantlin, Mike, 2723
Caouette, John, 2297
Caouette, Therese, 3497
CAP Properties Ltd., 3424
Capanna, Robert, 3019
Capasso, Michael, 2228
Capbarat, Patricia, 289
Capco Sales, Inc., 1804
Capece, Vincent G., Jr., 592
Capel, William, 3052
Caperton, Gaston, 2892
Capital Counsel, 3642
Capital One, 676, 3426
Capital One Bank, N.A., 1304, 1320, 3381
Capital Research & Management Co., 394
Capital Ventures of NV, 1585
Capitani, Steve, 3148
Capitol Aggregates, 3387
Capitol Federal Financial, 1251
Capobianco, Anthony J., 2108
Capodilupo, Larry, 1445
Caporale, Jay, 1464
Caporale, Wende, 2044
Capozzi Farms, 1918
Capozzi, Amelia, 1918
Capozzi, Edith, 1918
Capozzi, Frank, 1918
Capozzi, Lucy, 1918
Capozzi, Mildred, 1918
Cappelletti, Matthew, Jr., 2916, 3017
Cappello, Alexander, 3496
Cappelloni, Robert J., 307
Capps, Randy, 1289
Caprio, Tony, 2677
Capron, Jeffery P., 1372
Cara, Frank, 2228
Caranci, Kerry, 401
Caravello, Lorene, 1097
Carboneau, David K., 2867
Carbonell, Karelia Martinez, 729
Carbonneau, Daniel P., 1482
Cardenas, Jose A., 57
Cardin, Sanford, 2827
Cardin, Sanford "Sandy" R., 2829
Cardinal Health, Inc., 2677
Cardini, Filippo, 2473
Cardon, Helen Hemingway, 3396
Cardona, Evette M., 1075
Cardwell, Bickerton W., Jr., 860
Cardwell, R. Craig, 2611
Care Now, 3320
CareFirst Blue Cross Blue Shield, 3424
Carey, Amie, 999
Carey, Brian, 562
Carey, Charles P., 984
Carey, Henry H., 911
Carey, Jennifer L., 1693
Carey, John M., 2665
Carey, Mike, 2702
Carey, Philip N., 911
Carey, Rea, 660
Carfagna, Rita Murphy, 2744
Cargile, Samuel D., 1174
Cargill, Kenneth V., 1897
Cargill, Margaret A., 1689
Carillo, Gretchen Weisenburger, 431
Carl, Charles W., Jr., 2407
Carl, Molly, 3666
Carlan, Sarah W., 638
Carlin, Marti, 3321
Carlin, Stephanie Klingzell, 1274
Carlin, Wayne, 2674
Carlotti, C.M., 2321
Carls, William, 1582
Carlson, Brenda, 1848
Carlson, C. Kent, 3570
Carlson, Cathy, 2169
Carlson, Christopher A., 2756
Carlson, Gary L., 1223
Carlson, Herbert E., 2686
Carlson, Jay, 1580
Carlson, Jeff, 498
Carlson, Jennie P., 2709
Carlson, Mark, 2924
Carlson, Terri, 1558
Carlsson, Gunnar, 82
Carlston, Alice, 143
Carlston, Charles, 143
Carlston, Donal, 143
Carlston, Douglas G., 143
Carlston, Erin, 143
Carlston, Gary, 143
Carlton, David, 869
Carlton, Doyle E., III, 844
Carlton, Doyle E., Jr., 844
Carlton, Jerry, 276
Carlton, John M., Jr., 869
Carlton, Lisa, 754
Carlyle, Shannon McLin, 762
Carlyon, David, 2369
CarMax Auto Superstores, Inc., 3427
CarMax Business Services, LLC, 3427
Carmichael, James, 36
Carmody, Christine M., 598
Carmody, Timothy J., 1215
Carmola, Jack, 2561
Carmouche, David, 1302
Carnaroli, Craig R., 2926
Carnegie Corporation of New York, 674
Carnegie, Andrew, 2085, 2906
Carnell, J. Kevin, 1406
Carnes, Clifford, 1133
Carnes, Martha, 3266
Carnevale, Anthony, 2188
Carnevale-Henderson, Marisa, 842
Carney, Carole, 144
Carney, Jane, 264
Carney, Laura, 3607
Carney, Lloyd, 144
Carnielli, Sandra, 2295
Carnival Cruise Lines, Inc., 691
Carnivale, Nicholas, 1984
Caro, Robert A., 2194
Carol Electric Company, Inc., 146
Carolina East Medical Center, 3377
Carome, Kevin M., 847
Caron, Daniel, 564
Carpenter Revocable Trust, Agnes, 145
Carpenter, Alison, 1634
Carpenter, Andy, 1755
Carpenter, David R., 444
Carpenter, Elaine, 953
Carpenter, Karen H., 1523
Carpenter, Kay, 283
Carpenter, Matt, 492
Carpenter, Michael, 2662
Carpenter, Richard, 145
Carpenter, Robert, 1657
Carpenter, Thomas S., 1426
CARR Lane Manufacturing, 1818
Carr, Barbara Thiele, 3652
Carr, Catherine E., 232
Carr, Elliott, 1445
Carr, J. Anthony, 2963
Carr, Jim, 778
Carr, Joe, 1227
Carr, Joseph S., 1025
Carr, Kathleen D.H., 3453
Carr, Meredith G., 2706
Carr, Robert W., 2957
Carr, Steve, 948
Carrabba, Joseph A., 2681
Carragan, Craig, 564
Carraher, Ruth A., 534
Carreau, Robert A., 2407
Carrey Family Trust, 112
Carrey, James, 112
Carrick, Elizabeth, 1098
Carrick, John, 1914
Carrico, John D., 1946
Carrie, Ellen Zachry, 3387
Carrigan, Laura Cabot, 1442, 1443
Carringer, Jim, 2552
Carrington, Susan A., 894
Carroll, Charles, 363
Carroll, Howard W., Hon., 1083
Carroll, Jane C., 1977
Carroll, Jody, 1272
Carroll, Michael, 1294
Carroll, Paul, 3494
Carroll, Stephen D., 3678
Carroll, Stephen, Esq., 2932
Carroll, Wendy I., 1380
Carroll-Pankhurst, Cindie, 2673
Carruth, Anne S., 9
Carruth, Marlies, 1030
Carruthers, Sara P., 2710
Carse, Elizabeth, 609
Carson, Cecily M., 2086
Carson, Diane, 3503
Carson, Don, 1267
Carson, Edward S., 2086
Carson, Emmett D., 408
Carson, Judith M., 2086
Carson, Russell L., 2086
Cartagena, Luis, 2770
Cartee, Joseph B., 3
Carter Foundation Production Co., 3190
Carter, Adrianna, 2600
Carter, Amon G., 3190
Carter, Annie, 2682

Carter, C.J., 3431
Carter, E. Eugene, 657
Carter, Jennifer, 3521
Carter, Kathleen, 900
Carter, Larry, 1295, 1867
Carter, Lee A., 2694
Carter, Michael, 1156
Carter, Mollie H., 1263
Carter, N.B., 3190
Carter, Prudence L., 2191
Carter, Robert, 3290
Carter, S. Theresa, 2759
Carter, Steven M., 3625
Carter, Susan M., 877, 915
Carter, Travis J., 3178
Carter-Robertson, Kira, 1581
Cartier, Barbara, 103, 104
Cartiglia, Katherine Gilweit, 1872
Cartinella, Sherrie, 1876
Carto, David D., 2767
Cartwright, Herbert L., 3160
Carty, Blair, 76
Caruana, Sal, 2004
Carusi, Bruce, 1862
Carusi, Sue, 1862
Caruso, Donna, 714
Caruso, Frank, 2087
Caruso, Kim M., 830
Caruso, Mike, 2853
Caruso, Ruth, 2087
Caruth, W.W., III, 3261
Caruth, W.W., Sr., Mrs., 3261
Caruthers, Carol R., 1752
Carvel 1991 Trust, Agnes, The, 2088
Carvel Unitrust Remainderman, Thomas, 2088
Carvel, Agnes, 2088
Carvel, Thomas, 2088
Casamento, Laura, 2110
Cascade Natural Gas Corp., 2652
Cascarilla, Charles, 2230
Case, Donald, 613
Case, Gregory C., 963
Case, Jean N., 658
Case, Patti, 3504
Case, Peter G., 1322
Case, Stephen M., 658
Caselli, Richard J., 44
Casey Family Programs, 1414, 3500
Casey Trust, Iris, 2148
Casey, A. Michael, 120, 219
Casey, Annie E., 1353
Casey, Carol, 455
Casey, Carol W., 454
Casey, David, 3457
Casey, Edward G., 1509
Casey, James E. "Jim", 1353
Casey, Jean K., 219
Casey, Kathy, 505
Casey, Kevin M., 2921
Casey, Lyman H., 120
Casey, Marian M., 3324
Cash, Harvey Berryman, 3202
Cash, Michelle, 1979
Cash, Terry L., 3110
Cashaw, Allan, 2922
Cashdan, Lisa, 3417
Cashdin, Jeffrey, 3622
Cashill, Robert, 1984
Cashin, Arthur D., Jr., 2336
Cashion Family Foundation, John L., The, 351
Cashion Living Trust, Howard, 1206
Cashman, Chistopher, 2975
Cashman, Kathryn Batchelder, 2408
Casias, Ed, 537
Casini, Marlene A., 2689
Cason, Dallas G., 347, 397
Cassel, Christine K., 2192
Cassel, Rita Allen, 1900
Cassidy, Tom, 1175
Cassie, Beth, 2004
Cassinelli, Filippo, 3419
Casteel, Beth, 2923
Casteen, John T., III, 3436
Castel, P. Kevin, Hon., 2204
Caster, Marci, 3117
Castillo, Ernesto, 1857
Castillo, Gloria, 1014
Castle & Cooke, Inc., 338
Castle, Alfred L., 930
Castle, Courtney A., 582
Castle, Harold K.L., 929
Castle, Harold K.L., Mrs., 929
Castle, James H., 582
Castle, Jennie Y., 582
Castle, Jonatha Y., 582
Castle, Mary, 930
Castle, Mike, 3642
Castle, Samuel N., 930
Castle, William H., 582
Castleman, Marilyn, 2148
Castor, Bruce L., 3056
Castori, Pamela, 616
Castro, Ida, 3031
Castro, Martin R., 982
Castro, Ricardo A., 2343
Castruccio, Louis M., 294
Catalano, Antonio P., 3651
Catalina Marketing Corp., 716
Catalogue for Philanthropy, 676
Catalyst Foundation, Inc., 3424
Cate, Ruth L., 3097
Cates, David C., 1168
Cates, Rodney, 3287
Cates, Sheryl, 3287
Cates, Steve, 3378
Cathcart-Rake, Ruth, 1274
Catherwood, Susan W., 2988
Cathey, Catharine Mellon, 2998
Cathy, Donald M., 921
Cathy, S. Truett, 921
Catlin, John "Jack", 982
Cato, Jessica, 480
Caton, J.R., 2826
Cattan, Mary, 2332
Catto, Elizabeth Pettus, 480
Catto, Henry, 480
Catto, Roxana Gage, 3239
Catto, William Halsell, 480
Cattran, Cynthia L., 1576
Caufman, Ron, 3520
Caulfield, Gary, 933
Causby, Cindy, 2539
Causey, C. Chad, 1763
Cauthen, Irvin L., 3102
Cavagna, Joseph F., 1391
Cavalcanti, Glynda, 687
Cavaliere, Anthony J., 2932
Cavanah, Cindy, 1817
Cavanaugh, April, 1841
Cavanaugh, Rebecca B., 3434
Caven, Jay, 944
Caven, Jerry, 944
Caven, Mike, 944
Caven, Muriel, 944
Cavender, Richard, 1783
Cavendish, Michael, 3577
Caviness, Terry, 3163
Cawthon, Catherine A., 1618
Cay, Christopher, 912
Cayne, Richard, 1420
CBM Cos., Inc., 3603
CBM of Madison, Inc., 3603
CC Myers, Inc., 102
CDC of Health and Human Services Dept., 2167
Cearley, Michael, 1280
Cecil, Art, 1395
Cecil, Larry G., 2771
Cedar Rapids Bank & Trust, 1228
Cedillo-Perez, Liz, 3209
Cedlair Corp., 1388
Celer, Michael, 1052
Celico, Kristi P., 1127
Celio, Elizabeth, 1053
Celio, Elizabeth Lumpkin, 1053
Cellino, A.M., 2321
Cellular City, Ltd., 3327
Celstar Group, Inc., 2671
CEMEX Corp., 3191
Censullo, Marilyn A., 1517
Centaur, Inc., 2665
Centene Management Company, LLC, 1782
Centeno-Gomez, Diana, 2770
Center Care Health, 3377
Central Bank Illinois, 1022
Central Indiana Community Foundation, 1156
Central Shares Corp., 3145
Century 21, Inc., 2089
Century, Jane Friedman, 2391
Cerciello, Amy, 2118
Cerow, Michael S., 723
Cerruti, Dominique, 2336
Certain, Jackie, 1129
Certo, Matthew, 712
Cervantes, Jennifer, 2010
Cervenak, Chris, 1524
Cessna Aircraft Co., The, 803
Cessna Foundation, Inc., 3093
Cessna, Jodi, 2907
Cestello, Louis R., 1347
Cestone, Maria A., II, 2910
Cestone, Michele J., 2910
CFA Properties, Inc., 921
Ch2M Hill, 3505
Chace, Richard, 1885
Chadick, Gary R., 1237
Chadwick, Chris, Rev., 1382
Chadwick, Keith D., 2107
Chadwick, Laura Farish, 3228
Chaffee, Paul, 1662
Chahine, Toufic, 3280
Chaho, Joseph B., 585
Chaho, Michael B., 585
Chaifetz, Malcolm, 1960
Chait, Gerald, 2889
Challenge Foundation, Inc., 2873
Challenge Me Now, 2173
Chalmers, Bruce, 1887
Chaloupka, Judy, 1852
Chamberlain Group, Inc., 1005
Chamberlain, Bryce B., 1022
Chamberlain, Charles C., 2396
Chamberlain, Kathryn C., 2396
Chambers, Florence, 1304
Chambers, Karla S., 2846
Chambers, M. Susan, 74
Chambers, Michael, 2767
Chambers, Raymond G., 1965
Chameli, Kathleen C., 1244
Champer, Jeanne M., 1800
Chan, Cam, 305
Chan, Chi-Chao, 301
Chan, Ida Lopez, 157
Chan, Kenyon, 301
Chan, Michele, 148
Chan, Yvonne, 3451
Chance, Elizabeth B., 2004
Chandlee, Chad, 1216
Chandler, A., 3231
Chandler, Bert, 59
Chandler, Carol, 1498
Chandler, Don, 407
Chandler, Ellen B., 557
Chandler, Linda, 1191
Chandler, Richard B., Jr., 867
Chandler, Stephen M., 445
Chaney Enterprises, L.P., 628
Chaney, Carla, 3290
Chaney, Frances, 2840
Chaney, Francis H., II, 628
Chaney, Robert, 2840
Chang, Andrew, 934
Chang, Debbie, 842
Chang, Hemmie, 1472
Chang, Jae Min, 287
Chang, Sofia, 2466
Chang-Muy, Fernando, 3000, 3055
Chang-Rios, Karin, 1808
Channing, Susan Stockard, 747
Chano, Junko, 680
Chao Family Trust, 149
Chao, Amy, 149
Chao, Anne S., 3267
Chao, Elaine, 2066
Chao, Jessica, 2161
Chao, Ping, 149
Chao, Ryan, 1353
Chaolley Limited Partnership, 2703
Chapel, Diana, 3313
Chapelard, Frederic, 1899
Chapin, Michelle, 724
Chapin, William H., 3123
Chapla, Robert, 1586
Chaplin, Christina Stafford, 825
Chaplin, Chuck, 2297
Chaplin, Harvey R., 1558
Chapman, Alvah H., 717
Chapman, Betty Bateman, 717
Chapman, Brian, 1505
Chapman, Carl L., 1202
Chapman, Colleen, 1868
Chapman, Constance, 3527
Chapman, Daniel H., 3296
Chapman, Drupgyu Anthony, 2478
Chapman, H.A., 2808
Chapman, John S., 1024
Chapman, Mary K., 2808
Chapman, Patti, 2731
Chapman, Wyline Page, 717
Chapoton, John E., 656
Chappell, Norman P., 1160
Chaprnka, Karen A., 1623
Charaf, Ricardo J., 3419
Chardan Capital, 647
Charitable Remainder Trust, Rieker, 954
Charities Aid Foundation, 165
Charity Buzz, 647, 679
Charity Folks, Inc., Inc., 2336
Charles, Joseph, 2177
Charles, Marion Oates, 2146
Charles, Thomas, 2947
Charlestein, Gary, 2911
Charlestein, Morton L., 2911
Charlton Co., Harry, Inc., 1976

Charlton, Robert W., 1656
Charreton, Didier, 3170
Charter Charitable Foundation, 1896
Charter One Bank, 3067
Chartered Foundation, 746
Chartrand, Gary R., 719
Chartrand, Jeffrey, 719
Chartrand, Meredith, 719
Chartrand, Nancy J., 719
Chase Manhattan Bank, The, 2242
Chase Oil Co., 2009
Chase, Alfred E., 1446
Chase, Alice P., 2913
Chase, Anthony, 3267
Chase, Cara, 3378
Chase, David D., 2008
Chase, Deb, 2009
Chase, Edith, 564
Chase, Joe, 1580
Chase, Karla, 2009
Chase, Katherin Lee, 2008
Chase, Lavinia B., 1543
Chase, Lee J., III, 3120
Chase, Mack C., 2009
Chase, Marilyn Y., 2009
Chase, Missy, 3458
Chase, Richard, 2009
Chase, Robert, 2009
Chase, Susan L., 2950
Chase, William J., 954
Chasin, Charlie, 2315
Chasin, Laura, 2477
Chatam, Inc., 1893
Chatham Ventures, Inc., 2242
Chatman, Michael, 1783
Chatterjee, Dean Jay, 2782
Chatterton, James R., 3664
Chatzinoff, Howard, 2498
Chau, Micheline, 139, 306
Chau, Windon, 3315
Chaudoin, Don, 1205
Chavez, Joann, 1598
Chavez, John F., 287
Chavez, Marcie, 2011
Chazen Museum of Art, 2069
Chebbani, Ahmad, 1588
Checchia, Anthony P., 3019
Cheek, Yvonne, 1742
Cheers, Pennie Gonseth, 1241
Cheesman, Gary D., 1122
Cheetham, Philippa, 2445
Chehebar, Ezra A., 2172
Chehebar, Gabriel A., 2172
Chehebar, Josef A., 2172
Chehebar, Michael A., 2172
Chell, Jeffrey W., 2562
Chemaly, John P., 1505
Chemers, Martin M., 163
Chemical Investments, Inc., 2242
Chen, Albert, 301
Chen, Alice Huan-mei, 1459
Chen, Elizabeth McCoy, 319
Chen, Ida K., 2942
Chen, Stanley, 468
Chen-Courtin, Dorothy, 1505
Chenault, Kenneth I., 2034, 2066
Cheney Trust, Elizabeth F., 981
Cheney, Amy L., 2679
Cheney, Arta, 1729
Cheney, Jeffrey P., 3629
Cheney, Laura Stevenson, 3566
Cheng, Linda Y.H., 367
Cheng, Soua, 3606
Chenoweth, Chris, 207
Cherbec Advancement Foundation, 1752
Chernesky, Richard J., 2734
Chernick, Deborah, 1746
Chernick, Richard, 268
Chernin, David, 2092
Chernin, John, 2092
Chernin, Margaret, 2092
Chernin, Megan, 2092
Chernin, Peter, 2092
Chernoff, Carolyn, 2985
Chernoff, Julie, 1012
Cherry, Kimberley C., 3135
Cherundolo, John C., Hon., 1862
Chesapeake Energy Corporation, 3237
Chesebrough, Donna, 342
Chesebrough, Robert N., III, 342
Cheshire, Marjorie J. Rodgers, 1345
Chesney, James D., 3331
Chestang, Nicole M., 2188
Chester, Jack, 720
Cheston, Shelia, 3465
Cheu, Leslie A., 2474
Chevalier, Stephan J., 3670
Cheves, Bettye A., 849
Cheves, Cecil M., 849
Chevez, Cecil, 849
Chevron U.S.A., Inc., 28
Chewning, Thomas N., 3433
Chi, YoungSuk "YS", 1463
Chialdikas, Mike, 1034
Chiang, Anne, 468
Chiang, Antony, 3510
Chiang, Bessie, 2094
Chiang, Helen, 2094
Chiang, Michael, 2094
Chiar, Paul, 468
Chica Bonita, Inc., 2484
Chicago Community Trust, The, 983
Chicago Mercantile Exchange Trust, 984
Chicago Title Insurance Company, 1178
Chick-fil-A, Inc., 921
Chidester, Colleen, 1358
Chief Oil & Gas, LLC, 3330
Chien, Shu, 106
Chiesa, Melanie, 425
Chiesman, Allene R., 3115
Chifton Ltd Co., 3346
Chigier, Benjamin, 1464
Child Abuse Prevention Council, 161
Child, Rex, 1822
Childears, Linda, 488
Childers, Frank, 351
Childress, Dean, 3207
Childs, Bridget, 161
Childs, James E., Dr., 559
Childs, John D., 559
Childs, John W., 559
Childs, Kirsten, 2143
Childs, Richard S., Jr., 559
Childs, Sam, 562
Childs, Starling W., 559
Childs, William F., IV, 628
Chilman, Bill, 1647
Chilton, Greg, 157
Chime on Inc., 272
Chin, Wally, 933
Ching, Edric M., 931
Ching, Elizabeth Lau, 931
Ching, Gerry, Mrs., 938
Ching, Han Hsin, 931
Ching, Han Ping, 931
Ching, Hung Wo, 931
Ching, Shelli Mei Li, 931
Chinn, Susan, 2749
Chipman, Wayne, 1181
Chisnell, Michael, 2664
Chitwood, Melinda T., 3432
Chiu, Kevin Y.T., 2685
Chmura, Gary, Fr., 2786
Choate, Ed, 68
Chodorkoff, Betsy M., 3409
Choe, Martha, 3558
Choi, Audrey, 2315
Choksi, Armeane, 676
Chong, Martha, 571
Choo, Shinjoo, 3055
Chopus, Kelly, 3477
Choucair, Bechara, 1083
Chouinard, Malinda P., 362
Chouinard, Yvon, 362
Chow, Edward, 301
Chow, Ronald G., 260
Chowning, Glenn S., 2858
Choy, Michael K.K., 22
Chrisman, Lance, 1206
Christ Church, 3330
Christ, Chris T., 1579
Christensen, Allen D., 151
Christensen, Anker, 278
Christensen, Barbara, 1836
Christensen, C. Diane, 151
Christensen, Carmen M., 151
Christensen, Clay, 2828
Christensen, Douglas A., 2650
Christensen, Gary, 1739
Christensen, Keith, 3568
Christensen, Maren, 2322
Christensen, Sue E., 3618
Christenson, James E., 1624
Christenson, Nancy K., 2652
Christenson, Norma, 1706
Christian Alliance for Humanitarian Aid, 3269
Christian Foundation of the Triangle, The, 2863
Christian Health Ministries Foundation, 1299
Christian, Cheryl, 886
Christian, Dale, 3516
Christian, Paige, 2109
Christian, Ronald C., 2679
Christian, Ronald E., 1202
Christiansen, Mindy, 3677
Christianson, Megan, 1699
Christie, Elizabeth W., 2002
Christie, Ellen, 1472
Christie, James D., 2607
Christman, Chip, 2712
Christman, Marc, 1081
Christopher, Gail C., 1628
Christopher, Jack, 1758
Christopherson, Elizabeth G., 1900, 1982
Christopherson, Mark, 1694
Christopherson, Sue, 3631
Christy's Charity, 680
Christy, Alexandra, 2511
Christy, Debbi, 1189
Christy, Jennifer, 2732
Chroman, Susan E., 1249
Chronis, Amy, 569
Chronquist, Gladys, 3633
Chronquist, Harry, 3633
Chrystyn-Opperman, Julie, 350
Chrzan, Janet C., 3058
Chu, Benjamin K., 2106
Chu, Christina, 305
Chuah, Lucy, 2159
Chubb & Son, 102
Chugach Alaska Corp., 32
Chugach Alaska Regional Corp., 32
Chun, Miyoung, 275
Chun, Tammi, 933
Chupik, Colleen, 3494
Church, John R., 1697
Church, Phillip E., 2538
Church, Steve A., 1167
Church, Sylvia, 540
Churchill, Hugo, 2896
Churchill, Michelle, 407
Cicatiello, Anthony, 1990
Cicconi, James W., 3167
Cicerone, Ralph J., 2085
Cici, Michelle, 1694
Cigna, 3505
CIGNA Corp., 2917
Cimini, Ronald, 2947
Cimino, Anthony "Skip", 1979
Cimino, Audrey S., 1357
Cincinnati Foundation, Greater, The, 1141
Cindrich, Robert J., 2906
Cintani, Bill, 1847
Ciprich, Paula M., 2321
CIRI, Inc., 33
Cirillo, Ceil, 163
Cirone, Frank J., 3014
Cisneros, Joe, 2657
Cisneros, Suzanne Ortega, 2017
CITC, 33
CITGO Petroleum Corporation, 3179
Citibank, N.A., 2395
Citigroup, 2325
Citigroup UK, 2445
Citizens Bank, 1470
Citizens Bank Mid-Atlantic Charitable Foundation, The, 3067
Citizens Bank of Rhode Island, 3067
Citizens Bank of Southern Pennslyvania, 2952
Citizens Charitable Foundation, 3067
Citizens Savings Bank, 3067
Citizens Trust Co., 3067
City of Waterloo, 1234
Citybridge Foundation, 676
Civil War Preservation Trust, 3448
Clabaugh, Gavin T., 1645
Claborn, Jobey D., 3370
Cladis, Nick R., 747
Claflin, Will, 2658
Clain, Michael J., 2183
Claire Foundation, Lili, Inc., The, 3622
Clancy, Michael, 3056
Claneil Enterprises, Inc., 2918
Clannin, Robert J., 1353
Clapp, Haleh, 3542
Clapp, James N., II, 3542
Clapp, Margaret, 3542
Clapp, Matthew N., Jr., 3542
Clapp, Rebecca Greenleaf, 2444
Clapp, Tamsin O., 3542
Clapp, Wade, 2562
Clapptrap Trust, 1891
Clarian Health, 2562
Clarice, Michael, 1290
Clark Family Foundation, 202
Clark, Agenia, 3121
Clark, Andrew M., Dr., 2280
Clark, Angelica K., 359
Clark, Aubrey, 2221
Clark, Benic M., III, 3145
Clark, beth, 1152
Clark, Bobby, 502
Clark, Carol, 2915

Clark, Celeste A., 1628
Clark, Christine M., 2920
Clark, Claire, 393
Clark, Collette, 139
Clark, Dan, 1828, 1845
Clark, David G., 2920
Clark, David W., 2726
Clark, Edna McConnell, 2097
Clark, Etta, 3133
Clark, Frank E., 2096
Clark, Frank M., 982
Clark, G. Thomas, 2185
Clark, George M., III, 3125
Clark, H. Lawrence, 2097
Clark, Hollice, 989
Clark, J.H. Cullum, 3293
Clark, James McConnell, 2097
Clark, James McConnell, Jr., 2097
Clark, Jane Forbes, 2099
Clark, Jessie Wilcox, 591
Clark, John, 1448
Clark, John R., 1822
Clark, Jon, 394
Clark, Jonathan, 2696
Clark, Josh, 1185
Clark, Judy M., 2920
Clark, Kathy, 3316
Clark, Kevin, 1893
Clark, Kim, 1453
Clark, Lawrence S., 415
Clark, M. Craig, 3237
Clark, Malcolm N., 2611
Clark, Margot, 1171
Clark, Martha, 2578
Clark, Mary Jane, 474
Clark, Mary W., 3279
Clark, Midori, 535
Clark, Nita, 3209
Clark, Paul, 3163
Clark, Peggy, 72
Clark, Peter, 2331
Clark, Randy, 425
Clark, Richard J., 2721, 2745
Clark, Robert J., 2920
Clark, Robert Sterling, 2098
Clark, Roger E., 494
Clark, Susan Reed, 91
Clark, Teresa L., 1272
Clark, Thomas, 1289
Clark, Tim, 1154
Clark, Tina S., 1299
Clark, Trent, 948
Clark, W. Van Alan, 2097
Clark, William C., III, 1403
Clarke, Bonnie A., 1403
Clarke, Carol, 1909
Clarke, Dave, 1290
Clarke, Jesse, 1403
Clarke, Lois A., 3484
Clarke, Sally, 2148
Clarke, Steven W., 1403
Clarke, Stuart A., 1413
Clarke, William, 2540
Clarke, William C., III, 1403
Clarke, William C., III, Mrs., 1403
Clarkson Family Foundation, The, 2204
Clarkson, Bayard D., 2204
Clarkson, William, IV, 872
Clarno, Leona M., 3561
Class Act Arts, 1414
Class of 1961 Fund, 3494
Classen, Roger F., 2670
Claton, Larry, 2907
Clatpag Trust, 1891
Clatscatt Trust, 1891
Clattaur Trust, 1891
Clattecam Trust, 1891
Clattesad Trust, 1891
Claudepierre, Dale, 1616
Clauser, Ruth A., 3046
Clausing, Gretjen, 2985
Clausman, Linette, 10
Clauss, Ben, 3099
Clay, David, 1210
Clay, Jonathan C., 1977
Clay, Laura, 2821
Clay, Phillip L., 1631
Claybourn, Colleen, 3373
Claybourn, Joshua, 1202
Clayburn, D. Kent, 1872
Clayman, Caryn, 2024
Clayman, Edith Abramson, 2024
Clayman, Melvin, 2024
Claypool, Jim, 157
Clayton Holding Co., 1962
Clayton, B. Joe, 3128
Clayton, James L., 3128
Clayton, Janice K., 3128
Clayton, Kay, 3128
Clayton, Kevin T., 3128
Clayton, Lawrence, 2280
Clayton, Valerie, 2942
Cleary, Bernadette C., 1807
Cleary, Donald, 2038
Cleary, Mary Ann, 340
Cleary, Patrick, 257
Clebanoff, Jerry, 158
Clegg, Cynthia H., 592
Clement, Sally D., 1747
Clemente, James F., 3031
Clements Charitable Trust, 3195
Clements, Carolyn, 1184
Clements, Donna, 3195
Clements, Michael, 2632, 3195
Clemons, G. Scott, 59
Clennon, Bart, 3503
Cleveland, Barbara, 917
Cleveland, Judy A., 3503
Cleveland, Rose Ann, 656
Cleveland-Cliffs Inc., 2681
Cleven, Carol C., 705
Clevenger, Beth, 3589
Cleworth, Kim, 3489
Click, Betty J., 1253
Clif Bar & Co., 152
Cliff, Carolyn, 3493
Cliff, Ursula, 2224
Cliff, Walter C., 2224
Clifford, Charles H., Jr., 289
Clifford, Linda M., 2760
Clifford, Nancy L., 1171
Clifford, Robert C., 1726
Cliffs Natural Resources, 2681
Climie, Judy, 1180
Cline, Bud, 1616
Cline, Junior, 1805
Cline, Mike, 1129
Clinton Family Foundation, The, 3424
Clinton Investment Co., 3096
Clinton, Edward X., 983
Clobes, April M., 1581
Clorox Co., The, 153
Close, Anne Springs, 3111
Close, Derick S., 3111
Close, Elliott S., 3111
Close, Frances A., 3111
Close, H.W., 3111
Close, Katherine A., 3111
Close, M. Scott, 3111
Close, Nancy L., 788
Cloud, Amanda, 3352
Cloud, Kevin, 3326
Cloud, Laurel Iron, 2011
Clouse, Robert, 1607
Clover Capital Mgmt., 2655
Clow, Reggie, 1703
Cluck, Bruce W., 1013
Cluck, Frank D., Jr., 1013
Clunie, Heather, 1155
Cluster, Darryl W., 282
Clut, Bendon, 1859
Cluverius, James K., 3444
Clyde, Wilfred W., 102
Clyne, Richard A., 1863
CMGRP, Inc., 3424
CMRCC, Inc., 2242
Coach, Inc., 2100
Coakley, Sean, 1569
Coates, Elizabeth Huth, 3197
Coates, Philip, 2048
Coates, Thomas K., 1359
Coats, Dell, 340
Coats, Lonnell, 1921
Coatsworth, John H., 2467
Coatue Management, LLC, 2264
Cobb, Calvin Hayes, Jr., 661
Cobb, Carole, 1578
Cobb, Gerald, 3200
Cobb, Patrick, 1228
Cobb, Steve, 137
Cobb, Tyrus R., 863
Coberley, Charlotte, 1634
Coblentz, Lisa Y., 1358
Cobler, Larry, 1584
Coburn Survivor's Trust, 154
Coburn, Pip, 523
Coca-Cola Co., The, 864
Cochran Firm, The, 3424
Cochrane, Nick, 1215
Cocke, Frances F., 873
Cockerell, Martha, 1817
Cockrell, Ernie D., II, 3266
Cocotis, Paul A., 102
Codey, John, 2207
Coe, Charles R., Jr., 2821
Coe, Henry H.R., III, 3672
Coe, Henry H.R., Jr., 3672
Coe, Marty, 3672
Coe, Ross M., 2821
Coe, Ross M. "Rick", 2821
Coe, Ward I., 2821
Coehlo, Kenneth B., 1399
Coelho, Rosemarie, 1515
Coen, Beverly J., 2755
Coen, Steve, 1263
Coenen, Pamela A., 3620
Coffelt, Steve, 1663
Coffey, Deeda M., 2542
Coffey, Greg, 1010
Coffey, Shelby, III, 662
Coffey, Sherilee, 3498
Coffin, Alice S., 559
Coffin, Anne, 2408
Coffindaffer, Billy L., 3591
Coffman, Chad, 1155
Coffman, Cindy, 1836
Coffman, Faye, 1010
Coffman, Greg, 2686
Coffman, Jean, 1519
Coffman, Marcia, 1020
Cofrin, David H., 622
Cofrin, Edith Dee, 622
Cofrin, Gladys G., 622
Cofrin, Mary Ann H., 622
Cofrin, Mary Ann P., 622
Cofrin, Paige W., 622
Cogan, Gregory, 1450
Cogan, John F., Jr., 1450
Cogan, Jonathan, 1450
Cogan, Michele M., 1893
Cogan, Peter G., 1450
Coggin, Joan, Dr., 3119
Coggins, Christa, 2017
Coglianese, Marcy, 3642
Cogswell, Susan, 1616
Cogswell, Wilton W., III, 529
Cohan, Lucy, 2338
Cohee, Lynn, 1045
Cohen Foundation, John S., The, 721
Cohen Foundation, Sam L., 1327
Cohen Revocable Trust, Sonya, 2237
Cohen, Barton P., 1252
Cohen, Bennett, 3407
Cohen, Bette D., 1388
Cohen, Charlotte McKee, 3295
Cohen, David, 201
Cohen, David L., 2921
Cohen, Diana, 1012
Cohen, Elizabeth Ann, 721
Cohen, Emanuel, 1355
Cohen, Eric, 2465
Cohen, Holly B., 2979
Cohen, Howard, 2004
Cohen, Israel, 1355
Cohen, Janet L., 1892
Cohen, Jenny, 721
Cohen, Jeremy, 2074
Cohen, Jill R., 1892
Cohen, Joanne, 722
Cohen, Julie W., 2834
Cohen, Karen B., 2102
Cohen, Kenneth P., 2459, 2460
Cohen, Lea, 2103
Cohen, Linda, 2110
Cohen, Martin, 663
Cohen, Martin D., 1515
Cohen, Mary, 1252
Cohen, Michael, 2103
Cohen, N.M., 1355
Cohen, Naomi, 1355
Cohen, Perry L., 1892
Cohen, Philippa, 2074
Cohen, Rachel, 691
Cohen, Rachel F., 1892
Cohen, Rhoda R., 1467
Cohen, Rhonda, 2988
Cohen, Richard, 2283
Cohen, Richard B., 1892
Cohen, Richard S., 721
Cohen, Robert L., 1261
Cohen, Robert S., 565
Cohen, Russell A., 1467
Cohen, Sam L., 1327
Cohen, Sara, 2103, 2401
Cohen, Steven, 1464
Cohen, Steven A., 528
Cohen, William C., Jr., 1261
Cohn Foundation, Betsy and Alan, The, 2237
Cohn, Alan D., 2237
Cohn, Allan L., 1190
Cohn, Jacqueline, 1313
Cohn, Lisa Reckler, 528
Cohn, Ted J., 472
Cohon, Jared L., 2085, 2966
Cohrs Trust, Oscar, 2680

Cook, Charles W., Jr., 3129
Cook, Dave, 1587
Cook, Doug, 1616
Cook, Edward S., Jr., 3605
Cook, Frances, 3155
Cook, Gay, 483
Cook, Harold C., 3429
Cook, Karen S., 2402
Cook, Kathryn M., 3112
Cook, Langdon P., 570
Cook, Lauretta, 2539
Cook, Lucille T., 67
Cook, Mary McDermott, 3293
Cook, Philip I., 3017
Cook, Phyllis, 385
Cook, Royrickers, Dr., 4
Cook, Scott D., 263
Cook, Sean H., 1958
Cook, Trisha A., 975
Cook, Wallace L., 2126
Cook, Wayne S., 2396
Cook, William, 2788
Cook, Yvonne, 2968
Cooke Investment Group, 1156
Cooke Trust, William A., 3434
Cooke, Anna C., 932
Cooke, Catherine, 932
Cooke, William A., Incorporated, 3434
Cool, Jeanette, 314
Cooley, Garry E., 1192
Coolidge, Lawrence, 1529
Coombe, Michael A., 2658
Coombe, Tucker J., 2658
Coon, Cheryl F., 2843
Coon, Eli, 2843
Coon, James S., 2843
Cooney, C. Michael, 353
Cooney, Joan Ganz, 2357
Coons, Darryl E., 1705
Coons, Helen L., 2948
Cooper Charitable Lead Trust, Eric C., 2927
Cooper, Anita, 1067
Cooper, Ann, 2187
Cooper, Barbara, 2574
Cooper, Barry, 496
Cooper, Beckwith Archer, 870
Cooper, Brian, 3158
Cooper, Candace, 268
Cooper, Cary, 537
Cooper, David, 3589
Cooper, Diane, 3211
Cooper, Eric C., 2927
Cooper, Eva Aguirre, 1615
Cooper, Frederick E., 870
Cooper, Frederick E., Jr., 870
Cooper, Freny, 163
Cooper, Helen D., 870
Cooper, I. Wayne, 723
Cooper, J. Patterson, 2300
Cooper, Jeffrey, 1863
Cooper, Jim, 3589
Cooper, John W., 1998
Cooper, Johnson Joseph, 870
Cooper, Joseph H., 1834
Cooper, Lisa, 470
Cooper, Mae, 1166
Cooper, Margie, 193
Cooper, Robert, 2655
Cooper, Rochelle, 3052
Cooper, Susan E., 1599
Cooper-Siegel Foundation Charitable Lead Trusts, 2927
Cooperrider, Jon H., II, 2803
Coopersmith, Ari, 1902
Coopersmith, Jeffrey, 2505
Coopman, Katherine M., 379
Coopwood, Scott, 1760
Cooter, Mark, 3099
Cope, Andrew G., 3156
Cope, Judy, 2437
Copeland, A. Ray, 225
Copeland, Charles T.L., 639
Copeland, David L., 3350
Copeland, Gerret van S., 639
Copeland, Loretta M., 995
Copeland, Margot James, 2717, 2800
Copenhaver, John T., 3584
Coplan, Lee E., 1410
Copley Press Inc., The, 166
Copley, Helen K., 166
Copley, Lori, 2922
Copperwaite, Jason, 1155
Copple, E. Don, 949
Copple, Terry, 949
Coqui Development Co., 660
Corbett, Cornelia Gerry, 3228
Corbett, Jeannette M., 805
Corbin, Brian R., 2685
Corbin, Hunter W., 1944
Corbin, Ronald L., 3129
Corbin, S. Wells, 2407
Corbridge, Pam, 3390
Corcoran, Alison, 1549
Corcoran, James, 2206
Corcoran, Jane R., 1359
Corcoran, Mary, Dr., 1808
Corcoran, William W., 1448
Cordani, David M., 2917
Cordano, Michael D., 459
Cordeiro, Paula A., 264
CoreStates Financial Corp, 3055
Corey Delta Constructors, 102
Corfront, Linda, 2924
Corkery, Nancy W., 1351
Corleto, Richard, 339
Corlett, John R., 2770
Corley, Ginger A., 3274
Corley, Nolly E., 1508
Corman, Steven D., 2534
Corn, Elizabeth T., 858
Corneille, Barbara Berry, 111
Cornelius, Jeffrey, 3019
Cornell Trust, Peter C., 2340
Cornell, Alex, 1361
Cornell, Ann, 1361
Cornell, Ann D., 683
Cornell, Barbara, 2783
Cornell, George L., Jr., 1361
Cornell, Heather M., 2107
Cornell, Holly, 1361
Cornelson, George H., IV, 3096
Cornelson, Martin S., 3096
Cornett, Kathy, 3163
Cornille, Mary, 1450
Corning, Ursula, 2485
Cornish, John M., 1444, 1492
Cornwell, Joan, 1748
Cornwell, Ron, 1748
Corp, Rose Q., 1073
Corrado, Lorene A., 2124
Corrah, Tumani, 3516
Correll, Ada F., 871
Correll, Alston D., 871
Correll, Alston D., III, 871
Corrente, Judith-Ann, 2310
Corrigan, Daniel, 53
Corrigan, David R., 3209
Corrigan, Jennifer, 1115
Corrigan, John, 2317
Corrigan, Stephen M., 53
Corsello, Dan, 446
Corso, Cliff, 2297
Cortes, Francisca, 1524
Cortright, Michelle, 1583
Corvi, Carolyn, 3558
Corvin, Adele K., 430
Corvin, Dana A., 430
Corvin, Stuart, 430
Corwin, Randall D., 2666
Corwin/Moretrench, Arthur, 2228
Cosby, Lula, 2787
Cosentino, Guy, 2448
Cosentino, Julia Satti, 1455
Cosmo Co., 1388
Cosner, Chris, 1163
Coss, Benjamin R., 3457
Cossa, Joanne Hubbard, 2499
Cossyphas, Sherry, 1048
Costa, Anisa Kamadoli, 2463
Costa, Myrna, 448
Costas, Elizabeth, 2122
Costco Wholesale Corp., 131
Costello, Ann M., 2185
Costello, Marcy, 1740
Coster, Kevin, 751
Costigan, Joe, 2932
Cota, Stephanie, 312
Cote, Edmund J., Jr., 1562
Cote, Robert C., 1745
Cote, S. Ruggles, 1745
Cote, Samuel A., 1745
Cote-Ackah, Carra, 2454
Cotsen Library - Princeton, 2069
Cotsen, Lloyd, 167
Cotsen, Lloyd E., 77, 167
Cotsen, Margit, 167
Cotter, Colleen M., 2770
Cotter, Paula M., 1460
Cottingham, Joe, 1198
Cottingham, Patty, 2780
Cottingham, Robin, 2800
Cottrell, Frederick Gardner, 59
Couch, Kenneth R., 3109
Coudert, Cynthia, 2115
Coudert, Frederic R., III, 2115
Coudert, Margaret M., 2115
Coudert, Sandra, 2115
Coughlan, Gary P., 954
Coughlin, Catherine, 3167
Coulter, Chuck, 1218
Coulter, Susan Weeks, 176
Coulton, Claudia J., 2770
Counselman, Albert R., 1406
Counselman, Catherine R., 1406
Counselman, Charles C., 1406
Counselman, Margaret K., 1406
Counts, Andy, 2684
Courain, Jennifer R., 3474
Courain, Robert C., III, 3474
Courain, Robert C., Jr., 3474
Courain, Ruth D., 3474
Courtnage, Kathleen A., 1844
Courtnage, Larry J., 1844
Courtney, Charlene W., 619
Courtney, Dorothy, 170
Courtney, Karen, 1477
Courtois, Patricia, 727
Courts, Malon W., 860
Courts, Virginia Campbell, 860
Courville, Donna L., 391
Coury, Robert J., 3001
Cousins, Joselyn, 1867
Cousler-Emig, Julie, 3034
Coutant, Barry, 613
Coutinho, Candace, 3342
Covarrubias, Abel, 2010
Covenant Church of Pittsburgh, 3330
Coventry, Kim, 1002
Covington, George M., 1025
Covington, Marguerite, 823
Covitz, Lisa Adler, 960
Cowal, Sally Grooms, 2467
Cowan, Allison, 1833
Cowan, F. James, 3405
Cowan, Geoffrey, 87, 1833
Cowan, Jolyon Ellis, 721
Cowan, Noah, 176
Coward, E. Walter, Jr., 151
Cowden, W.H., Jr., 3318
Cowell, Janet, 2612
Cowell, Robert, 1636
Cowell, S.H., 168
Cowen, Jeanine M., 1557
Cowenhoven, Anna, 2524
Cowles Media Co., 317
Cowles, Anne C., 3510
Cowley, Paul, 1663
Cowper, Geoff, 3509
Cowsert, Susan, 1694
Cox Enterprises, Inc., 916
Cox Health, 3377
Cox, C. Lee, 379
Cox, Cathy, 863
Cox, Christopher, 1618
Cox, Cynthia, 1203
Cox, Harold D., 1459
Cox, Heather M., 3426
Cox, James M., Jr., 916
Cox, Jeanne, 2189
Cox, Jeff, 2723
Cox, Judith, 2203
Cox, Kathryn, 3015
Cox, Marilyn, 2814
Cox, Martha B., 2836
Cox, Michael J., 2899
Cox, Natalie, 2940
Cox, Ralph C., Jr., 1310
Cox, Robert F., Jr., 3008
Cox, Steven, 2655
Cox, Steven E., 2762
Cox, T.A., 1829
Cox, Thomas J., 482
Coy, Greg, 3507
Coy, Robert E., 448
Coye, Molly J., 550
Coyer, Steve, 543
Coyle, Bonnie S., 2986
Coyle, Bradford R., 3421
Coyle, Jim, 900
Coyle, Katherine G., 2806
Coyle, Landon, 1200
Coyne, Beth A., 3003
Coyne, Kevin, 1862
Coyne, Patrick P., 2887
Crabb, Wendy B., 928
Cracknell, Neil, 235
Craddock, Margaret, 3124
Craft, Carol L., 693
Craft, Jenny, 3679
Craft, Jimmy, 3113
Craft, Joy, 3113
Cragin, Charles L., 1340
Crahan, Michele McGarry, 2588
Craig, Charles S., 566
Craig, Chris, 1783
Craig, Debbie F., 2861

Curtis, Jackie, 1650
Curtis, Jacqueline, 1650
Curtis, Jay D., 2920
Curtis, John R., Jr., 3488
Curtis, Julie L., 2920
Curtis, Krysten, 156
Curtis, Kyle, 1650
Curtiss, Jacqueline DeWitt, 1650
Curtiss, Sarah, 2850
Curves International, Inc., 3253
Cusak, Michael, 2707
Cusenbary, Laura, 545
Cushing, Brenda J., 1211
Cushing, Margaret C., 2513
Cushing, Raymond L., 2683
Cushing, Robert T., 2407
Cushman, Dena, 3577
Cushman, Marjorie L., 175
Cushman, Stephen P., 175
Cussins, R. Donald, 1368
Custard, Linda P., 3262
Custer, G. Stanley, 3633
Custer, Todd W., 1144
Custer, Violet, 3633
Custom Nutrition Services, LLC, 65
Custom Shops, The, 1960
Cusumano, Michael, 162
Cutco Corporation, 2123
Cutco Cutlery, 2123
Cutco Cutlery Corp., 2123
Cutler, Kimberly, 2109
Cutler, Linda Beech, 391
Cutler, Scott, 2336
Cutler, Tracy, 2981
Cutshall, Pat, 1691
Cutter, Nancy L., 1885
Cutter, W. Bowman, III, 2402
Cutting, Carol Moore, 1559
Cuzzort, Pamela K., 3156
CVS Corp., 3068
CVS Pharmacy, Inc., 3068
Cwikiel, J. Wilfred, 1656
Cyphers, Judith B., 3481
Cyre, Jan, 3555
Czewski, Jim W., 3370

d'Adolf, Lila Gimprich, 2180
D'Agostino, John, 2331
D'Agostino, Max, 2124
D'Agostino, Sharon, 1948
D'Amato & Lynch, 2445
D'Amato, F. Marino, 591
D'Amato, June, 2487
D'Amato, Lawrence L., 2487
D'Amour, Charles L., 1456
D'Amour, Donald H., 1456
D'Angelo, Kara, 2350
D'Angelo, Peter P., 1956
D'Anniballe, Nick, 2227
D'Atri, E. Lang, 2788
d'Autremont, Gene, 2859
D'Elia, Lorraine, 215
D'Olier, H. Mitchell, 929
Dach, Leslie A., 74
Dachs, Alan B., 103
Dachs, Alan M., 104
Dachs, Lauren B., 103, 104
DaCosta, Igor, 2494
Dacotah Bank, N.A., 3117
Dadelahi, Samin, 3684
Dadisman, Carrol, 726
Dadisman, Mildred, 726
Dado, Craig, 378
Daetz, Alta, 1586
Daggett, Christopher J., 1990
Dahan Homes, Inc., 1364
Dahan, Haron, 1364
Dahl, Carol, 2857
Dahl, Cary, 3429
Dahl, Doris, 2819
Dahl, James H., 731
Dahl, Kathy, 726
Dahl, Richard J., 928
Dahl, William L., 731
Dahley Co., 1388
Dailey, Diane, 3580
Dailey, Julia, 2037
Dailey, Trent, 1129
Dain Rauscher Inc., 1730
Dain, Regina A., 2667
Dake, Gary C., 2108
Dakin, John, 543
Dal Pra, Marilee L., 57
Dalarossa, Daniel, 172
Dalarossa, Elza Harumi, 172
Dalbec, Keith, 2539
Dalby, Linda S., 1477
Dale, Angela Henkels, 2967
Dale, Berteline Baier, 2243
Dale, Brett M., 1008
Dale, Douglas, 441
Dale, Harvey, 2048
Dale, Lauren Lipcon, 2714
Dale, Tom, 992
Dalen, James, 65
Dales, Joanna Donnelly, 1626
Daley, John P., 2286
Daley, William M., 982
Dalio, Barbara, 567
Dalio, Devon, 567
Dalio, Matthew, 567
Dalio, Raymond T., 567
Dall'Olmo, Gail, 1616
Dallas Jewish Community Foundation, 2827
Dalton, Ann V., 738
Dalton, Dorothy U., 1592
Dalton, Mark, 538
Dalton, Robert, 349
Dalton, Sharon C., 550
Daly, Andrew, 543
Daly, Bernard, 2844
Daly, Charles U., 1040
Daly, Eileen F., 663
Daly, James J., 2075
Daly, Jim, 3520
Daly, Mary W.C., 3089
Daly, P. Niles, Jr., 3430
Dalzell, David B., Jr., 3579
Damato, Charles A., 2183
Dambach, Michael, 3063
Dambacher, Gary, 420
Damery, Sean, 503
Damis, James, 2878
Damm, Carla, 1254
Damme, Lora, 1851
Damner, Bert, 307
Damon, Brenden A., 1254
Damon, Donald H., 1254
Damon, Doneen Keemer, 630
Damon, Karen L., 1254
Damon, Kathleen J., 1254
Dan, Hideo, 1921
Dana Corporation, 1593
Dana Holding Corporation, 1593
Dana, Charles A., 2126
Dana, Charles A., III, 2126
Dana, Eleanor Naylor, 2126
Danastasio, Cody, 1785
Danastasio, Erin D., 1785
Danborn, Barb, 488
Dane, Herbert P., 1539
Danek, Sharon, 1663
Daniel International Corp., 3101
Daniel, Bill, 3201
Daniel, Charles E., 3101
Daniel, Christopher J., 3233
Daniel, D. Ronald, 2066
Daniel, Desmon, 1662
Daniel, Jamal, 3280
Daniel, James L., Jr., 3233
Daniel, Libby Stanfield, 2541
Daniel, Nicole C., 1298
Daniel, Rania, 3280
Daniel, Suzanne T., 3016
Daniel, Thomas F., 416
Daniel-Brima, Doris, 425
Daniels, Bill, 488
Daniels, Charles R., III, 2392
Daniels, Dianne J., 2056
Daniels, James C., 2107
Daniels, John, Jr., 3617
Daniels, Ron, 2858
Daniels, Ronald J., 1374
Daniels, Tim, 364
Danielson, Danny, 1158
Danielson, Dave, 3499
Danielson, Dick, 1225
Danielson, Donald C., 1204
Danielson, Patty, 1158
Daniely-Woolfolk, Eliza, 114
Dankenbrink, Kristine A., 2921
Dankers, Martha, 3511
Danksewicz, Jill Cosgrove, 1471
Danovitz, Burt, Ph.D., 2110
Danser, Gordon, 1979
Dantzler, Corey, 356
Danziger, Sheldon, 2402
DAR, Inc., 1804
Darcy, Thomas E., 203
Darden Restaurants, Inc., 732
Darden, Mary, 732
Dardess, Margaret B., 2600
Darling 2002 Charitable Lead Annuity Trust, William A., 1140
Darling, Bradford L., 485
Darling, John S., 733
Darling, Martha, 1576
Darling, Nancy A., 1140
Darling, Norma W., 733
Darling, Philip W., 1140
Darling, William A., 1140
Darling-Hammond, Linda, 2492
Darlow, Gillian, 1075
Darmon, Avital, 2051
Darnall, Tom, 2539
Darnell, Tommy, 1759
Daro, Deborah, 993
Daro, Phil, 348
Darr, Leslie M., 1301
Darr, William N., 1785
Darrah, S. Joseph, 3677
Darrah, Tim, 900
Darroch, Jacqueline, 2673
Darrow, Ben, 1115
Darrow, Jessica, 1115
Darrow, John S., 1115
Dart Foundation, William & Claire, 1594
Dart, Ariane L., 1594
Dart, Claire T., 1594
Dart, Kenneth B., 1594
Dart, Robert C., 1594, 3464
Dart, Stephen, 157
Dartley, Karen, 2128
Dartley, Peter, 2128
Dashefsky, Samuel, 3175
Dasher, Kevin, 1848
DaSilva, Maria, 1515
Dastugue, Michael, 3315
Daswani, Vivek A., 3419
Data Tresary Charitable Foundation, 679
Dater, Charles H., 2687
Dattner, Hezzy, 2168
Daucher, Lynn, 90
Daugherty, Barbara, 2496
Daugherty, Dick, 2612
Daugherty, F. Joe, 1835
Daugherty, J. Timothy, 1835
Daugherty, Josh, 1154
Daugherty, Michael, 1126
Daugherty, Robert B., 1835
Daugherty, Robert, III, 1835
Dauphinais, Roger, 1471
Dausch, Marie, 1191
Dautel, John, 2707
Davanne Realty Co., 1962
Davenport, Diana, 2106
Davenport, Elizabeth Beal, 3174
Davenport, James F., 2113
Davenport, Judith, 2966
Davenport, Maura, 1636
Davenport, Ronald R., Jr., 2993
David Farren, J., 1001
David, Betty, 2408
David, Charles Keith, 3363
David, Jessica, 3089
David, Laurence R., 3357
David, Leo, 178
David, Marlene, 1693
David, Ruth, 178
Davidovsky, Mario, 2262
Davidson, Betsy, 2245
Davidson, Bradford, 2245
Davidson, Daniel P., 2204
Davidson, Deb Kmon, 1402
Davidson, Frances, 3521
Davidson, Gwen, 1347
Davidson, J. Matthew, 2245
Davidson, Janet G., 1899
Davidson, Joan K., 2245
Davidson, Jonathan, 383
Davidson, Kulsum G., 2950
Davidson, Olga M., 2511
Davidson, Peter W., 2245
Davidson, Robert, 268
Davidson, Stuart, 2511
Davidson, Thomas, 537
Davidson, William, 378
Davies, Bill, 868
Davies, Christa, 963
Davies, Darlene, 122
Davies, Giles, 1398
Davies, John, 2111
Davies, Marjorie, 2782
Davies, Matthew M., 842
Davies, Rick, 1623
Davies, Trevor C., 986
Davies, Virginia L., 2001
Davis Charitable Lead Trust, M., 414
Davis Foundation, 3026
Davis, Ann S., 1576
Davis, Anne M., 1518
Davis, Barbara, 2731
Davis, Bill, 1115
Davis, Brenda S., 1949
Davis, Brian J., Hon., 722

Davis, Cari, 525
Davis, Caroline Bond, 932
Davis, Charles, 3245
Davis, Charlotte, 2644
Davis, Cindy, 74
Davis, D. Scott, 1353
Davis, Daniel, 2863
Davis, David, 361, 368
Davis, Deborah, 1365
Davis, Dee, 2521
Davis, Delta Anne, 3130
Davis, Don, 1272
Davis, Eleanor L., 2926
Davis, Elizabeth K., 2980
Davis, Florence, 2445
Davis, Fred L., 3120
Davis, Gary Bo, 1718
Davis, Graeme W., 232
Davis, H. Coleman, III, 1314
Davis, J. Homer, Rev., 3299
Davis, James C., 1365
Davis, James D., 12
Davis, James S., 1518
Davis, Jan, 1848
Davis, Jana, 3139
Davis, Jana J., 3129
Davis, Joe C., 3130
Davis, John H., 1457
Davis, John L., 1752
Davis, John Martin, 3275
Davis, Judy, 1753
Davis, Kassie, 984
Davis, Kathy, 1126, 1174
Davis, Kimberly J., 1365
Davis, Lant, 1203
Davis, Lori, 1519
Davis, M'Lea, 1758
Davis, Mark, 1186
Davis, Martha, 3414
Davis, Martin C., 3268
Davis, Mary, 1188
Davis, Mary W., 2429
Davis, Melissa M., 1752
Davis, Michael, 414
Davis, Michael L., 1697
Davis, Milton C., 8
Davis, Mimi Bailey, 2522
Davis, Nancy E., 547
Davis, Nancy I., 2924
Davis, Patricia, 685
Davis, Paul, 3299
Davis, Paul E., 1763
Davis, Paula, 2112
Davis, Rachelle, 3589
Davis, Richard A., 2811
Davis, Richard K., 2709
Davis, Robert T., 313
Davis, Robin A., 2780
Davis, Roger J., 2908
Davis, Ron, 543
Davis, Ronald, 1823
Davis, Russell R., Jr., 3083
Davis, Sadie, 1328
Davis, Sonya Meyers, 1803
Davis, Staige, 3417
Davis, Stephen A., 1457
Davis, Steven, 627
Davis, Susan, 832, 2950
Davis, Susan Brown, 3433
Davis, Tammy, 368
Davis, Terry, 2731
Davis, Terry C., Dr., 1306
Davis, Thomas P., 288
Davis, Tom C., 3349
Davis, Tom, Dr., 2662
Davis, Tony, 627
Davis, Virginia, 1163
Davis, W.R., 3174
Davis, Wendy, 2916
Davis, William, 1365
Davis, Wilma H., 1486
Davis, Winifred S., 885
Davis-Kusek, Jane, 1457
Davison Iron Works, Inc., 366
Davison, J. Scott, 1183
Davison, James, 1315
Davison, Richard H., 1551
Davison, William M., IV, 2988, 3019
Dawbarn, H.D. "Buz", 3429
Dawson, Judith M., 925
Dawson, Mackenzie, 574
Dawson, Melanie A., 2836
Dawson, Sue Ann, 2408
Dawson, Susan Scranton, 3057
Dawson, Tom, 2649
Day Pitney LLP, 1477
Day, Barbara Arnold, 1767
Day, Brandon, 1851
Day, Dana L., 1752
Day, Elizabeth Y., 1358
Day, Frank R., 1767
Day, H. Corbin, 12, 1944
Day, James C., 2822
Day, Jr. Trust, Rufus S., 2673
Day, Larry L., 45
Day, Lisa, 3503
Day, Martha Bonal, 1990
Day, Matt, Sr., 276
Day, Mike, 1360
Day, Nancy Sayles, 629
Day, Robert A., 276
Day, Rodney D., III, 2943
Day, Sherm, 863
Day, Stan, 1752
Day, Stanley R., Jr., 1752
Day, Tim, 3608
Day, Vivian W., 1752
Day, William, 1695
Dayton Hudson Corp., 1744
Dayton Power and Light Co., The, 2688
Dayton, Dawn, 3577
Dayton, Douglas J., 1690
Dayton, John, 888, 3262
Dayton, Mary L., 1747
Dayton, Mary Lee, 1747
Dayton, Wallace C., 1747
Dayton, Wendy W., 1690
Dayton, Wimberly Charlotte, 888
DDF 2005 Charitable Remainder Annuity Trust, 141
DDR Invesment Co., Inc., 1804
de Allesandrini, Enrico, 2513
de Alonso, Marcela Perez, 249
de Barona, Maryann Santos, 1130
de Beaumont, Pierre, 1366
de Goizueta, Olga C., 883
de Kay, Helen M., 998
de la Cruz, Mary, 1912
de la Fuente, Aura, 1041
de la Pena, Alfredo, 3006
De La Vega, Ralph, 3167
de Limur, Genevieve Bothin, 120
De Luca, Victor, 2335
De McCarty, Jack, 2825
De Miranda, Jay R., 179
De Miranda, Shirley Y., 179
de Pineres, Cristina Gutierrez, 2173
De Rivera, Ana Luisa Diez, 2264
de Roulet, Daniel C., 2350
de Roulet, Daniel C., Jr., 2350
de Roulet, Lorinda P., 2350
de Venoge, Marc, 2454
de Vries, Shlomit, 691
de Watteville, Irene, 2444
Deadrick, Chris, 1699
Deaktor, Michael W., 162
Dean, Anthony M., 968
Dean, Caroline W., 2130
Dean, Donna, 2390
Dean, Jimmy, 718
Dean, Roger, 1663
Dean, Terri, 3424
Dean, Thompson, III, 2130
Dean, Timothy, 2113
Dean, Tracey L., 3292
Dean, Trina R., 135
Dean, Victoria Seaver, 400
DeAscentis, Michael J., Jr., 2750
Deaton, Chad C., 3170
Deatrick, Deborah, 1336
Deaver Foundation, Delema, 2544
Deaver, Carolyn J., 656
Deaver, Kyle, 3378
DeBartolo Family Foundation, The, 734
DeBartolo Memorial Scholarship Foundation, Edward J., 734
DeBartolo, Cynthia R., 734
DeBartolo, Edward J., Jr., 734
DeBartolo, Lisa, 734
DeBartolo, Nikki, 734
DeBartolo, Tiffanie, 734
DeBauge, Jeff, 1257
Deberry, James A., 1776
DeBerry, Stephen, 273
DeBlasio, Alfred, Jr., 1984
DeBolt, Valerie, 1258
Debrowski, Tom, 312
DeBruyn, Nicolette, 975
DeBuse, Chip, 1847
Dec, Katherine, 3028
DeCabooter, Art, 57
Decaminada, Randy, 171
DeCamp, Cameron, 484
Decamp, Timothy L., 922
DeCardy, Chris, 357
DeCarolis, D.L., 2321
Decker, Ann, 768
Decker, Bettina L., 2184
Decker, Shirley Martin, 1647
Decker, Steve, 3591
Decker, Vicki, 1753
Deckert, Myrna, 3312
DeCoizart Charitable Trust, 2445
DeCrane, Vincent F., 2670
DeCuir, Laurie G., 1299
Deddens, Dave, 1141
Dedecker, Faith, 1022
Dedecker, Hayden, 1022
Dedman, Nancy, 3212
Dedman, Patricia Brown, 3212
Dedrick, George B., 1022
Dedrick, Imojean, 1184
Dee, Shelly H., 3263
Deeb, Matt, 3122
Deegan, Jennifer E., 1656
Deegan-Day, Joseph, 276
Deem, Becky, 3587
Deer Creek Foundation, 1789
Deer Park Road Corp., 486
Deere, Cynthia A. P., 3348
Deerfield Management Company, 2132
Deering, L. Patrick, 1406
Deering, Nicole, 2868
Dees, Joyce, 68
Dees, Maarton, 349
Deese, Carol, 957
Deetz, Randall J., 1144
Deevy, Brian, 488
DeFinnis, John E., Dr., 2908
DeFlavia, Laura, 3017
DeFoor, Byron, 3119
DeFord, Nicky, 537
deForest, Lydia Collins, 2133
DeFrancesco, Anne, 1426
DeFrantz, Anita L., 287
deFreitas, JoAnne, 2355
Degioia, John J., 2085
DeGraaf, John, 1919
DeGroodt, Patty, 3511
DeHaan Family Foundation, Christel, 1156
Dehaan, C.H., Dr., 3119
DeHaan, Christel, 1143
DeHaan, Keith A., 1143
DeHaan, Kirsten A., 1143
DeHaan, Timothy E., 1143
Dehmlow, Jonathan, 2732
Dehner, Richard J., 1240
DeHoyos, Rick, 3343
Deily, Linnet F., 3267
Deitsch, Ira, 1451
Deiwert, Ed, 1163
DeKarver, Martin, 315
Dekker, Hans, 1944
DeKruif, Robert M., 77
Del Monte, 952
del Rio, Carlos H., 3061
Delabretonne, Paula P., 1317
DeLan, Lisa, 218
Deland, Emme L., 2261
DeLaney, Beth, 2767
Delaney, Brenda, 1126
Delaney, Peter B., 2823
Delaney, Philip A., Jr., 727
Delaney, Rich, 2354
Delaney, Tammy, 545
Delaney, Wayne E., 3353
Delano, Mignon Sherwood, 1596
Delany, Brendan, 2926
Delany, Sean, 2122
Delaplaine, Bettie, 1367
Delaplaine, Edward S., 1367
Delaplaine, Edward S., II, 1367
Delaplaine, Elizabeth B., 1367
Delaplaine, George B., III, 1367
Delaplaine, George B., Jr., 1367
Delaplaine, James W., 1367
Delaplaine, John F., 1367
Delaplaine, John P., 1367
Delate, Edward M., 2904
Delaurenti, Charles J., II, 3514
Delavan Foundation, Nelson B., 661
Delaware Management Co., 3003
Delbanco, Andrew, 2459, 2460
Deleery, Seth, 3255
DeLeo, Jean T., 644
DeLeon, Dan C., 138
Delevati, Hank, 304
Delgado, Carlos Cruz, 3208
Delgado, Deivid, 22
Delgado, Jorge Cruz, 3208
Delgado, Louis, 2749
Delgado, Sonia, 1979
Delgato, Ximena A., 2524
DeLise, Laura, 757
Delisle, Raymond C., 485

Dell, Alexander, 3213
Dell, Michael, 3213
Dell, Susan, 3213
Della Bella, Michael, 619
Dellacca, David, 1154
Delo, Anne, 564
Deloach, Barbara, 1780
DeLoach, Frank, Jr., 866
DeLoach, Harris, 3098
DeLoache, William R., Jr., 3130
Deloitte & Touche LLP, 569
Deloitte & Touche USA LLP, 569
Deloitte Haskins & Sells, 569
Deloitte LLP, 569
Delong, Donald A., 1582
Delorey, Gail, 157
Delp, Lawrence F., 1541
Delp, Robert A., 1409
Delponte, Karen, 1501
DelSignore, Carl, 1368
DelSignore, Carmen P., 1368
Delta Dental Plan of Arkansas, Inc., 68
Delta Dental Plan of Kansas, Inc., 1255
Delta Dental Plan of Massachusetts, 1459
Deluca, Robert C., 3370
DeLucia, Michael S., 1890
Deluxe Corp., 2662
DeMaio, Stephen, 2281
DeMana, Jacqueline M., 459
DeMaria, Sissy, 729
DeMaria, Stacy L., 1483
DeMartini, James G.B., III, 412
Demartini, James G.B., III, 413
Demas, Olivia, 2655
Demashkieh, Rasha, 1590
Dembitzer, Fran, 2044
DeMera, Marie C., 1000
Deming, Wendy, 754
DeMoor, Barbara, 1595
Demopoulos, Harry B., 2146
DeMore, Dillon, 543
Demore, Timothy Allan, 3359
Demorest, Jon D., 369
DeMoss, Arthur S., 735
DeMoss, Charlotte, 735
DeMoss, Elizabeth J., 735
DeMoss, Nancy S., 735
DeMoss, Robert G., 735
DeMoss, Todd, 1240
Demoulas Super Markets, Inc., 1458
Demoulas, Arthur S., 1556
Demoulas, Arthur T., 1458
Dempsey, Austin M., 991
Dempsey, Bill, 2121
Dempsey, Ray C., 3181
Demsey, John D., 2287
Demtrak, Carolyn, 2107
DeMuth, Deb, 483
Demyan, Kirk C., 2952
den Hamer, Sandra, 176
Den Herder, Sue, 1591
DeNale, Carol A., 3068
Denault, Leo P., 1308
Denberg, Dawn, 1049
Denbo, Monte, 1181
Denbow, Don, 3305
Denczi, Barbara A., 2932
Dender, Washington C., 847
Denekas, Craig N., 1334
Denham, Robert E., 264, 2402
Denious, Robert W., 3019
Denison, Mary A., 1332
Denit, Helen P., 3435
Denius, F. Wofford, 3188
Denius, Franklin W., 3188
Denker, Jill, 1845
Denkers, Julie, 3392
Denkers, Stephen E., 3392
Denkers, Stephen G., 3392
Denkers, Susan E., 3392
Denlea, Leo E., Jr., 294
Denmark, David, 3146
Denmark, Ethel, 3100
Dennett, Marie G., 570
Denney, Emily, 623
Denney, Ronald, 3429
Dennin, Mike, 59
Dennis, Andre, 2976
Dennis, Jane, 1764
Dennis, Kimberly O., 389, 681
Dennis, Robin, 2737
Dennis, Russ, 990
Dennison, Phillip, 2685
Denny, Benjamin L., 1315
Denny, Charles M., Jr., 1748
Denova, James V., 2892
Denslow, Faith, 2773
Dental Services of Massachusetts Inc., 1459
Denton, A. Louis, 2887
Denton, David M., 3068
Denworth, Joanne R., 2948
Deon, Grace, Esq., 2900
Department of Education, 331
DePetro, Wyndsor, 617
DePillis, Mark S., 3056
DePizzo, Jason, 47
Depolo, Gary L., 111
Deposit Guaranty National Bank, 1770
DeProspero, Mike, 3591
DePuy Mitek, Inc., 1948
Derby, Alexandra, 309
Derby, Steven R., 2932
DeRenzo, Linda, 1513
DeRobles, Claudia, 3503
DeRodes, William J., 2798
Derose, Dan, 535
Derouen, D. Troy, 3248
Derr, Laraine, 35
Derrick, James V., Jr., 3274
Derry Publishing Co., 1536
Derry, Patrick T., 990
Dervish, Ahmet, Dr., 3597
DeSantis, Ann Ranae, 3214
Desantis, David, 1866
DeSantis, Robert J., 3214
Desaulniers, Dorothy, 3069
DesAutels, David, 1616
Desert Champions, 147
DeShazior, Samuel, 2655
DeShazo, Nikki, Hon., 3361
Deshong, Diane, 87
Deshong, Howard, III, 87
Deshong, Leonore, 87
DeSisto, Rena M., 2524
DesJardins, Linda Eich, 1703
Desler, Michael D., 445
Desmond-Hellmann, Susan, 3516
Desnoyers, Henry, 3117
DeSole, Gloria, 2108
Despasquale, Thomas, 3563
Despeaux, Kim, 1308
Desroches, Pascal, 2466
DesRuisseaux, Angela H., 1337
DesRuisseaux, David, 1337
DesRuisseaux, Libby, 1337
DesRuisseaux, Reid, 1337
Desser, Orley M., 960
Dessouky, Hilary, 362
Destler, William, Dr., 2185
deStwolinski, Elizabeth H., 1220
deStwolinski, Lance W., 1220
deStwolinski, Matthew, 1220
Detar, D. Scott, 3017
Detroit Edison Co., The, 1598
Dettmer, Dale, Esq., 723
Detweiler, John, 2900
Deupree, Ann T., 571
Deupree, Karolen, 571
Deupree, Kato, 571
Deupree, Richard R., III, 571
Deupree, Taylor, 571
Deupree, Thomas R., 571
Deur, Jan, 1586
Deutsch, Alvin, 328
Deutsch, David, 1369, 2359
Deutsch, Robert W., 1369
Deutsche Bank Americas, 2325
Deutsche Bank Americas Holding Corp., 2134
Dev, Vipul R., 279
Devanney, Timothy J., 611
DeVaughn, Richard, 2809
Developers, 1388
Development Mgmt., Inc., 524
Devereaux, Zilph P., 1771
Devereux, Barbara, 3385
Devereux, Michelle, 3385
DeVetter, Dennis, 3633
DeVetter, Roberta, 3633
DeVeydt, Wayne S., 1206
Devilbiss, Greg, 2707
deVillers, Rebecca, 2762
Devine, Tammy, 3109
DeVisser, Sherwood, 1648
Devitt, Ed, 2111
Devlin, John P., 2391
Devlin, Shawn L., 278
DeVoe, Sally A., 1175
DeVoge, Jarol A., 3054
DeVoll, Jennifer Fleming, 361
Devore, Helen S., 682
Devorris, Nancy, 2907
DeVos, Betsy, 1600
DeVos, Dick, 1600
Devos, Douglas L., 1671
DeVos, Elisabeth, 1600, 1658
DeVos, Richard M., Jr., 1600
Dew, Donald H., 2090
Dew, Patti, 3637
Dewald, Eric, 2908
Dewey, Fred, 2932
Dewey, Melvil, 2265
Dewire, Norman, Rev. Dr., 2689
DeWitt, Jack L., 1650
DeWitt, James Russell, 1650
DeWitt, Jim, 26, 1650
DeWitt, Lyne, 1650
DeWitt, Mary, 1650
DeWitt, Mary E., 1650
DeWitt, Melissa, 1650
DeWitt, Steve, 1650
DeWitt, Steven Lee, 1650
DeWyngaert, Richard, 1053
DeWyngaert, Susan, 1053
Dexter Shoe Co., 1340
Dey, Kimberly W., 933
Deyo, Richard A., 1489
DeYoung, Janet, 1591
DeYoung, Kevin, 3571
DFM Investment Co., Inc., 1804
Dhawan-Gray, Neetu, 1391
Dhillon, Janet, 3315
Dhimitri, Sandy, 2112
DHR Holdings, 679
Di Rita, Lawrence, 679
Diablo Contractors, Inc., 102
Diakov, Leanne, 1289
Diamente, Christine, 1899
Diamond, Chris, 545
Diamond, David A., 1850
Diamond, Irene, 2136
Diamond, Irvin F., 2007
Diamond, Ivan, 1344
Diamond, Jennifer, 2135
Diamond, Laraine, 2487
Diamond, Michael L., 2637
Diamond, Nell, 2135
Diamond, Robert E., III, 2135
Diamond, Robert E., Jr., 2135
Diamond, Sandra F., 801
Diana, Andrew J., 2888
Dias, Craig, 3510
Diaz, Angela, 3500
Diaz, David, 3179
Diaz, Kerry A., 805
Diaz, Manny, 2066
Diaz, Patricia J., 2094
Diaz, Rita, 361
Diaz-Infante, Alred, 157
DiBattista, Raymond, 2922
Dibble, Robert, 2134
Dick, C. Trafford, 2783
Dick, David, 1260
Dick, David, Dr., 1168
Dick, Edison, 661
Dick, Frank, 1634
Dick, Henry, 1764
Dick, Randy, 3587
Dick, Sylvia, 917
Dickens, Linda, 3364
Dickerson, Amina J., 1018
Dickerson, Lynn, 425
Dickerson, Rick, 1313
Dickey, Dave, 1227
Dickey, Jeb, 488
Dickinson, Elizabeth M., 180
Dickinson, Kristopher, 180
Dickinson, Martin C., 180
Dickman, J. Jerry, 2808
Dickson, Cary, 312
Dickson, David, 3378
Dickson, Greg, 479
Dickson, James, 2749
Dickson, Peggy, 1181
Dickson, R. Stuart, 1344
Dicovitsky, Gary, 1946
Dicus, John B., 1251, 1279
Dicus, John C., 1251
Didlake, Ralph, 1756, 1757
DiDomenico, Gregory, 993
Didomenico, Joseph, 261
Didriksen, Neil, 1369
Diederich, John, 991
Diederich, John H., 2915
Diehl, J. Ted, 947
Diehl, Ryan, 1260
Diener, Edward F., 1000
Diener, Marissa, 1000
Dienhart, Mark, 1738
Diermeier, Jeffrey J., 736
Diermeier, Julia M., 736
Diermeier, Julie M., 736
Diers, Melissa, 1836
Dietel, Kimberly R., 1468

Douglas, Anne, 186
Douglas, Brianna, 3098
Douglas, David W., 683
Douglas, Dianne, 312
Douglas, Jean, 683, 1361
Douglas, Kirk, 186
Douglas, Mark, 2794
Douglas, Peter, 186
Douglas, Ron, 1180
Douglas, Sarah, 2252
Douglas, Sioux, 35
Douglas, W. Leslie, 1361
Doupe, Allison J., 1714
Douzinas, Nancy R., 2376
Douzinas, Nancy Rauch, 2376
Douzinas, Ruth F., 2376
Dove Givings Foundation, 1420
Dovydenas, Elizabeth D., 1747
Dow Charitable Trust, Alden B., 1340
Dow, Grace A., 1597
Dow, Michael Lloyd, 1597
Dow, Peggy, 240
Dow, Peggy Ann, 409
Dow, Thomas, 3611
Dowd, Brian, 2880
Dowda, Tanya, 1710
Dower, Roger, 3648
Dowling, J. Robert, 1426
Dowling, Patrick, 137
Down, David, 378
Downey, Geraldine A., 2526
Downey, John A., 2485
Downey, Maria, 29
Downey, Matthew J., 1453
Downey, Paul C., 1453
Downham, Doreen, 611
Downie, Jocelyn, 2454
Downing, Terri, 3206
Downing, Tracy Toft, 1796
Downs, Dawn, 1750
Downs, Harry S., Dr., 863
Downs, Jeanne Floyd, 200
Downs, Patty Salo, 1677
Downs, Richard, 3363
Downton, Christine V., 2048
Doyal, Stephen D., 1794
Doyle, Christopher, 176
Doyle, Cynthia Tower, 2472
Doyle, Don, 3161
Doyle, Doug, 1861
Doyle, F. Patrick, 1861
Doyle, Frank, 2287
Doyle, Geoffrey, 976
Doyle, Gertrude R., 1861
Doyle, Jean, 1519
Doyle, John C., 1013
Doyle, Kay, 1505
Doyle, Marguerite, 976
Doyle, Melissa, 3666
Doyle, Michael, 976
Doyle, Nancy, 1861
Doyle, Patrick J., 2107
Doyle, Peter, 2071
Doyle, Richard P., 2074
Doyle, Robert M., 2472
Doyle, T. Lawrence, 1115
Doyle, William M., Jr., 994, 1249
Doyon Ltd., 34
Dozzi, Domenic P., 2935
Dozzi, Peter C., 2935
Dozzi, Theresa K., 2935
DPS Foundation, 528
Drabing, Darin B., 95
Drain, Scott, 1630
Drake, Erin, 328
Drake, Jamie, 2325
Drake, Michael V., 2106
Drake, Michael V., M.D., 139
Drake, Rodney, 2170
Drake, Skip, 1699
Drake, Susan, 3490
Dranow, Alan, 69
Draper, Stephen E., 922
Draper, Tom, 1623
Draughn, John, 3112
Drawdy, Larry, 1755
Dray, James R., 2410
Drayna, Dennis, 3155
Drebin, Allan R., 981
Dregne, Eric, 1216
Dreiss, Meredith Mitchell, 3297
Dreitzer, Albert J., 2144
Dreitzer, Mildred H., 2144
Drennan, James, 2704
Drennan, Joseph A., 2704
Dresher, James T., Jr., 1370
Dresher, James T., Sr., 1370
Dresher, Jeffrey M., 1370
Dresher, Joshua, 1370
Dresher, Patricia K., 1370
Dresher, Virginia M., 1370
Dressman, Mark, 3397
Drew, Everitt, 726
Drew, William F., Jr., 3112
Drewek, Mary anne, 1247
Dreyer, Susan, 1663
Dreyfus, Louis, 2145
Drezner, Julie Kenny, 157
Driehaus, Elizabeth, 1002
Driehaus, Richard H., 1002
Driessnack, Robert, 3527
Driessner, Johnnie, 2850
Driggers, John, 3524
Driker, Eugene, 1675
Drinkwater, Clover, 2109
Driscoll, Brent, 2123
Driscoll, Dawn-Marie, 823
Driscoll, John B., 1752
Driscoll, Margaret M., 3488
Driscoll, Timothy, 1885
Driscoll, W. John, 3559
Driskill, Lucienne, 1003
Driskill, Walter S., 1003
DRK Investment Co., Inc., 1804
Drobot, Joseph, 1004
Drobot, Judy, 1004
Drone, Jack, Dr., 1160
Drop in the Bucket, 3330
Drossner, Audrey B., 1348
Drossos, Eugenia, 1286
Drost, Charles Mitchell, 1303
Drost, William T., 1303
Drown, Joseph W., 187
Druckenmiller, Fiona, 2066
Drueding, James, 2936
Drueding, Richard, 2936
drugstore.com, inc., 65
Druley, Cynthia, 163
Drumm, Susan, 2232
Drummond, Lori, 3504
Dryco LLC., 826
Dryer, Ellen, 1004
DSD Realty, Inc., 1228
DTE Energy Ventures, Inc., 1598
du Pont, Edward B., 639
du Pont, Eleuthere I., II, 639
du Pont, M. Lynn, Dr., 639
du Pont, Pierre S., 639
du Pont, Pierre S., IV, 639
Duarte, Jose Tomas, 3208
Dubick, Mark A., 670
Dubois, Jacques E., 3673
DuBois, John J., 1022
DuBose, Ginger, 2822
Dubose, Sam, 2822
Dubose, Vivian N., 2822
DuBow, Michael, 722
Dubsky, Michael, Rev., 1387
Ducayet, Wally, 537
Ducceschi, Laura J., 3031
Duch, Mike, 3118
Duchossois Industries, Inc., 1005
Duchossois Technology Partners, LLC, 1005
Duchossois, Craig J., 1005
Duchossois, Kimberly T., 1005
Duchossois, Richard L., 1005
Duckmann, Stephanie, 1121
Duden, Mary G., 2926
Dudenhoeffer, John, 1128
Dudley, Ahrian Tyler, 22
Dudley, C.R., Jr., 22
Dudley, Gary C., 3274
Dudley, George H. T., 3419
Dudley, John D., 3610
Dudley, Louise M., 3428
Dudley, Mary C., 3610
Dudley, Michael, 1758
Dudley, Richard D., 3610
Dudley, Robert J., II, 3610
Dudley, Stewart R., 22
Dudnick, Andrew L., 191
Dudte, James J., 2803
Duer, Wendy, 278
Duermmeier, Christopher, 615
Duerr, Brad, 1125
Duesenberg, Mark H., 2697
Duff, Barbara, 535
Duff, Helen L., 1776
Duff, James C., 662
Duffell, Carol, 3347
Duffield, Sally, 1775
Duffin, Jacinda, 3609
Duffy, Barb, 2939
Duffy, Catherine, 235
Duffy, Dorothy B., 1402
Duffy, Joseph J., Jr., 1402
Duffy, Michael P., 161
Duffy, Paul, 2271
Duffy, Terrance A., 984
Dufresne, Michele, 3606
Dugas, Laura Jo, 3132
Dugas, Lynn King, 3132
Dugas, Pam, 3132
Dugas, Stephen H., 3132
Dugas, Wayne F., Jr., 3132
Dugas, Wayne F., Sr., 3132
Dugdale, Bill, 630
Duggan, Agnes B., 1283
Duggan, John, 562
Duggan, Teresa O'Shaugnessy, 1725
Duhl, Joanne, 2367
Duhme, Carol M., 1809
Duhme, David W., 1809
Duhme, Jeremy, 1809
Duke Energy, 2675
Duke, Doris, 2146
Duke, Jennifer Johnson, 811
Duke, Julie, 3148
Duke, Lisa Walker, 1719
Duke, Michael T., 74
Duke, Susan S., 3421
Dukes, David R., 410
Dula, Art, 3254
Dulaney, Betty Jo, 1760
Dulaney, Daryl, 1993
Duman, Louis J., 475
Dumas, Michael R., 3266
DuMouchel, William H., 1426
Dunaway, James R., 3357
Dunbar, Joe, 1131
Dunbar, Mary L., 1657
Dunbar, William, 672
Duncan, Barry, 3144
Duncan, Christina, 1053
Duncan, Dale, 1209
Duncan, Deborah L., 103, 104
Duncan, Debra Kay, 287
Duncan, George L., 1505
Duncan, Greg, 674
Duncan, John G., 2547
Duncan, Juanita, 162
Duncan, Mark D., 950
Duncan, Mary, 3227
Duncan, Sarah, 3511
Duncan, Susan M., 530
Duncan, W.W., 1395
Duncan, William G., Jr., 1288
Dunckel, Jeanette M., 471
Dunford, Albert, 162
Dunford, Lissa, 932
Dungan, Anna, 1146
Dunham Trust, John C., 1007
Dunham, Lynn, Dr., 2170
Dunham, R. James, 3008
Dunham, Robert H., 2613
Dunham, Scott, 342
Dunkelmann, Dianne, 2675
Dunkin, Craig, 1175
Dunkle, Terry K., 2922
Dunlap, Bonni, 3044
Dunlap, William H., 1878
Dunlavy, Teri, 1154
Dunleavy, Kathy, 3097
Dunleavy, Nancy Alba, 3006
Dunlop, Tim, 999
Dunn Construction, J.E., 1787
Dunn, Charles A., 783
Dunn, Debra L., 412
Dunn, Gregory W., 3151
Dunn, John, 25
Dunn, John M., 1205
Dunn, John S., Jr., 3216
Dunn, John S., Sr., 3216
Dunn, Kathryn, 3637
Dunn, Katie, 1663
Dunn, Kevin A., 1787
Dunn, Paige, 3521
Dunn, Peter, 2071
Dunn, Peter M., 2090
Dunn, Randy J., Dr., 2804
Dunn, Reagam, 3521
Dunn, Robert P., 1787
Dunn, Sarah, 2100
Dunn, Stephen D., 1787
Dunn, Steven D., 1787
Dunn, Terrence P., 1787
Dunn, Terry, 1787
Dunn, William H., Jr., 1787
Dunn, William H., Sr., 1787
Dunnan, D. Suart, Rev., 1360
Dunne, James, 2332
Dunne, James I., 2332
Dunne, James J., III, 2292
Dunne, Tiffany, 3
Dunning, Richard, 1607

Dunnington, Patricia, 2444
Dupkin, Carol N., 1371
Dupkin, Manuel, II, 1371
Duplessis, Ernest L., 1064
Dupree, Thomas H., Jr., 220
Dupree, Tracey, 1930
Duquette, Ron, 1660
Dura Medical Inc., 3320
Duran, Joe, 425
Durando, Jane Carlton, 844
Durchslag, Danielle, 2121
Durell, David, 1157
Durham, Andrew D., 3350
Durham, Brenton, 2232
Durham, Christine M., 2862
Durham, Cynthia Lambert, 2986
Durham, David R., 3350
Durham, Jolene, 1179
Durham, Lori, 2232
Durham, Sindy Shelton, 3350
Durham, Wendy H., 3350
Durie, John, 3352
Durkan, James, 1096
Durkee, Thomas V., 724
Durkin, Timothy, 3014
Duron, Rosalie, 2867
Durrant, Matthew, 2862
Durrill, Ginger, 3217
Durrill, Melissa, 3217
Durrill, Michele, 3217
Durrill, William R., 3217
Durrill, William R., Jr., 3217
Dusro, John A., Jr., 2932
Dutcher, Judi, 1684
Dutra Group, The, 102
Dutra, Craig J., 1453
Dutriac, Rick, 58
Dutton, Julia, 2948
Duval, Carol, 3161
Duvall, William C., 3349
Dvorak, Elizabeth, 712
Dvorak, Kevin J., 2653
Dworkis, Sam, 2038
Dwyer, Dean P., 166
Dwyer, Mary M., 1088
Dwyer, Mike, 1692
Dwyer, Rich, 1217
Dwyer, William J., 2381
Dye, Guilford, 160
Dye, James, 418
Dye, Kappy, 418
Dyer, Barbara, 666
Dyer, Betsy, 1766
Dyer, Kay, 2811
Dyer, Rick, 1593
Dyer, Sara R., 2765
Dyke, Elaine Van, 1888
Dykes, Martha Marshall, 895
Dykstra, Thomas, 1050
Dynamet Inc., 3028

Eagan, Gail, 1426
Eagan, Mark, 2108
Eagle-Tribune Publishing Co., 1536
Eagleman, David, 3303
Eagleton, Barbara, 1820
Eakes, Martin, 2160
Eakin, George, 1275
Eakins, Jon, 1146
Eakins, Ray, 1132
Eames, Cliff, 26
Ear, Sophal, 2121
Earhart, Anne G., 310
Earl, Anthony S., 1040
Earl, Orrin K., 361
Earl, Todd, 2809
Earle, Carol A., 1920
Earle, Dexter D., 1920
Earle, Linda, 2043
Earle, O. Perry, III, 2636
Earls, Michael, 1193
Early, Gerald, Dr., 1820
Early, Tom, 3343
Early, W. B., 2852
Easi, Inc., 1921
Easley, David C., 3648
Eason, Elizabeth, 838
Eason, Paul R., 3443
East Boston Savings Bank, 1460, 1517
East Rock Village, Inc., 1991
Eastburn, Dave, 1227
Eastburn, David, 1227
Eastdil Realty, Inc., LLC, 2207
Easterling, Stacey, 2673
Eastern Bank, 1461
Eastern Union Funding, 1902
Eastgate, Jeff Wyler, Inc., 2802
Eastham, Cathy, 3316
Eastham, G. Wayne, 3450
Eastman Chemical Co., 3133
Eastman, John, 551
Easton, James L., 287
Eaton Charitable Trust, W.E., 2332
Eaton Corp., 2692
Eaton Estate Trust, Hubert, 95
Eaton, Catherine I., 2693
Eaton, Cornelia, 361
Eaton, Jane E., 2332
Eaton, Joseph, 3252
Eaton, Kim, 1208
Eaton, Peggy, 3431
Eaton, Ruth, 3252
Eaton, Ruth Ann, 1705
Eaton, William C., 1539
Ebaugh, Emily, 2674
Ebb, Fred, 2149
Ebel, William E., 2006
Eberhard, Marie, 2751
Eberhardt, John E., Jr., 2907
Eberhart, James P., 1070
Eberhart, Mike, 1656
Eberhart, Ralph, 679
Eberle, Karl, 3621
Eberly, Kathy, 1960
Eberstein, Lanny, 389
Ebert, Michael G., 1611
Ebey, John G., 253
Eblen, Gary, 2539
Eblen, Jennie, 2540
Ebrhamimi, Alireza, 2030
Ebrom, Charles, 3387
Eby, Jeff, 3570
Eccles, Katie A., 439
Eccles, Spencer F., 439
Eccles, Tom, 2203
Echaveste, Maria, 139
Echolds, Leslie, 235
Echolds, Mike, 235
Eck, Jack, 543, 2232
Eckel, Fred, 2381
Eckerle, Mary, 1129
Eckert, Alfred C., III, 2873
Eckert, Karen, 1067
Eckert, Robert A., 243
Eckhardt, Laura, 2674
Eckhardt, Manah Kulp, 626
Eckhoff, James D., 1773
Eckholdt, Eric, 2118
Eckles, David, 935
Eckles, Morgan, 935
Eckley, Bonnie, 3511
Eckley, Brett, Dr., 3577
Eckloff, Ron, 1842
Eckstein, Richard J., 1492
Eckstrom, Elizabeth, 2842
Econome, Kathryn C., 439
Economou, James S., 276
Eddie, Gloria, 269
Eddie, Gloria Jeneal, 269
Eddington, Emily Ann, 3388
Eddington, Paul, 3388
Eddy, Charles R., 1539
Eddy, Edwin H., Jr., 2548
Eddy, Paula Fritz, 2939
Eddy, Susan, 1753
Eddy, Tristan, 1539
Edelblute, Ann, 3126
Edelheit, Aaron, 2827
Edelman, Cindy, 722
Edelman, Susan Datz, 722
Edelsohn, Lanny, 2233
Edelstein, Geoff, 441
Edelstone, Gary H., 192
Eder Annuity Trust, Andrew, 573
Eder Brothers, Inc., 573
Eder, Andrew J., 573
Eder, Andy, 1479
Eder, Eileen F., 573
Ederton, Liza T., 3466
Ederton, William A., 3466
Edgar, C. Ernest, 693
Edgar, Robert V., 2325
Edge, John H., 25
Edgerton, Larry, 3316
Edgman-Levitan, Susan, 1489
Edin, Kathryn, 2402
Edina Realty, Inc., 1694
Edison, Hope R., 1421
Edler, Dave, 3576
Edley, Christopher, 3516
Edlis, Stefan, 1009
Edmonds Charitable Remainder Trust, Mary Virginia, 2785
Edmonds, David B., 19
Edmonds, Maria N., 801
Edmonds, Pamela S., 2785
Edmondson, Susan J., 544
Edmunds, Matthew J., 2377
EDS Foundation, 249
Edson, Brad, 52
Edson, Bret, 52
Edson, Patricia, 52
Edwards, A.B. Kirk, 3219
Edwards, Adam B., 2993
Edwards, Anita Winsor, 2142
Edwards, Barbara A., 2391
Edwards, Berryman W., 3100
Edwards, Bob, 631
Edwards, Bruce, 268
Edwards, Carl, 2826
Edwards, Carolyn M., 28
Edwards, Charles W., 3493
Edwards, Chuck, 2539
Edwards, Claude D., 11
Edwards, David, 1316
Edwards, Donald, 3155
Edwards, Duncan, 2445
Edwards, Eddie, 1883
Edwards, George M., 3561
Edwards, Grace M., 1462
Edwards, Greg, 1300
Edwards, Gregory, 2734
Edwards, Gregory J., 2170
Edwards, Ishmell, Dr., 1760
Edwards, Jane, 631
Edwards, Joel, 2543
Edwards, John, 838
Edwards, John H., 2993
Edwards, Kee, 2737
Edwards, Kerry-Anne, 2326
Edwards, Mark, 838
Edwards, Michael M., 2993
Edwards, Monica, 1316
Edwards, Morris, 1158
Edwards, Paul B., 3666
Edwards, Phil, 2809
Edwards, Rodney, 2548
Edwards, Sharon, 3338
Edwards, T. Ashley, 1512
Edwards, Terry, 1250
Edwards, Trevor, 2865
Edwardson Charitable Lead Annuity Trust 2, Catherine O., 1092
Edwardson Charitable Lead Annuity Trust, Catherine O., 1092
Edwardson Family Foundation, 1092
Edwardson, Anne L., 1092
Edwardson, Catharine O., 1092
Edwardson, Shelly M., 1092
Efird, Claire, 2566
Efird, H. Timothy, II, 2560
Efromyson Fund, 1156
Egan, Brian, 1160
Egan, Dick, 3609
Egan, George, 808
Egan, J. Murray, 3048
Egan, Jennifer, 2050
Egan, Linda, 35
Egan, Mike F., 3191
Egbert, Marcia, 2736
Eggerlirg, Kristin, 1723
Eggert, James, 122
Eggertsson, Thrainn, 3436
Egli, John, Dr., 1170
Egly, Jane, 288
Egnot, Barbara, 2381
Ego, Kathleen, 613
Egolf, Monte, 1179
Ehlerman, P. Michael, 2893
Ehlers, Michael, 1714
Ehmcke, Lance D., 1240
Ehrenberg, Randy, 2112
Ehrgood, Kristin, 660
Ehrlich, Delia Fleishhacker, 199
Ehrlich, Jodi, 199
Ehrlich, John, Jr., 199
Ehrlich, Philip S., Jr., 471
El DuPont DE Nemours Co., 2562
Eichenberg, Ladorna, 188
Eichenberg, Robert, 188
Eichenberger, Steve, 1157
Eichold, Bernard H., Dr., 10
Eickelberger, Scott D., 2746
Eickmann, Margaret, 2874
Eifert, Donald A., 2609
Eilenberg, Moses, 2260
Eilers, Patrick C., 1088
Einhorn, Cheryl, 2150
Einhorn, David, 2150
Einhorn, Emily, 297
Einhorn, Jane, 391
Einhorn, Nancy, 3613
Einhorn, Peggi, 1949
Einhorn, Stephen, 3613
Einstandig, Jo, 1203
Einstein, Albert E., 739
Einstein, Birdie W., 739

Erler, Linda, 1162
Ernest, Robert, 1983
Ernst & Young, 3158
Ernst, John, 2027
Ernst, Katherine R., 1904, 1983
Ernst, Robert J., 1904
Erskine, Gary, 1175
Erstad, Shannon E.H., 948
Ervin, Charles, 2793
Ervin, Dean Wilson, 2118
Ervin, Glenda Lehman, 2798
Ervin, Le N., 2538
Ervin, Mark A., 1134
Erwert, Bill, 3530
Erwin, Anna P., 2578
Erwin, Kevin L., 823
Erwin, Peter, 2338
Escamilla, James, 1626
Eschhofen, Diana Moore, 2674
Escobar, F. Patrick, 287
Eshenbaugh, Jill, 155
Eskew, Michael L., 1353
Eskind, Richard J., 3129
Eskridge, Carl, 1857
Eskuche, Leslie M., 3393
Esmiol, Morris A., Jr., 529
Espaillat, Benigno, 1464
Espe, Marchell, 32
Espeland, Curtis E., 3133
Esping, Heather H., 3225
Esping, Perry E., 3225
Esping, William P., 3225
Espinosa, Gustavo, 993
Espinoza, Toni Beck, 162
Esposito, Anthony G., 2756
Espy, Jay, 1339
Esquenazi, Edmundo, 2173
Esquenazi-Shaio, Carolina, 2173
Esquivel, Eric, 3100
Esquivel, Marilyn B., 395
Esrey, William, 543
Esry, William C., 1817
Esser, Eloise, 1876
Esser, Julia Keough, 509
Esser, Richard B., 509
Essex, Willard, 1856
Essig Family Trust, 2148
Essig, Anne A., 2024
Essig, Rod, 3129
Essig, Stuart, 1945
Essman, Abbey, 3666
Essman, Adam, 3666
Essman, Ken, 3666
Essman, Marcy, 3666
Estep, David G., Col., 3468
Esterle, John, 462
Esterline, Bruce H., 3296
Esterson, Robin, 2473
Estes, Deborah Ann, 423
Estes, Scott, 1155
Estess, Sandra, 3261
Estey, Dede, 314
Estrada, Richard, 1299
Estrin, Mary Lloyd, 501
Estrin, Robert L., 501
Estrin, Zoe, 501
Etchart, Sarah, 1823
Etheridge, Frank S., III, 903
Etienne, Christine, 1578
Etscorn, Alice S., 1287
Etter, Dione, 1503
Ettinger, Barbara P., 574
Ettinger, Christian P., 574
Ettinger, Elsie, 574
Ettinger, Heidi P., 574
Ettinger, John R., 2207
Ettinger, Matthew P., 574
Ettinger, Richard P., 574
Ettinger, Richard P., Jr., 574
Ettinger, Virgil P., 574
Ettinger, Wendy W.P., 574
Etzel, Tim, 1279
Etzwiler, David D., 1993
Eude, Elisabeth, 1899
Evangelisti, Joseph, 3120
Evans Foundation, Charles, The, 2476
Evans, Arthur, 1511
Evans, Bonnie L. Pfeifer, 1925
Evans, Bridgitt, 538
Evans, Caswell A., Jr., 1459
Evans, Catherine Kobrinsky, 157
Evans, Charles, 1925, 2476
Evans, Charles, Jr., 1925
Evans, Dan, 2695
Evans, David L., 2156
Evans, Gareth, 1329
Evans, Jack, 1243, 1329
Evans, Jack B., 1222
Evans, Jean, 1329
Evans, Jeff, 3100
Evans, Joan, 3684
Evans, John, 425
Evans, John C., 2286
Evans, Kathryn, 3014
Evans, Kelli, 210
Evans, Kimberly H., 3275
Evans, Linda J., 912
Evans, Linda P., 3296
Evans, Lucia Brown, 2346
Evans, Megan A., 1262
Evans, Pamela S., 1539
Evans, Peggy, 2695
Evans, Roy Gene, 3202
Evans, Scott, 2191
Evans, Sian, 1329
Evans, Skip, 1257
Evans, Stephen, 2485
Evans, Thomas, 1445
Evans, Thomas H., 1378
Evans, Thomas J., 2695
Evans, Tina, 2705
Evans, Trevor, 1329
Evans, V. Lynn, 3124
Evans, William, 888
Evans-Tranum, Shelia, 3499
Evapco., Amex, 826
Evarts, Helen C., 2485
Evarts, William M., 2099
Eveillard, Elizabeth, 2263
Evenson, David, 2648
Everest, Christine Gaylord, 2813
Everett, Heidi J., 3480
Everett, Junella, 1203
Everett, Kathryn Brock, 2072
Everett, Margaret P., 2353
Evergreen Bancorp, Inc., 3549
Evergreen Bank, N.A., 3549
Everhart, Jennifer, 1618
Everhart, Thomas E., 275
Everhart, Thomas E., Dr., 276
Evers-Manly, Sandra, 3465
Eversole, Dan, 1647
Eves, David L., 1754
Ewald, Neal, 257
Ewbank, Mary, 1141
Ewing Autohaus, 3349
Ewing, Lorraine, 1154
Ewing, Lucinda B., 379
Ewing, S. Finley, III, 3349
Ewing, Stephen E., 1666
Exotic Metals Forming Co., 3536
Exxon Mobile, 36
Eychaner, Fred, 959
Eychner, Thomas D., 347, 397
Eyer, Robert J., 2922
Eyman, Amy, 2696
Eyre, Joe, 305
Ezerski, Ronald E., 1726

F & E Realty, 1962
Faanes, Mark, 3611
Fabems, A.L., 2791
Fabens, Andrew L., III, 2736
Faber, Doug, 368
Faber, Marilyn, 368
Fabian, Patricia, 991
Fabiano, James, II, 1662
Fabick Tractor Co., John, 1788
Fabick, Harry, 1788
Facchine, Thomas J., 2336
Facini, Deborah L., 2980
Fackler, Cynthia, 2342
Faerber, George O., 2762
Faessel, Steve, 83
Fagert, William, 2701
Fagnani, Laurie, 36
Fagot, Tom, 1845
Fagundes, Heather L., 317
Fahey, Richard, 412
Fahl, Greg, 1209
Faino, Laura Samberg, 3478
Fair, David R., 3030
Fair, Debra, 3148
Fair, F. Doyle, 1259
Fairbanks Charitable Lead Unitrust, 1927
Fairbanks, Betsy, 210
Fairbanks, David, 1845
Fairbanks, Jonathan B., 1145, 1927
Fairbanks, Marsha, 1842
Fairbanks, Richard M., 1145
Fairbanks, Richard M., III, 1927
Fairbanks, Shannon A., 1927
Fairbanks, Woods A., 1927
Fairchild, Marguerite, 3227
Faircloth Trust, Nancy B., 2519
Faircloth, Anne B., 2519
Faircloth, Nancy B., 2519
Fairfield, Freeman E., 2551
Fairfield, Jeffrey J., 3447
Fairmont Olympic Hotel, 3377
Fairview Nursing Care Center, Inc., 2254
Fairview Nursing Center Inc., 2255
Faks, Oni, 2484
Falahee, William P., 2245
Falatok, Andrew J., 3110
Falbaum, Rand, 1306
Falck, David P., 39
Falcone, Mark G., 475
Falder, Mike, 1129
Fales, Gilbert R., 3512
Falese, Robert D., 686
Falese, Robert D., Jr., 686
Falk Trust, Marian Citron, 3074
Falk, Jack, 697
Falk, Stephen, 2677
Fallis, Debra, 1311
Fallon, Bill, 2297
Fallon, James P., 70
Falls, Amy, 2160
Falsetto, Alicia, 3423
Fame Fashion House LLC., The, 2484
Family Doctors of Broward, 763
Fancy, Patricia L., 2197
Fanning, Robert R., Jr., 1464
Fansler Living Trust, 193
Fansler, D. Paul, 193
Fansler, Davis, 538
Fansler, Marlene, 193
Fant, Beth, 2010
Farash, Lynn, 2154
Farber, Erica, 2071
Farese, Conor, 194
Farese, Nancy R., 194
Farese, Robert, 194
Farese, Robert V., Jr., 194
Farish, Libbie Rice, 3228
Farish, William Stamps, 3228
Farkas, Janos, 2295
Farley, James S., 297
Farley, Katherine G., 2302
Farley, Kevin, 3414
Farley, Thomas, 2336
Farm Service Co., 111
Farm, Lis, 2876
Farmer, Scott, 386
Farmer, Terri L., 3601
Farmers Branch, 1960
Farmers Trust of Carlisle, 2952
Farmers Union Marketing & Processing Assoc., 1695
Farnsworth, Charles H., 1465
Farnsworth, Randall, 2342
Farnsworth, Sue Seibert, 3579
Farnsworth, Thomas C., 3120
Farnum, Amanda, 1390
Farquhar, David, 2863
Farr, Jim, 770
Farr, Kevin, 312
Farr, Leonard, 536
Farr, Olivia H., 1514
Farr, Walter S., 844
Farrance, Robert, Hon., 770
Farrar, Susan J., 163
Farrell, Cathy, 350
Farrell, J. David, 2916
Farrell, John, 2210
Farrell, John F., 1856
Farrell, Joseph, 1995
Farrell, Robert Michael, 3245
Farrington, Donna, 2900
Farrow, Jennifer Stafford, 825
Farrow, Stephen R., 1378
Farver, Constance, 1601
Farver, Herbert, 1601
Farver, Michael, 1601
Farver, Orville W., 1601
Farver, Patrick, 1601
Farver-Galiette, Cynthia, 1601
Farwell Trust, Ava W., 983
Fascitelli, Elizabeth Cogan, 2155
Fascitelli, Michael D., 2155
Fashion Exchange LLC., The, 2484
Faske, Howard, 3193
Fasken, Andrew A., 3229
Fasken, Paula, 3229
Fasken, Steve, 3229
Fasman, Kenneth H., Ph.D., 1424
Fasold, Sandra J., 340
Fast, Stephanie, 3158
Fath, Linda C., 2679
Fauber, Stuart C., 3454
Faucett, Sam, 11
Fauci, Anthony S., 2146
Fauliso, Anne Marie, 585
Faulkner, Karen, 1543

Faull, Gary F., 3514
Faull, Vicki, 3552
Fauntleroy, Elizabeth M., 3106
Fauth, Kristen, 3118
Favero, Joan, 401
Favre, Trent, 1764
Fawcett, Farrah, 195
Fawcett, Linda, 163
Fawley, Dan A., 2613
Fawn, Janis, 754
Fay, Cornelius Ryan, III, 1358
Fay, Paul, III, 2602
Fay-Bustillos, Theresa, 151
Fayard, Gary P., 864
Fayock, Daniel, 3018
Fead, Bob, 328
Feagin, Moses, 1769
Fearnside, Philip M., 1454
Fearon, Charles, 3000
Fearon, Robert H., Jr., 2090
Featherman, Sandra, 2942
Feathers, Elizabeth, 1438
Fecser, Frank, 2801
Feder, Abigail Jones, 2204
Feder, Franklin L. (Frank), 2882
Feder, Steven, 741
Feder, Susan, 2499
Federated Department Stores, Inc., 2726
Federico, Barbara, 1053
Federico, Kathleen, 1513
Fedor, John W., 1906
Fedorovich, Rick, 2655
Fedrick, Ronald M., 102
Fee Mission Council, 2731
Fee, Frank H., III, 768
Feed the Children, 3269
Feeley, Cathi, 2648
Feeney, Charles F., 2048
Feeney, James E., 2925
Feeney, Patricia G., 2706
Fehrs, Rebecca, 3447
Fehsenfeld, Fred M., Jr., 1151
Fehsenfeld, Suzanne, 1151
Feiberg, Ann Merriam, 564
Feigeles, Edward M., 809
Feigenbaum, Harvey, 1190
Feight, Brent, 1360
Fein, Dorothy, 2111
Fein, Edward, 2035
Feinberg, Mike, 360
Feinberg, Ross, 268
Feinstein, Michael, 328
Feintech Family Foundation, The, 196
Feintech, Irving, 196
Feintech, Lisa A., 196
Feintech, Wendy, 196
Feld, Alan R., 2051
Feldkemp, I.M., 3119
Feldman Charitable Lead Trust, Jacob, 2941
Feldman Foundation, The, 2941, 3230
Feldman Marital Trust, Jacob, 2941
Feldman, Daniel E., 3230
Feldman, Franklin, 2044
Feldman, Moses, 2941
Feldman, Robert L., 3230
Feldman, Ross, 2112
Feldman, Susan, 2941
Feldmann, Suzanne Mead, 3241
Feldstein, Daniel, 1928
Feldstein, David, 1928
Feldstein, George, 1928
Felhofer, Michael, 3609
Felich, Georgia D., 147
Felix, June, 2445
Fella, Leon, 2410
Fella, Robert H., 2410
Feller, Robert, 343
Fellman, Jennifer A., 1483
Fellows, Glenn, 2006
Fellows, Ryan, 1657
Fellows, William H., 2741
Fels, Samantha, 778
Fels, Samuel S., 2942
Feltes, Tom, 1845
Felton, John, Dr., 1187
Felts, Thomas J., Hon., 1147
Feminella, Ann, 2198
Feminist Women's Health Center, 1880
Fender, Laura, 1850
Feng, Michael, 2177
Fenig, Mickey, 390
Fenley, Gigi, 378
Fenn, Forrest, 679
Fenstemacher, Keith, 2110
Fenstermaker, Ginny, 1207
Fenton Art Glass Co., 3581
Fenton Gift Shops, Inc., 3581
Fenton, David C., 3581
Fenton, Joyce R., 947
Fenton, Michael D., 3581
Fenton, Randall R., 3581
Fenton, Steven, 947
Fenton, Thomas K., 3581
Feoli, Ludovico, 1316
Ferber, James W., 800
Ferdowsi, Farzin, 3129
Ferebee, David, Jr., 713
Ferebee, Percy, 2552
Ferenbach, Carl, 1482
Ferenbach, Judy, 1482
Ferens, Joseph F., Esq., 2923
Ferentz, JoAnne, 2908
Ferguson, Ellen Lee, 3513
Ferguson, Emily, 1233
Ferguson, Ernest E., 2540
Ferguson, Gary, 27
Ferguson, Gerene Dianne Chase, 2009
Ferguson, Hugh S., 3513
Ferguson, Jane Avery, 3513
Ferguson, Joan, 1760
Ferguson, Joe, 1851
Ferguson, John, 1193
Ferguson, John D., 3129
Ferguson, Judy, 1663
Ferguson, Julie, 900
Ferguson, Lori, 1270
Ferguson, Mary, 288
Ferguson, Randall, 1817
Ferguson, Richard, 2071
Ferguson, Sanford B., 2937
Ferguson, Stephen L., 1190
Ferland, Tina, 1581
Fernalld Trust, Kylee McVaney, 521, 542
Fernandez, Eduardo, 2780
Fernandez, Frank, 856
Fernandez, Henry L., 1126
Fernandez, James N., 2463
Fernandez, Jose, 2037
Fernandez, Judith, 1948
Fernandez, Nancy, 2037
Fernandez, Robert I., 3275
Fernos, Maria D., 3061
Ferraioli, Dominic, 2156
Ferraresi, Daniel J., 697
Ferrari, George P., Jr., 2112
Ferree, Robert B., IV, 3044
Ferreira, Marilyn, 159
Ferrell, Mark C., 3579
Ferrell, Paget, 2790
Ferrero, Thomas V., 2788
Ferriby, Robin D., 1588
Ferrie, Timothy, 2289
Ferris, Bruce, 1258
Ferro Corp., 2697
Ferro, Kevin, 2236
Ferro, Michael W., Jr., 982
Fertig, Alice, 2004
Fery, Sandra L. S., 948
Fesenmaier, Joe, 3611
Festivale Maritime, Inc., 691
Fetcher, Jay, 545
Fetchig Charitable Remainder Unitrust, Allie Morriss, 2578
Fett, David, 237
Fetterman, Annabelle L., 2599
Fetzer, Jeffrey A., 3008
Feuer, Michael, 674
Feulner, Edwin, Jr., 2028
Feuss, Bert, 408
Fewel, Scott, 2835
Fey, Grace, 1534
Fiakowski, Geraldine, 1352
Fiala, Robert A., 2792
Fibus Family Properties, LLC, 2698
Fibus, C. Kenneth, 2698
Fibus, M., 2698
Fica, Michelle, 564
Fidelity Charitable Gift Fund, 901, 2863
Fidelity Exploration & Production Co., 2652
Fidicuary Trust Co. Int'l., 1811
Fiduciary Trust Co. International, 2325
Field Trust, Daniel W., 1485
Field, Arthur Norman, 1912, 1981
Field, David J., 2945
Field, Jaimie, 2945
Field, Joseph, 2071
Field, Joseph M., 2945
Field, Margaret W., 564
Field, Marie H., 2945
Field, Marshall, IV, 1014
Field, Marshall, V, 1014
Field, Nancy E., 2945
Fielder, Ann C., 3275
Fields, Curtland E., 2002
Fields, Michael, 2805
Fields, Randolph, 1602
Fiery, Douglas A., 1360
Fifield, Helen D., 1512
Fifth Third Bank, 801, 1586, 2679, 2699
Fifth Third Bank, N.A., 2775
Figliola, Dan, 472
Figliuzzi, David, 2917
Figueredo, Jorge L., 321
Figueroa, Bruce, 3067
File, William H., 3577
Filene, Lincoln, 1468
Fili-Krushel, Patricia, 2322
Filice, Kay, 159
Fillit, Howard, 2233
Fillmore, Bill, 723
Filosa, Tracy Abedon, 1464
Financial Partners, 1156
Financial Trust Services, 2952
Finch, Doak, 743
Finch, Greg, 537
Finch, Robbin, 631
Finch, Robert, Jr., 3454
Finchem, Tim, 543
Findlay, Jack, 1616
Findlay, Marjorie M., 2918
Findlay, Sharyn, 1877
Findley, Kevin C., 279
Fine Line, LP, 3319
Fine, Art, 106
Fine, Roger S., 1949
Finear, David R., 355
Fineberg, Harvey V., 248, 2288
Finegan, Tim, 2805
Finerman, Ralph, 331
Finerty, Steve, 1802
Finestein, Russell, 2004
Finger, Suzette, 2524
Finigan, Barbara, 3077
Fink, Courtney, 2494
Fink, Richard, 1265
Finke, Jeff, 1180
Finke, Ron, 1817
Finkelstein, Mark, 2348
Finkle, Nancy, 2342
Finklestein, Michael, 577
Finlay, Duncan, Dr., 727
Finlay, Francis, 2445
Finlay, Karin K., 1884
Finlay, Louis E. "Ed", 3308
Finlay, Marcie, 2112
Finlay, Robert, 1884
Finlayson, Sharon, 1924
Finley Charitable Remainder Unitrust, R., 197
Finley, Ernest L., 197
Finley, J.B., 2946
Finley, Jim, 3607
Finley, John H., IV, 1529
Finley, Patrick T., 2740
Finley, Renee, 744
Finley, Ruth W., 197
Finley, Skip, 2071
Finn, Thomas L., 2680
Finneran, John G., Jr., 3426
Finnigan, Becky, 1724
Finocchiaro, Linda W., 469
Finucance, Flavia P., 576
Finucane, Anne M., 2524
Fiore, William J., 3453
Fioretti, Robert W., 1081
Fiorile, Michael J., 2071
FIP Corp., 577
Fireman, Paul, 1469
Fireman, Phyllis, 1469
Firestone, Joan, 2143
Firestone, Marc S., 1064
First American National Bank, 1770
First and Main, LLC, 524
First County Bank, 613
First Data Corp., 496
First Financial Bank, 2710, 2719
First Financial Northwest, Inc., 3514
First Giving, 2025
First Horizon National Corp., 3135
First National Bank, 494
First National Bank & Trust of Waynesboro, 2952
First National Bank and Trust of Newtown, 2900
First National Bank of Greencastle, 2952
First Republic Bank, 3072
First Savings Bank of Perkasie, 2900
First State Bank & Trust Co., 3647
First Tennessee Bank, 3137
First Tennessee Bank, N.A., 3140
First Tennessee National Corp., 3135
First Union Corp., 3055
First Union National Bank, 2616
FirstMerit Bank, N.A., 1643, 2655, 2788
Firszt, Anya, 3599

Firth, Edmee de M., 2145
Firth, Katherine V., 2145
Firth, Nicholas L.D., 2145
Fisackerly, Haley R., 1308
Fisch, Amy C., 206
Fisch, Ben, 3232
Fisch, Maytee R., 3232
Fisch, Sandra, 3232
Fisch, Stephanie, 3232
Fischbach, Gerald D., 2423
Fischbach, Nancy, 592
Fischer, Aaron, 1786
Fischer, Addison M., 165
Fischer, David T., 1588
Fischer, Dean R., 1235
Fischer, Elizabeth S., 370
Fischer, Jan, 1012
Fischer, Jennifer Atler, 528
Fischer, Kurt, 3516
Fischer, Larry, 992
Fischer, M. Peter, 1786, 1789
Fischer, Mark J., 3401
Fischer, Martha, 1789
Fischer, Martha C., 1786
Fischer, Matthew A., 1786
Fischer, Matthew G., 1789
Fischer, Michael P., 1786, 1789
Fischer, Richard, 1691
Fischer, Steven P., 203
Fischer, Teresa M., 1786
Fish and Mirtha G. Fish Trust, Ray C., 3233
Fish, Atsuko Toko, 1470
Fish, Edward Takezo, 1470
Fish, Emily, 1470
Fish, Kim Nedelman, 2787
Fish, Lawrence K., 1470
Fish, Leah Okajima Toko, 1470
Fish, Mirtha G., 3233
Fish, Raymond Clinton, 3233
Fishbein, Michael, 2905
Fishburne, Lynne, 434
Fisher 120 Wall, 2157
Fisher 92nd St., 2157
Fisher Brothers, 2157
Fisher Capital Assets, 2157
Fisher Charitable Trust, Zachary & Elizabeth, 2157
Fisher Fund, Doris and Donald, 1971
Fisher Park Lane Co., 2157
Fisher Scientific, 1893
Fisher Trust, Stanley D., 577
Fisher, A. Tony, 3097
Fisher, Andrew S., 2269
Fisher, Arnold, 2157
Fisher, Brian, 723
Fisher, Catherine M., 304
Fisher, Cheryl, 1155
Fisher, Donald G., 141
Fisher, Doris F., 141
Fisher, Elizabeth S., 370
Fisher, Elliott S., 1982
Fisher, Everett, 570
Fisher, Hinda N., 577
Fisher, Irwin E., 3129
Fisher, James A., 1121
Fisher, Janice B., 1121
Fisher, Jeff, 373
Fisher, John J., 141
Fisher, John W., 1121
Fisher, Joseph, 685
Fisher, Jud, 1121, 1134
Fisher, Kenneth, 2157
Fisher, Marvin N., 693
Fisher, Michael, 2037
Fisher, Nancy, 2722
Fisher, Peggy L., 1122
Fisher, Phillip W., 1588
Fisher, Rick, 3126
Fisher, Robert J., 370
Fisher, Terri, 3431
Fisher, Winston C., 2157
Fishman, C.J., 727
Fishman, David M., 2180
Fishman, Leora, 2180
Fishman, Richard G., 1298
Fisk, Barbara M., 687
Fisk, Kelly, 687
Fisker, Linda R., 39
Fisler, Christine M., 1489
Fister, Bruce, 2789
Fister, Christopher L., 2679
Fister, Kent D., 2789
Fitch, Orville, 1883
Fitgerald, Thomas J., 2603
Fitton, Chana, 1982
Fitton, James K., 2710
Fitts, David W., 1561
Fitzgerald Cleaning, 1517
Fitzgerald, Amber, 2809
Fitzgerald, Cantor, 1862
Fitzgerald, Donna M., 2116
Fitzgerald, Gail M., 1358
Fitzgerald, Judy, 1129
Fitzgerald, Katharine, 2111
Fitzgerald, L. Michael, 2110
Fitzgerald, Margaret Boles, 2286
Fitzgerald, Paul, Dr., 68
Fitzgerald, Stephen B., 2524
Fitzgerald, Teresa, 419
Fitzgerald, Thomas G., 1060
Fitzgerald, Timothy D., 2947
Fitzgerald-Schultz, Shannon, 1210
FitzGibbon, Thomas P., Jr., 968
Fitzgibbons, S. Dorothy Anne, 2167
Fitzmorris, Scott, 684
Fitzpatrick, Barry C., 180
Fitzpatrick, Frank, 1289
Fitzpatrick, Jack, 215
Fitzpatrick, Margaret M., 2917
Fitzpatrick, Sue, 1587
Fitzpatrick, Susan M., 1800
Fitzpatrick, Tim, 367
Fitzpatrick-Donahue, Anne, 2206
Fitzsimmons, Kelly, 2097
Fitzsimmons, Sue, 1387
Fitzsimons, Candace, 1578
Fitzsimons, Hugh A., Jr., 3247
FitzSimons, Michael J., 1656
Fiverson, Marjorie Gershwind, 2174
FJC, 2074
Flagg, Scott, 1505
Flaherty, Jay C., 1645
Flake, Floyd, Rev. Dr., 2167
Flambeau, Inc., 3655
Flamme, Larry, 1836
Flanagan Charitable Trust, Thomas & Esther, 2332
Flanagan, Esther C., 2332
Flanagan, Jennifer Z., 1432
Flanagan, Laura, 91
Flanagan, Margaret, 1462
Flanagan, Patricia J., 3089
Flanagan, Patrick, 2332
Flanagan, Patrick M., 1294
Flanagan, Sheila B., 611
Flanagan, Shiela B., 595
Flanagan, William, 3663
Flanders, Bryon, 347
Flanders, Byron, 397
Flanders, Fred J., 1823
Flanigan, James, 716
Flannery, Richard J., 3003
Flarsheim, Elizabeth, 3234
Flarsheim, Louis, 3234
Flather, Newell, 1523
Flatt, Stephen F., Dr., 3129
Flattery, Sarah, 1227
Flatto, Olivia Tournay, 2356
Flaville, Victoria K., 2926
Fleak, Michael L., 3587
Flederbach, Linda, 3017
Fleece, Joseph W., III, 801
Fleece, William H., 1016
FleetBoston Financial Foundation, 2524
Fleischer, Bruce M., 1582
Fleischer, Carl, 2158
Fleischer, Donald, 2158
Fleischer, Henry, 1582
Fleischer, Jennifer, 1856
Fleischer, Shirley, 2158
Fleischer, Steven, 2158
Fleischer, William R., 2158
Fleischmann, Brian F., 3650
Fleishans, Brendan, 1587
Fleishhacker, David, 199
Fleishhacker, Jeffrey, 199
Fleishhacker, Marc, 199
Fleishhacker, Mortimer, Jr., 199
Fleishhacker, Mortimer, Sr., 199
Fleishhacker, William, 199
Fleishman, Sue, 2466
Fleming, David, 630
Fleming, David W., 137
Fleming, Donald, 3009
Fleming, Ellen, 866
Fleming, Joseph M., 794
Fleming, Kim Tillotson, 2901
Fleming, Linda Rovder, Hon., 2922
Fleming, Michael, 117
Fleming, Michael E., Dr., 2474
Fleming, Stephen, 278
Fleming, Suzanne, 2799
Fletcher, Burton, 3484
Fletcher, Edward S., 122
Fletcher, Ernest "Bud", Jr., 2387
Fletcher, Fred, 1753
Fletcher, G. Paul, 3445
Fletcher, George P., 3678
Fletcher, James P., 288
Fletcher, Monique, 2177
Flick, Jeff, 3039
Flick, Robert, 400
Fliehman, Dennis W., 1581
Flinn, Irene, 44
Flinn, Robert S., 44
Flint, Anji, 1295
Flippin, John M., 3454
Fliss, Timothy S., Jr., 3598
Floch, Julie, 2122
Flood, Mary, M.D., Sr., 2269
Floren, Douglas C., 578
Florence, Bruce, 1282
Florence, Jeff Wyler, Inc., 2802
Florence, Priscilla, 287
Flores, Chio, 3502
Flores, Frank, 3465
Flores, Hector, 138
Flores, Kathryn Q., 3668
Flores, Kathy, 159
Flores, Ness, 3637
Flores-New, Fernando, 1611
Florez, Maria, 2368
Florida Institute of Technology, 918
Florida Sports Foundation, 750
Floridamae Vanderpool 2005 Trust, 996
Florio, Carl, 2223
Florio, Carl A., 2223
Flournoy Unitrust No. 2, Georgia T., 745
Flournoy, Bob, 3227
Flower, Walter C., III, 1310
Flowerree Residuary Marital Trust, 2845
Flowerree, Ann D., 2845
Flowerree, David R., 2845
Flowerree, Elaine D., 2845
Flowerree, John H., 2845
Flowerree, Robert E., 2845
Flowers Foods Bakeries Group, 952
Flowers, Bob, 3558
Flowers, Thomas I., 2225
Flowers, Walter J., 254
Flowers, Wilford, 3386
Floyd, Bart, 1218
Floyd, Charlotte B., 1348
Floyd, Mary Bell, 200
Floyd, William S., 200
Fluegel, Kari, 3052
Fluegel, Kathleen, 1702
Flug, Danielle, 2195
Flug, Laura, 2195
Flugaur, Rick, 3606
Fluor Corp., 3235
Fluor Foundation, The, 102
Flynn, Bryan, 351
Flynn, Nancy, 351
Flynn, Ruth S., 1069
Flynn, Steve, 107
Flynn-Learner, 2323
FMI - Management Consulting, 102
FMOL Health System, 3377
FMR Corp., 1889
Foege, William H., 251, 3500
Foellinger, Esther A., 1147
Foellinger, Helene R., 1147
Foerster, Susan, 525
Fogg, Sandra, 1428
Fogle, Brian, 1783
Foglia, Kymberly A., 1015
Foglia, Patricia A., 1015
Foglia, Vincent J., 1015
Foglia, Vincent W., 1015
Foisie, Michael R., 610
Foisie, Robert A., 610
Fojtasek, Travis, 1623
Folberg, Jay, 268
Folcroft Co., 1388
Foley, Dennis, 2498
Foley, Donald, 1569
Foley, James R., 2107
Foley, Jane, Dr., 331
Foley, John W., 2107
Foley, Linda K., 651
Foley, Melissa, 1519
Foley, Thomas, 1862
Foley, Tom, 1862
Foley, William, 2004
Folk, Craig, 823
Folkerts, Kevin, 1694
Folkstone Ltd., 890
Folland, Charles, 1822
Foltz, Charles D., 954
Folz, Cecilia, 543
Fomer, Margaret, 479
Fong, Albert, 151
Fong, Bobby, 301
Fonseca, Caio, 2245
Fonseca, Elizabeth K., 2245

Fonseca, Isabel, 2245
Fonseca, Quina, 2245
Fontanes, A. Alexander, 1502, 3554
Food Services of America, 1831
Foose, Randy, 1883
Foote, Virginia, 667
Foote-Hudson, Marilyn E., 2600
Foran, Kathee, 2210
Forbes, Herman, 1016
Forbes, Janice L., 371
Forbes, Moira, 2116
Forbes, Orcilla Zuniga, 2861
Forbs, Claudia, 2367
Forcum, Julie A., 1122
Ford Foundation, The, 502
Ford Motor Co., 2445
Ford, Alex, 2654
Ford, Allen, 2654
Ford, Allen H., 2654
Ford, Allyn C., 2846
Ford, Betty Jane, 2731
Ford, Charles, 2654
Ford, Charles K., 2654
Ford, Cynthia N., 1638
Ford, David Kingsley, 2654
Ford, David Knight, 2654
Ford, David, Jr., 2654
Ford, Dustin, 1225
Ford, Edsel, 2160
Ford, Elizabeth Brooks, 2654
Ford, Hallie E., 2846
Ford, Henry, 2160
Ford, James W., 1656
Ford, Jenice C. Mitchell, 1588
Ford, Jon, 1203
Ford, Kenneth W., 2846
Ford, Linda, 1182
Ford, Lise, 2654
Ford, Ned, 2654
Ford, Richard, 1649
Fordham, Kiki, 2480
Fore, Julian, 3421
Foreman Trust, 1083
Foreman, Barbara J., 1950
Foreman, Richard, 2071
Foreman, Richard A., 2071
Forer, David B., 2279
Forest Lawn Co., 95
Forester Offshore, 3642
Forgit, Cathy, 1723
Forman, Barry, 3570
Formicola, John, 261
Fornabaro, Michael, 2281
Fornear, Ben, 1691
Forner, Emira, 3503
Forney, Ann W., 19
Fornof, Pete, 1010
Forrest, Myra Gehert, 3017
Forrestel, Margaret, 1948
Forrester, Judy, 1817
Forrester, W. Thomas, 2764
Forsch, Randall T., 1584
Forshay, Wendy, 2450
Forsyth, Adrian, 3422
Forsyth, John D., 1246
Forsyth, William H., Jr., 2479
Forsythe, Garry V., 3127
Forte, Cheryl, 1472, 1508
Forte, Robin, 3237
Fortier, Chris, 2109
Fortin Foundation of Florida, 747
Fortin, Mary Alice, 747
Fortine Irrevocable Trust, Mary Alice, 747
Fortino, Barbara, 535
Fortino, Phil, 159
Fortis Benefits Insurance Co., 2047
Fortis Insurance Co., 2047
Fortis, Inc., 2047
Fortson, Benjamin J., 3185
Fortson, Edred, 2553
Fortune Foundation, Martha Murray, 497
Fortune Metal Group Inc., 1931
Fortune, Mike P., 3660
Fortune, Sheila M., 497
Foshee, Douglas L., 3267
Fosheim, Jon, 105
Foskey, Randall, 3487
Foss, Donald J., 2701
Foss, Donald J., Mrs., 2701
Foss, Walter R., 2701
Fossum, Lynn, 3505
Foster, Claude P., 3448
Foster, Diane, 3401
Foster, Fred L., 3102
Foster, Fred L., Jr., 2556
Foster, Leonard, 2796
Foster, Loleta Wood, Dr., 2541
Foster, Patricia A., 999
Foster, R. David, 3648
Foster, Richard N., 276
Foster, Rob, 1783
Foster, Stephen A., 2345
Foster, Steve, 2686
Foster, Therese, 996
Foster, Timothy, 2790
Foster, Tracy McFerrin, 1793
Foster, Trevor, 2790
Foster, Vicki, 3421
Foster, William, 1490, 2790
Fouad, Nadya, 3604
Fouberg, Rod, 3118
Foudree, Chuck, 1817
Fougnies, Douglas V., 45
Fouladi, A. Holly, 758
Foulkrod, Patricia G., 2956
Foundation Health Plan of Sacramento, 405
Foundation Jewish Philanthropies of Buffalo, 1902
Foundation of Integrated Services, 3548
Foundation, Samuel P. Pardoe, 1402
Fountain, Edmund M., Jr., 3238
Fountain, Karen, 2004
Fountain, Markland, 2850
Fountain, Nancy Frees, 3238
Fountain, W. Frank, 1588
Four Winds Casino Resort, 1657
Fournier, Alan P., 1932
Fournier, Jennifer L., 1932
Fournier, Lucinda Day, 276
Fournier, Susan, 3315
Fouss, Rob, 3587
Foutz, James R., 2923
Fowke, Benjamin G.S., III, 1754
Fowle, Stephen A., 630
Fowler Memorial Foundation, John Edward, 676
Fowler, Adrian Rhae, 3386
Fowler, Amber, 434
Fowler, Amy Goldman, 2181
Fowler, Cary, 2181
Fowler, Charles D., 2703
Fowler, Charlotte, 2703
Fowler, Charlotte A., 2703
Fowler, Dick, 945
Fowler, John C., 3668
Fowler, Lynn, 3188
Fowler, Pearl Gunn, 1372
Fowler, Peggy Y., 2867
Fowler, Rob, 900
Fowler, Robert D., 867
Fowler, Stephanie J., 2869
Fowler, W. Beal, 2986
Fowler, Willa Jo, 2809
Fowler-Spellman, Chann, 2703
Fox Channel Services LLC, 2562
Fox Mounsey, Anne E., 499
Fox, Alan C., 205
Fox, Ashton L., 2541
Fox, Becca Selvidge, 499
Fox, Belle, 3439
Fox, Beri, 3579
Fox, Beth, 3369
Fox, Christy B., 1789
Fox, Daveen, 205
Fox, Dennis, 1063
Fox, Eugene, 1998
Fox, Ingrid, 205
Fox, John F., Jr., 499
Fox, John M., 499
Fox, John M., Jr., 499
Fox, Kelley P., 499
Fox, Kevin, 205
Fox, Marcella F., 499
Fox, Sara, 205
Fox, Susan M., 331
Fox, Thomas F., 2289
Foxley, Zoe L., 501
Foy, Deborah, 477
Foy, Douglas J., 1121
Fradd, R. Brandon, 2445
Fraenkel, Barnet H., 3049
Fralick, Desiree, 2909
Fralick, William, 2787
Fralin, Robert P., 3432
Fram, Debra, 561
Framptom, Joseph H., 1286
Frampton Family Charitable Foundation, 2232
Frampton, Harry, III, 543
Francis, Carl, 2915
Francis, David R., 3457
Francis, Jonathan, 3366
Francis, Roger, 420
Franciscovich, Linda R., 2114
Franck, C. Duffy, Jr., 3147
Franckhauser, Margaret, 1883
Franco, Juan, 1847
Frandsen, Olaf, 1274
Frangiosa, Joseph D., 2926
Frank Foundation, Sidney, 2071
Frank, Alan W., 2071
Frank, Charles, 3655
Frank, Elizabeth T., 1972
Frank, George W., 2376
Frank, Jay L., 3129
Frank, John, 3023
Frank, Mariel, 3019
Frank, Mary, 3330
Frank, Michael, 2796
Frank, Michael J., 1803
Frank, Paul, 1314
Frank, Sidney E., 206
Frank, Stanley J. "Jack", Jr., 2687
Franke, Stephen L., 3615
Frankel Family LP, 1017
Frankel Living Trust, Matthew, 1017
Frankel, Bernard, 1017
Frankel, Bruce, 1604, 1605
Frankel, Jean, 1604, 1605
Frankel, Marya, 1017
Frankel, Matthew, 1017
Frankel, Miriam, 1017
Frankel, Peter, 1017
Frankel, Samuel, 1604
Frankel, Sandor, 2207
Frankel, Stanley, 1604
Frankel, Stuart, 1604
Frankenberg, Regina Bauer, 2162
Frankfort, Lew, 2100
Frankino, Samuel J., 2691
Franklin Holding Corp., 329
Franklin Holdings, Inc., 565
Franklin, Carmela Vircillo, 2263
Franklin, Douglas, Hon., 2685
Franklin, Fred W., 2613
Franklin, Jennifer, 1162
Franklin, John C., 3333
Franklin, Richard R., 748
Franklin, Tammy G., 748
Franklin, W. Stevens, 748
Franklin, Wilson P., 748
Franks, Betty, 2674
Frantz, Barbara, 1587
Frantz, Julie, 2850
Franz, Jennifer A., 2449
Fraser, Darryl M., 3465
Fraser, Ian H., 2485
Fraser, Jane, 3155
Fraser, Stu, 538
Frasier, Eleanor, 1817
Frattaroli, Tracey, 3168
Frauenthal, Harold, 1586
Frautschi, Walter Jerome, 3652
Frazee, Alexena, 3059
Frazell, Chad, 3644
Frazer, David R., 44
Frazier, Alexandra V. A., 3053
Frazier, Bob, 1272
Frazier, Evan S., 2968
Frazier, H. Matthew, 1953
Frazier, Janet, 1472
Frazin, Susan, 145
Freas, Donald, 2954
Freas, Lawrence, 2954
Frechette, Peter, 543
Freckman, Joanie C., 382
Frederick Trust, C. Lydia, 983
Frederick, Bob, 1848
Frederick, Brian R., 2683
Frederick, Cathey, 2815
Frederick, Charles, 2540
Frederick, Karen, 1505
Frederick, Ron, 2944
Frederikson, Dave, 3611
Free, Franci, 378
Freebairn Char Lead Annuity Trust, 1103
Freebairn, Elizabeth A., 1103
Freebairn, Kenneth T., 1103
Freebairn, William A., 1103
Freeburg, Carol, 1749
Freed, Allie S., 2163
Freed, Barbara, 1548
Freed, Elizabeth, 2163
Freed, Frances W., 2163
Freed, Gerald A., 2163
Freedland, Shirley, 1861
Freedland, Tzepah, 164
Freedman, James B., 410
Freedman, Kimberley, 1081
Freedman, Miriam, 2818
Freedman, Robert C., 2818
Freedman, Tony, 3505
Freedom Wireless Inc., 45
Freeland, Ben G., 3129
Freels, Gary W., 3610
Freeman, 3237

Gaalswyk, Kathy, 1703
Gabaldon, Eileen, 2013
Gabbard, Kevin, 1132
Gabbay, Carolyn Jacoby, 1481
Gaber, Steve, 2011, 2017
Gaberino, John A., Jr., 2831
Gabier, Russell L., 1612
Gabino, Mary A., 3061
Gabler, Karen A., 3593
Gabow, Patricia A., 1949
Gabran, Niclas, 2473
Gabriel, Nicholas M., 2160
Gacinski, John A., 2393
Gaddes, Richard, 2486
Gaddis, Larry R., 525
Gadomski, Robert E., 2986
Gadsden, William F., 1900
Gadus, Mary Beth, 1204
Gaede, Judy, 351
Gaede, Stan, 351
Gaerte, Stephen C., 1204
Gaffney, Joe, 3558
Gaffney, Rob, 543
Gafkay, Julie, 1606
Gage, Mike, 3305
Gage, Scott, Dr., 3597
Gagen, Tim, 537
Gager, James, 2287
Gagne, J. Leo, 563
Gagne-Holmes, Sara, 1336
Gagnon, Diane, 3414
Gagnon, Roberta, 1580
Gail Trust, 3472
Gain, Judy, 361
Gaither, Gloria, 1175
Gaither, James C., 333
Gaither, Linda, 3287
Galanes, Gloria, Dr., 1783
Galang, Astra Anderson, 359
Galantowicz, Barbara, 2731
Galantowicz, Mark, 2731
Galas, David, 3570
Galbraith, Anna Mae, 3014
Galbraith, James R., 251
Galbreath, David K., Jr., 2763
Galdenberg, Blauch, 2459
Gale, Fournier J., III, 19
Gale, Tom, 3296
Gall, Blake, 2909
Gallagher, Donald J., 2681
Gallagher, Gary W., 3448
Gallagher, James P., 2926
Gallagher, Karen K., 2674
Gallagher, Matthew D., 1374
Gallagher, Michael L., 1843
Gallagher, Ralph W., 2674
Gallagher, Richard S., 3646
Gallagher, William J., Esq., 2915
Galland, Michael S., 2800
Gallant, Allan, 3599
Gallatin, Ron, 2117
Gallegos, Victoria L., 1044
Gallen, Thomas A., Hon., 770
Galler, Beatrice, 2168
Galler, Lynne, 2168
Gallery, Robert E., 2524
Galli, Kathleen, 182
Galliher, Michael B., 1134
Gallivan, Mary, 2574
Gallman, Charles W., 2560
Gallo, Gregory M., 408
Gallo, Martha D., 733
Gallo, Ronald V., 394
Gallogly, Jim, 754
Galloway, Richard W., 693
Galloway-Tabb, Pamela Y., 662
Gallup, Nancy, 3527
Gallwas, Gerald E., 105
Gally, Susan D., 733
Galper, David, 1479
Galtney, Rob, 3266
Galtney, Robert F., 3240
Galtney, William F., Jr., 3240
Galvan, Bobby, Judge, 3196
Galvez, Fred, 3390
Galyen, Jeff, 1158
Gamache, Ed, 1663
Gamb, James, 363
Gamba, John, 823
Gambet, Daniel G., Fr., 3049
Gamble, George F., 213
Gamble, George T., 213
Gamble, James N., 97
Gamble, Jim, 213
Gamble, Joan L., 213
Gamble, Launce E., 213
Gamble, Launce L., 213
Gamble, Mark D., 213
Gamble, Mary S., 213
Gamble-Booth, Gwyneth, 2867
Gamboa, Gina, 3576
Gambrell, Sarah Belk, 2599
Gambrill, Anne J., 2556
Gambrinus Enterprises, 3630
Gammell, Tracy, 2858
Gamoran, Adam, 2191
Gamper, Albert, 1933
Gamper, Albert R., Jr., 1933
Gamper, Christopher, 1933
Gamper, Janice, 1933
Gandelot, Elizabeth Mower, 1004
Gandelot, Jon B., 1004
Gandia, Naomi, 647
Gandy, Greg, 525
Gang, Laura, 1545
Gangolli, Julian S., 80
Gannon, Tony, 3158
Gannon, William S., 2002
Gano, Charles H., 1656
Ganon, Shawn, 2359
Gans, Richard, Esq., 727
Gans, Stephen L., 2019
Ganshirt, Clark E., 1060
Gansler, Jill, 1388
Gansner, Andy, 3636
Gant, Gail, 3542
Gant, Steve, 3542
Ganz, Carole, 1443
Gappa, Jennifer, 1180
Garacochea, Stephanie L., 276
Garber, Dan, 1260
Garber, Eli S., 2061
Garber, Janine, 2795
Garber, Karlene Beal, 3174
Garber, Matt, 2907
Garber, Ross, 3159
Garber, Roy, 3683
Garber, Victor, 3678
Garcelon, Cherie, 1825
Garcetti, Eric, 388
Garcetti, Gil, 243, 388
Garcetti, Sukey, 388
Garcia, Angelo, 306
Garcia, Anne, 528
Garcia, Bo, 1581
Garcia, Brigitte, 329
Garcia, Carlos F., 729
Garcia, Dick, 1616
Garcia, Eugene E., 2161
Garcia, Francisco, 488
Garcia, Greg, 3330
Garcia, Guiomar, 660
Garcia, Jane, 138
Garcia, Juan Carlos, 2173
Garcia, Juan M., 260
Garcia, Juliet V., 2160
Garcia, Kristina, 999
Garcia, Marcela, 3312
Garcia, Ricardo, 3576
Garcia, Rosario, 3330
Garcia, Rosie, 43
Garcia, Sonja, 728
Garcia, Susan, 407
Garcia-Lathrop, Angie, 2524
Garcia-Tunon, Carlos, 2275
Gard, Christine Mary, 423
Gardey, Kim M., 1619
Gardiner, Becky, 419
Gardiner, Robert, 1514
Gardner Trust, A. Somers, 2148
Gardner, Cindy, 2322
Gardner, Denise, 982
Gardner, Edward T., III, 2705
Gardner, Emerson "Emo" N., Lt. Genl., 3468
Gardner, Frederick C., 1662
Gardner, George H., 2674
Gardner, Ginny, 3431
Gardner, J.B., 1192
Gardner, Jean, 3542
Gardner, Jill, 3542
Gardner, Lee H., 2705
Gardner, Lewis B., 2940
Gardner, Mahershall, 1146
Gardner, Peter J., 728
Gardner, Robert, 2835
Gardner, Robert, III, 2705
Gardner, Susanah A., 2705
Gardner, Timothy J., 623
Gardner, Warren, 591
Gardner-Goodno, Joan, 1705
Garen, Wendy, 359
Garey, Patrick, 2407
Garfield Trust, 2139
Garfield, Eugene, 2955
Garfield, Gary A., 3129
Garfield, Joshua, 2955
Garfield, Seth, 1453
Garfinkel, Barry H., 2427
Garfinkel, Steven, 1424
Gargan, Denise M, 3024
Gargaro, Eugene A., Jr., 1637
Gargiulo, Andrea, 1426
Garipoli, Rosemarie, 2101
Garland, Sheryl L., 3476
Garlanda, Victoria, 2436
Garlasco, Marc E., 2116
Garmey, Ronald, 2972, 3038
Garnett, Sandra, 530
Garniewski, John P., Jr., 3661
Garnsey, John, 543
Garofalo, John, 2655
Garofalow, Leigh, 2073
Garrett, Ezra, 367
Garrett, Jill, 349
Garrigan, Casey, 1851
Garriott, Helen, 2809
Garriott, Owen, 2809
Garris, Garry A., 2578
Garrison, Sandra L., 3268
Garrison, Susan, 3053
Garrison, Walter R., 3053
Garrity, Sheila, 3631
Garson, Palmer P., Mrs., 3470
Gart, Margie, 543
Garten, Jeffrey E., 550
Garth, Laura T., 1525
Garvin, Charles, Dr., 2733
Gary, Bob, 543
Gary, Leah S., 2760
Gary, Nancy, 526
Gary, Rob, 526
Gary, Samuel, 526
Garza, Alejandra, 1081
Garza, Danette, 1171
Garza, Nora, 484
Gasch, Daniel, 59
Gaskell, James, Dr., 2662
Gaskill, Joseph, 3030
Gaspar, Angie, 1045
Gass, Michelle, 3565
Gassman, Robert S., 2197
Gaston, Don, 2809
Gaston, Joe, 5
Gaston, Marilyn K., 1008
Gate Petroleum Company, 749
Gately, James, 3011
Gates Foundation, Bill and Melinda, 1971
Gates, Brad J., 877
Gates, Deborah, 3115
Gates, Janet G., 417
Gates, Jerry, 1176
Gates, John, 3405
Gates, K&L, 1568
Gates, Melinda French, 3516
Gates, Mimi Gardner, 2705, 3497
Gates, Moore, Jr., 1900
Gates, Nathan C., 417
Gates, Steven, 3370
Gates, William H. "Bill", III, 3516
Gates, William H., Sr., 3516
Gathers, Tom, 732
Gatins, Martin, 898
Gatins, Phillip, 898
Gattas, James, 3120
Gaucher, Harry S., 611
Gaudard, Cheryl, 1647
Gaudet, Caren Foisie, 610
Gaudet, Gregory H., 610
Gaudiani, Claire L., 2286
Gauldin, David T., II, 3429
Gault, Stanley C., 2740
Gauron, Paul R., 1518
Gause, Dick, 1135
Gaustad, Blaine, 1752
Gauthier, Kathryn "Kathy" L., 3468
Gautreau, David, 3014
Gavegnano, Richard, 1517
Gavegnano, Richard J., 1460
Gavin, Michael J., 2221
Gawande, Atul, 1538
Gay, Brigida C., 2126
Gay, Kevin, 1642
Gay, Tonee, 1848
Gayheart, Jack, 2707
Gayle, Helene D., 2390
Gaylord, Edith Kinney, 2811
Gaylord, Edward L., 2813
Gaylord, Thelma F., 2813
Gayner, Thomas S., 3433
Gaynor, Richard, 1204
Gazley, Martha, 2868
Gdovin, David, 2280
Gdowski, Tom, 1837
Gearen, John J., 1088

Geary, Bruce G., 2169
Geary, G. Stanton, 547
Geballe, Shelley, 1511
Gebbie, Marion B., 2170
Gebedou, Massie, 43
Geer, Sandy, 1214
Gegwich, Grant, 2932
Gehin-Scott, Gilbert A., 1986
Gehle, Misty, 3684
Geil, Gus, 2787
Geisenberger, Steve, 2981
Geiser, Jodi, 2675
Geisinger, Richard C., 764
Geismar, Ellen A., 3460
Geismar, Michael S., 3460
Geissler, Larry, 2733
Geithner, Peter, 667
Gelatt, Charles D., 3614
Gelatt, Daniel, 3614
Gelatt, Roberta K., 3614
Gelfand, Bertram, 1901
Geller, Alan, 1515
Geller, Maryana, 2465
Gellert, Annette, 214
Gellert, Carl, 215
Gellert, Celia Berta, 215
Gellert, Donald N., 2171
Gellert, Fred, 214
Gellert, Fred, Sr., 214
Gellert, G., 1957
Gellert, Gertrude E., 215
Gellert, Max E., 2171
Gellert, Robert J., 2171
Gelman 2001 Trust, Susan R., 1397
Gelman Charitable Lead Trust, Susan R., 1397
Gelman, Emmaia, 2441
Gelman, Felice, 2441
Gelman, Michael C., 1397
Gelman, Susan R., 1397
Gelman, Yoram, 2441
Geltzeiler, Michael S., 2336
Gelzer, Scott E., 3634
Gemma, Rick A., 2670
Gemuend, Markus, 216
Genco Masonry, Inc., 1381
GenCorp Foundation Inc., 2759
Genentech, 559
Genentech, Inc., 216, 365
General Atlantic Corp., 2048
General Atlantic Service Corp., 607
General Corporation, 3584
General Electric Foundation, 2407
General Mills, 952, 1743
General Mills, Inc., 1697
General Refractories Co., 3013
Genereux, Mark, 1226
Geneseo Lions Club, 1022
Genesis Endowment, 2173
Gengras Motor Cars, Inc., 580
Gengras, E. Clayton, Jr., 580
Gengras, Edith P., 580
Genn, Jonathan, 1376
Geno, Dennis R., 1652
Gentis, Laura, 1207
Gentsch, Richard A., 630
Gentzel, Tammy, 2909
Genuine Parts Co., 905
Genzyme Corp., 1988
Georgantas, Aristides, 1900
George, Alan, 3364
George, Alexander S., 3458
George, Armond R., 2253
George, Harry, III, 1358
George, Jeffrey Pilgram, 1698
George, Jonathan R., 1698
George, Penny Pilgram, 1698
George, Rick, 272
George, Robert P., 3601
George, Terrence R., 929
George, William W., 1698
Georgetown University, 2069
Georgia Medical Plan, Inc., 876
Georgia Power Co., 877
Georgia-Pacific Corp., 878
Gerace, John, 1487
Geraghty, Elisabeth, 981
Gerard, Anne, 2707
Gerard, Greg, Dr., 3119
Geras, Mary E., 2492
Gerber, Ann Rogers, 2012
Gerber, Daniel, 3051
Gerber, David, 1010
Gerber, Geoff, 2534
Gerber, Robert R., 2795
Gerbode, Frank A., 217
Gerbode, Sharon, 217
Gerdes, Stephanie, 1187
Geren, Pete, 3334
Gerene Furguson, 2009
Gerhard, Greg, 907
Gerhardt, Paul, 3488
Gerig, Kristina, 2662
Gerig, Stacey, 3316
Gering, William, 1357
Gerkin, Linda, 1184
Gerlach, Sue, 3662
Gerlock, Peg, 3555
Germ-Cramer, Kimberly, 2117
German, Deborah C., 712
German, Robert D., 2974
Germano, C. Dean, 138
Gernant, Michael L., 1022
Gerrard, Linda, 3587
Gerretse, Dale, 989
Gerry Foundation, 2111
Gersack, Jim, 3684
Gersh, Judah, 1832
Gershon, Elliot S., 960
Gershwind, Erik, 2174
Gerson, David, 2238
Gerspacher, Bill, 863
Gerstacker, Lisa J., 1653
Gerstenfeld, Donna, 676
Gerstle, Allan, 538
Gertmenian, Dennis, 137
Gerton, Jordan, 59
Gerwin, Naomi, 1415
Gery, Carolyn, 1130
Geske, Janine P., 3637
Gessner, Nancy, 2788
Getchell, Debra A., 1332
Gettens, James, 1512
Getter, Philip, 2499
Getty, Ariadne, 212
Getty, Gordon P., 218
Getty, John Paul, III, 212
Getty, William P., 2892
Getz, Jenifer, 2335
Getzinger, Karl, 2771
Geyelin, Erin, 1408
Gheens, C. Edwin, 1288
Ghelardi, Ellen Baker, 2886
Gherardi, Gai, 2043
Ghez, Ariana N., 2175
Ghez, Nomi P., 2175
GHF, Inc., 2952
Ghidinelli, Dan, 401
Ghidotti, Marian, 2558
Ghidotti, William, 2558
Gholston, J. Knox, 879
Ghubril, Saleem H., 2901
Ghuman, Minaski, 1187
Giacomin, Jon, 2677
Giammarino, Frank M., 1198
Gianelli, Mike, 425
Giangrasso, Chris, 2885
Gianninni, Julius, 154
Giannone, R. John, 3014
Giannuzzi, Donna, 714
Giant Eagle, Inc., 2889
Gibble, Mary, 1154
Gibbons, Christine, 2670
Gibbons, Lucia, 3055
Gibbons, Mary Jo, 1699
Gibbons, Miles J., Jr., 2501
Gibbs Die Casting Corp., 1167
Gibbs, Ellen Berland, 2161
Gibbs, James R., 416
Gibbs, Jason, 1241
Gibbs, Katie, 160
Gibbs, Sharon, 3099
Gibson, Becky, 1146
Gibson, Brian, 2348
Gibson, Cynthia D., 2021
Gibson, Dana, 1934
Gibson, Daniel, 2021
Gibson, Daniel F., 2021
Gibson, Donald, 2183
Gibson, Dunn & Crutcher LLP, 220
Gibson, Elizabeth A., 2021
Gibson, Frank B., Jr., 2599
Gibson, George C., 508
Gibson, Guy R., 371
Gibson, Harry, 1256
Gibson, Janell M., 2021
Gibson, Jayne, 1176
Gibson, Jennifer, 2021
Gibson, Jennifer L., 2021, 2091
Gibson, Jodie, 3315
Gibson, Joel T., 2021
Gibson, John F., 2021
Gibson, Lisa, 2686
Gibson, Mark, 3558
Gibson, Peter, 1934
Giddings, Paula, 2050
Gideon, Russ, 3364
Gidwani, Gita P., 2673
Gieck, Joe H., 3428
Gierach, Denice A., 1008
Giesel, William G., Jr., 2340
Gieske, Marguerite, 2784
Gietzen, Kenneth, 1584
Gifford, Helen G., 3440
Gifford, John K., 2113
Gifford, John, Mrs., 347
Gifford, Nanny G., 2936
Gifford, Rosamond, 2177
Giga, Aziz S., 3018
Gilb, Bob, 3502
Gilbert, Cal, 347, 397
Gilbert, Edward M., 2013
Gilbert, Jane, 2312
Gilbert, Jeffrey Z., 2312
Gilbert, Julanna V., 475
Gilbert, Louisa, 2312
Gilbert, Marion M., 2312
Gilbert, Roger, 2312
Gilbert, Samantha, 2160
Gilbert, Silvanus "Taco", Brig. Genl., 3468
Gilbert, William A., 1916, 3418
Gilbertsen, Jane, 3503
Gilbreath, Aimee, 201
Gilchrist Charitable Trust, Eric, 1245
Gilchrist, Alex, 1245
Gilchrist, Angus, 1245
Gildea, Scott, 2372
Gildred, Alison F., 381
Giles, Clark P., 3389, 3402
Giles, Jody, 1128
Giles, Patricia R., 925
Giles, Walter, 2161
Gilfillan, Christine Chambers, 1965
Gililland, Nancy, 1181
Gilkey, Glenn C., 3235
Gill, Barbara E., 2126
Gill, David M., 122
Gill, Eleanor, Dr., 1760
Gill, Elisabeth Childs, 559
Gill, James F., 2146
Gill, Phupinder, 984
Gill, Richard H., 22
Gill, Tim, 502
Gillen, Arlene, 1660
Gillen, Rex, 1660
Gillenwater, Bill, 1128
Gillepsie, Michael R., 2952
Giller, Yvette Birch, 335
Gillespie, Allan, 3561
Gillespie, Deborah, 1040
Gillespie, Lee Day, Mrs., 629
Gillespie, Nicole, Dr., 1955
Gillespie, Patrick B., 2975
Gillespie, Thomas D., 3464
Gillete, Gordon L., 830
Gillett, George, Jr., 543
Gilliam, Art, 3120
Gilliam, Franklin D., Jr., 114
Gilliam, Theopolis, 3441
Gilliam, Thomas, 2317
Gilliard, Michelle, 74
Gilliatt, Barbara, 1184
Gilligan, Edward P., 2034
Gilligan, Ellen M., 3637
Gilligan, Michael, 2286
Gilliland, Steve A., 1155
Gillingham, Todd, 3662
Gillis, Marjorie Bussmann, 595
Gillis, Neil J., 328
Gillmore, Travis W., 539
Gillotti, James, Esq., 3031
Gillum, Ira, 3299
Gillum, Roderick D., 1628
Gilman, Charles, III, 2178
Gilman, Martha S., 630
Gilmartin, James A., 2893
Gilmer, Emily, 3300
Gilmer, Stuart, 3300
Gilmore, Columbus, 904
Gilmore, Elizabeth Burke, 2306
Gilmore, Irving S., 1612
Gilmore, Jon, 1201
Gilmore, Robert, 2306
Gilmore, Scott, 498
Gilmore, Stacie, 498
Gilmore, William G., 221
Gilmore, William G., Mrs., 221
Gilmour, Allan D., 1588
Gilmour, Davie Jane, 2947
Giloth, Bob, 1353
Gilpin, Eddie, 1257
Gilreath, Perry, 3099
Gilsdorf, James R., 485
Gilson, Randy, 1856
Giltner, Thomas R., 3167

Gilweit, Martha Stout, 1872
Gimbel, Alva B., 2179
Gimbel, Bernard F., 2179
Gimbel, Leslie, 2179
Gimbel, Thomas S.T., 2179
Gimon, Eric, 248
Gimprich, Marvin, 2180
Gin, Julia, 1064
Gindi, Abraham, 2089
Gindi, Raymond, 2089
Gindi, Sam, 2089
Giner, A. Silvana, 1509, 1563
Gingerich, Dennis, Pastor, 714
Ginn, Alexander, 2706
Ginn, Ann L., 2706
Ginn, Janet K., 727
Ginn, Mary C., 2706
Ginn, Scott, 1305
Ginn, Walter P., 2706
Ginsberg, Gary L., 2466
Ginsberg, Judith, 2320
Ginsberg, Sonny, 1068
Ginsberg, Winston, 2473
Ginsburg, Violet, 386
Ginwright, Shawn A., 138
Gioia, Robert D., 2340
Giordano, Donna, 543
Giordano, Paul, 676
Giornelli, Lillian C., 917
Gipe, Dagmar Dunn Pickens, Mrs., 3216
Gipson, Carlton, 3511
Gipson, Fred, 2828
Gipson, Scott, 953
Girard, Judy, 1314
Girard, Linda McKinley, 2874
Girard, Patrick, 1549
Giron-Gordon, Terri, 2006
Giroux, Anne, 1636
Gislason, Jim, 1128
Gispanski, Thomas, 756
Gittell, Jody Hoffer, 1883
Giustini, Lou, 1360
Given, Stan, 725
Givens, Archie, Jr., 1717
Givens, Sarah K., 3121
Glab, Charlie, 1216
Glaceau, 37
Gladden, Gordon D., 1378
Gladden, Thomas, 3054
Gladish, Nina, 307
Gladson, Larry, 1228
Glaeser, Edward, 3516
Glance HR LLC, 797
Glancy, Alfred R., III, 1588
Glarner, Terrence, 1722
Glaros, Matthew, 1171
Glascock, Stephen L., 3094
Glaser, Barbara Linell, 2027
Glaser, D.J., 1257
Glaser, John, 3604
Glaser, Jonathan, 287
Glaser, Robert D., 3517
Glasgow Trust, Arthur, 3476
Glass, Kenneth E., 2559
Glass, Kerri, 581
Glass, Marybeth, 2825
Glass, Michael, 1589
Glass, Nancy J., 2559
Glasscock, J. Samuel, 3467
Glassman, Jeffrey, 451
Glassman, Jennifer, 2473
Glassman, Robert A., 1461
Glatfelter Charitable Lead Trust, Anne M., 2956
Glatfelter, Elizabeth, 2956
Glatt, Jordan, 1998
Glaub, Joseph, 3579
Glaxo Wellcome Americas Inc., 2600
GlaxoSmithKline Holdings (Americas) Inc., 2600
GlaxoSmithKline LLC F.K.A. SmithKline, 2957
Glazer, Avie, 750
Glazer, Bradford A., 1311
Glazer, Bryan, 750
Glazer, Edward, 750
Glazer, Jerome S., 1311
Glazer, Joel, 750
Glazer, Kevin, 750
Glazer, Margot, 775
Glazer, Shari Arison, 691
Gleaser, Mitch, 725
Gleason, James S., 224
Gleason, Janis F., 224
Gleason, Marty, 1227
Gleason, Nancy, 2170
Gleason, Todd R., 1727
Gleason, Tracy R., 224
Gleeson, Patrick, 340
Gleick, James, 692
Gleim, Sandy, 1201
Glen, John Fitten, 882
Glen, Molly K.D., 1861
Glen, Nancy J., 2952
Glenmede Trust Company, The, 2799
Glenn, Alston, 882
Glenn, Anne, 882
Glenn, Bernadette, 461
Glenn, Carrie Eugenia, 2560
Glenn, Jack, 882
Glenn, L., 2831
Glenn, Lee, 1852
Glenn, Lena Viola, 2560
Glenn, Lewis, 882
Glenn, Paul F., 225
Glenn, Robert, 882
Glenn, William D., 430
Glennon, Cathie, 2868
Glennon, Lauren Foisie, 610
Glick, Alvin L., 1574
Glick, Barry J., 1574
Glick, Carlton L., 1574
Glick, Eugene B., 1150
Glick, Jerrold L., 528
Glick, Marianne, 1126, 1150
Glick, Marilyn K., 1150
Glick, Nancy, 1083
Glick, Randal L., 1574
Glickstein, Alon, 158
Glide, Katrina D., 226
Glinn, Jim, 393
Global Leadership Foundation, 2399
Globe Oil and Refining Companies, 1725
Glosser, Daniel, 2922
Glosser, William L., Esq., 2922
Glover, Gordon, 1549
Gluck, Frederick W., 394
Gluck, Maxwell H., 227
Glyn, David R., 2961
Glynn, Christopher, 988
Godchaux, Justin A., 912
Goddard Trust, Adele H., 783
Goddard, Robert C., 905
Goddard, Teri, 490
Goddard, William R., Jr., 2822
Godeke, Steven, 2335
Godet, Eric, 725
Godfrey Jr. Charitable Lead Trust, D., 3618
Godfrey, Constance P., 3618
Godfrey, Dudley J., Jr., 3618
Godfrey, Gene, 886
Godlewski, Linda, 1093
Godley, Betty, 2088
Godsey, R. Kirby, 850
Godsil, Raymond D. (Tad), III, 1726
Godward, William W., 197
Goebel, 3505
Goedde, Bill, 1128
Goergen, B.J., 3330
Goeser, Greg, 58
Goettler, Ralph H., 2883
Goff, Laura, 309
Goff, Marcia, 2773
Goff, Phyllis, 1715
Goff, Robert A., 122
Goff, Stacey, 627
Gofrank, Shirley E., 1589
Goggans, Tommie J., III, 9
Goins, Charlynn, 2325
Goizueta, Javier C., 883
Goizueta, Roberto C., 883
Goizueta, Roberto S., 883
Gold Canyon Candle, 58
Gold, Dave, 229
Gold, David, 229
Gold, David B., 228
Gold, Elaine, 228
Gold, Emily, 228
Gold, Howard, 229
Gold, Jeff, 229
Gold, Judith, 2000
Gold, Katherine, 528
Gold, Sherry, 229
Gold, Sophia, 497
Gold, Steven A., 228
Gold-Bubier, Diane, 228
Gold-Lurie, Barbara, 228
Goldberg, Alan E., 2414
Goldberg, Avram J., 1421
Goldberg, Bradley, 2039
Goldberg, Brooke, 1311
Goldberg, Carol R., 1421
Goldberg, Ellen, 2301
Goldberg, Evan, 1311
Goldberg, Ira, 2044
Goldberg, Jay, 1729
Goldberg, Jay B., 2358
Goldberg, Jerome, 1327
Goldberg, Jordon, 3424
Goldberg, Kim Glazer, 1311
Goldberg, Miriam P., 2414
Goldberg, Robert, 1962
Goldberger, Leah, 2260
Golde, Helmut, 3546
Golden State Foods Corp., 235
Golden, Adolph, 2686
Golden, Alanna, 1097
Golden, Andrew K., 1979
Golden, Bradley, 1613
Golden, Donald L., 1613
Golden, James R., 3487
Golden, Joanne, 1647
Golden, Jonathan, 893
Golden, Kenneth M., 369
Golden, Marion, 1613
Golden, Michael, 893, 1613
Golden, Olivia, 2191
Golden, Randal E., 1613
Golden, Richard S., 1613
Golden, Sam, 3245
Golden, Web, 1256
Goldenburg, Blanche, 2460
Goldfarb, Allan, 3312
Goldhirsh Foundation, 658
Goldin, Claudia Brett, 476
Goldman 1997 Charitable Lead Annuity Trust, Richard, 1397
Goldman Charitable Trust, Sol, The, 2181
Goldman Children Trust, 2182
Goldman Fund, Richard and Rhoda, 1397
Goldman Grandchildren Trust, 2182
Goldman Sachs & Co., 970
Goldman, Dan, 2850
Goldman, Dorian, 2182
Goldman, Dorothy Tapper, 2194
Goldman, Herman, 2183
Goldman, Katja, 2182
Goldman, Kenneth J., 2385
Goldman, Lloyd, 2182
Goldman, Roger A., 552
Goldman, Sol, 2181
Goldner, Brian, 3077
Goldsberry, Yvonne, 1883
Goldsbury Charitable Trust, 3241
Goldsbury, Angela Aboltin, 3241
Goldsbury, Christopher, Jr., 3241
Goldschmidt, David M., 91
Goldseker, Ana, 1374
Goldseker, Deby, 1374
Goldseker, Morris, 1374
Goldseker, Sharna, 1374, 2074
Goldseker, Sheldon, 1374
Goldseker, Simon, 1374
Goldsmith, Donald A., 2181
Goldsmith, Harriet, 3099
Goldsmith, Harry, 3120
Goldsmith, Marcia, 2237
Goldstein, Albert, 3600
Goldstein, Charles A., 2238
Goldstein, Dorothy L., 2184
Goldstein, Eugene S., 3072
Goldstein, George S., 260
Goldstein, Jerome, 2184
Goldstein, Jerome R., 2184
Goldstein, Larry M., 3072
Goldstein, Merle F., 3072
Goldstein, Merle R., 3072
Goldstein, Michael L., 2183
Goldstein, Robert, 1314, 1472
Goldstein, Shephard, 1459
Goldstein, Stanley P., 3072
Goldstone, Elizabeth, 581
Goldstone, Steven F., 581
Goldy, Susan, 2324
Golf Tournament, 1483
Golichowski, Shirley, 1197
Golick, Ed, 1589
Golisano, B. Thomas, 2185
Golla, Clare, 1068
Golsby, Stephen W., 1039
Golson, William T., 498
Golston, Allan C., 3516
Gomby, Deanna, 245
Gomer, Adelaide P., 2349
Gomer, Brian D., 714
Gomez, Elizabeth M., 140
Gomez, Iris, 1486
Gomez, Jorge, 2677
Gomez, Ralph, 3196
Gomez, Victor, 1662
Gompers, Edward, 3579
Goncz, Edward J., 2937
Gonella, Carol, 1822
Gonnason, Jeff, 33
Gonter, Alex, 2151

Gonter, Joel, 2151
Gonter, Mark, 2151
Gonter, Neil, 2151
Gonter, Shlomo, 2151
Gonya, Jeffrey K., 1398
Gonz, Marena, 2221
Gonzales, Alberto R., Hon., 3129
Gonzales, Carmen, 3397
Gonzales, Douglas M., 1300
Gonzales, Judith, 1783
Gonzales, Nancy, 2191
Gonzalez, Alexander, 523
Gonzalez, Fernando, 159
Gonzalez, Jerry, 911, 2521
Gonzalez, Jose D., 3129
Gonzalez, Leni, 3421
Gonzalez, M. Lorena, 1722
Gonzalez, Maria, 1607
Gonzalez, Martha, 964
Gonzalez, Paola, 153
Gonzalez, Robert, 3291
Gonzalez, Robert J., Jr., 3291
Gonzalez, Shirley, 3291
Gonzalez, Will, 3051
Gonzalez-Falla, Celso M., 2178
Gonzalez-Falla, Sondra Gilman, 2178
Gonzalez-Mares, Elba, 340
Good Works Foundation, 2043
Good, Jon, 3099
Goodale, Jennifer P., 2477
Goodall, Amos, 2909
Gooden, Jerald B., 550
Goodey, Elodie Grant, 3181
Goodfellow, Charles C., 1909
Goodhardt, William A., 1388
Goodheart, Carol, 2526
Goodlatte, Maryellen, 3432
Goodman, Anne, 2770
Goodman, Carroll R., 3358
Goodman, Charles, 997
Goodman, Debra, 1578
Goodman, Dobert, 1902
Goodman, George J.W., 2050
Goodman, Jay, 3579
Goodman, John, 3518
Goodman, John A., 3518
Goodman, Kathy, 2733
Goodman, Leslie, 181
Goodman, Shawn, 3518
Goodman, Steven, 3256
Goodman, William R., III, 5
Goodnow, Charles, 1586
Goodrich Corp., 2561
Goodrich, Alexandra D., 13
Goodrich, Dennett W., 570
Goodrich, Gillian G., 13
Goodrich, Gillian W., 13
Goodrich, John A., 570
Goodrich, Marcia, 999
Goodrich, Mary B., 13
Goodrich, Ramsey W., 570
Goodrich, T. Michael, 13
Goodrich, T. Michael, II, 13
Goodson, Lief, 715
Goodson, Lief G., 715
Goodwin, Charles S., 1895
Goodwin, Linda, 2900
Goodwin, Peter, 2288
Google Inc., 231
Gooley, Richard, 3179
Goolsby, Allen C., III, 3474
Goorhouse, Mike, 1591
Gooss, Henry E., 2191
Gopalakrishnan, Adoor, 176
Gordan, Reginald E., Esq., 3476
Gorder, Charles F., 211
Gordijn, Peggy, 2038
Gordis, Jonathan, 2827
Gordis, Yonatan, Rabbi, 2827
Gordon Food Service Inc., 1610
Gordon, C. Scott, 2912
Gordon, Catherine Hutto, 258
Gordon, Christina M., 1475
Gordon, Courtney P., 2362
Gordon, David W., 405
Gordon, Elizabeth, 724
Gordon, Gail, 2326
Gordon, H. Don, 2896
Gordon, Hunter R., 2912
Gordon, James, 1268
Gordon, James D., 1610
Gordon, Jeff, Inc., 2562
Gordon, Jeffrey M., 2562
Gordon, Joel C., 3129
Gordon, John M., Jr., 1610
Gordon, Joseph K., 2912
Gordon, Josh, 2664
Gordon, Leila, 2912
Gordon, Lynn, 1166
Gordon, Michael, 290
Gordon, Michael S., 1475
Gordon, T. Duane, 2737
Gordon, Thomas J., 2793
Gordon, Wendy, 2389
Gordon, William C., 79
Gore, Cecelia, 3637
Goreham, Lucy, 1552
Gorelick, Jamie S., 1056
Goren, Nicky, 672
Goren, Paul, 348
Gorham, Mark, 2006
Gorham, Pat, 1703
Gorham, William, 373
Gorish, Frances M., 2495
Gorman, Christopher M., 2717
Gorman, Paul, 1735
Gormley, AnnChristine, 557
Gorovitz, Aaron, 724
Gorrie, Thomas M., 1949
Gorrissen, Nina M., 2250
Gorton, Slade, Sen., 2290
Gorzelanczyk, David, 2674
Gosch, Beth Kinsman, 2503
Goshgarian, Gerard, 1031
Goslee, Charles G., 1359
Gosnell, Jerry, 1587
Goss, Ann C., 3392
Goss, Ann Coit, 2841
Goss, Mary Jo, 2664
Gosselink, Julie, 1210
Gossett, John, 351
Gossett, Lyn, 351
Gostley-Hackett, Laurie, 2982
Goto, Greta L., 31
Gottesman Foundation, D.S. and R.H., 3071
Gottieb, Jaquelin, 876
Gottlieb, Adolph, 2187
Gottlieb, Art, 236
Gottlieb, Esther, 2187
Gottlieb, Lisa, 235
Gottschalk, Dinah, 3429
Gottschalk, Evan, 1180
Goudie, Mary, 659
Gough, Richard, 1135
Gough, Tom, 2109
Goughnour, Sam, 3589
Gould, Anna, 1476
Gould, Clara Lou, 2113
Gould, Donna R., 1477
Gould, Frederick Beau, 3545
Gould, Jason, 428
Gould, Joel, 1477
Gould, John W., 3000
Gould, Julie, 3545
Gould, Matthew, 1477
Gould, Michael, 676
Gould, Russ, 138
Gould, Russell S., 156
Govan, J. Gardner, 3618
Gow, Robert, 1657
Goward, Abigail, 2524
Gowen, H., II, 3521
Gowen, Herbert, 3521
Gowen, Laura, 3521
Gowen, Louisa, 3521
Gowen, William C., 3521
Goyins, Yvonne, 2005
Grabell, Neal, 2958
Graber, Richard W., 3601
Graber, Rick, 3627
Graber, Samuel W., 3292
Grabois, Neil R., 2237
Grabow, Raymond J., 2670
Grabowski, Debra S., 1885
Grabowski, Gary G., 3639
Grace Charitable Lea Ann Trust, Ann K., 46
Grace, Barb, 46
Grace, Charles B., III, 2479
Grace, Ellen D., 1747
Grace, Howard T., 46
Grace, Matt, 46
Grace, Mike, 159
Grade, Donald L., 3620
Gradert, Diana, 1217
Gradient, 1388
Grady, Caroline B., 705
Grady, Graham C., 1018
Grady, Jo Anne, 1849
Graebner, Nancy, 1584
Grafa, Trey, 3316
Graff, Jacob, 334
Graff, Kathleen, 3031
Graff, Nicole Bartner, 696
Graff, Pnina, 334
Grafman, Laura R., 57
Grafstein, Bernice, 232
Graham Marital Trust, Allen J., 3103
Graham, Allen J., 3103
Graham, Baxter, 1998
Graham, Carolyn, 1
Graham, Charles, 2185
Graham, Christine Vaughn, 3457
Graham, Daryl A., 630
Graham, Donald E., 663, 673
Graham, Garth, 550
Graham, John, 2604
Graham, John J., 1299
Graham, Katharine Meyer, 663
Graham, Kathryn G., 2345
Graham, Ken, 3259
Graham, Kerry, 3129
Graham, Leo, 401
Graham, Malcolm C., 2628
Graham, Mary, 673, 1056
Graham, Robert C., Jr., 2345
Graham, Robert H., 847
Graham, Robert M., 439
Graham, Ted, 2733
Graham, Terry, Ed.D., 9
Graham, William L., 3419
Grainger, David W., 1024
Grainger, Hally W., 1024
Grainger, William W., 1024
Gramshammer, Sheika, 543
Granahan, Laura, 1549
Grand Valley State University, 2069
Grand View Hospital, 3377
Grand, Debra L., 1061
Grande, Arlene, 1150
Grande, Thomas J., 1150
Grandell Rehabilitation, 2254, 2255
Grandinetti, Francis, 3042
Grandon, Carleen, 1222
Grandsand LLC, 2703
Grandt, Ken, 1837
Grandy, Edith G., 3449
Granger Associates, Inc., 1617
Granger Construction Co., 1617
Granger, Alton L., 1617
Granger, Donna, 1617
Granger, Janice, 1617
Granger, Jerry P., 1617
Granger, L. Keith, 7
Granger, Lynne, 1617
Granger, Ronald K., 1617
Granger, Stephen, 1471
Granholm, Gundrun, 2868
Granite Construction Co., 102
Grant Makers in Health, 3510
Grant Thornton LLP, 1026
Grant, A.J., 26
Grant, Celia, 1449
Grant, Chad, 3287
Grant, Dick, 3321
Grant, Doug, 351
Grant, Katharine R., 911
Grant, Kenneth, 1030
Grant, Leslie E., 1459
Grant, Mary D., 2190
Grant, Michael, 911
Grant, Sandy, 351
Grant, Stanley J. "Bud", 2167
Grant, Suzanne B., 637
Grant, William T., 2191
Grantmakers in Health, 2011
Granville, William "Billy", III, 3338
Grass Instrument Co., 232
Grass, Albert M., 232
Grass, Edgar, 1988
Grass, Ellen R., 232
Grass, Gayle C., 3549
Grass, Henry J., 232
Grassham, Jennifer, 2014
Grassi and Co., 2228
Grassi, Anthony P., 2081
Grassilli, Robert J., 215
Grasso, Richard, 2445
Grata, Mel, 2925
Gratopp, William C., 1590
Graunke, James, 363
Graunke, Terence M., 1060
Gravagno, Carole Haas, 3045
Gravatte, Trice, 3464
Graven, Irene C., 2475
Graver, Mark, 1141
Graves, Lary, 1198
Gravett, Guy M., 3461
Gravin, Jennifer, 655
Gravina, Amy, 708
Grawcock, Arthur, 1179
Gray, Barry A., Dr., 711
Gray, Barry A., Mrs., 711
Gray, Carolyn B., 2116
Gray, Christy E., 1820

Gray, Cindy, 1877
Gray, David, 711, 2515
Gray, Deborah Songer, 3577
Gray, Edward W.T., III, 2116
Gray, Frank T., 1411
Gray, Gretchen, 711
Gray, Harry B., 105
Gray, Herman B., 1666
Gray, Joseph, 711
Gray, Kathleen M., 2116
Gray, Laman A., Jr., Dr., 1288
Gray, Lucile J., 484
Gray, Marjorie S., 3352
Gray, Mark, 2071
Gray, Melanie, 3266
Gray, Paul, 333
Gray, Pearl, 162
Gray, Peter G., 2116
Gray, Robert, 711
Gray, Susan, 1464
Gray, Susanne, 1783
Gray, Taylor T., 2116
Gray, Thomas H., 819
Graybill, Cathryn Hunt, 2971
Grayson, Pegine, 269
Graziano, Robert V., 287
Great Lakes Higher Education Guaranty Corporation, 3118
Great Plains Natural Gas Co., 2652
Greatbatch, Ami, 2147
Greatbatch, Eleanor, 2147
Greatbatch, Tommie, 2147
Greatbatch, Warren, 2147
Greatbatch, Warren D., 2147
Greater New Orleans Foundation, 2368
Greathead, R. Scott, 2443
Greaves, Maryon, 162
Grebe, Michael W., 3601
Greco, Chris, 3648
Greco, Lois W., 3055
Greed, John R., 2317
Greehey, William E., 3307
Green Corporation, Joshua, 3521
Green Unitrust, G.M., 47
Green, Allan, 2233
Green, Allen P., 1790
Green, Arthur, 3017
Green, Brenda, 2840
Green, Carrie, 3568
Green, Cathy Obriotti, 3387
Green, Cecilia, 693
Green, Charles, 823
Green, Edith D., 3394
Green, Eleanor F., 2407
Green, George Mason, 47
Green, Georgie F., 1296
Green, Jasem, 3422
Green, Jennifer D., 30
Green, Josephine B., 1790
Green, Joshua, 3521
Green, Joshua, III, 3521
Green, Joshua, Mrs., 3521
Green, Karen R., 2986
Green, Kimberly, 751
Green, Lisa, 1930
Green, Lois C., 47
Green, Myra, 1459
Green, Nancy R., 2067
Green, Norman H., 162
Green, Richard C., 1793
Green, Rifka, 2255
Green, Steven J., 751
Green, Val A., 3394
Green, Val J., 3394
Greenawalt, W. Eileen, 475
Greenbaum, Robin, 1939
Greenberg, Allen, 1833
Greenberg, Alva G., 2179
Greenberg, Barbara R., 2385
Greenberg, Evan, 2880
Greenberg, Filomena M. D'Agostino, 2124
Greenberg, Irving "Yitz", Rabbi, 1479
Greenberg, Kenneth, 789
Greenberg, Michael, 789
Greenberg, Robert M., 3171
Greenberg, Roger, 789
Greenberg, Spencer, 2179
Greenberg, Stephen D., 2179
Greenblatt, Lewis, 92
Greenburg, Harry, 752
Greene, Arthur B., 1333, 2055
Greene, Christopher T., 2120
Greene, Donald J., 1449
Greene, Gayle, 160
Greene, Kim, 783
Greene, Lora, 1587
Greene, Michelle D., 2336
Greene, Paul F., 1501
Greene, Roger W., 1512
Greene, Steve, 2539
Greene, Trevor, 3502
Greene, Wade, 2477
Greenebaum, Mary Z., 2325
Greener, Sharon S., 1770
Greenfield, Janet, 633
Greenfield, Jerry, 3407
Greenhaven Assocs., 2489
Greenheck Marital Trust, Bernard A., 3620
Greenheck Survivor's Trust, Esther M., 3620
Greenhouse, Howard L., 3471
Greening, Ron, 3193
Greenlee, Amanda Link, 1762
Greenlight Capital, 2173
GreenPoint Bank, 3426
Greenslade, Mary Beth, 3104
Greenstreet, Yvonne, 3516
Greenup, Marion, 2423
Greenwall, Anna A., 2192
Greenwall, Frank K., 2192
Greenway, Hugh, 378
Greenwood Gardens, Inc., 1991
Greenwood, John T., 1022
Greer, Donna, 3269
Greer, Gayle, 488
Greer, Jack, 2680
Greer, Lucie C., 1752
Greer, Robert, 3591
Grefenstette, C.G., 2969
Greger, Ray, 312
Gregg, Bill, 1715
Gregg, Jason, 811
Gregg, Jody A., 1149
Gregg, Simon, 811
Gregg, Virginia C., 2108
Gregoria, Ric, 798
Gregorian, Lisa, 2466
Gregorian, Vartan, 2085
Gregory, C.E., III, 893
Gregory, Charles, 893
Gregory, Mary, 430
Gregory, Paul S., 1275
Gregory, R. Frederick, 3357
Gregory, Robert E., Jr., 3110
Gregory, Robert W., Jr., 482
Gregory, Susan, 2961
Gregory, Theophilus, 492
Gregory, Todd, 1662
Gregurich, Doug, 1182
Greifeld, Robert, 1401
Greig, Jerome "Jerry", 1302
Greig, Jim, 1154
Greiman, Soo, 1221
Grein, Thomas W., 1204
Greiner, Amy, 1207
Greiner, Jessica, 33
Greiner, John T., Jr., 2811
Greiner, Jola, 3494
Greiner, Julie, 2726
Greiner, Lindsay, 1225
Greisbaum, Kathy, 27
Greisgraber, Stephen, 2049
Greissing, Edward, 2167
Gremer, John, 1109
Gremore, Marie, 3641
Grenon, David, 1471
Grenrock, Gwyn L., 80
Gresham, Tom, 1760
Greshik, Joan, 1753
Grew Trust, Alma, 1478
Grey, Alex, 2043
Grey, Elizabeth Pardoe, 1522
Grey, Peter, 41
Greyhavens, Timothy, 3572
Greystone Funding Corp., 910
Grice, Cheryl, 1268
Gridley, William G., Jr., 559, 2408
Griege, Charles W., Jr., 3349
Griego, Linda, 357
Griego, Linda M., 359
Grier, Richard L., 3476
Grier, Rosey, 331
Griesbaum, Kathy, 27
Griesmer, Jim, 488
Griff, Christine, 2354
Griffey, Romey, 1290
Griffin, Beatrice C., 504
Griffin, Carl R., III, 1343
Griffin, Clarence A., 2563
Griffin, Clarence A., III, 2563
Griffin, Cynthia, 2868
Griffin, Danice C., 3648
Griffin, Elizabeth S., 2563
Griffin, Haynes G., 2563
Griffin, James, 3591
Griffin, Janet, 1246
Griffin, Jeffrey, 2563
Griffin, Katherine, 1178
Griffin, Pat, 504
Griffin, Sharon, 592
Griffin, Susan S., 3464
Griffinger, Theodore, 120
Griffith, H. Ronald, 1623
Griffith, John D., 1744
Griffith, Lawrence S.C., 2454
Griffith, R. Riggs, 2909
Griffiths, Kathleen, 1584
Griffiths, Paul "Stoney", III, 3044
Griggs, Denise M., 2740
Griglun, Thomas, 591
Grigsby, L. Lane, 1312
Grigsby, Peter, 1184
Grigsby, Todd William, 1312
Grill, Michael E., Dr., 1168
Grim, Arthur, 3059
Grim, Lawrence, Esq., 2900
Grimaldi, Joseph, 1464
Grimes, Anne W., 3185
Grimes, Connie, 2924
Grimes, Kelly, 2909
Grimes, Kim, 2924
Grimes, Kirk, 3235
Grimes, Michael, 1687
Grimes, Patti, 1373
Grimm, M. Sandlin, 700
Grimm, Valerie, 562
Grinspoon, Harold, 1479
Grinspoon, Winnie Sandler, 1479
Grissett, David, 2809
Grissom, S.L., 1053
Griswold, Scott A., 338
Grizzard, Robert, Jr., 3441
Grobman, Linda, 3056
Grodd, Barbara, 2344
Grodd, James, 2344
Groff, Mary E., 2960
Groff, Michael, 953
Groff, Peter, 360
Grogan, Ed, 3567
Grohs, Courtney, 3431
Grolier Club, 2069
Groll, Matthew A., 2883
Gropper, Mark, 3552
Grose, George R., 1388
Grose, Peter, 1388
Gross Irrevocable Trust, Meta G., 3076
Gross Trust, Rosalind, 583
Gross Trust, Virginia Fay, 3207
Gross Unitrust, Rosalind, 583
Gross, Arye, 162
Gross, Chaim, 2193
Gross, Charles H., 1634
Gross, Cynthia Squires, 62
Gross, Daniel, 2193
Gross, Daniel L., 139
Gross, Dov, 2193
Gross, Esther, 2193
Gross, Faigie, 2193
Gross, Gaila, 2829
Gross, Gregory S., 1083
Gross, Jody, 3401
Gross, Malcolm J., 3049
Gross, Pamela, 3555
Gross, Patrick W., 666
Gross, Pinchus, 2193
Gross, Pincus, 2193
Gross, Richard F., Dr., 1529
Gross, Steve, 441
Gross, Steven, 2188
Grossklaus, Charlie, 3611
Grossman, Adam D., 2827
Grossman, Daniel, 385
Grossman, Elizabeth Rice, 933
Grossman, Jay, 1412
Grossman, Jerome K., 637
Grossman, Nancy, 2408
Grossman, Pamela, 674, 1098
Grossman, Thomas, 3401
Groswold, Jerry, 503
Grote, Matthew, 1068
Grotemeyer, Kathy, 537
Grotke, Adam, 3480
Grout, Melinda, 3511
Grove, Jane, 1135
Grover, Jeff, 425
Groves, Anne, 1508
Groves, Bradford, 2767
Groves, Doug, 3193
Grubb, Kristen, 1724
Gruebele, Martin, 59
Gruel, John, 1623
Gruen, Julia, 2203
Gruening, Clark, 35
Grulke, Kara, 1587
Grumbach, Antonia M., 2504

Grumbacher, M.S., 2961
Grumbacher, Mary Jo, 2961
Grundfest, Julianne D., 71
Grundy, Joseph R., 2962
Gruss Settlor Trust, Joseph S., 753
Gruss Trust, Joseph S., 753
Gruss, Audrey B., 753
Gruss, Jean Fraser, 3155
Gruss, Martin D., 753
Gryphon International Growth, 3642
GTA Containers Inc, 1165
Guard, SuzanneClair, 2408
Guardian Protection Services, Inc., 3032
Guarnieri, Philip, 2111
Guastaferro, John, 83
Gudas, Elysia M., 2107
Gudas, Viki, 1657
Gudelsky, John, 1376
Gudelsky, Medda, 1376
Guelfi, Hillary Hedinger, 2849
Guernsey, Helen, 1221
Guernsey, Max E., 1221
Guerra, Fernando, Dr., 3341
Guerra, Lucas H., 1486
Guerrero, Ana, 2749
Guerrero, George, 492
Guertin, Pierre, 608
Guess, Francis, 3129
Guess, Mark, 2707
Guessoum, Nidhal, 3047
Guest, Richard L., 2919
Guest, Sandra M., 1768
Guethle, Kenneth, 1814
Guevara, Zac, 138
Guggenheim, Simon, 2194
Guggenheim, Simon, Mrs., 2194
Guggenhime, Andrew, 289
Guggenhime, Richard J., 289
Guglielmo, D. Anthony, 595
Guiabo, Paul L., 2516
Guiabo, Renee C., 2516
Guido, Patrick, 2642
Guidry, David, 1299
Guidugli, John J., 2710
Guilander f/b/o Trust, Robert M., 1791
Guilander, Robert, 1791
Guilarte, E. Andres, 807
Guilarte, Olga, 807
Guild, Alice F., 928
Guilford, Zeke, 729
Guill, Ernie T., Jr., 3454
Guillaume, Gabriel, 477
Guillies, Wendy, 1797
Guine, Joyce Davis, 368
Guinn, Linda A., 161
Gulbrandsen, Mary W., 3617
Gulick, Alice J., 2693
Gulick, Amy, 26
Gulick, Henry W., 2693
Gulick, Robin C., 3464
Gullen, David J., 44
Gulley, Philip G., 3044
Gulmi, James S., 3129
Gumbiner, Alis, 236
Gumbiner, Burke, 236
Gumbiner, Josephine S., 236
Gumbiner, Lee, 236
Gumness, Brian, 3620
Gumness, Sandra L., 3620
Gund, Ann L., 2708
Gund, Catherine, 2708
Gund, Geoffrey, 2708
Gund, George, 2708
Gund, George, III, 295
Gund, George, IV, 295, 2708
Gund, Zachary, 2708
Gundlach, Andrew, 2165, 2250
Gundlach, Roger, 2773
Gunkel, Alan, 1207
Gunn, Gail, 3430
Gunning, Thomas J., 1517
Gunsteens, Anne, 1390
Gunstone, Lauren, 1861
Gunter, Linda Hays, 3295
Gunzberg, Joan, 1012
Guon, Jane M., 355
Gupta, Ajay, 1969
Gupta, Ankur, 1969
Gupta, Nutan, 1969
Gupta, Pratima, 680
Gupta, Rakesh, 2541
Gupta, Sarita, 2139
Gupta, Saurabh, 488
Gurecky, Joe, 3245
Guren, Adam M., 2711
Guren, Debra Hershey, 2711
Gurieva, Diana M., 2038
Gurrado, Jerry, 1180
Gurwin, Eric, 2195
Gurwin, Joseph, 2195
Gushman, Richard W., II, 933
Gustafson, Mike, 1828
Gustawes, Todd, 272
Gustin, Marie, 585
Guterman, Stuart, 2106
Gutfleish, Ron, 2196
Gutfleish, Stacey, 2196
Guth, Jeremy, 2511
Guthman, Jack, 1009
Guthman, Sandra P., 1075
Guthrie, Carlton L., 1040
Guthrie, Sandra, 3054
Guthy, William R., 237
Gutierrez, Julie Weaks, 2006
Gutierrez, Laura F., 1003
Gutmann, Michael E., 2763
Gutterman, Leslie, 3062
Guttman, Charles, 2197
Guttman, Stella, 2197
Guttridge, Nicholas, 913
Guy, David H., Hon., 2107
Guy, Martha, 2599
Guyas, Vickie, 1170
Guylas, Joan D., 50
Guynn, Jack, 884, 917
Guyton, Dewey G., 3105
Guyton, Joan L., 3105
Guyton, Michelle, 497
Guzik, Nahum, 238
Guzman, Anita, 3014
Guzman, Mariano, 331
Guzman, Rick, 991
Gwaltney, Frank, 749
Gwaltney, Julia, 493
Gwin, Dean, 749
Gwyn, Mark R., 3129
Gyllenhaal, Anders, 317

H + H Excavation, 484
Ha, Paul, 1789
Haaff, Randall, 1128
Haas Charitable Trusts, Otto Haas & Phoebe W., 3011
Haas, Andrew, 3011
Haas, Chara C., 3045
Haas, Christina, 3011
Haas, David W., 3011
Haas, Elise S., 239
Haas, Frederick R., 3011
Haas, Janet, 3011
Haas, John C., 3011, 3045
Haas, Katherine, 3011
Haas, Leonard C., 3011
Haas, Michele, 2907
Haas, Miriam L., 239
Haas, Neill H., 2763
Haas, Otto, 3011
Haas, Peter E., 239
Haas, Phoebe W., 3011
Haas, Randy, 1847
Haas, Thomas W., 3011
Habbert, Helen Berkman, 1434
Habenicht, Brenda, 1162
Haber, Gary, 3126
Haber, Jeffry, 2106
Haber, Thomas R., 2600
Haber, William M., 438
Habig, Christopher, 2134
Hackbarth, James, 2564
Hackbarth, James P., 2564
Hacker, Bill, 1178
Hacker, Deanna, 1141
Hackett, Deborah, 1868
Hackett, James P., 1667
Hackett, Leo A., Esq., 2932
Hackett, Maggie, 1919
Hackett, R. Kevin, 1919
Hackett, Robert, 1909
Hackmann, Glen F., 3595
Hackworthy, John, 1185
Hadar Charitable Lead Trust, The, 2198
Hadar, Mica B., 2198
Hadar, Richard, 2198
Haddad Trust, Robert W. and Helen, 1153
Haddad, Angelo, 279
Haddad, Charles, Esq., 2893
Haddad, Richard A., 1168
Haddad, Robert W., Jr., 1153
Haddad, Tracy L., 1153
Haddeland, Pete, 1723
Hadden, Alexander M., 2513
Hadden, Alexander M., Mrs., 2513
Hadden, David, 1511
Haddon, Phoebe A., 2942
Haddon, Roger S., Jr., 2908
Haden, Patrick C., 270, 444
Hadhazy, Allan E., 784
Haedrich, Bill, 401
Hafez, Radwa, 1899
Hagan Endowment Foundation, The, 1792
Hagan Trust, The, 1792
Hagan, Dan, 1792
Hagberg, Marilyn J., 1240
Hagedorn Foundation, Horace, 2199
Hagedorn, Amy, 2199
Hagedorn, William, 2200
Hagen, Mardee, 3390
Hagen, Mary E., 1517
Hagenbuch, Diane S., 2756
Hager, Bob, 1723
Hager, Jim, 1710
Hager, Lindsay, 1607
Haggard, Charlie, 3328
Haggerty, Matthew E., Esq., 3031
Haggerty-Bearden, C. Gwen, 1672
Haggett, Robert M., 1511
Haglund, Brent M., 3654
Hagman, Lorri, 3497
Hagman, Paul, 2799
Hagny, Dennis, 3118
Hague, Valerie, 1179
Hahn, Gregory F., 1126
Hahn, Lowell, 1270
Haile Jr. Foundation, Carol Ann and Ralph V., 2675
Haile Trust, Ralph V., 2709
Haile, Ralph V., 2709
Hailey, Mary, 3641
Haines, Bruce S., 3030
Haines, David, Dr., 1168
Haines, Lana, 999
Haines, Pamela H., 1337
Hair, Charles M., 303
Haire, Susan L., 2538
Haisley, Jimmie Anne, 768
Haisley, Jimmie Anne, Dr., 2280
Hajny, Janet A., 1856
Hajra, Neel, 1576
Hajtman, L. Michael, 3256
Hakuta, Kenji, 674
Halbreich, Kathy, 2146
Halbritter, Barry, 2907
Halby, Peter C., 501
Halby, Will, 501
Hale, Mary, 3511
Haleen, Tobi, 1086
Halevy, Drew, 2376
Haley, Ben P., 1315
Haley, C. James, Jr., 3227
Haley, Carl T., 3129
Haley, Jeff, 2071
Halfhide, Jon, 401
Halfon, Ellen E., 2721
Halfon, Jay R., 2349
Haliday, Alfred C., Jr., 786
Hall Capital, 2817
Hall Family Investments, LLC, 3395
Hall, Aaron, 3395
Hall, Adam, 3395
Hall, Alan E., 3395
Hall, Annette, 3395
Hall, Anthony W., Jr., 3267
Hall, Beverly, 909
Hall, Brooks, Jr., 2817
Hall, Cami, 3395
Hall, Carol, 1187, 2143
Hall, Charlotte, 1668
Hall, Christian, 3395
Hall, Christoper E., 1426
Hall, Dan, 3207
Hall, Dave, 2570
Hall, David, 1668
Hall, David E., 1794
Hall, Dena M., 1559
Hall, Diane, 2848
Hall, Donald J., 1793
Hall, Donald J., Jr., 1794
Hall, E.A., 1793
Hall, Emily, 3395
Hall, Eric, 3395
Hall, Eugene C., 1776
Hall, Fred Jones, 2817
Hall, H. Andrew McMicking, 322
Hall, Henry, 609
Hall, James F., 1924
Hall, Jeannie, 3395
Hall, Jerry, 2331
Hall, Jim, 1157
Hall, John, 1156, 2796
Hall, Joseph C.M., 322
Hall, Joyce C., 1793
Hall, Karla D., 1598
Hall, Kathryn, 437
Hall, Kathryn A., 2302
Hall, Kay, 2850

Hall, Kim, 3395
Hall, Kirkland, 2817
Hall, Leslie Kelly, 1489
Hall, Lisa, 3267
Hall, Lyle G., 3042
Hall, Lyle G., Jr., 3042
Hall, Lyle G., Sr., 3042
Hall, Mary, 3133
Hall, Matthew A., 218
Hall, Maurice, 1758
Hall, Megan, 3042
Hall, Nancy, 2832
Hall, Nechie, 536
Hall, Prem, 3458
Hall, R.B., 1793
Hall, Roderick C.M., 322
Hall, Sophia, 3532
Hall, Thomas H., III, 918
Hall, William, 2048
Hall, William A., 1793
Hallam, Rob, 1253
Halldane, 1388
Hallenbeck, Alfred M., 2410
Haller, Albert G., 3522
Haller, Jim, 3378
Hallett, Jessie F., 1701
Hallett, Susan H., 3433
Halliday, Susan, 267
Halligan, Patrick, 2189
Halligan, Robert, 1983
Hallinan, Kathy, 2244
Hallingby, Julia H., 2201
Hallingby, Paul L., 2201
Hallman, Elisabeth, 140
Hallmark Cards, Inc., 1793, 1794
Hallock, Meloni M., 137
Hallock, Morris, 3115
Hallock, Robert B., 59
Halloin, Jeff, 3611
Halloran, Beth, 1717
Halloran, Harry, Jr., 2963
Hallquist, Carol, 1794
Halls, Tim, 1802
Hallstrom, Wyman P., III, 3083
Hallstrom, Wyman P., Jr., 3083
Halper, Deann, 2202
Halper, Murray, 2202
Halper, Robert, 2202
Halperin, Alan, 1055
Halperin, Mark, 240
Halperin, Philip W., 240, 409
Halperin, Robert, 240
Halperin, Ruth, 240
Halpern, Steven, 2144
Halpern, Susan U., 2426
Halsey, Karen, 2737
Halstead, Cathy, 206
Halstead, Peter, 206
Halter Foundation, Maurice, 1558
Halvorsen, Bradley W., 44
Halvorson, Newman T., Jr., 672
Hamblin, Brody, 3394
Hamblin, Dick, 3580
Hamblin, Holly, 3394
Hambrick, Thomas G., Jr., 3173
Hamburg, David, 2085
Hamel, Mark, 1742
Hamer, Mickey, 235
Hamerton-Kelly, Robert, 434
Hamill, Patrick, 498
Hamilton, B.A., 1286
Hamilton, Bud, 2017
Hamilton, Chris, 3148
Hamilton, David B., 2714
Hamilton, David F., 3153
Hamilton, Elizabeth, 3153
Hamilton, George, 682
Hamilton, John, 3153
Hamilton, Lisa M., 1353
Hamilton, M. Hayne, 3156
Hamilton, Neil, 2181
Hamilton, Peggy, 1589
Hamilton, Rose Lincoln, 3567
Hamilton, Scott, 505
Hamin, Leonard L., Sr., Dr., 3421
Hamlet, Virginia W., 3443
Hamm, Duke, 1158
Hamm, Harold, 2809
Hamm, Harold G., 1028
Hamm, Sue, 2809
Hamm, Sue A., 1028
Hamm, Sue Ann, 1028
Hammack, John A., 3296
Hammami, Hasan A., 718
Hamman, George, 3248
Hamman, Henry R., 3248
Hamman, Mary Josephine, 3248
Hamman, Russell R., 3248
Hammann, Conrad, 3580
Hammecker, Roy, 2366
Hammer, Kouhaila G., 1588
Hammer, Matt, 3568
Hammer/Pontchartrain Capital, M., LLC, 1314
Hammergren, John H., 321
Hammersmith, Suann D., 1634
Hammes, Robert M., 990
Hammett, Willie A., 2474
Hammill, Donald D., 3249
Hammond and Associates, 394
Hammond, Howell A., 2540
Hammond, Michael, 3467
Hammond, Philip W., 1367
Hammons, Brian, 1783
Hammons, Marva, 3499
Hamner, Millie, 537
Hamp, Steven K., 1588, 1631
Hamprick, Richard, 3442
Hamrich, Richard, Dr., 3444
Hamrick, Leslie Hille, 2816
Hamrock, Joseph, 2752
Hamus, Floyd, 3633
Hamus, Pat, 3633
Han, Amy, 1171
Han, Fang, 2423
Hanan, Benjamin, 754
Hanauer, Gerald, 3523
Hanauer, Leslie, 3523
Hanauer, Nick, 3523
Hanaway, Andrea, 3014
Hanback, Scott, 1130
Hancock, Allan G., 2907
Hancock, Gary, 3431
Hancock, John W., 1843
Hancock, Larry, 3587
Hancock, Margaret M. Augur, 3168
Hancock, Richard B., 381
Hand, Donna S., 903
Hand, Frances R., 755
Hand, Homer J., 755
Hand, Karen, 3433
Handel, Nancy H., 408
Handelman, Donald E., 2294
Handelman, Irving, 2407
Handelman, James H., 2294
Handelman, Richard, 2294
Handelman, Sara, 2407
Handelman, William R., 2294
Hander, Linda B., 1998
Handke, David P., Jr., 2736
Handler, Peter, 1051
Handy, Ned, 3089
Hanenburg, Edward, 1614
Hanes, F. Borden, Jr., 2565
Hanes, Frank B., Sr., 2565
Hanes, Norman, 1315
Hanes, R. Philip, Jr., 2565
Haney, Dale, 749
Hangs, George L., Jr., 2815
Hanifl, Kerry L., 1029
Hanifl, Paul H., 1029
Hanifl, Sharon M., 1029
Hanifl, Suzanne, 1029
Hanifl, Suzanne T., 1029
Hanisee, Robert, 106
Hank, Sheri, 1706
Hankin, Rockell N., 275
Hankins, James M., 829
Hanks, Jackson, 3364
Hanley, Andria, 729
Hanley, Janet, 1068
Hanley, William Lee, Jr., 1947
Hanlon, Tom, 3055
Hanlon, Victoria, 378
Hanna, Ashraf, 216
Hanna, Rod, 545
Hanna, Therese, 1757
Hanna, Troy M., 3110
Hanna, William, 267
Hannaford Bros. Co., 1330
Hannah, John R., 3341, 3347
Hannah, Kenneth, 3315
Hanneman, Judy, 305
Hanni, Carrie, 1157
Hannigan, Charlie, 2037
Hannigan, Michael R., 525
Hannon, Brian T., 2932
Hannon, James A., 242
Hannon, John, 1187
Hannon, William Herbert, 242
Hannum, Diane, 2331
Hanrahan, Dan, 1732
Hanrahan, Katherine, 3045
Hanratty, Janet L., 1344
Hans, Rick, 1109
Hans, William, 3655
Hansen, 826
Hansen Trust, Dane G., 1259
Hansen, Barbara, 2702
Hansen, Betty, 1241
Hansen, Bill, 1705
Hansen, Chip, Jr., 1583
Hansen, Dane G., 1259
Hansen, Darlene, 384
Hansen, David, 441
Hansen, G.W., 384
Hansen, Gretchen, 2964
Hansen, Inc., 2964
Hansen, K.N., Jr., 384
Hansen, K.N., Sr., 384
Hansen, Mary Dale, 2648
Hansen, Nancy Huston, 2973
Hansen, Nancy K., 2964
Hansen, Randy, 1614
Hansen, Teri A., 754
Hansen, Todd, 1836
Hansen, Walter, 384
Hansen, William Gregg, 2964
Hansen-Irps, Joy, 989
Hanson Aggregates West, Inc., 1673
Hanson, Alden Lee, 1597
Hanson, Bill, 1136
Hanson, Brian, 1224
Hanson, Calvin J., 448
Hanson, David J., 3654
Hanson, Kirk O., 412
Hanson, Lee, 1703
Hanson, Phillip J., 1817
Hanson, R. Reid, 850
Hanson, Sam, 1687
Hanson, Stephanie K., 2142
Hanson, Steve, 3552
Hanson, Virginia, 3296
Hanson, William C., 1633
Hanton, Jackie, 1590
Hanyu, Jiro, 680
Hapgood, Barbara, 574
Hapgood, Elaine P., 574
Hapgood, Matthew, 574
Hapke, Andrew, 267
Hapke, Claire, 267
Hapke, Norman, 267
Hapke, Norman F., Jr., 267
Hapke, Valerie Jacobs, 267
Hara, Julie, 1700
Hara, Julie S., 1713
Harabedian, Robert, 154
Haraksin, Tracy, 368
Haraldson, Beulah M., 3250
Harbers, Renee W., 3509
Harbeson, Ellen, 644
Harbour, Nancy, 29
Harckham, Janet, 246
Harcone 4 LLC, 809
Hard Rock Cafe International (USA) Inc., 756
Hard, Rachel, 1580
Hardacre, David, 167
Hardaway, Cathy Ann, 3031
Hardcastle, Jeff, 1584
Hardegree, William B., Jr., 903
Harder, Adam, 1207
Harder, Delmar S., 3524
Harder, Robert C., Dr., 1281
Hardesty, Donna J., 2814
Hardesty, F. Roger, 2814
Hardesty, Jane G., 885
Hardesty, Jean, 3578
Hardesty, Michelle, 2814
Hardgrove, Ian F., 1676
Hardie, David, 1868
Hardie, Donald, 888
Hardin Trust, Helen E., 3137
Hardin, Janie, 1157
Hardin, Katharine Harrison, 2599
Harding Service, LLC, 1965
Harding, Marty, 3662
Hardwick, Mark K., 1134
Hardy, Brent, 122
Hardy, Cary, 1998
Hardy, J. Michael, 3552
Hardy, John C., 1771
Hardy, S. Michael, 866
Hardy, Tammy, 3054
Hardy, Tom, 1136
Hardy, W. Marvin, IV, 842
Hare, Bonnie, 1133
Hare, Michael, 2958
Harenburg, Tom, 3642
Harford, Luke, 1344
Hargrave, Christine, 3579
Hargreaves, David D.R., 3077
Hargrove, Wade, 2071
Haring, Allen, 2203
Haring, Keith, 2203
Haring, Kristen, 2203

Harker, Martin, 1129
Harkleroad, Joe, 2707
Harkness, Calvin, 4
Harkness, Edward S., 2106
Harkness, Edward S., Mrs., 2106
Harkness, Stephen V., Mrs., 2106
Harla, JoAnne, 1945
Harlan, Leigh M., 2463
Harland, John H., 885
Harless, Jim, 3546
Harley-Davidson, Inc., 3621
Harlow, Thomas R., 2908
Harman, Janet E., 3273
Harman, Tim, 1176
Harmelink, Kevin, 1615
Harmon, Aaron, 2809
Harmon, Chris, 1128
Harmon, Claude C., 2815
Harmon, John Campbell, 3028
Harmon, Julia J., 2815
Harmon, Laura, 8
Harnden, Thomas, 2664
Harned, Dave, 1660
Harned, Elizabeth Quadracci, 3668
Harney, John, 3144
Harney, Pat, 1218
Harnick, Sheldon, 2252
Harnish, Mitch, 1207
Harold, Erica, 773
Harp-Jirschele, Mary, 3626
Harper Charitable Lead Annuity Trust, Louise G., 3528
Harper, Alan B., 3528
Harper, Andrew, 3411
Harper, Deb, 3510
Harper, Esther, 1998
Harper, Hugh, 2473
Harper, Jake, 3160
Harper, Morris, 2924
Harper, Philip S., 3411
Harper, Ralph E., 224
Harper, Sharon C., 57
Harper, Trude, 568
Harper-Taylor, Jeniffer, 1993
Harper-Wyman Co., 3411
Harpole, John C., 2479
Harr, Richard K., 2797
Harrah's Operating Co., Inc., 1860
Harral, William, III, 2887
Harrell, Deloris, 2604
Harrell, Shari, 2685
Harrell, William Larry, 3429
Harrigan-Hitz, Heather, 1187
Harrington, Daniel P., 2797
Harrington, Don, 327
Harrington, Kathleen, Sr., 1453
Harrington, Lydia L., 2781
Harrington, Tim, 1031
Harrington-Heide, Jane, 3628
Harris Associates, 993
Harris, Albert W., 982
Harris, Andrew L., 776
Harris, Carey A., 2896
Harris, Carla, 2315
Harris, Chris E., 2767
Harris, Clyde P., Jr., 2599
Harris, Connie, 419
Harris, Dee Ann, 2860
Harris, Don, 3304
Harris, Franco, 2966
Harris, George, 2282
Harris, Gillian, 1428
Harris, Henry U., III, 1565
Harris, Jane W., 991
Harris, Janet, 1759
Harris, Jerry, 167
Harris, Judy, 1203
Harris, Kay, 1219
Harris, Keecha, 2335
Harris, King W., 982
Harris, Kitty S., Dr., 3362
Harris, Kyle, 503
Harris, Lisa, 529
Harris, Loren S., 2275
Harris, Mariann, 287
Harris, Marie W., 1107
Harris, Mary, 179
Harris, Patricia E., 2066
Harris, Patti E., 2066
Harris, Paul N., 2717
Harris, Paul W., 3262
Harris, Richard M., 776
Harris, Sara D., 2915
Harris, Sarah, 1216
Harris, Scott, 1694
Harris, Susan G., 3436
Harris, Tim, 2683
Harris, W. Patrick, 3190
Harris, Walter, 1728
Harris, William, 723
Harrison, Angie, 943
Harrison, Avery, 2604
Harrison, Camille, 744
Harrison, Cassidy, 1864
Harrison, Connie, 1590
Harrison, Dan J., III, 3354
Harrison, David, 3546
Harrison, James I., III, 11
Harrison, Laurie Sands, 3340
Harrison, Lawrence M., 439
Harrison, Louise C., 472
Harrison, Marian P., 3324
Harrison, Mary Jane, 1184
Harrison, Michael, Pastor, 2799
Harrison, Nora Eccles Treadwell, 439
Harrison, Richard, Dr., 3597
Harrison, Robert S., 933
Harrison, Ron, 1132
Harrison, Sande Vincent, 3343
Harrison, Scott, 1705
Harrison, Verna, 142
Harrison, William T., Jr., 828
Harrold, Mary Beth, 1848
Harrop, Diane, 3684
Harry V. Quadracci 1998 Trust, 3668
Harryman, Robert J., 288
Hart, Barbara, 804
Hart, Bettieanne, 911
Hart, Christine, 2848
Hart, Darryl, 2540
Hart, Gary K., 167
Hart, Gladys, 2148
Hart, Karen Schwartz, 1981
Hart, Karl V., 1296
Hart, Ted, 3648
Hart, Thomas, 3054
Hart, W. Dehler, 3111
Harte, Christopher M., 3251
Harte, Edward, 3251
Harte, William, 3247
Harte, William S., 3251
Hartford, Scott, 2710
Hartgering, Bill, 268
Hartin, Susan F., 3229
Hartl, Deborah, 3503
Hartl, Leonard L., 3633
Hartl, Michael J., 611
Hartley, Indya, 2205
Hartley, Susan J., 1661
Hartley, Thomas D., 1803
Hartman, David, 1998
Hartman, Gena, 1200
Hartman, Gordon, 3252
Hartman, Gordon V., 3252
Hartman, Judith K., 2794
Hartman, Lynn Pike, 3014
Hartman, Margaret M., 3252
Hartman, Renee, 1186
Hartman, Robert, 1259
Hartman, Sid, 309
Hartman, Teri, 886
Hartman, Todd, 1685
Hartsband, Meryl, 3148
Hartshorn, Gary, 667
Hartwell, Mary Lynn, 948
Hartwell, Stephen, 661
Hartwig, Rose, 2850
Hartwig, Scott, 3052
Harty, Barbara A., 1101
Hartz, Greg, 2274
Hartz, Rayna, 33
Harvey, Ann, 513
Harvey, Cannon, 2232
Harvey, Constance, 513
Harvey, J. Dale, 461
Harvey, Laurel, 1398
Harvey, Lydia, 2232
Harvey, Mark, 513
Harvey, Nelson, 513
Harvey, Tanya, 992
Harvick, Kevin DeLana, 2574
Harward, Todd, 3099
Harwell, Aubrey B., Jr., Mr., 3129
Harwell, Jeffery, Jr., 3222
Harwood, Alice G., 500
Harwood, Amy W., 566
Harzan, Annette, 351
Harzan, John, 351
Hasbro, Inc., 3077
Hasburg, Charles, 591
Hasek, Jane, 1216
Hashemi, Nasrin, 241
Hashemi, Noosheen, 241
Hashimoto, Takehiko, 1495
Haskell, John E., 2090
Haskell, Molly, 2050
Haskin, Nancy, 1606
Haskins, Greg, Dr., 1836
Haslam, James A., III, 3138
Haslam, Susan B., 3138
Haslanger, Kathryn, 2106
Hassani, Hassan, 2030
Hasselbeck, Matthew, 635
Hasselbeck, Sarah, 635
Hassell, Raymond E., 3083
Hasselman, Michael W., 1144
Hasson, James, Jr., 758
Hastings, Diane F., 1332
Hastings, G. Richard, 1267
Hastings, Jennings, 630
Haston, Roger, 472
Hatch, Carol, 3607
Hatch, George, 1514, 1538
Hatch, Serena M., 1538
Hatch, Whitney, 1514, 1538
Hatcher, Claud A., 903
Hatcher, Susan, 2689
Hatfield, John S., 39
Hathaway, Harry L., 258
Hathaway, Phillips, 1394
Hatridge, Helen, 1817
Hattem, Gary S., 2134
Hatterscheidt Trusts, F.W., 3116
Hatterscheidt, Ruth K., 3116
Hattery, Max, 1180
Hattler, Denise M., 3453
Hattler, Hillary A., 3453
Hattler-Bramson, Andrea M., 3453
Hattman, David W., 1426
Hatton, Katherine, 1949
Hauck, William, 114
Haught, Anne Fehrenbacher, 1281
Haughy, Carey, 420
Haun, C. K., 948
Hauptman, Andrew, 2074
Hauptman, Ellen, 2074
Hauptman, Jeff, 1576
Hauser, Dick, 3609
Hauser, Pierre, 182
Hauser, Pierre, II, 2127
Hauswirth, Lisa Guggenhime, 289
Hautman, April, 1181
Haveman, Robert, 1658
Havens Living Trust, Westen, 2567
Havens, Charles Gerard, 2204
Haverlick, Brett, 2664
Haviland Plastic Products Co., 2772
Havner, Debi, 69
Hawaiian Electric Industries, Inc., 934
Hawk, Arlene F., 2661
Hawk, Bryan, 2661
Hawk, David, 3031
Hawk, Timothy, 2661
Hawker, Mary Stake, 1786
Hawkins Construction Co., 1838
Hawkins, Chaille W., 3358
Hawkins, Chris, 1838
Hawkins, Christopher R., 2075
Hawkins, Frances L., R.N., 1299
Hawkins, Fred, Jr., 1838
Hawkins, Fred, Sr., 1838
Hawkins, Jack, 770
Hawkins, Jay L., 950
Hawkins, John C., 630
Hawkins, John F., 2454
Hawkins, Kim, 1838
Hawkins, Lauren, 1384
Hawkins, Lawton, 864
Hawkins, Leslie, 3521
Hawkins, Matt, 3406
Hawkins, William, 864
Hawkins, Winsome, 909
Hawks, Richard, 2342
Hawley, Anne, 2146
Hawley, Nancy H., 2613
Hawley, Neil, 1280
Hawley, Philip M., 243
Hawn, Bruce Sams, 3342
Hawn, Caitlyn J., 3342
Hawn, Gates Helms, 2099
Hawn, Joe, Officer, 1168
Hawn, Nancy E., 3342
Hawn, Susan G., 3342
Hawthorne, Joan, 2648
Hay, Andrew MacKenzie, 2445
Hay, Carol S., 2091
Hayden, Carl, 2109
Hayden, John W., 2780
Hayden, Laureen, 3328
Hayden, Tim, 1128
Hayden, William B., 1024
Haydon, Richard L., 1862
Hayes, Anne, 3672
Hayes, Brad, 1189
Hayes, Brian, 1131
Hayes, Elaine Bryant, 2541

Hayes, Geralyn F., 1779
Hayes, Harrison F., 479
Hayes, J. Stoddard, Jr., Esq., 2915
Hayes, James C., 1748
Hayes, James D., 1702
Hayes, Jerry, 2027
Hayes, Jimmy W., 916
Hayes, Katherine D.R., 1702
Hayes, Patricia, 3372
Hayes, Robert M., 3467
Hayes, Shaun, 1820
Hayes, Stewart L., 1865
Hayes, Synnova B., 2056
Hayes, Tyan, 36
Haygood, Paul, III, 1310
Hayne, Nancy E., 3239
Hayne, Roxana Catto, 3239
Haynes, Dora Fellows, Mrs., 243
Haynes, Dorothy "Honey Bun", 933
Haynes, John Randolph, 243
Haynes, Lawrence E., 2925
Haynes, Lukas, 2306
Hayon, Beverly, 329
Hays, Charles D., 3604
Hays, Charles W., Jr., 1332
Hays, George W.S., 2771
Hayton, Allan, 34
Hayward, Archie B., Jr., 823
Hayward, Erik K., 1334
Hayward, Marilyn Rushworth, 630
Hayward, Stephen F., Dr., 3654
Hayworth-Hopp, Ashley, 1160
Hazard, Stephen, 1882
Hazeltine, Joyce, 3115
Hazen, Elizabeth, 59
HB Communications, 3505
HCA Inc., 3139
HCA—The Healthcare Co., 3139
HD Supply, 3505
Head, Martha, 543
Head, Randy, 1125
Head, Robert, 1045
Heald, Catherine Maclellan, Mrs., 3146
Healey, Kim A., 595
Healey, Otis M., 461
Health and Hospital Corp., 1156
Health Care Reit, Inc., 809
Health East Care Bethesda Hospital, 3377
Health Markets, 3198
Health Options, Inc., 744
Healy, Ann Marie, 2948
Healy, Bridget M., 2488
Healy, Cameron, 2848
Healy, Gary M., 744
Healy, Helen B., 474
Healy, John, 2541
Healy, Morley, 474
Healy, Thomas B., 2474
Healy, Thomas P., 1406
Healy, Tim, 2848
Hearsch, David, 1663
Hearst Argyle Television, 2071
Hearst Corp., 2445
Hearst, Joseph B., 3440
Hearst, William A., 3440
Heartland Trust Co., 2649
Heasley, Karen, 3039
Heasley, Lucas, 3039
Heasley-Treadwell, Christina, 3039
Heath Irrevocable Trust, Laura, 2724
Heath, G. Ross, Dr., 332
Heath, Jill Wells, 2612
Heath, Sheila, 2696
Heathwood, Desmond, 1487
Heatley, Alvin T., 3098
Heavin, Diane, 3253
Heavin, Gary, 3253
Heavin, Gary H., 3253
Heavin, Karen Nelson, 1189
Hebert, John, 1885
Hecht, Michael, 2428
Heck, Margaret Quirt, 3633
Heck, Patricia DelTorro, 565
Heckard, Tom, 1125
Heckman, Sally W., 2695
Heckscher, August, 2205
Heckscher, Martin A., 3019
Hedges, John, 1068
Hedinger, Blake H., 2849
Hedinger, Howard H., 2849
Hedinger, Nancy, 1924
Hedlund, Steven, Dr., 3438
Heeden, John L., 2630
Heekin, S., 3666
Heenan, Timothy S., 606
Heffelfinger, Royce, 1731
Heffernan, Hank, 3576
Heffernan, James B., 2668
Heffner, Kirsten, 943
Hefner, Keith, 2326
Heft, Crystal, 368
Heft, Jana C., 3643
Hefti, Marv, 1852
Hegarty, Michael, 2194
Hegarty, Neal R., 1645
Hegge, Cindy, 3540
Heginbotham, Stanley J., 2439
Hehir, Sara A., 897
Heide, Charles H., 624
Heide, Charles H., Jr., 624
Heide, Kathryn H., 624
Heide-Waller, Paula J., 624
Heidecorn, David, 2027
Heidt, Julia & Robert, 2780
Heidt, Julia Scripps, 2780
Heidtman Steel Products, Inc., 2665
Heien, Janet, 163
Heil, Jeffrey, 2146
Heil, Josephine, 964
Heilemann, Blackie, 3187
Heilemann, Paula, 3187
Heiling, Duane, 1731
Heilman, E. Bruce, 3477
Heiman/Fidelity Foundation, 559
Heimburger, Meredith, 3297
Heinburger, Elizabeth Holloway, 3264
Heine, Lucilee, 954
Heinegg, James G., 2391
Heinmiller, John C., 1741
Heinrich, Michael, 1218
Heinrich, Richard, 2044
Heinrichs, Haven S., 3340
Heinsheimer, Alfred M., 2326
Heinsheimer, Louis A., 2326
Heintz, Stephen B., 2389
Heinz, Alice, 3427
Heinz, Andre T., 2966
Heinz, Christopher, 2966
Heinz, Drue, 2966
Heinz, H. John, 2966
Heinz, Howard, 2966
Heinz, Sasha, 2966
Heinz, Teresa F., 2966
Heinz, Vira I., 2966
Heinze, Daniels, 1270
Heinze, Dyke, 1647
Heisen, Joann Heffernan, 1949
Heising, Mark W., 245
Heiskell, Marian S., 2451
Heisser, Amy, 1586
Heit, Philip, 2750
Heiting, Bill, 3633
Hejl, David, 58
Hejna, JoAnn, 1811
Helfen Wir, 3330
Helfet, David, 685
Helge, Kathleen, 1778
Helisek, Cynthia, 1673
Hellebuyck, Kathy, 1238
Heller, Alfred, 246
Heller, Clarence E., 246
Heller, Ellen M., 1416
Heller, Francie, 2297
Heller, Jill, 3648
Heller, Katherine, 246
Heller, Lesley, 765
Heller, Richard K., 2888
Heller, Ruth, 246
Hellerman, Brett D., 559
Hellman, Daryl A., 1461
Hellman, Mick, 385
Hellweg, Kurt D., 1785
Hellweg, Sheryl D., 1785
Hellweg, Tyler D., 1785
Helm, Lucy, 3565
Helm, Mark, 2810
Helman, Elizabeth Daisy, 1524
Helman, Frank G., 1343
Helmick, Neal, 1268
Helmken, John C., II, 912
Helms Bakeries, 247
Helms, Christopher A., 2752
Helms, William, 3
Helmsley Enterprises, Inc., 2207
Helmsley, Leona M., 2207
Helpenstell, Bonnie, 2871
Helpenstell, Emily, 2871
Helpenstell, Eric, 2871
Helpenstell, Lily, 2871
Helping Hand Sales Inc., The, 3424
Helsell, Frank P., 3556
Helsell, Peter F., 3556
Helsell, Virginia S., 3556
Helsell, William A., 3556
Helseth, Nancy L., 2842
Helstrom, Carl, 1947, 1968
Hembree, W.T., 1808
Hemenway, Robert E., 1793
Hemingway Foundation, 676
Hemingway, Ann, 3396
Hemingway, Henry S., 3396
Hemingway, Richard Keith, 3396
Hemingway, Shirley Stranquist, 3396
Hemmen, Pam, 1726
Hemmings, Collette, 2865
Hempstead, David M., 1588
Hemus, Simon, 2097
Henceroth, Alan, 537
Henderson, Allen Douglas, 758
Henderson, Anne W., 1752
Henderson, Barbara K., 758
Henderson, Bruce King Mellon, 2998
Henderson, Charles R., Jr., 2524
Henderson, Diann C., 56
Henderson, Dink, 725
Henderson, James D., II, 1886
Henderson, James L., Jr., 2553
Henderson, Jan, 1198
Henderson, Loise J., 3255
Henderson, Lucia, 758
Henderson, Patrick, 3683
Henderson, Pete, 1012
Henderson, Phillip, 2454
Henderson, Rhoe B., 2170
Henderson, Thomas, 1517
Henderson, Vincent, 1197
Hendler, Lee M., 1392
Hendrick Gordon Leasing, 2562
Hendrick Motorsports, 2562
Hendrick, Cal, 3316
Hendrick, Rick, 2562
Hendricks, Diane M., 3601
Hendricks, John C., 1400
Hendricks, John S., 1377, 2085
Hendricks, Maureen D., 1377
Hendrickson, Douglas, 1290
Hendrickson, John T., 1655
Hendrickson, Virginia, 1032
Hendriksen, Dick, 1836
Hendry, M.S., 3355
Henebry, Brian, 564
Henkel, Joe, 3196
Henkels & McCoy, Inc., 2967
Henkels, Barbara B., 2967
Henkels, Christopher B., 2967
Henkels, Paul M., Jr., 2967
Henle, David L., 2208
Henle, Joan C., 2208
Henley, Lisa, 2016
Henline, Carson S., 2628
Henneman, Jack, 1945
Hennessey, Jevera, 613
Hennessy, Anne Griffith, 886
Hennessy, Carole J., 1035
Hennessy, John, 333
Hennessy, Jonathan M., 1035
Hennessy, Matthew H., 1035
Hennessy, Michael P., 2596
Hennessy, Michael W., 986, 1035
Henney, Jane E., 2106
Hennig, Ruth G., 1514
Henning, Mary Jo, 1749
Henricks, Vern, 1268
Henricksen, Bob, 3352
Henriques, George, 1726
Henrotin Hospital, 1112
Henry, Alan, 3362
Henry, Brian L., 3133
Henry, Charles, Jr., 3014
Henry, Daniel T., 2034
Henry, Edward P., 2146
Henry, Frances Turner, 1302
Henry, Jeanette, 2773
Henry, Kim, 2828
Henry, Megan, 2410
Henry, Merton G., 1340
Henry, Patricia, 3542
Henry, Russ, 869
Henry-Keller, Piper, 3542
Hensel, Russel R., 3006
Hensell, Chip, 3580
Hensely, Darrel, 1817
Hensely, Sharon Elliott, 791
Hensleigh, Inez M., 1061
Hensley, Dick, 3445
Hensley, Jamie, 2707
Henson Foundation, Jane, 2210
Henson, Cheryl, 2210
Henson, Heather, 2210
Henson, James Maury "Jim", 2210
Henson, Jane, 2210
Henson, Richard A., 1378
Hensyn, Inc., 1991
Hentz, Kathryn Iacocca, 1487
Hepburn, Michael, 1948

Hepburn, Valerie, Dr., 863
Hepting, Robert, 1817
Hequembourg, Mark, 1286
Herbein, Kathleen D., 2893
Herbert, Allen, 1315
Herbert, Ann D., 2556, 3102
Herbert, Benjamin, 2197
Herbert, Dale M., 19
Herbert, Gavin S., 80
Herbert, Michael, 1255
Herbert, Peter A., 2197
Herbert, Robert M., 2412
Herbst, David A., 242
Herbst, George H., 842
Herczeg, Andrea, 1753
Herd, Jay, 3277
Herd, Patty, 3316
Herd, Tevis, 3160, 3229
Herd-Barber, Jacqueline, 3637
Herdendorf, Ann, 3616
Herding, George T., 3119
Herdman, Bruce W., 2948
Herdman, Roger C., 2167
Herendeen, Burniece, 2148
Hergert, Bob, 3642
Hergert, John P., 1081
Hering, Jennifer A., 1776
Herlache, John L., 3609
Herlihy, Edward D., 2490
Herlihy, Richard G., 211
Herlin, Cara P., 3373
Herlin, Jean T., 3373
Herman Miller Inc., 1624
Herman, Jeffrey, 3363
Herman, Mike, 543
Herman, Theodore, 2317
Herman, Theodore L., 2317
Herman, Thomas M., 2674
Hermance, Ronald E., 1942
Hermann, Diana P., 2408
Hermann, Natalie, 2148
Hermann, William M., 1588
Hermes, Brian, 3207
Hermes, Euler, 2574
Hermocillo, Jose, 405
Hernandez, Antonia, 114, 137
Hernandez, Carlos M., 3235
Hernandez, Enrique, Jr., 243
Hernandez, Jean, Dr., 3502
Hernandez, Jesus, 3502
Hernandez, Luz, 3051
Hernandez, Mario, Dr., 728
Hernandez, Ramona, 1548
Hernandez, Robert, 2880
Hernandez, Robert M., 2906
Hernandez, Sandra R., 114, 139
Hernandez, Victor Rivera, 3061
Hernreich, Robert, 543
Hero, Peter, 412
Herold, H. Robert, II, 1975
Herold, Matthew G., Jr., 1975
Heron, George, 1652
Herre, Tom, 3615
Herrera, Sharon Hays, 3295
Herrera, Yvette, 651
Herrick, David A., 3454
Herrick, Greg, 3587
Herrick, Jason, 3163
Herrick, John, 3107
Herrick, Scott, 1189
Herrick-Pacific Corporation, 377
Herring, Benjamin Ari, 1016
Herring, Carol P., 1979
Herring, J. Andrew, 1717
Herring, Kay, 1241
Herring, Margaret, 122
Herring, Paula, 3296
Herrington, Marilyn A., 2223
Herrington, Terri, 3142
Herrmann, Bryan, 363
Herrmann, Jon, 3051
Herron, John, 1308
Hershey Trust Co., 2952
Hershey, John R., III, 1360
Hershey, Loren W., 2711
Hershman, Peter, 618
Herskovitz, Amy, 2356
Herskowitz, Barry, 2017
Herst, Patricia U., 1979
Herterich, Karyn Kennedy, 767
Herterich, Morgan, 767
Herthaus, Donald H., 1942
Hertog, Roger, 2465
Hertzke, Lawrence, 484
Herzan, Alexandra, 2483
Herzberg, Pam, 1214
Herzog, Arie, 2193
Herzog, David, 2029
Herzstein, Albert H., 3256
Herzstein, Ethel Avis, 3256
Heslop, James G., 3
Hess Brothers Fruit Co, Inc., 952
Hess Foundation, The, 3053
Hess, Anne H., 650
Hess, Diana, 1098
Hess, Mandy L., 3601
Hess, Ray, 2907
Hess, Stephen, 2674
Hessel, David, 3173
Hesselbrock, Steve, 1295
Hessler, Deborah J., 712
Hessler, Kevin, 1358
Hester, Evette, 8
Hester, Lauren K., 665
Heth, Tim, 1223
Heth, Timothy M., 1217
Hetzner, Marc A., 497
Heuer, Michael A., 2659
Hewes, Bobby, 25
Hewey, Kristina B., 1351
Hewit, Randi, 2109
Hewitt, Chet P., 405
Hewitt, James, 1636
Hewitt, Patricia, 2022
Hewitt, Rosie, 1181
Hewitt, William D., 482
Hewlett, Flora Lamson, 248
Hewlett, Walter B., 248
Hewlett, William R., 248
Hewlett-Packard Co., 249
Hewsenian, Rosalind M., 2207
Hext Management, LLC, 3257
Hext, Jane, 3257
Hey, David R., 1114
Heyde, Lee, 1168
Heydlauff, Amy, 1584
Heydon, Michael, 1807
Heylin, Martha, 1069
Heyman Family LLC, Annette, 2212
Heyman, Annette, 2212
Heyman, Larry S., 2212
Heyman, Lazarus S., 2212
Heyman, Ronnie F., 2212
Heyman, Samuel J., 2212
Heyman, Stephen, 2326
Heyman-Layne, Carolyn, 29
Heymann, Claire Lynn, 1313
Heymann, Herbert, 1313
Heymann, Lila R., 1313
Heymann, Maurice, 1313
Heymann, Peter E., 1752
Heyneman, Tom S., 3679
Heynen, Cynthia, 1013
Heywood, Thomas A., 2892
HGJ Licensing, 2574
HGJ Licensing LLC, 2562
HHD, LLC, 1882
Hiam, Alexander W., 1565
Hiatt, Howard, 1538
Hiatt, Jane, 1759
Hibbing Taconite Co., 2681
Hickey, John, 1472
Hickey, John W., 3608
Hickey, William F., 2292
Hickman, David S., 1634
Hickman, Don, 1703
Hickman, Franklin J., 2801
Hickman, Linda, 3582
Hickman, Paula H., 1306
Hickman, Susanna B., 3488
Hickox, Charles V., Mrs., 2054
Hickox, Frances B., 2054
Hickox, James A.B., 2054
Hicks & Company, Jim, Inc., 192
Hicks Charitable Foundation, The, 2232
Hicks, Caitlyn, 1096
Hicks, Daniel K., Dr., 1382
Hicks, Greg, 1162
Hicks, Henry B., 3129
Hicks, Jennifer E., 192
Hicks, Jim, 192
Hicks, John E., Jr., 1096
Hicks, Michael E., 2759
Hicks, Neta, 192
Hicks, Paul, 3587
Hicks, Ruell L., Jr., 3112
Hicks, Valerie Bradley, 2801
Hicks, Wayland R., 192
Hieronimus, Jill M., 1392, 1393
Hieronymus, Mark, 10
Hiestand, F. Brian, 3487
Higashi, Taryn, 2480
Higdon, Lou, 41
Higdon, Theresa, 41
Higgins, Arabella, 696
Higgins, Arabella Bartner, 696
Higgins, Barbara, 1512
Higgins, Bob, 10
Higgins, Diane, 1854
Higgins, Julie, 2790
Higgins, Michael, 1578
Higgins, Ralph P., 2693
Higgins, Stephen D., 1708
Higgins, Trisha R., 2986
Higgins, William, 2263
Higgs, John R., 3429
Highet, Lea Paine, 2101
Highley, Randall M., 1077
Highmark Inc., 2968
Highmark West Virginia, Inc., 2968
Highsmith, Carol, 1171
Hightman, Carrie J., 2752
Hightower, Buckner, 3254
Hightower, James E., Jr., 1299
Highwoods Realty L.P., 1806
Hijkoop, Frans, 2307
Hilado, Tessa, 2354
Hilbert, Robert J., 492
Hilbrich, Gerald F., 712
Hild, Guy M., 2675
Hildebrand, Jeffrey D., 3258
Hildebrand, Melinda B., 3258
Hildebrandt, Leslie, 1573
Hildebrandt, Troy G., 3650
Hildner, Tim, 1606
Hilferty, Joan, 2975
Hilgers, Paul, 3386
Hill, Al G., Jr., 3260
Hill, Arthur B., 664
Hill, B. Harvey, Jr., 917
Hill, Catherine W., 1117
Hill, Cathy, 3401
Hill, Christopher, 823
Hill, Cleo, 501
Hill, Dale, 3259
Hill, Debbie, 2787
Hill, Debi, 1154
Hill, Elizabeth G., 139
Hill, Haines, 900
Hill, J. Tomilson, 538
Hill, James, 3326
Hill, Jaribu, 2335
Hill, Katherine P., 3324
Hill, Kent, 3245
Hill, Louis Fors, 1722
Hill, Louis W., Sr., 1722
Hill, Lyda, 3260
Hill, Margaret Hunt, 3260
Hill, Marion, 342
Hill, Mark E., 1126
Hill, Mary, 1192
Hill, Mary Jane, 2773
Hill, Mary Jo Gheens, 1288
Hill, Maud, 1722
Hill, Michael, 3071
Hill, Penny, 1616
Hill, Ranlyn Tiley, 330
Hill, Richard L., 3391
Hill, Scott, 1634, 2336
Hill, Stephen K., 867
Hill, Steve, 3558
Hill, Steve L., 1590
Hill, Virginia W., 48
Hill, Walter, Dr., 4
Hill, Williard, 2297
Hill-Scott, Karen, 359
Hillblom, Larry L., 250
Hillblom, Terry C., 250
Hillblom, Walter, 250
Hille, Jo Bob, 2816
Hille, Mary Ann, 2816
Hillegonds, Paul C., 1598, 1631
Hillelson, Louis, 2071
Hilliard Lyons Trust Co., 1287
Hilliard, Dozier, 770
Hilliard, Ethele, 3120
Hilliard, Thomas J., Jr., 2906
Hilliker, Don, 959
Hillis, Bob, 1836
Hillman, David McL., 2906
Hillman, Elsie H., 2969
Hillman, Henry L., 2969
Hillman, J.H., Jr., 2969
Hillock, Mickey, 3305
Hills, Linda T., 2906
Hills, Tom, 3115
Hillstrom, Michael C., 1060
Hillyer, Blair A., 2795
Hilsheimer, Cindy, 2750
Hilt, George, 1586
Hilt, Jack, 1586
Hilt, John, 1586
Hiltbrand, Bob, 2682
Hilton Foundation, Conrad, 1086
Hilton, Barron, 251
Hilton, Bob, 717

Hilton, Chris, 717
Hilton, Chris Chapman, 717
Hilton, Conrad N., 251, 1316
Hilton, Conrad N., III, 251
Hilton, Eric M., 251
Hilton, Michael F., 2755
Hilton, R. Robertson, 2736
Hilton, Stephen, 2118
Hilton, Steven M., 251
Hilton, William B., Jr., 251
Himmelfarb, Paul, 665
Himmelrich, Samuel, 1410
Himovitz, Robin Q. Pattis, 1073
Hinchey, John, 268
Hinck, Shelly, 1647
Hinderer, Walter, 2499
Hindes, J. Churchill, 3410
Hindle, David, 1562
Hindman, James M., 80
Hinds, Katherine, 785
Hindy, Stephen, 1344
Hine, Angela, 1642
Hine, Jennifer, 3571
Hine, Tiffany, 3580
Hiner, Travis, 1852
Hines, Christy, 1668
Hines, Donna, 3515
Hines, Dorothy S., 3090
Hines, Rodney, 3565
Hingst, Bob, 1131
Hinkle, William H., 252
Hinrichs, Robert S., 758
Hinson, Alex, Esq., 726
Hinson, Gertrude, 1387
Hinson, J.A., 800
Hinson, Michael, 3051
Hinson, W. Ron, 877
Hinton, Erin M., 2524
Hinton, Gregory P., 3008
Hintz, Melvin A., 3633
Hipp, Elizabeth Jane, 1250
Hipp, Michael J., 3650
Hipple, JR, 3476
Hiramoto, Patti, 157
Hirano Inouye, Irene, 2160
Hirano, Irene Y., 1631
Hires, William L., 2943
Hirrel, Richard J., 97
Hirrel, Tracy G., 97
Hirsch, Adam, 1908
Hirsch, Bruce A., 246
Hirsch, Dina, 655
Hirsch, Edward, 2194
Hirsch, Gladys Ottenheimer, 71
Hirsch, Joseph B., 71
Hirsch, Sanford, 2187
Hirsch, Wendy, 1007
Hirschberg, Jason, 3642
Hirschfeld, Benjamin G., 1839
Hirschfeld, Daniel J., 1839
Hirschfeld, David J., 1839
Hirschfeld, Michael A., 2694
Hirschfeld, Monya A., 1839
Hirschhorn, Barbara B., 1349, 1379
Hirschhorn, Daniel B., 1379
Hirschhorn, David, 1379
Hirschhorn, Michael J., 1349, 1379
Hirschy, Matthew G., 1123
Hirsh, Barry, 428
Hirt, Dana Westreich, 460
Hirt-Eggleston, Kaye, 1178
His Global Inc., 2232
His Way Homes, 1772
Hiscock, Dana W., 2079
Hitachi, Ltd., 666
Hitch, Henry H., 1900
Hitchcock, Nelson, 1143
Hitchcock, Todd, 1184
Hitchings, Roy, Jr., 1336
Hite, Haydn, 1864
Hite, Jessica, 1864
Hite, Lawrence, 2214
Hite, Lawrence D., 2214
HiteT, Marilyn, 1864
Hitt, Lisa, 869
Hittinger, J. Brian, 1171
Hittle, Ann, 3576
Hlavaty, Todd E., Dr., 1849
HNI Corp., 1223
Ho, Linda, 2040
Ho, Peter, 933, 938
Ho, Wayne, 2326
Ho, Y.C., 2094
Hoag, George Grant, 253
Hoag, George Grant, II, 253
Hoag, George Grant, III, 253
Hoag, Grace E., 253
Hoagland, Karl K., Jr., 1065
Hoagland, Sarah, 1065
Hoard, Steve, 3163
Hobart, Wendy C., 1260
Hobbs, Ben B., 1198
Hobbs, Christine, 1618
Hobbs, Larry A., 823
Hobbs, Robert B., Jr., 2943
Hobby Family Foundation, 480
Hoberman, Gerald, 1840
Hobick, Joy, 1817
Hoblitzelle, Esther T., 3262
Hoblitzelle, Karl St. John, 3262
Hobson, Mellody, 306
Hoch, Harry, 1837
Hochstein, Bernard, 2216
Hochstein, Michael, 2216
Hochstein, Miriam, 2216
Hochstein, Richard, 2216
Hochstein, Shaul, 960
Hochstein, Stephen, 2216
Hochwender, J. Michael, 2740
Hock, Doug, 493
Hockaday, Irvine O., Jr., 1793
Hocker, Sam L., 3279
Hockfield, Susan, 2085
Hodge, Clark, 725
Hodge, Glenn, 3327
Hodge, Janet A., 1008
Hodges, Brenda, 2861
Hodges, Diane L., 2001
Hodges, Don, 3207
Hodges, Lillia, 823
Hodges, Priscilla, 562
Hodgkins, William E., 1317
Hodgson, Joseph, 3597
Hodsdon, Ann, 1885
Hodshire, Jeremiah, 1620
Hodson, Harold, 1225
Hoechst Marion Roussel, Inc., 1988
Hoeck, James T., 1445
Hoefer, Bob, 1216
Hoefinghoff, Richard, 2680
Hoefle, Daniel C., 1885
Hoehn, Natasha, 409
Hoehn-Saric, R. Christopher, 648
Hoejland, Peter, 2064
Hoenlein, Malcolm, 2238
Hoensheid, Gary, 1616
Hoeschler, Linda L., 1722
Hoesterey, Brian, 1524
Hoesterey, Dawn, 1524
Hofer, Steven C., 3174
Hoff, Diana, 2869
Hoff, Susan S., 1685
Hoffberger, Judith R., 1409
Hoffen, Howard I., 2218
Hoffen, Sandra, 2218
Hoffer, Shannon, 3521
Hoffman, Alfred, Jr., 1326
Hoffman, Bill, 2071
Hoffman, Carol, 896
Hoffman, Daniel, 2050
Hoffman, David L., 1358
Hoffman, Dina, 163
Hoffman, Elisabeth, 1326
Hoffman, James, 2717
Hoffman, Jean Marie, Sr., 2680
Hoffman, Judy, 1067
Hoffman, Karen A., 77
Hoffman, Leonard R., 3350
Hoffman, Mabel, 609
Hoffman, Nancy E., Esq., 2108
Hoffman, Shay Shelton, 3350
Hoffman, Steven M., 2952
Hoffman, Therese H., 1090
Hoffman, Thomas F., 3054
Hofler, Thomas F., 3473
Hogan, David O., 2811, 2813
Hogan, Lori L., 1841
Hogan, Michael P., 1507
Hogan, Paul R., 1841
Hogan, Paul T., 2340
Hogan, Randall J., 1727
Hogan, Samalid, 1547
Hogarty, Daniel J., Jr., 2474
Hoge, Patrick, 678
Hogel, Carol C., 1006
Hogel, Catherine C., 1006
Hogel, Elisabeth, 1006
Hogen, Charles "Robin", 1949
Hogen, Mary, 21
Hogg, John, 3336
Hoglund, Forrest E., 3263
Hoglund, Sally R., 3263
Hogue, Thelma L., 4
Hoguet, Karen M., 2726
Hohenberg, Paul M., 2108
Hohlman, Cristina, 2132
Hohmann, Jere, 2900
Hohn, David C., 2270
Hoi, Samuel, 264
Hojnacki, William, 1197
Hokanson, Neil C., 378
Hoke, Steve, 384
Holbrook, Kevin, 538
Holbrook, Leah, 3576
Holbrook, Richard E., 1461
Holbrook, Sherry, 346
Holcomb, Douglas Clay, 2015
Holcomb, Gary, 2253
Holcomb, Larry, 2835
Holcombe, Marie, 2088
Holcombe, Paul A., Jr., 2600
Holcombe, Robert, Jr., 3111
Holden Trust, The, 2524
Holden, Henry R., 1445
Holder Construction Co., 887
Holder, Lofton, 2188
Holder-Price, Sue, 1130
Holding, Frank B., 2630
Holding, Thomas Charles, 1337
Holding, Wendy, 2335
Holdorf, Judi, 1217
Holdren, Thomas, 2747
Holefelder, Jack, Jr., 2932
Holen, Steve, 2651
Holiat, Lydia, 2932
Holiner, Hope, 2278
Hollabaugh, Beth, 2674
Holladay, Clay E., 1758
Hollan, Larry, 1184
Holland, Bernice, 3280
Holland, Jim, 1852
Holland, Marilyn M., 1840
Holland, Mary A., 1840
Holland, Max, 2552
Holland, Nancy L., 2753
Holland, Richard, 4
Holland, Richard D., 1840
Holland, Robert, Jr., 59
Holland, Stacy, 3055
Hollatz, Tom, 1731
Holleman, Brett, 1585
Holler, Denis, 1513
Holley, Jeffrey D., 1183
Holliday, Iris E., 3433
Holliday, Linda, 1703
Holliday, Susan, 1812
Holliman, Vonda, 1264
Hollingsworth, Elizabeth, 28
Hollingsworth, Susan Hunt, 2971
Hollins, Karen, 294
Hollis, Scott Burnham, 1760
Hollister, Don, 2707
Hollister, Lee, 393
Hollman, Daniel, 1806
Hollman, Don B., 1144
Holloman-Price Fdn., 2496
Holloway Revocable Trust, John D., 759
Holloway, Alan, 418
Holloway, Carolyn G., 3264
Holloway, E. Graham, 3264
Holloway, Janet M., 1803
Holloway, Janis, 2679
Holloway, John W., 759
Holloway, R. Kurtz, 2916
Hollowell, Sharon, 1142
Holly, LaShaunda, 10
Holm, Herbert W., 712
Holman, John W., III, 1944
Holman, John W., Jr., 1944
Holman, Robert, 1868
Holman, Tom, 1748
Holmberg, Dennis M., 2014
Holmberg, John, 493
Holmberg, Mr., 2219
Holmberg, Ruth S., 2451
Holmes, Amy, 315
Holmes, David A., 718
Holmes, Derek, 3327
Holmes, Edward A., 1946
Holmes, G. E., 2815
Holmes, Gordon, 2473
Holmes, Gregory, 232
Holmes, Hal, Jr., Dr., 3112
Holmes, Lisette E., 2113
Holmes, Louise, 2732
Holmes, Mary M., 2541
Holmes, Mitch, 1783
Holmes, Robert W., Jr., 1534
Holmlund, Mark, 378
Holmquist, Kareen, 3558
Holmquist, Marilyn L., 3656
Holoman, Smallwood, 1662
Holoubek, Phil, 1282
Holser, Leah, 3521
Holst, Stephen, 3683
Holsten, Diana L., 1122

Holston, Martin J., 249
Holt, Leon C., Jr., 3024
Holtel, Joseph A., 2762
Holthe, Jonathon, 1217
Holthouse, Colleen, 3265
Holthouse, Colleen M., 3265
Holthouse, Lisa, 3265
Holthouse, Michael H., 3265
Holton, JIm, 2331
Holton, Raymond B., 2986
Holyoke, Tom, 1852
Holzer, Alan, 2325
Holzer, Bambi, 260
Holzer, Erich, 1939
Holzer, Eva, 1939
Holzer, Robert, 1939
Holzer, Vivian, 1939
Hom, Winston, 391
Homa, Mike, 1850
Homan, Benjamin, Jr., 1033
Homan, David, 1731
Homchick, Craig, 3503
Home Instead, Inc., 1841
Home Towne Suites - Bowling Green LLC, 1818
Home Towne Suites - Clarksville LLC, 1818
Home, Richard, 3405
Homes, Richmond, 498
HON Industries Inc., 1223
Hon, Maria, 280
Honek, Mellow, 2010
Honeycutt, A.C., Jr., 2540
Honickman, Jeffrey A., 3029
Honickman, Lynne, 2970
Honickman, Marjorie, 3029
Honnold, Paul, 1214
Hood, James W., 1770
Hood, Jane Renner, 1834
Hood, Philip, 484
Hood, Robert, 2228
Hood, Robert C., 314
Hood, Teresa Rebozo, 807
Hoogeboom, Marge, 1585
Hoogendoorn, Case, 1068
Hoogland, Fredric, 1315
Hook, Jonathan, 59
Hook, Jonathan D., 1416
Hooker, Brian, 1930
Hooker, Craig, 1160
Hooser, Karen R., 2765
Hooton, Paula, 3233
Hoover, Anne, 1159
Hoover, Bob, 948
Hoover, Cynthia K., 1159
Hoover, David C., 1159
Hoover, Deborah D., 2740
Hoover, Dennis, 3259
Hoover, James E., 1159
Hoover, John, 2074, 3259
Hoover, Katherine C., 1159
Hoover, Mildred M., 1159
Hoover, Rebecca, 2562
Hoozer, Daniel Van, 235
Hope, Betsy, 2710
Hopkins, Ann, 869
Hopkins, C. Timothy, 948
Hopkins, Donald R., 1056
Hopkins, John, 408
Hopkins, John P., 483
Hopkins, Rachel Abrams, 3577
Hopkins, Ronnie, 900
Hopkins, Rusty, 900
Hopkins, Vince, 2680
Hopkinson, Sealy H., 1394
Hopper, Jim, 3494
Hopping, Andy, 1581
Hopwood, Andy P., 3181
Horan, David C., 2270
Hord, Janel, 2682
Hori, Jim, 407
Horizon Healthcare Services, Inc., 1940
Horn, Albert, Jr., 2674
Horn, Daniel L., 2668
Horn, Robyn, 75
Hornady, Ellen, 1837
Hornbach, Mike, 1141
Hornblower, Jonathan M., 3196
Horne, Eleanor, 1979
Horne, George B., 254
Horne, Mabel A., 1484
Horne, Steve, 1130
Horne, Timothy P., 254
Horner, Ann Marie, 1941
Horner, Carolyn, 1941
Horner, Duncan, 543
Horner, Gary C., Esq., 2922
Horner, Kathryn, 1941
Horner, Terry, 1941
Horner-Smith, Meghann, 1941
Horning, Chuck, 538
Hornsby, Doug, 1146
Hornsby, Kathy, 3488
Horntvedt, Jody, 1723
Horowitch, David, 2228
Horowitz, Alison, 2355
Horowitz, Ann P., 760
Horowitz, Dustin, 760
Horowitz, Joel J., 760
Horowitz, Margaret, 2220
Horowitz, Robert H., 2295
Horras, Nancy, 1227
Horsager, Naomi, 1689
Horsburgh, Christopher, 2724
Horst, Mary Lynn, 1849
Horton Fund, Alan & Beverley, 2780
Horton, Alice Kirby, 1952
Horton, David F., 2523
Horton, Gayle, 2855
Horton, Nancy, 2850
Horton, Neil, 1268
Horvitz, H. Robert, 3516
Hoshaw, Betsy, 1131
Hosking, John H., 1579
Hoskins, Richard J., 1081
Hosoda, Paul, 3531
Hospice of San Joaquin, 161
Hospira, Inc., 1034
Hosseini, Khaled, 255
Hosseini, Roya, 255
Hosseini, Sandra, 255
Host, Jerry, 1767
Hostek, Loren D., 3557
Hostetter, Amos B., Jr., 1433
Hostetter, Barbara W., 1433
Hostler, Lisa, 2981
Hotaling, Bruce, 3000
Hotchkiss, Craig, 1228
Hotel Americana, 2469
Hotz, Robert Lee, 678
Hotzler, Heidi, 2325
Hou, Grace B., 993
Houck, Gayle L., 2340
Houghton, Sean, 3414
Houkom, Betty, 823
Houle, Irene, 482
Houlihan, Cathy, 638
Houlihan, Robert W., 1240
Hourihan, Edward, Jr., 2154
House of Lloyd, Inc., 1267
House, F. Dewitt, Jr., 3443
House, Helen Fasken, 3229
House, Jim, 3304
House, Patricia, 248
Houseal, John, 1068
Houston, Alice, 1283
Houston, Gary, 3150
Houston, Jamie, 1759
Houston, Jamie G., III, 1767
Hovde Capital I, LLC, 3622
Hovde Financial, Inc., 3622
Hovde, Eric D., 3622
Hovde, Steven D., 3622
Hovey, Dawn, 1235
Hovland, Ann M., 475
How, Melissa, 1833
Howard Trust, Jack R., 2780
Howard, Barbara, 4, 867
Howard, Burgie, 1012
Howard, Christopher “Chris” B., Dr., 3468
Howard, Danette, 1174
Howard, David M., 1105
Howard, Don, 264
Howard, Horace, 1485
Howard, Janet, 3043
Howard, John L., 1024
Howard, Katherine Kelly, 1388
Howard, Kay, 3200
Howard, Marven E., 244
Howard, Melinda, 2844
Howard, Peter K., 3430
Howard, Randy, 1783
Howard, Robert G., 3043
Howard, Robert S., 1854, 3525
Howard, Roscoe, 448
Howard, Sam, 1642
Howard, Tim, 526
Howard, Wayne, 1395
Howard-Potter, Jack, 2780
Howatt, Thomas J., 3661
Howe, Calvin E., 2989
Howe, Dave, 2570
Howe, Debara, 1171
Howe, Eliza, 586
Howe, H.R., 2570
Howe, H.T., 2570
Howe, Isabel, 2050
Howe, Jacquelyn, 586
Howe, John, 586
Howe, Richard V., 1552
Howe, Ruth, 2148
Howe, Tina, 2143
Howell, Brad, 1131
Howell, Jim, 1583
Howell, Laverne, 3268
Howell, Martha C., 2101
Howell, Nancy B., 1906
Howell, Pam, 2790
Howell, Philip B., 2012
Howell, R. Rodney, 783
Howell, Ronald S., 3570
Howell, Winston, 726
Hower, Donovan E., Sr., 3448
Howes, Deborah S., 2127
Howett, Ciannat M., 872
Howie, Barbara L., 508
Howland, Edward M., 1539
Howland, John M., 3280
Howlin, Diane, 1584
Howrey, Matt, 1157
Hoy, Annette, 985
Hoy, Ariane, 1909
Hoy, James A., 2332
Hoy, James Sue, 2332
Hoy, Ronald R., 232
Hoyer, David, 3329
Hoyos, Jose, 43
Hoyt, Willma C., 2221
Hrabowski, Freeman A., III, 3500
HS Processing, LP, 2665
HSBC Bank USA, N.A., 2325, 2445
HSC Health Care Foundation, 1414
Hsia, Sven E., 2513
Hsiao, Gilbert, 325
HTOOB, Inc., 704
Htun, MaDoe, 3011
Huang, Alice S., 2390
Huang, Mikiko, Dr., 168
Huang, Shauna, 2882
Hubbard Foundation, 2574
Hubbard, Al, 543
Hubbard, Allan, 1174
Hubbard, Amy L., 1729
Hubbard, C. Mark, 1205
Hubbard, Hylan T., 3454
Hubbard, Jean, 361
Hubbard, Julie, 1098
Hubbard, Kenneth E., 7
Hubbard, Peggy, 2017
Hubbard, Robin, 502
Hubbert, Becky, 2020
Hubble, Butch, 2710
Hubbs, Donald H., 251
Huber, David R., 1940
Huber, Pat, 3431
Huber, Robert A., 282
Huber, Sandy, 1614
Hubert, A. Franklin, 2771
Hubscher, Chuck, 1647
Huckaby, Hank, 863
Huckenberg, Mark, 528
Huckin, Carol L., 3288
Huckins, Robert G., 3062
Huddleston, Bob, 1842
Hudetz, Frank C., 1008
Hudgins, Jeffrey, 822
Hudler, Carol, 3129
Hudner, Steve, 159
Hudson City Savings Bank, 1942
Hudson River Bank & Trust Co., 2223
Hudson, David T., 1754
Hudson, Edward R., Jr., 3185
Hudson, J. Clifford, 2160
Hudson, Jerry, 2922
Hudson, Laura J., 1332
Hudson, Mary R., 2881
Hudson, Paul, 2342
Hudson, Sonny, 3280
Hudson, Sue, 3356
Hudson-Jaccard Charitable Trust Fund, Aduh, 1272
Hudspeth, Larry, 301
Huebschen, Don, 3663
Huesman, Terri Donlin, 2762
Huey, Bruce E., 983
Huey, Ester, 3576
Huey, Jeanne W., 398
Huezo, Jeanette, 1422
Huff, Florida, 923
Huff, Olson, 2632
Huff, W.C., 303
Huffenus, Daniel S., 1042
Huffman, Gary T., 2756
Huggins, Anita, 1472
Hughes Medical Institute, Howard, 559
Hughes, Alan F., 3031

Hughes, Alana, 2829
Hughes, Arthur H., 661
Hughes, Baker, 3330
Hughes, Brian, 207
Hughes, Carolyn R., 1147
Hughes, Chris, 771
Hughes, David R., 2923
Hughes, Deborah L., 3357
Hughes, Geoffrey C., 2224
Hughes, Hattie Hyman, 207
Hughes, James S., 1453
Hughes, Jancie, 503
Hughes, Jeanne T., 1035
Hughes, John E., 986, 1035
Hughes, Katherine Nouri, 331
Hughes, Kim, 1152
Hughes, Leona, 695
Hughes, Mabel Y., 49
Hughes, Mark F., Jr., 2105
Hughes, Michael H., 3554
Hughey, Richard M., Jr., 1612
Hugo Neu Corp., 2323
Huizinga, Gretchen, 3509
Hulewicz, Mike, 1590
Hulings, Albert D., 1702
Hulings, Mary Andersen, 1702
Hull, Alan, 1756
Hull, John E., 2302
Hull, Kenneth, 1156
Hull, Ralph, 3308
Hullet, Diane Dow, 1597
Hulme, Christine J., 2763
Hulsman, Letty, 3419
Human Svcs. Corp., 1505
Humann, Phil, 754
Humber, Candace A., 378
Hume, Carol, 3605
Hume, Ivor Noel, 3605
Hume, Ivor Noel, Mrs., 3605
Humes, Brian K., 1818
Humes, Cori, 563
Humes, Jim, 1215
Humes, Kerry, Dr., 1063
Humiston, Mary E., 88
Hummel, Alethia, 999
Hummel, Carolyn, 1607
Hummel, Chad, 1943
Hummel, Charles F., 3605
Hummel, David R., 1943
Hummel, Jane, 1943
Hummel, Todd, 1943
Hummer, Philip Wayne, 1014
Hummer-Tuttle, Maria, 276
Humphrey, Louise, 726
Humphrey, Tom, 1636
Humphreys, Lewis H., 1795
Humphris, Robert R., 3448
Humphrys, Maureen, 3683
Hundley, Linda, 2578
Hungerpiller, James R., 912
Hunker, Fred D., 7
Hunsaker, Brain, 351
Hunsaker, Nancy, 351
Hunt, A. James, 2971
Hunt, Alexandra K., 2971
Hunt, Andrew McQ., 2971
Hunt, Avery S., 2971
Hunt, Bonnie B.K., 2971
Hunt, C. Giles, 2572
Hunt, Christopher M., 2971
Hunt, Daniel K., 2971
Hunt, Don, 2366
Hunt, Donald M., 2366
Hunt, Edward M., 2971
Hunt, Elizabeth H., 2971
Hunt, Evan McMasters, 2971
Hunt, Holly Bamford, 3495
Hunt, Joan, 1176
Hunt, John B., 2971
Hunt, Kathlee S., 3145
Hunt, Lila C., 2971
Hunt, Natasha, 342
Hunt, Penny, 1734
Hunt, Richard L., 389
Hunt, Richard M., 2971
Hunt, Roy A., 2971
Hunt, Roy A., III, 2971
Hunt, Stephanie E., 3209
Hunt, Torrence M., Jr., 2971
Hunt, Torrence W.B., 2971
Hunt, Tyler B., 2971
Hunt, Virginia, 1036
Hunt, William E., 2971
Hunter, A.V., 508
Hunter, Bruce, 2287
Hunter, Don, 1178
Hunter, Edwin F., III, 1307
Hunter, George Thomas, 3123
Hunter, Jack, 1127
Hunter, Shirley H., 3043
Hunter, Susan L., 2762
Hunter, Thomas, 1596
Hunter, Thomas A., 1590
Hunter-Ishikawa, Zen, 659
Hunting, Mary Anne, 1667
Huntington Bank, 3579
Huntington National Bank, The, 1586, 2679, 2788
Huntington, Al, 1133
Huntington, Robert H., Dr., 2793
Huntley, Allan, 1464
Hunzeker, Pam, 1847
Hupert, Ann, 3007
Hurd, Joseph D., Jr., 2907
Hurdelbrink, Laura, 3519
Hurlen Fund, Harold, 3494
Hurley, Cheryl, 2263
Hurley, Jay, 352
Hurley, ToniRae, 714
Huron Co., 1388
Hurst, Robert W., 3466
Hurt, Kathleen C., 461
Hurt, Sarah S., 461
Hurt, William H., 461
Hurtubise, Mark, 3526
Hurvis, Christina, 1037
Hurvis, J. Thomas, 1037
Hurvis, Julie A., 1037
Hurvis-Younkin, Sara, 1037
Hurwich, Cecelia, 91
Hurwitz, Barbara, 2254
Hurwitz, Benjamin A., 1094
Hurwitz, Kenneth D., 2056
Huschke, Kathryn Wise, 1649
Huseby, Sven, 574
Husid, Jackie, 1552
Huskey, Leon, 1180
Husmann, Joyce, 1135
Huss, David, 3150
Hussey, Alison, 714
Hussey, Bernice H., 3124
Hussey, Herbert E., 823
Huston, Charles L., III, 2973
Huston, Charles L., IV, 2973
Huston, Charles L., Jr., 2973
Huston, Joy, 2923
Huston, Morrison C., Jr., 3045
Huston, Ruth, 2973
Huston, Scott G., 2973
Hutaff, Lucile, 2541
Hutcheson, Dorothea W., 75
Hutcheson, John L., IV, 3141
Hutcheson, Karen, 75
Hutcheson, Mary E., 75
Hutcheson, Mary Ellen, 712
Hutcheson, Richard, 75
Hutcheson, Ryan, 2562
Hutcheson, Theodore M., Jr., 3141
Hutcheson, William L., 75
Hutchings, Jack, 1111
Hutchinson, Elaine S., 2275
Hutchinson, Howard G., 623
Hutchinson, Les, 1620
Hutchinson, Raymond J., 1611
Hutchinson, Robert E., 2616
Hutchinson, Susan E., 3196
Hutchison, Brad, 3278
Hutchison, Jeffrey, 2762
Hutchison, Laura, 653
Hutchison, Susan, 3562
Huth, Robert, Jr., 2982
Hutson, Chris, 1286
Huttenlocher, Daniel, 1056
Huttler, Stephen B., 1373
Hutto, Clare P., 258
Hutto, Eileen C., 258
Hutto, Scott W., 3112
Hutton, Ann, 2915
Hutton, Billy J., Jr., 2712
Hvalbukta Ans, 1524
Hwang Donor Advised Fund at Fuller, 2189
Hwang, Becky, 2189
Hwang, Sung Kook, 2189
Hwang, Sunny S., 281
Hwee, Koh Boon, 248
Hyams, Godfrey M., 1486
Hyams, Sarah A., 1486
Hybl, Kyle, 492
Hybl, William, 543
Hybl, William J., 492
Hyche, J. Tod, 3099
Hyde Park Nursing Home, Inc., 2254
Hyde, Lillia Babbitt, 1944
Hyduke, John, 1677
Hyla, Lee, 2262
Hyland, Carol, 3615
Hyland, M. Elise, 2940
Hylton, Donnie, 3471
Hyman, Alan L., 207
Hyman, Charles D. "Chuck", 722
Hyman, Howard L., 207
Hyman, Steven E., 2126
Hyndman, Thomas M., Jr., 3019
Hynek, Jacqueline, 3372
Hynek, Steven L., 3372
Hynnek, Julia L., 1702
Hyzer, Nancy, 990

Iacarella, Dawn, 1687
Iacoabelli, Jolie, 3401
Iacocca, Lido A. "Lee", 1487
Ibach, Teresa, 1842
Ibanez, Jose M., 954
Ibarguen, Alberto, 771
Ibarra, Ricardo, 312
Icap, 37
ICAP Securities USA LLC, 2562
Ieuter, Cal, 1642
Iger, Robert A., 181
Ignat, Brian, 2754
Ignat, Joseph, 2754
Ihrig, Frederick G., 485
Ilingworth, Calvin, 1160
IJO, 2562
Ikeda, Thomas M., 3531
ILC Holdings, Inc., 2266
Iler, Barbara Welles, 1529
Ilitch, Denise, 1666
Illinois Consolidated Telephone Co., 1053
IMA Financial Group Inc., The, 1261
Imboden, Connie E., 1347
IMF Civic Program, 676
Imhof, Mike, 543
Imhoff, Quincey, 202
Imhoff, Quincey T., 165
Imirizian, Maro, 3567
Imlay, Cindy, 888
Imlay, John P. "Scott", III, 888
Imlay, John P., Jr., 888
Imlay, Mary Ellen, 888
Imler, Fred, Sr., 2907
Immerwahr, John, Dr., 2502
Imondi, Deborah, 3093
IMPACT, 161
Impemba, Dominick, 2390
Imrie, Kent, 340
IMX, 3026
Inbar, Tomer, 2081
Ince, Max, 3356
Inch, Steve, 1861
Inch, Tara, 1861
Indeck, Jennifer, 696
Indeck, Jennifer Bartner, 696
Independence Blue Cross, 2975
Independence Communications, Inc., 2997
Independent Publications, Inc., 2997
Indiana Association Of Realtors, 1178
Indiana Energy, Inc., 1202
Indiana Plumbing Supply Co., Inc., 336
Indiana State Dept. of Health, 1156
Indiana Thrift for AIDS, 1156
Indianapolis Foundation, The, 1156
Indochino, 37
Industrial Tools Inc., 85
Indy Pride, 1156
Indyke, Dottie, 2017
Infield, Jack, 2909
Infinity Contact, 1228
INFOR, 3026
Infosoft Group, Inc., 679
Ingber, Adam F., 2355
Ingerman, Steven L., 2220
Ingmire, Robert E., 2436
Ingraham, Patricia, 2253
Ingram, Anna Storms, 2872
Ingram, Cynthia, 3443
Ingram, Lee Ann, 3121
Ingram, Mauri, 3571
Ingram, Patsy, 2552
Ingram, Robert A., 2600
Ingram, Scarlett, 1295
Ingwall, Teresa M., 2524
Inman, Douglas L., 1188
Inner City Broadcasting, 2071
Inserra, Robert, 1948
Insignares, Valerie L., 732
Insurance Management Associates, Inc., 1261
Int'l Merchandising Corp., 2562
Integra LifeSciences Corp., 1945
Intercon Overseas, Inc., 691
Interfaith Council, 613
Interfaith Hospitality, 3611
Intermedics, Inc., 757

Intermountain Gas Co., 2652
International Air Leases, Inc., 697
International Business Machines Corp., 2227
International Paper Co., 3142
International Risk Management, 3294
Interpacific Holdings, Inc., 2048
Interstate Power and Light Co., 3592
INTRUST Bank, N.A., 2806
Intuit Inc., 263
Inverso, Peter A., 1984
Iovine, Peter, 59
Iovino Charitable Lead Annuity Trust, The, 2228
Iovino, Mary, 2228
Iovino, Thomas, 2228
Iowa West Racing Assn., 1226
Ippel, Mary, 1687
Irace, Gregory, 1988
Irby, Charles L., 1770
Irgang, Tory, 2170
Irish, Ann K., 1656
Irish, Roberta P., 174
Irish, Thomas G., 174
Irvin, Nike, 137
Irvine, James, 264
Irvine, Tom, 982
Irving Consumer Products, 952
Irwin, Anna M., 2204
Irwin, Gail H., 2907
Irwin, Greg, 3684
Irwin, John N., III, 2026, 2504
Irwin, Kevin D., 1352
Irwin, Kevin W., Rev. Msgr., 650
Irwin, Robert J.A., 2120
Isaac, Amy E. Saltonstall, 1539
Isaacson, Kari, 3498
Isaacson, Walter, 2066
Isabella Bank and Trust, 1622
Isakson, Cherie, Rev., 1135
Isbell, Jim, 1155
Isbin, Sharon, 2049
Isetti, Duane, 161
Isgrig, Thomas R., 2758
Ish Shalom Trust, 2416
Isham, Duane, 2796
Isherwood, Elizabeth, 1453
Ishida, Takuzo, 1045
Isom, Ralph, 945
Israel, Allen D., 3490
Israelson, Bernice F., 1380
Israelson, Cynthia, 1380
Israelson, Max R., 1380
Israelson, Stuart G., 1380
Isroff, Richard, 2737
Istel, Andrea, 2234
Istel, John, 2234
Istel, Yves Andre, 2234
Istel, Yves-Andre, 2234
Itasca Medical Center Foundation, 1699
Itell, John P., 1360
Ito, Joi, 771, 1056
Iton, Anthony B., 138
Itsmyseat.com, 2001
Itzler, Ellen, 2019
Itzler, Jesse, 2019
Itzler, Peter, 2019
Iuliano, Susan, 1551
Ivanca, Tere, 1677
Ivanko, Marika, 1269
Ivens, Barbara J., 1611
Iverson, Brent, 59
Ives, Deborah M., 456
Ives, Mary, 1699
Ivory Residual Estate, 2332
Iwata, John C., 2227
Izzo, Anthony J., III, 1381
Izzo, Anthony J., Jr., 1381
Izzo, Scott D., 2998

J-Track LLC, 2228
Jablonski, Christine, 842
Jaborska, Dena Mottola, 1924
Jacangelo, Nicholas, 2335
Jacangelo, Nick, 2335
Jaccard Memorial Trust, A.H., 1272
Jaccard Memorial Trust, L.A., 1272
Jack, Jeffrey L., 1263
Jackson, Anthony, 3451
Jackson, Bill, 425
Jackson, Bruce, 2767
Jackson, Carol M., 628
Jackson, Catherine T., 3129
Jackson, Charles, 54
Jackson, Cobi, 2868
Jackson, Dauphen, 3300
Jackson, David, 3187
Jackson, David A., 2521
Jackson, David D., Hon., 3361
Jackson, Deborah C., 1461
Jackson, Deborah J., 1460
Jackson, Dorothy, 2058
Jackson, Douglas J., 19
Jackson, Eben, 3620
Jackson, Edgar B., 2770
Jackson, Elizabeth O., 854
Jackson, Emily Tow, 616
Jackson, Eugene W., 2953
Jackson, Franklin L., 1149
Jackson, Gayle P.W., 59
Jackson, Geoffrey W., 2953
Jackson, Jess S., 266
Jackson, John Henry, 1762
Jackson, John J., 2616
Jackson, Jon A., 3620
Jackson, Jonathon F., 1149
Jackson, Kate, 1296
Jackson, Kelvin, 3390
Jackson, Ken, 3503
Jackson, Kenneth T., 2286
Jackson, Kory, 1260
Jackson, Lloyd G., II, 2892
Jackson, Lori A., 682
Jackson, Marcy Zilber, 3670
Jackson, Maria C., 2851
Jackson, Marie-Louise, 2953
Jackson, Mark A., 1149
Jackson, Melissa S.A., 3670
Jackson, Michael L., 1149
Jackson, Peter D., 3620
Jackson, Robert, Hon., 1763
Jackson, Ronald, 1286
Jackson, Sally, 2366
Jackson, Shane M., 3670
Jackson, Sharon M., 1149
Jackson, Steven M., 3071
Jackson, Thomas H., 2154
Jackson, Victoria, 237
Jacksonville Jaguars, Ltd., 761
Jacob Associates, 102
Jacob, Beth M., 1744
Jacob, Dean L., 2733
Jacobowitz, Gerald N., 2111
Jacobs, Ann, 1528
Jacobs, Bill, 893
Jacobs, Christopher, 842
Jacobs, Debra M., 798
Jacobs, Evelyn, 401
Jacobs, Glenn, 1548
Jacobs, Joseph J., 267
Jacobs, Linda K., 2235
Jacobs, Lisbeth, 2237
Jacobs, Luke T., 2340
Jacobs, Margaret E., 267
Jacobs, Nancy, 1742
Jacobs, Paul E., 376
Jacobs, Russell C., III, 912
Jacobs, Todd, 1607
Jacobs, Violet J., 267
Jacobs, Violet Jabara, 267
Jacobs, Wesley, 1616
Jacobs, Yvonne, 543
Jacobsen, Brian, 2473
Jacobson, Carolyn, 651
Jacobson, Joanna, 1490
Jacobson, Jonathon, 1490
Jacobson, Joyce, 623
Jacobson, Knute, 3659
Jacobson, Lana, 1614
Jacoby, Jonathan, 1481
Jade, Hathaway F., 2918
Jaeckle, Fred, 809
Jaeger, Dick, 3607
Jaeger, Ellen, Dr., 948
Jafek, Bruce W., 479
Jaffe, Edwin A., 1491
Jaffe, Ira J., 1599, 1638
Jaffe, Lola, 1491
Jaffe, Mary H., 248
Jaffe, Meyer, 1491
Jaffe, Robert, 1491
Jaffe, Suzanne D., 59
Jaffenagler, Alissa, 1973
Jaffer, Fauzia, 763
Jaffer, Mohsin, 763
Jaharis, Kathryn, 2236
Jaharis, Mary, 2236
Jaharis, Michael, 2236
Jaharis, Michael, Jr., 2236
Jaharis, Steven, 2236
Jain, Kanika Virmani, 3270
Jain, Suman, 2399
Jain, Vinay K., 3270
Jakovic, Joseph M., 2902
Jakusz, Sharon, 3606
Jalonick, Mary M., 3209
Jamerson, Ellen P., 3454
James, Barbara L., 1626
James, Ellen, 268
James, Holly M., 1800
James, Juanita, 604
James, Neil, 993
James, Thomas M., 529
James, William R., 1770
James-Brown, Christine, 2191
Jamieson, Kathleen Hall, 87
Jamison, Karen, 3488
Jamison, Nelle Woods, 1857
Janc, Christopher M., 1008
Janes, Leah, 1154
Janke, Chris, 990
Jannarone, Gary, 1914
Jannusch, Rey, 1021
Janoush, Lucy, 1760
Jansen, Dan, 538
Jansen, Doug, Dr., 1179
Jansen, Elizabeth, 371
Jansen, Heather, 2680
Jansky, Dennis, 2655
Jansma, Rosy, 1168
Janssen Pharmaceutica Inc., 1948
Janz, James F., 3670
Janzen, Pete, 1710
Japanese American National Museum, 680
Jaquish, Gail A., 1865
Jarchow, Richard C., Sr., 764
Jardine, Robert A. "Drew", Jr., 1299
Jarecki, Donna M. C., 557
Jarecki, Gloria, 557
Jarecki, Nancy, 557
Jarnot, Chris, 543
Jarrett, Diane K., 2663
Jarrett, Joyce M., Dr., 3487
Jaskowiak, Scott E., 1799
Javits, Carla, 1511
Jay, Ann F., 1573
Jayapal, Pramila, 667
Jaynes, Lisa, 3378
Jayo, David, 3551
Jazwinski, Robert C., 2925
Jealous, Benjamin Todd, 385
Jeannero, Jane M., 1611
Jeans, Matthew M., 845
Jeep, Edward "Ed" L., 3468
Jeffcoat, Otis Allen, III, 3112
Jefferson, Ted, 2324
Jefferson, Thomas, 2649
Jeffress, Elizabeth G., 3442
Jeffress, Robert M., 3444
Jeffries, Dawn Harris, 988
Jeffries, Lynn, 2210
Jeffris, Thomas M., 3624
Jeld-Wen Co. of Arizona, 2852
Jeld-Wen Fiber Products, Inc. of Iowa, 2852
Jeld-Wen Holding, Inc., 2852
Jeld-Wen, Inc., 2852
Jelks, Bobby, 1306
Jendoco Construction Corp., 2935
Jenkin, Thomas M., 1860
Jenkins, Barbara, 484, 842
Jenkins, Beth Boney, 2599
Jenkins, Carlton, Dr., 1662
Jenkins, Carolyn S., 524
Jenkins, Cathy, 725
Jenkins, Christopher, 901
Jenkins, Christopher S., 524
Jenkins, David D., 524
Jenkins, Decosta E., 3129
Jenkins, Forrest N., 3120
Jenkins, Franklin Clay, 2616
Jenkins, George W., 804
Jenkins, Hugh, 3431
Jenkins, Jennifer, 10
Jenkins, Karen, 2795
Jenkins, Katha, 537
Jenkins, Laura Lee, 3346
Jenkins, Meredith, 2085
Jenkins, Rick, 484
Jenkins, Scott M., 2926
Jenkins, Susan, 2540
Jenkins, Thomas K., Hon., 2733
Jenkins, Tyrie Lee, 933
Jenkins, Wayne, Esq., 2689
Jenko, Mary E., 792
Jenks, John R., 264
Jenks, Vicki, 3606
Jennings, Cassandra, 391
Jennings, Dee, 394
Jennings, Elizabeth Cabell, 3425
Jennings, Frank G., 2231
Jennings, Judith, 1292
Jennings, Kevin, 2040
Jennings, Lisa, 1135
Jennings, Louise, 8
Jennings, Sherry, 252
Jennings, Toni, 842

Jensen, Ann, 3300
Jensen, Bob, 1217
Jensen, Gladys Margaret, 3194
Jensen, H. James, 3594
Jensen, Janet, 3198
Jensen, Janet Jarie, 3169
Jensen, Jeff, 3198
Jensen, Jeffrey J., 3194
Jensen, Jon, 2349
Jensen, Julie, 3192
Jensen, Julie J., 3194
Jensen, Lou Anne, 3198
Jensen, Lou Anne King, 3194
Jensen, Melissa Smith, 2785
Jensen, Ronald L., 3198
Jensen, Todd, 371
Jensen, Tom, 1701
Jenson, Lawrence, 3124
Jenson, Michael, 1832
Jeon, Brent, 280
Jeppson, Nancy, 1512
Jerde, Roxanne, 727
Jeremiah Project, 3330
Jeresaty, Robert M., 585
Jernagan, Luke, 2119
Jernigan, Matt, 1660
Jernstedt Trust, Dorothy, 377
Jernstedt, Derek, 377
Jernstedt, Dorothy, 377
Jernstedt, Jaci, 377
Jernstedt, Jennifer, 377
Jero, Paula, 3633
Jerviss, Shelly, 2231
Jessell, Thomas M., 1714
Jessen, Gwen, 1012
Jessup, James L., Jr., 3428
Jessup, Jim, 1201
Jeter, David, 1817
Jeter, Dennis, 1241
Jeter, James M., 869
Jett, E. Stephen, 3125
Jetter, Dean, 1188
Jewell, Bob, 2112
Jewell, Sally, 3551
Jewett, Harvey, 3116
Jewett, Jack B., 44
Jewish Communal Fund, 2574
Jewish Funders Network, 2827
Jewitt, Truda, 2188
JII Capital, Inc., 936
Jimenez, Carlos, 3579
Jimenez, Phillip, 1068
Jinkins, Laurie, 3567
Jinkins, Mark, 3609
JK Living Foundation, 272
JME Charitable Lead Trust, 2353
JME II Charitable Lead Trust, 2353
Joanem, John, 1031
Jobe, Kathy, 2796
Jobe, Warren Y., 917
Jobin-Leeds, Maria, 1422
Jobs, Laurene Powell, 1971
Jobst, Steven B., 393
Joffe, Gary, 3120
Joh, Erik Edward, 820
Johansen, David G., 3539
Johanson, Stephen H., 278
Johansson, Sarah A., 1592
Johns Hopkins Library, 2069
Johns, Christopher P., 367
Johns, Jay W., 3448
Johns, Karen B., 2671
Johns, Lisa R., 2969
Johns, Martha V., 2479
Johns, Sheryl L., 3267
Johns, Wendell, 1618
Johnson & Johnson, 1948
Johnson & Son, S.C., Inc., 3625
Johnson 1951 and 1961 Charitable Trusts, J. Seward, 811
Johnson Brothers Liquor Co., 1704
Johnson Charitable Lead Trust, Robert, 170
Johnson Foundation, Jimmie, 2562
Johnson Foundation, Robert Wood, 2011
Johnson, Abigail P., 1889
Johnson, Alan C., 170
Johnson, Ann L., 170
Johnson, Anthony S., 2503
Johnson, Ardes, 1748
Johnson, Arlyn T., 2714
Johnson, Asa J., 2240
Johnson, Betty W., 2241
Johnson, Brian C., 2830
Johnson, Candace, 1867
Johnson, Candace J., 506
Johnson, Carl J., 2974
Johnson, Carol R., 1098
Johnson, Carolyn E., 170
Johnson, Cary, 3259
Johnson, Chacona W., 1599
Johnson, Chandra Jenway, 2574
Johnson, Charles E., III, 1586
Johnson, Charles G., 482
Johnson, Charles W., Hon., 1656
Johnson, Cheri, 1751
Johnson, Chris, Mrs., 2578
Johnson, Christine D., 1850
Johnson, Christopher B., 3271
Johnson, Christopher W., 2241
Johnson, Colleen O., 2524
Johnson, Craig C., 170
Johnson, Darryl M., 3497
Johnson, David, 568
Johnson, David J., 1249
Johnson, David M., 3271
Johnson, David V., 1578
Johnson, Deb, 1215
Johnson, Deborah, 3471
Johnson, Deborah T., 3421
Johnson, Derrick, 2521, 2648
Johnson, Diana, 1323
Johnson, Donna M., 2391
Johnson, Douglas, 258
Johnson, Douglas R., 2280
Johnson, Dwayne, 2850
Johnson, E. Lynn, 1205
Johnson, Edward C., II, 1889
Johnson, Edward C., III, 1889
Johnson, Edward C., IV, 1889
Johnson, Elizabeth L., 1889
Johnson, Elsa, 779
Johnson, Elsa G., 803
Johnson, Eric, 1022
Johnson, Eric C., 170
Johnson, Eric S., 3428
Johnson, Evelyn, 3207
Johnson, Frank, 1336
Johnson, Gary D., 1726
Johnson, George G., 1588
Johnson, Gloria, 1704
Johnson, Gwendolyn Kess, 2714
Johnson, H. Fisk, III, 3625
Johnson, Hayden, 3193
Johnson, Heidi, 1705
Johnson, Helen May Marcy, 3546
Johnson, Henry P., 2288
Johnson, Holly, 1614
Johnson, Howard Marshall, 3229
Johnson, J.M. Hamlin, 2939, 3042
Johnson, James, 1812
Johnson, James M., 2240, 2794
Johnson, James Moore, 2240
Johnson, Janissa, 36
Johnson, Jean, 384
Johnson, Jeff, 3663
Johnson, Jennifer S., 2503
Johnson, Jerry L., 170
Johnson, Jesse, 538
Johnson, Jesse D., 2240
Johnson, Jessica, 2924
Johnson, Jill, 2830
Johnson, Jim, 420, 1132, 2632
Johnson, Jimmie, 2574
Johnson, Joan Jackson, 1581
Johnson, Johanna, 2714
Johnson, John, 1758
Johnson, John J., 3329
Johnson, John W., 3271
Johnson, Joseph C., 2219
Johnson, Joseph S., 983
Johnson, Judy, 1716
Johnson, Kate, 3190
Johnson, Katharine B., 854
Johnson, Kathryn, 1162
Johnson, Katrina, 31
Johnson, Keith W., 2241
Johnson, Kelly, 3511
Johnson, Kimala, 1228
Johnson, Kyle, 8
Johnson, L. Farnum, Jr., 3447
Johnson, Larry, 3163
Johnson, Lawrence A., 64
Johnson, Leigh, 1735
Johnson, Leslie A., 2219
Johnson, Lloyd K., 1705
Johnson, Louise U., 1972
Johnson, Lynn, 1704
Johnson, Lynne, 932
Johnson, M. Cole, 3464
Johnson, Margaret, 1500
Johnson, Margot A., 2974
Johnson, Marie, 613
Johnson, Mark L., 3190
Johnson, Mary Lou, 3503
Johnson, Matthew E., 2696
Johnson, Melissa, 734
Johnson, Michael, 1704, 1802
Johnson, Nadine, 1031
Johnson, Nancy, 2653
Johnson, Nancy Bellows, 3196
Johnson, Patricia, 2274
Johnson, Paul C., 1586
Johnson, Paula D., 1493
Johnson, Pete, 1760
Johnson, Preston L.C., 137
Johnson, Priscilla, 3023
Johnson, R. Milton, 3139
Johnson, Rafer, 287
Johnson, Rhett, 1699
Johnson, Richard S., 810
Johnson, Robert, 170, 1171
Johnson, Robert W., IV, 2241
Johnson, Robert Wood, 1949
Johnson, Robert Wood, IV, 2327
Johnson, Robin, 1704
Johnson, Russell, 3006
Johnson, Ruth, 3271
Johnson, Sally P., 1493
Johnson, Sally Patrick, 1493
Johnson, Samuel J., IV, 2714
Johnson, Samuel Lamont, 269
Johnson, Samuel, Jr., 408
Johnson, Scott, 1215
Johnson, Seth, 1326
Johnson, Shanna, 1587
Johnson, Sheila B., 3190
Johnson, Shielia, 64
Johnson, Si, 1626
Johnson, Spencer, 2050
Johnson, Stephen, 2555
Johnson, Stephen P., 1493
Johnson, Sunni, 854
Johnson, Suzanne Nora, 2290
Johnson, Thomas P., Jr., 2240
Johnson, Thomas Phillips, Jr., 2240
Johnson, Thomas Phillips, Sr., 2240
Johnson, Thomas S., 990
Johnson, Timothy, Dr., 2751
Johnson, Tina, 804
Johnson, Todd, 1704
Johnson, Tom, 850, 1061, 1178
Johnson, Tony, 1587
Johnson, Val B., 3405
Johnson, Walter S., 269
Johnson, Warren T., 483
Johnson, Weldon, 68
Johnson, Wendy S., 2521
Johnson, Whitney H., 3138
Johnson, Willard, 3271
Johnson, Willard T.C., 2241
Johnson, William, 1607
Johnson, William G., 2644
Johnson, Zach, 1228
Johnson, Zachary, 2714
Johnson-Drenth, Susan E., 2649
Johnson-Howell, April, 3648
JohnsonDiversey, Inc., 3625
Johnston, Bart A., 2259
Johnston, Carolyn, Dr., 1359
Johnston, Catherine I., 2265
Johnston, Cathy, 2027
Johnston, Emily, 1357
Johnston, Fred, 2686
Johnston, Frederick T., 768
Johnston, G. David, 25
Johnston, Gillian, 3156
Johnston, Hugh F., 2354
Johnston, J. Michael, 3537
Johnston, J.C., III, 2798
Johnston, James, 68
Johnston, Lavinia, 3156
Johnston, M. James, 1193
Johnston, Mark L., 1332
Johnston, Marybeth, 3537
Johnston, Michael, 3537
Johnston, Michael J., 2412
Johnston, Murray L., Jr., 3387
Johnston, Nancy K., 2763
Johnston, Neil C., 18
Johnston, Oscar, 2909
Johnston, Paul, 1170
Johnston, Penelope, 2125
Johnston, Peter E., 2762
Johnston, Renee, 1662
Johnston, Robert T., 3156
Johnston, Rosemary, 23
Johnston, S.K., Jr, 3156
Johnstone, Janet Jyll, 414
Joiner, Clint, 3150
Joiner, Katherine, 120
Jolliffe, Judy K., 1592
Jolly, Cynthia, 2632
Jolly, Mary S., 3105
Joly, Hubert, 1685
Jonassen, Hans B., 1299
Joncas, Steven, 1505

Jones Trust, Walter S. and Evan C., 1262
Jones, Andi, 571
Jones, Anthea, 700
Jones, B. Bryan, III, 1762
Jones, B. Bryan, IV, 1762
Jones, Belinda, 2702
Jones, Ben, 3255
Jones, Bernie, 1357
Jones, Bill, III, 866
Jones, Bobby, 3229
Jones, Carolyn, 1745
Jones, Carrie, 422
Jones, Charles I., Jr., 3584
Jones, Cheryl, 859, 1135
Jones, Cliff, 1817
Jones, Corinna, 2476
Jones, David, 2110
Jones, David A., 1284
Jones, David L., 1656
Jones, David R., 250, 2409
Jones, Denise R., 2091
Jones, Derek, 1176
Jones, Donald F., 59
Jones, Douglas L., 528
Jones, Erin, 727
Jones, Ernest, 1569
Jones, Felicia L., 4
Jones, Fletcher, 270
Jones, Fred, 2817
Jones, Geraldine M., 3054
Jones, Gussie, 2707
Jones, H. Lawrence, Dr., 3579
Jones, Hannah, 2865
Jones, Helayne B., 528
Jones, Hendrick, 1607
Jones, Herbert B., 3530
Jones, Hugh R., 1513
Jones, Irene, 347
Jones, J.K., 3290
Jones, Jack L., 1201
Jones, James H., 986
Jones, Jerry G., 2017
Jones, Jesse H., 3267
Jones, Jesse H., II, 3267
Jones, Jesse H., Mrs., 3267
Jones, John, 1129
Jones, John P., III, 3024
Jones, John T., 1831
Jones, Judith, 550
Jones, K. Malcom, 1880
Jones, Katherine J., 93
Jones, Kenneth M., 1896
Jones, Kenneth M., II, 1353
Jones, Kim Harris, 1064
Jones, L. Bevel, III, Bishop, 904
Jones, Landon Y., 1900
Jones, Lisa, 351
Jones, Lucy H., 2541
Jones, Lucy R., 1752
Jones, Margery M., 3529
Jones, Mary Eddy, 2817
Jones, Mary Shaddock, 1307
Jones, Mary T., 2529
Jones, Maurice D., 3632
Jones, Orville, III, 1857
Jones, Patricia A., 2973
Jones, Patrick, 351
Jones, Patti, 1152
Jones, Paul J., 3637
Jones, Paul Tudor, 2327
Jones, Paula R., 1030
Jones, Polly Swetland, 2781
Jones, Reginald N., 3477
Jones, Rhonda, 1209
Jones, Rich, 754
Jones, Rick, 340
Jones, Robert "Bob", 10
Jones, Rockwell, 2689
Jones, Ronald D., 3659
Jones, Sara Kelly, 2265
Jones, Scott K., 3526
Jones, Shelley, 11
Jones, Sherrie, 1616
Jones, Soni, 1158
Jones, Susan D., 571
Jones, Terrell, 2909
Jones, Tony, 2223
Jones, Victoria, 153
Jones, W. Alton, 3422
Jones, Wallace C., 592
Jones, Wilson R., 3643
Jones, Yonge R., 3104
Jones-Morrison, Gladys, 122
Joos, Ann, 707
Jordache Enterprises, Inc., 2318
Jordache Ltd., 2318
Jordan, Barbara M., 2918
Jordan, Brooke, 2119
Jordan, Ginny, 2119
Jordan, Gloria Perez, 1729
Jordan, J. Craig, 3018
Jordan, Jeff, 3330
Jordan, Jim, 2835
Jordan, Joe, 1758
Jordan, John R., Jr., 2599
Jordan, Joseph, 2880
Jordan, Karen, 1402
Jordan, Maria, 1646
Jordan, Nicole, 2119
Jordan, Robert, 1607
Jordan, Rodney W., 1722
Jordan, Ron, 1160
Jordan, Taylor, 2119
Jordan, Travis, 1402
Jordan, Vernon E., Jr., 2033
Jordan, Virginia W., 2119
Jordan, William Chester, 2459, 2460
Jordheim, Neil, 2649
Jorgensen, Arne, 3684
Jorgensen, Jay O., 1164
Jorgensen, Ove W., 1164
Jorgensen, Randy, 1603
Jorgensen, Ted, 2006
Jorgensen, Winifred M., 1164
Jorgenson, Erik, 1097
Jorgenson, Joel, Dr., 2649
Jorgenson, Judy, 3637
Jorgenson, Megan, 1097
Jornayvaz, Isla C., 3358
Joseph, Charles S., 744
Joseph, Elise E., 3221
Joseph, Erica N., 1359
Joseph, James A., Amb., 2211
Joseph, Margaret Elise Elkins, 3220
Joseph, Michael, 2826
Joseph, William D., 2783
Joshi, Avatar A., 1165
Joshi, Tenzing H., 1165
Joshi, Yatish J., 1165
Joslin, David C., 1611
Jostens, Inc., 1706
Journay, Rex, 1188
Journey, Dwight, 2810
Joyce, William L., 2120
Joyner, Pamela, 139
JP Morgan Chase, 272
JPIII Inc., 178
JPMorgan Chase, 2173
JPMorgan Chase Bank, N.A., 558, 956, 965, 982, 985, 990, 995, 998, 1011, 1016, 1033, 1036, 1043, 1057, 1059, 1071, 1072, 1091, 1095, 1110, 1306, 2009, 2096, 2129, 2162, 2190, 2200, 2242, 2285, 2325, 2417, 2418, 2433, 2445, 2577, 2655, 2679, 2716, 3072, 3180, 3335, 3642
JPMorgan Chase, N.A., 2131
Jreisat, Wijdan, 2679
JRO Charitable Lead Annuity Trust, 2675
JSW & JCW, LP, 845
JSwartz Charitable Lead Trust, 2455
Juarez, Ashley Smith, 719
Juarez, Gladys, 1099
Juarez, Rumaldo Z., 3196
Juba, George, 2890
Jubb, David, 221
Jubitz Investments, LP, 2853
Jubitz, Katherine H., 2853
Jubitz, M. Albin, Jr., 2853
Jubitz, Raymond G., 2853
Jubitz, Sarah C., 2853
Juchter, Elia, 2148
Juckett, J. Walter, 2404
Judd, Robert, 777
Judd, Sonali, 797
Judge, James J., 598
Judge, William, 2664
Judkins, Lafayette, 2611
Judlau Contracting, Inc., 2228
Judson, K. Leonard, 225
Judson, Sara, 1307
Jueptner, Peter, 2287
Juergens, Marty, 3504
Julander, Paula, 3393
Julian, Joseph, 2771
Julian, Paul C., 321
Julius, David, 1714
Julson, Althea, 2148
Jundi-Samman, Randa, Dr., 1590
Jung, Chris, 3118
Jungwirth, Helen, 3623
Juniata Valley Bank, 2952
Junior League, 1748
Junior League of Washington, 676
Juris, Hervey A., 2017
Jurkonis, Mary, 1868
Jurzykowski, Yolande L., 3491
Just Marketing, Inc., 2562
Just Rite Acoustics, Inc., 2562
Justesen, Joan, 2649
Justice-Moore, Kathleen, 333
Justin, Robert, 1589
Justis, Cleveland, 309
Justis, Jane Leighty, 512
Justis, Robert F., 512
Juzang, Angie, 1764
Juzwa, Heather, 3040
Jwell, Mary Louise Brown, 874

K N Energy, Inc., 510
K'Burg, Bill, 347, 397
Kaanon, Marian, 425
Kaare-Andersen, Soren, 2064
Kabbes, David G., 1779
Kabelin, Jerry, 1201
Kabler, Elizabeth K., 87
Kabler, Elizabeth R., 87
Kacer, Jim, 1330
Kachner, Michael J., 3632
Kackley, James R., 1624
Kadar, Avraham, 2319
Kadar, Einat, 2319
Kadar, Maya, 2319
Kadar, Nadav, 2319
Kade, Fritz, Jr., 2243
Kade, Max, 2243
Kaden, Debra A., 1540
Kaden, Lewis B., 2290
Kadinger, Suzanne, 1134
Kaemmer, Arthur W., 1702
Kaemmer, Frederick C., 1702
Kaemmer, Julia L., 1702
Kaemmer, Martha H., 1702
Kafer, David, 503
Kafka, Barbara, 676
Kahlert, Greg W., 1383
Kahlert, Roberta, 1383
Kahlert, William E., 1383
Kahn, Alan R., 2237
Kahn, Bruce, 1342
Kahn, David D., 1625
Kahn, Esther B., 1492
Kahn, Irving, 2237
Kahn, Julius "Sandy", III, 347
Kahn, Karen M., 91
Kahn, Malkie, 2061
Kahn, Stephen B., 91
Kahn, Todd, 2100
Kahn, William, 2108
Kaichen, Lisa M., 1310
Kaiser, Charles J., Jr., 3579
Kaiser, Heather G., 46
Kaiser, Kate, 46
Kaiser, Kay Lynn, 1184
Kaiser, Miranda M., 2389
Kaiserman Enterprises, LP, 2977
Kaiserman Marital Trust, Kevy K., 2977
Kaiserman, Hortense M., 2977
Kaiserman, Kenneth S., 2977
Kaiserman, Ronald L., 2977
Kaish, Morton, 2044
Kalama, Corbett A.K., 929
Kaldis, Catherine Daniel, 3233
Kalikow, N. Richard, 2206
Kalina, R. Terrence, 1052
Kalleward, Howard, 1592
Kalleward, Howard D., 1612
Kallman, Linda, 725
Kallstrom, Bob, 2741
Kalluski, Mary, 147
Kalnins, Vicki, 987
Kamal, Alex, 2132
Kamal, Terence, 2132
Kamas, John A., Rev., 2281
Kamen, Dean, 1882
Kamensky, Marvin, 983
Kaminsky, Gary J., 2213
Kaminsky, Gerald P., 2213
Kaminsky, Jaclyn, 2213
Kampfer, Merlin W., 44
Kampling, Patricia L., 3592
Kamps, Dick, 1586
Kanaan, Margaret Mary, 2950
Kanas, Elaine, 2244
Kanas, John A., 2244
Kandel, Eric R., 191
Kane, Brian, 1216
Kane, Brian J., 1244
Kane, Chad D., 3610
Kane, Elizabeth, 1056
Kane, Jacqueline P., 153
Kane, Jami S., 111
Kane, John C., 954
Kane, Mary, 2274
Kane, Maureen, 591

Kane, Micah A., 933
Kane, Michael, 2922
Kane, Michael F., 247
Kane, Patrick J., 2940
Kane, Susan, 363
Kane, Tina, 1699
Kaneta, Lester, 936
Kaneta, Marian, 936
Kansas Legal Services, Inc., 1281
Kantardjieff, Stefan A., 415
Kantner Charitable Trust, Woodrow A., 764
Kantner, Karen, 764
Kantner, Woodrow A., 764
Kantor, Connie, 718
Kao, Carly, 233
Kapitz, Jay, 158
Kapla, Liz, 1642
Kaplan and Family, Thomas, 901
Kaplan, Anne, 1041
Kaplan, Ashley Dorrance, 42
Kaplan, Burton B., 1041
Kaplan, Charles, 1041
Kaplan, Curt, 1041
Kaplan, David, 1041
Kaplan, Gabe, 607
Kaplan, Gary S., 3558
Kaplan, Gizelle, 2512
Kaplan, Harvey, 1707
Kaplan, Helen, 1707
Kaplan, Jean, 1041
Kaplan, Jo-An, 3081
Kaplan, Laura, 1707
Kaplan, Leah, 1707
Kaplan, Leonard J., 2640
Kaplan, Linda, 671
Kaplan, Louis, 671
Kaplan, Marjorie, 1707
Kaplan, Mark E., 1718
Kaplan, Martin S., 1474
Kaplan, Mary E., 2245
Kaplan, Michael, 1041, 2512
Kaplan, Morris, 1041
Kaplan, Myron, 2424
Kaplan, Rachel, 1707
Kaplan, Renee, 412
Kaplan, Richard D., 2245
Kaplan, Robert, 1041
Kaplan, Robert S., 2160
Kaplan, Ross, 1707
Kaplan, Susan A., 2326
Kaplan, Thomas, 901
Kaplan, Tobee W., 2640
Kaplan, Yitzcak, 2512
Kaplus, Laura Herzog, 2899
Kapnick, Jim, 1634
Kapoor, Nina, 354
Kapor, Mitchell, 273
Kapp, Constance Elizabeth Mellon, 2998
Kapp, Robert A., 3497
Kappner, Augusta Souza, 2492
Kappos, George, Jr., 2670
Karabim-Ahern, Rebecca, 563
Karaffa, Robert, 2731
Karaffa, Tracee, 2731
Karakul, Kurt, 2792
Karamanoukian, Alber K., 2001
Karangelen, Michael, 2473
Karaoglan, Alain, 2488
Karasik, Brenda-Lee, 3571
Karasin, Leslie, 3059
Karfunkel Family Foundation, 2093, 2217
Karfunkel, Ann, 2093
Karfunkel, Barry, 2217
Karfunkel, George, 2093
Karfunkel, Leah, 2217
Karfunkel, Michael, 2093, 2217
Karfunkel, Rene, 2093
Karfunkel, Robert, 2217
Karges, James M., 1690, 1747
Karibjanian, Nancy, 630
Karickhoff, Brenda C., 2466
Karim, Quarraisha Abdool, 2287
Karim, Salim S. Abdool, 3516
Karimi, Habibullah, 1432
Karinski, Edna, 162
Karl Hoblitzelle Trust, 3262
Karlawish, Jason H., 2192
Karmazin Foundation, Mel, 2071
Karmazin Trust, 2246
Karmazin Trust II, 2246
Karmazin, Bruce, 1053
Karmazin, Melvin, 2246
Karmin, Beth Kaplan, 1041
Karmin, Hannah, 1041
Karnes, Mark, 72
Karoff, H. Peter, 1734
Karoff, Peter, 3072
Karow, Andrew, 538
Karp, Daniel, 3303
Karp, Irene J., 1161
Karp, James S., 1161
Karp, Jane, 2035
Karp, Jason, 612
Karp, Richard, 2035
Karpf, Zac, 1853
Karpowicz, Paul, 2071
Karr, Carol J., 1615
Karr, Tim, 2947
Karras, Nolan, 3404
Karre, Paul J., 3142
Karwic, Michael B., 2915
Kasbarian, John, 2001
Kason Industries, Inc., 889
Kaspar, Mark, 3619
Kasper, Keith, 2948
Kasperzak, Mike, 305
Kass, Andy, 3662
Kass, Roger E., 3094
Kassewitz, Darcie Glazer, 750
Kasten, Rebecca, 2562
Kasten, Stan, 287
Kastler, Lesa, 3099
Kaswick, Jennifer, 227
Kaswick, Jon A., 227
Kaswick, Julie, 227
Kaszovitz, Robert, 2193
Katcher, Dorothy, 765
Katcher, Gerald, 765
Katcher, Jane, 765
Katchman, Don E., 2697
Kathman, Daniel, 2170
Katten Muchin Rosenman LLP, 1042
Katten Muchin Zavis, 1042
Katten Muchin Zavis Rosenman, 1042
Katterjohn, Eugene, Jr., 1286
Katz Charitable Income Trust, 1393
Katz Charitable Income Trust II, 1393
Katz, Abraham J., 889
Katz, Alexander S., 889
Katz, David, 889
Katz, Drew, 2019
Katz, Eleanor, 1393
Katz, Elizabeth Berylson, 1546
Katz, Esther, 889
Katz, Ezra, 778
Katz, Jeffrey, 1564
Katz, Joel A., 3108
Katz, Lawrence F., 2402
Katz, Marilyn, 2380
Katz, Martha, 876
Katz, Molly, Dr., 2679
Katz, Peter A., 889
Katz, Phyllis, 889
Katz, Robert, 543, 1546
Katz, Teller, Brant & Hild, 2802
Katzen, Seth J., 637
Katzenbach, Shirley S., 2296
Katzenberg, Susan B., 1374
Katzman, Julie T., 1056
Katzovicz, Roy, 2356
Kau, Zachary, 935
Kauffman, David, 2932
Kauffman, Ewing M., 1797
Kauffman, Julia Irene, 1797
Kauffman, Welz, 2499
Kaufman, Anne F., 1043
Kaufman, Dan, 867
Kaufman, Howard, 3108
Kaufman, Paula, 1463
Kaufmann, Al, 1647
Kaufmann, Marion Esser, 509
Kaufmann, Thomas C., 971
Kaufthal, Ilan, 1908
Kaur, Parvinder, 3351
Kaus, Jodi, 1268
Kauth, Laurie Bentson, 1684
Kavanaugh, Gerry, 1453
Kavanaugh, Robert, 161
Kavli, Fred, 275
Kawabe, Harry, 3531
Kawabe, Tomo, 3531
Kawamura, Takashi, 666
Kay, David R., 2183
Kay, Elizabeth D., 491
Kay, F. Stevon, 3102
Kay, Herma Hill, 385
Kay, Ina, 1384
Kay, Jack, 1384
Kay, Jami, 1267
Kay, Jane Craft, 3113
Kay, Lucy, 537
Kay, Martin, 3520
Kay, Sarah, 3442, 3444
Kay, Shelley Joan, 1384
Kaye, Alan, 312
Kaye, Judith S., Hon., 2427
Kaylie, Gloria W., 2247
Kaylie, Harvey, 2247
Kaylie, Roberta, 2247
Kayne, Alexander, 2758
Kayser, Kraig H., 2415
Kayton, Andrew H., 784
Kazahaya, Kenneth, Dr., 2919
Kazahaya, Masayuki, Dr., 2919
Kazee, Thomas A., 1205
Kazhe, Christina, Esq., 138
Kazma, Gerald, 766
Kazma, Leigh-Anne, 766
Kazma, Margaret, 766
Kazma, Michael, 766
Kazmaier, John, 2907
KCH Group, 647
Kcs Landscaping, 3505
KD Primus Trust, 2978
Keaffaber, Duane, 1146
Keaffaber, Jama, 1170
Kean Residuary Trust, Stewart B., 547
Kean, Beatrice Joyce, 1040
Kean, Stewart B., 547
Kean, Thomas H., 2085
Kean, Thomas H., Hon., 1900
Keane, Fay, 1583
Keane, John J., 2755
Keane, Marc, 2564
Kearins, Katie, 1802
Kearney, Catherine O'Malley, 2800
Kearney, Daniel P., 1040
Kearney, Dawn, 1160
Kearney, John P., 3031
Kearney, Michael, 131
Kearns, Becky, 3401
Kearny, Conor, 1549
Kears, David J., 114
Keast, Walter, 1235
Keathley, Duane, 279
Keating, Dwight M., 2892
Keating, Pollyanna, 373
Keating, Richard, 1067
Keck, Howard B., Jr., 276
Keck, Joe, 474
Keck, Katherine Cone, 324
Keck, Stephen M., 276
Keck, Theodore J., 276
Keck, W.M., III, 276
Keck, William M., 276
Keddy, Jim, 138
Keel, Jim, 3580
Keeler, Robert T., 2715
Keeley, Dawn, 2653
Keeling, J. Wayne, 2611
Keeling, James W., 978
Keely-Dinger, Kristen, 3122
Keemar, Cheryl Lee, 123
Keenan Trust, Kathy Ann, 560
Keenan, Francis, 2928
Keenan, Hilary, 560
Keenan, J. Patrick, 1849
Keenan, James F., 1172
Keenan, Julie, 1998
Keenan, Sue, 1170
Keene, Kim, 1128
Keene, Margaret, 400
Keene, Steven, 2006
Keeney, Anne Herold, 1975
Keeney, Elizabeth Marler, 2541
Keeney, Matthew Mayro, 1975
Keens, Catherine, 1995
Keep Memory Alive, 1314
Keep, Paul, 1615
Keet, Bonnie Falkenstine, 2248
Keet, Ernest E., 2248
Keet, Nancy, 2027
Keet, Nancy R., 2248
Keeton Hay Group, 3237
Keeton, Fred, 1860
Keever, Graham, 2540
Keffler, James, 831
Kehoe, Geoffrey, 1729
Keilitz, Dave, 1647
Keillor, Garrison, 2050
Keilman, Tom, 1171
Keilty, Nancy B., 1121
Keim, Melody, 2981
Keir, Anne Swayne, 431
Keiser, Michael, 3601
Keiser, Michael, Mrs., 3601
Keister, Rudy, 2684
Keith, Colleen Perry, 3097
Keith, Jayne, 2459, 2460
Kekst, Carol, 2249
Kekst, David J., 2249
Kekst, Gershon, 2249
Kekst, Joseph, 2249
Kela, Ajay, Dr., 450
Keleher, John, 3056

Keliipio, Kau'i, 452
Kelke, Linda, 1663
Kell, Betsy, 3611
Kellar Family Charitable Lead Trust, 3446
Kellar, Arthur, 3446
Kellar, Elizabeth, 3446
Kellar, Leslie Livingston, 893
Kellar, Lorrence, 2675
Kellar, Mary K., 3446
Kellar, Rick, 2741
Kelleher, David, 1156
Kelleher, Joan Negley, 3239
Kelleher, Steve, 2664
Kellen Foundation, A.M. & S.M., 2165
Kellen, Anna-Maria, 2250
Kellen, Michael, 2250
Kellen, Stephen M., 2250
Keller & Associates, J.J., Inc., 3626
Keller Charitable Remainder Annuity, 1627
Keller, Allison M., 276
Keller, Andrew J., 1627
Keller, Bernedine, 1627
Keller, Betsy, 307
Keller, Brian, 3626
Keller, Chad, 716
Keller, Charles C., 3054
Keller, Christina, 1615
Keller, Christina L., 1627
Keller, Dennis, 1398
Keller, Fred P., 1628
Keller, Frederick P., 1627
Keller, James, 1866
Keller, James J., 3626
Keller, John J. and Ethel D., 3626
Keller, Robert A., 408
Keller, Robert L., 3626
Keller, Sue, 1587
Keller, Thomas L., 3164
Keller, Williams, 1178
Keller-Krikava, Marne, 3626
Kellerman, Faye, 277
Kellerman, John, II, 1191
Kellerman, Jonathan, 277
Kellerman, Kelli, 135
Kelley, Bob, 1852
Kelley, Brian S., 1449
Kelley, Ed, 2811
Kelley, Gary, 1853
Kelley, Ken, 3163
Kellmanson, Mary, 700
Kellner, Mary, 3617
Kellner, Mary T., 3634
Kellner, Ted, 3617
Kellner, Ted D., 3605
Kellogg Foundation, 2011
Kellogg Foundation Trust, W.K., 1628
Kellogg LLC, 102
Kellogg Trust, Carrie Staines, 1628
Kellogg, Paul, 2099
Kellogg, Terry D., 7
Kellogg, W.K., 1628
Kelly Broadcasting Co., 278
Kelly Foundation, Dee, 3185
Kelly Television Co., 278
Kelly Trust, Eugene, 2231
Kelly, Ann M., 975
Kelly, Becky, 3429
Kelly, Beverly, 854
Kelly, Bronwen K., 1905
Kelly, Charles G., 1590
Kelly, Cynthia, 1541
Kelly, Daniel, 3627
Kelly, Denise, 1735
Kelly, Dennis J., 994
Kelly, Eric M., 805
Kelly, Eugene, 2231
Kelly, Frank, 1299, 2134
Kelly, G.G., LLC, 278
Kelly, Gregory G., 278
Kelly, J.S., LLC, 278
Kelly, James F., Jr., 122
Kelly, Jon S., 278
Kelly, Karen, 613
Kelly, Mike, 2604
Kelly, Paul, 2455
Kelly, Robert T., Jr., 1416
Kelly, Robin, 1286
Kelly, Scott J., 2688
Kelly, Thea, 1197
Kelly, Thomas E., 3229
Kelly, Thomas F., Dr., 2280
Kelly, Tom, 933
Kelly, William P., 2194
Kelly-Johnson, Susan, 1187
Kelmar, Steven B., 550
Kelsay, Amy, 1163
Kelsey 1968 Revocable Trust, Thomas V.A., 1504
Kelsey 1988 Revocable Trust, Elizabeth S., 1504
Kelsey, Elizabeth S., 1504
Kelsey, Heidi, 3173
Kelsey, Lea Dobbs, 1504
Kelsey, Margen S., 1504
Kelsey, Suzanne V.A., 1504
Kelsey, Thomas V.A., 1504
Kelsey, William C., 1504
Kelso, Betty Ann Stieren, 3197
Keltner, Tom, 537
Kemp, Beatrice W., 381
Kemp, James, 2680
Kemp, Kevin L., 952
Kemp, Michael F., 912
Kemper, Robin, 2181
Kemper, Timothy, 1983
Kempf, Christopher J., 2738
Kempton, John, 1583
Kenan, Anne, 603
Kenan, James G., III, 2577
Kenan, Thomas S., III, 2529, 2577
Kenan, William R., Jr., 2577
Kendall Charitable Remainder, Evelyn L., 705
Kendall Trust, Henry Way, 1494
Kendall, Andrew W., 1494
Kendall, Charles B., 1573
Kendall, David L., 1024
Kendall, Donald M., 2354
Kendall, Edward C., 59
Kendall, Henry, 1494
Kendall, Jacquelyn, 1031
Kendall, John P., 1494
Kendall, Nannie, 2794
Kendall, Philip A., 544
Kendall, Ted, III, 1763
Kendell, Kate, 385
Kendell, Kate, Esq., 138
Kendrick, Dorsey L., Dr., 595
Kendrick, Douglas, 468
Kendrick, James M., 2262
Kendrick, Kevin, 1642
Kendrick, Ruth, 468
Kendzior, Tony, 725
Kenlan, A. Jay, 3417
Kennard, Lydia H., 444
Kenneally, Jennifer, 2407
Kennebec Savings Bank, 1332
Kennedy Home, Catherine, Inc., The, 2578
Kennedy, Bruce, 2342, 2574
Kennedy, Christopher G., 982
Kennedy, Dave, 728
Kennedy, Dick, 1616
Kennedy, Donald P., 244
Kennedy, Edward A., III, 1003
Kennedy, George, 3654
Kennedy, Jack, 608
Kennedy, James C., 916
Kennedy, James O., 3145
Kennedy, Jim, Dr., 503
Kennedy, John, Jr., 268
Kennedy, Judith, 2166
Kennedy, Julie B., 1910
Kennedy, Kendel, 767
Kennedy, Kevin W., 2097, 2492
Kennedy, Kimberly, 767
Kennedy, Lesa, 2574
Kennedy, Michael, 2723
Kennedy, Neil M., 10
Kennedy, Parker S., 270
Kennedy, R. Michael, 2495
Kennedy, Susan, 1488
Kennedy, Traci, 1827
Kennedy, W. George, 767
Kennedy, William J., 1008
Kennedy-Olsen, Kathleen, 767
Kennelly, Dana Wedum, 1750
Kennelly, Karen A., 1151
Kennerly, Breann, 1661
Kennerly, Michael, 1661
Kennerly, Ross, 1661
Kennett, Shari, 1662
Kenney, Brigid E., 1107
Kenney, Donald J., 1459
Kenney, Siobhan, 88
Kenney, Suzanne, 1472
Kennickell, Al, Jr., 912
Kennifer, Rick, 157
Kenninger Trust, Ruth L., 1865
Kenninger, Steven C., 1865
Kenninger, Susan K., 1865
Kenny, Janice, 1436
Kenny, Maugha, 2502
Kenny, Peter M., 3605
Kent, Bob, 3587
Kent, Doug, 1852
Kenworthy, Charles, 148
Kenworthy, Harriet, 1646
Kenyon, James, III, 1832
Keogh, John, 2880
Keohane, Nannerl O., 2146
Keon, Margaret L., 1053
Keough, Bill, 2909
Keppy Memorial Trust, Walter & Carol, 1022
Kerby, Kendall S., 3488
Kerker, Michael A., 328
Kerkhoff, Rhonda, 1731
Kerman, Michael G., 905
Kern, Anita, 905
Kern, Deborah, 3627
Kern, Patricia E., 3627
Kern, Robert D., 3627
Kernon, Janet W., 211
Kerns, Pete, 420
Kerr, Michael T., 461
Kerr, W. David, 2923
Kerrey, Bob, 2470
Kersch-Schultz, Sheri, 3557
Kersey, Jenn, 1186
Kershow, Michael, 676
Kertzner, Daniel, 3089
Kervandjian, Heddy, 2909
Keshishian, Onnik, 2001
Kesselring, Charlotte, 2143
Kessler, David, 195
Kessler, Jim, 1257
Kester, Doris, 535
Kestner, R. Steven, 2764
Ketcham, Susan, 248
Ketchum, Stuart M., 447
Kettering, Glen L., 2752
Kettering, Virginia W., 2716
Keul, Jim, 1740
Keusch, Suzanne H., 2237
Keuther, Isabelle, 2148
Key, David G., 3216
Key, Lonnie, 687
Key, Robert, 687
KeyBank, 2407
KeyBank N.A., 2676, 2679, 2692, 2717, 2788, 2800
KeyBank, N.A., 2673
KeyCorp, 2717
Keys, Scott, 1214
Keyston, David, 2028
Keystone Foods Corp., 2904
Keystone Foods LLC, 2904
Keystone Foundation, The, 3587
Keywell, Bradley, 1049
Keywell, Kim, 1049
Kgabo, Molapo, 2731
Khalaf, Michel, 2307
Khan, Julius "Sandy", III, 397
Khan, Mehmood, 2354
Khan, Zia, 2390
Kheder, Susan, 1584
Khodakhah, Kamran, 232
Khor, Jacqueline, 156
Khouri, Naif A., 1598
Kia, Shirin, 3404
Kibbe, Sharon, 1150
Kick, Frank J., 2082
Kicklighter, Kurt, 267
Kido, Kenneth, 3426
Kidwell, Carla, 1128
Kidwell, Scott, 3316
Kiefer, Kathleen S., 1206
Kiefer, Kathryn, 1796
Kiefer, Markell, 1713
Kieffer, Maryanna L., 3485
Kieling, Nancy W., 1979
Kientz, Frank E., 3441
Kienz, Ethel, 3604
Kies, Peter S., 3595
Kieschnick, Michael, 91
Kiesel, Bill, 1163
Kiesling, Nita, 3287
Kieu, Quynh, 244
Kiewit, Peter, 1843
Kiger, Daniel, Rev., 2733
Kiger, Stephanie, 2017
Kiggens-Leifheit, Amber, 3633
Kihlman, Dale, 1295
Kikkoman Foods Foundation, 3666
Kilbride, James, 819
Kiley, Thomas R., 1426
Kilgore, Don, 1849
Kilgore, James, 1984
Kilgore, Ronald N., 1592, 1612, 1654
Killacky, John, 3417
Killebrew, Manuel, 1760
Killeen, Michael F., 2670
Killen, John V., 1541
Killian, Ann E., 2697
Killingsworth, Dorothy, 2604

Killion, Rick, 1226
Killmer, Walter J., Jr., 2437
Kilmer, Craig, 2907
Kilmer, Joe, 1175
Kilpin, Tim, 312
Kim Family Revocable Trust, 280
Kim, Andy, 1359
Kim, Byung, 170
Kim, Don-Won, 1495
Kim, Dong Koo, 280
Kim, Dong-Won, 1495
Kim, Geon Y., 281
Kim, Hyeok, 1722
Kim, Jeanne M., 281
Kim, Jinsoo, 1935
Kim, Randy, 251
Kim, Robert, 3162
Kim, Seong, 1935
Kim, Stephen, 1935
Kimball, Dena, 856
Kimball, H. Earle, 3079
Kimball, Jennifer, 2017
Kimball, Josh, 856
Kimball, Robert, 328
Kimberly, Dean, 1685
Kimberly-Clark Corporation, 952
Kimley-Horn, 3505
Kimmel, Margaret Mary, 2950
Kimmelman, Peter, 2136
Kimmet, Gary J., 224
Kimoto, Paul, 250
Kimsey, Frank C., Dr., 3140
Kind, Christina, 2483
Kind, Kenneth A., 2483
Kind, Patricia, 2483
Kind-Rubin, Valerie, 2483
Kindel, Maureen, 287
Kinder Morgan, Inc., 510
Kinder, David D., 3274
Kinder, Garry, 3207
Kinder, Nancy G., 3274
Kinder, Peter, 3417
Kinder, Richard D., 3274
Kindfuller, Andrew, 2483
Kindred, John J., III, 2200
King Charitable Trust, Cornelius L., 3080
King, Betty, 768
King, Betty S., 3475
King, C. Stephen, 3398
King, Carl B., 3275
King, Chuck, 1207
King, Curtis, Rev., 1382
King, David, 2632
King, Diana, 2251
King, Dorothy E., 3275
King, Florence E., 3275
King, George, 272
King, J. Dudley, Jr., 3100
King, James, 160
King, James P., 2455
King, Jeanne Anne, 2832
King, Kathy A., 3190
King, Kimberly Davis, 378
King, Lance, 502
King, Margaret B., 3633
King, Michael J., 215
King, Michele, 1192
King, Peter J., 1708
King, Roberta F., 1615
King, Russell S., 1708
King, Sandy, 1751
King, Stephen E., 1333, 2055
King, Steven, Sr., 3000
King, Susan Basil, 1748
King, Tabitha, 1333, 2055
King, Tom, 2632
King, Wendy, 1928
Kingma, Todd W., 1655
Kings Point Industries, Inc., 2195
Kingsland, Richard M., 445
Kingsley Fund, Sidney S., 2143
Kingsley, Charles, 551
Kingsley, Tony, 3063
Kingston, Wm., 1156
Kingzett, Robert, 2852
Kiniry, Sue, 2922
Kinner, Mark, 3679
Kinney, Jodona Morley, 1644
Kinning, Joseph, 1687
Kinnison, Tom, 3683
Kinray, Inc., 2476
Kinsel, Rick A., 2486
Kinsell, Stephen J., 1160
Kinship Trust Co., 681
Kintz, James P., 805
Kinzel, Judith, 2773
Kipp, Robert A., 1793
Kirbo, Bruce W., Jr., 869
Kirby, Allan P., Sr., 1952
Kirby, Charles A., 3125
Kirby, F.M., 1952
Kirby, F.M., II, 1952
Kirby, Jefferson W., 1952
Kirby, Nancy J., 3053
Kirby, S. Dillard, 1952
Kirby, Walker D., 1952
Kirch, Larry, 3631
Kirchheimer Trust, 1083
Kirgan, Mary Anne, 1404
Kirgan, Robert S., 1404
Kirk, Donald H., Jr., 1386
Kirk, Katy, 3431
Kirk, Kenneth C., 2940
Kirk, Patricia M., 1386
Kirk, Thomas H., 3450
Kirkbride, Cheryl M., 2798
Kirkish, Mark S., 3651
Kirkland 2004 Charitable Trust, 3143
Kirkland 2005 Charitable Trust, 3143
Kirkland 2007 Charitable Trust, 3143
Kirkland Foundation, Robert E. & Jenny D., 3150
Kirkland, Bedford F., 3143
Kirkland, Christopher, 3143
Kirkland, Jenny D., 3143
Kirkland, Robert, 3143
Kirkland, Robert E., 3150
Kirkpatrick, Frederick S., 1645
Kirkpatrick, Isabel, 823
Kirkpatrick, Kevin, 1178
Kirkpatrick, Shaun A., 44
Kirkpatrick, Timothy L., 7
Kirkwood, Amanda H., 219
Kirkwood, James, 2143
Kirkwood, John H., 219
Kirkwood, Wayne R., 714
Kirn, Chris, 992
Kirsch, James F., 2697
Kirsch, Susan, 2950
Kirschenbaum, Malcolm R., 662
Kirschner, E. Phil, 2818
Kirschner, Roberta L., 2818
Kirtland, Jennifer E., 3225
Kirtland, John E., 3225
Kirwin, Kelly, 1699
Kiser, Stephanie Norris, 2540
Kish, Joan, 1953
Kish, John C., 1953
Kishbaugh, James, 2908
Kishner, Judith Z., 2834
Kishner, Judy, 2833
Kislak, J.I., Inc., 769
Kislak, Jay I., 769
Kislak, Jean, 769
Kislak, Philip Thomas, 769
Kissam, L., 1298
Kissam, Luke, 1298
Kissel, Wendy, 2737
Kissene, Sandra, 1195
Kissinger, Cathy, 1607
Kistenbroker, David H., 1042
Kistler, Daniel G., 1061
Kistler, Walter, 3515
Kistler, Walter P., 3515
Kitch, Patti, 1176
Kitchelle Custom Homes, 237
Kitchens, Dean J., 220
Kitselman, Janet M., 2580
Kittle, Dwayne, 3431
Kittle, Robert, 3578
Kittredge, Lisa R., 1496
Kittredge, Michael J., 1496
Kiwanis Club of Bradenton, Inc., 770
Kjos, Andrew B., 2650
Kjos, David, 1750
Klahr, Suzanne Mckechnie, 2427
Klasen, Frazierita D., 2887, 3045
Klasky, Shel, 3494
Klatskin, Charles, 1954
Klatskin, Deborah, 1954
Klatskin, Lynne, 1954
Klatskin, Samuel, 1954
Klatsky, Arthur L., 1344
Klatzky, Howard T., 1693
Klauer, William R., Jr., 1216
Klauke, Joseph, 1064
Klaus, Jack, 1219
Klaus, Melynne, 1143
Klauser, Kenneth, 1921
Klavan, Ruchel Friedman, 177
Klavans, Nancy G., 1474
Kleban, Edward L., 2252
Kleberg, Caesar, 3276
Kleberg, Chris, 3276
Kleberg, Stephen J., 3276
Klecha, Roy W., Jr., 1590
Klee, Conrad C., 2253
Klee, Ted, 1099
Klee, Virginia, 2253
Klein Diamonds Inc., Julius, 2453
Klein Irrevocable Trust, Sara Dina, 2255
Klein, Abraham, 2254, 2255, 2453
Klein, Bella, 2453
Klein, Carine R., 3673
Klein, Christine Erion, 494
Klein, Danka, 1200
Klein, Elisabeth, 283
Klein, Freada Kapor, 273
Klein, Herbert C., 1497
Klein, James L., 283
Klein, Kenneth, 283
Klein, Linda S., 611
Klein, Lloyd E., 283
Klein, Michael, 115
Klein, Michele Gerber, 2279
Klein, Mordechai, 2254
Klein, Roger M., 1497
Klein, Ron, 2726
Klein, Sarah Dinah, 2254, 2255
Kleinheinz, John B., 3277
Kleinheinz, Marsha, 3277
Kleinschmidt, Amy, 1694
Kleissner, Alex, 2978
Kleissner, Andrea, 2978
Kleissner, Karl, 2978
Kleissner, Lisa, 2978
Kleist, Mark, 1614
Klemencic, Ron, 3548
Klemesrud, Mellony, 1241
Klemm, Connie, 1849
Klenck, Marilyn, 1205
Kleper, Ann-Louise, 1083
Klepfer, Robert O., Jr., 2637
Klepper, Heidi, 484
Kleppinger, David M., 2952
Kleptz, Melissa A., 2794
Kletscher, Joanne, 1680
Kleven, Cynthia F., 1676
Kline, Carolyn, 1176
Kline, Daniel L., 968
Kline, Gerald M., 284
Kline, Terrance A., 2898
Kline, William M., III, 3054
Klingenstein Fund, Esther A. and Joseph, 2258
Klingenstein, Andrew, 2256, 2258
Klingenstein, Andrew Davis, 1328
Klingenstein, Esther A., 2256
Klingenstein, Frederick A., 2256, 2257
Klingenstein, John, 1328, 2256
Klingenstein, Joseph, 2256
Klingenstein, Julie, 1328
Klingenstein, Kathy, 2258
Klingenstein, Patricia D., 2256
Klingenstein, Patricia Davis, 1328
Klingenstein, Paul, 1056
Klingenstein, Sharon L., 2256
Klingenstein, Susan, 2258
Klingenstein, Thomas, 2258
Klingenstein, Thomas Davis, 1328
Klingerman, Daniel A., 2947
Klink, Kathleen, 2710
Klismith, Tom, 3606
Klocko, Dan, 948
Klooster, Henry, 1586
Klopping, George, 347, 397
Klotnia, Diane, 1031
Klotzman, Jeff, 3287
Kluber, William, 1562
Klug, Jonathan P., 3167
Kluge, Mary Kay, 1008
Klugman, Rob, 528
Knall, David W., 1190
Knapik, Michelle, 617
Knapp, D. R., 2697
Knapp, David L., 1205
Knapp, George O., 2259
Knapp, George O., III, 2259
Knapp, John, 160
Knapp, Judy, 484
Knapp, Lauren Volgenau, 3485
Knapp, Paul, 1578
Knapp, Spencer, 3410
Knapp, W. Jared, III, 2259
Knauer, Joann, 1400
Knauer, Louise Whall, 1783
Knauf, Robert, 162
Knauss, Donald R., 153
Knecht, Alexander, 1102
Knedler, Marie, 1235
Kneeshaw, Warren, 376
Knell, Theresa N., 1394
Knepley, Katie, 407
Knez, Andrew, 1546
Knez, Debra S., 1546
Knez, Jessica, 1546

Knife & Son, L., Inc., 1545
Knife River Corp., 2652
Knight Inc., 510
Knight Trust, James A., 1630
Knight, Angela, 3604
Knight, Athelia, 653
Knight, Colleen, 1580
Knight, Dale A., 3586
Knight, James L., 771
Knight, John S., 771
Knight, Lynn, 1395
Knight, N. Scott, 2071
Knight, Penelope P., 2854
Knight, Philip H., 2854
Knight, Robert D., 714
Knight, Rory, 3047
Knight, Stephanie, 2868
Knight, Travis A., 2854
Knight, Warren, 268
Knight-Drain, Carol, 1630
Knighton, Maurine D., 2121
Knisley, Rex, 3009
Knispel, Lester, 428
Kniss, Lynee M., 288
Knitcraft, Inc., 2570
Knobel, Sara, 2112
Knobloch, Carla, 3183
Knock, Jan, 1241
Knoepfler, Charles A., 1240
Knoll, Jeffrey, 2741
Knoll, Tom, 2655
Knopman, Debra S., 2286
Knopoff, Alejandro, 613
Knopp, Theresa G., 3102
Knorr, Johnny, 2009
Knott, Ron, Fr., 1283
Knotts, Bradley, 1045
Knowles, C. Harry, 1955
Knowles, Janet H., 1955
Knowles, Joe, 1464
Knowles, Marie, 400
Knowles, Rachel Hunt, 2971
Knowlton, Austin E., 2720
Knowlton, Leslie, 569
Knox Charitable Lead Annuity Trust, George Ann, The, 890
Knox Charitable Lead Annuity Trust, Pat, The, 890
Knox, Boone A., 890
Knox, Jefferson B.A., 890
Knox, Julia P.R., 890
Knox, Ltd., 890
Knox, W. David, II, 3605
Knox, Wendell J., 1461
Knudsen, Richard, 1834
Knutson, Lisa A., 2780
Ko, Chung, 2189
Ko, Jensen, 2189
Kobara, John E., 137
Kober, Jane, 2797
Koblenzer, Dale, 2655
Koblik, Steven, Dr., 167
Koby, Eugene A., 2773
Koch Enterprises, Inc., 1167
Koch Industries, Inc., 1265
Koch Sons, George, Inc., 1167
Koch Sons, George, LLC, 1167
Koch Trusts for Charity, Fred C., 1264
Koch, Brad, 441
Koch, Charles G., 1265
Koch, David H., 1264, 1265
Koch, David M., 1167
Koch, Donald G., 2773
Koch, Elizabeth B., 1265
Koch, Fred C., 1265
Koch, Kevin R., 1167
Koch, Kimberly, 166
Koch, Mary R., 1265
Koch, Nancy J., 333
Koch, Priscilla, 2331
Koch, Robert J., 2888
Koch, Robert L., II, 1167
Koch, William C., Jr., Hon., 3129
Koch-Schumaker, Robyn, 2787
Koehm, Christopher J., 576
Koenig, Aaron, 2684
Koenig, Bradford, 285
Koenig, John, 1853
Koenig, Lauren, 285
Koepplinger, Suzanne, 1717
Koerber, Cyndy, 1836
Koester, Torin S., 3413
Koffler Corp., The, 3081
Koffler, Lillian, 3081
Kogod, Arlene R., 3479
Kogod, Robert P., 3479
Kohelet Yeshiva High School, 2979
Kohl, Ronald W., Dr., 2091
Kohler, Evangeline, 3629
Kohler, Herbert V., 3629
Kohler, Lillie B., 3629
Kohler, Marie C., 3629
Kohler, Mary S., 3669
Kohler, Terry J., 3669
Kohlwes, Gary F., 3514
Kohn, Al, 328
Kohn, Bill, 401
Kohout, Heather Catto, 480
Kohs, LaVerne R., 3633
Koirtyohann, Barbara, 1817
Kokot, Eugene V., 2251
Kolander, Jerry, 3287
Kolano, Edward, 2966
Kolb, Sandra Kiely, 2770
Kolba, Robert E., 3336
Kolber, Kari, 3211
Kolenda, Helena, 301
Kolendrianos, Harry T., 3430
Kolhmeir, J. Bleich, 2148
Kollman, Robert, 3287
Komos, Joseph P., 1796
Kompkoff, Gabriel, 32
Kompsi, Keith, 193
Konar, Howard, 2154
Kong, Albert, 443
Koniag, Inc., 36
Konigsberg, Julie E., 2727
Konneker, James R., 2541
Konner, Joan, 2412
Koo, Grace J., 2118
Koopman, Martin, 1836
Kooyker, Willem, 2310
Kopac, Matt, 626
Kopf, Robert Y., Jr., 3009
Kopko, Peter, 2663
Koplan, Jeffrey P., 1949
Kopper, Carolyn S., 532
Kora, Vidya, 1201
Koran, Ida, 1709
Korell, Brad, 1834
Korf, Larry, 1703
Korf, Mordechai, 772
Korf, Mordechai Y., 772
Korf, Nechama A., 772
Korff, Phyllis, 2237
Kornfeld, Emily Davie, 2261
Kornwasser Life Insurance, Mila, 390
Korolkiewicz, Linda, 562
Korologos, Ann McLaughlin, 2126
Korsmo, John, 3567
Kort, William B., 3438
Kortan, Ron, 1836
Korum Automotive Group, Inc., 3532
Korum Family Limited Partnership, 3532
Korum Investments, Jerry, 3532
Korum, Germaine R., 3532
Korum, Jerome, 3532
Korum, Jerry, 3532
Kos, Jeanne R., 713
Kosai, Aizo, 3531
Kosanovich, John, Dr., 1662
Kosarek, Charles L., Jr., 3176
Kosarek, Sherry, 3176
Kosarek, Willie J., 3176
Kosasa, Paul, 933
Koshal, Vipin, Dr., 2662
Kosinski, John, 2169
Kosman, Hod, 1852
Kosmin, M. Douglas, 2958
Koss, Blair, 2331
Kostanecki, Sheila K., 2400
Koster, Elaine, 255
Kostohryz, Thomas, 2662
Kostolansky, David J., 2685
Kostyack, Ray, 2004
Kotcamp, Kathy, 1283
Kotek, Jim, 3636
Kothari, Mitesh B., 1360
Kotik, Charlotta, 2187
Kott, Paul, 283
Kouroyen, Angela, 1877
Koury, Carol E., 1880, 1896
Koury, Frederick S., 1727
Koury, Michelle A., Dr., 2111
Koury-Jones, Carina, 1896
Koussevitzky, Olga, 2262
Koussevitzky, Serge, 2262
Kouvas, Patrice, 2685
Kovaleski, James, 3014
Kovar, Victoria, 1834
Kovarik, Emily, 1828
Kovash, Russell, Fr., 2651
Kovner, Bruce S., 1956
Kovner, Suzanne F., 1956
Kowach, John W., 3009
Kowalchuk, E. J., 3235
Kowalke, Kim, 2499
Kowalski, Michael J., 2463
Koyama, Todd, 3510
Kozakis, Chris M., 1513
Kozberg, Joanne Corday, 137
Kozberg, Lindsey C., 3496
Koziol, Jim, 3606
Kozlak, Jodeen A., 1744
Kpaa-Kaiser Permanente, 2001
Kracium, Mike, 1207
Krafft, Dennis, 1606
Kraft Foods Global, 952
Kraft Foods Global, Inc., 1064, 2562
Kraft Total, 2327
Kraft, Cynthia, 1257
Kraft, Dennis, 3116
Kraft, Rocky, 2758
Krahe, David, 2670
Kraiem, Elizabeth Leiman, 2237
Krakaur, Kenneth, 3471
Kral, Barbara H., 1840
Krall, Ron, 545
Kramer, Catherine, 773
Kramer, Christopher M., 2125
Kramer, Daniel R., 2125
Kramer, Diana, 282
Kramer, John, 1832
Kramer, Karl F., 282
Kramer, Kathleen McGrath, 282
Kramer, Keith, 1216
Kramer, Kevin, 1152
Kramer, Larry, 248
Kramer, Manuel, 1049
Kramer, Mary L., 1666
Kramer, Michael, 282, 3315
Kramer, P.S., 1799
Kramer, Sandra, 1063
Kramer, Susan, 1049
Krames, Crysta, 305
Krammer, Susan, 2840
Kramzer, Joyce A., 744
Krane, Hilary, 2865
Kranich, Michael, Sr., 2907
Kranwinkle, Mark, 3545
Kranwinkle, Sara, 3545
Kranz, Mary Jo, 1580
Kranzlin, Mary Ellen, 1402
Krapp, Elizabeth, 2981
Krarup, Irene, 2064, 2375
Krasner, Lee, 2363
Krasno, Richard M., 2577
Kratchman, Eden M., 2880
Kratovil, Edward, 3483
Kratz Foundation, 106
Kratz, Richard P., 106
Kraus, Laurence, 954
Krause, Claire, 1706
Krause, Lois, 3611
Krause, Richard A., 810
Krause, Robin, 2504
Krause, Stephen, 1063
Krauthammer, Charles, 669
Kraybill, Dave, 3017
Kreamer, Janice, 1797
Kreamer, Janice C., 2097
Kreckle, Kathryn A., 1628
Kreger, Shirley, 1221
Kreher, Rick, 1817
Kreid, Christopher, 1065
Kreiner, Charles F., Jr., 2120
Kreitzer, Joan, 2712
Krell, Joanne K., 1628
Krempa, Jerry, 3598
Krendl, Kathy, 2762
Krenicky, Kenneth, 3014
Krenzel, Sharla, 1280
Kresa, Kent, 276
Kresek, Bob, 305
Kresge, Cynthia L., 1631
Kresge, Sebastian S., 1631
Kresnak, Diane M., 1588
Kress, Amy C., 2774
Kress, Claude W., 2263
Kress, Rush H., 2263
Kress, Samuel H., 2263
Kretchmar, Brenda, 1766
Kretschmer, R. David, 1206
Kretsinger, Mary, 1257
Kretzschmar, Robert, Pastor, 1387
Kreuchauf, Katherine, 2700
Kreul, Juliana, 723
Kreul, Sandra, 757
Kreun, Curt, 2648
Kreutzer, Bob, 1280
Kriak, John M., 2922
Krick, Robert K., 3448
Krieg, Joanne, 1852
Krieger, John B., 2026
Krieger, Teresa R., 1582
Krieger-Burke, Teresa, 1582
Krigstein, Alan, 2975

Krikava, Michael, 1687
Krikorian, John, 1515
Kringlund, Pam, 3599
Kripp, Betty, 2896
Krishnamurti, Vasili, 2206
Kriss, Thomas, Dr., 1257
Kristofcak, Alexander, 2132
Kristoff, Sandy, 713
Kristol, William, 2465
Krodel, Greg, 1192
Kroeger, Dave, 3552
Kroeger, Eileen, 695
Kroeger, Paul, 1125
Kroell, Scott, 886
Kroes, Rich, 2027
Kroese, Mark, 3509
Kroger, William, 1086
Krohn, Rebecca, 1240
Krohn, S. D., 1676
Kromer, Megan, 3310
Kron, Judy, 484
Kron, Robert, 484
Krone, Bruce A., 2687
Krone, Dorothy G., 2687
Kronenberg, Alex, 2983
Kronenberg, Dorothy, 2983
Kronenberg, William, III, 2983
Kronick, Susan D., 771
Kroos, O.A., 3629
Krop, Pamela S., 1741
Kropf, Susan J., 2100, 2492
Kroske, Doug, 3099
Krosman, Susan M., 550
Krouse, Hillary, 774
Krouse, Rodger, 774
Krouse, Rodger R., 774
Krudop, Jim, 1
Krudy, Courtney, 1163
Krueger, Kurtiss R., 3659
Krueger, Steve, 1817
Krug, Daniel W., 2601
Krulewitch, Peter, 2113
Krull, Dana L., Mr., 1168
Krumm, Tim, 1218
Krumsiek, Barbara J., 672
Kruntorad, Virginia Blossom, 2668
Krupps, Philip, 992
Krupskas, Joan, 2233
Kruse, Anita, 3303
Kruse, Karl, 989
Kruse, Sarah, 3663
Krush, Phyllis J., 1155
Kubal, Elizabeth, 989
Kubera, Ronald, 3527
Kubert, Arthur J., 1572
Kubiak, Andy, 3662
Kubiak, Julie R., 947
Kubiak, Mark S., 947
Kubiak, Susan L., 947
Kubick, Jonathan J., 3619
Kubisch, Anne, 2846
Kubli, Tim, 419
Kucera, Matthew, 723
Kudas, Kris, 155
Kuechle, Scott, 2561
Kueffner, Eric, 35
Kuehnle, Edward, 716
Kuehnlein, Tim, 1587
Kuennen, Christa, 1246
Kuenzl, John E., 3630
Kuenzl, Norma, 3630
Kuenzli, Gwen, 2700
Kuerbis, Paul, 1955
Kuester, Dennis J., 3601
Kugley, Douglas D., 3107
Kuhlman, Randy, 1215
Kuhn, Dwight E., 2935
Kuhn, Hilda Albers, 1773
Kuhn, J. A., 2566
Kuhn, John A., 2566
Kuhn, Lori, 2739
Kuhn, Lucy S., 2566
Kuhn, Mark, 2533
Kuhn, Michael J., 1798
Kuhn, Richard W., 1008
Kuhn, Steven L., 1798
Kuhn, Thomas E., 1798
Kuhne, Jack, 2626
Kuhne, Lucy, 2626
Kuhne, William D.S., 2566
Kuhnley, Marc, 1694
Kuhns, Carole, 2773
Kuijpers, Roelfien, 2134
Kuiken, Tim, 1227
Kukla, Don, 1802
Kukla, Donald T., 1802
Kula, Donald T., 1802
Kulas, E.J., 2721
Kulas, Fynette H., 2721
Kulkarni, Bhushan, 1576
Kullman, Mary Caola, 1799
Kullman, Mary Ellen, 90
Kumar, Bandana, 2046
Kumar, Daryn, 425
Kumm, Dan, 1780
Kummer, Robert W., Jr., 270
Kundert, David J., 3637
Kuni Trust, Wayne D., 3533
Kuni, Joan E., 3533
Kuni, Wayne D., 3533
Kunick, Marlene Holly, 1651
Kunkel, John C., II, 2980
Kunkel, Molly, 2909
Kunkel, Paul A., 2980
Kunkel, Tom, 678
Kunkle, Lynn, 659
Kunnath, Richard M., 3548
Kunsman, Jason, 2674
Kuntz, Jean M., 2815
Kunze, Cliff, 1186
Kunze, Mel, 3369
Kunzman, Kenneth F., 1909
Kupfer, Lawrence, 3419
Kupferberg, Max L., 2487
Kuprion-Thomas, Sandra R., 3199
Kurack, Sandra M., 3549
Kuriyama, Shigehisa, 1495
Kurland, Gerald, 268
Kurmas, Steven E., 1598
Kuronen, Amy, 1693
Kurtz, Caroline Lupfer, 2725
Kurtz, David, 2984
Kurtz, Gregory P., 2670
Kurtz, Nancy, 1428
Kurtz, Robert M., Jr., 3155
Kurtz, Willis O., 2725
Kurzrok Foundation, The, 2675
Kusch, Jenifer, 1590
Kushner, Charles, 1957
Kushner, Jared, 1957
Kushner, Josh, 1957
Kushner, Nessia Sloane, 2205
Kushner, Seryl, 1957
Kusmer, James, 2764
Kustanbauter, Kay, 2909
Kuszaj, Elizabeth, 562
Kutak Rock LLP, 2297
Kutliroff, Susan, 1992
Kutz, Hattie, 637
Kutz, Milton, 637
Kuykendall, John, Rev. Dr., 1909
Kuzio, Keith S., 2947
Kuzma, Lisa, 2998
Kvamme, Damon, 286
Kvamme, E. Floyd, 286
Kvamme, Jean, 286
Kvamme, Todd, 286
Kvitek, Jesse, 3641
Kwiecinski, Henry, 2895
Kyle, Louis B., 954
Kyriakakis, Toni, 568
Kysor Industrial Corp., 3632
Kyte, Lawrence, 2751

L-3 Link Communications, 2280
L.C. Page Char Tr f/b/o Page Fam Char, 1651
La Dow, Anne M., 2780
La Forgia, Robert M., 3401
Laarman, Linda, 3609
LaBadie, Emily, 3666
Labaree, Aaron, 2345
Labaree, Frances, 2345
LaBate, Anne, 1979
LaBelle, John D., Jr., 611
Labenne, Andrew D., 3426
Laber, Ricky, 1618
Laborey, Annette, 2343
Labrie, Tom, 3117
Labry, Ed, 496
Lachowicz, Cheryl, 1862
Lachowicz, Theodore, 1862
Laciak, Geoff, 1187
Laclede Gas Co., 1799
LaCount, Robert, 3040
Lacouture, Dick, 503
LaCroix, Sara Morley, 1644
Lacrosse, Adernaline, 3026
Lacy Holdings Ltd., 3206
Lacy, Benjamin H., 1449
Lacy, Mark, 472
Lacy, Terri, 3266
Ladd, David J., 1468
Ladd, Donna J., 1468
Ladd, G. Michael, Jr., 1468
Ladd, Gene, 1180
Ladd, Kate Macy, 2288
Ladd, William L., 1468
Laderer, Theresa M., 2890
Lading, Phil, 1010
Ladner, John, 212
Laducer, Jim, 1722
LaDuke, Winona, 151
LaFayette, Aimee, 1868
Lafer, Fred S., 2035
Laff, Amy, 2144
Laffend, Jane, 554
Laffont 2009 Trust, 2264
Laffont, Philippe, 2264
Lafitte, Darrell, 3207
Lafitte, Michael, 3207
Lafrance, Dorothy, 1519
Lafrance, Richard L., 1453
Lafyatis, Robert, 1540
Lagasse, Emeril J., III, 1314
Lagerblade, Mary, 1063
Lageson, Angela D., 1727
Lagorio, Lisa, 364
LaGrange Memorial Health System, 993
Laguarda, Lucia, 167
Lahn, John L., 415
Lai, I.U., 301
Laidlaw, Kathleen Muir, 1627
Lail, Ernest R., 3442
Laine, Erick, 2123
Lainhant, Sharon W., 2142
Laiou, Evangelia, 1048
Laird, E. Cody, Jr., 872
Laird, John, 354
Laird, Linda, 907
Laird, Peter A., 1570
Laird, Tony, 1192
Lake City Bank, 1120
Lake County, 1031
Lake, Charlene, 3167
Lake, Eliza, 3059
Lake, Sonia, 1660
Lake, Thomas H., 1814
Lakewood Church, 3269
Lakey, Ronald L., 402
Lalli, Peter, 1988
Lalor, Willard A., 1498
Lalta, Brash, 753
LaLuzerne, Julie, 3649
Lam, Joseph, 468
LaMarche, Gara, 2048
LaMattina, John, 562
Lamb, Barbara, 2855
Lamb, Brenda, 2855
Lamb, Dorothy, 2855
Lamb, Frank, 2855
Lamb, Glenda, 1184
Lamb, James R., 596, 597
Lamb, Jim, 2855
Lamb, Nash, 3292
Lamb, Paula, 2855
Lamb, Peter, 2338
Lamb, Rick, Jr., 2855
Lamb, Stephen P., 630
Lambe, Christopher, 1718
Lamberg, Carol, 790
Lamberg, Pearl, 790
Lamberson Consulting, LLC, 102
Lambert Trust, Phyllis, 2074
Lambert, Blair, 340
Lambert, Clement T., 1567
Lambert, Cynthia A., 3650
Lambert, Ellen, 1966
Lambert, J. Hamilton, 3461
Lambert, J. William, 2618
Lambert, Jeffrey, 1671
Lambert, Jeffrey K., 1600
Lambert, Karen J., 850
Lambert, Peter, 2755
Lambert, Ron, 842
Lambert, Samuel W., 3418
Lambert, Samuel W., III, 1916, 1979
Lambert, Stephen J., 3103
Lambert, Susan R., 3103
Lambert, William L., 23
Lambright, Kris, 3502
Lambrou, Peter J., 2906
LaMendola, Sal, 1589
Lamkin, Janet W., 2524
Lamme, Cheryl, 1836
Lammers, James D., 1594
Lamont, Glenda G., 1165
Lamont, Sharon L., 1984
Lampe, Amy P., 3443
Lampert, Alan G., 1890
Lampton, Dorothy Lee, 1761
Lampton, Lee C., 1761
Lampton, Leslie B., 1761
Lampton, Leslie B., III, 1761
Lampton, Robert H., 1761
Lampton, William W., 1761

Lancaster, Sally R., 3296
Lancellot, Mike, 2123
Land O'Lakes, Inc., 1710
Landauer, Tracy Green, 2275
Lande, Sarah, 1217
Landers, Lynn, 73
Landers, Richard, 1917
Landes, Andrea C., 2106
Landes, Rodney, 73
Landesman, Debby, 1715
Landesman, Dodge, 574
Landesman, North, 574
Landin, Beth, 2109
Landis, Dave, 1847
Landis, H. Kel, 2599
Landis, John, 267
Landis, Susan S., 3577
Landman, Carole, 2205
Landmann, Barbara, 1899
Landreth, Lucinda, 3019
Landrum, Martha McDermott, 1316
Landry, Kim, 2932
Landry, Margaret, 363
Lands, Walker, 1772
Landsburg, William, 2958
Landwirth, Gary M., 775
Landwirth, Gregory D., 775
Landwirth, Henri, 775
Landwirth, Linda, 775
Landwirth, Theresa, 775
Landy, Laura K., 1982
Lane, Alexina, 738
Lane, Andrew, 2240
Lane, C.A., 503
Lane, Charles, 1001
Lane, Clifford, 2266
Lane, George H., III, 860
Lane, H. Merritt, III, 1299
Lane, Mildred, 2266
Lane, Randi, 2266
Lane, Robert J., Jr., 2270
Lane, Sandro, 35
Lane, Steven, 69
Laney, James T., 2286
Lang, Anne, 1026
Lang, Barbara, 672
Lang, Cathy, 1847
Lang, Janet, 65
Lang, Jeffrey R., 1134
Lang, Joseph, 3633
Lang, Lisa Marie, 26
Lang, Margaret A., 2345
Lang, Peter, 3642
Lang, Robert Todd, 2498
Lang, Todd, 2320
Lang, William, 2006
Langbauer, Del, 3524
Langbauer, Robert, 3524
Langdon, Larry R., 111
Lange, Duane, 1663
Lange, Joan, 2873
Lange, Louis G., 1344
Langeloth, Jacob, 2267
Langendorf, Stanley S., 289
Langenhorst, Dian, 1107
Langford, George, 232, 2534
Langford, Rob, 726
Langham, 368
Langley, Jim, Dr., 1848
Langley, Peter S., 1886
Langlois, Marie J., 3089
Langseth, Mark, 2850
Langstaff, David, 666
Langwell, Dennis J., 1502, 3554
Lanier, J. Hicks, 891
Lanier, J.W., 2824
Lanier, Richard S., 2477
Lanier, Sartain, 891
Lanigan, Bernard, Jr., 870
Lanjouw, Annette, 2040
Lankes, J. B., 2044
Lann, Danielle, Dr., 2105
Lanning, Morrie, 2649
Lanphear, Gail E., 1573, 1653
Lans, Bruce, 3663
Lansing, John S., 2265
Lansing, Sherry, 276, 290
Lansky, Gregg I., 3135
Lantis, Jeff, 1620
Lantrip, Mark S., 915
Lantum, Hoffman Moka, 2154
Lantz, Tom, 1132
Lanz, Jorge, 1136
Lanz, Lisa M., 1078
Lanzano, Steve, 2071
Lanznar, Howard S., 1042
Lapides, Leola, 163
LaPlace, William B., 2803
Lapostora, James, 3083
Larcen, Stephen, 562
Lare, Rebekah, 628
Largay, Dorothy F., 291
Large, Donald L., Jr., 7
Lario Oil and Gas Co., 1725
Lark, J. Andrew, 2122
Larkin, Amy S., 1363
Larkin, Richard, 232
Larkin, Terrence B., 1632
Larmett, James C., Mrs., 2513
Larner, Julie, 1136
Laros, Michael, 1124
Laros, Russell K., 2982
Laros, Russell K., III, 2982
Laros, Russell K., Jr., 2982
LaRosa, Ann, 1755
Larrowe, Mike, 3431
Larsen, Christine, 484
Larsen, Daniel, 122
Larsen, Daryl, 1599
Larsen, John A., 1711
Larsen, John E., 1711
Larsen, John O., 3592
Larsen, Karen R., 1711
Larsen, Katrina, 3662
Larsen, Mark, 1862
Larsen, Ralph S., 1949
Larson, Bernie, 162
Larson, Carol, 1115
Larson, Carol S., 357
Larson, Dexter, 1691
Larson, Donna, 999
Larson, Dorothy, 162
Larson, Dorothy M., 26
Larson, Eric B., 1588
Larson, Eva, 158
Larson, Geoff, 35
Larson, Jeff, 1262
Larson, Ken, 371
Larson, Margaret, 2650
Larson, Paul, 3576
Larson, Robert A., 3526
Larson, Scott, 3633
Larson, Steve, 1247
Larson, Timothy, 3637
LaSalle, Barbara B., 445
Lashbrook, Louanne, 1184
Lashley, Elinor Huston, 2973
Laska, Bev, 3606
Lasker, Nicole, 3611
Lasko, John C., 1958
Laskoski, Peggy, 3336
Laskow, Mark, 2906
Lasky, Mark, 3642
Laspa, Jude P., 103, 104
Lass, E. Donald, 802
Lassalle, Nancy N., 2268
Lastavica, Catherine, 1561
Lastavica, Catherine C., 1561
Lastowka, Joseph E., Jr., Esq., 2932
Lataif, Louis E., 1487
Latimer, Carol Rogers, 3144
Latimer, Douglas N., 3144
Latimer, Jay, 1832
Latimer, William H., III, 3144
Latona Associates Inc., 1893
LaTorre, Jean C., 592
Latshaw, Robert E., 2932
Latterell, Larry, 1699
Lattimer, William H., III, 3144
Lau, Constance H., 934
Lau, Michele, 321
Lau, Richard E., 564
Laub, Philippe, 2205
Laubscher, Leon, 3330
Lauder Charitable Trust, Estee, 2233
Lauder Companies, Estee, Inc., 2287
Lauder, Leonard A., 2233
Lauder, Ronald S., 2233, 2238
Lauderbach, William, 1573
Lauderbach, William C., 1653
Lauer, Brian, 3648
Lauer, Kay, 1257
Laulhere, Christine, 292
Laulhere, Gwen, 292
Laulhere, Larry, 292
Laulhere, Larry, Mrs., 292
Laulhere, Teresa, 292
Laulhere, Todd, 292
Laun, Susan, 376
Launders Marital Trust, Ruth C., 3447
Laureate Education, Inc., 648
Laurel Wilt Bank, Peter Smith, 2332
Laurence, Margaret, 1487
Laurino, Carl J., 3632
Lauritsen, Jeanne, 1216
Lauro, Shirley, 2143
Lauter, Lawrence G., 2796
Laux, Ronald, 1188
Lauzier, Paul, 3534, 3535
LaValley, Frederick J.M., 2962
Lave, Roy, 305
Lavender, Kevin P., 3129
Lavender, Martha G., 9
Laverack, Melissa W., 1567
Laverty, Robert, 1576
Lavery, David, 3083
Lavin, Arthur, M.D., 2770
Lavin, Richard P., 2750
Lavin, Thomas, 996
Lavine, Ann, 1753
Lavine, Steven, Dr., 167
Lavis, Victor, 81
Lavizzo-Mourey, Risa, 1949
Law, Douglas, 2899
Law, John, 3312
Lawford Co., 1388
Lawhorn, Ed, 3431
Lawler, Maggie, 1512
Lawler, Matthew J., 1240
Lawliss, Catherine H. Regan, 1936
Lawlor, Brian, 2071
Lawlor, Brian G., 2780
Lawlor, Stephen F., 1883
Lawner, Lilli, 2039
Lawrence, Barbara, 2000
Lawrence, Barbara A., 3492
Lawrence, Cara B., 483
Lawrence, David, Jr., 2161
Lawrence, Jeff, 293
Lawrence, Jill Piper, 3186
Lawrence, John T., III, 2694
Lawrence, Kathleen, Jr., 1660
Lawrence, Ken, 1272
Lawrence, Sandra A.J., 1793
Lawrence, Thomas W., III, 2584
Lawrence-Lightfoot, Sara, 2048
Laws, Diane, 866
Laws, Tom L., 950
Lawson, Andrea, 2173
Lawson, Barbara, 628
Lawson, Frederick Q., 3402
Lawson, Michael, 1203
Lawson, Peter Q., 3402
Lawson, Scott, 1847
Lawson, Tamara S., 3101
Lawther, Fonza Bell, 247
Lawton Company, William B., L.L.C., 1303
Lawton, Jack E., Jr., 1303
Lawton, Robert B., 242
Lawton, William B., 1303
Laycox, Devon, 120
Layman, Dan, 1125, 3429
Layne, Gloria G., 3434
Layne, Mark M., 3144
Layng, Jeffrey, 990
Layton, Greg, 1735
Layton, Matthew, 3510
Layton, Tom, 446
Lazar, Helen B., 2856
Lazar, Jack, 2856
Lazar, William B., 2856
Lazarof, Janice Taper, 433
Lazarus Charitable Fund, 1083
Lazarus, Ben, 3556
Lazarus, J. David, 3556
Lazarus, Katherine, 3556
LCNB National Bank, 2679
LCR-M Corp., 1006
Le Moal-Gray, Michele J., 2116
Leach, Brandon, 3299
Leach, Duane M., Dr., 3276
Leach, Gary J., 3299
Leach, Kenneth C., 2006
Leach, Nicole Rodriguez, 2134
Leadabrand, Frances, 1275
Leadform Est. LTD, 648
Leake, Michael T., 3464
Leal, Omar J., 3196
Leap, Roy, 1137
Lear Corp., 1632
Lear, Eric, 1984
Leary, Carol A., 1559
Leatherby, Russell, 283
Leatherman, Gary, 1179
Leatherman, J. Martin, 562
Leatherwood, Many, 2010
Leavens, Bill, 1959
Leavens, Nancy, 1959
Leavens, William B., III, 1959
Leavenworth, Elaine R., 954
Leavey, Dorothy E., 294
Leavey, Thomas E., 294
Leavitt, Sarah, 474
Leavitt, William, 474
Lebens, Michelle, 1850

Levis, William E., 2678
Levison, S. Jarvin, 876
Leviton, Susan, 1410
Levitt and Sons, Inc., 2275
Levitt, Abraham, 2275
Levitt, Alfred, 2275
Levitt, AnneMarie, 1960
Levitt, Jane, 1524
Levitt, Jim, 1524
Levitt, Matthew L., 1726
Levitt, Mortimer, 1960
Levitt, William, 2275
Levitt-Hirsch, Elizabeth, 1960
Levkovich, Natalie, 2948
Levy, Austin T., 1501
Levy, Carol, 3209
Levy, Craig, 1531
Levy, Damon, 1941
Levy, Daniel, 2389
Levy, David S., 162
Levy, Edward, 1902
Levy, Harold J., 2237
Levy, Jacob, 1902
Levy, Jerry, 2071
Levy, Karen, 2276
Levy, Kenneth, 2873
Levy, Leon, 2320
Levy, Meyer, 1515
Levy, Paul, 2276
Levy, Roberta Morse, 1531
Levy, Sarah K., 2282
Levy, Stan I., 1026
Levy-Pounds, Nekima, Esq., 1717
Lew, Ginger, 672
Lew, Kim Y., 2085
Lewellyn, Daryn, 1152
Lewin, Dan'l, 408
Lewis Family Foundation, Clark, 2868
Lewis Family Trust, 368
Lewis Foundation, Reginald F., The, 3424
Lewis, Andy, 537
Lewis, Carlotta, 3431
Lewis, Craig, 1394
Lewis, Craig C., 425
Lewis, Daniel E., 1201
Lewis, David, 1930
Lewis, David Baker, 1588
Lewis, David D., 3539
Lewis, Denise J., 1638
Lewis, Diana, 1763
Lewis, Diana D., 1709
Lewis, Donald McLeod, 2987
Lewis, Donna, 1357
Lewis, Earl, 2302
Lewis, Emma, 551
Lewis, Heather, 2710
Lewis, Jan, 1759
Lewis, Joanna M., 2887
Lewis, John, 1395
Lewis, John D., 1588
Lewis, John T., 487
Lewis, Karen J., 1917
Lewis, M. Todd, 1189
Lewis, Manuel M., 3083
Lewis, Marc, 1973
Lewis, Michael, 268
Lewis, Michaela, 1842
Lewis, Nancy, 1279
Lewis, Nathan, 363
Lewis, Philip E., 2302
Lewis, Renee, 313
Lewis, Rick, 1137
Lewis, Roderick W., 950
Lewis, Roland, 2326
Lewis, Sarah Elizabeth, 2494
Lewis, Shirley Long, 51
Lewis, Stephen R., Jr., 1734, 1748
Lewis, Tony, 491
Lewis, Vernie W., 3445
Lewis, Walter G., Rev., 650
Lewis-Sheets, Leslie, 1136
Leyba, Yvonne, 88
Leyden, Timothy M., 459
Leyden-Dunbar, Eleanor, 655
Leyhe, Denise, 3067
Li, Cheng, 667
Li, Esther, 165, 202
Li, Philip, 2098
Li, Romana, 676
Li, Yifei, 2390
Li-Cor of Lincoln LLC, 1574
Liang, Charles, 233
Liang, Matthew H., 1538
Liang, Patrick, 1873
Liang, Sara, 233
Liang, Stella, 1873
Liapis, Suzanne, 1721
Libby, John, 896
Liberman, Isaac, 2279
Liberty Building Co., 196
Liberty Mutual Group, 2967
Liberty Mutual Insurance Co., 1502
Libin, Jerome B., 2349
Liboff, Jerry, 31
Lichlyter, Craig, 1179
Lichtenberg, Nora, 671
Lichtenberg, William, 671
Lichtman, Jeff, 232
Liddell, Richard D., 2819
Lidemann, George L., 780
Lieb, Charles, 3619
Liebenson, Paul, 964
Liebherr, Paul, 3623
Liebman, Katherine, 2291
Liebman, Vance, 960
Liebscher, Anita, 2578
Liebscher, Robert, 3423
Lieder, Erick, 2864
Liedtke, Laurie L., 3288
Liedtke, Leslie Erb, 1599
Liefer, Diana McLean, 2997
Lienemann, Charlotte, 1846
Lienemann, Del, Jr., 1846
Lienemann, Del, Sr., 1846
Lienemann, Douglas, 1846
Lieske, Joanne, 1749
Liewald, Lisa, 3148
Lifshitz, Lisa, 910
Lifson, Todd J., 1717
Liftman, Alexandra C., 2524
Light Community Property Trust, William M., 3281
Light, Jack H., 3281
Light, Richard J., 2459, 2460
Light, Robert, 3063
Light, Rudy, 160
Light, William M., 3281
Lightle, Jared, 1783
Lightner, Larry, 3282
Lightner, Sue B., 3282
Ligon, Cheryl P., 2628
Lilja, Michael, 1746
Liljedahl, Kerdyle, 729
Lillevand, Peter, 269
Lilley, Jack B., 3353
Lillie, Charisse, 2322, 2921
Lillis, Chuck, 1580
Lilly Endowment, 1141
Lilly, Charlotte Johnson, 2714
Lilly, George, II, 869
Lilly, Ruth, 1173
Lim, Henry W., 1588
Liman, Lisa C., 2237
Limbach, George, 305
Limmer, Bryan, 3174
Limoli, Scott, 3567
Lin, Fu-Tyan, 3040
Lin, Maya, 2066
Linares, Lance, 163
Linbeck, Leo, III, 3266
Lincoln Avenue Realty Co., 2255
Lincoln, Brinton C., 2724
Lincoln, Constance P., 2724
Lincoln, G. Russell, 2724
Lincoln, James D., 2724
Lincoln, Kathryn, 1503
Lincy Foundation, The, 428
Lind, Cynthia H., 27
Lind, Deidre, 312
Lind, Martin, 484
Lindberg, Eric V., 2720
Lindberg, John C., 2720
Lindblom, Lance E., 2376
Lindell, Andrea R., 2758
Lindemann, Elizabeth, 2345
Lindemann, Frayda B., 780
Lindemann, George L., 780
Lindemann, George L., Jr., 780
Lindemann, Sloan N., 780
LindenLaub, Mark, 1124
Linder, Maureen, 1917
Lindgren, Anne H., 2479
Lindgren, Hedy K., 991
Lindley, Steven J., 3271
Lindley, Todd, 3520
Lindsay, Agnes M., 1890
Lindsay, Gary J., 2410
Lindsay, Howard, 2143
Lindsay, William N., III, 528
Lindsey, Margaret, 3365
Lindsey, Mark, 3536
Lindsey, Phyllis, 3536
Lindsey, Steven L., 1799
Lindsley, Janet, 833
Lindsley, William, 833
Lineback, Donald, 3155
Lineberger, Laura G., 2560
Linehan, Jerome, 1547
Linford, Rodney, 727
Ling, Walt, 1735
Lingenfelter, James S., 2803
Linhart, Deborah W., 2950
Link, Edwin A., 2280
Link, Edwin A., Mrs., 2280
Link, William M., Jr., 1762
Linke, Gordon F., 587
Linke, Jocelyn B., 587
Linn, Dawn M., 2947
Linnartz, John H., 1983
Linnartz, Victoria, 1904
Linnell, Jon, 1723
Linnen, Mary Lou, 1201
Linnert, Terrence G., 2561
Linquest, Eric, 1314
Linsley, Sarah, 1014
Linsmayer Revocable Trust, James B., 2585
Lintecum, Elaine, 317
Lintilhac Annuity Trust I, Claire D., 3412
Lintilhac Annuity Trust II, Claire D., 3412
Lintilhac, Claire Malcolm, 3412
Lintilhac, Crea S., 3412
Lintilhac, Louise S., 3412
Lintilhac, Paul S., 3412
Lintilhac, Philip M., 3412
Lintilhac, William S., 3412
Linton, Tina, 2664
Lintzenich, James C., 1174
Linville, Don, 1280
Linz, Brian J., 2943
Lipcon, Jesse, 2714
Lipcon, Patricia L. Johnson, 2714
Lipcon, Scott, 2714
Lipcon, Todd, 2714
Lipman, Robert S., 3129
Lipmanson Foundation, Margaret & Richard, 675
Lipoff, Norman H., 720
Lipp, Lee, Dr., 2648
Lippes, David, 3568
Lippman, Michael, 2422
Lipschutz, Lester, 2979
Lipton, Alan, 781
Lipton, Janice, 781
Lipton, Martin, 2490
Lischick, Karen E., 677
Lischick, Peter, 677
Lisi, Joan, 2335
Lisker, Marc, 3213
Lisker, Mitchell, 1902
Liss, Cathy, 2508
Lissau, W.R., 2831
Lissner Foundation, Herman, The, 2050
Lissner, Elaine, 358
Lissner, Gerda, 2281
List Trusts, Muriel & Robert, 1340
List, Bobye G., 2261
List, Stephen C., 1606
Lister, Alan, 2814
Listi, Frank, 235
Litchfield, Melanie, 3119
Litchfield, Rhonda, 3008
Litchfield, Ruth, 1246
Litow, Stanley S., 2227
Litt, Gordon, 2702
Littauer, Lucius N., 2282
Littel, John E., 3420
Litterman, Robert, 1949
Littick, Norma, 2783
Little, Dan, 2828
Little, Fletcher, 2866
Little, Teresa, 2407
Little, Tim, 2112
Littlefair, Andrew, 3321
Littlefield, Christopher J., 1211
Littlefield, James A., Dr., 3097
Littlejohns, Linda, 1945
Littles, Douglas M., 10
Littleton, Torrey B., 3209
Littman, Risa, 158
Littmann, Jeffrey C., 1675
Litton Industries, Inc., 3465
Litwin, Gordon N., 2409
Litwin, Leonard, 2283
Liu, Anna Luk, 301
Liu, Chiu-Chu, 233
Liu, Emily, 302
Liu, Emily F., 302
Liu, Hanmin, 1628
Liu, Justin, 302
Liu, Justin R., 302
Liu, Mimi W., 302
Liu, Peter, 151
Liu, Robert W., 302
Liu, Sara, 233

Live Nation Worldwide, Inc., 3108
Liveris, Andrew N., 1597
Livezey, Barbara, 1186
Livingston, Bess B., 893
Livingston, Bob, 1185
Livingston, Claudia M., 891
Livingston, Lanien, 34
Livingston, Mitchel D., 2757
Livingston, Randy, 354
Livingston, Roy N., 893
Livingston, Ruth Daily, 303
Livorna Investments, 102
Livsey, Charles H., 3402
Livsey, Herbert C., 3402
Lizza, Sandra R., 1998
LJS Revocable Trust, 2827, 2829
Llambelis, Lillian, 2326
Llewellyn, Carol, 95
Llewellyn, John, 95
Llewellyn, Rich, 117
Lloyd, Demi, 1267
Lloyd, Hannah, 1428
Lloyd, Harry J., 1267
Lloyd, Jeanette, 1267
Lloyd, Petrina A., 2935
Lloyd, Sophia, 1068
Lloyd, Susan, 3670
LMB Funding, 1974
Lo, Bernard, 2192
Lo, Hing-Har, 3431
Loadcraft Industries, Ltd., 3330
Lobach, David, 2986
Lobash, Catherine, 1816
Lobato, Kathryn, 257
Lobatz, Michael, Dr., 378
Lobdell, James, 2867
Lobel, Steven E., 2108
Lobert, Sandra, 2675
Locane, Jennifer, 2524
Locarni, Ida S., 1776
Lock, Bill, 3663
Lock, Pam, 1128
Lock, Sheri, 503
Locke, Deb, 1142
Locke, Jean, 1735
Lockett, Helen B., 361
Lockette, Elizabeth, 3401
Lockhart, G. Robert, 1881
Lockhart, Romona, 1881
Lockheed Martin Corp., 3284
Lockheed Martin Vought Systems, 3284
Locks, Sueyun Pyo, 2948
Lockwood, Dan, 1590
Locniskar, Dana M., 1588
Loda, Laura J., 3487
Lodestar Foundation, The, 676
Lodestone, 1388
Lodwig, Jeanette, 3558
Loeb, Ann R., 2479
Loeb, Michael, 268
Loeb, Rose, 3450
Loebner, Heather, 964
Loeffler, Kelly, 2336
Loeffler, Pauli, 2818
Loehr, Lulabelle, 1856
Loehr-Dols, Patricia, 1740
Loewe Foundation, 2143
Loewe, Frederick, 2284
Loewenstern, Richard, 3256
Loewenthal, Adlyn S., 561
Loewenthal, Ted, 561
Loewer, Deborah A., 3468
Lofquist, Gary, 3619
Loft, Richard, 303
Loftis, Jim, 2828
Loftis, Tom, 2787
Logan College of Chiropractic, 1232
Logan Foundation, Reva and David, 1002
Logan, Anne M., 206
Logan, Bill, 1012
Logan, Daniel, 1051
Logan, David, 1051
Logan, Harold R., 475
Logan, Harold R., Jr., 206
Logan, Jonathan, 1051
Logan, Kent, 543
Logan, Lyle, 1014
Logan, Richard, 1051
Logue, George E., Jr., 2947
Logue, James, III, 1618
Loh, Penn S., 1486
Lohide, Ruth, 1137
Lohman, Brett, 1022
Lohse, Jennifer, 47
Lohse, Linda, 47
Lohse, Patricia, 47
Lohse, Robert, 47
Loiacono, Nicholas A., 321
Loijens, Mari Ellen Reynolds, 408
Lokken, Jane, 3611
Lokken, Tena, 948
Lombard, Edward M., 1995
Lombardo, Philip J., 2071
LoMonaco, Paulette, 2197
Londis, Jeff, 3119
London, Bernard, 2228
Lonergan, Lauren, 1687
Lonergan, William, 1877
Loney, Chip, 1135
Long, Bob, 1647
Long, David H., 1502, 3554
Long, Dennis, 3520
Long, George A., 588
Long, Grace L., 588
Long, Ira M., 3125
Long, Jacob F., 51
Long, Joe R., 3285
Long, John F., 51
Long, Kathleen, 1586
Long, Milton, 304
Long, Mitchell, 3285
Long, Pat, 1256
Long, Peter, 114
Long, Phillip C., 2757
Long, Ruby, 3285
Long, Sallye, 3259
Long, Sidne J., 304
Long, Teresa L., 3285
Long, Thomas J., 304
Longbine, Jeff, 1262
Longbrake Trust, Mary, 1045
Longman, Laura J., 1979
Lonnes, Jerome L., 3447
Loo, Lamont, 3567
Loock Trust, Margaret, 3601
Loomes, Pat, 430
Loomis, Carol, 1833
Loomis, Peter, 2381
Looney, Ruth S., 3475
Loos, Jack, 3544
Loose, Harry Wilson, 3286
Loose, Rob, 1175
Lopez, Angel L. Saez, 3061
Lopez, Christopher, 3312
Lopez, David P., 408
Lopez, E. Zeke, 126
Lopez, Eleanor, 1591
Lopez, Humberto S., 65
Lopez, Jerry, 163
Lopez, Julia I., 156
Lopez, Lourdes, 2160
Lopez, Michael J., 126
Lopez, Susan, 2445
Lopez, Tina Starkey, 157
Lopez-Wessell, Cathy, 477
Lopez-Wessell, Irene, 477
Lopiccolo, Mary Beth, 2936
LoPresti, Pegi, 2429
Lord Baltimore Capital Corp., 1350
Lord, Charles, 1659
Lord, David, 1659
Lord, Heather, 1659
Lord, Nancy, 26
Lord, Richard, 1659
Lord, Susan Disney, 182
Lord-Wolff, Edith, 1659
Lordo, Lori, 2892
Lorence, Chris, 2366
Lorenz, Anton, 1343
Lorenz, Katherine, 3297
Lorenz, Nancy, 1185
Lorenz, Tina, 3607
Loretta, Hilary Kaplan, 1041
Loretto High School, 366
Loring, Angela, 1877
Loring, E. Amory, 1539
Loring, Jonathan B., 1501
Loring, Robert W., 1539
Lormand, Michael A., 3459
Lorton, George, 757
Los Angeles Olympic Organizing Comm., 287
Losch, William C., III, 3135
Loscuito, Deb, 3280
Losinger, Sarah McCune, 2993
Loucks, Donna, 2366
Louden, Nancy M., 2287
Louden, Thomas, 2689
Loughlin, Peter, 1885
Loughman 1997 Charitable Remainder Annuity Trust, Susan D., 182
Loughnane, Maureen, 1115
Loughran, Marcia B., 1415
Loughrey, F. Joseph, 1174
Loughridge, Mark, 2227
Louie, Gilman, 2290
Louie, May, 301
Louie, Sinclair, 301
Louis, Hank, 3401
Louis, Nelson, 2341
Lourd, Blaine, 272
Lourie, Kylee, 542
Louthan, Frank G., Jr., 3474
Love, Andrew Sproule, Jr., 3082
Love, Daniel Spoule, 3082
Love, Davis M., III, 3452
Love, Heather, 1265
Love, Jeff, 1130
Love, Kim, 3683
Love, Paula, 2820
Love, Robin B., 3452
Love, Steve, 2013
Love, Vincent B., 2177
Lovejoy, Mary F., 3089
Lovelace, John D., 3456
Lovelace, Richard M., 826
Lovelace, Sarah E., 3456
Lovell, Lura M., 65
Lovett, Tiffany W., 1621, 1645
Low, Sean, 3325
Lowder, Catherine, 894
Lowder, Charlotte, 894
Lowder, Gary, Dr., 3438
Lowder, Heather Anne, 894
Lowder, James K., 894
Lowder, Jarman F., 894
Lowder, Thomas H., 894
Lowe, Elizabeth, 359
Lowe, Ken, 2780
Lowe, Megan, 843
Lowe, Richard, 843
Lowe, Sandra Lois, 843
Lowe, Terry D., 83
Lowe, Tom, 3146
Lowell Museum Corp., 1505
Lowell, Bill, 3287
Lowell, Nan, 403
Lowell, Sara M., 310
Lowell, Wayne, 403
Lowell, William A., 1444
Lowenbery, Greg, 1227
Lowenthal, Paul, 729
Lowenthal, Steven R., 2594
Lower, Jackie, 1203
Lower, James Paul, 276
Lowery, Darlene, 2773
Lowes, 2562
Lowet, Henry A., 2282
Lowrie, Katie, 1214
Lowry, Glenn D., 2302
Lowry, Scott T., 1905
Lowy, Janey, 1967
Lowy, Philip B., 1967
Lox, William, 318
Loyce, James E., Jr., 329
Lozano, Jose, 2427
Lozano, Monica, 456, 2390
LRA, 1314
LSM Management, 2401
Lubar, David J., 3637
Lubash, Barbara N., 139
Lubbers, Arend, 1615
Lubberstedt, Wes, 1845
Lubchenco, Jane, 357
Lubleley, Michael D., 3471
Lucas, Arthur M., 866
Lucas, Benjamin F., II, 1394
Lucas, Donna, 156
Lucas, George W., Jr., 306
Lucas, Joy, 1047
Lucas, Lawrence R., 1060
Lucas, Matt, 419
Lucas, Peter, 1692
Lucas, Stuart E., 429
Lucasfilm Ltd., 306
Lucast, Jodi, 1694
Lucchese, John J., 1401
Luce, Clare Boothe, 2286
Luce, H. Christopher, 2286
Luce, Henry R., 2286
Lucent Technologies Inc., 1899
Lucero, Priscilla, 535
Lucht, Jennifer, Dr., 1168
Lucius, Jim, 1661
Luck, Suzanne, 1660
Luck, Ted, 1358
Lucksinger, Mike, 3259
Ludlam, Charles Stewart, 569
Ludwick, Christopher, 2988
Ludwig, Marianne, 1296
Ludwig, S. Peter, 2486
Luebke, Catherine, 1692
Luedeke, J. Barton, 1972
Luedeking, Otto, 2680
Luehring Irrevocable Trust, Ruth E., 1052
Luehring Trust, Marian D., 1052

Luers, William H., 2477
Lufrano, Robert, 744
Luger, Ellen Goldberg, 1697
Lugo, Rene Pinto, 3061
Luhman, Dave, 1130
Luhn, Dave, 3510
Lukas, Alan, 1326
Luke, Cathy, 933
Luke, John A., Jr., 3433
Luke, Lauren C., 3474
Lukens, Wanda C., 2794
Lukowski, Stanley J., 1461
Lumbert, Elizabeth, 1642
Lumpkin, Benjamin, 1053
Lumpkin, Benjamin I., 1053
Lumpkin, Besse Adamson, 1053
Lumpkin, Brent, 1307
Lumpkin, John R., 1949
Lumpkin, Mary G., 1053
Lumpkin, Richard Adamson, 1053
Lumpkin, Richard Anthony, 1053
Luna, Louis, 2011
Lund, Jay, 1678
Lund, Margaret McKee, 3295
Lund, Margaret T., 3645
Lundberg, Dana, 2091
Lundby, Sigrid, 3051
Lundebrek, Jan, 1740
Lundeen, Dean, 999
Lundell, Karin J., 2279
Lunder, Peter, 1324
Lundevall, Jessica Kaplan, 1041
Lundevall, Kaja, 1041
Lundin, Craig, 441
Lundin, Gloria, 990
Lungren, Daniel E., 270
Lungren, Lisa, 292
Lunn, Scott, 43
Lunney, J. Robert, 2269
Lunsford, Michael O., 1134
Luntz, Gregory W., 2788
Lupberger, Ed, 1763
Lupfer, Jonathan B., 2725
Lupfer, Sarah H., 2725
Lupica, Anne E., 2339
Luplow, Trish, 1662
Lupton, Carolyn C., 3288
Lupton, David, 3343
Lupton, T. Cartter, 3145
Lupton, T.C., Jr., 3288
Lupton, Tavenner C., III, 3288
Lurie, Ari A., 239
Lurie, Daniel L., 239
Luse, Bulah, 3289
Luse, Susan M., 1190
Luse, W.P., 3289
Lusk, Charles M., III, 3216
Lusk, E. Craig, 3326
Lussen, John F., 954
Lust, Angela, 3163
Lutgring, Michael D., 1305
Luther King Capital Management, 394
Luther, Cathy, 3642
Luther, Toby, 2846
Lutiger, Jim, 3662
Lutz, Garman, 3510
Lutz, Theodore C., 663
Lux, Miranda W., 307
Lyding, Sarah, 3496
Lyford, Shelley M., 458
Lygren, Rolf, 246
Lykins, Elizabeth Welch, 1667
Lyle, Janice, 87
Lyle, Jo, 1268
Lyman, Charles, 1725
Lynam, Fred C., 1335
Lynch, Edward, 1517
Lynch, Joe, 3504
Lynch, Linda, 1010
Lynch, M. Judith, 2957
Lynch, Maria M., 2519
Lynch, William, 2368
Lynehan, Linda, 1519
Lynham, John M., Jr., 3481
Lynn, Byran L., 279
Lynn, Cassie, 3121
Lynn, Edward R., 1246
Lynn, Elizabeth A., 1827
Lynn, Elizabeth R., 3094
Lynn, Heidi, 3415
Lynn, Jeff, 1827
Lynn, Joann, 3121
Lynn, Karen, 1211
Lyon, C.H. Randolph, 3595
Lyon, David, 1054
Lyon, Donna, 1054
Lyon, Linda, 1578
Lyons, Barbara, 1749
Lyons, Becky, 1141
Lyons, Bente S., 782
Lyons, Daniel M., 782
Lyons, Dianne M., 1243
Lyons, John, 1885
Lyons, Joseph, 2719
Lyons, Kristina E., 926
Lyons, Margaret, 2786
Lyons, Robert, Jr., 595
Lyons, Shaun B., 926
Lyons, Steve, 1137
Lyons, Thomas F., 1453

M & T Trust Co., 2501
M&T Bank, 2209, 2308, 2352, 2362, 2431, 2475, 2952
M&T Bank, N.A., 1404
M.D. Orthopaedics Inc., 1233
Ma'a, Stacie, 217
Maahs, Frederick J., 2921
Maar, William P., 1187
Maas, J. David, 1174
Mabry, Nancy, 2858
Mac Kinnon, George, 3633
MacAffer, John A., 2108
MacAllister, Lorissa K., 1627
MacAllister, Wesley, 1627
MacArthur Foundation, Catherine T., 1077
MacArthur Foundation, John D., 1077
MacArthur Foundation, John D. and Catherine T., 1002
MacArthur, C.J., 1055
MacArthur, Catherine T., 1056
MacArthur, Gina G., 1055
MacArthur, John D., 1056
Macaskill, Stephanie, 3414
Macauley, Alma Jane, 589
Macauley, Melinda Rice, 589
Macauley, Robert C., 589
Macauley, Robert C., Jr., 589
MacBride, Teri, 2947
Macchia, John, 1665
MacConnell, Diane, 1512
MacConnell, Gary, 1512
MacCowatt, Thomas H., 1944
MacCutcheon, James, 1356
Macdonald, Agnes, 2407
Macdonald, Anne F., 408
MacDonald, Beth, 1131
MacDonald, Brad, 1961
MacDonald, Corey Fuller, 1886
MacDonald, John A., 1793
Macdonald, Marg, 2943
MacDonald, Margaret, 1961
Macdonald, Maybelle Clark, 2859
MacDonald, Shirley, 1961
Macdonnell, Melissa M., 1502
MacDonnell, Melissa M., 3554
MacDougall, Peter, 394
MacFarlene, John, 1751
MacFie, Valerie A., 2432
Macgill, Frank S., 912
MacGovern, Rob, 630
Machamer, Susan, 704
Machones, Melinda, 1691
Macht, Amy, 1388
Macht, Philip, 1388
Macht, Sophia, 1388
Machtley, H. Ronald K., 3089
MacIlwinen, Frances G., 3103
MacIntosh, John, 2804
Macioce, Frank, 1998
Mack, Charlotte S., 385
Mack, Debra, 27
Mack, Dianne, 2204
Mack, John E., IV, 2113
Mack, John J., 2066, 2146
Mack, John W., 456
Mack, Marcie, Dr., 2809
Mack, Richard L., 1718
Mack, Roszell, III, 2188
Mack, Thomas, 27
Mackall, Corinne, 2771
Mackarey, Paula, 3031
Mackay, Calder M., 324
MacKay, Richard N., 324
Mackay, William, 221
Mackenzie, Alexander "Alec" R., 3468
MacKenzie, Andrew, 941
Mackenzie, Wendy, 2966
Mackie, Bert, 1028
MacKinnon, Kathleen, 1861
Macklem, Gary, 1663
Macklin, Tony, 2971
MacLachlan, Don, 3129
MacLaury, Bruce, 666
MacLean, Frederick R., 713
Maclean, Mary Ann, 1099
Maclellan, Christopher, 3146
Maclellan, Hugh O., Jr., 3146
Maclellan, R.L., Mrs., 3146
Maclellan, Robert H., 3146
Maclellan, Robert J., 3146
Maclin, Alan, 1687
Maclure, Mac, 1369
MacMaster, John, 1587
MacMillan, A.S. Pat, 3146
MacMillan, Courtney D., 461
MacMillan, Terrence A., 461
MacMillian, Jamie, 942
Macomber, Tom, 448
MacPhail, Carol S., 2950
MacPhee, Barbara C., 1310
MacPherson, Cathy, 3684
Macpherson, Cheryl, 3571
MacPherson, Rob, 1126
Macwell, 1388
Madden, Frank, 1946
Madden, Mark, 237
Madden, Mike, 3649
Madden, Sheryl, 1631
Madden, Sue Ellen, 3478
Madden, Todd, 1718
Maddock, Paul L., Jr., 566
Maddocks, Michael D., 3488
Maddox, Benjamin W., 2014
Maddox, Catherine M., 2014
Maddox, Don, 2014
Maddox, J.F, 2014
Maddox, James M., 2014
Maddox, Jay, 978
Maddox, Jennifer, 9
Maddox, John L., 2014
Maddox, Mabel S., 2014
Maddox, Patricia, 842
Maddox, Sue, 2014
Maddox, Susan, 2014
Maddox, Thomas M., 2014
Maddux, Gregory, 1866
Maddux, Kathleen, 1866
Mader, Cheryl, 3607
Mader, Steve, 1185
Madhaven, Ashok, 1917
Madhi, Shabir A., 3516
Madison Dearborn Partners, 1513
Madison, Nellie, 2858
Madonia, Eugene C., 3443
Madonia, Peter, 2390
Madrazo, Jesus, 1803
Madsen, Gary C., 1253
Madsen, Jacqueline, 36
Madsen, Sue Lanai W., 3510
Madzior, Aaron, 1652
Maertens, Mary, 1740
Maes, Dennis, Hon., 492
Maes, Donna, 535
Maestas, Steve, 2006
Magaram, Philip S., 187
Magargee, Susan, 2954
Magasinn, Vicki Fisher, 320
Magazine, Sarah, 1513
Magee, Allison, 471
Magee, David B., 2022
Magee, Frances W., 2022
Magee, Karen, 2466
Magee, Marc Porter, 2188
Mager, Reeva S., 2237
Magerman, David, 2979
Magerman, David M., 2979
Magers, Michael, 3222
Maggio-Calkins, Erin, 990
Maggos, Mark, 1067
Magnano, Robert J., 3426
Magno, Anthony M., 244
Magnolia Marine Transport Co., 1761
Magnus Asset Management Trust, The, 1058
Magnus, Alexander B., Jr., 1058
Magnus, Victoria, 1058
Magoon, Grace Previte, 1460
Magowan, Mark, 2205
Magrath, Charles, 2228
Magruder, Elaine, 3160
Maguire, Daniel, 1008
Maguire, Pamela Mitchell, 3297
Maguire, Robert, 1569
Maguire, Tobey, 607
Maharry, Shelly, 1217
Maher, Basil, 1937
Maher, Miriam Duffy, 1937
Mahler, Sue, 2689
Mahon, Grace M., 2947
Mahon, Nancy, 2287
Mahoney, Anne, 1547
Mahoney, Elaine, 187
Mahoney, Hildegarde E., 2126
Mahoney, Jackie, 2108

Mahoney, P. Michael, 3634
Mahowald, Douglas A., 2652
Mai-Weis, Frieda, 1274
Maier, Edward H., 3584
Maier, Pauline, 3584
Maier, William J., Jr., 3584
Maiers, Randy D., 1590
Maiers, Sarah, 1218
Maimone, Joseph A., 2873
Main, Brenda M., 1358
Maine, Donald, 1595
Maine, Eugenie W., 3447
Maino, Patricia McGee, 2820
Maislin, Stephen D., 3266
Maison Grande Assocs., 2416
Maiurro, Peter, 492
Majer, Sol, 390
Major League Baseball, 647
Major League Soccer, 37
Major, Bill, 2834
Major, John, 378
Major, Paul, 538
Majorkiewicz, Lucy, 2796
Majumder, Ranjit, 3591
Makagon, Kira, 238
Make-Up Art Cosmetics Inc., 2287
Makepeace Co., A. D., 1507
Makepeace, Christopher, 1507
Makode, Gail, 2297
Makoff, John, 58
Makovsky, Evan, 528
Makupson, Amyre, 1666
Malatos, Louisa, 3521
Malcolm, Joy Craft, 3113
Malcolm, Waynewright, 778
Malcom, Shirley M., 2966
Malcom, Susan, 81
Malczewski, Jim, 3642
Maldonado, Jeff, 2422
Maldonado, Maria, 2422
Maldonado, Melissa Lopez, 2422
Maldonado, Roger Juan, 2325
Malebra, James J., 1550
Malench, Joseph, 1010
Malenfant, David, 3161
Maletta, Matthew J, 80
Maley, Ryan, 1007
Malfavon, Marco, 1899
Malgieri, Patricia, 2185
Malhotra, Vinnie, 2466
Malicki, Beth, 1228
Malik, Andy, 809
Malin, Kathleen, 3089
Malinger, Kathleen M., 1097
Malinger, Kevin, 1097
Malinger, Lynette, 1097
Malinoski, Jean, 2331
Malkin, David, 2124
Malkin, Jessica A., 2124
Mallard, John E., 1249
Mallard, Wayne, 3471
Mallett, Amber, 943
Mallett, Jennifer, 2746
Mallin, Lisa, 493
Mallison, Andrew, 1772
Mallison, Vickie, 3229
Mallitz, David S., 734
Mallory, Michael A., 3424
Mallott, Amanda, 35
Malloy, Ken, 1227
Mallview, 1388
Malo, J. Kenneth, Jr., 522
Malo, John F., 522
Malo, Kathleen M., 522
Malone, Debi, 739
Malone, Eron, 638
Malone, Evan D., 514
Malone, Herbert J., Jr., 18
Malone, John C., 514
Malone, Leslie A., 514
Malone, Ocllo S., 16
Malone, Rob, 2655
Malone, Wallace D., Jr., 16
Malone, Wallace Davis, 16
Maloney, Carey, 2287
Maloney, Evan Coyne, 389
Maloney, Leslie, 2709
Maloney, Leslie P., 2709
Maloney, Timothy, 2709
Malott, Maxie A., 1122
Maloy, Jane, 2578
Maloy, Michael, 866
Malpass, Barbara, 1583
Maltby, Richard, Jr., 2252
Maltz, Daniel, 2727
Maltz, David, 2727
Maltz, Milton S., 2727
Maltz, Tamar, 2727
Maly, Paul J., 3651
Malyska, John N., 3453
Mancasola, John A., 318
Mancebo, Stephen, 1710
Mancini, Michelle M., 2894
Mancini, Pierluigi, 886
Mandel, Amy C., 2729
Mandel, Barbara A., 2729
Mandel, Florence, 2728
Mandel, Jack N., 2730
Mandel, Joseph C., 2728, 2730
Mandel, Lilyan, 2730
Mandel, Morton L., 2728, 2729, 2730
Mandel, Stacy L., 2729
Mandel, Thomas A., 2729
Mandelbaum, David, 1962
Mandelbaum, Michael, 1962
Mandelbaum, Moshe, 2357
Mandelbaum, Nathan, 1962
Mandelbaum, Philip, 1962
Mandelko, Patty, 1845
Mandell, Sarah Coade, 246
Mandella, Teresa, 161
Mandeville, Caroline, 2926
Mandeville, Josephine C., 2926
Mandeville, Nicole F., 662
Maness, Michael, 771
Manett, Bruce, 2674
Manfredi, Marilyn, 419
Mangan, Lawrence T., 2948
Mangelsdorf, Paul C., 59
Mangers, Dennis, 391
Mangione, Ellen J., 485
Mangold, Robert, 2187
Mangravite, Paula, 769
Mangun, Jan, 3429
Manhart, Marcia Y., 2806
Manhattan Beer Distributors, LLC, 3029
Manhattan Nursing Home Realty Inc., 2255
Manilla, Robert J., 1631
Manilow, Barbara Goodman, 997
Manilow, Barry, 328
Maniscalco, Benedict, 757
Manitoba Foundation, The, 2074
Manitowoc Company, 3632
Manjarres, Rodrigo, 1031
Mankins, Blair, 127
Manley Burke, LPA, 2769
Manley, Marie, 1657
Mann Foundation of Minnesota, Tedd & Roberts, The, 3114
Mann, Alison, 1923
Mann, Anastasia, 1923
Mann, David, 2782
Mann, Elizabeth N., 1145
Mann, Jacqueline, 1923
Mann, James E., 1923
Mann, Jennifer L., 2986
Mann, John, 1109
Mann, Sandra, 1888
Manner, James, Dr., 3040
Manners, J. Christopher, 2770
Manning, Bob, 492
Manning, Camille, 2358
Manning, Chuck, 1587
Manning, Jeanne, 866
Manning, Marilyn, 305
Manning, Nancy, 305
Manning, O. Raymond, Jr., 2541
Manning, Paul, 1131
Mannion, Gwyn, 2177
Manns, Jon, 1307
Manoogian, Richard A., 1637
Manriquez, Hank, 3503
Mans, Ray, Dr., 2876
Mansfield, Christopher C., 1502, 3554
Manske, Susan E., 1056
Mansour, John G., 288
Mansour, Lisa, 288
Mansuri, Dinaz, 1041
Manternach, Amy, 1216
Manton, Edwin, Sir, 2445
Manuel, Rick, 989
Manzke, Rob, 3606
Manzo, Cynthia, 703
Manzo, Robert, 703
Maples Burlingame, LLC, 190
Mapp, Karen L., 1486
Marable, Ned, 2578
Marano, Jean F., 2133
Marcacci, Donna, 988
Marcario, Rose, 362
Marcello, Beth, 2896
March 23, 2006 Trust, The, 636
March, Karen, 1945
March, Paul, 1197
Marchant, Ann Carol, 3477
Marchant, Danielle, 3503
Marchant, Robert E., 3477
Marchell, John, 2648
Marciano, Georges, 2357
Marcon, Fred R., 1963
Marcon, L. Charles, 2986, 3049
Marcon, Natalie, 1963
Marcu, Mihai, 2896
Marcus Pointe Baptist Church, 2562
Marcus, Dana, 205
Marcus, Emilie, Dr., 1463
Marcus, Gregory S., 3637
Marcus, Tom, 143
Marder, Ruth R., 1409
Mardigian, Arman, 1635
Mardigian, Edward S., 1635
Mardigian, Grant, 1635
Mardigian, Helen, 1635
Mardigian, Janet M., 1635
Mardigian, Matthew, 1635
Mardigian, Robert D., 1635
Mardirosian, Anahid, 2001
Maren, Peter, 725
Mares, Donald J., 483
Margerum, Sonya, 1130
Margo, Cynthia, 1699
Margolis, Barry H., 3266
Margolis, E. David, 2927
Margolis, James, 2986
Margolis, Nancy, 1576
Margulies, Martin Z., 785
Mariel, Serafin U., 2324
Marien, Marcia, 562
Marignoli, Kapi 'Olani K., 928
Marin, Lynda, 210
Marinakos, Plato A., 2975
Mariners Care, 647
Marinkovich, Tom, 488
Marino, Cheryl, 1964
Marino, John, 2792
Marino, Joseph, 1964
Marino, Robert A., 1940
Marion County Health Department, 1156
Marion General Hospital, 3377
Marion Merrell Dow Inc., 1988
Marion, Anne W., 3185
Marion, John L., 3185
Maritan Memorial Hospital, 3377
Mark, Florine, 1588
Mark, Howard, Dr., 3438
Mark, Thomas M., 783
Markel Corporation, 3363
Markel, Kate Levin, 1638
Markel, Virginia W., 211
Markell, Peter K., 1461
Marketplace One Foundation, 2863
Markey, Susan, 3546
Markham, Fred J., 3365
Markham, Nancy Louise Brown, 874
Markle, John, 2290
Markle, Mary, 2290
Markley, Allan, Dr., 1817
Markley, Larry, 2798
Markowitz, Teresa, 1353
Marks, Carolyn, 2291
Marks, Dennis A, 971
Marks, Edwin S., 2291
Marks, George E., 3006
Marks, Gerald, 651
Marks, Howard, 2207
Marks, J. Alan, 2018
Marks, James S., 1949
Marks, Judy, 1993
Marks, Melanie L., 912
Marks, Nancy A., 2291
Marks, Paul Camp, 861
Marks, Sam, 2134
Markward, David, Dr., 1063
Marley Trust, Kemper, 53
Marley, Ethel, 53
Marmelstein, Marvin, 1902
Marmor, Max, 2263
Marois, Ralph D., 1471
Maroney, C. Roderick, 639
Marotta, Justin, 2767
Marpat Foundation, 672
Marple, Anthony, 1336
Marquardt, Dorwin, 2649
Marquardt, Scott, 1740
Marquette Charitable Organization, 3104
Marquez, Bernadette, 515
Marquez, Timothy, 515
Marquis, Bryan, 3222
Marr, Dennis, 2381
Marr, Rob, 1209
Marriott Charitable Annuity Trust, J. Willard, 1390
Marriott, Alice S., 1390
Marriott, J. Willard, 1390
Marriott, J. Willard, Jr., 1390

Marriott, Richard E., 1390
Marriott, Stephen, 1390
Marrone, Matthew, 2113
Marrow, Eugene, 1485
Marryat, Karen, 1436
Mars Petcare, 3148
Mars, Linda, 3148
Mars, Lisa, 2376
Mars, Tom, 74
Marsalis, Delfeayo, 3303
Marsch, Susan, 2732
Marsh, Barnaby, 3047
Marsh, Eleanor, 1552
Marsh, George, Jr., 1472
Marsh, Gordon, 2187
Marsh, Jack, 662
Marsh, Linda, 2342
Marsh, Mel, 2787
Marsh, Peter R., 3538
Marsh, Richard S.T., 661, 3481
Marsh, Stephanie, 3469
Marshall, Colin S., 643
Marshall, David, 2539
Marshall, Douglas B., III, 3290
Marshall, Douglas B., Jr., 3290
Marshall, Dwight W., Jr., 1359
Marshall, Gary, 2293
Marshall, Ina, 2293
Marshall, Joe, 948
Marshall, John, 328
Marshall, Julie, 1852
Marshall, Kent, 2293
Marshall, Louise F., 54
Marshall, Regina, 1515
Marshall, Schuyler B., IV, 3340
Marshall, Shauna I., 385
Marshall, Stephanie Pace, 1018
Marshall, Thomas C., 187
Marshall, Thomas O., 895
Marshall, Thomas O., Mrs., 895
Marshall, Thurgood, Jr., 2160
Marshall, W. Gilman, 2293
Marshall-Blake, Lorina L., 2975
Marshall-King, Karen, 2148
Marsiglia, Nancy M., 1316
Marskbury, Logan, 1282
Marson, Ken, 3503
Marston, Wes, 725
Martel, Lysane, 2882
Martell, C. Michael, 1328
Martell, Sally, 1328
Martell, Sally Klingenstein, 2258
Martell, Sarah, 2258
Martella, Michael P., 727
Martens, Holley Fowler, 2703
Martens, Troy, 1215
Marter, Barbara J., 3147
Martex Fiber Southern Corp., 3060
Marth, Edward C., 3079
Martin Family Foundation, 1831
Martin Land Co., 3581
Martin, Alfred S., 786
Martin, Alison, 3655
Martin, Ann, 1837
Martin, Carla, 1763
Martin, Charles C., 3127
Martin, Christy, 2991
Martin, Daryn A., 80
Martin, Dustin, 865
Martin, E. Snow, Jr., 702
Martin, Elizabeth C., 786
Martin, G. Roxy, 786
Martin, Gail, 1292
Martin, Gary, 1061
Martin, George, 2991
Martin, George M., 191
Martin, Glenn E., 2326
Martin, J. Landis, 475
Martin, J.C., III, 3376
Martin, J.H., 1300
Martin, J.W., 2553
Martin, Jack, 1588
Martin, James, 2888
Martin, James G., 1344
Martin, Jane, 2689
Martin, Jerria, 4
Martin, John, 1130
Martin, John W., 3476
Martin, Kathryn, 2148
Martin, Kevin, 1208
Martin, Laura Keidan, 1042
Martin, Lawrence J., 3428
Martin, Leslee, 945
Martin, Lockheed, 3424
Martin, Luther N., Sr., 355
Martin, Malcolm E., 2200
Martin, Marcinda, 2147
Martin, Mike, 948
Martin, Moira B., 592
Martin, Murray D., 604
Martin, Patrick J., 787
Martin, Rebecca, 1752, 2991
Martin, Rodney E., 2599
Martin, Rodney O., 2488
Martin, Roger L., 412
Martin, Shannon, 2707
Martin, Shirley Moyers, 2816
Martin, Stephen D., 2689
Martin, Theodore E., 2097
Martin, Thomas, 1569
Martin, Valerie K., 3047
Martin, Webb F., 1645
Martin, William G., 2674
Martinelli, Monica, 2747
Martinez 2001 Trust, Guadalupe, 3291
Martinez, Carolina, 210
Martinez, Guadalupe, 3291
Martinez, Jorge, 771
Martinez, Jose, 3648
Martinez, Juan J., 771
Martinez, Leo, 2324
Martinez, Lilia, 3291
Martinez, Melanie, 1688
Martinez, Phyllis, 537
Martinez, Teressa, 3510
Martinez, Traci, Esq., 2689
Martinez-Rodriguez, Awilda L., 3457
Martino, Marilyn, 1551
Martino, Mary S., 2340
Martino, Phyllis, 3051
Martiny, Mary Anne, 3621
Marty, Trisha G., 2947
Martyak, Joseph, 933
Martyny, Milton D., 3017
Maruska, Jodi, 1837
Marva Smalls, Coastal Community
  Foundation, 3424
Marvald, Kenneth A., 2452
Marvin, David, 368
Marx Foundation, Virginia and Leonard,
  The, 308
Marx, Franz, 3142
Marx, Michael, 2750
Marx, Orion, 727
Marx, Victor Hugo, III, 15
Maryott, Brian, 155
Marziali, Eric A., 611
Marzouk, Shelby, 2205
Mascari, Parween S., 2892
Masco Corp., 1637
Masharawi, Rashid, 176
Masingill, W. Luther, 3125
Masiyiwa, Strive, 2390
Mason, Barry, Dr., 11
Mason, Beth, 702, 1208
Mason, Bob, Dr., 68
Mason, Dan, 2071
Mason, David, 2027
Mason, Jane Hemingway, 3396
Mason, John C., 1183
Mason, Linda A., 357
Mason, Louise, 1176
Mason, Marguerite F., 896
Mason, Raymond A., 1348
Mason, Robert, 1045
Mason, Sally F., 1190
Mason, Shelly R., 2925
Mason, Teresa, 3540
Mason, William Clarke, 2997
Massa, Cynthia, 3494
Massague, Joan, 2486
Massaro, George A., 1461
Massey, Betty, 3306
Massey, Harvey L., 712
Massey, John, 1852
Massey, Joseph, 3497
Massiano, Michael F., 2058
Massing, Michael, 678
Massmutual Financial Group, 1479
Masson, Richard, 3042
Masson, Robin, 2112
Massoni, Carol H., 1366
Massry, Mark, 1898
Massry, Morris, 2474
Mast, Allen, 904
Master Brand, 3505
Masterplan, Inc., 1388
Masters Gallery Foods, Inc., 952
Masters, Mark, 2767
Masters, Seth, 2502
Mastro, Randy M., 220
Mastropieri, Robert W., 1388
Masumoto, David Mas, 264
Matau, Karri, 3511
Matcheswalla, Mansoor, Dr., 3587
Matchett, Terri E., 1121
Mateyo, George, 2770
Mathers, G. Harold, 2294
Mathers, Leila Y., 2294
Matheson, Alline, 2054
Matheson, Bonnie B., 1597
Mathews, Bert, 3129
Mathews, Koshy, Rev. Dr., 3014
Mathews, Rebecca H., 2973
Mathey, Dean, 1916, 3418
Mathiasen, Jerry, 1226
Mathieson, Ann, 309
Mathieson, Peter F., 2901
Mathile, Clayton Lee, 2734
Mathile, MaryAnn, 2734
Mathile, Timothy, 2734
Mathios, Alan, 2112
Mathis, Betty K., 3352
Mathis, James E., Jr., 900
Mathis, William N., 3183
Mathur, Anshul, 3181
Mathurin Fund, The, 3494
Matias-Melendez, Dinorah, 2345
Matis, Nina B., 1084
Matisse Revocable Trust,
  Maria-Gaetana, The, 2295
Matisse, Maria-Gaetana, 2295
Matlack, Anne H., 3030
Matlack, Rex, 1274
Matoff, Rebecca, 133
Matos, Maria, 3055
Matson, Patti, 1833
Matsubayashi, Hoshu Y., Rev., 3531
Matsui Nursery, Inc., 311
Matsui, Takashi, 3531
Matsui, Toshikiyo Andy, 311
Matsui, Yasuko, 311
Matsuoka, Martha, 2335
Matt, Susan G., 2110
Mattel, Inc., 312
Mattern, L. Jeffrey, 2952
Mattern, Steve, 1716
Mattes, Martin, 1214
Mattessich, Michelle, 2004
Matthew, Steve, 2753, 2798
Matthews, Anne H., 903
Matthews, Beverly, 1158
Matthews, Dewayne, 1174
Matthews, Gail, 100
Matthews, John, 131
Matthews, Lois, 361
Matthews, N. Ross, 156
Matthews, Robert, 3067
Matthews, Sandi, 2599
Matthews, Susan, 3555
Matthews, Yvonne Alexander, 1400
Matthies, Katharine, 590
Matthiesen, Carrie N., 3304
Mattice, W. Scott, 3147
Mattone, Joseph M., 2167
Mattoon, Peter M., 3056
Mattson, Laurie, 1874
Matus, Kristi A., 550
Matweecha, Pamela, 3414
Mauceri, Lisa, 1149
Maude, Cathy, 1065
Mauer, Kent, 1665
Mauff, Erich, 2134
Maughan, Deryck C., Sir, 2445
Mauk, Anne S., 2259
Maunz, Bettina, 3162
Maupin, Emily, 372
Maupin, John E., Jr., Dr., 3129
Maurer, Carol, 3409
Maurer, Frederick, 2664
Maurer, K.C., 2479, 2494
Mauro, Albert P., Jr., 1794
Mauze, Abby Rockefeller, 2389
Mavrogordato, Helen S., 3100
Mavrovitis, Leo, 2049
Maxey, David, 2943
Maxfield, A. Melissa, 2921
Maxfield, W. Dale, Sr., 3127
Maxfield, William D., 3127
MAXIMUS, Inc., 3457
Maxson, Robert C., 90
Maxwell, Annie, 413
Maxwell, David O., 668
Maxwell, Jack M., III, 2943
Maxwell, Joan Hunt Scott, 2971
Maxwell, Joan P., 668
Maxwell, John, 2795
Maxwell, Patrick, 212
Maxwell, Robert W., 3196
May Department Stores Foundation,
  The, 2726
May, Betty R., 1762
May, Bruce, 2664
May, Carolyn B., 1341
May, Cindy S., 1762
May, Florence, 1154
May, Isabel, 752

May, Joan, 538
May, Karl, 3649
May, Linda J., 723
May, Linda K., 3352
May, Lou Adele, 3196
May, Martha, 1237
May, Nancy, 3304, 3310
May, Peter, 543, 752
May, Samuel D., 752
May, Thomas J., 598
May, William H., 105
Maybee, Terri R., 1794
Mayer, Beatrice Cummings, 2121
Mayer, Becky, 2173
Mayer, Bob, 1580
Mayer, Charles B., 1310
Mayer, Gregory C., 1083
Mayer, Jeffrey, 2134
Mayer, Jimmy, 2173
Mayer, Joe, 3567
Mayer, Mark, 1358
Mayer, Michael, 375
Mayer, Paul, 3641
Mayer, Richard H., 2922
Mayer, Susie, 2173
Mayerson Charitable Annuity Lead Trust, Manuel D., 2735
Mayerson Charitable Lead Trust, 2002 Arlene and Neal, The, 2735
Mayerson, Arlene B., 2735
Mayerson, Donna, 2735
Mayerson, Frederic H., 2735
Mayerson, Manuel D., 2735
Mayerson, Neal H., 2735
Mayerson, Rhoda, 2735
Mayes, Kent, 3273
Mayfair Medical Mgmt., 763
Mayfield, Jim, 160
Mayfield, Michael G., 394
Mayfield, Pinkie D., 663
Maynard, Olivia P., 1645
Mayo, Elizabeth B., 3100
Mayo, Rachel, 163
Mayor, Oliver Dewey, 3292
Mayr, George Henry, 2588
Mays, Cindy, 1217
Maytag, Fred, II, 1229
Maytag, Frederick L., III, 1229
Maytag, Kenneth P., 1229
Mayworm, Daniel E., 1088
Maza, Bruce A., 1284
Mazany, Terry, 982
Mazda Motor of America, 313
Mazda North American Opers., 313
Mazda Research & Development of North America, 313
Mazer, Magdalena, 1466
Mazer, Robert, 1466
Mazmanian, Daniel A., 243
Mazry, Ginny Solari, 163
Mazurkiewicz, Joe, Jr., 823
Mazza, David, 314
Mazzoula, Sandra, 161
Mazzullo, Theresa, 2154
MBIA Insurance Corp., 2297
McAbee, Heather, 3641
McAdam, Robert S., 732
McAdam, Sally Welker, 1809
McAdaragh, Pat, 1716
McAden, Jim, 3432
McAfee, Robert E., 1339
McAleese, Kevin, 3654
McAlexander, Dan, 904
McAllister, Bryan, 868
McAllister, Dale, 1214
McAllister, Lonnie J., 2541
McAllister, Michael, 268
McAllister, Sandy, 1395
McAnaney, Brian T., 2400
McAnaney, Edward G., 2400
McAnaney, Kevin G., 2400
McAndrews, Tom, 1214
McAniff, Peter, 361
McAninch, Janeen, 2859
McArtor, Kevin, 999
McAuliffe, E. Timothy, 2513
McAuliffe, Hawley Hilton, 251
McAvoy Trust, Agnes K., 971
McAvoy, Laura K., 303
McBeath, Faye, 3634
McBrayer, Katie, 1772
McBrayer, Keith, 2553
McBride, Anne V., 705
McBride, Jack, 3097
McBride, Mike, 948
McBroom, Amanda, 328
McBryde, Nowlin, 3318
McBurnett, Keith, 3259
McCabe, Christine A., 3502
McCabe, Daniel J., 2688
McCabe, James B., 921
McCabe, Kathleen, 2315
McCall, Donald J., 2538
McCall, Jennifer, 1214
McCall, Matthew, 417
McCallick, Frank, 3527
McCallum, Jim, 391
McCalpin, William F., 2211
McCammon, Stanley P., 3521
McCann Foundation, 2113
McCann, Nancy W., 2721, 2745
McCann, Sue Ellen, 462
McCanna, Michael, 32
McCarl, Steven, 2018
McCarrick, Theodore E., Cardinal, 3453
McCarroll, Steve, 25
McCartan, Michael, 1590
McCartan, Patrick F., 2721
McCarter, Fred, 1141
McCarthey, Sarah, 3397
McCarthy, A. Gregory, IV, 3453
McCarthy, Alexander, 1443
McCarthy, Ann M., 2340, 2503
McCarthy, Brian A., 2298
McCarthy, Christine M., 181
McCarthy, Denis, 1603
McCarthy, Eugenie Ross, 1809
McCarthy, George, 1503
McCarthy, Helen C., 1443
McCarthy, John, 294, 1012, 3054
McCarthy, John T., 564
McCarthy, John W., 3464
McCarthy, Juliana Allen, 1809
McCarthy, Kathleen L., 294
McCarthy, Kevin, 535
McCarthy, Louise Roblee, 1809
McCarthy, Margaret M., 550
McCarthy, Patrick, 1353
McCarthy, Priscilla, 2044
McCarthy, Robert, 1235
McCarthy, Roblee, Jr., 1809
McCarthy, Sarah S. P., 1975
McCarthy, Terri, 1674
McCarthy, Thomas A., 2917
McCarthy, Vincent, 1472
McCarty, Ned, 30
McCarty, Steve, 393
McCarty, Tom, 1842
McCary Foundation, Tom and Mary, 1748
McCauley, Michael, 2821
McCauley-Burrows, Mary, 2866
Mccausland, Alexander, 2589
McCausland, Thomas N., 1993
McCausland, Tim, 2111
McCaw, Craig O., 316, 3540
McCaw, Susan R., 3540
McCaw, Wendy P., 316
McCellon-Allen, Venita, 2657
McClafferty, Charles C., 1665
McClain Select Value, 3642
McClain, James, II, 3443
McClain, Jerry, 2723
McClain, Joseph S., 1344
McClain, Michael, 2670
McClanahan, Janine, 425
McClatchy Co., The, 317
McClean, Mary Gaylord, 2813
McCleary, Linda W., 1394
McCleary, Monique M., 2859
McCleery, William, Jr., 992
McClellan, Robert, 1067
McClelland, Scott, 1131
McClenahan, Patrick, 287
McCleskey, Edwin, 232
McClimon, Timothy J., 2033, 2034
McClintock, John R.D., 1473
McClintock, T.K., 2754
McCloud, William Bernard, 866
McCluiston, Deborah, 483
McClung, James F., Jr., 347, 397
McClung, Lori, 2770
McClure, Don, 493
McClure, Teri Plummer, 1353
McCluskey, John M., 1530
McClymont, Jim, 1849
McColgin, Alice, 1157
McColl, Robert, 667
McColl, Suzanne, 667
McCollister, Roger L., 1281
McCollum, Michael, 919
McConaughey, Camila, 272
McConaughey, Matthew, 272
McConn, Christiana R., 3358
McConn, Margaret E., 3338
McConnel, Gloria, 3125
McConnell, Alicia, 525
McConnell, Britt, 363
McConnell, C. Douglas, 1105
McConnell, Carl R., 318
McConnell, Charlotte, 1876
McConnell, Kathryn, 2539
McConnell, Leah F., 318
McConnell, September, 1209
McConnell, Stacey Willits, Esq., 2915
McConnell, William, 2723
McCorkle, Roger, 2876
McCormack, Elizabeth, 59
McCormack, Elizabeth J., 2048, 2477
McCormack, Jill A., 3425
McCormack, Kristen J., 1543
McCormack, Mike, 3178
McCormack, Wayne P., 564
McCormack, William, 1740, 1946
McCormick, Ben, 1301
McCormick, Charles, 999
McCormick, Jennifer, 1301
McCormick, Robert W., 3585
McCormick, Thomas P., 2054
McCosker, Pamela, 120
McCotter, Kevin, 1302
McCown, Sylvia, 1648
McCown, Teresa, 2712
McCoy, Anne, 319
McCoy, Bowen H., 319
McCoy, Carolyn, 2757
McCoy, Cathy, 1279
McCoy, Dena Woodard, 2877
McCoy, Dru, 1129
McCoy, James, 900
McCoy, Joanne R., 1358
McCoy, Michael, 3609
McCoy, Mike, 770
McCoy, Terri, 1157
McCracken, Carol, 747
McCracken, Merrick, 3162
McCrady, Christopher R., 2906
McCrady, Priscilla J., 2906
McCrae, Angela H., 3111
McCrary, Guy, 3316
McCraven, Paul A., 595
McCray, Ray, 161
McCrea, Colin, 2048
McCready, Al, 568
McCready, Mathilda Staunton Craig, 3044
McCrory, Ken, 1144
McCrory, Kenneth, 2896
McCrystal, Bill, 3427
McCuan, Suzanna, 1597
McCue, Howard M., III, 981, 1018
McCuiston, Stonewall, Dr., 989
McCulloch, Deb, 2771
McCulloch, Rob, III, 2771
McCullough, Lisa, 69
McCullough, P. Mike, 3168, 3296
McCully, A.C., 70
McCully, Michael, 1948
McCune Foundation, 2011
McCune, Barron P., Jr., 3054
McCune, Charles L., 2993
McCune, David F., 320
McCune, James, 3054
McCune, Sara Miller, 320
McCune, Stephanie, 484
McCurdy, Bob, 2447
McCurdy, Janet I., Esq., 1358
McCurdy, Jeffrey, 727
McCusker, Francis C., 3586
McCutchen, Mathew, 3557
McCutchen, Woodrow C., 2097
McDaniel, Marilyn J., 2923
McDaniel, Mark, 1618
McDaniel, Marvin, 1754
McDaniel, Sharon L., 3499
McDaniel, William, 3607
McDavid, Stephan L., 1771
McDavitt, Linda, 3310
McDemmond, Marie V., 1174
McDermott, Allison S., 2204
McDermott, C. David, 536
McDermott, Eugene, 3293
McDermott, Eugene, Mrs., 3293
McDermott, John, III, 2495
McDevitt, William G., III, 705
McDonald, Artemis, 3421
McDonald, Bill, 484
McDonald, Bob, 1877
McDonald, Charles Pat, 3255
McDonald, Craig, 1642
McDonald, Debbie, 948
McDonald, Donald D., 1113
McDonald, Douglas B., 1872
McDonald, Eric, 3287
McDonald, Evelyn M., 1113
McDonald, Frederick, 3085

McDonald, Frederick L., 1576
McDonald, Gregory C., 1831
McDonald, Hilary, 2265
McDonald, Hollie, 2932
McDonald, J., 3505
McDonald, Jennifer, 8
McDonald, Jill, 3355
McDonald, Jim, 2662
McDonald, Joe, Jr., 899
McDonald, Kevin, 537
McDonald, Kristen, 1666
McDonald, Martha Ann, 3287
McDonald, Micheal J., 2888
McDonald, Sam E., Jr., 1831
McDonald, Sheila, 1603
McDonald, Susan, 2642
McDonald, Susan Montgomery, 2747
McDonald, Sylvia, 3642
McDonald, Walter J., 2842
McDonnall, Jeffrey M., 1800
McDonnell, Alicia S., 1800
McDonnell, James S., III, 1800
McDonnell, John F., 516, 1800
McDonnell, Matthew J., 516
McDonnell, Patricia L., 516
McDonnell, Rich T., 2742
McDonough, Allison, 3635
McDonough, Bernard P., 3586
McDonough, Bill, 1764
McDonough, Diana Hattler, 3453
McDonough, Diane, 2112
McDonough, Joanne, 1998
McDonough, John J., 3635
McDonough, Kathleen, 630
McDonough, Kevin M., Rev., 1722
McDonough, Marilyn N., 3635
McDonough, Mark E., 1966
McDowell, John, Dr., 1290
McEachern, D.V., 3541
McEachern, Ida J., 3541
McElhinney, Christie, 483
McEllistrem, Michael, 1687
McElroy, Evan, 356
McElroy, Gregory E., 2919
McElroy, R.J., 1230
McEvily, Paul, 1910
McEvoy, Patrick, 3202
McEwen, Beatrice G., 562
McFadden, Bruce, 335
McFadden, Jeanmarie, 2315
McFaddin, Eugene H.B., 3381
McFadyen, Barbara Nicholson, 2329
McFall, F. Lawrence, 3430
McFarland Trust, C.E., 1299
McFarland Trust, D.A., 1299
McFarland, Barry, 1845
McFarland, Duncan, 2918
McFarland, John, 73, 1578
McFarland, Richard D., 1715
McFarlane, Brian, 349
McGarry, Kris, 1863
McGaughey, Frank, 897
McGee, B. Lee, 648
McGee, Chris, 1279
McGee, Dawn, 1825
McGee, Dean A., 2820
McGee, Marcella, 2868
McGee, Nancy, 3098
McGee, Shirley, 2539
McGee, Suzanne P., 3317
McGee, Vincent, 2345
McGehee, Hobson C., III, 1762
McGehee, Hobson C., Jr., 1762
McGeogh, Ed, 656
McGhee, Terry, 2696
McGill University, 2069
McGill, Charmaine D., 3188
McGill, Larry, 235
McGinn, Deborah E., 2191
McGinn, Fidelma, 3558
McGinness, James J., 3145
McGinness, Janet M., 2336
McGinnis, Jay M., 3679
McGinnis, John, 1395
McGlade, John E., 3024
McGladrey LLP, 826
McGlenn, Michael, 1807
McGlothlin, Everett, 3683
McGlothlin, Frances G., 3484
McGlothlin, James W., 3484
McGlothlin-Gayle, Martha, 3484
McGonagle, Dextra Baldwin, 2299
McGonigle, Cathy, 44
McGovern, Jean, 2297
McGowan, Archie, 1885
McGowan, David M., 1008
McGowan, Mark S., 744
McGowan, Stephen, 157
McGrail, Joseph A., Jr., 1550
McGrath, Christina, 492
McGrath, Dennis, 2826
McGrath, Kevin B., Jr., Hon., 2269
McGrath, L., 2757
McGrath, Patrick, 2796
McGrath, Raymond J., Hon., 2167
McGrath, Thomas F., III, 303
McGraw Charitable Lead Annuity Trust, Donald C., 2300
McGraw Charitable Trust, D., 2300
McGraw Foundation, 1060
McGraw Hill Companies, 2445
McGraw, A. William, 2741
McGraw, David W., 2300
McGraw, Donald C., 2300
McGraw, Donald C., III, 2300
McGraw, Regina, 1115
McGraw, Robert L.W., 2300
McGree, Elizabeth, 3576
McGregor, A. Bruce, 1562
McGregor, John S., 3605
McGregor, Katherine W., 1638
McGregor, Tracy W., 1638
McGrew, Mike, 1256
McGruder, Mary Helen, 900
McGuigan, Chris Ann, 1586
McGuinn, Ann M., 2906
McGuire, Allen, 3345
McGuire, Allen G., 3323
McGuire, Michael, 1026
McGuire, Patricia, 656
McGuire, Peggy, 3223
McGuire, Tina, 2540
McGuire, Tom, 2612
McGuire, Tricia L.M., 1640
McGurk, Thomas A., Jr., 1208
McHale, David R., 598
McHale, James E., 1628
McHarque, Jay, 754
McHugh, Alaistair C.H., 322
McHugh, Consuelo Hall, 322
McHugh, Frank, 641
McHugh, Theresa, 641
McIlvaine, Andrew M., 3054
McIlvaine, Breese, 3451
McIlvaine, George, 3684
McInaney, Nancy Clair Laird, 872
McInerny, Elizabeth DeCamp, 2131
McInerny, Ella, 938
McInerny, James D., 938
McInerny, Judith, 2109
McInerny, William H., 938
McInnes, Roderick R., 2534
McIntire, Christopher, 2805
McIntosh, Bruce A., 345
McIntosh, Frederick J., 345
McIntosh, James C., 929, 930
McIntosh, Jon, 345
McIntosh, Katie, 345
McIntosh, Ken, 1181
McIntosh, Thomas J., 345
McIntyre Financial Svcs., 3294
McIntyre, Daniel, 3063
McIntyre, James B., 1131
McIntyre, Shirley C., 3294
McIntyre, William S., 3294
McJett, Earl, 676
McKaig, Tom, 1180
McKay, Alexandra, 3499
McKay, Carol, 2231
McKay, Charles, 1133
McKay, Monika, 1316
McKay, Rich, 2297
McKean, Linda B., 1910
McKean, Quincy A.S., III, 1910
McKee Foods Corp., 3119
McKee, C. Steven, 3295
McKee, Clyde V., III, 3357
McKee, Evelyn, 3295
McKee, F. James, 3295
McKee, James T., 3295
McKee, Jay, 2078
McKee, John, 1755
McKee, Louis B., 3295
McKee, Lydia, 2232
McKee, Nina, 3464
McKee, Philip Russell, 3295
McKee, R. Brian, 3295
McKee, Robert E., 3295
McKee, Robert E., Inc., 3295
McKee, Robert E., IV, 3295
McKee, Rose A., 2892
McKee, Susan J., 3295
McKee, Virginia A., 2995
McKeen, Mark A., 3579
McKeever, Clark, 2809
McKelfresh, Greg, 1166
McKenna, Charles B., 1008
McKenna, Cheryl, 2683
McKenna, Laura K., 2483
McKenna, Wallace G., Jr., 3454
McKenney, Bruce J., 2894
McKenney, David M., 918
Mckenzie 2008, 368
Mckenzie, Barbara, 368
McKenzie, Charles "Lad", 2387
McKenzie, J. Michael, 3413
McKenzie, Mickey, 368
McKeone, Tod, 1845
McKeown, Daniel W., 1686
McKeown, Desmond, 1686
McKeown, Heidi, 1686
McKernan, R. Jack, Jr., 2947
McKesson Corp., 321
McKesson HBOC, Inc., 321
McKibben, Andrew, 1904
McKibben, Diana, 1904
McKiernan, Holiday Hart, 1174
McKim, Jim, 1683
McKinley, Mark, 2661
McKinney, Barbara Alexander, 3591
McKinney, Catherine A., 2996
McKinney, Tom, 1198
McKinnon, Michele A.W., 3476
McKinsey Company, 2574
McKinzie, Addie, 25
McKissack, Cheryl Mayberry, 1001
McKissick, Ellison Smyth, III, 3106
McKissock, David L., 796
McKnight Foundation, The, 1714, 1723
McKnight, Maude L., 1715
McKnight, William L., 1715
McKrill, Mike, 35
McLain, Adam, 2473
McLain, Kathleen G., 1359
McLain, Tim, 2747
McLanahan, Astride, 2907
McLanahan, Sara S., 2402
McLane, David H., 2362
McLaughlin Foundation, Edward & Patricia, 2071
McLaughlin, Beth, 3616
McLaughlin, Deborah A., 1453
McLaughlin, Douglas, 3684
McLaughlin, Edward F., 2071
McLaughlin, Gladys, 3549
McLaughlin, Justin, 1021
McLaughlin, Matthew T., 2434
McLaughlin, Sheila Ortega, 2017
McLaughlin, Virginia L., 3487
McLaughlin, William B., III, 3019
McLaughlin, William P., 1632
McLean Contributionship, The, 2912
McLean, Elizabeth P., 2997
McLean, Elizabeth R., 2997
McLean, Kerry, 263
McLean, Lisa, 2997
McLean, Marcia, 2477
McLean, Mary, 1797
McLean, Robert, 2997
McLean, Sandra, 2997
McLean, Sandra L., 2997
McLean, Susannah, 2997
McLean, Wendy, 2997
McLean, William L., III, 2997
McLean, William L., IV, 2997
McLean, William L., Jr., 2997
McLees, William, 2651
Mclellan, Richard, 1718
McLendon, Barbara, 2408
McLendon, William E., 867
McLeod, Alice, 1519
McLeod, Christopher, 2159
McLeod, James A.W., 2503
McLeod, Martha, 1888
McLeod, Tommy D., 39
McLoraine, Helen M., 505
McLoughlin, Hugh, Jr., 2171
McLoughlin, Mary Jo, 2350
McMahon, Bill, 2315
McMahon, John, 17
McMahon, John J., Jr., 884
McMahon, Pat, 1227
McMahon, Rob, 2199
McMahon, Ronald D., 378
McManemin, Megan, 538
McManus, Joseph, Capt., 3468
McMicking, Henry C., 322
McMicking, Joseph R., 322
McMillan, Bev, 2006
McMillan, Doug, 3672
McMillan, George, 4
McMillan, Kathleen M., 832
McMillan, Tia, 3580
McMillian, Hellen W., 687
McMillian, Lonnie M., 687
McMillian, Lonnie S., 687

McMillian, Priscilla, 2050
McMillin, John, 2265
McMillin, Kelly, 157
McMinn, Anne, 323
McMinn, Anne W., 323
McMinn, Charles, 323
McMinn, Charles J., 323
McMinn, Kimbela, 2539
McMullen, Justin, 2682
McMullen, Lori, 3683
McMullen, Mark, 3619
McMullen, Mark J., 3608
McMurdy Fund, Robert & Janet, 983
McMurray, Carson Reid, 3675
McMurray, John Thomas, 3675
McMurray, McCain Jay, 3675
McMurray, Tom, 3675
McMurray-Russ, Martha, 2538
McMurry, Mick, 3676
McMurry, Neil A., 3676
McMurry, Susie, 3676
Mcnabb, Charlene, 913
McNair, Alfred, 1755
McNair, Elaine, 3287
McNairy, Francine, 2981
McNamara, James, 2289
McNamara, Jennifer, 2270
McNamara, Julia M., Dr., 595
McNamara, Nicholas, 1512
McNamara, Peggy, 381
McNamer, Bruce, 2242
McNaughton, Brian R., 3549
McNaughton, Stan W., 3549
McNeal, A. Scott, 2948
McNeer, J. Frederick, 2831
McNeice, John, 1509
McNeice, John A., Jr., 1509
McNeil, Collin F., 2887
McNeil, Henry S., 2918
McNeil, Jennifer, 2918
McNeil, Kae, 3118
McNeil, Robert D., 2918
McNeil, Robert L., III, 2887
McNeil, Robert L., Jr., 2887
McNeil, Stanley, 3086
McNeil-Miller, Karen, 2614
McNeill, Dan K., 2541
McNeill, Omar Y., 630
McNeill, Paul, 1759
McNeill, William, 1290
McNicholas, Anthony J., III, 805
McNulty, Donna, 653
McNulty, John, Fr., 2786
McNulty, Stephen, 1436
McNutt, Gail, 3619
McNutt, Patricia, 3211
McOmber, Michelle S., 3405
McParland, Peter G., 3657
McPhee, Penelope "Penny", 856
McPheron, Philip, 2112
McPherson, Jeanne, 3568
Mcpherson, John, 1099
McPherson, Michael, 1459
McPherson, Michael S., 1098
McPherson, Sally, 2609
McQueen, Scott, 1215
McQueeney, Chris, 1154
McQuinn, JoAnn, 1198
McRae, James L., 1758
McRae, Patricia, 3526
Mcrae, Renee, 3544
McRae, Richard D., Jr., 1770
McRee, Mike, 1759
McReynolds, J. Scott, 2679
McShane, Joseph, 2066
McShane, Kelly Sweeney, 2760
McShepard, Randell, 2708
McSherry, Constance, 2894
McSpadden, Steve, 3201
McTeer, Victor, 1763
McTier, John, 869
McTiernan, Megan, 435
McVaney Investment Partnership, 521
McVaney Trust, Kevin Edward, 542
McVaney, C.Edward, 521
McVaney, Carole, 542
McVaney, Charles, 542
McVaney, Kevin E., 542
McVay, Cathy, 4
McVay, Donna, 1186
McVay, Scott, 1955
McVety, Meghan, 2915
McWain, Teresa L., 2656
McWane, C. Phillip, 17
McWane, Inc., 17
McWilliams, Alison, 1355
McWilliams, Terrence, 492
MDU Construction Services Grp., 2652
MDU Resources Group, Inc., 2652
Mead Johnson Nutrition Company, 1039
Mead, B. Kathlyn, 138
Mead, Christina Dykstra, 676
Mead, Elise G., 324
Mead, Giles W., 324
Mead, Jane W., 324
Mead, Parry W., 324
Meadows, Algur Hurtle, 3296
Meadows, Curtis W., Jr., 3296
Meadows, Karen L., 3296
Meadows, Robert A., 3296
Meadows, Virginia, 3296
Meadows-Efram, Corinne, 452
Meagher, Ann Chambers, 2113
Meagher, Kathryn, 363
Meagher, Laura, 2642
Meale, Al, 2908
Mealey, Carol-Ann, 2421
Meara, Michael, 163
Meares, Tracey L., 1040
Mebane, John G., Jr., 2529
Mecane, Joseph, 2336
Meck, Terrence, 2347
Medaris, Henry, 3219
Medford Multicare Center, 2255
Medford, Phil, 3227
Medford, William L., 3220, 3221
Medical Bridges, Inc., 3269
Medina Properties, Inc., 763
Medina, Monica, 1156
Medina, Terry, 163
Medina, Vicente, 727
Medina, Vincente, 727
Medley, Martha W., 3443, 3445
Medlin, George L., 2317
Medlock Trust, Mary L., 983
Medsker, Malinda, 1203
Medtronic Foundation, 1748
Medtronic, Inc., 757
Medusa Corp., 3191
Meduski, Richard P., 611
Medved, Denise, 3483
Medved, Jon J., 536
Medved, William, 3483
Medzegian, Jim, 3552
Medzie, Margaret, 2655
Meehan, Edward F., 3024
Meehan, Matthew, 729
Meehan, Shealagh, 352
Meehan, Susan, 1816
Meek, Brian, 401
Meek, Sue Ann, 3450
Meeker, David, 1988
Meeker, Robert D.C., Jr., 2296
Meekins, Lois, 73
Meeks, Elizabeth C., 849
Meeks, Elizabeth Cheves, 849
Meeks, Elsie, 1722
Meeks, Nia Ngina, 3051
Meeks, Ryan L., 849
Meelia, Mary J., 1510
Meelia, Richard J., 1510
Meenan, Jennifer Gamper, 1933
Meenan, Julie, 236
Meers, Elizabeth B., 2668
Meersman, Terrence R., 1689
Meese, Richard, 340
Meeske, Larry, 1063
Meh Holding Company, Ltd, 3252
Mehran, Alexander, 438
Mehta, Amit, 3540
Meier, Aileen, 1209
Meier, Anne R., 1904
Meier, Bill, 484
Meier, Charles R., 1983
Meier, Sharon, 1271
Meier, Walter C., 1904
Meijer, Douglas F., 1639
Meijer, Frederik G.H., 1639
Meijer, Hendrik O., 1639
Meijer, Inc., 1639
Meijer, Lena, 1639
Meijer, Mark D., 1639
Meili, Laurie, 502
Meiling, Dean, 1868
Meinerding, James, 1135
Meis, Robert F., 1240
Meisinger Trust, 368
Meixelsperger, Mary, 3644
Mekras, George D., 783
Melamed, Carol D., 663
Melamed, Leo, 984
Melbert, R. Barry, 1166
Melby, Diane, 3580
Melinson, James, 268
Melitschka, Bernice, 2771
Mellam, Laural D., 326
Mellencamp, Amy, 3410
Mellin, Dorothy, 1002
Mello, Lorraine, 1428
Mellon, 2900
Mellon, Armour N., 2998
Mellon, Paul, 2302
Mellon, Richard A., 2998
Mellon, Richard K., 2998
Mellon, Richard P., 2998
Mellon, Seward Prosser, 2998
Mellor, William (Chip) H., 3627
Melmed, Matthew, 2002
Melott, Debra, 2817
Melton, Campbell, 1760
Melton, Judy, 1158
Melville Corp., 3068
Melville, Dorothy, 1511
Melville, Ruth, 1511
Melville, Stephen, 1511
Menapace, Herman N., 2707
Menard 1979 Family Trust, 327
Menard, Barbara, 327
Menard, Bernard, 327
Menard, Joan, 1453
Menard, Marcel, 327
Menard, Mary, 327
Menard, Raymond N., 1501
Menasha Corp., 3636
Mendell, Ira L., 2303
Mendell, James, 2303
Mendell, Thomas G., 2303
Mendelsund, Judy, 2179
Mendenall, Paul, 3398
Mendenhall, Brad, 2809
Mendenhall, Bronco, 3398
Mendenhall, Diane, 1847
Mendenhall, Holly, 3398
Mendez, David Louis, 3267
Mendez-Morgan, Lily, 1486
Mendicina, Dan, 1274
Mendonca, Bob, 364
Mendoza, Adela, 3099
Mendoza, David, 2043
Mendoza, Gabriel Cruz, 3208
Mendoza, Natalie Camacho, 1722
Menefee, Charles E., Jr., 3104
Menefee, Tandy, 73
Menezes, M. Alia, 2304
Menezes, Mita N., 2304
Menezes, Pia A., 2304
Menezes, Tara A., 2304
Menezes, Victor J., 2304
Mengel, Andrea L., 2976
Menges, Glenda, 310
Mennicke, Michelle, 1726
Menser, Charles D., Jr., 846
Mensore, Tulane, 3579
MENTOR Network, The, 1513
Menzer, Cynthia, 2723
Menzies, Gretchen, 2918
Meoli, Anthony J., 1370
Meoli, Michael, 1370
Meoli, Virginia, 1370
Merage, David, 518, 519
Merage, Katherine, 518, 519
Merage, Laura, 519
Mercer, Elizabeth M., 328
Mercer, Ian, 1144
Mercer, Rebekah, 2305
Mercer, Robert, 2305
Merchan, Dario, 3179
Merchant, Jane, 1129
Merchant, Kathryn E., 2679
Merchants Bancshares, Inc., 3414
Merchants Bank, 3414
Merck & Co., Inc., 559, 1966
Merck, Serena S., 1514
Merculief, Boris, 27
Mercury Foundation of New York, 2386
Meredith, Donald W., 3009
Meridor, Sallai, 2465
Merillat, Nancy, 2674
Merillat, Orville D., 1640
Merillat, Richard D., 1640
Merillat, Ruth A., 1640
Meriman, Peter, 605
Merinoff, Charles, 1314
Merisotis, Jamie P., 1174
Meriwether, Karen, 2109
Merkin, Lauren K., 2051
Merksamer, Linda, 391
Merns, Marcy Syms, 1999
Merrick, Frank W., 2821
Merrick, Frank W. "Will", Jr., 2821
Merrick, Frank W., Mrs., 2821
Merrick, Randolph V., 1771
Merrick, Ward S., III, 2821
Merrifield, Ginny, 458
Merrild, Sonja, 1699
Merrill Lynch & Co., Inc., 2524

Merrill Lynch Trust Co., 801, 1958, 2325, 2723, 2986
Merrill Lynch, Pierce, Fenner & Smith Inc., 2336
Merrill, Blythe T., 2340
Merrill, Brooks, 58
Merrill, Joan B., 927
Merrill, John S., 1
Merrill, Mark B., 927
Merrill, Scott B., 927
Merriman, Michael, 2670
Merritt, Carrie, 407
Merritt, Edward J., 1517
Merritt, Raymond W., 3453
Mershon, Tracey, 1817
Mertz, Esther M., 788
Mertz, John, 3520
Mertz, Joyce, 2306
Mervis, Michael P., 3670
Merz, Lynn, 239
Merz, Steven P., 886
Meserve, Albert W., 2592
Meserve, Helen C., 2592
Meserve, Lauren, 2502
Meserve, Richard A., 275
Meservey, Patricia Maguire, 1464
Meshbane, Alice, 1150
Mesite, I. Margaret, 591
Mesite, Rose, 591
Mesker, David, 1789
Mesmer, Patti, 3118
Mesrobian, Peter, 3277
Messaro, Maureen, 2787
Messenger, Harold L., 2296
Messick, Rod, 2981
Messina, Salvadore, 1329
Messinger, Ruth, 2237
Messiqua, Gail P., 3472
Mestemacher, Carol, 1010
Meston, Susan, 1586
Mestres, Tony, 3558
Meszoly, Robin, 653
Metcalf, Paula, 1847
Metcalf, Tim, 315
Metheny, Richard, 2824
Metropolitan Life Insurance Co., 2307
Metropolitan Museum of Art, 2069
Metteauer, Melinda, 3457
Metz, Deborah T., 3429
Metz, Karen, 296
Metz, Michael, 3417
Metzger, Geneive Brown, 2445
Metzger, Moshe, 2037
Metzger, William C., 497
Metzger-Utt, Maddy, 3511
Metzler, Wesley J., 3677
Meurer, Mark, 3287
Meurer, Zeena M., 2328
Mews, Tom, 3641
Meyer, Agnes E., 672
Meyer, Alex A., 1222
Meyer, Bertram, 1967
Meyer, Dan, 1703
Meyer, Daniel, M.D., 3011
Meyer, David, 1120
Meyer, Erie H., 18
Meyer, Eugene, 672
Meyer, Fred G., 2861
Meyer, Gary, 1132
Meyer, James A., 2939
Meyer, Jane K., 2736
Meyer, Janis, 1257
Meyer, Joyce, 251
Meyer, Lawrence F., 162
Meyer, Lee R., Jr., 1758
Meyer, Leland, 3611
Meyer, Maggie, 373
Meyer, Melba Bayers, 2593
Meyer, Michael G., 1727
Meyer, Milton, 2594
Meyer, Natalie, 479
Meyer, Nicole, 1957
Meyer, Patricia, 3310
Meyer, Stephen, 540
Meyer, Steve, 947
Meyer, William, 2680
Meyer, William A., 805
Meyer-Ploeger, Amy, Dr., 1192
Meyercord, Champ, 10
Meyerhoefer, Trent M., 2692
Meyerhoff Charitable Income Trust, 1393
Meyerhoff Charitable Income Trust II, 1393
Meyerhoff Memorial Trusts, Rebecca, 1393
Meyerhoff Philanthropic Fund, Rebecca, The, 1393
Meyerhoff, Joseph, 1393
Meyerhoff, Joseph, II, 1392, 1393
Meyerhoff, Joseph, Mrs., 1393
Meyerhoff, Lenore P., 1392
Meyerkopf, Rick, 1330
Meyers, Evan, 1263
Meyers, Gail, 2205
Meyers, Howard, 3011
Meyers, Kathryn, 2205
Meyers, Ken, 1034, 1494
Meyersiek, Axel, 2473
Meyerson Foundation, David and Minnie, The, 2827
Mezzapelle, Michael G., 613
MGough, Dennis R., 2603
Mgrublian, Margaret, 361
MIBOR Service Corp., 1178
Micallef, Joseph S., 1719
Michael, Elsa B., 2862
Michael, Gary, 942
Michael, Loretta, 2604
Michael, Marcie, 1370
Michael, Mike, 2757
Michaelis, Elias K., 2233
Michaels, Jack, 1223
Michaels, John, 564
Michaelson, Jay, 2040
Michaelson, Terry, 2850
Micheli, Michael, 2747
Michell, Roy G., 1641
Michell, Roy G., Jr., 1641
Michell, William, 1641
Michels, Susan, 1705
Michelsen, Barbara, 3431
Michelson, Ellen A., 94
Michelson, Gary Karlin, 201
Michelson, Jere G., 1334
Michelson, Michael W., 94
Michener, James A., 2928
Michener, Lizanne, 2936
Michigan, Alan, 2183
Mickel, Buck A., 3101
Mickel, Charles, 3101
Mickens, Helen Pratt, 1581
Miclat, Joseph F., 2683
Micron Semiconductor Products, Inc., 950
Micron Technology, Inc., 950
Mid Shore Community Foundation, 255
Midcontinent Communications, 1716
Midcontinent Media, Inc., 1716
Middaugh, Amy, 1176
Middendorf, Alice C., 1394
Middendorf, J. William, Jr., 1394
Middendorf, Patricia A., 530
Middleditch, Leigh B., Jr., 3461
Middleton, Barbara, 1155
Middleton, Brook, 3423
Middleton, Carl, 3494
Middleton, John, 3511
Middleton, Mike, 628
Midkiff, Robin S., 925
Midland Tech LLC, 2228
Midwest Dental Products Corp., 3635
Midwest Maintenance and Construction, 2562
Midwest Trust Co., 1252
Miele, Christine Brock, 2072
Mielock, Douglas A., 1581
Mierlo, Chris van, 355
Miers, Fred, 2332
Miers, Frederic B., 2332
Miers, Gina, 11
Miers, Harriet, 3207
Mika, Susan, 1023
Miko, Paul, 2016
Milanese, Wendy A., 1917
Milas, Lawrence W., 2430
Milavetz, Diane, 158
Milbank, Jeremiah, 1947
Milbank, Jeremiah, III, 1947, 1968
Milbank, Katharine S., 1947
Milby, Charles D., Jr., 3248
Milby, Mary J., 3248
Milder, Daniel C., 1354
Milder, Donald B., 1354
Milder, Terri L., 1354
Mildren, Matt, 3330
Mildren, Nikki, 3330
Mildren, William, Sr., 2732
Mildren, William, Sr., Mrs., 2732
Milek, Shelley, 1753
Miles, Amy E., 3151
Miles, Gene, 1180
Miles, Jenny, 1191
Miles, John, 716
Miles, Lee L., 3390
Miles, Michael, 3312
Miles, Phoebe C., 634
Miley, Gwendolyn, 1948
Milgard, Mark, 3543
Milgard-DeGoede, Cari, 3543
Milgard-Rivera, Lori, 3543
Milhoan, Susan, 2232
Milhous, Gary, 192
Milias, Mary Ann, 471
Miligan, Stephen D., 459
Milinovich, Thomas G., 2924
Milken, Ferne, 331
Milken, Gregory A., 331
Milken, Lori A., 331
Milken, Lowell, 331
Milken, Michael, 331
Milken, Sandra, 331
Milken-Noah, Joni, 331
Millard, Alex, 3090
Millard, Katrina Gilbert, 2312
Miller Foundation, Joseph F., 1156
Miller Trust, Hazel, 3544
Miller, Adam, 2322
Miller, Adam L., 2921
Miller, Adonis E., 1547
Miller, Aishah, 3034
Miller, Allan R., 2574
Miller, Angie, 288
Miller, Ann T., 187
Miller, Arlene Michaels, 1107
Miller, Barbara H., 1081
Miller, Bill, 3356
Miller, Bonnie, 1848
Miller, Brian K., 3375
Miller, Bryan, 3256
Miller, C. Thomas, 1286
Miller, Catherine, 2686
Miller, Charlene, 2805
Miller, Christian, 120
Miller, Christopher, 2005
Miller, Clara, 2098, 2211
Miller, Constance Marks, 2291
Miller, Curtis, 3587
Miller, D. Byrd, III, 3097
Miller, Dan, 347, 397
Miller, David A., 2663
Miller, Denis, 1270
Miller, Diane, 2283
Miller, Diane Edgerton, 3422
Miller, Doris, 34
Miller, Edith D., 3056
Miller, Edward J., 1588
Miller, Edward M., 3486
Miller, Edwill B., 2308
Miller, Elinor, 1327
Miller, Emily, 1280
Miller, Eugene A., 1588, 1638
Miller, Fitzgerald, 2326
Miller, Frank R., 991
Miller, Fred, 3571
Miller, Georgette, 1129
Miller, Gerard, 3154
Miller, Harvey R., 2498
Miller, Herman, 1516
Miller, James D., 3475
Miller, James J., 51
Miller, James Ludlow, 1269
Miller, Jane E., 1843
Miller, Janet H., 3486
Miller, Janice McCoy, 319
Miller, Jean, 2864
Miller, Jennifer, 2830
Miller, Jenny, 37
Miller, Jerry D., 3223
Miller, Jim, 1623
Miller, Joe, 953
Miller, John A., 3102
Miller, John, Dr., 563
Miller, Joseph, Jr., 954
Miller, Joseph, Jr., Mrs., 954
Miller, JoZach James, 1269
Miller, Judy M., 251
Miller, Julia A., 2002
Miller, Karen, 1783
Miller, Katharine P., 1654
Miller, Katherine H., 1107
Miller, Kathy M., 279
Miller, Larry, 1616
Miller, Laura, 3171
Miller, Laura M., 3196
Miller, Laurence, 2043
Miller, Linda, 1845
Miller, Lonnie, 1852
Miller, Lori, 1832
Miller, Margaret G., 800
Miller, Mark, 2674
Miller, Marlene, 327
Miller, Mary Kathleen, 10
Miller, Maurice Lim, 138
Miller, Michael, 623
Miller, Michael H., 1211
Miller, Myron, 1516
Miller, Nancy, 1591

Miller, Oris, 408
Miller, P. Jon, 1154
Miller, Pam, 1240
Miller, Patricia A., 3615
Miller, Quincy, 3067
Miller, Rachel H., 2308
Miller, Randolph L., 2867
Miller, Robert C., 779
Miller, Roger, 2682
Miller, Ron, 988
Miller, Ronald W., Sr., 183
Miller, Rosa Copeland, 2950
Miller, Ruth, 2683
Miller, Sally Cheney, 3296
Miller, Sandy, 1154
Miller, Shakirah, 2005
Miller, Shar, 1171
Miller, Stephen B., 2633
Miller, Steve, 979
Miller, Stuart A., 778
Miller, Sue M., 1226
Miller, Susan, 2805
Miller, Tammy, 3530
Miller, Tim, 1226
Miller, Trina Dahl, 731
Miller, Vic, 1823
Miller, Walter E.D., 183
Miller, Warren Pullman, 1081
Miller, William I., 2492
Miller, William R., 2445
Miller, William S., 2294
Miller-Rosenstein, Gladys, 1980
Millesen, Judith, 2662
Millet, Mark, 1196
Millhouse, Barbara B., 2521
Millians, Philip, 904
Milligan, Cynthia H., 1628
Milligan, Gretchen, 394
Milligan, Gretchen Hartnack, 156
Milligan, Mardie, 2684
Milligan, Sharon, 2736
Millin, Steven G., 3615
Milling, R. King, 1316
Millis, Suzanne Storms, 2872
Millisor, Rob, 537
Millman, Ann, 1063
Mills, Bryan A., 1145, 1204
Mills, Catherine L., 3419
Mills, Frances Goll, 1643
Mills, Helen Crow, 22
Mills, Jim T., 3352
Mills, Karen, 354
Mills, Larry, 2858
Mills, Paul H., 1340
Mills, Robert K., 3145
Mills, Ruth B., 1135
Mills, Shannon, 1888
Millsap, Deborah, 2846
Millstein, Ira M., 2498
Millstone, Colleen, 1801
Millstone, Goldie G., 1801
Millstone, I.E., 1801
Millstone, Jennifer H., 2212
Millstone, Robert D., 1801
Milne, Christopher B., 1570
Milne, Marilyn, 3552
Milowski, Nicholas, 2207
Milstein, Edward, 607
Miltenberger, Gina, 2737
Milton, Janis, 96
Milward, John, 1282
Mims, Marcus, 2006
Mims, Rhoda, 2488
Minar, Clyde, 397
Minar, Clyde D., 347
Minard, Marcia, 1180
Mincey, Susan, 3206
Mindich, Eric M., 2302, 2309
Mindich, Stacey B., 2309
Miner, Mike, 393
Miner, Sharon, 3163
Miner-Swartz, Robin, 1581
Mines, Tom, 1589
Mink, John, 3621
Minneapolis Foundation, 1749
Minneola Co-op, 1234
Minner, Sam, 3431
Minnesota Life Insurance Co., 1739
Minnesota Mining and Manufacturing Co., 1676
Minnesota Twins, 647
Minnette, Dick, 1208
Minnich, Margaret W., 140
Minolta, Konica, 3505
Minow, Martha, 1056, 2427
Minto Communities, Inc., 789
Minton, Kim, 1163
Mintz, Joshua J., 1056
Mintz, Ward L.E., 2101
Mir, Gasper, III, 3266
Mirabito, John, 2107
Miramonti, Dina, 1603
Miranda, Adam, 2119
Miranda, Cameron, 2119
Miranda, Karen, 1099
Mirchandani, Nadine, 612
Mirolo, Amelita, 2738
Mirrer, Louise, 2237
Mirsepassi, Nadder, 371
Mirsky, Burton M., 2126
Mishler, Kent, 1187
Mishler, Kristi, 2648
Misiak, David G., 1726
Miskell, Eileen C., 1445
Mississippi Power Co., 1769
Mississippi Power Education Fdn., 1769
Mistry, Dinyar B., 367
Mitchell, Allyson, 3364
Mitchell, Amanda K., 865
Mitchell, Betsy, 3619
Mitchell, Brian Gregory, 3297
Mitchell, Cara, 900
Mitchell, Carleton Grant, 3297
Mitchell, Cleta, 3601
Mitchell, Cynthia W., 3297
Mitchell, Edward C., III, 865
Mitchell, Edward C., Jr., 865
Mitchell, George P., 3297
Mitchell, George Scott, 3297
Mitchell, Hilda, 3227
Mitchell, James, Dr., 2521
Mitchell, Jean, 1233
Mitchell, Jennifer B., 865
Mitchell, John, 1233
Mitchell, John Kirk, 3297
Mitchell, John P., Rev. Dr., 2002
Mitchell, Julie, 3163
Mitchell, Lori Read, 293
Mitchell, Mack C., Jr., 1344
Mitchell, Marcus W.H., Jr., 2538
Mitchell, Mark Douglas, 3297
Mitchell, Martha, 3663
Mitchell, Melanie, 1758
Mitchell, Michael Kent, 3297
Mitchell, Pam, 1227
Mitchell, Pat, 1180
Mitchell, Richard A., 2762
Mitchell, Robert H., 2769
Mitchell, Sarah Scott, 3297
Mitchell, Thomas N., 2048
Mitchell, Virginia C., 865
Mitchell, William, 2163
Mitchell, William E., 1332
Mitchell-Miller, Rochelle, 484
Mitchener, Frank, 1760
Mithoefer, Heather M., 2715
Mithoefer, Peter P., 2715
Mittal Steel USA Inc., 964
Mittal, Anuradha, 3407
Mittelstaedt, Darin, 3332
Mittelstaedt, Ronald J., 3332
Mittleman, Mary Sherman, 2419
Mitzel, David P., 2747
Miyanaga, Yutaka, 1070
Mizari Charity Fund, 1922
Mize, Ann, 1271
Mize, David C., 1271
Mizell, Diane, 391
Mizell, Robert, 3363
Moberg, Trish, 3641
MOC Holdco II, Inc., 2921
Moceri, Gregory, 1595
Moceri, Gregory C., 1595
Moceri, Margaret, 1595
Moceri, Margaret E., 1595
Mock, Janet, 2040
Mock, Max, 1168
Mockenhaupt, Robin E., 1949
Moczygemba, Jackie, 3247
Moderow, Joseph, 1353
Modic, Susan Schwabacher, 159
Modisett, Cori, 3187
Modisett, Leslie, 3187
Modugno, Patrick J., 251
Moe, Barbara, 3305
Moed, Sam, 2979
Moehle, Michael, 764
Moehling, John H., 357
MOEN, 3505
Moench, Jennifer L., 2752
Moentmann, Melanie, 1817
Moffett, Gary E., 2771
Moffett, George M., 840
Moffett, George M., II, 840
Moffett, Robert, Esq., 2986
Moffitt, Allen W., 146
Moffitt, Bill, 3568
Mohamad, Rahman, 2121
Mohammed, Basha G., 757
Mohl, William, 1308
Mohr, Matthew, 2649
Mohr, Ronnie, 1710
Mohraz, Judy Jolley, 57
Mohre, J. Craig, 2750
Mohrfeld, Cherie, 329
Moilanen, Phil, 1623
Moini, Ingrid A., 3482
Moise, Beth, 2017
Mokros, David, 515
Moldvay, Michael, 2796
Molella, Salvador, 2088
Molendorp, Dayton H., 1183
Moler, Edward, 2810
Molina, Mario J., 1056
Molina, Polo, 259
Molinari, Michael William, 1670
Moll, Robin Wright, 3574
Mollenberg, Trudy A., 2503
Molnar, Catherine, 408
Moloney, Jacqueline F., 1505
Moman, Anne, 11
Monahan, Michael, 604
Monahan, Michael T., 1588
Monahan, Richard, 3450
Monahan, Susan T., 1425
Monardo, Gregory G., 329
Monck, Ronald R., 718
Mondzelewski, Chris, 3148
Monfort Family Foundation, 484
Monfort, Charlie, 520
Monfort, Dick, 520
Monfort, Kenneth W., 520
Monfort, Myra, 520
Mongan, Tobias T., 3173
Monitello, Robert, 2770
Monk, Jon, 3401
Monk, Nancy J., 260
Monke, Sheila, 1836
Monnier, Ken, 2684
Monroe, Bill, 1663
Monroe, Marie, 3099
Monroe, Mark, 3488
Monroe, Rachel Garbow, 1416
Monroe, Ray, 3139
Monroe, Sandra W., 2541
Monsanto Co., 1803
Monsanto, Alda, 3419
Monse, Michelle D., 3275
Montague, Hazel G.M., 3141
Montalbano, Richard M., Sr., 1114
Montalvo, Maria, 3505, 3544
Montana Dakota Utilities Co., 2652
Monte, Constance, 2490
Montebello Trust, 1981
Montes de Oca, Ivonne, 408
Monteverde Group, 3579
Monteverdi, Manbin Khaira, 340
Montford, Debbie, 372
Montford, John, 372
Montford, Kaye C., 520
Montgomery County Dept. of Recreation, 1414
Montgomery, Barbara, 1749
Montgomery, Carolyn R., 1830
Montgomery, Edward E., 2686
Montgomery, Gerry, 1286
Montgomery, John D., 1260
Montgomery, Paul, 3133
Montgomery, Rebecca, 1769
Montgomery, Rosemary Storms, 2872
Montgomery, Stephanie Stenger, 1783
Montgomery, Stephen, 3487
Montgomery, Virginia, 2511
Montgomery, Walter S., Sr., 3096
Montgomery-Tabron, La June, 1628
Montoya, Eric, 498
Montoya, Melanie, 538
Montoya, Ronald E., 528
Montrone, Angelo, 1893
Montrone, Jerome, 1893
Montrone, Paul M., 1893
Montrone, Sandra G., 1893
Moody's Corp., 2297
Moody, Jacquelin A., 1672
Moody, Libbie Shearn, 3298
Moody, Melaine, Jr., 2782
Moody, Robert L., 3306
Moody, Robert L., Sr., 3298
Moody, Ross R., 3298
Moody, William Lewis, Jr., 3298
Moody-Dahlberg, Frances A., 3298
Mookherjee, Sati, 3571
Moon, Lawrence E., 1646
Moon, William, 2097
Mooney, Abigail S., 500
Mooney, Dee K., 950

Mooney, F. Steven, 500
Mooney, Gregory, 987
Mooney, James C., 3415
Mooney, Kay D., 550
Mooney, Michael E., 1468
Moor, M. Eugene, Jr., 7
Moore, Aaron, 1868
Moore, Albert W., 224
Moore, Ann S., 2492
Moore, Anne, 2325
Moore, Becky B., 708
Moore, Betty I., 333
Moore, Blanche Davis, 3299
Moore, Bruce, Jr., 3139
Moore, Carla, Hon., 2655
Moore, Cathy, 2612
Moore, Cindy, 1360
Moore, Claude, 3461
Moore, Clement C., II, 1396
Moore, Danielle H., 2054
Moore, Danielle Hickox, 747
Moore, David E., Sr., 2311
Moore, Dawn, 1087
Moore, Deborah L., 592
Moore, Dennis F., 2660
Moore, Doreen, 946
Moore, Dorothy, 2281
Moore, Eileen P., 2894
Moore, Elizabeth W., 1396
Moore, Gordon E., 333
Moore, Heather D., 1395
Moore, Jack, 3245, 3255
Moore, James, 3300
Moore, James L., 1770
Moore, Jim, 3356
Moore, John, 1188
Moore, Joseph L., 3240
Moore, Judith H., 1612
Moore, Judith Livingston, 2314
Moore, Katherine C., 2311
Moore, Kathy, 3158
Moore, Kenneth G., 333
Moore, Kevin S., 2099
Moore, Kristen L., 333
Moore, Laverne I., 2004
Moore, Lee Wayne, 3300
Moore, Leslie, 489, 3158
Moore, Lin, 11
Moore, Linda G., 3576
Moore, Lori A., 175
Moore, Lynne, 3193
Moore, Mackey, 1760
Moore, Marilyn, 831
Moore, Mark, 3187
Moore, Matthew W., 2219
Moore, Melanie, 3273
Moore, Meredith C., 1979
Moore, Nancy, 3606
Moore, Nancy Powell, 3324
Moore, Patrick C., 1763
Moore, Patrick K., 2933
Moore, Ralph, 729
Moore, Randolph G., 929
Moore, Richard, 2017
Moore, Richard W., 2311
Moore, Rick, 3546
Moore, Sara Giles, 897
Moore, Sarah Kaplan, 1041
Moore, Scott, 1685
Moore, Shabri, 1358
Moore, Stephen C., 805
Moore, Stephen F., 3129
Moore, Steven E., 333
Moore, Sue, 2723
Moore, Tammy R., 952
Moore, Taylor Frost, 2012
Moore, Thomas A., 2314
Moore, Thurston R., 3470
Moore, Timothy, 3501
Moore, Tom, 3300
Moore, Vicky, 3501
Moore, Vicky L., 2660
Moore, Walter M., IV, 3449
Moore, William Martin, 1289
Moore, Yvonne L., 2127
Moorehead, Jim, 160
Moorman, Bette D., 1752
Moorman, Carol E., 1060
Moot, Amey D., 2503
Moot, Richard E., 2503
Moot, Welles V., 2503
Mor, William, 1432
Mora, Carolyn, 3312
Morales, Amsi Y., 1505
Morales, Carlos, 3287
Morales, Hugo, 385
Morales, Jerry, 3316
Morales, Manuel A., Dr., 3061
Morales, Minerva, 3576
Moran, Asha Morgan, 2739
Moran, Caroline A., 2959
Moran, David, 3589
Moran, James, 2907
Moran, Janet, 1171
Moran, John R., 48
Moran, Marty, 2739
Moran, Patrick Michael, 3462
Moran, Sara S., 3034
Moran, Suzanne S., 3462
Moran, Tami Grigsby, 1312
Moran, William A., 3462
Morascyzk, Edward C., 3054
Morash, Douglas A., 1508
Moravec, F. Joseph, 656
Moravitz, Edward, 2889
Morby, Carolyn R., 1611
Morcos, Michael J., 1007
Mordell, Jayne S., 111
More, Pat, 1136
Moreau, Tom, 1660
Morehouse, Dean, 3563
Morehouse, K. Frank, 2652
Moreland, Steven, 1614
Morella, Constance A., Hon., 656
Morency, Jeanne L., 2856
Morency, Michael, 2856
Moreno, Albert F., 385
Moreno, Carlos R., Hon., 137
Moreno, Julie, 726
Moreno, Paula, 2160
Moretta, Daniel N., 2663
Morey, Lon, 1647
Morey, Sandra, 354
Morf, Darrel A., 1222
Morgan Library & Museum, 2069
Morgan Stanley, 2315
Morgan Stanley & Co. Inc., 2315
Morgan Stanley Dean Witter & Co., 2315
Morgan Stanley Group Inc., 2315
Morgan Stanley Smith Barney, 2986
Morgan Stanley, Dean Witter, Discover & Co., 2315
Morgan Trust, Russell Guy and Ruth Louise, 244
Morgan, Albert, 1270
Morgan, Bill, 3547
Morgan, Burton D., 2740, 2741
Morgan, Carol Varga, 3498
Morgan, Catherine A., 3301
Morgan, Christine R., 3301
Morgan, Dorothy, 562
Morgan, Erin M., 975
Morgan, J. Grey, 2630
Morgan, James A., 1517
Morgan, Karin W., 1408
Morgan, Karla, 2739
Morgan, Kim, 1580
Morgan, Lee M., 2739
Morgan, Leigh, 3516
Morgan, Leona, 1270
Morgan, Margaret Clark, 2741
Morgan, Marietta McNeill, 3463
Morgan, Michael C., 3301
Morgan, Paul F., 925
Morgan, Rob, 3099
Morgan, Ronnie, 3158
Morgan, Samuel L., 2204
Morgan, Samuel T., Jr., 3463
Morgan, Sara, 3547
Morgan, Sara S., 3301
Morgan, Sarah H., 3123
Morgan, Suzanne, 2741
Morgan, Tedd, 1753
Morgan, Victoria A., 2739
Morgan, William V., 3301
Morgan-Prager, Karole, 317
Morgenstern, Dan, 2301
Morgenthau, Robert P., 2161
Morger, Randal, 1823
Morgridge, Carrie, 642
Morgridge, John D., 642
Morgridge, John P., 642, 3617
Morgridge, Tashia, 642, 3617
Morgridge, Tashia F., 3617
Mori, Sandy Ouye, 329
Morial, Sybil H., 1302
Moriarty, Brunilda, 1944
Moriearty, Perry, 1715
Morille, Trish, 3355
Morino, Dana S., 2742
Morino, Mario M., 2742
Morino, Matthew, 2742
Moriuchi, N. Chiyo, 3030
Moriyama, Lisa, 1206
Morley, Burrows, Jr., 1644
Morley, Christopher, 1644
Morley, David H., 1644
Morley, George B., Jr., 1644
Morley, Katharyn, 1644
Morley, Michael, 1644
Morley, Peter, 1644
Morley, Peter, Jr., 1644
Morley, Ralph Chase, Sr., 1644
Morley, Ralph Chase, Sr., Mrs., 1644
Morning, John, 1645, 2002
Moroney, James M. "Jim", III, 3209
Moroney, Michael J., 2764
Morouse, James, 394
Morrell, Elner, 564
Morrell, Jim, 3504
Morrill, Richard L., 2460
Morris Family, Albert, 2771
Morris, Anne, 159
Morris, Anthony P., 599
Morris, Anthony, Esq., 2915
Morris, Courtney, 1616
Morris, Darren, 391
Morris, Dorothy M., 599
Morris, Earl W., 2864
Morris, Gabriella, 3055
Morris, Gabriella E., 1353
Morris, James F., 1359
Morris, James T., 355
Morris, Joseph W., 2828
Morris, Julie Lancaster, 3296
Morris, Leigh, 1171
Morris, Maria R., 2307
Morris, Michael G., 2656
Morris, P. Kevin, 272
Morris, Robert E., Jr., 599
Morris, Robert W., 3099
Morris, Sally, 1191
Morris, Stewart, Jr., 3308
Morris, Stewart, Sr., 3308
Morris, Susan T., 599
Morris, Susan W., 599
Morris, Tammy, 1837
Morris, Thomas Q., 2075, 2099
Morrison, Bill, 3488
Morrison, Emily Cade, 634
Morrison, Grace A., 1279
Morrison, Ian, 139
Morrison, J. Holmes, 3584
Morrison, Jerri L., 1910
Morrison, Larry, 3305
Morrison, M. Holly, 2908
Morrison, N. Jane, 1020
Morrison, Nina, 655
Morrison, Ralph R., 904
Morrison, Rebecca, 655
Morrison, Richard J., 598
Morrison, Robert L., 634
Morrison, Scot A., 1578
Morrissey, Joan S., 1008
Morrissey, Michael, 1867
Morrissey, Robert F., 706
Morrissey, Robert J., 706
Morrone, Colleen P., 2932
Morrow, Cynthia B., 2177
Morrow, Patrick, 2143
Morrow, Polly O'Brien, 604
Morrow, Sherry, 1842
Morrow, Teresa, 1717
Morse, Alan R., Jr., 1531
Morse, Carole E., 2867
Morse, Christine M., 1689
Morse, Eric Robert, 1531
Morse, Jennifer, 1531
Morse, Mary, 2110
Morse, Peter C., 1947
Morse, Susan, 2857
Morse, Timothy, 1531
Morss, Everett, Jr., 1539
Mortellaro, Janine, 2723
Mortensen, Sharon, 1642
Mortenson, David C., 1717
Morton, Franklin L., 3401
Morton, Jeff, 3325
Morton, John, 3539
Morton, S. Sidney, 347
Morton, Tina, 2985
Mory, Gene, 1170
Mosaic Company, Tho, 1718
Moscicki, Anna, 3684
Moscow, John, 2279
Moscrop, Tony, 3067
Moser, Bobby, 1628
Moser, Constance B., 698
Moser, Monica M., 1623
Moses & Yetta Charitable Trust, 2057
Moses, Leann O., 1316
Moses, Monte, 528
Mosher, Margaret C., 335
Mosher, Samuel B., 335
Mosher, Scott, 168
Moshier, Dusty, 1274
Mosier, Jerrilee K., 1193

Mosier, Lynn, 1869
Mosley, I. Sigmund, Jr., 888
Mosley, Ralph W., 3129
Moss Trust for Euluos Moss, Jack, 954
Moss, Andree K., 1316
Moss, Gerald, 1016
Moss, Jody, 1827
Moss, Lee C., 740
Moss, Lynda Bourque, 1722
Moss, Sara, 2287
Moss, William M., 3471
Most, Jordan, 1902
Mosteller, Karen, 714
Mosty, John, 3318
Moszkowski, Neal, 2473
Motamed, Margaret, 422
Motes, Holly, 948
Motiva, 3348
Motley, George B., 1539
Motley, John, 1010
Motley, Ronald L., 3107
Motley, Sandra D., 1899
Motorola Solutions, Inc., 1066
Motorola, Inc., 1066
Motorsports Authentics, 2562
Motorsports Charities, 2562
Motorsports Marketing, 2562
Motoyama, Stacie-Dee, 3504
Motsenbocker, Anne B., 3209
Mott, Charles Stewart, 1645
Mott, Kerry K., 276
Mott, Kevin, 1012
Mott, Maryanne, 452, 1645, 1646
Mott, Ruth R., 1646
Mott, Willard, 1597
Mottier, Bradley D., 822
Mottola, Maria, 2326
Mouawad, Fred, 1524
Mouch, Virginia, 1616
Mouden, Sip B., 1763
Moulds, Donald, 2106
Moulton, Amy, 1130
Moulton, Benjamin W., 1489
Moulton, Mari Beth C., 1418
Mounsey, Anne, 499
Mounsey, Peter, 499
Mount, Vivian, 488
Mountain, Janet, 3213
Mountain, Paul, 34
Mountcastle, Katharine B., 2521
Mountcastle, Katherine R., 2521
Mountcastle, Kenneth F., III, 2521
Mountcastle, Laura L., 2521
Mountcastle, Mary, 2521
Mountjoy, Michael B., 1288
Mourand, Don, 1636
Mourer, Ryan, 2331
Moutinho, Maria, 744
Movshon, Anthony, 1714
Mower, Darick E., 3391
Mower, Thomas E., 3391
Mower, Thomas W., 3391
Mowery, William, 1228
Mowrer, George, 2982
Mowrer, Gordon B., 2982
Mowry, Barbara, 1797
Moyer, Ariel C., 1366
Moyer, Charles I., 1259
Moyer, D. Scott, 2747
Moyer, Glenn E., 3059
Moyer, Scott, 2267
Moyers, Bill D., 2412
Moyers, Richard L., 672
Moylan, Laura, 953
Moynihan, Merrily, 580
Moynihan, Timothy J., 611
Mr. White LLC, 2476
Mrozek, Ernest J., 1008
Mrozik, Reiko, 1045
MSG Charitable Trust, 213
Mt. Washington Co-operative Bank, 1517
MTV Networks, 3424
Muchmore, Iris E., 1222
Muchnic, Daphne Nan, 1271
Muchnic, H.E., 1271
Muchnic, Helen Q., 1271
Muckel, John, 336
Muckel, Linda, 336
Mucklestone, Robert S., 3507
Mudd, Jane W., 3102
Mudge, Steve, 1010
Muegge, Linda, 1154
Muehlbauer, Brad J., 1167
Muehlbauer, James, 1205
Muehlbauer, James H., 1167
Muehleck, James K., 3443
Muehlhauser, Regina L., 264
Mueller, Aimee, 2037
Mueller, Bill, 1847
Mueller, Charles G., 1008
Mueller, Douglas, 2037
Mueller, Jack, 3401
Mueller, Linda, 1583
Mueller, Stacey, 1828
Mueller, Todd W., 1726
Muffo, John, 3431
Mufson, Kathleen Ryan, 604
Muhl, Shauna Sullivan, 916
Muhlbach, John L., Jr., 2663
Muir, Catherine L., 1627
Muir, David F., 1627
Muir, Elizabeth M., 1627
Muir, Lea Ann, 1627
Muir, William M, 1627
Muirhead, Nancy L., 2389
Mujica-Larson, Evelyn, 31
Mulcahy, Forrest, 767
Mulder, P. Haans, 1591
Mule, Edward A., 2316
Mulford, Nancy P., 3317
Mulholland, Donna A., 805
Mulholland, Soapy, 354
Mulka, John S., 2908
Mulkerin, Larry, 3561
Mullainathan, Sendhil, 1056
Mullane, William, 2799
Mullaney, Deborah, 2407
Mullaney, John J., 2754
Mullen Foundation, J.K., The, 522
Mullen, Anthony P., 2364
Mullen, Catherine S., 522
Mullen, John K., 522
Mullen, Mike, 2066
Mullenbrock, Craig M., 2763
Mullendore, Stuart L., 1360
Muller, Bob, 2604
Muller, Leonard J., 1114
Mulligan, Cathie, 2737
Mulligan, Donal Leo, 1697
Mulligan, Ed, 2686
Mulligan, John J., 1744
Mulligan, Larry, Hon., 2737
Mulligan, Terence P., 340
Mullikin, Phil, 1357
Mullin, Dave, 1632
Mullin, Dennis, 1268
Mullins, Shelley Dru, 2822
Mullins, Timothy P., 244
Mulot, Regis, 1549
Mulpas, Joe, 2688
Mulstay, John, 527
Mulvany, Kate, 613
Mulvihill, Heather, 2232
Mulvoy, James E., 1633
Mulvoy, Maree R., 1633
Munday, Heidi B., 1082
Munday, Reuben A., 1638
Mundel, Trevor, 3516
Mundy, David, 3302
Mundy, Gardner, 559
Mundy, Joe S., 3302
Mundy, John T., 3302
Mundy, Marion E., 3302
Mundy, Sue E., 3302
Munford, Julie, 1578
Munga, Susan, 2731
Mungenast Group Dealer Services, 1804
Mungenast, Barbara J., 1804
Mungenast, David F., 1804
Mungenast, David F., Jr., 1804
Mungenast, Kurt A., 1804
Mungenast, Raymond J., 1804
Munger, Wendy, 361
Muni, Craig, 2078
Munitz, Barry, Dr., 167
Munoz, Cecilia, 2048
Munro, Christopher R., 2859
Munro, Clark C., Jr., 2859
Munro, Clark C., Sr., 2859
Munro, David M., 2845
Munro, Don, 1763
Munro, Grant, 2743
Munro, Maurie M., 2859
Munro, Warner R., 2859
Munroe, Bobbie D., 793
Munroe, Ginny, 1176
Munroe, Jan H., 793
Munroe, Richard C., 793
Munroe, Richard G., 793
Munson, Arvid W., 3609
Munson, Ed, 83
Munson, Eddie R., 1666
Munson, Jon, 63
Munson, Josh, 1179
Munson, Linda J., 1925
Munzig, Judith, 85
Murabito, John M., 2917
Muraco, Julie, 2098
Muraki, David, 354
Murata, Tetsuo, 89
Murchison, Anne, 2578
Murdoch, Anne, 1012
Murdock, David H., 338
Murguia, Ramon, 1628
Murnane, Richard, 1098
Murnane, Tim, 1724
Murphy, Alissa, 1967
Murphy, Arthur, III, 1816
Murphy, Bill, 2112
Murphy, Brian F., 2744
Murphy, Bruce D., 2717, 2736
Murphy, David C., 2592
Murphy, Diana M., 866
Murphy, Edward, 1513
Murphy, Eileen, 638
Murphy, Frank, 2723
Murphy, Henry L., Jr., 1435, 1461
Murphy, John, 235
Murphy, John P., 2745
Murphy, Judith, 418
Murphy, Julia, 1816
Murphy, Kathleen, 1883
Murphy, Kevin K., 2893
Murphy, Mark, 1724
Murphy, Mary Holt Woodson, 2644
Murphy, Michael, 259
Murphy, Mike, 73
Murphy, Murlan J., Jr., 2744
Murphy, Pam, 2864
Murphy, Patrick T., 2336
Murphy, Patsy, 3380
Murphy, Patty, 1717
Murphy, Paul B., Jr., 3267
Murphy, Paul J., 2744
Murphy, Raymond M., 2744
Murphy, Richard, 661
Murphy, Robert J., 1887
Murphy, Roberta, 1816
Murphy, Scott, 3511
Murphy, Suzanne M., 2204
Murphy, Thomas, 1306, 2071
Murphy, Thomas J., 2113, 2935
Murphy, Timothy P., 3548
Murphy, William K., Esq., 2986
Murray, Corlis, 954
Murray, David, 3492
Murray, Douglas S., 461
Murray, Elizabeth, 461
Murray, Eulene H., 899
Murray, Eve-Lynne G., 461
Murray, Harry, Jr., 3578
Murray, Helen J., 1147
Murray, James D., 2185
Murray, James R., 461
Murray, Jason B., 2767
Murray, Jennifer, 394
Murray, Jim, 115
Murray, Joan D., 683
Murray, John F., Jr., 2392
Murray, Kantahyanee, 1391
Murray, Karen, 2761
Murray, Katharine L., 3492
Murray, Meghan, 3428
Murray, Michael J., 3047
Murschel, Catherine, 3115
Murthy Law Firm, 1399
Murthy, N.R. Narayana, 2160
Murthy, Sheela, 1399
Murthy, Srinivas, 1399
Muscarolas, Miriam, 456
Musgrave, Jeannette, 1805
Musgrave, Travis, 1282
Music Mastermind Inc., 2422
Music Today LLC, 2562, 2574
Mussato, Cheryl, 1262
Mussatt, Lynn, 3427
Musselman, Jamie P., 3049
Musselwhite, Stephen A., 3432
Musser, Clifton R., 501
Musser, Laura J., 1719
Musser, Marcie J., 501
Musser, Margaret K., 501
Musser, Robert W., 501
Mussman, Gaylord, 1836
Mustico, Michael, 2109
Musto, Catherine, 1578
Mutual of America Life Insurance Co., 2317
Mutual of Omaha Insurance Co., 1850
Muxlow, Paul, 1663
Muxlow, Tricia, 1663
Mwanza, Angela K., 2146
Mydna Media, Inc., 3159
Myers, Daria, 65
Myers, Dick, 1158

Myers, Donna, 1068
Myers, Douglas, 3487
Myers, Jack, 808
Myers, James A., 2658
Myers, James L., 1408
Myers, John, 1197
Myers, John C., IV, 808
Myers, June R., 808
Myers, Larry, 354
Myers, Max, 2823
Myers, Nellie, 1186
Myers, Paul, 808
Myers, Peter, 1443
Myers, Randolph, 2366
Myers, Randy W., 3488
Myers, Ronald, 2148
Myers, S. L., 837
Myers, Samford T., 10
Myers, Sue, 1357
Myers, Tim D., 2882
Myers, Vincent, 1910
Mylan Laboratories Inc., 3001
Mylan Pharmaceuticals, 3001
Mylander, George L., 2773
Myott, Shirley, 619
Myrhen, Trygve, 2232
Myrick, H. Gordon, 1764
Myrie, Sharon, 2079
Myska, Elizabeth, 1512

Nabisco Brands, Inc., 2613
Nabony, William, 901
Nachman, Gail, 1414
Nachshon, Shira, 195
Nada, Sherif A., 2472
Nadgwick, Rebecca J., 1835
Nadosy, Peter A., 2126, 2146, 2160
Nadwondny, Austin, 727
Naeve, Brian, 942
Nagel, David, 1395
Nagel, Rob D., 2492
Nagelkirk, Joan, 1663
Nager, Elizabeth, 2609
Nagle, Patricia Herold, 1975
Nagy, Louis, Jr., 33
Nahum, Edmond, Rabbi, 1898
Naify, Carlin, 391
Naiman, Norma Lee, 665
Nair, Mira, 176
Najarian, K. George, 2001
Najim, Harvey E., 3304
Najork, Susan, 2111
Nakano, Tsuyoshi, 3531
Nakash Holding LLC, 2318
Nakash, Avi, 2318
Nakash, Joseph, 2318
Nakash, Ralph, 2318
Nalty, Elizabeth S., 1316, 1319
Nalty, Jill K., 1319
Namee, Eric S., 1258
Namingha, Michael, 2017
Nance, Jessie, 2821, 2822
Nance, William, 2613
Nanci's Animal Rights Foundation, Inc., 184
Nanri, Takahiro, 680
Nanz, Barry, 1141
Napier, James H., 55
Nappi, Mark, 3052
Naragon, Frederic E., 2771
Nardella, Bruce, 1513
Narducci, Lucille Reed, 2670
Narodick, Sally, 3570
Narron, James W., 2599
Nartelski, Evelyn, 1648
Nartker, Joe, 1663
Narzissenfeld, Bruce, 830
Nascar, 2574
Nasdaq Stock Market, Inc., The, 1401
Nash Sports Club, Steve, 37
Nash, David, 1593
Nash, Helen, 2320
Nash, Jack, 2320
Nash, Joann, 37
Nash, Jonathan, 1539
Nash, Joshua, 2320
Nash, Martin, 767
Nash, Marvin, 1586
Nash, Rebecca, 1720
Nash, Stephen, 37
Nasr, Bassam, Dr., 1590
Nasr, Vali, 2389
Nass, Connie K., 1205
Nass, Marcia Thayer, 659
Natalicio, Diana, 2390
Nathan Barry Co., 1962
Nathan, Sandra, 309
Nathan, Walter R., 1083
Nathanson, Jeffrey, 1327
Nathoo, Raffiq, 2325
Nation, Fred, 1203
National Bank Of Indianapolis, 1178
National Bank of Indianapolis, The, 1156
National Beer Wholesalers Association, 1344
National City Bank, 1156, 1586, 2655, 2723, 2993
National Distributing Co., Inc., 1558
National Fish and Wildlife Foundation, 901
National Fuel Gas Company, 2321
National Gallery of Art, 2069
National Institute for the Severely Handicapped (NISH), 3326
National Machinery Co., 2748
National Machinery LLC, 2748
National Park Service, 318
National Science Foundation, 82
National Securities Corp., 1880
National Speaking of Women's Health, 2675
National Sporting Library, 2069
National University of Health Sciences, 1232
Nauman, Christopher J., 1540
Nava, Carolyn, 346
Navarrette, Steve, 1836
Navikas, David B., 3018
Navota, Katherine, 991
Nayak, Vasant, 1399
Naylor, Diane G., 3002
Naylor, Irvin S., 3002
Naylor, James, 1721
Naylor, Leah R., 3002
Naylor, S. Chester, II, 3002
Naylor, Sarah R., 3002
Nazarian, David, 341
Nazarian, Shulamit, 341
Nazarian, Soraya J., 341
Nazarian, Younes, 341
Nazem, Farzad, 241
NBC Universal, Inc., 2322
NBT Bank, N.A., 2332, 2365
NCL America, Inc., 2476
NCMIC Group, Inc., 1232
NCMIC Insurance Company, 1232
Neal, Alesha, 1191
Neal, Bruce, 3597
Neal, Karla, 3355
Neal, Richard, 268
Neal, Robert F., 1764
Neal, Shannon, 1097
Neal, Stephen C., 248
Neal, Susan Falck, 1158
Neal, Vivian, 2655
Neale, Gary, 545
Nearney Family Foundation, 3026
NEB Corp., 3664
Nebeker, Stephen B., 3402
Needham, Dorothy E., 2597
Needham, Eddie, 842
Needham, Jean, 3641
Needham, Judith, 1402
Needler, Michael S., 2700
Neel, Catherine, 2678
Neel, Hibbett, 1759
Neely, Greg, 1136
Neely, Mary M., 1573, 1653
Neely, Suzanne, 1762
Neely, Walter, 1756
Neenan, William B., 1509
Neese 1957 Trust, Margaret L., 3639
Neese Trust of 1954, Robert H., 3639
Neese, Robert H., 3639
Neese, Wendy L., 3639
Neeson, Heather Gael, 1009
Neff, Daniel A., 2490
Neff, David K., 1122
Neff, Jodi, 1049
Neff, Peter Gibbons, 840
Neff, Ralph, 1187
Nefsky, Robert, 1834
Negley, Nancy Brown, 3183
Nehrt, Sue, 1132
Neidorff, Michael F., 1782
Neighbors, Steven G., 941
Neihart, Connie, 1185
Neil, Gerard, 2648
Neilson, George W., 1721
Neisel, Bridgette, 2788
Neisloss, James, 1970
Neisloss, Stanley, 1970
Neisloss, Susan, 1970
Neiswander, D. Kirk, 2736
Nelms, Charlie, 1645
Nelson, Anna Spangler, 771
Nelson, Anne, 54
Nelson, Aune, 1067
Nelson, Brett, 1217
Nelson, Cathy, 384
Nelson, Charles F., 1172
Nelson, Charley, 1706
Nelson, Chris, 1971
Nelson, Cynthia, 1420
Nelson, David, 1751
Nelson, David W., 2651
Nelson, Deborah, 2612
Nelson, Faye Anderson, 1598
Nelson, Gary, 1221
Nelson, Gary D., 886
Nelson, Ginna, 3642
Nelson, Grace, 3003
Nelson, Greg, 160
Nelson, Helen P., 2928
Nelson, Janice, 1740
Nelson, John P., 1226
Nelson, Karen, 2868
Nelson, Kimberly A., 1697
Nelson, Larry R., 735
Nelson, Mark, 770, 1783
Nelson, Mary D., 3640
Nelson, Mary Goodwillie, 1667, 1674
Nelson, Melody S., 1359
Nelson, Michelle A., 3433
Nelson, P. Erik, 2928
Nelson, Randolph, 1420
Nelson, Steve, 2686
Nelson, Susie, 3579
Nelson, Thomas M., Rev., 1445
Nelson, Travis, 2473
Nelson, Victor D., 369
Nelson, Vince, 384
Nelson, W. Linton, ADM., 3003
Nelson, William R., 3476
Nemanic, Marc, 346
Nemec, Fred J., 3196
Nemeth, Joseph, 3607
Nemovicher, Sivan, 1900
Nepp, Dawn, 3126
Nerney, Tom & Jill, 3026
Nesbary, Dale K., 1586
Nesbitt, Cyndi, 1146
Nesbitt, Greg, 257
Nesbitt, Robert, 886
Nesbitt, William A., 3296, 3331
Nesh, Florence, 3004
Neshat, Shirin, 2494
Neshe, Dana, 1515
Ness, Ian, 2287
Nessier, Stephen, 467
Nestor, Lyndsey, 3589
Neth, Robert H., Jr., 1914
Nettles, Cory L., 3637
Nettles, Thomas A., IV, 11
Nettleton Trust, 1272
Network for Good, 3167
Neu, John L., 2323
Neu, Robert T., 2323
Neu, Wendy K., 2323
Neuberger, Gary, 3117
Neuberger, James A., 593
Neuberger, Marie S., 593
Neuberger, Roy R., 593
Neuberger, Roy S., 593
Neuenschwander, Jack L., 2763
Neufeld, Adele B., 2226
Neufeld, Jordan J., 2653
Neufeld, Lena, 2022
Neufeld, Peter, 2022
Neufeld, Shane, 2022
Neuharth, Jan, 662
Neuhoff, Elizabeth "Beth", 2071
Neuhoff, Joseph Boyd, 3202
Neuhoff, Patricia, 3142
Neuman, Dawn, 3623
Neumann, Roland M., 3669
Neumann, Roxann S., 3274
Neumann, Susan M., 606
Neumeister, Bill, 3511
Neumeyer, Marge, 1185
Neurath, Moshe, 1902
Neuro Rays Imaging, 647
Neurochem, Inc., 2233
Neurogena, 1948
Neurosurgery and Endovascular Associates, 37
Neutzling, Virginia, 2663
Nevas, Bernard, 594
Nevas, Leo, 594
Nevels, Reggie, 1129
Neverthirst, 3330
Neville, Richard, 268
Nevin, Janice E., 630
Nevin-Folino, Nancy, 1611
Nevlin, Linda K., 1065
New Balance Athletic Shoe, Inc., 1518
New Bidnis Inc., 2422

New Orleans Redevelopment Authority, 2368
New Orleans Wine and Food Experience, 1314
New York Cardiac Ctr., Inc., 1901
New York Mercantile Exchange, Inc., 2327
New York Stock Exchange LLC, 2336
NewAlliance Bancshares, Inc., 595
Newark Rotary Club, 2731
Newberry Library, 2069
Newberry, S. Lloyd, 866
Newby, L. Kristin, 623
Newcombe, Charlotte W., 1972
Newcomer, David C., 2674
Newcomer, Glen L., 2674
Newcomer, Phyllis, 3249
Newell, Mike, 278
Newell, Richard D., 3525
Newfarmer, Jerry, 2782
Newhall Land and Farming Co., The, 342
Newhall, Anthony, 342
Newhall, David, 342
Newhall, George A., 342
Newhall, Leila G., 342
Newhall, Roger, 342
Newhouse, Joseph P., 550
Newkirk, Glen, 2018
Newlands, David, 540
Newman, Cherish, 3399
Newman, Claudia, 3546
Newman, Eddie, 361
Newman, Elizabeth V., 2328
Newman, Gary, 3193
Newman, Harold, 2650
Newman, Howard, 2328
Newman, Howard H., 2328
Newman, J. Bonnie, 1174
Newman, Jill, 1552
Newman, John B., 2597
Newman, John H., 2905
Newman, Kelly D., 3399
Newman, Leslie, 637
Newman, Maryam R., 2328
Newman, Paul, 2707
Newman, Peter G., 2107
Newman, Richard, 2032
Newman, W.R., III, 1770
Newman, William T., Jr., Hon., 3421
Newmark, Craig Alexander, 169
Newsom, Jean, 661
Newsom, William A., 218
Newsome, Lenora, 73
Newson, Leslie A., 2372
Newsweb Corp., 959
Newsweek, Inc., 663
Newton, Blake T., III, 2391
Newton, Don, 1176
Newton, E. Anthony, 840
Newton, Jane, 2707
Newton, Tim, 2044
Newton, Virginia Shanteau, 1764
Next Chapter Holdings, 1073
Nexxus Group, The, 2562
Neyman, Craig, 357
NFL Charities, 2327
NFL Youth Football Fund, 2327
Ng, Chuck Man, 1931
Ng, John, 1931
Ng, Norman, 1931
Nganga, John, 2731
Nguen, Linh C., 1628
Ngunu, Grace, 1692
Nguyen, Nancy, 149
Niblick, Mark S., 1684
Nicely, Donna D., 3129
Nichinson, Brad, 340
Nicholas, Gregory C., 1242
Nicholas, Heidi, 2909
Nicholas, Henry T., III, 344
Nicholas, Mark, 3316
Nicholas, Victor, 34
Nicholls, S. Scott, Jr., 2513
Nichols Co., J.C., 1806
Nichols, Brad, 1198
Nichols, Chris, 1191
Nichols, James R., 1429, 1430
Nichols, Scott G., 278
Nichols, Thomas W., 2040
Nichols, W. Barrett, 1283
Nichols-Young, Stephanie, 3572
Nicholson, Chuck, 1759
Nicholson, Donald W., Jr., 630
Nicholson, James B., 1588, 1638
Nicholson, Jan, 2329
Nicholson, Jim, 488
Nicholson, Marion G., 2329
Nicholson, Nancy A., 1198
Nicholson, Shaun, 2707
Nichter, Susan, 1154
Nickel, Dirk, 1842
Nickel, Mark C., 2392
Nickell, Douglas R., 1812
Nickelson, Donald E., 270
Nickerson, Bruce G., 1336
Nickerson, Mathew D., 3554
Nickerson, Stephanie, 2204
Nickl, Wolfgang, 459
Nicklin, F. Oliver, 1014
Nicol, James, 540
Nicoli, David P., 623
Nicolla, Joseph, 647
Nicols, C. Christine, 3350
Nicorette, 2562
Niebla, J. Fernando, 244
Nieby Revocable Trust, Stanley, 770
Niederauer, Duncan L., 2336
Niedes, Pamela, 2693
Niegelsky, Leon, Jr., 2611
Niegos, Puff, 3163
Niehaus, Kate, 2330
Niehaus, Robert H., 2207, 2330
Nielsen, Katherine D., 1747
Nielsen, Willard D., 1949
Nielson, Jane, 2100
Nielson, Karen, 124
Nielson, Niel, 3146
Niemann, Craig, 1667
Niemeyer, Kenneth E., 18
Niemeyer, W. Phil, 3616
Niemi, William, 391
Niese, Rick, 2682
Niessen, Leo, Jr., 2598
Niessen, Linda C., 1459
Niester, Donna, 1590
Niester, Donna M., 1571
Nightingale, Kay, 3663
Niiya, Eddie, 352
NIKE, Inc., 2865
Nikitine, Vadim, 660
Niles Revocable Trust, Laura J., 597
Niles, Laura Janet, 597
Niley, Mildred, 2148
Nillson, Jenny Lind, 2050
Nilsen, Gunnar K., 275
Nipp, Charles R., 3526
Nippert Trust, Louise Dieterle, 2751
Nippert, Louis, 2751
Nippert, Louise D., 2751
NIR Group, The, 1974
Nisenson, Amy P., 3470
Niskanen, Linda, 1677
NiSource Corporate Services Co., 2752
Nisselson, Alan, 2183
Nita, Dan, 1860
Nitta, John, 3406
Nitta, Rick, 3406
Nix, David, 351
Nix, Virginia, 351
Noah, Sandi, 2759
Nobatian, Soleyman John, 154
Noble Royalties, Inc., 3237
Noble, Alice M., 2753
Noble, Cody, 2822
Noble, David D., 2753
Noble, Donald E., 2753
Noble, Donald, II, 2753
Noble, John W., 630
Noble, Kenneth E., 1042
Noble, Lloyd, 2822
Noble, Matthew, 2753
Noble, Russell, 2822
Noble, Ted, 1105
Nocco, Janinne, 1505
Noce, Walter W. "Bill", Jr., 139
Nochumson, Howard, 1112
Nodelman, Jordan, 617
Nodtvedt, Donald, 3430
Noell, Anne, 2868
Noethling, Rhodara Freyvogel, 2933
Nofer, George, 2895
Nohelty, Susan, 2274
Nohra, Jude, 2804
Nolan, Brian, 543
Nolan, James D., 1505
Nolan, Joseph R., Jr., 598
Noland, Mariam C., 1588
Noland, Sheri, 3568
Nolen, James S., 9
Noll, Pamela D., 2091
Noll, Patricia R., 345
Nolletti, David, 2559
Nolletti, Lara, 2559
Nolt, Sheryl Robins, 3477
Nolte, Anothy M., 3348
Noneman, Joan Carol, 423
Nong, Kristin D., 481
Nonomaque, Curt, 3377
Noon, Prudence J., 342
Noonan, Frank M., 1521
Noonan, Jay, 344
Noone, Laura Palmer, 1174
Nooyi, Indra K., 2354
Norberg, Eric, 1677
Norcia, Jerry, 1598, 1666
Norcross, Elizabeth, 926
Nord, Cindy, 2754
Nord, Eric Charles, 2754
Nord, Shannon, 2754
Nord, Walter G., 2754
Nord, Walter G., Mrs., 2754
Nordeen, Julie S., 3631
Nordeman, Anne, 2122
Nordic Group of Cos., Ltd., 3655
Nordson Corp., 2754, 2755
Nordt, John C., III, 783
Norfleet, Edward A., 2633
Norgard, Susanne, 160
Noriega, Arthur, IV, 757
Norland, Cynthia J., 2652
Norman Foundation, The, 2268
Norman, Alex, 236
Norman, Cynthia D., 1849
Norman, Eleanor, 562
Norman, Greg, Dr., 1131
Norman, Harold, 1209
Norman, Kenneth G., 2611
Norman, Terry, 1124
Norman, Virginia, 4
Normandin, Jim, 1247
Normandy Trust, 3224
Normile, Robert, 312
Nornamdeau, Daniel, 3418
Norquist, S. Griffin, Jr., 1767
Norrington, Margaret, 361
Norrington, Ralph, 361
Norris, David E., 1339
Norris, Jeff, 638
Norris, Jon L., 611
Norris, Stefan, 638
North American Foundation for University of Manchester, 2069
North Central Trust Co., 3631
North Side Bank & Trust Co., 2679
North Star Ventures, 1724
North, Aaron, 1797
North, Elizabeth Hendricks, 1377
Northam, Hazel, 2366
Northeast Nuclear Energy Co., 598
Northeast Utilities, 598
Northen, Mary Moody, 3306
Northern Engraving and Manufacturing Co., 3614
Northern Life Insurance Co., 2488
Northern Manhattan Nursing, 2255
Northern Trust Bank, 798
Northern Trust Bank of Florida, N.A., 801
Northern Trust Co., The, 1019
Northern Trust Company, The, 487, 982
Northrail, 1388
Northrop Grumman Corp., 3465
Northrop, Amanda, 1550
Northrop, Kaaren, 3609
Northrup, Thomas P., 3054
Northshore Mining Co., 2681
Northwest Christian Community Foundation, 2863
Norton, Alice, 1065
Norton, Allison, 3388
Norton, Dale, 1580
Norton, H. Wilbert, Jr., 662
Norton, Jim, 1720
Norton, Peter, 1720
Norton, Richard M., 1025
Norton, Robert E., II, 3601
Norton, Toby, 3388
Norville, Deborah, 2071
Norwick, Greg, 503
Nosbusch, Thomas D., 2652
Nostitz, Drewry H., Mrs., 2565
Nota, Chris, 354
Notis, Tzippy Friedman, 177
Notre Dame High School, 255
Notter, John L., 251
Novak, David C., 1293
Novak, Susan B., 1293
Novak, Wendy L., 1293
Novartis Inc., 2333
Novartis Pharmaceuticals Corp., 1973
Novick, Azriel, 2051
Novick, David, 3648
NoVo Foundation, 2865
Nowak, Betty, 3395
Nowak, Henry, 3395
Nowell, Brenda, 1758
Nowers Fund, Lola E., 842
Nowiszewski, Daniel, 1524
Nowlin, Kelly D., 2454

Nowlin, Newman R., 9
Nowling, Michael, 3510
Noyce Foundation, 175
Noyce Residual Trust, Robert N., 348
Noyce, Elizabeth B., 1334
Noyce, Pendred, 348
Noyce, Pendred E., 1334
Noyes, Charles F., 2335
Ntoumi, Francine, 3516
Nucor Corp., 2601
Null, Audrey C., 2771
Nulsen, Carol, 1683
Nulsen, David, 1683
Nunes, Mary Louise, 1453
Nunes, Paul, 562
Nuness, Al, 1706
Nunn, Sam, 2066
Nunnelly, James T., 1808
Nuorala, Kelsey L., 1656
Nusbaum, Jack H., 2105
Nuss, Henry, 3196
Nussbaum, Samuel R., M.D., 1206
Nusser, Martin, 1280
Nussle, Jim, 3516
NuStar Logistics, L.P., 3307
Nutter McClennen, 1568
Nutter McClennen & Fish LLP, 1427
Nutter, Mary, 2707
Nutting, William O., 3579
Nuzum, Rachel, 2106
NY Community Trust, 3424
Nyberg, Bruce E., 1588
Nye, Homer E., Dr., 1582
Nye, Mark, 948
Nye, Paul, 1176
Nyegaard, Kate, 306
Nygaard, Ellen, 3454
Nyman, George, 1605
Nyman, Jo Elyn, 1605
Nyman, Joelyn, 1604
Nypl, Milan, 3589
Nystrom, William B., 318

O' Connell, Karen, 1436
O' Meara, Tom, 1802
O'Beirne, Lisa, 2199
O'Boyle, Bonnie J., 2962
O'Brein, Charles, 3026
O'Brein, Mari, 3026
O'Brien, Alice, 3163
O'Brien, Ann, 2770
O'Brien, Bill, 3577
O'Brien, Cari, 1729
O'Brien, Edmund, 562
O'Brien, Ida, 250
O'Brien, James A., Esq., 2925
O'Brien, Jeanine, 2037
O'Brien, Jill, 299
O'Brien, John, 3119
O'Brien, John F., 2745
O'Brien, John P., 2770
O'Brien, Kevin, 2037
O'Brien, Michael G., 96
O'Brien, Michelle Atlas, 96
O'Brien, Mike, 989
O'Brien, Mimi, 2529
O'Brien, Norah M., 1638
O'Brien, Paul, 2925
O'Brien, Paul E., 2925
O'Brien, Thomas M., 2292
O'Brien, Tim, 3641
O'Brien, Tina, 2925
O'Brien, William, 617
O'Bryan, Kevin M., 2108
O'Bryan, Sean, 1603
O'Connell, Daniel, 2953
O'Connell, Jane B., 2269
O'Connell, Kathy, 2177
O'Connell, Robert E., 1246
O'Connell, Roseanne, 1428
O'Connor, Amy S., Esq., 2108
O'Connor, James J., 973
O'Connor, John, 1216, 3183
O'Connor, Kate Grubbs, 1025
O'Connor, Kathleen, 1449
O'Connor, Kristen K., 77
O'Connor, Mary Pat, 2382
O'Connor, Natalie Haden, 2588
O'Connor, Raymond, 1837
O'Connor, Rex, 1616
O'Connor, Richard D., 1332
O'Connor, Robert J., 991
O'Connor, Sarane R., 2054
O'Connor, Shelley, 2315
O'Connor, Timothy M., 522
O'Connor, Wendy, 3494
O'Data, Charles N., 2890
O'Day, David C., 2336
O'Donnell, Doris, 2883
O'Donnell, Joyce Christian, 125
O'Donnell, Mark, 2270
O'Donovan Trust A '86, Christine, 641
O'Farrell, Michael K., 163
O'Grady, Judith, 1945
O'Grady, Kathleen, 2339
O'Grady, Kathleen C., 2339
O'Grady, Shawn, 1697
O'Grady, Thomas B., 2339
O'Haire, Edward G., 2474
O'Halloran, Valerie, 3552
O'Hanlon, Dan, 1861
O'Hara, E. Lynne, 422
O'Hara, Elena Lynne, 422
O'Hara, John W., 422
O'Hara, Susan, 442
O'Hare, Tim, 2118
O'Kane, Margaret E., 1489
O'Keefe, Colleen, 1736
O'Keefe, Dan, 2787
O'Keefe, Dorothy, 3116
O'Keefe, Jeffrey, 1755
O'Keefe, Raymond, 2271
O'Kelly, D. Stafford, 954
O'Leary, Christopher, 1697
O'Leary, Denise M., 475
O'Leary, Kathleen, 2752
O'Maley, David B., 2756
O'Malley, Edward V., Jr., 44
O'Malley, Kristin, 1445
O'Mara, Lisa Pratt, 3433
O'Meara, Alice, 342
O'Meara, Steve, 257
O'Neil, Bob, 3666
O'Neil, Brian S., 1949
O'Neil, Jane R., 657
O'Neil, John J., 2409, 2428
O'Neil, Julie, 3666
O'Neil, Lidnsey, 2584
O'Neil, Mary Ann, 1647
O'Neill, Bob, 3666
O'Neill, Brian, 538
O'Neill, Dorothy K., 2760
O'Neill, James, 434
O'Neill, Jill, 1656
O'Neill, Jodi, 1178
O'Neill, John H., 2760
O'Neill, Julie, 3666
O'Neill, Meghan, 3666
O'Neill, Mike, 2071
O'Neill, Molly, 3666
O'Neill, Peter M., 2389
O'Neill, Rita R., 2652
O'Neill, Steven, 1784
O'Neill, Timothy, 2389
O'Neill, Wendy, 2389
O'Neill, William D., 611
O'Neill, William J., Jr., 2760
O'Rourke, James Joc, 1718
O'Rourke, William J., 2882
O'Shaughnessy, Chevonne E., 1725
O'Shaughnessy, Daniel J., 1725
O'Shaughnessy, Eileen A., 1725
O'Shaughnessy, Fran, 2707
O'Shaughnessy, I.A., 1725
O'Shaughnessy, John F., 1725
O'Shaughnessy, John F., Jr., 1725
O'Shaughnessy, Karen J., 1725
O'Shaughnessy, M., 3469
O'Shaughnessy, Mary Hurst, 3469
O'Shaughnessy, Terence P., 1725
O'Shaughnessy, William, 2071
O'Shea, Carole, 352
O'Shea, John P., 352
O'Shea, Mort, 1998
O'Shea, Peggy, 801, 2110
O'Sullivan, James J., 313
O'Tuel, Muriel Ward, 3112
Oak Assocs., 2655
Oak Foundation, 3424
Oak Tree Trust, 994
Oakes, T. Wayne, 3430
Oakey, Jean, 3458
Oakley, Eloy Ortiz, 156
Oakley, James E., III, 3138
Oakley, Jane, 1146
Oaks, Nancy, 216
Oakwood Homes, Inc., 1991
Oakwood Homes, LLC, 498
Oasis Center, 3121
Oates, Joyce Carol, 2194
Obata, Gyo, 1789
Obata, Kiku, 1820
Obenauer, Christie, 2653
Ober, Gayle M., 1698
Oberfeld, Neil, 528
Oberg, Greg, 3568
Obergfell, Brian, 2206
Oberlander, Eileen, 2146
Oberlander, Michael, 707
Oberlin College, 2069
Oberlin, Diane, 1164
Oberlin, E. Clifford, III, 2674
Oberlin, Wendy, 1144
Obermeyer, Michael, 1575
Obermeyer, Michelle Privat, 1575
Obregon, Sarah S., 2259
Obrist, John H., 2940
Obrow, Norman C., 187
Ocanas, J. Reymundo, 3
Oceanside Care Center, 2254, 2255
Ochs, Marilyn, 2609
Ochs, Rita, 490
Ochsner, Lena, 484
Odahowski, David A., 712
Odell, Helen Pfeiffer, 2602
Odell, Mary, 444
Odell, Robert Stewart, 2602
Odell, Virginia Fry, 579
Odendahl, Keith, 2862
Odgers, Richard, 446
Odille, Shelley Taylor, 2685
Odne, Kathleen L., 299
Odom, Carmen Hooker, 1489
Odom, James, 838
Oeken, Ashley Basile, 2770
Oelkers, Scott, 3406
Oelschlager, Debbbie, 3432
Oelschlager, Kathryn Krisch, 3432
Oertel, Anna J., 2773
Oestreicher, Sylvan, 2337
Oetinger, Judith F., 1121
Ofat, Theodore M., 2762
Office of Commissioner of Baseball, 3424
Offit, Sidney, 2050
Oftedal, Gunnhild, 349
Ogawa, Diane Harrison, 2006
Ogden, Henry M., 1998
Ogden, Margaret G., 2032
Ogden, Margaret H., 2338
Ogden, Marilynn, 2648
Ogden, Ralph E., 2338
Ogden, Roger, 2780
Ogie, Elizabeth C., 904
Ogilvie, Andrew, 2696
Oglesby, Sharon, 1218
Ogletree, Sandy, 3356
Ogren, Jennifer, 2488
Ogstrup-Pedersen, Anne-Margrete, 2375
Ohanesian, John R., 3496
Ohio National Financial Svcs., 2756
Ohio National Life Insurance Co., The, 2756
Ohio Power Co., 2657
Ohio State University, 2069
Ohlhausen, Katherine B., 625
Ohlsen, Ronald, 1069
Ohnmacht, Susan, 3342
Ohrstrom, Elias Buchanan, 1597
Oishei Consolidated Trust No. 1, 2340
Oishei Consolidated Trust No. 2, 2340
Oishei, John R., 2340
Okenica, Kathleen, 2297
Okeson, Ken, 2770
Oklahoma Gas and Electric Co., 2823
Okonjo-Iweala, Ngozi, Dr., 2390
Okonow, Dale, 2228
Okum, Nan, 363
Olafsson, Olaf, 2466
Olander, Chris, 1947, 1968
Olazabal, F. David, 729
Olberding, Julie, 2782
Olch, Bradley A., 3401
Old National Bank, 1182
Olderog, Karen, 1223
Oldford, Will G., Jr., 1590
Oldham, Morris Calvin, 3308
Olejniczak, Lon, 1228
Olekszyk, Danielle, 1666
Olesen, Eric, 3648
Oleson, Don, 1649
Oleson, Donald W., 1649
Oleson, Frances M., 1649
Oleson, Gerald, 1649
Oleson, Gerald E., 1649
Oleson, Gerald W., 1649
Olfers, Kristan, 3373
Olfers, Sarah H., 3373
Oliff, James E., 984
OLILVY, 647
Olin Corp., 2603
Olin, John A., 3621
Olinde, Gregory J., 1378
Oliphant, Grant, 2966
Olivares, Rosa, 2466
Olivarri, Leah Pagan, 3196
Olive, J. Terry, 3127

Oliveira, George, 1453
Oliveira, Ron, 3386
Oliver, Alan G., 3144
Oliver, Chris, 1129
Oliver, Elizabeth J., 2717
Oliver, Harry M., Jr., 1081
Oliver, John, 1104
Oliver, Leon J., 598
Oliver, Melvin, 320
Oliver, T. Richey, 3343
Oliverius, Maynard, 1279
Olivia, Blanchard C., 849
Oliwa, Suzanne, 1417
Olmert, Travis, 3099
Olmstead, Nancy, 65
Olmsted, George, 3468
Olmsted, Robert M., 1916, 3418
Olmsted, Sue, 3619
Oloffson, Richard, 1111
Olofson, Elizabeth, 2197
Olsen Charitable Trust, Christian, 794
Olsen, Ed, 2604
Olsen, Erik, 568
Olsen, Homer, 102
Olsen, Howard, 1852
Olsen, Jean B., 1691
Olsen, Lenoard R., Jr., 2983
Olsen, Polly M., 3507
Olsen, Ronald, 718
Olsen, Steve, 1853, 3607
Olson, Beverly Knight, 771
Olson, Catherine Grier, 2588
Olson, Dale, 1836
Olson, Darryl R., 1147
Olson, Douglas, 1187
Olson, Graham, 3633
Olson, Katy, 3606
Olson, Keith, 3498
Olson, Keith D., 1678
Olson, Kelley, 1753
Olson, Kris Kaiser, 3378
Olson, Lyndon, Jr., 3331
Olson, Mike, 1699
Olson, Rick, 1130
Olson, Teresa, 1706
Olson, Thomas L., 3608
Olson, William, 1847
Olsson, Walter, 1585
Olswang, Lesley B., 1190
Olthoff, Kay, 1586
Olwell, Carol, 3389
Olympia Trust, 2371
Oman, Darcy S., 3433
Oman, Richard H., 2765
Omnibus Charitable Trust, 2346
Omnicare, Inc., 2758
Omnicom Group, 3148
Omron Automotive Electronics, Inc., 1070
Omron Electronics Components, LLC, 1070
Omron Electronics Inc., 1070
Omron Electronics LLC, 1070
Omron Healthcare, Inc., 1070
One America, 2562
One Twelve Corp., 1962
Onifer, Karen, 158
Onley, Joy Hall, 1358
Onorato, Don, 2968
Onslow, Deborah, 2108
Opalenik, Maria L., 3374
Operation Days Work, 3158
Oplin, William F. (Bill), 2882
Oppegard, Donald, 2653
Oppenheim, Jane, 3031
Oppenheimer, Alan, 328
Oppenheimer, Steven, 2151
Oppens, Ursula, 2262
Opperman, Dwight D., 350
Opperman, Fane W., 350
Opperman, Vance K., 350
Optinuity Alliance Resources Corporation, 2297
Optivest Inc, 351
Optivest Properties, 351
Optivest Properties Protection, 351
Opus Corp., 1724
Opus, LLC, 1724
Orange Bowl Committee, 2206
Orange Wood Children's Fdn., 235
Oratz, Glenn, 378
Orbach, Dara, 1957
Orband, William J., Jr., 2253
Orchard Crossing III, 498
Orci, Eddie, 1866
Orci, Kim, 1866
Order of the Eastern Star, 2148
Ordiway, Robert, 3009
Oreck, Mira, 2827
Oregon Community Foundation, The, 2850
Oregon Ethiopian Community Organization, 3158
Oremus, Frederick L., 2762
Orenstein, Alexander, 2416
Orenstein, Brian A., 611
Oriel, Pat, 1573
Orkand, Donald, 3424
Orkand, Kim, 3424
Orlik, Darcy, 1647
Orosco, Ardena, 2011
Orosz, Joel, 1579
Orozco, Isaiah, 2345
Orozco, Leslie, 1662
Orr, Adele S., 3309
Orr, Arthur, 2253
Orr, Bartholomew, Rev., 1760
Orr, Bonnie, 2111
Orr, David, 357
Orr, Deano C., 3142
Orr, Franklin M., Jr., Dr., 332
Orr, Robert O., 2761
Orr, San W., Jr., 3601, 3661
Orr, Susan Packard, 357
Orr, Waldon H., 3309
Orrell, Paula, 364
Orrock, Nan Grogan, Hon., 911
Orsemigo, Paul R., 755
Orsinger, Genevieve McDavitt, 3310
Orsino, Jeannette M., 1426
Orszag, Peter R., 1949
Ort, Frances, 926
Ortberg, Robert K., 1237
Orth, Sarah, 363
Ortho Biotech Inc., 1948
Ortho Womens Health & Urology, 1948
Ortho-McNeil Pharmaceutical, Inc., 1948
Ortiz, Diane, 159
Ortiz, Jorge, 1031
Ortwein, Linda G., 1531
Orzechowski, Barbara F., 1240
Osagie, Emmanuel, 2923
Osberg, Sally, 412, 413
Osborn, Casey H., 3680
Osborn, Frederick H., III, 2113
Osborn, Gay, 1950
Osborn, Robin, 2106
Osborn, Stanley, 1709
Osborn, Susan J., 3680
Osborne Building Corp., 3147
Osborne Enterprises, Inc., 3147
Osborne, Dee, 2876
Osborne, Duncan E., 2007
Osborne, Karen, 2732
Osbourn, Teresa, 2604
Osco-Bingeman, Gigi, 465
Oseland, Lucille, 1212
Osgood, Kimberly, 2297
Oshei, Jean R., 2340
Oshei, R. John, 2340
Osheowitz, Michael W., 2188
Osheyack, Daniel J., 2466
Oshkosh Corp., 3643
Oshkosh Truck Corp., 3643
Oshlo, Rick, 537
Oshsner, Robert, 484
Osiason, Lee J., 729
Osmer, Patrick S., 59
Osmon, Dave, 1128
Osprey Investment Partners, 2655
Ostahowski, Mark, 1573
Ostrich, Rabbi David, 2909
Ostrie, Seth, 2037
Ostrow, Gary J., 1502, 3554
Otero, Maria, 1631
Otis, Clarence, Jr., 732
Otolski, Erin, 212
Ott, Alan W., 1653
Ott, Luther, 1759
Ottaway Jr. Trust, James, 2111
Otten, Laura, 2932
Ottenheimer, Gus, 71
Ottenheimer, Leonard J., 71
Otterlei, John, 2211
Ottersbach, Leah, 1292
Ottinger, Ronald, 348
Ottley, Marian W., 923
Ottmar, Steve, 2653
Ottosen, Barbara, 56
Ottosen, Barbara J., 56
Ottosen, Donald R., 56
Ouchi, William G., 251
Ouellett, Neal, 1885
Out of the Shell, LLC, 399
Outhwaite Revocable Trust, 1994 June G., The, 353
Outpost, 1388
Ouvrard, Hubert Pierre, 3438
Ouyalady Corporation, 2512
Oveland, Greg, 3326
Overdeer, Bill, 1209
Overholser, Geneva, 678
Overman, Bev, 1852
Overmyer, Michael, 1176
Overmyer-Velazquez, Mark, 2391
Overstreet, Jane, 1267
Overstreet, Jane, Dr., 487
Overton, Jeffery, 1866
Overton, Suellen, 1226
Owen, Bethany M., 1693
Owen, Brad, 1279
Owen, Gwen P., 3124
Owen, Jay L., 677
Owen, Mack, 3287
Owen, Mary M., 1675
Owen, Mike, 2543
Owen, Norman, 347, 397
Owen, Samantha, 408
Owen, Sarah, 823
Owens, Christopher, 2543
Owens, Donna, 2472
Owens, Elizabeth H., 3251
Owens, Kenneth R., 903
Owens-Illinois, Inc., 2678
Owlbear Industries Inc., 427
Ownbey, Ron, 68
Oxford League, Inc., The, 1893
Oxley, Kevin, 1623
Oxman, Stephen A., 2085
Oyens, Felix, 2069
Oyler, Tennyson S., 355
Ozbirn, Bob, 420
Ozer, Esra, 2882
Ozimek, Michael, 2407

P'Pool, William C., 1039
P.N.C. Bank, N.A., 1347
Pabalan, Steven S., 783
PACCAR, Inc., 2445
Pace, Peter, 2228
Pacesetter Systems, Inc., 757
Pacific Coast Construction Co., 215
Pacific Gas and Electric Co., 354
Pacific Gas and Electric Company, 367
Pacific Hospital Assn., 2866
Pacific Life Insurance Co., 355
Pacific Mutual Holding Co., 355
Pacific Technical Resources, 2562
Pacific Vascular Research Foundation, 186
PacificSource Health Plans, 2866
Paciulan, Eleanora, 1519
Pack, Gary, 3139
Pack, James, 867
Packard Foundation, David and Lucile, The, 332
Packard, David, 332, 357
Packard, Julie, 1683
Packard, Julie E., 332, 357
Packard, Lucile, 357
Packer Trust, Horace B., 3008
Packer, Don, 162
Packer, Horace B., 3008
Padar, Ed, 3266
Padgett, Joe, 714
Padgett, Joy, 2702
Padha, Adi, 569
Padmanabhan, Ram, 963
Pagan, Roberto, 3061
Pagano, Michael T., 2449
Page, Amy Hattler, 3453
Page, Arthur, 1539
Page, Clarence, 653
Page, David K., 1588
Page, Easter, 2790
Page, John, 235
Page, Kenneth R., 2479
Page, Lawrence, 231
Page, Lawrence C., Sr., 1651
Page, Louise Knapp, 2259
Page, Patrick, 2113
Pagonis, Koula, 1048
Pahl, Janet, 1868
Pahl, Leone M., 3594
Paige, Michele A., 2408
Pain, George H., 2603
Paine Foundation, Martin S., 2479
Paine, Peter, 2027
Painter, Dean E., Jr., 2599
Painter, William S., 1756
Pakradooni, Peter B., 2919
Palacios, Carlos, 163
Palandjian, Tracy, 2454
Palank, Angelica, 795
Palank-Sharlet, Angelica, 795
Palenchar, David J., 492
Palermo, James D., 734
Palfrey, John, 771

Paliotta, Mike, 2118
Palkhiwala, Akash, 376
Palladino, Charles F., 3017
Palladino, Steve, 1569
Palleon, Kim, 3656
Paller, Alan T., 1389
Paller, Channing, 1389
Paller, Marsha, 1389
Palm Beach Kennel Club, 3026
Palma, Robert A., 2762
Palmer, Bruce A., 2986
Palmer, Cynthia S., 1358
Palmer, David, 3662
Palmer, Denise, 1107
Palmer, Kelli E., 3428
Palmer, Mark, 3257
Palmer, Mary, 677
Palmer, Pauline E., 2058
Palmer, Rebekah T., 3134
Palmer, Rick, 3551
Palmer, Rogers, 677
Palmer, Roy, 1754
Palmer, Sheryl Rogers, 3339
Palmer, Susan, 3257
Palmer, Virginia, 600
Palmer-Erbs, Victoria, 1540
Palmisano, Samuel J., 2066, 2227
Palmore, Roderick A., 1697
Palumbo, A.J., 3009
Palumbo, Antonio J., 3009
Palumbo, Joseph, 3009
Palumbo, P.J., 3009
Palumbo, Steven, 3411
Paluzzi, Mary Bess, 11
Palzkill, Mary T., 971
Pamida, Inc., 3644
Pamperin, David Z., 3619
Panamaroff, Jon, 36
Panas, Gary, 331
Panatopoulos, Brady, 942
Pancoast, Terrence R., 2874
Pandl, Therese, 3619
Paneak, Raymond, 28
Panepinto, Robert, 724
Panico, Greg, 1948
Panigel, Michael, 1993
Pankonin, Lori, 1851
Pankonin, Phil, 1848
Pankow Family Trust of 1976, 3548
Pankow, Charles J., 3548
Pansing, Thomas R., 1840
Pantaleo, Peter, 2905
Pantalone, Brenda M., 2603
Panzirer, David, 2207
Panzirer, Walter, 2207
Papa, Barzella, 725
Papa, Joseph C., 1655
Papa, Mario J., 2156
Papandrea, Louis M., 2156
Papasan, Katie, 69
Pape, Jean W., 2287
Pape, Kathy, 2952
Pape, Stuart, 3424
Paperin, Stewart J., 2343
Papp, Rosellen C., 44
Pappas, Sarah, 816
Paquette, Heather, 1330
Paquette, Jennifer, 483
Paracha, Bilal, 1432
Paradis, Gina, 2331
Paradis, J.A., 1283
Paradise Beverages Inc., 85
Paragon Die & Engineering Co., 1627
Pardee Foundation, Elsa U., 1652
Pardee, Elsa U., 1653
Pardes, Herbert, 2290
Pardini, Jim, 193
Pardoe Trust, Helen P., 1522
Pardoe, Charles E., 1522
Pardoe, Charles H., II, 1522
Pardoe, Edward D., III, The Rev., 2479
Pardoe, Prescott Bruce, 1522
Pardoe, Samuel P., 1522
Parent, William M., 1436
Parilli, Orestes, 3179
Paris, Alex E., 3054
Paris, Kate, 3126
Paris, Nancy M., 876
Paris, Steven, Dr., 1888
Parish Irrevocable Trust, Suzanne U.D., 1654
Parish, Amy, 1896
Parish, Ivy, 1719
Parish, P. William, 1654
Parish, Preston L., 1654
Parish, Richard L., 796
Parish, Richard L., III, 796
Parish, Richard L., Jr., 796
Parish, Suzanne U.D., 1654
Park Clipper Leasing Associates, 2157
Park Grove Realty Co., 1388
Park National Bank, The, 2723
Park Roads Shopping Centerporter By, 2535
Park Terrace Care Center, 2254, 2255
Park, C.S., 408
Park, Charlotte, 3362
Park, Denten, 2010
Park, Hyun, 367
Park, Linda, 3558
Park, Roy H., 2349
Parker Foundation, Theodore Edson, The, 1505
Parker, Adelaide, 2407
Parker, Alan S., 588
Parker, Ann, 2578
Parker, Arthur H., 1543
Parker, David, 1472
Parker, DeAnne, 401
Parker, Desiree, 1701
Parker, Eugene J., 3104
Parker, John, 1290
Parker, John B., 2908
Parker, John S., 15
Parker, Jon, 3520
Parker, Josh, 2188
Parker, Kay, 3308
Parker, Latanae R., Jr., 783
Parker, Leroy, 1366
Parker, Linda J., 3434
Parker, Lyn, 1519
Parker, Maclyn T., 1127
Parker, Pam, 11
Parker, Patrick, 2028
Parker, Renee Brown, 2795
Parker, Richard, 1176
Parker, Richard C., 860
Parker, Robert S., 2632
Parker, Ruth F., 2773
Parker, Scott, 3318
Parker, Sean, 259
Parker, Theodore Edson, 1523
Parker, Timothy, 1614
Parker, Vickie, 1189
Parker, Virginia, 2612
Parker, Wilson H., 1
Parker-Moore, Jennifer, 1603
Parkerson, Alice B., 1316
Parkes, Freta, 3364
Parkinson, Catherine, 949
Parkinson, Geoffrey M., 596, 597
Parkinson, Molly O., 2479
Parkison, Kathy, Dr., 1160
Parks, Alan, 2844
Parks, Floyd L., 1612
Parks, Judy, 1851
Parks, Martin "Skip", 2387
Parks, Rosemary T., 1525
Parks, Sallie, 801
Parks, Shannon, 2882
Parks, T. David, 1525
Parks-Stamm, Elizabeth J., 1525
Parkview Christian Church, 996
Parkway, Reilly, 3333
Parman, Robert A., 2824
Parmelee, Brian, 268
Parmenter, Nancy, 1603
Parners Investing in Nursing's Future, 1940
Parr, Martha Sue, 1072
Parra, Ivan Kohar, 2521
Parravano, Carlo, 1966
Parris, Lori, 346
Parrish Medical Center, 3377
Parrish, Bill, 3158
Parrish, Cynthia V., 2710
Parrish, Debra L., 175
Parrish, Edna, 1229
Parrish, Lee H., 2710
Parrish, Margaret, 3158
Parrish, Tom, 3152
Parrott, James M., Jr., 2599
Parrott, Rex, 2733
Parrott, Vann K., 869
Parry, Frances, 2790
Parry, Gwyn P., 253
Parry, Virginia, 2749
Parry-Okeden, Blair, 916
Parsons, Anna, 946
Parsons, David W., 25
Parsons, Donald F., 637
Parsons, Marvin, 3589
Parsons, Mary Morton, 3470
Parsons, Morgan, 2683
Parsons, Ralph M., 359
Parsons, Richard D., 2390
Parsons, Rick, 69
Parsons, Robert W., Jr., 1944
Parsons, Roger B., 1944
Parsons, Stefani, 3504
Parsons, Stephen, 36
Parsons, Stu, 2723
Parsons, Susan E., 1167
Parthe, Mary, 1078
Partin, Ron, 2539
Partners Investing in Nursing's Future, 3476
Partridge, Barbara Leigh, 393
Partridge, H. Roy, Jr., 1339
Parzen, Ted, 373
Parzych, Cheryl A., 2950
Paschal, Justin, 259
Pascoe, Virgilio Perez, 900
Pascuzzi, Michael, 3113
Pashcow, Joel, 2476
Pashcow, Joel M., 1925
Paskoski, Joe, 805
Pasky, Cynthia J., 1588
Pasquerella, Mark, 1957
Pasquerilla, Mark E., 2922
Pass-Durham, Deborah S., 722
Passama, Gary, 419
Passe, Kevin, 1731
Passmore, Norm, 3498
Pastor, Ben, 3081
Patagonia Resources, LLC, 1524
Patagonia, Inc., 362
Patel, Jigs, 2445
Patel, Kiran C., 797
Patel, Pallavi C., 797
Patel, Sandip, 550
Patel, Sheetal, 797
Patel, Shilen, 797
Paterson, Jane R., 1040
Patience, 1388
Patillo, Bree, 884
Patillo, Kathleen B., 885
Patino, Douglas X., 1645, 3500
Patke, Susan, 1013
Patkotak, Crawford, 28
Patmon, Charles G., 161
Patmon, Dorothy N., 161
Patricia, Jenny, 2325
Patrick, Bill, 41
Patrick, Brian, 1828
Patrick, Charles F., 166
Patrick, Donna, 3589
Patrick, Geraldine A., 902
Patrick, Hilda B., 902
Patrick, Howard, 725
Patrick, Joseph E., Jr., 885, 902
Patrick, Joseph E., Sr., 902
Patrick, Mike, 393
Patrick, Shari L., 2390
Patrino, Melissa, 340
Pattee, Susan, 544
Patten, Kathryn M., 2763
Patten, Sammy, 749
Patterson Foundation, Cissy, 678
Patterson Trust No. 2, Robert, 601
Patterson Trust, Dorothy C., 798
Patterson, Alicia, 678
Patterson, Anne, 1269, 1349, 1350
Patterson, Aubrey Abbott, 1260
Patterson, Clara Guthrie, 601
Patterson, Craig W., 1269
Patterson, Cynthia B., 1498
Patterson, Deborah J., 1803
Patterson, Dorothy Clarke, 798
Patterson, Fleming, 3096
Patterson, Frances, 3099
Patterson, Jack, 1634
Patterson, James J., 798
Patterson, Jane, 1591
Patterson, John A., 1849
Patterson, Joyce, 3100
Patterson, Lisa, 1052
Patterson, Mark Elliot, 1269
Patterson, Melissa, 1646
Patterson, Patrick, III, 31
Patterson, Richard B., 1112
Patterson, Robert Leet, 601
Patterson, Robin F., 3480
Patterson, W.I., 3010
Pattillo Split Interest Trust, 905
Pattillo, H.G., 884
Pattillo-Cohen, Lynn L., 905
Pattis Family Investments, 1073
Pattis, Bette L., 1073
Pattis, Mark, 1073
Pattis, Mark R., 1073
Pattis, S. William, 1073
Patton Boggs, LLP, 3424
Patton, James B., 860
Patton, Jim, 3249
Patton, Sara L., 2798
Patyrak, Robert S., 3343
Paul, Douglas L., 2118

Paul, Josephine Bay, 2056
Paul, Linda, 1989
Paul, Marie, 31
Paule, Mike, 158
Pauley, Matt, 2707
Pauls, Celia M., 147
Paulsen, Thomas R., 1221
Paulson, Amanda Clark, 970
Paulson, Hank M., Jr., 2066
Paulson, Henry M., Jr., 970
Paulson, Henry Merritt, III, 970
Paulson, John, 2351
Paulson, Ken, 662
Paulson, Richard A., 2801
Paulson, Wendy J., 970
Pauly, Katie Kavanaugh, 3503
Pava, Jeremy, 1479
Pavlatos, Plato, 2787
Pavloff, Andrew, 2111
Pavloff, Jonathan, 2741
Pavlovsky, Yelena, 2371
Pawling Charitable Lead Annuity Trust, 2353
Paxson Morrison Eduction Fund, Hazelle, 792
Paxton Trust, Alice A., 2352
Paxton, Jay L., 309
Paxton, Jim, 159
Payless ShoeSource, Inc., 1253
Payne Family Foundation, 262
Payne, Brian, 1126
Payne, Christy, 3237
Payne, John, 1860
Payne, Marilyn, 167
Payne, Rebecca K., 262
Payne, Susan K., 3428
Paynter, Larry, 1157
Payson, Jonathan, 1464
PCCS, Inc., 3549
Peach, Richard, 1012
Peacock, Deborah, 2006
Peacock, Greg, 2265
Peak, Martha H., 1343
Peale Trust, Ruth S., 2353
Peale, John S., 2353
Pean, Jean Christophe, 312
Pearce, Gary B., 3268
Pearce, Rick, 2737
Pearl Assocs., 3376
Pearl, Julius, 131
Pearlman, Lowell R., 2540
Pearson Financial Group, 2863
Pearson Foundation, 255
Pearson, Cincy, 1896
Pearson, Jackie, 3163
Pearson, Jim, 1128
Pearson, Jonathan R., 1940
Pearson, Nils, 3249
Peca, Michael, 2078
Pechacek, Frank, 1235
Peck, Bob, 103, 104
Peck, Gary, 2947
Peck, Katherine, 502
Peck, M. Elaine, 1189
Peck, Marni L., 1244
Peck, Robert, 656
Peckham, Judith C., 2253
Peddicord, Kitty, 651
Peddie, Susannah, 725
Peden, Janet, 3245
Pedersen, Anne-Mare, 292
Pedersen, Kathryn, 545
Pederson, Sally, 1722
Pedigree Brand, 3148
Pedlow, Joyce, 3571
Pedroso, Luis, 1505
Pedrozzi, Mario, 364
Peebles, Jami S., 1783
Peebles, Sue, 1204
Peel, Madalynne L., 2825
Peeler, Clifford, 2606
Peeler, Larry, 2606
Peeples, Audrey R., 982
Peeples, P.G., Sr., 1282
Peeples, Vernon, 718
Peet, Shelly, 2755
Peetz, Sarah, 1847
Pegram, Jeffrey K., 2391
Peiffer, Garry L., 2700
Peine, Caroline F., 3313
Peirce, Mary, 2780
Peithmann, William A., 1118
Pejeau, Larry, 1124
Pekarek, Nancy K., 2957
Pekor, Allan J., 778
Pelaez, Marc Y.E., 2974
Pelissero, Deborah S., 335
Pelissero, Goodwin J., 335
Pelizzon, David, Col., 1078
Pellegrino, Frank, 2947
Pellegrino, James, 674
Pellegrom, Dan, 2673
Pelletier, David, 564
Pelletier, Jean, 1099
Pelletier, Marc S., 563
Pelletier, Sandra, 1883
Pelone, Frank, 2904
Pelster, Carla, 3567
Peltekian, Elizabeth M., 656
Peltier, Valerie S., 2325
Peltz, Charles, 1602
Pelzer, Robert E., 2333
Pemberton, Gayle, 2192
Pemberton, Gregory L., 1204
Pemberton, Margaret A., 1101
PEMCO Corp., 3549
PEMCO Mutual Insurance Co., 3549
PEMCO Technology Services, Inc., 3549
Pen, Sophia, 292
Pena, David B., 2044
Pence, Margaret Hall, 1793
Pence, Terry, 3201
Pender, Michael R., Jr., 727
Pendergast, Mary Louise Weyer, 1807
Pendergast, Thomas J., Jr., 1807
Pendergraft, Neal R., 1869
Pendergrass, David S., 2488
Pendleton, Ryan, 2664
Pendrey, J.C., Jr., 887
Penguin Group, 2562
Penick, Edward M., Sr., 71
Penland, Joe, Sr., 3314
Penland, Linda, 3314
Penn Security Bank & Trust Co., 3031
Penn, Anne, 37
Penn, J. Scottie, 2611
Penn, Magaly, 3099
Penn, Marian, 91
Penna, Katherine S., 2125
Pennell, Colleen, 294
Pennell, Karen, 3016
Penney Co., J.C., Inc., 3315
Penney Corp., J.C., Inc., 3315
Penney, Ron, 1783
Pennick, Aurie A., 1014
Pennington, C.B., 1317
Pennington, Claude B., III, 1317
Pennington, Daryl B., Jr., 1317
Pennington, Daryl B., Sr., 1317
Pennington, Hilary, 2160
Pennington, Irene W., 1317
Pennington, Sharon Palmer, 1317
Pennoyer, Christy, 2079, 2204
Pennoyer, Peter, 2504
Pennoyer, Robert, 2079
Pennoyer, Russell, 2191
Pennoyer, Russell P., 2026
Pennoyer, Tracy, 2079
Pennsylvania State Bank, 2952
Penrose, Spencer, 492
Penrose, Spencer, Mrs., 492
Pensec, Bob, 1175
Penson Financial Services, 1974
Pentair, Inc., 1727
Penton, Cat, 1225
People Magazine, 2476
Peoples Bank, The, 1275
Pepe, Cathy, 394
Pepin, Susan M., 57
Peppard, Denise, 3465
Pepper, Anthony M., 606
Pepper, J. Stanley, 1060
Pepper, Jane G., 2948
Peppes, Greg, 1255
Peppis, Paul, 424
Pepple, William, 2674
Pepsi Cola & National Brand Beverage, 2970
Pepsico, 2562, 3565
Pepsico, Inc., 186
PepsiCo, Inc., 2354
PepsiCola North America, 2574
Percontee, Inc., 1376
Percy, Brett, 2766
Percy, David, 2766
Percy, Kevin, 2766
Percy, Lisa, 1766
Percy-Falls, Jennifer, 2766
Perelman, Debra G., 2355
Perelman, Hope G., 2355
Perelman, Joshua G., 2355
Perelman, Raymond G., 3012, 3013
Perelman, Ronald O., 2355
Perelman, Steven G., 2355
Perenchio, A. Jerrold, 150
Perenchio, Margaret A., 150
Perera, Frederica, 1514
Peretto, Bo, 488
Peretz, Amiel M., 2068
Peretz, Anne, 2481
Peretz, Anne L., 2099
Peretz, Dylan M., 2068
Peretz, Michelle Young, 2068
Peretz, Taylor M., 2068
Perez, Beatriz, 864
Perez, Debra Joy, 1353
Perez, Eladio, 3179
Perez, Gloria, 1717
Perez, John, Comm., 363
Perez, Lillian, 1692
Perez, Paul, 722
Perez, Ray, 1274
Perfection Products, Inc., 2562
Perigo, Seth, 1163
Perille, Christopher, 1039
Perin, Keith, 1192
Perine, Jorli, 188
Perkin, Sylvia, 2607
Perkins, Benjamin F., 3678
Perkins, Donald, 1764
Perkins, Elvin, 1257
Perkins, Irene, 161
Perkins, Jayne, 1170
Perkins, Jimmie, 2874
Perkins, Maurice, 2673
Perkins, Paul, 161
Perkins, Susie, 1180
Perkins, Thomas J., 365
Perkins, William B., 1539
Perkins, William C., 1618
Perlman, Ira, 29
Perlman, Jeffrey F., 1979
Perlman, Nancy, 1328
Perlman, Noah, 2282
Permaul, Jane S., 301
Perna, Janet, 602
Perniconi, Mark J., 3548
Perot, Bette, 3317
Perot, H. Ross, 3317
Perot, H. Ross, Jr., 3317
Perot, Margot B., 3317
Perpich, Joseph G., 2192
Perpich, Michael J., Dr., 3438
Perraud, Steve, 3483
Perrigo Co., 1655
Perrin, Charles, 603
Perrin, Charles R., 603
Perrin, David B., 603
Perrin, Jeffrey L., 603
Perrin, Sheila, 603
Perrin, Sheila A., 603
Perrine, Esther M., 3238
Perrotte, Alisa, 1096
Perrotte, Andrew, 1096
Perrotty, P. Sue, 2893
Perry, Anthony, 993
Perry, Erinn, 3414
Perry, J. Marc, 3663
Perry, Jack, 1687
Perry, Jeff, 1203
Perry, Judy K., 62
Perry, Lorraine F., 136
Perry, Mauree Jane, 652
Perry, Peyton F., 2232
Perry, Richard J., Jr., 3622
Perry, Roger, 1616
Perry, Sam, 1849
Perry, Stephen A., 2788
Perry, Susan, 1464
Perry, Taylor, 3580
Perry, Wes, 3160
Perschevitch, Elizabeth, 366
Pershing Square Capital Mgmt., 2356
Pershing, Richard, 448
Persing, Melissa, 1751
Persinger, Darrell, 1132
Persinger, Kyle, 1129
Person, Norma J., 197
Personal Management Consultants Inc, 1866
Persons, Nona, 58
Persson, Vicky, 3552
Pertile, Anthony, 983
Pertzik, Marvin J., 2571
Peruggi, Regina S., 2204
Pessin, Fern, 613
Pestronk, Robert, 1646
Peszynski, Andrew F., 366
Peszynski, I.G., 366
Peter, Arthur L., 423
Peter, James B., Jr., 423
Peter, Joan C., 423
Peter, Joshua, 34
Peters, Andrew, 2078
Peters, Ann, 1883
Peters, Barbara, 1683
Peters, Barry, 3494

Pioneer Fund, The, 505
Piper Industries, Inc., 3186
Piper, Gretchen, 1717
Piper, Lynn, 3186, 3671
Piper, Mary, 3671
Piper, Paul, 3671
Piper, Paul P., 3671
Piper, Paul P., Jr., 3186
Piper, Paul P., Mrs., 3186
Piper, Paul P., Sr., 3186
Piper, Paul, Jr., 3186
Piper, Ronald K., 3671
Piper, Shirley, 3186
Piper, Virginia G., 57
Piper, William H., 1645
Pipp, Inc., 832
Piqunik Management Corp., 28
Piro, James J., 2867
Pisano, Carol, 2206
Pisano, Jane G., 243
Piselli, Elain, 1436
Piszek, Edward J., Jr., 2928
Piszek, Edward J., Sr., 2928
Piszek, George W., 2928
Piszek, William P., 2928
Pitcairn, Robert A., Jr., 2720
Pitkin, Sarah, 3471
Pitluk, Marvin J., 968
Pitman, Donne W., 2808
Pitman, Norman D., III, 18
Pitman, Norman D., Jr., 10
Pitney Bowes Inc., 604
Pitrone, Gina L., 3467
Pittelman, Carole, 2283
Pittman, Dana W., 1224
Pittman, Tom, 1760
Pitts, Francis Murdock, 2108
Pitts, Margaret A., 904
Pitts, William I.H., 904
Pittsburgh Steelers, 3026
Pivnick, Isadore, 430
Pivtorak Family Trust, 2371
Pivtorak, Vitaly, 2371
Pizzico, Kellie MacDonald, 1961
Places Inc., 628
Plager, Anna, 26
Plain, Brian, 1068
Plangere KCA Charitable Trust, The, 802
Plangere KRDJ Charitable Trust, The, 802
Plangere, Jules L., III, 802
Plangere, Jules L., Jr., 802
Plangere, Jules, Jr., 802
Plank, Desiree Jacqueline, 1363
Plank, Kevin A., 1363
Plank, Lollie Benz, 3684
Plank, Michael, 538
Plansoen, Hector L., 2608
Planters LifeSavers Co., 2613
Plass, Thyra, 3322
Plati, Crystal, 501
Platt, Daniel, 378
Platt, Susan, 1125
Platte Valley Medical Center, 484
Platter, Gerald, 1976
Platts, H. Gregory, 3481
Platts, Robin, 1370
Plautz, Dana, 2868
Plaxco, Barry, 3201
Playfair, Larry, 2078
Plaza Cleaning Service Co. II LP, 2157
Pledger, James E., Dr., 3292
Plemmons, Glenn, 2835
Plepler, Andrew D., 2524
Pletka, Irene, 2360
Pletka, Peter, 2360
Plevo, Frank, 1953
Plimpton, David L., 2204
Plisco, Mary Alice, 747
Plitt, Clarence M., 1404
Plotkin, Amanda, 2411
Plotkin, Carolyn, 2411
Plotkin, Fred, 2411
Plotkin, Janet, 2411
Plotkin, Jonathan, 2411
Plotts, David, 1359
Plough, Alonzo L., 1459
Plourde, Sally, 1519
Plukas, John M., 1461
Plum Corp., 2935
Plum, Susan Butler, 2197, 2427
Plumb, John K., 2225
Plumley, Mary Ann, 162
Plummer, Burke, 58
Plump, Jim, 1132
Plung, Louis, 2889
Plunkett, Ann C., 2966
Plunkett, L. Richard, 914
Plunkett, Mary, 3628
PNC, 2900, 3026
PNC Advisors, 3031
PNC Bank, 2788, 2996
PNC Bank, N.A., 1173, 1596, 1626, 2679, 2743, 2768, 2897, 2914, 2929, 2930, 2938, 2946, 2952, 2965, 2994, 2995, 2999, 3004, 3005, 3007, 3009, 3037, 3039, 3041, 3048, 3058
PNM Fund, 2016
Poage, Ray, 3174
Pobiner, Herbert, 1901
Pocalyko, Paul W., 3006
Pochal, Susan, 562
Pocilujko, Bill, 235
Podoll, Christopher J., 1249
Poe, Amy, 3383
Poe, Charles S., 3383
Poff, Jim, 3552
Pogue Foundation, The, 3207
Pogue, Ann, 3207
Pogue, Blake, 3207
Pogue, Jack, 3207
Pogue, John L., 2799
Pogue, Richard W., 2721
Pohl, Lynn, 1647
Pohl, Nicola, 59
Pohlad, Rebecca, 3555
Pohlman, Steve, 714
Poinier, Carol, 3014
Poirot, Rhonda, 3201
Poliak, Joan B., 3499
Policinski, Gene, 662
Polikov, Lee, 1848
Polinger Family Foundation, Howard & Geraldine, 1414
Polinger Family Trust, Geraldine, 1405
Polinger, Arnold Lee, 1405
Polinger, David Marc, 1405
Polinger, Geraldine, 1405
Polinger, Geraldine H., 1405
Polinger, Howard, 1405
Polinger, Jan, 1405
Polinger, Lorre Beth, 1405
Polisi, Joseph W., 2492
Polisseni, Gary, 2361
Polisseni, Gregory, 2361
Polisseni, Wanda, 2361
Polizzotto, Joseph, 2134
Polk Bros., Inc., 1075
Polk, Cheryl, 375
Polk, David D., 1075
Polk, Harry, 1075
Polk, Howard J., 1075
Polk, Morris G., 1075
Polk, Samuel H., 1075
Polk, Sol, 1075
Pollack, Anjali, 612
Pollack, Michael, 612
Pollak, Joseph E., 1399
Pollard, Alison, 1584
Pollard, Norval, 3287
Pollet, Paula D., 525
Polley, William, 420
Pollin, Lauren K., 1384
Pollinger, Amy, 2258
Pollock, Grace, 2362
Pollock, Lindsay Kathryn, 2362
Pollock, Robert, 2047
Pollock, S. Wilson, 2362
Pollpeter, Susan C., 2538
Polly, Linda, 3577
Polsky, Alex, 268
Polsky, Larry, 2584
Poltack, Rupal M., 1889
Poma, Frank, 1590
Pomerance, Mitchell, 1564
Pomerantz, Kathleen, 2256
Pomeroy, Claire, Dr., 405
Pomeroy, Katherine, 564
Pompa, Delia, 360
Pompadur, I. Martin, 2071
Pompetzki, George, 1988
Pon, Joseph M., 88
Ponce, Ana Marie, 157
Ponchick, Elizabeth T., 100
Ponchick, Elliot, 100
Pond, Tracie L., 1483
PonTell, Steve, 138
Pontikes, Melissa, 1044
Pontikes, Nicholas K., 1044
Ponting, Wendy, 3637
Pontzer, Deborah, 3042
Pool, Philip B., Jr., 2459, 2460
Poole, Chris, 268
Poole, Joe, 3488
Poole, John S., 3110
Poole, Steven W., 1611
Poonawala, Akbar, 2134
Poor, Mary A., 1427
Poore, Gary, 1259
Poore, Price, 1406
Poorman, Kevin, 1080
Pope Life Foundation, Lois, The, 779
Pope, Amanda Joyce, 2610
Pope, David, 1620
Pope, Ed, Rev., 3430
Pope, James Arthur, 2610, 3601
Pope, Joyce W., 2610
Pope, Juliette R., 2036
Pope, Kathy, 1607
Pope, Lois B., 779, 803
Pope, Lona, 900
Pope, Marsha, 1279
Pope, Paul D., 779
Pope, Sarah A., 2036
Popoff, Frank P., 2033
Popofsky, Mark, 676
Popp, Connie, 3604
Port, Clyde W., 3112
Port, Jennifer D., 554
Port, Neil, 2907
Portago, Carolina, 2358
Portago, Theodora, 2358
Portanova, Margarete Anne, 1509
Portaro, Sam A., Jr., Rev., 1081
Portcullis Partners, L.P., 3301
Porter Charitable Trust, Lucile, 1065
Porter, A. Alex, 2194
Porter, Andrew C., 2191
Porter, Barbara, 1735
Porter, Betty Robins, 3477
Porter, Biggs C., 3235
Porter, Charles, 2889
Porter, David, III, 3158
Porter, Ellen, 646
Porter, Grant, 2459, 2460
Porter, Keith, 1217
Porter, Martha A., 1101
Porter, Mary L., 2405
Porter, Patricia A., 3275
Porter, Reid, 646
Porter, Robert C., Jr., 2680
Porter, Robert, III, 2680
Porter, Susan J., 2780
Porteus, Beccy, 2686
Portland General Electric Co., 2867
Portnoi, Lee, 3158
Portnoy, James, 1064
Portoghese, Joseph D., 842
Portugal, Susan, 2524
Portz, Jay J., 1750
Portz, Ronny, 2803
Porzecanski, Arturo C., 2467
Posillico Foundation, 2228
Posillico, Paul, 2228
Posin, Esther, 2046
Poss, Todd, 3631
Post Traditional High Yield Fund, 3642
Post, Cynthia S., 1978
Post, Dave, 1587
Post, Gary, 605
Post, Glen F., III, 1978
Post, Ron, 2863
Post, Stephen G., 3047
Post-Newsweek Stations, 663
Poster, Dennis B., 552
Poteat, Jennifer, 1576
Poteat, Victor P., 693
Potter, Charles S., Jr., 1060
Potter, Charlie, 3654
Potter, Delcour S., 2271
Potter, Earl, Dr., 1703
Potter, Elizabeth Stone, 2408
Potter, Nancy, 2112
Pottruck, Emily Scott, 3401
Potts, Cheryl, 9
Potts, Thomas S., Jr., 9
Pouch, Robert H., 2289
Poucher, John S., 353
Poulos, Catherine M. Creticos, 1112
Poulson, Patricia D., 1122
Pouschine, Tatiana, 2026
Povich, Maurice R., 2476
Powell, Ann Lavelle, Esq., 3031
Powell, Ben H., Jr., 3324
Powell, Ben H., V, 3324
Powell, Ben H., VI, 3324
Powell, Beverly J., 1817
Powell, Christopher, 1403
Powell, Earl A., III, 656
Powell, Gary, 1783
Powell, Gregory, 1324
Powell, Kendall J., 1697
Powell, Kitty King, 3324
Powell, Laurence, 3146
Powell, Liz, 3648
Powell, Meredith, 1403

Powell, Myrtis, 2782
Powell, Paul W., 3339
Powell, Robbin C., 436
Powell, Scott, 1286
Powell, Stephen, 22
Powell, Weldon, 569
Power, Carla, 3158
Power, Christopher, 1263
Powers, Fred, 1154
Powers, Joe, 1735
Powers, John, 574
Powers, Judith, 801
Powers, Mary A., 1950
Powers, Norma, 2609
Powers, Pamela E., 3280
Powers, Paula, 378
Powers, Robert M., 2656
Powers, Robert P., 2657
Powers, Scott, 1152
Powers, William J., 2074
Poynor, Ed, 1219
Pozen, Robert C., 2106
PPG Industries, Inc., 3018
Pradere, John, 3681
Pradhan, Dora, 3430
Prager, Yossi, 2051, 2979
Prague, Andrew P., 1439
Prairie, Pam, 1616
Praiss, Thomas F., 2962
Pranger, Leigh, 1179
Pranschke, Leonard J., 1778
Prather, Pam, 2539
Prato, Greg, 2422
Pratt, Carolyn M., 1665
Pratt, Deborah R., 1536
Pratt, G. Michael, 2737
Pratt, Mike, 2326, 2409
Pratt, Nancy, 2954
Pratt, Roger, 1990
Praxair, Inc., 606
Pray, Barbara H., 2807
Pray, Donald E., 2807
Pray, Roger, 1022
Prchal, Douglass, 2653
Preble, Bob, 3520
Prechter, Patricia M., 1299
Precourt, Walt, 1718
Preece, William H., 954
Prehn, Toby, 942
Premier Bank and Trust, 3579
Premier Bank, N.A., 3616
Premier Dental Products Co., 2911
Premier Designs, 3207
Premier Medical Co., 2911
Prempas Trust, Helen, 993
Prendergast, S. Lawrence, 2002
Prescott, Heidi, 2508
Presley, Brian, 718
Pressberg, Gail, 661
Presser Foundation, Theodore, 3019
Presser, Theodore, 3019
Pressley, Kirk, 3
Pressman, Erica, 1405
Prestia, Carmine, 2909
Prestolite Wire Corp., 1893
Preston Ctr., 3158
Preston, Michael E., 665
Preston, Robert J., 2847
Preston, Seymour S., III, 2887
Preves, Donna Sue, 1113
Preves, Greg, 1113
Preves, Robert, 1113
Previn, Andre, 328
Prevost, Louis E., 2932
Prevratil, Joseph F., 90
Prewitt, Kenneth, 2191
Pricara, 1948
Price, Aimee Gamble, 213
Price, Allison, 373
Price, Andrew Francis, 3269
Price, Arthur L., 374
Price, Barbara, 260
Price, Carol B., 3472
Price, Dean, 1218
Price, Ella C., 361
Price, Glenda D., Dr., 1588
Price, Helen, 373
Price, Helen Smith, 864
Price, Herb, Dr., 1125
Price, Jennifer C., 2367
Price, Jo-Ann, 594
Price, Jody, 1674
Price, Jordan M., 2367
Price, Judy A., 1236
Price, Kimberly F., 1676
Price, Marcy, 2809
Price, Maxie, Jr., 867
Price, Michael, 543
Price, Michael F., 2367
Price, Michael R., 328
Price, Patricia A., 374
Price, Richard, 2009
Price, Robert, 373
Price, Sheila, 1068
Price, Sol, 131, 373
Price, Susan, 1189, 3269
Price, Theodore W., 3472
Price, Thomas, 2783
Price, Todd, 3269
Prichard, Peter S., 662
Prickett, Peter, 3642
Pridmore, Ken, 349
Priebe, Daniel, 1702
Priem, Susan, 2017
Priest, Eric, 3047
Priester, Brian, 1581
Priester, Susan, 3099
Prieto, Jose, 3312
Primary Health Management, Ltd., 3320
Primary Health, Inc., 3320
Prime, Meredith M., 2265
Prina, Dean, 528
Prince & Co., F.H., Inc., 1077
Prince Capital, 2173
Prince Charitable Remainder Unitrust, 1658
Prince Corp., 1658
Prince Foundation, 1600
Prince Living Trust, Elsa D., 1658
Prince Philanthropic Fund, Morton B. & Blance S., 960
Prince, Edgar D., 1658
Prince, Elsa D., 1658
Prince, Erik D., 1658
Prince, Frederick Henry, 1076, 1077
Prince, Frederick Henry, IV, 1076
Prince, John, III, 869
Prince, Larry L., 917
Prince-Troutman, Stacey, 724
Princeton University, 1398
Principi, Amy Wahlert, 1244
Pringle, Anne, III, 2943
Prinz, Beth Terdo, 704
Prior, Michael, 1464
Prior, Trudie J., 3419
Priour, Kyle, 3318
Pritchard, Elizabeth, 897
Pritchard, Margaret Beck, 3488
Pritchard, Ruth, 3580
Pritchett, Mark, 754
Pritzker Cousins Foundation, 1078
Pritzker Foundation, 1050, 1078
Pritzker, Adam Nicholas, 375
Pritzker, Isaac, 1050
Pritzker, Jacob, 1050
Pritzker, James, 1078
Pritzker, John A., 375
Pritzker, Joseph, 1050
Pritzker, Lisa, 375
Pritzker, Nicholas J., 1050, 1079
Pritzker, Noah Stone, 375
Pritzker, Penny, 1080
Pritzker, Regan, 1050
Pritzker, Rhoda, 1050
Pritzker, Susan S., 1050
Pritzker, Thomas J., 1079
Pritzlaff, Mary Dell, 1065
Privat, Jim, 1575
Privat, John, 1575
Privat, Monica Jo, 1575
Privat, Priscilla, 1575
Procter & Gamble Distributing, 952
Proctor, Curt, 1580
Proctor, Enola, 1065
Proctor, Harmon, 1
Proctor, Martin, 726
Proenza, Theresa, 2741
Proffitt, Kathy, 3119
Progressive Casualty Insurance Co., 2764
Progressive Logistics Services, LLC, 952
Progressive Specialty Insurance Company, 2764
Prohaska, Beth, 993
Prop, Leigh, 2757
Propp, Eleanor H., 2212
Propp, Ephraim, 2046
Propper, Susan, 537
Prosser, Michael H., 1240
Prosser, Sheri R., 3608
Prothro, Caren H., 3262
Protz, Bill, 716
Protz, Edward L., 3306
Provencher, Kenneth, 2866
Provident Bank Charitable Foundation, 2111
Provident Bank, The, 2679
Provizer, Marlene, 2326
Provost, David T., 1588
Prown, Jonathan, 3605
Pruden, J. Brooke, III, 3473
Pruden, Jonathan E., 3473
Pruden, Peter D., III, 3473
Pruden, Peter D., Jr., 3473
Pruden, Peter D., Sr., 3473
Prueter, Beverly, 2661
Pruett, Greg S., 367
Pruitt, Chris, 2893
Pruitt, Christopher, 3059
Pruitt, Larry, 2819
Prunaret Trust, Henri, 1473
Prunaret, Mildred Gardinor, 1473
Pruner, Dave, 3266
Prusak, Robert, 3683
Prusoff, William H., 913
Prussian, Gordon S., 1075
Prutz, Stan, 1300
Pry, Janet P., 2682
Pryce, Jennifer, 666
Pryde, Jim, 1817
Pryne, Jane, 3522
Pryor, Marcus Q., 2108
PSL Health Care Corporation, 483
Public Service Co. of New Hampshire, 598
Pucci, Gary T., 3658
Pucker, Gigi Pritzker, 1079
Puckett, John P., III, 3209
Puckett, Julie Phillips, 2015
Puckett, Lela Phillips, 2015
Puentes, George J., 2861
Puff, Randy, 1611
Puffer, Richard A., 3098
Pugh, Francis Nicholls, IV, 1318
Pugh, Francis T.N., III, 1318
Pugh, Francis T.N., IV, 1318
Pugh, Francis Tillou Nicholls, III, 1318
Pugh, Jo Ann Lewis, 1318
Pugh, JoAnn, 1318
Pugh, Larry, 1324
Pugh, Mary, 3558
Pugh, Michael L., 1318
Pugh, Michael Lewis, 1318
Pugh, Nancy, 1318
Pugh, Nancy Lewis Marie, 1318
Pulcini, John, 1205
Pulido, Maria Begona, 1013
Pullen-Venema, Elena, 3511
Pulles, Joanne, 3139
Pulliam, Myrta, 1126
Pulling, Thomas L., 2286
Pullman, George Mortimer, 1081
Pullman, Harriet Sanger, 1081
Pullum, J. Stephen, 786
Puls, Deana, 2776
Pumphrey, Steven C., 3502
Pung, Steve, 1647
Pung, Steven D., 1622
Pungello, Elizabeth P., 2533
Puntureri, Albert R., 2925
Purce, Thomas L., 3504
Purcell, Paul E., 3595
Purgason, Katherine B., 399
Purkey, Sheila L., 1374
Purnell, Katharine J., 461
Purnell, Kelley H., 461
Purnell, Mark L., 461
Purnell, Mary L., 461
Purnell, Molly, 461
Purnell, Richard W., 2974
Purnell, Susan K., 1359
Purohit, Manju, 9
Purser, Craig, 1344
Purvis, Debbie, 1770
Purvis, E. Gail, 3373
Purvis, Randy, 1623
Putnam, Larry, 1257
Putnam, Theodore I., 2120
Putnam-Walkerly, Kris, 2683
PW Financial Partners, 841
Pycik, John M., 1172
Pye, Elisa Stude, 3183
Pyle, Clint E., 826
Pyle, Ida M., 3381
Pyle, Joe, 3030
Pyles, John C., 2452
Pyott, David E.I., 80

Qiu, Jackie, 1576
Quackenbush, Christopher, 2292
Quackenbush, Gail, 2292
Quackenbush, Michael A., 2292
Quackenbush, Traci, 2292
Quad/Graphics, Inc., 3668
Quadracci, Elizabeth E., 3668
Quadracci, J. Joel, 3668
Quadrant Capital, 2173

Qualcomm Incorporated, 376
Quandt, William B., 661
Quane, Cindy, 129
Quantum Realtors Inc., 259
Quaresma, Laure, 3498
Quarles, Orage, III, 662
Quarles, Roger, 942
Quattrini, Raymond J., 2111
Queally, Kevin, 1564
Queen's Medical, The, 3377
Queen, Megan, 2733
Queens Nassau Nursing Home, 2254, 2255
Queensgate Co., 1388
Querna, Christie R., 3526
Querrey, Kimberly, 806
Quick, Patricia C., 2788
Quigg, Tom, 3520
Quigley, Ellen White, 1145
Quigley, Jill, 1255
Quill, Thomas H., Jr., 1501
Quillon, Robin, 2922
Quilty, Kevin J., 2113
Quimby, Hannah, 1338
Quimby, Rachelle, 1338
Quimby, Roxanne, 1338
Quin, J. Marvin, 2780
Quinlan, Annamarie, 2199
Quinlan, Michael J., 1340
Quinlan, Thomas E., 2940
Quinn, Barbara, 3015
Quinn, Cydney P., 2370
Quinn, Kenneth, 1248
Quinn, M.L., 3591
Quinn, Pat, 3611
Quinn, Sarah, 3015
Quinn, Stephen D., 2370
Quinn, Tim, 354
Quinn, Todd, 137
Quinn, Tom, 1832
Quinney, David E., 3402
Quinney, David E., III, 3402
Quinney, S.J., 3402
Quinones, Margarita, 2683
Quinson, Bruno A., 2408
Quint, Brian, 3552
Quintella, Antonio, 2118
Quiriconi, Margo, 1277, 1808
Quirk, Tom, 3058
Quiroz, Lisa Garcia, 2466
Quisenberry, Cynthia, 930
Quistad, Janice E., 250
Quistgaard, Jon, 1723
Quivey, M.B., 1853
Quivey, M.B., Mrs., 1853
Qwest Communications International Inc., 627

R G I Group Incorporated, 2355
R&R Investors Inc., 1236
R. & R. Realty Co., 1535
Raab, Emily, 3020
Raab, Isabel, 3020
Raab, Norman, 3020
Raab, Sara, 3020
Raab, Stephen, 3020
Raab, Whitney, 3020
Raabe, Bruce J., 416
Raabe, Dave, 1129
Rabb, Bruce, 2095
Rabb, James M., 1421
Rabb, Jane M., 1421
Rabe, Karen, 2251
Raben, Lucynda, 1255
Rabino, Kaynan, 691
Rabinowitz, Alan, 3155
Racette, Karen, 1626
Rachal, Ed, 3329
Racine, Andrew D., 2161
Racine, Peter M., 761
Racine, Ronald, 1471
Racing Rest of America II Inc., 647
Rackoff, Nancy L., 2906, 3010
RAD Investments Inc., 3252
Radar, Roger, 1657
Rader, Kae, 525
Radey, D. Neil, 2118
Radil, Sara Coffee, 1851
Radin, Edward C., 2396
Radler 2000, 3330
Radler 2000 Limited Partnership, 3330
Radler, Geoff, 3330
Radler, Graham C., 3330
Radler, Michael Evan, 3330
Radler, Michael G., 3330
Radler, Reinke, 3330
Radley, Jeanne R., 1809
Rados, Alexander, 415
Rados, Stephan A., 415
Radosevich, Rod, 1692
Rafal, Dyanne, 562
Raff, Martin, 191
Raga, Tom, 2688
Ragains, Ronald J., 1201
Ragan, Carolyn King, 906
Ragauss, Peter A., 3170
Rage, Patience, 2985
Ragland, W. Trent, Jr., 2599
Ragone, David V., 2286
Ragsdale, Joy, 2835
Ragusa, Philip, 2167
Rahal, William, 1914
Rahjes, Doyle D., 1259
Rahm, Susan Berkman, 1434
Rahmig, Marilyn, 1852
Rahn, James, 3627
Rainbolt, David, 2826
Rainbolt, Mike, 2835
Rainbow USA, Inc., 2172
Rainer Arnhold Trust, 337
Raines, Ann Haggerty, 2986
Raines, Jodee Fishman, 1599
Raines, Valerie, 2801
Rainey, Gregory P., 592
Rainey, Robert M., 2556, 3102
Rainger, Charles W., 2773
Rainoff, Elizabeth, 2350
Raintree, 1388
Raisbeck, James D., 3550
Raisbeck, Sherry L., 3550
Raja, Atul, 450
Raker, Tim, 1620
Rall, Gina H., 723
Rallis, Maria, 1048
Rallo, Eduardo, 408
Ralph, Bobby L., 3473
Ralsten, John, 3587
Ralston, Craig, 529
Ralston, Wind W., 126
Ramaker, Dave, 1642
Ramaker, David, 1597
Ramanathan, Prakash, 2253
Ramani, Sunder, 162
Ramapo Trust, 1912
Rambeau, Brenda, 907
Ramdas, Kavita, 2389
Ramer, Daniel E., 2763
Ramer, James, 1578
Ramer, Jarrod, 1179
Ramirez, Beatriz, 126
Ramlo, Randy A., 1243
Rammell, Art, 948
Ramos, Pedro, 2976
Ramos, Yulian, 2439
Ramos-Chertok, Maria, 309
Ramsay, Doug, Dr., 2747
Ramsay, Nonie B., 103, 104
Ramsburg, J. Ray, III, 1358
Ramsey, David I., 3201
Ramsey, Dean C., 3578
Ramsey, Douglas T., 3445
Ramsey, George, 1130
Ramsey, Henry, Jr., Hon., 385
Ramsey, Margaret A., 1530
Ramsey, Paul G., 2288
Ramsey, Priscilla D., 570
Ramsey, Richard H., 570
Ramsey, Richard L., 570
Ramsey, Sandy, 719
Ramstad, Edie, 1723
Ramunno, Lou, 2771
Ran, Shulamit, 2262
Rancho Road Development, 2157
Rand Realty and Development Co., 1075
Randall, Adam, 3021
Randall, Anthony L., 2372
Randall, Brett, 3021
Randall, Chris, 3021
Randall, Earl R., 3021
Randall, Heather, 2372
Randall, James, 2366
Randall, Rita, 3021
Randall, Robert P., 3021
Randall, Robin S., 3021
Randall-Mach, Cheryl, 1428
Randel, Don Michael, 2085
Randel, Vickie, 1256
Randell, David, Jr., 1415
Randhawa, Jessie, 3576
Randles, Steven G., 2747
Randolph, Carter, Dr., 2751
Randolph, Guy, Jr., 2751
Randolph, Jake, 821
Randolph, Jane R., 2751
Randolph, Robert M., 1529
Randolph, Strother, 900
Randolph, Whitney, 3338
Raneri, Stephanie A., 2479
Rangel, Mary, 1607
Rangel, Rebeca, 99
Ranger Investments, L.P., 2137
Rangos, Alexander, 3022
Rangos, Jenica, 3022
Rangos, Jill, 3022
Rangos, John G., Jr., 3022
Rangos, John G., Sr., 3022
Ranjani, Rakesh, 248
Rankin, R. Alex, 1283
Rankin, Thomas S., 1771
Ranney, George A., Jr., 1014
Ranney, Phillip A., 2803
Ransom, Kim, 1030
Rao, Amy, 398
Rao, Pravin, 1068
Raphael, Bob, 3552
Rapley, Diane, 143
Rapoport, Andrew, 2373
Rapoport, Audre, 3331
Rapoport, Bernard, 3331
Rapoport, Emily, 3331
Rapoport, Ida, 2373
Rapoport, Jed, 2607
Rapoport, Patricia, 3331
Rapoport, Ronald B., 3331
Rapp, Derek K., 1803
Rapp, Kathleen, 1226
Rapp, Marcia, 1615
Rappaport, Andrew, 380
Rappaport, Deborah, 380
Rappleyea, Holly, 2223
Rapson, Rip, 1631
Rasch, Jennifer, 2653
Rashford, John, Dr., 1001
Raskin, Roy, 2117
Raskin, Shelley, 2117
Raskob, Kathleen, 2006
Rasmuson, Edward, 29
Rasmussen, Astrid Kann, 2375
Rasmussen, Densel, 1837
Rasmussen, Hans Kann, 2375
Rasmussen, Kristian Kann, 2375
Rasmussen, Kristin, 1752
Rasmussen, Ralph, 3388
Rasmussen, Tom, 1357
Rasor, Linda, 3163
Rasulo, Jay, 181
Ratcliffe, James, 1030
Rateliff, Charles, 69
Rathbun-Gunn, Betsy, 3417
Rathjen, Carolyn P., 3317
Ratray, Peter, 2143
Ratshesky, A.C., 1531
Rattner, Amy, 638
Rattner, Andrew, 638
Rau, Amrish, 496
Rauch, David, 2376
Rauch, Louis J., 2376
Rauch, Lynn H., 1385
Rauch, Philip, 2376
Rauch, Philip J., 1385
Rauch, Philip J., Jr., 2376
Rauch, Ruth T., 2376
Raucher, Dana, 2073
Raudenbush, Stephen, 1098
Rauenhorst, Joe, 1724
Rauenhorst, Mark H., 1724
Rauh, James M., 2533
Rauter, Kristie, 3623
Rava, Susan R., 1789
Raver, Bill, 393
Raver, C. Cybele, 1098
Raver, Mark, 1198
Rawl, Julian, 2562
Rawlings, Jane L., 535
Rawlings, Lynn D., 1799
Rawlings, Steve, 1616
Rawlinson, Marion Clapp, 3542
Rawlinson, Maureen E., 136
Rawlinson, Rex J., 136
Rawls, Kaki, 724
Rawls, Olga Goizueta, 883
Ray, Bradford, 1294
Ray, Bradford T., 1294
Ray, Christine N., 3304
Ray, Cynthia Sineath, 2915
Ray, Frank, 3278
Ray, Gilbert T., 243
Ray, Helen, 900
Ray, Jim, 1158
Ray, Lisa, 69
Ray, Mike, 503
Ray, Rob, 2078
Ray, Stuart, 1294
Ray, Teresa, 1157
Raybould, Keith, 332
Rayl, Kristina, 631

Rayle, Terry, 1144
Raymer, Robert M., 2987
Raymo, Greg, 1740
Raymond James Trust Co., 801
Raymond, Carolyn M., 2997
Raymond, Jonathan, 429
Raymond, Larry, 1512
Raymond, Neil St. John, 1532
Raymond, Shirley, 1155
Raynolds, Robert, Dr., 547
Raythoen, 3363
Raza, Syed K., 78
RBC Capital Markets Corp., 1730
RBC Dain Rauscher Corp., 1730
RBC Dain Rauscher Inc., 397
RBS Alumini Association, 3424
RBS Citizens, N.A., 3067
RCI North American, 2562
Rea, George R., Jr., 1758
Reabold, Melissa, 1360
Read, Cheryl, 3139
Read, Jeff, 568
Read, Tyra, 714
Read, William A., 44
Reagan, Shirley P., 1315
Real Page, 3505
Real State Company, 560
Realsearch, 1388
Realty Investment Company, Inc., 1356
Reamer, Karen, 1749
Rebber, Stan, 1131
Rebling, Renee, 1227
Rebozo, Charles F., 807
Rebozo, Charles G., 807
Rebozo, Michael, 807
Rebozo, Thomas, Jr., 807
Rebozo, William, Jr., 807
Recanati Kaplan, Daphne, 901
Recanati-Kaplan Foundation, The, 901
Recasner, Anthony, 1316
Rechter, Ben R., 3129
Reck, Krista J., 624
Reckling, Isla C., 3358
Reckling, James S., 3358
Reckling, John B., 3358
Reckling, Stephen M., 3358
Reckling, T.R. "Cliff", IV, 3358
Reckling, T.R., III, 3358
Reckling, Thomas K., 3358
RECO Constructors, Inc., 3474
RECO Industries, Inc., 3474
Record, Linda, 2809
Recreational Equipment Inc., 3551
Red, Nancy Lynn, 3346
Redd, Dianne, 2868
Redd, Ellis S., 1205
Redd, Rainey D., 2933
Redden, Greg, 3055
Redding, Barb, 1603
Reddish, Cindi, 989
Reddy, Lakshmi, 1203
Reddy, Sushma, Dr., 1590
Reder, Robert F., 2408
Redfern, Jerry L., 1805
Redford, Jan L., 3324
Redick, John R., 3428
Reding, John, 3161
Redinger, Arthur, 1200
Redmond, Jerry, 1678
Redmond, Robin, 1081
Redna Inc., 182
Redwood Contracting, 2228
Redwood Neuroscience Institute, 82
Reece, Ken G., 2599
Reece, Patty, 1012
Reed, Bruce, 129
Reed, Burton, 1125
Reed, Charles C., 444
Reed, Cynthia, 3089
Reed, Doug, 1832
Reed, George, 2612
Reed, Jim, 1143
Reed, Joanne, 245
Reed, Joel, 899
Reed, Julie, 1515
Reed, Marsha L., 181
Reed, Michael E., 983
Reed, Rhoda Newberry, 1659
Reed, Robert, 329
Reed, Sydney, 3401
Reed, T.J., 3259
Reed, Thomas, 2890
Reeder, Ted, 1360
Rees, Nigel A., 321
Reese, Gary, 3319
Reese, Gilbert H., 2695
Reese, J. Gilbert, 2695, 2723
Reese, Louella H., 2695
Reese, Thomas O., 3538
Reese, Wayne, 1580
Reese, William, 1899
Reeve, Brenda, 1280
Reeve, Kenlon, 3394
Reeve, Thomas C., 540
Reeves, Bill, 2480
Reeves, Christy Oliver, 1302
Reeves, Katherine P., 3317
Reeves, Olivia, 1207
Reeves, Steven, 1156
Reeves, William Huntington, 2480
Reffett, Terry L., 1289
Reffner, Robert, 2655
Regal Entertainment Group, 3151
Regan, Amy H., 1936
Regan, James S., 1936
Regan, James S., III, 1936
Regan, John J., 1563
Regan, Patrick H., 1936
Regenberg, Lillian, 1711
Regiero, Angel, 3
Regino, Rita, 1376
Regions Bank, 5, 19, 1306
Regions Financial Corp., 19
Regions Morgan Keegan Trust, 19, 801
Regis Corp., 1732
Regis, Inc., 1732
Regnery, Eugenie F., 3104
Regnery, Particia L., 3104
Regnery, Walter C., 3104
Rehfeld, Bob, 35
Rehrig, Brian H., 1467
Rehtmeyer, Clint, 1021
Reich, Elaine M., 2220
Reich, Lilian, 2378
Reich, Margo, 3528
Reich, Seymour, 2378
Reich, Seymour D., 2283
Reichard, James, 2562
Reichheld, James H., 1505
Reid, Dan, 3498
Reid, Daniel, 2504
Reid, Delia, 329
Reid, E. Lewis, 250
Reid, Janet B., 2679
Reid, Jennifer, 3089
Reid, Robert J., 2014
Reidy, Ann Benson, 2232
Reidy, Janice, 1512
Reidy, Joseph, 1512
Reifenberg, Stephen, 1524
Reifenberg, Steve, 1524
Reik, Andrea, 2662
Reilly, Anson, 3333
Reilly, Asher, 3333
Reilly, Atlee, 3333
Reilly, Austin, 3333
Reilly, Axton, 3333
Reilly, Beverly A., 3333
Reilly, George, 1684
Reilly, Joseph, 2071
Reilly, Michael A., 3333
Reilly, Rosemary, 535
Reilly, Thom, 1860
Reilly, William, II, 990
Reiman Foundation, 2232
Reiman, Eric M., 44
Reiman, Roberta M., 3650
Reiman, Roy J., 3650
Reiman, Scott J., 3650
Reimann, Rella, 3568
Reimer, Doug, 1710
Rein, Gary D., 2221
Reinberger, Clarence T., 2765
Reinberger, Louise F., 2765
Reinberger, William C., 2765
Reinertson, Tara, 631
Reinhard, G. Douglas, 1368
Reinhardt, Aurelia A., 729
Reinhardt, Douglas E., 1332
Reinhardt, J. Alec, 2700
Reinhardt, Jim, 1852
Reinhart Partners, 3642
Reinhart, Marty, 3633
Reinharz, Jehuda, 2465
Reinhold, Henry, 2217
Reinhold, Paul E., 808
Reinhold, Rebecca L., 1285
Reiniche, Dominique, 864
Reininga, Daniel, 2331
Reinis, Richard G., 227
Reinke, Kristin, 231
Reinking, Craig, 3606
Reinsch, Lola C., 3421
Reinstadler, Ruppert, 2873
Reis, Judson, 2191
Reis, Kevin Michael, 3359
Reischman, Ann, 2801
Reiser, Margaret C., 885
Reiser, Robert E., Jr., 885
Reisman, Barbara, 1990
Reisman, Lonny, 550
Reiter, Bernard, 297
Reiter, Cody N., 1752
Reiter, Hayley M., 1752
Reiter, Kyle W., 1752
Reiter, Robert, 1261
Reitermann, Michael, 1993
Reithmeier, Roger, 990
Reitz, Susy, 1274
ReliaStar Bankers Security Life Insurance Co., 2488
ReliaStar Financial Corp., 2488
ReliaStar Life Insurance Co., 2488
ReliaStar United Services Life Insurance Co., 2488
ReMax of Georgia, 2173
Rembe, Toni, 446
Rembowski, Kathy, 1648
Remenapp, Donald, 3284
Remey, Don, 543
Remo, Dee Ann, 3433, 3476
Renard, James S., 3178
Rendahl, Joy, 568
Render, Cecilia H., 2755
Rendina Companies, 809
Rendina, Bruce A., 809
Rendina, David B., 809
Rendina, Lainie, 809
Rendina, Marji, 809
Rendina, Marjorie, 809
Rendina, Michael D., 809
Rendina, Richard M., 809
Rendina, Tricia, 809
Renditions Washington DC LLC, 628
Rengel, Paula J., 2773
Renier, Tom, 1677
Renjen, Punit, 569
Renken, Keith W., 444
Renner, Christopher, 574
Renner, Daniel S., 2766
Renner, Debra, 2766
Renner, J. Robert, 2766
Renner, Jill, 574
Renner, John W., 2766
Renner, Mary, 2766
Renner, R. Richard, 2766
Renner, Reid, 2766
Renner, Richard R., 2766
Renner, Robert, 2766
Renner, Steven, 2766
Renner, Sue, 518, 519
Renner, Tamara, 2766
Renner, Tara, 2766
Renner, Todd, 574
Renner, Trevor, 574
Renner-Yeomans, Jennie, 2766
Rennert, Irwin L., 3108
Rennie, Renate, 2467
Rennter, Jeff, 1848
Renoux, Kelly, 537
Renschler, Scott, 1356
Rentschler, Thomas, Jr., 2710
Renuart, Victor Eugene, Jr., Genl., 492
Renwick, Glenn M., 2764
Repensek, Jane, 3558
Repine, John E., 475
Repplier, Banning, 2408
Repplinger, William M., 501
Republic Die & Tool Co., 1958
Residual Charity Trust, W. Farnum, 3083
Resnansky, Kristin, 2347
Resnick & Sons, Jack, Inc., 2059
Resnick, Burton P., 2380
Resnick, Eric, 543
Resnick, Ira, 2380
Resnick, Ira M., 2379
Resnick, Jack, 2380
Resnick, Lynda, 331
Resnick, Paula S., 2379
Resnick, Pearl, 2380
Resnik, Leslie, 2745
Resor, Cynthia, 1292
Resptronics, Inc., 3023
Ressler, April, 2907
Retta, Hector, 3312
Rettenmier, Ross, 3511
Rettler, Tom, 3636
Reuland, Timothy J., 991
Reveley, W. Taylor, III, 2302
Revere, Elspeth A., 1056
Revocable Living Trust of Elmer J. Trulaske, 770
Revolution Studios, 2445
Rey-Hernandez, Cesar A., 3061
Reyes, Elias, 3226
Reyes, Elsie, 3579
Reyes, Jerome, 3098

Reyes, Juan J., 3061
Reygadas, Carlos, 176
Reykdal, Chris, 3502
Reynolds American, 2613
Reynolds Tobacco Co., R.J., 2613
Reynolds, Andrea L., 2113
Reynolds, C. Lockwood, 3481
Reynolds, Cathy, 205
Reynolds, Donald W., 1869
Reynolds, Edith, 564
Reynolds, Howard D., 212
Reynolds, Jonathan, 574
Reynolds, Josh, 2850
Reynolds, Kate B., 2614
Reynolds, Larry, 1845
Reynolds, Richard J., Jr., 911
Reynolds, Robert J., 309
Reynolds, Sigrid S., 3481
Reynolds, Susan, 1208
Reynolds, Thomas M., 3125
Reynolds-Cane, Dianne L., 3433
RFI Foundation Inc., 3424
Rhame, Donald, 859
Rhea, Martha, 1274
Rhea, Randall R., 3432
Rheault, Wendy, 1031
Rhee, Barbara R., 2270
Rhee, John, 2270
Rhines, Steven, 2822
Rhinesmith, Steffanie, 1145, 1204
Rhoads, Samuel V., 3030
Rhodehamel, William A., 1157
Rhodes, Arthur, 1084
Rhodes, Charlotte, 3163
Rhodes, Greg, 3504
Rhodes, Jeffrey J., 1084
Rhodes, Joan, 1195
Rhodes, Robert, 2736
RHP, Inc., 2349
Rhymes, Josephine, 1760
Rhynes, Lisa, 2830
Rhynhart, Erich, 1549
Ricchuito, David A., 3009
Ricci, A. Leo, 591
Ricci, Joann, 1316
Riccobene, Mary, 3586
Rice, Albert W., 1533
Rice, Bill, 2922
Rice, Charles L., Jr., 1316
Rice, Christopher B., 3348
Rice, Elizabeth, 2017
Rice, Henry F., 926
Rice, Jim, 3684
Rice, Joanne, 3343
Rice, John, 2942
Rice, Joseph A., 2194
Rice, Katherine D., 1702
Rice, Kathryn, 2407
Rice, Martin, 2407
Rice, Mary E., 1702
Rice, Mary Gage, 1533
Rice, Mary H., 1702
Rice, Michael N., 1651
Rice, Molly E., 1702
Rice, Motley, LLC, 3107
Rice, Nell M., 2566
Rice, Norm B., 3499
Rice, Ronald, 1290
Rice, Tim, 2688
Rich Products Corp., 2382
Rich, Barbara, 2126
Rich, Melinda, 2382
Rich, Robert E., Jr., 2382
Rich, Robert E., Sr., 2382
Rich, Stuart, 2905
Richard, Aurelie, 1099
Richard, Beth, 1085
Richard, Betty J., 1085
Richard, Elwood, 1085
Richard, Pessie, 2103, 2401
Richard, Robert J., 1246
Richards, Anna Jo, 1192
Richards, Bob, 441
Richards, Cecile, 2160
Richards, Charles, 2287
Richards, Cynthia, 2048
Richards, Elizabeth, 871
Richards, Gail, 1163, 2833
Richards, Gary, Dr., 1603
Richards, James R., 3454
Richards, Laura, 1647
Richards, Mabel Wilson, 382
Richards, Margaret T., 1745
Richards, Martin, 2524
Richards, Ron, 46
Richards, Roy, 908
Richards, Roy, Jr., 908
Richardson, Anne S., 3335
Richardson, Barb, 3502
Richardson, Barbara, 959
Richardson, Barbara B., 2541
Richardson, Charles, 1853
Richardson, Charles A., 934
Richardson, Christine, 484
Richardson, Connie, 1214
Richardson, Evelyn K., 1664
Richardson, Jacob, 1664
Richardson, Janie D., 1306
Richardson, Jannie, 525
Richardson, John, 551
Richardson, Katherine G., 933
Richardson, Kelly C., 371
Richardson, Louise, 2085
Richardson, M. Catherine, 2177
Richardson, Mary Ann, 1381
Richardson, Mary D., 1156
Richardson, Michael, 2584
Richardson, Nancy, 1218
Richardson, Peggy, 3421
Richardson, Sarah, 2822
Richardson, Sarah Beinecke, 2443
Richardson, Sid W., 3334, 3336
Richardson, Susan, 3069
Richardson, Tom, 1660
Richardson, William M., 3474
Richardson-Lowry, Mary B., 982
Richer, Bob, 3401
Riches, Scott, 305
Richins, Kent, 3684
Richman, Rae, 262
Richmond Memorial Hospital Foundation, 2616
Richmond, Bradford C., 732
Richmond, Christian T., 2874
Richmond, Frederick W., 1408
Richmond, Henry R., 2874
Richmond, Joseph W. "Rick", Jr., 3428
Richmond, Ruth B., 2874
Richmond, Sarah, 1623
Richter, Bill, 1268
Richter, Sid, 2223
Rickard, F.W., 1289
Rickard, Jean J., 653
Rickard, Polly Piper, 3186
Rickeman, Norman, 1717
Ricker, Michell, 1241
Ricker, Patricia, 792
Rickert, Mary, 401
Rickertson, Curt, 1845
Ricketts, Bob, 2909
Rico, Victoria B., 3182
Riddle, Pamela Cogan, 1450
Ridenour, Johnna, 175
Ridenour, Julie, 1667
Ridenour, Mark E., 2665
Rider, Anne, 758
Rider, Cynthia A., 1623
Rider, G. William, 3306
Rider, Mike, 306
Rider-Pool, Dorothy, 3024
Ridgefield High School Student Activity Account, 647
Ridgon, Henry, 900
Ridgway, Anne, 3446
Ridino, Robert, 163
Ridlen, Sue, Dr., 1125
Ridley, Nancy, 1647
Ridout, Kyle, 1136
Riedel, Walter G., III, 3357
Riegel, Amanda J.T., 2461
Rieger, Abraham, 2383
Rieger, Abraham Jacob, 2383
Rieger, David, 2383
Rieger, E. Annette, 3569
Rieger, John A., 2811
Rieger, Merri, Dr., 3552
Rieger, Rachel, 2383
Rieger, Roger A., 3569
Riemer, Terrin S., 3650
Riemke, John, 1127
Rieser, Len, 2942
Riesman, Robert, 1707
Rifai, Dana, 1171
Riffe, Susann, 1272
Rifkin, Francine, 1662
Rifkind, Richard A., 2194
Rifkind, Robert Gore, 383
Rifkind-Barron, Max, 383
Rigby, Kevin, 1973
Rigby, Nancy K., 916
Rigdon, Thomas M., 2825
Rigg, Remus, 1580
Rigg, Robert E., 2915
Riggio Foundation, The, 2368
Riggio, Leonard, 2368
Riggio, Louise, 2368
Riggs Conselman Michaels & Downes, Inc., 1406
Riggs, David W., 2610
Riggs, Earl, 823
Riggs, Earl, Mrs., 823
Riggs, Lisa, 2981
Riggs, Peggy, Dr., 1805
Riggs, Sheila, 1246
Riggs, Steve, 714
Rightmire, Karen, 3059
Rigney, John, 112
Rikard, Frank A., 20
Rikard, Glenn A., 20
Rikard, M.A., 20
Riker, Bernard, 1596
Riley, Amelia Q., 2926
Riley, Barbara W., 2926
Riley, Charles E., 3521
Riley, Emily C., 2926
Riley, Gerun, 129
Riley, Jennie, 1538
Riley, Katherine Murphy, 898
Riley, Kathleen, 897
Riley, Keith, 1273, 2741
Riley, Mabel Louise, 1534
Riley, Mark B., 891
Riley, Odell, 627
Riley, Thomas A., 2926
Riley-Chew, Dorothy, 2122
Rincones, Vanessa, 3052
Rindal, Edie Fleishhacker, 199
Rinde, Lisa, 3662
Rinder, Lawrence, 2494
Rindner, Edna, 1808
Ring, Frank, 2384
Ring, Freda, 2384
Ring, Leo, 2384
Ring, Louise, 2384
Ring, Michael, 2384
Ring, Timothy M., 1905
Ringel, Betsy, 1350
Ringel, Betsy F., 1349, 1379, 1409
Ringel, Deborah Taper, 433
Ringel, Neil, 1549
Ringelman, Roger, 3666
Ringenberg, Nicole M., 1803
Ringer, Bill, 1866
Rinker, Christopher R., 810
Rinker, David B., 810
Rinker, David S., 810
Rinker, Leighan R., 810
Rinker, M.E., Sr., 810
Rinne, Jennifer P., 1525
Riomax, Ltd., 3237
Riordan, Richard, 641
Rios, Tim, 264
Ripkey, Dawn, 3607
Rippel, Julius S., 1982
Rippeto, Doug, 543
Rishagen, Nancy, 328
Rishel, Philip S., 2923
Rising Sun Regional Foundation, 1141
Rising, Nelson, 276
Risk, Colleen M., 3377
Risley, Jeffrey, 1178
Risor, Bob, 73
Rissient, Pierre, 176
Ristau, Sherry, 1740
Ristine, Thomas H., 1145
Ritchie, Daniel L., 488
Ritchie, Shirley, 2606
RITE-HITE Corp., 3651
RITE-HITE Holding Corp., 3651
Ritsch, Malcolm E., Jr., 3459
Ritschard, Mike, 503
Ritschel, Debbie, 988
Rittenberg, Libby, 544
Ritter, Alan, 2020
Ritter, Alan I., 2020
Ritter, Beth, 626
Ritter, Geralyn S., 1966
Ritter, Jeannie, 2232
Ritter, Jonathan, 2020
Ritter, Michele, 803
Ritter, William D., 19
Rittgers, Rebecca, 210
Ritzel, Nancy, 2429
Ritzen, Jason, 3296
Rivas, Jose, 1735
Rivas-Ramos, Marti, 1171
Rivel, David, 2326
River City Bank, N.A., 278
Rivera, Chris, 3558
Rivera, Clara, 647
Rivera, Felipe, 3417
Rivera, Mariano, 647
Rivera, Ron J., 2006
Rivera, Ruben Morales, 3061
Riverbend Industries, LLC, 1234
Rivers, Edna, Mrs., 10
Riverway Co., 1733

Rivint, Zelma G., 3440
Rivitz, Jan, 1410
Rivlin, Alice M., 656
Rizk, Richard H., 3487
Rizley, Jerry W., 504
Rizzo, Cindy, 2040
Rizzo, Guy, 767
RJR Acquisition Corp., 2613
RJR Nabisco Holdings Corp., 2613
RJR Tobacco Intl., 2613
Roach, Joseph, 1687
Roach, Kevin L., Dr., 3438
Roach, Scott, 3580
Roach, Sonta, 34
Roane, Gay A., 3352
Roang, Sverre David, 3599
Roanhorse, Sherrick, 2011
Roark, Annmarie, 1505
Roarty, Susan, 1370
Robak, Kim, 1834
Robb, Harry, 957
Robb, J.Y., III, 3317
Robb, Patty, 957
Robb, Richard G., 2349
Robb, Sandy, 957
Robb, Sue, 957
Robb, Trish, 957
Robbins, Ashley, 1282
Robbins, Beverly, 607
Robbins, Bob, 1616
Robbins, Cathy, 492
Robbins, Clifton S., 607
Robbins, Edwin, 607
Robbins, Larry, 607, 1279
Robbins, Lawrence, 2386
Robbins, Patty, 261
Robbins, Regis T., 2758
Robe, Scott, 2662
Robenalt, Susan, 2689
Robers, Frank P., 2759
Roberson, Joseph, 1607
Roberston Fund, Jeanne and Sanford, 259
Robert Wood Johnson Charitable Trust, The, 1757
Robert, Cindy, 3538
Robert, Pilar Crespi, 2440
Robert, Stephen, 2440
Roberts Foundation, Flora, 2143
Roberts Fund, H. Clay and Sherry, 3494
Roberts Trust, Jess and Alta, 2844
Roberts Trust, Jessie Castle, 381
Roberts, Ann T., 608
Roberts, Annie Lee, 3361
Roberts, Brian K., 3441
Roberts, Carla, 1607
Roberts, Carol, 3672
Roberts, Carol L., 3142
Roberts, Don, 168
Roberts, Edward C., 608
Roberts, Emily Goodrich, 1188
Roberts, Frank, 999
Roberts, Jennifer P., 1299
Roberts, Jennifer S.D., 1445
Roberts, John B., 2485
Roberts, Karen, 1268
Roberts, Kathleen, 268, 727
Roberts, Lisa A., 1942
Roberts, Lorraine M., 2113
Roberts, Marc, 809
Roberts, Mark, 988
Roberts, Mark A., 1559
Roberts, Mary, 2868
Roberts, Mary Reed, 1861
Roberts, Nancy Elizabeth, 3168
Roberts, Patrick S., 2796
Roberts, Ralph J., 2921
Roberts, Ronald L., 3416
Roberts, Samuel, 396
Roberts, Shelly, 729
Roberts, Susan Bass, 1685
Roberts, Tempie, 1845
Roberts, Thomas, 2498
Roberts, Tom, 1152
Roberts, Virgil, 264
Roberts, William L., Jr., 3488
Robertshaw, Darren, 823
Robertson Foundation, 1971
Robertson, Charles S., 1904
Robertson, David, 26, 2867
Robertson, David A., 1468
Robertson, Dorothy B., 854
Robertson, Emily M., 687
Robertson, Geoffrey S., 1904, 1983
Robertson, Gregory B., 3444
Robertson, Harold G., 3140
Robertson, Joe, 2846
Robertson, John J., 1468
Robertson, Julia, 1904
Robertson, Julian H., Jr., 2464
Robertson, Marie H., 1904
Robertson, Mark, 3419
Robertson, W. Scott, 44
Robertson, Will, 3255
Robertson, William, 1983
Robertson, William J., 2798
Robertson, William S., 1904
Robeson, Mark D., 2740
Robfogel, Nathan J., 2154
Robins, E. Claiborne, 3477
Robins, E. Claiborne, Jr., 3477
Robins, Gregory C., 3477
Robinson, A.J., 918
Robinson, Ann, 393
Robinson, Barbara Paul, 2459, 2460
Robinson, Bob, 3579
Robinson, Branden, 1693
Robinson, Brandi, 2333
Robinson, Brenda, 1849
Robinson, Charles Nelson, 609
Robinson, Cheryl R., 136
Robinson, Chuck, 3571
Robinson, Constance K., 2977
Robinson, Craig, 407
Robinson, Craig P., 2322
Robinson, Curtis, 309
Robinson, David, 667
Robinson, Dennis W., 1503
Robinson, Diane, 360
Robinson, Donald G., 39
Robinson, Dorna M., 928
Robinson, Doug, 2732
Robinson, E.B., Jr., 1770
Robinson, Erica, 4
Robinson, Frank Brooks, 2906
Robinson, Guy N., 2513
Robinson, Homer, 2977
Robinson, Jack, 487
Robinson, Jack A., 1588
Robinson, Janet L., 2085
Robinson, Jean, 2953
Robinson, Jean A., 2901
Robinson, Jeffery P., 224
Robinson, Jesse, 1125
Robinson, Jill R., 1349, 1350, 1379
Robinson, Jim, 3606
Robinson, John H., 3190
Robinson, John R., 2505
Robinson, Jon, 1623
Robinson, Jonathan, 627
Robinson, Joseph R., 1646
Robinson, Judy, 3312
Robinson, Kenneth D., 800
Robinson, Kenneth S., Dr., 3124
Robinson, Kirk, 1180
Robinson, Kristy H., 3263
Robinson, Lynne, 1607
Robinson, Margaret, 2830
Robinson, Martha T., 3123
Robinson, Martin, 2210
Robinson, Melanie, 1370
Robinson, Melissa, 1808
Robinson, Michael, 1133
Robinson, Nicole R., 1064
Robinson, Perry, 2746
Robinson, R. Avery, 2387
Robinson, Ralph C., 3681
Robinson, Reggie, 1256
Robinson, Robert D., 1156
Robinson, Rowland P., 2505
Robinson, Sandy, 823
Robinson, Scott, 2795
Robinson, Stephanie, 1188
Robinson, Steve, 3503
Robinson, Sylvia B., 2505
Robinson, Teresa, 452
Robinson, Thomas E., 2794
Robinson, Torrence H., 3235
Robinson, William A., 250
Robinson, Winnie M., 2387
Robison, Annette S., 111
Robison, Eric, 1012
Robison, Laurie, 1581
Robison, M. Lavoy, 478
Robison, Mark A., 1123
Roblee Trust, Florence, 1809
Roboson, Cynthia J., 2289
Robson, Dwight D., 1513
Roby, Allan B, 1894
Roby, Barbara, 1894
Roby, David, 3030
Roby, David M., 1894
Roby, John C., 2767
Roby, Riley, 8
Roche, Bernard, 2885
Roche, Edward, 2388
Rochel, Tim, Sr., 2981
Rochelle, Anne Zachry, 3387
Rock, Arthur, 446
Rock, Patricia, 1541
Rockafellow, Michael, 3259
Rockdale Industries, Inc., 905
Rockefeller Charitable Trust, A.R., 2346
Rockefeller Trust Co., 2325
Rockefeller Trust Co., N.A., 682
Rockefeller Trust, A.M., 2346
Rockefeller, David, 2389
Rockefeller, David, Jr., 1322, 2390
Rockefeller, John D., III, 2389
Rockefeller, John D., Jr., 2389
Rockefeller, John D., Sr., 2390
Rockefeller, Justin, 2389
Rockefeller, Laurance S., 2389
Rockefeller, Martha Baird, 2389
Rockefeller, Nelson A., 2389
Rockefeller, Steven C., 2389
Rockefeller, Winthrop, 2389
Rockway, Dennis, 236
Rockwell Collins, Inc., 1237
Rodd, Allan K., 2701
Roddey, James C., 2993
Roddick Foundation, Andrew S., The, 3158, 3159
Roden, Elizabeth, 2888
Roderick, Blake, 992
Roderick, Willard, 2796
Rodgers, Blanche D., 1345
Rodgers, Gary, 537
Rodgers, Mary Anne, 357
Rodgers, Pamela, 1588
Rodgers, Theo C., 1345
Rodgers, W. Ralph, Jr., 869
Rodin, Judith, Dr., 2390
Rodish, Jane, 489
Rodman Five Realty Trust, 1535
Rodman Ford Sales, Inc., 1535
Rodman, Donald E., 1535
Rodman, Gene D., 1535
Rodman, Rica, 453
Rodrigo, Rohan, 656
Rodriguez, Aida, 2326
Rodriguez, Al, 394
Rodriguez, Arlene, 2335
Rodriguez, Edwin "Rod", Jr., 1316
Rodriguez, Mona, 2564
Rodriguez, Raul C., 157
Rodriguez, Ray, 771
Rodriguez, Ref, 360
Rodriguez, Sandra D., 3061
Rodriguez-Howard, Mayra, 1449
Roe, Anita, 960
Roeder, Susan, 1678
Roehl, Jerrald J., 2006
Roehrig, Sandi, 3615
Roell, William, 1949
Roembke, Greg, 1207
Roepstorff, Robbie B., 823
Roesch, Jane, 2883
Roesch, Jane H., 2896
Roest, Ted Vander, 2787
Roff, Andrew W., 2811
Roff, J. Hugh, Jr., 2811
Roger, David K., 2969
Rogers Children's Heritage Trust One, 3339
Rogers Children's Heritage Trust Two, 3339
Rogers Granchildren's Heritage Trust, 3339
Rogers Investment Corp., 1536
Rogers Towers, P.A., 826
Rogers, Adam, 1515
Rogers, Anthony J., 1236
Rogers, Anthony L., 729
Rogers, Charles, 1687
Rogers, Charles H., 2036
Rogers, Charley, 2539
Rogers, Charlie, 1687
Rogers, Christopher, 3616
Rogers, Clay, 326
Rogers, Dyke, 3163
Rogers, Florence L., 2618
Rogers, Greg, 1660
Rogers, Holly, 326
Rogers, Irving E., 1536
Rogers, J. Dickson, 3216
Rogers, John H., 3449
Rogers, Margot M., 1040
Rogers, Marilyn, 326
Rogers, Mark E., 1185
Rogers, Martha B., 1536
Rogers, Nancy, 1203
Rogers, Patrick, Hon., 993
Rogers, Richard L., 1638
Rogers, Robert M., 3339
Rogers, Robyn M., 3339
Rogers, Timothy, 326
Rogers, Tracy, 326

Rogerson, Thomas, 1539
Rohde, Jessica, 3414
Rohde, Mary Rita, 3576
Rohlf, Kathryn, 441
Rohlfing, Joan H., 925
Rohm, Jeanne Roccon, 328
Rohm, Robert F., Jr., 2225
Rohnert, Allison, 159
Rohr, George, 2051
Rohr, James, 2966
Rohr, Loren, 3200
Rohr, M., 1298
Rohr, Mark C., 1298
Rohr, Pamela, 2320
Rohr, Tom, 1186
Rohrbach, Peggy, 3672
Rohrer, Michelle, 216
Rohrick, Tom, Dr., 1852
Rohrig, Frederick W., 2663
Rohrig, Fredrick Dean, 3579
Rohrkaste, Michael K., 3643
Roitman, Daniel, 2173
Roitstein, Alex, Dr., 3597
Rojano, Ramon, 2612
Roland, Charles H., 1
Rolfe, Andrew, 2473
Rolland, Janna, 3546
Rolle, Katrina, 726
Rolle, Philip D., 1693
Roller, Dean H., 783
Roller, Jennifer, 2799
Roller, Mark C., 1183
Rolling, Ken, 2749
Rollins, Britton, 574
Rollnick, Ari, 729
Roma Bank, 1984
Romack, Bob, 1163
Romain, Ronald, 1205
Romano, Anthony J., 1965
Romano, Carol A., 1906
Romanoff, Mike, 2682
Rombach, Charles M., 3661
Romberger, Scott W., 3002
Rome, Ellen, 2673
Romeo, Randolph, 2539
Romero, Fatima, 3179
Romero, Kenneth, 2017
Romero, Wendy, 1060
Romero-Leggott, Valerie, 2011
Romig, Mark, 1314
Rommel, Rod, 3662
Romoser, David W., 3659
Rondeau, Terri, 1587
Rongers, Tina, 1171
Ronis, Robert J., 2801
Ronk, Alan E., 3432
Ronquist, Neal, 1616
Roob, Nancy, 2097
Roome, Peter W., 1950
Rooney, Debbie, 3417
Rooney, Emmy, 3100
Rooney, Joann, 3026
Rooney, John, 3026
Rooney, Kevin J., 2434
Rooney, Marianne, 2822
Rooney, Patrick, 2822
Rooney, Patrick T., 2811
Rooney, Peter, 1771
Rooney, Sean, 3026
Roos-Collins, Richard, 354
Roose, Gina, 1587
Root Charitable Trust, Susie M., 1272
Root, Judy, 2696
Root, Mary T., 866
Roothbert, Albert, 2391
Roothbert, Toni, 2391
Roper, Lynn, 1851
Rosa, Joseph J., 2472
Rosa, Karen L., 2145
Rosa, Margarita, 2161
Rosales, Guillermo, 69
Rosberg, Carl, 3429
Roscitt, Michelle W., 1985
Roscitt, Richard R., 1985
Roscoe, Jerry, 268
Rose & Kiernan, Inc., 2392
Rose Foundation, 528
Rose Trust, 363
Rose, Barbara, 1749
Rose, Camille, 989
Rose, Carolyn, 2789
Rose, Deborah, 2393
Rose, Deedie, 3262
Rose, Ella, 482
Rose, John, 3502
Rose, Kelly, 2819
Rose, Kristen L., 1711
Rose, Marianne Curtis, 1130
Rose, Melanie, 602
Rose, Nancy C., 1567
Rose, Ron, 1580
Rose, Sandra P., 2393
Rose, Sandy, 159
Rose, Sarah R. Frey, 1609
Rose, Susan, 320
Rose, Suzanne, 2819
Rose, Tricia, 2121
Rose, Walter B., 359
Rosemore, Inc., 1409
Rosen, Arlene, 1086
Rosen, Dennis, 1695
Rosen, Elaine D., 1631
Rosen, Sarah, 2122
Rosenbaum, Jeffrey N., 2108
Rosenberg, Barr, 386
Rosenberg, Beth, 2198
Rosenberg, Brian, 2459
Rosenberg, Brian C., 1748
Rosenberg, Cheryl, 910
Rosenberg, Dianne M., 2679
Rosenberg, Ellen, 2437
Rosenberg, Henry A., Jr., 1409
Rosenberg, Jennifer, 3440
Rosenberg, Joe, 1282
Rosenberg, Karen, 1832
Rosenberg, Kim, 2394
Rosenberg, Leona Z., 960
Rosenberg, Marvin, 386
Rosenberg, Mary, 386
Rosenberg, Max L., 385
Rosenberg, Patricia, 2017
Rosenberg, Ralph, 2394
Rosenberg, Ruth Blaustein, 1409
Rosenberg, Stephen, 910
Rosenberge, Charles, 351
Rosenberger, Gary, 2864
Rosenberry Charitable Term Trust, 1752
Rosenberry Jones Charitable Tust, Lucy, 1752
Rosenblatt, Lief D., 2051
Rosenblatt, Richard A., 2336
Rosenblatt, Toby, 156
Rosenblum, Ivan S., 2069
Rosenfeld, Barry, 1973
Rosenfeld, Rachel, 2193
Rosenfeld, Shea, 2193
Rosenfeldt, Paul, 3615
Rosengarten, James A., 2391
Rosenow, Penny, 999
Rosenstein, Anita May, 186
Rosenstein, Carl, 1980
Rosenstein, Neal, 1980
Rosenstein, Perry, 1980
Rosensweig, David, 616
Rosenthal Trust, Barbara Bakwin, 2395
Rosenthal, Ilene, 676
Rosenthal, James A., 2315
Rosenthal, John, 2265
Rosenthal, Jonathan, 2307
Rosenthal, Lynne, 1027
Rosenthal, Morris H., 2320
Rosenthal, Steven P., 1537
Rosenthal, William, Dr., 2395
Rosenthal, William, Mrs., 2395
Rosenwald Family Fund, W.H., 661
Rosenwald, Cindy, 1883
Rosequist, Ronald V., 174
Roser, Eleanor, 3389
Rosewood Corp., The, 3340
Rosin, Katharine S., 2409
Rosing, Wayne E., 291
Roskam, Robert, 1578
Roske, Mary Grace, 3558
Rosloniec, Michael, 1615
Rosner, Myron, 1908
Ross Fund, Sada, 3494
Ross, Alexander B., 2054
Ross, Bill, 1842
Ross, Catherine, 503
Ross, David, 1272
Ross, Dorothea Haus, 2396
Ross, Dorothy, 1663
Ross, Esther C., 72
Ross, Ford, 1279
Ross, George M., 3027
Ross, Jane, 72
Ross, Jody J., 1810
Ross, John S., 1810
Ross, Kevin E., 1559
Ross, Libby, 3421
Ross, Lyn M., 3027
Ross, M., 2831
Ross, Mary Caslin, 1947
Ross, Mellisa, 3588
Ross, Merry, 3027
Ross, MIchael, 3027
Ross, Philip A., 2825
Ross, R. J., 483
Ross, Rebecca, 714
Ross, Richard, Jr., 1025
Ross, Robert J., 2811
Ross, Robert K., 138
Ross, Robert, Dr., 1290
Ross, Samuel B., II, 3588
Ross, Samuel B., III, 3588
Ross, Sarane H., 2054
Ross, Spencer B., 3588
Ross, Stephen B., 2054
Ross, Susan S., 3588
Ross, William J., 2811
Rosse, Earle, 1877
Rossi, Craig Hall, 387
Rossi, Deborah, 346
Rossi, Ellen E., 3402
Rossi, Jack, 3582
Rossi, Joseph H., 595
Rossi, L. Jay, 387
Rossi, L. Jay, Mrs., 387
Rossi, Marjorie, 387
Rossi, Merilee, 387
Rossi, Moira Forbes, Countess, 2116
Rossi, Safford J., 387
Rossi, Sharon, 2003
Rossi, WJ, 725
Rossin, Ada E., 3028
Rossin, Peter C., 3028
Rossiter, Lois F., 3487
Rossiter, Rob, 1618
Roswell, Arthur E., 1349
Roswell, Elizabeth B., 1349
Rotan, Caroline P., 3228
Rotary Club of Columbus, 2731
Rotary Club of Elmbrook, 3666
Rotary Club of Upper Arlington, 2731
Rotenberg, Shannon Mabrey, 272
Roth and Co., Louis, 388
Roth, David H.O., 3182
Roth, Fannie, 388
Roth, Harry, 388
Roth, James J., 2317
Roth, Janet E., 3049
Roth, Louis, 388
Roth, Michael P., 388
Roth, Rachel, 388
Roth, Robert W., 1615
Roth, Sarah, 388
Roth-Fedida, Andrea, 388
Rothberg Trust, Samuel, 1082
Rothberg, Heidi B., 1082
Rothberg, Jean, 1082
Rothberg, Jean C., 1082
Rothberg, Jennifer Hoos, 2150
Rothberg, Lee Patrick, 1082
Rothberg, Michael, 1082
Rothberg, Samuel, 1082
Rothblatt, Ben, 1051
Rothe, Ann, 26
Rothe, Anne Richards, 795
Rothenberg, Lawrence, 773
Rothenberger, Steve, 1131
Rothkopf, Dick, 543
Rothman, Terry, 3606
Rothrock, Allyson, 3443
Rothrock, Donna, 2611
Rothschild, Nathaniel, 2377
Rothschild, Steven, 1717
Rothschild, Susan, 1428
Rothstein, Maks, 2397
Rothstein, Sergio, 2397
Rothweiler, Todd, 116
Rothwell, Sharon, 1637
Rotter, Steven J., 2380
Rotuck, Scott, 3591
Rotz, Ann Marie, 1360
Roumani, Nadia, 659
Rounds, Bruce, 3642
Rounsavall, Robert W., III, 1283
Rountree, Stephen D., 77
Rouse, Dudley L., Jr., 3296
Rouse, Elizabeth Meadows, 3296
Rouse, Eloise Meadows, 3296
Rouse, James, 1282
Roussin, Lucille A., 2101
Routh, Brad, 52
Roux, Henry, 305
Roux, Tina, 2496
Rover, Edward, 2290
Rover, Edward F., 2126
Rowan, Eleanor, 1986
Rowan, Henry M., 1986
Rowan, Virginia, 1309
Rowe, Bradley M., 3584
Rowe, Connie, 2771
Rowe, John J., 2757
Rowe, John W., 982, 2390
Rowe, Marshall, 1883

Rowe, Ramona C., 2540
Rowe, Rebecca, 1338
Rowe, Sara M., 3584
Rowe, Steven, 1883
Rowe, Thomas W., 3584
Rowell, Virginia, 801
Rowland, Benjamin A., Jr., 3415
Rowland, Daniel B., 3415
Rowland, Marilyn, 899
Rowland, Patricia M., 3440
Rowland, Pleasant T., 3652
Rowland, Robert, 3093
Rowland, Wendy G., 3415
Rowley, Lynn, 1175
Roy, Brittany D., 2142
Roy, Dillon, 2142
Roy, Judy, 1723
Roy, Lisa, 515
Roy, Ruby, M.D., 993
Royal Oak Foundation, 2069
Royal Trust, May Mitchell, 1661
Royal, Pamela J., 3433
Royal, Susan B., 2886
Royals Charities Inc., 647
Royalty, Andy, 1132
Royalty, Shelly S., 417
Roybal, Dolores E., 2011
Royce, Ginna, 3591
Royster, R. Randall, Esq., 2006
Rozeboom, Leon D., 1240
Rozek, Alex, 1500
Rozek, Gary, 1228
Rozek, Mimi, 1500
Rozenshteyn, Gary, 2355
Ruan, John, III, 1248
Rubega, Margaret, 1342
Rubeli, Maureen E., 60
Rubeli, Maureen M., 60
Rubeli, Paul E., 60
Ruben, Lawrence, 2060
Ruben, Richard, 2060
Rubenstein, Ernest, 2197
Rubenstein, Joshua S., 1042
Rubenstein, Terry M., 1392, 1393
Rubin Foundation, Samuel, Inc., 2398
Rubin, David M., 3045
Rubin, Donald, 2399
Rubin, Judith O., 2325
Rubin, L., 2254
Rubin, Martin A., 724
Rubin, Michael, 83
Rubin, Robert, 1472
Rubin, Samuel, 2398
Rubin, Shelley, 778, 2399
Rubinoff, Ira, Dr., 1398
Rubinow, Laurence P., 611
Rubinsztein-Dunlop, Halina, 106
Rubio, Luis, 2467
Ruble, Blaire, 2477
Ruble, Cindy S., 1579
Ruby, Burton B., 1201
Ruby, Diane, 346
Rucker, Fanon, 2782
Ruckle, James E., 1204
Rudd, David, 1598
Rudel, Jack N., 225
Rudel, Julius, 2499
Ruderman, Jay Seth, 1537
Ruderman, Marcia, 1537
Ruderman, Morton E., 1537
Ruderman, Todd Adam, 1537
Rudick, Ian, 3591
Rudnick, A.J., 10
Rudolph, Alexander S., 1101
Rudolph, Geoffrey E., 1101
Rudoy, Bruce F., 2965
Rudy, Paul, 1398
Rueff, Gail, 1142
Ruesga, G. Albert, Dr., 1316
Rueter, Marci, 3666
Ruffin Foundation, The, 3424
Ruggiero, Wendy L., 2596
Ruh, William J., 378
Ruhe, Thom, 1797
Ruhl, Roger L., 2687
Ruiz, Gisel, 74
Ruiz, Jesse H., 982
Ruiz-Healy, Catalina, 380
Rulon-Miller, William, 1955
Rumbough, J. Wright, Jr., 840
Rummel, Mason B., 1283
Rumsey, David, 2263
Rumsey, John, 1141
Rumsey, Todd C., 1147
Rumsfeld Foundation, Joyce and Donald, 679
Rumsfeld, Donald H., 679
Rumsfeld, Joyce P., 679
Rundquist, Rebecca, 1338
Runnells, Clive, III, 3245
Runyon, Richard M., 2429
Rupani, Amirali, 3209
Rupe, Arthur N., 389
Rupiper, Karla, 1848
Rupp, Adrienne, 1883
Rupp, George, 2288
Rupp, George E., 2286
Rupp, Gerald E., 2485
Ruppel, Phillip, 1216
Rupprecht, Daniel P., 1236
Rupprecht, Mark A., 1236
Rupprecht, Paul S., 1236
Rupprecht, Phyllis M., 1236
Rupprecht, Thomas P., 1236
Rusakov, Vitaliy V., 2882
Rusche, Joseph A., 1750
Rush, Mike, 1642
Rush, Scott R., 1655
Rush, Sherri, 1129
Rushing, Don, 3287
Rushing, Ted, 3287
Russel, Jim, 203
Russell, Cristine, 2106
Russell, David, Dr., 2809
Russell, G. Richard, 1843
Russell, George F., 680
Russell, Jackie, 1182
Russell, John C., 2418
Russell, Kimberly, 3433
Russell, Richard, 1260
Russell, Todd, 723
Russell, Tracy A., 420
Russo, Marcy, 2237
Russo, Ralph D., 2700
Russo, Robert A., 1492
Rust, Mary L., 2715
Rust, Randy, 3520
Ruth, David A., 1463
Ruth, Jim, 83
Rutherford, James, 1763
Rutherford, Mary, 1828
Rutherford, Peter, 3503
Rutherfurd, Winthrop, 2511
Rutherfurd, Winthrop, Jr., 2145
Rutkoff, Mally Z., 1083
Rutkowski, Walter F., 2906
Rutledge, Gary L., 1774
Rutledge, Kathleen, 1857
Rutter, David R., 1107
Rutter, Rebecca, 1877
Rutter, Twila, 2011
Ruvkun, Gary, Ph.D., 191
Ruyak, Kathy H., 2970
Ruzek, Mike, 3401
RWD Technologies, 1369
Ryals, Mike, 725
Ryan Enterprises Corp. of Illinois, 1087
Ryan Holding Corp. of Illinois, 1087
Ryan, Alice, 1395
Ryan, Colleen, 1202
Ryan, Corbett M.W., 1087
Ryan, Daniel M., 822
Ryan, Dave, 1171
Ryan, James D., Jr., 2410
Ryan, Joseph W., 3311
Ryan, Katrina W., 3682
Ryan, Kelly, 666, 3623
Ryan, M. Catherine, 1107
Ryan, Mary, 1455
Ryan, Michael, 3424
Ryan, Pamela M., 3368
Ryan, Patrick G., 1087
Ryan, Patrick G., Jr., 1087
Ryan, Patrick L., 1979
Ryan, Pete, 2331
Ryan, Richard, 2331
Ryan, Robert, 3014
Ryan, Robert J.W., 1087
Ryan, Shirley W., 1087
Ryan, Stephen, 105
Ryan, Susan Kirk, 637
Ryan, Thomas, 1808
Ryan, William J., 1334
Ryan, Yolanda V., 3311
Rybolt, Ryan M., 2679
Rydell, David R., 965
Ryder, Catherine, 1336
Ryder, E. Larry, 3443
Ryker, Debra B., 165, 202
Rynd, Mary Jane, 57
Ryzman, Abraham, 390
Ryzman, Betty, 390
Ryzman, Elie, 390
Ryzman, Rafael, 390
Ryzman, Zvi, 390

S.M.K.I. PTY LTD, 116
Saadeh, George, 122
Saal, Harry, 82
Saalfield, John I., 3042
Saar, Amy S., 2152
Sabal Co., 801
Sabarese, Michael, 441
Sabas, Jennifer Goto, 933
Sabatini, Dan, 1256
Sabban, Abdo, 659
Saber, Rosemary, 1428
Sabin Family Foundation, Andrew, 901
Sabin, Caroline J., 3324
Sabin, John, 658
Sabin, Mike, 2844
Sabourin, John P., 1779
Sabraw, Robert, 268
Sacchetta, James, 2983
Sacerdote, Grace, 722
Sacerdote, Matias, 1470
Sachs Trust, Henry, 529
Sachs, Gregory, 1998
Sachs, Henry, 529
Sachs, Keith, 2035
Sachs, Penelope, 1012
Sachs, Samuel, II, 2363
Sack, Michael, 451
Sackett, Deanna, 33
Sacks, Ian, 2473
Sacred Harvest Foundation, 2863
Saddi, Karim, 2473
Saddler, Michelle R. B., 1083
Sadecky, Toni L., 2890
Sadler, Dave, 1802
Sadow, Jenny Levis, 1065
Saeger, Cathy, 1836
Saenger, George W., 2540
Saesan, Goldie, 2924
Safeco Corp., 3554
Safeco Insurance Co., 3554
Saffell, Dennis, 503
Saga Communications, 2071
Sagat, Mary, 1549
Sage Publications, Inc., 320
Sage, David, 1197
Sage, Russell, Mrs., 2402
Sagehorn, David M., 3643
Sagen, Laura, 3499
Sager, Julie, 268
Sager, Mimi M., 3615
Sager, Thomas L., 630
Saggurti, Purna R., 2524
Sahara Coal Co., Inc., 1857
Sahlaney, Michael, Esq., 2922
Sahn, Edmond, 261
Sahney, Nitin, 2758
Sahnow, Robin, 35
Said, Abdul Aziz, 659
Saigh, Fred M., 1811
Saikami, Duane, 260
Saiki, Curtis, 933
Sailer, William, 376
Sain, Steve, 83
Saint James, Susan, 538
Sajdak, Robert A., 1582
Sajevic, Joe, 1836
Sajjad, Nabeela, 78
Sak, Elizabeth, 2119
Saka, Charles, 1987
Saka, Jeffrey, 1987
Saka, Raymond, 1987
Saka, Sammy, 1987
Sakac, Ann, Sr., 2495
Sakahara, Toru, 3531
Sakamoto, Marie, 931
Sakar International Inc., 1987
Sakellaris, Harry, 3456
Saks, Jane M., 2121
Sala, Angelica, 2139
Salamane, Denis J., 1942
Salamatof Native Association, 33
Salazar, Kathleen H., 444
Saleh, William B., 193
Salem, Albert, Jr., 757
Salgado, Sandy, 3
Salina, Paul G., 563
Salinas Valley Community Church, 3330
Salisbury, Tod P., Esq., 1358
Sallee, Jaclyn, 33
Salner, Rebecca, 408
Salo, Lynn D., 80
Salomon, Arthur R., 1282
Salomon, Lionel J., 2326
Salomon, Staci, 2286
Salsman, Gloria, 1241
Salter, Lee W., 318
Saltiel, Karen Fine, 867
Saltonstall, G. West, 1539
Saltz, Jack, 2060
Saltz, Leonard, Dr., 2060

Saltzman, Esther E., 1346
Saltzman, Rob, 117
Salva, Gary P., 592
Salvati, Mark, 1569
Salvatori, Kurt, 3054
Salzberg, Deborah Ratner, 672
Salzer, Richard L., Jr., 2192
Salzman, Ruth, 1908
Samad, Sam, 2677
Samaris, Shirley, 591
Samberg, Arthur, 3478
Samberg, Laura, 2403
Samberg, Rebecca, 2403, 3478
Sambunaris, Victoria, 2359
Samburg Family Foundation, 2827
Samerian Foundation, 1156
Samloff, Harold, 2510
Sammis, Cheri, 1662
Sammons, Todd, 1160
Samolczyk, Mark J., 2788
Sampaio, Jorge, 2085
Sample, Barbara, 1829
Sample, David F., 1829
Sample, Helen S., 1829
Sample, John Glen, 1829
Sample, Joseph S., 1829
Sample, Michael S., 1829
Sample, Miriam T., 1829
Sample, Patrick G., 1829
Sampson, Cynthia, 1326
Sampson, Elbert, 3000
Sampson, Gary, 36
Sampson, Holly C., 1693
Sampson, Tim, 3287
Sams, Alfred, III, 866
Sams, Earl C., 3342
Samson, Lori, 2880
Samstag, Gordon, 813
Samuel, Joe, 496
Samuels, Alexandra, 3053
Samuels, Barbara, 1102
Samuels, Deborah Addo, 1360
Samuels, Joseph T., Jr., 3428
Samuels, Robert H., 713
Samuels, Sherwin, 158
San Diego Habitat for Humanity, 2574
San Diego Union Shoe Fund, 166
San Francisco Film Society, 2095
San Francisco Foundation, The, 438
San Inocencio, Victor Garcia, 3061
San Joaquin County Office of Education Educational Foundation, 161
Sanchez, Frank I., 2749
Sanchez, Frank M., 287, 444
Sanchez, George & Mary Ann, 2780
Sanchez, Manolo, 3
Sanchez, Marisol, 1126
Sanchez, Philip, 2466
Sanchez, Sally, 1257
Sanchez, Thomasa, 724
Sanchez, Tricia Grigsby, 1312
Sand, Carolyn H., 683
Sand, Richard, 2452
Sand, Wesley, 2846
Sandbulte, Arend J., 1693
Sandburg, JoEllen, 1118
Sandefur, Charles C., 448
Sandelman, Jeffrey, 814
Sandelman, Sanford, 814
Sandelman, Susan, 814
Sander, Daniel J., 2710
Sander, Marcia, 304
Sandercott, Mark, 1742
Sanderhoff, Steen, 3648
Sanders, Cam, 1415
Sanders, Caroline J.S., 2620
Sanders, Charles A., 2600
Sanders, David, 2787, 3499
Sanders, Elizabeth, 1415
Sanders, Herman R., 2710
Sanders, Joanne, 351
Sanders, Joe, 1841
Sanders, Machelle, 3063
Sanders, Paul, 3308
Sanders, Sue, 1136
Sanders, Theresa, 3510
Sanders, Victoria B., 3419
Sanderson, Bill, 235
Sanderson, Carolyn, 1979
Sanderson, Don, 1620
Sanderson, Peggy, 3561
Sanderson, Valerie, 2682
Sanderson, Veronica, 1706
Sandhurst Associates, 2157
Sandler, Barbara, 382
Sandler, Ellen, 331
Sandler, Richard, 331
Sandler, Susan Rule, 95
Sandlin, Betty, 2552
Sandlin, Larry, 3291
Sandlin, Maria Louisa, 3291
Sandman, Dan D., 2906
Sandman, Jim, 672
Sandner, John F., 984
Sandness, Paul K., 2652
Sandoval, Arturo, 501
Sandoval, Niki, 394
Sandow, Darren, 2199
Sandoz Corp., 2333
Sandridge, Leonard W., Jr., 3428
Sandrock, Scott P., 2663
Sands, J. Clayton, 3340
Sands, Lee, 477
Sands, Patrick B., 3340
Sands, Stephen, 3340
Sands, Tim, 371
Sandstrom, Constance, 1336
Sanford, Brenda, 948
Sanford, Claire C., 926
Sanford, Gene, 1200
Sanford, Jo Anne, 2632
Sanford, Mary, 926
Sanford, Molly F., 3464
Sanfrey, Janis, 2799
Sanger, Beth T., 714
Sangster, Claudia, 343
Sanofi-Aventis US, LLC, 1988
Sansar Capital Foundation, 2159
Sant, Leo M., 2830
Sant, Maralynn V., 2830
Santana, Annabel, 2337
Santarone, Michael S., 826
Sante, B. Joanne, 957
Sante, Mike, 957
Santini, Connie P., 764
Santini, Leonard, 823
Santoni, Roland J., 458
Santoro, Brenda, 407
Santoro, Nancy, 261
Santulli, Margaret, 2019
Santulli, Richard, 2019
Sanzi, James, 3089
Sapoch, Jamie Kyte, 1916, 3418
Sapp, Richard, 378
Sapper, Jon, 257
Sarafian, Alex, 2001
Saran, Robin Kauffman, 637
Saratovsky, Kari Dunn, 658
Sardone, Frank, 1626
Sargeant, Kari, 989
Sargeant, Kimon Howland, 3047
Sargent, Karen Renner, 2766
Sargent, Melaney, 1157
Sargent, Nancy, 3609
Sargent, Sara Ann, 2922
Sarich, Jacquelyn A., 3605
Saridakis, Brenda R., 2670
Sarkella, Bill, 1663
Sarkeys, S.J., 2828
Sarkos, Janet, 2004
Sarmiento, Gil M., 1040
Sarnelli, Josephine, 1547
Sarofim, Allison, 2405
Sarofim, Christopher, 2405
Sarofim, Christopher B., 3183
Sarofim, Fayez, 186
Sarofim, Louisa S., 2405
Sarofim, Louisa Stude, 2405, 3183
Sarpolis, Keith, 1012
Sarra, Jon J., 2107
Sarratt, Mark, 1845
Sarrazin, Dorothy, 1731
Sarver, Fred K., 1296
Sarver, Gail, 1275
Sarver, Inc., 1275
Sarver, Robert G., 65
Sasakawa Peace Foundation, 680
Sasakawa Peace Foundation Tokyo, 680
Sasaki, Carol, 261
Sasaki, Glen, 261
SASL, 3365
Sasscer, Brian, 658
Sasser, Leslie E., 3221
Sasser, Leslie Keith Elkins, 3220
Sasso, William R., 2598
Sassoon, Rhonda, 395
Sassoon, Vidal, 395
Satchell, Ernest R., 1359
Sather, Timothy J., 1830
Satlof, Mark, 2166
Satrom, Jim, 2648
Satterlee, Ellen, 1674
Sattler, Bill, 3193
Saucerman, Pat, 3633
Sauer, Diane, 2685
Sauer, Gary B., 1736
Sauer, Patricia A., 1736
Sauers, Kim, 1201
Sauey, Floy A., 3655
Sauey, Todd L., 3655
Sauey, William R., 3655
Saugatuck Capital, 613
Sauke, Leon, 2478
Saul, Andrew, 2038
Saul, Denise, 2038
Saul, Dianne P., 1065
Saunders, Barry, 3098
Saunders, James C., 3441
Saunders, John E., 339
Saunders, Michael, 754
Saunders, Nancy A., 1534
Saunders, Rob, 1740
Saunders, Whitney G., 3473
Saurers, Judi, 2682
Sauter, Thomas R., 2366
Savage Administrative Trust, 396
Savage, Cheri, 394
Savage, Diana, 2674
Savage, Ronald J., 396
Savannah Electric Foundation, Inc., 877
Savas, Paul G., 2355
Save 2nd Base, 3026
Savedoff, Stuart H., 783
Savereide, John, 1742
Savido, Evelyn D., 2950
Savin Charitable Lead Trust, Muriel, 1989
Savin, Muriel, 1989
Savin, Nathan, 1989
Savin, Nathan E., 1989
Savin, Robert, 2035
Savings Bank of Manchester Foundation, Inc., 611
Savy, Joseph, 1451
Sawicki, Tracy A., 2472
Sawtell, Sarah, 2017
Sawyer, Brian, 1162
Sawyer, John D., 2719
Sawyer, Louise, 1500
Sax, Ellen, 2108
Saxena, Avinash, 3344
Saxena, Manoj, 3344
Saxena, Shubhada, 3344
Saybrook, Inc., 2853
Sayer, Evelyn W., 1737
Sayer, George W., 1737
Sayer, George, III, 1737
Sayer, John, 1737
Sayer, Michael Scott, 1737
Sayer, Patricia, 1737
Sayers, Donald D., 2644
Sayfer, Steven M., 2288
Saykaly, Ronald, Dr., 1282
Sayler, Alan P., 717
Sayler, Elizabeth Jubitz, 2853
Sayler, Lee B., 717
Sayler, Van C., 717
Sayler, Wyline Chapman, 717
Sayre, Sharon A., 3359
SBC Communications Inc., 3167
Scagliotti, Nackey & Robert, 2780
Scaife, David N., 2937
Scaife, Frances G., 2937
Scaife, Richard M., 2883
Scaife, Sara D., 2937
Scaife, Walter B., 347
Scales, Julie, 801
Scaling, Wilson, 3219
Scammahorn, Kamala Lightner, 3282
Scanlan, William, 3247
Scanlan, William J., 8
Scanlan, William, Jr., 3241
Scannell, Michael, 1550
Scannelli, Sandi, 723
Scardino, Frank P., 328
Scardino, Marjorie M., 1056
Scarff, Bill, 2787
Scarlett, Andrew S., 3152
Scarlett, Catherine M., 2107
Scarlett, Clifford, 2148
Scarlett, Dorothy F., 3152
Scarlett, Jennifer, 3152
Scarlett, Joseph H., Jr., 3152
Scarlett, Rob, 1742
Scarlett, Tara Anne, 3152
Scarsella, Julie, 2685
Scearce, Camden B., 3125
Schaal, Kevin E., Dr., 1382
Schachte, Margaret P., 3104
Schadt, Deborah O., 3120
Schaefer, Corinne, 1052
Schaefer, Emily K., 2541
Schaefer, John P., 59
Schaefer, Joseph M., Sr., 1052
Schafer, Amanda, 1647
Schafer, Betty R., 1421
Schafer, Judi, 3552

Schafer, Maureen, 1867
Schafer, Oscar S., 2406
Schafer, Sigrid U., 2406
Schaffer, Jan, 2811
Schaffler, Charles D., 3120
Schankler, Noah, 2310
Schankweiler, David, 2952
Schanzer, Ken, 543
Schapman, Laura, 1603
Scharbauer, Clarence, 3345
Scharbauer, Clarence, III, 3160
Scharbauer, Clarence, Jr., 3345
Schardt, Ralph, 296
Schastny, Peter, 3090
Schastok, Sara L., 1012
Schatz, Adrienne, 533
Schatz, David, 533
Schatz, Diane Maurer, 3409
Schatz, Douglas S., 533
Schatz, Jill E., 533
Schatz, Jill M., 533
Schatz, Myrna, 2178
Schatz, Susan, 2237
Schaupp, Mary G., 3608
Scheeler, C. Ron, 2599
Scheer, Brick, 1255
Scheer, Elizabeth L., 1299
Scheetz, Mick, 1178
Scheffe, Walter P., 2809
Scheffel, William N., 1782
Schell, Cathleen, 1652
Schell, Randall, 2366
Scheller, Richard H., 216
Schenck, Todd, 3390
Schendel, Richard, 3329
Schendel, Walter G., III, 2037
Schenk, Daniel, 1205
Schenk, Julie, 2830
Scheper, Charles R., 2679
Schepp, Florence L., 2408
Schepp, Leopold, 2408
Scherer, Thomas W., 3120
Scherer, Tim, 1660
Schervish, Thomas W., 2788
Schewel, Marc A., 3454
SCHI, 1922
Schiavoni, Mark A., 39
Schick, Kevin, 305
Schick, Peter G., 1802
Schick, Thomas, 2034
Schield, Darren, 426
Schier, Irene Reynolds, 911
Schierbeek, Robert H., 1600, 1671
Schierl, Carol A., 3608
Schierl, Michael J., 3608
Schierl, Paul J., 3608
Schiewetz, Richard F., 2774
Schiff, Charles O., 2784
Schiff, Hardin & Waite, 2353
Schiff, John J., III, 2784
Schiff, John J., Jr., 2784
Schiff, Stacy, 2194
Schiffer, Karen, 229
Schildberg Irrev. Trust, Sylvia K., 1238
Schildberg, Mark, 1238
Schildberg, Marlene, 1238
Schildberg, S.K., 1238
Schill, Michael H., 2427
Schilling, Joe, 3476
Schilling, Mike, 537
Schilling, Vicki, 2817
Schiltz, Laura A., 1240
Schimberg, Alice, 1083
Schinazi, Raymond F., 913
Schindler, Nicole, 3208
Schindler-Johnson, Elizabeth, 170
Schineller, Glenn, 2562
Schirmer, Henry, 2003
Schiro, Dorene, 26
Schissler, Nancy R., 3346
Schissler, Richard P., 3346
Schissler, Richard P., III, 3346
Schlachter, Jim, 2850
Schlafke, Ted, 3606
Schlag, Darwin W., 1814
Schleicher, William T., Jr., 987
Schlemmer, Robert N., 2794
Schlesinger, Harvey E., Hon., 722
Schlesinger, R. Diane, 84
Schlesinger, Stuart, 2254
Schlesinger, Thaleia, 1470
Schlesinger, William H., 2146
Schlessman, Dolores J., 530
Schlessman, Florence M., 530
Schlessman, Gary L., 530
Schlessman, Gerald L., 530
Schlessman, Lee E., 530
Schley, Scott, 1937
Schlichting, Nancy M., 1631
Schlieder, Edward G., 1319
Schliesman, Paul, 1701
Schlindwein, Paul C., II, 3610
Schlittler, William, 2810
Schlitz, Lloyd, 1290
Schloenbach, Steven, 2655
Schloesser, Jack, 3642
Schloss, Barry I., 1416
Schloss, Jeffrey P., 3047
Schlossman, Carol, 2649
Schlothauer, Barb, 1852
Schlott, Robert, 1226
Schlotterbeck, Steven T., 2940
Schlutz, Robert, 1225
Schmank, James, 1279
Schmeling, Pete, 3633
Schmid, Chris, 2753
Schmidhauser, Eric, 3158
Schmidhauser, Lucie, 3158
Schmidlapp, Jacob G., 2775
Schmidt Irrevocable Charitable Lead Annuity Trust, Jareen E., 3218
Schmidt Revocable Trust, Jareen E., 3218
Schmidt Trust, Geraldine, 3037
Schmidt, Anthony, 2262
Schmidt, Arthur J., 3665
Schmidt, Barbara, 203
Schmidt, Benno C., Jr., 1797
Schmidt, Buzz, 2211
Schmidt, Chad, 3153
Schmidt, Chester, 3153
Schmidt, Daniel P., 3601
Schmidt, Diane, 3422
Schmidt, Douglas M., 3153
Schmidt, Elizabeth, 3403
Schmidt, Eric, 398
Schmidt, Gerry, 3591
Schmidt, Jareen E., 3218
Schmidt, Jennifer L., 2774
Schmidt, John F., 40
Schmidt, Kris, 1634
Schmidt, Lynn D., 3018
Schmidt, Margaret, 40
Schmidt, Oscar, 2307
Schmidt, Raymond, 3665
Schmidt, Raymond E., 3665
Schmidt, Richard W., 482
Schmidt, Sandefur, 3403
Schmidt, Sarah E., 3153
Schmidt, Sophie, 398
Schmidt, Steven, 3153
Schmidt, Susan, 2835
Schmidt, Theodore, 3403
Schmidt, Theodore, Jr., 3403
Schmidt, Thomas A., 3665
Schmidt, Thomas, Sr., 1232
Schmidt, Tom, 40
Schmidt, Wendy, 398
Schmidt, William, 3665
Schmidt, William E., 3153
Schmidt, William J., 3665
Schmidt-Rogers, Lea, 3153
Schmit, Aaron, 2653
Schmitt, Alfons J., 2476
Schmitt, Arthur J., 1088
Schmitt, Caroline, 2566
Schmitt, Caroline F., 2410
Schmitt, Edward H., Jr., 991
Schmitt, Kilian J., 2410
Schmitt, Monty, 1720
Schmoke, Kurt, 2427
Schmoke, Kurt L., 2085
Schmuckal Land Co., 1664
Schmuckal, Arthur M., 1664
Schmuckal, Donald A., 1664
Schmuckal, Kevin P., 1664
Schmuckal, Paul M., 1664
Schnabel, Rockwell, Hon., 270
Schnadig, Dorothy D., 1089
Schnadig, Richard H., 1089
Schneeweiss, Stephen, 2090
Schneickert, Michael D., 361
Schneider Electric USA, Inc., 1099
Schneider, Charlene, 1849
Schneider, Henry, 1812
Schneider, Jane, 1812
Schneider, Joe, 1143
Schneider, John, 1218
Schneider, Kathryn, 2880
Schneider, Melvyn H., 1096
Schneider, Mildred, 2148
Schneider, Richard, 3522
Schneider, Ross M., 1812
Schneider, Scott N., 616
Schneidman, Richard, 2507
Schneidmiller, Gary T., 951
Schneidmiller, Gladys V., 951
Schneidmiller, Kevin E., 951
Schnitter, Julie, 364
Schnuck, Scott, 3082
Schnurmacher, Adolph, 2411
Schnurmacher, Ruth, 2411
Schnurr, Don, 1215
Schoen, John, 26
Schoenberg, Barbara H., 637
Schoenfelder, Brad, 1716
Schoenrich, Edyth H., 1391
Schoenthaler, Susan P., 94
Schoettler, Gail S., 483
Schoknecht, Kim, 190
Scholar, 1388
Scholin, Christopher A., Dr., 332
Scholl, Barry, 2106
Scholl, Dennis, 771
Scholting, Terri, 1848
Scholvinck, Marc, 115
Scholz, Denise, 1846
Schonherr, Mike, 354
School Employees Credit Union of Washington, 3549
Schooler, David R., 2776
Schooler, Dean, 2776
Schooler, Edith, 2686, 2776
Schooler, Heather L., 2776
Schooler, Matthew, 2776
Schooler, Seward, 2686
Schooler, Seward D., 2776
Schooler, Wesley, 2776
Schooley, Susan, 1638
Schools, Bob, 1330
Schoon, Rodney, 1179
Schoonmaker, Judith D., 592
Schoonmaker, Peter, 3683
Schoonmaker, Trevor, 2494
Schorr, Deb, 1847
Schoshinski, James J., 3608
Schott, John W., 3047
Schottenstein, Jay, 2777
Schottenstein, Jeffrey, 2777
Schottenstein, Jonathan, 2777
Schottenstein, Joseph, 2777
Schottenstein, Thomas H., 2778
Schrafft, Bertha E., 1543
Schrafft, William E., 1543
Schram, Gus W., III, 1303
Schrayer, Max R., II, 1083
Schreck, Albert R., 2022
Schreck, Celeste W., 2022
Schreck, Charles R., 2022
Schreck, Christine, 2022
Schreck, Edward, D.O., 2762
Schreck, Mason T., 2022
Schreck, Teresa Juarez, 2022
Schreck, Thomas A., 2022
Schreder, Carleen, 1119
Schreiber, Brian, 2029
Schreiber, Mark, 1257
Schreiber, Richard, 3487
Schreier, Alison, 814
Schreier, Andrew, 814
Schreier, Andrew M., 1912
Schreier, Edward G., 2336
Schreier, William S., 1912
Schrock, Bonnie, 1286
Schroder, Rod, 3163
Schroder, Soren, 1779
Schroeder, Denise, 1581
Schroeder, Emily, 221
Schroeder, Fu, 309
Schroeder, John C., 1205
Schroeder, Marybeth, 1012
Schroeder, Patricia, 3500
Schroeder, Sherrie, 711
Schroeder, Steve, 3662
Schroeder, Steven A., 264, 1734
Schrum, David F., 1160
Schubach, Carolyn, 3397
Schubert, Carroll, 3326
Schubert, Carroll W., 3326
Schuenemann, Latisha Bernard, 2893
Schuette, William D., 1653
Schuetz, Joachim, 2095
Schuetz, Lizabeth Rossi, 387
Schuh, Dale Robert, 3657
Schuh, Kevin, 3636
Schuiteman, Norma, 3504
Schul, Carole, 2737
Schulaner, Felice, 2100
Schulder, Michael, 2945
Schuler, E. Carroll, 3358
Schuler, Jack W., 1090
Schuler, Mary Jo, 1023, 1068
Schuler, Renate R., 1090
Schuler, Stephen G., 1023
Schuler, Tino H., 1090
Schulert, Andrew, 1047
Schulhof, Milford H., II, 485

Schuller, Gunther, 2262
Schultz Family Foundation, 3565
Schultz Family Foundation, Howard & Leslie, 2827
Schultz Foundation, Arthur B., 1402
Schultz, Adam, 1154
Schultz, Allen, 2793
Schultz, Allison, 2132
Schultz, Howard D., 3557
Schultz, John, 1589
Schultz, Joshua G., 2961
Schultz, Ken, 2832
Schultz, Michael, 1797
Schultz, Roger E., 3488
Schultz, Roxanne, 1622
Schultz, Sheri K., 3557
Schultz, Wendy, 3458
Schulz, Paul, 137
Schulze, Elizabeth, 1360
Schulze, Maureen, 1738
Schulze, Richard M., 1738
Schulze, Robert Ervin, 397
Schumacher, Andrew, 574
Schumacher, Austin J., 574
Schumacher, Kyle, 538
Schumacher, Lillian, Dr., 2793
Schumacher, Robert, 1611
Schuman, Dale N., 3526
Schumann Foundation, Florence and John, 1990
Schumann, Florence, 1990
Schumann, Florence F., 2412
Schumann, John, 1990
Schumann, John J., Jr., 2412
Schumann, R. Ford, 2412
Schumann, W. Ford, 2412
Schumm, David, 2674
Schupp, Joseph E., 1541
Schur, Anne, 3568
Schuster, Donald, 1647
Schusterman Family Foundation, Charles and Lynn, 2074
Schusterman, Charles, 2829
Schusterman, Lynn, 2827, 2829
Schusterman, Stacy, 2827
Schusterman, Stacy H., 2829
Schut, Evert, 349
Schutt, Laurisa S., 630
Schutt, Paul, 1576
Schutter, Mark, 2707
Schuur, Hendrik, 1623
Schwab, Maria, 3014
Schwabacher, Christopher C., 2183
Schwager, Joni S., 3044
Schwan's Home Services, 2562
Schwander, Stephen S., 2487
Schwart, Amy, 1885
Schwartz, Alan D., 2413
Schwartz, Alan E., 1588
Schwartz, Amy, 498
Schwartz, Barbara, 158
Schwartz, Barry F., 2355
Schwartz, Beth, 2476
Schwartz, Carol L., 3481
Schwartz, Carolyn, 561
Schwartz, David, 561
Schwartz, David A., 2003
Schwartz, David E., 830
Schwartz, Eric, 561
Schwartz, Henry L., 1912, 1981
Schwartz, Jack, 3538
Schwartz, Jane R., 2774
Schwartz, Jayson, 2476
Schwartz, Jodi D., 2490
Schwartz, Joel, 3331
Schwartz, Lois C., 1481
Schwartz, Lynda, 1150
Schwartz, Marc A., 129
Schwartz, Maria C., 1031
Schwartz, Richard W., 2774
Schwartz, Robert, 348
Schwartz, Ryan, 722
Schwartz, Seymour, 561
Schwartz, Stephen J., 250
Schwartz, Stephen L., 1912, 1981
Schwartz, Steve, 685
Schwartz, Vicki Trachten, 541
Schwarz, Beverly Rupe, 389
Schwarz, Colleen, 483
Schwarz, Eliza Ladd, 3090
Schwarz, Eric, 3090
Schwarz, F. William, III, 1590
Schwarz, Frederick A.O., III, 3090
Schwarz, Frederick A.O., Jr., 2048
Schwarz, H. Marshall, 3090
Schwarz, Henryk, 1991
Schwarz, Rae Paige, 3090
Schwarz, Stephen W., 912
Schwarz, Steven, 1991
Schwed, Roger, 2326
Schweizer, Felix E., 232
Schwendeman, Mark, 2732
Schweppe, Janet A., 1065
Schwerin, Anne-Marie Zell, 3498
Schwister, Ann M., 2679
Schwoeffermann, Catherine, 2221
Sciarra, Lorraine, 2502
Scientific Components Corp., 2247
Scinto, Nancy, 1107
Sciortino, Joe, 398
Scism, Anita, 69
Sclafani, Susan, 3451
Scoble, Fran, 361
Scolaro, Peter F., 1460
Scollins, Jay, 1564
Scop, Amy B., 140
Scopelliti, Joseph, 2908
Scoppetta, Nicholas, 2146
Scotford, John P., 2779
Scotford, John P., Jr., 2779
Scotford, John, Jr., 2779
Scotford, Judy, 2779
Scotford, Laura, 2779
Scotford, Laura L., 2779
Scotford, Stephen L., 2779
Scott Foundation, 3683
Scott Foundation, S & W, 102
Scott, Asaline, 1586
Scott, Betty J., 2825
Scott, Brian, 942
Scott, Bruce K., Maj. Genl., 3468
Scott, Carolyn, 1357
Scott, David A., 2921
Scott, David R., 1979
Scott, Douglas W., 3047
Scott, Edward, 3163
Scott, Eli, 494
Scott, Elizabeth Strother, 3458
Scott, Frederic W., Jr., 3428
Scott, H. Denman, Dr., 1501
Scott, Homer A., 3679
Scott, J.L., 942
Scott, Joseph B., 942
Scott, Lynette, 3679
Scott, Margaret, 3430
Scott, Mary Jo, 73
Scott, Mildred S., 3679
Scott, Patricia, 1749
Scott, Patrick, 3397
Scott, Peggy B., 1302
Scott, Ralph, 1400
Scott, Richard J., 1715
Scott, Sam, 3683
Scott, Sheila E., 2113
Scott, Stacy P., 2763
Scott, Taylor C., 1814
Scott, Tom, 2737, 3323
Scotten, Joyce, 1178
Scoville, Roger D., 1461
Scraberry, Missi, 3587
Scranton, Barb, 1181
Scranton, Charles W., 3415
Scranton, Joseph C., 3057
Scranton, Mary L., 3057
Scranton, Maryla, 3031
Scranton, Peter K., 3057
Scranton, S. Caitlin, 3057
Scranton, William W., 3057
Scranton, William W., III, 3057
Scribner, Norman O., 656
Scripps Co., E.W., The, 2780
Scripps Klenzing, Margaret, 2780
Scripps Vasquez, Virginia, 2780
Scripps, Cindy J., 2780
Scripps, Edward W. & Christy, 2780
Scripps, Henry R., 2780
Scripps, Paul K., 2780
Scripps, Robert P., 2780
Scripps, William H. & Kathryn, 2780
Scrivener, James, 724
Scroggins, Stacy, 73
Scull, Eliot, 3503
Scully, Arthur M., III, 2906
Scully, Doris, 1185
Scully, Terrance J., 1744
Scully, Timothy, Jr., 1344
Seacrest, Eric, 1849
Seagull Lighting, 3505
SEAKR Engineering, Inc., 531
Seal, Molly R., 3125
Seales, Mary, 1241
Sealey, Kim, 1220
Sealey, Pat, 1220
Seaman, Elizabeth, 3463
Seaman, Nancy M., 2413
Seaman, Richard N., 2740
Seaman, Stan, 979
Searcy, Valerie D., 877
Searengen, Kimberley, 1578
Searle, D. Gideon, 681
Searle, Daniel C., 681
Searls, Christine, 627
Sears, Anna L., 2781
Sears, Fred C., II, 630
Sears, Heather C., 1468
Sears, Lester M., 2781
Sears, Ruth P., 2781
Sears, Suzanne Harte, 1565
Sears, Todd, 2347
Seaton, David T., 3235
Seats Inc., 3655
Seaver, Carlton, 400
Seaver, Christopher, 400
Seaver, Martha, 400
Seaver, Michelle, 3099
Seaver, Patrick, 400
Seavey Trust, Thelma, 2148
Seawell, Chris, 2604
Seawell, David, 1301
Seawell, Katie, 1301
Seawell, Marjorie B., 1301
Seawell, Marjorie Beaird, 1301
Seawell, Susie, 1301
Seay, Mason, 1128
Seay, Yvonne D., 3577
Sebastian, Teresa, 732
Sechrest, Lee, 1489
Seckinger, Mark R., 2762
Secrest, Dorothy Gail, 372
Secrest, Tish, 2524
Securian Holding Co., 1739
Security National Trust Co., 3579
Sed, Karen Winner, 2925
Sedgwick, Michael B., 253
Sedwick, Dru A., 3032
Sedwick, Jay L., 3032
Sedwick, Linda, 3032
Sedzmak, Donna, 2771
Sedzmak, Joseph, 2771
Sedzmak, Joseph P., 2771
Seebold, Rhonda, 2908
Seedworks, 2199
Seely, Margaret, 3417
Seelye, Eugene, 3008
Seem, R.B., 3580
Segal, Amy R., 232
Segal, Barry, 1930
Segal, Dolly, 1930
Segal, George, 1992
Segal, Helen, 1992
Segal, Martin, 1930
Segal, Rena, 1992
Segal, Richard, 1930
Segal, Susan L., 2467
Segarra, Joseph W., 2382
Segel, Ronald, 1232
Seger, Andy, 1194
Seger, Audrey, 1194
Seger, Cynthia J., 1194
Seger, Kelly, 1194
Seger, Randolph L., 1194
Seger, Thomas W., 1194
Segers, Bo, 3148
Segerstrom, Clark, 420
Seget, Alan D., 2144
Seggelink, Luke, 3600
Seguin, Jennifer, 296
Seib, Karl E., 2099
Seiber, John, 180
Seiden, Norman, 1908
Seiden, Stephen, 1908
Seidenberg, Beatrix, 438
Seidenberg, Joseph, 1926
Seidenfaden, Jann, 2757
Seider, William M., 727
Seidl, Ann, 3597
Seidle, Charlene, 297
Seidner, Mary, 562
Seifert, Tom, 3494
Seifert-Russell, Margaret, 1133
Seigel, Fred, 1893
Seiling, Ric, 2078
Seitchik, Adam D., 1486
Seitz, Howard G., 1891
Sekermestrovich, Peter, 2835
Selby, Leland C., 596, 597
Selby, Marie, 816
Selby, Sandra F., Rev., 2655
Selby, William G., 816
Selden, Jo Hershey, 2711
Seldes, Marian, 2050
Seldes, Timothy, 2152
Selecky, Mary C., 3510
Select Energy, Inc., 598
Self, Catherine, 3122
Selian, Paul, 1550
Selig, Linda, 852

Seliger, Nancy, 3163
Seligman, Thomas K., 151
Selim, Francine, 160
Selim, Karen W., 3196
Selinger, Sam, 3510
Sell, Bradley N., 1360
Sell, Ed S., III, 850
Sellars, Guy, 1078
Sellars, John, 3659
Sellers, R. Scot, 495
Sellstrom, Carol W., 2239
Sellstrom, John L., 2239
Selman, Peter, 2445
Selsor, David, 2794
Selz Foundation, Inc., The, 2675
Selz, Joe, 71
Selzer, Herbert, 2173
Seman, Robert J., 2085
Semans, James D.B.T., 2529
Semel, Scott, 205
Seminoff, Nancy Wiseman, 1636
Semler, Bernard, 954
Semler, Jerry D., 1126
Semmes, Douglas R., 3347
Semmes, Douglas R., Jr., 3347
Semmes, Julia Yates, 3347
Semmes, Patricia A., 3347
Semmes, Thomas R., 3347
Semnani, Ghazelah, 3404
Semnani, Khosrow, 3404
Semnani, Khosrow B., 3404
Semnani, Taymour, 3404
Semrau, Kelly M., 3625
Sender, Adam, 817
Sender, Lenore, 817
Seneca Foods Corp., 2415
Senekjian, Harry, 3390
Seng, Kate, 1724
Seng, Tom, 1154
Senior, David M., 3406
Senkler, Robert L., 1739
Sens, Gene, 3552
Senske, Michael, 3627
Sentara Healthcare, 3467
Sentrilock,LLC, 1178
Sentry Insurance, 3657
Sentry Trust Co., 2952
Sepulveda, Eugene, 3273
Seramur, Brian, 3658
Seramur, Joan, 3658
Seramur, John C., 3658
Serck-Hanssen, Eilif, 648
Sergi, Kathy, 715
Sergi, Kathy J., 715
Sergi, Vincent A.F., 1042
Serino, Jim, 1623
Servillo, Gene, 1012
Sethman, Chad, 2924
Setlow, Carolyn E., 564
Settembrini, Joel, 746
Settle, Ernest, 1586
Settles, Jeremy, 2010
Setzer, Debra, 818
Setzer, Leonard R., 818
Setzer, Sidney, 818
Seubert, Pat, 3642
Seuthe, Brenda, 85
Severn Plumbing, 3505
Severns, Jerr, 1286
Severson, Katherine, 3567
Sevier, Marcus, 522
Sevier, Sheila, 522
Sewall, Elmina B., 1339
Seward, Diana, 2010
Sewell, Stace, 3218
Sewell, Stan, 3218
Sewell, Warren P., Jr., 914
Sexton, Leah Ann, 11
Sexton, Richard, 2445
Seybert, Henry, 3034
Seybold, Dorthea M., 1887
Seyle, David, 904
Seymour, Claudia, 2044
Seymour, Louise E., 1091
Seymour, Robert, 1768
SFX Escrow - Blood PSA, 1228
Shackelford, John, 839
Shackelford, Stephanie, 839
Shackelford, Stephanie W., 839
Shackelton, Scott, 269
Shade, Nancy, 1914
Shadwick, Gerald, 484
Shadwick, Jeannine, 484
Shaefer, William H., 2719
Shafer, Julie, 194
Shaffer, Cecile, 3035
Shaffer, David, 3035
Shaffer, Jack M., 3035
Shaffer, Michael A., 2674
Shaffer, Penelope S., 744
Shaffer, Quentin, 2466
Shaffer, Rebecca, 1981
Shaffer, Rose, 3035
Shaffer, Susan, 3035
Shaffir, Melvyn L., 2443
Shafir, Eldar, 1923
Shafir, Robert S., 2118
Shaheen, David, 1871
Shaheen, David M., 1871
Shaheen, Kari, 1662
Shaheen, Linda F., 1871
Shailor, Barbara A., 2263
Shainberg Endowment, Nathan & Dorothy, 2050
Shalom, Ish, 2416
Shamah, Amy, 3556
Shambach, John L., 1208
Shamel, Marlene, 2543
Shan, Helen, 604
Shands, Jay, 3227
Shaner, Troy K., 1215
Shank, Donna, 1263
Shank, Matthew D., Dr., 3421
Shanken, Leslie, 2101
Shanks, David, 3327
Shanks, Deb, 1125
Shanley, Frank E., 558
Shanley, Richard, 993
Shannon, Ann Dudley, 3610
Shannon, Darryl, 2078
Shannon, James C., III, 1505
Shannon, Kathleen, 2029
Shannon, Kathleen T., 363
Shannon, Kristin, 1314
Shannon, Michael, 543
Shannon, Wendy, 1735
Shapell Industries, 196
Shaper, C. Park, 510
Shapira, Anne L., 2870
Shapira, David S., 2889
Shapira, Elijahu, 2870
Shapiro, Brad, 133
Shapiro, Carol S., 3471
Shapiro, Charles, 1093
Shapiro, Isaac, 2477
Shapiro, Judith, 2459
Shapiro, Judith R., 2459, 2460
Shapiro, Mary, 1093
Shapiro, Molly, 1093
Shapiro, Morris R., 1093
Shapiro, Richard, Esq., 2111
Shapiro, Robert N., 1553
Shapiro, Roberta, 3385
Shapiro, Sarah H., 1379
Shapiro, Scott, 3558
Shapiro, Sharon Ellen, 1537
Shapiro, Stephen L., 2798
Shapiro, Stephen R., 471
Shapley, Rick, 726
Shar, Albert O., 1949
Share, Harvey, 3007
Sharfin, Ira, 2750
Sharkey, Christopher, 1356
Sharko, Matthew, 1097
Sharko, Michelle, 1097
Sharma, Deven, 2458
Sharman, Tanya E., 1090
Sharon, Ingrid, 3269
Sharp, David, 2662
Sharp, Eli R., 639
Sharp, Joan L., 630
Sharp, Leigh Ann, 1021
Sharp, Peggy, 945
Sharp, Rhonda, Dr., 1170
Sharp, Tom, 545
Sharpe, Ann M., Esq., 2108
Sharpe, Jerri Lynn Craft, 3113
Sharrock-Dorsten, Carolyn, 2674
Shashack, Will, 1010
Shattuck, Mayo A., II, 1407
Shatz, Carla, 2534
Shatz, Carla J., 1714
Shaughnessy, John, Jr., 1509
Shaver, Thomas, 1724
Shaw Trust, Evelyn, 1340
Shaw's Supermarkets, Inc., 3092
Shaw, Barb, 1162
Shaw, Cindy, 1764
Shaw, Dorothy, 1764
Shaw, Eric W., 1377
Shaw, George, 1286
Shaw, Glenn H., 892
Shaw, Jack R., 1190
Shaw, James W., 3110
Shaw, Jeff, 535
Shaw, Jennifer, 1559
Shaw, Joe, 2027
Shaw, Kathleen, 722
Shaw, L Stanley, 3505
Shaw, Lani A., 501
Shaw, Mark W., 2189
Shaw, Minor M., 3101
Shaw, Nancy Peterson, 892
Shaw, Patrick, 978
Shaw, Richard, 2890
Shaw, Richard W., 2008
Shaw, Roger D., Jr., 1783
Shaw, Sara Chase, 2008
Shaw, Sarah, 217
Shaw, Steve, 25
Shaw, William H., III, 892
Shawver, Mark, 364
Shay, Robert P., Jr., 2644
Shea Co., J.F., Inc., 402
Shea, Carey C., 2368
Shea, Greg, 1842
Shea, Jeremy C., 3600
Shea, John F., 402
Shea, Kristin, 2648
Shea, Lindsay D., 2511
Shea, Patrick Kelly, 3522
Shea, Peter O., 402
Shea-Ballay, Kathleen, 3046
Sheafer, Emma A., 2418
Sheahan, Casey, 362
Sheahan, Tim, 498
Sheble-Hall, Alexander, 3042
Sheboygan Beverage, Inc., 3630
Sheehan, Chris, 1545
Sheehan, Elizabeth, 1545
Sheehan, Gerald V., 1545
Sheehan, Jim, 3543
Sheehan, Joe, 1802
Sheehan, John, 1545
Sheehan, Joseph, 1802
Sheehan, Joseph E., 1895
Sheehan, Juliette K., 928
Sheehan, Margaret, 1545
Sheehan, Robert C., 2427
Sheehan, Timothy, 1545
Sheely, William Wallace, 3359
Sheenan, Janet, 1519
Sheerer, Marilyn, 2632
Sheets, Alice, 896
Sheets, Laura, 1131
Sheets, Ruth A., 1460
Sheetz, Brenda A., 1187
Shefts, Mark, 1974
Shefts, Wanda, 1974
Sheiffer, Steve, 3607
Shelby, Susan, 1472
Shelden, William W., Jr., 1588, 1638
Sheldon, Donald, 2754
Sheldon, Roy C., 301
Shelhamer, Betty S., 227
Shell Exploration & Production, 3348
Shell Offshore, Inc., 3237
Shell Oil Co., 28, 3348
Shell, Frederick E., 1598
Shell, John, 1163
Shelor, Cynthia M., 3432
Shelton, Allison Korman, 826
Shelton, Andrew B., 3350
Shelton, Bruce, 54
Shelton, Holly, 2702
Shelton, John, 1662
Shelton, Robert, 59
Shelton, Ruby W., 3350
Shelton, Ruth, 3229
Shelton, Sandra Waller, 1012
Shemanski, Alfred, 3560
Shemanski, Tillie, 3560
Shendo, Benny, Jr., 2011
Sheng, Kimberlee, 2868
Shennan, Jamie, 1832
Shepard, James D., 356
Shepard, John A., Jr., 3415
Shepard, Julia Sparkman, 656
Shepard, Mikki, 2306
Shepherd, Anne H., 3248
Shepherd, David W., 2219
Shepherd, Katherine B., 2672
Shepherd, Matthew, 73
Sheridan County YMCA, 3683
Sheridan, Don, 1241
Sheridan, Edward, 538
Sheridan, Eileen F., 394
Sheridan, Erica, 1663
Sheridan, John J., 973
Sheridan, Thelma, 2662
Sherman & Sterling, 2445
Sherman, Bruce, 3528
Sherman, Cindy, 2494
Sherman, John, 1797
Sherman, M. Eugene, 485
Sherman, Michael B., 1461

Sherman, Sandra Brown, 1952
Sherman, Scott D., 80
Sherman, Susan E., 2976
Sherman, Tom, 1307
Sherman, William S., 2419
Sherrard, William, 2623
Sherrer, Terrence, 2737
Sherrill, Joseph N., Jr., 3201
Sherry, Andrew, 771
Sherry, Fred, 2262
Sherwell, Jon P., 1378
Shevlin, Patricia A., 1088
Shewey, Bill, 2809
Shi, Theodore, 105
Shibata, Christy Rupert, 2322
Shibata, Myles, 933
Shield, Robin R., 3477
Shield-Taylor, Juliet E., 3477
Shields, Charlie, 1817
Shields, Joyce, 2097
Shields, Laura S., 1319
Shields, Patrick, 3544
Shields, Robert E., 1572
Shifflett, Todd, 3098
Shiflett, Laura, 3373
Shifman, Pamela, 2334
Shiller, Thomas, 2757
Shimer, Pete, 3558
Shin, Clara J., 385
Shingle, Alice K., 928
Shining D Farms, 1000
Shinkle, Debra A., 2665
Shinkman, Gillian C., 1361
Shinnick, William M., 2783
Shipley, Caroline C., 2342
Shipley, Seth, 1357
Shipp, Pam, 525
Shirai, Sandra, 569
Shireman, joe, 1155
Shires, Dana, 1756
Shirk, Gerald, 878
Shirk, Roland, 1142
Shirley, Johnna, 3098
Shiverick, Paul C., 2099
Shivers, Anna S. "Candy", 2540
Shm Shoes LLC., 2484
Shmerling, Michael D., 3129
Shoaff, Thomas, 3058
Shockley, Scott, 1121
Shoemaker, James R., Esq., 1358
Shoemaker, Linda J., 476
Shoemaker, Patricia, 1580
Shofe, Allen, 659
Sholler, Andrea, 2306
Shonk, Brian, 2696
Shoof, Thomas, 776
Shook, Charlie, 1130
Shook, Eric, 2793
Shook, Mark L., Rabbi, 1815
Shoolman, Edith Glick, 2420
Shoos, John, 1327
Shooshan, John G., 3421
Shore, Melanie, 725
Shores, Shirley A., 1358
Short, Jean R., 2625
Short, Marianne D., 1734
Short, Tracy, 3648
Short, William R., 867
Shorter, Kim, 2981
Shotton, Patricia J., 3449
Shoup, John, 1131
Shovelin, Julia M., 2560
Showalter, Craig R., 3684
Showden, Carisa, 143
Shows, Cali, Berthelot, Morris, LLP, 1314
Shrallow, Dale P., 3181
Shreve, Christine A., 1373
Shreves, Catherine, 1717
Shriver, Elizabeth, 1224
Shriver, Michael F., 2524
Shrock, Kelly, 1134
Shryock, Larry L., 3228
Shu Trading, Inc., 1023
Shuayb, Ahd, 78
Shuayb, Husam, 78
Shubert, Norman A., 1093
Shuey, Maura, 2991
Shuford, Alex, 1001
Shuford, Karen, 3289
Shuford, Karen L., 3262
Shuford, Lois, 1773
Shuler, Arlene, 2389, 2477
Shulman, Alison Bernstein, 652
Shulman, Stanley, 2290
Shulruff, Stuart P., 1042
Shultz, Herbert L., Jr., 2407
Shultz, Rowan, 2961
Shumaker, Albert L., 9
Shumaker, Dianne C., 1276
Shumaker, Eric A., 1276
Shumaker, Megan I., 1276
Shumaker, Paul K., 1276
Shumaker, Ronn, 1135
Shuman, Bonney Stamper, 866
Shuman, Erik, Esq., 723
Shuman, Stanley, 543
Shumate, Greg, 867
Shumski, Edward, 1755
Shumway, Brooks, 437
Shure, Alice, 1925
Shurts, Steve, 1703
Shute, Sharon, 2712
Shuter, Jack, 2731
Shuter, Pat, 2731
Shymanski, Richard W., 3153
Sibert, Ron, 1132
Sibley Irrevocable Trust, Effie Potts, 3323
Sibley, Hiram, 3323
Sibley, Horace, 923
Sibley, James M., 918
Sichting, Dan, 1152
Sickler, Judi, 1842
Sidden, Curt, 3622
Sidden, Jennifer, 3622
Sidford, James A., 2108
Sidnam, Caroline N., 2296
Sidoti, Paul A., M.D., 2269
Siebel, Kenneth F., 333
Siebel, Stacey, 404
Siebel, Thomas M., 404
Siebels, Jane M., 3047
Sieben, Todd W., 1022
Sieber-Benson, Vicki, 2876
Siebers, Steve, 992
Siebert, A.F., 3659
Siebert, Reginald L., 3659
Siegal, Edward G., 1453
Siegel Charitable Lead Trust, Naomi L., 2927
Siegel, Alan, 2461
Siegel, David, 544
Siegel, Herbert J., 2126
Siegel, Howard J., 984
Siegel, John E., 2147
Siegel, Larry, 3498
Siegel, Lynne F., 3533
Siegel, Marvin S., 2518
Siegel, Stephen, 2271
Siegel, Stuart C., 3433
Sieger, Diana R., 1615
Siegert, Kenneth V., 1504
Siegert, Robert F., 3648
Siegfried, Steve, 3026
Siegried, Carolyn, 364
Siegrist Construction, 484
Siegrist, Greg, 659
Siekerka, Michele N., 1984
Sielak, George, 28
Siemens, 3424
Siemens Corp., 1993
Sierra Pacific Industries, 406
Sierra Towers & Fresh Meadows, LLP, 2207
Sierra, J. Robert, 819
Sierra, John Robert, 819
Sierra, Jose L., 162
Sierra, Luis, 3181
Sierra, Mary, 819
Sieting, Janet, 1616
Sietsma, David, 801
Sieve, Marty, 1723
Sievers, Mark, 419
Sievertsen, Craig, 3498
Sifferlen, Ned J., 2688
Sigafoos, Kamilla, 2696
Sigelbaum, Harvey, 2399
Sigman, Marilyn, 26
Sigmon, Crosley Johnson, 2714
Sikes, Virginia P., Esq., 2985
Sikorski, Brad, 69
Silard, Timothy P., 385
Silber, Mark, 2423
Silberman, Samuel "Buddy", 2051
Silicon Valley Bank, 407
Silicon Valley Community Foundation, 259
Sill, Valerie J., 630
Sills, John W., III, 3429
Silsby, Andrew, 1332
Silsby, Paula D., 1340
Silva, Alicia Donahue, 352
Silva, Kevin D., 2297, 2488
Silver, Barbara, 614
Silver, Chelsea Hoopes, 619
Silver, Eli, 2051
Silver, F. Morris, 1830
Silver, Jane, 2136
Silver, Jean, 1428
Silver, Patti, 1027
Silver, Peter Milo, 614
Silver, Philip, 614
Silver, Philip Tyler, 614
Silver, R. Philip, 614
Silver, Richard, 268
Silverman, Barton M., 2976
Silverman, Fred, 309
Silverman, Greg, 2466
Silverman, Harold, 2324
Silverman, Irene Zambelli, 2101
Silverman, Robert, 1109
Silverman, Ross O., 1042
Silverman, Samuel B., 764
Silverman, Thomas N., 764
Silverson, Donald, 3017
Silverstein, Eileen S., 2020
Silverthorne, Iain, 340
Silverton Foundation, 3159
Silverton Partners, LP, 3368
Silvestri, Charles, 1867
Silwkowski, Mary B., 216
Silzle, Barbara J., 3053
Simches, Michael, 2220
Simensky, Edward, 1327
Simental, Santiago, 160
Simer, William A., 3526
Simmer, Mike, 3619
Simmermon, Marcia, 1175
Simmons, Adele, 65
Simmons, Angelica C., 342
Simmons, Bryan E., 2040
Simmons, Cecelia, 1051
Simmons, Cricket, 1852
Simmons, Elizabeth S., 1776
Simmons, Gwen, 3054
Simmons, Harris, 3389
Simmons, Jeffrey, 993
Simmons, Karen, 2915
Simmons, Karen A., 2915
Simmons, Marc, 2932
Simmons, Michael, 1126
Simmons, Omar, 1486
Simmons, Peter, 2146
Simmons, Thomas, Dr., 1808
Simmons, Tom, 1716
Simmons, William T., 2896
Simms, Cleo, 3432
Simms, Marsha, 2389
Simms, Rick, 499
Simon Trust, Ronald M., 2018
Simon, Deborah, 1156
Simon, Geri, 3313
Simon, Howard L., 2183
Simon, Janet, 2950
Simon, Jeffrey, 2804
Simon, Jennifer, 2702
Simon, Kenneth O., 22
Simon, Patsy, 3200
Simon, Peter, 105
Simon, Philip B., 191
Simon, R. Matthew, 973
Simon, Raymond F., 973, 1075
Simon, Renee B., Hon., 90
Simon, Ronald M., 410
Simon, Steven, 2018
Simon, Steven H., 410
Simon, Steven R., 147
Simon, Trinette, 2685
Simonds, Juliet L. Hillman, 2969
Simons DE TR I, Elizabeth, The, 245
Simons DE Trust II, Elizabeth, The, 245
Simons, Dolph, Jr., 1256
Simons, Elizabeth D., 245
Simons, James, 2423
Simons, James H., 245, 2423
Simons, Jim Marilyn, 2173
Simons, Marilyn, 2423
Simons, Robert, 1569
Simons, Susan W., 3129
Simonsen, Arnold J., 1094
Simonson, Elizabeth, 2548
Simonton, Steve, 3672
Simonyi, Charles, 3562
Simonyi, Lisa, 3562
Simpkins, Nancy, 1328, 2258
Simpson Charitable Trust, The, 3207
Simpson Family Charitable Foundation, 1748
Simpson Manufacturing Co., Inc., 411
Simpson, Barclay, 222, 411
Simpson, Brooks, 3570
Simpson, Dazelle D., 783
Simpson, Dean, 1751
Simpson, Jane, 2543
Simpson, K. Russell, 912
Simpson, Lin, 1215
Simpson, Louis A., 806

Simpson, Mike, 2712
Simpson, Scott, 73
Simpson, Sharon, 222
Simpson, Steve, 378
Simpson, W.H.B., 2626
Simpson, W.H.B., Mrs., 2626
Simpson-Godfrey, Diana, 2835
Sims, Carter, 3026
Sims, David L., 2919
Sims, Gretchen Crosby, 1040
Sims, Jenn, 3026
Sims, Lowery, 2043
Sims, Stephen, 919
Sinak, David L., 3251
Sinclair, Gloria J., 1024
Sinclair, Shea, 1280
Singer, Andy, 2737
Singer, Gary, 410
Singer, Larry, 1012
Singer, Linda, 268
Singer, Myer R., 1445
Singer, Paul E., 2424
Singh, Dinakar, 2425
Singh, Gopal, 3563
Singh, Gurpaul, 3351
Singh, Gurvinder P., 3351
Singh, Jagdish, 2787
Singh, Jill, 3563
Singh, Kamala, 3563
Singh, Rajeev, 3563
Singh, Ravi Mo, 2425
Singh, Sanjay, 2750
Singh, Sudhir, 3563
Singleton, David, 630, 2782
Singleton, Pamela, 2044
Singleton, Paul, 1128
Sinik, John, 2473
Sink, Brad S., 429
Sinnaeve, John, 1660
Sinsheimer, Alexander L., 1095
Sinsheimer, Alexandrine, 1095
Siocum, Michael C., 3426
Sioles, Elyse C., 61
Sioles, Harriet Z., 61
Sioles, Robert M., 61
Sippel, Thomas J., 1363
Siragusa, Alexander C., 1096
Siragusa, Isabel, 1096
Siragusa, John R., III, 1096
Siragusa, Ross D., 1096
Siragusa, Ross D., III, 1096
Siragusa, Sinclair C., 1096
Siritunga, Dilan, 2377
Sirot, Margaret, 320
Sirpurkar-Childress, Angha, 1432
Sirrine, John, 1581
Sisco, Martin, 3150
Sisisky, Mark P., 3433
Siska, Nancy, 1717
Sisley, Christine, 270
Sisson, Douglas L., 2998
Sistevans, Kiros, 2562
Sitarik, Denise, 1948
Sitt, David, 1898
Sitt, Eddie, 1898
Sizemore, Jeff, Rev., 1382
Sizemore, Patrecia, 2773
Sizer, John, 569
Sizer, Theodore, 1899
Sjostedt, Judy, 2968, 3587
Skadden, Arps, Slate, Meagher & Flom, 2427
Skaden Arps, 2445
Skagen, Ron, 3503
Skaggs, Robert C., Jr., 2752
Skaugstad, Chuck, 1218
Skedgell, Misty, 2466
Skeehan, Joseph W., 363
Skelly, Gertrude E., 820
Skelton, Brenda, 3659
Skelton, Joe, 2686
Skelton, Karen, 3368
Skelton, Marcie, 1772
Skelton, Robert M., 921
Skerpon, David B., 2952
Skilbred, Amy, 35
Skillman, Rose P., 1666
Skinner, Robert, 394
Skinner, Valerie Holloway, 3264
Skirvin, Brandi, 1282
Skiva International, Inc., 2172
Skjodt, Cynthia Simon, 1126
Skjonsby, Gregory, 351
Skjonsby, Mary, 351
Sklar, Linda, 752
Skoda, Gerald J., 2111
Skogen, Mark, 3619
Skoglund, Linda, 3662
Skoglund, Peter, 2118
Skoglund, Steve, 3641
Skoglund, William B., 991
Skoll, Jeffrey S., 412, 413
Skonberg, Lorena, 36
Skrutskie, Mike, 291
Slade, Jennifer K., 1167
Slade, Nicholas, 1722
Slager, David, 2377
Slagle, George, 3219
Slaight, Marsha D., 1785
Slaight, Tara L., 1785
Slaight, Thomas L., 1785, 1805
Slaight, Zachary D., 1785
Slamar, Charles, Jr., 1032
Slate, Jill, 3441
Slater, Tammy, 1207
Slater, Thomas C., 2922
Slattery, Anne, 564
Slattery, Barb, 1848
Slaughter, Chris, 394
Slavin, Peter, Dr., 809
Slawek, Joseph J., 1060
Slawson, Diana, 161
Slawson, Kathryn Aicher, 1323
Sledd, Robert C., III, 3433
Sleeman, John, 1344
Sleik, Tom, 3631
Slemp, C. Bascom, 2785
Slentz, Michael L., 1144
Slette, Gary, 1750
Slick, Rex, 1158
Slicker, John K., 67
Slifer, Beth, 2232
Slifer, Rodney, 543
Slifka, Barbara, 2428
Slifka, Barbara S., 2428
Slifka, Joseph, 2428
Slifka, Sylvia, 2428
Sliman, Jake, 1603
Slivia, Raymond, 1685
SLM Holding Corp., 1174
Sloan, Jake, 2205
Sloan, Jr. Charitable Lead Trust, O. Temple, 2628
Sloan, O. Temple, Jr., 2628
Sloan, Stephen R., 3401
Sloan, Steve, 2907
Sloan, Sue, 3018
Sloan, Todd, 2909
Sloane, Alexander, 2205
Sloane, Howard G. (Peter), 2205
Sloane, Virginia, 2205
Slocum, Caroline Gates, 1539
Sloenaker, James, 397
Sloneker, James, 347
Sloss, Deborah, 199
Sloss, Laura, 199
Sluder, Greenfield, 1442
Sluder, Hendrika, 1442
Slutsky, Lorie A., 2325
Sluys, Nancy M., 3409
Sluzewski, Jim, 2726
Slye, Terry, 1687
Smadbeck, Arthur J., 2205
Smadbeck, Jeffrey, 2205
Smadbeck, Lou, 2205
Smadbeck, Louis, Jr., 2205
Smadbeck, Mark, 2205
Smadbeck, Paul, 2205
Small Pond Investments, Ltd., 1524
Small, Cornelia, 2459, 2460
Small, George L., 1398
Small, J. Robert, 2174
Small, James, 3648
Small, John, Jr., 1176
Small, Mario, 1098
Small, Peggy, 1227
Smallwood, Thomas L., 3601
Smart, Allen J., 2614
Smart, Paul R., 2616
Smead, Ann, 543
Smedley, Sheryl, 4
Smiley, Butch, 3429
Smiley, Karl, 783
Smirich, John, 2381
Smirnov, Maxim, 2882
Smith Charitable Remainder Unitrust, Floyd, 3445
Smith Charitable Remainder Unitrust, Nancy M., 1775
Smith Charitable Trust, May and Stanley, 676
Smith Construction, C.D., Inc., 3660
Smith Corp., J M, 3109
Smith Family Foundation, Charles E., 960
Smith Foundation, Particia & William, 2332
Smith Investment LP, Robert & Pamela, 368
Smith Joint Charitable Remainder Unitrust, 1775
Smith Marital Trust, Robert Brookings, 1775
Smith Memorial Fund, 562
Smith Revocable Trust, Nancy Morrill, 1775
Smith Trust, Charles E., 3479
Smith, Adrienne, 1478
Smith, Alexander M., 3564
Smith, Anita S., 1150
Smith, Argile, 1755
Smith, B. Thomas, 1656
Smith, B.J., 2702
Smith, Banks M., 3371
Smith, Barry H., 2261
Smith, Bernadette Eyler, 2950
Smith, Bernice R., 3564
Smith, Beth K., 1277
Smith, Brad, 3558
Smith, Bradford K., 2467
Smith, Bradley, 2730
Smith, Bradley S., 2728, 2729
Smith, Brenda J., 492
Smith, Brent, 3631
Smith, Brian J., 3054
Smith, Bridget, 1662
Smith, Byron, 801
Smith, Camilla M., 2430
Smith, Carol Anne, Sr., 2786
Smith, Caroline, 3163
Smith, Cathy, 74
Smith, Charles E., 3479
Smith, Charles W., 253
Smith, Chris, 1286
Smith, Christine B., Dr., 3147
Smith, Clara Blackford, 3353
Smith, Clarice R., 3479
Smith, Clarke A., 417
Smith, Corey R., 3019
Smith, Cynthia, 3100
Smith, Dana W., 1546
Smith, Daniel D., 2989, 3025
Smith, Darnell, 744
Smith, David, 1209, 2689, 3325
Smith, David B., 3479
Smith, David Bruce, 960
Smith, David F., 2321
Smith, David L., 3160
Smith, David N., 2736
Smith, David, II, 493
Smith, Denise, 948
Smith, Dennis, 122
Smith, Derek, 2078
Smith, Donald R., 1965
Smith, Donna, 3587
Smith, Dorenda, 3364
Smith, Dorothea P., 902
Smith, Eileen O., 2896
Smith, Eleanor, 1352
Smith, Elizabeth B., 1486
Smith, Erin, 1163
Smith, Ethel Sergeant Clark, 2629
Smith, Evelyn A., 5
Smith, Fern, 268
Smith, Forrester M., III, 3371
Smith, Frank J., 3037
Smith, Fred W., 1869
Smith, Garrett K., 1240
Smith, Gary, 3522
Smith, Gary M., 3660
Smith, Gavin H., 3266
Smith, George D., Jr., 2430
Smith, George D., Sr., 2430
Smith, Gordon H., 2071
Smith, Greg, 83
Smith, Gregg, 1616
Smith, Gwendolyn A., 2932
Smith, H. William, Jr., 2332
Smith, Henry D., 3109
Smith, Herbert, III, 2169
Smith, Horace, 1547
Smith, Hugh, Dr., 1735
Smlth, J. Melvin, 1114
Smith, J. Michael, 739
Smith, James, 268, 2696
Smith, James Allen, 2098
Smith, James Campbell, 2785
Smith, Janaea, 1603
Smith, Jane, 3192
Smith, Jane Cavanaugh, 560
Smith, Janet, 1115
Smith, Jean Bixby, 137
Smith, Jean M., 1547
Smith, Jeffery T., 2221
Smith, Jeffrey, 1916
Smith, Jeffrey O., 3487
Smith, Jerry M., 903

Sorrells, Christopher, Dr., 3597
Sorrentino, Matthew R., Esq., 2986
Sosa, Liz, 1280
Soskin, William H., 91
Sosland, Morton I., 1793
Sosland-Edelman, Debbie, 1277
Sosnowski, Julie, 1596
Sotherden, Lucile, 2148
Sotirhos Nicholson, Pelagia, 2236
Sotiros, Diane, 1018
Soto-Harmon, Lidia, 672
Soulliere, Anne-Marie, 1889
Soupata, Lea N., 1353
Sources of Hope Foundation, 2173
Sousou, Ramez, 2473
Southcentral Foundation, 33
Southern Bancshares, Inc., 2630
Southern Bank & Trust Co., 2630
Southern Co., The, 915
Southern Comm Buildings, LLC, 1313
Southern Crushed Concrete, Inc., 1673
Southern Furniture Co. of Conover, Inc., 2531
Southern, Bill, 1260
Southstar, LP, 628
Southwestern Bell Corp., 3167
Soutus, Sonya, 864
Souza, Cynthia, 161
Sovereign Bank, 1541
Sovern, Michael I., 2048
Sox, Harold C., 1489
Soza, William, 3469
Space Mark Inc., 27
Spady, Bob, 1849
Spagnoletti, Joe, 1917
Spain, James, 1156
Spalding, Charles C., Jr., 932
Spalding, Philip F., 307
Spanbock, Marion, 2237
Spanbock, Maurice S., 2231
Spangler, C. Gregory, 2674
Spangler, Dean L., 2674
Spangler-Crawford, Diana, 2538
Spanier, David B., 2299
Spanier, Jonathan G., 2299
Spanier, Maury L., 2299
Spanton, Elisabeth, 1289
Spar, Debora, 2290
Sparber, Roy M., 2183
Sparby, David, 1754
Sparks, Candace "Candy", 487
Sparks, Gil, 3503
Sparks, Jackie, 1883
Sparks, Justice Keith F., Hon., 371
Sparks, Laura, 3011
Sparks, Mary Lee, 1053
Sparks, Robert D., 3154
Sparks, Willard D., 3154
Sparrow, Bradford, 1323
Sparrow, Paul, 662
Spartz, Margaret A., 1201
Spaulding, Karen Lee, 2340
Speakman-Yerick, Linda, 1179
Spearin, Preston and Burrows, Inc., 2228
Speas Co., 1813
Speas Unitrust, Alice J., 1813
Speas, Effie E., 1813
Speas, Victor E., 1813
Specialty Manufacturing Co., The, 1686
Speck, Samuel, III, 2683
Spector, Alfred, 231
Spedden, Sandra P., 1400
Speece, Arthur J., 3370
Speed, Linda S., 1136
Speedway Children's Charities, 2562
Speer, Lynnda L., 824
Speer, Mark, 1274
Speer, Richard M., 824
Speer, Roy M., 824
Speeth, Lauren, 190
Speh, Albert J., IV, 1097
Speh, Albert J., Jr., 1097
Speh, Claire R., 1097
Speh, Jonathan, 1097
Speh, Michael, 1097
Speir, Shannon G., 8
Spektor, Eryk, 2442
Spektor, Mira, 2442
Spell, Tara, 2514
Spellane, Thomas P., 2201
Spellings, Margaret, 3516
Spellman, Christina, 2296
Spence, Bryan, 1449
Spencer Foundation, 674
Spencer, Barbara A., 2548
Spencer, Denise K., 3100
Spencer, Don, 1583
Spencer, J.M., 2794
Spencer, John, 667
Spencer, Laura, 727
Spencer, Letitia A., 1839
Spencer, Lyle M., 1098
Spencer, M. Hunter, 2142
Spencer, Margaret Beale, 674, 2161
Spencer, Melinda, 3257
Spencer, Michael, 74
Spencer, Richard, 193
Spencer, Robert D., 2142
Spencer, Tim, 3257
Spencer, William M., III, 2142
Spensley, Michael S., 2454
Speranza, Paul S., Jr., 2497
Spero, Suzanne M., 1965
Spero, Thomas L., 3637
Sperry, Richard J., 3405
Spicer, Marian, 2684
Spiece, Trey, 43
Spiegel, David, 2103
Spiegel, Debra, 363
Spiegel, Eric A., 1993
Spiegel, Israel, 2103
Spiegel, Sarah, 2103
Spiegel, Steven, 1732
Spiegelman, Donald, 2212
Spielman, Ronald, 3607
Spiers, Mark, 537
Spika, Nicholas C., 3559
Spilotro, Saundra L., 1114
Spina, John, 1181
Spinks, Steve, 3099
Spinnato, John, 1988
Spira, David, 2193
Spirer, Kenneth, 1327
Spitaletta, Sabrina, 1988
Spitz, Edward A., 3102
Spitz, Julia, 2147
Spitzer Trust, Doreen, 2083
Spivey, Anita V., 1944
Splawn, Robert, M.D., 444
Spletzer, Art, 2674
Splinter, Michael R., 88
Spoelhof, Scott Alan, 1591
Spoelman, Roger, 349, 1586
Spohngellert, David B., 2171
Spolter, Jerry, 268
Spotanski, Micheal R., 1799
Spradling, J. Shannon, 1776
Spraggins, Joe, Genl., 1764
Spraggins, Marion, 3421
Sprague, Andy, 992
Sprague, James B., 1366
Sprague, Laurie Morse, 1531
Sprague, Ronald, 1924
Sprague, Seth, 2444
Sprague, William W., Jr., 1332
Sprauve-Martin, Margaret, 3419
Spray, Donna & Ed, 2780
Spray, Jane, 141
Spring Lake Park Lions Club, 1736
Spring Trust, Anna M., 381
Spring, M. Edward, 373
Springer, J. William, 2773
Springer, Kim, 513
Springgate, Susan, 1626
Springhouse Realty Co., 2953
Springs, Elliott W., 3111
Springs, Frances Ley, 3111
Springsted, Kirk, 1701
Sprint Nextel, 2562
Sprole, F. Russell, 2259
Sproul, Curt, 371
Sprowles, Jeffrey, 2900
Sprung, Sharon, 2044
Spurgeon, Mark, 3503
Spurlock, Doug, 384
Spurlock, Joyce, 384
Spurlock, Sandra, 3521
Spurrier, Clinton, 1241
Square D Co., 1099
Squeri, Stephen J., 2034
Squibb, James G., Jr., 3579
Squire Trust, Morris B., 2827
Squires, David, 2112
Squires, Deborah A., 62
Squires, Lena B., 62
Squires, William D., 62
Srodes, Ellen, 2950
Sroufe, Jon, 1168
SRYZ Corp., 390
SSR Charitable Lead Annuity Trust 2004, 1397
St. Andrews Presbyterian College, 2628
St. Boniface Hospital, 37
St. Clair, John G., 945
St. Clair, Yemana, 1338
St. Clair., Lucas, 1338
St. Francis Hospital, 1156
St. James Church, 2228
St. John's Community Foundation, 613
St. Joseph's Hospital, 757
St. Jude Medical, CRM Div., 757
St. Jude Medical, Inc., 1741
St. Luke Medical Staff, 363
St. Mary's Hospital, 2809
St. Paul Foundation, 1748
St. Paul's Episcopal Church Outreach Grant Council, 2731
Staab, Valari, 2322
Staack, Glenn, 649
Staadt, Gary, 1186
Staats Bibliotek Berlin, 2069
Stabler, Amelia Taper, 433
Stabler-Cordis, Sarah, 988
Stack, Edward W., 2099
Stack, Nina, 2597
Stackhouse Trust, Mary, 2447
Stackhouse, Lucinda, 28
Stackpole Carbon Co., 3042
Stackpole, Adelaide, 3042
Stackpole, Alice, 2407
Stackpole, Harrison C., 3042
Stackpole, J. Hall, 3042
Stackpole, Joseph, 609
Stackpole, R. Dauer, 3042
Stacy, Julie K., 3239
Stadleman, Kelly, 3589
Stadtler, Sander, 2594
Stadtmauer, Marisa, 1996
Stadtmauer, Richard, 1996
Stadtmueller, Gerald, 3630
Staebler, Rebecca, 3504
Staeck, Michael P., 3648
Stafford, Amanda, 3480
Stafford, Brian J., 1505
Stafford, Charles T., 886
Stafford, Charlotte, 825
Stafford, Earl W., Sr., 3480
Stafford, George, 305
Stafford, Inge P., 825
Stafford, John R., 825
Stager, Judy Manno, 2939
Staggers, Barbara C., 140
Staggs, Melanie, 137
Stahr, Don, 1259
Stairs, Michael, 3019
Stakely, Margaret, 3145
Staley, Catherine, 3043
Staley, Chuck, 1175
Staley, Franklin E.W., 1790
Staley, Roger, 2616
Staley, Sally J., 2770
Staley, Steven K., 2763
Staley, Stuart, 3043
Staley, Thomas F., 3043
Staley, Walter G., III, 1790
Stallard, Meg, 391
Stallings Foundation, 2574
Stallings, Mary M., 2809
Stamats, Amy, 1634
Stambaugh, Craig, 3488
Stambaugh, Jason, 1357
Stambaugh, Mary Ellen, 113
Stamelman, Andrew J., 1911
Stamford Hospital, 613
Stamm, Doug, 2861
Stammerjohn, Bettie B., 2924
Stamp, Joan Corson, 3579
Stamp, Lisa Collins, 795
Stamp, Trent, 189
Stamps, E. Roe, IV, 771
Stanback, Bruce, 2616
Stancati, Joe, 1593
Stancil, Mike, 3503
Standal, Bluebell, 939
Standish, Christine, 2108
Stanek, Bernard, 2559
Stanek, Mary Ellen, 3595
Stanfield, Mary, 1172
Stang, Debbie, 1716
Stangis, Dave, 1917
Stangler, Dane, 1797
Staniar, Burton B., 2080
Stanley Foundation, The, 1224
Stanley, Amanda G., 617
Stanley, David, 842
Stanley, Edmund A., Jr., 1413
Stanley, Janet T., 617
Stanley, Jeffrey A., 2670
Stanley, Jennifer, 1413
Stanley, Jill Hammer, 653
Stanley, Jim L., 2752
Stanley, Joseph H., 1224
Stanley, Justin A., Jr., 983
Stanley, Lincoln, 1224
Stanley, Lisa A., 1413
Stanley, Lynne E., 1224
Stanley, Morgan, 679

Stanley, Philip T., 617
Stanley, Richard H., 1224
Stanley, Tamiko L., 2950
Stannard, William B., 244
Stansbury, Tayloe, 263
Stansky, Jill M., 1551
Stantic, Lita, 176
Stanton, Charles E., 475
Stanton, John, 3558
Stanton, Marjorie, 562
Stanton, Robert E., 475
Stanton, Tom, 3331
Staph, Laura, 351
Staples, Cecil, 3364
Staples, Inc., 1549
Stapp, Carrie, 1142
Star Tribune Co., The, 317
Star, Sara Crown, 997
Star-Telegram Employees Fund, 3190
Stara, Dennis, 1851
Starbucks Coffee Co., 3565
Starbucks Corp., 3565
Starcher, Ann, 3582
Stardust Foundation of Arizona, 2448
Stark Carpet Corp., 2476
Stark, David, 2203
Stark, Donna, 1353
Stark, H.J. Lutcher, 3357
Stark, Jay W., 2980
Stark, John K., 2980
Stark, Kimberly, Dr., 2733
Stark, Mary, 2761
Stark, Michael, 2761
Stark, Nelda C., 3357
Stark, Peter, 2091
Starke, Frank, 1750
Starke, Lydia, 900
Starkey, Brad, 2682
Starkey, Claire, 3419
Starks, Daniel J., 1741
Starner, Margaret C., 783
Starr Foundation, 2445
Starr, Alice M., 2303
Starr, Elizabeth, 1
Starr, Loren M., 847
Stars for Children, 3333
Staryk, Ted, 1715
Stasch, Julia, 1056
State Bank & Trust Co., 2649
State Farm, 3424
State Street Bank & Trust Co., 1550, 3093
States, Jean, 1849
Staton, Faye, 3113
Staton, Jimmy D., 2752
Staub, Jonathan E., 928
Stauch, John L., 1727
Stauffer, M.J., 2773
Staunch, Linda J., 2599
Stautberg, Matt, 2726
Stautberg, Timothy E., 2780
Steadman, Janne, 1178
Steadman, Mary Jane, 3343
Steakley, John, 3139
Steals, Melvin H., Ph.D., 2890
Stechler, Bezalel Aryeh, 1997
Stechler, Gail, 1997
Stechler, Joseph, 1997
Steckler, Joan, 134
Stedham, Brenda S., 9
Stedman, Caryn, 3451
Steel City Corp., 2698
Steel Dynamics, Inc., 1196
Steel Technologies, Inc., 1294
Steel, Cooper, 826
Steel, Corinne, 2056
Steel, Danielle, 438
Steel, Pamela B., 2674
Steel, William, 2674
Steelcase Inc., 1667
Steele, Claude, 674
Steele, Claude M., 1056, 2402
Steele, George, 54
Steele, J. Donald, Jr., 2908
Steele, John M., 3139
Steele, Liana, 1837
Steele, Melinda, 708
Steele, Mike, 3503
Steele, Richard, 1652
Steele, Shelby, 3601
Steele, William G., Jr., 1878
Steen, Donald, 3349
Steen, Michael, 2747
Steenbergen, Ewout, 2488
Steenkamp, Zaldeus, 349
Steer, Dee, 3319
Steers, William C., 964
Steet, Franklin, 2712
Stefano, Ralph, 2097
Stefanski, Marc A., 2792
Steffan, Brian J., 3421
Steffel, Sheila, 1614
Steffen, Carolyn, 137
Steffens, Roger S., 877, 915
Stegall, Hugh H., Dr., 11
Stege, Bill, 1616
Stegeman, Klaus P., 1993
Steger, Charlie, 2939
Stegman, Harold, 1647
Stehling, James, 3318
Stehman, Catherine, 1387
Steiger, Mark, 2151
Steiger, Paul, 771
Steiger, Rod, 2798
Steigerwalt, Eric, 2307
Steill, Laurie, 1209
Stein, Carolyn Stafford, 825
Stein, Gretchen, 3662
Stein, Isaac, 264
Stein, Jason, 843
Stein, Mark S., 1314
Stein, Michael, 2406
Stein, Rhoda, 843
Stein, Richard H., 3265
Stein, Ronnit, 843
Stein, Sarah, 385
Steinberg, Joan E., 2315
Steinberg, Larry, 3045
Steinberg, Neil, 3089
Steinbock, R. Ted, 1283
Steinbrook, William M., Jr., 2873
Steiner Sports, 647
Steiner, Brent, 2798
Steiner, Jeff, 235
Steiner, Martin, 391
Steiner, Michael, 3505
Steiner, Ruth, 337
Steines, Ann Munson, 2726
Steinfield, Rebecca Morse, 1531
Steingart, Richard, 560
Steinhafel, Gregg W., 1744
Steinhagen, B.A., 1320
Steinhagen, Elinor, 1320
Steinhardt Foundation, Judy and Michael, 2074
Steinhardt, John, 2035
Steinhart, Corkin R., 713
Steinhauer, Bruce W., 1638
Steinman, Alan D., 1586
Steinmann Pharmacy, Inc., 2789
Steinmann, Jennifer, 569
Steinmann, Robert P., 2789
Steinmetz, Amy, 2103
Steinmetz, Bernat, 2103, 2401
Steinmetz, Bluma, 2222
Steinmetz, Herman, 2222
Steinmetz, Michael, 2103
Steinmetz, Micheal, 2103
Steinour, Patti, 2750
Steitz, J., 1298
Steitz, John M., 1298
Stelges, Tricia, 716
Stellar Group, The, 826
Stelzner, Dianna, 1223
Stembler, Bill, 866
Stemer, Susan, 667
Stemmerman, Marc, 2109
Stemoe, Gregory, 1687
Stenberg, Dave, 1845
Stenson, Tim, 2682
Stephanopoulos, George, 2071
Stephans, Joan R., 3028
Stephans, Peter N., 3028
Stephens, Barb, 1241
Stephens, Cerise, 2840
Stephens, David T., 1758
Stephens, Elton B., 24
Stephens, Elton B., Jr., 24
Stephens, James T., 24
Stephens, John, 3167
Stephens, Kathy Fong, 442
Stephens, Louise, 357
Stephens, Mel, 1632
Stephens, Michael D., 253
Stephens, Robert W., 3586
Stephens, Tegan, 1329
Stephenson, Ed, 159
Stephenson, Jack, 1683
Stephenson, Jody, 909
Stephenson, John W., 860
Stephenson, Roger T., 3656
Stephenson, Susan L., 3105
Stepka, Mathew, 231
Steriliz LLC, 2452
Sterioff, Eileen Kay, 2039
Sterkenburg, Ryan, 1616
Sterling, Donald T., 426
Sterling, Michelle, 376
Sterling, Rochelle H., 426
Sterling, Vanessa, 1144
Stern, Aaron, 2334
Stern, Abraham, 2260
Stern, Ann B., 3267
Stern, Beatrice, 2338
Stern, Beth, 2071
Stern, Donna, 1146
Stern, Elisabeth Ellen, 2338
Stern, Guy, 2499
Stern, H. Peter, 2338
Stern, Howard, 2071
Stern, Irvin, 1100
Stern, Joan O., 2338
Stern, John M., Jr., 1359
Stern, John Peter, 2338
Stern, Lynn S., 2179
Stern, Michael K., 1803
Stern, Nicholas S.G., 2179
Sternberg, Craig, 637
Sternberg, David, 1717
Sternberg, Paul, Jr., 15
Sternberg, William M., 1717
Sternberger, Sigmund, 2637
Sternleib, David F., 2204
Sternlieb, David, 2048
Stershic, Michael, 2986
Stetsenko, Elena, 771
Stetson, Anne, 1514
Stetson, Daniel T., 343
Steuer, Gary P., 475
Steuter, Al, 1851
Stevens 1997 Trust, Georgiana G., The, 219
Stevens, Alexandra Marie, 3359
Stevens, Carrie Ann, 2167
Stevens, Carroll, 2181
Stevens, Colin Michael, 3359
Stevens, Gene, 2700
Stevens, Georgiana G., 219
Stevens, Jeff Allan, 3359
Stevens, John M., 1366
Stevens, Karen, 2761
Stevens, Lehrue, Dr., 1307
Stevens, Marcella M., 1800
Stevens, Randall, Dr., 1203
Stevens, Sharon Ann, 3359
Stevens, Simon, 2106
Stevens, Tara, 3591
Stevens, W. Chandler, 2767
Stevens, William C., III, 3006
Stevens, William J., 7
Stevenson, Anne, 3566
Stevenson, Bayne, 754
Stevenson, Charles P., Jr., 2194
Stevenson, Jane, 3609
Stevenson, Jane Hetland, 3662
Stevenson, Mark, 2850
Stevenson, Mary H., 3566
Stevenson, Susan K., 660
Steward, Larry E., 1598
Stewart, Alana, 195
Stewart, Anna Mae, 2148
Stewart, Bill, 1280, 1845, 3520
Stewart, Catharine P., 1134
Stewart, Chester French, 2006
Stewart, Diana D., 2936
Stewart, Dorothy I., 361
Stewart, Jay, 3386
Stewart, Joseph M., 1628
Stewart, Leslie, 1878
Stewart, Marise M.M., 1645
Stewart, Marise Meynet, 452
Stewart, Mary E., 682
Stewart, Max, Jr., 1262, 3272
Stewart, Melanie, 3504
Stewart, Michael, 69
Stewart, Michael R., 1655
Stewart, Pat, 2876
Stewart, Renee, 1203
Stewart, Robert A., Jr., 1559
Stewart, Susie, 1136
Stewart, Verlena, 2737
Stewart, William C., 3032
Steyer, Hume R., 2130
Steyer, Thomas, 437
Stickney, James W., IV, 2540
Stiefel, John C., 290
Stieg, Edward C., 1582
Stieg, Elizabeth A., 1582
Stieren, Amy, 3197
Stierwalt, Mary, 1241
Stiker, Paul, 2406
Stiles, Eric, 1924
Stiles, Janet, 2552
Still, Susan K., 3432
Stiller, Shale D., 1411
Stilley, Patricia Moser, 3358

Stillman, Waddell W., 2194
Stillwater, Ann, 2766
Stillwell, Robert L., 3321
Stilwell, Leigh, 408
Stimpel, Richard J., 318
Stimpert, Cathy, 2767
Stinner, John, 1852
Stinnett, Maggie, 3378
Stinnett, William, III, 3100
Stinson, GeorgAnn, 3648
Stinson, Ken, 1835
Stinson, Marion, 3292
Stipe, Beth A., 3503
Stitely, David A., 2932
Stites, Elizabeth, 2673
Stitt, James E., 2123
Stitt, James, Jr., 2123
Stitt, John, 2123
Stiwinter, Karen, 2599
Stobbs, Larry, 1849
Stock Car Steel Aluminum Inc., 2574
Stock, Jim, 1141
Stock, John P., 445
Stockamp, Dale R., 2863
Stockamp, Gail, 2863
Stockbridge, Gary, 630
Stocker, Les, 361
Stockholm, Charles M., 217
Stockholm, Maryanna G., 217
Stockman, George E., 2674
Stockman, Robert B., Mrs., 2513
Stockton, Christy, 2868
Stockwell, John, Dr., 3110
Stoecker, Randy, 1548
Stoehr, Elizabeth, 1415
Stoering, Mark E., 1754
Stoffregen, Michael L., 1218
Stoga, Alan, 2467
Stokes, Caroline M., 2936
Stokes, Charles, 907
Stokes, Gary, 3510
Stokes, Patricia D., 2936
Stoller, Craig, 2772
Stoller, Russell, 2772
Stoller, Todd, 2772
Stolper, Michael, 1797
Stommes, Eric, 1703
Stone Charitable Trust, I. Stanley, 3605
Stone Mountain Industrial Park, Inc., 905
Stone, Alison, 3605
Stone, Amy M., 1102
Stone, Barbara S., 3664
Stone, Barbara West, 1102
Stone, Biz, 427
Stone, Carolyn, 3316
Stone, Chris, 21
Stone, Christopher, 427, 2343
Stone, David, 349, 1102, 1651, 1673
Stone, David L., Jr., 3443
Stone, Deborah, 1102
Stone, Donna D., 630
Stone, Edward C., Jr., 276
Stone, Eric P., 3664
Stone, Erica, 115
Stone, Guy Arnold, 211
Stone, Hannah, 3284
Stone, Holly, 1376
Stone, Hugh Lamar, III, 3343
Stone, James D., 1383
Stone, Jennifer, 1102
Stone, Jerry, 2540
Stone, Jessie V., 1102
Stone, Kathryn W., 1761
Stone, Livia, 427
Stone, Mary R., 812
Stone, Michael A., 1102
Stone, Norah Sharpe, 1102
Stone, Norman C., 1102
Stone, Patricia Grodd, 2344
Stone, Patricia H., 211
Stone, Peter E., 3664
Stone, Richard H., 211
Stone, S. Adam, 3664
Stone, Sandra, 1102
Stone, Sara, 1102
Stone, Sheldon M., 137
Stone, Stanley, 3605
Stone, Stanley, III, 3605
Stone, Steven, 268, 1102
Stone, Theresa M., 1324
Stone, Todd, 3150
Stone, W. Clement, 1102
Stone, William C., 812
Stoner, Joan, 346
Stoney, Mike, 3520
Stonitsch, Joan, 2737
Stonkus, Jim, 2664, 2796
Stookey, John Hoyt, 2098, 2099
Stoops, Reed, 35
Stop & Shop Cos., Inc., The, 1421
Stop & Shop Supermarket Co., The, 1421
Stophel, Glenn C., 3147
Stopper, Aaron, 1902
Storbeck, Cora, 1794
Storen, Stephen J., 2445
Storer, Bob, 35
Storey, Charles P., 3261
Stormer, JoAnn, 1735
Stormont-Vail Foundation, 3377
Storms, Howard, 364
Stortz, Lowell, 1684, 1717
Story, Bernard J., 2986
Storz, Robert Herman, 1854
Stott, Jonathan R., 2919
Stottlemyer, Deb, 2805
Stotz-Ghosh, Suprotik, 1626
Stouder, A.G., 2794
Stout, Catheryne, 2955
Stout, Christopher H., 1872
Stout, Conrad, 368
Stout, Lynne, 3054
Stout, Richard M., 1872
Stovall, Guy F., III, 3245
Stover, David, 2610
Stowe, Michael D., 1471
Stowers, Ryan, 2873
Strachan, Camille Jones, 1310
Strack, Denise, 333
Strader, Jim, 3587
Stradford, Laurel, 1030
Strafford, Maureen, 616
Strahs, Kenneth, 106
Strake, George W., 3256
Straleu and Co., 394
Straley, Peter F., 1559
Stranahan Trust, Mary, 1825
Stranahan, Abby, 2749
Stranahan, Ann, 2749
Stranahan, Daniel, 2749
Stranahan, Frank D., 2790
Stranahan, Mark, 2790
Stranahan, Mary, 1825
Stranahan, Mary C., 2749
Stranahan, Molly, 1825
Stranahan, Patrick, 2790
Stranahan, Patti, 2749
Stranahan, Robert, 2790
Stranahan, Robert A., 2790
Stranahan, Sarah, 2790
Strand, Eric H., 1453
Strandell, Peter, 1401
Stranden, 1388
Strandjord, Jeannine, 1797
Strange, Carol Martin, 2991
Strange, H. Lawrence, 2991
Strange, Karla, 3377
Strange, Lawrence, 2991
Strange, Merrill P., 3464
Strange, Peter S., 2679
Stranghoener, Lawrence, 1718
Stransky, Inc., 827
Stransky, Robert J., 827
Strasburg, Robert, 1719
Strasfield, Janice E., 2804
Strasner, Sherry, 3181
Strasser, Adam, 1125
Strassfield, Christina Mossaides, 2486
Stratford Ave. Trust, 1902
Stratton, John H., 1887
Stratton, Robert "Bob" A., Col., 3468
Straub, Dan, 2939
Strauch, Mary Helen, 1360
Straus Family Trust, 198
Straus, Faye, 198
Straus, Michael, 2494
Straus, Oscar S., III, 2479
Straus, Sandor, 198
Strautman, Jon, 1141
Straw, Nancy, 1751
Strawbridge, Robin, 199
Strawn, Jeff, 407
Strayer, Kelly, 1254
Strayer, Laurie, 653
Strayer, Steve, 2655
Strayhorn, Carole Keeton, 3386
Stredde, Sharon, 991
Street, David A., 3484
Street, Fay H., 3484
Street, James E., 510
Street, Nicholas D., 3484
Streeter, Mary Alice, 2798
Strein, Stefan, 1353
Streinger, Peter, 2037
Streisand, Barbra, 428
Streit, Alan E., 1254
Streng, William P., 3279
Stretch, Robert, 2789
Stretz, James, 1618
Strever, Harold B., Jr., 1221
Stribling, Clay, 3163
Stribling-Kivlan, Elizabeth Ann, 2513
Strickland, Ruth, 867
Strickland, Sandra, 867
Strickler, Jan, 1647
Strickler, William J., 1622
Stried, Amy W., 1752
Strietmann, William H., 2680
Strimbu, William J., 2925
Strimmenos, Sarah, 1147
Stringer, Howard L., 3129
Stringer, Howard, Sir, 2445
Stringfellow, Patty, 1160
Stripling, Kyle, 3259
Strisofksy, Pamela A., 2948
Stritzke, Jerry, 2100
Stroer, Glenn, 1274
Stroh, John, III, 1752
Stroh, Vivian Day, 1588
Strom, John D., 822
Stromberg, Jean Gleason, 248
Strong, Bente, 3481
Strong, Emily A., 1101
Strong, Gary, 391
Strong, Hattie M., 3481
Strong, Henry L., 3481
Strong, John D., Jr., 2807
Strong, John O., 244
Strong, L. Corrin, 3481
Strong, Lester, 348
Strong-Treister, Diane, 3582
Strosser, Ted, 2947
Stroud, Brandy, 1301
Strowd, Irene H., 2633
Strubinger, Gerald, Esq., 1232
Strubinger, Gerald, Jr., 1232
Structural Components, 826
Struewing, Herman, 1191
Strumpf, Linda B., 2207
Struyk, Robert J., 1715
Stryker, Jon L., 2040
Stryker, Mark, 3158
Stryker, Ronda E., 1626
Strynchuk, Lynne, 723
STSM, 486
Stuart, Bridge, 1868
Stuart, Duncan, 1642
Stuart, Dwight L., Jr., 429
Stuart, Elbridge A., 429
Stuart, Elbridge H., 429
Stuart, Elbridge H., III, 429
Stuart, Loraine, 340
Stuart, Mary H., 429
Stuart, Paulette, 535
Stuart, Sally Spradling, 1776
Stuart, Susan W., 2415
Stubbs, R. John, 3006
Stubsten, Douglas, 3527
Stuchin, Marcie, 2025
Stuchin, Miles M., 2025
Stuckey, John, 408
Stuckey, Trenton, 1144
Stucky, Steven, 2262
Stude, Herman L., 3183
Studebaker, Stacy, 26
Student Athletics Inc., 2019
Stueber, Frederick G., 2745
Stuermer, Sandra, 28
Stufflebeaum, Cheryl, 1219
Stuhr, Patricia, 3633
Stuit, Thomas, 1585
Stulman, Leonard, 1411
Stulsaft Testamentary Trust, Morris, The, 430
Stults, Dave, 1142
Stultz, Raquel, 1208
Stumne, Debra, 1694
Stumpe, Karen, 988
Stumpf, Melinda, 2986
Stunkel, Gene, 1866
Sturdivant, John, 1757
Sturgeon, Nancy G., 2613
Sturgis, Christine, 3360
Sturtz-Sreetharan, Cindi, 1045
Stutts, David, 3308
Stutzman, Jacki, 1187
Stutzman, John Max, 3677
Stutzman, Sandra, 379
Styberg, Ernest C., Jr., 3648
Styer, Elizabeth, 3006
Styers, Beth, 1176
Styres, Belinda, 1772
Su, Jane Jin Wen, 115
Suares, Rahamin "Rocky", 90
Suarez, Kiko, 1174

Subramanian, Sandhya, 2683
Succop, Benjamin S., 2538
Sudakoff Trust, Harry and Ruth, The, 828
Sudakoff, Harry, 828
Sudakoff, Ruth, 828
Sudbeck, Carol R., 355
Sudderth, Robert J., Jr., 3123
Suddes, Adele J., 3093
Suess, David, 1156
Sugai, Akinori, 680
Sugarman, Connie J., 637
Sugarman, Jay, 2450
Sugarman, Kelly, 2450
Suggs, D. Gray, 3102
Suggs, Michael, 1171
Sugiura, Go, 1045
Suits, Brenda L., 2524
Suki, Lenora, 2335
Sukolsky, Bob, 723
Sullivan, Algernon Sydney, Mrs., 1771
Sullivan, Carol, 3642
Sullivan, Carol H., 1088
Sullivan, Carolyn, 3219
Sullivan, Daniel L., 376
Sullivan, Dorothy G., 77
Sullivan, George Hammond, 1771
Sullivan, Irene, 801
Sullivan, Jack, 3642
Sullivan, John, 1717
Sullivan, John M., 3189
Sullivan, Katherine, 2566
Sullivan, Kerry H., 2524
Sullivan, Leonard W., 1453
Sullivan, Mariann, 2039
Sullivan, Mark, 1569
Sullivan, Martin, 2445
Sullivan, Mary, 1104
Sullivan, Mary Sneden, 1595
Sullivan, Michael F., 1725
Sullivan, Michelle, 3679
Sullivan, Nancy, 3488
Sullivan, Patrick, 1541
Sullivan, Sara O'Neill, 2760
Sullivan, Steve, 1178
Sullivan, T. Dennis, 1098, 2192
Sullivan, Thomas, 1647, 2495
Sullivan, Thomas H., 2434
Sullivan, William, 1595
Sultzbach, Don A., 2663
Sulzberger, Arthur Hays, 2451
Sulzberger, Arthur Ochs, 2451
Sulzberger, Iphigene Ochs, 2451
Sulzberger, Judith P., 2451
Sumberg, Richard, 1464
Sumerford, Rees, 866
Summer, Justin, 716
Summerfield, Elaine, 3433
Summerour, Robert B., Dr., 3119
Summers, Ahnise, 3364
Summers, Brett, 1395
Summers, Cindy, 3007
Summers, Dale T., 1358
Summers, Douglas J., 2452
Summers, Elisa Hill, 3260
Summers, James, 2011
Summers, Jayne C., 2452
Summers, John M., 2452
Summers, Todd D., 2452
Summerside, Paul, 3597
Summit Fund, LLC, The, 3484
Summy, Amy, 3399
Summy, Kelly, 1235
Sump, Randy, 1848
Sump, Scott, 1214
Sunbeam Development Corp., 689
Sunbeam Properties, Inc., 689
Sunbeam Television Corp., 689
Sunderland, Charles, 1278
Sunderland, James P., 1278
Sunderland, Kent, 1278
Sunderland, Lester T., 1278
Sunderland, Paul, 1278
Sunderland, William, 1278
Sundet, Sam, 3642
Sundheim, Jeffrey J., 2176
Sundin, Vanessa, 346
Sundram, Clarence J., 2483
Sundvold, Stephen, 268
Suniville, Thomas, 295
Sunoco, Inc., 3046
Sunrise Foundation, 281, 676
Sunrise Venture LLC, 2453
SunTrust Bank, 745, 786, 799, 801, 820, 846, 861, 863, 882, 895, 904, 917, 3454
SunTrust Banks, Inc., 707
Sunyecz, John A., 2923
Supahan, Terry, 257
Superior Metal Products, Inc., 2661
SUPERVALU INC., 1743
Suplisson, Angela "Angie" W., 3468
Supplee, Henderson, III, 3019
Suquet, Ileana, 1316
Suramek, Mae, 1292
Surls, Courtney L., 662
Suro, Robert, 243
Surrenda, David S., 1982
Suski, Richard, 611
Susquehanna Bank, 2952
Sussman, David, 1922
Sussman, Paul, 120
Sussman, Richard, 805
Sussman, Ted, 1336
Sustic, Mark, 2002
Sutcliffe, Louise, 2635
Suter, Tim, 999
Sutphin, Charles P., 1126
Sutter, Nedra, 1129
Sutton Foundation, Joe and Eileen, 2512
Sutton, David, 354
Sutton, Edmund, 667
Sutton, Heather, 2205
Sutton, Marion Mulligan, 2686
Sutton, Mark, 3142
Sutton, Rusty, 1845
Sutton, Zook, 397
Sutton, Zook, Hon., 347
Suzman, Mark, 3516
Suzor, Sandra Scott, 3679
Suzuki, Marcia, 287
Suzuki, Wendy, 1714
Svihovec, Linda, 2651
Swaback Charities, Mitchell, Inc., 2562
Swaback, Brad, 2562
Swager, Duane, II, 2896
Swaim, M. Mort, 23
Swain, Joyce, 842
Swain, Laura Taylor, Hon., 2204
Swan, Philip V., 361
Swan, Steve, 3571
Swango, Wilma, 1137
Swanson, Celia, 69
Swanson, Dennis, 2071
Swanson, Elizabeth, 1519
Swanson, Gordon, 378
Swanson, James R., 746, 980
Swanson, John W., II, 1586
Swanson, Laura, 1214
Swanson, Mark, 535
Swanson, Mark T., 980
Swanson, Marti, 1201
Swanson, Robert W., 1814
Swanson, Robert, Rev., 2922
Swantek, Sandra, 968
Swarthout, Andrew T., 534
Swartling, Tricia, 948
Swartz, Harold, 3581
Swartz, Jerome, Dr., 2455
Swartz, Judith W., 1553
Swartz, Kim, 195
Swartz, Neva, 3581
Swartz, Sidney W., 1553
Swartz, Sydney, 1553
Swarzman, Howard, 2283
Swayne, Judy K., 431
Swayne, Keith D., 431
Swearer, Dell Marie Shanahan, 1260
Swearngan, Chip, 496
Sweat, Bob, 770
Sweeney, Aileen, 309
Sweeney, Dennis, 351
Sweeney, Janet, 1179
Sweeney, Judith, 351
Sweeney, Linda Porr, 2981
Sweeney, Lois Irene, 347
Sweeney, Michael J., III, 886
Sweeney, Michelle, 2787
Sweeney, Mike, 2655
Sweeney, Paul, 2890
Sweeney, Ralph, 3099
Sweeney, Randall J., 2091
Sweeney, Taylor, 1225
Sweeney, Timothy M., 1505
Sweet, Judith V., 2110
Sweet, Midge, 911
Sweet, Robert W., Hon., 2204
Swensen, Thomas, 36
Swenson, Galen, 1274
Swenson, Judy P., 3556
Swenson, Karen, 2050
Swenson, Scott, 2653
Swensson, Macy D., 3143
Swetland, David Sears, 2781
Swetland, David W., 2781
Swetland, Mary Ann, 2781
Swift, Beth, 1642
Swift, Jack, 9
Swimmer, Joshua, 2923
Swindle, P.W., 2831
Swisher, Peggy E., 1818
Swiss, Rachel, 1583
Swistro, Christine, 1449
Switzer, Elise, 1342
Switzer, James L., Jr., 3096
Switzer, Jessica, 1342
Switzer, Patricia, 1342
Switzer, Patricia D., 1342
Switzer, Robert, 1342
Switzer, Toccoa W., 3096
Switzky, Gary, 3603
Sword, Elizabeth, 1361
Syed, Ike, 1432
Sylvan Learning Systems, Inc., 648
Sylvester, Cindy, 1178
Sylvester, Dan, 2747
Symens, Paul, 1695
Symes, Albert R., 1555
Symes, Barbara, 1555
Symes, Landers, 1555
Symes-Elmer, Arica, 1555
Symmes, F.W., 2636
Symmonds, Bob, 1257
Symonik, Beverly, 375
Syms, Lynn Tamarkin, 1999
Syms, Robert, 1999
Syms, Sy, 1999
Symson, Adam, 2780
Synder, Daniel, 1823
Synn, Alan, 483
Synovus Trust Co., 801
Synovus Trust Company, N.A., 20, 919
Sypher, Eleanor K., 2483
Syrek, Richard, 1662
Syrvalin, Kristine G., 2759
Sytsema, John M., 1586
Szabo, Cindy L., 630
Szabo, Raymond, 2693
Szalai, Veronika, 59
Szarell, Thelma, 2924
Szews, Charles L., 3643
Szigethy, Andrea, 2596
Szmit, Helena, 366
Szostak, Walter G., 1652
Szutu, Peter C., 90
Szwarc, Bernardo Pedro, 720

T and Company Moriarty, 2228
Tabankin, Margery, 428
Tabankin, Margery A., 2139
Tabasgo Foundation, The, 291
Tabat, Dawn, 3627
Taber, Jonathan, 2170
Taber, Nancy, 1579
Tabler, Michael Rex, 3534, 3535
Tabor, Albert S., 3324
Tabor, Kristin, 1832
Taccolini, Fred, 1636
Tackett, Maureen, 1593
Tada, Joni Eareckson, 3025
Taddonio, William, 3017
Taegel, Edwin, 3219
Taff, Cindy, 1192
Taft, Dudley S., 2757
Taft, John, 1730
Taft, Kathy, 2609
Tailwind, Ross, 3588
Tain, Catherine, 261
Taishoff Foundation, 2071
Tait, Donna F., 2932
Takach, Deborah E., 3054
Takacs, Jean, 2786
Takami, Andrew, 1136
Takanishi, Ruby, 2161
Taketa, Kelvin H., 933
Talamantes, Patrick J., 317
Talbert, Beth, 1589
Talbert, Lucina Noches, 1272
Talbert, Tukea, 1289
Talbot-Metz, Molly, 3097
Talbott, E. P., 2791
Talbott, Natalie, 306
Talbott, Nelson S., 2791
Taliaferro, Lilton R., Jr., 2975
Talkington, Margaret K., 3362
Tallant, Kevin, 900
Tallerico, Joe, 401
Talley, Johnnie, 393
Talley, Laura, 3611
Tallon, James R., 2106
Talltimber, 1388
Tally, Jessie, 2618
Talmide Chidishei Harim, 2254
Talpas, Jeffery, 3
Talsma, Kelly, 1832
Talton, Jimmy, 2612
Talton, Patricia, 3567
Tam, Kenneth C., 190

Tam, Nana, 2188
Tamboli, Kaizad, Dr., 1764
Tan, Lydia, 168
Tanaka, Susan, 2357
Tanakeyowma, Lilia M., 244
Tanami, Tatsuya, 680
Tananbaum, Doris, 2457
Tananbaum, Lisa, 2456
Tananbaum, Stanley, 2457
Tananbaum, Steve A., 2456
Tandon, Chandrika, 2458
Tandon, Lita, 2458
Tandon, Ranjan, 2458
Tandy, Anne Burnett, 3185
Tandy, Daniel W., 2336
Tanenbaum, Ann, 2237
Tang Industries, Inc., 1873
Tang, Cindy, 3607
Tang, Cyrus, 1873
Tang, Haeyoung K., 432
Tang, Kevin C., 432
Tang, Michael, 982
Tang, Oscar, 543
Tangvik, Beverly J., 1426
Taniguchi, Barry K., 933
Tanino, Katsumi, 3531
Tank, David, 1714
Tannehill, Jean, 3521
Tannehill, Rocky, 3521
Tannenbaum, Allison Atlas, 96
Tannenbaum, David, 96
Tannenbaum, Jeanne L., 2637
Tannenbaum, Leah Louise B., 2637
Tannenbaum, Nancy B., 2637
Tannenbaum, Sigmund I., 2637
Tannenbaum, Susan M., 2637
Tanner, Laurence A., 563
Tanner, Robin C., 3481
Tanous, Peter, 267
Tanski, Ronald J., 2321
Tantillo, Richard, 2110
Taormina, Jo Ann, 3063
Taormina, William, 83
Tapani, Traci, 1703
Taper, S. Mark, 433
Tapia, Tony, 477
Tarbox, Laura, 288
Tardi, Joseph, 2407
Tarella, David R., 647
Target Corp., 1744
Tarica, Mark E., 81
Tarica, Samuel, 81
Tarlton, Gregg, 235
Tarnoff, Jerome, 2279
Tarnoff, Michael B., 1083
Tarnok, Robert C., 2307
Tarpey, Randy, 2907
Tarpley, Billy, 68
Tarr, Bela, 176
Tarr, Greg, 1603
Tarrant, Deborah L., 3416
Tarrant, Megan, 3195
Tarrant, Richard E., 3416
Tarullo, Michael, 2689
Tarver, Sarah T., 3134
Tashjian, Adrienne V., 2001
Tate, Deborah Taylor, 3129
Tate, Harry B., 2826
Tate, Liz, 1126
Tate, William A., 11
Tateuchi, Atsuhiko, 3519
Tateuchi, Ina, 3519
Tatge, Jacklyn, 3183
Tatlock, Anne, 2085
Tatlock, Anne M., 2066
Tatman, Eula, 9
Tattersall, T. Kirk, 3433
Tatum, Jo, 1315
Tatum, Linda L., 299
Tatum, Lisa Skeete, 1979
Taub Revocable Trust, Henry, 2000
Taub, Henry, 2000, 2051
Taub, Ira, 2000
Taub, Marilyn, 2000
Taub, Steven, 2000
Tauber, Alfred I., 1412
Tauber, Ingrid D., 1412
Tauber, Laszlo N., 1412
Taubert, Bob, 1740
Tauck, Arthur C., III, 615
Tauck, Arthur C., Jr., 615
Tauck, Chuck, 615
Tauck, Peter, 615
Tauck, Robin, 615
Tauck, Tyler, 615
Taus, Ellen, 2390
Taussig, Brenda, 305
Tavares, Jose, 2204
Tavares, Jose A., 2204
Tavelli, Teresa, 943
Tavlin, Michael J., 1857
Tawes, Greg, 1359
Tawil, Saul, 1898
Tawill, Ralph, 1898
Taylor Char. Trust, Elizabeth, 1105
Taylor, A. Starke, Jr., 3349
Taylor, Betsy, 1413
Taylor, Chandler, 1802
Taylor, Charlie, 41
Taylor, Cheryl K., 1147
Taylor, Christine, 2355
Taylor, David, 3308
Taylor, Donald K., 1359
Taylor, Ed, Dr., 3502
Taylor, Fran, 1282
Taylor, Frank, 1687
Taylor, Gary, 268, 2696
Taylor, Gary J., 1308
Taylor, Glenn, 11
Taylor, Grant, 1128
Taylor, Gustavus F., 3605
Taylor, Heather Butler, 279
Taylor, Howard, 2865
Taylor, James A., 2881
Taylor, James Kahea, 1719
Taylor, Jane, 1719
Taylor, Jeff, 349
Taylor, Jeremy P., 1105
Taylor, Kate, 1564
Taylor, Kathryn, 437
Taylor, Kenneth N., 1105
Taylor, Kris, 3503
Taylor, Lauren C., 1359
Taylor, Linda Davis, 156
Taylor, Louis H., 1359
Taylor, Mark D., 1105
Taylor, Mary F., 2686
Taylor, Michael, 1618
Taylor, Michelle A., 630
Taylor, Nancy W., 2538
Taylor, Pat, 2796
Taylor, Paul, 1440, 1746
Taylor, Perry, 1141
Taylor, Peter W., 1105
Taylor, Robert C., Jr., 3145
Taylor, Robert M., 3245
Taylor, Robert N., 1147
Taylor, Shelley E., 2402
Taylor, Shelley M., 2881
Taylor, Stephen M., 1746
Taylor, Sue, 3527
Taylor, Teresa Jane, 2135
Taylor, Tommy, 754
Taylor, William G., 3111
TC Electric LLC, 2228
TD Bank, N.A., 3096
Tdub LLC, 2574
Teacher's Credit Union, 1197
Teachers Foundation, 3549
Teagle, Rowena Lee, 2459
Teagle, Walter C., 2459
Teagle, Walter C., III, 2459, 2460
Teagle, Walter C., Jr., 2459
Teague, Wil, 1128
Teal, James C., 1708
Teale, Jennifer, 3438
Teamer, Cheryl R., 1316
Teammates for Kids, 1866
Teammates for Kids Foundation, 2574
Teamup Team of Stars, 1414
Tebay, John, 3587
Tebbets, John, 954
Tebbetts, Jennell, 1257
Technical Marine Service, 261
Tecklenburg, Dorothy, 3054
TECO Energy, Inc., 830
TECT, 2559
Ted Arison Charitable Trust, 691
Tedesco, Francis, 886
Tedesco, Francis J., M.D., 863
Teel, K. Roger, Jr., 8
Teeter, Ann Rylie, 3501
Teeter, Geoff, 216
Teeter, Jennifer, 3501
Teeter, Jennifer M., 3501
Teeter, Roger, 3501
Teeter, Roger C., 3501
Tehan, Jean C., 3620
Teich, Pastor Andreas, 1652
Teisher, Jeanne, 2868
Teklits, Joseph, 2337
Telfer, Steve, 1133
Telfer, William, 3058
Tellado, Marta L., 2160
Telles, Cynthia, 137
Tellez, Kip, 3397
Tellez, Lorenzo, 3213
Tellor, Nancy JS, 1738
Tempero, Stephen, 1279
Tempest, Dixie, 1162
Temple, Ellen, 3227
Temple, L. Peter, Esq., 2915
Temple, Leslie P., 2947
Temple, Stanley A., Dr., 3654
Templeson Trust for robert Templeson, Herbert A., 2874
Templeton Religious Trust, 3047
Templeton World Charity Foundation, 3047
Templeton, Harvey M., III, 3047
Templeton, Herbert A., 2874
Templeton, John Marks, Jr., 3047
Templeton, John Marks, Sir., 3047
Templeton, Josephine "Pina", 3047
Templeton, Muriel, 3568
Templin, Daniel P., 999
Templin, Robert G., Jr., 672
Ten Pas, Paul H., 3629
Tenet Healthcare Foundation, 482
Tenhouse, Sharon, 992
Tennant, T. Michael, 867
Tennessee Higher Education Assn., 3121
Tenny, Barron "Buzz", 2325
Tennyson, Clark, 72
Tensiltech Corp., 1388
Tepper, Marge, 489
Teran, Javier Mier Y, 496
Tercek, Mark R., 285
Termine, Richard, 2210
Terracina, Roy, 3304
Terrano, Richard, 2252
Terrell, Fred, 2118
Terrill, Deb, 309
Terrill, Marc B., 1374
Terry, Carol, 608
Terry, Keith, 1012
Terry, Lee Ellen, 562
Tesher, Robert, Dr., 843
Tesjia, Kathee, 1744
Teskey, Kristen L., 2524
Tessen, Robert J., 3370
Testa, Barbara Ann, 2281
Teter, Betsy, 3097
Tetreault, Melissa, 1549
Teunon, Jennifer, 3542
Teutsch, Peter, 3575
Tevlin, Beth A.A., 1203
Tevrizian, Dickran, 268
Tewnion, Lewsley A., 2957
Texas IB Schools, 255
Texas Instruments Inc., 459
Texas Rangers Baseball Foundation, 272
Textron Inc., 3093
TFC Services, Inc., 3237
TFS Financial Corp., 2792
Thacher, Carry, 340
Thaler, Richard H., 2402
Thalhimer, Robert, 3433
Thalhimer, Robert L., 3476
Thalhimer, Sallie, 3458
Thaman, Mary, 2674
Thames, Brenda, 3099
Thames, Sydney E., 3342
Thanhouser, Sally P., Dr., 1371
Thannisch, George, 3227
Thatcher, Bill, 1215
Thatcher, K. Blake, 1070
Thatcher, Thomas D., II, 2204
Thatcher-Keller, Becky, 2653
Thaxton, Greg, 2755
Thayer, Gladys Brooks, 2075
Thayer, Larry R., 1445
Theam, Sophie, 1523
Theisen, Jim, 1216
Thelen, Alexander C. Von, 3448
Themistos, Thomas H., 1559
Therakos, Inc., 1948
Thernstrom, Abigail, 2873
Theune, Mary, 3669
Thewes Charitable Annuity Lead Trust, The, 1633
Thewes Trust, The, 1633
Thibault, George E., 2288
Thibodeau, Mia, 1693
Thiede, Patty, 1010
Thiel, paul, 378
Thiel, Peter, 434
Thieman, Frederick W., 2901
Thieme, Robert, 1773
Thigpen, Cindy, 3249
Thille, Nick, 393
Thilo, Sue, 948
Third Federal Savings and Loan Association, MHC, 2792
Thoelecke, Timothy N., 1060
Thogerson, Lynn, 886

Thomas, Bernie, 3502
Thomas, Blythe, 1263
Thomas, Carl M., 1288
Thomas, Catherine M., 840
Thomas, Cherryl T., 1075
Thomas, Colleen, 3592
Thomas, Deborah, 3077
Thomas, Emily, 831
Thomas, George I., 3570
Thomas, Glenn E., 1291
Thomas, Helen S., 831
Thomas, J. Darrell, 3621
Thomas, James A., 359
Thomas, James R., Jr., 1359
Thomas, Jamie, 2747
Thomas, Jane C., 1768
Thomas, Janice A., 672
Thomas, Jennifer S., 2006
Thomas, Joan, 1291
Thomas, Kathryn A., 1645
Thomas, L. Newton, 2892
Thomas, Lee B., 1291
Thomas, Linda, 1152
Thomas, M. Antoinette, 2479
Thomas, Marcia, 954
Thomas, Marisol, 2422
Thomas, Mary L., 3110
Thomas, Melody Murphy, 2744
Thomas, Nancy, 1257
Thomas, Nick, 1146
Thomas, Rob, 2422
Thomas, Robert, 2422
Thomas, Robert H., 3106
Thomas, Robert M., 2686
Thomas, Saint, 4
Thomas, Sandra D., 3584
Thomas, Sarah E., 2302
Thomas, Scott, 235
Thomas, Silva, 3465
Thomas, Thomas D., 3272
Thomas, Tim, 1286
Thomas, Tom, 1262
Thomas, William A., 831
Thomas, Worth, 1759
Thomases, Susan, 2166
Thomason, Jerry M., 2824
Thomason, Sandra, 1783
Thomasson, Patricia, 1758
Thompson Charitable Trust, B.R., The, 3134
Thompson Trust, Wade F.B., 2461
Thompson, Adella S., 3134
Thompson, Angela E., 2461
Thompson, Angela M., 3367
Thompson, Astrid I., 3549
Thompson, B. Ray, III, 3134
Thompson, B. Ray, Jr., 3134
Thompson, Barbara, Dr., 1817
Thompson, Betty E., 2231
Thompson, Bobby, 1257
Thompson, Brenda S., 3658
Thompson, C. Vance, 3134
Thompson, Carla D., 1628
Thompson, Carrie, 2846
Thompson, Charles A.Y., 2461
Thompson, Cherie F., 1316
Thompson, Cindy, 3567
Thompson, Corby D., 1126
Thompson, Cynthia J., 1762
Thompson, Daniel, 8
Thompson, Dick, 2835
Thompson, Don, 1176
Thompson, E. Arthur, 1834
Thompson, Elsie, 3424
Thompson, Gay, 823
Thompson, Harris R., 868
Thompson, Jack, 3116
Thompson, James, 662
Thompson, James R., 3367
Thompson, Jere W., Jr., 3209, 3262
Thompson, Jim, 1848, 2071
Thompson, Juanne J., 3134
Thompson, Judith, 2716
Thompson, Kathryn H., 624
Thompson, Kathy, 2686
Thompson, Kenneth R., II, 1463
Thompson, Kevin, 1576
Thompson, Kim, 168
Thompson, Levi T., Dr., 1576
Thompson, Marcia, 2409
Thompson, Margaret, 1306
Thompson, Margaret E., 1597
Thompson, Mark E., 3181
Thompson, Marnie, 2555
Thompson, Martin F., 3120
Thompson, Mary, 1849
Thompson, Michael A., 2906
Thompson, Michael C., 1314
Thompson, Michele, 1201
Thompson, Mildred, 471
Thompson, Milton O., 1126
Thompson, Paul W., Jr., 3430
Thompson, R. Wayne, 1255
Thompson, Radclyffe F., 3019
Thompson, Richard L., 1436
Thompson, Richard T., 823
Thompson, Sylvia, 3515
Thompson, Tracie, 2562
Thompson, W. Hayden, 2555
Thompson, Wade F.B., 2461
Thompson, William H., 2555
Thomsen, Carl J., 832
Thomsen, Danielle, 856
Thomsen, Frances D., 832
Thomsen, Robert J., 832
Thomson, Bonnie M., 435
Thomson, C. Jay, 435
Thomson, Clifford L., 435
Thomson, Irene, 1548
Thomson, Kris, 1706
Thomson, Lucy, 1644
Thomson, Robert F., II, 724
Thomson, Shannon M., 435
Thorn, Eugene A., III, 2663
Thornburg, Eric W., 592
Thornburg, Kent, 1135
Thornburg, Sarah Sparboe, 2540
Thorndike, William, Jr., 1722
Thorning, Susan, 122
Thornton, Matthew, Inc., 1888
Thornton, Ray, 3287
Thornton, Roger, 1197
Thornton, W. Gerald, 2628
Thornton, William S., 3215
Thorpe, James R., 1745
Thorpe, Merle, Jr., 661
Thorpe, Richard, 1745
Thorpe, Ron, 3451
Thorpe, Timothy, 1745
Thorton, Timothy, 1687
Thorton-Bias, Kathy, 3424
Thrall Car Manufacturing Co., 1005
Three Rivers Aluminum Co., 3021
Threet, Michael, 1867
Throckmorton, Dolly, 2924
Thun, Ferdinand, 3059
Thun, Peter, 3059
Thunderwood Co., 1388
Thurber, Emy, 305
Thurber, Jim, 305
Thurber, John, 3055
Thurber, Peter P., 1638
Thurlby, Ray, 1241
Thurman, Dianne S., 328
Thurman, John D., 1640
Thurow, Chuck, 1030
Thurston, Brad, 1185
Thurston, Lowell, 2733
Thurston, Robert, 1740
Thurston, Sheryl, 1135
Thurton, Harry A., Jr., 3476
Thye, Pamela M., 2296
Thygeson, N. Marcus, 114
Tibbals, Mike, 3211
Tibbs, Belva Denmark, 2770
Tibbs, Ester, 725
Tice, Merton, Jr., 3115
Tichenor, Lisa, 2071, 3328
Tichenor, McHenry, 2071
Tichenor, McHenry "Mac" T., Jr., 3328
Tichenor, McHenry "Taylor" T., III, 3328
Tichenor, Taylor, 3328
Tides Foundation, 1326, 2176
Tidmarsh, Karen MacCausland, 2526
Tidwell, Doris H., 3097
Tidwell, Sharon L., 1262
Tiede, Rob, 3098
Tierney, Brian X., 2656
Tierney, Hanne, 2210
Tierney, Kevin M., Sr., 1464
Tietz, Roger & Sue, 3611
TIFF ARP III, 3642
Tiffany & Co., 2463
Tiffany, Bob, 159
Tifft, Douglas, 2109
Tiger Asia Management, 2189
Tiger Conservation Fund, 2023
Tigerman, Charles S., 328
Tighe, Jack, 3031
Tilden Mining Co., 2681
Tilden, Joe, 3672
Tillema, John, 1160
Tillema, Nick, 1178
Tilles, Cap Andrew, 1815
Tilley, Donna, 3127
Tilley, Joshua, 2596
Tillson, David, 2205
Tilney, Elizabeth A., 3266
Tilney, Katherine R., 1702
Time Insurance Co., 2047
Time Warner Inc., 2466
Timmer, Steve, 2710
Timmerman, Douglas, 3603
Timmerman, Mark, 3603
Timmins, Norm, 315
Timpane, Michael, 3421
TINA, 477
Tinanoff, Norman A., 1459
Tinder, Tara Jean, 3663
Tindol, Perry, 867
Tiner, Stan, 1764
Ting, Carol, 429
Tingler, Randall L., 3434
Tingler, Wallace L., 3434
Tingley, Chad, 1102
Tinker, Edward Larocque, 2467
Tinkey, Jim, 1168
Tinkler, Philip, 1119
Tinney, Linda, 3175
Tinsley, E. Paul, 1471
Tint, Lawrence, 1955
Tippetts, J. Edward, 329
Tipton, Constance M., 2674
Tipton, Gwen I., 1127
Tipton, Tracy, 1127
Tireco, Inc., 302
Tirre, Lois, 2609
Tisch Hotels, Inc., 2469
Tisch, Alice M., 2468
Tisch, Andrew H., 2469
Tisch, Daniel R., 2469
Tisch, James S., 2469
Tisch, Joan H., 2469
Tisch, Jonathan M., 2469
Tisch, Laurence A., 2468
Tisch, Laurie M., 2469
Tisch, Steven E., 2469
Tisch, Thomas J., 2468, 2469
Tisch, Wilma S., 2468, 2469
Tisdale, Patricia, 381
Tishman, Dan, 538
Tishman, Daniel R., 2470
Tishman, Sheryl C., 2470
Titcomb, Daniel L., 1752
Titcomb, Frederick W., 1752
Titcomb, John W., Jr., 1752
Titley, Robert J.K., 2445
Tjaden, Kurt, 1851
TMF Health Quality Institute, 3370
Toal, Margaret L., 48
Tobias, David, 616
Tobias, Deborah Flanagan, 1199
Tobias, Eric, 1199
Tobias, Randall L., 1199
Tobias-Button, Paige N., 1199
Tobin, David J., 29
Tobin, John, 1649
Tocci, Michele C., 2062
Tocker, Barbara, 3369
Tocker, Darryl, 3369
Tocker, Phillip, 3369
Tocker, Phillip, Mrs., 3369
Tocker, Robert, 3369
Tocker, Terry, 3369
Todd, C. B., 3001
Todd, David M., 282
Todd, Jeremy, 1207
Todd, Kristin, 488
Todd, Mary, 368
Todd, Rick, 368
Todd, Ronald and Hazel, 2639
Todd, Shelly I., 1149
Todd, Thomas, 713
Tofle, Marla B., 340
Tognazzini, Roland E., Jr., 307
Tognazzini, Roland, Jr., 467
Tointon, Betty L., 539
Tointon, Bryan E., 539
Tointon, Robert G., 539
Tointon, William I., 539
Tokarsky, Michelle, Esq., 2922
Tokyo Club, 3497
Toll, Jennifer Bauer, 553
Toll, Martha A., 655
Tolle, Kirk, 1290
Tollefson, Darla, 3303
Tolley, Robert, 3578
Tolliver, Fred, 2805
Tolsma, Cynthia, 2952
Tomaino, Kimberly D., 2890
Tomasdottir, Halla, 3436
Tomasky, Susan, 2656
Tomassi, Kathy, 3684
Tomc, Richard W., 592
Tomei, Paula, 343
Tomenga, Walt, 1239

Tomera, Fred M., 1114
Tomich, Geraldine, 1867
Tomkins Industries, Inc., 540
Tomlin, Ann, 1290
Tomlins, Paula, 1274
Tompkins, Andy, 1263
Tompkins, Douglas R., 165, 202
Tompkins, Kristine M., 165
Tompkins, Kristine McDivitt, 202, 2081
Tompkins, Maureen C., 758
Tompkins, Richard, 2686
Toner, John G., 2674
Tonn, Sheri, 3567
Tonti, John E., 2771
Tontini, Nevio, 3503
Toohey, Alexandra, 2377
Toohey, Maureen, 1882
Toomey, Mary, 407
Topa Insurance Group, 85
Topek, Nathan H., 3256
Topfer, Alan, 3372
Topfer, Angela, 3372
Topfer, Mort, 3372
Topfer, Morton, 3372
Topfer, Richard, 3372
Topping, Robert G., 3488
Topps Us, 647
Torbert, Clay, 8
Torgersen, Carolyn, 3100
Torgow, Gary, 1588
Tornheim, Ken, 1045
Torres, Ernest C., Hon., 3089
Torres, Gerald, 650
Torres, Gregory, 1513
Torres, Robert, 3055
Torres, Wendel P., 525
Torres-Barron, Benjamin, 3312
Torrey, Kate, 2504
Torrington Area Foundation, 559
Torsone, Johnna G., 604
Tortorelli, Joseph L., 355
Tosh, Joseph N., II, 2890
Toth, Jim, 272
Touche, Peter, 2006
Toulouse, Sarah, 2888
Touma, Douglas S., 1590
Touradji, Pejman, 2471
Touradji, Shannon, 2471
Tourdot, Lynee, 3663
Tow, Claire, 616
Tow, Frank, 616
Tow, Leonard, 616
Towe, Neely D., 808
Towell, Todd, 472
Tower Land Co, LLC, 1303
Tower Living Trust, Peter, 2472
Tower, Elizabeth C., 2472
Tower, Peter, 2472
Tower, Peter, Inc., 2472
Towerbrook Capital Partners LP, 2473
Towey, Shawn, 3053
Towler, Fred, 3142
Towler, Susan B., 744
Towler, Vernon, 3473
Towles, Amor H., 2492
Town, Denice M., 3549
Townes, Charles H., 59
Townsend, Camilla, 227
Townsend, Christopher, 2307
Townsend, Margaret W., 3145
Townsend, Michele A., 355
Towson, G. Edward, II, 2540
Toy, Andrew, 3000
Trace Foundation, 2478
Tracery, 1388
Trachten, David, 541
Trachten, Gary, 541
Trachten, Morris, 541
Trachten, Sylvia, 541
Tracy, Alex, 1104
Tracy, Catherine, 992
Tracy, Don, 1104
Tracy, Jane, 1104
Tracy, Linda, 1104
Tracy, Liz, 1104
Tracy, Philip R., 2534
Tracy, Rob, 1104
trademark Metals Recycling LLC, 716
Traeger, Michele O'Shaughnessy, 1725
Trafelet, Remy W., 2207
Traggio, Anna, 2708
Trainer, B. Douglas, 3017
Trakinski, Amy, 2039
Tram Road Partners, LP, 3314
Trampke, Cam, 1152
Trandahl, Jeff, 2040
Tranquada, Robert E., 359
Transmaryland Co., 1388
Trant, Pat, 1207
Tranter, Thomas, Jr., 2109
Trapani, Kevin, 2521
Traubert, Brian S., 1079
Traubert, Bryan, 1080
Traubert, Bryan S., 1080
Trautman, David, 2723
Trautman, Dawn M., 355
Trautmann, Kristy, 2950
Travelstead, Chris, 3201
Traver, Charles, 1562
Travers, Martin, 1988
Travis, Anne, 1756
Travis, Anne B., 1757
Travis, Carol, 2112
Travis, June, 488
Travis, Robert, 2078
Travis, Tracey, 2287
Trawick, Carol, 1414
Trawick, James, 1414
Trawick, Ken W., 3329
Traylor Brothers, Inc., 102
Traylor, Michael T., 102
Traylor, Wilhelmina B., 3290
Traynor, Michael, 912
Treadway, Brandy, 3315
Treadwell Charitable Trust, Nora Eccles, 439
Treakle, Kay, 3524
Tredway, Dana, 545
Trees Trust, Edith L., 3048
Trees, George S., Jr., 983
Treff, Natalie, 1780
Tregoning, Daniel K., 1358
Treier, Merike, 2177
Tremaine, Burton G., III, 617
Tremaine, Burton G., Jr., 617
Tremaine, Burton G., Sr., 617
Tremaine, Emily Hall, 617
Tremaine, John M., 617
Tremaine, John M., Jr., 617
Tremaine, Sarah C., 617
Tremaine, Susan C., 617
Trembly, Jeff, 3642
Trenary, Lloyd R., 2819
Trent, Gina, 2273
Tressider, Susan Jackson, 2953
Tressler, Connie, 2908
Treumper, Mark, 1007
Treutel, David, Jr., 1764
Trevelyan-Hall, Kate, 322
Trew, Betsie, 3054
Trexler, Brad, 1273
Trexler, Harry C., 3049
Trexler, Mary M., 3049
Trezise, Robert L., Jr., 1581
Tri-Star Trust Bank, 1606
Triangle Trust, 2383
Triano, Victoria, The Rev., 563
Triantafillopoulos, Nick, 2759
Trice, Thomas L., IV, 1378
Trice, Win, 1395
Trieber, John, 2376
Trieu, Elizabeth, 3328
Trim Masters Inc., 1295
Trimble Revocable Living Trust, The, 3025
Trimble, Arch E., III, 3147
Trimble, Margaret Brown, 2989
Trimboli, Michael C., 827
Tripeny, Tony, 2109
Triplett, Deborah, 368
Triplett, R. Faser, 1768
Triplett, Tim, 368
Triplett, Vera, Dr., 1316
Tripp, Tracy, 3053
Tripp, Valerie, 3652
Tritch, Courtney, 1193
Triton Radio Networks, 2071
Troderman, Diane, 1479
Troesh, Carol, 1874
Troesh, Carrie, 1874
Troesh, Dennis, 1874
Troesh, Jeffrey, 1874
Troesh, Jon, 1874
Trojanowski, Robert S., 563
Tropper, Sam, 2151
Troska, Patrick J., 1728
Trost, Cathy, 662
Trost, Charles A., 3129
Troth, Diane, 293
Trotman, Mark, 1260
Trott, James C., 3160
Trotter, John, 268
Trottier, David, 2653
Troubetzkoy Trust, Ms., 2790
Troutman, Deanna, 2798
Trowbridge, Alice, 2947
Troxel, Douglas D., 481
Troxel, Kenneth D., 481
Troxel, Michael Douglas, 481
Troxel, Sergei George, 481
Troxell, William, 2429
Troy Financial Corp., 2474
Troy Savings Bank, The, 2474
Troyer, Doyle J., 952
Trubitt, Richard D., 3333
Trudell, Cynthia M., 2354
True, Bill, 3574
Trueb, Martin, 3077
Truemper, Mark E., 991
TrueNorth Companies, 1228
Truitt, Michael P., 1359
Truland Systems Corp., 3482
Truland, Mary W., 3482
Truland, Robert W., 3482
Trull, Florence M., 3373
Trull, R. Scott, 3373
Trull, R.B., 3373
Trulock, James, 1156
Truman, Darlene, 3580
Truman, Mildred Faulkner, 2475
Trumble, Susan McCune, 320
Trump Park Ave., LLC, 2476
Trump, Donald J., 2476
Trump, Donald J., Jr., 2476
Trump, Eric F., 2476
Trump, Ivanka M., 2476
Trunek, Bob, 3571
Trust A U/A of Ellison S. Mckissick, Jr., 3106
Trust, Lewis Elkins, 3000
Trustco Bank, 2407
Trustees of the Eastern Star Hall, 2148
Trustmark National Bank, 3149
Trutner, Elizabeth, 364
Trzcinski, Ronald, 2786
Tsang, Chui L., 301
Tse, Stephen, 391
Tseng, Vivian, 2191
Tsokris, Sue, 2354
Tsoumas, Richard, 1579
Tsoumas, Richard M., 1628
Tsui, John K., 3670
TT Trust, The, 1633
Tu, John, 443
Tu, Mary, 443
Tubb, Marilyn, 725
Tubbs, Charles B., 3374
Tubbs, Dave, 1663
Tubbs, Patricia A., 3374
Tubergen, Jerry L., 1600, 1671
Tuck, Kenneth, 3432
Tuck, W. Harold, 381
Tucker, Ben, 1415
Tucker, Carol, 1342
Tucker, Donald F., 1618
Tucker, Emily, 1415
Tucker, James, Rep., 1299
Tucker, John, 770
Tucker, Marcia Brady, 1415
Tucker, Mary M., 10
Tucker, Michael E., 1547
Tucker, Noah, 1415
Tucker, Phyllis, 1185
Tucker, Scott, 1168
Tucker, Toinette, 1415
Tudor, Katherine J., 3156
Tuetken, Doug, 1219
Tufano, Paul A., 2975
Tufaro Family Ltd. Partnership, 1524
Tufaro, David, 1524
Tufaro, Sharon, 1524
Tufenkian Import/Export Ventures, 2001
Tufenkian, David F., 2001
Tufenkian, James, 2001
Tuggle, Charles T., Jr., 3135
Tuggle, Clyde C., 864
Tuggle, Reginald, 2376
Tuininga, Heather, 3537
Tuitupou, Janeen Rossi, 387
Tukdarian, Eva M., 800
Tulchinsky, Igor, 620
Tulchinsky, Mina Joy, 620
Tulipana, Peter, 1226
Tull Metal and Supply Co., J.M., Inc., 917
Tull, J.M., 917
Tullar, Jill, 1128
Tulsky, James A., 2192
Tunney, Christine, 1007
Turani, Will, 3579
Turcik, John J., 2998
Turcotte, Jean Claire, 3196
Turino, James G., 2408
Turitz, Theodore, 1901
Turk, James C., 3475
Turk, Mark, 536
Turley, Elizabeth C., 3357

Turley, Stewart, 543
Turnage, Roxanne, 452
Turnbow, Walter, 69
Turnbull, Tom, 2674
Turner, Allen M., 1060
Turner, D. Abbott, II, 858
Turner, D.A., 858
Turner, Deborah F., 3129
Turner, Donna, 999
Turner, Elizabeth B., 858
Turner, Elizabeth T. Jones, 3168
Turner, George C., 2628
Turner, Greg, 1218
Turner, Isla Carroll, 3358
Turner, Jack B., 3129
Turner, James E., 2932
Turner, Joseph J., Jr., 3102
Turner, Kent Barbara, 2332
Turner, Laurey Stackpole, 3042
Turner, M. Terry, 3127
Turner, Madonna, 1282
Turner, Nancy Allen, 1282
Turner, P.E., 3358
Turner, Reginald M., 1588
Turner, Robert F., 2852
Turner, Ron, Sr., 1758
Turner, Shiloh, 2679
Turner, Thomas F., 2663
Turner, William B., 858
Turner, William L., 3577
Turngren, Lisa, 2087
Turock, David L., 835
Turock, Nancy G., 835
Turrell, Herbert, 2002
Turrell, Margaret, 2002
Tusch, Carol, 3142
Tutor-Saliba, 102
Tutrone, Ronald F., Jr., 1383
Tutt, R. Thayer, Jr., 492
Tuttle, Elbert F., 1567
Tuttle, Robert, 1882
Tuttleman, David Z., 3050
Tuttleman, Edna S., 3050
Tuttleman, Jan S., 3050
Tuttleman, Steven M., 3050
TUW Minerva Gundelfinger, 1272
Tweed, Robert E., 954
Tweed, Suzanna P., 729
Tweten, Margaret, 2648
Twigg, Robin, 1360
Twigg-Smith, Thurston, 938
Twing, Dale, 1607
Twisdale, Mark, 2632
Twitty, Jean, 1783
Twohig, Jack E., 3615
Tye, Eileen, 1558
Tye, John, 3287
Tye, Mike, 1842
Tyer, Susan, 1660
Tyler Corp., 3375
Tyler Technologies, Inc., 3375
Tyler, John E., III, 1797
Tyler, Kathleen, 1586
Tyler, Lucia, 2112
Tyler, Ron, 3361
Tyler, Stephen A., 3401
Tyler, William B., 1425
Tyner, Richard, 2011
Tyonek Native Corp., 33
Tyrrell, John E., 1219
Tysinger, Travis, 3429
Tyson, George E., II, 1754
Tyson, Michelle, 361
U S WEST, Inc., 627
U. S. Trust, 3330
U.S. Bank, N.A., 982, 1701, 1709, 1717, 1719, 1774, 1805, 1815, 1819, 1843, 2679, 2709, 2710, 2769, 2785, 2839, 2851, 2862, 2875, 3393, 3628, 3638
U.S. Department of Education, 129
U.S. Fish and Wildlife Service, 3654
U.S. National Bank, 2649
U.S. Oil Co., Inc., 3665
U.S. Trust Co., 2530
U.S. Trust Co., N.A., 831
U.S. Venture, Inc., 3665
UBP/Smith Barney, 3642
Ucelli, Loretta, 2357
UCLA Foundation, 2069
Udvardi, Michael, 2822
Udvarhelyi, I. Steven, 2975
Ueberroth, Peter V., 287
Uehling, Katherine D., 613
Uflacker, Curry, 3483
UGSC, 3198
Uhl, Chris, 1666
Uhlir, James R., 3570
UIC Construction LLC, 28
Uihlein, David V., Jr., 3601
Ukropina, James R., 276
Ulanow, Lisa, 665
Ulatowski, Adrian, 3619
Ulatowski, Lois E., 2495
Ulbrich, Mark, 2746
Ulf, Franklin E., 359
Ulich, David C., 204
Ullem, Scott B., 3598
Ullery, Mike, 1131
Ullmann, Glenn, 775
Ullmann, Lisa Landwirth, 775
Ulloa, Walter F., 287
Ullrich, Judy, 1141
Ulmer, Deborah L., 3476
Ulrich, S. M, 1407
Ulrich, Tim, 484
Umidi, Robert, Rev., 2110
Umlauf, Dale, 1751
Underberg, Terry, 1410
Underhill Charitable Trust, 2346
Underhill Foundation, 2346
Underwood, Carole, 3126
Underwood, Carrie, 3126
Underwood, Joanna D., 2098
Underwood, Robert, 1875
Unger, Catherine L., 137
Unger, Lee, 1759
Ungerleider, Jeane, 2481
Ungerleider, Steven, 204
Ungerleider-Mayerson, Joy G., 3071
Unilever Research, 2003
Unilever United States, Inc., 2003
Union Bank, N.A., 3512, 3541
United Bank, 3579
United Biosource Corp Speciality Cli, 680
United Cerebral Palsy, 161
United Coal Co., Inc., 3484
United Consulting, 1178
United Financial Bancorp, Inc., 1559
United Fire & Casualty Co., 1243
United Life Insurance Co., 1243
United Space Alliance, LLC, 3052
United Stations Radio Network, Inc., 2071
United Steel Deck, Inc., 1911
United way of Greater Milwaukee, 37
United Way of NYC, 2001
United Way of The Midlands, 1844
United Way of the NATL Capital Area, 676
United Western Medical Centers, 244
Universal Aide Society, 468
Universal Studios, Inc., 2322
University Hospital od Eastern Carolina, 3377
University of California-Berkeley, 2069
University of Florida, 799
University of Miami, 799
University of Mississippi Foundation, The, 1768
University of North Texas Health Science Center, 3370
University of Pennsylvania, 2069
University of South Carolina, 2069
University of Virginia, 2069
Univest, 2900
Univision Communications, Inc., 2071
Unterberg, Ann, 2325
Unterman, Tom, 137
Updike, Jim, 662
Upper Arlington Senior Fund, 2731
Upright, Arthur R., 2113
Upsher, Marilyn, 2817
Upton, Beth, 2747
Upton, John, 3538
Upton, Michelle, 3280
Uram, Thomas, 3054
Urano, Susan, 2662
Urbach Living Trust, Erika Rindler, 2237
Urbain, Charles M., 1039
Urban, Coryell, 2960
Urban, Karen O'Connor, 3196
Urbick, Alexandra, 163
Ureles, Alvin L., 2154, 2510
Urrutia, Roy, 3163
USA Group, Inc., 1174
USB Financial Services, 1165
Usera, Helen, 3115
USI Insurance, 3505
Usmonov, Djamshed, 176
Utter, Gail, 3292
Utterback, Ann M., 2014
Utz, Mark, 1735
Uy, Charmian, 3046
Uyeki, Bob, 418
Uyeki, Robert, 418

V.F. Corp., 2642
Vaccarezza, David, 161
Vadakin, Royale M., Rev. Msgr., 242
Vadja, David J., 2752
Vahe Nahabetian, 2001
Vahlberg, Vivian, 2811
Vahouny, Karen, 523
Vaid, Urvashi, 502
Valaas, Peter, 3503
Valadez, Judy, 292
Valandra, Kent T., 184
Valandra, Robert Louis, 184
Valavanis, Spero, 1187
Valde, Ellen, 1717
Valdes, Antonio, 3030
Valdes-Fauli, Jose, 729
Valdez, Katherine Osborn, 3324
Valdez, Kelley, 349
Valencia, Sarah, 408
Valente Foundation, George and Lena, The, 226
Valentine, Christine, 2479
Valentine, J. Randy, 3584
Valentine, Katrina A., 3586
Valentine, Phoebe V., 3053
Valentine, Sara, 841
Valera, Fernando, 3179
Valero Alamo Bowl, 2206
Valkirs, Gunars E., 937
Valkirs, JoRene, 937
Valley Bank & Trust Co., 2952
Valley Co., Inc., 1271
Valley, F. Wayne, 445
Valley, Gladys, 445
Valley, Tamara A., 445
Vallier, Robert, 1382
Vallier-Kaplan, Mary, 1459
Valone, Donald, 2939
Valosek, Elizabeth S., 3057
Van Aacken, Susan C., 389
van Agtmael, Emily, 676
van Ameringen, Arnold Louis, 2483
van Ameringen, Henry P., 2482, 2483
Van Andel Foundation, Jay and Betty, 1669
Van Baren, Gina, 1160
van Bergeijk, Chris, 933
van Beuren, Andrea, 3094
van Beuren, Archbold D., 3094
van Beuren, Barbara, 3094
van Beuren, Helene B., 3094
van Beuren, Hope Hill, 3094
Van Cleave, Julie, 3659
Van Clief, Mary Ann, 1912, 1981
Van de Wal, Eve, 2110
Van den Bergh Foods Co., 2003
Van Deuren, Richard A., 3627
Van Dire, Peter, 2900
Van Dorn, Walter G., 1544
Van Dusen, Barbara C., 1588
Van Fossen, E. Jane, 2689
Van Gorp, Stacy, 1230
Van Haren, W. Michael, 1674
Van Horne, Charles, 2391
Van Kley, Byron, 3538
Van Lee, Reggie, 2287
van Loben Sels, Ernst D., 446
Van Mill, Mike, 989
Van Milligen, Nancy, 1216
Van Mourick, Mark, 351
Van Mourick, Tricia, 351
Van Natta, Jennifer M., 259
Van Nelson, Robert, 1692
Van Ness, Paula, 564
Van Nortwick, Kimberly, 3674
Van Nortwick, Terry, 725
Van Orden, Alan, 948
Van Reken, Calvin P., 1585
Van Reken, Randall, 1585
Van Reken, Randall S., 1585
Van Reken, Stanley, 1585
Van Reken, Stanley R., 1585
Van Riper, Jeffrey L., 2415
Van Scoyoc, Sandi, 1888
Van Stone, James J., 1028
Van Tassel, Ann, 1586
Van Velson, Glenn, 1849
Van Vleck, James, 722
Van Vleck, Lisa, 1564
Van Wagoner, Randy, 2110
Van Woerkom, Dan, 3398
Vanaernam, Gary, 1225
Vanatta, Pam, 545
Vanbebber, Craig, 3284
Vance, Alex H., Jr., 608
Vance, Brian, 3504
Vance, James J., 3616
Vance, Sally, 1185
Vance, Sandy, 1162
Vance, Tim, 2686

Vance, Virginia G., 3096
VanCura, Sam, 2767
Vandemark, Jim, 2683
vanden Heuvel, Melinda Fuller, 1886
Vandenberg, Anne, 1218
Vandenberg, Bill, 501
Vandenberg, Dave, 2844
Vander Hart, Ginny, 1600
Vander Leest, Mary, 1743
Vander Ploeg, Mark, 1098
VanderHarst, Carol, 1652
Vanderhoef, Sheila, 1445
Vanderhoof, Joe, 2111
Vanderlaan, Michelle, 1068
VanderRoest, Stan M., 1611
Vanderslice, Michael, 3175
Vanderslice, Vicki, 3175
Vanderweide, Hannah J., 1671
Vanderweide, Katelyn S., 1671
Vanderweide, Suzanne C. Devos, 1671
Vanderweide, Suzanne DeVos, 1671
VanDeventer, Larry, 1877
VanEtten, Donald, 2387
Vanguard, 3642
Vanguard Group, 2986
VanHouten, Karen, 2111
VanHoy, Henry P., 2543
Vankavage, Ledy, 2038
VanMeter, Griffin, 1282
Vann, E.J., IV, 869
Vannata, Jerry B., 2826
VanNatta, Terry, 1192
Vanosky, Robert, 378
VanWinkle, Frederick, 907
VanWynkel, Tara F., 2706
Vapurciyan, Kirakos, 2001
Varela, Jesus, 126
Vargas, Belen, 456
Vargas, Marcos, 320
Vargas, Sandra L., 1748
Vargas, Sandy L., 1717
Varian, Nancy A., 2788
Varki Investments, Inc., 473
Varma, Vijay R., 2391
Varma, Vivek, 3565
Varmus, Harold, 3516
Varnum, Philip, 2857
Varoquiers, Carrie J., 321
Vasan, Usha, Dr., 3587
Vasek, Greg, 1851
Vashaw, Kirkland, 2674
Vasoli, Sandra C., 3006
Vasquez, Felicia & Virginia, 2780
Vasquez, Gilbert R., 287
Vasquez, Misael, 259
Vasseur, Ernest, 1031
Vasudevan, Deepa, 3034
Vaswani, Sanjay, 408
Vatnsdal, Lisa, 2049
Vatterott, John C., 2734
Vaughan, Chris, 1576
Vaughn, Cathryn E., 1878
Vaughn, David, 161
Vaughn, Dennis H., 1865
Vaughn, Doug, 1131
Vaughn, James M., Jr., 3254
Vaughn, Robert W., 1007
Vaux, Trina, 2988
Vazanna, Suzanne, 261
Vazquez, Desiree, 2459, 2460
Vazquez, Gilbert, 2203
Vazquez-Dedelow, Alexis, 1171
Veale, Carolyn, 1128
Veale, Harriet Ernst, 2797
Veale, Tinkham, II, 2797
Vear, Tom, 1636
Veasey, Zoe, 1562
Vecchie-Campbell, Donn, 1133
Vector Marketing Corp., 2123
Vectren Corp., 1202
Veeder, Sybil P., 2906
Veerman, Ralph D., 3025
Vega, Rosario, Sr., 2786
Vega-Marquis, Luz, 3500
Velamoor, Sesh, 3515
Velasco, Caridad, 697
Velasquez, Segundo, 1742
Velde, Betsy Vander, 1277
Velie, Carroll, 1608
Veliotes, Nicholas A., Amb., 661
Veller, Kevin S., 3416
Vellines, Wilson F., Jr., 3429
Velsini, Barbara, 2058
Velux Trust, The, 2375
Venkataraman, Bala, 2798
Venkatesan, Ravi, 2390
Ventulett, Thomas, 918
Ventura, Jo Ann, 2366
Venturella, John, 2737
Venuti, William, 713
Vera, Francesca, 161
Vera, John, 161
Vera, John R., 161
Vera, Ronald T., 137
Verbitsky, Nicholas, 2071
Verble, Kay W., 822
Verdieck, Kristen, 351
Verdin, Mary, 393
Vereb, Karen A., 2728, 2729, 2730
Veres, Keith A., 714
Vergara Trust, Lamar Bruni, 3246
Vergara, Lamar Bruni, 3376
Vering, Toni, 1836
Verizon Business Community Relation, 3424
Verlinde, Al, 1603
Vermie, Craig, 1228
Vermilye, W. Moorhead, 1395
Verner, Elizabeth H., 1771
Verner, Myrna, 3362
Vernon, Joe C., 3314
Veron, Heidi, 1811
Verplank, Monica, 1614
Verrochi, Paul M., 1560
Versa Cace Inc., 3119
Versfeld, Charlotte H., 854
Vesledahl, Dale, 1750
Veson, Eva D., 2376
Vestal, Richard, 1943
Vetter, Roman, 3624
Vettori, Diane S. A., Hon., 2685
VF Services, 647
VHA Gulf States, 3377
VHA Inc., 3377
VHA Southeast, 3377
Vice, Cynthia M., 7
Vice, Mark, 1142
Vick, Ross, 3328
Vickerman, Sue, 3504
Vickers, Clark L., 493
Vicklund, Traci L., 2292
Victory Memorial Park Foundation, 1910
Victory Wind-Down Company, 1031
Vidal, Kara K., 3274
Viera, Antonio Escudero, 3061
Vierk, Rich, 1847
Vierk, Richard J., 1834
Viersen, Sam K., Jr., 2830
Vietor, Lynn A., 257
Vietor, Vera P., 257
Viets, Hermann, 3627
Vigeland, Julie, 2851
Vigil, Alfredo, 2011
Vigness, Mary Katherine, 3328
Vijay, Madhu, 355
Viklund, Mark, 2292
Vilcek, Jan, 2486
Vilcek, Marica, 2486
Villa, David, 3500
Village Pantry, 2562
Villages of Hope Africa, 3330
Villaire, Michael, 260
Villamil, Marielena, 729
Villani, Allison, 1683
Villanueva, Maritza Rojas de, 3179
Villanueva, Marland, 1157
Villard, Vincent S., Jr., Mrs., 2513
Villarreal, Lydia M., 264
Villarreal, Noralisa, 3311
Villasuso, Raul, 1114
Villegas, Luis, 394
Villeneuve, James, 1774
Villenueve, James, 1344
Vinay, Michael, 2664
Vincent, Loree A., 641
Vincent, Richard A., 2762
Vinciguerra, Maggie, 2108
Viner, Edward, 1955
Viney, Jo, 3063
Viniar, Barbara A., 1395
Vining, Dick, 1203
Vinson, Laura, 3287
Viola, Roger K., 1279
Violich, Deanne Gillette, 467
Viray-Munoz, Belinda, 134
Virgin, Tom, 1128
Virginia American Industries, Inc., 3474
Virkler, Laura H., 1952
Virmani, Yash Paul, 3270
Virostek, Steve, 543
Visaggio, Joe, 1973
Visbal, J. Malcolm, 215
Viscardi, Molly Kreider, 3030
Vishnoi, Rohit, 1034
Viso, Olga, 2494
Visser, Anna, 368
Vissicchio, John A., 2470
Vistakon Pharmaceutical, 1948
Visual Communications Co., Inc., 396
Vitale, Jim, 978
Vitale, Joseph F., 2392
Vitale, Terri, 727
Vitlin, C., 3231
Vitlin, M., 3231
Vitlin, V., 3231
Vivino, Paul, Dr., 1453
Vleck, Roy Van, 1894
Voelkle, William, 2069
Voelz, Emil, 2796
Voelz, Shelley D., 1166
Vogel, Benjamin Charles, 3667
Vogel, Bob, 1634
Vogel, Charles, 268
Vogel, Charles H.E., 3667
Vogel, Kenneth E., 1260
Vogel, Rhona E., 3652
Vogel, Sarah, 1722
Vogelstein, Andrew, 2237
Vogelstein, Deborah H., 1379
Vogen, Kristin Carlson, 1032
Vogl, Tom, 3551
Vogler, John J., 2487
Vogler, Laura B., 2487
Vogt, Mary Anschuetz, 1065
Voigt, Thomas A., 2674
Voiland, Eugene J., 279
Vokolos-Zias, Ourania, 2205
Volgenau, Ernst, 3485
Volgenau, Lisa, 3485
Volgenau, Sara Lane, 3485
Volk, Edward, 1201
Volk, Tim, 3417
Volkema, Michael A., 1624
Volkman, Toby, 2286
Vollrath Co., LLC, The, 3669
Voltz, Susan A., 2297
Von Arx, Carol, 1809
Von Arx, Jeffrey Allen, 1809
Von Arx, Robyn Ann, 1809
Von Furstenberg, Alexandre, 2137
Von Furstenberg, Diane, 2137
Von Furstenberg, Tatiana, 2137
Von Gehr, Barbara, 3555
von Hassel, George A., 2204
Von Krusenstiern, Elizabeth R., 20
Von Krusenstiern, John, 20
von Trier, Lars, 176
Von Voigtlander, Jeffrey P., 1672
Vondra, Shawn, 1620
VonRosenstiel, Elaine, 3494
Voress, Judith, 3249
Vorhees, Charles A., 973
Vorhees, Marianne, 1134
Vorhis, David A., 1359
Voris, Scott, 991
Vorsatz, Mark, 190
Voth, Douglas, 2832
Vouras, Peter, Jr., 591
Vozar, Bonnie, 3372
Vradenburg, Alissa, 544
Vradenburg, Beatrice W., 544
Vradenburg, George A., 544
Vradenburg, Tyler, 544
Vrandenburg, George A., III, 544
Vrandenburg, George A., Jr., 544
Vreeland, Ann, 2674
Vroman, Rich, 3520
Vruwink, Dawn, 3623
Vukasin, George, 347, 397
Vyskocil, Mary Kay, 2325
Vyskocil, Nancy, 1723

W & W, Inc., 1818
Waage, Lori, 1749
Wachenheim, Chris A., 2489
Wachenheim, Edgar, III, 2489
Wachenheim, Lance R., 2489
Wachenheim, Sue W., 2489
Wachovia, 2900
Wachovia Bank, N.A., 613, 801, 2579, 2962, 3164
Wachovia Corp., 3055
Wachs, Joel, 2494
Wachtell, Herbert M., 2490
Wachtell, Lipton, Rosen & Katz, 2490
Wachtell, Wendy, 187
Wachter, Renee, 1693
Wackowski-Faria, Barbara, 1428
Waddell, Arin, 3679
Wade, Dennis, 3112
Wade, Jason, 1620
Wade, Jim, 3432
Wadge, Gordon R., 1310
Wadhams, Timothy J., 1637
Wadhwani, Kathleen E., 450
Wadhwani, Romesh T., 450

Warhola, Donald, 2494
Warm, David A., 1793
Warman, Michele S., 2302
Warmath, John T., Jr., 2637
Warner, Carre, 537
Warner, Ed, 3654
Warner, Gregory H., 2288
Warner, Guy R., 1296
Warner, John L., Jr., 3144
Warner, Marshall N., 3487
Warner, Norton, 1834
Warner, Philip, 2445
Warner, Richard, 2696
Warner, Valerie, 1168
Warnick, Robert, Rev., 1382
Warren, Andrew, 3431
Warren, Arete, 2516
Warren, Cheryl, 2037
Warren, Claire, 562
Warren, Dorian, 2139
Warren, James, 268
Warren, Jean M., 2831
Warren, John-Kelly C., 2831
Warren, Linda, 3401
Warren, Linda M., 2736
Warren, Robert P., 3439
Warren, Stephen K., 2831
Warren, W.K., Jr., 2831
Warren, William C., IV, 860
Warren, William K., 2831
Warren, William K., Mrs., 2831
Warren, William T., 41
Warrick, Meghan, 724
Warring, John, 3520
Warrington, John W., 2757
Warsh, Herman E., 452
Warsh, Michael, 452
Wartman, Carl, 3623
Warwar, Rebecca, 355
Warwick Community Bancorp, Inc., 2495
Wasem, Penny, 2696
Wasendorf, Amber, 1234
Wasendorf, Connie, 1234
Wasendorf, Russell R., Jr., 1234
Wasendorf, Russell R., Sr., 1234
Wasescha, Anna M., 592
Washburn, Earl, Dr., 405
Washburn, Steve, Dr., 3207
Washburne, Heather H., 3260
Washington Post Co., The, 663
Washington School Employees Credit Union, 3549
Washington Trust Bank, 3533
Washington Trust Co., The, 3095
Washington, A. Eugene, 1949
Washington, Dana, 1850
Washington, Eugene, 140
Washington, Kevin, 3558
Washington, Lara E., 2901
Washington, Marie Brooks, 137
Washington, Perry, 3100
Washington, Reginald L., 483
Washington, Vanessa L., 99
Wasielewski, Ana A., 3291
Wason, Paul K., 3047
Wasserman, Casey, 453
Wasserman, Edith B., 453
Wasserman, Lew R., 453
Wasserman, Lynne, 453
Wasson, Nathaniel P., 1008
Watanabe, Jeffrey N., 934
Watchowsky, Dale L., 1588
Water Project, Inc., The, 3330
Waterbury, James B., 1230
Waterman, Cecily, 438
Waterman, Darci, 3503
Waterman, Nancy J., 512
Waterman, Robert E., 59
Waters Fund, James L., 3040
Waters, James L., 1586
Waters, Judy, 867
Waters, Julie, 2112
Waters, Kim, 1758
Waters, Nina M., 722
Waters, Susan, 2027
Watkins, Barbara, 1068
Watkins, Carole, 2677
Watkins, Joy R., 726
Watkins, Julie, 503
Watkins, Linda, 948
Watkins, Nila C., 715
Watkins, Tony, 1286
Watlington, Stuart, 3430
Watson Clinic Foundation, 757
Watson Trust, William J., 983
Watson, Ann, 3558
Watson, Ashley B., 249
Watson, Ben, 503
Watson, Bill, 1868
Watson, Bud, 1282
Watson, Charles, 1771
Watson, Charles W., Esq., 2923
Watson, Debbie, 842
Watson, Eliza Jane, 1944
Watson, F. Jean, 3507
Watson, Geraldine F., 2389
Watson, Jamie, 340
Watson, Jared, 3558
Watson, Jeff, 3364
Watson, Jo-Ann, 1539
Watson, John S., Jr., 1979
Watson, Joseph W., 156
Watson, Karl H., Jr., 3191
Watson, Keith, 3093
Watson, Kelly, 3289
Watson, Kent, 2795
Watson, Kurt D., 1261
Watson, Roslyn M., 1486
Watson, Solomon, IV, 2427
Watson, Stephen, 2540
Watt, Alston, 869
Watt, Brenda, 1796
Watt, Robert A. "Bob", 3499
Watterson, Barbara N., 1448
Wattis Foundation, Paul L., 455
Wattis Trust, Phyllis C., 454
Wattles, Charles D., 1612
Wattlesworth, Roberta, 1246
Watts, Gail, 1178
Watts, Gary, 1753
Watts, Linda, 1764
Watts, Susan P., 3608
Watts, Wayne, 3167
Watumull, E., 939
Watumull, G.J., 939
Watumull, Gina, 939
Watumull, Rann J., 939
Watwood, Meredith, 122
Waugaman, Amber, 2259
Waugh, Seth, 2134
Waverly Plastics, Inc., 1221
Way, Griffith, 3497
Way, Joni B., 1289
Way, Paul, 1692
Wayne, Bob, 2947
Wayne, Daren, 900
Wayne, Valerie Rockefeller, 2389
Wayser, Joshua D., 1042
Wayside of Virginia Inc., 652
WBH Evansville, Inc., 1205
WBI Energy Midstream, LLC, 2652
WBI Energy Transmission, Inc., 2652
WBI Energy, Inc., 2652
WDI Corporation, 756
Weakley, Wendell W., Sr., 1768
Wean, Gordon B., 2685, 2799
Wean, Raymond John, Sr., 2799
Wean, Susanne C., 2906
Wearing, Betsy, 1274
Weatherhead, David Parmely, 1449
Weatherstone, Dennis, 618
Weatherstone, Marion, 618
Weaver Family Foundation, 621
Weaver, Francine Lavin, 621
Weaver, George, 1915
Weaver, Margaret, 3044
Weaver, Margaret W., 3189
Weaver, Paul J., 1618
Weaver, Sharon L., 3017
Weaver, Shirley, 1336
Webb, Angela, 3099
Webb, Anne B., 1351
Webb, Brey, 717
Webb, Byron, III, 992
Webb, Cindy, 1769
Webb, Cynthia, 154
Webb, Dale Chapman, 717
Webb, Del E., 64
Webb, Francis M., 1113
Webb, Fred K., Jr., 3456
Webb, George, 2543
Webb, Greg, 1307
Webb, Jeremy L., 1875
Webb, John H., 3447
Webb, Jon, 1606
Webb, Joyce A., 1008
Webb, Kenneth, 4
Webb, Kristy, 717
Webb, Lessie E., 3456
Webb, Lewis M., 1875
Webb, Lewis M., III, 1875
Webb, Louis A., 361
Webb, Margaret A., 1875
Webb, Marion L., 361
Webb, Marty, 3211
Webb, Mike, 3109
Webb, Pearl M., 1113
Webb, R. Davis, Jr., 1351
Webb, Robert D., 1455
Webber, Joan, 1673
Webber, Larry D., 1790
Webber, Neil, 3158
Webber, Russ, 3109
Webber, Thomas L., 2188
Webber, Wayne, 1673
Weber, Al, 2893
Weber, Arnold, 997
Weber, Carolyn, 2499
Weber, David, 3503
Weber, Doug, 1802
Weber, Frederick E., 1564
Weber, Gene, 2680
Weber, Jeff, 1067
Weber, Karl, 1636
Weber, Nicholas Fox, 551
Weber, Scott, 1010
Weber, Shen, 1692
Weber, Tammy A., 2947
Weber, W. Erik, 1144
Weber, Warren, 1226
Webster Bank, N.A., 591
Webster, David C., 3046
Webster, Edward, 3672
Webster, Edwin S., 1565
Webster, Wayne L., 1547
Weckbaugh, Heather, 522
Weckbaugh, John K., 522
Weckbaugh, Walter S., 522
Wedum, John A., 1750
Wedum, Maynard C., 1750
Weeber, Steve, 1218
Weeden Fund, Frank, 2496
Weeden, Alan N., 2496
Weeden, Bob, 2496
Weeden, Donald A., 2496
Weeden, Donald E., 2496
Weeden, Frank, 2496
Weeden, H. Leslie, 2496
Weeden, Jack D., 2496
Weeden, John D., 2496
Weeden, Norman, 2496
Weeden, William, 2496
Weeden, William F., 2496
Weeks, A. Ray, Jr., 867
Weeks, Bob, 1152, 1162
Weeks, Janis C., 232
Weeks, Lisa C., 1122
Weeldreyer, Robert, 1585
Weems, Carrie Mae, 2494
Weems, Diane Zabak, 886
Weems, Marianne, 2043
Weerasethakul, Apichatpong, 176
Wefald, Susan, 2139
Wege, Christopher M., 1674
Wege, Diana, 1674
Wege, Jonathan M., 1674
Wege, Peter M., 1674
Wege, Peter M., II, 1674
Wegehaupt, Kevin, 3117
Wegman, Daniel R., 2497
Wegman, Danny, 2452
Wegman, Joe, 1218
Wegman, Margaret F., 2497
Wegman, Robert B., 2497
Wehling, Katharine, 1187
Wehmeier, Sutter, 631
Wehrwein, Sven, 1717
Wei, James, 933
Weibrecht, Lisa, 2265
Weichers-Marshall, Ana, 248
Weichert, James A., 1708
Weidenbach, Joseph L., 1008
Weidenhammer, John P., 3059
Weidert, Steve, 1158
Weidman, John, 2252
Weidman, Shiela, 878
Weidner, Jared, 1176
Weidner, Thomas P., 1979
Weigand, Scott, 1860
Weigel, Karel, 1735
Weil, Andrew, 65
Weil, Christopher, 267
Weil, Gotshal & Manges LLP, 2498
Weil, Paul P., 1815
Weil, Richard L., 2297
Weiland, John H., 1905
Weiler, Anna, 1069
Weiler, Karen Buglisi, 2287
Weiler, Siegfried, 1069
Weiler, Skip, 2689
Weilnau, Sparky, 2773
Weinberg, Adam D., 2494
Weinberg, Donn, 1416
Weinberg, Eli, 2459, 2460
Weinberg, Harry, 1416
Weinberg, Penni M., 2728

Weinberg, Sharon L., 2237
Weinberger, Arianne, 647
Weinberger, Michael, 647
Weiner, Clifford M., 3367
Weiner, David, 2237
Weiner, Jon, 2019
Weingart, Ben, 456
Weingart, Stella, 456
Weingarten, Abraham, 2401
Weingarten, Charles Annenberg, 86, 87
Weingarten, David, 2401
Weingarten, Fay, 2401
Weingarten, Gregory Annenberg, 86, 87
Weingrod, Louise, 1948
Weinheimer, Eric, 1068
Weininger, Jerry, 2793
Weinman Family Foundation, 2332
Weinschenk, Fritz, 1343
Weinsheimer, William C., 1229
Weinstein, Alan, 2188
Weinstein, Daniel, 268
Weinstein, David A., 374
Weinstein, Herb, 2958
Weinstein, Hilary, 2480
Weintraub, Boris, 667
Weir, Billy, 919
Weir, Gordon, 2673
Weir, Mary, 1807
Weir, Shirley, 919
Weirauch, Bob, 3620
Weirether, Anne Marie, 589
Weisberg Charitable Lead Trust, Arthur & Joan, 3590
Weisberg, Arthur, 3590
Weisberg, Charles, 3590
Weisberg, Joan, 3590
Weisberg, Pamela, 3590
Weisberger, Gerald L., 469
Weise, Alisa K. F., 2837
Weise, Daniel W., 2837
Weise, David, 2837
Weise, David N., 2837
Weisenfeld, Jason, 2100
Weisenfeld, Patricia, 2423
Weiser, Esther, 2193
Weiser, John, 104
Weiser, John W., 103
Weiser, Mary H., 1588
Weiser, Naftali, 2193
Weiser, Wendy, 2662
Weishan, James J., 3657
Weisman, Jane, 1512
Weiss, Andrew, 1447
Weiss, Andrew M., 1447
Weiss, Arthur, 1604, 1625, 2117
Weiss, Bonnie, 1447
Weiss, Bonnie K., 1447
Weiss, Cora, 2398
Weiss, Daniel, 2398
Weiss, Daniel H., 2263
Weiss, David, 786
Weiss, Ellen, 2780
Weiss, Howard M., 1374
Weiss, Jane, 690
Weiss, Jeffrey W., 1322
Weiss, Jonathan V., 3487
Weiss, Judy, 2398
Weiss, Kurt C., Esq., 723
Weiss, Laurence, 2540
Weiss, Peter, 2398
Weiss, Robert E., 3275
Weiss, Suzanne, 1010
Weiss, Tamara, 2398
Weiss, Warren, 690
Weiss, William E., Jr., 3682
Weiss, William U., 3682
Weissberg Foundation, The, 676
Weissblum, Cynthia Rivera, 2188
Weisselberg, Allen, 2476
Weissman, Arie, 2040
Weissman, Harriet L., 2500
Weissman, Michael A., 2500
Weissman, Paul M., 2500
Weissman, Peter A., 2500
Weissman, Stephanie T., 2500
Weissmann, Gerald, 191
Weissmann, Jeffrey, 2217
Weitnauer, David, 872
Weits, Bracha, 2255
Weitz, Andrew S., 1855
Weitz, Anna, 3059
Weitz, Barbara V., 1855
Weitz, Kate Noble, 1855
Weitz, Meredith, 1855
Weitz, Roger, 1855
Weitz, Roger T., 1855
Weitz, Roy, 433
Weitz, Wallace R., 1840, 1855
Weizenbaum, Norman, 2889
Welborn, W. Miller, 3146
Welbourn, Dave, 1464
Welburn, Stuart, 2445
Welch Allyn, Inc., 2032
Welch, Dennis E., 2656, 2750
Welch, Larry, 371
Welch, Lisa, 3580
Welch, Marshall, III, 2947
Welch, Maryann, 3520
Welch, Mick, 723
Welch, Nancy, 44
Welch, Rebecca, 180
Weldon, Bill, 1154
Weldon, Linda, 1225
Weldon, Stephen, 1225
Welhorsky, Lynn C., 2412
Welker, Lisa, 1809
Welker, Virgil, 992
Well's Dairy Inc., 2574
Wellcome Trust, The, 2534
Welle, Paul, 1721
Weller, James T., Sr., 2925
Weller, Marcia K., 1144
Weller, Matt, 2689
Welles, Berkley, 2119
Welles, Christopher S., 2119
Welles, David K., 2119
Welles, David K., Jr., 2119
Welles, Georgia E., 2119
Welles, Hope J., 2119
Welles, Jeffrey F., 2119
Welles, Maud, 2119
Welles, Peter, 2119
Welles, Peter C., 2119
Welles, Rene, 2119
Welles, Ted, 2119
Welling, Eleanor, 2636
Welliver, Scott, 2109
Wellman, Arnold, 1353
Wellmark, Inc., 1246
Wellnitz, Paul, 2562
Wellons, Elizabeth Hobgood, 2599
WellPoint, Inc., 1206
Wells Annuity Trust, Ruth L., 2501
Wells Fargo, 2952, 2986
Wells Fargo Bank, 55
Wells Fargo bank, 259
Wells Fargo Bank, 356, 2565, 2962
Wells Fargo Bank Indiana, N.A., 1164, 1858
Wells Fargo Bank Minnesota, N.A., 1717, 2571
Wells Fargo Bank Northwest, N.A., 2572, 3392
Wells Fargo Bank Texas, N.A., 3201
Wells Fargo Bank West, N.A., 48
Wells Fargo Bank, N.A., 49, 315, 394, 852, 881, 896, 906, 923, 1169, 1856, 1915, 2516, 2517, 2518, 2520, 2523, 2526, 2527, 2528, 2530, 2532, 2536, 2537, 2544, 2545, 2546, 2547, 2548, 2549, 2550, 2551, 2552, 2553, 2554, 2556, 2557, 2558, 2566, 2567, 2568, 2569, 2573, 2575, 2576, 2579, 2580, 2581, 2582, 2583, 2585, 2586, 2587, 2588, 2589, 2590, 2591, 2592, 2593, 2594, 2595, 2597, 2598, 2602, 2603, 2605, 2607, 2608, 2614, 2615, 2617, 2619, 2620, 2621, 2622, 2623, 2624, 2625, 2626, 2627, 2629, 2631, 2634, 2635, 2636, 2638, 2639, 2641, 2643, 2645, 2646, 2649, 2903, 2949, 2987, 3033, 3159, 3166, 3215, 3322
Wells Fargo Private Client Services, 3553
Wells Fargo Trust Dept., 3309
Wells Fargo, N.A., 816
Wells Marital Trust, Frank, 2501
Wells Trust, Ethel B., 2022
Wells, Albert B., 2022
Wells, Christopher, 1403
Wells, Dawn E., 1876
Wells, DeAngeloa, 2867
Wells, George B., II, 2022
Wells, J. Kent, 2652
Wells, John, 1152
Wells, Karen, 2683
Wells, Kristen, 2022
Wells, Kristi, 839
Wells, Lindsey B., 1403
Wells, Nancy, 1189
Wells, Owen W., 1334
Wells, Patricia, 1841
Wells, Stephen L., 839
Wells, Susan, 33
Wells, Susan L., 2331
Wells, Susan M., 2022
Wells, Terry Lee, 1876
Welsh Construction, 1388
Welsh, David, 3173
Welsh, David D., 3173
Welsh, Jay, 268
Welsh, John J., 268
Welsh, Michael J., 2534
Welsh, Ray, 1851
Welstead, Marvin G., 1836
Welty, Claudia Scott, 1693
Welty, John D., 139
Welty, Steven Scott, 1170
Wenco, Inc. of North Carolina, 2852
Wenco, Inc. of Ohio, 2852
Wendelken, Cherie, 1439
Wendell, Sandi, 1851
Wendeln, Karen S., 2763
Wendeln, Tony, 2763
Wendl, Mary Grant, 2815
Wendling, Cheryl J., 1143
Wendt, Nancy J., 2852
Wendt, Roderick C., 2852
Wendy's of Montana Inc., 1831
Wenger, Brian, 1687
Wenger, Howard, 2798
Wennberg, David, 1489
Wenner, David L., 59
Wenner-Gren, Axel L., 2502
Wente, Tom, 1735
Wentling, Thomas L., Jr., 2906
Wentworth, Cynthia, 1880
Wentworth, Megan, 2868
Wenzel, John, 2376
Wenzel, Kenneth A., 829
Werdlow, Sean K., 1588
Werner Family Foundation, 3424
Werner, Mark, 2600
Werner, Mary Leach, 1307
Werner, William N., 1112
Wernig, Ruth, 138
Werring, Eden, 615
Wertern Division Of Mibor, 1178
Wertz, Donna, 351
Wertz, Richard, 1163
Wertz, Robert C., 2167
Wertz, Russell, 351
WesBanco Trust & Investment Services, Inc., 3579
Wescombe, Gary T., 105
Wesel, Marcy, 2732
Wesley, David Scott, 457
Wesley, Gregory, 3634
Wesley, Jonnie Lynn, 457
Wesley, Timothy Andrew, 457
Wesolowski, Timothy M., 2780
Wessell, Amy P., 477
Wessell, Leonard P., 477
Wessell, Leonard P., III, 477
Wessels, Kenneth, 1832
West Interactive Corp., 741
West Trusts, E. & J., 347
West, Brenda, 1817
West, Daniel, 1802
West, David M., 3448
West, Gary L., 458
West, James C., Jr., 3578
West, Joseph F., 1083
West, Ken, 535
West, Kristen, 3510
West, Laura, 3395
West, Madeline D., 1316
West, Mary Beth, 2492
West, Mary E., 458
West, Mary G., 629
West, Mary L., 458
West, Matt, 3395
West, Neal S., Esq., 2952
West, Rod K., 1308
West, Sharon Kelly, 2540
West, Terry W., 2828
Westbrook, Mary, 1218
Westbrook, Tracey, 722
Westby, David, Dr., 3520
Westergaard, Steadman, 2483
Westerhold, Mary, 1010
Westerland, Maureen, 537
Westerling, Richard S., 3151
Westermann, Mariet, 2302
Western Digital Corp., 459
Western Digital Technologies, Inc., 459
Western Massachusetts Electric Co., 598
Westfall, Heath, 3388
Westfall, John L., 3578
Westfall, Rebekah, 3388
Westfeldt, Thomas D., 1319
Westlake Hospital, 1114
Westlake, James L., 1819
Westlake, Nellie M., 1819
Westland Gardens Co., 1388

Westlund, Janice, 990
Weston Properties, Sam, Inc., 763
Weston, Coralie, 953
Weston, Sharon R., 1885
Westpac Banking Corp., 2001
Westreich, Anthony, 460
Westreich, Ruth, 460
Westreich, Stanley I., 460
Westriech, Lauren, 460
Westrope, 3505
Wetterau, Mark S., 235
Wettergren, David, 3662
Wettstein, Stacy, 1023
Weyehaeuser, Ian, 1752
Weyenberg, Tim, 3619
Weyerhaeuser, Benjamin D., 3559
Weyerhaeuser, C. Davis, 3559
Weyerhaeuser, F.T., 3559
Weyerhaeuser, Gail T., 3559
Weyerhaeuser, George H., 1752
Weyerhaeuser, Ian, 1752
Weyerhaeuser, Leilee, 1752
Weyerhaeuser, Robert M., 1752
Weyerhaeuser, W. Drew, 1752
Weyerhaeuser, Wendy, 1752
Weyerhaeuser, William T., 3559
Weyerhaeuser-Johnson, Jane, 1752
Weyerhauser, George H., Mrs., 1752
Weyers, Russell C., 3648
Weymouth, George, 2883
Weymouth, John, 3100
Weymouth, Theodore S., 1075
Weywrhaeuser, W. Drew, 3559
Whalen, David, 1195
Whalen, Karen, 496
Whalen, Michael, 369
Whalen, Tim, 3578
Whaley, James, 1993
Whaling, Tom, 3587
Whalton, Michael, 3580
Wham, S. Smith, 3102
Wharff, Carol B., 2732
Wharton, Clifton R., 2099
Wharton, Daniel B., 3587
Wharton, Dwayne, 3034
Whatley, Jon, 3196
WHDH-TV, Inc., 689
Wheat, Warren, 69
Wheelan, Belle S., 1174
Wheeler, James, 1478
Wheeler, James G., Jr., 3417
Wheeler, Jermaine, 2818
Wheeler, John R.C., 1584
Wheeler, Ken, 1286
Wheeler, Kevin J., 3129
Wheeler, Max E., 1001
Wheeler, Mimi, 1001
Wheeler, Robert L., 1647
Wheeler, Steven M., 44
Wheeless, Richard W., 2271
Whelan, Anita, 3424
Whelan, Catherine P., 3447
Whelan, Matthew, 415
Whelpley, John, 2123
Whelton, Joan M., 1443
Whetstone-Foltz, Patricia M., 713
Whetzel, Michelle, 630
Whichard, Mary, 2522
Whipple, Dan, 1157
Whipple, Earl D., 3047
Whipple, Gretchen, 1428
Whipple, Ken, 1588
Whipple, Mary, 72
Whipple, Mary Margaret, Hon., 3421
Whirlpool, 1314
Whisler, Ardyce, 1832
Whitaker, Anne, 1988
Whitaker, Janice M., 2600
Whitaker, Mae M., 1820
Whitaker, Vivian, 1189
Whitcup, Scott M., M.D., 80
White, A. Dennis, 2307
White, A. Scott, 823
White, Andy, 2773
White, Anne, 3503
White, Benjamin T., 923
White, Beth, 999
White, Bill, 1136
White, Brandon C., 3675
White, Carolyn A., 3442
White, Charles B., 3454
White, Chris, 1171
White, Claire Mott, 1621
White, Cyrus, 1699
White, Dale A., 1208
White, David E., 623
White, Diana, 3544
White, Diane L., 279
White, Edmund, 605
White, Gregory, 674
White, Hugh W., 1123
White, Jaleigh J., 1205
White, JoAnn, 2728, 2729, 2730
White, John D., 3329
White, John W., 921
White, Karen, 346
White, Kathleen M., 3196
White, Kathryn A. Weitz, 1840
White, Kathryn W., 1855
White, Keith, 3119
White, Kim, 1642
White, Lee, 1126
White, Linda, 3034
White, Linda A., 3053
White, Marcus, 3637
White, Mark, 1699
White, Michael H., 3651
White, Michael, Jr., 990
White, Miriam deQuadros, 322
White, Monica, 2331
White, Nancy G., 1790
White, Philip, 378
White, R. Elton, 754
White, Richard, 725
White, Richard L., 3054
White, Ridgeway H., 1621
White, Ridgway H., 1645
White, Russell E., 226
White, Sharon, 2754
White, Steve, 1917
White, Steven A., 2921
White, Susie, 2823
White, Thomas H., 2800
White, Thomas W., 3319
White, Vickie, 3292
White, Wayne, Dr., 1877
White, William S., 1621, 1645
White-Longworth, Stephenie, 1154
Whited-Howell, Mary Amelia, 2012
Whitehead, Andy, 687
Whitehead, Baruch, 2112
Whitehead, Cindy, 3287
Whitehead, Mark, 1847
Whitehead, Susan M., 687
Whitehill, Jim, 1620
Whiteleather, John, 1209
Whiteley, Sherry, 263
Whiteman, Lawrence E., 3042
Whitener, Sarah Ford, 2654
Whiteside, Carol, 405
Whiteside, Jeffrey W., 1202
Whiteside, Jennifer Tolle, 2599
Whitesman, Guy E., 823
Whitfield, Ed, 2555
Whitfill, Steve, 2809
Whitham, Mark, 2717
Whiting, Amy, 3296
Whiting, Giles, Mrs., 2504
Whiting, Len, 2907
Whiting, Macauley, Jr., 1597
Whitley, Steven R., 823
Whitley, Tracee, 1282
Whitlock, Jonathan, 990
Whitlock, R. Barnes, 1812
Whitman Charitable Remainder Trust, Catherine A., 1557
Whitman, Barbara, 2369
Whitman, C. Thomas, 3120
Whitman, Frederick C., 462
Whitman, Lars, 1627
Whitman, Leigh, 1321
Whitman, Lois, 2369
Whitman, Martin J., 2369, 2506
Whitman, Sara G., 1557
Whitman, Scott L., 211
Whitman, Wayne, 1321
Whitmore, Lynn, 1214
Whitmore, Richard, 156
Whitney, Ben, 1717
Whitney, Edward A., 3683
Whitney, Michael, 1878
Whitney, Todd, 2111
Whitney, Willis R., 2407
Whitridge, Serena M., 1514
Whitsitt, Jan, 3558
Whitsitt, William, 1823
Whitson, Betty, 484
Whitson, Nancy, 474
Whittaker, David, 2658
Whittaker, Harry W., 2658
Whittaker, Jim, 3421
Whittaker, Polly W., 2658
Whittaker, Sean, 2274
Whittaker, Thomas, 1691
Whittenberg, Russell T., 95
Whittenberger, Ethel B., 953
Whittle, Polly K., 3274
Whitworth, William B., 3196
Whitzel, Robin, 2840
Whorton, Brett, 921
Wible, Jeff, 1170
Wice, David H., 2942
Wichert, Sarah H., 3043
Wick, Emily R., 617
Wickert, Marilyn, 1180
Wickiser, Mike, 3663
Wicks, Mel, 3568
Wicks, Tom, 1764
Widdowson, Julia H., 3251
Widdup, Jeffrey, 2924
Wideman, Lillian, 4
Widener Memorial Foundation 2, 3056
Widener Memorial School Endowment, 3056
Widener, Peter A.B., 3056
Widger Trust, Leon P., 1877
Widing, J. William, III, 2893
Widner, Kenneth, 45
Widoff, Lissa, 1342
Wiebe, Nancy, 1255
Wieboldt, Anna Krueger, 1115
Wieboldt, Nancy, 1115
Wieboldt, William A., 1115
Wiechmann, Marcus, 1721
Wied, Elizabeth, 190
Wiederspan, Nancy, 1847
Wiegand, Ben, 841
Wiegand, Christine P., 2916
Wiegand, Phillips, 841
Wiegand, Phillips, Jr., 841
Wiegand, Ruth, 841
Wiegers Family Foundation, 2232
Wiegers, Betsy, 543
Wiegers, George A., 2232
Wiegert, Bob, 1227
Wiehl, Paul, 2662
Wielenga, Terilea J., 80
Wieman, Roberta, 338
Wieman, Russell G., 1026
Wiener, Ann, 2335
Wiener, Carolyn S., 2506
Wiener, Donald B., 1322
Wiener, Judy, 1759
Wiener, Malcolm H., 2506
Wiener, William B., Jr., 1322
Wienkers, Kevin, Dr., 3597
Wienkers, Kevin, Mrs., 3597
Wierda, Emilie, 1658
Wierda, Laurie S., 1650
Wierda, Laurie Sue, 1650
Wight, Russell, Jr., 2005
Wightman, Gail, 1845
Wightman, John, 1845
Wikert, Alinda H., 3260
Wikert, Cody M., 3260
Wikert, Margretta H., 3260
Wilbur, Deborah, 2342
Wilcox, John, 1831
Wilcox, Philip C., Jr., 661
Wilcox, Steven, 3662
Wilcox, Valerie Polisseni, 2361
Wilcox, William, 3603
Wilcoxson, Melvin, 1275
Wilczek, Ron, 3633
Wild Wings Foundation, 2346
Wildenthal, Kern, 3262
Wilder, H. Rodger, 1764
Wilder, Rick, Rev., 1382
Wilder, Roger, 1764
Wilder, Ruth E., 920
Wilder, Stephen F., 2391
Wilder, William, 920
Wildlife Care Center, 799
Wildrick, Eve B., 655
Wilds, Deborah J., Dr., 3502
Wiles, Rhonda, 1157
Wiles, Stephanie, 2112
Wiley Rein & Fielding, 2071
Wiley, Jennifer Volgenau, 3485
Wiley, Richard R., 2664
Wiley, Scott, 1225
Wiley, Tom, 2737
Wilfahrt, Barry, 2648
Wilfong, Diane, 1860
Wilford, Dan S., 3216
Wilfrid, Thomas N., 1972
Wilhoite, Charles, 2861
Wilkas, Anne M., 26
Wilkens, Michael T., 1243
Wilkerson, Betsy, 3526
Wilkerson, Dick, 3099
Wilkes, Robert W., 3102
Wilkie, Margot, 551
Wilkie, Valleau, Jr., 3336
Wilkin, Diana, 2071
Wilkins, Catherine, 3573
Wilkins, Jan, 3580

Wilkins, John W., Jr., 3229
Wilkins, Roger, 653
Wilkins, Zelene, 1627
Wilkinson, Bary, 463
Wilkinson, Brenda, 351
Wilkinson, Bruce, 463
Wilkinson, Cathy, 1590
Wilkinson, Darla J., 1771
Wilkinson, F. McKinnon, 2556, 2636
Wilkinson, Gerald, 351
Wilkinson, Guerin S., 463
Wilkinson, Joe B., 3343
Wilkinson, Marie, 954
Wilkinson, Stephen, Dr., 463
Wilkinson, Sue, 1847
Wilkinson, Teresa D., 3275
Wilkinson, Tom S., 463
Wilkinson, Warren S., 463
Wilkinson-Fannin, Lisa, 44
Wilks, Craig, 2710
Wilks, Farris, 3366
Wilks, Farris C., 3366
Wilks, JoAnn, 3366
Wilks, Sandra, 1107
Will, Dean, 2882
Will, George F., 3601
Willard Charitable Trust, Raymond & Alma, 2332
Willard Trust, Cecilia Young, 3382
Willard, Kirk, 3623
Willard, Magrieta L., 608
Willauer, Christian, 3059
Willens, Liliane, 1338
Willet, Linda A., 1940
Willett, Jeffrey, 1263
Willey, Stephanie T., 1359
Willhardt, Gary D., 1061
William, Kirk Harper, 3411
William, Susan Krenbiel, 1279
Williams Charitable Trust, Caroline, 983
Williams Charitable Trust, George J., 983
Williams Co., Gary, The, 526
Williams Energy Corp., Gary, 526
Williams Trust, Hobart W., 983
Williams, A. Damon, 3432
Williams, Andrea M., 2950
Williams, Angela, 1390
Williams, Ann Claire, 2085
Williams, Arthur A., 1567
Williams, Beatrice, 3383
Williams, Benjamin J., 1539
Williams, Benjamin S.J., 1140
Williams, Betty, 378
Williams, C. Wayne, 2108
Williams, Cad, 3364
Williams, Carolyn H., Hon., 1626
Williams, Catherine, 3030
Williams, Christopher H., 3433
Williams, Clarence, 391
Williams, Clyde, 2287
Williams, Craig M., 1541
Williams, Dave, 3606
Williams, David, 1817
Williams, David, II, 3129
Williams, Denice, 2326
Williams, Dennis R., 992
Williams, Dianne E., 562
Williams, Donna J., 991
Williams, Doris Carson, 2968
Williams, Dorothy L., 872
Williams, Dwight, 3567
Williams, E. Grainger, 71
Williams, Elizabeth, 3542
Williams, Emelie Melton, 2432
Williams, Ethel Isaacs, 805
Williams, Eva C., 2541
Williams, Evan, 1256
Williams, Frantz, Jr., 592
Williams, Grice E., 954
Williams, J. McDonald, 3262
Williams, James, 3558
Williams, Jay, 1620
Williams, Jerry, 1853
Williams, Jerry B., 3129
Williams, Jim, 371
Williams, Joel T., Jr., 3202
Williams, John, 1067
Williams, Johnathan, 360
Williams, Judee Ann, 3126
Williams, Julie Jones, 1065
Williams, Kate, 378
Williams, Kenna, 73
Williams, Kim, 2780
Williams, Kimberley S., 2113
Williams, Kristen E., 1500
Williams, Laird M., 872
Williams, Lamar, 3411
Williams, Lisa B., 897
Williams, Lynne, 489
Williams, Mark, 3273
Williams, Marva E., 968
Williams, Mary, 3504
Williams, Mary Alice, 1608
Williams, Michael J., 3657
Williams, Michael P., 1547
Williams, Mitch, 122
Williams, Nancy, 1218
Williams, Nash, 3654
Williams, Nat Chioke, Ph.D., 664
Williams, Noel Brown, 3139
Williams, Polly, 1567
Williams, Rainey, 2826
Williams, Raymond H., 471
Williams, Richard, 151, 2010
Williams, Richard S., Jr., 3436
Williams, Richard, Dr., 2543
Williams, Robert, 2071
Williams, Robert R., 59
Williams, Ronald K., 1610
Williams, Rosa Sternberger, 2637
Williams, Ruth E., 1264
Williams, Sarah, Esq., 801
Williams, Scott, 662
Williams, Sharon, 1817
Williams, Sherwin, 3505
Williams, Stacey, 1068
Williams, Stephen T., 2739
Williams, Thomas L., 2694
Williams, Tom, 1607
Williams, Vivien, 1735
Williams-Puccio, Kelly, 804
Williamson, Alexandra Bowes, 121
Williamson, Brian R., 2794
Williamson, Donald G., 1628
Williamson, Heidi, 2893
Williamson, James G., 563
Williamson, James J., 3630
Williamson, Keith H., 1782
Williamson, Marc, 3060
Williamson, Susan, 9
Williamson, W. Bland, 2807
Williamson, Wayne, 569
Willis North America, Inc., 102
Willis, Ann D., 2611
Willis, David, 1539
Willis, Gracia T., 2313
Willis, Joyce, 608
Willis, Kathryn, 867
Willis, Lois Cross, 2313
Willis, Mark, 1143
Willis, Sandy, 1663
Willman, J. Nolan, 1122
Willmoth-Carlson, Pam, 122
Willner, Peter, 2035
Willoughby, Jack, 2947
Willson, Janet, 508
Wilmans, Carlie, 454, 455
Wilmers, Robert G., 2446
Wilmington Trust Co., 629
Wilsey, Alfred S., Sr., 464
Wilsey, Diane B., 464
Wilsey, Michael W., 464
Wilson & Co., S.M., 809
Wilson, Andrew, 1696
Wilson, Angela B., 3441
Wilson, Anthony L., 877
Wilson, Becky, 3578
Wilson, Betty H., 1156
Wilson, Catherine M., 16
Wilson, Charles K., Jr., 3157
Wilson, Christina P., 378
Wilson, Clarence A., 3487
Wilson, Colleen, 216
Wilson, David, 556, 1374
Wilson, Dennis, 1142
Wilson, Diane M., 1851
Wilson, Dorothy Cheney, 3296
Wilson, Doug, Dr., 1359
Wilson, Dwayne A., 3235
Wilson, E. Miles, 1615
Wilson, Edwin G., Jr., 2611
Wilson, Frazier, 3348
Wilson, Gary, 2700
Wilson, Gayle, 359
Wilson, James C., Jr., 3109
Wilson, James E., 2686
Wilson, Jennifer, 2947
Wilson, Jennifer D., 2947
Wilson, John, 3451
Wilson, John H.T., 556
Wilson, John K., 1835
Wilson, John S. (Tripp), 2613
Wilson, Katherine C., 858
Wilson, Kenneth, 151
Wilson, Kerrie B., 672
Wilson, Kevin, 1039
Wilson, Lisa, 1215
Wilson, Mary M., 1675
Wilson, Matthew, 2991
Wilson, Michael, 1217
Wilson, Norman L., 473
Wilson, Olly W., Jr., 2262
Wilson, Pattye, 1766
Wilson, Paula, 2143
Wilson, Perry, 1771
Wilson, Raiann, 401
Wilson, Ralph C., Jr., 1675
Wilson, Randall, 1706
Wilson, Rebecca, 1105
Wilson, Robert A., 3157
Wilson, Robert F., 1383
Wilson, Robert W., 2507
Wilson, Rosine M., 3381
Wilson, Roxanne, 400
Wilson, Sandra W., 556
Wilson, Sarah F., 1696
Wilson, Spence, 3124
Wilson, Spence L., 3157
Wilson, Steve, 1609
Wilson, Steven, 3162
Wilson, Susan, Dr., 1808
Wilson, Suzanne M., Dr., 1955
Wilson, Tad, 1185
Wilson, V. Otis, Jr., 2538
Wilson, Velda, 1856
Wilson, Vera, 3019
Wilson, Warren, 1300
Wilson, Wayne, 287
Wilson, William, 556
Wilson-Moore, Elizabeth, 3157
Wilson-Oyelaran, Eileen B., Dr., 1626
Wilson-Scott, Dalila, 2242
Wilson-Taylor, Marti, 1486
Wilson-West, Carol, 3157
Wilt, Gary, 3119
Wilt, Priscilla, 2684
Wilton, Jane L., 2325
Wiltse, Tom, 1616
Wiltz, James W., 1726
Wimberley, Ruby J., 3357
Winans Company, C.H., 1906
Winant, Joan, 2152
Winant, John, 2152
Winbigler, Connie, 1580
Winblad, Ann, 1738
Winchester-Vega, Michele, Dr., 2111
Winder, Charles, 949
Winder, Phoebe, 1494
Windham, Diann, 3287
Windhorst, John, Jr., 1749
Windhorst, Peter, 1749
Window to Asia, 468
Windsor, 1388
Windway Capital Corp., 3669
Winebrenner-Nizam, Michelle, 497
Winestock, Jim, 1353
Wing, Keith M., 2890
Wing, Shelley, 1225
Wing-Berman, Molly, 3090
Wingard, Raymond R., 10
Wingate, Jo Stott, 869
Wingate, Roy S., 3357
Winger, Rodger, 1189
Wingo, Sherril L., 2609
Winiarski, Barbara, 466
Winiarski, Warren, 466
Winiberg, Siobhan, 496
Winkler, Charles P., M.D., 3459
Winkler, Clifford E., 3207
Winkler, Henry, 2782
Winn, Carie, 3606
Winn, Jack, 1124
Winn-Dixie Stores, Inc., 700
Winnard, Diane, 954
Winnell, Todd, 1656
Winner, Donna, 2925
Winowiecki, Ronald L., 1655
Winship, Susan, 1505
Winslow Tech Group, 3505
Winsor, Curtin, Jr., Hon., 2142
Winsor, Henry, 3000
Winsor, Monica, 2142
Winsor, Rebecca D., 2142
Winston, Bert F., III, 3358
Winston, Blake W., 3358
Winston, Harold R., 1242
Winston, Hathily Johnson, 269
Winston, Jim, 722
Winston, Joni R., 3650
Winston, L. David, 3358
Winter, Arthur, 1100
Winter, David K., 335
Winter, Dorothy, 1100
Winter, Elizabeth H., 2212
Winter, Emma, 1100
Winter, Marlene, 3552

Winter, William, Hon., 1763
Winters, Barbara, 1176
Winters, Peter, 905
Winterthur, 2069
Winthrop Trust, Amory, 2508
Winthrop, Inc., 1893
Winton, Randolph B., 2932
Wipple, Ross M., 72
Wirgau, Jessica, 3431
Wirginis, Terrence L., 2896
Wirshba, Lewis H., 2118
Wirth, Andy, 441
Wirth, Dyann, 2534
Wirtz, Mary, 3623
Wirz, Henry, 391
Wisbey, Ron, 448
Wischmeier, Priscilla, 1132
Wischmeier, Shawn, 1689
Wisconsin Dept. of Natural Resources, 3654
Wisconsin Dept. of Transportation, 3654
Wisconsin Power and Light Co., 3592
Wisdom, Grace, 2832
Wisdom, Peggy, 2832
Wise, Blake, 1400
Wise, Craig E., 2794
Wise, Janelle A., 946
Wise, Leslie, 1602
Wise, Phyllis M., 1949
Wiseman, Eric C., 2642
Wiseman, Rodney, 3370
Wiseman-Lewis, Frances, 83
Wisenbaker, Michael B., Jr., 3260
Wisenbaker, Wesley Hill, 3260
Wisenburg, Ralph, 2686
Wish You Were Here Productions, 647
Wishard Hospital, 1156
Wishcamper, Carol, 1339
Wishnafski, Diane, 595
Wismann, David, 1141
Wisne, Kathryn, 1578
Wisse, Ruth R., 2051
Wistar, Christy, 954
Wiswell, Byron C., 764
Witherby, Brenten, 990
Witherington, Hunter, 3124
Witherington, James D., Jr., 3124
Withers, Mettie, 702
Witkovski, Vicki F., 1844
Witmer, Chuck, 2909
Witorsch, Rafael, Dr., 3444
Witorsch, Raphael, 3442
Witt, Bruce, 1255
Witt, Jocelyn S., 587
Witt, John, 1832
Witt, John W., 122
Witt, Judy, 1012
Witt, Kyle D., 991
Witt, Richard A., 1850
Witt, Scott V., 826
Witt, Susan E. Ahrens, 1210
Wittchow, Scott, 3615
Wittenberg, Carol, 268
Wittenberg, Joel R., 1628
Witter & Co., Dean, 467
Witter, Dean, 467
Witter, Dean, III, 467
Witter, Dean, Mrs., 467
Witter, Malcolm G., 467
Witter, William P., 467
Witthoefft, Charles F., 3470
Wittig, Bob, 668
Witting, Paul, 1583
Wittink, Alicia P., 2349
Wittstein, Eric S., 2180
Wizig-Barrios, Renee, 3266
Wochner, Lee, 162
Woerner, John R., 523
Wohl, Frank, 1956
Wohlgemuth, Jay, 2834
Woidke, Eric, 2683
Wojahn, Jeff, 493
Wojan, Connie, 1583
Wojcik, Tim, 1837
Wojkowski, Dan, 178
Wolcott, Arthur S., 2415
Wolcott, Gregory, 2154
Wold, Clark, 3118
Woldar, Edwin, 2509
Woldar, Jay, 2509
Woldar, Paul, 2509
Woldar, Shirley, 2509
Wolden, Wayne, 1703
Woleske, Christine, 3619
Wolf, Avery C., 849
Wolf, Ben, 3540
Wolf, David, 390
Wolf, Don A., 3058
Wolf, Edward L., 2084
Wolf, Ellen, 2084
Wolf, Gerald, 2907
Wolf, Jeffrey, 2084
Wolf, Linda S., 982
Wolf, Luther H., III, 849
Wolf, Rebecca Medeiros, 159
Wolf, Robert B., 3010
Wolf, Stephanie R., 419
Wolf, Steven, 2084
Wolf, Thomas M., 2773
Wolfberg, David A., 783
Wolfe, Albert, 3587
Wolfe, Andrew Frey, 1696
Wolfe, Carol F., 1696
Wolfe, Daniel T., 1696
Wolfe, John J., 1775
Wolfe, Lawrence A., 1625
Wolfe, Molly Frey, 1696
Wolfe, Patricia A., 2905
Wolfe, Ray, 948
Wolfe, Wendy, 537
Wolfen, Werner, 145
Wolfensohn, James, 2085
Wolff, Gregory S., 611
Wolff, Henry, Jr., 131
Wolff, Holly, 2027
Wolff, J. Marshall, 2986
Wolff, Laura, 2098
Wolff, Paula, 1040
Wolford, Kate, 1714, 1715
Wolfson, David, 2039
Wolfwind, 1388
Wolfzorn, E. John, 2780
Wolk, David M., 2510
Wolk, Jeremy J., 2510
Wolk, Louis S., 2510
Wolk, Marvin L., 2510
Wolkowitz, Michael, 2278
Wollman, Jodie Lynn, 351
Wollons, Roberta, 1045
Wollowick, Gladys, 843
Wollowick, Janet Amy, 843
Woloshyn, Sonyia, 2002
Woloszyk, Carl, 1587
Wolpoff, Carol, 1417
Wolpoff, Harry K., 1417
Wolsey, Randy, 3330
Wolszczak, Jay, 756
Wolters, Kate Pew, 1667
Womac, Joe, 423
Womack, Christopher C., 915
Womble, Ralph H., 2565
Women's Center of San Joaquin County, 161
Wommack, Kent W., 1339
Wonacott, Jeff, 1616
Wonders, Clare Atkinson, 3196
Wong, Allene, 935
Wong, Colleen, 935
Wong, Frances, 1931
Wong, Huey, 301
Wong, Pausang, 301
Wong, Sharon, 1085
Wong, Winston F., 138
Woo, Michael, 301
Wood, Beth, 2232
Wood, Brandon C., 3547
Wood, Brenda K., 3547
Wood, Charles R., 619
Wood, David L., 504
Wood, Donald R., III, 3547
Wood, E. Jenner, III, 891, 904
Wood, Edna, 2407
Wood, Erica, 408
Wood, George, 2232
Wood, J. Kurt, 842
Wood, James, 2237
Wood, James C., III, 2674
Wood, Jeff, 2113
Wood, John F., 1790
Wood, Karen, 1215
Wood, Kate B., 1944
Wood, Ken, 1234
Wood, Phoebe A., 1288
Wood, Robert A., 1790
Wood, Robin, 2108
Wood, Roger, 3649
Wood, Ruth D., 26
Wood, Thomas, 2032
Wood, William P., 3368
Wood, Willis B., Jr., 243
Wood-Prince, Patrick, 1077
Wood-Prince, Patrick B., 1076
Woodard, Andrew, 2877
Woodard, Billy T., 2599
Woodard, Carlton, 2877
Woodard, Elizabeth H., 3428
Woodard, Joan, 2543
Woodard, Joan B., 59
Woodard, Joy, 2877
Woodard, Kim, 2877
Woodard, Kristen A., 2877
Woodard, Tod, 2877
Woodard, Tyson, 2877
Woodard, Walter A., 2877
Woodbourne Foundation, 2283
Woodburn, Connie, 2677
Woodburn, Joyce, 14
Woodbury, Evelyn, 1897
Woodcliff, Inc., 1991
Woodeshick, Kevin D., 2908
Woodford, Buckner, IV, 1282
Woodhouse, Charles E., 220
Woodhouse, Lorenzo E., 3410
Woodin, Peter, 268
Woodrow Foundation, 3510
Woodruff, Barbara McBeth, 315
Woodruff, Christopher S., 922
Woodruff, Dina, 922
Woodruff, Ethel I., 922
Woodruff, J. Barnett, 922
Woodruff, James W., 922
Woodruff, James W., III, 922
Woodruff, Judy, 2085
Woodruff, Judy C., 662
Woodruff, Katherine F., 922
Woods Trust, Adrian W., 1821
Woods, Alfred, 2005
Woods, Alfred L., 3488
Woods, Alison, 562
Woods, Bob, 278
Woods, Bonnie, 2110
Woods, C. Patrick, 1279
Woods, Cynthia R., 1828
Woods, David W., 102
Woods, Donna W., 1857
Woods, Emil, 2230
Woods, Francine, 342
Woods, Frank H., 1857
Woods, Frank H., Jr., 1857
Woods, H.A., 3295
Woods, Hank, 1847, 1857
Woods, Henry C., 1857
Woods, Henry Clay, III, 3150
Woods, J. Eric, 3100
Woods, James F., 1584
Woods, Janet, 3530
Woods, Kathryn Esping, 3225
Woods, Milton, 3515
Woods, Nelle C., 1857
Woods, Pam, 489, 3189
Woods, Richard A., 3426
Woods, Rodney, 3225
Woods, Skye, 315
Woods, Thomas C., IV, 1857
Woods, Thomas C., Jr., 1857
Woods, Ward W., 357
Woods, William S., 3430
Woodson Trust, Margaret C., 2644
Woodson, Margaret C., 2644
Woodson, Paul B., Jr., 2644
Woodward Communications, Inc., 1247
Woodward, Barbara Sullivan, 1247
Woodward, Kay E., Dr., 3110
Woodward, Kristin, 1247
Woodward, Robert B., 59
Woodward, Thomas, 1247
Woodward, Tina, 602
Woody, Dennis, Esq., 2932
Woodzell, Bruce, 3428
Wooley, Dudley, 1759
Woolf, Orien Levy, 3385
Woolhiser, Dale, 1828
Woolhiser, Michael, 1653
Woollam, Philip, 1309
Woollam, Tina Freeman, 1309
Woolsey, Holly, 723
Wooten, McKinley, 2632
Wooten, Rosalie O'Reilly, 1783
Wooten, Wilma, 1186
Wootton, Connie J., 2015
Worcel, Sonia, 2868
Worcester, Richard, 1200
Word at Work Foundation, The, 3666
Worden, Charles E., 1281
Worden, Joe, 1603
Workman, John L., 2758
Workman, M. James, Rev., 1440
Workman, Mike, 2702
Workman, Nicole, 2733
Workman, RaSheda, 4
Workneh, Claire, 1387
Worland, Brooke, 1163
World Childrens Fund-Europe (CH), 468
World Harvest Church, 468
World Reach, 2677
World Trade Ventures, Ltd., 889

Zamora, Rhonda, 2562
Zanden, Lisa Van der, 3325
Zanetti, Wayne, 2111
Zanger, Allene, 354
Zanghi, Phyllis, 2307
Zanone, Philip R., Jr., 3120
Zant, Julius D., 1359
Zappardino, Pam, 1357
Zarate, Barbara Clifton, 309
Zarcone, Dominick P., 3595
Zarcone, Michael, 2307
Zarrow, Edward, 2834
Zarrow, Henry H., 2833, 2834
Zarrow, Jack C., 2833
Zarrow, Stuart, 2833
Zarrow, Stuart A., 2834
Zarwin, Norman, 2958
Zastrow, Jim, 1693
Zatyrka, Sasha, 560
Zauher, Jim, 401
Zausner, Meryl, 2333
Zaw-Mon, Caroline Hunt, 2971
Zayas, Andrea, 360
Zeckhauser, Sally H., 1498
Zeff, Anne L., 790
Zeglis, John, 1176
Zehnder, W. Don, 1606
Zeidler, Jeanne, 3487
Zeilinger, Bob, 1606
Zeisel, H., 2049
Zeitlin, Jide, 2146
Zeldenrust, Robert, 1607
Zeldin, Claudia, 3060
Zeldin, Jessica, 3060
Zeldin, Martin, 3060
Zeldin, Stephanie, 3060
Zeldin, Sybille, 3060
Zeldlin, Claudia, 3060
Zeleny, Dennis, 3046
Zeljo, Jon E., 2529
Zell, Helen H., 1119
Zell, Joann L., 1119
Zell, John, 722
Zell, Kellie, 1119
Zell, Matthew M., 1119
Zell, Samuel, 1119
Zelle, Julie B., 1713
Zeller, David J., 1032
Zeller, Joyce, 2044
Zellerbach, Charles R., 471
Zellerbach, Jennie B., 471
Zellerbach, Thomas H., 471
Zellerbach, William J., 471
Zellers, Jeff, 2746
Zelnak, Judy D., 2647
Zelnak, Stephen P., Jr., 2647
Zeltwanger, Ron, 1176
Zemanek, Christine, 3543
Zendt Charitable Trust, George, 1112
Zeneca Inc., 623
Zeng, Yu "Gary", 301
Zentz, Robert W., 648
Zerhouni, Elias A., 3516
Zervigon, Luis, 1316
Zerzan, Tom, 1988
Zeugner, Mary Z., 3425
Zeuli, Kimberly, 3487
Zeve, Roberta, 541
Zhang, Ji-Qiang, 3422
Zia Co., The, 3295
Ziccolella, Vincent, 2271
Zickler, Judith, 1419
Zickler, Judy, 1419
Zickler, Leo E., 1419
Zide, Teri Ann, 2732
Ziegenbein, Jeff, 1843
Ziegeweid, Joy, 2427
Ziegler, Arthur P., Jr., 2883
Ziegler, Craig C., 139
Zielinski, Joseph, 958
Zielke, Bill, 1193
Zieman, Mark, 317
Ziese, Kristen, 1160
Ziff Investment Partnership LP II, 2515
Ziff, Daniel M., 2515
Ziff, Leslie, 2515
Ziff, Ted, II, 2909
Ziffren, John, 287
Ziger, Steven G., 1347
Zilber, Joseph J., 3670
Zilber, Ltd., 3670
Zilber, Marilyn, 3670
Zilber, Vera J., 3670
Zilkha, Ezra K., 1968
Zillmer, Chelsea M., 975
Zimdars, John, 3659
Zimmer, Bernie, 58
Zimmer, Ida, 2732
Zimmer, Mary, 1730
Zimmer, Michael V., 3657
Zimmer, Scott, 1606
Zimmerman Family Trust, No. 1, 1249
Zimmerman, Clara, 940
Zimmerman, Diane L., 2273
Zimmerman, Hans, 940
Zimmerman, Jane, 2035, 2909
Zimmerman, John W., 540
Zimmerman, Kenneth, 1990
Zimmerman, Lee E., 537
Zimmerman, Ron, 2035
Zimski, Patrick, 3027
Zingale, Daniel, 138
Zink, Frank, 638
Zink, Kenneth E., 1641
Zinn, Douglas, 2577
Zinsmeyer, Jeffrey W., 2139
Zipf, Cindy, 1924
Zipperly, Cynthia H., 10
Zippert, Carol, Dr., 4
Zitzelsberger, Terrie, 1647
Zobell, Barbara, 436
Zobell, Karen, 436
Zoccola, William L., 3120
Zoffer, Jerome, 2062
Zoghbi, Huda Yahya, 1714
Zollett, Scott, 2737
Zollner, Fred, 1858
Zollo, Margaret G., 903
Zondag, Sharon, 2982
Zook, Thomas W., 2701
Zoretic, Richard C., 3420
Zornoza, Simon, 1550
Zottoli, Steven J., 232
Zubay, Cori, 888
Zuccaro, Edward J., 1916
Zuccaro, Edward R., 3418
Zuccaro, Teri, 1216
Zucco, Donato, Dr., 2922
Zuccotti, John E., 2146
Zuchero, Sandra, 2916
Zucker, Benjamin, 2046
Zuckerman, Jane L., 2107
Zugazagoitia, Julian, 2494
Zuill, Cummings V., 2048
Zukerman, Ed, 2470
Zumstein, Ron, 1298
Zuppas, Nitsa, 404
Zurbay, Donald, 1741
Zurek, Thomas M., 1183
Zurier, Samuel D., 3062
Zuskin, Lauren, 574
Zuskin, Morey, 574
Zwald, Robert L., 876
Zweifler, Michael, Dr., 68
Zwilich, Ellen Taaffe, 2194
Zwirn, Randy H., 1993

GEOGRAPHIC INDEX

Foundations in boldface type make grants on a national, regional, or international basis; the others generally limit giving to the city or state in which they are located. For local funders with a history of giving in another state, consult the "see also" references at the end of each state section.

ALABAMA

Andalusia: Andalusia 1
Anniston: Community 9
Birmingham: BBVA 3, Caring 7, Day 12, Goodrich 13, Hawkins 14, **International 15**, Malone 16, McWane 17, Regions 19, Rikard 20, Stephens 24
Dothan: Wiregrass 25
Indian Springs: Smith 22
Mobile: **Atlantis 2**, Brown 5, Community 10, Meyer 18
Montgomery: Caddell 6, Central 8, Simpson 21
Northport: Community 11
Selma: Black 4
Summerdale: Snook 23

see also 70, 687, 700, 804, 821, 849, 860, 878, 894, 914, 915, 1667, 1778, 2521, 2593, 2603, 2681, 2885, 3018, 3052, 3181, 3466, 3505

ALASKA

Anchorage: Alaska 26, Aleut 27, Arctic 28, Atwood 29, Block 30, Bristol 31, Chugach 32, CIRI 33, Koniag 36, **Nash 37**
Fairbanks: Doyon 34
Juneau: Juneau 35

see also 324, 442, 512, 2717, 3181, 3235, 3490, 3513, 3524, 3531, 3572

AMERICAN SAMOA

see 1948

ARIZONA

Mesa: Prayer 58
Paradise Valley: Sioles 61
Phoenix: Ahearn 38, APS 39, Flinn 44, Grace 46, Hill 48, Hughes 49, Long 51, Marketplace 52, Marley 53, Napier 55, Ottosen 56, Piper 57, Squires 62
Prescott: Christian 41, Webb 64
Scottsdale: Dorrance 42, Freedom 45, Rubeli 60, Stardust 63
Tucson: Barton 40, Every 43, Green 47, Jasam 50, Marshall 54, **Research 59**, Weil 65

see also 3, 82, 99, 263, 550, 631, 856, 878, 1035, 1206, 1220, 1245, 1707, 1724, 1860, 1864, 2008, 2033, 2034, 2242, 2315, 2348, 2727, 2863, 2872, 3076, 3119, 3359, 3397, 3420, 3491, 3572, 3575, 3621

ARKANSAS

Arkadelphia: Ross 72
Bentonville: Wal-Mart 74
El Dorado: Union 73
Gurdon: Cabe 67
Little Rock: Frueauff 70, Ottenheimer 71
Rogers: Buck 66
Sherwood: Delta 68
Siloam Springs: **Windgate 75**
Springdale: Endeavor 69

see also 235, 627, 631, 878, 1103, 1278, 1298, 1308, 1710, 1763, 1869, 1872, 2211, 2521, 2656, 2677, 2808, 2815, 3018, 3109, 3120, 3275, 3284, 3360, 3598

CALIFORNIA

Agoura Hills: Community 158, **Hilton 251**
Aliso Viejo: Nicholas 344
Anaheim: Anaheim 83
Aptos: Community 163
Arroyo Grande: Brisco 127
Auburn: Placer 371
Bakersfield: Brown 132, Kern 279
Bayside: Humboldt 257
Berkeley: **Arkay 91**, **Parsemus 358**, Trio 440
Beverly Hills: Ahmanson 77, Bohnett 117, Brandman 125, Congregation 164, Douglas 186, Eisner 189, Fawcett 195, Feintech 196, Fuserna 212, **Guthy-Jackson 237**, i.am.angel 259, Just 272, Leichtman 298, Smith 415, Sterling 426, Van Nuys 447
Brea: Family 192
Burbank: Disney 181, Disney 182
Burlingame: Elfenworks 190
Carlsbad: Tippett 436, West 458
Chico: North 346
Claremont: Philanthropy 368
Corte Madera: Metta 329
Costa Mesa: **Lingnan 301**
Culver City: Chan 148
Daly City: Gellert 215
Dana Point: Mediathe 325, Optivest 351
Danville: Quest 377
Davis: Glide 226
El Segundo: **Mattel 312**, **Mercer 328**
Emeryville: Clif 152
Encinitas: Bravo 126, **Leichtag 297**, Rancho 378
Encino: Carpenter 145, Muskin 339, Price 374
Fairfield: Solano 419
Fountain Valley: Tu 443
Freestone: **Warsh 452**
Fremont: **Cuore 172**, Fremont 207, Green 233
Fresno: Fansler 193
Gardena: Liu 302
Geyserville: Hinkle 252, Jackson 266
Glendale: Community 162, McCoy 319
Goleta: **Las 291**
Grass Valley: True 442
Hayward: **Alalusi 78**
Hollister: Community 159
Indian Wells: Champions 147
Irvine: Allergan 80, **Beckman 105**, Beckman 106, Bonner 118, GSF 235, Helms 247, Klein 283, Mazda 313, Shepherd, 403, Western 459
Kentfield: **Gleason 224**
La Habra: Institute 260
La Jolla: Foundation 203, Menard 327, Price 373
Lafayette: Berry 111
Laguna Beach: Laguna 288, **Marisla 310**, Swayne 431
Lake Forest: McBeth 315
Livermore: Pedrozzi 364
Long Beach: Archstone 90, Gumbiner 236, Laulhere 292
Los Alamitos: Adams 76, CEC 146
Los Altos: **Beavers 102**, Chao 149, Heising-Simons 245, Los Altos 305, Noyce 348, **Packard 357**
Los Angeles: Anderson 85, **Annenberg 86**, Arnall 92, Atlas 96, **Better 112**, **Broad 129**, California 137, California 138, Chartwell 150, Coburn 154, Cotsen 167, Dart-L 177, **DJ & T 184**, Drown 187, Found 201, **Foundation 204**, Gibson 220, **Grass 232**, Haynes 243, **Keck 276**, Kellerman 277, LA84 287, Lansing 290, Leavey 294, Military 330, Morris 334, Murdock 338, **Nazarian 341**, Parsons 359, Partners 360, Patagonia.org 362, Rifkind 383, Roth 388, Ryzman 390, Sassoon 395, **Seaver 400**, Taper 433, UniHealth 444, Wallis 451, Wasserman 453, Weingart 456, WHH 461
Los Gatos: Berry 110
Manhattan Beach: Windsong 465
Marina del Rey: Richards 382
Menlo Park: Hewlett 248, Rossi 387
Mill Valley: **Gellert 214**, Horne 254
Modesto: Stanislaus 425
Monterey: Community 157, Ransom 379
Moraga: Soda 418
Moss Landing: Monterey 332
Mountain View: **Google 231**, Guzik 238, Intuit 263, Silicon 408
Napa: Mead 324, Napa 340
Newport Beach: Carlston 143, Curci 173, Eichenberg 188, Noll 345, Pacific 355, Simon 410
North Hills: Boeckmann 116
Novato: Marin 309
Oakland: Braddock 123, California 139, **Clorox 153**, **Kapor 273**, Northern 347, Scaife 397, Valley 445
Ontario: Kim 280
Orinda: Barth 101, GirlSMART 222, Simpson 411
Oxnard: **Kavli 275**, Samuelsson 392
Palm Springs: Anderson 84
Palo Alto: American 82, **Floyd 200**, Hewlett 249, **Moore 333**, Schmidt 398, Skoll 412, Skoll 413, **Special 422**, **Wadhwani 450**
Palos Verdes Estates: Wesley 457
Palos Verdes Peninsula: De Miranda 179

COLORADO

CONNECTICUT

DELAWARE

639, McHugh 641, Morgridge 642, Morse 643, Pinkerton 645, Prairie 646, Sylvan 648, Terk 649
Wimington: Brookwood 624

see also 70, 74, 518, 519, 695, 878, 1373, 1407, 1541, 1919, 1972, 2075, 2242, 2315, 2488, 3018, 3019, 3055, 3067, 3466

DISTRICT OF COLUMBIA

Washington: Bauman 650, Berger-Marks 651, Bernstein 652, Block 653, Bou 654, **Butler 655**, Cafritz 656, **Carter 657**, **Case 658**, **El-Hibri 659**, Flamboyan 660, **Foundation 661**, **Freedom 662**, Graham 663, **Hill 664**, Himmelfarb 665, **Hitachi 666**, **Institute 667**, Jovid 668, Krauthammer 669, Lehrman 670, Lichtenberg 671, Meyer 672, Monarch 673, **National 674**, National 675, New Futures 676, Palmer 677, Patterson 678, Rumsfeld 679, **Sasakawa 680**, **Searle 681**, Stewart 682, **Wallace 683**, Wallace 684, **Wyss 685**

see also 70, 74, 76, 107, 112, 181, 182, 220, 231, 232, 241, 245, 249, 252, 263, 268, 295, 312, 313, 316, 336, 380, 410, 413, 480, 509, 550, 567, 569, 587, 604, 636, 694, 756, 817, 864, 878, 962, 970, 1009, 1064, 1066, 1076, 1092, 1224, 1264, 1291, 1293, 1322, 1346, 1350, 1352, 1355, 1356, 1363, 1367, 1372, 1373, 1377, 1384, 1389, 1390, 1397, 1399, 1401, 1405, 1417, 1419, 1452, 1741, 1896, 1927, 1936, 1953, 1956, 1972, 2003, 2033, 2034, 2045, 2073, 2118, 2242, 2278, 2290, 2303, 2307, 2317, 2322, 2349, 2354, 2356, 2373, 2375, 2391, 2393, 2400, 2424, 2427, 2451, 2466, 2508, 2522, 2610, 2706, 2742, 2760, 2791, 2865, 2917, 2941, 2959, 3004, 3033, 3071, 3093, 3179, 3181, 3184, 3280, 3319, 3320, 3411, 3426, 3435, 3457, 3462, 3466, 3479, 3480, 3481, 3482, 3499, 3525, 3575, 3590, 3603, 3622, 3661

FLORIDA

Aventura: **Arison 691**
Bal Harbour: Greenburg 752
Boca Raton: **Kazma 766**, Krouse 774, Moos 790, Sandelman 814, Sunburst 829, TWS 836
Bonita Springs: A. & R. 686
Boynton Beach: Plangere 802, **Skelly 820**
Bradenton: Kiwanis 770
Cape Coral: Cape Coral 714
Captiva: Stafford 825
Clearwater: Pinellas 801
Coconut Creek: Minto 789
Coconut Grove: Green 751
Coral Gables: Coral Gables 729, Dunspaugh-Dalton 738, Kennedy 767, Macdonald 783
Delray Beach: Benjamin 699, Lattner 776, Life 779
Fernandina Beach: Burton 711
Fleming Island: Reinhold 808
Fort Lauderdale: **Campbell 713**, Feder 741, Henderson 758, Leiser 777, Palank 795, Thomsen 832, Tippett 833, Turock 835
Fort Myers: Southwest 823
Fort Pierce: Alpha 687, King 768
Gainesville: Community 725
Golden Beach: Lipton 781
Havana: Munroe 793
Highland Beach: Erdle 740
Hobe Sound: Bell 698
Homestead: DiMare 737
Jacksonville: Bi-Lo/Winn-Dixie 700, Blanksteen 701, Chartrand 719, Community 722, Finch 743, Florida 744, Focus 746, Gate 749, Jacksonville 761, Morningstar 791, River 811, **Samstag 813**, Setzer 818, Stellar 826
Jupiter: Bartner 696, Rendina 809
Key Biscayne: Margulies 785
Key Largo: Bohnert 703
Key West: Around 692
Lakeland: Blanton 702, Burnetti 709, Carlton 715, Morrison 792, Publix 804
Longboat Key: Wiegand 841
Manalapan: Pope 803
Melbourne: Community 723, Einstein 739
Miami: **Chester 720**, Katcher 765, **Knight 771**, Korf 772, Lennar 778, Rebozo 807
Miami Beach: Batchelor 697, Horowitz 760, Sender 817
Miami Lakes: Kislak 769
N. Miami: Ansin 689
Naples: Diermeier 736, Franklin 748, Martin 787, Querrey 806, Sage 812
North Miami: Applebaum 690
North Palm Beach: Olsen 794, Parish 796
Odessa: Speer 824
Orlando: Brown 707, Cohen 721, Community 724, Darden 732, Flournoy-Theadcraft 745, Hard 756, Holloway 759, Martin 786, Peterson 799, Phillips 800
Palm Beach: Burns 710, Fortin 747, Tsunami 834, **Whitehall 840**
Palm Beach Gardens: Azeez 694, Burnett 708, Kantner 764, Lyons 782, MAH 784
Pembroke Pines: Wollowick 843
Ponte Vedra Beach: Dahl 731, Landwirth 775, Sontag 822
Port Saint Lucie: Boston 705
Punta Gorda: Charlotte 718, Stransky 827
Sarasota: Bank 695, Community 727, Kramer 773, Mertz 788, Patterson 798, Selby 816, Sudakoff 828
South Miami: Ware 838
St. Petersburg: Catalina 716, Chapman 717, Snell 821
Stuart: Booth 704, Thomas 831
Tallahassee: Community 726
Tampa: Atkins 693, Conn 728, DeBartolo 734, Glazer 750, **Heartbeat 757**, **Patel 797**, Sierra 819, TECO 830, Walter 837
Tavernier: Wright 845
Venice: Gulf 754
Vero Beach: Darling 733
Wauchula: Woodbery 844
West Miami Beach: Lindemann 780
West Palm Beach: Bradley 706, **DeMoss 735**, Gruss 753, Hand 755, Quantum 805, Rinker 810
Weston: **Jaffer 763**
Winter Park: Bush 712, Jacobsen 762, Wells 839, Winter 842

see also 3, 16, 19, 70, 123, 181, 541, 550, 565, 567, 569, 622, 860, 878, 915, 958, 980, 1011, 1016, 1019, 1064, 1066, 1073, 1094, 1101, 1161, 1206, 1237, 1314, 1376, 1380, 1459, 1528, 1553, 1594, 1621, 1659, 1661, 1668, 1670, 1671, 1696, 1718, 1724, 1774, 1809, 1829, 1858, 1904, 1915, 1917, 1950, 1961, 1963, 1974, 2033, 2034, 2075, 2118, 2212, 2236, 2238, 2242, 2259, 2280, 2300, 2322, 2354, 2380, 2382, 2415, 2447, 2488, 2516, 2526, 2528, 2577, 2581, 2593, 2605, 2608, 2617, 2619, 2699, 2726, 2727, 2728, 2760, 2779, 2886, 3015, 3027, 3052, 3078, 3081, 3090, 3108, 3109, 3132, 3153, 3156, 3161, 3191, 3235, 3320, 3411, 3420, 3447, 3466, 3524, 3596, 3635, 3671, 3674

GEORGIA

Alpharetta: EZ 874
Atlanta: Abreu 846, AIM 847, Atlanta 852, Baker 853, Bancker-Williams 854, Blank 856, Burke 859, Campbell 860, Camp-Younts 861, **Coca 864**, Colston 865, Cooper 870, Correll 871, Dobbs 872, Exposition 873, Garden 875, Georgia 876, Georgia 877, **Georgia 878**, Gholston 879, Gholston 880, Gilbert 881, Glenn 882, Goizueta 883, Harland 885, Healthcare 886, Holder 887, **Imlay 888**, Katz 889, Lanier 891, Livingston 893, Lowder 894, Marshall 895, Mason 896, Moore 897, Murphy 898, Murray 899, Pitts 904, Ragan 906, Raoul 907, Rockdale 909, **Rosenberg 910**, Southern 915, Trailsend 916, Tull 917, Wilder 920, WinShape 921, Woodward 923
Bremen: Sewell 914
Brunswick: Sapelo 911
Carrollton: Richards 908
Clayton: Orianne 901
Columbus: Amos 848, Amos-Cheves 849, Bradley 858, **Pickett 903**, Weir 919, Woodruff 922
Dalton: Community 868
Decatur: **Guanacaste 884**, Patrick 902
Duluth: Community 867
Gainesville: North 900
Kennesaw: University 918
Macon: Anderson 850, Bowen 857
Marietta: Ligon 892
Saint Simons Island: Communities 866
Savannah: Savannah 912
Sharpsburg: Cobb 863
Stone Mountain: Pittulloch 905
Thomasville: Community 869
Thomson: Knox 890
Tucker: Schinazi 913

see also 16, 19, 20, 52, 70, 74, 235, 263, 356, 496, 550, 604, 622, 625, 700, 736, 748, 771, 776, 793, 804, 975, 1064, 1066, 1206, 1353, 1549, 1550, 1594, 1624, 1697, 1774, 1794, 1803, 1871, 1896, 1993, 2020, 2033, 2034, 2118, 2178, 2242, 2317, 2488, 2521, 2526, 2545, 2553, 2555, 2699, 2726, 2755, 2759, 3018, 3033, 3109, 3134, 3162, 3181, 3311, 3397, 3411, 3420, 3452, 3457, 3466, 3632, 3650, 3671

GUAM

see 1948

HAWAII

Honolulu: Atherton 925, Baldwin 926, Castle 930, Ching 931, Cooke 932, Hawaii 933, Hawaiian 934, Kahiau 935, Kaneta 936, McInerny 938, **Watumull 939**, Zimmerman 940
Kailua: Castle 929, Makana 937
Kapolei: Campbell 928
Lahaina: Buehner 927

see also 20, 142, 198, 206, 217, 291, 304, 310, 326, 431, 481, 1416, 1661, 1704, 1859, 2007, 2760, 2848, 3406

IDAHO

Boise: Adams 941, Albertson 942, Cunningham 946, Idaho 948, Jeker 949, **Micron 950**, Supervalu 952
Caldwell: Whittenberger 953
Eagle: Caven 944
Garden City: Angels 943
Idaho Falls: CHC 945
Post Falls: Schneidmiller 951
Sandpoint: Equinox 947

see also 99, 182, 513, 627, 631, 836, 927, 1278, 1594, 1710, 1722, 1750, 1803, 1827, 2242, 2415, 2717, 2856, 2866, 2971, 3339, 3396, 3452, 3490, 3524, 3526, 3572, 3575

ILLINOIS

Arlington Heights: Magnus 1058
Aurora: Community 991, Dunham 1007
Barrington: Oberweiler 1069
Bloomington: Funk 1021
Buffalo Grove: Simonsen 1094
Carol Stream: **Tyndale 1105**
Champaign: Diener 1000
Chicago: Ackermann 955, Adams 956, Alphawood 959, **American 960**, Angell 962, Aon 963, ArcelorMittal 964, Bergstrom 965, Bersted 966, Bersted 967, Bobolink 970, Boothroyd 971, Brach 973, Burk 977, Chartered 980, Cheney 981, Chicago 982, Children's 983, CME 984, Coldwell 985, Coleman 986, Comer 987, Conduit 994, Copeland 995, Crown 997, de Kay 998, Donnelley 1001, Driehaus 1002, **Driskill 1003**, Dryer 1004, Edlis-Neeson 1009, Eisenberg 1011, Field 1014, Foglia 1015, Forbes 1016, Frankel 1017, Fry 1018, Frye 1019, Fulk 1020, Grant 1026, Guthman 1027, Hamm 1028, Hanifl 1029, Harper 1030, Hendrickson 1032, Homan 1033, Hughes 1035, Hunt 1036, Jackson 1038, **Joyce 1040**, Katten 1042, Kaufman 1043, Lars 1047, **Lascaris 1048**, Lefkofsky 1049, Libra 1050, Logan 1051, Lyon 1054, **MacArthur 1056**, Maddox 1057, McCauley 1059, Pangburn 1071, Parr 1072, Pierce 1074, Polk 1075, Prince 1076, Prince 1077, Pritzker 1078, Pritzker 1079, Pritzker 1080, Pullman 1081, Reese 1083, Rosen 1086, Ryan 1087, Seymour 1091, Shapiro 1093, Sinsheimer 1095, Siragusa 1096, **Spencer 1098**, Stern 1100, Stewart 1101, Sumac 1103, VNA 1107, Walter 1110, Ward 1111, Washington 1112, Wieboldt 1115, Woods 1117, Zell 1119
Countryside: FDC 1013
Danville: Cadle 979
Decatur: **Buffett 975**, Ullrich 1106
Deerfield: **Mondelez 1064**, Rhodes 1084, **Walgreens 1109**
Dundee: McGraw 1060
Edwardsville: Edwardsville 1010
Evanston: Evanston 1012
Geneseo: Geneseo 1022
Glencoe: Schnadig 1089
Glenview: Johnson 1039
Godfrey: Monticello 1065, Nelson 1067
Gurnee: **Abbott 954**
Highland Park: Kaplan 1041, Pattis 1073
Hinsdale: Community 993
Kankakee: Community 989
LaGrange: Schmitt 1088
Lake Forest: **Grainger 1024**, Grant 1025, Hospira 1034, MacArthur 1055, Schuler 1090
Lake Zurich: Allegretti 958
Mahomet: Yowell 1118
Mattoon: Lumpkin 1053
Moline: Moline 1063
Monmouth: Mellinger 1061
Mount Sterling: Tracy 1104
Naperville: Albert 957
Northbrook: Dunard 1006, Hurvis 1037
Northfield: **Kobe 1045**
Oak Brook: Duchossois 1005
Oak Park: Good 1023, Oak Park 1068, Stone 1102
Oakbrook Terrace: Westlake 1114
Orland Park: Cord 996
Palatine: Kenny's 1044, Square 1099
Palos Heights: Brennan 974
Peoria: Community 988, Redhill 1082
Quincy: Community 992
Rockford: C.W.B. 978, Community 990
Rosemont: Speh 1097
Schaumburg: Blowitz 968, **Motorola 1066**, Omron 1070
Sycamore: DeKalb 999
Waukegan: Healthcare 1031
West Chicago: Richard 1085
Westmont: Amicus 961
Wheaton: Buonacorsi 976, DuPage 1008, Luehring 1052
Wilmette: Shamrock 1092
Winthrop Harbor: Webb 1113

---

see also 40, 70, 166, 235, 240, 268, 345, 396, 540, 549, 550, 565, 569, 631, 655, 677, 733, 736, 766, 806, 878, 1140, 1182, 1205, 1223, 1244, 1286, 1325, 1459, 1550, 1585, 1648, 1697, 1701, 1707, 1710, 1727, 1729, 1791, 1794, 1796, 1803, 1809, 1855, 1860, 1917, 1963, 1993, 2003, 2033, 2034, 2054, 2065, 2075, 2118, 2119, 2231, 2236, 2242, 2305, 2307, 2315, 2317, 2322, 2327, 2354, 2369, 2386, 2415, 2427, 2603, 2623, 2627, 2638, 2677, 2699, 2706, 2720, 2758, 2812, 2838, 3001, 3007, 3018, 3066, 3067, 3073, 3074, 3076, 3078, 3086, 3088, 3181, 3372, 3457, 3500, 3593, 3598, 3621, 3624, 3635, 3644, 3663

INDIANA

Anderson: Madison 1175
Auburn: DeKalb 1144
Avon: Hendricks 1157
Batesville: Ripley 1191
Bloomfield: Greene 1152
Bluffton: Wells 1207
Carmel: Globe 1151, Tobias 1199
Columbia City: Whitley 1209
Columbus: Haddad 1153
Connersville: Fayette 1146
Corydon: Harrison 1155
Covington: Western 1208
Evansville: Community 1128, Koch 1167, Old 1182, Vectren 1202, Welborn 1205
Fort Wayne: Auer 1120, Brotherhood 1123, Cole 1127, Darling 1140, Foellinger 1147, Kuhne 1169, Master 1177, Schwab 1193, Steel 1196
Franklin: Johnson 1163
Greencastle: Putnam 1189
Greenfield: Hancock 1154
Greensburg: Decatur 1142
Hartford City: Blackford 1122
Indianapolis: Central 1126, DeHaan 1143, Fairbanks 1145, FSJ 1149, Glick 1150, Health 1156, Hoover 1159, Jorgensen 1164, Lilly 1173, **Lumina 1174**, MIBOR 1178, OneAmerica 1183, Regenstrief 1190, Walther 1204, WellPoint 1206
Jasper: Seger 1194
Jeffersonville: Jasteka 1161
Kokomo: Community 1131
Lafayette: Community 1130
LaGrange: LaGrange 1170
Lawrenceburg: Dearborn 1141
Liberty: Union 1200
Ligonier: Noble 1179
Logansport: Cass 1125
Madison: Community 1133
Marion: Community 1129
Merrillville: Legacy 1171
Michigan City: Unity 1201
Mooresville: Kendrick 1166
Muncie: Ball 1121, Community 1134
Nashville: Brown 1124
New Albany: Community 1136
New Castle: Henry 1158
Noblesville: Crosser 1139
North Vernon: Jennings 1162
North Webster: Shoop 1195
Paoli: Orange 1184
Plymouth: Marshall 1176
Portland: Portland 1188
Rensselaer: Jasper 1160
Rising Sun: Ohio 1181
Rochester: Northern 1180
Rockville: Parke 1186
Rushville: Rush 1192
Seymour: Community 1132
South Bend: Joshi 1165, Leighton 1172, TCU 1197
Spencer: Owen 1185
Terre Haute: Froderman 1148, Wabash 1203
Tipton: Tipton 1198
Valparaiso: Porter 1187
Vevay: Community 1137
Warsaw: Kosciusko 1168
Winchester: Community 1135

---

see also 70, 497, 771, 812, 878, 959, 964, 1040, 1099, 1211, 1325, 1353, 1401, 1657, 1697, 1710, 1858, 1860, 1865, 2054, 2075, 2242, 2314, 2562, 2627, 2656, 2657, 2665, 2679, 2699, 2709, 2717, 2752, 2772, 3005, 3007, 3037, 3041, 3058, 3153, 3181, 3420, 3598, 3624, 3644

IOWA

Boone: Beckwith 1213
Cedar Falls: Peregrine 1234
Cedar Rapids: Hall-Perrine 1222, Johnson 1228, **Rockwell 1237**, United 1243, Wallace 1245
Chariton: South 1241
Clarinda: Clarinda 1214
Clive: NCMIC 1232
Council Bluffs: Iowa 1226, Pottawattamie 1235
Davenport: Bechtel 1212
Des Moines: Wellmark 1246, World 1248
Dubuque: Community 1216, Wahlert 1244, Woodward 1247
Durant: Iowa 1225
Fairfield: Jefferson 1227, Zimmerman 1249
Fort Dodge: Community 1215
Greenfield: Schildberg 1238
Grinnell: Ahrens 1210
Iowa City: Community 1218
Manchester: Delaware 1219
Mason City: Stebens 1242
Muscatine: Community 1217, HNI 1223, Holthues 1224
Newton: Maytag 1229
Rippey: Schroeder 1239
Sioux City: deStwolinski 1220, Siouxland 1240
Waterloo: Guernsey 1221, McElroy 1230
Wayland: On 1233
West Des Moines: Aviva 1211, R & R 1236

---

see also 99, 481, 512, 627, 878, 992, 1063, 1064, 1099, 1278, 1353, 1585, 1678, 1697, 1710, 1722, 1729, 1803, 1843, 1850, 1860, 1989, 2623, 3007, 3018, 3411, 3527, 3592, 3598, 3624, 3638, 3644, 3650

KANSAS

Atchison: **Muchnic 1271**
Emporia: Emporia 1257, Jones 1262
Garden City: Western 1280
Hays: Rush 1273
Hutchinson: Hutchinson 1260
Lawrence: Beach 1250, Douglas 1256, Western 1281
Leawood: Skillbuilders 1277
Logan: Hansen 1259
Manhattan: Manhattan 1268
Olathe: **Shumaker 1276**
Overland Park: Cohen 1252, **Lloyd 1267**, Sunderland 1278
Phillipsburg: Morgan 1270
Prairie Village: Miller 1269, Nettleton 1272
Salina: Salina 1274

Smith Center: Sarver 1275
Topeka: Capitol 1251, Collective 1253, Damon 1254, Topeka 1279
Wichita: Delta 1255, Farah 1258, Insurance 1261, Kansas 1263, Koch 1264, Koch 1265

---

see also 70, 99, 539, 540, 565, 569, 771, 776, 878, 957, 1034, 1206, 1211, 1477, 1710, 1727, 1779, 1794, 1795, 1797, 2815, 2863, 2888, 3093, 3272, 3313, 3420, 3505, 3644, 3647

KENTUCKY

Crestwood: Good 1289
Lexington: Blue 1282, Campbell 1285, USA 1296
Louisville: Brown 1283, C.E. 1284, Etscorn 1287, Gheens 1288, J & L 1291, Kentucky 1292, Lift 1293, Steel 1294
Maysville: Hayswood 1290
Nicholasville: Trim 1295
Paducah: Community 1286

---

see also 70, 216, 771, 878, 1099, 1161, 1167, 1182, 1205, 1206, 1223, 1353, 1407, 1593, 1594, 1670, 1701, 1727, 2242, 2521, 2577, 2613, 2656, 2661, 2677, 2679, 2680, 2694, 2699, 2709, 2714, 2717, 2772, 2885, 2914, 2940, 3018, 3109, 3127, 3153, 3235, 3420, 3466, 3598, 3644

LOUISIANA

Baton Rouge: Albemarle 1298, Baton Rouge 1300, Blue 1302, Clement 1305, Grigsby 1312, Pennington 1317
Lafayette: Heymann 1313, Pugh 1318
Lake Charles: Burton 1303, Community 1307
Metairie: Whitman 1321
New Orleans: Baptist 1299, Chambers 1304, Entergy 1308, Freeman 1309, German 1310, Glazer 1311, Lagasse 1314, New Orleans 1316, Schlieder 1319, Steinhagen 1320
Ruston: Lincoln 1315
Shreveport: Beaird 1301, Community 1306, Wiener 1322

---

see also 70, 313, 499, 700, 841, 878, 1206, 1288, 1628, 1718, 1763, 1803, 1860, 1978, 2012, 2075, 2211, 2242, 2521, 2656, 2845, 3018, 3108, 3420, 3426, 3505, 3598, 3632

MAINE

Augusta: Kennebec 1332, Maine 1336
Bangor: King 1333
Bar Mills: Narragansett 1337
Belfast: Switzer 1342
Boothbay Harbor: **Walter 1343**
Camden: Golden 1329
Ellsworth: Lynam 1335
Freeport: Sewall 1339
Harrison: Aicher 1323
Kennebunk: Somers 1341
Oakland: Borman 1325
Portland: Alfond 1324, **Catalyst 1326**, Cohen 1327, Davis 1328, Hannaford 1330, Horizon 1331, Libra 1334, Quimby 1338, Smith 1340

---

see also 65, 547, 550, 638, 708, 845, 871, 1206, 1431, 1439, 1443, 1467, 1468, 1476, 1518, 1524, 1529, 1554, 1568, 1621, 1683, 1885, 1887, 1890, 1894, 2075, 2081, 2135, 2391, 2444, 2505, 2522, 2717, 2971, 3092, 3375, 3420

MARIANAS (COMMONWEALTH OF)

---

see 1948

MARYLAND

Baltimore: Adams 1345, Baker 1347, **Blaustein 1349**, Blaustein 1350, **Casey 1353**, Croft 1362, Cupid 1363, Dahan 1364, Dresher 1370, Goldseker 1374, Hirschhorn 1379, Macht 1388, Meyerhoff 1392, Meyerhoff 1393, Middendorf 1394, Plitt 1404, Rembrandt 1407, Rosenberg 1409, Straus 1410, Stulman 1411
Bel Air: **ABMRF 1344**
Bethesda: **Cohen 1355**, Cornell 1361, **de Beaumont 1366**, Fowler 1372, Izzo 1381, Mann 1389, Marriott 1390, **Morningstar 1397**, Mustard 1400, Trawick 1414
Brooklandville: Kentfields 1385
Chestertown: Moore 1396
Chevy Chase: Polinger 1405, Zickler 1419
Columbia: **Braitmayer 1351**
Cumberland: DelSignore 1368
Easton: Mid-Shore 1395, Richmond 1408, Town 1413, Tucker 1415
Ellicott City: Kirk 1386
Frederick: Community 1358, Delaplaine 1367
Gaithersburg: Ceres 1354, Wolpoff 1417
Gambrills: **Jehovah 1382**
Hagerstown: Community 1360
Hampstead: Lutheran 1387
Hanover: Davis 1365
Hunt Valley: Bunting 1352, **Northern 1402**
Lutherville: Battye 1348, Murthynayak 1399
North Bethesda: Tauber 1412
Owings Mills: Dupkin 1371, **Weinberg 1416**
Phoenix: Maryland 1391
Riderwood: **Mpala 1398**
Rockville: Freeman 1373, NASDAQ 1401
Salisbury: Community 1359, Henson 1378
Silver Spring: Commonweal 1356, Gudelsky 1376, Hendricks 1377, Kay 1384
Sparks: Wright 1418
Sykesville: Kahlert 1383
Towson: **Ames 1346**, Deutsch 1369, Israelson 1380, Osprey 1403, RCM & D 1406
Westminster: Community 1357

---

see also 70, 74, 142, 404, 457, 473, 550, 587, 628, 648, 653, 654, 656, 672, 677, 835, 975, 1066, 1206, 1459, 1541, 1565, 1594, 1697, 1710, 1912, 1961, 1972, 1983, 2075, 2118, 2352, 2376, 2508, 2760, 2847, 2994, 3002, 3004, 3019, 3020, 3022, 3039, 3382, 3420, 3426, 3435, 3466, 3479, 3482, 3505, 3589, 3603, 3632

MASSACHUSETTS

Agawam: Grinspoon 1479
Amherst: Colombe 1452, Felix 1466
Arlington: Sanborn 1540
Bedford: Gould 1476
Belmont: Franklin 1472
Beverly: Symes 1555
Beverly Farms: Levy 1501
Boston: Adams 1423, Alden 1425, Arbella 1426, Archibald 1427, Babson 1429, Babson 1430, Balfour 1431, **Barr 1433**, Berkman 1434, Boynton 1437, Brooks 1440, Cabot 1442, Cabot 1443, Calderwood 1444, Chase 1446, Child 1447, Clarke 1448, Clipper 1449, Cogan 1450, Cole 1451, **Conservation 1454**, DentaQuest 1459, Edwards 1462, Farnsworth 1465, Filene 1468, Fish 1470, **Germeshausen 1474**, Gordon 1475, Gould 1477, Grew 1478, Hazard 1480, High 1482, Horne 1484, Hyams 1486, **Iacocca 1487**, **Foundation 1489**, Jacobson 1490, **Kahn 1492**, Kendall 1494, Kittredge 1496, **Lalor 1498**, Learning 1500, Liberty 1502, Linden 1504, Magee 1506, McNeice 1509, Melville 1511, MENTOR 1513, **Merck 1514**, Miller 1516, New 1518, Noonan 1520, Noonan 1521, Pardoe 1522, Parker 1523, Perpetual 1526, Peters 1527, Ratshesky 1531, Raymond 1532, Rice 1533, Riley 1534, Rogers 1536, Sailors' 1539, Santander 1541, Schrafft 1543, Shattuck 1544, **Sociological 1548**, **State 1550**, Swan 1552, Swartz 1553, Thee 1556, Verrochi 1560, Vingo 1561, Webber 1563, Weber 1564, Webster 1565, Wells 1566, Windover 1568
Braintree: Tye 1558
Brockton: Howard 1485
Cambridge: Access 1422, **Barakat 1432**, **Bruner 1441**, **Lincoln 1503**
Chelmsford: Demoulas 1458
Concord: Winning 1569
Danvers: Essex 1464
Edgartown: **Patagonia 1524**
Falmouth: **Brabson 1438**
Foxboro: Meelia 1510, Rodman 1535
Framingham: MetroWest 1515, Staples 1549
Groveland: Wadleigh 1562
Hadley: Rx 1538
Holliston: Williams 1567
Hyde Park: Blue 1436
Jamaica Plain: Currents 1455
Kingston: Sheehan 1545
Lexington: Kim 1495
Lincoln: Kelsey 1493, Ramsey 1530
Lowell: Lowell 1505
Lynn: Eastern 1461
Needham: **Adelson 1424**
New Bedford: Association 1428, Community 1453
Newburyport: Newburyport 1519
Newton: **Elsevier 1463**, Herbert 1481, Ruderman 1537, Smith 1546, Two 1557
Newtonville: Massachusetts 1508
North Andover: Gardinor 1473
Northampton: **Sweet 1554**, **Xeric 1570**
Peabody: East 1460
Pittsfield: **A Child 1420**
Plainville: Honey 1483
Plymouth: Perennial 1525
Salem: Phillips 1529
South Boston: Mount 1517
Springfield: D'Amour 1456, Davis 1457, Smith 1547
Stockbridge: Jaffe 1491
Sudbury: Sudbury 1551
Waban: Krieger 1497
Wakefield: Phelps 1528
Waltham: Fields 1467, Fireman 1469, Inavale 1488
Wareham: Makepeace 1507
Wellesley: Brooks 1439
West Springfield: United 1559
Westborough: Francis 1471
Weston: Aaron 1421
Worcester: Memorial 1512
Yarmouth Port: Bilezikian 1435
Yarmouthport: Cape Cod 1445

---

see also 30, 70, 74, 88, 232, 237, 240, 254, 263, 268, 348, 404, 447, 547, 559, 567, 584, 586, 598, 604, 607, 622, 629, 636, 638, 643, 651, 673, 675, 689, 705, 706, 789, 809, 878, 970, 994, 1047, 1053, 1066, 1101, 1102, 1211, 1224, 1253, 1308, 1330, 1331, 1342, 1351, 1377, 1404, 1417, 1621, 1697, 1741, 1747, 1779, 1880, 1886, 1889, 1890, 1893, 1894, 1902, 1921, 1931, 1932, 1971, 1977, 1983, 1991, 2033, 2034, 2075, 2081, 2118, 2130, 2166, 2201, 2212, 2236, 2242, 2249, 2300, 2307, 2315, 2348, 2354, 2375, 2387, 2393, 2420, 2421, 2427, 2444, 2446, 2449, 2455,

2472, 2473, 2476, 2481, 2488, 2505, 2526, 2562, 2608, 2704, 2714, 2725, 2754, 2755, 2759, 2769, 2913, 2921, 2941, 2971, 2972, 2977, 3023, 3038, 3063, 3064, 3067, 3070, 3071, 3077, 3090, 3092, 3130, 3270, 3409, 3411, 3413, 3420, 3457

MICHIGAN

Ada: Van Andel 1669
Adrian: Merillat 1640
Allegan: Perrigo 1655
Almont: Four 1603
Alpena: Community 1587
Ann Arbor: Ann Arbor 1576, Knight 1630, RNR 1659
Ann Harbor: Anderson 1575
Battle Creek: Binda 1579, **Kellogg 1628**
Bay City: Pardee 1652
Bay Harbor: Bay Harbor 1578
Birmingham: Alix 1572, Frankel 1605
Blissfield: Farver 1601
Bloomfield Hills: Carls 1582, **Erb 1599**, Legion 1633, Michell 1641
Cedar: Schmuckal 1664
Chelsea: Chelsea 1584
Clinton Township: Webber 1673
Coldwater: Branch 1580
Detroit: Community 1588, DTE 1598, Jubilee 1624, Mardigian 1635, McGregor 1638, Royal 1661, Skillman 1666
East Jordan: Charlevoix 1583
Flint: **Isabel 1621**, Mills 1643, **Mott 1645**, Mott 1646
Frankenmuth: Frankenmuth 1606
Fremont: Fremont 1607, **Gerber 1611**
Fruitport: Van 1670
Grand Haven: Grand Haven 1614
Grand Rapids: Davenport 1595, Family 1600, Frey 1608, Frey 1609, G. 1610, Grand Rapids 1615, Keller 1627, Meijer 1639, Steelcase 1667, Vanderweide 1671, Wege 1674
Grosse Pointe Farms: Wilson 1675
Harbor Springs: Baiardi 1577
Hillsdale: Hillsdale 1620
Holland: Community 1591, Onequest 1650, Prince 1658
Howell: Von 1672
Jackson: Alro 1574, Jackson 1623, Sigmund 1665
Kalamazoo: Dalton 1592, Delano 1596, Gilmore 1612, Kalamazoo 1626, Parish 1654
Lansing: Capital 1581, Granger 1617, Great 1618
Marlette: Technical 1668
Marquette: Marquette 1636
Mason: Dart 1594
Midland: **Allen 1573**, Dow 1597, Midland 1642, **Pardee 1653**
Mount Pleasant: Isabella 1622, Mount Pleasant 1647
Muskegon: Community 1586
New Buffalo: Pokagon 1657
Petoskey: Petoskey 1656
Port Huron: Acheson 1571, Community 1590
Rochester: Community 1589
Roscommon: Roscommon 1660
Saginaw: Hebert 1619, Morley 1644, Nartel 1648, Saginaw 1662
Sandusky: Sanilac 1663
Southfield: Golden 1613, Lear 1632
Sylvan Lake: Christian 1585
Taylor: Masco 1637
Tecumseh: Lenawee 1634
Traverse City: Grand 1616, Oleson 1649
Troy: Farwell 1602, Frankel 1604, **Kresge 1631**, Page, 1651
Van Buren Township: Dana 1593
Warren: Kahn 1625

see also 50, 97, 463, 505, 540, 604, 771, 832, 878, 957, 1004, 1040, 1043, 1074, 1119, 1182, 1298, 1697, 1710, 1754, 1932, 1958, 2040, 2211, 2242, 2369, 2575, 2590, 2656, 2665, 2681, 2699, 2717, 3007, 3018, 3067, 3411, 3624, 3644

MINNESOTA

Bayport: **Andersen 1678**
Bemidji: Neilson 1721, Northwest 1723
Bloomington: **O'Shaughnessy 1725**, Riverway 1733
Duluth: Alworth 1677, Depot 1691, Duluth 1693, Johnson 1705
Eden Prairie: Cargill 1689
Edina: **Kaplan 1707**, **Porter 1729**
Fergus Falls: West 1751
Golden Valley: **Pentair 1727**
Grand Rapids: Grand Rapids 1699
Hutchinson: Southwest 1740
Little Falls: Initiative 1703
Long Lake: Sayer 1737
Mankato: Andreas 1679
Minneapolis: Beim 1683, Dayton 1690, Donaldson 1692, Edina 1694, Frey 1696, General 1697, George 1698, Greystone 1700, Jostens 1706, **King 1708**, Larsen 1711, Marbrook 1713, **McKnight 1714**, McKnight 1715, Midcontinent 1716, Minneapolis 1717, Nash 1720, Phillips 1728, RBC 1730, Regis 1732, Robina 1734, Schulze 1738, SUPERVALU 1743, Target 1744, Thorpe 1745, **Trust 1746**, W.M. 1747, Wallin 1748, Wedum 1750, Xcel 1754
Minnetonka: Opus 1724, WCA 1749
North St. Paul: Sauer 1736
Plymouth: **Mosaic 1718**
Redwood Falls: Farmers 1695, Redwood 1731
Richfield: Best 1685
Rochester: Rochester 1735
St. Louis Park: Avocet 1680
St. Paul: 3M 1676, Bahl 1681, Boss 1686, Briggs 1687, Butler 1688, Hallett 1701, HRK 1702, Johnson 1704, Koran 1709, Land 1710, Musser 1719, Northwest 1722, **Patterson 1726**, Securian 1739, **St. Jude 1741**, Sundance 1742, **Weyerhaeuser 1752**
Wayzata: Bentson 1684
Winona: Winona 1753

see also 94, 99, 228, 350, 459, 627, 771, 832, 878, 964, 1040, 1064, 1101, 1223, 1224, 1401, 2176, 2231, 2242, 2415, 2488, 2548, 2562, 2571, 2580, 2582, 2585, 2586, 2615, 2621, 2648, 2649, 2681, 2706, 2739, 2885, 3592, 3598, 3624, 3644, 3655, 3662

MISSISSIPPI

Biloxi: Biloxi 1755
Greenville: King's 1766
Gulfport: Gulf 1764, Mississippi 1769
Hernando: Community 1760
Jackson: Center 1757, Community 1759, Ergon 1761, Feild 1762, Foundation 1763, Regions 1770
Meridian: Community 1758
Oxford: Sullivan 1771
Ridgeland: Bower 1756, Luckyday 1767, Walker 1772
University: Mississippi 1768

see also 70, 700, 771, 878, 915, 1308, 1594, 1628, 1710, 1860, 2211, 2521, 2759, 3120, 3154, 3235, 3466

MISSOURI

Carthage: Boylan 1776
Clayton: Guilander 1791, Ross 1810, Tilles 1815
Columbia: Hagan 1792
Fenton: Fabick 1788
Independence: Truman 1817
Kansas City: Brace 1777, Butler 1780, Curry 1784, Dunn 1787, Green 1790, Hall 1793, Hallmark 1794, Humphreys 1795, **Kauffman 1797**, Nichols 1806, Pendergast 1807, Prime 1808, Speas 1813, Trudy 1816
Kirkwood: St. Louis 1814
Saint Louis: Moneta 1802
Springfield: Community 1783, Darr 1785, Musgrave 1805, Schneider 1812
St. Louis: Albers/Kuhn 1773, Anheuser 1774, Bellwether 1775, Breen 1778, Bunge 1779, Canfield 1781, Centene 1782, **Deer 1786**, Gateway 1789, Innovative 1796, Kuhn 1798, Laclede 1799, **McDonnell 1800**, Millstone 1801, **Monsanto 1803**, Mungenast 1804, Roblee 1809, Saigh 1811, Walker 1818, Westlake 1819, Whitaker 1820, Woods 1821

see also 46, 70, 99, 235, 553, 568, 627, 631, 707, 833, 878, 957, 992, 1064, 1099, 1113, 1167, 1206, 1269, 1272, 1276, 1278, 1477, 1550, 1621, 1697, 1710, 1860, 2038, 2042, 2077, 2242, 2603, 2699, 2726, 2751, 2840, 2888, 3082, 3234, 3286, 3320, 3420, 3598, 3621, 3624, 3644, 3650, 3682

MONTANA

Arlee: High 1825
Billings: Sample 1829, Wendy's 1831
Bozeman: Cross 1822
Helena: Greater 1823, Montana 1828
Lakeside: Lynn 1827
Missoula: Silver 1830
Whitefish: Whitefish 1832

see also 88, 362, 513, 636, 1278, 1377, 1683, 1695, 1697, 1722, 2048, 2520, 2628, 3490, 3524, 3572, 3644, 3679

NEBRASKA

Fremont: Fremont 1836
Grand Island: Grand Island 1837
Hastings: Wilson 1856
Kearney: Hirschfeld 1839, Kearney 1842
Lexington: Lexington 1845
Lincoln: Cooper 1834, Lienemann 1846, Lincoln 1847, Nebraska 1851, Woods 1857
North Platte: Mid-Nebraska 1849
Omaha: **Buffett 1833**, Daugherty 1835, Hawkins 1838, Holland 1840, Home 1841, Kiewit 1843, Kim 1844, Mutual 1850, Storz 1854, Weitz 1855, Zollner 1858
Papillion: Midlands 1848
Scottsbluff: Oregon 1852, Quivey 1853

see also 70, 99, 222, 355, 386, 458, 496, 627, 731, 1099, 1220, 1226, 1240, 1278, 1710, 3223, 3644

NEVADA

Crystal Bay: Shaheen 1871
Henderson: EBV 1862, Troesh 1874
Incline Village: Parasol 1868
Las Vegas: Bendon 1859, Caesars 1860, Engelstad 1863, Harris 1864, Maddux 1866, Nevada 1867, **Reynolds 1869**, **Tang 1873**, Webb 1875
Reno: Doyle 1861, Stout 1872, Wells 1876

Zephyr Cove: Jaquish 1865

see also 64, 99, 263, 269, 465, 778, 878, 936, 941, 1167, 1206, 1314, 1993, 2242, 2317, 3018, 3320, 3420

NEW HAMPSHIRE

Concord: Alexander 1877, Charter 1880, Endowment 1883, HNH 1888, Up 1896
Hampton: Penates 1893
Hanover: Byrne 1879
Keene: Panjandrum 1892
Loudon: Mosaic 1891
Lyme: Roby 1894
Manchester: Bean 1878, DEKA 1882, Lindsay 1890, Smyth 1895
Nashua: Finlay 1884
North Conway: Ham 1887, Woodbury 1897
Portsmouth: Foundation 1885
Rye Beach: Fuller 1886
Salem: Johnson 1889
Wolfeboro: **Christian 1881**

see also 70, 222, 313, 578, 598, 610, 878, 1016, 1206, 1308, 1330, 1342, 1426, 1431, 1444, 1467, 1468, 1489, 1504, 1522, 1529, 1536, 1541, 1554, 1565, 1567, 1774, 2075, 2155, 2769, 2969, 2971, 3067, 3092, 3420

NEW JERSEY

Brick: Roscitt 1985
Bridgewater: **Sanofi 1988**
Camden: Campbell 1917
Cherry Hill: Hummingbird 1943
Clifton: Feldstein 1928
Deal: Ahavat 1898
East Hanover: **Novartis 1973**
Eatontown: Ezra 1926
Edison: Nandansons 1969, Saka 1987
Englewood: Beer 1907, Holzer 1939
Englewood Cliffs: Unilever 2003
Far Hills: Gamper 1933, Gibson 1934
Florham Park: Kushner 1957, Stadtmauer 1996
Fort Lee: Syms 1999
Hackensack: Buehler 1915
Hamburg: Levitt 1960
Hopewell: Bunbury 1916
Iselin: **Siemens 1993**
Jersey City: Eisenreich 1922, Fortune 1931
Lawrenceville: Princeton 1979
Livingston: Earle 1920, Hawthorne 1937
Long Branch: Brothers 1913
Long Valley: Leavens 1959
Montclair: Schumann 1990, Turrell 2002
Montvale: Onyx 1974
Moonachie: Tufenkian 2001
Moorestown: **Knowles 1955**
Morristown: Jones 1950, Kirby 1952, MCJ 1965, **Rippel 1982**
Mountainside: Schwarz 1991
Murray Hill: **Alcatel 1899**, Bard 1905
New Brunswick: **Johnson 1948**
Newark: Horizon 1940, Newark 1971, Wight 2005
Newfield: Capozzi 1918
North Bergen: Snyder 1995
North Brunswick: Segal 1992
Paramus: Hudson 1942, Point 1977
Passaic: **American 1902**
Pennington: Elias 1923, Fenwick 1929, Kish 1953, Lasko 1958, MacDonald 1961, Neisloss 1970, Post 1978, Savin 1989
Pittstown: Catholic 1919
Plainsboro: Integra 1945
Princeton: **Allen 1900**, Bonner 1909, Evans 1925, Harbourton 1936, **Horner 1941**, **JM 1947**, **Johnson 1949**, Kovner 1956, **Milbank 1968**, **Newcombe 1972**
Rancocas: Rowan 1986
Randolph: Grace 1935
Red Bank: Banbury 1904, Robertson 1983
Ridgewood: Marcon 1963
Ringwood: Brotherton 1914
River Edge: Marino 1964
Robbinsville: Roma 1984
Roselle: Bauer 1906
Rumson: Borden 1910
Short Hills: **Pfeiffer 1975**
Summit: Bouras 1911, Fournier 1932, Summit 1998
Teaneck: **Berrie 1908**, Brookdale 1912, **Puffin 1980**, **Ramapo 1981**, Stechler 1997, Taub 2000
Tenafly: Allied 1901
Teterboro: Klatskin 1954
Trenton: Environmental 1924
Warren: Hyde 1944
Watchung: Focus 1930
Wayne: **International 1946**
West Orange: Mandelbaum 1962, Pierson 1976
Westfield: Baker 1903, Fairbanks 1927, Westfield 2004
Whitehouse Station: Merck 1966
Woodcliff Lake: Eisai 1921
Wyckoff: Meyer 1967

see also 12, 70, 164, 181, 203, 547, 550, 554, 601, 686, 694, 703, 796, 802, 825, 845, 878, 910, 998, 1064, 1066, 1206, 1325, 1331, 1377, 1380, 1407, 1469, 1482, 1497, 1541, 1549, 1550, 1678, 1697, 1774, 1860, 2053, 2075, 2089, 2118, 2122, 2133, 2163, 2184, 2191, 2218, 2241, 2242, 2297, 2310, 2323, 2327, 2329, 2356, 2367, 2372, 2385, 2400, 2447, 2455, 2465, 2498, 2506, 2527, 2564, 2569, 2576, 2597, 2598, 2620, 2635, 2704, 2755, 2888, 2910, 2985, 3011, 3019, 3023, 3055, 3066, 3067, 3080, 3093, 3221, 3420, 3426, 3479, 3604

NEW MEXICO

Albuquerque: Albuquerque 2006, Pierce 2016
Artesia: Chase 2009
Hobbs: Maddox 2014
Las Cruces: Community 2010
Santa Fe: Aurora 2007, B.F. 2008, Con 2011, Frost 2012, Garfield 2013, Phillips 2015, Santa Fe 2017, Simon 2018

see also 3, 65, 99, 410, 473, 488, 497, 513, 627, 878, 1035, 1053, 1206, 1220, 1628, 1697, 1754, 1864, 2405, 2486, 2677, 2815, 3033, 3235, 3312, 3316, 3320, 3420, 3572, 3673

NEW YORK

Albany: Community 2108, Family 2153
Amherst: Alfiero 2031, **Buffalo 2078**, Henry 2209, Lee 2270, Miller 2308, Pollock 2362, Snayberger 2431
Armonk: **IBM 2227**, MBIA 2297, Yudelson 2514
Auburn: Stardust 2448
Bangall: Animal 2038
Bedford: Naomi 2319, Newman 2328
Bedford Hills: Sidewalk 2422, **Weeden 2496**
Bellmore: Levy 2276
Binghamton: Hoyt 2221, Klee 2253, Link 2280
Bohemia: Lane 2266
Briarcliff Manor: **Gutfleish 2196**
Bronx: New Yankee 2324
Brooklyn: B'Chaya 2057, Cohen 2103, **Discount 2139**, EMB 2151, Gross 2193, Hps 2222, **Klein 2254**, Kochov 2260, Kornfeld 2261, Moore 2312, Rachel 2371, Rieger 2383, S & W 2401, Shalom 2416, Wilson 2507, Yashar 2512
Buffalo: **Cummings 2120**, Oishei 2340, Paxton 2352, Rich 2382, Truman 2475, Wells 2501, Western 2503
Canandaigua: Ontario 2342
College Point: IF 2228
Corona: **Klein 2255**
Dobbs Ferry: Liberal 2278
Dunkirk: Northern 2331
East Greenbush: Rose 2392
Elmira: Aequus 2028
Forest Hills: Palmer 2348
Garden City: Brooks 2075, Overhills 2346, Rauch 2376
Getzville: Tower 2472
Glen Head: Barker 2054
Glens Falls: Beach 2058
Great Neck: Butler 2081
Hauppauge: Capri 2084, Initial 2231
Horseheads: Community 2109
Hudson: Hudson 2223
Hudson Falls: Sandy 2404
Ithaca: Community 2112, Legacy 2274, Park 2349
Jamestown: Chautauqua 2091, Gebbie 2170, Holmberg 2219, Hultquist 2225
Jericho: Coudert 2115
Johnson City: Community 2107
Katonah: Dartley 2128, Samberg 2403
Kings Point: Kaylie 2247
Lake Placid: Adirondack 2027, Lake Placid 2265
Lloyd Harbor: Shoreland 2421, Swartz 2455
Long Island City: **Henson 2210**, Rosenthal 2395
Lowville: Pratt 2366
Mamaroneck: **Animal 2039**
Marion: Seneca 2415
Melville: Hite 2214, Kanas 2244, **Pershing 2356**
Middle Village: **Friends 2167**
Monsey: Benmen 2061, Sunrise 2453
Montgomery: Community 2111
Mount Kisco: **Mathers 2294**
Mountainville: Ogden 2338
New Hyde Park: Litwin 2283
New York: 100 2019, Abelard 2022, **Abraham 2023**, Access 2025, Achelis 2026, **AIG 2029**, **Alavi 2030**, American 2033, **American 2034**, American 2035, Anderson 2036, **Arcus 2040**, Aresty 2041, Aronson 2042, Art 2043, Artists 2044, Asen 2045, Assael 2046, Assurant 2047, Atlantic 2048, Authors 2050, **AVI 2051**, AYN 2052, Azrak 2053, Barking 2055, Bay 2056, Belfer 2059, Belfer 2060, Berg 2062, Betesh 2063, Bikuben 2064, Black 2065, **Bloomberg 2066**, Blum 2067, **Breslauer 2069**, Brillo-Sonnino 2070, Broadcasters 2071, Brock 2072, Bronfman 2073, **Bronfman 2074**, Brownstone 2077, Bullitt 2079, Burton 2080, **Bydale 2082**, Canaday 2083, **Carnegie 2085**, Carson 2086, Caruso 2087, Century 2089, Chernin 2092, Chesed 2093, Chiang 2094, Cinereach 2095, Clark 2096, **Clark 2097**, **Clark 2098**, Clark 2099, Coach 2100, Coby 2101, Cohen 2102, Coleman 2104, Collins 2105, **Commonwealth 2106**, Cote 2114, **Credit 2118**, Cricket 2119, **Cummings 2121**, Cummings 2122, D'Agostino 2124, Dammann 2125, **Dana 2126**, Daphne 2127, de Coizart 2129, Dean 2130, DeCamp 2131, Deerfield 2132, deForest 2133, **Deutsche 2134**, Diamond 2136, Diller 2137, DiMenna 2138, Dobkin 2140, **Dramatists 2143**, Dreitzer 2144, Dreyfus 2145, **Duke 2146**, Ebb 2149, Einhorn 2150, **Eppley 2152**, Fascitelli 2155, Fisher 2157, Fleischer 2158, **Flowering 2159**, **Ford 2160**, **Foundation 2161**, **Frankenberg 2162**, Freed 2163, Freeman 2164, French 2165, Friedman 2166, Galler 2168, Gellert 2171, Gemj 2172, **Genesis 2173**, Gershwind 2174, Giant 2176, **Gilman 2178**, Gimbel 2179, **Gimprich 2180**, **Goldman 2181**, **Goldman 2182**, Goldman 2183, Goldstein 2184, **Gottlieb 2187**, Gould 2188, Grace 2189,

Grant 2190, **Grant 2191**, **Greenwall 2192**, **Guggenheim 2194**, Gurwin 2195, Guttman 2197, Hadar 2198, Hagedorn 2200, Hallingby 2201, Halper 2202, Haring 2203, Havens 2204, Heckscher 2205, Heisman 2206, Helmsley 2207, Henle 2208, **Heron 2211**, Heyman 2212, High 2213, Hochstein 2216, Hod 2217, Hoffen 2218, Horowitz 2220, **Hughes 2224**, Hycliff 2226, Imago 2230, Institute 2232, **Institute 2233**, Istel 2234, Jaharis 2236, Jewish 2237, Jewish 2238, Johnson 2239, Johnson 2240, Johnson 2241, **JPMorgan 2242**, **Kade 2243**, **Kaplan 2245**, Karmazin 2246, Kekst 2249, Kellen 2250, **King 2251**, Kleban 2252, Klingenstein 2256, Klingenstein 2257, **Klingenstein 2258**, Knapp 2259, **Koussevitzky 2262**, **Kress 2263**, Laffont 2264, Langeloth 2267, Lassalle 2268, Lavelle 2269, Lee 2271, Leeds 2272, Leeman 2273, Levitt 2275, Liberman 2279, Lissner 2281, Littauer 2282, Loewe 2284, Luce 2285, **Luce 2286**, **M.A.C. 2287**, **Macy 2288**, Marine 2289, Markle 2290, Marks 2291, **Matisse 2295**, **Mayday 2296**, McCarthy 2298, McGonagle 2299, McGraw 2300, Meadmore 2301, **Mellon 2302**, Mendell 2303, Menezes 2304, Mercer 2305, **Mertz 2306**, **MetLife 2307**, Mindich 2309, Monteforte 2310, Moore 2313, Moore 2314, Morgan 2315, Mule 2316, Mutual 2317, Nakash 2318, **Nash 2320**, NBC 2322, Neu 2323, New York 2325, New York 2326, New York 2327, Nicholson 2329, Niehaus 2330, Novartis 2333, NoVo 2334, **Noyes 2335**, NYSE 2336, Oestreicher 2337, O'Grady 2339, Ong 2341, **Open 2343**, Ostgrodd 2344, **Overbrook 2345**, Palette 2347, Paulson 2351, Perelman 2355, **Peterson 2357**, Petrie 2358, Planning 2359, Pletka 2360, **Pollock 2363**, **Porticus 2364**, Price 2367, Project 2368, Purple 2369, Quinn 2370, Randall 2372, Rapoport 2373, Rasmussen 2375, Regals 2377, Reich 2378, Resnick 2379, Resnick 2380, Ring 2384, Rivendell 2385, Robbins 2386, Roche 2388, **Rockefeller 2389**, **Rockefeller 2390**, Roothbert 2391, Rose 2393, Rosenberg 2394, Rothstein 2397, **Rubin 2398**, **Rubin 2399**, Ruffin 2400, **Sage 2402**, Sarofim 2405, Schafer 2406, **Schepp 2408**, Scherman 2409, Schnurmacher 2411, Schumann 2412, Schwartz 2413, SDA 2414, **Shatford 2417**, Sheafer 2418, Sherman 2419, Shoolman 2420, Simons 2423, Singer 2424, Singh 2425, Sirus 2426, Slifka 2428, Smith 2430, Snyder 2433, Society 2434, Sorel 2437, **Soros 2439**, Source 2440, **Sparkplug 2441**, Spektor 2442, Sperry 2443, Sprague 2444, St. George's 2445, St. Simon 2446, Stackhouse 2447, Sugarman 2450, Sulzberger 2451, **Surdna 2454**, Tandon 2458, **Teagle 2459**, Teagle 2460, Thompson 2461, Tiffany 2463, Tiger 2464, **Tikvah 2465**, Time 2466, **Tinker 2467**, Tisch 2468, Tisch 2469, Tishman 2470, **Towerbrook 2473**, **Trust 2477**, **Tsadra 2478**, Tuttle 2479, **Unbound 2480**, Union 2481, van Ameringen 2482, van Ameringen 2483, V'hanun 2484, Vidda 2485, Vilcek 2486, Voya 2488, Wachtell, 2490, **Wallace 2492**, **Warhol 2494**, Weil, 2498, **Weill 2499**, **Wenner 2502**, Whiting 2504, Wiener 2506, Woodcock 2511, **Youth 2513**, Ziff 2515

North Rose: Marshall 2293

North Tonawanda: East 2147

Norwich: Norwich 2332, Post 2365, Smith 2429

Olean: Cutco 2123

Oriskany: Eastern 2148

Pawling: Peale 2353

Pelham: Countess 2116, Patrina 2350

Pittsford: Golisano 2185, Polisseni 2361

Plainview: Ghez 2175

Port Washington: Marley 2292

Poughkeepsie: Community 2113

Pound Ridge: Box 2068

Purchase: **PepsiCo 2354**, Tananbaum 2456, Wachenheim 2489

Queens: Augustine 2049

Rochester: Farash 2154, **Ross 2396**, Schmitt 2410, Summers 2452, Wegman 2497, Wolk 2510

Rockville Centre: Stark 2449, Winley 2508

Roslyn Harbor: Hagedorn 2199

Rye Brook: Andor 2037, Moore 2311, Tananbaum 2457

Sag Harbor: Vogler 2487

Sagaponack: Touradji 2471

Saranac Lake: Keet 2248

Saratoga Springs: Ferraioli 2156, Solomon 2436

Schenectady: Schenectady 2407

Skaneateles: Allyn 2032

South Salem: **Abba's 2021**

Stamford: Robinson 2387

Staten Island: Geary 2169

Suffern: Wagner 2491

Syracuse: Chapman 2090, Gifford 2177, Snow 2432

Tarrytown: 1848 2020, **Diamond 2135**, Donner 2142

Troy: Troy 2474

Uniondale: Widgeon 2505

Utica: Community 2110

Warwick: Warwick 2495

White Plains: **Jabara 2235**, **Skadden 2427**, Weissman 2500

Williamsville: National 2321

Woodbury: Abramson 2024, Cramer 2117, Trump 2476, Woldar 2509

Wynantskill: Rhodes 2381

Yonkers: Carvel 2088

---

see also 3, 12, 70, 74, 92, 112, 121, 141, 149, 150, 169, 174, 177, 181, 206, 212, 220, 222, 230, 231, 235, 252, 263, 277, 295, 312, 325, 326, 334, 337, 362, 365, 370, 386, 390, 395, 404, 432, 434, 473, 496, 509, 518, 541, 547, 548, 550, 551, 552, 554, 555, 556, 557, 565, 566, 567, 579, 581, 587, 589, 593, 594, 596, 599, 601, 602, 604, 607, 612, 616, 618, 619, 633, 636, 647, 650, 651, 655, 680, 690, 691, 692, 696, 701, 703, 719, 731, 740, 741, 752, 753, 756, 765, 772, 773, 774, 780, 782, 787, 790, 796, 803, 806, 814, 817, 825, 827, 834, 835, 836, 864, 878, 889, 910, 955, 956, 970, 994, 997, 998, 1006, 1009, 1016, 1017, 1033, 1036, 1053, 1055, 1064, 1066, 1070, 1082, 1093, 1095, 1100, 1101, 1102, 1206, 1211, 1224, 1253, 1264, 1308, 1311, 1322, 1323, 1330, 1346, 1350, 1364, 1377, 1384, 1392, 1393, 1396, 1401, 1407, 1408, 1415, 1416, 1434, 1439, 1447, 1450, 1455, 1467, 1481, 1482, 1491, 1493, 1500, 1537, 1541, 1545, 1550, 1554, 1565, 1621, 1625, 1670, 1675, 1681, 1697, 1707, 1774, 1779, 1862, 1872, 1882, 1891, 1893, 1896, 1899, 1903, 1904, 1908, 1911, 1912, 1914, 1922, 1923, 1925, 1926, 1928, 1932, 1936, 1942, 1944, 1953, 1954, 1956, 1957, 1960, 1962, 1965, 1968, 1970, 1971, 1972, 1977, 1983, 1985, 1986, 1991, 1996, 1999, 2000, 2001, 2003, 2007, 2516, 2519, 2526, 2527, 2529, 2532, 2569, 2577, 2581, 2627, 2638, 2704, 2714, 2717, 2722, 2726, 2728, 2758, 2760, 2777, 2865, 2881, 2882, 2884, 2885, 2886, 2910, 2927, 2929, 2941, 2945, 2955, 2969, 3020, 3023, 3066, 3067, 3071, 3080, 3085, 3090, 3178, 3179, 3180, 3181, 3191, 3311, 3351, 3411, 3420, 3426, 3447, 3457, 3478, 3479, 3590, 3596, 3598, 3622, 3635, 3650, 3682

NORTH CAROLINA

Asheville: Community 2540, Glass 2559

Belmont: Howe 2570

Chapel Hill: Brady 2533, Kenan 2577, Morgan 2596, Strowd 2633

Charlotte: Adams 2516, **Bank 2524**, Beckman 2526, Bergen 2527, Byrum 2535, Christopher 2537, Dalton 2542, Deaver 2544, Ferebee 2552, Gambrill 2556, Goodrich 2561, Griffin 2563, Hanes 2565, Harvest 2566, Hoffman 2569, Humphrey 2571, **Johnson 2574**, Levine 2584, McCausland 2589, Meyer 2593, Needham 2597, Nucor 2601, Olin 2603, Plansoen 2608, Richmond 2616, Shingleton 2624, Short 2625, Simpson 2626, Smith 2629, Symmes 2636

Concord: Gordon 2562

Conover: Bolick 2531

Durham: Biddle 2529

Fayetteville: Cumberland 2541, Rogers 2618

Gastonia: Glenn 2560

Greensboro: Fund 2555, Tannenbaum 2637, Toleo 2640, VF 2642

Hendersonville: Community 2539

Littleton: Bailey 2522

Mocksville: Davie 2543

Morganton: Community 2538

Mount Olive: Southern 2630

Ocean Isle Beach: Hackbarth 2564

Raleigh: Anonymous 2519, North Carolina 2599, Pope 2610, Rex 2612, Sloan 2628, State 2632, Zelnak 2647

Reidsville: Reidsville 2611

Research Triangle Park: **Burroughs 2534**, North 2600

Salisbury: Peeler 2606, Woodson 2644

Southern Shores: Outer 2604

Tryon: Polk 2609

Wilmington: Kennedy 2578

Winston Salem: Katz 2576, Linsmayer 2585, Roberts 2617, Sutcliffe 2635, Wrasse 2645

Winston-Salem: Adams 2517, Allen 2518, Arkwright 2520, Babcock 2521, Balin 2523, Bettman 2528, Billingsley 2530, Borun 2532, Caine 2536, Dobbs 2545, Duke 2546, Duncan 2547, Eddy 2548, Emma 2549, Everett 2550, Fairfield 2551, Fortson 2553, French 2554, Garrow 2557, Ghidotti 2558, Havens 2567, Helb 2568, Hunt 2572, Hunter 2573, Kanitz 2575, Kistler 2579, Kitselman 2580, Kramer 2581, Krost 2582, **Laffin 2583**, Lynum 2586, Marsh 2587, Mayr 2588, McNeil 2590, Merrick 2591, Meserve 2592, Meyer 2594, Moretz 2595, Niessen 2598, Odell 2602, Paddock 2605, Perkin 2607, Reynolds 2613, Reynolds 2614, Ribenack 2615, Rose 2619, Sanders 2620, Sandt 2621, Schmuhl 2622, Sherrard 2623, Sites 2627, Stahlberg 2631, Stuart 2634, Templin 2638, Todd 2639, Towne 2641, Wann 2643, Wyly 2646

---

see also 70, 235, 313, 338, 358, 550, 567, 677, 698, 731, 738, 743, 771, 775, 789, 791, 833, 860, 870, 878, 1034, 1099, 1223, 1401, 1525, 1594, 1727, 1860, 1917, 1929, 1952, 2082, 2118, 2120, 2349, 2391, 2413, 2699, 2863, 2888, 2959, 3018, 3063, 3106, 3109, 3264, 3382, 3409, 3430, 3445, 3452, 3456, 3466, 3467, 3505

NORTH DAKOTA

Bismarck: MDU 2652, North Dakota 2653

Fargo: Fargo 2649, Larson 2650

Grand Forks: Community 2648

Williston: Martell 2651

---

see also 99, 627, 771, 1695, 1710, 1716, 1722, 1729, 1750, 1754, 3644

OHIO

Akron: Akron 2655, Bernard 2667, Freygang 2704, Orr 2761

Amherst: Nord 2754

Athens: Athens 2662

Barberton: Barberton 2664, Tuscora 2796

Beachwood: Andrews 2659, Maltz 2727

Bedford Heights: **Brush 2673**

Bratenahl: Sears 2781

Brooklyn: Calhoun 2676

Bryan: Bryan 2674
Bucyrus: Community 2682
Canton: Austin 2663, Stark 2788
Chagrin Falls: Talbott 2791
Cincinnati: Anderson 2658, Building 2675, Cincinnati 2679, Cincinnati 2680, Dater 2687, Emery 2694, Fifth 2699, Haile, 2709, Johnson 2714, Keeler 2715, Knowlton 2720, Macy's 2726, Mayerson 2735, Nippert 2751, Ohio 2756, Ohio 2757, **Omnicare 2758**, Ryan 2769, Schmidlapp 2775, Scripps 2780, Seasongood 2782, Skyler 2784, Slemp 2785, Steinmann 2789
Cleveland: Abington 2654, **Bingham 2668**, Brentwood 2670, Cliffs 2681, **Eaton 2692**, Gund 2708, KeyBank 2717, Kulas 2721, Lincoln 2724, Mandel 2728, **Mandel 2729**, Mandel 2730, McGregor 2736, Munro 2743, Murphy 2745, O'Neill 2760, Reinberger 2765, Renner 2766, Saint 2770, Third 2792, White 2800, Woodruff 2801
Cleveland Heights: Eaton 2693
Columbus: American 2656, American 2657, Mirolo 2738, NiSource 2752, Osteopathic 2762, Schooler 2776, Schottenstein 2777, Schottenstein 2778
Concord Township: Hershey 2711
Coshocton: Coshocton 2686
Dayton: **Benedict 2666**, Brethen 2671, Dayton 2688, Gardner 2705, Kettering 2716, Mathile 2734, Schiewetz 2774
Dublin: Brown 2672, **Cardinal 2677**, **Marafiki 2731**
Eaton: Home 2712
Elyria: Community 2683
Fairlawn: **OMNOVA 2759**
Findlay: Findlay 2700
Hamilton: Hamilton 2710, Knoll 2719
Haviland: Samaritan 2772
Highland Heights: **Lerner 2722**
Hudson: Morgan 2740, Morgan 2741
Lancaster: Fairfield 2696
Lima: Ar-Hale 2661
Loudonville: Young 2803
Mansfield: Richland 2767
Marietta: Marietta 2732
Marion: Marion 2733
Mayfield Heights: Ferro 2697, Fowler 2703
Mayfield Village: Progressive 2764
Middletown: Middletown 2737
Milford: Wyler 2802
Nelsonville: Foundation 2702
New Albany: New Albany 2750
New Philadelphia: Tuscarawas 2795
Newark: Evans 2695, Licking 2723
Niles: Fibus 2698
Pepper Pike: Murphy 2744, Veale 2797
Perrysburg: Charities 2678
Piqua: Piqua 2763
Poland: Scotford 2779
Powell: Delaware 2689
Rocky River: Morino 2742
Rome: Dodero 2691
Salem: Salem 2771
Salineville: Angels 2660
Sandusky: Sandusky 2773
Seven Hills: Spirit 2786
Sidney: Community 2684
Springfield: Llewellyn 2725, Springfield 2787
Tiffin: National 2748, Tiffin 2793
Toledo: Bates 2665, **Needmor 2749**, Stranahan 2790
Troy: Troy 2794
University Heights: Ginn 2706
Warren: Wean 2799
Westlake: Nordson 2755
Wooster: Foss 2701, **Noble 2753**, Wayne 2798
Xenia: Greene 2707
Yellow Springs: Morgan 2739, YSI 2805
Youngstown: Community 2685, Youngstown 2804
Zanesville: Murphy 2746, Muskingum 2747, Roggecora 2768, Shinnick 2783

---

see also 62, 76, 166, 540, 550, 631, 715, 771, 878, 889, 902, 961, 1040, 1099, 1202, 1206, 1253, 1290, 1298, 1415, 1434, 1593, 1621, 1670, 1675, 1697, 1710, 1727, 1774, 1917, 1961, 2075, 2242, 2315, 2451, 2847, 2863, 2925, 2971, 3018, 3023, 3067, 3181, 3191, 3420, 3446, 3462, 3527, 3579, 3581, 3586, 3587, 3598, 3621, 3624, 3644

OKLAHOMA

Alva: Wisdom 2832
Ardmore: Noble 2822
Enid: Cherokee 2809
Muskogee: Kirschner 2818
Newkirk: Peel 2825
Norman: Liddell 2819, Sarkeys 2828
Oklahoma City: Dolese 2810, **Ethics 2811**, Gaylord 2813, Jones 2817, McGee 2820, Merrick 2821, Oklahoma 2823, Parman 2824, Presbyterian 2826
Tulsa: Adams 2806, Bernsen 2807, Chapman 2808, Freese 2812, Hardesty 2814, Harmon 2815, Hille 2816, **ROI 2827**, **Schusterman 2829**, Viersen 2830, Warren 2831, Zarrow 2833, Zarrow 2834

---

see also 70, 99, 180, 711, 878, 1028, 1594, 1869, 1902, 2015, 2242, 2656, 2661, 3078, 3126, 3154, 3170, 3292, 3321, 3397, 3505, 3598

OREGON

Beaverton: Knight 2854, **NIKE 2865**
Bend: Macdonald 2859
Corvallis: Benton 2835, Simple 2871
Eugene: PacificSource 2866, Woodard 2877
Florence: Western 2876
Hermiston: Leonard 2858
Jacksonville: Chaney 2840
Klamath Falls: Jeld 2852
Lake Oswego: Lamb 2855, TeamCFA 2873
Lakeview: Daly 2844
Medford: Maxey 2860, Morris 2864
Portland: Braemar 2836, Burning 2837, Castle 2839, Coit 2841, Collins 2842, Coon 2843, Flowerree 2845, Glory 2847, Healy 2848, Hedinger 2849, I Have 2850, Jackson 2851, Jubitz 2853, Lazar 2856, **Lemelson 2857**, Meyer 2861, Michael 2862, PGE 2867, Portland 2868, Renaissance 2869, Shapira 2870, Storms 2872, Templeton 2874, West 2875, Wyss 2878
Roseburg: Caddock 2838, Ford 2846
Tigard: Mission 2863

---

see also 36, 99, 118, 142, 180, 216, 221, 235, 324, 614, 627, 649, 878, 1159, 1237, 1278, 1710, 1722, 2242, 2440, 2528, 2572, 2717, 2969, 3277, 3490, 3498, 3513, 3524, 3554, 3566, 3572

PENNSYLVANIA

Allentown: Baker 2886, Lehigh Valley 2986, Rider 3024, Trexler 3049
Altoona: Central 2907
Ambler: Copernicus 2928
Bala Cynwyd: **Lee 2984**, Perelman 3012, Perelman 3013
Beaver: Beaver 2890
Berwick: Central 2908
Bethlehem: Brooks 2899, Laros 2982, Shaffer 3035
Blue Bell: Henkels 2967
Bridgeville: II-VI 2974
Bristol: Grundy 2962
Bryn Mawr: Ludwick 2988
Butler: Sedwick 3032
Canonsburg: Mylan 3001
Colmar: North 3006
Conshohocken: Pierce 3015
Conshokocken: Feldman 2941
Doylestown: Bucks 2900, Seybert 3034
East Earl: Pilgrim 3016
Easton: Staley 3043
Erwinna: Tuttleman 3050
Exton: Lazarich 2983
Gladwyne: Drueding 2936
Harrisburg: Foundation 2952, Kunkel 2980
Haverford: Presser 3019
Hershey: Glatfelter 2956
Holicong: Raab 3020
Huntingdon Valley: Golden 2958
Johnstown: Community 2922
King of Prussia: Arkema 2885
Lampeter: **M.E. 2989**, **Riverside 3025**
Lancaster: Ferree 2944, Lancaster 2981, Shuman 3036
Malvern: Field 2945
McMurray: Rossin 3028
Media: **Botstiber 2898**
Murrysville: **Respironics 3023**
Narbeth: Kohelet 2979
Norristown: Child 2916
Philadelphia: **ACE 2880**, Ames 2884, Berwind 2894, Betz 2895, Burgess 2903, **Cardiovascular 2905**, CIGNA 2917, Clareth 2919, Comcast 2921, Fels 2942, First 2948, **Firth 2949**, Garfield 2955, GlaxoSmithKline 2957, Grumbacher 2961, Honickman 2970, Independence 2975, Independence 2976, Kaiserman 2977, Leeway 2985, Lewis 2987, Martin 2991, Merchants 3000, Penn 3011, Ross 3027, Scattergood 3030, Seebe 3033, Stoneleigh 3045, Sunoco 3046, Union 3051, Wells 3055, **Zeldin 3060**
Phoenixville: Phoenixville 3014
Pittsburgh: Adams 2881, **Alcoa 2882**, Allegheny 2883, Bayer 2888, Beacon 2889, Benedum 2892, Birmingham 2896, Black 2897, Buhl 2901, Buncher 2902, **Carnegie 2906**, Cestone 2910, Chase 2913, Chenault 2914, Cooper 2927, Davis 2929, Davis 2930, Degenstein 2931, Donahue 2933, Dozzi 2935, DSF 2937, Duff 2938, EQT 2940, Finley 2946, FISA 2950, Goshen 2959, Harris 2965, Heinz 2966, Highmark 2968, Hillman 2969, Hunt 2971, Hunt 2972, **KL 2978**, McCune 2993, McKaig 2994, McKee 2995, McKinney 2996, Mellon 2998, Mendel 2999, Nesh 3004, Noll 3005, O'Brien-Veba 3007, Palumbo 3009, Patterson 3010, **PPG 3018**, Rangos 3022, Smith 3037, Sneath 3038, Snee 3039, Society 3040, Somerville 3041, Staunton 3044, Trees 3048, United 3052, Wilson 3058
Plymouth Meeting: Charlestein 2911, Claneil 2918, Widener 3056
Pottstown: Pottstown 3017
Quakertown: 100 2879
Radnor: Female 2943, Groff 2960, Nelson 3003
Reading: Berks 2893
Rydal: Saramar 3029
Saint Marys: Elk 2939
Scranton: Scranton 3031, Willary 3057
Sewickley: Hansen 2964
Sharon: Community 2925
St. Marys: Stackpole 3042
State College: Centre 2909
Uniontown: Community 2923
Villanova: Rooney 3026
Washington: Washington 3054
Wayne: Barra 2887, Charter 2912, Delaware 2932, Huston 2973, McLean 2997
Waynesburg: Community 2924
Wellsboro: Packer 3008
West Chester: Chester 2915

West Conshohocken: Calvert 2904, Connelly 2926, Halloran 2963, **Templeton 3047**, Valentine 3053
Wexford: Randall 3021
Williamsport: First 2947
Willow Grove: Fourjay 2953
Wyomissing: Freas 2954, Wyomissing 3059
York: Naylor 3002
Youngsville: Clark 2920

see also 70, 87, 396, 434, 469, 497, 505, 549, 550, 555, 565, 568, 573, 639, 655, 685, 686, 698, 771, 774, 834, 841, 878, 1006, 1053, 1064, 1073, 1084, 1194, 1298, 1365, 1407, 1416, 1434, 1541, 1550, 1594, 1621, 1707, 1710, 1860, 1902, 1917, 1919, 1941, 1943, 1952, 1961, 1966, 1972, 2033, 2034, 2075, 2118, 2171, 2220, 2236, 2242, 2259, 2276, 2297, 2307, 2308, 2315, 2321, 2322, 2352, 2362, 2381, 2391, 2400, 2415, 2431, 2483, 2488, 2499, 2501, 2506, 2544, 2568, 2598, 2607, 2617, 2620, 2629, 2661, 2699, 2755, 2759, 3067, 3109, 3133, 3161, 3162, 3382, 3404, 3596, 3598, 3621, 3632

PUERTO RICO

San Juan: Puerto Rico 3061

see also 3, 660, 1948, 2034, 2677, 3068

RHODE ISLAND

Cranston: Decedric 3069
East Providence: Masonic 3083
Newport: van Beuren 3094
Pawtucket: Hasbro 3077
Providence: Bernhardt 3062, Biogen 3063, Bird 3064, Bliss 3065, Chamberlain 3066, DeLoura 3070, **Dorot 3071**, Elms 3072, Estate 3073, Falk 3074, Gross 3076, Hecht 3078, King 3080, Koffler 3081, Love 3082, McCabe 3084, McDonald 3085, McNeil 3086, Parmelee 3088, Rhode Island 3089, Schwarz 3090, Seymour 3091, Shaw's 3092, Textron 3093
Riverside: Citizens 3067
Westerly: Kimball 3079, Washington 3095
Woonsocket: CVS 3068

see also 70, 566, 776, 836, 1076, 1342, 1353, 1431, 1448, 1467, 1468, 1480, 1501, 1529, 1541, 1554, 1727, 1894, 1977, 2075, 2155, 2196, 2394, 2755, 3214, 3673

SOUTH CAROLINA

Anderson: Foothills 3102
Belton: WebbCraft 3113
Charleston: Motley 3107
Chester: Lutz 3105
Clinton: Bailey 3096
Easley: McKissick 3106
Fort Mill: Springs 3111
Greenville: Community 3099, Daniel 3101, Graham 3103
Hartsville: Byerly 3098
Hilton Head Island: Community 3100
Murrells Inlet: Waccamaw 3112
Spartanburg: Black 3097, Smith 3109, Spartanburg 3110
Sullivans Island: Joanna 3104, Singing 3108

see also 70, 235, 771, 778, 804, 849, 856, 860, 878, 888, 908, 1001, 1099, 1298, 1904, 1917, 2081, 2508, 2521, 2556, 2566, 2603, 2626, 2636, 2646, 2754, 2759, 2886, 3018, 3133, 3235, 3420, 3445, 3466

SOUTH DAKOTA

Aberdeen: Hatterscheidt 3116, Schwab 3117, South 3118
Rapid City: Chiesman 3115
Sioux Falls: Brenden-Mann 3114

see also 70, 99, 222, 627, 771, 1240, 1246, 1695, 1710, 1716, 1722, 1729, 1754, 2517, 3644

TENNESSEE

Chattanooga: Alumni 3119, Benwood 3123, Chattanooga 3125, Hurlbut 3140, Hutcheson 3141, Lyndhurst 3145, **Maclellan 3146**, Osborne 3147, Tucker 3156
Franklin: Pedigree 3148
Hendersonville: CIC 3127
Kingsport: Eastman 3133
Knoxville: Clayton 3128, Elgin 3134, Haslam 3138, Regal 3151
Memphis: Assisi 3120, Briggs 3124, First 3135, Hardin 3137, **International 3142**, Sparks 3154, Stuttering 3155, Wilson 3157
Nashville: Baptist 3122, Checotah 3126, Community 3129, Davis 3130, Dugas 3132, Frist 3136, HCA 3139, Phillips 3149, **Scarlett 3152**, Schmidt 3153
Parsons: Ayers 3121
Union City: Kirkland 3143, Latimer 3144, Promethean 3150

see also 5, 19, 70, 74, 647, 704, 804, 841, 849, 860, 878, 944, 1099, 1206, 1213, 1697, 1961, 1978, 2075, 2138, 2317, 2516, 2521, 2603, 2656, 2677, 2699, 2751, 2885, 3264, 3420, 3457, 3466, 3484, 3598, 3644, 3682

TEXAS

Abilene: Shelton 3350
Aledo: Reilly 3333
Amarillo: Amarillo 3163, Engler 3223
Austin: **A Glimmer 3158**, A Glimmer 3159, Cain 3188, Conley 3201, **Dell 3213**, Fifth 3231, Hammill 3249, KDK-Harman 3273, Long 3285, Orr 3309, Professional 3326, Saxena 3344, **Tingari-Silverton 3368**, Tocker 3369, Toma 3370, Topfer 3372, Wright 3386
Beaumont: Penland 3314, Ward 3381
Boerne: Sikh 3351
Bryan: Astin 3166, Dougherty 3215, Plass 3322
Burnet: Hill 3259
Centerville: Wallrath 3380
Colleyville: Holloway 3264
Corpus Christi: Behmann 3176, Coastal 3196, Durrill 3217, Moore 3299, Rachal 3329, Sams 3342
Corsicana: Navarro 3305
Dallas: AT&T 3167, Augur 3168, Baron 3171, Bass 3172, Beasley 3175, Bickel 3178, Booth 3180, Collins 3199, Constantin 3202, Criswell 3207, Dallas 3209, Dedman 3212, Embrey 3222, Esping 3225, Flarsheim 3234, Hill 3260, Hillcrest 3261, Hoblitzelle 3262, Hoglund 3263, **Jiv 3270**, Jones 3272, King 3275, Lightner 3282, Littauer 3283, Lockheed 3284, Loose 3286, Lupton 3288, Luse 3289, McDermott 3293, McIntyre 3294, Meadows 3296, Peine 3313, Pickens 3321, QuadW 3328, Richardson 3335, Richter 3337, Rosewood 3340, Shelter 3349, Smith 3353, Sturgis 3360, Summerlee 3361, Thompson 3367
Dripping Springs: Burch 3184
Eastland: Thirteen 3366
El Paso: McKee 3295, **Paso 3312**, Stevens 3359
Fairview: Martinez 3291
Fort Worth: Alcon 3161, Alcon 3162, Burnett 3185, Carter 3190, Deakins 3210, Edwards 3218, Kleinheinz 3277, Philecology 3319, Proctor 3325, Psalm 3327, **Radler 3330**, Richardson 3334, Richardson 3336, Waggoner 3379
Galveston: Moody 3298, Northen 3306
Georgetown: Chisholm 3193
Granbury: Edwards 3219
Houston: **Baker 3170**, Baxter 3173, **Bolivar 3179**, **BP 3181**, Brown 3183, Cain 3189, CEMEX 3191, Community 3200, Cruz-Diez 3208, DeSantis 3214, Dunn 3216, Elkins 3220, Elkins 3221, Erol 3224, Farish 3228, Fish 3233, Frees 3238, Galtney 3240, Goodman 3242, Greentree 3244, Hachar 3246, Hamman 3248, Heinlein 3254, Herzstein 3256, Hildebrand 3258, Holthouse 3265, **Houston 3266**, Houston 3267, **International 3269**, Johnson 3271, Kinder 3274, **Levant 3280**, **Marshall 3290**, Morgan 3301, Mundy 3302, Music 3303, **Oldham 3308**, P 3311, Powell 3324, Rockwell 3338, Schissler 3346, Shell 3348, Simmons 3352, Smith 3354, Smith 3355, Sterling 3358
Irving: B.E.L.I.E.F. 3169, Chasdrew 3192, **Chrest 3194**, College 3198, Feldman 3230, Fluor 3235, NAPE 3237, **VHA 3377**
Kerrville: Cailloux 3187, Peterson 3318
Kingsville: Kleberg 3276
Laredo: Vergara 3376
Longview: Crain 3206
Lubbock: Lubbock 3287, South 3356, Talkington 3362
Lufkin: Fairchild 3227
McKinney: DeBusk 3211, Task 3363
Midland: Abell 3160, Beal 3174, Fasken 3229, Moore 3300, Permian 3316, Potts 3323, Scharbauer 3345
Odessa: Hext 3257
Onalaska: Williams 3383
Orange: Stark 3357
Palacios: Trull 3373
Palestine: Texas 3364
Paris: L. 3278, Lennox 3279
Plano: Penney 3315, Perot 3317, Tyler 3375, Woolf 3385
Richmond: Henderson 3255
Rockport: Howell 3268
San Angelo: San Angelo 3343
San Antonio: Anderson 3164, Brackenridge 3182, Coates 3197, Cowden 3205, Gage 3239, Goldsbury 3241, Halsell 3247, Harte 3251, Hartman 3252, Light 3281, Najim 3304, NuStar 3307, Orsinger 3310, Saint 3341, Semmes 3347, Tomerlin 3371, Willard 3382, Zachry 3387
Sherman: Mayor 3292, **PHM 3320**
Texarkana: Texas 3365
The Woodlands: Haraldson 3250, Mitchell 3297, RDM 3332
Tyler: Clements 3195, Ezekiel 3226, Fisch 3232, Rogers 3339
Waco: C.I.O.S. 3186, Heavin 3253, Rapoport 3331, Waco 3378
West University Place: Tubbs 3374
Wharton: Gulf 3245

see also 3, 67, 70, 74, 80, 88, 263, 291, 313, 358, 372, 435, 480, 493, 550, 569, 604, 612, 646, 776, 778, 847, 864, 985, 1034, 1057, 1064, 1070, 1071, 1072, 1091, 1092, 1099, 1167, 1194, 1206, 1237, 1261, 1298, 1308, 1320, 1353, 1401, 1407, 1418, 1594, 1621, 1710, 1754, 1774, 1776, 1794, 1917, 1978, 1983, 1993, 2009, 2015, 2033, 2034, 2059, 2118, 2178, 2211, 2231, 2242, 2305, 2315, 2317, 2322, 2348, 2354, 2405, 2488, 2549, 2656, 2677, 2760, 2808, 2815, 2838, 2863, 2885, 2886, 2888, 3001, 3018, 3052, 3133, 3420, 3426, 3457, 3590, 3621, 3632, 3671

UTAH

Highland: Mendenhall 3398
Lehi: Yamagata 3406
Lindon: Ashton 3388
Ogden: Dialysis 3390, Hall 3395

Park City: Green 3394, Park 3401
Salt Lake City: Bamberger 3389, Eccles 3392, Eskuche 3393, Hemingway 3396, McCarthey 3397, Quinney 3402, Schmidt 3403, Semnani 3404, Utah 3405
Springville: Earth 3391
Wellsville: Morrell 3399

see also 74, 99, 136, 488, 513, 627, 685, 927, 1206, 1278, 1917, 1941, 2033, 2034, 2073, 2242, 2315, 2370, 2536, 2717, 2839, 2862, 3572

VERMONT

Burlington: General 3410
Grafton: Windham 3418
Marshfield: Block 3409
Middlebury: Vermont 3417
Putney: McKenzie 3413
Shelburne: Lintilhac 3412
South Burlington: **Ben 3407**, Merchants 3414
South Londonderry: Rowland 3415
Weston: Harper 3411
Winooski: Tarrant 3416

see also 70, 610, 758, 1036, 1308, 1330, 1342, 1431, 1467, 1468, 1493, 1529, 1554, 1565, 1879, 1890, 1894, 1920, 2002, 2075, 2083, 2164, 2240, 2303, 2717, 3001, 3067, 3080

VIRGIN ISLANDS

Charlotte Amalie: Community 3419

see also 699, 1948

VIRGINIA

Annandale: Twinkling 3483
Arlington: Arlington 3421, Samberg 3478, Smith 3479
Bristol: United 3484
Charlottesville: **Blue 3422**, **Brown 3424**, Charlottesville 3428, Eiriksson 3436, Lee-Jackson 3448, MLG 3460, Oak 3466, **WestWind 3486**
Christiansburg: Community 3431
Danville: Community 3430, Maude 3456
Emporia: Greensville 3441
Fairfax: **Loyola 3453**, Moore 3461
Falls Church: **Longview 3451**, **Northrop 3465**, **Olmsted 3468**
Glen Allen: Metropolitan 3459
Herndon: Launders 3447
Leesburg: O'Shaughnessy-Hurst 3469
Louisa: Cooke 3434
Lynchburg: Lynchburg 3454
Manassas: Kellar 3446
Marshall: **Bosack 3423**
Martinsville: Harvest 3443, Keesee 3445
McLean: Capital 3426, **Fox 3439**, Moran 3462, Volgenau 3485
Newport News: MAIHS 3455
Norfolk: Lincoln 3449, Pruden 3473
Pulaski: Richardson 3475
Reston: **Foundation 3438**, MAXIMUS 3457, Stafford 3480, **Truland 3482**
Richmond: Cabell 3425, CarMax 3427, Community 3433, Denit 3435, Gwathmey 3442, Jeffress 3444, Love 3452, Memorial 3458, Morgan, 3463, Parsons 3470, **Price 3472**, RECO 3474, Richmond 3476, Robins 3477
Roanoke: Community 3432
Springfield: Strong 3481
Staunton: Community 3429
Suffolk: Obici 3467
Virginia Beach: AMERIGROUP 3420, Gifford 3440
Warrenton: Loeb 3450, Northern 3464
Williamsburg: Williamsburg 3487, Williamsburg 3488
Woodbridge: Potomac 3471

see also 70, 74, 107, 142, 154, 235, 263, 336, 337, 370, 395, 396, 434, 569, 586, 604, 636, 653, 656, 672, 677, 745, 791, 836, 861, 864, 870, 878, 950, 952, 970, 1064, 1085, 1206, 1326, 1356, 1372, 1373, 1377, 1383, 1394, 1419, 1549, 1565, 1678, 1727, 1747, 1774, 1904, 1935, 1985, 1993, 2031, 2080, 2081, 2125, 2130, 2142, 2303, 2305, 2354, 2400, 2508, 2519, 2521, 2550, 2589, 2610, 2624, 2625, 2627, 2656, 2657, 2722, 2755, 2760, 2764, 2785, 2847, 2932, 2940, 2945, 3004, 3093, 3109, 3184, 3306, 3409, 3411, 3515, 3661

WASHINGTON

Bainbridge Island: Bainbridge 3494
Bellevue: Jones 3530, **Luke 3537**, Smith 3564
Bellingham: Whatcom 3571
Edmonds: Corvias 3505
Ephrata: Lauzier 3534, Lauzier 3535
Everett: Everett 3511, Fales 3512, Intermec 3527
Freeland: Arise 3493
Friday Harbor: San Juan 3555
Hoquiam: Grays 3520
Kirkland: Anderson 3492, McCaw 3540
Lake Tapps: **Children's 3501**
Medina: Eggnog 3509, Lochland 3536, **Singh 3563**
Mercer Island: Jones 3529
Olympia: Community 3504
Puyallup: Korum 3532
Redmond: **Foundation 3515**
Renton: First 3514, Renton 3552
Richland: Three 3568
Seattle: Ackerley 3489, Allen 3490, Almi 3491, Biller 3496, Blakemore 3497, Casey 3499, Casey 3500, College 3502, Discuren 3507, Echo 3508, Ferguson 3513, **Gates 3516**, **Glaser 3517**, Goodman 3518, **Goodwin 3519**, Green 3521, Howard 3525, **Ji 3528**, Kawabe 3531, Maxwell 3539, McEachern 3541, Medina 3542, Miller 3544, Moccasin 3545, Northwest 3546, OneFamily 3547, PEMCO 3549, Raisbeck 3550, Richardson 3553, Safeco 3554, Satterberg 3556, Schultz 3557, Seattle 3558, Shemanski 3560, Simonyi 3562, **Starbucks 3565**, Stevenson 3566, Tudor 3569, Washington 3570, **Wilburforce 3572**, Wilkens 3573, Wright 3574, Wrigley 3575
Sequim: Haller 3522
Shoreline: Hanauer 3523
Spokane: Empire 3510, Inland 3526
Sumner: REI 3551
Tacoma: Bamford 3495, Dimmer 3506, Harder 3524, Milgard 3543, Sequoia 3559, Tacoma 3567
Vancouver: Kuni 3533, Marsh 3538, Pankow 3548
Walla Walla: Blue 3498, Sherwood 3561
Wenatchee: Community 3503
Yakima: Yakima 3576

see also 32, 36, 99, 235, 324, 406, 429, 448, 550, 604, 614, 627, 645, 685, 878, 951, 1029, 1206, 1223, 1278, 1353, 1575, 1594, 1621, 1683, 1697, 1710, 1722, 1827, 1917, 2021, 2171, 2242, 2415, 2526, 2603, 2717, 2779, 2837, 2855, 2856, 2861, 2863, 3018, 3020, 3077, 3235, 3359, 3420

WEST VIRGINIA

Beckley: Beckley 3577
Charles Town: McCormick 3585
Charleston: Five 3582, Maier 3584
Clarksburg: Burnside 3578
Huntington: Weisberg 3590
Martinsburg: Eastern 3580
Morgantown: Your 3591
Parkersburg: McDonough 3586, Parkersburg 3587, Ross 3588
Parsons: Tucker 3589
Wheeling: Community 3579
Williamstown: Fenton 3581

see also 70, 704, 878, 1167, 1368, 1373, 1875, 2242, 2521, 2656, 2681, 2699, 2732, 2766, 2840, 2892, 2940, 2994, 3001, 3018, 3039, 3161, 3162, 3397, 3420, 3466

WISCONSIN

Appleton: U.S. 3665
Arcadia: Wanek 3667
Baraboo: Sauey 3655
Belleville: CBM 3603
Beloit: Neese 3639, Stateline 3663
Brillion: Ariens 3594
Brookfield: Rowland 3652, Siebert 3659
Eau Claire: Eau 3611
Fond du Lac: Fond du Lac 3615, Smith 3660, Stone 3664
Fort Atkinson: Fort 3616
Green Bay: BayCare 3597, Cornerstone 3608, Green Bay 3619, Pamida 3644
Hudson: St. Croix 3662
Janesville: Community 3607, Jeffris 3624
Kohler: Kohler 3629
La Crosse: Elmwood 3614, La Crosse 3631
Lyons: **Wagner 3666**
Madison: Alliant 3592, Blooming 3599, Fund 3617, Hovde 3622, Sand 3654
Manitowoc: Manitowoc 3632
Marshfield: Marshfield 3633
Milwaukee: **Baird 3595**, Baker 3596, Bock 3600, **Bradley 3601**, Center 3604, Chipstone 3605, Einhorn 3613, Godfrey 3618, Harley 3621, Kloss 3628, McBeath 3634, McDonough 3635, Milwaukee 3637, Murray 3638, Nelson 3640, Pick 3646, Pritchett 3647, Reiman 3650, RITE-HITE 3651, Schlegel 3656, Zilber 3670
Neenah: Bemis 3598, Brown 3602, Keller 3626, Menasha 3636
New Richmond: New 3641
Oshkosh: Kuenzl 3630, Oshkosh 3642, Oshkosh 3643
Plover: Seramur 3658
Racine: Johnson 3625, Racine 3648
Sheboygan: Windway 3669
Stevens Point: Community 3606, Sentry 3657
Sturgeon Bay: Door 3609, Raibrook 3649
Sussex: Windhover 3668
Waukesha: Kern 3627
Waupaca: Anthony 3593
Wausau: Dudley 3610, Greenheck 3620, Spire 3661
Wauwatosa: Pettit 3645
Wisconsin Rapids: Incourage 3623

see also 99, 128, 235, 379, 604, 624, 655, 677, 736, 878, 957, 974, 1034, 1040, 1064, 1110, 1206, 1244, 1247, 1353, 1545, 1678, 1691, 1693, 1695, 1697, 1702, 1704, 1710, 1711, 1727, 1729, 1750, 1754, 1881, 1896, 1917, 2242, 2317, 2415, 2526, 2586, 2677, 2755, 2759, 3007, 3018, 3420

WYOMING

Casper: McMurry 3676
Cody: Cody 3672
Jackson: Dubois 3673, Furrer 3674, Marine 3675, Weiss 3682
Laramie: Wyoming 3684
Powell: Moyer 3677

INTERNATIONAL GIVING INDEX

List of terms: Names of countries, continents, or regions used in this index are drawn from the complete list below. Terms may appear on the list but not be present in the index.

Index: In the index itself, foundations are listed under the countries, continents, or regions in which they have demonstrated giving interests or made charitable contributions. Within these country or regional groupings, foundations are arranged by state location, abbreviated name, and sequence number.

Afghanistan
Africa
Albania
Algeria
Andorra
Angola
Anguilla
Antarctica
Antigua & Barbuda
Arctic Region
Argentina
Armenia
Aruba
Asia
Australia
Austria
Azerbaijan
Bahamas
Bahrain
Balkans, The
Bangladesh
Barbados
Belarus
Belgium
Belize
Benin
Bermuda
Bhutan
Bolivia
Bonaire
Bosnia-Herzegovina
Botswana
Brazil
British Virgin Islands
Brunei
Bulgaria
Burkina Faso
Burma (Myanmar)
Burundi
Cambodia
Cameroon
Canada
Cape Verde
Caribbean
Cayman Islands
Central Africa
Central Africa Republic
Central America
Central Asia and the Caucasus
Chad
Chile
China
Colombia
Commonwealth of the Northern Mariana Islands
Comoros
Congo
Costa Rica
Croatia
Cuba
Curacao
Cyprus
Czech Republic
Democratic Republic of the Congo
Denmark
Developing countries
Djibouti
Dominica
Dominican Republic
East Africa/Horn of Africa
East Asia
East Jerusalem
East Timor
Eastern & Central Europe
Ecuador
Egypt
El Salvador
England
Equatorial Guinea
Eritrea
Estonia
Ethiopia
Europe
Federated States of Micronesia
Fiji
Finland
France
French Guiana
Gabon
Gambia
Georgia (Republic of)
Germany
Ghana
Gibraltar
Global programs
Greater Antilles
Greece
Greenland
Grenada
Guadeloupe
Guatemala
Guernsey
Guinea
Guinea-Bissau
Guyana
Haiti
Honduras
Hong Kong
Hungary
Iceland
India
Indonesia
Iran
Iraq
Ireland
Isle of Man
Israel
Italy
Ivory Coast
Jamaica
Japan
Jersey
Jordan
Kazakhstan
Kenya
Kiribati
Kosovo
Kuwait
Kyrgyzstan
Laos
Latin America
Latvia
Lebanon
Leeward Islands
Lesotho
Lesser Antilles
Liberia
Libya
Liechtenstein
Lithuania
Luxembourg
Macau
Macedonia
Madagascar
Malawi
Malaysia
Maldives
Mali
Malta
Marshall Islands
Martinique
Mauritania
Mauritius
Mexico
Middle East
Moldova
Monaco
Mongolia
Montenegro
Montserrat
Morocco and the Western Sahara
Mozambique
Namibia
Nauru
Nepal
Netherlands
Netherlands Antilles
New Caledonia
New Zealand
Nicaragua
Niger
Nigeria
North Korea
North Africa
Northern Ireland
Norway
Oceania
Oman
Pakistan
Palau
Panama
Papua New Guinea
Paraguay
Peru
Philippines
Poland
Portugal
Qatar
Romania
Russia
Rwanda
Saint Kitts-Nevis
Saint Lucia
Saint Vincent & the Grenadines
Samoa
Sao Tome and Principe
Saudi Arabia
Scandinavia
Scotland
Senegal

Serbia
Seychelles
Sierra Leone
Singapore
Slovakia
Slovenia
Solomon Islands
Somalia, Somaliland and Puntland
South Africa
South America
South Asia
South Korea
South Sudan
Southeast Asia
Southern Africa
Soviet Union (Former)
Spain
Sri Lanka
Sub-Saharan Africa
Sudan
Suriname
Swaziland
Sweden
Switzerland
Syria
Tahiti
Taiwan
Tajikistan
Tanzania, Zanzibar and Pemba
Thailand
Togo
Tonga
Trinidad & Tobago
Tunisia
Turkey
Turkmenistan
Turks & Caicos Islands
Tuvalu
Uganda
Ukraine
United Arab Emirates
United Kingdom
Uruguay
Uzbekistan
Vanuatu
Vatican City
Venezuela
Vietnam
Wales
West Bank/Gaza
Western Africa
Windward Islands
Yemen
Yugoslavia (Former)
Zambia
Zimbabwe

Afghanistan
Massachusetts: Barakat 1432

Africa
California: Alalusi 78, Annenberg 86, CW 176, Grass 232, Hilton 251, Lee 295, Open 349, Roth 388
Georgia: Bancker-Williams 854, Coca 864, Georgia 878
Illinois: Libra 1050
Kansas: Lloyd 1267
Maine: Catalyst 1326
Minnesota: Porter 1729, Sundance 1742
Missouri: Monsanto 1803
New York: Abraham 2023, Arcus 2040, Carnegie 2085, Clark 2098, Ford 2160, IBM 2227, JPMorgan 2242, Open 2343, PepsiCo 2354, Rockefeller 2390, Unbound 2480
Oregon: Lemelson 2857, NIKE 2865
Pennsylvania: Alcoa 2882, Huston 2973, PPG 3018
Tennessee: International 3142, Maclellan 3146
Virginia: Loyola 3453
Washington: Children's 3501, Gates 3516, Starbucks 3565
Wisconsin: Wagner 3666

Albania
New York: Trust 2477

Angola
Texas: Baker 3170, International 3269

Antarctica
New York: Tinker 2467

Argentina
California: Conservation 165, Foundation 202, Mattel 312
Colorado: First 496
Illinois: Mondelez 1064, Motorola 1066
Minnesota: Mosaic 1718
Missouri: Monsanto 1803
New York: American 2034, Deutsche 2134, JPMorgan 2242
Texas: Bolivar 3179

Armenia
New York: Trust 2477

Asia
California: Alalusi 78, Annenberg 86, Christensen 151, CW 176, Hilton 251, International 261, Open 349, Spencer 424
Connecticut: Praxair 606
Georgia: Georgia 878
Illinois: Libra 1050
Missouri: Monsanto 1803
New York: Abraham 2023, Ford 2160, Freeman 2164, IBM 2227, JPMorgan 2242, Open 2343, PepsiCo 2354
Oregon: Lemelson 2857
Pennsylvania: Alcoa 2882, PPG 3018
Tennessee: Maclellan 3146
Virginia: Blue 3422, Loyola 3453
Washington: Gates 3516, Starbucks 3565

Australia
California: Christensen 151, Las 291, Mattel 312
Colorado: First 496
Florida: Jaffer 763, Samstag 813
Georgia: Coca 864
Illinois: Mondelez 1064
Massachusetts: State 1550
New York: American 2034, Commonwealth 2106
Pennsylvania: Alcoa 2882
Texas: BP 3181, Tingari-Silverton 3368

Austria
Colorado: Avenir 473, First 496
Iowa: Rockwell 1237
Massachusetts: State 1550
New York: Kade 2243
Pennsylvania: Alcoa 2882, Botstiber 2898, Respironics 3023

Azerbaijan
New York: Trust 2477

Bahamas
New York: Credit 2118
Ohio: Marafiki 2731

Bangladesh
New York: PepsiCo 2354
Oregon: NIKE 2865

Belarus
New York: Trust 2477

Belgium
Illinois: Motorola 1066
Massachusetts: State 1550

Belize
Wisconsin: Wagner 3666

Bermuda
Virginia: Truland 3482
Wisconsin: Wagner 3666

Bolivia
Wisconsin: Wagner 3666

Bosnia and Herzegovina
New York: Trust 2477

Brazil
California: Cuore 172, Mattel 312, Thiel 434
Connecticut: Praxair 606
Illinois: Mondelez 1064, Motorola 1066
Michigan: Kellogg 1628
Minnesota: Mosaic 1718
Missouri: Monsanto 1803
New York: Credit 2118, Deutsche 2134, JPMorgan 2242, MetLife 2307, Overbrook 2345
Oregon: NIKE 2865
Pennsylvania: Alcoa 2882, KL 2978

Bulgaria
New York: Trust 2477

Burkina Faso
Missouri: Monsanto 1803

Cambodia
Massachusetts: Grinspoon 1479
Minnesota: McKnight 1715
New York: Matisse 2295

Canada
Alaska: Nash 37
California: Mattel 312, Thiel 434
Colorado: Kinder 510
Florida: Jaffer 763
Illinois: Joyce 1040, Mondelez 1064, Motorola 1066
Iowa: Rockwell 1237
Maryland: ABMRF 1344
Massachusetts: Kendall 1494, State 1550, Sweet 1554
Michigan: Erb 1599
Minnesota: Andersen 1678, Mosaic 1718, Patterson 1726
Missouri: Monsanto 1803
New Jersey: Horner 1941
New York: American 2034, Bronfman 2074, Buffalo 2078, Commonwealth 2106, Credit 2118, Cummings 2120, Deutsche 2134, Guggenheim 2194, IBM 2227, JPMorgan 2242, M.A.C. 2287, Mayday 2296, PepsiCo 2354, Shatford 2417, Tsadra 2478
North Carolina: Burroughs 2534
Ohio: Eaton 2693, OMNOVA 2759
Pennsylvania: Alcoa 2882, Carnegie 2906, Respironics 3023
Texas: Summerlee 3361
Washington: Starbucks 3565, Wilburforce 3572

Caribbean
California: CW 176
Colorado: General 501
Minnesota: Porter 1729
New York: Ford 2160, Guggenheim 2194, Open 2343
Pennsylvania: Alcoa 2882
Virginia: Loyola 3453, WestWind 3486

Cayman Islands
Massachusetts: State 1550

Central America
California: Arntz 93

Colorado: General 501
Minnesota: Porter 1729
New Mexico: Aurora 2007
Pennsylvania: Alcoa 2882
Wisconsin: Wagner 3666

Central Asia
New York: Open 2343

Chile
California: Allende 79, Conservation 165, Foundation 202, Marisla 310, Mattel 312
Georgia: Coca 864
Massachusetts: Patagonia 1524
Minnesota: Mosaic 1718
Missouri: Monsanto 1803
New York: Deutsche 2134, JPMorgan 2242, Weeden 2496

China
Alabama: Atlantis 2
California: Alalusi 78, Applied 88, Hewlett 248, Lingnan 301, Mattel 312, Scovel 399
Georgia: Coca 864
Illinois: Motorola 1066
Kansas: Lloyd 1267
Massachusetts: Lincoln 1503
Minnesota: Mosaic 1718
Missouri: Monsanto 1803
Nevada: Tang 1873
New Jersey: American 1902
New York: American 2034, Carnegie 2085, PepsiCo 2354, Rockefeller 2389
Ohio: Cardinal 2677, OMNOVA 2759
Pennsylvania: Alcoa 2882
Texas: BP 3181
Virginia: Blue 3422
Washington: Starbucks 3565

Colombia
California: Fund 210
Georgia: Coca 864
Missouri: Monsanto 1803
New York: Genesis 2173, JPMorgan 2242

Costa Rica
Florida: Community 725
Georgia: Guanacaste 884

Croatia
New York: Trust 2477

Cyprus
Illinois: Lascaris 1048
Texas: Chrest 3194

Czech Republic
New York: Trust 2477

Denmark
Pennsylvania: Respironics 3023

Developing Countries
California: Rivendell 384
Massachusetts: Conservation 1454
New Jersey: International 1946
Ohio: Brush 2673
Oregon: Lemelson 2857, NIKE 2865
Texas: PHM 3320
Virginia: Loyola 3453
Washington: Gates 3516

Dominican Republic
Ohio: Cardinal 2677, Marion 2733

East Jerusalem
District of Columbia: Foundation 661
New York: Jabara 2235, Sparkplug 2441

Eastern Africa
Texas: Radler 3330

Eastern Asia
New York: Luce 2286

Eastern Europe
California: CW 176
Michigan: Mott 1645
New York: Open 2343, Trust 2477
Tennessee: Maclellan 3146

Ecuador
California: Fund 210
New York: Overbrook 2345

Egypt
New York: Jabara 2235

El Salvador
Florida: Kazma 766

England
California: Guthy-Jackson 237
District of Columbia: Butler 655
Florida: Jaffer 763
Illinois: Buffett 975, Motorola 1066
New Jersey: Horner 1941
New York: Berg 2062, Goldman 2181
Ohio: Lerner 2722
Texas: A Glimmer 3158

Estonia
New York: Trust 2477

Ethiopia
California: Christensen 151
Massachusetts: Barr 1433
Texas: A Glimmer 3158

Europe
California: Annenberg 86, Applied 88
Georgia: Coca 864, Georgia 878
Illinois: Libra 1050
Massachusetts: Lincoln 1503, State 1550
Missouri: Monsanto 1803
New York: IBM 2227, JPMorgan 2242, Kade 2243, Kress 2263
Pennsylvania: Alcoa 2882, PPG 3018
Texas: BP 3181
Washington: Gates 3516, Starbucks 3565

Finland
New York: Towerbrook 2473

France
California: Mattel 312, Thiel 434
Connecticut: Albers 551
Illinois: Mondelez 1064, Motorola 1066
Iowa: Rockwell 1237
Massachusetts: State 1550
New York: American 2034, Tsadra 2478
Ohio: OMNOVA 2759
Pennsylvania: M.E. 2989
Virginia: Price 3472

Georgia
New York: Trust 2477

Germany
California: Mattel 312
Colorado: First 496
Illinois: Mondelez 1064
Massachusetts: State 1550
New York: American 2034, Kade 2243, Weill 2499
Pennsylvania: Respironics 3023
Texas: BP 3181

Ghana
New York: PepsiCo 2354
Ohio: Noble 2753

Global Programs
California: Hilton 251, Packard 357
Colorado: Society 534
District of Columbia: Case 658
New York: Clark 2098, Open 2343, Rockefeller 2390

Greece
Colorado: First 496
Illinois: Lascaris 1048
Massachusetts: Memorial 1512

Guatemala
California: International 261
District of Columbia: Palmer 677
Missouri: Monsanto 1803
Texas: International 3269

Haiti
Massachusetts: Barr 1433
Michigan: Kellogg 1628
Texas: International 3269

Honduras
Iowa: Wahlert 1244
Minnesota: Pentair 1727
Missouri: Monsanto 1803
New Hampshire: Christian 1881
Ohio: Noble 2753
Texas: International 3269

Hong Kong
California: Lingnan 301, Mattel 312
New York: American 2034

Hungary
California: Mattel 312
New York: Trust 2477

Iceland
Virginia: Eiriksson 3436

India
California: Applied 88, Hewlett 248, International 261, Mattel 312, Wadhwani 450
Connecticut: Praxair 606, SCA 612
Florida: Jaffer 763, Patel 797
Hawaii: Watumull 939
Illinois: MacArthur 1056
Kansas: Lloyd 1267
Massachusetts: Barakat 1432, Barr 1433, State 1550
Minnesota: Mosaic 1718
Missouri: Monsanto 1803
New York: American 2034, Bloomberg 2066, Flowering 2159, MetLife 2307, PepsiCo 2354, Tandon 2458, Tsadra 2478
Ohio: OMNOVA 2759
Oregon: NIKE 2865
Pennsylvania: KL 2978, Pilgrim 3016
Texas: Dell 3213, Jiv 3270, Oldham 3308
Washington: Foundation 3515, Singh 3563

Indonesia
California: Mattel 312
Illinois: Mondelez 1064
Missouri: Monsanto 1803

Iran
New York: Jabara 2235

Iraq
New York: Jabara 2235

Ireland
Massachusetts: State 1550
Texas: A Glimmer 3158

Israel
California: David 178, Leichtag 297, Nazarian 341, Rifkind 383, Sassoon 395
Colorado: Merage 519
District of Columbia: Foundation 661

Florida: Arison 691, Chester 720, Greenburg 752, Wollowick 843
Georgia: Rosenberg 910
Illinois: American 960, Crown 997, Stern 1100
Louisiana: Wiener 1322
Maryland: Ames 1346, Blaustein 1349, Cohen 1355, Dahan 1364, Meyerhoff 1393, Morningstar 1397, Polinger 1405, Weinberg 1416
Massachusetts: Grinspoon 1479
Minnesota: Kaplan 1707
Missouri: Millstone 1801
New Jersey: Berrie 1908, Syms 1999
New York: Abba's 2021, Assael 2046, AVI 2051, Berg 2062, Bronfman 2074, Bydale 2082, Cote 2114, Cummings 2121, Dobkin 2140, Gimprich 2180, Goldman 2182, Klein 2254, Klein 2255, Littauer 2282, Nash 2320, Sparkplug 2441, Tikvah 2465, Tisch 2469
North Carolina: Kramer 2581
Ohio: Maltz 2727, Mandel 2729, Omnicare 2758
Oklahoma: ROI 2827, Schusterman 2829
Rhode Island: Dorot 3071, King 3080
Texas: Feldman 3230
Virginia: Samberg 3478

Italy
California: Mattel 312, Parsemus 358, Thiel 434
Georgia: Coca 864
Idaho: Micron 950
Illinois: Buffett 975, Mondelez 1064
Massachusetts: State 1550
New Jersey: Berrie 1908
New York: American 2034, Goldman 2181, Towerbrook 2473
Pennsylvania: Huston 2973
Texas: Bolivar 3179

Japan
California: Applied 88, Mattel 312
District of Columbia: Sasakawa 680
Georgia: Coca 864
Illinois: Kobe 1045
Massachusetts: State 1550
New York: American 2034
Texas: BP 3181
Washington: Goodwin 3519

Jordan
New York: Jabara 2235

Kazakhstan
New York: Trust 2477

Kenya
California: Christensen 151, International 261
Florida: DeMoss 735, Jaffer 763
Maryland: Mpala 1398, Northern 1402
Missouri: Monsanto 1803
Ohio: Marafiki 2731, Noble 2753
Oregon: NIKE 2865

Kosovo
New York: Rockefeller 2389, Trust 2477

Kyrgyz Republic
California: Christensen 151
New York: Trust 2477

Laos
California: McConnell 318
Illinois: Walgreens 1109
Minnesota: McKnight 1715

Latin America
California: CW 176, Fund 210, Grass 232, Hewlett 248, Open 349
District of Columbia: Wallace 683
Georgia: Bancker-Williams 854, Coca 864, Murphy 898
Illinois: Libra 1050
Massachusetts: Lincoln 1503, Merck 1514
Michigan: Mott 1645
Minnesota: Sundance 1742
Missouri: Monsanto 1803
New York: Clark 2098, Deutsche 2134, Ford 2160, Guggenheim 2194, IBM 2227, JPMorgan 2242, MetLife 2307, Open 2343, Overbrook 2345, Tinker 2467, Weeden 2496
Oregon: Lemelson 2857
Virginia: Blue 3422, Loyola 3453, WestWind 3486
Washington: Starbucks 3565

Latvia
New York: Trust 2477

Lebanon
District of Columbia: El-Hibri 659
New York: Jabara 2235

Lithuania
New York: Trust 2477

Luxembourg
Massachusetts: State 1550

Macedonia
New York: Trust 2477

Malawi
Missouri: Monsanto 1803
Texas: International 3269

Malaysia
California: Mattel 312

Mexico
California: Arntz 93, Christensen 151, Fund 210, Marisla 310, Mattel 312
Colorado: General 501
District of Columbia: Palmer 677
Illinois: MacArthur 1056, Mondelez 1064, Motorola 1066
Maine: Golden 1329
Michigan: Kellogg 1628
Missouri: Monsanto 1803
New York: American 2034, Deutsche 2134, JPMorgan 2242, MetLife 2307, Overbrook 2345, PepsiCo 2354, Tinker 2467
Ohio: Cardinal 2677
Pennsylvania: Alcoa 2882
Texas: International 3269, Paso 3312, Summerlee 3361
Washington: Ji 3528

Middle East
California: Alalusi 78, CW 176, Firedoll 198, Open 349
District of Columbia: El-Hibri 659, Foundation 661
Kansas: Lloyd 1267
Massachusetts: State 1550
New York: Arcus 2040, Clark 2098, Ford 2160, JPMorgan 2242
Pennsylvania: PPG 3018
Tennessee: Maclellan 3146
Washington: Starbucks 3565

Moldova
New York: Trust 2477

Mongolia
New York: Trust 2477

Montenegro
New York: Rockefeller 2389, Trust 2477

Namibia
Ohio: Noble 2753

Nepal
California: McConnell 318
New York: Tsadra 2478

Netherlands
California: Thiel 434
Kansas: Lloyd 1267
Massachusetts: State 1550
New Jersey: American 1902
New York: American 2034

New Zealand
New York: Commonwealth 2106

Nicaragua
Ohio: Noble 2753

Nigeria
Illinois: MacArthur 1056
Oregon: NIKE 2865

Northern Africa
New York: Jabara 2235

Northern Ireland
Pennsylvania: M.E. 2989

Oceania
California: CW 176, Packard 357
Missouri: Monsanto 1803

Pakistan
Massachusetts: Barakat 1432

Papua New Guinea
California: Christensen 151

Paraguay
Alaska: Nash 37
Missouri: Monsanto 1803
Oregon: NIKE 2865

Peru
California: Fund 210
New York: Deutsche 2134, JPMorgan 2242, MetLife 2307
Washington: Foundation 3515

Philippines
Georgia: Coca 864
Illinois: Mondelez 1064
Missouri: Monsanto 1803
Texas: BP 3181, International 3269
Wisconsin: Wagner 3666

Poland
California: Mattel 312, Peszynski 366
Illinois: Motorola 1066
Massachusetts: State 1550
New York: Trust 2477
Pennsylvania: Copernicus 2928

Qatar
Massachusetts: State 1550

Romania
New York: Trust 2477

Russia
Georgia: Coca 864
Illinois: MacArthur 1056, Mondelez 1064
Michigan: Mott 1645
Minnesota: Sundance 1742
New York: Carnegie 2085, Trust 2477, Weeden 2496
Pennsylvania: Alcoa 2882

Scotland
Georgia: Imlay 888
Illinois: Driehaus 1002
New York: Weill 2499

Serbia
New York: Rockefeller 2389, Trust 2477

Sierra Leone
Maine: Catalyst 1326

Singapore
California: Applied 88
Idaho: Micron 950
Illinois: Motorola 1066
Massachusetts: State 1550
New York: American 2034, Flowering 2159

Slovakia
New York: Trust 2477

Slovenia
New York: Trust 2477

South Africa
Massachusetts: State 1550
Michigan: Mott 1645
Missouri: Monsanto 1803
New York: Mellon 2302
Ohio: Noble 2753

South America
California: Foundation 202, Smith 416
Connecticut: Praxair 606
Georgia: Georgia 878
Minnesota: Porter 1729
New Mexico: Aurora 2007
Pennsylvania: Alcoa 2882
Virginia: Blue 3422
Washington: Gates 3516
Wisconsin: Wagner 3666

South Korea
California: Applied 88
Massachusetts: State 1550
New York: MetLife 2307

South Sudan
Texas: Radler 3330

Southeastern Asia
California: Open 349
New York: Arcus 2040, Luce 2286, Open 2343, Rockefeller 2390
Virginia: Loyola 3453

Southern Africa
Michigan: Kellogg 1628
New York: Heron 2211
Wisconsin: Sand 3654

Southern Asia
California: Hewlett 248, Packard 357

Soviet Union
District of Columbia: Wallace 683
Maryland: Weinberg 1416

Spain
California: Mattel 312
Illinois: Mondelez 1064
New York: American 2034

Sri Lanka
California: International 261
Pennsylvania: KL 2978

Sub-Saharan Africa
California: Hewlett 248, Packard 357
Massachusetts: Barr 1433
New York: Carnegie 2085

Sweden
Pennsylvania: Respironics 3023

Switzerland
California: Foundation 204
District of Columbia: Wyss 685
Massachusetts: State 1550
New York: Bloomberg 2066
Texas: Levant 3280

Syria
New York: Jabara 2235

Taiwan
California: Applied 88
Massachusetts: State 1550
New York: American 2034

Tajikistan
California: Christensen 151
New York: Trust 2477

Tanzania
Florida: DeMoss 735, Jaffer 763
Minnesota: King 1708, McKnight 1715
Oregon: NIKE 2865

Thailand
California: International 261, Mattel 312
District of Columbia: Sasakawa 680
Missouri: Monsanto 1803
Ohio: OMNOVA 2759

Timor-Leste
Texas: Tingari-Silverton 3368

Turkey
California: Christensen 151
Texas: Chrest 3194

Turkmenistan
New York: Trust 2477

Uganda
Alaska: Nash 37
Florida: DeMoss 735
Minnesota: McKnight 1715
Missouri: Monsanto 1803
Oregon: NIKE 2865
Washington: Luke 3537

Ukraine
Michigan: Mott 1645
New York: Trust 2477

United Kingdom
California: Google 231, Mattel 312, Peszynski 366, Thiel 434
Colorado: First 496
District of Columbia: Butler 655
Illinois: Mondelez 1064
Iowa: Rockwell 1237
Kansas: Lloyd 1267
Massachusetts: Foundation 1489, State 1550
Missouri: Monsanto 1803
New York: American 2034, Commonwealth 2106, Diamond 2135, PepsiCo 2354, St. George's 2445, Towerbrook 2473, Unbound 2480
Oregon: Wyss 2878
Pennsylvania: M.E. 2989
Texas: BP 3181
Virginia: Bosack 3423, Fox 3439
Washington: Starbucks 3565

Uruguay
Missouri: Monsanto 1803

Uzbekistan
New York: Trust 2477

Vanuatu
California: Christensen 151

Venezuela
Texas: Bolivar 3179

Vietnam
Minnesota: McKnight 1715

West Bank/Gaza (Palestinian Territories)
District of Columbia: Foundation 661
New York: Jabara 2235, Sparkplug 2441

Yemen
New York: Jabara 2235

Zambia
Oregon: NIKE 2865

Zimbabwe
Pennsylvania: Pilgrim 3016

TYPES OF SUPPORT INDEX

List of terms: Terms for the major types of support used in this index are listed below with definitions.

Index: In the index itself, foundation entries are arranged under each term by state location, abbreviated name, and sequence number. Foundations in boldface type make grants on a national, regional, or international basis. The others generally limit giving to the state or city in which they are located.

Advocacy: cash grants for services related to advocacy, including advocating for better assistance in various program areas (for example school reform, full access to health care, legal reform, environmental clean-up work, etc.) and providing assistance in planning advocacy campaigns.

Annual campaigns: any organized effort by a nonprofit to secure gifts on an annual basis; also called annual appeals.

Building/renovation: money raised for construction, renovation, remodeling, or rehabilitation of buildings; may be part of an organization's capital campaign.

Camperships: funding to organizations to provide partial or full tuition subsidies to enable participants who would not otherwise be financially able to participate in fee-based camping programs.

Capital campaigns: a campaign, usually extending over a period of years, to raise substantial funds for enduring purposes, such as building or endowment funds.

Cause-related marketing: linking gifts to charity with marketing promotions. This may involve donating products which will then be auctioned or given away in a drawing with the proceeds benefiting a charity. The advertising campaign for the product will be combined with the promotion for the charity. In other cases it will be advertised that when a customer buys the product a certain amount of the proceeds will be donated to charity. Often gifts made to charities stemming from cause-related marketing are not called charitable donations and may be assigned as expenses to the department in charge of the program. Public affairs and marketing are the departments usually involved.

Computer technology: grants to acquire, upgrade or develop computer technology. Includes hardware, software, peripherals, systems, networking components and mobile devices.

Conferences/seminars: a grant to cover the expenses of holding a conference or seminar.

Consulting services: professional staff support provided by the foundation to a nonprofit to consult on a project of mutual interest or to evaluate services (not a cash grant).

Continuing support: a grant that is renewed on a regular basis.

Curriculum development: grants to schools, colleges, universities, and educational support organizations to develop general or discipline-specific curricula.

Debt reduction: also known as deficit financing. A grant to reduce the recipient organization's indebtedness; frequently refers to mortgage payments.

Donated equipment: surplus furniture, office machines, paper, appliances, laboratory apparatus, or other items that may be given to charities, schools, or hospitals.

Donated land: land or developed property. Institutions of higher education often receive gifts of real estate; land has also been given to community groups for housing development or for parks or recreational facilities.

Donated products: companies giving away what they make or produce. Product donations can include periodic clothing donations to a shelter for the homeless or regular donations of pharmaceuticals to a health clinic resulting in a reliable supply.

Emergency funds: a one-time grant to cover immediate short-term funding needs on an emergency basis.

Employee matching gifts: a contribution to a charitable organization by a corporate employee which is matched by a similar contribution from the employer. Many corporations support employee matching gift programs in higher education to stimulate their employees to give to the college or university of their choice. In addition, many foundations support matching gift programs for their officers and directors.

Employee volunteer services: an ongoing coordinated effort through which the company promotes involvement with nonprofits on the part of employees. The involvement may be during work time or after hours. (Employees may also volunteer on their own initiative; however, that is not described as corporate volunteerism). Many companies honor their employees with awards for outstanding volunteer efforts. In making cash donations, many favor the organizations with which their employees have worked as volunteers. Employee volunteerism runs the gamut from school tutoring programs to sales on work premises of employee-made crafts or baked goods to benefit nonprofits. Management of the programs can range from fully-staffed offices of corporate volunteerism to a part-time coordinating responsibility on the part of one employee.

Employee-related scholarships: a scholarship program funded by a company-sponsored foundation usually for children of employees; programs are frequently administered by the National Merit Scholarship Corporation which is responsible for selection of scholars.

Endowments: a bequest or gift intended to be kept permanently and invested to provide income for continued support of an organization.

Equipment: a grant to purchase equipment, furnishings, or other materials.

Exchange programs: usually refers to funds for educational exchange programs for foreign students.

Faculty/staff development: grants to institutions or organizations to train or further educate staff or faculty members

Fellowships: usually indicates funds awarded to educational institutions to support fellowship programs. A few foundations award fellowships directly to individuals.

Film/video/radio: grants to fund a specific film, video, or radio production.

General/operating support: a grant made to further the general purpose or work of an organization, rather than for a specific purpose or project; also called unrestricted grants.

Grants to individuals: awards made directly by the foundation to individuals rather than to nonprofit organizations; includes aid to the needy. (See also "Fellowships," "Scholarships—to individuals," and "Student loans—to individuals.")

In-kind gifts: a contribution of equipment, supplies, or other property as distinct from a monetary grant. Some organizations may also donate space or staff time as an in-kind contribution.

Income development: grants for fundraising, marketing, and to expand audience base.

Internship funds: usually indicates funds awarded to an institution or organization to support an internship program rather than a grant to an individual.

Land acquisition: a grant to purchase real estate property.

Lectureships: see "Curriculum development."

Loaned talent: an aspect of employee volunteerism. It differs from the usual definition of such in that it usually involves loaned professionals and executive staff who are helping a nonprofit in an area involving their particular skills. Loaned talents can assist a nonprofit in strategic planning, dispute resolution or negotiation services, office administration, real estate technical assistance, personnel policies, lobbying, consulting, fundraising, and legal and tax advice.

Loans: see "Program-related investments/loans" and "Student loans—to individuals."

Loans—to individuals: assistance distributed directly to individuals in the form of loans.

Management development/capacity building: grants for salaries, staff support, staff training, strategic and long-term planning, capacity building, budgeting and accounting.

Matching/challenge support: a grant which is made to match funds provided by another donor. (See also "Employee matching gifts.")

Mission-related investments/loans: Market-rate loans or other investments (as distinguished from grants) to organizations to finance projects related to the foundation's stated charitable purpose and interests. Organizations invested in may be for-profit entities.

Operating budgets: see "General/operating support."

Pro bono services: pro bono services rendered by a company, professional services firm, intermediary,association or individual professional leveraging the core competencies and expertise of the professional(s) engaged to meet the client's need.

Pro bono services-advocacy: pro bono consulting assistance related to advocacy, including advocating for better services in various program areas (for example school reform, full access to health care, legal reform, environmental clean-up work, etc.) and providing assistance in planning advocacy campaigns that will follow current legal guidelines preventing certain kinds of advocacy by nonprofits

Pro bono services-board: pro bono consulting assistance in board effectiveness assessment, board recruitment process design, board reporting, meeting facilitation, executive coaching, and performance review.

Pro bono services-communications/public relations: pro bono consulting assistance in external communications and public relations, including but not limited to assistance with the development of an annual report, brochure, newsletter design, and/or public service announcement.

Pro bono services-financial management: pro bono consulting assistance in financial management, including but not limited to program cost analysis, financial audit, financial controls assessment and design, budgeting process design, pricing strategy, and purchase and supply chain audit.

Pro bono services-fundraising: Pro bono consulting assistance in programs or projects directly relating to fundraising. These may include event planning and production, executive fundraising coaching, donor segmentation, in-kind opportunity assessment, capital campaign design and management, and the development of capital campaign materials.

Pro bono services-human resources: pro bono consulting assistance in the area of human resources, including a strategic assessment and recommendations for a human resources plan, organizational diversity plan, performance management system, back office systems implementation, staff compensation and incentive plan, staff training and development plan, and an internal communications plan.

Pro bono services-interactive/website technology: pro bono consulting assistance in website technology, including the design and development of a basic website, interactive website, intranet, and extranet.

Pro bono services-legal: pro bono consulting assistance in the area of legal support, including donation of legal services in court situations, review of various legal documents, including those related to incorporation and other law, justice, and counsel issues.

Pro bono services-marketing/branding: pro bono consulting assistance in marketing and branding. Programs or projects may cover issues such as a program marketing, organizational positioning and key messages, visual identity or re-naming.

Pro bono services-medical: pro bono consulting assistance in the medical area, including donation of medical services and equipment.

Pro bono services-strategic management: pro bono consulting assistance in the area of strategic management, including the development of a strategic plan, refined mission, environmental and sustainability policy and plan, internal capacity assessment, strengths, weaknesses, opportunities, and threats analysis, competitive analysis, earned income business plan, geographic expansion plan, and logic model design

Pro bono services-technology infrastructure: pro bono consulting assistance in technology infrastructure such as donor database implementation, the development of an organizational IT plan, installation of office networking, remote IT access set up, and program database implementation.

Professorships: a grant to an educational institution to endow a professorship or chair.

Program development: grants to support specific projects or programs as opposed to general purpose grants.

Program evaluation: grants to evaluate a specific project or program; includes awards both to agencies to pay for evaluation costs and to research institutes and other program evaluators.

Program-related investments/loans: a loan is any temporary award of funds that must be repaid. A program-related investment is a loan or other investment (as distinguished from a grant) made by a foundation to another organization for a project related to the foundation's stated charitable purpose and interests.

Public relations services: may include printing and duplicating, audio-visual and graphic arts services, helping to plan special events such as festivals, piggyback advertising (advertisements that mention a company while also promoting a nonprofit), and public service advertising.

Publication: a grant to fund reports or other publications issued by a nonprofit resulting from research or projects of interest to the foundation.

Renovation projects: see "Building/renovation."

Research: usually indicates funds awarded to institutions to cover costs of investigations and clinical trials. Research grants for individuals are usually referred to as fellowships.

Scholarship funds: a grant to an educational institution or organization to support a scholarship program, mainly for students at the undergraduate level. (See also "Employee-related scholarships.")

Scholarships—to individuals: assistance awarded directly to individuals in the form of educational grants or scholarships. (See also "Employee-related scholarships.")

Seed money: a grant or contribution used to start a new project or organization. Seed grants may cover salaries and other operating expenses of a new project. Also known as "start-up funds."

Special projects: see "Program development."

Sponsorships: endorsements of charities by corporations; or corporate contributions to all or part of a charitable event.

Student aid: see "Fellowships," "Scholarships—to individuals," and "Student loans—to individuals."

Student loans—to individuals: assistance awarded directly to individuals in the form of educational loans.

Technical assistance: operational or management assistance given to nonprofit organizations; may include fundraising assistance, budgeting and financial planning, program planning, legal advice, marketing, and other aids to management. Assistance may be offered directly by a foundation staff member or in the form of a grant to pay for the services of an outside consultant.

Travel awards: funding to organizations to provide awards to individuals to cover transportation and/or out-of-town living expenses while attending a conference or completing a period of studt or special project. Enrollment in a college or university is not a requirement.

Use of facilities: this may include rent free office space for temporary periods, dining and meeting facilities, telecommunications services, mailing services, transportation services, or computer services.

Advocacy

Illinois: Allegretti 958
Nebraska: Cooper 1834
New Hampshire: Finlay 1884

Annual campaigns

Alabama: BBVA 3, Black 4
Arizona: Green 47, Hughes 49, Napier 55
Arkansas: Cabe 67, Endeavor 69, Frueauff 70
California: **Applied 88**, Aratani 89, Atlas 96, Bank 99, Bannerman 100, Barth 101, Bechtel 103, Bechtel, 104, Bengier 109, Clif 152, Community 157, Community 161, Disney 181, Dolby 185, Gellert 215, Getty 218, GGS 219, Haas 239, Hand 241, Jackson 266, Lucas 306, McClatchy 317, Outhwaite 353, Price 373, Simpson 411, Taper 433, **Wilkinson 463**
Colorado: **Daniels 488**, Donnell 491, **Gill 502**, Mullen 522, Schlessman 530, Summit 537, Telluride 538, Yampa 545
Connecticut: Meriden 591, Neuberger 593, Senior 613
Delaware: **AstraZeneca 623**, CenturyLink-Clarke 627, Chaney 628, Lennox 638, Sylvan 648
Florida: Bi-Lo/Winn-Dixie 700, Brown 707, Burns 710, Catalina 716, **Chester 720**, Coral Gables 729, Erdle 740, Greenburg 752, Thomas 831, Wollowick 843
Georgia: Camp-Younts 861, Exposition 873, Georgia 877, **Georgia 878, Imlay 888**, Knox 890, Livingston 893, Marshall 895, Moore 897, Sapelo 911, Southern 915
Hawaii: Atherton 925, Kaneta 936
Illinois: Brach 973, Crown 997, Duchossois 1005, Dunard 1006, Frankel 1017, Kenny's 1044, Logan 1051, Lumpkin 1053, Speh 1097, Square 1099, Tracy 1104, Webb 1113
Indiana: Ball 1121, Brotherhood 1123, Central 1126, DeHaan 1143, Fairbanks 1145, Koch 1167, Kuhne 1169, Tipton 1198
Iowa: Guernsey 1221, Maytag 1229, Wahlert 1244
Kansas: Capitol 1251, Collective 1253, Hutchinson 1260, Sunderland 1278, Topeka 1279
Kentucky: Community 1286
Louisiana: Albemarle 1298, Freeman 1309
Maine: Alfond 1324, Borman 1325, Somers 1341
Maryland: **Cohen 1355**, Delaplaine 1367, Freeman 1373, Gudelsky 1376, Henson 1378, Hirschhorn 1379, Macht 1388, Meyerhoff 1393, **Morningstar 1397**, Richmond 1408, Rosenberg 1409, Straus 1410, Tucker 1415, Zickler 1419
Massachusetts: **Barr 1433**, **Brabson 1438**, Cabot 1443, Cape Cod 1445, Davis 1457, Demoulas 1458, Eastern 1461, Grinspoon 1479, **Kahn 1492**, Krieger 1497, Massachusetts 1508, Miller 1516, Santander 1541, Smith 1546, Williams 1567
Michigan: Community 1589, Dana 1593, Dart 1594, Family 1600, Farver 1601, Gilmore 1612, Granger 1617, **Isabel 1621**, Masco 1637, Morley 1644, Oleson 1649, Onequest 1650, Sanilac 1663, Schmuckal 1664, Van Andel 1669, Vanderweide 1671, Wege 1674
Minnesota: **Andersen 1678**, Briggs 1687, Butler 1688, Donaldson 1692, Frey 1696, Greystone 1700, HRK 1702, **Kaplan 1707**, Larsen 1711, Marbrook 1713, Nash 1720, Opus 1724, **O'Shaughnessy 1725**, RBC 1730, Regis 1732, Riverway 1733, Securian 1739, Winona 1753
Mississippi: Community 1759, Ergon 1761, Mississippi 1769, Regions 1770, Walker 1772
Missouri: Butler 1780, Centene 1782, Community 1783, Laclede 1799, Millstone 1801, Musgrave 1805
Nebraska: Fremont 1836, Hawkins 1838, Oregon 1852, Storz 1854, Zollner 1858
Nevada: Parasol 1868
New Hampshire: Ham 1887, Penates 1893
New Jersey: Banbury 1904, Holzer 1939, Kirby 1952
New Mexico: Santa Fe 2017
New York: Adirondack 2027, Allyn 2032, American 2033, **American 2034**, Barker 2054, Berg 2062, Community 2112, **Diamond 2135**, Farash 2154, Fisher 2157, Freed 2163, Gebbie 2170, Goldman 2183, Heyman 2212, High 2213, Hultquist 2225, Johnson 2240, Knapp 2259, Lee 2271, McGonagle 2299, Mendell 2303, Monteforte 2310, Moore 2311, National 2321, Norwich 2332, NYSE 2336, Rich 2382, Ruffin 2400, Scherman 2409, Schmitt 2410, Schnurmacher 2411, Sulzberger 2451, Thompson 2461, **Towerbrook 2473**, Vidda 2485, Wachenheim 2489, Wachtell, 2490
North Carolina: Bolick 2531, Ferebee 2552, Goodrich 2561, Hanes 2565, Meyer 2594, Olin 2603, Reynolds 2613, Southern 2630
North Dakota: MDU 2652, North Dakota 2653
Ohio: Anderson 2658, Andrews 2659, Ar-Hale 2661, Brown 2672, Cliffs 2681, Community 2682, Dater 2687, Ferro 2697, Fifth 2699, Kettering 2716, KeyBank 2717, Kulas 2721, Macy's 2726, Maltz 2727, Marion 2733, Mayerson 2735, Murphy 2744, Murphy 2745, National 2748, Nippert 2751, NiSource 2752, Nordson 2755, Ohio 2756, **OMNOVA 2759**, Progressive 2764, Reinberger 2765, Salem 2771, Scotford 2779, Sears 2781, Tiffin 2793, Tuscarawas 2795
Oklahoma: Adams 2806, Chapman 2808, Hille 2816, McGee 2820, Merrick 2821, Oklahoma 2823, **Schusterman 2829**, Zarrow 2834
Oregon: Benton 2835, Flowerree 2845, Macdonald 2859, Portland 2868, Woodard 2877
Pennsylvania: **Alcoa 2882**, Ames 2884, Arkema 2885, Baker 2886, Bucks 2900, Buncher 2902, Centre 2909, Charlestein 2911, CIGNA 2917, Community 2923, Ferree 2944, Freas 2954, Hunt 2971, Huston 2973, **KL 2978**, Lazarich 2983, Martin 2991, Patterson 3010, Pottstown 3017, **PPG 3018**, Rangos 3022, Stackpole 3042, Washington 3054, Wyomissing 3059, **Zeldin 3060**
Rhode Island: Biogen 3063, McDonald 3085
South Carolina: Bailey 3096, Springs 3111
Tennessee: First 3135, Frist 3136, HCA 3139, Hutcheson 3141, Phillips 3149, Schmidt 3153, Tucker 3156, Wilson 3157
Texas: Abell 3160, Augur 3168, Bickel 3178, Brown 3183, Burch 3184, Cailloux 3187, Carter 3190, Coates 3197, Fisch 3232, Fish 3233, Fluor 3235, Hamman 3248, Hammill 3249, Herzstein 3256, Hill 3260, Hoglund 3263, **Houston 3266**, Houston 3267, Kinder 3274, Light 3281, Lightner 3282, Lockheed 3284, Luse 3289, **Marshall 3290**, Martinez 3291, McDermott 3293, McKee 3295, Moore 3299, Penney 3315, Rosewood 3340, Sams 3342, Sterling 3358, Trull 3373, Waggoner 3379, Willard 3382, Zachry 3387
Vermont: Tarrant 3416, Windham 3418
Virginia: Pruden 3473, RECO 3474
Washington: Dimmer 3506, Everett 3511, Fales 3512, **Gates 3516**, Harder 3524, Milgard 3543
West Virginia: Eastern 3580, Maier 3584, McDonough 3586
Wisconsin: Alliant 3592, **Baird 3595**, Bemis 3598, **Bradley 3601**, Cornerstone 3608, Elmwood 3614, Johnson 3625, Marshfield 3633, Neese 3639, Oshkosh 3643, Pettit 3645, Pick 3646, Sauey 3655, U.S. 3665, Windhover 3668

Building/renovation

Alabama: Community 9, Community 10
Arizona: APS 39, Green 47, Marshall 54, Napier 55, Piper 57, Webb 64
Arkansas: Cabe 67, Endeavor 69, Frueauff 70, Ross 72
California: Ahmanson 77, Aratani 89, Ayrshire 97, Bank 99, Bannerman 100, Bechtel 103, Bechtel, 104, Beynon 113, Bothin 120, Brisco 127, Community 157, Community 161, Copley 166, Cowell 168, **DJ & T 184**, Dolby 185, Eisner 189, Finley 197, Firedoll 198, Fremont 207, Fusenot 211, Gellert 215, Gilmore 221, Gold 228, GSF 235, Haas 239, Hannon 242, Hewlett 249, **Hilton 251**, Hoag 253, Humboldt 257, Jackson 266, Jones 270, **Keck 276**, Kelly 278, Kern 279, Kvamme 286, LA84 287, Lesher 299, **Lingnan 301**, Los Altos 305, Lucas 306, Marin 309, **McConnell 318**, Outhwaite 353, Parsons 359, Pasadena 361, Patron 363, **Peszynski 366**, PG&E 367, Rancho 378, Rossi 387, Sacramento 391, Samuelsson 392, San Luis 393, Santa Barbara 394, Shasta 401, Sonora 420, Taper 433, Valley 445, Weingart 456, Wilsey 464
Colorado: Animal 472, Ballantine 474, Bonfils 475, **Daniels 488**, El Pomar 492, Foundation 498, Griffin 504, Marquez 515, Mullen 522, Rose 528, Seay 532, Stratton 536, Summit 537, Vradenburg 544, Yampa 545

Connecticut: 1772 547, **Calder 558**, Community 562, Community 563, Connecticut 564, **Deupree 571**, Matthies 590, NewAlliance 595, **Praxair 606**, Roberts 608

Delaware: AEC 622, Chaney 628, Delaware 630, Kutz 637, Lennox 638, Longwood 639

District of Columbia: Bou 654, Graham 663

Florida: Bank 695, Benjamin 699, Bi-Lo/Winn-Dixie 700, Bush 712, Chapman 717, Conn 728, Coral Gables 729, Kennedy 767, **Knight 771**, Munroe 793, Phillips 800, Pinellas 801, Publix 804, Quantum 805, Reinhold 808, Selby 816, Southwest 823, Thomas 831

Georgia: Abreu 846, Amos 848, Amos-Cheves 849, Atlanta 852, Campbell 860, Community 867, Exposition 873, EZ 874, **Georgia 878**, Harland 885, **Imlay 888**, Knox 890, Lanier 891, Livingston 893, Marshall 895, Moore 897, Pitts 904, Sewell 914, Trailsend 916, Tull 917, University 918, Woodward 923

Hawaii: Atherton 925, Baldwin 926, Campbell 928, Castle 930, Cooke 932, McInerny 938

Idaho: Angels 943, CHC 945, Cunningham 946, Idaho 948

Illinois: Adams 956, Bersted 966, Brach 973, Chicago 982, Coleman 986, Community 991, Community 992, Crown 997, DeKalb 999, DuPage 1008, Edwardsville 1010, Field 1014, Frankel 1017, **Grainger 1024**, Hunt 1036, Jackson 1038, Kaufman 1043, Logan 1051, Omron 1070, Pritzker 1078, Speh 1097, Square 1099, Walter 1110, Webb 1113

Indiana: Ball 1121, Brotherhood 1123, Brown 1124, Central 1126, Cole 1127, Community 1129, Community 1131, Community 1132, Community 1133, Community 1134, Community 1136, Dearborn 1141, Decatur 1142, DeKalb 1144, Fairbanks 1145, Fayette 1146, Froderman 1148, Harrison 1155, Hendricks 1157, Henry 1158, Jennings 1162, Johnson 1163, Koch 1167, Kosciusko 1168, Kuhne 1169, LaGrange 1170, Legacy 1171, Madison 1175, Marshall 1176, Master 1177, Noble 1179, Northern 1180, Old 1182, Orange 1184, Portland 1188, Putnam 1189, Rush 1192, Seger 1194, Steel 1196, Tipton 1198, Unity 1201, Wabash 1203, Welborn 1205, Wells 1207, Western 1208

Iowa: Ahrens 1210, Clarinda 1214, Community 1217, Guernsey 1221, Hall-Perrine 1222, HNI 1223, Iowa 1226, Jefferson 1227, Maytag 1229, McElroy 1230, Siouxland 1240, Stebens 1242, Wahlert 1244

Kansas: Beach 1250, Capitol 1251, Collective 1253, Delta 1255, Douglas 1256, Farah 1258, Hansen 1259, Sunderland 1278, Topeka 1279

Kentucky: Blue 1282, Brown 1283, Etscorn 1287, Gheens 1288, Hayswood 1290, Trim 1295

Louisiana: Albemarle 1298, Beaird 1301, Community 1306, Entergy 1308, Freeman 1309, Pennington 1317, Steinhagen 1320

Maine: Alfond 1324, Borman 1325, Hannaford 1330, King 1333, Libra 1334

Maryland: **Ames 1346**, **Blaustein 1349**, **Cohen 1355**, Community 1358, Croft 1362, Dresher 1370, Fowler 1372, Gudelsky 1376, Henson 1378, Meyerhoff 1393, Middendorf 1394, Mid-Shore 1395, Rembrandt 1407, Richmond 1408, Rosenberg 1409, Straus 1410, Tucker 1415, **Weinberg 1416**, Zickler 1419

Massachusetts: **Barr 1433**, Berkman 1434, Boynton 1437, Cabot 1443, Clipper 1449, Community 1453, Davis 1457, DentaQuest 1459, Eastern 1461, Farnsworth 1465, Levy 1501, Massachusetts 1508, Miller 1516, Pardoe 1522, Parker 1523, Phelps 1528, Riley 1534, Sailors' 1539, Santander 1541, Smith 1546, United 1559, Wadleigh 1562, Webster 1565, **Xeric 1570**

Michigan: Alro 1574, Capital 1581, Community 1586, Community 1589, Community 1590, Community 1591, Dalton 1592, Dana 1593, Dart 1594, Davenport 1595, Dow 1597, Farver 1601, Frankenmuth 1606, Fremont 1607, Gilmore 1612, Grand Rapids 1615, Grand 1616, **Isabel 1621**, Jackson 1623, Kahn 1625, Keller 1627, Knight 1630, Lenawee 1634, Marquette 1636, Masco 1637, McGregor 1638, Merillat 1640, Midland 1642, Morley 1644, Mount Pleasant 1647, Oleson 1649, Perrigo 1655, Petoskey 1656, Pokagon 1657, Saginaw 1662, Sanilac 1663, Steelcase 1667, Vanderweide 1671, Wege 1674

Minnesota: **Andersen 1678**, Dayton 1690, Depot 1691, Donaldson 1692, Edina 1694, Greystone 1700, Johnson 1705, **King 1708**, Land 1710, Larsen 1711, Marbrook 1713, McKnight 1715, Midcontinent 1716, Neilson 1721, Opus 1724, Regis 1732, Riverway 1733, Rochester 1735, **Trust 1746**, WCA 1749

Mississippi: Community 1759, Mississippi 1769

Missouri: Anheuser 1774, Boylan 1776, Centene 1782, Community 1783, Curry 1784, Dunn 1787, Gateway 1789, Green 1790, Hall 1793, Hallmark 1794, Laclede 1799, Musgrave 1805, Speas 1813, Walker 1818, Whitaker 1820

Montana: Lynn 1827, Silver 1830, Whitefish 1832

Nebraska: Fremont 1836, Hawkins 1838, Hirschfeld 1839, Kearney 1842, Kiewit 1843, Lexington 1845, Lincoln 1847, Midlands 1848, Mid-Nebraska 1849, Mutual 1850, Oregon 1852, Storz 1854, Zollner 1858

Nevada: Caesars 1860, **Reynolds 1869**, **Tang 1873**

New Hampshire: Alexander 1877, Bean 1878, Ham 1887, Johnson 1889, Lindsay 1890, Penates 1893

New Jersey: Banbury 1904, Beer 1907, Borden 1910, Buehler 1915, Bunbury 1916, Campbell 1917, Hudson 1942, Hyde 1944, Kirby 1952, Leavens 1959, Robertson 1983, Summit 1998, Turrell 2002, Westfield 2004

New Mexico: Chase 2009, Maddox 2014

New York: Adirondack 2027, **Alavi 2030**, Allyn 2032, American 2033, Anderson 2036, **Arcus 2040**, Barker 2054, Brooks 2075, Carvel 2088, Chapman 2090, Chautauqua 2091, Clark 2099, Community 2107, Community 2109, Community 2110, Community 2112, **Cummings 2120**, Cutco 2123, **Deutsche 2134**, **Diamond 2135**, East 2147, Family 2153, Ferraioli 2156, Freed 2163, Gebbie 2170, Gifford 2177, Goldman 2183, Golisano 2185, Heckscher 2205, High 2213, Hoyt 2221, Hudson 2223, Hultquist 2225, Jaharis 2236, **JPMorgan 2242**, Knapp 2259, Legacy 2274, Liberman 2279, MBIA 2297, **Nash 2320**, Northern 2331, Norwich 2332, Ong 2341, Ring 2384, Robinson 2387, **Ross 2396**, Schenectady 2407, Seneca 2415, Snow 2432, Sulzberger 2451, Thompson 2461, Time 2466, Tisch 2469, Truman 2475, Tuttle 2479, Vidda 2485, Wachenheim 2489, Western 2503, Widgeon 2505

North Carolina: Adams 2517, Bolick 2531, Dalton 2542, Duncan 2547, Ferebee 2552, French 2554, Glass 2559, Glenn 2560, Hanes 2565, Hunt 2572, Kramer 2581, Meyer 2594, North Carolina 2599, Olin 2603, Outer 2604, Polk 2609, Reidsville 2611, Reynolds 2614, Smith 2629, Southern 2630, State 2632, Strowd 2633, Tannenbaum 2637

North Dakota: Fargo 2649, MDU 2652, North Dakota 2653

Ohio: Abington 2654, American 2656, Anderson 2658, Ar-Hale 2661, Barberton 2664, **Benedict 2666**, **Bingham 2668**, Brown 2672, Bryan 2674, Cincinnati 2679, Cliffs 2681, Community 2682, Community 2685, Coshocton 2686, Dater 2687, Delaware 2689, Dodero 2691, **Eaton 2692**, Emery 2694, Evans 2695, Fairfield 2696, Ferro 2697, Fifth 2699, Findlay 2700, Fowler 2703, Greene 2707, Hershey 2711, Knoll 2719, Kulas 2721, Licking 2723, Maltz 2727, Marietta 2732, Marion 2733, Mayerson 2735, Middletown 2737, Morgan 2739, Murphy 2744, Murphy 2745, Muskingum 2747, Nippert 2751, NiSource 2752, Nord 2754, Nordson 2755, Ohio 2756, Ohio 2757, **OMNOVA 2759**, Piqua 2763, Reinberger 2765, Richland 2767, Saint 2770, Salem 2771, Sandusky 2773, Scotford 2779, Scripps 2780, Sears 2781, Slemp 2785, Stark 2788, Troy 2794, Tuscarawas 2795, Wayne 2798, White 2800, Young 2803, Youngstown 2804, YSI 2805

Oklahoma: Adams 2806, Bernsen 2807, Chapman 2808, Gaylord 2813, Hille 2816, McGee 2820, Merrick 2821, Noble 2822, Oklahoma 2823, Sarkeys 2828, **Schusterman 2829**, Viersen 2830, Warren 2831

Oregon: Benton 2835, Braemar 2836, Ford 2846, Hedinger 2849, Jeld 2852, Macdonald 2859, Meyer 2861, Western 2876, Woodard 2877

Pennsylvania: **Alcoa 2882**, Arkema 2885, Bucks 2900, Buncher 2902, Central 2908, Centre 2909, Cestone 2910, Chase 2913, Chester 2915, Claneil 2918, Community 2923, Community 2924, Community 2925, Connelly 2926, DSF 2937, Elk 2939, Ferree 2944, Finley 2946, First 2947, FISA 2950, Fourjay 2953, Grundy 2962, Hunt 2971, **KL 2978**, Laros 2982, Lehigh Valley 2986, McCune 2993, McLean 2997, Mellon 2998, Mylan 3001, Patterson 3010, Penn 3011, Phoenixville 3014, Pierce 3015, Pottstown 3017, **PPG 3018**, Presser 3019, Rossin 3028, Snee 3039, Stackpole 3042, Trexler 3049, Union 3051, Washington 3054, Widener 3056, Wyomissing 3059

Rhode Island: CVS 3068, Hasbro 3077, Kimball 3079, McNeil 3086, Rhode Island 3089, Shaw's 3092, Textron 3093, van Beuren 3094, Washington 3095

South Carolina: Bailey 3096, Byerly 3098, Community 3100, Daniel 3101, Graham 3103, Joanna 3104, Lutz 3105, Spartanburg 3110, Springs 3111

Tennessee: Benwood 3123, Briggs 3124, CIC 3127, First 3135, Frist 3136, HCA 3139, Lyndhurst 3145, Osborne 3147, Phillips 3149, Tucker 3156, Wilson 3157

Texas: Abell 3160, Amarillo 3163, Bass 3172, Beasley 3175, **Bolivar 3179**, Brown 3183, Cailloux 3187, Carter 3190, Coates 3197, Collins 3199, Community 3200, Constantin 3202, Dallas 3209, Elkins 3220, Elkins 3221, Embrey 3222, Fisch 3232, Fish 3233, Fluor 3235, Gage 3239, Gulf 3245, Hamman 3248, Herzstein 3256, Hext 3257, Hill 3260, Hillcrest 3261, Hoblitzelle 3262, Hoglund 3263, **Houston 3266**, Houston 3267, Kinder 3274, King 3275, Light 3281, Lightner 3282, Littauer 3283, Lubbock 3287, Luse 3289, **Marshall 3290**, Martinez 3291, Mayor 3292, McDermott 3293, McKee 3295, Meadows 3296, Moody 3298, Northen 3306, **Oldham 3308**, Peterson 3318, Rachal 3329, Richardson 3334, Rogers 3339, Rosewood 3340, Sams 3342, San Angelo 3343, Simmons 3352, Smith 3353, Sterling 3358, Sturgis 3360, Summerlee 3361, Topfer 3372, Waco 3378, Waggoner 3379, Ward 3381, Willard 3382, Wright 3386, Zachry 3387

Utah: Eccles 3392, Eskuche 3393, Hemingway 3396

Vermont: Merchants 3414, Tarrant 3416, Vermont 3417, Windham 3418

Virginia: AMERIGROUP 3420, **Bosack 3423**, Cabell 3425, Gwathmey 3442, **Loyola 3453**, Lynchburg 3454, Morgan, 3463, Northern 3464, Parsons 3470, Potomac 3471, Pruden 3473, Robins 3477, United 3484

Washington: Ackerley 3489, Allen 3490, Anderson 3492, Bainbridge 3494, Community 3503, Dimmer 3506, Grays 3520, Green 3521, Inland 3526, Kawabe 3531, Korum 3532, McEachern 3541, Medina 3542, Milgard 3543, Renton 3552, San Juan 3555, Seattle 3558, Sherwood 3561

West Virginia: Beckley 3577, Community 3579, Eastern 3580, Maier 3584, McDonough 3586, Parkersburg 3587

Wisconsin: Alliant 3592, Ariens 3594, Bemis 3598, **Bradley 3601**, Community 3606, Community 3607, Cornerstone 3608, Dudley 3610, Eau 3611, Elmwood 3614, Incourage 3623, Jeffris 3624, Johnson 3625, Manitowoc 3632, Milwaukee 3637, Neese 3639, Oshkosh 3642, Pettit 3645, Pick 3646, U.S. 3665

Wyoming: McMurry 3676, Weiss 3682

Capital campaigns

Seattle 3558, Sherwood 3561, **Wilburforce 3572**, Wright 3574
West Virginia: Beckley 3577, Eastern 3580, Fenton 3581, Maier 3584, McDonough 3586, Parkersburg 3587
Wisconsin: **Baird 3595**, Bemis 3598, Community 3607, Cornerstone 3608, Dudley 3610, Eau 3611, Harley 3621, Johnson 3625, La Crosse 3631, Manitowoc 3632, Milwaukee 3637, Murray 3638, Neese 3639, Oshkosh 3642, Pettit 3645, Pick 3646, Zilber 3670
Wyoming: McMurry 3676, Weiss 3682

Cause-related marketing

New York: Voya 2488

Computer technology

Pennsylvania: First 2947
Wisconsin: Green Bay 3619

Conferences/seminars

Alabama: Community 9, **International 15**
Alaska: Alaska 26, CIRI 33
Arkansas: Cabe 67, Endeavor 69
California: American 82, Annenberg 87, Aratani 89, Archstone 90, Atlas 96, Ayrshire 97, Blue 114, California 138, California 140, **Christensen 151**, Community 157, Community 161, **Ellison 191, Foundation 202, Fund 210, Gellert 214, Glenn 225**, Jacobs 267, **Kapor 273, Lawrence 293, Lingnan 301**, Los Altos 305, Marin 309, McClatchy 317, **Moore 333**, North 346, Pacific 355, Placer 371, Samuelsson 392, Silicon 408, Sonora 420, **Special 422**, Stuart 429, Taper 433, True 442, **Warsh 452**
Colorado: Animal 472, Donnell 491, Foundation 498, **General 501, Gill 502**, Leighty 512, Piton 526, Summit 537, Vradenburg 544, Yampa 545
Connecticut: Aetna 550, Connecticut 564, Deloitte 569, Middlesex 592, Palmer 600
Delaware: AEC 622
District of Columbia: Bauman 650, Bernstein 652, **Foundation 661, Searle 681**
Florida: Benjamin 699, Bi-Lo/Winn-Dixie 700, Conn 728, Coral Gables 729, Darden 732, Winter 842
Georgia: Baker 853, Communities 866, Georgia 876, Georgia 877, **Georgia 878**, Healthcare 886, Pitts 904, Savannah 912
Idaho: Albertson 942
Illinois: Brach 973, Coleman 986, Community 988, Edwardsville 1010, Frankel 1017, Hughes 1035, **Joyce 1040, Tyndale 1105**
Indiana: Ball 1121, Brown 1124, Central 1126, Community 1129, Community 1133, Community 1134, Community 1136, Fayette 1146, Hancock 1154, Harrison 1155, Health 1156, Henry 1158, LaGrange 1170, **Lumina 1174**, Noble 1179, Orange 1184, Tipton 1198, Unity 1201, Welborn 1205
Iowa: Ahrens 1210, Community 1217, Guernsey 1221, Maytag 1229, Siouxland 1240
Kansas: Capitol 1251, Hutchinson 1260, Salina 1274
Louisiana: Community 1306
Maine: Horizon 1331, Maine 1336, Smith 1340, Somers 1341
Maryland: **Casey 1353**, Community 1359, **de Beaumont 1366**, Macht 1388, Rembrandt 1407
Massachusetts: **Barr 1433, Bruner 1441**, Cape Cod 1445, **Iacocca 1487, Kahn 1492**, Massachusetts 1508, Melville 1511, Parker 1523, Sheehan 1545
Michigan: Ann Arbor 1576, Branch 1580, Community 1587, Fremont 1607, Gilmore 1612, Hillsdale 1620, Lenawee 1634, **Mott 1645**, Mount Pleasant 1647, Pokagon 1657
Minnesota: Farmers 1695, Grand Rapids 1699, Greystone 1700, Northwest 1722, Northwest 1723, Southwest 1740, **St. Jude 1741, Trust 1746**, Winona 1753
Mississippi: Community 1759, Foundation 1763
Missouri: Community 1783, Green 1790, **Kauffman 1797, Monsanto 1803**, St. Louis 1814
Nebraska: Midlands 1848, Mid-Nebraska 1849, Nebraska 1851
Nevada: Nevada 1867
New Hampshire: Alexander 1877, Bean 1878, Endowment 1883
New Jersey: **Allen 1900**, Brookdale 1912, Brotherton 1914, Integra 1945, Kirby 1952, **Knowles 1955**, Merck 1966, **Milbank 1968, Ramapo 1981**, Summit 1998, Westfield 2004
New Mexico: Con 2011, Frost 2012
New York: Achelis 2026, **American 2034, Arcus 2040, AVI 2051**, Bay 2056, Berg 2062, **Bronfman 2074, Carnegie 2085**, Chautauqua 2091, Community 2107, Community 2109, Community 2110, Cricket 2119, **Cummings 2121, Foundation 2161**, Gifford 2177, **Goldman 2182, Grant 2191**, Initial 2231, **Institute 2233, JPMorgan 2242**, Klingenstein 2256, **Kress 2263**, Lake Placid 2265, **Macy 2288**, Ong 2341, **Peterson 2357, Porticus 2364**, Rauch 2376, **Rockefeller 2389, Rockefeller 2390, Sage 2402, Sparkplug 2441, Tinker 2467**, Vilcek 2486, Voya 2488, **Wallace 2492, Warhol 2494, Wenner 2502**, Western 2503, Widgeon 2505
North Carolina: **Bank 2524**, Biddle 2529, Brady 2533, Cumberland 2541, Eddy 2548, French 2554, Glass 2559, Meserve 2592, North Carolina 2599, Outer 2604, Polk 2609, Rogers 2618, Strowd 2633, Tannenbaum 2637
North Dakota: Community 2648, North Dakota 2653
Ohio: Athens 2662, Austin 2663, Barberton 2664, **Bingham 2668**, Brentwood 2670, **Cardinal 2677**, Coshocton 2686, Foundation 2702, Gund 2708, Hamilton 2710, Kulas 2721, Licking 2723, Marietta 2732, Marion 2733, Morgan 2740, Morgan 2741, Muskingum 2747, Nord 2754, O'Neill 2760, Scripps 2780, Tiffin 2793, Tuscora 2796
Oklahoma: Bernsen 2807, Cherokee 2809, **Ethics 2811, Schusterman 2829**, Zarrow 2833
Pennsylvania: **Alcoa 2882**, Baker 2886, Bayer 2888, Berks 2893, Bucks 2900, Centre 2909, Chester 2915, CIGNA 2917, Claneil 2918, Comcast 2921, Community 2924, Copernicus 2928, First 2947, FISA 2950, Pottstown 3017, Scranton 3031, Society 3040, Staunton 3044, **Templeton 3047**, Tuttleman 3050
Puerto Rico: Puerto Rico 3061
Rhode Island: Rhode Island 3089
South Carolina: Community 3099, Spartanburg 3110
Tennessee: Assisi 3120, Benwood 3123, First 3135, Stuttering 3155
Texas: Hext 3257, **Houston 3266**, Houston 3267, McKee 3295, Moody 3298, Moore 3299, Richardson 3334, San Angelo 3343, Sterling 3358, Summerlee 3361, Tocker 3369
Utah: Hemingway 3396
Vermont: Lintilhac 3412, Windham 3418
Virginia: **Bosack 3423, Longview 3451**, Moore 3461, **WestWind 3486**
Washington: **Glaser 3517**, Grays 3520, **Ji 3528**, Jones 3530
West Virginia: Beckley 3577, Community 3579
Wisconsin: Alliant 3592, **Bradley 3601**, Community 3606, Community 3607, Harley 3621, Marshfield 3633, Oshkosh 3642, Racine 3648, Sand 3654, St. Croix 3662
Wyoming: Wyoming 3684

Consulting services

Alabama: Black 4
Alaska: Alaska 26
Arkansas: Ross 72
California: Atlas 96, Buell 134, California 137, Clif 152, Community 157, Community 161, Cowell 168, Fox 205, **Fund 210**, Gerbode 217, Heller 246, Humboldt 257, Jacobs 267, **Kapor 273**, Kern 279, Marin 309, Mosher 335, North 346, **Packard 357**, Placer 371, San Luis 393, Sonora 420, Truckee 441, True 442
Colorado: Donnell 491, Foundation 498, **Gill 502**, Leighty 512, Rose 528, Telluride 538, Vradenburg 544
Connecticut: Community 562, Community 563, Connecticut 564, Palmer 600
District of Columbia: Meyer 672
Florida: Bush 712, Community 722, Conn 728, Greenburg 752, Gulf 754, Quantum 805, Southwest 823, Winter 842
Georgia: Communities 866
Hawaii: Cooke 932, Hawaii 933
Illinois: **Abbott 954**, Chicago 982, Community 989, Community 993, Edwardsville 1010, Frankel 1017, Oak Park 1068, Speh 1097
Indiana: Ball 1121, Central 1126, Community 1132, Community 1133, Community 1134, Foellinger 1147, Hancock 1154, Harrison 1155, Health 1156, Henry 1158, Jennings 1162, Johnson 1163, LaGrange 1170, **Lumina 1174**, Marshall 1176, Noble 1179, Northern 1180, Orange 1184, Putnam 1189, Tipton 1198
Iowa: Community 1216, Community 1217, Iowa 1226, Stebens 1242
Kentucky: Blue 1282, C.E. 1284
Maryland: Baker 1347, **Casey 1353**, Community 1359, Fowler 1372, Goldseker 1374, Straus 1410
Massachusetts: **Barr 1433**, Cape Cod 1445, Clipper 1449, Davis 1457, Essex 1464, Melville 1511, Parker 1523, Sudbury 1551
Michigan: Charlevoix 1583, Community 1586, Fremont 1607, Gilmore 1612, Jackson 1623, Marquette 1636, Midland 1642, Mount Pleasant 1647, Pokagon 1657
Minnesota: Butler 1688, Duluth 1693, Northwest 1723, Phillips 1728, Riverway 1733, Rochester 1735, **Trust 1746**
Mississippi: Community 1758, Foundation 1763
Missouri: Community 1783, Pendergast 1807
Nebraska: Lincoln 1847, Nebraska 1851, Woods 1857
Nevada: Nevada 1867
New Hampshire: Alexander 1877, Bean 1878
New Jersey: **Allen 1900**
New York: Allyn 2032, **Arcus 2040, Bronfman 2074, Clark 2097**, Community 2107, Community 2109, Community 2110, Community 2112, Cricket 2119, Cummings 2122, Ferraioli 2156, **Friends 2167**, Hoyt 2221, Initial 2231, New York 2325, O'Grady 2339, **Porticus 2364**, Rauch 2376, **Rockefeller 2389, Teagle 2459**
North Carolina: Meserve 2592, North Carolina 2599, Outer 2604, Reidsville 2611
Ohio: Ar-Hale 2661, Athens 2662, Brentwood 2670, Dater 2687, Findlay 2700, Foundation 2702, Kulas 2721, Morgan 2741, Murphy 2745, Muskingum 2747, O'Neill 2760, Saint 2770, Stark 2788
Oklahoma: Cherokee 2809, Hille 2816, Sarkeys 2828, **Schusterman 2829**
Oregon: Mission 2863, Woodard 2877
Pennsylvania: Barra 2887, Berks 2893, Central 2908, Chester 2915, Claneil 2918, **KL 2978**, North 3006, Penn 3011, Pottstown 3017, Scranton 3031
Puerto Rico: Puerto Rico 3061
Rhode Island: Rhode Island 3089
South Carolina: Byerly 3098, Community 3100, Spartanburg 3110
Tennessee: Assisi 3120, **Maclellan 3146**
Texas: Hext 3257, **Houston 3266**, Meadows 3296, Northen 3306, San Angelo 3343
Utah: Hemingway 3396
Vermont: Vermont 3417, Windham 3418
Virginia: Arlington 3421, Community 3429, Robins 3477

Washington: Community 3504, Tacoma 3567, Whatcom 3571, **Wilburforce 3572**
West Virginia: Beckley 3577, Community 3579
Wisconsin: Siebert 3659, St. Croix 3662

Continuing support

Alabama: Regions 19
Alaska: Alaska 26, CIRI 33
Arizona: Hughes 49, Piper 57, Webb 64
Arkansas: Cabe 67, Frueauff 70
California: **Amado 81**, Anderson 84, **Applied 88**, Aratani 89, AS&F 95, Atlas 96, Bechtel, 104, Berry 111, Blue 114, Buell 134, California 137, California 140, Campbell 142, **Christensen 151**, Community 157, Community 158, Community 161, Community 163, Disney 181, **DJ & T 184**, Eisner 189, Firedoll 198, **Foundation 202**, **Fund 210**, Fusenot 211, **Gellert 214**, Gellert 215, Genentech 216, Getty 218, GGS 219, Gilmore 221, Gold 228, Gumbiner 236, Haas 239, Hannon 242, Heller 246, Hewlett 248, **Hilton 251**, **Kapor 273**, Kern 279, Kirchgessner 282, Kvamme 286, Lesher 299, **Lingnan 301**, Livingston 303, Lucas 306, Lux 307, Marin 309, McClatchy 317, McKesson 321, Milken 331, Noyce 348, Pacific 354, Pacific 355, **Packard 357**, Patron 363, PG&E 367, Placer 371, Plum 372, Quest 377, Rancho 378, Rifkind 383, Rosenberg 385, San Luis 393, Silicon 408, Soda 418, Solano 419, Sonora 420, **Special 422**, Streisand 428, Stuart 429, Stulsaft 430, Truckee 441, vanLoben 446, **Warsh 452**, **Wilkinson 463**, Wilsey 464, Zellerbach 471
Colorado: Ballantine 474, Brett 476, Burt 479, Colorado 483, Comprecare 485, Donahue 490, Donnell 491, El Pomar 492, **Gill 502**, **Kinder 510**, Marquez 515, Pikes 525, Schlessman 530, Stratton 536, Summit 537, Vradenburg 544, Yampa 545
Connecticut: Community 563, Fry 579, Neuberger 593, NewAlliance 595, Northeast 598, Perrin 603
Delaware: **AstraZeneca 623**, CenturyLink-Clarke 627, Day 629, Delaware 630, Edwards 631, Lennox 638
District of Columbia: Bauman 650, Jovid 668, Stewart 682, **Wallace 683**
Florida: Batchelor 697, Bi-Lo/Winn-Dixie 700, Brown 707, Catalina 716, Chapman 717, Conn 728, Dunspaugh-Dalton 738, Erdle 740, Florida 744, Greenburg 752, Henderson 758, Jacksonville 761, Kramer 773, Landwirth 775, Macdonald 783, Morrison 792, Pinellas 801, Thomas 831
Georgia: Bancker-Williams 854, **Coca 864**, Georgia 877, **Georgia 878**, Knox 890, Livingston 893, Pitts 904, Sapelo 911, Southern 915, WinShape 921
Hawaii: Campbell 928, Hawaiian 934, McInerny 938
Idaho: Idaho 948, **Micron 950**
Illinois: **Abbott 954**, Bersted 966, Blowitz 968, Boothroyd 971, Chicago 982, Community 993, Crown 997, Dunard 1006, Frankel 1017, Fry 1018, **Grainger 1024**, Guthman 1027, **Joyce 1040**, **Mondelez 1064**, Omron 1070, Polk 1075, Prince 1076, Schmitt 1088, Siragusa 1096, Speh 1097, Square 1099, Stern 1100, Webb 1113, Wieboldt 1115
Indiana: Brown 1124, Cole 1127, DeHaan 1143, Fairbanks 1145, Foellinger 1147, Harrison 1155, Health 1156, Hendricks 1157, Henry 1158, **Lumina 1174**, Old 1182, Owen 1185, WellPoint 1206
Iowa: Aviva 1211, Community 1217, Guernsey 1221, Maytag 1229, **Rockwell 1237**, Wellmark 1246
Kansas: Capitol 1251, Collective 1253, Hansen 1259, Hutchinson 1260, Kansas 1263, Koch 1265, Skillbuilders 1277, Sunderland 1278, Topeka 1279
Louisiana: Baptist 1299, Beaird 1301, Community 1306, Grigsby 1312
Maine: Libra 1334, Somers 1341
Maryland: Blaustein 1350, Commonweal 1356, Delaplaine 1367, Deutsch 1369, Fowler 1372, Freeman 1373, Henson 1378, Macht 1388, Meyerhoff 1393, NASDAQ 1401, Polinger 1405, Rembrandt 1407, Town 1413, Zickler 1419
Massachusetts: Arbella 1426, Boynton 1437, Cape Cod 1445, Clipper 1449, Davis 1457, DentaQuest 1459, Fireman 1469, Hyams 1486, **Kahn 1492**, Kelsey 1493, Krieger 1497, Levy 1501, Liberty 1502, MetroWest 1515, New 1518, Ratshesky 1531, Sailors' 1539, Santander 1541, Schrafft 1543, Sheehan 1545, **State 1550**, **Xeric 1570**
Michigan: Dalton 1592, Dana 1593, Dart 1594, DTE 1598, Family 1600, Farver 1601, Fremont 1607, Gilmore 1612, **Isabel 1621**, Keller 1627, McGregor 1638, Morley 1644, **Mott 1645**, Mott 1646, Oleson 1649, Pokagon 1657, Sanilac 1663, Skillman 1666, Vanderweide 1671
Minnesota: Best 1685, Briggs 1687, Butler 1688, Donaldson 1692, George 1698, Greystone 1700, HRK 1702, **Kaplan 1707**, Larsen 1711, Marbrook 1713, Minneapolis 1717, **Mosaic 1718**, Nash 1720, **O'Shaughnessy 1725**, **Patterson 1726**, RBC 1730, Riverway 1733, Sayer 1737, **St. Jude 1741**, **Trust 1746**, Wedum 1750, Winona 1753
Mississippi: Community 1759, Community 1760, Foundation 1763, Gulf 1764, Mississippi 1769
Missouri: Anheuser 1774, Butler 1780, Centene 1782, Community 1783, Curry 1784, Hallmark 1794, Laclede 1799, Millstone 1801, **Monsanto 1803**, Musgrave 1805, Pendergast 1807, Truman 1817
Montana: Montana 1828
Nebraska: Midlands 1848, Weitz 1855, Zollner 1858
Nevada: Caesars 1860
New Hampshire: Alexander 1877, Fuller 1886, Penates 1893, Smyth 1895
New Jersey: **Alcatel 1899**, **Allen 1900**, Banbury 1904, Beer 1907, **Berrie 1908**, Bonner 1909, Borden 1910, Holzer 1939, Horizon 1940, Kirby 1952, **Knowles 1955**, Princeton 1979, Schumann 1990, Turrell 2002
New Mexico: Albuquerque 2006, Frost 2012, Santa Fe 2017
New York: Adirondack 2027, **Alavi 2030**, **American 2034**, American 2035, Barker 2054, Bay 2056, Berg 2062, **Carnegie 2085**, Century 2089, Chautauqua 2091, **Clark 2097**, **Clark 2098**, Clark 2099, Coach 2100, Community 2107, Countess 2116, Cricket 2119, Dammann 2125, Daphne 2127, Deerfield 2132, **Deutsche 2134**, **Diamond 2135**, Ferraioli 2156, **Ford 2160**, **Foundation 2161**, Gebbie 2170, **Gilman 2178**, Gimbel 2179, **Goldman 2182**, Goldman 2183, Guttman 2197, Haring 2203, **Heron 2211**, Hultquist 2225, Hycliff 2226, Johnson 2240, **JPMorgan 2242**, **Kaplan 2245**, Klingenstein 2256, Knapp 2259, Lake Placid 2265, Lee 2271, Link 2280, MBIA 2297, **Mellon 2302**, **Mertz 2306**, **MetLife 2307**, Moore 2311, Morgan 2315, New York 2326, **Noyes 2335**, O'Grady 2339, **Open 2343**, Ostgrodd 2344, Park 2349, Patrina 2350, **PepsiCo 2354**, Rapoport 2373, Rich 2382, **Rockefeller 2390**, Scherman 2409, Schnurmacher 2411, Schumann 2412, Sirus 2426, Sulzberger 2451, **Surdna 2454**, **Teagle 2459**, Tiffany 2463, Tiger 2464, Tisch 2469, Troy 2474, Tuttle 2479, Vidda 2485, Voya 2488, **Weeden 2496**
North Carolina: Adams 2517, Bailey 2522, **Bank 2524**, Brady 2533, Caine 2536, Eddy 2548, Goodrich 2561, Meyer 2594, North Carolina 2599, Olin 2603, Polk 2609, Reidsville 2611, Reynolds 2613, Strowd 2633
North Dakota: MDU 2652
Ohio: American 2656, Ar-Hale 2661, Athens 2662, Austin 2663, **Bingham 2668**, Brentwood 2670, Brown 2672, **Cardinal 2677**, Community 2685, Coshocton 2686, Dater 2687, Dayton 2688, Delaware 2689, **Eaton 2692**, Fairfield 2696, Fifth 2699, Foundation 2702, Fowler 2703, Gund 2708, KeyBank 2717, Kulas 2721, Macy's 2726, Morgan 2741, Murphy 2744, Murphy 2745, Nippert 2751, NiSource 2752, Nord 2754, Nordson 2755, **OMNOVA 2759**, Salem 2771, Sears 2781, Stranahan 2790, Tuscarawas 2795, Wayne 2798, YSI 2805
Oklahoma: Hille 2816, Kirschner 2818, Oklahoma 2823, **Schusterman 2829**, Viersen 2830
Oregon: Benton 2835, Caddock 2838, Jackson 2851, PGE 2867, Templeton 2874
Pennsylvania: **Alcoa 2882**, Arkema 2885, Baker 2886, Bayer 2888, Beacon 2889, Burgess 2903, **Carnegie 2906**, Central 2908, Cestone 2910, Claneil 2918, Comcast 2921, Community 2922, Connelly 2926, Copernicus 2928, Fels 2942, First 2947, First 2948, FISA 2950, Fourjay 2953, Heinz 2966, Highmark 2968, Hillman 2969, Hunt 2971, Martin 2991, Mellon 2998, Patterson 3010, Phoenixville 3014, **PPG 3018**, Rider 3024, Scranton 3031, Trexler 3049, Union 3051, Valentine 3053, Washington 3054, Wyomissing 3059
Puerto Rico: Puerto Rico 3061
Rhode Island: Biogen 3063, CVS 3068, **Dorot 3071**, Hasbro 3077, Textron 3093, Washington 3095
South Carolina: Black 3097, Byerly 3098, Daniel 3101, Foothills 3102, Lutz 3105, Singing 3108, Smith 3109, Spartanburg 3110
Tennessee: Baptist 3122, Benwood 3123, Eastman 3133, Lyndhurst 3145, Phillips 3149, **Scarlett 3152**, Wilson 3157
Texas: Abell 3160, Augur 3168, Bass 3172, Brown 3183, Burch 3184, Cailloux 3187, Carter 3190, Coates 3197, Embrey 3222, Esping 3225, Fisch 3232, Fish 3233, Frees 3238, Hamman 3248, Herzstein 3256, **Houston 3266**, Houston 3267, KDK-Harman 3273, Kinder 3274, Light 3281, Lockheed 3284, Lubbock 3287, Luse 3289, **Marshall 3290**, Martinez 3291, McDermott 3293, McKee 3295, Meadows 3296, Moore 3299, Northen 3306, Orsinger 3310, Richardson 3334, Rockwell 3338, Rosewood 3340, Sams 3342, Simmons 3352, Topfer 3372, Trull 3373, Waggoner 3379, Willard 3382, Wright 3386
Utah: Bamberger 3389, Hemingway 3396
Vermont: Lintilhac 3412
Virginia: AMERIGROUP 3420, Arlington 3421, Capital 3426, CarMax 3427, Community 3431, Community 3433, Moore 3461, Pruden 3473, Samberg 3478, **WestWind 3486**, Williamsburg 3487
Washington: Blue 3498, Casey 3499, Dimmer 3506, Ferguson 3513, **Foundation 3515**, **Gates 3516**, Harder 3524, Kawabe 3531, Renton 3552, Safeco 3554, **Starbucks 3565**, Tacoma 3567, **Wilburforce 3572**
West Virginia: Eastern 3580, Tucker 3589
Wisconsin: Alliant 3592, Bemis 3598, **Bradley 3601**, Community 3606, Cornerstone 3608, Elmwood 3614, Green Bay 3619, La Crosse 3631, Manitowoc 3632, Marshfield 3633, McBeath 3634, Milwaukee 3637, Oshkosh 3642, Oshkosh 3643, Sentry 3657, U.S. 3665, Windhover 3668
Wyoming: McMurry 3676, Scott 3679, Weiss 3682, Wyoming 3684

Curriculum development

Alabama: BBVA 3, Community 9, Community 10
Arizona: Webb 64
Arkansas: Cabe 67, Endeavor 69
California: **Amado 81**, **Applied 88**, Aratani 89, Archstone 90, Atlas 96, Bechtel 103, Bechtel, 104, Cowell 168, Crail 170, Fleishhacker 199, **Gellert 214**, Genentech 216, Haas 239, Heller 246, **Hilton 251**, **Kapor 273**, **Keck 276**, Kern 279, **Lingnan 301**, Marin 309, Mazda 313, Noyce 348, Rancho 378, **Rivendell 384**, **Rupe 389**, Sonora 420, **Special 422**, Taper 433, UniHealth 444, Versacare 448, Wilsey 464
Colorado: Animal 472, Community 484, **Crowell 487**, Donahue 490, **Kinder 510**, Leighty 512, Piton 526, Rose 528, Schlessman 530, Stratton 536, Summit 537, Yampa 545
Connecticut: **Calder 558**, Community 563, Connecticut 564, Deloitte 569, Pitney 604
District of Columbia: Bauman 650, Block 653

Florida: Burns 710, Henderson 758, **Knight 771**, Thomas 831
Georgia: Abreu 846, Communities 866, **Imlay 888**, Livingston 893
Hawaii: Atherton 925, Campbell 928, Castle 930
Idaho: Albertson 942, Idaho 948, **Micron 950**, Whittenberger 953
Illinois: Chicago 982, Coleman 986, Community 992, Edwardsville 1010, Evanston 1012, Field 1014, Frankel 1017, Fry 1018, Hughes 1035, Logan 1051, **Motorola 1066**, Polk 1075, Speh 1097, Stone 1102, Tracy 1104
Indiana: Ball 1121, Central 1126, Community 1132, Community 1134, Community 1135, Hancock 1154, Harrison 1155, Hendricks 1157, Jennings 1162, Madison 1175, Old 1182, Orange 1184, Owen 1185, TCU 1197, Tipton 1198, Tobias 1199, Welborn 1205, Western 1208
Iowa: Iowa 1226, Maytag 1229, Wellmark 1246
Kansas: Douglas 1256, Hutchinson 1260, Sarver 1275, **Shumaker 1276**
Kentucky: Good 1289
Louisiana: Albemarle 1298, Baptist 1299, Community 1306
Maine: Horizon 1331, Libra 1334, Somers 1341
Maryland: **Braitmayer 1351, de Beaumont 1366**, Deutsch 1369, Mid-Shore 1395, NASDAQ 1401, Polinger 1405, Wright 1418, Zickler 1419
Massachusetts: Clarke 1448, Essex 1464, **Kahn 1492**, Liberty 1502, Riley 1534, Santander 1541, Sheehan 1545, Smith 1546, Staples 1549
Michigan: Anderson 1575, Binda 1579, Community 1591, Dart 1594, Davenport 1595, DTE 1598, Fremont 1607, Grand 1616, Keller 1627, Mount Pleasant 1647, Oleson 1649, Pokagon 1657, Sanilac 1663, Wege 1674
Minnesota: 3M 1676, Best 1685, Duluth 1693, Edina 1694, Grand Rapids 1699, Larsen 1711, **O'Shaughnessy 1725**, Phillips 1728, **Trust 1746**, West 1751, Xcel 1754
Mississippi: Community 1758, Community 1759, Foundation 1763
Missouri: Boylan 1776, Community 1783, Green 1790, **Kauffman 1797, Monsanto 1803**, St. Louis 1814
Montana: Silver 1830
Nebraska: Hirschfeld 1839, Mid-Nebraska 1849
New Jersey: **Allen 1900**, Horizon 1940, Merck 1966, Princeton 1979, Westfield 2004
New Mexico: Frost 2012, Maddox 2014
New York: Achelis 2026, Adirondack 2027, Anderson 2036, **Arcus 2040**, Aronson 2042, **AVI 2051**, Berg 2062, **Bronfman 2074, Carnegie 2085**, Community 2107, Community 2109, Community 2110, Community 2112, **Deutsche 2134**, Freeman 2164, **Friends 2167, Genesis 2173**, Gifford 2177, Gould 2188, Haring 2203, Heckscher 2205, High 2213, Hoyt 2221, **JPMorgan 2242**, Kornfeld 2261, **Macy 2288**, Oishei 2340, Patrina 2350, **Peterson 2357, Porticus 2364, Rockefeller 2390**, Schnurmacher 2411, **Sparkplug 2441, Teagle 2459**, Troy 2474
North Carolina: Brady 2533, Caine 2536, Community 2540, Eddy 2548, North Carolina 2599, North 2600, Olin 2603, Polk 2609
North Dakota: Community 2648
Ohio: Ar-Hale 2661, Athens 2662, Austin 2663, Barberton 2664, **Bingham 2668**, Brentwood 2670, Bryan 2674, Coshocton 2686, Fairfield 2696, Foundation 2702, Fowler 2703, Hershey 2711, KeyBank 2717, Licking 2723, Marion 2733, Middletown 2737, Morgan 2740, Morgan 2741, Murphy 2745, Nippert 2751, Nordson 2755, O'Neill 2760, Saint 2770, Scripps 2780, Sears 2781, Slemp 2785, Springfield 2787, Troy 2794, YSI 2805
Oklahoma: Cherokee 2809, **Ethics 2811**, Hille 2816, **Schusterman 2829**
Oregon: Braemar 2836, PGE 2867
Pennsylvania: **Alcoa 2882**, Baker 2886, Bayer 2888, Buhl 2901, Cestone 2910, Claneil 2918, Community 2924, Community 2925, Fels 2942, Highmark 2968, **KL 2978**, Pottstown 3017, Scranton 3031, Staley 3043, Staunton 3044, **Templeton 3047**, Tuttleman 3050
Puerto Rico: Puerto Rico 3061
Rhode Island: McDonald 3085, McNeil 3086
South Carolina: Byerly 3098, Community 3100, Daniel 3101, Spartanburg 3110
Tennessee: Assisi 3120, **International 3142, Scarlett 3152**, Wilson 3157
Texas: Alcon 3162, AT&T 3167, Brown 3183, Coates 3197, Esping 3225, Fasken 3229, Fluor 3235, **Houston 3266**, Houston 3267, Light 3281, **Marshall 3290**, McDermott 3293, Meadows 3296, Northen 3306, Orsinger 3310, Powell 3324, Rockwell 3338, Sterling 3358, Summerlee 3361, Waggoner 3379, Willard 3382
Utah: Hemingway 3396
Vermont: Merchants 3414, Vermont 3417, Windham 3418
Virginia: Arlington 3421, Community 3429, **Longview 3451**, Memorial 3458, Samberg 3478, Strong 3481
Washington: Ackerley 3489, Blue 3498, Grays 3520, **Ji 3528**, Jones 3530, Safeco 3554
West Virginia: Eastern 3580, Tucker 3589
Wisconsin: **Bradley 3601**, Community 3606, Community 3607, Green Bay 3619, Harley 3621, La Crosse 3631, Stateline 3663
Wyoming: Scott 3679

Debt reduction

Arkansas: Cabe 67
California: Ahmanson 77, Marin 309
Delaware: AEC 622
Illinois: Frankel 1017
Iowa: Community 1217
Kansas: Hutchinson 1260
Kentucky: Community 1286
Maryland: Meyerhoff 1393
Michigan: Dalton 1592, Gilmore 1612, Knight 1630
Minnesota: Riverway 1733
Missouri: Dunn 1787
New Hampshire: Ham 1887
New Jersey: Banbury 1904, Hyde 1944
New York: Lee 2271
North Carolina: Southern 2630, Strowd 2633
Pennsylvania: Patterson 3010, Trees 3048
Tennessee: Phillips 3149
Texas: Herzstein 3256, **Houston 3266**, Lightner 3282, Meadows 3296, Sterling 3358
Wisconsin: Blooming 3599, Cornerstone 3608

Donated equipment

Indiana: TCU 1197

Donated land

Illinois: McGraw 1060

Donated products

California: Clif 152, **Clorox 153**, Western 459
Florida: Glazer 750
Illinois: **Mondelez 1064, Walgreens 1109**
Kansas: Delta 1255
Minnesota: **Mosaic 1718**
New Jersey: **Johnson 1948, Novartis 1973, Sanofi 1988**
Ohio: **Cardinal 2677**
Texas: Alcon 3161

Emergency funds

Alabama: Community 9, Community 10
Alaska: Alaska 26
Arizona: Green 47, Hughes 49, Webb 64
Arkansas: Cabe 67, Frueauff 70, Ross 72, Wal-Mart 74
California: Anaheim 83, AS&F 95, Campbell 142, Community 157, Community 160, Cowell 168, Crail 170, Firedoll 198, Gumbiner 236, **Hilton 251**, Humboldt 257, **Lawrence 293**, Marin 309, Military 330, Rancho 378, Sacramento 391, Santa Barbara 394, Sonora 420, Taper 433
Colorado: Animal 472, Burt 479, Community 484, Donahue 490, El Pomar 492, **General 501, Gill 502**, Stratton 536, Vradenburg 544, Yampa 545
Connecticut: Community 562, Community 563
District of Columbia: Block 653, Lichtenberg 671
Florida: Bush 712, Chapman 717, Community 722, Community 727, Conn 728, Coral Gables 729, Erdle 740, Greenburg 752, Gulf 754, **Knight 771**, Peterson 799, Quantum 805, Reinhold 808, **Skelly 820**, Southwest 823, Winter 842, Wollowick 843
Georgia: Camp-Younts 861, **Coca 864**, Community 867, Georgia 877, Moore 897, Savannah 912, Southern 915
Hawaii: **Watumull 939**
Idaho: Idaho 948
Illinois: **Abbott 954**, Community 990, Driehaus 1002, Edwardsville 1010, Field 1014, Frankel 1017, Libra 1050, Oberweiler 1069, Siragusa 1096, Speh 1097, Square 1099
Indiana: Brown 1124, Central 1126, Community 1129, Community 1130, Community 1132, Community 1133, Community 1134, Community 1136, Decatur 1142, Fayette 1146, Harrison 1155, Hendricks 1157, Henry 1158, Johnson 1163, LaGrange 1170, Madison 1175, Marshall 1176, Noble 1179, Northern 1180, Porter 1187, Tipton 1198, Wabash 1203, WellPoint 1206, Wells 1207, Western 1208, Whitley 1209
Iowa: Community 1217, Guernsey 1221, Maytag 1229, McElroy 1230, United 1243, Wahlert 1244
Kansas: Capitol 1251, Douglas 1256, Salina 1274, Skillbuilders 1277, Sunderland 1278, Topeka 1279
Kentucky: C.E. 1284, Community 1286
Louisiana: Community 1306, New Orleans 1316
Maine: Libra 1334
Maryland: Blaustein 1350, Community 1358, Community 1359, Meyerhoff 1393, Mid-Shore 1395
Massachusetts: **Barr 1433**, Berkman 1434, Cape Cod 1445, Clipper 1449, Community 1453, Davis 1457, Essex 1464, Fields 1467, Fireman 1469, Kelsey 1493, Massachusetts 1508, Santander 1541, Swan 1552, Weber 1564
Michigan: Ann Arbor 1576, Charlevoix 1583, Community 1586, Community 1589, Community 1590, Community 1591, Dalton 1592, Dana 1593, Farver 1601, Frankenmuth 1606, Fremont 1607, Gilmore 1612, Kalamazoo 1626, Morley 1644, Mount Pleasant 1647, Pokagon 1657, Saginaw 1662, Sanilac 1663
Minnesota: **Andersen 1678**, Duluth 1693, Edina 1694, Grand Rapids 1699, Greystone 1700, Midcontinent 1716, Northwest 1723, Riverway 1733, Rochester 1735, WCA 1749, Winona 1753
Missouri: Community 1783, Green 1790, Hall 1793, **Kauffman 1797**, Millstone 1801, Speas 1813
Montana: Montana 1828, Silver 1830, Whitefish 1832
Nebraska: Grand Island 1837, Hirschfeld 1839, Kearney 1842, Lincoln 1847, Mutual 1850
Nevada: Nevada 1867
New Hampshire: Endowment 1883, Fuller 1886, Penates 1893
New Jersey: **Allen 1900**, Banbury 1904, **Berrie 1908**, Kirby 1952, Princeton 1979, Summit 1998, Westfield 2004
New Mexico: Santa Fe 2017
New York: **American 2034**, Anderson 2036, Chautauqua 2091, Community 2107, Community 2109, Community 2110, Community 2112, **Dramatists 2143**, Farash 2154, Gifford 2177,

Gottlieb 2187, High 2213, Lee 2271, Ontario 2342, Rapoport 2373, **Ross 2396**, Schnurmacher 2411, Smith 2429, St. George's 2445, Sulzberger 2451, Truman 2475, **Weeden 2496**, Wells 2501, Western 2503

North Carolina: Community 2539, Duncan 2547, Ferebee 2552, Hanes 2565, Meyer 2594, North Carolina 2599, Outer 2604, Reidsville 2611, Rogers 2618, Smith 2629, Tannenbaum 2637

North Dakota: Fargo 2649

Ohio: Ar-Hale 2661, Austin 2663, Brown 2672, Cincinnati 2679, Community 2682, Fairfield 2696, Foundation 2702, Gund 2708, Hamilton 2710, Mayerson 2735, Middletown 2737, Murphy 2744, National 2748, Nordson 2755, Richland 2767, Saint 2770, Scripps 2780, Slemp 2785, Stark 2788, Tiffin 2793, Troy 2794, Wayne 2798, White 2800, Woodruff 2801, Youngstown 2804, YSI 2805

Oklahoma: Bernsen 2807, Hille 2816, Sarkeys 2828, **Schusterman 2829**, Viersen 2830

Oregon: Meyer 2861, Templeton 2874

Pennsylvania: **Alcoa 2882**, Arkema 2885, Brooks 2899, Centre 2909, Cestone 2910, Community 2923, Community 2925, Fourjay 2953, Huston 2973, Lehigh Valley 2986, McKee 2995, Merchants 3000, Patterson 3010, **PPG 3018**, Tuttleman 3050, Union 3051, Wyomissing 3059, **Zeldin 3060**

Puerto Rico: Puerto Rico 3061

Rhode Island: Kimball 3079, Rhode Island 3089

South Carolina: Community 3099, Spartanburg 3110

Tennessee: Assisi 3120, Baptist 3122, Wilson 3157

Texas: Amarillo 3163, Augur 3168, **BP 3181**, Cailloux 3187, Carter 3190, **Chrest 3194**, Dallas 3209, Edwards 3218, Elkins 3220, Elkins 3221, Embrey 3222, Hammill 3249, Hext 3257, **Houston 3266**, Kinder 3274, Light 3281, Lockheed 3284, Lubbock 3287, **Marshall 3290**, McKee 3295, Meadows 3296, Moore 3299, Permian 3316, Rachal 3329, San Angelo 3343, Simmons 3352, Sterling 3358, Waggoner 3379, Willard 3382

Utah: Hemingway 3396

Vermont: Vermont 3417

Virginia: Arlington 3421, **Bosack 3423**, Community 3432, Community 3433, Lynchburg 3454, Pruden 3473

Washington: Allen 3490, Community 3504, Grays 3520, Green 3521, **Starbucks 3565**, Tacoma 3567

West Virginia: McDonough 3586, Parkersburg 3587, Your 3591

Wisconsin: Alliant 3592, Community 3607, Cornerstone 3608, Dudley 3610, Green Bay 3619, Incourage 3623, Milwaukee 3637, Oshkosh 3642, Pick 3646, Stateline 3663, U.S. 3665

Wyoming: McMurry 3676

Employee matching gifts

Alabama: Regions 19

Arizona: Napier 55, Piper 57

Arkansas: Union 73, Wal-Mart 74

California: Bechtel 103, Bechtel, 104, **Beckman 105**, California 137, California 138, Campbell 142, **Clorox 153**, College 156, Copley 166, Crail 170, Disney 181, Hewlett 248, Hewlett 249, **Hilton 251**, Intuit 263, Irvine 264, Jacobs 267, **Keck 276**, Marin 309, **Mattel 312**, McClatchy 317, **McConnell 318**, McKesson 321, Pacific 355, **Packard 357**, PG&E 367, Sierra 405, Stuart 429, UniHealth 444, Weingart 456, Western 459

Colorado: Colorado 483, El Pomar 492, Encana 493, **First 496**, **Gill 502**, **Kinder 510**, Piton 526, Tomkins 540

Connecticut: Aetna 550, Deloitte 569, NewAlliance 595, Northeast 598, Pitney 604, **Praxair 606**

Delaware: CenturyLink-Clarke 627

Florida: Bi-Lo/Winn-Dixie 700, Bush 712, Darden 732, **Knight 771**, Publix 804, Quantum 805

Georgia: Blank 856, **Coca 864**, Georgia 877, Goizueta 883

Hawaii: Hawaiian 934

Idaho: **Micron 950**

Illinois: Aon 963, Chicago 982, Community 988, Crown 997, Donnelley 1001, Duchossois 1005, Field 1014, **Joyce 1040**, Lumpkin 1053, **MacArthur 1056**, **Mondelez 1064**, Omron 1070, Polk 1075, Prince 1076, Prince 1077, Siragusa 1096, **Spencer 1098**, Square 1099, Tracy 1104

Indiana: Koch 1167, **Lumina 1174**, Owen 1185, TCU 1197, Unity 1201, Vectren 1202, WellPoint 1206

Iowa: Aviva 1211, Community 1217, **Rockwell 1237**

Kansas: Capitol 1251, Delta 1255, Topeka 1279

Louisiana: Albemarle 1298, Community 1306

Maryland: **Blaustein 1349**, Freeman 1373, Mid-Shore 1395, Rembrandt 1407

Massachusetts: Arbella 1426, Eastern 1461, **Elsevier 1463**, Liberty 1502, Santander 1541, **State 1550**

Michigan: Dana 1593, DTE 1598, Fremont 1607, Frey 1609, Gilmore 1612, Grand Rapids 1615, Kalamazoo 1626, **Kellogg 1628**, **Kresge 1631**, Masco 1637, McGregor 1638, Morley 1644, **Mott 1645**, Skillman 1666, Steelcase 1667

Minnesota: 3M 1676, Donaldson 1692, General 1697, HRK 1702, Jostens 1706, Land 1710, McKnight 1715, Midcontinent 1716, Northwest 1722, **Pentair 1727**, RBC 1730, Sayer 1737, Securian 1739, **St. Jude 1741**, SUPERVALU 1743, Xcel 1754

Mississippi: Mississippi 1769, Regions 1770

Missouri: Anheuser 1774, Bunge 1779, Butler 1780, Hallmark 1794, **Kauffman 1797**, Laclede 1799, **Monsanto 1803**

Nebraska: Lincoln 1847, Mutual 1850, Nebraska 1851

Nevada: **Reynolds 1869**

New Jersey: Bard 1905, Campbell 1917, Horizon 1940, **JM 1947**, **Johnson 1949**, **Milbank 1968**, Unilever 2003

New York: American 2033, **Arcus 2040**, Assurant 2047, **Bronfman 2074**, **Carnegie 2085**, **Clark 2098**, Coach 2100, **Dana 2126**, **Deutsche 2134**, **Duke 2146**, **Ford 2160**, **Heron 2211**, **IBM 2227**, **JPMorgan 2242**, **Kress 2263**, Littauer 2282, **Luce 2286**, **Macy 2288**, MBIA 2297, **MetLife 2307**, Mutual 2317, New York 2325, Novartis 2333, NYSE 2336, **Open 2343**, Park 2349, **PepsiCo 2354**, **Rockefeller 2389**, **Rockefeller 2390**, **Sage 2402**, **Surdna 2454**, **Teagle 2459**, Voya 2488, **Wallace 2492**

North Carolina: **Bank 2524**, Goodrich 2561, Olin 2603, Reynolds 2613, VF 2642

North Dakota: MDU 2652

Ohio: Austin 2663, **Cardinal 2677**, Charities 2678, Cliffs 2681, Coshocton 2686, **Eaton 2692**, KeyBank 2717, Macy's 2726, Middletown 2737, Nord 2754, Nordson 2755, Ohio 2756, **OMNOVA 2759**, Progressive 2764, Scripps 2780, YSI 2805

Oklahoma: Noble 2822, Oklahoma 2823

Oregon: Flowerree 2845, Ford 2846, Meyer 2861, Mission 2863

Pennsylvania: **ACE 2880**, **Alcoa 2882**, Arkema 2885, Buhl 2901, CIGNA 2917, Connelly 2926, GlaxoSmithKline 2957, McCune 2993, Penn 3011, **PPG 3018**

Rhode Island: Biogen 3063, Citizens 3067, Hasbro 3077, Textron 3093

South Carolina: Bailey 3096

Tennessee: First 3135, HCA 3139, **International 3142**, Lyndhurst 3145

Texas: Abell 3160, AT&T 3167, **Baker 3170**, **BP 3181**, Brown 3183, Fluor 3235, **Houston 3266**, Houston 3267, Meadows 3296, NuStar 3307, Rachal 3329, Rosewood 3340, Shell 3348

Vermont: **Ben 3407**

Virginia: AMERIGROUP 3420, Capital 3426, CarMax 3427, **Northrop 3465**

Washington: Casey 3500, Everett 3511, **Gates 3516**, Intermec 3527, Safeco 3554, **Starbucks 3565**

West Virginia: McDonough 3586

Wisconsin: Alliant 3592, **Baird 3595**, Bemis 3598, Harley 3621, Johnson 3625, Keller 3626, Menasha 3636, Sentry 3657, U.S. 3665, Windhover 3668, Zilber 3670

Wyoming: Scott 3679

Employee volunteer services

Arkansas: Wal-Mart 74

California: Allergan 80, **Clorox 153**, GSF 235, Intuit 263, **Mattel 312**, McClatchy 317, McKesson 321, Silicon 407, Western 459

Colorado: **First 496**

Connecticut: Aetna 550, Pitney 604, **Praxair 606**

Delaware: Burt's 626, CenturyLink-Clarke 627

District of Columbia: **Hitachi 666**

Florida: Darden 732, Minto 789

Georgia: **Georgia 878**

Idaho: **Micron 950**

Illinois: Aon 963, **Mondelez 1064**, **Motorola 1066**

Indiana: Koch 1167, Vectren 1202, WellPoint 1206

Iowa: Aviva 1211, Wellmark 1246

Kansas: Capitol 1251

Louisiana: Albemarle 1298, Blue 1302

Maryland: Rembrandt 1407

Massachusetts: Arbella 1426, Liberty 1502, **State 1550**

Michigan: DTE 1598

Minnesota: 3M 1676, General 1697, Land 1710, **Mosaic 1718**, RBC 1730, Securian 1739, Xcel 1754

Missouri: Anheuser 1774, Butler 1780, Hallmark 1794

Nebraska: Mutual 1850

Nevada: Caesars 1860

New Jersey: **Alcatel 1899**, Campbell 1917, Horizon 1940

New York: American 2033, Coach 2100, **Credit 2118**, **Deutsche 2134**, **JPMorgan 2242**, MBIA 2297, **MetLife 2307**, Morgan 2315, NYSE 2336, **PepsiCo 2354**, Voya 2488

North Carolina: **Bank 2524**, Goodrich 2561, VF 2642

North Dakota: MDU 2652

Ohio: **Cardinal 2677**, Dayton 2688, **Eaton 2692**, KeyBank 2717, Macy's 2726, Nordson 2755, **OMNOVA 2759**, Scripps 2780

Pennsylvania: **ACE 2880**, **Alcoa 2882**, CIGNA 2917, Comcast 2921, EQT 2940, **PPG 3018**

Rhode Island: Citizens 3067, CVS 3068

Tennessee: First 3135, HCA 3139, **International 3142**

Texas: AT&T 3167, **BP 3181**, Fluor 3235, Penney 3315

Virginia: CarMax 3427

Washington: Intermec 3527, **Starbucks 3565**

Wisconsin: Alliant 3592, **Baird 3595**, Harley 3621, Menasha 3636

Employee-related scholarships

Alabama: BBVA 3

Arkansas: Wal-Mart 74

California: Blue 114, Brooks 131, **Clorox 153**, Disney 181, **Mattel 312**, McKesson 321, Mosher 335, Sacramento 391, Sierra 406

Connecticut: Conway 565, Northeast 598

Florida: Erdle 740

Georgia: **Georgia 878**, Weir 919

Illinois: **Abbott 954**, Omron 1070, Speh 1097, Square 1099

Indiana: Community 1132, Harrison 1155, Jennings 1162, Koch 1167

Iowa: Siouxland 1240

Kansas: Koch 1265, Topeka 1279

Kentucky: Blue 1282

Louisiana: Albemarle 1298

Maine: Hannaford 1330

Massachusetts: D'Amour 1456, Santander 1541

Michigan: Community 1591, Dana 1593, Grand Rapids 1615, Lenawee 1634, Steelcase 1667

Minnesota: Donaldson 1692, Farmers 1695, General 1697, Jostens 1706, **Patterson 1726, Trust 1746**
Missouri: Butler 1780, Hall 1793
Montana: Montana 1828
New Jersey: Campbell 1917, **Siemens 1993**, Unilever 2003
New Mexico: Chase 2009
New York: **AIG 2029**, American 2033, Community 2108, Community 2109, **MetLife 2307**, **PepsiCo 2354**, **Teagle 2459**
North Carolina: **Bank 2524**, Goodrich 2561, North Carolina 2599, Nucor 2601, Reynolds 2613
North Dakota: MDU 2652
Ohio: American 2657, **Cardinal 2677**, Cliffs 2681, Fairfield 2696, Fifth 2699, Macy's 2726, National 2748, **OMNOVA 2759**, Scripps 2780, YSI 2805
Oklahoma: Noble 2822
Pennsylvania: **Alcoa 2882**, Arkema 2885, Berks 2893, Calvert 2904, Community 2925, **PPG 3018**
Rhode Island: CVS 3068, Textron 3093
South Carolina: Spartanburg 3110
Texas: Dallas 3209, Fluor 3235, **Houston 3266**, Richardson 3336, Simmons 3352
Virginia: Lynchburg 3454
Washington: Intermec 3527
West Virginia: Tucker 3589
Wisconsin: Alliant 3592, Bemis 3598, Johnson 3625, Sauey 3655, Sentry 3657, Windhover 3668

Endowments

Arizona: Green 47, Hughes 49, Napier 55, Piper 57, Stardust 63
Arkansas: Cabe 67, Endeavor 69, Frueauff 70, Ross 72
California: Ahmanson 77, Aratani 89, Ayrshire 97, **Beavers 102**, Beynon 113, Community 160, Community 161, Copley 166, Finley 197, Fremont 207, Gellert 215, Haas 239, **Hilton 251**, Jacobs 267, Jones 270, Kern 279, Kirchgessner 282, Lucas 306, McClatchy 317, **McConnell 318**, Mosher 335, North 346, Stanislaus 425, Wasserman 453, **Wilkinson 463**
Colorado: **Malone 514**, Schlessman 530, Summit 537, Yampa 545
Connecticut: NewAlliance 595, Senior 613
District of Columbia: Lichtenberg 671
Florida: Batchelor 697, Chapman 717, Community 722, Dunspaugh-Dalton 738, Greenburg 752, Kennedy 767, **Knight 771**, Rinker 810, Southwest 823, Thomas 831
Georgia: Baker 853, Campbell 860, Exposition 873, Glenn 882, Knox 890, Lanier 891, Livingston 893, Marshall 895, Savannah 912
Hawaii: **Watumull 939**
Idaho: Cunningham 946
Illinois: Adams 956, Crown 997, Dunard 1006, Frankel 1017, **Grainger 1024**, Logan 1051, Monticello 1065, Omron 1070
Indiana: Ball 1121, Community 1133, Fairbanks 1145, Fayette 1146, Henry 1158, Jennings 1162, LaGrange 1170, Northern 1180, Owen 1185, TCU 1197, Unity 1201, Wabash 1203, Whitley 1209
Iowa: Community 1217, deStwolinski 1220, Guernsey 1221, Jefferson 1227, Maytag 1229, Stebens 1242, Wallace 1245, World 1248
Kansas: Beach 1250, Hutchinson 1260, Salina 1274, Sunderland 1278
Kentucky: Blue 1282, C.E. 1284, Community 1286
Louisiana: Community 1306, Freeman 1309, New Orleans 1316
Maine: Alfond 1324, King 1333, Libra 1334
Maryland: **Blaustein 1349**, Delaplaine 1367, Henson 1378, Hirschhorn 1379, Meyerhoff 1393, Middendorf 1394, Tucker 1415, Zickler 1419
Massachusetts: **Barr 1433**, Berkman 1434, **Brabson 1438**, Cabot 1443, Demoulas 1458, Eastern 1461, Fields 1467, Grinspoon 1479, Hazard 1480, **Kahn 1492**, Krieger 1497, Webster 1565
Michigan: Branch 1580, Charlevoix 1583, Community 1589, Dow 1597, Fremont 1607, Grand 1616, Lenawee 1634, Mount Pleasant 1647, Roscommon 1660, Wege 1674
Minnesota: Grand Rapids 1699, **Kaplan 1707**, Larsen 1711, Marbrook 1713, Opus 1724, **O'Shaughnessy 1725**, Riverway 1733, Sayer 1737
Mississippi: Community 1759, Community 1760, Sullivan 1771
Missouri: Centene 1782, Community 1783, Curry 1784, Green 1790, Saigh 1811, Walker 1818
Montana: Whitefish 1832
Nebraska: Fremont 1836, Nebraska 1851, Oregon 1852
Nevada: Parasol 1868
New Hampshire: Ham 1887, Johnson 1889
New Jersey: **Allen 1900**, Banbury 1904, Beer 1907, Brotherton 1914, Holzer 1939, Kirby 1952, **Newcombe 1972**
New York: Adirondack 2027, **Arcus 2040**, Brooks 2075, Community 2109, Community 2110, Community 2111, Cutco 2123, Eastern 2148, **Ford 2160**, **Foundation 2161**, Gebbie 2170, **Gilman 2178**, Goldman 2183, Heyman 2212, High 2213, Jaharis 2236, Knapp 2259, Littauer 2282, Markle 2290, McGonagle 2299, **Mellon 2302**, Mendell 2303, Moore 2311, Ruffin 2400, Schmitt 2410, Shoreland 2421, Simons 2423, Sulzberger 2451, Vidda 2485, Widgeon 2505
North Carolina: Community 2540, Dalton 2542, Deaver 2544, Hanes 2565, Kenan 2577, Levine 2584, Meyer 2594, North Carolina 2599, Outer 2604, Strowd 2633
North Dakota: Community 2648, North Dakota 2653
Ohio: American 2656, Andrews 2659, Ar-Hale 2661, **Bingham 2668**, Community 2685, Eaton 2693, Fairfield 2696, Findlay 2700, Foundation 2702, Hershey 2711, Maltz 2727, Marietta 2732, Marion 2733, Morgan 2740, Murphy 2744, Muskingum 2747, **OMNOVA 2759**, Osteopathic 2762, Renner 2766, Richland 2767, Scotford 2779, Scripps 2780, Slemp 2785, Steinmann 2789, Wayne 2798, YSI 2805
Oklahoma: Cherokee 2809, Hille 2816, Kirschner 2818, McGee 2820, Presbyterian 2826, Sarkeys 2828, Viersen 2830, Warren 2831
Oregon: Benton 2835, Jackson 2851, Jeld 2852, Macdonald 2859, Western 2876
Pennsylvania: Bucks 2900, Chester 2915, Claneil 2918, Copernicus 2928, Ferree 2944, Fourjay 2953, Hansen 2964, Hillman 2969, Hunt 2971, **KL 2978**, Lancaster 2981, McCune 2993, McKinney 2996, McLean 2997, Phoenixville 3014, Pierce 3015, Shaffer 3035, Trees 3048, Wyomissing 3059
Rhode Island: van Beuren 3094
South Carolina: Bailey 3096, Daniel 3101, Graham 3103, Springs 3111
Tennessee: Assisi 3120, Eastman 3133, First 3135, Phillips 3149, Tucker 3156, Wilson 3157
Texas: Brackenridge 3182, Burch 3184, Cain 3188, Carter 3190, Constantin 3202, Dunn 3216, Elkins 3220, Elkins 3221, Fairchild 3227, Fish 3233, Fluor 3235, Gulf 3245, Herzstein 3256, Hill 3259, Hoglund 3263, **Houston 3266**, Houston 3267, Kinder 3274, Light 3281, McDermott 3293, Richardson 3334, Sterling 3358, Sturgis 3360, Waggoner 3379
Virginia: Cabell 3425, Community 3429, Robins 3477
Washington: Ackerley 3489, Blue 3498, Community 3503, Dimmer 3506, Everett 3511, Harder 3524, Milgard 3543, Renton 3552, Sherwood 3561
West Virginia: Eastern 3580, Maier 3584, Tucker 3589, Your 3591
Wisconsin: Community 3607, Cornerstone 3608, Johnson 3625, Marshfield 3633, Neese 3639, Oshkosh 3642, Pick 3646, Racine 3648, St. Croix 3662
Wyoming: McMurry 3676

Equipment

Alabama: Andalusia 1, Community 9, Community 10, **International 15**
Alaska: Alaska 26
Arizona: Every 43, Hughes 49, Piper 57, Webb 64
Arkansas: Cabe 67, Delta 68, Endeavor 69, Frueauff 70, Ross 72
California: Ahmanson 77, Allergan 80, Ayrshire 97, Bannerman 100, Bothin 120, **Christensen 151**, Community 157, Community 160, Community 161, Community 162, Copley 166, Cowell 168, Crail 170, **DJ & T 184**, Eisner 189, Firedoll 198, Fleishhacker 199, Fremont 207, Fusenot 211, **Gellert 214**, Gellert 215, Gilmore 221, GSF 235, Gumbiner 236, Haas 239, Heller 246, Hewlett 249, **Hilton 251**, Hoag 253, Humboldt 257, Jones 270, **Keck 276**, Kelly 278, Kern 279, Kirchgessner 282, Kvamme 286, LA84 287, Lesher 299, Livingston 303, Lux 307, Marin 309, **Mattel 312**, **McConnell 318**, McKesson 321, Mead 324, Mosher 335, Outhwaite 353, Pacific 355, Parsons 359, Pasadena 361, Patron 363, Perkins 365, Rancho 378, Rossi 387, Samuelsson 392, San Luis 393, Santa Barbara 394, Shasta 401, Silicon 407, **Smith 416**, Sonora 420, **Special 422**, Taper 433, Treadwell 439, Truckee 441, True 442, Versacare 448, Weingart 456, Witter 467
Colorado: Bonfils 475, Burt 479, Community 484, Comprecare 485, **Crowell 487**, **Daniels 488**, El Pomar 492, Foundation 498, Mullen 522, Rose 528, Schlessman 530, Stratton 536, Summit 537, Telluride 538, Vradenburg 544, Yampa 545
Connecticut: Community 562, Community 563, Connecticut 564, **Deupree 571**, Matthies 590, Middlesex 592, NewAlliance 595, Palmer 600, **Praxair 606**, Roberts 608
Delaware: AEC 622, Brown 625, Chaney 628, Delaware 630, Edwards 631, Lennox 638, Longwood 639
District of Columbia: Graham 663, Stewart 682
Florida: Bank 695, Benjamin 699, Bi-Lo/Winn-Dixie 700, Burns 710, Bush 712, Cape Coral 714, Charlotte 718, Community 727, Conn 728, Florida 744, Glazer 750, Kennedy 767, Macdonald 783, Munroe 793, Phillips 800, Pinellas 801, Publix 804, Quantum 805, Reinhold 808, Selby 816, Southwest 823, Thomas 831, **Whitehall 840**, Wollowick 843
Georgia: Abreu 846, Amos-Cheves 849, Atlanta 852, Communities 866, Community 867, Exposition 873, Georgia 876, Georgia 877, **Georgia 878**, Harland 885, Mason 896, North 900, Pitts 904, Savannah 912, University 918, Woodward 923
Hawaii: Atherton 925, Campbell 928, Castle 930, Cooke 932, McInerny 938
Idaho: CHC 945, Cunningham 946, Idaho 948, Whittenberger 953
Illinois: Brach 973, Chicago 982, Coldwell 985, Coleman 986, Community 988, Community 989, Community 990, Community 991, Community 992, Crown 997, DeKalb 999, DuPage 1008, Edwardsville 1010, Field 1014, Frankel 1017, **Grainger 1024**, McCauley 1059, **Motorola 1066**, Oberweiler 1069, Polk 1075, Seymour 1091, Speh 1097, Stern 1100, VNA 1107, Walter 1110, Washington 1112, Webb 1113
Indiana: Auer 1120, Ball 1121, Brown 1124, Cass 1125, Central 1126, Cole 1127, Community 1129, Community 1130, Community 1131, Community 1133, Community 1134, Dearborn 1141, Decatur 1142, DeKalb 1144, Fairbanks 1145, Froderman 1148, Hancock 1154, Harrison 1155, Health 1156, Hendricks 1157, Henry 1158, Jennings 1162, Johnson 1163, Kendrick 1166, Kosciusko 1168, Kuhne 1169, LaGrange 1170, Legacy 1171, Madison 1175, Marshall 1176, Noble 1179, Northern 1180, Orange 1184, Porter 1187, Portland 1188, Rush 1192, Steel 1196, Tipton 1198, Unity 1201, Vectren 1202, Wabash 1203, Welborn 1205, Wells 1207, Western 1208
Iowa: Ahrens 1210, Clarinda 1214, Community 1217, Iowa 1226, Jefferson 1227, Maytag 1229, McElroy

1230, Siouxland 1240, Stebens 1242, Wahlert 1244
Kansas: Capitol 1251, Delta 1255, Douglas 1256, Hansen 1259, Hutchinson 1260, **Lloyd 1267**, Manhattan 1268, Salina 1274, Sunderland 1278
Kentucky: Blue 1282, Brown 1283, Community 1286, Etscorn 1287, Gheens 1288, Good 1289, Hayswood 1290, Trim 1295
Louisiana: Beaird 1301, Community 1306, Schlieder 1319, Steinhagen 1320
Maine: Borman 1325, Horizon 1331, King 1333, Libra 1334, Lynam 1335, Maine 1336, Somers 1341
Maryland: **Ames 1346**, Baker 1347, Community 1359, Dresher 1370, Fowler 1372, Freeman 1373, Gudelsky 1376, Henson 1378, Macht 1388, Meyerhoff 1393, Mid-Shore 1395, **Weinberg 1416**
Massachusetts: Boynton 1437, Cape Cod 1445, Clarke 1448, Clipper 1449, Davis 1457, DentaQuest 1459, East 1460, Essex 1464, Farnsworth 1465, **Kahn 1492**, Levy 1501, Pardoe 1522, Parker 1523, Riley 1534, Smith 1546, United 1559, Wadleigh 1562
Michigan: Branch 1580, Capital 1581, Community 1587, Community 1589, Community 1590, Community 1591, Dalton 1592, Dana 1593, Dart 1594, Delano 1596, Dow 1597, Farver 1601, Fremont 1607, Gilmore 1612, Grand Haven 1614, Grand 1616, **Isabel 1621**, Jackson 1623, Kalamazoo 1626, Lenawee 1634, Marquette 1636, McGregor 1638, Merillat 1640, Midland 1642, Morley 1644, Mount Pleasant 1647, Oleson 1649, Petoskey 1656, Pokagon 1657, Royal 1661, Saginaw 1662, Sanilac 1663, Steelcase 1667, Wege 1674
Minnesota: Beim 1683, Farmers 1695, Greystone 1700, **King 1708**, Land 1710, Marbrook 1713, McKnight 1715, Midcontinent 1716, Minneapolis 1717, Neilson 1721, Riverway 1733, Thorpe 1745, **Trust 1746**, Winona 1753
Missouri: Boylan 1776, Community 1783, Curry 1784, Dunn 1787, Gateway 1789, Green 1790, Hall 1793, Hallmark 1794, Laclede 1799, **Monsanto 1803**, Musgrave 1805, Speas 1813
Montana: Lynn 1827, Sample 1829, Whitefish 1832
Nebraska: Fremont 1836, Hirschfeld 1839, Kearney 1842, Kiewit 1843, Lexington 1845, Lincoln 1847, Midlands 1848, Mid-Nebraska 1849, Zollner 1858
Nevada: Nevada 1867, **Reynolds 1869**
New Hampshire: Alexander 1877, Bean 1878, Ham 1887, Lindsay 1890, Smyth 1895
New Jersey: Banbury 1904, Borden 1910, Brotherton 1914, Buehler 1915, Campbell 1917, Hyde 1944, Integra 1945, Kirby 1952, Leavens 1959, Summit 1998, Turrell 2002, Westfield 2004
New Mexico: Frost 2012, Maddox 2014
New York: Achelis 2026, Allyn 2032, Anderson 2036, Barker 2054, Berg 2062, Brooks 2075, Chautauqua 2091, Community 2107, Community 2109, Community 2110, Community 2112, Community 2113, **Cummings 2120**, East 2147, Family 2153, Ferraioli 2156, Freed 2163, Gebbie 2170, **Genesis 2173**, Gifford 2177, Golisano 2185, Heckscher 2205, Hoyt 2221, Hudson 2223, Hultquist 2225, Klee 2253, Lake Placid 2265, Legacy 2274, McGonagle 2299, Northern 2331, Norwich 2332, Ong 2341, **Porticus 2364**, Rapoport 2373, Robinson 2387, **Ross 2396**, Schenectady 2407, Schmitt 2410, Schnurmacher 2411, Snow 2432, Tisch 2469, **Towerbrook 2473**, Troy 2474, Truman 2475, Tuttle 2479, Wells 2501, Western 2503, Widgeon 2505
North Carolina: Adams 2517, Bailey 2522, Brady 2533, Community 2539, Community 2540, Duncan 2547, Ferebee 2552, French 2554, Ghidotti 2558, Glass 2559, Glenn 2560, Hanes 2565, Hunt 2572, Katz 2576, North Carolina 2599, Olin 2603, Outer 2604, Polk 2609, Reidsville 2611, Reynolds 2614, Rogers 2618, Sanders 2620, Smith 2629, Southern 2630, Strowd 2633, Tannenbaum 2637
North Dakota: Fargo 2649, MDU 2652, North Dakota 2653
Ohio: Anderson 2658, Austin 2663, Barberton 2664, **Bingham 2668**, Brentwood 2670, Brown 2672, Bryan 2674, Cincinnati 2679, Community 2682, Community 2684, Community 2685, Coshocton 2686, Dater 2687, Delaware 2689, **Eaton 2692**, Emery 2694, Fairfield 2696, Fifth 2699, Fowler 2703, Greene 2707, Hershey 2711, Kettering 2716, Kulas 2721, Licking 2723, Marietta 2732, Marion 2733, Mathile 2734, Middletown 2737, Morgan 2739, Murphy 2744, Murphy 2745, Muskingum 2747, National 2748, Nordson 2755, Orr 2761, Piqua 2763, Reinberger 2765, Richland 2767, Saint 2770, Salem 2771, Sandusky 2773, Scripps 2780, Sears 2781, Slemp 2785, Springfield 2787, Stark 2788, Tiffin 2793, Troy 2794, Tuscarawas 2795, Tuscora 2796, Wayne 2798, White 2800, Young 2803, Youngstown 2804, YSI 2805
Oklahoma: Bernsen 2807, Cherokee 2809, Hardesty 2814, Hille 2816, McGee 2820, Noble 2822, Oklahoma 2823, Presbyterian 2826, Sarkeys 2828, Viersen 2830
Oregon: Benton 2835, Braemar 2836, Castle 2839, Collins 2842, Ford 2846, Jeld 2852, Meyer 2861, Mission 2863, Western 2876
Pennsylvania: **Alcoa 2882**, Arkema 2885, Baker 2886, Bayer 2888, Brooks 2899, Bucks 2900, Central 2908, Centre 2909, Cestone 2910, Chase 2913, Child 2916, Claneil 2918, Community 2922, Community 2923, Community 2924, Community 2925, Connelly 2926, Degenstein 2931, DSF 2937, Elk 2939, Fels 2942, Finley 2946, First 2947, First 2948, FISA 2950, Foundation 2952, Fourjay 2953, Grundy 2962, Highmark 2968, Huston 2973, Laros 2982, Lehigh Valley 2986, McCune 2993, McLean 2997, Mellon 2998, Nelson 3003, Patterson 3010, Penn 3011, Phoenixville 3014, **PPG 3018**, Presser 3019, Snee 3039, Stackpole 3042, Trees 3048, Trexler 3049, Union 3051, Washington 3054, Wells 3055, Widener 3056, Wyomissing 3059
Puerto Rico: Puerto Rico 3061
Rhode Island: McDonald 3085, McNeil 3086, Rhode Island 3089, Textron 3093
South Carolina: Byerly 3098, Community 3099, Community 3100, Daniel 3101, Graham 3103, Lutz 3105, Smith 3109, Spartanburg 3110, Springs 3111
Tennessee: Assisi 3120, Benwood 3123, First 3135, HCA 3139, **International 3142**, Phillips 3149
Texas: Abell 3160, Amarillo 3163, Bass 3172, **Bolivar 3179**, Cailloux 3187, Carter 3190, Coastal 3196, Community 3200, Constantin 3202, Dallas 3209, Edwards 3218, Elkins 3220, Elkins 3221, Embrey 3222, Esping 3225, Farish 3228, Fisch 3232, Fluor 3235, Gulf 3245, Hamman 3248, Herzstein 3256, Hext 3257, Hillcrest 3261, Hoblitzelle 3262, Hoglund 3263, **Houston 3266**, Houston 3267, King 3275, Light 3281, Lightner 3282, Lubbock 3287, Luse 3289, **Marshall 3290**, Martinez 3291, McDermott 3293, McKee 3295, Meadows 3296, Moody 3298, Moore 3299, **Oldham 3308**, Orsinger 3310, Penney 3315, Peterson 3318, Rachal 3329, Rapoport 3331, Richardson 3334, Sams 3342, San Angelo 3343, Simmons 3352, Smith 3353, Sterling 3358, Sturgis 3360, Summerlee 3361, Tocker 3369, Trull 3373, Waco 3378, Waggoner 3379, Ward 3381, Wright 3386, Zachry 3387
Utah: Ashton 3388, Bamberger 3389, Eccles 3392, Eskuche 3393, Green 3394, Hemingway 3396
Vermont: Merchants 3414, Tarrant 3416, Vermont 3417
Virginia: **Bosack 3423**, Cabell 3425, Community 3429, Community 3431, Community 3432, Community 3433, Gwathmey 3442, **Loyola 3453**, Lynchburg 3454, Memorial 3458, Morgan, 3463, Northern 3464, Parsons 3470, Pruden 3473, Robins 3477
Washington: Anderson 3492, Bainbridge 3494, Blue 3498, Community 3503, Dimmer 3506, Everett 3511, Grays 3520, Inland 3526, Intermec 3527, Kawabe 3531, Korum 3532, Lauzier 3534, McEachern 3541, Milgard 3543, Renton 3552, Seattle 3558, Tacoma 3567, **Wilburforce 3572**, Yakima 3576
West Virginia: Beckley 3577, Community 3579, Eastern 3580, Maier 3584, McDonough 3586, Parkersburg 3587, Your 3591
Wisconsin: Alliant 3592, **Bradley 3601**, Community 3606, Community 3607, Cornerstone 3608, Dudley 3610, Eau 3611, Green Bay 3619, Incourage 3623, Johnson 3625, La Crosse 3631, Marshfield 3633, Milwaukee 3637, New 3641, Oshkosh 3642, Racine 3648, Seramur 3658, Stateline 3663, U.S. 3665, **Wagner 3666**, Windway 3669
Wyoming: McMurry 3676, Moyer 3677

Exchange programs

California: Aratani 89, **Lingnan 301**, Mazda 313
Colorado: Summit 537, Yampa 545
Indiana: Henry 1158
Iowa: Clarinda 1214
Michigan: Community 1586
New York: Berg 2062, **Clark 2098**, Freeman 2164, **Kade 2243, Trust 2477**
North Carolina: Smith 2629
Ohio: Murphy 2745
Texas: **Houston 3266**

Faculty/staff development

Louisiana: Blue 1302

Fellowships

Alabama: **International 15**
Alaska: CIRI 33
Arizona: Piper 57
California: American 82, Aratani 89, **Christensen 151**, Clif 152, Fleishhacker 199, Genentech 216, **Glenn 225, Grass 232**, Hand 241, Haynes 243, Hillblom 250, **Hilton 251**, Jones 270, Kelly 278, **Lingnan 301**, Lux 307, Mazda 313, **Packard 357**, Parsons 359, Price 373, **Rupe 389**
Colorado: Donnell 491
Connecticut: Childs 559, Deloitte 569
District of Columbia: **Institute 667, National 674**, Patterson 678, **Searle 681**
Florida: Benjamin 699, **Knight 771, Skelly 820**
Georgia: Abreu 846, **Coca 864**
Idaho: **Micron 950**
Illinois: Crown 997, Frankel 1017, **Grainger 1024, MacArthur 1056**, Monticello 1065, Schmitt 1088, Siragusa 1096, **Spencer 1098**, Washington 1112
Indiana: Fairbanks 1145
Iowa: Maytag 1229, McElroy 1230
Kansas: Capitol 1251
Kentucky: Etscorn 1287, Good 1289
Maine: Smith 1340, Switzer 1342
Maryland: **Casey 1353, de Beaumont 1366**, Deutsch 1369, Meyerhoff 1393, NASDAQ 1401, Richmond 1408
Massachusetts: **Barr 1433**, Berkman 1434, Cabot 1443, **Iacocca 1487, Kahn 1492**, Kim 1495, **Lalor 1498, Lincoln 1503**, Smith 1547
Michigan: **Kellogg 1628**
Minnesota: McKnight 1715, **St. Jude 1741**
Missouri: **Kauffman 1797**
New Jersey: **Allen 1900, Berrie 1908, JM 1947, Knowles 1955**, Merck 1966, **Milbank 1968, Newcombe 1972, Puffin 1980**
New Mexico: Frost 2012
New York: Aronson 2042, Art 2043, Berg 2062, **Commonwealth 2106**, Community 2110, **Cummings 2121, Diamond 2135, Foundation 2161**, Freeman 2164, **Friends 2167**, Goldman 2183, **Grant 2191, Guggenheim 2194**, Heckscher 2205, High 2213, **IBM 2227**, Jewish 2237, Klee 2253, Klingenstein 2256, **Klingenstein 2258**,

Film/video/radio

General/operating support

Michigan: Alro 1574, Branch 1580, Capital 1581, Community 1589, Dalton 1592, Dana 1593, Dart 1594, Delano 1596, Dow 1597, DTE 1598, **Erb 1599**, Family 1600, Farver 1601, Farwell 1602, Four 1603, Fremont 1607, Gilmore 1612, **Isabel 1621**, Isabella 1622, Jackson 1623, Jubilee 1624, Kahn 1625, Kalamazoo 1626, Keller 1627, **Kellogg 1628**, Knight 1630, **Kresge 1631**, Lear 1632, Legion 1633, Lenawee 1634, Masco 1637, McGregor 1638, Merillat 1640, Mills 1643, Morley 1644, **Mott 1645**, Mott 1646, Nartel 1648, Oleson 1649, Parish 1654, Perrigo 1655, Pokagon 1657, Prince 1658, Royal 1661, Skillman 1666, Steelcase 1667, Technical 1668, Van Andel 1669, Vanderweide 1671, Von 1672, Wege 1674, Wilson 1675

Minnesota: 3M 1676, **Andersen 1678**, Avocet 1680, Best 1685, Boss 1686, Butler 1688, Dayton 1690, Depot 1691, Duluth 1693, Edina 1694, Frey 1696, General 1697, George 1698, Greystone 1700, HRK 1702, Initiative 1703, Johnson 1705, Jostens 1706, **King 1708**, Koran 1709, Land 1710, Larsen 1711, Marbrook 1713, McKnight 1715, Minneapolis 1717, **Mosaic 1718**, Nash 1720, Northwest 1722, Opus 1724, **O'Shaughnessy 1725**, **Pentair 1727**, Phillips 1728, RBC 1730, Redwood 1731, Regis 1732, Riverway 1733, Securian 1739, **St. Jude 1741**, SUPERVALU 1743, Target 1744, Thorpe 1745, WCA 1749, Winona 1753, Xcel 1754

Mississippi: Community 1759, Community 1760, Ergon 1761, Feild 1762, Foundation 1763, Gulf 1764, Mississippi 1769, Regions 1770, Sullivan 1771, Walker 1772

Missouri: Anheuser 1774, Bunge 1779, Butler 1780, Canfield 1781, Centene 1782, Community 1783, Curry 1784, Dunn 1787, Fabick 1788, Hall 1793, Hallmark 1794, **Kauffman 1797**, Laclede 1799, Millstone 1801, **Monsanto 1803**, Musgrave 1805, Nichols 1806, Ross 1810, Schneider 1812, Speas 1813, Truman 1817, Walker 1818

Montana: Lynn 1827, Wendy's 1831, Whitefish 1832

Nebraska: **Buffett 1833**, Cooper 1834, Grand Island 1837, Hawkins 1838, Hirschfeld 1839, Kiewit 1843, Lincoln 1847, Mutual 1850, Nebraska 1851, Weitz 1855, Woods 1857, Zollner 1858

Nevada: Caesars 1860, Nevada 1867, Parasol 1868

New Hampshire: Alexander 1877, Bean 1878, Byrne 1879, Foundation 1885, Fuller 1886, HNH 1888, Panjandrum 1892

New Jersey: **Alcatel 1899**, Baker 1903, Banbury 1904, Bard 1905, Beer 1907, **Berrie 1908**, Borden 1910, Bunbury 1916, Campbell 1917, Elias 1923, Gamper 1933, Gibson 1934, Harbourton 1936, Horizon 1940, Hudson 1942, Integra 1945, Kirby 1952, Mandelbaum 1962, MCJ 1965, Merck 1966, Onyx 1974, Post 1978, Princeton 1979, Saka 1987, **Sanofi 1988**, Savin 1989, Schumann 1990, Schwarz 1991, **Siemens 1993**, Syms 1999, Turrell 2002, Unilever 2003, Wight 2005

New Mexico: Albuquerque 2006, B.F. 2008, Chase 2009, Con 2011, Maddox 2014, Santa Fe 2017

New York: 1848 2020, **Abba's 2021**, Abelard 2022, Access 2025, Achelis 2026, Adirondack 2027, Aequus 2028, Alfiero 2031, American 2033, **American 2034**, Anderson 2036, Animal 2038, **Animal 2039**, **Arcus 2040**, Assurant 2047, AYN 2052, Barker 2054, Barking 2055, Bay 2056, Berg 2062, Black 2065, Box 2068, Bronfman 2073, **Bronfman 2074**, **Buffalo 2078**, Butler 2081, **Bydale 2082**, **Carnegie 2085**, Carson 2086, Caruso 2087, Century 2089, Chapman 2090, Chautauqua 2091, Chiang 2094, **Clark 2097**, Clark 2099, Coach 2100, Community 2107, Community 2108, Community 2112, Countess 2116, **Credit 2118**, Cricket 2119, **Cummings 2121**, Dammann 2125, Daphne 2127, Dean 2130, Deerfield 2132, **Deutsche 2134**, **Discount 2139**, Dobkin 2140, Donner 2142, **Dramatists 2143**, Dreitzer 2144, Dreyfus 2145, Farash 2154, Fisher 2157, **Ford 2160**, **Foundation 2161**, Freed 2163, Freeman 2164, **Friends 2167**, Gebbie 2170, Gifford 2177, **Gilman 2178**, Gimbel 2179, **Goldman 2182**, Goldman 2183, Golisano 2185, Grant 2190, Guttman 2197, Hadar 2198, Hagedorn 2200, Hallingby 2201, **Henson 2210**, **Heron 2211**, High 2213, Hochstein 2216, Hudson 2223, Hultquist 2225, Hycliff 2226, **IBM 2227**, **Jabara 2235**, Johnson 2240, **JPMorgan 2242**, **Kaplan 2245**, Kaylie 2247, Keet 2248, **King 2251**, Klingenstein 2256, Knapp 2259, Lake Placid 2265, Lavelle 2269, Liberman 2279, Lissner 2281, Litwin 2283, Luce 2285, **Luce 2286**, Marine 2289, Marks 2291, **Mathers 2294**, **Mertz 2306**, **MetLife 2307**, Mindich 2309, Moore 2311, Morgan 2315, Mule 2316, Mutual 2317, Nakash 2318, **Nash 2320**, NBC 2322, New York 2326, New York 2327, **Noyes 2335**, NYSE 2336, O'Grady 2339, Oishei 2340, Ong 2341, **Open 2343**, Ostgrodd 2344, **Overbrook 2345**, Park 2349, Paxton 2352, **PepsiCo 2354**, **Porticus 2364**, Rapoport 2373, Rasmussen 2375, Rauch 2376, Regals 2377, Rich 2382, Roche 2388, **Rockefeller 2389**, **Rockefeller 2390**, Rose 2392, Rothstein 2397, **Rubin 2398**, Ruffin 2400, Sandy 2404, Schenectady 2407, Scherman 2409, Schmitt 2410, Schnurmacher 2411, Schumann 2412, Seneca 2415, **Shatford 2417**, Shoolman 2420, Shoreland 2421, Simons 2423, Sirus 2426, Snayberger 2431, Snyder 2433, Spektor 2442, Sprague 2444, Sulzberger 2451, Sunrise 2453, **Surdna 2454**, Tananbaum 2457, Thompson 2461, Tiffany 2463, Tiger 2464, Time 2466, **Towerbrook 2473**, **Tsadra 2478**, Tuttle 2479, van Ameringen 2482, van Ameringen 2483, Vidda 2485, Wachtell, 2490, Wagner 2491, **Wallace 2492**, Warwick 2495, **Weeden 2496**, Weil, 2498, Widgeon 2505, **Youth 2513**

North Carolina: Adams 2517, Babcock 2521, Bailey 2522, **Bank 2524**, Bettman 2528, Billingsley 2530, Bolick 2531, Brady 2533, Caine 2536, Cumberland 2541, Davie 2543, Everett 2550, Fairfield 2551, Fund 2555, Glenn 2560, Goodrich 2561, Griffin 2563, Harvest 2566, Helb 2568, Howe 2570, Hunt 2572, Katz 2576, Kistler 2579, **Laffin 2583**, Meyer 2594, Niessen 2598, North Carolina 2599, Olin 2603, Perkin 2607, Polk 2609, Reidsville 2611, Rogers 2618, Sanders 2620, Sherrard 2623, Shingleton 2624, Sites 2627, Smith 2629, Southern 2630, Stahlberg 2631, Strowd 2633, Stuart 2634, Tannenbaum 2637, VF 2642, Wann 2643, Woodson 2644, Zelnak 2647

North Dakota: MDU 2652, North Dakota 2653

Ohio: American 2656, Andrews 2659, Angels 2660, Ar-Hale 2661, Austin 2663, **Bingham 2668**, Brentwood 2670, Brethen 2671, Brown 2672, **Brush 2673**, Charities 2678, Cliffs 2681, Community 2683, Community 2685, Dater 2687, Dayton 2688, Dodero 2691, **Eaton 2692**, Eaton 2693, Evans 2695, Fairfield 2696, Ferro 2697, Fifth 2699, Findlay 2700, Foss 2701, Foundation 2702, Fowler 2703, Gardner 2705, Ginn 2706, Gund 2708, Kettering 2716, KeyBank 2717, Knoll 2719, Knowlton 2720, Kulas 2721, Macy's 2726, Maltz 2727, Mandel 2728, **Mandel 2729**, Marietta 2732, Marion 2733, Mathile 2734, Mayerson 2735, Morgan 2739, Morgan 2740, Morgan 2741, Murphy 2744, Murphy 2745, Murphy 2746, Muskingum 2747, National 2748, **Needmor 2749**, Nippert 2751, **Noble 2753**, Nord 2754, Ohio 2756, **Omnicare 2758**, **OMNOVA 2759**, Orr 2761, Progressive 2764, Reinberger 2765, Richland 2767, Saint 2770, Samaritan 2772, Schottenstein 2777, Scotford 2779, Scripps 2780, Sears 2781, Skyler 2784, Springfield 2787, Stark 2788, Third 2792, Veale 2797, Youngstown 2804

Oklahoma: Adams 2806, Chapman 2808, Harmon 2815, Hille 2816, McGee 2820, Merrick 2821, Noble 2822, Oklahoma 2823, **Schusterman 2829**, Viersen 2830, Warren 2831, Zarrow 2833, Zarrow 2834

Oregon: Benton 2835, Braemar 2836, Burning 2837, Caddock 2838, Castle 2839, Ford 2846, Hedinger 2849, Jeld 2852, Lazar 2856, Macdonald 2859, Meyer 2861, Michael 2862, Mission 2863, Morris 2864, **NIKE 2865**, PacificSource 2866, PGE 2867, Renaissance 2869, Templeton 2874, Woodard 2877, Wyss 2878

Pennsylvania: **ACE 2880**, Adams 2881, Allegheny 2883, Ames 2884, Arkema 2885, Baker 2886, Barra 2887, Beacon 2889, Beaver 2890, Birmingham 2896, Black 2897, Bucks 2900, Buncher 2902, Burgess 2903, Central 2908, Centre 2909, Cestone 2910, Charlestein 2911, Chase 2913, Chenault 2914, Chester 2915, Child 2916, CIGNA 2917, Claneil 2918, Clareth 2919, Comcast 2921, Community 2925, Connelly 2926, Dozzi 2935, DSF 2937, Feldman 2941, Fels 2942, Ferree 2944, Finley 2946, First 2947, First 2948, FISA 2950, Foundation 2952, Fourjay 2953, Freas 2954, Goshen 2959, Grundy 2962, Hansen 2964, Harris 2965, Heinz 2966, Henkels 2967, Highmark 2968, Honickman 2970, Hunt 2971, Huston 2973, Independence 2975, Independence 2976, **KL 2978**, Kunkel 2980, Martin 2991, McKinney 2996, Mellon 2998, Mendel 2999, Mylan 3001, Nelson 3003, O'Brien-Veba 3007, Patterson 3010, Penn 3011, Phoenixville 3014, Pierce 3015, Pilgrim 3016, Pottstown 3017, **PPG 3018**, Raab 3020, Randall 3021, **Respironics 3023**, Rider 3024, Rossin 3028, Saramar 3029, Scranton 3031, Sedwick 3032, Shaffer 3035, Society 3040, Trees 3048, Trexler 3049, Tuttleman 3050, Union 3051, United 3052, Valentine 3053, Washington 3054, Wilson 3058, Wyomissing 3059, **Zeldin 3060**

Puerto Rico: Puerto Rico 3061

Rhode Island: Biogen 3063, Citizens 3067, **Dorot 3071**, Estate 3073, Hasbro 3077, Kimball 3079, Masonic 3083, McDonald 3085, McNeil 3086, Rhode Island 3089, Seymour 3091, Shaw's 3092, Textron 3093, van Beuren 3094, Washington 3095

South Carolina: Black 3097, Byerly 3098, Joanna 3104, McKissick 3106, Singing 3108, Smith 3109, Springs 3111

Tennessee: Alumni 3119, Assisi 3120, Baptist 3122, Briggs 3124, CIC 3127, Eastman 3133, First 3135, HCA 3139, Hutcheson 3141, **International 3142**, Lyndhurst 3145, Phillips 3149, Regal 3151, **Scarlett 3152**, Tucker 3156, Wilson 3157

Texas: Abell 3160, Anderson 3164, Astin 3166, Augur 3168, Baron 3171, Bass 3172, Beal 3174, Beasley 3175, Bickel 3178, **BP 3181**, Brown 3183, Burch 3184, Burnett 3185, Cailloux 3187, Carter 3190, CEMEX 3191, Coastal 3196, Coates 3197, Collins 3199, Community 3200, Dallas 3209, Deakins 3210, Edwards 3218, Edwards 3219, Embrey 3222, Erol 3224, Fairchild 3227, Fasken 3229, Fisch 3232, Fish 3233, Flarsheim 3234, Fluor 3235, Frees 3238, Gage 3239, Goldsbury 3241, Goodman 3242, Gulf 3245, Hachar 3246, Hamman 3248, Heavin 3253, Herzstein 3256, Hext 3257, Hill 3260, Hoglund 3263, Holloway 3264, **Houston 3266**, Houston 3267, **International 3269**, KDK-Harman 3273, Kinder 3274, Lightner 3282, Littauer 3283, Lockheed 3284, Long 3285, Lubbock 3287, Luse 3289, **Marshall 3290**, Martinez 3291, Mayor 3292, McDermott 3293, McKee 3295, Meadows 3296, Moore 3299, Morgan 3301, Northen 3306, NuStar 3307, Orsinger 3310, P 3311, Peine 3313, Penney 3315, Peterson 3318, **PHM 3320**, Powell 3324, QuadW 3328, Rachal 3329, Rapoport 3331, Reilly 3333, Richardson 3334, Richardson 3335, Rockwell 3338, Rogers 3339, Rosewood 3340, Sams 3342, San Angelo 3343, Shell 3348, Shelter 3349, Simmons 3352, Sterling 3358, Sturgis 3360, Talkington 3362, Topfer 3372, Trull 3373, Tyler 3375, **VHA 3377**, Waggoner 3379, Willard 3382

Utah: Ashton 3388, Bamberger 3389, Eccles 3392, Eskuche 3393, Hemingway 3396, Quinney 3402

Vermont: **Ben 3407**, Lintilhac 3412, McKenzie 3413, Tarrant 3416, Vermont 3417, Windham 3418

Virginia: AMERIGROUP 3420, Arlington 3421, **Blue 3422**, Capital 3426, Charlottesville 3428, Community 3429, Community 3431, Community 3432, Community 3433, **Foundation 3438**, Lee-Jackson 3448, MAXIMUS 3457, Memorial 3458, Metropolitan 3459, Moore 3461, **Olmsted**

3468, Potomac 3471, Pruden 3473, RECO 3474, Robins 3477, Samberg 3478, Stafford 3480, Strong 3481, **Truland 3482**, Twinkling 3483, United 3484, **WestWind 3486**, Williamsburg 3487

Washington: Arise 3493, Bainbridge 3494, Blue 3498, Casey 3499, Casey 3500, Community 3503, Community 3504, Corvias 3505, Dimmer 3506, Everett 3511, Fales 3512, Ferguson 3513, First 3514, **Gates 3516, Glaser 3517, Goodwin 3519**, Grays 3520, Haller 3522, Harder 3524, Inland 3526, **Ji 3528**, Kawabe 3531, Korum 3532, Lochland 3536, Medina 3542, Milgard 3543, Northwest 3546, OneFamily 3547, PEMCO 3549, REI 3551, Renton 3552, Safeco 3554, Seattle 3558, Smith 3564, **Starbucks 3565**, Tacoma 3567, Whatcom 3571, **Wilburforce 3572**

West Virginia: Eastern 3580, Fenton 3581, Maier 3584, McCormick 3585, McDonough 3586, Tucker 3589, Weisberg 3590

Wisconsin: Ariens 3594, **Baird 3595**, BayCare 3597, Bemis 3598, **Bradley 3601**, Chipstone 3605, Community 3606, Community 3607, Cornerstone 3608, Door 3609, Dudley 3610, Einhorn 3613, Elmwood 3614, Fort 3616, Johnson 3625, Keller 3626, Kuenzl 3630, La Crosse 3631, Manitowoc 3632, Marshfield 3633, McBeath 3634, McDonough 3635, Menasha 3636, Neese 3639, Oshkosh 3642, Oshkosh 3643, Pamida 3644, Pettit 3645, Pick 3646, RITE-HITE 3651, Sand 3654, Sauey 3655, Sentry 3657, Smith 3660, St. Croix 3662, U.S. 3665, Wanek 3667, Windhover 3668, Zilber 3670

Wyoming: Cody 3672, McMurry 3676, Perkins 3678, Scott 3679, Weiss 3682, Whitney 3683, Wyoming 3684

Grants to individuals

Alaska: Alaska 26, CIRI 33, Koniag 36

Arkansas: Wal-Mart 74

California: **Alalusi 78**, California 140, Carlston 143, CEC 146, **CW 176, Ellison 191**, Fleishhacker 199, **Foundation 202**, Foundation 203, Guzik 238, Humboldt 257, Optivest 351, Picerne 369, Rancho 378, Rest 381, Rosenberg 386, Sonora 420

Colorado: Colorado 482, Helmar 505, Sachs 529, SEAKR 531, Society 534

Connecticut: Colburn-Keenan 560, Senior 613

Delaware: **AstraZeneca 623**, CenturyLink-Clarke 627

Florida: Community 722, Coral Gables 729, DeBartolo 734, Erdle 740, Hard 756, King 768

Georgia: Amos-Cheves 849, **Rosenberg 910**, Southern 915

Hawaii: Ching 931

Illinois: **Abbott 954**, de Kay 998, Driehaus 1002, **Walgreens 1109**

Indiana: Hendricks 1157

Iowa: United 1243, World 1248

Kansas: Damon 1254, Jones 1262, Salina 1274

Kentucky: Kentucky 1292

Maryland: **Casey 1353**

Massachusetts: **A Child 1420**, Association 1428, Cape Cod 1445, Kim 1495, Weber 1564, **Xeric 1570**

Michigan: Four 1603, Pardee 1652

Minnesota: Koran 1709

Missouri: Butler 1780

New Jersey: **American 1902**, Feldstein 1928, **Knowles 1955, Puffin 1980, Sanofi 1988**, Segal 1992

New York: **Abba's 2021, Animal 2039**, Art 2043, Artists 2044, Broadcasters 2071, Collins 2105, Community 2109, Ebb 2149, **Gottlieb 2187**, Havens 2204, **Henson 2210**, Kleban 2252, Klingenstein 2256, **Koussevitzky 2262**, Lissner 2281, **Luce 2286**, Marine 2289, **Open 2343, Pollock 2363, Schepp 2408, Skadden 2427, Soros 2439, Sparkplug 2441**, St. George's 2445, Tuttle 2479, **Wenner 2502**

North Carolina: Beckman 2526, Eddy 2548, Strowd 2633

Ohio: Foss 2701, Marietta 2732, National 2748, Samaritan 2772, Scripps 2780, Tuscarawas 2795

Oregon: I Have 2850

Pennsylvania: Berks 2893, **Cardiovascular 2905, Carnegie 2906**, Community 2925, Female 2943, Honickman 2970, Leeway 2985, Merchants 3000, Presser 3019, **Templeton 3047**

Rhode Island: Rhode Island 3089

Tennessee: Hurlbut 3140, Stuttering 3155

Texas: Alcon 3161, Heinlein 3254, Lockheed 3284, Penney 3315, Perot 3317, Sikh 3351, South 3356, Task 3363, Texas 3364, **VHA 3377**

Vermont: Vermont 3417

Virgin Islands: Community 3419

Virginia: Arlington 3421, Community 3433

Washington: **Ji 3528**, Tudor 3569

Wisconsin: BayCare 3597, Marshfield 3633, **Wagner 3666**

Wyoming: Cody 3672, Perkins 3678

Income development

Alabama: Central 8

California: Ahmanson 77, Aratani 89, Placer 371, **Special 422**, Truckee 441

Colorado: Pikes 525

Georgia: Healthcare 886

Hawaii: Kaneta 936

Illinois: Chicago 982, Coleman 986, Evanston 1012, Oak Park 1068

Indiana: Community 1132, Putnam 1189, Tipton 1198

Iowa: Community 1217

Kansas: Capitol 1251

Kentucky: C.E. 1284

Maryland: Baker 1347, Straus 1410

Massachusetts: Lowell 1505

Michigan: Ann Arbor 1576

Minnesota: West 1751

New York: Community 2108, New York 2325, Rapoport 2373, Western 2503

North Carolina: Community 2540, Cumberland 2541

Ohio: Foundation 2702, Ginn 2706, Morgan 2739, O'Neill 2760, Wean 2799

Oregon: Meyer 2861, Mission 2863

Pennsylvania: Centre 2909, **KL 2978**, McCune 2993

Texas: **Houston 3266**, Littauer 3283, **Marshall 3290**, Meadows 3296, Rockwell 3338

Vermont: Vermont 3417

Virginia: Robins 3477

Washington: Allen 3490, Bainbridge 3494, Casey 3500, Grays 3520, Satterberg 3556

In-kind gifts

Alabama: Black 4, Community 10

Arkansas: Union 73

California: Fox 205, **Kapor 273, Lawrence 293, Mattel 312, McConnell 318**, North 346, Sierra 405, Western 459, **World 468**

Colorado: El Pomar 492, Summit 537

Connecticut: SBM 611

Florida: Coral Gables 729, Darden 732, Glazer 750, Jacksonville 761, Peterson 799

Georgia: **Georgia 878**, Savannah 912

Illinois: Community 988, **Mondelez 1064, Walgreens 1109**

Indiana: Ball 1121, Community 1134, Fayette 1146, Jennings 1162, LaGrange 1170, Noble 1179, Old 1182

Iowa: Community 1217, World 1248

Kansas: Collective 1253, Topeka 1279

Maryland: Henson 1378, Mid-Shore 1395

Massachusetts: Cape Cod 1445

Michigan: Branch 1580, Community 1591, Hillsdale 1620

Minnesota: 3M 1676, **Mosaic 1718**, Northwest 1723

Missouri: Truman 1817

Nebraska: Fremont 1836, Mutual 1850

Nevada: Parasol 1868

New Hampshire: Ham 1887

New Jersey: **Novartis 1973**

New York: **MetLife 2307, PepsiCo 2354**

North Carolina: Cumberland 2541, Goodrich 2561

North Dakota: Fargo 2649

Ohio: **Cardinal 2677, Eaton 2692**, Muskingum 2747, **OMNOVA 2759**, Stark 2788

Oklahoma: **Schusterman 2829**

Oregon: Portland 2868

Pennsylvania: EQT 2940

Puerto Rico: Puerto Rico 3061

South Carolina: Community 3099, Spartanburg 3110

Tennessee: **International 3142**, Regal 3151

Texas: Alcon 3161, **Houston 3266, Marshall 3290**, McKee 3295, Sams 3342

Utah: Hemingway 3396

Washington: Community 3504, Grays 3520, San Juan 3555, Whatcom 3571

Wisconsin: Community 3607, Marshfield 3633, Windway 3669

Internship funds

Alaska: Alaska 26, CIRI 33, Doyon 34, Koniag 36

California: **Lingnan 301**, Lux 307, Parsons 359, **Rupe 389**

Colorado: Leighty 512

Connecticut: **Deupree 571**

Florida: Benjamin 699, Community 722, Greenburg 752, **Skelly 820**

Illinois: Frankel 1017, Lumpkin 1053, McGraw 1060, Monticello 1065, Oberweiler 1069, Speh 1097

Iowa: Maytag 1229, McElroy 1230, World 1248

Kansas: Capitol 1251, Skillbuilders 1277

Kentucky: C.E. 1284

Maine: Horizon 1331

Maryland: Deutsch 1369

Massachusetts: **Kahn 1492**, Kendall 1494

Minnesota: Thorpe 1745

New Jersey: Brotherton 1914, Buehler 1915, **JM 1947**, Merck 1966, **Newcombe 1972**

New Mexico: B.F. 2008

New York: Aronson 2042, Goldman 2183, Heckscher 2205, High 2213, **Kress 2263**, Levitt 2275, **Luce 2286**, Morgan 2315, O'Grady 2339, **Open 2343**, Patrina 2350, **Peterson 2357**, Sulzberger 2451

North Carolina: **Bank 2524**, Eddy 2548, North 2600, Polk 2609, Strowd 2633, Tannenbaum 2637

Ohio: Gund 2708, Morgan 2740, Muskingum 2747, Nippert 2751, Scripps 2780, Sears 2781, Seasongood 2782

Oklahoma: **Schusterman 2829**

Oregon: Benton 2835, Macdonald 2859

Pennsylvania: Centre 2909, Fels 2942, Independence 2975, Society 3040, Tuttleman 3050

Rhode Island: **Dorot 3071**, Textron 3093

South Carolina: Community 3099

Tennessee: **Scarlett 3152**, Tucker 3156

Texas: **Houston 3266**, QuadW 3328, Summerlee 3361

Washington: Blue 3498

West Virginia: Eastern 3580

Wisconsin: **Bradley 3601**, Community 3607

Land acquisition

Arizona: Webb 64

Arkansas: Cabe 67

California: Ahmanson 77, Ayrshire 97, Cowell 168, Firedoll 198, **Foundation 202**, Gold 228, Marin 309, Mead 324, **Moore 333, Packard 357**, Rancho 378, Santa Barbara 394

Colorado: Ballantine 474, El Pomar 492, Summit 537

Delaware: AEC 622, Lennox 638, Longwood 639

District of Columbia: **Wallace 683**
Florida: Bush 712, Coral Gables 729, Reinhold 808, Selby 816
Georgia: Campbell 860
Illinois: Chicago 982, Edwardsville 1010, Field 1014, Frankel 1017, Nelson 1067, Oberweiler 1069
Indiana: Auer 1120, Brown 1124, Central 1126, Cole 1127, Harrison 1155, Hendricks 1157, Kendrick 1166, LaGrange 1170, Noble 1179, Unity 1201
Iowa: Community 1217, Maytag 1229, Stebens 1242
Kansas: Sunderland 1278
Kentucky: Brown 1283, C.E. 1284
Louisiana: Community 1306
Maine: King 1333, Libra 1334, Somers 1341
Maryland: Meyerhoff 1393, Mid-Shore 1395
Massachusetts: **Barr 1433**, Cape Cod 1445, Davis 1457, Fields 1467, Kelsey 1493, Parker 1523, Sheehan 1545, **Sweet 1554**, **Xeric 1570**
Michigan: Anderson 1575, Dalton 1592, Frey 1609, Gilmore 1612, Grand Haven 1614, Grand Rapids 1615, Jackson 1623, Mount Pleasant 1647, Oleson 1649, Pokagon 1657
Minnesota: Greystone 1700, **King 1708**, Marbrook 1713
Missouri: Boylan 1776, Green 1790, Hall 1793
Montana: Sample 1829
Nebraska: Hirschfeld 1839, Kiewit 1843, Lincoln 1847, Midlands 1848, Mid-Nebraska 1849
New Hampshire: Fuller 1886, Ham 1887, Panjandrum 1892, Penates 1893
New Jersey: Hyde 1944, Kirby 1952
New Mexico: Maddox 2014
New York: Adirondack 2027, Community 2110, **Cummings 2120**, Ferraioli 2156, Freeman 2164, Gifford 2177, Hultquist 2225, Schenectady 2407, Thompson 2461, **Weeden 2496**, Western 2503
North Carolina: Bailey 2522, Ferebee 2552, Glass 2559, Hanes 2565, Tannenbaum 2637
Ohio: Barberton 2664, Fairfield 2696, Gund 2708, Kulas 2721, Maltz 2727, Muskingum 2747, Richland 2767, Salem 2771, Scotford 2779, Sears 2781, Stark 2788, Wayne 2798
Oklahoma: Hille 2816, McGee 2820, Viersen 2830
Oregon: Woodard 2877
Pennsylvania: Claneil 2918, First 2947, Grundy 2962, Martin 2991, McCune 2993, McLean 2997, Mellon 2998, Patterson 3010, Penn 3011, Trexler 3049
Rhode Island: Rhode Island 3089, Seymour 3091, van Beuren 3094
Tennessee: Benwood 3123, Lyndhurst 3145, Tucker 3156
Texas: Amarillo 3163, Brown 3183, Cailloux 3187, Carter 3190, Constantin 3202, Herzstein 3256, Hext 3257, Hillcrest 3261, Hoblitzelle 3262, **Houston 3266**, Houston 3267, Kinder 3274, McDermott 3293, Meadows 3296, Moody 3298, Richardson 3334, San Angelo 3343, Sterling 3358, Summerlee 3361
Utah: Eccles 3392
Vermont: Lintilhac 3412
Virginia: Robins 3477, **WestWind 3486**
Washington: Community 3503, Ferguson 3513, Grays 3520, Green 3521, **Ji 3528**, Sherwood 3561, Tacoma 3567
West Virginia: Eastern 3580
Wisconsin: Community 3606, Dudley 3610, Milwaukee 3637, U.S. 3665
Wyoming: Moyer 3677

Loans—to individuals

Florida: Benjamin 699
Minnesota: Northwest 1723, Southwest 1740
New York: Authors 2050
Ohio: Samaritan 2772

Management development/capacity building

Alabama: BBVA 3, Central 8, Community 9, Community 10
Arizona: Piper 57
Arkansas: Cabe 67, Wal-Mart 74
California: Ahmanson 77, Aratani 89, Atlas 96, Bechtel 103, Bechtel, 104, Blue 114, California 137, California 138, Campbell 142, Clif 152, Community 157, Community 160, Community 161, Community 163, Cowell 168, Eisner 189, Fox 205, **Fund 210**, Gerbode 217, **Hilton 251**, Humboldt 257, **Kapor 273**, Kern 279, Laguna 288, Lesher 299, **Lingnan 301**, McCune 320, Napa 340, North 346, Noyce 348, Pacific 354, Pacific 355, **Packard 357**, Placer 371, Rancho 378, **Rivendell 384**, Rosenberg 385, Sacramento 391, San Luis 393, Silicon 408, Soda 418, Solano 419, Sonora 420, **Special 422**, Stuart 429, Truckee 441, UniHealth 444, Weingart 456
Colorado: Bonfils 475, **Crowell 487**, Leighty 512, Pikes 525, Rose 528, Summit 537, Vradenburg 544
Connecticut: Community 562, Connecticut 564, Middlesex 592, NewAlliance 595
Delaware: Edwards 631, Longwood 639
District of Columbia: Cafritz 656, **El-Hibri 659**, Jovid 668, Meyer 672, Wallace 684
Florida: Bush 712, Charlotte 718, Community 723, Community 724, Conn 728, Florida 744, Henderson 758, **Knight 771**, Quantum 805, Southwest 823, Winter 842
Georgia: Camp-Younts 861, Communities 866, **Georgia 878**, Healthcare 886, Moore 897, North 900
Hawaii: Atherton 925, Castle 929, Cooke 932, Hawaii 933
Idaho: Idaho 948
Illinois: Chicago 982, Community 990, Community 992, Community 993, Evanston 1012, Guthman 1027, Kaplan 1041, Libra 1050, Lumpkin 1053, Oak Park 1068, Pierce 1074, Polk 1075, Speh 1097, Stone 1102, Tracy 1104
Indiana: Ball 1121, Community 1128, Community 1132, Community 1133, Community 1136, Fairbanks 1145, Foellinger 1147, Harrison 1155, Health 1156, Johnson 1163, LaGrange 1170, **Lumina 1174**, Noble 1179, Porter 1187, Tipton 1198
Iowa: Community 1216, Community 1217, Iowa 1226, Wellmark 1246
Kansas: Capitol 1251, Douglas 1256, Farah 1258, Kansas 1263, Salina 1274, **Shumaker 1276**
Kentucky: Blue 1282, C.E. 1284
Louisiana: Beaird 1301, Blue 1302, Community 1306, New Orleans 1316
Maine: Cohen 1327, Maine 1336, Sewall 1339
Maryland: Baker 1347, **Casey 1353**, Community 1359, **de Beaumont 1366**, Mid-Shore 1395, Zickler 1419
Massachusetts: Access 1422, **Barr 1433**, Cape Cod 1445, Community 1453, Davis 1457, DentaQuest 1459, Essex 1464, Kendall 1494, Lowell 1505, Melville 1511, Smith 1546, Sudbury 1551
Michigan: Ann Arbor 1576, Capital 1581, Community 1586, Community 1590, **Erb 1599**, Fremont 1607, Knight 1630, Lenawee 1634, **Mott 1645**, Mott 1646, Mount Pleasant 1647, Pokagon 1657, Steelcase 1667
Minnesota: Larsen 1711, Northwest 1722, Northwest 1723, Phillips 1728, Rochester 1735, Winona 1753
Mississippi: Community 1760, Foundation 1763
Missouri: Bellwether 1775, Community 1783
Montana: Whitefish 1832
Nebraska: Cooper 1834, Fremont 1836, Lincoln 1847, Nebraska 1851
New Jersey: **Allen 1900**, **Berrie 1908**, Elias 1923, **JM 1947**, Merck 1966, **Rippel 1982**, Westfield 2004
New Mexico: Con 2011, Santa Fe 2017
New York: **American 2034**, **Arcus 2040**, **Clark 2097**, Clark 2099, Community 2108, Community 2109, Community 2110, Community 2112, Community 2113, **Credit 2118**, Cricket 2119, **Cummings 2121**, DeCamp 2131, **Deutsche 2134**, **Ford 2160**, **Frankenberg 2162**, **Genesis 2173**, Gould 2188, Johnson 2240, **JPMorgan 2242**, **MetLife 2307**, **Nash 2320**, New York 2325, New York 2326, Oishei 2340, Ong 2341, Park 2349, **PepsiCo 2354**, **Porticus 2364**, Rapoport 2373, Sheafer 2418, **Sparkplug 2441**, **Surdna 2454**, Tiger 2464, Tower 2472, van Ameringen 2483
North Carolina: **Bank 2524**, Brady 2533, Community 2539, Community 2540, Cumberland 2541, Davie 2543, Goodrich 2561, North Carolina 2599, Reidsville 2611, Rex 2612, Strowd 2633, Tannenbaum 2637
North Dakota: Fargo 2649
Ohio: Abington 2654, Ar-Hale 2661, Athens 2662, **Bingham 2668**, Fairfield 2696, Fifth 2699, Findlay 2700, Fowler 2703, Ginn 2706, Kettering 2716, Maltz 2727, Mayerson 2735, Morgan 2739, Morgan 2741, O'Neill 2760, Osteopathic 2762, Reinberger 2765, Richland 2767, Saint 2770, Sandusky 2773, Sears 2781, Tuscarawas 2795, Wayne 2798, Wean 2799, Youngstown 2804
Oklahoma: Cherokee 2809, Hille 2816, Sarkeys 2828, Viersen 2830
Oregon: Ford 2846, Meyer 2861, Mission 2863, **NIKE 2865**
Pennsylvania: **Alcoa 2882**, Baker 2886, Barra 2887, Benedum 2892, Bucks 2900, Buhl 2901, Chester 2915, Claneil 2918, First 2948, Heinz 2966, Highmark 2968, Independence 2975, **KL 2978**, Lancaster 2981, Lehigh Valley 2986, McCune 2993, North 3006, Penn 3011, Phoenixville 3014, Pottstown 3017, Staunton 3044
Puerto Rico: Puerto Rico 3061
Rhode Island: CVS 3068, Rhode Island 3089
South Carolina: Black 3097, Community 3100, Daniel 3101
Tennessee: Assisi 3120, Benwood 3123, **Scarlett 3152**
Texas: Alcon 3162, Amarillo 3163, Booth 3180, **Chrest 3194**, Dallas 3209, **Houston 3266**, KDK-Harman 3273, King 3275, Meadows 3296, Orsinger 3310, Powell 3324, Rockwell 3338, San Angelo 3343, Simmons 3352, Tocker 3369, Trull 3373, Waco 3378
Vermont: **Ben 3407**, Vermont 3417
Virginia: Arlington 3421, Capital 3426, Northern 3464, Robins 3477, Samberg 3478, Williamsburg 3487
Washington: Allen 3490, Blue 3498, Casey 3500, Community 3503, Grays 3520, Inland 3526, Medina 3542, Satterberg 3556, Sherwood 3561, Tacoma 3567, Whatcom 3571, **Wilburforce 3572**
West Virginia: Eastern 3580, Parkersburg 3587
Wisconsin: Community 3607, Green Bay 3619, Incourage 3623, Johnson 3625, Marshfield 3633, Milwaukee 3637, Oshkosh 3642, St. Croix 3662, Zilber 3670
Wyoming: Scott 3679, Wyoming 3684

Matching/challenge support

Alabama: BBVA 3, Central 8, Community 9, Community 10, **International 15**, McWane 17
Alaska: Alaska 26
Arizona: Every 43, Grace 46, Hill 48, Piper 57, Webb 64
Arkansas: Cabe 67, Frueauff 70, Ross 72, Wal-Mart 74, **Windgate 75**
California: Ahmanson 77, AS&F 95, Atlas 96, Ayrshire 97, Bannerman 100, **Beavers 102**, Bechtel, 104, Buell 134, California 137, Campbell 142, **Christensen 151**, Community 157, Community 158, Community 160, Community 162, Cowell 168, Crail 170, Drown 187, Eisner 189, Firedoll 198, Fox 205, Fusenot 211, **Gellert 214**, Gerbode 217, Getty 218, Good 230, Gumbiner 236, Haas 239, Hewlett 248, **Hilton 251**, Humboldt 257, Irvine 264, Jacobs 267, Jones 270, **Kapor 273**, **Keck 276**, Kern 279, Kirchgessner 282, Kvamme 286, LA84 287, Lesher 299, Livingston 303, Los Altos 305, Lux 307, Marcled 308, Marin 309, McClatchy 317,

McConnell 318, Mead 324, Newhall 342, North 346, Noyce 348, Outhwaite 353, **Packard 357**, Parsons 359, Placer 371, **Rivendell 384**, Roth 388, Sacramento 391, San Luis 393, Santa Barbara 394, Sonora 420, **Special 422**, **Spencer 424**, Stulsaft 430, Taper 433, True 442, Valley 445, Versacare 448, **Warsh 452**, Weingart 456, WHH 461

Colorado: Bright 477, Burt 479, Colorado 482, Colorado 483, Community 484, **Daniels 488**, Donnell 491, **Gill 502**, Leighty 512, Marquez 515, Pikes 525, Rose 528, Schlessman 530, Serimus 533, Summit 537, Telluride 538, Vradenburg 544

Connecticut: Aetna 550, **Calder 558**, Community 563, Connecticut 564, Ensworth 575, Matthies 590, Middlesex 592, NewAlliance 595, Palmer 600

Delaware: AEC 622, Brown 625, Chaney 628, Edwards 631, Lennox 638, Longwood 639

District of Columbia: Bauman 650, Block 653, Cafritz 656, **Foundation 661**, Graham 663, **Hitachi 666**, Lichtenberg 671, Meyer 672, Palmer 677, **Wallace 683**, Wallace 684

Florida: Bank 695, Batchelor 697, Bi-Lo/Winn-Dixie 700, Bush 712, Cape Coral 714, Charlotte 718, Community 722, Conn 728, Coral Gables 729, Darden 732, Dunspaugh-Dalton 738, Henderson 758, Jacksonville 761, Jacobsen 762, Kennedy 767, **Knight 771**, Landwirth 775, Phillips 800, Quantum 805, Reinhold 808, **Skelly 820**, Southwest 823, TECO 830, Thomas 831, Winter 842, Wollowick 843

Georgia: Abreu 846, Anderson 850, Campbell 860, Community 868, Georgia 876, Harland 885, Knox 890, Livingston 893, Moore 897, North 900, Sapelo 911

Hawaii: Atherton 925, Castle 930, Cooke 932, McInerny 938

Idaho: CHC 945, Idaho 948

Illinois: Chicago 982, Children's 983, Coleman 986, Community 988, Community 989, Community 990, Community 991, Community 992, Community 993, Crown 997, DeKalb 999, Driehaus 1002, Dunard 1006, DuPage 1008, Field 1014, Frankel 1017, Grant 1025, Guthman 1027, Hughes 1035, Libra 1050, Logan 1051, Lumpkin 1053, **MacArthur 1056**, McCauley 1059, Oak Park 1068, Oberweiler 1069, Pritzker 1078, Speh 1097, Square 1099, **Tyndale 1105**, VNA 1107, Washington 1112

Indiana: Ball 1121, Brown 1124, Cass 1125, Central 1126, Cole 1127, Community 1129, Community 1131, Community 1132, Community 1133, Community 1134, Community 1136, Dearborn 1141, Decatur 1142, DeHaan 1143, DeKalb 1144, Fairbanks 1145, Glick 1150, Hancock 1154, Harrison 1155, Hendricks 1157, Henry 1158, Jasper 1160, Jennings 1162, Johnson 1163, Koch 1167, Kosciusko 1168, Kuhne 1169, LaGrange 1170, Legacy 1171, **Lumina 1174**, Madison 1175, Marshall 1176, Noble 1179, Northern 1180, Portland 1188, Putnam 1189, Ripley 1191, Rush 1192, TCU 1197, Tipton 1198, Wabash 1203, Welborn 1205, Wells 1207, Western 1208, Whitley 1209

Iowa: Ahrens 1210, Community 1217, Hall-Perrine 1222, Iowa 1226, Maytag 1229, McElroy 1230

Kansas: Capitol 1251, Douglas 1256, Hutchinson 1260, Kansas 1263, Topeka 1279

Kentucky: Blue 1282, Brown 1283, Etscorn 1287, Hayswood 1290, Trim 1295

Louisiana: Baptist 1299, Blue 1302, Community 1306, German 1310, New Orleans 1316, Steinhagen 1320

Maine: Alfond 1324, Cohen 1327, Horizon 1331, King 1333, Sewall 1339, Somers 1341, **Walter 1343**

Maryland: **Blaustein 1349**, **Braitmayer 1351**, Commonweal 1356, Dresher 1370, Fowler 1372, Freeman 1373, Goldseker 1374, Henson 1378, Meyerhoff 1393, Middendorf 1394, Mid-Shore 1395, Plitt 1404, Polinger 1405, Rembrandt 1407, Rosenberg 1409, Stulman 1411, Town 1413, Tucker 1415, **Weinberg 1416**, Wright 1418, Zickler 1419

Massachusetts: **Barr 1433**, Berkman 1434, Cabot 1443, Cape Cod 1445, Clarke 1448, Clipper 1449, Davis 1457, Fields 1467, Hyams 1486, **Iacocca 1487**, Kelsey 1493, Linden 1504, Melville 1511, Miller 1516, New 1518, Parker 1523, Riley 1534, Sailors' 1539, Sheehan 1545, Smith 1546, Sudbury 1551, **Sweet 1554**, United 1559

Michigan: Ann Arbor 1576, Branch 1580, Capital 1581, Community 1586, Community 1589, Community 1590, Dalton 1592, Dart 1594, Dow 1597, **Erb 1599**, Fremont 1607, Gilmore 1612, Grand Haven 1614, Grand 1616, Hillsdale 1620, Jackson 1623, Kalamazoo 1626, Keller 1627, **Kellogg 1628**, Midland 1642, Morley 1644, **Mott 1645**, Mott 1646, Mount Pleasant 1647, Oleson 1649, Petoskey 1656, Pokagon 1657, Saginaw 1662, Vanderweide 1671, Wege 1674

Minnesota: Frey 1696, HRK 1702, Initiative 1703, **King 1708**, Land 1710, Larsen 1711, Marbrook 1713, McKnight 1715, Neilson 1721, Northwest 1723, **O'Shaughnessy 1725**, **Porter 1729**, Riverway 1733, Rochester 1735, **Trust 1746**, Wedum 1750, Winona 1753

Mississippi: Community 1758, Community 1759, Community 1760, Foundation 1763, Gulf 1764

Missouri: Anheuser 1774, Community 1783, Curry 1784, Gateway 1789, Green 1790, **Kauffman 1797**, **Monsanto 1803**, Musgrave 1805, Saigh 1811, Speas 1813, Truman 1817

Montana: Silver 1830, Whitefish 1832

Nebraska: Daugherty 1835, Fremont 1836, Grand Island 1837, Hirschfeld 1839, Kearney 1842, Kiewit 1843, Lexington 1845, Lincoln 1847, Mutual 1850, Nebraska 1851, Storz 1854, Woods 1857

Nevada: Nevada 1867, Parasol 1868, **Tang 1873**

New Hampshire: Bean 1878, Fuller 1886, Ham 1887, HNH 1888, Lindsay 1890

New Jersey: **Berrie 1908**, Borden 1910, Brookdale 1912, Brotherton 1914, Buehler 1915, Bunbury 1916, Campbell 1917, Hyde 1944, **JM 1947**, **Johnson 1949**, Leavens 1959, MCJ 1965, **Newcombe 1972**, **Ramapo 1981**, Summit 1998, Turrell 2002, Westfield 2004

New Mexico: Frost 2012, Maddox 2014, Santa Fe 2017

New York: Abelard 2022, Achelis 2026, Adirondack 2027, Allyn 2032, **Arcus 2040**, Bay 2056, **Bydale 2082**, Carvel 2088, Chautauqua 2091, Community 2107, Community 2109, Community 2110, Community 2112, **Credit 2118**, **Cummings 2120**, Cummings 2122, Cutco 2123, **Deutsche 2134**, Dreyfus 2145, Freeman 2164, Gebbie 2170, Gifford 2177, Golisano 2185, Heckscher 2205, **Heron 2211**, Hoyt 2221, Jaharis 2236, Johnson 2240, Kaylie 2247, Lake Placid 2265, Langeloth 2267, Legacy 2274, Littauer 2282, **Luce 2286**, **Macy 2288**, **Mellon 2302**, **Mertz 2306**, Northern 2331, O'Grady 2339, Oishei 2340, Ong 2341, Park 2349, **Porticus 2364**, Pratt 2366, Rapoport 2373, Rauch 2376, Robinson 2387, **Rockefeller 2389**, **Ross 2396**, Schenectady 2407, Scherman 2409, Schnurmacher 2411, Schumann 2412, Snow 2432, Sprague 2444, **Teagle 2459**, Tower 2472, Troy 2474, Truman 2475, van Ameringen 2482, Western 2503

North Carolina: Bailey 2522, Biddle 2529, Brady 2533, Community 2539, Community 2540, Cumberland 2541, Davie 2543, Eddy 2548, French 2554, Fund 2555, Glass 2559, Glenn 2560, Goodrich 2561, Hanes 2565, Kenan 2577, Levine 2584, Meserve 2592, North 2600, Outer 2604, Polk 2609, Reidsville 2611, Reynolds 2614, Rogers 2618, Simpson 2626, Smith 2629, Strowd 2633, Tannenbaum 2637

North Dakota: Fargo 2649, North Dakota 2653

Ohio: Akron 2655, Ar-Hale 2661, Austin 2663, Barberton 2664, **Benedict 2666**, **Bingham 2668**, Brentwood 2670, Bryan 2674, **Cardinal 2677**, Charities 2678, Cincinnati 2679, Community 2682, Community 2683, Community 2685, Coshocton 2686, Delaware 2689, **Eaton 2692**, Fairfield 2696, Gund 2708, KeyBank 2717, Kulas 2721, Licking 2723, Macy's 2726, Maltz 2727, Marietta 2732, Mathile 2734, Mayerson 2735, Middletown 2737, Morgan 2739, Morgan 2740, Morgan 2741, Murphy 2744, Murphy 2745, Muskingum 2747, Nord 2754, O'Neill 2760, Reinberger 2765, Richland 2767, Saint 2770, Sandusky 2773, Scotford 2779, Scripps 2780, Sears 2781, Stark 2788, Stranahan 2790, Tiffin 2793, Troy 2794, Wayne 2798, Young 2803, YSI 2805

Oklahoma: Adams 2806, Bernsen 2807, Chapman 2808, Cherokee 2809, Hardesty 2814, Hille 2816, McGee 2820, Merrick 2821, Noble 2822, Sarkeys 2828, **Schusterman 2829**

Oregon: Collins 2842, Ford 2846, Jeld 2852, Lamb 2855, Macdonald 2859, Meyer 2861, Michael 2862, Mission 2863

Pennsylvania: **Alcoa 2882**, Arkema 2885, Baker 2886, Benedum 2892, Berks 2893, Brooks 2899, Bucks 2900, Buncher 2902, Central 2908, Centre 2909, Cestone 2910, Claneil 2918, Community 2924, Community 2925, Connelly 2926, Degenstein 2931, DSF 2937, Elk 2939, EQT 2940, Fels 2942, Finley 2946, First 2947, First 2948, FISA 2950, Foundation 2952, Fourjay 2953, Freas 2954, Highmark 2968, Huston 2973, Independence 2976, **KL 2978**, Lehigh Valley 2986, Martin 2991, McKinney 2996, McLean 2997, Mellon 2998, North 3006, Penn 3011, Phoenixville 3014, Pottstown 3017, Presser 3019, Scranton 3031, Seybert 3034, Stackpole 3042, Staunton 3044, **Templeton 3047**, Trexler 3049, Willary 3057, Wyomissing 3059, **Zeldin 3060**

Puerto Rico: Puerto Rico 3061

Rhode Island: **Dorot 3071**, Kimball 3079, McNeil 3086, Rhode Island 3089, Textron 3093

South Carolina: Bailey 3096, Byerly 3098, Community 3099, Community 3100, Daniel 3101, Graham 3103, Joanna 3104, Spartanburg 3110, Springs 3111

Tennessee: Assisi 3120, Benwood 3123, Davis 3130, HCA 3139, Lyndhurst 3145, **Maclellan 3146**, Osborne 3147, Phillips 3149, Schmidt 3153, Wilson 3157

Texas: Abell 3160, Amarillo 3163, AT&T 3167, Bass 3172, Brown 3183, Cailloux 3187, Carter 3190, **Chrest 3194**, Constantin 3202, Dallas 3209, Dunn 3216, Edwards 3218, Embrey 3222, Fasken 3229, Fisch 3232, Fish 3233, Goldsbury 3241, Gulf 3245, Hamman 3248, Hext 3257, Hillcrest 3261, Hoblitzelle 3262, Hoglund 3263, **Houston 3266**, Kinder 3274, Lightner 3282, Littauer 3283, Long 3285, Lubbock 3287, **Marshall 3290**, Mayor 3292, McDermott 3293, Meadows 3296, Moody 3298, Orsinger 3310, Permian 3316, Peterson 3318, Powell 3324, Rapoport 3331, Richardson 3334, Rockwell 3338, Rogers 3339, Rosewood 3340, Sams 3342, San Angelo 3343, Sikh 3351, Simmons 3352, South 3356, Sterling 3358, Sturgis 3360, Summerlee 3361, Tomerlin 3371, Topfer 3372, Trull 3373, Waco 3378, Zachry 3387

Utah: Eccles 3392

Vermont: Lintilhac 3412, Windham 3418

Virginia: **Blue 3422**, Cabell 3425, Charlottesville 3428, Community 3431, Community 3433, Gwathmey 3442, **Longview 3451**, **Loyola 3453**, Lynchburg 3454, Moore 3461, Morgan, 3463, Potomac 3471, Samberg 3478, **WestWind 3486**

Washington: Ackerley 3489, Allen 3490, Community 3503, Community 3504, Dimmer 3506, **Goodwin 3519**, Grays 3520, Harder 3524, Korum 3532, Medina 3542, Milgard 3543, Northwest 3546, San Juan 3555, Sherwood 3561, Tacoma 3567, **Wilburforce 3572**

West Virginia: Beckley 3577, Community 3579, Eastern 3580, Maier 3584, McDonough 3586, Parkersburg 3587, Your 3591

Wisconsin: Alliant 3592, Blooming 3599, **Bradley 3601**, Community 3606, Community 3607, Cornerstone 3608, Dudley 3610, Eau 3611,

Elmwood 3614, Green Bay 3619, Incourage 3623, Jeffris 3624, Keller 3626, La Crosse 3631, Marshfield 3633, McBeath 3634, Milwaukee 3637, Oshkosh 3642, Pamida 3644, Racine 3648, Rowland 3652, Siebert 3659, St. Croix 3662, Stateline 3663, U.S. 3665, Zilber 3670
Wyoming: Moyer 3677, Scott 3679, Wyoming 3684

Mission-related investments/loans

California: California 137, California 138, Cowell 168, Jacobs 267, **Kapor 273**, McCune 320, Silicon 408, Skoll 412
Colorado: **General 501**
District of Columbia: **Hitachi 666**
Florida: **Knight 771**
Illinois: Donnelley 1001
Indiana: Central 1126
Louisiana: Beaird 1301, Community 1306
Maine: Switzer 1342
Maryland: **Casey 1353**
Massachusetts: Hyams 1486, **Merck 1514**
Michigan: Kalamazoo 1626, **Kellogg 1628**
Minnesota: West 1751
Missouri: Community 1783
New York: **Deutsche 2134**, **Heron 2211**, **Noyes 2335**, Oishei 2340, Park 2349, Rasmussen 2375, **Rockefeller 2389**
North Carolina: Babcock 2521
Ohio: Stranahan 2790
Oregon: Meyer 2861
Pennsylvania: **KL 2978**, Lancaster 2981
Texas: KDK-Harman 3273
Vermont: Vermont 3417
Virginia: **Blue 3422**
Washington: Seattle 3558

Pro bono services - legal

Illinois: Polk 1075
Maine: Cohen 1327

Pro bono services - medical

Maine: Cohen 1327

Professorships

California: Ayrshire 97, Jones 270, **Kavli 275**, Kirchgessner 282, **Lingnan 301**, **Rupe 389**, Treadwell 439
Connecticut: Deloitte 569
Delaware: AEC 622
Florida: Benjamin 699, Dunspaugh-Dalton 738
Georgia: Mason 896, Pitts 904
Idaho: **Micron 950**
Illinois: Coleman 986, Crown 997, Frankel 1017, **Grainger 1024**, Square 1099
Indiana: Ball 1121
Iowa: Maytag 1229, McElroy 1230
Kansas: Capitol 1251
Kentucky: Etscorn 1287
Maryland: **de Beaumont 1366**, Meyerhoff 1393, Middendorf 1394, Richmond 1408
Massachusetts: **Iacocca 1487**
Minnesota: Marbrook 1713
Mississippi: Community 1759
Nebraska: Hirschfeld 1839, Weitz 1855
New York: Berg 2062, Freeman 2164, Heyman 2212, **Kade 2243**, **Kress 2263**, **Luce 2286**, Oishei 2340, **Open 2343**, Ruffin 2400, Simons 2423
North Carolina: Eddy 2548, North 2600
Ohio: Brown 2672, Kulas 2721, Maltz 2727, Scripps 2780
Oklahoma: McGee 2820, Noble 2822, Presbyterian 2826, Sarkeys 2828, **Schusterman 2829**
Oregon: Woodard 2877
Pennsylvania: **Botstiber 2898**, Independence 2976, **Respironics 3023**
Puerto Rico: Puerto Rico 3061
Tennessee: First 3135
Texas: Brown 3183, Burch 3184, Cain 3188, Carter 3190, Dunn 3216, Fish 3233, **Houston 3266**, Kinder 3274, McDermott 3293, Sterling 3358, Summerlee 3361, Waggoner 3379
Vermont: Lintilhac 3412
Washington: Anderson 3492
West Virginia: Maier 3584
Wisconsin: **Bradley 3601**

Program development

Alabama: BBVA 3, Black 4, Caring 7, Central 8, Community 9, Community 10
Alaska: Alaska 26, CIRI 33
Arizona: APS 39, Every 43, Flinn 44, Hill 48, Hughes 49, Piper 57, **Research 59**, Stardust 63, Webb 64
Arkansas: Cabe 67, Endeavor 69, Frueauff 70, Ross 72, Wal-Mart 74, **Windgate 75**
California: **Allende 79**, Allergan 80, **Amado 81**, Anaheim 83, Anderson 84, **Applied 88**, Aratani 89, Archstone 90, **Arkay 91**, Arntz 93, AS&F 95, Atlas 96, Ayrshire 97, Bank 99, Bannerman 100, Bechtel 103, Bechtel, 104, Berry 111, Blue 114, Bohnett 117, Buell 134, California 137, California 139, California 140, Campbell 142, Carlston 143, **Christensen 151**, Clif 152, **Clorox 153**, College 156, Community 157, Community 158, Community 160, Community 161, Community 162, Community 163, Cowell 168, Crail 170, Disney 181, Drown 187, Eisner 189, Firedoll 198, Fleishhacker 199, **Foundation 202**, Fox 205, Fremont 207, Friedman 208, **Fund 210**, Gamble 213, **Gellert 214**, Gellert 215, Genentech 216, Gerbode 217, Gold 228, **Google 231**, GSF 235, Gumbiner 236, Haas 239, Hannon 242, Heller 246, Hewlett 248, **Hilton 251**, Hoag 253, Humboldt 257, Intuit 263, Irvine 264, Jackson 266, Jacobs 267, Johnson 269, **Kapor 273**, **Keck 276**, Kelly 278, Kern 279, Kirchgessner 282, LA84 287, Laguna 288, Langendorf 289, **Lawrence 293**, Lesher 299, **Lingnan 301**, Los Altos 305, Lucas 306, Lux 307, Marcled 308, Marin 309, **Marisla 310**, **Mattel 312**, Mazda 313, McClatchy 317, McCune 320, McKesson 321, Mead 324, **Moore 333**, Mosher 335, Napa 340, Newhall 342, North 346, Noyce 348, Outhwaite 353, Pacific 354, Pacific 355, **Packard 357**, Parsons 359, PG&E 367, Plum 372, Rancho 378, **Rivendell 384**, Rosenberg 385, Roth 388, **Rupe 389**, Sacramento 391, Samuelsson 392, San Luis 393, Santa Barbara 394, Shea 402, Sierra 405, Sierra 406, Silicon 407, Silicon 408, **Smith 416**, Soda 418, Solano 419, Sonora 420, **Special 422**, **Spencer 424**, Stanislaus 425, Streisand 428, Stuart 429, Stulsaft 430, Taper 433, Trio 440, Truckee 441, True 442, UniHealth 444, Valley 445, Versacare 448, Weingart 456, **Wilkinson 463**, Wilsey 464, Witter 467, Zellerbach 471
Colorado: Animal 472, Bonfils 475, Brett 476, Bright 477, Colorado 483, Community 484, Comprecare 485, **Crowell 487**, **Daniels 488**, Donnell 491, El Pomar 492, Fortune 497, Foundation 498, **General 501**, **Gill 502**, Kaufmann 509, **Kinder 510**, Leighty 512, Maki 513, Marquez 515, **National 523**, Piton 526, Rose 528, Schlessman 530, Serimus 533, Southern 535, Stratton 536, Summit 537, Telluride 538, Vradenburg 544, Yampa 545
Connecticut: Aetna 550, **Albers 551**, Bender 554, **Calder 558**, Community 562, Community 563, Connecticut 564, **Deupree 571**, Ensworth 575, Fisher 577, Fry 579, Hoffman 585, Long 588, Matthies 590, Middlesex 592, NewAlliance 595, Northeast 598, Palmer 600, Perrin 603, Pitney 604, **Praxair 606**, Roberts 608, Robinson 609, Inc. 616
Delaware: 18 621, **AstraZeneca 623**, Brown 625, Burt's 626, CenturyLink-Clarke 627, Chaney 628, Delaware 630, Edwards 631, Kutz 637, Lennox 638, Longwood 639, Sylvan 648
District of Columbia: Bauman 650, Bernstein 652, Block 653, **Butler 655**, Cafritz 656, Graham 663, **Hitachi 666**, Jovid 668, Lichtenberg 671, Meyer 672, Palmer 677, Stewart 682, **Wallace 683**, Wallace 684
Florida: Bank 695, Batchelor 697, Benjamin 699, Bi-Lo/Winn-Dixie 700, Brown 707, Burns 710, Bush 712, Cape Coral 714, Catalina 716, Charlotte 718, Community 722, Community 723, Community 724, Community 725, Community 727, Conn 728, Darden 732, **DeMoss 735**, Dunspaugh-Dalton 738, Erdle 740, Florida 744, Glazer 750, Greenburg 752, Gulf 754, Hard 756, Henderson 758, Jacksonville 761, Jacobsen 762, Kennedy 767, **Knight 771**, Landwirth 775, Macdonald 783, Munroe 793, **Patel 797**, Peterson 799, Phillips 800, Publix 804, Quantum 805, Southwest 823, Thomas 831, **Whitehall 840**, Winter 842
Georgia: Abreu 846, Amos-Cheves 849, Anderson 850, Atlanta 852, Bancker-Williams 854, **Coca 864**, Communities 866, Community 867, Community 868, Exposition 873, EZ 874, Georgia 876, Georgia 877, **Georgia 878**, Glenn 882, Goizueta 883, Harland 885, Healthcare 886, **Imlay 888**, Knox 890, Lanier 891, Marshall 895, Mason 896, North 900, Raoul 907, Sapelo 911, Southern 915, Trailsend 916
Hawaii: Atherton 925, Baldwin 926, Campbell 928, Castle 929, Castle 930, Cooke 932, Hawaii 933, Hawaiian 934, Kaneta 936, McInerny 938
Idaho: Albertson 942, Cunningham 946, Idaho 948, **Micron 950**, Whittenberger 953
Illinois: Allegretti 958, Aon 963, ArcelorMittal 964, Bergstrom 965, Blowitz 968, Boothroyd 971, Brach 973, Cheney 981, Chicago 982, Coleman 986, Comer 987, Community 988, Community 989, Community 990, Community 992, Community 993, Crown 997, Donnelley 1001, Driehaus 1002, Dunard 1006, DuPage 1008, Edwardsville 1010, Evanston 1012, Field 1014, Frankel 1017, Fry 1018, **Grainger 1024**, Guthman 1027, Hospira 1034, Hughes 1035, Hunt 1036, **Joyce 1040**, Kaplan 1041, Kaufman 1043, Kenny's 1044, Lumpkin 1053, **MacArthur 1056**, **Mondelez 1064**, **Motorola 1066**, Nelson 1067, Oak Park 1068, Omron 1070, Polk 1075, Prince 1076, Pritzker 1078, Pullman 1081, Reese 1083, Seymour 1091, Siragusa 1096, Speh 1097, Stern 1100, Stone 1102, Tracy 1104, **Tyndale 1105**, VNA 1107, Walter 1110, Washington 1112
Indiana: Ball 1121, Brotherhood 1123, Brown 1124, Cass 1125, Central 1126, Community 1128, Community 1129, Community 1131, Community 1133, Community 1134, Community 1135, Community 1136, Dearborn 1141, Decatur 1142, DeHaan 1143, DeKalb 1144, Fairbanks 1145, Foellinger 1147, Glick 1150, Greene 1152, Hancock 1154, Harrison 1155, Health 1156, Hendricks 1157, Henry 1158, Jennings 1162, Johnson 1163, Koch 1167, Kosciusko 1168, Kuhne 1169, LaGrange 1170, Legacy 1171, **Lumina 1174**, Madison 1175, Marshall 1176, Master 1177, Noble 1179, Northern 1180, Old 1182, Orange 1184, Parke 1186, Porter 1187, Portland 1188, Putnam 1189, Rush 1192, TCU 1197, Tipton 1198, Tobias 1199, Unity 1201, Vectren 1202, Welborn 1205, WellPoint 1206, Wells 1207, Western 1208
Iowa: Ahrens 1210, Clarinda 1214, Community 1217, Iowa 1226, Maytag 1229, McElroy 1230, **Rockwell 1237**, Siouxland 1240, United 1243, Wahlert 1244, Wellmark 1246
Kansas: Capitol 1251, Collective 1253, Delta 1255, Douglas 1256, Farah 1258, Hutchinson 1260, Insurance 1261, Kansas 1263, Koch 1265, **Lloyd 1267**, Manhattan 1268, Salina 1274, Skillbuilders 1277, Topeka 1279, Western 1280
Kentucky: Blue 1282, C.E. 1284, Community 1286, Gheens 1288, Hayswood 1290, Trim 1295

Constantin 3202, Dallas 3209, Elkins 3220, Elkins 3221, Embrey 3222, Esping 3225, Fairchild 3227, Farish 3228, Fasken 3229, Fisch 3232, Fish 3233, Flarsheim 3234, Fluor 3235, Frees 3238, Goldsbury 3241, Gulf 3245, Hext 3257, Hillcrest 3261, Hoblitzelle 3262, Hoglund 3263, Holloway 3264, **Houston 3266**, Houston 3267, KDK-Harman 3273, Kinder 3274, King 3275, Light 3281, Lightner 3282, Littauer 3283, Long 3285, Lubbock 3287, **Marshall 3290**, Martinez 3291, McDermott 3293, McKee 3295, Meadows 3296, Moody 3298, Moore 3299, Morgan 3301, Northen 3306, **Oldham 3308**, Orsinger 3310, **Paso 3312**, Penney 3315, Permian 3316, Powell 3324, QuadW 3328, Rapoport 3331, Richardson 3334, Richardson 3335, Rockwell 3338, Rosewood 3340, Sams 3342, San Angelo 3343, Sikh 3351, Simmons 3352, Smith 3353, South 3356, Sterling 3358, Sturgis 3360, Summerlee 3361, Tocker 3369, Topfer 3372, Trull 3373, **VHA 3377**, Waco 3378, Waggoner 3379, Wright 3386, Zachry 3387

Utah: Ashton 3388, Hemingway 3396

Vermont: **Ben 3407**, Lintilhac 3412, Merchants 3414, Tarrant 3416, Vermont 3417, Windham 3418

Virginia: AMERIGROUP 3420, Arlington 3421, **Blue 3422, Bosack 3423**, Capital 3426, CarMax 3427, Community 3429, Community 3432, Community 3433, Gwathmey 3442, **Longview 3451**, Lynchburg 3454, MAXIMUS 3457, Memorial 3458, Moore 3461, Northern 3464, **Northrop 3465**, Potomac 3471, Pruden 3473, RECO 3474, Robins 3477, Samberg 3478, Strong 3481, United 3484, **WestWind 3486**, Williamsburg 3487

Washington: Ackerley 3489, Allen 3490, Blue 3498, Casey 3499, Casey 3500, Community 3503, Community 3504, Dimmer 3506, Everett 3511, Fales 3512, Ferguson 3513, **Foundation 3515, Gates 3516, Glaser 3517**, Grays 3520, Inland 3526, Jones 3530, Kawabe 3531, Korum 3532, Medina 3542, Milgard 3543, Northwest 3546, PEMCO 3549, Renton 3552, Safeco 3554, **Starbucks 3565**, Tacoma 3567, Whatcom 3571, **Wilburforce 3572**

West Virginia: Beckley 3577, Community 3579, Eastern 3580, Maier 3584, McDonough 3586, Parkersburg 3587, Tucker 3589, Your 3591

Wisconsin: Alliant 3592, **Baird 3595**, Bemis 3598, Blooming 3599, **Bradley 3601**, Community 3606, Community 3607, Cornerstone 3608, Door 3609, Dudley 3610, Eau 3611, Fond du Lac 3615, Green Bay 3619, Harley 3621, Incourage 3623, Johnson 3625, Keller 3626, Kern 3627, Kohler 3629, La Crosse 3631, Marshfield 3633, McBeath 3634, Milwaukee 3637, Oshkosh 3642, Oshkosh 3643, Pamida 3644, Pettit 3645, Racine 3648, Rowland 3652, Sand 3654, Siebert 3659, Stateline 3663, Windway 3669, Zilber 3670

Wyoming: McMurry 3676, Scott 3679, Weiss 3682, Wyoming 3684

Program evaluation

Alabama: Community 9, Community 10

Alaska: Alaska 26

Arkansas: Endeavor 69

California: Anderson 84, Archstone 90, Atlas 96, Bechtel, 104, Blue 114, California 137, California 138, California 139, California 140, **Christensen 151**, Community 163, Firedoll 198, **Fund 210**, Heller 246, **Hilton 251**, Irvine 264, Johnson 269, **Kapor 273**, Kern 279, **Lawrence 293**, Los Altos 305, Marcled 308, Marin 309, Mosher 335, Noyce 348, **Packard 357**, Placer 371, Price 373, Sacramento 391, Sierra 405, Soda 418, Sonora 420, **Special 422**, Stuart 429, UniHealth 444, Zellerbach 471

Colorado: Colorado 483, **Daniels 488, National 523**, Piton 526, Rose 528, Serimus 533, Summit 537, Vradenburg 544

Connecticut: Community 563, Connecticut 564, Middlesex 592

District of Columbia: Block 653, Cafritz 656, Jovid 668, Wallace 684

Florida: Charlotte 718, Conn 728, **Knight 771**, Macdonald 783, Quantum 805, Winter 842

Georgia: Communities 866, Healthcare 886, North 900

Hawaii: Atherton 925, Castle 929, Castle 930, Cooke 932

Illinois: Chicago 982, Community 990, Community 993, Evanston 1012, Fry 1018, **Joyce 1040**, Libra 1050, Lumpkin 1053, Polk 1075, Reese 1083, Stone 1102, VNA 1107

Indiana: Ball 1121, Central 1126, Community 1128, Community 1132, Fairbanks 1145, Foellinger 1147, Harrison 1155, Health 1156, Johnson 1163, LaGrange 1170, **Lumina 1174**, Orange 1184

Kansas: Delta 1255, Douglas 1256, Kansas 1263, **Shumaker 1276**

Louisiana: Baptist 1299, Beaird 1301, Blue 1302, New Orleans 1316

Maine: Horizon 1331, Maine 1336

Maryland: **Blaustein 1349, Casey 1353, Cohen 1355, de Beaumont 1366**, Straus 1410

Massachusetts: **Barr 1433**, Davis 1457, Essex 1464, **Kahn 1492**, Kelsey 1493, Melville 1511, Miller 1516, Sheehan 1545, Smith 1546, Sudbury 1551

Michigan: Community 1591, Four 1603, Fremont 1607, Gilmore 1612, Jackson 1623, **Kellogg 1628, Mott 1645**, Mott 1646, Mount Pleasant 1647

Minnesota: Duluth 1693, McKnight 1715, Northwest 1723, Phillips 1728, Riverway 1733, Sundance 1742, WCA 1749, Winona 1753

Missouri: Community 1783, Hall 1793, Hallmark 1794, **Kauffman 1797, Monsanto 1803**

Montana: Silver 1830

Nebraska: Lincoln 1847, Woods 1857

New Hampshire: Alexander 1877, Bean 1878

New Jersey: **Allen 1900, Johnson 1949**

New Mexico: Con 2011

New York: Achelis 2026, Anderson 2036, **Arcus 2040, Carnegie 2085, Clark 2097, Commonwealth 2106**, Community 2107, Community 2109, Community 2110, Community 2112, **Cummings 2121, Ford 2160**, Gifford 2177, **Goldman 2182**, Golisano 2185, Gould 2188, **Grant 2191**, Heckscher 2205, **Heron 2211**, Johnson 2240, Kornfeld 2261, Langeloth 2267, **Macy 2288, MetLife 2307**, New York 2325, O'Grady 2339, Oishei 2340, Rapoport 2373, Rauch 2376, **Sparkplug 2441**, Tiger 2464, Tower 2472, Voya 2488, **Wallace 2492**

North Carolina: Brady 2533, Community 2539, Community 2540, Cumberland 2541, North Carolina 2599, Reidsville 2611, Rex 2612, Reynolds 2614, Strowd 2633, Tannenbaum 2637

Ohio: Findlay 2700, Ginn 2706, Marion 2733, Morgan 2741, O'Neill 2760, Saint 2770, Sandusky 2773, Springfield 2787, Stranahan 2790, Wean 2799

Oklahoma: Chapman 2808, Cherokee 2809, Hardesty 2814, Merrick 2821, Sarkeys 2828

Oregon: Caddock 2838

Pennsylvania: Barra 2887, Buhl 2901, Chester 2915, Claneil 2918, Community 2924, DSF 2937, First 2948, FISA 2950, Heinz 2966, Hunt 2971, Mellon 2998, Penn 3011, Phoenixville 3014, Staunton 3044, Wells 3055

Rhode Island: **Dorot 3071**, Rhode Island 3089

South Carolina: Black 3097, Byerly 3098, Community 3100, Daniel 3101

Tennessee: Assisi 3120, **Maclellan 3146, Scarlett 3152**, Wilson 3157

Texas: Cailloux 3187, **Chrest 3194, Houston 3266**, Meadows 3296, Orsinger 3310, **Paso 3312**, Rockwell 3338, Rosewood 3340, San Angelo 3343

Vermont: Vermont 3417

Virginia: Community 3429, Northern 3464, Robins 3477, Samberg 3478, Williamsburg 3487

Washington: Allen 3490, Casey 3499, Casey 3500, Inland 3526, Medina 3542, Tacoma 3567, **Wilburforce 3572**

Wisconsin: Community 3607, Dudley 3610, Eau 3611, Green Bay 3619, Milwaukee 3637, St. Croix 3662, Stateline 3663, Zilber 3670

Wyoming: Wyoming 3684

Program-related investments/loans

Alabama: Community 10

Arkansas: Cabe 67

California: Ahmanson 77, **Broad 129**, Burns 136, California 137, California 138, **Conservation 165**, Cowell 168, Friedman 208, **Hilton 251**, Jacobs 267, Los Altos 305, Marin 309, **Moore 333**, Mosher 335, Napa 340, Noyce 348, **Packard 357**, Skoll 412, Specialty 423, Taper 433, UniHealth 444, Weingart 456

Connecticut: Dalio 567

District of Columbia: **Case 658**

Florida: Bush 712, Community 722, **Knight 771**, Phillips 800

Georgia: Lanier 891, University 918

Illinois: **Abbott 954**, Blowitz 968, Children's 983, Coleman 986, Community 990, Donnelley 1001, Dunham 1007, **MacArthur 1056**, Prince 1076, Rosen 1086, Washington 1112, Wieboldt 1115

Indiana: Community 1130, Decatur 1142, Jennings 1162, Putnam 1189

Kentucky: C.E. 1284

Maine: Libra 1334, Maine 1336

Maryland: **Blaustein 1349, Casey 1353**, Ceres 1354, Goldseker 1374, Plitt 1404

Massachusetts: Berkman 1434, Fireman 1469, Grinspoon 1479, Hyams 1486, Kelsey 1493, Melville 1511, Pardoe 1522, Parker 1523

Michigan: Community 1586, Community 1590, Family 1600, Fremont 1607, Grand Rapids 1615, Kalamazoo 1626, **Kellogg 1628, Kresge 1631**, Meijer 1639, **Mott 1645**, Pokagon 1657, Skillman 1666

Minnesota: Initiative 1703, Larsen 1711, McKnight 1715, Minneapolis 1717, Northwest 1722, Northwest 1723, Southwest 1740, West 1751

Mississippi: Community 1758, Regions 1770

Missouri: Community 1783, Hall 1793, **Kauffman 1797**

Nebraska: Kiewit 1843, Woods 1857

New Hampshire: HNH 1888

New Jersey: **Johnson 1949**

New Mexico: Maddox 2014

New York: **Alavi 2030, AVI 2051, Bloomberg 2066**, Clark 2099, Community 2107, Community 2110, Community 2112, **Deutsche 2134**, Einhorn 2150, **Ford 2160**, Gebbie 2170, **Heron 2211, Institute 2233, Jabara 2235, JPMorgan 2242, Kaplan 2245**, Lake Placid 2265, **Mertz 2306, MetLife 2307**, Oishei 2340, **Open 2343**, Park 2349, Planning 2359, **Rockefeller 2390, Surdna 2454**, van Ameringen 2483, **Weeden 2496**, Western 2503, Wilson 2507

North Carolina: Babcock 2521

Ohio: Barberton 2664, Findlay 2700, Gund 2708, Hamilton 2710, Marietta 2732, Morgan 2741, Murphy 2745, Muskingum 2747, Nord 2754, Richland 2767, Saint 2770, Wean 2799

Oklahoma: Hardesty 2814, Harmon 2815, Presbyterian 2826, Warren 2831

Oregon: **Lemelson 2857**, Meyer 2861

Pennsylvania: Berks 2893, Buhl 2901, Central 2908, Community 2922, Elk 2939, First 2947, Hansen 2964, Hillman 2969, **KL 2978**, McCune 2993, Mellon 2998, Penn 3011

Puerto Rico: Puerto Rico 3061

Rhode Island: Rhode Island 3089

Tennessee: Benwood 3123, Tucker 3156

Texas: Burnett 3185, C.I.O.S. 3186, **Chrest 3194**, Heinlein 3254, **Houston 3266**, Meadows 3296, Orsinger 3310, **PHM 3320**, Richardson 3334, Rockwell 3338

Vermont: Vermont 3417

Virginia: **Blue 3422**, Robins 3477
Washington: **Gates 3516**, Tacoma 3567, Washington 3570
Wisconsin: **Bradley 3601**, Incourage 3623, Oshkosh 3642
Wyoming: Whitney 3683

Public relations services

Rhode Island: Citizens 3067

Publication

Alabama: Community 9, Community 10
Alaska: Alaska 26
Arkansas: Ross 72
California: California 140, **Foundation 202, Gellert 214**, Gellert 215, Heller 246, **Hilton 251, Lingnan 301**, Noyce 348, Rancho 378, Sacramento 391, **Smith 416**, Sonora 420, Stuart 429, Taper 433, Truckee 441, **Warsh 452**, Witter 467
Colorado: Colorado 483, **Crowell 487**, Donnell 491, Rose 528, Society 534
Connecticut: **Albers 551**, Connecticut 564, Matthies 590, Palmer 600
Delaware: AEC 622
District of Columbia: Bauman 650, **Foundation 661, Searle 681**
Florida: Charlotte 718
Georgia: Georgia 876, Healthcare 886
Idaho: Whittenberger 953
Illinois: Brach 973, Community 992, Driehaus 1002, Frankel 1017, Logan 1051, Pritzker 1078, **Tyndale 1105**
Indiana: Ball 1121, Brown 1124, Central 1126, Froderman 1148, Harrison 1155, Henry 1158, **Lumina 1174**, Marshall 1176, Orange 1184
Iowa: Maytag 1229, Wellmark 1246
Kansas: Douglas 1256, Farah 1258, Hansen 1259, Salina 1274
Louisiana: Steinhagen 1320
Maine: Smith 1340
Maryland: **Casey 1353**, Community 1358, **de Beaumont 1366**, Macht 1388, Meyerhoff 1393
Massachusetts: **Kahn 1492**, Kelsey 1493, **Lincoln 1503**, Melville 1511, **Xeric 1570**
Michigan: Ann Arbor 1576, Community 1590, Dart 1594, Gilmore 1612, Hillsdale 1620, Mount Pleasant 1647, Saginaw 1662
Minnesota: Duluth 1693, Greystone 1700, **Trust 1746**
Montana: Whitefish 1832
Nebraska: Nebraska 1851
Nevada: Nevada 1867
New Jersey: **JM 1947**, Merck 1966, **Milbank 1968, Puffin 1980**, Westfield 2004
New Mexico: Frost 2012, Santa Fe 2017
New York: Abelard 2022, Achelis 2026, Adirondack 2027, Anderson 2036, **Arcus 2040**, Berg 2062, **Carnegie 2085**, Chautauqua 2091, **Clark 2098**, Community 2109, Community 2112, **Foundation 2161, Grant 2191**, Initial 2231, Johnson 2240, **Kaplan 2245**, Klingenstein 2256, **Kress 2263**, Littauer 2282, **Macy 2288, MetLife 2307**, New York 2325, **Open 2343, Rockefeller 2390, Ross 2396, Sage 2402**, Snow 2432, **Sparkplug 2441, Wallace 2492, Warhol 2494, Wenner 2502**, Western 2503, Widgeon 2505
North Carolina: Brady 2533, Cumberland 2541, North Carolina 2599, Outer 2604, Polk 2609, Rogers 2618
North Dakota: Community 2648, North Dakota 2653
Ohio: Fairfield 2696, Foundation 2702, Gund 2708, Marion 2733, Murphy 2745, Muskingum 2747, Nord 2754, Saint 2770, Springfield 2787, YSI 2805
Oklahoma: **Schusterman 2829**
Pennsylvania: Bucks 2900, Centre 2909, Claneil 2918, Comcast 2921, Community 2924, Copernicus 2928, Foundation 2952, Fourjay 2953, Lehigh Valley 2986, McLean 2997, Patterson 3010, Scranton 3031, **Templeton 3047**, Washington 3054
Puerto Rico: Puerto Rico 3061
Rhode Island: **Dorot 3071**, Rhode Island 3089
Tennessee: Assisi 3120, Stuttering 3155
Texas: Hext 3257, **Houston 3266**, Houston 3267, Meadows 3296, Moody 3298, Moore 3299, Richardson 3334, Sikh 3351, Sterling 3358, Summerlee 3361, Trull 3373, Waggoner 3379
Vermont: Vermont 3417
Virginia: Community 3431, **Longview 3451**, Northern 3464
Washington: **Gates 3516, Ji 3528**
Wisconsin: **Bradley 3601**, Manitowoc 3632, Marshfield 3633, New 3641, U.S. 3665

Research

Alabama: BBVA 3, Black 4, Community 9, **International 15**
Alaska: CIRI 33
Arizona: Flinn 44, Hughes 49, Napier 55, **Research 59**, Webb 64
Arkansas: Cabe 67, Ross 72
California: American 82, Annenberg 87, **Arkay 91**, Bechtel, 104, **Beckman 105**, Beckman 106, Bengier 109, Blue 114, California 137, California 139, California 140, **Christensen 151, Ellison 191**, Fremont 207, **Gellert 214**, Gellert 215, Genentech 216, **Glenn 225, Grass 232**, Hand 241, Haynes 243, Heller 246, Hillblom 250, **Hilton 251**, Hoag 253, Irvine 264, Johnson 269, **Kavli 275, Keck 276**, Kirchgessner 282, Kvamme 286, **Lingnan 301**, Marcled 308, Marin 309, Mazda 313, McKesson 321, Mead 324, Milken 331, **Moore 333**, Murdock 338, North 346, Noyce 348, Pacific 355, **Packard 357**, Parsons 359, Patron 363, Plum 372, Rifkind 383, Rossi 387, **Rupe 389**, Samuelsson 392, **Seaver 400, Smith 416, Special 422**, Stuart 429, Taper 433, Treadwell 439, Valley 445, **Warsh 452**, Wasserman 453, Witter 467
Colorado: Ballantine 474, Bonfils 475, Colorado 483, Comprecare 485, Donnell 491, Kaufmann 509, **Malone 514, National 523**, Rose 528
Connecticut: Aetna 550, Bender 554, Childs 559, Colburn-Keenan 560, Community 563, Connecticut 564, Deloitte 569, **Deupree 571**, Palmer 600, Patterson 601, Inc. 616
Delaware: AEC 622
District of Columbia: Bauman 650, **Foundation 661**, Jovid 668, Lehrman 670, **Searle 681**, Stewart 682, **Wallace 683**
Florida: Bi-Lo/Winn-Dixie 700, **Campbell 713**, Greenburg 752, Hard 756, **Skelly 820, Whitehall 840**, Winter 842, Wollowick 843
Georgia: Blank 856, Georgia 876, Healthcare 886, **Imlay 888**, Mason 896
Hawaii: Atherton 925, Hawaii 933
Idaho: **Micron 950**
Illinois: Blowitz 968, Boothroyd 971, Chicago 982, Coldwell 985, Coleman 986, Community 990, Duchossois 1005, Frankel 1017, **Grainger 1024, Joyce 1040**, Kaufman 1043, Logan 1051, **MacArthur 1056**, Oberweiler 1069, Pritzker 1078, Redhill 1082, Reese 1083, Seymour 1091, Sinsheimer 1095, **Spencer 1098**, Washington 1112, Webb 1113
Indiana: Ball 1121, Fairbanks 1145, Foellinger 1147, Harrison 1155, Hendricks 1157, Henry 1158, Koch 1167, **Lumina 1174**, Marshall 1176, Orange 1184, Regenstrief 1190, TCU 1197, Walther 1204, WellPoint 1206
Iowa: Maytag 1229, McElroy 1230, Siouxland 1240, Wallace 1245
Kansas: Koch 1264, Koch 1265
Kentucky: Brown 1283, C.E. 1284, Gheens 1288, Good 1289
Louisiana: Baptist 1299, Blue 1302, Community 1306, Grigsby 1312, New Orleans 1316, Schlieder 1319, Steinhagen 1320
Maine: Alfond 1324, Cohen 1327, King 1333, Libra 1334, Maine 1336, Somers 1341
Maryland: **ABMRF 1344, Casey 1353, de Beaumont 1366**, Deutsch 1369, Gudelsky 1376, Macht 1388, Meyerhoff 1393, NASDAQ 1401, Wright 1418, Zickler 1419
Massachusetts: Alden 1425, **Barr 1433**, Berkman 1434, **Brabson 1438, Bruner 1441, Conservation 1454, Iacocca 1487, Kahn 1492**, Kendall 1494, Levy 1501, **Lincoln 1503**, Melville 1511, New 1518, Parker 1523, Smith 1546, **Sociological 1548**, Webster 1565, Williams 1567
Michigan: Ann Arbor 1576, Community 1586, Dalton 1592, Dart 1594, Dow 1597, Frey 1609, **Gerber 1611, Kresge 1631**, Morley 1644, Mount Pleasant 1647, **Pardee 1653**, Pokagon 1657, Royal 1661
Minnesota: Duluth 1693, Edina 1694, Farmers 1695, Greystone 1700, Marbrook 1713, **McKnight 1714**, Northwest 1723, **O'Shaughnessy 1725, St. Jude 1741, Trust 1746**, West 1751
Missouri: Bellwether 1775, Community 1783, **Kauffman 1797, McDonnell 1800**, Millstone 1801, **Monsanto 1803**, Saigh 1811, Speas 1813, St. Louis 1814
Montana: Whitefish 1832
Nebraska: Lincoln 1847, Midlands 1848, Weitz 1855
Nevada: Caesars 1860, **Reynolds 1869**
New Hampshire: Endowment 1883, Johnson 1889
New Jersey: **Allen 1900**, Banbury 1904, **Berrie 1908**, Brookdale 1912, Brotherton 1914, Buehler 1915, Elias 1923, Feldstein 1928, Horizon 1940, Hummingbird 1943, Hyde 1944, **JM 1947, Johnson 1949**, Kirby 1952, **Knowles 1955**, Merck 1966, **Milbank 1968, Ramapo 1981, Rippel 1982**, Summit 1998, Westfield 2004
New Mexico: Con 2011, Maddox 2014
New York: Achelis 2026, **AVI 2051**, Bay 2056, Berg 2062, **Bronfman 2074**, Butler 2081, **Carnegie 2085**, Carvel 2088, **Clark 2098, Commonwealth 2106**, Community 2109, **Cummings 2120, Cummings 2121, Dana 2126**, Diller 2137, **Eppley 2152**, Ferraioli 2156, **Foundation 2161**, Freeman 2164, Gifford 2177, **Goldman 2182**, Goldman 2183, **Grant 2191, Greenwall 2192**, Heckscher 2205, Heyman 2212, Hite 2214, Initial 2231, **Institute 2233**, Jaharis 2236, Johnson 2240, **Kaplan 2245**, Kekst 2249, Klingenstein 2256, Knapp 2259, Kornfeld 2261, **Kress 2263**, Lee 2271, Link 2280, Littauer 2282, Litwin 2283, **Luce 2286, Mathers 2294, Mayday 2296**, McGonagle 2299, **Mellon 2302, MetLife 2307**, New York 2325, NYSE 2336, Oishei 2340, **Open 2343, Peterson 2357, Porticus 2364, Rockefeller 2390, Sage 2402**, Schenectady 2407, Schnurmacher 2411, Simons 2423, Smith 2430, **Sparkplug 2441**, Tiffany 2463, **Tinker 2467**, Tisch 2469, Vidda 2485, Vilcek 2486, Vogler 2487, Voya 2488, **Wallace 2492, Warhol 2494, Wenner 2502**
North Carolina: Allen 2518, Bailey 2522, Brady 2533, **Burroughs 2534**, Duncan 2547, Eddy 2548, French 2554, Goodrich 2561, **Laffin 2583**, Meyer 2594, North Carolina 2599, Olin 2603, Rogers 2618, Smith 2629, Sutcliffe 2635
North Dakota: Community 2648, North Dakota 2653
Ohio: Akron 2655, Athens 2662, Brentwood 2670, Brown 2672, Bryan 2674, **Cardinal 2677**, Dodero 2691, Gund 2708, Kettering 2716, Kulas 2721, Maltz 2727, Marietta 2732, Marion 2733, Murphy 2745, Muskingum 2747, Nippert 2751, **Omnicare 2758**, Reinberger 2765, Ryan 2769, Saint 2770, Scripps 2780, Sears 2781, Seasongood 2782, Springfield 2787, Stark 2788, Wayne 2798, Woodruff 2801
Oklahoma: Adams 2806, Chapman 2808, Hardesty 2814, Hille 2816, McGee 2820, Merrick 2821, Noble 2822, Presbyterian 2826, Sarkeys 2828, **Schusterman 2829**, Warren 2831
Oregon: Collins 2842, Jackson 2851

Pennsylvania: **Alcoa 2882**, Beaver 2890, Berks 2893, Betz 2895, Brooks 2899, Buhl 2901, **Cardiovascular 2905**, Centre 2909, Cestone 2910, Chester 2915, Claneil 2918, Community 2924, DSF 2937, Ferree 2944, Huston 2973, **KL 2978, Lee 2984**, Lewis 2987, McLean 2997, Mellon 2998, Patterson 3010, Penn 3011, Pottstown 3017, Raab 3020, Rossin 3028, Scranton 3031, Society 3040, **Templeton 3047**, Tuttleman 3050, Widener 3056

Puerto Rico: Puerto Rico 3061

Rhode Island: McNeil 3086

Tennessee: Assisi 3120, Davis 3130, Frist 3136, Wilson 3157

Texas: Abell 3160, Alcon 3162, Bass 3172, **BP 3181**, Brackenridge 3182, Brown 3183, Cain 3188, Carter 3190, **Chrest 3194**, Coates 3197, Collins 3199, Dunn 3216, Edwards 3218, Elkins 3220, Elkins 3221, Esping 3225, Farish 3228, Fish 3233, Fluor 3235, Hamman 3248, Hext 3257, Hoglund 3263, Holloway 3264, **Houston 3266**, Houston 3267, Light 3281, Lightner 3282, Lockheed 3284, **Marshall 3290**, Mayor 3292, McDermott 3293, McKee 3295, Meadows 3296, Moody 3298, Moore 3299, QuadW 3328, Richardson 3334, Rosewood 3340, San Angelo 3343, Sikh 3351, South 3356, Sterling 3358, Sturgis 3360, Summerlee 3361, Waggoner 3379, Willard 3382

Utah: Dialysis 3390, Eccles 3392, Hemingway 3396

Vermont: Lintilhac 3412

Virginia: AMERIGROUP 3420, **Bosack 3423**, Jeffress 3444, **Longview 3451**, Northern 3464, RECO 3474, Samberg 3478, Williamsburg 3487

Washington: Allen 3490, Anderson 3492, Casey 3499, Casey 3500, Dimmer 3506, **Foundation 3515, Gates 3516, Ji 3528**, Pankow 3548, Washington 3570, **Wilburforce 3572**

Wisconsin: Alliant 3592, **Bradley 3601**, Community 3606, Eau 3611, Incourage 3623, Manitowoc 3632, Milwaukee 3637, Pettit 3645, Sand 3654, Windway 3669

Scholarship funds

Alabama: BBVA 3, Black 4, Central 8, Community 9, Community 10, McWane 17, Simpson 21

Alaska: CIRI 33

Arizona: Flinn 44, Grace 46, Hill 48, Marshall 54, Napier 55, Stardust 63, Webb 64

Arkansas: Cabe 67, Endeavor 69, Frueauff 70, Ross 72, Wal-Mart 74

California: Ahmanson 77, Allergan 80, Anderson 85, Aratani 89, Ayrshire 97, Bank 99, Barth 101, **Beavers 102**, Bechtel 103, Bechtel, 104, Berry 111, Beynon 113, Blue 114, Brisco 127, Brocchini 130, California 137, California 140, **Clorox 153**, College 156, Community 158, Community 160, Community 161, Community 162, Copley 166, Cummings 171, Disney 181, Drown 187, Finley 197, Fremont 207, **Gellert 214**, Gellert 215, Hannon 242, Heller 246, **Hilton 251**, Hoag 253, Humboldt 257, Jacobs 267, Jones 270, Kelly 278, Kirchgessner 282, Langendorf 289, Lesher 299, **Lingnan 301**, Lucas 306, Lux 307, Marin 309, **Mattel 312**, Mazda 313, McClatchy 317, **McConnell 318**, McKesson 321, McMicking 322, Milken 331, Mosher 335, Napa 340, Newhall 342, North 346, Parsons 359, Pedrozzi 364, PG&E 367, Placer 371, Plum 372, Price 373, Rancho 378, Richards 382, **Rivendell 384, Rupe 389**, Sacramento 391, Santa Barbara 394, Shasta 401, Silicon 408, Simpson 411, Solano 419, Sonora 420, **Special 422**, Taper 433, UniHealth 444, Valley 445, Versacare 448, Wasserman 453

Colorado: Community 484, **Crowell 487**, Donahue 490, El Pomar 492, Kaufmann 509, Schlessman 530, Summit 537, Telluride 538, Tomkins 540, Vradenburg 544

Connecticut: Aetna 550, Community 562, Connecticut 564, Conway 565, Deloitte 569, **Deupree 571**, Palmer 600, **Praxair 606**, Saybrook 610

Delaware: Brown 625, Chaney 628

District of Columbia: Cafritz 656, **Carter 657**, Lehrman 670, New Futures 676

Florida: Ansin 689, Benjamin 699, Bi-Lo/Winn-Dixie 700, Blanton 702, Cape Coral 714, Catalina 716, **Chester 720**, Community 722, Community 724, Community 725, Community 727, Conn 728, Coral Gables 729, Darden 732, Erdle 740, Florida 744, Greenburg 752, Gulf 754, Jacksonville 761, Jacobsen 762, Kennedy 767, King 768, Kiwanis 770, Macdonald 783, Morrison 792, Pinellas 801, **Samstag 813, Skelly 820**, Southwest 823, Thomas 831, TWS 836, Winter 842, Woodbery 844

Georgia: AIM 847, Amos-Cheves 849, Baker 853, Bancker-Williams 854, Bowen 857, **Coca 864**, Exposition 873, EZ 874, Georgia 877, **Georgia 878**, Glenn 882, Goizueta 883, **Imlay 888**, Moore 897, Pitts 904, Savannah 912

Hawaii: Campbell 928, Castle 930, Hawaii 933, McInerny 938

Idaho: Cunningham 946, Idaho 948, **Micron 950**, Whittenberger 953

Illinois: ArcelorMittal 964, Boothroyd 971, Brach 973, Coleman 986, Community 988, Community 990, Community 991, Community 992, Crown 997, Dunard 1006, Dunham 1007, DuPage 1008, Frankel 1017, **Grainger 1024**, Hospira 1034, Hughes 1035, Moline 1063, Monticello 1065, Omron 1070, Polk 1075, Pullman 1081, Redhill 1082, Schmitt 1088, Siragusa 1096, Speh 1097, Square 1099, Stone 1102, Tracy 1104, Ward 1111, Washington 1112, Webb 1113

Indiana: Brown 1124, Central 1126, Community 1130, Community 1131, Community 1132, Community 1133, Community 1134, Community 1135, Community 1136, Decatur 1142, Fayette 1146, Froderman 1148, Hancock 1154, Henry 1158, Jasper 1160, Jennings 1162, Johnson 1163, Kosciusko 1168, LaGrange 1170, Legacy 1171, Madison 1175, Master 1177, Noble 1179, Northern 1180, Parke 1186, Portland 1188, Putnam 1189, Rush 1192, Shoop 1195, TCU 1197, Tipton 1198, Unity 1201, Wabash 1203, WellPoint 1206, Western 1208

Iowa: Aviva 1211, Clarinda 1214, Community 1216, Community 1217, deStwolinski 1220, Maytag 1229, McElroy 1230, **Rockwell 1237**, Siouxland 1240, Stebens 1242, Wahlert 1244

Kansas: Capitol 1251, Collective 1253, Delta 1255, Hansen 1259, Hutchinson 1260, Insurance 1261, Koch 1265, **Lloyd 1267**, Rush 1273, Salina 1274, Sarver 1275, Topeka 1279

Kentucky: Blue 1282, C.E. 1284, Community 1286, Etscorn 1287, Gheens 1288, Good 1289, Hayswood 1290, Steel 1294, Trim 1295

Louisiana: Community 1306, Entergy 1308, Grigsby 1312

Maine: Alfond 1324, Borman 1325

Maryland: Commonweal 1356, Community 1358, Community 1360, **de Beaumont 1366**, Dresher 1370, Gudelsky 1376, Henson 1378, Macht 1388, Meyerhoff 1393, Mid-Shore 1395, Osprey 1403, Rembrandt 1407, Richmond 1408, Straus 1410

Massachusetts: Arbella 1426, Babson 1430, Berkman 1434, Cabot 1443, Cape Cod 1445, Clarke 1448, Community 1453, Demoulas 1458, East 1460, Eastern 1461, Essex 1464, Gordon 1475, Grinspoon 1479, Herbert 1481, **Kahn 1492**, Kelsey 1493, Krieger 1497, Levy 1501, Liberty 1502, Makepeace 1507, New 1518, Phelps 1528, Ramsey 1530, Rogers 1536, Schrafft 1543, Sheehan 1545, Williams 1567, **Xeric 1570**

Michigan: Alro 1574, Ann Arbor 1576, Binda 1579, Branch 1580, Charlevoix 1583, Christian 1585, Community 1586, Community 1587, Community 1588, Community 1589, Community 1590, Community 1591, Dart 1594, Farwell 1602, Four 1603, Frankenmuth 1606, Fremont 1607, Gilmore 1612, Grand Haven 1614, Grand 1616, Hillsdale 1620, Jubilee 1624, Kahn 1625, Kalamazoo 1626, Keller 1627, Lear 1632, Lenawee 1634, Marquette 1636, Midland 1642, Mills 1643, Mount Pleasant 1647, Perrigo 1655, Petoskey 1656, Pokagon 1657, Roscommon 1660, Royal 1661, Saginaw 1662, Schmuckal 1664, Steelcase 1667, Van Andel 1669, Wege 1674

Minnesota: 3M 1676, Best 1685, Donaldson 1692, Duluth 1693, General 1697, Koran 1709, Marbrook 1713, Northwest 1723, Opus 1724, **O'Shaughnessy 1725, Pentair 1727**, Regis 1732, SUPERVALU 1743, Thorpe 1745, **Trust 1746**, WCA 1749, Wedum 1750, West 1751

Mississippi: Community 1759, Community 1760, Gulf 1764, Mississippi 1769, Regions 1770, Sullivan 1771

Missouri: Anheuser 1774, Centene 1782, Community 1783, Curry 1784, Green 1790, Humphreys 1795, Millstone 1801, Musgrave 1805, Saigh 1811, St. Louis 1814, Tilles 1815, Truman 1817

Montana: Lynn 1827, Whitefish 1832

Nebraska: Grand Island 1837, Hawkins 1838, Hirschfeld 1839, Lincoln 1847, Midlands 1848

Nevada: Caesars 1860, Nevada 1867, Parasol 1868, **Tang 1873**

New Hampshire: Alexander 1877, Fuller 1886, Lindsay 1890, Penates 1893, Smyth 1895

New Jersey: **Allen 1900**, Bard 1905, Brotherton 1914, Hudson 1942, Integra 1945, **Newcombe 1972**, Princeton 1979, **Siemens 1993**, Summit 1998, Syms 1999, Turrell 2002, Unilever 2003

New Mexico: Albuquerque 2006, B.F. 2008, Chase 2009, Santa Fe 2017

New York: Achelis 2026, Adirondack 2027, Allyn 2032, Aronson 2042, Berg 2062, Brooks 2075, **Buffalo 2078**, Carvel 2088, Coach 2100, Community 2107, Community 2109, Community 2110, Community 2111, Community 2113, Cutco 2123, **Diamond 2135**, Farash 2154, Fisher 2157, Freeman 2164, Gebbie 2170, Goldman 2183, Heckscher 2205, High 2213, Hudson 2223, Jaharis 2236, Kekst 2249, Knapp 2259, Lake Placid 2265, Lavelle 2269, Lee 2271, **Luce 2286**, McGonagle 2299, Mendell 2303, **MetLife 2307**, Moore 2311, Morgan 2315, National 2321, New York 2325, New York 2327, Northern 2331, Norwich 2332, NYSE 2336, Oishei 2340, Ong 2341, **Open 2343**, Park 2349, Patrina 2350, Robinson 2387, Roothbert 2391, Rose 2392, Ruffin 2400, Schenectady 2407, Schnurmacher 2411, Seneca 2415, Snow 2432, Spektor 2442, Sulzberger 2451, **Towerbrook 2473**, Truman 2475, Voya 2488, Wachenheim 2489, Wachtell, 2490, Weil, 2498

North Carolina: Adams 2517, Bergen 2527, Biddle 2529, Brady 2533, Caine 2536, Community 2540, Cumberland 2541, Davie 2543, Eddy 2548, Ferebee 2552, French 2554, Goodrich 2561, Harvest 2566, Kramer 2581, **Laffin 2583**, Mayr 2588, Meserve 2592, Meyer 2594, Needham 2597, Niessen 2598, North Carolina 2599, North 2600, Olin 2603, Outer 2604, Perkin 2607, Polk 2609, Reynolds 2613, Rogers 2618, Sanders 2620, Southern 2630, Sutcliffe 2635, Tannenbaum 2637, Wyly 2646

North Dakota: Community 2648, Fargo 2649, MDU 2652, North Dakota 2653

Ohio: Akron 2655, American 2656, Austin 2663, Barberton 2664, Bates 2665, **Benedict 2666**, Brown 2672, **Cardinal 2677**, Charities 2678, Cliffs 2681, Community 2682, Community 2683, Community 2684, Coshocton 2686, Dater 2687, Delaware 2689, **Eaton 2692**, Evans 2695, Fairfield 2696, Fifth 2699, Findlay 2700, Foundation 2702, Greene 2707, Gund 2708, Hamilton 2710, Kettering 2716, KeyBank 2717, Knoll 2719, Licking 2723, Macy's 2726, Maltz 2727, Marietta 2732, Marion 2733, Middletown 2737, Morgan 2740, Murphy 2744, Muskingum 2747, National 2748, Nippert 2751, Nordson 2755, **OMNOVA 2759**, Renner 2766, Richland 2767, Ryan 2769, Saint 2770, Salem 2771, Sandusky 2773, Sears 2781, Slemp 2785, Stark 2788, Steinmann 2789, Tiffin 2793, Troy 2794, Tuscarawas 2795, Wayne 2798, Young 2803, YSI 2805

Oklahoma: Hille 2816, Kirschner 2818, McGee 2820, Oklahoma 2823, Sarkeys 2828, **Schusterman 2829**, Zarrow 2834

Oregon: Benton 2835, Castle 2839, Collins 2842, Hedinger 2849, Jeld 2852, Macdonald 2859, Michael 2862, Morris 2864, PGE 2867, Renaissance 2869, West 2875

Pennsylvania: **ACE 2880**, **Alcoa 2882**, Baker 2886, Bayer 2888, Beaver 2890, Berks 2893, **Botstiber 2898**, Bucks 2900, Buncher 2902, Centre 2909, Cestone 2910, Charlestein 2911, Chester 2915, CIGNA 2917, Claneil 2918, Comcast 2921, Community 2923, Community 2925, Connelly 2926, Duff 2938, Elk 2939, EQT 2940, First 2947, Foundation 2952, Fourjay 2953, Freas 2954, Harris 2965, Henkels 2967, Independence 2975, Independence 2976, Lancaster 2981, Lehigh Valley 2986, O'Brien-Veba 3007, Packer 3008, Pilgrim 3016, **PPG 3018**, Presser 3019, Randall 3021, Saramar 3029, Scranton 3031, Sneath 3038, Society 3040, United 3052, Washington 3054, **Zeldin 3060**

Rhode Island: Citizens 3067, CVS 3068, DeLoura 3070, McNeil 3086, Rhode Island 3089, Textron 3093

South Carolina: Bailey 3096, Community 3099, Foothills 3102, McKissick 3106, Smith 3109, Spartanburg 3110, Waccamaw 3112

South Dakota: Hatterscheidt 3116, Schwab 3117, South 3118

Tennessee: Benwood 3123, CIC 3127, Davis 3130, Eastman 3133, First 3135, Frist 3136, HCA 3139, Kirkland 3143, Osborne 3147, Phillips 3149, Promethean 3150, Regal 3151, Tucker 3156, Wilson 3157

Texas: Abell 3160, Amarillo 3163, AT&T 3167, Augur 3168, B.E.L.I.E.F. 3169, **Baker 3170**, Bickel 3178, **BP 3181**, Brackenridge 3182, Brown 3183, Cailloux 3187, Cain 3188, Carter 3190, Coastal 3196, Community 3200, Constantin 3202, Dallas 3209, DeBusk 3211, Edwards 3219, Esping 3225, Fairchild 3227, Fasken 3229, Fisch 3232, Fish 3233, Fluor 3235, Hamman 3248, Haraldson 3250, Herzstein 3256, Hext 3257, Hill 3260, Hoglund 3263, **Houston 3266**, Houston 3267, Kinder 3274, Long 3285, Lubbock 3287, Luse 3289, **Marshall 3290**, Martinez 3291, McDermott 3293, McKee 3295, Moody 3298, Moore 3299, Morgan 3301, Navarro 3305, Penney 3315, Permian 3316, Powell 3324, QuadW 3328, Reilly 3333, Rogers 3339, South 3356, Sterling 3358, Sturgis 3360, Texas 3364, Trull 3373, Waco 3378, Waggoner 3379, Wallrath 3380

Utah: Bamberger 3389, Eccles 3392, Eskuche 3393, Green 3394

Vermont: Lintilhac 3412, McKenzie 3413, Merchants 3414, Tarrant 3416

Virginia: Arlington 3421, Charlottesville 3428, Community 3429, Community 3430, Community 3431, Community 3432, Lynchburg 3454, Memorial 3458, Moore 3461, **Northrop 3465**, Potomac 3471, Pruden 3473, RECO 3474, Strong 3481, United 3484

Washington: Anderson 3492, Bainbridge 3494, Casey 3499, Community 3504, Dimmer 3506, Everett 3511, **Gates 3516**, Korum 3532, Lochland 3536, Milgard 3543, PEMCO 3549, Renton 3552, San Juan 3555, Tudor 3569, Whatcom 3571

West Virginia: Beckley 3577, Community 3579, Maier 3584, Parkersburg 3587, Tucker 3589, Your 3591

Wisconsin: Alliant 3592, Ariens 3594, Blooming 3599, **Bradley 3601**, Center 3604, Community 3606, Community 3607, Fond du Lac 3615, Green Bay 3619, Harley 3621, Incourage 3623, Johnson 3625, Kern 3627, La Crosse 3631, Marshfield 3633, Milwaukee 3637, Neese 3639, Oshkosh 3642, Sentry 3657, St. Croix 3662, Stateline 3663, **Wagner 3666**, Windway 3669

Wyoming: McMurry 3676, Scott 3679

Scholarships—to individuals

Alabama: Andalusia 1, Central 8, Hawkins 14, Smith 22

Alaska: Alaska 26, Aleut 27, Arctic 28, Bristol 31, Chugach 32, CIRI 33, Doyon 34, Koniag 36

Arizona: Christian 41, Grace 46

Arkansas: Buck 66, Endeavor 69, Union 73

California: Anaheim 83, Brooks 131, Community 163, Fansler 193, Hand 241, Humboldt 257, Kern 279, Kimbo 281, Leavey 294, Los Altos 305, Marin 309, Matsui 311, Northern 347, Optivest 351, Pedrozzi 364, Price 373, Sacramento 391, San Luis 393, Santa Barbara 394, Scaife 397, Shasta 401, Silicon 408, Simon 410, Sonora 420, Stanislaus 425

Colorado: Colorado 482, **Daniels 488**, Denver 489, Griffin 504, Norwood 524, Sachs 529, Seay 532, Telluride 538, Yampa 545

Connecticut: Community 562, Community 563, Connecticut 564, Eder 573, Grampy's 582, Meriden 591, Saybrook 610, SBM 611

Delaware: Chaney 628

District of Columbia: **Freedom 662**

Florida: Benjamin 699, Blanton 702, Charlotte 718, Community 724, Community 727, DeBartolo 734, Erdle 740, Hand 755, Kantner 764, King 768, Life 779, Martin 786, Martin 787, Morrison 792, **Patel 797**, Pinellas 801, **Samstag 813**, Selby 816, Southwest 823, Sunburst 829

Georgia: Amos-Cheves 849, Cobb 863, Community 869, Savannah 912, WinShape 921

Hawaii: Atherton 925, Hawaii 933, Kaneta 936, Zimmerman 940

Idaho: Jeker 949, **Micron 950**

Illinois: **Abbott 954**, Community 990, Community 991, Edwardsville 1010, Geneseo 1022, **Kobe 1045**, **Lascaris 1048**, Mellinger 1061, Oak Park 1068, Schuler 1090

Indiana: Blackford 1122, Brown 1124, Cass 1125, Central 1126, Cole 1127, Community 1128, Community 1130, Community 1131, Community 1132, Community 1133, Community 1134, Community 1136, Dearborn 1141, Decatur 1142, DeKalb 1144, Fayette 1146, Harrison 1155, Hendricks 1157, Johnson 1163, Joshi 1165, Kendrick 1166, LaGrange 1170, Legacy 1171, Madison 1175, Marshall 1176, Noble 1179, Orange 1184, Owen 1185, Parke 1186, Portland 1188, Shoop 1195, TCU 1197, Tipton 1198, Union 1200, Wabash 1203, Wells 1207, Western 1208, Whitley 1209

Iowa: Clarinda 1214, Delaware 1219, Iowa 1225, Iowa 1226, Jefferson 1227, Schroeder 1239, Siouxland 1240

Kansas: Douglas 1256, Hansen 1259, Hutchinson 1260, Jones 1262, Salina 1274, Sarver 1275, Topeka 1279

Kentucky: Blue 1282, Hayswood 1290

Louisiana: Baton Rouge 1300, Burton 1303

Maryland: Adams 1345, Community 1358, Community 1359

Massachusetts: Cape Cod 1445, D'Amour 1456, Edwards 1462, Essex 1464, Honey 1483, MetroWest 1515, Phillips 1529, Smith 1547, Sudbury 1551, Williams 1567

Michigan: Charlevoix 1583, Community 1587, Community 1588, Community 1589, Community 1590, Frankenmuth 1606, Fremont 1607, **Gerber 1611**, Grand Haven 1614, Grand Rapids 1615, Grand 1616, Hebert 1619, Hillsdale 1620, Jackson 1623, Kalamazoo 1626, Legion 1633, Marquette 1636, Mount Pleasant 1647, Petoskey 1656, Pokagon 1657, Saginaw 1662, Sigmund 1665

Minnesota: Alworth 1677, Duluth 1693, Grand Rapids 1699, Initiative 1703, Land 1710, Northwest 1723, Redwood 1731, Wallin 1748, Winona 1753

Mississippi: Community 1759

Missouri: Guilander 1791, Walker 1818, Westlake 1819

Montana: Montana 1828

Nebraska: **Buffett 1833**, Fremont 1836, Grand Island 1837, Kearney 1842, Lexington 1845, Mid-Nebraska 1849, Nebraska 1851, Oregon 1852

Nevada: Doyle 1861

New Hampshire: Alexander 1877, Foundation 1885, Ham 1887, Woodbury 1897

New Jersey: Baker 1903, **Knowles 1955**, Lasko 1958, Merck 1966, Princeton 1979, **Siemens 1993**, Wight 2005

New Mexico: Albuquerque 2006, Chase 2009, Maddox 2014, Simon 2018

New York: Adirondack 2027, Barking 2055, Bikuben 2064, Broadcasters 2071, **Buffalo 2078**, Chautauqua 2091, Community 2107, Community 2109, Community 2111, Hadar 2198, Henry 2209, **King 2251**, Lake Placid 2265, Morgan 2315, Northern 2331, Norwich 2332, **Open 2343**, **PepsiCo 2354**, Post 2365, **Rockefeller 2390**, **Schepp 2408**, **Shatford 2417**, Snayberger 2431, Sperry 2443, **Youth 2513**

North Carolina: Community 2539, Community 2540, Cumberland 2541, Davie 2543, Deaver 2544, Eddy 2548, Fairfield 2551, Ferebee 2552, Ghidotti 2558, McNeil 2590, North Carolina 2599, Nucor 2601, Outer 2604, Polk 2609, Schmuhl 2622, Sloan 2628, State 2632, Tannenbaum 2637, Towne 2641, Wyly 2646

North Dakota: Fargo 2649, North Dakota 2653

Ohio: Ar-Hale 2661, **Brush 2673**, Bryan 2674, Community 2682, Community 2683, Community 2684, Coshocton 2686, Delaware 2689, Fairfield 2696, Gardner 2705, Marietta 2732, Marion 2733, Middletown 2737, Munro 2743, Murphy 2746, Muskingum 2747, National 2748, Piqua 2763, Richland 2767, Samaritan 2772, Scripps 2780, Shinnick 2783, Slemp 2785, Springfield 2787, Stark 2788, Tuscarawas 2795, Tuscora 2796, YSI 2805

Oregon: Benton 2835, Daly 2844, Ford 2846, Leonard 2858, Western 2876

Pennsylvania: Beaver 2890, Berks 2893, Berwind 2894, **Botstiber 2898**, **Carnegie 2906**, Central 2908, Chester 2915, Clareth 2919, Comcast 2921, Community 2922, Community 2923, Community 2924, Community 2925, Elk 2939, EQT 2940, Foundation 2952, II-VI 2974, Lazarich 2983, Lewis 2987, McKaig 2994, Noll 3005, O'Brien-Veba 3007, Phoenixville 3014, Shuman 3036, Society 3040, Washington 3054

Puerto Rico: Puerto Rico 3061

Rhode Island: Masonic 3083, Rhode Island 3089

South Carolina: Bailey 3096, Community 3100, Spartanburg 3110

South Dakota: Hatterscheidt 3116

Tennessee: Alumni 3119, CIC 3127, **Scarlett 3152**

Texas: Astin 3166, College 3198, Fasken 3229, Hachar 3246, Hamman 3248, Haraldson 3250, Hill 3259, Reilly 3333, Sikh 3351, Texas 3364

Utah: Bamberger 3389

Vermont: General 3410, Rowland 3415, Windham 3418

Virginia: Arlington 3421, **Brown 3424**, Community 3430, Community 3433, **Foundation 3438**, Lee-Jackson 3448, Lincoln 3449, Lynchburg 3454, Maude 3456, **Olmsted 3468**, United 3484

Washington: Arise 3493, Blakemore 3497, Blue 3498, Community 3503, Corvias 3505, Everett 3511, Grays 3520, Haller 3522, Kawabe 3531, Lauzier 3535, Lochland 3536, Maxwell 3539, PEMCO 3549, Tacoma 3567, Tudor 3569

West Virginia: Burnside 3578, Eastern 3580, McCormick 3585, Parkersburg 3587, Tucker 3589

Wisconsin: Alliant 3592, Ariens 3594, Community 3607, Fort 3616, Fund 3617, Green Bay 3619, Incourage 3623, Kohler 3629, La Crosse 3631, Marshfield 3633, Menasha 3636, Milwaukee 3637, Nelson 3640, Oshkosh 3642, Racine 3648, St. Croix 3662

Wyoming: Cody 3672, Wyoming 3684

Seed money

Alabama: Central 8, Community 9, Community 10
Arizona: Flinn 44, Hughes 49, Webb 64
Arkansas: Cabe 67, Endeavor 69, Ross 72
California: Aratani 89, **Arkay 91**, Ayrshire 97, Bannerman 100, California 140, **Christensen 151**, Community 157, Community 160, Community 162, Cowell 168, Crail 170, Drown 187, Eisner 189, Firedoll 198, **Foundation 202, Fund 210, Gellert 214**, Good 230, Heller 246, Humboldt 257, Irvine 264, Jacobs 267, Johnson 269, **Kapor 273**, Kirchgessner 282, **Lingnan 301**, Los Altos 305, Lux 307, Marin 309, Mead 324, Napa 340, Newhall 342, Parsons 359, Rancho 378, **Rivendell 384**, Rossi 387, **Rupe 389**, Sacramento 391, **Seaver 400**, Silicon 408, Sonora 420, **Special 422, Spencer 424**, Stanislaus 425, Taper 433, Trio 440, Truckee 441, True 442, **Wilkinson 463**, Witter 467
Colorado: Animal 472, Brett 476, Colorado 483, Community 484, Comprecare 485, Foundation 498, **General 501**, Pikes 525, Piton 526, Society 534, Stratton 536, Summit 537, Telluride 538, Yampa 545
Connecticut: **Albers 551**, Community 563, Connecticut 564, **Deupree 571**, Ensworth 575, Matthies 590, NewAlliance 595, Palmer 600
Delaware: Delaware 630, Kutz 637, Longwood 639
District of Columbia: Bauman 650, **Butler 655, El-Hibri 659**, Graham 663, Jovid 668, **Wallace 683**
Florida: Community 722, Community 724, Community 727, Conn 728, Henderson 758, Kennedy 767, **Knight 771**, Landwirth 775, Lennar 778, Macdonald 783, Quantum 805, Reinhold 808
Georgia: Abreu 846, Anderson 850, Bancker-Williams 854, Community 867, Community 868, Georgia 876, Livingston 893, North 900
Hawaii: Atherton 925, Baldwin 926, Campbell 928, Castle 929, Castle 930, Cooke 932, McInerny 938
Idaho: Cunningham 946, Idaho 948, Whittenberger 953
Illinois: Community 988, Community 989, Community 990, Community 991, Community 992, DeKalb 999, Driehaus 1002, DuPage 1008, Evanston 1012, Field 1014, Frankel 1017, Grant 1025, Guthman 1027, Kaufman 1043, Libra 1050, Lumpkin 1053, Mellinger 1061, Oak Park 1068, Prince 1076, Speh 1097, Stern 1100, VNA 1107, Washington 1112, Webb 1113
Indiana: Brown 1124, Cass 1125, Central 1126, Cole 1127, Community 1129, Community 1130, Community 1131, Community 1132, Community 1133, Community 1134, Community 1136, Dearborn 1141, Decatur 1142, Fairbanks 1145, Hancock 1154, Harrison 1155, Health 1156, Hendricks 1157, Henry 1158, Jasper 1160, Johnson 1163, LaGrange 1170, Legacy 1171, **Lumina 1174**, Marshall 1176, Noble 1179, Northern 1180, Portland 1188, Putnam 1189, Ripley 1191, Rush 1192, Tipton 1198, Unity 1201, Wabash 1203, Wells 1207, Western 1208, Whitley 1209
Iowa: Ahrens 1210, Community 1216, Community 1217, Iowa 1226, Maytag 1229, McElroy 1230, Siouxland 1240, Wellmark 1246
Kansas: Capitol 1251, Delta 1255, Farah 1258, Hutchinson 1260, **Lloyd 1267**, Salina 1274, Skillbuilders 1277, Topeka 1279
Kentucky: Blue 1282, C.E. 1284, Good 1289
Louisiana: Baptist 1299, Beaird 1301, Community 1306, Freeman 1309, German 1310, New Orleans 1316, Steinhagen 1320
Maine: Golden 1329, Horizon 1331, King 1333, Libra 1334, Somers 1341, **Walter 1343**
Maryland: Baker 1347, **Braitmayer 1351**, Commonweal 1356, Community 1358, Community 1359, Community 1360, **de Beaumont 1366**, Deutsch 1369, Goldseker 1374, Macht 1388, Meyerhoff 1393, Mid-Shore 1395, Richmond 1408, Straus 1410, Town 1413, Tucker 1415, Zickler 1419
Massachusetts: Access 1422, Alden 1425, Berkman 1434, Boynton 1437, **Brabson 1438**, Cape Cod 1445, Community 1453, **Conservation 1454**, Davis 1457, Essex 1464, Farnsworth 1465, Fields 1467, Fireman 1469, **Kahn 1492**, Kelsey 1493, Kendall 1494, Levy 1501, Melville 1511, Parker 1523, Ratshesky 1531, Riley 1534, Smith 1546, Wadleigh 1562, Williams 1567, **Xeric 1570**
Michigan: Ann Arbor 1576, Binda 1579, Capital 1581, Carls 1582, Charlevoix 1583, Community 1586, Community 1587, Community 1588, Community 1589, Community 1590, Community 1591, Dalton 1592, Davenport 1595, Dow 1597, **Erb 1599**, Fremont 1607, Frey 1609, Gilmore 1612, Grand Haven 1614, Grand Rapids 1615, Grand 1616, Hillsdale 1620, Jackson 1623, Kalamazoo 1626, Keller 1627, **Kellogg 1628**, Marquette 1636, McGregor 1638, Midland 1642, Morley 1644, **Mott 1645**, Mount Pleasant 1647, Petoskey 1656, Saginaw 1662, Sanilac 1663, Steelcase 1667
Minnesota: Duluth 1693, Farmers 1695, Greystone 1700, Initiative 1703, Land 1710, Midcontinent 1716, Minneapolis 1717, Musser 1719, Northwest 1723, **Patterson 1726**, Rochester 1735, **St. Jude 1741, Trust 1746**, Wedum 1750, West 1751, **Weyerhaeuser 1752**
Missouri: Butler 1780, Community 1783, **Deer 1786**, Green 1790, **Monsanto 1803**, Speas 1813, St. Louis 1814, Truman 1817
Nebraska: Fremont 1836, Hirschfeld 1839, Kearney 1842, Kiewit 1843, Lexington 1845, Lincoln 1847, Midlands 1848, Mid-Nebraska 1849, Weitz 1855, Woods 1857
Nevada: Nevada 1867, Parasol 1868
New Hampshire: Alexander 1877, Bean 1878, Fuller 1886, Ham 1887
New Jersey: **Allen 1900**, Banbury 1904, Borden 1910, Brookdale 1912, Brotherton 1914, Environmental 1924, **Johnson 1949**, Leavens 1959, MCJ 1965, Princeton 1979, **Puffin 1980, Ramapo 1981**, Schumann 1990, Summit 1998, Turrell 2002, Westfield 2004
New Mexico: Con 2011, Frost 2012, Maddox 2014, Santa Fe 2017
New York: Abelard 2022, Achelis 2026, Adirondack 2027, Allyn 2032, Anderson 2036, Bay 2056, **Bronfman 2074**, Chautauqua 2091, Clark 2099, Community 2107, Community 2108, Community 2109, Community 2110, Community 2112, Community 2113, **Cummings 2120, Cummings 2121**, Cummings 2122, Dammann 2125, **Deutsche 2134**, Family 2153, Ferraioli 2156, **Foundation 2161**, Gebbie 2170, Gifford 2177, **Gimprich 2180, Goldman 2182**, Goldman 2183, Golisano 2185, Gould 2188, Heckscher 2205, Hycliff 2226, **Institute 2233, Kaplan 2245**, Klingenstein 2256, Kornfeld 2261, Lake Placid 2265, Legacy 2274, Littauer 2282, McGonagle 2299, **Mertz 2306, Nash 2320**, New York 2325, New York 2326, Northern 2331, **Noyes 2335**, O'Grady 2339, Oishei 2340, Patrina 2350, **Porticus 2364**, Rapoport 2373, Rauch 2376, Roche 2388, **Rockefeller 2389, Rockefeller 2390, Ross 2396, Rubin 2398**, Schenectady 2407, Snow 2432, **Sparkplug 2441**, Thompson 2461, **Tinker 2467**, Tower 2472, Truman 2475, van Ameringen 2482, van Ameringen 2483, Vidda 2485, Vogler 2487, **Weeden 2496**, Wells 2501, **Wenner 2502**, Western 2503
North Carolina: Biddle 2529, Community 2539, Cumberland 2541, Duncan 2547, Ferebee 2552, Glenn 2560, Hanes 2565, Kenan 2577, Kramer 2581, Meserve 2592, Meyer 2594, North 2600, Outer 2604, Polk 2609, Rex 2612, Reynolds 2614, Rogers 2618, Smith 2629, Strowd 2633, Tannenbaum 2637
North Dakota: North Dakota 2653
Ohio: Akron 2655, Anderson 2658, Ar-Hale 2661, Austin 2663, Cincinnati 2679, Community 2683, Community 2684, Coshocton 2686, Dater 2687, Delaware 2689, Eaton 2693, Evans 2695, Fairfield 2696, Findlay 2700, Gund 2708, Hamilton 2710, Hershey 2711, Licking 2723, Macy's 2726, Marietta 2732, Marion 2733, Mayerson 2735, Middletown 2737, Morgan 2740, Muskingum 2747, Nord 2754, Nordson 2755, Piqua 2763, Richland 2767, Saint 2770, Sandusky 2773, Schmidlapp 2775, Scripps 2780, Sears 2781, Slemp 2785, Springfield 2787, Stark 2788, Troy 2794, Wayne 2798, White 2800, Woodruff 2801, YSI 2805
Oklahoma: **Ethics 2811**, Merrick 2821, Noble 2822, **Schusterman 2829**
Oregon: Collins 2842, Flowerree 2845, Lamb 2855, Lazar 2856, Meyer 2861, **NIKE 2865**, Templeton 2874, Western 2876, Woodard 2877
Pennsylvania: Allegheny 2883, Benedum 2892, Berks 2893, Buhl 2901, Central 2908, Centre 2909, Cestone 2910, Claneil 2918, Community 2924, DSF 2937, EQT 2940, Fels 2942, Finley 2946, First 2947, FISA 2950, Foundation 2952, Fourjay 2953, Huston 2973, **KL 2978**, Laros 2982, Lehigh Valley 2986, Martin 2991, McCune 2993, McLean 2997, Mellon 2998, Nelson 3003, Patterson 3010, Penn 3011, Phoenixville 3014, Presser 3019, Scranton 3031, Seybert 3034, Shaffer 3035, Stackpole 3042, Staunton 3044, Tuttleman 3050, Valentine 3053, Widener 3056, Wyomissing 3059
Rhode Island: **Dorot 3071**, Kimball 3079, Rhode Island 3089
South Carolina: Black 3097, Byerly 3098, Community 3099, Community 3100, Daniel 3101, Spartanburg 3110, Springs 3111
Tennessee: Benwood 3123, Davis 3130, **International 3142**, Lyndhurst 3145, Osborne 3147, Phillips 3149, **Scarlett 3152**, Wilson 3157
Texas: Abell 3160, Amarillo 3163, Burnett 3185, Cailloux 3187, Carter 3190, Coastal 3196, Embrey 3222, Fish 3233, Flarsheim 3234, Hext 3257, Hoblitzelle 3262, **Houston 3266**, Lubbock 3287, **Marshall 3290**, McDermott 3293, McKee 3295, Meadows 3296, Moody 3298, Permian 3316, Peterson 3318, Rapoport 3331, Richardson 3334, Rockwell 3338, San Angelo 3343, Sikh 3351, Simmons 3352, South 3356, Sterling 3358, Summerlee 3361, Tomerlin 3371, Trull 3373, Waco 3378, Waggoner 3379, Ward 3381
Vermont: Lintilhac 3412, Vermont 3417, Windham 3418
Virginia: Arlington 3421, Charlottesville 3428, Community 3431, Community 3432, Community 3433, **Longview 3451**, Lynchburg 3454, Memorial 3458, Samberg 3478
Washington: Community 3503, Ferguson 3513, **Foundation 3515, Goodwin 3519**, Grays 3520, Harder 3524, Inland 3526, **Ji 3528**, Jones 3530, Kawabe 3531, Northwest 3546, **Starbucks 3565**, Tacoma 3567, Washington 3570, **Wilburforce 3572**
West Virginia: Beckley 3577, Community 3579, Eastern 3580, Parkersburg 3587, Tucker 3589, Your 3591
Wisconsin: Alliant 3592, Community 3606, Community 3607, Dudley 3610, Eau 3611, Fond du Lac 3615, Green Bay 3619, Incourage 3623, Johnson 3625, Kohler 3629, La Crosse 3631, McBeath 3634, Milwaukee 3637, New 3641, Oshkosh 3642, Racine 3648, Siebert 3659, St. Croix 3662, Stateline 3663, U.S. 3665
Wyoming: McMurry 3676, Wyoming 3684

Sponsorships

Alabama: BBVA 3
Arkansas: Wal-Mart 74
California: Allergan 80, **Applied 88**, GSF 235, **Mattel 312**, Sierra 406
Connecticut: Aetna 550, Deloitte 569, NewAlliance 595, Northeast 598, Pitney 604
Delaware: Sylvan 648
Georgia: **Coca 864**, Georgia 877, **Georgia 878**
Idaho: **Micron 950**
Illinois: **Mondelez 1064**, Square 1099
Indiana: Brotherhood 1123, Koch 1167, Steel 1196, Vectren 1202, WellPoint 1206

Kansas: Collective 1253
Kentucky: Trim 1295
Louisiana: Blue 1302
Massachusetts: DentaQuest 1459, Eastern 1461, **State 1550**
Michigan: DTE 1598, Isabella 1622
Minnesota: Farmers 1695, **Mosaic 1718**, Opus 1724, **St. Jude 1741**, SUPERVALU 1743
Missouri: Bunge 1779, Centene 1782
Montana: Wendy's 1831
Nevada: Caesars 1860
New Jersey: Bard 1905, Horizon 1940, Integra 1945
New York: American 2033, Century 2089, **Deutsche 2134**, **JPMorgan 2242**, MBIA 2297, NYSE 2336, Rich 2382, Voya 2488
North Carolina: Goodrich 2561
Ohio: KeyBank 2717, National 2748, Ohio 2756, **Omnicare 2758**
Oklahoma: Oklahoma 2823
Oregon: PGE 2867
Pennsylvania: **Alcoa 2882**, Comcast 2921, EQT 2940
Rhode Island: Biogen 3063, Citizens 3067, Textron 3093
Tennessee: First 3135, Regal 3151
Texas: **BP 3181**, Penney 3315
Virginia: AMERIGROUP 3420, United 3484
Washington: Korum 3532
Wisconsin: Johnson 3625, Pamida 3644, Sentry 3657

Student loans—to individuals

California: Community 162, Santa Barbara 394, Shasta 401
Colorado: Colorado 482
Florida: Benjamin 699
Georgia: **Pickett 903**
Illinois: Mellinger 1061
Indiana: Whitley 1209
Maryland: Plitt 1404
Massachusetts: Cape Cod 1445
Michigan: Mount Pleasant 1647
Minnesota: Redwood 1731
Mississippi: Feild 1762
Missouri: Speas 1813
New York: **Alavi 2030**, Community 2111, Ontario 2342
North Dakota: Martell 2651
Ohio: Shinnick 2783, Stark 2788
Pennsylvania: Clareth 2919, Community 2925
South Carolina: Springs 3111
Tennessee: Latimer 3144
Texas: Hachar 3246
Wyoming: Perkins 3678, Whitney 3683

Technical assistance

Alabama: Black 4, Central 8, Community 9
Alaska: Alaska 26
Arizona: Every 43, Piper 57
Arkansas: Frueauff 70
California: Ahmanson 77, Archstone 90, **Arkay 91**, Atlas 96, Blue 114, Buell 134, California 137, California 138, California 140, Community 157, Community 160, Community 162, Community 163, Cowell 168, Firedoll 198, Fleishhacker 199, Fox 205, **Fund 210**, **Gellert 214**, Gellert 215, Gerbode 217, Gumbiner 236, Heller 246, **Hilton 251**, Humboldt 257, Irvine 264, Jacobs 267, Johnson 269, **Kapor 273**, Kern 279, Kirchgessner 282, Lesher 299, Los Altos 305, Marin 309, **Mattel 312**, **McConnell 318**, McCune 320, Napa 340, North 346, Noyce 348, Parsons 359, Placer 371, Rancho 378, Sacramento 391, San Luis 393, Sierra 405, Soda 418, Sonora 420, Stuart 429, Trio 440, Truckee 441, True 442, UniHealth 444, **Warsh 452**, Zellerbach 471
Colorado: Animal 472, Bonfils 475, Brett 476, Colorado 483, **Crowell 487**, Donnell 491, **General 501**, Leighty 512, Piton 526, Rose 528, Summit 537, Telluride 538, Vradenburg 544
Connecticut: Community 562, Community 563, Connecticut 564, Ensworth 575, Middlesex 592
Delaware: AEC 622, Delaware 630, Edwards 631
District of Columbia: Bauman 650, Cafritz 656, Jovid 668, Meyer 672
Florida: Burns 710, Bush 712, Community 722, Conn 728, Florida 744, Henderson 758, Kennedy 767, **Knight 771**, Macdonald 783, Quantum 805, Southwest 823
Georgia: Communities 866, Healthcare 886, North 900
Hawaii: Atherton 925, Castle 929, Castle 930, Cooke 932, Hawaii 933
Illinois: Bersted 966, Chicago 982, Community 990, Community 993, Field 1014, Frankel 1017, Fry 1018, Guthman 1027, Lumpkin 1053, McGraw 1060, Polk 1075, Prince 1076, Reese 1083, Siragusa 1096, Speh 1097
Indiana: Ball 1121, Brown 1124, Central 1126, Community 1129, Community 1132, Community 1133, Community 1134, Decatur 1142, DeKalb 1144, Fairbanks 1145, Foellinger 1147, Hancock 1154, Health 1156, Henry 1158, Johnson 1163, LaGrange 1170, Legacy 1171, **Lumina 1174**, Marshall 1176, Noble 1179, Orange 1184, Putnam 1189, Rush 1192, Unity 1201, Wells 1207
Iowa: Ahrens 1210, Community 1216, Community 1217, Maytag 1229
Kansas: Capitol 1251, Hutchinson 1260, Kansas 1263
Kentucky: Blue 1282, C.E. 1284
Louisiana: Baptist 1299, Beaird 1301, Community 1306, New Orleans 1316
Maine: Libra 1334, Maine 1336
Maryland: Baker 1347, **Blaustein 1349**, **Casey 1353**, Community 1359, Dresher 1370, Freeman 1373, Goldseker 1374, Straus 1410
Massachusetts: Access 1422, **Barr 1433**, Cape Cod 1445, Clipper 1449, Community 1453, **Conservation 1454**, Davis 1457, DentaQuest 1459, Essex 1464, Farnsworth 1465, Hyams 1486, **Kahn 1492**, Kelsey 1493, Melville 1511, MetroWest 1515, Riley 1534, Sheehan 1545, **Sweet 1554**, United 1559, **Xeric 1570**
Michigan: Branch 1580, Capital 1581, Charlevoix 1583, Community 1587, Community 1588, Community 1590, Community 1591, Fremont 1607, Frey 1609, Gilmore 1612, Grand Rapids 1615, Grand 1616, Jackson 1623, Kalamazoo 1626, **Kellogg 1628**, **Kresge 1631**, Marquette 1636, Midland 1642, **Mott 1645**, Mott 1646, Mount Pleasant 1647, Oleson 1649, Petoskey 1656, Saginaw 1662, Sanilac 1663
Minnesota: Duluth 1693, Grand Rapids 1699, Initiative 1703, McKnight 1715, Minneapolis 1717, Northwest 1722, Northwest 1723, Rochester 1735, Securian 1739, Southwest 1740, Sundance 1742, **Trust 1746**, West 1751, Winona 1753
Mississippi: Foundation 1763, Gulf 1764
Missouri: Community 1783, Gateway 1789, Hall 1793, Hallmark 1794, Roblee 1809
Montana: Whitefish 1832
Nebraska: Lexington 1845, Lincoln 1847, Midlands 1848, Woods 1857
Nevada: Nevada 1867
New Hampshire: Alexander 1877, Endowment 1883, Foundation 1885
New Jersey: Harbourton 1936, Horizon 1940, **Johnson 1949**, MCJ 1965, Princeton 1979, Summit 1998, Westfield 2004
New Mexico: Con 2011, Frost 2012, Santa Fe 2017
New York: Abelard 2022, Achelis 2026, Adirondack 2027, **Arcus 2040**, Bay 2056, **Bronfman 2074**, **Carnegie 2085**, **Clark 2097**, Clark 2099, Community 2107, Community 2108, Community 2109, Community 2110, Community 2112, Cricket 2119, Cummings 2122, **Deutsche 2134**, Ferraioli 2156, **Foundation 2161**, Gifford 2177, **Heron 2211**, Hoyt 2221, Initial 2231, **JPMorgan 2242**, **Kaplan 2245**, **Mertz 2306**, New York 2325, New York 2326, O'Grady 2339, Ong 2341, **Open 2343**, **Porticus 2364**, Rapoport 2373, Rauch 2376, **Rockefeller 2389**, **Rockefeller 2390**, Scherman 2409, **Sparkplug 2441**, Tiger 2464, Tower 2472, Tuttle 2479, van Ameringen 2483, **Wallace 2492**, Western 2503
North Carolina: Brady 2533, Community 2539, Community 2540, Cumberland 2541, Eddy 2548, Meserve 2592, North Carolina 2599, Outer 2604, Reidsville 2611, Rex 2612, Reynolds 2614, Smith 2629
North Dakota: Fargo 2649
Ohio: Ar-Hale 2661, Athens 2662, Barberton 2664, **Bingham 2668**, Bryan 2674, Cincinnati 2679, Community 2683, Community 2685, Fairfield 2696, Findlay 2700, Foundation 2702, Gund 2708, Marietta 2732, Marion 2733, Mayerson 2735, Morgan 2739, Morgan 2741, Muskingum 2747, Nord 2754, Nordson 2755, O'Neill 2760, Richland 2767, Saint 2770, Scripps 2780, Springfield 2787, Stark 2788, Tiffin 2793, Wean 2799, YSI 2805
Oklahoma: Cherokee 2809, **Ethics 2811**, Hille 2816, Merrick 2821, Sarkeys 2828, **Schusterman 2829**
Oregon: Ford 2846, Meyer 2861, Portland 2868
Pennsylvania: Baker 2886, Benedum 2892, Birmingham 2896, Brooks 2899, Buhl 2901, Central 2908, Centre 2909, Cestone 2910, Chase 2913, Claneil 2918, Community 2923, Community 2924, Connelly 2926, Fels 2942, Ferree 2944, FISA 2950, Foundation 2952, Heinz 2966, Huston 2973, **KL 2978**, McCune 2993, Mellon 2998, Merchants 3000, North 3006, Penn 3011, Phoenixville 3014, Scranton 3031, Tuttleman 3050, Wells 3055
Puerto Rico: Puerto Rico 3061
Rhode Island: **Dorot 3071**, Rhode Island 3089, Textron 3093
South Carolina: Black 3097, Byerly 3098, Community 3099, Community 3100
Tennessee: Assisi 3120, Baptist 3122, Benwood 3123, Lyndhurst 3145
Texas: Burnett 3185, Cailloux 3187, Chasdrew 3192, **Chrest 3194**, Edwards 3218, Hext 3257, **Houston 3266**, KDK-Harman 3273, Meadows 3296, Moody 3298, Moore 3299, Orsinger 3310, **Paso 3312**, Rockwell 3338, San Angelo 3343, Simmons 3352, Summerlee 3361, Trull 3373, Waco 3378
Vermont: Vermont 3417, Windham 3418
Virginia: Arlington 3421, Community 3433, **Longview 3451**, Lynchburg 3454, Samberg 3478
Washington: Allen 3490, Blue 3498, Casey 3499, Casey 3500, Community 3503, Ferguson 3513, **Gates 3516**, **Glaser 3517**, Inland 3526, Sherwood 3561, Tacoma 3567, Whatcom 3571, **Wilburforce 3572**
West Virginia: Beckley 3577, Community 3579, Tucker 3589
Wisconsin: Community 3607, Dudley 3610, Eau 3611, Green Bay 3619, Incourage 3623, Marshfield 3633, McBeath 3634, Milwaukee 3637, St. Croix 3662
Wyoming: McMurry 3676, Wyoming 3684

Travel awards

Hawaii: Hawaii 933

Use of facilities

Massachusetts: **State 1550**
North Carolina: Goodrich 2561

SUBJECT INDEX

List of terms: Terms used in this index conform to the Foundation Center's Grants Classification System's comprehensive subject area coding scheme. The alphabetical list below represents the complete list of subject terms found in this edition. "See also" references to related subject areas are also provided as an additional aid in accessing the giving interests of foundations in this volume.

Index: In the index itself, foundation entries are arranged under each term by state location, abbreviated name, and sequence number. Foundations in boldface type make grants on a national, regional, or international basis. The others generally limit giving to the state or city in which they are located.

Accessibility/universal design
Adult education—literacy, basic skills & GED
Adult/continuing education
Adults
Adults, men
Adults, women
African Americans/Blacks
Aging
Aging, centers/services
Agriculture
Agriculture, community food systems
Agriculture, farm bureaus/granges
Agriculture, farm cooperatives
Agriculture, farmlands
Agriculture, sustainable programs
Agriculture/food
Agriculture/food, government agencies
Agriculture/food, public education
Agriculture/food, reform
Agriculture/food, research
Agriculture/food, single organization support
AIDS
see also AIDS, people with
AIDS research
AIDS, people with
Alcoholism
ALS
ALS research
Alzheimer's disease
Alzheimer's disease research
American Red Cross
Animal population control
Animal welfare
Animals/wildlife
Animals/wildlife, alliance/advocacy
Animals/wildlife, association
Animals/wildlife, bird preserves
Animals/wildlife, clubs
Animals/wildlife, endangered species
Animals/wildlife, fisheries
Animals/wildlife, formal/general education
Animals/wildlife, preservation/protection
Animals/wildlife, public education
Animals/wildlife, research
Animals/wildlife, sanctuaries
Animals/wildlife, single organization support
Animals/wildlife, special services
Animals/wildlife, training
Animals/wildlife, volunteer services
Anthropology/sociology
Anti-slavery/human trafficking
Aquariums
Art & music therapy
Arthritis
Arthritis research
Arts
see also dance; film/video; museums; music; performing arts; theater; visual arts
Arts councils
Arts education
Arts, administration/regulation
Arts, alliance/advocacy
Arts, artist's services
Arts, association
Arts, cultural/ethnic awareness
Arts, equal rights
Arts, folk arts
Arts, formal/general education
Arts, information services
Arts, management/technical assistance
Arts, multipurpose centers/programs
Arts, public education
Arts, research
Arts, services
Arts, single organization support
Asians/Pacific Islanders
Assistive technology
Asthma
Asthma research
Astronomy
Athletics/sports, academies
Athletics/sports, amateur leagues
Athletics/sports, baseball
Athletics/sports, basketball
Athletics/sports, equestrianism
Athletics/sports, football
Athletics/sports, golf
Athletics/sports, school programs
Athletics/sports, soccer
Athletics/sports, Special Olympics
Athletics/sports, training
Athletics/sports, water sports
Athletics/sports, winter sports
Autism
Autism research
Big Brothers/Big Sisters
Biology/life sciences
Biomedicine
Biomedicine research
Bisexual
Blind/visually impaired
Botanical gardens
Botanical/horticulture/landscape services
Botany
Boy scouts
Boys
Boys & girls clubs
Boys clubs
Brain disorders
Brain research
Breast cancer
Breast cancer research
Buddhism
Business school/education
Business/industry
Camp Fire
Cancer
Cancer research
Cancer, leukemia
Cancer, leukemia research
Catholic agencies & churches
Catholic federated giving programs
Cemeteries/burial services
Cerebral palsy
Charter schools
Chemistry
Child development, education
Child development, services
Children
Children, adoption
Children, day care
Children, foster care
Children, services
Children/youth
Children/youth, services
Chiropractic
Chiropractic research
Christian agencies & churches

Civil liberties, advocacy
Civil liberties, death penalty issues
Civil liberties, due process
Civil liberties, first amendment
Civil liberties, freedom of information
Civil liberties, freedom of religion
Civil liberties, reproductive rights
Civil liberties, right to life
Civil rights, race/intergroup relations
see also civil/human rights
Civil rights, voter education
Civil/human rights
Civil/human rights, advocacy
Civil/human rights, aging
Civil/human rights, alliance/advocacy
Civil/human rights, association
Civil/human rights, disabled
Civil/human rights, equal rights
Civil/human rights, immigrants
Civil/human rights, LGBTQ
Civil/human rights, minorities
Civil/human rights, public policy
Civil/human rights, reform
Civil/human rights, women
Community development, business promotion
Community development, citizen coalitions
Community development, civic centers
Community development, neighborhood associations
Community development, neighborhood development
Community development, public/private ventures
Community development, service clubs
Community development, small businesses
Community development, women's clubs
Community/economic development
Community/economic development, alliance/advocacy
Community/economic development, equal rights
Community/economic development, formal/general education
Community/economic development, management/technical assistance
Community/economic development, public education
Community/economic development, public policy
Community/economic development, research
Community/economic development, single organization support
Community/economic development, volunteer services
Computer science
Consumer protection
Courts/judicial administration
Crime/abuse victims
Crime/law enforcement
Crime/law enforcement, formal/general education
Crime/law enforcement, government agencies
Crime/law enforcement, management/technical assistance
Crime/law enforcement, missing persons
Crime/law enforcement, police agencies
Crime/law enforcement, public education
Crime/law enforcement, reform
Crime/law enforcement, research
Crime/law enforcement, single organization support
Crime/violence prevention
see also domestic violence; gun control
Crime/violence prevention, abuse prevention
see also child abuse; domestic violence
Crime/violence prevention, child abuse
Crime/violence prevention, domestic violence
Crime/violence prevention, gun control
Crime/violence prevention, sexual abuse
Crime/violence prevention, youth
Cystic fibrosis
Cystic fibrosis research
Deaf/hearing impaired
Dental care
Dental school/education
Developmentally disabled, centers & services
Diabetes
Diabetes research
Digestive diseases
Disabilities, people with
Disasters, 9/11/01
Disasters, fire prevention/control
Disasters, floods
Disasters, Hurricane Katrina
Disasters, preparedness/services
Disasters, search/rescue
Diseases (rare)
Dispute resolution
Down syndrome
Ear, nose & throat diseases
Ear, nose & throat research
Economic development
Economic development, visitors/convention bureau/tourism promotion
Economically disadvantaged
Economics
Education
Education, association
Education, community/cooperative
Education, computer literacy/technology training
Education, continuing education
Education, drop-out prevention
Education, e-learning
Education, early childhood education
Education, equal rights
Education, ESL programs
Education, ethics
Education, formal/general education
Education, fund raising/fund distribution
Education, gifted students
Education, management/technical assistance
Education, public education
Education, public policy
Education, reading
Education, reform
Education, research
Education, services
Education, single organization support
Education, special
Electronic communications/Internet
Elementary school/education
Elementary/secondary education
Elementary/secondary school reform
Employment
Employment, job counseling
Employment, labor unions/organizations
Employment, retraining
Employment, services
Employment, sheltered workshops
Employment, training
Employment, vocational rehabilitation
End of life care
Engineering
Engineering school/education
Engineering/technology
Environment
see also energy; natural resources
Environment, administration/regulation
Environment, air pollution
Environment, alliance/advocacy
Environment, association
Environment, beautification programs
Environment, climate change/global warming
Environment, energy
Environment, forests
Environment, formal/general education
Environment, government agencies
Environment, information services
Environment, land resources
Environment, legal rights
Environment, management/technical assistance
Environment, natural resources
Environment, plant conservation
Environment, pollution control
Environment, public education
Environment, public policy
Environment, recycling
Environment, reform
Environment, research
Environment, single organization support
Environment, toxics
Environment, waste management
Environment, water pollution
Environment, water resources
Environmental and resource rights
Environmental education
Epilepsy research
Eye diseases
Eye research
Family services
Family services, adolescent parents
Family services, counseling
Family services, domestic violence
Family services, parent education
Financial services
Financial services, credit unions
Food banks
Food distribution, groceries on wheels
Food distribution, meals on wheels
Food services
Food services, congregate meals
Foundations (community)
Foundations (private grantmaking)
Foundations (private independent)
Foundations (private operating)
Foundations (public)
Gay men
Genetic diseases and disorders
Genetic diseases and disorders research
Geology
Geriatrics
Geriatrics research
Gerontology
Girl scouts
Girls
Girls clubs
Goodwill Industries
Government/public administration
Graduate/professional education
Health care
Health care, administration/regulation
Health care, alliance/advocacy
Health care, association
Health care, clinics/centers
Health care, cost containment
Health care, emergency transport services
Health care, EMS
Health care, equal rights
Health care, ethics
Health care, financing
Health care, formal/general education
Health care, fund raising/fund distribution
Health care, government agencies

Offenders/ex-offenders, probation/parole
Offenders/ex-offenders, rehabilitation
Offenders/ex-offenders, services
Offenders/ex-offenders, transitional care
Optometry/vision screening
Organ research
Orthodox agencies & churches
Orthopedics
Palliative care
Parasitic diseases research
Parkinson's disease
Pediatrics
Pediatrics research
Performing arts
Performing arts (multimedia)
Performing arts centers
Performing arts, ballet
Performing arts, choreography
Performing arts, dance
Performing arts, education
Performing arts, music
Performing arts, music (choral)
Performing arts, music composition
Performing arts, music ensembles/groups
Performing arts, opera
Performing arts, orchestras
Performing arts, theater
Performing arts, theater (musical)
Pharmacology research
Pharmacy/prescriptions
Philanthropy/voluntarism
Philanthropy/voluntarism, administration/regulation
Philanthropy/voluntarism, alliance/advocacy
Philanthropy/voluntarism, association
Philanthropy/voluntarism, information services
Philanthropy/voluntarism, management/technical assistance
Philosophy/ethics
Physical therapy
Physical/earth sciences
Physically disabled
Physics
Planetarium
Political science
Population studies
Poverty studies
Pregnancy centers
Prostate cancer
Prostate cancer research
Protestant agencies & churches
Protestant federated giving programs
Psychology/behavioral science
Public affairs
Public affairs, association
Public affairs, citizen participation
Public affairs, equal rights
Public affairs, finance
Public affairs, information services
Public affairs, political organizations
Public affairs, public education
Public affairs, reform
Public affairs, research
Public health
Public health school/education
Public health, bioterrorism
Public health, clean water supply
Public health, communicable diseases
Public health, environmental health
Public health, epidemiology
Public health, hygiene
Public health, obesity
Public health, occupational health
Public health, physical fitness
Public health, sanitation
Public health, STDs
Public policy, research
Public utilities, sewage
Public utilities, water
Recreation
Recreation, adaptive sports
Recreation, association
Recreation, camps
Recreation, centers
Recreation, community
Recreation, fairs/festivals
Recreation, parks/playgrounds
Recreation, public policy
Religion
see also Jewish agencies & temples; Protestant agencies & churches; Catholic agencies & churches
Religion, association
Religion, formal/general education
Religion, interfaith issues
Religion, public policy
Religious federated giving programs
Reproductive health
Reproductive health, abortion clinics/services
Reproductive health, family planning
Reproductive health, prenatal care
Reproductive health, sexuality education
Residential/custodial care
Residential/custodial care, group home
Residential/custodial care, hospices
Residential/custodial care, senior continuing care
Rural development
Safety, automotive safety
Safety, education
Safety/disasters
Safety/disasters, public education
Safety/disasters, volunteer services
Salvation Army
Scholarships/financial aid
Science
see also biological sciences; chemistry; computer science; engineering/technology; marine science; physical/earth sciences
Science, formal/general education
Science, public education
Science, research
Secondary school/education
see also elementary/secondary education
Sex workers
Sickle cell disease
SIDS (Sudden Infant Death Syndrome) research
Single parents
Social entrepreneurship
Social sciences
see also anthropology/sociology; economics; political science; psychology/behavioral science
Social sciences, equal rights
Social sciences, ethics
Social sciences, formal/general education
Social sciences, government agencies
Social sciences, interdisciplinary studies
Social sciences, public policy
Social sciences, research
Space/aviation
Speech/hearing centers
Spine disorders research
Spirituality
Student services/organizations
Substance abuse, prevention
Substance abuse, services
Substance abuse, treatment
Substance abusers
Surgery
Surgery research
Teacher school/education
Terminal illness, people with
Theological school/education
Theology
Transgender and gender nonconforming
Transportation
Tropical diseases
United Ways and Federated Giving Programs
Urban League
Urban/community development
Utilities
Veterinary medicine
Veterinary medicine, hospital
Visual arts
Visual arts, architecture
Visual arts, art conservation
Visual arts, design
Visual arts, painting
Visual arts, photography
Visual arts, sculpture
Vocational education
Vocational education, post-secondary
Vocational school, secondary
Voluntarism promotion
Volunteers of America
Web-based media
Welfare policy/reform
Women
see also civil/human rights, women; reproductive rights
Women, centers/services
YM/YWCAs & YM/YWHAs
Young adults
Young adults, female
Young adults, male
Youth
Youth development
Youth development, adult & child programs
Youth development, agriculture
Youth development, alliance/advocacy
Youth development, business
Youth development, centers/clubs
Youth development, citizenship
Youth development, community service clubs
Youth development, equal rights
Youth development, formal/general education
Youth development, intergenerational programs
Youth development, public policy
Youth development, reform
Youth development, religion
Youth development, research
Youth development, scouting agencies (general)
Youth development, services
Youth development, volunteer services
Youth, pregnancy prevention
Youth, services
Zoos/zoological societies

Accessibility/universal design

Ohio: Nordson 2755

Adult education—literacy, basic skills & GED

Alabama: Community 10
Arkansas: Wal-Mart 74
California: Ahmanson 77, Community 162, Lux 307, Marin 309, Pacific 355, Sacramento 391, Weingart 456
Colorado: El Pomar 492
Connecticut: Pitney 604
District of Columbia: Block 653, Cafritz 656, Meyer 672
Florida: Bank 695
Georgia: Atlanta 852, Harland 885
Illinois: Community 988, Field 1014, Polk 1075
Indiana: Ball 1121, Harrison 1155
Iowa: Siouxland 1240
Louisiana: Community 1306
Maryland: Fowler 1372, Rosenberg 1409
Massachusetts: Kelsey 1493, Ratshesky 1531, **State 1550**
Michigan: Jackson 1623, Knight 1630, Roscommon 1660
Minnesota: RBC 1730
Nevada: Nevada 1867
New Mexico: Santa Fe 2017
New York: Community 2108, Cummings 2122, Dreyfus 2145, Grant 2190, Northern 2331, **Rubin 2399**
Ohio: Findlay 2700, **OMNOVA 2759**, Reinberger 2765, Richland 2767
Pennsylvania: Fourjay 2953, McCune 2993, Stackpole 3042, Union 3051
Texas: Booth 3180, Coastal 3196, Fisch 3232, Hoblitzelle 3262, King 3275, Lubbock 3287, Meadows 3296, Sterling 3358, Trull 3373, Wright 3386
Virginia: Arlington 3421, Moore 3461, Strong 3481
Washington: Blue 3498, Community 3503, Grays 3520, Renton 3552
West Virginia: Parkersburg 3587
Wisconsin: Cornerstone 3608

Adult/continuing education

California: **Applied 88**, Marcled 308
Colorado: El Pomar 492
Connecticut: Connecticut 564, Long 588, Palmer 600, Pitney 604
District of Columbia: Cafritz 656
Hawaii: Hawaii 933
Illinois: Coleman 986, Community 988, Polk 1075
Louisiana: Albemarle 1298
Massachusetts: Hyams 1486, **State 1550**
Michigan: Midland 1642
Missouri: Truman 1817
Nevada: Nevada 1867
New Jersey: **Newcombe 1972**
New York: Initial 2231, **JPMorgan 2242**
North Carolina: Cumberland 2541, Goodrich 2561
Ohio: Richland 2767
Pennsylvania: **Alcoa 2882**, Connelly 2926, EQT 2940, Stackpole 3042
South Carolina: Spartanburg 3110
Texas: Constantin 3202, Edwards 3218, Hillcrest 3261, Hoblitzelle 3262, Meadows 3296, South 3356
Vermont: Vermont 3417
Washington: Community 3503, Renton 3552, Seattle 3558, Tacoma 3567, Yakima 3576
Wisconsin: Milwaukee 3637

Adults

Alabama: Black 4
Arizona: Webb 64
Arkansas: Ross 72
California: Ahmanson 77, Aroha 94, Community 157, **Gellert 214**, Gerbode 217, Lesher 299, Marcled 308, Napa 340, Newhall 342, Patron 363, Silicon 408, **Special 422**, Taper 433, Weingart 456
Colorado: Colorado 483, Rose 528, Summit 537
Connecticut: Community 562, Community 563, **Deupree 571**
District of Columbia: Jovid 668, Patterson 678
Florida: Landwirth 775, Pinellas 801, Quantum 805, Winter 842
Georgia: Abreu 846
Illinois: Blowitz 968, Chicago 982, Fry 1018, Siragusa 1096
Indiana: Brown 1124, Community 1132, Community 1134, **Lumina 1174**
Iowa: Stebens 1242
Kansas: Kansas 1263, Topeka 1279
Maine: Horizon 1331
Maryland: **Casey 1353**, Community 1360, Fowler 1372, Stulman 1411
Massachusetts: Essex 1464, MetroWest 1515, **State 1550**
Michigan: Fremont 1607, Grand Rapids 1615, Midland 1642, Sanilac 1663
Minnesota: Beim 1683, General 1697, Larsen 1711, Rochester 1735
Mississippi: Community 1760, Gulf 1764
Nebraska: Kearney 1842
New Hampshire: Foundation 1885
New Jersey: **Allen 1900**, Hyde 1944, **JM 1947**
New York: **Commonwealth 2106**, Community 2107, Johnson 2240, Langeloth 2267, **MetLife 2307**, **Nash 2320**, **Noyes 2335**, **Overbrook 2345**, **Soros 2439**, Western 2503
North Carolina: Babcock 2521, Glenn 2560, North Carolina 2599, North 2600, Reidsville 2611
Ohio: **Brush 2673**, Cincinnati 2679, Fairfield 2696, O'Neill 2760, Saint 2770, Youngstown 2804
Oklahoma: Hardesty 2814, Hille 2816
Pennsylvania: Birmingham 2896, Connelly 2926, First 2948, Mellon 2998, Phoenixville 3014, Staunton 3044
South Carolina: Lutz 3105
Tennessee: Baptist 3122, **Maclellan 3146**, **Scarlett 3152**, Wilson 3157
Texas: Bass 3172, Embrey 3222, Hoglund 3263, McDermott 3293, Orsinger 3310, Rockwell 3338, Wright 3386
Virginia: Williamsburg 3487
Washington: **Gates 3516**
Wisconsin: Green Bay 3619, La Crosse 3631, Marshfield 3633, Milwaukee 3637, New 3641, Pettit 3645, St. Croix 3662
Wyoming: McMurry 3676

Adults, men

Alabama: Black 4
Arizona: Webb 64
California: California 140, Fleishhacker 199, Gerbode 217, Lesher 299, Patron 363, Weingart 456
Colorado: Summit 537
District of Columbia: Jovid 668
Georgia: Abreu 846
Illinois: Blowitz 968, Chicago 982, Fry 1018
Iowa: Stebens 1242
Michigan: Grand Rapids 1615, Midland 1642, Sanilac 1663
Mississippi: Community 1760
Nebraska: Midlands 1848, Woods 1857
New Hampshire: Lindsay 1890
New Jersey: **Allen 1900**
New York: Community 2107
North Carolina: Glenn 2560, Reidsville 2611
Ohio: Fairfield 2696, O'Neill 2760
Oklahoma: Hardesty 2814
Pennsylvania: Phoenixville 3014
Tennessee: Wilson 3157
Texas: Bass 3172, Embrey 3222, Hoglund 3263, Orsinger 3310, Rockwell 3338
Washington: **Gates 3516**
Wisconsin: Marshfield 3633

Adults, women

Alabama: Black 4
Arizona: Webb 64
California: California 140, Community 161, Fleishhacker 199, Gerbode 217, Gumbiner 236, Lesher 299, Patron 363, Weingart 456
Colorado: Summit 537
District of Columbia: Jovid 668
Georgia: Abreu 846
Illinois: Blowitz 968, Chicago 982, Fry 1018
Indiana: Brown 1124
Iowa: Stebens 1242
Kansas: Topeka 1279
Louisiana: New Orleans 1316
Michigan: Grand Rapids 1615, Midland 1642, Mount Pleasant 1647, Sanilac 1663, Van Andel 1669
Mississippi: Community 1760
Montana: Montana 1828
Nebraska: Midlands 1848, Woods 1857
Nevada: Wells 1876
New Hampshire: Lindsay 1890
New Jersey: **Allen 1900**, **Newcombe 1972**
New York: **Clark 2098**, Community 2107, Johnson 2240, **Noyes 2335**, **Sparkplug 2441**
North Carolina: Glenn 2560
Ohio: **Brush 2673**, Fairfield 2696, O'Neill 2760
Oklahoma: Hardesty 2814
Pennsylvania: Phoenixville 3014
Tennessee: Wilson 3157
Texas: Bass 3172, **Chrest 3194**, Embrey 3222, Hoglund 3263, Orsinger 3310, Rockwell 3338
Washington: **Gates 3516**
Wisconsin: Marshfield 3633

African Americans/Blacks

Alabama: Black 4, Community 10
Arizona: Webb 64
California: California 137, California 138, California 140, Community 157, Cowell 168, Fleishhacker 199, **Gellert 214**, Gerbode 217, Gumbiner 236, Lesher 299, Weingart 456
Colorado: Colorado 483, Sachs 529
District of Columbia: Cafritz 656, Jovid 668
Florida: **Knight 771**
Illinois: Chicago 982, Fry 1018, **Mondelez 1064**, Siragusa 1096
Indiana: Health 1156, **Lumina 1174**
Iowa: Siouxland 1240
Maryland: **Casey 1353**
Massachusetts: Access 1422, Hyams 1486
Michigan: Ann Arbor 1576, Grand Rapids 1615, **Kellogg 1628**, Midland 1642, Sanilac 1663
Minnesota: Minneapolis 1717, Northwest 1722, Phillips 1728
Mississippi: Community 1760, Foundation 1763
Missouri: Anheuser 1774, Centene 1782
Nebraska: Woods 1857
New Hampshire: Lindsay 1890
New Jersey: **Allen 1900**, Hyde 1944
New Mexico: Santa Fe 2017
New York: **Bloomberg 2066**, **Cummings 2121**, **Discount 2139**, **Ford 2160**, Haring 2203, Langeloth 2267, **Macy 2288**, **MetLife 2307**, New York 2326, **Noyes 2335**, **Open 2343**, **Sparkplug 2441**

North Carolina: Glenn 2560, North Carolina 2599, Reidsville 2611, Strowd 2633
Ohio: Akron 2655, Cincinnati 2679, Community 2683, O'Neill 2760, Saint 2770, Springfield 2787
Oklahoma: Hille 2816
Pennsylvania: Birmingham 2896, First 2948, Heinz 2966, **PPG 3018**, Staunton 3044
Tennessee: Baptist 3122, Wilson 3157
Texas: Dallas 3209, McDermott 3293, Moore 3299, Sterling 3358
Virginia: **Brown 3424**
Wisconsin: Community 3607, Green Bay 3619, La Crosse 3631

Aging

Alabama: Black 4, Community 10
Arizona: Webb 64
Arkansas: Cabe 67, Ottenheimer 71
California: Ahmanson 77, Allergan 80, Anaheim 83, Archstone 90, Ayrshire 97, Brandman 125, California 137, California 140, Community 157, Community 162, Eisner 189, Gerbode 217, Gilmore 221, **Glenn 225**, Gumbiner 236, Lesher 299, Marin 309, Military 330, Outhwaite 353, Pacific 355, Pasadena 361, Patron 363, Sacramento 391, San Luis 393, Solano 419, Sonora 420, Taper 433, True 442, Weingart 456
Colorado: Bright 477, Burt 479, Colorado 483, Comprecare 485, **Daniels 488**, El Pomar 492, Hunter 508, Kaufmann 509, Rose 528, Summit 537
Connecticut: Community 562, Community 563, Connecticut 564, Long 588, NewAlliance 595, Palmer 600, Senior 613
Delaware: Delaware 630, Kutz 637, Palmer 644
District of Columbia: Cafritz 656, Lehrman 670
Florida: Bank 695, Bush 712, Cape Coral 714, Charlotte 718, Community 722, Community 723, Community 724, Community 725, Community 727, Coral Gables 729, Gate 749, Greenburg 752, Patterson 798, Pinellas 801, Selby 816, Winter 842
Georgia: Community 867, Marshall 895, Pitts 904
Hawaii: Hawaii 933
Illinois: **Abbott 954**, Allegretti 958, Blowitz 968, Chicago 982, Community 988, de Kay 998, Diener 1000, Evanston 1012, Field 1014, Logan 1051, Oak Park 1068, Reese 1083, Seymour 1091, Siragusa 1096, Square 1099, Washington 1112, Webb 1113
Indiana: Community 1133, Community 1134, Community 1135, Harrison 1155, Putnam 1189
Iowa: Community 1216, Siouxland 1240, Stebens 1242, Wahlert 1244
Kansas: Delta 1255, Hutchinson 1260, Manhattan 1268, Nettleton 1272
Louisiana: Blue 1302, Community 1306, Entergy 1308, Steinhagen 1320
Maine: **Walter 1343**
Maryland: Community 1360, Fowler 1372, Stulman 1411, **Weinberg 1416**
Massachusetts: Association 1428, Boynton 1437, Clipper 1449, Essex 1464, Farnsworth 1465, Kelsey 1493, MetroWest 1515, Sailors' 1539, Sanborn 1540, Swan 1552, Wadleigh 1562, Williams 1567
Michigan: Ann Arbor 1576, Charlevoix 1583, Community 1590, Community 1591, Fremont 1607, Grand Rapids 1615, Hillsdale 1620, Midland 1642, Mount Pleasant 1647, Prince 1658, Saginaw 1662, Sanilac 1663, Steelcase 1667, Van Andel 1669
Minnesota: **Andersen 1678**, Beim 1683, Minneapolis 1717, Northwest 1723, Rochester 1735, Southwest 1740
Mississippi: Community 1760, Foundation 1763
Missouri: Community 1783, Dunn 1787, Humphreys 1795, Moneta 1802, Truman 1817
Nebraska: Kearney 1842, Lincoln 1847, Oregon 1852, Woods 1857
Nevada: Caesars 1860, Nevada 1867
New Jersey: Beer 1907, Horizon 1940, **Johnson 1949**, Kirby 1952, **Ramapo 1981**, **Rippel 1982**, Summit 1998
New Mexico: Con 2011, Frost 2012, Maddox 2014, Santa Fe 2017
New York: Artists 2044, **Clark 2098**, **Commonwealth 2106**, Community 2107, Community 2108, **Cummings 2120**, Dreyfus 2145, Eastern 2148, Hagedorn 2200, Litwin 2283, McGonagle 2299, **MetLife 2307**, **Nash 2320**, New York 2326, Northern 2331, **Skadden 2427**, Tuttle 2479, van Ameringen 2483, Western 2503
North Carolina: Balin 2523, Community 2539, French 2554, Glenn 2560, Kennedy 2578, North Carolina 2599, Paddock 2605, Peeler 2606, Reidsville 2611, Strowd 2633
North Dakota: MDU 2652, North Dakota 2653
Ohio: Abington 2654, Akron 2655, **Cardinal 2677**, Cincinnati 2679, Cincinnati 2680, Fairfield 2696, McGregor 2736, Middletown 2737, Muskingum 2747, O'Neill 2760, Richland 2767, Saint 2770, Stark 2788, Youngstown 2804
Oklahoma: Hille 2816
Pennsylvania: Berks 2893, Birmingham 2896, Community 2925, Connelly 2926, Elk 2939, EQT 2940, Female 2943, First 2948, Highmark 2968, Independence 2976, McLean 2997, North 3006, Phoenixville 3014, Pierce 3015, Scranton 3031, Snee 3039
Rhode Island: Kimball 3079
Tennessee: Baptist 3122, Community 3129, Wilson 3157
Texas: Bass 3172, Baxter 3173, Carter 3190, Coastal 3196, Dallas 3209, Embrey 3222, Frees 3238, Hammill 3249, Hillcrest 3261, Hoblitzelle 3262, Holloway 3264, King 3275, Lightner 3282, McDermott 3293, Meadows 3296, Moody 3298, Orsinger 3310, Permian 3316, Sterling 3358, Wright 3386
Virginia: AMERIGROUP 3420, Arlington 3421, Lynchburg 3454, Williamsburg 3487
Washington: Community 3503, Inland 3526, Kawabe 3531, Tacoma 3567, Yakima 3576
Wisconsin: Green Bay 3619, Keller 3626, La Crosse 3631, Marshfield 3633, McBeath 3634, Milwaukee 3637, Oshkosh 3642, Pamida 3644, Racine 3648, Stateline 3663
Wyoming: McMurry 3676

Aging, centers/services

Alabama: Community 10, Community 11
Arizona: Piper 57
Arkansas: Ottenheimer 71
California: Anaheim 83, Bothin 120, Brocchini 130, California 137, California 140, Community 162, **Gellert 214**, Gellert 215, **McConnell 318**, Parsons 359, Placer 371, Sacramento 391, Santa Barbara 394, Sonora 420
Colorado: Comprecare 485, El Pomar 492, Stratton 536, Summit 537
Connecticut: Community 562, Community 563, Connecticut 564, Long 588, Palmer 600, Senior 613, Weatherstone 618
Delaware: Palmer 644
District of Columbia: Cafritz 656, Lehrman 670
Florida: Bank 695, Community 722, Greenburg 752, Gulf 754, Minto 789, Patterson 798, Pinellas 801, Selby 816, Sudakoff 828
Georgia: Marshall 895, Pitts 904
Hawaii: Hawaii 933
Idaho: CHC 945
Illinois: Chicago 982, Community 988, Evanston 1012, Field 1014, Logan 1051, Omron 1070, Siragusa 1096, Yowell 1118
Indiana: Blackford 1122, Central 1126, Community 1129
Iowa: Siouxland 1240, Wahlert 1244
Kansas: Hutchinson 1260, Insurance 1261
Louisiana: Community 1306, Steinhagen 1320
Maryland: Community 1358, Fowler 1372, **Weinberg 1416**
Massachusetts: Boynton 1437, Clipper 1449, East 1460, Farnsworth 1465, Sailors' 1539, Swan 1552, Wadleigh 1562
Michigan: Ann Arbor 1576, Fremont 1607, Hillsdale 1620, Prince 1658
Minnesota: **Andersen 1678**, Rochester 1735, Thorpe 1745, WCA 1749
Missouri: Truman 1817
Nebraska: Hirschfeld 1839, Home 1841, Lincoln 1847
Nevada: Caesars 1860, Nevada 1867
New Hampshire: Foundation 1885
New Jersey: Beer 1907, Hyde 1944, **Johnson 1949**, **Ramapo 1981**
New Mexico: Frost 2012, Maddox 2014, Santa Fe 2017
New York: Artists 2044, Community 2108, Community 2110, Community 2111, Coudert 2115, **Cummings 2120**, Dreyfus 2145, Gifford 2177, New York 2325, New York 2326, Northern 2331, Tuttle 2479, Vidda 2485, Western 2503
North Carolina: Balin 2523, Community 2539, Cumberland 2541, French 2554, Kennedy 2578, Meserve 2592
North Dakota: North Dakota 2653
Ohio: Akron 2655, Bryan 2674, Cincinnati 2680, Community 2685, Fairfield 2696, Greene 2707, Macy's 2726, Marietta 2732, McGregor 2736, Ohio 2756, Richland 2767, Stark 2788, Steinmann 2789
Oklahoma: Zarrow 2834
Oregon: Benton 2835, Macdonald 2859, Meyer 2861, PGE 2867
Pennsylvania: Connelly 2926, Fourjay 2953, Golden 2958, McLean 2997, Rossin 3028, Saramar 3029, Shaffer 3035, Snee 3039, Trexler 3049
Rhode Island: Kimball 3079
South Carolina: Springs 3111
Tennessee: Community 3129
Texas: Abell 3160, Amarillo 3163, Bass 3172, Carter 3190, Coastal 3196, Frees 3238, Heavin 3253, Hillcrest 3261, Hoblitzelle 3262, King 3275, Meadows 3296, Smith 3354, Wright 3386
Virgin Islands: Community 3419
Virginia: AMERIGROUP 3420, Arlington 3421, Lynchburg 3454, Metropolitan 3459
Washington: Blue 3498, Community 3503, Inland 3526, Kawabe 3531, Renton 3552, Tacoma 3567
Wisconsin: Incourage 3623, Keller 3626, McBeath 3634, Milwaukee 3637, Pamida 3644, Pettit 3645

Agriculture

California: **Foundation 202**, Heller 246, Newhall 342, Sierra 406
Delaware: Burt's 626
District of Columbia: **Wallace 683**
Illinois: **Buffett 975**, **Mondelez 1064**
Indiana: Johnson 1163
Iowa: Iowa 1225, World 1248
Kentucky: Trim 1295
Massachusetts: **Conservation 1454**
Michigan: **Kellogg 1628**
Minnesota: Alworth 1677, Farmers 1695, **Mosaic 1718**, Nash 1720
Missouri: **Monsanto 1803**
New Jersey: **International 1946**
New York: **Eppley 2152**, **Ford 2160**, **Noyes 2335**
North Carolina: Griffin 2563
Ohio: Bryan 2674, Greene 2707
Texas: Meadows 3296
Washington: **Gates 3516**, Lauzier 3534, **Starbucks 3565**

Agriculture, community food systems
California: Clif 152
Louisiana: Community 1306
Minnesota: **Mosaic 1718**
Vermont: **Ben 3407**

Agriculture, farm bureaus/granges
Missouri: **Monsanto 1803**

Agriculture, farm cooperatives
Wisconsin: Blooming 3599

Agriculture, farmlands
Arkansas: Wal-Mart 74
California: Clif 152
Illinois: **Buffett 975**
Minnesota: Farmers 1695, **Mosaic 1718**
Missouri: **Monsanto 1803**
Pennsylvania: Brooks 2899
Texas: Behmann 3176

Agriculture, sustainable programs
Arkansas: Wal-Mart 74
California: Clif 152, Tomkat 437
Delaware: Burt's 626
Minnesota: Farmers 1695, Land 1710
New York: Anderson 2036
Wisconsin: Blooming 3599

Agriculture/food
Alabama: Central 8
California: Clif 152, McClatchy 317, **Packard 357**, **Warsh 452**
Florida: Batchelor 697, Hard 756
Georgia: Ligon 892
Idaho: Supervalu 952
Maryland: Croft 1362
Massachusetts: Brooks 1440, **Conservation 1454**, Makepeace 1507, Thee 1556
Michigan: **Kellogg 1628**, Petoskey 1656
Minnesota: Farmers 1695, Land 1710
New Hampshire: Alexander 1877
New Jersey: **Allen 1900**, Saka 1987
New York: Laffont 2264, Levitt 2275, **PepsiCo 2354**
North Dakota: Fargo 2649
Pennsylvania: Sunoco 3046
Rhode Island: Citizens 3067
Texas: Halsell 3247, King 3275, Lockheed 3284
Vermont: Windham 3418
Washington: Empire 3510, Grays 3520, Seattle 3558
Wisconsin: Kuenzl 3630

Agriculture/food, government agencies
Michigan: Roscommon 1660

Agriculture/food, public education
Michigan: Roscommon 1660
Missouri: **Monsanto 1803**

Agriculture/food, reform
North Carolina: Community 2540

Agriculture/food, research
California: **Warsh 452**
Missouri: **Monsanto 1803**

Agriculture/food, single organization support
Michigan: Roscommon 1660

AIDS
California: De Miranda 179, Marin 309, Sacramento 391, Sierra 405, Traina 438, Weingart 456
Colorado: **Gill 502**
Connecticut: Connecticut 564, Long 588, Palmer 600
District of Columbia: Cafritz 656
Florida: Bank 695, **Campbell 713**
Georgia: **Coca 864**
Hawaii: McInerny 938
Illinois: Community 988, Evanston 1012, Field 1014, Fry 1018, Polk 1075, Washington 1112
Indiana: Health 1156
Michigan: Roscommon 1660
Minnesota: HRK 1702
Nevada: Nevada 1867, Shaheen 1871
New Mexico: Frost 2012, Santa Fe 2017
New York: Community 2108, Daphne 2127, Diller 2137, Ebb 2149, **Ford 2160**, Hagedorn 2200, Haring 2203, **M.A.C. 2287**, Marshall 2293, McCarthy 2298, New York 2325, Tisch 2469, van Ameringen 2482
North Carolina: Cumberland 2541
Ohio: Anderson 2658, Gund 2708, Macy's 2726, Stark 2788
Pennsylvania: Union 3051
Rhode Island: Rhode Island 3089
Texas: Burnett 3185, Hoblitzelle 3262, Holloway 3264, **International 3269**, King 3275, Meadows 3296, Moody 3298, Sterling 3358, Wright 3386
Vermont: Vermont 3417
Virginia: Community 3433, MAXIMUS 3457
Washington: Community 3503, **Gates 3516**, Tacoma 3567
Wisconsin: McBeath 3634, Milwaukee 3637

AIDS research
California: **Beckman 105**, Tang 432
Connecticut: Ensworth 575, Long 588, Palmer 600
Florida: **Campbell 713**
Illinois: Community 988, Washington 1112
Michigan: Roscommon 1660
Nevada: Nevada 1867
New Jersey: Kirby 1952
New Mexico: Frost 2012
New York: Haring 2203, McCarthy 2298
Ohio: Anderson 2658, Gund 2708, Macy's 2726, Stark 2788
Pennsylvania: Union 3051
Texas: Meadows 3296, Moody 3298, Sterling 3358
Washington: Tacoma 3567

AIDS, people with
Alabama: Black 4, Community 10
Arizona: Webb 64
California: Community 157, **Hilton 251**, Patron 363, Taper 433, Weingart 456
Colorado: Bright 477
Connecticut: Community 562
Delaware: AEC 622
District of Columbia: Cafritz 656
Florida: Southwest 823
Georgia: Abreu 846
Illinois: Field 1014, Fry 1018, Siragusa 1096, Washington 1112
Indiana: Health 1156
Minnesota: HRK 1702, Phillips 1728
New Hampshire: Lindsay 1890
New Jersey: Hyde 1944, Kirby 1952, MCJ 1965
New Mexico: Con 2011, Santa Fe 2017
New York: **Ford 2160**, Haring 2203, New York 2326, **Open 2343**, **Sparkplug 2441**, van Ameringen 2482
North Carolina: Glenn 2560, North Carolina 2599
Ohio: Akron 2655, Saint 2770, White 2800
Oklahoma: Hille 2816
Pennsylvania: First 2948
Tennessee: Baptist 3122
Texas: Abell 3160, Dallas 3209, Embrey 3222, Holloway 3264, McDermott 3293, Sterling 3358
Washington: **Gates 3516**
Wisconsin: Cornerstone 3608, Green Bay 3619, Milwaukee 3637

Alcoholism
California: Sacramento 391, Sierra 405, Sonora 420
Colorado: Comprecare 485, **Daniels 488**
Connecticut: Palmer 600
Illinois: Community 988
Iowa: Siouxland 1240
Maryland: **ABMRF 1344**
New Jersey: Borden 1910
New Mexico: Santa Fe 2017
New York: Achelis 2026, Western 2503
Ohio: Andrews 2659, Coshocton 2686, Hamilton 2710, Murphy 2745, Woodruff 2801, Youngstown 2804
Pennsylvania: Connelly 2926, Stackpole 3042
Tennessee: Davis 3130
Texas: Coastal 3196, Hoblitzelle 3262, Meadows 3296, Wright 3386
Vermont: Vermont 3417
Washington: Community 3503
Wisconsin: McBeath 3634

ALS
Pennsylvania: Betz 2895, Charlestein 2911

ALS research
Connecticut: Inc. 616
Oklahoma: Adams 2806

Alzheimer's disease
California: Brown 132, Eichenberg 188
Illinois: Eisenberg 1011
Louisiana: Heymann 1313
Maine: Borman 1325
Michigan: Nartel 1648
Nevada: Caesars 1860
New Jersey: Evans 1925
New York: **Institute 2233**, **MetLife 2307**
North Carolina: Stahlberg 2631
Pennsylvania: Grumbacher 2961, Somerville 3041
Texas: Holloway 3264, King 3275, Smith 3354
Virginia: Richmond 3476
Wisconsin: Green Bay 3619

Alzheimer's disease research
Colorado: Kaufmann 509
Michigan: Dart 1594, **Erb 1599**
New York: D'Agostino 2124, **MetLife 2307**
Oklahoma: Hille 2816

American Red Cross
Alabama: Andalusia 1
Arkansas: Wal-Mart 74
California: Eichenberg 188, Hewlett 249, Kelly 278, Lucas 306, Pacific 355, PG&E 367
Colorado: **First 496**
Florida: Darden 732, Wollowick 843

Animal population control

Animal welfare

Animals/wildlife

Animals/wildlife, alliance/advocacy

Animals/wildlife, association

Animals/wildlife, bird preserves

Animals/wildlife, clubs

Animals/wildlife, endangered species

Animals/wildlife, fisheries

Animals/wildlife, formal/general education

Animals/wildlife, preservation/protection

Animals/wildlife, public education

Animals/wildlife, research

Texas: Kleberg 3276

Animals/wildlife, sanctuaries
Alaska: Alaska 26
California: Campbell 142
New York: **Arcus 2040**, Winley 2508

Animals/wildlife, single organization support
Michigan: Roscommon 1660

Animals/wildlife, special services
California: Dickinson 180
Michigan: Roscommon 1660
New York: **Arcus 2040**

Animals/wildlife, training
Minnesota: **Patterson 1726**

Animals/wildlife, volunteer services
Michigan: Roscommon 1660
Minnesota: **Patterson 1726**

Anthropology/sociology
California: Getty 218
New York: **Wenner 2502**

Anti-slavery/human trafficking
California: **Google 231**

Aquariums
Illinois: Stewart 1101
Maryland: RCM & D 1406
Pennsylvania: **PPG 3018**
Virginia: MAIHS 3455
Washington: Ferguson 3513

Art & music therapy
New York: Community 2108
Rhode Island: CVS 3068

Arthritis
California: Braddock 123
Florida: Patterson 798
New Jersey: Hummingbird 1943
Ohio: Marion 2733
Oklahoma: Parman 2824
Pennsylvania: Adams 2881, Somerville 3041

Arthritis research
California: Treadwell 439
Florida: Sontag 822
Pennsylvania: Seebe 3033

Arts
Alabama: BBVA 3, Black 4, Central 8, Community 9, Community 10, Community 11, Day 12, Goodrich 13, McWane 17, Regions 19, Stephens 24
Alaska: CIRI 33
Arizona: Dorrance 42, Flinn 44, Green 47, Hill 48, Long 51, Marshall 54, Piper 57, Stardust 63
Arkansas: Cabe 67, Ross 72
California: Ahmanson 77, Allergan 80, **Amado 81**, Anaheim 83, **Annenberg 86**, **Applied 88**, Ayrshire 97, Berry 111, Blum 115, Bowes 121, Brittingham 128, **Broad 129**, Brocchini 130, California 137, Chartwell 150, Clif 152, **Clorox 153**, Coburn 154, Community 157, Community 158, Community 159, Community 160, Community 162, Community 163, Copley 166, Dickinson 180, Disney 181, Disney 183, Douglas 186, Drown 187, Eichenberg 188, Finley 197, Fleishhacker 199, Fremont 207, Friend 209, Fusenot 211, **Gellert 214**, Gerbode 217, Glide 226, Gluck 227, Good 230, **Google 231**, GSF 235, Guzik 238, Heller 246, Helms 247, Hewlett 248, Hinkle 252, Hoag 253, Humboldt 257, **Keck 276**, Kern 279, Kim 280, Kvamme 286, Laguna 288, Langendorf 289, Lansing 290, Laulhere 292, Lesher 299, Liu 302, Long 304, Los Altos 305, Lucas 306, Marin 309, **Mattel 312**, Mazza 314, McBeth 315, McClatchy 317, **McConnell 318**, McCoy 319, Menard 327, **Mercer 328**, Mosher 335, **Nazarian 341**, Newhall 342, Nicholas 343, Pacific 355, **Packard 357**, Pasadena 361, Plum 372, Price 374, Pritzker 375, **Qualcomm 376**, Rancho 378, Ransom 379, Rifkind 383, Sacramento 391, San Luis 393, Santa Barbara 394, Sassoon 395, **Seaver 400**, Shasta 401, Sierra 406, Silicon 407, Simpson 411, Smith 417, Solano 419, Sonora 420, **Spencer 424**, Stanislaus 425, Streisand 428, Stulsaft 430, Swayne 431, Taper 433, Tippett 436, Truckee 441, Tu 443, Van Nuys 447, **Wadhwani 450**, Wallis 451, Wattis 454, Wattis 455, WHH 461, **Wilkinson 463**, Wilsey 464, Wrather 469
Colorado: **Avenir 473**, Ballantine 474, Bonfils 475, Catto 480, Change 481, Community 484, El Pomar 492, Erion 494, Grand 503, Griffin 504, **Kinder 510**, **Merage 519**, Monfort 520, Pikes 525, Summit 537, Telluride 538, Vail 543, Vradenburg 544, Yampa 545
Connecticut: **Albers 551**, Bender 554, Common 561, Community 562, Community 563, Connecticut 564, Dennett 570, **Deupree 571**, **Educational 574**, Ensworth 575, Fisher 577, Gengras 580, Goldstone 581, Grampy's 582, Hoffman 585, Linke 587, Long 588, Matthies 590, Middlesex 592, Neuberger 593, NewAlliance 595, Old 599, Palmer 600, Perrin 603, Roberts 608, SBM 611, **Tremaine 617**, Weatherstone 618, Wood 619
Delaware: AEC 622, Chaney 628, Delaware 630, **Gloria 634**, Longwood 639, Morgridge 642, Sylvan 648, Terk 649
District of Columbia: Bauman 650, Bernstein 652, Bou 654, Cafritz 656, Graham 663, Lehrman 670, Lichtenberg 671
Florida: Ansin 689, **Arison 691**, Around 692, Bank 695, Bartner 696, Batchelor 697, Blanksteen 701, Brown 707, Bush 712, Cape Coral 714, Chapman 717, Charlotte 718, Community 722, Community 723, Community 724, Community 725, Community 726, Community 727, Coral Gables 729, Darden 732, Darling 733, DeBartolo 734, DiMare 737, Finch 743, Florida 744, Green 751, Gulf 754, Jacksonville 761, Katcher 765, **Knight 771**, Landwirth 775, Lattner 776, Leiser 777, Lindemann 780, Martin 786, Mertz 788, Phillips 800, Pinellas 801, Selby 816, Snell 821, Southwest 823, Sudakoff 828, TECO 830, Tippett 833, Tsunami 834, TWS 836
Georgia: Anderson 850, Atlanta 852, Bradley 858, Campbell 860, Communities 866, Community 867, Community 868, Community 869, Dobbs 872, Georgia 877, **Georgia 878**, Gilbert 881, Harland 885, Holder 887, Knox 890, Lanier 891, Livingston 893, Murphy 898, Murray 899, North 900, Savannah 912, Tull 917, Woodruff 922, Woodward 923
Hawaii: Atherton 925, Baldwin 926, Castle 930, Hawaii 933, McInerny 938, **Watumull 939**
Idaho: CHC 945, Cunningham 946, Idaho 948, Supervalu 952, Whittenberger 953
Illinois: Albert 957, Allegretti 958, Alphawood 959, Angell 962, Aon 963, Boothroyd 971, Brach 973, Burk 977, C.W.B. 978, Cadle 979, Chicago 982, Community 988, Community 989, Community 990, Community 991, Community 992, Crown 997, DeKalb 999, Donnelley 1001, Driehaus 1002, Dunard 1006, DuPage 1008, Edwardsville 1010, Evanston 1012, Field 1014, Frankel 1017, Fry 1018, Fulk 1020, Geneseo 1022, **Grainger 1024**, Guthman 1027, Harper 1030, **Joyce 1040**, Katten 1042, Lars 1047, Lefkofsky 1049, Logan 1051, Lumpkin 1053, Maddox 1057, Moline 1063, Oak Park 1068, Omron 1070, Pattis 1073, Polk 1075, Prince 1076, Prince 1077, Pritzker 1079, Pritzker 1080, Ryan 1087, Schuler 1090, Shapiro 1093, Siragusa 1096, Square 1099, Walter 1110, Ward 1111, Woods 1117, Zell 1119
Indiana: Auer 1120, Ball 1121, Blackford 1122, Brown 1124, Central 1126, Cole 1127, Community 1128, Community 1129, Community 1130, Community 1131, Community 1132, Community 1133, Community 1134, Community 1135, Community 1136, Community 1137, Dearborn 1141, Decatur 1142, DeHaan 1143, DeKalb 1144, Fayette 1146, Glick 1150, Greene 1152, Haddad 1153, Hancock 1154, Harrison 1155, Hendricks 1157, Henry 1158, Jasper 1160, Jasteka 1161, Jennings 1162, Johnson 1163, Jorgensen 1164, Joshi 1165, Koch 1167, Kuhne 1169, LaGrange 1170, Legacy 1171, Lilly 1173, Madison 1175, Marshall 1176, Noble 1179, Northern 1180, Ohio 1181, Orange 1184, Owen 1185, Porter 1187, Portland 1188, Putnam 1189, Ripley 1191, Rush 1192, TCU 1197, Tipton 1198, Tobias 1199, Unity 1201, Wabash 1203, Wells 1207, Western 1208, Whitley 1209
Iowa: Ahrens 1210, Aviva 1211, Bechtel 1212, Community 1215, Community 1217, Community 1218, Hall-Perrine 1222, HNI 1223, Jefferson 1227, Maytag 1229, McElroy 1230, **Rockwell 1237**, Siouxland 1240, South 1241
Kansas: Beach 1250, Cohen 1252, Collective 1253, Douglas 1256, Emporia 1257, Hutchinson 1260, Insurance 1261, Koch 1264, Koch 1265, Manhattan 1268, Miller 1269, **Muchnic 1271**, Salina 1274, Sunderland 1278, Topeka 1279
Kentucky: Blue 1282, Campbell 1285, Community 1286, Gheens 1288, Kentucky 1292, Trim 1295
Louisiana: Albemarle 1298, Beaird 1301, Community 1306, Freeman 1309, Glazer 1311, Grigsby 1312, Heymann 1313, New Orleans 1316, Steinhagen 1320
Maine: Alfond 1324, Borman 1325, Cohen 1327, Golden 1329, Hannaford 1330, Kennebec 1332, King 1333, Libra 1334, Quimby 1338, **Walter 1343**
Maryland: Baker 1347, **Blaustein 1349**, Community 1357, Community 1358, Community 1359, Community 1360, Delaplaine 1367, Freeman 1373, Henson 1378, Kentfields 1385, Macht 1388, Marriott 1390, Meyerhoff 1393, Mid-Shore 1395, Moore 1396, **Morningstar 1397**, RCM & D 1406, Richmond 1408, Rosenberg 1409, Straus 1410, Trawick 1414, Tucker 1415, Wright 1418, Zickler 1419
Massachusetts: Arbella 1426, Babson 1430, **Barr 1433**, Brooks 1439, **Bruner 1441**, Cabot 1442, Cabot 1443, Cape Cod 1445, Cogan 1450, Community 1453, Davis 1457, Essex 1464, Filene 1468, Fish 1470, Grinspoon 1479, Herbert 1481, Inavale 1488, Jaffe 1491, Levy 1501, Liberty 1502, Lowell 1505, Miller 1516, Noonan 1520, Parker 1523, Phelps 1528, Ramsey 1530, Ratshesky 1531, Riley 1534, Rodman 1535, Santander 1541, Schrafft 1543, Shattuck 1544, Smith 1546, Sudbury 1551, Two 1557, United 1559, Verrochi 1560, Webber 1563, Webster 1565, Williams 1567, Windover 1568, **Xeric 1570**
Michigan: Ann Arbor 1576, Baiardi 1577, Bay Harbor 1578, Binda 1579, Branch 1580, Charlevoix 1583, Community 1586, Community 1587, Community 1588, Community 1589, Community 1590, Community 1591, Dalton 1592, Dana 1593, Delano 1596, Dow 1597, DTE 1598, **Erb 1599**, Family 1600, Farver 1601, Farwell 1602, Fremont 1607, Frey 1609, Gilmore 1612, Grand Rapids

Arts councils
California: Irvine 264
Florida: Brown 707
North Carolina: Reynolds 2613
North Dakota: MDU 2652
Tennessee: Eastman 3133
Texas: Jones 3272
Wisconsin: Wanek 3667

Arts education
Alabama: Stephens 24
Arkansas: **Windgate 75**
California: Eisner 189, Gluck 227, Parsons 359, Rifkind 383, **Wadhwani 450**
Colorado: **Kinder 510**
District of Columbia: Bernstein 652
Florida: Bush 712
Illinois: Alphawood 959, Community 988, Edlis-Neeson 1009, Guthman 1027, Stewart 1101
Iowa: **Rockwell 1237**, Siouxland 1240
Louisiana: Albemarle 1298, Lagasse 1314
Maine: Horizon 1331
Maryland: **Blaustein 1349**
Massachusetts: Alden 1425, Filene 1468, Ramsey 1530, Ratshesky 1531
Michigan: Community 1586, Roscommon 1660
Minnesota: **Pentair 1727**, Xcel 1754
Missouri: **Monsanto 1803**
New Hampshire: Fuller 1886
New Jersey: Horizon 1940
New Mexico: Santa Fe 2017
New York: Aronson 2042, Bay 2056, Hadar 2198, Haring 2203, Heckscher 2205, **JPMorgan 2242**, Loewe 2284, O'Grady 2339, **Surdna 2454**, **Teagle 2459**, Tiffany 2463
North Carolina: Bergen 2527
Ohio: Ginn 2706, Hershey 2711
Oregon: PGE 2867
Pennsylvania: Baker 2886, Presser 3019, Washington 3054
South Carolina: WebbCraft 3113
Tennessee: HCA 3139
Texas: Bass 3172, King 3275, NuStar 3307
Vermont: McKenzie 3413
Virginia: CarMax 3427
Washington: Renton 3552, Tacoma 3567
West Virginia: Eastern 3580
Wisconsin: Harley 3621

Arts, administration/regulation
Connecticut: **Albers 551**, Robinson 609
Oregon: Ford 2846

Arts, alliance/advocacy
California: Parsons 359
Georgia: Camp-Younts 861
Maryland: Baker 1347
New York: Diller 2137, **Surdna 2454**

Arts, artist's services
California: Picerne 369
Connecticut: **Albers 551**
Michigan: **Kresge 1631**
New York: **Warhol 2494**
Texas: Northen 3306

Arts, association
New York: Loewe 2284, **Surdna 2454**
Ohio: Ohio 2756

Arts, cultural/ethnic awareness
Alaska: Aleut 27, CIRI 33, Doyon 34
California: **Christensen 151**, Irvine 264, Kelly 278, Liu 302, Mazda 313, **Packard 357**
Georgia: Abreu 846, Livingston 893
Hawaii: Kahiau 935
Illinois: Omron 1070
Indiana: Central 1126, Noble 1179, Old 1182
Kentucky: Community 1286, Trim 1295
Michigan: DTE 1598, Mott 1646
Minnesota: 3M 1676, HRK 1702, Marbrook 1713, **Pentair 1727**, RBC 1730
Nebraska: Lincoln 1847
New Jersey: Horizon 1940
New York: American 2033, Assael 2046, **Jabara 2235**, **Rockefeller 2389**, **Rubin 2399**, Shoreland 2421, St. Simon 2446, **Surdna 2454**
Ohio: American 2656, Nordson 2755, **OMNOVA 2759**, Tiffin 2793
Pennsylvania: Berks 2893, EQT 2940
Rhode Island: **Dorot 3071**
Texas: Kleinheinz 3277, **Levant 3280**
Utah: Semnani 3404
Virginia: Community 3431
Washington: **Goodwin 3519**, Miller 3544
Wisconsin: Green Bay 3619

Arts, equal rights
Minnesota: Xcel 1754
Pennsylvania: **PPG 3018**

Arts, folk arts
California: Irvine 264
Texas: Morgan 3301
Washington: Yakima 3576

Arts, formal/general education
California: Aroha 94
Florida: Burns 710
Louisiana: Community 1306
Michigan: Webber 1673
Minnesota: HRK 1702
New Jersey: Point 1977
Ohio: Skyler 2784

Arts, information services
Connecticut: **Albers 551**

Arts, management/technical assistance
Connecticut: **Albers 551**

Arts, multipurpose centers/programs
California: Barth 101, Frank 206, Irvine 264
Maine: Quimby 1338
Massachusetts: Ramsey 1530
Minnesota: Winona 1753

Arts, public education
Connecticut: **Albers 551**
Kansas: **Shumaker 1276**
Michigan: Roscommon 1660
Tennessee: Tucker 3156

Arts, research
Connecticut: **Albers 551**
Florida: Horowitz 760

Arts, services
California: Parsons 359
Connecticut: **Albers 551**

Arts, single organization support
California: Zellerbach 471
Connecticut: **Albers 551**
Louisiana: Community 1306
Minnesota: HRK 1702

Asians/Pacific Islanders
Alabama: Community 10
Arizona: Webb 64
California: California 137, California 140, Community 157, Cowell 168, Fleishhacker 199, Gerbode 217, Kimbo 281, Lesher 299, Liu 302, Taper 433, Weingart 456
District of Columbia: Cafritz 656, Jovid 668
Illinois: Chicago 982, Fry 1018
Indiana: **Lumina 1174**
Iowa: Siouxland 1240
Massachusetts: Access 1422, Hyams 1486
Michigan: Grand Rapids 1615, **Kellogg 1628**
Minnesota: Minneapolis 1717, Phillips 1728
Nebraska: Woods 1857
New Hampshire: Lindsay 1890
New Jersey: **Allen 1900**
New Mexico: Santa Fe 2017
New York: **Ford 2160**, **MetLife 2307**, **Noyes 2335**, Ong 2341, **Sparkplug 2441**
North Carolina: North Carolina 2599
Ohio: Community 2683, O'Neill 2760
Pennsylvania: First 2948
Wisconsin: Community 3607, La Crosse 3631

Assistive technology
Massachusetts: Liberty 1502
Rhode Island: CVS 3068

Asthma
California: Beynon 113, HealthCare 244
Rhode Island: CVS 3068

Asthma research
Georgia: Raoul 907

Astronomy
Arizona: **Research 59**
California: **Las 291**
Ohio: Skyler 2784

Athletics/sports, academies
Delaware: Hasselbeck 635
Massachusetts: New 1518

Athletics/sports, amateur leagues
California: Brocchini 130, **Foundation 204**, LA84 287, **Mattel 312**
Colorado: **Daniels 488**
Florida: Dahl 731, Glazer 750
Iowa: R & R 1236
Kentucky: Trim 1295
Massachusetts: Phelps 1528
Michigan: Alro 1574
Missouri: Centene 1782
Montana: Wendy's 1831

New York: New Yankee 2324, Truman 2475
Tennessee: First 3135
Wisconsin: Ariens 3594, Johnson 3625

Athletics/sports, baseball
Iowa: Jefferson 1227
Michigan: Roscommon 1660
Montana: Wendy's 1831
Nebraska: Hawkins 1838
Ohio: Ar-Hale 2661

Athletics/sports, basketball
Michigan: Roscommon 1660

Athletics/sports, equestrianism
California: Cole 155
Michigan: Van 1670
New Hampshire: Mosaic 1891
New York: Warwick 2495
Pennsylvania: Goshen 2959, Naylor 3002

Athletics/sports, football
Florida: Glazer 750
Michigan: Roscommon 1660

Athletics/sports, golf
Florida: Blanton 702
Iowa: R & R 1236
Maryland: Rembrandt 1407
Michigan: Roscommon 1660
New York: Fisher 2157
Texas: NuStar 3307

Athletics/sports, school programs
California: Eisner 189, **Foundation 204**, Sierra 406
Maryland: Cupid 1363
Michigan: Roscommon 1660
New York: Freed 2163, Heckscher 2205
Ohio: Piqua 2763
Rhode Island: CVS 3068
Wisconsin: Bemis 3598

Athletics/sports, soccer
Indiana: Rush 1192
Maryland: Hendricks 1377
Michigan: Roscommon 1660

Athletics/sports, Special Olympics
California: Anaheim 83, Kelly 278, **Mattel 312**
Minnesota: **Patterson 1726**
Pennsylvania: Packer 3008

Athletics/sports, training
California: LA84 287
Indiana: Rush 1192
Michigan: Roscommon 1660
New York: Freed 2163
Texas: Moore 3299

Athletics/sports, water sports
Florida: Community 725
Ohio: Coshocton 2686
Oregon: Benton 2835

Athletics/sports, winter sports
Colorado: Vail 543
Maine: Libra 1334

Autism
New Jersey: Focus 1930
New York: Karmazin 2246, Rosenthal 2395
Pennsylvania: FISA 2950
Virginia: MAIHS 3455

Autism research
New Jersey: Focus 1930
New York: Simons 2423
North Carolina: Stahlberg 2631
Wisconsin: New 3641

Big Brothers/Big Sisters
California: GSF 235
Florida: Gate 749
Georgia: **Coca 864**
Illinois: Jackson 1038
Kansas: Capitol 1251
Missouri: Darr 1785
New Jersey: **Alcatel 1899**
New York: **Credit 2118**
Ohio: American 2656, Dayton 2688
Pennsylvania: Comcast 2921, Lazarich 2983, Patterson 3010
Wisconsin: Manitowoc 3632, Oshkosh 3643
Wyoming: Moyer 3677

Biology/life sciences
Arizona: Flinn 44
California: **Beckman 105**, **Christensen 151**, **Ellison 191**, **Glenn 225**, **Grass 232**, **Keck 276**, Pacific 355
Florida: **Whitehall 840**
Massachusetts: **Sweet 1554**
Michigan: Hillsdale 1620
Minnesota: Alworth 1677
New Jersey: **Allen 1900**, Banbury 1904
New York: **Eppley 2152**, **Institute 2233**, **Kade 2243**, **Mathers 2294**, McGonagle 2299, Newman 2328
North Carolina: **Burroughs 2534**
Texas: Dunn 3216, Elkins 3221

Biomedicine
California: **Beckman 105**, **Broad 129**, **Ellison 191**, **Grass 232**, Sierra 405
Minnesota: Alworth 1677
Missouri: St. Louis 1814
New Jersey: Kirby 1952
New York: **Cummings 2120**, **Eppley 2152**, **Kade 2243**, McGonagle 2299, Smith 2430
Oregon: Collins 2842
Pennsylvania: DSF 2937
Virginia: Jeffress 3444
Wisconsin: McBeath 3634

Biomedicine research
California: **Ellison 191**
Louisiana: Schlieder 1319
Massachusetts: **Adelson 1424**
New York: New York 2325
Texas: Halsell 3247

Bisexual
California: Weingart 456

Michigan: Grand Rapids 1615

Blind/visually impaired
Alabama: Black 4, Community 11
Arizona: Webb 64
California: Community 157, Fusenot 211, **Hilton 251**, Kelly 278, Kirchgessner 282, Lesher 299, McBeth 315, Patron 363, Smith 415, Taper 433, Weingart 456
Colorado: Hunter 508
Connecticut: Dennett 570
District of Columbia: Cafritz 656
Florida: Boston 705, Greenburg 752, Pinellas 801, Southwest 823, Thomas 831
Georgia: Abreu 846
Illinois: Adams 956, Chicago 982, Dryer 1004, Luehring 1052, Siragusa 1096
Kansas: Emporia 1257
Maryland: Battye 1348
Michigan: Grand Rapids 1615, Sanilac 1663
Nebraska: Midlands 1848
Nevada: Nevada 1867
New Hampshire: Lindsay 1890
New Jersey: Hyde 1944
New York: Blum 2067, Community 2108, D'Agostino 2124, deForest 2133, Hagedorn 2200, **Open 2343**, Pollock 2362, **Ross 2396**
North Carolina: Cumberland 2541, Hoffman 2569, North Carolina 2599, Shingleton 2624
Ohio: Cincinnati 2679, Fairfield 2696, Licking 2723, O'Neill 2760, Springfield 2787
Oklahoma: Hardesty 2814, Hille 2816
Pennsylvania: Chase 2913, Child 2916, Connelly 2926, First 2948, Mendel 2999, Patterson 3010, Phoenixville 3014
Texas: Abell 3160, Alcon 3162, Dallas 3209, McDermott 3293, Moore 3299
Virginia: Memorial 3458
West Virginia: Weisberg 3590
Wisconsin: Cornerstone 3608, Green Bay 3619, La Crosse 3631

Botanical gardens
Arizona: Ottosen 56
California: **Smith 416**
Florida: Batchelor 697, DiMare 737
Georgia: Exposition 873, **Imlay 888**
Iowa: Beckwith 1213, Guernsey 1221
Michigan: Meijer 1639
Missouri: Bellwether 1775
New Mexico: B.F. 2008
New York: Butler 2081, **Goldman 2181**, Hagedorn 2200, Widgeon 2505
North Carolina: Rogers 2618
Oregon: Flowerree 2845
Pennsylvania: Feldman 2941, Ludwick 2988, Randall 3021
Texas: Bass 3172, Dedman 3212, Waggoner 3379
Washington: **Goodwin 3519**

Botanical/horticulture/landscape services
Maryland: Moore 1396
Michigan: Keller 1627
Missouri: **Monsanto 1803**
New York: Tiffany 2463
Texas: Richardson 3335
Wisconsin: Harley 3621

Botany
Minnesota: Alworth 1677

Boy scouts
Alabama: Caring 7
California: AS&F 95, Bell 107, GSF 235
Florida: Batchelor 697, Brown 707
Illinois: Luehring 1052
Iowa: HNI 1223
Kansas: Insurance 1261, Morgan 1270
Kentucky: Trim 1295
Massachusetts: Magee 1506
Michigan: Lear 1632, Perrigo 1655, Roscommon 1660
Minnesota: Xcel 1754
Missouri: Centene 1782, Fabick 1788, Musgrave 1805
Nebraska: Hawkins 1838, Quivey 1853, Zollner 1858
North Carolina: Bolick 2531
Ohio: Dayton 2688, Ohio 2756, Schiewetz 2774
Texas: Conley 3201
Virginia: Moore 3461, United 3484
Wisconsin: **Baird 3595**
Wyoming: Dubois 3673

Boys
Alabama: Black 4, Community 10
Arizona: Webb 64
California: California 140, **Clorox 153**, Community 161, Cowell 168, Gumbiner 236, Lesher 299, Patron 363, Simpson 411, Weingart 456
Georgia: Abreu 846
Illinois: Chicago 982, Evanston 1012, Fry 1018
Iowa: Stebens 1242
Michigan: Grand Rapids 1615, Sanilac 1663
Minnesota: **O'Shaughnessy 1725**
Mississippi: Community 1760
Missouri: Saigh 1811
Nebraska: Midlands 1848
New Jersey: **Allen 1900**, Hyde 1944
New York: Community 2107, Heckscher 2205, **MetLife 2307**, **Ross 2396**
North Carolina: Glenn 2560
Ohio: Fairfield 2696, Hershey 2711, O'Neill 2760
Oklahoma: Hardesty 2814, Hille 2816
Pennsylvania: Birmingham 2896, Child 2916, Heinz 2966, Pilgrim 3016
Tennessee: **Scarlett 3152**, Wilson 3157
Texas: Bass 3172, McDermott 3293, Moore 3299, Orsinger 3310, Rockwell 3338
Washington: **Gates 3516**
Wisconsin: Marshfield 3633

Boys & girls clubs
Arizona: Rubeli 60
Arkansas: Wal-Mart 74
California: AS&F 95, Beynon 113, California 140, Carney 144, Laulhere 292, Pacific 354, Pacific 356, Quest 377, Samuelsson 392
Connecticut: Dennett 570, Hall 584, Meriden 591
Delaware: Brown 625
Florida: Ansin 689, Bell 698, Darden 732, Feder 741, Fortin 747, Jacobsen 762, Morrison 792, Rebozo 807, Stafford 825, Sudakoff 828, Walter 837
Georgia: Correll 871, Woodruff 922
Illinois: Chartered 980, Katten 1042
Indiana: Crosser 1139, Lilly 1173, WellPoint 1206
Kansas: Capitol 1251
Louisiana: Community 1306
Maine: Kennebec 1332
Maryland: Community 1360
Massachusetts: Chase 1446, Demoulas 1458, Eastern 1461, Fish 1470, Liberty 1502, Staples 1549, Webster 1565, Winning 1569
Michigan: Dana 1593, Dart 1594
Minnesota: Best 1685, Opus 1724
Missouri: Centene 1782, Musgrave 1805, Schneider 1812
Montana: Wendy's 1831
Nebraska: Hawkins 1838
New Jersey: Campbell 1917, Gibson 1934, Jones 1950, Kish 1953
New York: Coudert 2115, Mule 2316, Wells 2501
Ohio: American 2656, Cliffs 2681, Third 2792
Pennsylvania: Comcast 2921, Rider 3024
South Carolina: McKissick 3106, Smith 3109
Tennessee: Clayton 3128, Regal 3151, Schmidt 3153
Texas: Clements 3195, Conley 3201, Edwards 3219, Holthouse 3265, Peine 3313
Virginia: United 3484
Washington: Goodman 3518, PEMCO 3549
Wisconsin: Alliant 3592, **Baird 3595**, Incourage 3623, Manitowoc 3632, RITE-HITE 3651, Sentry 3657, Zilber 3670
Wyoming: Moyer 3677

Boys clubs
California: Samuelsson 392
New York: Widgeon 2505
Rhode Island: Chamberlain 3066, Kimball 3079

Brain disorders
North Carolina: Stahlberg 2631

Brain research
California: Hillblom 250
Florida: Sontag 822
Massachusetts: **Adelson 1424**
Missouri: **McDonnell 1800**
New York: **Dana 2126**

Breast cancer
California: HealthCare 244
Delaware: **AstraZeneca 623**
Illinois: Omron 1070
Massachusetts: Arbella 1426
Michigan: Nartel 1648
Nevada: Shaheen 1871
New Jersey: Beer 1907
New York: Coach 2100
Ohio: Macy's 2726
Pennsylvania: CIGNA 2917, Rooney 3026

Breast cancer research
California: **Parsemus 358**
Nevada: Shaheen 1871
Texas: Smith 3355

Buddhism
New Jersey: Jones 1950
New York: **Tsadra 2478**
Washington: Almi 3491

Business school/education
Alaska: CIRI 33
California: Braddock 123, Halperin 240
Connecticut: Deloitte 569
Illinois: Coleman 986
Indiana: Steel 1196
Iowa: United 1243
Maryland: Adams 1345
Michigan: DTE 1598, Grand Haven 1614, Morley 1644
Minnesota: 3M 1676
New Hampshire: Penates 1893
New Mexico: Frost 2012
North Dakota: MDU 2652
Ohio: Fifth 2699, Morgan 2740, Stark 2788, Third 2792, Troy 2794
Oregon: Woodard 2877
South Carolina: McKissick 3106
Texas: **A Glimmer 3158**, Abell 3160, Fluor 3235, Hillcrest 3261
Washington: Jones 3530
Wisconsin: Baker 3596

Business/industry
Alabama: BBVA 3
California: Bank 99, Foundation 203
Delaware: Sylvan 648
Georgia: Holder 887
Kansas: Collective 1253, Insurance 1261
Michigan: DTE 1598
Minnesota: Securian 1739, Xcel 1754
New Jersey: **Sanofi 1988**
New York: Coach 2100, **Deutsche 2134**, NYSE 2336
Ohio: Morino 2742
Oregon: **Lemelson 2857**
Pennsylvania: EQT 2940
Rhode Island: Washington 3095
Tennessee: Eastman 3133
Texas: Penney 3315
Washington: PEMCO 3549

Camp Fire
Washington: PEMCO 3549

Cancer
Alabama: Caddell 6
California: **Beckman 105**, Braddock 123, Brown 132, Coburn 154, Curci 174, Eichenberg 188, Fawcett 195, Frank 206, Genentech 216, McKesson 321, Outhwaite 353, Wrather 469, Zafiropoulo 470
Colorado: Tomkins 540
Connecticut: Bauer 553, Robbins 607
Delaware: **AstraZeneca 623**
District of Columbia: Stewart 682
Florida: Bi-Lo/Winn-Dixie 700, Gate 749, Greenburg 752, Lennar 778, Minto 789, Olsen 794, Rendina 809, Stafford 825
Georgia: Burke 859, Cooper 870, Georgia 877
Hawaii: Buehner 927
Illinois: Coleman 986, Community 988, Frye 1019, Hospira 1034, Hughes 1035, Katten 1042, Luehring 1052, Rhodes 1084
Indiana: Kosciusko 1168, WellPoint 1206
Kansas: **Lloyd 1267**
Kentucky: Campbell 1285, Trim 1295
Maryland: RCM & D 1406, Wolpoff 1417
Massachusetts: Demoulas 1458, Herbert 1481, Kittredge 1496, Sanborn 1540
Michigan: Dana 1593, **Pardee 1653**, Perrigo 1655, Van 1670
Minnesota: Johnson 1704
Mississippi: Ergon 1761, Mississippi 1769
Nebraska: Midlands 1848
Nevada: Nevada 1867
New Jersey: Horizon 1940, Hyde 1944, Jones 1950, **Rippel 1982**
New Mexico: Santa Fe 2017
New York: Abramson 2024, Alfiero 2031, Belfer 2059, Carvel 2088, Diller 2137, **Goldman 2182**, Hagedorn 2200, Johnson 2241, Lane 2266, McGonagle 2299, Mindich 2309, New York 2325, Ostgrodd 2344, Palette 2347, Singer 2424
North Carolina: Fortson 2553, Gordon 2562, Sutcliffe 2635
Ohio: Bates 2665, **Eaton 2692**, Fibus 2698
Oregon: Collins 2842

Cancer research

Cancer, leukemia

Cancer, leukemia research

Catholic agencies & churches

Catholic federated giving programs

Cemeteries/burial services

Cerebral palsy

Charter schools

Chemistry

Child development, education

Child development, services

Children

Children, adoption

Children, day care

Children, foster care

Children, services

Children/youth

Children/youth, services

Johnson 2239, **JPMorgan 2242**, Karmazin 2246, Klee 2253, Klingenstein 2257, Lane 2266, Lee 2270, Leeman 2273, Legacy 2274, Levitt 2275, Litwin 2283, Marks 2291, Marley 2292, **MetLife 2307**, Moore 2312, Moore 2313, Mutual 2317, New York 2325, New York 2326, Norwich 2332, Ontario 2342, Price 2367, Regals 2377, Resnick 2379, Roche 2388, Rose 2392, **Ross 2396**, Rothstein 2397, Samberg 2403, Sandy 2404, Schwartz 2413, Seneca 2415, Snayberger 2431, Snow 2432, Snyder 2433, Sugarman 2450, **Teagle 2459**, Tiger 2464, Vidda 2485, Voya 2488, Warwick 2495, Weissman 2500, Western 2503, Woldar 2509

North Carolina: Balin 2523, Billingsley 2530, Community 2540, Cumberland 2541, Dalton 2542, French 2554, Ghidotti 2558, Glenn 2560, Gordon 2562, Hanes 2565, Hoffman 2569, Hunt 2572, Kistler 2579, Meserve 2592, Meyer 2593, Moretz 2595, Morgan 2596, Niessen 2598, North 2600, Odell 2602, Olin 2603, Paddock 2605, Peeler 2606, Perkin 2607, Richmond 2616, Smith 2629, Strowd 2633, Symmes 2636, Templin 2638, Woodson 2644

North Dakota: Community 2648, Fargo 2649, North Dakota 2653

Ohio: Akron 2655, Anderson 2658, Brown 2672, Calhoun 2676, Charities 2678, Cincinnati 2679, Cliffs 2681, Community 2685, Coshocton 2686, Dater 2687, Dodero 2691, **Eaton 2692**, Fairfield 2696, Foundation 2702, Freygang 2704, Gund 2708, Hamilton 2710, Hershey 2711, Johnson 2714, Licking 2723, Llewellyn 2725, Marietta 2732, Mathile 2734, Murphy 2744, Murphy 2745, Muskingum 2747, Nippert 2751, Nord 2754, Nordson 2755, Ohio 2756, Reinberger 2765, Richland 2767, Salem 2771, Samaritan 2772, Skyler 2784, Stark 2788, Troy 2794, White 2800, Youngstown 2804

Oklahoma: Bernsen 2807, Hardesty 2814, Peel 2825, **Schusterman 2829**, Viersen 2830

Oregon: Braemar 2836, Castle 2839, Ford 2846, Jackson 2851, Jubitz 2853, Lamb 2855, Meyer 2861, Michael 2862, Mission 2863, PGE 2867, Renaissance 2869, Templeton 2874

Pennsylvania: **Alcoa 2882**, Black 2897, Buhl 2901, Child 2916, CIGNA 2917, Comcast 2921, Community 2922, Community 2924, Connelly 2926, Cooper 2927, Delaware 2932, Drueding 2936, DSF 2937, Elk 2939, Ferree 2944, Fourjay 2953, Freas 2954, Grumbacher 2961, Grundy 2962, Heinz 2966, Lancaster 2981, Ludwick 2988, McLean 2997, Mellon 2998, Nelson 3003, Packer 3008, Patterson 3010, Rangos 3022, Scranton 3031, Seybert 3034, Shaffer 3035, Snee 3039, Stackpole 3042, Staley 3043, Staunton 3044, Trees 3048, Trexler 3049, Tuttleman 3050, Widener 3056, Wilson 3058, **Zeldin 3060**

Rhode Island: Chamberlain 3066, Gross 3076, Kimball 3079, McNeil 3086, Rhode Island 3089

South Carolina: Bailey 3096, Community 3099, Joanna 3104, Motley 3107, Singing 3108, Spartanburg 3110

South Dakota: Chiesman 3115

Tennessee: Briggs 3124, Clayton 3128, Dugas 3132, Kirkland 3143, Osborne 3147, Wilson 3157

Texas: **A Glimmer 3158**, A Glimmer 3159, Abell 3160, Amarillo 3163, Augur 3168, Bass 3172, Beal 3174, Beasley 3175, Behmann 3176, Booth 3180, Cailloux 3187, Coastal 3196, Collins 3199, Conley 3201, Constantin 3202, Cowden 3205, Crain 3206, **Dell 3213**, Edwards 3219, Elkins 3220, Elkins 3221, Esping 3225, Fasken 3229, Fisch 3232, Fish 3233, Frees 3238, Goldsbury 3241, Goodman 3242, Gulf 3245, Halsell 3247, Hamman 3248, Hillcrest 3261, Hoblitzelle 3262, Holthouse 3265, Johnson 3271, King 3275, Lennox 3279, Lightner 3282, Littauer 3283, Lubbock 3287, Lupton 3288, McDermott 3293, McKee 3295, Meadows 3296, Moore 3299, Najim 3304, Penland 3314, Proctor 3325, Rachal 3329, RDM 3332, Richardson 3335, Rockwell 3338, Rosewood 3340, Saint 3341, Sams 3342, Shelton 3350, Simmons 3352, Smith 3353, Sterling 3358, Thompson 3367, Topfer 3372, Trull 3373, Vergara 3376, Waco 3378, Waggoner 3379, Ward 3381, Willard 3382, Williams 3383, Wright 3386

Utah: Bamberger 3389, Eskuche 3393, Hall 3395, Hemingway 3396

Vermont: Harper 3411, McKenzie 3413, Vermont 3417

Virgin Islands: Community 3419

Virginia: AMERIGROUP 3420, Arlington 3421, Community 3432, Community 3433, Lynchburg 3454, MAXIMUS 3457, Memorial 3458, Moran 3462, Robins 3477, Samberg 3478, United 3484

Washington: Anderson 3492, Blue 3498, Casey 3500, Community 3503, Discuren 3507, Echo 3508, Kawabe 3531, Lauzier 3534, **Luke 3537**, McEachern 3541, Milgard 3543, Miller 3544, OneFamily 3547, San Juan 3555, Satterberg 3556, Schultz 3557, Seattle 3558, Shemanski 3560, Tacoma 3567, Whatcom 3571

West Virginia: Eastern 3580, Parkersburg 3587

Wisconsin: **Baird 3595**, BayCare 3597, Elmwood 3614, Incourage 3623, La Crosse 3631, Manitowoc 3632, McBeath 3634, Milwaukee 3637, Oshkosh 3642, Pettit 3645, Pritchett 3647, Sauey 3655, Stateline 3663, Stone 3664, **Wagner 3666**, Windhover 3668

Wyoming: McMurry 3676, Scott 3679, Wyoming 3684

Chiropractic

Missouri: St. Louis 1814

Chiropractic research

Iowa: NCMIC 1232

Christian agencies & churches

Alabama: Brown 5

Arizona: Jasam 50, Long 51, Marketplace 52

California: Berry 111, Bonner 118, Braddock 123, CEC 146, Chao 149, De Miranda 179, Helms 247, Kimbo 281, Kvamme 286, Muckel 336, Noll 345, North 346, **Open 349**, Optivest 351, Philanthropy 368

Colorado: **Crowell 487**, Esther 495, Galena 500, McDonnell 516, Morgan 521, Norwood 524, Seay 532, Tomkins 540, TYL 542

Connecticut: Daycroft 568, Dennett 570, Floren 578, Gengras 580

Delaware: **Gloria 634**, Pinkerton 645, Prairie 646, Rivera 647

Florida: A. & R. 686, Burns 710, Chapman 717, DeBartolo 734, **DeMoss 735**, DiMare 737, Einstein 739, Lattner 776, Martin 786, Morrison 792, Reinhold 808, Snell 821, Tippett 833, Walter 837, Wells 839, Wiegand 841, Woodbery 844, Wright 845

Georgia: Amos 848, Amos-Cheves 849, Campbell 860, Cooper 870, Schinazi 913, Wilder 920, WinShape 921

Hawaii: Kaneta 936

Idaho: Caven 944

Illinois: Hendrickson 1032, Lars 1047, Luehring 1052, Richard 1085, Shamrock 1092, **Tyndale 1105**, Webb 1113

Indiana: Brotherhood 1123, Froderman 1148, FSJ 1149, Haddad 1153, Master 1177, Seger 1194

Iowa: Beckwith 1213, Schildberg 1238, Stebens 1242

Kansas: **Lloyd 1267**

Kentucky: Etscorn 1287, Lift 1293

Maryland: Mustard 1400, Tucker 1415

Massachusetts: Perennial 1525, Rogers 1536, Williams 1567

Michigan: Christian 1585, Family 1600, Farwell 1602, G. 1610, Granger 1617, Jubilee 1624, Legion 1633, Mardigian 1635, Merillat 1640, Michell 1641, Oleson 1649, Onequest 1650, Prince 1658, Roscommon 1660, Vanderweide 1671

Minnesota: Andreas 1679, Hallett 1701, Redwood 1731

Mississippi: Ergon 1761, Feild 1762, Walker 1772

Missouri: Canfield 1781, Fabick 1788, Musgrave 1805, Woods 1821

Nebraska: Quivey 1853

Nevada: Troesh 1874, Webb 1875

New Hampshire: **Christian 1881**, Penates 1893

New Jersey: Bauer 1906, Bonner 1909, Jones 1950, Kish 1953, Marino 1964, Post 1978, Roma 1984, Snyder 1995

New York: Aresty 2041, Brillo-Sonnino 2070, Brock 2072, Kanas 2244, Marine 2289, MBIA 2297, Rhodes 2381

North Carolina: Bolick 2531, Everett 2550, Fortson 2553, Glenn 2560, Harvest 2566, Hoffman 2569, Howe 2570, Kennedy 2578, Moretz 2595, Shingleton 2624, Sites 2627, Sloan 2628, Templin 2638

Ohio: Ar-Hale 2661, Bates 2665, Brethen 2671, Dater 2687, Orr 2761, Piqua 2763, Samaritan 2772, Steinmann 2789, Veale 2797, Young 2803

Oklahoma: Gaylord 2813, Harmon 2815, Jones 2817, Liddell 2819, Peel 2825

Oregon: Caddock 2838, Flowerree 2845, Mission 2863

Pennsylvania: Beaver 2890, Clark 2920, Degenstein 2931, Finley 2946, Hunt 2972, Huston 2973, **M.E. 2989**, McKee 2995, Packer 3008, Pilgrim 3016, Rangos 3022, Sedwick 3032, Snee 3039, Staley 3043, Wilson 3058

Rhode Island: Parmelee 3088

South Carolina: Bailey 3096, Community 3099, McKissick 3106, Smith 3109, Springs 3111

Tennessee: Elgin 3134, Haslam 3138, Latimer 3144, **Maclellan 3146**, Osborne 3147, Schmidt 3153

Texas: Augur 3168, Baxter 3173, Behmann 3176, C.I.O.S. 3186, Clements 3195, Criswell 3207, Dougherty 3215, Edwards 3218, Elkins 3221, Greentree 3244, Heavin 3253, Hext 3257, Howell 3268, Martinez 3291, McKee 3295, Moore 3299, Penland 3314, **PHM 3320**, Plass 3322, Rachal 3329, Reilly 3333, Richter 3337, Shelton 3350, Thirteen 3366, Vergara 3376

Utah: Eskuche 3393, Schmidt 3403

Vermont: Harper 3411

Virginia: Stafford 3480, **Truland 3482**

Washington: **Children's 3501**, Goodman 3518, Green 3521, **Luke 3537**, OneFamily 3547

Wisconsin: BayCare 3597, Center 3604, Hovde 3622, Windhover 3668

Wyoming: Christian 3671, Seven 3680

Civil liberties, advocacy

California: McCune 320, Streisand 428, **Warsh 452**

District of Columbia: Block 653

Illinois: Libra 1050

Missouri: **Deer 1786**

New York: 1848 2020, **Cummings 2121**, **Gimprich 2180**, **Overbrook 2345**

Civil liberties, death penalty issues

California: **Fund 210**

District of Columbia: **Butler 655**

Civil liberties, due process

California: vanLoben 446

Georgia: Sapelo 911

Illinois: Libra 1050

Civil liberties, first amendment

District of Columbia: Block 653, **Freedom 662**

New York: Klingenstein 2256
Ohio: Scripps 2780

Civil liberties, freedom of information

District of Columbia: **Freedom 662**

Civil liberties, freedom of religion

New York: Anderson 2036

Civil liberties, reproductive rights

California: Dolby 185, Gerbode 217, Gumbiner 236, **Packard 357**, Taper 433
Colorado: **General 501**
Connecticut: **Educational 574**
District of Columbia: Cafritz 656
Illinois: Libra 1050
Maryland: **Cohen 1355**
Michigan: Grand Rapids 1615
Minnesota: Nash 1720, Phillips 1728
Missouri: **Deer 1786**, Roblee 1809
Nebraska: **Buffett 1833**
New York: Anderson 2036, **Bydale 2082**, **Clark 2098**, Gimbel 2179, Hallingby 2201, New York 2325, New York 2326, **Noyes 2335**, **Overbrook 2345**, Scherman 2409
Ohio: **Brush 2673**
Pennsylvania: Claneil 2918, Patterson 3010

Civil liberties, right to life

Delaware: **Gloria 634**
Florida: Carlton 715
Wisconsin: Ariens 3594

Civil rights, race/intergroup relations

Alabama: BBVA 3
California: California 137, Humboldt 257, Irvine 264, Mazda 313
Connecticut: **Praxair 606**
District of Columbia: Meyer 672
Florida: Chapman 717, **Knight 771**
Illinois: Field 1014, Polk 1075
Maryland: Hirschhorn 1379
Massachusetts: Hyams 1486
Michigan: Community 1588, Grand Rapids 1615, **Mott 1645**
Minnesota: Duluth 1693, Initiative 1703, Minneapolis 1717, Musser 1719
Missouri: **Deer 1786**, Roblee 1809
New Mexico: Santa Fe 2017
New York: **Ford 2160**, New York 2326
North Carolina: Cumberland 2541
Ohio: Gund 2708, Richland 2767
Pennsylvania: Union 3051
Texas: Meadows 3296
Vermont: **Ben 3407**
Wisconsin: Milwaukee 3637

Civil rights, voter education

California: **Arkay 91**, Bohnett 117, Streisand 428
New York: **Carnegie 2085**, **Cummings 2121**

Civil/human rights

California: **Arkay 91**, Craigslist 169, Gerbode 217, Gibson 220, McCune 320, Skoll 413, Streisand 428, vanLoben 446
District of Columbia: Block 653, Cafritz 656, Meyer 672, **Wyss 685**
Georgia: Sapelo 911
Illinois: Community 988, Katten 1042, Lefkofsky 1049, Libra 1050
Iowa: Holthues 1224
Kansas: Hutchinson 1260, **Shumaker 1276**, Western 1281
Maryland: **Cohen 1355**
Massachusetts: Berkman 1434, Eastern 1461
Minnesota: Briggs 1687, Minneapolis 1717, Rochester 1735
Missouri: Community 1783
New Hampshire: Panjandrum 1892
New Jersey: Elias 1923
New York: **Arcus 2040**, Bullitt 2079, **Bydale 2082**, Diamond 2136, **Ford 2160**, Hycliff 2226, **Open 2343**, **Overbrook 2345**, **Rubin 2398**, Scherman 2409, **Skadden 2427**, Wagner 2491
North Carolina: Cumberland 2541
Ohio: Sears 2781
Pennsylvania: FISA 2950
Texas: Embrey 3222, Rapoport 3331, Sikh 3351
Vermont: **Ben 3407**, Block 3409, Vermont 3417
Wisconsin: Windway 3669

Civil/human rights, advocacy

California: **Fund 210**
District of Columbia: **Hill 664**
Illinois: Libra 1050
New Jersey: **Allen 1900**, Elias 1923
New York: 1848 2020, Abelard 2022, **Cummings 2121**, **Overbrook 2345**, Scherman 2409, **Skadden 2427**, van Ameringen 2482
Ohio: Akron 2655
Pennsylvania: CIGNA 2917

Civil/human rights, aging

District of Columbia: Cafritz 656
Maryland: Stulman 1411
Michigan: Grand Rapids 1615
Minnesota: Minneapolis 1717
New Mexico: Santa Fe 2017
New York: New York 2325, New York 2326

Civil/human rights, alliance/advocacy

California: **Fund 210**
Illinois: Libra 1050
New York: Cricket 2119, New York 2326

Civil/human rights, association

New York: Wilson 2507

Civil/human rights, disabled

Illinois: Reese 1083
Kansas: Beach 1250
Michigan: Grand Rapids 1615
Minnesota: Minneapolis 1717, Phillips 1728
New Mexico: Santa Fe 2017
New York: New York 2325, New York 2326
Pennsylvania: FISA 2950, **Riverside 3025**

Civil/human rights, equal rights

California: Pacific 355
Florida: Florida 744
Michigan: DTE 1598
New York: **Cummings 2121**, Hagedorn 2199, **IBM 2227**, Morgan 2315, NoVo 2334, **PepsiCo 2354**
Ohio: KeyBank 2717
Pennsylvania: CIGNA 2917
Wisconsin: Alliant 3592, **Baird 3595**

Civil/human rights, immigrants

Arkansas: Endeavor 69
California: Firedoll 198, Rosenberg 385, vanLoben 446
District of Columbia: Cafritz 656
Illinois: Sumac 1103
Michigan: Grand Rapids 1615
Minnesota: Minneapolis 1717, Phillips 1728
New Mexico: Santa Fe 2017
New York: **Carnegie 2085**, New York 2325, New York 2326, Wagner 2491
Vermont: **Ben 3407**

Civil/human rights, LGBTQ

California: Bohnett 117, vanLoben 446
Colorado: **Gill 502**
Florida: Feder 741
Michigan: Grand Rapids 1615
Minnesota: Phillips 1728
New Mexico: Santa Fe 2017
New York: **Arcus 2040**, Johnson 2240, New York 2325, New York 2326

Civil/human rights, minorities

California: vanLoben 446
District of Columbia: Cafritz 656
Michigan: Grand Rapids 1615
Minnesota: Minneapolis 1717, Phillips 1728
New Jersey: Elias 1923
New Mexico: Santa Fe 2017
New York: New York 2325, New York 2326, Scherman 2409, Wagner 2491

Civil/human rights, public policy

Illinois: Libra 1050

Civil/human rights, reform

Illinois: Libra 1050

Civil/human rights, women

California: vanLoben 446
District of Columbia: Cafritz 656
Kentucky: Kentucky 1292
Michigan: Grand Rapids 1615
Minnesota: Minneapolis 1717, Phillips 1728
New Mexico: Santa Fe 2017
New York: **Bydale 2082**, **Jabara 2235**, New York 2325, New York 2326, NoVo 2334

Community development, business promotion

Arkansas: Wal-Mart 74
California: Bank 99
Indiana: Central 1126
Missouri: **Kauffman 1797**
Nebraska: Hawkins 1838
North Carolina: Olin 2603
Ohio: Dayton 2688
Pennsylvania: Merchants 3000
Texas: Sterling 3358
Wisconsin: Wanek 3667

Community development, citizen coalitions

California: California 140
Colorado: Colorado 483
Florida: Gulf 754
New Mexico: Santa Fe 2017
New York: Cricket 2119, **Mertz 2306**
Ohio: **Needmor 2749**, Seasongood 2782

Community development, civic centers

Pennsylvania: Adams 2881
Texas: Herzstein 3256
Washington: Miller 3544

Community development, neighborhood associations

Indiana: Blackford 1122, Community 1129

Community development, neighborhood development

Alabama: BBVA 3, Goodrich 13
California: Irvine 264, North 346, Silver 409
Colorado: Pikes 525
Connecticut: Middlesex 592
District of Columbia: Graham 663
Florida: Gulf 754, **Knight 771**
Georgia: Communities 866, Georgia 877
Idaho: Idaho 948
Illinois: Evanston 1012, **MacArthur 1056**, Moline 1063, Oak Park 1068
Indiana: Central 1126, Community 1130, Community 1134, Legacy 1171, Western 1208, Whitley 1209
Maryland: Goldseker 1374
Massachusetts: Melville 1511
Michigan: DTE 1598, Jubilee 1624, **Kellogg 1628**, Mount Pleasant 1647, Prince 1658
Minnesota: Opus 1724
Mississippi: Community 1758, Community 1759
Missouri: Butler 1780
Nebraska: Kiewit 1843, Lexington 1845, Oregon 1852
New York: Community 2109, **Deutsche 2134**, **Heron 2211**, **JPMorgan 2242**, Levitt 2275, Truman 2475, Wagner 2491
North Carolina: **Bank 2524**
Ohio: Community 2683, Greene 2707, Saint 2770, Seasongood 2782, Third 2792
Oregon: Western 2876
Pennsylvania: Allegheny 2883, Beaver 2890, Berks 2893, Chester 2915, Community 2924, Washington 3054, Wells 3055
South Carolina: Community 3100
Tennessee: Community 3129, Eastman 3133
Texas: AT&T 3167, Burnett 3185, Dallas 3209, Hill 3259, Houston 3267, Rockwell 3338
Virginia: Community 3429, Community 3431, Oak 3466
Washington: Blue 3498, Community 3503, Inland 3526, Lauzier 3534
West Virginia: Beckley 3577, Eastern 3580
Wisconsin: Green Bay 3619, Harley 3621, Marshfield 3633, Zilber 3670

Community development, public/private ventures

Minnesota: Initiative 1703
Wyoming: Wyoming 3684

Community development, service clubs

California: Carney 144
New York: Miller 2308

Community development, small businesses

Arkansas: Wal-Mart 74
California: Bank 99, Clif 152, Firedoll 198, Intuit 263
Connecticut: Northeast 598
Georgia: **Georgia 878**
Illinois: Coleman 986
Indiana: Old 1182
Massachusetts: Babson 1430
Minnesota: Northwest 1723
Missouri: **Kauffman 1797**
New York: **Deutsche 2134**, **JPMorgan 2242**
North Carolina: **Bank 2524**
Ohio: KeyBank 2717
Pennsylvania: Merchants 3000
Virginia: Capital 3426
Washington: Seattle 3558

Community development, women's clubs

California: Buell 134
Michigan: Roscommon 1660

Community/economic development

Alabama: BBVA 3, Black 4, Central 8, Community 10, Community 11, Meyer 18
Alaska: Alaska 26
Arizona: Long 51, Ottosen 56, Stardust 63
Arkansas: Endeavor 69, Ottenheimer 71, Ross 72, Union 73, Wal-Mart 74
California: Allergan 80, Ayrshire 97, Bank 99, California 137, Community 157, Community 160, Community 163, Friedman 208, Fuserna 212, **Gellert 214**, Genentech 216, Gerbode 217, Hand 241, Hewlett 248, Hosseini 255, Humboldt 257, Intuit 263, Jacobs 267, **Kapor 273**, Kelly 278, Leavey 294, Los Altos 305, Marin 309, Matsui 311, **McConnell 318**, McCune 320, McMinn 323, Nicholas 343, Parsons 359, Pasadena 361, Placer 371, Rancho 378, Sacramento 391, San Luis 393, Santa Barbara 394, **Scovel 399**, Shasta 401, Sierra 405, Silicon 407, Silicon 408, Soda 418, Solano 419, Sonora 420, Thomson 435, Truckee 441, Weingart 456, Western 459
Colorado: Brett 476, Community 484, El Pomar 492, Grand 503, Pikes 525, Piton 526, Southern 535, Stratton 536
Connecticut: Community 562, Community 563, Connecticut 564, Ensworth 575, Howe 586, Long 588, Matthies 590, Middlesex 592, NewAlliance 595, Northeast 598, Palmer 600, **Praxair 606**
Delaware: Burt's 626, Chaney 628, Delaware 630, Morgridge 642
District of Columbia: Bernstein 652, Cafritz 656, **Case 658**, **Hill 664**, Lehrman 670, Meyer 672
Florida: Ansin 689, Bank 695, Bell 698, Charlotte 718, Community 723, Community 724, Community 726, Community 727, Coral Gables 729, Florida 744, Fortin 747, Glazer 750, Lattner 776, Phillips 800, Plangere 802, Quantum 805, Rinker 810, Selby 816, Southwest 823, TWS 836
Georgia: Anderson 850, Atlanta 852, **Coca 864**, Communities 866, Community 867, Community 868, **Georgia 878**, Glenn 882, Lanier 891, Livingston 893, North 900
Hawaii: Atherton 925, Castle 929, Hawaii 933, Hawaiian 934
Idaho: Adams 941, CHC 945
Illinois: Angell 962, Aon 963, Chartered 980, Chicago 982, Coleman 986, Community 988, Community 990, Community 992, DeKalb 999, Edwardsville 1010, Evanston 1012, Field 1014, Funk 1021, Geneseo 1022, Jackson 1038, **Mondelez 1064**, Oak Park 1068, Polk 1075, Square 1099, Tracy 1104, Ward 1111
Indiana: Ball 1121, Blackford 1122, Brown 1124, Cass 1125, Central 1126, Community 1128, Community 1129, Community 1131, Community 1132, Community 1133, Community 1135, Community 1136, Community 1137, Dearborn 1141, Decatur 1142, DeKalb 1144, Fairbanks 1145, Fayette 1146, Greene 1152, Hancock 1154, Harrison 1155, Hendricks 1157, Henry 1158, Jasper 1160, Jennings 1162, Johnson 1163, Kuhne 1169, LaGrange 1170, Legacy 1171, Marshall 1176, Noble 1179, Northern 1180, Ohio 1181, Old 1182, Owen 1185, Parke 1186, Portland 1188, Putnam 1189, Ripley 1191, Tipton 1198, Union 1200, Unity 1201, Vectren 1202, Wabash 1203, Welborn 1205, Wells 1207, Whitley 1209
Iowa: Aviva 1211, Clarinda 1214, Community 1215, Community 1216, Community 1217, Delaware 1219, Holthues 1224, Iowa 1226, Maytag 1229, Siouxland 1240, South 1241
Kansas: Capitol 1251, Douglas 1256, Hutchinson 1260, Insurance 1261, Manhattan 1268, Topeka 1279
Kentucky: Blue 1282, Campbell 1285, Community 1286
Louisiana: Albemarle 1298, Baton Rouge 1300, Community 1306, Grigsby 1312, Heymann 1313, New Orleans 1316
Maine: Golden 1329, Kennebec 1332, Narragansett 1337
Maryland: Adams 1345, Community 1358, Community 1359, Croft 1362, Delaplaine 1367, DelSignore 1368, Mid-Shore 1395, NASDAQ 1401
Massachusetts: Arbella 1426, **Barr 1433**, Brooks 1439, **Bruner 1441**, Cape Cod 1445, Clarke 1448, Clipper 1449, Community 1453, East 1460, Hyams 1486, Liberty 1502, Lowell 1505, Miller 1516, Mount 1517, Newburyport 1519, Parker 1523, Riley 1534, Rogers 1536, Santander 1541, Sudbury 1551
Michigan: Alro 1574, Ann Arbor 1576, Branch 1580, Capital 1581, Charlevoix 1583, Community 1586, Community 1588, Community 1589, Community 1590, Community 1591, Delano 1596, Dow 1597, DTE 1598, Farver 1601, Four 1603, Frankenmuth 1606, Fremont 1607, Frey 1609, Gilmore 1612, Grand Haven 1614, Grand Rapids 1615, Grand 1616, Hillsdale 1620, Isabella 1622, Jackson 1623, Kalamazoo 1626, **Kellogg 1628**, **Kresge 1631**, Lenawee 1634, Midland 1642, Morley 1644, **Mott 1645**, Mott 1646, Petoskey 1656, Pokagon 1657, Saginaw 1662, Sanilac 1663, Schmuckal 1664, Steelcase 1667, Van Andel 1669, Vanderweide 1671, Wege 1674
Minnesota: Dayton 1690, Duluth 1693, Grand Rapids 1699, HRK 1702, Initiative 1703, Johnson 1705, Land 1710, Larsen 1711, Marbrook 1713, McKnight 1715, Midcontinent 1716, Minneapolis 1717, **Mosaic 1718**, Neilson 1721, Northwest 1722, Opus 1724, **Pentair 1727**, RBC 1730, Redwood 1731, Riverway 1733, Rochester 1735, Securian 1739, Southwest 1740, **St. Jude 1741**, Target 1744, West 1751, Xcel 1754
Mississippi: Foundation 1763, Gulf 1764, King's 1766, Mississippi 1769
Missouri: Anheuser 1774, Boylan 1776, Butler 1780, Centene 1782, Community 1783, Dunn 1787, Hall 1793, Moneta 1802, Musgrave 1805, Nichols 1806, Truman 1817
Montana: Wendy's 1831
Nebraska: Grand Island 1837, Kearney 1842, Kiewit 1843, Lexington 1845, Midlands 1848, Mid-Nebraska 1849, Nebraska 1851, Oregon 1852, Weitz 1855, Woods 1857
Nevada: Harris 1864, Nevada 1867, Parasol 1868
New Jersey: **Allen 1900**, Campbell 1917, Capozzi 1918, Elias 1923, Levitt 1960, MCJ 1965, Princeton 1979, **Sanofi 1988**, Summit 1998, Unilever 2003, Westfield 2004
New Mexico: Chase 2009, Pierce 2016, Santa Fe 2017
New York: Adirondack 2027, Allyn 2032, American 2033, **American 2034**, Assurant 2047, Carson 2086, Chautauqua 2091, **Clark 2098**, Community 2107, **Deutsche 2134**, DiMenna 2138, **Discount 2139**, **Ford 2160**, Gebbie 2170, Grant 2190, Hagedorn 2200, Hallingby 2201, Hudson 2223, Johnson 2239, **JPMorgan 2242**, **Kaplan 2245**, Klingenstein 2257, Legacy 2274, Marshall 2293, MBIA 2297, **Mertz 2306**, **MetLife 2307**, National 2321, NBC 2322, New York 2325, New York 2326, Nicholson 2329, Northern 2331, NoVo 2334, NYSE 2336, Oishei 2340, Peale 2353, **Pershing 2356**, Polisseni 2361, Quinn 2370, Rauch 2376, Robinson 2387, **Rockefeller 2390**, Sandy 2404, Schenectady 2407, Scherman 2409, Sherman 2419, Snow 2432, **Sparkplug 2441**, **Surdna**

2454, Thompson 2461, Vidda 2485, Wegman 2497, Wells 2501, Western 2503
North Carolina: Babcock 2521, **Bank 2524**, Beckman 2526, Biddle 2529, Community 2538, Community 2539, Community 2540, Cumberland 2541, Dalton 2542, Goodrich 2561, **Johnson 2574**, Kitselman 2580, Outer 2604, Polk 2609, Reynolds 2613, Reynolds 2614, Smith 2629, Tannenbaum 2637, VF 2642
North Dakota: Community 2648, Fargo 2649, Larson 2650, MDU 2652, North Dakota 2653
Ohio: Akron 2655, American 2656, Bryan 2674, Calhoun 2676, Cincinnati 2679, Community 2682, Community 2684, Coshocton 2686, Dayton 2688, Delaware 2689, **Eaton 2692**, Eaton 2693, Fairfield 2696, Ferro 2697, Fifth 2699, Foundation 2702, Gund 2708, Haile, 2709, Hamilton 2710, Knoll 2719, **Mandel 2729**, Marietta 2732, Middletown 2737, Murphy 2745, Muskingum 2747, National 2748, New Albany 2750, NiSource 2752, Orr 2761, Piqua 2763, Richland 2767, Roggecora 2768, Sandusky 2773, Sears 2781, Stark 2788, Stranahan 2790, Third 2792, Troy 2794, Tuscarawas 2795, Wayne 2798, Wean 2799, Wyler 2802, Young 2803
Oklahoma: Cherokee 2809, Hille 2816, Jones 2817
Oregon: Benton 2835, Flowerree 2845, Ford 2846, Jeld 2852, Meyer 2861, Woodard 2877
Pennsylvania: Bayer 2888, Benedum 2892, Berks 2893, Bucks 2900, Central 2907, Centre 2909, Chase 2913, CIGNA 2917, Claneil 2918, Community 2922, Community 2923, Community 2925, Connelly 2926, Davis 2930, Degenstein 2931, Delaware 2932, EQT 2940, Fels 2942, First 2947, First 2948, Foundation 2952, Grumbacher 2961, Grundy 2962, Hunt 2971, **KL 2978**, Lancaster 2981, Laros 2982, Lazarich 2983, Lehigh Valley 2986, Mellon 2998, Packer 3008, Perelman 3013, **PPG 3018**, Rider 3024, Scranton 3031, Snee 3039, Stackpole 3042, Union 3051, Willary 3057
Puerto Rico: Puerto Rico 3061
Rhode Island: Citizens 3067, Elms 3072, Rhode Island 3089, Textron 3093, Washington 3095
South Carolina: Bailey 3096, Byerly 3098, Community 3100, Foothills 3102, Graham 3103, Joanna 3104, Lutz 3105, Spartanburg 3110, Springs 3111, Waccamaw 3112
Tennessee: Assisi 3120, Clayton 3128, Community 3129, Eastman 3133, Lyndhurst 3145, Phillips 3149, Wilson 3157
Texas: Abell 3160, Alcon 3162, AT&T 3167, Behmann 3176, Bickel 3178, Booth 3180, **BP 3181**, Cailloux 3187, Chisholm 3193, Coastal 3196, Collins 3199, Dedman 3212, **Dell 3213**, Embrey 3222, Fluor 3235, Frees 3238, Herzstein 3256, Hoblitzelle 3262, Kinder 3274, Lightner 3282, Long 3285, Loose 3286, Lubbock 3287, Mayor 3292, McDermott 3293, Meadows 3296, Moody 3298, Northen 3306, NuStar 3307, Peine 3313, Permian 3316, Professional 3326, Rapoport 3331, Rockwell 3338, Sams 3342, San Angelo 3343, Shell 3348, Simmons 3352, Smith 3353, Sterling 3358, Texas 3364, Trull 3373, Waco 3378, Williams 3383
Utah: Eskuche 3393, Green 3394, Park 3401
Vermont: **Ben 3407**, Lintilhac 3412, Tarrant 3416, Vermont 3417, Windham 3418
Virgin Islands: Community 3419
Virginia: AMERIGROUP 3420, Arlington 3421, Cabell 3425, Capital 3426, Charlottesville 3428, Community 3431, Community 3433, Harvest 3443, Launders 3447, Loeb 3450, Love 3452, Lynchburg 3454, MAXIMUS 3457, Northern 3464, Richardson 3475, Williamsburg 3488
Washington: Casey 3500, Community 3503, Community 3504, Corvias 3505, First 3514, **Gates 3516**, Grays 3520, Haller 3522, Inland 3526, **Luke 3537**, Renton 3552, San Juan 3555, Seattle 3558, Sherwood 3561, **Starbucks 3565**, Tacoma 3567, Yakima 3576
West Virginia: Community 3579, McDonough 3586, Parkersburg 3587, Ross 3588
Wisconsin: Alliant 3592, **Baird 3595**, Center 3604, Fond du Lac 3615, Fort 3616, Green Bay 3619, Harley 3621, Incourage 3623, Johnson 3625, Kuenzl 3630, Marshfield 3633, Milwaukee 3637, Oshkosh 3642, Oshkosh 3643, Pettit 3645, Racine 3648, Raibrook 3649, Sauey 3655, Sentry 3657, St. Croix 3662, Stateline 3663, Stone 3664, U.S. 3665, Wanek 3667
Wyoming: Moyer 3677, Scott 3679, Whitney 3683, Wyoming 3684

Community/economic development, alliance/advocacy

New York: Cricket 2119, Scherman 2409

Community/economic development, equal rights

New York: **Mertz 2306**

Community/economic development, formal/general education

California: Weingart 456

Community/economic development, management/technical assistance

California: Irvine 264
Louisiana: Entergy 1308

Community/economic development, public education

California: JAMS 268

Community/economic development, public policy

California: JAMS 268, Soda 418

Community/economic development, research

Massachusetts: **Sociological 1548**

Community/economic development, single organization support

Michigan: Roscommon 1660

Community/economic development, volunteer services

Iowa: Schildberg 1238

Computer science

California: Craigslist 169, **Google 231**, **Keck 276**, Western 459
Idaho: **Micron 950**
Minnesota: Alworth 1677
New Jersey: **Siemens 1993**
New York: **IBM 2227**
Ohio: Community 2682
Pennsylvania: Comcast 2921

Consumer protection

Ohio: Akron 2655
Wisconsin: CBM 3603

Courts/judicial administration

California: JAMS 268, Opperman 350

Crime/abuse victims

Alabama: Black 4, Community 11
Arizona: Webb 64
California: Community 157, Community 161, **Fund 210**, **Gellert 214**, Gumbiner 236, Lesher 299, Simpson 411, Weingart 456
Colorado: Hunter 508
Connecticut: **Deupree 571**
District of Columbia: Cafritz 656
Florida: Bush 712, Landwirth 775, Southwest 823
Georgia: Abreu 846
Illinois: Field 1014
Iowa: Stebens 1242
Maryland: Ceres 1354, Community 1360
Michigan: Grand Rapids 1615, Midland 1642, Sanilac 1663
Minnesota: Larsen 1711
Nebraska: Midlands 1848, Woods 1857
New Hampshire: Foundation 1885, Lindsay 1890
New Jersey: Hyde 1944
New York: Community 2107, van Ameringen 2483
North Carolina: Glenn 2560, North Carolina 2599, Reidsville 2611
Ohio: Fairfield 2696, O'Neill 2760, Saint 2770, Springfield 2787, Youngstown 2804
Pennsylvania: Birmingham 2896, Phoenixville 3014, Staunton 3044
Tennessee: Baptist 3122, Wilson 3157
Texas: Abell 3160, Dallas 3209, Embrey 3222, Fluor 3235, Hoglund 3263, McDermott 3293, Moore 3299
Virginia: Memorial 3458
Wisconsin: Cornerstone 3608, Green Bay 3619, Marshfield 3633

Crime/law enforcement

Louisiana: New Orleans 1316
Michigan: Grand Haven 1614, Hillsdale 1620, Roscommon 1660
Minnesota: Briggs 1687
New York: Goldman 2183, Liberal 2278, **Open 2343**, Western 2503
Ohio: Coshocton 2686, Gund 2708, Stark 2788
Pennsylvania: Delaware 2932, Union 3051
Texas: Bickel 3178, Meadows 3296

Crime/law enforcement, formal/general education

Michigan: Roscommon 1660

Crime/law enforcement, government agencies

Indiana: Dearborn 1141
Michigan: Roscommon 1660

Crime/law enforcement, management/technical assistance

Michigan: Roscommon 1660

Crime/law enforcement, missing persons

Michigan: Roscommon 1660

Crime/law enforcement, police agencies

Iowa: Guernsey 1221
Michigan: Roscommon 1660

New York: Brownstone 2077, Fisher 2157, Tananbaum 2457
Wisconsin: Alliant 3592

Crime/law enforcement, public education
Michigan: Roscommon 1660

Crime/law enforcement, reform
District of Columbia: **Butler 655**

Crime/law enforcement, research
Pennsylvania: **Lee 2984**

Crime/law enforcement, single organization support
Michigan: Roscommon 1660

Crime/violence prevention
Alabama: Community 10
California: California 140, Humboldt 257, Taper 433
Illinois: **Joyce 1040**, Oak Park 1068
Indiana: Welborn 1205
Iowa: Community 1215
Louisiana: Baptist 1299
Minnesota: Duluth 1693, Midcontinent 1716
Mississippi: Community 1758
Missouri: Roblee 1809, Truman 1817
New Jersey: **Johnson 1949**
New York: Gifford 2177
Ohio: **OMNOVA 2759**
Washington: PEMCO 3549

Crime/violence prevention, abuse prevention
Alabama: Community 10
California: Boys 122, Drown 187, Eisner 189, Fremont 207
Florida: Pinellas 801
New York: Community 2108, **Ford 2160**, Seneca 2415
Pennsylvania: First 2948
Texas: Bass 3172, **Dell 3213**, King 3275, Meadows 3296

Crime/violence prevention, child abuse
California: Boys 122, Fansler 193, Fremont 207, Gold 228, Gumbiner 236
Colorado: Brown 478
Delaware: Delaware 630
Florida: Ware 838
Illinois: **Driskill 1003**
Kentucky: Trim 1295
New York: 1848 2020, Cummings 2122, **Duke 2146**, Seneca 2415
Ohio: National 2748
Oklahoma: **Schusterman 2829**
Oregon: Ford 2846
Pennsylvania: Claneil 2918
Tennessee: Regal 3151
Texas: Dallas 3209, **Dell 3213**, Goldsbury 3241, King 3275, Meadows 3296, Najim 3304, Topfer 3372
Virginia: MAXIMUS 3457
Washington: Renton 3552

Crime/violence prevention, domestic violence
California: Ahmanson 77, **Allende 79**, Blue 114, Fremont 207, Gumbiner 236, Trio 440
Connecticut: Community 563
Florida: Bush 712
Illinois: Polk 1075, Washington 1112
Indiana: Kosciusko 1168
Iowa: Siouxland 1240
Kansas: **Shumaker 1276**
Michigan: Ann Arbor 1576
Minnesota: Midcontinent 1716, Minneapolis 1717, Phillips 1728
Missouri: Roblee 1809
Nebraska: Woods 1857
New Jersey: MCJ 1965
New Mexico: Chase 2009, Santa Fe 2017
New York: New York 2325
Ohio: White 2800
Pennsylvania: Claneil 2918, FISA 2950, Staunton 3044
Texas: King 3275, Meadows 3296, Sterling 3358
Washington: Renton 3552

Crime/violence prevention, gun control
Illinois: **Joyce 1040**
New Jersey: MCJ 1965

Crime/violence prevention, sexual abuse
California: Hand 241
New York: Caruso 2087
Pennsylvania: FISA 2950

Crime/violence prevention, youth
California: Anaheim 83, Sierra 405, Weingart 456
Connecticut: Inc. 616
Florida: Bank 695, Gate 749
Georgia: Sapelo 911
Illinois: Community 988, **MacArthur 1056**
Michigan: Hillsdale 1620, Skillman 1666
Nebraska: Mutual 1850
New Jersey: Borden 1910
New York: Achelis 2026, Cummings 2122
North Carolina: Cumberland 2541
Ohio: Anderson 2658, Dater 2687
Oregon: Meyer 2861
Pennsylvania: Highmark 2968, Hunt 2971
Texas: Constantin 3202
Wisconsin: Milwaukee 3637

Cystic fibrosis
California: Wesley 457
Ohio: Piqua 2763
Virginia: **Truland 3482**
Wisconsin: **Baird 3595**

Cystic fibrosis research
California: Brunswick 133

Deaf/hearing impaired
Arizona: Webb 64
California: Gumbiner 236, Lesher 299, Patron 363, Taper 433, Weingart 456
Colorado: Hunter 508
District of Columbia: Cafritz 656
Florida: Pinellas 801, Southwest 823
Georgia: Abreu 846
Illinois: Adams 956
Indiana: Community 1132
Kansas: Emporia 1257
Michigan: Fremont 1607, Grand Rapids 1615, Midland 1642, Sanilac 1663
Nebraska: Midlands 1848
New Hampshire: Lindsay 1890
New Jersey: Hyde 1944, Kirby 1952
New York: Community 2108, **Ross 2396**
North Carolina: North Carolina 2599
Ohio: Cincinnati 2679, Fairfield 2696, O'Neill 2760, Saint 2770, Springfield 2787
Oklahoma: Hardesty 2814, Hille 2816
Pennsylvania: Connelly 2926, First 2948, Phoenixville 3014
Tennessee: Baptist 3122, Wilson 3157
Texas: Abell 3160, Baxter 3173, Dallas 3209, McDermott 3293, Moore 3299
Virginia: Memorial 3458
Wisconsin: La Crosse 3631

Dental care
Arkansas: Delta 68
California: California 140, Livingston 303, Pacific 355, Patron 363
District of Columbia: Meyer 672
Florida: Florida 744, King 768
Georgia: Cobb 863
Illinois: Community 993, Healthcare 1031, VNA 1107
Iowa: Wellmark 1246
Kansas: Delta 1255
Massachusetts: DentaQuest 1459
Minnesota: **Patterson 1726**
New Hampshire: Endowment 1883, HNH 1888
New York: Ontario 2342
Ohio: Austin 2663, Skyler 2784
Oregon: Ford 2846
Pennsylvania: Highmark 2968
Texas: Hillcrest 3261, Meadows 3296
Wisconsin: McBeath 3634

Dental school/education
California: California 140
Kansas: Delta 1255
Massachusetts: DentaQuest 1459
Minnesota: **Patterson 1726**
New York: Rhodes 2381
Virginia: **Foundation 3438**

Developmentally disabled, centers & services
Arkansas: Wal-Mart 74
California: GSF 235, **Special 422**
Colorado: **Daniels 488**
Connecticut: NewAlliance 595
Florida: Minto 789, Olsen 794, Pinellas 801, Walter 837
Georgia: Goizueta 883
Illinois: Omron 1070, Seymour 1091
Indiana: Henry 1158
Iowa: United 1243
Massachusetts: East 1460, Liberty 1502
Michigan: Jubilee 1624, Perrigo 1655
Missouri: Centene 1782
Nevada: Caesars 1860
New York: Rose 2392, Warwick 2495
North Carolina: Kennedy 2578
Ohio: Ohio 2756
Oregon: PGE 2867
Pennsylvania: CIGNA 2917
Texas: Heavin 3253, Mundy 3302, Penney 3315, Proctor 3325
Virginia: AMERIGROUP 3420, MAXIMUS 3457
Washington: Everett 3511, Safeco 3554

Diabetes
California: Hillblom 250, McKesson 321, Mead 324
Florida: Patterson 798
Illinois: FDC 1013
Indiana: WellPoint 1206

Diabetes research

Digestive diseases

Disabilities, people with

Disasters, 9/11/01

Disasters, fire prevention/control

Disasters, floods

Disasters, Hurricane Katrina

Disasters, preparedness/services

Disasters, search/rescue

Diseases (rare)

Dispute resolution

Down syndrome

Ear, nose & throat diseases

Ear, nose & throat research

Economic development

Economic development, visitors/convention bureau/tourism promotion

Economically disadvantaged

Economics

Education

Education, association

Education, community/cooperative

Education, computer literacy/technology training

Education, continuing education

Education, drop-out prevention

Education, e-learning

Education, early childhood education

Louisiana: Blue 1302
Massachusetts: **Barr 1433**, Davis 1457, Santander 1541, Sheehan 1545, Smith 1546
Michigan: Branch 1580, Hillsdale 1620, **Kellogg 1628**, Skillman 1666, Steelcase 1667
Minnesota: 3M 1676, Frey 1696, **King 1708**, Minneapolis 1717, Opus 1724, **O'Shaughnessy 1725**
Mississippi: Community 1760, Foundation 1763
Missouri: Hall 1793
Nebraska: Mutual 1850
New Jersey: Borden 1910, Hyde 1944, MCJ 1965, Schumann 1990, Turrell 2002
New York: Community 2113, **Foundation 2161**, **Genesis 2173**, Goldman 2183, Guttman 2197, Heckscher 2205, **IBM 2227**, Initial 2231, Rauch 2376, Roche 2388, Seneca 2415, Sirus 2426, Tower 2472
North Carolina: Community 2538, Reynolds 2614, Smith 2629
Ohio: American 2656, Cincinnati 2679, Fairfield 2696, Gund 2708, Hershey 2711, Middletown 2737, Nord 2754, Ohio 2756, Reinberger 2765, Richland 2767, Stark 2788, Wean 2799, White 2800
Oregon: Templeton 2874
Pennsylvania: Claneil 2918, Community 2925, Connelly 2926, Mellon 2998, Seybert 3034
Rhode Island: Textron 3093
South Carolina: Community 3099, Springs 3111
Tennessee: Benwood 3123, Davis 3130
Texas: Bass 3172, King 3275, McDermott 3293, Meadows 3296, Powell 3324, Wright 3386
Vermont: Vermont 3417
Virginia: Capital 3426
Washington: Ackerley 3489, Community 3503, Renton 3552, Seattle 3558, Yakima 3576
Wisconsin: McBeath 3634, Milwaukee 3637, Siebert 3659, Stateline 3663
Wyoming: Christian 3671

Education, equal rights

New York: **Genesis 2173**

Education, ESL programs

Arkansas: Wal-Mart 74
Rhode Island: Textron 3093
Tennessee: **International 3142**
Washington: Seattle 3558

Education, ethics

California: **Rupe 389**
Colorado: **Daniels 488**

Education, formal/general education

Florida: **Chester 720**
Illinois: **Motorola 1066**
Louisiana: Community 1306
Michigan: Roscommon 1660
New York: **Genesis 2173**
Texas: KDK-Harman 3273

Education, fund raising/fund distribution

Alabama: Snook 23
California: Skywords 414
Colorado: Monfort 520
New Jersey: Merck 1966
New York: 100 2019
Ohio: Kulas 2721
Pennsylvania: Stackpole 3042
Texas: Rogers 3339, Sterling 3358

Education, gifted students

Colorado: **Malone 514**

Education, management/technical assistance

Hawaii: Castle 929
New York: **Genesis 2173**, Kornfeld 2261

Education, public education

California: Noyce 348, Stuart 429
Colorado: **National 523**
Hawaii: Castle 929
Illinois: Dryer 1004, **MacArthur 1056**, Reese 1083
Louisiana: Community 1306
Maryland: **Blaustein 1349**
Massachusetts: Colombe 1452, Sanborn 1540
Missouri: Schneider 1812
New Mexico: Santa Fe 2017
New York: Freeman 2164, New York 2325
Ohio: Greene 2707, **Noble 2753**
South Carolina: Foothills 3102
Texas: Meadows 3296, **Paso 3312**, Powell 3324
Washington: **Gates 3516**

Education, public policy

California: **Rupe 389**, Stuart 429
Colorado: Foundation 498
Hawaii: Castle 929
Maryland: Straus 1410
Michigan: Frey 1608
Missouri: **Kauffman 1797**
New York: Cricket 2119
Texas: KDK-Harman 3273
Virginia: **Longview 3451**

Education, reading

Arkansas: Wal-Mart 74
California: Ahmanson 77, **Applied 88**, Bank 99, **Better 112**, Crail 170, Lux 307, **Mattel 312**, Mazda 313, Quest 377, Sacramento 391, Weingart 456
Colorado: El Pomar 492
Connecticut: NewAlliance 595, Pitney 604
Delaware: Morgridge 642
District of Columbia: Meyer 672
Florida: Bank 695, Florida 744, Glazer 750, Jacksonville 761
Georgia: Atlanta 852, **Georgia 878**, Pittulloch 905
Hawaii: Hawaii 933
Illinois: Community 988, Polk 1075
Indiana: Ball 1121, Decatur 1142, Old 1182, TCU 1197, Unity 1201, Vectren 1202
Iowa: Siouxland 1240
Kentucky: Blue 1282
Louisiana: Community 1306, Entergy 1308
Maryland: Fowler 1372
Massachusetts: Kelsey 1403, Ramsey 1530, Staples 1549
Michigan: Grand Rapids 1615, Jackson 1623, Pokagon 1657, Skillman 1666
Minnesota: Jostens 1706, RBC 1730
Nevada: Nevada 1867
New York: **Carnegie 2085**, Daphne 2127, Dreyfus 2145, **Genesis 2173**, **IBM 2227**, **JPMorgan 2242**, Kornfeld 2261, Northern 2331
North Carolina: Davie 2543, Morgan 2596, North 2600
Ohio: Charities 2678, Nordson 2755, **OMNOVA 2759**, Richland 2767, Scripps 2780
Oregon: Benton 2835, PGE 2867
Pennsylvania: Comcast 2921, EQT 2940, Stackpole 3042, Union 3051
Rhode Island: Textron 3093
Tennessee: Eastman 3133, **International 3142**
Texas: Booth 3180, Coastal 3196, Hoblitzelle 3262, Long 3285, Lubbock 3287, Meadows 3296, Sterling 3358, Wright 3386
Virginia: Arlington 3421, Capital 3426, MAXIMUS 3457, **Northrop 3465**, Strong 3481
Washington: Community 3503, Safeco 3554, Seattle 3558
West Virginia: Parkersburg 3587
Wisconsin: Sauey 3655, Sentry 3657

Education, reform

California: Johnson 269, **Rupe 389**, Stuart 429
Colorado: **Daniels 488**, Foundation 498
Hawaii: Castle 929
Maryland: **Blaustein 1349**
Missouri: Roblee 1809
New York: Achelis 2026, **Carnegie 2085**, Cricket 2119, **Foundation 2161**, **Genesis 2173**, **JPMorgan 2242**
North Carolina: Goodrich 2561
Ohio: Nordson 2755

Education, research

California: **Seaver 400**, Stuart 429
Colorado: **National 523**
District of Columbia: **National 674**
Florida: Dahl 731
Idaho: **Micron 950**
Illinois: **Spencer 1098**
Louisiana: Community 1306
Massachusetts: Kim 1495
Michigan: Mount Pleasant 1647
New York: Bay 2056, **Ford 2160**, **Grant 2191**, Initial 2231
Ohio: Gund 2708
Pennsylvania: **Lee 2984**
Texas: Hammill 3249, Northen 3306, Sterling 3358
Wisconsin: **Bradley 3601**

Education, services

Arkansas: Wal-Mart 74
California: **Mattel 312**, Quest 377
Colorado: Donnell 491, **Kinder 510**
Connecticut: NewAlliance 595, Pitney 604
Florida: Ansin 689, Darden 732, Lennar 778
Georgia: **Coca 864**
Illinois: Tracy 1104
Indiana: Vectren 1202
Iowa: HNI 1223
Massachusetts: **Barr 1433**, Eastern 1461, Liberty 1502, Ratshesky 1531
Michigan: DTE 1598
Minnesota: 3M 1676, **Andersen 1678**, RBC 1730, Xcel 1754
Missouri: **Kauffman 1797**
New York: **Deutsche 2134**, **JPMorgan 2242**, **MetLife 2307**, Seneca 2415, **Wallace 2492**
North Carolina: Goodrich 2561, Peeler 2606
Ohio: **OMNOVA 2759**
Oregon: I Have 2850
Pennsylvania: **Alcoa 2882**, Black 2897
Rhode Island: Textron 3093
Texas: KDK-Harman 3273
Utah: McCarthey 3397
Virginia: Capital 3426, MAIHS 3455
Washington: Safeco 3554, Sherwood 3561, Yakima 3576

Education, single organization support

Alabama: Snook 23
California: Siebel 404

Employment, labor unions/organizations

Employment, retraining

Employment, services

Employment, sheltered workshops

Employment, training

Employment, vocational rehabilitation

End of life care

Engineering

Engineering school/education

Engineering/technology

Environment

Environment, administration/regulation

Environment, air pollution

Environment, alliance/advocacy

Environment, association

Environment, beautification programs

Environment, climate change/global warming

Environment, energy

Environment, forests

Environment, formal/general education

Environment, government agencies

Louisiana: Wiener 1322
Michigan: **Kresge 1631**

Environment, information services

California: **Kapor 273**

Environment, land resources

California: Adams 76, Barth 101, Clif 152, Disney 181, **Foundation 202**, Glide 226, Lucas 306, Pacific 354, PG&E 367, Siebel 404, Winiarski 466
Connecticut: Northeast 598
Delaware: Lennox 638
Florida: Darden 732
Georgia: **Georgia 878**, Richards 908
Illinois: Community 989, Nelson 1067
Iowa: **Rockwell 1237**
Maryland: Rembrandt 1407
Massachusetts: **Barakat 1432**, **Barr 1433**, Pardoe 1522, Raymond 1532, **Sweet 1554**
Michigan: Baiardi 1577, Community 1586, Pokagon 1657
Minnesota: Land 1710, Xcel 1754
Nevada: Caesars 1860
New York: Anderson 2036, Bullitt 2079, Butler 2081, Tiffany 2463, Woodcock 2511
Oregon: Burning 2837
Pennsylvania: **ACE 2880**, **Alcoa 2882**, Brooks 2899
Rhode Island: van Beuren 3094
South Carolina: McKissick 3106
Tennessee: First 3135
Virginia: **WestWind 3486**
Washington: REI 3551
Wisconsin: Sand 3654

Environment, legal rights

Wisconsin: Bock 3600

Environment, management/technical assistance

Pennsylvania: Brooks 2899

Environment, natural resources

Alabama: BBVA 3, Goodrich 13
Alaska: Alaska 26, Juneau 35
Arizona: Dorrance 42
Arkansas: Ross 72
California: Barth 101, Bechtel, 104, Braddock 123, **Christensen 151**, Clif 152, **Conservation 165**, Firedoll 198, **Foundation 202**, **Gellert 214**, Gold 228, Heising-Simons 245, Heller 246, Hewlett 248, Mazda 313, McCaw 316, Mead 324, Pacific 355, **Packard 357**, Patagonia.org 362, PG&E 367, Sacramento 391, True 442, Wallis 451, Western 459, Witter 467
Colorado: Catto 480, El Pomar 492, **General 501**, Maki 513, Summit 537
Connecticut: Bok 555, Community 562, Palmer 600
Delaware: Burt's 626, Day 629
District of Columbia: Cafritz 656, **Wallace 683**
Florida: Bank 695, Batchelor 697, Burton 711, Darden 732, Tsunami 834
Georgia: Bancker-Williams 854, Correll 871, Georgia 877, **Georgia 878**, Richards 908, Trailsend 916
Hawaii: Hawaii 933
Idaho: CHC 945
Illinois: Bersted 967, Bobolink 970, Community 988, Donnelley 1001, Lumpkin 1053, **MacArthur 1056**, McGraw 1060, Nelson 1067, Pierce 1074, Prince 1076
Indiana: Dearborn 1141, Owen 1185, Vectren 1202
Iowa: Maytag 1229, **Rockwell 1237**, Wallace 1245
Kansas: Topeka 1279
Kentucky: Campbell 1285
Louisiana: Community 1306, Grigsby 1312
Maine: Borman 1325, Golden 1329, Quimby 1338
Maryland: Rembrandt 1407, Town 1413
Massachusetts: Archibald 1427, **Barr 1433**, **Conservation 1454**, Fields 1467, High 1482, Kelsey 1493, Kendall 1494, Makepeace 1507, Miller 1516, Raymond 1532, Sheehan 1545, **Sweet 1554**
Michigan: Ann Arbor 1576, Baiardi 1577, Carls 1582, Community 1589, Dow 1597, DTE 1598, Hillsdale 1620, Jubilee 1624, Knight 1630, **Kresge 1631**, **Mott 1645**, Wege 1674
Minnesota: 3M 1676, **Andersen 1678**, Beim 1683, Dayton 1690, Marbrook 1713, **Mosaic 1718**, Northwest 1723, Robina 1734, SUPERVALU 1743, W.M. 1747, **Weyerhaeuser 1752**, Xcel 1754
Mississippi: Mississippi 1769
Missouri: Anheuser 1774, Bellwether 1775, Laclede 1799
Montana: High 1825, Montana 1828
Nevada: Caesars 1860
New Hampshire: Fuller 1886, Mosaic 1891, Roby 1894
New Jersey: Borden 1910, Harbourton 1936, Hyde 1944, **International 1946**, Kirby 1952, **Sanofi 1988**, Unilever 2003
New Mexico: Albuquerque 2006, Frost 2012, Santa Fe 2017
New York: Abelard 2022, Anderson 2036, Butler 2081, Canaday 2083, Carson 2086, de Coizart 2129, **Duke 2146**, Family 2153, **Ford 2160**, Freeman 2164, Henle 2208, Hudson 2223, **Hughes 2224**, Johnson 2239, **Kaplan 2245**, Litwin 2283, **Overbrook 2345**, Overhills 2346, Rasmussen 2375, **Rockefeller 2389**, Scherman 2409, Snow 2432, Sprague 2444, Tiffany 2463, **Tinker 2467**, **Trust 2477**, **Weeden 2496**, Widgeon 2505, Wilson 2507, Ziff 2515
North Carolina: Borun 2532, Cumberland 2541, Glass 2559, Hanes 2565, Polk 2609, VF 2642
North Dakota: MDU 2652
Ohio: American 2656, Anderson 2658, Athens 2662, Charities 2678, Community 2684, Eaton 2693, Gund 2708, Lincoln 2724, Maltz 2727, Stark 2788, Talbott 2791, Troy 2794
Oregon: Burning 2837, Flowerree 2845, Jubitz 2853, Meyer 2861
Pennsylvania: **Alcoa 2882**, Brooks 2899, Claneil 2918, Community 2922, EQT 2940, First 2947, McLean 2997, Mellon 2998, Penn 3011, Scranton 3031, Wyomissing 3059
Rhode Island: Kimball 3079, Love 3082, Rhode Island 3089, Washington 3095
Tennessee: Community 3129, Dugas 3132, First 3135
Texas: **BP 3181**, Fluor 3235, Lennox 3279, Meadows 3296, Northen 3306, Pickens 3321, Potts 3323, Sterling 3358
Vermont: **Ben 3407**, Block 3409, Harper 3411, Vermont 3417
Virginia: **Blue 3422**, Community 3431, Oak 3466
Washington: Community 3503, Ferguson 3513, Harder 3524, **Ji 3528**, Moccasin 3545, Northwest 3546, REI 3551, Tacoma 3567, **Wilburforce 3572**, Yakima 3576
Wisconsin: Alliant 3592, Bemis 3598, Bock 3600, Harley 3621, Johnson 3625, Milwaukee 3637, U.S. 3665
Wyoming: Wyoming 3684

Environment, plant conservation

California: PG&E 367
Maine: Sewall 1339
Maryland: Cornell 1361
Minnesota: Land 1710
Pennsylvania: Brooks 2899
Vermont: Windham 3418

Environment, pollution control

California: Campbell 142, Clif 152, **Lawrence 293**
Illinois: DuPage 1008
Maryland: Community 1358, Rembrandt 1407
Michigan: **Mott 1645**
Missouri: **Monsanto 1803**
Pennsylvania: **Alcoa 2882**, Washington 3054
Wisconsin: Johnson 3625

Environment, public education

California: Campbell 142, Heller 246, Pacific 354, **Packard 357**
Florida: Batchelor 697
Minnesota: Xcel 1754
New York: Northern 2331
Texas: Bass 3172
Washington: Seattle 3558

Environment, public policy

California: Campbell 142, Heller 246, **Kapor 273**
District of Columbia: **Searle 681**
Georgia: Sapelo 911
Hawaii: Castle 929
Massachusetts: **Merck 1514**
Michigan: **Kresge 1631**
New York: **Bydale 2082**, **Cummings 2121**
Pennsylvania: **Alcoa 2882**, Brooks 2899

Environment, recycling

California: **Kapor 273**
Georgia: **Coca 864**, **Georgia 878**
Michigan: Pokagon 1657
Missouri: Anheuser 1774
Pennsylvania: **Alcoa 2882**, EQT 2940
Tennessee: **International 3142**

Environment, reform

Louisiana: Wiener 1322
New York: **Cummings 2121**

Environment, research

Alaska: Alaska 26
California: Campbell 142, **Christensen 151**, Heller 246, **Smith 416**
Colorado: Catto 480
Florida: Batchelor 697, Katcher 765
Massachusetts: **Barakat 1432**, Colombe 1452
Minnesota: Alworth 1677
New York: **Bydale 2082**, Tiffany 2463
Pennsylvania: Brooks 2899, Martin 2991
Washington: **Ji 3528**

Environment, single organization support

California: Campbell 142
Pennsylvania: Brooks 2899

Environment, toxics

California: California 140, Campbell 142, **Marisla 310**
Georgia: Sapelo 911
Maine: Golden 1329
Massachusetts: **Merck 1514**
New York: **Noyes 2335**
Pennsylvania: Brooks 2899

Environment, waste management

California: California 140, Clif 152
New Jersey: Unilever 2003
Pennsylvania: **Alcoa 2882**

Environment, water pollution

California: California 140, Campbell 142
Georgia: **Coca 864**, Georgia 877
Massachusetts: Lowell 1505
Michigan: Community 1586
Minnesota: Initiative 1703
Missouri: **Monsanto 1803**
New York: Anderson 2036, **PepsiCo 2354**
Pennsylvania: Brooks 2899
Tennessee: **International 3142**
Washington: Seattle 3558

Environment, water resources

California: Campbell 142, **Conservation 165**, Firedoll 198, **Google 231**, **Hilton 251**, Pacific 355, Patagonia.org 362
Connecticut: Common 561, Northeast 598
Florida: Darden 732, Lennar 778, Ware 838
Georgia: **Coca 864**, Sapelo 911
Hawaii: Castle 929
Iowa: **Rockwell 1237**
Massachusetts: **Barakat 1432**, Bilezikian 1435, Lowell 1505, **Sweet 1554**
Michigan: **Erb 1599**, Jubilee 1624
Minnesota: Land 1710, **Mosaic 1718**, **Pentair 1727**, **Porter 1729**, Xcel 1754
Mississippi: Mississippi 1769
Missouri: Anheuser 1774
New Jersey: Unilever 2003
New York: Anderson 2036, Butler 2081, Coudert 2115, Northern 2331, Park 2349, **PepsiCo 2354**, Scherman 2409, Tiffany 2463
Oregon: Burning 2837
Pennsylvania: **ACE 2880**, **Alcoa 2882**, Brooks 2899, Martin 2991
Washington: Northwest 3546, **Starbucks 3565**
Wisconsin: Sand 3654

Environmental and resource rights

Illinois: Libra 1050
New York: **Cummings 2121**

Environmental education

Alabama: BBVA 3
Alaska: Alaska 26
California: **Applied 88**, Campbell 142, Lee 296, Pacific 354, Pacific 355, PG&E 367, Sacramento 391, Swayne 431
Colorado: **Kinder 510**
District of Columbia: **Wallace 683**
Florida: Darden 732, Gulf 754
Georgia: **Georgia 878**
Hawaii: Hawaii 933
Illinois: DuPage 1008
Indiana: Vectren 1202
Louisiana: Grigsby 1312
Maine: Horizon 1331, Quimby 1338
Maryland: Middendorf 1394, Rembrandt 1407
Michigan: DTE 1598, Mills 1643
Minnesota: Xcel 1754
Missouri: Anheuser 1774
Montana: High 1825
New York: Butler 2081, Canaday 2083, de Coizart 2129, Johnson 2240
Ohio: American 2656
Oregon: Burning 2837
Pennsylvania: **Alcoa 2882**, Bayer 2888, EQT 2940, McLean 2997, **PPG 3018**
South Carolina: Singing 3108
Tennessee: **International 3142**
Texas: Fluor 3235
Wisconsin: Alliant 3592, Ariens 3594, Blooming 3599, Bock 3600, Harley 3621

Epilepsy research

New York: Klingenstein 2256

Eye diseases

California: **Beckman 105**, Kirchgessner 282
Kentucky: Etscorn 1287
Massachusetts: Memorial 1512
New York: de Coizart 2129, **Friends 2167**, Lavelle 2269
North Carolina: Templin 2638
Ohio: Marion 2733
Pennsylvania: Fourjay 2953, Perelman 3013
Texas: Alcon 3161, Alcon 3162
Utah: Green 3394

Eye research

Alabama: **International 15**
California: **Beckman 105**, Hillblom 250, Kirchgessner 282
Indiana: Glick 1150
New Jersey: **Pfeiffer 1975**
New York: de Coizart 2129
North Carolina: Hoffman 2569, Templin 2638
Texas: Alcon 3161, Alcon 3162, Tomerlin 3371

Family services

Alabama: Central 8, Community 10
Arizona: Hughes 49, Long 51, Stardust 63
Arkansas: **Windgate 75**
California: Anderson 84, Bothin 120, Brandes 124, California 140, Community 162, Crail 170, Cummings 171, **Gellert 214**, GSF 235, Gumbiner 236, HealthCare 244, Humboldt 257, Hutto 258, Jacobs 267, Johnson 269, Kelly 278, Laulhere 292, Leichtman 298, Lesher 299, Marcled 308, Napa 340, Newhall 342, Outhwaite 353, Pacific 355, **Packard 357**, Parsons 359, Pasadena 361, PG&E 367, Quest 377, Sacramento 391, Sierra 405, Smith 415, Sonora 420, Taper 433, Thomson 435, Trio 440, Weingart 456, Western 459, Wrather 469
Colorado: Colorado 483, El Pomar 492, Marquez 515, Piton 526, Rose 528, SEAKR 531, Stratton 536, Summit 537
Connecticut: Colburn-Keenan 560, Community 562, Community 563, Connecticut 564, Ensworth 575, Long 588, Matthies 590, Palmer 600
District of Columbia: Cafritz 656, **Hill 664**, Meyer 672
Florida: Bank 695, Brown 707, Burns 710, Carlton 715, Chapman 717, Community 723, Community 725, Community 726, Community 727, Conn 728, Florida 744, Gate 749, Jacksonville 761, Kennedy 767, **Knight 771**, Landwirth 775, Pinellas 801, Sudakoff 828, Wiegand 841
Georgia: Campbell 860, WinShape 921
Hawaii: Buehner 927, Hawaiian 934
Illinois: Bersted 967, Chartered 980, Community 988, Community 990, Evanston 1012, McCauley 1059, Oak Park 1068, Pierce 1074, Polk 1075, Schnadig 1089, Seymour 1091, Speh 1097, Tracy 1104
Indiana: Ball 1121, Blackford 1122, Central 1126, Community 1129, Foellinger 1147, Marshall 1176, Portland 1188, Steel 1196
Iowa: Beckwith 1213, Community 1217, Guernsey 1221, Siouxland 1240
Kansas: Skillbuilders 1277, Topeka 1279
Kentucky: J & L 1291, Lift 1293
Louisiana: Albemarle 1298, Community 1306, Entergy 1308, Grigsby 1312
Maine: Somers 1341
Maryland: Ceres 1354, Community 1360, Cupid 1363, Polinger 1405, Straus 1410
Massachusetts: Arbella 1426, Association 1428, Community 1453, East 1460, Eastern 1461, Franklin 1472, Gould 1477, Hazard 1480, Hyams 1486, Kelsey 1493, Liberty 1502, Linden 1504, MENTOR 1513, New 1518, Peters 1527, Ratshesky 1531, Riley 1534, Sailors' 1539, Weber 1564
Michigan: Ann Arbor 1576, Branch 1580, Charlevoix 1583, Community 1589, Community 1590, Family 1600, Fremont 1607, Frey 1609, Grand Rapids 1615, Hillsdale 1620, Kalamazoo 1626, Knight 1630, Onequest 1650, Prince 1658, Saginaw 1662, Skillman 1666, Vanderweide 1671
Minnesota: Butler 1688, Cargill 1689, Duluth 1693, General 1697, Grand Rapids 1699, HRK 1702, Initiative 1703, **Kaplan 1707**, **King 1708**, Minneapolis 1717, **Pentair 1727**, Phillips 1728, RBC 1730, Rochester 1735, Sundance 1742, Target 1744, Thorpe 1745, WCA 1749, West 1751
Mississippi: Community 1759, Ergon 1761, Foundation 1763
Missouri: Centene 1782, Hall 1793, Hallmark 1794, Roblee 1809
Nebraska: Lincoln 1847, Mutual 1850, Woods 1857
Nevada: Bendon 1859, Nevada 1867
New Hampshire: Alexander 1877
New Jersey: Borden 1910, Bunbury 1916, Hyde 1944, **Johnson 1949**, **Sanofi 1988**, Schwarz 1991
New Mexico: Frost 2012
New York: Achelis 2026, Allyn 2032, Andor 2037, Assurant 2047, Brillo-Sonnino 2070, Canaday 2083, **Clark 2098**, Coach 2100, Community 2110, **Credit 2118**, Dammann 2125, Daphne 2127, Deerfield 2132, deForest 2133, Heckscher 2205, IF 2228, **JPMorgan 2242**, Kaylie 2247, Lee 2270, MBIA 2297, **MetLife 2307**, Moore 2312, New York 2325, Northern 2331, Rauch 2376, Rose 2392, Sirus 2426, Tiger 2464, Western 2503
North Carolina: **Bank 2524**, Cumberland 2541, Gordon 2562, Katz 2576, Kistler 2579, Moretz 2595, VF 2642
Ohio: Akron 2655, Ar-Hale 2661, Austin 2663, Bates 2665, Community 2682, Community 2684, Dater 2687, **Eaton 2692**, Fifth 2699, Foundation 2702, Greene 2707, Mathile 2734, Middletown 2737, Nordson 2755, O'Neill 2760, Richland 2767, Saint 2770, Scripps 2780, Stark 2788, White 2800, Youngstown 2804
Oregon: Jubitz 2853, Meyer 2861, PGE 2867, Storms 2872
Pennsylvania: CIGNA 2917, Claneil 2918, Delaware 2932, First 2947, Fourjay 2953, Hansen 2964, Heinz 2966, Highmark 2968, Honickman 2970, Hunt 2972, Mellon 2998, Pilgrim 3016, Seybert 3034, Staley 3043, Staunton 3044, Wells 3055
Rhode Island: Parmelee 3088, Rhode Island 3089, Textron 3093, Washington 3095
South Carolina: Lutz 3105, Springs 3111
Tennessee: HCA 3139
Texas: Abell 3160, Amarillo 3163, Baron 3171, Bass 3172, Cailloux 3187, Coastal 3196, Esping 3225, Fluor 3235, Frees 3238, Heavin 3253, Hill 3259, Holthouse 3265, King 3275, Lubbock 3287, Meadows 3296, Rockwell 3338, Saint 3341, Sterling 3358, Thompson 3367, Trull 3373, Waco 3378, Ward 3381, Wright 3386
Utah: Hemingway 3396
Vermont: Harper 3411, Merchants 3414, Vermont 3417
Virgin Islands: Community 3419
Virginia: AMERIGROUP 3420, CarMax 3427, Community 3429, Community 3432, Lynchburg 3454, MAXIMUS 3457, MLG 3460, Moran 3462, Northern 3464, Samberg 3478

Washington: Blue 3498, Casey 3500, Community 3503, Discuren 3507, Goodman 3518, Green 3521, Medina 3542, Safeco 3554, Satterberg 3556, Tacoma 3567, Whatcom 3571
West Virginia: Eastern 3580, Parkersburg 3587, Your 3591
Wisconsin: Anthony 3593, Incourage 3623, La Crosse 3631, McBeath 3634, Milwaukee 3637, New 3641, Pamida 3644, Pritchett 3647, Raibrook 3649, Sauey 3655

Family services, adolescent parents

California: Trio 440
New Mexico: Santa Fe 2017
Pennsylvania: FISA 2950
Texas: Topfer 3372

Family services, counseling

Pennsylvania: Staunton 3044

Family services, domestic violence

Alabama: Central 8
California: Blue 114, Braddock 123, Shea 402, Simpson 411, Trio 440
Georgia: **Georgia 878**
Illinois: Alphawood 959
Massachusetts: Eastern 1461, Franklin 1472
Missouri: Truman 1817
Nebraska: Mutual 1850
New Mexico: Santa Fe 2017
New York: Coach 2100, Wolk 2510
North Carolina: Kennedy 2578
Ohio: Reinberger 2765
Oregon: PGE 2867
Pennsylvania: Chase 2913, FISA 2950
Texas: Heavin 3253, Shelter 3349
Virginia: CarMax 3427, Obici 3467
Washington: OneFamily 3547
Wisconsin: Johnson 3625, Sauey 3655

Family services, parent education

Georgia: Goizueta 883
Indiana: Noble 1179
Iowa: Wellmark 1246
Michigan: **Mott 1645**
New York: Cummings 2122, MBIA 2297
Ohio: **OMNOVA 2759**
Oregon: PGE 2867
Rhode Island: CVS 3068
Texas: Topfer 3372
Washington: Yakima 3576

Financial services

California: Marcled 308, Soda 418
New York: **Heron 2211**, **JPMorgan 2242**, **MetLife 2307**
Washington: **Gates 3516**

Financial services, credit unions

California: Marcled 308

Food banks

Arkansas: Wal-Mart 74
California: **Applied 88**, California 140, Genentech 216, GSF 235, Mazda 313
Colorado: **First 496**
Connecticut: Aetna 550, NewAlliance 595
Delaware: CenturyLink-Clarke 627
Florida: Bi-Lo/Winn-Dixie 700, Darden 732, Olsen 794
Illinois: **Mondelez 1064**, Omron 1070
Indiana: Crosser 1139, Kuhne 1169
Louisiana: Albemarle 1298
Maryland: Battye 1348, Moore 1396
Massachusetts: Arbella 1426, Clipper 1449, Eastern 1461, Liberty 1502, Williams 1567
Michigan: Delano 1596, Pokagon 1657
Minnesota: General 1697, Land 1710, SUPERVALU 1743
Nebraska: Mutual 1850
New Hampshire: Woodbury 1897
New Jersey: Hummingbird 1943, Unilever 2003
New York: **American 2034**, **Credit 2118**, MBIA 2297, **MetLife 2307**, Morgan 2315, **PepsiCo 2354**, Sprague 2444, Wegman 2497
North Carolina: **Bank 2524**
Ohio: American 2656, Dayton 2688, Macy's 2726, Marion 2733, Reinberger 2765, Samaritan 2772
Oklahoma: Parman 2824
Oregon: Coit 2841, PGE 2867
Pennsylvania: **ACE 2880**, Adams 2881, Bayer 2888, Community 2924, Patterson 3010, Trexler 3049
Rhode Island: Hasbro 3077, Kimball 3079, Textron 3093
Tennessee: Regal 3151
Texas: Bass 3172, Coastal 3196, Fisch 3232, King 3275, South 3356
Virginia: Morgan, 3463, United 3484
Washington: Intermec 3527, Renton 3552
Wisconsin: Bemis 3598, Pamida 3644, Windhover 3668

Food distribution, groceries on wheels

Texas: King 3275

Food distribution, meals on wheels

Arkansas: Wal-Mart 74
California: California 140, Fusenot 211
Florida: Tippett 833, Walter 837
Michigan: Dana 1593, DTE 1598
Missouri: Curry 1784
Nevada: Caesars 1860
New York: **American 2034**
North Carolina: Kennedy 2578
Ohio: Freygang 2704
South Carolina: Smith 3109
Texas: Bass 3172, South 3356

Food services

Arkansas: Wal-Mart 74
California: **Applied 88**, Braddock 123, Clif 152, Genentech 216, GSF 235, Humboldt 257, Kelly 278, Pacific 355, **Packard 357**, Sacramento 391, Sonora 420, Weingart 456
Colorado: El Pomar 492
Connecticut: Aetna 550, NewAlliance 595
Delaware: CenturyLink-Clarke 627, Palmer 644
District of Columbia: Cafritz 656
Florida: Batchelor 697, Bi-Lo/Winn-Dixie 700, Community 723, Darden 732, Gate 749, Glazer 750
Illinois: Community 988, Field 1014, **Mondelez 1064**, Stern 1100
Indiana: Community 1130
Iowa: Wellmark 1246
Kansas: **Lloyd 1267**
Kentucky: Lift 1293
Maryland: Fowler 1372, **Weinberg 1416**
Massachusetts: Arbella 1426, Clipper 1449, East 1460, Ramsey 1530, Winning 1569
Michigan: Hillsdale 1620, Jubilee 1624, Masco 1637, Pokagon 1657, Skillman 1666
Minnesota: Duluth 1693, General 1697, Land 1710, **Mosaic 1718**, Nash 1720, RBC 1730, SUPERVALU 1743, Target 1744
Missouri: **Monsanto 1803**, Mungenast 1804
Nebraska: Mutual 1850
Nevada: Caesars 1860, Nevada 1867
New Jersey: Bonner 1909, Campbell 1917, Unilever 2003
New Mexico: Frost 2012, Santa Fe 2017
New York: American 2033, **American 2034**, **Credit 2118**, **JPMorgan 2242**, **M.A.C. 2287**, Morgan 2315, New York 2325, **PepsiCo 2354**, Solomon 2436, Stark 2449
North Carolina: Balin 2523, **Bank 2524**, Gambrill 2556, Griffin 2563
Ohio: American 2656, Macy's 2726, Marion 2733, Mathile 2734, Murphy 2744, Stark 2788
Oregon: PGE 2867
Pennsylvania: **ACE 2880**, Community 2924, Community 2925, Fourjay 2953, Goshen 2959, North 3006, Pierce 3015
Rhode Island: Hasbro 3077, Textron 3093
South Carolina: Lutz 3105, Smith 3109
Tennessee: HCA 3139, **International 3142**
Texas: Coastal 3196, Edwards 3218, Fluor 3235, Hillcrest 3261, **International 3269**, Sterling 3358, Sturgis 3360, Trull 3373, Williams 3383
Vermont: Vermont 3417
Virginia: AMERIGROUP 3420, Arlington 3421, CarMax 3427, Lynchburg 3454, MAXIMUS 3457, Twinkling 3483, United 3484
Washington: Community 3503, Fales 3512, Haller 3522, Safeco 3554, Tacoma 3567
Wisconsin: Anthony 3593, Bemis 3598, Harley 3621, Milwaukee 3637, Windhover 3668

Food services, congregate meals

Texas: King 3275

Foundations (community)

Arizona: APS 39, Stardust 63
Arkansas: Ross 72
California: Cush 175, Irvine 264, Quest 377, Wallis 451
District of Columbia: Monarch 673
Florida: Bell 698, Brown 707, Burton 711, Flournoy-Theadcraft 745, Minto 789, Morrison 792, Reinhold 808, Sierra 819, Sunburst 829
Georgia: **Imlay 888**, Richards 908, Rockdale 909
Hawaii: Kahiau 935
Idaho: Schneidmiller 951
Illinois: Good 1023
Indiana: Glick 1150, Vectren 1202
Kansas: Capitol 1251
Louisiana: Community 1306, Pugh 1318
Maine: Lynam 1335
Maryland: Hendricks 1377, Henson 1378, Mann 1389
Massachusetts: Felix 1466
Michigan: Acheson 1571, Jubilee 1624, Meijer 1639, RNR 1659, Schmuckal 1664
Minnesota: Andreas 1679, Sayer 1737
Montana: Silver 1830
New Jersey: Bauer 1906, Levitt 1960
New York: Allyn 2032, American 2033, **American 2034**, Cutco 2123, Marshall 2293, Moore 2311
North Carolina: Kitselman 2580, Levine 2584, Sherrard 2623, Todd 2639
Ohio: Bates 2665, Gardner 2705, Haile, 2709, Knoll 2719, Morgan 2739, **Noble 2753**, Seasongood 2782, Young 2803
Oklahoma: McGee 2820
Pennsylvania: Black 2897, Grumbacher 2961
South Carolina: Foothills 3102
Tennessee: Ayers 3121, Chattanooga 3125, Hurlbut 3140, Osborne 3147

Texas: **BP 3181**, Dedman 3212, **Levant 3280**, Loose 3286, Morgan 3301, Peine 3313
Utah: Park 3401
Washington: **Goodwin 3519**, Whatcom 3571
Wisconsin: Greenheck 3620, Oshkosh 3643, Pritchett 3647, Stone 3664
Wyoming: Dubois 3673

Foundations (private grantmaking)
Arizona: Marshall 54
California: Blum 115, Feintech 196, Metta 329, Opperman 350, Skywords 414
Colorado: Esther 495, **Merage 519**, **National 523**
Connecticut: Bauer 553
Florida: Fortin 747, Green 751, Kantner 764, Krouse 774, Lipton 781, Rendina 809, Sender 817
Illinois: Funk 1021, Pritzker 1079, Walter 1110
Maryland: Kay 1384
Massachusetts: **Iacocca 1487**, Inavale 1488, Jacobson 1490
Michigan: Dalton 1592, Farver 1601
Minnesota: **Trust 1746**
Missouri: Humphreys 1795
Nebraska: Lienemann 1846
New York: 100 2019, Brownstone 2077, Coleman 2104, Diller 2137, Einhorn 2150, Halper 2202, **Heron 2211**, Imago 2230, **Matisse 2295**, Mercer 2305, Moore 2314, Polisseni 2361, Regals 2377, Schwartz 2413
North Carolina: Christopher 2537
Oklahoma: Wisdom 2832
Pennsylvania: Wilson 3058
Texas: Cain 3189, Jones 3272, L. 3278, Shelton 3350
Utah: Semnani 3404
Virginia: Lee-Jackson 3448

Foundations (private independent)
California: **Leichtag 297**
Illinois: Bersted 967
Mississippi: Walker 1772

Foundations (private operating)
California: **Packard 357**
Maine: Aicher 1323

Foundations (public)
California: Burns 135, Irvine 264, **Rupe 389**
Colorado: Ballantine 474
Connecticut: Macauley 589
Florida: Minto 789
Maine: Narragansett 1337
Michigan: RNR 1659
Minnesota: Johnson 1704
New York: **Pershing 2356**, Sulzberger 2451, Touradji 2471, Trump 2476
Pennsylvania: CIGNA 2917
Tennessee: Clayton 3128
Texas: **Jiv 3270**
Utah: Semnani 3404
Virginia: **Price 3472**

Gay men
Alabama: Black 4
California: Weingart 456
Michigan: Grand Rapids 1615

Genetic diseases and disorders
Minnesota: Alworth 1677
New York: Hallingby 2201
Pennsylvania: CIGNA 2917

Genetic diseases and disorders research
New York: Singh 2425

Geology
Colorado: Society 534
Minnesota: Alworth 1677
New York: Tiffany 2463
North Carolina: Olin 2603

Geriatrics
California: Archstone 90, Hillblom 250
Colorado: Burt 479, **Daniels 488**
New Jersey: **Rippel 1982**
Ohio: McGregor 2736, Steinmann 2789
Virginia: Richmond 3476

Geriatrics research
California: **Glenn 225**
New Jersey: **Pfeiffer 1975**, **Rippel 1982**

Gerontology
California: Archstone 90, **Ellison 191**
Maryland: Stulman 1411
New Jersey: **Rippel 1982**

Girl scouts
California: Bechtel, 104
Georgia: **Coca 864**
Michigan: Lear 1632, Perrigo 1655
Missouri: Darr 1785
New Jersey: **Alcatel 1899**
New York: Mutual 2317, Wells 2501
Ohio: Dayton 2688
Oklahoma: Peel 2825
Pennsylvania: **Alcoa 2882**, FISA 2950
Wisconsin: Schlegel 3656

Girls
Alabama: Black 4, Community 10
Arizona: Webb 64
California: **Allende 79**, California 140, **Clorox 153**, Community 161, Cowell 168, Fleishhacker 199, Gerbode 217, **Google 231**, Gumbiner 236, LA84 287, Lesher 299, **Mattel 312**, Patron 363, PG&E 367, Roth 388, San Luis 393, Simpson 411, Weingart 456
Colorado: Community 484, Summit 537
District of Columbia: Cafritz 656
Florida: Community 725
Georgia: Abreu 846
Illinois: Chicago 982, Evanston 1012, Field 1014, Fry 1018, **Motorola 1066**, Siragusa 1096
Indiana: Noble 1179
Iowa: Stebens 1242
Maryland: Community 1359
Massachusetts: Essex 1464
Michigan: Fremont 1607, Frey 1608, Grand Rapids 1615, Knight 1630, Midland 1642, Mount Pleasant 1647, Sanilac 1663
Minnesota: **O'Shaughnessy 1725**
Mississippi: Community 1760
Missouri: Saigh 1811
Montana: Montana 1828
Nebraska: Midlands 1848, Weitz 1855
New Jersey: **Allen 1900**, Hyde 1944
New York: Community 2107, Heckscher 2205, **MetLife 2307**, New York 2325, NoVo 2334, **Open 2343**, **Overbrook 2345**, Patrina 2350, **Ross 2396**
North Carolina: Community 2540, Glenn 2560, Strowd 2633
Ohio: **Brush 2673**, Fairfield 2696, Hershey 2711, O'Neill 2760, Richland 2767, Youngstown 2804
Oklahoma: Hardesty 2814, Hille 2816
Oregon: **NIKE 2865**
Pennsylvania: **Alcoa 2882**, Birmingham 2896, Child 2916, Connelly 2926, FISA 2950, Heinz 2966, Phoenixville 3014, Pilgrim 3016, Staunton 3044, Valentine 3053
Tennessee: **Scarlett 3152**, Wilson 3157
Texas: Bass 3172, Embrey 3222, Frees 3238, McDermott 3293, Moore 3299, Orsinger 3310, Rockwell 3338
Vermont: Harper 3411
Washington: **Gates 3516**, **Singh 3563**, Tacoma 3567
West Virginia: Community 3579
Wisconsin: Community 3607, Marshfield 3633, Milwaukee 3637, Oshkosh 3642

Girls clubs
California: Samuelsson 392, Simpson 411
New York: Voya 2488

Goodwill Industries
Arkansas: Wal-Mart 74
Iowa: United 1243
Louisiana: Community 1306

Government/public administration
California: Sacramento 391, Taper 433
Connecticut: Palmer 600
Illinois: Chicago 982, Community 988, Geneseo 1022, McCauley 1059
Indiana: Central 1126, Cole 1127, Harrison 1155, Henry 1158, Marshall 1176
Iowa: Siouxland 1240, Stebens 1242
Kansas: Hansen 1259, Topeka 1279
Louisiana: Freeman 1309
Michigan: Charlevoix 1583, Community 1587, Community 1588, Fremont 1607
Minnesota: Duluth 1693, Rochester 1735
Nebraska: Fremont 1836, Grand Island 1837
Nevada: Nevada 1867
New Jersey: Kirby 1952
New York: Aequus 2028, Chautauqua 2091, **Clark 2098**, **Ford 2160**, New York 2325, Pratt 2366, Robinson 2387, **Tinker 2467**
North Carolina: Fairfield 2551, Ferebee 2552, Hunt 2572
North Dakota: Fargo 2649
Ohio: Coshocton 2686, Gund 2708, Murphy 2745, Richland 2767, Salem 2771, Seasongood 2782, Stark 2788
Pennsylvania: Grundy 2962
Rhode Island: Rhode Island 3089
Texas: Abell 3160, Booth 3180, Carter 3190, Loose 3286, McDermott 3293, Meadows 3296
Utah: Hemingway 3396
Virginia: Arlington 3421, Community 3431
Washington: Tacoma 3567
Wisconsin: La Crosse 3631, McBeath 3634, Milwaukee 3637

Graduate/professional education
Alaska: CIRI 33
California: Genentech 216, Johnson 269
Florida: Blanksteen 701
Minnesota: **Patterson 1726**

Health care

Health care, administration/regulation

Health care, alliance/advocacy

Health care, association

Health care, clinics/centers

Health care, cost containment

Health care, emergency transport services

Health care, EMS

Health care, equal rights

Health care, ethics

Health care, financing

Health care, formal/general education

Health care, fund raising/fund distribution

Health care, government agencies

Health care, HMOs

California: California 139
Texas: **Dell 3213**

Health care, home services

California: California 140, Livingston 303
Connecticut: Senior 613
Illinois: VNA 1107
Maryland: Lutheran 1387, Maryland 1391
New York: Community 2108
Ohio: Reinberger 2765
Pennsylvania: McLean 2997
Virginia: MAXIMUS 3457
Wisconsin: Dudley 3610

Health care, infants

California: Livingston 303, Patron 363
Colorado: Kaufmann 509
Connecticut: Aetna 550
District of Columbia: Stewart 682
Indiana: WellPoint 1206
Michigan: **Gerber 1611**
New Hampshire: Foundation 1885
Texas: **Dell 3213**, Topfer 3372
Washington: **Gates 3516**

Health care, information services

New Jersey: Horizon 1940
New York: High 2213
Ohio: Osteopathic 2762

Health care, insurance

Alabama: Community 10
California: Blue 114, California 139, **Packard 357**
Indiana: WellPoint 1206
Massachusetts: DentaQuest 1459
New Hampshire: HNH 1888
New Jersey: **Johnson 1949**
North Carolina: Reynolds 2614
Ohio: Austin 2663
Virginia: AMERIGROUP 3420

Health care, management/technical assistance

Massachusetts: DentaQuest 1459

Health care, organ/tissue banks

Georgia: Mason 896
Kentucky: Etscorn 1287
Texas: **Bolivar 3179**

Health care, patient services

California: Allergan 80, Eichenberg 188, Genentech 216, GSF 235, McKesson 321, Patron 363
Connecticut: Aetna 550
Delaware: **AstraZeneca 623**
Florida: Florida 744, Glazer 750, Lennar 778
Georgia: Burke 859
Maryland: Maryland 1391
Minnesota: HRK 1702
Nevada: Caesars 1860
New York: Mutual 2317
North Carolina: Olin 2603
Ohio: **Cardinal 2677**, **Eaton 2692**, Samaritan 2772
Pennsylvania: CIGNA 2917, Highmark 2968, North 3006, Rossin 3028
Rhode Island: CVS 3068
Tennessee: Regal 3151
Texas: **Bolivar 3179**, Coastal 3196, **Dell 3213**
Wisconsin: Manitowoc 3632

Health care, public policy

California: Blue 114
Connecticut: Aetna 550
Florida: Florida 744
Maine: Maine 1336
Massachusetts: DentaQuest 1459
New Jersey: **Milbank 1968**
New York: **Cummings 2121**

Health care, reform

California: Blue 114
Michigan: **Kellogg 1628**
New York: **Cummings 2121**
Pennsylvania: North 3006

Health care, research

California: Mead 324
Florida: Morningstar 791
Illinois: Richard 1085
Louisiana: Lincoln 1315
Virginia: AMERIGROUP 3420

Health care, rural areas

California: California 140
New Jersey: **Rippel 1982**
New York: **Friends 2167**
North Carolina: Reynolds 2614
Texas: King 3275

Health care, single organization support

Ohio: **Lerner 2722**

Health care, support services

California: Patron 363, Solano 419
Illinois: VNA 1107
Maryland: Maryland 1391
Minnesota: **King 1708**
Texas: **Bolivar 3179**, **International 3269**, **Paso 3312**

Health care, volunteer services

Illinois: Katten 1042

Health organizations

Alabama: Meyer 18
California: Curci 174, Dolby 185, Fremont 207, Kelly 278, Mellam 326, Metta 329, Napa 340, Wallis 451, Westreich 460, Wilsey 464
Colorado: McDonnell 516
Delaware: **AstraZeneca 623**, Day 629
District of Columbia: Cafritz 656, Meyer 672
Florida: Bradley 706, Carlton 715, Hard 756, Holloway 759, Minto 789, Olsen 794, Speer 824
Georgia: Lowder 894, Woodward 923
Hawaii: Ching 931
Illinois: Bersted 966, Duchossois 1005, Funk 1021, Lyon 1054, Stern 1100
Indiana: Haddad 1153
Louisiana: Heymann 1313, Wiener 1322
Maine: Borman 1325, Davis 1328
Maryland: Osprey 1403
Massachusetts: **Barakat 1432**, **Elsevier 1463**, Inavale 1488, Massachusetts 1508, McNeice 1509, Meelia 1510, Two 1557
Michigan: Baiardi 1577, Delano 1596, Farver 1601, Farwell 1602, Frankel 1604, Royal 1661, Van 1670, Von 1672, Wilson 1675
Minnesota: Schulze 1738, **St. Jude 1741**
Mississippi: Biloxi 1755, Feild 1762
Missouri: Pendergast 1807, Speas 1813, Tilles 1815
Nebraska: Kim 1844
New Hampshire: Foundation 1885
New Jersey: Catholic 1919, Earle 1920, Harbourton 1936, **International 1946**, Kish 1953, MacDonald 1961, Nandansons 1969
New York: **Abba's 2021**, Access 2025, American 2035, Belfer 2059, **Dana 2126**, Dartley 2128, Fleischer 2158, Friedman 2166, Kanas 2244, Leeds 2272, Marshall 2293, Mercer 2305, National 2321, Newman 2328, Palette 2347, **Pershing 2356**, Touradji 2471, Trump 2476, Union 2481, Wolk 2510
North Carolina: Garrow 2557, Helb 2568, Linsmayer 2585, Simpson 2626, Southern 2630, Stahlberg 2631
Ohio: Freygang 2704, Haile, 2709, Mandel 2728, Piqua 2763, Renner 2766, Sears 2781
Oklahoma: Adams 2806, Cherokee 2809
Pennsylvania: Cooper 2927, Grumbacher 2961, Highmark 2968, Rooney 3026, Somerville 3041
Tennessee: Chattanooga 3125
Texas: Cailloux 3187, Conley 3201, Fasken 3229, Hill 3260, **Radler 3330**, Thompson 3367, Tyler 3375, Willard 3382
Vermont: Vermont 3417
Virginia: RECO 3474
Washington: Lauzier 3534, Smith 3564
Wisconsin: Incourage 3623, Murray 3638

Health organizations, association

Alabama: Stephens 24
Arizona: Barton 40, Hill 48, Jasam 50, Marshall 54
California: Blum 115, Braddock 123, Bravo 126, Cush 175, Eichenberg 188, Fansler 193, Fusenot 211, Gibson 220, Gold 229, Helms 247, **Hilton 251**, Kvamme 286, McBeth 315, **Nazarian 341**, Philanthropy 368, Price 374, Pritzker 375, Rossi 387, Sacramento 391, Sassoon 395, Sierra 405, Smith 415, Smith 417, Sonora 420, Treadwell 439, West 458
Colorado: Colorado 483, Comprecare 485, El Pomar 492, Monfort 520, Mullen 522, Norwood 524, Summit 537, Yampa 545
Connecticut: Aronson 552, Bridgemill 556, Community 563, Connecticut 564, Craig 566, Dalio 567, Dennett 570, Ensworth 575, Goldstone 581, Long 588, Meriden 591, Palmer 600, Robbins 607
Delaware: Delaware 630, Freygish 633
District of Columbia: Lehrman 670
Florida: Applebaum 690, Bank 695, Community 727, DeBartolo 734, DiMare 737, King 768, Mertz 788, Moos 790, Pope 803, Reinhold 808, Rendina 809, Sierra 819, Thomas 831, TWS 836, Wollowick 843
Georgia: Bradley 858, Camp-Younts 861, Georgia 876, Savannah 912, Woodruff 922
Hawaii: Atherton 925, Baldwin 926, Cooke 932, McInerny 938
Idaho: Jeker 949
Illinois: Boothroyd 971, Community 988, Community 991, Evanston 1012, Hendrickson 1032, Luehring 1052, Magnus 1058, McCauley 1059, Oberweiler 1069, Pattis 1073, Polk 1075, Shapiro 1093, Webb 1113
Indiana: Ball 1121, Central 1126, Community 1133, Fayette 1146, Froderman 1148, Northern 1180, Parke 1186
Iowa: Maytag 1229, Siouxland 1240
Kansas: Hutchinson 1260, **Muchnic 1271**

Kentucky: Blue 1282, Gheens 1288
Maine: Alfond 1324, King 1333
Maryland: Battye 1348
Massachusetts: Sailors' 1539, Williams 1567
Michigan: Ann Arbor 1576, Community 1586, Community 1587, Community 1588, Dart 1594, Four 1603, Frankel 1605, Fremont 1607, Grand Rapids 1615, Hillsdale 1620, **Kellogg 1628**, Lenawee 1634, Mardigian 1635, Marquette 1636, McGregor 1638, Michell 1641, Morley 1644, Prince 1658
Minnesota: George 1698, Johnson 1704
Mississippi: Community 1759
Missouri: St. Louis 1814
Nevada: Jaquish 1865, Nevada 1867
New Hampshire: Bean 1878
New Jersey: Bauer 1906, Borden 1910, Eisai 1921, Evans 1925, Fournier 1932, Hyde 1944, Levitt 1960, Mandelbaum 1962, MCJ 1965, Meyer 1967, Neisloss 1970, Pierson 1976, **Ramapo 1981**, Snyder 1995, Syms 1999
New Mexico: Frost 2012, Phillips 2015, Santa Fe 2017
New York: 100 2019, Abramson 2024, Black 2065, **Buffalo 2078**, Chernin 2092, Cohen 2102, **Cummings 2121**, D'Agostino 2124, Diller 2137, Dobkin 2140, Fascitelli 2155, **Gilman 2178**, **Goldman 2181**, Goldman 2183, Heisman 2206, Henle 2208, Heyman 2212, Litwin 2283, McGraw 2300, New York 2325, Perelman 2355, Regals 2377, Resnick 2379, Rhodes 2381, **Ross 2396**, Sandy 2404, Schnurmacher 2411, Schwartz 2413, Sugarman 2450, Summers 2452, Tananbaum 2457, Thompson 2461, Tisch 2468
North Carolina: French 2554, Glass 2559, Odell 2602, Smith 2629
North Dakota: Fargo 2649
Ohio: Akron 2655, Barberton 2664, Calhoun 2676, Community 2683, Community 2684, Dodero 2691, Fairfield 2696, Hamilton 2710, Murphy 2745, Nord 2754, Richland 2767
Oklahoma: Bernsen 2807, Chapman 2808, Hardesty 2814, Parman 2824, Zarrow 2833
Oregon: Benton 2835
Pennsylvania: Ames 2884, Betz 2895, Central 2907, Community 2922, Community 2923, Dozzi 2935, Drueding 2936, Elk 2939, Foundation 2952, Fourjay 2953, Hunt 2972, Patterson 3010, Ross 3027, Scranton 3031, Snee 3039, Tuttleman 3050, **Zeldin 3060**
Rhode Island: Kimball 3079, Rhode Island 3089
South Carolina: Spartanburg 3110
Tennessee: Clayton 3128, Community 3129, Davis 3130
Texas: Astin 3166, Behmann 3176, Dallas 3209, Deakins 3210, Dunn 3216, Elkins 3220, Elkins 3221, Engler 3223, Greentree 3244, Henderson 3255, Hillcrest 3261, Hoglund 3263, Holthouse 3265, Howell 3268, Kinder 3274, Lightner 3282, Loose 3286, Lubbock 3287, Luse 3289, McDermott 3293, Rachal 3329, Richardson 3334, Richter 3337, Shelton 3350, Smith 3355, South 3356, Sturgis 3360, Toma 3370, Waggoner 3379, Wright 3386
Utah: Ashton 3388, Semnani 3404
Vermont: Harper 3411
Virginia: Community 3432, Kellar 3446, Metropolitan 3459
Washington: McEachern 3541, Schultz 3557, Seattle 3558, Shemanski 3560, Tacoma 3567
West Virginia: Beckley 3577
Wisconsin: BayCare 3597, McBeath 3634, McDonough 3635, Milwaukee 3637, Pettit 3645, Stateline 3663, U.S. 3665, Zilber 3670
Wyoming: Cody 3672, Wyoming 3684

Health organizations, equal rights

Florida: Jacobsen 762

Health organizations, fund raising/fund distribution

Minnesota: Johnson 1704

Health organizations, public education

California: California 139
Minnesota: **St. Jude 1741**
South Carolina: Black 3097

Health organizations, public policy

California: California 139

Health organizations, reform

California: Blue 114

Health organizations, research

Massachusetts: Gardinor 1473
Michigan: **Gerber 1611**

Health sciences school/education

Alaska: CIRI 33
Mississippi: Ergon 1761
New York: **Macy 2288**
Virginia: AMERIGROUP 3420

Heart & circulatory diseases

California: **Beckman 105**, Treadwell 439
Connecticut: Connecticut 564
Delaware: **AstraZeneca 623**
Florida: Greenburg 752, Speer 824
Illinois: Community 988, Katten 1042, Omron 1070
Indiana: WellPoint 1206
Michigan: Nartel 1648
Minnesota: **St. Jude 1741**
Mississippi: Mississippi 1769
Nevada: Nevada 1867
New Jersey: Horizon 1940, **Rippel 1982**
New York: Wegman 2497
Pennsylvania: Highmark 2968
Rhode Island: CVS 3068
Texas: NuStar 3307, Sterling 3358, Wright 3386
Virginia: **Truland 3482**
Washington: Corvias 3505

Heart & circulatory research

California: **Beckman 105**, Treadwell 439
Illinois: Community 988
Indiana: Leighton 1172
Nevada: Nevada 1867
New Jersey: **Rippel 1982**
Pennsylvania: **Cardiovascular 2905**
Texas: Goldsbury 3241, Sterling 3358, Tomerlin 3371

Hemophilia

Connecticut: Colburn-Keenan 560

Higher education

Alabama: BBVA 3, Brown 5, Caddell 6, Community 10, Hawkins 14, McWane 17, Smith 22
Alaska: Aleut 27, Arctic 28, Atwood 29, Bristol 31, Chugach 32, CIRI 33, Doyon 34, Koniag 36
Arizona: APS 39, Barton 40, Christian 41, Flinn 44, Grace 46, Hill 48, Hughes 49, Marley 53, Marshall 54, Ottosen 56, Squires 62, Stardust 63, Weil 65
Arkansas: Cabe 67, Frueauff 70, Ottenheimer 71, Ross 72, Wal-Mart 74
California: Ahmanson 77, Annenberg 87, **Applied 88**, Bank 99, Barth 101, **Beavers 102**, Beckman 106, **Better 112**, Beynon 113, Blum 115, Braddock 123, Brandman 125, Brisco 127, Burns 136, California 140, Chartwell 150, College 156, Community 162, Cotsen 167, Craigslist 169, Dolby 185, Douglas 186, Eichenberg 188, Gellert 215, Genentech 216, Gluck 227, Gold 229, **Google 231**, Guzik 238, Halperin 240, Hannon 242, Heller 246, Helms 247, Hewlett 248, Hutto 258, Jones 270, **Kapor 273**, **Keck 276**, Kellerman 277, Koenig 285, Lansing 290, Leichtman 298, **Lingnan 301**, Liu 302, Los Altos 305, Lucas 306, Marcled 308, Matsui 311, McBeth 315, McCoy 319, McKesson 321, McMicking 322, Mosher 335, Muckel 336, Mulago 337, Murdock 338, Opperman 350, Parsons 359, Pedrozzi 364, Pritzker 375, Quest 377, Rossi 387, Sacramento 391, Sassoon 395, Scaife 397, Shasta 401, Solano 419, Specialty 423, Tang 432, Tu 443, Valley 445, Van Nuys 447, Wallis 451, Wasserman 453, Weingart 456, Wesley 457, Westreich 460, **Wilkinson 463**, Wrather 469
Colorado: Change 481, Colorado 482, Donnell 491, El Pomar 492, Griffin 504, Hewit 506, Kaufmann 509, **Kinder 510**, Marquez 515, Puksta 527, Seay 532, Telluride 538, Tointon 539, Tomkins 540, Trachten 541
Connecticut: **Albers 551**, Bauer 553, Bridgemill 556, Colburn-Keenan 560, Connecticut 564, Conway 565, Craig 566, Dalio 567, Deloitte 569, Eder 573, Fisher 577, Floren 578, Hoffman 585, Howe 586, Linke 587, Neuberger 593, **Niles 596**, Palmer 600, Pitney 604, **Praxair 606**, Robbins 607, Saybrook 610, Inc. 616
Delaware: Kendeda 636, Lennox 638, McHugh 641, Sylvan 648
District of Columbia: Bou 654, Cafritz 656, **Carter 657**, Lichtenberg 671, Rumsfeld 679, **Searle 681**, **Wyss 685**
Florida: Ansin 689, Applebaum 690, Bank 695, Batchelor 697, Bell 698, Bi-Lo/Winn-Dixie 700, Blanksteen 701, Blanton 702, Bohnert 703, Bradley 706, Brown 707, Burnett 708, Burnetti 709, Burton 711, **Chester 720**, Community 724, Community 725, Community 727, Dahl 731, Darden 732, DeBartolo 734, Diermeier 736, DiMare 737, Dunspaugh-Dalton 738, Erdle 740, Florida 744, Gulf 754, Hand 755, Katcher 765, **Kazma 766**, Kislak 769, Kiwanis 770, Lennar 778, Martin 786, Martin 787, Morrison 792, Patterson 798, Plangere 802, Rinker 810, River 811, Sandelman 814, Selby 816, Southwest 823, Stransky 827, Sunburst 829, Thomsen 832, Tippett 833, Turock 835, Walter 837, Ware 838, Wollowick 843
Georgia: AIM 847, Amos 848, Amos-Cheves 849, Anderson 850, Baker 853, Bowen 857, Bradley 858, Campbell 860, Camp-Younts 861, Cobb 863, **Coca 864**, Colston 865, Cooper 870, Correll 871, Exposition 873, Georgia 877, **Georgia 878**, Goizueta 883, **Guanacaste 884**, Holder 887, Katz 889, Knox 890, Marshall 895, Murphy 898, Patrick 902, Pitts 904, Pittulloch 905, Ragan 906, Sapelo 911, Trailsend 916, Tull 917, University 918, Weir 919, Woodruff 922
Hawaii: Makana 937, Zimmerman 940
Idaho: Cunningham 946, Jeker 949, **Micron 950**
Illinois: Bersted 967, Brach 973, CME 984, Coldwell 985, Coleman 986, Comer 987, Community 988, Community 991, Copeland 995, Dunard 1006, Foglia 1015, Funk 1021, Grant 1026, Hendrickson 1032, Homan 1033, Hurvis 1037, Jackson 1038, Katten 1042, **Kobe 1045**, Lars 1047, **MacArthur 1056**, Maddox 1057, Magnus 1058, McGraw 1060, Mellinger 1061, Monticello 1065, Omron 1070, Pattis 1073, Polk 1075, Pritzker 1079, Ryan 1087, Schuler 1090, Shapiro 1093, Siragusa 1096, Ullrich 1106, Walter 1110, Webb 1113
Indiana: Auer 1120, Ball 1121, Brotherhood 1123, Brown 1124, Cole 1127, Community 1130,

Community 1131, Community 1135, Fayette 1146, Froderman 1148, Glick 1150, Harrison 1155, Jasper 1160, Johnson 1163, Jorgensen 1164, Kuhne 1169, LaGrange 1170, Leighton 1172, Lilly 1173, **Lumina 1174**, Marshall 1176, Master 1177, Old 1182, OneAmerica 1183, Parke 1186, Portland 1188, Regenstrief 1190, Tobias 1199, Union 1200, Vectren 1202

Iowa: Aviva 1211, Delaware 1219, Hall-Perrine 1222, HNI 1223, Maytag 1229, McElroy 1230, R & R 1236, Schroeder 1239, United 1243, Wahlert 1244, Wallace 1245, Woodward 1247

Kansas: Capitol 1251, Hansen 1259, Hutchinson 1260, Insurance 1261, Koch 1264, Koch 1265, Miller 1269, **Muchnic 1271**, Rush 1273, Sunderland 1278

Kentucky: Brown 1283, Campbell 1285, Etscorn 1287, Gheens 1288, J & L 1291, Trim 1295

Louisiana: Baton Rouge 1300, Burton 1303, Community 1306, Freeman 1309, Grigsby 1312, Heymann 1313, Pugh 1318, Schlieder 1319

Maine: Alfond 1324, Borman 1325, **Catalyst 1326**, Hannaford 1330, King 1333

Maryland: Bunting 1352, Community 1358, Community 1359, Dahan 1364, Davis 1365, Delaplaine 1367, DelSignore 1368, Dupkin 1371, Gudelsky 1376, Hendricks 1377, Henson 1378, Macht 1388, Meyerhoff 1393, Middendorf 1394, NASDAQ 1401, **Northern 1402**, RCM & D 1406, Rembrandt 1407, Rosenberg 1409, Tucker 1415, Wright 1418, Zickler 1419

Massachusetts: Aaron 1421, Archibald 1427, Berkman 1434, Brooks 1439, Cabot 1443, Calderwood 1444, Clarke 1448, D'Amour 1456, Demoulas 1458, Eastern 1461, Edwards 1462, **Elsevier 1463**, Grew 1478, Herbert 1481, High 1482, Inavale 1488, **Foundation 1489**, Jacobson 1490, Jaffe 1491, Krieger 1497, Liberty 1502, Phelps 1528, Schrafft 1543, Smith 1547

Michigan: **Allen 1573**, Alro 1574, Ann Arbor 1576, Binda 1579, Charlevoix 1583, Dart 1594, Davenport 1595, Dow 1597, DTE 1598, Farver 1601, Farwell 1602, Grand Rapids 1615, Hillsdale 1620, **Isabel 1621**, Jubilee 1624, Kahn 1625, **Kresge 1631**, Lear 1632, Mardigian 1635, McGregor 1638, Mills 1643, Morley 1644, Oleson 1649, Onequest 1650, Perrigo 1655, Petoskey 1656, RNR 1659, Wege 1674, Wilson 1675

Minnesota: 3M 1676, Andreas 1679, Boss 1686, Briggs 1687, Duluth 1693, Farmers 1695, Frey 1696, Greystone 1700, Jostens 1706, Land 1710, Midcontinent 1716, Opus 1724, **Patterson 1726**, **Pentair 1727**, Regis 1732, Rochester 1735, Securian 1739

Mississippi: Community 1759, Ergon 1761, Feild 1762, Luckyday 1767, Mississippi 1768, Mississippi 1769, Sullivan 1771

Missouri: Anheuser 1774, Boylan 1776, Breen 1778, Butler 1780, Centene 1782, Hall 1793, Humphreys 1795, Millstone 1801, Musgrave 1805, Schneider 1812, Tilles 1815, Walker 1818

Montana: Wendy's 1831

Nebraska: Hawkins 1838, Hirschfeld 1839, Kiewit 1843, Lienemann 1846, Lincoln 1847, Midlands 1848, Oregon 1852, Quivey 1853, Wilson 1856, Zollner 1858

Nevada: Caesars 1860, Doyle 1861, Jaquish 1865, **Reynolds 1869**, **Tang 1873**, Troesh 1874, Webb 1875

New Hampshire: Ham 1887, Lindsay 1890, Penates 1893, Roby 1894, Smyth 1895, Woodbury 1897

New Jersey: **Alcatel 1899**, **Allen 1900**, Baker 1903, Banbury 1904, **Berrie 1908**, Bonner 1909, Brookdale 1912, Buehler 1915, Campbell 1917, Earle 1920, Eisai 1921, Fortune 1931, Gibson 1934, Holzer 1939, Jones 1950, **Knowles 1955**, Kovner 1956, Kushner 1957, Levitt 1960, Mandelbaum 1962, Merck 1966, Neisloss 1970, **Newcombe 1972**, Point 1977, Post 1978, **Ramapo 1981**, **Sanofi 1988**, **Siemens 1993**, Syms 1999, Taub 2000

New Mexico: B.F. 2008, Chase 2009, Frost 2012, Maddox 2014

New York: **AIG 2029**, Alfiero 2031, Allyn 2032, American 2033, **American 2034**, Belfer 2059, Blum 2067, Box 2068, **Breslauer 2069**, Bronfman 2073, Brooks 2075, Brownstone 2077, Burton 2080, Carson 2086, Carvel 2088, Century 2089, Chernin 2092, Coach 2100, Community 2107, Community 2110, Cramer 2117, Cutco 2123, Dartley 2128, Dean 2130, **Deutsche 2134**, **Diamond 2135**, Diller 2137, Dobkin 2140, Einhorn 2150, Farash 2154, Fascitelli 2155, Fleischer 2158, **Ford 2160**, Gellert 2171, Gershwind 2174, Gifford 2177, **Goldman 2181**, Goldstein 2184, Gould 2188, **Gutfleish 2196**, Hallingby 2201, Heckscher 2205, Henle 2208, Heyman 2212, High 2213, Holmberg 2219, **Hughes 2224**, Hultquist 2225, Hycliff 2226, IF 2228, Imago 2230, **Institute 2233**, Jaharis 2236, Johnson 2241, **JPMorgan 2242**, **Kade 2243**, Kanas 2244, Kaylie 2247, Kekst 2249, Kellen 2250, **King 2251**, Klingenstein 2256, Klingenstein 2257, Lake Placid 2265, Lee 2270, Leeds 2272, Levy 2276, Liberman 2279, Littauer 2282, Loewe 2284, **Luce 2286**, MBIA 2297, McGonagle 2299, **Mellon 2302**, Mendell 2303, Menezes 2304, **MetLife 2307**, Miller 2308, Moore 2312, Moore 2314, Morgan 2315, Mule 2316, Mutual 2317, Nicholson 2329, Northern 2331, Norwich 2332, Oishei 2340, Ostgrodd 2344, Overhills 2346, Park 2349, **PepsiCo 2354**, Pletka 2360, Price 2367, Purple 2369, Rasmussen 2375, Reich 2378, Rhodes 2381, Ring 2384, Rose 2392, Rose 2393, Rosenberg 2394, **Rubin 2398**, **Rubin 2399**, Ruffin 2400, Sandy 2404, **Schepp 2408**, Schmitt 2410, Schumann 2412, Schwartz 2413, SDA 2414, Seneca 2415, Shoreland 2421, Singh 2425, Sirus 2426, Smith 2430, Snayberger 2431, Snow 2432, Spektor 2442, Stardust 2448, Summers 2452, Swartz 2455, Tananbaum 2456, **Teagle 2459**, Teagle 2460, Time 2466, Tisch 2468, Tisch 2469, Truman 2475, Vilcek 2486, Wachenheim 2489, Warwick 2495, Weissman 2500, Wells 2501, Whiting 2504, Widgeon 2505, Wiener 2506

North Carolina: Allen 2518, Anonymous 2519, **Bank 2524**, Biddle 2529, Bolick 2531, Byrum 2535, Caine 2536, Christopher 2537, Community 2539, Cumberland 2541, Dalton 2542, Deaver 2544, Dobbs 2545, Duke 2546, Gambrill 2556, Goodrich 2561, Hanes 2565, Harvest 2566, Havens 2567, Howe 2570, Humphrey 2571, Hunter 2573, Kanitz 2575, Kenan 2577, Mayr 2588, McNeil 2590, Meserve 2592, Niessen 2598, North 2600, Nucor 2601, Odell 2602, Olin 2603, Perkin 2607, Reynolds 2613, Roberts 2617, Rogers 2618, Sandt 2621, Schmuhl 2622, Shingleton 2624, Short 2625, Simpson 2626, Sloan 2628, Smith 2629, Southern 2630, State 2632, Tannenbaum 2637, Towne 2641, Woodson 2644

North Dakota: Larson 2650, MDU 2652, North Dakota 2653

Ohio: American 2656, American 2657, Andrews 2659, Ar-Hale 2661, Bates 2665, Bryan 2674, Calhoun 2676, Charities 2678, Cliffs 2681, Coshocton 2686, Dater 2687, Dayton 2688, **Eaton 2692**, Emery 2694, Evans 2695, Ferro 2697, Fifth 2699, Foss 2701, Freygang 2704, Gund 2708, Haile, 2709, Knoll 2719, Knowlton 2720, Kulas 2721, **Lerner 2722**, Lincoln 2724, Llewellyn 2725, Mandel 2728, **Mandel 2729**, Middletown 2737, Mirolo 2738, Morgan 2739, Morgan 2740, Murphy 2745, National 2748, Nord 2754, Ohio 2756, Reinberger 2765, Renner 2766, Richland 2767, Roggecora 2768, Schmidlapp 2775, Scotford 2779, Shinnick 2783, Skyler 2784, Stark 2788, Talbott 2791, Third 2792, Tiffin 2793, Veale 2797

Oklahoma: Bernsen 2807, Chapman 2808, Gaylord 2813, Merrick 2821, Noble 2822, Oklahoma 2823, Parman 2824, Viersen 2830

Oregon: Castle 2839, Chaney 2840, Collins 2842, Flowerree 2845, Jubitz 2853, Knight 2854, **Lemelson 2857**, Leonard 2858, Meyer 2861, Michael 2862, PGE 2867, Renaissance 2869, Woodard 2877

Pennsylvania: **ACE 2880**, Adams 2881, **Alcoa 2882**, Ames 2884, Arkema 2885, Baker 2886, Bayer 2888, Beacon 2889, Berks 2893, Berwind 2894, Betz 2895, Black 2897, Bucks 2900, Calvert 2904, CIGNA 2917, Community 2925, Connelly 2926, Davis 2929, Dozzi 2935, DSF 2937, Elk 2939, EQT 2940, Feldman 2941, Ferree 2944, First 2947, Fourjay 2953, Freas 2954, Garfield 2955, Glatfelter 2956, Groff 2960, Grumbacher 2961, Grundy 2962, Hansen 2964, Hunt 2971, II-VI 2974, Kaiserman 2977, McCune 2993, McKaig 2994, Mendel 2999, Naylor 3002, O'Brien-Veba 3007, Palumbo 3009, Patterson 3010, Perelman 3012, Perelman 3013, **PPG 3018**, Presser 3019, Randall 3021, Rangos 3022, **Respironics 3023**, Ross 3027, Saramar 3029, Scranton 3031, Sedwick 3032, Stackpole 3042, Trexler 3049, Wyomissing 3059, **Zeldin 3060**

Rhode Island: Biogen 3063, CVS 3068, Gross 3076, Koffler 3081, Love 3082, Masonic 3083, Schwarz 3090, Textron 3093, Washington 3095

South Carolina: Bailey 3096, Community 3099, Daniel 3101, Joanna 3104, Lutz 3105, McKissick 3106, Smith 3109, Spartanburg 3110, WebbCraft 3113

South Dakota: Hatterscheidt 3116, Schwab 3117, South 3118

Tennessee: Ayers 3121, Clayton 3128, Eastman 3133, First 3135, Hardin 3137, Haslam 3138, Regal 3151, **Scarlett 3152**, Schmidt 3153, Wilson 3157

Texas: Abell 3160, Anderson 3164, AT&T 3167, B.E.L.I.E.F. 3169, Behmann 3176, Bickel 3178, Booth 3180, **BP 3181**, Cain 3188, Carter 3190, Coastal 3196, Coates 3197, Collins 3199, Community 3200, Constantin 3202, Criswell 3207, Elkins 3220, Elkins 3221, Engler 3223, Fisch 3232, Fish 3233, Fluor 3235, Greentree 3244, Gulf 3245, Hachar 3246, Hamman 3248, Heavin 3253, Hillcrest 3261, Hoblitzelle 3262, Johnson 3271, Jones 3272, Kleberg 3276, Lennox 3279, Long 3285, Martinez 3291, McDermott 3293, McKee 3295, Mitchell 3297, Moore 3299, Morgan 3301, Navarro 3305, NuStar 3307, Penney 3315, Perot 3317, Peterson 3318, Potts 3323, QuadW 3328, Rachal 3329, Reilly 3333, Richardson 3334, Richardson 3336, Richter 3337, Rogers 3339, Rosewood 3340, Schissler 3346, Shelton 3350, Smith 3353, Smith 3355, Sterling 3358, Stevens 3359, Talkington 3362, Texas 3364, Texas 3365, Trull 3373, Tubbs 3374, Vergara 3376, Wallrath 3380, Wright 3386, Zachry 3387

Utah: Bamberger 3389, Eccles 3392, Eskuche 3393, Green 3394, McCarthey 3397, Quinney 3402, Schmidt 3403, Semnani 3404, Yamagata 3406

Vermont: General 3410, Harper 3411, McKenzie 3413, Tarrant 3416, Vermont 3417

Virginia: AMERIGROUP 3420, **Bosack 3423**, Cabell 3425, Denit 3435, Kellar 3446, Launders 3447, Lee-Jackson 3448, Lincoln 3449, Maude 3456, Moore 3461, Morgan, 3463, Northern 3464, **Northrop 3465**, **Price 3472**, Richardson 3475, **Truland 3482**, United 3484

Washington: Anderson 3492, Bamford 3495, Biller 3496, Blakemore 3497, Blue 3498, Community 3503, Dimmer 3506, Discuren 3507, Ferguson 3513, Green 3521, Jones 3530, Lauzier 3534, Lauzier 3535, Maxwell 3539, McCaw 3540, PEMCO 3549, Richardson 3553, Shemanski 3560, Tacoma 3567, Washington 3570, Wrigley 3575, Yakima 3576

West Virginia: Burnside 3578, Maier 3584, Parkersburg 3587

Wisconsin: Alliant 3592, Ariens 3594, **Baird 3595**, Bemis 3598, **Bradley 3601**, Chipstone 3605, Einhorn 3613, Elmwood 3614, Fund 3617, Incourage 3623, Johnson 3625, Kohler 3629, La Crosse 3631, Manitowoc 3632, Menasha 3636, Milwaukee 3637, Neese 3639, Nelson 3640, Oshkosh 3642, Pettit 3645, Pritchett 3647, RITE-HITE 3651, Sauey 3655, Sentry 3657,

Seramur 3658, Siebert 3659, Stateline 3663, Windhover 3668, Windway 3669, Zilber 3670
Wyoming: Dubois 3673, Perkins 3678, Whitney 3683

Higher education reform

Louisiana: Community 1306

Higher education, college

Arizona: Dorrance 42
California: California 140, Zafiropoulo 470
Colorado: Denver 489
Connecticut: Perna 602
Illinois: Stewart 1101
Iowa: Woodward 1247
Louisiana: Community 1306
Minnesota: Bahl 1681
Missouri: Curry 1784
New York: Brillo-Sonnino 2070, Gould 2188, Hadar 2198
North Carolina: Moretz 2595, Needham 2597
South Carolina: Foothills 3102
Texas: Plass 3322
Washington: Sherwood 3561
Wisconsin: Bock 3600

Higher education, college (community/junior)

California: California 140, Hewlett 248
Idaho: Albertson 942
Louisiana: Community 1306
Maryland: Lutheran 1387
Minnesota: **Patterson 1726**
New Hampshire: Byrne 1879
New York: Stardust 2448, Truman 2475
North Carolina: North 2600
Oregon: Leonard 2858
Washington: **Gates 3516**

Higher education, university

California: Boeckmann 116, Carney 144, Carpenter 145, Eichenberg 188, Foundation 203, Lee 296, Siebel 404, Versacare 448
Colorado: Trachten 541
Connecticut: Bok 555, Floren 578
Florida: A. & R. 686, Atkins 693, Feder 741, Stellar 826
Illinois: Pritzker 1079, Rhodes 1084, Rosen 1086, Stewart 1101
Louisiana: Community 1306
Maryland: Lutheran 1387
Massachusetts: **Patagonia 1524**, Phelps 1528
Minnesota: Bentson 1684, Johnson 1704, Nash 1720, Wallin 1748, Wedum 1750
Missouri: Darr 1785, Schneider 1812
Montana: Greater 1823
New Jersey: Gamper 1933, Savin 1989
New Mexico: Simon 2018
New York: Hadar 2198, Initial 2231, Newman 2328, Purple 2369, Rothstein 2397, Spektor 2442, St. George's 2445
North Carolina: Arkwright 2520, Borun 2532, Needham 2597
Ohio: Fibus 2698, Ryan 2769, Seasongood 2782
Pennsylvania: **Botstiber 2898**, Copernicus 2928, McKaig 2994, Nesh 3004, Rooney 3026
Texas: Durrill 3217, Edwards 3219, Harte 3251, Kleinheinz 3277, **Levant 3280**, South 3356
Virginia: MAIHS 3455
Washington: **Goodwin 3519**
Wisconsin: McDonough 3635

Hinduism

New Jersey: Nandansons 1969
New York: Tandon 2458

Hispanics/Latinos

Alabama: Black 4
Arizona: Webb 64
California: California 137, California 140, Community 157, Cowell 168, Fleishhacker 199, Gerbode 217, Gumbiner 236, Lesher 299, San Luis 393, Simpson 411, Weingart 456
Colorado: Colorado 483, Rose 528, Summit 537
Connecticut: Connecticut 564
District of Columbia: Cafritz 656, **Carter 657**, Jovid 668
Illinois: Chicago 982, Fry 1018, **Mondelez 1064**, Siragusa 1096, Sumac 1103
Indiana: Health 1156, **Lumina 1174**
Iowa: Siouxland 1240, Wahlert 1244
Massachusetts: Access 1422, Hyams 1486
Michigan: Grand Rapids 1615, **Kellogg 1628**
Minnesota: Minneapolis 1717, Northwest 1722, Phillips 1728
Mississippi: Community 1760
Missouri: Anheuser 1774
Nebraska: Midlands 1848, Woods 1857
New Hampshire: Lindsay 1890
New Jersey: **Allen 1900**, Hyde 1944
New Mexico: Con 2011, Santa Fe 2017
New York: Aresty 2041, **Ford 2160**, Haring 2203, Langeloth 2267, **Macy 2288**, **MetLife 2307**, New York 2326, **Noyes 2335**, **Open 2343**, **Sparkplug 2441**, van Ameringen 2483
North Carolina: Glenn 2560, North Carolina 2599, Reidsville 2611, Strowd 2633
Ohio: Cincinnati 2679, Community 2683, O'Neill 2760, Saint 2770
Oklahoma: Hille 2816
Oregon: Benton 2835
Pennsylvania: Connelly 2926, First 2948, Laros 2982, Phoenixville 3014
Tennessee: Baptist 3122, **Maclellan 3146**
Texas: Abell 3160, Embrey 3222, Frees 3238, Long 3285, McDermott 3293, Moore 3299, **Paso 3312**, Rockwell 3338, Sterling 3358
Wisconsin: Community 3607, Green Bay 3619, Marshfield 3633

Historic preservation/historical societies

Alaska: CIRI 33
Arizona: Marley 53
Arkansas: Union 73
California: Brisco 127, Community 157, Community 160, Community 163, Mazda 313, Placer 371, Sacramento 391, San Luis 393, Smith 417
Colorado: El Pomar 492, Summit 537
Connecticut: 1772 547, Connecticut 564, Middlesex 592
Delaware: Chaney 628
Florida: Bank 695, Charlotte 718, Coral Gables 729, Selby 816, Southwest 823
Georgia: Community 868, Cooper 870, Exposition 873, Livingston 893
Hawaii: Hawaii 933
Illinois: Alphawood 959, Community 988, Community 990, Driehaus 1002, Luehring 1052
Indiana: Community 1131, Community 1135, Decatur 1142, Harrison 1155, Jasper 1160, Parke 1186, Unity 1201
Iowa: HNI 1223
Kansas: Morgan 1270
Kentucky: Brown 1283, Campbell 1285
Louisiana: Chambers 1304
Maine: Horizon 1331, Narragansett 1337
Maryland: Baker 1347, Community 1357, Community 1358, Community 1359, Delaplaine 1367
Massachusetts: Archibald 1427, Community 1453, Makepeace 1507, Williams 1567
Michigan: Carls 1582, Community 1591, Jackson 1623, Oleson 1649, Petoskey 1656
Minnesota: Boss 1686, Marbrook 1713
Mississippi: Gulf 1764
Missouri: Truman 1817
Montana: Greater 1823
Nebraska: Quivey 1853
New Hampshire: Johnson 1889
New Jersey: Brotherton 1914, Kirby 1952, Westfield 2004
New Mexico: Albuquerque 2006
New York: Adirondack 2027, American 2033, **American 2034**, Berg 2062, Butler 2081, Hudson 2223, **Kaplan 2245**, Marshall 2293, New York 2325, Norwich 2332, **Pershing 2356**, Snow 2432, Thompson 2461, Truman 2475, **Trust 2477**, Warwick 2495, Wilson 2507
North Carolina: Fairfield 2551, Gambrill 2556, Hanes 2565, Meserve 2592, Outer 2604, Perkin 2607, Smith 2629, Tannenbaum 2637
Ohio: Akron 2655, Bryan 2674, Community 2685, Dater 2687, Murphy 2745, Nordson 2755, Richland 2767, Schiewetz 2774, Stark 2788, Troy 2794, Youngstown 2804
Oklahoma: McGee 2820
Pennsylvania: Allegheny 2883, Berks 2893, Claneil 2918, Community 2923, Dozzi 2935, First 2947, Lehigh Valley 2986, McCune 2993, McLean 2997, Patterson 3010, Scranton 3031
Rhode Island: Rhode Island 3089, van Beuren 3094
South Carolina: Graham 3103, Joanna 3104, Spartanburg 3110
Tennessee: Community 3129
Texas: Collins 3199, Herzstein 3256, Hoblitzelle 3262, Lubbock 3287, McDermott 3293, Meadows 3296, Northen 3306, Smith 3354, Sterling 3358, Summerlee 3361, Ward 3381
Vermont: Block 3409, Vermont 3417, Windham 3418
Virginia: Cabell 3425, Community 3429, Community 3431, Gwathmey 3442, Lee-Jackson 3448, Morgan, 3463, Parsons 3470, **Price 3472**, **Truland 3482**, Williamsburg 3488
Washington: Blue 3498, Community 3503, Grays 3520, Inland 3526, Renton 3552, Seattle 3558, Tacoma 3567
West Virginia: Community 3579, Parkersburg 3587
Wisconsin: Bemis 3598, Chipstone 3605, Community 3607, Green Bay 3619, Incourage 3623, Jeffris 3624, Johnson 3625, Milwaukee 3637, Murray 3638, Raibrook 3649, Rowland 3652, Spire 3661

Historical activities

California: Muckel 336, **Wilkinson 463**
Delaware: Chaney 628
Florida: Walter 837
Hawaii: Castle 930
Illinois: Pritzker 1078
Indiana: Orange 1184
Massachusetts: Vingo 1561
New York: Alfiero 2031, Aresty 2041, Rhodes 2381, Solomon 2436
North Carolina: Bolick 2531
Pennsylvania: Ferree 2944
Tennessee: HCA 3139
Texas: King 3275

History/archaeology

Alaska: CIRI 33
New York: Family 2153, **Kress 2263**, Littauer 2282, **Wenner 2502**
North Carolina: Cumberland 2541

Ohio: Murphy 2745
Oregon: PGE 2867
Texas: Coastal 3196, Meadows 3296, Northen 3306, Summerlee 3361
Washington: Community 3503
Wisconsin: **Bradley 3601**

Holistic medicine

Arizona: Weil 65
Tennessee: Baptist 3122

Home accessibility modifications

Rhode Island: Shaw's 3092

Homeless

Alabama: Black 4, Community 10
Arizona: Hill 48, Webb 64
Arkansas: Cabe 67
California: Ahmanson 77, California 137, California 140, Community 157, Community 161, Community 162, Gilmore 221, Gumbiner 236, **Hilton 251**, Lesher 299, Marin 309, Parsons 359, Patron 363, Sacramento 391, San Luis 393, Silicon 408, Sonora 420, Taper 433, Weingart 456
Colorado: Colorado 483, **Daniels 488**, El Pomar 492, Hunter 508, Rose 528, Summit 537
Connecticut: Community 562, Connecticut 564
District of Columbia: **Butler 655**, Cafritz 656, **Hill 664**, Himmelfarb 665, Jovid 668
Florida: Bank 695, Bush 712, Community 725, Landwirth 775, Pinellas 801, Southwest 823
Georgia: Abreu 846, EZ 874, Tull 917
Illinois: Chicago 982, Community 988, Evanston 1012, Field 1014, Pierce 1074, Polk 1075, Prince 1076, Siragusa 1096, VNA 1107, Washington 1112
Indiana: Community 1132, Community 1134, Henry 1158
Iowa: Siouxland 1240, Stebens 1242, Wahlert 1244
Kansas: Topeka 1279
Louisiana: Community 1306
Maryland: Ceres 1354, **Cohen 1355**, Community 1360, Dresher 1370, Fowler 1372
Massachusetts: Clipper 1449, Essex 1464, Fireman 1469, Kelsey 1493, Liberty 1502, Linden 1504, Melville 1511, Smith 1546
Michigan: Ann Arbor 1576, Grand Rapids 1615, McGregor 1638, Midland 1642, Sanilac 1663, Schmuckal 1664, Skillman 1666, Van Andel 1669
Minnesota: Duluth 1693, Frey 1696, Larsen 1711, Minneapolis 1717, Phillips 1728
Missouri: Roblee 1809
Nebraska: Midlands 1848, Woods 1857
Nevada: Nevada 1867
New Hampshire: Foundation 1885, Lindsay 1890
New Jersey: Borden 1910, Hyde 1944, **Johnson 1949**, MCJ 1965
New Mexico: Con 2011, Frost 2012, Santa Fe 2017
New York: Clark 2096, **Clark 2098**, Community 2107, Cummings 2122, **Discount 2139**, Langeloth 2267, Litwin 2283, **MetLife 2307**, New York 2326, NYSE 2336, Rapoport 2373, Sidewalk 2422, Troy 2474, van Ameringen 2483, Western 2503
North Carolina: Community 2539, Cumberland 2541, Glenn 2560, North Carolina 2599, Reidsville 2611, Strowd 2633
North Dakota: North Dakota 2653
Ohio: Akron 2655, Cincinnati 2679, Fairfield 2696, Johnson 2714, Marion 2733, Murphy 2744, Nord 2754, Nordson 2755, O'Neill 2760, Osteopathic 2762, Saint 2770, Springfield 2787, Stark 2788, White 2800
Oklahoma: Hardesty 2814, Hille 2816
Oregon: Benton 2835
Pennsylvania: Connelly 2926, Drueding 2936, First 2948, Fourjay 2953, Independence 2976, North 3006, Phoenixville 3014, Staunton 3044, Union 3051
Rhode Island: Kimball 3079
Tennessee: Baptist 3122, Wilson 3157
Texas: Abell 3160, Baron 3171, Baxter 3173, Coastal 3196, Dallas 3209, Embrey 3222, Fluor 3235, Frees 3238, Hoblitzelle 3262, Holloway 3264, King 3275, McDermott 3293, Meadows 3296, Moore 3299, Orsinger 3310, Rockwell 3338, Sterling 3358, Sturgis 3360, Waco 3378, Wright 3386
Virginia: Launders 3447, Lynchburg 3454
Washington: Community 3503, **Gates 3516**, Safeco 3554, Tacoma 3567
West Virginia: Eastern 3580
Wisconsin: Cornerstone 3608, Green Bay 3619, La Crosse 3631, Milwaukee 3637, Pettit 3645, Stateline 3663

Homeless, human services

Arizona: Stardust 63
California: Ahmanson 77, **Applied 88**, Bank 99, Bothin 120, California 140, CEC 146, Fremont 207, **Hilton 251**, Muckel 336, Pacific 355, Parsons 359, Sacramento 391, Siebel 404, Silicon 407, Sterling 426, Weingart 456
Colorado: **Daniels 488**, El Pomar 492, **First 496**
Connecticut: Community 563, Connecticut 564, Ensworth 575, NewAlliance 595
Delaware: CenturyLink-Clarke 627
District of Columbia: Cafritz 656, Himmelfarb 665, Meyer 672
Florida: Alpha 687, Bank 695, Batchelor 697, Chapman 717, Cohen 721, Lennar 778
Georgia: Colston 865, Tull 917
Idaho: Angels 943
Illinois: Brach 973, Chicago 982, Community 988, Evanston 1012, Field 1014, Pierce 1074, Polk 1075, Seymour 1091, Siragusa 1096, Stern 1100
Kansas: Topeka 1279
Louisiana: Community 1306
Maryland: Fowler 1372
Massachusetts: Arbella 1426, Clipper 1449, East 1460, Fireman 1469, Liberty 1502, Linden 1504, Melville 1511, Smith 1546
Michigan: Ann Arbor 1576, Masco 1637, Perrigo 1655, Skillman 1666, Steelcase 1667
Minnesota: Duluth 1693, Thorpe 1745
Mississippi: Ergon 1761
Missouri: Fabick 1788, Hall 1793
Nebraska: Mutual 1850
Nevada: Nevada 1867
New Jersey: Borden 1910, Harbourton 1936, Hyde 1944, **Johnson 1949**
New Mexico: Frost 2012, Santa Fe 2017
New York: Community 2108, Deerfield 2132, **Deutsche 2134**, Dreitzer 2144, Mutual 2317, New York 2325, New York 2326, Sidewalk 2422, Stark 2449
North Carolina: **Bank 2524**, Community 2539, Cumberland 2541
Ohio: Brethen 2671, Charities 2678, Mathile 2734, Murphy 2744, Osteopathic 2762, Stark 2788, White 2800
Oregon: PGE 2867
Pennsylvania: Community 2925, Connelly 2926, Fourjay 2953, Union 3051
Rhode Island: Kimball 3079, Rhode Island 3089, Textron 3093
Texas: Coastal 3196, Fluor 3235, Goldsbury 3241, Meadows 3296, NuStar 3307, Shelter 3349, Sterling 3358, Sturgis 3360, Trull 3373, Wright 3386
Vermont: Vermont 3417
Virginia: Lynchburg 3454, MAXIMUS 3457
Washington: Blue 3498, Community 3503, Grays 3520, Medina 3542, Renton 3552, Safeco 3554, Seattle 3558, Tacoma 3567
Wisconsin: Johnson 3625, Keller 3626, Milwaukee 3637, Sauey 3655, Stateline 3663

Horticulture/garden clubs

Florida: Wright 845
Michigan: Meijer 1639
Nebraska: Kearney 1842
Pennsylvania: EQT 2940

Hospitals (general)

Alabama: Caring 7
Arizona: Hill 48, Jasam 50
Arkansas: Cabe 67, Frueauff 70, Wal-Mart 74
California: Allergan 80, Beynon 113, Bonner 118, Burns 136, California 140, Chartwell 150, Community 162, Curci 173, Douglas 186, Fusenot 211, **Gellert 214**, Gellert 215, HealthCare 244, Hoag 253, Lansing 290, Laulhere 292, Livingston 303, **Mattel 312**, Mazda 313, Menard 327, Metta 329, Mulago 337, Patron 363, Philanthropy 368, Pritzker 375, Smith 417, Sonora 420, UniHealth 444, Van Nuys 447, Versacare 448, Wasserman 453, Weingart 456, Wrather 469
Colorado: El Pomar 492, Kaufmann 509
Connecticut: Abramowitz 548, Aetna 550, Aronson 552, Bender 554, Community 563, Dennett 570, Floren 578, Hoffman 585, Long 588, Meriden 591, Palmer 600, **Praxair 606**, SBM 611, Wood 619
Delaware: Palmer 644, Pinkerton 645
Florida: Ansin 689, Applebaum 690, Batchelor 697, Bi-Lo/Winn-Dixie 700, Brown 707, Community 725, Dahl 731, Dunspaugh-Dalton 738, Glazer 750, Greenburg 752, Kantner 764, Kramer 773, Moos 790, Reinhold 808, Setzer 818, **Skelly 820**, Speer 824, Tippett 833, Walter 837, Wollowick 843
Georgia: Atlanta 852, Camp-Younts 861, **Coca 864**, **Imlay 888**, Katz 889, Livingston 893, Marshall 895
Illinois: C.W.B. 978, Children's 983, Comer 987, Community 991, Diener 1000, Foglia 1015, Katten 1042, Kenny's 1044, Parr 1072, Pattis 1073, Prince 1076, Pritzker 1079, Rosen 1086, Siragusa 1096, Square 1099, Ward 1111, Webb 1113
Indiana: Ball 1121, Cole 1127, Community 1131, Crosser 1139, Dearborn 1141, Jasper 1160, Marshall 1176, Rush 1192, WellPoint 1206
Iowa: HNI 1223
Kansas: Hansen 1259, Insurance 1261, Miller 1269, Sarver 1275, Sunderland 1278
Louisiana: Albemarle 1298, Blue 1302
Maine: Alfond 1324, Hannaford 1330
Maryland: DelSignore 1368, Henson 1378, Israelson 1380, Izzo 1381, Kahlert 1383, Kay 1384, RCM & D 1406, Wolpoff 1417
Massachusetts: Alden 1425, Arbella 1426, Calderwood 1444, Demoulas 1458, Fireman 1469, Gardinor 1473, Herbert 1481, **Iacocca 1487**, **Foundation 1489**, Jaffe 1491, Kittredge 1496, McNeice 1509, New 1518, Rogers 1536, Sanborn 1540, Smith 1546, Tye 1558, Webber 1563, Weber 1564, Webster 1565, Windover 1568
Michigan: **Allen 1573**, Baiardi 1577, Carls 1582, Dart 1594, Hillsdale 1620, Morley 1644, Perrigo 1655, Van Andel 1669, Webber 1673, Wege 1674, Wilson 1675
Minnesota: **Andersen 1678**, Bentson 1684, Dayton 1690, Greystone 1700, **King 1708**, Land 1710, Robina 1734
Mississippi: Biloxi 1755, Ergon 1761
Missouri: Brace 1777, Butler 1780, Centene 1782, Fabick 1788, Green 1790, Hallmark 1794
Nebraska: Hirschfeld 1839, Kearney 1842, Lienemann 1846, Midlands 1848
Nevada: Caesars 1860, Webb 1875
New Hampshire: Finlay 1884

New Jersey: Bauer 1906, **Berrie 1908**, Capozzi 1918, Catholic 1919, Fortune 1931, Hummingbird 1943, Hyde 1944, Integra 1945, **Johnson 1949**, Jones 1950, Mandelbaum 1962, Meyer 1967, Neisloss 1970, Pierson 1976, Point 1977, **Rippel 1982**, Schwarz 1991, Taub 2000
New Mexico: Phillips 2015
New York: **American 2034**, Beach 2058, Box 2068, Brooks 2075, Brownstone 2077, Burton 2080, Carvel 2088, Coach 2100, Coleman 2104, Community 2107, Community 2110, Cramer 2117, **Cummings 2120**, Cummings 2122, Cutco 2123, Deerfield 2132, **Deutsche 2134**, Diller 2137, DiMenna 2138, Ferraioli 2156, Fisher 2157, Gershwind 2174, Gifford 2177, Goldstein 2184, Hallingby 2201, Helmsley 2207, Heyman 2212, Hudson 2223, Hycliff 2226, **Institute 2233**, Jaharis 2236, Johnson 2241, Klingenstein 2256, Klingenstein 2257, Lane 2266, Liberman 2279, Litwin 2283, Marshall 2293, McGonagle 2299, Miller 2308, Mindich 2309, Morgan 2315, Mule 2316, Neu 2323, Northern 2331, Norwich 2332, Oestreicher 2337, Perelman 2355, Polisseni 2361, Pollock 2362, Price 2367, Regals 2377, Ring 2384, Rose 2392, Rosenthal 2395, Sandy 2404, Schafer 2406, SDA 2414, Sherman 2419, Society 2434, Stardust 2448, Tisch 2468, Trump 2476, Warwick 2495, Wegman 2497, Weissman 2500, Ziff 2515
North Carolina: **Bank 2524**, French 2554, Helb 2568, Hoffman 2569, Kistler 2579, Merrick 2591, Plansoen 2608, Sloan 2628, Southern 2630
North Dakota: MDU 2652
Ohio: American 2656, Anderson 2658, Athens 2662, Brentwood 2670, **Cardinal 2677**, Cliffs 2681, Coshocton 2686, Dater 2687, Dodero 2691, **Eaton 2692**, Fairfield 2696, **Lerner 2722**, Lincoln 2724, Murphy 2745, Muskingum 2747, National 2748, Ohio 2756, **OMNOVA 2759**, Reinberger 2765, Richland 2767, Troy 2794
Oregon: Jeld 2852, Michael 2862
Pennsylvania: Ames 2884, Betz 2895, Charter 2912, Dozzi 2935, Drueding 2936, Groff 2960, Grundy 2962, Highmark 2968, Laros 2982, McLean 2997, Packer 3008, Palumbo 3009, Patterson 3010, **Respironics 3023**, Rossin 3028, Saramar 3029
Rhode Island: Bird 3064, Bliss 3065, CVS 3068, Hasbro 3077, Kimball 3079, Koffler 3081, Schwarz 3090, Textron 3093, Washington 3095
South Carolina: Daniel 3101
South Dakota: Brenden-Mann 3114
Tennessee: First 3135, Regal 3151, Wilson 3157
Texas: Augur 3168, **Bolivar 3179**, Carter 3190, Coastal 3196, Constantin 3202, Dunn 3216, Elkins 3220, Elkins 3221, Fasken 3229, Fish 3233, Greentree 3244, Hamman 3248, Heavin 3253, Henderson 3255, Hillcrest 3261, Hoblitzelle 3262, Holloway 3264, McDermott 3293, McIntyre 3294, McKee 3295, Potts 3323, Richter 3337, Sterling 3358, Sturgis 3360
Utah: Eskuche 3393, Schmidt 3403
Vermont: Merchants 3414
Virginia: Denit 3435, **Truland 3482**
Washington: Anderson 3492, Community 3503, Dimmer 3506, Moccasin 3545, Shemanski 3560, Tacoma 3567, Wilkens 3573
Wisconsin: **Baird 3595**, Incourage 3623, Neese 3639, Pettit 3645, Schlegel 3656, Windhover 3668
Wyoming: Cody 3672, Furrer 3674

Hospitals (specialty)

Arizona: Ottosen 56
Arkansas: Cabe 67, Delta 68
California: Dickinson 180, Found 201, HealthCare 244, Kellerman 277, Patron 363, Pritzker 375, Tang 432, UniHealth 444
Colorado: Fox 499
Connecticut: Aronson 552, Meriden 591, Robbins 607
Florida: DiMare 737, Holloway 759, Speer 824, Stafford 825, Turock 835
Georgia: Colston 865
Illinois: de Kay 998, Frye 1019, Luehring 1052, Parr 1072
Kansas: Koch 1264, Miller 1269, Morgan 1270
Massachusetts: Cole 1451, **Kahn 1492**
Michigan: Acheson 1571, Golden 1613, Van 1670
Mississippi: Feild 1762
Missouri: Millstone 1801, Woods 1821
Nebraska: Hawkins 1838
Nevada: Troesh 1874
New Jersey: **Rippel 1982**
New York: Abramson 2024, Alfiero 2031, Andor 2037, Carvel 2088, Cramer 2117, Johnson 2241, Niehaus 2330, Robbins 2386
North Carolina: Christopher 2537, Gordon 2562, Roberts 2617
Ohio: Freygang 2704, Keeler 2715, Nippert 2751, Skyler 2784
Pennsylvania: Mendel 2999, Nesh 3004
Rhode Island: Hecht 3078
Texas: Alcon 3162, Edwards 3219, Kinder 3274, Smith 3355
Washington: Anderson 3492

Housing/shelter

Alabama: BBVA 3, Central 8
Arkansas: Wal-Mart 74
California: Allergan 80, **Applied 88**, Bank 99, Clif 152, Community 157, Cowell 168, Genentech 216, Glide 226, GSF 235, **Hilton 251**, Humboldt 257, i.am.angel 259, McMinn 323, **Packard 357**, Santa Barbara 394, Silicon 407, Weingart 456
Colorado: Community 484, **First 496**, Fox 499, Pikes 525
Connecticut: Fisher 577, NewAlliance 595, SBM 611
Delaware: Longwood 639
District of Columbia: **Butler 655**, Cafritz 656, Graham 663
Florida: Bush 712, Community 723, Community 725, Community 726, Gate 749, Munroe 793, Pinellas 801
Georgia: **Georgia 878**
Idaho: Angels 943
Illinois: Allegretti 958, Brach 973, Community 990, Dunham 1007, FDC 1013, Lyon 1054, Oak Park 1068, Pierce 1074
Indiana: Central 1126, Community 1130, Unity 1201, Vectren 1202
Kansas: Capitol 1251, Douglas 1256
Kentucky: Blue 1282
Louisiana: Beaird 1301, Community 1306, Entergy 1308, New Orleans 1316
Maryland: Community 1358, **Weinberg 1416**
Massachusetts: Boynton 1437, Brooks 1440, Community 1453, East 1460, Eastern 1461, Makepeace 1507, Santander 1541
Michigan: Community 1591, Delano 1596, Great 1618, Masco 1637
Minnesota: **Andersen 1678**, Edina 1694, Frey 1696, Marbrook 1713, Minneapolis 1717, Northwest 1723, Opus 1724, Sundance 1742, Target 1744
Mississippi: Mississippi 1769
Missouri: Anheuser 1774, Butler 1780, Moneta 1802, Roblee 1809
Montana: Lynn 1827
Nebraska: Weitz 1855
Nevada: Stout 1872
New Hampshire: Finlay 1884, Woodbury 1897
New Jersey: Catholic 1919, Hudson 1942, Roma 1984
New Mexico: Santa Fe 2017
New York: **Abba's 2021**, Assurant 2047, Bikuben 2064, **Deutsche 2134**, Hagedorn 2200, **JPMorgan 2242**, Legacy 2274, **MetLife 2307**, NYSE 2336, Project 2368, Stark 2449, Troy 2474
North Carolina: Babcock 2521, **Bank 2524**, Reynolds 2614
North Dakota: Fargo 2649
Ohio: American 2656, **Eaton 2692**, Fairfield 2696, Fifth 2699, Home 2712, Knoll 2719, Nordson 2755, Sears 2781
Oregon: Simple 2871
Pennsylvania: Bayer 2888, Chase 2913, Claneil 2918, North 3006, Phoenixville 3014, Scranton 3031, Wells 3055
Puerto Rico: Puerto Rico 3061
Rhode Island: Citizens 3067, Rhode Island 3089, Textron 3093, Washington 3095
Tennessee: HCA 3139
Texas: Baron 3171, Coastal 3196, Fisch 3232, Fluor 3235, King 3275, Littauer 3283, Permian 3316, Plass 3322, **Radler 3330**
Utah: Mendenhall 3398
Vermont: Vermont 3417
Virginia: Arlington 3421, Capital 3426, Pruden 3473
Washington: Bainbridge 3494, Medina 3542, Miller 3544, Renton 3552, Seattle 3558, Yakima 3576
Wisconsin: Alliant 3592, Brown 3602, Dudley 3610

Housing/shelter, aging

Texas: Topfer 3372

Housing/shelter, development

California: California 137, Marin 309, Parsons 359, Sacramento 391, Taper 433
Colorado: El Pomar 492
Connecticut: Connecticut 564, Ensworth 575, Goldstone 581
Delaware: Delaware 630, Kendeda 636
District of Columbia: Cafritz 656
Florida: Batchelor 697, Selby 816
Georgia: Atlanta 852, EZ 874, **Georgia 878**, Tull 917
Illinois: Chicago 982, Driehaus 1002, Evanston 1012, Omron 1070, Square 1099
Indiana: Brotherhood 1123, Vectren 1202
Kansas: Hutchinson 1260
Louisiana: Albemarle 1298, Entergy 1308, Pugh 1318, Steinhagen 1320
Maryland: Fowler 1372, Rembrandt 1407
Massachusetts: Clipper 1449, Farnsworth 1465, Hyams 1486, Melville 1511, Parker 1523, Phelps 1528, Riley 1534, **Xeric 1570**
Michigan: Grand Rapids 1615, Kalamazoo 1626, Knight 1630, Masco 1637
Minnesota: Butler 1688, Duluth 1693, Frey 1696, McKnight 1715, Midcontinent 1716, Rochester 1735, Thorpe 1745
Missouri: Anheuser 1774, Curry 1784, Hall 1793, Truman 1817
Nebraska: Weitz 1855, Woods 1857
New Hampshire: Bean 1878
New Jersey: Borden 1910
New York: Chautauqua 2091, **Credit 2118**, **Deutsche 2134**, **Ford 2160**, Grant 2190, **JPMorgan 2242**, New York 2325, New York 2326, Warwick 2495, Western 2503
North Carolina: Cumberland 2541
Ohio: American 2656, **Eaton 2692**, Gund 2708, Hamilton 2710, Morgan 2739, Murphy 2744, National 2748, Ohio 2756, Stark 2788
Oregon: Meyer 2861, Portland 2868
Pennsylvania: EQT 2940, McCune 2993, Union 3051, Wells 3055
Rhode Island: Citizens 3067
Tennessee: Community 3129, Davis 3130, HCA 3139, Lyndhurst 3145
Texas: Constantin 3202, Frees 3238, Hillcrest 3261, Hoblitzelle 3262, Meadows 3296
Virginia: Community 3433, Oak 3466

Ullrich 1106, Walter 1110, Ward 1111, Webb 1113, Woods 1117, Zell 1119

Indiana: Auer 1120, Ball 1121, Blackford 1122, Brotherhood 1123, Brown 1124, Cass 1125, Central 1126, Community 1128, Community 1129, Community 1130, Community 1131, Community 1132, Community 1133, Community 1134, Community 1135, Community 1136, Community 1137, Crosser 1139, Darling 1140, Dearborn 1141, Decatur 1142, DeKalb 1144, Fairbanks 1145, Fayette 1146, Froderman 1148, Glick 1150, Globe 1151, Greene 1152, Hancock 1154, Harrison 1155, Health 1156, Hendricks 1157, Henry 1158, Hoover 1159, Jasper 1160, Jennings 1162, Johnson 1163, Koch 1167, Kuhne 1169, LaGrange 1170, Legacy 1171, Leighton 1172, Madison 1175, Marshall 1176, Noble 1179, Northern 1180, Ohio 1181, Old 1182, OneAmerica 1183, Orange 1184, Owen 1185, Parke 1186, Porter 1187, Portland 1188, Putnam 1189, Ripley 1191, Rush 1192, Seger 1194, Tipton 1198, Union 1200, Unity 1201, Wabash 1203, Wells 1207, Whitley 1209

Iowa: Ahrens 1210, Aviva 1211, Clarinda 1214, Community 1215, Community 1217, Community 1218, Hall-Perrine 1222, HNI 1223, Holthues 1224, Iowa 1226, Johnson 1228, Maytag 1229, McElroy 1230, On 1233, Siouxland 1240, South 1241, United 1243, Wahlert 1244, Woodward 1247, Zimmerman 1249

Kansas: Beach 1250, Capitol 1251, Collective 1253, Damon 1254, Douglas 1256, Emporia 1257, Hutchinson 1260, Insurance 1261, Manhattan 1268, Miller 1269, Morgan 1270, Salina 1274, Sarver 1275, Skillbuilders 1277, Topeka 1279, Western 1281

Kentucky: Blue 1282, Brown 1283, Campbell 1285, Community 1286, Etscorn 1287, Gheens 1288, J & L 1291, Lift 1293, Steel 1294, Trim 1295

Louisiana: Albemarle 1298, Beaird 1301, Clement 1305, Community 1306, Freeman 1309, Glazer 1311, Grigsby 1312, Heymann 1313, New Orleans 1316, Pennington 1317, Pugh 1318, Steinhagen 1320, Wiener 1322

Maine: Alfond 1324, Borman 1325, Golden 1329, Hannaford 1330, Kennebec 1332, King 1333, Libra 1334, Lynam 1335, Narragansett 1337, Sewall 1339, Somers 1341, **Walter 1343**

Maryland: Adams 1345, Battye 1348, Bunting 1352, **Casey 1353**, Ceres 1354, **Cohen 1355**, Commonweal 1356, Community 1357, Community 1358, Community 1359, Community 1360, Dahan 1364, Dresher 1370, Dupkin 1371, Fowler 1372, Freeman 1373, Goldseker 1374, Hirschhorn 1379, Kahlert 1383, Kay 1384, Kirk 1386, Macht 1388, Marriott 1390, Meyerhoff 1392, Meyerhoff 1393, Middendorf 1394, Mid-Shore 1395, Moore 1396, **Morningstar 1397**, Murthynayak 1399, Mustard 1400, Osprey 1403, Straus 1410, Tauber 1412, Trawick 1414, Tucker 1415, **Weinberg 1416**, Zickler 1419

Massachusetts: **A Child 1420**, Aaron 1421, Arbella 1426, Archibald 1427, Babson 1429, **Barakat 1432**, Berkman 1434, Bilezikian 1435, Blue 1436, Boynton 1437, Brooks 1440, Cabot 1442, Cabot 1443, Cape Cod 1445, Chase 1446, Clarke 1448, Clipper 1449, Cogan 1450, Community 1453, Currents 1455, Davis 1457, Demoulas 1458, East 1460, Eastern 1461, **Elsevier 1463**, Essex 1464, Felix 1466, Fireman 1469, Fish 1470, Francis 1471, Gardinor 1473, **Germeshausen 1474**, Gordon 1475, Gould 1477, Grinspoon 1479, Hazard 1480, Herbert 1481, Horne 1484, Howard 1485, Hyams 1486, Inavale 1488, Jacobson 1490, Jaffe 1491, Krieger 1497, Levy 1501, Liberty 1502, Lowell 1505, Massachusetts 1508, Meelia 1510, Memorial 1512, MENTOR 1513, Miller 1516, Mount 1517, New 1518, Newburyport 1519, Noonan 1520, Noonan 1521, Pardoe 1522, Parker 1523, Perpetual 1526, Peters 1527, Rice 1533, Riley 1534, Rodman 1535, Rogers 1536, Sailors' 1539, Santander 1541, Sudbury 1551, Swartz 1553, United 1559, Wadleigh 1562, Webber 1563, Weber 1564, Webster 1565, Wells 1566, Williams 1567, Windover 1568

Michigan: Acheson 1571, Alix 1572, Alro 1574, Ann Arbor 1576, Baiardi 1577, Bay Harbor 1578, Binda 1579, Branch 1580, Capital 1581, Charlevoix 1583, Chelsea 1584, Community 1586, Community 1587, Community 1588, Community 1589, Community 1590, Community 1591, Dalton 1592, Dana 1593, Dart 1594, Delano 1596, Dow 1597, DTE 1598, Farver 1601, Farwell 1602, Frankel 1604, Fremont 1607, Frey 1608, Frey 1609, Gilmore 1612, Grand Rapids 1615, Granger 1617, Hillsdale 1620, Jackson 1623, Jubilee 1624, Kahn 1625, Keller 1627, Knight 1630, **Kresge 1631**, Lear 1632, Lenawee 1634, Mardigian 1635, Marquette 1636, Masco 1637, McGregor 1638, Merillat 1640, Michell 1641, Midland 1642, Mills 1643, Morley 1644, **Mott 1645**, Mount Pleasant 1647, Nartel 1648, Oleson 1649, Onequest 1650, Page, 1651, Perrigo 1655, Petoskey 1656, Pokagon 1657, RNR 1659, Saginaw 1662, Sanilac 1663, Schmuckal 1664, Skillman 1666, Steelcase 1667, Technical 1668, Van Andel 1669, Van 1670, Vanderweide 1671, Von 1672, Webber 1673, Wege 1674, Wilson 1675

Minnesota: **Andersen 1678**, Andreas 1679, Avocet 1680, Beim 1683, Best 1685, Boss 1686, Briggs 1687, Butler 1688, Cargill 1689, Dayton 1690, Duluth 1693, Edina 1694, Frey 1696, General 1697, Greystone 1700, Initiative 1703, Johnson 1705, **Kaplan 1707**, Land 1710, Larsen 1711, Marbrook 1713, Midcontinent 1716, Minneapolis 1717, **Mosaic 1718**, Nash 1720, Neilson 1721, Opus 1724, Phillips 1728, **Porter 1729**, RBC 1730, Redwood 1731, Regis 1732, Riverway 1733, Rochester 1735, Schulze 1738, Securian 1739, **St. Jude 1741**, Sundance 1742, Target 1744, Thorpe 1745, **Trust 1746**, WCA 1749, Wedum 1750, Winona 1753

Mississippi: Community 1759, Ergon 1761, Feild 1762, Gulf 1764, King's 1766, Mississippi 1768, Mississippi 1769, Walker 1772

Missouri: Albers/Kuhn 1773, Anheuser 1774, Boylan 1776, Brace 1777, Centene 1782, Community 1783, Curry 1784, Dunn 1787, Fabick 1788, Green 1790, Hall 1793, Hallmark 1794, Humphreys 1795, Kuhn 1798, Laclede 1799, Millstone 1801, Moneta 1802, **Monsanto 1803**, Mungenast 1804, Musgrave 1805, Nichols 1806, Pendergast 1807, Speas 1813, Tilles 1815, Trudy 1816, Truman 1817, Woods 1821

Montana: High 1825, Lynn 1827, Montana 1828, Sample 1829, Silver 1830

Nebraska: Cooper 1834, Fremont 1836, Grand Island 1837, Hawkins 1838, Hirschfeld 1839, Holland 1840, Home 1841, Kearney 1842, Kiewit 1843, Kim 1844, Lexington 1845, Lienemann 1846, Lincoln 1847, Midlands 1848, Mid-Nebraska 1849, Mutual 1850, Quivey 1853, Storz 1854, Weitz 1855, Woods 1857

Nevada: Bendon 1859, Caesars 1860, Doyle 1861, Engelstad 1863, Jaquish 1865, Maddux 1866, Nevada 1867, Parasol 1868, **Reynolds 1869**, **Tang 1873**, Troesh 1874, Webb 1875, Wells 1876

New Hampshire: Alexander 1877, Bean 1878, Charter 1880, Finlay 1884, Ham 1887, Lindsay 1890, Penates 1893, Woodbury 1897

New Jersey: Banbury 1904, Bard 1905, Beer 1907, **Berrie 1908**, Borden 1910, Bouras 1911, Brotherton 1914, Campbell 1917, Catholic 1919, Earle 1920, Eisai 1921, Evans 1925, Fairbanks 1927, Fenwick 1929, Fournier 1932, Gibson 1934, Harbourton 1936, Hawthorne 1937, Hudson 1942, Hummingbird 1943, Hyde 1944, **International 1946**, Jones 1950, Kish 1953, Klatskin 1954, Leavens 1959, Levitt 1960, MacDonald 1961, Marcon 1963, Marino 1964, MCJ 1965, Meyer 1967, Nandansons 1969, Neisloss 1970, Pierson 1976, Point 1977, Princeton 1979, **Ramapo 1981**, Roma 1984, Rowan 1986, **Sanofi 1988**, Schumann 1990, Snyder 1995, Syms 1999, Taub 2000, Tufenkian 2001, Turrell 2002, Unilever 2003, Westfield 2004

New Mexico: Albuquerque 2006, Chase 2009, Frost 2012, Garfield 2013, Maddox 2014, Phillips 2015, Pierce 2016, Santa Fe 2017, Simon 2018

New York: 100 2019, Abelard 2022, **Abraham 2023**, Abramson 2024, Adirondack 2027, **Alavi 2030**, Alfiero 2031, Allyn 2032, American 2033, **American 2034**, Andor 2037, Aresty 2041, Assurant 2047, Atlantic 2048, **AVI 2051**, Barker 2054, Beach 2058, Belfer 2059, Blum 2067, Box 2068, Brillo-Sonnino 2070, Broadcasters 2071, **Bronfman 2074**, Brownstone 2077, Bullitt 2079, Carson 2086, Carvel 2088, Century 2089, Chapman 2090, Chautauqua 2091, **Clark 2098**, Clark 2099, Cohen 2103, Community 2107, Community 2109, Community 2110, Community 2113, **Credit 2118**, **Cummings 2120**, Cummings 2122, D'Agostino 2124, Dartley 2128, Dean 2130, Deerfield 2132, deForest 2133, **Deutsche 2134**, Diller 2137, DiMenna 2138, Dobkin 2140, Donner 2142, Dreitzer 2144, Dreyfus 2145, Eastern 2148, Farash 2154, Fascitelli 2155, Ferraioli 2156, Fleischer 2158, **Ford 2160**, French 2165, Gebbie 2170, Gellert 2171, Giant 2176, Gifford 2177, **Gimprich 2180**, **Goldman 2181**, Goldman 2183, Grace 2189, Grant 2190, Gurwin 2195, **Gutfleish 2196**, Hagedorn 2200, Hallingby 2201, Halper 2202, Heisman 2206, Helmsley 2207, Henle 2208, Heyman 2212, Hochstein 2216, Hoyt 2221, Hultquist 2225, Hycliff 2226, **IBM 2227**, IF 2228, Istel 2234, Jaharis 2236, Johnson 2239, Johnson 2240, Johnson 2241, Kanas 2244, **Kaplan 2245**, Karmazin 2246, Kaylie 2247, Keet 2248, **King 2251**, Klee 2253, **Klein 2254**, Klingenstein 2257, Knapp 2259, Laffont 2264, Lee 2270, Lee 2271, Leeds 2272, Leeman 2273, Legacy 2274, Levy 2276, Liberman 2279, Litwin 2283, **M.A.C. 2287**, Marine 2289, Marks 2291, MBIA 2297, McGonagle 2299, McGraw 2300, Mendell 2303, Menezes 2304, Mercer 2305, **MetLife 2307**, Monteforte 2310, Moore 2311, Moore 2312, Moore 2313, Moore 2314, Morgan 2315, Mule 2316, Mutual 2317, **Nash 2320**, National 2321, New Yankee 2324, New York 2325, New York 2326, New York 2327, Newman 2328, Nicholson 2329, Norwich 2332, NYSE 2336, Oestreicher 2337, Oishei 2340, Ong 2341, Palette 2347, Paulson 2351, Perelman 2355, **Pershing 2356**, Pollock 2362, Purple 2369, Rapoport 2373, Regals 2377, Reich 2378, Resnick 2379, Rich 2382, Ring 2384, Roche 2388, Rose 2392, Rose 2393, Rosenberg 2394, Ruffin 2400, Samberg 2403, Sandy 2404, Schafer 2406, Scherman 2409, Schmitt 2410, Schnurmacher 2411, Schwartz 2413, SDA 2414, Shalom 2416, Sherman 2419, Singer 2424, Snyder 2433, Society 2434, Source 2440, Spektor 2442, Sprague 2444, Stardust 2448, Sugarman 2450, Summers 2452, Tananbaum 2456, Tananbaum 2457, Teagle 2460, Thompson 2461, Tiger 2464, Tisch 2468, Tisch 2469, Touradji 2471, Troy 2474, Truman 2475, Trump 2476, **Unbound 2480**, van Ameringen 2482, Vidda 2485, Vogler 2487, Wachenheim 2489, Wachtell, 2490, Wagner 2491, Warwick 2495, Wegman 2497, Weil, 2498, Weissman 2500, Wells 2501, Western 2503, Widgeon 2505, Woldar 2509, Wolk 2510, Woodcock 2511, Yudelson 2514, Ziff 2515

North Carolina: Adams 2516, Adams 2517, Bailey 2522, Balin 2523, **Bank 2524**, Bettman 2528, Billingsley 2530, Bolick 2531, Borun 2532, Community 2538, Community 2539, Community 2540, Cumberland 2541, Dalton 2542, Duncan 2547, Fairfield 2551, Fortson 2553, Gambrill 2556, Ghidotti 2558, Glass 2559, Glenn 2560, Goodrich 2561, Gordon 2562, Griffin 2563, Hanes 2565, Howe 2570, Humphrey 2571, Hunt 2572, Hunter 2573, **Johnson 2574**, Kitselman 2580, Kramer 2581, **Laffin 2583**, Levine 2584, Linsmayer 2585, McCausland 2589, Meserve 2592, Meyer 2593, Moretz 2595, Niessen 2598, North Carolina 2599, Odell 2602, Olin 2603, Outer 2604, Paddock 2605, Perkin 2607, Polk 2609, Reynolds 2614,

Rogers 2618, Rose 2619, Sanders 2620, Shingleton 2624, Short 2625, Simpson 2626, Smith 2629, State 2632, Stuart 2634, Symmes 2636, Tannenbaum 2637, Templin 2638, Toleo 2640, VF 2642, Wann 2643, Woodson 2644

North Dakota: Community 2648, Fargo 2649, MDU 2652, North Dakota 2653

Ohio: Abington 2654, Akron 2655, American 2656, Ar-Hale 2661, Athens 2662, Austin 2663, Bates 2665, Bernard 2667, **Bingham 2668**, Brethen 2671, Building 2675, Calhoun 2676, Charities 2678, Cincinnati 2679, Cliffs 2681, Community 2682, Community 2683, Community 2684, Community 2685, Dater 2687, Dayton 2688, Delaware 2689, Dodero 2691, **Eaton 2692**, Eaton 2693, Emery 2694, Evans 2695, Fairfield 2696, Ferro 2697, Fibus 2698, Fifth 2699, Findlay 2700, Freygang 2704, Gund 2708, Haile, 2709, Hamilton 2710, Johnson 2714, Kettering 2716, KeyBank 2717, Knoll 2719, Kulas 2721, Licking 2723, Llewellyn 2725, Maltz 2727, Mayerson 2735, McGregor 2736, Middletown 2737, Morgan 2739, Murphy 2744, Murphy 2745, Muskingum 2747, National 2748, New Albany 2750, Nippert 2751, NiSource 2752, **Noble 2753**, Nord 2754, Nordson 2755, Ohio 2756, Ohio 2757, **OMNOVA 2759**, Orr 2761, Piqua 2763, Richland 2767, Saint 2770, Samaritan 2772, Sandusky 2773, Schmidlapp 2775, Scripps 2780, Seasongood 2782, Springfield 2787, Stark 2788, Stranahan 2790, Talbott 2791, Tiffin 2793, Troy 2794, Tuscarawas 2795, Tuscora 2796, Veale 2797, Wayne 2798, White 2800, Young 2803, Youngstown 2804

Oklahoma: Adams 2806, Bernsen 2807, Chapman 2808, Cherokee 2809, Dolese 2810, Freese 2812, Gaylord 2813, Hardesty 2814, Harmon 2815, Hille 2816, Merrick 2821, Noble 2822, Oklahoma 2823, Parman 2824, Sarkeys 2828, **Schusterman 2829**, Viersen 2830, Warren 2831, Zarrow 2833, Zarrow 2834

Oregon: Braemar 2836, Castle 2839, Chaney 2840, Coit 2841, Flowerree 2845, Glory 2847, Jackson 2851, Jeld 2852, Jubitz 2853, Macdonald 2859, Meyer 2861, Michael 2862, Mission 2863, PacificSource 2866, PGE 2867, Portland 2868, Renaissance 2869, Shapira 2870, Storms 2872, Templeton 2874, Woodard 2877, Wyss 2878

Pennsylvania: 100 2879, Ames 2884, Barra 2887, Bayer 2888, Beaver 2890, Benedum 2892, Birmingham 2896, Black 2897, Bucks 2900, Buncher 2902, **Carnegie 2906**, Central 2908, Centre 2909, Charlestein 2911, Charter 2912, Chase 2913, Chester 2915, CIGNA 2917, Claneil 2918, Community 2922, Community 2923, Community 2924, Connelly 2926, Cooper 2927, Degenstein 2931, Delaware 2932, Donahue 2933, Dozzi 2935, Drueding 2936, DSF 2937, Elk 2939, Finley 2946, First 2947, First 2948, **Firth 2949**, FISA 2950, FISA 2950, Foundation 2952, Fourjay 2953, Freas 2954, Garfield 2955, Goshen 2959, Grumbacher 2961, Halloran 2963, Henkels 2967, Hillman 2969, Hunt 2971, Hunt 2972, Huston 2973, Independence 2976, Kunkel 2980, Lancaster 2981, Laros 2982, Lazarich 2983, Lehigh Valley 2986, McCune 2993, McKee 2995, McKinney 2996, Mellon 2998, North 3006, Palumbo 3009, Patterson 3010, Perelman 3012, Phoenixville 3014, Pierce 3015, **PPG 3018**, Raab 3020, **Riverside 3025**, Ross 3027, Saramar 3029, Scranton 3031, Sedwick 3032, Seybert 3034, Shaffer 3035, Smith 3037, Somerville 3041, Stackpole 3042, Staunton 3044, Sunoco 3046, Trexler 3049, Tuttleman 3050, Union 3051, United 3052, Washington 3054, Willary 3057, Wilson 3058, Wyomissing 3059

Rhode Island: Biogen 3063, Bliss 3065, Citizens 3067, Kimball 3079, Masonic 3083, McNeil 3086, Parmelee 3088, Rhode Island 3089, Schwarz 3090, Textron 3093, van Beuren 3094, Washington 3095

South Carolina: Bailey 3096, Community 3099, Community 3100, Daniel 3101, Graham 3103, Joanna 3104, Motley 3107, Singing 3108, Smith 3109, Spartanburg 3110

Tennessee: Assisi 3120, Ayers 3121, Briggs 3124, CIC 3127, Clayton 3128, Community 3129, Dugas 3132, Eastman 3133, Elgin 3134, First 3135, Frist 3136, Haslam 3138, Hutcheson 3141, **International 3142**, Latimer 3144, Osborne 3147, Phillips 3149, Regal 3151, Sparks 3154, Tucker 3156

Texas: **A Glimmer 3158**, Abell 3160, Alcon 3161, Alcon 3162, Amarillo 3163, Anderson 3164, AT&T 3167, Augur 3168, **Baker 3170**, Baron 3171, Bass 3172, Beal 3174, Beasley 3175, Behmann 3176, **Bolivar 3179**, Booth 3180, **BP 3181**, Brown 3183, Burch 3184, Burnett 3185, C.I.O.S. 3186, Cain 3189, Carter 3190, CEMEX 3191, Chasdrew 3192, Chisholm 3193, Coastal 3196, Collins 3199, Community 3200, Conley 3201, Constantin 3202, Cowden 3205, Dallas 3209, Deakins 3210, Dedman 3212, DeSantis 3214, Durrill 3217, Edwards 3218, Edwards 3219, Embrey 3222, Engler 3223, Esping 3225, Ezekiel 3226, Farish 3228, Fasken 3229, Feldman 3230, Fisch 3232, Fish 3233, Fluor 3235, NAPE 3237, Greentree 3244, Halsell 3247, Hamman 3248, Hammill 3249, Heavin 3253, Henderson 3255, Herzstein 3256, Hext 3257, Hill 3260, Hillcrest 3261, Hoblitzelle 3262, Hoglund 3263, Holloway 3264, Holthouse 3265, **Houston 3266**, Houston 3267, Howell 3268, **Jiv 3270**, Johnson 3271, Kinder 3274, King 3275, Lennox 3279, Light 3281, Lightner 3282, Littauer 3283, Lockheed 3284, Loose 3286, Lubbock 3287, Lupton 3288, Luse 3289, **Marshall 3290**, Martinez 3291, Mayor 3292, McIntyre 3294, Meadows 3296, Moody 3298, Moore 3299, Moore 3300, Mundy 3302, NuStar 3307, Orr 3309, Orsinger 3310, **Paso 3312**, Penland 3314, Penney 3315, Permian 3316, Perot 3317, Pickens 3321, Potts 3323, Powell 3324, Proctor 3325, Rachal 3329, RDM 3332, Reilly 3333, Richardson 3334, Richter 3337, Rockwell 3338, Rosewood 3340, Saint 3341, San Angelo 3343, Scharbauer 3345, Schissler 3346, Shelton 3350, Simmons 3352, Smith 3353, Smith 3355, Sturgis 3360, Talkington 3362, Texas 3364, **Tingari-Silverton 3368**, Trull 3373, Vergara 3376, Waco 3378, Waggoner 3379, Ward 3381, Willard 3382, Woolf 3385, Wright 3386, Zachry 3387

Utah: Bamberger 3389, Eccles 3392, Eskuche 3393, Hall 3395, Park 3401, Quinney 3402, Schmidt 3403, Semnani 3404

Vermont: **Ben 3407**, Harper 3411, Merchants 3414, Tarrant 3416, Vermont 3417

Virginia: Arlington 3421, Cabell 3425, CarMax 3427, Charlottesville 3428, Community 3429, Community 3430, Community 3431, Community 3432, Denit 3435, **Foundation 3438**, Gifford 3440, Greensville 3441, Gwathmey 3442, Kellar 3446, Launders 3447, Loeb 3450, Love 3452, Lynchburg 3454, Maude 3456, MAXIMUS 3457, Memorial 3458, Morgan, 3463, Northern 3464, Obici 3467, O'Shaughnessy-Hurst 3469, Parsons 3470, Pruden 3473, RECO 3474, Richardson 3475, Smith 3479, United 3484, **WestWind 3486**, Williamsburg 3488

Washington: Allen 3490, Anderson 3492, Arise 3493, Bainbridge 3494, Bamford 3495, Biller 3496, Blue 3498, **Children's 3501**, Community 3503, Community 3504, Dimmer 3506, Eggnog 3509, Everett 3511, Fales 3512, Ferguson 3513, First 3514, **Gates 3516**, Goodman 3518, Grays 3520, Green 3521, Haller 3522, Howard 3525, Inland 3526, Jones 3529, Kawabe 3531, Korum 3532, Lauzier 3534, **Luke 3537**, McCaw 3540, McEachern 3541, Milgard 3543, Moccasin 3545, OneFamily 3547, PEMCO 3549, Raisbeck 3550, Renton 3552, Safeco 3554, San Juan 3555, Satterberg 3556, Schultz 3557, Seattle 3558, Shemanski 3560, Sherwood 3561, Tacoma 3567, Wilkens 3573, Wrigley 3575, Yakima 3576

West Virginia: Beckley 3577, Community 3579, Fenton 3581, McDonough 3586, Parkersburg 3587, Ross 3588, Your 3591

Wisconsin: Alliant 3592, Anthony 3593, Ariens 3594, **Baird 3595**, Baker 3596, BayCare 3597, Bemis 3598, Brown 3602, Chipstone 3605, Community 3606, Community 3607, Cornerstone 3608, Door 3609, Dudley 3610, Eau 3611, Fond du Lac 3615, Fort 3616, Green Bay 3619, Greenheck 3620, Harley 3621, Hovde 3622, Incourage 3623, Johnson 3625, Keller 3626, Kloss 3628, Kuenzl 3630, La Crosse 3631, Manitowoc 3632, McBeath 3634, McDonough 3635, Milwaukee 3637, Murray 3638, Neese 3639, New 3641, Pettit 3645, Pick 3646, Pritchett 3647, Racine 3648, Raibrook 3649, Sauey 3655, Schlegel 3656, Siebert 3659, St. Croix 3662, Stateline 3663, Stone 3664, U.S. 3665, **Wagner 3666**, Wanek 3667, Windhover 3668, Windway 3669, Zilber 3670

Wyoming: Dubois 3673, Marine 3675, McMurry 3676, Moyer 3677, Scott 3679, Surrena 3681, Wyoming 3684

Human services, alliance/advocacy

Ohio: Nordson 2755

Human services, emergency aid

Alabama: Community 10
California: Anaheim 83
Idaho: Idaho 948
Indiana: Central 1126, Portland 1188
Iowa: Community 1215
Minnesota: Koran 1709
Rhode Island: Rhode Island 3089
Texas: Fluor 3235

Human services, equal rights

Minnesota: Larsen 1711
New York: NoVo 2334

Human services, financial counseling

Alabama: BBVA 3
Arkansas: Wal-Mart 74
California: Bank 99, Fremont 207, Intuit 263
Colorado: **First 496**
Indiana: Old 1182
Louisiana: Entergy 1308
Maryland: NASDAQ 1401
Massachusetts: Eastern 1461, Santander 1541
Minnesota: RBC 1730
Nebraska: Mutual 1850
New York: **Deutsche 2134**, **JPMorgan 2242**, **MetLife 2307**, NYSE 2336, Voya 2488
North Carolina: **Bank 2524**
Ohio: KeyBank 2717
Oregon: **NIKE 2865**
Pennsylvania: **PPG 3018**
Tennessee: First 3135
Virginia: Capital 3426

Human services, gift distribution

Tennessee: Regal 3151

Human services, mind/body enrichment

Arkansas: Wal-Mart 74
Minnesota: **Trust 1746**
Nevada: Caesars 1860
New Jersey: **Rippel 1982**
New York: Hultquist 2225

Human services, personal services

California: Santa Barbara 394

Human services, reform

Human services, transportation

Humanities

Immigrants/refugees

Immunology

Immunology research

Independent living, disability

Indigenous peoples

Infants/toddlers

Infants/toddlers, female

Infants/toddlers, male

Interactive games
Minnesota: Best 1685

International affairs
California: **Cuore 172**, **CW 176**, **Foundation 202**, **International 261**, Sassoon 395, Skoll 413, **Wadhwani 450**
District of Columbia: **Institute 667**
Iowa: Holthues 1224
Michigan: Jubilee 1624
New York: Donner 2142, Einhorn 2150, **Ford 2160**, **M.A.C. 2287**, Ogden 2338, **Sparkplug 2441**, **Tinker 2467**
North Carolina: Kramer 2581
Pennsylvania: **Botstiber 2898**, Field 2945
Rhode Island: **Dorot 3071**
Texas: **A Glimmer 3158**
Wisconsin: **Bradley 3601**

International affairs, arms control
New York: **Carnegie 2085**, **Rubin 2398**
Vermont: Block 3409

International affairs, foreign policy
New York: **Rubin 2398**, **Tinker 2467**, Wiener 2506
Ohio: Veale 2797
Wisconsin: **Bradley 3601**

International affairs, goodwill promotion
California: Chao 149
Kentucky: C.E. 1284
Maine: **Walter 1343**
Minnesota: Duluth 1693
New Jersey: Fairbanks 1927
New York: Freeman 2164, **Tinker 2467**, Wiener 2506

International affairs, information services
Massachusetts: Colombe 1452

International affairs, national security
New York: **Carnegie 2085**, **Peterson 2357**

International affairs, research
District of Columbia: Rumsfeld 679

International affairs, U.N.
New York: Marshall 2293

International agricultural development
New York: **Jabara 2235**

International conflict resolution
District of Columbia: **El-Hibri 659**
Illinois: **Buffett 975**

International democracy & civil society development
District of Columbia: **El-Hibri 659**

International development
California: **Google 231**, Roth 388
Delaware: Sylvan 648
Florida: Green 751, **Patel 797**
Hawaii: **Watumull 939**
Massachusetts: **Patagonia 1524**
Minnesota: Minneapolis 1717, **Weyerhaeuser 1752**
New York: Assael 2046, Donner 2142, **Jabara 2235**, **Tsadra 2478**
Pennsylvania: **ACE 2880**
Texas: Reilly 3333
Washington: **Gates 3516**
Wisconsin: Hovde 3622

International economic development
California: Hewlett 248
Illinois: Shamrock 1092
Minnesota: **Porter 1729**
New York: **Ford 2160**, **Jabara 2235**, **Open 2343**, **Rockefeller 2390**
Texas: **PHM 3320**
Washington: **Glaser 3517**, **Starbucks 3565**

International exchange
New York: **Jabara 2235**, **Trust 2477**

International human rights
California: **Alalusi 78**, **Better 112**, **Google 231**
Colorado: **General 501**
District of Columbia: **El-Hibri 659**
Florida: Around 692, **Patel 797**
Illinois: Libra 1050, **MacArthur 1056**, Magnus 1058
Iowa: Holthues 1224
Maine: **Catalyst 1326**
Maryland: **Blaustein 1349**, Blaustein 1350, **Cohen 1355**
New Jersey: Harbourton 1936
New York: **Ford 2160**, Mendell 2303, **Open 2343**, **Overbrook 2345**, Rivendell 2385, **Rubin 2398**, **Sparkplug 2441**
Pennsylvania: Scranton 3031
Texas: McDermott 3293

International migration/refugee issues
Georgia: Rockdale 909
New York: **Kaplan 2245**, Sherman 2419, **Sparkplug 2441**

International peace/security
California: Craigslist 169, Firedoll 198
Colorado: **General 501**
District of Columbia: **El-Hibri 659**, **Foundation 661**, **Wyss 685**
Illinois: **MacArthur 1056**
Iowa: Holthues 1224
Kansas: **Shumaker 1276**
Maine: **Catalyst 1326**
Maryland: **Morningstar 1397**
Massachusetts: Colombe 1452
Minnesota: Duluth 1693, **Weyerhaeuser 1752**
New York: **Carnegie 2085**, **Rockefeller 2389**, **Rubin 2398**, Wiener 2506
Ohio: Eaton 2693

International relief
California: **Alalusi 78**, **Applied 88**, **World 468**
Connecticut: Macauley 589
District of Columbia: **El-Hibri 659**
Florida: **Patel 797**
Georgia: Amos-Cheves 849
Illinois: Katten 1042
Indiana: Brotherhood 1123, Crosser 1139
Iowa: On 1233
Maryland: Hirschhorn 1379
Michigan: Jubilee 1624
New York: Achelis 2026, Donner 2142, Sherman 2419
North Carolina: Bolick 2531
Pennsylvania: **ACE 2880**, **Zeldin 3060**
Texas: **A Glimmer 3158**, **BP 3181**, **International 3269**, Trull 3373
Utah: Semnani 3404
Wisconsin: **Wagner 3666**

International studies
California: Hewlett 248, **Lingnan 301**
Georgia: Livingston 893
New York: Freeman 2164, **Luce 2286**

Intersex
California: Weingart 456

Islam
California: **Alalusi 78**
District of Columbia: **El-Hibri 659**
Florida: **Jaffer 763**
New York: **Alavi 2030**, **Jabara 2235**
Utah: Semnani 3404

Jewish agencies & synagogues
Arkansas: Ottenheimer 71
California: Arnall 92, Blum 115, Brunswick 133, Congregation 164, Dart-L 177, David 178, Douglas 186, Friend 209, Gold 228, Gold 229, Guzik 238, Kellerman 277, Lansing 290, Leichtman 298, Milken 331, Morris 334, **Nazarian 341**, Pritzker 375, Rifkind 383, Ryzman 390, Sassoon 395
Colorado: **Merage 519**, Rose 528, Trachten 541
Connecticut: Abramowitz 548, Aronson 552, Common 561, Eder 573, Neuberger 593, Nevas 594, Robbins 607
Delaware: 18 621
District of Columbia: Bernstein 652, Krauthammer 669, Lehrman 670
Florida: Applebaum 690, Azeez 694, Blanksteen 701, **Chester 720**, Cohen 721, Einstein 739, Erdle 740, Feder 741, Greenburg 752, Horowitz 760, Katcher 765, Kislak 769, Korf 772, Landwirth 775, Lipton 781, Lyons 782, Minto 789, Moos 790, Sandelman 814, Sender 817, Setzer 818, Wollowick 843
Georgia: **Rosenberg 910**, Schinazi 913
Illinois: **American 960**, Crown 997, Forbes 1016, Guthman 1027, Katten 1042, Logan 1051, Pattis 1073, Polk 1075, Pritzker 1079, Redhill 1082, Reese 1083, Shapiro 1093, Stern 1100
Kansas: Cohen 1252
Maine: Cohen 1327
Maryland: **Blaustein 1349**, Dahan 1364, Freeman 1373, Gudelsky 1376, Hirschhorn 1379, Israelson 1380, Kay 1384, Meyerhoff 1392, Meyerhoff 1393, **Morningstar 1397**, Polinger 1405, Straus 1410, Tauber 1412, Tucker 1415
Massachusetts: Aaron 1421, Berkman 1434, Child 1447, Fireman 1469, Grinspoon 1479, Herbert 1481, Jacobson 1490, Jaffe 1491, Krieger 1497, Ratshesky 1531, Ruderman 1537, Swartz 1553
Michigan: Frankel 1604, Kahn 1625, Nartel 1648
Minnesota: Bentson 1684, Johnson 1704, **Kaplan 1707**, Phillips 1728, Regis 1732
Missouri: Kuhn 1798, Millstone 1801
New Jersey: Ahavat 1898, **American 1902**, Beer 1907, **Berrie 1908**, Brothers 1913, Eisenreich 1922, Evans 1925, Ezra 1926, Holzer 1939, Klatskin 1954, Kushner 1957, Mandelbaum 1962, Marino

Jewish federated giving programs

Journalism school/education

Kidney diseases

Kidney research

Labor rights

Language (classical)

Language (foreign)

Language/linguistics

Law school/education

Law/international law

Leadership development

Legal services

Texas: Bickel 3178, Wright 3386
Vermont: Harper 3411
Wisconsin: Milwaukee 3637, RITE-HITE 3651

Legal services, public interest law
California: vanLoben 446
Georgia: Sapelo 911
New Jersey: Evans 1925
Pennsylvania: Independence 2976

Lesbians
Alabama: Black 4
California: Weingart 456
Pennsylvania: Staunton 3044

LGBTQ
Alabama: Black 4
Arizona: Webb 64
California: Bohnett 117, California 137, California 140, Community 157, Fleishhacker 199, Gerbode 217, Gumbiner 236, Lesher 299, PG&E 367, San Luis 393, Weingart 456
Colorado: **Gill 502**
District of Columbia: Cafritz 656
Florida: Burns 710
Illinois: Chicago 982, Field 1014, Logan 1051, Washington 1112
Massachusetts: Currents 1455, Hyams 1486, Two 1557
Michigan: Grand Rapids 1615
Minnesota: Larsen 1711, Phillips 1728
Montana: Montana 1828
New Hampshire: Foundation 1885
New Jersey: Hyde 1944
New Mexico: Santa Fe 2017
New York: **Arcus 2040**, **Ford 2160**, Haring 2203, Johnson 2240, Langeloth 2267, Luce 2285, McCarthy 2298, **MetLife 2307**, New York 2326, **Open 2343**, **Overbrook 2345**, Palette 2347, **Sparkplug 2441**, van Ameringen 2482
Ohio: Akron 2655, KeyBank 2717
Oklahoma: Hille 2816
Pennsylvania: First 2948, Staunton 3044
Texas: Chasdrew 3192, Dallas 3209, Richardson 3335
Wisconsin: La Crosse 3631, Milwaukee 3637

Libraries (academic/research)
Massachusetts: Calderwood 1444

Libraries (public)
Alabama: Brown 5
California: Braddock 123, Community 158, Community 162, Farese 194, Genentech 216, Kelly 278, Klein 283, Simpson 411, WHH 461
Colorado: **Kinder 510**
Connecticut: **Praxair 606**, Weatherstone 618
Florida: Glazer 750
Illinois: Lumpkin 1053
Indiana: Auer 1120, Marshall 1176
Iowa: Beckwith 1213, HNI 1223, Schildberg 1238, United 1243, Woodward 1247
Kentucky: Trim 1295
Maine: King 1333, Smith 1340
Maryland: Moore 1396
Massachusetts: Brooks 1439, Grew 1478, Memorial 1512, Santander 1541
Michigan: Pokagon 1657, Steelcase 1667
Minnesota: Land 1710, Regis 1732
Missouri: Centene 1782, **Monsanto 1803**
New Jersey: Savin 1989
New York: Brownstone 2077, Gellert 2171, Sherman 2419, Truman 2475, Western 2503
North Carolina: Community 2538, Hackbarth 2564, Hoffman 2569, Southern 2630
North Dakota: MDU 2652
Ohio: Ohio 2756, Young 2803
Pennsylvania: Degenstein 2931, EQT 2940, Packer 3008, Patterson 3010, **PPG 3018**
Rhode Island: Washington 3095
Texas: King 3275
Virginia: United 3484
Washington: Allen 3490, Ferguson 3513, Safeco 3554, Seattle 3558
Wisconsin: Alliant 3592, Manitowoc 3632, Neese 3639, Windhover 3668

Libraries (special)
Colorado: Brown 478
Pennsylvania: Randall 3021
Texas: Fish 3233, Lupton 3288

Libraries, archives
New York: **Carnegie 2085**

Libraries/library science
California: Ahmanson 77, Anaheim 83, Community 160, Kline 284, Rifkind 383, Sonora 420
Colorado: El Pomar 492
Connecticut: Community 562, Community 563, Palmer 600
Florida: Community 725
Idaho: Idaho 948, Whittenberger 953
Indiana: Portland 1188, Shoop 1195, Unity 1201
Massachusetts: **Elsevier 1463**, Herbert 1481
Michigan: Community 1587, Dow 1597, Fremont 1607, Hillsdale 1620
Nebraska: Grand Island 1837, Kearney 1842
New York: Adirondack 2027, Barker 2054, Brooks 2075, Chapman 2090, Chautauqua 2091, Cohen 2102, Community 2110, Hallingby 2201, Keet 2248, Lake Placid 2265, Miller 2308, Northern 2331, Pollock 2362, Snow 2432, Wachenheim 2489
North Carolina: Cumberland 2541, Gambrill 2556, Hunt 2572, Shingleton 2624, Smith 2629
Ohio: Dater 2687, Middletown 2737, Murphy 2745, Muskingum 2747, Reinberger 2765, Richland 2767, Troy 2794
Oklahoma: Viersen 2830
Oregon: Ford 2846
Pennsylvania: Buhl 2901, Chester 2915, McCune 2993, McLean 2997, Scranton 3031, Snee 3039, Stackpole 3042
Rhode Island: Rhode Island 3089
Texas: Coastal 3196, Constantin 3202, Meadows 3296, Rachal 3329, Sterling 3358, Sturgis 3360, Tocker 3369, Trull 3373
Vermont: Vermont 3417
Virginia: **Bosack 3423**, Community 3431, Lynchburg 3454
Washington: Community 3503, **Gates 3516**, Tacoma 3567, Yakima 3576
West Virginia: Parkersburg 3587, Tucker 3589

Literature
Alaska: CIRI 33
California: Gellert 215, Rosenberg 386
Florida: Chapman 717
Illinois: Alphawood 959, Cheney 981, Logan 1051, **Tyndale 1105**
Kentucky: Kentucky 1292
Minnesota: Land 1710
Missouri: **Monsanto 1803**
New York: **Kade 2243**, Littauer 2282, Whiting 2504
North Carolina: Cumberland 2541
Pennsylvania: Randall 3021
Washington: Seattle 3558, Yakima 3576

Lung diseases
Georgia: Raoul 907
Pennsylvania: Somerville 3041

Lung research
Georgia: Raoul 907
Pennsylvania: **Respironics 3023**

Lupus research
New York: Johnson 2241
Wisconsin: Milwaukee 3637

Marine science
California: **Beckman 105**, **Grass 232**, **Keck 276**, **Marisla 310**, Monterey 332, **Packard 357**
Florida: Bank 695
Maine: Hannaford 1330
New Jersey: Banbury 1904
New York: Link 2280, Marine 2289, **Tinker 2467**

Mathematics
Alaska: CIRI 33
Arizona: APS 39
California: American 82, **Applied 88**, Baker 98, Crail 170, Hewlett 249, **Keck 276**, Noyce 348, Western 459
Connecticut: NewAlliance 595
Idaho: **Micron 950**
Illinois: **Motorola 1066**
Indiana: Old 1182
Iowa: **Rockwell 1237**
Maryland: Rembrandt 1407
Michigan: DTE 1598, Grand Haven 1614
Minnesota: 3M 1676, Alworth 1677, **Andersen 1678**, **Pentair 1727**, Securian 1739, **St. Jude 1741**, Xcel 1754
Missouri: **Kauffman 1797**, **Monsanto 1803**
New Jersey: **Knowles 1955**, Merck 1966, **Siemens 1993**
New York: **Deutsche 2134**, **IBM 2227**, Simons 2423
North Carolina: Goodrich 2561
Ohio: Nordson 2755, **OMNOVA 2759**
Oklahoma: Oklahoma 2823
Oregon: PGE 2867
Pennsylvania: **Alcoa 2882**, Bayer 2888, EQT 2940, **PPG 3018**
Rhode Island: Biogen 3063
Tennessee: Eastman 3133
Texas: AT&T 3167, Fluor 3235
Virginia: CarMax 3427, **Northrop 3465**
Wisconsin: Bemis 3598

Media, film/video
California: Craigslist 169, **CW 176**, Disney 181, Fleishhacker 199, Lucas 306, Skywords 414
Colorado: Summit 537
Florida: Bank 695, Gulf 754
Illinois: **MacArthur 1056**
Kentucky: Kentucky 1292
Minnesota: Best 1685, Land 1710
New Jersey: Evans 1925, **Puffin 1980**
New York: Cinereach 2095, **Cummings 2121**, **Ford 2160**, Resnick 2380, Time 2466, Vilcek 2486

Ohio: Akron 2655
Tennessee: Regal 3151
Washington: Seattle 3558

Media, journalism

California: Craigslist 169
Florida: **Knight 771**
New York: **Cummings 2121**, Time 2466

Media, print publishing

District of Columbia: Patterson 678
Florida: **Knight 771**
New York: **Cummings 2121**, Park 2349, Snow 2432
Ohio: Scripps 2780
Texas: **PHM 3320**

Media, radio

California: Roth 388
Colorado: Catto 480
Florida: Around 692
Massachusetts: Memorial 1512
Missouri: Centene 1782
Montana: Greater 1823
Nebraska: Weitz 1855
New York: **Cummings 2121**
Ohio: Morgan 2739
Texas: Criswell 3207, Heavin 3253
Washington: Seattle 3558

Media, television

California: Disney 181
Florida: Brown 707, Leiser 777
Iowa: Aviva 1211
Kentucky: Campbell 1285
Massachusetts: Filene 1468
Minnesota: Land 1710
New Jersey: Gamper 1933, Syms 1999
New York: **Cummings 2121**, D'Agostino 2124, **MetLife 2307**, Park 2349, Smith 2430, Time 2466
Texas: Heavin 3253
Washington: PEMCO 3549

Media/communications

California: Bohnett 117, Coburn 154, Disney 181, **Google 231**, Mediathe 325, Price 374, Roth 388
Florida: Cohen 721, Jacksonville 761
Illinois: Logan 1051, **MacArthur 1056**
Massachusetts: Santander 1541
Minnesota: **Andersen 1678**, Best 1685
Montana: Greater 1823
New York: Alfiero 2031, Beach 2058, Broadcasters 2071, **Cummings 2121**, Diller 2137, **Ford 2160**, Kellen 2250, **King 2251**, Mercer 2305, **Open 2343**, Park 2349, Schumann 2412, Time 2466
Ohio: Reinberger 2765, Seasongood 2782
Oklahoma: **Ethics 2811**
Oregon: Coit 2841
Pennsylvania: Arkema 2885
Texas: Meadows 3296, Wright 3386
Vermont: Harper 3411
Washington: Community 3503, **Glaser 3517**, Yakima 3576

Medical care, bioethics

New York: **Greenwall 2192**, Littauer 2282

Medical care, community health systems

California: California 140, Livingston 303, Patron 363
Illinois: Healthcare 1031
Indiana: Kosciusko 1168
Massachusetts: MetroWest 1515
Michigan: Schmuckal 1664
New Jersey: **Rippel 1982**
Ohio: **Cardinal 2677**, Ginn 2706, Osteopathic 2762
Oklahoma: Presbyterian 2826
Pennsylvania: Phoenixville 3014, Pottstown 3017
Virginia: Williamsburg 3487

Medical care, in-patient care

Michigan: McGregor 1638
Missouri: Mungenast 1804
New York: Countess 2116, Vidda 2485

Medical care, outpatient care

California: Community 159, Patron 363
Minnesota: **King 1708**
New York: Kellen 2250

Medical care, rehabilitation

California: Anaheim 83, Livingston 303, Patron 363, Sierra 405, Weingart 456
District of Columbia: Cafritz 656
Florida: Chapman 717
Illinois: Coleman 986, Community 988, Prince 1076
Indiana: Kosciusko 1168
Massachusetts: Demoulas 1458
Michigan: Fremont 1607
Minnesota: **Patterson 1726**
Missouri: St. Louis 1814
Nevada: Nevada 1867
New Jersey: Beer 1907, Hyde 1944, **Milbank 1968**
New York: Achelis 2026, Cummings 2122, NYSE 2336, **Ross 2396**, Western 2503
North Carolina: Cumberland 2541, Ribenack 2615
Ohio: Dater 2687, Murphy 2745
Pennsylvania: Community 2925, FISA 2950, Fourjay 2953
Rhode Island: CVS 3068
South Carolina: McKissick 3106
Texas: Constantin 3202, Edwards 3219, Hillcrest 3261, Hoblitzelle 3262, McKee 3295, Meadows 3296, South 3356, Sterling 3358, Wright 3386
Washington: Community 3503

Medical research

California: Baker 98, Bell 107, **Broad 129**, Curci 174, Frank 206, **Grass 232**, **Hilton 251**, Mazda 313, Mellam 326, Outhwaite 353, **Parsemus 358**, Patron 363, Rifkind 383, Streisand 428, **Thiel 434**, Valley 445, WHH 461
Florida: Alpha 687, Batchelor 697, Community 725, Gruss 753, Ware 838
Georgia: Schinazi 913
Illinois: **Driskill 1003**, Fulk 1020, **Grainger 1024**, Lefkofsky 1049
Indiana: Haddad 1153
Maryland: **ABMRF 1344**, Tauber 1412
Massachusetts: **Adelson 1424**, **Kahn 1492**, Smith 1546
Michigan: Royal 1661
Mississippi: Center 1757
Missouri: **McDonnell 1800**, Trudy 1816
New Hampshire: Foundation 1885, Woodbury 1897
New Jersey: **Berrie 1908**, Brotherton 1914, Feldstein 1928, Integra 1945, MacDonald 1961, **Pfeiffer 1975**
New York: Capri 2084, **Dana 2126**, Diamond 2136, **Duke 2146**, **Eppley 2152**, Friedman 2166, Helmsley 2207, Hycliff 2226, Keet 2248, Kekst 2249, **Mayday 2296**, MBIA 2297, McGraw 2300, Naomi 2319, Schmitt 2410, Wachtell, 2490, Woldar 2509
North Carolina: **Laffin 2583**, Lynum 2586
Ohio: Akron 2655, Maltz 2727, Reinberger 2765, Sears 2781
Oklahoma: Sarkeys 2828
Oregon: Knight 2854, Macdonald 2859
Pennsylvania: Drueding 2936, DSF 2937, Rangos 3022
Texas: Bass 3172, Farish 3228, Najim 3304, NuStar 3307, Pickens 3321, RDM 3332, Thompson 3367, Tomerlin 3371
Utah: Green 3394
Washington: Seattle 3558, Smith 3564
Wisconsin: Milwaukee 3637

Medical research, association

North Carolina: Fortson 2553

Medical research, formal/general education

Indiana: Regenstrief 1190

Medical research, information services

Indiana: Regenstrief 1190

Medical research, institute

Arizona: Flinn 44, Marshall 54
California: Arnall 92, **Beckman 105**, Bell 107, Brandman 125, Burns 136, Carpenter 145, Chan 148, Douglas 186, Drown 187, Gibson 220, **Glenn 225**, Gold 229, **Guthy-Jackson 237**, Hillblom 250, Hoag 253, **Keck 276**, Kvamme 286, Laulhere 292, McMinn 323, Milken 331, Opperman 350, Philanthropy 368, **Qualcomm 376**, Smith 415, Treadwell 439, Wasserman 453, West 458
Colorado: Kaufmann 509
Connecticut: Bender 554, Childs 559
District of Columbia: Lehrman 670, Monarch 673
Florida: Applebaum 690, DeBartolo 734, DiMare 737, Greenburg 752, Kramer 773, Life 779, Wollowick 843
Georgia: Georgia 876, Livingston 893, Savannah 912
Hawaii: Hawaii 933
Illinois: Blowitz 968, Coldwell 985, Hughes 1035, Reese 1083, Shapiro 1093, Sinsheimer 1095, Washington 1112
Indiana: Leighton 1172, Regenstrief 1190
Iowa: Wallace 1245
Kansas: **Muchnic 1271**
Maryland: Cupid 1363
Massachusetts: Alden 1425, Community 1453, Swartz 1553, Webster 1565
Michigan: Alix 1572, Golden 1613, **Pardee 1653**
Minnesota: Alworth 1677, Greystone 1700, **McKnight 1714**
Missouri: Bellwether 1775, St. Louis 1814
Nevada: **Reynolds 1869**
New Hampshire: Johnson 1889
New Jersey: **Allen 1900**, Banbury 1904, Capozzi 1918, Focus 1930, Hummingbird 1943, Kirby 1952, **Ramapo 1981**
New York: 100 2019, Achelis 2026, American 2035, Belfer 2059, Blum 2067, Cramer 2117, **Cummings 2120**, D'Agostino 2124, **Eppley 2152**, Johnson 2239, Johnson 2241, **Kade 2243**, Karmazin 2246, Klingenstein 2256, Knapp 2259, Kornfeld 2261, Lane 2266, Litwin 2283, McGonagle 2299, Oishei 2340, Ostgrodd 2344, Rasmussen 2375, Regals 2377, SDA 2414, Smith 2430, Tisch 2469, Trump 2476, Vilcek 2486

North Carolina: Allen 2518, **Burroughs 2534**, Eddy 2548, Gordon 2562, Sutcliffe 2635
Ohio: Akron 2655, Dodero 2691, Licking 2723
Oklahoma: Gaylord 2813, Merrick 2821, Noble 2822, Presbyterian 2826, Warren 2831
Oregon: Collins 2842
Pennsylvania: Buncher 2902, McCune 2993, Widener 3056
Rhode Island: Falk 3074, Gross 3076
Tennessee: Davis 3130
Texas: Cain 3188, Coates 3197, Dunn 3216, Edwards 3218, Elkins 3220, Elkins 3221, Fish 3233, Hamman 3248, Hillcrest 3261, Lightner 3282, McDermott 3293, McKee 3295, Moody 3298, Potts 3323, Smith 3355, South 3356, Sturgis 3360, Waco 3378
Utah: Dialysis 3390, Semnani 3404
Vermont: Harper 3411
Virginia: Jeffress 3444
Washington: Anderson 3492, Biller 3496, Dimmer 3506, Kuni 3533, Wilkens 3573
Wisconsin: Hovde 3622, Seramur 3658

Medical school/education

Alabama: Andalusia 1
Arizona: Weil 65
California: California 140, Genentech 216, McKesson 321
Connecticut: Aetna 550
Florida: Applebaum 690, King 768, Macdonald 783, Parish 796, Speer 824
Georgia: Cobb 863, Georgia 876, Katz 889
Illinois: Homan 1033, Pritzker 1079, Sinsheimer 1095, Washington 1112
Indiana: Ball 1121, Kendrick 1166
Iowa: Siouxland 1240
Massachusetts: Gardinor 1473
Minnesota: Alworth 1677
Missouri: Speas 1813, St. Louis 1814
New Jersey: Feldstein 1928, Hyde 1944, Integra 1945, **Johnson 1949**, **Pfeiffer 1975**, **Ramapo 1981**
New York: Belfer 2059, Belfer 2060, Collins 2105, Community 2108, **Cummings 2120**, **Goldman 2182**, **Institute 2233**, Jaharis 2236, Kanas 2244, Klingenstein 2257, **Klingenstein 2258**, Kornfeld 2261, **Macy 2288**, McGonagle 2299, Resnick 2380, Vilcek 2486
Ohio: Brentwood 2670, Munro 2743, Ryan 2769
Oklahoma: Presbyterian 2826
Oregon: Collins 2842
Pennsylvania: Garfield 2955, Perelman 3012, **Respironics 3023**
Rhode Island: CVS 3068
Texas: Alcon 3162, Elkins 3221, Gulf 3245, Hoblitzelle 3262, Luse 3289, Meadows 3296, Moody 3298, South 3356
Utah: Bamberger 3389
Virginia: Moore 3461
Washington: Stevenson 3566
Wisconsin: McBeath 3634

Medical specialties

Illinois: Siragusa 1096
Michigan: Vanderweide 1671
New Jersey: Bard 1905

Medical specialties research

Louisiana: Pennington 1317

Medicine/medical care, public education

California: Livingston 303, Patron 363
Illinois: Healthcare 1031
Louisiana: Blue 1302
Massachusetts: DentaQuest 1459, MetroWest 1515
Rhode Island: CVS 3068

Men

Alabama: Black 4
Arizona: Webb 64
California: California 140, Gerbode 217, Lesher 299, Patron 363, Weingart 456
District of Columbia: Jovid 668
Illinois: Chicago 982, Fry 1018
Indiana: Community 1134, Henry 1158
Iowa: Stebens 1242
Kansas: Hutchinson 1260
Michigan: Grand Rapids 1615, Midland 1642, Sanilac 1663
Mississippi: Community 1760, Gulf 1764
New Jersey: **Allen 1900**, Hyde 1944
New York: Community 2107, **MetLife 2307**, Ostgrodd 2344
North Carolina: Glenn 2560, Reidsville 2611
Ohio: Cincinnati 2679, Fairfield 2696, O'Neill 2760
Oklahoma: Hardesty 2814, Hille 2816
Pennsylvania: Birmingham 2896, Phoenixville 3014, Staunton 3044
Tennessee: Wilson 3157
Texas: McDermott 3293, Orsinger 3310, Rockwell 3338
Washington: **Gates 3516**
Wisconsin: Marshfield 3633

Mental health, addictions

District of Columbia: Himmelfarb 665
Oklahoma: Liddell 2819

Mental health, association

Maryland: Stulman 1411
New Jersey: Jones 1950
New York: Mule 2316
Texas: Potts 3323

Mental health, clinics

Illinois: Community 993
Texas: P 3311

Mental health, counseling/support groups

California: Trio 440
Florida: Florida 744
Illinois: Community 993, Healthcare 1031
New York: Freed 2163
Texas: Rockwell 3338
Washington: Renton 3552

Mental health, depression

California: Traina 438
Michigan: Frankel 1605
Minnesota: RBC 1730
New Jersey: Horizon 1940
New York: **Klingenstein 2258**

Mental health, disorders

California: Traina 438
Maryland: Tauber 1412
Minnesota: RBC 1730
New Jersey: **Johnson 1949**
New York: Freed 2163
Texas: Rockwell 3338

Mental health, grief/bereavement counseling

California: Livingston 303
Pennsylvania: Highmark 2968
Wisconsin: **Baird 3595**

Mental health, schizophrenia

Maryland: Stulman 1411

Mental health, smoking

Indiana: WellPoint 1206
New Jersey: **Johnson 1949**

Mental health, treatment

Alabama: Community 9
Florida: Diermeier 736
Georgia: Pittulloch 905
Hawaii: Hawaii 933
Illinois: Healthcare 1031
Maryland: **Blaustein 1349**, Stulman 1411
Massachusetts: Community 1453
Minnesota: RBC 1730, **Weyerhaeuser 1752**
Montana: Lynn 1827
New York: Tower 2472, van Ameringen 2483
North Carolina: Reynolds 2614
Ohio: Reinberger 2765
Pennsylvania: Staunton 3044
Texas: Rockwell 3338

Mental health/crisis services

California: Annenberg 87, Aroha 94, Atlas 96, Fremont 207, **Gellert 214**, HealthCare 244, **Hilton 251**, Livingston 303, Pacific 355, Patron 363, Sacramento 391, Sierra 405, Sonora 420, Truckee 441
Colorado: Colorado 483, Comprecare 485, Summit 537
Connecticut: Community 562, Community 563, Connecticut 564
District of Columbia: Cafritz 656, Meyer 672
Florida: Bank 695, Community 727, Florida 744, Gulf 754, Macdonald 783, Pinellas 801, Southwest 823, Walter 837
Illinois: Blowitz 968, Community 988, DuPage 1008, Field 1014, Polk 1075, Stern 1100
Indiana: Blackford 1122, Central 1126, Community 1129, Community 1130, Henry 1158, Kosciusko 1168, Unity 1201
Iowa: Siouxland 1240
Kansas: Hutchinson 1260, Manhattan 1268
Kentucky: Gheens 1288, Hayswood 1290
Louisiana: Community 1306
Maryland: Blaustein 1350
Massachusetts: Brooks 1440
Minnesota: **Andersen 1678**, Nash 1720, RBC 1730, Thorpe 1745
Nebraska: Kearney 1842, Kim 1844, Midlands 1848, Mutual 1850
Nevada: Caesars 1860, Nevada 1867
New Hampshire: Alexander 1877, Foundation 1885
New Jersey: Borden 1910, Horizon 1940, Hyde 1944, **Johnson 1949**
New Mexico: Frost 2012, Santa Fe 2017
New York: Barker 2054, Cummings 2122, Dammann 2125, Goldman 2183, Legacy 2274, New York 2325, Tower 2472, van Ameringen 2483, Western 2503
North Carolina: Cumberland 2541, Reynolds 2614, Smith 2629
North Dakota: North Dakota 2653
Ohio: Akron 2655, Athens 2662, Austin 2663, Coshocton 2686, Fairfield 2696, Licking 2723, Morgan 2741, Richland 2767, Woodruff 2801
Oklahoma: Bernsen 2807, Zarrow 2833

Mental health/crisis services, association

Mental health/crisis services, hot-lines

Mental health/crisis services, public education

Mental health/crisis services, public policy

Mental health/crisis services, rape victim services

Mental health/crisis services, research

Mental health/crisis services, suicide

Mentally disabled

Microfinance/microlending

Middle schools/education

Migrant workers

Military/veterans

Military/veterans' organizations

Minorities

Minorities/immigrants, centers/services

Mobile media

Mormon agencies & churches

Multiple sclerosis

Multiple sclerosis research

Museums

Museums (art)

Museums (children's)

Museums (ethnic/folk arts)

Texas: Orr 3309
Washington: **Goodwin 3519**

Museums (history)

Indiana: Kuhne 1169
Michigan: Nartel 1648, Parish 1654
Oklahoma: Gaylord 2813
Pennsylvania: Mendel 2999

Museums (marine/maritime)

California: Outhwaite 353
Florida: Kislak 769
Nebraska: Lincoln 1847
Virginia: **Truland 3482**

Museums (natural history)

Illinois: Angell 962, Comer 987, Ward 1111
New York: D'Agostino 2124, **Gilman 2178**, Keet 2248, Klingenstein 2257
Pennsylvania: Dozzi 2935
Utah: Bamberger 3389
Virginia: **Price 3472**
Washington: Stevenson 3566

Museums (science/technology)

Alabama: McWane 17
Arizona: Dorrance 42
California: Bengier 109
Connecticut: Northeast 598
Illinois: **Motorola 1066**
Massachusetts: **Brabson 1438**
Michigan: DTE 1598, Lear 1632
Minnesota: 3M 1676
New Jersey: Buehler 1915
North Carolina: Goodrich 2561, VF 2642
Ohio: Cliffs 2681
Pennsylvania: Bayer 2888, **PPG 3018**
Rhode Island: Biogen 3063

Museums (specialized)

California: Dickinson 180, Kelly 278
Colorado: **Avenir 473**
Florida: Kislak 769
Minnesota: **Patterson 1726**
New York: Solomon 2436, Sulzberger 2451
Pennsylvania: Kunkel 2980
Virginia: Lee-Jackson 3448, Moore 3461
Wisconsin: Zilber 3670

Museums (sports/hobby)

Michigan: Wilson 1675

Mutual aid societies

Indiana: Haddad 1153

Native Americans/American Indians

Alabama: Black 4
Alaska: Aleut 27, Arctic 28, Bristol 31, Chugach 32, CIRI 33, Doyon 34, Koniag 36
Arizona: Webb 64
California: California 137, California 140, **Christensen 151**, Community 157, Cowell 168, Fleishhacker 199, Gumbiner 236, Weingart 456
District of Columbia: Jovid 668
Florida: Thomas 831
Illinois: Chicago 982, Siragusa 1096
Indiana: **Lumina 1174**
Iowa: Siouxland 1240, Wahlert 1244
Massachusetts: Access 1422
Michigan: Grand Rapids 1615, **Kellogg 1628**, Pokagon 1657
Minnesota: Cargill 1689, Duluth 1693, Land 1710, Minneapolis 1717, Northwest 1722, Phillips 1728
Mississippi: Community 1760
Montana: Montana 1828
Nebraska: Midlands 1848, Woods 1857
New Hampshire: Lindsay 1890
New Jersey: **Allen 1900**, **Johnson 1949**
New Mexico: Con 2011, Frost 2012, Santa Fe 2017
New York: Atlantic 2048, Langeloth 2267, **Macy 2288**, **MetLife 2307**, **Noyes 2335**, **Ross 2396**, Ruffin 2400, **Sparkplug 2441**
North Carolina: Cumberland 2541, Meyer 2593, North Carolina 2599
Oregon: Benton 2835
Pennsylvania: First 2948
Tennessee: Baptist 3122
Texas: McDermott 3293
Virginia: Arlington 3421
Washington: Allen 3490
Wisconsin: Community 3607, Green Bay 3619

Neighborhood centers

Alabama: Community 10
Massachusetts: Hazard 1480
New York: McCarthy 2298, Rivendell 2385
Washington: Renton 3552

Nerve, muscle & bone diseases

California: Brocchini 130
Pennsylvania: Highmark 2968

Nerve, muscle & bone research

Wisconsin: Milwaukee 3637

Neuroscience

California: **Grass 232**
Florida: Greenburg 752
Minnesota: Alworth 1677, McKnight 1715
New York: **Dana 2126**
Pennsylvania: DSF 2937

Neuroscience research

Massachusetts: **Adelson 1424**
Minnesota: **McKnight 1714**
New Jersey: Integra 1945
New York: Klingenstein 2256

Nonprofit management

Alabama: Central 8
California: California 140, Irvine 264, Placer 371, San Luis 393, Shasta 401
Florida: Bush 712, Charlotte 718
Hawaii: Hawaii 933
Louisiana: Community 1306
Massachusetts: **Bruner 1441**, Cape Cod 1445
Michigan: Knight 1630
Minnesota: Initiative 1703, West 1751
Mississippi: Mississippi 1769
New Mexico: Santa Fe 2017
New York: **American 2034**, Community 2113, Union 2481
North Carolina: Community 2540
Ohio: **Mandel 2729**, Morino 2742
Pennsylvania: Community 2924
Rhode Island: Rhode Island 3089
Texas: King 3275, Rockwell 3338
Virginia: Lynchburg 3454

Nursing care

Alabama: Andalusia 1
California: Patron 363, Weingart 456
Delaware: **AstraZeneca 623**
Florida: King 768
Illinois: VNA 1107, Washington 1112
Iowa: Siouxland 1240
Massachusetts: MetroWest 1515
Missouri: Musgrave 1805, St. Louis 1814
New Jersey: **Johnson 1949**
North Carolina: Griffin 2563, Ribenack 2615
Ohio: Murphy 2745
Pennsylvania: Fourjay 2953, Independence 2976
Texas: Abell 3160, Gulf 3245, Meadows 3296
Utah: Bamberger 3389
Wisconsin: McBeath 3634

Nursing home/convalescent facility

Illinois: Washington 1112
Michigan: **Isabel 1621**
Minnesota: Midcontinent 1716
Pennsylvania: McLean 2997

Nursing school/education

California: California 140, Dickinson 180, McKesson 321
Florida: Florida 744
Illinois: Walter 1110, Washington 1112
Iowa: Schildberg 1238
Minnesota: Alworth 1677
Mississippi: Biloxi 1755
Missouri: Musgrave 1805, St. Louis 1814
New York: Community 2108, **Macy 2288**, Post 2365
North Carolina: Rogers 2618, Sutcliffe 2635
Ohio: Steinmann 2789, Tuscora 2796
Oregon: Collins 2842, Leonard 2858
Pennsylvania: Independence 2975, Independence 2976, Nesh 3004
Texas: Abell 3160
Virginia: Greensville 3441, Metropolitan 3459, Moore 3461, Richmond 3476

Nutrition

Arkansas: Wal-Mart 74
California: California 140, Fremont 207, Just 272, Sierra 405
Colorado: El Pomar 492
Connecticut: Aetna 550
Delaware: Delaware 630
Florida: Florida 744, Gate 749, Jacksonville 761
Georgia: **Coca 864**
Illinois: Community 988, FDC 1013, Hospira 1034, **Mondelez 1064**
Indiana: Health 1156, Welborn 1205
Iowa: Wellmark 1246
Louisiana: Blue 1302, Community 1306
Massachusetts: Eastern 1461, Kelsey 1493, New 1518
Michigan: **Allen 1573**, **Gerber 1611**
Minnesota: General 1697, Land 1710, **Mosaic 1718**, SUPERVALU 1743
Mississippi: Community 1760
Missouri: **Monsanto 1803**
Nevada: Caesars 1860
New Jersey: Campbell 1917, Horizon 1940, **Pfeiffer 1975**, Unilever 2003

New York: Assurant 2047, Dreyfus 2145, Freed 2163, Levitt 2275, Morgan 2315, NYSE 2336, Palette 2347, **PepsiCo 2354**
North Carolina: **Bank 2524**, Cumberland 2541
Pennsylvania: Highmark 2968, Independence 2975, North 3006
Rhode Island: Citizens 3067
Texas: Meadows 3296, **Paso 3312**
Virginia: AMERIGROUP 3420, CarMax 3427, MAXIMUS 3457, MLG 3460
Washington: **Gates 3516**, **Starbucks 3565**
Wisconsin: Blooming 3599, McBeath 3634, Milwaukee 3637

Obstetrics/gynecology
California: California 140, HealthCare 244

Offenders/ex-offenders
Alabama: Black 4
Arizona: Webb 64
California: California 140, Community 157, **Fund 210**, Rosenberg 385, Taper 433, Weingart 456
District of Columbia: Cafritz 656, Jovid 668
Illinois: Chicago 982, Field 1014, Siragusa 1096
Massachusetts: Access 1422, Essex 1464
Minnesota: Larsen 1711
New Jersey: Kirby 1952
New York: Achelis 2026, Langeloth 2267, **Open 2343**, Ostgrodd 2344, van Ameringen 2483
North Carolina: North Carolina 2599, Reidsville 2611
Ohio: O'Neill 2760
Oklahoma: Hardesty 2814, Hille 2816
Tennessee: Baptist 3122
Texas: Orsinger 3310
Wisconsin: Milwaukee 3637

Offenders/ex-offenders, prison alternatives
California: California 140, **Fund 210**
New York: Achelis 2026

Offenders/ex-offenders, probation/parole
California: California 140

Offenders/ex-offenders, rehabilitation
California: California 140
Minnesota: **Trust 1746**
Ohio: Reinberger 2765

Offenders/ex-offenders, services
California: California 140
New York: Ostgrodd 2344

Offenders/ex-offenders, transitional care
California: California 140

Optometry/vision screening
California: Livingston 303
Florida: Florida 744, Glazer 750
Illinois: Healthcare 1031
New York: **Deutsche 2134**, Ontario 2342
Pennsylvania: Phoenixville 3014
Texas: Alcon 3162

Organ research
Georgia: Mason 896

Orthodox agencies & churches
Kansas: Farah 1258
New Jersey: Bouras 1911
New York: Jaharis 2236

Orthopedics
District of Columbia: **Wyss 685**
North Carolina: Christopher 2537
Pennsylvania: Widener 3056

Palliative care
California: Archstone 90, UniHealth 444
New Jersey: **Johnson 1949**, **Milbank 1968**
New York: Chiang 2094, Kornfeld 2261, Littauer 2282, **Open 2343**
Texas: **Jiv 3270**

Parasitic diseases research
Washington: **Gates 3516**

Parkinson's disease
Ohio: Marion 2733
Wisconsin: Milwaukee 3637

Pediatrics
California: Genentech 216, HealthCare 244, Zafiropoulo 470
Florida: Applebaum 690
Iowa: Peregrine 1234
Kentucky: Etscorn 1287
Michigan: **Gerber 1611**
New Jersey: **Sanofi 1988**
New York: Morgan 2315, **Ross 2396**
North Carolina: Gambrill 2556, Gordon 2562
Pennsylvania: Rangos 3022
Rhode Island: CVS 3068, Hasbro 3077
Texas: **Jiv 3270**, Topfer 3372
Virginia: Richmond 3476

Pediatrics research
Colorado: Kaufmann 509
Michigan: **Gerber 1611**
New Jersey: **Pfeiffer 1975**

Performing arts
Alabama: Caddell 6
Alaska: Atwood 29, CIRI 33, Juneau 35
California: Ahmanson 77, **Clorox 153**, Community 162, Douglas 186, Fleishhacker 199, Fremont 207, Getty 218, Guzik 238, Hewlett 248, Irvine 264, **McConnell 318**, Opperman 350, **Packard 357**, Parsons 359, Placer 371, Plum 372, Sacramento 391, Simpson 411, Sonora 420, Tu 443, Wallis 451, Wasserman 453, Wattis 455, WHH 461, Zellerbach 471
Colorado: El Pomar 492, Fortune 497, Summit 537
Connecticut: **Albers 551**, Bender 554, Fisher 577, Neuberger 593, NewAlliance 595, Palmer 600, Roberts 608
District of Columbia: Cafritz 656, Lichtenberg 671
Florida: Bank 695, Bartner 696, Dunspaugh-Dalton 738, Kramer 773, Leiser 777, Life 779, Lindemann 780, **Samstag 813**, Selby 816
Georgia: Community 867, Livingston 893, Tull 917
Illinois: Chicago 982, Community 988, Katten 1042, Kaufman 1043, Maddox 1057, Pangburn 1071, Polk 1075, Ryan 1087, Simonsen 1094
Indiana: Auer 1120, Darling 1140
Iowa: Aviva 1211, McElroy 1230
Kansas: Hutchinson 1260, Insurance 1261, Salina 1274, Topeka 1279
Kentucky: Kentucky 1292
Louisiana: Community 1306, Grigsby 1312
Maryland: Baker 1347, Freeman 1373, Polinger 1405
Massachusetts: **Barr 1433**, Berkman 1434, Herbert 1481, Jaffe 1491, Santander 1541
Michigan: Ann Arbor 1576, Community 1589, Dalton 1592, DTE 1598, Frankel 1604, Fremont 1607, Gilmore 1612, Grand Rapids 1615, Hillsdale 1620, Keller 1627, Masco 1637, Morley 1644, Pokagon 1657, Skillman 1666, Wege 1674
Minnesota: **Andersen 1678**, Boss 1686, Duluth 1693, General 1697, Land 1710, Marbrook 1713, Thorpe 1745, Xcel 1754
Mississippi: Community 1759, Feild 1762
Missouri: Centene 1782, Gateway 1789, Hall 1793, Hallmark 1794, **Monsanto 1803**
Nebraska: Holland 1840, Kearney 1842, Midlands 1848, Weitz 1855, Woods 1857
New Hampshire: Fuller 1886, Johnson 1889, Woodbury 1897
New Jersey: Holzer 1939, Horizon 1940, Hyde 1944, Kirby 1952, Levitt 1960, Point 1977
New Mexico: Maddox 2014, Santa Fe 2017
New York: American 2033, **American 2034**, Assael 2046, Blum 2067, Brock 2072, **Clark 2098**, **Duke 2146**, **Ford 2160**, Goldman 2183, **Henson 2210**, Lassalle 2268, Liberman 2279, Loewe 2284, **Mellon 2302**, Purple 2369, Resnick 2379, Scherman 2409, Sheafer 2418, Tisch 2468, **Trust 2477**, Western 2503
North Carolina: Adams 2517, Billingsley 2530, Cumberland 2541, Odell 2602, Smith 2629
Ohio: Akron 2655, Anderson 2658, Andrews 2659, Dayton 2688, Emery 2694, Haile, 2709, Knoll 2719, Kulas 2721, Middletown 2737, Morgan 2739, Murphy 2745, Muskingum 2747, Nordson 2755, **OMNOVA 2759**, Reinberger 2765, Stark 2788, Youngstown 2804
Oregon: Benton 2835, Jackson 2851, Meyer 2861
Pennsylvania: Baker 2886, Burgess 2903, Claneil 2918, EQT 2940, Ferree 2944, Garfield 2955, Independence 2976, McCune 2993, McLean 2997, Penn 3011, **PPG 3018**, Saramar 3029, Washington 3054
Rhode Island: Rhode Island 3089
South Carolina: Graham 3103
Tennessee: Benwood 3123, Eastman 3133
Texas: Carter 3190, Deakins 3210, Dedman 3212, Fish 3233, Hoblitzelle 3262, King 3275, Littauer 3283, McIntyre 3294, Moody 3298, Music 3303, Proctor 3325, Richardson 3334, Rosewood 3340, Sterling 3358, Wright 3386
Utah: Quinney 3402, Schmidt 3403
Virginia: Arlington 3421, **Fox 3439**, Gifford 3440
Washington: Allen 3490, Blue 3498, Community 3503, Echo 3508, McEachern 3541, Renton 3552, Safeco 3554, Sherwood 3561, Tacoma 3567, Yakima 3576
West Virginia: Tucker 3589
Wisconsin: **Baird 3595**, Baker 3596, Incourage 3623, Johnson 3625, Kohler 3629, Milwaukee 3637, Pick 3646, RITE-HITE 3651, Sentry 3657, Stateline 3663

Performing arts (multimedia)
Illinois: Alphawood 959
New York: **Cummings 2121**

Performing arts centers
Alabama: Stephens 24
Arizona: Hughes 49
California: Carpenter 145, Irvine 264, Liu 302, Pacific 355

Connecticut: Inc. 616
Florida: **Patel 797**
Kansas: Capitol 1251
Maryland: Baker 1347, Freeman 1373
Massachusetts: Fireman 1469
Missouri: Centene 1782
New Hampshire: Penates 1893
New Jersey: Gamper 1933
New York: Belfer 2059, Fisher 2157, Heyman 2212, Hycliff 2226, St. Simon 2446, Wegman 2497
Pennsylvania: Grumbacher 2961
Texas: Bass 3172
Washington: Wright 3574

Performing arts, ballet

California: Baker 98, Irvine 264
Connecticut: Bender 554
Florida: Ansin 689
Georgia: Holder 887
Illinois: Pangburn 1071
Minnesota: Thorpe 1745
Missouri: Centene 1782
New Jersey: Point 1977
New York: **Hughes 2224**, Lassalle 2268, Slifka 2428, Ziff 2515
Pennsylvania: Adams 2881, Patterson 3010
Virginia: **Price 3472**
Wisconsin: **Baird 3595**, Einhorn 3613

Performing arts, choreography

Kentucky: Kentucky 1292

Performing arts, dance

California: Fleishhacker 199, Hewlett 248, Irvine 264, Plum 372
Colorado: Vail 543
Connecticut: Roberts 608
District of Columbia: Cafritz 656
Florida: Bank 695
Illinois: Alphawood 959, Cheney 981, Community 988, Prince 1077
Iowa: Siouxland 1240
Louisiana: Community 1306
Maryland: Mann 1389
Minnesota: Thorpe 1745
New Jersey: **Puffin 1980**
New York: **Clark 2098**, **Duke 2146**, **Ford 2160**, **Mertz 2306**, Scherman 2409, **Trust 2477**, Western 2503, Ziff 2515
North Carolina: Biddle 2529
Ohio: Coshocton 2686, Murphy 2745
Washington: Seattle 3558
Wisconsin: Bemis 3598, Milwaukee 3637

Performing arts, education

California: Roth 388
Florida: Mertz 788
Illinois: Dunard 1006
Indiana: Community 1130
Kentucky: Campbell 1285
Massachusetts: **Kahn 1492**
Missouri: Curry 1784
New York: Gellert 2171, Heckscher 2205, Lassalle 2268
North Dakota: Larson 2650
Tennessee: Tucker 3156
Vermont: McKenzie 3413

Performing arts, music

Alabama: Caddell 6
California: Fleishhacker 199, Getty 218, Heller 246, Hewlett 248, **Mercer 328**, Plum 372, Price 374, Roth 388, Sonora 420, **Wadhwani 450**
Colorado: El Pomar 492, Summit 537, Vail 543
District of Columbia: Cafritz 656, Krauthammer 669
Florida: Blanton 702, Katcher 765
Georgia: Katz 889
Illinois: Alphawood 959, Cheney 981, Community 988, Dunard 1006
Indiana: Community 1130, Crosser 1139, Joshi 1165
Iowa: Siouxland 1240
Michigan: Community 1589, Dalton 1592
Minnesota: **Andersen 1678**, Duluth 1693, RBC 1730, Xcel 1754
Missouri: Boylan 1776
New Hampshire: Smyth 1895
New Jersey: Holzer 1939
New Mexico: Santa Fe 2017
New York: Carvel 2088, **Clark 2098**, Community 2108, **Deutsche 2134**, **Duke 2146**, **Ford 2160**, Gellert 2171, Kellen 2250, **Koussevitzky 2262**, Lassalle 2268, Moore 2313, Sarofim 2405, Scherman 2409, Sorel 2437, **Trust 2477**, **Weill 2499**, Western 2503
North Carolina: Adams 2517, Bergen 2527, Biddle 2529, Gambrill 2556, Stuart 2634
Ohio: American 2656, Kulas 2721, Licking 2723, Muskingum 2747, Youngstown 2804
Pennsylvania: Central 2907, Presser 3019
Vermont: McKenzie 3413
Washington: Community 3503, Seattle 3558

Performing arts, music (choral)

Illinois: Prince 1077
Pennsylvania: Patterson 3010
Wyoming: Christian 3671

Performing arts, music composition

Kentucky: Kentucky 1292

Performing arts, music ensembles/groups

New York: **Sparkplug 2441**

Performing arts, opera

Arizona: Hill 48, Hughes 49
California: Baker 98, Dolby 185, Good 230, Irvine 264, Leichtman 298
Colorado: **Avenir 473**
Florida: Bartner 696, Leiser 777, Lindemann 780
Georgia: Woodruff 922
Illinois: Dunard 1006, Maddox 1057, Pangburn 1071, Prince 1077
Iowa: Woodward 1247
Louisiana: Community 1306
Maine: Borman 1325
Massachusetts: **Brabson 1438**, Calderwood 1444, **Kahn 1492**
Minnesota: Boss 1686
New Hampshire: Penates 1893, Smyth 1895
New York: Cohen 2102, Gellert 2171, Ghez 2175, **Hughes 2224**, Lassalle 2268, Lissner 2281, **Weill 2499**
Ohio: Ohio 2756
Pennsylvania: Patterson 3010
Tennessee: HCA 3139, Schmidt 3153
Texas: Littauer 3283, Schissler 3346
Washington: Hanauer 3523
Wisconsin: **Baird 3595**

Performing arts, orchestras

Alabama: Caddell 6, Stephens 24
Arizona: Stardust 63
California: Dolby 185, Eichenberg 188, Heller 246, Irvine 264, Rifkind 383, Simpson 411, Zafiropoulo 470
Colorado: Griffin 504
Delaware: Sylvan 648
Florida: Bartner 696, Blanton 702, Brown 707, Chapman 717, Snell 821, Walter 837
Illinois: Dunard 1006, Maddox 1057, Pangburn 1071, Prince 1077
Indiana: Auer 1120, OneAmerica 1183
Louisiana: Community 1306
Maryland: RCM & D 1406
Massachusetts: Arbella 1426, **Brabson 1438**, Calderwood 1444, Cogan 1450, Fish 1470, Grew 1478, Liberty 1502
Michigan: Alro 1574, Dana 1593, Lear 1632
Minnesota: 3M 1676, Nash 1720, Thorpe 1745
Missouri: Centene 1782, Curry 1784, Hallmark 1794
Montana: Wendy's 1831
Nebraska: Holland 1840, Lienemann 1846
New Hampshire: Smyth 1895
New Mexico: Garfield 2013
New York: Gellert 2171, Resnick 2380, Schmitt 2410, Sorel 2437
North Carolina: Smith 2629
Ohio: Ar-Hale 2661, Charities 2678, Cliffs 2681, **Eaton 2692**, Ohio 2756, Young 2803
South Carolina: Daniel 3101
Tennessee: First 3135
Texas: P 3311, Plass 3322, Potts 3323, Schissler 3346, Willard 3382
Wisconsin: Pick 3646

Performing arts, theater

Alabama: Caddell 6
Arizona: Stardust 63
California: **Applied 88**, Barth 101, Douglas 186, Fleishhacker 199, Hewlett 248, Irvine 264, Lansing 290, Plum 372, Pritzker 375, Sacramento 391, Sierra 406, Tippett 436
Colorado: El Pomar 492, Summit 537
Connecticut: Hall 584
Delaware: Sylvan 648
District of Columbia: Cafritz 656
Florida: Ansin 689, Bank 695, Brown 707, Community 722, Dunspaugh-Dalton 738, Mertz 788
Georgia: Anderson 850, Blank 856
Illinois: Alphawood 959, Cheney 981, Guthman 1027, Katten 1042, Pangburn 1071, Polk 1075, Prince 1077
Indiana: Parke 1186
Iowa: Siouxland 1240, Stebens 1242, United 1243
Kansas: Hutchinson 1260
Kentucky: Kentucky 1292
Louisiana: Community 1306
Massachusetts: Calderwood 1444, **Kahn 1492**, Symes 1555
Michigan: Ann Arbor 1576, Community 1586, Dana 1593, Grand Rapids 1615, Hillsdale 1620
Minnesota: Boss 1686, Marbrook 1713
Missouri: Hallmark 1794
Montana: Silver 1830, Wendy's 1831
New York: Blum 2067, **Clark 2098**, Diller 2137, **Dramatists 2143**, **Duke 2146**, **Ford 2160**, **Gilman 2178**, Istel 2234, Kleban 2252, Lassalle 2268, Loewe 2284, Miller 2308, Mindich 2309, Randall 2372, Scherman 2409, Solomon 2436, Stardust 2448, Sugarman 2450, Time 2466, **Trust 2477**, **Weill 2499**, Western 2503
North Carolina: Biddle 2529, Smith 2629, VF 2642
North Dakota: MDU 2652

Ohio: Cliffs 2681, **Eaton 2692**, Murphy 2745, National 2748
Pennsylvania: Adams 2881, Patterson 3010, Randall 3021
South Carolina: Lutz 3105
Tennessee: Regal 3151
Texas: Sterling 3358
Virginia: **Fox 3439**, **Price 3472**
Washington: Biller 3496, Community 3503, Tacoma 3567, Wright 3574
West Virginia: Eastern 3580
Wisconsin: Bemis 3598, Incourage 3623

Performing arts, theater (musical)
Louisiana: Community 1306
New York: Ebb 2149, **Weill 2499**

Pharmacology research
California: **Parsemus 358**

Pharmacy/prescriptions
California: Patron 363
Colorado: El Pomar 492
Indiana: Kosciusko 1168
Minnesota: Alworth 1677
Ohio: **Cardinal 2677**
Rhode Island: CVS 3068

Philanthropy/voluntarism
California: Berry 110, Family 192, **Floyd 200**, Gerbode 217, Hand 241, Hewlett 248, Irvine 264, Kern 279, **Packard 357**, Rappaport 380, Stone 427, **Wadhwani 450**
Colorado: **Gill 502**, Leighty 512, Merage 518, **Merage 519**
Florida: Community 725
Georgia: North 900
Illinois: Amicus 961, Logan 1051, Pritzker 1079
Indiana: Central 1126, Community 1129, Greene 1152, Legacy 1171
Kansas: Western 1281
Maryland: Israelson 1380, Kentfields 1385
Michigan: Anderson 1575, Frey 1609, Onequest 1650
Minnesota: Butler 1688, Southwest 1740
Missouri: Ross 1810
New Hampshire: Byrne 1879
New Jersey: Meyer 1967
New Mexico: Chase 2009
New York: **Bloomberg 2066**, **Breslauer 2069**, Donner 2142, **Ford 2160**, Helmsley 2207, **Unbound 2480**
North Carolina: Meserve 2592
Ohio: Morino 2742, Sears 2781
Rhode Island: Hasbro 3077
Washington: Almi 3491, Yakima 3576

Philanthropy/voluntarism, administration/regulation
California: Irvine 264

Philanthropy/voluntarism, alliance/advocacy
Washington: **Gates 3516**

Philanthropy/voluntarism, association
California: Irvine 264, Los Altos 305

Philanthropy/voluntarism, information services
California: Irvine 264

Philanthropy/voluntarism, management/technical assistance
California: **Packard 357**

Philosophy/ethics
Alaska: CIRI 33
California: **Rupe 389**

Physical therapy
Indiana: Kosciusko 1168
Minnesota: **Patterson 1726**
Rhode Island: CVS 3068

Physical/earth sciences
California: **Beckman 105**, **Keck 276**
Florida: Selby 816, Sunburst 829
Minnesota: Alworth 1677
New York: **Eppley 2152**, **Kade 2243**
Pennsylvania: Society 3040
Virginia: Jeffress 3444

Physically disabled
Alabama: Black 4, Community 11
Arizona: Webb 64
Arkansas: Cabe 67
California: Ahmanson 77, **Better 112**, Community 157, **Gellert 214**, Gumbiner 236, Lesher 299, Outhwaite 353, Patron 363, San Luis 393, Weingart 456
Colorado: Hunter 508, Summit 537
Connecticut: **Deupree 571**, Gross 583
District of Columbia: Cafritz 656
Florida: Jacobsen 762, Southwest 823
Georgia: Abreu 846
Illinois: Blowitz 968, Siragusa 1096
Indiana: Brown 1124, Henry 1158
Iowa: Community 1216
Maryland: Community 1360, Fowler 1372
Michigan: Fremont 1607, Midland 1642, Sanilac 1663
Missouri: Saigh 1811
Nebraska: Midlands 1848
New Hampshire: Foundation 1885, Lindsay 1890
New Jersey: Hyde 1944
New York: Achelis 2026, Black 2065, Community 2107, **MetLife 2307**, **Nash 2320**, **Ross 2396**
North Carolina: Glenn 2560, North Carolina 2599, Reidsville 2611, Strowd 2633
Ohio: Cincinnati 2679, Fairfield 2696, KeyBank 2717, O'Neill 2760, Richland 2767, Saint 2770, Springfield 2787, Youngstown 2804
Oklahoma: Hardesty 2814, Hille 2816
Oregon: Benton 2835
Pennsylvania: Child 2916, Connelly 2926, First 2948, Independence 2976, Lazarich 2983, North 3006, Phoenixville 3014
Tennessee: Baptist 3122, Wilson 3157
Texas: Abell 3160, Bass 3172, Dallas 3209, Hartman 3252, Holloway 3264, McDermott 3293, Moore 3299, Orsinger 3310, Proctor 3325
Washington: Wilkens 3573
Wisconsin: Green Bay 3619, La Crosse 3631, Marshfield 3633

Physics
Arizona: **Research 59**
California: **Beckman 105**
Minnesota: Alworth 1677
New Jersey: **Siemens 1993**
New York: **IBM 2227**

Planetarium
Illinois: Ward 1111

Political science
Massachusetts: Colombe 1452
New York: Aequus 2028, Littauer 2282, **Tinker 2467**
Wisconsin: **Bradley 3601**

Population studies
California: Hewlett 248, **Packard 357**
New York: **Weeden 2496**
North Carolina: Cumberland 2541

Poverty studies
California: Rosenberg 385
Texas: **Marshall 3290**

Pregnancy centers
California: California 140
Florida: Carlton 715
New York: Spektor 2442
Texas: Potts 3323

Prostate cancer
New Jersey: Evans 1925

Prostate cancer research
Kansas: Koch 1264
New York: Thompson 2461

Protestant agencies & churches
Alabama: Stephens 24
Arizona: Barton 40, Long 51
Arkansas: Cabe 67, Union 73
California: Boeckmann 116, Kimbo 281, McCoy 319, Philanthropy 368, Smith 417, Versacare 448
Colorado: Norwood 524, TYL 542
Connecticut: Meriden 591, Old 599
Delaware: Brookwood 624
District of Columbia: Bou 654
Florida: Alpha 687, Bank 695, Bell 698, Booth 704, Burnett 708, Burnetti 709, Finch 743, Holloway 759, Speer 824, Stafford 825
Georgia: Amos 848, Baker 853, Campbell 860, Camp-Younts 861, Colston 865, Gholston 880, Marshall 895, Patrick 902, Pitts 904, Ragan 906, Sewell 914
Hawaii: Atherton 925
Illinois: Brennan 974, Copeland 995, Frye 1019, Hunt 1036, Luehring 1052, Pierce 1074, **Tyndale 1105**, Yowell 1118
Indiana: Darling 1140, Master 1177, Parke 1186
Iowa: Stebens 1242
Louisiana: Burton 1303, Chambers 1304
Maryland: DelSignore 1368, **Jehovah 1382**, Lutheran 1387, Osprey 1403
Massachusetts: Inavale 1488, Perennial 1525
Michigan: Mills 1643, Technical 1668, Vanderweide 1671
Minnesota: Andreas 1679, Dayton 1690
Mississippi: Luckyday 1767, Mississippi 1768
Missouri: Breen 1778, Humphreys 1795, Trudy 1816
Nebraska: Lienemann 1846
New Jersey: Kish 1953, Lasko 1958, Point 1977, Snyder 1995
New York: deForest 2133, Grace 2189, IF 2228, Kanas 2244, Kellen 2250, Miller 2308, Mule 2316, Peale 2353, **Shatford 2417**, Vidda 2485

North Carolina: Byrum 2535, Community 2538, Dalton 2542, Griffin 2563, Helb 2568, Humphrey 2571, Peeler 2606, Plansoen 2608, Rogers 2618, Simpson 2626, Sites 2627, Sloan 2628
Ohio: Knoll 2719, Scotford 2779
Oklahoma: Bernsen 2807
Pennsylvania: Black 2897, Connelly 2926, Huston 2973, Smith 3037, Stackpole 3042, Staley 3043
South Carolina: Lutz 3105
Tennessee: Clayton 3128, Hutcheson 3141, **Maclellan 3146**, Wilson 3157
Texas: Anderson 3164, Astin 3166, C.I.O.S. 3186, Cain 3188, Coates 3197, Community 3200, Crain 3206, Criswell 3207, Dedman 3212, Ezekiel 3226, Henderson 3255, Johnson 3271, Mundy 3302, **Oldham 3308**, Orr 3309, Perot 3317, Potts 3323, Psalm 3327, RDM 3332, Rogers 3339, Shelton 3350, Sterling 3358, Ward 3381, Williams 3383
Vermont: Harper 3411
Virginia: Love 3452, MAIHS 3455
Washington: Bamford 3495
Wisconsin: Kern 3627, Murray 3638, Siebert 3659
Wyoming: Christian 3671, Surrena 3681

Protestant federated giving programs

Illinois: Ackermann 955, Hunt 1036
Texas: Astin 3166
Wisconsin: Siebert 3659

Psychology/behavioral science

California: Traina 438
New York: **Grant 2191**
Pennsylvania: Staunton 3044

Public affairs

Alabama: Black 4
California: Allergan 80, Blum 115, Genentech 216, Gerbode 217, Murdock 338, Pacific 355, Silicon 408
Colorado: Pikes 525
Delaware: **Gloria 634**
District of Columbia: **Searle 681**, Wallace 684
Florida: Gulf 754, Phillips 800
Georgia: Livingston 893
Illinois: Crown 997, Field 1014, Square 1099, Stern 1100
Indiana: Ball 1121, Koch 1167, Legacy 1171, Madison 1175, Noble 1179, Rush 1192, Tipton 1198, Vectren 1202, Wells 1207, Whitley 1209
Iowa: Aviva 1211, Clarinda 1214, Maytag 1229
Kansas: Koch 1264
Kentucky: Blue 1282
Louisiana: New Orleans 1316
Maine: Hannaford 1330
Maryland: **Casey 1353**, Community 1358
Massachusetts: Cabot 1442, Cabot 1443, Clipper 1449, Liberty 1502, Parker 1523
Michigan: Ann Arbor 1576, Capital 1581, Community 1588, Dart 1594, Hillsdale 1620, Masco 1637
Minnesota: Land 1710, **Mosaic 1718**, RBC 1730, Rochester 1735, Securian 1739, **St. Jude 1741**, Winona 1753
Missouri: Hallmark 1794, **Monsanto 1803**
Nebraska: Grand Island 1837, Lincoln 1847
Nevada: Caesars 1860, **Reynolds 1869**
New Jersey: Mandelbaum 1962, Schumann 1990
New Mexico: Santa Fe 2017
New York: Abelard 2022, American 2033, **American 2034**, **Clark 2098**, Community 2110, Donner 2142, Johnson 2240, **JPMorgan 2242**, **Mellon 2302**, **MetLife 2307**, NBC 2322, Novartis 2333, Schnurmacher 2411, Snyder 2433
North Carolina: Beckman 2526, Community 2539, North Carolina 2599
North Dakota: Fargo 2649, Larson 2650
Ohio: Akron 2655, Athens 2662, Cliffs 2681, Dayton 2688, Delaware 2689, Eaton 2693, Ferro 2697, Findlay 2700, Gund 2708, KeyBank 2717, Murphy 2745, Nordson 2755, **OMNOVA 2759**, Scripps 2780, Springfield 2787
Oklahoma: Kirschner 2818
Oregon: Jeld 2852
Pennsylvania: Arkema 2885, Community 2922, Hunt 2971, McKinney 2996, **PPG 3018**, Scranton 3031
Rhode Island: Rhode Island 3089, Seymour 3091
South Carolina: Joanna 3104
Tennessee: Eastman 3133
Texas: AT&T 3167, Booth 3180, Brown 3183, Burch 3184, **Houston 3266**, Meadows 3296, Penney 3315, Permian 3316, Scharbauer 3345
Utah: Park 3401
Vermont: Harper 3411, Vermont 3417
Washington: Seattle 3558
Wisconsin: Alliant 3592, Bemis 3598, **Bradley 3601**, Windway 3669

Public affairs, association

Maryland: Goldseker 1374

Public affairs, citizen participation

California: **Arkay 91**, **Kapor 273**, Patagonia.org 362, Santa Barbara 394
District of Columbia: Block 653
Florida: Gulf 754, **Knight 771**
Illinois: Evanston 1012
Indiana: Putnam 1189
Louisiana: Baptist 1299, Community 1306
Michigan: Ann Arbor 1576
Minnesota: RBC 1730
Missouri: **Deer 1786**, Roblee 1809
Nevada: Nevada 1867
New Mexico: Santa Fe 2017
New York: **Ford 2160**, **Peterson 2357**, Schumann 2412, **Surdna 2454**
Ohio: Coshocton 2686, Middletown 2737, Morino 2742, Nordson 2755
Rhode Island: **Dorot 3071**
Vermont: **Ben 3407**
Wisconsin: **Bradley 3601**, McBeath 3634

Public affairs, equal rights

Florida: Horowitz 760

Public affairs, finance

Illinois: **Joyce 1040**
Massachusetts: Jaffe 1491
New York: **Peterson 2357**

Public affairs, information services

Alaska: Alaska 26
Massachusetts: **Lincoln 1503**

Public affairs, political organizations

Illinois: **Joyce 1040**

Public affairs, public education

Massachusetts: **Lincoln 1503**

Public affairs, reform

California: Rosenberg 385

Public affairs, research

California: Rappaport 380
Massachusetts: **Lincoln 1503**, **Sociological 1548**

Public health

Alabama: BBVA 3
Arkansas: Wal-Mart 74
California: Allergan 80, **Annenberg 86**, California 138, California 140, Fremont 207, McKesson 321, Patron 363, Santa Barbara 394, UniHealth 444
Connecticut: Aetna 550, Inc. 616
Delaware: **Gloria 634**
District of Columbia: Palmer 677
Florida: Florida 744
Georgia: Georgia 876, Healthcare 886
Illinois: Hospira 1034, Pritzker 1080, Reese 1083
Indiana: Decatur 1142, Legacy 1171, WellPoint 1206
Iowa: Wellmark 1246
Kansas: Kansas 1263, Topeka 1279
Kentucky: Community 1286
Louisiana: Blue 1302, Community 1306
Maryland: **de Beaumont 1366**
Massachusetts: MetroWest 1515
Minnesota: **Andersen 1678**
Mississippi: Community 1760
New Jersey: Horizon 1940, **Johnson 1949**
New York: **Bloomberg 2066**, Brownstone 2077, Carson 2086, **Friends 2167**, **MetLife 2307**, **Open 2343**, **PepsiCo 2354**
North Carolina: North 2600
Ohio: Austin 2663, **Cardinal 2677**, Ginn 2706, Osteopathic 2762
Oregon: PacificSource 2866
Pennsylvania: CIGNA 2917, Highmark 2968, Independence 2975, North 3006, Phoenixville 3014, Pottstown 3017
Rhode Island: Textron 3093
South Carolina: Black 3097
Texas: **International 3269**, P 3311, Rockwell 3338
Virginia: AMERIGROUP 3420, Loeb 3450
Washington: **Gates 3516**
Wisconsin: Harley 3621

Public health school/education

California: California 140
Georgia: Georgia 876
New York: **Macy 2288**

Public health, bioterrorism

Maryland: **de Beaumont 1366**

Public health, clean water supply

California: **Hilton 251**
District of Columbia: **Wallace 683**
Georgia: **Coca 864**
Illinois: **Buffett 975**
Minnesota: **Pentair 1727**
Missouri: **Monsanto 1803**
New York: **PepsiCo 2354**
Washington: **Gates 3516**, **Starbucks 3565**

Public health, communicable diseases

California: California 140
Indiana: WellPoint 1206
Maryland: **de Beaumont 1366**

Recreation, community
Colorado: Brown 478
Florida: Woodbery 844
Indiana: Shoop 1195
Louisiana: Community 1306
New Jersey: Roma 1984
Texas: Schissler 3346

Recreation, fairs/festivals
Alabama: Caddell 6
California: Sierra 406
Kentucky: Trim 1295
Michigan: Pokagon 1657
Ohio: Dayton 2688
Pennsylvania: EQT 2940
Wisconsin: Bemis 3598

Recreation, parks/playgrounds
Alabama: Community 10
Arizona: Freedom 45
California: Community 160, Pacific 354, PG&E 367, Valley 445
Connecticut: **Deupree 571**
Florida: Coral Gables 729, Darden 732, Selby 816
Indiana: Blackford 1122, Community 1129, Marshall 1176, Rush 1192
Iowa: Ahrens 1210, Siouxland 1240
Kentucky: Trim 1295
Maryland: Rembrandt 1407
Michigan: Pokagon 1657
Minnesota: Land 1710
Mississippi: Community 1758
Missouri: Gateway 1789, Whitaker 1820
New York: Butler 2081, **Credit 2118**, Hallingby 2201, Heckscher 2205, Northern 2331, Thompson 2461, Tiffany 2463
Ohio: Bryan 2674, Slemp 2785
Pennsylvania: **Alcoa 2882**, CIGNA 2917, Packer 3008, Randall 3021
Rhode Island: CVS 3068, Hasbro 3077
Texas: Coastal 3196, Dallas 3209, Richardson 3335
Utah: Green 3394
Virginia: CarMax 3427
Washington: Miller 3544, Seattle 3558
Wisconsin: Schlegel 3656, Windhover 3668

Recreation, public policy
California: Ahmanson 77

Religion
California: **Alalusi 78**, Aratani 89, Fusenot 211, **Hilton 251**, Marin 309, **Rivendell 384**
Colorado: **Crowell 487**
Connecticut: Adams 549, Howe 586, Palmer 600
Florida: Community 725, **Jaffer 763**, Landwirth 775, Lattner 776, MAH 784, Pinellas 801, Reinhold 808, Rinker 810, Sierra 819
Georgia: Bradley 858, Community 868, North 900, Savannah 912, WinShape 921
Illinois: Burk 977, Cadle 979
Indiana: Brotherhood 1123, Fayette 1146, Koch 1167, Wabash 1203, Welborn 1205
Kentucky: Blue 1282, Steel 1294
Louisiana: Glazer 1311
Maine: Lynam 1335, Narragansett 1337
Maryland: **Ames 1346**, Community 1358, Tucker 1415
Massachusetts: **A Child 1420**, Demoulas 1458, Kittredge 1496, Thee 1556
Michigan: Alix 1572, Isabella 1622
Minnesota: **Trust 1746**
Mississippi: Foundation 1763
Missouri: Dunn 1787, Green 1790, Ross 1810
Nebraska: Daugherty 1835
New Jersey: Bonner 1909, Brotherton 1914, Capozzi 1918, Catholic 1919, Hyde 1944, Pierson 1976, Saka 1987
New York: **Abba's 2021**, Achelis 2026, Clark 2096, Cohen 2103, Galler 2168, **Klein 2254**, Littauer 2282, MBIA 2297, Nakash 2318, Smith 2429, Sorel 2437, Tishman 2470, Vogler 2487, Weil, 2498
North Carolina: Adams 2517, Community 2538, Duncan 2547, Garrow 2557, Harvest 2566, Krost 2582, Niessen 2598, North Carolina 2599
Ohio: Bryan 2674, Community 2685, **Omnicare 2758**, Renner 2766
Oregon: Flowerree 2845, Mission 2863
Pennsylvania: Central 2907, Community 2922, Davis 2929, Foundation 2952, Hunt 2971, **Riverside 3025**, Scranton 3031, **Templeton 3047**, Washington 3054
Rhode Island: Estate 3073, King 3080, Parmelee 3088
Tennessee: CIC 3127, Sparks 3154
Texas: Edwards 3218, Elkins 3220, Elkins 3221, Hamman 3248, Henderson 3255, Hildebrand 3258, **Houston 3266**, Lupton 3288, Moody 3298, **PHM 3320**, Rogers 3339, Scharbauer 3345, Sikh 3351, Sterling 3358, Trull 3373
Utah: Mendenhall 3398
Virginia: Community 3431
Washington: Lochland 3536, Miller 3544, Moccasin 3545, Shemanski 3560
Wisconsin: BayCare 3597, Marshfield 3633, Siebert 3659
Wyoming: Furrer 3674, McMurry 3676

Religion, association
Tennessee: **Maclellan 3146**

Religion, formal/general education
Maryland: Mustard 1400
Virginia: Keesee 3445

Religion, interfaith issues
District of Columbia: **El-Hibri 659**
Kansas: **Shumaker 1276**
Kentucky: J & L 1291
Maine: **Catalyst 1326**
Maryland: **Ames 1346**, Hirschhorn 1379
New Jersey: **Berrie 1908**
New York: **Cummings 2121**, **Ford 2160**
North Carolina: Gambrill 2556
Texas: **PHM 3320**
Utah: Semnani 3404

Religion, public policy
New York: **Tikvah 2465**

Religious federated giving programs
Florida: Speer 824
Illinois: Pritzker 1079, Richard 1085, **Tyndale 1105**
Michigan: Merillat 1640
New York: Halper 2202
Texas: Perot 3317

Reproductive health
California: California 140, **Packard 357**, Roth 388
Colorado: **General 501**
Illinois: Grant 1025, **MacArthur 1056**
Iowa: Wellmark 1246
New York: **Ford 2160**, **Open 2343**
Pennsylvania: Pilgrim 3016
Texas: **Jiv 3270**, **PHM 3320**
Virginia: AMERIGROUP 3420, Oak 3466

Reproductive health, abortion clinics/services
New York: Anderson 2036

Reproductive health, family planning
Arizona: Hughes 49
California: California 140, **Gellert 214**, Gold 228, Hewlett 248, **Packard 357**
Colorado: **Avenir 473**, **General 501**
Connecticut: Community 563, **Educational 574**, Palmer 600
District of Columbia: Cafritz 656
Florida: Bank 695
Illinois: Community 988, Kaufman 1043, Prince 1076
Maryland: Moore 1396
Massachusetts: Kelsey 1493, **Lalor 1498**
Michigan: Delano 1596
Nebraska: **Buffett 1833**
New Jersey: Borden 1910
New York: Anderson 2036, **Clark 2098**, Moore 2311, Ostgrodd 2344, Scherman 2409, Woodcock 2511
North Carolina: Cumberland 2541, Griffin 2563
Ohio: **Brush 2673**
Oklahoma: McGee 2820
Pennsylvania: Claneil 2918, Union 3051
Texas: Hill 3260
Vermont: Vermont 3417
Virginia: **WestWind 3486**
Washington: Blue 3498, Community 3503, **Gates 3516**, Moccasin 3545
Wisconsin: Milwaukee 3637, Windhover 3668

Reproductive health, prenatal care
California: California 140
Florida: Burns 710
Indiana: WellPoint 1206
Iowa: Wellmark 1246
Pennsylvania: Highmark 2968
Virginia: AMERIGROUP 3420

Reproductive health, sexuality education
California: California 140
Minnesota: HRK 1702
New York: Anderson 2036, **Ford 2160**

Residential/custodial care
California: Carney 144
Florida: Walter 837
Georgia: Goizueta 883, Tull 917
Hawaii: Hawaii 933
Illinois: Allegretti 958, Parr 1072, Seymour 1091
Iowa: United 1243
Maryland: Maryland 1391
Michigan: Delano 1596
Minnesota: Sauer 1736
North Carolina: Hunter 2573
Ohio: Ohio 2756
Oklahoma: Liddell 2819
Texas: Mundy 3302, Proctor 3325
Virginia: Obici 3467

Residential/custodial care, group home
Mississippi: Ergon 1761

Residential/custodial care, hospices

Alabama: Community 11
California: Community 162, **Keck 276**, Sacramento 391, Santa Barbara 394, Sonora 420, Weingart 456
Colorado: El Pomar 492, Summit 537
Connecticut: Connecticut 564, Palmer 600
Delaware: Palmer 644
District of Columbia: Cafritz 656
Florida: Bank 695, Community 727, Kantner 764, Stellar 826
Illinois: Foglia 1015, Frye 1019, Ryan 1087
Indiana: Kosciusko 1168
Iowa: United 1243
Kansas: Hutchinson 1260
Maryland: Tucker 1415, Wolpoff 1417
Massachusetts: Demoulas 1458, East 1460, Shattuck 1544
Michigan: Hillsdale 1620, Pokagon 1657, Schmuckal 1664, Von 1672, Wilson 1675
Missouri: Mungenast 1804
New Hampshire: Penates 1893
New Mexico: Frost 2012
New York: High 2213, McGraw 2300, Northern 2331, Warwick 2495, Western 2503
North Carolina: Bolick 2531, Christopher 2537, Cumberland 2541, Gambrill 2556, Kennedy 2578, Moretz 2595, VF 2642
Ohio: Brethen 2671, Community 2682, Johnson 2714, McGregor 2736, Muskingum 2747, Troy 2794, Youngstown 2804
Pennsylvania: Fourjay 2953
South Carolina: Lutz 3105
Texas: Fisch 3232, Hill 3260, Meadows 3296, Potts 3323, Sterling 3358, Wright 3386
Washington: Blue 3498, Community 3503, Renton 3552, Tacoma 3567
Wisconsin: Green Bay 3619, McBeath 3634, Wanek 3667, Windhover 3668

Residential/custodial care, senior continuing care

California: California 140
New York: Eastern 2148
North Carolina: Balin 2523
Pennsylvania: DSF 2937
South Carolina: Bailey 3096

Rural development

Hawaii: **Watumull 939**
Michigan: **Kellogg 1628**, **Mott 1645**
Minnesota: Land 1710, Musser 1719
Nebraska: Kiewit 1843
New Jersey: **International 1946**
New York: **Ford 2160**
North Carolina: Cumberland 2541
Pennsylvania: Stackpole 3042
Texas: King 3275, Meadows 3296
Wyoming: Wyoming 3684

Safety, automotive safety

Massachusetts: Arbella 1426
Ohio: Progressive 2764

Safety, education

Alabama: Caring 7
Indiana: Decatur 1142
Missouri: **Monsanto 1803**
Ohio: Angels 2660
Virginia: Oak 3466

Safety/disasters

Alabama: McWane 17
California: **Hilton 251**, Humboldt 257, Napa 340, Shasta 401, **Wadhwani 450**
Connecticut: Palmer 600
District of Columbia: **Sasakawa 680**
Florida: Glazer 750, MAH 784, Southwest 823
Georgia: **Georgia 878**
Illinois: **Motorola 1066**
Indiana: Noble 1179
Iowa: Jefferson 1227, Siouxland 1240
Kansas: Damon 1254, Manhattan 1268
Kentucky: C.E. 1284
Louisiana: New Orleans 1316
Massachusetts: Liberty 1502
Michigan: Ann Arbor 1576
Minnesota: **Andersen 1678**
Missouri: **Monsanto 1803**
New York: Andor 2037, Freed 2163, **PepsiCo 2354**
North Dakota: Fargo 2649
Ohio: American 2656, **Cardinal 2677**, Coshocton 2686, NiSource 2752, **OMNOVA 2759**
Oregon: **NIKE 2865**
Pennsylvania: **Alcoa 2882**
Texas: Coastal 3196, Elkins 3221, Meadows 3296
Virginia: Arlington 3421, Community 3429
Washington: Community 3503, **Gates 3516**, Renton 3552, Safeco 3554
Wisconsin: Alliant 3592, Anthony 3593, Community 3607, Dudley 3610

Safety/disasters, public education

Wisconsin: Dudley 3610

Safety/disasters, volunteer services

Virginia: Greensville 3441

Salvation Army

Alabama: Caring 7
Arkansas: Wal-Mart 74
California: Eichenberg 188, Siebel 404
Connecticut: Meriden 591, Northeast 598
Delaware: Palmer 644
Florida: Walter 837
Georgia: Georgia 877
Illinois: Ackermann 955, Frye 1019, Luehring 1052, **Mondelez 1064**
Kansas: Sarver 1275
Kentucky: Campbell 1285
Louisiana: Community 1306
Maryland: Battye 1348
Massachusetts: Liberty 1502, McNeice 1509
Michigan: Sigmund 1665
Minnesota: Target 1744
Mississippi: Ergon 1761
Missouri: Boylan 1776, Fabick 1788, Musgrave 1805
New York: Brock 2072, deForest 2133, Johnson 2239, Solomon 2436
North Carolina: Gambrill 2556, Helb 2568, Olin 2603, Peeler 2606, Plansoen 2608, Sites 2627, Southern 2630, Templin 2638, Zelnak 2647
Ohio: Brethen 2671, Dayton 2688, **Eaton 2692**, National 2748, NiSource 2752
Oklahoma: Oklahoma 2823, Parman 2824
Pennsylvania: **Firth 2949**, Hunt 2972, Rider 3024
Rhode Island: Chamberlain 3066, Hecht 3078, Parmelee 3088
Tennessee: First 3135
Texas: Anderson 3164, Heavin 3253, Moore 3299, Potts 3323, Shelton 3350
Virginia: United 3484
Wisconsin: Anthony 3593, Bemis 3598, Murray 3638, Oshkosh 3643

Scholarships/financial aid

Alaska: CIRI 33
Arizona: Ahearn 38, Marshall 54
Arkansas: Union 73
California: College 156, Disney 181
Colorado: Puksta 527, Tomkins 540
Connecticut: **Deupree 571**
District of Columbia: Block 653
Florida: Atkins 693, Hand 755, Jacobsen 762, Morrison 792, **Skelly 820**
Georgia: Anderson 850, **Coca 864**
Hawaii: Zimmerman 940
Indiana: Blackford 1122, Community 1135, Harrison 1155, Jasper 1160, Marshall 1176, Shoop 1195, Wells 1207
Iowa: Jefferson 1227
Kansas: Salina 1274
Massachusetts: Ramsey 1530
Michigan: Community 1586
Minnesota: Xcel 1754
Missouri: Anheuser 1774, Tilles 1815
Nevada: Shaheen 1871, **Tang 1873**
New Jersey: Grace 1935, Rowan 1986
New York: **Buffalo 2078**, Heckscher 2205, Jewish 2237, Kleban 2252, Knapp 2259, Rhodes 2381, Roothbert 2391, Society 2434
North Carolina: Ferebee 2552, Kanitz 2575, Meserve 2592
Ohio: Charities 2678, Delaware 2689, Foundation 2702, Murphy 2746
Oregon: Shapira 2870
Pennsylvania: Chester 2915, Duff 2938, **PPG 3018**
Texas: AT&T 3167, B.E.L.I.E.F. 3169, **BP 3181**, College 3198, Penney 3315
Washington: Echo 3508

Science

Arizona: APS 39, **Research 59**
California: **Applied 88**, Bechtel, 104, **Beckman 105**, **Broad 129**, Buell 134, Crail 170, Hewlett 249, **Kavli 275**, **Keck 276**, McMicking 322, **Moore 333**, Nicholas 343, Noyce 348, Pacific 355, **Packard 357**, Parsons 359, Western 459
Colorado: Change 481
Connecticut: NewAlliance 595, Palmer 600
Delaware: CenturyLink-Clarke 627
Florida: Chapman 717, Sudakoff 828
Illinois: **Grainger 1024**, Lars 1047, **Motorola 1066**
Iowa: **Rockwell 1237**
Kansas: Koch 1264, **Shumaker 1276**
Louisiana: Community 1306, Grigsby 1312
Michigan: Dow 1597, DTE 1598
Minnesota: 3M 1676, Alworth 1677, **Andersen 1678**, **Pentair 1727**, **St. Jude 1741**, Xcel 1754
Missouri: Albers/Kuhn 1773, **Kauffman 1797**, **McDonnell 1800**, **Monsanto 1803**
Nebraska: Daugherty 1835
New Hampshire: DEKA 1882
New Jersey: Banbury 1904, Buehler 1915, Feldstein 1928, **Knowles 1955**, Merck 1966, **Siemens 1993**
New Mexico: Santa Fe 2017
New York: **Dana 2126**, **Deutsche 2134**, **Guggenheim 2194**, **IBM 2227**, **Sparkplug 2441**
North Carolina: Goodrich 2561, Moretz 2595, North 2600
Ohio: NiSource 2752, **OMNOVA 2759**, Piqua 2763
Oklahoma: Oklahoma 2823
Oregon: PGE 2867, Western 2876
Pennsylvania: **Alcoa 2882**, Arkema 2885, Bayer 2888, Buhl 2901, EQT 2940, Lehigh Valley 2986, **PPG 3018**, **Templeton 3047**

Rhode Island: Biogen 3063
Tennessee: Eastman 3133, **International 3142**
Texas: AT&T 3167, Bass 3172, Brown 3183, Conley 3201, Elkins 3220, Elkins 3221, Fluor 3235, Hoblitzelle 3262, Mitchell 3297, Moody 3298, Sturgis 3360
Vermont: McKenzie 3413
Virginia: **Bosack 3423**, CarMax 3427, Jeffress 3444, **Northrop 3465**
Washington: Allen 3490, Bainbridge 3494, Simonyi 3562
West Virginia: Weisberg 3590
Wisconsin: Bemis 3598

Science, formal/general education

California: Genentech 216
Hawaii: Kahiau 935
Idaho: **Micron 950**
Iowa: **Rockwell 1237**
Kansas: Koch 1264
Minnesota: 3M 1676, Xcel 1754
Missouri: **Monsanto 1803**
New Jersey: Merck 1966, **Siemens 1993**
New York: **IBM 2227**
Ohio: NiSource 2752, Nordson 2755
Pennsylvania: **PPG 3018**
Texas: Fluor 3235, KDK-Harman 3273

Science, public education

California: **Las 291**
Washington: Simonyi 3562

Science, research

California: **Ellison 191**, Mazda 313, **Seaver 400**
Michigan: **Gerber 1611**
Missouri: **McDonnell 1800**
New Jersey: **Berrie 1908**, Brotherton 1914
New York: **Mathers 2294**, Oishei 2340, Rose 2393, Simons 2423, Swartz 2455
Ohio: Community 2685
Pennsylvania: Central 2907
Vermont: Lintilhac 3412
Washington: Washington 3570

Secondary school/education

Arkansas: Wal-Mart 74
California: Ahmanson 77, Bannerman 100, Brocchini 130, Carlston 143, Gellert 215, **Gleason 224**, **Kapor 273**, **Keck 276**, **McConnell 318**, Mosher 335, Parsons 359, PG&E 367, Quest 377, Shea 402, Sierra 406, **Wadhwani 450**, Weingart 456
Colorado: Donnell 491, Mullen 522, Summit 537
Connecticut: Community 563, Connecticut 564, Palmer 600
Delaware: Brookwood 624
District of Columbia: Bou 654, Cafritz 656, Meyer 672
Florida: Ansin 689, Bank 695, Darden 732, Finch 743, Martin 786, Parish 796, Rendina 809, Selby 816, Stellar 826, Walter 837
Georgia: Campbell 860, Camp-Younts 861, Goizueta 883, Sewell 914, Tull 917, WinShape 921
Idaho: **Micron 950**
Illinois: Ackermann 955, Bersted 967, Brach 973, Chicago 982, Coleman 986, Community 988, Field 1014, Fry 1018, Omron 1070, Webb 1113
Indiana: Ball 1121, Harrison 1155, Marshall 1176
Iowa: McElroy 1230, R & R 1236, Wahlert 1244
Kentucky: Gheens 1288
Louisiana: Community 1306, Pennington 1317
Maryland: **Braitmayer 1351**, Commonweal 1356
Massachusetts: East 1460, Phelps 1528, Rogers 1536, Schrafft 1543
Michigan: **Kellogg 1628**, Morley 1644
Minnesota: Greystone 1700
Missouri: Centene 1782, Hall 1793
Nebraska: Mutual 1850
New Jersey: Hyde 1944, Jones 1950, **Knowles 1955**, **Siemens 1993**
New Mexico: Simon 2018
New York: Bay 2056, Carvel 2088, Coach 2100, Community 2113, **Credit 2118**, Deerfield 2132, **Ford 2160**, **Genesis 2173**, Initial 2231, Kanas 2244, Kaylie 2247, Kellen 2250, Morgan 2315, Mutual 2317, NBC 2322, Oishei 2340, Ruffin 2400, **Shatford 2417**, Tisch 2469, Warwick 2495, Wegman 2497, Western 2503
North Carolina: **Bank 2524**, Biddle 2529, Griffin 2563, Hunt 2572, Kanitz 2575, Kenan 2577, Mayr 2588, Niessen 2598, Smith 2629
North Dakota: MDU 2652
Ohio: Andrews 2659, Ar-Hale 2661, **Benedict 2666**, Charities 2678, Cliffs 2681, Coshocton 2686, Dayton 2688, Dodero 2691, **Eaton 2692**, Gund 2708, **Noble 2753**, Nord 2754, Piqua 2763, Richland 2767, Samaritan 2772, Third 2792, White 2800
Oregon: **NIKE 2865**, TeamCFA 2873
Pennsylvania: Charlestein 2911, Claneil 2918, Connelly 2926, Lazarich 2983, Ludwick 2988, Penn 3011, Saramar 3029, Sneath 3038, Stackpole 3042
Rhode Island: Biogen 3063, Kimball 3079
South Carolina: Smith 3109, WebbCraft 3113
Tennessee: Benwood 3123, Lyndhurst 3145, Regal 3151
Texas: AT&T 3167, Bass 3172, Booth 3180, Cain 3188, Constantin 3202, Crain 3206, Hillcrest 3261, Hoblitzelle 3262, McDermott 3293, Morgan 3301, Peterson 3318, Rockwell 3338, Sterling 3358, Trull 3373
Utah: McCarthey 3397
Vermont: Vermont 3417
Virginia: Lee-Jackson 3448
Washington: Ackerley 3489, **Gates 3516**, PEMCO 3549
Wisconsin: Ariens 3594, **Baird 3595**, McBeath 3634, Milwaukee 3637, Pettit 3645, Schlegel 3656, Siebert 3659, Wanek 3667

Sex workers

California: Weingart 456

Sickle cell disease

Illinois: Kenny's 1044

SIDS (Sudden Infant Death Syndrome) research

Colorado: Kaufmann 509

Single parents

Alabama: Black 4, Community 10, Community 11
Arizona: Webb 64
California: Community 157, Gumbiner 236, Lesher 299, Marcled 308, Patron 363, Weingart 456
Colorado: Summit 537
District of Columbia: Cafritz 656, Jovid 668
Florida: Southwest 823
Georgia: Abreu 846
Maryland: Community 1360
Massachusetts: Kelsey 1493
Michigan: Grand Rapids 1615, **Kellogg 1628**, Midland 1642, Sanilac 1663
Mississippi: Community 1760
Nebraska: Midlands 1848
New York: Community 2107
North Carolina: Glenn 2560, North Carolina 2599, Reidsville 2611
Ohio: Fairfield 2696, O'Neill 2760, Youngstown 2804
Oklahoma: Hardesty 2814
Pennsylvania: First 2948, Phoenixville 3014, Pilgrim 3016
Tennessee: Wilson 3157
Texas: Embrey 3222, Hoglund 3263, McDermott 3293, Orsinger 3310, Rockwell 3338
Wisconsin: Community 3607, Green Bay 3619, La Crosse 3631, Marshfield 3633

Social entrepreneurship

California: Skoll 412
Georgia: **Georgia 878**
Minnesota: Sundance 1742
Nevada: EBV 1862
New York: **MetLife 2307**, Niehaus 2330, **Pershing 2356**
Oregon: **NIKE 2865**
Pennsylvania: Baker 2886
Texas: **PHM 3320**
Washington: **Starbucks 3565**

Social sciences

California: Haynes 243, **Lingnan 301**, Sacramento 391
District of Columbia: **Searle 681**
Illinois: Community 988, Edlis-Neeson 1009
Kentucky: Kentucky 1292
Maryland: **Ames 1346**
New York: **Ford 2160**, **Grant 2191**, **Guggenheim 2194**, Littauer 2282, **Luce 2286**, **Sage 2402**
Ohio: Morino 2742
South Dakota: Chiesman 3115
Vermont: Windham 3418
Virginia: Lynchburg 3454
Washington: Bainbridge 3494

Social sciences, equal rights

Tennessee: Assisi 3120

Social sciences, ethics

California: **Rupe 389**
Tennessee: Assisi 3120

Social sciences, formal/general education

Massachusetts: Colombe 1452

Social sciences, government agencies

Massachusetts: Colombe 1452

Social sciences, interdisciplinary studies

New York: **Grant 2191**

Social sciences, public policy

Alaska: Alaska 26
California: Heising-Simons 245
Colorado: Catto 480
Maine: Smith 1340
Massachusetts: Colombe 1452
Montana: High 1825
New Hampshire: Endowment 1883
New York: Mercer 2305
Pennsylvania: Halloran 2963
Washington: Bainbridge 3494

Social sciences, research

New York: **Grant 2191**

Space/aviation
California: Braddock 123
Michigan: Parish 1654
New Jersey: Buehler 1915
New York: Link 2280
North Carolina: Goodrich 2561
Texas: Heinlein 3254, Thompson 3367

Speech/hearing centers
California: Patron 363
Michigan: Carls 1582
North Carolina: Eddy 2548, Smith 2629
Texas: **Bolivar 3179**

Spine disorders research
District of Columbia: **Wyss 685**

Spirituality
Kansas: **Shumaker 1276**
Maryland: Delaplaine 1367
Minnesota: Marbrook 1713
New York: **Cummings 2121**
Texas: QuadW 3328

Student services/organizations
Connecticut: Nevas 594
New York: Heckscher 2205, Wagner 2491
Washington: Grays 3520

Substance abuse, prevention
Alabama: Community 10
California: Community 157, GGS 219
Delaware: Delaware 630
Florida: Chapman 717, Community 725
Michigan: Perrigo 1655
Minnesota: **Andersen 1678**
Missouri: Roblee 1809
New Mexico: Santa Fe 2017
New York: Achelis 2026
Ohio: Reinberger 2765
Pennsylvania: Staunton 3044
Texas: Goldsbury 3241

Substance abuse, services
California: Anaheim 83, Drown 187, Gellert 215, Patron 363, Santa Barbara 394, Sierra 405, Sonora 420, Weingart 456
Colorado: **Daniels 488**, El Pomar 492
Connecticut: Community 562, Community 563, Connecticut 564
District of Columbia: Cafritz 656, Meyer 672
Florida: Pinellas 801
Illinois: Community 988, Community 993, Field 1014, Grant 1025, Rosen 1086
Indiana: Community 1130, Welborn 1205
Iowa: Siouxland 1240
Kansas: Hutchinson 1260, Topeka 1279
Massachusetts: Parker 1523
Michigan: Fremont 1607, Jackson 1623, Skillman 1666
Minnesota: Butler 1688
Nebraska: Oregon 1852
Nevada: Nevada 1867
New Hampshire: Fuller 1886
New Jersey: Borden 1910, Hyde 1944, **Johnson 1949**, Princeton 1979
New Mexico: Chase 2009, Frost 2012, Maddox 2014
New York: deForest 2133, New York 2325, Northern 2331, Tower 2472, Western 2503
North Carolina: Cumberland 2541, Reynolds 2614
Ohio: Coshocton 2686, Hamilton 2710, Richland 2767, Stark 2788, Troy 2794, Woodruff 2801
Pennsylvania: Connelly 2926, Fourjay 2953, Snee 3039, Stackpole 3042, Staunton 3044, Union 3051
Tennessee: Davis 3130
Texas: Abell 3160, Coastal 3196, Constantin 3202, Hillcrest 3261, Meadows 3296, Sterling 3358, Trull 3373, Wright 3386
Vermont: Vermont 3417
Virginia: Williamsburg 3487
Washington: Casey 3499, Community 3503, Tacoma 3567
West Virginia: Eastern 3580
Wisconsin: McBeath 3634, Milwaukee 3637

Substance abuse, treatment
California: Wrather 469
Illinois: Rosen 1086
Maryland: Lutheran 1387
Montana: Lynn 1827
Ohio: Reinberger 2765
Pennsylvania: Staunton 3044
Texas: **International 3269**
Wisconsin: Stone 3664

Substance abusers
Alabama: Black 4
Arizona: Webb 64
California: Ahmanson 77, Community 157, Gumbiner 236, **Hilton 251**, Lesher 299, Patron 363, Weingart 456
Colorado: Summit 537
Connecticut: Community 562
District of Columbia: Cafritz 656, Jovid 668
Florida: Southwest 823
Georgia: Abreu 846
Indiana: Brown 1124
Maryland: Community 1360
Michigan: Midland 1642, Sanilac 1663
Minnesota: Larsen 1711
Nebraska: Midlands 1848
New Hampshire: Lindsay 1890
New Jersey: Hyde 1944, Kirby 1952
New York: Achelis 2026, Community 2107, Langeloth 2267, **Open 2343**, Tower 2472
North Carolina: Glenn 2560, North Carolina 2599, Reidsville 2611
Ohio: Fairfield 2696, O'Neill 2760, Saint 2770
Oklahoma: Hardesty 2814, Hille 2816
Pennsylvania: Birmingham 2896, First 2948, Phoenixville 3014, Staunton 3044
Tennessee: Baptist 3122, Wilson 3157
Texas: Abell 3160, Hoblitzelle 3262, McDermott 3293, Moore 3299, Orsinger 3310
Virginia: Williamsburg 3487
Wisconsin: Cornerstone 3608, Green Bay 3619, La Crosse 3631

Surgery
Minnesota: **St. Jude 1741**

Surgery research
New Jersey: Integra 1945

Teacher school/education
Alabama: BBVA 3
Arkansas: Wal-Mart 74
Delaware: Sylvan 648
Hawaii: Castle 930
Idaho: **Micron 950**
Missouri: Roblee 1809
New Jersey: **Knowles 1955**, Merck 1966, **Siemens 1993**
New York: **Carnegie 2085**, **Credit 2118**, Heckscher 2205, **JPMorgan 2242**, Naomi 2319, Roothbert 2391
Pennsylvania: **Alcoa 2882**
Vermont: Rowland 3415
Virginia: **Longview 3451**, Moore 3461

Terminal illness, people with
Alabama: Black 4, Community 11
Arizona: Webb 64
Arkansas: Cabe 67
California: Community 157, Gilmore 221, Weingart 456
Colorado: Summit 537
Florida: Landwirth 775
Georgia: Abreu 846
Illinois: Blowitz 968
Indiana: Orange 1184
Iowa: Wahlert 1244
Michigan: Midland 1642
Nebraska: Midlands 1848
New York: **Open 2343**
North Carolina: Glenn 2560, North Carolina 2599, Reidsville 2611
Ohio: Fairfield 2696, O'Neill 2760, Saint 2770
Oklahoma: Hardesty 2814, Hille 2816
Pennsylvania: First 2948, Phoenixville 3014
Tennessee: Baptist 3122, Wilson 3157
Texas: Holloway 3264, McDermott 3293, Orsinger 3310
Wisconsin: Green Bay 3619

Theological school/education
California: Brunswick 133, **Rivendell 384**
Colorado: **Crowell 487**
Hawaii: Atherton 925
Illinois: Ackermann 955, MacArthur 1055
Indiana: Master 1177
Michigan: Christian 1585, Jubilee 1624, Schmuckal 1664
Mississippi: Ergon 1761
Missouri: Breen 1778, Fabick 1788
New York: Century 2089, Grace 2189, Kekst 2249, **Luce 2286**, **Nash 2320**, Resnick 2380
North Carolina: Bolick 2531, Byrum 2535, Everett 2550, Woodson 2644
Ohio: Munro 2743, Schottenstein 2777
Oklahoma: Presbyterian 2826
Pennsylvania: Beacon 2889, Charlestein 2911
Tennessee: Latimer 3144
Texas: C.I.O.S. 3186, Criswell 3207, Henderson 3255, Trull 3373
Virginia: Denit 3435
Washington: Kawabe 3531
Wyoming: Christian 3671

Theology
New York: **Luce 2286**

Transgender and gender nonconforming
Alabama: Black 4
California: Weingart 456

Transportation
California: Craigslist 169
Colorado: El Pomar 492
Connecticut: Palmer 600

Tropical diseases

United Ways and Federated Giving Programs

Urban League

Urban/community development

Utilities

Veterinary medicine

Veterinary medicine, hospital

Visual arts

Visual arts, architecture

Visual arts, art conservation

Visual arts, design

Visual arts, painting

Connecticut: **Albers 551**
Kentucky: Kentucky 1292
New York: **Gottlieb 2187**

Visual arts, photography

Kentucky: Kentucky 1292
New Jersey: Segal 1992
New York: Hite 2214

Visual arts, sculpture

Missouri: **Deer 1786**
New York: **Gottlieb 2187**

Vocational education

Alaska: Arctic 28, Bristol 31, Chugach 32, CIRI 33, Doyon 34
California: Lux 307, Sacramento 391
Colorado: El Pomar 492
Connecticut: Connecticut 564
District of Columbia: Jovid 668, Lehrman 670, Meyer 672
Florida: Bank 695
Illinois: Dunham 1007, Polk 1075
Kansas: Hansen 1259
Massachusetts: Kelsey 1493, Ratshesky 1531, Staples 1549, **State 1550**
Minnesota: **Pentair 1727**
New Jersey: **Alcatel 1899**
New York: Cummings 2122, Goldman 2183
North Carolina: Cumberland 2541, Nucor 2601
Ohio: KeyBank 2717, Murphy 2745, Richland 2767, Troy 2794
Oregon: Daly 2844
Pennsylvania: Scranton 3031, Stackpole 3042
Texas: Constantin 3202, Hext 3257, Hillcrest 3261, Hoblitzelle 3262
Virginia: CarMax 3427
Washington: Safeco 3554, Yakima 3576
Wisconsin: Nelson 3640

Vocational education, post-secondary

Alaska: Aleut 27, Koniag 36
Michigan: Grand Haven 1614
North Carolina: Wrasse 2645

Vocational school, secondary

California: California 140

Voluntarism promotion

California: **Clorox 153**, Irvine 264, **McConnell 318**, Sacramento 391, Sonora 420
Colorado: El Pomar 492, Leighty 512
Connecticut: Community 562
District of Columbia: Cafritz 656
Illinois: Community 988, Hughes 1035
Indiana: TCU 1197, Whitley 1209
Kansas: Hutchinson 1260
Massachusetts: Lowell 1505
Michigan: Hillsdale 1620, **Kellogg 1628**, **Mott 1645**
Minnesota: Rochester 1735
New Jersey: **Johnson 1949**
New York: **American 2034**, **Credit 2118**, Northern 2331
North Carolina: Cumberland 2541
Ohio: Cincinnati 2679, Nordson 2755
Oklahoma: **Schusterman 2829**
Pennsylvania: **Carnegie 2906**, Comcast 2921, EQT 2940, Scranton 3031, Stackpole 3042
Rhode Island: Rhode Island 3089
Texas: Abell 3160, Meadows 3296
Washington: Community 3503, Tacoma 3567
Wyoming: Wyoming 3684

Volunteers of America

Louisiana: Community 1306

Web-based media

New York: **Cummings 2121**

Welfare policy/reform

District of Columbia: **Searle 681**
New York: Achelis 2026

Women

Alabama: Black 4
Arizona: Webb 64
Arkansas: Wal-Mart 74
California: **Allende 79**, Allergan 80, Ayrshire 97, Bannerman 100, Buell 134, California 137, California 140, Community 161, **Gellert 214**, Gerbode 217, **Google 231**, Gumbiner 236, Lesher 299, **Marisla 310**, Military 330, Patron 363, PG&E 367, Roth 388, San Luis 393, Sonora 420, Streisand 428, Swayne 431, Taper 433, Weingart 456
Colorado: Community 484, Summit 537
Connecticut: Aetna 550, Community 562, Connecticut 564, Pitney 604
Delaware: AEC 622
District of Columbia: Berger-Marks 651, Cafritz 656, **Carter 657**, **Hill 664**, Jovid 668, Lichtenberg 671
Florida: Bank 695, Bi-Lo/Winn-Dixie 700, Bush 712, Carlton 715, Community 725
Georgia: Abreu 846, Bancker-Williams 854, **Coca 864**, EZ 874, **Georgia 878**
Illinois: Blowitz 968, Chicago 982, Community 988, Evanston 1012, Field 1014, Fry 1018, Katten 1042, Monticello 1065, Polk 1075, Siragusa 1096, Washington 1112
Indiana: Brown 1124, Community 1134, Health 1156, Henry 1158, Whitley 1209
Iowa: Stebens 1242, Wahlert 1244
Kansas: Collective 1253, Skillbuilders 1277, Topeka 1279
Kentucky: Kentucky 1292
Louisiana: Beaird 1301, Community 1306
Maryland: **Cohen 1355**, Community 1359, Dresher 1370
Massachusetts: Access 1422, Association 1428, Essex 1464, Fireman 1469, Franklin 1472, Grinspoon 1479, Kittredge 1496, Swan 1552, Swartz 1553
Michigan: DTE 1598, Fremont 1607, Frey 1608, Grand Rapids 1615, Knight 1630, Midland 1642, Mount Pleasant 1647, Sanilac 1663
Minnesota: Duluth 1693, Phillips 1728, WCA 1749
Mississippi: Community 1760
Missouri: Butler 1780, Roblee 1809
Nebraska: Woods 1857
Nevada: Nevada 1867
New Hampshire: Panjandrum 1892
New Jersey: **Allen 1900**, Borden 1910, Hyde 1944, MCJ 1965, **Rippel 1982**
New Mexico: Con 2011, Frost 2012, Santa Fe 2017
New York: **Bydale 2082**, **Clark 2098**, Coach 2100, Community 2107, Community 2109, Daphne 2127, Dobkin 2140, Dreitzer 2144, **Flowering 2159**, **Ford 2160**, Jewish 2237, **Macy 2288**, **MetLife 2307**, NoVo 2334, **Noyes 2335**, Ostgrodd 2344, **Overbrook 2345**, Patrina 2350, **PepsiCo 2354**, Roche 2388, **Rubin 2398**, **Unbound 2480**, Wagner 2491
North Carolina: Community 2540, Cumberland 2541, Glenn 2560, Niessen 2598, North Carolina 2599, Peeler 2606, Reidsville 2611, Smith 2629, Strowd 2633
Ohio: Akron 2655, **Brush 2673**, Cincinnati 2679, Community 2683, Fairfield 2696, Gund 2708, Macy's 2726, Morgan 2739, Murphy 2745, O'Neill 2760, Richland 2767, Saint 2770, White 2800
Oklahoma: Hardesty 2814, Hille 2816
Oregon: Portland 2868
Pennsylvania: **Alcoa 2882**, Bayer 2888, Birmingham 2896, Claneil 2918, Connelly 2926, Drueding 2936, Female 2943, First 2948, FISA 2950, Independence 2976, Leeway 2985, Phoenixville 3014, Pilgrim 3016, **PPG 3018**, Staunton 3044, Valentine 3053
Rhode Island: Textron 3093
Tennessee: Wilson 3157
Texas: Bass 3172, **Chrest 3194**, Edwards 3218, Embrey 3222, Frees 3238, Henderson 3255, Lightner 3282, McDermott 3293, Orsinger 3310, Richardson 3335, Rockwell 3338, Shelter 3349, Sterling 3358, Waco 3378
Vermont: Harper 3411
Virginia: Arlington 3421, Lynchburg 3454, Oak 3466
Washington: Arise 3493, Biller 3496, Community 3503, **Gates 3516**, Tacoma 3567
West Virginia: Community 3579
Wisconsin: Community 3606, Community 3607, La Crosse 3631, Marshfield 3633, Oshkosh 3642

Women, centers/services

California: **Allende 79**, Buell 134, California 140, Gumbiner 236, **Marisla 310**, Sonora 420
Connecticut: Community 562
District of Columbia: Cafritz 656, Meyer 672
Florida: Bank 695, Pinellas 801
Georgia: Bancker-Williams 854
Illinois: Chicago 982, Polk 1075, Schuler 1090
Louisiana: Beaird 1301
Maryland: Ceres 1354
Massachusetts: Hazard 1480, Swan 1552, Williams 1567
Michigan: Knight 1630
Minnesota: Butler 1688, Minneapolis 1717
Missouri: Roblee 1809
Nevada: Nevada 1867
New Hampshire: Charter 1880
New Jersey: Borden 1910
New Mexico: Frost 2012
New York: Coach 2100, Dobkin 2140, Dreyfus 2145, **Ford 2160**, **Jabara 2235**, New York 2325, NoVo 2334, Patrina 2350, Roche 2388, Rosenthal 2395, Western 2503
North Carolina: Cumberland 2541, Smith 2629
Ohio: Gund 2708, Murphy 2745, Richland 2767, Schmidlapp 2775
Oregon: Portland 2868
Pennsylvania: Community 2924, Connelly 2926, FISA 2950, Pilgrim 3016, Tuttleman 3050, Valentine 3053, **Zeldin 3060**
Texas: Edwards 3218, Simmons 3352, Waco 3378
Virginia: Lynchburg 3454
Washington: Arise 3493, Community 3503, OneFamily 3547
Wisconsin: Milwaukee 3637, Pettit 3645, Windhover 3668

YM/YWCAs & YM/YWHAs

Alabama: Brown 5, McWane 17
California: Anderson 85, AS&F 95, Braddock 123, California 140, Fusenot 211, Klein 283, Thomson 435, Zafiropoulo 470
Connecticut: Meriden 591
Delaware: Pinkerton 645

Florida: Batchelor 697, Brown 707, Chapman 717, Finch 743, Jacksonville 761, Kiwanis 770, Munroe 793, Reinhold 808, Sierra 819, Sudakoff 828
Georgia: Amos-Cheves 849
Illinois: Bersted 967, Foglia 1015, Good 1023, Lars 1047, **Mondelez 1064**, Tracy 1104, Walter 1110
Indiana: Jorgensen 1164, Kuhne 1169, Vectren 1202, WellPoint 1206
Iowa: Bechtel 1212, Guernsey 1221, HNI 1223, Schildberg 1238, Stebens 1242, United 1243
Kentucky: Campbell 1285, Etscorn 1287, Trim 1295
Louisiana: Community 1306
Maine: Hannaford 1330, Kennebec 1332
Maryland: Community 1360, Macht 1388
Massachusetts: Berkman 1434, East 1460, Honey 1483
Michigan: Acheson 1571, Dalton 1592, Granger 1617, Mills 1643, Schmuckal 1664
Minnesota: General 1697, Midcontinent 1716, **Porter 1729**
Missouri: Schneider 1812
Montana: Silver 1830, Wendy's 1831
Nebraska: Hirschfeld 1839, Midlands 1848, Quivey 1853, Zollner 1858
Nevada: Troesh 1874
New Jersey: Bauer 1906, Horizon 1940
New York: American 2033, Brock 2072, Chapman 2090, **Deutsche 2134**, Hultquist 2225, **JPMorgan 2242**, Norwich 2332, Rose 2392, Wells 2501
North Carolina: Bolick 2531, French 2554, Harvest 2566, Humphrey 2571, Kennedy 2578, Moretz 2595, Morgan 2596, Reynolds 2613, Ribenack 2615, Symmes 2636, Woodson 2644
Ohio: Ar-Hale 2661, **Eaton 2692**, Haile, 2709, National 2748, Nippert 2751, Ohio 2757, Schiewetz 2774, Schmidlapp 2775
Oklahoma: Viersen 2830
Pennsylvania: 100 2879, Black 2897, CIGNA 2917, Comcast 2921, Degenstein 2931, Grumbacher 2961, Kunkel 2980, Laros 2982, Pottstown 3017, **PPG 3018**, Rossin 3028, Sedwick 3032, Wilson 3058
Rhode Island: Kimball 3079, Shaw's 3092, Washington 3095
South Carolina: Bailey 3096, Lutz 3105, Smith 3109
Tennessee: Clayton 3128, HCA 3139, Regal 3151
Texas: Bass 3172, Beasley 3175, Moore 3299, Schissler 3346, Sterling 3358
Utah: Green 3394, Schmidt 3403
Virginia: AMERIGROUP 3420, Greensville 3441, United 3484
Washington: Bamford 3495, Discuren 3507, REI 3551, Safeco 3554
Wisconsin: Alliant 3592, **Baird 3595**, Elmwood 3614, Manitowoc 3632, Neese 3639, Oshkosh 3643, Raibrook 3649, RITE-HITE 3651, Schlegel 3656, Sentry 3657, Smith 3660, Spire 3661
Wyoming: Surrena 3681

Young adults

Alabama: Black 4, Community 10, Malone 16
Arizona: Webb 64
Arkansas: Cabe 67
California: Ahmanson 77, Ayrshire 97, California 140, Community 157, Eisner 189, **Gellert 214**, Gerbode 217, Gumbiner 236, **Hilton 251**, Johnson 269, Lesher 299, Marcled 308, Napa 340, Patron 363, San Luis 393, Taper 433, Weingart 456
Colorado: Colorado 483, Summit 537
Connecticut: Connecticut 564, **Deupree 571**
District of Columbia: Cafritz 656, Jovid 668
Florida: Bush 712, Landwirth 775, Southwest 823
Georgia: Abreu 846, Camp-Younts 861
Idaho: Whittenberger 953
Illinois: Blowitz 968, Chicago 982, Fry 1018, Mellinger 1061, Siragusa 1096
Indiana: Community 1134, **Lumina 1174**
Iowa: McElroy 1230, Stebens 1242
Maryland: Ceres 1354, Community 1360
Massachusetts: **Barr 1433**, Essex 1464, MetroWest 1515, Smith 1546, **State 1550**
Michigan: Grand Rapids 1615, Midland 1642, **Mott 1645**, Sanilac 1663
Minnesota: **O'Shaughnessy 1725**
Mississippi: Community 1760, Gulf 1764
Missouri: Westlake 1819
Nebraska: Midlands 1848
New Hampshire: Lindsay 1890
New Jersey: **Allen 1900**, Hyde 1944, **Knowles 1955**
New York: Aronson 2042, Canaday 2083, **Clark 2097**, **Clark 2098**, Clark 2099, Community 2107, Cummings 2122, Gould 2188, **Nash 2320**, Price 2367, **Sparkplug 2441**
North Carolina: Glenn 2560, North Carolina 2599, Reidsville 2611
Ohio: **Brush 2673**, Cincinnati 2679, Fairfield 2696, O'Neill 2760, Saint 2770
Oklahoma: Hardesty 2814, Hille 2816
Pennsylvania: Birmingham 2896, Connelly 2926, Heinz 2966, Ludwick 2988, Mellon 2998, Phoenixville 3014, Staunton 3044
Tennessee: Baptist 3122, **Maclellan 3146**, **Scarlett 3152**, Schmidt 3153, Wilson 3157
Texas: Abell 3160, AT&T 3167, Hill 3259, Hoglund 3263, McDermott 3293, Moore 3299, Orsinger 3310, Rockwell 3338
Virginia: **Brown 3424**, **WestWind 3486**
Washington: **Gates 3516**
Wisconsin: Green Bay 3619, La Crosse 3631, Marshfield 3633, Milwaukee 3637

Young adults, female

Arizona: Webb 64
California: Community 161, Gerbode 217, Gumbiner 236, Patron 363, Simpson 411, Weingart 456
District of Columbia: Jovid 668
Georgia: Abreu 846
Illinois: Blowitz 968, Chicago 982, Fry 1018, Monticello 1065
Maryland: **Cohen 1355**
Massachusetts: Essex 1464
Michigan: Knight 1630, Midland 1642, Sanilac 1663
Minnesota: **O'Shaughnessy 1725**
Mississippi: Community 1760
Montana: Montana 1828
New Jersey: **Alcatel 1899**, **Allen 1900**
New York: **Clark 2097**, Community 2107, Gould 2188, **MetLife 2307**, New York 2325, **Overbrook 2345**, Patrina 2350
Ohio: **Brush 2673**, Fairfield 2696, O'Neill 2760
Oklahoma: Hardesty 2814
Pennsylvania: Child 2916, Phoenixville 3014
Tennessee: Wilson 3157
Texas: Bass 3172, Embrey 3222, McDermott 3293, Moore 3299, Rockwell 3338
Washington: **Gates 3516**
Wisconsin: Marshfield 3633

Young adults, male

Alabama: Black 4
Arizona: Webb 64
California: Gerbode 217, Gumbiner 236, Patron 363, Weingart 456
District of Columbia: Jovid 668
Georgia: Abreu 846
Illinois: Blowitz 968, Chicago 982, Fry 1018
Michigan: Midland 1642, Sanilac 1663
Minnesota: **O'Shaughnessy 1725**
Mississippi: Community 1760
New Jersey: **Allen 1900**
New York: **Clark 2097**, Community 2107, Gould 2188, **MetLife 2307**
Ohio: **Brush 2673**, Fairfield 2696, O'Neill 2760
Oklahoma: Hardesty 2814
Pennsylvania: Child 2916, Phoenixville 3014
Tennessee: Wilson 3157
Texas: Bass 3172, McDermott 3293, Moore 3299, Rockwell 3338
Washington: **Gates 3516**
Wisconsin: Marshfield 3633

Youth

Alabama: Black 4, Community 10, Community 11
Arizona: Every 43, Piper 57, Webb 64
Arkansas: Cabe 67
California: Anaheim 83, Ayrshire 97, Boys 122, California 140, **Clorox 153**, Community 157, Community 159, Community 161, Cowell 168, Fansler 193, **Gellert 214**, Gilmore 221, Gumbiner 236, **Hilton 251**, Johnson 269, Klein 283, Lesher 299, Marcled 308, Mazda 313, McKesson 321, Napa 340, Outhwaite 353, Pacific 354, Pacific 355, Parsons 359, Pasadena 361, Patron 363, Roth 388, San Luis 393, Sierra 405, Sierra 406, Silicon 408, Simpson 411, Solano 419, Stanislaus 425, Taper 433, Weingart 456
Colorado: Colorado 483, Donnell 491, Hunter 508, **Kinder 510**, Summit 537
Connecticut: Community 562, Community 563, Connecticut 564, Fry 579, Perrin 603, Saybrook 610
District of Columbia: Cafritz 656, **Hill 664**, Jovid 668, New Futures 676, Palmer 677
Florida: Cape Coral 714, Community 723, Community 727, Glazer 750, Jacksonville 761, Kennedy 767, Southwest 823, Winter 842
Georgia: Community 867, **Georgia 878**, Tull 917
Idaho: Whittenberger 953
Illinois: Aon 963, Blowitz 968, Community 990, Evanston 1012, Field 1014, Guthman 1027, **Motorola 1066**, Siragusa 1096
Indiana: Brown 1124, Community 1130, Community 1133, Community 1135, Fayette 1146, Foellinger 1147, Hancock 1154, **Lumina 1174**, Northern 1180, Portland 1188, Putnam 1189, Whitley 1209
Iowa: Community 1216, McElroy 1230, **Rockwell 1237**, Siouxland 1240
Kansas: Insurance 1261, Manhattan 1268, Topeka 1279
Kentucky: Lift 1293
Maryland: Community 1359, Community 1360, Dresher 1370, Fowler 1372, Rembrandt 1407, Wright 1418
Massachusetts: **Barr 1433**, Cabot 1442, Essex 1464, **Germeshausen 1474**, Kelsey 1493, Liberty 1502, MENTOR 1513, Smith 1546, Staples 1549
Michigan: Community 1589, Community 1590, Fremont 1607, Grand Rapids 1615, Grand 1616, Granger 1617, **Kellogg 1628**, Lenawee 1634, Midland 1642, Saginaw 1662, Sanilac 1663, Skillman 1666, Steelcase 1667
Minnesota: Avocet 1680, Beim 1683, Best 1685, Land 1710, Larsen 1711, Northwest 1723, **O'Shaughnessy 1725**, RBC 1730, Rochester 1735, Sundance 1742
Mississippi: Community 1760
Missouri: Canfield 1781, Dunn 1787, **Monsanto 1803**, Saigh 1811
Nebraska: Grand Island 1837
Nevada: Shaheen 1871
New Hampshire: Foundation 1885, Lindsay 1890
New Jersey: **Alcatel 1899**, **Allen 1900**, Hyde 1944, Kirby 1952
New Mexico: Con 2011
New York: Achelis 2026, Canaday 2083, **Clark 2097**, **Clark 2098**, Community 2107, **Credit 2118**, Cricket 2119, Cummings 2122, **Deutsche 2134**, **Ford 2160**, Gould 2188, Haring 2203, Johnson 2240,

Luce 2285, Morgan 2315, New Yankee 2324, New York 2326, **Open 2343**, Ostgrodd 2344, **Ross 2396**, Ruffin 2400, Seneca 2415, Tower 2472, Troy 2474, van Ameringen 2483
North Carolina: Cumberland 2541, Davie 2543, Glass 2559, Glenn 2560, North Carolina 2599, Reidsville 2611, Strowd 2633
North Dakota: Fargo 2649, North Dakota 2653
Ohio: Abington 2654, Brethen 2671, **Brush 2673**, **Cardinal 2677**, Cincinnati 2679, Community 2682, Community 2683, Dayton 2688, Fairfield 2696, Mathile 2734, Morgan 2739, **Noble 2753**, Nord 2754, Nordson 2755, O'Neill 2760, Saint 2770, Springfield 2787, Stark 2788, Troy 2794, Youngstown 2804
Oklahoma: Hardesty 2814, Hille 2816
Oregon: Benton 2835, Ford 2846, Templeton 2874
Pennsylvania: Baker 2886, Bayer 2888, Birmingham 2896, Child 2916, Connelly 2926, First 2948, Highmark 2968, Ludwick 2988, McLean 2997, Mellon 2998, Phoenixville 3014, Pilgrim 3016, Staunton 3044
Tennessee: Baptist 3122, **International 3142**, **Maclellan 3146**, Wilson 3157
Texas: Amarillo 3163, AT&T 3167, B.E.L.I.E.F. 3169, Bass 3172, **Chrest 3194**, Constantin 3202, Hoblitzelle 3262, McDermott 3293, Moore 3299, Orsinger 3310, **Paso 3312**, Powell 3324, Rockwell 3338, Sterling 3358, Waco 3378
Virginia: Lynchburg 3454, MAXIMUS 3457, **Northrop 3465**, **WestWind 3486**, Williamsburg 3487
Washington: Everett 3511, **Gates 3516**, Safeco 3554
West Virginia: Community 3579, Eastern 3580
Wisconsin: La Crosse 3631, Marshfield 3633, Milwaukee 3637, New 3641, Oshkosh 3642, Pamida 3644, Racine 3648, St. Croix 3662, Stateline 3663

Youth development

Alabama: Black 4
Alaska: **Nash 37**
Arkansas: Cabe 67
California: **Allende 79**, Anaheim 83, Anderson 84, Bechtel, 104, Berry 110, California 138, California 140, **Clorox 153**, Community 162, Community 163, Cowell 168, Family 192, Fuserna 212, Gamble 213, GGS 219, Gold 228, **Hilton 251**, Just 272, LA84 287, Langendorf 289, **Mattel 312**, Napa 340, Pacific 354, **Packard 357**, Picerne 369, Placer 371, Roth 388, Shasta 401, Sierra 405, Truckee 441, Zellerbach 471
Colorado: Community 484, Craig-Scheckman 486, **Daniels 488**, Piton 526, Seay 532
Connecticut: NewAlliance 595, Tauck 615
Delaware: Pinkerton 645, Sylvan 648
District of Columbia: Block 653, **Hill 664**
Florida: Alpha 687, Cape Coral 714, Gulf 754, Reinhold 808
Georgia: Amos-Cheves 849, Campbell 860, **Coca 864**, Communities 866, Community 868, **Georgia 878**, Goizueta 883, Tull 917, WinShape 921
Hawaii: Atherton 925, Castle 929, Kaneta 936
Idaho: Adams 941, Equinox 947
Illinois: Angell 962, Aon 963, CME 984, Jackson 1038, Speh 1097, Stone 1102, Tracy 1104, Ullrich 1106, Zell 1119
Indiana: Community 1128, Community 1129, Community 1132, Community 1136, Decatur 1142, DeKalb 1144, Harrison 1155, Hendricks 1157, LaGrange 1170, Lilly 1173, Northern 1180, Old 1182, Tipton 1198, Unity 1201, Welborn 1205
Iowa: Community 1215, Community 1218, Jefferson 1227, **Rockwell 1237**
Kansas: Hutchinson 1260
Louisiana: New Orleans 1316
Maine: Alfond 1324
Maryland: Ceres 1354, Mid-Shore 1395, Polinger 1405
Massachusetts: Babson 1429, Blue 1436, Cabot 1442, Cabot 1443, Eastern 1461, Essex 1464, Grinspoon 1479, Sheehan 1545, **State 1550**, United 1559, **Xeric 1570**
Michigan: Branch 1580, Community 1586, Delano 1596, DTE 1598, Farver 1601, Gilmore 1612, Granger 1617, Kalamazoo 1626, Mills 1643, Mott 1646, Mount Pleasant 1647, Petoskey 1656, Sanilac 1663, Van Andel 1669
Minnesota: 3M 1676, Hallett 1701, Jostens 1706, Land 1710, McKnight 1715, Northwest 1723, Opus 1724, RBC 1730, Securian 1739, Southwest 1740, **Trust 1746**
Mississippi: Community 1759, Luckyday 1767, Regions 1770
Missouri: Butler 1780, Green 1790, Truman 1817, Woods 1821
Montana: Lynn 1827
Nebraska: Grand Island 1837, Oregon 1852, Zollner 1858
New Hampshire: Fuller 1886
New Jersey: **Alcatel 1899**, **Allen 1900**, Bunbury 1916, Campbell 1917, Hawthorne 1937, **Horner 1941**, Leavens 1959
New Mexico: Chase 2009, Maddox 2014
New York: **Clark 2097**, Community 2107, Community 2109, East 2147, Family 2153, Gifford 2177, **Grant 2191**, Hagedorn 2200, Heckscher 2205, Holmberg 2219, Johnson 2239, **JPMorgan 2242**, Luce 2285, Mendell 2303, **MetLife 2307**, Neu 2323, New York 2325, Northern 2331, NYSE 2336, Robbins 2386, Schenectady 2407, Seneca 2415, Trump 2476, Yudelson 2514
North Carolina: **Bank 2524**, Bettman 2528, North Carolina 2599, Outer 2604
North Dakota: Fargo 2649
Ohio: Building 2675, Findlay 2700, Knoll 2719, Marion 2733, Morgan 2739, Orr 2761, Reinberger 2765, Scotford 2779, Sears 2781, Third 2792, Wyler 2802
Oregon: Ford 2846, Hedinger 2849, Jubitz 2853
Pennsylvania: **Alcoa 2882**, Allegheny 2883, Berks 2893, Chester 2915, Claneil 2918, First 2947, Rangos 3022, **Templeton 3047**, United 3052
Rhode Island: CVS 3068, Estate 3073, McDonald 3085, Schwarz 3090, Textron 3093
Tennessee: HCA 3139
Texas: **Dell 3213**, Edwards 3219, Esping 3225, Herzstein 3256, Hill 3259, King 3275, Littauer 3283, Moody 3298, NuStar 3307, Orr 3309, **Paso 3312**, Penney 3315, Richardson 3335, Rosewood 3340, Smith 3353, Topfer 3372, Tyler 3375
Virginia: Capital 3426, CarMax 3427, Community 3433, **WestWind 3486**
Washington: Bainbridge 3494, Casey 3500, PEMCO 3549, Renton 3552, Seattle 3558, **Starbucks 3565**, Yakima 3576
West Virginia: Five 3582
Wisconsin: Bemis 3598, Elmwood 3614, Green Bay 3619, Harley 3621, Incourage 3623, Kern 3627, Milwaukee 3637, Oshkosh 3643

Youth development, adult & child programs

Arizona: Piper 57
California: **Applied 88**, Community 160, Fox 205, Pacific 355, Solano 419
Connecticut: Pitney 604
Indiana: Fayette 1146, Vectren 1202
Louisiana: Community 1306
Maryland: Rosenberg 1409
Massachusetts: Liberty 1502
Minnesota: **King 1708**, RBC 1730
New Jersey: **Alcatel 1899**
New York: **MetLife 2307**, Seneca 2415
North Carolina: **Bank 2524**
Ohio: Bryan 2674
Oregon: **NIKE 2865**
Pennsylvania: EQT 2940, **PPG 3018**
Rhode Island: Textron 3093
Texas: Fluor 3235, Lupton 3288
Virginia: CarMax 3427
Washington: Everett 3511

Youth development, agriculture

Iowa: Beckwith 1213
Minnesota: Land 1710
Missouri: **Monsanto 1803**
Ohio: Bryan 2674

Youth development, alliance/advocacy

New York: Cricket 2119

Youth development, business

Arkansas: Wal-Mart 74
Florida: Brown 707, Kiwanis 770
Georgia: **Georgia 878**
Indiana: Jorgensen 1164
Maryland: Rembrandt 1407
Michigan: Dana 1593, Davenport 1595
Minnesota: Midcontinent 1716
New Jersey: **Alcatel 1899**
New York: **Credit 2118**, **MetLife 2307**, Voya 2488
North Carolina: Olin 2603
Ohio: **Eaton 2692**
Pennsylvania: **Alcoa 2882**, EQT 2940
Tennessee: HCA 3139
Texas: Penney 3315
Washington: PEMCO 3549
Wisconsin: Alliant 3592, Ariens 3594

Youth development, centers/clubs

California: California 140, Community 160, Fusenot 211, Parsons 359, Quest 377, Ransom 379
Florida: Community 727
Illinois: Luehring 1052
Louisiana: Community 1306, Pennington 1317
Massachusetts: Verrochi 1560
Michigan: Oleson 1649
Minnesota: **King 1708**
Mississippi: Mississippi 1769
Missouri: Mungenast 1804
New York: **Credit 2118**
North Carolina: Billingsley 2530
Ohio: Slemp 2785
Texas: Jones 3272
Washington: Dimmer 3506, Satterberg 3556

Youth development, citizenship

California: Fox 205
Delaware: Sylvan 648
Missouri: Roblee 1809
Nevada: Nevada 1867
Ohio: Coshocton 2686, Middletown 2737
Pennsylvania: Connelly 2926, Nelson 3003
Virginia: Community 3431
Wisconsin: **Bradley 3601**, McBeath 3634

Youth development, community service clubs

Massachusetts: Cape Cod 1445
New York: Marshall 2293
Ohio: Ohio 2757
Tennessee: HCA 3139

FOUNDATION NAME INDEX

Numbers following the foundation names refer to the entry sequence numbers in the Descriptive Directory section. The codes (FD) and (FD2) indicate whether the foundation appeared in the previous edition of *The Foundation Directory* or *The Foundation Directory Part 2.*

100 Acre Wood Foundation, PA, **2879** (FD2)
100 Mile Man Foundation Inc., The, NY, **2019** (FD2)
1772 Foundation, Inc., CT, **547** (FD)
18 Pomegranates Inc., DE, **621** (FD2)
1848 Foundation, NY, **2020** (FD2)

307 Brady Foundation, OK, *see* 2812
3M Foundation, MN, **1676** (FD)

A Child Waits Foundation, MA, **1420** (FD2)
A Glimmer of Hope Foundation - Austin, TX, **3159** (FD2)
A Glimmer of Hope Foundation, TX, **3158** (FD)
A. & R. Charitable Foundation, Inc., FL, **686** (FD2)
Aaron Foundation, The, MA, **1421** (FD)
Abba's Ambassadors, Inc., NY, **2021** (FD2)
Abbott Foundation, Clara, The, IL, **954** (FD)
Abelard Foundation Inc., The, NY, **2022** (FD2)
Abell-Hanger Foundation, TX, **3160** (FD)
Abington Foundation, The, OH, **2654** (FD)
ABMRF/The Foundation for Alcohol Research, MD, **1344** (FD)
Abraham Foundation, Alexander, The, NY, **2023** (FD2)
Abramowitz Family Foundation, CT, *see* 548
Abramowitz Foundation, Kenneth and Nira, CT, **548** (FD2)
Abramson-Clayman Foundation, NY, **2024** (FD2)
Abreu Charitable Trust, M & F, GA, *see* 846
Abreu Charitable Trust, May P. & Francis L., GA, **846** (FD2)
Access Capital Foundation, NY, **2025** (FD2)
Access Strategies Fund, Inc., MA, **1422** (FD2)
ACE Charitable Foundation, PA, **2880** (FD)
ACE INA Foundation, PA, *see* 2880
Achelis Foundation, The, NY, **2026** (FD)
Acheson Foundation, James C., MI, **1571** (FD2)
Ackerley Foundation, Ginger and Barry, WA, **3489** (FD)
Ackermann Memorial Fund, G.A., IL, **955** (FD2)
Adams Charitable Foundation, Arthur F. & Alice E., NC, **2516** (FD)
Adams Charitable Foundation, Judith and Jean Pape, The, OK, **2806** (FD)
Adams Charitable Trust, Marjorie C., IL, **956** (FD2)
Adams Foundation Inc., PA, **2881** (FD2)
Adams Foundation, Hop & Mae, The, ID, **941** (FD2)
Adams Foundation, Inc., Ellen H., CT, **549** (FD2)
Adams Foundation, Inc., William L. and Victorine Q., The, MD, **1345** (FD2)
Adams Legacy Foundation, CA, **76** (FD2)
Adams Memorial Fund, Frank W. & Carl S., MA, **1423** (FD)
Adams Trust, Charles E. & Caroline J., MA, *see* 1423
Adams-Mastrovich Family Foundation, NC, **2517** (FD)
Adelson Medical Research Foundation, Dr. Miriam and Sheldon G., MA, **1424** (FD)
Adirondack Community Trust, NY, *see* 2027
Adirondack Foundation, NY, **2027** (FD)
Administers of the Berwick Health and Wellness Fund, PA, *see* 2908
AEC Trust, The, DE, **622** (FD)
Aequus Institute, NY, **2028** (FD2)
Aetna Foundation, Inc., CT, **550** (FD)
Aetna Life & Casualty Foundation, Inc., CT, *see* 550
Ahavat Haim Vachesed, NJ, **1898** (FD2)
Ahearn Family Foundation, AZ, **38** (FD)
Ahmanson Foundation, The, CA, **77** (FD)
Ahrens Foundation, Claude W. & Dolly, The, IA, **1210** (FD)
Aicher Family Foundation, Inc., ME, **1323** (FD)
AIG Foundation, Inc., NY, **2029** (FD)
AIM Foundation, GA, **847** (FD)
Akron Community Foundation, OH, **2655** (FD)
Alalusi Foundation, CA, **78** (FD)
Alaska Conservation Foundation, AK, **26** (FD)
Alavi Foundation, NY, **2030** (FD)
Albemarle Foundation, LA, **1298** (FD)
Albers Foundation, Inc., Josef and Anni, The, CT, **551** (FD)
Albers Foundation, Inc., Josef, CT, *see* 551
Albers/Kuhn Family Foundation, MO, **1773** (FD2)
Albert Charitable Foundation, J.R., IL, **957** (FD)
Albertson Foundation, Inc., J. A. & Kathryn, ID, **942** (FD)
Albuquerque Community Foundation, NM, **2006** (FD)
Alcatel-Lucent Foundation, NJ, **1899** (FD)
Alcoa Foundation, PA, **2882** (FD)
Alcoholic Beverage Medical Research Foundation, MD, *see* 1344
Alcon Cares, Inc., TX, **3161** (FD2)
Alcon Foundation, Inc., The, TX, **3162** (FD)
Alden Trust, John W., MA, **1425** (FD2)
Aleut Foundation, The, AK, **27** (FD)
Alexander & Baldwin Foundation, HI, **924** (FD)
Alexander Eastman Foundation, NH, **1877** (FD)
Alfiero Family Charitable Foundation, NY, **2031** (FD)
Alfond Foundation, Harold, ME, **1324** (FD)
Alice Manufacturing Company, Inc. Foundation, SC, *see* 3106
Alix Foundation, Jay & Maryanne, MI, *see* 1572
Alix Foundation, The, MI, **1572** (FD)
Allegheny Foundation, PA, **2883** (FD)
Allegretti Foundation, Inc., Fred & Jean, IL, **958** (FD)
Allen Charitable Trust, Phil N., NC, **2518** (FD2)
Allen Family Foundation, Paul G., The, WA, **3490** (FD)
Allen Foundation, Inc., MI, **1573** (FD)
Allen Foundation, Inc., Rita, NJ, **1900** (FD)
Allende Foundation, Isabel, The, CA, **79** (FD)
Allergan Foundation, The, CA, **80** (FD)
Alliant Energy Foundation, Inc., WI, **3592** (FD)
Allied Educational Foundation, NJ, **1901** (FD2)
Allyn Foundation, Inc., NY, **2032** (FD)
Almi Foundation, Inc., WA, **3491** (FD)
Alpha Foundation, Inc., FL, **687** (FD)
Alphawood Foundation, IL, **959** (FD)
Alro Steel Foundation, The, MI, **1574** (FD)
Alumni Achievement Awards, Inc., TN, **3119** (FD2)
Alworth Memorial Fund, Marshall H. and Nellie, MN, **1677** (FD)
Amado Foundation, Maurice, CA, **81** (FD)
Amarillo Area Foundation, Inc., TX, **3163** (FD)
Amateur Athletic Foundation of Los Angeles, CA, *see* 287
American Electric Power Foundation, OH, **2656** (FD)
American Electric Power System Educational Trust Fund, The, OH, **2657** (FD2)
American Express Charitable Fund, NY, **2033** (FD)
American Express Foundation, NY, **2034** (FD)
American Friends of Even Yisroel Charitable Foundation, NJ, **1902** (FD2)
American Friends of the Hebrew University Charitable Common Fund, Inc., NY, **2035** (FD2)
American Friends of the National Institute for Psychobiology in Israel, IL, **960** (FD2)
American Institute of Mathematics, CA, **82** (FD2)
AMERIGROUP Foundation, VA, **3420** (FD)
AmerUs Group Charitable Foundation, IA, *see* 1211
Ames Charitable Trust, Harriett, PA, **2884** (FD)
Ames Foundation, Inc., Kathryn, The, MD, **1346** (FD)
Amicus Foundation, IL, **961** (FD)
Amos Family Foundation, Daniel P., GA, **848** (FD)
Amos Foundation, Inc., Daniel P. and Shannon L., GA, *see* 848
Amos-Cheves Foundation, Inc., GA, **849** (FD)
AmSouth Foundation, MS, *see* 1770
Anaheim Community Foundation, CA, **83** (FD2)
Andalusia Health Services Inc., AL, **1** (FD2)
Andersen Corporate Foundation, MN, **1678** (FD)
Anderson Children's Foundation, Irene W. & Guy L., CA, **84** (FD)
Anderson Foundation, Inc., Peyton, The, GA, **850** (FD)
Anderson Foundation, Marion & John E., CA, **85** (FD)
Anderson Foundation, Paul M., MI, **1575** (FD2)
Anderson Foundation, Robert A. and Kathey K., TX, **3164** (FD2)
Anderson Foundation, WA, **3492** (FD)
Anderson Foundation, William P., OH, **2658** (FD2)
Anderson-Rogers Foundation, Inc., NY, **2036** (FD2)
Andor Capital Management Foundation, NY, **2037** (FD)
Andreas Foundation, L. & N., MN, **1679** (FD)
Andrews Foundation, The, OH, **2659** (FD2)
Angell Family Foundation, Paul M., IL, **962** (FD)
Angels Among Us, Inc., ID, **943** (FD2)
Angels on Track Foundation, The, OH, **2660** (FD2)
Anheuser-Busch Foundation, MO, **1774** (FD)
Animal Assistance Foundation, CO, **472** (FD)
Animal Farm Foundation, Inc., NY, **2038** (FD2)
Animal Welfare Trust, NY, **2039** (FD2)
Ann Arbor Area Community Foundation, MI, **1576** (FD)
Ann Arbor Area Foundation, MI, *see* 1576
Anna Fund, Inc., The, FL, **688** (FD)
Annenberg Foundation Trust at Sunnylands, The, CA, **87** (FD)
Annenberg Foundation, CA, **86** (FD)

Bemis Company Foundation, WI, **3598** (FD)
Ben & Jerry's Foundation, Inc., VT, **3407** (FD)
Bender Foundation, Inc., Morris S. & Florence H., The, CT, **554** (FD2)
Bendon Family Foundation, NV, **1859** (FD2)
Benedict Foundation for Independent Schools, The, OH, **2666** (FD2)
Benedum Foundation, Claude Worthington, PA, **2892** (FD)
Bengier Foundation, The, CA, **109** (FD)
Benjamin Foundation, Inc., Bennie & Martha, The, FL, **699** (FD2)
Benmen Fund, NY, **2061** (FD2)
Benton County Foundation, OR, **2835** (FD2)
Bentson Foundation, MN, **1684** (FD)
Benwood Foundation, Inc., TN, **3123** (FD)
Berg Foundation, Inc., David, The, NY, **2062** (FD)
Bergen Foundation, Frank and Lydia, NC, **2527** (FD)
Berger-Gerald Marks Foundation, Edna, DC, *see* 651
Berger-Marks Foundation, The, DC, **651** (FD2)
Bergstrom Inc. Charitable Foundation, IL, **965** (FD)
Berkman Charitable Trust, Allen H. and Selma W., The, MA, **1434** (FD)
Berks County Community Foundation, PA, **2893** (FD)
Bernard Foundation, Ralph L. & Florence A., OH, **2667** (FD2)
Bernhardt Foundation, Helene and Bertram, RI, **3062** (FD2)
Bernsen Foundation, Grace & Franklin, OK, **2807** (FD)
Bernstein Family Foundation, DC, **652** (FD2)
Bernstein Family Foundation, Leo M., DC, *see* 652
Berrie Foundation, Russell, The, NJ, **1908** (FD)
Berry Foundation, C.J., CA, **110** (FD2)
Berry Foundation, Lowell, The, CA, **111** (FD)
Bersted Foundation, Alfred, IL, **966** (FD)
Bersted Foundation, Grace, IL, **967** (FD2)
Berwind Foundation, Inc., Charles G., PA, **2894** (FD2)
Best Buy Children's Foundation, MN, *see* 1685
Best Buy Foundation, MN, **1685** (FD)
Betesh Family Foundation, Inc., Eddie and Rachelle, The, NY, **2063** (FD)
Bethlehem Area Foundation, PA, *see* 2986
Better and Better Foundation, VT, **3408** (FD)
Better U, CA, **112** (FD2)
Bettman Foundation, Francis & Monte, NC, **2528** (FD2)
Betz Foundation, Theodora B., PA, **2895** (FD2)
Beynon Foundation, Kathryne, The, CA, **113** (FD2)
Bi-Lo/Winn-Dixie Foundation, Inc., FL, **700** (FD)
Bickel & Brewer Foundation, TX, **3178** (FD)
Bickel & Brewer Legal Foundation, TX, *see* 3178
Biddle Foundation, Mary Duke, The, NC, **2529** (FD)
Bikuben Foundation New York, Inc., The, NY, **2064** (FD2)
Bilezikian Family Foundation, Inc., MA, **1435** (FD)
Biller Family Foundation, Sheri & Les, WA, **3496**, *see* 3496 (FD)
Billingsley Foundation, Charle & Ruth, NC, **2530** (FD2)
Biloxi Regional Medical Center, Inc., MS, **1755** (FD2)
Binda Foundation, Guido A. & Elizabeth H., MI, **1579** (FD)
Bingham Foundation, William, The, OH, **2668** (FD)
Biogen Foundation, Inc., RI, *see* 3063
Biogen Idec Foundation Incorporated, RI, **3063** (FD)
Bird Trust, Lizzie & Edward V., RI, **3064** (FD2)
Birmingham Foundation, The, PA, **2896** (FD)
Black & Allon Fuller Fund, Harry S., NY, **2065** (FD2)
Black Belt Community Foundation, Inc., The, AL, **4** (FD2)
Black Charitable Trust, Elizabeth S., PA, **2897** (FD2)
Black Foundation, Inc., Mary, SC, **3097** (FD)
Blackford County Community Foundation, Inc., IN, **1122** (FD2)
Blair County Community Endowment, PA, *see* 2907
Blakemore Foundation, WA, **3497** (FD)
Blank Family Foundation, Arthur M., The, GA, **856** (FD)
Blanksteen Foundation, Goldie & David, FL, **701** (FD2)
Blanton Charitable Foundation, Inc., Hilda Sutton & William D., FL, **702** (FD2)
Blaustein Foundation, Inc., Jacob and Hilda, The, MD, **1349** (FD)
Blaustein Foundation, Inc., Morton K. and Jane, The, MD, **1350** (FD)
Bliss Estate Trust, Frederick S., RI, **3065** (FD)
Block Foundation Inc., Harris & Frances, VT, **3409** (FD2)
Block Foundation, Herb, DC, **653** (FD)
Block Foundation, Richard L. and Diane M., AK, **30** (FD2)
Bloomberg Family Foundation, Inc., The, NY, *see* 2066
Bloomberg Philanthropies, NY, **2066** (FD)
Blooming Prairie Foundation, Inc., WI, **3599** (FD2)
Blowitz-Ridgeway Foundation, The, IL, **968** (FD)
Blue Cross and Blue Shield of Florida Foundation, FL, *see* 744
Blue Cross and Blue Shield of Louisiana Foundation, LA, **1302** (FD)
Blue Grass Community Foundation, Inc., KY, **1282** (FD)
Blue Grass Foundation, Inc., KY, *see* 1282
Blue Hills Bank Charitable Foundation Inc., MA, **1436** (FD2)
Blue Knight Foundation, The, IL, **969** (FD)
Blue Moon Fund, Inc., VA, **3422** (FD)
Blue Mountain Area Foundation, WA, *see* 3498
Blue Mountain Community Foundation, WA, **3498** (FD)
Blue Shield of California Foundation, CA, **114** (FD)
Blum Family Foundation, CA, **115** (FD)
Blum Foundation, Inc., Edith C., NY, **2067** (FD)
BOA Client Foundation, FL, *see* 695
Bobolink Foundation, The, IL, **970** (FD)
Bock Foundation, John C., WI, **3600** (FD2)
Boeckmann Charitable Foundation, CA, **116** (FD2)
Bohnert Foundation, Inc., FL, **703** (FD2)
Bohnett Foundation, David, CA, **117** (FD)
Bok Family Foundation, The, CT, **555** (FD)
Boles Family Foundation, OH, **2669** (FD2)
Bolick Foundation, The, NC, **2531** (FD)
Bolivar Foundation, Inc., Simon, TX, **3179** (FD)
Bonfils-Stanton Foundation, CO, **475** (FD)
Bonner Foundation, Clark and Nancy, CA, **118** (FD2)
Bonner Foundation, Inc., Corella & Bertram F., The, NJ, **1909** (FD)
Booth Ferris Foundation, TX, **3180** (FD)
Booth Foundation, Inc., FL, **704** (FD)
Boothroyd Foundation, Charles H. and Bertha L., IL, **971** (FD2)
Borden Memorial Foundation, Mary Owen, NJ, **1910** (FD)
Borgman Family Foundation, CA, **119** (FD2)
Borman Family Foundation, The, ME, **1325** (FD2)
Borun Foundation, Harry H. and Anna, NC, **2532** (FD2)
Bosack and Bette M. Kruger Charitable Foundation, Inc., Leonard X., VA, **3423** (FD)
Boss Foundation, The, MN, **1686** (FD2)
Boston Center for Blind Children, Inc., FL, **705** (FD2)
Bothin Foundation, CA, **120** (FD)
Botstiber Foundation, Dietrich W., The, PA, **2898** (FD)
Bou Family Foundation, Inc., DC, **654** (FD2)
Boulder Historical Society Trust, IL, **972** (FD2)
Bouras Foundation, Inc., Nicholas J. and Anna K., The, NJ, **1911** (FD)
Bowen Trust, R. A., The, GA, **857** (FD2)
Bower Foundation, Inc., The, MS, **1756** (FD)
Bowes Family Foundation, CA, **121** (FD2)
Box of Rain Foundation, The, NY, **2068** (FD2)
Boylan Foundation, Helen S., MO, **1776** (FD2)
Boynton Fund, John W., MA, **1437** (FD2)
Boys and Girls Aid Society of San Diego Ltd., CA, **122** (FD2)
Boys and Girls Foundation, CA, *see* 122
BP Amoco Foundation, Inc., TX, *see* 3181
BP Foundation, Inc., TX, **3181** (FD)
Brabson Library & Educational Foundation, MA, **1438** (FD2)
Brace Charitable Trust, William J., MO, **1777** (FD2)
Brach Foundation, Helen V., IL, **973** (FD)
Brackenridge Foundation, George W., TX, **3182** (FD)
Braddock Charitable Foundation, Robert C. & Lois C., CA, **123** (FD2)
Bradley Foundation, Inc., Lynde and Harry, The, WI, **3601** (FD)
Bradley, Jr. Charitable Fund, Harry L., FL, **706** (FD)
Bradley-Turner Foundation, Inc., GA, **858** (FD)
Brady Education Foundation, Inc., NC, **2533** (FD)
Brady Foundation, Inc., W.H., NC, *see* 2533
Braemar Charitable Trust, OR, **2836** (FD)
Braitmayer Foundation, The, MD, **1351** (FD2)
Branch County Community Foundation, MI, **1580** (FD)
Brandes Foundation, Linda, CA, **124** (FD)
Brandman Foundation, Saul, CA, **125** (FD)
Bravo Foundation, The, CA, **126** (FD2)
Breen Charitable Foundation, Marion I., MO, **1778** (FD)
Brenden-Mann Foundation, Blythe, SD, **3114** (FD)
Brenden-Mann Foundation, SD, *see* 3114
Brennan Family Charitable Trust, The, IL, **974** (FD2)
Brentwood Foundation, OH, **2670** (FD)
Breslauer Foundation, Inc., B. H., NY, **2069** (FD2)
Brethen Foundation, Robert H., The, OH, **2671** (FD2)
Brett Family Foundation, CO, **476** (FD)
Bridgemill Foundation, CT, **556** (FD)
Briggs and Morgan Foundation, MN, **1687** (FD2)
Briggs Foundation, Inc., Thomas W., TN, **3124** (FD)
Bright Mountain Foundation, CO, **477** (FD2)
Brightwater Fund, The, CT, **557** (FD)
Brillo-Sonnino Family Foundation, NY, **2070** (FD2)
Brisco Foundation, Leo A. and Minta L., CA, **127** (FD2)
Bristol Bay Native Corp., Education Foundation, AK, **31** (FD2)
Brittingham Family Foundation, CA, **128** (FD)
Broad Foundation, Eli & Edythe, The, CA, **129** (FD)
Broad Foundation, The, CA, *see* 129
Broadcasters Foundation of America, NY, **2071** (FD)
Broadcasters Foundation, Inc., NY, *see* 2071
Brocchini Family Foundation, Albert & Rina, CA, **130** (FD2)
Brock Foundation, The, NY, **2072** (FD2)
Broderbund Foundation, CA, *see* 143
Bronfman Family Foundation, Inc., Edgar M., The, NY, *see* 2073
Bronfman Foundation, Samuel, The, NY, **2073** (FD)
Bronfman Philanthropies, Inc., Andrea and Charles, The, NY, **2074** (FD)
Brookdale Foundation, The, NJ, **1912** (FD)
Brooks Family Charitable Foundation, MA, *see* 1439
Brooks Family Foundation, MA, **1439** (FD2)
Brooks Foundation, Cora L., PA, **2899** (FD2)
Brooks Foundation, Gladys, NY, **2075** (FD)
Brooks Foundation, Harold, MA, **1440** (FD)
Brooks Foundation, Sunshine, CA, **131** (FD2)
Brookwood Foundation, DE, **624** (FD2)
Brotherhood Mutual Foundation Inc., IN, **1123** (FD2)
Brothers Ashkenazi Foundation, Inc., The, NJ, **1913** (FD)
Brotherton Charitable Foundation, Fred J., NJ, **1914** (FD)
Brotherton Foundation, Inc., Fred J., NJ, *see* 1914
Brown Charitable Foundation, Stokes and Sarah, AL, **5** (FD2)
Brown County Community Foundation, Inc., IN, **1124** (FD)
Brown Family Charitable Fund, Inc., Bennett A., DE, *see* 625
Brown Family Foundation Inc., Robert and Susan, The, WI, **3602** (FD2)
Brown Family Foundation, CO, *see* 478
Brown Family Foundation, Tim & Libby, CO, **478** (FD2)
Brown Family Foundation, Warren, OH, **2672** (FD2)
Brown Foundation, Inc., James Graham, KY, **1283** (FD)
Brown Foundation, Inc., Mary Alice and Bennett, DE, **625** (FD2)
Brown Foundation, Inc., The, TX, **3183** (FD)
Brown Foundation, Milton V., NY, **2076** (FD2)

Charlotte Community Foundation, Inc., FL, **718** (FD)
Charlotte County Foundation, Inc., FL, *see* 718
Charlottesville Area Community Foundation, VA, **3428** (FD)
Charlottesville-Albemarle Community Foundation, VA, *see* 3428
Charter Charitable Foundation, NH, **1880** (FD2)
Charter Foundation, The, PA, **2912** (FD)
Chartered Foundation, The, IL, **980** (FD2)
Chartrand Foundation, Inc., The, FL, **719** (FD)
Chartwell Charitable Foundation, CA, **150** (FD)
Chasdrew Fund, The, TX, **3192** (FD)
Chase Charity Foundation, Alfred E., MA, **1446** (FD)
Chase Foundation, NM, **2009** (FD)
Chase Manhattan Foundation, The, NY, *see* 2242
Chase Trust, Alice P., PA, **2913** (FD2)
Chattanooga Ophthalmological Foundation, TN, **3125** (FD2)
Chautauqua Region Community Foundation, Inc., NY, **2091** (FD)
CHC Foundation, ID, **945** (FD2)
Checotah Animal Town & School Cats Foundation, The, TN, **3126** (FD)
Chelsea Health and Wellness Foundation, The, MI, **1584** (FD)
Chenault, Jr. Agricultural Foundation, C.C., PA, **2914** (FD2)
Cheney Foundation, Elizabeth F., IL, **981** (FD)
Chernin Family Foundation, Inc., The, NY, **2092** (FD)
Cherokee Strip Community Foundation, OK, **2809** (FD)
Chesed Foundation of America, NY, **2093** (FD)
Chester County Community Foundation, PA, **2915** (FD)
Chester Foundation, Jack, FL, **720** (FD)
Chiang Foundation, Y.C. Ho/Helen & Michael, The, NY, **2094** (FD)
Chicago Community Trust, The, IL, **982** (FD)
Chico Community Foundation, CA, *see* 346
Chiesman Foundation for Democracy, Inc., SD, **3115** (FD2)
Child Development Center, PA, *see* 2916
Child Development Foundation, PA, **2916**, *see* 2916 (FD2)
Child Relief International Foundation, MA, **1447** (FD)
Children's Care Foundation, The, IL, **983** (FD)
Children's Chance for Life, WA, **3501** (FD2)
Children's Health Fund, CA, *see* 381
Childs Memorial Fund for Medical Research, Jane Coffin, The, CT, **559** (FD)
Ching Foundation, Hung Wo & Elizabeth Lau, HI, **931** (FD)
Chipstone Foundation, WI, **3605** (FD2)
Chisholm Trail Communities Foundation, The, TX, **3193** (FD2)
Chrest Foundation, Inc., TX, **3194** (FD2)
Christensen Fund, The, CA, **151** (FD)
Christian Foundation, Taylor, NH, **1881** (FD2)
Christian Health Ministries, LA, *see* 1299
Christian Mission Concerns of Tennessee, Inc., WY, **3671** (FD)
Christian Missionary Scholarship Foundation, MI, **1585** (FD2)
Christian Scholarship Foundation, AZ, **41** (FD2)
Christopher Memorial Charity Fund, Louis J., NC, **2537** (FD)
Chugach Heritage Foundation, AK, **32** (FD)
CIC Foundation, Inc., TN, **3127** (FD)
CIGNA Foundation, PA, **2917** (FD)
Cincinnati Foundation for the Aged, The, OH, **2680** (FD)
Cincinnati Foundation, Greater, The, OH, **2679** (FD)
Cinereach Ltd., NY, **2095** (FD)
CIRI Foundation, The, AK, **33** (FD)
Citizens Charitable Foundation, RI, **3067** (FD)
Claneil Foundation, Inc., PA, **2918** (FD)
Clareth Fund: The Philadelphia Association of Zeta Psi Fraternity, The, PA, **2919** (FD2)
Clarinda Foundation, The, IA, **1214** (FD)
Clark Charitable Fund, NY, *see* 2096
Clark Charitable Trust, Frank E., NY, **2096** (FD2)
Clark Foundation, Edna McConnell, The, NY, **2097** (FD)
Clark Foundation, Inc., PA, **2920** (FD2)
Clark Foundation, Inc., Robert Sterling, NY, **2098** (FD)
Clark Foundation, The, NY, **2099** (FD)
Clarke Trust, John, The, MA, **1448** (FD)
Clayton Family Foundation, The, TN, **3128** (FD)
Clement Foundation, Inc., Christen Elizabeth, LA, **1305** (FD)
Clements Family Foundation, The, TX, **3195** (FD2)
Cleveland-Cliffs Foundation, The, OH, *see* 2681
Clif Bar Family Foundation, CA, **152** (FD)
Cliffs Foundation, The, OH, **2681** (FD)
Clipper Ship Foundation, Inc., MA, **1449** (FD)
Clisby Charitable Trust, The, VA, *see* 3437
Clorox Company Foundation, The, CA, **153** (FD)
CME Group Foundation, IL, **984** (FD)
Coach Foundation, Inc., NY, **2100** (FD)
Coastal Bend Community Foundation, TX, **3196** (FD)
Coates Charitable Foundation of 1992, Elizabeth Huth, TX, **3197** (FD)
Cobb Educational Fund, Ty, GA, **863** (FD)
Coburn Foundation, James and Paula, The, CA, **154** (FD2)
Coby Foundation, Ltd., The, NY, **2101** (FD2)
Coca-Cola Foundation, Inc., The, GA, **864** (FD)
Cody Medical Foundation, WY, **3672** (FD2)
Cogan Family Foundation, MA, **1450** (FD)
Cohen Charitable Fund Part One, Barton P. and Mary Davidson, KS, **1252** (FD)
Cohen Foundation, Inc., Karen B., NY, **2102** (FD2)
Cohen Foundation, Naomi and Nehemiah, MD, **1355** (FD)
Cohen Foundation, Sam L., ME, **1327** (FD)
Cohen LD Family Foundation, Inc., NY, **2103** (FD2)
Cohen Trust, John and Golda, FL, **721** (FD)
Coit Family Foundation, The, OR, **2841** (FD2)
Colburn-Keenan Foundation, Inc., CT, **560** (FD2)
Coldwell Foundation, Lizanell and Colbert, IL, **985** (FD2)
Cole Charitable Pria Foundation, Ben And Rose, MA, **1451** (FD2)
Cole Foundation for Horses Inc, Teddy, CA, **155** (FD2)
Cole Foundation, Inc., Olive B., IN, **1127** (FD)
Coleman Foundation, Chase and Stephanie, The, NY, **2104** (FD)
Coleman Foundation, Inc., The, IL, **986** (FD)
Collective Brands Foundation, KS, **1253** (FD)
College Access Foundation of California, The, CA, **156** (FD)
College First Foundation, TX, **3198** (FD2)
College Spark Washington, WA, **3502** (FD)
Collins Family Foundation, Inc., Calvert K., TX, **3199** (FD)
Collins Foundation, Inc., Calvert K., TX, *see* 3199
Collins Foundation, Joseph, NY, **2105** (FD)
Collins Medical Trust, OR, **2842** (FD2)
Colombe Foundation, MA, **1452** (FD)
Colorado Masons Benevolent Fund Association, CO, **482** (FD)
Colorado Trust, The, CO, **483** (FD)
Colston Foundation, Inc., Edward, The, GA, **865** (FD2)
Columbia Gas Foundation, OH, *see* 2752
Columbia/HCA Healthcare Foundation, Inc., TN, *see* 3139
Columbine Foundation for the Grand Foundation, CO, *see* 503
Combined International Foundation, IL, *see* 963
Comcast Foundation, The, PA, **2921** (FD)
Comdisco Foundation, IL, *see* 1044
Comer Science & Education Foundation, IL, **987** (FD)
Commercial Federal Charitable Foundation, CA, *see* 99
Common Sense Fund Inc., The, CT, **561** (FD)
Common Stream, MA, *see* 1455
Commonweal Foundation, Inc., MD, **1356** (FD)
Commonwealth Fund, The, NY, **2106** (FD)
Communities of Coastal Georgia Foundation, Inc., GA, **866** (FD)
Community Fdn. of Delaware County, OH, *see* 2689
Community Foundation Alliance, Inc., IN, **1128** (FD)
Community Foundation for Crawford County, OH, **2682** (FD)
Community Foundation for Monterey County, CA, **157** (FD)
Community Foundation for Muskegon County, MI, **1586** (FD)
Community Foundation for Northeast Georgia, GA, **867** (FD)
Community Foundation for Northeast Michigan, MI, **1587** (FD)
Community Foundation for Oak Park, CA, **158** (FD2)
Community Foundation for San Benito County, CA, **159** (FD)
Community Foundation for South Central New York, Inc., The, NY, **2107** (FD)
Community Foundation for Southeast Michigan, MI, **1588** (FD)
Community Foundation for Southeastern Michigan, MI, *see* 1588
Community Foundation for the Alleghenies, The, PA, **2922** (FD)
Community Foundation for the Greater Capital Region, Inc., The, NY, **2108** (FD)
Community Foundation for the Ohio Valley, Inc., WV, **3579** (FD)
Community Foundation in Jacksonville, The, FL, *see* 722
Community Foundation of Brevard County, Inc., FL, *see* 723
Community Foundation of Brevard, FL, **723** (FD)
Community Foundation of Burke County, NC, **2538** (FD)
Community Foundation of Cape Cod, The, MA, *see* 1445
Community Foundation of Carroll County, Inc., MD, **1357** (FD)
Community Foundation of Central Florida, Inc., FL, **724** (FD)
Community Foundation of Central Illinois, IL, **988** (FD)
Community Foundation of Central Wisconsin, Inc., WI, **3606** (FD)
Community Foundation of East Mississippi, MS, **1758** (FD2)
Community Foundation of Eastern Connecticut, CT, **562** (FD)
Community Foundation of Elmira-Corning and the Finger Lakes, Inc., The, NY, **2109** (FD)
Community Foundation of Fayette County, PA, **2923** (FD)
Community Foundation of Fort Dodge and United Way, IA, **1215** (FD)
Community Foundation of Frederick County, MD, Inc., The, MD, **1358** (FD)
Community Foundation of Grand Forks, East Grand Forks and Region, ND, **2648** (FD)
Community Foundation of Grant County, IN, **1129** (FD)
Community Foundation of Greater Dubuque, IA, **1216** (FD)
Community Foundation of Greater Jackson, MS, **1759** (FD)
Community Foundation of Greater Johnstown, The, PA, *see* 2922
Community Foundation of Greater Lafayette, The, IN, **1130** (FD)
Community Foundation of Greater Lorain County, The, OH, *see* 2683
Community Foundation of Greater Muscatine, IA, **1217** (FD2)
Community Foundation of Greater New Britain, CT, **563** (FD)
Community Foundation of Greater Rochester, MI, **1589** (FD2)
Community Foundation of Greater South Wood County, Inc., WI, *see* 3623
Community Foundation of Greene County, Pennsylvania, PA, **2924** (FD2)
Community Foundation of Greenville, Inc., SC, **3099** (FD)

Community Foundation of Henderson County, Inc., NC, **2539** (FD)
Community Foundation of Herkimer & Oneida Counties, Inc., The, NY, **2110** (FD)
Community Foundation of Howard County, Inc., The, IN, **1131** (FD)
Community Foundation of Jackson County, Inc., The, IN, **1132** (FD2)
Community Foundation of Johnson County, IA, **1218** (FD)
Community Foundation of Kankakee River Valley, IL, **989** (FD2)
Community Foundation of Lorain County, The, OH, **2683** (FD)
Community Foundation of Madison and Jefferson County, Inc., IN, **1133** (FD)
Community Foundation of Mendocino County, Inc., The, CA, **160** (FD)
Community Foundation of Middle Tennessee, Inc., TN, **3129** (FD)
Community Foundation of Muncie and Delaware County, Inc., The, IN, **1134** (FD)
Community Foundation of North Central Florida, Inc., FL, **725** (FD)
Community Foundation of North Central Pennsylvania, PA, *see* 2939
Community Foundation of North Central Washington, WA, **3503** (FD)
Community Foundation of North Florida, Inc., The, FL, **726** (FD)
Community Foundation of North Louisiana, The, LA, **1306** (FD)
Community Foundation of Northeast Alabama, AL, **9** (FD)
Community Foundation of Northeast Florida, Inc., The, FL, *see* 722
Community Foundation of Northern Illinois, IL, **990** (FD)
Community Foundation of Northwest Georgia, Inc., GA, **868** (FD)
Community Foundation of Northwest Mississippi, MS, **1760** (FD)
Community Foundation of Orange and Sullivan, Inc., NY, *see* 2111
Community Foundation of Orange County, Inc., NY, **2111** (FD2)
Community Foundation of Portage County, Inc., WI, *see* 3606
Community Foundation of Randolph County, Inc., IN, **1135** (FD2)
Community Foundation of San Joaquin, CA, **161** (FD2)
Community Foundation of Santa Cruz County, The, CA, *see* 163
Community Foundation of Sarasota County, Inc., The, FL, **727** (FD)
Community Foundation of Shelby County, The, OH, **2684** (FD)
Community Foundation of Shreveport-Bossier, LA, *see* 1306
Community Foundation of Sidney and Shelby County, The, OH, *see* 2684
Community Foundation of South Alabama, The, AL, **10** (FD)
Community Foundation of South Georgia, Inc., GA, **869** (FD)
Community Foundation of South Puget Sound, The, WA, **3504** (FD)
Community Foundation of Southeastern Connecticut, Inc., The, CT, *see* 562
Community Foundation of Southeastern Massachusetts, MA, **1453** (FD)
Community Foundation of Southern Indiana, IN, **1136** (FD)
Community Foundation of Southern New Mexico, NM, **2010** (FD)
Community Foundation of Southern Wisconsin, Inc., WI, **3607** (FD)
Community Foundation of Southwest Georgia, Inc., GA, *see* 869
Community Foundation of Southwest Louisiana, LA, **1307** (FD)
Community Foundation of St. Clair County, MI, **1590** (FD)
Community Foundation of Switzerland County, Inc., IN, **1137** (FD)
Community Foundation of the Central Blue Ridge, The, VA, **3429** (FD)
Community Foundation of the Chemung County Area and Corning Community Foundation, The, NY, *see* 2109
Community Foundation of the Dan River Region, VA, **3430** (FD)
Community Foundation of the Eastern Shore, Inc., MD, **1359** (FD)
Community Foundation of the Fox River Valley, IL, **991** (FD)
Community Foundation of the Holland/Zeeland Area, The, MI, **1591** (FD)
Community Foundation of the Lowcountry, SC, **3100** (FD)
Community Foundation of the Mahoning Valley, OH, **2685** (FD)
Community Foundation of the New River Valley, The, VA, **3431** (FD2)
Community Foundation of the Ozarks, MO, **1783** (FD)
Community Foundation of the Quincy Area, IL, **992** (FD2)
Community Foundation of the Verdugos, CA, **162** (FD2)
Community Foundation of the Virgin Islands, VI, **3419** (FD)
Community Foundation of Tompkins County, NY, **2112** (FD)
Community Foundation of Washington County Maryland, Inc., MD, **1360** (FD)
Community Foundation of West Alabama, AL, **11** (FD)
Community Foundation of West Kentucky, KY, **1286** (FD)
Community Foundation of Western North Carolina, Inc., The, NC, **2540** (FD)
Community Foundation of Western Pennsylvania and Eastern Ohio, PA, **2925** (FD)
Community Foundation of Western Virginia, VA, **3432** (FD)
Community Foundation Santa Cruz County, CA, **163** (FD)
Community Foundation Serving Greeley and Weld County, CO, **484** (FD)
Community Foundation Serving Richmond & Central Virginia, The, VA, **3433** (FD)
Community Foundation, Inc., MO, *see* 1783
Community Foundation, Inc., The, FL, **722** (FD)
Community Foundation, The, LA, *see* 1306
Community Foundations of the Hudson Valley, NY, **2113** (FD)
Community Hospital Foundation, TX, **3200** (FD2)
Community Memorial Foundation, IL, **993** (FD)
Compass Bank Foundation, AL, *see* 3
Compassionate Spirit Foundation, Inc., IN, **1138** (FD2)
Comprecare Foundation, CO, **485** (FD2)
Con Alma Health Foundation, Inc., NM, **2011** (FD)
Conduit Foundation, The, IL, **994** (FD)
Congregation Joseph Jacob Abraham, CA, **164** (FD2)
Conley Foundation, Gene, TX, **3201** (FD2)
Conn Memorial Foundation, FL, **728** (FD)
Connecticut Community Foundation, The, CT, **564** (FD)
Connelly Foundation, PA, **2926** (FD)
Conservation Land Trust, The, CA, **165** (FD)
Conservation, Food and Health Foundation, Inc., MA, **1454** (FD)
Constantin Foundation, Inc., The, TX, **3202** (FD)
Constellation Energy Group Foundation, Inc., MD, *see* 1407
Conway Scholarship Foundation, Inc., Carle C., CT, **565** (FD2)
Cook Inlet Region, Inc. Foundation, The, AK, *see* 33
Cooke Foundation, Ltd., HI, **932** (FD)
Cooke Foundation, William A., VA, **3434** (FD2)
Coon Family Foundation, OR, **2843** (FD2)
Cooper Charitable Foundation, Inc., Frederick E. Cooper and Helen Dykes, GA, **870** (FD2)
Cooper Foundation, NE, **1834** (FD)
Cooper Industries Foundation, TX, **3203** (FD)
Cooper-Siegel Family Foundation, The, PA, **2927** (FD)
Copeland Foundation, Leslie & Loretta, IL, **995** (FD)
Copernicus Society of America, PA, **2928** (FD2)
Copley Foundation, Helen K. and James S., CA, **166** (FD)
Copley Foundation, James S., CA, *see* 166
Coral Gables Community Foundation, FL, **729** (FD)
Coral Gables Foundation, The, FL, *see* 729
Cord Vanderpool Foundation, IL, **996** (FD2)
Cornell Douglas Foundation, Inc., MD, **1361** (FD2)
Cornell Trust, Peter C., FL, **730** (FD2)
Cornerstone Foundation of Northeastern Wisconsin Inc., WI, **3608** (FD)
Cornerstones for Kids, TX, **3204** (FD2)
Correll Family Foundation, Inc., The, GA, **871** (FD)
Corvias Foundation, WA, **3505** (FD)
Coshocton Foundation, OH, **2686** (FD)
Cote Foundation Inc., Berthe M., NY, **2114** (FD2)
Cotsen Family Foundation, CA, **167** (FD)
Coudert Foundation, Frederic R., NY, **2115** (FD)
Countess Moira Charitable Foundation, The, NY, **2116** (FD)
Covington Community Foundation, Inc., IN, *see* 1208
Cowden Charitable Foundation, Faye L. and William L., TX, **3205** (FD)
Cowell Foundation, S. H., CA, **168** (FD)
Cox, Jr. Foundation, Inc., James M., GA, *see* 916
Craig Family Foundation, Inc., C. S., CT, **566** (FD2)
Craig-Scheckman Family Foundation, CO, **486** (FD2)
Craigslist Charitable Fund, CA, **169** (FD)
Crail-Johnson Foundation, CA, **170** (FD)
Crain Foundation, The, TX, **3206** (FD)
Cramer Family Foundation, Inc., Gerald and Daphna, The, NY, **2117** (FD)
Cramer Family Foundation, Inc., Gerald B., NY, *see* 2117
Crane-Rogers Foundation, The, DC, *see* 667
Credit Suisse Americas Foundation, NY, **2118** (FD)
Credit Suisse First Boston Foundation Trust, NY, *see* 2118
Cricket Island Foundation, NY, **2119** (FD)
Cricket Island Foundation, The, NY, *see* 2119
Criswell Foundation, Inc., W.A., TX, **3207** (FD)
Croft Foundation Inc., L. Gordon, MD, **1362** (FD2)
Cross Charitable Foundation, Inc., MT, **1822** (FD)
Crosser Family Foundation, Inc., IN, **1139** (FD2)
Crowell Trust, Henry P. and Susan C., CO, *see* 487
Crowell Trust, The, CO, **487** (FD)
Crown Family Philanthropies, IL, *see* 997
Crown Memorial, Arie and Ida, IL, **997** (FD)
Cruz-Diez Foundation, TX, **3208** (FD2)
Cumberland Community Foundation, Inc., NC, **2541** (FD)
Cummings Foundation, Inc., James H., NY, **2120** (FD)
Cummings Foundation, James G., CA, **171** (FD2)
Cummings Foundation, Nathan, The, NY, **2121** (FD)
Cummings Memorial Fund, Frances L. & Edwin L., The, NY, **2122** (FD)
Cunningham Foundation, Inc., Laura Moore, ID, **946** (FD)
Cuore Foundation, CA, **172** (FD2)
Cupid Foundation, Inc., The, MD, **1363** (FD)
Curci Family Foundation, John, CA, **173** (FD)
Curci Foundation, Shurl & Kay, The, CA, **174** (FD)
Currents of Change, Inc., MA, **1455** (FD)
Curry Family Foundation, The, MO, **1784** (FD2)
Curtis Fund, The, VT, *see* 3410
Curves Community Fund, Inc., The, TX, *see* 3253
Cush Automotive Charitable Foundation, CA, *see* 175
Cush Family Foundation, The, CA, **175** (FD2)
Cutco Foundation Inc., NY, **2123** (FD2)
CVS Caremark Charitable Trust, Inc., RI, **3068** (FD)
CVS/pharmacy Charitable Trust, Inc., RI, *see* 3068
CW Film Foundation, Inc., CA, **176** (FD2)

Floyd Family Foundation, CA, **200** (FD2)
Fluor Foundation, The, TX, **3235** (FD)
Focus Autism, Inc., NJ, **1930** (FD)
Focus on Excellence, Inc., FL, **746** (FD2)
Foellinger Foundation, Inc., IN, **1147** (FD)
Foglia Family Foundation, IL, **1015** (FD)
Fond du Lac Area Foundation, WI, **3615** (FD)
Foothills Community Foundation, SC, **3102** (FD)
Forbes Charitable Trust, Herman, IL, **1016** (FD2)
Ford Family Foundation, The, OR, **2846** (FD)
Ford Foundation, NY, **2160** (FD)
Forest Lawn Foundation, CA, *see* 95
Fort Atkinson Community Foundation, WI, **3616** (FD)
Fort Pierce Memorial Hospital Scholarship Foundation, Inc., FL, *see* 768
Fort Worth Burn Foundation, TX, **3236** (FD2)
Forte American Heroes Fund, TX, **3237** (FD2)
Fortin Foundation, Mary Alice, The, FL, **747** (FD)
Fortis Foundation, NY, *see* 2047
Fortson Charitable Trust, Ed & Claude, NC, **2553** (FD2)
Fortune Education Foundation, Inc., NJ, **1931** (FD)
Fortune Foundation, Inc., Sheila, CO, **497** (FD2)
Foss Memorial Employees Trust, Donald J., OH, **2701** (FD2)
Found Animals Foundation, Inc., CA, **201** (FD)
Foundation for Appalachian Ohio, The, OH, **2702** (FD2)
Foundation for Child Development, NY, **2161** (FD)
Foundation for Deep Ecology, CA, **202** (FD)
Foundation for Educational Excellence, CO, **498** (FD)
Foundation for Enhancing Communities, The, PA, **2952** (FD)
Foundation for Enterprise Development, CA, **203** (FD2)
Foundation for Global Sports Development, The, CA, **204** (FD2)
Foundation for Informed Medical Decisions Foundation, MA, *see* 1489
Foundation for Middle East Peace, DC, **661** (FD2)
Foundation for Roanoke Valley, VA, *see* 3432
Foundation for Seacoast Health, NH, **1885** (FD)
Foundation for the Future, WA, **3515** (FD)
Foundation for the Mid South, MS, **1763** (FD)
Foundation Northwest, WA, *see* 3526
Foundation of the Litton Industries, VA, *see* 3465
Foundation of the Pierre Fauchard Academy, VA, **3438** (FD2)
Foundation, Inc., Jones, KS, *see* 1262
Four County Community Foundation, MI, **1603** (FD2)
Four County Foundation, MI, *see* 1603
Fourjay Foundation, PA, **2953** (FD)
Fournier Family Foundation, The, NJ, **1932** (FD)
Fowler Family Foundation, Char and Chuck, The, OH, **2703** (FD)
Fowler Family Foundation, Charles and Charlotte, OH, *see* 2703
Fowler Memorial Foundation, John Edward, MD, **1372** (FD)
Fox Family Foundation, CO, **499** (FD2)
Fox Family Foundation, Frieda C., CA, **205** (FD)
Fox Foundation, William and Eva, The, VA, **3439** (FD2)
Francis Community Health Care, Inc., Saint, MA, **1471** (FD2)
Frank Foundation, Sidney E., The, CA, **206** (FD)
Frankel Family Foundation, IL, **1017** (FD)
Frankel Foundation, Samuel & Jean, MI, **1604** (FD)
Frankel Health and Research Foundation, Samuel and Jean, The, MI, **1605** (FD)
Frankenberg Foundation, Regina Bauer, The, NY, **2162** (FD)
Frankenmuth Area Community Foundation, Greater, MI, *see* 1606
Frankenmuth Community Foundation, MI, **1606** (FD2)
Franklin Foundation, Wilson P. & Anne W., FL, **748** (FD2)
Franklin Square House Foundation, MA, **1472** (FD)
Freas Foundation, Inc., PA, **2954** (FD2)
Freed Foundation, The, NY, **2163** (FD)
Freedom Forum, Inc., The, DC, **662** (FD)
Freedom Wireless Foundation, AZ, **45** (FD2)
Freeman Foundation, Ella West, The, LA, **1309** (FD)
Freeman Foundation, Inc., Carl M., The, MD, **1373** (FD)
Freeman Foundation, NY, **2164** (FD)
Frees Foundation, The, TX, **3238** (FD)
Freese Family Foundation, Inc., OK, **2812** (FD2)
Fremont Area Community Foundation, MI, **1607** (FD)
Fremont Area Community Foundation, NE, **1836** (FD)
Fremont Area Foundation, The, MI, *see* 1607
Fremont Bank Foundation, CA, **207** (FD)
French Foundation, Marina Kellen, NY, **2165** (FD)
French Fund, Samuel & Katharine, NC, **2554** (FD)
French Fund, Samuel H. French III and Katharine Weaver, NC, *see* 2554
Frey Charitable Trust, Twink, MI, **1608** (FD)
Frey Foundation, MI, **1609** (FD)
Frey Foundation, MN, **1696** (FD)
Freygang Foundation, Walter Henry, OH, **2704** (FD2)
Freygish Foundation, DE, **633** (FD)
Friedman Family Foundation, CA, **208** (FD)
Friedman New York Foundation for Medical Research, Gerald J. and Dorothy R., The, NY, **2166** (FD)
Friend Family Foundation, Eugene, The, CA, *see* 209
Friend Family Foundation, The, CA, **209** (FD)
Friends of the Congressional Glaucoma Caucus Foundation, Inc., NY, **2167** (FD)
Frist Foundation, Dorothy Cate & Thomas F., The, TN, **3136** (FD)
Frist Medical Foundation, The, TN, *see* 3136
Froderman Foundation, Inc., The, IN, **1148** (FD)
Frost Foundation, Ltd., The, NM, **2012** (FD)
Frueauff Foundation, Inc., Charles A., AR, **70** (FD)
Fry Foundation, Lloyd A., IL, **1018** (FD)
Fry Memorial Trust, L. P., CT, *see* 579
Fry Memorial Trust, Lily Palmer, CT, **579** (FD2)
Frye Foundation, Charles F. & Esther M., IL, **1019** (FD2)
FSJ Foundation, Inc., IN, **1149** (FD2)
Fulk Family Foundation, Inc., IL, **1020** (FD)
Fuller Foundation, Inc., The, NH, **1886** (FD)
Fully Invested Foundation, The, UT, *see* 3398
Fund for Democratic Communities, The, NC, **2555** (FD2)
Fund for Nonviolence, CA, **210** (FD)
Fund for Wisconsin Scholars, Inc., WI, **3617** (FD)
Fund for Wisconsin Scholarship, Inc., WI, *see* 3617
Funk Foundation, Paul A., IL, **1021** (FD2)
Furrer Foundation, WY, **3674** (FD2)
Fusenot Charity Foundation, Inc., Georges and Germaine, CA, **211** (FD2)
Fuserna Foundation, CA, **212** (FD)

G. II Charities, MI, **1610** (FD)
Gage Foundation, Alfred S., The, TX, **3239** (FD2)
Gainesville Community Foundation, FL, *see* 725
Galena Foundation, The, CO, **500** (FD)
Galler Research Foundation Inc., Marc, NY, **2168** (FD2)
Galtney Foundation, The, TX, **3240** (FD2)
Gamble Foundation, The, CA, **213** (FD2)
Gambrill Foundation, NC, **2556** (FD2)
Gamper Foundation, Albert and Janice, NJ, **1933** (FD2)
Garden Foundation, Allan C. and Leila J., GA, **875** (FD2)
Gardinor-Prunaret Foundation, MA, **1473** (FD2)
Gardner Foundation, OH, **2705** (FD2)
Garfield Foundation, Eugene, The, PA, **2955** (FD2)
Garfield Street Foundation, NM, **2013** (FD2)
Garrow Family Charitable Foundation, NC, **2557** (FD2)
Gate Foundation, Inc., The, FL, **749** (FD2)
Gates Foundation, Bill & Melinda, WA, **3516** (FD)
Gates Foundation, William H., WA, *see* 3516
Gateway Foundation, MO, **1789** (FD)
Gaylord Foundation, E. L. and Thelma, OK, **2813** (FD)
Geary Foundation, Bruce G., NY, **2169** (FD)
Gebbie Foundation, Inc., NY, **2170** (FD)
Gellert Family Foundation, Fred, The, CA, **214** (FD2)
Gellert Family Trust, Leopold R., NY, **2171** (FD2)
Gellert Foundation, Carl Gellert and Celia Berta, The, CA, **215** (FD)
Gellert Foundation, Carl, The, CA, *see* 215
Gemj Chehebar Foundation, NY, **2172** (FD2)
Genentech Foundation, CA, **216** (FD)
General Education Fund, Inc., VT, **3410** (FD)
General Mills Foundation, MN, **1697** (FD)
General Service Foundation, CO, **501** (FD)
Geneseo Foundation, IL, **1022** (FD2)
Genesis Foundation Inc., NY, **2173** (FD)
Gengras, Jr. Foundation, Inc., E. Clayton and Edith P., CT, **580** (FD2)
George Family Foundation, MN, **1698** (FD)
Georgetown Area Community Foundation, The, TX, *see* 3193
Georgia Health Foundation, Inc., GA, **876** (FD2)
Georgia Power Foundation, Inc., GA, **877** (FD)
Georgia Scientific and Technical Research Foundation, GA, *see* 918
Georgia-Pacific Foundation, Inc., GA, **878** (FD)
Gerber Companies Foundation and The Gerber Baby Food Fund, The, MI, *see* 1611
Gerber Foundation, The, MI, **1611** (FD)
Gerbode Foundation, Wallace Alexander, CA, **217** (FD)
German Protestant Orphan Asylum Association Foundation, LA, **1310** (FD2)
Germeshausen Foundation, Inc., MA, **1474** (FD)
Gershwind Family Foundation, The, NY, **2174** (FD)
Getty Family Foundation, The, CA, *see* 212
Getty Foundation, Ann and Gordon, The, CA, **218** (FD)
GGS Foundation, CA, **219** (FD)
Gheens Foundation, Inc., The, KY, **1288** (FD)
Ghez Foundation, Nomi P., The, NY, **2175** (FD2)
Ghidotti Foundation, William & Marian, NC, **2558** (FD)
Gholston Foundation, J. Knox, GA, **879** (FD2)
Gholston Foundation, J. William, GA, **880** (FD2)
Gholston Trust, J. William, GA, *see* 880
Giant Eagle Foundation, The, PA, *see* 2889
Giant Steps Foundation, The, NY, **2176** (FD2)
Gibson Family Foundation, NJ, **1934** (FD)
Gibson, Dunn & Crutcher Foundation, The, CA, **220** (FD)
Gifford Charitable Corporation, Rosamond, The, NY, **2177** (FD)
Gifford Foundation, Helen G., VA, **3440** (FD2)
Gifford Foundation, Lee A. & Helen G., The, VA, *see* 3440
Gifford Foundation, The, NY, *see* 2177
Gilbert, Jr. Charitable Fund, Price, GA, **881** (FD)
Gill Foundation, The, CO, **502** (FD)
Gilman, Jr. Foundation, Inc., Sondra & Charles, NY, **2178** (FD2)
Gilmore Foundation, Irving S., MI, **1612** (FD)
Gilmore Foundation, William G., The, CA, **221** (FD)
Gimbel Foundation, Inc., Bernard F. and Alva B., NY, **2179** (FD)
Gimprich Family Foundation, Inc., NY, **2180** (FD2)
Gindi Associates Foundation, Inc., NY, *see* 2089
Ginn Charitable Trust, Frank Hadley Ginn and Cornelia Root, The, OH, **2706** (FD2)
Ginn Foundation, The, OH, *see* 2706
GirlSMART Literacy Program, CA, **222** (FD2)
GLA Foundation, CA, **223** (FD2)
Glaser Foundation, The, WA, *see* 3517
Glaser Progress Foundation, WA, **3517** (FD)
Glass Family Foundation, Inc., NC, *see* 2559
Glass Foundation, Inc., NC, **2559** (FD)
Glatfelter III Family Foundation, Anne & Philip, PA, **2956** (FD)
Glaxo Wellcome Foundation, The, NC, *see* 2600
GlaxoSmithKline Foundation, PA, **2957** (FD)
Glazer Family Foundation, Inc., FL, **750** (FD)
Glazer Foundation Inc., Jerome S., LA, **1311** (FD2)
Gleason Family Foundation, CA, **224** (FD)
Gleason Foundation, CA, *see* 224
Glendale Community Foundation, CA, *see* 162

Glenn Charitable Foundation, Jack and Anne, GA, **882** (FD)
Glenn Foundation for Medical Research, Inc., CA, **225** (FD)
Glenn Foundation for Medical Research, Inc., Paul F., CA, see 225
Glenn Foundation, Inc., Carrie E. and Lena V., The, NC, **2560** (FD2)
Glick Foundation Corporation, Eugene and Marilyn, IN, **1150** (FD)
Glide Foundation, Thornton S., Jr. and Katrina D., CA, **226** (FD)
Global Film Initiative, The, CA, see 176
Globe Foundation Limited, IN, **1151** (FD2)
Globe Foundation, The, WA, see 3495
Gloria Dei Foundation, DE, **634** (FD)
Glory Foundation, OR, **2847** (FD)
Gluck Foundation, Inc., Maxwell H., CA, **227** (FD)
Godfrey Foundation Inc., Dudley and Constance, WI, **3618** (FD2)
Goizueta Foundation, The, GA, **883** (FD)
Gold Foundation, David B., The, CA, **228** (FD)
Gold Foundation, Sheila, CA, **229** (FD)
Golden Family Foundation, Donald & Norma, MI, **1613** (FD2)
Golden Rule Foundation, Inc., The, ME, **1329** (FD2)
Golden Slipper Club Uptown Home for the Aged, PA, **2958** (FD2)
Goldman Charitable Trust, Lillian, The, NY, **2181** (FD)
Goldman Family Foundation, Inc., Joyce and Irving, NY, **2182** (FD)
Goldman Foundation, Herman, NY, **2183** (FD)
Goldman Foundation, Inc., Irving, NY, see 2182
Goldsbury Foundation, The, TX, **3241** (FD)
Goldseker Foundation of Maryland, Inc., Morris, MD, **1374** (FD)
Goldseker Foundation, MD, see 1374
Goldstein Family Foundation, The, NY, **2184** (FD)
Goldstone Family Foundation, The, CT, **581** (FD)
Golisano Foundation, B. Thomas, The, NY, **2185** (FD)
Golub Foundation, Inc., Neil and Jane, NY, **2186** (FD2)
Good Heart Work Smart Foundation, IL, **1023** (FD)
Good Samaritan Foundation, Inc., KY, **1289** (FD)
Good Works Foundation, The, CA, **230** (FD)
Goodman Foundation, The, WA, **3518** (FD2)
Goodman-Abell Foundation, TX, **3242** (FD)
Goodrich Charitable Foundation, Mike and Gillian, AL, see 13
Goodrich Foundation, Inc., The, NC, see 2561
Goodrich Foundation, Mike and Gillian, AL, **13** (FD)
Goodrich Foundation, NC, **2561** (FD)
Goodwin Tateuchi Foundation, Atsuhiko and Ina, The, WA, **3519** (FD)
Google Foundation, CA, **231** (FD)
Gordon Children's Foundation, Jeff, The, NC, **2562** (FD)
Gordon Family Foundation, MA, **1475** (FD)
Gordon Foundation, Jeff, The, NC, see 2562
Gordon, Jr. Foundation, W. K., The, TX, **3243** (FD2)
Goshen Hill Foundation, Inc., PA, **2959** (FD2)
Gottlieb Foundation, Inc., Adolph and Esther, NY, **2187** (FD)
Gould Charitable Foundation, Inc., Anna, MA, **1476** (FD2)
Gould Charitable Foundation, The, MA, **1477** (FD2)
Gould Foundation, Edwin, NY, **2188** (FD)
Gould Youth & Family Learning Association, Inc., Allen, DC, see 676
GPOA Foundation, LA, see 1310
Grace and Mercy Foundation, Inc., The, NY, **2189** (FD)
Grace Charity Foundation Inc., NJ, **1935** (FD2)
Grace Foundation, William M. & Ann K., AZ, **46** (FD)
Graff Family Foundation, CA, see 334
Graham Foundation, The, SC, **3103** (FD)
Graham Fund, Philip L., DC, **663** (FD)
Grainger Foundation Inc., The, IL, **1024** (FD)
Grampy's Charities, CT, **582** (FD2)
Grand Forks Community Foundation, Greater, The, ND, see 2648
Grand Foundation, CO, **503** (FD)
Grand Haven Area Community Foundation, Inc., MI, **1614** (FD)
Grand Island Community Foundation, Inc., NE, **1837** (FD)
Grand Rapids Area Community Foundation, MN, **1699** (FD)
Grand Rapids Community Foundation, MI, **1615** (FD)
Grand Rapids Foundation, The, MI, see 1615
Grand Traverse Regional Community Foundation, MI, **1616** (FD)
Granger Foundation, MI, **1617** (FD)
Grant Foundation, Charles M. & Mary D., NY, **2190** (FD2)
Grant Foundation, William T., NY, **2191** (FD)
Grant Healthcare Foundation, IL, **1025** (FD)
Grant Thornton Foundation, IL, **1026** (FD)
Grass Foundation, The, CA, **232** (FD2)
Grays Harbor Community Foundation, WA, **3520** (FD)
Great Lakes Capital Fund Nonprofit Housing Corporation, MI, **1618** (FD)
Greater Montana Foundation, The, MT, **1823** (FD2)
Greater Morgantown Community Trust, Inc., WV, see 3591
Green Bay Community Foundation, Inc., Greater, WI, **3619** (FD)
Green Earth Charitable Organization, CA, **233** (FD2)
Green Family Foundation, Inc., FL, **751** (FD)
Green Foundation, Allen P. & Josephine B., MO, **1790** (FD)
Green Foundation, George Mason and Lois C., The, AZ, **47** (FD)
Green Foundation, Joshua, WA, **3521** (FD)
Green Foundation, Val A. Green and Edith D., UT, **3394** (FD2)
Green Mountain Coffee Roasters Foundation, VT, see 3408
Greenberg Foundation, Monica and Hermen, MD, **1375** (FD2)
Greenburg May Foundation, Inc., FL, **752** (FD)
Greene County Community Foundation, Inc., IN, see 1152
Greene County Community Foundation, OH, **2707** (FD)
Greene County Foundation, Inc., IN, **1152** (FD2)
Greene Giving, OH, see 2707
Greenheck Foundation, B.A. and Esther, WI, **3620** (FD2)
Greensville Memorial Foundation, VA, **3441** (FD2)
Greensville Memorial Hospital, VA, see 3441
Greentree Fund, The, TX, **3244** (FD2)
Greenwall Foundation, The, NY, **2192** (FD)
Grew Family Charitable Foundation, MA, **1478** (FD2)
Greystone Foundation, The, MN, **1700** (FD)
Griffin Endowment, The, NC, **2563** (FD2)
Griffin Foundation, Inc., The, CO, **504** (FD)
Griffin Foundation, Kenneth and Anne, The, IL, see 969
Grigsby Foundation, Merice "Boo" Johnson, The, LA, **1312** (FD)
Grinspoon Charitable Foundation, Harold, The, MA, **1479** (FD)
Groff Surgical and Medical Research and Education Charitable Trust, Mary E., The, PA, **2960** (FD2)
Groskinsky Foundation, MT, **1824** (FD2)
Gross Foundation, Harold & Rebecca H., CT, **583** (FD2)
Gross Foundation, Inc., NY, **2193** (FD)
Gross Foundation, Maurice R. & Meta G., RI, **3076** (FD2)
Group Health Foundation of Greater St. Louis, MO, see 1814
Grousbeck Family Foundation, CA, **234** (FD)
Grumbacher Foundation, M. S., The, PA, **2961** (FD2)
Grundy Foundation, The, PA, **2962** (FD2)
Gruss Foundation, Audrey and Martin, FL, **753** (FD)
GSF Foundation, CA, **235** (FD)
Guanacaste Ventures U.S., Inc., GA, **884** (FD)
Gudelsky Family Foundation, Inc., Homer and Martha, The, MD, **1376** (FD)
Guernsey Charitable Foundation, Max and Helen, IA, **1221** (FD)
Guggenheim Memorial Foundation, John Simon, NY, **2194** (FD)
Guilander Scholarship Trust, Anna M., MO, **1791** (FD2)
Gulf Coast Community Foundation of Venice, FL, see 754
Gulf Coast Community Foundation, FL, see 754
Gulf Coast Community Foundation, Inc., FL, **754** (FD)
Gulf Coast Community Foundation, MS, **1764** (FD)
Gulf Coast Medical Foundation, TX, **3245** (FD)
Gumbiner Foundation, Josephine S., The, CA, **236** (FD)
Gund Foundation, George, The, OH, **2708** (FD)
Gurwin Foundation Inc., J., NY, **2195** (FD2)
Gutfleish Foundation, Ron and Stacey, NY, **2196** (FD)
Guthman Fund, Leo S., The, IL, **1027** (FD)
Guthy-Jackson Charitable Foundation, The, CA, **237** (FD)
Guttman Foundation, Inc., Stella and Charles, NY, **2197** (FD)
Guzik Foundation, The, CA, **238** (FD)
Gwathmey Memorial Trust, Richard and Caroline T., VA, **3442** (FD)
H.E.I. Charitable Foundation, HI, see 934
Haas Fund, Mimi and Peter, CA, **239** (FD)
Haas Fund, Miriam and Peter, CA, see 239
Hachar Charitable Trust Fund, D. D., TX, **3246** (FD)
Hackbarth Foundation, Inc., James and Pauline, NC, **2564** (FD2)
Hadar Foundation, Richard and Mica, The, NY, **2198** (FD2)
Hadar Foundation, The, NY, see 2198
Haddad Foundation, Inc., Robert and Helen, IN, **1153** (FD2)
Hagan Scholarship Foundation, The, MO, **1792** (FD2)
Hagedorn Foundation, NY, **2199** (FD)
Hagedorn Fund, NY, **2200** (FD)
Haile, Jr. Foundation, Carol & Ralph, OH, see 2709
Haile, Jr./U.S. Bank Foundation, Carol & Ralph, OH, **2709** (FD)
Hall Family Foundation, MO, **1793** (FD)
Hall Foundation, Alan and Jeanne, The, UT, **3395** (FD)
Hall Foundation, Charles H., CT, **584** (FD2)
Hall Foundation, Inc., MS, **1765** (FD)
Hall Foundation, Inc., The, IA, see 1222
Hall-Perrine Foundation, The, IA, **1222** (FD)
Haller Foundation, Albert, WA, **3522** (FD)
Hallett Charitable Trust, Jessie F., MN, **1701** (FD2)
Hallett Charitable Trust, MN, see 1701
Hallingby Family Foundation, Inc., The, NY, **2201** (FD2)
Hallmark Corporate Foundation, MO, **1794** (FD)
Halloran Foundation, The, PA, **2963** (FD2)
Halper Foundation, Robert & Deann, The, NY, see 2202
Halper Foundation, Robert, The, NY, **2202** (FD2)
Halperin Foundation, Robert and Ruth, CA, **240** (FD)
Halsell Foundation, Ewing, The, TX, **3247** (FD)
Ham Charitable Foundation, Inc., Kendal C. & Anna, NH, **1887** (FD2)
Hamilton Community Foundation, Inc., The, OH, **2710** (FD)
Hamm Foundation, Harold G. and Sue Ann, IL, **1028** (FD)
Hamman Foundation, George and Mary Josephine, TX, **3248** (FD)
Hammill Foundation, Donald D., TX, **3249** (FD2)
Hanauer Foundation, Nick and Leslie, The, WA, **3523** (FD)
Hancock County Community Foundation, Inc., IN, **1154** (FD2)
Hand Foundation, Inc., The, FL, **755** (FD2)
Hand Foundation, The, CA, **241** (FD)
Hanes Foundation, John W. and Anna H., The, NC, **2565** (FD)
Hanifl Foundation, Paul and Suzanne, IL, **1029** (FD2)

Hunter Trust, Inc., A. V., CO, **508** (FD)
Huntingdon, Jr. Charitable Trust, K., OH, **2713** (FD2)
Hurlbut Memorial Fund, Orion L. & Emma B., TN, **3140** (FD)
Hurvis Charitable Foundation, Inc., IL, **1037** (FD)
Huston Foundation, The, PA, **2973** (FD)
Hutcheson Foundation, Hazel Montague, TN, **3141** (FD2)
Hutchinson Community Foundation, KS, **1260** (FD)
Hutto Patterson Charitable Foundation, CA, **258** (FD)
Hyams Foundation, Inc., The, MA, **1486** (FD)
Hyams Fund, Sarah A., MA, see 1486
Hycliff Foundation, NY, **2226** (FD2)
Hyde and Watson Foundation, The, NJ, **1944** (FD)

I Have a Dream Foundation - Oregon, OR, **2850** (FD2)
i.am.angel Foundation, CA, **259** (FD2)
Iacocca Family Foundation, The, MA, **1487** (FD)
Iacocca Foundation, The, MA, see 1487
IASD Health Care Foundation, The, IA, see 1246
IBM International Foundation, NY, **2227** (FD)
IBM South Africa Projects Fund, NY, see 2227
Idaho Community Foundation, ID, **948** (FD)
IF Foundation, The, NY, **2228** (FD)
II-VI Foundation, PA, **2974** (FD)
II-VI Incorporated Foundation, PA, see 2974
IMA Foundation, KS, see 1261
Imagine 247 Foundation, NY, **2229** (FD2)
Imago Dei Foundation, Inc., NY, **2230** (FD)
Imlay Foundation, Inc., The, GA, **888** (FD)
Inavale Foundation, Inc., MA, **1488** (FD)
Incourage Community Foundation, Inc., WI, **3623** (FD)
Independence Blue Cross Foundation, PA, **2975** (FD)
Independence Community Foundation, MO, see 1817
Independence Foundation, PA, **2976** (FD)
Indiana Energy Foundation, Inc., IN, see 1202
Informed Medical Decisions Foundation, Inc., MA, **1489** (FD)
ING Foundation, NY, see 2488
Initial Teaching Alphabet Foundation, NY, **2231** (FD2)
Initiative Foundation, MN, **1703** (FD)
Inland Northwest Community Foundation, WA, **3526** (FD)
Innovative Technology Education Fund, MO, **1796** (FD2)
Institute for Depression Studies and Treatment, NY, **2232** (FD2)
Institute for Healthcare Advancement, CA, **260** (FD)
Institute for the Study of Aging, Inc., NY, **2233** (FD2)
Institute of Current World Affairs, Inc., DC, **667** (FD2)
Insurance Management Associates Foundation, KS, **1261** (FD2)
Integra Foundation, Inc., The, NJ, **1945** (FD)
Intermec Foundation, WA, **3527** (FD)
International Foundation, The, NJ, **1946** (FD)
International Humanity Foundation, CA, **261** (FD2)
International Medical Outreach, Inc., TX, **3269** (FD)
International Palace of Sports, Inc., IN, see 1195
International Paper Company Foundation, TN, **3142** (FD)
International Retinal Research Foundation, Inc., AL, **15** (FD)
Intrepid Philanthropy Foundation, CA, **262** (FD)
Intuit Foundation, The, CA, **263** (FD)
Iovino Family Foundation, The, NY, see 2228
Iowa Foundation for Agricultural Advancement, IA, **1225** (FD2)
Iowa West Foundation, IA, **1226** (FD)
Irvine Foundation, James, The, CA, **264** (FD)
Isaacs Brothers Foundation, The, CA, **265** (FD)
Isabel Foundation, The, MI, **1621** (FD)
Isabella Bank & Trust Foundation, MI, **1622** (FD2)
Israelson Family Foundation, Inc., MD, **1380** (FD2)
Istel Foundation, Inc., Y. A., NY, **2234** (FD2)
Itzler Family Foundation, The, NY, see 2019
Izzo Family Foundation, MD, **1381** (FD2)

J & L Foundation, The, KY, **1291** (FD)
Jabara Charitable Trust, Violet, The, NY, **2235** (FD2)
Jackson Charitable Trust, Marion Gardner, IL, **1038** (FD)
Jackson Community Foundation, MI, **1623** (FD)
Jackson County Community Foundation, The, MI, see 1623
Jackson Family Foundation, Inc., The, CA, **266** (FD)
Jackson Foundation, Greater, MS, see 1759
Jackson Foundation, The, OR, **2851** (FD)
Jacksonville Jaguars Foundation, FL, **761** (FD)
Jacobs Family Foundation, Inc., CA, **267** (FD)
Jacobsen Charitable Foundation Inc., Hans & Cay, FL, **762** (FD2)
Jacobson Family Trust Foundation, The, MA, **1490** (FD)
Jaffe Foundation, The, MA, **1491** (FD2)
Jaffer Foundation, Mohsin & Fauzia, FL, **763** (FD)
Jaharis Family Foundation, Inc., The, NY, **2236** (FD)
JAMS Foundation, CA, **268** (FD)
Janssen Ortho Patient Assistance Foundation, Inc., NJ, see 1948
Jaquish & Kenninger Foundation, The, NV, **1865** (FD2)
Jasam Foundation Fund B, AZ, **50** (FD)
Jasper Foundation, Inc., IN, **1160** (FD2)
Jasteka Foundation, IN, **1161** (FD2)
Jefferson County Community Foundation, Greater, IA, **1227** (FD2)
Jeffress Memorial Trust, Thomas F. and Kate Miller, VA, **3444** (FD)
Jeffris Family Foundation, Ltd., WI, **3624** (FD)
Jehovah-Jireh Foundation, Inc., MD, **1382** (FD2)
Jeker Family Trust, ID, **949** (FD)
Jeld-Wen Foundation, The, OR, **2852** (FD)
Jeld-Wen, Wenco Foundation, OR, see 2852
Jenkins Foundation, Inc., George W., FL, see 804
Jennings County Community Foundation, Inc., IN, **1162** (FD2)
Jensen Family Foundation, Inc., J., TX, see 3194
Jensen Foundation, Janet Jarie, TX, see 3169
Jewish Foundation for Education of Women, NY, **2237** (FD)
Jewish Renaissance Foundation Inc., NY, **2238** (FD)
Ji Ji Foundation, The, WA, **3528** (FD)
Jiv Daya Foundation, TX, **3270** (FD)
JM Foundation, The, NJ, **1947** (FD)
Joanna Foundation, The, SC, **3104** (FD2)
Johnson & Johnson Patient Assistance Foundation, Inc., NJ, **1948** (FD)
Johnson Brothers Charitable Foundation, The, MN, see 1704
Johnson Charitable Foundation, Willard and Ruth, The, TX, **3271** (FD)
Johnson County Community Foundation, Greater, IN, see 1163
Johnson County Community Foundation, Inc., IN, **1163** (FD)
Johnson Family Foundation, Lynn, The, MN, **1704** (FD2)
Johnson Family Foundation, NY, see 2240
Johnson Family Foundation, OH, **2714** (FD2)
Johnson Foundation, Inc., Willard T. C., NY, **2241** (FD)
Johnson Foundation, Jimmie, NC, **2574** (FD)
Johnson Foundation, Lloyd K., MN, **1705** (FD)
Johnson Foundation, NY, **2239** (FD2)
Johnson Foundation, Robert Wood, The, NJ, **1949** (FD)
Johnson Foundation, Thomas Phillips and Jane Moore, The, NY, **2240** (FD)
Johnson Foundation, Walter S., CA, **269** (FD)
Johnson Foundation, Zach, IA, **1228** (FD2)
Johnson Fund, Edward C., NH, **1889** (FD)
Johnson Fund, Inc., SC, WI, see 3625
Johnson Giving, Inc., SC, WI, **3625** (FD)
Johnson Memorial Trust, John Alfred & Oscar, NY, see 2239
Johnson Nutrition Foundation, Mead, IL, **1039** (FD)
Jones Charitable Trust, Margery, WA, **3529** (FD2)
Jones Family Foundation, Fred, OK, **2817** (FD)
Jones Foundation, Fletcher, The, CA, **270** (FD)
Jones Foundation, Fred and Mary Eddy, The, OK, see 2817
Jones Foundation, Herbert B., The, WA, **3530** (FD)
Jones Foundation, Inc., W. Alton, VA, see 3422
Jones Foundation, The, CA, see 270
Jones Foundation, Walter S. and Evan C., KS, **1262** (FD)
Jones Fund, Blanche & George, NJ, **1950** (FD2)
Jones Testamentary Trust, Walter S. and Evan C., TX, **3272** (FD)
Jorgensen Foundation Inc., Ove W., IN, **1164** (FD2)
Joshi Foundation Inc, Georgina, The, IN, **1165** (FD)
Jostens Foundation, Inc., The, MN, **1706** (FD)
Jovid Foundation, DC, **668** (FD2)
Joyard Foundation, The, CA, **271** (FD2)
Joyce Foundation, The, IL, **1040** (FD)
JPMorgan Chase Foundation, The, NY, **2242** (FD)
JSMF, MO, see 1800
Jubilee Foundation, MI, **1624** (FD)
Jubitz Family Foundation, OR, **2853** (FD)
Juneau Community Foundation, AK, **35** (FD2)
Just Keep Livin Foundation, CA, **272** (FD2)
Justice for Athletes, CA, see 204

K21 Health Foundation, IN, see 1168
Kade Foundation, Inc., Max, NY, **2243** (FD)
Kahiau Foundation, The, HI, **935** (FD2)
Kahlert Foundation, Inc., The, MD, **1383** (FD2)
Kahn Charitable Foundation, Esther B., MA, **1492** (FD2)
Kahn Family Foundation, MI, see 1625
Kahn Foundation, D. Dan and Betty, The, MI, **1625** (FD2)
Kaiserman Foundation, Kevy K. & Hortense M., PA, **2977** (FD2)
Kalamazoo Community Foundation, The, MI, **1626** (FD)
Kalamazoo Foundation, MI, see 1626
Kanas Family Foundation, John and Elaine, NY, **2244** (FD)
Kaneta Charitable Foundation, HI, see 936
Kaneta Foundation, HI, **936** (FD2)
Kanitz Scholarship Memorial Fund, Louis J. & Golda I., NC, **2575** (FD2)
Kankakee River Valley Foundation, IL, see 989
Kansas Health Foundation, KS, **1263** (FD)
Kansas Health Foundation/Kansas Health Trust, KS, see 1263
Kantner Foundation, Inc., FL, **764** (FD2)
Kaplan Family Foundation, Mayer and Morris, IL, **1041** (FD)
Kaplan Family Foundation, MN, **1707** (FD2)
Kaplan Family Foundation, The, NC, see 2640
Kaplan Fund, Inc., J. M., The, NY, **2245** (FD)
Kapor Center for Social Impact, CA, **273** (FD)
Kapor Foundation, Mitchell, CA, see 273
Karmazin Foundation, Mel, NY, **2246** (FD)
Katcher Family Foundation, Inc., The, FL, **765** (FD)
Katten Muchin Rosenman Foundation, Inc., IL, **1042** (FD)
Katten Muchin Zavis Rosenman Foundation, Inc., IL, see 1042
Katz Foundation, Abraham J. & Phyllis, GA, **889** (FD)
Katz Foundation, H.L., NC, **2576** (FD2)
Katz Memorial Fund, Harry, NC, see 2576
Kauffman Foundation, Ewing Marion, MO, **1797** (FD)
Kaufman Dance Foundation, Glorya, CA, **274** (FD)
Kaufman Memorial Trust, Chaim, Fanny, Louis, Benjamin and Anne Florence, The, IL, **1043** (FD2)
Kaufmann Foundation, Marion Esser, CO, **509** (FD)
Kavli Foundation, The, CA, **275** (FD)
Kawabe Memorial Fund, WA, **3531** (FD2)
Kawabe Trust, Harry S., WA, see 3531
Kay Family Foundation, Inc., The, MD, **1384** (FD)
Kaylie Foundation, Inc., Harvey & Gloria, The, NY, **2247** (FD)
Kazma Family Foundation, FL, **766** (FD)
KBR Charitable Trust, NC, see 2614
KDK-Harman Foundation, TX, **3273** (FD)

Leeds Family Foundation, NY, **2272** (FD)
Leeman Foundation, Inc., Stephen & May Cavin, NY, **2273** (FD2)
Leeoma Charitable Trust, CO, **511** (FD)
Leeway Foundation, The, PA, **2985** (FD2)
Lefkofsky Family Foundation, The, IL, **1049** (FD)
Legacy Foundation of Tompkins County, NY, **2274** (FD2)
Legacy Foundation, Inc., IN, **1171** (FD)
Legion Foundation, The, MI, **1633** (FD)
Lehigh Valley Community Foundation, PA, **2986** (FD)
Lehrman Foundation, Inc., Jacob and Charlotte, DC, **670** (FD)
Leichtag Foundation, The, CA, **297** (FD)
Leichtman and Arthur E. Levine Family Foundation, Lauren B., CA, **298** (FD)
Leighton Foundation, Inc., Judd, IN, **1172** (FD)
Leighty Foundation, The, CO, **512** (FD2)
Leiser Foundation, Inc., Josephine S., FL, **777** (FD2)
Lemelson Foundation, The, OR, **2857** (FD)
Lenawee Community Foundation, MI, **1634** (FD)
Lennar Foundation, FL, **778** (FD)
Lennox Foundation, DE, **638** (FD)
Lennox Foundation, Martha, David & Bagby, TX, **3279** (FD)
Leominster-Croft Foundation, Inc., MD, *see* 1362
Leonard Foundation, Red and Gena, OR, **2858** (FD2)
Lerner Foundation, The, OH, **2722** (FD)
Lesher Foundation, Dean & Margaret, CA, **299** (FD)
Leslie Foundation Irrevocable Trust, MN, **1712** (FD2)
Levant Foundation, The, TX, **3280** (FD)
Levin Family Foundation, The, OR, *see* 2869
Levine Family Foundation, Howard and Irene, CA, **300** (FD)
Levine Foundation, Leon, The, NC, **2584** (FD)
Levitt Foundation, Inc., Mortimer, NJ, **1960** (FD)
Levitt Foundation, Inc., NY, **2275** (FD)
Levy Family Foundation, Paul and Karen, The, NY, **2276** (FD)
Levy Foundation, Inc., June Rockwell, MA, **1501** (FD)
Lewis Jr. Charitable Foundation, Carol Sutton & William M., The, NY, **2277** (FD)
Lewis Memorial Fund, Mabelle McLeod, PA, **2987** (FD2)
Lexington Community Foundation, NE, **1845** (FD2)
Liberal Do-Gooder Foundation, The, NY, **2278** (FD2)
Liberman Foundation, Inc., Bertha & Isaac, NY, **2279** (FD2)
Liberty Mutual Foundation, Inc., The, MA, **1502** (FD)
Libra Foundation, ME, **1334** (FD)
Libra Foundation, The, IL, **1050** (FD)
Lichtenberg Family Foundation, Inc., DC, **671** (FD2)
Lichtenberg Foundation, William R. & Nora, DC, *see* 671
Licking County Foundation, OH, **2723** (FD)
Liddell Foundation, Robert Clay, OK, **2819** (FD2)
Lienemann Charitable Foundation, Inc., NE, **1846** (FD2)
Life Foundation Inc., Lois Pope, FL, **779** (FD)
Lift A Life Foundation, Inc., KY, **1293** (FD)
Light Charitable Trust, Jack H. & William M., TX, **3281** (FD)
Lightner Sams Foundation, Inc., Larry, TX, **3282** (FD)
Ligon Foundation, The, GA, **892** (FD2)
Lilly Philanthropic Foundation, Ruth, IN, **1173** (FD)
Lincoln Community Foundation, Inc., NE, **1847** (FD)
Lincoln Family Foundation, G.R., The, OH, **2724** (FD)
Lincoln Foundation, Inc., MA, *see* 1503
Lincoln Foundation, Inc., NE, *see* 1847
Lincoln Health Foundation, LA, **1315** (FD)
Lincoln Institute of Land Policy, MA, **1503** (FD)
Lincoln-Lane Foundation, The, VA, **3449** (FD)
Lindemann Charitable Foundation II, FL, **780** (FD)
Linden Foundation Inc., The, MA, **1504** (FD)
Lindsay Trust, Agnes M., NH, **1890** (FD)
Lingnan Foundation, CA, **301** (FD)
Lingnan University, Trustees of, CA, *see* 301
Link Foundation, The, NY, **2280** (FD)
Linke Foundation, Gordon F. and Jocelyn B., CT, **587** (FD2)
Linsmayer Foundation Trust, James B., NC, **2585** (FD2)
Lintilhac Foundation, VT, **3412** (FD)
Lipton Foundation, FL, **781** (FD2)
Lissner Foundation, Inc., Gerda, NY, **2281** (FD2)
Littauer Educational Trust, Helen Irwin, TX, **3283** (FD2)
Littauer Foundation, Inc., Lucius N., The, NY, **2282** (FD)
Litwin Foundation, Inc., The, NY, **2283** (FD)
Liu Foundation, RM, The, CA, **302** (FD)
Livingston Foundation, Inc., GA, **893** (FD2)
Livingston Memorial Foundation, CA, **303** (FD)
Llewellyn Foundation, The, OH, **2725** (FD)
Lloyd Charitable Trust, Harry J., KS, **1267** (FD)
Lochland Foundation, The, WA, **3536** (FD)
Lockheed Martin Vought Systems Employee Charity Fund, TX, **3284** (FD)
Loeb Foundation, Inc., Jesse and Rose, The, VA, **3450** (FD2)
Loewe Foundation, Inc., Frederick, NY, **2284** (FD2)
Logan Foundation, Reva and David, IL, **1051** (FD)
Long Foundation for the Arts, Joe and Teresa L., The, TX, *see* 3285
Long Foundation, George A. & Grace L., CT, **588** (FD2)
Long Foundation, Inc., John F., AZ, **51** (FD)
Long Foundation, The, TX, **3285** (FD2)
Long Foundation, Thomas J., CA, **304** (FD)
Longview Foundation for Education in World Affairs and International Understanding, Inc., VA, **3451** (FD2)
Longwood Foundation, Inc., DE, **639** (FD)
Loose Trust, Harry Wilson, TX, **3286** (FD2)
Los Altos Community Foundation, CA, **305** (FD)
Louisiana Child Caring Foundation, Inc., LA, *see* 1302
Love Conservation Foundation, Edward K., RI, **3082** (FD2)
Love, III Foundation, Davis, VA, **3452** (FD)
Lowder Foundation, Thomas H. and Jarman F., The, GA, **894** (FD)
Lowell Community Foundation, Greater, MA, **1505** (FD)
Loyola Foundation, Inc., The, VA, **3453** (FD)
Lubbock Area Foundation, Inc., TX, **3287** (FD)
Lucas Family Foundation, George, CA, **306** (FD)
Lucasfilm Foundation, CA, *see* 306
Luce Charitable Trust, Theodore, NY, **2285** (FD)
Luce Foundation, Inc., Henry, The, NY, **2286** (FD)
Lucent Technologies Foundation, NJ, *see* 1899
Luckyday Foundation, The, MS, **1767** (FD)
Ludwick Foundation, Christopher, PA, **2988** (FD2)
Ludwick Institute, The, PA, *see* 2988
Luehring Foundation, Wesley, IL, **1052** (FD2)
Luke 12:48 Foundation, WA, **3537** (FD)
Lumina Foundation, IN, **1174** (FD)
Lumpkin Family Foundation, The, IL, **1053** (FD)
Lupton Family Foundation, T. C., TX, **3288** (FD2)
Luse Foundation, W. P. & Bulah, TX, **3289** (FD2)
Lutheran Home and Hospital Foundation, Inc., MD, **1387** (FD2)
Lutz Foundation, Clarence H. and Anna E., SC, **3105** (FD2)
Lux Foundation, Miranda, CA, **307** (FD2)
Lynam Trust, Hattie A. and Fred C., ME, **1335** (FD2)
Lynch Scholarship Foundation, John B., DE, **640** (FD2)
Lynchburg Community Trust, Greater, VA, **3454** (FD)
Lyndhurst Foundation, TN, **3145** (FD)
Lynn Foundation, Elizabeth A., MT, **1827** (FD2)
Lynum Trust, Edith H., NC, **2586** (FD2)
Lyon Leukemia Foundation, Robert, The, IL, **1054** (FD2)
Lyons Foundation, Daniel M. Lyons & Bente S., FL, **782** (FD)
M Health Foundation, The, CA, *see* 329
M.A.C. AIDS Fund, The, NY, **2287** (FD)
M.A.C. Global Foundation, The, NY, *see* 2287
M.A.C.H. Foundation, The, WA, *see* 3491
M.E. Foundation, The, PA, **2989** (FD)
MacArthur Family Charitable Foundation, IL, **1055** (FD2)
MacArthur Foundation, John D. and Catherine T., The, IL, **1056** (FD)
Macauley Foundation, Inc., The, CT, **589** (FD2)
MacDonald Family Foundation, Inc., Bradley T., The, NJ, **1961** (FD2)
MacDonald Family Foundation, Inc., The, NJ, *see* 1961
Macdonald Foundation, Inc., Dr. John T., FL, **783** (FD)
Macdonald Fund, Maybelle Clark, OR, **2859** (FD)
Macht Foundation, Inc., Morton and Sophia, MD, **1388** (FD2)
Maclellan Foundation, Inc., The, TN, **3146** (FD)
Macy Jr. Foundation, Josiah, NY, **2288** (FD)
Macy's Foundation, OH, **2726** (FD)
Maddox Foundation, J. F, NM, **2014** (FD)
Maddox Trust, Web, IL, **1057** (FD)
Maddux Foundation, NV, **1866** (FD2)
Madison County Community Foundation, IN, **1175** (FD)
Magee Trust, George W.P., MA, **1506** (FD2)
Magnus Charitable Trust, IL, **1058** (FD)
MAH Foundation, Inc., FL, **784** (FD2)
MAHADH Foundation, The, MN, *see* 1702
Maier Foundation, Inc., WV, **3584** (FD)
Maier Foundation, Sarah & Pauline, WV, *see* 3584
MAIHS Foundation, VA, **3455** (FD2)
Maine Health Access Foundation, ME, **1336** (FD)
Makana Aloha Foundation, The, HI, **937** (FD2)
Makepeace Neighborhood Fund, MA, **1507** (FD2)
Maki Foundation, CO, **513** (FD2)
Malone Family Foundation, AL, **16** (FD2)
Malone Family Foundation, The, CO, **514** (FD)
Maltz Family Foundation, Milton and Tamar, The, OH, **2727** (FD)
Mandel Family Foundation, Joseph and Florence, The, OH, **2728** (FD)
Mandel Family Foundation, Morton and Barbara, The, OH, **2729** (FD)
Mandel Foundation, Jack N. and Lilyan, OH, *see* 2730
Mandel Foundation, Jack, Joseph, and Morton, OH, **2730** (FD)
Mandel Foundation, Joseph and Florence, The, OH, *see* 2728
Mandel Foundation, Morton and Barbara, OH, *see* 2729
Mandelbaum Foundation, The, NJ, **1962** (FD2)
Manhattan Community Foundation, Greater, KS, **1268** (FD)
Manitowoc Company Foundation, The, WI, **3632** (FD2)
Mann-Paller Foundation, Inc., MD, **1389** (FD2)
Marafiki Global Aids Ministry, OH, **2731** (FD2)
Marbrook Foundation, MN, **1713** (FD)
Marcled Foundation, The, CA, **308** (FD)
Marcon Foundation, Inc., NJ, **1963** (FD)
Mardigian Foundation, Edward & Helen, MI, **1635** (FD)
Margulies Foundation, Inc., Martin Z., FL, **785** (FD2)
Marietta Community Foundation, OH, **2732** (FD)
Marin Community Foundation, CA, **309** (FD)
Marine Society of the City of New York, The, NY, **2289** (FD2)
Marine Ventures Foundation, Inc., WY, **3675** (FD2)
Marino Family Foundation, Inc., Joseph and Cheryl, NJ, **1964** (FD2)
Marion Community Foundation, Inc., OH, **2733** (FD)
Marisla Foundation, The, CA, **310** (FD)
Marketplace One Foundation, The, AZ, **52** (FD)
Markle Foundation, John and Mary R., The, NY, *see* 2290
Markle Foundation, The, NY, **2290** (FD)
Marks Family Foundation, Nancy and Edwin, NY, **2291** (FD)
Marks Family Foundation, NY, *see* 2291
Marley Foundation, Inc., Jacob, The, NY, **2292** (FD2)
Marley Foundation, Kemper and Ethel, The, AZ, **53** (FD)
Marquette Community Foundation, MI, *see* 1636
Marquette County Community Foundation, MI, **1636** (FD2)

Marquez Foundation, CO, *see* 515
Marquez Foundation, Timothy & Bernadette, CO, **515** (FD)
Marriott Foundation, J. Willard and Alice S., The, MD, **1390** (FD)
Marriott Foundation, J. Willard, The, MD, *see* 1390
Marsh Foundation, Edward N. and Margaret G., NC, **2587** (FD2)
Marsh Foundation, Peter R., WA, **3538** (FD)
Marshall County Community Foundation, Inc., IN, **1176** (FD)
Marshall Family Foundation, NY, **2293** (FD2)
Marshall Foundation, AZ, **54** (FD)
Marshall Foundation, Mattie H., GA, **895** (FD2)
Marshall, Jr. Family Foundation, Douglas B., TX, **3290** (FD)
Marshfield Area Community Foundation, WI, **3633** (FD2)
Martell Memorial Foundation, C.F., ND, **2651** (FD2)
Martin Charitable Trust, G. Roxy & Elizabeth C., FL, **786** (FD2)
Martin Family Foundation, Patrick J., The, FL, **787** (FD2)
Martin Family Foundation, The, PA, **2990** (FD2)
Martin Foundation, George & Miriam, PA, **2991** (FD)
Martinez Foundation, Guadalupe and Lilia, The, TX, **3291** (FD)
Maryland Home & Community Care Foundation, MD, **1391** (FD2)
Masco Corporation Charitable Trust, MI, *see* 1637
Masco Corporation Foundation, MI, **1637** (FD)
Mason Fund, Carlos and Marguerite, The, GA, **896** (FD)
Masonic Grand Lodge Charities of Rhode Island, Inc., RI, **3083** (FD2)
Massachusetts Maternity & Foundling Hospital Corporation, MA, **1508** (FD2)
Master Works Foundation, Inc., IN, **1177** (FD2)
Mathers Charitable Foundation, G. Harold & Leila Y., The, NY, **2294** (FD)
Mathile Family Foundation, OH, **2734** (FD)
Matisse Charitable Foundation, Pierre and Tana, NY, **2295** (FD)
Matsui Foundation, CA, **311** (FD)
Mattel Children's Foundation, CA, **312** (FD)
Mattel Foundation, CA, *see* 312
Matthews Fund, The, PA, **2992** (FD2)
Matthies Foundation, Katharine, CT, **590** (FD)
Maude Charitable Trust, J. T. - Minnie, VA, **3456** (FD)
Maxey Foundation, Leightman, The, OR, **2860** (FD2)
MAXIMUS Foundation, Inc., VA, **3457** (FD2)
Maxwell Foundation, Edmund F., WA, **3539** (FD2)
Mayday Fund, The, NY, **2296** (FD)
Mayerson Foundation, Manuel D. & Rhoda, OH, **2735** (FD)
Mayor Foundation, Oliver Dewey, TX, **3292** (FD)
Mayr Trust, George Henry, NC, **2588** (FD)
Maytag Family Foundation, F., The, IA, **1229**, *see* 1229 (FD)
Mazda Foundation (USA), Inc., The, CA, **313** (FD2)
Mazza Foundation, Sam, The, CA, **314** (FD)
MBIA Foundation, Inc., NY, **2297** (FD)
McBeath Foundation, Faye, WI, **3634** (FD)
McBeth Foundation, CA, **315** (FD)
McCabe Catholic Charities, RI, **3084** (FD2)
McCarthey Dressman Education Foundation, The, UT, **3397** (FD2)
McCarthy Foundation, Inc., Brian A., NY, **2298** (FD)
McCauley Charitable Trust, Luther T., IL, **1059** (FD2)
McCausland Charitable Trust, Alexander, NC, **2589** (FD)
McCaw Foundation, Craig and Susan, The, WA, **3540** (FD)
McCaw Foundation, Wendy P., CA, **316** (FD)
McClatchy Company Foundation, CA, **317** (FD2)
McConnell Foundation, The, CA, **318** (FD)
McCormick Scholarship Fund, Robert W., WV, **3585** (FD2)
McCoy Charitable Foundation, Bowen H. and Janice Arthur, CA, **319** (FD)
McCune Foundation, PA, **2993** (FD)
McCune Foundation, The, CA, **320** (FD)
McDermott Foundation, Eugene, The, TX, **3293** (FD)
McDonald Trust, Frederick, RI, **3085** (FD2)
McDonnell Family Foundation, CO, **516** (FD)
McDonnell Foundation, James S., MO, **1800** (FD)
McDonough Foundation, Inc., Bernard, WV, **3586** (FD)
McDonough Foundation, WI, **3635** (FD2)
McEachern Charitable Trust, D. V. & Ida, WA, **3541** (FD)
McEachern Charitable Trust, Ida J., WA, *see* 3541
McElroy Trust, R. J., IA, **1230** (FD)
McGee Foundation, Inc., The, OK, **2820** (FD)
McGonagle Foundation, Inc., Dextra Baldwin, NY, **2299** (FD)
McGraw Foundation, Inc., Donald C., The, NY, **2300** (FD)
McGraw Wildlife Foundation, Max, IL, **1060** (FD2)
McGregor Foundation, The, OH, **2736** (FD)
McGregor Fund, MI, **1638** (FD)
McHugh-O'Donovan Foundation, Inc., Frank, DE, **641** (FD)
McInerny Foundation, HI, **938** (FD)
McIntyre Foundation, Shirley & William S., TX, **3294** (FD2)
MCJ Amelior Foundation, The, NJ, **1965** (FD)
MCJ Foundation, The, NJ, *see* 1965
McKaig Foundation, Lalitta Nash, PA, **2994** (FD)
McKee for the Poor Fund, Virginia A., PA, **2995** (FD2)
McKee Foundation, Robert E. and Evelyn, TX, **3295** (FD2)
McKenzie Family Charitable Trust, VT, **3413** (FD)
McKesson Foundation, Inc., CA, **321** (FD)
McKesson HBOC Foundation, Inc., CA, *see* 321
McKinney Charitable Foundation, William V. and Catherine A., PA, **2996** (FD2)
McKissick Foundation, Ellison S. and Noel P., SC, **3106** (FD)
McKnight Endowment Fund for Neuroscience, The, MN, **1714** (FD)
McKnight Foundation, The, MN, **1715** (FD)
McLean Contributionship, The, PA, **2997** (FD)
McMicking Foundation, CA, *see* 322
McMicking Foundation, Joseph R., The, CA, **322** (FD)
McMinn Foundation, CA, **323** (FD)
McMurry Foundation, The, WY, **3676** (FD)
McNeice, Jr. Charitable Foundation, John A., MA, **1509** (FD2)
McNeil Foundation, Colonel Stanley R., RI, **3086** (FD)
McNeil Scholarship Trust, John N. McNeil and Stella, NC, **2590** (FD2)
McVaney Family Foundation, CO, *see* 542
McVaney-Fernalld Family Foundation Trust, CO, *see* 521
McWane Foundation, AL, **17** (FD)
MDU Resources Foundation, ND, **2652** (FD)
Mead Foundation, Giles W. and Elise G., CA, **324** (FD)
Meadmore 2002 Trust, Clement, NY, *see* 2301
Meadmore Foundation, Clement, The, NY, **2301** (FD2)
Meadowlark Foundation, CO, **517** (FD)
Meadowood Foundation, MN, *see* 1690
Meadows Foundation, Inc., The, TX, **3296** (FD)
Mediathe Foundation, Inc., CA, **325** (FD2)
Medina Foundation, WA, **3542** (FD)
Meelia Family Foundation, The, MA, **1510** (FD)
Meijer Foundation, The, MI, **1639** (FD)
Mellam Family Foundation, CA, **326** (FD)
Mellinger Educational Foundation, Inc., Edward Arthur, IL, **1061** (FD)
Mellon Foundation, Andrew W., The, NY, **2302** (FD)
Mellon Foundation, Richard King, PA, **2998** (FD)
Melville Charitable Trust, The, MA, **1511** (FD)
Memorial Foundation for Children, VA, **3458** (FD)
Memorial Foundation for the Blind Inc., MA, **1512** (FD2)
Memorial Homes for the Blind, MA, *see* 1512
Menard Family Foundation, CA, **327** (FD)
Menasha Corporation Foundation, WI, **3636** (FD)
Mendel Charitable Trust, Solomon & Sylvia, PA, **2999** (FD2)
Mendell Family Fund Inc., The, NY, **2303** (FD2)
Mendell Fund, Inc., Ira L. & Margaret P., The, NY, *see* 2303
Mendenhall Foundation, Holly and Bronco, The, UT, **3398** (FD2)
Mendocino County Community Foundation, Inc., CA, *see* 160
Menezes Foundation, Inc., The, NY, **2304** (FD2)
MENTOR Network Charitable Foundation, Inc., The, MA, **1513** (FD2)
Merage Foundation, Andre & Katherine, CO, **518** (FD)
Merage Foundation, David and Laura, CO, **519** (FD)
Mercer Family Foundation, NY, **2305** (FD)
Mercer Foundation, Johnny, The, CA, **328** (FD)
Merchants Bank Foundation, Inc., VT, **3414** (FD2)
Merchants Fund, PA, **3000** (FD2)
Merck Fund, John, The, MA, **1514** (FD)
Merck Institute for Science Education, Inc., NJ, **1966** (FD)
Meriden Foundation, The, CT, **591** (FD)
Meridian Charitable Foundation, Inc., MA, *see* 1460
Merillat Foundation, Orville D. & Ruth A., MI, **1640** (FD)
Merrick Foundation, The, OK, **2821** (FD)
Merrick Medical Equip. Trust, Bette M., NC, **2591** (FD2)
Mertz Charitable Trust, Esther M., FL, **788** (FD2)
Mertz Gilmore Foundation, NY, **2306** (FD)
Mertz-Gilmore Foundation, Joyce, NY, *see* 2306
Meserve Memorial Fund, Albert & Helen C., NC, **2592** (FD2)
MetLife Foundation, NY, **2307** (FD)
Metropolitan Health Foundation, Inc., VA, **3459** (FD2)
MetroWest Community Health Care Foundation, Inc., MA, *see* 1515
MetroWest Health Foundation, MA, **1515** (FD)
Metta Fund, CA, **329** (FD)
Meyer Charitable Fund, Inc., Erie Hall, AL, **18** (FD)
Meyer Charitable Trust, Fred, OR, *see* 2861
Meyer Charitable Trust, Melba Bayers, NC, **2593** (FD2)
Meyer Foundation, Eugene and Agnes E., DC, **672** (FD)
Meyer Fund, Milton and Sophie, NC, **2594** (FD2)
Meyer Memorial Foundation, Inc., Aaron and Rachel, NJ, **1967** (FD)
Meyer Memorial Trust, OR, **2861** (FD)
Meyerhoff Foundation, Inc., Lyn P., The, MD, **1392** (FD2)
Meyerhoff Fund, Inc., Joseph, The, MD, **1393** (FD)
MIBOR Foundation, Inc., IN, **1178** (FD2)
Michael Foundation, Herbert I. and Elsa B., OR, **2862** (FD2)
Michell Charitable Foundation and Trust, Roy G., MI, **1641** (FD2)
Michelson Foundation, The, CA, *see* 94
Michigan Capital Fund for Non-Profit Housing Corporation, MI, *see* 1618
Micron Technology Foundation, Inc., ID, **950** (FD)
Mid-America Foundation, MO, *see* 1784
Mid-Nebraska Community Foundation, Inc., NE, **1849** (FD)
Mid-Shore Community Foundation, Inc., MD, **1395** (FD)
Midcontinent Foundation, MN, *see* 1716
Midcontinent Media Foundation, MN, **1716** (FD2)
Middendorf Foundation, Inc., MD, **1394** (FD)
Middlesex County Community Foundation, Inc., CT, **592** (FD)
Middletown Community Foundation, OH, **2737** (FD)
Midland Area Community Foundation, MI, **1642** (FD)
Midland Foundation, MI, *see* 1642
Midlands Community Foundation, NE, **1848** (FD2)
Milbank Foundation for Rehabilitation, NJ, *see* 1968
Milbank Foundation, NJ, **1968** (FD)
Milgard Family Foundation, Gary & Carol, WA, *see* 3543
Milgard Family Foundation, Gary E., WA, **3543** (FD)
Military Women In Need Foundation, CA, **330** (FD2)
Milken Family Foundation, The, CA, **331** (FD)

Miller Design Foundation, Herman, MI, *see* 1624
Miller Family Foundation, Nathan & Isabel, IL, **1062** (FD2)
Miller Foundation, Hazel, WA, **3544** (FD2)
Miller Foundation, Herman and Frieda L., MA, **1516** (FD)
Miller Trust, Edwill B., NY, **2308** (FD2)
Miller-Mellor Association, KS, **1269** (FD2)
Mills Fund, Frances Goll, MI, **1643** (FD2)
Millstone Foundation, MO, **1801** (FD2)
Milwaukee Foundation, Greater, WI, **3637** (FD)
Milwaukee Foundation, WI, *see* 3637
Mindich Family Foundation, The, NY, **2309** (FD)
Minneapolis Foundation, The, MN, **1717** (FD)
Minnesota Mining and Manufacturing Foundation, MN, *see* 1676
Minto Foundation, Inc., FL, **789** (FD2)
Mirolo Charitable Foundation, OH, **2738** (FD2)
Mirolo Foundation, OH, *see* 2738
Mission Increase Foundation, OR, **2863** (FD)
Mississippi Common Fund Trust, MS, **1768** (FD)
Mississippi Power Foundation Inc., MS, **1769** (FD)
Mitchell Foundation, Cynthia & George, The, TX, **3297** (FD)
Mittal Steel USA Foundation, Inc., IL, *see* 964
MLG Foundation, The, VA, **3460** (FD)
Mobile Community Foundation, The, AL, *see* 10
Moccasin Lake Foundation, WA, **3545** (FD)
Moline Foundation, The, IL, **1063** (FD)
Monarch Fund, DC, **673** (FD)
Mondelez International Foundation, The, IL, **1064** (FD)
Moneta Group Charitable Foundation, MO, **1802** (FD2)
Monfort Charitable Foundation, CO, *see* 520
Monfort Family Foundation, CO, **520** (FD)
Monsanto Fund, MO, **1803** (FD)
Montana Community Foundation, MT, **1828** (FD)
Montana Good Works Foundation, MT, *see* 1825
Monteforte Foundation, Inc., The, NY, **2310** (FD)
Monterey Bay Aquarium Research Institute, CA, **332** (FD2)
Montgomery Area Community Foundation, Inc., AL, *see* 8
Monticello College Foundation, The, IL, **1065** (FD)
Moody Foundation, The, TX, **3298** (FD)
Moore and Blance Davis Foundation, Allen Lovelace, TX, **3299** (FD)
Moore Charitable Foundation, Claude, The, VA, **3461** (FD)
Moore Charitable Foundation, Wayne & Jo Ann, TX, **3300** (FD)
Moore Charitable Trust, Clement C. Moore II and Elizabeth W. Y., The, MD, **1396** (FD2)
Moore Family Foundation, David and Katherine, NY, **2311** (FD)
Moore Family Foundation, Inc., Edward S., NY, **2312** (FD)
Moore Foundation, Blanche Davis, The, TX, *see* 3299
Moore Foundation, Gordon and Betty, CA, **333** (FD)
Moore Foundation, Inc., Marion, NY, **2313** (FD)
Moore Foundation, Sara Giles, The, GA, **897** (FD)
Moore Foundation, Tom and Judy, The, NY, **2314** (FD)
Moos Foundation, Paul, FL, **790** (FD2)
Moran Family Foundation, VA, **3462** (FD2)
Moretz Foundation Trust, Inc., O. Leonard, NC, **2595** (FD2)
Morgan Charitable Foundation, Albert Morgan and Leona A., KS, **1270** (FD2)
Morgan Creek Foundation, NC, **2596** (FD)
Morgan Family Foundation, OH, **2739** (FD)
Morgan Foundation, Burton D., The, OH, **2740** (FD)
Morgan Foundation, Margaret Clark, The, OH, **2741** (FD)
Morgan Foundation, Pete, CO, **521** (FD)
Morgan Foundation, TX, **3301** (FD)
Morgan Stanley Foundation, Inc., NY, **2315** (FD)
Morgan Stanley Foundation, NY, *see* 2315
Morgan, Jr. Trust, Marietta McNeill Morgan & Samuel Tate, VA, **3463** (FD)
Morgridge Family Foundation, DE, **642** (FD)
Morino Foundation, OH, *see* 2742
Morino Institute, OH, **2742** (FD2)
Morley Brothers Foundation, MI, *see* 1644
Morley Foundation, MI, **1644** (FD2)
Morningstar Foundation, The, FL, **791** (FD2)
Morningstar Foundation, The, MD, **1397** (FD)
Morrell Family Charities, UT, **3399** (FD2)
Morris Family Foundation, OR, **2864** (FD2)
Morris Foundation, Inc., Jay, CA, **334** (FD)
Morrison Foundation, Inc., Glenn W. & Hazelle Paxson, FL, **792** (FD2)
Morse Foundation, Martha, The, DE, **643** (FD2)
Mosaic Company Foundation, MN, **1718** (FD)
Mosaic Fund, The, NH, **1891** (FD)
Mosher Foundation, Samuel B. and Margaret C., CA, **335** (FD)
Mosher Foundation, Samuel B., CA, *see* 335
Mosher Foundation, The, CA, *see* 335
Motley Foundation Inc., Mark Elliott, The, SC, **3107** (FD2)
Motorola Foundation, IL, *see* 1066
Motorola Solutions Foundation, IL, **1066** (FD)
Mott Foundation, Charles Stewart, MI, **1645** (FD)
Mott Foundation, Ruth, MI, **1646** (FD)
Mount Pleasant Area Community Foundation, MI, **1647** (FD2)
Mount Pleasant Community Foundation, MI, *see* 1647
Mount Saint Clare Education Foundation, IA, **1231** (FD2)
Mount Washington Charitable Foundation, Inc., MA, **1517** (FD2)
Moyer Foundation, Willard H., WY, **3677** (FD)
Mpala Wildlife Foundation, Inc., MD, **1398** (FD2)
Muchnic Foundation, KS, **1271** (FD2)
Muckel Foundation, John and Linda, CA, **336** (FD2)
Mulago Foundation, CA, **337** (FD)
Mule Family Foundation, NY, **2316** (FD2)
Mullen Foundation, J. K., CO, **522** (FD2)
Mundy Family Foundation, The, TX, **3302** (FD)
Mungenast Foundation, Inc., David and Barbara, The, MO, **1804** (FD2)
Mungenast Foundation, Inc., The, MO, *see* 1804
Munro Scholarship Trust, Grant, OH, **2743** (FD2)
Munroe Foundation, Richard C., FL, **793** (FD2)
Murdock Institute for Business & Culture, David H., CA, **338** (FD)
Murphy Family Foundation, The, OH, **2744** (FD2)
Murphy Foundation, John P., OH, **2745** (FD)
Murphy Foundation, Katherine John, GA, **898** (FD)
Murphy Residuary Trust, T. R., OH, **2746** (FD2)
Murray Foundation, Harry and Virginia, WI, **3638** (FD2)
Murray Foundation, Stuart & Eulene, GA, **899** (FD)
Murthy Foundation, Inc., The, MD, *see* 1399
Murthynayak Foundation, Inc., The, MD, **1399** (FD2)
Musgrave Foundation, MO, **1805** (FD)
Music Doing Good, Inc., TX, **3303** (FD2)
Muskegon County Community Foundation, Inc., MI, *see* 1586
Muskin Family Foundation, CA, **339** (FD2)
Muskingum County Community Foundation, OH, **2747** (FD)
Musser Fund, Laura Jane, The, MN, **1719** (FD)
Musser Fund, The, MN, *see* 1719
Mustard Seed Foundation, MD, **1400** (FD2)
Mutual of America Foundation, NY, **2317** (FD)
Mutual of Omaha Foundation, NE, **1850** (FD)
Mylan Charitable Foundation, The, PA, **3001** (FD)

Najim Family Foundation, Harvey E., TX, **3304** (FD)
Nakash Family Foundation, NY, **2318** (FD)
Nandansons Charitable Foundation, Inc, NJ, **1969** (FD2)
Naomi Prawer Kadar Foundation, Inc, The, NY, **2319** (FD2)
Napa Valley Community Foundation, CA, **340** (FD)
Napier Foundation, James H., The, AZ, **55** (FD2)
Napier Foundation, The, AZ, *see* 55
Narragansett Number One Foundation, ME, **1337** (FD2)
Nartel Family Foundation, MI, **1648** (FD2)
Nartel Foundation, Werner and Ruth, MI, *see* 1648
NASDAQ OMX Group Educational Foundation, Inc., MD, **1401** (FD)
Nasdaq Stock Marked Educational Foundation, Inc., The, MD, *see* 1401
Nash Family Foundation, NY, **2320** (FD)
Nash Foundation, Steve, AK, **37** (FD)
Nash Foundation, The, MN, **1720** (FD2)
Nashville Community Foundation, Inc., TN, *see* 3129
National Academy of Education, The, DC, **674** (FD)
National Endowment for Financial Education, CO, **523** (FD2)
National Fuel Gas Company Foundation, NY, **2321** (FD)
National Literacy Program Fund, CA, *see* 222
National Machinery Foundation Inc., OH, **2748** (FD)
National Public Education Foundation, DC, **675** (FD2)
Navarro County Educational Foundation, TX, **3305** (FD2)
Naylor Family Foundation, PA, **3002** (FD)
Nazarian Family Foundation, Y. & S., CA, **341** (FD)
NBC Universal Foundation, NY, **2322** (FD)
NCMIC Foundation, Inc., IA, **1232** (FD)
NDCF, ND, *see* 2653
Nebraska Community Foundation, NE, **1851** (FD2)
Needham Foundation, Robert Sidney, NC, **2597** (FD2)
Needmor Fund, The, OH, **2749** (FD)
Neese Family Foundation, Inc., WI, **3639** (FD2)
NEFE, CO, *see* 523
Neilson Foundation, George W., MN, **1721** (FD)
Neisloss Family Foundation, Inc., The, NJ, **1970** (FD2)
Nelson Foundation, Grace S. & W. Linton, PA, **3003** (FD)
Nelson Foundation, James & Aune, IL, **1067** (FD)
Nelson Scholarship Fund, Victor & Mary D., WI, **3640** (FD2)
Nesh Charitable Trust, Florence, PA, **3004** (FD2)
Nettleton Foundation, George H., KS, **1272** (FD2)
Nettleton Home, George H., KS, *see* 1272
Neu Family Foundation, Inc., John and Wendy, The, NY, **2323** (FD)
Neuberger Foundation, Inc., Roy R. and Marie S., CT, **593** (FD)
Nevada Community Foundation, Inc., NV, **1867** (FD)
Nevas Family Foundation, Inc., Leo & Libby, CT, *see* 594
Nevas Family Foundation, Inc., Leo, CT, **594** (FD2)
New Albany Community Foundation, OH, **2750** (FD2)
New Balance Foundation, MA, **1518** (FD)
New Britain Foundation for Public Giving, CT, *see* 563
New Futures, DC, **676** (FD2)
New Orleans Foundation, Greater, The, LA, **1316** (FD)
New Richmond Area Community Foundation, The, WI, **3641** (FD)
New Yankee Stadium Community Benefits Fund, Inc., The, NY, **2324** (FD)
New York Community Trust, The, NY, **2325** (FD)
New York Foundation, NY, **2326** (FD)
New York Jets Foundation, Inc., NY, **2327** (FD2)
New York Stock Exchange Foundation, Inc., NY, *see* 2336
NewAlliance Foundation, Inc., CT, **595** (FD)
Newark Charter School Fund, Inc., NJ, **1971** (FD)
Newburyport Society for the Relief of Aged Women, Inc., MA, **1519** (FD2)
Newcombe Foundation, Charlotte W., The, NJ, **1972** (FD)
Newhall Foundation, Henry Mayo, The, CA, **342** (FD)
Newman Family Foundation, Inc., Howard and Maryam, The, NY, **2328** (FD)
Newport Fed Charitable Foundation, RI, **3087** (FD2)
Nicholas Endowment, CA, **343** (FD)
Nicholas, III Foundation, Henry T., CA, **344** (FD)
Nichols Company Charitable Trust, MO, **1806** (FD2)

Nicholson Foundation, The, NY, **2329** (FD)
Niehaus Foundation, Robert and Kate, The, NY, **2330** (FD)
Niessen, Jr. Charitable Trust, Leo, NC, **2598** (FD2)
NIKE Foundation, OR, **2865** (FD)
NIKE P.L.A.Y. Foundation, OR, *see* 2865
Niles Foundation, Henry E., CT, **596** (FD)
Niles Foundation, Laura J., CT, **597** (FD)
Nippert Charitable Foundation, Inc., L. and L., OH, **2751** (FD)
NiSource Charitable Foundation, OH, **2752** (FD)
Noble Charitable Foundation, Inc., Donald E. and Alice M., OH, *see* 2753
Noble County Community Foundation, IN, **1179** (FD)
Noble Foundation, Inc., Donald and Alice, OH, **2753** (FD)
Noble Foundation, Inc., Samuel Roberts, The, OK, **2822** (FD)
Nokomis Foundation, MI, *see* 1608
Noll Foundation, Inc., CA, **345** (FD)
Noll Foundation, John H., PA, **3005** (FD2)
Noonan Memorial Fund, Deborah Munroe, MA, **1520** (FD2)
Noonan Memorial Research Fund, Deborah Munroe, MA, **1521** (FD2)
Noonan Trust, Frank M., MA, *see* 1521
Nord Family Foundation, The, OH, **2754** (FD)
Nordson Corporation Foundation, The, OH, **2755** (FD)
North Carolina Community Foundation, NC, **2599** (FD)
North Carolina GlaxoSmithKline Foundation, Inc., The, NC, **2600** (FD)
North Dakota Community Foundation, ND, **2653** (FD)
North Fork Foundation, VA, *see* 3426
North Georgia Community Foundation, GA, **900** (FD)
North Penn Community Health Foundation, PA, **3006** (FD)
North Valley Community Foundation, CA, **346** (FD)
Northeast Michigan Community Foundation, MI, *see* 1587
Northeast Utilities Foundation, Inc., CT, **598** (FD)
Northen Endowment, Mary Moody, TX, **3306** (FD)
Northern California Scholarship Foundation and the Scaife Scholarship Foundation, The, CA, *see* 347
Northern California Scholarship Foundation, The, CA, **347** (FD)
Northern Chautauqua Community Foundation, Inc., NY, **2331** (FD2)
Northern Indiana Community Foundation, Inc., IN, **1180** (FD)
Northern Kenya Fund, MD, **1402** (FD2)
Northern Piedmont Community Foundation, VA, **3464** (FD)
Northrop Grumman Foundation, The, VA, **3465** (FD)
Northstar Partners Scholarship Fund, MN, *see* 1748
Northwest Area Foundation, MN, **1722** (FD)
Northwest Fund for the Environment, WA, **3546** (FD2)
Northwest Minnesota Foundation (NWMF), MN, **1723** (FD)
Norwich Foundation, Greater, The, NY, **2332** (FD2)
Norwood Foundation, The, CO, **524** (FD)
Novak Foundation, Inc., David C. and Wendy L., The, KY, *see* 1293
Novartis Patient Assistance Foundation, Inc., NJ, **1973** (FD)
Novartis US Foundation, NY, **2333** (FD)
NoVo Foundation, NY, **2334** (FD)
Noyce Foundation, The, CA, **348** (FD)
Noyes Foundation, Inc., Jessie Smith, NY, **2335** (FD)
Nucor Foundation, NC, **2601** (FD)
NuStar Foundation, TX, **3307** (FD)
NYSE Euronext Foundation, Inc., NY, **2336** (FD)

O'Brien-Veba Scholarship Trust, PA, **3007** (FD2)
O'Grady Foundation, NY, **2339** (FD2)
O'Neill Foundation, Inc., William J. and Dorothy K., The, OH, **2760** (FD)
O'Shaughnessy Foundation, Inc., I. A., MN, **1725** (FD)
O'Shaughnessy-Hurst Memorial Foundation, The, VA, **3469** (FD)
O'Shea Foundation, The, CA, **352** (FD2)
Oak Hill Fund, VA, **3466** (FD)
Oak Park/River Forest Community Foundation, IL, **1068** (FD)
Oberweiler Foundation, IL, **1069** (FD2)
Obici Foundation, Inc., VA, *see* 3467
Obici Healthcare Foundation, Inc., VA, **3467** (FD)
Odell Fund, Robert S. & Helen P., NC, **2602** (FD)
Odell Fund, Robert Stewart and Helen Pfeiffer, NC, *see* 2602
Oestreicher Foundation, Inc., Sylvan and Ann, NY, **2337** (FD)
Ogden Foundation, Inc., Ralph E., NY, **2338** (FD)
OGE Energy Corp. Foundation, OK, *see* 2823
Ohio County Community Foundation, Inc., IN, **1181** (FD2)
Ohio MedCenter Foundation, Inc., OH, *see* 2733
Ohio National Foundation, The, OH, **2756** (FD)
Ohio Valley Foundation, The, OH, **2757** (FD2)
Oishei Foundation, John R., The, NY, **2340** (FD)
Oklahoma Gas and Electric Company Foundation, Inc., OK, **2823** (FD)
Old National Bank Foundation, Inc., IN, **1182** (FD)
Old Stones Foundation, Inc., The, CT, **599** (FD)
Oldham Little Church Foundation, TX, **3308** (FD)
Oleson Foundation, MI, **1649** (FD)
Olin Corporation Charitable Trust, NC, **2603** (FD)
Olmsted Foundation, George and Carol, The, VA, **3468** (FD)
Olsen 1990 Private Foundation, C., FL, **794** (FD2)
Omnicare Foundation, OH, **2758** (FD)
OMNOVA Solutions Foundation, Inc., OH, **2759** (FD)
Omron Foundation, Inc., IL, **1070** (FD)
On His Path, IA, **1233** (FD)
OneAmerica Foundation, Inc., The, IN, **1183** (FD)
OneFamily Foundation, WA, **3547** (FD2)
Onequest Foundation, MI, **1650** (FD)
Ong Family Foundation, The, NY, **2341** (FD2)
Ontario Children's Foundation, NY, **2342** (FD2)
Ontario Children's Home, NY, *see* 2342
Onyx and Breezy Foundation, NJ, **1974** (FD2)
Open Doors International, Inc., CA, **349** (FD)
Open Society Institute, NY, **2343** (FD)
Opperman Foundation, Dwight D., The, CA, **350** (FD)
Optivest Foundation, CA, **351** (FD2)
Opus Foundation, MN, **1724** (FD)
Oral Health Services Foundation, Inc., MA, *see* 1459
Orange County Community Foundation, Inc., IN, **1184** (FD)
Oregon Trail Community Foundation, Inc., NE, **1852** (FD)
Orianne Society, The, GA, **901** (FD2)
Original Sorenson Legacy Foundation, UT, **3400** (FD)
Orr Charitable Trust, Waldon H. and Adele, TX, **3309** (FD2)
Orr Family Foundation, Robert O. and AnnaMae, OH, **2761** (FD)
Orsinger Foundation, Genevieve and Ward, TX, **3310** (FD)
Orsinger Foundation, Genevieve McDavitt, TX, *see* 3310
Osborne Foundation, Inc., Weldon F., TN, **3147** (FD)
Oshkosh Area Community Foundation, WI, **3642** (FD)
Oshkosh Corporation Foundation, Inc., WI, **3643** (FD2)
Oshkosh Foundation, WI, *see* 3642
Oshkosh Truck Foundation, Inc., WI, *see* 3643
Osprey Foundation, The, MD, **1403** (FD)
Osteopathic Heritage Foundations, OH, **2762** (FD)
Ostgrodd Foundation, Inc., The, NY, **2344** (FD2)
Ottenheimer Brothers Foundation, AR, **71** (FD2)
Ottley Trust-Atlanta, Marian W., GA, *see* 923
Ottosen Family Foundation, The, AZ, **56** (FD)
Our Community's Foundation, WV, *see* 3587
Our Family for Families First, Inc., WA, *see* 3505
Outer Banks Community Foundation, Inc., NC, **2604** (FD)
Outhwaite Charitable Trust, June G., CA, **353** (FD)
Overbrook Foundation, The, NY, **2345** (FD)
Overhills Foundation, NY, **2346** (FD)
Owen County Community Foundation, IN, **1185** (FD2)

P Twenty-One Foundation, The, TX, **3311** (FD2)
Pacific Forest & Watershed Lands Stewardship Council, CA, **354** (FD)
Pacific Life Foundation, CA, **355** (FD)
Pacific Mutual Charitable Foundation, CA, *see* 355
Pacific Source Health Plan, OR, *see* 2866
Pacific Youth Foundation, CA, **356** (FD)
PacificSource Charitable Foundation, Inc., OR, *see* 2866
PacificSource Foundation for Health Improvement, OR, **2866** (FD)
Packard Foundation, David and Lucile, The, CA, **357** (FD)
Packer Foundation Inc., Horace B., PA, **3008** (FD2)
Paddock Foundation, Jerome & Mildred, NC, **2605** (FD2)
Paducah Area Community Foundation, KY, *see* 1286
Page, Sr. Family Charitable Foundation, Lawrence C., MI, *see* 1651
Page, Sr. Family Charitable Foundation, Rose and Lawrence C., MI, **1651** (FD2)
Palank Memorial Foundation, Inc., Paul, FL, **795** (FD)
Palette Fund, Inc., The, NY, **2347** (FD)
Palmer Foundation, Inc., Pat, NY, **2348** (FD2)
Palmer Foundation, The, DC, **677** (FD)
Palmer Fund, Frank Loomis, CT, **600** (FD)
Palmer Home, Inc., DE, **644** (FD2)
Palumbo Charitable Trust, A. J. & Sigismunda, PA, **3009** (FD)
Pamida Foundation, WI, **3644** (FD)
Pangburn Foundation, The, IL, **1071** (FD2)
Panjandrum Foundation, The, NH, **1892** (FD)
Pankow Foundation, Charles, WA, **3548** (FD)
Parasol Community Foundation, Inc., NV, *see* 1868
Parasol Tahoe Community Foundation, NV, **1868** (FD)
Pardee Cancer Treatment Fund of Bay County, MI, **1652** (FD2)
Pardee Foundation, Elsa U., MI, **1653** (FD)
Pardoe Foundation, Samuel P., MA, **1522** (FD2)
Parish Foundation, Richard Laurence, The, FL, **796** (FD2)
Parish Foundation, Suzanne D., MI, *see* 1654
Parish Foundation, Suzanne Upjohn Delano, MI, **1654** (FD)
Park City Foundation, The, UT, **3401** (FD2)
Park Foundation, Inc., NY, **2349** (FD)
Parke County Community Foundation, Inc., IN, **1186** (FD)
Parker Foundation, Theodore Edson, The, MA, **1523** (FD)
Parkersburg Area Community Foundation, WV, **3587** (FD)
Parman Foundation, Robert A., OK, **2824** (FD2)
Parmelee Foundation, John W., RI, **3088** (FD2)
Parr Trust, Martha Sue, IL, **1072** (FD)
Parsemus Foundation, CA, **358** (FD2)
Parsons Foundation, Mary Morton, The, VA, **3470** (FD)
Parsons Foundation, Ralph M., The, CA, **359** (FD)
Partners for Developing Futures, Inc., CA, **360** (FD)
Pasadena Community Foundation, CA, **361** (FD)
Pasadena Foundation, CA, *see* 361
Paso del Norte Health Foundation, TX, **3312** (FD)
Patagonia Sur Foundation, The, MA, **1524** (FD2)
Patagonia.org, CA, **362** (FD)
Patel Family Foundation, Inc., Drs. Kiran & Pallavi, FL, **797** (FD)
Patrick Family Foundation, Inc., GA, **902** (FD2)
Patrina Foundation, NY, **2350** (FD2)
Patron Saints Foundation, The, CA, **363** (FD)
Patterson Charitable Fund, W. I., PA, **3010** (FD2)
Patterson Dental Foundation, MN, *see* 1726
Patterson Foundation, Alicia, DC, **678** (FD2)

Racine County Area Foundation, Inc., WI, *see* 3648
Radler Foundation, The, TX, **3330** (FD)
Rafiki Aids Ministry, OH, *see* 2731
Ragan and King Charitable Foundation, GA, *see* 906
Ragan Charitable Foundation, Carolyn King, GA, **906** (FD2)
Raibrook Foundation, WI, **3649** (FD)
Raisbeck Foundation Trust, James D. and Sherry, WA, **3550** (FD)
Ramapo Trust, NJ, **1981** (FD)
Ramsey McCluskey Family Foundation, The, MA, **1530** (FD2)
Rancho Santa Fe Community Foundation, CA, *see* 378
Rancho Santa Fe Foundation, CA, **378** (FD)
Randall Foundation, Charity, PA, **3021** (FD2)
Randall Theatrical Fund, Inc., Tony, NY, **2372** (FD2)
Rangos Charitable Foundation, John G., PA, **3022** (FD2)
Ransom Foundation, Nancy Buck, CA, **379** (FD)
Raoul Foundation, W. G., GA, **907** (FD2)
Rapoport Family Foundation, The, NY, **2373** (FD2)
Rapoport Foundation, Bernard and Audre, TX, **3331** (FD)
Rappaport Family Foundation, CA, **380** (FD2)
Rashbi, Aishel, NY, **2374** (FD2)
Rasmussen Foundation, V. Kann, NY, **2375** (FD)
Ratshesky Foundation, A.C., MA, **1531** (FD2)
Rauch Foundation, NY, **2376** (FD)
Raymond Family Foundation, MA, **1532** (FD2)
RBC Dain Rauscher Foundation, MN, *see* 1730
RBC Foundation USA, MN, **1730** (FD)
RCI Foundation, IN, *see* 1143
RCM & D Foundation, The, MD, **1406** (FD2)
RDM Positive Impact Foundation, TX, **3332** (FD)
Rebozo Foundation, Inc., Carmen, FL, **807** (FD)
RECO Foundation, The, VA, **3474** (FD2)
Redhill Foundation - Rothberg Family Charitable Trust, IL, *see* 1082
Redhill Foundation - Sam and Jean Rothberg Family Charitable Trust, IL, **1082** (FD)
Redwood Area Communities Foundation, Inc., MN, **1731** (FD2)
Reese Health Trust, Michael, IL, **1083** (FD)
Reese Hospital Foundation, Michael, IL, *see* 1083
Regal Foundation, TN, **3151** (FD)
Regals Foundation, NY, **2377** (FD)
Regenstrief Foundation, Inc., IN, **1190** (FD)
Regions Bancorporation Foundation, AL, *see* 19
Regions Financial Corporation Foundation, AL, **19** (FD)
Regions Foundation, MS, **1770** (FD)
Regis Foundation, MN, **1732** (FD)
REI Foundation, The, WA, **3551** (FD)
Reich Fund, The, NY, **2378** (FD2)
Reidsville Area Foundation, NC, **2611** (FD)
Reilly Family Foundation, The, TX, **3333** (FD2)
Reiman Charitable Foundation, Inc., WI, *see* 3650
Reiman Foundation, Inc., WI, **3650** (FD)
Reinberger Foundation, The, OH, **2765** (FD)
Reinhold Foundation, Inc., Paul E. & Ida Klare, FL, *see* 808
Reinhold Foundation, Inc., Paul E. & Klare N., FL, **808** (FD2)
Rembrandt Foundation, Inc., MD, **1407** (FD)
Renaissance Foundation, The, OR, **2869** (FD)
Rendina Family Foundation, The, FL, **809** (FD2)
Renner Foundation, OH, **2766** (FD2)
Renton Community Foundation, WA, **3552** (FD)
Research Corporation for Science Advancement, AZ, **59** (FD)
Resnick Foundation, Inc., Ira M., The, NY, **2379** (FD)
Resnick Foundation, Jack and Pearl, The, NY, **2380** (FD2)
Respironics Sleep and Respiratory Research Foundation, PA, **3023** (FD)
Rest Haven Preventorium for Children, Inc., CA, **381** (FD2)
Rex Endowment, John, NC, **2612** (FD)
Reynolds American Foundation, NC, **2613** (FD)
Reynolds Charitable Trust, Kate B., NC, **2614** (FD)
Reynolds Foundation, Donald W., NV, **1869** (FD)
Reynolds Foundation, R. J., NC, *see* 2613
Rhode Island Community Foundation, The, RI, *see* 3089
Rhode Island Foundation, The, RI, **3089** (FD)
Rhodes Family Foundation, Jeffrey J., IL, **1084** (FD)
Rhodes Memorial Fund, Lawrence I. & Blanche H., NY, **2381** (FD2)
Ribenack Charitable Trust, Dorothy N., NC, **2615** (FD)
Rice Charitable Foundation, Albert W., MA, **1533** (FD)
Rich Family Foundation, NY, **2382** (FD)
Rich Foundation, NY, *see* 2382
Richard Benevolent Foundation, IL, **1085** (FD2)
Richards Foundation, Inc., The, GA, **908** (FD2)
Richards Scholarship Fund, Mabel Wilson, The, CA, **382** (FD2)
Richards, Jr. Foundation for Charitable Giving, Roy, GA, *see* 908
Richardson Benevolent Foundation, C. E., VA, **3475** (FD2)
Richardson Charitable Trust, Anne S., TX, *see* 3335
Richardson Foundation, Sid W., TX, **3334** (FD)
Richardson Fund, Anne S., TX, **3335** (FD)
Richardson Irrevocable Trust, M. Valeria, WA, **3553** (FD)
Richardson Memorial Fund, Sid, TX, **3336** (FD2)
Richfood Foundation, The, ID, see 952
Richland County Foundation of Mansfield, Ohio, The, OH, *see* 2767
Richland County Foundation, OH, **2767** (FD)
Richmond Community Foundation, Greater, VA, *see* 3433
Richmond Community Foundation, Inc., NC, **2616** (FD)
Richmond Foundation, Inc., Frederick W., MD, **1408** (FD2)
Richmond Memorial Health Foundation, VA, **3476** (FD)
Richter Charitable Trust, Adam, TX, **3337** (FD2)
Rider-Pool Foundation, PA, **3024** (FD2)
Rieger Charitable Foundation Trust, The, NY, **2383** (FD)
Rifkind Foundation, Robert Gore, CA, **383** (FD2)
Rikard Charitable Trust, M.A., AL, **20** (FD2)
Riley Foundation, Mabel Louise, The, MA, **1534** (FD)
Riley Foundation, The, MA, *see* 1534
Ring Foundation, Inc., The, NY, **2384** (FD2)
Rinker, Sr. Foundation, Inc., Marshall E., FL, **810** (FD)
Ripley County Community Foundation, Inc., IN, **1191** (FD2)
Rippel Foundation, Fannie E., NJ, **1982** (FD2)
RITE-HITE Corporation Foundation Inc., WI, **3651** (FD)
Rivendell Foundation, NY, **2385** (FD2)
Rivendell Stewards' Trust, CA, **384** (FD)
River Branch Foundation, FL, **811** (FD)
Rivera Foundation, Mariano, DE, **647** (FD2)
Riverside Foundation Charitable Trust, The, PA, **3025** (FD)
Riverway Foundation, MN, **1733** (FD2)
RNR Foundation, Inc., MI, **1659** (FD2)
Robbins Family Foundation, The, CT, **607** (FD2)
Robbins Foundation, Inc., CT, *see* 607
Robbins Foundation, Larry, NY, *see* 2386
Robbins Foundation, NY, **2386** (FD)
Roberts Foundation, Inc., Edward C. & Ann T., CT, **608** (FD2)
Roberts, Jr. Trust, Percival, NC, **2617** (FD)
Robertson Foundation for Government Inc., NJ, **1983** (FD2)
Robina Foundation, MN, **1734** (FD)
Robins Foundation, VA, **3477** (FD)
Robinson Fund, Charles Nelson, CT, **609** (FD2)
Robinson-Broadhurst Foundation, Inc., NY, **2387** (FD)
Roblee Foundation, Joseph H. & Florence A., MO, **1809** (FD)
Roby Charitable Trust, Allan B. & Frances M., The, NH, **1894** (FD2)
Roche Relief Foundation, Edward & Ellen, NY, **2388** (FD2)
Rochester Area Community Foundation, Greater, MI, *see* 1589
Rochester Area Foundation, MN, **1735** (FD)
Rockdale Foundation Inc., The, GA, **909** (FD)
Rockdale Fund for Social Investment, Inc., GA, *see* 909
Rockefeller Brothers Fund, Inc., NY, **2389** (FD)
Rockefeller Foundation, The, NY, **2390** (FD)
Rockford Community Foundation, IL, *see* 990
Rockwell Collins Charitable Corporation, IA, **1237** (FD)
Rockwell Fund, Inc., TX, **3338** (FD)
Rodman Ford Sales, Inc. Charitable Trust, MA, **1535** (FD2)
Rogers Charitable Trust, Florence, NC, **2618** (FD2)
Rogers Family Foundation, MA, **1536** (FD)
Rogers Foundation, The, TX, **3339** (FD)
Roggecora Memorial Foundation, OH, **2768** (FD)
ROI Community, Inc., OK, **2827** (FD)
Roma Bank Community Foundation, Inc., NJ, **1984** (FD2)
Rooney Foundation, Kelly, The, PA, **3026** (FD2)
Roothbert Fund Inc., The, NY, **2391** (FD2)
Roscitt Family Foundation, The, NJ, **1985** (FD2)
Roscommon County Community Foundation, MI, **1660** (FD2)
Rose & Kiernan Charitable Foundation, Inc., NY, **2392** (FD2)
Rose Community Foundation, CO, **528** (FD)
Rose Foundation, Deborah, The, NY, **2393** (FD)
Rose Pf F/B/O Asia Connection, E. K., NC, **2619** (FD)
Rosen Foundation, Michael Alan, IL, **1086** (FD2)
Rosenberg Foundation, CA, **385** (FD)
Rosenberg Foundation, Inc., Henry and Ruth Blaustein, The, MD, **1409** (FD)
Rosenberg Foundation, Inc., Murray & Sydell, GA, **910** (FD)
Rosenberg Foundation, Kim and Ralph, The, NY, **2394** (FD2)
Rosenberg Foundation, Murray M., GA, *see* 910
Rosenberg Fund, Anna Davidson, CA, *see* 386
Rosenberg Memorial Fund, Dorothy Sargent, CA, **386** (FD2)
Rosenthal Family Foundation, Barbara & William, NY, **2395** (FD2)
Rosewood Foundation, The, TX, **3340** (FD)
Ross Family Foundation, John S., MO, **1810** (FD2)
Ross Family Fund, PA, **3027** (FD)
Ross Foundation Inc., The, WV, **3588** (FD)
Ross Foundation, Dorothea Haus, The, NY, **2396** (FD)
Ross Foundation, John S. & Jody J., MO, *see* 1810
Ross Foundation, Lynn & George M., PA, *see* 3027
Ross Foundation, The, AR, **72** (FD)
Rossi Family Foundation, CA, **387** (FD2)
Rossin Foundation, PA, **3028** (FD2)
Roth Family Foundation, CA, **388** (FD)
Rothstein Charitable Youth Trust, Maks & Lea, The, NY, **2397** (FD2)
Rowan Family Foundation, Inc., Henry M., NJ, **1986** (FD)
Rowland Foundation Inc., The, VT, **3415** (FD)
Rowland Foundation, Inc., Pleasant T., WI, **3652** (FD)
Royal Foundation, May Mitchell, MI, **1661** (FD2)
Rubeli Foundation Inc., Maureen and Paul, AZ, **60** (FD2)
Rubin Foundation, Inc., Samuel, NY, **2398** (FD)
Rubin Foundation, Inc., Shelley & Donald, The, NY, **2399** (FD)
Rude Foundation, Inc., Raymond C., NV, **1870** (FD2)
Ruderman Family Charitable Foundation, MA, *see* 1537
Ruderman Family Foundation, MA, **1537** (FD)
Ruffin Foundation, Inc., Peter B. & Adeline W., NY, **2400** (FD)
Rumsfeld Foundation, DC, **679** (FD)
Rupe Foundation, Arthur N., CA, **389** (FD)
Rupe Foundation, CA, *see* 389

Rush County Community Foundation, Inc., IN, **1192** (FD2)
Rush Educational Trust, David and Mary P., KS, **1273** (FD2)
Rx Foundation, MA, **1538** (FD)
Ryan Foundation, Albert J., The, OH, **2769** (FD2)
Ryan Foundation, Patrick G. & Shirley W., IL, **1087** (FD)
Rylander Memorial Library Trust, WI, **3653** (FD)
Ryzman Foundation, Inc., CA, **390** (FD)

S & W Foundation, Inc., NY, **2401** (FD2)
Sachs Foundation, CO, **529** (FD)
Sacramento Region Community Foundation, CA, **391** (FD)
Sacramento Regional Foundation, CA, *see* 391
Safeco Insurance Fund, WA, **3554** (FD)
Sage & Dice Foundation, The, FL, **812** (FD)
Sage Foundation, Russell, NY, **2402** (FD)
Saginaw Community Foundation, MI, **1662** (FD)
Saigh Foundation, The, MO, **1811** (FD)
Sailors' Snug Harbor of Boston, Inc., MA, **1539** (FD2)
Saint Luke's Foundation of Cleveland, Ohio, OH, **2770** (FD)
Saint Susie Charitable Foundation, TX, **3341** (FD)
Saka Family Foundation, Charles and Brenda, The, NJ, **1987** (FD)
Salem Community Foundation, Inc., OH, **2771** (FD)
Salina Community Foundation, Greater, KS, **1274** (FD)
Samaritan Foundation, OH, **2772** (FD2)
Samberg Family Foundation, VA, **3478** (FD)
Samberg Foundation, Rebecca and Arthur, The, NY, **2403** (FD)
Sample Foundation, Inc., The, MT, **1829** (FD2)
Sams Foundation, Inc., Earl C., TX, **3342** (FD)
Samstag Fine Arts Trust, Gordon, FL, **813** (FD2)
Samuelsson Foundation, Harriet H., CA, **392** (FD)
San Angelo Health Foundation, TX, **3343** (FD)
San Juan Island Community Foundation, WA, **3555** (FD)
San Luis Obispo County Community Foundation, CA, **393** (FD)
Sanborn Foundation for the Treatment and Cure of Cancer, Inc., Elizabeth and George L., MA, **1540** (FD2)
Sand County Foundation, Inc., WI, **3654** (FD2)
Sandelman Foundation, FL, **814** (FD2)
Sanders Charitable Trust No. II, Caroline J. S., NC, **2620** (FD2)
Sandoz Foundation of America, NY, *see* 2333
Sandt Trust, Kurt, NC, **2621** (FD2)
Sandusky/Erie County Community Foundation, OH, **2773** (FD)
Sandy Hill Foundation, The, NY, **2404** (FD)
Sanilac County Community Foundation, MI, **1663** (FD2)
Sanofi Foundation for North America, NJ, **1988** (FD)
Sanofi-aventis Patient Assistance Foundation, NJ, *see* 1988
Santa Barbara Foundation, CA, **394** (FD)
Santa Fe Community Foundation, NM, **2017** (FD)
Santander Bank Foundation, MA, **1541** (FD)
Sapelo Foundation, Inc., The, GA, **911** (FD)
Sapelo Island Research Foundation, Inc., GA, *see* 911
Saramar Charitable Fund, The, PA, **3029** (FD2)
Sarasota County Community Foundation, Inc., The, FL, *see* 727
Sarkeys Foundation, OK, **2828** (FD)
Sarofim Foundation, Louisa Stude, NY, **2405** (FD)
Sarver Charitable Trust, KS, **1275** (FD)
Sasakawa Peace Foundation U.S.A. Inc, DC, **680** (FD)
Sassoon Foundation, Vidal, CA, **395** (FD2)
Satterberg Foundation, WA, **3556** (FD2)
Sauer Children's Renew Foundation, MN, **1736** (FD2)
Sauey Family Foundation, W. R. and Floy A., WI, **3655** (FD2)
Savage Charitable Foundation, CA, **396** (FD)
Savannah Community Foundation, The, GA, **912** (FD)
Savannah Foundation, The, GA, *see* 912
Savin Foundation, Rueben & Muriel, NJ, **1989** (FD2)
Saxena Foundation Inc, TX, **3344** (FD2)
Saybrook Charitable Trust, CT, **610** (FD)
Sayer Charitable Foundation, The, MN, **1737** (FD2)
SBC Foundation, TX, *see* 3167
SBM Charitable Foundation, Inc., CT, **611** (FD)
SCA Charitable Foundation, CT, **612** (FD2)
Scaife Charitable Foundation, PA, *see* 2937
Scaife Scholarship Foundation, CA, **397** (FD2)
Scarlett Family Foundation, TN, **3152** (FD)
Scattergood Behavioral Health Foundation, PA, **3030** (FD)
Schafer Family Foundation, NY, **2406** (FD)
Scharbauer Foundation Inc, TX, **3345** (FD)
Schelzi Family Foundation, The, MA, **1542** (FD2)
Schenectady Foundation, The, NY, **2407** (FD)
Schepp Foundation, Leopold, NY, **2408** (FD2)
Scherman Foundation, Inc., The, NY, **2409** (FD)
Schiewetz Foundation, Inc., The, OH, **2774** (FD)
Schildberg Foundation, IA, **1238** (FD2)
Schinazi and Family Foundation, Inc., Raymond F., GA, **913** (FD2)
Schissler Charitable Foundation, TX, *see* 3346
Schissler Foundation, The, TX, **3346** (FD2)
Schlegel Foundation, Oscar C. & Augusta, WI, **3656** (FD2)
Schlessman Family Foundation, Inc., CO, **530** (FD2)
Schlessman Foundation, Inc., CO, *see* 530
Schlieder Educational Foundation, Edward G., LA, **1319** (FD)
Schmidlapp Fund, C., OH, *see* 2775
Schmidlapp Fund, Charlotte R., OH, **2775** (FD2)
Schmidt Family Foundation, The, CA, **398** (FD)
Schmidt Family Foundation, Theodore & Elizabeth, UT, **3403** (FD2)
Schmidt Foundation, Inc., William E., TN, **3153** (FD2)
Schmitt Foundation, Arthur J., IL, **1088** (FD)
Schmitt Foundation, Inc., Kilian J. and Caroline F., The, NY, **2410** (FD2)
Schmuckal Family Foundation, Art and Mary, The, MI, **1664** (FD2)
Schmuhl Scholarship Fund Trust, Milton and Leonore, The, NC, **2622** (FD2)
Schnadig-Belgrad Foundation, The, IL, **1089** (FD2)
Schneider Foundation, MO, **1812** (FD2)
Schneidmiller Family Foundation, Inc, ID, **951** (FD2)
Schnurmacher Foundation, Inc., Adolph & Ruth, NY, **2411** (FD)
Schooler Family Foundation, OH, **2776** (FD2)
Schottenstein Foundation C, Saul, OH, **2778** (FD2)
Schottenstein Foundation, Jay and Jean, The, OH, **2777** (FD)
Schottenstein Foundation, Jay L., OH, *see* 2777
Schrafft Charitable Trust, William E. Schrafft and Bertha E., MA, **1543** (FD)
Schroeder Trust, Dale D., IA, **1239** (FD2)
Schuler Family Foundation, IL, **1090** (FD)
Schultz Family Foundation, WA, **3557** (FD)
Schulze Family Foundation, Richard M., MN, **1738** (FD)
Schumann Center for Media and Democracy, Inc., The, NY, *see* 2412
Schumann Fund for New Jersey, Inc., The, NJ, **1990** (FD)
Schumann Media Center, Inc., The, NY, **2412** (FD)
Schusterman Family Foundation, Charles and Lynn, OK, **2829** (FD)
Schwab Foundation, Inc., Olin B. and Desta, IN, **1193** (FD2)
Schwab Memorial Foundation, Edward L., SD, **3117** (FD2)
Schwartz Family Foundation, NY, **2413** (FD)
Schwarz Family Foundation, F. A. O., RI, **3090** (FD2)
Schwarz Foundation, NJ, **1991** (FD)
Scotford Foundation, OH, **2779** (FD2)
Scott Foundation, Homer A. & Mildred S., WY, **3679** (FD)
Scovel Foundation, Inc., Drs. Janene and Tom, CA, **399** (FD2)
Scranton Area Foundation, Inc., The, PA, **3031** (FD)
Scripps Howard Foundation, OH, **2780** (FD)
SDA Foundation, The, NY, **2414** (FD)
Seacor Foundation, FL, **815** (FD)
SEAKR Foundation, CO, **531** (FD2)
Searle Freedom Trust, DC, **681** (FD)
Sears-Swetland Family Foundation, The, OH, **2781** (FD2)
Sears-Swetland Foundation, The, OH, *see* 2781
Seasongood Good Government Foundation, Murray and Agnes, OH, **2782** (FD2)
Seattle Foundation, The, WA, **3558** (FD)
Seaver Institute, The, CA, **400** (FD)
Seay Foundation, CO, **532** (FD)
SECU Foundation, NC, *see* 2632
Securian Foundation, MN, **1739** (FD)
Sedwick Foundation, The, PA, **3032** (FD)
Seebe Trust, Frances, PA, **3033** (FD2)
Segal Foundation, George & Helen, NJ, **1992** (FD)
Seger Memorial Foundation, Inc., Steven M., IN, **1194** (FD2)
Selby Foundation, William G. Selby and Marie, FL, **816** (FD)
Semmes Foundation, Inc., TX, **3347** (FD)
Semnani Family Foundation, UT, **3404** (FD)
Semnani Foundation, UT, *see* 3404
Sender Charitable Trust, FL, **817** (FD2)
Seneca Foods Foundation, NY, **2415** (FD)
Senior Services of Stamford, Inc., CT, **613** (FD2)
Sentry Foundation, Inc., WI, *see* 3657
Sentry Insurance Foundation, Inc., WI, **3657** (FD)
Sequoia Foundation, WA, **3559** (FD)
Seramur Family Foundation Inc., WI, **3658** (FD2)
Serimus Foundation, CO, **533** (FD)
Setzer Family Foundation Inc., FL, **818** (FD2)
Seven Pillars Foundation, WY, **3680** (FD)
Sewall Foundation, Elmina B., ME, **1339** (FD)
Sewell Foundation, Inc., Warren P. & Ava F., GA, **914** (FD2)
Seybert Institution for Poor Boys and Girls, Adam and Maria Sarah, PA, **3034** (FD2)
Seybert Institution, PA, *see* 3034
Seymour Foundation, W. L. & Louise E., IL, **1091** (FD2)
Seymour Trust, George Dudley, RI, **3091** (FD2)
SFC Charitable Foundation, SC, *see* 3108
Shaffer Family Charitable Trust, PA, **3035** (FD)
Shaheen Foundation, Inc., David and Linda, The, NV, **1871** (FD)
Shalan Foundation, Inc., The, CA, *see* 108
Shalom Ish Foundation, The, NY, **2416** (FD2)
Shamrock Foundation, IL, **1092** (FD2)
Shapira Charitable Foundation, Anne & Eli, OR, **2870** (FD2)
Shapiro Foundation, Inc., Charles and M. R., IL, **1093** (FD)
Shapiro Foundation, Inc., Fern G. Shapiro, Morris R. Shapiro, and Charles, IL, *see* 1093
Share Foundation, KS, *see* 1267
Shasta Regional Community Foundation, CA, **401** (FD)
Shatford Memorial Trust, J. D., NY, **2417** (FD2)
Shattuck Charitable Trust, Clinton H. & Wilma T., The, MA, **1544** (FD2)
Shaw's Market Trust Fund, RI, *see* 3092
Shaw's Supermarket Charitable Foundation, RI, **3092** (FD2)
Shea Company Foundation, J. F., CA, **402** (FD2)
Sheafer Charitable Trust, Emma A., NY, **2418** (FD2)
Sheehan Family Foundation, MA, **1545** (FD)
Shell Companies Foundation, Inc., TX, *see* 3348
Shell Oil Company Foundation, TX, **3348** (FD)
Shelter Golf, Inc., TX, **3349** (FD2)
Shelton Family Foundation, TX, **3350** (FD)
Shemanski Testamentary Trust, Alfred & Tillie, WA, **3560** (FD2)
Shenango Valley Foundation, PA, *see* 2925

Shepherd, Sower, Sentinel and Scholar Foundation, CA, **403** (FD2)
Sherman Foundation, Murray G. & Beatrice H., NY, **2419** (FD2)
Sherrard Foundation, Bill & Susan, The, NC, **2623** (FD2)
Sherwood Trust, WA, **3561** (FD)
Shingleton Trust, Newton B., NC, **2624** (FD2)
Shinnick Educational Fund, William M., OH, **2783** (FD2)
Shire Philanthropic Foundation, CA, *see* 434
Shoolman Children's Foundation, Edith Glick, The, NY, **2420** (FD)
Shoop Sports and Youth Foundation Inc., IN, **1195** (FD2)
Shoreland Foundation, The, NY, **2421** (FD)
Short, Jr. Trust, Shelton H., NC, **2625** (FD)
Shumaker Family Foundation, The, KS, **1276** (FD)
Shuman Scholarship Fund Trust, Robbins, The, PA, **3036** (FD2)
Sidewalk Angels Foundation, NY, **2422** (FD2)
Siebel Foundation, Thomas and Stacey, The, CA, **404** (FD)
Siebert Lutheran Foundation, Inc., WI, **3659** (FD)
Siemens Foundation, NJ, **1993** (FD)
Sierra Foundation, Inc., FL, **819** (FD2)
Sierra Health Foundation, CA, **405** (FD)
Sierra Pacific Foundation, CA, **406** (FD)
Sigmund Foundation, Bill and Vi, MI, **1665** (FD)
Sikh Spirit Foundation, Inc., The, TX, **3351** (FD2)
Silicon Valley Bank Foundation, The, CA, **407** (FD2)
Silicon Valley Community Foundation, CA, **408** (FD)
Silver Family Foundation, CT, **614** (FD)
Silver Foundation, Barbara, CT, *see* 614
Silver Foundation, Morris & Helen, MT, **1830** (FD2)
Silver Giving Foundation, The, CA, **409** (FD)
Silver Lining Foundation, The, CA, *see* 409
Silverton Foundation, TX, *see* 3368
Simmons Foundation, The, TX, **3352** (FD)
Simon Charitable Foundation, The, NM, **2018** (FD2)
Simon Family Foundation, Ronald M., CA, *see* 410
Simon Foundation for Education and Housing, CA, **410** (FD)
Simons Foundation, The, NY, **2423** (FD)
Simonsen Family Charitable Foundation, Inc., Arnold, IL, **1094** (FD2)
Simonyi Fund for Arts and Sciences, Charles and Lisa, WA, **3562** (FD)
Simonyi Fund for Arts and Sciences, Charles, WA, *see* 3562
Simple Actions Family Foundation, OR, **2871** (FD2)
Simpson Foundation, CA, *see* 411
Simpson Foundation, The, AL, **21** (FD2)
Simpson Foundation, The, NC, **2626** (FD)
Simpson PSB Fund, CA, **411** (FD)
Simson Foundation, Inc., Walter H., NJ, **1994** (FD2)
Singer Foundation, Paul E., The, NY, **2424** (FD)
Singh Family Foundation, NY, **2425** (FD)
Singh Family Foundation, WA, **3563** (FD2)
Singing for Change, SC, **3108** (FD2)
Sinsheimer Fund, Alexandrine and Alexander L., The, IL, **1095** (FD)
Sioles Family Foundation, Milton & Harriet, AZ, **61** (FD2)
Siouxland Community Foundation, IA, **1240** (FD)
Siouxland Foundation, IA, *see* 1240
Siragusa Foundation, The, IL, **1096** (FD)
Sirus Fund, The, NY, **2426** (FD)
Sites Designated Charities Trust, NC, **2627** (FD2)
Sites Foundation, Venette and Mabel, NC, *see* 2627
Skadden Foundation, NY, **2427** (FD)
Skadden, Arps, Slate, Meagher & Flom Fellowship Foundation, NY, *see* 2427
Skelly Charitable Foundation, Gertrude E., The, FL, **820** (FD)
Skillbuilders Fund, KS, **1277** (FD2)
Skillman Foundation, The, MI, **1666** (FD)
Skoll Foundation, The, CA, **412** (FD)
Skoll Global Threats Fund, CA, **413** (FD)
Skyler Foundation, OH, **2784** (FD2)
Skywords Family Foundation, CA, **414** (FD)
Slemp Foundation, The, OH, **2785** (FD)
Slifka Foundation, Inc., Joseph & Sylvia, NY, **2428** (FD)
Sloan, Jr. Foundation, Carole C. and O. Temple, NC, **2628** (FD)
Smith Charitable Foundation, Clara Blackford Smith & W. Aubrey, TX, **3353** (FD)
Smith Charitable Foundation, Mary Alice, The, TX, **3354** (FD)
Smith Family Foundation, Charles E., VA, **3479** (FD)
Smith Family Foundation, Richard and Susan, MA, **1546** (FD)
Smith Foundation Inc., C. D., WI, **3660** (FD2)
Smith Foundation, Frank J., PA, **3037** (FD2)
Smith Foundation, Inc., R. C., NY, **2429** (FD)
Smith Foundation, J.M., SC, **3109** (FD)
Smith Foundation, Lester and Sue, The, TX, *see* 3355
Smith Foundation, Lester M., The, WA, **3564** (FD2)
Smith Foundation, Lon V., CA, **415** (FD)
Smith Foundation, Margaret Chase, The, ME, **1340** (FD)
Smith Foundation, The, TX, **3355** (FD)
Smith Fund, Horace, The, MA, **1547** (FD2)
Smith Fund, Inc., George D., NY, **2430** (FD)
Smith Horticultural Trust, Stanley, The, CA, **416** (FD)
Smith Memorial Fund, Ethel Sergeant Clark, NC, **2629** (FD)
Smith Scholarship Foundation, Inc., J. Craig and Page T., AL, **22** (FD2)
Smith-Walker Foundation, CA, **417** (FD2)
SmithKline Beecham Foundation, PA, *see* 2957
Smyth Trust, Marion C., NH, **1895** (FD2)
Snayberger Memorial Foundation, Harry E. and Florence W., NY, **2431** (FD2)
Snayberger Memorial Foundation, NY, *see* 2431
Sneath Trust, Dorothy Melcher, PA, **3038** (FD2)
Snee-Reinhardt Charitable Foundation, PA, **3039** (FD)
Snell Family Foundation, Randolph, FL, **821** (FD2)
Snook Foundation, AL, **23** (FD)
Snow Foundation, Inc., John Ben, The, NY, **2432** (FD2)
Snyder Foundation, Helen M., The, NJ, **1995** (FD2)
Snyder Fund, Valentine Perry, NY, **2433** (FD)
Society for Analytical Chemists of Pittsburgh, PA, **3040** (FD2)
Society of Economic Geologists Foundation, Inc., CO, **534** (FD)
Society of the Friendly Sons of Saint Patrick in the City of New York, The, NY, **2434** (FD2)
Sociological Initiatives Foundation, Inc., MA, **1548** (FD2)
Soda Foundation, Y & H, CA, **418** (FD)
Solano Community Foundation, CA, **419** (FD2)
Solomon Charitable Foundation, Doris and Daniel, NY, **2435** (FD2)
Solomon Testamentary Trust, Alfred Z., NY, **2436** (FD)
Somers Foundation, Inc., Virginia Hodgkins, ME, **1341** (FD2)
Somerville Charitable Trust, Graham and Thelma, PA, **3041** (FD2)
Sonora Area Foundation, CA, **420** (FD)
Sontag Foundation, Inc., FL, **822** (FD)
Sorel Charitable Organization, Inc., Elizabeth & Michel, The, NY, **2437** (FD2)
Sorenson Legacy Foundation, The, UT, *see* 3400
Soroka Charitable Trust, William, CA, **421** (FD)
Soros Charitable Foundation, NY, **2438** (FD)
Soros Fellowships for New Americans, Paul & Daisy, NY, **2439** (FD)
Soros Foundation, Paul & Daisy, NY, *see* 2439
Sound Federal Savings and Loan Association Charitable Foundation, NJ, *see* 1942
Source of Hope Foundation, NY, **2440** (FD)
South Central Iowa Community Foundation, IA, **1241** (FD)
South Dakota Education Access Foundation, SD, **3118** (FD)
South Plains Foundation, TX, **3356** (FD2)
Southdown Foundation, TX, *see* 3191
Southern Bank Foundation, NC, **2630** (FD)
Southern Colorado Community Foundation, CO, **535** (FD)
Southern Company Charitable Foundation, Inc., GA, **915** (FD)
Southwest Florida Community Foundation, Inc., The, FL, **823** (FD)
Southwest Initiative Foundation, MN, **1740** (FD)
Southwest Louisiana Community Foundation, LA, *see* 1307
Southwest Minnesota Foundation, MN, *see* 1740
Sovereign Bank Foundation, MA, *see* 1541
Sparkplug Foundation, The, NY, **2441** (FD2)
Sparks Foundation, The, TN, **3154** (FD2)
Spartanburg County Foundation, The, SC, **3110** (FD)
Speas Foundation, Victor E., MO, **1813** (FD)
Special Hope Foundation, The, CA, **422** (FD)
Specialty Foundation, CA, **423** (FD)
Speech Foundation of America, TN, *see* 3155
Speer Foundation, Roy M., FL, **824** (FD)
Speh Foundation, Albert J. & Claire R., IL, **1097** (FD)
Spektor Family Foundation, Inc., NY, **2442** (FD2)
Spencer Foundation, The, IL, **1098** (FD)
Spencer Foundation, W. L. S., The, CA, **424** (FD)
Sperry Fund, The, NY, **2443** (FD)
Spire Foundation, Inc., Nancy Woodson, WI, **3661** (FD)
Spirit Foundation, The, NY, *see* 2334
Spirit Services, Inc., OH, **2786** (FD)
Sprague Educational and Charitable Foundation, Seth, The, NY, **2444** (FD)
Spring Leaf Foundation, NY, *see* 2229
Springfield Foundation, The, OH, **2787** (FD)
Springs Close Foundation, Inc., The, SC, **3111** (FD)
Springs Foundation, Inc., SC, *see* 3111
Square D Foundation, IL, **1099** (FD)
Squires Educational Foundation, Inc., William D., The, AZ, **62** (FD2)
St. Croix Valley Foundation, WI, **3662** (FD)
St. George's Society of New York, NY, **2445** (FD)
St. Jude Medical Foundation, MN, **1741** (FD)
St. Louis Health Foundation, Greater, MO, **1814** (FD2)
St. Simon Charitable Foundation, Inc., NY, **2446** (FD)
Stackhouse Foundation, Mary Reinhart, NY, **2447** (FD2)
Stackpole-Hall Foundation, PA, **3042** (FD)
Stadtmauer Family Foundation, Inc., Marisa & Richard, NJ, **1996** (FD)
Stafford Family Foundation, The, VA, *see* 3480
Stafford Foundation, John R. and Inge P., The, FL, **825** (FD2)
Stafford Foundation, VA, **3480** (FD2)
Stahlberg Foundation, Joseph H., NC, **2631** (FD2)
Staley Foundation, Thomas F., PA, **3043** (FD2)
Stanislaus Community Foundation, CA, **425** (FD)
Staples Foundation for Learning, Inc., MA, *see* 1549
Staples Foundation, Inc., MA, **1549** (FD)
Star Tribune Foundation, CA, *see* 317
Starbucks Foundation, The, WA, **3565** (FD)
Stardust Foundation of Central New York, The, NY, **2448** (FD)
Stardust Foundation, Inc., AZ, **63** (FD)
Stark Charitable Foundation, Howard E., NY, **2449** (FD2)
Stark Community Foundation, OH, **2788** (FD)
Stark County Foundation, Inc., The, OH, *see* 2788
Stark Foundation, Nelda C. and H. J. Lutcher, TX, **3357** (FD)
State Employees' Credit Union Foundation, NC, **2632** (FD)
State Street Foundation, Inc., MA, **1550** (FD)
Stateline Community Foundation, The, WI, **3663** (FD2)
Staunton Augusta Waynesboro Community Foundation, VA, *see* 3429

True North Foundation, CA, **442** (FD)
Truland Foundation, VA, **3482** (FD)
Trull Foundation, The, TX, **3373** (FD)
Truman Foundation, Mildred Faulkner, NY, **2475** (FD2)
Truman Heartland Community Foundation, MO, **1817** (FD)
Trump Foundation, Donald J., The, NY, **2476** (FD)
Trust for Mutual Understanding, NY, **2477** (FD)
Trust for the Meditation Process, MN, **1746** (FD2)
Tsadra Foundation, NY, **2478** (FD)
Tsunami Foundation, FL, **834** (FD)
Tu Foundation, John and Mary, CA, **443** (FD2)
Tubbs Charitable Trust, Charles B. and Patricia A., TX, **3374** (FD)
Tucker Community Foundation, WV, **3589** (FD)
Tucker Foundation, Inc., Marcia Brady, MD, **1415** (FD2)
Tucker Foundation, TN, **3156** (FD)
Tudor Foundation, The, WA, **3569** (FD2)
Tufenkian Foundation, The, NJ, **2001** (FD2)
Tull Charitable Foundation, The, GA, **917** (FD)
Turn the Corner Foundation, NY, *see* 2462
Turner Charitable Foundation, TX, *see* 3358
Turock Family Foundation, The, FL, **835** (FD2)
Turrell Fund, NJ, **2002** (FD)
Tuscarawas County Community Foundation, OH, **2795** (FD2)
Tuscora Park Health & Wellness Foundation, OH, **2796** (FD2)
Tuttle Fund, Isaac H., NY, **2479** (FD)
Tuttleman Family Foundation, PA, **3050** (FD2)
Twinkling Eyes Foundation, The, VA, **3483** (FD2)
Two Sisters and a Wife Foundation, Inc., MA, **1557** (FD)
TWS Foundation, The, FL, **836** (FD)
Tye Medical Aid Foundation, Ray, MA, **1558** (FD)
TYL Foundation, CO, **542** (FD)
Tyler Foundation, TX, **3375** (FD2)
Tyndale House Foundation, IL, **1105** (FD)

U.S. Oil/Schmidt Family Foundation, Inc., WI, *see* 3665
U.S. Venture/Schmidt Family Foundation, Inc., WI, **3665** (FD)
Ullrich Foundation Trust, John, IL, **1106** (FD)
Unbound Philanthropy, NY, **2480** (FD)
UniHealth Foundation, CA, **444** (FD)
Unilever United States Foundation, Inc., NJ, **2003** (FD)
Union Benevolent Association, PA, **3051** (FD2)
Union County Community Foundation, Inc., AR, **73** (FD2)
Union County Foundation, Inc., IN, **1200** (FD2)
Union Square Fund, NY, **2481** (FD)
United Charitable Foundation, MA, **1559** (FD2)
United Coal Company Charitable Foundation, VA, *see* 3484
United Community Foundation, Inc., WI, *see* 3607
United Company Charitable Foundation, The, VA, **3484** (FD)
United Fire Group Foundation, IA, **1243** (FD)
United Space Alliance Foundation, PA, **3052** (FD2)
Unity Foundation of La Porte County, Inc., IN, **1201** (FD)
Universal Studios Foundation, Ltd., NY, *see* 2322
University Financing Foundation, Inc., The, GA, **918** (FD)
UNOVA Foundation, The, WA, *see* 3527
Up The River Endeavors Inc., NH, **1896** (FD2)
USA Equestrian Trust Inc., KY, **1296** (FD2)
Utah Medical Association Foundation, UT, **3405** (FD2)
Utica Foundation, Inc., NY, *see* 2110

V and V Foundation, OH, *see* 2797
V'hanun Foundation Inc., Rachum, The, NY, **2484** (FD2)
Vail Valley Foundation, Inc., CO, **543** (FD)
Valentine Foundation, PA, **3053** (FD2)
Valley Foundation, Wayne & Gladys, CA, **445** (FD)
van Ameringen Foundation, H., NY, **2482** (FD)
van Ameringen Foundation, Inc., NY, **2483** (FD)
Van Andel Foundation, Steve & Cindy, MI, *see* 1669
Van Andel Foundation, Steve, MI, **1669** (FD)
van Beuren Charitable Foundation, Inc., RI, **3094** (FD)
Van Kampen Boyer Molinari Charitable Foundation, MI, **1670** (FD)
van Loben Sels Foundation, CA, *see* 446
van Loben Sels/RembeRock Foundation, CA, **446** (FD)
Van Mourick Foundation, Mark, The, CA, *see* 351
Van Nuys Foundation, I. N. & Susanna H., CA, **447** (FD)
VanderWeide Family Foundation, MI, **1671** (FD)
VanderWeide Foundation, Robert & Cheri, MI, *see* 1671
Veale Foundation, The, OH, **2797** (FD)
Vectren Foundation, Inc., IN, **1202** (FD)
Vergara Trust, Lamar Bruni, TX, **3376** (FD)
Vermont Community Foundation, VT, **3417** (FD)
Verrochi Family Charitable Trust, MA, **1560** (FD2)
Versacare, Inc., CA, **448** (FD)
VF Foundation, The, NC, **2642** (FD)
VHA Foundation, Inc., TX, **3377** (FD)
VHA Health Foundation, Inc., The, TX, *see* 3377
Vidda Foundation, The, NY, **2485** (FD)
Viersen Family Foundation, Inc., Sam, OK, **2830** (FD)
Vietor Trust, Vera P., CA, **449** (FD2)
Vilcek Foundation, Inc., The, NY, **2486** (FD)
Vingo Trust III, The, MA, **1561** (FD)
Visiting Nurse Association of Chicago, IL, *see* 1107
VNA Foundation, IL, **1107** (FD)
Vogler Foundation, Inc., Laura B., The, NY, **2487** (FD2)
Volgenau Foundation, The, VA, **3485** (FD2)
Von Blon Family Charitable Foundation, The, IL, **1108** (FD2)
Von Voigtlander Foundation, Ted & Jane, MI, **1672** (FD)
Voya Foundation, NY, **2488** (FD)
Vradenburg Foundation, Bee, CO, **544** (FD2)

W.M. Foundation, MN, **1747** (FD)
Wabash Valley Community Foundation, Inc., IN, **1203** (FD)
Waccamaw Community Foundation, SC, **3112** (FD)
Wachenheim Foundation, Sue and Edgar, NY, **2489** (FD)
Wachovia Regional Foundation, PA, *see* 3055
Wachtell, Lipton, Rosen & Katz Foundation, NY, **2490** (FD)
Waco Foundation, TX, **3378** (FD)
Wadhwani Foundation, CA, **450** (FD)
Wadleigh Foundation, Inc., George C., MA, **1562** (FD)
Wadleigh Home for Aged Men, Inc., George C., MA, *see* 1562
Waggoner Charitable Trust, Crystelle, TX, **3379** (FD)
Wagner Foundation, Ltd., R. H., WI, *see* 3666
Wagner Foundation, Ltd., The, WI, **3666** (FD)
Wagner Foundation, Rose and Sherle, NY, **2491** (FD2)
Wahlert Foundation, IA, **1244** (FD2)
Wal-Mart Foundation, AR, *see* 74
Wal-Mart Foundation, Inc., The, AR, **74** (FD)
Walgreens Assistance, Inc., IL, **1109** (FD)
Walker Foundation, Earl E. Walker and Myrtle E., The, MO, **1818** (FD)
Walker Foundation, MS, **1772** (FD)
Walker Foundation, W. E., MS, *see* 1772
Wallace Foundation, The, NY, **2492** (FD)
Wallace Genetic Foundation, Inc., DC, **683** (FD)
Wallace Global Fund II, DC, **684** (FD)
Wallace Research Foundation, IA, **1245** (FD)
Wallace-Reader's Digest Funds, NY, *see* 2492
Wallach Foundation, Miriam G. and Ira D., NY, **2493** (FD)
Wallin Education Partners, MN, **1748** (FD)
Wallis Foundation, CA, **451** (FD)
Wallrath Educational Foundation, Richard, TX, **3380** (FD)
Walmart Foundation, The, AR, *see* 74
Walter & Lorenz Foundation, Inc., ME, *see* 1343
Walter Corporation Foundation, Jim, FL, *see* 837
Walter Family Trust, Byron L., IL, **1110** (FD2)
Walter Foundation, Inc., Otto and Fran, ME, **1343** (FD)
Walter Foundation, The, FL, **837** (FD)
Walther Cancer Foundation, Inc., IN, **1204** (FD)
Walther Cancer Institute Foundation, Inc., IN, *see* 1204
Wanek-Vogel Foundation, Ltd., The, WI, **3667** (FD)
Wann Foundation, Ralph J., NC, **2643** (FD2)
Ward Foundation, A. Montgomery, IL, **1111** (FD)
Ward Heritage Foundation, Mamie McFaddin, TX, **3381** (FD)
Ware Foundation, The, FL, **838** (FD)
Warhol Foundation for the Visual Arts, Andy, The, NY, **2494** (FD)
Warren Foundation, William K., The, OK, **2831** (FD)
Warsh-Mott Legacy, CA, **452** (FD)
Warwick Savings Foundation, NY, **2495** (FD2)
Washington County Community Foundation, Inc., PA, **3054** (FD)
Washington Research Foundation, WA, **3570** (FD)
Washington Square Health Foundation, Inc., IL, **1112** (FD)
Washington Trust Charitable Foundation, The, RI, **3095** (FD2)
Wasserman Foundation, CA, **453** (FD)
Waterbury Foundation, The, CT, *see* 564
Wattis Foundation, Paul L., CA, **454** (FD2)
Wattis Foundation, Phyllis C., CA, **455** (FD)
Watumull Foundation, HI, **939** (FD2)
Wayne County Community Foundation, OH, **2798** (FD)
Wayne County Foundation, Inc., Greater, OH, *see* 2798
WCA Foundation, MN, **1749** (FD)
Wean Foundation, Raymond John, The, OH, **2799** (FD)
Weatherstone Family Foundation, Inc., The, CT, **618** (FD)
Webb Family Foundation, Inc., NV, **1875** (FD2)
Webb Foundation, Del E., AZ, **64** (FD)
Webb Foundation, IL, **1113** (FD2)
WebbCraft Family Foundation, Inc., The, SC, **3113** (FD2)
Webber 1985 Charitable Trust, Vila B., MA, **1563** (FD2)
Webber Foundation, Wayne and Joan, The, MI, **1673** (FD)
Weber Charities Corporation, Frederick E., The, MA, **1564** (FD2)
Webster Foundation, Edwin S., MA, **1565** (FD)
Wedum Foundation, J.A., MN, **1750** (FD)
Weeden Foundation, NY, **2496** (FD)
Wege Foundation, The, MI, **1674** (FD)
Wegman Charitable Foundation, Robert B., NY, *see* 2497
Wegman Family Charitable Foundation, The, NY, **2497** (FD)
Weil Foundation, The, AZ, **65** (FD)
Weil, Gotshal & Manges Foundation Inc., NY, **2498** (FD)
Weill Foundation for Music, Inc., Kurt, NY, **2499** (FD2)
Weinberg Foundation, Inc., Harry and Jeanette, The, MD, **1416** (FD)
Weingart Foundation, CA, **456** (FD)
Weir Scholarship Foundation Trust, Shirley and Billy, GA, **919** (FD2)
Weisberg Family Foundation, Inc., Arthur and Joan, WV, **3590** (FD2)
Weiss Foundation, Andrew and Bonnie, The, MA, *see* 1447
Weiss Foundation, Inc., William E., WY, **3682** (FD2)
Weissman Family Foundation Inc., Paul and Harriet, The, NY, **2500** (FD)
Weissman Family Foundation, Paul M., The, NY, *see* 2500
Weitz Family Foundation, NE, **1855** (FD)
Welbilt Corporation Foundation, WI, *see* 3632
Welborn Baptist Foundation, Inc., IN, **1205** (FD)
Welborn Foundation, Inc., IN, *see* 1205
Wellmark Foundation, The, IA, **1246** (FD)
WellPoint Foundation, Inc., IN, **1206** (FD)
Wells County Foundation, Inc., The, IN, **1207** (FD)
Wells Family Foundation, Inc., FL, **839** (FD2)
Wells Fargo Regional Foundation, PA, **3055** (FD)
Wells Foundation, Franklin H. & Ruth L., NY, **2501** (FD2)
Wells Foundation, George W., MA, **1566** (FD2)
Wells Foundation, Terry Lee, NV, **1876** (FD2)